Who Was Who in America

Biographical Titles Currently Published by Marquis Who's Who

Who's Who in America
Who's Who in America derivatives:
  Who's Who in America Junior & Senior High School Version
  Geographic/Professional Index
  Who's Who in America Classroom Project Book
Who Was Who in America
  Historical Volume (1607-1896)
  Volume I (1897-1942)
  Volume II (1943-1950)
  Volume III (1951-1960)
  Volume IV (1961-1968)
  Volume V (1969-1973)
  Volume VI (1974-1976)
  Volume VII (1977-1981)
  Volume VIII (1982-1985)
  Volume IX (1985-1989)
  Volume X (1989-1993)
  Index Volume (1607-1993)
Who's Who in the World
Who's Who in the East
Who's Who in the Midwest
Who's Who in the South and Southwest
Who's Who in the West
Who's Who in Advertising
Who's Who in American Education
Who's Who in American Law
Who's Who in American Nursing
Who's Who of American Women
Who's Who of Emerging Leaders in America
Who's Who in Entertainment
Who's Who in Finance and Industry
Who's Who in Religion
Who's Who in Science and Engineering
Index to Who's Who Books
The Official American Board of Medical Specialties
  Directory of Board Certified Medical Specialists

Who Was Who in America ®

with World Notables

Volume X
1989-1993

MARQUIS
Who'sWho

A Reed Reference Publishing Company
121 Chanlon Road
New Providence, New Jersey 07974 U.S.A.

Published by Marquis Who's Who, a Reed Reference Publishing Company. Copyright © 1993 by Reed Publishing (USA) Inc. All rights reserved. No part of this publication may be reproduced, stored in a retrieval system or transmitted in any form or by any means—including, but not limited to, electronic, mechanical, photocopying, recording or otherwise—or used for any commercial purpose whatsoever without the prior written permission of the publisher and, if publisher deems necessary, execution of a formal license agreement with publisher. For information, contact Marquis Who's Who, 121 Chanlon Road, New Providence, New Jersey 07974, 1-800/621-9669.

Sandra S. Barnes—Publisher
Peter E. Simon—Senior Vice President, Database Publishing
Leigh Yuster—Associate Publisher
Paul Canning—Editorial Director
Frederick Marks—Senior Managing Editor
Harriet Tiger—Senior Editor

Library of Congress Catalog Card Number 43-3789
International Standard Book Numbers 0–8379–0222–3 (set)
                      0–8379–0220–7 (volume X)
                      0–8379–0221-5 (Index volume)

Manufactured in the United States of America

Table of Contents

Preface

The publication of Volume X of *Who Was Who in America* is an important step forward in the growth of a series of biographical reference books that seek to reflect both American history and the genealogical heritages of this country. The sketches are of deceased biographees in *Who's Who in America* as well as our regional and topical library.

The *Was* books (to use the shortened form by which they are better known) display the distinctive characteristics that have made *Who's Who in America* both an internationally respected reference work, and a household word in the country of its origin. Sketches not only were prepared by information supplied by the biographees themselves, but were approved and frequently revised by the subjects before being printed in a Marquis publication. As a result, many sketches contain personal data unavailable elsewhere. The preface to the first volume of *Who's Who in America* selected this fact as one of the volume's outstanding characteristics, and stated: "The book is autobiographical, the data having been obtained from first hands." Similarly, *Who Was Who in America* is largely autobiographical. Although condensed to the concise style that Marquis Who's Who has made famous, the sketches contain essential facts. Inclusion of date of death and place of interment completes the sketches.

In continuing improvements introduced in previous volumes of *Who Was Who in America*, this volume includes sketches of some Marquis biographees known to be 93 years of age or older. Lacking current information regarding these individuals, we make such inclusions in the hope that our apologies will be accepted should errors occur. These sketches are denoted by asterisks. Sketches of recently deceased world notables also are included, particularly of those international figures whose careers had a direct bearing on the courses of recent American history.

The result is far more than a biographical directory of some 122,000 deceased American notables within the covers of ten volumes. *Who Was Who in America* contains a vital portion of American history from the early days of the colonies to 1993. It is the autobiography of America.

Key to Information

[1] GIBSON, OSCAR JULIUS, [2] physician, medical educator; [3] b. Syracuse, N.Y., Aug. 31, 1918; [4] s. Paul Oliver and Elizabeth H. (Thrun) G.; [5] m. Judith S. Gonzalez, Apr. 28, 1939; [6] children: Richard Gary, Matthew Cary, Samuel Perry. [7] BA magna cum laude, U. Pa., 1940; MD, Harvard U., 1944. [8] Diplomate Am. Bd. Internal Medicine, Am. Bd. Preventive Medicine. [9] Intern Barnes Hosp., St. Louis, 1944-49, resident, 1950-66; clin. assoc. Nat. Heart Inst., NIH, Bethesda, Md., 1966-68; chief resident medicine U. Okla. Hosps., 1968-69; asst. prof. community health Okla. Med. Ctr., 1969-70, assoc. prof., 1970-74, prof., chmn. dept., 1974-80; dean U. Okla. Coll. Medicine, 1978-82; v.p. med. staff affairs Bapt. Med. Ctr., Oklahoma City, 1982-86, exec. v.p., 1986-88, chmn., 1988-92; [10] mem. governing bd. Ambulatory Health Care Consortium, Inc., 1979-80; mem. Okla. Bd. Medicolegal Examiners, 1985-1991. [11] Contbr. articles to profl. jours. [12] Bd. dirs., v.p. Okla. Arthritis Found., 1982-1990; trustee North Central Mental Health Ctr., 1985-1992. [13] Served with U.S. Army, 1955-56. [14] Recipient R.T. Chadwick award NIH, 1968; Am. Heart Assn. grantee, 1985-86, 88. [15] Former fellow Assn. Tchrs. Preventive Medicine; former mem. Am. Fedn. Clin. Research, Assn. Med. Colls., AAAS, AMA, Masons, Shriners, Sigma Xi. [16] Republican. [17] Roman Catholic. [18] Avocations: swimming, weight lifting, travel. [19] Home: Oklahoma City [20] Died August 15, 1992; buried Tulsa, Okla.

KEY

[1]	Name
[2]	Occupation
[3]	Vital Statistics
[4]	Parents
[5]	Marriage
[6]	Children
[7]	Education
[8]	Professional certifications
[9]	Career
[10]	Career Related
[11]	Writings and creative works
[12]	Civic and political activities
[13]	Military
[14]	Awards and fellowships
[15]	Professional and association memberships, Clubs and Lodges
[16]	Political affiliation
[17]	Religion
[18]	Avocations
[19]	Home
[20]	Death Information

Table of Abbreviations

The following abbreviations and symbols are frequently used in this book

†Recently deceased biographees selected for *Who Was Who in America* without the participation of the next of kin due to publication deadlines.

*Non-current sketches of *Who Was Who in America* biographees who were born 93 or more years ago.

AA, A.A. Associate in Arts, Associate of Arts
AAAL American Academy of Arts and Letters
AAAS American Association for the Advancement of Science
AAHPER Alliance for Health, Physical Education and Recreation
AAU Amateur Athletic Union
AAUP American Association of University Professors
AAUW American Association of University Women
AB, A.B. Arts, Bachelor of
AB Alberta
ABA American Bar Association
ABC American Broadcasting Company
AC Air Corps
acad. academy, academic
acct. accountant
acctg. accounting
ACDA Arms Control and Disarmament Agency
ACLU American Civil Liberties Union
ACP American College of Physicians
ACS American College of Surgeons
ADA American Dental Association
a.d.c. aide-de-camp
adj. adjunct, adjutant
adj. gen. adjutant general
adm. admiral
adminstr. administrator
adminstrn. administration
adminstrv. administrative
ADP Automatic Data Processing
adv. advocate, advisory
advt. advertising
AE, A.E. Agricultural Engineer
A.E. and P. Ambassador Extraordinary and Plenipotentiary
AEC Atomic Energy Commission
aero. aeronautical, aeronautic
aerodyn. aerodynamic
AFB Air Force Base
AFL-CIO American Federation of Labor and Congress of Industrial Organizations
AFTRA American Federation of TV and Radio Artists
AFSCME American Federation of State, County and Municipal Employees
agr. agriculture
agrl. agricultural
agt. agent
AGVA American Guild of Variety Artists
agy. agency
A&I Agricultural and Industrial
AIA American Institute of Architects
AIAA American Institute of Aeronautics and Astronautics
AICPA American Institute of Certified Public Accountants
AID Agency for International Development

AIDS Acquired Immune Deficiency Syndrome
AIEE American Institute of Electrical Engineers
AIM American Institute of Management
AIME American Institute of Mining, Metallurgy, and Petroleum Engineers
AK Alaska
AL Alabama
ALA American Library Association
Ala. Alabama
alt. alternate
Alta. Alberta
A&M Agricultural and Mechanical
AM, A.M. Arts, Master of
Am. American, America
AMA American Medical Association
amb. ambassador
A.M.E. African Methodist Episcopal
Amtrak National Railroad Passenger Corporation
AMVETS American Veterans of World War II, Korea, Vietnam
anat. anatomical
ann. annual
ANTA American National Theatre and Academy
anthrop. anthropological
AP Associated Press
APO Army Post Office
apptd. appointed
Apr. April
apt. apartment
AR Arkansas
ARC American Red Cross
archeol. archeological
archtl. architectural
Ariz. Arizona
Ark. Arkansas
ArtsD, ArtsD. Arts, Doctor of
arty. artillery
AS American Samoa
AS Associate in Science
AS Associate of Applied Science
ASCAP American Society of Composers, Authors and Publishers
ASCE American Society of Civil Engineers
ASHRAE American Society of Heating, Refrigeration, and Air Conditioning Engineers
ASME American Society of Mechanical Engineers
ASPCA American Society for the Prevention of Cruelty to Animals
assn. association
assoc. associate
asst. assistant
ASTM American Society for Testing and Materials
astron. astronomical
astrophys. astrophysical
ATSC Air Technical Service Command
AT&T American Telephone & Telegraph Company
atty. attorney
Aug. August
AUS Army of the United States

aux. auxiliary
Ave. Avenue
AVMA American Veterinary Medical Association
AZ Arizona

B. Bachelor
b. born
BA, B.A. Bachelor of Arts
BAgr, B.Agr. Bachelor of Agriculture
Balt. Baltimore
Bapt. Baptist
BArch, B.Arch. Bachelor of Architecture
BAS, B.A.S. Bachelor of Agricultural Science
BBA, B.B.A. Bachelor of Business Administration
BBC British Broadcasting Corporation
BC, B.C. British Columbia
BCE, B.C.E. Bachelor of Civil Engineering
BChir, B.Chir. Bachelor of Surgery
BCL, B.C.L. Bachelor of Civil Law
BCS, B.C.S. Bachelor of Commercial Science
BD, B.D. Bachelor of Divinity
bd. board
BE, B.E. Bachelor of Education
BEE, B.E.E. Bachelor of Electrical Engineering
BFA, B.F.A. Bachelor of Fine Arts
bibl. biblical
bibliog. bibliographical
biog. biographical
biol. biological
BJ, B.J. Bachelor of Journalism
Bklyn. Brooklyn
BL, B.L. Bachelor of Letters
bldg. building
BLS, B.L.S. Bachelor of Library Science
Blvd. Boulevard
BMW Bavarian Motor Works (Bayerische Motoren Werke)
bn. batallion
B.& O.R.R. Baltimore & Ohio Railroad
bot. botanical
BPE, B.P.E. Bachelor of Physical Education
BPhil, B.Phil. Bachelor of Philosophy
br. branch
BRE, B.R.E. Bachelor of Religious Education
brig. gen. brigadier general
Brit. British, Brittanica
Bros. Brothers
BS, B.S. Bachelor of Science
BSA, B.S.A. Bachelor of Agricultural Science
BSBA Bachelor of Science in Business Administration
BSChemE Bachelor of Science in Chemical Engineering
BSD, B.S.D. Bachelor of Didactic Science
BST, B.S.T. Bachelor of Sacred Theology
BTh, B.Th. Bachelor of Theology
bull. bulletin
bur. bureau
bus. business
B.W.I. British West Indies

CA California
CAA Civil Aeronautics Administration
CAB Civil Aeronautics Board
CAD-CAM Computer Aided Design-Computer Aided Model
Calif. California
C.Am. Central America
Can. Canada, Canadian
CAP Civil Air Patrol
capt. captain
CARE Cooperative American Relief Everywhere
Cath. Catholic
cav. cavalry
CBC Canadian Broadcasting Company
CBI China, Burma, India Theatre of Operations
CBS Columbia Broadcasting Company
CCC Commodity Credit Corporation
CCNY City College of New York
CCU Cardiac Care Unit
CD Civil Defense
CE, C.E. Corps of Engineers, Civil Engineer
cen. central
CENTO Central Treaty Organization
CERN European Organization of Nuclear Research
cert. certificate, certification, certified
CETA Comprehensive Employment Training Act
CFL Canadian Football League
ch. church
ChD, Ch.D. Doctor of Chemistry
chem. chemical
ChemE, Chem.E. Chemical Engineer
Chgo. Chicago
chirurg. chirurgical
chmn. chairman
chpt. chapter
CIA Central Intelligence Agency
Cin. Cincinnati
cir. circuit
Cleve. Cleveland
climatol. climatological
clin. clinical
clk. clerk
C.L.U. Chartered Life Underwriter
CM, C.M. Master in Surgery
CM Northern Mariana Islands
C.&N.W.Ry. Chicago & North Western Railway
CO Colorado
Co. Company
COF Catholic Order of Foresters
C. of C. Chamber of Commerce
col. colonel
coll. college
Colo. Colorado
com. committee
comd. commanded
comdg. commanding
comdr. commander
comdt. commandant
commd. commissioned
comml. commercial
commn. commission
commr. commissioner

compt. comptroller
condr. conductor
Conf. Conference
Congl. Congregational, Congressional
Conglist. Congregationalist
Conn. Connecticut
cons. consultant, consulting
consol. consolidated
constl. constitutional
constn. constitution
constrn. construction
contbd. contributed
contbg. contributing
contbn. contribution
contbr. contributor
contr. controller
Conv. Convention
coop. cooperative
coord. coordinator
CORDS Civil Operations and Revolutionary Development Support
CORE Congress of Racial Equality
corp. corporation, corporate
corr. correspondent, corresponding, correspondence
C.&O.Ry. Chesapeake & Ohio Railway
coun. council
C.P.A. Certified Public Accountant
C.P.C.U. Chartered Property and Casualty Underwriter
CPH, C.P.H. Certificate of Public Health
cpl. corporal
C.P.R. Cardio-Pulmonary Resuscitation
C.P.Ry. Canadian Pacific Railway
CRT Cathode Ray Terminal
C.S. Christian Science
CSB, C.S.B. Bachelor of Christian Science
C.S.C. Civil Service Commission
CT Connecticut
ct. court
ctr. center
CWS Chemical Warfare Service
C.Z. Canal Zone

D. Doctor
d. daughter
DAgr, D.Agr. Doctor of Agriculture
DAR Daughters of the American Revolution
dau. daughter
DAV Disabled American Veterans
DC, D.C. District of Columbia
DCL, D.C.L. Doctor of Civil Law
DCS, D.C.S. Doctor of Commercial Science
DD, D.D. Doctor of Divinity
DDS, D.D.S. Doctor of Dental Surgery
DE Delaware
Dec. December
dec. deceased
def. defense
Del. Delaware
del. delegate, delegation
Dem. Democrat, Democratic
DEng, D.Eng. Doctor of Engineering
denom. denomination, denominational
dep. deputy
dept. department
dermatol. dermatological

desc. descendant
devel. development, developmental
DFA, D.F.A. Doctor of Fine Arts
D.F.C. Distinguished Flying Cross
DHL, D.H.L. Doctor of Hebrew Literature
dir. director
dist. district
distbg. distributing
distbn. distribution
distbr. distributor
disting. distinguished
div. division, divinity, divorce
DLitt, D.Litt. Doctor of Literature
DMD, D.M.D. Doctor of Medical Dentistry
DMS, D.M.S. Doctor of Medical Science
DO, D.O. Doctor of Osteopathy
DPH, D.P.H. Diploma in Public Health
DPhil, D.Phil. Doctor of Philosophy
D.R. Daughters of the Revolution
Dr. Drive, Doctor
DRE, D.R.E. Doctor of Religious Education
DrPH, Dr.P.H. Doctor of Public Health, Doctor of Public Hygiene
D.S.C. Distinguished Service Cross
DSc, D.Sc. Doctor of Science
D.S.M. Distinguished Service Medal
DST, D.S.T. Doctor of Sacred Theology
DTM, D.T.M. Doctor of Tropical Medicine
DVM, D.V.M. Doctor of Veterinary Medicine
DVS, D.V.S. Doctor of Veterinary Surgery

E, E. East
ea. eastern
E. and P. Extraordinary and Plenipotentiary
Eccles. Ecclesiastical
ecol. ecological
econ. economic
ECOSOC Economic and Social Council (of the UN)
ED, E.D. Doctor of Engineering
ed. educated
EdB, Ed.B. Bachelor of Education
EdD, Ed.D. Doctor of Education
edit. edition
EdM, Ed.M. Master of Education
edn. education
ednl. educational
EDP Electronic Data Processing
EdS, Ed.S. Specialist in Education
EE, E.E. Electrical Engineer
E.E. and M.P. Envoy Extraordinary and Minister Plenipotentiary
EEC European Economic Community
EEG Electroencephalogram
EEO Equal Employment Opportunity
EEOC Equal Employment Opportunity Commission
E.Ger. German Democratic Republic
EKG Electrocardiogram
elec. electrical
electrochem. electrochemical
electrophys. electrophysical
elem. elementary
EM, E.M. Engineer of Mines
ency. encyclopedia

Eng. England
engr. engineer
engring. engineering
entomol. entomological
environ. environmental
EPA Environmental Protection Agency
epidemiol. epidemiological
Episc. Episcopalian
ERA Equal Rights Amendment
ERDA Energy Research and Development
  Administration
ESEA Elementary and Secondary Education
  Act
ESL English as Second Language
ESPN Entertainment and Sports
  Programming Network
ESSA Environmental Science Services
  Administration
ethnol. ethnological
ETO European Theatre of Operations
Evang. Evangelical
exam. examination, examining
Exch. Exchange
exec. executive
exhbn. exhibition
expdn. expedition
expn. exposition
expt. experiment
exptl. experimental
Expwy. Expressway

F.A. Field Artillery
FAA Federal Aviation Administration
FAO Food and Agriculture Organization
  (of the UN)
FBI Federal Bureau of Investigation
FCA Farm Credit Administration
FCC Federal Communications Commission
FCDA Federal Civil Defense
  Administration
FDA Food and Drug Administration
FDIA Federal Deposit Insurance
  Administration
FDIC Federal Deposit Insurance
  Corporation
FE, F.E. Forest Engineer
FEA Federal Energy Administration
Feb. February
fed. federal
fedn. federation
FERC Federal Energy Regulatory
  Commission
fgn. foreign
FHA Federal Housing Administration
fin. financial, finance
FL Florida
Fl. Floor
Fla. Florida
FMC Federal Maritime Commission
FOA Foreign Operations Administration
found. foundation
FPC Federal Power Commission
FPO Fleet Post Office
frat. fraternity
FRS Federal Reserve System
Frwy. Freeway

FSA Federal Security Agency
Ft. Fort
FTC Federal Trade Commission

G-1 (or other number) Division of General
  Staff
GA, Ga. Georgia
GAO General Accounting Office
gastroent. gastroenterological
GATT General Agreement of Tariff and
  Trades
GE General Electric Company
gen. general
geneal. genealogical
geod. geodetic
geog. geographic, geographical
geol. geological
geophys. geophysical
gerontol. gerontological
G.H.Q. General Headquarters
GM General Motors Corporation
GMAC General Motors Acceptance
  Corporation
G.N.Ry. Great Northern Railway
gov. governor
govt. government
govtl. governmental
GPO Government Printing Office
grad. graduate, graduated
GSA General Services Administration
Gt. Great
GTE General Telephone and Electric
  Company
GU Guam
gynecol. gynecological

HBO Home Box Office
hdqrs. headquarters
HEW Department of Health, Education and
  Welfare
HHD, H.H.D. Doctor of Humanities
HHFA Housing and Home Finance Agency
HHS Department of Health and Human
  Services
HI Hawaii
hist. historical, historic
HM, H.M. Master of Humanics
HMO Health Maintenance Organization
homeo. homeopathic
hon. honorary, honorable
Ho. of Dels. House of Delegates
Ho. of Reps. House of Representatives
hort. horticultural
hosp. hospital
HUD Department of Housing and Urban
  Development
Hwy. Highway
hydrog. hydrographic

IA Iowa
IAEA International Atomic Energy Agency
IBM International Business Machines
  Corporation
IBRD International Bank for Reconstruction
  and Development

ICA International Cooperation
  Administration
ICC Interstate Commerce Commission
ICU Intensive Care Unit
ID Idaho
IEEE Institute of Electrical and Electronics
  Engineers
IFC International Finance Corporation
IGY International Geophysical Year
IL Illinois
Ill. Illinois
illus. illustrated
ILO International Labor Organization
IMF International Monetary Fund
IN Indiana
Inc. Incorporated
Ind. Indiana
ind. independent
Indpls. Indianapolis
indsl. industrial
inf. infantry
info. information
ins. insurance
insp. inspector
insp. gen. inspector general
inst. institute
instl. institutional
instn. institution
instr. instructor
instrn. instruction
internat. international
intro. introduction
IRE Institute of Radio Engineers
IRS Internal Revenue Service
ITT International Telephone & Telegraph
  Corporation

JAG Judge Advocate General
JAGC Judge Advocate General Corps
Jan. January
Jaycees Junior Chamber of Commerce
JB, J.B. Jurum Baccalaureus
JCB, J.C.B. Juris Canoni Baccalaureus
JCD, J.C.D. Juris Canonici Doctor, Juris
  Civilis Doctor
JCL, J.C.L. Juris Canonici Licentiatus
JD, J.D. Juris Doctor
jg. junior grade
jour. journal
jr. junior
JSD, J.S.D. Juris Scientiae Doctor
JUD, J.U.D. Juris Utriusque Doctor
jud. judicial

Kans. Kansas
K.C. Knights of Columbus
K.P. Knights of Pythias
KS Kansas
K.T. Knight Templar
KY, Ky. Kentucky

LA, La. Louisiana
L.A. Los Angeles
lab. laboratory
lang. language
laryngol. laryngological
LB Labrador

LDS Church Church of Jesus Christ of Latter Day Saints
lectr. lecturer
legis. legislation, legislative
LHD, L.H.D. Doctor of Humane Letters
L.I. Long Island
libr. librarian, library
lic. licensed, license
L.I.R.R. Long Island Railroad
lit. literature
LittB, Litt.B. Bachelor of Letters
LittD, Litt.D. Doctor of Letters
LLB, LL.B. Bachelor of Laws
LLD, L.L.D. Doctor of Laws
LLM, L.L.M. Master of Laws
Ln. Lane
L.&N.R.R. Louisville & Nashville Railroad
LPGA Ladies Professional Golf Association
LS, L.S. Library Science (in degree)
lt. lieutenant
Ltd. Limited
Luth. Lutheran
LWV League of Women Voters

M. Master
m. married
MA, M.A. Master of Arts
MA Massachusetts
MADD Mothers Against Drunk Driving
mag. magazine
MAgr, M.Agr. Master of Agriculture
maj. major
Man. Manitoba
Mar. March
MArch, M.Arch. Master in Architecture
Mass. Massachusetts
math. mathematics, mathematical
MATS Military Air Transport Service
MB, M.B. Bachelor of Medicine
MB Manitoba
MBA, M.B.A. Master of Business Administration
MBS Mutual Broadcasting System
M.C. Medical Corps
MCE, M.C.E. Master of Civil Engineering
mcht. merchant
mcpl. municipal
MCS, M.C.S. Master of Commercial Science
MD, M.D. Doctor of Medicine
MD, Md. Maryland
MDiv Master of Divinity
MDip, M.Dip. Master in Diplomacy
mdse. merchandise
MDV, M.D.V. Doctor of Veterinary Medicine
ME, M.E. Mechanical Engineer
ME Maine
M.E.Ch. Methodist Episcopal Church
mech. mechanical
MEd., M.Ed. Master of Education
med. medical
MEE, M.E.E. Master of Electrical Engineering
mem. member
meml. memorial
merc. mercantile

met. metropolitan
metall. metallurgical
MetE, Met.E. Metallurgical Engineer
meteorol. meteorological
Meth. Methodist
Mex. Mexico
MF, M.F. Master of Forestry
MFA, M.F.A. Master of Fine Arts
mfg. manufacturing
mfr. manufacturer
mgmt. management
mgr. manager
MHA, M.H.A. Master of Hospital Administration
M.I. Military Intelligence
MI Michigan
Mich. Michigan
micros. microscopic, microscopical
mid. middle
mil. military
Milw. Milwaukee
Min. Minister
mineral. mineralogical
Minn. Minnesota
MIS Management Information Systems
Miss. Mississippi
MIT Massachusetts Institute of Technology
mktg. marketing
ML, M.L. Master of Laws
MLA Modern Language Association
M.L.D. Magister Legnum Diplomatic
MLitt, M.Litt. Master of Literature
MLS, M.L.S. Master of Library Science
MME, M.M.E. Master of Mechanical Engineering
MN Minnesota
mng. managing
MO, Mo. Missouri
moblzn. mobilization
Mont. Montana
MP Northern Mariana Islands
M.P. Member of Parliament
MPA Master of Public Administration
MPE, M.P.E. Master of Physical Education
MPH, M.P.H. Master of Public Health
MPhil, M.Phil. Master of Philosophy
MPL, M.P.L. Master of Patent Law
Mpls. Minneapolis
MRE, M.R.E. Master of Religious Education
MS, M.S. Master of Science
MS, Ms. Mississippi
MSc, M.Sc. Master of Science
MSChemE Master of Science in Chemical Engineering
MSF, M.S.F. Master of Science of Forestry
MST, M.S.T. Master of Sacred Theology
MSW, M.S.W. Master of Social Work
MT Montana
Mt. Mount
MTO Mediterranean Theatre of Operation
MTV Music Television
mus. museum, musical
MusB, Mus.B. Bachelor of Music
MusD, Mus.D. Doctor of Music
MusM, Mus.M. Master of Music
mut. mutual
mycol. mycological

N. North
NAACP National Association for the Advancement of Colored People
NACA National Advisory Committee for Aeronautics
NAD National Academy of Design
NAE National Academy of Engineering
NAFE National Association of Female Executives
N.Am. North America
NAM National Association of Manufacturers
NAPA National Association of Performing Artists
NARAS National Academy of Recording Arts and Sciences
NAREB National Association of Real Estate Boards
NARS National Archives and Record Service
NAS National Academy of Sciences
NASA National Aeronautics and Space Administration
nat. national
NATAS National Academy of Television Arts and Sciences
NATO North Atlantic Treaty Organization
NATOUSA North African Theatre of Operations
nav. navigation
NB, N.B. New Brunswick
NBA National Basketball Association
NBC National Broadcasting Company
NC, N.C. North Carolina
NCAA National College Athletic Association
NCCJ National Conference of Christians and Jews
ND, N.D. North Dakota
NDEA National Defense Education Act
NE Nebraska
NE, N.E. Northeast
NEA National Education Association
Nebr. Nebraska
NEH National Endowment for Humanities
neurol. neurological
Nev. Nevada
NF Newfoundland
NFL National Football League
Nfld. Newfoundland
NG National Guard
NH, N.H. New Hampshire
NHL National Hockey League
NIH National Institutes of Health
NIMH National Institute of Mental Health
NJ, N.J. New Jersey
NLRB National Labor Relations Board
NM New Mexico
N.Mex. New Mexico
No. Northern
NOAA National Oceanographic and Atmospheric Administration
NORAD North America Air Defense
Nov. November
NOW National Organization for Women

N.P.Ry. Northern Pacific Railway
nr. near
NRA National Rifle Association
NRC National Research Council
NS, N.S. Nova Scotia
NSC National Security Council
NSF National Science Foundation
NSW New South Wales
N.T. New Testament
NT Northwest Territories
numis. numismatic
NV Nevada
NW, N.W. Northwest
N.W.T. Northwest Territories
NY, N.Y. New York
N.Y.C. New York City
NYU New York University
N.Z. New Zealand

OAS Organization of American States
ob-gyn obstetrics-gynecology
obs. observatory
obstet. obstetrical
Oct. October
OD, O.D. Doctor of Optometry
OECD Organization of European
  Cooperation and Development
OEEC Organization of European
  Economic Cooperation
OEO Office of Economic Opportunity
ofcl. official
OH Ohio
OK Oklahoma
Okla. Oklahoma
ON Ontario
Ont. Ontario
oper. operating
ophthal. ophthalmological
ops. operations
OR Oregon
orch. orchestra
Oreg. Oregon
orgn. organization
ornithol. ornithological
OSHA Occupational Safety and Health
  Administration
OSRD Office of Scientific Research and
  Development
OSS Office of Strategic Services
osteo. osteopathic
otol. otological
otolaryn. otolaryngological

PA, Pa. Pennsylvania
P.A. Professional Association
paleontol. paleontological
path. pathological
PBS Public Broadcasting System
P.C. Professional Corporation
PE Prince Edward Island
P.E.I. Prince Edward Island
PEN Poets, Playwrights, Editors, Essayists
  and Novelists (international association)
penol. penological
P.E.O. women's organization (full name not
  disclosed)
pers. personnel

pfc. private first class
PGA Professional Golfers' Association of
  America
PHA Public Housing Administration
pharm. pharmaceutical
PharmD, Pharm.D. Doctor of Pharmacy
PharmM, Pharm.M. Master of Pharmacy
PhB, Ph.B. Bachelor of Philosophy
PhD, Ph.D. Doctor of Philosophy
PhDChemE Doctor of Science in Chemical
  Engineering
PhM, Ph.M. Master of Philosophy
Phila. Philadelphia
philharm. philharmonic
philol. philological
philos. philosophical
photog. photographic
phys. physical
physiol. physiological
Pitts. Pittsburgh
Pk. Park
Pkwy. Parkway
Pl. Place
Pla. Plaza
P.&L.E.R.R. Pittsburgh & Lake Erie
  Railroad
P.O. Post Office
PO Box Post Office Box
polit. political
poly. polytechnic, polytechnical
PQ Province of Quebec
PR, P.R. Puerto Rico
prep. preparatory
pres. president
Presbyn. Presbyterian
presdl. presidential
prin. principal
proc. proceedings
prod. produced
prodn. production
prof. professor
profl. professional
prog. progressive
propr. proprietor
pros. atty. prosecuting attorney
pro tem pro tempore
PSRO Professional Services Review
  Organization
psychiat. psychiatric
psychol. psychological
PTA Parent-Teachers Association
ptnr. partner
PTO Pacific Theatre of Operations, Parent
  Teacher Organization
pub. publisher, publishing, published
pub. public
publ. publication
pvt. private

quar. quarterly
qm. quartermaster
Q.M.C. Quartermaster Corps
Que. Quebec

radiol. radiological
RAF Royal Air Force
RCA Radio Corporation of America

RCAF Royal Canadian Air Force
RD Rural Delivery
Rd. Road
R&D Research & Development
REA Rural Electrification Administration
rec. recording
ref. reformed
regt. regiment
regtl. regimental
rehab. rehabilitation
rels. relations
Rep. Republican
rep. representative
Res. Reserve
ret. retired
Rev. Reverend
rev. review, revised
RFC Reconstruction Finance Corporation
RFD Rural Free Delivery
rhinol. rhinological
RI, R.I. Rhode Island
RISD Rhode Island School of Design
Rm. Room
RN, R.N. Registered Nurse
roentgenol. roentgenological
ROTC Reserve Officers Training Corps
RR Rural Route
R.R. Railroad
rsch. research
Rte. Route
Ry. Railway

S. South
s. son
SAC Strategic Air Command
SAG Screen Actors Guild
SALT Strategic Arms Limitation Talks
S.Am. South America
san. sanitary
SAR Sons of the American Revolution
Sask. Saskatchewan
savs. savings
SB, S.B. Bachelor of Science
SBA Small Business Administration
SC, S.C. South Carolina
SCAP Supreme Command Allies Pacific
ScB, Sc.B. Bachelor of Science
SCD, S.C.D. Doctor of Commercial Science
ScD, Sc.D. Doctor of Science
sch. school
sci. science, scientific
SCLC Southern Christian Leadership
  Conference
SCV Sons of Confederate Veterans
SD, S.D. South Dakota
SE, S.E. Southeast
SEATO Southeast Asia Treaty Organization
SEC Securities and Exchange Commission
sec. secretary
sect. section
seismol. seismological
sem. seminary
Sept. September
s.g. senior grade
sgt. sergeant
SHAEF Supreme Headquarters Allied
  Expeditionary Forces

SHAPE Supreme Headquarters Allied
  Powers in Europe
S.I. Staten Island
S.J. Society of Jesus (Jesuit)
SJD Scientiae Juridicae Doctor
SK Saskatchewan
SM, S.M. Master of Science
So. Southern
soc. society
sociol. sociological
S.P. Co. Southern Pacific Company
spl. special
splty. specialty
Sq. Square
S.R. Sons of the Revolution
sr. senior
SS Steamship
SSS Selective Service System
St. Saint, Street
sta. station
stats. statistics
statis. statistical
STB, S.T.B. Bachelor of Sacred Theology
stblzn. stabilization
STD, S.T.D. Doctor of Sacred Theology
Ste. Suite
subs. subsidiary
SUNY State University of New York
supr. supervisor
supt. superintendent
surg. surgical
svc. service
SW, S.W. Southwest

TAPPI Technical Association of the Pulp
  and Paper Industry
Tb. Tuberculosis
tchr. teacher
tech. technical, technology
technol. technological
Tel. & Tel. Telephone & Telegraph
temp. temporary
Tenn. Tennessee
Ter. Territory
Terr. Terrace
Tex. Texas
ThD, Th.D. Doctor of Theology
theol. theological
ThM, Th.M. Master of Theology
TN Tennessee
tng. training
topog. topographical
trans. transaction, transferred
transl. translation, translated
transp. transportation
treas. treasurer
TT Trust Territory
TV television
TVA Tennessee Valley Authority
TWA Trans World Airlines
twp. township
TX Texas
typog. typographical

U. University
UAW United Auto Workers

UCLA University of California at Los
  Angeles
UDC United Daughters of the Confederacy
U.K. United Kingdom
UN United Nations
UNESCO United Nations Educational,
  Scientific and Cultural Organization
UNICEF United Nations International
  Children's Emergency Fund
univ. university
UNRRA United Nations Relief and
  Rehabilitation Administration
UPI United Press International
U.P.R.R. United Pacific Railroad
urol. urological
U.S. United States
U.S.A. United States of America
USAAF United States Army Air Force
USAF United States Air Force
USAFR United States Air Force Reserve
USAR United States Army Reserve
USCG United States Coast Guard
USCGR United States Coast Guard Reserve
USES United States Employment Service
USIA United States Information Agency
USMC United States Marine Corps
USMCR United States Marine Corps
  Reserve
USN United States Navy
USNG United States National Guard
USNR United States Naval Reserve
USO United Service Organizations
USPHS United States Public Health Service
USS United States Ship
USSR Union of the Soviet Socialist
  Republics
USTA United States Tennis Association
USV United States Volunteers
UT Utah

VA Veterans' Administration
VA, Va. Virginia
vet. veteran, veterinary
VFW Veterans of Foreign Wars
VI, V.I. Virgin Islands
vice pres. vice president
vis. visiting
VISTA Volunteers in Service to America
VITA Volunteers in Technical Service
vocat. vocational
vol. volunteer, volume
v.p. vice president
vs. versus
VT, Vt. Vermont

W, W. West
WA Washington (state)
WAC Women's Army Corps
Wash. Washington (state)
WAVES Women's Reserve, US Naval
  Reserve
WCTU Women's Christian Temperance
  Union
we. western
W. Ger. Germany, Federal Republic of
WHO World Health Organization

WI Wisconsin
W.I. West Indies
Wis. Wisconsin
WSB Wage Stabilization Board
WV West Virginia
W.Va. West Virginia
WY Wyoming
Wyo. Wyoming

YK Yukon Territory
YMCA Young Men's Christian Association
YMHA Young Men's Hebrew Association
YM & YWHA Young Men's and Young
  Women's Hebrew Association
yr. year
YT, Y.T. Yukon Territory
YWCA Young Women's Christian
  Association

zool. zoological

Alphabetical Practices

Names are arranged alphabetically according to the surnames, and under identical surnames according to the first given name. If both surname and first given name are identical, names are arranged alphabetically according to the second given name.

Surnames beginning with De, Des, Du, however capitalized or spaced, are recorded with the prefix preceding the surname and arranged alphabetically under the letter D.

Surnames beginning with Mac and Mc are arranged alphabetically under M.

Surnames beginning with Saint or St. appear after names that begin Sains, and are arranged according to the second part of the name, e.g. St. Clair before Saint Dennis.

Surnames beginning with Van, Von or von are arranged alphabetically under letter V.

Compound hyphenated surnames are arranged according to the first member of the compound. Compound unhyphenated surnames are treated as hyphenated names.

Many hyphenated Arabic names begin Al–, El–, or al–. These names are alphabetized according to each biographee's designation of last name. Thus Al–Bahar, Mohammed may be listed either under Al–or under Bahar, depending on the preference of the listee.

Parentheses used in connection with a name indicate which part of the full name is usually deleted in common usage. Hence Abbott, W(illiam) Lewis indicates that the usual form of the given name is W. Lewis. In such a case, the parentheses are ignored in alphabetizing and the name would be arranged as Abbott, William Lewis. However, if the name is recorded Abbott, (William) Lewis, signifying that the entire name William is not commonly used, the alphabetizing would be arranged as though the name were Abbott, Lewis. If an entire middle or last name is enclosed in parentheses, that portion of the name is used in the alphabetical arrangement. Hence Abbott, William (Lewis) would be arranged as Abbott, William Lewis.

Who Was Who in America

ABBE, GEORGE BANCROFT, author; b. Somers, Conn., Jan. 28, 1911; s. Harry Allen Grant and Aida (Kittredge) A.; m. Barbara Rossiter, Sept. 22, 1934. Student, Cushing Acad., 1928; B.A., U. N.H., 1933; M.A., U. Iowa, 1938. Tchr. lit., writing Mt. Holyoke Coll., Yale U., Columbia U., U. Iowa, U. Maine, U. Pitts., Wayne U., Springfield Coll., U. N.H.; staff writers confs. U. N.H., Idaho State Coll., Corpus Christi (Tex.) Fine Arts Colony, Wooster (Ohio) Coll., Western Mass., State of Maine, Cape Cod, others; co-dir. New Eng. Writers Conf., Suffield (Conn.) Acad.; faculty Tchrs. Coll. Conn., New Britain, 1955-57; asst. prof. English Russell Sage Coll., 1958-64, assoc. prof. English, 1964-67, resident author, 1958-67; prof. humanities, writer-in-residence State Univ. Coll., Plattsburgh, N.Y.; dir. Champlain Writers Conf. Mem. editorial bd. Book Club for Poetry; adv. editor: Poetry Public; author: Voices in the Square, 1938, Dreamer's Clay, 1940, Wait for These Things, 1940, Letter Home, 1945, Mr. Quill's Crusade, 1948, The Wide Plains Roar, 1954, Bird in the Mulberry, 1954, Poetry, the Great Therapy, 1956, The Incandescent Beast, 1957, The Winter House, 1957, One More Puritan, 1960; play The Adomatic Man, 1960; The Collected Poems of George Abbe, 1935-61, 1961, Stephen Vincent Benet on Writing, 1964, You and Contemporary Poetry: An Aid-to-Appreciation, 1964, The Larks, 1965, The Non-conformist, 1966, The Funeral, 1967, Shatter the Day, 1968, Yonderville, 1969, Dreams and Dissent, New Poems, 1961-70, 1971, Abbe and Benét, 1973, The Pigeon Lover (fiction-biography), 1981; editor: Hill Wind, 1935; Contbr. short stories and poems to books, mags., lit. publs.; rec. artist, Folkways Corp., poems, Two hour rec. of poems, Library of Congress. Recipient Shelley Meml. award, 1956. Mem. Poetry Soc. Am. Home: Plattsburgh N.Y. Died Mar. 15, 1989; buried Guilford, Conn. †

ABBOTT, BERENICE, photographer; b. Springfield, Ohio, July 17, 1898; d. Charles E. and Alice (Bunn) A. Student, Ohio State U., 1917-18, Kunstschule, Berlin, 1923; hon. doctorate degree, U. Maine, 1971, Smith Coll., 1973, New Sch. Social Research, 1981, Bowdain Coll., 1982, Bates Coll., 1981. Photography asst. Man Ray, Paris, 1923-25; owner photog. studio Paris, 1926-29; profl. portrait photographer; returned to N.Y., 1929; specialized in documentary and portrait photography; photographer Fed. Arts Project, N.Y.C., 1930-39. Exhbns. include, Mus. Modern Art, N.Y.C., Smithsonian Instn., Washington, Marlborough Gallery, N.Y., Lunn Gallery, Washington, Bklyn. Mus., Art Inst. Chgo., Vision Gallery, Boston, N.Y. Pub. Libr., Oct-Jan, 1989-90; works represented in permanent collections Mus. Modern Art, N.Y.C., Met. Mus. Art, N.Y.C., Mus. Fine Arts, Boston, Smithsonian Instn., Washington, Art Inst. Chgo., Mus. Fine Arts, Houston, San Francisco Mus. Art, Bibliothèque Nationale, Paris, N.Y. Pub. Libr.; books include Changing New York, 1939, Greenwich Village Today and Yesterday, 1949, A Portrait of Maine, 1968, Berenice Abbott Photographs, 1970, Guide to Better Photography, 1941, 53, The View Camera Made Simple, 1948, The World of Atget, 1964, Berenice Abbott American Photographer, 1982. Recipient Friends of Photography award, 1983, Internat. Erice prize for Photography, 1987. Mem. Am. Acad. Inst. Arts Letters (hon.). Home: Monson ME Died Dec. 10, 1991. †

ABBOTT, CHARLES HOMER, rope company executive; b. Houston, Dec. 29, 1909; s. Charles Howard and Lela (Hunt) A.; m. Jane Millikin, Apr. 5, 1940; children: Edwin Hunt, John Millikin, Betsy, Fred Hardy. Student, U. Nebr., 1928-29; A.B., Yale U., 1932; LL.B., St. Lawrence U., 1938. Employed sales dept. U.S. Indsl. Alcohol Co., N.Y.C., 1932-33, Nat. Distillers Products Corp., 1933-42; O.P.A.; field operations officer Fuel Rationing div., 1942-43; asst. to adminstr. in charge of price bds. O.P.A., 1946-47; sp. sales rep. Gt. Lakes Steel Corp., 1947-49; Southeastern mgr. Gen. Plywood Corp., 1949-51, gen. sales mgr., 1951-52, v.p., 1952-55; sales mgr. panel and door div. Atlas Plywood Corp., gen. mgr., 1956-58; v.p. marketing Stylon Corp., Milford, Mass., 1958-62; dir. Stylon Corp., 1959-63, Samson Cordage Works, Boston, 1962-76; pres. Samson Cordage Works, 1963-75, chmn. bd., 1975-76; chmn. bd. Samson Ocean Systems, Inc., 1976-79, ret., 1979; pres., chmn. exec. com. Cordage Inst., 1977-79. Served to lt. USN, 1943-46. Mem. Harvard Club, Yale Club (assoc.), Phi Delta Theta, Phi Delta Phi. Home: Weston Mass. Deceased. †

ABBRUZZESE, ALBERT VINCENT, JR., investment executive, educator; b. Boston, May 14, 1950; s. Albert Vincent Sr. and Angelina (Guerrerio) A. BS, Boston Coll., 1972; postgrad., N.Y. Inst. Fin., 1977. Account executive Prudential-Bache Securities, New Orleans, 1976-77; investment exec. Shearson Am. Express, New Orleans, 1977-82; portfolio mgr. E.F. Hutton, Inc., New Orleans, 1982-87; v.p. investments Prudential-Bache Securities, New Orleans, 1987-88; pres. investments Dean Witter Reynolds, New Orleans, 1988-89; adj. prof. fin. Tulane U., New Orleans, from 1980. Bd. dirs. ACLU, New Orleans, 1985-88, Mental Health Assn. of Greater New Orleans, 1985-88, Mental Health Assn. in La., from 1985; pres. Park Timbers Homeowners Assn., New Orleans, 1984-86. Mem. Internat. Assn. Fin. Planners (assoc.). Democrat. Roman Catholic. Home: Quincy Mass. Died March 3, 1989.

ABE, SHINTARO, Japanese government official; b. Apr. 29, 1924; Mem. Japanese Ho. of Reps., from 1958; pvt. sec. to Prime Minister Nobusuke Kishi, 1957-58; former dep. sec.-gen. Liberal Democratic Party, former v.p. diet policy com., chmn. diet policy com., 1976-77, chmn. policy affairs research council, 1979-81, chmn. exec. council, sec. gen., 1989; minister of Agr. and Forestry, 1974-76; chief cabinet sec., 1977-78; minister of Internat. Trade and Industry, 1981-82; minister of Fgn. Affairs, 1982-86; former polit. reporter Mainichi newspaper; mem. internat. adv. council Inst. Internat. Studies. Died May 16, 1991. Home: Tokyo Japan

ABEGG, EUGENE, banker; b. Blakesburg, Iowa, Oct. 10, 1897; s. Walter and Katherine (Smith) A.; m. Florence McCaig, June 7, 1922; 1 child, Margery Finch. Ed. pub. schs. Clk. Ottumwa Nat. Bank, 1916; clk., then cashier Kenwood Nat. Bank, Chgo., 1917-29; v.p. Hyde Park Kenwood Nat. Bank, Chgo., 1929-31; pres. South Side Trust & Savs. Bank, Chgo., 1931-32; cashier Ill. Nat. Bank & Trust Co., Rockford, 1932-35, pres., from 1935; bd. dirs. numerous cos. Trustee Rockford Meml. Hosp. *

ABEL, THEODORE, educator; b. Lodz, Poland, Nov. 24, 1896; s. Theodore and Jadwiga (Lorenz) A.; m. Theodora Mead, Nov. 9, 1923; children: Peter, Caroline, Zita. MA, Columbia U., 1925, PhD, 1939. Asst. prof. U. Ill., 1925-29; mem. faculty Columbia U., 1929-51, prof., 1950-51; prof. Hunter Coll., from 1951, chmn. dept. sociology & anthropology, from 1950. Author: Systematic Sociology in Germany, 1929, Why Hitler Came Into Power, 1938. Served in Polish Army, 1918-21. Mem. Ea. Sociol. Soc. *

ABEL, WILLARD EDWARD, agriculturist, consultant; b. Vancouver, Wash., Aug. 10, 1906; s. Charlie Edward and Julia (Wilson) A.; m. Hazel Belle Shoemaker, Nov. 1, 1930; 1 son, David. A.A., Centralia Jr. Coll., 1927. With Westin Hotels & Resorts (formerly Western Internat. Hotels), 1925-71; successively room clk., asst. mgr., mgr. Western Internat. Hotels Co., 1930-53, v.p., 1953-62, sr. v.p., 1963-71; pres., gen. mgr. Hotel Sir Francis Drake, San Francisco, 1947-59; exec. v.p. St. Francis Hotel Corp., 1959-61, pres., 1961-72; also dir.; pres. Internat. Western Hotels Ltd., 1965-71, Ellis O'Farrell Garage Corp., 1965-76; v.p. Western Internat. Mgmt. Co., Hoteles Biltmore de Guatemala; sr. v.p., dir. Western Internat. Hotels Co., to 1970; cons. in field; farmer, apple grower, Sebastopol, Calif. Served in AUS, 1941-46; lt. col. Q.M. Mem. Am. Hotel and Motel Assn. (pres. 1965, pres., dir. ednl. inst.), Calif. Hotel Assn. (past pres., dir.), San Francisco C. of C. (dir.). Home: Sebastopol Calif. Deceased. †

ABERNATHY, MABRA GLENN, political science educator; b. Birmingham, Ala., Nov. 25, 1921; s. James Robert and Lynia Esther (Vines) A.; m. Nancy Katherine Perry, Sept. 6, 1949; children: M. Glenn, T. Duncan, Richard C. B.S., Birmingham-So. Coll., 1942; M.A., U. Ala., 1947; Ph.D., U. Wis., 1953. Asst. city mgr. Mountain Brook, Ala., 1947-48; instr. polit. sci. U. Ala., 1948-49; mem. faculty dept. polit. sci. U. S.C., Columbia, 1951-90; Olin D. Johnston prof. polit. sci. U. S.C., 1977-86, disting. prof. emeritus, 1986-90; vis. asst. prof. U. Wis., 1959-60; vis. prof. U. Southampton (Eng.), 1982. Author The Right of Assembly and Association, 1961, 2d edit., 1981, Civil Liberties Under the Constitution, 5th edit, 1989; co-editor: The Carter Years, 1984. Served with USAF, 1942-46. Methodist. Club: Kosmos (Columbia). Home: Columbia S.C. Died June 6, 1990; buried Birmingham, Ala.

ABERNATHY, RALPH DAVID, clergyman; b. Linden, Ala., Mar. 11, 1926; s. W.L. and Louivery (Bell) A.; m. Juanita Odessa Jones, Aug. 31, 1952; children: Juandalynn Ralpheda, Donzaleigh Avis, Ralph David III, Kwame Luthuli. B.S., Ala. State Coll., 1950; M.A. in Sociology, Atlanta U., 1951; LL.D., Allen U., S.C., 1960, Southampton Coll., L.I. U., 1969, Ala. State U., Montgomery, 1974; D.D. (hon.), Morehouse Coll., 1971, Kalamazoo Coll., 1978. Personnel counselor, instr. social sci. Ala. State Coll., 1951; ordained to ministry Bapt. Ch., 1948; pastor First Bapt. Ch., Montgomery, Ala., 1951-61, West Hunter St. Bapt. Ch., Atlanta, 1961-90. Author: And The Walls Came Tumbling Down, 1989. Organizer Montgomery Improvement Assn., 1955, initiator bus. boycott, Montgomery, 1955, an organizer, 1957; since financial sec.-treas. So. Christian Leadership Conf., v.p. at large, then pres., 1968-77; leader Poor People's Campaign, Resurrection City, Washington, 1968; chmn. Commn. on Racism and Apartheid; addressed UN, 1971; mem. Atlanta Ministers Union; organizer, chmn. Operation Breadbasket, Atlanta; mem. adv. com. Congress of Racial Equality; participant World Peace Council Presdl. Com. Meeting, Santiago, Chile, 1972; active local ARC, Am. Cancer Soc., YMCA. Recipient Peace medal German Democratic Republic, 1971. Mem. NAACP, Kappa Alpha Psi, Phi Delta Kappa. Club: Mason (32 deg.). Home: Atlanta Ga. Died Apr. 17, 1990. †

ABKOWITZ, MARTIN AARON, ocean engineering educator, physicist; b. Revere, Mass., Sept. 19, 1918; s. Max and Annie (Weise) A.; m. Davette Eisenstein, Mar. 9, 1947; children: Janis Lynne, Mark David, Suzanne Jill. S.B. in Naval Architecture, Mass. Inst. Tech., 1940; A.M. in Physics, Harvard, 1949, Ph.D. in Physics, 1953. Naval architect David Taylor Model Basin, 1940-42, physicist, 1946-49; faculty MIT, 1949-88, prof. ocean engring., 1959-88, prof. emeritus, from 1988; cons. engr., from 1949, Fulbright lectr., Denmark, 1962-63, France, 1971-72, Israel, 1979. Served to capt. AUS, 1942-46. Recipient Humboldt award, 1990. Mem. Soc. Naval Architects and Marine Engrs., Sigma Xi. Home: Lexington Mass. Deceased. †

ABRAMS, TALBERT, aviator, photogrammetrist, instrument manufacturer, scientific consultant and explorer; b. Tekonsha, Mich., Aug. 17, 1895; s. William Blodgett and Sarah Elizabeth (Bruner) A.; m. Leota Fry, Jan. 15, 1923 (dec. Feb. 1978). Student, U.S. Naval Aero. Sch., Pensacola, Fla., 1917; D.Sc. (hon.), Mich. Coll. Mining and Tech., 1952; D.Eng. (hon.), Mich. State U., 1961; LL.D. (hon.), Western Mich. U., 1971. U.S. transport pilot signed by Orville Wright, Air Mail Service, 192O, Mich. Aero. Service Corp., 1921; v.p. Mich. Airways, 1922; pres. Abrams Aerial Survey Corp., Lansing, Mich., 1923-58, chmn., bd. dirs., from 1958; pres. Abrams Aircraft Corp., 1936-44, Abrams Instrument Corp. (merged with Curtiss-Wright Corp., 1937-61, Airlandia, Inc., from 1954, Aerial Explorers Corp., from 1961; sci. cons. Curtiss- Wright Corp.; founder Abrams Research & Test Center, Mich., 1955; mapped Isle Royale, 1929, also large areas for U.S. Govt., 1917—, P.R., 1935-37, Dominican Republic, W.I., 1940-41, Cuba, 1935-44, for Liberian Survey Firestone Plantations Co.; mem. U.S. Navy-NSF Operation Deep Freeze, 1963-67; numerous aerial surveys fgn. countries; del. several internat. congresses; served in civilian capacity for USMC, U.S. Army, USAF, USN.; Pres. Talbert & Leota Abrams Found., from 1960. Author: The Essentials of Aerial Surveys and Photo Interpretation (used as textbook USMC, Army and Navy). Donor Talbert Abrams award, Am. Soc. Photogrammetry, from 1944; donor Talbert and Leota Abrams Planetarium to Mich. State U., 1961, Meridian-Base Line Surveyors Park (hist. site) to State of Mich., 1967; donated Stratoplane Explorer to Nat. Air Mus., Smithsonian Instn., Washington. Served with aviation sect. USMC, 1917-19; Served with aviation sect. U.S. Army AC Res., 1924-34. Recipient Civilian Service award U.S. Army; Order Arctic Realm USAF, Alaska; Hon. Centennial award Mich. State U., 1955; Community Service award City of Lansing, Mich., 1962; Order of Magellan Circumnavigators Club, 1963; apptd. indsl. ambassador State Mich., 1958; named to OX-5 Aviation Hall of Fame, 1972; Antartic mountain named Abrams Mountain, 1966. Mem. NAM (nuclear energy com.), ASCE, Mich. Soc. Civil Engrs. (hon.), Am. Soc. Photogrammetry (pres. 1951, hon. life mem.), Mich. Engring. Soc. (hon.), Detroit Soc. Engrs., Mich. Soc. Profl. Engrs. (hon.), Am. Congress Surveying and Mapping (hon), Soc. of South Pole, Australian Inst. Cartographers, Quiet Birdmen, Soc. Am. Mil. Engrs., Am. Ordnance Assn. (past v.p.), Am. Legion, VFW, First Marine Aviation Force Vets. Assn., Last Man Pioneer Air Mail Club, Chi Epsilon (hon.), Pi Tau Sigma (hon.), Tau Beta Pi (hon). Clubs: Masons (N.Y.C.), Rotary (N.Y.C.), Explorers (N.Y.C.), Wings

(N.Y.C.); Lansing Engrs, City (dir.), Lansing Country, Circumnavigators. Home: Lansing Mich. †

ABRELL, RONALD LANE, education educator; b. Coal City, Ind., Mar. 14, 1934; s. Osce W. and Pauline A. A.; B.S., Ind. State U., 1959, M.S., 1962; Ed.D., Mont. State U., 1972; m. JoAnn Barnhizer, Mar. 31, 1963; 1 son, Lane. Tchr. social scis. Shelbyville (Ind.) High Sch., 1959-62, Broad Ripple High Sch., Inspls., 1962-67, North Putnam Sch. Corp., Bainbridge, Ind., 1967-68; coordinator student teaching in Chgo., Western Ill. U., Macomb, Ill., 1968-73; prof. edn. Coll. Edn., Macomb,from 1973, dir. student teaching, chmn. ednl. field experiences, 1973-81, asst. to dean, 1981-83; pres. Am. Nat. Bus. Hall of Fame,from 1983. Served with U.S. Army, 1953-55. Mem. Ill. Assn. Tchr. Educators (pres. 1978-79, chmn. legis. com. 1977-78, 79-80), Am. Assn. Sch. Adminstrs., Assn. Supervision and Curriculum Devel., Horace Mann League, N. Am. Soc. Tng. and Devel., Am. Mgmt. Assn., Am. Assn. Community and Jr. Colls., Assn. Tchr. Educators, World Future Soc., Phi Delta Kappa. Democrat. Club: Elks. Author: Strictly for Student Teachers, 1973; contbr. articles to profl. jours. Deceased. Home: Matteson Ill. †

ACCETTURA, GUY, electrical products manufacturing company executive; b. Ceglie del Campo, Italy, Feb. 23, 1919; came to U.S., 1928; s. Vito L. and Maria (Roppo) A.; m. Mabel G. Blindell, May 11, 1946; children—Raymond V., Paul G., Carl J., Janet Rosalie, Linda Margaret. Student, Ill. Inst. Tech., 1936-38; B.S. cum laude in Commerce, De Paul U., 1948. With Western Electric Co., 1936-66, 69-82, dir. orgn. planning, 1964-65, v.p., 1965-66, v.p. mfg., Newark,, 1969-76, exec. v.p., 1976-79, sr. exec. v.p., 1979-82, also bd. dirs.; v.p., gen mgr. Bell Telephone Labs., Murray Hill, N.J., 1966-69. Mem. Columbus Water Planning Commn., 1963-64; Bd. dirs., pres. YM/YWCA of Newark and Vicinity, 1973-74; trustee, exec. com. N.J. Symphony Orch.; trustee, exec. com., sec. N.J. Symphony Hall; trustee Western Electric Fund, 1971-76, Rutgers U. Found., 1977-78, Bucknell U., 1981-91, Acting Co., 1981-87. Served with AUS, 1942-46, ETO. Decorated Bronze Star. Mem. NAM, Columbus C. of C. (dir. 1963-64), Pi Gamma Mu. Club: Rotarian. Home: Wyckoff N.J. Died Oct. 20, 1991; buried Mahwah, N.J.

ACE, GOODMAN, writer; b. Kansas City, Mo., Jan. 15, 1899; m. Jane Sherwood, 1928. Began career as cub reporter Kansas City Jour.-Post, later became movie and play reviewer; writer Easy Aces radio show, 1928-45; chief writer Danny Kaye program; supr. comedy programs CBS, 1946, charge devel. new radio programs; writer Tallulah Bankhead's radio program The Big Show, 1950-52; permanent guest radio show Jane Ace, Disc Jockey, 1951-52; head writer Milton Berle, 1952-55, also TV columnist Saturday Rev.; head writer Perry Como show, 1955-59. Prodr., writer variety shows, five CBS spectaculars; creator CBS Open House, 1960. *

ACERRA, ANGELO THOMAS, bishop; b. Memphis, Nov. 7, 1925. Student, St. Benedict's, Atchison, Kans., Cath. U. Am., St. Mary's U., San Antonio, U. No. Colo., Angelicum, Rome. Ordained priest Roman Cath. Ch., 1950. Titular bishop of Lete; aux. bishop Mil. Vicariate, 1983-90. Home: Alexandria Va. Died July 26, 1990.

ACKER, DAVID DE PEYSTER, engineer, educator; b. Newark, Oct. 12, 1921; s. David De Peyster and Lillian Mulford (Gillmor) A.; m. Lillian Radcliff Work, Apr. 9, 1949; children: Suzanne Clark, Maritta Fairchild. BS in Mech. Engring., Rutgers U., 1948, MS, 1950 . Tool designer Wright Aero. Corp., Paterson, N.J., 1940-42; design engr. Am. Tool Engring. Co., N.Y.C., 1942; asst. to chief engr. Bright Star Battery Co., Clifton, N.J., 1945-46; instr. mech. engring. Rutgers U., 1948-51, Va. Polytech. Inst., summer 1950; with N.Am. Rockwell Corp., El Segundo, Calif., 1951-70, mem. sr. tech. staff, sr. v.p. research and engring., 1966-70; staff engr., dir. def. research and engring. Office Sec. Def., Washington, 1970-73; sr. mem. research staff, asso. dean adminstrn., prof. mgmt. Def. Systems Mgmt. Coll., Ft. Belvoir, Va., 1973—; instr., vis. lectr. UCLA, 1957-68; lectr. various univs. Served with AUS, 1942-45. Decorated Bronze Star medal, others; recipient Cert. of Merit Electronic Industries Assn., 1974, Outstanding Performance award Def. Systems Mgmt. Coll., 1975-81, Exceptional Performance award, 1982-90, Comdr.'s award for Civilian Svc., 1986, Cert. Appreciation mfg. mgmt. com. Nat. Security Indsl. Assn., 1983, Cert. Appreciation Nat. Cryptologic Sch., 1986. Mem. ASME (chmn. exec. com. mgmt. div., 1973-74, mem. gen. engring. dept., policy bd. 1975-81, nat. membership devel. com. 1978-82, coun. on engring. 1981-83, Gantt Bd. of Awards 1983-92, chmn. 1983-84, Centennial medal, other awards), Am. Soc. Engring. Edn., Soc. Mfg. Engrs., Sigma Xi. Presbyterian (elder). Author: Skill in Communication, a Vital Element in Effective Management, 1980, 2d edit., 1990; A History of the Defense Systems Management College: Center of Excellence in Acquisition Management Education and Research, 1986; contbr. over 200 articles to profl. lit. Deceased. Home: McLean Va. †

ACKERLY, S(AMUEL) SPAFFORD, physician; b. Blkyn., May 20, 1895; s. George Briggs and Nancy Spafford (Brown) A.; m. Carita Clark, Oct. 17, 1925; children: William Clark, Carita Jane, Nancy Lavinia, Elizabeth Spafford. AB, Wesleyan U., 1921; MD, Yale U., 1925. Intern N.Y. Hosp., 1926; clin. dir. Worcester State Hosp., 1928-30; asst. prof., rsch. assoc. Yale Inst. Human Rels., 1930-32; dir. Louisville Mental Hygiene Clinic, from 1932; prof. psychiatry U. Louisville, 1932-63, Disting. prof., from 1963, chmn. dept., 1947-63, psychiatrist in residence, from 1963; chief svc. Norton Psychiat. Clinic, 1949-63. Trustee Louisville Pub. Libr., 1950-60. With inf. U.S. Army, 1917-20. Recipient John S. Guggenheim rsch. fellowship, 1959. Fellow ACP, Am. Orthopsychiat. Assn., Am. Psychiat. Assn., Coll. Am. Psychiatrists; mem. Am. Acad. Child Psychiatry, Am. Acad. Psychoanalysis, Am. Acad. Neurology, So. Med. Assn., Ky. Psychiat. Assn., Louisville Art Ctr. Assn., others. *

ACKERMAN, HARRY S., television executive, producer; b. Albany, N.Y., Nov. 17, 1912; s. Harold and Anna (Flannery) A.; m. Elinor Donahue, Apr. 21, 1961; children—Brian, Peter, James, Christopher; children by previous marriage—Susan, Stephen. A.B., Dartmouth, 1935. Free-lance writer and actor, 1935-36; radio dir. Young & Rubicam, N.Y.C., 1936-42, radio prodn. head, 1942-45, v.p. charge radio programs, 1945; exec. producer CBS, N.Y.C., 1948; dir. network programs CBS, Hollywood, Calif., 1948; v.p., dir. TV and radio CBS, Hollywood, 1949-51, v.p. charge TV, 1951-55; exec. dir. spl. prodns. CBS-TV, 1956-57; pres. Ticonderoga Prodns., ind. producer TV, 1957-58; v.p., exec. producer Screen Gems Pictures Corp. div. Columbia Pictures Industries, Inc., 1958-73; head Harry Ackerman Prodns.; v.p. Capitol Pictures, Inc., Hollywood; spl. radio cons. U.S. Treasury, 1944-46. Co-creator TV shows The Flying Nun, Bewitched. Bd. dirs. TV Acad. Found.; trustee, mem. exec. com. Motion Picture and TV Fund. Mem. Acad. TV Arts and Scis. (past pres. Los Angeles, past nat. pres.), Manuscripts Soc. (charter, dir.), Am. Arbitration Assn. Club: Dartmouth So. Calif. Home: North Hollywood Calif. Died Feb. 3, 1991.

ACKLEN, GERALD GILL, journalist; b. Portland, Oreg., Dec. 9, 1907; s. Gerald Jasper and Josephine (Gill) A.; m. Ruth Dinges, Sept. 7, 1940; children: Ruthann Acklen de la Vega, Linda Jo Acklen Chieffo, Gerald Craig, Daniel William. BS, U. Oreg., 1942. Tchr. schs., 1935-39; sch. prin., Madras, 1940-42, Grants Pass, Oreg., 1942-45; life ins. underwriter Mut. of N.Y., Grants Pass, 1945-69; wire editor Daily Courier, Grants Pass, 1950-61, sports and city editor, 1961-63, regional editor, sports, 1963-65, sports, 1963-77, hist. editor, 1977-92; news corr. for AP, also for UPI, 1950-76, Oreg. Jour., 1942-82, Oreg. Sports, 1950-76; publicity dir. So. Oreg. Horse Racing Assn., 1978-81. Pres., Josephine County Diabetes Assn., 1976-79, program chmn., 1979-92; bd. dirs. Oreg. affiliate Am. Diabetes Assn., 1981-1 bd. dirs. Josephine County Community Concert Assn., 1946-68, pres., 1961-64; scoutmaster Boy Scouts Am., Grants Pass, 1942-45, mem. troop com., 1945-48; mem. ofcl. bd. Methodist Ch., 1959-65, 70-82, head usher, 1949-87; mem. Grants Pass Centennial Commn., 1983-85. Lodge: Masons. Deceased. Home: Grants Pass Oreg. †

ACUFF, ROY CLAXTON, singer, fiddler, bandleader; b. Maynardville, Tenn., Sept. 15, 1903; s. Neill and Ida (Carr) A.; m. Mildred Louise Douglas, Dec. 25, 1936 (dec.); 1 son, Roy Neil. Ed. pub. schs., Knoxville, Tenn. Co-owner Acuff-Rose Pub. Co., Hickory Records. Profl. singer, musician, Doc Hower's Medicine Show, then performer with his band The Crazy Tennesseans (name later Smoky Mountain Boys), Sta. WNOK, Knoxville, Tenn., rec. artist, Columbia Records, 1936, Mem. Grand Ole Opry radio program, from 1938, 1st appearance with Smoky Mountain Boys on Grand Ole Opry, 1938, appeared with Grand Ole Opry, 1938-92 ; songs include The Precious Jewel, Great Speckled Bird, Wabash Cannonball, Wreck on the Highway, Night Train to Memphis, Beneath the Lonely Mountain of Clay; albums include Roy Acuff and His Smoky Mountain Boys, Greatest Hits, How Beautiful Heaven Must Be, King of Country, Smoky Mountain Memories, That's Country, Greatest Hits Vol. II; film appearances include Grand Ole Opry, 1940, Hi Neighbor, 1942, My Darling Clementine, 1943, Sing, Neighbor Sing, 1944, Cowboy Canteen, 1944, Night Train to Memphis, 1946; yearly tours for, U.S.O., 1949-71. Nominee for gov. Tenn., 1948. Named to Country Music Hall of Fame, 1962; recipient Grammy Lifetime Achievement award, 1987, Nat. Medal of Arts award, 1991. Home: Nashville Tenn. Died Nov. 22, 1992. †

ACZEL, THOMAS, chemist; b. Nagykanizsa, Hungary, Dec. 18, 1930; came to U.S., 1959; s. Joseph Aczel and Elisabeth (Fischer) Vajda-Aczel; m. Mollie Goodman, July 15, 1962; children: Joseph Israel, Stephen Max, Elisabeth Anne, Bettina Vera. DSc, U. Trieste, Italy, 1954. Tech. cons. Aquila Refinery, Trieste, 1954-55, Rome, 1955-58; rsch. chemist rsch. div. Humble Oil and Refining Co. (now Exxon Rsch. and Engrg. Co.), Baytown, Tex., 1959-63, sr. rsch. chemist, 1963-66; rsch. specialist Exxon Rsch. & Engring. Co., Clinton, N.J., 1966-68, rsch. assoc., 1968-76, sr. rsch. assoc., 1976-83, sci. advisor, 1983-86, sci. advisor corp. rsch. Analytical Scis. Lab., from 1986; cons. Oak Ridge (Tenn.) Nat. Lab., 1975-76. Author numerous book chpts., articles U.S. and fgn. publs.; editorial bd. Mass Spectroscopy Revs., 1981-85, Energy and Fuels, from 1990. Bd. dirs. Baytown Friends Sterling Libr., Baytown Symphony Orch., 1975-78. Recipient Profl. award Baytown Soc. Profl. Engrs. and Chemists, 1967. Mem. Am. Chem. Soc. (bd. dirs. S.E. Tex. sect. 1975, 78, 79, chmn. edn. com. 1979-81, chmn. sect. 1982, nat. counsellor 1986-87, chmn. membership com. div. petroleum chemistry 1987-90, div. fuels, chmn.-elect, 1990, Best Paper award div. fuels 1969, Profl. award S.E. Tex. sect. 1978, Nat. award 1989, Thomas Aczel year ly award for excellence in chem. edn. established in his name by S.E. chpt.), ASTM (chmn. rsch. div. IV sect. M 1971-89, sec. com. E-14, 1979-80, chmn. com. 1982-83, editor spl. publ. 1983), Am. Soc. for Mass Spectrometry (charter, chmn. nominating com. 1979-80, bd. dirs. 1982-83). Jewish. Died May 19, 1991; buried Houston, Tex.

ADAM, MALCOLM, life insurance executive; b. Phila., Feb. 21, 1895; s. James and Elizabeth (Evans) A.; m. Margaret E. Redheffer, June 12, 1928; children: Adrienne E. Sharples, Margaret E. LLB, Temple U., 1920. Bar: Pa. 1920. Associated with Penn Mut. Life Ins. Co., Phila., from 1911, v.p. in charge ops., 1937-49, pres., 1949-61, chmn. bd., 1961-62, chmn. exec. com., from 1962; lectr., later prof. ins. law Temple U., 1921-27. Trustee Penn Mut. Life Ins. Co. Phila.; dir. Fidelity-Phila. Trust Co., Phila.; formerly regional v.p. Navy League of U.S., 4th Naval Dist., World War II. Mem. Life Ins. Assn. Am., Nat. Indsl. Conf. Bd., St. Andrew's Soc. *

ADAM, THOMAS RITCHIE, political science educator; b. Brechin, Scotland, May 7, 1900; came to U.S., 1930; s. Thomas Beat and Janet (Robertson) A. Student, Merchiston Castle Sch., 1914-18; MA with honors in history, U. Edinburgh, 1923, LLB, 1924; student, Gray's Inn, Inns of Court, London, 1925. Assoc. chmn. Devel. and Migration Commn., Commonwealth of Australia, Melbourne, 1926-30; assoc. prof. polit. sci. Occidental Coll., Calif., 1930-37; field rep. Am. Assn. for Adult Edn., N.Y.C., 1937-39; prof. polit. sci. NYU, 1949-90. Author: The Civic Value of Museums, 1937, Museums and Popular Culture, 1938, Popular Education for International Understanding, 1949, Modern Colonialism: Institutions and Policies, 1955, Government and Policies in Africa, South of the Sahara, 1959. Lt. col. The Black Watch, British Armed Forces, 1939-45; mil. asst. to dep. chief of Imperial Gen. Staff (British), 1944. Decorated Officer of the Order of Orange Nassau (with swords) Holland, 1945. Mem. Am. Polit. Sci. Assn., Phi Beta Kappa. Home: New York N.Y. Died Oct. 13, 1990.

ADAMS, CHARLES ARTHUR, municipal financial analyst; b. Caldwell, Idaho, July 25, 1933; s. John Woodrow and Eileen (Vail) A.; BA, Coll. Idaho, 1962; m. Susan Rae Donovan, Jan. 30, 1960; children: Michael C., Teresa M. Sales mgr. Hoppins Ins. Agy., Nampa, Idaho, 1961-63; auditor Indsl. Indemnity Ins. Co., Boise, Idaho, 1964-65, Argonaut Ins. Co., Portland, 1966-67; br. mgr. Am. Mut. Ins. Co., Portland, 1968-70; underwriting mgr. Alaska Pacific Assurance Co., Juneau, 1970-73; pres. A.I.M. Ins. Inc., Anchorage, 1973-78, pres. parent co. A.I.M. Corp., 1977-78, also sr. v.p. A.I.M. Internat., Tokyo, 1975-78; fin. officer City of Petersburg (Alaska), 1978, City of Homer (Alaska), 1979; fin. analyst Municipality of Anchorage, from 1980; community adv. bd. KSKA, from 1983. Vol. in corrections, State of Alaska, 1981; mem. central com. Libertarian Party of Alaska, 1981-84, vice chmn., from 1985, chmn., Anchorage, 1982-83. Sgt. maj. AUS, USARSF 1952-76, ret. Mem. Resource Devel. Council Alaska, Homebuilders Alaska (dir. 1974-78), Homeowners Warranty Council Alaska (v.p. 1977), Porsche Club Am., Airborne Assn., VFW, Am. Legion, Spl. Forces Decade Assn., Alaska Council Sports Car Clubs (dir. 1976-78), Alaska World Affairs Council (chmn. fin. and devel. com. 1983-84, dir. from 1984, univ. and coll. liaison com. from 1985). Clubs: Toastmasters (named Summit Club Speaker of Yr. 1969), Wednesday Club, Captain Cook Athletic. Lodge: KC. Author: fin. procedures and master policy to insure constrn. of Alaska pipeline. Deceased. Home: Anchorage AK †

ADAMS, EVA BERTRAND, management consultant; b. Wonder, Nev.; d. Verner Lauer and Cora (Varble) A. B.A., U. Nev.; M.A., Columbia, 1937; LL.B., Washington Coll. Law, 1948; LL.M., George Washington U., 1950; LL.D., U. Portland, 1966, U. Nev., 1967; J.D., Am. U., 1969. Bar: Nev. and D.C. bars 1950. Tchr. Las Vegas High Sch.; asst. dean Women, instr. English U. Nev., 1937-40; administrv. asst. to Sen. Pat McCarran, 1940-54, Sen. Ernest Brown, 1954, Sen. Alan Bible, 1954-61; dir. Bur. of Mint, Washington, 1961-69; mgmt. cons., from 1969; dir. Fund Mgmt. Co. Omaha, Teletrip Co.; Mem. Commn. on White House Fellows, 1970-73; mem. adv. com. on rights and responsibilities of women Sec. HEW, 1974-76; mem. nat. bd. Med. Coll. Pa. Mem. Washoe and St. Mary's Hosp. Guild; bd. dirs. Politecnic U.P.R. Mem. Am., Fed., Nev., D.C. bar assns., Nat. Exec. Secs. Assn. (hon.), Am. Women in Radio and TV, Reno C. of C., Senate Secs. Assn. (pres. 1943-44), Bus. and Profl. Women Assn., Cap and Scroll, Kappa Alpha Theta, Kappa Phi, Kappa Delta Pi. Clubs: Am. Newspaper Women's, Soroptomist, 1925 F Street. Home: Reno Nev. Died Aug. 23, 1991. †

ADAMS, FANEUIL, lawyer; b. Concord, Mass., May 11, 1898; s. Edward Brinley and Rebecca (Ames) A.; m. Rose A. Bradley, Oct. 14, 1922 (dec. July 1923); m. Susanne C. Root, June 25, 1925; children: Faneuil, B. Dunkin. AB, Harvard U., 1919, LLB, 1922. Bar: Mass. 1922. Practiced law Boston, from 1922; ptnr. Hill, Barlow, Goodale & Adams; trustee Cambridge Savs. Bank. Author: (with Hall) Massachusetts Law of Landlord and Tenant, The AIA Contradct Documents and the Law. Served as aspirant French Army, World War I. Mem. ABA, Mass Bar Assn., Boston Bar Assn., others. *

ADAMS, JAMES EDWARD, academic dean; b. Lee's Summit, Mo., July 5, 1898; s. David William Henry and Annie Lee (Alley) A.; m. Conradina Henrietta Lommel, Aug. 23, 1924. AB, William Jewell Coll., 1920; MS, Purdue U., 1922; student, U. Wis., 1924; PhD, Iowa State Coll., 1936. Mem. staff Ind. Agrl. Expt. Sta., 1922-23; instr. chemistry N.D. Agr. Coll., 1923-25; soil technologist, plant biochemist U.S. Dept. Agr., S.C., Tex., 1928-42; sr. agronomist, supt. Delta Expt. Sta., Miss., 1942-46; head dept. agronomy Tex. A&M Coll., 1946-55, dean agr., 1955-56; dean agr., dir. Agrl. Expt. Sta. Agrl. Ext. U. Nev., 1956-63; agrl. rsch. adminstr. AID, Amman, Jordan, from 1963. With U.S. Army, 1918. Fellow Am. Soc. Agronomy, AAAS; mem. Future Farmers Am., Soil Sci. Soc. Am., Tex. Acad. Sci., Am. Chem. Soc., Sigma Xi, others. *

ADAMS, JOHN ALLAN STEWART, geochemist, educator; b. Independence, Mo., Nov. 1, 1926; s. George Carroll and Eva (Stewart) A.; m. Anne Donchin, Apr. 8, 1949 (div. 1973); children: Joanne Athena, John Allan Stewart Jr., David Donchin, Christopher Barth. PhB, U. Chgo., 1946, BS, 1948, MS, 1949, PhD, 1951. Project assoc., lectr. geochemistry U. Wis., 1951-54; mem. faculty Rice U., 1954-92, prof. geology, 1960-88, prof. geochemistry emeritus, 1988-92, chmn. dept., 1965-71. Am. exec. editor: Geochimica et Cosmochimica Acta, 1960-66; Author: (with John J.W. Rogers) Fundamentals of Geology, 1966; Editor: (with W.M. Lowder) The Natural Radiation Environment, 1964, 73. Served with USNR, 1945-46. NSF sr. postdoctoral fellow, 1960. Fellow Am. Inst. Chemists, Geol. Soc. Am., Sigma Xi; mem. Geochem. Soc., Am. Chem. Soc., Am. Assn. Petroleum Geologists (Disting. lectr. 1955). Home: Houston Tex. Died Feb. 10, 1992. †

ADAMS, JOHN EVI, psychiatry educator; b. Durham, N.C., May 23, 1937; s. Joseph Edison and Katherine (Smith) A.; m. Ann Carver Absalom, Apr. 17, 1965; children: Christopher Dylan, Gregory Carter. BA, Swarthmore Coll., 1959; postgrad., U. N.C., 1959-60; MD, Cornell U., 1964. Diplomate Am. Bd. Psychiatry and Neurology. Intern in medicine Vanderbilt U. Hosp., Nashville, 1964-65; resident in psychiatry Stanford (Calif.) U. Med. Ctr., 1965-68, research fellow in psychiatry, 1967-68, asst. prof. psychiatry, 1970-74; prof., chmn. dept. psychiatry Coll. Medicine U. Fla., Gainseville, from 1974; spl. asst. to dir. NIMH, Bethesda, 1968-69, assoc. dir. manpower and tng., 1969-70; vis. scholar Inst. Psychiatry Maudsley Hosp., London, 1984-85; psychiatrist-in-chief Shands Hosp., Gainesville, 1974—; cons. VA Med. Ctr., Gainesville, from 1974; sr. examiner Am. Bd. Psychiatry and Neurology, Chgo., from 1979. Editor: Coping and Adaption, 1974; contbr. articles to profl. jours. Served to surgeon USPHS, 1968-70. NIMH, Nat. Inst. Alcohol Abuse & Alcoholism research and tng. grantee, Rockville, Md., from 1970. Fellow Am. Psychiat. Assn. (vice chmn. rsch. council from 1984), Am. Coll. Psychiatrists, So. Psychiat. Assn.; mem. AAAS, Am. Assn. Chmn. of Depts. Psychiatry (pres. 1983-84), Am. Psychosomatic Soc. Democrat. Club: Heritage (Gainesville). Home: Gainesville Fla. Died Apr. 14, 1989.

ADAMS, JOHN JOSEPH, lawyer; b. Marshalltown, Iowa, June 25, 1916; s. Thomas Edward and Susan (Watson) A.; m. Virginia McCabe, Sept. 21, 1940; children: John Thomas, James McCabe, Ann Virginia. B.A., U. Mich., 1938, J.D., 1940. Bar: Iowa 1940, Ohio 1942, U.S. Dist. Ct. (no. dist.) Ohio 1942, U.S. Ct. Appeals (6th cir.) 1947, U.S. Supreme Ct. 1948. Law clk. to justice U.S. Supreme Ct., Washington, 1940-41; assoc., then ptnr. Squire, Sanders & Dempsey, Cleve., 1941-89; bd. dirs. various cos. Contbr. articles to legal publs. Served to capt. JAGD U.S. Army, 1943-46, ETO. Mem. ABA, Cleve. Bar Assn., Cuyahoga County Bar Assn., Ohio Bar Assn., Indsl. Relations Research Assn. Republican. Clubs: Union, Westwood Country; Ct. Nisi Prius (Cleve.). Home: Cleveland Ohio Died July 23, 1989; buried Woodlawn Cemetry, Toledo.

ADAMS, LEONIE, poet; b. Bklyn., Dec. 9, 1899; d. Charles Frederick and Henrietta (Rozier) Adams; m. William E. Troy, June 3, 1933 (dec. 1961). A.B., Barnard Coll., 1922; D.Litt., N.J. Coll. for Women, 1950. Instr. writing and poetry NYU, N.Y.C., 1930-32; instr. writing and poetry Sarah Lawrence Coll., 1933-34, Bennington Coll., 1935-37, 41-44; lectr. N.J. Coll. for Women, 1946-48, Columbia U., N.Y.C., 1947-68; vis. prof. poetry U. Wash., 1961, 69, Purdue U., Ind., 1971-72; cons. poetry Library of Congress, Washington, 1948-49; fellow in letters Library of Congress, 1949-55; mem. staff Breadloaf Writers Conf., 1956-58. Author: Those Not Elect, 1925, High Falcon, 1929, Poems, A Selection, 1954; editor: Lyrics of Francois Villon, 1932. Recipient Harriet Monroe award, Shelley Meml. award, 1954, Bolingen prize in poetry, 1955, Brandeis medal and award for poetry, 1969; Guggenheim fellow, 1928-30; fellow Acad. Am. Poets, 1959; grantee Nat. Council for Arts, 1966-67, Nat. Found. for Arts, 1966-67; Fulbright lectr., France, 1955-56. Mem. Nat. Inst. Arts and Letters (award 1949, sec. 1959-61). Club: P.E.N. Home: New Milford Conn. Died June 27, 1988. †

ADAMS, NORMAN ILSLEY, JR., physicist; b. Winthrop, Mass., Sept. 20, 1895; s. Norman Ilsley and Mabel Estelle (George) A.; B.A., Yale U., 1917, Ph.D., 1923; m. Genevieve A. Sloan, July 28, 1926; children: Norman Ilsley, Harry Bell. Engr. dept. devel. and research AT&T, N.Y.C., 1923-24; mem. faculty Yale U., New Haven, 1925-85, prof. physics, 1944-64, prof. emeritus, 1964-85; vis. prof. U. Idaho, 1964, U. Del., 1965, Central Wash. State Coll., 1967; cons. engr. in radio broadcasting, 1927-85 . Served as 2d lt., 301st Heavy Tank Bn., A.E.F., France, 1918; dir. Eatontown Signal Lab., Fort Monmouth, N.J., 1941-43; ret. rank lt. col. Registered profl. engr. (communications), Conn. Decorated Legion of Merit. Fellow Am. Phys. Soc.; mem. Res. Officers Assn., Ret. Officers Assn., Mil. Order World Wars, Order Lafayette, Gamma Alpha, Phi Beta Kappa, Sigma Xi. Republican. Episcopalian. Clubs: Appalachian Mountain; New Haven Lawn. Author: Principles of Electricity (with L. Page), 1931; Electrodynamics (with L. Page), 1940. Died Mar. 19, 1985. Home: Gainesville Fla. †

ADAMS, PAUL LINCOLN, lawyer; b. Sault Ste. Marie, Mich., Apr. 9, 1908; s. John M. and Angela Moloney A.; m. Ruth Karpinski, July 28, 1934; children: Mary Louise, Susan Elizabeth, Katherine Whitcomb, Barbara Ann. AB, U. Mich., 1930, MA, 1931, LLB, 1936. Bar: Mich. 1936. Pvt. practice Sault Ste. Marie, 1936-90; mayor City of Sault Ste. Marie, 1938-42; with Bd. Econ. Warfare, Washington, 1943-44; mem. Mich. State Social Welfare Commn., 1949; chmn. Sault Ste. Marie Charter Commn., 1950; regent U. Mich., 1956-57; atty. gen. State of Mich., 1958-61; justice Mich. Supreme Ct., 1962, 64-72, Mich. Ct. of Appeals, 1973. Mem. Phi Eta Sigma, Phi Beta Kappa. Home: Laingsburg Mich. Died Nov. 23, 1990.

ADAMS, PHELPS HAVILAND, former public relations executive; b. Boston, Dec. 14, 1902; s. Henry Ethelbert and Mary Aurora (Haviland) A.; m. Ruth E. Hollinger, June 18, 1928. Student, U. Colo., 1919-22; B.Litt., Columbia U., 1924; student, London Sch. of Econs., 1924, The Sorbonne, Paris, France, 1925. Columbia corr. N.Y. Herald, 1923; reporter N.Y. Sun, 1926, then Washington corr., 1929-50, sent to Palestine, Trans-Jordan, Syria and Lebanon to do spl. series entitled The Truth About Palestine, Oct.-Dec. 1937; war corr. aboard U.S.S. Enterprise, off Japan, April 1945; spl. asst. to asst. to chmn. U.S. Steel Corp., 1950-55, exec. dir. public relations and asst. to chmn., 1955-57, v.p. public relations, 1957-63, adminstrv. v.p. public relations, 1964-67; Pres. Litchfield Park (Ariz.) Library Assn., 1970-71. Bd. dirs. Ch. at Litchfield Park (Ariz.), 1984. Recipient Freedoms Found. Honor award, 1950; Gold Plate award Am. Acad. Achievement, 1967. Mem. Pub. Relations Seminar (chmn. 1959-60), Sigma Delta Chi. Clubs: Alfalfa, Gridiron (pres. 1948) (Washington); Wigwam Golf and Country (Litchfield Park, Ariz.). Home: Litchfield Park Ariz. Died Jan. 13, 1991.

ADAMS, RAYMOND WILLIAM, English educator; b. Elgin, Ill., May 7, 1898; s. Alfred Franklyn and Etta (Fisk) A.; m. Mary Charlotte Garth, June 25, 1927. AB, Beloit Coll., 1920; AM, U. N.C., 1921, PhD, 1928. Instr. in English U. N.C., 1924-29, asst. prof., 1929-36, assoc. prof., 1936-39, prof., from 1939, acting chmn. English dept., 1945-46, 54-55; vis. prof. NYU, 1952, Alumni lectr., Phi Beta Kappa lectr. Beloit Coll., 1960. Editor: Walden (Thoreau), 1930; contbr. biography of Thoreau, other biographies to Dictionary of Am. Biography; also articles to jours. Rsch. fellow Gen. Edn. Bd., 1934-35; recipient disting. svc. award Beloit Coll., 1960. Mem. Medieval Acad. Am., Assn. Men of Kent and Kentish Men, MLA, Archeol. Soc. N.C., N.C. Coun. Tchrs. English, others. *

ADAMS, RICHARD DONALD, export executive, naval reserve officer; b. Ambridge, Pa., June 14, 1909; s. Arthur David and Mary May (Patterson) A.; m. Lorene M. Hoffer, Nov. 19, 1950; children: David Byron, April Annette. B.S. in Mech. and Elec. Engring., U.S. Naval Acad., 1932. Registered profl. engr., Calif. Commd. ensign U.S. Navy, 1932; active duty, 1932-37, 41-46; mem. Res., 1937-41, 46-69; advanced through grades to rear adm., 1963, rep. of comdt. 12th Naval Dist., 1964-66, dep. comdr. Wester Sea Frontier, 1966-69; ret. With Superior Diesel Engine Co., 1937-41; owner, mgr. Overseas Indsl. Services (exporters machinery and indsl. supplies), San Francisco, from 1952, R.D. Adams Co. (mfrs. agts.), San Francisco, from 1946. Decorated Army Disting. Unit citation, Navy Res. medal with 3 bronze stars, other campaign and area ribbons. Mem. ASME, Navy League U.S., Naval Res. Assn., U.S. Naval Acad. Found., Naval Order of U.S. (comdr.), U.S. Naval Acad. Alumni Assn., Ret. Officers Assn. Lodge: Masons (32 deg.). Home: San Bruno Calif. Deceased. †

ADAMS, RICHARD EDWARD, manufacturing executive; b. Sullivan, Mo., June 25, 1936; s. Woodrow Carl and Helen Elizabeth A.; student public schs., Normandy, Mo.; m. Janet Marie Vie, Apr. 23, 1955; children: Paul Matthew, Dawn Kathleen, Mark Edward. Salesman, Bevo Realty Co., St. Louis, 1955-61; archtl. draftsman Saul Dien-Architect, Olivette, Mo., 1961-63; prefabrication draftsman County Lumber Co., Hazelwood, Mo., 1963-64; mgr. engring. dept. So. Cross Lumber Co., Hazelwood, 1964-72, prodn. mgr., 1972-75; gen. mgr., sales mgr. Chromalloy Bldg. Products, Hazelwood, 1975-81; v.p., dir. U.S. ops. Gainsborough Hardware Industries, Inc., Chesterfield, Mo., 1981; archtl. and design cons. Committeeman, Boy Scouts Am., 1975-78, cubmaster, 1976-77; co-chmn. United Way, 1973-78. Recipient Homer award St. Louis Home Builders Assn., 1969, Product Presentation award, 1977, Product Mgmt. award, 1978. Mem. Hoo-Hoo Internat., Compass Orgn. (founder). Roman Catholic. Deceased. Home: Chesterfield Mo. †

ADAMSTONE, FRANK BELTON, educator; b. Listowel, Ont., Can., Dec. 10, 1896; s. William Murrell and Birdie Elizabeth (Smith) A.; m. Edith Margaret Lawson, June 30, 1925; 1 child, Ruth Evelyn. BA, U. Toronto, 1921, MA, 1922, PhD, 1924. With Royal Ont. Mus. geol. expdn., 1919-20; biol. survey Lake Nipigon, 1921-23; instr. zoology U. Ill., 1924-27, assoc., 1927-35, asst. prof., 1935-39, assoc. prof., 1939-44, prof., from 1944; chmn. exec. com. dept. zoology U. Ill., 1947, acting head, 1948, head dept., 1949-57, chmn. divsn. biol. scis., 1953. Author: Laboratory Manual of Vertebrate Embryology (with W. Shumway), 1939, Introduction to Vertebrate Embryology (with W. Shumway), 1953; also articles. Fellow AAAS; mem. Am. Soc. Zoologists, Am. Assn. Anatomists, Sigma Xi, others. *

ADIKES, JOHN, banker; b. Jamaica, N.Y., July 15, 1894; s. Thomas and Catherine (Fitzgibbon) A.; m. Ann Linz, Mar. 17, 1925; children: John, Avis Ann, Thomas. LLB, NYU, 1915; LLD (hon.), St. John's U., 1960. Mem. firm Street, Hanavan & Adikes, 1923-26; trustee Jamaica Savs. Bank, 1926-44, exec. v.p., 1944-45, pres., from 1945; mem. Queens adv. com. Chase Manhattan Bank. Former mem. Bd. Higher Edn. City of N.Y. Mem. Queens C. of C., Savs. Bank Assn. State N.Y. *

ADLER, BENJAMIN, consulting engineer; b. N.Y.C., Nov. 10, 1903; s. William and Rose A.; m. Beatrice Ross, June 30, 1938; children: Elizabeth Jan (Mrs. Geoffreey Picket), Susan Lois (Mrs. Victor Bers), Pamela Ann, Jane Winifred. EE, Poly. Inst. Bklyn., 1926, D Eng (hon.), 1967. Registered profl. engr., N.Y. Geophys. rsch. engr. Phillips Petroleum Co., 1926-28; rsch. engr. RCA, 1928-30, comml. engring. mgr., 1931-44; chief facilities engr. ABC, 1944-48, also cons. engr. TV broadcasting and comms.; pres., dir. engring. Adler Electronics, Inc., New Rochelle, N.Y., 1948-63; v.p. Litton Industries, 1963-65; pres. Royfax div. Litton Industries, Paramus, N.J., 1965-68; self-employed cons. engr. Larchmont, N.Y., 1968-90; acting pres. Poly. Inst., Bklyn., 1969-71; chmn. bd. Transworld Svcs., Inc., L.A., 1970-90; past bd. dirs. Aberdeen Mfg. Co., Inc., N.Y.C., Polychrome Cor., Comtech Labs., Inc. Chmn. com. of TV repeaters TV, 1959; chmn. engring. com. Com. All channel Broadcasting, 1963-64; rep. industry adv. com. FCC, 1961. Trustee emeritus, corp. bd. Poly, Inst. N.Y.; bd. dirs. Ctr. for Environment and Man, Hartford, 1973-90. Recipient Disting. Alumnus award Poly.Inst. Bklyn., 1965. Past fellow AAAS, IEEE (life); past mem. NSPE, Electronic Industries Assn. (v.p. 1952-65), Soc. Motion Picture and TV Engrs. Home: Larchmont N.Y. Died Apr. 16, 1990; cremated.

ADLER, KURT, psychoanalyst; b. Nieder Florstadt, Germany, Apr. 10, 1907; s. Herman and Augusta (Seligman) A.; M.D., Frankfurt, Germany, 1931; m. Edna Mae Mannion, Sept. 30, 1939; children: Karen Adler Evans, Constance Adrienne, Audrey Lynn; came to U.S., 1937, naturalized, 1941. Intern, Mcpl. Hosp., Munich, Germany, 1931-32; resident Univ. Psychiat. Hosp., Heidelberg, Germany, 1932-33, Salpêtrière, Paris, 1933-34; instr., research asst. Path. Inst. U. Istanbul (Turkey), 1934-36; practice neurology and psychiatry, N.Y.C., 1937-42, Jamaica, N.Y., from 1946, psychoanalysis, 1953-92; mem. staff Queens Gen., Triboro hosps., 1946-67; cons. Queens Hosp. Center, 1967-92; cons. psychiatry Jamaica Hosp., 1952-92. Served to lt. col. AUS, 1942-46. Diplomate Am. Bd. Psychiatry and Neurology. Fellow Am. Psychiat. Assn. (life), Am. Acad. Psychoanalysis, AAAS; mem. Am. Acad. Neurology, N.Y. Acad. Scis. Deceased. Home: Jamaica N.Y. †

ADLER, NORMAN ABNER, lawyer, broadcasting and advertising executive; b. N.Y.C., Oct. 8, 1909; s. Isaac Julius and Anna (Bluestein) A.; m. Leona Kleban, June 28, 1934; children—John Robert, Louise Rachel. B.A., NYU, 1930; J.D., Yale, 1933. Bar: N.Y. bar 1933. Asso. mem. firm Rosenberg, Goldmark & Colin, N.Y.C., 1933-38; spl. asst. to U.S. atty. gen., anti-trust div. Dept. Justice, 1938-45; asst. gen. atty. RCA, 1945-48; gen. atty. Columbia Records, 1948-55; v.p. charge Columbia Record Club, 1955-60; exec. v.p. Columbia Records (div. CBS), 1960-66; v.p., gen. mgr. CBS Ednl. Services Div., 1966-67; v.p., gen. exec. CBS, Inc., 1967-71; chmn. exec. com. Wunderman Ricotta & Kline,

1971-74. Mng. editor Yale Law Jour., 1932-33. Recipient Cullen prize for excellence in legal scholarship Yale, 1931. Mem. Fed. Bar Assn., Assn. Bar City N.Y., Order of Coif, Phi Beta Kappa Assos., Phi Beta Kappa. Home: La Jolla Calif. Died Dec. 2, 1989.

AFFLECK, RAYMOND TAIT, architect, educator; b. Penticton, B.C., Can., Nov. 20, 1922; s. John Earnest and Barbara (Tait) A.; m. Betty Ann Henley, Sept. 16, 1952; children: Graham (dec.), Neil, Jane, Gavin, Ewan. BArch, McGill U., 1947, DSc (hon.), 1984; postgrad., Eidgenossische Technische Hochschule, Zurich, Switzerland, 1948; LLD, U. Calgary, 1972; Dr. Tech. hon., N.S. Tech. U., 1976; LLD (hon.), Concordia U., Montreal, 1988. Asst. architect McDougall, Smith, Fleming, Montreal, Que., Can., 1948-49, Vincent Rother Assocs., Montreal, 1950-52; architect, prin. Affleck Desbarats Dimakopoulos Lebensold Sise, Montreal, 1952-70, Arcop Assocs., Montreal, from 1970; asst. prof. McGill U., Montreal, 1954-58, vis. prof., from 1960; design cons. Nat. Capital Commn., Ottawa, Ont., Can., 1965-75, Wascana Centre Authority, Regina, Can., from 1979; mem. archtl. design com. City of Dorval, Can., 1960-62; mem. explorations jury Can. Council, Ottawa, 1970-76. Prin. works include: Place Bonaventure, 1968 (Massey medal 1972), Stephen Leacock Bldg., 1966 (Massey medal 1972), Arts and Culture Centre, 1967, Market Sq., 1983, Maison Alcan, 1983. Recipient Can. Centennial medal Govt. of Can., 1967; recipient Aga Khan award for architecture, 1980, Crédit Foncier award for bldg. preservation Maison Alcan, 1984, Internat. award for innovative design Internat. Council Shopping Ctrs., 1984; The Ray Affleck Design Prize established in his memory Sch. Architecture Mc Gill U. Fellow Royal Archtl. Inst. Can. (Gold medal in architecture posthumous award 1989); mem. Royal Can. Acad. (academician), Order of Architects of Que. (medal of honor 1983, Prix d'excellence award 1984), Ont. Assn. Architects, Assn. Architects N.Y., Assn. Architects Calif. Clubs: Faculty (McGill U.); Mt. Royal Tennis (Montreal). Home: Westmount Que., Can. Died Mar. 16, 1989; buried Massawippi Cemetery, Eastern Twp., Que.

AHEARN, VINCENT PAUL, trade association manager; b. Nashville, Sept. 8, 1896; s. John Thomas and Julia Ann (Hardiman) A.; m. Mary Belle Geary, Jan. 12, 1925; children: Julia Ann, Patricia Geary, Vincent Paul. LLB, Georgetown U., 1920. With Nat. Sand and Gravel Assn., from 1921, exec. sec., 1926, then mining dir.; mining dir. Nat. Ready Mixed Concrete Assn., Nat. Indsl. San Assn.; pres. Am. Trade Assn. Execs., 1942-43, Wash. Trade Assn. Execs., 1942-43; chmn. mfg. trade group Nat. Indsl. Coun., 1941; mem. bd. trustees Indsl. Hygiene Found.; industry mem. Nat. War Labor Bd.; exec. dir. Pres.'s Conf. on Indsl. Safety; indsl. rels. cons. Econ. Coop. Adminstrn. With USN, World War I. Mem. Am. Legion, Delta Chi. *

AIDEKMAN, ALEX, food company executive; b. 1915. Salesman Good Deal Market Co., Irvington, N.J., until 1942; owner, salesman Uniondale Foods Inc., 1946-55; founder, pres., dir. Wakefern Food Corp., 1955-67; chmn. bd. Supermarkets Operating Co. (merged into Supermarkets Gen. Corp.), Woodbridge, N.J., 1956-66; chmn., bd. dirs. Supermarkets Operating Co. (merged into Supermarkets Gen. Corp,), 1966-86, chmn. emeritus, exec. bd. dirs., 1986-87. Leader Food Industry Coun. United Jewish Appeal; trustee Jewish Community Found. MetroWest; philanthropies include Aidekman Rsch. Ctr. for Molecular Rsch., Rutgers U., an arts ctr. at Tufts U., rsch. professorship in neurology Mt. Sianai Hosp., N.Y.C. Served to 1st lt. AUS, 1942-46. Home: Woodbridge N.J. Died Dec. 14, 1990.

AIKEN, WILLIAM DAVID, lawyer; b. Sunnyside, Wash., Aug. 28, 1923; s. William Jerome and Louisa Gertrude (Nichols) A.; student Wash. State U., 1941-43, 46-47; JD, George Washington U., 1949; m. Dorothy Louise Snyder, May 28, 1948; children: Katherine Aiken Schwartz, Mary L. Aiken Fishback, Sally S. Aiken Fetterer, Jerome Ross. Admitted to Wash. bar, 1951; asso. firm Chaffee & Aiken, Sunnyside, Wash., 1951-60; sole practice law, Sunnyside, 1960—; mcpl. judge City of Sunnyside, 1951-58; justice of peace Yakima County, Wash., 1951-58. Mem. Yakima County Civil Service Com., 1969—, chmn., 1975-77; mem. Yakima County Boundary Rev. Bd., 1985—, Selective Service Bd. 31 Yakima and Klickitat Counties, 1982—. Served to with U.S. Army, 1943-46, lt. col. JAG Wash. State Guard. Decorated Bronze Star. Mem. ABA, Wash. State Bar Assn. (exec. com. family law sect. 1974-76), Yakima County Bar Assn. (pres. 1985-86), Am. Judicature Soc., Am. Acad. Polit. and Social Sci. Episcopalian. Clubs: Masons (32 deg.), Shriners, Coll., Seattle. Home: Sunnyside Wash.

AIKINS, LINCOLN JAMES, college dean; b. Windham, Maine, Dec. 7, 1898; s. James Edward and Cora Ellen (Harlow) A.; m. Marion Emily Cousins, Aug. 23, 1925; children: Ann Gordon Draper, Jean Ellen. AB, Bates Coll., 1919, AM, 1935; student, Hart Theol. Sem., U. Colo.; EdD, Mont. State Coll., 1958. Instr. English Berea Coll., 1919-20; prin. high sch. Maine, 1921-27; registrar, dean Billings (Mont.) Poly. Inst., 1928-40; dean Dawson County Jr. Coll., Glendive, Mont., 1949-52; supt. schs. Glendive, 1942-45; dean basic curricula Ea. Mont. Coll. Edn., from 1945, registrar, 1945-55, v.p., from 1957. Mem. AAUP, NEA, Mont. Edn. Assn., N.W. Assn. Jr. Colls., Phi Delta Kappa. *

AILEY, ALVIN, choreographer; b. Rogers, Tex., Jan. 5, 1931; s. Alvin and Lula E. (Cliff) A. Student, UCLA, 1949-50, Los Angeles City Coll., 1950-51, San Francisco State Coll., 1952-53, Lester Horton Dance Group, Los Angeles, 1949-51, 53; with, Hanya Holm, N.Y.C., 1954-55, Martha Graham, 1956, others; acting student with, Stella Adler, 1960-62; with, Milton Katselas, 1961; hon. degree, Princeton U., Bard Coll., Adelphi U., Cedar Crest Coll.; DFA, Long Island U., 1987. Disting. prof. Manhattan Community Coll., 1985-86. Choreographer, Lester Horton Dance Group, from 1953; formed Alvin Ailey Am. Dance Theater, 1958-89; performed numerous festivals, 1959—, Australian, S.E. Asian tour, 1962, World Festival Negro Arts, Dakar, Senegal, 1966, East and West Africa, 1967, Russia, 1970, world tour, 1977, S.Am., 1978, 81; actor, 1961—; choreographer, dancer TV, 1954—, also motion pictures; performances include The Carefree Tree, 1956, Sing Man Sing, 1956, Show Boat, 1957, Jamaica, 1957, Call Me by My Rightful Name, Tiger Tiger Burning Bright, Talking To You; choreographed: musicals African Holiday; operas Leonard Bernstein's Mass; spls. for TV including Solo for Mingus, 1979, Memoria, 1979; spl. co. performances include inaugural eve gala for Pres., 1977, White House State Dinner, 1978, King of Morocco in Marrakesh, 1979; created numerous maj. works for co., also for Joffrey Ballet, Harkness Ballet, Am. Ballet Theater, Bat-Dor, Ballet Internat. de Caracas, Paris Opera Ballet, Aterballeto, Royal Danish Ballet, London Festival Ballet, Pitts. Ballet, La Scala Opera Ballet. Recipient Springarn medal, 1976, Mayor's Award of Art and Culture, 1977, Capezio award, 1979, UN Peace Medal, 1982, A. Philip Randolph award, 1984, Monarch award Nat. Council for Culture and Art, 1984, Assn. Coll. Univ. & Community Arts Admintrs. merit award, 1984, Internat. Soc. Performing Arts Adminstrs. merit award, 1984, Samuel H. Scripps Am. Dance Festival award, 1987, Kennedy Ctr. Honor, 1988, Handel Medallion City of N.Y.; named Disting. New Yorker, Bowery Bank, 1984. Home: New York N.Y. Died Dec. 1, 1989; buried L.A.

AINBINDER, SEYMOUR, real estate consultant; b. Bklyn., July 10, 1928; s. Max and Sonia Rose (Alterman) A.; m. Rose Beatrice Cooper, Jan. 14, 1951; children—Michael Cooper, Jonathan Cooper. Student Rutgers U., 1955-56, Upsala Coll., 1957-58. Store mgr. S. Klein Dept. Stores, N.Y.C., 1947-60; v.p. Allied Dept. Stores, N.Y.C., 1960-72, Arlen Shopping Ctrs., N.Y.C. and Chattanooga, 1972-77; owner, mgr. Ainbinder Assocs., Houston, 1977-80; ptnr. Ainbinder Bramalea Co., Houston, 1980-82; real estate cons., owner Scads, Inc., Houston, 1982—; owner, mgr. Cards and Things, Houston, Scad's Gift Shop. Club: Westwood Country. Home: Houston Tex.

AITKEN, WILLIAM INGLIS, lawyer; b. Lincoln, Nebr., Oct. 4, 1896; s. Martin Inglis and Clara Elizabeth (Carmody) A.; m. Helen Mary Cook, Sept. 22, 1923; children: Martha Elizabeth Greer, Mary Greer, Nancy Weir Senger. AB, U. Nebr., 1918; LLB, Harvard U., 1921. Bar: Nebr. 1921. Mem. law firm Woods, Aitken & Aitken, from 1921; v.p., dir. mem. exec. com. Lincoln Tel. & Tel. Co.; dir., mem. exec. com. Addressograph-Multigraph Corp., Cleve.; bd. dirs. various cos. 2d lt. U.S. Army, 1918-19, 2d lt. USAR, 1919-24. Mem. ABA, Nebr. State Bar Assn., Lincoln Bar Assn., Ind. Pioneers Telephone Assn., others. Republican. Congregationalist. *

ALBERDING, CHARLES HOWARD, petroleum and hotel executive; b. Clayville, N.Y., Mar. 5, 1901; s. Charles and Doris (Roberts) A.; m. Bethine Wolverton, May 2, 1930; children: Beth Ann, Mary Katherine, Melissa Linda. EE, Cornell U., 1923. Lab. asst., draftsman, operator Producers & Refiners Corp., Parco, Wyo., 1923-25; engr., cracking plant supt. Imperial Refineries, Ardmore, Okla., Eldorado, Ark., 1925-27; head fgn. operating dept. Universal Oil Products Co., London, Eng., Ploesti, Roumania, Rangoon, Burma, Venice, Italy, 1927-33; head operating, service depts., Chgo. hdqrs. Universal Oil Products Co., 1933-42; pres., dir. Paradise Inn, Inc., Jokake Inn, Inc., Vinoy Park Hotel Co., Holiday Hotel Corp., Alsonett Hotels, Sabine Irrigation Co., Sabine Canal Co., Tides Hotel Corp., Harmony Oil Corp., London Square Corp., Petroleum Spltys., Lincoln Lodge Corp., Peabody Hotel Corp., Memphis, Hermitage Hotel Co., Nashville, Royal Palms Inn, Inc., Torrey Pines Inn, La Jolla, Calif., Charleston First Corp.; petroleum cons., dollar-per-yr. man WPB, 1942-43; dist. dir. petroleum refining Petroleum Adminstrn. for War, 1943-45. Presdl. councilor Cornell U.; bd. govs. Endowment Found., Heritage Trust. Named to Athletic Hall of Fame Cornell U., 1988. Mem. Scorpion. Republican. Congregationalist. Clubs: Valley (Phoenix); Kenilworth (Chgo.), Cornell (Chgo.); Sunset Country (St. Petersburg, Fla.), Bath (St. Petersburg, Fla.); Tides Country (pres., dir.), Rolling Greens Golf (pres., dir.), Sunrise Golf (Sarasota, Fla.) (pres., dir.). Home: Kenilworth Ill. Died Mar. 14, 1989.

ALBERTS, IRWIN N., publishing company executive. Pres., chief exec. officer Panini USA, N.Y.C.; also sr. v.p. adminstrn. and devel. Macmillan Pub., N.Y.C. Home: East Hampton N.Y. Died Apr. 18, 1991.

ALBRECHT, RALPH GERHART, lawyer; b. Jersey City, Aug. 11, 1896; s. J. Robert and Gertrude A.F. (Richter) A.; m. Aillinn Leffingwell; 1 child, Peter Leffingwell. AB, U. Pa., 1919; LLB, Harvard U., 1923. Bar: N.Y. 1924, U.S. Supreme Ct. 1927. Sr. ptnr. Peaslee, Brigham, Albrecht & McMahon, N.Y.C., 1933-60, counsel, from 1961; spl. asst. to U.S. atty. gen. and assoc. trial counsel to Justice Robert H. Jackson, Nuernberg War Crimes Trial, 1945-46; asst. dir. OSS, 1945; others. Co-author: America Next, 1940. With USNRF, 1918; with N.Y. N.G., 1924-30; comdr. USNR, 1941-45. Fellow Am. Geog. Soc.; mem. ABA, Assn. Bar City N.Y., Mcpl. Art Soc., Inter-Am. Bar Assn., Internat. Bar Assn., Am. Soc. Internat. Law, Internat. Law Assn., Goethe House, Nat. Legal Aid Assn., Legal Aid Soc., others. *

ALBRITTON, CLAUDE CARROLL, JR., geologist, dean; b. Corsicana, Tex., Apr. 7, 1913; s. Claude C. and Iris (Stapleton) A.; m. Jane Christman, Aug. 5, 1944; children: Jane DeHart, Claude C., Elizabeth Ann Scott. A.B., B.S., So. Meth. U., 1933; A.M., Harvard U., 1934, Ph.D. (J.B. Woodworth fellow 1935-36), 1936. From instr. to assoc. prof. geology So. Methodist U., 1936-47, prof., 1947-78, dean faculty Coll. Arts and Scis., 1952-57, dean Grad. Sch., 1957-71, chmn. bd. publs., 1968-78, vice provost for library devel., 1971-73, W.B. Hamilton prof. geology, 1955-78, dean libraries, 1973-78; v.p., sr. scientist Inst. Study of Earth and Man, from 1978, chmn. bd. publs., 1968-78, exec. sec. Colophon, 1971-78; dir. Grad. Research Center, Inc., 1961-64, Sci. Info. Inst., 1964-72; geologist U.S. Geol. Survey, 1942-49; Rosenbach fellow in bibliography U. Pa., 1969-70; cons. NSF, 1977-80; mem. U.S. Nat. Com. History of Geology, chmn., 1980-81; corr. mem. Internat. Com. History of Geol. Scis., from 1972. Author: The Abyss of Time, 1980, Catastrophic Episodes in Earth History, 1988, (with others) Origin of The Qattara Depression, Egypt, 1988; co-author: The Midland Discovery, 1955, Guidelines and Standards for the Education of Secondary School Teachers of Science and Mathematics, 1971, The Prehistory of Nubia, 1968; editor and co-author: The Fabric of Geology, 1964, Uniformity and Simplicity, 1965, Filosofia de la Geologia, 1970, Philosophy of Geohistory, 1975; editor: Jour. Grad. Research Center, 1960-70; adv. editor for geology: Arno Press, 1976-80; author articles for Ency. Brit., 1975. Chmn. scholarship selection com. Chance Vought Aircraft Corp., 1955-63; mem. com. geosci. and man Internat. Union Geol. Socs., U. Cambridge, Eng., 1971; mem. exec. com. John E. Owens Found., from 1955; trustee E. de Golyer Found., 1958-66. Recipient DeWitt medal, 1933. Mem. Dallas Coun. World Affairs (past bd. dirs.), AAAS (chmn. sect. E 1968, mem. philosophy of sci. and math. edn. 1970), Geol. Soc. Am. (councillor 1957-69, chmn. joint tech. program com. 1973, chmn. div. history of geology 1976-77, chmn. div. archeol. geology 1982-83, award div. history of geology 1983-88, archaeol. geology award 1988), Paleontol. Soc. (councillor 1956-62), Am. Assn. Petroleum Geologists, Am. Geol. Inst. (chmn. liberal arts panel 1963-66), Soc. Econ. Paleontologists and Mineralogists, Tex. Acad. Sci., Philos. Soc. Tex., Phi Beta Kappa, Sigma Xi (com. on lectureships 1976-82), Kappa Alpha. Methodist. Club: Cadence. Home: Dallas Tex. Died Nov. 1, 1988; buried Hillcrest Meml. Pk., Dallas.

ALCORN, HOWARD WELLS, state official; b. Suffield, Conn., May 14, 1901; s. Hugh M. and Cora Terry (Wells) A.; m. Bertha Eloise Pinney, Oct. 28, 1927; children: Carolyn Hatheway, Elizabeth Wells, Dorcas Terry. A.B., Dartmouth, 1923; student, Harvard Law Sch., Yale Law Sch. Bar: Conn. 1926. Judge Suffield Town Ct., 1929-43; exec. sec. to Gov. Conn., 1943; judge Superior Ct. Conn., 1943-59, chief judge, 1959-61; justice Supreme Ct. Conn., 1961-70, chief justice, 1970-71, state referee, 1971-92; Dir. 1st Nat. Bank of Suffield, 1928-51, v.p., 1934-51; chmn. zoning commn. Suffield, 1928-43; mem. Conn. Ho. Reps., 1927-29, 31, speaker, 1931, floor leader Conn. Senate, 1933; chmn. Republican Town Com., Suffield, 1928-33; alt. del.-at-large Rep. Nat. Conv., 1932. Mem. ABA, Conn. Bar Assn., Hartford County Bar Assn. (treas. 1934-36), SAR, Sons Union Vets., Antiquarian and Landmarks Soc. (pres. 1936-40), Suffield Grange. Congregationalist. Clubs: Mason, Hartford. Home: Suffield Conn. Died Aug. 10, 1992. †

ALCORN, HUGH MEADE, JR., lawyer; b. Suffield, Conn., Oct. 20, 1907; s. Hugh M. and Cora Terry (Wells) A.; m. Janet Hoffer, Oct. 21, 1933 (dec.); children: Thomas Glenn (dec.), Janet Eileen; m. Marcia Powell, Apr. 14, 1955. A.B., Dartmouth, 1930; LL.B., Yale, 1933; LL.D., U. Hartford, 1974. Bar: Conn. bar 1933. Ptnr. Alcorn, Bakewell & Smith (now Tyler, Cooper & Alcorn), Hartford, from 1933; asst. state's atty. Hartford County, 1935-42; state's atty., 1942-48; dir. United Bank & Trust Co., Hartford.; Mem. Conn. Ho. of Reps., 1937, 39, Rep. floor leader, 1939, speaker, 1941; chmn. Suffield Rep. Town Com., 1938-53; mem. Conn. Rep. State Central Com., 1948-57; del. Rep. Nat. Conv., 1940, 48, 52, 56, 60, alternate, 1944, vice chmn. arrangements com., 1956; mem. Rep. Nat. Com. from Conn., 1953-61, vice chmn., 1956-57, chmn., 1957-59, gen. counsel, 1960-61; Rep. floor leader constl. conv.,

1965. Mem. Am. Coll. Trial Lawyers, ABA, Conn. Bar Assn. (pres. 1950-51), Hartford County Bar Assn., Sons Union Vets., Conn. Soc. S.A.R., Suffield Grange, Apollo Lodge, Phi Beta Kappa. Republican. Conglist. Club: Anglers (N.Y.C.). Lodges: Masons, Elks (N.Y.C.); Rotary (Hartford) (pres. 1949-50). Home: Suffield Conn. Deceased. †

ALDRICH, DANIEL GASKILL, JR., university chancellor; b. Northwood, N.H., July 12, 1918; s. Daniel Gaskill and Marian (Farnum) A.; m. Jean Hamilton, Aug. 23, 1941; children: Daniel Gaskill III, Elizabeth, Stuart Hamilton. B.S., U.R.I., 1939, D. Sc. (hon.), 1960; M.S., U. Ariz., 1941, D.H.L. (hon.), 1985; Ph.D., U. Wis., 1943, D.Sc. (hon.), 1982; D.H.L., U. Redlands, 1978, Chapman Coll., 1980, Nat. U., 1981. Rsch. chemist U. Calif. Citrus Expt. Sta., Riverside, 1943-55; chmn. dept. soils and plant nutrition U. Calif., Davis and Berkeley, 1955-59; univ. dean agr. U. Calif.-Berkeley, 1959-62; chancellor U. Calif.-Irvine, 1962-84, chancellor emeritus, 1984-90; acting chancellor U. Calif., Riverside, 1984-85, Santa Barbara, 1986-87; apptd. Pres. Agrl. Task Force to Zaire, 1985; former head nat. study on population and food, NSF; dir. Pacific Mut. Co. Mem. exec. bd. Orange County council Boy Scouts Am.; bd. dirs. Big Brothers Orange County, SRI Internat., Internat. Vol. Services; trustee Pacific Sch. Religion. Served as maj., inf. AUS; lt. col. Res. Mem. AAAS (past pres. Pacific div.), Western Soc. Soil Sci. (pres.), Am. Soc. Agronomy (dir.), Nat. Acad. Scis. (agrl. edn. policy com., commn. on edn. in agr. and nat. resources), Nat. Assn. State Univs. and Land-Grant Colls., Soil Conservation Soc., Soil Sci. Soc. Am., Am. Soc. Hort. Sci. Mem. United Ch. Christ. Home: Laguna Niguel Calif. Died Apr. 9, 1990.

ALDRIN, EDWIN EUGENE, aviator, aviation consultant; b. Worcester, Mass., Apr. 12, 1896; s. Carl J. and Anna (Nelson) A.; m. Marion G. Moon, Mar. 22, 1924; children: Madeline Ross, Fay Ann, Edwin E. AB, Clark U., 1915; grad. study, Worcester Poly. Inst., 1916; MS, MIT, 1917, DSc, 1928. Commd. 2d lt. CAC U.S. Army, 1917, various mil. positions, resigned as capt., 1917-28; lt. col. Army A.F., 1942; assigned to Air Staff, chief SADU Sea Search Attack Devel. Unit; transferred to fgn. duty, 1943; asst. chief staff ops., air insp. Hdqrs. 13th A.F., 1944; chief All Weather Flying Ctr. Wright Field; chmn. Airports & Airport Fire Protection NFPA, 1949; comdr. Atlas Sky Merchant, first Round-the World Merchandising Flight, 1948; ret. USAF. Author papers on airport fuels; supervised revision of C.N. Monteith's Simple Aerodynamics; contbr. articles to profl. jours. Deocrated Air medal with oak leaf cluster; Commendatore Order Crown of Italy. Fellow AIAA, AAAS, Royal Aero. Soc., ASME; mem. Soc. Automotive Engrs., ASTM, Nat. Aero. Assn., Aero Club France, Am. Legion, Sigma Xi. *

ALEXANDER, JOHN DAVIS, SR., lawyer; b. Holland Island, Md., May 10, 1899; s. Harvey George and Nancy Harper (Sheetz) A.; m. Mildred Lillian Ebelein, Nov. 2, 1946; children: Dorothy (Mrs. Joseph David Watson), John Davis. BS, St. John's Coll., 1920; LLB, U. Md., 1924. Sole practice; instr. Balt. U. Law Sch., 1928-68. Served with USMCR, World War I. Clubs: Engineering, Barristers. Home: Glen Arm Md. Deceased. †

ALEXANDER, JOHN FRANK, tenor; b. Meridian, Miss.; s. Charles Curtis and Eva (Ogburn) A.; m. Sue Travis, Aug. 10, 1952; 1 dau., Cindy Sue. Student, Duke U., 1941-43; B.Mus., Cin. Conservatory Music, 1949; D.Performing Arts, U. Cin., 1968. Disting. prof. voice and opera U. Cin., 1974-91. Tenor with NBC TV Opera, 1956-59, N.Y.C. Opera, 1957-61, leading tenor, Met. Opera Co., 1961-91, leading tenor with Phila. Lyric Opera, Pitts. Opera, Ft. Worth Opera, New Orleans Opera, Vancouver (B.C., Can.) Opera, Vienna Staatsoper, Covent Garden, London, Vienna Volksoper, San Francisco Opera, Opera Co. Boston, Chgo. Lyric Opera, Houston Grand Opera, others; recs. include Norma, Beethoven's 9th Symphony, others; soloist with Phila. Orch., Chgo. Symphony Orch., London Symphony Orch., others. Served with USAAF, 1944-46. Mem. Am. Guild Mus. Artists (gov.). Congregationalist. Clubs: Dutch Treat (N.Y.C.); Manhasset Bay Yacht. Home: Cincinnati Ohio Died Mar. 8, 1991. †

ALEXANDER, JOHN HEALD, lawyer; b. Denver, Nov. 15, 1904; s. Harry Heald and Margaret (McGowan) A.; m. Edna Perkins, Aug. 28, 1926; children: John Heald Jr., Judith, Anne. A.B., Yale, 1926, LL.B., 1928. Bar: N.Y. 1929, N.J. 1943, D.C. 1966. Formerly sr. ptnr. firm Mudge, Rose, Guthrie, Alexander & Ferdon, N.Y.C., now counsel; chmn. Pres.'s Task Force on Bus. Tax, 1969-70. Mem. Am., N.Y. State bar assns., Assn. Bar City N.Y., Am. Law Inst. Clubs: Yale (N.Y.C.); Baltusrol Golf (Springfield, N.J.). Home: New York N.Y. Deceased. †

ALEXANDER, LOUIS, writer, educator; b. N.Y.C., Mar. 15, 1917; s. Louis I. and Gertrude (Seydel) A.; m. Paulette Marlowe, Dec. 23, 1948 (div. Dec. 1968); children: Kathryn, Marjory; m. Mildred Nootsie Crowe, Aug. 8, 1976. B.S. in Mktg., U. Newark, 1941; M. Letters in Journalism, U. Houston, 1961. Reporter, county editor Houston Chronicle, 1947-57; free-lance writer for mags. and newspapers, 1957-90; instr., then asst. prof. journalism U. Houston, 1954-82; corr. Wall Street Jour., 1959-75, Newsweek, 1964-90, Nat. Pub. Radio, 1972-80; pres. All News Is Local, Inc., pubs. Carolina's Bus. Weekly, Asheville, N.C. Author: Beyond the Facts, 1975, 2d edit., 1982. Mem. Bellaire Parks and Recreation Commn., 1957-60; mem. fin. subcom. Sch. Adv. Com., Bellaire, 1976-77; mem. citizens adv. bd. Met. Transit Authority, 1978-83. Served with USAAF, 1942-45; to capt. USAF, 1951-52; lt. col. Res. Decorated D.F.C., Air medal with three oak leaf clusters. Mem. Am. Soc. Journalists and Authors, Nat. Conf. Editorial Writers, Western Carolina Entrepreneurial Council (pres. 1986-87), SCORE, Press Club (Houston).Died Oct. 22, 1990. Home: Richmond Tex. †

ALEXANDER, W(ALTER) BOYD, college official; b. Phila., June 28, 1898; s. George Black and Isabelle Herron (Ferson) A.; m. Ellen Priscilla Dunn, Aug. 3, 1918 (dec. Apr. 1964); children: Joanne Stern, Rodney Boyd. Student Williamson Sch. Mech. Trades, Drexel Inst., 1915-18, 1918; BS in Edn., U. Pa., 1925, MA, 1927; LiitD, Antioch Coll., 1963. Journeyman carpenter, 1918-19, bldg. contractor, 1919-20; instr. math. Vet.'s Bur. Dept. Temple U., 1920-24; instr. indsl. arts high sch. Collingswood, N.J., 1924-25; dir. vocat. edn. Norristown, Pa., 1925-26; dir. edn. Phila. YMCA, 1926-29; assoc. pers. dir. Antioch Coll., 1929-32, vocat. counselor, instr. math., 1932-34, asst. prof. edn., 1935-36, assoc. prof., 1936-41; prof. edn. Antioch Coll., from 1941, asst. to pres., 1936-38, dean adminstrn., 1938-55, dean of faculty, 1956-63, acting pres., 1939-40, 47-48, v.p., 1941-63, v.p., dean faculty emeritus, cons., from 1963. Trustee Wilberforce U., from 1961. Fellow AAAS, Am. Geog. Soc.; mem. North Cen. Assn. Schs. & Colls., Ohio Coll. Assn., Am. Humanist Assn., others. *

ALEXANDER, WILLIAM PATTERSON, agriculture executive; b. New Haven, July 29, 1893; s. Arthur Chambers and Mary Elizabeth (Hillenbrand) A.; m. Alice Renton Bond, Feb. 27, 1919; children: William Patterson, Benjamin Bond, Henry Arthur, Alice Renton. M.S., Yale U.; postgrad. U. Hawaii. Dir. research EWA Plantation, Hawaii, 1920-27; gen. adminstr. Gomez-Mena, Hauana, Cuba, 1927-29; gen. mgr. Grove Farm Co., Lihue, Hawaii, 1929-54, ret. Author: Irrigation, 1924; Grove Farm-100 Years, 1965. Contbr. articles to profl. jours. Chmn., YMCA, Honolulu, 1959-65; adv. bd. Salvation Army, 1955-65; pres. Hawaiian Hist. Soc., 1955-92, Hawaiian Mission Children's Soc., 1925; regent U. Hawaii, 1940-52. Served with USN, 1917-1919. Paul Harris fellow, 1983; mem. C. of C. Kauai, C. of C. Honolulu. Republican. United Ch. Christ. Clubs: Waikiki Yacht, Pacific, Outrigger. Lodges: Rotary, Masons. Deceased. Home: Honolulu Hawaii †

ALFANGE, DEAN, lawyer; b. Constantinople, Dec. 2, 1897; came to U.S., 1901; m. Thalia Perry, Aug. 11, 1929; children—Whitman, Dean. A.B., Hamilton Coll., 1922; LL.B., Columbia U., 1925. Bar: N.Y, U.S. Supreme Ct. 1925. Since practiced in N.Y.C.; chmn. N.Y.C. Appeals Bd., SSS; Chmn. Enemy Alien Hearing Bd. So. Dist. N.Y.; mem. N.Y. State Bd. Inquiry in Longshore Industry; founder Legion for Am. Unity, 1940; mem. exec. com. Citizens for Victory; dir. Better Understanding Found. for Religious and Racial Tolerance, Greek War Relief Assn.; nat. chmn. Emergency Com. to Save Jewish People of Europe; chmn. N.Y. State Quarter Horse Racing Commn., 1971-73, Am. Christian Palestine Com. of Greater N.Y.; Chmn. Fgn. Lang. Speakers Bur. Dem. Presdl. Campaign Com., 1940; Dem. candidate for Congress 17th N.Y. Dist., 1941; nominated for gov. N.Y., Am. Labor Party, 1942; chmn. Liberal and Labor Com. which founded Liberal party State of N.Y., 1944, Israel Anniversary Celebration Com., 1949. Author: My Creed This Week mag. and Reader's Digest The Horse Racing Industry, 1976. Trustee Fashion Inst. Tech., N.Y., United Greek Orthodox Charities, Archdiocesan Greek Cathedral of Holy Trinity, N.Y.; pres. LaGuardia Meml. Settlement House. Recipient Freedom Found. Award, 1960; Theodore Roosevelt Meml. award for non-fiction book The Supreme Court and the National Will, 1937; Donor scholarship endowments Hamilton Coll. to promote democratic govt. and religious understanding; elected to Settlement House Hall of Fame, 1986. Mem. Nat. Inst. Social Scis., Am. Acad. Polit. and Social Sci., UN Assn. (dir.), NAACP, Am., N.Y. bar assns., Am. Legion, Nat. Inst. Social Scis., Am. Hellenic Congress (nat. chmn.), Order of Ahepa (past nat. pres.), Am. Quarter Horse Assn. (racing com.), Grand St. Boys Assn., United Hunts Assn., Phi Beta Kappa, Pi Delta Epsilon, Delta Sigma Rho. Clubs: Mason, Elk, Turf and Field, Economic of N.Y, Circus Saints and Sinners; Governor's (N.Y.) (exec. com.). Home: New York N.Y. Died Oct. 24, 1989; cremated.

ALFORD, ANDREW, consulting engineer; b. Samara, USSR, Aug. 5, 1904; m. Helen Glaser, Apr. 3, 1930. AB, U. Calif., 1924, postgrad,, 1924-26; postgrad,, Calif. Inst. Tech., 1927-28; D in Applied Sci. (hon.), Ohio U., 1975. Registered profl. engr., Mass. Lab. worker Fox Film Co., Beverly Hills, Calif., 1929-31; engr. Mackay Radio and Telegraph Co. subs. ITT, 1934-41; head Air Navigation Lab. of ITT, 1941-43; leader antenna group Radio Research Lab. Harvard U., Cambridge, Mass., 1943-44; head direction finder and antenna div. Radio Research Lab. Harvard U., Cambridge, 1944-45; pres. Andrew Alford Cons. Engrs., Woburn, Mass., from 1945, Alford Mfg. Co., Woburn, from 1948. Inventor loop antenna, equi-signal glide path, null reference glide path, wide aperature localizer system, VOR system. Recipient Automated Measurements Career award Automatic R.F. Techniques Group, 1986. Fellow IEEE (presdl. cert. of merit 1948, Pioneer award 1965, mem. various coms.); mem. N.Y. Acad. Scis. Home: Saugus Mass. Died Feb. 11, 1992. †

ALFRIEND, JOHN SAMUEL, banker; b. Norfolk, Va., July 6, 1897; s. Richard Jeffery and Mary Emily (Hulme) A.; m. Harriet Lucille Sanderlin, June 17, 1922; children: Anne Bolling Abbitt, Susan Bland Bevan. Ed. pub. schs., Norfolk; student, Norfolk Acad., 1911-14; grad., Am. Inst. Banking. Messenger Nat. Bank Commerce Norfolk, 1914, clerical worker, until 1931, cashier, 1931-36, asst. to pres., 1936-37, exec. v.p., dir., 1937-42, pres., 1942-59, chmn. bd., 1959-62, CEO, 1959-62; chmn., CEO Va. Nat. Bank, 1963-64, chmn. exec. com., from 1964; dir. numerous corps. With USMC, World War I. Decorated Purple Heart; recipient King's Medal for Svc. in Cause of Freedom, 1946, disting. svc. award Va. C. of C., 1959, Meritorious Pub. Svc. citation USN, 1962. Mem. Va. Bankers Assn., Am. Bankers Assn., Norfolk C. of C., Order First Families Va., SAR, others. *

ALKER, GEORGE, JR., radiology educator; b. Budapest, Hungary, Oct. 22, 1929; came to U.S., 1949; s. George Sr. and Helen (Varosy) A.; m. June Braun, May 17, 1958; 1 child, John. BS, Allegheny Coll., 1952; MD, U. Buffalo, 1956. Intern E.J. Meyer Meml. Hosp., Buffalo, 1956-57, resident in radiology, 1957-60; attending radiologist Erie County Med. Ctr., Buffalo, from 1962; prof., chmn. dept. radiology SUNY at Buffalo, from 1981; cons. neuroradiology Buffalo VA Med. Ctr., from 1962. Co-author: 4 books; contbr. articles to profl. jours. Mem. traffic safety bd. Erie County, Buffalo, 1988-89. Capt. M.C., U.S. Army, 1960-62; maj. USAR, 1957-65. Recipient Cert. of Appreciation N.Y. Coalition Safety Belt Use, 1989. Mem. Am. Coll. Radiology, Am. Soc. Neuroradiology, Cervical Spine Rsch. Soc. (sec. 1988-89), Buffalo Radiol. Soc. (pres. 1976-77), Hungarian Med. Assn. Am. (pres. elect 1989). Republican. Roman Catholic. Home: Buffalo N.Y. Died Dec. 31, 1991.

ALLAN, RUPERT MORTIMER, JR., public relations executive; b. St. Louis, Oct. 25, 1912; s. Rupert Mortimer and Edna Bates Weil Allan. B.A., Washington U., St. Louis, 1933; postgrad., U. Toulouse, France, 1934-35; M.A., Oxford (Eng.) U., 1937. Master Taylor Sch. Boys, Clayton, Mo., 1938-41; book reviewer St. Louis Post-Dispatch, 1940-41; writer Sta. KSD, St. Louis, 1941; polit. affairs officer Dept. State, 1945-46; asst. dir. public relations Universal-Internat. Studios, Universal City, Calif., 1946-47; asst. continental mgr. Motion Picture Assn. Am., Paris, 1947-49; West Coast corr. Flair mag., 1949; a West Coast editor Look mag., 1950-55; v.p. Arthur P. Jacobs Co. pub. relations, Beverly Hills, Calif., 1955-60; ptnr. ICPR and predecessors, pub. relations, Los Angeles and Beverly Hills, 1960-77; exec. v.p. Stone/Hallinan Assos. Inc., Public Relations, from 1978; hon. consul of Monaco in Los Angeles, from 1976; trustee The Actors Studio, from 1985. Mem. adv. bd. Brody Arts Fund, from 1986. Served as lt. comdr. USNR, 1942-45. Democrat. Episcopalian. Home: Beverly Hills Calif. Died Aug. 24, 1991; cremated.

ALLEN, BEULAH REAM, physician, academic dean; b. Dingle, Idaho, Jan. 26, 1897; d. William Dewine and Nora Ellen (Crockett) Ream; m. Henderson Wilcox Allen, Sept. 27, 1937; children: Lee, Henderson Wilcox. RN, Ill. Tng. Sch. for Nurses, 1922; AB, U. Utah, 1928; MD, U. Calif., San Francisco, 1932. Intern Children's Hosp., San Francisco, 1931-32; resident, chief resident St. Luke's Hosp., Manila, Philippines, 1932-34; med. officer charge Mary J. Johnston Hosp., Manila, 1934-35, 37-41; Japanese war prisoner Baguio and Manila, 1941-45; pvt. practice San Leandro, Calif., 1945-47, Palo Alto, San Francisco, 1947-61; tchr. supervised family rels. classes, from 1951; dean Coll. Nursing Brigham Young U., from 1961. Recipient Medal of Freedom, 1945. Mem. Am. Acad. Sci., Calif. Med. Assn., Santa Clara Med. Assn., Am. Acad. Gen. Practice, Alpha Epsilon Iota. Mem. LDS Ch. *

ALLEN, DAVID, vocational school educator; b. Los Angeles, Aug. 10, 1919; B.A., Long Beach State Coll., 1957; M.A., Los Angeles State Coll., 1958; Ed.D., U. Calif. at Los Angeles, 1962; m. Lucille Mary Scott, May 22, 1944; children: Bruce Robert, Bonnie Lynn. Line service mechanic Pan Am. World Airways, 1946-56; instr. Los Angeles Trade-Tech. Coll., 1952-56; spl. supr. Bur. Indsl. Edn., Calif. Dept. Edn., 1956-60; supr. tradetech. tchr. edn. U. Calif. at Los Angeles, 1960-92, lectr. Sch. Edn., 1962-92, assoc. dir. Div. Vocat. Edn., 1967-92; cons. ednl. adv. com. Calif. Instn. for Men, Ventura Sch. for Girls, 1961-92, Nat. Council Vocat. Edn., 1967; dir. nat. conf. curriculum devel. in vocat. and tech. edn. U.S. Office Edn., 1969. Served with USNR, 1944-46. Recipient citation of service Dept. Corrections State of Calif., 1966, certificate of award FAA, 1967, Presdl. Distinguished Service and medal award for aviation research FAA-Dept. Transp., 1971; named Man of

Year, Aviation Technician Edn. Council, 1969; Calif. Ships award. Fellow Soc. Licensed Aircraft Engrs. and Technologists Gt. Britain; mem. Am. Vocat. Assn., Calif. Indsl. Edn. Assn. (past treas.), Nat. Soc. Study of Edn., Epsilon Pi Tau (Laureate citation 1965), Phi Delta Kappa. Author: Handbook for Beginning Teachers, 1957; A Guide for Developing Electronic Courses, 1958; Simulation and Program Development Strategies, 1967; Automatic Controls, An Instructor's Guide, 1962; Polysensory Learning Through Multi-Media Instruction in Trade and Technical Education, 1968; Air Traffic Control, A Feasibility Study, 1970; Curriculum Development for Inhalation Therapy, 1971; Clean Air Through Automotive Emission Center, 1972; Analysis and Synthesis for a Vocational Student Information System, 1972; Suggested Models for Solutions to Current Vocational Education Problems, 1972; A Survey of Text Materials Used in Aviation Maintenance Schools, 1974; A Survey of the Aviation Mechanics Occupation, 1974; Principles of Adult, Vocational, and Technical Education, 1975; Social and Academic Characteristic Assessments of Black Inner-City High School Students; An Analysis of Alternatives for Payment to States under Public Law 94-482, 1978; Principles and Practices of Vocational Education, 1979; The Instructional Processes in Vocational Education, 1980; A Guide for Professional Development, 1981; contbr. articles to profl. jours., chpt. to yearbook. Deceased. Home: Los Angeles Calif. †

ALLEN, EDWARD JONES, educator, labor-management arbitrator; b. Canon City, Colo., July 30, 1898; s. J. Henry and Jennie (Jones) A.; m. Fanny C. Sheldon, Aug. 19, 1921; children: Betty, Carolyn Turner, Robert Edward. BA, Colo. Coll., 1921; AM, Columbia U., 1923, PhD, 1936. Tchr. econs. & history high sch., Twin Falls, Idaho, 1921-22; asst. econs. dept. Columbia U., 1922-24; officer of instrn. Columbia U. Ext., 1924-27; asst. to dir. univ. ext. Columbia U., 1927-28; acting. dir. Seth Low Jr. Coll. Columbia U., 1928-31, dir., 1931-36; dean Coll. Arts and Scis., prof. econs. U. Maine, 1936-41; dean Coll. Arts and Scis., prof. econs. U. Denver, 1941-47, dean acad. adminstrn., prof. econs., 1947-49; dean coll. prof. econs. Earlham Coll., 1949-51; chmn. 11th Regional WSB, 1951-53; arbitrator labor mgmt. disputes, 1953-54; assoc. dir. Joint Coun. on Econ. Edn., 1955-59; prof. econs. State Univ. Coll., Plattsburgh, N.Y., from 1959; instr. econs. CCNY, 1923-27; part-time instr. various other instns. With SATC. Mem. Am. Econ. Assn., NEA, Am. Edn. Fellowship, Am. Arbitration Assn., Ind. Conf. on Higher Edn., Nat. Acad. Arbitrators, Beta Theta Pi. *

ALLEN, GEORGE, former professional football coach, football analyst; b. Detroit, Apr. 29, 1922; s. Earl R. and Loretta (Hannigan) A.; m. Etty L. Lumbroso, May 26, 1951; children: George, Gregory, Bruce, Jennifer. B.A., M.A., U. Mich.; postgrad., U. So. Calif. Formerly football coach Morningside Coll., Sioux City, Iowa, Whittier (Calif.) Coll.; coach defense Chicago Bears; head coach Los Angeles Rams, 1978; head coach, v.p., gen. mgr. Washington Redskins (Nat. Football Conf.), 1971-77; football commentator and analyst CBS Sports, 1979-82; coach and gen. mgr. Chgo. Blitz, 1982-83; coach Ariz. Wranglers, Phoenix, 1983-84; gen. mgr. Ariz. Wranglers, 1984-85; football commentator and analyst CBS Sports, 1985-90; football coach Calif. State U., Long Beach, 1989-90. Chmn. Pres.'s Council on Phys. Fitness and Sports, 1980-87; chmn., chief exec. officer Nat. Fitness Found. Home: Long Beach Calif. Died Dec. 31, 1990. †

ALLEN, HERBERT, steel company executive; b. Ratcliff, Tex., May 2, 1907; s. Jasper and Leona (Matthews) A.; m. Helen Daniels, Aug. 28, 1937; children: David Daniels (dec.), Anne (Mrs. Jonathan Taft Symonds), Michael Herbert. B.S. in Mech. Engring., Rice U., 1929. Registered profl. engr., Tex. Engaged in research, 1929-31; with Cameron Iron Works, Inc. (and predecessor), Houston, from 1931; v.p. engring. and mfg. Cameron Iron Works, Inc. (and predecessor), 1942-50, v.p., gen. mgr., 1950-66, pres., 1966-73, chmn. bd., 1973-77. Bd. govs. Rice U., Houston, 1949-64, trustee, 1964-76, chmn., 1972-76. Named Inventor of the Yr., Houston Patent Attys. Assn., 1977, 88; recipient Gold medal for Disting. Svc., Rice U. Alumni Assn., 1975, Disting. Achievement award Offshore Tech. Conf., 1990. Hon. mem. ASME (Petroleum Div. award 1977); mem. Nat. Acad. Engring., Am. Inst. Mining, Metall. and Petroleum Engrs., Am. Petroleum Inst., Tex. Soc. Profl. Engrs. (named Engr. of Year 1961), Houston C. of C. (bd. dirs. 1952-54, v.p. 1954-55, dir.-at-large 1962), Houston Engring. and Sci. Soc., Tau Beta Pi. Episcopalian. Clubs: River Oaks Country, Petroleum, Ramada, Houston, Bayou (Houston); Metropolitan (N.Y.C.). Home: Houston Tex. Deceased. †

ALLEN, IRWIN, motion picture writer, producer, director; b. N.Y.C., June 12; s. Joseph and Eva (Davis) A. Student, CCNY, Columbia U. Radio news commentator KLAC, Hollywood, Calif.; syndicated newspaper columnist, motion picture editor Atlas Features Syndicate, Hollywood; lit. agt. motion pictures; television producer, commentator Hollywood. Prodn. exec.: Double Dynamite; assoc. producer: Where Danger Lives; co-producer: A Girl in Every Port; producer, dir., screenplay writer: The Sea Around Us (Bet Documentary film Academy award 1952); producer: Dangerous Mission, When Time Ran Out; writer, producer, dir.: Animal World; producer, dir., co-writer screenplay: The Story of Mankind; producer, co-writer screenplay: The Big Circus; producer, dir., co-writer: The Lost World, Voyage to the Bottom of the Sea, Five Weeks in a Balloon, City Beneath the Sea; producer, dir. spl. action sequences The Towering Inferno (David Donatello award and Academy Awards for photography and song), 1974, The Poseidon Adventure (Academy Award for Best Song (The Morning After) 1972); producer, dir.: The Swarm; Beyond the Poseidon Adventure; creator, producer: TV series Land of The Giants, Lost in Space, The Time Tunnel, Voyage to the Bottom of the Sea, Swiss Family Robinson, Code Red; producer: TV movies Memory of Eva Ryker, Adventures of the Queen, The Time Travellers, Flood, Fire, The Return of Captain Nemo, Hanging by a Thread, Cave-In, The Night the Bridge Fell Down, Alice in Wonderland, Outrage. Recipient Internat. Laurel award Motion Picture Exhibitors, Blue Ribbon award for excellent motion picture prodn. Box Office mag. (5 times), Merit award So. Calif. Fedn. Womans Clubs (5 times); named NATO Producer of Yr., Fox Showman of Yr. Home: Malibu Calif. Died Nov. 2, 1991; buried Mt. Sinai Meml. Pk., L.A.

ALLEN, JAMES R., air force officer, business executive; b. Louisville, Nov. 17, 1925; s. James Smoot and Ruth (Rodgers) A.; m. Kathryn Lewis; children: Jeffrey, Kathryn. B.S. in Mil. Engring, U.S. Mil. Acad., 1948; postgrad., Army Command and Gen. Staff Coll., 1959-60, Indsl. Coll. Armed Forces, 1964-65; M.S. in Bus. Adminstrn, George Washington U., 1965. Commd. 2d lt. USAF, 1948, advanced through grades to gen., 1977; mem. flying tng. classes Randolph AFB, Tex., Nellis AFB, Nev., 1948-49; with 18th Fighter Group P.I., 1949-51; aide to comdr. Fifth Air Force, Korea, 1951; mem. 71st Fighter Squadron, Greater Pitts. Airport, 1951-53; co. tactical officer U.S. Mil. Acad., West Point, N.Y., 1953-56; flight comdr., squadron ops. officer 53d Fighter Day Squadron, Ramstein Air Base, Germany, 1956-58; with Directorate Plans Hdqrs. U.S. Air Forces in Europe, 1958-59; with directorate Plans Hdqrs. USAF, Pentagon, 1960, asst. dep. dir. plans, 1968-69; dep. dir. plans and policy Directorate of Plans, dep. chief staff plans and operations, 1969-72; comdr. 4th Tactical Fighter Squadron, Eglin AFB, Fla., 1965; dep. comdr. for operations 12th Tactical Fighter Wing, Cam Ranh Bay, Vietnam, 1965-67, 3615th Pilot Tng. Wing, Craig AFB, Ala., 1967-68; comdr. 19th Air Div., Carswell AFB, Tex.; asst. dep. chief staff for ops. SAC, Offutt AFB, Nebr., 1972-73; chief staff SAC, Offutt AFB, from 1973; supt. USAF Acad., 1974-77; chief staff SHAPE, 1977-79; dep. comdr.-in-chief U.S. European Command, 1979-81; comdr.-in-chief Mil. Airlift Command, 1981-83, ret., 1983; chmn., chief exec. officer Internat. Planning and Analysis Ctr., Inc., 1983-90, vice chmn., from 1990; pres., chief exec. officer CAE-Link Corp., 1990-91. Decorated D.S.M. with oak leaf cluster, Legion of Merit with two oak leaf clusters, D.F.C. with one oak leaf cluster, Bronze Star, Air medal with eleven oak leaf clusters, Air Force Commendation medal with one oak leaf cluster, Army Commendation medal; comdr. French Ordre Nationale du Mérite; Sudanese Order of the Two Niles. Home: Alexandria Calif. Died Aug. 11, 1992. †

ALLEN, J(OSEPH) GARROTT, surgeon, educator; b. Elkins, W.Va., June 5, 1912; s. James Edward and Susan H. (Garrott) A.; m. Dorothy O. Travis, July 15, 1940 (div. 1968); children: Barry Worth, Edward Henry, Nannette (Mrs. Antonio Alarcón), Lester Travis, Joseph Garrott; m. Kathryn L. Shipley, Dec. 27, 1968; children: Robert Kelman, Grant Frederick, Susan. Student, Davis and Elkins Coll., 1930-32; AB, Washington U., St. Louis, 1934; MD, Harvard, 1938. Diplomate: Am. Bd. Surgery (mem. bd. 1958-64). Intern Billings Hosp., U. Chgo., 1939; asst. resident surgery U. Chgo., 1940-44, instr. surgery, 1943-47, asst. prof., 1947-48, asso. prof., 1948-51, prof., 1951-59; research asso. metall. labs. Manhattan Project, 1944-46; group leader Argonne Nat. Lab., 1946-59; prof. Sch. Medicine, Stanford U., 1959-77; active emeritus, from 1977; exec. dept. surgery, 1959-61; mem. surgery study sect. USPHS, 1955-59. Author: (with others) Surgery-Principles and Practice, 1957, 4th edit., 1970, Shock and Transfusion, Therapy, 1959, The Epidemiology of Hepatitis, 1972, also sci. papers.; Editor: (with others) Peptic Ulcer, 1959; co-editor: (with others) Family Health Ency, 1970; chief editor: (with others) Archives of Surgery, 1960-70; mem. editorial bd.: (with others) Lab World, 1978. Trustee Am. Youth Found., 1954-67; Mem. NRC, 1950-54; Mem. standards com. Am. Assn. Blood Banks, 1958. Recipient prize for protamine sulfate/heparin work Chgo. Surg. Soc., 1940; John J. Abel prize for research irradiation injury Am. Assn. Pharmacology and Exptl. Therapeutics, 1948; Ednl. award Am. Assn. Blood Banks, 1954; Gold medal for original research Ill. Med. Soc., 1948, 52; Samuel D. Gross award Pa. Acad. Surgery, 1955; First Merit award Chgo. Tech. Securities Council, 1955; First John Elliott award Am. Assn. Blood Banks, 1956; citation Washington Alumni Assn., 1960; Ford Found. grant, 1986-87. Fellow AAAS; Mem. Soc. Exptl. Biology and Medicine, Am. Physiol. Soc., A.C.S. (chmn. com. blood and allied problems), Internat. Surg. Group (founder), AMA (Gold medal for original research 1948), Am. Surg. Assn., Soc. Clin. Surgery (sec. 1958-60), S.F. Surg. Soc., Soc. Univ. Surgeons, Am. Cancer Soc. (chmn. com. cancer therapy), Western, Pacific Coast surg. assns., Surg. Infection Soc. (founder mem. 1980), Halsted Soc., Alpha Omega Alpha. Home: Stanford Calif. Died Jan. 10, 1992; buried Elkins, W.Va.

ALLEN, KATHERINE YARNELL, state legislator; b. Pueblo, Colo., June 17, 1925; d. Paul and Gladys deFord (Meffley) Yarnell; m. William Allen, Jr., Sept. 20, 1947; children: Susan M. Southwick, Mary K., Barbara D. A.B. in Econs., U. Denver, 1947. State legislator Wash. House of Reps., Olympia, 1983-92. Pres. Edmonds Sch. Dist. #15 Sch. Bd., Lynnwood, Wash., 1976, mem., 1973-77; mayor pro-tem, Edmonds, mem. Edmonds City Council, 1977-83. Recipient Thanks Badge, Totem Girl Scout Council, 1980, named Disting. Girl Scout, 1985; recipient Outstanding Service award Dist. PTA, 1978; Living Legend award Edmonds Sch. Dist. #15, 1985. Mem. LWV, AAUW, Elected Washington Women, Women's Polit. Caucus. Republican. Presbyterian. Deceased. Home: Edmonds Wash. †

ALLEN, ROGER WILLIAMS, university dean; b. Birmingham, Ala., Mar. 20, 1897; s. Charles Morehead and Nannie Arabella (Thomson) A.; m. Margaret Ann Church, Nov. 22, 1927; children: Patsy Jane, Roger W. BS, Auburn U., 1918, MS, 1919; AM, U. Mich., 1921; PhD, Columbia U., 1927. Chemist D.C. Pickard, cons. chemists, summer 1917, E.I. Du Pont de Nemours & Co., Washburn, Wis., summer 1918, CWS, Cleve., 1918, Ala. State Chem. Lab., Auburn, 1919, U.S. Dept. Entomology, summer 1921, Inecto, Inc. and Marinello Co., N.Y.C., 1926-28; prof. chemistry Howard Coll., Birmingham, 1921-22, 23-26; prof. chemistry Auburn U., 1928-41, dean Sch. Sci. and Lit., from 1941. Author: Fundamentals of Chemistry, 1930. Dir. fund drive Auburn Community Chest, 1940. Mem. Ala. Acad. Sci., Ala. Ednl. Assn., Sigma Xi, Phi Kappa Phi, Phi Lambda Upsilon, Omicron Delta Kappa, Delta Sigma Pi, Alpha Epsilon Delta, Pi Kappa Alpha, Phi Eta Sigma. Home: Auburn Ala. Died Mar. 15, 1990.

ALLEN, ROY O., JR., architect; b. Sayre, Pa., Mar. 14, 1921; s. Roy O. and Lyndall (Harding) A.; m. Marion Marshall Taylor, Dec. 12, 1964; 1 child, Michael; children by previous marriage: Jeffrey, Gary, Leslie. BS in Architecture, Pa. State U., 1943. Procedures engr. Curtis-Wright Corp., 1942-45; with Skidmore, Owings & Merrill, N.Y.C., 1946-92, past gen. ptnr.; Fellow AIA, Mus. Modern Art, Nat. Golf Links Club (S. Hampton, L.I.), Univ. Club, Met. Club, Links Club. Home: New York N.Y. Died Mar. 25, 1992.

ALLEN, THOMAS OSCAR, oil and gas consulting executive; b. Weimar, Tex., Dec. 8, 1914; s. Dee Hansworth and Anna (Uzzell) A.; m. Ninette Marie Smith, Aug. 23, 1938; children: Thomas E., Jean Allen-Ikeson. B.S. in Elec. Engring, Tex. A&M, 1936; grad., Army Command and Gen. Staff Coll., 1943. With Humble Oil & Refining Co. (Exxon Co. U.S.A.), Houston, 1936-58; supervising petroleum engr. Humble Oil & Refining Co. (Exxon Co. U.S.A.), 1949-53, sr. supervising petroleum engr., 1953-58; research mgr. petroleum prodn. research div. Jersey Prodn. Research Co. (Exxon Co.), Tulsa, 1958-63; sr. research assoc. Jersey Prodn. Research Co. (Exxon Co.), 1965; pres. Oil and Gas Cons. Internat., Inc., Tulsa, 1965-84, chief exec. officer, from 1984. Co-author: Production Operations, Vols. 1-2, 1978, 3d edit., 1989. Served to maj. AUS, 1942-46. Mem. AIME (disting. lectr. 1966-67), Am. Petroleum Inst. (chmn. prodn. com. south dist. 1955-56, chmn. nat. subcom. for Hall of Petroleum, Smithsonian Instn. 1961-67), Am. Petroleum Inst. Home: Tulsa Okla. Died Nov. 8, 1989; buried Calvary Cemetery, Tulsa.

ALLGOOD, CLARENCE WILLIAM, federal judge; b. Birmingham, Ala., Sept. 12, 1902; s. Robert Veneable and Patricia (Robinson) A.; m. Marie Maxwell, June 27, 1927; 1 son, Clarence William. Student, Howard Coll., 1921-23; B.S., Ala. Poly. Inst., 1926; LL.B., Brimingham Sch. Law, 1941. Bar: Ala. 1941. Referee in bankruptcy U.S. Dist. Ct. No. Ala., 1937-61; U.S. dist. judge No. Dist. Ala., 1961-91, sr. dist. judge.; Dir. Fidelity Mortgage Co. Ala., Fidelity Fed. Savs. and Loan Assn. Author articles; contbr. textbooks. Mem. counsel profl. relations Am. Hosp. Assn., 1950-52; chmn. Ala. Hosp. Trustee Assn., 1951; Chmn. trustees South Highland Infirmary, Birmingham, 1945-55; trustee Crippled Childrens Hosp. and Clinic, from 1941, pres., 1958; trustee Ala. Soc. Crippled Children and Adults, 1946-48. Mem. Am., Ala., Birmingham bar assns., Pi Kappa Alpha, Sigma Delta Kappa, Blue Key. Clubs: Mason (Birmingham), Shriner (Birmingham), Elk. (Birmingham), Civitan (Birmingham). Home: Birmingham Ala. Died Nov. 30, 1991; buried Elmwood Cemetery, Birmingham.

ALLISON, B. R., conservationist, consultant; b. Rockwell City, Iowa, Nov. 12, 1915; s. Bert Ross and Florence June (Anderson) A.; m. Bernice Dwyer, May. 3, 1936; children: Camille Allison Miller, Gere Lynne Allison Brown, Michael R. Student, George Peabody Coll., 1938-39. With Civilian Conservation Corps, 1934; park supt. Tenn. Dept. Conservation, Nashville, 1940-47, dir. div. state parks, 1947-49; exec. dir. Tenn. Rural Electric Coop. Assn., Nashville, 1949-51; owner, mgr. Highland Rim Nursery-Buck Allison Inc., Nashville,

1951-75; commr. Tenn. Dept. Conservation, Nashville, 1975-79; cons., chmn. bot. com. Tenn. Bot. Gardens, Nashville, 1958-62; park commr. Metro Nashville Bd. Parks, Nashville, 1964-72; pres. Tenn. Nurserymen's Assn., Nashville, 1958; sr. fellow Am. Inst. Park Dirs., 1948. Contbr. articles to jours. in field. Bd. dirs. Nashville Boy's Club, 1971; bd. dirs. Nashville Children's Mus., 1971-73; mem. Hist. Commn., Nashville, 1981-83; pres. Tenn. Hist. Soc., 1981-83. Served with USN, 1943-45. Recipient Athens award Smithsonian Instn., 1960. Life mem. Tenn. Conservation League; life. mem. Nature Conservancy; life mem. Am. Forestry Assn.; mem. Am. Masters Foxhounds Assn., Am. Legion. Democrat. Roman Catholic. Home: Nashville Tenn. Deceased. †

ALLISON, FRAN, radio and television actress; b. LaPorte City, Iowa; m. Archie Levington. Student, Coe Coll., Cedar Rapids, Iowa. Tchr. pub. schs. Iowa, began entertainment career as radio singer, 1934; began entertainment career as radio singer Chgo., 1937; prin. radio role Aunt Fanny on Breakfast Club; TV role Kukla, Fran, and Ollie, 1947-57; Fran Allison show WGTN-TV, 1958-60; guest appearances TV shows, 1960-89. Home: New York N.Y. Died June 13, 1989.

ALLISON, IRL, pianist, music educator; b. Warren, Tex., Apr. 8, 1896; s. John Van and Mary Cleona (Richardson) A.; m. Jessie Johnson, July 3, 1918; children: Mary J., John, Irl, Lucile Ockey. AB, Baylor U., 1915, AM, 1922; MusD, Southwestern Conservatory, Dallas, 1947; LLD, Hardin-Simmons U., 1954; student, Chgo. Mus. Coll., 1919, Columbia U., 1920-21, 1942, U. Tex., 1943; MusD (hon.), Houston Conservatory, 1954. Dean music Rusk Coll., 1918-19; instr. piano Baylor Coll. for Women, 1921-23; dean fine arts Montezuma Coll., 1923-27; dean music Hardin-Simmons U., 1927-34; pres. Nat. Guild Piano Tchrs., Am. Coll. Musicians, from 1934. Author: Through the Years, Our George; also articles. Co-founder, donor grand prize Van Cliburn Internat. Quadrennial Piano Competition. Founder Golden Rule peace movement, originator World Peace Programs (radio), 1948. Mem. Music Tchrs. Nat. Assn., Music Educators Nat. Coun., Nat. Music Coun. *

ALLRED, EVAN LEIGH, chemistry educator; b. Deseret, Utah, May 22, 1929; s. Leigh Richmond and Louise (Cowley) A.; m. Barbara Klea Hawkins, Apr. 21, 1955; children: Kevin Michael, Richard Paul, Steven Leigh and Craig Lynn (twins). B.S., Brigham Young U., 1951, M.S., 1956; Ph.D., UCLA, 1959. Research chemist Phillips Petroleum Co., Bartlesville, Okla., 1951-54; instr. chemistry U. Wash., 1960-61; sr. research chemist Rohm & Haas Co., Phila., 1961-63; asst. prof. chemistry U. Utah, 1963-67, asso. prof., 1967-70, prof., 1970-91. David P. Gardner faculty fellow, 1976; NSF postdoctoral fellow, 1959-60. Mem. Am. Chem. Soc., Sigma Xi, Phi Kappa Phi. Mem. Ch. of Jesus Christ of Latter Day Saints. Home: Salt Lake City Utah Died 1991. †

ALLSMAN, PAUL T., government official; b. Kansas City, Mo., June 24, 1898; s. Charles C. and Martha Ann (Trekell) A.; m. Velma C. Hawkins, Sept. 15, 1926; children: Paul L., Rosemary F. Snow. BS in Mining & Metallurgy, U. Ariz., 1924, EM, 1937. Chemist United Verde Copper Co., Clarkdale, Ariz., 1925; chief chemist United Verde Copper Co., Jerome, 1926-31, engr., 1932-34, chief sampler, 1935; chief sampler United Verde br. Phelps Dodge Corp., Jerome, 1935-36, acting gen. foreman open pit, 1936; asst. mining engr. U.S. Bur. Mines divsn. office, 1936-37, assoc. mining engr., 1938-39; mining engr. charge mining divsn. office Salt Lake City, 1940-42, prin. mining engr., 1942-45; chief mining br., 1945-49, chief mining divsn. Region IV, Denver, 1950-51, regional dir. Region V, Mpls., 1952-54, regional dir. Region VII, Knoxville, Tenn., 1954; asst. regional dir. for minerals all Ea. states, from 1955; then staff rsch. mining engr. U.S. Bur. Mines, Washington. With U.S. Army, 1918. Mem. Am. Inst. Mining & Metall. Engrs., Sigma Tau, Sigma Chi. *

AL-MAKTUM, SHEIKH RASHID IBN SAID (SHEIKH RASHID BIN SAID AL-MAKTUM), ruler of Dubai, vice president and prime minister United Arab Emirates; b. 1914; s. Sheikh Said bin Maktum; married; 5 children; ed. privately. Ruler of Dubai, 1958-90; v.p. United Arab Emirates, 1971-90, prime minister, 1979-90. Home: Abu Dhabi United Arab Emirates

ALMENDROS, NESTOR, cinematographer; b. Barcelona, Spain, Oct. 30, 1930; s. Hermino and Maria (Cuyas) A. PhD, Havana (Cuba) U., 1955; student cinematography and film editing, CCNY, 1956; student cinematoraphy and film editing, Centro Sperimentale di Cinematografia, Rome, 1957. Tchr. Spanish Vassar Coll., 1957-59. Dir. documentary films for ICAIC, Cuba, 1959-61; films photographed include La Collectioneuse, 1966, My Night At Maud's, 1969 (Best cinematography award Nat. Assn. Film Critics), The Wild Child, 1969 (Best Photography award U.S. Assn. Film Critics), Claire's Knee, 1970, The Story of Adele H, 1975, The Marquise of O, 1975, Madame Rosa, 1977, The Last Metro, 1980 (Best Photography award French Acad. Motion Picture Arts and Techniques), Days of Heaven, 1979 (Best Cinematography award Am. Acad. Motion Picture Arts and Scis., U.S. Assn. Film Critics), Kramer vs Kramer, 1980, The Blue Lagoon, 1980, Sophie's Choice, 1982 (Best Photography award N.Y. Film Critics), Pauline at the Beach, 1983, Confidentially Yours, 1984, Places in the Heart, 1984, Heartburn, 1986; co-producer, co-dir. documentary film Nobody Listened, 1988; dir. photography Nadine, 1987, New York Stories (Martin Scorsese's segment), 1989, Billy Bathgate, 1991; author: A Man with a Camera, 1980; co-dir., co-writer: Improper Conduct, 1984. Decorated chevalier Order Arts and Letters, France, 1976. Mem. Am. Soc. Cinematographers. Home: New York N.Y. Died Mar. 4, 1992.

ALPER, JONATHAN LOUIS, theatre executive; b. Washington, Sept. 14, 1950; s. Jerome M. and Janet (Levy) A. BA, Amherst Coll., 1971; cert., Webber-Douglas Acad., London, 1974. Lit. mgr., dir. Folger Theatre Group, Washington, 1975-78; artistic assoc. Manhattan Theatre Club, N.Y.C., from 1980; dramaturg Sundance (Utah) Playwriting Conf., 1982, 84, 85, 86. Dir.: plays Alls Well That Ends Well, 1976, Teeth N'Smiles, 1977, Hamlet, 1978, Safe House, 1978, In the Valentine Lounge, 1986, Death of a Buick, 1987. Mem. Phi Beta Kappa. Home: New York N.Y. Deceased. †

ALPERT, GEORGE, lawyer; b. Boston, Mar. 24, 1898; s. William and Gertrude (Cline) A.; m. Gertrude R. Levin, Jan. 1, 1922; children: William, Leonard, Richard. LLB magna cum laude, Boston U., 1918; LLD, Brandeis U., 1953; MS (hon.), Bradford-Durfee Tech. Inst., 1956; DHL, Yeshiva U., 1959. Bar: Mass. 1919. Practiced law Boston, from 1919; sr. ptnr. Alpert and Alpert, 1947-56; asst. dist. atty. Suffolk County, 1924-27; pres., dir. N.Y., N.H. & H. R.R. Co., from 1956, chmn., from 1957. Trustee Brandeis U., Franklin Hosp.; co-chmn. United Jewish Appeal, 1946; bd. overseers Albert Einstein Coll. Medicine. Mem. ABA, Mass. Bar Assn., Boston Bar Assn., Waltham Bar Assn., Nat. Planning Assn., others. *

ALSAKER, ELWOOD CECIL, meat packing company executive; b. Rosholt, S.D., Oct. 31, 1924; s. Conrad Peter and Edla Victoria (Wass) A.; m. Virginia Cumming, Sept., 1947. B.B.A., U. Minn., 1948. With George A. Hormel & Co., Austin, Minn., from 1948; sr. v.p., treas. George A. Hormel & Co.; dir. First Bank of Austin, Minn., Hormel Found. Bd. dirs. Austin YMCA. Served with U.S. Army, 1944-46. Republican. Lutheran. Club: Austin Country (bd. dirs.). Home: Austin Minn. Died June 14, 1989; buried Graceland Cemetery, White Rock, S.D.

ALSDORF, JAMES WILLIAM, manufacturing executive; b. Chgo., Aug. 16, 1913; s. Anthony James and Camilie (Lederer) A.; m. Barbara Brach, Aug. 17, 1935 (div. Jan 2, 1950); children: Gregg, Lynne, Jeffery, James; m. Marilynn Markham, 1952. Student, Wharton Sch. Finance and Commerce, U. Pa., 1932-34. Chmn., dir. Alsdorf Internat. Ltd., Chgo.; Pres, and dir. A.J. Alsdorf Corp. (exporters and internat. mchts.); chmn. emeritus Cory Food Services, Inc. (mfrs.), Chgo.; also past officer, dir. subsidiaries and divs. Fresh'nd-Aire Co., Nicro Steel Products Co., Autopoint Co., Chgo.; dir., chmn. exec. com., v.p., sec. Grindmaster of Ky., Inc.; past. pres., treas., dir. Cory Sales Corp., Chgo., Cory Coffee Service Plan, Inc., Chgo., Cory Coffee Service Plan, Toronto, Ont., Can.; pres., dir. Cory AG, Zurich, Switzerland, Cory AG (and subsidiary), Cory Kaffee Serviceplan, Zurich; past treas., dir. Cory Corp. (Can.) Ltd., Toronto, Ont.; dir. Cory Still Internat. Ltd., London, Unarco Industries, Inc., Hyatt Internat. Corp., Chgo.; past dir. NK Cory AB, Stockholm, Sweden, NK Cory AB (and subsidiaries); Cory Coffee Service A/S, Oslo, Norway, OY Cory Coffee Service AB, Helsinki, Finland; past chmn. bd., dir. Flavor-Seal Corp., Chgo.; past pres., dir. Mitchell Mfg. Co. (and subsidiaries), Chgo. Mem. nat. com. U. Art Mus., U. Calif., Berkeley; mem. exec. com. of adv. council Snite Mus. Art, U. Notre Dame; mem. citizens bd. U. Chgo.; mem. collectors com. Nat. Gallery Art, Washington; asso. Rehab. Inst. Chgo.; mem. Mid-Am. com. Internat. Bus. and Govt. Cooperation, Inc.; mem. univ. library council Northwestern U. Library, Evanston, Ill.; past mem. of Gov. Ill.'s Com. Trade Expansion.; Pres., dir. Alsdorf Found., Chgo.; past bd. dirs. World Wildlife Fund, Washington; mem. 1001 club; trustee Menninger Found. of Topeka; past chmn., life trustee, life gov., disting. benefactor, chmn. nominating com., vice chmn. exec. com. Art Inst. Chgo.; bd. dirs., v.p. Sarah Siddons Soc., Chgo.; life trustee benefactor Indpls. Mus. Art; opus mem. Ravinia Festival Assn.; subscribing mem. Am. Craftsmen's Council, N.Y.C.; vis. com. div. humanities U. Chgo.; mem. adv. bd. Martin D'Arcy Gallery Art, Loyola U., Chgo.; mem. Far Eastern Studies com. U. Chgo., also Pres.'s Fund com.; past governing mem. Orchestral Assn.; life mem. Field Mus. Natural History, Chgo.; mem. internat. council Mus. Modern Art, N.Y.C.; v.p., vice chmn., contbg. mem., trustee com. Am. Assn. Museums, Washington; bd. govs Dumbarton Oaks; vice chmn. fine arts adv. com. Fed. Res. Bd.; mem. Renaissance Soc., U. Chgo.; founding mem. Old Masters Soc., Chgo.; sponsor Friends of Park; mem. Sustaining Fellows, mem. Textile Soc. Art Inst. Chgo.; trust asso. Chgo. Community Trust; mem. Cultural Affairs Com. USIA. Named to Wisdom Hall of Fame; recipient Wisdom Award of Honor, 1979, Centennial award Art Inst. Chgo., 1979; Bicentennial Arts Award medal King Gustav Adolph of Sweden. Mem. Chgo. Hort. Soc., Oriental Ceramics Soc., Am. Assn. Mus., Archaeol Inst. Am., Nat. Geog. Soc., Newcomen Soc. N.Am., Nat. Housewares Mfrs. Assn. Chgo. (pres. 1949-51, dir., mem. exec. com.), Gen. Alumni Bd. U. Pa., Northwestern U. Assos., Friends of Art of Northwestern U. (patron Block Gallery), Ordre des Compagnons du Beaujolais, Antiquarian Soc. (life), Chgo. Council Fine Arts (bus. adv. com.), Contemporary Art Circle Chgo. (founding mem.), Newberry Library Assn., Chgo. Hist. Soc. (life, gov.), Friends Asia House Gallery, Asia Soc., Chinese Art Soc. Am., Oriental Inst. of U. Chgo. (assoc., mem. adv. council), Friends Chgo. Public Library (mem. centennial com.), The Orientals, Archives Am. Art, Smithsonian Instn. (sustaining), Chgo. Public Sch. Art Soc., Nat. Trust Hist. Preservation, Wedgewood Soc. Chgo. (dir.), Soc. Contemporary Art (sponsor), Chgo. Council Fgn. Relations (mem. Chgo. com.), Friends of Neuberger Mus. (Purchase, N.Y.), Friends of Am. Mus. in Britain (N.Y.C.), Met. Mus. Art (nat. asso.), Historic Pullman Found. (sustaining), David and Alfred Smart Gallery of U. Chgo. (supporting), Chgo. Open Lands Project (governing), Sigma Chi (award 1975). Clubs: Executives (Chgo.) (past dir.), Chicago (Chgo.), The Arts (Chgo.) (dir., mem. exhbns. com., chmn. nominating com.), University of Pa. (Chgo.) (past dir.), Tavern (Chgo.) (past gov.), Casino (Chgo.), President's of Loyola U. (Chgo.); Sunset Ridge Country (Northbrook, Ill.); Post and Paddock (Arlington Heights, Ill.) (dir., exec. com.). Home: Winnetka Ill. Died Apr. 21, 1990.

ALSOP, JOSEPH WRIGHT, JR., writer; b. Avon, Conn., Oct. 11, 1910; s. Joseph Wright Sr. and Corinne Douglas (Robinson) A.; m. Susan Mary Jay Patten, Feb. 16, 1961 (div. 1978). Grad., Groton Sch., 1928; AB, Harvard U., 1932. Mem. staff N.Y. Herald Tribune, N.Y.C., 1932-35; Mem. staff Washington, 1936-37, freelance writer; Mellon lectr. Nat. Gallery Art, 1978. Author: (with Robert E. Kintner) (syndicated column on politics) The Capital Parade for N.Am. Newspaper Alliance, 1937-40, (with Turner Catledge) The 168 Days, 1938, (with Robert E. Kintner) Men Around the President, 1938, American White Paper, 1940, (with Stewart Alsop) We Accuse, 1955, The Reporter's Trade, 1958, From the Silent Earth, 1964, FDR A Centenary Remembrance, 1982, The Rare Art Traditions, 1982, (column) Matter of Fact, syndicated through N.Y. Herald Tribune, 1945-58, (column) Washington Post, then Los Angeles Times Syndicate, 1958-74; contbr. to mags. including New Yorker, N.Y. Rev. Books. Commd. lt. USN, 1940; joined Am. Vol. Air Group as aide to Gen. Chennault; captured by Japanese at Hong Kong, held prisoner until June 1942; then was exchanged and returned to U.S.; became civilian lend lease adminstr. to China, Dec. 1942, Chunking; capt. 14th Air Force and mem. staff of Gen. Chennault 1943-45. Decorated Legion of Merit, Chinese Cloud Banner. Club: Knickerbocker (N.Y.C.). Home: Washington D.C.

ALWAY, ROBERT HAMILTON, pediatrician, educator; b. University Place, Nebr., Dec. 10, 1912; s. Frederick J. and Eva M. K. (Cook) A.; m. Sophia Chamberlin, May 21, 1942; children: Anne, Mary K., Frederick R., Joan, Theodore. BS, U. Minn., 1937, MD, 1940. Instr., assoc. prof. U. Utah, 1942-49; assoc. prof. pediatrics Stanford, 1949-52; prof. pediatrics U. Colo., 1953-55, Stanford, 1955-90; dean, 1958-64; med. dir. Stanford Convalescent Home, 1956-60, Stanford U. Hosp., 1975-90. Commonwealth Fund fellow Guy's Hosp., London Eng., 1964-65; nat. adv. council Nat. Inst. Child Health and Human Devel., 1963-67. Mem. Am. Acad. Pediatrics, Am. Pediatric Soc., Cal. Acad. Medicine, Royal Soc. Medicine, Chi Psi, Nu Sigma Nu, Alpha Omega Alpha. Home: Oak Harbor Wash. Died Oct. 26, 1990; cremated.

ALZADO, LYLE MARTIN, former professional football player; b. Bklyn., Apr. 3, 1949. B.A., Yankton (S.D.) Coll., 1971. Profl. football player Denver Broncos, 1971-79, Cleve. Browns, 1979-82, Los Angeles Raiders, 1982-85; fought Muhammed Ali in exhbn. match, Denver, 1979. Host radio sports talk show, Sta. KWBZ, Denver, 1976-77. Colo. hon. head coach Spl. Olympic Program for Retarded; vol. staff Children's Hosp.; co-chmn. Bike-a-thon for Cystic Fibrosis, Read-a-thon; hon. chmn. Walk for Mankind; hon. nat. sports com. Muscular Dystrophy, Arapahoe County chmn.; bd. dirs. Am. Cancer Soc.; mem. Fight for Life St. Anthony's Hosp.; active juvenile delinquent program and Police Athletic League of Denver Police Dept., active civic orgn. fund raising. Recipient Earl Hartman Meml. award as outstanding defensive lineman on Denver Broncos, 1975; Byron Whizzer White Humanitarian award Nat. Football League, 1977; Friend of Youth award Optimists Internat., 1978; named Man of Year Denver Jaycees, 1976; Man of Year Nat. Football League, 1977; AFC Defensive Player of Yr., 1977; All-Pro Defensive Lineman, 1977. Home: El Segundo Calif. Died June 14, 1992. †

AMBERG, RAYMOND MICHAEL, hospital administrator; b. St. Paul, Aug. 24, 1895; s. John Adam and Rose Ann (Keogh) A.; m. Margaret Helen McHugh, Aug. 1, 1925; children: John Raymond, Mary Ellen Kelley. PhC, U. Minn., 1920. Asst. hosp. mgr. U. Minn. Hosps., 1924-29, hosp. mgr., 1929-32, asst. dir., 1932-35, supt., dir., 1935-64, prof. hosp. adminstrn.

Sch. Pub. Health, 1946-64; exec. dir. Hosp. Planning for Met. Mpls., from 1964.; cons. U.S. State Dept., Vietnam, 1964. Fellow Am. Coll. Hosp. Adminstrs.; mem. Am. Hosp. Assn., Am. Pub. Health Assn., Am. Assn. Med. Colls., Univ. Hosp. Execs. Coun., Minn. Hosp. Assn., others. *

AMINO, LEO, sculptor, designer; b. Japan, June 26, 1911; came to U.S., 1929; s. Ichiju and Yufu A.; m. Julie Blumberger, 1947; 1 dau., Eriko. Student, NYU, Am. Artists Sch. tchr. sculpture Black Mountain (N.C.) Coll., 1946, 50; formerly tchr. sculpture Cooper Union, N.Y.C. One man shows include, Montross Gallery, 1940, Artists' Gallery, 1940-43, Clay Club Gallery, 1941, Bonestell Gallery, 1945, Sculptors Gallery, 1946-49, Sculpture Center, 1951, 52, 54, 57, 71, 73, Art Alliance, Phila., 1951, East Hampton Gallery, 1969, 70; represented in, Mus. of Modern Art, Massillon Mus., Addison Gallery, Am. Art, U. Neb., Grand Rapids Mus., Olsen Found., New Haven, Tex. State Coll., Women, Des Moines Art Center, Whitney Mus. Am. Art, Provincetown, Mass., Rutgers U., New Brunswick, N.J., Nat. Mus. Am. Art, Smithsonian Instn., also pub. and pvt. collections. Home: New York N.Y. Died Dec. 1, 1989; cremated.

AMORY, ROBERT, JR., lawyer; b. Boston, Mar. 2, 1915; s. Robert and Leonore (Cobb) A.; m. Mary Armstrong, June 17, 1938; children: Robert III, Daniel. A.B., Harvard, 1936, LL.B., 1938. Bar: N.Y. 1939, N.H. and Mass. 1946, D.C. 1965. Practiced in N.Y.C., 1938-40; prof. law and accounting Harvard Law Sch., 1946-52; dep. dir. CIA, 1952-62; chief internat. div. Bur. Budget, 1962-65; mem. NSC Planning Bd., 1953-61; mem. firm Corcoran, Foley, Youngman & Rowe, Washington, 1965-72; sec., gen. counsel Nat. Gallery Art, Washington, 1973-80; U.S. del. Bermuda Conf., 1953, Bangkok, 1955; trustee Arena Stage, 1961-85; bd. overseers Harvard U., 1963-69; mem. adv. council Sch. Advanced Internat. Studies, Johns Hopkins U.; mem. Cambridge Sch. Com., 1949-51; treas. Washington Cathedral Found., 1969-77. Author: Surf and Sand, 1947, Materials on Accounting, 1949. Entered Army as pvt. 1941; commanded amphibian engr. battalion and regiment New Guinea and Philippine campaigns; discharged as col. 1946; lt. col. Armor Mass. N.G., 1946-51. Mem. Am. Law Inst. (life), Harvard Alumni Assn. (pres. 1961-62, dir. 1959-63, 75-77), Harvard Law Sch. Alumni Assn, pres. 1974-76). Clubs: Metropolitan (Washington), Cosmos (Washington); Chevy Chase, Cruising of America. Home: Washington DC Died Apr. 19, 1989.

AMOS, JOHN BEVERLY, insurance company executive; b. Enterprise, Ala., June 5, 1924; s. John Shelby and Mary Helen (Mullins) A.; m. Elena Diaz-Verson, Sept. 23, 1945; children: John Shelby, II, Maria Teresa. Ed., U. Miami, Fla., 1947, LL.D., 1979; J.D., U. Fla., 1949; LLD (hon.), U. West Fla., Mercer U. Bar: Fla. 1949. Pvt. practice Ft. Walton Beach, Fla., 1949-55; founder, 1955, Am. Family Life Assurance Co., Columbus, Ga., 1955; former pres., now chmn. bd., chief exec. officer Am. Family Corp. Past pres. Goodwill Industries, Columbus; past chmn. 3d Dist. Ga. Democratic Com.; trustee Morris Brown Coll., Atlanta, Roosevelt Warm Springs (Ga.) Found., Hughston Sports Medicine Found., Inc., Columbus; mem. nat. com. Nat. Mus. Jewish History, Phila.; vice chmn. Nat. Bipartisan Polit. Action Com.; bd. dirs. Met. Columbus Urban League; mem. bd. visitors Boston U. Sch. Medicine, Walter F. Gerge Coll. Law, Mercer. U., Macon, Ga.; mem. pres. adv. bd. Duke U., Durham, N.C., mem. bd. overseers Duke Comprehensive Cancer Ctr.; chmn. Sch. of Ams. Columbus Support Group, Ft. Benning, Ga.; mem. numerous civic bds. and orgns. Named Man of Yr., Ga. Conf. African Meth. Episcopal Ch., 1984, NAACP, 1985, Georgian of Yr. Ga. Assn. Broadcasters, 1986; recipient Disting. Service award Small Bus. Council Am., 1985, Disting. Citizen award Chattahoochee council Boy Scouts Am., 1985. Mem. Mem. Nat. Assn. Mfrs. (bd. dirs.), Nat. Assn. Life Cos. (v.p.), Fla. Bar Assn. Roman Catholic. Clubs: Metropolitan (N.Y.C.); Big Eddy (Columbus), Harmony (Columbus). Home: Columbus Ga. Deceased. †

AMRAM, PHILIP WERNER, lawyer; b. Phila., Mar. 14, 1900; s. David Werner and Beulah (Brylawski) A.; m. Emilie S. Weyl, Dec. 18, 1924; children—Mariana B., David Werner, III.; m. Helen M. Costello, June 5, 1982. A.B., U. Pa., 1920; B.S.A., Pa. State Coll., 1922; LL.B. cum laude, U. Pa., 1927. Bar: Pa. 1927, D.C. 1945. Practiced as mem. law firm of Wolf, Block, Schorr & Solis-Cohen, Phila., 1927-42; mem. Amram, Hahn & Sundlun (and successor firms), Washington; tchr. Pa. practice and practice ct. U. Pa. Law Sch., 1929-42; in charge aviation activities, as chief internat. air transport div. Bd. Econ. Warfare, Washington, 1942; chief rep. S. Pacific area, 1943, spl. asst. to Atty. Gen. U.S. in charge litigation against, Standard Oil Co., N.J., 1943-45; also spl. adviser to Alien Property Custodian.; Mem. civil procedural rules com. Supreme Ct. Pa., from 1938, chmn., 1958-82, chmn. emeritus, 1986; chmn. adv. com. to U.S. Commn. on Internat. Rules of Jud. Procedure, 1959-66; mem. adv. rules com. U.S. Dist. Court, Eastern Dist. Pa., Circuit Ct. of Appeals, 1939-42; mem. State Dept. Adv. Com. on Internat. Pvt. Law, 1964-76, vice chmn., 1971-76; Ofcl. U.S. observer Hague Conf. Internat. Pvt. Law, 1956, 60, mem. ofcl. delegation, 1964, 68, 72, 76, chmn. delegation, 1972. Author: Amram's Pennsylvania Common Pleas Practice, 7th edit, 1970, New Federal Rules in Pennsylvania, 1938, Goodrich-Amram Pennsylvania Procedural Rules Service, 1940-80; Editor-in-chief: U. Pa. Law Rev, 1926-27; contbr. law revs. Assoc. trustee law sch. U. Pa., 1959-76; Pres. United Community Services of Washington, 1956-68, La Fondation de l'Ecole Française Internationale de Washington, 1966-76. Served as 2d lt. inf. U.S. Army, World War I. Decorated officier French Legion of Honor, comdr. Ordre des Palmes Academiques. Mem. Am. Law Inst., Mil. Order Fgn. Wars, ABA (prize for pvt. internat. law 1983), Fed. Bar Assn., Internat. Bar Assn., state and local bar assns., Order of Coif, Phi Kappa Phi. Club: Cosmos. Home: Washington DC Died Apr. 20, 1990; buried Loveladies, N.J.

ANDERBERG, EDWARD CLARENCE, banker; b. N.Y.C., Nov. 28, 1918; s. Eberhard I. and Selma (Bogren) A.; m. Carol Kirkwood, Oct. 12, 1951; children—Thomas, Robert, Karen, Stephen. B.S., NYU, 1951, M.B.A., 1966. With Green Point Savs. Bank, Bklyn., from 1935, asst. sec., 1954-60, asst. v.p., 1960-66, v.p., 1966-67, exec. v.p., 1967-82, pres., 1982-86, also bd. dirs. Bd. mgrs. Greenpoint br. YMCA, from 1970, chmn. world service com., from 1967 . Served with AUS, 1942-46. Died Jan. 9, 1992; buried Pinelawn (N.Y.) Meml. Pk.

ANDERL, STEPHEN, clergyman; b. Chippewa Falls, Wis., July 13, 1910; s. Henry A. and Katherine (Schneider) A.; B.A. magna cum laude St. John's U., 1932, M.Div., 1974; postgrad. Catholic U. Am., 1940; Ph.D., World U., 1982; D.D., Partasarathy Acad., Madras, India, 1984. Ordained priest Roman Catholic Ch., 1936; curate in Wisconsin Rapids, Wis., 1936-37; chaplain Villa St. Joseph, LaCrosse, Wis., 1942-49; pastor in Spring Valley, Wis., 1949-52, Hewitt, Wis., 1952-53, Assumption Parish, Durand, Wis., 1953-82; tchr., guidance counselor, vice prin. Aquinas High Sch., La Crosse, Wis., 1937-49. Censor books, clergy examiner, vicar gen. for religious Diocese of La Crosse, 1951-66; vicar forane Durand Deanery, 1953-82; mem. commn. on worship and sacraments 3d Diocesan Synod, 1955; spl. research cons. 4th Diocesan Synod, 1985-86; diocesan chaplain Boy Scouts Am., Girl Scouts U.S.A., 1936-49; diocesan dir. Young Christian Workers, 1940-50; chaplain XII World Jamboree Boy Scouts, 1967, Nat. Jamboree Boy Scouts Am., 1969, 73; Wis. state chaplain COF, 1986-92; mem. Diocesan Clergy Personnel Bd., 1970-74; exec. sec. Cath. Youth Orgn., Diocese of La Crosse, 1938-49; diocesan dir. Sodality, 1938-49; cons. Central Commn. of Diocese of LaCrosse for Implementation of Vatican Council. Mem. exec. com. Chippewa Valley council Boy Scouts Am., mem. nat. Cath. com. on scouting, from 1974, vice chmn. diocesan Cath. com. on scouting; housing commr., La Crosse, 1948-49; Nat. Coun., BSA; mem. Gov.'s Com. on Children and Youth, 1957-63; adviser Wis. Youth Com., 1960-92; mem. State Comprehensive Mental Health and Retardation Planning Com., Durand Community Council; dir. West Central Wis. Community Action Agy., OEO; bd. dirs. La Crosse Diocesan Bd. Edn., La Crosse Diocesan Cath. Social Agy., Inc., Silver Waters council Girl Scouts U.S.A.; founder, dir. West Central Wis. Community Action Agy. Decorated Knight Grand Commdr. Mil. Order of the Holy Sepulchre, 1986, Confederation of the Chivalry, 1986, Knight Grand Commdr., Order of the Rainbows, 1987, Legion of Honor, Cath. Order of Foresters, 1988; created domestic prelate with title of right reverend msgr. by Pope John XXIII, 1962; recipient Silver Beaver award Boy Scouts Am., 1968; St. George award, 1969; St. Ann. award Girl Scouts U.S., 1980, citation West Cap, 1975; God and Youth medal Nat. Cath. Youth Coun., Mother Seton medal Nat. Cath. Coun. of Women. Mem. Wis. Geneol. Soc., Am. Acad. Religion, Wis. Acad. Arts, Sci. and Letters, Am. Numis. Soc., Collectors of Religion on Stamps, Christian Writers Assn., Internat. Acad. Intellectuals. Lodge: K.C. (4th degree; chaplain Durand council 1953-82, John F. Kennedy council from 1984, faithful friar Pope John XXIII gen. assembly 1960-82, Bishop Sheen assembly from 1984, Knight of St. George 1990). Author: Technique. of the Catholic Action Cell, 1942; Papal Teaching on Catholic Action, 1946; The Religious and Catholic Action, 1947; Catholic Action, a Responsibility of the School, 1948; Parish of the Assumption, Life and Times of the Mystical Christ in Durand, 1960. Contbr. articles to religious mags. and jours. Deceased. Home: Eau Claire Wis. †

ANDERSON, ARNOLD STUART, lawyer; b. N.Y.C., June 4, 1934; s. David and Mary (Bilgoray) A.; m. Barbara Sapkowitz, Oct. 1, 1955; children: David Jay, Randi Lee. B.A., CCNY, 1956; J.D., Columbia U., 1959. Bar: N.Y. 1959, U.S. Supreme Ct. 1971. Gen. atty., office gen. counsel FAA, Washington, 1960-61; assoc. Fly, Shuebruck, Blume & Gaguine, N.Y.C., 1962-63; asst. counsel N.Y. Moreland Commn. on Alcoholic Beverage Control Law, N.Y.C., 1963-64; assoc. Winthrop, Stimson, Putnam & Roberts, N.Y.C., 1964-79; v.p., gen. counsel Woolworth Corp., N.Y.C., 1979-80, sr. v.p., gen. counsel, 1980-82, exec. v.p. adminstrn., gen. counsel, 1982-91; asst. counsel investigation into jud. conduct Supreme Ct. Appellate Div. 2d Dept., 1970; bd. dirs. F.W. Woolworth Ltd. (Can.), Woolworth Mexicana S.A. de C.V. (Mex.), Kinney Shoe Corp., Kinney Can., Inc., Richman Bros. Co., Holtzman's Little Folk Shop, Inc. Author: (with R.S. Taft) N.Y. Practice Series, Personal Taxation, Vol. I, 1975; contbr. (with R.S. Taft) articles to profl. jours. Asst. counsel investigation jud. conduct Supreme Ct. Appellate. Mem. ABA, Fed. Bar Assn., N.Y. State Bar Assn., Assn. of Bar of City of N.Y. Home: New York N.Y. Died Mar. 27, 1991; buried Mt. Lebanon Cemetery, Glendale N.Y.

ANDERSON, CARL DAVID, physicist; b. N.Y.C., Sept. 3, 1905; s. Carl David and Emma Adolfina (Ajaxson) A.; m. Lorraine Elvira Bergman; children—Marshall David, David Andrew. BS, Calif. Inst. of Tech., 1927, PhD magna cum laude, 1930; ScD (hon.), Colgate U., 1937, Gustavus Adolphus Coll., 1963; LLD (hon.), Temple U., 1948. Coffin research fellow Calif. Inst. Tech., 1927-28, teaching fellow in physics, 1928-30, research fellow in physics, 1930-33, asst. prof. physics, 1933-37, asso. prof., 1937-39, prof., 1939-76, prof. emeritus, from 1976, chmn. div. physics, math. and astronomy, 1962-70; researcher on x-ray photoelectrons, 1927-30, on gamma rays and cosmic rays, from 1930. Awarded gold medal Am. Inst. of City of N.Y., 1935; Nobel prize in physics, 1936; Elliott Cresson medal of the Franklin Inst., 1937; John Ericsson medal Am. Soc. Swedish Engrs., 1960. Mem. Am. Phys. Soc., Am. Philos. Soc., Nat. Acad. Scis., Sigma Xi, Tau Beta Pi. Home: San Marino Calif. Died Jan. 11, 1991.

ANDERSON, CHARLES ALFRED, geologist; b. Bloomington, Calif., June 6, 1902; s. Amel Andrew and Mary (Lyman) A.; m. Helen Argall, July 25, 1927; 1 child, Robert A. Student, Riverside Jr. Coll., 1920-22; AB, Pomona Coll., 1924, DSc, 1960; PhD, U. Calif., Berkeley, 1928. Instr. U. Calif., Berkeley, 1928-30, asst. prof., 1930-38, assoc. prof., 1938-42; with U.S. geol. Survey, Washington, 1942-90, chief mineral deposits br., 1953-58, chief geologist, 1959-64; rsch. geologist U.S. geol. Survey, Menlo Park, Calif., 1964-90; mem. exec. com. div. earth scis. NRC, 1956-59. Contbr. articles to sci. jours. Past fellow Geol. Soc. Am. (councilor 1946-49), Mineral. Soc. Am.; past mem. AIME, Am. Acad. Arts and Scis., Soc. Econ. Geologists (v.p. 1959), Geophys. Union, Geochem. Soc., Nat. Acad. Scis., Cosmos (Washington). Home: Menlo Park Calif. Died Jan. 17, 1990.

ANDERSON, CHARLES ARNOLD, sociologist, educator; b. Platte, S.D., Jan. 13, 1907; s. Edward Thomas and Edith (Orvis) A.; m. Mary Jean Bowman, July 18, 1942; 1 son, Lloyd Barr. B.A., U. Minn., 1927, M.A., 1928, Ph.D., 1932; Ph.D. (hon.), U. Stockholm, 1978. Faculty U. Minn., 1929, Harvard U., 1930-35, 43, Iowa State U., 1936-43, U. Ky., 1945-58; various U.S. govt. assignments, 1944-45; faculty U. Calif. at Berkeley, 1948-49; vis. prof. U. Lund, Sweden, 1954-55; Fulbright scholar Uppsala (Sweden) U., 1955-56; prof. U. Chgo., from 1958, also dir. Comparative Edn. Ctr., 1958-73; cons. UNESCO, Ford Found., World Bank, OECD; vis. prof. U. Stockholm, 1974, U. London, 1975. Author: Social Selection in Education and Economic Development, 1983; co-author: Where Colleges are and Who Attends, 1973; editor Am. Jour. Sociology, 1967-73; joint editor: Education, Economy and Society, 1961, Education and Economic Development, 1965; contbr. articles to profl. jours. Mem. Comparative Edn. Soc. (pres.), Swedish Royal Acad. Sci., Phi Beta Kappa, Sigma Xi. Home: Chicago Ill. Deceased. †

ANDERSON, DEWEY, economist; b. Grand Forks, N.D., Jan. 14, 1897; s. Hans D. and Amalia B. (Peterson) A.; m. Erma Sams, June 30, 1920; children: Harry, June. AB, Stanford U., 1927, MA, 1928, PhD, 1932. Exec. Prisoner of War Work & Relief, Poland and Baltic States, 1921-24; exec. Am. sect. European Student Relief, Russia, 1924-27; mem. faculty Stanford U., and dir. Stanford-Alaska Ednl. Study, 1930-34; mem. Calif. legislature, 1935-37; dir. rsch. econ. problems John Randolph & Dora Haynes Foudn., L.A., 1936-38; codir. Inst. Occupational Rsch. Stanford U.; budgeteer, by appt. Gov.-Elect Calif., 1938-39; adminstr. State Relief Adminstrn., Calif., 1939; econ. counsel, exec. sec. Temporary Nat. Econ. Com., 1939-41; chief Am. hemisphere divsn. Bd. Econ. Warfare, Washington, 1942; chief supply & transport divsn. Office Fgn. Relief & Rehab. Ops., Dept. State, 1943; mem. food adv. com. War Food Adminstrn., 1943; chief field ops. UNRRA, 1944; exec. sec. Small Bus. Com. U.S. Senate, 1945; exec. dir. Pub. Affairs Inst. *

ANDERSON, ERNEST LEROY, lumber company executive; b. Logan, Utah, Aug. 11, 1910; s. Anthon Edward and Nora (Egbert) A.; m. Grace Rasmussen, Sept. 8, 1936; children: Robert Monte, Kristen Anderson Bennett, Ross Carl. B.S., Utah State U., 1937. With Anderson Lumber Co., Ogden, Utah, from 1929, pres., chief exec. officer, 1963-79; chmn. bd. Anderson Lumber Co., from 1979; mgr. Pioneer Wholesale Supply Co., 1960-61, chmn. bd., from 1979; pres. Bonneville Lumber Co.; adv. bd. No. div. First Security Bank Utah; mem. nat. adv. council, mem. bus. partners program Utah State U., Logan. Pres. Logan C. of C., 1954; chmn. Logan City Planning Commn., 1957. Mem. Nat. Lumber Dealers Assn. (bd. dirs. 1974-75), Intermountain Lumber Dealers Assn. (bd. dirs. 1951-54), Mountain States Lumber Dealers Assn. (pres. 1967), Ogden C. of C. (treas. 1966), Old Main Soc. (past pres., mem. pres.'s club), Ogden Golf and Country Club, Ambassador Athletic Club, Rotary (past pres. Logan chpt.), Sigma Chi (life), Alpha Kappa Psi. Home: Salt Lake City Utah Died Jan. 27, 1988; buried Mt. Olivet, Salt Lake City.

ANDERSON, FORREST HOWARD, former governor of Montana; b. Helena, Mont., Jan. 30, 1913; s. Oscar A. and Nora (O'Keefe) A.; m. Margaret Evelyn Samson, Jan. 24, 1941; children: Margaret Louise Anderson Templin, Arlee Joan Anderson Taylor, Newell Burke. Student, U. Mont.; LLB, Columbia U., 1938. Bar: Mont. 1938. Practiced in Helena, 1938-52; county atty. Lewis and Clark County, Helena, 1945-47; assoc. justice Supreme Ct. Mont., Helena, 1953-57; spl. counsel indsl. accident fund State of Mont., Helena, 1947-49, atty. gen., 1957-69, gov., 1969-72. Mem. Mont. Ho. of Reps., 1943-45. Mem. Masons (32d degree), Shriners, Elks, Eagles, Moose, Phi Delta Theta. Democrat. Methodist. Home: Helena Mont. Died July 21, 1989; buried Helena, Mt.

ANDERSON, GEORGE WALTER, film critic, columnist; b. Arnold, Pa., Jan. 21, 1932; s. Francis Edgar and Margaret Neil (Crytzer) A.; m. Nancy Kathleen Link, Nov. 11, 1961; children: Scott Elliott, Holly Kathleen. BA, Duquesne U., 1955. Reporter Valley News Dispatch, Tarentum, Pa., 1958-69; film critic PItts. Post-Gazette, 1969-92; tchr. film course Duquesne U., Pitts., 1975, U. Pitts., 1976-79, 80. Writer (newspaper column) Valley News Dispatch, 1959-69, Pitts. Post-Gazette, 1969-92. Pres. Allegheny Classic Film Soc., New Kensington, Pa., 1965-68, Allegheny Valley Concert Assn., New Kensington, 1967-68. 1st lt. U.S. Army, 1955-57. Mem. Variety Club (bd. dirs. 1979-81). Democrat. Home: Pittsburgh Pa. Died Sept. 5, 1992. †

ANDERSON, GRACE MERLE, sociology educator; b. London, Eng., Oct. 31, 1923; d. Ernest William and Nettie May (Harwood) A. B.A., McMaster U., 1961, M.A., 1964, LL.D., 1985; Ph.D., U. Toronto, Ont., Can., 1971. Chemist Wolsey, Leicester, Eng., 1944-47; head chemist Wolsey of Can., Quebec City, Que., Can., 1947-50; chemist L. B. Holliday, Montreal, Que., 1950-53; mem. tech. staff Can. Baptist Overseas Mission, Costa Rica and Bolivia, 1954-60; asst. prof. sociology Acadia U., N.S., 1963-67; assoc. prof. sociology and anthropology Wilfrid Laurier U., Waterloo, Ont., 1970-77, prof., from 1977; adj. prof. U. Waterloo, from 1974. Author: Town Lake Road: Urban Fringe Poverty in Nova Scotia, 1967, A Selected Bibliography on Portuguese Immigration, 1970, Networks of Contact: The Portuguese and Toronto, 1974, A Future to Inherit: Portuguese Communities in Canada, 1976, Non-Milk Cookbook, 1976, 2d edit., 1977, Spanish-Speaking Immigrants in Selected Canadian Cities, 1977, The Leadership Years, 1987; contbr. to Can. Ency. Mem. Can. Assn. Sociology and Anthropology, Soc. for Sci. Study Religion, Can. Ethnic Studies Assn. Baptist. Home: Waterloo Ont., Can. Died Oct. 19, 1989; buried Waterloo, Ont., Can.

ANDERSON, HAROLD H(OMER), psychologist; b. Dakota City, Nebr., Oct. 23, 1897; s. Samuel Lilley and Mary (Inglis) A.; m. Gladys Marie Lowe, June 30, 1927; children: Janet Lowe Twente, Theodore Inglis. SB, Harvard U., 1922; Diplome, Rousseau Inst., Geneva, Switzerland, 1928; Cert. de Pedagogie, U. Geneva, 1928, PhD, 1929. Rsch. asst. prof. psychology Iowa Child Welfare Rsch. Sta. State U. Iowa, 1929-36; specialist in emergency nursery schs. U.S. Office Edn. & Fed. Emergency Relief Adminstrn., Washington, 1934; asst. prof. U. Ill., 1936-41, assoc. prof., 1941-46; prof. psychology & head dept. Mich. state U., 1946-55, rsch. prof., from 1955; tchr. summer sch. various univs. Editor: Creativity and its Cultivation, 1959. Fulbright rsch. prof. psychology U. Frankfurt am Main, Germany, 1953-54. Fellow APA, Am. Orthopsychiat. Assn., AAAS, Am. Edn. Rsch. Assn.; mem. Midwestern Psychol. Assn., Mich. Psychol. Assn., Soc. for Rsch. in Child Devel., Soc. for Psychol. Study of Social Issues, others. *

ANDERSON, HOWARD CLEVENGER, lawyer; b. Gloucester, N.J., Dec. 3, 1910; s. Howard C. and Bertha M. (Ducey) A. AB, Princeton U., 1931; LLB, Howard U., 1934. Assoc. Root, Clark, Buckner & Ballantine, N.Y.C., 1934-46; atty. We. Electric Co., Inc., N.Y.C., 1946-56, gen. solicitor, 1956-58; v.p., gen. counsel Chesapeake & Potomac Telephone cos. of Washington, Va., Md., 1958-75; ptnr. Debevoise & Liberman, Washington, 1976-77; counsel Dewey, Ballantine, Bushby, Palmer & Wood, Washington and N.Y.C., 1977-90. Mem. ABA, Bar Assn. D.C., Bar Assn. City N.Y., Met. Club, Chevy Chase Club (Washington), Princeton Club (N.Y.C.), Phi Beta Kappa. Home: Washington D.C. Deceased.

ANDERSON, IVAN DELOS, impressionist painter; b. Yankton, S.D., Feb. 13, 1915; s. Albert and Elizabeth (Cooper) A.; m. Bette Stanley, Feb. 19, 1944; 1 son, Greg. B.A., Yankton Coll., 1937; diploma cosmetology, Poly. Coll., Los Angeles, 1939. Designer Ivan of Hollywood, Calif., 1938-40, House of Westmore, Hollywood, 1946-47; v.p. Nutri-Tonic Corp., Hollywood, 1948-59. Author; illustrator: Creative Hairshaping and Hairstyling, 1947 (Best Litho Textbook of Yr. award Am. Lithography Soc. 1948), Hairstyling, 1948; one-man exhbns. include, Falco Gallery, Sherman Oaks, Calif., 1967, Cagle Galleries, Lubbock, Tex., 1974, Norton Simon's Hunt-Wesson Gallery, Fullerton, Calif., 1974, Huney Gallery, San Diego, 1975, The Gallery, Catalina Island, Calif., 1975, Expressions Gallery, Newport Beach, Calif., 1976, Moulton Playhouse, Laguna Beach, Calif., 1977, group exhbns. include, Festival of Arts, Laguna Beach, (1973-74), Chaffey Coll., Cucamonga, Calif., (1974), Art-A-Fair Festival, Laguna Beach, 1975, 76, 77, Laguna Beach Mus., 1974, 75, 76; represented in permanent collections Mus. Modern Art, N.Y.C., Los Angeles Mus., Buffalo Bill Hist. Mus. Cody, Wyo., Roy Rogers Mus., Victorville, Calif., Library of Congress, Los Angeles Children's Hosp., also numerous pvt. collections including, Ronald Reagan, John Wayne, Mary Pickford; posters commd. include Hopalong Cassidy, 1976, Catalina Island Casino, 1977, Laguna Beach, 1977; paintings commd. for Anderson's Children of World Serigraph series, 1975-76; paintings commd. Secrets and Boy with Big Hat, 1983. Served with AUS, 1941-46. Recipient Gold trophy Grand Nat., 1940, Best Portrait of Yr. award Wilshire Ebel Club, 1967, Best of Show Catalina Art Festival, 1967, Grand Prize United Meth. Ch., Los Angeles, 1969, Wrigley award P.K. Wrigley, 1968, 1st prize Catalina Art Festival, 1976. Mem. Art-a-Fair. Home: Laguna Beach Calif. Died Jan. 22, 1991; buried Forest Lawn, Glendale, Calif.

ANDERSON, J. BLAINE, federal judge; b. Trenton, Utah, Jan. 19, 1922; s. Leslie Howard and Theo Ellen (Stocking) A.; m. Grace Little, Nov. 14, 1944; children—J. Eric, J. Blaine, Leslie Ann, Dirk Brian. Student, U. Idaho, 1940-41, U. Wash., 1945-46; LL.B., U. Idaho, 1949; J.D. (hon.), Lewis and Clark Coll., 1978. Bar: Idaho bar 1949. Practiced in Blackfoot, 1949-71; partner firm Furchner and Anderson (and predecessor law firms), 1955-71; U.S. dist. judge Dist. Idaho, Boise, 1971-76; U.S. circuit judge U.S. Ct. Appeals, 9th Circuit, 1976-88. Chmn. Idaho Air Pollution Commn., 1959-60. Served with USCG, 1942-45. First Recipient Faculty award of Legal Merit, U. Idaho Coll. Law, 1974. Fellow Am. Coll. Trial Lawyers; mem. Am. Bar Assn. (mem. ho. of dels. 1959-60, 64-71, gov. 1971-74, mem. council gen. practice sect. 1962-66, 70-71, mem. adv. bd. editors Jour. 1969-71), Idaho State Bar (bd. commrs. 1958-61, pres. 1960-61, chmn. unauthorized practice of law com. 1955-58), S.E. Idaho Dist. Bar (pres. 1957-58), Am. Judicature Soc. (dir. 1961-66), Am. Coll. Probate Counsel. Home: Boise Idaho Died Apr. 16, 1988; buried Morris Hill Cemetery, Boise, Idaho.

ANDERSON, PAUL N(ATHANIEL), business executive; b. Jamestown, N.Y., Sept. 10, 1898; s. Frank O. and Amelia S. (Norquist) A.; m. Cecile K. Ogren, June 21, 1922; children: Paul Nathaniel, Frank Olaus, Daniel Ogren, Raymond Quintus, John Timothy. Student, Phillips Andover Acad., 1915-18; BS, MIT, 1922. Treas., asst. supt. Empire Case Goods Co., Jamestown, 1922-34; pres., gen. mgr. Dahlstrom Metallic Door Co., 1934-61; pres., gen. mgr. Dahlstrom Mfg. Corp., from 1961, also dir.; bd. dirs. Bank of Jamestown, Jamestown Furniture Mfg. Bldg. Commr. Bd. Pub. Utilities, Jamestown, 1930-48; trustee Chautauqua (N.Y.) Instn., Lakeview Cemetery Assn., Jamestown. Mem. Nat. Assn. Mfrs., Jamestown Mfg. Assn. *

ANDERSON, ROBERT ALEXANDER, corporate executive; b. Honolulu, June 6, 1894; s. Robert Willis and Susan Alice (Young) A.; m. Margaret Leith Center, Nov. 14, 1919; children: Robert Alexander, David Leith, Allen Willis, Pamela Susan. ME, Cornell U., 1916. Apprentice Westinghouse Electric Mfg. Co., East Pittsburgh, Pa., 1916-17; rsch. dept. Isko Co., Chgo., 1919-21; chief engr. McClellan Refrigerating Co., Chgo., 1921-23; sales engr., then dept. mgr., treas., v.p., pres., chmn. bd. The Hawaii Corp., from 1923; pres., dir. Bishop Trust Co., Ltd.; dir. various corps. Bd. dirs., past pres. Honolulu Symphony; bd. dirs. Leahi Hosp. 1st lt. USAAF, 1917-19. Mem. Am. Soc. Refrigeration Engrs., ASCAP, Downtown Improvement Assn., others. *

ANDERSON, ROBERT BERNERD, lawyer, former secretary of the Treasury; b. Burleson, Tex., June 4, 1910; s. Robert Lee and Elizabeth (Haskew) A.; m. Ollie Mae Anderson, Apr. 10, 1935; children: James Richard, Gerald Lee. Student, Weatherford Coll., Tex., 1927; LL.B., U. Tex., 1932; LL.D., McMurry Coll., Tex., 1950, Tex. Christian U., 1951; Litt.D., Mid.-Western U., Tex., 1951. Bar: Tex. 1932. Sole practice law Fort Worth, from 1932; mem. Tex. Ho. of Reps., 1932; asst. atty. gen. Tex., 1932-33; prof. law U. Tex., Austin, 1933-34; tax commr. State of Tex., 1934-37, racing commr., 1934-37, mem. State Tax Bd., 1934-37; chmn., exec. dir. Tex. Unemployment Commn., 1936-37; sec. Dept. Navy, 1953-54; dept. sec. Dept. Def., 1954-55; pres. Ventures Ltd., N.Y.C. and Toronto, 1955-57; sec. Dept. Treasury, 1957-61; ptnr. Loeb, Rhoades & Co., N.Y.C., 1961-73, Anderson & Pendleton, Washington, from 1980; chmn. Robert B. Anderson Co. Ltd., from 1971, Am. Gas & Chem. Co. Ltd.; dir. Intercontinental Trailsea Corp. Chmn. bd. overseers Eisenhower Coll.; mem. nat. exec. bd. Boy Scout Am., Bus Council. Decorated cross of Order of Boyaca Colombia; decorated Most Exalted Order of White Elephant Thailand, medal of Freedom, 1955, Grand Cross Ct. of Honour, 1959; recipient Tex. award, 1954, Navy Disitng. Pub. Service award, 1955, Army Exceptional Service award, 1955, Air Force Civilian Service award, 1955; named Texan of Yr., 1955. Mem. Nat. Geog. Soc. (life), Washington Nat. Cathedral Navy League Am., ABA, Assn. Bar City N.Y., The Chancellors, Phi Delta Phi. Clubs: Metropolitan, University (N.Y.C.); Greenwich (Conn.) Country; Lodges: Order of DeMolay; Masons. Home: New York N.Y. Died Aug. 19, 1989.

ANDERSON, SIGURD, judge; b. Arendal, Norway, Jan. 22, 1904; came to U.S., 196, naturalized, 1915; s. Karl and Bertha (Broten A.; m. Vivian Walz, Apr. 3, 1937; 1 child, Kristin Karen. BA cum laude, U. S.D., 1931, LLB cum laude, 1937; LLD, Yankton Coll., 1953, Gettysburg Coll., 1958. States atty. Day County S.D., 1939-41; asst. atty. gen. State of S.D., 1941-43, atty. gen., 1947-51, gov., 1951-55; mem. FTC, 1955-64; pvt. practice law Webster, S.D., 1964-67; judge 5th Jud. Cir. S.D., 1967-75; chmn. Mo. River States Com., 1953-55. Bd. dirs. Am. Norwegian Mus.; bd. advisers N.E. Mental health, Aberdeen, S.D.; mem. adv. coun. Civil War Centennial Commn. lt. comdr. USNR, World War II. Recipient DAR Americanism medal for contbns. to state and nation by fgn.-born citizen, 1958, Alumni Achievement award U. S.D., 1979, Outstanding Alumni award Augustana Acad., 1979; hometown's airport named in his honor. Mem. ABA, Am. Judicature Soc., Fed. Bar Assn., S.D. Bar Assn., Coun. Former Govs., S.D. Judges Assn., S.D. Hist. Soc., Norwegian-Am. Hist. Assn., S.D Ornitholoigists Union, U. S.D Alumni Assn., Masons 33 degree, Shriner , Kiwanis, Sons of Norway, Order Ea. Star, VFW, Am. Legion, Phi Beta Kappa, Delta Theta Phi, Pi Kappa Delta, Lambda Chi Alpha hon. . Home: Webster S.C. Died Dec. 21, 1990.

ANDERSON, THOMAS F(OXEN), biophysics educator, researcher; b. Manitowoc, Wis., Feb. 7, 1911; s. Anton Oliver and Mabel (Foxen) A.; m. Wilma Fay Ecton, Dec. 28, 1937; children: Thomas Foxen Jr., Jessie Dale. BS, Calif. Inst. Tech., 1932, PhD, 1936; postgrad., U. Munich, 1932-33. Instr. chemistry U. Chgo., 1936-37; instr. in botany U. Wis., Madison, 1937-39, instr. in phys. chemistry, 1939-40; RCA fellow NRC, 1940-42; assoc. Johnson Found., U. Pa., Phila., 1942-46, mem. faculty, from 1946, prof. biophysics, from 1958; sr. mem. Inst. for Cancer Research, Phila., 1958-76, sr. mem. emeritus, from 1976; mem. study sect. NIH, Bethesda, Md., 1961-78; chmn. U.S. Nat. Com. for Pure and Applied Biophysics, 1965-69. Assoc. editor Virology, 1960-66; mem. editorial bd. Intervirology, 1972-85, Bacteriological Revs.; contbr. articles to profl. jours. Research grantee Office Naval Research, 1946-52, NSF, 1952-75; Fulbright fellow Inst. Pasteur, 1955-57, Guggenheim fellow, 1955-57, recipient Silver medal, 1957. Fellow AAAS; mem. NAS (chmn. sect. genetics 1985-88), Electron Microscope Soc. Am. (pres. 1955, Disting. award 1982), Internat. Fedn. Electron Microscope Socs. (pres. 1960-64), Biophys. Soc. (pres. 1965), Am. Soc. Naturalists, Deutsche Gesselschaft for Elektronenmikroskopie, Societé Francaise de Microscopie Electronique (hon.), Sigma Xi, Pi Alpha Tau. Club: Phila. Cricket. Home: Philadelphia Pa. Died Aug. 11, 1991; buried Amherst, Wis.

ANDERSON, THOMAS LEIGHTON, advertising executive; b. Lindsay, Ont., Dec. 19, 1895; s. Thomas and Margaret A. (Stuart) A.; m. Gladys A. Blake, Sept. 20, 1918; children: Joan P., Richard J. Jeweler, optician Vandusen & Anderson, Toronto, 1915-20; copywriter, account exec. Advt. Svc. Co., Toronto, 1920-28; v.p., mgr. Cockfield, Brown & Co., Ltd., Toronto, 1928-42, v.p., mng. dir., 1942-56, pres., 1956-58, chmn. bd., from 1958; pres. Gaylord Printing Co., Ltd., Toronto; v.p. Sayvette Ltd. dept. stores, Can. With RAF, 1918. *

ANDERSON, TOTTON JAMES, political science educator; b. Beirut, May 26, 1909; s. Samuel M. and Agatha (Totton) A.; m. Frances Elizabeth Moore, Aug. 17, 1934. A.B., U. Calif. at Berkeley, 1930, M.A., 1931; Ph.D., U. So. Calif., 1946. Registrar, dean Ventura (Calif.) Coll., 1935-42, 46-47; mem. faculty U. So. Calif., from 1947, prof. polit. sci., 1958-83, Disting. emeritus prof., from 1983, chmn. dept. polit. sci., 1957-60, 64-66, assoc. dean div. social scis. Coll. Letters, Arts and Scis., 1966-69, cons. prof. Sch. Bus., from 1975; vis. prof. U. Hawaii, summer 1958; Disting. vis. prof. U. San Diego, 1978-79; polit. cons., from 1960; exec. com. Calif. Constl. Revision Commn., 1964-73; chmn. exec. com. Calif. Legis. Intern Program, 1957-71; mem. Mayor Los Angeles Community Redevel. Adv. Com., 1966-68; asso. dir. Nat. Center Edn. in Politics, 1954-55; regional dir. Citizenship Clearing House, 1959-63; Trustee Coro Found., 1959-72. Co-author: Introduction to Political Science, 4th edit., 1983, Western Politics, 1958, Bibiliography on Western Politics, 1958, Politics in the American West, 1969, Political Dynamiting, 1970; contbg. author: Cooperation and Conflict: Readings in American Federalism, 1969; contbr. articles to profl. jours. Served to lt. col. USAAF, 1943-45, to col. USAF 1954-69. Decorated Bronze Star. Mem. Am. Polit. Sci. Assn., Western Polit. Sci. Assn. (pres. 1952-53), Am. Acad. Polit. and Social Scis., Phi Beta Kappa (pres. Alpha Alumni Assn. in So. Calif. 1964-66). Home: San Diego Calif. Died Jan. 28, 1992.

ANDREJEVIC, MILET, painter; b. Petrovgrad, Yugoslavia, Sept. 25, 1925; came to U.S., 1958, naturalized, 1961; s. Dimitrije and Jelena (Dragicevic) A.; m. Helen Bardeen, Apr. 30, 1955; 1 son, Mark. B.F.A., Belgrade Acad. Fine Arts, 1944, M.F.A., 1950. Instr. NYU, 1965-66, Bklyn. Coll., 1974-76, N.Y. Academy Art, from 1985; asst. prof. Pratt Inst., from 1981. One man shows, Green Gallery, N.Y.C., 1961, 63, Goldowsky Gallery, N.Y.C., 1970, 71, 72, 76, R. Schoelkopf Gallery, N.Y.C., 1981, group shows include, Whitney Mus. Anns., N.Y.C., 1963, 64, 65, Mus. Modern Art, N.Y.C., 1977, Hirsch & Adler Gallery, N.Y.C., 1980, Phila. Acad., 1981, Am. Acad. and Inst. Arts and Letters, 1984; represented in permanent collections, Whitney Mus., Hirschorn Mus., Washington, Met. Mus., N.Y.C., U. Tex., Austin, U. Va., Charlottesville, R.I. Sch. Design, Allentown Mus., U. N.C.; mem., The Green Gallery, N.Y.C., 1961-64, Bellamy Goldowsky Gallery, N.Y.C., 1970-79, Robert Schoelkopf Gallery, N.Y.C., from 1979. Nat. Endowment for Arts grantee, 1976; Ingram Merrill Found, grantee, 1980; The N.Y. Found. for Arts grantee, 1985. Mem. Nat. Acad. Design. Home: New York N.Y. Died Oct. 20, 1989.

ANDREWS, M(AURICE) NELL, lawyer; b. Lafayette, Ga., Dec. 24, 1894; s. Oty Payne and Ada (Frazier) A.; m. Foy Rhyne, Dec. 23, 1921; children: Alexander Rhyne, Ann Elizabeth. LLB, U. Ga., 1916; student, U. Edinburgh, Scotland, 1918-19. Bar: Ga. 1916. Practiced law Lafayette; asst. solicitor gen. Rome Cir., 1925-29, solicitor gen., 1929-32; asst. U.S. atty. No. Dist. Ga., Atlanta, 1934-38; spl. asst. to Atty. Gen. U.S. Anti-trust Divsn., 1939-40, chief trial sect., criminal divsn., 1940-42; chief trial atty. SEC, 1938-39; U.S. dist. atty. No. Dist. Ga., 1942-46; U.S. judge, 1949-50. 1st lt. inf. U.S. Army, 1917-19; capt. JAG Res. Decorated Silver Star World War I. Mem. Ga. Bar Assn., Am. Legion. *

ANDREWS, THELMA, librarian; b. Lampass, Tex., Mar. 10, 1904; d. Athelston and Emily (Adams) A. BA, Hardin-Simmons U., 1925; MA, State U. Iowa, 1928; grad., Libr. Sch. U. Chgo., 1945. Librarian Hardin-Simmons U., 1926-56; dir. Abilene Pub. Libr., 1956-71; vis. lectr. Grad. Sch. Libr. Sci., U. Tex., summers 1964-67. Mem. Tex. Libr. Assn. (past pres., named disting. librarian 1971). Home: Abilene Tex. Died Sept. 3, 1989.

ANGELL, JAMES WATERHOUSE, economist; b. Chgo., May 20, 1898; s. James Rowland and Marion Isabel (Watrous) A.; m. Jane Norton Grew, Oct. 19, 1923; children: James Grew, Edward Dexter. AB, Harvard U., 1918, AM, 1921, PhD, 1924; postgrad., U. Chgo., 1919-20. Asst. in econs. U. Chgo., 1919-20; instr. in econs. Harvard U., 1921-22, 23-24; lectr. in econs. Columbia U., 1924-26, assoc. prof., 1926-31, prof., from 1931. Author: The Theory of International Prices, 1926, The Recovery of Germany, 1929, 32, Der Wiederaufbau Deutschlands, 1930, Financial Foreign Policy of U.S., 1933, The Behavior of Money, 1936, Investment and Business Cycles, 1941; co-author: Measures for International Economic Stability, 1951; contbr. articles to profl. jours. Fellow Am. Acad. Arts & Scis.; mem. Am. Econ. Assn., Econometric Soc., Royal Econ. Soc., Acad. Polit. Sci., Coun. Fgn. Rels., Phi Beta Kappa. *

ANSPACH, CHARLES LEROY, educator; b. Fremont, Ohio, Mar. 5, 1895; s. Phillip Noble and Amanda (Loose) A.; m. Mary Fisher, Sept. 10, 1916; children: Vivian Mardele, Lillian Katherine. AB, Ashland Coll., 1919, AM, 1920, LLD, 1944; AM, U. Mich., 1923, PhD, 1930; LLD, Ferris Inst., 1959; LHD, No. Mich. Coll., 1959; LittD, Central Mich. U., 1959. Registrar Ashland Coll., 1923-26; fellow U. Mich., 1926-27; dean Ashland Coll., 1926-30; head dept. edn. Ea. Mich. Coll., 1930-34, dean adminstrn., 1934-35; pres. Ashland Coll., 1935-39, pres. emeritus, from 1939. Bd. regents Ea. Mich. U.; bd. visitors Freedoms Found.; others. Mem. Mich. Schoolmasters Club, NEA, Pi Kappa Delta, others. *

ANTON, NICHOLAS GUY, consulting physicist, engineer; b. Trieste, Austria, Dec. 14, 1906; came to U.S., 1926, naturalized, 1943; s. Joseph and Ann (Mandle) A.; m. Bernice Irene Skripsky, June 19, 1932; children: Joan Carol Anton Pearlman, Linda Elaine Anton Kincaid, Nanci Helen Anton Bobrow. Grad., Tech. Inst. Leonardo da Vinci, 1926; student, Columbia U., 1926-28. Various engring. positions Duovac Radio Tube Corp., Bklyn., 1928-31; pres., chmn. bd. Electronic Labs., Inc., Bklyn., 1931-32; founder, gen partner in charge mfg., factory engring. Amperex Electronics Products, 1932-48; pres., dir. research, devel., engring. Anton Electronic Labs., Bklyn., 1948-61; chmn. bd. Anton Imco Corp., 1959-61; founder, pres., dir. research, devel. EON Corp., Bklyn., 1961-78; cons., lectr. N.Y.C., 1978-79; pres., chmn. Dosimeter Corp., 1963-75; lectr. L.I. U., 1969-78; indsl. tech. cons. AEC for UN Internat. Conf. on Peaceful Uses of Atomic Energy, Geneva, 1955; Mem. Pres.'s Conf. on Indsl. Safety, 1967-92, Albert Gallatin Assos., NYU, 1951-54; Centennary com. Poly. Inst. Bklyn., 1963-64, U.S. Nat. UN Day Com., 1972-74, 76. Contbr. numerous articles, papers to profl. lit.; achievements include patents for Art of Utilizing Molybdenum, Radiation Indicator, Electron Tube Heat Dissipating Radiator, Double Profile Grinder, Radiation Detector Tube, Power Supply Circuits for Radiation Detectors, Radiation Detectors, Variable Voltage Regulator, Radiation Detector and Indicator, Method of Fabricating Radiation Detectors, Electron Emitters, Ruggedized Anode Construction, Air Particle Monitor, Geiger Mueller Counter Tube, Radiation Dosimeter, Micro-Miniature Beta Gamma Detector, Method and Apparatus for Developing Thermoplastic Resin Type Film, Pulsed Source High Speed Dry-Process Photographic Printer Processor, (with others) Meter Protective Device, Printerd Circuit Connector, Light Powered Switch, Range Measuring Apparatus Using Radioactive Material. Recipient Cert. of Appreciation, Office of Pres.; inducted into Wisdom Hall of Fame, Wisdom Soc. Fellow IEEE, Am. Phys. Soc., N.Y. Acad. Scis., N.Y. Acad. Medicine (asso.), AAAS, Am. Philos. Soc.; mem. ASME, Am. Math. Soc., Am. Soc. for Nondestructive Testing, Electronic Industries Assn. (past chmn. various coms.), Am. Standard Assn. Jewish. Clubs: Unity, Engineers. Home: Pompano Beach Fla. Died June 10, 1992. †

ANTOON, A(LFRED) J(OSEPH), theatrical director; b. Lawrence, Mass., Dec. 7, 1944; s. Alfred Joseph and Josephine Katherine (Saba) A. Student, Jesuit Sem., Lenox, Mass., 1962-65, Yale Drama Sch.; B.A., Boston Coll., 1968, D.H.L. (hon.), 1973. Theatrical director. Broadway prodns. include: That Championship Season, 1973 (Tony award, Drama Desk award, Drama Critics award), Much Ado About Nothing, 1973, The Good Doctor, The Effect of Gamma Rays on Man in the Moon Marigolds, Dance of Death, Trelawny of the Wells, The Rink; off-Broadway prodns. include: The Art of Dining, 1980 (Obie award), Cymbeline; London prodns. include: Subject to Fits, That Championship Season; television prodns. include: Much Ado About Nothing, Hereafter. Home: New York N.Y. Died Jan. 22, 1992. †

APOSTLE, HIPPOCRATES GEORGE, mathematics educator; b. Tyrnavos, Greece, Jan. 1, 1910; came to U.S.,, naturalized, 1922; s. George C. and Aspasia (Tzartzanos) A.; m. Margaret Wylie, 1968. B.A., Columbia, 1933, M.A., 1935; postgrad., U. Chgo., 1935-39; Licence en Philosophie, Laval U., Can., 1941; Ph.D. in Philosophy, Harvard, 1943. Asst. prof. math. and physics W. Va. Wesleyan Coll., 1942-43; asst. prof. math. U. Rochester, 1943-45; asst. prof. math. and philosophy Amherst Coll., 1945-47; asst. prof. philosophy U. Chgo., 1947-48; prof. math. Grinnell Coll., from 1948, Steele prof., from 1961; pub. The Peripatetic Press. Author: Aristotle's Philosophy of Mathematics, 1952, College Algebra, 1954, A Survey of Basic Mathematics, 1960, Aristotle's Metaphysics, 1967, Aristotle's Physics, 1969, Aristotle's Ethics, 1975, Aristotle's Categories and Propositions, 1980, Aristotle's Posterior Analytics, 1981, Aristotle's On the Soul, 1982, Aristotle Selected Works, 1983, Aristotle's Politics, 1986, Aristotle's Poetics, 1990. Home: Grinnell Iowa Died July 18, 1990; buried Hazelwood Cemetery, Grinnell, Iowa.

APPEL, KENNETH ELLMAKER, psychiatrist; b. Lancaster, Pa., May 15, 1896; s. John Wilberforce and Ella Julia (Roberts) A.; m. Madeleine Hunt, Sept. 2, 1921; children: Joan, Katharine. AB, Franklin and Marshall Coll., 1915; AM, Harvard U., 1916, PhD, 1918, MD, 1924. Resident U. Pa. Hosp., 1924-26; asst. phys. dept. nervous & mental diseases Pa. Hosp., 1926-29, cons., chief neuropsychiat. clin. outpatient dept., 1930; asst. prof. psychiatry Med. Sch. U. Pa., 1931-46, prof. clin. psychiatry, 1941-47, then prof. emeritus, chmn. dept. psychiatry; asst. psychiatrist U. Pa. Hosp., 1931-46; then dir. clinic for functional diseases; cons. psychiat. to ednl. instns. Author books in field. Mem. AMA, Am. Psychiat. Assn., Coll. Physicians Phila., Am. Neurol. Soc., Am. Psychoanalysis Soc., others. *

APPLETON, DONALD, paper manufacturing executive; b. Haverhill, Mass., Apr. 20, 1894; s. Edmund K. and Alice (Kelly) A.; m. Nathalie Arnold, Dec. 17, 1920; children: Alix (Mrs. Bernard J. Hasson Jr.), Lucy (Mrs. Frank Potter), John; m. 2d, Agnes Bailey Nov. 4, 1950. Grad., Phillips Acad., Andover, mass., 1914; BS, Harvard U., 1918. Paper mgr., 1920-89; with Oxford Paper Co., 1937-89; v.p., dir. Oxford Paper Co., N.Y.C., 1957-89, also mem. exec. com.; past bd. dirs. Nashwaak Pulp & Paper Co., Ltd. Capt., 31st F.A., U.S. Army, 1918. Past mem. Tech. Assn. Pulp and Paper Industry, Harvard Club (N.Y.C.), Moraine Country (Dayton, Ohio). Home: Greens Farms Conn. Died Mar. 21, 1989.

ARBOGAST, ZOLLIE O., JR., lawyer; b. Kansas, Ill., June 6, 1929; s. Zollie O. and Helen (Ryan) A.; m. Mary Anita Stewart, June 2, 1951 (dec.); children—Daniel Steven, Alane Annette. Student, Eastern Ill. State U., 1947-49; JD, Chgo.-Kent Coll. Law, 1952. Bar: Ill. bar 1952. Practiced in Marshall, 1952-63, Casey, from 1967; county judge Clark County, Ill., 1958-64; assoc. judge 5th Jud. Circuit Ill., 1964-67, cir. judge, from 1988; partner firm Partlow & Arbogast, 1967-75; individual practice law Casey, 1976-80, 81-88; partner firm Arbogast & Arbogast. Mem. Am., Ill., Clark County bar assns., Phi Alpha Delta. Republican. Mem. Christian Ch. Club: Mason. Home: Casey Ill. Died Nov. 28, 1989.

ARCOMANO, JOSEPH PETER, radiologist; b. Bklyn., June 7, 1924; s. Frank and Mary G. (Mugavero) A.; m. Ellen I. Gustafson, June 4, 1949; children—Peter, Lisa, Paul. B.S., U. Chgo., 1946, M.D., 1949. Diplomate: Am. Bd. Radiology. Intern Greenpoint Hosp., 1949; resident in radiology L.I. Coll. Hosp., 1952-55; practice medicine specializing in radiology Bklyn., 1955-60, Huntington, N.Y., from 1960; mem. staff Northport VA Hosp., Nassau County Med. Center, Mercy Hosp., St. Charles Hosp., Mather Meml. Hosp., Sagamore Children's Hosp.; asso.prof. radiology Sch. Medicine, N.Y. U., 1967-70; prof. radiology Med. Sch., State U. N.Y., Stony Brook, from 1977; dir. radiology North Shore Med. Group, from 1970; dir. sch. radiologic tech. Northport VA Hosp.; mem. X-Ray Technician Bd. of Examiners, N.Y. State, 1964-69. Contbr. articles to radiol. jours. Served with U.S. Army, 1942-45; with M.C., 1950-52, Korea. Recipient Dir.'s Outstanding Service award Northport VA Hosp., 1972, 77. Fellow Am. Coll. Radiology; mem. AMA (Physicians Recognition award 1969, 72, 77), Radiol. Soc. N. Am., Am. Roetngen Ray Soc., Soc. Nuclear Medicine, Am. Soc. Compensation Medicine, 38th Parallel Med. Soc. Korea. Roman Catholic. Home: Huntington N.Y. Died Sept. 8, 1987.

ARDEN, EVE (EUNICE GUEDENS), actress; b. Mill Valley, Calif., Apr. 30, 1912; d. Charles Peter and Lucille Frank Quedens; m Edward G Bergen div. 1948 ; adopted children: Liza Constance; m. Brooks West, Aug 24, 1951 dec. 1984 ; 1 child, Douglas Brooks; 1 adopted child, Duncan Paris. Student pub schs. Actress: N.Y. shows Shubert Ziegfield Follies, 1933, Very Warm for May, Two for the Show, Let's Face It, 1941; motion pictures include Stage Door, 1938; Cover Girl, 1944, The Doughgirls, 1944, Mildred Pierce, 1945, Goodbye My Fancy, 1951, We're Not Married, 1952, Anatomy of a Murder, 1959, Dark at the Top of the Stairs, 196, Sergeant Deadhead, 1965, Grease, 1978, Under the Rainbow, 1981, Grease II, 1982; TV movies Alice in Wonderland, 1983; radio series Our Miss Brooks, 1948, TV series, 1952. Recipient Emmy award, 1953, Sarrah Siddons award as Actress of Yr in Hello Dolly, Chgo., 1967-68. Home: Beverly Hills Calif. Died Nov. 12, 1990.

AREL, BULENT, composer; b. Istanbul, Turkey, Apr. 23, 1919; came to U.S.,, naturalized, 1973; Grad., Ankara State Conservatory, 1947. Tchr. Ankara, Turkey, 1945-51; music dir. Radio Ankara, 1951-59, 63-65; formerly research asst. (Rockefeller Found. grantee) Columbia-Princeton Electronic Music Center; mem. faculty Yale U., 1961-62, 65-70; founder, dir. Yale U. Electronic Music Studio, 1965; prof. music, dir. Electronic Music Studios, SUNY, Stony Brook, 1971-89; vis. prof. Columbia U. Works include symphonies, ballets, chamber and theatre music, electronic music, instrumental works, electronic music including Electronic Music No. 1, 1960; Mimiana I, II, III, 1968, 69, 73; film score Out of Into, 1972, also others; recs. for Stereo Electronic Music No. 1, CRI, Columbia, Finnadar, Opus One. Recipient Nat. Endowment for Arts awards (2); N.Y. State research grantee. Home: East Setauket N.Y. Died Nov. 24, 1990; cremated.

ARLT, GUSTAVE OTTO, educational executive; b. Lock Haven, Pa., May 17, 1895; s. Hans and Helene Bertha (Hoffman) A.; m. Gusti Herrman, June 25, 1920; 1 child, Marlene. AB, U. Chgo., 1915, AM, 1929, PhD, 1931; LLD, U. Calif. Instr. German Ind. U., 1923-24; asst. prof. DePauw U., 1924-29; assoc. prof. Ind. U., 1931-35; prof. German UCLA, 1935-61, assoc. dean grad. divsn., 1950-57, dean, 1958-61, dean emeritus, 1962, chmn. dept. Germanic langs., 1935-44, chmn. fgn. lang. group, 1940-44; pres. Coun. Grad. Schs. in U.S., Washington, from 1961. Editor: Das Schiff des Heils, 1933, Jacobowsky und der Oberst, 1945, Der Abiturientenag, 1948; editor, translator numerous other texts. 1st sgt. U.S. Army, 1917-23. Deocrated Officers Cross Order of Merit. Mem. Hist. Soc. So. Calif., L.A. Chamber Symphony Soc., MLA Am., Soc. Advancement Scandinavian Study, Am. Musicol. Soc., Calif. Folklore Soc., Am. Assn. Tchrs. German, others. *

ARMISTEAD, PARKES, banker; b. Franklin, Tenn., July 21, 1893; s. George Harrison and Jessie (Parkes) A.; m. Katherine Moore, Apr. 12, 1917. Student, Vanderbilt U. Asst. cashier Broadway Nat. Bank, 1918-23; asst. cashier 1st Am. Nat. Bank, Nashville, 1923-27, asst. v.p., 1927-29, v.p., 1929-35, exec. v.p., 1935-48, pres., 1948-57, chmn. bd. dirs., from 1957; bd. dirs. numerous corps. Trustee Vanderbilt U. *

ARMITAGE, ROBERT ERNEST, molding company executive; b. Lawrence, Mass., Sept. 22, 1926; s. Ernest and Elsie A. (Volkman) A.; m. Virginia Boocock, May 28, 1949; children—Barbara Ann Armitage Chidsey, James Robert, David Allen. B.S.A., Bentley Coll., 1946. Sr. auditor Patterson, Teele & Dennis, Boston, 1945-53; chief acct. Sprague Electric Co., North Adams, Mass., 1953-65; asst. treas. Sprague Electric Co., 1965-68, sr. fin. officer, treas., 1968-73, sr. v.p. fin., treas., 1973-85, dir., 1968-85; v.p. fin. Lakewood Industries, Inc. and its divs., Pittsfield, Mass., from 1985, Poly-Matrix Inc, Pittsfield, Mass., 1985-86, Syntronics, Inc., 1985-86, Lakewood Mold Co. Inc., 1985-86, Lakewood Industries, Inc., from 1986; treas. Sprague Electric Co. Credit Union, 1953-68; mem. adv. bd. Berkshire Bank &

Trust, North Adams, 1972-85. Bd. dirs., treas. No. Berkshire Santa Fund, North Adams, from 1958; corporator North Adams Regional Hosp., 1959-83; bd. dirs. No. Berkshire YMCA, 1960-82, pres., 1970-72; mem. adv. bd. Salvation Army, North Adams, 1968-83. Recipient Francis H. Hayden Meml. award No. Berkshire C. of C., 1973; Disting. Service award No. Berkshire YMCA, 1973. Mem. Am. Inst. CPAs, Mass. Soc. CPAs. Methodist. Lodge: Masons (North Adams). Home: North Adams Mass. Died Oct. 19, 1989; cremated.

ARMOR, JAMES BURTON, retail drug company executive; b. Pauls Valley, Okla., Sept. 14, 1926; s. James Dennis and Maida Bland (Beckham) A.; m. Mary Ann Stump, Sept. 4, 1948; children: James Burton, Nancy Diane, John Andrew, Jeffrey David. Student, La. Tech. U., 1944-45, Duke U., 1945-46; BS in Mktg., Okla. U., 1948. With J.C. Penney Co., 1948-73, store mgr., 1960-62; merchandising coordinator Hdqrs. J.C. Penney Co., N.Y.C., 1962-64; mdse. mgr. J.C. Penney Co., 1964-70; dir. store ops. Thrift Drug Co. (div. J.C. Penney), Pitts., 1971-73; v.p. Thrift Drug Co. (div. J.C. Penney), 1974-75, exec. v.p., 1975-80, pres., 1980-87; ret., 1987. Mem. North Caldwell (N.J.) Sch. Bd., 1968-69, North Caldwell Planning and Zoning Bd., 1969-70; assoc. program mem. U. Pitts. Grad. Sch., 1980-91 , exec. com., 1984-87; trustee Allegheny Health, Edn. and Research Corp. (Allegheny Gen Hosp.), 1984; bd. dirs. Retail Drug Inst. of L.I.U. Coll. Pharmacy; div. chmn. United Way of S.W. Pa., 1984-85; bd. dirs. Better Bus. Bur. Western Pa., 1985-89. Served with USN, 1944-46. Named Chain Drug Retailer of Yr. Chain Drug Rev., 1986. Mem. Bus. Assn. Regional Indsl. Devel. Corp. (pres. 1978-80), Nat. Assn. Chain Drug Stores (dir. 1980-87, exec. com. 1982-86), Phi Delta Theta. Republican. Presbyn. Home: Pittsburgh Pa. Died Jan. 10, 1992. †

ARMOUR, RICHARD (WILLARD), writer, educator; b. San Pedro, Calif., July 15, 1906; s. Harry Willard and Sue (Wheelock) A.; m. Kathleen Fauntleroy Stevens, Dec. 25, 1932; children—Geoffrey Stevens, Karin Elizabeth. AB, Pomona Coll., 1927, LittD, 1972; AM, Harvard U., 1928, PhD, 1933; LittD, Coll. of Ozarks, 1944; LHD, Whittier Coll., 1968, So. Calif. Coll. Optometry, 1972; LLD, Coll. Idaho, 1969, Claremont Men's Coll., 1974. Instr. in English U. Tex., 1928-29, Northwestern U., 1930-31; Dexter Scholar (research fellow) from Harvard at John Forster Library, Victoria and Albert Museum, London, 1931; prof. English, head div. of modern langs. Coll. of the Ozarks, 1932-33; Am. lectr. U. Freiburg, Germany, 1933-34; asst. prof., asso. prof. and prof. English Wells Coll., 1934-45; prof. English Scripps Coll. and Claremont Grad. Sch., 1945-63; dean of faculty Scripps Coll., 1961-63, Balch lectr. in English lit., 1963-66, dean and prof. emeritus, from 1966; Chancellor's lectr. Calif. State U. and Colls., 1964-68; writer-in-residence U. Redlands, 1974, Stanford U., 1965; vis. prof. Whittier Coll., 1975; served as Am. specialist abroad for U.S. State Dept., 1964, 66, 67, 68, 70; Fund Advancement Edn.; faculty fellow, 1953-54; Carnegie vis. prof. English U. Hawaii, 1957; leader of European tours, summers, 1926-31. Author: of numerous books, including Barry Cornwall, 1935, (with Raymond F. Howes) Coleridge the Talker, 1940, Yours for the Asking, 1942, Golf Bawls, 1946, Writing Light Verse, 1947, For Partly Proud Parents, 1950, It All Started with Columbus, 1953, Light Armour, 1954, It All Started with Europa, 1955, It All Started with Eve, 1956, Twisted Tales from Shakespeare, 1957, Nights with Armour, 1958, It All Started with Marx, 1958, Drug Store Days, 1959, The Classics Reclassified, 1960, Golf Is a Four-Letter Word, 1962, Armour's Almanac, 1962, The Medical Muse, or What to Do Until the Patient Comes, 1963, Through Darkest Adolescence, 1963, Our Presidents, 1964, The Year Santa Went Modern, 1964, American Lit Relit, 1964, An Armoury of Light Verse, 1964, The Adventures of Egbert the Easter Egg, 1965, Going Around in Academic Circles, 1965, Animals on the Ceiling, 1966, Punctured Poems, 1966, It All Started with Hippocrates, 1966, It All Started with Stones and Clubs, 1967, A Dozen Dinosaurs, 1967, Odd Old Mammals, 1968, My Life with Women, 1968, English Lit Relit, 1969, On Your Marks: A Package of Punctuation, 1969, A Diabolical Dictionary of Education, 1969, All Sizes and Shapes of Monkeys and Apes, 1970, A Short History of Sex, 1970, Who's in Holes?, 1971, Writing Light Verse and Prose Humor, 1971, All in Sport, 1972, Out of My Mind, 1972, The Strange Dreams of Rover Jones, 1973, It All Started with Freshman English, 1973, Going Like Sixty: A Lighthearted Look at the Later Years, 1974, Sea Full of Whales, 1974, The Academic Bestiary, 1974, The Spouse in the House, 1975, The Happy Bookers: A History of Librarians and Their World, 1976, It All Would Have Startled Columbus, 1976, It All Started with Nudes: An Artful History of Art, 1977, Strange Monsters of the Sea, 1979, Insects All Around Us, 1981; Anyone for Insomnia?, 1982; Educated Guesses, 1983; Have You Ever Wished You Were Something Else?, 1983; mem. editorial bd.: The Writer; contbr. regular feature to Quote, The Weekly Digest; contbr. articles and poems to nat. mags. Trustee Claremont Men's Coll., Claremont McKenna Coll., 1968—. Served as 2d lt. inf. Res. Corps U.S. Army, 1927-37; active duty in Antiaircraft Arty. 1942-46; lt. col., detailed to War Dept. Gen. Staff (mem.) 1944-46; col. U.S. Army Res. Decorated Legion of Merit with oak leaf cluster. Mem. Modern Lang. Assn. Am., Am. Assn. Univ. Profs., Calif. Writers Guild, P.E.N., Phi Beta Kappa. Conglist. Home: Claremont Calif. Died Feb. 28, 1989; cremated.

ARMSTRONG, DONALD BUDD, JR., advertising and marketing consultant; b. N.Y.C., June 23, 1915; s. Donald Budd and Eunice (Burton) A.; m. Marion Lee Rising, Aug. 9, 1940 (div. Jan. 1955); children: Judith Lee, Keir Alexander, Donald Budd III; m. Eleanor Dippel Sinclair, Jan. 1955. BA, Harvard, 1937. Jr. exec. trainee Lehn & Fink Inc., N.Y.C., 1937-39; advt. rsch. Young & Rubicam Inc., 1939-45; assoc. dir. rsch. McCann-Erickson Inc., N.Y.C., 1946-48; dir. rsch. McCann-Erickson Inc., 1949-51; v.p. charge rsch., mem. adv. com. advt. plans, 1951-55, chmn. creative plans bd., 1956, v.p. for mktg. svcs., chmn. mktg. plans bd., 1957, asst. to the pres., coord. of profl. svcs., 1958, v.p. in charge acct. planning and mktg. svcs., 1959-63; chmn. bd. McCann-Erickson (Can.) Ltd., 1959-63, Communications Affiliates Inc., N.Y.C., 1960-61; mem. corp. staff, sr. v.p., assoc. dir. J. Walter Thompson Co., N.Y.C., 1963-73; advt. and mktg. cons., 1976-90; Communications Affiliates Inc., N.Y.C., 1960-61. Author: Dynamics of Mass Media. Mem. Copy Rsch. coun., Advt. Rsch. Found., Am. Assn. Advt. Agys. (standing com. on rsch.), Am. Assn. Pub. Opinion Rsch. Mem. Am. Mktg. Assn. (v.p. 1952), Hasty Pudding of 1776, Lampoon, Harvard (N.Y.C.), Sleepy Hollow Country Club. Home: Ponte Vedra Fla. Died Apr. 17, 1990.

ARMSTRONG, EDWARD GABRIEL, banker; b. Enfield, Conn., Sept. 16, 1897; s. G. Allingham and Harriet (Hurlburt) A.; m. Barbara Morrison Eaton, July 24, 1922; children: Edward A., Lucia Williams. BS, Trinity Coll., 1921. With Lomas & Nettleton Co., New Haven, 1921-25; with Union & New Haven Trust Co., from 1925, head trust dept., from 1945, dir., from 1947, sr. v.p., 1959-63, vice chmn. bd., chmn. trust com., from 1963. Mem. Conn. Bankers Assn., Soc. Colonial Wars Conn., Newcomen Soc., others. *

ARMSTRONG, GEORGE ROBERT, utility executive; b. Terre Haute, Ind., Oct. 6, 1898; s. Fred and Cornelia (Woolsey) A.; m. Emma Thorne, May 20, 1930. BS, Rose Poly Inst., 1921. Engr. constrn. Louisville Gas & Electric Co., 1922-29, gen. supt. constrn., 1929-39, gen. supt., 1939-48, exec. v.p., 1948-57, pres., 1957-63, chmn. of the bd., from 1963; pres. Ohio Valley Transmission Corp., East Cen. Nuclear Group; v.p. Ind.-Ky. Electric Corp.; dir. 1st Nat. Lincoln Bank Louisville, Va. Carolina Chem. Corp., Ohio Valley Electric Corp., Ky. Trust Co., others. With U.S. Army, World War I. Mem. Am. Inst. Elec. Engrs., others. *

ARMSTRONG, PHILIP B(ROWNELL), anatomist, educator; b. Rutherford, N.J., Mar. 26, 1898; s. Samuel Eugene and Isabella Augusta (Gott) A.; m. Marion Louise Schmuck, Sept. 7, 1932; children: Peter Brownell, Samuel Currie. BS, Mass. State Coll., 1921; MD, Cornell U., 1926. Instr. Cornell U., 1926-28, asst. prof., 1928-37; Rockefeller fellow Cambridge U., Sir William Dunn Inst. Biochem., 1934-35; prof. anatomy U. Ala. Sch. Medicine, 1937-38, SUNY, Syracuse, from 1938; anatomist Nat. Bd. Med. Examiners, from 1939; clk. Corp. Marine Biol. Lab., 1940-42, trustee from 1946, dir. from 1950; dir. Gen. Biol. Supply House; mem. corp. Woods Hole Oceanographic Instn., from 1950. Contbr. articles to profl. jours. Mem. Fulbright Fellowship Com. NRC, 1960. Mem. Am. Zool. Soc., Am. Anat. Assn., Am. Physiol. Soc., Harvey Soc., Phi Sigma Kappa, Sigma Xi, others. *

ARMSTRONG, RICHARD LEE, geological sciences educator; b. Seattle, Aug. 4, 1937; s. Donald William and Bernice Hilda (Alwood) A.; m. Julia Anderson McNeely, Sept. 7, 1961 (div. Feb. 1989); children: Katherine Elizabeth, Jonathan Karl, Rebecca Lynne. B.S., Yale U., 1959, Ph.D., 1964. Acting instr. to assoc. prof. Yale U., New Haven, 1962-73; assoc. prof. geol. scis. U. B.C., Vancouver, Can., 1973-76, prof., from 1976. Contbr. chpts. to books and articles to profl. jours. NSF fellow, 1963-64; Morse and Guggenheim fellow, 1968-69. Fellow Royal Soc. Can., Geol. Assn. Can. (pres. Cordilleran sect. 1975-76, Logan medal 1990), Geol. Soc. Am. (pres. Cordilleran sect. 1985-86); mem. Geochem. Soc., Am. Geophys. Union, Internat. Assn. for Volcanology and Chemistry of the Earths Interior (chmn. working group radiogenic isotopes 1984-87). Home: Vancouver Can. Deceased. †

ARNESON, ROBERT CARSTON, sculptor, educator; b. Benicia, Calif., Sept. 4, 1930. B.A. in Edn, Calif. Coll. Arts and Crafts, 1954; M.F.A. Mills Coll, 1958; student ceramics with, Antonio Prieto. Instr. design Mills Coll., 1960-62; prof. art U. Calif.-Davis, 1962-91, prof. emeritus, 1991-92. One man shows, various galleries, U.S. and London, retrospective exhbn., Mus. Contemporary Art, Chgo., also San Francisco Mus. Art, 1974, Robert Arneson: A Retrospective-Des Moines Art Ctr., 1986, Hirshhorn Mus. and Sculpture Garden, Washington, 1986, Portland Art Mus., 1987, Oakland Mus., Calif., 1987; exhibited in group shows, U. Calif. Art Mus., Berkeley, 1967, Johnson Wax Collection, touring U.S. and Europe, 1968-73, Whitney Mus. Am. Art, N.Y.C., 1969, 81-82, Mus. Contemporary Crafts, N.Y.C., 1971, Mus. Modern Art, Kyoto, also Tokyo, Japan, 1971-72, Crocker Art Mus., Sacramento, 1981, San Francisco Mus. Modern Art, 1982; represented in permanent collections, San Francisco Mus. Modern Art, Oakland (Calif.) Art Mus., Santa Barbara (Calif.) Mus. Art, U. Calif. Art Mus., Berkeley, Nat. Mus. Modern Art, Kyoto, Utah Mus. Fine Arts, Salt Lake City, Stedlijk Mus., Amsterdam, Holland. Recipient Am. Acad. and Inst. of Arts and Letters award, 1991. Home: Davis Calif. Died Nov. 2, 1992. †

ARNOFF, E. LEONARD, college dean, management scientist; b. Cleve., Oct. 15, 1922; s. David and Lena (Mentz) A.; m. Ann Edith Kolisch, Aug. 21, 1948; children: Janice Lee (dec.), Susan Renee Arnoff Spohr. B.S., Western Res. U., 1943; M.S, Case Inst. Tech., 1948; Ph.D., Calif. Inst. Tech., 1951. Mathematician, hydrodynamicist Naval Ordnance Test Station, Pasadena, Calif., 1950-51; mathematician, aero. research scientist NACA, Cleve., 1951-52; prof. ops. research Case Inst. Tech., Cleve., 1952-61; cons. Japanese Govt., U.S. Dept. State, summer 1959; prin., nat. dir. planning and ops. services Ernst & Whinney (C.P.A.s), Cleve., 1960-83; prof. bus. adminstrn., dean Coll. Bus. Adminstrn. U. Cin., from 1983; instr. Case Inst. Tech., 1946-48; teaching fellow, Inst. scholar Calif. Inst. Tech., 1948-51; pres. Arnoff & Assocs., from 1988. Author: Introduction to Operations Research, 17th printing, 1957, (Co-author) also articles.; textbooks.; Editor: Mgmt. Sci, 1955-70. Co-pres. Cleveland Heights PTA, 1964-65; vis. com. Case Western Res. U., 1980-83; bd. dirs. Camp Fire, Inc., Panorama Services and Products, Jr. Achievement of Cin. Served with inf. AUS, 1943-46. Decorated Bronze Star, Purple Heart with 2 oak leaf clusters. Fellow Ops. Research Soc. Am., AAAS; mem. Inst. Mgmt. Scis. (internat pres. 1968-69), N.Am. Soc. Corporate Planning, Inst. Mgmt. Cons., Math. Assn. Am., U.S. Figure Skating Assn., Sigma Xi, Omicron Delta Kappa, Beta Alpha Psi., Omega Rho (internat. pres. 1982-84), Beta Gamma Sigma, Delta Sigma Pi. Clubs: Plaza Figure Skating (Cleve.) (pres. 1971-73), Cleve. Skating (Cleve.), Masons (Cleve.) (master 1961-62). Home: Sanibel Fla. Deceased. †

ARNOLD, ARTHUR Z., educator; b. Armavir, Georgia, Mar. 1, 1898; came to U.S., 1914; naturalized, 1925.; s. Leonid Chehadze Z. and Vera (Arnashvilli) B.; m. Marie Barbara Blain, July 28, 1925. AB, George Washington U., 1926; LLB, Hamilton Coll., 1922; MS, Columbia U., 1928, PhD, 1937. Instr. econs. CCNY, 1928-38; mem. faculty NYU, from 1935, asst. prof., 1941-43, assoc. prof., 1943-46, prof. econs. Washington Sq. Coll. Arts & Scis., Grad. Sch., from 1946; cons., economist, statistician, from 1932. Author: Banks, Credit and Money in Soviet Russia, 1937, Curbing Inflation Through Taxation (with others), 1944; also articles. Mem. Am. Econ. Assn., Royal Econ. Soc., Am. Statis. Assn., Acad. Polit. Sci., Am. Assn. Univ. Profs., Biometric Soc., AAAS. *

ARNOLD, EVERETT JOHN, life insurance company executive; b. Wisconsin Rapids, Wis., Dec. 4, 1932; s. John George and Margaret Elizabeth (Schroder) A.; m. Bernadeen Evelyn Yonko, June 25, 1955; children—Karoline Kay, Richard Bert. B.B.A. in Acctg., U. Wis., 1958. C.P.A., Wis. Asst. state auditor Wis. Dept. Audit, 1958-61; with Nat. Guardian Life Ins. Co., Madison, Wis., from 1961; v.p., dir. adminstrn. Nat. Guardian Life Ins. Co., 1969-73, exec. v.p., dir. adminstrn., 1973-74, exec. v.p., treas., from 1974. Mem. budget com., loaned exec. Madison United Way; adv. bd. Madison YWCA; mem. peer rev. com. Wis. Chiropractors Assn. Served with AUS, 1953-54, Korea. Mem. Wis. Soc. C.P.A.s, Life Office Mgmt. Assn. (asso.), Madison C. of C., Nat. Rifle Assn. (life), Beta Alpha Psi. Clubs: Kiwanis, Maple Bluff Country. Home: Waunakee Wis. Died July 24, 1989; buried Madison, Wis.

ARNOLD, MORRIS FAIRCHILD, bishop; b. Mpls., Jan. 5, 1915; s. LeRoy and Kate (Fairchild) A.; m. Harriet Borda Schmidgall, Jan. 1978; children by previous marriage: Jaqueline Fairchild (Mrs. Arnold Crocker), William Morris. B.A. magna cum laude, Williams Coll., 1936; M.Div. cum laude, Episcopal Theol. Sch., 1940; D.D., Kenyon Coll., 1961, Williams Coll., 1972. Ordained priest Episcopal Ch., 1940; priest-in-charge St. John's Ch., Saugus, Mass., 1940-43; chaplain U.S. Army, 1943-45; rector Grace Ch., Medford, Mass., 1945-50; Episcopal students chaplain Tufts Coll., Boston, 1945-50; rector Christ Ch., Cin., 1950-72; consecrated suffragan bishop, 1972; suffragan bishop Episcopal Diocese of Mass., 1972-92. Del. to Anglican Congress from So. Ohio, 1954; dep. to 7 Gen. Convs. of Episcopal Ch., 1958-70; co-founder U.S. Ch. and City Conf., 1959, pres., 1964-66; mem. Joint Commn. on Edn. for Holy Orders, 1961-68; program and budget com. of Episcopal Ch., 1961-70, 77-80; pres. Council of Chs. of Greater Cin., 1961-63; treas. Cin. Met. Area Religious Coalition, 1968-72; trustee ARC, 1957-63, Family Service, 1962-71, Better Housing League, 1951-72; mem. Cathedral Deans Assn., 1955-72; mem. steering com. Urban Bishop's Coalition, 1977-82. Mem. Soc. for the Relief of Aged or Disabled Clergymen (v.p. 1972-82), Alumni Assn. Episcopal Theol. Sch. (pres. 1969-72), Phi Beta Kappa, Delta Phi. Home: Belmont Mass. Died Dec. 3, 1992. †

ARRAU, CLAUDIO, concert pianist; b. Chillan, Chile, Feb. 6, 1903; widowed; children: Carmen, Mario (dec.), Christopher. Endowed as child prodigy by Chilean Govt. to study at, Stern Conservatory, Berlin, with Martin Krause, 1912-18. Made debut in Berlin, 1915, London debut, 1920; toured Germany, Europe, S.Am., 1st U.S. Tour, 1923-24; returned permanently, 1941, toured USSR, 1929, 30, 68, Australia, 1947, 57, 62, 68, 70, 74, South Africa, 1949, 52, 56, Japan, 1965, 68, 72, 79, 82, 84, 87, Israel, 1950, 52, 58, 60, 64, 67, 71, 72; presented 32 Beethoven piano sonatas in N.Y., 1953, 62; toured world many times; recorded major piano works of Debussy, Beethoven, Brahms, Chopin, Liszt, Schumann, Schubert, Mozart; 25 CD Arrau Collection by Philips Rec., 1991. Decorated chevalier Order Arts and Letters, comdr. Legion of Honor (France); Deutsches Verdienst Kreuz Ger.; recipient Liszt prize, 1913, 14; Ibach prize, 1917; Grand Prix Internat. des Pianistes at Geneva, 1927; Internat UNESCO Music prize, 1983; streets named in honor Santiago and Chillan. Home: Munich Germany Died June 9, 1991.

ARROWSMITH, WILLIAM AYRES, classics educator, translator, writer; b. Orange, N.J., Apr. 13, 1924; s. Walter Weed and Dorothy (Ayres) A.; m. Jean Reiser, Jan. 10, 1945 (div. 1980); children: Nancy, Beth. BA, Princeton U., 1947, PhD, 1954; BA (Rhodes scholar), Oxford (Eng.) U., 1951, MA, 1958; LLD (hon.), Loyola U., 1968; LHD (hon.), St. Michael's Coll., Burlington, Vt., 1968; DLitt (hon.), Westminster Coll., Fulton, Mo., 1969, Dartmouth Coll., 1970, Dickinson Coll., 1971, Lebanon Valley Coll., 1973; DLH (hon.), U. Detroit, 1973, Grand Valley State Coll., 1973, Syracuse U., 1982, Carnegie-Mellon U., 1974, Daniel Webster Coll., Nashua, N.H., 1989. Instr. classics Princeton U., 1951-53; instr. classics and humanities Wesleyan U., Middletown, Conn., 1953-54; asst. prof. classics and humanities U. Calif., Riverside, 1954-56; mem. faculty U. Tex., Austin, 1958-70; prof. classics U. Tex., 1959-70, chmn. dept., 1964-66, univ. prof. arts and letters, 1965-70; prof. classics, univ. prof. Boston U., 1971-76; vis. Henry McCormick prof. dramatic lit. Sch. Drama Yale U., 1976-77; prof. writing seminars and classics Johns Hopkins U., 1977-81; presdl. prof. Georgetown U., Washington, 1981; David B. Kriser prof. humanities NYU, 1983-84; Robert W. Woodruff prof. of classics and comparative lit. Emory U., Atlanta, 1982-86; univ. prof., prof. classics Boston U., from 1986; ednl. cons. Ford Found., 1970-71; cons. Leadership Tng. Inst., Office of Edn., 1970-71; vis. prof. humanities M.I.T., spring 1971; lectr. Folger Shakespeare Library, Washington, 1981; fellow Center Advanced Studies, Wesleyan U., 1967, Battelle Meml. Inst., Seattle, 1968; founding editor Chimera, 1942-44, Hudson Rev., 1948-60, Arion, Jour. Classical Culture, 1962—; adv. editor Tulane Drama Rev., 1960-67, Delos, A Jour. of Translation, 1987-90; adv. bd. Mosaic, from 1967, Yeats-at-the-Abbey Theatre, Dublin, Ireland, from 1988, Beacon, from 1991; sr. classics editor Hellas, from 1991; mem. exec. com. Nat. Translation Center, 1965-70; mem. faculty, mem. bd. Nat. Humanities Faculty, 1972-74; mem. Acad. Lit. Studies, 1975, Internat. Council on Future of the Univ. Translator: (Petronius) The Satyricon, 1959, (Euripides) The Bacchae, Cyclops, Heracles, Orestes and Hecuba, 1960, (Aristophanes) The Birds, 1961, Clouds, 1962, (with R. Shattuck) The Craft and Context of Translation, 1962, (with D. S. Carne-Ross, Cesare Pavese) Dialogues with Leucò, 1965, (Cesare Pavese) Hard Labor, 1976, (M. Antonioni) That Bowling Alley on the Tiber, 1985, (Montale) The Storm and other Things, 1985, (Montale) The Occasions, 1987; editor: Image of Italy, 1961, Five Modern Italian Novels, 1964; gen. editor: The Greek Tragedy in New Translation (33 vols.), from 1973, Alcestis (Euripides), 1975; gen. editor, translator. Friedrich Nietzsche, Unmodern Observations, 1990; contbr. numerous articles to profl. jours. With AUS, 1943-46. Fellow Woodrow Wilson Found., 1947-48, Guggenheim Found., 1957-58, Prix de Rome sr. research fellow Am. Acad. Rome, 1956-57, Rockefeller fellow in humanities, 1980-81; Phi Beta Kappa vis. scholar, 1964-65; recipient Longview award for criticism, 1960, Bromberg award for excellence in teaching U. Tex., 1959, Morris L. Ernst award for excellence in teaching, 1962, Piper Prof. award for disting. teaching, 1966, Harbison award for disting. teaching, 1971, award for lit. Am. Acad. and Nat. Inst. Arts and Letters, 1978, Landon Translation prize, 1986, Shestack Poetry prize, 1987, Internat. Montale prize, 1990. Mem. PEN, Assn. Am. Rhodes Scholars, Phi Beta Kappa. Democrat. Home: Brookline Mass. Died Feb. 20, 1991.

ARRUPE, PEDRO, clergyman; b. Bilbao, Spain, Nov. 14, 1907; s. Marcelino and Dolores (Gondra) A. Student, State U. Madrid, 1927; Jesuit Seminaries, Oña, Spain, 1932, Marneffe, Belgium, 1933, Valkenburg, Holland, 1936, St. Mary's Coll., 1937, St. Stanislaus Tertlanship, 1938. Entered Soc. of Jesus, Loyola, Spain, 1927; ordained priest Roman Catholic Ch., 1936; rector, master of novices Jesuit Novitiate, Hiroshima, Japan, 1942-54; provincial superior Japan, 1954-65; vice chancellor Sophia U., Tokyo, 1956-64; prof., 1956-64; gen. Soc. of Jesus Rome, Italy, 1965-83; pres. Union Superiors Gen., 1967-82. Author: Yo Vivi La Bomba Atomica, 1952, Este Japon increible, 1954, Christo No Michi, Kyosan-Shugi, Miyo So.io Hito Wo, Xaverio No Shingen, Xaverio No Sugata, Wakaki Seidai No Atau, El P. Arrupe en Colombia, 1968, Fe cristiana y compromiso misionero, 1969, The Visit of Fr. General to the English Province, 1970, Escala an Espana, 1970, Jesuit General in the Philippines, 1971, Witnessing to Justice, 1972, Nuestra vida consagrada, 1972, Hacia un mundo en cambio, 1972, Men for Others, 1973, A Planet of Heal, 1975, Pioneers of the Spirit, 1976, La vida religiosa ante un reto historico, 1978, Hambre de pan y de Evangelio, 1978, Challenge to Religious Life Today, 1979, Justice with Faith Today, 1980, Cartas del Padre Arrupe, 1980, L'Esperance ne trompe pas, 1981, La Identidad del Jesuita, 1981, La Iglesia de Hoy y del Futuro, 1982. Home: Rome Italy Died Feb. 5, 1991; buried Campo Verano Cemetery.

ARTHUR, JEAN, actress; b. N.Y.C., Oct. 17, 1908; m. Frank Ross, 1932. Student pub. schs., N.Y. Actress in motion pictures under contract with Paramount Pictures, 1929-31; in 14 plays in stock cos. and on Broadway, N.Y.C., 1931-34, motion pictures, Hollywood, 1934—; actress appearing in Whole Town's Talking, Mr. Deeds Goes to Town, You Can't Take It With Your, Mr. Smith Goes to Washington, Only Angels Have Wings, Too Many Husbands, The Plainsman, Easy Swing, Talk of the Town, The More the Merrier, Impatient Years, 1944. Home: Hollywood Calif. Died June 19, 1991.

ARTHUR, RANSOM JAMES, psychiatrist, educator; b. N.Y.C., Dec. 5, 1925; s. Ransom James and Barbara Remick A.; m. Frances Nickolls, Dec. 18, 1954; children: Jane, Shelley. A.B. with honors, U. Calif., Berkeley, 1947; M.D. cum laude, Harvard U., 1951. Intern Mass. Gen. Hosp., Boston, 1951-52; teaching fellow Harvard Med. Sch., 1951-54; resident in pediatrics Children's Med. Center, Boston, 1952-54; resident in psychiatry Queens Hosp., Honolulu, 1954-55; commd. lt U.S. Navy, 1958, advanced through grades to capt., 1968; resident U.S. Naval Hosp., Bethesda, Md., 1957-60; comdg. officer U.S. Naval Med. Neuropsychiat. Res. Unit, San Diego, 1963-74; prof. psychiatry, assoc. dean Sch. Medicine; dir. Neuropsychiat. Inst. Hosp. and Clinics, UCLA, 1974-79; dean Sch. Medicine, U. Oreg., Portland, 1979-83; prof. UCLA, from 1983; chief of staff Brentwood VA Hosp., Los Angeles, from 1983; cons. Founder Masters' Swimming, 1970, nat. chmn., 1970-72, nat. chmn. goals and objectives, from 1972. Author: An Introduction to Social Psychiatry, 1971; contbr. articles to profl. jours.; mem. editorial bd.: Mil. Medicine, from 1972, Am. Jour. Psychiatry, 1975-79. Served with USMCR, 1943-46. Decorated Legion of Merit (2). Mem. Am. Coll. Psychiatrists, Am. Psychiat. Assn., Royal Soc. Medicine, AMA (Physicians Recognition award), Assn. Am. Med. Colls., Assn. Mil. Surgeons, Phi Beta Kappa, Sigma Xi. Home: Los Angeles Calif. Died Oct. 28, 1989.

ARZT, MAX, rabbi, educator; b. Poland, Mar. 20, 1897; came to U.S., 1902; naturalized, 1915; s. Hyman and Anna (Grossbach) A.; m. Esther Podolsky, Mar. 7, 1922; children: Miriam Teplitz, David, Raphael. BS, CCNY, 1918; MA, Columbia U., 1921; MHL, Jewish Theol. Sem. Am., 1921, DHL, DD, 1934, 50. Rabbi Temple Beth El, Stamford, Conn., 1921-24, Temple Israel, Scranton, Pa., 1924-39; dir. field activities, assoc. prof. practical theology Jewish Theol. Sem., 1939-51, vice chancellor, from 1951, Israel Goldstein prof. practical theology, from 1962. Author: Justice and Mercy, 1963; contbg. editor Judaism quar. Pres. Rabbinical Assembly Am., 1939, exec. com. United Synagogue Am.; mem. exec. com. N.Y. Bd. Rabbis. *

ASCHENBORN, HANS JURGEN, librarian, administrator; b. Windhoek, S. Africa, Aug. 19, 1920; s. Hans Anton and Emmy (Bredow) A.; m. Helga C. Hermenau, Apr. 17, 1947; 4 children. B.A., Univ. S. Africa, 1950; M.A. in Library Sci., U. Pretoria, 1957, Ph.D., 1966. Dept. head U. Pretoria, 1947-49, 52-59, Transvaal Provincial Library Services, Pretoria, 1948-52; dep. dir., dir. State Library, Pretoria, from 1959; mem. Nat. Library Adv. Council, Nat. Adv. Bd. Library and Info. Sci.; adv. bd. Nat. Libraries. Author: Stimmen deutscher Dichter, 1949; Titelbeskrywing, 1956; Sachkatalogisierung seit Trebst, 1957; Staatsbib der ZAR, 1970. U.S. State Dept. grantee, 1961-62, Can. Council Leadership grantee, 1961-62. Hon. fellow Internat. Info. Mgmt. Congress, Machine Readable Cataloguing (council mem.); mem. S. African Library Assn., S. African Inst. Library and Info. Sci. (council mem.); assoc. mem. S. African Acad. vir Wetenskap en Kuns. Died Oct., 1986, Pretoria, South Africa. Died Oct. 3, 1986; interred Kameldrif, Pretoria. Home: Pretoria Republic of South Africa

ASCHENBRENNER, KARL, educator, philosopher; b. Bison, Kans., Nov. 20, 1911; s. John and Elisabeth Nathalia (Schnell) A.; m. Margaret Marie Kerr, Jan. 19, 1937; children: Lisbeth, Peter, John. A.B., Reed Coll., 1934; M.A., U. Calif.-Berkeley, 1938, Ph.D., 1940. Instr. philosophy Reed Coll., 1940-42; mem. faculty U. Calif.-Berkeley, from 1946, prof. philosophy, from 1959, chmn. philosophy, 1960-63, chmn. dept. design, 1964-65; vis. lectr. Amerika Inst., U. Munich, 1950. Co-editor, translator: (Baumgarten) Reflections on Poetry, 1954, Aesthetic Theories, 1965; author: The Concepts of Value, 1971, The Concepts of Criticism, 1974, Analysis of Appraisive Characterization, 1983, Companion to Kant's Critique of Pure Reason, 1983, The Concept of Coherence in Art, 1985; also articles, reviews in field. Del. Internat. Congress Aesthetics, 1956, 60, 64, 72, 76, 80. Served to lt. USNR, 1943-46. Guggenheim fellow Vienna and London, 1956-57; Fulbright research fellow U. Munich, 1963-64; sr. fellow Nat. Endowment for Humanities, 1972; exchange scholar Inst. Cultural Relations, Budapest, Hungary, 1974-75, 77. Mem. Brit. Soc. Aesthetics, Phi Beta Kappa. Club: University Faculty (Berkeley). Home: Los Angeles Calif. Died July 4, 1988; buried Budapest, Hungary.

ASHBAUGH, JOHN HARVEY, manufacturing executive; b. Inpls., Sept. 1, 1897; s. John Harvey and Clara Belle (Wilson) A.; m. Elsie Hobday, Aug. 4, 1934; 1 child, Sara Jane. Student Blies Elec. Sch., Carnegie Tech. Night Sch., 1918-21. Apprentice Westinghouse Electric Mfg. Co., 1918-19, positions various depts., 1919-32, with appliance divsn., from 1932, dir. conversion appliance divsn. to wartime prodn., 1932, v.p., 1944-57; bd. dirs. various cos. *

ASHBY, HUGH C(LINTON), transportation company executive; b. Slaughters, Ky., Oct. 23, 1934; s. Clint and Ruth Helen (Orton) A.; m. Alma Joyce Atwood, Dec. 23, 1960; children: Forrest W., Sarah C. B.S., Murray State U., 1960. Tchr. Pub. Schs., Paducah, Ky., 1960-62; budget analyst Ky. Dept. Fin., Frankfort, 1962-64; dir. div. of rates Ky. Dept. Motor Transp., Frankfort, 1964-68; dir. rates and budgets Am. Transit Corp., St. Louis, 1968-71, v.p. adminstrn., 1971-76, exec. v.p., 1976-89; pres. ATC Mgmt. Corp., St. Louis, 1989-91. Served with USAF, 1954-58. Home: Saint Louis Mo. Died Dec. 1991. †

ASHBY, JACK LANE, cattle rancher; b. Berkeley, Calif., Apr. 3, 1911; s. Shirley Joshua and Lola (McKellips) A.; m. Patricia Robbins, June 17, 1936; children: Peter Robbins, Robert Lane (dec.), Richard William, Charlotte Brownlie, Sarah Robbins. AB, Stanford U., 1933. Investment banker with E.F. Hutton & Co., San Francisco, 1933-35, Eastland & Co., 1935-39, Irving Lundborg & Co., 1939-40; indsl. financing with Comml. Investment Trust Co., 1940-41; joined with Kaiser Steel Corp., Oakland, Calif., 1941, v.p. gen. mgr., 1948-59, pres., 1959, later vice chmn., dir.; former chmn. Kaiser Resources Ltd.; past dir. Nat. Indsl. Conf. Bd. Past mem. Am. Iron and Steel Inst. (past hon. mem. bd.), Calif. Cattlemen's Assn., Calif. C. of C. (past dir.), L.A. C. of C., San Francisco C. of C., Oakland C. of C., Claremont Coutnry Club (Oakland), Family, Pacific-Union (San Francisco), Marrakesh Country (Palm Desert, Calif.), Delta Kappa Epsilon. Home: Palm Desert Calif. Died Jan. 7, 1990.

ASHBY, ROBERT SAMUEL, lawyer; b. Crawfordsville, Ind., July 9, 1916; s. William Wallace and Nellie (Graybill) A.; m. Susan Gatch, June 4, 1949; children: Jean G., Willis G. A.B. with highest honors, Ind. U., 1938; LL.B. magna cum laude, Harvard, 1941. Bar: Ind. 1941, N.Y. 1942. Assoc. firm Carter, Ledyard & Milburn, N.Y.C., 1941-42; partner firm Barnes & Thornburg, Indpls., from 1946; dir. Ind. Nat. Corp.; bd. dirs. Inland Container Corp., Altamil Corp., Indiana Knitwear Corp., Ulrich Chemical, Inc., Nixon Enterprises. Editor: Harvard Law Rev, 1941; Contbr. articles to tax and legal jours. Chmn. bd. of govs. Indpls. Mus. Art, 1960-88. Served to lt. comdr. USNR, 1942-46; The English Speaking Union (pres. Ind. chpt.), trustee Krannit Charitable Trust (chmn. Com. Foreign Relations). Mem. ABA, Ind. Bar Assn., Indpls. Bar Assn., Assn. of Bar of City of N.Y., Bar Assn. 7th Fed. Cir., Meridian Hills Country Club, Phi Beta Kappa, Sigma Nu. Clubs: Indianapolis Dramatic, Contemporary, University. Home: Indianapolis IN Died Nov. 29, 1989; buried Cemetery Ladoga, Ind.

ASHCROFT, DAME PEGGY (DAME EDITH MARGARET EMILY HUTCHINSON), actress; b. Dec. 22, 1907; d. William Worsley and Violet Maud (Bernheim) A.; m. Rupert Hart-Davis, 1929 (dissolved); m. Theodore Komisarjevsky, 1934 (dissolved); m. Jeremy Hutchinson, 1940 (dissolved 1966); children: Nicholas, Liza. Ed. Croydon and Central Sch. of Speech Tng., Albert Hall, London; D.Litt. (hon.), Oxford U., 1961, Leicester U., 1964; D.Lit. (hon.), London U., 1965, Warwick U., 1966, Cambridge U., 1972, Bpen U., 1986, Bristol U., 1986, Reading U., 1986. Debuted at Birmingham Repertory Theatre, 1926; mem. Royal Shakespeare Co., Stratford and London, 1960-64, dir., from 1968. Appeared in theatrical prodns. including Edward My Son, 1946, The Heiress, 1948, The Deep Blue Sea, 1952, Hedda Gabler, 1955, The Seagull, 1964, Days in the Trees, 1966, Ghosts, 1967, Delicate Balance, 1968, Landscape, 1969, Katherine of Aragon in Henry VIII, The Plebeians, 1970, The Lovers of Viorne (Evening Standard Best Actress award 1972), 1971, Lloyd George Knew My Father, 1972, Old Times, 1972, John Gabriel Borkman, 1975, Happy Days, 1975, Old World, 1976, Watch on the Rhine, 1980, Family Voices, 1981, All's Well That Ends Well, 1981, A Perfect Spy, 1987; in films including The Wandering Jew, Thirty-Nine Steps, 1935, The Nun's Story, 1951, Sunday Bloody Sunday, 1971, Three into Two Won't Go, Passage to India (Acad. award 1984), Madame Sousatzka, 1988, She's Been Away (Venice Festival award); TV appearances include Cream in My Coffee, Caught on a Train, 1980, The Jewel in the Crown, 1984, The Heat of the Day, 1990. Decorated Dame of Order

Brit. Empire, 1956; recipient King's Gold medal Norway. Died June 14, 1991. Home: London Eng.

ASHER, EUGENE LEON, historian, educator; b. Cleve., Nov. 23, 1929; s. Samuel H. and Dorothy Denise (LePon) A.; A.B., UCLA, 1952, M.A., 1955, Ph.D, 1958; postgrad. (Fulbright fellow) U. Paris, 1956-57, U. Toulouse, 1957; m. Bonnie Jane Anderson, June 9, 1956; children: Allyson Elizabeth, Christine Marie. Asst. prof. history U. Wichita (Kans.), 1957-59; mem. faculty history Calif. State U.-Long Beach, 1959-67, 71-92, prof., chmn. dept. history, 1971-76, exec. asst. to pres., 1976-80, exec. officer, 1980-92, dir. univ. relations, 1984-92; exec. dir. KLON-FM public radio, 1981-92; dir. Am. Hist. Assn. History Edn. Project, 1968-75; prof. history Ind. U., Bloomington, 1969-71. Pres., Casa Dorado Mng. Agt. Inc., Palm Springs, Calif., 1975. Vice chmn. Long Beach Am. Revolution Bicentennial Commn., 1973-76; co-chmn. history adv. panel, mem. Calif. State Social Scis. Commn., 1965-68; chmn. Joint Anglo-U.S. Commn. Confs. History, Dept. State, 1972-75; trustee Los Angeles Theater Ctr., 1983-92, v.p. bd. trustees, 1985-86, pres. 1986-87, chmn. bd. 1987-92. Trustee Sloan Found. Notre Dame U. Program; Am. Council Learned Socs. fellow, 1962-63, 66-67; Social Sci. Research Council grantee, 1962, 66-67; HEW grantee, 1969-75. Mem. Soc. History Edn. (chmn bd. 1972-78), Am. Hist. Assn., Nat. Council Social Studies, Orgn. Am. Historians, Societe d'Histoire Moderne et Contemporaine, Phi Beta Kappa Alumni Assn. (council Calif. 1979-92, v.p. 1982-84, pres. 1984-86). Author: The Resistance to the Maritime Classes: the Survival of Feudalism in the France of Colbert, 1960: (with others) A Framework for the Social Sciences: Report of the Statewide Social Science Study Commission, 1968. Contbr. articles to profl. publs.; producer film: Oil: The Pioneering Years, 1978. Deceased. Home: Long Beach Calif. †

ASHFORTH, ALBERT C., banker; b. Toronto, Ont., Can., Mar. 6, 1893; s. William and Mary (Hall) A.; m. Annetta Lillian Ross, Sept. 5, 1921; 2 sons. Student pub. schs., Toronto. Jr. Bank of Hamilton, Toronto, 1909; with Dominion Bank, Toronto, from 1910, various positions, to gen. mgr., v.p., dir., 1910-55, pres., 1955-60; bd. dirs. Can. Life Assurance Co.; v.p. Corp. Investors Ltd.; dir. various corps. Bd. regents Victoria U. Mem. Can. C. of C., Bd. Trade Can., Masons. *

ASHMEAD, JOHN, JR., educator, author; b. N.Y.C., Aug. 22, 1917; s. John and Mildred (Hinkel) A.; m. Ann Wheeler Harnwell, Oct. 15, 1949; children: John III, Graham Gaylord, Gaylord Harmwell, Louisa Harral, Theodora Wheeler. BA magna cum laude, Harvard U., 1938, MA, 1941, PhD, 1950. Mem. faculty Haverford Coll., 1947-92, prof. English, 1961-92, chmn. dept., 1973-92; lectr. English Bryn Mawr Coll., 1949; lectr. English and history Athens (Greece) Coll., 1956-57; Fulbright lectr. Am. Studies Osaka (Japan) U. Fgn. Studies, 1955-56, Nat. Chengchi U. and Taiwan Normal U., Taipei, 1960-61, Banaras (India) Hindu U., 1964-65; mem. Nat. Adv. Coun. Teaching English as a Fgn. Lang., 1962-67; pres. Fellows of Am. Studies Phila., 1968-69; chmn. Sch. and Coll. Conf. English, N.Y.C., 1966-68; U.S. del Brit. Coun. Conf. Teaching English Lit. Overseas, Cambridge, Eng., 1962. Author: (novel) The Mountain and the Feather, 1961, (textbook) English 12, 1967; editor short stories, articles, revs. Chief regional judge for Pa. and N.Y., Book of Month Club Writing Fellowship contest, 1966. Lt. USNR, 1942-46, PTO. Decorated Commendation medal; grantee Am. Coun. Learned Soc., 1960, Am. Inst. Indian Studies, 1964-65, Asia Soc., 1964-65, Ford Found., 1964. Mem. Modern Lang. Assn. (chmn. Oriental-Western lit. rels. conf. group 1966), Am. Studies Assn., Assn. Asian Studies, Machine Transp. Soc., Soc. Archtl. Historians, Nat. Coun. Tchrs. English, Phi Beta Kappa. Home: Haverford Pa. Died Feb. 7, 1992; body donated to sci.

ASHMORE, ROBERT THOMAS, former congressman, lawyer; b. Greenville County, S.C., Feb. 22, 1904; s. John Thomas and Lena (Smith) A.; m. Willie Vance Linthicum; 1 child, Nancy Vance. Grad., Furman U., 1927. Practiced in Greenville, S.C., from 1928; pros. atty. Greenville County Ct., 1930-52; mem. 83d-90th congresses from 4th S.C. Dist., Washington, 1953-68; pvt. practice, Greenville, from 1969. Chmn. S.C. Appalachian Coun. Govts., 1970-72, mem. exec. com., from 1970. Officer U.S. Army, 1942-46, col. USAR ret. Mem. U.S. Jaycees (past v.p.), S.C. Jaycees (organizer, 1st pres.), Greenville Jaycees (past bd. dirs., v.p., pres.), Res. Officers Assn., Am. Legion (comdr. Greenville 1972), Woodmen of World, Greenville Exch. Club (past pres.), Men's Garden Club (past pres.), Elks. Democrat. Baptist. Home: Greenville S.C. Died Oct. 4, 1989.

ASIMOV, ISAAC, biochemist, author; b. Petrovichi, Russia, Jan. 2, 1920; came to U.S., 1923; s. Judah and Anna Rachel (Berman) A.; m. Gertrude Blugerman, 1942 (div. 1973); children: David, Robyn Joan; m. Janet Jeppson, 1973. BS, Columbia U., 1939, MA, 1941, PhD, 1948; holder 14 hon. degrees. Faculty Boston U. Sch. Medicine, from 1949, assoc. prof. biochemistry, 1955-79, prof., from 1979. Books include: I, Robot, 1950, The Stars, Like the Dust, 1951, Foundation, 1951, Foundation and Empire, 1952, Currents of Space, 1952, Second Foundation, 1953, Caves of Steel, 1954, The

Naked Sun, 1957; textbook Biochemistry and Human Metabolism, rev. edit, 1957; Nine Tomorrows, 1959, The Words of Science, 1959, Realm of Numbers, 1959, The Living River, 1960, Kingdom of the Sun, 1960, Realm of Measure, 1960, Wellsprings of Life, 1960, Words from Myths, 1961, Realm of Algebra, 1961, Words in Genesis, 1962, Fact and Fancy, 1962, Words on the Map, 1962, Search for the Elements, 1962, Words from the Exodus, 1963, The Human Body, 1963, The Genetic Code, 1963, View from a Height, 1963, Kite that Won the Revolution, 1963, Human Brain, 1964, A Short History of Biology, 1964, Adding a Dimension, 1964, A Short History of Chemistry, 1865, The Greeks, 1965, Of Time and Space and Other Things, 1965, The New Intelligent Man's Guide to Science, 1965, Fantastic Voyage, 1966, The Noble Gases, 1966, The Neutrino, 1966, The Roman Republic, 1967, Understanding Physics, 1966; Is Anyone There?, 1967, To the Ends of the Universe, 1967, Mars, 1967, Egyptians, 1967, Asimov's Mysteries, 1968, Science, Numbers and I, 1968, Stars, 1968, Galaxies, 1968, A Whiff of Death, 1968, Near East, 1968, Asimov's Guide to the Bible, vol. 1, 1968, vol. 2, 1969, The Dark Ages, 1968, Words from History, 1968, Photosynthesis, 1969, The Shaping of England, 1969, Twentieth Century Discovery, 1969, Nightfall and Other Stories, 1969, Opus 100, 1969, ABC's of Space, 1969, Great Ideas of Science, 1969, Solar System and Back, 1970, Asimov's Guide to Shakespeare (2 vols.), 1970, Constantinople, 1970, ABC's of the Ocean, 1970, Light, 1970, The Stars in Their Courses, 1971, Where Do We Go from Here?, 1971, What Makes the Sun Shine?, 1971, The Sensuous Dirty Old Man, 1971, The Best New Thing, 1971, Isaac Asimov's Treasury of Humor, 1971, The Hugo Winners, Vol. 2, 1971, The Land of Canaan, 1971, ABC's of the Earth, 1971, The Left Hand of the Electron, 1972, The Gods Themselves, 1972, Asimov's Guide to Science, 1972, More Words of Science, 1972, ABC's of Ecology, 1972, The Early Asimov, 1972, The Shaping of France, 1972, The Story of Ruth, 1972, Asimov's Annotated Don Juan, 1972, The Shaping of North America, 1973, Today and Tomorrow and, 1973, Jupiter, the Largest Planet, 1973, Please Explain, 1973, How Did We Find Out About Numbers, 1973, How Did We Find Out About Dinosaurs, 1973, The Tragedy of the Moon, 1973, Asimov on Astronomy, 1974, The Birth of the United States, 1974, Before the Golden Age, 1974, Our World in Space, 1974, How Did We Find Out About Germs, 1974, Asimov's Annotated Paradise Lost, 1974, Tales of the Black Widowers, 1974, Earth: Our Crowded Spaceship, 1974, Asimov on Chemistry, 1974, How Did We Find Out About Vitamins, 1974, Of Matters Great and Small, 1975, The Solar System, 1975, Our Federal Union, 1975, How Did We Find Out about Comets, 1975, Science Past—Science Future, 1975, Buy Jupiter and Other Stories, 1975, Eyes on the Universe, 1975, Lecherous Limericks, 1975, Heavenly Host, 1975, The Ends of the Earth, 1975, How Did We Find Out About Energy, 1975, Asimov on Physics, 1976, Murder at the ABA, 1976, How Did We Find Out About Atoms, 1976, The Planet That Wasn't, 1976, The Bicentennial Man and Other Stories, 1976, More Lecherous Limericks, 1976, More Tales of the Black Widowers, 1976, Alpha Centauri, The Nearest Star, 1976, How Did We Find Out About Nuclear Power, 1976, Familiar Poems Annotated, 1977, The Collapsing Universe, 1977, Asimov on Numbers, 1977, How Did We Find Out About Outer Space, 1977, Still More Lecherous Limericks, 1977, Hugo Winners, Vol. II, 1977, The Beginning and the End, 1977, Mars, The Red Planet, 1977, The Golden Door, 1977, The Key Word and Other Mysteries, 1977, Asimov's Sherlockian Limericks, 1977, One Hundred Great Science Fiction Short Short Stories, 1978, Quasar, Quasar, Burning Bright, 1978, How Did We Find Out About Earthquakes, 1978, Animals of the Bible, 1978, Life and Time, 1978, Limericks: Too Gross, 1978, How Did We Find Out About Black Holes?, 1978, Saturn and Beyond, 1979, In Memory Yet Green, 1979, Opus 200, 1979, Extraterrestrial Civilizations, 1979, How Did We Find Out About Our Human Roots?, 1979, The Road to Infinity, 1979, A Choice of Catastrophes, 1979, Isaac Asimov's Book of Facts, 1979, The Science Fictional Solar System, 1979, The Thirteen Crimes of Science Fiction, 1979, How Did We Find Out About Antarctica?, 1979, Casebook of the Black Widowers, 1980, How Did We Find Out About Oil?, 1980, In Joy Still Felt, 1980, Microcosmic Tales, 1980, Who Dun It?, 1980, Seven Deadly Sins of Science Fiction, 1980, The Annotated Gulliver's Travels, 1980, How Did We Find Out About Coal, 1980, In the Beginning, 1981, Asimov on Science Fiction, 1981, Venus: Near Neighbor of the Sun, 1981, How Did We Find Out About Solar Power?, 1981 How Did We Find Out About Volcanoes?, 1981, Views of the Universe, 1981, The Sun Shines Bright, 1981, Change, 1981, A Glossary of Limericks, 1982, How Did We Find Out About Life in the Deep Sea, 1982, The Complete Robot, 1982, Laughing Space, 1982, Exploring the Earth and the Cosmos, 1982, How Did We Find Out About the Beginning of Life, 1982, Foundations Edge, 1982, How Did We Find Out About the Universe, 1982, Counting the Eons, 1983, The Winds of Change and other Stories, 1983, The Roving Mind, 1983, The Measure of the Universe, 1983, The Union Club Mysteries, 1983, Norby, the Mixed-Up Robot, 1983, How Did We Find Out About Genes, 1983, The Robots of Dawn, 1983, X Stands for Unknown, 1984, Norby's Other Secret, 1984, How Did We Find Out About

Computers, 1984, Opus 3000, 1984, Banquet of the Black Widowers, 1984, Limericks for Children, 1984, Asimov's New Guide to Science, 1984, How Did We Find Out About Robots, 1984, Asimov's Guide to Halley's Comet, 1985, Exploding Suns, 1985, Norby and the Lost Princess, 1985, How Did We Find Out About the Atmosphere, 1985, The Edge of Tomorrow, 1985, The Subatomic Monster, 1985, The Disappearing Man and Other Stories, 1985, Robots and Empire, 1985, Norby and The Invaders, 1985, How Did We Find Out About DNA?, 1985, The Alternate Asimovs, 1986, The Dangers of Intelligence, 1986, How Did We Find Out About the Speed of Light, 1986, Best Science Fiction of Isaac Asimov, 1986, Best Mysteries of Isaac Asimov, 1986, Foundation and Earth, 1986, Robot Dreams, 1986, Norby and the Queen's Necklace, 1986, Far as Human Eye Could See, 1987, How Did We Find Out About Blood, 1987, Past, Present and Future, 1987, How Did We Find Out About Sunshine?, 1987, How to Enjoy Writing, 1987, Norby Finds a Villain, 1987, Fantastic Voyage II, 1987, How Did We Find Out About the Brain?, 1987, Did Comets Kill the Dinosaurs?, 1987, Beginnings, 1987, Asimov's Annotated Gilbert and Sullivan, 1988, How Did We Find Out About Superconductivity?, 1988, Other Worlds of Isaac Asimov, 1988, Relativity of Wrong, 1988, Prelude to Foundation, 1988, Azazel, 1988, Norby Down to Earth, 1988, How Did We Find Out About Microwaves, 1989, Asimov's Galaxy, 1989, The Asimov Chronicles, 1989, The Tyrannosaurus Prescription, 1989, Asimov On Science, 1989, Nemesis, 1989, Asimov's Chronology of Science and Discovery, 1989, How Did We Find Out About Photosynthesis, 1989, Norby and Yobo's Great Adventure, 1989, Puzzles of the Black Widowers, 1990, Norby and the Oldest Dragon, 1990, Frontiers, 1990, Out of the Everywhere, 1990, Robot Visions, 1990, How Did We Find Out About Lasers, 1990, Nightfall, 1990, Complete Stories, Vol. I, 1990, The March of the Millennia, 1990, The Secret of the Universe, 1991, How Did We Find Out About Neptune, 1991, How Did We Find Out About Pluto, 1991, Asimov's Chronology of the World, 1991, Asimov Laughs Again, 1992, (with Janet Asimov) Norby and the Court Jester. Served as cpl. U.S. Army, 1945-46. Recipient James T. Grady award Am. Chem. Soc., 1965, AAAS-Westinghouse Sci. Writing award, 1967, five Hugo awards, three Nebula awards. Democrat. Home: New York N.Y. Died Apr. 6, 1990.

ASNES, MARVIN ARTHUR, manufacturing company executive; b. New Brunswick, N.J., May 18, 1928; s. Louis and Esther (Mirsky) A.; m. Norma Ketay, Sept. 27, 1959; children: Anthony Ketay, Andrew Edwin, James Louis. BS, MIT, 1949; MBA, Harvard U., 1951. Rsch. asst. Harvard Bus. Sch., 1951-52; asst. to pres. Clay Adams, N.Y.C., 1954-57, v.p., 1957-59, exec. v.p., 1959-64; dir. Becton Dickinson & Co., Rutherford, N.J., 1964-87, pres. LSE div., 1965-69, group v.p., 1968-72, exec. v.p. parent co., 1972-74, chief oper. officer, 1974-87, pres., 1980-87; bd. dirs. Harper and Row, N.Y.C., GTE, Stamford, Conn., Gen. Am. Investors Co., N.Y.C. Patentee centrifuge, also other lab. equipment and supply items. Mem. vis. com. Sloan Sch. Mgmt., MIT, 1971-75, MIT Vis. Commn. Sponsored Rsch., 1975-81; bd. dirs. N.Y.C. Ballet Inc., 1980-87, Stanley M. Isaacs Neighborhood Ctr., Inc., 1968-79; trustee Mt. Sinai Sch. Medicine, 1978-87, Camp Madison-Felivia, N.Y.C., 1964-72; trustee, treas. Bank Street Coll. Edn. 1st lt. USAF, 1952-54. Mem. Hosp. Industries Mfrs. Assn., Sci. Apparatus Makers Assn., Instrument Soc. Am., Harvard Club, Tau Beta Pi. Home: New York N.Y. Died Mar. 13, 1987; buried Greenwich, Conn.

ATHA, JOSEPH SAMUEL, coffee company executive; b. Grayville, Ill., Feb. 18, 1898; s. Frank Perry and Edith Louise (Shaw) A.; m. Ethel B. Shufflebotham, Jan. 13, 1923; children: Ethelyn Chase, Elaine Merriman, Donald J. Student, U. Kans., 1916-18; DFA (hon.), Kansas City Art Inst., 1953. With J.A. Folger & Co., Kansas City Mo., from 1918, chmn. bd., from 1961; also dir. Chairman Nat. Coffee Assn., from 1963. Pres. Jackson County Soc. Crippled Children, 1942-43; pres. Kansas City Art Inst., 1954, trustee, from 1944; trustee Drury Coll., Kansas City Philharm. Orch., Midwest Rsch. Inst. With U.S. Army, 1918. Decorated chevalier Order Leopold II, 1959. Mem. Sigma Alpha Epsilon. *

ATKINS, CRAIG STARBUCK, judge, lawyer; b. Greensboro, N.C., Aug. 17, 1903; s. Benjamin F. and Neva O. (Starbuck) A.; m. Margaret Elinor Denty, June 30, 1926 (dec.); children: Craig Starbuck, Constance (Mrs. John E McShulskis); m. 2d., Lucille Helen Formen, May 28, 1971. AB, George Washington U., 1923, LLB, 1925. Bar: D.C. 1925. Atty. U.S. Bd. Taxz Appeals, 1927-37; atty. Office of Chief Counsel IRS, 1937-49, asst. chief counsel, 1954-55; tax adviser to Greek Govt. and ECA Mission to Greece, 1949-51; judge Tax Ct. of U.S., 1955-72. Home: Bethesda Md. Died June 2, 1990.

ATKINS, THOMAS LEE, human resources development specialist; b. Chgo., Dec. 4, 1921; s. Samuel Merritt and Alphonsine Marie (La Londe) A.; B.A., U. Notre Dame, 1943; postgrad. Cath. U. Am., 1947-51; m. Marylin E. Bowman, Dec. 19, 1966; children: Elizabeth Ann, Catherine Marie. Ordained priest, Roman Cath. Ch., 1951; asst. pastor Saginaw (Mich.) Sts. Peter &

Paul Ch., 1951-54, St. Helen Ch., Saginaw, 1954-58; chaplain VA Hosp., Saginaw, 1954-58, USNR Tng. Ctr., Bay City, Mich., 1958-64; pastor Sebewaing (Mich.) St. Mary's Nativity Ch., 1958-63; tng. specialist Bur. Personnel Services, Mich. Employment Security Commn., 1974-88. Bd. dirs. Saginaw Valley Indian Assn., from 1972, pres., 1981-87. Served with USNR, 1943-46. Mem. Social Workers Roundtable (pres. 1969-74), SAR (Mich. soc. state chaplain from 1988, state sec. from 1988, membership chmn. from 1989). Portrait editor, Notre Dame DOME, 1942; lit. editor Sacred Heart Gothic, 1946-47. Died Sept. 13, 1990. Home: Detroit Mich.

ATKINSON, ARTHUR JOHN, physician; b. Chgo., Dec. 4, 1900; s. William James and Bertha (Behn) A.; m. Inez Hill, Apr. 27, 1929; children—Inez, Arthur John. B.S. and M.S., U. Chgo., 1921; M.D., Rush Med. Coll., 1924. Asso. in pharmacology and physiology U. Chgo., 1920-24; intern Presbyn. Hosp., 1924-25; med. resident Cook County, 1926-27; specialist in internal medicine, from 1926; assoc. in medicine Rush Med. Coll., 1925-31; asst. physician Presbyn. Hosp., 1926-30; mem. faculty Northwestern U., from 1931; prof. medicine; attending physician Northwestern Meml. Hosp., from 1931. Mem. Am. Gastroenterol. Assn., AMA, Central Soc. for Clin. Research, Inst. of Medicine of Chgo., Chgo. Soc. Internal Medicine, Am. Coll. Gastroenterology, Chgo. Med. Soc. Clubs: Mid-America (Chgo.), Chicago Yacht (Chgo.). Home: Chicago Ill. Died Aug. 28, 1989.

ATKINSON, CHARLES HARRY, clergyman, church executive; b. Hampton, N.B., Can., Mar. 21, 1894; s. Frank Newton and Frances Elinda (Elliott) A.; m. Gertrude Irene Edwards, Sept. 5, 1922; children: Arthur G., Kathleen E., Carl E., Irene Vaughan. AB, Acadia U., 1922; BD, Andover Newton Theol. Sem., 1926. Jr. officer Royal Bank Can., 1910-15; ordained to ministry Bapt. ch., 1922; assoc. pastor Clarendon St. Ch., Boston, 1922-24; pastor 1st Ch., Livermore Falls, Maine, 1924-28, Medford, Mass., 1928-38; pastor Brunswick St. Ch., Fredericton, N.B., 1938-41; sec. edifice funds and bldg. counsel Am. Bapt. Home Mission Soc., N.Y.C., 1941-53; exec. dir. Bur. Ch. Bldg. Nat. Coun. Chs. Christ, 1953-56; editor Protestant Church, from 1956; assoc. editor Christian Herald mag., from 1956. Author: Building and Equipping for Christian Education, How to Get Your Church Built; also articles. 1st lt. Can. Army, 1915-19. Decorated Mil. Cross; recipient Elbert M. Conover Meml. award Ch. Architecture Guild, 1956. Mem. Ch. Architects Guild Am. *

ATKINSON, FREDERICK GRISWOLD, department store executive; b. Aspinwall, Pa., Dec. 5, 1904; s. John Frederick and Dee (Griswold) A.; m. Joyce Mallory Hill, May 25, 1934; 1 son, Frederick (dec.). Student, Columbia Coll., 1922-26. With Cities Service Co. N.Y., 1926-34; with Procter & Gamble Co. of Cin., 1935-40, R.H. Macy & Co., Inc., N.Y.C., 1940-70; v.p. for personnel administrn. R.H. Macy & Co., Inc., 1948-67, sr. v.p., dir., 1967-70, cons., 1970-72; trustee Seamen's Bank for Savs., N.Y.C., 1955-72; chmn. Am. Retail Fedn. Employee Relations Com., 1951-55; chmn. personnel adv. council Nat. Indsl. Conf. Bd., 1952-53; mem. labor-mgmt. Manpower Policy Com., U.S. Dept. Labor. Pres. bd. trustees St. Paul's Am. Ch., Rome, Italy, St. James Am. Ch., Florence, Italy; pres. bd. of fgn. parishes Nat. Episcopal Ch.; trustee Gen. Theol. Sem., N.Y.C., 1965-75, Roosevelt Hosp., Aspen Valley Hosp., Aspen Valley Med. Found., Voice Found., N.Y.C.; bd. dirs. U.S. Com. for UNICEF; chmn., pres. Kunkel Found., Palm Beach, Fla., 1987-90. Served as col. USAF, 1942-45; brig. gen. USAF Res., from 1945; spl. cons. to sec. Air Force, 1950-51. Decorated D.S.M. for outstanding performance in position of high responsibility, World War II. Fellow Internat. Acad. Mgmt. (Geneva); mem. Am. Mgmt. Assn. (dir., v.p. personnel div. 1954-56, hon. life mem.), Delta Upsilon. Clubs: Union, Pilgrims of U.S. (N.Y.C.); Army and Navy (Washington); Everglades (Palm Beach, Fla.). Home: Palm Beach Fla. Died May 5, 1991; buried Ch. of the Heavenly Rest, N.Y.C.

ATTWOOD, JAMES ALBERT, insurance company executive; b. Detroit, June 1, 1927; s. Albert Messenger and Tyyne Marie (Koskela) A.; m. Pauline Veryl Ellwood, June 18, 1955; children: Terry Jo, James Albert, Dorothy Tyyne, Katherine Pauline. B.A., U. Mich., 1950; student, Ohio State U., 1952-53, Salmon Chase Coll. Law, 1952-53. With Equitable Life Assurance Soc. U.S., N.Y.C., 1950-56, 61-83, v.p., 1966-68, sr. v.p., 1969-72, exec. v.p., 1973-77, exec. v.p., chief ins. officer, 1977-79, exec. v.p., chief investment officer, 1980-83, dir., 1973-83; chmn., pres., chief exec. officer, trustee Mut. Life Ins. Co. N.Y., N.Y.C., 1983-89, also dir.; partner Hewitt Assocs., Libertyville, Ill., 1956-61; chmn. MONY Reins.; dir. Monyco, Inc., Sherwin-Williams Co., Am. Council Life Ins.; bus. exec. in residence Mt. Holyoke Coll., 1976; vis. prof. polit. sci. Hunter Coll., CUNY, 1977-78. Mem. Bronxville (N.Y.) Bd. Edn., 1972-77; v.p. Adoption Service Westchester, 1964-70; deacon, elder Bronxville Ref. Ch., 1973-78, 83-87; adv. dir. Internat. Found. Employee Benefit Plans, 1973-77; bd. dirs. Coll. of Ins., 1983—, N.Y. Theol. Sem., 1985-87, Suomi Coll., 1987—, Com. for Econ. Devel., 1987—, N.Y.C. Partnership, 1987—. Served with USNR, 1945-46; with USAF, 1952-53. Fellow Soc. Actuaries (dir. 1979-82, v.p. 1983-85); mem. Am. Acad. Actuaries (dir. 1978-81), Internat. Assn. Actuaries, Am. Pension Conf. (steering com. 1970-73), Health Ins. Assn. Am. (bd. dirs.), Life Office Mgmt. Assn. (bd. dirs.), N.Y. C. of C. (bd. dirs.), Phi Beta Kappa, Phi Kappa Phi, Phi Eta Sigma. Clubs: University, The Links (N.Y.C.); Siwanoy Country (Bronxville). Home: Bronxville N.Y. Died Oct. 31, 1989; buried Reformed Ch. of Bronxville, N.Y.

ATTWOOD, STEPHEN S(TANLEY), university dean; b. Cleve., May 29, 1897; s. William Rix and Mary (Hamilton) A; m. Frieda Diekhoff, June 8, 1927; children: Stanley William, Julia Clemence. BS, U. Mich., 1918, MS, 1923. Profl. engr., Mich. Engr. Packard Motor Car Co., 1919-20; mem. faculty elec. engring. dept. U. Mich., from 1920, prof. elec. engring., from 1937, chmn. dept., 1953-58, dean coll. engring., from 1958; various summer part-time positions. Contbr. articles to profl. jours. Fellow IRE, Am. Inst. Elec. Engrs.; mem. Am. Soc. Engring. Edn., Engring. Soc. Detroit, Sigma Xi, others. *

ATTWOOD, WILLIAM, journalist; b. Paris, July 14, 1919; s. Frederic and Gladys (Hollingsworth) A.; m. Simone Cadgene, June 22, 1950; children—Peter, Janet Hoglund, Susan. A.B., Princeton U., 1941. Corr. N.Y. Herald Tribune in Paris and with UN Bur., 1946-49; European corr. Colliers mag., 1949-51; European editor Look mag., 1951-54, nat. editor, 1955-57, fgn. editor, 1957-61; U.S. ambassador to Guinea, 1961-63; spl. adviser U.S. del. UN, 1963-64; U.S. ambassador to Kenya, 1964-66; editor-in-chief, v.p. Cowles Communications, Inc., N.Y.C., 1966-70; pres., pub. Newsday, Inc., Garden City, N.Y., 1970-78; chmn. bd. Newsday, Inc., 1978-79; adj. prof. journalism C. W. Post Coll., 1980, Yale U., 1981; mem. John F. Kennedy presdl. campaign staff, 1960; regional alumni trustee Princeton, 1967-71; trustee Kress Found., 1971-80; bd. dirs. CARE; mem. exec. com. Am. Com. U.S.-Soviet Relations; mem. U.S. del. UNESCO Gen. Conf., 1978. Author: The Man Who Could Grow Hair, 1949, Still the Most Exciting Country, 1955, (with George B. Leonard, Jr. and J. Robert Moskin) The Decline of the American Male, 1958, The Reds and the Blacks, 1967, The Fairly Scary Adventure Book, 1969, Making It Through Middle Age: Notes While in Transit, 1982, The Twilight Struggle: Tales of the Cold War, 1987; numerous articles for the New Yorker, Saturday Evening Post, Reader's Digest, Nation, Time, Esquire and other nat. mags. Mem. New Canaan (Conn.) Town Council. Served to capt. AUS, 1941-45. Recipient Nat. Headliners award, 1955, 57, George Polk Meml. award, 1956, N.Y. Newspaper Guild Page One award, 1960. Mem. Council Fgn. Relations, Overseas Devel. Council. Democrat. Clubs: Century, Princeton of N.Y.C, Country of New Canaan. Home: New Canaan CT Died Apr. 4, 1989; buried New Canaan, Conn.

ATWOOD, EDWARD WILSON, lawyer; b. Portland, Maine, June 27, 1897; s. Thomas W.W. and Grace E. (Tobie) A.; m. Luena Hutchinson, Sept. 1, 1927; children: Thomas W.W., Luena A. Whitaker. Student, Bowdoin Coll., 1916-17; LLB, Boston U., 1922. Bar: Maine 1922. Pvt. practice Portland; mem. Pierce, Atwood, Scribner, Allen & McKusick, Portland. Mem. Maine Ho. of Reps. from Portland dist., 1923-25. 2d lt. U.S. Army, 1917-19; AEF in France. Mem. ABA, Maine Bar Assn., Psi Upsilon. *

ATWOOD, WILLIAM, food products company executive; b. Springfield, Mass., 1927. Grad., U. Mass., Amherst, 1954, U. Mass., Amherst, 1956. Pres. A.D. Makepeace Co., Wareham, Mass., now pres., chief exec. officer, also bd. dirs.; former vice chmn. Ocean Spray Cranberries Inc., Plymouth, Mass., also bd. dirs.; past pres., dir. Cape Cod Cranberry Growers Assn.; bd. dirs. Sandwich Coop. Bank, Farm Credit Bank, Springfield, Mass. Mem. bldg. com. Upper Cape Regional Vocat. Sch.; chmn. bldg. com. Wareham Police Sta. Served with USN, W.W. II. Mem. Kittansett Golf Club (bd. govs.), Elks, Masons. Home: Marion MA Died Sept. 1, 1991; buried West Barnstable, Mass.

AUGUSTINE, SISTER MARY, college president; b. Milw., May 29, 1896; d. John P. and Elizabeth (Stumpf) Scheele. AB, Cath. U., 1918; AM, Marquette U., 1931, PhD, 1939. Tchr. secondary schs., 1934-36; instr., prof. edn. Alverno Coll., from 1940, asst. dean, 1946-48, pres., from 1948. Author: Educational Aspects of Spiritual Writing, 1940, That They May Have Life, 1952, That They May Know the Way, 1953, That They May Grow in Grace, 1955, That They May Believe in God's Love, 1961; contbr. articles to religious & ednl. publs. Mem. religious congregation Sch. Sisters of St. Francis. *

AURBACH, GERALD DONALD, research institute administrator; b. Cleve., Mar. 24, 1927; s. Philip S. and Lenora (Weinberg) A.; m. Hannah Leah Rose, Oct. 16, 1960; children: Elissa G., Pamela K. B.A., U. Va., 1950, M.D., 1954. Intern New Eng. Ctr. Hosp., Boston, 1954-55, resident in medicine, 1955-56, USPHS fellow, 1956-59; commd. officer USPHS, 1959-88, med. dir., 1966-88; research assoc. Nat. Inst. Arthritis, Metabolism and Digestive Diseases, NIH, HHS, Bethesda, Md., 1959-61, sr. investigator, 1961-64, chief sect. on mineral metabolism, 1965-73, chief metabolic diseases br., 1973-91; mem. endocrinology study sect. div. rsch. grants NIH, 1968-70; mem. program organizing com. 3d Internat. Congress Endocrinology, sec., treas., 4th Congress; Gordon Wilson lectr. Am. Clin. and Climatol. Assn., 1973; Staige Davis Blackford lectr. U. Va., 1986; Henry Turner lectr. U. Okla., 1987; Royal Soc. Medicine Burroughs Wellcome vis. prof., 3 weeks 1989; Sandoz lectr. Can. Soc. Endocrinology and Metabolism, 1989; vis. prof. Mayo Clinic, 1990. Assoc. editor: Endocrinology, 1968-72; vol. editor: Handbook of Physiology; editor-in-chief: Vitamins and Hormones, from 1982; contbr. articles on clin. and basic endocrine research to profl. jours. Recipient John Horsley Meml. prize U. Va., 1960, Andre Lichtwitz prize French Nat. Inst. for Med. Rsch., 1968, Meritorious Service award USPHS, 1969, Gairdner Internat. award, 1983, Centennial Disting. Alumnus award U. Va., 1988, Disting. Svc. medal USPHS, 1988, Charles R. Fenwick Outstanding Alumnus award U. Va. Club of Washington, 1989. Fellow AAAS; mem. NAS, Am. Soc. Clin. Investigation (editorial com. 1971-76), AMA, Am. Fedn. Clin. Research, Assn. Am. Physicians, Endocrine Soc. (v.p. 1978-79, council 1983-86, pres. elect 1987, pres. 1988-89, Edwin B. Astwood lectr. award 1985), Am. Soc. Biol. Chemists, Internat. Soc. Endocrinology (exec. com.), Laurentian Hormone Conf. (v.p.), Am. Soc. Bone and Mineral Research (William F. Neuman award 1981), Internat. Conf. on Calcium Regulating Hormones, Inc. (bd. dirs.), Peripatic Club, Alpha Omega Alpha. Home: Potomac Md. Died Nov. 4, 1991; buried ADAS Israel Cemetery, Washington.

AUTORI, FRANCO, orchestra conductor; b. Naples, Italy, Nov. 29, 1903; came to U.S., 1928, naturalized, 1936; s Michelangelo and Marta Martucci Autoriello; m. Paola Lawn, 1928 dec 1946 ; m. Lygia Berezynska, Jan. 27, 1948. Orch. condr. Pa. Grand Opera Co., 1928, Chgo. Civic Opera Co., Ravinia Opera Co., 1928-32; condr. Sinfonietta of Dallas, 1932-34; staff condr. The Fed. Music Project, N.Y.C., 1934-36; musical dir., condr. Philharm. Orch., Buffalo, 1936-45; assoc. condr. N.Y. Philharm. Symphony Soc., 1949-59; musical dir., condr. Tulsa Philharm. Soc., 1961-71; condr. Dallas Symphony, summers 1932-34; musical dir., condr. Chautauqua Symphony Orch., summers 1944-52; guest condr. NBC Symphony, 1946, State Radio Symphony Orch., Buenos Aires, others; condr. concerts, opera, Poland, 1947-48. Home: Tulsa Okla. Died Oct. 16, 1990.

AWALT, FRANCIS GLOYD, lawyer; b. Laurel, Md., Jan. 3, 1895; s. Frank W. and Effie Whitworth (Young) A.; m. Jaffa Beatrice Haslup, July 26, 1919; children: Francis Gloyd, Gilbert Haslup. Grad., Balt. Poly. Inst., 1914; LLB, U. Md., 1917. Bar: Md. 1917, D.C. 1936, U.S. Supreme Ct. 1925, U.S. Ct. Appeals (D.C. cir.) 1939. With Marbury & French, Balt., 1917; asst. gen. counsel, then gen. counsel Balt. Ordnance Claims Bd., 1919; asst. chief, then chief award sect. Bd. Contract Adjustment, 1920; spl. asst. to sec. treasury Washington, 1920-27; 2d dep. comptr. currency & gen. counsel to comptr., 1922-28, 1st dep. and gen. counsel, 1928-32, 33-36, acting comptr., 1932-33; then mem. firm Awalt, Clark & Sparks, Washington. 2d lt. field aty. U.S. Res. Corps, 1918. *

AXTHELM, PETE, columnist, author; b. N.Y.C., Aug. 27, 1943; s. Ralph Axthelm and Marjorie Axthelm Scholly; 1 dau., Megan. B.A., Yale U., 1965. Racing writer, columnist, N.Y. Herald Tribune, N.Y.C., 1965-66; staff writer, Sports Illus., 1966-68; sports editor, Newsweek, N.Y.C., 1968-73, columnist, contbg. editor, from 1973; commentator, NBC Sports, N.Y.C., 1980-85; NFL commentator ESPN, from 1987; author: The Modern Confessional Novel, 1967, (with William F. Talbert) Tennis Observed, 1969, (with O. J. Simpson) O.J.: Education of a Rich Rookie, 1971, The City Game, 1971, The Kid, 1978. Recipient Page One award Newspaper Guild; Nat. Headliners award; Silver Gavel award Am. Bar Assn.; Schick award; Eclipse award. Mem. Nat. Turf Writers Assn., Nat. Pro Football Writers Assn. Home: New York N.Y. Died Feb. 2, 1991.

AYCOCK, EZRA KENNETH, state official, educator, physician; b. Pinewood, S.C., Mar. 23, 1927; s. Robert James and Helen Beatrice (Geddings) A.; m. Mary Echo Cook, June 4, 1954; children: Doris Dawson, Ezra Kenneth. A.B., Duke U., 1950; M.D., Med. Coll. S.C., 1954; M.P.H., Harvard U., 1964. Diplomate: Am. Bd. Preventive Medicine, Am. Bd. Pediatrics. Intern Columbia (S.C.) Hosp., 1954-55; resident in pediatrics Children's Hosp., Los Angeles, 1955-56, Med. Coll. Hosp., Charleston, S.C., 1956-57; pvt. practice medicine specializing in pediatrics Columbia, 1957-63; asst. dir. S.C. Maternal and Child Health div. S.C. Bd. Health, Columbia, 1963-67; state health officer, sec. exec. com. S.C. Maternal and Child Health div. S.C. Bd. Health, 1967-73; dir. Charleston Co. Health Dept., 1965-67; chmn. S.C. Pollution Control Authority, 1967-70; commr. S.C. Dept. Health and Environ. Control, Columbia, 1973-77; chmn. pub. health services adminstrn. U. S.C., 1977-80; dir. West Ala. Health Dist., from 1980; clin. prof. preventive medicine Med. U. Ala. Contbr. numerous articles to profl. jours. Fellow Am. Coll. Preventive Medicine, Am. Pub. Health Assn. (pres., exec. and governing councils So. Br.); mem. AMA, S.C. Pub. Health Assn., Assn. State and Terr. Health Officers (sec.-treas., pres., chmn. com. relations with affiliates), Ala. Med. Assn., Columbia, S.C. med. socs., Am. Acad. Pediatrics, S.C. Pediatric Assn., S.C. Acad. Gen. Practice, S.C. State Employees Assn., Alpha Omega Alpha. Home: Tuscaloosa Ala. Died Oct. 23, 1989; buried Tuscaloosa, Ala.

AYER, SIR ALFRED JULES, philosopher, educator, writer; b. Oct. 29, 1910; s. Jules Louis Cyprien A.; m. Grace Isabel Renee Lees, 1932; 2 children; m. Alberta Constance Chapman (Dee Wells), 1960 (div. 1983, remarried Apr. 26, 1989); 1 child; m. Vanessa Mary Addison Lawson Salmon (dec.). Scholar, Eton Coll.; scholar with honors 1st class in Lit. Hum., Christ Church Oxford, 1932, M.A., 1936; Dr. hon., U. Brussels, 1962; D.Litt. hon., East Anglia, 1972, U. Trent, London U., Durham U.; DHL hon., Bard Coll., 1983. Lectr. in philosophy Christ Church, 1932-35, research student, 1935-44; fellow Wadham Coll., Oxford, Eng., 1944-46, hon. fellow, 1957, dean, 1945-46; Grote prof. philosophy of mind and logic U. London, 1946-59, dean arts faculty, 1950-52; Wykeham prof. logic U. Oxford, 1959-78; fellow New Coll., U. Oxford, 1959-78, hon. fellow, 1980; fellow Wolfson Coll., 1978-83; hon. fellow Coll. U. London, 1979; vis. prof. NYU, 1948-49, CCNY, 1961-62, Surrey U., 1978, Bard Coll, from 1986; Montgomery fellow Dartmouth Coll., 1982-83. Editor: The Humanist Outlook, 1968; author: Metaphysics and Common Sense, 1969, Russell and Moore: The Analytical Heritage, 1971, Probability and Evidence, 1972, Russell, 1972, Bertrand Russell as a Philosopher, 1973 (Brit. Acad. lectr.), The Central Questions of Philosophy, 1974, Part of My Life, 1977, Perception and Identity, 1979 (Festschrift reply to critics), Hume, 1980, Philosophy in the Twentieth Century, 1982, Freedom and Morality, 1984, More of My Life, 1984, Wittgenstein, 1985, Voltaire, 1986, Thomas Paine, 1988; contbr. articles to profl. jours.; lectr.: William James, Harvard U., 1970, John Dewey, Columbia U., 1970, Gifford, St. Andrews, 1972-73; author: Language, Truth and Logic, 1936, 1946, The Foundations of Empirical Knowledge, 1940, Thinking and Meaning, 1947 (Inagural lectr.); editor: (with Raymond Winch) British Empirical Philosophers, 1952; author: Philosophical Essays, 1954, The Problem of Knowledge, 1956; editor: Logical Positivism, 1959; author: Privacy, 1960 (Brit. Acad. lectr.), The Concept of a Person and Other Essays, 1963, Man As a Subject for Science, 1964 (Auguste Comte lectr.), The Origins of Pragmatism, 1968. Mem. Central Advisory Council for Edn., 1963-66; pres. ind. Adoption Soc., 1965—. Served in Welsh Guards, 1940-45; served to capt. Welsh Guards, 1940-45, Attache at HM Embassy, Paris 1945. Decorated Chevalier de la Legion d'Honneur, 1977; decorated Order of Cyril and Methodius, 1st class Bulgaria, 1977. Mem. Humanist Assn. (pres.), Modern Lang. Assn., Internat. Inst. Philosophy (chmn. Booker Prize Com. 1978), Am. Acad. Arts and Scis. (hon.), Royal Danish Acad. Scis. and Letters (fgn. mem.). Home: London England Died June 27, 1989; buried Le Beausset, France.

AYMAR, GORDON CHRISTIAN, portrait painter; b. East Orange, N.J., July 24, 1893; s. William Howard and Maud (Christian) A.; m. Margaretta Kneass White, Jan. 24, 1920 (dec.); children—Carol Penrhyn Aymar Armstrong, Barbara Aymar Earle, Gordon Christian (dec.). A.B., Yale U., 1914; postgrad., Sch. Mus. Fine Arts, Boston, 1917. Art dir. J. Walter Thompson, N.Y.C., 1920-30; art dir., v.p. Compton Advt. Agy., N.Y.C., 1930-45; cons. designer, portrait work, 1945-59, lectr. in field. Exhibited, Darien Library, Darien Art Festival, Housatonic Art League, New Milford, Conn., Rowayton (Conn.) Art Center, Conn. Classic Arts, Nat. Acad., Christ Ch., Redding, Conn., Bridgeport (Conn.) Mus. Art, Sci. and Industry, Am. Watercolor Soc., Canton (Ohio) Art Inst., Boise (Idaho) Art Inst., Charles and Emma Frye Mus., Seattle, Abilene (Tex.) Fine Arts Mus., Orlando (Fla.) Art Assn., Columbia (S.C.) Mus. Art, Davenport (Iowa) Municipal Art Gallery, Moore Coll. Art, Phila., Arnot Art Gallery, Elmira, N.Y., Baldwin-Wallace Coll., Berea, Ohio, Brooks Meml. Art Gallery, Memphis, Phoenix Art Mus., Century Assn., Yale Club, N.Y.C., Nat. Arts Club, Dayton Art Inst., Montreal (Can.) Mus. Art, Royal Soc. Painters in Water Colour, London, Washington (Conn.) Art Assn., Kent (Conn.) Art Assn., The Gallery, House of Books, Kent, Pomperaug Valley Art League, Southbury, Conn., Gunnery Sch., Washington, Conn., portraits in permanent collections, Am. Cyanamid Co., N.Y., Madison Ave. Presbyn. Ch., N.Y.C., Nat. Council Chs., N.Y.C., Phillips Acad., Andover, Mass., Union Theol. Sem., N.Y.C., Racquet Club, N.Y.C., Little Mgmt. Co., N.Y.C., Bennett Coll., Milford, N.Y., Lazarus Co., Columbus, Ohio, South Kent (Conn.) Sch., Loomis Chaffee Sch., Windsor, Conn., Temple of Justice, Olympia, Wash., Yale U. Art Gallery, New Haven, Neurol. Inst., N.Y.C., Middlebury (Vt.) Coll., Drew U., Madison, N.J., India House, Young & Rubicam, Ogilvy and Mather, N.Y.C., Pratt Inst., Bklyn., Art Dirs. Club, others, photographs in permanent study coll., Mus. Modern Art, N.Y.; art dir., Darien Hist. Soc.; Author: An Introduction to Advertising Illustration, 1930, Bird Flight, 1934, Start 'Em Sailing, 1941, Treasury of Sea Stories, 1944, (with Gordon C. Aymar, Jr.) Second Book on Sailing, 1960, (with Margaretta W. Aymar) Michael Sails the Mud Hen, 1960, Yacht Racing Rules and Tactics, 1954, 7th edit, 1973, The Art of Portrait Painting, 1967. Chmn. Park and Recreation Com., rep. town meetings, Darien, Conn., 1952-58. Served as lt. (j.g.) USNR, World War I. Recipient award Nat. Soc. Art Dirs., 1951. Mem. N.Y. Art Dirs. Club (adv. bd., past pres., Hall of Fame 1975), Nat. Soc. Art Dirs. (charter pres., bd.), Am. Watercolor Soc. (dir. 1960-61, 1st v.p. 1961-62), Kent Art Assn. (exec. com., exhbn. com.). Club: Salmagundi (N.Y.C.). Home: South Kent Conn.

AYRE, HENRY GLENN, university dean; b. Centralia, Ill., July 29, 1898; s. John Aaron and Bertha Angeline (Guymon) A.; m. Virginia Lee Neftzger, June 14, 1928. EdB, So. Ill. U., 1925; MSc, U. Mich., 1928; PhD, Peabody Coll. for Tchrs., 1937. Tchr. rural schs. Marion County, Ill., 1919-21; tchr. math, physics High Sch., Carterville, Ill., 1924-25, Benton, Ill., 1925-27, Waukegan, 1928-36; asst. prof. math Western Ill. U., 1937-43, assoc. prof., dir. Gen. Coll., 1943-46, head dept., dir. Gen. Coll., 1951-58, prof. math., dean Sch. Arts & Scis., from 1950. Author: Basic Mathematical Analysis, 1950, (with Rothwell Stephens) Analytic Geometry-Two and Three Dimensions, 1956. Fellow AAAS; mem. Nat. Coll. Tchrs. Math., Cen. Assn. Sci. & Math. Tchrs., Ill. Coun. Tchrs. Math., NEA, Assn. Higher Edn., Nat. Geog. Soc., Math. Assn. Am., Am. Assn. Colls. Tchr. Edn. *

BABCOCK, EDWARD C. See VAN HEUSEN, JAMES

BACHMAN, WALTER CRAWFORD, marine engineer, consultant; b. Pitts., Dec. 24, 1911; s. Clarence E. and Mary Elizabeth (Crawford) B.; m. Helen Elizabeth Van Cleaf, Mar. 25, 1938; children—Van Cleaf, Elizabeth Crawford Bachman Ramjoué. B.S. in Indsl. Engring, Lehigh U., 1933, M.S., 1935. Tchr. mech. engring. Lehigh U., 1935-36; marine engr. Fed. Shipbldg. and Dry Dock Co., 1936, Gibbs & Cox, Inc., N.Y.C., 1936-70; chief engr. Gibbs & Cox, Inc., 1958-63, v.p., chief engr., 1963-70; marine cons. Short Hills, N.J., from 1970. Fellow ASME; mem. Nat. Acad. Engring. (mem. marine bd. 1967-75), Soc. Naval Architects and Marine Engrs., Am. Soc. Naval Engrs., N.Y. Acad. Scis. Home: Short Hills N.J. Died Mar. 1, 1991; buried Greewood Cemetery, Bklyn., N.Y.

BACHRACH, BRADFORD K., photographer; b. Worcester, Mass., Nov. 8, 1910; s. Louis Fabian and Dorothy Deland (Keyes) B.; m. Rosamond Esselen, Feb. 19, 1939 (dec. Apr. 1992); children: Susan Prentiss, William Bradford, Dorothy Locke, Laura Keyes. Grad., Phillips Exeter Acad., 1929; A.B., Harvard, 1933. With Bachrach, Inc., Watertown, Mass., from 1933; v.p., dir. Bachrach, Inc., from 1938, pres., 1955-77. Served to lt. USNR, 1943-45. Mem. Mass. Soc. Mayflower Descs. Unitarian. Club: Harvard (N.Y.C.). Home: Wellesley Mass. Died Sept. 10, 1992. †

BACKSTROM, LATHROP GUSTAF, paint and varnish manufacturer; b. Green Bay, Wis., Oct. 6, 1895; s. Frank G. and Selma C. (Nord) B.; m. Geraldine Brown, Apr. 2, 1921; children: Lathrop Gustaf, Raymond (twins). Grad., Kansas City Jr. Coll., 1917; LLB, Kansas City Sch. Law, 1921. Acct. City Ice Co., Kansas City, 1919-26; with Cook Paint & Varnish Co., Kansas City, Mo., from 1926, v.p., 1935-42, exec. v.p., 1942-46, pres., 1946-60, chmn., from 1960; bd. dirs. various cos. Bd. regents Rockhurst Coll. With U.S. Army, World War I. Mem. Nat. Paint, Varnish & Lacquer Assn., Kansas City C. of C., Phi Alpha Delta. *

BACKUS, JIM (JAMES GILMORE BACKUS), actor, writer; b. Cleve., Feb. 25, 1913; s. Russell Gould and Daisy (Gilmore-Taylor) B.; m. Henriette Kaye (Henny Backus), Jan. 14, 1943. Student, Ky. Mil. Sch., Louisville, U. Sch., Cleve., Am. Acad. Dramtic Arts, N.Y.C. Broadway, radio motion pictures Cleve., 1933-36, on radio, N.Y.C., 1936-44; actor with Keenan Wynn in Hitch Your Wagon, Too Many Heroes, 1944-46; with Alan Young Created Updyke caricature, 1946; then moved to Hollywood with show; star radio show Jim Backus show; motion picture include Rebel Without a Cause, 1955, Ice Palace, 1959, Brothers Grimm, 1962, Magic Carpet, 1971; played opposite Joan Davis in TV series, I Married Joan; in TV series Jim Backus Show, 1960, star of Talent Scouts, TV program, summer 1962; appeared in TV series Gilligan's Island, 1967, also Magoo's Classics; night clubs include Las Vegas, 1967; writer, prodr. of Mooch, 1971; author: (with Henriette Kaye) Rocks on the Roof, What Are You Doing After the Orgy, 1962, Only When I Laugh, 1965, Back to Backus, Backus Strikes Back, Forgive Us Our Digressions, also 2 motion pictures, numerous TV and radio shows. Home: Bel Air Calif. Died July 3, 1989.

BACON, EDWARD ALSTED, government official; b. Milw., June 24, 1897; s. Frank Rogers and Ellen (Alsted) B.; m. Lorraine Goodrich Graham, Feb. 17, 1920; children: Lorraine Graham, Edward Alsted, Ellen Alsted. AB, Harvard U., 1920. Shop employee Cutler-Hammer, Inc., Milw., 1920-22, asst. sec., 1922-26; served to v.p. 1st Wis. Nat. Bank, Milw., 1926-32; v.p., treas. Wis. Bankshares Corp., 1928-32, dir., 1928-34; comptr. Cutler-Hammer, Inc., 1934-37; pres. Smith Steel Foundry Co., Milw., 1937-42; asst. to Sec. Army for Canal Zone Affairs; dep. asst. Sec. Army; chmn. exec. coun. Air Coordinating Com., 1953-60. With USMC, 1918, USNR, 1941-46. Mem. Am. Legion, Elks, others. *

BACON, ERNST, musician; b. Chgo., May 26, 1898; s. Charles S. and Maria von (Rosthorn) B.; m. Mary Prentice Lillie, 1927; children—Margaret Frances and Joseph Rosthorn; m. Analee Camp, 1937; children—Paul Ernest Bacon, Arthur Bacon; m. Moselle Camp, 1952; 1 child, Madeline K.; m. Ellen Wendt, 1972; 1 child, David Ernst. Student, Northwestern U., U. Chgo.; M.A., U. Calif., 1935; studied privately with, Alexander Raab, Glenn D. Gunn, Ernest Bloch, Karl Weigl. Appeared in concerts in U.S. and Europe; mem. faculty Eastman Sch. of Music, Hamilton Coll., Converse Coll.; founder Bach festival of Carmel, Calif., 1935; supr., condr. Fed. Music Project, San Francisco, 1935-37; dean Sch. of Music, Converse Coll., Spartanburg, S.C., 1938-45; dir. New Spartanburg Festival, 1939-45; dir. Sch. Music, Syracuse U., 1945-47, composer-in-residence then prof. emeritus. Composer 2 symphonies, 2 piano concertos, 4 orchestral suites; Fables for orch. and narrator; short oratorios By Blue Ontario's Shore, Usania, Requiem, Ecclesiastes; symphony with narrator Great River (text Paul Horgan); orch. suites Ford's Theatre, From These States; 2 orch. elegies Marin and To Ansel Adams; music play A Tree on the Plains (text Paul Horgan); music to The Tempest; music-comedy Take Your Choice; 2 trios, 2 quintets, organ Spirits and Places; also works for piano, 2 pianos, ch. music, 2 ballets; author: 100 Fables, Words on Music, Notes on the Piano, The Honor of Music, Advice to Patrons, Imaginary Dialogues. Recipient Bispham, Ditson Award and League of Composers Louisville Commns.; Pulitzer fellowship, 1932; 3 Guggenheim fellowships; Campion citation; grant-citation Nat. Inst. of Arts and Letters; grant-citation Am. Soc. Authors, Composers and Publishers. Home: Orinda Calif. Died Mar. 16, 1990; buried Orinda, Calif.

BACON, FRANCIS, painter; b. Dublin, Ireland, 1909. Self-taught painter. One-man shows include London, 1949, N.Y.C., 1953; exhbns. include Venice Biennale (Italy), 1954, Marlborough Fine Art, London, 1960, 63, 65, 67, 83, 85, 89, 90,Tale Gallery, London, Mannheim, Turin, Zurich, Amsterdam, 1962, Hamburg, Stockholm, Dublin, 1965, Solomon Guggenheim Mus., N.Y.C., 1963, Art Inst. Chgo., 1963, Comtemporary Arts Assn., Houston, 1963, Galerie Maeght, Paris, 1966, 89, Marlborough, N.Y., 1968, 80, 87, 89, 90, Grand Palais, Paris, 1971, Kunsthalle, Dusseldorf, Germany, 1972, Met. Mus. Art, N.Y.C., 1975, Marlborough Galerie, Zurich, 1975, Musée Cantini, Marseilles, France, 1976, Museo de Arte Moderna, Mexico, 1977, Museo de Arte Comtemporenco, Caracas, Venezuela, 1977, Galerie Claude Bernard, Paris, 1977, Nat. Mus. Modern Art, Tokyo, Kyoto, Nagoya, 1983, Galerie Beyeler, Basle, 1987, Cen. House of Artists, New Treyakov Gallery, Moscow, 1988, Marlborough, Tokyo, 1988-89, Hirshorn Mus., Washington, 1988-90, Tate Gallery, London, 1988-90, Staatsgalerie, Stuttgart, 1988-89, National Galerie, Berlin, 1988-89, L.A. County Mus. Art, 1988-90, Mus. Modern Art, N.Y., 1988-90; prin. works include: Three Studies for Figures at the Base of a Crucifixion, 1944, Crucifixion, 1965, 72, 73, 86-86, 87; single oil paintings: Man with Dog, 1953, Study After Velazquez's Portrait of Pope Innocent X, 1953, Two Figures, 1953, Study for a Portrait, 1957, Study of the Human Body, 1982. Recipient Rubens prize City of Siegen, 1967, award Carnegie Inst., Pitts., 1967. Home: London Eng. Died Apr. 28, 1992. †

BACON, J. RAYMOND, management professional; b. Chgo., Aug. 11, 1906; s. Elmer Winfield and Alma C. (Romburg) B.; diploma in commerce Northwestern U., 1943; M.A., Western U., 1950; Ph.D. in Bus. Adminstrn. (hon.), Colo. State Christian Coll., 1972; m. Florence I. Burdine, Nov. 5, 1927 (dec. Nov. 1960); 1 dau., Grace Florence (Mrs. John W. Bacher); m. 2d, Margaret Austin, Nov. 30, 1963. Asst. mgr. King Woodworking Co., Chgo., 1926-34; dept. head Montgomery Ward & Co., Chgo. and Albany, N.Y., 1935-40; v.p., gen. mgr. O. D. Jennings & Co., Chgo., 1940-48; exec. v.p. Rockola Mfg. Co., Chgo., 1948-54; pres., treas., dir. F. H. Noble & Co., Chgo., 1954-67; pres., dir. F. H. Noble & Co. (Can.) Ltd., 1956-67; mng. dir. F. H. Noble & Co. (Ireland), Belfast, No. Ireland, 1963-67; pres., dir. Draftette Co., Hemet, Calif., 1967-86. Mem. Am. Mgmt. Assn., Soc. for Advancement Mgmt., A.I.M. (asso.), YMCA, Art Inst. Chgo. (life), Hemet C. of C., Calif. Mfrs. Assn. Presbyn. Kiwanian (past pres.). Deceased. Home: Hemet Calif. †

BADGER, RICHARD MCLEAN, chemistry educator; b. Elgin, Ill., May 4, 1896; s. Joseph Stillman and Carrie Mabel (Hewitt) B.; m. Virginia Alice Sherman, July 8, 1933; children: Anthony Sherman, Jennifer Hewitt. Student, Northwestern U., 1916-17, 19; BS, Calif. Inst. Tech., 1921, PhD, 1924; internat. rsch. fellow in chemistry, Univs. Gottingen and Bonn, Germany, 1928-29. Asst. prof. chemistry Calif. Inst. Tech., Pasadena, 1929-38, assoc. prof., 1938-45, prof., from 1945; lectr. in chemistry U. Calif., 1931. Contbr. articles to profl. jours. John Simon Guggenheim Meml. Found. fellow, 1960-61. Fellow Am. Phys. Soc., Am. Acad. Arts & Scis.; mem. Nat. Acad. Scis., Sigma Xi. *

BAER, BENJAMIN FRANKLIN, federal official, criminologist; b. Peoria, Ill., Jan. 2, 1918; s. Henry and

Emma (Siebenthal) B.; m. Dorothea Frances Heisman, Mar. 20, 1942; children: Marc Bradley, Meredith Jan, Bartley Benjamin F. B.A., San Diego State U., 1941; M.S.W., U. So. Calif., 1947, postgrad., 1964. Camp dir. Probation Dept., Los Angeles, 1942-47; staff Calif. Dept. Corrections, Sacramento, 1947-54; assoc. warden San Quentin, 1954-60; dir. Dept. Corrections State of Iowa, Des Moines, 1960-64, Correctional Decision Info. Project, Sacramento, 1965-67; dep. commr., chmn. youth commn. Minn. Dept. Corrections, St. Paul, 1967-72; staff U.S. Parole Commn., 1972; commr. U.S. Parole Commn., Washington, 1981-91; chmn. U.S. Parole Commn., 1982-91; ex-officio mem. U.S. Sentencing Commn., 1985-91; bd. dirs. Adv. Correctional Council, Washington, 1982-91, Nat. Inst. Corrections, 1982-91; mem. Pres. Kennedy's Juvenile Deliquence Commn., 1961-63. Author (with Harlan Hill) California Correctional Information System: Preliminary Information System Design, 1967. Mem. Am. Correctional Assn., Assn. Paroling Authorities Internat. Home: Rockville Md. Died Apr. 9, 1991; buried Peoria, Ill.

BAER, FRANCIS SHAW, banker; b. Medford, Mass., Mar. 9, 1893; s. John Willis and Lora (Van Dusen) R.; m. Georgiana Drummond, May 31, 1918; chidren: Mary Schweizer, Georgiana Johnston. AB, Occidental Coll., 1914, LLD, 1956. V.p. Hunter-Dulin Co., 1922-24; pres. Baer-Brown-Parsons Co., 1924-29; v.p. Security-1st Nat. Bank, 1929; pres. Pacific Co., 1930-34, Pacific Fin. Corp., 1934-42; vice chmn. bd. dirs., mem. exec. com. Bank of Am. Nat. Trust & Savs. Assn., San Francisco, 1942, sr. vice chmn. bd. dirs., 1945-49; sr. v.p., dir., mem. exec. com. Bankers Trust Co. N.Y., 1949-55, exec. v.p., mem. exec. com., dir., 1955-56, chmn. exec. com., 1956-58; chmn. bd. dirs. 1st Western Bank & Trust Co., 1959-61; chmn. bd. United Calif. Bank, San Francisco, from 1961; chmn. bd. Allied Concord Fin. Corp., N.Y.; bd. dirs. Celanese Corp. Am., Raymond Internat., Inc. Lt. (j.g.) USNRF, 1917-18. *

BAHMER, ROBERT H., archivist; b. Gardena, N.D., Sept. 27, 1904; s. Henry J. and Ida (Becker) B.; m. Viva L. Robbins, Jan. 10, 1931; children: Henry W., Kathryn J., Clifford L. Student, U. N.D., 1922-23; AB, N.D. State Tchrs. Coll., 1928; AM, U. Colo., 1929; PhD, U. Minn., 1941. Instr. Jr. Coll., Ironwood, Mich., 1932-34; sec. to Congressman Frank Hook, 1934-36; archivist Nat. Archives, 1936-42, Navy Dept., 1942, War Dept., 1943-48; asst. archivist U.S. Nat. Archives, 1948-56; dep. archivist of the U.S., 1956-66, archvist of the U.S., 1966-68; past. sec. gen. Internat. Coun. on Archives. Past mem. Soc. Am. Archivists, Am. Hist. Assn., The Westerners. Home: Chevy Chase Md. Died Mar. 14, 1990.

BAIL, PHILIP MILO, university president; b. Boonsville, Mo., June 26, 1898; s. Philip Dunleavy and Mollie (Powell) B.; m. Josephine Scott Hayden, Dec. 28, 1920. AB, Mo. Valley Coll., 1926; AM, State U. Ind., 1928, PhD, 1931; numerous hon. degrees. Tchr. high sch. Minn. and Iowa, 1920-28; prin. U. Iowa High Sch., Iowa City, 1928-31; supr. high schs. Dist. 27, Hibbing, Minn., 1931-35; pres. Chevy Chase Jr. Coll., Washington, 1935-40; dean coll. edn. Butler U., Indpls., 1940-48; dir. Univ. Coll., 1945-58; pres. Mcpl. Univ. Omaha, 1948-65; vis. lectr. U. Iowa, summers 1932-39. Milo Bail Student Ctr. named in his honor Omaha U. Mem. Assn. Am. Colls., Newcomen Soc., NEA, Nat. Assn. Sec. Sch. Prins., Dept. Suprs., Am. Assn. Sch. Admisntrs., others. *

BAILEY, FREDERICK EUGENE, JR., polymer scientist; b. Bklyn., Oct. 8, 1927; s. Frederick Eugene and Florence (Berkeley) B.; m. Mary Catherine Lowder, May 7, 1979. B.A., Amherst Coll., 1948; M.S., Yale U., 1950, Ph.D., 1952. Sr. chemist Union Carbide Rsch. Devel., 1952-59, group leader, 1959-62, asst. dir., 1962-69; mgr. mktg. rsch. Union Carbide, N.Y.C., 1969-71; sr. rsch. scientist Union Carbide, South Charleston, W.Va., 1971-91; sr. sci. cons. specialty chems. div. Union Carbide, South Charleston, 1991; adj. prof. chemistry dept. U. Charleston, Morris Harvey Coll., 1962-63, 65; mem. grad. faculty W.Va. U., 1959-61; chmn. Gordon Rsch. Conf. on Polymers, 1972, 84; mem. Gordon Rsch. Conf. Coun.; vice chmn. Gordon Rsch. Conf. on Foams, 1990, chmn., 1992. Author: Poly(ethylene Oxide), 1976, Alkylene Oxides and Their Polymers, 1990; editor: Initiation of Polymerization, 1983; (with K.N. Edwards) Urethane Chemistry and Applications, 1981; (with A. Eisenberg) Interactions in Macromolecules, 1986; patentee in field. Addison Brown scholar Amherst Coll., 1948; Forrest Jewett Moore fellow, 1949. Fellow AAAS, Am. Inst. Chemists (cert. chemist, Chem. Pioneer award 1987), N.Y. Acad. Scis.; mem. Am. Chem. Soc. (chmn. divisional officer caucus 1980-85, chmn. div. polymer chemistry 1976, councilor div. 1978-90, com. sci. 1978, 82-83, gen. sec. Macromolecular Secretariat 1978, divisional activities com. 1980-86, sec. divisional activities com. 1986, com. on coms. 1987-90, bd. dirs. 1990-91, candidate for pres. 1991, Outstanding Sci. Achievement award Kanawha Valley sect. 1988, Disting. Svc. award Div. Polymer Chemistry, 1991). Republican. Episcopalian. Club: Tennis (Charleston, W.Va.). Home: Charleston W.V. Died Aug. 8, 1991; inurned; St. Matthew's Ch. Columbarium, Charleston, W.Va.

BAILEY, GEORGE GILBERT, lawyer; b. Wheeling, W.Va., Dec. 1, 1913; s. George Alfred and Anna Gibson (Rose) B.; m. Lucretia Anne Tucker, Aug. 5, 1944; children—Barbara Anne, Bruce Tucker, John Preston. A.B., W.Va. U., 1935, LL.B., 1937. Bar: W.Va. bar 1937. Practiced in Wheeling; partner firm Bailey, Byrum & Vieweg; city solicitor Wheeling, 1955-72; Pres., dir. Central Union Co. Pres. Oglebay Inst., 1958-60; sec. Sandscrest Found., from 1954; vice-chancellor Episcopal Diocese of W.Va. Served with USCGR, 1942-45. Fellow Am. Bar Found.; mem. ABA (ho. of dels. 1964-79, gov. 1974-77), W.Va. Bar Assn. (pres. W.Va. 1962-63), Ohio County Bar Assn. (pres. 1957), State Bar Assn. (pres. 1963-64), Am. Coll. Trial Lawyers, Am. Judicature Soc., Am. Legion, Symposiarchs, Theta Chi, Phi Delta Phi. Democrat. Home: Wheeling W.Va. Died Feb. 1, 1989; buried Lawrencefield Churchyard, Wheeling, W.Va.

BAILEY, JACK BLENDON, computer company executive; b. Ft. Worth, Aug. 17, 1925; s. Claude E. and Lalla (Davis) B.; m. Alma Herod. A.B., Okla. State U., 1943, A.M., 1951; LL.B., Columbia, 1948. Bar: Okla. bar 1949. Asso. firm Farmer, Woolsey, Flippo & Bailey, Tulsa, 1949-72; partner Farmer, Woolsey, Flippo & Bailey, 1951-72; vice-pres., gen. counsel Telex Corp., Tulsa, 1972-88. Served with AUS, 1943-45. Mem. Am., Okla. bar assns. Home: Tulsa Okla. Died June 4, 1989; buried Anson, Tex.

BAILEY, PEARL, singer; b. Newport News, Va., Mar. 29, 1918; d. Joseph James B.; m. John Randolph Pinkett, Jr., Aug. 31, 1948 (div. Mar. 1952); m. Louis Bellson, Jr., Nov. 19, 1952. Student pub. schs., Phila.; B.A. in Theology, Georgetown U., Washington, D.C., 1985, L.H.D. (hon.). Singer, from 1933; vocalist various popular bands; stage debut in St. Louis Woman, N.Y.C., 1946; role in Broadway musical Hello Dolly, 1967-68, Arms and the Girl, House of Flowers, Bless You All, Duey's Tale, Hurry Up America, and Spit; albums include: Bad Old Days, Cole Porter Song Book, Echoes of an Era; motion pictures include: Variety Girl, Carmen Jones, St. Louis Blues, Porgy and Bess, Isn't It Romantic, Norman, Is That You, That Certain Feeling, All the Fine Young Cannibals, The Landlord, Lost Generation; contract artist, Coral Records, Columbia Records, Decca; night club engagements, N.Y.C., Boston, Hollywood, Las Vegas, Chgo., London, from 1950; star Pearl Bailey Show, ABC-TV, 1970-71; guest artist various TV programs; Spl. Tony award for Hello, Dolly 1967-68; author: Raw Pearl, 1969, Pearlie Mae, Talking to Myself, 1971, Pearl's Kitchen, 1973, Duey's Tale, 1975, Hurry Up, America and Spit, 1976. Spl. rep. U.S. delegation to UN from 1975. Recipient Donaldson award, 1956. March of Dimes award 1968, Centennial award AAUW, 1988; named Entertainer of the Year Cue Magazine, 1967, 1968, U.S.O. Woman of the Year, 1969; recipient citation from Mayor John V. Lindsay of N.Y.C. Home: Lake Havasu Ariz. Died Aug. 17, 1990; buried Rolling Green Meml. Pk., near Phila.

BAILEY, THOMAS DAVID, educator; b. Lugoff, S.C., Oct. 31, 1897; s. Samuel David and Mary Julia (Campbell) B.; m. Burness McConnell, Aug. 25, 1921; children: Billie McNab, Mary Julia Shealy. AB, Wofford Coll., 1919; MAE, U. Fla., 1939; LLD, Fla. So. Coll., 1949. Prin. Govan (S.C.) Schs., 1919-20; pres. Thomas Indsl. Inst., De Funiak Springs, Fla., 1920-24; prin. Winyan High Sch., Georgetown, S.C., 1924-28; supervising prin. Ocala (Fla.) Pub. Schs., 1939-43, Tampa (Fla.) Pub. Schs., 1943-47; sec. pub. rels. Fla. Edn. Assn., Tallahassee, 1947-48; state supt. pub. instrn. State of Fla., from 1949; mem. various state ednl. coms. Mem. Nat. Coun. Chief State Sch. Officers, NEA, Fla. Congress Parents & Tchrs., Fla. Edn. Assn., Assn. Sec. Sch. Prins., others. *

BAILEY, WILLIAM JOHN, chemistry educator; b. East Grand Forks, Minn., Aug. 11, 1921; s. Ross and Erva (Stewart) B.; m. Mary Caroline Worsham, Aug. 27, 1949; children: Caroline Jane, John Robert, Barbara Ann, Arthur D. B Chemistry, U. Minn., 1943; PhD, U. Ill., 1946. Arthur D. Little postdoctoral fellow MIT, Cambridge, 1946-47; asst. prof. chemistry Wayne State U., Detroit, 1947-49, assoc. prof., 1949-51; rsch. prof. organic chemistry U. Md., College Park, 1051-89; chmn. Gordon Rsch. Conf. on Organic Reactions, 1960;; mem. postdoctoral selection com. NSF, 1963-66; mem. NRC adv. com. on elastomers to U.S. Army Natick Labs., 1961-67, chmn. com. on macromolecular chemistry, 1967-79; U.S. rep. macromolecular div. Internat. Union Pure and Applied Chemistry, 1967-81; Robert A. Welch lectr., 1971; Rauscher Meml. lectr. Rensselaer Poly. Inst., 1976; Gossett award lectr. N.C. State U., 1983. Author books on polymers, also 200 articles; mem. editorial bd. Jour. Organic Chemistry, 1957-63, Macromolecular Synthesis, 1960-89, Record Chem. Progress, 1950-70, Jour. Macromolecular Sci. Chemistry, 1966-89, Jour. Polymer Sci., 1967-89, Macromolecules, 1967-72, Chem. Tech., 1972-89, Current Abstracts Chemistry, 1972-89, Index Chemicus, 1972-89, Polymer Sci. and Tech., 1972-89, Chem. and Engring. News, 1974-76, 79, 81. Recipient Fatty Acid Producers Rsch. award, 1955, Disting. Alumnus award U. Minn., 1976; rsch. grantee Gulf Oil Found., 1971. Mem. AAAS, Am. Chem. Soc. (dir.-at large 1973, 77-82, pres. 1975, chmn. bd. 1979, 81, Witco polymer chemistry award 1977, award in applied polymer chemistry 1986), Chem. Soc. Washington (pres. 1961, svc. award 1969, Hillebrand prize 1984), Am. Inst. Chemists (D.C. Inst. honor scroll 1975), Am. Oil Chemists Soc., Coun. Sci. Soc. Pres. (exec. bd. 1975-77), Fedn. Material Socs. (trustee 1976-80), Phi Beta Kappa, Sigma Xi (ann. achievement award U. Md. chpt. 1979), Phi Kappa Phi, Alpha Chi Sigma. Home: University Park Md. Died Dec. 17, 1989.

BAIN, GEORGE WILLIAM, geology educator; b. Lachute, Quebec, May 8, 1901; came to U.S., 1922, naturalized, 1934; s. James and Margaret (McFaul) B.; m. Anne Elizabeth Kahrs, Sept. 18, 1926; children: Elizabeth Anne, Iris Louise, Bruce Kahrs. BSc, McGill U., 1921, MSc, 1923; PhD, Columbia, 1927; AM (hon.), Amherst Coll., 1941. Field asst. Geol. Survey of Can., 1921-24; asst. to Vt. State Geologist, 1925; asst. prof.geology U. Vt., 1925-26; instr. advancing Hitchcock prof. mineralogy and geology Amherst Coll., 1926-66; prof. emeritus, 1966-91; dir. Pratt Mus. of Amherst Coll., from 1948; cons. geologist Vt. Marble Co., 1927-39; took numerous assignments with Internat. Exec. Svc. Corps, Philippines, Taiwan, Iran, Brazil. Author: Marble Deposits of Newfoundland, 1937, Flow of Time Through the Connecticut Valley, 1943. Geologist U.S. War Dept. Served with Can. O.T.C., 1916-18. Received British Assn. medal McGill U., 1921, President's Gold medal of Can. Inst. Mining and Metallurgy, 1926; U.S. War Dept. Commendation for Exceptional Civilian Svc., 1946. Mem. Geol. Soc. Am., Mineral Soc. Am., Soc. Econ. Geologists, Am. Inst. Mining and Metall. Engrs., Geol. Soc. of S. Africa, Can. Inst. Mining and Metall., Sigma Xi. Home: Amherst Mass. Died June 11, 1991; buried Amherst, Mass.

BAIN, WILLIAM JAMES, architect; b. New Westminster, B.C., Can., Mar. 27, 1896; s. David and Annie Wilson (Forrester) B.; m. Mildred Worline Clark, May 29, 1924; children: Robert Clark, William James, Jr., Nancy Ann (Mrs. Edward George Lowry III). Student, U. Pa., 1919-21; student in, Europe, 1922. Employed in Boston, N.Y., Los Angeles; Employed in Seattle, 1922-24, practice architecture, 1924-85; mem. firm Naramore, Bain, Brady and Johanson, 1943-85; Mem. Nat. Pub. Adv. Panel for Archtl. Services, 1968-69; regional adv. bd. SBA. Prin. works include Nat. FDA Bldg, Washington, Washington Bldg., Seattle; assoc. architect: 1st Nat. Bank of Missoula (Mont.), U. Wash. Med. Sch., Seattle, IBM Bldg., Seattle, Seattle 1st Nat. Bank, Seattle Post Intelligencer, Batelle Research Centers, addition to Mayo Clinic, Rochester, Minn., Kingdome, 1979-85 ; also numerous residences in Wash., Oreg., Idaho, Mont. and B.C. Bd. dirs. Salvation Army.; past mem. Seattle Housing Adv. Bd.; pres. Arthritis Found. Western Wash., 1968; trustee Seattle Urban Renewal. Served with 117th Field Signal Bn., attached to 166th Inf., Rainbow Div. U.S. Army, 1917-18. Fellow AIA (jury of fellows 1950-55, mem. bd. past pres. Wash. chpt., sec. coll. fellows 1966, Seattle pres. 1968); mem. English Speaking Union (mem. bd. 1964-70, 78-85), C. of C. (mem. exec. com. 1968-69, dir. 1960-70, treas. 1965, constrn. man of year 1966), Am. Arbitration Assn. Clubs: Rainier (dir.), Rotary, Washington Athletic, Seattle Tennis. Home: Seattle Wash. Died Jan. 21, 1985. †

BAINBRIDGE, JOHN, writer; b. Monticello, Minn., Mar. 12, 1913; s. William Dean and Bess (Lakin) B.; m. Dorothy Alice Hazlewood, June 2, 1936; children: Jonathon, Janet. B.S., Northwestern U., 1935. Mem. editorial staff The New Yorker, 1938-92. Contbr. numerous Profiles to The New Yorker, articles to other nat. publs.; Author: Little Wonder, or The Reader's Digest and How It Grew, 1946, The Wonderful World of Toots Shor, 1951, Biography of an Idea, 1952, Garbo, 1955, The Super-Americans, 1961, Like a Homesick Angel, 1964, Another Way of Living, 1968, English Impressions, 1981; contbr. to Goumet mag., 1972-92. Mem. Authors Guild. Club: Coffee House (N.Y.C., N.Y.). Home: Bath Eng. Died Nov. 12, 1992. †

BAINER, ROY, dean, agricultural engineer; b. nr. Ottawa, Kans., Mar. 7, 1902; s. Harry M. and Clara Ellen (Nitcher) B.; m. Lena Mae Cook, May 29, 1926; 1 dau., La Nelle. B.S., Kans. State Coll., 1926, M.S., 1929; LL.D., U. Calif., 1969; D.Engring, Kans. State U., 1983. Instr. Kans. State Coll., 1926-27, asst. prof., 1927-29; asst. prof., agrl. engr. U. Calif.-Davis, 1929-37, assoc. prof., 1937-45, assoc. agrl. engr., 1937-43, agrl. engr., from 1943, prof. agrl. engring., from 1945, chmn. div., 1947-61, asst. dean engring., 1952-61, assoc. dean, 1961-62, dean, 1962-69, dean emeritus, from 1969, founder univ. Engring. Coll., founder The Higgins Libr. at univ.; Cons. Brit. Ministry Agr., 1945, U.S. Army, Japan, 1948; asso. dir. mechanization center FAO of UN, Chile, 1958, cons., Peru, 1961, 62, 63-64, 65, 66, 69; cons. Dept. State in Laos, 1966, Kasetsart U., Bangkok, Thailand, 1966; cons. to minister agr., Brazil, 1969, Spain, 1971-72; cons. Arya-Mehr U. Tech., Iran, 1975, Guanajuato U., Mexico, 1977, Malawi, 1978; hon. prof. Agrarian U., Peru, 1964; mem. agr. bd. Nat. Acad. Sci.-NRC, 1957-62; mem. at large NRC; resource person Library Congress, from 1972. Co-author: Principles of Farm Machinery; Contbr. articles to profl. jours. Recipient McCormick Gold Medal for outstanding achievement agrl. engring., Disting. Svc. award Am. Soc. Sugar Beet Technologists, 1960, Disting. Svc.

award Kans. State U., 1960, Disting. Svc. award U. Mo., 1962; named to Hall of Fame Kans. State U., 1989. Roy Bainer Hall named in his honor at Engring. Coll. Mem. Am. Soc. Agrl. Engrs. (past pres.), Nat. Acad. Engring., Am. Soc. Engring. Edn. (Vincent Bendix gold medal 1962), Calif. Acad. Sci., Sigma Xi, Phi Mu Alpha, Gamma Sigma Delta, Tau Beta Pi. Republican. Methodist. Clubs: Commonwealth, Faculty, Rotary (past pres. Davis). Home: Davis Calif. Died Jan. 24, 1990; buried Davis, Calif.

BAKER, ALTON WESLEY, management educator, corporate administrator; b. Chickasha, Okla., May 28, 1912; s. Charles Wesley and Frances Cornelia (Hennington) B.; m. Mary Elizabeth Dill, June 4, 1938; children: Don Wesley, Viki Joan. B.B.A., U. Tex., 1936; A.M., George Washington U., 1947; Ph.D., Ohio State U., 1952; degree, Cambridge U. Assoc. prof. Ohio State U., 1947-54; prof., chmn. dept. mgmt. So. Meth. U., 1954-92; prof. Southwestern Legal Found. U. Tex.; prof. Southwestern Grad. Sch. Banking; div. head Fairchild Corp.; chmn. bd. Dill Mfg. Corp.; dir. research Ohio State U. Research Found., U.S. and Orient; Chmn. bd. regional postmaster selection U.S. Post Office Service, 1969-92 ; cons. to postmaster gen., 1968-92 ; cons. to industry in, U.S. and S.Am.; cons. S.W. Legal Found., S.W. Grad. Sch. Banking; prof. Air U.; dir. research intelligence SAC, USAF, Far East. Author: numerous publs. including Supervisor and His Job, 3d ed, 1978, internat. edit., 1979, Management: Small Manufacturing Plants, 1955. Chmn. bd. dirs. So. Meth. U. Retirement System, Inc. Mem. Acad. Mgmt. Clubs: Country (Dallas), Rotary (Dallas). Home: Dallas Tex. Died Aug. 17, 1992. †

BAKER, GERTRUDE MARGARET, physical education educator; b. Rochester, N.Y., Apr. 28, 1894; d. William and Mary Theresa (Eberle) B. Diploma hygiene and phys. edn., Wellesley Coll., 1915; BS in Edn., U. Minn., 1922, MA, 1929; EdD, Columbia U., 1946. Faculty U. Minn., from 1921, prof. phys. edn. for women, dir. dept., from 1945; cons. curriculum reorgn. Minn., 1948-50. Author: Graded Lessons in the Fundamentals of Physical Education, 1938, (with others) The Modern Teacher of Physical Education, 1940; contbr. articles to profl. jours. Fellow Am. Acad. Phys. Edn.; mem. Am. Assn. Health, Phys. Edn. and Recreation (honor award fellow 1957, chmn. nat. coms. 1946-61, sec. nat. rsch. sect. 1935-37), Minn. Assn. Health, Phys. Edn. and Recreation (honor award 1958, pres. 1925-26), Ctrl. Dist. Assn. Health, Phys. Edn. and Recreation (honor award fellow 1954, pres. 1925-26), Nat. Assn. Phys. Edn. Coll. Women (treas. 1944-46, chmn. com. trends as affect phys. edn. women 1951-55), Ctrl. Assn. Phys. Edn. Coll. Women (pres. 1946-47), League of Women Voters, Women's Inter Club Coun. Mpls. (pres. 1949-52), Pi Lambda Theta, Kappa Delta Pi, Rotarian (pres. Mpls. womens 1941-42). *

BAKER, MILTON G., school administrator; b. Phila., Aug. 24, 1896; s. Frank Robertson and Sallie (Dimmock) B.; m. May Porter Hagenbuch, Apr. 29, 1924; 1 child, Ann Porter (Mrs. Winslow Martin). Student, Brown Prep. Sch., 1911-14, St. John's Coll., 1915-17; LLD, Gettysburg Coll., Temple U., Norwich U.; PdD, LaSalle Coll., 1956. Pres., supt. Valley Forge Mil. Acad., 1928-92; bd. dirs. Mil Colls. and Schs. U.S. past pres., S.R., v.p., Mil. Order World Wars, past commdr. Pa. chpt., nat. commdr. 1950-51, Commonwealth Pa. Armory, Franklin Inst., Freedoms Found. Gettysburg Battle Centennial Commn.; chmn. Commonwealth Pa. Mil Commn., 1952-58. Trustee Old Eagle Sch., Stafford, Pa., Temple U., Gen. George Catlett Marshall Found., Lexington, Va., Gen. Douglas MacArthur Meml. Found., Norfolk, Va.; vice chmn. bd. advs. Villanova U.; bd. dirs. Freedom Found. Gettysburg Battle Centennial Commn.; chmn. U.S. Nat. Commn., UNESCO, 1953-55, del.-at-large 1953-58; chmn. inauguration Gov. of Pa., 1963; chmn. Scott for Senate com. (Pa.) 1964 With U.S. Army, 1917-21; commdg. gen. Nat. Guard Pa. 1943-46;gen. U.S. dir. civil Defense, Phila., 1941-42, commnd. lt. gen. 1957. Decorated by U.S, Brazil, Nicaragua, Belgium, Ecuador, Bulgaria, France; recipient Order of Merit (Italy), 1959. Fellow Co. Mil. Historians, Internat. Coll. Surgeons; mem. Navy League U.S. (Phila. coun.), Am. Ch. Union (v.p.), Assn. U.S. Army (pres. 1960-63), Pa. C. of C. (bd. dirs.), Am. Legion, Am. Assn. Jr. Colls., Assn. Am. Colls., Old Guard City of Phila., Mil. Order Loyal Legion, St. Andrews Soc., Hist. Soc. of Pa., Reserve Officers Assn. of U.S., Franklin Inst. Pa., Valley Forge Hist. Soc., Pa. Soc. of N.Y., Nat. Assn. Secondary Sch. Prins., Mil. Order Fgn Wars, Brotherhood of St. Andrew, Newcomers Soc. of Eng., Devon Horse Show Assn. (bd. dirs.), Mason (32 degree), Union League (N.Y.C., Phila.), Capitol Hill Club (Washington), Army Navy Club, Penn Club (Phila.), St. David's Golf Club, British Officers Club, Rolling Rock Club (Ligonier Pa.), Surf Club (Miami Beach), Bald Peak Colony (N.H.). *

BAKER, WALTER CUMMINGS, banker; b. Oneida, N.Y., Mar. 29, 1893; s. William and Fannie E. (Wallace) B.; m. May Ida Case, Sept. 15, 1921 (dec. 1946); m. Lois Wurtele, May 25, 1951. BS, Union Coll., 1915, LLD (hon.), 1955. Salesman Bond & Mortgage Guarantee Co., Bklyn., 1915-18; with Guaranty Trust Co. N.Y., 1919-58, asst. trust officer, 1925-28, trust officer, 1928-45, v.p., 1945-58; bd. dirs. J.J. Newberry Co. Life trustee Union Coll., chmn. bd. trustees, 1941-63; govt. Union U., treas., from 1938; trustee, v.p., fellow in perpetuity Met. Mus. Art; trustee Archaeol. Inst. Am., treas., 1948-64, hon. life fellow, pres. N.Y. soc., 1951-54. With USN, 1918-19. Mem. Master Drawings Assn., Nat. Inst. Social Scis., Psi Upsilon. *

BALAKIAN, NONA HILDA, editor, book critic; b. Istanbul, Turkey; came to U.S., 1926; d. Diran and Koharig (Panossian) B. B.A., Barnard Coll., 1942; M.S. in Journalism, Columbia U., 1943. Mem. editorial bd. N.Y. Times Book Rev., N.Y.C., 1943-88; book reviewer Sunday and daily N.Y. Times, 1943-87, lit. cons., from 1988; cons. in field; mem. book selection com. Books-Across-the-Sea, 1978-86; mem. Pulitzer Prize jury (for nonfiction), 1977, for poetry, 1979, 81, Hopwood Award jury (for essays), 1979. Contbr. revs., articles, essays to various lit. mags.; Author: Critical Encounters: Literary Views and Reviews, 1953-1977, 1978; editor: (with Charles Simmons) The Creative Present: Notes on Contemporary American Fiction, 1963; editorial bd.: Ararat Quar., 1970-80. Recipient Humanities award Rockefeller Found., 1981. Mem. PEN (exec. bd. 1973-80), Nat. Book Critics Circle (founding; exec. bd. from 1974, sec. 1974-76), Authors Guild. Home: New York N.Y. Died Apr. 6, 1991.

BALASSA, BELA, economist, educator; b. Budapest, Hungary, Apr. 6, 1928; came to U.S., 1957, naturalized, 1962; s. George and Charlotte (Andreics) B.; m. Carol Ann Levy, June 12, 1960; children: Mara, Gabor. Diplomkaufmann, Acad. Fgn. Trade, Budapest, 1948; Dr. iuris rerumque Politicarum, U. Budapest, 1951, hon. doctorate, 1991; PhD in Econs, Yale, 1959; honorary doctorate, U. Paris, 1988. Asst., later assoc. prof. Yale U., 1959-67; adviser, later cons. econs. dept. IBRD, from 1966; prof. polit. economy Johns Hopkins U., 1967-91, prof. emeritus, 1991; vis. prof. U. Calif., Berkeley, 1961-62, Columbia U., 1963-64; econ. adviser to internat. orgns. and fgn. govts., cons. to govt. and industry, from 1963. Author: The Hungarian Experience in Economic Planning, 1959, The Theory of Economic Integration, 1961, Trade Prospects for Developing Countries, 1964, Economic Development and Integration, 1965, Trade Liberalization among Industrial Countries: Objectives and Alternatives, 1967, Studies in Trade Liberalization, 1967, The Structure of Protection in Developing Countries, 1971, European Economic Integration, 1975, Policy Reform in Developing Countries, 1977, Industrial Development in Thailand, 1980, Development Strategies in Semi-Industrial Economies, 1982, The Newly-Industrializing Countries in the World Economy, 1981, Turkey: Industrialization and Trade Strategy, 1982; Morocco: Industrial Incentives and Export Promotion, 1984, Change and Challenge in the World Economy, 1985, Toward Renewed Economic Growth in Latin America, 1986, Adjusting to Success: Balance of Payments Policy in East Asia, 1987, Changing Trade Patterns in Manufactured Goods: An Econometric Investigation, 1988, Japan in the World Economy, 1988, New Directions in the World Economy, 1989, Comparative Advantage, Trade Policy and Economic Development, 1988, Economic Policies in Pacific Area Developing Countries, 1991; contbg. editor: Changing Patterns in Foreign Trade and Payments, 1964, 70, 77, Economic Progress, Private Values and Public Policy: Essays in Honor of William Fellner, 1977; Economic Incentives, 1985. Rockefeller fellow, 1957-58; Relm Found. grantee, 1958; Ford Found. dissertation fellow, 1958-59; Social Sci. Research Council grantee, 1963; NSF grantee, 1970-74, Prix Rossi of the Académie des sciences morales et politiques (Paris), 1980; Bernhard Harms Prize Kiel Inst. of World Economies, 1984; V.K. Ramaswami Meml. Lectr. (New Delhi), 1986; Bohm-Bawerk Vis. Prof. U. Innsbruck, 1987. Mem. Am. Econ. Assn., Econometric Soc., Royal Econ. Soc., Assn. Comparative Econ. Studies (pres. 1979-80), Hungarian Acad. Scis. Home: Washington DC Died May 10, 1991; buried Washington.

BALASSA, LESLIE LADISLAUS, chemical executive, consultant; b. Bacsfoeldvar, Vojvodina, Yugoslavia, Sept. 6, 1903; came to U.S., 1926; s. Bela Adalbertus and Bella (Grosz-Gyoery) B.; m. Alice Mabel Hussey, Dec. 1, 1933; children: John, Paul. PhD, U. Vienna, Austria, 1926. Rsch. mgr. E.I. duPont de Nemours, Phila. and Flint,, Mich., 1927-43; rsch. dir. U.S. Finishing Co., Providence, 1943-49; exec. v.p. Aula Chem. Corp., Jersey City and Elizabeth, N.J., 1949-57; mgr. textile colors rsch. Geigy Chems. Corp., Ardsley, N.Y., 1957-60; pres. Lescarden Ltd., Goshen, N.Y., 1960-80; vice chmn. bd. Lescarden Ltd., N.Y.C., 1980-92; pres. Balassa Rsch. Assocs., Blooming Grove, N.Y., 1980-92, HFM, Inc., Blooming Grove, 1987-92; pres. Balchem Corp., Slate Hill, N.Y., 1957-64, bd. dirs., Lescarden Corp., N.Y.C., HFM, Inc., Blooming Grove. Contbr. numerous articles to profl. jours.; inventee in field. Mem. Mid-Hudson Peace Network, Cornwall, N.Y., from 1984. Mem. Am. Chem. Soc. (emeritus), Chemists Club. Democrat. Home: Claremont Calif. Died July 2, 1992. †

BALCH, GLENN O., author; b. Venus, Tex., Dec. 11, 1902; s. Glenn Olin and Edith (Garrison) B.; m. Faula Mashburn (div. 1935); 1 dau., Betty Lou; m. Elise Kendall, May 15, 1937; children—Lynne Kendall, Mary, Olin. Student, North Tex. State Tchrs. Coll., Denton, 1921-23, U. Tex., 1923-24; A.B., Baylor U., 1924; postgrad., Columbia, 1937. Bank clerk, 1923-24; forest ranger U.S. Forestry Svc., 1924; newspaper reporter, traveling corr. Idaho Daily Statesman, Boise, 1926-29; free-lance mag. writer and publicity, from 1929; asst. to U.S. Sen. John Thomas (Idaho) prior to W.W. II. Author: Riders of the Rio Grande, 1937, Tiger Roan, 1938, Hide-rack Kidnapped, 1939, Indian Paint, 1942 (made into movie), Wild Horse, 1946, Viking Dog, 1948, Christmas Horse, 1949, Lost Horse, 1950 (Boys' Club Book award 1951), Winter Horse, Squaw Boy, Midnight Colt, Indian Saddle-Up, 1953, Little Hawk and The Free Horses, 1956, The Brave Riders, 1958, White Ruff, Horses, 1959, Horse in Danger, 1960, The Stallion King, 1960, Spotted Horse, 1961, Stallion's Foe, 1962, The Runaways, 1963, Guide to Western Horseback Riding, 1965, The Book of Horses, 1966, Keeping Horse, 1966, The Flaxy Mare, 1967, Horse of Two Colors, 1968, Buck, Wild, 1976; many books transl. into fgn. langs.; contbr. to periodicals. Served to lt. col. USAAF, 1941-45, CBI. Recipient George Washington Meml. awards Freedoms Found., 1954, 56, 57, Recognition award for contbn. to Idaho children Idaho Libr. Assn., 1989; featured in Idaho Authors Rm. Boise Pub. Libr. Home: Boise ID Died Sept. 16, 1989; cremated.

BALDWIN, HANSON WEIGHTMAN, author, editor; b. Balt., Mar. 22, 1903; s. Oliver Perry and Caroline (Sutton) B.; m. Helen Bruce, June 8, 1931; children: Barbara, Bruce, Elizabeth. Student, Boys' Latin Sch., Balt.; BS, U.S. Naval Acad., 1924. Commd. ensign USN, 1924, advanced through grades to lt. (j.g.), served aboard battleships and a destroyer, resigned, 1927; police reporter, gen. assigment reporter Balt. Sun, 1928-29; with N.Y. Times, 1929-91, mil. and naval corr., 1937-42, mil. editor, 1942-91. Author: (with W.F. Palmer) Men and Ships of Steel, 1935, The Caissons Roll-A Military Survey of Europe, 1938, Admiral Dealth, 1939, What the Citizen Should Know About the Navy, 1941, United We Stand, 1941, Strategy for Victory, 1942, The Price of Power, 1948, Great Mistakes of the War, 1950, Sea Fights and Shipwrecks, 1955, The Great Arms Race, 1958, World War I: An Outline History, 1962, Battles Lost and Won: Great Campaigns of World War II, 1966, Strategy for Tomorrow, 1970; editor: (with Shepard Stone) We Saw It Happen, 1938; contbr. to N.Y. Times mag., U.S. Naval Inst. Procs., Harpers, Atlantic Monthly, Sat. Evening Post. Recipient Pulitzer Prize, 1942. Home: New York N.Y. Died Nov. 13, 1991.

BALDWIN, JACK NORMAN, microbiology educator; b. Nephi, Utah, Dec. 6, 1919; s. Ernest Frank and Eva (Christison) B.; m. Adell Holmgren Cheney, Sept. 6, 1946; children—Marian Adell, Jack Norman, Eva Lee. B.A., U. Utah, 1942, M.A., 1947; Ph.D., Purdue U., 1950. Research asso. Purdue U., 1948-50; asst. prof. Ohio State U., Columbus, 1950-56; asst. prof. Ohio State U., 1956-60, prof., 1960-63; prof. U. Ky., Lexington, 1963-67; prof. dept. microbiology U. Ga., Athens, 1967-84; ret, 1985. Contbr. articles to profl. jours. Served with AUS, 1942-45. Mem. Am. Soc. Microbiology, Soc. Gen. Microbiology, Soc. Exptl. Biology and Medicine, AAAS, Sigma Xi, Phi Lambda Upsilon. Mem. LDS Ch. Home: Saint George UT Died Nov. 4, 1989; buried St. George, Utah.

BALDWIN, PAUL CLAY, business executive; b. Tully, N.Y., May 19, 1914; s. Fred Lynn and Grace Ann (Clay) B.; m. Margaret Mary Fargo, Nov. 2, 1940 (dec. July 1970); children: Barbara F., Paul Clay, Robert F.; m. Doris Walsh, May 20, 1972. BS, Syracuse U., 1936; MS, Inst. Chemistry, 1938, PhD, 1940; ScD, Lawrence U., 1972. With Scott Paper Co., 1940-77, tech. dir., prodn. supr., 1940-46, gen. plant mgr., 1946-51, asst. v.p., 1951-53, v.p., 1953-57, v.p. mfg., engring. and research, 1957-60, exec. v.p. mfg., engring. and research, 1960-62, exec. v.p., 1962-68, vice chmn., dir., 1968-77; vice chmn., dir. Gilman Paper Co., 1981-86; past chmn. bd. Brunswick Pulp & Paper Co.; cons. to paper industry, Devon, Pa.; Chmn. corp. adv. council Syracuse U.; chmn. bd. Research Corp.; dir.-at-large Syracuse Pulp and Paper Found.; former chmn. bd., exec. com. Am. Paper Inst.; chmn. bd. trustees Inst. Paper Chemistry. Recipient Honor award U. Maine Pulp and Paper Found., 1972. Fellow TAPPI; mem. World Affairs Council Phila., Tau Beta Pi, Phi Kappa Psi, Alpha Chi Sigma, Pi Mu Epsilon. Clubs: Aronimink; Union League (Phila.); Radnor Hunt; Anglers (N.Y.). Home: Rose Valley PA Died Nov. 11, 1990.

BALL, C(HARLES) OLIN, educator, association official; b. Abilene, Kans., Mar. 30, 1893; s. Charles Asa and Ellen (Markley) B.; m. Madeline Esther Hoopes, Jan. 1, 1920; 1 child, Bette Neilson. AB, George Washington U., 1920, MS, 1922, PhD, 1926; student, Cambridge U., U. Chgo. Rsch. technician Nat. Canners Assn., 1919-22; technician, group supr. Am. Can Co., 1922-30, asst. mgr., asst. to dir. rsch., 1930-41; tecch. dir. Owens-Ill. Can Co., 1942-44; cons. food tech. Maumee, Ohio, 1947-49; editor Food Tech. mag., 1947-50, editor emeritus, from 1950; prof. food tech., rsch. specialist Rutgers U., 1949-63, chmn. dept. food sci., 1959-63, emeritus prof., from 1963; v.p. Avi Pub. Co., from 1963. Author books on kinetics of food sterilzation. Served with Kan. N.G. on Mexican border, 1916; capt. U.S. Army, 1917-19. Founding mem. Inst. Food

Technologists; mem. Nat. Canners Assn., N.Y. Acad. Scis., AAAS, Sigma Xi, others. *

BALL, LUCILLE, actress; b. Jamestown, N.Y., Aug. 6, 1911; d. Henry D. and Desiree (Hunt) B.; m. Desi Arnaz, Nov. 30, 1940 (div. 1960); children: Lucie Desiree, Desiderio Alberto IV; m. Gary Morton, Nov. 19, 1961. Ed. high sch., dramatic sch., studied with John Murray Anderson. Pres. Desilu Prodns., Inc., 1962-67, Lucille Ball Prodns., 1967—. Motion picture actress, 1934—; pictures include Broadway thru a Keyhole, 1933, Blood Money, 1933, Moulin Rouge, 1933, Roman Scandals, 1933, Nana, 1934, Bottoms Up, 1934, Hold that Girl, 1934, Bulldog Drummond Stikes Back, 1934, The Affairs of Cellini, 1934, Kid Millions, 1934, Broadway Bill, 1934, Jealousy, 1934, Men of the Night, 1934, Fugitive Lady, 1934, Carnival, 1935, Roberta, 1935, Old Man Rhythm, 1935, Top Hat, 1935, The Three Musketeers, 1935, I Dream Too Much, 1935, Chatterbox, 1936, Follow the Fleet, 1936, The Farmer in the Dell, 1936, Bunker Bean, 1936, That Girl from Paris, 1936, Don't Tell the Wife, 1937, Stage Door, 1937, Joy of Living, 1938, Go Chase Yourself, 1938, Having a Wonderful Time, 1938, The Affairs of Annabel, 1938, Room Service, 1938, The Next Time I Marry, 1938, Annabel Takes a Tour, 1938, Beauty for the Asking, 1939, Twelve Crowded Hours, 1939, Panama Lady, 1939, Five Came Back, 1939, That's Right You're Wrong, 1939, The Marines Fly High, 1940, Too Many Girls, 1940, A Guy, a Girl and Gob, 1940, Look Who's Laughing, 1941, Valley of the Sun, 1942, The Big Street, 1942, Seven Days Leave, 1942, DuBarry Was a Lady, 1943, Best Foot Forward, 1943, Thousands Cheer, 1943, Meet the People, 1944, Without Love, 1945, Abbott and Costello in Hollywood, 1945, Ziegfeld Follies, 1946, The Dark Corner, 1946, Easy to Wed, 1946, Two Smart People, 1946, Lover Come Back, 1946, Lured, 1947, Her Husband's Affairs, 1947, Sorrowful Jones, 1949, Easy Living, 1949, Miss Grant Takes Richmond, 1949, Fuller Brush Girl, 1950, Fancy Pants, 1950, Magic Carpet, 1950, The Long, Long Trailer, 1954, Forever Darling, 1956, The Facts of Life, 1960, Critic's Choice, 1963, A Guide for the Married Man, 1967, Yours, Mine and Ours, 1968, Mame, 1974; star TV shows I Love Lucy, 1951-55, The Lucy Show, 1962-68, Here's Lucy, 1968-73, Life With Lucy, 1986; starred on Broadway in Wildcat; TV movie appearances include Stone Pillow, 1985. Recipient Emmy award for best comedienne, 1952, 55, 67, 68; Golden Apple award, 1973; Ruby award, 1974; Entertainer of Yr. award, 1975; inducted into Television Acad. Hall of Fame, 1984. Presbyterian. Home: Los Angeles CA Died Apr. 26, 1989.

BALL, WILLIAM, theatre producer, director; b. Chgo., Apr. 29, 1931; s. Russell and Catherine (Gormaly) B;. A.B., Fordham U.; M.A. (NBC/RCA fellow), Carnegie Inst. Tech.; Ph.D. (hon.), Carnegie-Mellon U., 1979. Founder, gen. dir. Am. Conservatory Theatre, 1965-86. Appearances with Oreg. Shakespeare Festival, 1950-53, Antioch Shakespeare Festival, 1954, Group 20 Players, 1956, San Diego Shakespeare Festival, 1955, Arena Stage, Washington, 1957-58; in Broadway and on tour Back to Methuselah, 1958, Six Characters in Search of An Author, 1959, Cosi Fan Tutte, 1959, The Inspector General, 1960, Porgy and Bess, 1961, Midsummer Night's Dream, 1963; with off-Broadway, N.Y.C. Center Opera Co. in The Misanthrope, The Lady's Not for Burning, The Country Wife; directing debut with Ivanov, 1958 (Obie award); dir. A Month in the Country, 1956-58, Under Milkwood, 1956-61, Six Characters in Search of An Author, 1963; appeared in The Tempest, Stratford (Conn.) Festival, 1964, Yeoman of the Guard, Stratford, Can.; librettist, dir.: Natalia Petrovna, N.Y.C. Center Opera Co., 1964, Tartuffe for Lincoln Center Repertory Co., 1965. Recipient Tony award, 1979; Fulbright scholar to Eng., 1953-54; Ford Found. Director's grantee, 1959; commn. for Natalia Petrovna, 1964. Home: San Francisco Calif. Died July 30, 1991. †

BALLARD, EDWARD GOODWIN, philosophy educator, author; b. Fairfax, Va., Jan. 3, 1910; s. James W. and Margaret (Lewis) G.; m. Lucy McIver Watson, Nov. 22, 1938; children: Susanne Ballard Dowouis, Lucy Eve Ballard Armentrout Ma, Edward Marshall. B.A., Coll. William and Mary, 1931; diploma, U. Montpelier, France, 1933; M.A., U. Va., 1936, Ph.D., 1946; postgrad., U. Sorbonne, Paris, 1951, Harvard U., 1931-32. Asst. prof. English Va. Mil. Inst., 1939-41; asst. in philosophy U. Va., 1941-42; asst. prof. philosophy Tulane U., 1946-52, assoc. prof., 1952-56, prof., 1956-77, W. R. Irby prof. philosophy, from 1977, emeritus, 1980; vis. prof. Yale U., 1963-64, La. State U. at Baton Rouge, 1969, U. Mo., 1981, U. of South, 1981-82; mem. selection com. Woodrow Wilson fellowship, 1966-69; selection panel Nat. Endowment for Humanities, 1970-74; Bd. dirs. Center Advanced Research in Phenomenology, from 1979. Author: Art and Analysis, 1957, Socratic Ignorance, 1965, Philosophy at the Cross Roads, 1971, Man and Technology: Toward the Measurement of a Culture, 1978, Principles of Interpretation, 1983; Philosophy and the Liberal Arts , 1989; editorial bd. So. Jour. Philosophy, 1963-78, Research in Phenomenology, from 1969, Tulane Studies in Philosophy, 1970-80; cons. editor: Continental Thought series, U. Ohio Press, from 1979, Current Continental Research, Univ. Press Am., from 1980; contbr. articles to philos. jours. Served to comdr. USNR, 1942-46; Res., ret., 1970, PTO. Grantee Tulane U., 1959-60, 68-69. Mem. So. Soc. Philosophy and Psychology (pres. 1967), Am. Philos. Assn., AAAS, Am. Metaphys. Soc., P.E.P, Husserl Cir., Heidegger Cir. Home: El Cerrito Calif. Died Sept. 8, 1989; buried Fairfax, Va.

BALLARD, HAROLD EDWIN, professional hockey executive; b. 1903; m. Dorothy (dec.); 3 children. Former mgr. Sea Fleas amateur hockey team, West Toronto (Ont., Can.) Nationals jr. team; mgr., later pres. Jr. Toronto Marlboros; dir. Maple Leaf Gardens; pres., owner Toronto Maple Leafs., from 1972. Home: Toronto Can. Died Apr. 11, 1990; buried Park Lawn Cemetery, Toronto, Can.

BALLMAN, DONALD KARL, chemical company executive; b. Indpls., Apr. 18, 1910; s. Frank E. and Fern (Armstrong) B.; m. Eliazabeth Margaret Jerome, Nov. 19, 1938; children: Donald Karl, Brenda Katherine. Student, Butler U., 1926-28; AB in Chemsitry, U. Ind., 1931, MS in Chemistry, 1935. Salesman Dow Chem. Co., Midland, Mich., 1935-43, mgr. Dowicide sales, 1943, mgr. tech. svc. and devel., 1943-45, asst. gen. sales mgr., 1945-49, gen. sales mgr., 1949-57, dir. sales, 1957-61, v.p., 1959-68, v.p. charge mktg., purchasing and distbn., 1961-68, sr. v.p., 1968-89, mem. exec. com., 1962-89, mem. fin. com., 1968-89, also dir.; pres. Ventures Investment and Fin. Co. div. Dow, 1969-89; past. bd. dirs. Dorco Packaging Corp., Dow Chem. Can. Ltd., Dow Chem. Fin. Corp. Past mem. Am. Chem. Soc., Comml. Chem. and Devel. Assn., Soc. Chem. Industry (Am. sect.), Union League, Canadian (N.Y.C.). Home: Midland Mich. Died May 31, 1989.

BALLOU, PAUL HOLTON, banker; b. Chester, Vt., Aug. 7, 1897; s. Henry Lincoln and Carrie (Hubbard) B.; m. Grace Fullerton Carpenter, Dec. 25, 1924; children: Carolyn Susan Smith, Paul Carpenter. Grad., Culver Mil. Acad., 1915; student, Amherst Coll., 1915-16, U.S. Mil. Acad., 1918-19; AB, Yale U., 1920. Asst. treas. Chester Savs. Bank, 1934-36, treas., 1936-38; mgr. Chester office Vt. Savs. Bank, 1938-45, pres., 1945-58; chmn. bd., dir. Vt. Nat. Savs. Bank, from 1958. Trustee Meml. Clinic, Chester Acad.; mem. Vt. Legislature, 1931-33. With Am. Field Svc., 1917; 1st lt. U.S. Army, 1942-45. Decorated Croix de Guerre. *

BALMER, THOMAS JAMES, metal products company executive; b. Chgo., Sept. 9, 1913; s. Edwin and Katharine (MacHarg) B.; m. Eleanor Eliza Hamant, Oct. 19, 1935 (dec. Nov. 1976). Grad., Choate Sch., 1931; AB, Harvard U., 1935; postgrad., MIT, 1942-43, NYU, 1946-48. Mem. pub. rels. staff N.Y. Stock Exch., N.Y.C., 1939-57; account exec. Fiscal Info. Svc., N.Y.C., 1957-61; acocunt supr. Dudley-Anderson Yutzy, N.Y.C., 1961-68; corp. sec., dir. pub. rels. MSL Industries Inc., Beverly Hills, Calif., 1968-91; cons. pub. rels. Pacific Am. Industries, Calif. Shopping Ctrs., Inc. Exeter Oil Co. Ltd. Author: Investment Facts About Common Stocks and Cash Dividends, 1947, Do. Electronics Companies Need a New Kind of Public Relations?, 1967. Dir. fund raising Dobbs Ferry (N.Y.) Hosp., 1964. With AUS, 1942-46. Recipient Oscar award Fin. World Nat. Contest, 1970. Mem. Nat. Investor Rels. Inst., Am. Soc. Corp. Sec., New Eng. Soc. City N.Y., Harvard Club (N.Y.C.), Sigma Alpha Epsilon. Home: Santa Monica Calif. Deceased.

BALSLEY, IROL WHITMORE, management educator; b. Venus, Nebr., Aug. 22, 1912; d. Sylvanus Bertrand and Nanna (Carson) Whitmore; m. Howard Lloyd Balsley, Aug. 24, 1947. B.A., Nebr. State Coll., Wayne, 1933; M.S., U. Tenn., 1940; Ed.D., Ind. U., 1952. Tchr. high schs. Osmond and Walthill, Nebr., 1934-37; asst. prof. Ind. U., 1942-49; lectr. U. Utah, 1949-50, Russell Sage Coll., 1953-54; prof. office adminstrn. La. Tech. U., 1954-65, also head dept. office adminstrn., 1963-65; prof. bus. edn. Tex. Tech U., 1965-72, prof. edn., 1972-75; prof. adminstrv. services U. Ark., Little Rock, 1975-80, prof. emeritus, 1980-89; adj. prof. Hardin-Simmons U., Abilene, Tex., 1980-81; coordinator USAF clk.-typist tng. program Pa. State U., 1951, instr., head office tng. sect. TVA, 1941-42; editorial asst. South-Western Pub. Co., 1940-41. Author: (with Wanous) Shorthand Transcription Studies, 1968; (with Robinson) Integrated Secretarial Studies, 1963; (with Wood and Whitmore) Homestyle Baking, 1973; Century 21 Shorthand, Vol. I, 1974, (with Robert Hoskinson) Vol. II, 1974; Self-Paced Learning Activities for Century 21 Shorthand, Vol. I, 1977; High Speed Dictation, 1980, Where On Earth?, 1986. Mem. Nat. Bus. Edn. Assn. (past pres. research found.), Adminstrv. Mgmt. Soc., Nat. Collegiate Assn. Secs. (co-founder, past pres., nat. exec. sec. 1976-81), Pi Lambda Theta, Delta Pi Epsilon (past nat. sec.), Beta Gamma Sigma, Phi Delta Kappa, Pi Omega Pi, Sigma Tau Delta, Alpha Psi Omega, Delta Kappa Gamma. Home: Bradenton Fla. Died Apr. 4, 1989; buried Wayne, Nebr.

BALTER, ROBERT BRANDON, geotechnical engineer; b. N.Y.C., Jan. 30, 1925; s. Louis Ephraim and Ella (Allerhand) B.; m. Barbara Gene Lilienfield, June 19, 1949; children: Terri Lynn Balter Feinblum, Lori Ann Balter Levine, Steven David, Arthur Allen, Edward Gary. Student, Bklyn. Poly. Inst., 1943-44; BCE, Cath. U. Am., 1948; MS, Harvard U., 1949. Jr. constrn. engr. U.S. Govt., Washington, 1948; soils engr. J.E. Greiner Co., Balt., 1949-54, sr. soils engr., 1955-57, chief soils engr., 1958-63; cons. engr., Balt., 1963-65; pres. The Robert B. Balter Co., Owings Mills, Md., 1965-82; instr. soil mechanics and found. engring. Johns Hopkins U., Balt., 1955-56. Contbr. articles to profl. jours. Trustee Har Sinai Congregation, 1969-82, pres., 1976-77; bd. dirs. Har Sinai Sr. Citizens Housing Corp., 1973-82, pres., 1975-82; bd. dirs. Har Sinai West Corp., 1981-82. Recipient award State of Md., 1971, 73, 74, 76, 77. Fellow ASCE, Am. Cons. Engrs. Coun. (Engring. Excellence award 1969, 72); mem. NSPE, ASTM, Internat. Soc. Soil Mechanics and Found. Engrs., Am. Soc. for Technion (bd. dirs. 1972-82), Harvard Club, Md. Yacht Club., Tau Beta Pi. Home: Baltimore Md. Died Dec. 4, 1982; buried Har Sinai Cemetery.

BANCROFT, HARDING FOSTER, newspaper executive; b. N.Y.C., Dec. 29, 1910; s. Francis Sidney and Beatrice F. (Jordan) B.; m. Jane Northrop, July 2, 1936 (dec.); children: Alexander, Mary Jane Bancroft Collins, Harding F., Catherine; m. Edith Merrill, 1986. A.B., Williams Coll., 1933, LL.D., 1981; LL.B., Harvard U., 1936; LL.D., Wilmington Coll., 1968. Bar: N.Y. 1937. Atty. Searle James & Crawford, N.Y.C., 1936-41, OPA, Washington, 1941-43, Lend Lease Adminstrn., Washington and North Africa, 1943; chief div. UN Polit. Affairs, Dept. State, 1945; dir. Office UN Polit. and Security Affairs; U.S. dep. rep. UN Collective Measures Com., with personal rank of minister, 1950-53; legal adviser ILO, Geneva, 1953-56; sec. New York Times Co., 1956-63, exec. v.p., 1963-74, vice-chmn., 1974-76, also dir., 1961-76; mem. U.S. del. to 21st UN Gen. Assembly, with rank of ambassador. Bd. dirs. Greer Children's Community, 1969-78, Ralph Bunche Inst. UN; trustee Williams Coll., 1968-81, Sarah Lawrence Coll., 1960-70; trustee Carnegie Endowment for Internat. Peace, 1964-81, vice-chmn., 1970-81; trustee Carnegie Corp. N.Y., 1966-78, vice-chmn., 1974-78; trustee Clark Art Inst., 1971-87, pres., 1977-87, Found. Center, 1975-79; bd. mgrs. N.Y. Bot. Garden, 1975-86; mem. adv. bd. WNET/13 Ednl. TV; bd. govs. N.Y.C. Center Music and Drama, 1975-77. Served as lt. USNR, 1943-45. Mem. Fgn. Policy Assn. (dir. 1969-77). Club: Century Assn. Home: Boca Grande Fla. Died Feb. 6, 1992.

BANDY, WILLIAM THOMAS, JR., French language educator; b. Nashville, May 11, 1903; s. William Thomas and Margaret (Villines) B.; m. Alice Scudder Burghardt, Nov. 5, 1929 (dec. Mar. 1970); children: Jane B. McWilliams, William Thomas III, Peter Burghardt, Helen Margaret B. Spiegelman, Carol Villines B. Oberdorfer, Cynthia Palmer B. O'Brien; m. Carol D. Poggenburg, Oct. 20, 1970. BA, Vanderbilt U., 1923; postgrad., U. Grenoble, France, 1924, U. Paris, 1925, 26-27; MA, Vanderbilt U., 1926; postgrad., U. Ill., 1927-28, U. Strasbourg, France, 1928; PhD, Peabody Coll. for Tchrs., 1931. Prof. French, chmn. dept. modern langs. Stephens Coll., Columbia, Mo., 1931-36; mem. faculty U. Wis., Madison, 1936-68, prof. French, 1949-68, prof. emeritus, 19668-89, chmn. dept. French and Italian, from 1959, chmn. div. humanities, 1958-61, mem. Inst. for Rsch. in Humanities, 1962-63; disting. prof. French, dir. Ctr. for Baudelaire Studies, Vanderbilt U., Nashville, 1968-73, disting. prof. emeritus, 1973-89. Author: Baudelaire Judged by His Contemporaries, 1933, Baudelaire en 1848, 1946, Baudelaire Devant Ses Contemporains, 1957; editor: Edgar Allan Poe, Seven Tales, 1971, Charles Baudelaire, Edgar Allan Poe: sa vie et ses ouvrages, 1973; compiler: A World-Index of Baudelaire's Poems, 1939. Lt. comdr. USNR, 1942-36, comdr. Res. ret. Decorated chevalier Ordre Arts et Lettres; fellow Am. Field Svc., 1928-30; Fulbright rsch. scholar, 1955-56. Mem. MLA (exec. coun.), AaUP, Am. Assn. Tchrs. French, Soc. for Lit. History France. Home: Nashville Tenn. Died July 6, 1989; buried Wayne, Maine.

BANKS, ROBERT LOUIS, research chemist; b. Piedmont, Mo., Nov. 24, 1921; s. James Arthur and Maude Lelia (McAllister) B.; m. Mildred Kathleen Lambeth, Aug. 30, 1947; children: Susan Lee, Mary Kathleen, Melissa Ann. Student, S.E. Mo. State Coll., 1940-42; BSChemE, U. Mo., Rolla, 1944, BSChemE (hon.), 1976, D. Engring. (hon.), 1988; MS, Okla. State U., 1953. Process engr. Coop. Refinery, Coffeyville, Kans., 1944-45; research chemist Phillips Petroleum Co., Bartlesville, Okla., 1946-66; research assoc. Phillips Petroleum Co., 1967-80, sr. research assoc., 1980-85; cons., from 1985. Patentee crystalline polypropylene, 1983. Recipient Okla. Chemist award, 1974, award Am. Inst. Chemists, 1981, Perkin medalist, 1987. Mem. Am. Chem. Soc. (award in petroleum chemistry 1979, mem. adv. bd. for petroleum research fund 1981-86), N. Am. Catalysis Soc. Methodist. Clubs: Masons, Elks, Hillcrest Country, Sunset Country and Golf. Home: Bartlesville OK Died Jan. 3, 1989; buried Bartlesville, Okla.

BANNER, FRANKLIN COLEMAN, journalism educator; b. Unionville, Mo., Aug. 10, 1895; s. Winfield Scott and Rebecca (Roberts) B. AB, BJ, U. Mo., 1919, AM, 1920; D of Journalism, U. London, 1925. Reporter Kansas City Jour., 1920-22; mem. editorial staff Chgo. Jour., Chgo. Daily News, 1922-24, London Chronicle, 1925; fgn. corr. Am. newspapers, 1925; head dept. journalism Pa. State U., from 1926, prof., then prof. emeritus. Mem. Royal Inst. Journalists, Press Congress of World, Am. Assn. Schs. & Depts.

Journalism, Am. Assn. Tchrs. Journalism, Nat. Com. on Rsch. in Journalism, Sch. Adv. Com. Pa. Newspaper Pubs. Assn., others. *

BANZHAF, CLAYTON HARRIS, retail company executive; b. Buffalo, Dec. 24, 1917; s. Joseph Maxmillian and Elizabeth (Harris) B.; m. Dolores J. Gavins, Dec. 30, 1962; children by previous marriage: Barbara Banzhaf Grimmett, Debra Banzhaf York, William Clay. M.B.A., U. Chgo., 1954. With Sears, Roebuck & Co., 1936-81, corp. asst. treas., 1958-60; sr. asst. treas. Sears, Roebuck & Co., Chgo., 1961-74; treas. Sears, Roebuck & Co., 1975-81, v.p., 1976-81, also dir.; pres., chief exec. officer Sears Roebuck Acceptance Corp., Wilmington, Del., 1963-72; dir. Sears Roebuck Acceptance Corp., 1972-81; former treas. Fleet Maintenance Inc., Lifetime Foam Products, Inc., Sears Fin. Corp., Sears Internat. Fin. Co., Sears Roebuck Internat. Inc., Sears Roebuck Overseas, Inc., Sears Roebuck de P.R. Inc., Terminal Freight Handling Co., Tower Ventures, Inc.; former dir., chmn. audit com. Barclays Am. Corp.; former dir. Banco de Credito Internacional S.A., Homart Devel. Co., Lake Shore Land Assn., Inc., Sears Overseas N.V., Western Forge Corp.; former officer other subs. Mem. com. banking, monetary and fiscal affairs U.S. C. of C., 1969-74; mem. exec. com. Chgo. Area coun. Boy Scouts Am., 1963-68, adv. bd., 1969-81; bd. dirs. Coun. Community Svcs., Chgo., 1975-77, United Way Met. Chgo., 1977-81; trustee Elmira (N.Y.) Coll., 1975-81; mem. com. on allied health evaluation and accreditation AMA, 1978-85; mem. bus. adv. coun. U. Ill., Chgo., 1978-81; mem. adv. bd. Coll. Health Related Professions, U. Fla., Gainesville, 1985-90. Decorated Army Commendation medal. Mem. Fin. Execs. Inst. (pres. Chgo. 1972-73, nat. dir., exec. com. 1975-78, Midwest area v.p. 1977-78), Am. Assembly Collegiate Schs. Bus. (continuing accreditation com.), U. Chgo. Alumni Assn. (dir. 1966-67, v.p. 1968, pres. 1969, alumni council Grad. Sch. Bus. 1969, pres. 1972-75). Republican. Presbyterian. Clubs: Hound Ears, Long boat Key, Sarabay Country, Medinah Country. Home: Blowing Rock N.C. Died Oct. 31, 1990; cremated.

BARBA, PHILIP S(TANLEY), pediatrician; b. Phila., Aug. 25, 1895; s. William P. and Lettia F. (Bishop) B.; m. Martha Webb Purcell, June 19, 1920; children: William Philip, Virginia Parker. BS, Princeton U., 1917; MD, U. Pa., 1923. Diplomate Am. Bd. Pediatrics. Intern Germantown (Pa.) Hosp., 1923-24, dir. dept. pediatrics, 1945-46; chief Svc. Roxborough Meml., Phila., 1939-56; attending pediatrician St. Christophers Hosp., 1948-56; assoc. prof. pediatrics grad. sch. medicine U. Pa., from 1945, assoc. prof. preventive medicine and pediatrics med. sch., from 1956, assoc. dean Sch. Medicine, 1958-65. Vice chmn. nat. com. White House Conf. Children & Youth, 1960. Mem. AMA, Am. Acad. Pediatrics, Phila. Pediatric Soc., Pa. State Med. Soc., Phila. County Med. Soc., Assn. Am. Med. Colls., Am. Pediatric Soc. *

BARBER, RED (WALTER LANIER BARBER), sports broadcaster, writer; b. Miss., 1908; m. Lylah Barber. Former broadcaster U. Fla.; former broadcaster Cin. Reds baseball games Sta. WLW, Cin.; broadcaster Bklyn. Dodgers, 1939-53, N.Y. Yankees, 1954-66; now commentator Morning Edit. Nat. Pub. Radio, Washington. Author: The Broadcasters, 1970, Nineteen Forty-seven: When All Hell Broke Loose in Baseball, 1982, 4 others. Home: Washington D.C. Died Oct. 22, 1992. †

BARDEEN, JOHN, physicist, educator; b. Madison, Wis., May 23, 1908; s. Charles Russell and Althea (Harmer) B.; m. Jane Maxwell, July 18, 1938; children—James Maxwell, William Allen, Elizabeth Ann Bardeen Greytak. BS, U. Wis., 1928, MS, 1929; PhD, Princeton U., 1936; 16 hon. degrees. Geophysicist Gulf Research & Devel. Corp., Pitts., 1930-33; mem. Soc. Fellows Harvard U., 1935-38; asst. prof. physics U. Minn., 1938-41; with Naval Ordnance Lab., Washington, 1941-45; research physicist Bell Telephone Labs., Murray Hill, N.J., 1945-51; prof. physics, elec. engring. U. Ill., Urbana, 1951-75, emeritus, from 1975; mem. Pres.'s Sci. Adv. Com., 1959-62, White Ho. Sc. Coun., 1980's. Co-inventor transistor leading to modern electronics; co-developer (with Leon Cooper and Robert Schrieffer) superductivity theory. Recipient Ballantine medal Franklin Inst., 1952; John Scott medal Phila., 1955; Fritz London award, 1962; Vincent Bendix award, 1964; Nat. Medal Sci., 1966; Morley award, 1968; medal of honor IEEE, 1971; Franklin medal, 1975; co-recipient Nobel prizes in physics, 1956 and 72; Presdl. medal of Freedom, 1977; Lomonosov medal Soviet Acad. Scis., 1987; $3 million faculty position endowed by Sony Corp. established in his honor at U. Ill. Fellow Am. Phys. Soc. (Buckley prize 1954, pres. 1968-69); mem. Am. Acad. Arts and Sci., IEEE (hon.), Am. Philos. Soc., Royal Soc. Gt. Britain (fgn. mem.), Acad. Sci. USSR (fgn. mem.), Indian Nat. Sci. Acad. (fgn.), Japan Acad. (hon.), Pakistan Acad. Sci. (fgn.), Austrian Acad. Sci. (corr.), Hungarian Acad. Sci. (fgn.). Home: Champaign Ill. Died Jan. 30, 1991; buried Forest Hill Cemetery, Madison, Wis.

BARFIELD, THOMAS HARWELL, army officer; b. Lineville, Ala., Jan. 20, 1917; s. Jesse Morton and Janie Isobel (Davis) B.; m. Beri Harrison Young, Aug. 16, 1941; children: Thomas H., Jane Young. Grad., Marion Mil. Inst., 1935; A.B., U. Ala., 1937; M.S., George Washington U., 1962; grad., Nat. War Coll., 1960; L.H.D., Judson Coll., 1980. Commd. 2d lt. U.S. Army, 1938, advanced through grades to maj. gen., 1969; assigned U.S. Forces in S. Pacific, World War II, Gen. Hdqrs. Far East Command in Occupation of Japan; then UN Command in Korea; assigned Army Gen. Staff, 1945-48, 60-62, U.S. Army Air Def. Command, 1952-53, 62-64, 68-71, Joint Chiefs Staff, 1967-68, U.S. Army Air Def. Center, 1953-56, 65-66, 8th U.S. Army, Korea, 1966-67, N. Am. Air Def. Command, 1969-75; pres. Marion Mil. Inst., 1976-83. Decorated Army Commendation medal with oak leaf cluster, Bronze Star, Meritorious Service medal, Legion of Merit with 3 oak leaf clusters, Distinguished Service medal. Mem. Phi Gamma Delta. Home: Marion Ala. Deceased. †

BARGER, HAROLD, educator, economist; b. London, Eng., Apr. 27, 1907; came to U.S., 1939; s. George and Florence E. (Thomas); m. Anne Macdonald Walls, July 8, 1937; m. 2d, Gwyneth Evans Kahn, Dec. 10, 1955. BA, Cambridge (Eng.) U., 1930; PhD, London Sch. Econs., 1937. Lectr. U. Coll., London, 1931-36, 38-39, asst. prof., 1943-47, assoc. prof., 1947-54, prof. econs., 1954-75, emeritus, 1975-89, chmn. dept., 1961-64; staff Nat. Bur. Econ. Rsch., 1940-54. Author: Money, Banking and Public Policy, 1962, The Management of Money, 1964, others. lst lt. OSS, AUS, 1943-45. Past mem. AAUP, Am. Econ. Assn. Home: Chatham N.Y. Died Aug. 9, 1989.

BARGMANN, VALENTINE, mathematics and physics educator; b. Berlin, Apr. 6, 1908; came to U.S., 1937, naturalized, 1943; s. Abram and Rosa (Rosenblatt) B.; m. Sophie Goldberg, July 21, 1941. Student, U. Berlin, 1926-32; PhD, U. Zurich, Switzerland, 1936. Mem. Inst. for Advanced Study, Princeton, N.J., 1937-46; vis. lectr. Princeton U., 1946-47, assoc. prof. math. physics, 1948-57, prof., 1957-89; assoc. prof. U. Pitts., 1948. Mem. Am. Phys. Soc., Am. Math. Soc., Sigma Xi. Home: Princeton N.J. Died July 21, 1989.

BARIL, OFIER L(UDGER), chemistry educator; b. Spencer, Mass., July 21, 1898; s. Arthur J. and Luce C. (David) B.; m. Blanche G. St. Denis, Aug. 27, 1928; children: Pauline, Jeanne, Jeannette, Elain, Olier, Estelle, Madeleine, Paul, Raymond, David. AB, Holy Cross Coll., 1920, AM, 1923; MS, Columbia U., 1927; PhD, Clark U., 1943. Tchr. sci. West Boylston (Mass.) High Sch., 1920-21, Morrisville (Vt.) People's Acad., 1921-22; instr. in chemistry Holy Cross Coll., Worcester, Mass., 1922-27, lectr., 1927-28, asst. prof., 1928-36, prof., 1936-43, dir. rsch., prof. organic chemistry, from 1943; biochemist Fallon Clinic, Worcester, from 1944. Contbr. articles to Jour. Am. Chem. Soc., Jour. Chem. Edn. With U.S. Army, World War I. Mem. Am. Chem. Soc., Am. Assn. Clin. Chemists, Am. Ordnance Assn., Internat. Commn. for Uniform Methods Sugar Analysis. *

BARKAN, ALEXANDER ELIAS, labor union official; b. Bayonne, N.J., Aug. 9, 1909; s. Jacob and Rachel (Perelmen) B.; m. Helen Stickno, May 10, 1942; children: Lois, Carol. PhB, U. Chgo., 1933. With Textile Workers Organizing Com., 1937; organizer Textile Workers Union Am., 1938, sub-regional dir., 1938-42, polit. action dir., 1947-55; vets. dir. CIO community services dir., 1945; exec. dir. N.J. CIO Council, 1946; asst. dir. polit. edn. com. AFL-CIO, Washington, 1955-57, dep. dir. , 1957-63, dir. 1963-81. Served with USNR, 1942-45. Home: Chevy Chase Md. Died Oct. 18, 1990.

BARKE, (JAMES) ALLEN, automobile manufacturing company executive; b. Rhodes Green, Eng., Apr. 16, 1903; s. James Edward and Emma (Livsey) B.; m. Doris Marian Bayne, 1937 (dec. 1952); children: Marian (Mrs. Alan Clegg) David, Harry; m. Marguerite Amy Sutcliffe, 1953; 1 stepchild, Marguerite. Student, Manchester (Eng.) Coll. Tech. With Ford Morot Co., Ltd., 1932-90, mng. dir., 1962-63; mng. dir., chief exec. officer Ford Morot Co., Ltd., London, 1963-90, vice chmn., 1965-90; Gov. London Grad. Sch. Bus. Studies. Past fellow Brit. Inst. Mgmt.; past mem. Soc. Motor Mfrs. and Traders Ltd. (past mem. coun), Royal Automobile Club. Home: Ingatestone Essex England Deceased.

BARKER, GEORGE GRANVILLE, writer; b. Essex, England, Feb. 26, 1913; s. George and Marion Frances (Taaffe) B.; m. Jessica Woodward, Nov. 1933; children: Anthony, Anastasia (twins). Student, Regents Street Poly., London, 1929. Chair English lit. Tohoku U., Japan, 1939; lectr., vis. prof. Oxford Cambridge Univs., U. Wis., 1971-72. Author: 30 Preliminary Poems, 1933, Alanna Autumnal, 1933, Poems, 1935, Calamiterror, 1937, Lament and Triumph, 1940, Janus, 1940, Sacred and Secular Elegies, 1943, Eros in Dogma, 1944, News of the World, 1950, The Dead Seagull, 1950, A Vision of Beasts and Gods, 1954, The True Confession George Barker, 1957, (play) The View from Blind I, 1962, Dreams of a Summer Night, 1966, The Golden Chains, 1968, runes and Rhymes and Tunes and Chimes, 1970, To Aylsham Fair, 1970, When I Get up at Morning, 1970, Essays, 1970, Poems of Places and People, 1970, The Alphabetical Zoo, 1972, In Memory of David Archer, 1973, Dialogues etc., 1976. Arts fellow York U., 1966-67. Mem. soc. Authors of London, Poetry Soc. Oxford U. (elected patron 1953). Home: Norfolk Eng. Died Oct. 27, 1991; buried St. Mary's Ch., Norfolk, Eng.

BARKER, LESLIE PAXTON, physician; b. Elba, Idaho, 1901; s. A.J. and Eliabeth (Stauffer) B.; m. Katherine Buckhout Bonnell, Jan. 28, 1953. MD, Columbia U. Dir. dermatology St. Luke's Hosp., also St. Barnabas Hosp., 1942-67, past cons. dermatologist; past. cons. dermatologist Presbyn. Hosp., Columbia Med. Ctr., both N.C.Y.; clin. prof. dermatology Columbia Coll. Physicians and Surgeons, 1955-67, past spl. lectr. Contbr. articles to med. jours. Past mem. AMA, Am. Dermatol.Soc., N.Y. Dermatol. Soc., N.Y. Acad. Medicine, Soc. Investigative Dermatology, Acad. Dermatology. Home: Pound Ridge N.Y. Died June 3, 1990.

BARKER, W. GARDNER, food company executive; b. Brookline, Mass., May 27, 1913; s. Charles Miller and Lila Brookhouse (Rice) B.; m. Milda Allen, June 20, 1935; children: Sue Brookhouse Barker Gray,, William Gardner Jr., Elizabeth H. Barker Gubersky, Bruce Allen. AB, Harvard U., 1935; postgrad., Stanford U., 1936; MS, MIT, 1937. Various positions to mgr. market exploration Lever Bros. Co., 1937-48, dir. new products, 1848-50; exec. v.p., bd. dirs. Simoniz Co., Chgo., 1950-56; v.p. new products Thomas J. Lipton, Inc., Englewood Cliffs, N.J., 1956-57, exec. v.p., 1957-58, pres., chief exec. officer, 1959-72, chmn. bd., chief exec. officer, 1973-78, chmn. fin. com., 1978, also bd. dirs.; chmn. bd. Thomas J. Lipton, Ltd., Can. Mem. devel. com. MIT Corp. Lt. (j.g.) USNR, 1943-46. Mem. AIM, Grocery Mfrs. Am. (bd. dirs. 1966-69), Am. Mktg. Assn., Consumer Rsch. Inst. (bd. dirs.), Tea Assn. U.S.A. (bd. dirs. 1958-63, pres. 1960-62), Tea Coun. U.S.A. (bd. dirs. from 1961, chmn. 1963-65, 67-69, 71-73, treas. 1969-71, from 1977), Cruising Club Am., N.Y. Yacht Club, Brook Club, Sales Execs. Club, Harvard Club, Country Club Boston, Indian Harbor Yacht Club (Conn.), Pleon Yacht Club, Ea. Yacht Club (Marblehead, Mass.). Episcopalian. Home: Marblehead Mass. Died Nov. 2, 1990; buried Brookline, Ma.

BARLOW, R(EUEL) R(ICHARD), educator, journalist; b. Monticello, Wis., Apr. 28, 1894; s. Joseph Henry and Martha (Wallace) B.; m. Alice Townsend, Sept. 28, 1921 (div. Jan. 1956); children: Richard, Mary Alice Persche, Townsend, Charlotte Matthews; m. Rose Turner Martin, Sept. 4, 1956; 1 adopted son, Leon. Diploma, Wis. Acad., Madison, 1912; AB, U. Wis., 1918; AM, U. Ill., 1929. Reporter Madison Democrat, 1912-16; reporter, news editor La Crosse (Wis.) Leader-Press, 1916; state capitol reporter Wis. State Jour., 1919-20; asst. city editor Mpls. Tribune, 1925-26; mgr. KSTP radio sta., Mpls.-St. Paul, 1926-27; inst. journalism U. Minn., 1920-25; mem. faculty U. Ill., from 1927, prof. journalism, 1937-63, prof. emeritus, from 1963. Author: New Survey of Journalism (with G.F. Mott and others), 1950; also articles. Mem. Ill. Press Assn., Am. Assn. Tchrs. Journalism, Sigma Delta Chi, Kappa Tau Alpha. *

BARNARD, KATHLEEN RAINWATER, business educator; b. Wayne City, Ill., Dec. 28, 1927; d. Roy and Nina (Edmison) Rainwater; BS, So. Ill. U., 1949, MS, 1953; postgrad. Ind. U., 1953; PhD, U. Tex., 1959; m. Donald L. Barnard, Aug. 17, 1947 (div. Mar. 1973); children: Kimberly, Jill. Tchr. pub. high sch., Wayne City, Ill., 1946-51; faculty asst., lectr. Vocat. Tech. Inst., So. Ill. U., Carbondale, 1951-53; lectr. bus. edn. Northwestern U., Chgo., 1953-55; chmn. dept. bus. adminstrn. San Antonio Coll., 1955-60; chmn. dept. bus. edn. DePaul U., Chgo., 1960-62; chmn. dept. bus. Loop Coll. (now Harold Washington Coll.), City Colls. Chgo., 1962-67, prof., 1968—, exec. sec., bd. dirs. credit union, 1975-78; cons., evaluator Ill. Program for Gifted Children, State Demonstrator Center, Oak Park (Ill.) Pub. Schs.; cons. First Nat. Bank Chgo., 1974; ednl. cons. Ency. Brit., 1969. Cons. edn. and tng. div. Continental Ill. Nat. Bank & Trust Co., Chgo., 1967, Victor Corp., from 1965; cons. IBM, Inc., summer 1968. Mem. North Central Bus. Edn. Assn., Nat. Bus. Edn. Assn., Chgo. Assn. Commerce and Industry, Delta Kappa Gamma, Pi Omega Pi, Alpha Delta Pi (sponsor), Sigma Phi (sponsor), Delta Pi Epsilon (pres. Alpha Theta chpt. 1958). Contbg. author: College Typewriting, 1960; Business Correspondence, 1962. Died Nov., 1991. Home: Niles Ill.

BARNES, RUSSELL C., foreign news analyst; b. Huntington, Ind., Aug. 31, 1897; s. James F. and Lucy A. (Stewart) B.; m. Constance Ingalls, Oct. 1, 1927; children: Lucie J. Barnes Seymour, John J. A.B., U. Mich., 1920. Fgn. corr. Detroit News, 1925-31, 41-53, Washington corr., 1931-32; fgn. news columnist, radio commentator Detroit News Sta. WWJ, 1932-41, London corr., 1941, fgn. news analyst, 1953-70, contbr. articles, from 1970; lectr. fgn., domestic politics Oakland U., 1942; dir. OWI (Cairo Bur.), 1943; asst. to Am. ambassador to Egypt, 1943; Am. press officer Cairo and Tehran confs., 1943; dir. psychol. warfare bur. Allied Force Hdqrs., Algiers and Caserta, 1944-45. Recipient exceptional Civilian Service medal War Dept. Mem. Phi

Delta Theta. Home: Birmingham MI Died Jan. 10, 1989; buried Birmingham, Ala.

BARNETT, MARGUERITE ROSS, university president; b. Charlottesville, Va., May 21, 1942; d. Dewey Ross and Mary (Douglass) Barnett; m. Stephen A. Barnett, Dec. 18, 1962 (div.); 1 child, Amy Dubois; m. Walter Eugene King, June 30, 1980. AB in Polit. Sci., Antioch Coll., 1964; MA in Polit. Sci., U. Chgo., 1966, PhD in Polit. Sci., 1972. Lectr. U. Chgo., 1969-70; Asst. prof. Princeton U., N.J., 1970-76; prof., chmn. Howard U., Washington, 1976-80; prof. polit. sci., politics and edn. Tchrs. Coll., Columbia U., N.Y.C., 1980-83; vice chancellor CUNY, 1983-86; chancellor U. Mo., St. Louis, 1986-90; pres. U. Houston, from 1990; bd. dirs. Overseas Devel. Coun., Washington, Monsanto Co., Sallie Mae. Author: The Politics of Cultural Nationalism in South India, 1976. Editor 4 books on edn. and pub. policy. Bd. dirs. Pub. Edn. Assn., N.Y.C., from 1985, Arts and Edn. Coun., Mo. Hist. Soc., Houston Opera Soc., 1991; mem. adv. bd. Houston Symphony, 1991; mem. Civic Progress; exec. bd. Boy Scouts of Am., Symphony Soc.; trustee Mo. Botanical Garden. Recipient John D. Levy award Am. Jewish Congress, 1988, Lamplighter award Pub. Rels. Soc. Am., St. Louis chpt., 1989, Sammy Davis Jr. award; named Outstanding Educator of Yr. St. Louis Sentinel Newspaper, 1989, Woman of Yr. St. Louis Variety Club, 1989. Mem. Am. Polit. Sci. Assn. (mem. exec. council 1977-78), Council on Fgn. Relations. Home: Houston Tex. Died Feb. 26, 1992.

BARNEY, LAWRENCE DAVIS, business executive; b. Milw., Feb. 21, 1906; s. Robert Davis and Anna Vickers (Longhorn) B.; m. Dorrit Astrom, Dec. 28, 1929; children: Joan Elizabeth, Lawrence Davis. AB, U. Wis., 1927. Exec. office auditor Singer Sewing Machine Co., N.Y.C., 1927-30; with Wis. Alumni Rsch. Found., Madison, Wis., 1930-44, bus. mgr., 1934-44; past pres. Hoffmann-LaRoche, Inc., past chmn. bd.; past. bd. dirs. Hoffmann-La Roche, Fidelity Union Trust Co., Union Bag & Paper Corp., Colonial Life Ins. Co. Past mem. Pharm. Mfrs. Assn. (past bd. dirs.), Dairymen;s Country Club (Boulder Junction, Wis.), U., Drug and Chem. (N.Y.C.), Essex (Newark, n.J.), Madison (Wis.), Gold (Montclair, N.J.). Home: Upper Montclair N.J. Died June 25, 1989.

BARNEY, WILLIAM JOSHUA, JR., contracting and construction executive; b. N.Y.C., Aug. 17, 1911; s. William Joshua and Lilian C. (Warner) B.; m. Priscilla S. Payne, Feb. 10, 1940. Grad., Choate Sch., 1929; B.S., Yale U., 1933. Registered profl. engr., N.Y. With W. J. Barney Corp. (gen. contractors), N.Y.C., from 1933, sec., 1948-52, exec. v.p., then pres., 1952-71, chmn. bd., from 1971; pres., trustee W. J. Barney Found., Inc., from 1958. Bd. dirs. Nat. Horse Show Assn. Am., Ltd., 1956-89, emeritus hon. life dir., chmn; dir. U.S. Equestrian Team, Inc., 1956-89, hon life dir.; assisted in establishment Nat. Horse Show Found., 1982; bd. dirs. N.Y. Heart Assn., Inc., 1959-70; trustee Colony Found., from 1962, Allen-Stevenson Sch., 1968-89, dir. emeritus; employer trustee Metal Lather Local 46 Funds, 1952-84. Served from lt. (j.g.) to comdr. USNR, 1940-45. Recipient award of merit Nat. Horse Show Found., 1987. Fellow ASCE; mem. ASPCA (bd. mgrs. 1959-77), Soc. Cin., U.S. Srs. Golf Assn., Soc. Colonial Wars, Am. Horse Shows Assn. (hon. life mem., Walter Devereaux Sportsmanship award 1991), Yale Club, Univ. Club, Madison Square Garden Club, Union Club, Church Club, Country of Fairfield Club, Fairfield Country Hunt Club, Ekwanok Country Club, Meadows Country Club. Home: Southport Conn. Died Mar. 20, 1991; buried Woodlawn Cemetery, Westchester, N.Y.

BARNHART, WILLIAM RUPP, clergyman, religion educator; b. Saegerstown, Pa., Feb. 7, 1903; s. John L. and Emma A. (Rupp) B.; m. Eleanor Welch Lyles, Sept. 1, 1927 (dec. July 1981); children: Eleanor Hoyle, Joanne Sanford. A.B., Johns Hopkins U., 1923; A.M., Columbia U., 1924; student, Union Theol. Sem., 1923-25, 1926-27; D.D., Pacific U., 1938. Student asst. Madison Ave. Presbyn. Ch., N.Y.C., 1926-27; prof. philosophy and religion Pacific U., Oreg., 1927-30; head dept. religion Hood Coll., Frederick, Md., 1930-47; head dept. religion and philosophy Hood Coll., 1947-58; minister Circular Congregational Ch., Charleston, S.C., 1958-68; minister emeritus Circular Congl. Ch., from 1968; exec. sec. Fedn. of Chs., Washington, 1940-41; ordained to ministry Congl. Ch., 1930; mem. Potomoc Synod of Evang. and Ref. Ch., 1930-58; past mem. Edn. and Research of Fed. Council of Churches of Christ in Am.; mem. Inter-Faith com. on Religious Life in Nation's Capital, 1940-42; lectr. religious emphasis weeks at various univs. and colls.; weekly religious broadcaster, 1958-80; mem. Md.-Del. Council Chs., 1942-58, Univ. Christian Mission Team sent out by Fed. Council Chs. of Christ, 1946-49, preaching mission teams; lectr. ministerial confs. Contbr. articles to religious jours. Bd. dirs. Community Chest, Washington, 1940-42; trustee S.C. State Coll., from 1972. Mem. Am. Philos. Assn., Nat. Assn. Bibl. Instrs., Charleston Ministerial Assn. (pres. 1964). Clubs: University (Balt.); Interchurch (Washington) (pres. 1948-49); Rotary (Charleston, S.C.), Charleston Country (Charleston, S.C.). Home: Boston Mass. Died Sept. 3, 1989; buried Greensburg, Pa.

BARON, SALO WITTMAYER, historian, educator; b. Tarnow, Austria, May 26, 1895; came to U.S., 1926; s. Elias and Minna (Wittmayer) B.; m. Jeannette G. Meisel, June 12, 1934; children: Shoshana Baron Tancer, Tobey Baron Gitelle. PhD, U. Vienna, 1917, D. in Polit. Sc., 1922, JD, 1923; ordained Rabbi, Jewish Theol. Sem., Vienna, 1920; DHL (hon.), Hebrew Union Coll., Cin., 1944, Spertus Coll., Chgo., 1975, Jewish Theol. Sem. Am., 1983; LLD (hon.), Dropsie U., 1962; LittD (hon.), Rutgers U., 1963, Columbia U., 1964; golden doctorate Vienna, 1969; PhD (hon.), U. Tel-Aviv, 1970, Hebrew U., Jerusalem, 1975; LHD (hon.), Yeshiva U., 1975, Bard Coll., 1979, SUNY-Stony Brook, 1985, Hobart Coll., 1986. Lectr. history Juedisches Paedagogium, Vienna, 1919-25; vis. lectr. Jewish Inst. Religion, N.Y.C., 1926; prof. history, acting librarian Jewish Inst. Religion, 1927-30, dir. dept. advanced studies, 1928-30; prof., Miller Chair of Jewish history Columbia U., 1930-63, prof. emeritus, from 1963; dir. Ctr. of Israel and Jewish Studies, Columbia U., 1950-68, dir. emeritus, from 1968; Rauschenbusch lectr. Colgate-Rochester Div. Sch., 1944; vis. prof. history Jewish Theol. Sem., 1954-71, Hebrew U., Jerusalem, 1958, Rutgers U., 1964-69; vis. prof. dept. religious studies Brown U., 1966-68; Pres. Conf. Jewish Social Studies, 1941-55, 59-68, hon. pres., 1955-59, from 68; pres. Jewish Cultural Reconstrn., Inc., 1947-80; chmn. commn. survey Nat. Jewish Welfare Bd., 1947-49; chmn. library information Am. Jewish Com.; mem. citizens fed. com. edn. U.S. Dept. Edn., 1947-52; chmn. cultural adv. com. Conf. Jewish Material Claims against Germany, 1953-55; corr. mem. internat. com. for sci. history mankind UNESCO, from 1953. Author: Die Judenfrage auf dem Wiener Kongress, 1920, Die Politische Theorie Ferdinand Lassalle's, 1923, Azariah de Rossi's Attitude to Life, 1927, The Israelitic Population under the Kings (Hebrew), 1933, A Social and Religious History of the Jews, 3 vols, 1937, rev. edit. vols. I-XVIII, 1952-83, Bibliography of Jewish Social Studies, 1938-39, 1941, The Jewish Community, 3 vols, 1942, Modern Nationalism and Religion, 1947, The Jews of the United States, 1790-1840, (with Joseph L. Blau), (3 vols.), 1963, The Russian Jew under Tsars and Soviets, 1964, rev. edit., 1976, paperback edit., 1987, History and Jewish Historians, 1964, Ancient and Medieval Jewish History: Essays, 1972, Steeled by Adversity: Essays and Addresses on American Jewish Life, 1971, The Contemporary Relevance of History, 1986; Editor: Jewish Studies in Memory of G.A. Kohut, 1935, Jewish Social Studies, quar, 1939—, Essays on Maimonides, 1941, (with George S. Wise) Violence and Defense in the Jewish Experience, 1977, (with Isaac E. Barzilay) Jubilee Vol. of American Academy for Jewish Research, 2 vols, 1980; Contbr. articles to various publs. Trustee Jewish Inst. Religion, 1937-55; pres. acad. council Hebrew U., 1940-50; bd. govs. U. Tel-Aviv, from 1968, U. Haifa, from 1971. Decorated knight Order of Merit Republic of Italy, 1972; Akiba award Am. Jewish Com., 1987; Salo Wittmayer Baron professorship in Jewish history, culture and society named in his honor Columbia U., 1979; hon. fellow Oxford Ctr. for Postgrad. Hebrew Studies, 1983, Mus. for Jewish Diaspora, Tel Aviv, 1984. Fellow Am. Acad. Jewish Research (pres. 1940-43, 58-63, 67, 69-79, hon. pres. from 1980), Am. Acad. Arts and Scis.; mem. Am. Jewish Hist. Soc. (pres. 1953-55), Am. Hist. Assn., Soc. Bibl. Lit. Home: New York N.Y. Died Nov. 25, 1989; buried Acacia Cemetery, N.Y.C.

BARR, STRINGFELLOW, author, lecturer; b. Suffolk, Va., Jan. 15, 1897; s. William Alexander and Ida (Stringfellow) B.; m. Gladys Baldwin, Aug. 13, 1921. BA, U. Va., 1916, MA, 1917; postgrad., Oxford U., U. Ghent, Belgium, 1919-21, 22-23; BA, MA, diplome, U. Paris, 1922. Asst. prof. modern European history U. Va., 1924-27, assoc. prof., 1927-30, prof., 1930-37; vis. prof. liberal arts U. Chgo., 1936-37; pres., mem. bd. visitors & gov. St. John's Coll., 1937-46; pres. Found. for World Govt., 1948-58; vis. prof. polit. sci. U. Va., 1951-53; prof. humanities Newark Coll. Rutgers U., 1955-64; adv. editor Va. Quar. Rev., 1926-30, 34-37, editor, 1930-34; adv. editor Britannica edit. Great Books, 1944-46; active in World Govt. orgns. since 1940. Author: Mazzini-Portrait of an Exile, 1935, Pilgrimage of Western Man, 1949, Let's Join the Human Race, 1950, Citizens of the World, 1952, Copydog in India, 1955, The Kitchen Garden Book, 1956, Purley Academic, 1958, The Will of Zeus, 1962, The Three Worlds of Man, 1963; also articles. With U.S. Army, 1917-19. Mem. Am. Soc. Historians, Phi Beta Kappa, Raven Soc. *

BARRETT, ALAN HILDRETH, physics educator; b. Springfield, Mass., June 7, 1927; s. Raymond L. and Sibyl (Jesseman) B.; m. Virginia McCulloch, Sept. 3, 1949; children—Richard Alan, Bonnie Jean. B.S., Purdue U., 1950; M.S., Columbia, 1953; Ph.D. in Physics, 1956. Postdoctoral rsch. fellow U.S. Naval Rsch. Lab., Washington, 1956-57; lectr., rsch. assoc. U. Mich., 1957-61; assoc. prof. MIT, Cambridge, 1961-65, prof. elec. engring., 1965-87, prof. physics, then emeritus prof., from 1987; advisor, cons. NASA, NSF, NIH, Nat. Radio Obs., Nat. Astronomy and Ionosphere Ctr. Mem. editorial bd. Astrophys. Jour., 1971-74. With USN, 1944-46. Co-recipient Count Rumford award Am. Acad. Scis., 1971; Alexander von Humboldt sr. scientist award, 1986; Guggenheim fellow, 1977-78. Mem. Am. Astron. Soc., Internat. Astron. Union, Internat. Sci. Radio Union, Am. Geophys. Union, Am. Acad. Arts and Scis. Home: Center Harbor N.H. Died July 3, 1991; buried at sea.

BARRETT, EDWARD WARE, magazine publisher; b. Birmingham, Ala., July 3, 1910; s. Edward Ware and Lewis Robertson (Butt) B.; m. Mason Daniel, Nov. 25, 1939; children: Margo Mason, Lisa Lewis. Student, U. Dijon, France, summer 1930; AB, Princeton U., 1932; LLD, Bard Coll., 1950. Reporter, editor various news orgns., 1933-42; dir. overseas ops. OWI, 1942-46; editorial dir. Newsweek mag., 1946-50; asst. sec. state for pub. affairs U.S. Dept. State, Washington, 1950-52; exec. v.p. Hill and Knowlton, Inc., 1953-56; dean Columbia U. Grad. Sch. Journalism, N.Y.C., 1956-68; dir. Communications Inst., Acad. Ednl. Devel., 1969-77; pub., editorial chmn. Columbia Journalism Rev., N.Y.C., 1975-82, pub. emeritus, 1982-89; mem. Presdl. Study Commn. on Internat. Radio Broadcasting, 1972-73; juror Nat. Mag. Awards, from 1965, duPont-Columbia Survey and Awards, from 1968; trustee Corrs. Fund, from 1959; bd. dirs. Pub. Affairs Press, Atlantic Coun.; founder Columbia Journalism Rev., 1961. Author: Truth Is Our Weapon, 1953; co-author: Educational Television—Who Should Pay?, 1968; editor: This Is Our Challenge, 1958, Journalists in Action, 1963. Recipient Carr Van Anda award Ohio U., 1967, Mass Media award Am. Jewish Com., 1969, Maria Moors Cabot prize Columbia U., 1969, Kappa Tau Alpha award U. Ill., 1972, award Columbia U. Sch. Journalism Alumni, 1973. Mem. Fgn. Policy Assn. (bd. dirs.), Coun. Fgn. Rels., Century Assn. (N.Y.C.), Met. Club (Washington), Cap and Gown (Princeton), Round Hill Club (Greenwich, Conn.). Home: Greenwich Conn. Died Oct. 23, 1989; interred Christ Ch. Meml. Garden, Greenwich, Conn.

BARRETT, JAMES LEE, screenwriter; b. Charlotte, N.C., Nov. 19, 1929; s. James Hamlin and Anne (Blake) B.; m. Merete Engelstoft, June 1960; children: Jessica, Penelope, Birgitte, Christian, David. Ed., Furman U., Pa. State U., Columbia U., Art Students League. Screenwriter, from 1955. Screenwriter: (motion pictures) D.I. (Marine Corps Combat Corrs. Assn. award), The Greatest Story Ever Told, Bandolero, The Undefeated, Shenandoah, tick...tick...tick, The Cheyenne Social Club, The Green Berets, Something Big, Fools' Parade, Hank, Smokey and the Bandit; (TV films) The Awakening Land (Am. Women in Radio and TV cert. commendation), Belle Starr, Stubby Pringle's Christmas (Humanities nomination), The Day Christ Died, Angel City, Mayflower: The Pilgrim Experience, The Defiant One's, Stagecoach (Award from Nat. Cowboy Hall of Fame and Western Heritage Soc.), Poker Alice, April Morning, Jesse; creator (TV series) Our House, Vengeance, The Quick and The Dead; playwright: Shenandoah (Tony award for best musical book); developed for TV: In The Heat of The Night. Served with USMC, 1950-52. Mem. Writers Guild Am., Dramatists Guild, Acad. Motion Picture Arts and Scis. Home: San Luis Obispo CA Died Oct. 15, 1989; cremated.

BARRNETT, RUSSELL JOFFREE, medical educator; b. Boston, July 27, 1920; s. Thomas Warren and Dora G. (Shopmick) B.; children: Russell J., William T., Elissa. AB, Ind. U., 1943; MD, Yale, 1948. Intern Beth Israel Hosp., Boston, 1948-49; fellow Harvard Med. Sch., Boston, 1949-51, instr., 1951-53, assoc., 1953-55, asst. prof. anatomy, 1955-59; assoc. prof. Yale Med. Sch., New Haven, 1959-62, prof. anatomy, 1962-89, dir. grad. studies, 1967-89, chmn. dept., 1968-89; mem. com. on growth NRC, 1954-56, mem. dir. biology and agr., 1967-89; vis. investigator Rockefeller Inst.; adviser div. biology and medicine AEC, med. edn. and rsch. WHO. Assoc. editor Anat. Record, 1962-67, Jour. Histochemists, 1963-89, Jour. Ultrastructure Rsch., 1965-89, Annales D'Histochemie, 1963-89. Bd. dirs. Am. Child Guidance Found. With AUS, 1943. Past mem. AAAS, Am. Assn. Electron Microscopy (pres. 1973-74), Am. Assn. Anatomy, Histochem. Soc. (pres. 1962), Cell Biology Soc., Biophys. Soc., Sigma Xi. Home: Hamden Conn. Died Aug. 21, 1989.

BARRON, BRYTON, writer, lecturer; b. Doon, Iowa, Dec. 6, 1898; s. Hiram H. and Emma J. Barron (grandparents); A.B., Sioux Falls Coll., 1922; B.Litt. (Rhodes scholar at Pembroke Coll. 1920-23), Oxford (Eng.) U., 1923, diploma in econ. and polit. sci., 1922; m. Ella Rosalie Lillibridge, Dec. 31, 1922 (dec. Jan. 24, 1983); children: Bebe, Roger L.; m. Louisa H. Stanton, Dec. 20, 1983. Editorial writer Daily Argus-Leader, Sioux Falls, S.D., 1923-25; div. chief, bur. edn., editor monthly mag. for tchrs., author lang. manual, Philippines, 1925-28; asst. editor Dept. State, Washington, 1929, chief pub. sect., 1929-40, asst. chief div. research and publs., 1940-44, chief of treaty staff, adv. on treaty affairs, 1944-50, research historian, 1950-56; pub. Crestwood Books, 1962-66, sr. editor, 1966-72; lectr. on fgn. affairs throughout the U.S., 1956—. Founder, treas., gen. mgr. Dept. State Fed. Credit Union, 1935-42; founder, pres. Dept. State Recreation Assn., 1935. Active conservative causes; charter mem. Reagan Presdl. Task Force, 1988, Rep. Senatorial Inner Circle, 1987. Recipient award Am. Acad. Public Affairs Los Angeles, 1964, Liberty award Congress Freedom, 1959; award Young Ams. Against Communism, 1964; Disting. Alumnus award Sioux Falls Coll., 1972. Mem. Acad. Model Aeros. (nat. sec. 1952, Superior Service award

1979), Fla. Modelers Assn. (sec.-treas. 1969-74), Gold Coast Free Flighters (sec. 1976-82). Author: Inside the State Department, 1956; The Untouchable State Department, 1962, rev. as State Department: Blunders or Treason?, 1965; co-author: Dream Becomes a Nightmare: The UN Today, 1964; The Inhumanity of Urban Renewal, 1965; compiler: Trouble Abroad: An Independent Survey of World Affairs, 1965; Heaven on Earth for 60 Years: The Lifelong Romance of Ella Lilbridge and Bryton Barron-Their Adventures, their Writings, their Revelations of Washington Political Intrigues, 1983; editor newsletter for sr. citizens, 1983-85; contbr. articles to mags. and newspapers; co-author (with wife) series of lang. textbooks; played leading role in release of secret Yalta Papers. Barron papers in Library U. Oreg. Deceased. Home: Hialeah Fla.

BARRON, LOUIS, publishing company executive; b. Erie, Pa., June 21, 1919; s. Newman and Sonia (Grefenson) B.; m. Wilma Dinowitzer, Dec. 9, 1941 (div. 1959); children: Geoffrey Warlock, Tovey, Jillian; m. Muriel Winona Townsend, June 22, 1959; 1 child, David Linnell. AB, U. Chgo., 1939; student, Columbia U., 1943-44, NYU, 1945-50. Assoc. editor Bibliography of Am. Lit., N.Y.C., 1944-50; librarian Grolier Info. Service, N.Y.C., 1950-58; exec. editor Worldmark Press, N.Y.C., 1958-64; v.p., sr. editor Praeger Pubs., N.Y.C., 1964-69; v.p., editor-in-chief Universe Books, N.Y.C., 1970-89; editor-in-chief Barnes & Noble Books, N.Y.C., 1989-90. Editor: Worldmark Encyclopedia of the Nations (5 vols.), 1960, 63, Styles in Art (12 vols.), 1971-78; John Heartfield, 1977; Goya, 1979 (Charles Rufus Morey award 1981); How to Grow Science, 1980 (Outstanding Academic Book award 1982). Republican. Home: New York N.Y. Died Aug. 13, 1990; buried Downsville, N.Y.

BARTELL, GERALD AARON, corporate executive, arts advocate; b. Chgo., May 20, 1914; s. Benjamin and Lena (Tartakowsky) Beznor; m. Joyce Meta Jaeger, Nov. 2, 1941; children: Jeffrey Bruce, Denis Paul, Laura Beth, Jane Alice, Thad Edward and Thomas Hunter (twins). Ph.B., U. Wis., 1937, M.A., 1939, postgrad. Law Sch., 1939-40. Radio actor, dir., producer, 1932-47; faculty dept. radio edn. U. Wis., Madison, 1937-47, assoc. prof., 1946; founder Bartell Broadcasting Corp., Milw., 1947; pres. Bartell Broadcasting Corp., 1947-65; chmn., pres., pub. Macfadden-Bartell Corp., N.Y.C., 1962-65, pres., pub., chmn., 1962-65; pub., chmn. Bartell Media Corp., N.Y.C., 1965-68; writer Letters from the Pub. Pagent Mag., 1964-67; writer broadcaster Wis. Arts Reports, 1972-75; founder, chmn. Am. Med. Bldgs., Inc., Milw., 1966-74; founder TeleHaiti, Port-au-Prince, 1959, TeleCuracao, 1960, Tele-Aruba, 1963; former pres. Netherlands Antilles Broadcasting Corp. Producer, performer children's radio programs, records, TV movies. Pres. Classic Theatre, Inc., Madison, Wis., from 1976; producer, performer The Shakespeare Digest; pres. Emerald Realty Co., Milw., from 1965; co-founder Select Entertainment Corp., L.A. (formerly Telstar Corp.), chmn. from 1981; co-founder, dir Country Music TV, L.A., Las Vegas Entertainment Network, L.A.; dir. C.E.L. Inc., N.Y.C. (formerly Corp. for Entertainment and Learning), from 1973, nat. com. Opt-in-Am., 1989-90; chmn., Wis. Found. for Arts, from 1974; former mem. bus. com. for the arts Am. Coun. of Arts; chmn. Albert Schweitzer Found. for Charity and Edn., Zurich, 1966-68; radio TV advisor to Hubert Humphrey, 1964; former bd. dirs. Am. Council Arts, N.Y.C.; founding chmn. Wis. Arts Bd., 1973. Served to lt. (j.g.) USNR, 1942-45. Named to Hall of Fame Wis. Broadcasters' Assn., 1990; Rockefeller fellow NBC, N.Y.C. and Chgo., 1938, recipient State of Wis. Governor's Award (posthumously) 1992. Mem. U. Wis. Alumni Assn. (Disting. Svc. award 1978), U. Wis. Pres. Club (charter mem.), Opt in Am. (nat. com. 1989-90), Phi Kappa Phi. Unitarian. Home: Madison Wis. Died July 27, 1990; buried Forest Hill Cemetery, Madison, Wis.

BARTEMEIER, LEE H(ENRY), psychiatrist; b. Muscatine, Iowa, Sept. 12, 1895; s. John Albert and Katherine (Schaab) B.; m. Elizabeth Haltigan, Nov. 23, 1921; children: Mary Elizabeth Hurley, John Albert, Katharine Schaab Roney. AB, Cath. U. Am., 1914, AM, 1916; MD, Georgetown Med. Coll., 1920. Intern, resident Henry Ford Hosp., Detroit, 1920-24; rsch. student Henry Phipps psychiat. clinic, Johns Hopkins Hosp., 1924-26; vol. asst. instr. neurol. anatomy Johns Hopkins Hosp., 1925-26; rsch. student Harper Hosp. psychiat. clinic, Detroit, 1926-30; instr. mental hygiene dept. nursing Harper Hosp., 1926-33, assoc. staff mem., 1926-47; instr. Chgo. Inst. for Psychoanalysis, 1938-39; dir. profl. staff Haven Sanitarium, Rochester, Mich., 1942-54; assoc. prof. psychiatry Wayne U. Med. Sch., Detroit, 1944-54; cons. in psychiatry USPHS, 1947; mem. vis. staff Henry Ford Hosp., Detroit, 1924-54; lectr. U. Mich., 1947-54; med. dir. The Seton Psychiat. Inst., from 1954; clin. prof. psychiatry U. Md. Trustee Salk Inst. Biol. Studies, from 1962; mem. Md. Bd. Health & Mental Hygiene, from 1961. Fellow ACP, Am. Orthopsychiat. Assn., Am. Psychoanalytic Assn., Internat. Psychoanalytic Assn., Cen. Neuropsychiat. Assn., others. *

BARTH, EARL E., physician; b. Olivet, S.D., May 1, 1901; s. Albert and Matilda (Boegler) B.; m. Ella M. Jensen, Feb. 26, 1927; 1 dau., Barbara B. Myers. AB, North Central Coll., Naperville, Ill., 1922, DSc (hon.), 1968; MD, Northwestern U., 1928. Diplomate Am. Bd. Radiology (trustee, mem. bd. 1958-64). Practice medicine and surgery, from 1928; faculty Northwestern U., from 1931, dir. x-ray dept., from 1936, assoc. prof. radiology, 1948-53, prof., 1953-69, emeritus prof., 1969, chmn. dept. of radiology, 1957-69, acting chmn., 1969-72, cons., from 1972; radiologist Passavant Meml. Hosp., Chgo., from 1936; cons. radiology VA Research Hosp., Commonwealth Edison Co., Peoples Gas, Light and Coke Co., Ill. Bell Telephone Co.; vis. prof. radiology Mayo Clinic, 1960; Am. del. Internat. Congresses Radiology, 1962, 65, 69, 73. Contbr. articles med. jours. Mem. radiation com. NRC-Nat. Acad. Scis.; Treas. 5th Inter-Am. Congress Radiology; del., chmn. U.S. delegations to Internat. Congresses Radiology, Montreal, 1962, Rome, 1965, Tokyo, 1969, Madrid, 1973, Goldmedalist, 1973. Served as comdr. M.C. USNR, World War II. Grubbe gold medalist Chgo. Med. Soc., 1967. Fellow Acad. Internat. Medicine; mem. AMA, Chgo., Ill. med. socs., Inst. Medicine of Chgo., Societa Italiana di Radiologia Medica and Medicina Nucleare (hon. mem.), Am. Roentgen Ray Soc. (past v.p. and chmn. exec. council, pres. 1962-63), Radiol. Soc. N.Am., Am. Coll. Radiology (chmn. bd. of chancellors 1957-60, pres. 1960-61, gold medalist 1962), Chgo. Roentgen Soc. (past pres.), Am. Assn. Ry. Surgeons, Inter-Am. Coll. Radiology, Nipon Radiol. Soc. (hon.), Phi Chi, Alpha Omega Alpha. Presbyterian. Home: Evanston Ill. Died Feb. 11, 1990.

BARTH, ERNEST, chemical company executive; b. Vienna, Austria, Feb. 17, 1926; s. Jacob and Regina (Hecht) B.; m. Rita Spiegel, Dec. 30, 1951; 1 dau., Karen Nina. Pres., Continental Fertilizer Corp., N.Y.C., also v.p. Continental Ore Corp., 1953-72; pres. Agrico Internat., Inc., Tulsa and N.Y.C., 1972-73; pres. Beker Internat. Corp., Greenwich, Conn., also sr. v.p. Beker Industries, 1973-75; v.p. Philipp Bros./Engelhard Minerals & Chem. Corp., N.Y.C., 1975-77; sr. v.p. Beker Industries Corp., Greenwich, 1977-79; pres., dir. Superfos Am., Inc., Greenwich, 1979-85, chmn. bd., chief exec. officer, 1985-86; pres. Superfos Investments Ltd., Greenwich, 1985-86 ; dir. Mineral GMBH, Hamburg, Germany, Minex Corp. subs., Greenwich, 1978-92; dir. affiliated cos.; cons. Chemie Linz AG of Austria, Balfour Maclaine Internat. Group—Wall St. Plaza. Mem. White House Food for Peace Council, 1962; co-chmn. U.S. Indsl. Mission to Korea, 1962. Clubs: Board Room (N.Y.C.); Burning Tree Country, Belle Haven (Greenwich, Conn.); Longboat Key (Sarasota, Fla.). Deceased. Home: Greenwich Conn. †

BARTHELME, DONALD, author; b. Phila., 1931; s. Donald and Helen (Bechtold) B.; m. Marion Knox, May 26, 1978; children: Anne, Katharine. Entertainment reporter, critic Houston Post, from 1955; later dir. Contemporary Arts Mus., Houston; Disting. vis. prof. English CCNY, 1974, 75; Cullen prof. English U. Houston, 1980's. Author 15 books incl.: (novels) Snow White, 1967, Unspeakable Practices, Unatural Acts, 1968, The Dead Father, 1975, Paradise, 1986, The King, 1990) published posthumously); short stories Come Back, Dr. Caligari, 1964, City Life, 1970, Sadness, 1972; stories Guilty Pleasures, 1974, Amateurs, 1976, Great Days, 1979, Sixty Stories, 1981, Overnight to Many Distant Cities, 1983, Forty Stories, 1987; author, illustrator (children's book) The Slightly Irregular Fire Engine (Nat. Book award). With U.S. Army, 1953-54. Recipient Nat. Inst. Arts and Letters award, 1972, Rea award for Short Story, 1988; Guggenheim fellow, 1966; Meml. scholarship for writing students established at U. Houston in his name. Mem. PEN, Authors Guild, Authors League Am., Am. Acad. and Inst. Arts and Letters. Home: New York N.Y. Died July 23, 1989.

BARTHOLOME, PETER WILLIAM, bishop; b. Bellechester, Minn., Apr. 2, 1893; s. Nicholas and Catherine (Jacobs) B. AB, Campion Coll., 1914; student, St. Paul Theol. Sem., 1914-17, Apollinaire U., Rome, 1928-30. Ordained priest Roman Cath. Ch., 1917. Curate St. John's Ch., Rochester, Minn., 1917-19; prof. Latin, Greek, philosophy St. Mary's Coll., Winona, Minn., 1919-28; chaplain Sisters of St. Francis Motherhouse, Rochester, 1930-33; pastor St. John's Ch., Caledonia, Minn., 1933-36; dir. Soc. for Propagation of Faith & Confraternity of Christian Doctrine, Rochester, 1936-39; state chaplain KC, 1936-39; pastor St. John's, Rochester, 1939-42; coadjutor bishop St. Cloud, Minn., 1941-53, bishop, from 1953. Pres. Nat. Cath. Rural Life Conf., 1954-56. Apptd. by Pope Pius XII as Asst. at Pontifical Throne, 1954. *

BARTLETT, GENE EBERT, former divinity school president; b. Elkins, W.Va., Apr. 18, 1910; s. Genus Ebert and Susan Jessie (Lyon) B.; m. Jean Kenyon, June 30, 1937; children: David Lyon, Marion Elizabeth Bartlett Van Arsdell, Randall Kenyon, Stephen James, Sarah Margaret. AB, Denison U., 1931, DD (hon.), 1952; BD, Colgate-Rochester Div. Sch., 1935; LLD (hon.), U. So. Calif., 1962; LHD (hon.), Kenyon Coll., 1968; DD (hon.), Colgate U., 1969. Ordained to ministry Bapt. Ch., 1934. Pastor, Syracuse, N.Y., 1937-42, Columbia, Mo., 1942-47, Evanston, Ill., 1947-53; pastor, 1st Bapt. Ch., L.A., 1953-60; pres. Colgate-Rochester (N.Y.) Div. Sch., 1960-70; pastor 1st Bapt. Ch., Newton Centre, Mass., 1970-80; pres. emeritus Colgate-Rochester, Bexley Hall, Crozer Theol. Sem., 1981-89, pastorin residence, 1983-89; Beecher lectr. Yale U., 1961; speaker Chgo. Sunday Evening Club, from 1959; univ. preacher Rockefeller Chapel, U. Chgo., from 1947; preaching missions to Korea and Japan for USAF, 1954; pres. Am. Bapt. Ch. in U.S.A., 1972-73; mem. bd. edn. Am. Bapt. Conv., 1943-52, mem. gen. coun., from 1959; mem. univ. Christian mission Nat. Coun. Chs., 1942-52. Author: The News in Religion, 1947, The Audacity of Preaching, 1962; also chpt. to book. Bd. dirs. Ch. Fedn. L.A.; trustee Berkeley (Calif.) Bapt. Div. Sch., Stephens Coll., Columbia. Mem. Univ. Club, Kappa Sigma. Home: Rochester N.Y. Died Nov. 3, 1989; buried Medina, N.Y.

BARTLETT, RUHL JACOB, historian, educator; b. Webster, W.Va., Jan. 24, 1897; s. Adolphus J. and Mary Anne (Shroyer) B.; m. Lela May Work, Aug. 30, 1924. AB, Ohio U., 1920; AM, U. Cin., 1923; PhD, Ohio State U., 1927. Tchr. high sch. history Piqua, Ohio, 1920-21, Norwood, Ohio, 1921-23; instr. U. Iowa, 1925-26, Ohio State U., 1927; asst. prof. history Tufts U., 1927-32, prof., head dept. history, 1932-56, dean Grad. Sch., 1938-39, dean Fletcher Sch. Law & Diplomacy, 1944-45, prof. Fletcher Sch., from 1944; taught summer terms La. State U., Ill. State Tchrs. Coll., Hyannis State Tchrs. Coll., U. Wyo., Ohio State U. Author: John C. Fremont and the Republican Party, The League to Enforce Peace, The Record of American Diplomacy, People and the Politics of Latin America, Policy and Power: Two Centuries of American Foreign Policy. With USN, 1918. Mem. Am. Hist. Assn., Miss. Valley Hist. Assn., So. Hist. Assn., others. *

BARTOL, GEORGE E, III, office supplies manufacturing company executive; b. Phila., Apr. 20, 1921; s. George E. and Mary (Rush) B.; m. Mary Farr, June 18, 1943; children: Blair Bartol McInnes, Mary Rush Bartol Wolfzon, Victoria Bartol Vallely, Katherine Bartol Lunt. BA, Princeton U., 1943. With Hunt Mfg. Co., Phila., 1946-83, pres., chief exec. officer, 1957-69, chmn. bd., chief exec. officer, 1969-73, 75-83; exec. dep. sec. commerce Commonwealth of Pa., Harrisburg, 1973-75; bd. dirs. 3d Dist. Fed. Res. Bank. Bd. dirs. Urban Affairs Partnership, World Affairs Coun. Phila., Phila. Hist. Soc., Phila. Acad. Natural Scis., Phila. Met. YMCA; chmn. bd. mgrs. Franklin Inst.; trustee Oldfields Sch., Glencoe, Md., 1966-74; mem. Phila. Internat. Steering Com. Lt. (j.g.) USN, 1943-45. Mem. Writing Instruments Mfrs. Assn. (pres. 1960-62), Mayflower Soc., Racquet Club (Phila.), Princeton Club, Gulph Mills Club, Phila. Club. Home: New York N.Y. Deceased.

BARTON, ALAN RAYMOND, utility executive; b. West Haven, Conn., Feb. 6, 1925; s. Alan Raymond and Edith Beatrice (Muicahy) B.; student Ga. Inst. Tech., 1944; B.Mech. Engring., Tulane U., 1946; B.E.E., Auburn U., 1948; M.B.A., U. Ala., 1979; m. Peggy Finneran, Feb. 11, 1952 (dec. Apr. 1980); children: Alan, Mary Rae, Elizabeth, William. With Ala. Power Co., Birmingham, 1948-80, v.p., 1964-69, sr. v.p., 1969-75, exec. v.p., 1975-80, also dir.; pres. Miss. Power Co., Gulfport, 1980-92, now also chief exec. officer, dir. Served to lt. (j.g.) USNR, 1943-47. Mem. IEEE. Roman Catholic. Deceased. Home: Gulfport Miss. †

BARZMAN, BEN FRANK, screenwriter; b. Toronto, Ont., Can., Oct. 12, 1910; came to U.S., 1926; s. Aaron and Bess Gertrude (Turoffsky) B.; m. Norma Levor; children: Luli, John, Aaron, Daniel, Paul, Marco, Suzanne Genevieve. BA, Reed Coll., 1938. Screenwriter for various cos. including RKO, MGM, 20th Century-Fox, Los Angeles, 1938-49; screenwriter London and Paris, 1949-79. Author: Echo X, 1960 (Sci. Fiction Writer award), (with Norma Barzman) Rich Dreams, 1982; screenwriter of over 30 films. Named Officer in Order of Arts and Letters, Ministry of Culture, Paris, 1985. Mem. Writers Guild of Am. West, Phi Beta Kappa. Home: West Hollywood Calif. Died Dec. 15, 1989. †

BASKERVILLE, CHARLES, artist; b. Raleigh, N.C., Apr. 16, 1896; s. Charles and Mary Boylan (Snow) B. Student, Tome Sch., 1912-15, Cornell U. Coll. Architecture, 1919; student Art Student League, Acad. Julien, Paris. Illustrator for mags. & advertisements, 1921-30, mrual & screen specialist, 1930-34, portrait painter, 1934; then mural and portrait painter, murals in many Am. homes, lounge of S S. America, others. Exhibited 60 portraits AAF heroes Nat. Gallery Art, Washington, 1944; ofcl. artist to paint Air Corps heroes & gens. 1st lt. inf. U.S. Army, World War I; lt. col. U.S. Army Air Corps, 1942-45. Decorated Silver Star, Order Purple Heart with Oak Leaf Cluster, Victory Medal with four bronze battle clasps, Legion of Merit. Mem. Am. Artists Profl. League, Nat. Soc. Mural Painters, others. *

BASSETT, HARRY HOOD, banker; b. Flint, Mich., May 6, 1917; s. Harry Hoxie and Jessie Marie (Hood) B.; m. Florence Schust Knoll, June 22, 1958; children: Harry Hood, George Rodney, Patrick Glenn. B.S., Yale U., 1940. Asst. trust officer First Nat. Bank, Palm Beach, Fla., 1940-42; chmn. bd. 1st Nat. Bank, Palm Beach, Fla., 1965-71; asst. v.p. First Nat. Bank, Miami, 1947-48, v.p., 1948-56, asst. to pres., 1951-62, pres., 1962-66, chmn. bd., 1966-76, chmn. exec. com., 1959-66; chmn. bd. Southeast Banking Corp., Miami, 1967-82;

chmn., exec. com. Southeast Banking Corp., from 1974; bd. dirs. S.E. Banking Corp. Mem. Orange Bowl Com.; chmn. bd. trustees emeritus U. Miami. Served as pilot Civil Coastal Patrol (anti-submarine), 1941-42; 1st lt. USAAF, 1944-46. Decorated Air medal. Episcopalian. Clubs: Links, River (N.Y.C.); Biscayne Bay Yacht (Fla.); Bohemian (San Francisco); Metropolitan (Washington). Home: Miami Fla. Deceased. †

BASYE, PAUL EDMOND, lawyer, educator; b. Nappanee, Ind., Oct. 2, 1901; s. Otto and Carrie C. (Wynekoop) B.; m. Margaret Louise deClercq, June 13, 1931; children: Charles E., John P. AB, U. Mo., 1923; JD, U. Chgo., 1926; LLM, U. Mich., 1943, SJD, 1946; DSc (hon.), U. Mo., 1984. Bar: Mo., 1926, Calif., 1945. Pvt. practice law Kansas City, Mo., 1926-42, San Francisco, 1944-48, Burlingame, Calif., 1948-92; asst. prof. law U. Kansas City, 1938-42; prof. Hastings Coll. Law, U. Calif., San Francisco, 1948-92; prof. law, summer sessions Stanford U., Calif., 1950, U. Tex., 1956, U. So. Calif., Los Angeles, 1963, 65; ptnr. Basye & Golden, San Mateo, Calif., 1984-92. Author: Clearing Land Titles, 1953, 2d edit., 1970; (with Lewis M. Simes) Problems in Probate Law Including a Model Probate Code, 1946; contbr. articles to legal jours. Mem. ABA (chmn. sect. real property, probate and trust law 1965-66), Calif. Bar Assn. (lectr. continuing edn. program), Order of Coif, Phi Beta Kappa. Home: San Mateo Calif. Deceased. †

BATEMAN, FRANK B(RACE), investment banker; b. Grenloch, N.J., Nov. 20, 1897; s. Frederic Harlan and Ellen (Brace) B.; m. Dorothy Hawkins, June 29, 1932; children: Barbara Ellen, Brace John. War diploma, Cornell U., 1919. Sales mgr. Bateman Mfg. Co. and successor cos., 1919-30; dir., v.p., vice chmn. Blair & Co., Inc., N.Y.C., 1930-55; pres., dir. Fla. Growth Co., Fla. Growth Fund, Inc.; mng. ptnr. Frank B. Bateman, Ltd., investment co., Palm Beach, Fla.; bd. dirs. various corps. With U.S. Army, 1918. *

BATES, JOHN LOREN, public utilities executive; b. Beeville, Tex., Dec. 24, 1898; s. Mack Warren and Myra (Wilder) B.; m. Alline Ellison, June 12, 1929. Student, Tex. A&M Coll., 1916-17; LLD, U. Corpus Christi, 1958. With Cen. Power & Light Co., from 1923; mgr. Cen. Power & Light Co., McAllen and Mission, Tex.; distbn. engr., asst. dist. mgr., dist. mgr. Cen. Power & Light Co., San Benito; v.p., divsn. mgr. Cen. Power & Light Co., Victoria, Tex.; v.p. Cen. Power & Light Co., 1923-54, gen. mgr., from 1940, then chmn.; dir. numerous corps. Mem. Navy League U.S., C. of C., Rotary, others. *

BAUER, DALE ROBERT, publisher; b. Evanston, Ill., June 10, 1928; s. Valentine H. and Lutie (Jacobsen) B.; m. Sheila Gregory, Feb. 1955 (div. Aug. 1982); children: Richard Gregory, Courtney Anne; m. Peggy Kent, June 1986. BS in Econs., U. Pa., 1954. Pub. Med. World News, N.Y.C., 1966-72; group pub., v.p. McGraw-Hill, Inc., N.Y.C., 1972-76; pres. Billboard Pub., N.Y.C., 1976-78; pres. Standard Rate & Data Service, Inc., Wilmette, Ill., 1978-85, chmn. bd., 1985-88; group v.p. Macmillan, Inc., N.Y.C., 1981-88; pres. Edgewater Mgmt., Inc., Vero Beach, Fla., from 1989; bd. dirs. ADM Corp., Stamford, Conn. Served to lt. (j.g.) USNR, 1946-52, Korea. Mem. Univ. Club (N.Y.C.), John's Island Club, Quogue Field Club (N.Y.). Republican. Episcopalian. Home: Vero Beach Fla. Deceased. †

BAUER, WALTER E(MIL), university dean; b. Chgo., July 22, 1897; s. Anton Ernst and Anna Teresa (Schwotzer) B.; m. Clara Hedwig Brauer, Feb. 14, 1925 (dec. Mar. 1956); children: Walter Richard, Johanna Emily, Sharon Elizabeth, Susan Marie; m. Della Marie Krentz, Dec. 14, 1957. Student, Concordia Theol. Sem., St. Louis, 1917-21; AM, Columbia U., 1922; student, Harvard U., 1922-23; PhD, Cornell U., 1932. Ordained to ministry Luth. Ch., 1923. Pastor Trinity Luth. Ch., Scarsdale, N.Y., 1923-26; instr. history Valparaiso U., 1926-29, asst. prof. history, 1929-33, assoc. prof., 1933-40, prof., from 1940, head dept. history, from 1946, dean Coll. Arts & Scis., 1946-57, dean faculty, 1946-62, dean emeritus of faculty, from 1962. Author: In Thy Light, 1944, God and Caesar, 1959. Bd. dirs. Valparaiso Pub. Libr. Mem. Am. Soc. Ch. History, NEA, Am. Hist. Soc., Pi Gamma Mu. *

BAUHOF, RUDOLF, accountant; b. Canton, Ohio, Jan. 6, 1902; s. Ralph Addison and Florence (Smith) B.; m. Adelaide Cash, July 7, 1965; children—Barbara Sue (Mrs. James L. Barth), Robert Hamilton. A.B., Mt. Union Coll., 1924. C.P.A., Ohio. Indsl. accountant with two cos. now part L.T.V. Corp., 1924-28; assoc. Ernst & Whinney, CPAs,, Cleve., from 1928; ptnr. Ernst & Whinney, CPAs,, from 1946. Mem. AICPA, Ohio Soc. CPAs, Sigma Nu, Psi Kappa Omega, Beta Alpha Psi. Clubs: Union, Country, Mid-day. Home: Cleveland Ohio Died Feb. 11, 1989; buried Westlawn Cemetery, Canton.

BAUMER, FRANKLIN L., history educator; b. Johnstown, Pa., May 10, 1913; s. Herman E. and Anna (Dibert) B.; m. Margarita Thieler, June 22, 1936 (dec.); children—Constance (dec.), Joanna.; m. Bodil Bruus Fullerton, Mar. 4, 1983. A.B., Yale U., 1934, Ph.D., 1938; student, London (Eng.) U., 1935-36. Prof. history Yale U., New Haven, from 1954, Randolph W. Townsend prof. history, 1963-83, prof. emeritus, 1983, dir. grad. studies in history, 1951-60. Author: The Early Tudor Theory of Kingship, 1940, 2d edit., 1966, Main Currents of Western Thought, 1952, 4th rev. edit., 1978, Religion and the Rise of Scepticism, 1960, 69, Intellectual Movements in Modern European History, 1965—, Modern European Thought, 1977, Spanish edit., 1985; contbr. articles to profl. jours., also Dictionary of the History of Ideas, 1973. Guggenheim fellow, 1945-46; faculty fellow Fund for Advancement Edn., 1953-54. Mem. Am. Hist. Assn., Hist. Sci. Soc. Episcopalian. Home: Hamden Conn. Died Sept. 14, 1990.

BAUMGARTNER, LEONA, physician; b. Chgo., Aug. 18, 1902; d. William J. and Olga (Leisy) B.; m. Nathaniel M. Elias, 1942 (dec. 1964); m. Alexander D. Langmuir, 1970. AB, U. Kans., 1923, DS, 1925; postgrad., Kaiser Wilhelm Inst., Munich, Fed. Republic Germany, 1928-28; PhD, Yale U., 1932, MD, 1934, LLD (hon.), 1970; DSc (hon.), Women's Coll., 1950, NYU, 1954, Russell Sage Coll., 1955, Smith Coll., 1956, Western Coll. Women, 1960, U. Mass., 1963, U. Mich., 1967, McMurray Coll., 1967, N.Y. Med. Coll., 1968, Clark Coll., 1969; LHD (hon.), Keuka Coll., 1963; LLD (hon.), Skidmore Coll., 1959, Oberlin Coll., 1965. Diplomate Am. Bd. Pediatrics, Am. Bd. Preventive Medicine and Pub. Health. Mem. faculty Colby Community High Sch., Kans., 1923-24; mem. faculty Kans. City Jr. Coll., 1925-26, U. Mont., 1926-28; intern, then asst. resident, asst. in pediatrics N.Y. Hosp. and Cornell Med. Coll., 1934-36; lectr. nursing edn. Columbia U., 1939-42; with N.Y.C. Dept. Health, 1937-62, commr. health, 1954-62; exec. dir. N.Y. Found., 1953-54; assoc. chief U.S. Children's Bur., Fed. Security Agy., 1949-50, cons., 1950-56; mem. faculty Med. Coll., Cornell U., 1939-66, mem. pediatrics and pub. health faculty, 1957-66; vis. lectr. maternal and child health Med. Sch. Pub. Health, Harvard U., 1948-62; vis. prof. social medicine Harvard Med. Sch., Boston, 1966-76; asst. adminstr. Office Tech. Coop. and Research, AID, Dept. State, 1962-65; exec. dir. Med. Care and Edn. Found., Inc., Boston, 1968-72; adviser French Ministry Health, 1945, Indian minister health, 1955; mem. exch. mission to USSR, 1958; lectr. for Tokyo Met. Govt., 1961; mem. nat. adv. counc. Peace Corps, 1961-63. Contbr. med. and sci. articles to profl. jours. Bd. dirs. N.Y. Fund for Children; trustee coun. U. Mass., from 1973; trustee New Sch. Social Rsch., N.Y.C., 1966-74, adv. coun., from 1964. Recipient Elizabeth Blackwell award Hobart and William Smith Colls., 1961, Samuel J. Crumbine award Kans. Pub. Health Assn., 1961, Wilbur Lucius Cross medal Grad. Sch. Assn. of Yale U., 1970, Pub. Welfare Gold medal Nat. Acad. Scis., 1977, others; univ. fellow Yale U. 1930-31; Sterling fellow Yale U., 1931-32. Mem. Harvey Soc., History Sci. Soc., Am. Assn. History Medicine, Am. Pub. Health Assn. (pres. 1958-59, Albert Lasker award 1954), Am. Acad. Pediatrics, Am. Pediatric Soc., Child Welfare League Am. (bd. dirs.), Nat. Social Welfare Assembly (v.p.), Nat. Conf. Social Work (exec. com.), Nat. Health Council (pres. 1956), Am. Acad. Arts and Scis., N.Y. Acad. Medicine, Inst. Medicine of Nat. Acad. Sci., Mortar Bd., Phi Beta Kappa, Sigma Xi, Pi Beta Phi, Phi Sigma. Home: Chilmark Mass. Died Jan. 15, 1991; cremated.

BAXTER, JAMES PHINNEY, III, educator; b. Portland, Maine, Feb. 15, 1893; s. James Phinney Jr. and Nelly Furbish (Carpenter) B.; m. Anne Holden Strang, June 21, 1919 (dec. May 1962); children: James Phinney IV, Arthur Brown, Stephen Bartow. AB, Williams Coll., 1914, AM, 1921; AM, Harvard U., 1923, PhD, 1926; LLD, Harvard and Amherst, 1938, U. Me. and Wesleyan U., 1939, Hobart Coll., 1942; Bowdoin Coll., 1944; LittD, Syracuse U., 1945; LHD, Case Inst. of Tech., 1948, Am. Internat. Coll., 1954; LLD, Williams Coll., 1947, Kenyon Coll., 1949, Columbia U., 1954, Brown U., 1956, U. Rochester, 1960; DSc, Union Coll., 1949. With Indsl. Fin. Corp., N.Y.C., 1914-15; instr. history Colo. Coll., 1921-22; Harvard traveling fellow, 1924-25; instr. history Harvard U., 1925-27, asst. prof., 1927-31, assoc. prof., 1931-36, prof., 1936-37; master Adams House, 1931-37; pres. Williams Coll., 1937-61, pres. emeritus, from 1961; ednl. adviser U.S. Mil. Acad.; lectr. Lowell Inst., Naval War Coll., Cambridge U. Author: The Introduction of the Ironclad Warship, 1933, Scientists Against Time, 1946. Mem. bd. overseers Harvard U.; trustee Williams Coll., 1934-37; term trustee MIT, 1956-61. Winner 1947 Pulitzer prize in history. Fellow AAAS, Coun. Fgn. Rels.; mem. Am. Coun. Edn., Am. Hist. Assn., Am. Antiquarian Soc., Am. Soc. Internat. Law, Am. Polit. Sci. Assn., others. *

BAYLOR, HUGH MURRAY, musician; b. What Cheer, Iowa, Apr. 8, 1913; s. John Thomas and Elizabeth (Murray) B.; m. Elisabeth A. Barbou, Sept. 1, 1937; children: Denis A., Michael G., Stephen M. BA, U. Iowa, 1934, MA, 1936, PhD, 1950; diplôme d'exécution, Conservatoire Americain, Fontainebleau, France, 1938; studies with, Robert Casadesus, Marcel Dupre, Hughette Dreyfus, Nadia Boulanger. Asst. U. Iowa, 1934-37; prof. music, chmn. dept. William Penn Coll., Oskaloosa, Iowa, 1937-42; prof. music Knox Coll., Galesburg, Ill., 1942-92; disting. service prof. Knox Coll., 1959-80, prof. emeritus, 1980-92, chmn. music dept., 1969-76. Composer chamber music, songs and comic opera; editor piano music; contbr. articles to profl. jours. Mem. Phi Beta Kappa, Pi Kappa Lambda. Home: Galesburg Ill. Died June 3, 1992. †

BAYS, KARL DEAN, business executive; b. Loyall, Ky., Dec. 23, 1933; s. James K. and Myrtle (Criscillis) B.; m. Billie Joan White, June 4, 1955; children: Robert D., Karla. BS, Eastern Ky. U., 1955, LLD (hon.), 1977; MBA, Ind. U., 1958; DCS (hon.), Union Coll., Ky., 1971. With Am. Hosp. Supply Corp., Evanston, Ill., 1958-85, pres., bd. dirs., 1970, chief exec. officer, 1971-85, chmn. bd., 1974-85; chmn. bd. Baxter Internat., Deerfield, Ill., 1985-87; chmn., chief exec. officer Whitman Corp., Chgo., 1987-89, also bd. dirs.; bd. dirs. Amoco Corp., Delta Air Lines, Inc., Am. Productivity and Quality Ctr. Trustee emeritus Duke U., Northwestern U.; life mem. bd. dirs. Lake Forest Hosp. Served with USMCR, 1955-57. Recipient Trojan MBA Achievement award U. So. Calif., 1972, Horatio Alger award, 1979, Disting. Alumni Service award Ind. U., 1977; named Outstanding Alumnus Eastern Ky. U., 1973, Mktg. Man of Year Sales and Mktg. Execs. Assn. Chgo., 1977, Outstanding Chief Exec. Officer in hosp. and health-care supplies industry, Fin. World, 1981-82, 85, Outstanding Chief Exec. Officer in hosp. supply industry, Wall St. Transcript, 1980, 84. Clubs: Econ., Comml., Mid-Am. (Chgo.); Glen View; Old Elm, Onwentsia. Home: Lake Forest Ill. Died Nov.6, 1989.

BAZIN, GERMAIN RENE MICHEL, writer, lecturer; b. Paris; s. Charles and Laurence (Mounier-Poutht) B.; m. Countess Heller Bielozerkowka, 1946. Student, St. Croix d'Orléans, st. Croix Neuilly; Docteur ès Lettres, Coll. de Pontlevoy, Sorbonne; hon. degreess Lettres, U. Rio de Janeiro (Brazil), Villanova U. Univ. prof., curator paintings and drawings Louvre Mus., 1937-50, chief curator paintings and drawins, 1951-65; dir. restoration paintings Mus. of France, 1965; prof. museology dept. Louvre Sch., 1941, also dir. writing lab., lectr.; past rsch. prof. York U., Toronto, Ont., Can. Author: Mont Saint-Michel, 1932, Fra Angelico, 1941, 48, Crépusule des Images, 1946, Corot, 1942, 51, l'Epoque Impresionniste, 1949, l'Architecture religieuse baroque au Brésil, 1957, Histoire générale de l'Art, 1951, 58, 63, Chefs d'oeuvres au Louvre, 1958, French Impressionists in the Louvre, 1959, Ermitage Écoles èstrangères, 1958, Gallery of Flowers, 1960, Aleijadinho, 1963, The Loom of Art, 1961, The Museum Age, 1967, World Sculpture, 1968, The Baroque Age, 1968, La Peinture d'avant Garde, 1969, others; contbr. articles to French and fgn. mags. Capt., inf., French Army, 1939-44. Decorated officer Légion d'Honneur, commandeur Arts et Lettres (France); Order of Leopold, grand officer Couronne Belge (Belgium); Order of Santiago (Portugal); Order Merit Republic of Italy; officer Cruzeiro do Sul (Brazil), Pole-Star (Sweden), others. Past mem. Latin-Am. Unio, Inter-Allied Cir. Paris, Cercle Union, Also numerous acads. Roman Catholic. Home: Paris France Died May 3, 1990.

BEADLE, GEORGE WELLS, biology educator, academic administrator; b. Wahoo, Nebr., Oct. 22, 1903; s. Chauncey Elmer and Hattie (Albro) B.; m. Marion Cecile Hill, Aug. 22, 1928 (div. 1953); 1 son, David; m. Muriel Barnett, Aug. 12, 1953; 1 stepson, Redmond James Barnett. B.S., U. Nebr., 1926, M.S., 1927, D.Sc., 1949; Ph.D., Cornell U., 1931; M.A., Oxford (Eng.) U., 1958, D.Sc. (hon.), 1959; D.Sc., Yale U., 1947, Northwestern U., 1952, Rutgers U., 1954, Kenyon Coll., 1955, Wesleyan U., 1956, Birmingham U., 1959, Pomona Coll., 1961, Lake Forest Coll., 1962, U. Rochester, 1963, U. Ill., 1963, Brown U., 1964, Kans. State U., 1964, U. Pa., 1964, Wabash Coll., 1966, Syracuse U., 1967, Loyola U., Chgo., 1970, Hanover Coll., 1971, Eureka Coll., 1972, Butler U., 1973, Gustavus Adolphus Coll., 1975, Ind. State U., 1976; LL.D., U. Calif. at Los Angeles, 1962, U. Miami, 1963, Brandeis U., 1963, Johns Hopkins U., 1966, Beloit Coll., 1966, U. Mich., 1969; D.H.L., Jewish Theol. Sem. Am., 1966, DePaul U., 1969, U. Chgo., 1969, Canisius Coll., 1969, Knox Coll., 1969, Carroll Coll., 1971, Roosevelt U., 1971; D. Pub. Service, Ohio No. U., 1970. Teaching asst. Cornell U., 1926-27, experimentalist, 1927-31; NRC fellow Calif. Inst. Tech., 1931-33, instr., 1933-35; guest investigator Institut de Biologie, physico-chimique, Paris, 1935; asst. prof. genetics Harvard U., 1936-37; prof. biology (genetics) Stanford U., 1937-47; prof. biology and chmn. div. biology Calif. Inst. Tech., 1946-60, acting dean faculty, 1960-61; pres., trustee, prof. biology U. Chgo., 1961-68, pres. emeritus, William E. Wrather Distinguished Service prof., hon. trustee, 1969-75, prof. emeritus, 1975; dir. Inst. Biomed. Research, AMA, Chgo., 1968-70; Eastman vis. prof. Oxford U., 1958-59; mem. Pres.'s Sci. Adv. Council, 1960; hon. pres. 12th Internat. Congress Genetics, 1968. Author: (with Alfred H. Sturtevant) An Introduction to Genetics, 1939, Genetics and Modern Biology, 1963, (with Muriel B. Beadle) The Language of Life, 1966 (Edison award best sci. book for youth 1967). Hon. trustee Mus. Sci. and Industry, Chgo.; trustee Calif. Inst. Tech., 1969-75; adv. bd. Robert A. Welch Found., from 1971. Recipient Lasker award Am. Pub. Health Assn., 1950; Dyer award, 1951, Emil C. Hansen prize Denmark, 1953; Albert Einstein Commemorative award in sci., 1958; Nobel Prize in medicine and physiology (with Edward L. Tatum and Joshua Lederberg), 1958; Am. Cancer Soc. nat. award, 1959; Kimber Genetics award NAS, 1960; Priestley Meml. award, 1967; Donald Forsha

Jones medal, 1972; Order St. Olaf. Mem. AAAS (pres. 1955), Nat. Acad. Scis. (council 1969-72), Am. Philos. Soc., Am. Acad. Arts and Scis., Genetics Soc. Am. (pres. 1946), Genetical Soc. Gt. Britain, Indian Soc. Genetics and Plant Breeding, Indian Nat. Sci. Acad. (hon.), Chgo. Hort. Soc. (pres. 1968-71, trustee 1971-76), Royal Soc. London, Danish Royal Acad. Scis., Japan Acad. (hon.), Inst. Lombardo Sci. and Letters (Milan, Italy), Phi Beta Kappa (hon.), Sigma Xi. Home: Pomona CA Died, 1989.

BEALS, JOHN D(AVID), lawyer; b. N.Y.C., Jan. 19, 1896; s. John D. and Mary Helen (Nicholson) B.; m. Anna E. Lohman, Jan. 26, 1924; 1 child, Julia B. Lewis. AB, Columbia U., 1917, LLB, 1921. Bar: N.Y. 1921. Practiced law N.Y.C., from 1921; ptnr. Beals & Nicholson, 1921-53, Towsend & Lewis, from 1958; pres. dir. 1220 Park Av. Corp.; sec., dir. A.W. McDonald Inc.; mem. com. Uptown divsn. Chase Manhattan Bank. Pres. Am. Soc. Prevention Cruelty to Animals, 1948-52. Mem. Assn. Bar City of N.Y., ABA, N.Y. State Bar Assn., N.Y. Co. Lawyers Assn., others. *

BEAN, JACOB, museum curator; b. Stillwater, Minn., Nov. 22, 1923; s. William Bronson and Lurain (Eichten) B. Student, Harvard U., 1941-45. Chargé de mission Cabinet des Dessins Musée du Louvre, Paris, 1957-60; chargé de mission honoraire Musée du Louvre, from 1960; asst. curator charge drawings Met. Mus. Art, 1960-62, assoc. curator, 1962, curator, 1963-92, curator emeritus, from 1992; adj. prof. fine arts NYU, 1967-80. Author: Les Dessins Italiens de la Collection Bonnat, 1960, 100 European Drawings in The Metropolitan Museum of Art, 1964, Italian Drawings in the Art Museum, Princeton University, 1966, Dessins Français du Metropolitan Museum, 1973, 17th Century Italian Drawings in The Metropolitan Museum of Art, 1979, 15th and 16th Century Italian Drawings in The Metropolitan Museum of Art, 1982, 15th-18th Century French Drawings in The Metropolitan Museum of Art, 1986; co-author: Drawings from New York Collections I, The Italian Renaissance, 1965, II, The Seventeenth Century in Italy, 1967, III, The Eighteenth Century in Italy, 1971, Le Dessin à Rome au XVII siècle, 1988, 18th Century Italian Drawings in The Metropolitan Museum of Art, 1990; assoc. editor: Master Drawings mag., 1962-92. Fellow Brit. Acad. (corr.), Athenaeum (London), Turf Club (London). Home: New York N.Y. Deceased. †

BEARD, JAMES FRANKLIN, English language educator; b. Memphis, Feb. 14, 1919; s. James Franklin and Anna (Shipley) B.; m. Eleanor Mary Williams, May 26, 1945; children: Anne S. Greene, Mary W. A.B., Columbia U., 1940, M.A., 1941; Ph.D., Princeton U., 1949. Instr. English Princeton U., 1943-48; instr. Dartmouth Coll., 1948-51, asst. prof., 1951-55; asst. prof. English Clark U., Worcester, Mass., 1955-57, assoc. prof., 1957-61, prof., from 1961, chmn. dept., 1980-84, research prof., from 1987. Editor: The Letters and Journals of James Fenimore Cooper, Vol. I and II, 1960, Vols. III, IV, 1964, Vols. V, VI, 1968; editor-in-chief: the Writings of James Fenimore Cooper, from 1980. Guggenheim fellow, 1952-53, 58-59; Nat. Endowment Humanities sr. fellow, 1967-68; grantee, 1971-72; Am. Antiquarian-NEH fellow, 1979. Mem. Am. Antiquarian Soc., MLA, N.Y. State Hist. Assn., AAUP, Am. Studies Assn., Bibliog. Soc. Am., Soc. Textual Editing, Phi Beta Kappa. Democrat. Home: Worcester Mass. Died Dec. 14, 1989; buried Bristol, Tenn.

BEARD, WILLIAM KELLY, publishing consultant; b. Germantown, Pa., Aug. 11, 1898; s. William K. and Vida (Fleming); m. Florence Wynkoop, Mar. 16, 1929 (dec.); children: Helen, William Kelly III; m. 2d., Emily Mathias. BS, U. Pa., 1919. With The McGraw-Hill Pub. Co., 1924-49, v.p., 1945-49; pres. Assoc. Bus. Publs., 1949; past cons. in field. With O.T.S., U.S. Army, 1918. Mem. S.R., Sons Colonial Wars, U. Club (N.Y.C.), St. Andrews Golf, Fox Meadow Tennis (Scarsdale, N.Y.), Psi Upsilon, Sigma Delta Chi, Alpha Delta Sigma. Home: Scarsdale N.Y. Died Mar. 22, 1990.

BEASLEY, WILLIAM HOWARD, III, holding company executive; b. Dallas, Oct. 1, 1946; s. William Howard, Jr. and Doris Ann (Waddell) B.; m. Jean Childers, June 10, 1972; children: William Howard, IV, Scott Childers, Elizabeth Anne. AB with distinction (Scholar-Athlete award 1966), Duke U., 1968; MBA, U. Tex., Austin, 1969, PhD, 1971. Interviewer disting. execs. Nat. Ednl. TV, Austin, 1969; mem. faculty U. Tex., 1968-71; spl. asst. to sec., dep. sec. Treasury Dept., 1971-73; dir. Republican staff U.S. Senate com. on banking, housing, and urban affairs, 1973-75; spl. asst. to pres. N.W. Industries, Inc., Chgo., 1975-78; vice chmn. bd. Velsicol Chem. Corp., Chgo., 1978-79; pres., chief exec. officer Velsicol Chem. Corp., 1979-81, Beasley Enterprises, from 1979; chmn., chief exec. officer Lone Star Technologies, Dallas, from 1985; bd. dirs. Aon Corp., Centel Corp. Enterprises, Inc., Dallas. Dir. The Acorn Fund; adv. council Coll. Bus. Administrn., U. Tex., Austin; trustee Northwestern U., Evanston, Ill.; mem. N.Y. Council Foreign Relations. Served with USAF, 1968-70. Mem. Young Pres.' Orgn. Republican. Presbyterian. Clubs: Union League (Chgo.); Chicago. Home: Dallas Tex. Died Nov. 1, 1990; buried Dallas.

BEATTY, PATRICIA JEAN, author; b. Portland, Oreg., Aug. 26; d. Walter Marcus and Jessie Pauline (Miller) Robbins; m. Carl G. Uhr, July 31, 1975; 1 child by previous marriage, Ann Alexandra. BA, Reed Coll., 1944. Tchr. English and history Coeur d'Alene (Idaho) High Sch., 1947-50; librarian DuPont Co., Wilmington, Del., 1952-53; mem. library staff Riverside (Calif.) Public Library, 1953-57; tchr. creative writing UCLA, 1968-69, U. Calif., Riverside, 1967-68. Author 52 children's books (11 with Dr. John L. Beatty): The Indian Canoe Maker, 1960, Who Comes to King's Mountain?, 1975, At the Seven Stars, 1965, Campion Towers, 1966, Hail Columbia, 1970, A Long Way to Whiskey Creek, 1971, Red Rock Over the River, 1973, Something to Shout About, 1976, By Crumbs, It's Mine, 1976, I Want My Sunday, Stranger, 1977, Wait for Me, Watch for Me, Eula Bee, 1978, Lacy Makes a Match, 1979, That's One Ornery Orphan, 1980, Lupita Mañana, 1981, Eight Mules From Monterey, 1982, Jonathan Down Under, 1982, Melinda Takes a Hand, 1983, Turn Homeward, Hannalee, 1984, The Coach That Never Came, 1985, Behave Yourself, Bethany Brant, 1986, Charley Skedaddle, 1987 (Scott O'Dell award for Hist. Fiction), Be Ever Hopeful Hannalee, 1988, Sarah and Me and the Lady from the Sea, 1989, (with Phillip Robbins) Eben Tyne, Powdermonkey, 1990, Jayhawker, 1991, Who Comes with Cannons?, 1993, numerous others; also numerous translations. Established the John and Patricia Beatty award through Calif. Libr. Assn. to encourage writing of children's books about culture and heritage of Calif. Recipient 15 awards for books, also award for disting. body of work So. Calif. Coun. Children's Lit., 1988. Mem. AAUW, Soc. Children's Book Writers, The Thursday Group, Zonta Club, Delta Kappa Gamma (hon.). Democrat. Home: Riverside Calif. Died July 9, 1991; cremated.

BEATY, ERNEST ALBERT, foreign language educator; b. Lancaster, S.C., Jan. 19, 1898; s. Robert Thomas and Mary Elizabeth (Davis) B.; m. Margaret Lyon Clark, Mar. 17, 1925; children: Martha Lyon Barton, Mary Davis. AB, Davidson Coll., 1924; MA, U. S.C., 1923; BD, Columbia U., 1924, MA, 1927. Instr. English U. Tenn., 1924-25; instr. Latin Washington Sq. Coll., NYU, 1927-28; mem. faculty Davidson Coll., 1925-27, from 1928, prof. Latin and German, from 1932, prof. Latin, 1934-37, W.R. Grey prof. Latin and German, from 1958; mem. Mecklenburg County (N.C.) Bd. Health, from 1939—; chmn. Mecklenburg County (N.C.) Sanatorium, 1951-53; pres. Mecklenburg County (N.C.) Tb and Health Assn., 1946, Davidson chpt. ARC, 1938-44; mem. social svc. com. Charlotte (N.C.) Meml. Hosp., from 1948. Contbr. articles to profl. jours. Mayor, Davidson, 1940-51, commr., 1953-57; commr. Mecklenburg County, 1951-53; bd. mgrs. Chronic Disease Hosp. Unit of Charlotte-Mecklenburg, Hosp. Authority; chmn. bd. Davidson Relief Soc., from 1953; trustee Charlotte C.C. System, Montreat-Anderson Coll.; bd. dirs. Davidson Heart Assn., Davidson Cancer Soc. Mem. Classical Assn., Am. Panel Arbitrators, Scabbard and Blade, Omicron Delta Kappa, Delta Phi Alpha, Eta Sigma Pi, Sigma Upsilon, Quadwranglers Club (Davidson). Democrat. Presbyterian. *

BEAULAC, WILLARD L., government official; b. Pawtucket, R.I., July 25, 1899; s. Sylvester C. and Lena Eleanor (Jarvis) B.; m. Catherine Hazel Arrott Greene, Feb. 25, 1935; children: Noel J., Joan C., Nancy A., Willard L., Jr. Student, Brown U., 1916-18; B in Fgn Svc., Georgetown U., 1921, LLD (hon.), 1949. Clk. Bur. Internal Revenue, 1921; vice consul Tampico, 1921-23, Puerto Castilla, 1923-24; consul Arica, 1925; sec. Am. Delegation and asst. sec. Plebiscitory Commn. Tacna-Arica Arbitration, 1926; 3d sec. Port-au-Prince, 1927; 2d sec. Managua, 1928-33; 2d sec. San Salvador, 1940, counselor of embassy, 1940-41; counselor gen. Div. of Am. Republics, 1937; 1st sec. Havana, 1933-37; asst. chief Div. of Latin Am. Affairs, 1924, Madrid, 1941-44; amb. to Paraguay, 1944-47, Colombia, 1947-51, Cuba, 1951-53, Chile, 1953-56, Argentina, 1956-60; adviser Am. del., 2d Regional Conf. of Am. States; del. 9th Internat. Conf. Am. States, Bogota; Colombia, 1948; adv. to Am. del. 4th Meeting of Consultation of Ministers of Fgn. Affairs of Am. States, 1951; past. dep. comdt. for fgn. affairs Nat. War Coll. Author: Career Ambasssador, 1951. Home: Fairfax Va. Died Aug. 25, 1990.

BEBOUT, JOHN WILLIAM, lawyer; b. Newark, Ohio, Apr. 10, 1898; s. Edmund and Bessie (Hobbs) B.; m. Vonda F. Eley, Sept. 15, 1924; children: Bonnie Lou Wening, Barbara Ann Farley. AB, Ohio State U., 1921, LB, 1923. Bar: Ohio. Sr. mem. Boxell, Bebout, Torbet & Potter, from 1950; instr. Coll. Law, U. City Toledo, 1926-45; lectr. on fed. estate taxes at bar insts., from 1945; dir., sec. numerous indsl. corps.; exec. sec. Funeral Dirs. Assn. Northwestern Ohio, from 1935. Author: (with J. W. Yager) Ohio Inheritance Tax, 1950; contbr. articles to profl. jours. Active local United Appeal, Luth. Orphans and Old Folks Home. Fellow Am. Bar Found., Ohio Bar Found., Am. Coll. Probate Counsel; mem. ABA (ho. of dels. from 1958), Ohio Bar Assn. (chmn. probate and trust law com. 1940-52, exec. com. 1952-58, coun. dels. 1958-60), Am. Trial Lawyers Assn., Toledo C. of C., Delta Theta Phi, Masons, Toledo Club, Inverness Club (Toledo). Lutheran. *

BECHTEL, STEPHEN DAVISON, engineering company executive; b. Aurora, Ind., Sept. 24, 1900; s. Warren A. and Clara (West) B.; m. Laura Adaline Peart, Sept. 7, 1923 (dec.); children: Stephen Davison, Barbara Bechtel Davies. Student engring., U. Calif., LL.D. (hon.), 1954; LL.D., Loyola U., 1958, Golden Gate U., 1976; D.Eng., U. Pacific, 1966, Washington U., 1976, Carroll Coll., 1983; D.Pub. Service, U. San Francisco, 1982. Registered profl. engr., Calif. Gen. constrn. bus. with father, 1919; with W.A. Bechtel Co., v.p., 1925-36, pres., 1936; 1st v.p., dir. Six Cos., Inc. (builders), Hoover Dam, 1931-36; co-organizer, dir. Bechtel-McCone Corp., 1937-46; during World War II, chmn. Calif. Shipbldg. Corp., Wilmington; dir. Marinship Corp., Sausalito, Calif.; sr. dir. Bechtel Group; pres., dir. Lakeside Corp.; adv. com. Export-Import Bank U.S., 1969-74; mem. dirs. adv. council Morgan Guaranty Trust Co. N.Y.; mem. Bus. Adv. Council, U.S. Dept. Commerce, 1950-60, chmn., 1958-59, mem. bus. council, from 1961. Mem. Pres.'s Adv. Com. on Nat. Hwy. Program, 1954-55; sr. mem. The Conf. Bd.; bd. dirs. emeritus Stanford Research Inst.; trustee Ford Found., 1960-70; chmn. San Francisco Bay Area Council, 1961-63, trustee, from 1946. Served with 20th Engrs., AEF, U.S. Army, World War I. Decorated Order of Cedar (Lebanon), knight Order of St. Sylvester (Holy See), knight comdr. Ct. Honor, officer Am. Soc. Order St. John of Jerusalem; recipient John Fritz gold medal and cert., 1961, Nat. Def. Transp. award, 1960, Achievement award Bldg. Industry Conf. Bd., San Francisco, 1951; Moles award for outstanding achievement in constrn., 1952; Alumni Assn. award, 1951; Alumnus of Yr., U. Calif., 1952; 1st Internat. Achievement award World Trade Club, 1970; 1st Outstanding Alumnus award U. Calif. Bus. Adminstrn. Alumni Assn., 1970; Golden Beaver award for mgmt., 1963; Forbes Mag. award, 1957; named Calif. Industrialist of Yr., Calif. Mus. Sci. and Industry, 1968; Berkeley citation U. Calif. Coll. Engring., 1975; Golden Plate award Am. Acad. Achievement, 1976; Narariya Star of Merit, Govt. Indonesia, 1976; William F. Knowland Meml. award New Oakland Com., 1978; Good Scout award Boy Scouts Am., 1978; Man of Yr. award Brazilian-Am. C. of C., 1981; named to Nat. Bus. Hall Fame, 1976, Internat. Exec. of Yr., Brigham Young U. Sch. Mgmt., 1978, Humanitarian of Yr. Easter Seal Soc. of Alameda County, 1984, Citizen Diplomacy award, Internat. Visitors Ctr., 1986, Alexis de Toqueville award United Way, 1987, Disting. Alumni award Marcus A. Foster Ednl. Inst., 1987. Mem. Am. Petroleum Inst., ASCE, Soc. Naval Architects and Marine Engrs., Cons. Constructors Council Am., World Affairs Council No. Calif., Calif. Inst. Assocs., Moles, Beavers, Beta Theta Pi (Oxford Cup 1987). Republican. Methodist. Clubs: Pacific Union (San Francisco), Commonwealth (San Francisco), Press and Union League (San Francisco), Engineers (San Francisco), Stock Exchange (San Francisco), Bohemian (San Francisco); California (Los Angeles); Claremont Country (Oakland, Calif.); Cypress Point (Monterey Peninsula, Calif.); Links, Sky (N.Y.C.). Lodges: Masons (33 deg.); Shriners. Home: San Francisco Calif. Died Mar. 14, 1989.

BECK, DWIGHT MARION, bible educator, clergyman; b. Adrian, Mich., July 2, 1893; s. Jonas Marion and Hallie Agnes (Clement) B.; m. Mildred Jean Lugg, June 28, 1918; children: Charles, Janice Barton. AB, Syracuse U., 1918; STB, Boston U., 1922, PhD, 1928; student divinity sch., Harvard U., 1922-24. Ordained to ministry Meth. Ch., 1921. Pub. sch. tchr. Mt. Morris, N.Y., 1912-14; tchr., athletic coach Cazenovia (N.Y.) Sem., 1918-19; supply pastor Rockefeller Meml. Meth. Ch., Syracuse, N.Y., 1916-19; min. Congl. Ch., Nahant, Mass., 1919-1924; prof. English bible Mount Union Coll., Alliance, Ohio, 1924-30; prof. bible Syracuse (N.Y.) U., from 1930, chmn. dept. bible and religion, 1933-59, fng. student adviser, from 1964; summer session tchr. Boston U., 1925, 31, 32, 36, Scarritt Coll., 1958; vis. prof. Oberlin Sch. Theology, summer 1960, Colgate U., 1960, Iliff Sch. Theology, summer 1961, Randolph-Macon Woman's Coll., 1962-63; mem. Central (N.Y.) Conf. Meth. Ch. Author: (with E.P. Booth) New Testament Studies, 1942, Through the Gospels to Jesus, 1954, Later New Testament Letters, 1961; assoc. editor Jour. Bible and Religion, 1952-60, acting editor, 1955-56, book editor, 1956-58; contbr. articles to religious jours. Mem. AAUP, Nat. Assn. Biblical Instrs. (treas. 1942-46, pres. 1947-48), Soc. Biblical Lit. and Exegesis, Am. Sch. Oriental Rsch., Phi Beta Kappa, Phi Kappa Phi, Theta Chi Beta, Theta Alpha. *

BECK, ROBERT HOLMES, history and philosophy educator; b. N.Y.C., Nov. 25, 1918. AB, Harvard U., 1939; PhD in History and Philos. Edn., Yale U., 1942. Instr. history and philos. edn. U. Rochester, 1942-43; asst. prof. U. Kansas City, 1946-47; prof. history and philos. edn. U. Minn., Mpls., 1947-91, Regents prof. history and philosophy edn., 1977-89. Author: A Social History of Education, 1965, Change and Harmonization in European Education, 1971, Aeschylus: Playwright Educator, 1975, Beyond Pedagogy, 1980; co-author: Curriculum in the Modern Elementary School, 1953, The Changing Structure of Europe, 1970; contbr. articles to profl. jours. Mem. Philos. Edn. Soc. (pres. 1961), Soc. Profs. Edn. (pres. 1970), Hist. Edn. Soc., Am. Edn. Studies Assn. Home: Minneapolis Minn. Died Dec. 31, 1991; interred in Mpls.

BECK, SIMONE SIMCA, cooking educator, author; b. Bain Freville, Normandy, France, July 7, 1904. Grad., La Varenne Sch., Paris. Chef, tchr. Paris, 1930-37; co-owner, mgr. cooking school, Paris, 1960-70. Author: (with Julia Child) Mastering the Art of French Cooking, Vol. 1, 1961, Vol. II, 1970; Simca's Cuisine, 1972, New Menus from Simca's Cuisine, 1979. Mem. Cercle Gourmettes (Paris). Home: Chateauneuf France Died Dec. 20, 1991. †

BECKER, GEORGE JOSEPH, educator, author; b. Aberdeen, Wash., Apr. 19, 1908; s. George Joseph and Ella (Fox) B.; m. Marion Kelleher, Aug. 25, 1932; children: John, Dennis, Michael. B.A., U. Wash., 1929, M.A., 1930, Ph.D., 1937. Mem. faculty Immaculate Heart Coll., Los Angeles, 1934-39, Los Angeles City Coll., 1939-42; translator War Dept., 1942-45; mem. faculty Swarthmore Coll., 1945-70, chmn. dept. English, 1953-70, Alexander Griswold Cummins prof. English, 1961-70; mem. faculty Western Wash. U., Bellingham, 1970-74, acting chmn. dept. English, 1973; Fulbright lectr. Am. lit. and civilization U. Bordeaux, U. Lille, 1956-57; Fulbright lectr. Am. lit., Pau, summer, 1963, Chmn. selection com. pre-doctoral Fulbright grants to, Gt. Britain, 1958. Author: John Dos Passos, 1974, Shakespeare's Histories, 1977, Realism in Modern Literature, 1980, D.H. Lawrence, 1980, Master European Realists of the Nineteenth Century, 1982, James A. Michener, 1983, Academic Progression, 1990; also articles on Am. novelists of social criticism; translator: Jean-Paul Sartre, Anti-Semite and Jew, 1948; editor, translator: Documents of Modern Literary Realism, 1963, Paris Under Siege, 1870-1871, 1969, Paris and The Arts, 1851-1896, 1971. Fulbright research grantee to Spain, 1963-64. Mem. Phi Beta Kappa. Home: Bellingham Wash. Died Dec. 22, 1989; buried Evergreen-Washelli Cemetery, Seattle.

BECKER, NORMAN OTTO, surgeon; b. Fond du Lac, Wis., Jan. 16, 1918; s. John H. and Ottilie A. (Graf) B.; m. Mildred Murdoch, June 20, 1943; children: Mary Gail, James Murdoch, Julia Brown, Constance Marjorie. B.A., U. Wis., 1940, M.D., 1943. Diplomate Am. Bd. Surgery. Intern, resident, chief resident in surgery Cleve. Met. Hosp., 1943-49; asst. clin. prof. surgery U. Wis.; surgeon Assoc. Physicians, Fond du Lac., Wis., 1949-88. Chmn. bd. dirs., mem. exec. com. U. Wis. Found., from 1983; pres. Citizens Council of U. Wis. Ctr. Served with USNR, 1944-46, PTO. Fellow ACS (bd. govs.); mem. Wis. Med. Soc., Fond du Lac County Med. Soc., AMA, U. Wis. Alumni Assn. (past pres., Disting. Service award 1976), Wis. Surg. Soc. (past pres.). Lutheran. Lodge: Fond du Lac Rotary (past pres., Paul Harris fellow). Home: Fond Du Lac Wis. Deceased. †

BECKERS, WILLIAM KURT, investment banker; b. Elberfeld, Germany, May 2, 1900; came to U.S., 1902, naturalized, 1914; s. William Gerard and Antoinette (Pothen) B.; m. Annadel Kelly, Apr. 20, 1929 (dec. July 1985); children: Antoinette (Mrs. Robert W. Macnamara), Annadel (Mrs. James Timpson). B.A., Yale U., 1924; student, Columbia Grad. Sch. Econs., 1925. With Spencer Trask & Co., N.Y.C., 1925, ptnr., 1929; ptnr. Hornblower & Weeks (merger with Spencer Trask & Co.), Loeb, Rhoads (merged with Hornblower & Weeks); then sr. v.p. Shearson Lehman Bros., E.F. Hutton (merger with previous firms); dir. Mohawk Paper Mills, Inc. Bd. govs. N.Y. Stock Exchange, 1938-42, 44-47, vice chmn. bd., 1947-50. Republican. Episcopalian. Clubs: Univ, Maidstone. Home: East Hampton N.Y. Died Aug. 10, 1989; buried East Hampton, N.Y.

BECKETT, SAMUEL, writer; b. Dublin, Ireland, Apr. 13, 1906; s. William Frank and Mary Roe Beckett; m. Suzanne Dechevaux-Dumesnil. B.A., Trinity Coll., Dublin, 1927, M.A., 1931, D.Litt. (hon.), 1959. Lectr. English Ecole Normale Superieure, Paris, 1928-30; lectr. French Trinity Coll., Dublin, 1930-32. Author: (poems) Whoroscope, 1930, Echo's Bones, 1935, Collected Poems in English and French, 1977; (essay) Proust, 1931; (short stories) More Pricks Than Kicks, 1934, Four Novellas, 1945; (novels) Murphy, 1938, Watt, 1944, Company, 1980; novels in French Molloy, 1951, Malone Dies, 1951, The Unnamable, 1953, How It Is, 1961, Imagination Dead Imagine, 1965, Mercier and Camier, 1945, Company, 1980, Worstward Ho, 1983; plays in French Waiting for Godot, 1952, Endgame, 1956; plays for radio All That Fall, 1956, Embers, 1958, Words and Music, 1959, Cascando, 1962; (plays) Krapp's Last Tape, 1958, Happy Days, 1961, Play, 1963 (Obie award), Breath, 1970, Not I, 1972, Rockaby, 1981, That Time, 1972, Theater 1, Theater 2, 1960; short stories in French Nouvelle et Textes pour Rien, 1950, Film, 1963, Ill Seen Ill Said, 1981; TV play Ghost Trio and...But the Clouds, 1976. Recipient Prix Formentor, 1961; Nobel prize for lit., 1969; Grand Priz National du Théâtre (France), 1975. Mem. Am. Acad. Arts and Scis. (hon.). Home: Paris France Died Dec. 22, 1989; buried Montparnasse Cemetery, Paris.

BEDFORD, CLAY PATRICK, SR., aircraft and electronics industry executive; b. Benjamin, Texas, Aug. 25, 1903; m. Catherine Ann Bermingham; children—Clay P. II, Peter, Ann. Grad., Rensselaer Poly. Inst., 1924, D.Engring. (hon.), 1971. With Kaiser (and affiliates in heavy constrn., shipbldg., automobiles, aircraft), 1925-76; pres. Kaiser Aerospace & Electronics Corp., until 1976; exec. v.p. Kaiser-Frazer Corp.; Served as asst. to dir. fed. def. moblzn., 1951-52, asst. to sec. of def., 1952, Washington. Hon. trustee Rensselaer Poly. Inst.; trustee emeritus St. Mary's Coll., Moraga, Calif., Ednl. Facilities Lab., N.Y.C., Am. Grad. Sch. Internat. Mgmt., Glendale, Ariz., Calif. Coll. Arts and Crafts, Oakland, Calif. Mem. Civil Engrs. Soc., Alpha Tau Omega. Clubs: Paradise Valley Country, Claremont Country; Royal and Ancient Golf (St. Andrews, Scotland). Home: Paradise Valley Ariz. Died Oct. 26, 1991; buried Oakland, Calif.

BEEBE, GEORGE HOLLIS, newspaper editor; b. Pittsfield, Mass., Mar. 1, 1910; s. George Hatch and Lila (Brainard) B.; m. Helen Plato Lewis, Aug. 14, 1938. BS, Boston U., 1932. With Billings (Mont.) Gazette, 1933-43; joined Miami (Fla.) Herald, 1944, mng. editor, 1951-66, sr. mng. editor, 1966-72, assoc. pub., 1972. Mem. Inter-Am. Press Assn. (chmn. exec. com. 1969-77), Am. Assn. Sunday and Feature Editors (pres. 1950), AP Mng. Editors Assn. (bd. dirs. 1958-64, pres. 1965), Am. Soc. Newspaper Editors (a founder, chmn., exec. dir. world press freedom com. from 1976). Home: Miami Shores Fla. Died Apr. 26, 1990; Miami, Fla.

BEEBE, ROBERT PARK, career officer, yacht designer; b. Fort McKinley, P.I., Nov. 21, 1909; s. Royden Eugene and Sara Reid (Park) B.; m. Lucy Maude Ord, Oct. 21, 1933 (dec. Dec. 1960); 1 dau., Lucy Cresap Ord; m. Linford B. Donovan, July 6th, 1963. B.S., U.S. Naval Acad., 1931; M.A., Boston U., 1957; grad., Naval War Coll., 1958. Commd. ensign U.S. Navy, 1931, advanced through grades to capt., 1950; comdr. U.S.S. Sitkoh Bay, 1953, Bombing Squadron 12, 1942; assigned Office Naval Intelligence, 1952; dept. chief staff, J-2 staff comdr. in chief Alaska, 1954-56; chmn. naval warfare Naval War Coll., 1957-58, head advanced study group, 1957; dir. Gen. Line and Naval Sci. Sch., U.S. Naval Postgrad. Sch., 1958-61; designer yachts. Author: Voyaging under Power, 1975; Contbr. articles on yachts and yacht design, also politico-mil. affairs. Mem. U.S. Naval Inst. Club: N.Y. Yacht. Home: Carmel Calif. Died Aug. 19, 1988; Military burial San Diego, Calif.

BEECH, KEYES, journalist; b. Pulaski, Tenn., Aug. 13, 1913; s. Walter William and Leona (Cardin) B.; m. Linda Mangelsdorf, June 15, 1951 (div. Feb. 1969); children: William Keyes, Jr., Barnaby C., Walter; m. Yuko Horiguchi, July 11, 1973; 1 child, Hannah Keyes. Student pub. schs., St. Petersburg, Fla. Copyboy, reporter Evening Independent, St. Petersburg, 1930-37; reporter Akron (Ohio) Beacon Jour., 1937-43, Honolulu Star-Bull., 1945-47; fgn. corr. Chgo. Daily News, Tokyo, Hong Kong, 1947-77; bur. chief Los Angeles Times, Bangkok, Thailand, 1979-82; free-lance writer Bethesda, Md., from 1982. Author: (with others) The U.S. Marines on Iwo Jima, (with others) Uncommon Valor, Tokyo and Points East, 1954, Not Without the Americans, 1971. Served as sgt. USMC, 1943-45, PTO. Recipient Pulitzer Prize, 1950, Sigma Delta Chi award, 1950; Nieman fellow Harvard U., 1952-53. Clubs: Fgn. Corr. (Tokyo and Bangkok); Cosmos (Washington). Home: Bethesda Md. Died Feb. 15, 1990.

BEERS, FRANKLIN ARTHUR See CRONQUIST, ARTHUR JOHN

BEERS, WILLIAM O., food company executive; b. Lena, Ill., May 26, 1914; s. Ernest and Rosa (Binz) B.; m. Mary Elizabeth Holmes (dec.); m. Frances Lemaux Miller, Feb. 17, 1954; children: Marila Beers Beatty, Barbara Ann Beers Guzzardo, Mary Elizabeth Beers Sumner, Richard W., Duncan R. Miller. With Kraft, Inc., 1937-79, dir., 1965-85, pres., 1968-73, chmn. bd., chief exec. officer, 1972-79; pres. Kraft Foods, 1965-68. Past pres. Wis. Alumni. Research Found.; mem. U. Wis. Found. Mem. Bus. Council (hon.). Clubs: Chicago, Old Elm (Chgo.). Home: Scottsdale Ariz. Died Apr. 19, 1992.

BEETZ, JEAN, lawyer, Canadian supreme court justice; b. Montreal, Que., Mar. 27, 1927; s. Jean and Jeanne (Cousineau) B. B.A., U. Montreal, 1947, LL.L., 1950, LL.D. (hon.), 1977; B.A., Honor Sch. Jurisprudence, Oxford (Eng.) U., 1953, M.A., 1958; LL.D. (hon.), U. Ottawa, 1975, York U., 1983, U. Sherbrooke, 1987; D.C.L. (hon.), Windsor U., 1978. Bar: Called to Que. bar 1950. Practiced in Montreal, 1950-51; mem. faculty U. Montreal Faculty Law, 1953-73, prof. Constl. law, 1966-73, dean, 1968-70; spl. counsel on constl. matters to prime minister Can., 1968-71; justice Que. Ct. Appeals, 1973-74; puisne judge Supreme Ct. Can., 1974-88. Contbr. to legal publns. Rhodes scholar, 1951; hon. fellow Pembroke Coll., Oxford U.; companion Order Can. Fellow Royal Soc. Can. Home: Montreal Can. Deceased. †

BEG, MIRZA ABDUL BAQI, theoretical physicist; b. Etawah, India, Sept. 20, 1934; s. Mirza Abdul Hai and Sarah (Khan) B.; m. Nancie Stager Kress, Nov. 7, 1958. B.Sc. with honours; D.J.S., Govt. Sci. Coll., Karachi, Pakistan, 1951; M.Sc., Karachi U., 1954; Ph.D., U. Pitts., 1958. Research fellow U. Birmingham, Eng., 1958-60; research asso. Brookhaven Nat. Lab., 1960-62, cons., from 1965, mem. high energy adv. com., 1975-78; mem. Inst. Advanced Study, Princeton, 1962-64; mem. faculty Rockefeller U., 1964-90, prof. physics, 1968-90; vis. positions at U. Calif.-Berkeley, Argonne Nat. Lab., Niels Bohr Inst., U. Wash., Scuola Normale Superiore, Pisa, Italy, Stanford U., UCLA, Centro de Investigacion del Instituto Politecnico Nacional, Mexico; sr. vis. scientist European Ctr. for Nuclear Research, Geneva, Switzerland, 1972; trustee Aspen Ctr. Physics, 1981-87, mem. adv. bd., from 1987. Editor Comments on Nuclear Particle Physics, 1984-90; contbr. articles to profl. jours. Fellow Am. Phys. Soc., N.Y. Acad. Scis. Home: New York N.Y. Died Jan. 30, 1990; buried Aspen, Colo.

BEGEMAN, MYRON LOUIS, university educator; b. Corydon, Iowa, Sept. 9, 1893; s. Louis and Magdelene (Thuman) R.; m. Hazel Lucile Flagler, July 15, 1919; children: Robert Louis, Jean Lucile. Student, Iowa State Tchrs. Coll., 1909-12; BME, AB, U. Mich., 1915, MS, 1922. Registered profl. engr., Tex. Apprentice in machine shops Studebaker Corp., Detroit, 1915-16; asst. supt. Ransom & Randolph Co., Toledo, 1917, Wagner Mfg. Co., Cedar Falls, Iowa, 1919-21; instr. U. Mich., 1921-23, asst. prof. mech. engring., 1923-24; chief mech. engr. Carey & Esselstyn, Detroit, 1924-25, Miss. Glass Co., St. Louis, 1925-32; assoc. prof. mech. engring. U. Tex., 1932-38, prof., from 1938, chmn. dept., 1947-49, 53-57; rsch. engr. Def. Rsch. Lab., from 1946. Author: Manufacturing Processes, 1942, rev., 1947, 52, 57, 63; cons. editor Production Handbook, 1946, 58; contbr. articles to profl. jours. lt. col. U.S. Army, WWI, 1942-44. Fellow AAAS, ASME; mem. NSPE, Am. Soc. for Metals, Am. Soc. Tool and Mfg. Engrs. (nat. edn. award 1960), Internat. Inst. Welding (Am. coun.), Am. Soc. Engring. Edn. (chmn. indsl. engr. div. 1948-49), Tex. Acad. Sci., Am. Welding Soc. (ednl. com. from 1948, resistence welding com. from 1960), Phi Kappa Phi, Tau Beta Pi, Pi Tau Sigma, Sigma Xi, Phi Mu Alpha, Univ. Club, Rotary, Mason. Presbyterian. *

BEGIN, MENACHEM, Israeli prime minister; b. Brest-Litovsk, Russia, Aug. 16, 1913; s. Zeev-Dov and Hassia Begin; m. Aliza Arnold; 3 children. MJ, U. Warsaw. Head Betar Zionist Youth Movement, Poland, from 1939; served with Polish Army, arrested by Russians, 1940, held in concentration camp in Siberia, 1940-41, released under Stalin-Sikorski agreement and joined Polish Army in USSR, discharged upon arrival in Palestine (now Israel), 1942, led freedom movement against Brit. rule in Palestine as comdr.-in-chief of Irgun Zvai Leumi in Israel, 1942; co-founder Herut (Freedom) Movement in Israel, 1948, chmn.; mem. Knesset, from 1948; minister without portfolio Govt. of Israel, 1967-70, prime minister, 1977-83, minister of def., 1980-81. Author: The Revolt: Personal Memories of the Commander of Irgun Zvei Leumi, 1949, The White Nights, 1957, 77, In the Underground, 1978. Joint chmn. Likud (Unity) Party, 1973-84. Recipient Nobel Peace Prize, 1978. Home: Jerusalem Israel Died Mar. 9, 1992.

BEHRENDS, RALPH EUGENE, physicist, educator; b. Chgo., May 20, 1926; s. Oluf and Marie-Thérèse (Ichtertz) B.; B.S., U.S. Naval Acad., 1947; Ph.D., UCLA, 1956; m. Ana L. Duran, June 29, 1954 (div.); 1 son, Jon Carlo; m. 2d, Marlene I. Bowman, Oct. 7, 1961 (div.); 1 dau., Kendra Ralene. Instr., U. Calif. at Los Angeles, 1956-57; asst. physicist Brookhaven Nat. Lab., 1957-59; NSF fellow Inst. for Advanced Study, Princeton U., N.J., 1959-60; research asso. U. Pa., Phila., 1960-61; asst. prof. physics Belfer Grad. Sch. Sci. Yeshiva U., N.Y.C., 1961-62, asso. prof., 1962-66, prof., 1966-78, prof. physics, N.Y.C., 1978-86, chmn. dept., 1982-86. Served as ensign USN, 1947-50. NSF research grantee, 1962-70. Mem. Am. Phys. Soc. Democrat. Contbr. articles on theory elementary particles to tech. jours., books. Died May 29, 1990. Home: New York N.Y.

BEISE, S. CLARK, banker; b. Windom, Minn., Oct. 13, 1898; s. Henry C. and Blanche (Johnson) B.; m. Virginia Carter, Jan. 27, 1934; children: Sally Ann, Carter Clark. B.S., U. Minn., 1923; LL.D. (hon.), St. Mary's Coll. of Calif., 1960. Clk. Mpls. Trust Co., 1922-24; nat. bank examiner Office Comptroller of Currency, Washington, 1924-27, 33-36; trust officer Peoples Nat. Bank, Jackson, Mich., 1927-30, Nat. Bank of Jackson, 1930-33; with Bank of Am. Nat. Trust and Savs. Assn., San Francisco, 1936-63, sr. v.p., 1951-54, pres., 1954-63, chmn. exec. com., 1963-69, also hon. dir.; mem. Bus. Council, Washington, 1959-86; chmn. San Francisco Bay Area Council, 1963-65. Mem. adv. coun. San Francisco Planning and Urban Renewal Assn., 1968-75; hon. chmn., hon. life mem. Golden Gate chpt. ARC; trustee Com. for Econ. Devel., 1954-71, hon. trustee; mem. coun. Stanford Rsch. Inst. Served with U.S. Army, World War I. Decorated Order of Merit (Italy); recipient Outstanding Achievement award U. Minn., 1955, Econ. Statesmanship award Seattle U., 1957; named One of Fifty Foremost Businessmen of Am. Forbes Mag., 1957, Calif. Industrialist of Yr. Calif. Mus. Sci. and Industry, 1963. Home: Hillsborough Calif. Died Oct. 21, 1989; buried Cypress Lawn Cemetery, Colma, Calif.

BEITTEL, ADAM DANIEL, clergyman; b. Lancaster, Pa., Dec. 19, 1898; s. William Henry and Jennie Ann

(Chesser) B.; m. Ruth Stoner Fox, Aug. 22, 1925; children: Daniel Charles, William Fox. AB, Findlay (Ohio) Coll., 1922, LLD, 1963; AM, Oberlin Coll., 1924; BD, U. Chgo., 1925, PhD, 1929; LLD, Findley Coll., 1963, Beloit Coll., 1964. Min. Community Ch., Columbus, Mont., 1925-27; prof. religion Earlham Coll., 1929-32; min. Collegeside Ch., Nashville, 1932-35; prof. sociology Guilford Coll., 1936-45, dean, 1937-45; pres. Talladega Coll., 1945-52; dean chapel, prof. religion Beloit Coll., 1953-60; pres. Tougaloo Coll., 1960-64, pres. emeritus, from 1964; min. United Ch. of Christ, from 1964; program dir. Miss. program Am. Friends Svc. Com.; bd. mem. So. Regional Coun., Miss. Coun. Human Rels.; mem. Nat. Citizens Com. Community Rels.; sec. Miss. adv. com. U.S. Commn. Civil Rights. *

BELCHER, JOHN CHESLOW, sociologist, educator; b. Tulsa, Feb. 26, 1920; s. John Cheslow and Blanche (Renfrow) B.; m. Patricia Lucile Yates, Nov. 25, 1948; children: Meriwyn, John Christopher, Laura McGee, Matthew, Glenda Strickland. B.S., Okla. State U., 1943; M.A., La. State U., 1945; Ph.D., U. Wis., 1950. Asst. prof. sociology U. Miss., Oxford, 1947-49; assoc. prof. rural sociology Okla. State U., Stillwater, 1949-55; prof. sociology U. Ga., Athens, 1955-84, prof. emeritus, from 1984; columnist Courier-Herals, Dublin, Ga., from 1985; vis. prof. sociology U. P.R., Rio Piedras, 1969; Fulbright prof. demography Universidad Nacional Pedro Henriquez Urena, Dominican Republic, 1971-72; Cons. in rural sociology UN Devel. Program, Dominican Republic, 1969; cons. div. physician manpower NIH, 1971-72, Universidad de la Republica, Montevideo, Uruguay, 1978, 79; dir. profl. seminars for ex-grantees U.S. Dept. State, Dominican Republic, 1973, 74, 75, 76, 77, 78, 79, Guatemala, 1978, 79; Fulbright Rsch. prof. Inst. Nacional de Estatica, Dominican Republic, 1979-80; cons. CII-Viviendas, Dominican Republic, from 1985. Author: (with King) 1950, (with Morland, Balswick and Rubin) Social Problems in the United States, 1975; also chpts. in books, articles in profl. jours. Recipient Michael award U. Ga., 1967; Tribute of Appreciation Internat. Communication Agy., 1980; Research grantee Health Info. Found., 1959; Research grantee U.S. Dept. Agr., 1956-58; Research grantee So. Appalachian Studies, 1959-60; Research grantee USPHS, 1964-67; Research grantee Agrl. Devel. Council, 1966-68; Research grantee Nat. Inst. Child Health and Human Devel., 1971-73; Research grantee So. Edn. Found., 1974-75; Research grantee EPA, 1974-75; Research grantee Adminstrn. on Aging, HEW, 1975-76. Mem. Population Reference Bur., Am. Sociol. Soc., Rural Sociol. Soc., So. Sociol. Soc. Home: Dublin Ga. Died Aug. 3, 1990; buried Northview Cemetery, Dublin, Ga.

BELCHER, TAYLOR GARRISON, American diplomat; b. S.I., N.Y., July 1, 1920; s. Taylor and Miriam (Frazee) B.; m. Edith Anthony, Oct. 22, 1942; children: Anthony, Taylor Garrison III. BA, Brown U., 1941. Joined Fgn. Svc., U.S. Dept. State, Washington, 1946; diplomatic sec. Am. Embassy, Mexico City, 1947-50; consul Am. Embassy, Glascow, Scotland, 1950-54; internat. affairs officer U.S. Dept. State, 1954-57, dir. West Coast affairs Bur. Inter-Am. Affairs, 1961-64; consul Am. Embassy, Nicosia, Cyprus, 1957-58, consul gen., 1958-60; assigned to Can. Nat. Def. Coll., Kingston, Ont., 1960-61; U.S. amb. to Cyprus, 1964-69; to Peru, Lima, 1969-74; pres. Garrison's Landing Assn., Garrison Sta. Plaza Corp., Inc. Nat. chmn. Cyprus Relief Fund Am., Cyprus Children's Fund; trustee Putnam County Hist. Soc., Hamilton Fish Meml. Libr., Malcolm K. Gordon Sch. Lt. USNR, 1942-45. Mem. Fgn. Svc. Assn. Home: Garrison-on-Hudson N.Y. Died Aug. 6, 1990; Garrison, N.Y.

BELFORD, WILLIAM WIESS, pediatrician; b. Georgetown, Tex., Nov. 24, 1897; s. Charles Sanford and Mary Emily (Carothers) B.; m. Elizabeth Russell, Oct. 8, 1925; children: Mary Engler, Martha Root. AB, Southwestern U., 1918; MD, Johns Hopkins U., 1922. Intern New Haven Hosp., 1922-23; intern then resident St. Louis Childrens Hosp., 1923-26; instr. pediatrics Washington U. Med. Sch., St. Louis, 1924-25; pvt. practice pediatrics San Diego, from 1926; attending pediatrician San Diego County, Mercy, Childrens, Grossmont, Sharp Meml., Scripps Meml., Chula Vista Community Hosps.; cons. Calif. Crippled Children's Svcs., U.S. Navy Hosp.; San Diego del. White House Conf. Children and Youth, 1960; active 6th Pan Am. Congress Pediatrics, 1960. Fellow Am. Acad. Pediatrics (chmn. Calif. 1954-58, nat. pres. 1959-60); mem. AMA, Calif. Med. Soc., San Diego County Med. Soc., Am. Heart Assn., Am. Cancer Soc., San Diego Tb Assn., Southwestern Pediatric Soc., San Diego Acad. Medicine (pres. 1957), Phi Delta Theta, Phi Chi. Episcopalian. *

BELL, JOHN STEWART, physicist; b. Belfast, Ireland, July 28, 1928; s. John and Mary Ann (Brownlee) B.; m. Mary Bell. BSc in Exptl. Physics, Queen's U., Belfast, 1948; BSc in Math. Physics, Queen's U., 1949, DSc (hon.), 1988; PhD, U. Birmingham, England, 1956; ScD (hon.), Trinity Coll., Dublin, 1988. Physicist U.K. Atomic Energy Rsch. Establishment, Harwell, 1949-53, 54-60; with dept. math physics U. Birmingham, 1953-54; physicist CERN, Geneva, from 1960, SLAC, Stanford U., 1963-64. Author: Speakable and Unspeakable in Quantum Mechanics, 1987; contbr. numerous articles to profl. jours. Recipient Reality Found. prize, 1982, Dirac medal Inst. of Physics, 1988, Dannie Heineman prize Am. Physics Soc., 1989. Fellow Royal Soc. of London (Hughes medal 1989); mem. Am. Acad. Arts and Scis. (hon. fgn.). Home: Geneva Switzerland Died Oct. 1, 1990; buried St. Georges Cemetery, Geneva.

BELL, ROBERT EDWARD, physics educator; b. New Malden, Eng., Nov. 29, 1918; s. Edward R. and Edith (Rich) B.; m. Jeanne Atkinson, July 5, 1947; 1 child, Alison Ann. B.A., U. B.C., 1939, M.A., 1941; Ph.D., McGill U., 1948. Radar developer Nat. Research Council, Ottawa, Can., 1941-45; nuclear researcher Chalk River Nuclear Labs., 1946-52; prof. physics McGill U., Montreal, Que., 1956-83; Rutherford prof. McGill U., 1960-83, dir. Foster Radiation Lab., 1960-69, vice dean arts and sci., 1964-67, dean Faculty Grad. Studies and Research, 1969-70, prin., vice chancellor, 1970-79; dir. Arts, Scis. and Tech. Centre, Vancouver, B.C., 1983-85. Fellow Am. Phys. Soc., Royal Soc. (London), Royal Soc. (Can.) (pres. 1978-81); mem. Canadian Assn. Physicists (pres. 1965-66). Home: Delta Can. Deceased. †

BELL, ROBERT PAUL, university president; b. Charlottesville, Ind., Sept. 28, 1918; s. Paul H. and Emma Adaline (Overman) B.; m. Margaret Cora Strattan, Apr. 3, 1942; children: Paul Strattan, Barbara Ann. BS, Ball State Tchrs. Coll., 1940; MCS, Ind. U., 1942, EdD, 1952. Tchr. bus. Pendleton High Sch., Ind., 1940-41; grad. asst. Sch. Bus., Ind. U., 1941-42; instr. U.S. Naval Tng. Sch., 1942-44, Lab. Sch., Sch. Edn., Ind. U., 1944-47; mem. faculty Ball State U., Muncie, from 1947, prof. head dept. bus., 1954-61, prof. bus. edn., dean div. fine and applied arts, 1961-65; dean Coll. Bus., 1964-73, v.p. bus. affairs, treas., 1972-81, univ. pres., from 1981; dir. Muncie Fed. Savs. & Loan Assn. Author: Instructional Materials in Accounting, 1948, Instructional Materials in Typewriting, 1963, 2d edit., 1972; also articles.; editor: Ball State Commerce Jour, from 1954. Div. chmn. Muncie United Fund, 1962-63; bd. dirs. Delaware County Soc. Crippled, from 1963, United Way, from 1973, Community Found. of Muncie and Delaware County, Ball Meml. Hosp., 1982-84 (and 4 subs., from 1984), The Community Found. of Muncie and Del. County, Inc.; dir. Minnetrista Cultural Ctr., from 1988. Mem. Nat. Bus. Tchrs. Assn. (1st v.p. 1960), N. Central Bus. Edn. Assn. (pres. 1963), Nat. Bus. Edn. Assn. (bd. dirs. 1963), Future Bus. Leaders Am. (Ind. adviser 1954-61), NEA, Ind. Tchrs. Assn., Nat. Thrift Com., Blue Key, Exchange Club (pre. Muncie 1962-63), Rotary (hon.), Delta Pi Epsilon, Pi Omega Pi, Sigma Tau Gamma., Beta Gamma Sigma, Sigma Iota Epsilon. Home: Muncie Ind. Died Feb. 28, 1992.

BELL, WILLIAM HENRY, lawyer; b. Yenangyaung, Burma, Dec. 15, 1926; came to U.S., 1932; s. William R. and Beulah Joyce (Girsham) B.; m. Rita Ely, 1950; children: Sharon, Martin, David, Leta. BA, Duke U., 1947; BBA, Texas A&I U., 1950; JD, Tulsa U., 1954; DHL (hon.), Okla. Christian Coll., 1973. Bar: Okla. 1954, U.S. Dist. Ct. (no. dist.) 1954, U.S. Ct. Appeals (10th cir.). 1954, U.S. Supreme Ct. 1968. Assoc. John Rogers, Tulsa, 1954-64; ptnr. Rogers and Bell, Tulsa, from 1964; Bd. dirs. Bank Okla., Tulsa, Red River Oil Co. Trustee Hillcrest Med. Ctr., Okla., 1964-88, Okla Med. Research Found., 1964-88, Trinity U., 1967-88, various colls. and univs.; past pres., chmn. Tulsa Area United Way; past pres. Tulsa Edn. Found., Tulsa Med. Edn. Found., others. Served with USNR, 1944-46. Recipient Disting. Service award U.S. Jr. C. of C., 1961, Medallion Boys Clubs Am., 1962; named Man of Yr. Downtown Tulsa Unlimited, 1973, Outstanding Layman Okla. State Med. Assn., 1983; named to Okla. Hall of Fame, 1974; Disting. Service award Trinity U., 1988. Fellow Am. Bar Found., Am. Coll. Probate Counsel, Southwestern Legal Found. , Okla. Bar Found. (past pres.); mem. ABA (resource devel. council), Fed. Energy Bar Assn., Okla. Bar Assn. (past pres.), Tulsa County Bar Assn. (past pres., outstanding jr. mem. 1960, outstanding sr. mem. 1972). Republican. Episcopalian. Clubs: So. Hills, Summit, Tulsa. Home: Tulsa Okla. Died Sept. 16, 1988; buried Tulsa, Okla.

BELLAMY, PETER, drama critic, lecturer; b. Cleve., Nov. 9, 1914; s. Paul and Marguerite Scott (Stark) B.; m. Jean Margaret Dessel, Mar. 11, 1939; children: Sheila Jean, Stephen Paul, John Stark II, Christopher Aladdin, Nicole Loughman. Student, Harvard U., 1932-36. Comml. editor Des Moines Register, 1936-37; mem. staff Cleve. News, 1938-60, gossip columnist, soc. editor, until 1960; mem. staff Cleve. Plain Dealer, from 1960, entertainment editor, drama critic, from 1962; lectr. Shakespeare and criticism Western Res. U., 1963-64. Author: The Amish, 1971. Trustee Neighborhood Settlement Assn., 1952-64; pres. bd. Glenville Community Center, 1952-54; bd. dirs. Nationalities Service Center, 1961-65, Elinor T. Rainey Inst., 1958-60, Golden Age Center, 1961-64. Served with USNR, 1945-46. Mem. Nat. Council Tchrs. English, Am. Theatre Critics Assn., Cleve. Press Club (pres. 1960-62). Episcopalian (vestryman). Clubs: Lambs (N.Y.C.); Cleve. Play House. Home: Cleveland OH Died Jan. 6, 1989; buried Lakeview Cemetery, Cleve.

BELLAMY, RALPH REXFORD, actor; b. Chgo., June 17, 1904; s. Charles Rexford and Lilla Louise (Smith) B.; m. Alice Delbridge, 1926 (div. 1930); m. Catherine Willard, 1931 (div. 1945); children: Lynn, Willard; m. Ethel Smith, 1945 (div. 1947); m. Alice Murphy, 1949. Student high sch. Appeared with William Owen in Shakespeare and the classics, 1921, Old Matt and Wash Gibbs, The Shepherd of the Hills, Chautaupua Road Co., 1922; with stock companies, Madison, Wis., Evansville, Ind., 1922-23, traveling repertoire, Beach & Jones Co., 1924, John Winninger Repertoire Co., 1925, stock companies in numerous other cities, including, St. Joseph, Mo., Ft. Wayne and Terre Haute, Ind., 1923-28, 30; played leading parts, dir. own co., Des Moines, Nashville, Evanston, Ill., 1926-1930; actor stock cos., Jamestown, Rochester, and Freeport, N.Y., 1929-30; starred in N.Y.C. prodn. Roadside, 1930; also starred in plays including N.Y.C. prodn. Oh Men! Oh Women!, 1954; starred in play Sunrise at Campobello, on Broadway, 1958-59; on tour play, 1959, 60, (Tony award 1950, Delia Austrian award 1950, N.Y. Critics award 1950, 1st Ann. Best Actor award Acad. Radio and TV Arts and Scis. 1950), in movie based on play Sunrise At Campobello, 1960; and has appeared in 107 motion pictures, 1930—, including The Secret Six, 1931, Wildgirl, 1931, Airmail, 1932, By Persons Unknown, Beauty's Daughter, Dangerous Intrigue, Tradewinds, 1945, The Awful Truth, 1947 (Acad. award nomination), Hands Across the Table, 1949, His Girl Friday, 1950, The Courtmartial of Billy Mitchell, 1952, Divebomber, 1954, Carefree, 1955, Let's Get Married, Straight From the Shoulder, The Professionals, 1966, Rosemary's Baby, 1968, Cancel My Reservation, 1970, Oh God, 1977, Trading Places, 1983, Amazon Women on the Moon, 1988, Coming to America, 1988, The Good Mother, 1988, Pretty Woman, 1990; starred in N.Y. stage prodns. Tomorrow the World, 1943-44, State of the Union, 1945-47, Detective Story, 1949-50; producer, dir. N.Y. stage prodn. Pretty Little Parlor, N.Y.C., 1944; weekly TV series Man Against Crime, 1949-54; guest star appearances TV dramatic programs including Climax, Theatre Guild of Air, Philco Playhouse, Hallmark, General Electric, Phillip Morris, Playhouse 90, 1954—; radio guest maj. programs; narrator Victor record albums Rubaiyat of Omar Khayam, Leaves of Grass, Stories and Songs of the Civil War; starred in TV series Eleventh Hour, 1963-64, Man Against Crime, 1949-54; NBC documentary Hope-Ship, Saigon, South Vietnam, 1962; narrator 13-week TV series One to One for Episcopal Ch., 1962 (Emmy award); co-star TV series The Survivors, 1968-69, The Most Deadly Game series, ABC-TV, 1970—, The Hunter, 1971—, Moneychangers; appeared as Franklin D. Roosevelt in TV mini-series The Winds of War (Emmy nomination), other TV mini-series include Fearful Decision, 1955 (Emmy nomination), War and Remembrance, Christine Cromwell, Missiles of October, 1974 (Emmy nomination); appeared in TV movies Condominium; also guest star various TV shows including Wheels, The Millionaire, L.A. Law, 1988, Matlock, 1988; author: When the Smoke Hit the Fan, 1979. Presdl. appointee nat. bd. U.S.O., 1958-60; mem. Pres.'s Com. on 50th Anniversary Dept. Labor, 1962; vice chmn. nat. campaign. ARC, 1963; chmn. N.Y. Regional NCCJ Brotherhood Week, 1963; founder, past mem. Calif. Arts Commn.; bd. dirs. People-to-People Project Hope, Theatervision, 1972-73. Recipient award of merit State of Israel, 1968; 1st Ann. Hal Roach Entertainment award, 1989. Mem. Actors Equity Assn. (pres. 1952-64, now pres. emeritus, life), Acad. Motion Picture Arts and Scis. (bd. dirs. 1982-84, Achievement and Humanitarian award 1986), Screen Actors Guild (founder, 1st bd. dirs., Outstanding Achievement and Humanitarian award 1983), Am. Arbitration Assn. (dir. 1962-64), Dutch Treat Club, Players Club (N.Y.C., bd. dirs. 1958-64, life), Lambs Club (N.Y.C., coun. 1952-56). Home: Los Angeles Calif. Died Nov. 21, 1991. †

BELLINGER, ALFRED RAYMOND, foreign language educator; b. Durham, Pa., July 24, 1893; s. Hiram Paulding and Elizabeth Dwight (Raymond) B.; m. Charlotte Blake Brinsmade, June 26, 1920; children: Peter F., Rossiter R., Hilda Gewin, Mary Davenport, Elizabeth Miller. BA, Yale U., 1917, PhD, 1925; student, Am. Sch. Classical Studies, Athens, 1926. Instr. classics Yale Coll., 1920-26, asst. prof., 1926-33, assoc. prof., 1933-39, Lampson prof. Latin, 1930-62, Lampson prof. Latin emeritus, from 1966, acting dean, 1953-54; fellow Saybrook Coll., from 1933; mem. exec. com. Am. Sch. Classical Studies, Athens, 1947-50, chmn. mng. com., 1961-62; bd. dirs. Am. Coun. Learned Socs., 1946-49; mem. Inst. Advanced Study, 1960-61; mem. bd. scholars Dumbarton Oaks, from 1948, vis. scholar, 1963-64; mem. joint conf. bd. Com. on Internat. Exchange of Persons, 1949-51. Author: The Coins, Dura Final Report VI, 1949, The End of the Seleucids, 1949; editor of reports Excavation of Dura-Europos since 1932; Yale Classical Studies, Vols. VI-X, 1939-47. Fellow Royal Numis. Soc. London (hon., Gold medal 1955); mem. Am. Philol. Assn., Archeol. Inst. (v.p.), Am. Numis. Soc. (Huntington medal 1943), German Archaeol. Inst. (corr.), Internat. Numis. Commn. (hon.). *

BELLINGER, JOHN DOOLEY, banker; b. Honolulu, May 13, 1923; s. Eustace L. and Lei (Williams) B.; m. Joan Simms, Apr. 7, 1945; children: Dona, Jan, Neil. Student, U. Hawaii, 1941-42, LLD (hon.), 1982; LHD (hon.), Hawaii Loa Coll., 1986. With First Hawaiian Bank (and predecessor), Honolulu, from 1942, chmn., chief exec. officer, from 1969, also bd. dirs.; chief exec. officer, chmn. bd. First Hawaiian, Inc., Honolulu; also bd. dirs. First Hawaiian, Inc.; chmn., chief exec. officer First Hawaiian Credit Corp.; chmn. chief exec. officer, dir. 1st Hawaiian Leasing, Inc.; dir. Alexander & Baldwin, Honolulu, Matson Nav. Co., Hawaiian Telephone Co., Restaurant Suntory, U.S.A., Halekulani Corp.; mem. Gov.'s adv. bd. Underwater Cable Transmission Project. Chmn. Japan-Hawaii Econ. Coun.; chmn., bd. dirs. Pacific Internat. Ctr. for High Tech.; bd. dirs. North Hawaii Community Hosp., Inc.; civilian aide to sec. Army for Hawaii; chmn. U.S. Army Civilian Adv. Steering Com.; trustee Francis H.I. Brown Found., Punahou Sch., Japan-Am. Inst. Mgmt. Sci. Fund; hon. trustee Bishop Mus.; bd. dirs. East-West Ctr. Found. With AUS, 1946-47; bd. govs. Japanese Cultural Ctr. Hawaii. Decorated Disting. Civilian Service Medal Sec. of Army, 1980; recipient Am. Acad. of Achievement Golden Plate Award, 1970, Disting. Citizen award Congl. Medal of Honor Soc., 1981; decorated ProPatria award, 1984, Torch of Liberty award Anti-Defamation League of B'nai B'rith, 1984, Businessman of Yr. award Hawaiian Bus./Profl. Assn., 1984; Gen. Creighton W. Abrams medal, David Malo award Rotary Club Honolulu, 1986, Community Relations award of excellence Dept. Army, 1987; 3d Class Order Rising Sun, 1985; named Hawaii Disting. Citizen, Boy Scouts Am. Aloha coun., 1987; named to Honolulu Dist. of Edn. Hall of Fame, Disting. Leadership award U. Hawaii Found. Trustees, 1989, numerous others. Mem. Hawaii C. of C. (bd. dirs.), Assn. U.S. Army, Navy League, Assn. Res. City Bankers, Hawaii Bankers Assn. Clubs: Hawaiian Civic, Oahu Country, Waialae Country (Honolulu) (bd. dirs., past pres.); The 200 (treas., past pres.). Home: Honolulu Hawaii Died Sept. 17, 1989; Nat. Meml. Cemetery of the Pacific. Honlulu, Hawaii.

BELLINO, CARMINE SALVATORE, accountant, government investigator; b. Elizabeth, N.J., July 26, 1905; s. Frank and Frances (Lafaso) B.; m. Santina I. Novello, June 6, 1936 (dec. 1979); children: Francis, Robert, Joseph, Mary Catherine, Mary Joan, Mary Sandra, Maryan Joyce.; m. Catherine Tripodi DiGiacomo, Aug. 20, 1983; stepchildren: Joseph, Melchior, Elizabeth, John. B.C.S. with honors in Acctg., NYU, 1928. C.P.A., N.J., D.C., N.Y. Acct. Mills & Co., N.Y.C., 1927-34; spl. agt. acct., also adminstrv. asst. to dir. FBI, 1934-45; asst. dir. RFC, 1945-46, War Assets Adminstrn., 1946-47; pvt. practice acctg. Washington and N.Y.C., 1947-62; resident agt. Wright Long & Co., N.Y.C., 1951-60; resident partner Wright Long & Co., 1964-70; chief investigator select com. on 1972 presdl. campaign activities U.S. Senate, 1973-74; chief investigator U.S. Senate Judiciary Com., 1979-81; spl. cons. to Pres. John F. Kennedy, 1961-63, to Pres. Lyndon B. Johnson, 1963-64; mem. bd. contract appeals AEC, 1964-70; acct. cons. to various U.S. congressional coms., Washington, 1947-60, 64-74. Served to lt. col. USAAF Res. Mem. AICPA, D.C. Soc. CPAs, Soc. Former Spl. Agts. FBI. Lodge: K.C. (4 deg.). Home: Coconut Creek Fla. Died Feb. 29, 1990.

BELLPORT, BERNARD PHILIP, consulting engineer; b. LaCrosse, Kans., May 25, 1907; s. Bernard P. and Louise H. (Groves) B.; m. Elsy V. Johnson, June 11, 1931 (dec. Mar. 1954); children: Louise Bellport Garcia, Bernard Philip; m. Mabelle W. Kandolin, Sept. 26, 1955. B.S. in Mining Engring, Poly. Coll. Engring., Oakland, Calif., 1927. Registered profl. engr., Colo. Mining engr. Western U.S., 1927-28; engr.-geologist St. Joseph Lead Co., 1928-31; with Phoenix Utility Co., 1931-32, Mont. Hwy. Commn., 1932-35, Bur. Reclamation, 1936-72; regional dir. region 2, Calif., 1957-59; asso. chief engr. region 2, Calif., Denver, 1959-63; chief engr. region 2, Calif., 1963-70, dir. design and constrn., 1970-72; practice as engring. cons., from 1972; arbitrator Constrn. Arbitration Panel, State of Calif. Recipient Distinguished Service award Dept. Interior; Golden Beaver for engring.; named Man of Year Am. Pub. Works Assn., 1970. Mem. Nat. Acad. Engring., U.S. Commn. Large Dams (chmn. 1971-72), Internat. Commn. Irrigation, Drainage and Flood Control, ASCE (pres. Colo. 1966), Am. Arbitration Assn., Rossmoor Engrs. Club, Internat. Water Resources Assn., Hon. Order Ky. Cols., Chi Epsilon (hon.). Episcopalian. Clubs: Masons (32 deg.), Shriners, Round Hill Country. Home: Walnut Creek Calif. Deceased. †

BEMIS, JAMES R(OSBOROUGH), lumber manufacturer; b. Prescott, Ark., Oct. 25, 1898; s. William Noyes and Elizabeth (Rosborough) B.; m. Jane Simpson, Aug. 16, 1947; children: Lucy Piper, Edward, Harold, Andrew Hastings, Marita Jane. Student, Shenandoah Valley Acad., 1915-17, Va. Mil. Inst., 1917-18, U. Wis., 1919. Lumber salesman St. Louis, 1920-21, wholesale lumber bus., 1921-29; wholesale lumber bus. Prescott, 1929-33; lumber mfr., 1933; pres. Ozon Lumber Co., Prescott, from 1929, Prescott & Northwestern R.R., from 1935. Mem. So. Pine Assn., Nat. Lumber Mfrs. Assn., Ark. C. of C., Sigma Chi. *

BENDER, RALPH EDWARD, agricultural educator; b. nr. Waldo, Ohio, Dec. 29, 1910; s. George Edward and Nina Amelia (Almendinger) B.; m. Harriett Louise Anspaugh, June 10, 1937; children: John Edward, Susan Jane. B.S. in Agr, Ohio State U., 1933, M.A., 1941, Ph.D., 1947. Tchr. vocat. agr. Anna (Ohio) High Sch., 1933-37; instr. dept. agrl. edn. Ohio State U.; also tchr. vocat. agr. Canal Winchester High Sch., 1937-47, asst. prof., 1947-48, assoc. prof., 1948-51, chmn. dept. agrl. edn., 1948-78, prof., 1951-78, emeritus prof., 1978-90; vis. prof. Auburn U., 1954, U. Calif., 1957, Colo. State U., 1959, 61, 68, Cornell U., 1962, Pa. State U., 1964, Kans. State U., 1979; U.S. AID specialist Tchr. Edn. Study in Brazil, 1967, 74; external examiner U. Sierra Leone, 1975; cons. Ohio Adv. Council for Vocat. Edn., 1980-85; cons.-specialist div. vocat. edn. U.S. Office Edn., 1969, 70; cons. nat. bd. dirs. Future Farmers Am., 1976-77. Co-author: The FFA and You-Your Guide to Learning, 1972, 74, 79; co-author: Adult Education in Agriculture, 1972; contbg. author: AVA Yearbook, The Individual and His Education, 1972. Mem. troop com. Boy Scouts; pres. Jr. Fair Bd. Ohio, 1929-30; pres. 50 Year Club Ohio State Fair, 1985; pres. Bd. of Edn.; mem. adv. com. Sch. Edn., Cornell U., 1942-67. Named to Ohio Agrl. Hall of Fame, 1982. Mem. Am. Vocat. Assn. (life mem.; nat. v.p. 1967-70, pres. agrl. edn. div. 1967-70, Outstanding Service award 1971), Ohio Vocat. Agrl. Assn. (pres. 1945-46), Am. Assn. Tchr. Educators in Agr. (pres. 1957-58, Distinguished Teaching award 1969), Central Regional Agrl. Edn. Conf. (pres. 1963-64), Ohio Vocat. Assn. (pres. 1946-47), Ohio Sch. Bd. Assn., Future Farmers Am. (pres. Ohio 1929-30, nat. v.p. 1930-31, VIP citation 1978), NEA, Nat. Vocat. Agr. Tchrs. Assn., Ohio Safety Council, Ohio Edn. Assn., Ohio Assn. Adult Edn., Farm Bur., Grange, Alpha Zeta, Gamma Sigma Delta, Phi Delta Kappa, Phi Kappa Phi, Phi Eta Sigma, Omicron Tau Theta. Methodist. Clubs: Mason, Lions (pres. 1959), Ohio State U. Faculty, Pres.'s. Home: Canal Winchester Ohio Died Feb. 11, 1990; buried Franklin Hills Meml. Gardens, Ohio.

BENDETSEN, KARL ROBIN, business executive, lawyer; b. Aberdeen, Wash., Oct. 11, 1907; s. Albert M. and Anna (Bentson) B.; m. Billie McIntosh, 1938; 1 son, Brookes McIntosh; m. Maxine Bosworth, 1947; 1 dau., Anna Martha; m. Gladys Ponton de Arce Heurtematte Johnston, 1972. A.B., Stanford U., 1929, J.S.D., 1932. Bar: Calif., Oreg., Ohio, N.Y., Wash., D.C., U.S. Supreme Ct. Practiced law Aberdeen, Wash., 1932-40; mgmt. counsel, 1946-47; cons. spl. asst. to sec. U.S. Dept. Def., 1948; asst. sec. Dept. Army, 1948-50, under sec., 1950-52; dir. gen. U.S. R.R.s, 1950-52; chmn. bd. Panama Canal Co., 1950-54; counsel Champion Papers, 1952-53, v.p. Tex. div., 1953-55, v.p. ops., 1955-60, chmn. bd., pres., chief exec. officer, 1960-67; dir. Westinghouse Electric, 1961-80; chmn., pres., chief exec. officer Champion Internat., 1967-72; dir. N.Y. Stock Exchange, 1972-82; chmn. exec. com. Champion Internat., 1973-75; spl. U.S. rep. with rank of ambassador to W.Ger., 1956, spl. U.S. ambassador to Philippines, 1956; chmn. adv. com. to sec. Dept. Def., 1962; vice chmn. Def. Manpower Commn., 1974-76; bd. overseers Hoover Instn.; chmn. panel on Strategic Def. Initiative for Pres. Reagan, 1980-84. Directed evacuation of Japanese from West Coast, 1942. Served to col. U.S. Army, 1940-46; spl. rep. sec. of war to Gen. MacArthur 1941. Decorated D.S.M. with oak leaf cluster, Silver Star, Legion of Merit with 2 oak leaf clusters, Bronze Star with 3 oak leaf clusters and Combat V, Army Commendation medal with 3 oak leaf clusters, medal of Freedom; Croix de Guerre with Palm; officer Legion of Honor (France); Croix de Guerre with palm (Belgium); mem. Order Brit. Empire; recipient Disting. Civilian Service medal. Mem. Theta Delta Chi. Episcopalian. Clubs: Links (N.Y.C.), Metropolitan (N.Y.C.), Brook (N.Y.C.); Chicago; Washington Athletic (Seattle); Bohemian (San Francisco), Pacific Union (San Francisco); F Street (D.C.), Georgetown (D.C.); Everglades (Palm Beach, Fla.), Bath and Tennis (Palm Beach, Fla.). Home: Washington DC Died June 28, 1989.

BENJAMIN, HAROLD (RAYMOND WAYNE), educator; b. Gilmanton, Wis., Mar. 27, 1893; s. Herbert Samuel and Harriet Louise (Locke) B.; m. Georgiana Kessi, Aug. 26, 1919 (dec. Apr. 1958); children: Harold Herbert, Georgiana Olive Faulkner, William Francis. Grad., Oreg. Normal Sch., 1915; AB, U. Oreg., 1921, AM, 1924; PhD, Stanford U., 1927; LLD, Drake U., 1955; LittD, Pacific U., 1962. Prin. Salem Heights Elem. Sch., 1915-16; supt. schs. Umatilla, Oreg., 1920-22; editor Umatilla Spokesman, 1921-22; asst. prof. edn. U. Oreg., 1922-25; teaching fellow Stanford U., 1925-27, dir. practice teaching, 1927-31, assoc. prof., 1928-31; prof. edn. & asst. dean Coll. Edn. U. Minn., 1931-38, dir. Ctr. for Continuation of Study, 1936-37; Minn. state dir. adult edn., 1933-34, 36-37; prof. edn., dir. Coll. Edn., dean summer quarter U. Colo., 1937-39; dean. Coll. Edn., dean summer quarter U. Md., 1939-51; prof. edn. George Peabody Coll. Tchrs., 1951-58, emeritus, from 1958; disting. svc. prof. edn. Glassboro State Coll., from 1962; cons., lectr. numerous schs. Author: True Faith and Allegiance, 1950, Building a National System of Education (in Korean), 1955, others; editor: Democratic Administration of Higher Education, 1950. Served in World Wars I and II. *

BENNER, NOLAN PAUL, foundation executive; b. Hoffman, Pa., Mar. 24, 1893; s. Ulysses F. and Mary Ann (Remaly) B.; m. Nettie Ludwig, Mar. 8, 1919; children: Bettie J. Garrettson, Nolan Paul. Student, Lehigh U. Trustee Texler Found., Allentown, Pa., from 1934, exec. dir., from 1947; pres. Cia. Minera Lehigh, S.A., Cuba, from 1956; bd. dirs. Lehigh Valley Trust Co. Trustee Allentown Art Mus. With Pa. N.G.; capt. U.S. Army, World War I. *

BENNETT, CLARENCE EDWIN, educator; b. Providence, May 23, 1902; s. George Wilfred and Clara Freeman (Wright) B.; m. Ruth Nason, Sept. 8, 1928; children: Muriel N. Bennett McAlister, Ronald Stokes. PhB, Brown U., 1923, MS, 1924, PhD, 1930. Instr. physics Brown U., 1923-31, MIT, 1931-34; asst. prof. physics U. Maine, Orono, 1934-38, assoc. prof., 1938-40, prof., 1940-70, prof. emeritus, cons., 1970-92, head dept. physics, 1939-67; with Office Naval Rsch., 1946-56; mem. Nat. Acad. Sci. adv. panel Nat. Bur. Standards, 1959-62. Author: Physics, 1935, Physics Without Math, 1949, First Year College Physics, 1954, Physics Problems, 1958. Fellow AAAS, Am. Phys. Soc. (chmn. N.E. sect.); mem. Am. Inst. Physics (counselor Maine), Am. Assn. Physics Tchrs., Optical Soc. Am., AAUP, Am. Soc. Engring. Edn. (physics editor), Phi Beta Kappa, Sigma Xi, Phi Kappa Phi, Tau Beta Pi, Sigma Pi Sgima (exec. com.), Mason. Home: Orono Maine Died Dec. 19, 1990.

BENNETT, DOROTHEA, genetics educator, researcher; b. Honolulu, Dec. 27, 1929; d. James William and Anna Marie (Schorling) B. BA, Barnard Coll., 1951; PhD, Columbia U., 1956; MD (hon.), Uppsala (Sweden) U. Rsch. assoc. Columbia U., N.Y.C., 1956-62; asst. prof. genetics Cornell U. Med. Sch., N.Y.C., 1962-65, assoc. prof., 1965-71, prof., 1971-76; mem. staff Sloan Kettering Inst. Cancer Rsch., N.Y.C., 1976-86; prof. U. Tex., Austin, 1986-90; mem. bd. sci. overseers Jackson Lab., Bar Harbor, Maine, 1975-89. Contbr. over 150 articles to profl. jours. NSF, NIH grantee. Home: Austin Tex. Died Aug. 16, 1990; cremated.

BENNETT, ELMER FRANK, lawyer; b. Longmont, Colo., Sept. 17, 1917; s. Herbert A. and Jessie C. (Wharton) B.; m. Gertrude A. Turner, Sept. 9, 1939 (dec. 1972); children: John H., Kathryn H.; m. Jewell Brooks Middleton, 1982. A.B., Colo. State Coll. Edn., 1938; LL.B., Stanford U., 1941. Bar: D.C. 1947. Adminstrv. work War Dept., 1942-48; trial atty. FTC, 1948-51; legal adviser, exec. sec. U.S. Senator Eugene D. Millikin of Colo., 1951-53; legis. counsel Dept. Interior, 1953-56, asst. to sec. interior, 1956-57, gen. counsel, 1957-58, undersec., 1958-61; mem. firm Ely, Duncan & Bennett, 1961-66; gen. counsel U.S. Pub. Land Law Rev. Commn., 1966-70; spl. asst. to dir. Office Emergency Preparedness, Exec. Office of Pres., Washington, 1970-71, gen. counsel, asst. dir., 1971-73; trustee pension and health benefit trusts, from 1978. Adminstrv. asst. to chmn. resolutions com. Republican Nat. Conv., 1952. Mem. Am. (chmn. mineral law sect. 1965-66), Fed. bar assns., Blue Key, Phi Alpha Delta, Phi Alpha Theta. Republican. Episcopalian. Home: Rehoboth Beach Del. Died July 10, 1989; buried Park Lawn Meml. Park, Rockville, Md.

BENNETT, HARRY, chemical consultant; b. N.Y.C., May 28, 1895; s. Louis and Esther (Cohen) B.; m. Rose Michaels, Feb. 6, 1921; children—Helene M., Marilyn S. (Mrs. L. Ziegler). BSChemE, NYU, 1917. Pres. Bennett-Rosendahl Co., Inc. (cons.), Miami Beach, Fla.; dir. B.R. Lab., Miami Beach; Chmn. Chem. Forum, Miami Beach. Author or chief editor over 50 reference books on chemistry including: The Chemical Formulary, 28 vols., from 1932, The Chemical and Technical Dictionary, Ency. of Chemical Trademarks and Synonyms. Mem. Am. Inst. Chemists, Am. Chem. Soc., Am. Assn. Textile Chemists and Colorists, N.Y. Acad. Scis., Soc. Cosmetic Chemists, Inst. Chem. Engrs., Inst. Food Tech., Royal Inst. Chemistry, Oil Chem. Soc., Am. Ceramic Soc., Soc. Plastics Engrs., Am. Inst. Chem. Engrs., Tau Beta Pi. Home: Miami Beach Fla. Died July 20, 1990.

BENNETT, IVAN LOVERIDGE, JR., physician, educator; b. Washington, Mar. 4, 1922; s. Ivan Loveridge and Ruby (Jenrette) B.; m. Martha Rhodes, June 24, 1944; children: Susan, Paul Bruce, Katherine, Jeffrey Ivan. A.B., Emory U., 1943, M.D., 1946. Diplomate: Am. Bd. Internal Medicine, 1954. Intern Grady Meml. Hosp., Atlanta, 1946-47, chief resident physician, 1951-52; fellow in pathology Johns Hopkins Hosp., Balt., 1949-50; asst. resident physician Duke Hosp., Durham, 1950-51; asst. in pathology Johns Hopkins U., Balt., 1949-50, asso. prof. medicine, 1954-57, prof., 1957-58, Baxley prof. pathology, dir. dept. pathology, 1958-66; asst. in medicine Emory U., New Orleans, 1951-52; asst. prof. internal medicine Yale U., New Haven, 1952-54; dep. dir., acting dir. Office Sci. and Tech., Exec. Office of Pres., Washington, 1966-69, cons., 1963-70, from 1976; v.p. health affairs NYU, 1969, prof., from 1970, exec. v.p., 1976; dir. NYU Med. Ctr., 1969-73, provost, 1973-82; dean Sch. Medicine NYU, 1970-82, acting pres. univ., 1979-81; asst. pathologist Johns Hopkins Hosp., 1949-50, physician, cons. in bacteriology, 1954-58, pathologist-in-chief, 1958-68; asso. physician Grace-New Haven Hosp., 1952-54; attending physician West Haven VA Hosp., 1953-54; cons. in medicine Loch Raven VA Hosp., 1955-58, Clin. Center, USPHS, Bethesda, Md., 1955-58, Balt. City Hosps., 1954-58, cons. in pathology, 1958-66; lectr. in field; dir. Technicon Corp., from 1974, Group Health Inc., from 1976; mem. Pres.'s Sci. Adv. Com., 1966-70, Commn. on Epidemiological Survey, Armed Forces Epidemiology Bd.; research contract dir. Army Chem. Corps; mem. bd. sci. counselors Nat. Inst. for Dental Research; member exec. com. div. med. scis.; mem. bd. sci. advisers Armed Forces Inst. Pathology; mem. bd.

medicine Nat. Acad. Scis., 1967-70; mem. panel on Sci. and Tech., Com. on Sci. and Astronautics, U.S. Ho. of Reps., from 1969; mem. def. sci. bd. Dept. Def., 1974-77; mem. numerous profl., sci. adv. groups, coms.; mem. long range planning com. Johns Hopkins U., 1965-66; mem.-at-large exec. planning com. U. Okla., 1967-68, bd. visitors, 1968-70; mem. vis. com. bd. overseers Harvard U., 1974-76; mem. vis. com. U. Mass., 1974-75; bd. dirs. Pub. Health Inst. City of N.Y., Inc., from 1969; trustee Milton Helpern Library of Legal Medicine, 1969-76, chmn., 1971; trustee Med. Library Center N.Y., Better Bellevue Assn., 1969; mem. Health Research Council City of N.Y., from 1972; men's com. Japan Internat. Christian U. Found., from 1972; chmn. interim bd. govs. N.Y. County Health Services Rev. Orgn., 1974-76; adv. bd. Assn. Pathology Chmn., from 1977; med. panel N.Y. State Commn. Jud. Conduct, from 1977; adv. com. health manpower Health Planning Council N.Y., from 1977; adv. com. program sci. and tech. policy Grad. Sch. Pub. Adminstrn., N.Y. U., 1978; adv. council Nat. Hypertension Assn., from 1979; adv. council gt. neglected diseases of mankind program Rockefeller Found., from 1978. Author tech. articles sci. jours.; editorial bd.: Principles of Internal Medicine, 1954-69, Clin. Research, 1954-56, Bull. Johns Hopkins Hosp., 1960-66, Ann. Rev. Medicine, 1965-66, Jour. Biochem. and Molecular Pathology, 1947-67, Lab. Investigation, 1966-69; editorial adv. bd. Sci. Year, 1974-77; adv. bd. Tech. in Soc., An Internat. Jour. Served to lt. (j.g.) USNR, 1947-49. Recipient Francis Gilman Blake award Yale U., 1954; Gordon Wilson medal, 1958; Arun Bannerjee medal Calcutta U., 1963; Duke Med. Center Alumni award, 1971; Emory U. Med. Alumni Assn. award, 1972; Abraham Flexner award for disting. service to med. edn., 1978. Fellow A.C.P., N.Y. Acad. Scis. (com. on Office of Tech. Assessment from 1978), Am. Soc. Clin. Pathologists, Am. Coll. Osteopathic Internists (hon.), Am. Acad. Arts and Scis.; mem. Soc. Exptl. Biology and Medicine, Am. Fedn. Clin. Research (pres. 1957-58), Am. Soc. Clin. Investigation, Assn. Am. Physicians, AMA, Biomed. Engring. Soc., Am. Assn. Pathologists and Bacteriologists, Am. Soc. Exptl. Pathology, Am. Clin. and Climatol. Assn., Inst. Medicine (charter, chmn. health policy bd. 1973, fin. com. 1977), Am. Assn. Immunologists, Internat. Acad. of Pathology (council 1964-66), Johns Hopkins Med. Soc. (pres. 1963-64), Research Pathologists Am., Balt. City Med. Soc., Md. Soc. Pathologists (council 1965-66), Am. Council Edn. (dir. 1976-78), Orgn. Univ. Health Center Adminstrs., Mental Health Soc. Westchester County, Med. Soc. County N.Y. (comitia minora from 1970, bd. censors from 1971, del. to ho. of dels. Med. Soc. State N.Y. from 1973, pres. 1975-76, trustee from 1976), Am. Assn. Profs. Pathology, Am. Acad. Polit. and Social Sci., Acad. Polit. Sci., Assn. Am. Med. Colls. (chmn. council deans 1974, chmn. assn. 1976, fin. com. from 1976), Am. Assn. Higher Edn., Tokyo Soc. Internal Medicine (hon.), Am. Pub. Health Assn., N.Y. Cancer Soc., Harvey Soc., Phi Beta Kappa, Sigma Xi, Omicron Delta Kappa, Alpha Omega Alpha, Sigma Chi, Phi Chi. Clubs: Century Assn., Cosmos. Home: New York N.Y. Died July 21, 1990.

BENNETT, JOAN, actress; b. Palisades, N.J., Feb. 27, 1910; d. Richard and Adrienne (Morrison) B.; m. John Marion Fox, 1926 (div. Aug. 1928); 1 dau., Diana; m. Gene Markey (writer), Mar. 16, 1932 (div. 1937); 1 dau., Melinda; m. Walter Wanger, 1940 (div. 1965); children: Stephanie, Shelley; m. David Wilde, Feb. 14, 1978. Ed., pvt. schs. Miss Chandor's and Miss Hopkins, N.Y.C., St. Margaret's, Waterbury, Conn., L'Ermitage, Versailles, France. Lectr. The Bennett Playbill, 1971-73. Made stage debut in Jarnegan with father, 1928; appeared in 73 films including Little Women, 1933, Man Hunt, 1941, The Woman in the Window, 1944, Scarlet Street, 1946, The Macomber Affair, 1947, Father of the Bride, 1950, Father's Little Dividend, 1951; TV movies Suddenly Love, 1978, A House Possessed, 1980, Divorce Wars, 1981; stage plays Stage Door, 1938, Love Me Little, Janus, Pleasure of His Company, Jane, The Man Who Came to Dinner, The Boy Friend, Butterflies are Free; TV series, also Never Too Late, London, 1963-64; Author: (with Lois Kibbee) The Bennett Playbill, 1970. Home: Scarsdale N.Y. Died Dec. 7, 1990.

BENNETT, JOSIAH WHITNEY, government official; b. Cambridge, Mass., Nov. 18, 1916; s. Josiah Clark and Annie (Whitney) B.; m. Chou Nien-tz'u, Sept. 20, 1940; children: Ann Bennett Spence, Jean Bennett DeCoste. Student, Harvard U., 1934-35, Yenching U., China, 1937, U. Chgo., 1938. With War Dept., 1942-46, USIS Nanking China, Tel Aviv, Israel and Washington, 1946-56; polit. counselor State Dept., Lagos, Nigeria, 1961-64; dep. dir. East Asian affairs, 1964-66; country dir. for Republic of China, 1966-67; dir. for Malaysia and Singapore, 1970-71, Vietnam Working Group, Washington, 1971-72; minister-counselor for polit. affairs Am. Embassy, Saigon, 1972-75; sr. fgn. svc. insp. Washington, 1975-77; cons. Dept. State, 1979-92; dep. province sr. adviser, Vinh Long, Vietnam, 1968-69; diplomat-in-residence Kans. State U., 1969-70. Recipient Republic of Vietnam Medal of Merit, 1969, Meritorious award AID, 1970. Mem. Am. Polit. Sci. Assn., Am. Fgn. Svc. Assn. Home: Marco Island Fla. Died Feb. 22, 1992.

BENNETT, LOUIS LOWELL, social welfare consultant; b. N.Y.C., Jan. 15, 1909; s. Maurice and Sarah (Brown) B.; m. Estelle Goldman, June 8, 1929; children—Peter Charles, Richard. LL.B., St. John's U., 1931, B.S., 1939; M.S., Sch. Social Work, Columbia U., 1941. Bar: N.Y. bar 1931, Fed. bar 1931. Dir. evening session St. John's U., 1927-41; practiced in N.Y.C., 1931-71; asst. regional dir. U.S. Office Community War Services, N.Y., 1941-45; exec. dir., organizer Vets. Service Center, N.Y.C., 1944-45; cons. to adminstr., regional housing expediter Nat. Housing Agy., Washington, also N.Y.C., 1945-47; asst. exec. dir. Am. Jewish Com., N.Y.C., 1947-49; exec. dir. N.Y. Assn. for New Ams., 1949-52; asst. exec. vice chmn. Nat. United Jewish Appeal, 1952-56; exec. dir. Jewish Child Care Assn. of N.Y., 1956-60; asst. exec. dir. Comm. Council Greater N.Y., 1960-62; regional rep. Office of Aging, HEW, N.Y.C., 1962-65; prin. Welfare Adminstrn. regional rep. Bur. Family Services, 1965-67; dep. regional commr., dep. equal employment opportunities rep. Social and Rehab. Service, 1967-70; prof., dean students, chmn. dept. student personnel services Baruch Coll., CUNY, 1970-72; cons. War Manpower Commn., 1942-44; lectr. Columbia U. Sch. Social Work, 1942-70; lectr., condr. insts. at numerous colls. and univs.; adv. bd. N.Y. State Health Preparedness Commn., 1943; hon. dep. commr. N.Y. State Dept. Social Welfare, 1950; cons. N.Y. State CD Commn., 1950, U.S. Office Edn., 1952-53; bd. dirs. Child Welfare League Am., 1960-62; mem. bd. Assn. Children's Instns. N.Y. State, 1956-60; mem. joint bd. com. Council Social Work Edn.-Nat. Assn. Social Workers, 1960-67; mem. com. psychiat. services for children N.Y.C. Dept. Hosps., 1962-65; mem. examining panel N.Y.C. Civil Service Commn., 1956-72, N.Y. State Civil Service Commn., 1968-72; mem. N.Y. Gov.'s Com. Aging, 1971-72; cons. N.Y. State Office for Aging, 1971; del. 1971 White House Conf. Aging. Contbr. numerous articles to profl. publs. Recipient Superior Service award HEW, 1968. Mem. Nat. Assn. Social Workers (mem. bd. N.Y.C. chpt. 1956-73, Fla. chpt. from 1973, nat. treas., nat. bd. 1959-61), Am. Bar Assn., Am. Public Welfare Assn., Am. Soc. Public Adminstrn. (sr.), Columbia U. Sch. Social Work Alumni Assn. (pres. 1945-48), Acad. Cert. Social Workers, Council Social Work Edn. (v.p., mem. bd., exec. com.), Nat. Council Juvenile Ct. Judges (asso.), Am. Arbitration Assn., Nat. Conf. Social Work, Nat. Conf. Lawyers and Social Workers (co.-chmn. 1965-70, hon. mem.). Home: Miami Beach Fla. Died Dec. 25, 1991; buried Menorah Gardens Cemetery, Miami Beach.

BENNETT, ROBERT RUSSELL, composer, conductor; b. Kansas City, Mo., June 15, 1894; s. George Robert and May (Bradford) B.; m. Louise Edgerton Merrill, Dec. 29, 1919; 1 child, Jean. Studied with Carl Busch and Nadia Boulanger, Paris, Berlin, Vienna, London, for 5 yrs. Played violin, piano and trombone Kansas City, 1908-16; copyist, orchestrator, composer of music N.Y.C., 1916-26; composer and conductor Europe, 1926-29, 32, Hollywood, Calif., 1935-40; composer, conductor and commentator various radio stas., N.Y.C., from 1940; composer and conductor various tv films, from 1950. Author in field. Recipient fellowship John Simon Guggenheim Meml. Found., 2 Victor prizes for symphonic works. Mem. ASCAP, Nat. Assn. Am. Composers and Conductors (pres. 1947), Bohemians (v.p. 1950), Tennis Club (L.A.), West Side Tennis (N.Y.). *

BENOIST, JEAN-MARIE JULES, educator, author, journalist, researcher; b. Paris, Apr. 4, 1942; s. Jean Adrien and Suzanne (Guesde) B.; m. Nathalie Isabelle Bréaud, Oct. 16, 1964 (div. 1979); children: Fabrice, Alienor, Sylvain; m. 2d, Catherine Cecile Dewavrin, Sept. 27, 1979; children: Olivier Alexis, Alexis Emmanuel. B.A. in Philosophy, Sorbonne, 1963, B.A. in Arts, 1963, M.A., 1965, Agregation, 1966; student Ecole Normale Supérieure, Paris, 1963-66. Prof. philosophy, Lycee London, 1966-70; cultural attaché French Embassy, London, 1970-74; sr. lectr. College de France, Paris, 1974-81, assoc. prof.in history and modern civilization, 1981-90; dir. essay series Presses Universitaires de France, Paris, from 1979; founder Conservative Think Tank Forum, 1984, 1979; sr. research fellow Monde et Entreprise, from 1983; founder, chmn. CERIS (European Ctr. for Internat. Relations and Strategy), 1984; vis. lectr. Harvard U., NYU, Georgetown U., War Coll., Washington, others. Author: Marx est Mort, 1970; La Revolution Structurale, 1975 (French Acad. award, paperback 1980, pub. U.S. under title The Structural Revolution); Tyrannie du Logos, 1975; Pavane pour une Europe Defunte, 1976 (paperback 1978); Les Nouveaux Primaires, 1978; Un Singulier Programme, 1978; Chronique de Décomposition du PCF, 1979 (French Acad. award), La Génération Sacrifiee, 1980 (French Acad. award), Le Devoir D'Opposition, 1982; editor: John Donne, 1983; L'Identité , 1983; Figures de Baroque, 1983; Les Outils de la Liberté, 1985; SDI and Deterrence, 1987; Chirac: Homme d'Etat, 1988; mem. editorial bd. La Revue des Deux Mondes, 1988; columnist Le Quotidien de Paris, from 1981; contbr. articles to publs. including Le Figaro, le Monde, Critique, Wall Street Jour., Washington Post. Gen. election Union Democratie Française candidate against Marchais, Val de Marne, 1978; mem. Nat. Com. for Giscard's Re-election; mem. Nat. Council of Rally for French Republic; French mem. of Com. for Free World. Mem. Am. Legion. Roman Catholic. Clubs: Le Siècle, Savile (London), PEN (nat. com.); Travellers (Paris). Died Aug. 1, 1990. Home: Neuilly sur Seine France

BENSON, BARRY T., exporter; b. Fannin County, Tex., Nov. 28, 1894; s. Nesbit and Cornelia (Johnston) B.; m. Juanita Plant, May 19, 1919; m. Grace Turner Homsher, May 10, 1947. Student, Wall Tng. Sch., Honey Grove, Tex., 1910-11, Spear Jr. Coll., 1912-13, YMCA Sch. Commerce, 1924-27. Employee telephone & electric cos., 1911-17; then salesman, sales mgr. motor car cos.; engr. electric & comm. cos., 1919-34; engring. expert FCC, 1935-37; asst. trade commr. Bur. Fgn. & Domestic Commerce, 1937, Calcutta, 1937; trade commr., 1938; consul, fgn. svc. officer, cons. sec. Diplomatic Svc., 1939; consul, 2d sec. Bogota, 1941; acting comml. attache, 1943; various other diplomatic positions to 1948; liaison officer between Am. Embassy and Econ. Commn. for Asia and Far East, UN; charge d'affaires, 1948; mem. U.S. delegation to com. of whole of Far East Commn. of UN, 1949; del., adv. UN Econ. Commn. for Asia and Far East, Singapore, 1949; comml. attache, 1st sec. U.S. Embassy, London, 1950; 1st sec. Am. Embassy, Mexico, 1951-52; fgn. trade cons. With USN, 1917-19. Mem. VFW, Masons, Elks. *

BENSON, GEORGE STUART, university chancellor; b. Okla. Ter., Sept. 26, 1898; s. Stuart Felix and Emma (Rogers) B.; m. Sallie Ellis Hockaday, July 2, 1925 (dec. 1980); children: Mary Ruth, Fannie Lois.; m. Marguerite O'Banion, Feb. 22, 1983. B.S., Okla. A. and M. Coll., Stillwater, 1924; A.B., Harding Coll., 1925, LL.D., 1932; M.A., U. Chgo., 1931; LL.D., Knox Coll., 1948, Waynesburg Coll., Okla. Christian Coll., 1968, Freed-Hardeman Coll., 1981. Tchr. rural schs. Okla., 1918-21; high sch. prin., 1924-25; missionary and tchr. South China, 1925-36; prof. English Nat. Sun Yat Sen U., Canton, China, 1929-30; editor Oriental Christian, Canton, 1929-36; founder, trustee and pres. Canton Bible Sch., 1930-36; pres. Harding Coll., 1936-65, pres. emeritus, 1965-91; chancellor Okla. Christian Coll., 1956-64, chief exec. officer, 1964-67; chancellor Ala. Christian Coll., Montgomery, 1975-86, Faulkner U., Montgomery, from 1986; Tchr., authority on Oriental religions and philosophy. Writer: syndicated weekly newspaper column Looking Ahead, 1942-85; producer: radio program Land of the Free (now Behind the News), 1942-85; Contbr. to religious publs. and secular mags. Pres. Ark. Pub. Expenditure Council, 1942-44, 52-56; dir. Nat. Thrift Com., Inc.; Mem. Nat. Com. for Religion and Welfare Recovery, 1939; appointed by Pres. Eisenhower to advisory bd. U.S. Mcht. Marine Acad., Kings Port, N.Y., 1953-56; pres. Nat. Edn. Program, Searcy, Ark., 1942-85; chmn. bd. Zambia Christian Secondary Sch., Kalomo, 1966-84; mem. nat. adv. bd. Am. Security Council, from 1975; mem. Pres. Reagan's Task Force. Recipient numerous awards Freedoms Found., Horatio Alger award, 1981; named to Okla. Hall of Fame, 1972, Dewey County Hist. Soc. Hall of Fame, 1989, Arkansan of Yr., 1953-54, others. Mem. C. of C., AIM, Pi Kappa Delta. Mem. Ch. of Christ. Club: Kiwanian. Home: Searcy Ark. Died Dec. 15, 1991.

BENTLEY, CLAUDE, artist; b. N.Y.C., June 9, 1915; m. Frances Julia Norman, Apr. 6, 1957. Student, Northwestern U., 1932-34, Art Inst. Chgo., 1945-49. instr. Art Inst. Chgo., 1959-61. Designer: Plaza Del Lago Shopping Center, Wilmette, Ill.; Exhbns. include, Corcoran Gallery Art, 1953, 59, San Francisco Mus. Art, 1960, Whitney Mus. Am. Art, N.Y.C., 1955, Art Inst. Chgo., 1941, 48, 50-66, 68, Sarasota (Fla.) Art Assn., 1959; represented in permanent collections, including, U. Ill., Met. Mus. Art, N.Y.C., Denver Art Mus., Art Inst. Chgo., Santa Barbara Mus., Ill. State Mus., Springfield, Santa Fe Art Mus., Albuquerque Mus.; works include: mural at, Hotel De La Borda, Taxco, Mexico, murals at, 3600 Lake Shore Dr., Chgo.; artist in residence, Layton Sch. Art, Milw., 1956-59. Served with AUS, 1941-45. Recipient prizes Govt. France, 1971, prizes Sarasota Art Assn., 1959, prizes Art Inst. Chgo., 1949, 50, 55, 63, prizes Met. Mus. Art, 1952, prizes Denver Art Mus., 1954, 60. Home: Santa Fe N.Mex. Deceased. †

BERGEN, THOMAS JOSEPH, lawyer, nursing home executive, association executive; b. Prairie du Chien, Wis., Feb. 7, 1913; s. Thomas Joseph and Emma Marilla (Grelle) B.; m. Jean Loraine Bowler, May 29, 1941 (dec. Aug. 1972); children—Kathleen Bergen McElwee, Eileen Bergen Bednarz, Patricia Bergen Buss, Thomas Joseph, Patrick Joseph, John Joseph. Student, U. Wis., 1930-32; J.D., Marquette U., 1937, postgrad., 1937-38. Bar: Wis. 1937, U.S. Supreme Ct. 1972. Practice law Milw., from 1937; exec. sec. Wis. Assn. Nursing Homes, 1957-71; legal counsel, exec. dir. Am. Coll. Nursing Home Adminstrs., Milw., 1967-68; sec., dir. Bayside Nursing Home, Milw., from 1967; pres., dir. N.W. Med. Ctrs., Inc., Milw., from 1968, Northland Med. Ctrs., Inc., Milw., from 1968; treas., exec. dir. Nat. Geriatrics Soc., Milw., from 1971; pres. Sen. Joseph R. McCarthy Found., Inc., 1983, pres. bd., from 1979; mem. program planning com. Nat. Conf. on Aging del. to conf., 1974; panel speaker Nat. Justice Found. Conv., 1974; v.p. Western Goals U.K., London, from 1988. Editor: Silver Threads, Wis. Assn. Nursing Homes publ., 1963-71, News Letter, Am. Coll. Nursing Home Adminstrs., 1967-68; Views and News, Nat. Geriatrics Soc., from 1971; founder, editor Senator Joseph R. McCarthy Ednl. Soc. monthly newsletter, from 1987; mem. editorial bd. Educational Gerontology, 1973-85; contbr. articles to nursing home publs. and profl. jours. Bd. dirs., treas. Nat. Geriatrics Ednl. Soc., from 1971; bd.

dirs., pres. Wis. Justice Found., from 1971; founder, pres. Senator Joseph R. McCarthy Ednl. Found., Inc., 1983. Served with AUS, 1943, 44. Recipient Merit award Wis. Assn. Nursing Homes, 1962, Outstanding Leadership award Nat. Geriatrics Soc., 1976, Disting. Svc. citation Nat. Geriatrics Soc., Inc., 1989. Mem. ABA, Wis. Bar Assn., Milw. Bar Assn. (pres., exec. dir.), Real Estate Profls. Assn. (pres. 1974), Am. Med. Writers Assn., Western Goals UK (hon. v.p. 1988—), Delta Theta Phi, Delta Sigma Rho. Roman Catholic. Home: Wauwatosa Wis. Died Sept. 23, 1992; buried Milw.

BERGER, EVELYN MILLER, psychologist; b. Hanford, Calif., Nov. 7, 1896; d. George A. and Margaret (Ross) Miller; m. Jesse Arthur Berger, June 16, 1939. AB, Stanford U., 1921, AM, 1930; PhD, Columbia U., 1932; PdD, U. Pacific, 1961. Cert. psychologist, Calif.; cert. Am. Bd. Examiners in Profl. Psychology and Counseling. Sch. tchr., prin. Panama City, 1918-19; exec. sec. girls' work M.E. Ch., Chile, Argentina, 1921-23; tchr. Spanish San Jose High Sch., 1923-30, Coll. Pacific, Stockton, Calif., 1929, 30; dean of women, assoc. prof. Spanish Allegheny Coll., 1932-36; dean of women U. Idaho, 1936-38, State Coll. San Diego, 1938-39; lectr. adult study groups mental hygiene and guidance Alameda, Berkely, Albany, 1942-44; pres. Calif. Conf. W.S.C.S. (Meth.) 1942, divsn. East Bay Psychol. Ctr., Okla., 1944; tchr. counseling, consultant in psychology Berkely Baptist divsn. sch. Contbr. articles and short stories to profl. jours. Fellow APA, Internat. Coun. Psychologists, Mental Health Soc. No. Calif., Western Psychol. Assn., Coun. on Family Rels., P.E.O., Kappa Delta Pi, Pi Lambda Theta, Gamma Phi Beta. Methodist. *

BERGHOF, HERBERT, actor, director, educator; b. Vienna, Sept. 13, 1909; s. Paul and Regina Berghof; m. Alice Hermes (div.); m. Uta Hagen. Student, U. Vienna, Vienna State Acad. Dramatic Art; pupil of, Alexander Moissi, Max Reinhardt, Lee Strasberg. Charter mem. Actors Studio, N.Y.C.; Theatrical appearances include Don Carlos, 1927; resident mem. St. Gallen Repertory Co., Zurich, 1927-29; mem. Deutsches Volks Theatre, theatre in cler Josefstadt, Vienna, 1929-30; performed Berlin and Salzburg festivals, 1930-33, 33-38; appeared in Romeo and Juliet, Journey's End, The Doctor's Dilemma, Hamlet, All God's Chillun got Wings, Crime for Crime, Six Characters in Search of an Author, An American Tragedy, Everyman, Ghosts, As You Like It, Candida; dir. The Melody That Got Lost, Vienna; N.Y.C. debut as King Lear, 1941; appearance in Criminals; dir. From Vienna; actor, dir. Reunion in New York, rev. version From Vienna, 1940; actor in France, 1941, Nathan the Wise, 1943, Twelfth Night, 1942, Winter Soldiers, 1942, The Russian People, 1942, The Innocent Voyage, 1943, Oklahoma, 1943, Jacobowsky and the Colonel, 1944, The Man Who Had All the Luck, 1944, Little Women, 1944, The Beggars are Coming to Town, 1945, St. Lazare's Pharmacy (tour), 1945, The Mayor of Zalemea, 1946, Temper the Wind, 1946, The Whole World Over, 1947, Ghosts, 1948, Hedda Gabler, 1948, Miss Liberty, 1949, Torquato Tasso, 1949, The Lady From the Sea, 1950, Guardsman, 1951, Tovarich, 1952, The Deep Blue Sea, 1952; numerous stock appearances; dir. The Key, 1947, Rip Van Winkle, 1947, Waiting for Godot, N.Y.C., 1956-57, Protective Custody, 1956, The Infernal Machine, 1958, Twelfth Night, 1959, The Queen and the Rebels, 1959; dir., actor The Affairs of Anatol; appeared in the Andersonville Trial, 1959, Krapp's Last Tape, 1960, Oppenheimer, Lincoln Center, 1969; dir. Do Know The Milky Way?, 1961, This Side of Paradise, 1962, Seize the Day, Tomorrow, Kaspar, Poor Murderer (Broadway), 1976; film appearances include Assignment Paris, 1952, Diplomatic Courier, 1952, Five Fingers, 1952, Red Planet Mars, 1952, Fraûlein, 1958, An Affair of the Skin, 1963, Cleopatra, 1963, Harry and Tonto, 1974, Those Eyes, Those Lips, 1981, Voices, 1986; numerous radio and TV appearances; tchr. acting Columbia, New Sch. Social Research, Neighborhood Playhouse, Am. Theatre Wing: founder, dir. HB Studio, 1945, HB Playwrights Found., 1964. Mem. SAG, AFTRA, Actors Equity Assn. Home: New York N.Y. Died Nov. 5, 1990.

BERGSTROM, NATHAN HOUGH, paper company executive; b. Neenah, Wis., Apr. 25, 1895; s. Dedrick W. and Sarah (Hough) B.; m. Agnes E. Birdsall, June 12, 1919; children: Alice P. Moore, Marjorie S. Moore, Natalie J. Rindal. Student, Lawrence Coll., 1912-16. With Bergstrom Paper Co., Neenah, from 1916, dir., from 1919, treas., 1921-28, sec., 1928-43, v.p., sec., 1943-44, v.p., 1944-48, pres., 1948-62, chmn. bd., from 1962. With U.S. Army, 1917-19. Mem. Am. Paper & Pulp Assn., Printing Paper Mfrs. Assn., Newcomen Soc. *

BERKO, STEPHAN, physicist, educator; b. Oradea, Rumania, Dec. 16, 1924; came to U.S., 1947; BA, U. Va., 1950, PhD, 1953. Asst. prof. U. Va., Charlottesville, 1954-57, assoc. prof., 1958-60, prof. physics, 1960-61; prof. physics Brandeis U., Waltham, Mass., 1961-91, William R. Kenan Jr. prof., 1978-91, chmn. dept. physics, 1965-67, 71-74; vis. scientist Solid State Physics Inst., U. Paris, 1968; internat. lectr. on positron and positronium physics. Contbr. articles to profl. jours. NRC postdoctoral fellow Princeton U., 1953-54, Sloan Found. fellow Bohr Inst., Copenhagen, 1958, 59, Guggenheim fellow Laue Langevin Inst., Grenoble, France, 1976-77. Fellow Am. Acad. Arts and Scis., Am. Phys. Soc.; mem. NAS, Phi Beta Kappa. Home: Wellesley Mass. Died May 15, 1991.

BERLIN, DON R., aeronautical executive; b. Romona, Ind., June 13, 1898; s. Charles Norton and Maude Easter (Mull) B.; m. Helen Elizabeth Hents, Feb. 16, 1926; 1 child, Donald Edward. BSME, Purdue U., 1921, D in Engring. (hon.), 1953. Asst. aerodynamics lab. U.S. Army Air Corps, 1921-26; project engr., chief draftsman Douglas Aircraft, Santa Monica, Calif., 1926-29; chief engr. Valley Mfg. Co., Glendale, Calif., 1929, Northrop Corp., 1929-32, Northrop Aircraft, Inglewood, Calif., 1932-34; project engr., chief engr., dir. engring. Curtiss-Wright Airplane divsn., Buffalo, 1934-42; dir. aircraft devel. Fisher Body divsn. GM Corp., Detroit, 1942-45; dir. installation engring. sect. Allison Divsn., Inpls., 1945-47; v.p. engring. & contracts McDonnell Aircraft Corp., St. Louis, 1947, exec. v.p., 1949-51; v.p., gen. mgr. McDonnel Aircraft Corp., 1951-52; pres., dir. Vertol Aircraft Corp., Morton, Pa., 1953-60; chmn. exec. com., 1953-55, chmn. bd. dirs., 1955-60; v.p., gen. mgr. Vertol divsn. Boeing, 1960-62, v.p., cons., 1962-63; v.p. Curtiss-Wright Corp., Wood Ridge, N.J., from 1963. Fellow AIAA, Am. Ordnance Assn.; mem. Soc. Automotive Engrs., Am. Helicopter Soc., A.F. Assn. *

BERLIN, IRVING, composer; b. Russia, May 11, 1888; came to U.S., 1893; s. Moses and Leah (Lipkin) Baline; m. Dorothy Goetz, Feb. 1913 (dec. July 1913); m. Ellin Mackay, Jan. 4, 1926 (dec.); children: Mary Ellin Berlin Barrett, Linda Berlin Emmet, Elizabeth Berlin Peters. Ed. pub. schs., N.Y.C.; hon. degrees, Bucknell U., Temple U., Fordham U. Pres. The Irving Berlin Music Corp. Writer, composer popular songs: Alexander's Ragtime Band, Oh How I Hate to Get Up in the Morning, When I Lost You, When I Leave the World Behind, What'll I Do?, All Alone, Remember, Reaching for the Moon, Always, Because I Love You, At Peace With the World, Russian Lullaby, Music Box Revues, Coconuts, Ziegfeld Follies, Me, Any Bonds Today, White Christmas; musical comedy revue This is the Army; film musical Easter Parade; stage musicals Annie Get Your Gun, Miss Liberty, Call Me Madam, Mr. President, 1962; also various others; total songs composed about 800. Served as sgt. Infantry, at Camp Upton, L.I. Recipient Presdl. Medal of Freedom, 1977, Medal of Merit for This Is The Army; Lawrence Langer award for disting. lifetime achievement in Am. theater, 1978; Congl. Gold medal for God Bless America; decorated Legion of Honor (France). Clubs: Lambs, Friars. Lodges: Masons, Shriners, Elks. Home: New York N.Y. Died Sept. 22, 1989; buried Woodlawn Cemetery, N.Y.

BERNAL, IGNACIO, archaeologist; b. Paris, Feb. 13, 1910; s. Rafael Bernal and Rafaela García Pimentel; m. Sofia Verea, Oct. 14, 1944; children: Ignacio, Rafaela, Carlos, Concha. LL.D., U. Mex., 1949; M.A., Cambridge (Eng.) U., 1975; M.A. hon. degrees, U. Calif., St. Mary's U., San Antonio, U. Americas. Prof. anthropology U. Mex., 1948-76; dir. Nat. Inst., Mexico City, 1968-71, Mus. Anthropology, Mexico City, 1962-77; vis. prof. anthropology U. Tex., 1954, U. Calif., 1958, Harvard U., 1961, Cambridge U., 1975-76, Sorbonne U., Paris, 1955-56, U. Madrid, 1964, U. Rome, 1966. Author: A History of Mexican Archaeology, The Olmec World, others; contbr. 267 articles on archaeology and history to profl. jours. Decorated officer Royal Order Orange-Nassau, Netherlands; officer Legion of Honor; comdr. Legion of Honor, France; comdr. Order of Merit, Italy; officer Order of Crown, Belgium; comdr. Order of Merit, Ger.; officer Royal Order of Danebrog, Denmark; comdr. Order of Merit, Senegal; comdr. Royal Victoria Order, Eng.; comdr. Star of Yugoslavia. Mem. U.S. Nat. Acad. Scis. (fgn. assoc.), El Colegio Nacional, Academia de la Historia, Academia de la Lengua. Roman Catholic. Home: Mexico City Mex. Deceased. †

BERNARDI, THEODORE C., architect; b. Korcula, Dalmatia, Yugoslavia, Oct. 3, 1903; came to U.S., 1912; s. John A. and Vincenza (DePolo) B.; m. Beatrice Boot, Aug. 1947; children—Gene, Joan Bernardi Breece. B.A., U. Calif.-Berkeley, 1924, postgrad., 1925. Lic. architect, Calif. Draftsman, designer, architect Wurster, Bernardi & Emmons, San Francisco, 1923-43, ptnr., 1944-64, exec. v.p., 1964-73, cons., from 1974; lectr. U. Calif.-Berkeley, 1954-71; chmn. archtl. design com. San Francisco Housing Authority, 1965-69; chmn. Reynolds Award Jury, Colo., 1968. Archtl. works include: Cowell Coll. U. Calif.-Santa Cruz, First Unitarian Ch. of Berkeley, Strawberry Canyon Recreation Facility U. Calif.-Berkeley. Fellow AIA (Award of Merit 1956, San Francisco chpt. award of Merit 1957, Archtl. Firm award 1965, Collaborative Achievement award 1966, Award of Merit 1966); mem. San Francisco Planning and Urban Research, World Affairs Council. Club: Commonwealth (San Francisco); Faculty (Berkeley). Died Jan. 10, 1990. Home: Sausalito Calif.

BERNAT, EUGENE, textile manufacturing executive; b. Budapest, Aug. 18, 1896; came to U.S., 1903, naturalized, 1910; s. Emile and Emma (Fried) B.; m. Elva I. Packer, Apr. 25, 1926; children: William A., Geoffrey E. BS, Harvard U., 1920. With Emile Bernat & Sons Co., Jamaica Plain, Mass., from 1920; pres. Emile Bernat & Sons Co., Jamaica Plain, from 1939. Mem. Am. Assn. Textile Chemists and Colorists, Chinese Art Soc. Am., Mason. *

BERNDT, REXER, college executive; b. Bellefontaine, Ohio, Mar. 9, 1920; m. Geraldine Cowman; children: Elizabeth, Katherine, Rexer Jr. (dec.). Pres. Ft. Lewis Coll., Durango, Colo., 1969-91. Home: Durango Colo. Died June 25, 1991; cremated.

BERNER, NORMAN ARTHUR, minister; b. Guelph, Ont., Can., Oct. 8, 1910; s. Ulrich Rudolf and Clara Anna (Nieghorn) B.; m. Ruth Marguerite Ludwig, Apr. 14, 1941; children: Carole, Suzanne, Heather. Grad., Waterloo Lutheran Sem., 1938; B.A., Waterloo Coll., U. Western Ont., 1935; D.D., Waterloo Luth. U., 1972. Ordained to ministry Luth. Ch. Am., 1938; pastor Brantford-Woodstock Parish, 1938-45, Morrisburg Parish, 1945-46; editor United Luth. Publ. House, Phila., 1946-50; mgr. Luth. Ch. Supply Store, Kitchener, Ont., 1950-54; asst. to pres. Evang. Luth. Synod of Can., 1955-62, Eastern Can. Synod, Luth. Ch. Am., Kitchener, 1963-79; vice pastor Zion Luth. Ch., Stratford, Ont., 1979-80, St. Stephen Luth. Ch., Kitchener, Ont., 1984; Sec., v.p. Can. Luth. Council, 1954-66; pres. Luth. Council in, Can., 1978-80; exec. dir. Luth. Ch. Can. Found., 1980-85; mem. bd. social missions United Luth. Ch. in Am., 1958-62; sec. Can. sect. Luth. Ch. Am., 1969-75; mem. Joint Commn. on Inter-Luth. Relationships, 1969-78, Commn. on Luth. Merger, 1978-81; mem. exec. com. Can. Council Chs., 1968-72, pres., 1972-76; del. Luth. World Fedn. Conf. on Social Responsibility, Vienna, 1969; observer Luth. World Fedn. Assembly, Mpls., 1957, Union Am. Hebrew Congregations Biennial Conv., N.Y.C., 1973; bd. dirs. Can. Luth. World Relief, 1978-80; mem. Luth. Ch. Am. Seminar on Japan., 1972; observer, cons. Gen. Commn. on Ch. Union, Can., 1968-72; fraternal del. World Council Chs. Assembly, Nairobi, 1975, visitor, Vancouver, 1983; synod staff ofcl. Luth. Ch. Am. div. for Mission in N.Am., 1970-79; bd. govs. Waterloo Luth. U., 1960-62; stewardship cons. Eastern Synod, Evang. Luth. Ch. in Can., 1986-88; chaplain Kitchener-Waterloo Hosps., 1983-90. Home: Kitchener Can. Died Apr. 29, 1991. †

BERNER, T. ROLAND, lawyer, corporation executive; b. N.Y.C., Sept. 23, 1909; s. Irwin Rolston and Cecile (Olin) B.; m. Rosalie Leventritt, Mar. 24, 1938; children: Edgar Rolston, Rosalie Berner Fedoruk, Winifred Berner Parker, Thomas Roland, Richard Olin. B.S., Harvard U., 1931; LL.B., Columbia U., 1935. Bar: N.Y. 1936. Assoc. Cravath, DeGersdorff, Swaine & Wood, N.Y.C., 1935-42; sole practice N.Y.C, 1946-70; chmn. bd., pres. Curtiss-Wright Corp., Wood Ridge, N.J., 1960-90, chief exec. officer, 1965-80; chmn. bd. Dorr-Oliver, Inc.; dir., exec. com. Amerace Corp., GAF Corp. Bd. dirs. Young Audiences, Inc., Bus. Com. for the Srts, Edgar M. Leventritt Found.; founder Leventritt Piano Competition; trustee Carnegie Corp., Marlboro Music Sch. Served to lt. comdr. USNR, 1942-45. Recipient Navy Meritorious Pub. Service citation. Mem. Bar Assn. N.Y.C., Am. Ordnance Assn., Air Force Assn., Assn. U.S. Army, Nat. Security Indsl. Assn., Soc. Automotive Engrs. Episcopalian. Clubs: Harvard, Highland Country, Economic (N.Y.C.); Nat. Aviation (Washington). Home: Fort Lee N.J. Died Mar. 18, 1990.

BERNERS, EDGAR HUBERT, architect; b. Port Washington, Wis., Jan. 6, 1898; s. Hubert Joseph and Catherine (Peters) B.; m. Rose Zita Davis, Aug. 18, 1923; children: Edgar D., Mary (Mrs. Thomas Kishler). B.S. in Archtl. Engring., U. Ill., 1921. Registered architect, Wis., Minn., Mich., Ill., Mo., N.D., La.; registered profl. engr., Wis. Architect, engr. Foeller, Schober & Stephenson, Green Bay, Wis., 1922-26; engr. Truscon Steel Co., Youngstown, Ohio, 1926-28; ptnr. Foeller, Schober, Berners, Green Bay, 1928-46, Berners, Schober & Kilp, Green Bay, 1946-92; pres. Nat. Council Archtl. Registration Bds., 1952-53. Prin. works include St. Norbert Abbey, Depere, Wis., St. John's Hosp., Springfield, Ill., St. Elizabeth's Hosp., Belleville, Ill., St. Vincent Hosp., Green Bay, St. Mary's Hosp., Green Bay, Sacred Heart Hosp., Eau Claire, Wis., U. Wis. Coll. Engring. Electrical Engring. Chem. Engring. Civil Engring., Wis. Ctr. Bldg., numerous other hosps., schs. Mem. Wis. Registration Bd. Architecture and Engring., Madison, 1950-74, chmn. archtl. div., 1964-74. Served with USN, 1918. Recipient Abbot Pennings Founder award St. Norbert Abbey, De Pere, Wis., 1983; Dr. Nathan Ricker fellow dept. architecture U. Ill., Urbana, 1984-85; Paul Harris fellow Rotary Internat., Evanston, Ill., 1984. Fellow AIA (nat. bd. dirs. 1952-55); mem. Wis. Soc. Architects (past pres., merit award 1950), Nat. Soc. Profl. Engrs., Am. Legion. Roman Catholic. Lodges: K.C. (Dr. Henney award Wis. council 1955), Elks, Rotary. Deceased.*

BERNHEIM, ELINOR KRIDEL (MRS. LEONARD H. BERNHEIM), social welfare volunteer; b. N.Y.C., June 26, 1907; d. Alexander Hayes and Irma (Hernsheim) Kridel; m. Leonard H. Bernheim. B.A., Vassar Coll., 1928; postgrad., N.Y. Sch. Social Work, 1947-48. Mem. bd. and council Assn. for Aid for Crippled Children, from 1941; trustee Fedn. Jewish Philanthropies,

N.Y.C., from 1942; v.p. Fedn. Jewish Philanthropies, 1955-58, chmn. women's div. fund raising drive, 1943, 44, 49, chmn. women's bd., 1955-58, hon. chmn., from 1958, v.p., from 1971; pres. bd. Jewish Assn. Neighborhood Ctrs., 1948-52; dir. Nat. Jewish Welfare Bd., from 1944, chmn. women's div., 1954-61, hon. chmn. women's bd., from 1961; mem. bd. com. Nat. Conf. for Social Welfare, 1947-51, v.p., 1949-51, chmn. edn. and recreation div., from 1959; adv. com. vol. services VA, 1947-61; bd. dirs. United Neighborhood Houses of N.Y.C., 1949-53; mem. bd. Nat. Council on Social Work Edn., 1952-54, mem. nat. citizens com. on careers, 1961-65; mem. bd. Nat. Assembly Social Policy and Devel.; pres. bd. Mosholu Montefiore Community Center, 1958-70; bd. dir. Associated YM and YWHA's of Greater N.Y., 1958-60, assoc. chmn., 1960-69, co-chmn., from 1970; pres. Community Council Greater N.Y., 1970-78, chmn. bd., from 1978; adv. bd. Columbia Univ. Sch. Social Work, 1968-78; bd. dirs. Community Service Soc., 1961-78; mem. N.Y. State Welfare Conf., 1961-63, Nat. Conf. Social Welfare, 1963, Gov. N.Y. State Com. Children and Youth, 1963; co-chmn. Dimitri Mitropolous Internat. Music Competition, 1961-63; bd. dirs. Young Concert Artists, from 1968; mem. Mayor's Screening Panel to Bd. Higher Edn., N.Y.C., 1964; v.p. Nat. Jewish Welfare Bd., 1967-71, Columbia Univ. Sch. Social Work, from 1968; mem. N.Y.C. chpt. Nat. Council on Alcoholism; mem. N.Y.C. Mayor's Office for Vol. Action, 1975, Nat. Homemakers Service Council, 1980; bd. dirs. Lavanburg Corner House Found., 1981, Brookdale Inst. on Aging, 1983; founder Elinor K. Bernheim awards, 1980; co-founder Florence G. Heller Research Ctr. Author articles in field. Recipient Gen. award N.Y. State Welfare Conf., 1958; Bi-Centennial medal Columbia U., 1956; Frank L. Weil award Nat. Jewish Welfare Bd., 1960; Research Inst. citation Nat. Conf. Jewish Center Workers, 1961; Blanche Ittleson award, 1963; Naomi Lehman Meml. Found. award, 1966; caring New Yorker award Community Council Greater N.Y., 1982; citation of honor Nat. Council Jewish Women; citation of honor Mosholu Montefiore Community Ctr., 1985. Clubs: Women's City, Cosmopolitan (N.Y.C.). Home: New York N.Y. Died Oct. 9, 1992. †

BERNSTEIN, DAVID, surgeon; b. Minsk, Russia, Oct. 20, 1910; came to U.S., 1912, naturalized, 1932; s. George and Anna (Rossoff) B.; m. Dorothy Ashery, Sept. 2, 1937; children—Helen Miriam Berman Young, Herbert Jacob. B.S., N.Y. U., 1930, M.D., 1935. Intern Bellevue Hosp.-N.Y. U., N.Y.C., 1935-37; resident in ear, nose, throat and facial plastic surgery Bellevue Hosp.-N.Y. U., 1937-39; clin. prof. otorhinolaryngology, chief of plastic surgery N.Y. U. Med. Center, from 1966; chief otolaryngology service Maimonides Med. Center, from 1966; cons. otorhinolaryngol. plastic surgery VA Hosp., N.Y.C.; attending otolaryngologist plastic surgery Bellevue-N.Y. U. Hosp.; pres., exec. com. of med. staff Met. Geriatric Center, 1974-75, mem. joint com. bd. trustees, from 1975; cons. Coney Island Hosp. Contbr. articles to profl. jours., sci. papers to meetings. Served to maj. M.C. AUS, 1944-46. Recipient Meritorious Service award N.Y. U., 1977; named hon. police surgeon N.Y.C., 1979. Fellow Am. Acad. Ophthalmology and Otolaryngology, Am. Acad. Facial, Plastic and Reconstructive Surgery, Am. Assn. Cosmetic Surgeons, Internat. Coll. Surgeons; mem. N.Y., Vienna acads. medicine, N.Y. U. Med. Sch. Alumni Assn. (pres. 1974-75), N.Y. U. Alumni Fedn. (dir.), Phi Beta Kappa. Jewish (adv. com. to bd. trustees temple). Clubs: N.Y. U, Medallion (pres. 1980). Home: Brooklyn N.Y. Died Jan. 15, 1988.

BERNSTEIN, LEONARD, conductor, pianist, composer; b. Lawrence, Mass., Aug. 25, 1918; s. Samuel Joseph and Jennie (Resnick) B.; m. Felicia Montealegre Cohn, Sept. 9, 1951 (dec. June 1978); children: Jamie, Alexander, Nina. A.B., Harvard U., 1939; grad., Curtis Inst. Music, 1941; studied conducting with, Fritz Reiner and Serge Koussevitzky; studied piano with, Helen Coates, Heinrich Gebhard, and Isabella Vengerova; numerous hon. degrees from various colls. and univs. Asst. to Serge Koussevitzky at Berkshire Music Center, 1942; asst. condr. N.Y. Philharmonic Symphony, 1943-44; condr. N.Y.C. Symphony, 1945-48; frequent condr. Israel Philharmonic Orch., from 1947, mus. adviser, 1948-49; faculty Berkshire Music Center, 1948-55, head conducting dept., 1951-55; prof. music Brandeis U., 1951-56; co-condr. with Dimitri Mitropoulos of N.Y. Philharmonic, 1957-58, music dir., 1958-69; Charles Eliot Norton prof. poetry Harvard, 1972-73. Condr. major orchs. of U.S., Europe in tours, 1946-90, opera at La Scala, Milan, also Met. Opera, N.Y.C. and Vienna State Opera; shared transcontinental tour in U.S. with Serge Koussevitzky and Israel Philharmonic, 1951; toured Europe with Vienna Philharmonic Orch., 1970, gala Bicentennial tour, Am. and Europe with N.Y. Philharmonic, 1976; condr. 6-city tour of U.S., summer 1986; condr. Israel Philharm. Orch. in celebration of its 50th anniversary, N.Y.C., Sept. 1986, world-wide telecast Berlin celebration concerts, 1989, laureate condr., 1988, pres. English Bach Festival 1977—, London Symphony Orch. 1987—, condr. commemorative concert marking 50th anniversary Nazi invasion of Poland, 1989; artistic co-chmn. Pacific Music Festival, Sapporo, Japan, 1990; works include Clarinet Sonata, 1942, Seven Anniversaries for Piano, 1942, Song Cycle, I Hate Music, 1943, Four Anniversaries for Piano, 1948, Song Cycle, La Bonne Cuisine, 1949; Symphony Number 1-Jeremiah, 1942, Symphony Number 2-The Age of Anxiety, 1949, Symphony Number 3, Kaddish, Beethoven symphony Number 9, 1989; composer, librettist 1-act opera Trouble in Tahiti, 1952; Chichester Psalms, for mixed chorus, boys' choir, orch., 1965; score for musical show On The Town; ballets Fancy Free, 1944, Facsmile, 1946; Dybbuk, 1974; incidental score for prodn. Peter Pan, 1950, The Lark, 1957; mus. score for Broadway prodn. Wonderful Town, 1953; Broadway musicals Candide, 1956, West Side Story, 1957; film On the Waterfront, 1954; songs Afterthought, Silhouette, 1951, Two Love Songs, 1949; Serenade, for violin and string orch. with percussion, 1954, Five Anniversaries for Piano, 1964; Mass, theatre piece for singers, players and dancers, 1971; Dybbuk Variations, Suites No. 1 and 2, from ballet by Jerome Robbins, 1974; Songfest, a cycle of Am. poems for six singers and orch., 1977; overture for orch. Slava!, 1977; Three Meditations, from Mass, for cello and orch., 1977; Divertimento for Orchestra, 1980, A Musical Toast for Orchestra, 1980; Halil for flute and orch., 1980; A Quiet Place (opera), 1983; Thirteen Anniversaries for piano, 1988; Arias and Barcarolles, for piano duet and singers, 1988; Missa Brevis, for singers and percussion, 1988, Concerto for Orchestra (Jubilee Games 1986-89), 1989, Dance Suite for brass quintet, 1990; author: The Joy of Music, 1959 (Christopher award), Leonard Bernstein's Young People's Concerts for Reading and Listening, 1962, rev. edit., 1970, The Infinite Variety of Music, 1966, The Unanswered Question: Six Talks at Harvard, 1976. Findings, 1982. Founder Bernstein Edn. Through the Arts Fund, 1990. Recipient Emmy award for Young People's Concerts, 1960, for Outstanding Classical Music Program, Leonard Bernstein and the N.Y. Philharm., 1976, The Handel Medallion, 1977, Lifetime Achievement Grammy award, 1985, Gold medal Am. Acad. Arts and Letters, 1985, Gold medal Britain Royal Philharm. Soc., 1987, Grammy award for best cast show album West Side Story, 1986, Edward MacDowell medal, 1987, Johannes Brahms prize, 1988, Star of People's Friendship medalovt. East Germany, 1989, Praemium Imperiale award for life achievement Govt. Japan, 1990; apptd. laureate condr. Philharm. for life; festival produced in his honor by London Symphony Orch. in cooperation with Barbican Ctr., 1986; decorated commandeur du Légion d'Honneur (France), 1986; festival Bernstein at 70 produced in his honor by Boston Symphony Orch., Tanglewood, 1988. Home: New York N.Y. Died Oct. 14, 1990; buried Greenwood, Bklyn.

BERNSTEIN, MARVER HILLEL, political science educator, academic administrator; b. Mankato, Minn., Feb. 7, 1919; s. Meyer M. and Esther (Alpert) B.; m. Sheva Rosenthal, Sept. 19, 1943. B.A., M.A., U. Wis., 1940; Ph.D. in Politics, Princeton U., 1948; D.H.L., Jewish Theol. Sem., 1975, Northeastern U., 1978, Duquesne U., 1978, Brandeis U., 1983, Balt. Hebrew Coll., Hebrew Union Coll., 1984. Budget examiner U.S. Bur. Budget, 1942-46; mem. faculty Princeton U., 1947-72, prof. polit. and pub. affairs, 1958-72, chmn. dept. politics, 1961-64; assoc. dir. Woodrow Wilson Sch., 1962-64; dean Woodrow Wilson Sch. Pub. and Internat. Affairs, 1964-69; pres. Brandeis U., Waltham, Mass, 1972-83; Univ. prof. Georgetown U., Washington, 1983-89; dir. New Eng. Mchts. Nat. Bank, Bank New Eng. N.A., 1973-83; cons. orgn., adminstrn. state and fed. agys. State Controller of Israel, 1953-57, A.I.A., 1968-70; asso. staff dir. spl. com. fed. conflict of interest laws Assn. Bar City N.Y., 1958-60; mem. Adminstrv. Conf. U.S., 1961-62, Rockefeller Pub. Service Awards Selection Com., 1964-69; mem. Nat. B'nai B'rith Hillel Found., from 1966, chmn., 1969-75, hon. chmn., from 1975. Author: Regulating Business by Independent Commission, 1955, The Politics of Israel, 1957, The Job of the Federal Executive, 1958, (with Walter Murphy, others) American Democracy, 1951-73. Chmn. Pub. and Sch. Employees' Grievance Procedure Study; mem. Commn. N.J., 1967; mem. N.J. Apportionment Commn., 1968-69, Mass. Ethics Commn., 1978-82, U.S. Holocaust Meml. Council, 1980-86 ; hon. trustee Am. Jewish Hist. Soc., 1985—, Joint Distbn. Com., 1978-88, Found. for Jewish Studies, 1985-89; bd. dirs. WGBH Ednl. Found., 1972-83, WETA, 1984-89; pres. Nat. Fedn. for Jewish Culture, 1982-86, Am. Profs. Peace in Mid. East, 1985-89. Fellow Am. Acad. Arts and Scis.; mem. Nat. Acad. Pub. Adminstrn., Am. Polit. Sci. Assn., Am. Soc. Pub. Adminstrn., Cosmos Club. Home: Washington DC Died Mar. 1, 1990.

BERNSTEIN, PAUL MURRAY, lawyer; b. N.Y.C., Dec. 24, 1929; s. Emanuel Klein and Anne Krasner-Glauber; m. Mae Piccirilli, June 10, 1950; children: Jane Shapiro, Richard. BA, Columbia U., 1951, LLB, 1953. Bar: N.Y. 1953, U.S. Dist. Ct. (so. and ea. dists.) N.Y. 1953, U.S. Supreme Ct. 1969, U.S. Ct. Appeals (4th, 5th, 6th and 9th cirs.). Assoc. Chadbourne Parke W&W, N.Y.C., 1953-63; gen. mgr. Saks Fifth Ave, N.Y.C., 1964-68; ptnr. Kreindler & Kreindler, N.Y.C., 1969-83; sr. ptnr. Bernstein Litowitz Berger & Grossmann, N.Y.C., 1983-90; frequent lectr. in field. Columnist N.Y. Law Jour., 1972-85; author numerous articles. Trustee Fed. Bar Council. Harlan Fiske Stone scholar Columbia Law Sch. Mem. ABA, Assn. of Bar of City of N.Y., Practicing Law Inst. Home: Bellmore N.Y. Died Aug. 15, 1990; buried Woodlawn Cemetery, Bronx, N.Y.

BERNSTEIN, RICHARD BARRY, scientist, chemistry educator; b. N.Y.C., Oct. 31, 1923; s. Simon and Stella Ruth (Grossman) B.; m. Norma Bianca Olivier, Dec. 17, 1948; children: Neil David, Minda Dianne, Beth Anne, Julie Lynn. AB, Columbia Coll., N.Y.C., 1943, MA in Chemistry, 1946; PhD in Chemistry, Columbia U., N.Y.C., 1948; DSc (hon.), U. Chgo., 1988. From asst. prof. to assoc. prof. chemistry Ill. Inst. Tech., Chgo., 1948-53; from assoc. prof. to prof. U. Mich., Ann Arbor, 1953-63; prof. U. Wis., Madison, 1963-67, Daniells prof. chemistry, 1967-73; Doherty prof. chemistry U. Tex., Austin, 1973-77; Higgins prof. natural scis., dept. chemistry Columbia U., 1977-82; sr. v.p. Occidental Petroleum Research Corp., Irvine, Calif., 1982-83; prof. chemistry UCLA, 1983-90; researcher Manhattan Project, S.A.M. Labs., Columbia U., 1942-46; Hinshelwood lectr. Oxford (Eng.) U., 1980 . Author: Chemical Dynamics Via Molecular Beams and Lasers, 1982, (with R.D. Levine) Molecular Reaction Dynamics, 1974, Molecular Reaction Dynamics and Chemical Reactivity, 1987; editor: Atom-Molecule Collision Theory, 1979, U.S. editor: Chem. Physics Letters, 1978-81, 85-90. Served with C.E. U.S. Army, 1944-46. A.P. Sloan fellow, 1956-60, NSF fellow, 1960-61; Fairchild Disting. scholar Calif. Inst. Tech., 1986, 90; recipient Robert A. Welch Award in Chemistry, 1988, Nat. Medal of Sci., 1989. Fellow AAAS, Am. Acad. Arts and Scis., Am. Phys. Soc.; mem. Nat. Acad. Scis. (Chem. Scis. award 1985), Am. Chem. Soc. (Debye award 1981, Langmuir award 1988, Gibbs medal 1989). Home: Los Angeles Calif. Died July 8, 1990; buried Santa Monica, Calif.

BERRIDGE, WILLIAM ARTHUR, economist; b. Lynn, Mass., Apr. 13, 1893; s. Frank and Sadie May (Brown) B.; m. Ruth Reid, Jan. 24, 1918; children: Katherine Sohler, Ruth Margaret. AB, Harvard U., 1914, AM, 1919, PhD, 1922. Instr. math. Harvard U., 1915-17, instr. econs., 1920-22; asst. to assoc. prof. Brown U., 1922-27, dir. rsch. Bur. Bus. Rsch., 1923-27; cons. economist Met. Life Ins. Co., 1924-27, economist, 1927-61; cons. economist Great Barrington, Mass., from 1961. Author: Cycles of Unemployment in the U.S., 1923, Purchasing Power of the Consumer (with E.A. Winslow and R.A. Flinn), 1925, others. Maj. Coast Arty. Res. Corps, World War I. Fellow Am. Statis. Assn.; mem. Am. Econ. Assn., Royal Statis. Soc., Royal Econ. Soc., Market Rsch. Coun., Am. Risk & Ins. Assn., Conf. Bus. Economists, Am. Fin. Assn., Economists Nat. Com. on Monetary Policy, others. *

BERRY, RICHARD CHISHOLM, industrial materials manufacturing executive, researcher; b. Salem, Mass., July 14, 1928; s. Kenneth Bliss and Georgia Ellen (Chisholm) B.; m. Louise Spaulding, June 9, 1951; children: Donald, Pamela, Robin, Christopher, Judith. BSChemE, MIT, 1948, MSChemE, 1949. With Rogers (Conn.) Corp., 1949-92, devel. engr., 1949-55, mgr. fibrous product devel., 1955-57, mgr. product devel., 1957-63, tech. dir., 1963-66, v.p. R & D, 1966-80, v.p. tech., 1980-86, sr. v.p. tech., 1986-92. Contbr. articles on advanced polymeric materials to profl. jours.; patentee in field. Chmn, adv. coun. Quinebaug Valley Community Coll., Danielson, Conn., 1971-75, pres. Found., 1972-76; mem. bd. trustees Community Colls., Hartford, Conn., 1973-84; mem. Bd. Higher Edn., Hartford, 1977-83. Recipient Civic Achievement award Danielson C. of C., 1977. Mem. IEEE, Internat. Electronic Packaging Soc., Am. Chem. Soc., Am. Inst. Chem. Engring. Republican. Home: Danielson Conn. Deceased. †

BERTHEAU, CESAR JORDAN, banker; b. San Francisco, June 5, 1897; s. Cesar and Anita (Jordan) B.; m. Bernard M. Cameron, Nov. 28, 1941. AB, U. Calif., 1919. Mgr. L.A. office Am. Nat. Co. San Francisco, 1925-28; v.p., N.Y.C. rep. Am. Nat. Co., Am. Trust Co. San Francisco, 1928-30; v.p., dir. Pacific Trust Co., Am. Pacific Corp., N.Y.C., 1928-30; v.p. Marine Midland Trust Co., 1930-47; pres., dir. Fidelity Safe Deposit Co., N.Y.C., 1939-47; pres. chmn. exec. com., dir. Anchorage Homes, Inc., Westfield, Mass., 1947; exec. v.p., dir. Peoples Trust Co. Bergen County, Hackensack, N.J., 1948-51, pres., CEO, 1951-60, chmn. bd., from 1960. Bd. fellows Fairleigh Dickinson U., 1960-63. 2d lt. arty. AUS, 1918-19. Mem. Soc. Calif. Pioneers, Psi Upsilon. *

BERUH, JOSEPH, drama and film producer; b. Pitts., Sept. 27, 1924; s. William Israel and Clara (Parnes) B.; children: David Marshall, William Israel. B.F.A., Carnegie Inst. Tech., 1950. Ptnr. Lansbury/Beruh Prodns., N.Y.C., from 1969. Producer numerous plays including Leave It to Jane, 1959, Long Days Journey into Night, 1970, Godspell, 1971, Promenade, 1969, Waiting for Godot, 1971, Comedy, 1973, Gypsy, 1975, The Night That Made America Famous, 1976, The Magic Show, 1974, American Buffalo, 1977, N.Y.C., Cat's Pajamas, 1963, Nourish the Beast, 1973, Kittiwake Island, 1960, Young, Gifted and Black, 1965, Trains, 1969, The Enclave, 1974, Blasts and Bravos, Gypsy, London; producer films including Godspell, 1973, Blue Sunshine, 1977, Squirm, 1976, The Wild Party, 1974, He Knows You're Alone, 1979, The Clairvoyant, 1982. Served with AUS, 1943-46. Recipient Alumni Merit award Carnegie-Mellon U., 1987. Mem. League of N.Y. Theatres. Home: New York N.Y. Died 1990. †

BESS, GORDON CLARK, cartoonist; b. Richfield, Utah, Jan. 12, 1929; s. Claude Lee and Maude (Clark) B.; m. Joanne Elizabeth Vaught, July 9, 1955; children—Susan, Richard, Deborah. Student, Hailey (Idaho) High Sch. Combat artist 1st div. U.S. Marine Corps, Korea, 1951-52; cartoon editor Leatherneck Mag., Washington, 1953-56; art dir. Crest-Craft Co., Cin., 1957-67; vol. adj. tchr. Boise Pub. Schs. Creator: syndicated comic strip Redeye, Boise, Idaho, 1967-88. Served with USMC, 1948-56. Recipient Alfred award (France) for best humor comic strip, 1976. Mem. Nat. Cartoonists' Soc., Newspaper Comics Council. Home: Boise Idaho Died Nov. 24, 1989; buried Morris Hill Cemetery, Boise, Idaho.

BEST, JOHN STEVENS, lawyer; b. Arlington Heights, Ill., May 18, 1906; s. Bruce Taylor and Genevieve (Stevens) B.; m. Pamelia Laurence, July 9, 1934 (dec.); children: Pamelia, Bruce, Mary Best Bartelt; m. Helen Meredith, June 26, 1958. A.B., U. Wis., 1928, LL.B., 1930. Bar: Wis. 1930; C.P.A., Wis. Practiced law Milw., from 1938; assoc. Lecher, Michael, Whyte & Spohn, 1938-43; mem. firm Michael, Best & Friedrich, and predecessors, Milw., 1943-89; income tax counsel, gen. counsel Wis. Tax Commn., 1930-38. Mem. Am., Wis., Milw. bar assns., Sigma Nu, Alpha Kappa Psi, Phi Alpha Delta, Beta Gamma Sigma, Order of Coif. Clubs: Milwaukee, University (Milw.). Home: Menominee Falls Wis. Died Nov. 9, 1989; buried Wis. Meml. Pk., Brookfield.

BETO, GEORGE JOHN, minister, educator; b. Hysham, Mont., Jan. 19, 1916; s. Louis H. and Margaret (Witsma) B.; m. Marilynn Knippa, Mar. 5, 1943; children—Dan, Lynn, Mark, Beth. Student, Concordia Coll., Milw., 1930-35, Concordia Sem., St. Louis, 1935-37, 38-39; B.A., Valparaiso U., 1938; M.A., U. Tex., 1944, Ph.D., 1955; DD, Concordia Seminary, 1989. Ordained to ministry Luth. Ch., 1943. Instr. Concordia Coll., Austin, Tex., 1939-49, pres., 1949-59; vis. instr. U. Tex., 1944; pres. Concordia Theol. Sem., Springfield, Ill., 1959-62; dir. Tex. Dept. Corrections, Huntsville, 1962-72; Disting. prof. Sam Houston State U., Huntsville, 1972-91; dir. 1st Nat. Bank, Palestine. Sec. Tex. Bd. Corrections, 1953-59; mem. Ill. Parole and Pardon Bd., 1961-62, Tex. Youth Coun., 1975-88; chief of chaplains Tex. Youth Commn.; Am. del. UN Conf. on Prevention Crime and Treatment Offender, Kyoto, Japan, 1970, Geneva, 1975, Milan, 1985; mem. commn. on correctional facilities and svcs. ABA; mem. Tex. Constl. Revision Commn., 1973-74. Recipient medal for devel. ednl. system Tex. prison system Tex. Heritage Found., 1958, Disting. Alumnus award U. Tex., 1971, U. Valparaiso; Takeuchi fellow, Japan, 1990. Mem. Am. Correctional Assn. (past pres., E.R. Cass award 1972), Phi Delta Kappa, Alpha Delta Kappa. Lutheran. Home: Austin Tex. Died Dec. 4, 1991; buried State Cemetery, Austin, Tex.

BETTELHEIM, BRUNO, psychologist, educator, author; b. Vienna, Austria, Aug. 28, 1903; came to U.S., 1939, naturalized, 1944; s. Anton and Paula (Seidler) B.; m. Trude Weinfeld, May 14, 1941; children: Ruth, Naomi, Eric. Ph.D., U. Vienna, 1938. Research assoc. Progressive Edn. Assn., U. Chgo., 1939-41; assoc. prof. psychology Rockford (Ill.) Coll., 1942-44; asst. prof. ednl. psychology U. Chgo., 1944-47, assoc. prof., 1947-52, prof., 1952-73, Stella M. Rowley Disting. Svc. prof. edn., prof. psychology and psychiatry, 1963-73; head Sonia Shankman Orthogenic Sch., U. Chgo., 1944-73. Author: (with Morris Janowitz) Dynamics of Prejudice, 1950, Love is Not Enough: The Treatment of Emotionally Disturbed Children, 1950, Symbolic Wounds, 1954, Truants from Life, 1955, The Informed Heart, 1960, Dialogues with Mothers, 1962, The Empty Fortress, 1967, The Children of the Dream, 1969, A Home for the Heart, 1974, The Uses of Enchantment, 1976, Surviving, 1979, (with Karen Zelan) On Learning to Read: The Child's Fascination with Meaning, 1982, Freud and Man's Soul, 1983, A Good Enough Parent, 1987, Freud's Vienna and Other Essays, 1990; contbr. articles, essays to popular, profl. publs. Fellow Am. Psychol. Assn., Am. Orthopsychiat. Assn.; mem. Am. Philos. Assn., AAUP, Am. Sociol. Assn., Chgo. Psychoanalytic Soc., Am. Acad. Edn. Democrat. Home: Silver Spring Md. Died Mar. 13, 1990.

BETTS, ISAAC FRANKLIN, banker; b. Thomasville, Ala., Dec. 5, 1897; s. Isaac Franklin and Mamie (Tarry) B.; m. Oweta Stallings, June 9, 1927; 1 child, Eugene Stallings Miller. AB, So. Meth. U., 1921; ABA, Rutgers U., 1941. Chief examiner Fed. Res. Bank, Dallas, 1922-39, Continental-Am. Bank & Trust Co., Shreveport, La., 1939-47; pres. Am. Nat. Bank of Beaumont, Tex., from 1947; dir. Midwestern Ins. Co., Tulsa, Houston br. Fed. Res. Bank of Dallas, Tex. Rsch. League, Tex. Bur. Econs. Understanding; mem. fed. adv. coun. Fed. Res. System. Contbr. articles to profl. jours. Trustee So. Meth. U. Mem. Am. Bankers Assn., U.S. C. of C. (dir.), Kappa Alpha, Mason, Rotary. Methodist. *

BETTS, ROBERT BUDD, advertising agency executive; b. Easton, Pa., Nov. 28, 1922; s. James A. and Vanetta (Rickards) B.; m. Emilie Woehrle, July 21, 1945; children—Dorothy Brooks, Anne Louise, Robert Budd. BS, Harvard U., 1944. Editor Harcourt, Brace; producer documentary films; pres., creative dir. William Esty & Co., N.Y.C., from 1967; hon. chmn. bd. William Esty Co., N.Y.C. Author: Along the Ramparts of the Tetons, 1978, In Search of York, 1985. Served with U.S. Army, WWII, ETO. Decorated Bronze Star medal. Clubs: Lost Tree (North Palm Beach, Fla.); Sky (N.Y.C.). Home: New York N.Y. Died Mar. 10, 1989; buried Kelly, Wyo.

BEUVE-MERY, HUBERT, journalist; b. Paris, Jan. 5, 1902; s. Hubert and Josephine (Tanguy) B-M.; m. Genevieve Deloye, Sept. 27, 1928; children: Jean-Jacques, Paul, Andre, Pierre. BA, Sch. Lit.; LLD, Law Sch. Paris. Dir. judicial and econ. sect. French Inst. Prague, 1928-39; corr. Temps, Prague, 1934-38; mgr. Le Monde, also dir. publs., 1944-69. Author: La Theorie des Pouvoirs publics, d'apres Francois de Vittoria et ses Rapports avec le Droit public contemporain, Vers la plus grande Allemagne, 1939; Reflexions politiques, 1932-52, Le Suicide de la IVe Republique, 1958; Onze ans de regne, 1958-69 vus par Sirius, 1974. Mem. adminstrv. council French Press Agy; pres. Ctr. for Formation of Journalists. Decorated comdr. Nat. Chilian Order of Merit, Greek Nat. Order of Phoenix, Nat. Order Senegal, grand officer Nat. Danish Order of Danneborg, Order of Lion of Finland. Mem. Acad. Wine Bordeaux. Home: Paris France Died, 1989; buried in Cimetiere de Montparnasse Paris.

BEVEN, THOMAS D., railroad executive; b. New Orleans, Dec. 23, 1898; s. Charles T. and Mary Ann (Farrell) B.; m. Mabel Hamilton Reich, June 24, 1920; children: William Farrell, Stephen Peter. Student pub. schs., New Orleans and Jackson, Miss. Messenger, caller and clk. I.C. R.R., New Orleans, 1912-14; clk. I.C. R.R., McComb, Miss., 1916-17, 20-21; switchman I.C. R.R., McComb, 1921, traveling auditor, 1922-23, yardmaster, 1924, gen. yardmaster, 1925-29, trainmaster, 1929-35, supt., 1935-38; gen. mgr. Elgin, Joliet & Ea. Rlwy. Co., 1939-41, v.p., 1941-46; pres., dir. Elgin, Joliet & Ea. Rlwy. Co., from 1946. 1st lt. USMC, 1917-20. Mason, Traffic Club, Union League Club, Chgo. Club, Western Rlwy. Club (past pres.), South Shore Country Club, Chgo. (Ill.) Athletic Assn., Duquesne Club (Pitts.). Democrat. Episcopalian. *

BEVILACQUA, JOSEPH A., state supreme court chief justice; b. Providence, Dec. 1, 1918; s. John and Angelica (Inonnoti) B.; m. Josephine Amato, 1946; children—John J., Angelica H., Joseph A., Mary Ann. B.A., Providence Coll., 1940; J.D., Georgetown U., 1948. Bar: R.I. Asst. adminstr. charitable trusts dept. R.I. Atty. Gen.'s Office, 1950-54; mem. R.I. Ho. of Reps., from 1955, dep. majority leader, 1965-66, majority leader, 1966-68, speaker, 1969; chief justice R.I. Supreme Ct., until 1985. Mem. R.I. Democratic Com., 1950-54; del. Dem. Nat. Conv., 1968. Served as 1st lt. U.S. Army, 1941-46. Home: Providence R.I. Died June 21, 1989.

BEVIS, JOSEPH C., marketing research executive; b. Harrison, Ohio, Jan. 16, 1910; s. Joseph C. and Helen S. (Norton) B.; m. Betsy Ross, Dec. 9, 1934; children—Joseph Ross, James Norton, Cheryl Ann, Beverly Jean. A.B., Miami U., Oxford, Ohio, 1931; M.A., Northwestern U., 1932; student, Ohio State U., 1931. Made pioneer telephone survey of radio audience, 1932; employee, then mgr. hardware and farm implement store Harrison, 1932-34; dir. surveys of relief population research div. Fed. Emergency Relief Adminstrn. (and successor orgn. WPA), 1934-40; with Opinion Research Corp., Princeton, N.J., 1940-70, v.p., 1945-57, pres., 1957-60, 65-67, chmn., chief exec. officer, 1960-70. Mem. Am. Mktg. Assn., Am. Assn. for Pub. Opinion Research, Market Research Council N.Y., Sigma Alpha Epsilon. Home: Stuart Fla. Died June 5, 1990; body donated to science.

BEWKES, EUGENE GARRETT, foundation executive; b. Paterson, N.J., Feb. 12, 1895; s. Lambert and Cornelia (Gardenier) B.; m. Helen Van Vlaanderen, June 20, 1918; children: Elizabeth Kate Ratcliff, Jean Carol Jerome, Eugene Garrett Jr. BA, Colgate U., 1919; BD, Yale U., 1922; PhD, Edinburgh U., Scotland, 1924; LLD, Colgate U., 1945, Syracuse U., 1950, Bowling Green State U., 1964, St. Lawrence U., 1965; LHD, Bucknell U., 1949; ScD, Clarkson Coll. Tech., 1947. Min. 1st Congl. Ch., Norwood, Mass., 1924-27; assoc. prof. philosophy Colgate U., 1927-29, prof., head dept., 1929-31, dean students, 1931-33, head Sch. Philosophy & Religion, 1934-45; dir. St. Lawrence County Nat. Bank. Sec. bd. trustees Colgate U., 1934-45; asst. dir., then dir. Bur. Manpower Utilization War Manpower Commn., 1943-45; pres. St. Lawrence U., Canton, N.Y., 1945-63; dir. edn. Edward John Found., from 1963. Mem. Assn. Colls. & Univs. State of N.Y., Am. Philos. Assn., Creighton Philos. Club, Phi Beta Kappa, others. *

BEWLEY, LOYAL VIVIAN, electrical engineer consultant; b. Republic, Wash., Dec. 19, 1898; s. Frank W. and Sadie M. (Harvey) B.; m. Mary Katheryne McAuley, Oct. 17, 1923; children: Robert Lynn, Donald Thomas. Student, Battersea Poly., London, 1919; BS, U. Wash., 1923; MS, Union Coll., 1927; student advanced course, GE Co., 1923-26. Elec. engr., from 1923; design engr. GE Co., 1923-28, rsch. engr., 1928-40; prof., head dept. elec. engring. Lehigh U., 1940-62, dean of engring., 1954-62; cons. engring. edn. GE Co., from 1962; commandant Allentown Sch. of Res. Officers. Author: Alternating Current Machinery, 1949, Flux Linkages and Electro-magnetic Induction, 1952, Tensor Analysis of Electric Circuits and Machines, 1961; contbr. tech. papers and articles to profl. jours. Sgt. U.S. Army, 1917-19, Col. U.S. Army, 1942-46. Decorated Silver star, Bronze star. Fellow IEEE (best paper prize 1931, Lamme medal 1963); mem. Sigma Xi, Tau Beta Pi, Eta Kappa Nu. *

BEZAZIAN, PAUL D., advertising agency executive; b. Providence, Mar. 29, 1906; s. John B. and Daisy (Babasinian) B.; m. Florence Irene Bell, Sept. 9, 1933; children: John P., Paulette F., Harold A. BA, Oberlin Coll., 1927. Salesman Meyer Connor & Co., Chgo., 1927-31; sales mgr. Credit Firm, Chgo., 1931-36; ptnr. Bezazian & Sutherland, Niles Center, Ill., 1936-37; mgr., ptnr. Bezazian Bros., Chgo., 1937-40; mng. ptnr., treas. Burton Browne Advt., Chgo., 1941-88. Club: Gaslight (chmn. bd. dirs., chmn. exec. com. 1975-76). Home: Chicago Ill. Died Oct. 11, 1988; cremated.

BHARATI, AGEHANANDA, anthropologist, educator; b. Vienna, Austria, Apr. 20, 1923; came to U.S., 1956, naturalized, 1968; s. Hans and Margarete Helene (von May) Fischer. A.B. in Ethnology and Indology, Oriental Inst. and Ethnol. Inst., U. Vienna, 1948; Acharya (Ph.D.), Samnyasa Mahavidyalaya, India, 1951. Lectr. in German Delhi (India) U., 1951; hon. reader in philosophy Benares Hindu U., India, 1951-54; guest prof. comparative religion Nalanda (India) Inst. Postgrad. Buddhist Studies, 1954-55; vis. prof. comparative religion Mahamukuta Royal Buddhist Acad., Bangkok, Thailand, 1955-56; Asia Found. vis. prof. U. Tokyo, 1956-57, Kyoto, Japan, 1956-57; research asso. Far Eastern Inst., U. Wash., Seattle, 1957-60; asst. prof. anthropology Syracuse (N.Y.) U., 1961-64, asso. prof., 1964-68, Ford-Maxwell prof. Asian studies, 1968-91, chmn. dept. anthropology, 1971-80; ordained to Hindu Samnyasi Order of Monks, India, 1951; lectr. various Am. univs., from 1956, U. Goettingen, Germany, 1970, U. Heidelberg, Germany, 1971, U. Stockholm, 1968; Rose Morgan Distinguished vis. prof. U. Kans., Lawrence, 1970; Fulbright prof. Marburg U., West Germany, 1987; coordinator 9th Internat. Congress of Anthrop. and Ethnol. Scis., Chgo., 1973. Author: The Ochre Robe, 1963, A Functional Analysis of Indian Thought and Its Social Margins, 1964, The Tantric Tradition, 1966 (transl. German, Italian), The Asians in East Africa: Jayhind and Uhuru, 1972, The Light at the Center: Context and Pretext of Modern Mysticism, 1976, Great Tradition and Little Traditions: Indological Investigations in Cultural Anthropology, 1978, Hindu Views and Ways and the Hindu-Muslim Interface, 1981, Indology and Science, 1989, The Absent Arbiter, 1992; editor: Tibet Soc. Bull., 1974-81; co-editor: World Anthropology, 1973; contbr. numerous book revs. and articles on cultural anthropology, religion and the history of Occidental and Oriental philosophy to lit. mags. and scholarly Am., Brit. and German jours.; contbr. numerous book chpts. on Oriental religion and cultural anthropology. Grantee NIMH, 1964, Am. Inst. Ceylonese Studies, 1970-71; Fulbright teaching scholar, West Germany, 1987. Fellow Am. Anthrop. Assn., Soc. Applied Anthropology, Royal Anthrop. Inst. of Gt. Britain and Ireland, Royal Asiatic Soc.; mem. Assn. for Asian Studies, Am. Oriental Soc., Wash. Anthrop. Soc., Soc. Sci. Study of Religion, Mensa Internat., Tibet Soc. (dir. 1975—), Mind Assn. Home: Rochester N.Y. Died May 14, 1991; cremated.

BIANCOLLI, LOUIS, writer; b. N.Y.C., Apr. 17, 1907; s. Carmine and Achilla (Montesano) B.; m. Edith Rattner, 1933 (dec. 1957); 1 dau., Margaret (Mrs. Murray Weissbach); m. Jeanne Mitchell, 1958; children: Lucy, Amy. AB, N.Y. U., 1935, AM, 1936; postgrad., Columbia U., 1936-38, Am. Council Learned Socs. grant for studies Russian, Intensive Lang. Programs, 1943. Music critic, N.Y. World-Telegram and Sun, 1928-66, annotator, N.Y. Philharmonic Soc., 1941-49; author: (with Robert Bagar) The Concert Companion, 1947, The Book of Great Conversations, 1948, The Victor Book of Operas, 1949, The Analytical Concert Guide, 1951, (with Mary Garden) Mary Garden's Story, 1951, (with Kirsten Flagstad) The Flagstad Manuscript, 1952, The Opera Reader, 1953, The Mozart Handbook, 1954, (with Herbert F. Peyser) Masters of the Orchestra, 1954, (with Ruth Slenczynska) Forbidden Childhood, 1957, (with Roberta Peters) A Debut at the Met, 1967; Translator: Boris Godounoff libretto from Russian, 1952, 64; in blank verse Dante's Divine Comedy, 1966, (with Thomas Scherman) The Beethoven Companion, 1972; libretto: (with Thomas Scherman) Italian opera Ezio (Handel), 1972, Poro (Handel), 1977, Introduction to Am. edit. Greek collection of letters of Dimitri Mitropoulos, 1972; Contbr. (with Thomas Scherman) articles to mags., music brochures. Recipient achievement award NYU Grad. Sch. Alumni Assn., 1985. Mem. Music Critics Circle, Phi Beta Kappa. Home: New Preston Conn. Died June 13, 1992. †

BICKFORD, GEORGE PERCIVAL, lawyer; b. Berlin, N.H., Nov. 28, 1901; s. Gershon Percival and Lula Adine (Buck) B.; m. Clara L. Gehring, Apr. 6, 1933 (dec. Dec. 1985); 1 dau., Louise G. Boyd; m. Jessie B. McGaw, May, 1986 (div. Nov. 1988). A.B. cum laude, Harvard, 1922, LL.B., 1926. Bar: Ohio 1926. Since practiced in Cleve.; asso. firm Arter & Hadden, partner, from 1940; instr. Hauchung U., Wuchang, China, 1922-23; instr. taxation Western Res. Law Sch., 1940-47; lectr. Indian history and culture Cleve. Coll., 1948-50; gen. counsel FHA, Washington, 1958-59; hon. consul of India, from 1964; Mem. Cleve. Moral Claims Commn., 1935-37. Mem. Cuyahoga County Rep. Exec. Com., 1948-58, 60-91; Trustee Am. U. in Cairo; vis. com. fine arts dept. Harvard, 1962-68, 72-78; trustee, former v.p. Cleve. Mus. Art; trustee Cleve. Inst. Art.; mem. Nat. Com. for Festival of India in U.S., 1985; mem. adv. com. Asia Soc. Houston, 1986. Served with Ohio N.G., 1926-29; from capt. to lt. col. JAG dept. AUS, 1942-46. Decorated Legion of Merit. Mem. Am., Ohio, Cleve. bar assns., Cleve. Council World Affairs (trustee). Episcopalian (standing com. Diocese Ohio 1951-63, chancellor 1962-77). Clubs: Union (Cleve.), Rowfant (Cleve.), Cleve. Skating; Army and Navy (Washington); Harvard (N.Y.C.). Home: Cleveland Ohio Died Oct. 14, 1991. †

BICKFORD, JOHN VAN BUREN, coal company executive; b. Roanoke, Va., 1934; m. Loretta Scott; children: John, Jr., Cameron. Grad., Va. Poly Inst., 1955. Mgr. sales office Westmoreland Coal Sales Co., Charlotte, N.C., 1961-69; dist. mgr. Westmoreland Coal Sales Co., Cin., 1969-74; v.p. Westmoreland Coal Sales Co., Phila., 1974-81, pres., 1981-91; bd. dirs. Ea. Coal and Coke Co. Home: Devon PA Died June 28, 1991.

BIDEZ, EARLE FELTON, railroad executive; b. Carrollton, Ga., Oct. 22, 1897; s. Rene Victor and Mary Robert (Felton) B.; m. Thelma Calhoun, Sept. 4, 1916; children: Earle Calhoun, William Alexander, Mirian Elizabeth Clark. Student pub. schs., Rockmart, Ga. With C. of Ga. Rlwy. Co., 1917, chief clk., auditor disbursements, 1937-43, asst. to comptr., 1943-48, exec. asst. on staff of pres., 1948-50, v.p., 1951-59, exec. v.p., from 1960; exec. v.p., dir. Ocean S.S. Co. of Savannah, South Western R.R. Co.; pres., dir. Port Wentworth Corp., Crossgate Homes; dir. Atlanta Terminal Co., Macon Terminal Co., Midland Properties Co., Ctrl. of Ga. Rlwy. Co., Empire Land Co., Chattham Terminal Co., Ctrl. of Ga. Motor Transport Co., Savannah & Atlanta Rlwy. Co., Liberty Nat. Bank and Trust Co. Mem. C. of C., Savannah Rotary, Savannah Yacht and Country Club, Oglethorpe Club. Methodist. *

BIELER, ANDRE (CHARLES BIELER), painter; b. Lausanne, Switzerland, Oct. 8, 1896; s. Charles and Blanche (Merle d'Aubigne) B.; m. Jeannette Meunier, Apr. 27, 1931; children—Nathalie, Sylvie, Andre, Peter. Student, Stanstaed Acad., 1909-15, Art Students League, Woodstock, N.Y., 1919-20; LL.D. (hon.), Queen's U., Kingston, Ont., Can., 1969. Later head dept. art history, studio classes; instr. summer sch. Banff, Alta., Can., 1940; public lectr. Nat. Gallery Can., Ottawa, Ont., 1941; Can. del. opening Nat. Gallery, Washington, 1941; coordinator through Fulbright Found. for 1st Conf. Can. Artists (later called Kingston Conf.)leading to founding of Fedn. Can. Artists. Painter: Island of Orleans, Que., Can., 1926-30; with Beaver Hall group, Montreal, Que., 1930-36, one-man shows throughout Can., 1926—; apptd. resident artist Queen's U., Kingston, 1936; commd. murals include works for, Aluminum Co. Can., 1945, Vets.' Bldg., Ottawa, 1954, Aluminum Co., Japan, Tokyo, 1968. Co-founder, 1st dir. Agnes Etherington Art Centre, Queens U., Kingston, Ont. Served with Can. Inf., 1915-19. Recipient Centennial medal for service to Can., 1967; decorated Order of Can., 1988; subject of biography by Frances K. Smith, 1980. Mem. Ont. Soc. Artists, Can. Group Painters, Can. Soc. Painters in Water-Color, Can. Soc. Graphic Art, Royal Can. Acad., Fedn. Can. Artists (1st pres.). Clubs: Queen's, Faculty. Home: Kingston Ont., Can. Died Dec. 1, 1989; buried Glenhaven Meml. Garden, Kingston, Ont., Can.

BIEMESDERFER, DANIEL L(UKE), college president; b. Kissel Hill, Pa., Jan. 19, 1894; s. Horace Norvin and Clara (Weidler) B.; m. Elva Lutz Walter, June 28, 1922; children: Robert Walter, Charles Daniel, Martha Anne. AB, Franklin & Marshall Coll., 1921; AM, U. Pa., 1931; LittD, Muhlenberg Coll., 1943; ScD, Franklin & Marshall Coll., 1949. Tchr. Warwick twp., Lancaster County, Pa., 1911-15; prin. Christiana Boro, Lancaster County, 1917-19, Strasburg Boro, Lancaster County, 1919-20; tchr. Mauch Chunk High Sch., 1921-22; supervising prin. Mt. Joy Boro schs., 1922-24, Manor-Millersville Sch., 1924-43; pres. State Tchrs. Coll., Millersville, from 1943. With U.S. Army, World War I. Mem. NEA, Pa. Edn. Assn., Cliosophic Soc., Phi Beta Kappa, others. *

BIERKOE, GEORGE OLAF, clergyman, educator; b. Bklyn., July 2, 1895; s. Johan Arnt and Alvilde (Boe) Bjerkoe; m. Eleanor Tupper, June 21, 1933; children: Priscilla, Barbara. AB, Muhlenberg Coll., Allentown, Pa., 1922; LittD, Muhlenberg Coll., 1946; BD, Luth. Theol. Sem., Mount Airy, Pa., 1925; AM, NYU, 1935. Ordained to ministry Luth. Ch., 1925. With Endicott-Johnson Co., N.Y.C., 1914-17; social worker Luth. Ch., N.Y.C., 1923; pastor Ch. of the Good Shepherd, Bellaire, N.Y., 1925-35; instr. Boston YMCA, 1936-38, Stoneleigh Coll., Rye, N.H., 1937; founder, pres., trustee Endicott Jr. Coll., Beverly, Mass. With U.S. Army. Mem. Greater Boston Cooperative Soc., Beverly (Mass.) C. of C., Beverly YMCA, Phi Kappa Tau, Rotary. Republican. *

BIESER, IRVIN GRUEN, lawyer; b. Dayton, Ohio, June 15, 1902; s. Charles William and Flora Sophia (Gruen) B.; m. Catharine Mary French, Apr. 14, 1936; children: Catharine Black, Irvin Gruen, Jr. B.S. cum laude, Harvard U., 1924, LL.B., 1927. Bar: Ohio 1927. Practiced in Dayton; sr. ptnr. Bieser, Greer & Landis, and predecessors, 1932-74, of counsel, 1974-89; dir. Midwest Securities Investment, Inc., City Transit Co.; v.p., dir. Everybody's Office Outfitters, Inc., 1931-69; dir. emeritus Dayton Power & Light Co., 1958-73; mem. standing com. on gen. principles of law recognized by community of nations and spl. com. on rev. UN charter World Peace Through Law Center. Author: Origin and Rise of the Republican Party, 1924. Founder, trustee, now trustee emeritus Miami Valley Hosp., pres., 1948-54; trustee emeritus Hosp. Care Corp., S.W. Ohio, from 1939, pres., 1956-58, chmn., 1958-60; trustee Dayton Art Inst., 1954-76, sec., 1956, v.p., 1967; trustee Dayton Philharmonic Orch. Assn., 1963-70; trustee Frank M. Tait Found., 1959—, pres., 1980-89. Mem. Internat. Bar Assn., ABA, Ohio Bar Assn. (past mem. coms. on taxation, jud. reform), Dayton Bar Assn. (pres. 1957-58), Am. Judicature Soc., Dayton Lawyers Club (trustee), Dayton Law Library Assn. (trustee, pres. 1969-72), Alpha Sigma Phi. Republican. Lutheran. Clubs: Rotary (Dayton), Dayton Country (Dayton), Moraine Country (Dayton), Harvard (Dayton) (past pres.), Racquet (Dayton); Masons. Home: Dayton Ohio Died Sept. 15, 1989; buried Woodland Cemetery, Dayton.

BIGART, HOMER, journalist; b. Hawley, Pa., Oct. 25, 1907; s Homer S. and Anna Schardt B.; m. Alice Weel, July 6, 1963 dec. Jan. 1969 ; m. Else Holmelund Minarik, Oct. 3, 1970; stepchild, Brooke Minarik. War corr. N.Y. Herald Tribune, 1942-45, roving corr., 1945-55; fgn. corr. N.Y. Times, 1955-63, nat. corr., 1963-72. Recipient Pulitzer prize for Pacific war reporting, 1945, Korean war articles, 1951. Home: Barrington N.H. Died Apr. 16, 1991.

BIGLEY, GEORGE ARTHUR, financial company executive; b. Sabina, Okla., Oct. 8, 1898; s. Roy and Martha (West) B.; m. Esther Mary O'Brien, Sept. 11, 1928; children: Martha Bigley Kenyon, Richard Ryan. AB, Ind. U., 1921. CEO, chmn. bd. dirs. Pacific Fin. Corp., Detroit, from 1962; pres., dir. Merchants Bank Detroit, Mich., from 1933; bd. dirs. Transamerica Corp., Pacific Fin. Corp.; pres., dir. Mero Investments Corp., from 1953. Mem. Detroit Club, Detroit Athletic Club, Country of Detroit Club, Lochmoor Club (Detroit), Grosse Pointe Yacht Club, Country of Fla. Club (Delray). *

BILLINGS, WILLIAM HOWARD, chief justice; b. Kennett, Mo., Aug. 21, 1921; s. James V. and Leora (Sapp) B. LLB, U. Mo., 1952, BGS, 1988. Bar: Mo., U.S. Dist. Ct. (ea. dist.) Mo., U.S. Supreme Ct. Ptnr. McHaney, Billings & Welman, Kennett, 1952-66; judge 35th jud. cir., Kennett, 1966-73, so. dist. Mo. Ct. Appeals, Springfield, 1973-82; judge Supreme Ct. Mo., Jefferson City, from 1982, chief justice, 1987-89; lectr. Mo. State Hwy. Patrol, 1971-72. Pres., v.p. bd. curators U. Mo., Columbia, 1965-74. Capt. USMCR, 1942-45. Mem. ABA, Mo. Bar Assn., Dunklin County (Mo.) Bar Assn., Am. Legion, VFW, Amvets, Masons, Order of Coif, Phi Delta Phi, Pi Kappa Alpha. Methodist. Home: Jefferson City Mo. Deceased. †

BILLINGSLEA, CHARLES, army officer; b. Chgo., May 16, 1914; s. Charles and Mabel Billingslea; m. Bettina Hill, Dec. 17, 1939; 1 child, Charles. BS, U.S. Mil. Acad., 1936; grad., Army War Coll., 1953, Nat. War Coll., 1958; grad. Advanced Mgmt. Program, Harvard, 1957. Commd. 2d lt. U.S. Army, 1936, advanced through grades to maj. gen., 1963; various assignments U.S. and Hawaii, 1936-41; with II Corps and Allied Forces Hdqrs., Eng., 1942, Hdqrs. USAAF 1st Brit. Parachute Brigade, 5th Army, Morocco, Algeria and, Tunisia, 1942-43; exec. pathfider Parachute Brigade, Sicily, Italy, 1943; exec. officer 504th parachute Inf., Eng. and Italy, 1943-44; regtl. comdr. 325th Glider Inf., Eng., Cen. Europe and Berlin, 1944-45; chief staff 82d Airborne Div., 1945-46; with plans sect. Army Field Force, Ft. Monroe, Va., 1946-49; mem. staff and faculty Command and Gen. Staff Sch. and War Coll., 1949-51; assigned ORO, Korea and Washington, 1951-52; chief plans SHAPE, Paris, 1953-56; dep. chief European region OSD, ISA, Washington, 1958-61; dep. chief staff 8th U.S. Army, Korea, 1961-62; assigned Hdqrs. 2d Div., Ft. Bragg, N.C., 1962; comdg. gen. 2d Inf. Div., Ft. Benning, Ga., 1962-64; then dep. comdg. gen. Combat Devel. Command, Ft. Belvoir, Va. Decorated D.S.C. with oak leaf cluster, Bronze Star medal with oak leaf cluster, Army Commendation ribbon with oak leaf cluster; Fouragerre (Belgium); Orange Lanyard, knight 4th class Militarie Willems Order (Netherlands); Red Star (Russia); Korean Order Merit 3d class. Past Mem. Assn. U.S. Army, Rotary. Home: Fort Belvoir Va. Died Mar. 15, 1989.

BINGHAM, CURTIS HARRY, investment banker; b. Rockford, Ill., Nov. 3, 1898; s. Charles and Lola (Curtis) B.; m. Mary Decker, Aug. 12, 1922; children: Mary Jane, Charles, Richard. BS, Oreg. State Coll., 1921. With Bingham, Walter & Hurry, Inc., L.A., from 1933, pres., bd. dirs., from 1933. Bd. dirs. Travelers Aid of L.A., Soc. for Prevention Cruelty to Animals. Mem. Nat. Assn. Securities Dealers (gov.), Investment Bankers Assn. Am. (gov., chmn. Calif. group, past pres.), Bond Club (L.A., past pres.). *

BIRCH, ALBERT FRANCIS, geophysicist, educator; b. Washington, Aug. 22, 1903; s. George Albert and Mary Clayton (Hemmick) B.; m. Barbara Channing, July 15, 1933; children: Anne Campaspe, Francis Sylvanus, Mary Narcissa. BSEE, Harvard U., 1924, MA, 1929; PhD, 1932, ScD hon., 1982. Engr. N.Y. Telephone Co., 1924-26; instr., tutor physics Harvard U., 1931-34, rsch. assoc. geophysics, 1932-37, asst. prof., 1937-43, assoc. prof., 1943-46, prof., 1946-74, emeritus, 1974-92; on leave MIT, 1941-42, Sturgis-Hooper prof. geology, 1948; Sherman Fairchild disting. scholar Calif. Inst. Tech., 1975; editor: Handbook of Physical Constants. Comdr. USNR, 1942-45. Decorated Legion of Merit; recipient Arthur L. Day medal Geol. Soc.; William Bowie medal Am. Geophys. Union, 1960, Nat. medal of Sci., 1968, Vetlesen prize Columbia U., 1969, Bridgman medal AIRAPT, 1983. Fellow Royal Astron. Soc. (gold medal 1973), Am. Phys. Soc., Am. Acad. Arts and Sci., Geol. Soc. Am. (pres. 1964, Penrose medal 1969, Geol. Soc. London); mem. Am. Geophys. Union, Seismol. Soc. Am., Nat. Acad. Sci., Am. Philos. Soc., Sigma Xi. Home: Cambridge Mass. Died Jan. 31, 1992.

BIRD, WILLIAM RUSSELL, club executive; b. Elwood, Ind., Sept. 3, 1898; s. Elmer Ellsworth and Margaret (Thomas) B.; m. Martha Ann Farr, May 21, 1935. Student, Washington U., St. Louis, 1925-27; LLB, John Marshall Law Sch., 1947. Bar: Ill. 1947. Order clk. Wagner Electric Mfg. Co., St. Louis, 1917-18; acct., chief clk. to gen. yardmaster Terminal R.R. Assn. St. Louis, 1918-20; asst. to local auditor Alton & So. R.R., East St. Louis, Ill., 1920-22; sec. to dist. sales mgr. Am. Locomotive Co., St. Louis, 1922-29, sales rep., 1929-35; asst. sec. Internat. Assn. Lions Clubs, Chgo., 1946, sec., 1947-63, gen. counsel, from 1963. Mem. ABA, Delta Theta Phi. *

BIRKENSTEIN, LILLIAN RAY, ornithologist; b. Phila., Oct. 9, 1900; d. Morris and Stella (Schloss) Rosenzweig; B.A. (coll. scholar), Wellesley Coll., 1922; student U. Pa., 1920-21, Northwestern U., 1936-37, Instituto Allende (Mexico), 1951-55, Academia Hispana-Americana (Mexico), 1960-68; m. George Ulman Birkenstein, Sept. 2, 1922; children: Dorothy (Mrs. Jose Vidargas), Jean (Mrs. Atlee Washington). Pres., Anker-Holth Mfg. Co., Port Huron, Mich., 1944-51; researcher local Spanish and tribal Indian names of Mexican birds, from 1952; vol. librarian, San Miguel Allende, Mex., 1954-64, tchr. ornithology Institute Allende, San Miguel Allende, 1973. Bd. dirs. Public Library San Miguel Allende, 1954-67, Hot Breakfasts for Sch. Children, San Miguel, 1957-61. Mem. San Miguel Allende Audubon Soc. (founder 1967, pres. 1967-71, dir. 1971-88), Am. Soc. Mfg. Engrs. (hon. life), Am. Ornithologists Union, Cooper Ornithol. Soc., Linnaean Soc., Wilson Ornithol. Soc., Cornell Lab. Ornithology, Mexican Natural History Soc. (from dir. 1972), Mexican Ornitholog. Soc. (dir.), Internat. Com. for Bird Preservation (treas. Mexican sect. from 1968), Women's Aux. AIME (hon.). Clubs: San Miguel Allende Garden (1st v.p. from 1971); Golf Malanquin. Author: Native Names of Mexican Birds, 1981. Contbr. articles to various publs. Died July 13, 1988; buried San Miguel Allende. Home: San Miguel Allende Mex.

BIRNBAUM, STEPHEN NORMAN, magazine editor, broadcaster; b. N.Y.C., Mar. 28, 1937; s. Louis M. and Ruth L. (Kreisel) B.; m. Alexandra Mayes, Dec. 28, 1972. B.A., Columbia U., 1957. Founder Chamberlain Properties, N.Y.C., 1960-67; creative dir. DePerri Advt., Inc., N.Y.C., 1967-72; mng. editor Fodor's Travel Guides, N.Y.C., London, 1972-75; editor Diversion Mag., Titusville, N.J., 1975-76; editorial dir. Diversion Mag., N.Y.C., from 1976; travel editor Golf Mag., 1973-87, Esquire, 1976-79, N.J. Monthly Mag., 1977; travel commentator CBS Radio Network, from 1977; travel editor Today Show NBC, 1977-79, Good Morning America, ABC, 1982-86, CBS Morning News, 1986-87; editor Harper Collins, from 1977; editor/commentator Birmbaum Audio Travel Guides pub. by Warner Audio, 1985-88; travel editor Playboy mag., 1979-82, 84-85, Good Housekeeping mag., from 1982, Prodigy, 1987-89; travel commentator Ind. Network News, 1981. Syndicated columnist Chgo. Tribune/N.Y. News Syndicate, 1978 from; editorial dir. Sojourn mag., from 1978, Fair Lanes Mag., from 1979, Direct mag., 1981-84, Philip Morris mag., 1984-85, Time Off mag., 1985-86, Revlon's Perspectives mag., 1985-88, Light mag., 1985-86, Instant mag., 1987-88. Served with USCG, 1958-66. Mem. Soc. Am. Travel Writers, N.Y. Travel Writers, Golf Writers Am. Home: New York N.Y. Died Dec. 20, 1991; cremated.

BISCHOFF, ELMER, artist, educator; b. Berkeley, Calif., July 9, 1916; s. John A. and Elna (Nelson) B. BA, U. Calif.-Berkeley, 1938, MA, 1939; DFA (hon), Otis Art Inst., Parsons Sch. Design, 1983, San Francisco Art Inst., 1985; DFA (hon.), Calif. Coll. Arts and Crafts, 1989. Instr. San Francisco Art Inst., 1940's, chmn. grad. program, 1957-63; from instr. art dept. to prof. emeritus U. Calif.-Berkeley, 1963-85. Represented permanent collections Art Inst. Chgo., Mus. Modern Art, U. Kans. Mus. Art, Whitney Mus. Am. Art, Met. Mus. Art., N.Y.C., Rockefeller Inst., New Sch. Art Ctr.,

N.Y.C., San Francisco Mus. Art, Corcoran Galley Art, Washington, Hirshhorn Mus.; also pvt. collections; permanent exhibit, John Berggruen Gallery, San Francisco. Served with USAAF, 1942-46, ETO. Grantee Ford Found., 1959; grantee Nat. Inst. Arts and Letters, 1963; recipient Disting. Teaching award Coll. Art Assn., 1983. Mem. Nat. Acad. Design, Am. Acad. and Inst. Arts and Letters. Home: Berkeley Calif. Died Mar. 2, 1991; buried Berkeley.

BISHOP, DONALD FRANCIS, investment counselor; b. Phila., Oct. 8, 1897; s. Clarence Meecham and Harriet Baxter (Pierce) B.; m. Janet Redman, Feb. 10, 1923; children: Nancy Janet, Jane. Student, U. Pa., 1922-23. Investment banker Eastman, Dillon & Co., Phila., 1920-36; investment counselor Bishop & Co., Phila., 1936-41; v.p. Provident Trust Co., Phila., 1941-46; pres. Bishop & Herdberg, Inc., from 1946. Trustee Rittenhouse Fund. Mem. Fin. Analysts. *

BISHOP, JOHN H., lawyer; b. Monterey, Va., Jan. 14, 1896; s. Vergil B. and Mary Jane (Miller) B.; m. Mildred Charleen, 1928. LLB, U. Va., 1918. Bar: Ill. 1920. Practiced law Chgo., from 1920; ptnr. Fink, Lowes & Bishop, Chgo., 1920-28, Woods & Bishop, Chgo., 1928-30, Bishop & Burdett, 1930-35, 45-46, Bishop, Mitchell, Burdett, 1935-45, Bishop, Burdett, Falasz & Doherty, from 1946; bd. dirs. numerous cos. Mem. ABA, Ill. Bar Assn., Chgo. Bar Assn. *

BISHOP, MORIAN HOOVER, investment banker; b. State Center, Iowa, July 15, 1896; s. Joseph Marshall and Maud (Hoover) B.; m. Alice McLean, June 25, 1927; children: John M., Martha Ann Gately. AB, U. Minn., 1916. With M.H. Bishop & Co., Mpls., from 1929, ptnr., from 1957; pres. Lakedale Telephone Co., from 1945; bd. dirs. Regan Bakeries, Timesavers, Inc., N.W. Plastics, Inc. Bd. govs. Midwest Stock Exch., 1960-62. With U.S. Army, World War I. Mem. Am. Legion, Nat. Assn. Securities Dealers, Investment Bankers Assn. Am. *

BISHOP, ROBERT, museum director, art educator; b. Readfield, Maine, Aug. 25, 1938; s. Charles and Muriel (Webber) B. Ph.D. in Am. Culture, U. Mich., 1975. Mgr. publs. Greenfield Village and Henry Ford Mus., Dearborn, Mich., 1966-74, mus. editor, 1974-76; adj. prof. art history U. Mich., Dearborn, 1977, Ann Arbor, 1975-77; dir. Mus. Am. Folk Art, N.Y.C., from 1976; adj. prof. art and art edn. NYU, from 1980. Author, designer: Centuries and Styles of the American Chair, 1640-1970, 1973, 83, How to Know American Antique Furniture, 1973, Guide to American Antique Furniture, 1973, American Folk Sculpture, 1974, New Discoveries in American Quilts, 1975; author: The Borden Limner and His Contemporaries, 1976, Treasurers of American Folk Art, 1979; co-author, designer: America's Quilts and Coverlets, 1972, American Painted and Decorated Furniture, 1972, The American Clock, 1976, A Gallery of Amish Quilts, 1976; co-author: World Furniture, 1979, The World of Antiques, Art and Architecture in Victorian America, 1979, Folk Painters of America, 1979, A Gallery of American Weathervanes and Whirligigs, 1980, (with Lipman and Warren) Young America, A Folk Art History, 1986, (with Houck) All Flags Flying, 1986; editor, picture editor other books. Bd. dirs. N.Y.C. Coun. Mus., from 1978, Koreshan Unity, Estero, Fla., from 1978, Pioneer Ednl. Found., Estero, from 1978; trustee Opportunity Resources, N.Y.C., from 1979, Grove House, Coconut Grove, Fla., from 1977; chmn. bd. dirs. ISALTA, N.Y.C., from 1980; bd. dirs., mem. exec. com. Arts and Bus. Coun., Inc. Recipient Impresario award creative writing Internat. Cultural Soc., 1975, Silver medal Internat. Film and TV Festival, 1978. Home: New York N.Y. Died Sept. 22, 1991; buried Readfield, Maine.

BISSELL, JEAN GALLOWAY, federal judge; b. Due West, S.C., June 9, 1936; d. Robert Stone and Clara Elizabeth (Agnew) Galloway; m. Gregg Claude Bissell, June 11, 1969. Student, Erskine Coll., 1952-54; BS magna cum laude, U. S.C., 1956, LLB, 1958; LLD (hon.), Converse Coll., 1976, Furman U., 1987. Bar: S.C. 1958. With Haynsworth, Perry, Bryant, Marion and Johnston, Greenville, S.C., 1958-71; ptnr. McKay, Sherrill, Walker & Townsend, Columbia, S.C., 1971-76; sr. v.p., gen. counsel S.C. Nat. Bank, Columbia, 1976-80, exec. v.p., gen. counsel, 1980-81, vice chmn., chief adminstrv. officer, gen. counsel, 1981-84; sr. v.p., gen. counsel S.C. Nat. Corp., Columbia, 1976-80, exec. v.p., gen. counsel, 1980-81, vice chmn., chief adminstrv. officer, gen. counsel, 1981-84, dir., 1982-84; cir. judge U.S. Ct. Appeals Fed. Cir., Washington, 1984-90; lectr sch. law U. S.C., 1971-78, 80-84. Mem. adv. coun. S.C. State Library, 1971-76, Erskine Coll., 1971-74, Columbia Coll., 1974-78, Furman U., 1972-84; mem. pres.'s nat. adv. coun. U. S.C., 1981-84; mem. bd. Columbia Philharm. Orch., 1975-78, Greater Columbia Community Rels. Coun., 1976-79; regent Leadership S.C., 1979-81; mem. merit selection panel S.C. Pub. Svc. Commn., 1980-84; chmn. Richland County Pub. Libr., 1975-78; mem. S.C. Libr. Bd., 1982-84; mem. bd. S.C. Coun. Econ. Edn., 1984. Recipient Disting. Svc. award S.C. Library Assn., 1973, 1st ann. Friend of Librarians award, 1976, Algernon Sydney Sullivan award, Disting. Alumnus award U. S.C. Coll. Bus. Adminstrn., 1988, Mary Mildred Sullivan award, 1989. Mem. ABA, S.C. Bar Assn. Clubs: City Tavern (Washington), Cosmos Club (Washington). Home: Washington D.C. Died Feb. 4, 1990; buried Due West, S.C.

BIXBY, R. BURDELL, lawyer; b. Schenectady, Oct. 11, 1914; s. Raymond O. and Mabel A. (Rumsey) B.; m. Anne M. Hardwick, Oct. 25, 1941; 1 son, Robert Hardwick. A.B., Colgate U., 1936; LL.B., Albany Law Sch., 1940, J.D., 1968. Bar: N.Y. 1940. Partner firm Dewey, Ballantine, Bushby, Palmer & Wood, N.Y.C., 1955-85; Asst. sec. gov. State N.Y., 1948-50, exec. asst., 1950-52, sec., 1952-54; sec.-treas. N.Y. State Thruway Authority, 1950-60, chmn., sec., treas., 1960-61, chmn., sec., 1961-74; permanent pres. N.Y. State Electoral Coll. of 1972. Trustee Hudson City Savs. Instn., N.Y.; treas. N.Y. State Republican Com., 1959-61. Served with USAAF, 1942-46. Mem. ABA, Am. Legion. Lodge: Masons. Home: Hudson N.Y. Died Jan. 16, 1991; buried Cedar Park Cemetery, Hudson. N.Y.

BIZINSKY, (HYMAN) ROBERT, artist; b. Atlanta, June 17, 1915; m. Eleanor Anita Guggenheim, 1952. Grad. high sch., Atlanta; student, High Mus. Art, Atlanta, 1936-42; studied with Hans Hofmann, 1942-46, studied with Louis Bouche, 1942-46, studied with Eves Brayer, 1946-50, studied with Emile-Othon Friesz. Mem. art staff Atlanta Constn., 1936-42; columnist The Pacer newspaper, L.A., 1952-55; mem. staff art dept. Beverly Hills (Calif.) Adult Edn., 1955-75. Exhibited in group shows at High Mus. Art, Atlanta, 1944, 45, Nat. Gallery Art, Washington, 1945, Riverside Mus., 1945, Provincetown (Mass.) Mus., 1946, Prix de la Critique, 1948, Pershing Hall, Paris, 1948, Foyer Montparnasse, Paris, 1948, European Ctr., Paris, 1948, Gallery Sainte-Placide, Paris, 1949, Gallery Casteluche, Paris, 1949, traveling exhbn., France, North Africa, Germany, Finland, 1950-51, Gallery Else Clausen, Paris, 1950-51, Societé Nat. des Beaux-Arts, 1950-51, Gallery Zak, Paris, 1950-51, L.A. County Mus. Art, 1952, Francis Lynch Gallery, L.A., 1953, All-City Art Festival, L.A., 1954, Brentwood Art Festival, 1957, pvt. exhbns., 1960-75, others; permanent collection in Nat. Mus. of U.S. Army, Washington, Army Med. Mus., Washington; commd. by U.S. Army to paint historical murals documenting 1st Armored Div., 1942, Feingarten Galleries, L.A., 1990, Armory show, N.Y.C., 1992, Pepperdine U. Art Gallery, One-Man Retrospective, Malibu, Calif., 1992. Appointed mem. Mayor's Art Community Adv. Com. of L.A., 1966. With U.S. Army, 1942-46. Recipient commendation medal from US Army and Red Cross, 1946, Bronze medal All-City Art Festival, 1954; Huntington Hartford Found. scholar, 1951-52. Home: Los Angeles Calif. Died Feb. 20, 1982.

BLACK, C(HARLES) WARREN, business executive; b. Balt., 1898; s. Charles G. and Laura (Slick) B.; m. Alice Maxwell, 1927; children: Charles W. Jr., Alice Mangels. Grad., Johns Hopkins U., 1917. With Arundel Corp., Balt., from 1919, from asst. chief engr. to exec. v.p., 1919-55, pres., 1955-63, chmn., CEO, from 1963, also bd. dirs.; pres. dir. Md. Slag Co., Balt.; bd. dirs. various cos.; corporator Savs. Bank Balt. 2d lt. engrs. ORC, 1919. Mem. ASCE, Soc. Am. Mil. Engrs., Nat. Slag Assn., Balt. Assn. Commerce. *

BLACK, CYRIL EDWIN, history, international affairs educator; b. Bryson City, N.C., Sept. 10, 1915; s. Floyd Henson and Zarafinka (Kirova) B.; m. Corinne Manning, June 30, 1951; children: James Manning, Christina Ellen. Student, U. Besancon, 1934-35, U. Berlin, summer 1935; A.B., Duke U., 1936; A.M., Harvard U., 1937, Ph.D., 1941; Litt.D. (hon.), Ursinus Coll., 1978. Mem. faculty Princeton U., 1939-86, asst. prof., 1946-49, assoc. prof., 1949-54, prof. history, 1954-86, Duke prof. Russian history, 1961-70, Shelby Collum Davis prof. in European history, 1972-83, emeritus James S. McDonnell Disting. prof. history, until 1989, dir. Ctr. Internat. Studies, 1968-85; fellow Behavioral Studies Center, 1960-61; officer Dept. State, 1943-44, fgn. service aux. officer assigned, Eastern Europe, 1944-46; mem. U.S. del. UN Commn. Investigation Concerning Greek Frontier Incidents, 1947; adviser, alt. U.S. mem. subcommn. on prevention discrimination and protection minorities, 1949-52, mem. U.S. del. to observe Soviet elections, 1958; civilian faculty Nat. War Coll., 1950; vis. fellow Wilson Center, 1982-83. Author: Establishment of Constitutional Government in Bulgaria, 1943, Twentieth Century Europe: A History, (with E.C. Helmreich), 4th edit., 1972, The Dynamics of Modernization, 1966, (with R.A. Falk, K. Knorr, O.R. Young) Neutralization in World Politics, 1968, (with others) The Modernization of Japan and Russia, 1975, (with others) The Modernization of China, 1981, Understanding Soviet Politics: The Perspective of Russian History, 1986; Editor: (with others) Challenge in Eastern Europe, 1954, Rewriting Russian History, 1956, The Transformation of Russian Society, 1960, (with T.P. Thornton) Communism and Revolution, 1964, (with R.A. Falk) The Future of the International Legal Order, 4 vols, 1969-72, Comparative Modernization: A Reader, 1975; Contbr. to profl. jours. Mem. Am. Hist. Assn., Am. Polit. Sci. Assn., Council Fgn. Relations. Home: Princeton N.J. Died July 18, 1989; buried Princeton (N.J.) Cemetery.

BLACK, EUGENE ROBERT, banker; b. Atlanta, May 1, 1989; s. Eugene Robert and Gussie (Grady) B.; m. Susette Heath, Jan. 25, 1930; children: Elizabeth Black Campbell, Eugene Robert, William Heath. Grad., U. Ga., 1917; LLD (hon.), U. Chattanooga, 1951, Columbia U., 1954, Oglethorpe U., 1955, Syracuse U., 1957, Macalester Coll., 1959, U. Ark., 1959, Rutgers U., 1959, Yale U., 1960, Princeton U., 1960, Harvard U., 1960, Williams Coll., 1960, Manchester U., Eng., 1961, Bishops U., Can., 1961, Emory U., 1962, Oxford U., 1962, U. Sussex, 1962; Dr. Econs. & Social Scis., U. Hamburg, Fed. Republic Germany, 1962; DPA, Northeastern U., 1962. Employed Harris, Forbes & Co., Atlanta, 1931-33, asst. v.p., 1933; with Chase Nat. Bank, N.Y.C., 1933-47, 2d v.p., 1933-37, v.p., 1937-47; exec. dir. for U.S. Internat. Bank for Reconstrn. and Devel., Wash., 1947-49; pres., chmn. exec. dirs. Internat. Bank for Reconstrn. and Devel., 194-62; chmn., pres. Internat. Fin. Corp., 1961-62; dir., cons. Chase Manhattan Bank, 1963-70; cons. Am. Express Co., 1970-92; chmn. bd. Blackwell Land Co. Inc., Scandinavian Securities Corp.; mem. adv. bd. Colonial Fund, Inc., Colonial Growth Shares, Inc., Colonial Income Fund, Inc.; dir. Warner Communications Inc., Corporate Property Investors; chmn., dir. Howmet Corp.; cons. Internat. Tel. & Tel. Co.; mem. World Bank Pension Fund. Author: The Diplomacy of Economic Development, Alternative in Southeast Asia. Trustee, chmn. bd. Pierpont Morgan Libr., Johns Hopkins; trustee Conservation Found., Population Coun., Inc.; dir. Atlantic Coun., Project Hope, Internat. Exec. Svc. Corps.; mem. bd. trustees, also pres. Am. Shakespeare Festival; chmn. men's adv. com. Girls Clubs Am.; vice-chmn. Planned Parenthood-World Population; mem. bd. overseers vis. com. Harvard U. Ctr. Internat. Affairs. Mem. Phi Beta Kappa. Home: Brooklyn N.Y. Died Feb. 20, 1992.

BLACK, JAMES FRANCIS, radiation technology company executive; b. Butte, Mont., Jan. 15, 1919; s. William Joseph and Agnes Leona (Tillman) B.; m. Edna Frances Zekevich, Oct. 15, 1955; children—Claudia Edna, Gregory James. B.Sc., U. Calif.-Berkeley, 1940; M.A., Princeton U., 1943, Ph.D., 1943. Group leader Exxon Research and Engring. Co., Linden, N.J., 1945-56, research assoc., 1956-59, sr. research assoc., 1959-67, sci. advisor, 1967-83; pres. Applied Radiation Tech. Inc., Chatham, N.J., 1983-88; vice chmn. adv. com. on isotopes and radiation AEC, Washington, 1959-64, N.J. Commn. on Radiation Protection, Trenton, 1958-61; mem. select com. Nat. Weather Service, NRC, Washington, 1979-80. Contbr. articles to profl. jours.; patentee in field. Fellow AAAS, Explorers Club; mem. Am. Nuclear Soc. (chmn. isotopes 1968-69), Am. Chem. Soc., Am. Meteorol. Soc. Republican. Roman Catholic. Clubs: N.Y. Sailing (N.Y.C.); Appalachian Mountain (Boston). Home: Chatham N.J. Died Dec. 15, 1988; buried Gates of Heaven Cemetery, East Hanover, N.J.

BLACK, LEON DAVID, JR., lawyer; b. Saluda, S.C., Nov. 11, 1926; s. Leon David and Ruth W. (Wheeler) B.; m. Margaret Louise Flynn, Dec. 1, 1956; children: Rebecca Black Freeman, David, Julia Black Downey. BA, Miami U., Oxford, Ohio, 1948; LLB, Yale U., 1952. Bar: Fla. 1952, U.S. Dist. Ct. (so. dist.) Fla. 1954, U.S. Ct. Appeals (5th cir.) 1966, (11th cir.) 1981. U.S. Supreme Ct. 1972. Ptnr. Brigham, Black, Niles & Wright, 1952-58, Kelly, Black, Black, Byrne, Craig & Beasley, P.A. and predecessor firms, Miami, Fla., 1958-92. Chmn. bd. Heart Assn. of Greater Miami, 1976-78; bd. dirs. Am. Heart Assn. of Greater Miami, from 1979. Lt. USNR, 1944-46. Fellow Am. Coll. Trial Lawyers; mem. ABA (chmn. com. on condemnation, zoning and property use litigation, litigation sect. coun. 1985-87), Internat. Soc. Barristers, Fla. Bar, Dade County Bar Assn. Congregationalist. Clubs: Biscayne Bay Yacht, Royal Palm Tennis, Riviera Country, Miami, Ocean Reef. Contbr. chpts., articles to profl. publs. in field. Deceased. Home: Miami Fla. †

BLACK, MATTHEW WILSON, educator; b. Altoona, Pa., Apr. 14, 1895; s. William George and Della Gertrude (Yeager) B.; m. Dorothy S. Dinsmore, June 20, 1929; children: Anne Bockee, Matthew W. AB, Pa. State U., 1915; AM, U. Pa., 1916, PhD, 1928. Tchr. English lit., instr. English U. Pa., 1916-18, 19-23, asst. prof., 1923-43, assoc. prof., 1933-49, prof., from 1939; external examiner Swarthmore Coll., 1939-41; dir. drama sec. English Inst., Columbia U., 1929. Author: The Life and Works of Richard Braithwait, 1928, Elizabethan and 17th Century Lyrics, 1938, Typical Elizabethan Plays (with Felix E. Schelling), 1949, others; editor: Variorum Richard II, 1955, Richard II in Pelican series. With U.S. Army, 1918. Mem. MLA, Shakespeare Soc. Phila., Phi Kappa Phi, Sigma Phi Epsilon. *

BLACK, SAMUEL PAUL WEST, neurosurgery educator; b. Barbourville, Ky., Dec. 19, 1916; s. Read Postlethwaite and Louise (West) B.; m. Betty Lohman, Dec. 23, 1944; children—Susan Postlethwaite, John Sheldon, Nancy Read, Samuel Paul West. B.S., Yale U., 1940; M.D., Johns Hopkins U., 1943. House officer gen. surgery New Haven Hosp., 1944, 46-47; resident neurol. surgery Yale U., New Haven, 1948-50, instr. neurosurgery, 1950-52, asst. prof., 1952-55; prof. neurosurgery U. Mo., Columbia, 1955-82, prof. emeritus, 1982-90, dir. intracranial aneurysm study dept. pathology, from 1982; vis. scholar Green Coll. Oxford U., 1982. Contbr. articles to profl. jours. Served with USNR, 1944-46. George H. Knight fellow Yale U., 1947-48. Mem. New Eng. Neurosurg. Soc. (exec. com.

1953-55), Am. Assn. Neurol. Surgeons, A.C.S., Assn. Research in Nervous and Mental Disease, So. Neurosurgical Soc., Mo. Med. Soc., Mo. Neurosurg. Soc. (v.p. 1980-81), Sigma Xi. Clubs: Austrian Mountain, Pithotomy; Rotary (Columbia) (pres. 1981-82). Home: Columbia Mo. Died June 9, 1990.

BLACK, WENDELL WILSON, lawyer; b. Everett, Wash., Apr. 15, 1896; s. William W. and Mollie (Neil) B.; m. Marion Mitchell, June 22, 1921 (dec. Feb. 1932); m. Helen Meisnest, May 5, 1934; children: William W., Keith M. LLB, U. Wash., 1920. Bar: Wash. 1920, U.S. Supreme Ct. 1944. With Seattle br. Fed. Res. Bank, 1920-25; practiced law Seattle, from 1925; ptnr. Holman, Marion, Black, Perkins & Coie and predecessor firms, 1943-64; counsel Holman, Marion, Perkins, Cole & Stone, 1965; sec. Puget Sound Power & Light Co., 1944-55; bd. dirs. Puget Sound Savs. & Loan Assn., 1928-31. With U.S. Army, 1917-19. Mem. ABA, Wash. Bar Assn., Seattle-King County Bar Assn., Am. Judicature Soc., Am. Legion, others. *

BLACK, WILLIAM ALBERT, educator; b. Greene County, Mo., Nov. 25, 1897; s. Albert Gallatin and Jenny L. (Montgomery) B.; m. Marea Belfield, Nov. 7, 1920; 1 child, William Vincent. BS, Kans. State Tchrs. Coll., 1926, MS, 1934; PhD, U. Colo., 1942. Tchr. high sch. Blue Mound, Kans., 1926-27; tchr. Ft. Scott (Kans.) Jr. Coll., 1934-41; supt. schs. Uniontown, Kans., 1927-33; instr. U. Colo., 1941-42; pres. Pueblo (Colo.) Jr. Coll., 1942-45; dir. jr. colls. & curriculum Wash. State Coll., Olympia, 1945-47; head dept. edn., psychology & philosophy Kans. State Coll. Pittsburg, 1947-64, prof. edn. & psychology, from 1964; vis. prof. univs. Colo., Okla., Iowa. Author: (with Zeran, others) The Teacher and His Job, 1953. Pres. Pueblo Civic Symphony, 1944-45. Mem. NEA, Colo. Jr. Coll. Assn., Colo.-Wyo. Acad. Sci., Am. Assn. Jr. Colls., Kans. Tchrs. Assn., Am Legion. *

BLACKALL, ERIC ALBERT, literary critic; b. London, Oct. 19, 1914; came to U.S., 1958; naturalized, 1965; s. Frederick and Lillie (Stanger) B.; m. Jean Hargrave Frantz, June 25, 1960; 1 child, Roger Nicholas. Student, Latymer Upper Sch., London; B.A., Gonville and Caius Coll., Cambridge (Eng.) U., 1936, M.A., 1940; Litt. D., Cambridge U., 1960; Ph.D., U. Vienna, Austria, 1938. Lectr. English lang. and lit. U. Bâle, Switzerland, 1938-39; lectr. German Cambridge U., 1939-58; vis. prof. German lit. Cornell U., 1957-58, chmn. dept. German lit., 1958-65, Avalon Found. prof. in humanities, 1965-67, Schurman prof. German lit., 1967-85, prof. emeritus, 1985-89; dir. Soc. for the Humanities, 1981-84; vis. prof. U. Heidelberg, Germany, 1968, King's Coll., U. London, 1988, 89. Author: Adalbert Stifter, 1948, The Emergence of German as a Literary Language, 1959, 2d edit., 1978, Die Entwicklung des Deutschen zur Literatursprache, 1966, Goethe and the Novel, 1976, The Novels of the German Romantics, 1983; editor, translator: Goethe: Wilhelm Meister's Apprenticeship, 1989; articles, revs. German studies. Decorated Cross Honor for Sci. and Art 1st class Austria, 1973; Order of Merit 1st class (W.Ger.), 1985; recipient J.G. Robertson prize in German Studies U. London, 1962; Guggenheim fellow, 1965-66. Fellow Am. Acad. Arts and Scis., Am. Philos. Soc.; mem. Modern Lang. Assn., English Goethe Soc., Am. Assn. Tchrs. German, AAUP, Phi Beta Kappa. Home: Ithaca N.Y. Died Nov. 16, 1989; buried Ithaca, N.Y.

BLACKBIRD, WILLIAM N., state supreme court justice; b. Coalgate, Okla., May 26, 1894; s. Robert and Agnes (Phillips) B.; m. Anne Courtney, 1915; m. Daisey Hawley, Dec. 1, 1954. Student, Okla. Sch. Mines, 1914, Okmulgee Law Sch., 1922-27. County judge Okmulgee County, Okla., 1933-43, dist. judge, 1943-53; assoc. justice Supreme Ct. Okla., from 1953, later chief justice. Mem. Okla. Bar Assn., Masons. *

BLACKMAN, JOHN H., JR., insurance company executive; b. West Pittston, Pa., Jan. 5, 1893; s. John Hughes and May (Allen) B.; m. Emily Fuller, Nov. 17, 1919 (dec. 1958); children: Joan Harvey, Ruth Schooley; m. June A. Therien, June 9, 1962. BS, Yale U., 1914. With Mut. Life Ins. Co., N.Y.; then chmn. bd. Investors Syndicate Life Inst. & Annuity Co., Mpls.; bd. dirs. Investors Diversified Svcs. Inc. Mem. exec. coun., trustee Episc. Dioceses Bethlehem, Pa.; trustee Lawrenceville Sch. Capt. U.S. Army, World War I. Decorated Silver Star. Mem. Wyo. Hist. & Geol. Soc., Masons, others. *

BLAIK, EARL HENRY, manufacturing corporation executive; b. Detroit, Feb. 15, 1897; s. William Douglas and Margaret Jane B.; m. Merle McDowell, Oct. 20, 1924; children: William McDowell, Robert McDowell. A.B., Miami U., Oxford, Ohio, 1918, LL.D. (hon.), 1959; B.S., U.S. Mil. Acad., 1920; student, Cav. Sch., Fort Riley, Kans., 1920-21; D.H.L., Dartmouth Coll., 1977. Commd. 1st lt. cav. U.S. Army; served with 8th Cav., 1922-23, resigned, 1923; mem. firm W.D. and E.H. Blaik (builders), Dayton, Ohio, 1923-34; head football coach Dartmouth Coll., 1934-40; part time football coach U.S. Mil. Acad., West Point, 1927-34; dir. athletics, chmn. athletic bd. U.S. Mil. Acad., 1949-58; serving as lt. col. U.S. Army, 1943, col. cav., 1944; v.p., dir. Avco Corp., N.Y.C., 1959-60; dir., chmn. exec. com. Avco Corp., from 1960; chmn. exec. com. Blaik Oil Co., Oklahoma City. Author, contbr. to mags. Trustee John F. Kennedy Library; mem. adv. bd. McArthur Meml. Found.; sponsor Hampton Inst. Named Coach of the Yr., 1946; Coach of Yr. Washington Touchdown Club, 1953; named to Nat. Football Hall of Fame, 1959; recipient State of Va. Sportsman Club award Touchdown Club of N.Y. award, 1958, Gold Medal award Nat. Football Found. and Hall of Fame, 1966, Presdl. Medal of Freedom award, 1986. Mem. Assn. Grads. U.S. Mil. Acad. (hon. trustee), Assn. U.S. Army (adv. bd.), Beta Theta Pi, Tau Kappa Alpha. Clubs: Blind Brook (N.Y.), Metropolitan (N.Y.); Burning Tree (Washington); La Quinta (Palm Desert, Calif.). Home: Colorado Springs Colo. Died May 6, 1989. †

BLAISDELL, GEORGE GRANT, business executive; b. Bradford, Pa., June 5, 1895; s. Philo C. and Sarah (Grant) B.; m. Miriam Barcroft, Feb. 21, 1922; children: Harriett Wick, Sarah Blauser; m. Barbara Thompson, Apr. 20, 1957. Student Ricker Classical Inst., Horace Mann Sch. Gen. mgr. Blaisdell Machinery Co., Bradford, 1917-20; owner Blaisdell Oil Co., Bradford, 1930-50; pres. Zippo Mfg. Co., from 1933, also treas., dir.; pres., Blaisdell Bros., N.Y.C., 1936-37; dir. Bradford Nat. Bank, from 1950. *

BLAIZE, HERBERT AUGUSTUS, prime minister of Grenada; b. Feb. 26, 1918, Island of Carriacou; s. James and Mary Blaize; m. Venetia Blaize, 1946; 6 children. Ed. Grenada Boys' Secondary Sch., Law Soc. Eng. Solicitor; M.P., after 1957, minister for trade and prodn., 1957-60, chief minister, 1960-61, 62-67, premier, 1967, mem. opposition to Coup of 1979, prime minister, 1984-89. Died Dec. 19, 1989; buried Hillsborough, Carraicou, Grenada. Home: Saint George's Grenada

BLAKE, AMANDA, actress; b. Buffalo, 1931; m. Frank Gilbert, 1967. Appeared in TV series Gunsmoke, 1956-69; films include: Battleground, 1950, Lili, 1953, About Mrs. Leslie, 1954, High Society, 1956. Home: Los Angeles Calif. Died Aug. 16, 1989.

BLAKEY, ART, drummer; b. Pitts., Oct. 11, 1919; m. Ann Arnold; children: Akira, Kenji; 7 children from previous marriages; 6 adopted children. Hon. doctorate, Berklee Coll. Music, 1987. Drummer with various groups, including Jame Murray, Pitts., early 1940s, Mary Lou Williams, 1942, Fletcher Henderson, 1943-44, Billy Eckstine, 1944-47, Lucky Millinder, 1949, Buddy DeFranco Quartet, 1951-53; founder, drummer The Jazz Messengers, 1955-90; toured with Giants of Jazz, 1971-72. Albums include Backgammon, Buhaina, Child's Dance, Gypsy Folk, In My Prime, vol. I, In This Korner, Jazz Messengers, Keystone 3, Night in Tunisia, Reflections in Blue, 'S Make It, Straight Ahead, Thermo with Hubbard, Shorter, Fuller, Art Blakey with Thelonius Monk, Not Yet, (with Dr. John and David Newman) Bluesiana Triangle, 1990. Recipient New Star award Down Beat Critics, 1953, Grammy award for best jazz instrumental performance group, 1984, Golden Record, 1985, Charly Parker award Northsea Festival, 1989. Home: New York N.Y. Died Oct. 16, 1990.

BLALOCK, HUBERT MORSE, JR., sociology educator; b. Balt., Aug. 23, 1926; s. Hubert Morse and Helen Dorothy (Welsh) B.; m. Ann Bonar, Aug. 13, 1951; children: Susan Lynn, Kathleen Ann, James Welsh. A.B., Dartmouth Coll., 1949; M.A., Brown U., 1953; Ph.D., U. N.C., 1954. Instr. sociology U. Mich., Ann Arbor, 1954-57, asst. prof., 1957-61; assoc. prof. Yale U., 1961-64; prof. U. N.C., Chapel Hill, 1964-71; prof. U. Wash., Seattle, 1971-89, prof. emeritus, 1989. Author: Social Statistics, rev. 2d edit., 1979, Causal Inferences in Nonexperimental Research, 1964, Theory Construction, 1968, Toward a Theory of Minority Group Relations, 1967, Intergroup Processes, 1979, Black-White Relations in the 1980's, 1979, Conceptualization and Measurement in the Social Sciennces, 1982, Basic Dilemmas in the Social Sciences, 1984, Power and Conflict, 1989, Understanding Social Inequality, 1991. Served with USN, 1944-46. Fellow Am. Acad. Arts and Scis., Am. Statis. Assn.; mem. Nat. Acad. Sci., Am. Sociol. Assn. (pres. 1978-79). Home: Seattle Wash. Died Feb. 8, 1991; buried Hansville, Wash.

BLANCHARD, RALPH HARRIS, financial executive; b. Niagara Falls, N.Y., June 27, 1895; s. Herman Kingsley and Alice Amanda (Tucker) B.; m. Margaret Huntington Hooker, June 30, 1924 (div. 1944); children: Sara Erickson, Susan Bliss; m. Grace Alma Godolphin. AB, Cornell U., 1917. With Nat. Carbon Co., Niagara Falls, 1919; asst. to pres. Nat. Thrift Bond Corp., 1920-21; bank employee Power City Trust Co., Niagara Falls, 1921-24; exec. sec. Community Chest, Niagara Falls, 1924-28; adminstrv. dir. Community Chests & Couns., Inc., N.Y.C., 1928-43, exec. dir., 1943-60. 2d lt. ORC, 1918. Mem. NASW, Delta Sigma Rho. *

BLANK, SAMUEL, business executive; b. N.Y.C., Apr. 23, 1896; s. Morris and Jennie (Polonsky) B.; m. Beatrice Miller, June 20, 1915; children: Marion Frehling, Rose Kramer, Jerome. Chmn. bd. Nat. Brands, Inc. and affiliated cos., Miami, Fla.; chmn. bd. Nat. Beverages, Inc., Pepsi-Cola Bottling Co. of Lakeland, Inc., Seaboard Warehouse Terminals, Inc., Miami; ptnr. State Beverages, Miami. Trustee U. Miami, Mt. Sinai Hosp. Mem. Nat. Beer Wholesalers Assn. Am., Beer Industry Fla., others. *

BLATNIK, JOHN A., congressman, educator; b. Chisholm, Minn., Aug. 17, 1911; s. John and Margaret (Kochevar) B.; m. Gisela Hager, Apr. 9, 1955; children: Thomas, Sephanie, Valerie. BE cum laude, Winona State Tchrs. Coll., 1935; student, U. Chgo., summer 1938; postgrad. in pub. adminstrn., U. Minn., 1941-42. Tchr. country sch., 1930-31; ednl. adviser Civilian Conservation Corps, Superior Nat. Forest, Minn., 1935-37; chem. instr. Chisholm (Minn.) High Sch., 1937-39; asst. to St. Louis County (Minn.) Supt. Schs., 1939-41; mem. Minn. State Senate, 1941-46, 80th-93d U.S. Congresses from 8th Minn. Dist.; dir. Former Mems. Congress. Co-founder, past chmn. Dem. Study Com.; former chmn. N.E. Minn. Rehab. Com., 1940-42, Minn. Dem. nat. committeeman, 1962-72; chmn. Minn. delegation Dem. Nat. Conv., 1968; active Boy Scouts Am. With Intelligence and Office Strategic Svcs., USAAF, 1946. Decorated Bronze Star medal with oak leaf cluster, Air medal; recipient Gold Key award as outstanding young man in community, 1941, Bernard M. Baruch Prize, 1968, Water Conservation and Mgmt. award Minn. Izaak Walton League, 1970. Mem. VFW, Minn. Am.-Jugoslav Assn. (state pres. 1939-41), Izaak Walton League, Am. Legion, Am. Vets. Com., Kappa Delta Pi. Mem. Democratic-Farmer-Labor party. Roman Catholic. Home: Forest Heights Md. Died Dec. 18, 1991.

BLAUSTEIN, MORTON K., petroleum company executive; m. Mary Jane Blaustein; 2 children from previous marriage: Susan Berlow, Jeanne Bokor; 2 stepchildren: Sandra Carter, Taylor Lucas. PhD, Stanford U., 1955. With Am. Trading and Prodn. Corp., Balt., 1951-90, v.p., 1968-70, pres., 1970-73, chmn. bd., chief exec. officer, dir., 1973-90. Former chmn., mem. bd. Balt. br. Am. Jewish Com., nat. v.p. 9 yrs; past bd. dirs. Park Sch., Sinai Hosp., Johns Hopkins. U.; adminstrv. coun. Jacob Blaustein Inst. Advancement of Human Rights (established in his honor). Mem. Nat. Petroleum Coun., Advt. Coun. (pub. policy com.). Home: Pikesville Md. Died Dec. 17, 1990.

BLECKER, MICHAEL JOHN, university president; b. Chgo., May 11, 1931; s. Michael M. and Ida Camille (Witt) B. A.B., Harvard U., 1953; postgrad. St. John's Sem., 1956-60; Ph.D., U. Wis., 1964. Ordained Priest, Roman Catholic Ch., 1960. Instr. dept. history St. John's U., Collegeville, Minn., 1960-61, asst. prof., 1964-70, assoc. prof., 1971, chmn. dept. theology, 1967-79, pres., 1971-82; pres. Grad. Theol. Union, Berkeley, Calif., 1982-89. Assoc. editor Am. Benedictine Rev., 1969-89. Contbr. articles to Am. Benedictine Rev., Speculum, Liberal Edn., Studi Senesi. Bd. dirs. Holy Names Coll., Oakland, Calif., 1983-89; mem. Nat. Conf. Cath. Bishops Commn. on Orthodox/Roman Catholic Dialog, 1969-82. Mem. Nat. Assn. Ind. Colls. and Univs. (bd. dirs. 1979-82). Club: Athenien-Nile (Oakland, Calif.). Died June 7, 1989. Home: Berkeley Calif. †

BLINKS, LAWRENCE ROGERS, biologist, educator; b. Michigan City, Ind., Apr. 22, 1900; s. Walter Moulton and Ella Little (Rogers) B.; m. Anne Catherine Hof, July 27, 1928; children—John Rogers, David (dec.), Samuel (dec.). Student, Kalamazoo Coll., 1918-19, Stanford U., 1920-21; B.S., Harvard U., 1923, M.A., 1925, Ph.D., 1926. Asst. in gen. physiology Rockefeller Inst., N.Y.C., 1926-31, assoc., 1931-33; assoc. prof., then prof. Stanford U., Calif., 1933-65; prof. U. Calif.-Santa Cruz, 1965-72; dir. Hopkins Marine Sta., Pacific Grove, Calif., 1943-65; asst. dir. NSF, Washington, 1954-55. Contbr. articles to sci. publs. Fellow Guggenheim Found., 1939-40, Fulbright Found., 1957. Fellow Am. Acad. Arts and Scis., AAAS, Calif. Acad. Sci.; mem. Nat. Acad. Scis., Western Soc. Naturalists (pres. 1950), Am. Soc. Plant Physiologists (Stephen Hales award), Soc. Gen. Physiologists (pres. 1952). Club: Faculty (Stanford). Home: Carmel Calif. Died Mar. 4, 1989; cremated.

BLINN, KEITH WAYNE, legal educator; b. Hutchinson, Kans., July 28, 1917; s. Alonzo Cary and Clifton (Wright) B.; m. Ellen Young, Aug. 31, 1940; children—John Randolph, Stephen David. A.B., Washington and Lee U., 1940; J.D. (Sterling fellow), Yale U., 1951. Bar: Wis. 1941, Tex. 1953, N.Y. 1966, Conn. 1976. Atty. TVA, 1942, NLRB, 1942-46; prof. law U. N.D., 1946-52; vis. prof. law U. Idaho, 1952; sr. v.p., gen. counsel Continental Oil Co., N.Y.C., 1962-77; prof. law U. Houston, 1977-85; vis. prof. engring. U. Calif., Irvine, 1984-90; dir. Commonwealth Oil Refining Co., Haldor Topsoe Inc., Am. Legal Fedn.; lectr., seminar participant, from 1964; arbitrator Am. Arbitrator Assn., from 1961, Fed. Mediation and Conciliation Ser., from 1981; Atty. adviser OPA, 1951; chmn. regional enforcement commn. WSB, Mpls., 1952. Author: Cases and Materials on Federal Energy Regulations, Readings on International Energy Transactions and Internat. Petroleum Exploration and Exploitation Agreements: Legal, Economic and Policy Aspects, Legal and Ethical Concepts in Engineering, 1989, Legal and Ethical Concepts in Engineering, 1989. Mem. bd. zoning appeals, Bellaire, Tex., 1957, mem. city council, 1959. Mem. Am. Bar Assn., Assn. Bar City N.Y., Order of Coif, Phi

Delta Phi. Episcopalian (vestryman). Clubs: Stamford (Conn.); Yacht; Wee Burn Country (Darien, Conn.); Bristol (R.I.) Yacht; Univ. (Irvine, Calif.). Home: Irvine Calif. Died May 15, 1990.

BLISS, ANTHONY ADDISON, lawyer; b. N.Y.C., Apr. 19, 1913; s. Cornelius Newton and Zaidee (Cobb) B.; m. Barbara Field, Dec. 22, 1937 (div. Dec. 1941); 1 dau., Barbara Last; m. Jo Ann Sayers, June 9, 1942 (div. July 1967); children: Eileen Bliss Andahazy, Anthony Addison, John Wheeler; m. Sally Bralley, July 24, 1967; children: Mark Bralley, Timothy Newton. BA, Harvard U., 1936; LLB, U. Va., 1940. Bar: N.Y. 1943. Cons. mem. Milbank, Tweed, Hadley & McCloy, N.Y.C.; ret. trustee U.S. Trust Co. N.Y.; hon. chmn. Nat. Corp. Fund for Dance Inc.; former mem. council Nat. Endowment for Arts. Bd. dirs. Met. Opera Assn., 1949-91, pres., 1956-67, gen. mgr., 1974-85; trustee Portledge Sch.; chmn. bd. Found. for Joffrey Ballet, 1970-91; bd. dirs. Am. Arts Alliance. Served in USNR, 1942-45. Decorated Air medal. Mem. ABA, Internat. Bar Assn., N.Y. State Bar Assn., Nassau County Bar Assn., Assn. of Bar of City of N.Y., Creek Club, Beaver Dam Winter Sports Club. Home: Oyster Bay N.Y. Died Aug. 10, 1991. †

BLOCH, HERMAN SAMUEL, chemist; b. Chgo., June 15, 1912; s. Aaron and Esther (Broder) B.; m. Elaine J. Kahn, July 4, 1940; children—Aaron N., Janet L. (Mrs. Daniel Martin), Merry D. (Mrs. Robert L. Jones). B.S., U. Chgo., 1933, Ph.D., 1936. With UOP, Inc., Des Plaines, Ill., 1936-77; asso. dir. research UOP, Inc., 1964-73, dir. catalysis research, 1973-77; Cons. in field; chmn. com. phys. scis. Ill. Bd. Higher Edn., 1969-71. Author. Co-inventor biogradable detergent; holder, co-holder over 200 patents. Commr. Housing Authority Cook County, from 1966, chmn., 1971; chmn. Skokie (Ill.) Human Relations Commn., 1965-71; pres. bd. edn. Skokie Sch. Dist. 68, 1962-63; trustee Skokie Library Bd., from 1981. Recipient E.V. Murphree award indsl. and engring. chemistry Am. Chem. Soc., 1974; Eugene J. Houdry award Catalysis Soc., 1971; I-R 100 award Indsl. Research mag., 1973; named to Skokie Hall of Fame, 1989. Hon. mem. Am. Inst. Chemists (honor scroll 1957, Chem. Pioneer award 1989); mem. Am. Chem. Soc. (chmn. bd. 1973-77), AAAS (v.p. for chemistry 1970), Nat. Acad. Scis., Soc. Chem. Industry, Ill. Acad. Sci., N.Y. Acad. Sci., U. Chgo. Alumni Assn. (Profl. Achievement award 1988), Chemists Club Chgo., Phi Beta Kappa (pres. Chgo. 1968-69), Sigma Xi. Home: Skokie Ill. Died June 16, 1990; buried Shalom Cemetery, Palatine, Ill.

BLOCH, RAY E., business executive; b. Marshallville, Ohio, Sept. 10, 1894; s. Charles E. and Margaret (Stotler) B.; m. Rhea Garman, Dec. 16, 1915; 1 child, Mary Ellen. With Mohawk Rubber Co., from 1913; pres., gen. mgr., dir. Mohawk Rubber Co., Akron, 1935, then chmn. bd.; also with Mohawk Rubber Co. N.Y., Inc., from 1935. Mem. Akron C. of C., Newcomen Soc. *

BLOCK, MARVIN AVRAM, physician; b. Buffalo, Jan. 11, 1903; s. Robert and Sarah (Sernoffsky) B.; m. Lillian Kevitt, Nov. 29, 1933. BS, MD, SUNY, Buffalo, 1925; student, U. Vienna, Austria, 1931. Intern Buffalo Gen. Hosp., 1924-25, mem. staff, from 1951; intern Buffalo City Hosp., 1925-26; mem. faculty SUNY-Buffalo Med. Sch., from 1927, now prof. emeritus clin. medicine; practice medicine specializing in internal medicine, 1945—, practice medicine specializing in alcoholism and addictive diseases, 1950—; bd. mgrs. Meyer Meml. Hosp., Buffalo, 1943-44, U. Buffalo Rehab. Ctr., 1949-51; vis. lectr. U. Nev., U. Tex., U. Utah Sch. Alcohol Studies, McMaster U., Inst. Alcohol, U. Colo. Sch. Alcohol Studies, Columbia Sch. Social Studies, U. Miss. Sch. Alcohol Studies, U. Witwatersrand, South Africa, U. Capetown, South Africa, U. Stellenbosch, South Africa, U. Melbourne, Australia; cons. South Africa Nat. Council Alcoholism, 1960, Australian Council Alcoholism, 1960, New Zealand Council Alcoholism, 1960, Dept. Hosps. and Med. Facilities of AMA, 1964, Malvern (Pa.) Inst., B.C. Project of Am. Psychiat. Assn., NIMH, Buffalo Police Dept., Dept. Health, N.Y. State Motor Vehicle Bur.; founder N.Y. State Council Coms. Alcoholism, 1950, pres., 1954-60; pres. Western N.Y. Com. Edn. Alcoholism, 1954-59, bd. dirs., from 1949; bd. dirs. Nat. Council Alcoholism, v.p., 1963; adv. bd. Erie dean acad. affairs SUNY, from 1964; dean County Mental Health Assn., Internat. Inst. Alcoholism; adv. com. narcotics N.Y. State Dept. Health, N.Y. State Dept. Mental Hygiene; NSF del. Am.-Japanese Conf. on Addictions, 1964. Author: Alcohol--Its Facets and Phases; numerous other works in field. Mem. exec. com. Erie County Community Welfare Council, 1963; bd. dirs. Buffalo and Erie County Community Chest, 1956-60, Rosa Coplon Home and Infirmary, Jewish Fedn. Social Service, Nat. Council Joint Distbn.; pres. Marvin A. and Lillian K. Block Found.; trustee Buffalo & Erie County Pub. Library, from 1979. Recipient M. & R. award Am. Acad. Gen. Practitioners, 1953, Buffalo Evening News award, 1955, citation of merit Malvern Inst., 1962, Wisdom Award of Honor, Wisdom Soc., 1966, Nat. Medal Achievement, Am. Med. Soc. Alcoholism, 1972; hon. fellow Clifford C. Furnas Coll., Faculty SUNY-Buffalo, 1973. Fellow Am. Pub. Health Assn., N.Y. State Pub. Health Assn., Assn. Am. Med. Colls.; mem. AAAS, AMA (chmn. com. alcoholism council mental health), N.Y. State Med. Soc. (chmn. subcom. alcoholism and narcotics pub. health com.), Erie County Med. Soc. (chmn. spl. com. problems alcoholism), Buffalo Acad. Medicine, Am. Acad. Polit. and Social Scis., N.Y. Acad. Scis., N.Y. State Soc. Med. Research, Am. Geriatrics Soc., Western N.Y. Geriatrics Soc., Profl. Assn. Alcoholism, World Med. Assn., Brit. Soc. Study Alcoholism, N.Y. State Assn. Professions, Acad. Psychosomatic Medicine, Buffalo Fine Arts Acad., Buffalo Philharmonic Orch. Soc., Buffalo Chamber Music Soc., Erie County Soc. Prevention Cruelty Animals, Am. Jewish Physicians Com., Cleve. Health Mus., Salvation Army Assn., Am. Jewish Com., Alumni Assn. SUNY-Buffalo, Am. Red Mogen David for Israel, Zionist Orgn. Am., Am. Edn. Found., Maimonides Med. Soc., Am. Med. Soc. on Alcoholism (v.p.), Buffalo Council World Affairs (bd. dirs. 1975), Life & Death Transition Soc. (bd. dirs. from 1980). Clubs: Automobile (Buffalo); Westwood Country (Williamsville, N.Y.). Lodge: B'nai B'rith. Home: Buffalo N.Y. Died Feb. 28, 1989; buried Buffalo.

BLODGETT, RALPH HAMILTON, economist, educator; b. North Adams, Mass., Dec. 25, 1905; s. Charles Raymond and Lillian (Morits) B.; m. Loretta Neunfeldt, June 14, 1930 (dec. Dec. 1957); children: Moyra Loretta (Mrs. James F. Schaeffner), Sandra Elizabeth (Mrs. Stuart A. McIntosh); m. Margaret Adkins, July 18, 1958. B.S. in Econs, U. Vt., 1927; A.M., Syracuse U., 1928; Ph.D., U. Pa., 1933. Grad. asst. econs. Syracuse U., 1927-28; instr. econs. Valparaiso U., 1928-29; instr., asst. prof. econs. U. Pa., 1929-37; asst. prof. econs. U. Ill., 1937-41, assoc. prof., 1941-45, prof., 1945-50; prof. econs. U. Fla., Gainesville, 1950-76, prof. emeritus, 1976, acting head econs. dept., 1964-65; bd. editors U. Fla. Social Sci. Monograph Series; vis. prof. econs. U. So. Calif., summer, 1949; econ. cons., expert witness various law firms; econ. cons. TVA, 1959-61, NASA, 1964-65, HUD, 1965-67. Author: Cyclical Fluctuations in Commodity Stocks, 1935, Principles of Economics, 1941, rev. edit., 1946, 51, Comparative Economic Systems, 1944, 49, Our Expanding Economy: An Introduction, 1955; co-author: An Economic Question Book, 1931, Contemporary Economic Problems, 1932, Getting and Earning, 1937, Economics: Principles and Problems, 1937, rev. edits., 1942, 48, Current Economic Problems, 1939, 1947, Comparative Economic Development, 1956, Fluctuations in General Business, 1977; Author numerous articles and monographs in econs. Mem. Am. Econ. Assn., So. Econ. Assn., Midwest Econ. Assn. (v.p. 1946-47), AAUP, Univ. Profs. for Acad. Order, Am. Contract Bridge League (life master), Phi Beta Kappa, Omicron Delta Epsilon, Sigma Alpha Epsilon, Alpha Kappa Psi, Beta Gamma Sigma. Democrat. Episcopalian. Clubs: U. Fla. Bridge, Gainesville Golf and Country, Heritage. Home: Gainesville Fla. Died Dec. 19, 1988; buried Evergreen Cemetery, Gainesville, Fla.

BLOOM, ALLAN, political science educator; b. Indpls., Sept. 14, 1930; s. Allan and Malvina Dorothea (Glasner) B. AB, U. Chgo., 1949, AM, 1953, PhD, 1955; exchange fellow, U. Paris, 1953-55; postgrad., Heidelberg U., Fed. Republic Germany, 1957. Reader U. Paris, 1954-55; lectr. liberal arts U. Chgo., 1955-60; vis. asst. prof. polit. sci. Yale U., 1962-63; from asst. prof. to assoc. prof. govt. Cornell U., 1963-70; prof. polit. sci. U. Toronto, 1970-79; prof. Com. on Social Thought and the Coll., U. Chgo., 1979-92; vis. prof. U. Tel Aviv, 1969, Hautes Etudes Paris, 1984-92. Author: Shakespeare's Politics, 1964, The Closing of the American Mind, 1987, Giants and Dwarfs, 1990; editor: Confronting the Constitution, 1990; translator, commentator Plato, Rousseau. Recipient Clark Disting. Teaching award, 1967, prix Jean Jacques Rousseau, City of Geneva, 1987; fellow Rockefeller Found., 1957-58, Cornell Soc. Humanities, 1968-69, Guggenheim Found., 1975-76. Home: Chicago Ill. Died Oct. 7, 1992. †

BLOUGH, CARMAN GEORGE, accountant; b. Johnstown, Pa., Nov. 11, 1895; s. Silas S. and Mary Alice (Wertz) B.; m. Lillie Katherine Flory, Aug. 17, 1922; 1 child, Elizabeth Jean Martin. AB, Manchester Coll., 1917, LLD, 1944; MA, U. Wis., 1922; student, Harvard U., 1932-33. Tchr., 1917-22; with Wis. State Tax Commn., 1922-27; dir. budget State of Wis., 1927-29; prof. U. N.D., 1929-33, Armour Inst. Tech., 1933-34; chief acct. SEC, 1934-38; ptnr. Arthur Andersen & Co., Chgo., 1938-42; dir. procurement policy divsn. War Prodn. Bd.; adj. prof. acctg. Columbia U., 1947-61; vis. lectr., prof. various instns.; cons. various orgns. Author: Practical Applications of Accounting Standards, 1957; also articles. Mem. AICPA, Am. Acctg. Assn., Delta Sigma Pi, Beta Gamma Sigma, Beta Alpha Psi. *

BLOUNT, CHARLES, JR., business executive; b. N.Y.C., Jan. 25, 1897; s. Charles and Mildred Arnold (Bernheimer) B.; m. Mercedes Marshall, Feb. 26, 1927; children: Lorna Claire, Mercedes Elena. Ed., Bovee Sch. and Choate Sch.; AB, Harvard U., 1918. With United Piece Dye Works, various locations, from 1919; gen. mgr. United Piece Dye Works, from 1936, exec. v.p. in charge of reorgn., 1937, pres., dir., from 1944. Author: A Workable Plan for Settlement of Industry-Labor Disputes, 1946. With USNR, 1917-19. Mem. Am. Assn. Textile Chemists and Colorists, Mil. Order World War. *

BLOUSTEIN, EDWARD J., university administrator, law educator; b. N.Y.C., Jan. 20, 1925; s. Samuel and Celia (Einwohner) B.; m. Ruth Ellen Steinman, Oct. 6, 1951 (dec.); children: Elise, Lori. B.A., N.Y. U., 1948; B. Phil. (Fulbright Scholar), Wadham Coll., Oxford (Eng.) U., 1950; Ph.D., Cornell U., 1954, J.D., 1959. Bar: N.Y. 1959, Vt. 1971. Polit. analyst State Dept., 1951-52; instr. logic and philosophy Cornell U., 1954-55; prof. law NYU Law Sch., 1961-65; pres. Bennington (Vt.) Coll., 1965-71, Rutgers U., 1971-89. Mem. Nat. Assn. State Univs. and Land Grant Coll. (chmn 1984), Phi Beta Kappa. Home: Piscataway N.J. Died Dec. 19, 1989.

BLUM, VIRGIL CLARENCE, political science educator; b. Defiance, Iowa, Mar. 27, 1913; s. John Peter and Elizabeth (Rushenberg) B. Student, Creighton U., 1932-34; AB, St. Louis U., 1938, MA, 1945; postgrad., U. Chgo., 1950-51; PhD, St. Louis U., 1954. Joined Soc. of Jesus, 1934; ordained priest Roman Catholic Ch., 1947. Tchr. Campion High Sch., Prairie du Chien, Wis., 1941-44; asst. prof. Creighton U., 1953-56; mem. faculty Marquette U., 1956-90, prof. polit. sci., 1961-78, chmn. dept., 1961-65, 70-71; past bd. dirs. Santa Fe Comms., Inc. Author: Freedom of Choice in Education, 1958, Freedom in Education, 1965, Education: Freedom and Competition, 1967, Catholic Education: Survival of Demise, 1969, Parent Power for Tuition Grants, 1971, Catholic Parents-Political Eunuchs, 1972, also articles. Chmn. Children's Equal Opportunmities Com., 1965-71; mem. exec. com. Citizens for ednl. Freedom, 1964-76; bd. dirs., 1964-90; founder Catholic League for Religious and Civil Rights; pres. Catholic League for Religious and Rights; bd. dirs. Thomas J. White Found., 1983-90. Past mem. Am., Polit. Sci. Assn., Am. Judicature Soc., Midwest Polit. Sci. Assn., Nat. Coun. on Religion and Pub. Edn. Home: Milwaukee Wis. Died Apr. 5, 1990; buried Milw.

BLUME, PETER, artist; b. Russia, Oct. 27, 1906; came to U.S., 1911, naturalized, 1921; s. Harry and Rose (Gopin) B.; m. Grace Douglas Gibbs Craton, Mar. 9, 1931. Student pub. schs., Art Student Ednl. Alliance, N.Y.C., 1919-24, Art Students League, N.Y.C., Beaux Arts. Exhibited at Daniel Gallery, N.Y.C., 1926-31, Cleve., Columbus, Phila., Detroit, Balt., San Francisco, Buffalo, and Whitney museums, Mus. Modern Art, N.Y.C., Century of Progress Expn., Chgo., Internat. Venice, Italy, Julien Levy Gallery, Currier Gallery, Manchester, N.H., Wadsworth Atheneum, Hartford, Conn., Kennedy Gallery, N.Y.C., 1968, Danenberg Gallery, 1970, Coe Kerr Gallery, 1974, Dinten Fass Gallery, 1980, retrospective exhbn. Wadsworth Atheneum, 1964, Mus. Contemporary Art, Chgo., 1976, New Britain (Conn.) Mus. Am. Art, 1982, Mead Mus., Amherst Coll., 1985; subject of book Peter Blume by Frank Anderson Trapp, 1987. Recipient first prize Carnegie Art, 1934, 2d purchase award Artists for Victory Exhbn. Met. Mus. of Art, 1942, for his South of Scranton Exhbn., Durlacher Bros., 1947; Guggenheim Found. fellow, 1932, 36. Mem. Am. Acad. Nat. Inst. Arts and Letters, A.N.A. Home: Sherman Conn. Died Nov. 30, 1992. †

BLUMENTHAL, ANDRE, metals company executive; b. N.Y.C., Jan. 23, 1904; s. Sidney and Lucy (Picard) B.; m. Mildred Wimpfheimer, Nov. 23, 1927; children: William, Thomas, Elizabeth. Grad., Ethical Culture Sch., 1921; B.A., Yale U., 1925. With Sidney Blumenthal & Co., Inc., 1926-57, dir., 1930-57, pres., 1953; pres. Norwalk Powdered Metals, Inc., 1958-82; Pres. Textile Research Inst., 1952-53, Conn. Hosp. Planning Commn., 1971-72; pres. Conn. Hosp. Assn., 1956, now hon. mem. Pres. Norwalk Hosp., 1960-62, then hon. trustee; chmn. Conn. Bd. Mental Health, 1957-59; chmn. adv. bd. Conn. Mental Health Center, 1965-69; hon. dir. Greater Norwalk Community Council; former pres., dir. Norwalk Hosp.; former pres. Conn. Hosp. Planning Commn.; sec. Yale Coll. Class of 1925, from 1975. Commdr. USNR, World War II. Home: Norwalk Conn. Died Sept. 22, 1989.

BLUMENTHAL, SIDNEY, educator, physician; b. N.Y.C., June 24, 1909; s. Jacob and Lena (Uhran) B.; m. Elaine Levy, Apr. 4, 1953; childen: Patricia, Peggy. BS, U. La., 1930, MD, 1933. Diplomate Am. Bd. Pediatrics (chmn. sub-bd. pediatric cardiology). Intern Milw. Children's Hosp., 1933-34; resident Mt. Sinai Hosp., N.Y.C., 1934-36; pvt. practice pediatrics N.Y.C., 1950-58, Babies Hosp., N.Y.C., 1955-70; prof. clin. pediatrics Columbia Coll. Phys. and Surg., 1959-70; prof. pediatric cardiology U. Miami, Fla., 1970-90; dean postgrad. med. edn. U. Miami, 1970-74; vis. prof. pediatric cardiology Nat. Taiwan U., Taipei, 1964. Chmn. coun. on rheumatic fever and congenital heart disease Am. Heart Assn. Lt. col. M.C., AUS, 1942-45. Decorated Bronze Star. Mem. Alpha Omega Alpha. Home: Miami Fla. Died June 19, 1990.

BLUMGART, HERRMAN L(UDWIG), physician; b. Newark, July 19, 1895; s. David and Sophie (Hiller) B.; m. Margaret Stein, July 18, 1931; 1 child, Ann. SB, Harvard U., 1917, MD, 1921, ScD (hon.), 1962. Diplomate Am. Bd. Internal Medicine and Cardiology. Intern Peter Bent Brigham Hosp., 1921-22; asst. Thorndike Meml. Lab. Boston City Hosp., 1924-28; assoc. prof. medicine Harvard U., 1928-46, prof. medicine, 1946-62, then prof. emeritus; cons. various orgns. Col.

MC U.S. Army, 1943-46. Decorated Legion of Merit with oak leaf cluster; recipient Gold Heart award Am. Heart Assn. Fellow ACP, Am. Coll. Cardiology; mem. Am. Soc. Clin. Investigation, Assn. Am. Physicians, Am. Physiol. Soc., Am. Acad. Arts & Scis., Soc. Cons. of World War II, AMA, others. *

BOAS, ROBERT SANFORD, investment banker; b. N.Y.C., May 21, 1923; s. Benjamin W. and Ruth (Hirschman) B.; m. Marjorie Marks, June 23, 1946; children: Richard, Susan, Andrew. AB, Cornell U., 1945; AB hon. degree, Western State Coll. Law, 1973. Exec. v.p. Carl Marks & Co., Inc., N.Y.C., 1946-53; chmn. bd. Carl Marks & Co., Inc., from 1953; pres. CMNY Capital Co., from 1961; v.p. Carl Marks Found., from 1958, STEE CED, from 1989; trustee Com. for Econ. Devel., 1989-92. Chmn. North Shore Univ. Hosp., Manhasset, N.Y., 1972-92, pres., 1973-77; assoc. bd. dirs. Met. Opera, United Jewish Appeal, United Cerebral Palsy Research and Ednl. Found.; bd. dirs. Joint Distbn. Com. With AUS, 1943-44. Mem. Nat. Assn. Securities Dealers, Nat. Securities Traders Assn. Clubs: Fresh Meadow Country, Palm Beach Country, Harmonie, India Ho., Masons. Home: Great Neck N.Y. Died June 22, 1992. †

BOAST, WARREN BENEFIELD, electrical engineer; b. Topeka, Dec. 13, 1909; s. Charles W. and Lulu (Robinson) B.; m. Ruth J. Hansen, Nov. 28, 1936; children: Richard, Charles, Thomas. B.E.E., U. Kans., 1933, M.S., 1934; Ph.D., Iowa State Coll., 1936. Asst. elec. engring. Iowa State U., 1934, prof., head dept., 1954-75, prof. emeritus, from 1975; Anson Marston distinguished prof. engring., 1964; pres. Nat. Electronics Conf., 1967; U.S. del. Internat. Electrotech. Commn., Aix-les Bains, France, 1964. Author: Illumination Engineering, 1942, 53, Principles of Electric and Magnetic Fields, 1948, 56; Spanish transl. Técnica de la Iluminación Eléctrica, 1965; Principles of Electric and Magnetic Circuits, 1950, 57, Vector Fields, 1964, Japanese transl. parts I and II, 1967; contbr. to: McGraw-Hill Ency. Sci. and Tech, 1960, 66, 71, 77, 82, Reinhold Ency. Physics, 1966, 74, 85, Standard Handbook for Electrical Engrs., 12th edit, 1987; patentee in field; research on electro-acoustic transducers. Recipient Faculty citation, 1971; Marston medal, 1980. Fellow IEEE (Meritorious award of Edn. Soc. 1978, Centennial medal 1984), Illuminating Engring. Soc.; mem. Am. Soc. Engring. Edn., Sigma Xi, Eta Kappa Nu, Tau Beta Pi. Home: Ames Iowa Deceased. †

BOATWRIGHT, PURVIS JAMES, JR., association executive; b. Augusta, Ga., Nov. 8, 1927; s. Purvis James and Louise Ferguson B.; m. Nancy Blakely, Aug. 3, 1951; children: Cynthia, Purvis James III, Carolyn. Student, Ga. Inst. Tech., Wofford Coll. Exec. sec. Carolina Golf Assn., 1959-69; asst. dir. U.S. Golf Assn., Far Hills, N.J., 1969-81, exec. dir. rules and competitions, from 1981; sec. World Coun. of Golf. Author revision of Rules of Golf, recodifying Decisions on Rules of Golf, 1987. Recipient Richardson award Golf Writers Assn. Am., 1990; inducted to Carolinas Golf Hall of Fame, S.C. Athletic Hall of Fame, Wofford Coll. Hall of Fame. Named one of 100 Heroes of the 1st Century of Golf in Am. Mem. Somerset Hills Country Club (Bernardsville, N.J.). Home: Far Hills N.J. Died Apr. 5, 1991; buried Golf House, Far Hills, N.J.

BOBBITT, ARCHIE NEWTON, lawyer; b. Eckerty, Ind., Sept. 3, 1895; s. Irvin and Ida Mae (Newton) B.; m. Frances Bringle Adams, Aug. 21, 1921. Student, Cen. Normal Coll., 1913, 15, 19; LLB, Benjamin Harrison Law Sch., 1927, Ind. U. Bar: Ind. 1927. Various positions, to 1927; practiced law Inpls., from 1927; sr. mem. Bobbitt, Martz & Beattey, 1942-51; city atty., 1943-44, corp. coun., 1944-48; judge Supreme Ct. Ind., 1951-63; sr. mem. Ruckelshaus, Bobbitt & O'Connor, Inpls., from 1964. With USN, World War I. Mem. ABA, Inpls. Bar Assn., Lawyers Assn. Inpls., N.Am. Gasoline Tax Conf., Sigma Delta Kappa. *

BOBROVNIKOFF, NICHOLAS THEODORE, astronomer; b. Russia, Apr. 29, 1896; came to U.S., 1924; naturalized, 1930; s. Theodore Basil and Helena (Gavriloff) B.; m. Mildred Gwynne Sharrer, June 25, 1930; children: David Porter, Jean Inglis, Stephen Peters. Student, Inst. Mining Engrs., Petrograd, 1914-17, U. Prague, 1921-24; PhD, U. Chgo., 1927. Martin Kellogg fellow Lick Obs., Calif., 1927-29; Natural Rsch. fellow U. Calif., 1929-30; asst. prof. astronomy Ohio Wesleyan U., 1930-34, assoc. prof., from 1934; assoc. prof. astronomy Ohio State U., 1935-45, prof., from 1945; acting dir. Perkins Obs., Ohio Wesleyan U., Ohio State U., 1935-37, dir., 1937-52. Author: (monograph) Halley's Comet in Its Apparition of 1909-11, 1931; also numerous articles. Mem. AAAS, Am. Astron. Soc., Am. Geophys. Union, History of Sci. Soc., Internat. Astron. Union, Internat. Geophys. Year, Royal Astron. Soc., Sigma Xi. *

BOCK, ROBERT M., university dean, science administrator; b. Preston, Minn., July 26, 1923; s. Glen E. and Hilda (Snyder) B.; m. Ruth Golbien, Sept. 21, 1947; children—Karen, Susan. B.S., U. Wis., 1949, Ph.D. in Chemistry, 1952; postgrad., Calif. Inst. Tech., 1955, Cambridge (Eng.) U., 1961. Mem. faculty U. Wis., Madison, 1952-89, prof. molecular biology, 1965-89, dean Grad. Sch., 1967-89, prof. emeritus, 1989, dir. univ. industry rsch. programs, from 1989; mem. exec. com. Nat. Assn. State U. and Land Grant Colls., 1979, chmn. council on research policy and grad. edn., 1978; chmn. com. on young research faculty in sci. and engring. NRC, 1979; mem. com. nat. needs biomed. and behavioral research personnel Nat. Acad. Scis., chmn. basic biomed. sci. panel, 1985; mem. adv. council NIH div. research resources, 1986—. Contbr. profl. jours. Sci. adviser Gov. of Wis., from 1969. With U.S. Army, World War II. Mem. Am. Chem. Soc. (chmn. div. biol. chemistry from 1974), Soc. Exptl. Biologists (chmn. public affairs com.), Assn. Grad. Schs. (pres. 1972-73), Sigma Xi (pres. Wis. Soc. 1972). Home: Madison Wis. Died July 2, 1991.

BOCKHOFF, HARRY W, tool manufacturing executive; b. Indpls., Apr. 5, 1895; s. William Frederick and Julia (Kloecker) B.; m. Harriett E. Luscomb, Aug. 17, 1918; children: Phyllis (Mrs. John E. Crane), William Frederick II, Camilla Ann (Mrs. John E. Ellis). Student, U. Ill., 1919, Cornell U., 1920. With Nat. Automatic Tool Co, Inc., Richmond, Ind., from 1916, v.p., mgr., 1918-28, past pres., chmn., from 1958; dir. Second Nat. Bank, Richmond, Sta. WKBV, Richmond. Active Richmond's Com. of 100. Mem. Nat. Machine Tool Builders Assn., Elk Club, Rotary, Columbia (Indpls.). *

BOCKUS, HENRY L., physician; b. Newark, Del., Apr. 18, 1894; s. William Jones and Luella (Whiteman) B.; m. Rosalynd Foss, Jan. 13, 1935; 1 child, Barbara Ann. MD, Jefferson Med. Coll., 1917, DSc., 1958; DSc., Dickenson Coll., 1946, U. Pa., 1961. Diplomate Am. Coll. Physicians., Am. Bd. Internal Med., Phila. Coll. Physicians. Resident physician Lenox Hill Hosp., N.Y.C., 1920-21; private practice Phila., 1921; internist specializing in gastro-intestinal disorders and as gastroenterologist; organizer stomache clinic Grad. Hosp. U. Pa., from 1921; prof. gastroenterology U. Pa., Phila., from 1931, prof. and chmn. dept. medicine, 1949-60; prof. medicine emeritus U. Pa., from 1960; cons. physician Grad. Hosp.; hon. civiliancons. surgeon gen. USN; chmn., bd. dirs. MEDICO; v.p. bd. dirs. CARE; cons. gastroenterologist Bryn Mawr Hosp., Abington Meml. Hosp., Phila. Naval Hosp.; hon. prof. medicine U. Antioquia (Columbia), 1964; chmn. World Congress in Gastroenterology, Washington, 1958; mem. bd. trustees Jefferson Med. Coll. Author: Gastrenterology, 3 vols., 1943-46, Postgraduate gastroenterology, 1950; mem. editorial bd. Jour. of Gastroenterology; contbr. articles to profl. jours. Lt. M.C., USN, 1917-19; with 7th rgt. USMC in Cuba. Decorated Comdr. Order Hipolito Unahue (Peru), Order al Merite de Chile; recipient Caldwell medal Am. Reentgen Ray Soc., 1950, Strittmater awardPhila. County Med. Soc., 1951, Modern Med. award for achievement, 1962. Fellow Am. Coll. Physicians, Royal Soc. Arts, London, Nat. Acad. Med., Mex. (hon.); hon. mem. Gastrolenterol. Assns. of Ctrl. Am., Chile, Cuba, Venezuela, Peru, Brazil, Argentina, Uruguay, Spain, India, Belgium, Germany, Columbia, Organization Mundialde Gastroenterologia (pres. 1958-62, hon. pres. from 1962), Am. Gastroenterol. Assn. (past pres., Friedenwald medal 1962), AMA (former chmn. sect. gastroenterology and proctology), Pathologic Soc.; hon. assoc. Am. Proctologic Assn., Alpha Omega Alpha, Phila. Country Club, University Club (Phila.). *

BODIAN, DAVID, anatomist, educator; b. St. Louis, May 15, 1910; s. Harry and Tillie (Franzel) B.; m. Elinor Widmont, June 26, 1944; children: Helen, Marion, Brenda, Alexander, Marc Oliver. BS, U. Chgo., 1931, PhD, 1934, MD, 1937; LHD (hon.), Johns Hopkins U., 1987. Asst. in anatomy U. Chgo., 1935-38; NRC fellow medicine U. Mich., 1938; anatomy Johns Hopkins, 1939-40; asst. prof. anatomy Western Res. U., 1940-41; research on problems poliomyelitis, faculty dept. epidemiology Johns Hopkins, 1942-57; assoc. prof. epidemiology Johns Hopkins (Sch. Hygiene and Pub. Health), 1946-57, prof. anatomy, dir. dept., 1957-76, prof. neurobiology dept. otolaryngology, 1976-85, emeritus prof., from 1985; tech. com. poliomyelitis vaccine USPHS, 1957-64; vaccine adv. com. Nat. Found., 1956-60; cons. NIH, mem. bd. sci. counselors, div. biol. standards, 1957-59; mem. bd. sci. advisers Nat. Inst. of Neurol. Diseases, 1968-73. Author: Neural Mechanisms in Poliomyelitis, 1942; mng. editor Am. Jour. Hygiene, 1947-57; assoc. editor Virology, 1957-60, Anat. Record, 1968-72, Exptl. Neurology, 1971-75; mem. editorial bds. Jour. Comparative Neurology, 1966-73; contbr. science articles profl. jours. Served as lt. USNR, World War II. Recipient E. Mead Johnson award in pediatrics Am. Acad. Pediatrics, 1941. Mem. NAS, AAAS, Am. Assn. Anatomists (pres. 1971-72), Am. Acad. Arts and Scis., Am. Philos. Soc. (Karl Spencer Lashly award 1985), Am. Physiol. Soc., Neurosci. Soc., Assn. Rsch. Nervous and Mental Diseases, Soc. Française de Neurologie (hon.), Anat. Soc. Gt. Britain and Ireland (hon.), Mex. Soc. Anatomy (hon.), Delta Omega Hon. Pub. Health Soc. (Alpha chpt.), Phi Beta Kappa, Sigma Xi. Home: Baltimore Md. Died Sept. 18, 1992. †

BOE, JASON DOUGLAS, former state senator, optometrist; b. L.A., Mar. 10, 1929; s. Christian J. and Lillian (Eggers) B.; m. Kathryn Lynette Reule, June 1, 1952; children: Eric, Peter, Brian. BA, Pacific Luth. U., 1951; OD, Pacific U., 1955. Pvt. practice, Reedsport, Oreg., 1955-90. Contbr. articles to profl. jours. Mem. Oreg. Ho. of Reps., 1964-70, minority whip, 1967, minority leader, 1969; mem. Oreg. Senate, 1970-80, pres., 1973-80; mem. exec. bd. Nat. Conf. State Legislators, 1976-79, pres., 1978-79; mem. Edn. Commn. States, from 1973; co-chmn. Oreg. Emergency Bd., 1973-81; mem. Adv. Commn. Intergovtl. Rels., 1978. Mem. Am. Optometric Assn., Reedsport C. of C. Democrat. Lutheran. Home: Reedsport Oreg. Died Mar. 20, 1990; Scottsburg, Oreg.

BOGGS, MARION A., clergyman; b. Liberty, S.C., Sept. 21, 1894; s. Marcus Addison and Lucy (Dunwoody) B.; m. Lelia F. Kabler, Sept. 12, 1922; 1 child, Marion A., Jr. AB, Davidson Coll., 1915; BD, Union Theol Sem., 1919; DD, Ark. Coll., 1929. Ordained to ministry Presbyn. Ch., 1919. Assoc. pastor Grace Convent Ch., Richmond, Va., 1919-20; pastor First Presbyn. Ch., Dermott, Ark., 1920-25; pastor First Ch., Blytheville, Ark., 1925-30, Hot Springs, Ark., 1930-39; pastor Second Ch., Little Rock, Ark., 1939-62; assoc. pastor First Presbyn. Ch., Pensacola, Fla., from 1962; moderator Synod of Ark., 1935, Gen. Assembly Presbyn. Ch., 1960-61; rep. Presbyn. Ch., Oxford Conf. on Life and Work, 1937; rep. Presbyn. Ch., U.S. Nat. Coun. Chs.; mem. exec. com. on World Missions. Mem. Newcomen Soc., Eng., Mason, K.T. Ind. Dem., Little Rock Rotary. *

BOHLEN, JOE MERL, sociology educator, consultant; b. Dubuque, Iowa, June 1, 1919; s. Chris David and Loretta Florence (Hess) B.; m. Helen Jean Gardner, Sept. 10, 1941 (div. 1968); children—Chris G., Richard E.; m. Nancy Jerome Loveland, Dec. 23, 1970; stepchildren—David W., Sally D. B.S., Iowa State U., 1947, M.S., 1948, Ph.D., 1954. Instr. sociology Coll. of Agr. Iowa State U., Ames, 1947-51, asst. prof. sociology, 1951-55, assoc. prof. sociology, 1955-58, prof. sociology, from 1958; research cons. Agr. Inst., Republic of Ireland, Dublin, from 1965. Contbr. articles to profl. jours. Served with USN, 1943-46, PTO. Recipient Wilton Park award, 1973. Mem. Rural Sociol. Soc. (mem., chmn. com. selection of outstanding theses awards, 1964-68), Sigma Xi, Alpha Kappa Delta, Gamma Sigma Delta, Phi Delta Kappa, Phi Kappa Phi. Democrat. Home: Ames Iowa Died Mar. 10, 1989.

BOHMAN, GEORGE VROOM, speech educator; b. Princeton, Ill., Sept. 24, 1908; s. Oscar William and Rachel Maude (Vroom) B.; m. Gladys Presley, June 22, 1940; children—Robert Presley, Eric James. A.B., Monmouth Coll., 1929; M.A., U. Wis., 1934, Ph.D., 1947. Instr. speech Dakota Wesleyan U., 1930-33, asst. prof., head dept., 1933-37; instr. pub. speaking Dartmouth, 1937-39, asst. prof., 1939-47, chmn. dept. pub. speaking, 1941-45, dir. speech in Naval English V-12 course, 1943-45; prof. speech Wayne State U., Detroit, 1947-78, prof. emeritus, 1978, grad. chmn., 1947-55, chmn., 1955-73. Co-author: History of the First Presbyterian Church of Princeton, Ill, 1937; editor, author: History of the First Congregational Church, Royal Oak, Mich, 1967; contbr. The Congregationalist; contbr. articles to speech and hist. jours. Mem. Hanover (N.H.) Democratic Town Com., 1944-47, chmn., 1946-47; Trustee Congl. Found. for Theol. Studies, 1963-70, 71-74, chmn., 1966-70; lectr. Congl. history and polity Congl. Library, 1978. Mem. AAUP, Speech Communication Assn. (chmn. com. on microfilm and microcard materials 1949-50, com. on history Am. pub. address 1952-55, com. on problems in speech edn. in colls. and univs. 1942-45), Eastern Pub. Speaking Conf. (sec.-treas. 1942-45), Central States Speech Assn., Ill., Bureau County (Ill.) hist. socs., Nat. Assn. Congl. Christian Chs. (exec. com. 1955-56, 59-62, chmn. 1961-62, moderator 1957-58, chmn. past moderators 1968, 85), Pi Kappa Delta (nat. council 1934-37), Tau Kappa Alpha, Phi Kappa Phi, Gamma Omicron Mu, Delta Sigma Rho. Congregationalist (del. Gen. Council 1954-56; moderator Mich. State Assn. 1961-62, exec. com. Mich. conf. 1962-73, editor Mich. Conglist. 1977-89). Home: Royal Oak Mich. Died Jan. 18, 1989; buried Princeton, Ill.

BOHN, J(ACOB) LLOYD, physicist, educator; b. Lickdale, Pa., Nov. 16, 1896; s. Henry and Percida (Bordner) B.; m. Florence Lucy Cushman, Jan. 1, 1926. BS, Pa. State Coll., 1924; student, Harvard U., 1924-26; PhD, Calif. Inst. Tech., 1928. Tchr. pub. schs. Pa., 1916-17, 19-20; tching. asst. Pa. State Coll., 1923-24; rsch. asst. Harvard Cancer Commn., Cambridge, Mass., 1924-26; rsch. physicist Fogg Art Mus., Harvard, Cambridge, Mass., 1925-26, summer 1929; tching. asst. Calif. Inst. Tech., 1926-27, rsch. asst., 1927-28; physicist Shell Oil Co., summer 1927; instr. Temple U., 1938-31, asst. prof., 1931-36, assoc. prof., 1936-43, prof., 1943-64, chmn. dept. physics, 1951-63, prof. emeritus of physics, from 1964, rsch. prof. physics, from 1964; prof. U. Pa., summer 1946-47; participant atomic tests Mercury, Nev., 1952-53, V-2 flights White Sands, N.Mex., 1949-50; had micrometeorite equipment in Explorer I satellite. Contbr. articles to profl. jours.; patentee. With USAF, 1917-19. Mem. IEEE, AAAS, Am. Inst. Aeros. and Astronautics, Am. Phys. Soc., Accoustical Soc. Am., Am. Assn. Physics Tchrs., Am. Assn. U. Profs., Franklin Inst., Physics Club Phila. (pres. 1955-56), Pa. Conf. Coll. Physics Tchrs. (pres. 1956), Blue Key Club, Pierian Sodality Club, Sigma Pi Sigma, Sigma Xi, Phi

Kappa Phi, Phi Mu Alpha, Kappa Kappa Psi. Mem. Reformed Ch. *

BOHROD, AARON, artist; b. Chgo., Nov. 21, 1907; s. George and Fannie (Feingold) B.; m. Ruth Bush, Dec. 27, 1929; children: Mark, Georgi (Mrs. Stephen Rothe), Neil. Student, Crane Coll., Chgo., 1925-26, Art Inst. Chgo., 1927-29, Art Students League, N.Y.C., 1930-32; D.F.A., Ripon Coll., 1960. Artist in residence So. Ill. U., 1942-43, U. Wis.-Madison, 1948-73; With War Art Unit (South Pacific War Area, on Govt. assignment); served as artist war corr. Life mag., Normandy, Cherbourg, Eng., Luxembourg, Germany, 1943-45. Painted series pictures of Kansas City for Mo. Documentary Art Project, 1946, series on Pitts. for Pa. Documentary Art Project, 1947, series on Mich. for Mich. Documentary Art Project, 1947, series of symbolic still life paintings for Look mag., Great Religions of America, 1957-60; represented in permanent collections, Met. Mus. Art, Whitney Mus. Am. Art, N.Y.C., Art Inst. Chgo., Bklyn. Mus., Boston Mus. Art, Pa. Acad. Art, Corcoran Mus., Washington, Swope Gallery Art, Terre Haute, Butler Art Inst., Youngstown, U. Ariz., Walker Art Center, Mpls., Norton Art Inst., Telfair Art Acad., Fla., Davenport (Iowa) Art Inst., Library of Congress, Witte Meml. Mus., San Antonio, Springfield (Mass.) Mus. Fine Arts, New Britain (Conn.) Art Mus., Detroit Inst. Arts, Miller Art Center, Sturgeon Bay, Wis., Wichita State U., Mich. State U., Hartford Gallery Modern Art, Finch Coll., N.Y., Milw. Art Center, Oshkosh Pub. Mus., Madison Art Center, U. Ill., Miami U., Bergstrom Art Center, Neenah, Wis., U. Maine, Ball State U., So. Ill. U., Clinton (Ill.) Art Center, U. Mo., Ohio U., St. Lawrence U., Mac Nider Mus., Albrecht Gallery, St. Joseph, Mo., U. Wyo., U. Pitts., U. Wis. Fox Valley, Menasha Philippines Nat. Mus., Manila, Hadassah Hosp., Tel Aviv, Hirschhorn Mus., Washington, Elvejhem Art Center, U. Wis., Wis. Med. Soc., Madison, Beloit (Wis.) Coll., Okla. Art Ctr., Oklahoma City, San Diego Mus. (Calif.), permanent collections, State Capitol, Madison, U. Maine, represented in Cleve. Mus. Art, Detroit Art Inst., Syracuse U., Naples, Fla. Art Ctr., U. Pitts., Haggerty Mus. Marquette U., Milw., Lakeview Mus. Arts and Scis., Peoria, Ill., Rahr-West Mus., Kenosha, Wis., Minn. Mus. Art, St. Paul, Phoenix Mus. Art; murals include Madison Main Libr., Hawthorne (Ill.) Race Track, U.S. Post Office brs., Vandalia, Ill., Galesburg, Ill., Clinton, Ill.; author: A Decade of Still Life, 1966; paintings reproduced in Time, Life, Fortune, Holiday, Coronet and Esquire mags.; illustrator: A Pottery Sketch Book, U. Wis. Press, 1959, Wisconsin Sketches, (with Robert Gard), 1973, Figure Sketches with Essays and E.E. Elliott and Howard E. Wooden, 1990. Recipient Carr landscape prize, 1935; recipient Tuthill watercolor prize, 1935, Logan prizes and Art Inst. medals, 1937-45, Brower prize Art Inst. Chgo., 1947, 84, hon. mention San Francisco Golden Gate Expn., 1939, hon. mention Carnegie Internat. Exhbn., 1939, first award of merit Calif. Water Color Soc., 1940, first prize Phila. Water Color Soc., Pa. Acad. Fine Arts, 1942, 5th Purchase prize Artists for Victory Expn., Met. Mus. Art, 1942, Corcoran 2d prize, W.A. Clark prize and silver medal, 1943, prize Am. Nat. Acad., 1951, 53, 1st prize Profl. Art Exhbn., Ill. State Fair, 1955, hon. mention Miami Nat. Ceramic Exhbn., 1956, Saltus Gold medal NAD, 1961; Hassam Purchase award, 1962; Kirk Meml. award, 1965; Fine Arts award Gov. Wis., 1969; Guggenheim fellow in creative art, 1936-37, 37-38. Home: Madison Wis. Died Apr. 3, 1992.

BOLAND, THOMAS ALOYSIUS, archbishop; b. Orange, N.J., Feb. 17, 1896; s. John Peter and Ellen (O'Rourke) B. AB, AM, Seton Hall U., 1919, LLD (hon.), 1940; DD, North Am. Coll., 1923. Tchr. moral theology and cannon law Immaculate Conception Sem., Darlington, N.J., 1923-38; chancellor Archdiocese of Newark, 1938-40; titular bishop of Hirina, aux. to Archbishop of Newark and rector of Immaculate Conception Sem., 1940-47; bishopof Patterson Diocese, N.J., 1947-53; archbishop of Newark, from 1953. *

BOLDREY, EDWIN BARKLEY, neurological surgeon, educator; b. Morgantown, Ind., July 17, 1906; s. Edwin H. and Florence B. (Barkley) B.; m. Helen B. Eastland, June 16, 1932; children—Nancy J., Edwin E., Susan E. A.B., De Pauw U., 1927; M.A., Ind. U., 1930, M.D., 1932; M.Sc., McGill U., 1936. Diplomate: Am. Bd. Neurol. Surgery (dir. 1958-64). Intern Montreal Gen. Hosp., 1932-34, admitting officer, spl. grad. student pathology, 1934-35; research fellow Montreal Neurol. Inst., 1935-36, 40, house officer neurology and neurol. surgery, 1936-37, fellow neuropathology, 1938, resident neurology and neurol. surgery, 1939; mem. faculty U. Calif. Sch. Medicine, from 1940, instr. surgery, 1940-44, asst. clin. prof. surgery, 1944-47, asst. clin. prof. neurol, surgery, 1947-48, asso. prof. neurol. surgery, 1948-60, prof., 1960-74, prof. emeritus, from 1974, chmn. dept., 1951-56, neurol. surgeon-in-chief of hosps., 1951-56; attending neurol. surgeon Langley Porter Clinic, 1945-74; cons. neurol. surgeon San Francisco Shriner's Hosp. for Crippled Children, from 1948, US Naval Hosp., Camp Pendleton, Calif., VA, Washington, San Francisco Hosp., 1951-86 , Parks AFB Hosp., 1955-58, May T. Morrison Rehab. Center, 1956-62, Ft. Riley VA Hosp., from 1957, Travis AFB Hosp., from 1958, Barrow Neurol. Inst., Phoenix, Letterman Gen. Hosp., USN Hosp., San Diego; lectr. neurol. surgery Oakland Naval Hosp., from 1966; cons. Nat. Inst. Neurol. Disease and Blindness, 1960-64; cons. Nat. Inst. Neurol. Disease and Stroke, 1966-73, chmn. research tng. grant com., 1967-70, mem. nat. adv. council, 1973-77; nat. adv. NINCDS Council mem. dist. rev. com. Calif. Bd. Med. Examiners, 1969-76; mem. nat. clin. adv. United Cerebral Palsy, 1953-63, bd. dirs., San Francisco, 1958-78, mem. med. adv. bd., 1961-78; adv. council neurol. surgery A.C.S., 1956-61; cons. USPHS Hosps., 1966-82 ; mem. med. adv. bd. Epilepsy Found., 1966-76; bd. dirs. Princeton Conf. Cerebrovascular Disease, 1970-74, Neurol. Scis. Found. of Portland, Oreg., from 1978. Author articles; contbr. med. books, encys. Recipient Royer award, 1970. Fellow A.C.S.; mem. A.M.A., Assn. for Research and Nervous and Mental Disease, Pan Pacific Surg. Assn. (v.p. 1975, 78), Am. Neurol. Assn., Am. Acad. Neurol. Surgery (pres. 1958-59, historian 1970-81), Soc. Neurol. Surgeons (pres. 1965-66, historian 1970-84), Am. Assn. Neurol. Pathology, AAAS, Harvey Cushing Soc. (v.p. 1964-65, parliamentarian 1975, 76), N.Y., Calif. acads. sci., Calif. Acad. Medicine, Can. Neurol. Soc., San Francisco Neurol. Soc. (a founder, pres. 1948-49, 80-81), Can. Neurosurg. Soc., Western Neurosurg. Soc. (a founder, pres. 1964-65), Am. Trauma Soc. (founding mem.), Calif. Assn. Neurol. Surgery (founder), N. Calif. Acad. Clin. Oncology, Am. Heart Assn., Phi Delta Theta, Phi Chi, Alpha Omega Alpha. Clubs: Commonwealth (San Francisco), University (San Francisco). Home: Palo Alto Calif. Died June 6, 1988; buried Washington Cemetery, Elrod, Ind.

BOLES, EWING THOMAS, investment banker; b. Williamstown, Ky., May 4, 1895; s. John R. and Sarah Sheriff (McGowan) B.; m. Katherine Dwyer, June 19, 1920; children: Ewing Thomas, Jr., Helen Anne (Mrs. W.B. Hardy Jr.). Student, U. Ill., 1915, Coll. Law U. Ky., 1916-17; AB, Centre Coll., 1916. Assoc. Halsey, Stuart & Co., Chgo., 1926-29; sales mgr. BancOhio Securities Co., Columbus, Ohio, 1929-35, pres., 1935; pres., dir. The Ohio Co. (formerly BancOhio Securities Co.), Columbus, Ohio, 1942-64, chmn. bd., from 1964; dir. Arro Expansion Bolt Co., Atlas Realty Inc., Hadson Ohio Oil Co., Nat. Bldg Corp., Ohio River Collieries Co., Ohio Valley Pub. Co., Mid-Continent Mfg. Co., Brodhead-Garrett Co., Huber-Warco Co., Hartman Elec. Mfg. Co., White-Haines Optical Co., Federated Pubs. Inc., Techno Fund, Inc. Chmn. Bd, Trustees Centre Coll. Mem. Investment Dealers Ohio, Investment Bankers Assn. Am. (past pres.), Nat. Assn. Securities Dealers, Inc. (gov.), Columbus Athletic Club, Phi Kappa Tau (past nat. pres.). *

BOLET, JORGE, musician, educator; b. Havana, Cuba, Nov. 15, 1914; s. Antonio and Adelina Tremoleda B. Artist diploma, MusB, Curtis Inst. Music. From asst. prof. to prof. piano Curtis Inst. of Music, 1938-42; prof. music Ind. U. Sch. Music, 1968-90; head piano dept. Curtis Inst. Music, 1977-90; rec. artist RCA Records, 1972-74, Everest Records, 1962, Remington Records, 1954, Genesis Records, 1972. Concert pianist European debut, 1936; concert tours in U.S., South Am., Europe, Asia, Australia, Africa; piano soloist with symphony orchs. including Boston Symphony, Chgo. Symphony, Berlin Philharm., Cleve. Orch., San Francisco Symphony, Phila. Orch., Vienna Symphony, London Philharm., Oslo Philharm., and others; soloist in music festivals including Ravinia Ill. Summer Concerts, Hollywood Calif. Bowl, Vienna Austria Festival, and others. 2d lt. AUS, 1945-46. Recipient Naumburg award, 1937, Josef Hofmann award Curtis Inst., 1938, Record of the Yr. award Stereo Rev. Mag., 1973. Home: Fuenterrabia Spain Died Oct. 16, 1990.

BOLGER, WILLIAM FREDERICK, business executive; b. Waterbury, Conn., Mar. 13, 1923; s. George V. and Catherine (Leary) B.; m. Marjorie Tilton, Dec. 17, 1949; children: Catherine A., Margaret J. Grad., George Washington U., 1949; LittD, St. Bonaventure Coll., Norwich U. Various positions Post Office Dept., Washington, 1941-78, dep. postmaster gen.; regional postmaster gen. NW region Post Office Dept., N.Y.C.; postmaster gen. Post Office Dept., Washington, 1978-84; vice chmn. Gray & Co. Pub. Communications Internat., Washington, 1984-86; pres. Air Transport Assn. Am., Washington, 1986-88; chmn. TCOM Systems Inc., Washington, 1987-89; bd. dirs. Bausch & Lomb, Rochester, N.Y. Mem., past pres. Wolf Trap Found., Washington, from 1982; mem. Fed. City Council, Washington, 1987-88, Washington Bd. Trade, 1987-88; nat. adv. bd. Am. U., Washington; trustee Norwich U., Northfield, Vt.; bd. dirs. Spl. Olympics. With U.S. Army Air Corps, 1942-45. Named Comdr. Order Orange/Nassau, Queen Beatrix, Netherlands, 1982; recipient Heinrich von Stephen medal Ministry Posts and Telecommunications, Fed. Republic Germany, 1982. Mem. Leukemia Soc. Am. (pres. Nat. Capital area chapter 1985-87, Spiral Life award 1981). Roman Catholic. Clubs: Army-Navy Country (Arlington, Va.); Internat. Washington. Home: Alexandria Va.

BOLINGER, DWIGHT LEMERTON, language educator; b. Topeka, Aug. 18, 1907; s. Arthur Joel and Gertrude (Ott) B.; m. Louise Ida Schrynemakers, July 1, 1934 (dec. Apr. 1986); children: Bruce Clyde, Ann Celeste Bolinger McClure. BA summa cum laude, Washburn Coll., 1930, LittD (hon.), 1964; MA, U. Kans., 1932; PhD, U. Wis., 1936. Instr. U. Wis., Madison, 1936, Kansas City (Mo.) Jr. Coll., 1937; assoc. prof. Washburn Coll., Topeka, 1937-44; from asst. prof. to prof. U. So. Calif., Los Angeles, 1944-60, head dept. Spanish, Italian and Portuguese, 1947-59; prof. Spanish U. Colo., Boulder, 1960-63; prof. Romance langs. and lits. Harvard U., Cambridge, Mass., 1963-73, prof. emeritus, 1973; vis. prof. emeritus Stanford (Calif.) U., 1977-92. Author 16 books including: Interrogative Structures of American English, 1957, Forms of English, 1965, Aspects of Language, 1968, 2d edit. 1975, co-author 3d edit., 1981, The Phrasal Verb in English, 1971, Degree Words, 1972, Meaning and Form, 1977, Language: The Loaded Weapon, 1980 (George Orwell award Nat. Coun. Tchrs. English 1981), Intonation and Its Parts, 1986, (with others) Modern Spanish, 1960, Intonation and Its Uses, 1989; joint chmn. of hon. edit. adv. bd. Ency. of Lang. and Linguistics, 1992. Sterling fellow in linguistics Yale U., 1943-44, research fellow in speech Haskins Labs., 1956-57, fellow Ctr. for Advanced Study in Behavioral Scis., 1969-70. Fellow AAAS, Brit. Acad. (corr.); mem. N.Y. Acad. Scis. (hon. life), Royal Spanish Acad. (corr.), Am. Assn. Tchrs. of Spanish and Portuguese (pres. 1960), Linguistic Soc. Am. (pres. 1972), Linguistic Assn. Can. and U.S. (pres. 1975-76). Home: Palo Alto Calif. Died Feb. 23, 1992, buried Alta Mesa Cemetery, Palo Alto, Calif.

BOLLES, BLAIR, corporation executive, journalist; b. St. Louis, Feb. 26, 1911; m. Mona Byrnina Dugas, Apr. 19, 1941; children: Edmund B., Charles DeV., Zoe L., Harry P. Student, Yale U., 1929-30, 31-32. Wrote for newspapers and mags., 1925-32; tchr. Gunston Sch., Centreville, Md., 1930-31; in advt. office Palais Royal Dept. Store, Washington, 1932; reporter Washington Sun, also Washington Herald, 1933; congl. corr. Universal Service, 1934, 34-35; rewrite man. N.Y. Am., 1934; with Washington Star, 1935-44; successively as writer on N.R.A. and A.A.A. diplomatic corps; dir. Washington bur. Fgn. Policy Assn., 1944-51, Washington corr., 1951-53; U.S. editor France Actuelle, 1952-53; European corr. Toledo Blade, 1953-56, assoc. editor, 1957-59; v.p. mktg., water div. Fairbanks, Morse and Co., 1959-64; v.p. govt. relations Colt Industries Inc., 1964-67, 68-77, v.p. internat., 1966-68, adviser to pres., 1977-82, sr. rep. Chief Exec. Office, 1982-86, also chmn. vol. polit. com. Polit. Action Com., 1975-84; regular contbr. Washingtoniana, Sunday edit. N.Y. Times, 1938; contbr. on fgn. affairs N.Am. Newspaper Alliance; reg. contbr. on polit. affairs Toronto Star Weekly; polit. writer for mags., from 1936; spl. adviser FAO Conf., UN, Copenhagen, 1946; chmn. steering com. Com. for Effective Capital Recovery, 1971-84; chmn. exec. com. Com. for Reform Double Taxation of Investment.; chmn. steering com. Coalition for Uniform Product Liability Law, 1981-85. Author: America's Chance of Peace, 1939, Arctic Diplomacy, 1948, Military Establishment of the United States, 1949, U.S. Military Policy, 1950, Tyrant from Illinois, 1951, How To Get Rich in Washington, 1952, Armed Road to Peace, 1952, The Big Change in Europe, 1958, Men of Good Intentions, 1960, Corruption in Washington, 1961; contbr. to nat. mags. Dir. Ctr. for Continuing Edn., Washington, from 1975. Decorated Royal medal of St. Olav, Norway. Mem. Am. Soc. Naval Engrs., A.I.M., Nat. Security Indsl. Assn., Anglo-Am. Press Assn. Paris. Roman Catholic. Clubs: Cosmos (Washington); Yale (N.Y.C.). Home: Bethesda Md. Died Jan. 26, 1990; cremated.

BOLLING, RICHARD, congressman; b. N.Y.C., May 17, 1916; s. Richard Walker and Florence Easton B.; m. Nona Bolling; 1 child, Andrea; stepchildren: Jimmy Akin, John Akin. AB, U. of South, 1937, AM, 1939; postgrad., Vanderbilt U., 1939-40; LLD hon. , Rockhurst Coll., 1971. Dir. student activities and vets. affairs U. Kansas City, 1946-47; nat. vice-chmn. Am. Vets. Com., 1947-48; mem 81st-97th Congresses from 5th Mo. Dist.; chmn. select com. on coms. U.S. Ho. of Reps., 1973-74, chmn rules com., 1978-82, mem. steering and policy com. of Democratic Caucus; fellow Ctr. for Advanced Studies, Wesleyan U., 1962-64; vis. prof. polit. sci. U. Mo., Kansas City; prof. politics Boston Coll. Author: House Out of Order, 1965, Power in the House, 1968, rev. edit., 1974; co-author: with John Bowles America's Competitive Edge: How to Get Our Country Moving Again, 1982. Lt. col. AUS, 1941-46, PTO. Recipient Congl. Disting. award Am Polit. Sci. Assn., 1961; named to Sports Illustrated 25th Anniversary All-Am. Football Team. Mem. Phi Beta Kappa. Democrat. Episcopalian. Home: Kansas City Mo. Died Apr. 20, 1991.

BOLLMEIER, EMIL WAYNE, manufacturing company executive; b. Hurst, Ill., Jan. 16, 1925; s. Emil Philip and Flossie Louise (Swain) B.; m. Nancy Lee Mercier, Feb. 9, 1972; children—David Wayne, Ann Louise, Paul Wesley. B.S. in Chem. Engring, U. Nebr., 1947; postgrad., U. Minn., 1949-51. With 3M Co., St. Paul, 1947-82; div. v.p. electro products div. 3M Co., 1965-72, group v.p. elec. products group, 1973-83, mem. 3M ops. com.; chief exec. officer, gen. ptnr. C-TEK Ltd. Partnership, from 1983; pres. Dynex Research, Inc., from 1983; chmn. bd., pres. Global Thermoelectric Power Systems Ltd., 1985-86. Patentee in field. Mem. Planning Commn., Mendota Heights, Minn., 1960-65; chmn. Republican Party, Dakota County, Minn., 1965-68. Served with USNR, 1945-46. Fellow IEEE; mem.

Nat. Elec. Mfrs. Assn. (bd. govs.), Sigma Xi, Sigma Tau. Presbyterian. Home: Saint Paul Minn. Died Sept. 8, 1989.

BOLSTER, CALVIN MATHEWS, naval officer, aeronautic engineer; b. Ravenna, Ohio, Aug. 17, 1897; s. William Harvey and Lottie Josephine (Mathews) B.; m. Agnes Elizabeth Ryan, Jan. 5, 1925; children: Carolyn Elizabeth, Dennis Richard, Mary Agnes. BS, U.S. Naval Acad., 1919; student, U.S. Naval Acad. Postgrad Sch., 1920-21; MSin Naval Construction, MIT, 1923; MS in aeronautical engring., Calif. Inst. Tech., 1936. Commd. ensign USN, 1919, advances through grades to rear adm., 1949; worked in rigid airship devel., helium repurification, 1923-25, airplane hook-on equipment, 1929-32, naval aviator (LTA) and (HTA), active in rsch. and construction programs on aeronautical features, aircraft carriers and jet assisted take off equipment, 1940-45; dep., asst. chief naval rsch. U.S. Navy Dept., 1947-49, asst. chief rsch. and devel. Bur. Aero., 1949-51, chief naval rsch., 1951-53; coord. devel. Gen. Tire & Rubber Co., 1954-62; dir. indsl. rsch. and devel. Aerojet-Gen. Corp., Elmonte, Calif., from 1962. Decorated Legion of Merit, Hon. Comdr. Mil. Order of Brit. Empire. Mem. AIAA, Cosmos Club (Washington). *

BOLTON, FREDERICK ROLSHOVEN, lawyer; b. Detroit, Sept. 27, 1896; s. Edwin Cyrus and Therese (Rolshoven) B.; m. Mabel Carey, Dec. 28, 1925; 1 child, Ann Therese (Mrs. Norman Dodge). Engr., U. Mich., 1918; LLB, Detroit Coll. Law, 1921; BE, Wayne State U., 1927; MA, U. Detroit, 1931. Bar: Mich. 1921. Mem. Shock, Bolton & Graham, Detroit, 1937-60; ptnr. Lacy, Lawson, Kirkby, Bolton & Hoffman, Detroit, from 1960; gen. counsel Nat. Auto and Flat Glass Dealers Assn., Detroit Glass Dealers Assn., TV Svc. Assn. Mich. Inc. Dir. Square Deal Refrigeration, Inc., Esco Engring. Corp., Woolf Aircraft Products, Inc.; dir., sec-treas. Detroit and Mich. Artists Meml. Inc. Ensign USNRF, World War I.; comdr. USNR, World War II. Mem. ABA, Mich. Bar Assn., Detroit Bar Assn., Am. Soc. Assn. Execs., Assn. Execs. Mich. (v.p. 1957), Mich. Execs. Forum (chmn. 1957), Judge Advocates Assn. (1st v.p. 1961-62, pres. 1962-63), Soc. Automotive Engrs., Am. Legion (past comdr.), Mil. Order World Wars (regional comdr.), Mason, Detroit Athletic Club, Detroit Golf Club, Harmonie Club, Savoyard Club (Detroit), Outrigger Canoe Club (Honolulu), Army and Navy Club, Nat. Assn. Execs. (Washington), Delta Theta Phi (nat. chancellor 1957-59). Republican. Episc. *

BOLZ, SANFORD HEGLEMAN, lawyer, consultant; b. Albany, N.Y., May 3, 1915; s. August Joseph and Etta (Hegleman) B.; m. Joyce Barbara Farbstein, Nov. 24, 1940; children: Diane Miriam, Jody. A.B. with honors, Cornell U., 1935, LL.B., 1938. Bar: N.Y. 1939, U.S. Supreme Ct. 1946, D.C. 1947, Calif. 1961. Research asst. N.Y. State Law Revision Commn., 1938-39; assoc. firm Cohen, Cole, Weiss & Wharton, N.Y.C., 1939-41; appeals atty. NLRB, Washington, 1941-43; enforcement atty. OPA, Washington, 1943-44; chief counsel transp. and shipping Lend-Lease, Fgn. Econ. Adminstrn., Washington, 1944-46; sole practice law Washington, 1946-60, 65-68; ptnr. Abramson & Bolz, Salinas, Calif., 1960-65; gen. counsel Empire State C. of C., Albany, N.Y., 1969-78; sr. v.p., gen. counsel Empire State C. of C., 1978-80; employee benefits cons., lectr., labor arbitrator; Washington counsel Am. Jewish Congress, 1948-60, Am. Jewish Com., 1965-68, U.S. Supreme Ct. Briefs on Constl. Law. Dem. candidate for Congress from 12th Dist. Calif., 1964. Mem. Am. Bar Assn., Calif. Bar Assn., Phi Beta Kappa, Phi Kappa Phi, Delta Sigma Rho. Jewish. Home: Slingerlands N.Y. Died Aug. 5, 1991.

BOMMARITO, PETER, union president; b. Detroit, May 17, 1915; m. Dorothy Bommarito. Grad. high sch. With Uniroyal Inc. (formerly U.S. Rubber), 1939-42, 45-89; with United Rubber, Cork, Linoleum and Plastic Workers Am. AFL-CIO, Akron, Ohio, 1948-89; local v.p. United Rubber, Cork, Linoleum and Plastic Workers Am., Akron, Ohio, 1955-57, local pres., 1957-60; internat. v.p. United Rubber, Cork, Linoleum and Plastic Workers Am., Akroe, Ohio, 1960-66; internat. pres. United Rubber, Cork, Linoleum and Plastic Workers Am., Akron, Ohio, 1966-89; v.p., mem. exec. coun. AFL-CIO, Akron, Ohio, 1969-89; mem. exec. com. Internat. Fedn. Chem. and Gen. Workers Union. Labor vice chmn. United Fund, Akron, 1962, past hon. trustee; past mem. adv. bd. Salvation Army; past trustee Akron Area Sr. Citizens. With USMCR, 1942-45. Past mem. Goodyear Hunting Fishing Club. Home: Akron Ohio Died Sept. 18, 1989.

BOND, JOHN REED, magazine editor; b. Muncie, Ind., July 25, 1912; s. Raymond W. and Mary E. (Reed) B.; m. Margaret Elaine Knaack, May 27, 1950; children: Marilee W. Bond Nudo, John Reed; m. Mercedes Bond. Grad., GM Inst., 1937. Design engr. Oldsmobile div. GM, 1937-39, White Truck, 1939-40; design engr. Studebaker, 1940-43, Airesearch, 1940-50; Airesearch McCulloch Motors, 1950-52; pres., editor Bond Pub. Co., Inc., pubs. Road & Track mag., Newport Beach, Calif., 1952-72; Author: Sports Cars in Action, 1954; tech. editor: Alumnium in Automobiles, 1957. Mem. Soc. Automotive Engrs., Sports Car Club Am. (life). Home: Escondido Calif. Died July 20, 1990; Escondido, Calif.

BOND, JOSEPH FRANCIS, textile company executive; b. Troy, N.Y., Feb. 17, 1927; s. John A. and Catherine (Waters) B.; m. Jane A. Powers, Oct. 4, 1952; children: Joseph Francis, Mary Marcia, John Matthew, Mary Louise. BBA, Siena Coll., Loudonville, N.Y., 1950. With Behr-Manning, Inc., Troy, 1950-57; with Gen. Electric Co., 1957-60, Gen. Aniline and Film Corp., Rensselaer, N.Y., 1960-62; controller Macmillian, Inc., 1963-67, v.p., 1966-67, sr. v.p. fin., 1967-75, exec. v.p.; v.p., treas. Cone Mills Inc., Greensboro, N.C., 1975-79, exec. v.p., treas., 1979-84, vice chmn., treas., 1984-92, also bd. dirs.; bd. dirs. No. region Wachovia Bank and Trust Co. Bd. dirs. Greensboro United Way, 1976-78, Cerebral Palsy Sch., Greensboro, 1978-92; bd. regents Inst. Mgmt. Acctg., 1976-79. Served with USNR, 1945-46. Mem. Fin. Execs. Inst. (bd. dirs. 1980-83), Nat. Assn. Accts., Greensboro C. of C. (bd. dirs. 1979-80), N.C. Textile Found. (bd. dirs. 1979-92), Am. Textile Mfg. Inst. (econ. policy com. 1985-92). Club: Greensboro Country. Deceased. Home: Greensboro N.C. †

BOND, MAURICE CHESTER, economic and marketing educator; b. Thetford, Vt., July 5, 1897; s. Ernest Champion and Alice Sophia (Kinney) B.; m. Flora Holway, June 25, 1921; children: Philip Gardner, William Bradford, Robert Dewey. Tchr. Morrisville, N.Y., 1920-23; instr. Cornell U., Ithaca, N.Y., 1926-28, asst. prof. mktg., 1928-34, prof. mktg., 1934-64, prof. emeritus, from 1964; agrl. economist Extension Svc. USDA, 1931, 36, Que. (Can.) Dairy Commn., 1932, dairy sect. Agrl. Adjustment Adminstrn. USDA, 1934, Agrl. Expt. Sta., P.R., 1936; rsch. work Coop. Grange League Fedn. Exchange Inc., 1943; rsch. dir. N.Y. State Commn. on Agr., 1945; cons. Fed. Extension Svc. USDA, 1948-49, P.R. Adv. Food Commn., 1953-54; dir. Extension N.Y. State Colls. Agr. and Home Econs., 1954-62; extension cons. Coll. Agr. U. Phillipines, Laguna, 1962-64; chmn. USDA State Emergency Planning Com., 1962-64, Nat. Extension Sub-com. Mktg. Edn., 1954-57, Nat. Extension Com. Orgn. and Policy, 1958-61. Author: (with Van B. Hart and L.C. Cunningham) Farm Management and Marketing, 1942; contbr. articles to profl. jours. Active Nat. 4-H Club Found. Recipient USDA Superior award, 1957; rsch. fellow U. Vt., 1924-25. 2nd lt. Inf., U.S. Army, 1918. Mem. Internat. Assn. of Agrl. Economists, Am. Farm Econ. Assn., Sigma Xi, Phi Kappa Phi, Phi Mu Delta, Alpha Zeta, Epsilon Sigma Phi. *

BONDY, PHILIP LEDERER, cigar company executive; b. N.Y.C., Mar. 12, 1910; s. Richard C. and Bessie (Gross) B.; m. Rae Emily Parish, Sept. 30, 1938; children: Sally Rae (Mrs. William T. Herndon), Susan Ann (Mrs. David Gordon Willoughby), Richard C., Sandra Lee. Student, Choate Sch., 1924-28. Salesman Gen. Cigar Co., Inc., N.Y.C., 1929-49, v.p., 1946-61, dir., 1949-90, sr. v.p., 1961-70, exec. vp., 1970-75, vice chmn. bd., 1975-90. Mem. Brit. Admiralty Del., 1942-46. Recipient King's medal for svc. in cause of freedom, 1946. Past mem. Masters of Foxhounds Assn., Goldens Bridge Hounds, Cigar Inst. Am. (past bd. dirs.), Sales Execs. Club (N.Y.C.), Waccabuc Country (N.Y.), Desert Forest Golf (Carefree, Ariz.). Home: Waccabuc N.Y. Died June 23, 1990.

BONDY, ROBERT EARL, social welfare administrator; b. Dover, Minn., Aug. 13, 1895; s. Robert William and Hannah Ida (Glidden) B.; m. Ruth Dunn, Sept. 10, 1917; children: Ruth Eleanor, Robert Earl; m. Marjorie Knapp Workman, Sept. 18, 1948; stepchildren: Ann Workman Sheldon, Jenny Workman, Julia Workman Sterrett. Grad., U. Chgo., 1917. Mgr. social svc. bur. C. of C., Columbus, Ohio, 1917-18; with ARC, Washington, 1919-39; dir. field svc., dept. civilian relief, lake dist. ARC, Cleve., 1919-20; asst. mgr. S.W. divsn. ARC, St. Louis, 1920-22; nat. dir. war svc. ARC, Washington, 1922-27, mgr. ea. area, 1927-31, nat. dir. disaster relief, 1931-39, dir. reconstruction Miss. Valley Flood Relief, 1927; dir. drought relief ea. states ARC, 1930-31, exec. dir. cotton distribution program, 1932-33, dir. relief ops. spring floods, 1936, assoc. gen. dir. Ohio-Mississippi Valley Flood Ops., 1937; Am. del. to League of RC Socs., Internat. Conf. on Disaster Reliefand Nursing ARC, Paris, 1937; dir. relief ops. New England hurricane ARC, 1938; dir. pub. welfare District of Columbia ARC, Washington, 1939-41, adminstr. svcs. to Armed Forces, 1941-46; went on adminstrv. trips to European and Pacific war theaters ARC, 1943, 44, 45; dir. Nat. Social Welfare Assembly, N.Y., from 1946; chmn. adv. coun. on participation of nat. orgns., mid-century White House Conf. on children and youth; vice-chmn. 1960 White House Conf. on children and youth; chmn. sect. religion White House Conf. on Aging. Contbr. articles to profl. jours. Pres. Montgomery County Civic Fedn., 1933-35; chmn. Nat. Social Work Coun., N.Y.C., 1940-45; chmn. welfare and consumer interest com. Dist. of Columbia Coun. of Def., 1940-41; chmn. Nat. Com. on Svc. to Vets., 1944-46; cons. F.C.D.A., U.S. Dept. of State, 1951-53; mem. bd. Am. Immigration Conf.; mem. adv. bd. U.S. Displaced Persons Commn.,1948-53; chmn. Health and Welfare Adv. Coun., AFL-CIO Community Svcs. Com., from 1959; mem. bd. exec. com. Nat. Health and Welfare Retirement Assn., from 1957; mem. various coms. on Nat. Coun. Chs. of Christ; mem. consultation on role of chs. in social svc. World Coun. of Chs., 1962. With U.S. Army, 1918. Mem. Am. Assn. Social Workers, Nat. Conf. Social Welfare, Am. Pub. Welfare Assn., Phi Gamma Delta, Sigma Delta Chi. *

BONE, ROBERT GEHLMANN, university president; b. Springfield, Ill., June 2, 1906; s. Eugene E. and Alice (Gehlmann) B.; m. Karin Levanius, Sept. 26, 1944; children: John Levanius, Robert Gehlmann. AB, Coll. of Wooster, 1928; AM, U. Ill., 1932, PhD, 1937; certificate, U. Freiburg-in-Breisgau, Germany, 1938; LLD, Lincoln Coll., 1966; Ill. State U., 1968. Tchr. Am. Coll., Alexandria, Egypt, 1928-31; acting dir., 1930-31; prof. history, dir. forensics Lincoln (Ill.), 1932-34; instr. history U. Ill., 1934-42; prof. history, head dept. Shrivenham Am. U., Eng., 1945-46; prof. history U. Ill., 1951-56; dir. div. spl. svcs. for war vets, 1947-52, dir. div. gen. studies, 1946-52; acting dean Coll. Edn., 1952-53; asst. provost, 1954-56; pres., emeritus Ill. State U. (Normal), 1956-67; vis. prof. Coll. of Wooster, 1969-71; cons. Ford Found. Campaign chmn. Tb Seal, 1966-67; pres. bd. dirs. Adlai E. Stevenson Lectures on Internat. Affairs, 1965-67, David Davis Meml. Home, 1960-65. Author: Ancient History, 1939, rev. edit., 1955, Shrivenham American University, 1946. Bd. dirs. Inst. Oriental Students (Brent House) Chgo., 1938-48, YMCA, 1946-56; mem. Civil War Centennial Commn.; exec. com. Ill. Lincoln Sesquicentennial Commn. Mem. nat. com. on standards Nat. Council for Accrediting Tchr. Edn., mem. commn. on colls. and univs. North Central Assn.; bd. dirs. Ill. Certification Bd., 1958-62; chmn. Ill. Commn. Coll. Testing, 1959-67; trustee Winston Churchill Coll., Pontiac, Ill., 1965-71; bd. dirs. Multiple Sclerosis Assn., 1965-91, Ill. State U. Found.; trustee Eureka (Ill.) Coll., 1968-71; bd. regents Lincoln Acad. Ill., chancellor, 1968-71. Served as maj. A.C., AUS, 1942-46; ETO. Recipient Centennial Yr. Alumni awrad Coll. of Wooster, 1966; Educator of Yr. award Ill. Edn. Assn., 1966; Spl. Edn. award Ill. Congress Parents and Tchrs., 1966; Spl. Citizen award McLean County Jaycees, 1967, Outstanding Citizen award for Normal, 1968, Active Sr. Citizen award Kiwanis Club, 1976, Spirit of McLean County award, 1986; named Laureate of the Lincoln Acad. of Ill., 1979; Paul Harris fellow. Mem. Assn. State Colls. and Univs. (dir. 1963-67), Am. Assn. Colls. Tchr. Edn., Archeol. Inst. Am., NEA, Am. Assn. Higher Edn. (dir., nat. pres. 1956-57, Am., Ill. (v.p., dir. 1972-91, adv. com. for state archives) hist. socs., Am. Assn. Coll. Tchrs. of Edn. (nat. com. on tchr. edn.), Ill. Geneal. Soc. (dir. 1972-91), Huguenot Soc. Am., Magna Charta Barons, SAR, Phi Kappa Delta, Phi Kappa Phi, Zeta Psi, Phi Alpha Theta, Chi Gamma Iota, Kappa Theta Gamma, Phi Kappa Epsilon, Phi Alpha Phi, Phi Delta Theta, Alpha Tau Alpha, Alpha Phi Omega, Omicron Delta Kappa, Phi Eta Sigma. Presbyterian. Home: Normal Ill. Died Jan. 13, 1991; buried Oak Ridge Cemetery.

BONGARTZ, ROY, writer; b. Providence, Dec. 8, 1924; s. Royal and Emma Asplund B.; m. Cecilia Leigh, June 15, 1955; 1 child, Joe Michael. MA, Miami U., Oxford, Ohio, 1951, BA, 1950. Author: play The Applicant, 1961, stories Twelve Chases on West Ninety-Ninth Street, 1965; contbr stories, articles to Sat. Evening Post, New Yorker, Nation, N.Y. Times, others. With AUS, 1943-46. Home: Foster R.I. Deceased.

BONNELL, HETTIE HAZLETT, past member Republican National Committee; b. Wheeling, W.Va., Feb. 4, 1898; d. Edward and Jessie (List) Hazlett; m. Robert Owen Bonnell, June 23, 1923; children: Edwina Hazlett Havens, Robert Owen. Student, Smith Coll., 1916-17; BS in Social Sci., Carnegie Inst. Tech., 1920. Recreational dir. nat. YWCA, 1919; survey staff, spl. field rep. Nat. Child Labor Com., 1920-21; exec. sec. Children's Code Commn., W.Va., 1921-23; 1st woman chmn. U.S. Assay Commn., 1953; pioneer Ten O'Clock Club for Rep. presdl. campaigns, 1948, 52; v.p. Md. Fedn. Rep. Women, 1954-56; orgd., taught polit. workshops, 1954; vice chmn. Rep. State Cent. Com.; mem. Rep. Nat. Com. for Md., 1958-65. Author: Political Primer, 1954. Co-chmn. Orthopedic Workshop for Handicapped, Arnes Hosp., St. Louis; nat. bd. Women's Med. Coll. Pa.; mem. bd. Balt. Family and Children's Soc., Children's Hosp. Sch., James Lawrence Kernan Children's Hosp.; mem. bd. Jr. League of St. Louis, Balt.; pioneer, past chmn. Svc. Men's Club. Episcopal Diocese of Md. Methodist (mem. bd., exec. com.). *

BONNELL, JOHN SUTHERLAND, minister; b. P.E.I., Can., Jan. 10, 1893; came to U.S., 1935; s. Abraham and Catherine (Cameron) B.; m. Bessie Louise Carruthers, June 1923; children: George Carruthers, Catherine Cameron, Elizabeth Louise, Jessie Margaret. BA, Dalhousie U., Halifax, N.S., 1919, LLD, 1967; BD, Pine Hill Div. Hall, Halifax, N.S., 1927, DD, 1934; LLD, Washington and Jefferson Coll., 1943, U. N.B., 1958, St. Dunstan's Roman Cath. U., P.E.I., Can., 1963; LittD (hon.), Dickinson Coll., 1960; DD, Lafayette Coll., 1950; DLitt, Acadia U., Can., 1972. Ordained to ministry Presbyn. Ch., 1922. Pastor St. Andrew's Ch., St. John, N.B., Can., 1923-29, Westminster Ch., Winnipeg, Can., 1929-35; pastor Fifth Ave Presbyn. Ch., N.Y.C., 1935-62, minister emeritus; pres. N.Y. Theol. Sem., N.Y.C., 1966-69; lectr. Theol. Sem., Princeton, N.J., 1938-60; on goodwill preaching mission to Britain, spl. del. to Gen. Assembly of Ch. of Scotland (Edinburgh) from Presbyn. Ch. in the U.S.A., 1941; Sprunt lectr. Union Theol. Sem., Richmond, Va., 1943; chancellor's lectr., Queens U., Kingston, Ont. Can.,

1944; Norton lectr., So. Bapt. Theol. Sem., Louisville, 1944; Ashlin lectr. 1st Presbyn. Ch., Morresville, N.C., 1949; Perkins lectr. 1st Meth. Ch., Wichita Falls, Tex., 1950; Charles Cluadius Beam lectr. 1st Presbyn. Ch. Charlotte, N.C., 1953; Weber Meml. lectr. Moravian Theol. Sem., Bethlehem, Pa., 1956; Edward lectr. Shadyside Ch., Pitts., 1958. Author numerous books including What Are You Living For, 1950, The Practice and Power of Prayer, 1954, Heaven and Hell: No Escape From Life, 1958, I Believe in Immortality, 1959, Certainties for Uncertain Times, 1962, Do You Want to be Healed?, 1968, Presidential Profiles, 1971; contbr. articles to profl. jours. Recipient The King's medal for svc. in cause of freedom King George VI, 1949. Mem. Protestant Coun. N.Y. (pres. 1961), Can. Soc. N.Y. (pres. 1959-60), NCCJ (co-chmn. religious commn.), Can Club, Univ. Club (N.Y.C.). Home: New York N.Y. Died Feb. 23, 1992.

BOOHER, EDWARD E., publishing executive; b. Dayton, Ohio, July 29, 1911; s. Wilfred Elsworth and Cora Maybelle (Middlestader) B.; m. Agnes Martin Whitaker, 1961. A.B., Antioch Coll., 1936; Dr. Humanities and Lit. (hon.), Rutgers U., 1979. Interviewer, sec. N.Y. State Employment Service, N.Y.C., 1935; joined McGraw-Hill Book Co., Inc., 1936, became v.p., 1944, also bd. dirs., 1951, exec. v.p., 1954-60, pres., 1960-68, chmn. bd., chief exec. officer, 1968-70; pres. books and edn. services group McGraw-Hill, Inc., 1970-76; dir. Nat. Enquiry Into the Prodn. and Dissemination of Scholarly Knowledge, Am. Council Learned Socs., 1976-78; publishing cons., from 1978; pres. Holtzbrinck Pub. Group; bd. dirs. Scholastica mags, Sci. Am. mag., Henry Holt & Co., W.H. Freeman & Co.; chmn. Motown Publishing Group. Clubs: Century, Nassau. Home: Kennett Square Pa. Died Sept. 29, 1990.

BOOKBINDER, JACK, artist, educator; b. Odessa, Russia, Jan. 15, 1911; came to U.S., 1922; s. Israel and Rebecca (Biener) B.; m. Bella Braverman, Sept. 16, 1936; children: Michael Richard, Carl Fredric. Student, Pa. Acad. Fine Arts, 1930-34; B.S. in Edn., U. Pa., 1934; M.F.A., Tyler Sch. Art, Temple U., Phila., 1946; D.F.A. (hon.), Moore Coll. Art, Phila., 1976. Lectr. art history Barnes Found., Merion, Pa., 1937-44; lectr. art edn. U. Pa., 1946-59; lectr. art history Pa. Acad. Fine Arts, 1949-61; lectr. art edn. Pa. State U., summer 1950; dir. art edn. Phila. Pub. Schs., 1959-77; instr. painting and lithography Kutztown (Pa.) State Coll., summer 1962; juror nat. and local art exhbns. Exhibited one-man shows Pa. Acad. Fine Arts, Phila., 1948, 52, Phila. Art Alliance, Phila., 1954, 64, Woodmere Mus. Phila., 1955, Nessler Art Gallery, N.Y.C., 1961, William Penn Meml. Mus., Harrisburg, 1974, Gross-McLeaf Gallery, Phila., 1976, Long Beach Island Found., N.J., 1980, Marjorie Cahn Gallery, Los Gatos, Calif., 1980, Peale House, Pa. Acad. Fine Arts, Phila., 1984; group shows include Rochester Print Club, N.Y., 1948, Royal Acad., London, 1962, Met. Mus. Art, N.Y.C., 1966, Palacio de Bellas Artes, Mexico City, 1968, Artists Equity Exhbn., Tel Aviv, Israel, 1978, U. Del., 1980, Phila. Print Club, 1980, Phila. Art Alliance, 1981, Art Soc. of Internat. Monetary Fund (3 man show), Washington, 1984, Art Soc. Internat. Monetary Fund, Washington, 1984; Tribute exhbn. Sunshine Found., Phila., 1986; represented in permanent collections, Pa. Acad. Fine Arts, Phila. Mus. Art, Library of Congress, Nat. Gallery of Art, Washington, Yale U. Art Gallery, New Britain (Conn.) Inst., Temple U., Kutztown State Coll., Converse Coll., S.C., Mus. Fine Arts, Abilene, Tex., Reading (Pa.) Mus. and Art Gallery, Frye Mus., Seattle, Widener Coll., Chester, Pa., Bradley U., Peoria, Ill., Gulf Coast Art Ctr., San Jose (Calif.) Mus. Art, Lafayette (Ind.) Art Ctr.; author: Invitation to the Arts, 1944, Compton's History of Sculpture, 1957 edit.; producer, performer: TV shows Art and the Artist, Artists U.S.A., Profiles in Art, others, 1955-76. Recipient Gen. Alumni award Temple U., 1964; recipient Super-achiever award Juvenile Diabetes Found., 1976, numerous other awards including John J. Newman award Nat. Soc. Painters in Casein and Acrylic, 1980, 1st prize in oil painting Phila. Sketch Club, 1981, Thornton Oakley Meml. award Phila. Water Color Club, 1984, Best of Show award Artsits Guild of Del. Valley, Phila., 1987. Mem. NAD, Am. Watercolor Soc., Nat. Soc. Painters in Casein and Acrylics (v.p.), Allied Artists Am., Audubon Artists Am. (Grumbacher Gold medal 1982), Phila. Watercolor Club (v.p. Charles Taylor award 1981, Pennell Meml. prize 1983). Home: Philadelphia Pa. Died June 9, 1990; cremated.

BOOKER, HENRY GEORGE, engineering, mathematics educator; b. Barking, Essex, Eng., Dec. 14, 1910; came to U.S., 1948, naturalized, 1952; s. Charles Henry and Gertrude Mary (Ratcliffe) B.; m. Adelaide Mary McNish, July 9, 1938; children—John Ratcliffe, Robert William, Mary Adelaide, Alice. Student, Palmer's Sch., Grays, Essex, 1921-30; B.A., Christ's Coll., Cambridge, 1933, Ph.D., 1936; Guggenheim fellow, Cambridge U., 1954-55. Fellow Christ's Coll., 1935-48; sci. officer Ministry Aircraft Prodn., London, 1940-45; lectr. Cambridge U., 1945-48; prof. elec. engring. Cornell U., 1948-65, dir. sch. elec. engring., 1959-63; assoc. dir. Center Radio Physics and Space Research; prof. engring. and applied math., 1962-65; prof. applied physics U. Calif. at San Diego, from 1965; hon. prof. Wuhan U., People's Republic China, from 1981. Author: An Approach to Electrical Science, 1959, A Vector Approach to Oscillations, 1965, Energy in Electromagnetism, 1982, Cold Plasma Waves, 1984 (Chinese edit. 1985), also sci. papers on radio wave propagation. Jr. intermediate and sr. county scholarships Essex, Eng., 1920-30; Entrance scholarship Christ's Coll., 1930; Allen scholarship, 1934-35; Smith's prize, 1935; Duddell, Kelvin and instn. premiums Instn. Elec. Engrs., London, 1948-50. Fellow IEEE; mem. Nat. Acad. Scis., Internat. Union Radio Sci. (hon. pres. from 1979), Sigma Xi. Home: La Jolla Calif. Died Nov. 1, 1988; buried El Camino Meml. Pk, San Diego.

BOOMSLITER, PAUL COLGAN, educator; b. Urbana, Ill., Oct. 24, 1915; s. George Paul and Alice (Colgan) B.; m. Patricia A. Flynn Himes, July 19, 1968; children: Paula Elise, Ann Dekker, Sara Ransone, Paul Lon, Mary Elizabeth Himes, Peter Edmund Himes. A.B., W.Va. U., 1935; postgrad., La. State U., 1937; M.A., U. Iowa, 1938; Ph.D., U. Wis., 1942; postgrad., Northwestern U., 1948. Asst. prof. Goucher Coll., Balt., 1940-46; asst. prof. Cornell U., 1946-48; prof. SUNY, Albany, 1948-79; chmn. speech pathology and audiology SUNY, 1969-73; research asso. prof. Albany Med. Coll., 1968-76; profl. dir. Northeastern N.Y. Speech Center, 1958-63, cons., 1963-76; profl. dir. Capital Area Speech Center, from 1976; cons. speech pathology and audiology Albany VA Hosp., 1956-76, Albany Study Center for Learning Disabilities, 1963-76, Albany Child Guidance Center, from 1963, N.Y. State Dept. Mental Hygiene, from 1969. Author: The Referential Search Organ, 1960, The Boomsliter-Creel Test of Tonal Processing, 1965, Language Capacity and Language Learning, 1970; Contbr. articles profl. jours. Served with USAAF, 1942-46. Recipient certificate of clin. competence in speech Am. Speech and Hearing Assn., 1950. Fellow Am. Speech and Hearing Assn., Acoustical Soc. Am.; mem. AAAS, N.Y. State, Capital Area speech and hearing assns., N.Y. Acad. Scis., Modern Lang. Assn., Phi Beta Kappa. Episcopalian. Home: Albany N.Y. Deceased. †

BOOSKTAVER, ALEXANDER, investment consultant; b. Sag Harbor, N.Y., Apr. 11, 1911; s. Samuel and Jennie (Lekus) B.; m. Dorothy Ravitt, Sept. 3, 1936; 1 child, Richard. Student bus. adminstrn., NUY, 1933-34; grad., Am. Inst. Banking, 1936. With trust dept. Hanover Bank, N.Y.C., 1930-41; with comptroller's dept. Schroder Trust Co., N.Y.C., 1941-46; v.p., comptroller Amalgamated Bank N.Y., 1946-56; controller, dir. invesmtnet dept. Internat. Ladies Garment Workers Union, N.Y.C., 1956-61; dir. invemstment dept. AFL-CIO, Washington, 1961-68; v.p. instl. rels. Anchor Corp., Eliazbeth, N.J., 1968-69; pres. PMH Mgmt. Corp., Seaford, N.Y., 1969-73; sr. v.p. Midwest Mortgage Co., Miami, Fla., 1973-76; investment cons., 1976-89; past bd. dirs. Peoples Nat. Bank of Md., Suitland, Hebrew Inst. L.I. Past editorial adv. bd. Pension World. Mem. adv. com. housing and urban devel. AID, 1963-68; mem. adv. bd. Nat. Found. Health, Welfare and Pension Plans, 1963-68. Home: Miami Beach Fla.

BOOTH, HENRY SCRIPPS, foundation executive; b. Detroit, Aug. 11, 1897; s. George Gough and Ellen (Scripps) B.; m. Carolyn E. Farr, Sept. 27, 1924; children: Stephen Farr, David Gagnier, Cynthia B. Ballantyne, Melinda B. Hubbard, Martha B. Jacobs. BArch, U. Mich., 1924. Exec. dir., chmn. bd. trustees Cranbrook Found., from 1946; dir. Booth Newspapers, Inc., Detroit News. Hon. pres. Oakland Citizens League; pres. Civic Rsch., Cranbrook Acad. Art, Cranbrook Music Guild. *

BOOTH, ROBERT EDMOND, librarian, educator, angelologist; b. Bridgeport, Conn., May 21, 1917; m. Ada Margaret Pfohl, Aug. 19, 1944; children: Ellen Caroline, Margaret Anne. A.B., Wayne State U., 1941; B.S. in L.S, Columbia U., 1942; A.M. in L.S, U. Mich., 1943; Ph.D., Western Res. U., 1960. Jr. asst. Detroit Public Library, 1943-44; editor, bibliographer Univ. Microfilms, Ann Arbor, Mich., 1944-46; reference librarian Peabody Inst. Library, Balt., 1946-47; assoc. librarian MIT, 1947-56; research assoc., instr. Sch. Library Sci., Western Res. U., Cleve., 1956-60; assoc. prof. div. library sci. Wayne State U., Detroit, 1960-64; prof., dir. Wayne State U., 1964-84, prof. emeritus, 1984-92; ptnr. Booth Media Assocs., 1983-87; producer, host Grosse Pointe Cable TV, 1986-89; cert. arbitrator Better Bus. Bur., 1987-89; cons. to various libraries, govt. agys. and profl. orgns., 1954-92; cons., mem. exec. com. Communication Info. System for Unemployed, 1983-87; del. to Library Assn. Australia, summers, 1971, 73, 77; vice chmn. Mich. Libr. Consortium, 1978-79; mem. adv. com. tng. and rsch. U.S. Bur. Libr. and Ednl. Tech., 1971-73. Author: Culturally Disadvantaged, 1967, Index to Poverty, Human Resources and Manpower Information, 1967, Index to Minority Group Employment Information, 1967, (with M. Ricking) Handbook for Task Analysis, 1972, Personnel Utilization in Libraries, 1974. Bd. dirs. Services for Older Citizens, 1984-90, Cathedral Terr., 1985-92; vestryman Christ Ch. (Episcopal), Grosse Pointe, 1989-92. Recipient 25 Yr. Disting. Svc. award, 1991; named Disting. Alumnus U. Mich. Sch. Library Sci., 1977, Disting. Alumnus Case-Western Res. U. Sch. Library Sci., 1979. Mem. ALA, Mich. Library Assn. (pres. 1970-71, Mich. Librarian of Yr. 1979-80), Spl. Libraries Assn. (disting. service award Mich. chpt. 1984), Assn. Am. Library Schs., Friends of Detroit Pub. Library (bd. dirs.), Founders Soc. Detroit Inst. Arts, Book Club of Detroit, English Speaking Union (first v.p. Detroit br. 1987-89, dep. chair region VI 1988-92). Clubs: Prismatic, Grosse Pointe Sr. Men's, Grosse Pointe Men's Garden. Home: Grosse Pointe Mich. Died May 15, 1992. †

BOOTHE, VIVA BELLE, educator; b. Tyler, Tex., Jan. 27, 1893; d. John and May Estelle (McCarty) Boothe. AB, U. Tex., 1918; AM, U. Pa., 1920, PhD, 1923. Head dept. econs. and sociology Elmira (N.Y.) Coll., 1923-28; asst. prof. bus. rsch. Ohio State U., 1928-30, assoc. prof., 1930-33, prof., 1933-62; acting dir. Bur. Bus. Rsch., 1936-41, dir. Bur. Bus. Rsch., 1941-62, editor publs., from 1936; statis. clk. U.S. Food Adminstrn., 1918; statistician War Industries Bd., 1918-19, Joint Congl. Commn. of Agrl. Inquiry, 1921; editorial asst. Annals of Am. Acad. Polit. and Social Scis., 1919-23; prof. sociology U. Tex., summer 1924, N.Y. State Tchrs. Coll., Albany, summer 1927. Editor: Bull. Bus. Rsch.; author: The Political Party as a Social Process, 1923, Salaries and Cost of Living in Universities and Colleges, 1932, Seasonability of Employment in Ohio Industries, 1942, Average Wages in Ohio Industries, 1947. Mem. AAUP, AAUW, Am. Statis. Assn., Am. Econ. Assn., Assn. U. Burs. Bus. and Econ. Rsch. (pres. 1954-55), Phi Beta Kappa, Phi Chi Theta, Beta Gamma Sigma, Altrusa (internat. pres. 1959-61). Democrat. Methodist. *

BORDALLO, RICARDO JEROME, former governor of Guam; b. Sumay, Guam, Dec. 11, 1927; s. Baltazar Jerome and Josephine Torres (Pangelinan) B.; m. Madeleine Zeien, June 20, 1953; 1 child, Deborah Bordallo Gerber. Student U. San Francisco, 1948-50. Owner, operator Toyota dealership, Guam, 1956-1974, Ricky's Enterprises, 1956-1975; pub. Pacific Jour., Guam, 1966; chmn., dir. Family Fin. Co., 1959-74; mem. Guam Legislature, 1956-70, elected minority leader 8th Guam Legislature, 1964, chmn. Democratic Party of Guam, 1960-63, 1971-73, del. to Nat. Dem. Conv., 1964, 68, gov. of Guam, 1974-78, 1982-86. Bd. dirs. Marianas Assn. for Retarded Children, 1962-64, Navy League of Guam, 1965-73; vice chmn., bd. dirs. ARC; active Guam Tourist Commn., 1963-65, Guam Spl. Olympics orgn. Mem. Guam C. of C., 1960-73. Lodge: Lions (pres. 1956). Died Jan. 31, 1990; buried Pigo Cemetery, Agana, Guam. Home: Agana GU

BORDEN, HENRY, barrister, solicitor; b. Halifax, N.S., Can., Sept. 25, 1901; s. Henry Clifford and Mabel (Ashmere) Barnstead B.; m. Jean Creelman MacRae, June 1, 1929; children—Robert, Ann, Perry, Mary Jean, Henry. B.A., McGill U., 1921; postgrad., Dalhousie Law Sch., 1922-24, LL.D., 1968; B.A. (Rhodes Scholar), Exeter Coll., Oxford, 1926; LL.D., St. Francis Xavier U., 1960, U. Toronto, 1972; D.C.L., Acadia U., 1960. Bar: Lincoln's Inn, London 1927, N.S 1927, Ont., 1927, King's Counsel 1938. With Royal Bank Can., 1921-22; gen. counsel Dept. Munitions and Supply, Ottawa, 1939-42; chmn. Wartime Industries Control Bd., Ottawa; co-ordinator of controls Dept. Munitions and Supply, 1942-43; past lectr. corp. law Osgoode Hall Law Sch.; sr. mem. Borden, Elliot, Kelley & Palmer, 1936-46; chmn. Royal Commn. on Energy, 1957-59; dir. Can. Imperial Bank of Commerce, 1946-71; pres. Brascan Ltd. (formerly Brazilian Traction, Light & Power Co. Ltd.), 1946-63; dir. Ball Can., 1948-74, Can. Investment Fund Ltd., 1950-78, IBM Can. Ltd., 1952-78, Massey-Ferguson Ltd., 1956-77; chmn. Brascan Ltd. (formerly Brazilian Traction, Light & Power Co. Ltd.), 1963-65; dir. British Newfoundland Corp. Ltd., 1963-73; pres. British Newfoundland Corp. Ltd. (Brinco), 1965-67, chmn., 1965-69; pres., chmn. Churchill Falls Labrador Corp., 1965-67; chmn. Can. bd. Norwich Union Ins. Socs., 1938-76; dir. Brascan, 1946-75. Co-author: Handbook of Canadian Company Law, 1931; Editor: Robert Laird Borden, His Memoirs, 1938, Letters to Limbo, (by Sir Robert L. Borden), 1971. Past pres., then dir., mem. exec. com. Royal Agrl. Winter Fair; chmn., bd. govs. U. Toronto, 1964-68, hon. chmn. bd. govs., 1968-71; hon. trustee Royal Ont. Mus. Decorated comdr. Order St. Michael and St. George, 1943; grand officer Nat. Order So. Cross Brazil, 1962; Centennial medal, 1967; medal of service Order Can., 1969. Mem. Phi Kappa Pi. Mem. Anglican Ch. Clubs: York (Toronto). Home: Toronto Can. Died May 6, 1989; cremated.

BORGSTROM, GEORG ARNE, educator, scientist, author; b. Gustav Adolf, Sweden, Apr. 5, 1912; came to U.S., 1956, naturalized, 1962; s. Algot and Anna (Littorin) B.; m. Greta Ingrid Stromback; children: Lars, Gerd Borgstrom Linder, Sven. B.S., U. Lund, Sweden, 1932, M.S., 1933; D.Sc., U. Lund, 1939. Asso. prof. plant physiology U. Lund, 1940-43; head Inst. Plant Research and Food Storage, Nynashamn, Sweden, 1941-48, Swedish Inst. Food Preservation Research, Goteborg, 1948-56; prof. Swedish Inst. Food Preservation Research, 1953-56; prof. food sci. Mich. State U., 1956-81, prof. geography, 1966-81, prof. emeritus, 1981. Author: The Transverse Reactions of Plants, 1939, Japan's World Success in Fishing, 1964, The Hungry Planet, 1965, 2d edit., 1972, Principles of Food Science, 2 vols., 1968, 76, Too Many—A Study of Earth's Ecological Limitations, 1969, 2d edit., 1970, Harvesting the Earth, 1973, Focal Points—A Food Strategy for the Seventies, 1973, The Food and People Dilemma, 1973;

editor: Fish as Food, 4 vols., 1960-64; Editor: Atlantic Ocean Fisheries, 1961. Recipient Internat. Socrates prize, 1968, Disting. Faculty award Mich. State U., 1969; Lit. Merit prize Swedish Authors Found., 1973; J.A. Wahlberg Gold medal, 1974; Internat. award Inst. Food Technologists, 1975. Fellow World Acad. Arts and Scis., Royal Swedish Acads. Scis., Engring. and Agrl. Scis.; mem. 25 sci. and tech. acads. and profl. orgns. Home: Goteborg Sweden Died Feb. 7, 1990; buried Boras, Sweden.

BORLAND, BARBARA DODGE (MRS. HAL BORLAND), author; b. Waterbury, Conn.; d. Harry G. and Grace (Cross) Dodge; student Oberlin U., 1922-23, Columbia U. Sch. Journalism, 1923; m. 2d, Hal Borland, Aug. 10, 1945 (dec. Feb. 1978); 1 dau., Diana (Mrs. James C. Thomson, Jr.). Editorial cons. various pubs., 1923-35; condr. Writers Workshop, N.Y.C., 1934-38; writer, also collaborator with husband, fiction for Colliers, McCalls, Good Housekeeping, Cosmopolitan, Redbook, others, 1946-56; garden columnist Berkshire Eagle, Pittsfield, Mass., 1960. Recipient Distinguished Alumna award St. Margaret's Sch., 1972. Congregationalist. Mem. Authors League Am. Author: The Greater Hunger, 1962 (chosen Ambassador Book, English Speaking Union 1963); This is the Way My Garden Grows ... and This is the Way My Garden Cooks, 1986; contbr.: New England: The Four Seasons, 1980; editor: Twelve Moons of the Year (by Hal Borland), 1979. Died Feb. 11, 1991. Home: Salisbury Conn.

BORNEMANN, ALFRED HENRY, economist, educator; b. Queens, N.Y., Nov. 30, 1908; s. Ernest and Carrie (Wolters) B.; m. Bertha Kohl, Aug. 20, 1938; 1 son, Alfred Richard. Student, U. Goettingen, summer 1929; B.A. cum laude, NYU, 1933, M.A., 1937, Ph.D., 1941; cert. with honors, Indsl. Coll. Armed Forces, 1963. Accountant Cities Service Co., 1923-33, Am. Water Works & Electric Co., Inc., 1934-40; teaching fellow NYU, 1940-41; instr. Rutgers U., 1941-44; vis. lectr. NYU, 1944-45, Bklyn. Coll., summer 1945; asst. prof. Boston U., 1945-46, L.I. U., 1946-48; assoc. prof. Muhlenberg Coll., 1948-50, Fla. State U., 1950-51; prof., head econs. and bus. adminstrn. dept. Norwich U., 1951-58; chmn. dept. mgmt. St. Francis Coll., 1958-60; prof. economics, bus. adminstrn. C.W. Post Coll. of L.I. U., 1960-66; mem. faculty City U. N.Y.-Hunter, Kingsborough, 1967-74, Fairleigh Dickinson U., 1966, 75, CUNY-Bklyn. Coll., 1977-78, St. Francis Coll., 1978-79; self-employed, from 1979. Author: J. Laurence Laughlin: Chapters in the Career of an Economist, 1940, Fundamentals of Industrial Management, 1963, Essentials of Purchasing, 1974, Fifty Years of Ideology: A Selective Survey of Academic Economics in the United States 1930 to 1980, 1981; Letters from a German Family: The Bornemann Correspondence in Historical Context, 1988; Contbr. articles to profl. jours. Mem. Am. Acctg. Assn., Acad. Mgmt., Am. Econ. Assn., Am. Finance Assn., Bus. History Conf., Vt. Hist. Soc., Thomas Wolfe Soc., Alpha Kappa Psi (dep. councilor 1953-54, dist. dir. 1954-67, regional dir. 1962, chmn. expansion com. 1956-62, chmn. history com. 1965-68), Omicron Delta Epsilon, Pi Gamma Mu. Home: Englewood N.J. Died Apr. 26, 1991.

BORTZ, EDWARD LEROY, physician; b. Greensburg, Pa., Feb. 10, 1896; s. Adam Franklin and Anna Margaret (Wineman) B.; m. Margaret Sophia Welty, Dec. 27, 1926; 1 child, Walter Michael. Student, Pa. State Coll., 1915-17; AB, Harvard, 1919; MD, Harvard Med. Sch., 1923; LLD (hon.), Hahnemann Med. Coll., 1948; grad. study pathology, U. Vienna, Erdheim's Clinic (Vienna), Christeller's Clinic (Berlin), 1925-26; DSc, Pa. Military Coll., 1950. Diplomate Am. Bd. Internal Medicine, 1937. Intern Lankenau Hsop., 1923-25; spl. work pathology Mayo Clinic, 1925, U. Ill. Med. Sch., 1925; instr. dept. pathology U. Pa. Sch. Medicine, 1930-32; assoc. prof. medicine Grad. Sch. Medicine, U. Pa., from 1932; chief med. svc. B Lankenau Hosp., 1932-61, sr. con. in medicine, from 1961, pres. med. staff, from 1949. Author: Diabetes Control; editor: The Cyclopedia of Medicine, Surgery and Specialties; contbr. numerous articles on nutrition, metabolism and geriatrics. Hon. med. cons. to surgeon gen. USN; mem. med. adv. bd. Nat. Resources Security Bd.; cons. Coun. on Nat. Emergency Med. Svc.; advisor White House Conf. on Aging. Served as pilot Army Air Corps, WWI; capt. M.C., U.S.N. with marines in Iwo Jima, and in atomic bomb area, WWII. Recipient meritorious svc. medal Commonwealth of Pa. for work on pneumonia commn. of State Med. Soc., 1939, gold medal Am. Geriatrics Soc., 1960, Am. Med. Writers' Assn., 1961. Mem. Coll. of Physicians of Phila., Am. Coll. Physicians (gov. Ea. Pa., regent from 1949), AMA (chmn. coun. on sci. assembly 1944-47, chmn. com. on nat. emergency svc. 1946-47, in charge sci. program Centennial Celebration Atlantic City 1947, v.p. 1946, pres. 1947), Am. Clin. and Climatol. Assn., Phila. County Med. Soc. (life mem., pres. 1940-41), Pa. State Med. Soc. (hon.), Alpha Omega Alpha, Soc. of Internal Medicine of Med. Assn. of the Argentine (fgn. corr. mem.), Am. Geriatrics Soc. (pres. 1960-61). *

BOSKOWSKY, WILLY, musician; b. Vienna, Austria, 1909. Student, Vienna Acad. Music. Violinist Vienna Philharm. Orch., 1933-79, condr. New Yr.'s concerts, 1955-79, concertmaster, 1936-79; head violin dept Vienna Acad. Music, 1935; founder Boskovksy Trio, 1937, Boskovsky Quartet, 1948; mem Vienna Octet; tours throughout world. Home: Vienna Austria Died Apr. 23, 1991.

BOUCHE, LOUIS, artist; b. N.Y.C., Mar. 18, 1896; s. Henri Louis and Marie Antoinette (Bernard) B.; m. Marian Wright, Nov. 26, 1921; children: Jane, Michael (dec.). Student, La Grande Chaumiere, Colarossi, Paris, 1910-15, Art Students' League, N.Y.C., 1915-16. Represented by murals in Internat. Music Hall, Rockefeller Ctr., N.Y.C., atty. gen's. office Justice Bldg., Washington, Interior Bldg., Washington; represented in collections of Met. Mus. of Art, Whitney Mus., Am. Acad. Arts and Letters, numerous others; painting McSorley's Bar, purchased by U. Nebr., Shooting Gallery purchased by Pa. Acad. Fine Arts; mural decorations Eisenhower Found., Abilene, Kans.; author: Robert Henri (with William Yarrow), 1921. Served in USNR, WW. Recipient John Sanford Saltus prize and medal, 1915, John Simon Guggenheim Fellowship for Painting, 1933, Carol H. Beck gold medal Pa. Acad. Fine Arts, 1944, National Academician. Mem. N.A.D. (sec. 1959, corr. sec. 1963, instr. art sch.), Nat. Inst. Arts and Letters (v.p. from 1959). Democrat. Roman Catholic. *

BOUDIN, LEONARD B., lawyer; b. N.Y.C., July 20, 1912; s. Joseph and Clara (Hessner) B.; m. Jean Roisman, Feb. 28, 1937; children: Michael, Kathy. B.S.S., CCNY, 1933; LL.B., St. John's U., 1935; postgrad. (hon. fellow) U. Pa. Law Sch., 1974; LLD (hon.) Colby Coll., 1989. Bar: N.Y. 1936, U.S. Supreme Ct. 1949, U.S. Ct. Appeals (1st cir.) 1951, (2d cir.) 1944, D.C. 1951, all other fed. cirs., U.S. Dist. Ct. (so. dist.) N.Y. 1939, U.S. Dist. Ct. (ea. dist.) N.Y. 1964, D.C. 1957, U.S. Ct. Claims 1953, U.S. Ct. Mil. Appeals 1973, U.S. Customs Ct. 1956, U.S. Treasury Dept. 1962. Legal counsel, Labor Bd. Mems. War Labor Bd., 2nd region, N.Y. 1944; vis. prof. Harvard Law Sch., 1970-71, Yale Sch. Law, 1974, U. Calif.-Berkeley, 1975; prof. U. So. Calif., Los Angeles, 1976; disting. vis. prof. Hofstra Sch. Law, 1978; vis. lectr. U. Colo., Boulder, 1979; vis. prof. U. Wash., Seattle, 1980; vis. prof. constl. and internat. litigation Stanford Law Sch., 1985; regents lectr. Boalt Hall U. Calif. Law Sch., 1986; Beijing, Shanghai Univs., 1987; sr. mem. firm Rabinowitz Boudin, Standard, Krinsky & Lieberman, N.Y.C., 1948; gen. counsel Bill of Rights Found., Nat. Emergency Civil Liberties Com., Nat. Emergency Civil Liberties Found. Contbr. articles to profl. jours. Recipient Tom Paine award Nat. Emergency Civil Liberties Com., 1980; Fowler Harper fellow Yale Law Sch., 1984; Ralph Shikes fellow Harvard Law Sch., 1980. Mem. Am. Law Inst., Assn. Bar City N.Y., Nat. Lawyers Guild, Am. Law Inst., Am. Soc. Internat. Law, Am. Fgn. Law Assn. Clubs: Harvard, Marshal Chess. Died Nov. 24, 1989. Home: New York N.Y.

BOUFFARD, PAUL HENRI, barrister; b. Quebec, Apr. 5, 1895; s. Pierre and E. (Vachon) B.; m. Margaret Hatchett, Aug. 21, 1918; children: Mariette Duchesne, Patricia Gosselin, Charles. Edn., Que. Sem. and Laval U. Apptd. Can. Senate, 1946; ptnr. Bouffard, Turgeon, Amyot, Choquette & Lesage, from 1952; v.p. Adminstrn. & Trust Co., Stanstead & Sherbrooke Inc. Co., Sterling Ins. Co.; dir. St. Lawrence Columbian & Metals Corp., Merrill Mining Island Corp., Ltd., Wabasso Cotton Co., Ltd., Dow Brewery, Ltd., Montreal Life Co., Ritz-Carlton Hotel (Montreal), Champlain Paper Box Co., Royal Bank of Can., Provincial Transport Co., Nat. Drug & Chem. Co., St. Lawrence Cement Co., Interprovincial Freezers Ltd., Merit Ins. Co., La Compagnie France-Film, Que. Freezers Ltd., La Compagnie D'Autobus de Que., Merrill Island Co., Ltd., Can. Gen. Fund, N.Am. Fund of Can., Ltd., Standard Paper Box Co., Ltd., Gen. Baking Co., Ltd., Gelco Co., Gen. Baking Co. Gov. Sch. Commerce Que.; trustee Laval U. Hon. col. C.O.T.C., Laval U. Comdr. ORder St. Gregory the Great. Clubs: Garrison, Cercle Universitaire (Que.), Country (Ottawa). Liberal. Roman Catholic. *

BOULWARE, LEMUEL RICKETTS, industrial executive; b. Springfield, Ky., June 3, 1895; s. Judson A. and Martha Price (Ricketts) B.; m. Norma Brannock, Dec. 28, 1935 (dec. 1987). A.B., U. Wis., 1916; L.H.D., Center Coll., 1953; LL.D., Carroll Coll., 1954, Union Coll., 1957; ScD., Clarkson Coll., 1962; D.Edn. in Econs. (hon.), Hillsdale (Mich.) Coll., 1980. Tchr. bus. adminstrn. U. Wis., 1916-17; tchr. Bklyn. night schs., 1919-20; comptroller E. W. Bliss Co., Hastings (Mich.) div., 1919; purchasing agt., factory mgr. H. B. Sherman Mfg. Co., Battle Creek, Mich., 1920-25; gen. sales mgr. Easy Washing Machine Corp., Syracuse, N.Y., 1925-35; v.p., gen. mgr. Carrier Corp., Syracuse, 1936-39, Celotex Corp., Chgo., 1940-42; asst. to chmn. WPB, 1942; dep. comptroller shipbuilding WPB, 1942-43; operations vice chmn. WPB, 1943-44; mem. prodn. exec. com. and standardization of shipbuilding design com. of Combined Chiefs of Staff; with Gen. Electric Co. as marketing cons. and in charge affiliated mfg. cos., 1945; v.p., 1945-47, in charge employee, community and union relations, 1947-56, v.p. public and employee relations, 1956-59, v.p. cons. relations services, 1959-61. Author: The Truth about Boularism: Trying To Do Right Voluntarily, 1969, What You Can Do about Inflation, Unemployment, Productivity, Profit and Collective Bargaining, 1972; lectr., writer, cons. Served as capt., inf. U.S. Army, 1917-19. Recipient Medal of Merit for War Service; Distinguished Am. Citizen award Harding Coll., 1963, Individual Achievement award Freedoms Found., 1986. Baptist. Clubs: Century (Syracuse); Blind Brook (Purchase, N.Y.); Round Hill (Greenwich, Conn.); Gulfstream Golf (Fla.); Gulfstream Bath and Tennis. Home: Delray Beach Fla. Died Nov. 7, 1990.

BOURAS, HARRY, artist; b. Rochester, N.Y., Feb. 13, 1931; s. Harry James and Alice (LaPriesse) B.; m. Arlene Marie Aklin, Aug. 18, 1951; 1 dau., Lorraine Ann. B.A., U. Rochester, 1951; postgrad., U. Chgo., 1955-56; M.F.A., U. Ill., 1978. Artist-in-residence U. Chgo., 1962-64, Columbia Coll., Chgo., 1964-89; faculty Northwestern U., 1965-67. host weekly radio program Critic's Choice, Sta. WFMT, from 1965; paintings and sculptures world-wide; exhibited in numerous one-man shows U.S., fgn. countries, from 1956; represented in permanent collections Mus. Modern Art, N.Y.C., Art Inst. Chgo., Rochester, N.Y., Tokyo, important sculpture works, Chgo., Aspen, Detroit, N.Y., New Delhi, Tokyo.; Bd. dirs. Creative Student Writers Found.; author numerous articles on art; former guest critic for The Chgo. Tribune. Recipient Pauline Palmer award Chgo. Art Inst., 1962, Logan Gold medal for sculpture, 1964; Hokin Found. grantee, 1969; Guggenheim Found. fellow, 1971-72. Club: Arts of Chgo. Home: Evanston Ill. Died July 15, 1990.

BOURNE, PHILIP WALLEY, architect; b. Boston, Nov. 30, 1907; s. Frank A. and Gertrude (Beals) B.; m. Mary Elliot Nicholson, June 15, 1932; children: Sallie Bourne Harrison, Philip Elliot (dec.), Jonathan F. Student in architecture, M.I.T., 1925-30, Harvard U. Sch. City Planning, 1933-34. Planner housing div. Pub. Works Adminstrn., 1934-37, U.S. Housing Authority, Washington, 1937-46; housing adviser Hawaii Housing Authority, Honolulu, 1938-39; housing cons. Republic of Haiti, 1949; internat. housing cons. Dept. State, 1950-51; dir. planning Mass. State Housing Bd., Boston, 1952-53; practice architecture Boston, from 1953; propr. The Boston Athenaeum. Recent works include, Peabody Mus., Salem, Mass., Salem Savs. Bank, Concord (Mass.) Library, G.M. Jones Meml. Library, Salem. Chmn. Mass. Art Commn., 1965-77; Trustee Trustees of Reservations, Mass. Commr. Mass. Designer Rev. Bd., 1965-66. Fellow AIA (dir. New Eng. regional council 1967-70, nat. dir. 1967-70); mem. Boston Soc. Architects (pres. 1964-66), Nat. Assn. Housing Ofcls., Am. Guild Organists. Episcopalian. Clubs: Cosmos (Washington); St. Anthony (N.Y.C.); Harvard (Boston); Union Boat, Eastern Yacht. Home: Salem Mass. Deceased. †

BOUVIER, JOHN ANDRE, JR., lawyer, corporate executive, legal and financial consultant; b. nr. Ocala, Fla., May 16, 1903; s. John Andre and Ella (Richardson) B.; m. Helen A. Schaefer, June 6, 1928 (dec. 1983); children: Helen Elizabeth (Mrs. William Spencer), John Andre III, Thomas Richardson; m. Barbara Carney; children: Mark B. Carney, Kevin P. Carney. Student, Davidson Coll., 1922-24; AB, U. Fla., 1926, LLB, 1929, JD, 1969; MBA, Northwestern U., Evanston, Ill., 1930; LHD (hon.), Windham Coll., 1977; D of Commerce (hon.), Ft. Lauderdale Coll., 1985. Bar: Fla. bar 1929. Practiced in Gainesville, 1929, Miami, 1930—; specialist corp., real estate and probate law, cons. atty.; gen. counsel Patterson & Maloney, Ft. Lauderdale; chmn. exec. com. Permutit Co., 1964-73; chmn. bd. Prosperity Co.; vice chmn. bd. Ward Indsl. Corp.; chmn. bd., pres. Pantex Mfg. Corp., Nat. Leasing Inc., Miami; pres. Knaust Bros., Inc., K-B Products Corp., Iron Mountain Atomic Storage Vaults, Inc., West Kingsway, Inc., East Kingsway, Inc., South Kingsway, Inc.; pres., dir. Ace Solar Constrn. Co., Southport Apts., BMB Devel. Co., Hendricks Devel. Corp.; sec. 50th St. Heights, Inc., Knight Manor, Inc., Dade Constrn. Co. (all Miami), Karen Club Apt. Hotel, Ft. Lauderdale, C&S Banking Corp., Landmark Banking Corp. Fla., Farquhar Machinery Co., BMB Devel. Corp., Hendricks Isle Devel. Corp. Author monographs, newspaper articles in field. Bd. dirs. Syracuse Govtl. Research Bur.; dir., sec. Wilson Garden Apts. Inc. Commr., Dade County council Boy Scouts Am.; chmn. Malecon Com. Dade County; mem. Planning Council Zoning Bd. Miami; chmn. Coxsackie-Athens Area Redevel. Com.; vice chmn. Nat. Parkinson Found.; bd. dirs., trustee Miami Boys Clubs; trustee Windham Coll., Westminster Manor, Gateway Terrace. Mem. Internat. Platform Assn., Am. Judicature Soc., ABA, Fla. Bar Assn., Dade County Bar Assn., Broward County Bar Assn., Miami C. of C., Sigma Chi (Order of Constantine). Presbyterian. Clubs: Miami Beach Rod and Reel, Riviera Country, Ft. Lauderdale Yacht, Skaneateles (N.Y.) Country, Ponte Vedra Country, Tower, Capitol Hill. Lodge: Masons, Shriners, Elks, Rotary. Home: Fort Lauderdale Fla. Died Mar. 29, 1989; buried Blowing Rock, N.C.

BOVAIRD, DAVIS D(OUTHETT), petroleum equipment executive; b. Bradford, Pa., Sept. 27, 1896; s. William J. and Anna L. (Davis) B.; m. Florence Hettinger, Sept. 21, 1921; children: Ruthanna, William J., Mary Florence. Student, Coll. of Emporia, 1914-17, LLD; AB, U. Mich., 1918, BS in ME, 1920. Field salesman Bovaird Supply Co., Tulsa, 1920-22; plant mgr. Bovaird Supply Co., Independence, Kans., 1922-27; v.p., treas. Bovaird Supply Co., Independence, 1927-49, pres., 1949-

62, chmn. bd. dirs., from 1962; dir. Pub. Svc. Co. of Okla., First Nat. Bank & Trust Co., Tulsa, Pennzoil Co. of Pa. Trustee U. Tulsa; dir., chmn. bd. Hillcrest Med. Ctr. Mem. Am. Petroleum Inst., Petroleum Equipment Suppliers Assn. (dir.), Kappa Sigma, Tulsa Club, So. Hills Country Club. Presbyterian. *

BOVET, DANIEL, physiologist; b. Neuchatel, Switzerland, 1907; s. Pierre and Amy (Babut) B.; m. Filomena Nitti, 1938; 1 son. DSc, U. Geneva; hon. doctorates, U. Palermo, U. Rio de Janeiro, others. Asst. in physiology U. Geneva, 1928-29; asst. Inst. Pasteur, Paris, 1929-39, dir. lab., 1939-47; dir. labs. therapeutic chemistry Istituto Superiore di Sanità, Rome, 1947-64; prof. pharmacology U. Sassari, 1964-71; prof. psychobiology U. Rome, 1971-82, hon. prof., 1982-92; dir. lab. psychobiology and psychopharmacology Consiglio Nazionale della Richerche, 1969-75. Author: (with others) Structure chimique et activité pharmacodynamique des medicaments du système nerveux vegetatif, 1948; (with others) Curare and Curare-like Agents, 1959; (with others) Controlling Drugs, 1974. Recipient Nobel prize for physiology and medicine, 1957; decorated grand officer Order Italian Republic. Mem. Accademia Nazionale dei Lincei, Royal Soc. (Eng.) (fgn.). Home: Rome Italy Died Apr. 8, 1992. †

BOVEY, EDMUND CHARLES, business executive; b. Calgary, Alta., Can., Jan. 29, 1916; s. Charles A. and Dorothy (Smith) B.; m. Margaret Snowdon, Jan. 29, 1941; children: Charles Gordon, Myra. Student, Victoria (B.C., Can.) Coll., 1931, U. B.C., 1935; LLD (hon.), U. Toronto, 1986. Joined No. Ont. Natural Gas Co. Ltd. (subsequently Norcen Energy Resources Ltd), 1959; v.p. Norcen Energy Resources Ltd., 1960-65, pres., 1965-74, chief exec. officer, chmn. exec. com., 1968-81; chmn. bd. TeleFilm Can., 1974-81; appointed chancellor U. Guelph, 1989; dir. Argus Corpl Ltd., NN Life Ins. Co. Can., Griffith Labs. Inc., Chgo., Griffith Labs. Can. Ltd., Mercedes-Benz Can. Ltd., Guardian-Morton Shulman Precious Metals Inc., Value Investment Corp.; chmn. Ont. govt. commn. on future devel. of univs. of Ont., 1984, Fed. Task Force on Funding Arts in Can., 1985. Past pres. Art Gallery Ont., Art Gallery Found., Can. Fedn. Friends of Mus., World Fedn. Friends Mus.; bd. dirs. Canadian Exec. Service Overseas; chmn. Toronto Econ. Devel. Corp., exec. com. Toronto Design Exchange; past chmn. Council for Bus. and Arts in Can.; bd. dirs. Nat. Ballet Can.; bd. dirs., v.p. Roy Thompson Hall, The Banff Centre for the Arts, Nat. Ballet Sch., Canadian Liver Found.; vice chmn. Internat. Council Mus. Modern Art; past chmn. The Wellesley Hosp. U. Guelph; hon. mem. nat. coun. Boy Scout Can. Decorated Officer Order of Can. Mem. Can. Gas Assn. (past pres., dir.). Mem. Anglican Ch. (past warden). Clubs: Rosedale Golf, Granite, Toronto, York, (Toronto). Home: Willowdale Can. Died Apr. 25, 1990.

BOWDITCH, EBENEZER FRANCIS, educational consultant; b. Framingham Center, Mass., June 4, 1912; s. John Perry and Alice (Bradford) B.; m. Anna Mitchel Hale, Aug. 3, 1935; children: Ebenezer Francis, Susan Hale, Nathaniel Hale. Student, Milton (Mass.) Acad., 1925-31; AB, Harvard U., 1925. Tchr. athletics and sci. Shady Hill Sch., Cambridge, Mass., 1933-35; tchr. Milton Acad., 1935-37; asst. dean of freshmen Harvard Coll., 1937-39; headmaster Park Sch., Indpls., 1939-41, Lake Forest (Ill.) Acad., 1941-51; dean of students MIT, 1951-56, spl. adviser to the pres., 1956-57; adminstrv. dir. Rsch. Soc. for Creative Altruism, 1957-58; ednl. cons., 1958-90. Mem. AD and Hasty Pudding clubs of Harvard, Cum Laude Soc. at Milton Acad., Havard Club (N.Y.C.). Republican. Home: Rye Beach N.H. Died Feb. 6, 1990.

BOWEN, HOWARD ROTHMANN, economist; b. Spokane, Wash., Oct. 27, 1908; s. Henry G. and Josephine (Menig) B.; m. Lois B. Schilling, Aug. 24, 1935; children: Peter Geoffrey, Thomas Gerard. BA, Wash. State U., 1929, MA, 1933; PhD, U. Iowa, 1935; postdoctoral, U. Cambridge and London Sch. Econs., 1937-38; hon. doctorate, Carnegie-Mellon U., Claremont Grad. Sch.Coe Coll., Coll. of Santa Fe, Cornell Coll., Drake U., Grinnell Coll., Knox Coll., Loras Coll., Loyola U. of Chgo., Marycrest Coll., Ohio State U., Towson State U., Union Coll., U. Ill., U. Pacific, U. Tulsa, Williams Coll., Blackburn Coll., Augustana Coll., Whitman Coll. Instr. to assoc. prof. econs. U. Iowa, 1935-42; chief economist joint com. in internal revenue taxation U.S. Congress, 1942-44; chief economist Irving Trust Co., 1945-47; dean, prof. econs. Coll. Commerce and Bus. Adminstrn., U. Ill., 1947-52; prof. econs. Williams Coll., 1952-55; pres. Grinnell (Iowa) Coll., 1955-64, U. Iowa, Iowa City, 1964-69; prof. econs. Claremont Grad. Sch., 1969-84, pres., chancellor Claremont U. Ctr., 1970-75, R. Stanton Avery prof. econs. and edn., 1974-84, emeritus prof., 1984-89; dir. Bankers Life Co. Des Moines; policy elected dir. Tchrs. Ins. and Annuity Assn. and Coll. Retirement Equities Fund, then trustee TIAA-CREF; past dir. Common Fund, 1969-75; mem. U.S. Tax Mission to Japan, 1949; econ. cons. Nat. Council Chs., 1949-53; chmn. Gov.'s Commn. Econ. and Social Trends in Iowa, 1958; mem. Fed. Adv. Com. Intergovtl. Relations, 1961-64; chief U.S. Aid Mission to Thailand, 1961; chmn. Nat. Citizen's Com. Tax Revision and Reduction, 1963, chmn. Nat. Commn. Tech., Automation and Econ. Progress, 1964-66; mem. task force higher ednl fin. Nat. Coun. Ind. Colls. and Univs., 1973-74; mem. study group on condition of excellence in Am. higher edn. U.S. Office Edn., 1983-85. Author: English Grants in Aid, 1939, Iowa Income, 1934, Unemployment Compensation Applied to Iowa, 1936, Toward Social Economy, 1948, 2d edit., 1977, Social Responsibilities of the Businessman, 1953, Graduate Education in Economics, 1953, Christian Values and Economic Life, 1954, (with Garth L. Mangum) Automation and Economic Progress, 1966, The Finance of Higher Education, 1968, (with Gordon Douglass) Efficiency in Liberal Education, 1971, Investment in Learning, 1977, Academic Compensation, 1978, The Costs of Higher Education, 1980, The State of the Nation and The Agenda for Higher Education, 1982 (Ness prize best book on liberal edn.), (with Jack H. Schuster) American Professors: A National Resource Imperiled, 1986, Academic Recollections; An Autobiography, 1988; also over 300 pamphlets and articles; editor, contbr. Evaluationg Performance for Accountability, 1974; editorial bd. Jour. Higher Edn., 1972-81, Change mag., 1979-89. Past trustee LeMoyne-Owen Coll., Argonne Univs. Assn. (chmn. 1967-69), Occidental Coll., Nat. Commn. on Accrediting; past bd. visitors Tulane U.; trustee Grinnell Coll., 1975-86, Claremont Univ. Ctr., 1980-86. Social Sci. Research Council fellow for study in Eng., 1937-38; Carnegie Found. for Advancement Teaching fellow, 1980-81; recipient awards for leadership in higher edn. Nat. Council Ind. Colls. and Univs., 1975, N.Y. Assn. Colls. and Univs., 1976,. Nat. Assn. Student Personnel Adminstrs., 1981, Council Ind. Colls., 1983, 1983, Disting. Service to Edn. award Council for Advancement Edn., 1985, Assn. Instl. Research, 1987, Disting. Alumnus awards U. Iowa, Wash. State U.; Bowen Hall Med. Sci. Bldg. at U. Iowa named in his honor; endowed lectureship in his name Claremont Grad. Sch.; H.R. and Lois Bowen Sci. Bldg. at Grinnell Coll. named in his honor. Mem. Am. Fin. Assn. (pres. 1950), Am. Assn. Higher Edn. (pres. 1975), Am. Econ. Soc., Western Econ. Assn. (pres. 1977), Nat. Acad. Edn., Assn. Study Higher Edn. (pres. 1980), Phi Kappa Phi, Beta Gamma Sigma, Phi Beta Kappa. Home: Claremont Calif. Died Dec. 22, 1989; cremated.

BOWEN, J(EAN) DONALD, language professional, educator; b. Malad, Idaho, Mar. 19, 1922; s. John David and Lillian (Larson) B.; m. Catherine Holley, May 27, 1948; children: David James, Douglas Ray, Dale Eugene, Christina Lee, Karen Lucy. A.B., Brigham Young U., 1944; M.A., Columbia U., 1949; Ph.D., U. N.Mex., 1952. Instr. Duke U., Durham, N.C., 1952-53; sci. linguist Fgn. Service Inst., Washington, 1953-58; prof. English UCLA, 1958-87, emeritus, 1987; co-dir. Philippine Ctr. for Lang. Study, UCLA, 1958-63, field dir. Survey of Lang. Use and Lang. Teaching in Ea. Africa, 1968-70; vis. prof. Am. U. Cairo, 1974-77, Ain Shams U., 1976-77. Author: Patterns of English Pronunciation, 1975, (with others) Adaptation in Language Teaching, 1978, Patterns of Spanish Pronunciation, 1960, The Sounds of English and Spanish, 1965, The Grammatical Structures of English and Spanish, 1965, English Usage, 1983, TESOL Techniques and Procedures, 1985; author, editor: (with others) Studies in Southwest Spanish, 1976, Linguistics in Oceania, 1971, Language in Ethiopia, 1976; contbr. articles to profl. jours. Served with U.S. Army, 1943-46. Mem. Linguistic Soc. Am., MLA, TESOL. Mem. LDS Ch. Home: Los Angeles Calif. Died Jan. 23, 1989; buried City Cemetery, Brigham, Utah.

BOWERS, ALBERT, pharmaceutical company executive; b. Manchester, Eng., July 16, 1930; came to U.S., 1954; s. Albert and Mary (Munn) B.; m. Gwynn C. Akin, Dec. 1985. BS in Chemistry, London U., 1951; PhD in Organic Chemistry, U. Manchester, 1954. Group rsch. leader Syntex S.A., Mexico City, 1956-64, assoc. dir. chem. rsch., 1960-61, 61, dir. chem. rsch., Syntex rsch. div., v.p. mktg, 1964; v.p. internat. div. Syntex, 1964-67; v.p. Syntex Corp., Palo Alto, Calif., 1965, bd. dirs., 1968, pres., chief oper. officer, 1976-80, pres., chief exec. officer, 1980-82, chmn., chief exec. officer, 1981-89, chmn. bd., 1989-90; pres. Syntex Labs., Inc., 1967-73, Syntex USA, 1967-82; bd. dirs. Clorox Co. Contbr. articles to profl. jours.; patentee in selective fluorination of steroids, corticoid compounds synthesis, norethindrone synthesis; originator 120 patents. Active Calif. Bus. Roundtable, Bus. Higher Edn. Forum, Rockefeller U. Coun.; founding mem. U. Calif., San Francisco Found.; mem. exec. com. Bay Area Coun.; mem. Conf. Bd.; mem. adv. coun. SRI Internat.; trustee adv. bd. Beckman Ctr. for History of Chemistry. Recipient Sci. prize Mex. Acad. Sci., 1964; Fulbright fellow Wayne State U., 1954-55; CEO awards Wall St. Transcript, 1983, 87, 88. Home: Menlo Park Calif. Died July 26, 1990; buried Skylawn Meml. Pk., San Mateo, Calif.

BOWERS, FREDSON THAYER, educator; b. New Haven, Apr. 25, 1905; s. Fredson Eugene and Hattie (Quigley) B; m. Hyacinth Sutphen, Nov. 11., 1924; children: Fredson, Joan Stout, Stephen, Peter; m. Nancy Hale, Mar. 16, 1942. PhB, Brown U., 1925, LittD, 1970; PhD, Harvard U., 1934; LittD, Clark U., 1970; LHD, U. Chgo., 1973. Instr. English, tutor modern langs. Harvard U., Boston, 1926-36; instr. English Princeton U., 1936-38; asst. prof. English U. Va., Charlottesville, 1938-46, assoc. prof., 1946-48, prof. English, 1948-50; professorial lectr. English, U. Chgo., 1950-65, chmn. dept., 1961-68, Linden Kent prof. Lit., 1968-75; prof. emeritus Chgo., from 1975; dean faculty arts scis. U. Chgo., 1968-69; Fulbright fellow advanced research, U.K., 1952-53; Sanders reader in bibliography Cambridge (Eng.) U., 1958, James Lyell reader in bibliography Oxford U., 1959; Guggenheim fellow, 1958-59, 71-72; regional chmn. Woodrow Wilson Nat. Fellowship Found., 1956-59; Phi Beta Kappa vis. scholar, 1962-63; vis. fellow All Souls Coll., Oxford, 1972, 74; resident Villa Serbelloni Research and Conf. Ctr., 1970, 72; fellow Commoner Churchill Coll., Cambridge, 1975. Author: Principles of Bibliographical Description, 1949, On Editing Shakespeare and Elizabethan Dramatists, 1955, Textual and Literary Criticism, 1959, Bibliography and Textual Criticism, 1964, Essays in Bibliography, Texts and Editing, 1975; editor: Studies in Bibliography, 1949—, Dramatic Works of Thomas Dekker, 4 vols., 1953-61, Whitman's Manuscripts for 1860 Leaves of Grass, 1955, Pelican Shakespeare Merry Wives of Windsor, 1963, Works of Christopher Marlowe, 2 vols., 1973, rev. 1981, Vladimir Nabokov Lectures, 3 vols., 1980-83; textual editor: Centenary edit. Hawthorne, 11 vols., 1962-74, U. Va. edit. Stephen Crane, 10 vols., 1969-75, ACLS edit. William James, 17 vols., 1975-88; gen. editor: Dramatic Works in the Beaumont and Fletcher Canon, 10 vols., from 1966, Elizabethan Dramatists, 1987, Jacobean and Caroline Dramatists, 1987; contbr. articles to profl. jours. Served as comdr. USNR, 1942-45, Washington. Recipient Bicentennial medal Brown U., 1964, Thomas Jefferson award, U. Va., 1971, Julian P. Boyd award for Documentary Editing, 1986. Fellow Am. Acad. Arts and Scis.; corr. fellow Brit. Acad; mem. S. Atlantic Modern Lang. Assn. (pres. 1969), MLA (exec. council 1963-67), Bibliog Soc. (Gold Medal 1968), London, Bibliog. Soc. Am., of U. Va., of Oxford, Soc. for Textual Scholarship (pres. 1985). Club: Elizabethan (Yale U.). Home: Charlottesville Va. Died Apr. 11, 1991.

BOWLES, EDWARD LINDLEY, consulting engineer, educator; b. Westphalia, Mo., Dec. 9, 1897; s. Samuel Addison and Julia Johnson B.; m. Lois Wuerpel, June 17, 1922; children: Edmund Addison, Frederick Wuerpel. BS, Washington U., 1920; MS, MIT, 1922; DSc, Norwich U., 1945. Registered profl. engr., Mass. Radio editor Boston Evening Transcript, 1921-22; asst. dept. elec. engring. MIT, 1920-21, instr., 1921-25, asst. prof. elec. communications, 1925-27, assoc. prof., 1927-37, prof., 1937-63, charge communication div. dept. elec. engring., 1947-52, mem. patent com., dir., cons. prof. elec. communications, 1947-52, cons. prof., 1952-63, prof. emeritus, 1963-90; cons. elec. patent matters; charter mem., sec. microwave sect. Nat. Def. Rsch. Coun., 1940-42; cons. sec. war, 1942-47; cons. communications and radar USAAF, 1943, operational and organizational problems, 1944; sci. cons. USAF, 1947-51; sci. warfare adviser weapons evaluation group Office Sec. Def., 1950-52, cons. sec. army, 1951-52; gen. cons. Raytheon Co., Lexington, Mass., 1947-66; cons. then spl. asst. to pres. Analex Corp., Boston, 1964-67; chmn. bd., pres. Info. Transfer Corp., 1968-70. Patentee in field. Chmn. bd. adhoc adv. com. on VHF-UHF, TV allocations Senate Com. Interstate and Fgn. Commerce, 1956-58; mem. panel on patents Commerce Tech. Adv. Bd. Army; mem NAS-NRC Rsch. Bd. for Nat. Security, 1945; past trustee, mem. exec. com. Bentley Coll.; past charter trustee Kodaly Musical Tng. Inst.; trustee Newton-Wellesley Hosp., 1981-9; life mem. Boston Mus. Fine Arts. 2d lt. F.A., U.S. Army, 1918. Decorated D.S.M., Presdl. Medal of Merit; named comdr Order Brit. Empire; recipient disting. alumni citation Washington U., 1955. Fellow IEEEE fellowship award IRE 1947 , Am. Phys. Soc., Am. Acad. Arts and Scis. v.p. 1954-56 ; mem. AAAS, Soc. Promotion Engring. Edn., Ops. Rsch. Soc., Westphalia Hist. Soc. charter , St. Botolph Club Boston , Cosmos Club Washington , Sigma Xi. Home: Wellesley Hills Mass. Died Jan. 5, 1990.

BOWMAN, JOHN WICK, clergyman; b. Brownsville, Pa., Aug. 3, 1894; s. Winfield Scott and Maggie Moore (Wicks) B.; m. Alma Louise Coles, June 2, 1919; children: John Scott, Margaret Louise, Douglas Coles. AB cum laude, Wooster (Ohio) Coll., 1916, DD, 1951; AM, Princeton U., 1919; BD (fellow in Bibl. theology), Princeton Theol. Sem., 1920; PhD, So. Baptist Theological Seminary, Louisville, 1930; postgrad, U. Zurich, 1936; DD, Waynesburg Coll., 1943, U. St. Andrews, Scotland, 1951. Ordained minister Presbyn. Ch. in U.S.A., 1919. Evangelistic and ednl. missionary Punjab Mission, India, 1920-36; guest prof. N.T. Western Theol. Sem., Pitts., 1936-37, assoc. prof., 1937-38, meml. prof. N.T. lit. and exegesis, 1938-44; Robert Dollar prof. N.T. interpretation San Francisco Theol. Sem., 1944-61; assoc. min. United Ch., Sun City, Ariz., from 1964; lectr. Union Theol. Sem., N.Y.C., 1955, 64, Fulbright prof. Christianity, Internat. Christian U., Tokyo, 1957-58; lectr. So. Bapt. Theol. Sem., 1957, 58, Union Theol. Sems., Tokyo and Manila, Silliman U., Dumaguete City, P.I., 1958. Author: several books including The Gospel for the Mount, 1957, General Epistles, 1962, Jesus' Teaching in Its Environment, 1963; contbr. Tools for Bible Study, 1956, New Peake Commentary, 1961, Interpreters Bible Dictionary, 1963; contbr. articles to religious publs. Adv. bd. Revision Am. Standard Version Old and New Testaments. Co-winner Abingdon-Cokesbury award for best religious book, 1948. Mem. Soc. Bibl. Lit. and Exegesis (pres. Pacific Coast br. 1947-48), Nat. Assn. Bibl. Instrs., Societas Novi Testamenti Studiorum, Phi Beta Kappa, Chi Alpha. Presbyterian. *

BOWMAN, WESLEY ELLSWORTH, illustrative photographer; b. Aberdeen, S.D., Aug. 3, 1898; s. William Samuel and Alice Ott (Claridge) B.; m. Margaret Galloway, Aug. 3, 1926; children: Margaret Alice Brown, David Galloway. Grad., Wayland Acad., Beaver Dam, Wis., 1923; M in Photography, Profl. Photographers Am., 1946, 64. Apprentice Chgo. Comml. Photographic Co., 1924-28; pres., owner Wesley Bowman Studio, Inc., Chgo., from 1928, Wesley Bowman, Inc., Chgo., from 1956; pioneer negative-positive system color photography; guest lectr. Winona Sch. Photography, 1956-62; judge internat., nat., state comml. photog. exhbns., 1957-62. Commr. Kenilworth (Ill.) Park Bd., 1947-53; pres. Village Kenilworth, 1953-57; chmn. Kenilworth Plan Commn., 1957-62; mem. dept. info. and promotion Episcopal Diocese Chgo.; trustee Wayland Acad., Canterbury House of Northwestern U.; chmn. bd. trustees Winona Sch. Photography; chmn. bldg. com. for nat. hdqrs. bldg. Profl. Photographers Am.; mem. adv. bd. Rochester Inst. Tech.; treas. Canterbury House, Northwestern U. With U.S. Army, 1917-19. Recipient awards Art Dirs. Club Chgo., 1944, 52-54, award Affiliated Advt. Agy. Network, 1960; Disting. Svc. award Ind. Photog. Assn., 1954, S.W. Photog. Assn., 1957. Mem. Profl. Photographers Am. (dir. exec. bd. 1955-61, sec.-treas. 1962, pres. 1963-64), Chgo. Photog. Guild (pres. 1939-45, dir. 1945-52), Camerascraftsmen Am. Inst. British Photographers, Kenilworth Club, Westmoreland Country Club (Wilmette, Ill.), Dairymans Country Club (Boulder Junction, Wis.). Republican. Episcopalian. *

BOYCE, WILLIAM GEORGE, museum director emeritus, educator; b. Fairmont, Minn., July 25, 1921; s. William Irving and Nellie Hazel (Goetz) B.; m. Joan Palmer, July 29, 1949; children: Todd William, Robyn Jo, Timothy Palmer. B.S., U. Minn., 1949, M.Ed., 1952; postgrad., Mills Coll., Oakland, Calif., 1954-55. Clk. 1st Nat. Bank, Fairmont, 1939-41; high sch. and jr. coll. tchr. Worthington, Minn., 1949-57; mem. faculty U. Minn., Duluth, 1957-85; prof. art, dir. Tweed Mus. Art, 1969-85. Author: David Ericson, 1963, also mus. exhbn. catalogues. Served with USNR, 1941-45. Decorated Naval Commendation medal; Ford Found. grantee, 1954-55. Mem. NEA (life), Am. Assn. Mus., Midwest Mus. Conf. (v.p. Minn. chpt. 1967-70), Minn. Art Edn. Assn. (pres. 1963-65). Democrat. Episcopalian. Home: Duluth Minn. Died Apr. 12, 1992. †

BOYD, DAVID MILTON, process control executive; b. St. Louis, Jan. 5, 1918; s. David M. and Josephine (Drake) B.; m. Louise VanDeventer, June 11, 1941; children—Gwendolyn Boyd Graybar, David Garrison, Barbara Josephine. BSChemE, U. Colo., 1941, hon. doctorate, 1950. With Barratt Chem. Co., 1941-42, Blaw Knox Constrn. Co., 1942-43, Eastern States Petroleum Co., 1943-45, Monsanto Chem. Co., 1945-46, Oak Ridge Nat. Labs., 1946-48; mgr. instrument engrg. design and svc. Universal Oil Products Co., Des Plaines, Ill., from 1948. Contbr. articles profl. jours.; Contbg. author: McGraw Hill Handbook of Separation Techniques; 160 patents. Clarendon Hills (Ill.) del. to West Suburban Transit Bd. Recipient Instrument Soc. Am. Sperry award Chgo. Tech. Socs. Council, 1957, Disting. Engring. Alumnus award U. Colo., 1970; Honeywell internat. award Inst. Measurement and Control, London, Eng., 1981. Fellow Instrument Soc. Am. (mem. admissions com., mem. recommended practices com., chmn. nat. meeting 1979), ASME; sr. mem. IEEE; mem. Am. Inst. Chem. Engrs., Am. Chem. Soc., Sigma Alpha Epsilon. Presbyn. (elder). Club: Ruth Lake Country (Hinsdale, Ill.). Home: Clarendon Hills Ill. Died Dec. 18, 1990.

BOYD, DAVID PRESTON, surgeon; b. Paisley, Scotland, July 1, 1914; came to U.S., 1928, naturalized, 1941; s. John and Christina (Johnson) B.; m. Mignon Finch, June 24, 1939; children—David Preston, Lew Finch, John Hamilton. Student, Glasgow U., 1930-32; M.D., McGill U., 1938; Postgrad. work in surgery, Montreal (Que., Can.) Gen. Hosp., 1938-42. Diplomate Am. Bd. Surgery, Am. Bd. Thoracic Surgery. Practice surgery Amsterdam, N.Y., 1942-47; surg. staff Lahey Clinic div. Lahey Found., Boston, from 1948; also chmn. emeritus dept. thoracic and cardiovascular surgery. Lahey Clinic div. Lahey Found.; historian Lahey Clin. Found.; lectr. surgery Harvard U. Mem. editorial bd. Chest, from 1966, Year book of Cancer; contbr. articles to profl. jours. Trustee, mem. exec. com. Pine Manor Jr. Coll.; trustee Lahey Found.; pres. Countway Library Assocs., Harvard U. Fellow A.C.S., Am. Surg. Assn., Soc. Thoracic Surgeons, Royal Coll. Surgeons Can.; mem. Internat. Cardiovascular Soc., Internat. Soc. Surgery, A.M.A., Am. Assn. for Thoracic Surgery, Am. Thoracic Soc., New Eng., Boston surg. socs., Am. Heart Assn., Am. Coll. Chest Physicians (pres. 1971-72, historian), Am. Assn. History Medicine, Soc. for Vascular Surgery. Presbyn. (elder). Clubs: The Country (Brookline, Mass.); Wellesley (Boston). Home: Wellesley Hills Mass. Died Mar. 5, 1989; buried Wellesley, Mass.

BOYD, ELISE STEPHENS, rural health project administrator; b. Nashville, Sept. 21, 1930; d. Elbert Montgomery and Elise (Robin) Stephens; m. Herschel Livingston Boyd, Dec. 22, 1951; children: Patrick Stephens, David Stephens. Gen. acad. diploma Ward-Belmont Coll., Nashville, 1950, U. Chattanooga, 1951; BS in Human Svcs. Mgmt., U. Tenn., 1976. Project dir. Jackson County Rural Health Project, Scottsboro, Ala., 1978-86; sec. Marion County Speech and Hearing Bd. Dirs., South Pittsburg, Tenn., 1975-76, pres., 1976-78; bd. dirs. North Ala. Health Edn. and Resource Ctr., Huntsville, Ala., 1979-82; council mem. North Ala. Health Systems Agy., Madison, Ala., 1980-82; pres. Jackson County Home Health Adv. Bd., Scottsboro, from 1980; mem. interdisciplinary adv. council Sch. Nursing, U. Ala., Birmingham, 1983-84, Marshall-Jackson Mental Health Adv. Bd., Guntersville, Ala., from 1980. Vice pres. Care Assurance System for Aged and Homebound, Scottsboro, 1982-84; bd. stewards Citizens for Industry, Scottsboro, 1983-84. Mem. AAUW, Orgn. Active Women-Stevenson, Ala. Rural Health Assn. (sec. 1981-83, v.p. 1983-84), Nat. Assn. Community Health Ctrs. Nat. Rural Primary Care, Assn. Am. Rural Health Assn., Scottsboro/Jackson County C. of C. (bd. dirs. 1983-85, Outstanding Citizen award 1985), Stevenson County C. of C. (sec. 1982-84). Club: DAR (Scottsboro). Died Jan. 19, 1986. Home: Scottsboro Ala.

BOYDEN, ALAN ARTHUR, educator; b. Milw., June 16, 1897; s. Arthur and Carrie (Wheeler) B.; m. Mabel Josephine Gregg, Sept. 15, 1923; children: Alan Arthur, Douglas Gregg, Mabel Maxon (Mrs. Thomas Ralph Davenport), Cornelia Wheeler (Mrs. Richard Thum). A.B., U. Wis., 1921, Ph.D., 1925. With Rutgers U., 1925-86, New Brunswick, N.J., 1925-86; instr., asst. prof., asso. prof. Rutgers U., 1925-44, prof., 1944-62, prof. emeritus, 1962-86, acting chmn. dept. zoology, 1947-48, chmn., 1954-59; Fulbright lectr. Queen Mary's Coll. U. London, 1960-61, 67-68; Rose Morgan vis. prof. U. Kans., 1964; Co-founder, chmn. Bur. Biol. Research, 1936-39; founder, dir. Serological Mus., 1948-62, dir. emeritus, 1971-86, editor, 1948-86. Author: Perspectives in Zoology. Served with U.S. Army, 1918. Recipient Distinguished Service citation Beloit Coll., 1970; Am. Cancer Soc. grantee, 1957-58, 58-59; NSF grantee, 1957-59. Fellow AAAS, N.Y. Acad. Scis., N.Y. Zool. Soc.; mem. Am. Soc. Naturalists, Am. Assn. Immunologists, Classification Soc., Soc. Systematic Zoology, Systematics Assn., Franklin Twp. Hist. Soc., Blackwell Mills Canal House Assn. (treas. 1971-86), English Speaking Union (pres. New Brunswick br. 1960-62), Rockingham Assn. Home: Princeton N.J. Died July 1986. †

BOYDEN, WILLARD NEWHALL, insurance executive; b. Chgo., Mar. 6, 1897; s. Francis Willard and Anna (Newhall) B.; m. Angela Johnston, May 1, 1931; children: Lucia, Johnston Newhall, Thomas Newhall. Student, Evanston Acad., 1914-15; BA, Williams Coll., 1919. Clk., bookkeeper, traveling rep. W. H. Perrine & Co., Chgo. Bd. Trade, 1919-21; with bond dept. No. Trust Co., 1921-24; salesmen, investment analyst Marshall Field, Glore, Ward & Co., 1924-30; joined Continental Casualty Co. and Continental Assurance Co., Chgo., 1930; v.p., dir., sec., exec. com. Continental Casualty Co. and Continental Assurance Co.; v.p., sec., dir. Transportation Ins. Co., Chgo.; Chmn. fin. sect. Am. Life Conf., 1950-51; chmn. Mid-Western Ins. Voluntary Credit Restraint Com., 1951-52. Mem. Chgo. Crime Commn.; dir. Chgo. chpt. ARC; mem. bd. trustees Williams Coll.; pres. Soc. of Alumni of Williams Coll., 1952-54. 2d lt. U.S. Army, 1918. Mem. Chi Psi., Univ. Club (Chgo.), Onwentsia Club (Lake Forest). Presbyterian. Republican. *

BOYNE, EDWIN MCKINLEY, dean; b. Marlette, Mich., July 18, 1897; s. George and Ida A. (Jones) B.; m. Vera M. Martens, June 23, 1923; children: John E., Phillip M., Robert W., Frederick J. BA, Alma (Mich.) coll., 1920; MA, U. Mich., 1926; PhD, Mich. State U., 1948. Athletic coach Midland, Mich., 1920-23; prin. schs. Midland, Manistee, 1923-28; jr. coll. instr. Muskegon, Mich., 1928-37; supt. schs. Mason, Mich., 1937-46; supt. Dependents Sch., Berlin, Germany, 1946-47; prof. edn., dir. student teaching Mankate (Minn.) State Coll., 1948-56, dean sch. grad. studies, from 1957; vis. prof. U. Fla., 1956-57. Chmn. Ingham County (Mich.) OPA, 1942-43; mem. city planning commn., Mason, MIch., 1944. With U.S. Army, 1918. Mem. NEA, Phi Delta Kappa, Mason, Kiwanis (past pres.). Presbyterian (elder). *

BRADEN, WALDO W., emeritus speech educator; b. Ottumwa, Iowa, Mar. 7, 1911; s. Wilbern C. and Stella (Warder) B.; m. Dana Crane, Aug. 18, 1938; 1 child, Helen Dana. B.A., Penn Coll., 1932; M.A., U. Iowa, 1938, Ph.D., 1942. Tchr. Fremont (Iowa) High Sch., 1933-35, Mt. Pleasant High Sch., 1935-38; tchr. speech Iowa Wesleyan Coll., 1938-40, dean students, 1942-43, 45-46; asso. prof. speech La. State U., Baton Rouge, 1946-51; prof. La. State U., 1951-73, Boyd prof., 1973-79, Boyd prof. emeritus, from 1979, chmn., 1958-76; vis. prof. Washington U., summer 1952, Mich. State U., summer 1953, U. Pacific, summer 1965, Calif. State Coll., Fullerton, 1969. Author: (with Gary) Public Speaking, 1951, rev. edit., 1963, (with Brandenburg) Oral Decision-Making, 1955, (with Genring) Speech Practices, 1958, Public Speaking: Essentials, 1966, (with Thonssen and Baird) Speech Criticism, 1970; editor: Speech Methods and Resources, 1961, rev. edit., 1972, The Speech Teacher, 1967-69, Oratory in the Old South, 1970, Oratory in the New South, 1979, Representative American Speeches, 1970-80, Oral Tradition in the South, 1983, Abraham Lincoln Public Speaker, 1988; contbr. articles to profl. jours. Served with AUS, 1943-45. Mem. Speech Communication Assn. (council from 1954, exec. sec. 1954-57, pres. 1962, Disting. Ser. award 1978), So. Speech Assn. (pres. 1969-70), Pi Kappa Delta, Delta Sigma Rho, Tau Kappa Alpha, Omicron Delta Kappa. Methodist. Home: Columbia Mo. Died 1992. †

BRADFIELD, RICHARD, agronomist; b. West Jefferson, Ohio, Apr. 20, 1896; s. Bayard Taylor and Martha Anderson (Truitt) B.; m. Ethel May Hill, June 21, 1923; 1 child, Richard; 2d m. Hannah Amelia Stillman, Aug. 6, 1926; children: Robert Browning, Stillman, David Maurice, Patricia Jane, James Worthington. AB, Otterbein Coll., Westerville, Ohio, 1917; DSc, Otterbein Coll., 1941; PhD, Ohio State U., 1922; summer student, U. Wis., 1923. Tchr. sci. and math. Fairfield Twp. High Sch., Madison County, Ohio, 1917-18; asst. to assoc. prof. soils U. Mo., 1920-30; prof. soils Ohio State U., 1930-37; prof. soil tech. Cornell U., 1937-61, prof. emeritus, from 1961, head dept. agronomy, 1937-55; Guggenheim fellow Kaiser Wilhelm Inst. for Physikalishe und Electrochemie, Berlin, Dahlem, 1927-28; dir. agr. in Far East for Rockefeller Found., 1955-57, trustee, 1957-61, spl. cons., 1962—; cons. soil scientist USDA, 1941-52; U.S. del. to 3d Internat. Congress of Soil Sci., Oxford, Eng., 1935; mem. Rockefeller Found. Mexican Agrl. Commn., 1941-55; advisor U.S. del., 3d Inter-Am. Conf. on Agr., Caracas, 1945; F.A.O. Com. on Agrl. Prodn., 1946, 47; faculty rep., bd. trustees Cornell U., 1944-48. Mem. editorial bd.: Jour. Am. Soc. Agronomy, from 1940; cons. editor: Soil Sci., from 1935. Mem. com. on plant and crop ecology Nat. Rsch. Coun., 1950-53; mem. Nat. Soil Rsch. Com., 1950-52; mem. vis. com. biology dept. Brookhaven Nat. Lab., 1951-53; mem. U.S. Agrl. Mission to U.K., 1946. Fellow AAAS (v.p., chmn. sect. Ohio 1941), Am. Soc. Agronomy (v.p. 1941, pres. 1942); mem. Soil Sci. Am. (pres. 1937), Internat. Soc. Soil Sci. (pres.), Sigma Xi, Alpha Zeta, Rotary. *

BRADFORD, R(ICHARD) KNOX, railroad executive; b. Pine Bluff, Ark., May 30, 1896; s. James Turner and Helen Sparks (Knox) B.; m. Jane Elizabeth Campbell, Feb. 20, 1920; children: Helen Clair Wasley, Jane Elizabeth. Student, Randolph Macon Acad., Bedford, Va., 1911-12. With Rock Island R.R., Des Moines, 1913-23, St. Louis Southwestern Ry., 1915-16; trainmaster Rock Island, Amarillo, Tex., 1923; staff officer, various positions Denver & Rio Grande Western R.R., Denver; loaned as spl. examiner of railroad loans to railroad div. Reconstrn. Fin. Corp., Washington, 1938-39; asst. gen. mgr. Rio Grande Western R.R., Denver, 1939; exec. asst. to trustees Salt Lake City, 1942-47; v.p. D. & R. G. W. R.R., Salt Lake City, 1947-55; v.p. traffic D. & R. G. W. R.R., Denver, 1955-63, sr. v.p., from 1963; pres., dir. Rio Grande Land Co.; dir. Denver Market & Produce Terminal, Inc., Denver Union Terminal Railway Co. Mem. Newcomen Soc., Alta Club, Denver Club, Mile Hi Club, Denver Country Club, Uion League Club (Chgo.), Garden of the Gods Club (Colorado Springs, Colo.). Republican. *

BRADLEY, DAVID GILBERT, theology educator; b. Portland, Oreg., Sept. 1, 1916; s. Rowland Hill and Edith (Gilbert) B.; m. Gail Soules, Mar. 19, 1940 (dec. 1982); 1 child, Katherine Ann Bradley Johnson; m. Lorene L. Greuling, Dec. 27, 1984. A.B., U. So. Calif., 1938; postgrad., Drew Theol. Sem., 1938-39; B.D., Garrett Theol. Sem., 1942; M.A., Northwestern U., 1942; Ph.D., Yale U., 1947; postgrad., Sch. Oriental and African Studies, U. London, 1955-56. Asst. prof. religion, chaplain Western Md. Coll., 1946-49; mem. faculty dept. religion Duke U., Durham, 1949-92; prof. Duke U., 1970-86; retired, 1986; vis. prof. Garrett Sem., summer 1960, U. Va., summer 1969, U. N.C., Chapel Hill, 1970; mem. N.C. Conf. United Meth. Ch.; mem. Fulbright-Hays sr. screening com., religion, 1966-68. Author: A Guide to the World's Religions, 1963, Circles of Faith, 1966, The Origins of the Hortatory Materials in the Letters of Paul, 1977; contbr. articles to profl. jours. Pres. Durham Civic Choral Soc., 1959-60; mem. citizens adv. com. Durham Urban Renewal Program, 1965-67; treas. Durham Arts Council, 1968-69; pres. Durham Savoyards Ltd., 1976-77. Gt. Religions Fund fellow South and East Asia, 1969-70. Mem. Am. Acad. Religion (nat. program chmn. 1958, pres. So. sect. 1964), N.C. Tchrs. Religion (pres. 1961), Am. Soc. Study of Religion (sec. 1966-69, editor newsletter 1973-92), Assn. Asian Studies, AAUP (pres. Duke U. chpt. 1971-72), Soc. Internat. Devel. (chpt. sec.-treas. 1983-85). Democrat. Home: Durham N.C. Died Sept. 19, 1992. †

BRADLEY, DAVID RALL, SR., newspaper publisher; b. Toledo, Aug. 4, 1917; s. Henry D. and Alta Katherine (Rall) B.; m. Shirley Wyeth, Dec. 27, 1941; children: Margaret, Natalie, Henry, David Rall. A.B., U. Wis., 1939. Advt. salesman Bridgeport Times-Star, Conn., 1939-40, Headley-Reed Co., N.Y.C., 1941, Kelly-Smith Co., Chgo., 1942-43; nat. advt. mgr. News-Press & Gazette, St. Joseph, Mo., 1946; dir. News-Press & Gazette, 1947-88, sec.-treas., prodn. mgr., 1948-57, pub., 1956-81, pres., 1972-81, chmn. bd., 1972-88; dir.

Landmark Communications, Norfolk, Va.; pres. St. Joseph Indsl. Devel. Co.; chmn. bd. St. Joseph Cablevision, Macon Cablevision, Mo., WSAV-TV, Savannah, Ga., SDTV, Inc., Sioux Falls, S.D.; dir. Broadcasters Miss., Inc., Jackson, WECT-TV, Wilmington, N.C.; former dir., vice chmn. AP. Mem. Am. Newspaper Pubs. Assn., Newspaper Advt. Bur. (past dir.), Chi Psi. Presbyterian. Clubs: Masons; Country, Benton (St. Joseph). Home: Saint Joseph Mo. Died Mar. 6, 1988; buried St. Joseph Meml. Pk. Cemetery.

BRADLEY, HAROLD WHITMAN, history educator, state legislator; b. Greenwood, R.I., July 9, 1903; s. Harold and Lillian (Whitman) B.; m. Elizabeth Forbes, Aug. 28, 1940; 1 dau., Anne (Mrs. Philip Gronbach); m. Pearle E. Quinn, Dec. 5, 1947; 1 son, David. A.B., Pomona Coll., 1925, A.M., 1926; Ph.D., Stanford U., 1932. Tchr. Burbank High Sch., 1926-27; instr. Santa Barbara State Tchrs. Coll., 1929-30; instr. in history Stanford U., 1930-36, asst. prof., 1936-42, assoc. prof., 1942-45; asst. prof. history U. Wash., 1938-39; dean and prof. history Claremont (Calif.) Grad. Sch., 1945-53, prof. history, 1953-54; prof. history Vanderbilt U., 1954-72, prof. emeritus, from 1972, chmn. dept., 1954-62; lectr. in history U. Tenn., Nashville, 1973-78; Mem. Tenn. Ho. of Reps., 1964-72; Mem. com. on Am. History in Schs. and Colls., 1943. Author: The American Frontier in Hawaii, 1942, The United States 1492-1877, 1972, The United States Since 1865, 1973; Mem. bd. editors: Pacific Hist. Rev, 1940-54, Miss. Valley Hist. Rev, 1946-49; Contbr. to: Ency. Brit., Collier's Ency. Yearbook. Alternate del. Democratic Nat. Conv., 1952; mem. Charter Revision Commn. Nashville-Davidson County, from 1978. Recipient Albert J. Beveridge Meml. prize Am. Hist. Assn., 1943. Mem. Am., So. hist. assns., Orgn. Am. Historians, Am. Studies Assn. (pres. Ky.-Tenn. chpt. 1956-57, nat. council 1972-75), Phi Beta Kappa. Democrat (mem. Davidson County exec. com. 1960-62). Methodist. Home: Nashville Tenn. Died Dec. 7, 1990.

BRADLEY, NORMAN ROBERT, lawyer; b. Phila., May 24, 1917; s. William A. and Eliza (Gwinnutt) B.; m. Sharlee Merner Elsworth, June 24, 1978; children: Christine Bradley Jensen, Evelyn, Joan Bradley Masover, Suzy Elsworth Heithcock. A.B., U. Ala., 1939; J.D. with honors, Dickinson Sch. Law, 1942. Bar: Pa. 1942. Practice law Phila., 1946-82; ptnr. firm Saul, Ewing, Remick & Saul, Phila., 1963-82, head litigation dept., 1964-82; lectr. trial practice Temple U., 1974-75; mem. Commn. Jud. Selection, Retention and Eval., chmn. Com. Eval. Fed. Judges, 1979; mem. adv. bd. Acad. Advocacy to 1982; arbitrator for Am. Arbitration Assn., Calif. Pub. Employment Relations Bd., Calif. Mediation/Conciliation Service, Marin County (Calif.) Bar Assn. Mem. editorial bd. Dickinson Law Rev., 1941-42. Mem. budget rev. com. United Fund Phila. and vicinity, 1965-70, mem. central allocations com., 1968-70; trustee Unitarian Soc. Germantown, 1965-68; bd. dirs. World Affairs Council, Phila., 1975-79, mem. adv. bd., 1979-82; trustee, mem. exec. com. World Affairs Council No. Calif., chmn. Marin Steering com., 1985-86; mem. Marin County Grand Jury, 1985, chmn. law and justice com. Served to lt. USNR, 1942-46. Mem. ABA (life), Pa. Bar Assn. (life), Phila. Bar Assn. (life), Phila. Assn. Def. Counsel (v.p. 1978, pres. 1979), ACLU, Phi Beta Kappa, Theta Chi. Democrat. Clubs: Mt. Tam Racquet (Larkspur, Calif.); Tiburon (Calif.) Yacht; Sons in Retirement (San Rafael, Calif.). Home: Ross Calif. Died Aug. 22, 1991.

BRADSHAW, MELVIN B., insurance company executive; b. Peoria, Ill., 1922; grad. Bradley U., 1949; postgrad. Harvard U., 1968. Chmn. bd., chief exec. officer Liberty Mut. Ins. Co., Liberty Mut. Fire Ins. Co., Liberty Life Assurance Co. of Boston (all Boston), Liberty Mut. (Bermuda) Ltd., Liberty Mut. Mgmt. (Bermuda) Ltd., Hamilton; chmn. bd. Helmsman (Underwriting) Ltd., London, Liberty Mut. Ins. Co. (Mass.) Ltd., London; dir. Nat. Shawmut Bank of Boston, Shawmut Corp. Died 1991. Home: Newton Mass. †

BRADY, GEORGE K(EYPORTS), English language educator; b. Ft. Leavenworth, Kans., Oct. 16, 1893; s. Col. Jasper Ewing and Virginia Nelles (Wright) B.; m. Margaret Gordon, Apr. 12, 1919; children: Margaret, Virginia, Betty Ann. AB, U. Ill., 1915; AM, Harvard U., 1919; PhD, U. Ill., 1923. Prof. English Toledo U., 1923-25; asst. prof. English U. Ky., 1925-26, assoc. prof., 1926-37, prof. English, from 1937, dir. fgn. students orientation program; mem. Cultural Sci. Mission to Tokyo, Japan, 1948. 1st lt. U.S. Army, 1916-18. Mem. AAUP, Modern Lang. Assn., Phi Beta Kappa. *

BRAGG, JEFFERSON DAVIS, dean; b. Alexandria, La., Oct. 31, 1896; s. Jefferson Davis and Mary (Hilton) B.; m. Mildred Kathleen Rogers, July 23, 1919; children: Jefferson Davis, Mary Owens Stokes. AB, La. Coll., 1917; MA, Baylor U., 1924; PhD, U. Tex., 1938. Asst. prin. Bastrop (La.) High Sch., 1917-18; tchr. history and math. Pineville (La.) High Sch., 1919-20; tchr. history Waco (Tex.) High Sch., 1924-25; faculty mem. Baylor U., from 1925, prof., from 1945, chmn. dept. history, 1949-64, dean of men, 1931-33, dean of the grad. sch., from 1960. Author: Louisiana in the Confederacy, 1941. Mem. bd. Water Commrs., City of Waco, 1945-55; pres. S.W. Athletic Conf., 1951-53. Mem. So. Hist. Assn., Tex. State Hist. Assn., Mississippi Valley Hist. Assn., Am. Studies Assn., Alpha Chi (hon.), Pi Gamma Mu. Democrat. Baptist. *

BRAIS, F(RANCOIS) PHILIPPE, lawyer; b. Montreal, Que., Oct. 18, 1894; s. Narcisse Emilien and Blanche (Brunet) B.; m. Louise Dore, Feb. 24, 1925; children: J. Philippe, Louise Vaillancourt, Francoise Helene, Michelle Brault, Lucile. Student, Ste Marie de Monnoir Coll., St. Johns, Que., McGill U., Montreal; LLD (hon.), U. Montreal, 1945. Bar: Province of Quebec, 1917. Assoc. firm Brais, Campbell, Mercier & Pepper, Advs.; pres. Gen. Theatres Ltd., Quebec, Les Cinemas Odeon Ltee; dir. Woods Mfg. Co., Ltd., Wabassco Cotton Co., Ltd., Sun Life Assurance Co. of Can., Montreal Trust Co., Fraser Cos. Ltd., Can. Pacific Ry. Co., Can. Iron Foundries, Ltd., Golden Eagle Refining Co. of Can. Ltd.; chmn. bd. Banque Canadienne Nationale; dir. Can. Investment Fund, Ltd., Can. Fund, Inc.; chmn. Rediffusion, Inc.; mem. adv. bd. Sun Ins. Office Ltd., Patriotic Assurance Co., Ltd., London & County Ins. Co. Ltd., others. Apptd. to Legis. Coun. P.Q., 1940; vice chmn. Wartime Info. Bd., 1941-45; mem. Dominion Exec. and Joint Chmn., Quebec div., Nat. War Fin. Com., 1941-45; gov. Montreal Children's Hosp., Children's Meml. Hosp., Royal Edward Laurentian Hosp.; chmn. bd. govs. French Federated Charities, 1944-45; vice chmn. Can. Disaster Relief Fund, Inc.; nat. dir. Can. Coun. Christians and Jews; created King's Counsel, 1927; Batonnier Gen. of Province of Quebec, 1949-50. Mem. Can. Bar Assn. (pres. 1944-45), Montreal Bd. Trade (hon. life mem.), ABA, Mount Royal Club, St. Denis Club, Montreal Reform Club, Garrison (Quebec) Club, Seigniory Club, Rideau Club (Ottawa, Ont.). Roman Catholic. *

BRAISLIN, GORDON STUART, banker; b. Bklyn., Jan. 13, 1901; s. William C. and Alice (Cameron) B.; m. Esther Elizabeth Hamm, July 26, 1935 (dec. Sept. 1989); children: Elizabeth Cameron, Alice Stevenson, Gordon Stuart, William Stevenson. A.B., Cornell U., 1923. With Prudence Co., Inc., N.Y.C., 1924-30; pres. Realty Assocs. Mgmt., Inc., N.Y.C., 1931-38; founder Gordon S. Braislin, Inc., 1938; pres. (merged into Braislin, Porter & Baldwin, Inc., N.Y.C., Bklyn. and Westchester County, N.Y. 1942, merged into Braislin, Porter & Wheelock, Inc., N.Y.C., 1942-49, (Braislin, Porter & Wheelock, Inc.), 1949-65; trustee Dime Savs. Bank N.Y., 1946-76, chmn. trustees, chief exec. officer, 1965-74, vice chmn., 1975-76, mem. adv. council, from 1976; dir. Savs. Bank Trust Co., 1969-75; trustee Savs. Bank Life Ins. Fund, 1968-76, chmn., 1973-75. Trustee Bodman Found., Achelis Found.; bd. dirs., finance com. Am. Bible Soc.; trustee Bklyn. Inst. Arts and Scis., 1966-75; pres. N.Y. Eye and Ear Infirmary, 1961-77; trustee Roosevelt Hosp., 1961-77; bd. dirs. Bklyn. Eye and Ear Hosp., 1956-61, Community Blood Council Greater N.Y., 1963-76, Downtown Bklyn. Devel. Assn., 1965-75; founding mem. N.Y. Blood Ctr.; dir. Am. Bible Soc.; mem. operating com. Interch. Center, 1959-72; bd. mgrs. dept. missions Episcopal Diocese N.Y., 1956-60. Recipient Gold medal, 1973, Citizen's award Med. Soc. N.Y. County, 1975. Mem. Savs. Banks Assn. N.Y. State (dir. 1965-75), Soc. Colonial Wars, Phi Beta Kappa. Clubs: University, St. Nicholas Soc. (N.Y.C.); Brooklyn; Quaker Hill Country (Pawling, N.Y.). Home: New York N.Y. Died Apr. 3, 1990; buried Green Wood Cemetery, Bklyn.

BRANCH, CHARLES HENRY HARDIN, physician; b. Hopkinsville, Ky., Feb. 14, 1908; s. Charles Henry Hardin and Elisabeth Collins (Reed) B.; m. Erma Smith, Dec. 11, 1937; children—Robert Hardin, Alan Henry. A.B., U. Fla., 1928; M.D., Tulane U., 1935. Intern So. Pacific Hosp., San Francisco, 1935-36; prof., head dept. psychiatry U. Utah Coll. Medicine, 1948-70; emeritus clin. prof. U. So. Calif., from 1971; dir. Am. Bd. Psychiatry and Neurology, sec.-treas., 1961, pres., 1962; mem. nat. adv. mental health council NIMH, 1957-61, spl. cons., from 1961; nat. cons. psychiatry to surgeon gen. USAF, 1959-62; cons. psychiatry and neurology consultants br. Office Surgeon Gen., Dept. Army, from 1962; profl. adv. bd. Internat. Com. against Mental Illness. Mem. editorial bd. Am. Jour. Forensic Psychiatry; mem. editorial bd. emeritus Clin. Psychiatry News. Fellow A.C.P., Am. Geriatrics Soc., Am. Psychiat. Assn. (council, sec., pres. 1962-63), Royal Soc. Medicine, Am. Coll. Forensic Psychiatry; mem. , Nat. Assn. Mental Health (profl. adv. bd., dirs., pres. research found. 1965-69), AAAS, Pan Am. Med. Assn., Intermountain Psychiat. Assn., Nat. Acad. Religion and Mental Health, Sigma Xi. Home: San Diego Calif. Died June 22, 1990; buried Santa Barbara, Calif.

BRANCH, JUDSON B., insurance company executive. With Nat. Life Ins. Co. U.S.A., 1929-34; with Allstate Ins. Cos., Skokie, Ill., 1934-72, sr. v.p., 1954-57, pres., CEO, 1957-66, chmn. bd., CEO, 1966-72; past chmn. bd. Allstate Enterprises Stock Fund, Inc.; past bd. dirs. Allstate Ins. Co., Allstate Life, Alstadt Internat., Zurich, Switzerland, Nat. Coun. on Alcoholism; past chmn. Evanston Hosp. Assn.; past trustee Savs. and Profit Sharing Pension Fund Sears, Roebuck & Co. Employees. named Mktg. Man of Yr. Chgo. chpt. Am. Mktg. Assn., 1960; recipient Disting. Svc. award Fedn. Ins. Counsel, 1966. Mem. Econ. Club., Chgo., Mid-Am. Comml., Execs., Skokie Country, Sunset Ridge Country, Pauma Valley Country. Home: Northbrook Ill. Died Oct. 30, 1989.

BRAND, NEVILLE, actor; b. Kewanee, Ill., Aug. 13, 1921. Appeared in films D.O.A., 1949; Halls of Montezuma, 1951, Stalag 17, 1953, Riot in Cell Block Seven, 1954, Mohawk, 1955, The Tin Star, 1957, Cry Terror, 1958, Five Gates to Hell, 1959, The Scarface Mob, 1960, Huckleberry Finn, 1960, Birdman of Alcatraz, 1962, That Darn Cat, 1965, The Desperados, 1968, Scalawag, 1973, Cahill, U.S. Marshall, 1973, The Deadly Trackers, 1973, Psychic Killer, 1973, The Ninth Configuration, 1980, Without Warning, 1980; other shows appeared on TV in Laredo, 1965, The Captain and the Kings, The Seekers. Served with AUS, 1938-48. Home: Los Angeles Calif. Died Apr. 16, 1992.

BRAND, RAY MANNING, lawyer; b. N.Y.C., May 6, 1922; s. David and Mary (Honigman) B.; m. Edythe Bernstein, Sept. 17, 1928; children: Clifford, David, Patrice, Allison. LL.B., St. John's U., 1946. Bar: N.Y. 1946, U.S. Dist. Ct. (ea. and so. dists.) N.Y. 1947, U.S. Supreme Ct. 1961. Chmn., sr. ptnr. Brand & Brand, Garden City, N.Y., 1949-91; lectr. criminal law Nassau County Bar Assn. Mem. exec. com. Nassau County Dem. County Com., from 1960; chmn. Dem. Town Com., 1955-58. Capt. USAF, 1943-46. Decorated Air medal with 4 oak leaf clusters. Mem. N.Y. State Bar Assn., Nassau County Bar Assn., Assn. Trial Lawyers Am., N.Y. State Trial Lawyers Assn., Nassau County Criminal Bar Assn. (past pres.), Nat. Assn. Criminal Def. Attys., Internat. Platform Assn., Pine Hollow Country Club (East Norwich, N.Y.), Frenchmens Creek Club (North Palm Beach, Fla.), Masons. Died June 29, 1991. Home: Jericho N.Y.

BRANDON, ARTHUR LEON, educational consultant; b. Philippi, W.Va., May 18, 1898; s. Frank V. and Laura (Zinn) B.; m. Margaret C. Weddell, Mar. 12, 1923. BA, Broaddus Coll., 1927, D of Humane Letters, 1962; MA, Bucknell U., 1927; LLD, Okla. Bapt. U., 1936. Prof. journalism and English Okla. Bapt. U., 1927-29; asst. prof. bus. English, dir. publicity Bucknell U., 1929-33, asst. to pres., dir. pub. rels., 1933-35; exec. asst., assoc. dir. Youth Commn. of Am. Coun. on Edn., 1935-39; dir. pub. rels., assoc. prof. journalism U. Tex., 1939-43; dir. spl. svcs. Vanderbilt U., 1943-45; dir. U. rels., prof. journalism U. Mich., 1946-57; dir. Univ. Devel. Coun., 1953-57; v.p. for u. rels. NYU, 1957-64, spl. asst. to pres. and chancellor, from 1964; exec. com. Inst. Social Rsch., Ann Arbor, 1947-57; mem. publs. coun. NYU Press, from 1958, chmn., 1960-62; chmn. policy bd. Inst. Econ. Affairs, N.Y., from 1962; com. pub. rels. N.Y.C. Coun. Higher Edn., from 1958, chmn., 1960-62; chmn. ad hoc commn. standards and accreditation svcs. for blind Am. Found. Blind. Author: Post-war Problems of American Colleges, 1944; co-author: How Fare American Youth, 1938; contbr. articles to various ednl. jours. Trustee Bucknell U., 1951-56, from 1963, adv. com. on econs., bus. adminstrn., from 1959, mem. devel. coun., from 1961; trustee Alderson-Broaddus Coll., 1936-40, chmn. adv. bd. govs., from 1959. Seaman USN, WWI. Mem. Am. Coll. Pub. Rels. Assn. (pres. 1944-46, v.p. 1941-44, disting. svc. award 1947, outstanding achievement award 1957, nat. program chmn. 1960, keynote speaker 1963), NYU Hon. Soc., Phi Kappa Sigma, Sigma Delta Chi, N.Y. U. Club, U. Faculty Club, Univ. Press. of Mich. Club (sec. 1946-53). Baptist. *

BRANDT, CARL GUNARD, educator; b. Ludington, Mich., Sept. 20, 1897; s. Charles H. and Mary (Carlson) B. LLB, U. Mich., 1921, LLM, 1922. Bar: Wis. 1922, Ill. 1929. Mem. faculty dept. speech U. Mich., 1920-28; prof. English and chmn. dept. English U. Mich., Coll. Engring., from 1937; lectr. in speech U. Mich., Coll. of Lit., Sci. and the Arts, from 1937; bus. mgr. Oratorical Assn. Lecture Course, from 1933. Co-editor: Selected American Speeches on Basic Issues. Mem. Speech Assn. Am., Am. Soc. for Engring. Edn., Delta Sigma Rho, Delta Theta Phi, Mason. Presbyterian. *

BRANDT, WILLY, former chancellor of Federal Republic of Germany; b. Lübeck, Germany, Dec. 18, 1913; m. Carlotta Thorkildson, 1941; 1 dau., Ninja; m. 2d, Rut Hansen, 1948; children: Peter, Lars, Matthias; m. 3d, Brigitte Seebacher, 1983. Student, Latin Sch., Lübeck; student history, U. Oslo, Norway; abitur Johanneum; Dr. (hon.), U. Pa., Harvard, Yale, St. Andrews, Oxford U.; LL.D., U. Md., 1960; hon. degree, Moscow State U., 1989. Journalist Norway, Sweden, 1933-45; journalist Scandinavian newspapers, press cooperator diplomatic rep. Berlin, 1945-47; chief editor Berlin Stadtblatt, 1950-51; mem. House of Reps., Berlin, 1950-66; governing mayor West Berlin, 1957-66; fgn. minister, dep. chancellor Fed. Republic Germany, Bonn, 1966-69, chancellor, 1969-74; mem. German Bundestag, 1949-57, 61-92; pres. German Bundesrat, 1957-58, v.p., 1958-59; pres. Deutscher Staedtetag (Conf. German mayors), 1958-63; mem. European Parliament, 1979-83. Chmn. bd. dirs. Berliner Bank. Rep. in Berlin, directive com. Social Dem. Party, 1948-49, mem. provincial com., Berlin, 1950-63, dep. chmn., 1954-58, 1950-70, chmn., 1958-63, dep. chmn., Germany, 1962-64, party chmn., 1964-87, candidate for chancellorship, 1961, 65; pres. Socialists Internat., 1976-92; chmn. Ind. Commn. on Devel. Issues, 1977-80; hon. chmn. Party of Dem. Socialism, Berlin, 1990-92. Author: Peace Politics in

Europe, 1968; The Ordeal of Co-Existence, 1963; Begegnung mit Kennedy, 1964; People and Politics 1960-75, 1978; Frauenheute, 1978; Links und Frei, 1982, Erinnerungen, 1989. Hon. pres. provincial com. German Red Cross; chmn. governing bodies Free U. Tech. U. Berlin. Decorated Grosses Verdienstkreuz (Germany); Star of Uprising 1st Class (Jordan); grand cross Order of St. Olaf (Norway); grand cross Order of King of Greece; recipient Freedom House award, 1961, Nobel Peace prize, 1971, Reinhold Niebuhr award, 1972, Aspen Inst. Humanities Studies prize, 1973, numerous others. Mem. S.S. Soc. Berlin, Soc. Germany Indivisable (exec. com.), German Hort. Soc., Bonn Germann Soc. Fgn. Politics, Soc. Christian-Jewish Coop., Ernest Reuter Soc., German Soc. UN, Max Planck Gesellschaft (senator). Home: Bonn Germany Died Oct. 8, 1992. †

BRANSCOMB, HARVIE, chancellor; b. Huntsville, Ala., Dec. 25, 1894; s. Lewis Capers and Nancy (McAdory) B.; m. Margaret Vaughan, June 15, 1921; children: Harvie, Ben Vaughan, Lewis McAdory. BA, Birmingham-So. Coll., 1914, DLitt; Rhodes scholar, Oxford U., 1914-17, BA and MA; PhD, Columbia U., 1924, LLD (hon.), 1954; LLD (hon.), Southwestern Coll., 1954, Brandeis U., 1958, Northwestern U., 1958; DLH, Hebrew Union Coll.; LHD, So. Methodist U., 1961. Adj. prof. philosophy So. Meth. U., 1919-20, assoc. prof. N.T., 1920-21, prof., 1921-25; prof. N.T. Divinity Sch., Duke U., 1925-45, dean, 1945-46, dir. librs., 1934-41, chmn. div. of ancient langs. and lits., 1937-44; chancellor Vanderbilt U., 1946-63, chancellor emeritus, from 1963; ednl. cons. Internat. Bank for Reconstrn. and Devel., 1963-64; chmn. U.S. Nat. Commn. for UNESCO, from 1963; vice chmn. U.S. Delegation to UNESCO Gen. Conf., 1964; mem. Nat. Adv. Health Coun.; dir. Libr. Project of Assn. Am. Colls., 1937-38. Editor: The Am. Oxonian, 1943-46, Jesus and the Law of Moses, 1930, The Teachings of Jesus, 1931, The Gospel of Mark, 1937, Teaching with Books, 1940. Bd. dirs. Colonial Williamsburg (Va.) Gen. Edn. Bd., Cordell Hull Found. for Internat. Edn.; chmn. Commn. of Am. Libr Assn. to Brazil, 1945; chmn. U.S. Adv. Commn. for Ednl. Exchange, 1947-51; with commn. for relief in Belgium, 1914-15. Pvt. F.A., O.T.S., 1918. Recipient Medaille du Roi Albert, Medaille de la Reine, Belgium, Order So. Cross, Brazil. Mem. Soc. Bibl. Lit. and Exegesis, Assn. of Am. Rhodes Scholars, ALA, Am. Coun. on Edn. (chmn. commn. on edn. and internat. affairs), Sigma Alpha Epsilon, Phi Beta Kappa, Cumberland Club, Belle Meade Country Club, Century Assn. Club (N.Y.). Methodist. *

BRATBY, JOHN R.A., painter, author; b. July 19, 1928; s. George Alfred and Lily (Randall) B.; m. Jean Cooke, 1953 (div.); 4 children; m. Patti Prime, 1977. Ed. Kingston Art Sch., Royal Coll. Art, London; DLitt (hon), U. Birmingham. Works exhibited in Tate Gallery, London, Nat. Gallery Can., Nat. Gallery New South Wales, Mus. Modern Art, N.Y.C., Walker Art Gallery, Arts Council, Glasgow Mus. Art, numerous others; numerous one-man exhbns.; rep.: Pittsburgh Internat. Festival, 1955, 57, Venice Biennale, 1956; executed painting for film The Horse's Mouth, 1958; author: Breakdown, 1960, Breakfast and Elevenses, 1961, Brake-Pedal Down, 1962, Break 50 Kill, 1963, Stanley Spencer, 1969, The Devils, 1984, Apocryphal Letters by Edward Lowerby, 1985; maj. exhbn. Nat. Portrait Galley, 1991; editor-in-chief Art Quarterly, 1987-92. Recipient Guggenheim Nat. award, 1956, 58. Died July 20, 1992. Home: Hastings Eng. †

BRAUDE, JACOB MORTON, justice, writer; b. Chgo., Dec. 13, 1896; s. Emil and Anna (Kaplan) B.; m. Adele Covy Englander, Feb. 22, 1946; children: Ann, Jane (Mrs. David M. Berkson). AB cum laude, U. Mich., 1918; grad., Northwestern, 1919; JD, U. Chgo., 1920. Bar: Ill. 1920. Atty. Chgo., 1920-27; counsel Nat. Jewelers Bd. Trade, 1927-33; asst. atty. gen., assoc. dir. fin. State of Ill., 1933-34; judge Mcpl. Ct., Chgo., 1934-56; presiding judge Chgo. Boys' Ct., 1938-45; judge Cir. Cts. Ill., Cook County, from 1956; chief justice, 1960-61; Lectr. juvenile delinquency. Author: I Like Bad Boys, 1939, Speakers Encyclopedia of Stories, Quotations and Anecdotes, 1955, Braude's Second Encyclopedia of Stories, Quotations and Anecdotes, 1957, Braude's Handbook of Humor for All Occassions, 1958, New Treasury of Stories for Every Speaking and Writing Occassion, 1959, Speaker's Encyclopedia of Humor, 1961, Lifetime Speaker's Encyclopedia, 2 vols., 1962, Quips, Quotes and Anecdotes, 1963, Braude's Treasury of Wit and Humor, 1964, Complete Speaker's and Toastmaster's Library, 9 vols., 1965; contbr. mags. Active Citizens Com. on Parole; pres. Portal Ho. Clinic for Treatment Alcoholics, Chgo. Commn. Alcoholism, Org. which supports Am. Boys' Commonwealth, Deborah Boys' Club, Albany Park Boy's Club, Camp Wooster; nat. v.p. Com. for advancememt Am. Judaism, 1954-55; chmn. Chgo. divsn. Am. Jewish Com.; chmn. bd. Judge Bishop Bernard J. Sheil Youth of Yr. award, from 1952; del.-at-large Chgo. Coun. Social Agys.; v.p. Chgo. Conf. for Youth; active Citizens Com. Loyola U.; adv. bd. Chgo. Nat. Coun. Family Rels., World Youth, Nat. Assn. for Gifted Children, St. Leonard's House; bd. dirs. Jewish Children's Bur., Big Bro. Assn. Ill., Juvenile Protective Assn. Served as 2d lt. F.A., U.S. Army, 1918. Mem. ABA, Ill. Bar Assn., Chgo. Bar Assn., Am. Judicature Soc. Chgo. (pres.), Ill. (pres. from 1950), acads. criminology, Soc. Midland Authors, Decalogue Soc., Ill. Soc. for Mental Hygiene (v.p.), Mil. Order World Wars, Am. Legion, 40 and 8, City Club, Standard Club (Chgo.), Masons (past master), Beta Phi. Democrat. Jewish. *

BRAZELTON, FRANK ALEXANDER, optometry educator; b. Chgo., May 22, 1926; s. Frank Alexander and Katharine (Keating) B.; m. Margaret Bernice Shean, Aug. 15, 1948 (div. 1971); children: Stephen, Martin, Claire, Kathleen. B in Vision Sci., Los Angeles Coll. Optometry, 1950, OD, 1951; MS in Edn., U. So. Calif., 1975. Asst. prof. So. Calif. Coll. Optometry, Fullerton, 1955-58, assoc. prof., 1958-65, prof. optometry, from 1965, dean acad. affairs, 1984-85, assoc. dean faculty affairs, from 1985. Author: Handbook for Optometric Educators, 1978; also articles. Served with USNR, 1943-46, PTO. Fellow Am. Acad. Optometry (diplomate in low vision, sec.-treas. 1982-84, pres. from 1986); mem. AAAS, AAUP. Democrat. Roman Catholic. Home: Covina Calif. Deceased. †

BRECHER, EDWARD MORITZ, author; b. Mpls., July 20, 1911; s. Hans and Rhodessa (Roston) B.; m. Ruth Ernestine Cook Stilson, Dec. 27, 1941 (dec. 1966); children—William Earl, John Samuel, Jeremy Hans. Student, U. Wis. Exptl. Coll., 1928-30; BA magna cum laude, Swarthmore Coll., 1932; MA, U. Minn., 1934; postgrad., Brown U., 1934-35. Writer Compton's Pictured Ency., Chgo., 1936-37; research supr. U.S. Senate Com. on Interstate Commerce, 1938-41; research supr., asst. to chmn. FCC, Washington, 1941-46; asso. editor Consumer Reports, N.Y.C., 1947-51; editor Tech. Assistance Adminstrn., UN, 1951-52; free lance writer, from 1952; Lectr. on sex research and illicit drugs various colls. and med. schs., from 1969; mem. ad hoc com. Treatment and Prevention of Drug Addiction and Drug Abuse, Washington, 1970; cons. to Ford Found., 1975-77, Kinsey Inst., 1986-87. Author: (with Ruth E. Brecher) Medical and Hospital Benefit Plans, 1961, (with Ruth E. Brecher and others) Consumers Union Report on Smoking and the Public Interest, 1963, (with Ruth E. Brecher) An Analysis of Human Sexual Response, 1966, The Rays: A History of Radiology in the U.S. and Canada, 1968, The Sex Researchers, 1969, expanded edit, 1979, Licit and Illicit Drugs, 1972, Methadone Treatment Manual, 1973, Health Care in Correctional Institutions, 1975, Treatment Programs for Sex Offenders, 1977, Love, Sex, and Aging: A Consumers Union Report, 1984; appeared in lead role Ripple of Time, 1974, Les Amies, 1978. Justice of peace Town of Cornwall, Conn., from 1966, mem. bd. fin. 1963-74, mem. bd. assessors, 1974-78. Recipient George Polk Meml. award, Robert T. Morse Meml. award Am. Psychiat. Assn., 1971, Ellie award Am. Soc. Mag. Editors, 1975, (with wife) Albert Lasker Meml. award Lasker Found., 1963, (with wife) Robert T. Morse Writer's award Am. Psychiat. Assn. Fellow Soc. Sci. Study of Sex; mem. Nat. Assn. Sci. Writers, Yelping Hill Assn. Home: West Cornwall Conn. Died Apr. 1, 1989; cremated.

BRECK, HENRY C(USHMAN), investment banker; b. Oakland, Calif., Mar. 3, 1893; s. Samuel and Florence Mabel (Coffin) B.; m. Dorothy Reynolds, Dec. 10, 1917; 1 child, Henry Reynolds. BS, U. Calif., 1914, grad. student, 1915. Sec. to mem. Fed. Res. Bd., Washington, 1916-17; asst. to U.S. fin. rep. Peace Conf., Paris, 1919; asst. to Fed. Res. agt. Fed. Res. Bank, San Francisco, 1920-21; exec. asst. to agt. gen. for reparations payments Berlin, 1924-26; with J. & W. Selgman & Co.; mem. N.Y. Stock Exchange, from 1926; v.p., dir., chmn. exec. com. Tri-Continental Fin. Corp.; v.p., dir., mem. exec. com. Tri-Continental Corp.; dir. Holly Sugar Corp.; mem. U.S. adv. com. Royal Exchange Assurance; mem. U.S. bd. of Comml. Union Groups of Fire Ins. Cos. Treas. Rec. for the Blind, N.Y.C. 1st lt. U.S. Army, 1917-19. Mem. Alpha Delta Phi, Phi Delta Phi, Phi Beta Kappa, Beta Gamma Sigma, Piping Rock Club (L.I.), Racquet and Tennis Club, River Club, Links Club, Brook Club (N.Y.C.). Episcopalian. *

BREEDEN, EDWARD LEBBAEUS, JR., lawyer, state senator; b. Norfolk, Va., Jan. 28, 1905; s. Edward L. and Cora Lee (McCloud) B.; m. Willie Holland, Sept. 8, 1928 (dec.); m. Virginia Hurt Sneed, Apr. 16, 1966. Student, Hampden-Sydney Coll., LL.D. (hon.), 1973; student, George Washington U. Law Sch. Bar: Va. 1927. Mem. Va. State Ho. of Dels., 1936-44, Va. Senate, 1944-72; past pres., chmn. bd. 1st Va. Bank of Tidewater; dir. Va. Port Authority, 1st Va. Life Ins. Co., 1st Va. Banks Inc. (trustee emeritus); trustee, past pres. Hunter Found.; bd. dirs. Med. Ctr. Hosps., Norfolk; mem. Va. Adv. Legis. Coun., 1944, chmn., 1946; mem. Va. Gov.'s Adv. Bd. on Budget, 1968-72. Mem. Am., Va., Norfolk-Portsmouth bar assns., Kappa Sigma. Presbyn. (elder). Clubs: Virginia, Norfolk Yacht and Country, Harbor (Norfolk). Home: Norfolk Va. Died June 1, 1990; buried Norfolk, Va.

BREITEL, CHARLES D., lawyer, judge; b. N.Y.C., Dec. 12, 1908; s. Herman L. and Regina D. (Zuckerberg) B.; m. Jeanne S. Hollander, Apr. 9, 1927; children: Eleanor Breitel Alter, Sharon H. (dec.), Vivian H. A.B., U. Mich., 1929; LL.B., Columbia U., 1932, LL.D. (hon.), 1978; LL.D., L.I. U., 1953, Yeshiva U., 1974, N.Y. Law Sch., 1975, Siena Coll., 1980; L.H.D. (hon.), Hebrew Union, 1979; LL.D. (hon.), Union U., 1986. Bar: N.Y. 1933. Assoc. Moers & Rosenschein, 1933, Engelhard, Pollak, Pitcher, Stern & Clarke, 1934-35; dep. asst. dist. atty., staff Thomas E. Dewey, 1935-37; dep. asst. dist. atty. for spl. rackets investigations, 1938-41; chief Indictment Bur., 1941; asso. with Dewey pvt. law practice, 1942; counsel to Gov. Dewey, 1943-50; apptd. justice State Supreme Ct., 1950; assoc. justice Appellate Div., First Dept., 1952-66; judge Ct. Appeals State N.Y., 1967-73, chief judge, 1974-78; of counsel Proskauer Rose Goetz & Mendelsohn, N.Y.C., 1978-85; adj. prof. Columbia Sch. Law, 1963-69; also mem. bd. visitors. Mem. Pres.'s Commn. on Law Enforcement and Adminstrn. of Justice, 1965-67; mem. Fed. Commn. on Internat. Rules Jud. Procedure, 1958-66, N.Y. State Post War Pub. Works Planning Commn., 1943-45, Joint Legis. Com. on Interstate Cooperation (adminstr.), 1946, Gov's Com. on State Ednl. Program, 1945-47, Commn. Mcpl. Revenues and Reduction of Taxes, 1945-46; mem. adminstrv. tribunal Inter-Am. Devel. Bank, 1982-88; mem. jud. panel Ctr. Pub. Resources, from 1982. Mem. exec. com. N.Y. chpt. Am. Jewish Com., also mem. nat. bd. govs.; chmn. 20th Century Fund Task Force, 1979. Fellow Am. Soc. Arts and Scis., Am. Bar Found. (hon.); mem. Am. Law Inst., Inst. Jud. Adminstrn., Assn. Bar City N.Y. (past v.p.), N.Y. County Lawyers Assn., ABA, N.Y. State Bar Assn. Club: Century (N.Y.C.). Lodge: B'nai B'rith. Home: New York N.Y. Died Dec. 1, 1991; cremated.

BREM, THOMAS HAMILTON, physician; b. C.Z., 1910. MD, Johns Hopkins, 1937. Intern Johns Hopkins Hosp., Balt., 1937-38; asst. pathology Stanford, 1938-39; resident physician L.A. County Gen. Hosp., 1939-41, past. mem. attending staff; past cons. VA Hosp., Long Beach, Calif.; past physician-in-chief L.A. County Hosp.; past prof., head dept. medicine U. So. Calif. Capt. AUS, 1542-45. Past fellow ACP; past mem. AMA, Assn. Am. Physicians, Alpha Omega Alpha. Home: Los Angeles Calif. Died Mar. 8, 1990.

BRENEMAN, GERALD MYERS, physician, educator; b. Lancaster, Pa., July 11, 1924; s. Ira Stetler and Emma Ruth (Myers) B.; m. Patricia Jane Waurzyniak, July 1, 1950; children: Christopher, Hilary Ann. B.S., Franklin and Marshall Coll., 1944; M.D., Jefferson Med. Coll., 1949. Diplomate Am. Bd. Internal Medicine, Am. Bd. Cardiovascular Disease. Intern Henry Ford Hosp., Detroit, 1949-50, resident in internal medicine, 1952-54, resident in cardiovascular diseases, 1954-55, assoc. physician div. cardiovascular diseases, 1955-74, sr. assoc. physician, 1974-89; past clin. asst. prof. medicine U. Mich. Author, co-author sci. papers. Trustee Mich. Heart Assn., from 1968, pres., 1971-72. Served with M.C., USNR, 1950-52. Fellow ACP, Am. Coll. Cardiology, Am. Coll. Chest Physicians; mem. Phi Beta Kappa, Alpha Omega Alpha. Republican. Methodist. Clubs: Franklin Racquet (Mich.); Oakland County Sportsmen's (Waterford, Mich.). Home: Farmington Hills Mich. Died Aug. 21, 1990; cremated.

BRENEMAN, WILLIAM RAYMOND, educator; b. Indpls., June 3, 1907; s. William Trytle and Minnie Nell (Stephenson) B.; m. Mary Alice Petty, Sept. 13, 1930; children: William Louis, Raymond Bruce, Miriam Eilene. AB, Ind. Central Coll., 1930, LLD, 1962; PhD, Ind. U., 1934. NRC fellow U. Wis., 1934-35; instr. zoology Miami U., Oxford, Ohio, 1935-36; mem. faculty Ind. U., 1936-92, Waterman prof. zoology, 1962-92, chmn. dept. zoology, 1966-68; spl. rsch. avian endocrinology. Author: Animal Form and Function, 1954; also rsch. articles. Recipient Liever award for disting. teaching Ind. U., 1955. Fellow Ind. Acad. Sci.; mem. AAAS, Am. Soc. Zoologists, Poultry Sci. Assn., World Poultry Congress, N.Y. Acad. Scis., Sigma Xi. Home: Bloomington Ind. Died Jan. 31, 1992.

BRENNER, EDWARD JOHN, lawyer; b. Wisconsin Rapids, Wis., June 26, 1923; s. Edward Charles and Lillian (Hephner) B.; m. Jane Segrest, June 1, 1951; children: Beverly, Douglas, Carolyn, Mary. BS in Chem. Engring, U. Wis., 1947, MS, 1948, JD, 1950. Bar: Wis. 1950, D.C. 1970, Va. 1971. Chem. engr. Esso Standard Oil Co., 1950-53; with Esso Research and Engring. Co., 1953-64, asst. dir. legal div., 1960-64; U.S. commr. patents, 1964-69; v.p., asst. to pres. Gen. Instrument Corp., 1969-70; pvt. practice patent law Arlington, Va., 1970-92. Served with U.S. Army, 1944-46. Mem. Am., Wis., Va. Bar Assns., Bar Assn. D.C., Am., N.J. Patent Law Assns., Am. Chem. Soc. Home: Punta Gorda Fla. Died June 15, 1992. †

BRESLIN, GEORGE M(ONTGOMERY), lawyer; b. L.A., Oct. 7, 1895; s. Thomas Peter and Mary Agnes (Murphy) B.; m. Katharine O'Brien, May 21, 1919 (dec. 1924); 1 child, George Montgomery; m. Agnes Gertrude Scully, Sept. 9, 1926; children: Marie, Anne, Janet, Barbara, Eileen, Carolyn. LLB, U. So. Calif., 1917; LLD (hon.), Loyola U., L.A., 1924. Bar: Calif. 1917. Mem. Smith & Breslin, L.A., 1917-34; pvt. practice, 1934-39; mem. Bodkin, Breslin & Luddy, from 1939; pres., dir. Standard Packing Co., from 1938; dir. Calif. Bank, from 1939. Mem. bd. regents Loyola U., L.A., 1932-50. Ensign USNRF, 1917-19. Deocrated Knight of Malta. Mem. ABA, Calif. State Bar Assn., L.A. Bar Assn. (past pres.), Native Sons Golden West, Hist. Soc. So. Calif., Phi Delta Phi, Elk (past exalted ruler), K.C., Calif. Club, Bel-Air Ray Club, Newman Club. Republican. *

BREWER, EDWARD EUGENE, tire and rubber company executive; b. Findlay, Ohio, July 19, 1925; s. William B. and Edna (Hurrel) B.; m. Joyce K. Josephsen, Feb. 7, 1948; children: Stephen, Rebecca, Mary, Sara, Debra. B.S. in Mech. Engring., Purdue U., 1949. With Cooper Tire & Rubber Co., Findlay, 1949-56, v.p., 1956-70, exec. v.p., 1970-77, pres., chmn. bd., 1977-82, chmn. bd., chief exec. officer, from 1982. Home: Clearwater Fla. Died Aug. 9, 1992. †

BREWTON, JOHN E., educator; b. Brewton, Ala., Dec. 18, 1898; s. John Edmund and Mamie (Solomon) B.; m. Sara Westbrook, Apr. 12, 1924; 1 child, Betty. AB, Howard Coll., Birmingham, Ala., 1922; student, Columbia U., summer 1923; AM, George Peabody Coll. for Tchr., Nashville, Tenn., 1931; PhD, George Peabody Coll. for Tchr., 1933. Instr. English Howard Coll., summer 1922; head English dept. Leon High Sch., Tallahassee, Fla., 1924-25; instr. Fla. State Coll. for Women, summer 1925; supt. Quincy (Fla.) Pub. Schs., 1925-34; profl. asst. div. surveys and field svcs. George Peabody Coll. for Tchrs., 1934-35; dir. bur. of rsch. Louisville (Ky.) Pub. Schs., 1935-37; instr. U. Louisville, 1936-37, Emory U., Atlanta, summer 1937; prof. edn. and assoc. dir., dir. surveys and field svcs. George Peabody Coll. Tchrs., 1937-42, prof. edn., dean of Grad. Sch., acting dir. div. surveys, 1943-45, acting pres., 1944-45, dir. divsn. surveys and field svcs., 1945-51, head English dept., from 1951; cons. to dept. edn. Fisk U., Nashville, Tenn., 1940-44; dir. so. rural life coun. sponsored jointly by George Peabody Coll. for Tchrs., Vanderbilt U., Scarritt Coll. and Fisk U., 1943-49. Editor: Jour. of Fla. Edn. Assn., 1928-29; compiler: Gaily We Parade, 1940, Bridled With Rainbows, 1949, Christmas Bells Are Ringing, 1951, Sing a Song of Seasons, 1955, Birthday Candles Burning Bright, 1960; author: Index to Children's Poetry, 1942, 1st Supplement, 1954, 2d Supplement, 1965; also author, co-author or compiler textbooks. Mem. Com. on So. Regional Studies and Edn., Am. Ednl. Rsch. Assn., NEA (rural edn. dept., dept. suprs. and dist. instrn.), Phi Delta Kappa. *

BRICE, ASHBEL GREEN, publishing company executive; b. York, S.C., July 21, 1915; s. John Steele and Claudia Wilkie (Moore) B. A.B., Columbia U., 1936, M.A., 1937; postgrad., Duke U., 1937-39. Instr. dept. English Duke, Durham, N.C., 1939-45, North Tex. State Tchrs. Coll., 1940, Coll. City N.Y., summers 1937-42; joined Duke U. Press, 1945, asst. editor, 1945-47, editor, asso. dir., 1947-51, dir., editor, 1951-81. Mem. Assn. Am. U. Presses (dir. 1965-66). Democrat. Presbyterian. Home: Durham N.C. Died Dec. 15, 1988.

BRICKWEDDE, FERDINAND GRAFT, physicist; b. Balt., Mar. 26, 1903; s. Ferdinarnd Henry and Virginia (Graft) B.; m. Marion Langhorne Howard, July 28, 1934; children: Marion Virginia (dec.), Ruth Lance Cooper, Langhorne Virginia. AB, Johns Hopkins, 1922, MA, 1924, PhD, 1925. Rsch. assoc. Nat. Bur. Standards, Washington, 1925-26; chief low temperature lab, 1926-46, chief thermodynamics sect., 1946-52, chief heat and power div., 1946-56, cons. to dir., 1957-62; part-time prof. physics U. Md., 1942-56; dean Coll. Chemistry and Physics, prof. chemistry and physics Pa. State U., 1956-63; Evan Pugh rsch. prof. physics, 1963-68, Evan Pugh rsch. prof. physics emeritus, 1968—; on leave of absence U. Cal. Radiation Lab., Livermore, 1952-53; initiated NBS Cryogenic Engring. Lab., Boulder, Colo., headed group designed liquefaction plant, 1950-53; cons. Los Alamos Sci. Lab., 1948-72; mem. NRC div. math. and phys. scis., 1944-47, mem. exec. com., 1945, mem. commn. on very low temperature physics Internal Union Pure and Applied Physics, 1948-57; mem. Commn. 1 for cryophysics and cryoengring. in Internat. Inst. Refrigeration, 1957-72, also v.p. Commn. 1, mem. U.S. nat. com., 1957-63; chmn. com. on Physics Abstracts Am. Inst. Physics, 1959-67; mem. adv. com. on thermonetry Internat. Com. Weights and Measures, 1958—, chmn. 2 internat. working groups in thermonetry, 1962-67, pres. adv. com., 1965-68; mem. NRC evaluation panel, heat div. Nat. Bur. Standards, 1974-77. Co-discover of a heavy isotope of hydrogen, deuterium; contbr. articles in fields physics and phys. chemistry. Am. del. Internat. Union Pure and Applied Physics, Amsterdam, 1948, 10th Internat. Congress on Refrigeration, Copenhagen, 1959, 11th Congress, Munich, 1963. Recipient Hillebrand prize Chem. Soc. Washington, 1940; Washington Acad. award, 1941. Fellow Am. Phys. Soc. (mem. council 1940-43, treas. div. chem. physics 1952-58, bd. editors for Phys. Rev. 1952-54), Acoustical Soc. Am., AAAS, Wash. Acad. Scis. (v.p. 1939); mem. Am. Chem. Soc. Am. Assn. Physics Tchrs., Philos. Soc. Washington (pres. 1939), Am. Inst. Physics (assoc. editor Jour. Chem. Physics 1935-37, Physics of Fluids 1960-62), Sigma Xi (pres. D.C. prof. chpt. 1950-51), Mason, Cosmos Club (Washington). Home: University Park Pa. Died Mar. 29, 1989; buried Memorial Park, State Coll., Pa.

BRIDENBAUGH, CARL, historian, writer; b. Phila., Aug. 10, 1903; s. Charles Herbert and Mabel (Corbin) B.; m. Jessica Hill, Sept. 8, 1931 (dec. 1943); m. 2d Roberta Haines Herriott, June 17, 1944. BS, Dartmouth Coll., 1925, Litt.D, 1958; student, U. Pa., 1925-27; AM, Harvard U., 1930, PhD, 1936; AM, Brown U., 1963; LHD, R.I. Coll., 1976. Instr. English and history MIT, 1927-29, 30-34, asst. prof. history, 1934-38; assoc. prof. history Brown U., Providence, 1938-42, Univ. prof., 1962-69; lectr. history Coll. William and Mary, 1945-46; dir. Inst. Early Am. History and Culture, Williamsburg, Va., 1945-50; Margaret Byrne prof. Am. history U. Calif., Berkeley, 1950-62; specialist U.S. State Dept., India, 1956; mem. adminstrv. bd. Papers of Benjamin Franklin, 1970-92; mem. Hist. Am. Bldgs. Survey, 1957-62; cons. Am. civilization to U.S. Nat. Commn. for UNESCO, 1957-60, Commn. for Humanities, 1962-64. Author: Cities in the Wilderness, 1938, (with Jessica Bridenbaugh) Rebels and Gentlemen, 1942, Peter Harrison, 1949, Seat of Empire, 1950, Colonial Craftsman, 1950, Myths and Realities, 1952, Cities in Revolt, 1955, Mitre and Sceptre, 1962, Vexed and Troubled Englishmen, 1590-1640, 1968, (with Roberta Bridenbaugh) No Peace Beyond the Line, 1971, Silas Downer: Forgotten Patriot, 1974, Fat Mutton and Liberty of Conscience, Society in Rhode Island 1636-1690, 1974, others; contbr. revs. to papers. Lt. comdr. USNR, 1942-44. Recipient award Internat. Berkeley Soc., 1977, Merit award Am. Soc. State and Local History, 1952, 75; fellow Ctr. for Advanced Study in Behavioral Scis., 1965-66; Guggenheim fellow, 1958, 62, 68. Fellow Royal Hist. Soc., Am. Acad. Arts and Scis., R.I. Hist. Soc.; mem. Am. Philos. Soc., Am. Antiquarian Soc., Am. Hist. Assn. (pres. 1962), Soc. Cincinnati (hon.), Colonial Soc. Mass., Mass. Hist. Soc., Providence Art Club, Phi Beta Kappa. Home: Providence R.I. Died Jan. 6, 1992.

BRIDGES, HARRY (ALFRED RENTON BRIDGES), union official; b. Melbourne, Australia, July 28, 1901; s. Alfred Ernest and Julia (Dorgan) B.; m. Agnes Brown, Dec., 1923; 1 child, Jacqueline; m. 2d, Nancy Berdico; children: Julie Ellen, Robert Alfred; m. 3d, Noriko Sawada; 1 child, Katherine. Edn., St. Brennan's Parochial Sch., Melbourne. Joined Internat. Longshoremen's Assn., 1920; leader strike against Pacific Coast shipowners, 1934; past pres. Pacific Coast dist. Internat. Longshoremen's Assn.; organizer Maritime Fedn. of Pacific, 1935, later pres. Dist. Coun. 2; joined Internat. Longshoremen's and Warehousemen's Union, 1937, past pres. Author: (pamphlet) Women in War, 1943; writer column On the Beam appearing in the Dispatcher, 1943-90. Commr. San Francisco Port Commn., 1970-90; v.p. Internat. Liaison Forum of Peace Forces, 1977-90. Past mem. San Francisco Port Authority, 1970-90. Home: San Francisco Calif. Died Mar. 30, 1990.

BRIGGS, FRANK P., senator, editor; b. Armstrong, Mo., Feb. 25, 1894; s. Thomas H. and Susan Almira (Pyle) B.; m. Catherine Allen Shull, May 28, 1916; children: Thomas Frank, Eugene Allen, Darlene Ruth, Betty Barbara, Dorothy Catherine. Student, Ctrl. Coll., Fayette, Mo., 1911-14; BJ, U. Mo., 1915. Editor Fayette (Mo.) Democrat-Leader, 1915; city editor Moberly (Mo.) Monitor-Index, 1916-17; editor Trenton (Mo.) Times, 1917-18, city editor, 1919; night editor Shawnee (Okla.) Morning News, 1919-23; editor and owner Macon (Mo.) Chronicle-Herald, from 1924; mayor City of Macon, 1933; asst. sec. Interior Fish and Wildlife, from 1961; mem. Mo. State Senate, 1933-45, pres., 1941-45; appointed U.S. Senator from Missouri to fill unexpired term of Harry S. Truman; mem. Mo. Conservation Commn., from 1947; mem. Internat. Commn. for North Atlantic Fisheries, from 1961. Recipient Disting. Public Svc. award Sch. Journalism, U. Mo., 1958. Mem. Sigma Delta Chi, Masons (grand master Mo. 1957-58), Elks, Rotarian, Nat. Press (Washington D.C.). *

BRIGGS, HERBERT WHITTAKER, international law educator; b. Wilmington, Del., May 14, 1900; s. Frederic Foyé and Eleanore Ashton (Lewis) B.; m. Virginia Elizabeth Yoder, Dec. 22, 1977; children: Sarah Ashton, Deborah Anne, Jeffrey Peter, Lucinda Moseley. AB, W.Va. U., 1921; PhD, Johns Hopkins U., 1925; postgrad., Acad. Internat. Law, The Hague, The Netherlands, 1925-27, 29. Instr. polit. sci. Johns Hopkins U., Balt., 1925-26; C.R.B. fellow in internat. law, Brussels, 1926-27; mem. rsch. staff Fgn. Policy Assn., N.Y.C., 1927-28; acting assoc. prof. polit. sci. Oberlin (Ohio) Coll., 1928-29; asst. prof. govt. Cornell U., Ithaca, N.Y., 1919-37, prof., 1937-47, prof. internat. law, 1947-69, Goldwin Smith prof. internat. law emeritus, 1969-90, chmn. dept. govt., 1946-51; lectr. Acad. Internat. Law, 1958, 69, U.S. Naval War Coll., 1955, 56, 58; guest lectr. Turkish Inst. Internat. Law, U. Istanbul, U. Ankara, Turkish Gen. Staff War Acad., 1947; Fulbright lectr. U. Copenhagen Law Faculty, 1951, 53; mem. Internat. Law Commn., UN, 1962-66; U.S. del. Vienna Conf. on Law of Treaties, 1968; of counsel to Honduras, Spain, Chile, Libya, and Can. before Internat. Ct. Justice; mem. Anglo-French Ct. Arbitration on Continental Shelf, 1975-78. lectr. Acad. Internat. Law, 1958, 69, U.S. Naval War Coll., 1955, 56, 58; guest lectr. Turkish Inst. Internat. Law, U. Istanbul, U. Ankara, Turkish Gen. Staff War Acad., 1947; Fulbright lectr. U. Copenhagen Law Faculty, 1952-53; mem. Internat. Law Commn., UN, 1962-66; U.S. del. Vienna Conf. on Law of Treaties, 1968; of counsel to Honduras, Spain, Chile, Libya, and Can. before Internat. Ct. Justice; mem. Anglo-French Ct. Arbitration on Continental Shelf, 1975-78. Fellow Am. Acad. Arts and Scis.; mem. Internat. Inst. Law, Am. Soc. Internat. Law (pres. 1959-60, bd. editors Am. Jour. Internat. Law from 1939, editor-in-chief 1955-62). Home: Ithaca N.Y. Died Jan. 6, 1990; cremated.

BRIGGS, JOHN GURNEY, JR., music critic, editor; b. High Point, N.C., Feb. 17, 1916; s. John Gurney and Hazel Irene (Harmon) B.; m. Elizabeth Balée Westmoreland, Dec. 23, 1938 (dec. 1980); children—Robert Ragan, Mary Curtis. Student, U. N.C., 1932-35; grad., Curtis Inst. Music, 1938. Music editor, NBC, 1938-40; music critic: N.Y. Post, 1940-49; editor: Etude music mag., 1949-52; music critic N.Y. Times, 1952-60; sr. writer, Smith, Kline & French Labs., Phila., 1961-70; writer Camden (N.J.) Courier-Post, 1970-89, ret.; program annotator, Phila. Orch., 1963-71; Author: The Collector's Tchaikovsky, 1959, Leonard Bernstein: The Man, His Work and His World, 1961, The Collector's Beethoven, 1962, Requiem for a Yellow Brick Brewery, 1969; Contbr. articles and short stories to mags. Served with AUS, 1943-46. Mem. Athenaeum of Phila., Phila. Art Alliance, Pa. Hort. Soc. Episcopalian. Home: Pennsauken N.J. Died Aug. 9, 1990.

BRILL, HENRY, psychiatrist, educator; b. Bridgeport, Conn., Oct. 6, 1906; s. August Michael and Gussie (Kissel) B.; m. Wenonah Beale, Apr. 17, 1948; children: Michael Henry, Jean Malcolm; 1 dau. by previous marriage, Helen Elizabeth (Mrs. Charles Broxmeyer). B.A., Yale U., 1928, M.D., 1932. Intern, resident Pilgrim State Hosp., West Brentwood, N.Y., 1932-38, clin. dir. hosp., 1942-50, dir., 1958-74; from instr. to clin. prof. Albany (N.Y.) Med. Coll., 1952-54; professorial lectr. State U. Med. Center at Syracuse; lectr. history psychiatry Columbia Med. Sch., from 1957; dir. Craig Colony, Sonyea, N.Y., 1950-52; clin. prof. psychiatry Downstate Med. Center at Stonybrook, from 1973; from asst. to 1st dep. commr. N.Y. State Dept. Mental Hygiene, 1952-64; regional dir. N.Y. State Dept. Mental Hygiene, L.I., 1974-76; cons. N.Y. State Dept. Mental Hygiene, 1976-90; adminstr. N.Y. State Mental Hygiene Research Program, 1952-64; charge narcotic treatment program, N.Y. State, 1958-64; vice chmn. N.Y. State Narcotic Addiction Control Commn., 1966-68; chmn. com. clin. drug. evaluation NIMH, 1960-65; com. drug dependence NRC, 1959-73; mem. expert panel drug dependence WHO, from 1968; chmn. com. hallicinogenic drugs FDA-NIMH, 1960-70; mem. com. sedatives, stimulating and hallucinogenic drugs FDA, 1969-78; chmn. methadone evaluation com. Columbia Sch. Pub. Health, 1966-73; chmn. Narcotic Addiction Control Commn. Suffolk County, N.Y., 1968-73; FDA Methadone Com.; mem. Nat. Commn. on Marijuana and Drug Abuse, 1971-73; pres. Research Found. Mental Hygiene, Inc., 1976-78; chmn. N.Y. State Drug Abuse Adv. Com., from 1980. Fellow Am. Psychiat. Assn. (life, council 1964-68, chmn. com. nomenclature and statistics 1960-73); mem. AMA (chmn. com. drug dependence and alcoholism 1962-72), Am. Coll. Neuropsychopharmacology (pres. 1969), Internat. Coll. Psychopharmacology, Eastern Psychiat. Research Assn., Am. Psychopath. Assn. (pres. 1972). Home: Islip N.Y. Died June 17, 1990; buried Bay Shore, N.Y.

BRINIG, MYRON, author; b. Mpls.; s. Maurice and Rebecca (Coin) B. Student, NYU and Columbia U., 1917-21. Author: Singermann, 1929, Wide Open Town, 1931, This Man Is My Brother, 1932, The Flutter of an Eyelid, 1933, Out of Life, 1934, Sun Sets in the West, 1935, The Sisters, 1937, May Flavin, 1938, Anne Minton's Life, 1939, All of Their Lives, 1941, The Family Way, 1942, The Gamble Takes a Wife, 1943, You and I, 1945, Hour of Nightfall, 1947, No Marriages in Paradise, 1949, Footsteps on the Stair, 1950, The Sadness in Lexington Avenue, 1951, Street of the Three Friends, 1953, The Looking-Glass Heart, 1958. Home: New York N.Y. Died May 13, 1991.

BRINKER, JOHN HENRY, industrial equipment company executive; b. Cleve., May 31, 1914; s. John Henry and Marion (Crawford) B.; m. Virginia Grosvenor Bryant, Feb. 10, 1940; children: Ann Grosvenor, Lynn Crawford, John Henry. AB, U. Rochester, 1936; MBA with high distinction, Harvard U., 1947. Sales engr. Pfaulder Co., Rochester, N.Y., 1937-42; gen. sales mgr., dir. mktg. A.O. Smith Corp., Milw., 1947-55, gen. mgr., 1955-59, v.p. corp., 1959; v.p. mktg. A.O. Smith Corp., Chgo., 1965-71; pres. A.O. Smith Corp., Houston, 1971-72; pres. A.O. Smith-Harvestore Products, Inc., Arlington Heights, Ill., 1972-77, also chmn. bd. dirs.; exec. v.p. J.I. Case Co., Racine, Wis., 1959-60; exec. v.p. Cherry Burrell Corp., 1960-64; pres. Glascote Products, Inc., Cleve., 1964-65; bd. dirs. Howard-Harvestore Ltd., Harleston, Eng., First Bank & Trust Co., Arlington Heights. Chmn. fund appeal St. Mary's Hosp., 1956; trustee U. Rochester. Lt. comdr. USNR, 1942-46. Mem. Ill. C. of C. (dir.), Chgo. Club, Ramada Club. Presbyterian (elder). Home: Montgomery Tex. Died Sept. 16, 1991. †

BRIXEY, JOHN CLARK, mathematics educator; b. Mounds, Okla., June 28, 1904; s. Albin Monroe and Ethel Lillian (Buchanan) B.; m. Dorothea B. Morrison, Dec. 26, 1926; children—John Clark, Dorothy Jane (Mrs. George W. Ingels); m. Neoma Jo Durkee, Aug. 18, 1979. B.A., U. Okla., 1924, M.A., 1925; Ph.D., U. Chgo., 1936. Mem. faculty U. Okla., from 1925, prof. math., 1947-74, emeritus, from 1974; cons. prof. biostatistics and epidemiology U. Okla. Med. Center, 1960-74, adj. prof. emeritus, 1974—. Author: (with R.V.

Andree) Modern Trigonometry, 1955, Fundamentals of College Mathematics, rev. edit, 1961. Recipient award excellence teaching U. Okla., 1956. Mem. Am. Math. Soc., Math. Assn. Am. (bd. govs. 1951-52, sec. Okla.-Ark. sect. 1939-51), Phi Beta Kappa, Sigma Xi. Democrat. Mem. Disciples of Christ Ch. (past elder). Home: Norman Okla. Died Feb. 23, 1989.

BRIZGYS, VINCENTAS, bishop; b. Plyniai, Lithuania, Nov. 10, 1903; came to U.S., 1952, naturalized, 1959; s. Mathew and Mary (Vikelis) B. Student, Priests Sem., Gizai, Lithuania, 1921-27; Dr. Philosophy and Canon Law, Gregorian U., Rome, 1935. Ordained priest Roman Catholic Ch., 1927; parish priest Lithuania, 1927-30; mem. faculty Priests' Sem., 1936-40; rector Interdiocesan Priest's Sem., Kaunas, Lithuania, 1940-41; dean, prof. Theol. Faculty, State's U., Kaunas, 1941-44; ordained bishop of Bosano and aux. bishop of Kaunas, 1940; served in France, Spain, Portugal, 1947-51, Archdiocese of Chgo. and diocese of, Joliet, Ill., from 1951; Cons. Commn. for Bishop and Adminstrs. Diocese Preparing Vatican II Ecumenic Council, 1960-61; asst. pastoral care Holy Cross Hosp., Chgo., 29 yrs. Mem. AAAS, Pax Romana. Club: K.C. Home: Chicago Ill. Died Apr. 23, 1992; buried St. Casimir Cemetery, Chgo.

BROADY, K(NUTE) O(SCAR), education educator; b. Pitzer, Iowa, May 8, 1898; s. George Augustus and Mary (Brown) B.; m. Lois Thelma Pedersen, Dec. 28, 1932; children: Karen Margaret, Paula Marie, Merritt Pedersen. BS, Washburn Coll., 1920; MA, U. Chgo., 1927; PhD, Columbia U., 1930. Teacher rural sch., Plains, Kans., 1916-17; science teacher Lincoln (Kans.) High Sch., 1920-22, prin., 1922-24; supt. pub. schs. Sylvan Grove, Kans., 1924-26; assoc. prof. sch. admnstrn. U. Nebr., 1928-31, prof. sch. adminstrn., 1931-41, prof. sch. adminstrn. and dir. univ. extension, 1941-60, dir. univ. extension and head ctr. for continuing edn., 1959-63; prof. edn. U. Ala., from 1964; sec. Internat. Cont. Corr. Edn., 1938, pres. 1948; mem. Survey Staff Wash. State Ednl. Survey, 1946, D.C. Ednl. Survey, 1948; mem. U.S. Nat. Commn. UNESCO; vis. expert, cons. Edn. Divsn. U.S. Forces, Austria, 1947, F.O.A., Turkey, 1954, ECA, Jamaica, 1961, USAID Venezuela, 1963. Co-author: (with M.A. Stoneman and A.D. Brainard) Construction, Modernization, Renovation and Repair of Twelve Grade School Plants, 1949, (with others) Your Life Plans and The Armed Forces, 1955. Served as pvt. U.S. Army, 1917. Mem. AAUP, Phi Delta Kappa. Presbyterian. *

BROCKELBANK, WILLIAM JOHN, lawyer, university professor; b. Ont., Can., Mar. 13, 1895; s. William and Mary (Hunter) B.; m. Mary Chambers, July 29, 1922 (div. 1937); 1 dau. Frank Leslie; m. Naomi Lorene Campbell, July 8, 1839 (div. 1941); m. Esther Norie, Aug. 17, 1945. Student, Pickering Coll., Newmarket, Ont., Can., 1913-15; AB, Haverford (Pa.) Coll., 1919; LLB, Harvard U., 1923; Barrister at Law, Lincoln's Inn, 1928; Docteur en Droit, Univ. de Paris, 1934. Bar: Idaho 1944. Assoc. prof. law U. Ala., 1923-24, prof. law, 1928-31; lectr. law U. Pitts., 1924-25; sec. Internat. Corp. Co., Paris, France, 1925-28; practiced law Paris, 1934-35; prof. law U. Kans., 1935-40; practiced law Vancouver, B.C., 1940-42; lectr. govt. U. B.C., 1941-42; vis. prof. law U. Kansas City, 1942-43; assoc. prof. law U. Idaho, 1943-45, prof. law, from 1945; vis. prof. law U. P.R., 1954-55, 62-63; spl. lectr. on law for Dept. of State, Haiti, 1958-59, Uniform Laws Commr. for Idaho since 1947. Author: Interstate Enforcement of Family Support, 1960, The Community Property Law of Idaho, 1963; contbr. law reviews. Served with ARC 1918-19. Officier d'Académie (France); mem. AAUP, Order of Coif, Phi Beta Kappa, Phi Delta Phi, Masons. Democrat. Unitarian. *

BROCKEY, HAROLD, department store executive; children: Mrs. Joel Goldberg, Mrs. Lewis Kravitz. Chmn. bd., dir. Rich's Inc., Atlanta; v.p. Federated Stores. Mem. Nat. Retail Assn., Rotary. Home: Atlanta Ga. Died June 21, 1991.

BRODY, SAMUEL MANDELL, architect; b. Plainfield, N.J., Aug. 9, 1926; s. Joseph Edward and Mary Eleanor (Greenberg) B.; m. Sally Rich Rosenthal, June 9, 1954; children: Elizabeth, David, Daniel. B.A., Dartmouth Coll., 1947; M.Arch., Harvard U., 1950. Partner Davis, Brody & Wisniewski, N.Y.C., 1952-66, Davis, Brody & Assos., N.Y.C., 1966-92; adj. prof. Cooper Union Sch. Architecture, 1962-85; vis. prof. Davenport chair Yale U. Sch. Architecture, 1974; vis. prof. U. Pa., 1976; vis. lectr. Harvard U., N.Y. State U., Buffalo, Ball State U., Yale U., R.I. Sch. Design, Walker Art Center. Prin. works include Riverbend Houses, 1966, East Midtown Plaza, 1968, U.S. Pavilion, Osaka, 1970, Waterside, 1974, Hampshire Coll. Athletic/Recreation Center, 1975, L.I. U. Bklyn. Center, 1960-70, Time Inc. Conf. Ctr., 1983, Brown U. Geology/Chemistry Ctr., 1983, Bklyn. Bot. Gardens, 1989, Brown U. Dormitories, 1991, Harvard Med. Sch. E. Quadrangle Rsch. Facility, 1992. Served with USN, 1943-45. Recipient Arnold W. Brunner prize Nat. Inst. Arts and Letters, 1975; Louis Sullivan award, 1977. Fellow AIA (Archtl. Firm award 1975, medal of honor N.Y. chpt.). Jewish. Clubs: Rembrandt (Brooklyn Heights, N.Y.); Century Assn. (N.Y.C.). Home: Brooklyn N.Y. Died July 28, 1992. †

BROMFIELD, DONALD COLEMAN, bank executive, realtor; b. Plainfield, N.J., July 26, 1893; s. Lawrence B. and Edith (Dalziel) B.; m. Helen Phipps, April 20, 1920; children: Genevieve, Edith, Donald. Student, pub. schs. of Denver. Salesman, later jr ptnr. Wilson Cranmer & Co. investment bankers; mem. N.Y. Stock Exchange, 1913-28; pres. Producers Livestock Credit Corp.; v.p., dir. Fin. Indsl. Fund. Past gov. nat. ARC. Served as 1st lt. U.S. Army, 1917-19. Decorated Purple Heart. Mem. Denver Club, Country Club of Denver. Republican. Episcopalian. *

BRONFMAN, ALLAN, distilling corporation executive; b. Brandon, Manitoba, Can., Dec. 21, 1895; s. Ekiel and Minnie (Elman) B.; m. Lucy Bilsky, June 28, 1922; children: Edward M., Peter F., Mona Sheckman (dec.). BA, U. Manitoba, 1915, LLB, 1919; PhD honoris causa, Hebrew U. of Jerusalem, 1957. Called to bar of Manitoba, 1919. With Andrews, Andrews, Burbridge & Bastedo, Winnipeg, 1919-24; with Distillers Corps.-Seagrams, Ltd., Montreal, from 1924, v.p., from 1934; v.p. Distillers Corp., Ltd., Montreal, Calvert Distillers, Ltd., Amherstberg, Ont., Seco Investments, Ltd., Montreal; dir. Joseph E. Seagram & Sons, Ltd.; mem. bd. dirs. Surgeon's Hall of Fame, Internat. Coll. Surgeons, Chgo. Pres. Jewish Orphanage and Children's Aid Western Can., 1921-24; exec. com. Fedn. Jewish Philanthropies, Montreal, 1925-27, vice-chmn., 1927-28, chmn., 1928-31, trustee, from 1925; pres. campaign to raise funds for Jewish Gen. Hosp., Montreal, 1929, pres. of hosp., 1933-55, hon. pres., mem. exec. com., chmn. joint conf. com., from 1955; mem. nat. coun. Boy Scouts of Can.; hon. chmn. Que. Soc. Crippled Children, 1935-60; bd. trustees YW and YMHA, 1958; hon. v.p., mem. Dominion Coun. Can. Jewish Cong.; mem. nat. exec. com. United Jewish Agencies; nat. coun., nat. exec. Zionist Orgn. Can., from 1950, nat. chmn. Herzl 50th yr. commemoration; chmn. first combined Jewish Appeal Campaign Montreal, 1941; nat. pres. Can. Friends of Hebrew U. of Jerusalem, from 1944, mem. bd. govs., from 1950, dept. chmn. 1955; nat. chmn. for can. of Israel's Tenth Anniversary Celebrations, 1958-59; bd. dirs. Assn. for Paraplegics, Concerts Symphoniques, Montreal Festivals, Montreal Opera Guild; trustee Ency. Judaica Rsch Found. Named Israel Bond Man of Yr., 1964; decorated Chevalier Legion of Honor, 1949, Grand Cross del Merito Order Malta, 1948; recipient Can. Humanitarian award B'nai B'rith, 1958. Mem. Order of St. John of Jerusalem (assoc. officer brother), McGill U. Alumni Assn., Pi Lambda Phi, Masons, Montefiore Club, Elm Ridge Golf and Country Club (Montreal), Royal Automobile Can. Club. Orthodox Jewish. *

BRONSON, PATRICIA ANN, mathematics educator; b. Leesville, La., Mar. 15, 1931; d. Glenn Cecil and Allie Lee (Copeland) Packer; student Northwestern State U., 1948-51; B.A., George Peabody Coll., 1960, M.A., 1962; m. John Orville Bronson, Jr., June 11, 1966; children: Richard Wayne McCoy, Victoria Patricia Elizabeth, Glenn Charles Stephen. Tchr., Nashville Met. Schs., 1962-65, Calhoun Tech. Jr. Coll., Decatur, Ala., 1965-67; asst. prof. math. Chesapeake Coll., Wye Mills, Md., 1967-89. Mem. Math. Assn. Am., Nat. Council Tchrs. Math., AAUP, Miss., S.C. hist. socs., La. Hist. Assn., Am. Math. Assn. Two-Yr. Colls., Md. Math. Assn. Two-Yr. Colls., Theta Sigma Upsilon, Delta Kappa Gamma. Democrat. Episcopalian. Club: Order Eastern Star. Author: Index of the Census of 1850, Orangeburg and Pickens Districts, S.C., 1974. Died 1989. Home: Wye Mills Md. †

BROOKS, CHANDLER MCCUSKEY, physiology educator; b. Waverly, W.Va., Dec. 18, 1905; s. Earle Amos and Mary (McCuskey) B.; m. Nelle Irene Graham, June 25, 1932. A.B., Oberlin Coll., 1928; M.A., Princeton U., 1929, Ph.D., 1931; D.Sc. (hon.), Berea Coll., 1970; D.Sci. (hon.), SUNY, 1986. NRC fellow, teaching fellow Harvard Med. Sch., 1931-33; instr., then asso. prof. physiology Johns Hopkins Med. Sch., 1933-48; prof. physiology and pharmacology, chmn. dept. L.I. Coll. Medicine, 1948-50; prof. physiology, chmn. dept. State U. N.Y. Downstate Med. Center, Bklyn., 1950-72; prof., dir. grad. edn. State U. N.Y. Downstate Med. Center, 1956-66; dean State U. N.Y. Downstate Med. Center (Grad. Sch.), 1966-72; acting pres. State U. N.Y. Downstate Med. Center (Med. Center), 1969-71, Disting. prof., from 1971; vis. prof. Tokyo and Kobe (Japan) med. schs., 1961-62, U. Otago, Dunedin, New Zealand, 1975; vis. scholar U. Aberdeen, Scotland, 1973-74; hon. mem. faculty Catholic U., Santiago, Chile.; mem. study sects. NIH, 1949-69. Author: (with others) Excitability of the Heart, 1955, Humors, Hormones and Neural Secretions, 1962, (with Kiyomi Koizumi) Japanese Physiology, Past and Present, 1965; editor: (with P.F. Cranefield) The Historical Development of Physiological Thought, 1959, (with others) Cerebrospinal Fluid and the Regulation of Ventilation, 1965, The Changing World and Man, 1970, (with H.H. Liu) The Sinoatrial Pacemaker of the Heart, 1972, (with K.K. Koizumi) Integrations of Autonomic Reactions, 1972; founder, editor-in-chief: Jour. of Autonomic Nervous System, 1978-86. Trustee Internat. Found., from 1972, chmn. grants com., from 1973. Decorated Order of Rising Sun 3d class Japan; cited Internat. Physiol. Congress, 1965; Guggenheim fellow, 1946-48; Rockefeller fellow, 1950; China Med. Bd. N.Y. fellow, 1961-62. Fellow Ctr. Theol. Inquiry; mem. NAS, AAAS (council 1950-65), Harvey Soc. (pres. 1965, N.Y. Heart Assn. (council 1965-75), Am. Soc. Pharmacology and Exptl. Therapeutics, Internat. Brain Research Orgn., Nat. Soc. Med. Research, Royal Soc. Medicine, N.Y. Acad. Scis., Soc. Exptl. Biology and Medicine, Soc. Study Internal Secretions, Soc. Study Nervous and Mental Diseases, Am. Coll. Cardiology, Am. Coll. Pharmacology and Chemotherapy, Am. Inst. Biol. Scis., AMA (spl. affiliate), Am. Physiology Soc., Phi Beta Kappa, Sigma Xi, Alpha Omega Alpha; hon. mem. Nat. Acad. Medicine Buenos Aires, Cardiology Soc. Argentina, biol. socs. Montevideo, Uruguay, Inst. Hist. Medicine and Med. Research New Delhi, Alumni Assn., Coll. Medicine Downstate Med. Center. Home: Princeton N.J. Died Nov. 29, 1989; buried Greenwood Cemetery, Wheeling, W.Va.

BROOKS, EDWARD PENNELL, fund trustee; b. Westbrook, Maine, July 11, 1895; s. Harry Danielson and Bertha (Pennell) B.; m. Carol Butler Wright, June 19, 1922; children: Beverly Floe, Carol Pihl, Robert Wright. BS, MIT, 1917; DSc, Drexel Inst. Tech., 1958. With Sears, Roebuck & Co., 1927-51, v.p. factories, 1939-51, dir., 1941-52; dean Sch. Indsl. Mgmt., MIT, 1951-59; dir. Colonial Growth & Energy Fund, Colonial Fund, Inc., Plymouth Cordage Co.; trustee Am. Optical Co., Savs. & Profit Sharing Pension Fund Sears, Roebuck & Co. Employees; mem. corp. MIT, 1940-45. 1st lt. U.S. Army, 1917-19, AEF. Decorated D.S.C.; recipient Medal of Freedom. Fellow Am. Acad. Arts and Scis.; mem. Delta Upsilon, Chgo. Club, Commonwealth Club, Comml. Club (Chgo.), St. Botolph Club, Union Club (Boston), Anglers Club (N.Y.C.). *

BROOKS, FRANK PICKERING, physician, physiologist; b. Portsmouth, N.H., Jan. 2, 1920; s. Frank Edwin and Florence Isabel (Towle) B.; m. Emily Elizabeth Marden, July 5, 1942; children: William Bradley, Sally Elizabeth, Robert Pickering. AB, Dartmouth Coll., 1941; MD, U. Pa., 1943, ScD in Medicine, 1951; D Honoris Causa, U. Aix-Marseille, 1987. Intern Hosp. U. Pa., Phila., 1944; resident Hosp. U. Pa., 1944-46; USPHS research fellow Jefferson Med. Coll., 1951-52; instr. U. Pa., 1952-53, asst. prof., 1954-60, assoc. prof., 1960-70, prof. medicine and physiology, 1970-90, prof. emeritus, 1990-91, chief gastrointestinal sect., 1972-75, acting chief, 1986-89; sr. lectr. in physiology U. Edinburgh, Scotland, 1955-56; research assoc. VA Center, Los Angeles, 1966-67; mem. Nat. Commn. on Digestive Diseases, 1977-79; mem. council NIADDK, 1983-86; mem. career awards com. VA, 1983-87. Author: The Control of Gastrointestinal Function, 1970, Gastrointestinal Pathophysiology, 2d edit, 1979, Peptic Ulcer Disease, 1985; editor: Digestive Diseases and Scis., 1982-87. Served to lt. (j.g.) USNR, 1946-48. Recipient Bologna Day medal World Congress Gastroenterology, 1988; Research Career Devel. award Nat. Inst. Arthritis, Metabolism and Digestive Diseases, 1964-70. Mem. Am. Gastroent. Assn. (pres.-elect 1979-80, pres. 1980-81, Friedenwald medal 1988), Am. Physiol. Soc. (chmn. gastrointestinal sect. 1966), Brit. Soc. Gastroenterology (hon.), Am. Pancreatic Assn. (pres. 1980-81), Am. Clin. Climatological Assn. (v.p. 1984), Alpha Omega Alpha (hon.), Belgian Soc. Gastroent. Assn. (Broheé medal 1985). Republican. Episcopalian. Club: Union League Phila. Home: Wynnewood Pa. Died Mar. 18, 1991. †

BROOKS, JAMES, artist; b. St. Louis, Oct. 18, 1906; s. William Rodolphus and Abigail (Williamson) B.; m. Mary MacDonald, 1938; m. Charlotte Park, Dec. 22, 1947. Student, So. Meth. U., 1923-25, Art Students League, 1927-31; studied with, Wallace Harrison, 1945. Instr. Pratt Inst., N.Y.C., 1948-55; faculty Columbia U., 1946-48, Queens Coll., N.Y.C., 1966-69, New Coll., 1965-67, U. Pa., Phila., 1971; Andrew Carnegie prof. Cooper Union, N.Y.C.; vis. critic advanced painting Yale U., New Haven, 1955-60; vis. artist New Coll., Sarasota, Fla., 1965-67. One-man shows include Peridot Gallery, N.Y.C., 1950-53, Borgenicht Gallery, N.Y.C., 1954, Stable Gallery, N.Y.C., 1957, 59, Kootz Gallery, N.Y.C., 1961, 63, 64, Phila. Art Alliance, 1966, Martha Jackson Gallery, N.Y.C., 1968, 71, 72, 75, Berenson Gallery, Miami, Fla., 1969, Galleria Lorenzelli, Milan and Bergamo, Italy, 1975, Carone Gallery, Ft. Lauderdale, Fla., 1976, Robinson Gallery, Houston, 1976, Lerner-Heller Gallery, N.Y.C., 1978, Gruenebaum Gallery, N.Y.C., 1979, 80, 81, 83, 86, Montclair (N.J.) Mus., 1978, Dan Flavin Art Inst., Bridgehampton, N.Y., 1985, Century Assn., N.Y.C., 1988, Berry-Hill Galleries, 1989; exhibited Retrospective Exhbn. at Whitney Mus. Am. Arts, N.Y.C., 1963-64, at Dallas Mus. Fine Arts, 1972, Martha Jackson Gallery and Finch Coll. Mus. Art, N.Y.C., 1975, Portland (Maine) Mus. Art, 1983, The Heckscher Mus., Huntington, N.Y., 1988; artist in residence, Am. Acad., Rome, 1963; exhibited, Rose Art Mus., Brandeis U., Walker Art Center, Mpls., UCLA, Balt. Mus., Mus. Modern Art, Washington, 1963, Whitney Mus., Modern, Bklyn., Met., Guggenheim museums, Art Inst. Chgo., Nat. Gallery, Washington, numerous others, also Tokyo, Sao Paulo, Basle, Munich, Milan, London, Berlin, Brussels, Paris, Barcelona, Perth, Australia, 1958; executed murals, Little Falls (N.J.) Post Office, Woodside (L.I.) Library, LaGuardia Airport. Bd. govs. Skowhegan Sch. Art. Recipient prizes Pitts. Internat., 1952, prizes Mobil Oil Hdqrs., Fairfax, Va., prizes Art Inst. Chgo., 1957, 62; Guggenheim fellow, 1967-68; Nat. Endowment for

Arts grantee, 1973; recipient 86th Ann. Artists Gold medal Nat. Arts Club, 1985. Mem. Am. Acad. Inst. Arts and Letters. Club: Century (N.Y.C.). Home: Springs N.Y. Died Mar. 10, 1992.

BROOKS, RICHARD, writer, director; b. Phila., May 18, 1912. Student, Temple U. Radio writer, narrator, commentator NBC; author screenplays for motion pictures including: Brute Force, Swell Guy, White Savage; original author Crossfire, To the Victor; writer, collaborator Storm Warning, Key Largo, Mystery Street; dir., author Elmer Gantry (Acad. award for screen play 1961), The Brothers Karamazov, Cat on a Hot Tin Roof, Sweet Bird of Youth, Deadline, U.S.A., Battle Circus, Last Hunt, Something of Value; dir. Take the High Ground, Flame and the Flesh, Catered Affair, Looking for Mr. Goodbar, 1977; dir., collaborator Last Time I Saw Paris; producer, dir., The Blackboard Jungle, 1955; writer Lord Jim, Wrong is Right, 1982; dir., writer: Professionals, In Cold Blood; author: novels The Producer, Brick Fox Hole, Boiling Point; also motion pictures The Happy Ending, 1969, Dollars, 1971, Bite the Bullet, 1975, Fever Pitch, 1985. Recipient Lifetime Achievement award Writers Guild Am. W., Dirs. Guild Am., 1990. Home: Beverly Hills Calif. Died Mar. 11, 1992.

BROOKS, ROBERT ROMANO RAVI, economics educator; b. Rome, Dec. 5, 1905; parents Am. citizens; m. Mary Elizabeth Storer, May 31, 1929; children—Patricia Skidmore, Robin Bruce Stirling, Johathan Storer. Ph.B., Wesleyan U., 1926; B.A., Oxford U., 1928; Ph.D., Yale U., 1935. Instr. econs. Wesleyan U., 1929-32; instr. indsl. relations Yale U., New Haven, 1931-37; dean New Haven Labor Coll., 1935-37; instr. summer sch. for women workers Bryn Mawr Coll., 1936; asst. prof. econs. Williams Coll., Williamstown, Mass., 1937-45, dean, 1946-63, Orrin Sage prof. econs., 1946-63, 68-71, prof. emeritus, 1971-92; co-founder, dir. Ctr. Devel. Econs., 1959-63; apptd. cultural attache U.S. embassy, New Delhi, India, 1963-68; chmn. bd. dirs. U.S. Ednl. Found., New Delhi, 1963-68; instr. labor relations U. Calif., 1940; labor adviser WPB, 1940-41; dir. labor office OPA, 1942-44, sr. exec. officer, 1945, dep. adminstr. info., 1946; founder, exec. dir. Tuition Exchange, Inc., 1947-63; mem. New Eng. Wage Stablzn. Enforcement Commn., 1950-51. Author: When Labor Organizes, 1937, Unions of Their Own Choosing, 1938, As Steel Goes, 1940, Williamstown, The First Two Hundred Years, 1953, American Studies in India, 1966, Love in a Pasture, 1968, Williamstown: Twenty Years Later, 1974, (with Vishnu Wakankar) Stone Age Painting in India, 1975, Sicilian Rebel, 1979, A Tumult of Years, 1983; contbr. articles to profl. jours.; editor Am. Rev., New Delhi, 1963-68, Exploration and Research Stone Age Painting in India, from 1971; inventor new method for restoring stone age paintings. Trustee Bennington Coll.; bd. dirs. Mass. Higher Edn. Assistance Corp.; moderator Williamstown Town Meetings, 1969-71. Recipient Pres.' Cert. of Merit award, 1947; Rhodes scholar, 1926. Mem. Phi Beta Kappa. Home: Nyack N.Y. Died Jan. 28, 1992.

BROOKS, ROBERT WILLIAM, banker; b. Bloomfield, N.J., Nov. 1, 1935; s. William George and Marion Agnes (Carter) B.; m. Margaret Caroll Snider, Nov. 11, 1961; children: Robert Scott, Elizabeth Ann. B.S., Lebigh U., 1957. With Chemical Bank, N.Y.C., from 1957, exec. v.p., from 1983. Served with USAF, 1958-60. Mem. N.Y. Credit and Fin. Mgmt. Assn., Nat. Comml. Fin. Assn. (dir. from 1982). Republican. Roman Catholic. Club: Canoe Brook Country. Home: Chatham N.J. Deceased. †

BROPHY, JAMES JOHN, physicist, university official; b. Chgo., June 6, 1926; s. James J. and Ella Helen (Nerad) B.; m. Muriel Ann Johnson, Aug. 26, 1949; children: James J., John R., Thomas C. B.S. in Elec. Engring, Ill. Inst. Tech., 1947, M.S. in Physics, 1949, Ph.D. in Physics, 1951. Research physicist Armour Research Found. of Ill. Inst. Tech., 1951-53, supr. solid state physics, 1953-56, asst. dir. physics div., 1956-61, dir. tech. devel. of Found., 1961-63, v.p. for tech. devel., 1963-66; acad. v.p. Ill. Inst. Tech., 1967-76; sr. v.p. Inst. Gas Tech., Chgo., 1976-80; v.p. rsch. U. Utah, Salt Lake City, 1980-91, emeritus prof. physics, emeritus prof. elec. engring., from 1991; trustee Underwriters Labs., Inc. Author: Semiconductor Devices, 1965, Basic Electronics for Scientists, 1966, 5th edit., 1990; co-author: Electronic Processes in Materials, 1963; Co-editor: Organic Semi-conductors; Contbr. articles to profl. jours. Fellow Am. Phys. Soc.; mem. AAAS, Western Soc. Engrs., Sigma Xi. Home: Salt Lake City Utah Deceased. †

BROSS, JOHN ADAMS, lawyer, government consultant; b. Chgo., Jan. 17, 1911; s. Mason and Isabel Foster (Adams) B.; m. Priscilla Prince, June 1936; children: Wendy, John, Justine; m. Joanne Bass, Oct. 28, 1947; 1 son, Peter F. AB, Harvard U., 1933, LLB, 1936. Bar: N.Y. 1938. Sole practice N.Y.C., 1936-42, 46-49; assoc. firm Parker & Duryee, N.Y.C., ptnr., from 1941; asst. gen. counsel U.S. High Commr. to Germany, 1949-51; U.S. govt. cons. fgn. affairs, 1951-57, from 1960; advisor, coordinator Am. embassy, Bonn, Germany, 1957-59; dep. to dir. of central intelligence for programs evaluation CIA, 1963-71; staff mem. task force on nat. mil. establishment Hoover Commn., 1948. Chmn. bd. dirs. Cen. Atlantic Environment Ctr., from 1971; trustee Conservation Found., from 1986; bd. dirs. World Wild Life Fund U.S. Conservation Found. Served to col. USAAF, 1942-46. Decorated Legion of Merit, Bronze Star medal; Order Brit. Empire; King Christian X Medal of Liberty. Mem. Assn. of Bar of City of N.Y. (chmn. com. state legislation 1946-49), Council on Fgn. Relations N.Y. Clubs: Metropolitan (N.Y.C.), Harvard (N.Y.C.); Alibi. Home: McLean Va. Died Oct. 16, 1990; buried Peterborough, N.H.

BROWER, ROBERT CLARK, state judge; b. Fullerton, Nebr., Oct. 12, 1896; s. Martin I. and Ella (Clark) B.; m. Lenore Heyrock, May 19, 1923; children: John M., Helen Porter, Thomas D. Student, U. Nebr., 1914-17; LLB, U. Mich., 1919. Bar: Nebr. 1919, Mont. 1920. Lawyer Kalispell, Mont., 1920-22, Fullerton, 1922-61; atty. Noffsinger & Walchli, 1920-22; mem. firm Kemp & Brower, 1922-49; pvt. practice, 1949-51; mem. firm Brower & Brower, 1951-61; judge Supreme Ct. Nebr., from 1961; v.p. Fullerton Nat. Bank. Mem. Nebr. Legislature, 1953-57. Mem. Phi Alpha Delta, Elk. *

BROWN, ALLEN WEBSTER, bishop; b. La Fargeville, N.Y., July 22, 1908; s. Nicholas H. and Edith (Haller) B.; m. Helen Belshaw, July 5, 1930; children: Allen Webster, Raymond Dutson, Reed Haller, Elizabeth E. BA, Syracue U., 1930; ThB, Phila Div. Sch., 1934, ThM, 1937; DD, Nashotah House, 1955, LLD, 1973; LHD, Siena Coll., 1974. Ordained deacon and priest Episocpal Ch., 1934. Rector St. Johns Ch., Richfield Springs, N.Y., 1934-40, St. Mark's Ch., Malone, N.Y., 1940-42, Christ Ch., Hudson, N.Y., 1942-53; dean All Sts. Cathedral, Albany, N.Y., 1953-59; suffragan bishop Diocese of Albany, 1959-61, bishop, 1961-74; mem. house dept. Episcopal Ch., 1943, 46, 49, 52, 55; mem. Archbishop's Anglican Orthodox Internation Commn., 1968-70; mem. exec. coun. Episcopal Ch., 1970-73. Author: The Inner Fire, 1977; editor: The Anglican, 1945-47. Mem. Mayor's Adv. Coun., Hudson, 1952-53; mem. Chancellor's Panel on Univ. Purposes, 1970-90; ; past trustee St. Agnes Sch., Child's Hosp., St. Margaret's Home, Housae Sch., St. Francis Homes, Nelson House. Past mem. NAACP. Home: Elka Park N.Y. Died Jan. 19, 1990.

BROWN, ARTHUR, microbiology educator; b. N.Y.C., Feb. 12, 1922; s. Samuel S. and Ida (Hoffman) B.; m. Elaine Belaief, Dec. 24, 1947; children: Karen A., Kenneth M., Stephen S., David P. B.A., Bklyn. Coll., 1943; postgrad., U. Ky., 1946-47; Ph.D. (fellow), U. Chgo., 1950; Ph.D. sr. postdoctoral fellow, U. Geneva, Switzerland, 1964. Diplomate: Am. Bd. Microbiology. Research assoc. U. Chgo., 1951; instr. microbiology SUNY, 1951-55; br. chief virology lab. Ft. Detrick, Frederick, Md., 1955-69; head dept. microbiology, prof. U. Tenn., 1969-88, disting. service prof., 1983-89, prof. emeritus, 1989; vis. prof. Georgetown U., 1967-68, George Washington U., 1957-69, U. Md., 1957-59, U. Wash., Seattle, 1986, 88; mem. tng. grants com. NIH, 1969-73; cons. virus cancer program Nat. Cancer Inst., 1970-74; cons. Oak Ridge Nat. Labs., from 1972; exptl. viral study sect. NIH, 1979-83; mem. life scis. panel NRC, from 1986. Contbr. articles to profl. jours. Bd. dirs. YMCA, Frederick, Md., 1959-61. Served to 1st lt. USAAF, 1943-46. Macebearer U. Tenn., 1975; Chancelor's scholar, 1979. Fellow Am. Acad. Microbiology; mem. Am. Soc. Microbiology, Am. Soc. Virology, Soc. Exptl. Biology and Medicine, Am. Assn. Immunologists, Infectious Disease Soc. Am., Am. Assn. Cancer Research, AAAS. Jewish (pres. congregation). Club: Masons. Home: Knoxville Tenn. Deceased. †

BROWN, ARTHUR HUNTINGDON, government official; b. Huntingdon, Que., Dec. 15, 1895; s. Rev. S. and Florence (Dalgleish) B.; m. Regina Margaret Milliken, July 28, 1926; children: Robert Ronald, Alice Jean, James Harold. Student, U. Toronto, 1913-15, Wetmore Hall Law Sch., Regina, Sask., 1919-22. Bar: Sask. 1922. Lawyer Sask., 1922-29; sec.-treas., legal adviser Can. Farm Loan Bd., Ottawa, 1929-39; mem., chmn. Dependents' Allowance Bd., Ottawa, 1939-42; mem. dependents' bd. trustees Dept. Nat. Def., 1942-45; chief exec. officer, legal adviser Dept. Labor, 1943, asst. dep. minister labor, 1951-53, dep. minister labor, 1953-60; vice chmn. Wartime Labor Rels. Bd., 1945-48; chmn. Can. Labor Rels. Bd., from 1963; Can. govt. rep. governing body ILO, Geneva, 1953-57, chmn., 1955-56; dir. Can. br. Internat. Labour Office, from 1961. Served with F.A., Can. Army in France, WWI. Decorated Order Brit. Empire, 1943. Mem. United Church of Can. *

BROWN, BEN HILL, JR., consultant; b. Spartansburg, S.C., Feb. 8, 1914; s. Ben Hill and Clara Twitty (Colock) B.; m. Barbara B. Burt, Mar. 3, 1940 (div.); children: Ben Hill III, Barbara Middleton, Calra Colcock, Hardee Burt; m. naomi Huber, June 27, 1970. AB, Wofford Coll., 1935; JD, George Washington U., 1939. Bar: S.C. 1959. Pvt. practice Spartanburg, 1939-41; asst. to legal adviser Dept. of State, 1946-49, dep. asst. sec. for congl. Rels., 1949-55; assigned Nat. War Coll., 1955-56; dir. U.S. Ops. Mission to Iraq, 1956-58, U.S. Ops. Mission to Libya, 1959-60; consul gen. Turkey, Istanbul, 1960-64; U.S. ambassador to Liberia, 1964-69; diplomat-in-residence Northwestern U., 1969-70; pvt. cons. St. Alexandria, Va., 1971-89; attended UN Gen. Assembly as adviser, 1947, mem. survey mission to Germany, 1948, mem. U.S. del. to Intergovtl. Conf. to draft agreement establishing Internat. Authority for the Ruhr, 1948; vice chmn. U.S. del. to UN Conf. on Trade and Devel., 1964. Called active duty as res. officer, 1941; served mil. govt. Italy, Supreme Hdqrs., Allied Expeditionary Forces, in Eng., France and Germany; dep. chief, acting chief legal br. Office Mil. Govt. (U.S. Zone), Germany, 1945-46; inactive duty as lt. col. Judge Adv. Gen. Dept., 1946. Decorated Legion of Merit, Bronze Star medal. Mem. Spartanburg Bar Assn., Masons, Phi Delta Phi, Kappa Alpha Order, Pi Kappa Delta, Chi Beta Phi, Sigma Upsilon, Blue Key. Episcopalian. Home: Alexandria Va. Died May 25, 1989.

BROWN, BRENDAN F., jurist, legal educator; b. Sioux City, Iowa, Oct. 19, 1898; s. Matthew Francis and Bertha Isabella (Brady) B. AB, Creighton U., Omaha, Nebr., 1921, LLB, 1924; LLM, Cath. U. Am., 1925, JUB and JUL, 1926, JUD, 1927; D. Philosophy in Law, Oxford U., 1932; spl. law rsch. student, Harvard U., 1937-38. Bar: Nebr. 1924, D.C. 1925, U.S. Supreme Ct., U.S. Ct. Claims, U.S. Ct. Customs and Patent Appeals, 1939. With Root, Clark, Buckner & Ballantine, N.Y.C., summer 1939, Smart & Von Sneidern, 1940-41; spl. rsch. work as spl. asst. to atty. gen. Dept. Justice, 1946; chief of opinions and regulations sect. Post Office Dept., 1948; instr. in English, history and Latin Creighton U., 1921-23; instr. in law Cath. U. of Am., 1926-27, 32-40, assoc. prof., acting dean, 1942-46, prof. law, 1946-54, dean, 1949-54; prof. law Loyola U. of So., New Orleans, from 1954; legal adviser law firm Urciolo, Miller, Platshen & Urciolo, Washington; chancellor Boswell Inst. New Orleans; dir. Legal Inst., Regional Offices, Va.; gen. reporter 6th Internat. Congress of Comparative Law, Hamburg, Germany, 1962; jud. cons. chief prosecution Internat. Mil. Tribunal for Far East, war crimes trial, Tokyo, Japan, 1946-48. Author: The Natural Law Reader, 1960, Crimes Against International Law (with Joseph B. Keenan), 1950; contbr. numerous articles to law bulls. and publs., also many book reviews. Recipient Creighton U. Alumnus of Yr. award, 1963, Disting. Alumnus Outstanding Achievement award in the field of law Cath. U. of Am., 1963. Mem. AAUP, Internat. Assn. for Philosophy Law and Social Philosophy (Am. sect.), Inter-Am. Bar Assn., Fed. Bar Assn. (dist. v.p., mem. nat. coun.), ABA, Nebr. Bar Assn., D.C. Bar Assn., La. Bar Assn., New Orleans Bar Assn., Bar City of N.Y., Am. Law Inst., La. Law Inst., Riccobono Seminar Roman Law Am. (past sec.), Assn. Am. Law Schs. (chmn. Round Table coun. jurisprudence 1956-57), Canon Law Soc. of Am. (past v.p.), St. Thomas More Soc. of Am. (pres.), Am. Soc. Internat. Law, Am. Soc. Legal Hist. (v.p. 1956-57), Cath. Assn. for Internat. Peace, Am. Cath. Hist. Assn., Am. Cath. Philos. Assn., UN League of Lawyers (former mem. exec. com. US. Divsn.), Oxford Cath. Assn., St. Catherine Soc. Oxford, Am. Legion, Krewe of Virgilians, Alpha Pi Omicron (hon.), Alpha Sigma Nu, Delta Sigma Rho, Gamma Eta Gamma, Blue Key, Alpha Delta Gamma, Harvard Club, Nat. Lawyers (Washington), Round Table (New Orleans). *

BROWN, COURTNEY C., university dean; b. St. Louis, Oct. 15, 1904; s. Alexander Hanks and Joan (MacCallum) B.; m. Marjorie Warren Lawbaugh, Nov. 26, 1930; children: Joanne Brown Lyman, Roxanne B. Warren, Courtney Warren. MD, Dartmouth Coll., 1926; PhD, Columbia U., 1940; LLD, Miami U., Oxford, Ohio, 1959; DBA (hon.), U. Sherbrooke, Que., Can., 1967. With various stock exch. firms and Bankers Trust Co., N.Y.C., 1926-35; assoc. dir. rsch. Chase Nat. Bank, N.Y.C., 1941-42; v.p. CCC, USDA, Washington, 1942-43; dep. dir. Equipment Bur., WPB, Washington, 1943-44; chief div. war supply and resources U.S. Dept. State, Washington, 1943-45; vice chmn. President's Famine Emergency Com., Washington, 1946; economist, asst. to chmn. bd. Standard Oil Co. N.J., 1946-54; instr., lectr. Columbia U., N.Y.C., 1937-41, dean Grad. Sch. Bus., 1954-69, v.p. for bus., 1955-57; George E. Warren prof. bus. policy, 1963-70, Paul Garrett prof. pub. policy and bus. responsibility, 1970-71, founder, editor Columbia Jour. World Bus., 1965-72; creator, participant Let's Talk Business, NBC-TV, 1962-65; bd. dirs. CBS, U.P. Corp., Assoc. Dry Goods Corp.; mem. West Side adv. bd. Chem. Bank N.Y. Trust Co.; bd. govs. N.Y. Stock Exch., 1959-62; chmn. Gov.'s Com. on Minimum Wage in N.Y. State, 1965; mem. President's Commn. on Internat. Trade and Investment Policy, 1970-71. Author 9 books, including Liquidity and Instability, 1940, (autobiography) The Dean Meant Business, 1983; contbg. author: Contemporary Economic Problems and Trends, 1941, Symbols and Values, 1954, Political Economy of American Foreign Policy, 1955, The Director Looks at His Job, 1957, Journey toward Understanding, 1958, The Creative Interface, 1968, Putting the Corporate Board to Work, 1976, Beyond the Bottom Line, 1979; editor: World Business, Promise and Problems, 1970. Exec. dir. Am. Assembly, 1955-56, chmn. bd. trustees, 1969-79; trustee Columbia U.; a founder, then hon. trustee Coun. for Fin. Aid to Edn.; mem. N.Y. adv. bd. Salvation Army, 1965-69. Mem. Acad. Polit. Sci. (trustee), Scarsdale Golf Club, Century Assn. Congregationalist. Home: Scarsdale N.Y. Died Apr. 28, 1990; buried Kensico Cemetery.

BROWN, EDWARD JAMES, foreign language educator; b. Chgo., July 12, 1909; s. Edward James and Marie (O'Neill) B.; m. Catherine Stillman Cossum, Oct. 7, 1941; 1 dau., Meredith Ann Brown Loring. A.B., U. Chgo., 1933, A.M., 1946; Ph.D., Columbia U., 1950. From instr. Russian to prof. Brown U., 1947-65, chmn. dept. Slavic langs., 1960-65; prof. Russian, chmn. dept. Slavic langs. and lits. Ind. U., Bloomington, 1965-69; prof. Slavic langs. Stanford U., 1969-91; Mem. Am. Com. Slavists, 1958; del. IV Internat. Congress Slavists, 1958; cons. Fgn. Area Fellowship Program, 1964-66; cons. grants Am. Council Learned Socs., 1964-71; mem. Joint Com. Slavic Studies, 1964-65, 67-71; exec. com. Inter-Univ. Com. Travel Grants, 1965-67. Author: The Proletarian Episode in Russian Literature, 1953, reissued, 1971, Russian Literature Since the Revolution, 1963, rev., 1969, 3d rev. edit., 1982, Stankevich and His Moscow Circle, 1966; editor: Major Soviet Writers: Essays in Criticism, 1973, Mayakovsky: A Poet in the Revolution, 1973. Served with USAAF, 1943-45. Rockefeller fellow, 1946; Am. Council Learned Socs. fellow, 1946-47; Howard fellow, 1955-56; exchange prof. to USSR Am. Council Learned Socs.-Acad. Scis. Program, fall 1963; sr. fellow Russian Inst., Columbia U., 1969, vis. prof., 1981; vis. prof. Harvard U., 1982; Stanford U. Humanities Ctr. fellow, 1987-88. Mem. MLA, Am. Assn. Tchrs. Slavic and Eastern European Langs. (pres. 1966), Am. Assn. Advancement Slavic Studies (pres. 1967-70), Phi Beta Kappa. Home: Stanford Calif. Died Jan. 9, 1991; cremated.

BROWN, ESTHER LUCILE, author, lecturer; b. Manchester, N.H.; d. Charles Wesley and Nellie (Morse) B. B.A. with spl. honors, U. N.H., 1920; Ph.D. in Social Anthropology, Yale, 1929; LL.D., Skidmore Coll., 1950. Asst. prof. social sci. U. N.H., 1926-29; research assoc. Russell Sage Found., N.Y.C., 1930-45, dir. dept. studies in professions, 1945-48, exec. program planning and direction, 1948-63; writer, lectr., cons., 1963-76; vis. prof. U. Wis.-Madison, 1970; cons. for WHO, 1952-53. Author: The Professional Engineer, 1935, Social Work as a Profession, 4th edit, 1942, Nursing as a Profession, 2d edit, 1940, Physicians and Medical Care, 1934, Lawyers and the Promotion of Justice, 1938, Lawyers, Law Schools and the Public Service, 1948, Nursing for the Future (translated into Swedish, Portuguese, Japanese), 6th edit, 1953, (with Milton Greenblatt and Richard H. York) From Custodial to Therapeutic Patient Care in Mental Hospitals, 1955, Newer Dimensions of Patient Care: Part I, The Use of Physical and Social Environment of the Hospital for Therapeutic Purposes, 1961, Part II, Improving Staff Motivation and Competence in the General Hospital, 1962, Part III, Patients as People, 1964, Newer Dimensions of Patient Care, vol. 1 (translated into Japanese), 1965, Nursing Reconsidered: A Study of Change, Part I, 1970, Part II, 1971 (translated into Japanese), also numerous articles. Social Sci. Research Council fellow in France, 1929-30. Hon. life mem. Nat. League for Nursing; mem. Am. Sociol. Assn., Soc. Applied Anthropology. Home: San Francisco Calif. Died July 6, 1990.

BROWN, H. EMMETT, foreign service officer; b. Grand Rapids, Mich., Apr. 28, 1897; s. Frank Holmes and Leola (Schwingle) B.; m. Ruth Margaret Owen, June 29, 1922; children: Hugh Sheldon, Marcia Mary Crosman. BS, U. Rochester, 1918; AM, Columbia, 1929, EdD, 1938. Tchr. various pvt. and pub. schs., 1918-28; tchr. sci. Lincoln Sch. Tchrs. Coll.; instr. natural scis. Tchrs. Coll. Columbia, 1928-44; prof. sci., head dept. N.Y. State Coll. for Tchrs., Buffalo, 1944-52; Fulbright lectr. Rangoon, Burma, 1950-51; edn. officer Mut. Security Adminstrn. Mission to China, Taipei, Taiwan, 1952-57; chief edn. div. U.S. Ops. Mission to Afghanistan, 1957-62; with U.S. AID Mission, Mogadiscio Somal Republic, ret. 1964. Author: (with E. C. Schwachtgen) Physics, the Story of Energy, 1949, 54, Community Schools of Taiwan, 1956; gen. editor: Science of Pre-Flight Aeronautics, 1942. Fellow AAAS; mem. AAUP, Nat. Coun. Elem. Sch. (pres. 1950-51), Nat. Assn. Rsch. Sci. Teaching, Nat. Sci. Tchrs. Assn. Unitarian. *

BROWN, J. CALVIN, mechanical engineer, lawyer; b. Pomona, Calif., Jan. 12, 1896; s. James Calhoun and Lily May (Nichols) B. ME, Calif. Inst. Tech., 1917; LLB, Hamilton Coll., 1921, LLM, 1922; spl. courses, Southwestern U., U. So. Calif. Bar: Calif. Mech. engr., cons. Gage Aircraft Co., L.A., Chico, Calif., 1917-30. Contbr. articles to tech. and patent subjects. Chmn. Engrs. 7th War Loan Drive; appeal agt. Selective Svc. System, WWII. Mem. Internat. Adventures (v.p.), U.S. Supreme Ct. Bar, ABA (various coms.), Calif. Bar Assn., Calif. State Bar Assn., Ill. Bar Assn., D.C. Bar Assn., L.A. Bar Assn. (past chmn. patent sect.), Am. Patent Law Assn. (chmn. So. Calif. sect. 1941-43, v.p. 1945-49), L.A. Patent Law Assn. (pres. 1942-44), Am. Soc. M.E. (pres. 1950-51), Newcomen Soc. of Great Britain, Soc. of Motion Picture and TV Engrs., Pi Tau Sigma, L.A. Athletic Club, Town Hall Club. *

BROWN, KARL, editor; b. Long Island, Kans., Jan. 13, 1895; s. Leonidas T. and Eva D. (Robb) B. AB, U. Kans., 1920; BS, N.Y. State Libr Sch., Albany, 1925. Instr. Iowa State Coll., Ames, 1920-23; asst. N.Y. Pub. Libr., 1925-40, assoc. bibliographer, 1940-48, acting editor, 1948-50, editor, 1950-54; freelance editor, bibliographer, from 1954; cons. St. Martin's Press, N.Y.C., from 1956; libr. cons. Reynolds Libr., Rochester, N.Y., 1929-30; editor Libr. Jour., N.Y., 1943-51, cons., 1959-64; spl. editor libr. sci. Webster's New Internat. Dictionary, from 1960; indexer, bibliographer Antiquarian Press, N.Y.C., 1961-65; editor libr. terms G. & C. Merriam Co., 1961-65. Author: Guide to the Reference Collections of the New York Public Library, 1941; compiler, editor: American Library Directory, 1930-48; editorial advisor ency. Crowell-Collier, N.Y.; contbr. articles to profl. jours. Mem. ALA (reprint expediter 1959-62, com. reprinting bd. Acquisitions Libr. Materials), N.Y. Libr. Assn. (v.p.). Republican. Episcopalian. *

BROWN, LESLIE EDWIN, educator; b. Whiting, Iowa, June 4, 1898; s. William Gaylor and Cora Ann (Me-Kim) B.; m. Evangeline Henika, Aug. 9, 1924. Student, Grinnell Coll., 1916-17, 18-19; AB, U. Wis., 1921; AM, Columbia, 1930. High sch. prin. Brown's Valley, Minn., 1922-24; supt. schs. Brown's Valley, 1924-27, Monticello, Minn., 1927-29; dir., tchr. Windward Sch., White Plains, N.Y., 1930-37; regional supr. Emergency Adult Edn. Program N.Y. State, 1937-39; dir. Community Sch. for Adults, Lincoln Libr., Springfield, Ill., 1939-44; instr. edn., dir. dept. debating and pub. discussion U. Wis., 1945-47; prof. adult edn. Western Res. U., from 1948, exec. officer dept. edn., 1958-59, acting chmn. dept. edn., 1964-65; dean adminstrn. Cleve. Coll., 1948-63, acting dean, 1953-56, dean, from 1963; mem. bd. edn. Chagrin Falls, Ohio, from 1960, pres., 1961. Author articles, monographs. Mem. Adult Edn. Assn., United States (v.p. 1957-58), N. Ctrl. Assn. (mem. TV com.), Cleve. Adult Edn. Coun. (past chmn.), ALA, Ohio Adult Edn. Assn., Phi Beta Kappa, Omicron Delta Kappa, Delta Sigma Pi, Phi Delta Kappa, Kiwanis. Episcopalian. *

BROWN, MARTIN PARKS, state senator; b. Hart, Ga., Nov. 29, 1914; s. Heber C. and Hattie (Parks) B.; m. Joyce Winn, 1938; children: Jerry Parks, Sandra Joyce, Martin Boyce. Mcht., cotton farmer, fertilizer dealer; mem. Ga. Ho. of Reps., 1961-66, Ga. Senate, from 1968. With U.S. Army, 1943-46, ETO. Decorated Battle Star. Democrat. Baptist. Home: Hartwell Ga. Deceased. †

BROWN, PAUL, football executive; b. Norwalk, Ohio, Sept. 7, 1908. Ed., Ohio State U., Miami U., Ohio. Coach, Severn, Md., 1930-32; coach football and basketball Massillon (Ohio) High Sch., 1932-41; coach Ohio State U., Columbus, 1941-43, Great Lakes Coll., 1944-45; coach profl. football team Cleve. Browns, 1946-62; coach profl. football team Cin. Bengals, 1968-76, v.p., gen. mgr., 1976-91. Home: Cincinnati Ohio Died Aug. 5, 1991; buried Marrillon, Ohio.

BROWN, PAUL HOWARD, management consultant; b. Commerce, Ga., July 3, 1906; s. John Glenn and Carrie H. (Holcomb) B.; m. Mildred Chesnutt, June 6, 1935; children: Beverly Louise (Mrs. Paul F. Goree, Jr.), Virginia Elaine (Mrs. Harold W. Lochner, Jr.). Student, U. Ga., 1927-28. Cost acct. Morse Bros. Lubmer Co., 1926-30, office mgr., sales mgr., 1930-35; br. mgr. Seaboard Fin. Corp., 1935-38, Gen. Fin. Corp., Evanston, Ill., 1938; successively regional mgr., v.p. Gen. Fin. Corp., Orlando, Fla., 1938-62, exec. v.p., 1962-63, chmn., CEO, 1963-70; mgt. cons. Orlando, Fla., 1970-89; past pres. Brown Bros. Farms, Inc.; past v.p. C.N.A. Fin.Corp. Mem. Orlando Country Club, Univ. (Orlando). Methodist. Home: Orlando Fla. Died Sept. 25, 1990.

BROWN, RHETT DELFORD (HARRIETT BROWN), artist, educator; b. Atlanta, Nov. 12, 1924; d. Robert J. and Irene (Fox) Gurney; B.A., Duke U., 1944; m. William A. Cone, Oct. 1945 (div. Nov. 1960); children: Peggy, Carol; m. 2d Robert Delford-Brown, Mar. 21, 1963. Actress in stock and community theatres, N.H. and N.Y., 1950-59; founder, dir. Cricket Theatre, N.Y.C., 1959-63; producer Happenings and Events, London, Nice, France, Great Neck, N.Y., 1963-70; co-founder Gt. Bldg. Crack-Up Gallery, N.Y.C., 1969-71, gallery dir., 1971-76; instr. L.I. U., 1978-79, Am. Inst. Textile Art, Pine Manor Coll., Chestnut Hill, Mass., Spring 1978, 79, 80; studio artist Embroiderers Guild Am., N.Y.C., 1973-88; died, 1988; exhibited work in one-woman show: Gt. Bldg. Crack-Up, N.Y.C., 1974; exhibited in group shows: Erotics Gallery, N.Y.C., 1975-80, Union Carbide Invitational, 1978, U. Del., Wilmington, 1980, Brookfield (Conn.) Craft Center, 82, Abigail Adams Mus., N.Y.C., 1982, Culdane Ctr., Brookline, Mass., 1982; represented in permanent collections: Smithsonian, Inst. Contemporary Art, London; exhibited Textile Art Retrospective Gaston County Mus., Dallas, N.C., 1960-65. Co-chmn., Friends of Jackson Sq. Park, N.Y.C.; bd. dirs. The Ridiculous Theatrical Co., N.Y.C., 1977-88, Brookfield Craft Ctr. Cert. tchr. mixed-media stitchery, Valentine Mus., Richmond, Va. Mem Embroiderers Guild Am. (acquisition com.), Nat. Standards Council, Am. Inst. Textile Art (dir.), Coll. Art Assn., Woman's Art Caucus. Died Sept. 18, 1988. Home: New York N.Y. †

BROWN, THOMAS MCPHERSON, physician; b. Washington, June 29, 1906; s. Thomas Janney and Elsie (Palmer) B.; m. Olive H. Young, July 6, 1937; 1 dau., Gael McPherson. A.B., Swarthmore Coll., 1929; M.D., Johns Hopkins, 1933. Successively intern, asst. resident, chief resident medicine Johns Hopkins Hosp., 1933-37, 39-40; research rheumatic fever Rockefeller Inst. Hosp., N.Y.C., 1937-39; from asso. medicine to asst. prof. medicine Johns Hopkins, 1939-46; chief medicine VA Hosp., Washington, 1946-48; Eugene Meyer prof. medicine, chmn. dept. medicine, also dir. arthritis research unit George Washington U., 1948-70; co-dir. Rehab. Research and Tng. Center, 1965-70; also chief of medicine George Washington U. Hosp., 1948-70; founder, dir. Arthritis Inst. Nat. Hosp, Arlington, from 1970; Bd. dirs. Eugene and Agnes Meyer Found., Swarthmore Found., Sidwell Friends Sch. Author articles in gen. clin. medicine, infectious and tropical diseases.; also author related infectious hypersensitivity concept of mechanism rheumatoid arthritis and rheumatic diseases. Served to lt. col. M.C. AUS, 1942-45. Recipient Ivy medal Swarthmore Coll., 1929, Joshua Lippincott fellow, 1929; Dennison Strong fellow Johns Hopkins, 1929-33. Fellow A.C.P.; mem. Soc. Clin. Investigation, Am. Clin. and Climatological Soc., So. Soc. Clin. Research, Phi Beta Kappa, Sigma Xi, Alpha Omega Alpha, Phi Kappa Psi. Mem. Soc. of Friends. Home: Arlington Va. Died Apr. 17, 1989.

BROWN, WILLIAM F., editor, publisher; b. Chgo., Dec. 5, 1904; s. Thomas J. and Ellen (Walsh) B.; m. Vonne Ellen Windchy, June 14, 1941; children; Ellen Catherine, Barbara Ann, William F. Student, DePaul U. With Am. Field, 1922-90, stenographer, registrar, 1924, field trial reporter, 1925, asst. editor, 1927, bus. mgr., 1931, editor, 1940; pres. Am. Field Pub. Co., Chgo., 1943-90; past pub., editor Am.. Field, Chgo. Author: The Field Trial Primer, 1934, A. F. Hochwalt Biography, 1940, How To Train Hunting Dogs, 1942, Rod and Gun Calendar, 1944, Retriever Gun Dogs, 1945, Field Trails, 1947, National Field Trial Champions, 1956-66, 66; contbr. sect. on dogs to Ency. Americana, sect. on sport hunting to Ency. Brit.; contbr. articles to various publs. Roman Catholic. Home: Chicago Ill. Died Apr. 21, 1990.

BROWN, WILLIAM LACY, genetic supply company executive; b. Arbovale, W.Va., July 16, 1913; s. Tilden L. and Mamie Hudson (Orndoff) B.; m. Alice Hevener Hannah, Aug. 17, 1941; children: Alicia Anne, William Tilden. BA, Bridgewater Coll., Va., 1936; MS, Washington U., St. Louis, 1939, PhD, 1941; PhD (hon.), Drake U., 1980, DSc (hon.), 1987; PhD (hon.), W.Va. U., 1989. Cytogeneticist Dept. Agr., Washington, 1941-42; dir. maize breeding Rogers Bros. Co., Olivia, Minn., 1942-45; with Pioneer Hi-Bred Internat., Inc., Des Moines, 1945-83, v.p., dir. corp. research, 1965-75, pres., 1975-79, chief exec. officer, 1975-81, chmn., dir., 1979-83; dir. Am. Farmland Trust, Winrock Internat; extramural prof. botany Washington U., 1957-65; mem. Gov. Iowa Sci. Adv. Coun., 1977-89. Co-author: Corn, 1987, Its Early Fathers, 1987; author papers maize cytogenetics, evolution, germplasm conservation. Bd. regents Nat. Colonial Farm. Trustee Accokeek Found., Washington; bd. regents Bridgewater (Va.) Coll. Fulbright advanced research scholar Imperial Coll. Tropical Agr., Trinidad, 1952-53; Univ. fellow Drake U., 1981; recipient Disting. Alumni award Bridgewater Coll., 1980, Disting. Alumni award Washington U., 1981, Henry Shaw medal Mo. Bot. Garden, 1986, Iowa Gov.'s Sci. medal, 1987; named Citizen of Yr. Johnston C. of C., 1991. Fellow Am. Soc. Agronomy, Iowa Acad. Sci. (dir., disting. fellow award); mem. AAAS, Nat. Acad. Scis. (chmn. bd. on agr. 1983-89), Am. Genetics Soc., Can. Genetics Soc., Am. Genetics Assn., Am. Inst. Biol. Scis., Bot. Soc. Am., Soc. Econ. Botany (Disting. Econ. Botanist award 1980), Crop Sci. Soc. Am. (pres. 1982, Genetics and Plant Breeding award for industry 1986), Phi Beta Kappa, Sigma Xi. Mem. Soc. of Friends. Home: Johnston Iowa Died Mar. 8, 1991; body donated to science.

BROWNE, DIK, cartoonist; b. N.Y.C., Aug. 11, 1917; m. Joan Kelly (dec.); children: Bob, Chris, Sally. Studied at, Cooper Union. Copyboy, staff artist N.Y. Jour. Am., 1936-41; staff artist Newsweek, 1941-42; advt. artist Johnstone and Cushing Art Agts., N.Y.C., 1946-54. Comic strip artist Hi And Lois, 1954—; comic strip artist, writer Hagar the Horrible, from 1973 author: (with Mort Walker) Land of Lost Things, 1973, Hagar the Horrible, 1973, Wit and Wisdom of Hagar the Horrible, 1974, The Best of Hagar, 1981, The Very Best of Hagar, 1982, (with Christopher Browne) Hagar the Horrible's Very Nearly Complete Viking Handbook, 1985, Best of Hagar, 1985, Hagar Hits the Mark, Happy Hour, Helga's Revenge, Midnight Munchies, My Feet Are Really Drunk, On The Loose, On the Rocks, Sack Time, Simple Life, Hagar at Work, Hear No Evil, Hagar and the Golden Maiden, (with Mort Walker) All Hi and Lois Books, also numerous others. Served with AUS, World War II. Recipient Banshee Silver Lady award, 1962, Elzie Segar award, 1975, Best Non-Brit. Internat. Cartoon award, 1983, Best Overseas Cartoon award, 1986, Overseas Origin Cartoonist award, 1987, all Cartoonist Club of Gt. Britain, 1st ann. Max and Moritz Preis Bester Comic-Kunstler award, Comic Salon, Erlangen, Fed. Republic Germany, 1984. Mem. Nat. Cartoonists Soc. (pres. 1963-65, Reuben awards 1962, 73, Best Humor Strip Cartoonist (for Hi & Lois) 1959, 60, (for Hagar) 72, 77, 85, 87, Elzie Segar award, 1973), Nat. Comics Council. Home: Sarasota Fla. Died June 4, 1989.

BROWNELL, SAMUEL MILLER, educator; b. Peru, Nebr., Apr. 3, 1900; s. Herbert and May (Miller) B.; m. Esther Delzell, June 23, 1927; children: Richard, Dorothy (Mrs. Bryce Templeton), Jane (Mrs. K. Cheek), Ruth (Mrs. Thomas Green). AB, U. Nebr., 1921, LLD, 1963; AM, Yale U., 1924, PhD, 1926; BL, Shurtleff Coll., 1954; EdD, Tufts U., 1954; LLD, U. Denver, 1954, Harding Coll., 1955, Cen. Coll., 1955, U. S.D., 1955, High Point Coll., 1956, Wayne State U., 1959, U. Nebr., 1963, Mich. State U., 1963; PedD, Bradley U., 1955; EdD, Western Mich. U., 1956; LHD, Doane Coll., 1966. Prin. Demonstration High Sch. State Tchrs. Coll., Peru, 1921-23; asst. prof. edn. N.Y. State Coll. Tchrs., 1926-27; supt. schs. Grosse Pointe, Mich., 1927-38; vis. prof. ednl. adminstrn. Yale, 1937-38, prof. ednl. adminstrn. Grad. Sch., 1938-53, part-time prof. urban edn. adminstrn., 1966-70, sr. cons. in. edn., 1970-73; pres. New Haven State Tchrs. Coll., 1947-53; U.S. commr. edn., 1953-56; supt. pub. schs. Detroit, 1956-66; part-time prof. edn. U. Conn., 1966-70; lectr. U. Wis., 1927, 39, Cornell U., 1930, 41, Harvard, 1931-35, U. So. Calif., 1940, 49, 56, 59, U. Mich., 1942, 44. Author: Progress in Educational Administration, 1935, Urban Education, 1972; contbr. articles to profl. jours., and author numerous sch. surveys. Vice chmn. U.S. del UNESCO, Montevideo, Uruguay, 1954, U.S. rep. Conf. Ministers of Edn. of Ams., Lima, Peru, 1956; chmn. U.S. del. Internat. Conf. on Edn., Geneva, 1960. Past mem. Mayflower Soc., Phi Beta Kappa, Phi Delta Kappa, Kappa Phi Kappa. Home: New Haven Conn. Died Oct. 12, 1990.

BROWNING, FRANK MILTON, financier, sales executive; b. Ogden, Utah, Oct. 17, 1897; s. Jonathan Edmund and Mary (Jones) B.; m. Eugenia Hanson, June 16, 1923; children: Frances Marie Smith, Roderick Hanson, Phillip Holbrook. Student pub. schs., Ogden. Organizer, pres. Browning Chevrolet, Co., from 1933, Budget Fin. and Ins. Co., from 1947; organizer, chmn. Bank of Ben Lomond; chmn. Bank of Utah; pres. J.E. Browning Co.; dir. Deseret News Pub. Co., Salt Lake City. State senator Utah, from 1959; mem. nat. bank adv. com. to the Comptr. of the Currency; Utah state chmn. John F. Kennedy Meml. Libr. Fund. Served as pilot U.S. A.A.C., Eng., France, Germany, 1917-19, disch. 2d lt.; comdr. Persian Gulf Ordnance Depot, Iran, 1943, U.S. Ordnance Dept., 1941-46, disch. as col. Mem. Ogden C. of C. (pres. 1934), Automobile Old Timers Club of Am., Rotary (Ogden). *

BROWNING, IBEN, biophysicist, climatologist, inventor; b. Vanderbilt, Tex., Jan. 9, 1918; s. Bede and Lugilla (McCormick) B.; m. Florence A. Pinto, July 30, 1945; 1 dau., Evelyn. B.S., S.W. Tex. State Tchrs. Coll., 1937; M.A., U. Tex., 1947, Ph.D. in Physiology, Genetics and Bacteriology, 1948. Tutor in physiology U. Tex., Austin, 1937-38; technician U. Tex., 1938-39, instr. biology, 1946-47; pres. Tex. Cedar Products Co., 1940-41; cons. climatologist Mitchell Hutchins/Paine Webber, from 1975; Nat. Research fellow in biophysics U. Pa., Phila., 1948-49; asst. biologist M.D. Anderson Hosp., Houston, 1949-52, asst. prof., 1950-52; devel. physicist Am. Optical Co., 1952-54; supr. optics div. Bell Aircraft Corp., 1954-57; staff mem., scientist Sandia Lab., Albuquerque, 1957-60; prin. investigator Panoramic Research Co., Palo Alto, Calif., 1960-64; exec. dir. Thomas Bede Found., Los Altos, Calif. and Albuquerque, from 1963; pres. Sydnor-Barent Scanner Corp., Albuquerque, from 1971; cons. in various fields to numerous bus. and fin. instns. and research orgns. Author: (with N. Winkless) Climate and the Affairs of Men, 1975, Robots on Your Doorstep, 1978, (with Evelyn Garriss) Past and Future History: A Planner's Guide, 1982; editor The Browning Newsletter, from 1977; holder numerous U.S. and fgn. patents. Served with USAAF, 1941-45. Mem. AAAS. Home: Sandia Park N.Mex. Died July 18, 1991; buried Sandia Mtns.

BROWNLEE, RICHARD SMITH, historian; b. Brookfield, Mo., Mar. 12, 1918; s. Ellis Crance and Mary Margaret (Shore); m. Alice Lucille Rowley, Oct. 31, 1942; children: Richard Smith, III, Margaret Ann. A.B., U. Mo., Columbia, 1939, B.J., 1940, M.A. in History, 1950, Ph.D., 1955. Asst. prof. history extension div. U. Mo., Columbia, 1950-60; asst. dir. adult edn. U. Mo., 1950-60; sec., dir. State Hist. Soc. Mo., Columbia, 1960-85; mem. Mo. Records Commn., from 1967, Civil War Centennial Commn., 1961-65, Historic Sites Adv. Commn., 1961-81, State Capitol Restoration Commn., 1967, Am. Revolution Bicentennial Commn., 1976-78, Nat. Hist. Publs. and Records Commn., from 1978; cultural dir. Mo. Pavilion, N.Y. World's Fair, 1962. Author: Gray Ghosts of the Confederacy, 1959; editor: Missouri Hist. Rev, 1960-85, A Catalogue of Specialized Libraries of Missouri, 1962; co-editor: Messages and Proclamations of Governors James T. Blair and John M. Dalton, 1961-64. Served with AUS, 1941-42; to capt. USAAF, 1942-45. Mem. Am. Hist. Assn., Mississippi Valley Hist. Soc., So. Hist. Assn., Mo. Press Assn., Mo. Mus. Assocs. (founding mem.), Acad. Mo. Squires, Friends of U. Mo. State Hist. Soc. Libraries, Am. Legion, Phi Beta Kappa, Kappa Tau Alpha, Sigma Nu. Presbyterian. Club: Mo. Country. Home: Columbia Mo. Deceased. †

BRUBACHER, JOHN SELLER, university professor; b. Easthampton, Mass., Oct. 18, 1898; s. Abram Royer and Rosa (Haas) B.; m. Winifred Wemple, Aug. 12, 1924; children: John W., Paul W. AB, Yale, 1920; LLB, Harvard, 1923; PhD, Columbia, 1927. Bar: Mass. 1923. Instr. edn. Dartmouth, 1924-25; assoc. in edn. Columbia U., 1925-27, asst. prof., 1928; asst. prof. history and philosophy of edn. Yale U., 1928-34, assoc. prof., 1934-46, prof., 1946-59, Reuben Post Halleck prof. history and philosophy of edn., 1948; dir. four coll. study Conn. Dept. Edn., 1959-60; prof. edn. U. Mich., Ann Arbor, from 1960; vis. prof. Am. U. of Beirut, Lebanon, 1951-52, 56-57; Fulbright prof. Kyushu U., Fukuoka, Japan, 1957. Author: Modern Philosophies of Education, 1939, History of the Problems of Education, 1947, (with Willis Rudy) Higher Education in Transition, 1958, Bases for Policy in Higher Education, 1965; editor: Henry Barnard on Education, 1931, The Public School and Spiritual Values, 1944, Eclectic Philosophy of Education, 1951; content editor: Library of Edn. Mem. NEA, AAUP, Philosophy of Edn. Soc. (pres. 1942-46), Nat. Soc. Coll. Tchrs. Edn. (pres. 1963), Phi Beta Kappa, Phi Delta Kappa, Kappa Delta Pi. Conglist. (deacon). *

BRUCE, LOUIS ROOKS, lawyer; b. Onondaga Indian Reservation, Dec. 30, 1906; s. Louis R. and Nellie (Rooks) B.; m. Anna Jennings Wikoff, Nov. 19, 1930; children: Charles Wikoff, Katherine (Mrs. William H. Huxtable), Donald Kenneth. BA, Syracue U., 1930. Owner, operator dairy farm Richfield Springs, N.Y., 1930-34; N.Y. state dir. Indian projects NYA, 1935-42; edn. and youth dir. Dairymen's League Coop. Assn., 1946-55; v.p. Compton Advt., N.Y.C., 1955-59; with FHA, aslo N.Y. State Housing Authority, 1959-69; commr. Indian Affairs, Washignton, 1969-89; Past bd. dirs. Yale Broadcasting Co.; founder, past exec. dir. Nat. Congress Indian Affairs; founder, past bd. dirs. Arrow, Inc. Recipient Freedom's Found. award, 1949, Liberty Bell award Otsego County (N.Y.) Bar Assn., 1970. Mem. Assn. Am. Indian Affairs, Indian Coun. Five (Achievement award), N.Y. state Village Indian Assns., Mid Ea. Coops., Farm Bur. Fedn., Nat. Grange, Syracuse U. Alumni Assn. (Achievement award 1970), Rotary, Masons, Zeta Psi (pres. 1962-64), Sigma Delta Chi. Methodist (trustee, lay leader). Home: Richfield Springs N.Y. Died May 20, 1989.

BRUETSCH, WALTER L., physician; b. Singen, Hohentwiel, Germany, Nov. 25, 1896; came to U.S., 1924, naturalized, 1930.; s. Ludwig and Bertha (Wagner) B. AB, Fridericianum Coll., Davos, Switzerland, 1917; MD, U. Freiburg, Germany, 1922; grad. student, U. Vienna, 1931. Intern U. Hosps. of Hamburg, 1923-24; asst. physician and pathologist Ctrl. State Hosp., Indpls., 1925-30, dir. psychiat. rsch., 1930-38, head of the rsch. dept., from 1938; asst. prof. dept. nervous and mental diseases Ind. U. Sch. Medicine, 1931-37, clin. prof. neurology and psychiatry, from 1937. Mem. bd. editors, Excerpta Medica, section on neurology and psychiatry, pub. under auspices U. of Amsterdam, Netherlands, from 1948, Neuropsiquiatria, Jour. Neuropathology and Exptl. Neurology; author: Syphilitic Atrophy, 1952, Cerebral Arteriosclerosis, 1953; articles on rsch. in dementia praecox. Spl. cons. USPHS, Washington, from 1937. Recipient award Laymen's League Against Epilepsy, for describing rheumatic epilepsy-sequel of rheumatic fever, 1940. Mem. AMA, Am. Neurol. Assn., Am. Acad. Neurology, Am. Psychiat. Assn., Soc. Medico-Psychologique Paris (hon. mem.), Woodstock Club. *

BRUMBAUGH, GRANVILLE MARTIN, lawyer; b. St. Louis, Mar. 10, 1901; s. Noah J. and Rosa (Flory) B.; m. Sophia Waldman, June 19, 1926; children: Mary Ann Brumbaugh Hellmuth, Granville Martin, John. EE, Lehigh U., 1922; LLB, George Washington, 1925. Bar: N.Y., 1927. Asst. examiner U.S. Patent Office, 1922-25; assoc. Redding, Greeley, O'Shea & Campbell, 1925-34; ptnr. Hoguet, Neary & Campbell, N.Y.C., 1934-46; successor firm Campbell, Brumbaugh, Free & Graves (now Brumbaugh, Graves, Donohue & Raymond), 1946-92. Mem. bd. fin., Westport, Conn., 1947-48, town meeting rep., 1949-55. Mem. ABA, Am. Patent Law Assn., N.Y. Patent Law Assn. (pres. 1953-54), Assn. Bar City N.Y., Downtown Assn. Club (N.Y.C.), Country Club (Fairfield, Conn.), Phi Delta Phi, Phi Delta Theta. Home: Westport Conn. Died Mar. 9, 1992.

BRUN, EDMOND ANTOINE, educator; b. Saint Cannat, France, Dec. 31, 1898; s. Antoine Marius and Marie (Villecrose) B.; m. Suzanne Vincent, Sept. 8, 1923. BSc, U. Marseille, 1921, MS (fellowship nat. competitive test), 1923; DSc., Paris, 1934. Prof. spl. courses Lycee Nice, 1925-30, Parisian Lycee, 1930-42; lectr. then prof. fluid mechanics Faculte des Scis., from 1942; dir. Laboratoire d'Aerothermique, prof. Ecole Nationale Superieure de l'Aeronautique, from 1942. Author articles and books on aerodynamic heating convection, flight and icing of aircraft. Mem. Armed Forces, 1917-19. Decorated chevalier Legion of Honor, officer Military Merit (Brazil), comdr. Palmes Academiques, Laureate Acad. Scis. Fellow AIAA, Royal Area Soc.; fgn. fellow Nat. Acad. Scis., Internat. Astronautics Acad., Soc. Francaise des Thermiciens (pres.). *

BRUNDAGE, JOHN DENTON, insurance company executive; b. Newark, Mar. 28, 1919; s. Edgar Ray and Salome (Denton) B.; m. Ann Lounsbury, Nov. 29, 1941; children—Elizabeth Ann Bush, Susan Thorpe, Patricia Copley, John. A.B., Princeton U., 1941. C.L.U. Agy. asst. Bankers Nat. Life Ins. Co., Montclair, N.J., 1945-46, asst. to pres., 1953-54, adminstrv. v.p., 1955-57, exec. v.p., 1957-58, pres., dir., 1958-71; sales promotion mgr. Mut. Benefit Life Ins. Co., Newark, 1946-47, regional supt. agys., 1948-50, dir. agys., 1950-52; agy. mgr. Mut. Benefit Life Ins. Co., N.Y.C., 1952-53; chmn., dir. Palisades Life Ins. Co., New City, N.Y., 1965-71; chmn., pres., dir. Ga. Internat. Life, Atlanta, 1972-74; pres., dir. Dominion Trust Life, Houston, 1972-74; chmn., chief exec. officer Globe Life Ins. Co., Chgo., 1974-77, 79-84, pres., 1977-79, chmn., pres., 1980-84; v.p. Protectogon, Inc., from 1984; dir. Geneva Life, Gt. Equity Life. Chmn. Montclair Urban Coalition, 1969-70; chmn. bd. Am. Heart Assn., 1962-65, chmn., 1980-83; bd. govs. Chgo. Heart Assn., from 1976; trustee Sch. of the Ozarks, from 1976. Served to lt. comdr. USNR, 1940-45. Recipient Gold Heart award Am. Heart Assn., 1965, Citizens award for distinguished community service N.J. Acad. Medicine, 1964. Fellow Life Office Mgmt. Assn.; mem. Nat. Assn. Life Underwriters, Am. Coll. Life Underwriters. Clubs: Princeton (N.Y.C.); Short Hills (N.J.); Indian Hill (Winnetka); Chgo; Quadrangle (Princeton). Home: Winnetka Ill. Died Oct. 27, 1989.

BRUNER, WILLIAM WALLACE, banker; b. Orangeburg, S.C., Nov. 6, 1920; s. Robert Raysor and Bessie (Livingston) R.; children: William W., Thomas W., James L. CPA, S.C. Accountant J. W. Hunt & Co. (C.P.A.'s), Columbia, S.C., 1945-48; with First Nat. Bank S.C., Columbia, 1948-84; sr. v.p. First Nat. Bank S.C., 1961-64, pres., 1964-84, also chmn. bd., dir.; chmn. bd. S.C. Nat. Corp., Columbia, 1984-85, dir., 1984-87; pres. First Bankshares Corp. S.C. 1969-84; dir. Spartan Mills, Spartanburg, S.C. Treas. United Fund Columbia, 1958-59, bd. dirs., 1956- 58, chmn. large firms div., 1965, bd. dirs. treas., 1956-57; chmn. chpt. ARC, 1958-60, nat. fund vice chmn., 1960-61; trustee Providence Hosp., Columbia, chmn. fin. com., 1978-79, chmn. bd. trustees, 1980-82, 1986-88; trustee Bus. Partnership Found. U. S.C., Columbia, sec.-treas., 1972-73, chmn., 1984-85; treas. S.C. Soc. Crippled Children and Adults, 1967-70, v.p., 1970-71, pres., 1971-72; trustee Columbia Museums Art and Sci., from 1981. Lt. comdr. USNR, 1941-45. Mem. Am. Inst. CPA's, S.C. Assn. CPA's, Columbia C. of C. (treas. 1961, v.p. 1962), Urban League Columbia (bd. dirs.), Am. Bankers Assn. (adv. com. on fed. legislation 1966-71, governing council 1972-74, bd. dirs. 1972-73, trustee fund for edn. in econs. 1976-77, chmn. 1977), S.C. Bankers Assn. (v.p. 1967-68, pres. 1970-71), U.S. C. of C. (banking, monetary and fiscal affairs com. 1977-79), Phi Beta Kappa, Beta Gamma Sigma, Sigma Nu. Methodist. Home: Columbia N.C. Deceased. †

BRUNNER, KARL, economist; b. Zurich, Switzerland, Feb. 16, 1916; s. William and Ida (Maulaz) B.; m. Rosmarie Enderle, Sept. 20, 1945. Student, U. Zurich, 1934-37, London Sch. Econs., 1937-38; PhD (hon.), U. Louvain, Belgium. Past rsch. assoc. Swiss Nat. Bank; past econ. adviser Swiss Watch C. of C.; past mem. faculty U. Calif., L.A., Ohio State U., U. Bern, U. Rochester, N.Y.; also past dir. Ctr. for Rsch. Govt. Policy and Bus. U. Rochester; founder Jour. Money, Credit and Banking, Jour. Monetary Econs. Past mem. Am. Econ. Assn. Home: Rochester N.Y. Died May 9, 1989.

BRUNO, ANGELO J., supermarket company executive; b. Birmingham, Ala., May 29, 1922; married. With Brunos Inc., Birmingham, Ala., from 1946, chief oper. officer, dir.; chmn., chief exec. officer Brunos Inc. Served with U.S. Army, 1943-46. Home: Birmingham Ala. Died 1991. †

BRUNSON, WILLIAM REEDER, banker; b. Meridian, Miss., Jan. 23, 1895; s. John Howard and Helen (Lathan) B.; m. Lucille Boswell, Feb. 29, 1928; 1 child, William Reeder. Student pub. schs. Pres., gen. mgr. Brunson Furniture Co., 1928-32; pres. White System, Inc., 1932-37; v.p. Indsl. Fin. & Thrift Corp., New Orleans, 1937-49; pres. Indsl. Fin. & Thrift Corp., 1949-60, hon. chmn. bd., dir., from 1960; pres. Am. Credit Co., Colonial Fin. & Thrift, Tenn.; dir. First Fin. & Thrift Corp., Chattanooga, Tenn. and Rome, Ga. Lt. U.S. Army, WWI. Mem. Am. Indsl. Bankers Assn. (pres. 1950-51), Elk, Mason. Presbyterian. *

BRUSSEL-SMITH, BERNARD, artist, educator; b. N.Y.C., Mar. 1, 1914; s. Raymond and Belle (Epstein) B.-S.; m. Mildred Cornfeld, Sept. 25, 1937; 1 son, Peter. Student, Penn Acad. Fine Arts, 1931-36. Art dir. Geyer Publs., 1939-42; head advt. dept. Chance-Voight Aircraft Co., 1942-44; art dir. Noyes & Sproul, 1944-45; free lance wood engraver, from 1945; instr. Cooper Union, Bklyn. Mus., Phila. Mus. Sch. Art, N.A.D., Coll. City N.Y. Prints included in collections, Library of Congress, Carnegie Inst., N.Y. Pub. Library, U. Ill., Phila. Mus., Smithsonian Instn., Boymans Mus., Rotterdam, Nat. Collection, Bklyn. Mus., Sterling Library Yale U., Fairleigh Dickinson W. LIbrary. Recipient Frank Hartley Anderson award, 1948, Am. Artist Group award, 1948, John Taylor Arms Meml. prize, 1970, Samuel Morse award, 1976, Cannon award, 1981; asso. Nat. Acad., 1952. Clubs: Art Directors,

Type Directors, Dutch Treat. Home: Bedford Hills N.Y. Died May 8, 1989; buried Bedford Hills.

BRYAN, CURTIS FRANCE, banker; b. Sapulpa, Okla., Feb. 29, 1896; s. Vaughn Rohrer and Bessie Lucas (France) B.; m. Lulu Frances Smith, May 22, 1924; 1 child, Frances Joan. Edn. pub. schs. Asst. sec.-treas. Mileage Gasoline Co., 1914-16; gen. mgr. Quality Oil & Gasoline Co., 1916-18; resident mgr. Biery Oil Co., 1919-20; pres., gen. mgr. Union Oil Refining Co., 1920; ind. producer of oil, 1920-25; pres. Bryan & Emery, Inc., 1925-27; pres., dir. Bryan Petroleum Corp., 1927-50; chmn. bd. Admiral State Bank, 1954-65, Community State Bank, Tulsa, Okla., from 1955; pres., dir. Toklan Oil (formerly Royalty Corp.), 1937-55. Sgt. U.S. Army, 1918; col. AUS, 1942-46. Awarded Legion of Merit, U.S. Mem. Ind. Petroleum Assn. Am., Mason, Tulsa Club, So. Hills Country Club, Lyford Cay Club (Nassau). Republican. Unitarian. *

BRYAN, WILHELMUS B(OGART), JR., educator; b. Washington, Oct. 9, 1898; s. Wilhelmus Bogart and Emily (Pentland) B.; m. Elizabeth Carter, July 27, 1945; children: Wilhelmus Bogart, Katharine M. Grad., Phillips Acad., Andover, Mass., 1916; AB, Princeton, 1920, AM, 1924; student, Princeton Theol. Sem., U. Minn.; DHL (hon.), Macalester Coll., 1952. Ordained to ministry Presbyn. Ch., 1924. Asst. pastor 1st Presbyn. Ch., Princeton, N.J., 1924-31; pastor for Presbyn. students Princeton; organizer, dir. Westminster Found., Princeton, 1931-38; dir. Blake Sch. boarding dept., Hopkins, Minn., 1939-46; dean Macalester Coll., St. Paul, 1946-51; dir. Mpls. Sch. of Art, 1951-62; dir. emeritus; dir. Atlanta Art Assn., 1962-65. Chmn. Ga. Art Commn. Mem. Nat. Assn. Schs. Art (pres.), Mason, Clubs: Rotary (Atlanta), Minneapolis, Princeton of N.Y. Democrat. *

BRYANT, EDWARD KENDALL, civil engineer; b. Norwood, Mass., Apr. 13, 1902; s. Edward Andem and Alice Elizabeth (Crandell) B.; m. Tamara Herne, Nov. 23, 1966; children—Edward Andem, John Dixon. C.E., Rensselaer Poly. Inst., 1925. Engr. William S. Lozier, Rochester, N.Y., 1924-28; prin. John L. Weber, Inc., Trenton, N.J., 1928-30; owner, operator Edward K. Bryant (Cons. Engr.), Mt. Holly, N.J., 1930-42; project engr. Tippetts Abbett McCarthy Stratton, N.Y.C., 1946-56; partner Tippetts Abbett McCarthy Stratton, N.Y.C., 1956-73; owner, operator Edward K. Bryant (Cons. Engr.), Chevy Chase, Md., from 1974. Served to comdr. Civil Engr. Corps USN, 1942-46. Mem. ASCE, Am. Cons. Engrs. Council, Soc. for Internat. Devel., Am. Arbitration Assn., Soc. Am. Mil. Engrs., Theta Chi. Republican. Episcopalian. Club: Army and Navy (Washington). Home: Chevy Chase Md. Died July 22, 1991.

BRYANT, REECE L(AWRENCE), poultry husbandman; b. Omaha, Ill., Aug. 23, 1898; s. Gnar Orman and Eva (Knight) B.; m. Lottye Phillips, June 26, 1923. Student, Western Ky. State Teachers Coll., 1921; BS, U. of Ky., 1923; MS, Cornell U., 1926, PhD, 1928. Instr. in Agr. Western Ky. State Teachers Coll., 1923-25; asst. prof. poultry husbandry Va. Poly Inst., 1928-41, assoc. prof., 1941-46; asst. poultry husbandman Va. Agr. Expt. Sta., 1929-41, assoc. poultry husbandman, 1941-46; prof. poultry husbandry, chmn. dept. N.D. State U.; poultry husbandman N.D. Agrl. Expt. Sta., from 1946; mem. N.D. Poultry Improvement Bd., tech. com. N. Ctrl. States Poultry Breeding Project. Author articles in sci. jours. and Expt. Sta. bulls. Served with USNR, 1918. Mem. Poultry Sci. Assn., N.D. Acad. Sci., Alpha Zeta, Masons (past master), Order Eastern Star (past patron), Lions (Blacksburg, Va. and Fargo, N.D.). Methodist. *

BUBB, HENRY AGNEW, savings and loan association executive; b. Williamsport, Pa., Mar. 26, 1907; s. Harry A. and Marjorie (Wheeler) B.; m. Elizabeth Black, June 26, 1929; 1 child, Barbara Elizabeth (Mrs. John C. Dicus). Student, U. Kans., 1924-27; D.B.A. in Bus. (hon.), Washburn U. Chmn. bd. Capitol Fed. Savs. and Loan Assn., Topeka; former chmn. and dir. Mortgage Guaranty Ins. Corp. of Milw.; chmn. emeritus MGIC Investment Corp., Milw.; dir. Columbian Nat. Title Ins. Co., Topeka, Capitol Funds, Inc., Topeka, Security Benefit Group Cos., Topeka; former chmn. Fed. Home Loan Bank of Topeka; former vice chmn. MGIC Indemnity Corp., N.Y.; former dir. MGIC Fin. Corp., MGIC Mortgage Co., Milw.; past pres. Mid-West Savings and Loan Conf.; past trustee Am. Savs. and Loan Inst.; mem. adv. com. of savs. and loan bus. Treasury Dept.; past mem. task force Fed. Home Loan Bank Bd., Washington. Past sr. mem., chmn. Kans. State Bd. Regents; past chmn. Kans. Edn. Commn.; past chmn. Higher Edn. Loan Program; former dir. Shawnee County ARC, former chmn. numerous charitable drives, chmn., mem. war loan and victory fund coms.; past vice chmn., mem. Topeka Planning Bd.; past chmn. Topeka Housing and Planning Com.; mem. Fiscal Adv. Bd. Topeka; chmn. United Fund; bd. regents Washburn U.; nat. chmn. Young Republican Nat. Fedn., 1937-38; del. Rep. Nat. Conv., 1964; nat. chmn. Citizens for Reagan, 1968; former trustee Inst. Fiscal and Polit. Edn., N.Y.C.; trustee U. Kans. Endowment Assn.; bd. dirs., past pres. Downtown Topeka, Inc. Recipient award Treasury Dept., 1946, Wisdom award of honor, Disting. Service citation, Higher Edn. Leadership prize, Fred Ellsworth medal U. Kans., Disting. Kansan award Native Sons and Daus., 1974, Bubb Light Circle Washburn U., 1980, others. Disting. fellow Internat. Union Bldg. Socs. and Savs. and Loan Assns.; mem. U.S. League Savs. Instns. (chmn. legis. com. 1954-63, legis. cons., exec. com. 1949-63, pres. 1949-50), Kans. Savs. and Loan League (past pres.), U.S. League Savs. Assns. (sr. adv. group com. on polit. action), Topeka C. of C. (past pres., dir.), Kans. U. Alumni Assn. (past nat. pres.), Newcomen Soc. N. Am., S.A.R., 35th Div. Assn., Sigma Chi (past pres. alumni chpt., named Significant Sig 1977), Alpha Kappa Psi. Episcopalian (past sr. warden). Lodges: Masons (Disting. Service award 1968, 33 deg., potentate), Jester (past dir., grand cross Ct. Honor), Rotary (Paul Harris fellow 1986), Sojourners. Clubs: Topeka Country (past pres., past dir.); Cabiri; Garden of the Gods (Colorado Springs, Colo.); Paradise Valley Country (Ariz.). Home: Topeka Kans. Died Jan. 10, 1989; buried Topeka.

BUCHANAN, JOHN MURDOCH, fish products producer; b. Steveston, B.C., July 21, 1897; s. Donald and Christie Ann (Morrison); m. Mildred Abercrombie, March 14, 1925; 2 children. BA, U. B.C., 1917. Fishing bus. Steveton, B.C., 1917-20; with firm of auditors, 1920-21, Cedar's Ltd. lumber mfrs., 1921-27; with British Columbia Packers, Ltd., from 1928, sec.-treas., 1932, gen. mgr., 1935, v.p., gen. mgr., 1941, pres., 1946-56, chmn. bd., 1956-58, chmn. bd., pres., 1958-64, dir., chmn. policy com., from 1964; bd. dirs. MacMillan, Bloedel and Powell River Ltd., Can. Imperial Bank of Commerce, Pacific Coast Fire Ins. Co.; adv. bd. Can. Trust Co., Huron & Erie Mortgage Corp. Mem. Vancouver Club, Faculty Club, U. Vancouver Club (hon.). Mem. United Ch. of Can. *

BUCHIN, IRVING D., orthodontist, educator; b. N.Y.C., Feb. 17, 1920; s. David and Lillian (Polowick) B.; m. Jean Jacobs, May 18, 1941; sons: Peter Jay, John David. D.D.S., N.Y. U., 1943; postgrad., U. Detroit, 1949, Tenple U., 1951. Diplomate: Am. Bd. Orthodontics. Practice dentistry limited to orthodontics N.Y.C., from 1946; chief of orthodontics Jewish Chronic Disease Hosp., 1955-57; orthodontist Jewish Meml. Hosp., 1950; asst. vis. dental surgeon City Hosp., 1946; mem. panel of orthodontists N.Y.C. Dept. Health, from 1949; constituent, mem. adv. bd. N.Y.C. Dept. Health (Bur. Dentistry), from 1972; orthodontist U. Hosp., Boston U., Meml. Hosp. Mass., 1963-68; cons. div. dentistry, dept. surgery Children's Hosp. Phila., from 1979; lectr., clinician in postgrad. edn. ADA (Am. Assn. Orthodontists); instr. Charles H. Tweed Found. Orthodontic Research, 1964-73, dir., pres. Eastern sect., 1972-73; vis. asso. prof. orthodontics Boston U. Sch. Medicine; asso. prof. orthodontics U. Pa. (Sch. Dental Medicine), 1967-73, prof., 1974-89; guest lectr. Columbia U., Fairleigh Dickinson U., Baylor U., N.Y. U., Howard U., Tufts U., U. So. Calif., U. Toronto, U. Caracas (Venezuela), from 1969; cons., mem. orthodontic peer rev. com. 11th dist. N.Y. State; bd. dirs. Angle Orthodontists Research and Edn. Found., from 1981. Constituent editor Am. Jour. Orthodontics contbr. articles to dental jours., textbooks. Inventor Buchin cephalometric template for facial measurements. Served to capt. Dental Corps AUS, 1943-46. Fellow Am. Coll. Dentists, Chas. H. Tweed Internat. Found. for Orthodontic Research; mem. Eastern Assn. Strang-Tweed Study Groups (sec. 1951-57), Am. Assn. Orthodontists (council on orthodontic edn. from 1982), Am. Acad. Dental Medicine, Internat. Assn. Dental Research, Pierre Fauchard Acad., N.Y. Acad. Scis., Fedn. Dentaire Internationale, N.E. Soc. Orthodontists (pres. 1977-78, chmn. exam bd. preceptee accreditation, del. Am. Assn. Orthodontists, constituent editor 1972-75, edn. com. from 1972, bd. censors 1979-83), Edward H. Angle Soc. Orthodontics (nat. treas. 1970-75, dir. 1981-87, editor Eastern component 1966-74, pres. 1972-73), Angle Orthodontists Research and Edn. Found. (dir. 1981). Clubs: Muttontown Golf and Country, Univ. Pa. Faculty. Home: Forest Hills N.Y. Died Mar. 30, 1989; buried Long Island, N.Y.

BUCHLER, JUSTUS, philosopher, educator; b. N.Y.C., Mar. 27, 1914; s. Samuel and Ida (Frost) B.; m. Evelyn Urban Shirk, Feb. 20, 1943; 1 dau., Katherine Urban Tessen. BS, CCNY, 1934; MA, Columbia U., 1935, PhD, 1939. Lectr. philosophy Columbia U., 1937-42; instr. philosophy Bklyn. Coll., 1938-43; faculty Columbia U., 1942-71, prof. philosophy, 1956-71, Johnsonian prof., 1959-71, chmn. dept. philosophy, 1964-67, chmn. Contemporary Civilization program in coll., 1950-56; disting. prof. philosophy SUNY-Stony Brook, 1971-81, disting. prof. emeritus, 1981. Author: Charles Peirce's Empiricism, 1939, (with J.H. Randall Jr.) Philosophy: An Introduction, 1942, (with others) The Philosophy of Bertrand Russell, 1944, Toward a General Theory of Human Judgment, 1951, 2d rev. edit., 1979, Studies in the Philosophy of Charles Sanders Peirce, 1952, A History of Columbia College on Morningside, 1954, Nature and Judgment, 1955, The Concept of Method, 1961, Metaphysics of Natural Complexes, 1966, The Main of Light: On the Concept of Poetry, 1974; editor: (with B. Schwartz) The Obiter Scripta of George Santayana, 1936, The Philosophy of Peirce: Selected Writings, 1940, (with Randall and Shirk) Readings in Philosophy, 1946, (with others) Introduction to Contemporary Civilization in the West, 2 vols, 1946, (with Randall) Chapters in Western Civilization, 2 vols, 1948. Mem. Am. Philos. Assn., ACLU (vice chmn. nat. acad. freedom com. 1958-64). Home: Garden City N.Y. Died Mar. 19, 1991.

BUCKLER, WILLIAM EARL, English and American literature educator; b. Loretto, Ky., Oct. 10, 1924; s. William Oscar and Mary (Hiestand) Buckler. A.B., U. Ky., 1944, M.A., 1946; Ph.D., U. Ill., 1949. Asst. prof. English and Am. lit. NYU, N.Y.C., 1953-57, assoc. prof., 1957-59, prof., from 1959, assoc. dean Washington Sq. Coll., 1958-60, dean Washington Sq. Coll., 1960-69, vice chancellor univ., 1969-70; frequent lectr. on Sunrise Semester program Sta. WCBS-TV; founder Thomas Hardy Soc. NYU. Author: numerous books including Matthew Arnold's Books: Toward a Publishing Dairy, 1958, Prose of the Victorian Period, 1958, The Literature of England, 1966, The Major Victorian Poets, 1973, The Victorian Imagination, 1980, On the Poetry of Matthew Arnold, 1982, The Poetry of Thomas Hardy, 1983, Matthew Arnold Prose, 1983, Man and His Myths: Tennyson's Idylls of the King in Critical Context, 1984, Poetry and Truth in Robert Browning's The Ring and the Book, 1985, Walter pater: Three Major texts, 1986, Walter Pater: The Critic as Artist of Ideas, 1987; numerous articles; former editor The Victorian Newsletter. Am. Philos. Soc. fellow, 1957; Fulbright fellow, 1949-50; Ford Found. fellow, 1951-52. Mem. MLA. Home: New York N.Y. Died Feb. 25, 1990; buried Loretto Motherhouse, Nerinx, Ky.

BUCKLEY, EMERSON, conductor, music director; b. N.Y.C., Apr. 14, 1916; s. Wendell and Minnie E. (Buckley) B.; m. Mary Henderson, May 27, 1948; children: Robert Allen, Richard Edward. BA, Columbia U., 1936; LHD, U. Denver, 1959; MusD (hon.), Nova U., 1980. Mem. faculty U. Denver, 1956, Columbia, 1957-58, Manhattan Sch. Music, 1958-70, Temple U., 1970, N.C. Sch. Arts, 1971. Music dir. Columbia Grand Opera, 1936-38, Palm Beach (Fla.) Symphony and Chorus, 1938-41, N.Y.C. Symphony, 1941-42, San Carlo Opera, 1943-45, WOR-MBS, N.Y.C., 1945-54, Marquis de Cuevas Ballet, 1950, Mendelssohn Glee Club, N.Y.C., 1954-63, P.R. Opera Festival, 1954-58, Symphony of the Air, also Empire State Mus. Festival, 1955, Chgo. Opera, 1956, Tagarazuka Dance Theatre, also Greek Theatre, Los Angeles, 1958, Chautauqua Festival, N.Y., 1960, music and artistic dir., Miami (Fla.) Opera Guild, 1950-86, Central City (Colo.) Opera, 1956-69, music dir., condr., Ft. Lauderdale Symphony, 1963-88, music dir., Seattle Opera, 1964, condr., N.Y.C. Opera, 1955-78, Duluth (Minn.), New Orleans and Balt. Operas, from 1970, Phila. Lyric Opera, San Francisco Opera, from 1975, Houston, Milw., Tulsa operas, from 1976, Madrid Opera, 1983, Met. Opera of Caracas, Venezuela, 1977-81, Philharmonic Orch. Fla., 1984, Teatro Petruzzelli, Bari, Orch. Sinfonia dell'Emilia Romagna Arturo Toscanini, Parma and Modena, Arena, Verona, 1985, Torino, Pesaro, Genova Opera, Italy, Beijing, Bayrische Rundfunk Orch., Munich, London Symphony, 1986, Vienna Philharmonic and Vienna Staatsoper, 1985-87, Argentina Teatro Colon Opera, Opera Colo., 1987; Guest appearances with various orchs. including Toronto (Ont., Can.) Philharmonic, Mpls. Symphony, Miami Symphony, P.R. Symphony, Mex. Symphony, Maracaibo (Venezuela) Symphony, Seoul (Korea) Philharmonic, Phoenix Symphony, Boston Symphony, Montreal Symphony, Houston Symphony, N.J. Symphony, Dallas Symphony, Los Angeles Philharm., Hollywood Bowl, New World Festival; dir.: world premiers of Am. operas including The Ballad of Baby Doe, 1956, Gallantry, 1958, He Who Gets Slapped, 1959, The Crucible, 1961, Gentlemen Be Seated, 1963, Lady from Colorado, 1964, Minutes 'Till Midnight, 1982; recordings for, Deutsche Grammophon, M-G-M, Columbia, Composers Records Inc., London-Polydor, Decca, Heliodor; condr. 1st Luciano Pavarotti film Yes, Giorgio for MGM, numerous TV shows, (movie) Distant Harmony, 1987. Recipient Fox prize Columbia Coll., 1936, Alice M. Ditson Condr.'s award, 1964, Colo. Ambassadors Sash, 1965, Gold Chair award Cen. City Opera, 1965, Am. Patroit award Fla., 1971, John Jay award, 1984, chevalier Order Arts and Letters (France), 1970. Mem. Nat. Assn. Am. Composers and Condrs. Club: Masons. Home: North Miami Beach Fla. Died Nov. 18, 1989; buried Vista Gardens, Miami, Fla.

BUEHLER, CALVIN A., chemistry educator; b. Stone Creek, Ohio, Nov. 29, 1896; s. Philip E. and Mary (Froelich) B.; m. Catherine B. McCallem, Dec. 21, 1963. BS in Chem. Engring., Ohio State U., 1919, MS, 1920, PhD, 1922; advanced study, U. Chgo., 1924. Rsch. chemist Barrett Co., Phila., 1918-19; duPont fellow Ohio State U., 1921-22; asst. prof. chem U. Tenn., 1922-25, assoc. prof., 1925-28, prof., from 1928, disting. svc. prof., from 1962, head dept. chem., 1940-62; mem. staff Ohio State U., summers, 1928, 29; researcher for Chem. Warfare Svc., 1946-48; researcher for medicinals Nat. Insts. of Health, 1958-63. Author articles in field. Dir. So. Appalachian Sci. Fair, 1954-55. Recipient So. Chemist award, 1950. Mem. AAAS, AAUP, Am. Chem. Soc. (sec.-treas., East Tenn. sect., 1930-40, chmn. 1947), Tenn. Acad. Sci. (chmn. Chem. sect. 1943), Irving Club. Presbyterian. *

BUFFINGTON, FRANCIS STEPHAN, engineering educator, consultant; b. Allegany, N.Y., May 14, 1916; s. Henry Clay and Marguarite Ann (Stephan) B.; m.

Marjorie Irma Hills, Aug. 26, 1939; children—Francis Stephan, Roger Hills. B.S., MIT, 1938, D.Sc., 1951. Registered profl. engr., Calif. Mem. research staff MIT, Cambridge, 1940-41, research asst., 1947-51; from asst. prof. to prof. Calif. Inst. Tech., Pasadena, Calif., from 1951; assoc. dean Calif. Inst. Tech., Pasadena, 1975-84; cons. in field. Contbr. chpt. to book, articles to profl. jours. Served to capt. U.S. Army, 1942-45. Mem. Am. Phys. Soc., Am. Soc. for Metals, Sigma Xi (pres. chpt. 1962-67). Republican. Clubs: Athenaeum. Home: Flintridge Calif. Died Apr. 23, 1989; buried Westwood Vets. Cemetery, L.A.

BUKOWSKI, ARTHUR F., priest, educator; b. Bay City, Mich., Oct. 30, 1905; s. Frank S. and Constance (Luczak) B. Student, St. Joseph's Sem., Grand Rapids, Mich., 1924-28; AB, Cath. U., Washington, 1928, AM, 1929; student, Sulpician Sem., Washington, 1929-33. Ordained priest Roman Cath. Ch., 1933. Dean Auinas Coll., Grand Rapids, 1934-37, pres., 1937-89. Past mem. Am. Cath. Sociol. Soc.. Home: Grand Rapids Mich. Died Oct. 10, 1989.

BULLEN, ADELAIDE KENDALL (MRS. KENNETH SUTHERLAN BULLEN), anthropologist; b. Worcester, Mass., Jan. 12, 1908; d. Oliver Sawyer and Grace (Marble) Kendall; A.B. cum laude, Radcliffe Coll., 1943; postgrad. Harvard U., 1943-48, 50; m. Ripley Pierce Bullen, July 25, 1929 (dec. Dec. 1976); children: Dana Ripley II, Pierce Kendall; m. 2d, Kenneth Sutherland Bullen, Mar. 22, 1980. Research anthropologist Health Center, Radcliffe Coll., 1943-44, Fatigue Lab., Harvard U. Grad. Sch. Bus. Adminstrn., 1944-46; civilian cons. in anthropology U.S. War Dept., 1946; anthropologist Peabody Mus., Harvard U., 1946-48, Fla. State Mus., 1949-92. Fellow Am. Anthrop. Assn., AAAS, Royal Anthrop. Inst. London, Soc. Applied Anthropology; mem. Am. Assn. Phys. Anthropologists, Am. Psychosomatic Soc., N.Y. Acad. Scis., Authors League Am., Authors Guild, Soc. Research in Child Devel. Clubs: Gainesville Golf and Country. University Women's, Gainesville Woman's. Author: New Answers to the Fatigue Problem, 1956, paperback edit., 1980; also articles in field; contbg. editor Anthropology, Handbook of Latin American Studies, 1969-71. Deceased. Home: Gainesville Fla. †

BUNNELLE, ROBERT ELLSWORTH, newspaper publisher; b. Urbana, Ohio, Aug. 21, 1903; s. Elmer Ellsworth and Olivemay (Colbert) B.; m. Margaret Elizabeth Harrison, Oct. 30, 1926 (dec.); m. Frances McKay Peace, Aug. 23, 1962. Student, Wittenberg Coll., 1921-23, Northwestern U., 1924. Reporter Lynchburg (Va.) News, Asheville (N.C.) Times; also mng. editor Bristol (Va.) Bull., 1925-31; with A.P., 1931-54; beginning as editor A.P., Atlanta; successively chief of bur., mng. exec. A.P., London, Eng.; chief bur. A.P., Can., 1931-49; gen. exec. A.P., N.Y.C., 1949-54; chmn. bd., pub. Asheville Citizen-Times, 1954-74, pres., 1958-74; dir. Multimedia, Inc. Mem. N.C. Hwy. Commn., 1957-61; pres. Greater Asheville Council, Council, 1962-64; Trustee Meml. Mission Hosp., 1968-69. Mem. N.C. Press Assn. (pres. 1962-63), Am. Corrs. Assn. (pres. London 1943-44), Parliamentary Press Gallery Assn. (dir. 1950-51), Asheville C. of C. (pres. 1967), Phi Kappa Psi. Clubs: Biltmore Forest Country (Pawleys Island, S.C.), Mountain City (Pawleys Island, S.C.) (pres. 1959), Litchfield Country (Pawleys Island, S.C.). Home: Pawleys Island S.C. Died May 30, 1988.

BUNNEY, WILLIAM E., pharmaceutical manufacturing executive; b. Tacoma, Wash., May 24, 1902; s. William Harry and Agnes L. (Stephenson) B.; m. Nora O. Null, Sept. 17, 1927; children: William Edward, Benjamin Stephenson. BS, Mont. State Coll., 1924; PhD, U. Ill., 1927. Sr. chemist Antitoxin Vaccine Lab. Mass. Dept. of Health, 1927-30; assoc. dir. Bur. of Labs. Mich. Dept. of Health, 1930-38; dir. biol. products prodn. E.R. Squibb & Sons, 1938-42, dir. biol. labs., 1942-43, mfg. labs., 1943-52, dir., 1946-52, v.p., 1953-54, v.p., dir. mfg. worldwide, 1952-54; tech. dir. Squibb Chem. div. Olin Mathieson Chem. Corp., 1954-55, v.p., dir. mfg. ops., 1955-92; dir. Nat. Bank N.J. Leader U.S. Russia Exch. Mission, 1962; mem. adv. bd. Rutgers U. Rsch., Grad. Instrn. Mem. Nat. Planning Coun., New Brunswick C. of C. (pres. 1950-52), Am. Assn. Immunologists, Am. Chem. Soc., Am. Pub. Health Assn., Soc. Exptl. Biology and Medicine, Soc. of Am. Bacteriologists, AAAS, , Univ. Club (N.Y.C.), Sigma Chi, Sigma Xi, Phi Lambda Upsilon. Republican. Baptist. Home: Millstone N.J. Died Jan. 8, 1992.

BUNSHAFT, GORDON, architect; b. Buffalo, May 9, 1909; s. David and Yetta (Bunshaft) B.; m. Nina Elizabeth Wayler, Dec. 2, 1943. B.Arch., M.I.T., 1933, M.Arch. (fellow), 1935; D.F.A. (hon.), U. Buffalo, 1962. Chief designer Skidmore, Owings & Merrill, N.Y.C., 1937-42; ptnr. Skidmore, Owings & Merrill, N.Y.C., Chgo., San Francisco, until 1979, Portland, Oreg., 1949-79; Vis. com. Sch. Architecture, M.I.T., 1940-42, Harvard U., 1954-60, Yale U., 1959-62; mem. Pres.'s Commn. on Fine Arts, 1963-72; former trustee Carnegie Mellon U., Pitts.; trustee, mem. internat. council Mus. Modern Art. Ptnr. charge design: Fifth Ave. br. Mfrs. Trust Co, Lever House-Park Ave., both N.Y.C., Conn. Gen. Life Ins. Co and Emhart Hdqrs., Hartford, H.J. Heinz Co., Ltd, Hayes Park, Middlesex, Eng., Banque Lambert, Brussels, Beinecke Rare Book and Manuscript Libr. at Yale U., Reynolds Metals Co. Bldg, Richmond, Va., new wing at Albright-Knox Art Gallery, Buffalo, Chase Bank, N.Y.C., Lyndon Baines Johnson Libr., 1971 and Sid W. Richardson Hall, U. Tex., Austin, Hirshhorn Mus. and Sculpture Garden, Washington, 1074, Am. Can Co, Greenwich, Conn., 140 Broadway, N.Y.C., Philip Morris Factory, Richmond, Va., Nat. Comml. Bank, Jeddah, Saudi Arabia, Haj Terminal and Support Complex, Jeddah Internat. Airport. Served As maj. C.E. AUS, 1942-46. Recipient M.I.T. and Rotch travelling fellowships for study Europe and N. Africa, 1935-37, Brunner award Am. Acad. and Inst. Arts and Letters, 1955, Gold medal Am. Acad. and Inst. Arts and Letters, 1984, medal of honor N.Y. chpt. AIA, 1961, Chancellor's medal U. Buffalo, 1969, Pritzker Architecture prize, 1988. Academician NAD; Fellow AIA; mem. Am. Acad. and Inst. Arts and Letters, Buffalo Fine Arts Acad. (hon.). Home: New York N.Y. Died Aug. 6, 1990; buried Buffalo.

BURCH, DEAN, lawyer; b. Enid, Okla., Dec. 20, 1927; s. Bert Alexander and Leola (Atkisson) B.; m. Patricia Meeks, July 7, 1961; children: Shelly Burch Bennett, Dean, Dianne Burch Butterfield. LL.B., U. Ariz., 1953. Bar: Ariz. 1953, D.C. 1975. Asst. atty. gen. Ariz., 1953-54; adminstrv. asst. to Sen. Barry Goldwater, 1955-59; mem. firm. Dunseath, Stubbs & Burch, Tucson, 1959-69, Pierson, Ball & Dowd, 1975-87; dir. gen. Internat. Telecommunications Satellite Orgn. (Intelsat), Washington, 1987-91; dep. dir. Goldwater for President Com., 1963-64; chmn. Republican Nat. Com., 1964-65; mgr. Goldwater for Senate Campaign, 1968; chief of staff George Bush Vice Presdl. Campaign, 1980; sr. adv. Reagan-Bush Com., 1980; counsellor to Pres. Nixon 1974, to Pres. Ford, 1975; apptd. by Pres. Reagan as chmn. U.S. del. to 1st session on use of geostationary satellite orbit and planning of space service World Adminstrv. Radio Conf., Geneva, 1985; named chmn. FCC by Pres. Nixon. Mem. Ariz. Bd. Regents, 1969-70. Served with AUS, 1946-48. Mem. Blue Key, Phi Delta Theta. Home: Potomac Md. Died Aug. 4, 1991.

BURDICK, CHARLES LALOR, chemical engineer; b. Denver, Apr. 14, 1892; s. Frank Austin and Anna (Lalor) B.; m. Alison Ward, 1938; children: Lalor, Cynthia. BS, Drake U., 1911, LLD (hon.), 1970; BS, MIT, 1913, MS, 1914; postgrad., Kaiser Wilhelm Inst., Berlin, and Univ. Coll., London, 1914-16; PhD, U. Basel, Switzerland, 1915; DSc (hon.), U. Del., 1955; DEng (hon.), Widener Coll., 1976. Research asso. in chemistry Mass. Inst. Tech. and Cal. Inst. Tech., 1916-17; metall. engr. Guggenheim Bros., N.Y. and, Chile, 1919-24; v.p. and cons. engr. Anglo-Chilean Consol. Nitrate Corp., 1924-28; with E.I. du Pont de Nemours, 1929-57; in various positions as asst. chem. dir., ammonia dept., spl. asst. to pres., chmn. bds. in E.I. du Pont de Nemours, Mexico of; DuPont (S.A., and), Cia. Mexicana de Explosives. Mem. exec. com. Internat. Planned Parenthood Fedn., 1962-68; pres. Christiana Found., 1960-73; exec. dir., trustee Lalor Found., Wilmington, C. Lalor Burdick Lecture Fund of MBL, Woods Hole, Mass., from 1985; founding dir. U. Del. Rsch. Found.; hon. life mem. Del. Acad. Medicine; bd. dirs. Planned Parenthood-World Population, 1961-67. 1st lt. Ordnance div. U.S. Army, 1917-18. Fellow AAAS; mem. N.Y. Acad. Sci. (life), Am. Inst. Chem. Engrs., Am. Assn. Planned Parenthood Profls., Soc. Study Fertility (Eng.) (Marshall medal 1984), Wilmington Club, Greenville Country Club, Phi Beta Kappa. Home: Wilmington Del. Died Dec. 11, 1989; buried Lower Brandywine Cemetery, Wilmington, Del.

BURDICK, QUENTIN NORTHROP, senator; b. Munich, N.D., June 19, 1908; s. Usher Lloyd and Emma (Robertson) B.; m. Marietta Janecky, Mar. 18, 1933 (dec. Mar. 1958); children: Jonathan, Jan Mary, Jennifer, Jessica; m. Jocelyn Birch Peterson, July 7, 1960; 1 child, Gage (dec.); stepchildren: Leslie, Birch. B.A., U. Minn., 1931, LL.B., 1932. Bar: N.D. 1932. Practiced in Fargo, 1932-58; mem. 86th Congress, N.D. at large, 1958-60; U.S. senator from N.D., 1960-92; chmn. Senate environ. and pub. works com., agr. appropriations subcom. 86th-102d Congresses; mem. appropriations, Indian affairs, aging coms.; candidate for lt. gov., 1942, for gov., 1946, for U.S. Senator, 1956. Founder Senate Rural Health Caucus. Mem. Sons of Norway, Sigma Nu. Democrat. Congregationalist. Clubs: Mason, Elk, Eagle, Moose. Home: Fargo N.D. Died Sept. 8, 1992. †

BURGESS, HAROLD DEMPSTER, lawyer; b. Dundee, Ill., July 10, 1894; s. John W. and Sadie E. (Dempster) B.; m. Mary Ellen Evans, Sept. 16, 1964. Ed. pub. schs., Beatrice, Nebr.; student, U. Colo., 1913-14, U. Nebr., 1914-17; A.B. in absentia, U. Nebr., 1920; student, U. Chgo., 1920-21. Bar: Ill. 1921. Since practiced in Chgo.; of counsel Keck, Mahin, Cate. Mem. Am., 7th Circuit, Ill., Chgo. bar assns., Legal Club Chgo., Law Club. Republican. Episcopalian. Clubs: Metropolitan (Chgo.); Edgewood Valley Country (LaGrange). Home: Hinsdale Ill. Died Mar. 9, 1989. †

BURGESS, MAGNUS MALLORY, manufacturing executive; b. Detroit, Mich., Dec. 7, 1896; s. Magnus and Janet (Williamson) B.; m. Blanche Irene Reynolds, July 30, 1919; 1 child, Nancy Irene (Mrs. Thomas Stedman Torgerson). Factory time keeper C.R. Wilson Body Co., Detroit, 1911, asst. sec., 1919, sec., 1921, treas., asst. mgr. and dir., 1923-24; sec., treas. Detroit Floor Board Co., Detroit, 1920-22; with Murray Corp. Am., Detroit, 1924-25; gen. mgr. C. Haines Wilson Investment Co., Detroit, 1925-29; treas. Towle Aircraft Co., Detroit, 1929-30; v.p. and dir. No. Mich. Investment Co., Detroit, 1926-30, No. Mich. Holding Co., Detroit, 1926-30; v.p., treas., dir. and gen. mgr. Sheller Mfg. Corp., Portland, Ind., 1929-32, chmn. bd. and pres., 1932-53; dir. E.W. Bliss Co., Canton, Ohio. Clubs: Bloomfield Hills Country, Detroit, Detroit Golf, Detroit Athletic, Grosse Pointe Yacht, Oakland Hills Country, Recess, Question, Chicago Golf, Chicago Racquet, Tavern Chicago, Indian Creek, Miami Beach. Lodges: Mason 32 degree (Shriner). Home: Bloomfield Hills Mich. Died Aug. 14, 1953; interred Woodlawn Cemetery, Detroit.

BURKAT, LEONARD, music executive, writer; b. Boston, July 21, 1919; s. Hyman Aaron and Sophie (Cooper) B.; m. Marion Frances Gumner, June 23, 1940; children: Howard, Susan Burkat Trubey, Caroline Burkat Hall. Student, Columbia U., 1941, Harvard U., 1944-46. Asst. chief Boston Pub. Libr. Music Dept., 1937-47; librarian, asst. to music dir., prin. artistic adminstrv. officer Boston Symphony Orch., Inc., Boston and Lenox, Mass., 1947-63; dir. Columbia Masterworks Records, v.p. Columbia Records Div., v.p. Columbia Records Group CBS, Inc., N.Y.C., 1963-73; owner Leonard Burkat Program Note Service, Danbury, Conn., 1975-92; cons., speaker numerous orgns. Contbr. numerous articles to Boston Globe, Boston Evening Transcript, N.Y. Times, Mus. Quarterly, Notes, others; contbr. New Grove Dictionary of American Music; writer numerous concert program notes, album liner notes. Decorated Chevalier Order of Arts and Letters of French Republic, 1987. Mem. Am. Musicol. Soc., Am. Symphony Orch. League, Chamber Music Am., Music Critics Assn., Music Library Assn., Sonneck Soc. Home: Danbury Conn. Died Aug. 23, 1992. †

BURKE, JOE, professional baseball executive; m. Mary B. Burke; children: Joe, Mary Ann, Jimmy, John, Alice, Bobby, Vincent. From ticket mgr. to bus. mgr. to gen. mgr. Louisville Colonels, 1948-60; from asst. gen. mgr. to bus. mgr. to treas. to v.p. Washington Senators (now Tex. Rangers), 1961-73; v.p. bus. Kansas City (Mo.) Royals, 1973-74, exec. v.p., gen. mgr., 1974-81, pres., from 1981, also dir.; chmn. com. on divisional play, mem. com. on expansion, schedule, div. of receipts, player relations Am. League. Named Major League Exec. of Yr. Sporting News, 1976; recipient Mr. Baseball award 7th Ann. Kansas City Baseball Award Dinner, 1978. Home: Kansas City Mo. Deceased. †

BURKE, JOHN GARRETT, historian of science, educator; b. Boston, Aug. 12, 1917; s. Edmund Joseph and Catherine Cecelia (Barry) B.; m. Mary Margaret Porter, Oct. 13, 1945 (dec.); children: Alison (Mrs. John Mitchell Ball), Kevin, Eileen; m. Ann. S. Bartlett, Dec. 13, 1986. B.S., M.I.T., 1938; M.A., Stanford U., 1960, Ph.D., 1962. Metallurgist Bethlehem Steel Co., Johnstown, Pa., Houston, 1938-41; v.p. Cummins Diesel Engines, Inc., Pitts., 1945-48; pres. Dry Ice Converter Corp., Tulsa, 1949-58; asst. prof. history UCLA, Los Angeles, 1962-67; assoc. prof. UCLA, 1967-71, prof., 1971-81, prof. emeritus, 1981-89, dean social scis., 1970-73, dean Coll. Letters and Sci., 1974-77. Author: Origins of the Science of Crystals, 1966, Atoms, Blacksmiths and Crystals, 1967, The Science of Minerals in the Age of Jefferson, 1978, Cosmic Debris: Meteorites in History, 1986; editor: The New Technology and Human Values, 1966, 1972, Technology and Change, 1980, The Uses of Science in the Age of Newton, 1983, Science and Culture in the Western Tradition, 1987; contbr. articles to profl. jours. Served with AUS, 1941-42; Served with USAAF, 1943-45. Decorated Air medal with one oak leaf cluster.; Recipient Abbott Payson Usher award, 1967; NSF grantee, 1965-68; Nat. Endowment Humanities grantee, 1973, 74, 78; Guggenheim fellow, 1979-80. Fellow AAAS; mem. Am. Hist. Assn., History of Sci. Soc. (treas. 1971-75), Soc. History of Tech. (mem. exec. council 1974-79), ASME, History and Heritage Commn. Home: Tulsa Okla. Died Feb. 21, 1989. †

BURKE, JOHN MILES, manufacturing corporation executive; b. Glendale, Calif., Nov. 5, 1938; s. Avery John and Dorice Katherine (Davidson) B.; m. Barbara Dinsmore Gibbs, Feb. 23, 1963; 1 dau., Elena Katherine. B.A. in Econs., Claremont Men's Coll., 1961; B.S. in Engring., Stanford U., 1961; M.B.A., UCLA, 1965, Ph.D. in Bus. Mgmt., 1968. With Litton Industries, 1968-72; gen. mgr. Heim Universal Bearing div. Rockwell Internat., 1972-76; group v.p. auto splty. group W.R. Grace, 1976-78; pres., chief exec. officer Automotive and Consumer Group, Loctite Corp, Cleve., 1978-84; pres., chief exec. officer, dir. Hauserman Inc., 1984-89. Mem. vis. com. Weatherhead Sch. of Mgmt., Case Western Res. U. Mem. Motor and Equipment Mfrs. Assn. (dir.), Union Club Cleve. Home: Hudson Ohio Died June 21, 1990; buried Glendale, Calif.

BURKE, THOMAS FRANCIS, communication company executive; b. Newton, Mass., Jan. 27, 1929; s. Thomas James and Mary Ann (McFarland) B.; m. Mary E. Sughrue, Nov. 12, 1955; children: Thomas J., Robert F., Maureen E., Daniel R., Paul J., Sheila Rose, John P. A.B. magna cum laudein Econs., Boston Coll., 1951,

M.A. in Econs., 1959; cert. with honors in acctg., Bentley Coll. Acctg. and Fin., 1954. Asst. chief acct. Hollingsworth & Whitney Co., Boston, 1951-54; asst. controller CBS Electronics, Danvers, Mass., 1954-61; asst. comptroller M/A-Com, Inc., Burlington, Mass., 1961-64, comptroller, 1964-78, v.p. fin. and treas., 1978-82, exec. v.p. adminstrn. and fin., 1982-86, also bd. dirs., chief oper. officer, 1986, pres., chief exec. officer, 1987, chmn. bd., 1989; bd. dirs. Aritech Corp., Associated Industries Mass. Author: periodicals Budgetary Control, 1959, Fin. Planning, 1961. Mem. Town Com. re Revaluation, Stoneham, Mass., 1969; mem. St. Vincent de Paul Soc., Stoneham, 1968, mem. fin. com., Andover, Mass., 1973; mem. Boston Coll. Fides. Mem. Fin. Execs. Inst., Nat. Assn. Accts., Treasurers Assn., Am. Mgmt. Assn., Boston Coll. Alumni Assn. Roman Catholic. Lodge: K.C. Home: North Andover Mass. Died Sept. 21, 1989; buried North Andover.

BURKLEY, GEORGE GREGORY, physician, naval officer; b. Pitts., Aug. 29, 1902; s. Frank George and George and Anna (O'Donnell) B.; m. Isabel Winburn, Nov. 30, 1933; children: Isabel B. Michael Starling, Nancy A. Leo Denlea, George W., Richard M. BS, U. Pitts., 1926, MD, 1928, DSc, 1963; postgrad., U. Minn., 1929-32. Diplomate Nat. Bd. Med. Exam. Intern St. Francis Hosp., Pitts., 1928-29; resident fellow internal medicine Mayo Clinic, 1929-32; fellow cardiology U. Pitts., 1933-34; asst. prof. medicine, 1934-41; practice medicine, specializing internal medicine and cardiology Pitts., 1934-41; commd. lt. comdr. M.C. USN, 1941; advanced through grades to vice adm., 1964, served in S. Pacific, 1942-44; chief medicine naval hosps. Charleston, S.C., Memphis, Newport, R.I., Portsmouth, Va., 1946-57; comdg. officer Naval Dispensary Washington, 1959-61; physician to Pres. John F. Kennedy, 1961-63, to Pres. Lyndon B. Johnson, 1963-69. Mem. vis. com. Sch. Medicine, U. Pitts. Fellow ACP; mem. AMA, Pitts. Acad. Medicine, Alpha Omega Alpha, Phi Sigma. Home: Boulder Colo. Died Jan. 2, 1991; buried Arlington Nat. Cemetery.

BURLESON, OMAR, lawyer, former congressman; b. Anson, Tex., Mar. 19, 1906; s. Joseph and Bettie (Couch) B. Student, Abilene (Tex.) Christian Coll., 1924-26, Hardin-Simmons U., 1926-27; LLD, Cumberland U., 1929. County atty. Jones County, Tex., 1931-35; county judge, 1935-41; spl. agent FBI, 1940-41; sec. Congressman Sam Russell, 1941-42; gen. counsel Nat. Capitol Housing Authority, Washington, 1942; mem. 80th-95th Congresses from 17th Tex. Dist. Pres. Tex. Welfare Assn., 1936-38, County Judges and Commrs Assn. of Tex. Served to lt. comdr. USN, 1942-46, PTO. Mem. Lions Internat. dist. gov. Lions Clubs, Masons. Democrat. Home: Lubbock Tex. Died May 14, 1991.

BURNETT, HAMILTON S(ANDS), justice; b. Jefferson City, Tenn., Aug. 20, 1895; s. J.M. and Caroline (Sands) B.; m. Mary Griffin, Oct. 10, 1923 (dec. 1952); children: Jamie Knox, Adeline Sands, Hamilton Sands; m. Marjie Beaman, Dec. 1953 (dec. July 5, 1964). AB, Carson-Newman Coll., 1916; LLB, U. Va., 1920, LLD (hon.), 1948. Bar: Tenn. 1920. Pvt. practice Knoxville, 1920-34; atty. Poore, Testerman & Burnett; cir. judge Knoxville, Tenn., 1932-42; judge Tenn. Ct. of Appeals, 1942-47; assoc. justice Supreme Ct. Tenn., Nashville, 1947, justice, 1947-63, chief justice, from 1963. Pres. Empty Stocking Fund, Knoxville, from 1943; trustee Carson-Newman Coll. (chmn.). Mem ABA, Tenn. Bar Assn., Am. Judicature Soc., Knoxville C. of C., YMCA, Order of Coif, Phi Delta Phi, Masons (33 degrees, Shriner), Kiwanian. Democrat. Baptist. *

BURNETTE, NANCY EVERITT, retail company executive; b. Hackettstown, N.J., Jan. 8, 1932; d. Isaac Dill and Bess Louise (Lamson) Everitt; m. Robert W. Burnette, June 6, 1979; children: Elizabeth, James, Samuel. BA, Wellesley Coll., 1953; MA, U. Calif., Berkeley, 1968. Investment officer U.S. Trust, N.Y.C., 1953-55, Wells Fargo, San Francisco, 1968-74; U. Calif., 1974-78; corp. sec., asst. treas. Lucky Stores Inc., Dublin, Calif., 1978-83; bd. dirs. Yosemite Lab., Berkeley. Mem. Fedn. Fin. Analysts, Chartered Fin. Analysts, Am. Soc. Corp. Secs., Security Analysts San Francisco, Women's Forum West, Fin. Club. Home: Oakland Calif. Died Nov., 1983.

BURNS, JAMES FRANCIS, financial advisor; b. N.Y.C., Sept. 28, 1922; s. Martin and Ellen (Lavelle) B.; m. Irene M. O'Reilly, Nov. 22, 1951; children: Mary Ellen, Michael, Betty Anne, Maureen. B.B.A. in Acctg., Iona Coll., New Rochelle, N.Y., 1944; M.B.A. in Fin., NYU, 1950. C.P.A., N.Y. Audit mgr. Price Waterhouse & Co., C.P.A.s, N.Y.C., 1944-63; treas., controller United Brands Co., N.Y.C., 1963-74; v.p., chief fin. officer C.D. Mallory & Co., N.Y.C., 1976-79; controller Gen. Host Co., N.Y.C., 1974-76; v.p. fin. Dairylea Coop. Inc., Pearl River, N.Y., 1979-82; fin. tax adv. Tallman, N.Y., 1982-88. Vice chmn. bd. lay trustees Iona Coll.; treas., lector St. Aedan Roman Cath. Ch., Pearl River. Mem. Am. Inst. C.P.A.s, N.Y. State Soc. C.P.A.s. Republican. Club: Pearl River Nauraushaun Swim (past pres., dir.). Home: Pearl River N.Y. Died Dec. 22, 1988; buried Ascension Cemetery, Monsey, N.Y.

BURNS, JOHN LAWRENCE, investments company executive; b. Watertown, Mass., Nov. 16, 1908; s. Michael P. and Ellen (Holihan) B.; m. Beryl M. Spinney, Aug. 29, 1937 (dec. May 1991); children: John Spinney, Lara Burns Cunningham. B.S., Northeastern U., 1930, D.B.A. (hon.), 1957; Sc.D., Harvard U., 1934. Supt. wire div. Republic Steel Corp., 1934-42; vice chmn. exec. com., coordinating partner Booz, Allen & Hamilton, 1942-57; pres. RCA, 1957-62; vice chmn. bd. Cities Service Co., 1965-66, chmn. bd., 1966-68; pres. John L. Burns & Co., N.Y.C., from 1968; ret. chmn. bd. trustees Magnavox Govt. and Indsl. Electronics Co. Chmn. emeritus, bd. dirs. Boys' Clubs Am.; mem. corp. Northeastern U. Mem. Com. for Econ. Devel. (hon. trustee). Clubs: Round Hill (Greenwich, Conn.); Blind Brook (Portchester, N.Y.); Sky (N.Y.C.), Econ. (N.Y.C.). Home: Greenwich Conn. Deceased. †

BURR, DONALD DAVID, business executive; b. N.Y.C., Apr. 20, 1923; m. Anne Marie Scheitlie, June 28, 1975; children by previous marriage: Cynthia Parry, Cory Howell. Account exec. Bache & Co., 1946-47; gen. mgr. LaPlaya Products, Inc., 1948-52; gen. sales mgr. Hazel Bishop, Inc., 1952-54, v.p. mktg., 1954, pres., 1955-57, also dir.; pres. Parry Labs., Inc., 1957-61, also dir.; v.p., dir. Am. Motor Scooter Corp., 1960-61; dir. Tracey Enterprises, Inc., 1960-61; v.p. Faberge, Inc., 1961-63, exec. v.p., 1963-64; v.p. Parfum Lorle, Inc., 1961-64, Odell Co., Inc., 1962-64; v.p. mktg. Yardley of London, Inc., 1964-66, exec. v.p., 1966-68, pres., 1968-69, also dir.; chmn., pres. Burr Corp., 1970-72; chmn. Am. Pharm. Co., Inc., Devon Products Co., Inc., Trylon Products Co. Inc., 1970-72; chmn. bd. Brandwynne Burr Advt., Inc., N.Y.C., 1972-80, Cyncory Investments, N.Y.C., from 1976; pres. D.D. Burr Investors Group, from 1982; dir. Yardley & Co., Ltd., London, 1967-69. Trustee Big Bros. Inc. of N.Y., 1974—. Served with USNR, 1942-44; as lt. (j.g.) USCGR, 1944-46. Clubs: New York Athletic; Devon Yacht (Amagansett, L.I.); Maidstone (East Hampton, L.I., N.Y.). Home: East Hampton N.Y. Died Feb. 1, 1990; buried Cedar Lawn Cemetery, East Hampton.

BURROUGHS, WALTER LAUGHLIN, publisher; b. Bridgewater, S.D., Aug. 21, 1901; s. William S. and Bertha (Laughlin) B.; m. Hazel Georgia Sexsmith, June 1, 1925 (dec. Oct. 1970); 1 child, Toni (Mrs. Philip Schuyler Doane); m. Lucy Bell, Feb. 28, 1972. BA, U. Wash., 1924; postgrad., U. Calif., Berkeley, 1925-28. Dir. publs. U. Calif., Berkeley, 1925-28; gen. mgr. North Pacific Gravure Co., Seattle, 1928-30; gen. mgr. Crocker Union Lithograph and Pub. Co., L.A., 1930-41; co-founder Bantam Books, L.A., 1938; ind. book pub. with Merle Armitage, 1938-42; Pacific coast rep. H.W. Kaster & Sons, L.A., 1941-42; exec. v.p. Eldon Industries Los Angeles, 1946-62; corp. pres., pub. Orange Coast Daily Pilot, Newport Beach, Costa Mesa, Huntington Beach, Calif., 1948-65, chmn. bd., 1965-68; pres. Orion Mgmt. Corp. Chmn. bd. dirs. emeritus Children's Hosp. Orange County; trustee Jefferson Trust, Western World Med. Found., Irvine, Calif.; active Ctr. for the Performing Arts. Col. U.S. Army, 1942-45. Honored (with late E.J. Power) for role in bringing U. Calif. to Irvine with dedication of Founders Ct. on campus, 1978. Mem. Soc. Profl. Journalists, Bohemian Club, Jonathan Club, Newport Harbor Yacht Club, Newport Beach Country Club, Center Club (Costa Mesa), Nat. Press Club, Rotary, Sigma Delta Chi (nat. pres.). Died Sept. 17, 1990; buried at sea. Home: Newport Beach Calif.

BURROW, WILLIAM FITE, SR., lawyer, oil executive; b. Milan, Tenn., July 2, 1907; s. Richmond Jarold and Nancy (Jackson) B.; m. Josephine Worsham, Oct. 12, 1938 (div. 1967); children: William Fite, Nancy Marian, Bruce Raguet, Christopher Randolph; m. Marjorie Hanley, Mar. 7, 1968. AB, Vanderbilt U., 1929; LLB, Yale U., 1931; postgrad, Harvard U., 1931-32, Cambridge U., Eng., 1932. Bar: Tex., 1932. Assoc. Turner, Rodgers and Winn, Dallas, 1932-37; sr. ptnr. Worsham, Burrow and Worsham, Dallas, 1938-47, Leake, Henry, Golden & Burrow, et al, Dallas, 1948-72, Burrow and Bass, P.C., Dallas, 1972-91; pres. Big D Theatre Co., 1955-72, Dallaco Oil and Gas, Inc., 1977-88; dean Jefferson U. Law Sch., 1935-36. Author: A Time for Change, 1990; contbr. articles to profl. jours. Tex. rep. Brit. govt.'s Civilian Tech. Corp., 1941; Dem. candidate for Congress, 1946; founder 1st Eisenhower Rep. Club in U.S., 1951; mem. grad. bd. Yale Law Sch., 1955-60; alumni bd. dirs. Vanderbilt U., 1959-63; bd. dirs. Yale Law Sch. Fund; trustee St. Mark's Sch. of Tex., 1958-65; vestryman, chmn. dept. social relations Episc. Diocese of Dallas. Col. U.S. Army, World War II. Decorated Legion of Merit, Bronze Star with oak leaf cluster, Croix de Guerre with palm (Belgium), Medaile Liberté (France). Mem. Am. Arbitration Assn. (nat. panel arbitrators), ABA, Tex. Bar Assn. (chmn. pub. utilities com., assoc. editor jour. 1939-42), Dallas Bar Assn. (v.p., chmn. grievance com.), Jr. Bar Assn. Dallas (pres.), SAR, SCV, Dallas Interacial Com., Anglo-Tex. Soc. (chmn.), Yale Law Sch. Assn. (exec. com. 1958-65), Alpha Tau Omega, Phi Delta Phi. Clubs: Yale (past pres.), Vanderbilt (past pres.), Idlewild, Crescent, Dallas Petroleum, Brook Hollow Golf; Garden of the Gods (Colorado Springs), Broadmoor Golf. Home: Dallas Tex. Died June, 1991. †

BURRUD, WILLIAM JAMES, film producer; b. Hollywood, Calif., Jan. 12, 1925; s. Leland John and Emma Jane (Lindsey) B.; m. Marlene Ann Dorman, Dec. 30, 1975; children: John William, Robert Scott. BS, U. So. Calif., 1947. Debuted as child actor in road show prodn. Music in the Air, 1932; later under contract to 20th Century Fox, Columbia Pictures, Metro-Goldwyn-Mayer; owner, operator Bill Burrud Prodns., Inc., L.A., 1954—; producer TV shows (series) Animal World, World of the Sea, Safari to Adventure, Wildlife Adventure, Islands in the Sun, Challenging Sea, Treasure, True Adventure, Vagabond, Wanderlust, Wonderful World of Women, (TV spls.) Open Heart Surgery, Swingin' Fling, This Nation Israel, Tora, Tora, Tora, Is There an Ark?, Where Did All the Animals Go?, Baja: Great New Adventure, Centerfold Pets, also 11 2-hour adventure/wildflie/treasure spls., others; producer motion picture Masai; author: Animal Quiz. Chmn. Alumni Fund U. So. Calif.; participant forum and conv. Nat. Coun. on Alcoholism, San Diego, 1977; bd. dirs. Sea World. With USN, WWII. Star with his name implanted on Hollywood Walk of the Stars, 1977. Home: Huntington Beach Calif. Died July 12, 1990; buried Riverside Nat. Cemetery, Riverside Calif.

BURSK, EDWARD COLLINS, editor; b. Lancaster, Pa., Apr. 16, 1907; s. John Howard and Sarah Katharine (Mull) B.; m. Catherine Hertzler Irwin, June 26, 1930; children: Edward Collins, John Howard, Christopher Irwin. Student, Mercerburg Acad., 1923-24; AB, Amherst Coll., 1928; AM, Harvard, 1929. Instr. Greek and Latin Darmouth, 1931-33; pres. J.H. Bursk Co., 1933-41; instr. Greek, econs. Franklin and Marshall Coll., 1941-42; instr. bus. adminstrn. Harvard, 1942, asst. prof., 1943, assoc. prof., 1946-51, prof., 1953-67; mng. editor Harvard Bus. Rev., 1943-47, editor, 1947-90; past. chmn. Internat. Mgmt. & Mktg. Group, Inc.; past pres. Intermark, Inc.; past bd dirs. Newsome & Co., Inc., Gum Products, Inc., N.Am. Invemstnet Fund N.V., N.Am. Bank Stock Fund N.V., Rumford Ins. Co., Underwriters Investment Corp., Conf. Svc. Corp., Interliving Corp., Hamilton Internat. Corp. Author: Text and Cases in Marketing: A Scientific Approach, 1962, Cases in Marketing Management, 1965; co-author: Advanced Cases in Marketing Management, 1968; editor: Thinking Ahead for Business, 1952, Getting Things Done in Business, 1953, How to Increase Executive Effectiveness, 1953, The Management Team, 1954, Human Relations for Management, 1956, Business and Religion, 1959, Planning the Future Strategy of Your Business, 1956; co-editor: The World of Business, 1962, New Decision-Making Tools for Managers, 1963, Modern Marketing Strategy, 1964, Salesmanship and Sales Force Management, 1971. Named to Distbn. Hall of Fame, 1962. Past mem. Internat. Mktg. Rsch. and Planning Dirs. (past coun.), Internat. Mktg. Inst. (past ednl. dir.), Am. Mktg. Assn. (v.p. mktg. mgmt. 1962-63), Kappa Theta, Phi Beta Kappa, Delta Tau Delta. Home: Langhorne Manor Pa. Died Feb. 12, 1990; buried Cohasset, Mass.

BURT, WAYNE VINCENT, oceanographer, educator; b. South Shore, S.D., May 10, 1917; s. John David and Mary Pearle (McDuffee) B.; m. Grace Louise DuBois, Jan. 15, 1941; children: John Alan, Christine Louise, Laurence W., Darcy Jean. B.S. in Math, Pacific Coll., 1939; M.S., UCLA, 1948, Ph.D. in Phys. Oceanography, 1952; D.Sc. (hon.), George Fox Coll., Newberg, Oreg., 1963. Instr. Oreg. high schs., 1939-42; material engr. Kaiser Co., Inc., Wash. State, 1942; instr. math. U. Oreg., 1946; asst. Scripps Instn., 1946-48, assoc. oceanographer, 1948-49; asst. prof. oceanography, research oceanographer Chesapeake Bay Inst., Johns Hopkins, 1949-53, asst. dir., 1953; research oceanographer dept. oceanography U. Wash., 1953-54; assoc. prof. oceanography Oreg. State U., Corvallis, 1954-59, prof., chmn. dept., 1959-67, assoc. dean research, 1967-76, assoc. dean oceanography, 1976-78, 81, emeritus prof., 1981, dir. marine sci. center, 1964-72; oceanographer London br. Office Naval Research, U.S. Navy, 1979-80; sci. attache Am. Embassy, New Delhi, India, 1986-87; Mem. sci. expdns. to Eastern tropical Pacific Ocean Scripps Instns. Oceanography, 1955, 58, Can. Hudson expdn., 1970, Brit. Royal Soc. expdns., 1972, 77, 78, German expdn., 1973, Japanese expdn., 1975; rep. XIV Limnology Congress, Vienna, Austria, 1959; rep. to UN Research Vessel Forum, Tokyo, Japan, 1961; rep. UNESCO Inter-govtl. Oceanographic Commn., Paris, 1965; mem. Nat. Adv. Com. on Oceans and Atmosphere, 1971-75. Editor: Wiley-Intersci. series Wastes in the Oceans, 1982-85; contbr. articles to profl. jours. Trustee George Fox Coll., 1970-73. Served to lt. USNR, 1942-46; comdr. Res. Recipient Alumni Disting. Prof. award Oreg. State U., 1968, Centennial award, 1968; Gov.'s Scientist award Oreg. Mus. Sci. and Industry, 1969; Man of Yr. award Willamette Valley Research Council, 1971; Burt Hall named in his honor Oreg. State U., 1987; Alumnus of Yr. award George Fox Coll., 1988. Fellow Am. Meteorol. Soc. (council 1969-71, exec. com. 1972); mem. Am. Geophys. Union (pres. oceanography sect. 1964, ocean sci. award 1984), Am. Soc. Limnology and Oceanography (pres. Pacific sect. 1958, editorial bd. 1963-64). Home: Corvallis Oreg. Died Aug. 24, 1991; buried Oak Lawn Cemetery, Corvallis, Oreg.

BURTON, CHARLES WESLEY, manufacturing executive; b. Balt., Nov. 26, 1897; s. Charles W. and Eurith Ann Hargest (Leach) B.; m. Nildred M. Meyer, July 12, 1922; children: Charles L., Mildred (Mrs. Lee S. Pyles), William Kenneth, Phyllis (Mrs. Fielding Watson). Grad., Balt. City Coll.; AB, St. John's Coll., 1918. CPA, Md. CPA Haskins & Sells, 1922-29; accountant Anchor Post Products, Balt., 1929-37; treas. Anchor Post Products, 1938-45, v.p., 1945-50, exec. v.p., 1950-56, pres., 1956-59, chmn. bd., pres., from 1959, also bd. dirs.; dir. Indsl. Corp. of Baltimore City; adv. bd. Liberty Mutual Ins. Co.; Bd. mgrs. YMCA Schs. Served as 2d lt., inf., US Army, World War I. Mem. Balt Assn. Commerce, Md. Assn. CPAs, Fin. Execs. Inst., NAM, Kappa Alpha, Enterprise Club, Sherwood Forest Club, Balt. Country Club, Kiwanis. *

BURTON, SCOTT, artist; b. Greensboro, Ala., 1939. Art studies with Leon Berkowitz, Washington; with Hans Hofmann, Provincetown, Mass., 1957-59; BA, Columbia U., 1962; MA, NYU, 1963. One-man shows include Finch Coll., N.Y., 1971, Whitney Mus. Am. Art, 1972, Am. Theater Lab, N.Y., 1972, Artists Space, N.Y., 1975, Solomon R. Guggenheim Mus., N.Y.C., 1976, Droll/Kolbert Gallery, N.Y.C., 1977, Brooks Jackson Gallery Iolas, N.Y.C., 1978, Protetch-McIntosh Gallery, Washington, 1979, Daniel Weinberg Gallery, San Francisco, 1980, Los Angeles, 1986, Univ. Art Mus. U. Calif., Berkeley, 1980, Dag Hammarskjold Plaza Sculpture Garden, N.Y.C., 1981, Max Protetch Gallery, N.Y.C., 1981, 82, 85, 86, McIntosh-Drysdale Gallery, Houston, 1984, Balt. Mus. Art, 1986; exhibited in group shows at U. Iowa Mus. Art, Iowa City, 1970, Whitney Mus. Am. Art, 1975, 81, 85, Akademie der Kunste, West Berlin, Fed. Republic Germany, 1976, Kassel, Fed. Republic Germany, 1977, 82, Mus. Am. Found. for Arts, Miami, Fla., 1977, Inst. Contemporary Art U. Pa., Phila., 1977, Solomon R. Guggenheim Mus., 1978, Neuberger Mus. SUNY at Purchase, 1979, Marian Goodman Gallery, N.Y.C., 1980, Myers Fine Arts Bldg. SUNY at Plattsburgh, 1981, MIT, Cambridge, 1981, 83, Art Inst. Chgo., 1982, San Francisco Mus. Modern Art, 1982, Hirshhorn Mus. and Sculpture Garden Smithsonian Instn., Washington, 1983, 84, Artpark, Lewiston, N.Y., 1983, Tate Gallery, London, 1983, Kunsthalle, Bern, Switzerland, 1983, Milw. Art Ctr., 1983, Mus. Art R.I. Sch. Design, Providence, 1984, Mus. Modern Art, N.Y.C., 1984, Los Angeles County Mus. Art, 1985, 86, Carnegie Inst., Pitts., 1985, Cin. Mus. Art, 1986, Marisa del Re Gallery, N.Y.C., 1986, Mus. Art, Ft. Lauderdale, Fla., 1986, various others; represented in permanent collections Art Mus. Princeton U., Chase Manhattan Art Collection, N.Y.C., Cin. Art Mus., Dallas Mus. Art, Detroit Inst. Arts, Solomon R. Guggenheim Mus., Joslyn Art Mus., Omaha, La Jolla Mus. Contemporary Art, Los Angeles County Mus. Art, La. Mus., Humleback, Denmark, Mellon Bank, Pitts., Milw. Art Ctr., Mobil Corp., Mus. Contemporary Art, Los Angeles, Mus. Modern Art, N.Y.C., Phila. Mus. Art, Rolling Stone Mag., N.Y.C., Tate Gallery, London, Univ. Art Mus. U. Calif., Berkeley, Walker Art Ctr., Mpls., Whitney Mus. Am. Art; prin. works include atrium furniture, plantings and floor design Equitable Ctr. Tower West Bldg, N.Y.C., atrium seating, lower lobby seating Arts and Media Tech. Facility MIT, Pearlstone Park City of Balt.; subject of various articles. Home: New York N.Y. Died Dec. 29, 1989. †

BURTT, EVERETT JOHNSON, economic consultant; b. Jackson, Mich., Aug. 6, 1914; s. Everett Johnson and Eve Mildred (Meisenhelter) B.; m. Cynthia Webb, June 15, 1940; children—Michael Coburn, Judith. A.B., Berea Coll., 1935; M.A., Duke, 1937, Ph.D., 1950. Instr. econs. U. Me., 1939-41; instr. Denver U., 1941-42; labor market analyst War Manpower Commn., 1942-43; employment analyst U.S. Bur. Labor Statistics, Boston, 1946-47; asst. prof. Boston U., 1947-52, asso. prof., 1952-57, prof. econs., 1957-80, prof. emeritus, 1980; chmn. dept. Boston U. (Coll. Liberal Arts and Grad. Sch.), 1952-68, chmn. all-univ. dept., 1956-68, acting chmn. dept. econs., 1971-74; asso. dir. Manpower Inst., 1974-75. Author: Labor Markets, Unions and Government Policies, 1963, Plant Relocation and the Core City Worker, 1967, Social Perspectives in the History of Economic Theory, 1972, Labor in the American Economy, 1979; Contbr. profl. periodicals, reports. Served with U.S. Army, 1943-46. Mem. Am. Econ. Assn., Indsl. Relations Research Assn. (pres. Boston 1966-67), AAUP, Phi Beta Kappa (hon. Boston U. chpt. 1981). Home: North Easton Mass. Died Feb. 24, 1989; buried Canton, Mass.

BURWELL, LEWIS CARTER, JR., airline executive; b. Charlotte, N.C., Apr. 23, 1908; s. Lewis Carter and Saida Stoney (Jones) B.; m. Edith Branson, Nov. 6, 1942; children: Margaret S. Barnhardt (dec.), Lewis Carter III, Henry M., Robert E.L., Edith Lynne Abraham. A.B. cum laude, U. South, 1928; C.L.U., Wharton Sch., U. Pa., 1934. Pres. Plans Inc., Charlotte and Houston, 1930-42; chmn. Plans Inc., Washington, 1960; pres. Resort Airlines, Pinehurst, N.C., 1946-51, Miami, Fla., 1946-51; v.p. Flying Tiger Line, Washington, 1951-57; chmn. bd. Overseas Nat. Airways, Washington, 1957-60, Pinehurst Airlines, 1973-86; dir. Airlift Internat., Miami, Wilson-Murrow Cos., Washington, Air Shipping Agys., Ltd., London, Eng. Author: Scrapbook, 1947, The Climb is Fun, 1984. Trustee U. South, 1932-35. Served to col. USAAF, 1942-46. Decorated Bronze Star, Air medal with 2 oak leaf clusters, D.F.C. with 2 oak leaf clusters U.S.; Y'un Hui medal; Grand Star of Honor Republic of China). Named Hon. Command Pilot, Chinese Air Force. Episcopalian. Clubs: Pinehurst Country, Green Valley Country. Home: Greenville S.C. Died Feb. 10, 1988; interred Arlington Nat. Cemetery. †

BUSCH, AUGUST A., JR., beverage executive; b. St. Louis, Mar. 28, 1899; s. August A. Sr. and Alice (Zisemann) B.; m. Margaret Snyder, Mar. 11, 1981 (dec.); 10 children from previous marriages. Ed., Smith Acad.; LL.D. (hon.), St. Louis U., 1969. With Mfrs. Ry. Co., Lafayette South Side Bank and Trust Co.; gen. supt. Anheuser-Busch, Inc., St. Louis, 1924-26, 6th v.p., gen. mgr., 1926-31, 2d v.p., gen. mgr., 1931-34, 1st v.p., gen. mgr., 1934-41, pres., 1946-72, chmn. bd., 1956-77; chief exec. officer Anheuser-Busch Cos., Inc., St. Louis, 1971-75, hon. chmn. bd., 1977-89; mem. brewing industry adv. com. WPB, 1942; pres., chmn. bd., chief exec. officer St. Louis Cardinals, 1953—; chmn. Mfrs. Ry. Co., St. Louis Refrigerator Car Co.; bd. dirs. Centerre Trust Co., Gen. Am. Life Ins. Co., Centerre Bank, St. Louis. Chmn. pub. relations com. United Fund St. Louis, from 1964; chmn. bd. Civic Progress, Inc., 13 years, St. Louis U. Devel. Fund drive; bd. dirs. St. Louis Municipal Opera; chmn. St. Louis Bicentennial Celebration Com. Served as col. Ordnance Dept. AUS, 1942-45. Recipient Fleur-de-Lis award St. Louis U., 1960; named Man of Year St. Louis Globe-Democrat, 1961; Man and Boy award nat. bd. Boys' Clubs Am., 1966; Citizen No. 1 award Press Club Met. St. Louis, 1967; Man of Year award So. Calif. Retail Liquor Dealers Assn., 1971; hon. commodore USCG Aux., 1972. Clubs: St. Louis Country (St. Louis), Racquet (St. Louis), Old Warson (St. Louis), Log Cabin (St. Louis), Bridlespur Hunt (St. Louis); Rolling Rock (Ligonier, Pa.). Home: Saint Louis Mo. Died Sept. 29, 1989; buried St. Louis.

BUSCH, NIVEN, novelist, screenwriter; b. N.Y.C., Apr. 26, 1903; s. Briton Niven and Christine (Fairchild) B.; m. Sonia Frey, 1926 (div. 1934); m. Teresa Wright, May 12, 1942 (div. 1952); m. Carmencita Baker, Mar. 14, 1956 (div. Sept. 1969); m. Suzanne Te Roller de Sanz, Dec. 8, 1973; children: Peter, Briton, Terence, Mary, Jerry, Joseph, Nicholas and Liza (twins). Student, Princeton U., 1924-25. Assoc. editor Time mag., N.Y.C., 1925-31; assoc. editor, contbr. New Yorker mag., N.Y.C., 1924-31; screenwriter Warner Brothers, 20th Century-Fox, Metro-Goldwyn-Mayer, Paramount, Universal studios, RKO, Hollywood, Calif., 1931-52; story editor Sam Goldwyn Prodns., Hollywood, 1940-42; ind. film producer Hollywood, 1946-52; ind. screenwriter, novelist San Francisco, from 1952; regents' prof. English and fine arts U. Calif., Irvine, 1970, 71, 75, San Diego, 1972, Berkeley, 1977; lectr. dept. humanities Princeton U., 1985, 86. Author: Twenty-One Americans (originally pub. New Yorker mag.), 1930; (novels) The Carrington Incident, 1941, Duel in the Sun, 1944, They Dream of Home, 1944, Day of the Conquerors, 1946, The Furies, 1948, The Hate Merchant, 1953, The Actor, 1955, California Street, 1958, The San Franciscans, 1961, The Gentleman from California, 1965, The Takeover, 1977, No Place For a Hero, 1976, Continent's Edge, 1980, The Titan Game, 1989; (screenplays) In Old Chicago, 1937 (Acad. award nomination), The Westerner, 1940, Pursued, 1946, The Capture, 1946, The Postman Always Rings Twice, 1946, Distant Drums, 1951, Man from the Alamo, 1952, The Moonlighter, 1953, The Treasure of Pancho Villa, 1955, The Crowd Roars, Scarlet Dawn, College Coach, Babbitt, The Man with Two Faces, He Was Her Man, The Big Shakedown, Off the Record, The Angels Wash Their Faces, Belle Starr, others. Mem. Acad. Motion Picture Arts and Scis., Authors Guild, Writers Guild Am. West. Republican. Episcopalian. Clubs: Presidio Army Golf (San Francisco); Princeton (N.Y.C.). Home: San Francisco Calif. Died Aug. 25, 1991; buried San Francisco.

BUSH, BEVERLY, association executive, artist; b. Kelso, Wash.; d. Edward Lawrence and Gunild Hedvig (Hansen) Stover; m. William Bush, Jan. 8, 1944. B.A., U. Wash.; student, Art Student's League, Nat. Acad. Design. Exec. sec., from 1958. Nat. exhbns. include, Audubon Artists, N.A.D., Nat. Assn. Women Painters, USA 59; rep. pvt. colls. with Artists Equity Assn., Inc., from 1956. Mem. Zeta Phi Eta. Home: Anchorage Alaska Died Aug. 17, 1990; buried Evergreen Washelli Meml. Pk., Seattle.

BUSH, FREDERIC ANDREW, oil industry executive, geologist, consultant; b. Silver City, N.Mex., Mar. 10, 1904; s. Frederic Andrew and Elizabeth (Argenbright) B.; m. Margaret Devlin, Aug. 4, 1928; 1 dau., Margaret E. Bush Brooks. A.B., Stanford University, 1925. Paleontologist Atlantic Oil Prodn. Co., 1925; stratigrapher Sinclair Oil & Gas Co., 1926-30, chief geologist, 1930-32; chief geologist Sinclair Prairie Oil Co., 1932-45, Sinclair Oil Corp., 1945-50; v.p. Sinclair Can. Oil Co.; dir. Sinclair Oil Corp.; pres., dir. Sinclair Internat. Oil Co., chmn. bd., 1968; v.p., dir. Sinclair Petroleum Co., to 1968; dir., v.p. Cambridge Royalty Co.; dir. Cambridge Petroleum Royalties Ltd.; petroleum cons. from 1986; mem. exec. com. bd. advisors paleontol. sect. Am. Mus. Natural History, until 1968. Fellow Geol. Soc. Am., Explorers Club; mem. Am. Assn. Petroleum Geologists, Société Geologique de France, Am. Petroleum Inst., Petroleum Exploration Soc., N.Y. Acad. Sci., Audubon Soc., English Speaking Union. Club: Shenorock Shore (Rye, N.Y.). Home: Greenwich Conn. Died Oct. 9, 1989.

BUSTEED, ROBERT CHARLES, botany educator; b. Milan, Ind., Sept. 4, 1907; s. Robert and Emma (Elble) B.; m. Ada Flora Kohlerman, June 6, 1931; children—Philip Gene, Robert Louis, Richard Charles, Wallace Bruce. Student, Hanover Coll., 1925-27; A.B., Ind. U., 1930, M.A., 1932, Ph.D., 1936. Grad. asst. botany dept. and U., 1930-33, tutor, 1934-35, instr., 1935-36; prof., head dept. biology Appalachian State Tchrs. Coll., 1937-45; prof. botany, chmn. sci. div. U. Ga., Savannah div., 1946-48; prof., head dept. biology, chmn. sci. div., grad. council West Tex. State Coll., from 1948; Faculty sponsor West Tex. State chpt. Tex. Collegiate Acad. Sci.; Mem. adminstrv. council Kilgore Research Center, from 1967. Dir. Am. Brittany Spaniel Club, 1946; Dist. commr. Boy Scouts Am., Boone, N.C., 1944-46. Mem. Texas Coll. Tchrs. Assn., Tex. Panhandle Sci. Council (dir. 1959, pres. 1967- 68), Ind. Acad. Sci., Sigma Xi, Theta Kappa Nu, Alpha Phi Omega (sponsor), Beta Beta Beta (sponsor). Lutheran. Clubs: Mason (Boone), Lion (Boone) (pres.). Home: Canyon Tex. Died June 23, 1988.

BUTCHER, DEVEREUX, association executive; b. Radnor, Pa., Sept. 24, 1906; s. Henry Clay and Constance (Devereux) B.; m. Mary Frances Taft, Dec. 13, 1935; 1 son, Russell Devereux. Grad., St. George's Sch., Pa. Acad. Fine Arts, 1928. Free lance writer, photographer, 1936-39; editorial asst. Am. Forests mag. Am. Forestry Assn., 1941-42; exec. sec. Nat. Parks Assn., 1942-50, field rep., 1950-57; founding editor Nat. Parks Mag., 1942-57; editor, pub. Nat. Wildlands News, 1959-62; dir. Hawk Mountain Sanctuary Assn., 1963-80, John Burroughs Meml. Assn., 1965-80; Mem. adv. com. on conservation Sec. Interior, 1952-53. Author: Exploring Our National Parks and Monuments, 1947, Exploring the National Parks of Canada, 1951, Seeing America's Wildlife in Our National Refuges, 1955, Exploring Our National Wildlife Refuges, 1963, Our National Parks in Color, 1964; Co-author photographer: Knowing Your Trees, 1963-78; painter landscapes nat. parks, nature monuments. Mem. Wilderness Soc., Defenders Wildlife (sec. 1947-59), Nat. Parks Assn. Home: Gladwyne Pa. Died May 22, 1991; buried Swan Point Cemetery, R.I.

BUTCHER, HAROLD, journalist; b. Colcester, England, May 9, 1893; s. Alfred James and Clara Alice (Buckingham) B.; m. Elizabeth Van Dyke Ford, June 23, 1934; children: John Beverly, Geoffrey, Elizabeth Tertia. Ed., Royal Grammar Sch., Colcester, Eng. Feature storywriter for Brit. papers and daily cables to London Daily Herald, 1930-37; features in New York Times, Travel Mag., Daily Herald (London), Catholic Herald (London); v.p. Assn. Fgn. Press Correspondents in U.S., 1937-39; convocation lectr. Mo., Wis., Wayne, Northwestern, and Minn. Univs., 1940; editor Yavapai Co. Messenger, 1952-56; writer articles on religion, travel. Author articles for Am. and Brit. publs.; contbr. to "You Americans" 1939, Ency. Brittanica, numerous Catholic mags. Santa Fe rep. N.C.W.C. News Svc., Washington, The American Organist, S.I.; N.Y. Pres. Santa Fe Chamber Music Soc., 1961-62; founder, commentator Prescott Cultural Ctr. of the Air Radio program, 1948-52. Mem. Gallery of Living Catholic Authors. *

BUTCHER, HOWARD, III, investment banker; b. Ardmore, Pa., Jan. 28, 1902; s. Howard Jr. and Margaret (Keen) B.; m. Elizabaeth Crosswell McBee Jan.8, 1936 (dec. Oct. 1972); children: Howard IV, McBee, Jonathan; m. Elizabeth Shryock, June 1973. BA, U. Pa., 1923, LLD (hon.), 1967; PhD in Civil Law (hon.), St. Joseph's Coll., 1968; LLD (hon.), PMC Colls., 1969. Cert. investment banker. Sr. ptnr. Butcher and Sherrerd, Phila., 1948-68; chmn. emeritus Butcher and Singer Inc., Phila., from 1968. Home: Villanova Pa. Died June 19, 1991; buried Ch. of the Redeemer, Bryn Mawr, Pa.

BUTLER, ROY FRANCIS, classics educator; b. Atlanta, May 4, 1914; s. Roy Edward and Mae (Kenner) B.; m. Barbara Goehring Scott, Nov. 17, 1943; children: Roy Francis, John Scott. A.B. (Chattanooga Times scholar), U. Chattanooga, 1935; M.A. (Latin scholar), U. Tenn., 1938; Ph.D. (Univ. scholar), Ohio State U., 1942. Instr. U. Tenn., 1946, Ohio State U., 1946-47; asst. prof. U. Tenn., 1947, 48; faculty Baylor U., Waco, Tex., 1947-84; prof. classics Baylor U., 1952-84, chmn. dept. classics, 1958-84, prof., chmn. emeritus, from 1984. Author: Vocabulary Building Through Etymology, 1948, Handbook of Medical Terminology, 1957, 71, The Meaning of Agapao and Phileo in the Greek Testament, 1977, (with others) Epigrams of Martial, 1987, American Poetry Anthology, 1990; editorial cons.: Dorland's Illustrated Medical Dictionary, 1965, 74; contbr. articles to profl. jours. Served with USAAF, 1942-45. Mem. Am. Philol. Assn., Linguistic Soc. Am., Am. Oriental Soc., Classical Assn. Middle West and South, N.Y. Acad. Scis., AAAS, Mensa, Phi Kappa Phi, Blue Key. Home: Waco Tex. Deceased. †

BUTT, HOWARD EDWARD, supermarket executive; b. Memphis, Apr. 9, 1895; s. Charles C. and Florence (Thornton) B.; m. Mary Elizabeth Holdsworth, Dec. 5, 1924; children: Howard Edward, Charles C., Margaret Eleanor William Crook. Developed and owned, pres. and chmn. bd. H.E. Butt Grocery Co., Corpus Christi, Tex., 1920-71. Established H.E. Butt Found., 1934, widely known philanthropist and civic leader. With

U.S. Navy. Mem. Mason (33 deg.). Baptist. Home: Corpus Christi Tex. Died Mar. 12, 1991; buried Kerrville, Tex.

BUTTENWIESER, BENJAMIN JOSEPH, banker; b. N.Y.C., Oct. 22, 1900; s. Joseph L. and Caroline (Weil) B.; m. Helen Lehman, Oct. 2, 1929; children: Lawrence Benjamin, Carol (dec.), Peter Lehman, Paul Arthur. BA, Columbia U., 1919, LLD, 1977. Adv. dir. Lehman Bros., Kuhn Loeb, Inc.; past U.S. asst. high commr., Germany. Trustee Fedn. Jewish Philanthropic Soc., Columbia, Lenox Hill Hosp., N.Y.C. Police Found., Charles H. Revson Found. Mem. Midday Club, Columbia Club, Univ. Club (N.Y.C.), Century County Club (White Plains, N.Y.). Home: New York NY Died Dec. 31, 1991.

BUTTERFIELD, LANDER W(ESTGATE), lawyer; b. Chgo., Sept. 8, 1897; s. William W. and Katherine (Dutton) B.; m. Guinevere Youngs, Oct. 2, 1931; children: Julie Ann (Mrs. Robert G. Crowder), Landra Jane. Student, Dartmouth, 1915-16, Northwestern, 1919-21; AB, U. Mich., 1919; JD, Stanford U., 1922. Bar: Calif. 1923, Ill. 1953. Atty. A.T. & S.F. Ry, Calif., 1923-52; gen. atty, Chgo., from 1952. Served as 2d lt. F.A., U.S. Army, 1918-19. Mem. ABA, Calif. State Bar Assn. Episcopalian. *

BUTTERWORTH, FRANK WILLOUGHBY, III, naval officer, engineering consultant; b. Phila., June 29, 1937; s. Frank Willoughby II and Kathryn (Hering) B.; m. Janet Marie DeVylder, May 4, 1963; children: Frank W. IV, Elizabeth Lyn, Lori Anne. BS, U.S. Naval Acad., 1958. Commd. ensign USN, 1958, advanced through grades to Rear Adm.; engr. officer USS Narwhal USN, Groton, Conn., 1967-70; exec. officer USS John. C. Calhoun USN, Charleston, S.C., 1970-72; cmdg. officer USS Billfish USN, Groton, 1973-76; comdr. submarine Squadron Three USN, San Diego, 1978-80; comdr. submarine Group Two USN, Groton, 1983-85; sr. mem. Nuclear Propulsion Examining Bd. U.S. Pacific Fleet, Pearl Harbor, Hawaii, 1976-78, chief of staff, comdr. submarine force, 1980-82; asst. dep. under sec. defense (internat. programs and tech. transfer) Dept. Defense, Washington, 1982-83, asst. dep. chief naval ops. (submarine warfare) Office of Chief Naval Ops., 1985-87; sr. v.p. ASTA Engring., Inc., Phila., 1987-88; dir. submarine systems analysis RES Ops. Physical Dynamics Inc., Arlington, Va., 1988. Decorated Legion of Merit, 1980, 82, 85, 87, Meritorious Service medal, 1976, 78. Mem. U.S. Naval Inst., Navy League U.S., Naval Submarine League. Republican. Roman Catholic. Home: Annandale Va. Died Oct. 9, 1988; buried Arlington Nat. Cemetery.

BUTTERWORTH, OLIVER, English language educator, author; b. Hartford, Conn., May 23, 1915; s. Paul McMillan and Clarabel (Smith) B.; m. Miriam Ford Brooks, June 30, 1940; children: Michael, Timothy, Dan, Kate Butterworth de Valdez. BA, Dartmouth Coll., 1937; MA, Middlebury Coll., 1947. Tchr. Latin and English, Kent Sch., 1937-48; instr., asst. prof. English, Hartford Coll. for Women, 1948-59, assoc. prof., 1959-69, prof., 1969-90. Author: (juveniles) The Enormous Egg, 1956, The Trouble with Jenny's Ear, 1960 (award Herald-Tribune Spring Festival of Books), The Enormous Egg, 1971 (selected for Lew Carrol Bookshelf), The Narrow Passage, 1973. Bd. dirs. Hartford Stage Co.; vol. Hartford Ballet, Barnstromers; mem. bd. numerous civic groups, including Mark Twain Meml. Home: West Hartford Conn. Died Sept. 17, 1990; W. Hartford, Conn.

BUTTLE, EDGAR ALLYN, judge; b. N.Y.C., May 7, 1903; s. Norman Alexander and Ella Tice (Collins) B.; m. Erika Lucille Heydolph, Aug. 9, 1931; 1 dau., Dagmar Jo Ann. A.B., Columbia U., 1928; J.D., N.Y.U., 1931; J.S.D., N.Y. U., 1935; postgrad., Princeton U., 1945. Bar: N.Y. 1933, D.C. 1948. Spl. asst. atty. gen. N.Y. State, 1933; law assoc. George Gordon Battle, 1936-49; N.Y. regional counsel War Assets Adminstrn., 1946-48; spl. asst. to atty. gen. of U.S., antitrust div., 1950-52; trial counsel Finch & Schaefler, N.Y.C., 1952-56; adminstrv. law judge FTC, 1959-73, lectr. fed. trial practice; sr. fed. adminstrv. law judge, U.S.; presiding hearing officer adminstrv. trials Dade County, Fla.; chmn. bd. Buttle-Baker Chem. Corp., 1953-56; mem. adv. com. on vets. re-employment Dept. Labor; fed. referee Appeals Council Social Security Adminstrn., 1956-59. Author: The Perplexities of Trade Regulation, 1956, The Search for Administrative Justice, published 1958, A Guide to the Law and Legal Literature of Peru, (in collaboration with Library of Congress), 1947, Trial Problems in Antitrust Litigation, 1953; also articles to law jours. Served as comdr. USNR, 1942-45; navy liaison officer Selective Service Hdqrs., 1943-45, N.J. and Del. Decorated Army Commendation medal; recipient Distinguished Service award FTC; named hon. adm. Tex. Navy. Mem. S.R., SAR, Fed. Adminstrv. Law Judges Conf. (pres. 1961-62), World Assn. Judges, ABA, Fed. Bar Assn. (exec. council 1947-48, chmn. adminstrv. law com. 1962-63, 65-66), VFW, Delta Sigma Phi, Phi Delta Phi. Episcopalian. Club: Princeton of South Fla. Home: Miami Fla. Died 1990. †

BUYSKE, DONALD ALBERT, pharmaceutical executive, scientist; b. Milw., Aug. 30, 1927; s. George S. and Agnes (Chuppa) B.; m. Jo Kessel, Aug. 28, 1952 (div. June 1980); children: Gail, Donna, Jo, Steven. B.S. in Chemistry, Drury Coll., 1949; M.S. in Biochemistry, U. Wis.-Madison, 1952, Ph.D., 1954. Mem. chemistry faculty Duke U., Durham, N.C., 1954-56; head dept. exptl. therapeutics Lederle Labs., Pearl River, N.Y., 1956-65; dir. rsch. Ayerst Labs., Montreal, Que., Can., 1965-69; v.p. R & D Warner Lambert, Morris Plains, N.J., 1969-80; v.p. Johnson & Johnson, New Brunswick, N.J., 1980-81; sr. v.p. S.C. Johnson and Son, Racine, Wis., 1981-84; founder, chief exec. officer, chmn. Somerset Pharms., Denville, N.J., 1984-90; cons. Chem. Venture Capitol, N.Y.C., 1985-90; dir. Micro Tech., Milw., Wind Point Ptnrs., Racine, Venture Capitol Inc., Milw. Contbr. articles to profl. jours. Advisor, Muscular Dystrophy, N.Y.C., 1975-77, NSF, Washington, 1975-90; bd. dirs. St. Claire's Hosp., Denville, N.J., 1977-81, U.S.-Hungarian Trade Coun., Washington, 1975-90. With U.S. Army, 1945-47. Mem. Am. Soc. Microbiology (editor 1975-83, Editors award 1983), Am. Soc. Pharmacology, Am. Chem. Soc., N.Y. Acad. Scis., AAAS. Republican. Home: West Palm Beach Fla. Died Dec. 8, 1990; buried Cuddebackville, N.Y.

BYAM, MILTON SYLVESTER, library consultant; b. N.Y.C., Mar. 15, 1922; s. Charles and Sybil J. (Williams) B.; m. Yolanda Shervington, Jan. 18, 1947; 1 child, Roger. BS in Social Scis., City Coll., N.Y., 1947; MS, Columbia U., 1949, postgrad., 1968; postgrad., N.Y. U., 1950-51. With Bklyn. Pub. Library, 1947-68, chief pub. services, 1961-65, dep. dir., 1965-68; chmn. dept. library sci. St. Johns U., 1968-72; dir. D.C. Public Library, 1972-74, Queens Borough Pub. Library, Jamaica, N.Y., 1974-79; pres. Byam et al Consultants Inc., from 1979; tchr. history of libraries, humanities, lit., social sci. lit. Pratt Inst., Sch. Library Sci., Bkyln., 1956-67; tchr. pub. library adminstrn. St. Johns U. Grad. Sch., 1956-68; co-chmn. Bklyn. Citizens Com. for Nat. Library Week, 1959-60; trustee Bookmobile Services Trust, 1968, New York Reference and Resources Council, 1969-72, 74-79; cons./adviser to High John, U. Md. Grad. Library Sch., 1969-70; mem. adv. council Cath. Library Assn., 1968-72; mem. adv. com. dept. library sci. Queens Coll.; examiner, dir. positions N.Y. N.J. State Civil Service Dept., 1966-80. Contbr. articles to profl. jours. Vestryman Grace Ch., Jamaica, 1968-69; mem. Commn. on Urban Affairs, Diocese of L.I., 1971-72; mem. Flushing Suburban Civic Assn., 1953, pres., 1964, fin. sec., 1983; mem. Community Planning Bd. 15A, 1967-68; bd. dirs. Queens Coun. on Arts, Queens coun. Boy Scouts Am.; mem. Queens chpt. ARC, from 1979, v.p., 1986-87; pres. Queens Coun. for Social Welfare, 1979-84, v.p., 1985-87; mem. Jamaica Hosp. Nursing Home. With AUS, 1943-45. Decorated Bronze Star medal; recipient Savannah State Coll. Library award, 1964, Friends of Library award Bklyn. Pub. Library, 1968, commendation D.C. Library Services and Constrn. Act Adv. Council, 1974, resolution of commendation bd. trustees D.C. Pub. Library, 1974, certificate of appreciation Personnel Dept., City of Phila., 1974, plaque for outstanding community service Queens Alumni chpt. Delta Sigma Theta, 1974, Brotherhood awards NCCJ, 1977, Brotherhood awards St. Albans Civic Improvement Assn., 1977, award Queens Interfaith Clergy Council, 1977, award Municipal Officers Club of D.C., 1974, award ARC, 1978, award Greater Jamaica C. of C., 1979. Mem. ALA, N.Y. State Library Assn. (chmn. intellectual freedom com. 1968-72), New York Library Club (dir. 1956-57, 69-71). Episcopalian. Clubs: Jamaica Rotary (pres. 1978), Archons of Colophons, Melvil Dui Chowder and Marching Soc. Home: Flushing N.Y. Died July 14, 1991.

BYERLY, THEODORE CARROLL, zoology educator, government official; b. Melbourne, Iowa, May 3, 1902; s. William Henry and Lulu May (Crook) B.; m. Helen Frances Freeman, May 31, 1929 (dec.); children: Carroll (Mrs. N. Holcomb), David, Nora (Mrs. T.D. Bolita); m. Imogene J. McCarthy, Aug. 7, 1967. AB, U. Iowa, 1923, MS, 1925, PhD, 1926. Instr. zoology U. Mich., 1926-28, Hunter Coll., 1928-29, Peabody Coll., 1927-28, Howard U., 1929-30; physiologist div. animal husbandry Bur. Animal Industry, Dept. Agr., from 1929, sr. poultry husbandman charge poultry husbandry investigation, from 1941, chief animal husbandry div., from 1947; asst. dir. livestock research Agrl. Research Service, 1955-57, dep. adminstr., 1957-62, adminstr. coop. state exptl. sta. service, 1962-63; adminstr. Coop. State Research Service, 1963-69; coordinator environmental quality activities Dept. Agr., 1969-73, cons., from 1973; prof. U. Md., 1937-41, adj. prof., 1976-87; cons. Winrock Internat. Center Livestock Research and Tng., 1975-82; chmn. div. biology and agr. NCR, 1963-65; mem. U.S. Nat. Commn. for UNESCO, 1954-60; chmn. U.S. delegation Internat. Conf. Rational Use Biosphere, 1968, Nat. Com. for Man and Biosphere, 1968-79; tech. adviser to U.S. delegation UN Conf. on Human Environment, Stockholm, Sweden, 1972. Recipient Superior Service award U.S. Dept. Agr., 1953; Disting. Service award, 1965; Spl. award, 1972; elected to Sci. Hall of Fame, Agrl. Rsch. Svc., 1990. Fellow AAAS, Poultry Sci. Assn. (Borden award 1943, pres. 1960-61), Am. Soc. Animal Sci.; mem. Am. Inst. Biol. Scis. (Disting. Svc. award 1979), Am. Soc. Zoologists (emeritus), Soc. Exptl. Biology and Medicine (emeritus), Acad. Medicine, D.C., Am. Poultry Hist. Assn. (Hall of Fame 1983), World Affairs Coun., Friends Agrl. Rsch. Beltsville, USDA-ARS Science Hall of Fame. Democrat. Club: Cosmos (Washington). Home: Greenbelt Md. Died May 17, 1990; buried St. John Episcopal Ch., Beltsville, Md.

BYWATERS, JERRY, artist, educator, art museum director; b. Paris, Tex., 1906; s. Porter A. and Hattie (Williamson) B.; m. Mary McLarry, Nov. 3, 1930; children: Jerry, Dick. B.A., So. Meth. U., 1927; student, Art Students League, N.Y.C., 1927; studied in, Mexico. Europe. Prof. art So. Meth. U., from 1936, head dept. art, 1965-67; dir. Dallas Mus. Fine Arts, 1943-64; founder, dir. Jerry Bywaters Research Collection on Am. Art and Architecture, So. Meth. U., from 1981; painter, printmaker, lectr. art, from 1930; art critic Dallas News, 1933-39; art editor Southwest Rev., Dallas, 1950-60. Home: Dallas Tex. Deceased. †

CACCIA, HAROLD ANTHONY (LORD CACCIA), diplomat; b. India, Dec. 21, 1905; s. Anthony and Fanny Theodora (Birch) C.; m. Anne Catherine Barstow, Oct. 4, 1932; children: David, Clarissa, Antonia. Student, Eton, Trinity Coll., Oxford, Eng.; Laming Travelling fellow, Queen's Coll., Oxford, 1928. Entered Her Majesty's Diplomatic Svc., 1929-65; assigned Peking China, 1932; fgn. office, 1935, asst. pvt. sec. to sec. of state, 1936, assigned Athens Greece, resident minister N. Africa, 1943; allied control commn. Italy, 1943-44; then polit. adviser to gen. officer, comdg. officer comdr. in chief Land Forces, Greece, 1944, asst. under-sec. state, 1946, dep. under-sec. state, 1949; Brit. high commr. Austria, 1950-54; Brit. ambassador, 1951-54, dep. under-sec. state Fgn. Office, 1954-56, permanent under-sec. state, 1962-65, Brit. ambassador to U.S., Washington, 1956-61; provost Eton Coll., Windsor, England, 1965-77. Created Baron of Abernant, 1965, lord prior Order of St. John, 1969. Chmn. ITT (U.K.) Ltd.; dir. Orion Bank, Prudential Assurance, Ltd., Fgn. and Colonial Eurotrust. Decorated knight grand cross Most Disting. Order St. Michael and St. George, Royal Victorian Order; grand cross Order St. John Jerusalem; Austrian Grosses Goldenes Ehrenzeichen am Bande. Fellow Trinity Coll. (hon.), Queen's Coll., 1974. Home: Powys Wales Died Oct. 31, 1990; buried St. Mauritius, Altmawr.

CADY, HOWARD STEVENSON, editor; b. Middlebury, Vt., July 28, 1914; s. Frank William and Marian (Kingsbury) C.; m. Marjory Arnold, Dec. 31, 1938; children: Peter, Janet (Mrs. James Hutchinson), Susan (Mrs. Timothy Y. Hayward), Anne (Mrs. Andrew M. Jackson), Ellen. A.B., Middlebury Coll., 1936. With editorial dept. The Macmillan Co., N.Y.C., 1937-41; mng. editor Stephen Daye Press, Brattleboro, Vt., 1941-42; editor Doubleday & Co., Inc., N.Y.C., San Francisco, 1942-52; editor-in-chief Little Brown & Co., Inc., Boston, 1952-54, Henry Holt & Co., N.Y.C., 1954-57; editor-in-chief, v.p., dir. G. P. Putnam's Sons, 1957-62; gen. mgr., editor-in-chief gen. book div. Holt, Rinehart & Winston, Inc., 1962-64; exec. editor David McKay Co., Inc., 1964-68; sr. editor, v.p. Wm. Morrow & Co., Inc., 1968-84, cons. editor, 1984-90; cons. editor Adler & Adler, Bethesda, Md., 1986-87; lectr. editing and publishing Sch. Gen. Studies, Columbia U., 1958-60. Served with OSS, 1943-45, with AUS, 1945-46. Home: Middlebury Conn. Died Nov. 4, 1990.

CAFFEY, JOHN, physician; b. Castle Gate, Utah, Mar. 30, 1895; s. Benjamin Franklin and Katherine (MacLean) C.; m. Sidneth Earle, Mar. 27, 1942. AB, U. Mich., 1916, MD, 1919. Med. and relief work with ARC, Serbia, Poland, 1920-21; mem. Am. Relief Commn., Russia, 1922-23; from asst. to assoc. prof. clin. pediatrics Coll. Phys. and Surg., Columbia, 1928-53, prof. clin. pediatrics, 1952, prof. radiology, 1953-61, prof. emeritus radiology; from asst. to pediatrician Babies Hosp., N.Y.C., 1928-55; cons. radiologist Presbyn. Hosp., N.Y.C.; vis. prof. radiology and pediatrics Univ. Pitts.; radiologist Pitts. Children's Hosp. Author: Pediatric X-Ray Diagnosis, 1945. Mem. Am. Pediatric Soc., Am. Roentgen Ray Soc. (hon.), Am. Orthopedic Assn. (hon.), Royal Soc. Medicine (London, hon.). *

CAGE, JOHN, composer; b. Los Angeles, Sept. 5, 1912; s. John Milton and Lucretia (Harvey) C.; m. Xenia Kashevaroff, June 7, 1935 (div. 1945). Student, Pomona Coll., 1928-30; pupil, Richard Buhlig, Adolph Weiss, Henry Cowell, Arnold Schoenberg; hon. degree, Calif. Inst. Arts, 1986. Faculty Cornish Sch., Seattle, 1936-38, Sch. Design, Chgo., 1941-42; tchr. composition New Sch. for Social Research, N.Y.C., 1955-60; musical dir. Merce Cunningham and Dance Co., N.Y.C., 1944-66; fellow Center Advanced Studies, Wesleyan U., Middletown, Conn., 1960-61; composer-in residence U. Cin., 1967; research prof. and asso. Center Advanced Studies, U. Ill., Urbana, 1967-69; Charles Eliot Norton prof. poetry Harvard U., 1988-89; mem. bd., past pres. Cunningham Dance Found.; mem. Found. for Contemporary Performance Arts. Dir. concert percussion music sponsored by Mus. Modern Art and League Composers, 1943; commd. by Ballet Soc. to write The Seasons, 1947, by Donaueschinger Musiktage to write work for two prepared pianos 34'46. 766 for Two Pianists, 1954, by Montreal Festivals Soc. to write work for full orch. Atlas Eclipticalis, 1961, by Serge Koussevitsky Music Found. in Library of Congress to write work. Cheap Imitation for Full Orch., 1972; Lecture on the Weather for 12 speaker-vocalists (tape and film in collaboration with Maryanne Amacher and Luis

Frangella), 1975, by Seiji Ozawa and Boston Symphony Orch. in collaboration with 5 other Am. orchs. and NEA to write Renga with Apartment House 1776 for orch., four quartets and eight soloists, 1976, by Metz Centre Européen pour la Recherche Musicale to write 30 pieces for 5 orchs., 1981 by Frankfurt Opera to write Europeras 1&2, by Cabrillo Festival to write Dance 4/ Orchs., 1982, by radio Bremen to write A House Full of Music, 1982, by Suntory Internat. Program to write Etcetera 2/4 Orchs., 1986, y Boston Symphony Orch. and the Fromm Found. to write 101, 1989, by Almeida Festival to write Europeras 3 and 4, 1990; recorded Fontana Mix on magnetic tape for Studio di Fonologia, Milan, Italy, 1958; organized group of musicians and engrs. for making music directly on magnetic tape, 1951; produced (with Lejaren Hiller) HPSCHD for seven harpsichords and 52 computer generated tapes, 1967-69; author: (with Kathleen O'Donnell Hoover) The Life and Works of Virgil Thomson, 1958, Silence, 1961, A Year from Monday, 1967, (with Alison Knowles) Notations, 1969, (with Lois Long and Alexander H. Smith) Mushroom Book, 1972, M, 1973, Writings Through Finnegans Wake, 1978, Empty Words, 1979, 83, For the Birds, Themes and Variations, X, I-VI, 1990; Graphic works include Not Wanting to Say Anything About Marcel, 1969, (with Calvin Sumsion) Seven Day Diary, Score Without Parts, 17 Drawings by Thoreau, Signals, 1978, Changes and Disappearances, 1979, On the Surface, 1980. Recipient award for extending boundries musical art Nat. Acad. Arts and Letters, 1949; recipient 1st prize Woodstock Art Film Festival for score of Works of Calder, 1951, ann. award from the People to People Com. on Fungi, 1964; Thorne Music Fund grantee, 1967-69; Carl Sczuka prize for Roaratorio, an Irish Circus on Finnegans Wake, 1979, Poses Creative Arts award Brandeis U., 1983, Laurate Kyoto prize Inamori Found. Acad., 1989; Guggenheim fellow, 1949; named Charles Eliot Norton Prof. of Poetry, Harvard U. 1988-89; commdr. Order of Arts and Letters French Ministry of Culture. Mem. ASCAP, N.Y. Mycol. Soc. (founder), Nat. Acad. Arts and Letters, Am. Acad. Arts and Scis., AAAL. Home: New York N.Y. Died Aug. 12, 1992. †

CAHALAN, (JOHN) DONALD, psychology educator; b. Lewistown, Mont., Oct. 3, 1912; s. Daniel Emmett and Emma Cecilia (Robinson) C.; m. Ellen Margaret Johnson, Aug. 19, 1933; children: Carolyn Cahalan Cooper, Michael. B.A., State U. Iowa, 1937, M.A., 1938; Ph.D., George Washington U., 1968. Assoc. prof. psychology and social sci., dir. Opinion Research Ctr., U. Denver, 1946-49; research dir. Attitude Assessment, Dept. Army, 1949-52; research cons. to univ. and govt. research groups, 1952-57; chief project dir. W.R. Simmons and Assocs., N.Y., 1957-59; pres. ARB Surveys, Inc., N.Y.C., 1959-62; exec. v.p. Nowland & Co., Greenwich, Conn., 1962-64; program dir. social research group George Washington U., 1964-70; from adj. prof. to prof. behavioral scis. in residence, also dir. social research group Sch. Pub. Health, U. Calif., Berkeley, 1970-78, prof. pub. health emeritus, 1978-92; vis. colleague Sch. Pub. Health, U. Hawaii, 1978-79. Author: Problem Drinkers: A National Survey, 1970, (with Ira H. Cisin and Helen M. Crossley) American Drinking Practices, 1969, (with Robin Room) Problem Drinking Among American Men, 1974, Understanding America's Drinking Problem, 1987, An Ounce of Prevention: Strategies for Solving Tobacco, Alcohol, and Drug Problems, 1991, Digging for Irish Roots: How to Search for Your Ancestors, 1991, also articles. Mem. Mayor's Commn. Human Relations, Denver, 1947-48. Served with USNR, 1943-46. NIMH grantee, 1970. Mem. Am. Psychol. Assn., Soc. Psychol. Study Social Issues, Am. Sociol. Soc., Soc. Study of Social Problems, Am. Pub. Health Assn. (Lifetime Achievement award 1991), Am. Assn. Pub. Opinion Rsch. (sec.-treas. 1969-73), Sigma Xi. Home: Berkeley Calif. Died Oct. 27, 1992. †

CAIN, JAMES CLARENCE, physician; b. Kosse, Tex., Mar. 19, 1913; s. Thomas Marshall and Aileen (Jackson) C.; m. Ida May Wirtz, June 6, 1938; children-Stephaine Cannon (Mrs. Karl H. Van D'Elden), Mary Lucinda (Mrs. William Carleton Moore), Katherine May (Mrs. Jerry Wayne Snider), James Alvin. B.A., U. Tex., 1933, M.D., 1937; M.S., U. Minn., 1948. Diplomate: Pan Am. Med. Assn. Intern Protestant Episcopal Hosp., Phila., 1937-39; instr. pathology U. Tex. Med. Sch., 1939-40; fellow in internal medicine Mayo Found., Rochester, Minn., 1940-41, 46-48; mem. dept. medicine Mayo Clinic, Rochester, 1948, head of sect. gastroenterology and internal medicine, 1966-70; prof. medicine U. Minn., Mayo Med. Sch. until 1978; personal physician to Pres. Johnson, from 1946; Mem. nat. adv. heart council NIH; pres. Minn. Bd. Med. Examiners, 1971, 72; chmn. nat. adv. commn. for selection drs., dentists and allied med. personnel SSS, adviser to dir., 1969-70; mem. Nat. Adv. Commn. on Med. Manpower; cons. to surgeon gen. Dept. Army; mem. spl. med. adv. group to VA, from 1976; mem. adv. com. Bur. Drugs, FDA, 1973-75. Contbr. articles to profl. jours., chpts. to books. Chmn. Johnson for Pres. vols., Minn., 1964; nat. steering com. City Innovation, 1989. Recipient Ashbel Smith Distinguished Alumnus award U. Tex. Med. Sch., 1969. Mem. Soc. Med. Cons. Armed Forces (pres.), AAAS, AMA (vice chmn. council on nat. security, recipient Billings Gold medal award 1963), So. Minn. Med. Assn., Minn. Internal Medicine Soc. (council), A.C.P. (life mem., gov. for Minn.), Am. Gastroenterol. Assn., Am. Assn. Study Liver Disease, Am. Fedn. Clin. Research, Am. Assn. History Medicine, Fedn. State Med. Bds. U.S., U. Tex. Med. Sch., Mayo Clinic alumni assns., IEEE, Am. Radio Relay League, Amateur Radio Emergency Corps, Sigma Xi, Delta Kappa Epsilon, Alpha Kappa, Alpha Epsilon Delta. Baptist. Home: Rochester Minn. Died Feb. 1, 1992; buried Rochester, Minn.

CALDWELL, JAMES RUSSELL, rubber manufacturer; b. Enfield, Conn., Sept. 28, 1896; s. Thomas Bernard and Elizabeth (Cummings) C.; m. Madeleine Loomis, June 12, 1918; children: Barbara (Mrs. William F. Miller), Jean (Mrs. Earl H. Mabry). Student, Georgetown U., 1914-15, Trinity Coll., Hartford, Conn., 1916-17. Indsl. engr. Fisk Rubber Co., 1917-19; factory mgr., v.p. Seamless Rubber Co., 1919-30; factory mgr. C.F. Church Mfg. Co., 1931-32; pres., gen. mgr. Wooster Rubber Co., 1932-58; chmn. exec. com. Wooster Rubber Co. (name changed to Rubbermaid Inc. 1957), 1958-65; chmn., bd. dirs. Rubbermaid Inc., 1960-65. Chmn. Wayne County Rep., Fin. Com.; v.p. Boca Raton Community Hosp. Served with USN, 1918. Recipient Horation Alger medal Am. Schs. and Colls. Assn., 1962. Mem. Nat. Housewares Mfg. Assn. (dir.), Nat. Sales Execs., Merchants and Manufacturers (Chgo.), Cleve. Athletic Club, Royal Palm Yacht Country Club. Presbyterian. *

CALDWELL, OLIVER JOHNSON, educator, former government official; b. Foochow, China, Nov. 16, 1904; s. Harry Russell and Mary Belle (Cope) C.; m. Eda Joslin Holcombe, June 29, 1935; children: Eda Joslyn (Mrs. Edmund Becker), Gail Edna (Mrs. Roland Smith). Student, U. Wash., 1922-23; A.B., Oberlin Coll., 1926, M.A., 1927; student music, aesthetics, 1927-29; student, Army Civil Affairs Tng. Sch., U. Chgo., 1943; L.H.D., Baldwin-Wallace Coll.; LL.D., Ithaca U., Albright Coll. Head social scis. Harvey Sch., Hawthorne, N.Y., 1929-35; assoc. prof. English U. Amoy, China, 1935-36; prof. English U. Nanking, China, 1936-37; acting head dept. fgn. langs. U. Nanking, 1937-38; pub. relations officer Asso. Bds. Christian Colls. in China, 1938-43; chief student br., fed. programs br., div. exchange of persons Dept. State, 1947-51; chief program devel. staff ednl. exchange service U.S. Internat. Information Adminstrn., 1951-52; asst. commr. internat. edn., dir. div. internat. edn. U.S. Office Edn., later acting asso. commr., 1952- 64; vis. prof. comparative edn. U. Md., 1964-65; dean internat. services So. Ill. U., Carbondale, 1965-69; prof. higher edn. So. Ill. U., 1969-73, prof. emeritus, from 1973; author, cons., from 1973. Author: A Secret War-Americans in China 1944-45, 1972; Collaborator: The Task of the Universities in a Changing World; Contbr. 250 articles to profl. and popular jours., also symposium; govtl. papers and personal papers in Hoover Instn. for Study of War, Revolution and Peace. Mem. sch. bd., Falls Church, 1952-56; assisted U. Nanking move through gorges Yangtze River to Chengtu after Japanese attack. Served from capt. to maj., OSS, AUS, 1943-45. Mem. various profl. assns. Methodist. Club: Rotarian. Home: Cobden Ill. Deceased. †

CALHOUN, ROBERT LOWRY, theologian, educator; b. St. Cloud, Minn., Dec. 30, 1896; s. David Thomas and Lida Brooks (Toomer) C.; m. Ella Clay Wakeman, Dec. 24, 1923; children: David Wakeman, Edward Thomas Davidson, Robert Maurice, Harriet Huddleston. BA, Carleton Coll., 1915, LLD, 1946; BD, Yale U., 1918, MA, 1919, PhD, 1923; DD, U. Chgo., 1941, Oberlin Coll., 1944, Princeton U., 1957. Instr. philosophy and edn. Carleton Coll., Ill., 1921-23; from instr. to assoc. prof. hist. theology Yale U., New Haven, Conn., 1923-36, prof. hist. theology, from 1936; spl. lectr. Yale U., 1934, Ohio Wesleyan U., 1935, Colgate-Rochester Theol. Sem., 1937, Princeton U., 1938, 43, Theol. Sem. of the Reformed Chs. in the U.S., 1940, Jewish Theol. Sem. of Am., 1940, U. Va., 1941, Pacific Sch. of Religion, 1942, Harvard U., 1943, 44, Vanderbilt U., 1944, U. Chgo., 1947, Notre Dame Law Sch., 1959; Netherlands-Am. Exchange prof. U. Amsterdam 1952-53; Ayer lectr. Colgate Rochester Theol. Sem., 1958; Danforth lectr. Cornell U., 1958-59. Author, co-author books including God and the Common Life, 1935, reissued 1954, Work and Vocation, 1954. Mem. AAUP (1st v.p. 1954-56), Am. Philos. Assn., Am. Acad. Arts and Scis., Phi Beta Kappa, Delta Sigma Rho, Book and Bond Club (Yale). Congretionalist. *

CALLAGHAN, MORLEY EDWARD, author; b. Toronto, Ont., Can., 1903; s. Thomas and Mary (Dewan) C.; m. Lorrete Florence, 1929; 2 children. Student St. Michael's Coll.; B.A., U. Toronto, 1925, LL.D., 1966, U. Western Ont., 1965; Litt.D. (hon.), U. Windsor, 1973. Author: (novels) Strange Fugitive, 1928; Native Argosy, 1929; It's Never Over, 1930; No Man's Meat, 1931; Broken Journey, 1932; Such is My Beloved, 1934; They Shall Inherit the Earth, 1935; More Joy in Heaven, 1936; Now that April's Here, 1937; Jake Baldwin's Vow (for children), 1948; The Varsity Story, 1948; The Loved and the Lost, 1955; The Man with the Coat, 1955; A Many Coloured Coat, 1960; A Passion in Rome, 1961; That Summer in Paris, 1963; Morley Callaghan Vols. I and II, 1964; A Fine and Private Place, 1975; Close to the Sun Again, 1975; No Man's Meat and the Enchanted Pimp, 1978, A Wild Old Man on the Road, 1988; short stories publ. in the New Yorker, Sat. Evening Post, Harper's Bazaar. Recipient Canadian Council medal, 1966; Royal Bank Can. award, 1970; decorated companion Order of Can., 1983. Roman Catholic. Died Aug.25, 1990. Home: Toronto Can.

CALLAGHAN, WILLIAM MCCOMBE, naval officer; b. Oakland, Calif., Aug. 8, 1897; s. Charles William and Rose (Wheeler) C.; m. Helen Louise Brunett, Aug. 24, 1921 (dec. 1970); children: Jane Callaghan Gude, William McCombe Jr.; m. Martha Harper (dec. 1973); m. Sarah Duerson. BS, U.S. Naval Acad., 1918; MSEE, Columbia U., 1925. Commd. ensign USN, 1918, advanced through grades to rear adm., 1945; instr. marine engring. U.S. Naval Acad., Annapolis, Md.; war plans officer for logistics Pacific Fleet; comdr. USS Mo.; chief Naval Transp. Svc.; comdr. amphibious forces Pacific Fleet; comdr. all naval forces in Far East; v.p. Am. Export Lines, from 1957; chmn. maritime transp. rsch. bd. NAS. Decorated Legion of Merit, Knight of Malta, Order of Rising Sun (Japan), Order of White Elephant (Thailand), Order of Boyaca (Brazil), also others. Roman Catholic. Home: Chevy Chase Md. Died July 8, 1991; Arlington Nat. Cemetery.

CALLAWAY, FULLER EARLE, JR., manufacturer; b. LaGrange, Ga., Jan. 1, 1907; s. Fuller Earle and Ida Jane (Cason) C.; m. Alice Hinman Hand, Aug. 6, 1930; children: Fuller Earle III, Ida Cason Callaway Hudson. Ed., Ga. Inst. Tech., Eastman Bus. Sch. N.Y.; LL.D., LaGrange Coll., 1971; L.H.D., Mercer U., 1980; LL.D., Morris Brown Coll., 1982; D.Sc., U. Ala.-Birmingham, 1984. Treas., Valley Waste Mills, 1927; treas., gen. mgr. Truline, Inc., 1928; dir. Callaway Mills, 1932-46, pres., treas., 1935-36, pres., 1936-45, ret., 1945-59; chmn. bd., chief exec. officer Callaway Mills Co., 1959-61, pres., chief exec. officer, 1961-65, chmn., chief exec. officer, 1965-68; chmn. Callaway Mills, Inc., 1961-68, pres., 1962-65; chmn. Internat. Leasing Corp., 1961-65, pres., 1962-65; pres. Internat. Products & Services, Inc., 1965-70, 76-78, chmn., 1970-78; propr. Hills & Dales; chmn. bd., pres. Charitable Services Co., from 1978. Trustee Callaway Found., 1943-76, Fuller E. Callaway Found., 1923-76, Ga. Tech. Research Inst., Ga. Tech. Found., Callaway Ednl. Assn., 1943-76; past dir. West Ga. council Boy Scouts Am. Commd. capt. Ga. State Guard, 1942; comdg. Troup County Co., lt. col., comdg. 3d Bn. 1943; transferred to D.O.L. 1944; a.d.c., staff gov. Ga. 1943-71. Recipient Silver Beaver award Boy Scouts Am., 1939; Paul Harris fellow. Fellow Textile Inst. (Eng); mem. Ga. Textile Mfrs. Assn. (treas., v.p., pres. 1938-39, dir.), Am. Textile Mfrs. Inst. (chmn. 1945, v.p., dir., chmn. 1947-48), Phi Delta Theta. Democrat. Baptist. Clubs: Masons, Rotary, Field, Long Boat Key Golf, Capital City, Highland Country, Piedmont Driving, Big Eddy. Home: La Grange Ga. Deceased. †

CALLIHAN, HARRIET K., medical society executive; b. Chgo., Feb. 8, 1930; d. Harry Louis and Josephine (Olstad) Kohlman; m. Clair Clifton Callihan, Dec. 17, 1955; 1 child, Barbara Clair Callihan. BA, U. Chgo., 1951, MBA, 1953. Personnel dir. Leo Burnett Co., Chgo., 1953-57, John Plain & Co., 1957-62, Follett Pub. Co., 1962-64, Needham, Harper & Steers, N.Y.C., 1966-68, Bell, Boyd, Lloyd, Haddad & Burns, 1964-66, Hume, Clement, Hume & Lee, 1968-70; owner, operator PersD, 1970-75; exec. dir. Inst. Medicine Chgo., from 1975, mng. editor ofcl. med. publ. Proceedings, from 1975. Sec./treas. Interagy. Council on Smoking and Disease. Mem. Chgo. Soc. Assn. Execs., Conf. Med. Soc. Execs. Greater Chgo. (pres.), Am. Med. Writers Assn. (pres., v.p. publicity club), Nat. Sci. Writer's Assn., Lincoln Park Zool. Soc., Field Mus. Soc. Natural History, Nat. Soc. Fund Raising Exec. Profl. Conv. Mgrs. Assn., Chgo. Council Fgn. Relations, Chgo. Connection, Met. Chgo. Coalition Aging, Midwest Pharm. Advt. Club. Clubs: Westmoreland Country, Michigan Shores, Cliffdwellers. Deceased. Home: Chicago Ill. †

CALVERT, JAMES HENRY, business executive; b. Widnes, England, Oct. 22, 1898; s. Albert Ellis and Annie (Spencer) C.; m. Carolyn Rice, Sept. 29, 1923; children: James Spencer, David Rice, Jonathan, Richard. Student, Wade Deacon Sch., Widnes, England. Mdse. mgr. C.F. Hovey Co., Boston, 1925-29, Jordan Marsh Company, 1930-32; chmn. Joske Bros. Co. dept. store, San Antonio, Tex., from 1932; dir. Alamo Nat. Bank; trustee Southwest Rsch. Found., Trinity U. Methodist. *

CAMBIO, FRANK CAESAR, lawyer; b. Providence, Aug. 14, 1895; s. Camillo Guiseppe and Maria Sophia (Mercurio) C.; m. Adelina Benevenga, June 11, 1923; children: Maria Alberta, Frank Caesar. AB, Brown U., 1917; student, Harvard Law Sch., 1918-20. Bar: R.I. 1922. Pvt. practice Providence, from 1922; atty. Godfrey & Cambio, from 1925; asst. atty. gen. Providence, 1938-40; chmn. R.I. Bd. Bar Examiners, from 1964, R.I. Bd. Tax Equalization; mem. bd. tax assessment review City of Providence; mem. commn. on reapportionment Ho. of Reps.; candidate atty. gen. for R.I., 1954. Dir. United Fund Inc., Federal Hill House. Mem. ABA, R.I. Bar Assn. (pres. 1957-58), Aurora Civic Assn., Republican Club of R.I. (v.p.). *

CAMERON, COLIN CAMPBELL, produce company and land development executive; b. Paia, Hawaii, Feb. 2,

1927; s. J. Walter and Frances (Baldwin) C.; m. Margaret Hartley, Aug. 25, 1951 (dec. Apr. 1986); children: Douglas, Richard, Margaret, Frances; m. Pamela Andelin, Nov. 24, 1991. AB, Harvard U., 1950, MBA, 1953. Chmn., pres. Maui Land & Pineapple Co., Inc., from 1969; chmn. Kapalua Land Co., Ltd., from 1974, Maui Pineapple Co. Ltd.; v.p., bd. dirs. Haleakala Ranch Co., Ltd.; pres., bd. dirs. Maui Pub. Co. Ltd., pubs. Maui News; bd. dirs. Bank of Hawaii, Maui Electric Co., Ltd., High Tech. Devel. Corp., Bancorp Hawaii, Hawaiian Trust Co. Ltd. Bd. dirs., mem. exec. com. Lahaina Restoration Found.; v.p. J. Walter Cameron Ctr., also chmn. long-range planning com; chmn. Maui Econ. Devel. Bd.; bd. dirs. Nature Conservancy Hawaii. With USNR, 1945-46. Mem. Pacific Basin Econ. Coun., North Pacific Assn., Honolulu Coun. Fgn. Rels., Pacific Club. Home: Paia Hawaii Deceased. †

CAMPBELL, ARTHUR RUSSELL, oil company executive; b. Manheim, Pa., May 1, 1898; s. Abraham L. and Minnie M. (Wisegarver) C.; m. Margaret N. Youtz; children: Arthur R., Robert G., Richard L.; m. Harriette Harding Wood, May 1, 1963. Grad., high sch. CPA Pa., N.Y. Officer Lancaster (Pa.) Iron Works Inc., Lancaster Brick Co., DeValt Products Co., Garbed Oil Co.,, 1927-55; ptnr. Harder and Campbell, 1944-48; indsl. cons. N.Y.C., 1944-48; v.p. Exec. Svc. Corp., N.Y.C., 1949-52, mem. renegotiation Bd., 1956-62; pres. Garbed Oil Co., Mt. Joy, Pa., from 1962. Served with Air Svc., U.S. Army, 1917-18. Mem. Fin. Execs. Inst., Am. Inst. Accts., Am Legion, Masons. Republican. Episcopalian. *

CAMPBELL, JAMES ARTHUR, chemistry educator; b. Elyria, Ohio, Oct. 1, 1916; s. James Allen and Helen (Metcalf) C.; m. Dorothy Carnell, Nov. 12, 1938; children: Kathleen Annette Campbell Fischer, Christine Campbell North. AB, Oberlin Coll., 1938, DSc (hon.), 1988; MSc, Purdue U., 1939; PhD, U. Calif., Berkeley, 1942; DSc (hon.), Beaver Coll., 1972, Harvey Mudd Coll., 1987. Instr. U. Calif., Berkeley, 1942-45; researcher Manhattan Project, 1943-45; prof. Oberlin Coll., 1945-57; program dir. NSF, 1956-57; prof. chemistry, chmn. dept. Harvey Mudd Coll., Claremont, Calif., from 1957, prof. emeritus, 1987, dean faculty, 1974-75; dir. chem. edn. material study Harvey Mudd Coll. and U Calif.-Berkeley, 1960-63; Sci. adviser UNESCO, Asia, 1969-70; adviser Ford, Sloan, Danforth Founds., Research Corp.; lectr. AAAS-Znaniye (USSR) Exchange, 1973; vis. prof. U. Nairobi, 1983; Fulbright lectr. Punjab U., India; AAAS exchange prof. People's Republic China. Author: (with L.E. Steiner) General Chemistry, 1955, Why Do Chemical Reactions Occur?, 1965, Chemical Systems, 1970, Teacher's Guide to Chemical Systems, 1970, (with Barbara Burke) Chemistry, The Unending Frontier, 1978; Columnist Jour. Chem. Edn., 1972-79. Mem. Vols. for Vital English; active vol. Claremont Meals on Wheels. Recipient James Flack Norris award N.E. sect. Am. Chem. Soc., 1963; Mfg. Chemists award, 1963; So. Calif. Industry award, 1965; Fund for Advancement Edn. fellow Cambridge U., 1952-53; Guggenheim fellow Kyoto U., also Cambridge U., 1963-64; Nat. Sci. Faculty fellow Harvard, 1970-71; resident scholar Villa Serbelloni, 1972; vis. prof. Chinese U., Hong Kong, 1975-76. Mem. AAAS, AAUP, Am. Chem. Soc. (Sci. Apparatus Makers award 1972), Chem. Soc.; Claremont Rotary. Mem. Soc. of Friends. Home: Claremont Calif. Died May 22, 1989; body donated to science.

CAMPBELL, JAMES MARSHALL, university dean; b. Warsaw, N.Y., Sept. 30, 1895; s. William Henry and Catherine Rose (McGinn) C. AB, Hamilton Coll., 1917; student, Princeton U., 1917-18; MA, Catholic U. of Am., 1920, PhD, 1923. Ordained priest Roman Catholic Ch., 1926. Asst. in Greek Catholic U. of Am., Washington, 1920, instr. to assoc. prof. classics, 1921-34, prof. Greek and Latin, dean of Coll., from 1934; dir. Pacific Coast branch, Catholic U. summer sessions, San Rafael, Calif. from 1932. Author numerous books and articles; assoc. editor The Catholic University Patristic Studies. Served as Corpl., 345th Machine Gun Co., 87th divsn., 1918-19; mem adv. bd. Dunbarton Coll., Washington D.C. Mem. Am. Philol. Assn., Mediaeval Acad. Am., Phi Beta Kappa, Phi Beta Kappa Assocs. Domestic Prelate, 1959. *

CAMPBELL, JOHN TUCKER, secretary of state; b. Calhoun Falls, S.C., Dec. 12, 1912; s. John Brown Gordon and Mary (Tucker) C.; m. Gertrude Davis, Jan. 4, 1936; children: James Gordon. Student, U. S.C., 1941-42. Pres. Campbell Drug Stores, Columbia, S.C., from 1938; mem. Columbia City Coun., 1954-58, 66-70, mayor, 1970-78; sec. state State of S.C., 1978-90. Served with USAAF, 1943-46. Mem. S.C. Pharm. Assn. (dir. 1971-73), Nat. League Cities, S.C. Mcpl. Assn. (pres. 1972-73), Mason (Shriner), Optimist Internat. (state gov. 1964-65), Palmetto. Methodist. Home: Columbia S.C. Died Aug. 26, 1991; buried Columbia, S.C.

CAMPBELL, MARGARET AMELIA, nursing educator; b. Vancouver, B.C., Can., June 27, 1923; d. Ivan Glen and Helen Kathleen (Davis) C. B.A., U. B.C., 1947, B.A.Sc. in Nursing, 1948; M.S. in Nursing, Western Res. U., 1955; Ed.D., Columbia U., 1970. Staff nurse, asst. head nurse Vancouver Gen. Hosp., 1948-49; instr., sr. adminstrv. instr. Vancouver Gen. Hosp. Sch. Nursing, 1949-54; from instr. to prof. Sch. Nursing, U. B.C., 1955-88; cons. curriculum devel. nursing schs. Recipient award of distinction nursing div. Alumni Assn. U. B.C., 1988, cert. of merit, 1990. Mem. Registered Nurses Assn. B.C. (Award of Excellence 1987), Can. Nurses Found., Can. Assn. Univ. Schs. Nursing. (hon. life Western region). Home: Vancouver Can. Died Jan. 29, 1992. †

CAMPBELL, RICHARD ARTHUR, architect; b. Bklyn., May 1, 1930; s. William J. and Dorothy T. (Regan) C.; m. Françoise Marie Botrot, Nov. 14, 1972; children: Scott, Carene. BArch, U. Oreg., 1956; MArch, Yale U., 1961. Cert. Nat. Coun. Archtl. Registration Bds. Designer Wilmsen, Endicott, Eugene, Oreg., 1956, Skidmore, Owings and Merrill, Portland, Oreg., 1958-60, 61-64; prin. Campbell-Yost-Grube, P.C., Portland, 1964-85; lectr. Yale U., U. Oreg. Grad. Sch., Portland State U., Portland Art Mus., Lewis and Clark Coll., Portland; mem. numerous design award juries. Ian Lewis traveling fellow, 1959-60. Fellow AIA (9 design awards); mem. Multnomah Athletic Club, West Hills Racquet Club. Home: Portland Oreg. Died Nov. 17, 1985.

CAMPBELL, ROBERT KENNETH, utilities company executive; b. Chgo., June 20, 1930; s. Donald E. and Jeanette A. Campbell; m. Alvina Oblinger; children: John E., Thomas L., Joseph A. BS in Engring, Ill. Inst. Tech., 1952; MS in ME, U. Ill., 1956; MBA, U. Chgo., 1958; JD, Loyola U., 1962. Registered profl. engr., Ill. With AT&T Techs. Inc., 1957-77, dir. mfg., 1969-71, gen. mgr. Reading (Pa.) Works, 1971-72, gen. mgr. Allentown Works, 1972-77; pres. Pa. Power & Light Co., Allentown, 1977-90, chmn., 1987-90; chief exec. officer Pa. Power and Light Co., Allentown, 1979-90, also bd. dirs.; bd. dirs. Harsco Corp., Consolidated Rail Corp.; mem. Pa. Econ. Devel. Partnership Bd., Lehigh Valley Partnership, also pres.; mem. bd. govs., vice chmn. Edison Electric Inst., Inst. Nulcear Power Ops., Electric Power Rsch. Inst., Am. Nuclear Energy Coun., Assn. Edison Illuminating Cos., Advanced Reactor Corp., U.S. Coun. for Energy Awareness; chmn. bd. govs. Nuclear Mgmt. and Resources Coun. V.p. Minsi Trails coun. Boy Scouts Am., also bd. govs.; bd. govs. eastern Pa. chpt. The Nature Conservancy, Pa. Environ. Coun., Lehigh Valley Bus. Conf. on Health Care, Whitaker Found.; mem. pres.' coun. Allentown Coll. St. Francis de Sales; trustee Ill. Inst. Tech. Served with U.S. Army, 1953-55. Mem. ASME, NSPE, Pa. Soc. Profl. Engrs., Ill. Bar Assn., Pa. Bus. Roundtable, Pa. Chamber Bus. and Industry (past chmn.), Pa. Soc. (past pres.), Sigma Xi, Tau Beta Pi. Presbyterian. Clubs: Lehigh Country (Allentown); Saucon Valley Country (Bethlehem, Pa.). Home: Allentown Pa. Died June 19, 1990. †

CAMPBELL, WILLIS L., insurance executive; b. Spokane, Washington, Feb. 17, 1898; s. John P. and Elizabeth (McEachran) C.; m. Catherine Thompson, Sept. 24, 1924; children: James R., Thomas J. BBA, U. Washington, 1922. Ptnr. Dean Witter & Co.; mem. N.Y. Stock Exchange, 1926-42; v.p., treas. Gen. Ins. Co. of Am., 1st Nat. Ins. Co. of Am., Gen. Am. Corp., Seattle, 1946-52, pres., dir., from 1952; pres., dir. Safeco Ins. Co. of Am., Safeco Life Ins. Co.; dir. Boeing Co.; trustee Washington Mutual Savings Bank. Trustee Seattle Art Mus., Seattle Found. Served as lt. col. Gen. Staff Corps, U.S. Army, 1942-46. Mem. Greater Seattle, Inc., Seattle C. of C., Rainier Club, University Club, Seattle Golf Harbor Club, Seattle Tennis Club. Episcopalian. *

CAMPION, FRANK DAVIS, editorial and public relations executive; b. Columbus, Ohio, Oct. 30, 1921; s. Edward Winslow and Ruth Baird (Johnson) C.; m. Ann Cornell, 1948 (div. 1963); children—Frank Davis, Ann Baird; m. Georgene A. Haney, July 30, 1964; children—Katherine Weller, Geoffrey Mills. BA with honors, Yale U., 1943. Reporter, editor Life mag., 1945-60; copywriter Young and Rubicam, 1961-68; pub. relations exec. N.Y. Stock Exchange, 1968-70; communications dir. Am. Med. Assn., Chgo., 1970-77; spl. asst. for pub. relations AMA, Chgo., 1978-84, dir. AMA consumer book program, 1985-88. Author: The AMA and U.S. Health Policy Since 1940, 1984. served with U.S. Army, 1943-45. Decorated Bronze Star. Mem. Pub. Relations Soc. Am. Club: Indian Hill. Home: Winnetka Ill. Died July 20, 1989.

CANGELOSI, VINCENT EMANUEL, university dean, educator; b. Baton Rouge, Feb. 5, 1928; s. Philip Vincent and Angelina Elizabeth (Roccaforte) C.; m. Mary Jean Johnson, Feb. 23, 1952; children: Philip William, Phyllis Ann, Angyln Marie, Mary Jean, Joan. B.S., La. State U., 1954, M.B.A., 1956; Ph.D. in Econs, U. Ark., 1961; postdoctorate, Carnegie-Mellon U., 1964. Instr., then asst. prof. U. Ark., 1956-59; instr. La. State U., 1959-60; asso. prof. U. Ark., 1960-65, U. Tex., 1965-67; from prof. to prof. emeritus La. State U., Baton Rouge, from 1967, prof. quantitative bus. analysis, 1984-86, chmn. dept. quantitative methods, 1970-74, dean jr. div., 1975-84; pres., chief exec. officer, dir. First Met. Mortgage Corp.; dir. Met. Bank & Trust, First Met. Fin. Corp.; Chmn. bd. vis. Postal Service Inst.; spl. cons. Postmaster Gen., 1968; adj. prof. quantitative methods U. Southwestern La., 1987—. Editor: Mathematics and Quantitative Methods Series, 1967, Compound Statements and Mathematical Logic, 1967, Basic Statistics - A Real World Approach, 1976, 3d edit., 1983; Contbr. to World Book Ency. Served with AUS, 1950-52. Fellow Decision Scis. Inst. (1st Ann. Disting. Service award 1970); mem. Phi Eta Sigma, Phi Kappa Phi; Beta Gamma Sigma Pi Gamma Mu, Pi Tau Pi, Alpha Kappa Psi. Club: Rotary. Home: Baton Rouge La. Died Oct. 19, 1988; buried Greenoaks Meml. Pk., Baton Rouge, La.

CANNON, MRS. GRANT G. See JOHNSON, JOSEPHINE WINSLOW

CANTIN, MARC, biomedical educator; b. Que., Can., July 8, 1933; s. Leopold and Lucienne (Pouliot) C.; m. Feliciana Faraco, June 20, 1967; children: Bernard, Marc, Phillippe. BA, Laval U., 1953, MD, 1958; PhD, U. Montreal, 1962. Cert. pathologist. Lectr. U. Chgo., 1962-65; asst. prof. U. Montreal, Que., 1965-68, assoc. prof., 1968-73, prof., 1973-90; dir. lab. patho-biology Clin. Rsch. Inst. Montreal, 1980-90, dir. Hypertension Rsch. Group, 1984-90. Editor: The Secratory Process, 1977, Hypertension, 1981. Capt. Mil. Flight Area, 1957-62. Recipient Rsch. Achievement award Am. Heart Assn., 1988. Fellow Royal Soc. Can. Home: Montreal Can. Died June 18, 1990.

CAPLAN, HARRY, classics educator; b. Hoag's Corners Rensselaer County, N.Y., Jan. 7, 1896; s. Jacob and Sarah (Tolchin) C. AB, Cornell U., 1916, AM, 1917, PhD, 1921. Instr. pub. speaking Cornell U., Ithaca, N.Y., 1919-23, from instr. to prof. classics, from 1919, chmn. dept. classics, 1929-46, Goldwin Smith prof. classical langs. and lit., from 1941; vis. prof. summers U. Wis., 1925, U. Mich., 1932, Northwestern U., 1938, Stanford U., 1942, 48, U. Chgo., 1945, Columbia U., 1946; fellow Ctr. for Advanced Studies Wesleyan U., 1962-63, 64. Author, editor: Gianfrancesco Pico della Mirandola On The Imagination, 1930; Mediaeval Artes Praedicandi, 1934; Mediaeval Artes Praedicandi- A Supplementary Hand list, 1936; Rhetorics ad Herennium, 1954; (with H.H. King) Pulpit Eloquence-English, 1955; (with H.H. King) Pulpit Eloquence-German, 1956; asst. editor Quar. Jour. Speech, 1923; joint editor Cornell Sudies in Classical Philolgy; contbr. articles and reviews in fields of classical and medieval lit. Fellow John Simon Guggenheim Meml. Found., 1928-29 (studying medieval rhetoric in librs. of Europe), also 1956. Served in U.S. Army W.W.I, 1918-19. Grad. scholar archeology and comparative philology Cornell U., 1916-17, grad. fellow in Latin and Greek, 1917-18. Fellow Mediaeval Acad. Am.; mem. MLA, AAUP, Am. Philol. Assn. (pres. 1955), Speech Assn. Am., Renaissance Soc. Am., Linguistic Soc. Am., Classical Assn. of England and Whales, Phi Beta Kappa, Phi Eta Sigma, Delta Sigma Rho, Phi Delta Kappa, Phi Kappa Phi. Jewish. *

CAPLES, JOHN, advertising agency executive; b. N.Y.C., May 1, 1900; s. Byron H. and Edith Jessie (Richards) C.; m. Dorothy N. Dickes, Aug. 16, 1957. Student, Columbia U., 1918-19; B.S., U.S. Naval Acad., 1924. With engring. dept. N.Y. Telephone Co., 24-25; advt. writer Ruthrauff & Ryan, Inc., 1925-27; writer, exec. Batten, Barton, Durstine & Osborn, Inc., N.Y.C., 1927-41, v.p., 1941-82, creative dir. emeritus, 1982; tchr. advt. Grad. Sch. Bus. Columbia U., 1952-53. Author: Tested Advertising Methods, 1932, rev. 1974, Advertising for Immediate Sales, 1936, Advertising Ideas, 1938, Making Ads Pay, 1957, How to Make Your Advertising Make Money, 1981; co-author: Copy Testing, 1939; Author: two advertisements (including: They Laughed When I Sat Down at the Piano) included in book The 100 Greatest Advertisements; Columnist: book Direct Marketing mag, 1972—; Contbr. to book: The Advertising Handbook, 1950, Saturday Rev.; various advt. trade jours. Mem. council of judges Advt. Hall of Fame, 1963-72; pub. relations counsel Girl Scouts U.S.A., from 1973; Mem. nat. adv. council Episcopal Ch. Found., from 1968; mem. pub. relations com. Nat. Multiple Sclerosis Soc., from 1969. Served as seaman USNRF, 1918; from lt. comdr. to comdr. USNR, 1942-45. Recipient Ann. award Nat. Assn. Direct Mail Writers, 1969, Ann. Leadership award Hundred Million Club, 1972; named to Copywriters Hall of Fame, 1973; Advt. Hall of Fame, 1977. Mem. Market Research Council N.Y., Copy Research Council N.Y., Direct Mktg. Creative Guild, Naval Acad. Assn., Alpha Delta Sigma. Clubs: Univ. (N.Y.C.), Dutch Treat (N.Y.C.), Players (N.Y.C.). Home: New York N.Y. Died June 10, 1990; buried Mt. Hope Cemetery, Hastings-on-Hudson, N.Y.

CAPLES, WILLIAM GOFF, lawyer, former college president; b. Pitts., Oct. 4, 1909; s. William Goff and Alice Keller (Thomas) C.; m. Julia D. Pringle, Oct. 3, 1936; 1 child, Pamela Gunning Wilkes; m. Jean Coburn Dunbar, Dec. 1, 1945; children: William Goff, Cynthia Keller Mull. PhB, Kenyon Coll., 1930, LLD (hon.), 1961; JD, Northwestern U., 1933; LLD (hon.), Loyola U., Chgo., 1969. Bar: Ill. 1933. Practiced in Chgo., 1933-38; gen. atty. Continental Casualty Co.; v.p. Nat. Casualty Co., 3938-42; mgr. indsl. rels. Inland Steel Co., 1946-50, v.p., 1953-68; pres., bd. dirs. Inland Steel Container Co., 1950-53; pres. Kenyon Coll., Gambier, Ohio, 1968-75, pres. emeritus, 1975-89; of counsel Vedder, Price, Kaufman & Kammholz, Chgo., 1975-89; bd. dirs. Buckeye Internat., Inc. Mem. adv. coun. Sch. Indsl. and Labor Rels., Cornell U., 1960-64; mem.

Chgo. Bd. Edn., pres., 1961; mem. nat. adv. com. Manpower Devel. and Tng. Act, 1962-89; mem. President's Adv. Com. on Labor and Mgmt. Policy; mem. adv. com. civilian pers. mgmt. Dept. Army; bd. dirs. United Charities, Chgo., pres. 1954-56; trustee Kenyon Coll.; bd. visitors Air U., 1972-75; exec. dir. Chgo. Commn. on Econ. Devel., 1976-79. Lt. col. C.E., AUS, 1942-46. Mem. NAM (v.p. 1954-61), Better Govt. Assn., Indsl. Rels. Assn. Chgo. (pres. 1951-52), Am. Mgmt. Assn., Am. Iron and Steel Inst. (chmn. com. indsl. rels. 1958-61), Am. Arbitration Assn. (bd. dirs.), Univ. Club, Tavern Club, Commonwealth Club, Comml. Club, Met. Club (Washington), Phi Beta Kappa. Home: Chicago Ill. Died Dec. 4, 1989; buried Gambier, Ohio.

CAPRA, FRANK, producer, motion picture director; b. Palermo, Italy, May 18, 1897; came to U.S. at age of 6; s. Salvatore C.; m. Lucille Warner, 1933 (dec. 1984); children: Thomas, Frank Jr, Lucille. Ed., Calif. Inst. Tech. Pres. Acad. of Motion Picture Arts and Sciences, 4 times, 1935-39, pres. Screen Dirs. Guild, 3 times, 1938-40, 1959. Producer motion pictures, from 1921; produced, directed: The Strong Man, Submarine, Flight, Dirigible, American Madness, Platinum Blonde, Lady for a Day, It Happened One Night, Mr. Deed Goes to Town, 1936, Mr. Smith Goes to Washington, 1939, Lost Horizon, Broadway Bill, You Can't Take It With You, Meet John Doe, 1941, Arsenic and Old Lace, It's a Wonderful Life, 1947, State of the Union, Riding High, Here Comes the Groom, A Hole in the Head, Pocketful of Miracles, 1961; dir. TV spl. 50th Anniversary Columbia Pictures, ABC-TV, 1975; made series of army orientation films Why We Fight; produced, directed Rendevous in Space, 1964; author: The Name Above The Title, 1971. Bd. dirs. Calif. Inst. Tech. Served as pvt., advancing to 2d lt. U.S. Army, World War I; commd. maj. U.S. Army, 1942; discharged with rank of col. 1945. Decorated D.S.M., Legion of Merit; Order British Empire; recipient 3 Academy awards (Oscars) for best direction of year, 1934, 36, 38; twice produced pictures which received Acad. award as best of the year; Lifetime Achievement award Am. Film Inst., 1982; recipient, Nat. Medal of Arts, 1986. Home: La Quinta Calif. Died Sept. 3, 1991; buried Coachella Valley Cemetery, Calif.

CARBONE, JOHN VITO, physician; b. Sacramento, Dec. 13, 1922; s. Vito and Prima Marie (Demaria) C.; m. Gene Elizaeth Grinslade, Sept. 1, 1946; children: John Vito, Jerome, James. A.B., U. Calif., Berkeley, 1945; M.D., U. Calif., San Francisco, 1948. Intern San Francisco Gen. Hosp., 1948-49, sr. asst. resident, 1950-51, asst. chief med. svc., 1958-60, chief blue med. svc., 1960-61; resident dept. metabolism Walter Reed Army Hosp., 1952-54; Giannini fellow in medicine, 1954-55; asst. resident in medicine U. Calif. Med Center, San Francisco, 1949-50; chief resident U. Calif. Med Center, 1950-51, instr., 1951-52, fellow, 1954-55, asst. prof., 1955-60; assoc. prof. U. Calif. Med. Ctr., 1960-66, chief gastroenterology div., 1961-66, prof. medicine, from 1966. Contbr. numerous articles to med. jours. Served to capt. M.C. USAR, 1952-54. Recipient Gold Headed Cane award U. Calif. Sch. Medicine, 1948, Acad. Senate Teaching award, 1959, Disting. Teaching award, 1968, 69; named Alumnus of Yr., 1976. Fellow A.C.P.; mem. Am. Fedn. Clin. Research, Calif. Soc. Internal Medicine, Am. Gastroenterology Assn., Western Soc. Clin. Investigation, Soc. Exptl. Biology and Medicine, AMA, Western Soc. Physicians, Phi Beta Kappa, Alpha Omega Alpha. Home: San Rafael Calif. Deceased. †

CARDMAN, CECILIA, artist; b. Soveria Mannelli, Italy; d. Samuel and Maria (Mendicino) Cardman. B.F.A., U. Colo., 1934, B.A., 1934; student Instituto dei Belli Arte, Naples, Italy, 1921-23, Denver Art Mus., 1930-31, studied with Leon Kroll, Nat. Acad., 1945-46, others. Head dept. painting Mesa Coll., Grand Junction, Colo., 1930-40; one-man shows: Naples, Italy, Grist Mill Gallery, Chester, Vt., Bergdorf-Goodman, 1978, Jarvis Gallery, Sandwich, Mass., 1975, Elliott Mus., Stuart, Fla., Grand Junction, Colo., 1981; group shows include: Nat. Arts Club, 1975-76, Nat. Acad., 1945, Knickerbocker Artists, 1979, Nelson Gallery, 1937-38, Denver Art Mus., 1924-25, Nat. League Am. Pen Women, 1979, Grand Central Art Gallery, 1977, Am. Artist Profl. League, 1979-80; one-woman show Elliott Mus., Stuart, Fla., 1988. Recipient numerous awards. Mem. Jackson Heights Art Club (1st prize 1982, 2d prize 1983), Pen & Brush (dir. admissions, Emily Nichols Hatch award 1982, 1st prize 1983, pres. 1987-88), Coll. Women's Club, Salmagundi Club (Lay Jury prize 1979), Nat. League Am. Pen Women (dir.; 1st br. v.p.), Sumi-e Soc. (prize 1982, recipient soc. award 1987), Ky. Watercolor Soc., Artist Fellowship, Inc., Knickerbocker Artists, Catherine Lorillard Wolfe Art Club (pres., dir., Best in Show award 1980, named Woman of the Year 1987), Am. Artists Profl. League (nat. dir.), Allied Artists Am. (dir. publicity, bd. dirs. 1983-86), Nat. Cowboy Hall of Fame, Western Heritage Ctr. Roman Catholic. Died 1989. Home: Jackson Heights N.Y. †

CARGILL, OTTO ARTHUR, JR., lawyer; b. Oklahoma City, May 30, 1914; s. Otto Arthur and Delia Ann (Arnold) C.; m. Rebecca Kay; children: Carole Sue Cargill Lash, Henson, Christina Cargill Best, John Russell, Angela Beth, Kima Leigh, Jennifer Ann. LL.B., Cumberland U., 1934. Bar: Okla. 1935, U.S. Dist. Ct. (we. dist.) Okla. 1935, U.S. Dist. Ct. (no. dist.) Okla. 1956, U.S. Dist. Ct. (ea. dist.) Okla. 1957, U.S. Ct. Appeals (10th cir.) 1944, U.S. Supreme Ct. 1938. Sole practice Oklahoma City, from 1935. Pres. Buffalo Breeders Am. Inc. Served with U.S. Army, 1943. Fellow Internat. Acad. Trial Lawyers; mem. Oklahoma City C. of C., ABA, Okla. Bar Assn., Oklahoma County Bar Assn., Assn. Trial Lawyers Am., Okla. Trial Lawyers Assn. (pres. 1947, 63), Am. Bd. Trial Advs., Nat. Assn. Criminal Def. Lawyers (co-chmn. membership com. 1971), Am. Judicatue Soc., Law-Sci. Acad. Am. (founding mem. Gold medal award). Democrat. Baptist. Club: Petroleum. Home: Edmond Okla. Deceased. †

CARLEN, RAYMOND NILS, steel company executive, consultant; b. Rockford, Ill., May 3, 1919; s. Charles and Hannah (Nystrom) C.; m. Jean Lovejoy, June 15, 1946; children: Cynthia Jean, Susan Joy. B.S. in Metall. Engring, U. Ill., 1942; M.S. in Bus. Adminstrn, U. Chgo., 1950. With Joseph T. Ryerson & Son, Inc., Chgo., 1946-83, v.p. Eastern region, 1963-64, exec. v.p., 1964-68, pres., 1968-76, chmn. bd., 1976-78, also dir.; sr. v.p. Inland Steel Co., Chgo., 1976-78, vice chmn., 1978-82; pres. Aarjoy Inc., Oakbrook, Ill., 1982-89, also dir.; dir. Am. Nat. Bank and Trust of Chgo., Hinsdale Fed. Savs. & Loan Assn., Ill., Grant Sq. Agy., Kewaunee Sci. Corp., Lindberg Corp. Mem. Ill. Emergency Resources Planning Com., 1964; chmn. Ill. Council on Econ. Edn., 1982-83; Chmn. Hinsdale (Ill.) Community Caucus, 1963-64; chmn. bd. counselors Chgo. Council Boy Scouts Am., 1981-83; pres. Chgo. area council Boy Scouts Am., 1970-74; active fund raising U. Chgo., Loyola U., Chgo., Passavant Meml. Hosp., Met. Crusade of Mercy.; Bd. dirs. Hinsdale Community House, 1957-60, Hinsdale PTA, 1957-60; mem. adv. council U. Chgo., from 1960; adv. council Coll. Engring., U. Ill., 1952-80. Served to maj. C.E. AUS, 1942-45, ETO. Mem. Chgo. Assn. Commerce and Industry, Ill. C. of C. (Leadership award 1961), Exec. Program Club Chgo. Clubs: Chicago Golf (Wheaton, Ill.) (pres. 1965, 66, dir. 1960-67, 74-76, 80-82); Hinsdale (Ill.) Golf; Chicago (Chgo.), Commerical (Chgo.), Economic (Chgo.). Home: Oak Brook Ill. Died Apr. 22, 1989.

CARLSON, ANDERS JOHAN, educator, engineer; b. St. Peter, Minn., Aug. 3, 1894; s. John Sven and Mary Mathilda (Anderson) C.; m. Louise Josephine Thorson, Sept. 26, 1925; children: Anders Johnston, John Stanley, Mary Louise Hanes. BS, U. Minn., 1916, CE, 1917, MS, 1925; PhD, U. Calif., 1929. Profl. petroleum engr., Calif. Instr. sch. mines U. Minn., 1917-19, asst. prof., 1919-26; cons. engr., mine expert Minn. Tax Commn., 1918-26; rsch. asst., jr. rsch. fellow Am. Petroleum Inst., 1927-31; lectr. coll. mining U. Calif., 1926-30, assoc. prof., 1930-42, prof. petroleum engring., 1942-43, prof. petroleum engring. div. mineral tech., from 1943, chmn. div., 1949-53; Ednl. supr. ESMWT, 1941-45; ops. analyst USAAF, 1945. Author rsch. paper Inorganic Environment in Kerogen Transformation, 1937. Mem. Am. Petroleum Inst., AAAS, Am. Chem. Soc., Sigma Xi, Tau Beta Pi, Alpha Sigma Phi, Sigma Rho, Pi Epsilon Tau, Scabbard and Blade, Clubs: Engrs. (Mpls.), Faculty (Berkeley), Univ. (Oakland, Calif.). *

CARLSON, EDGAR MAGNUS, clergyman, educator; b. Amery, Wis., July 12, 1908; s. David and Hilda (Swanson) C.; m. Ebba Edquist, July 11, 1934; children: David Jon, Joanna Linda, Samuel Edquist. Ordained to ministry Lutheran Ch., 1933; pastor Mount Olivet Luth. Ch., Mpls., 1933-37; prof. Bible and ethics Gustavus Adolphus Coll., 1937-42; asst. prof. ch. history and English Bible Augustana Theol. Sem., 1942-44; pres. Gustavus Adolphus Coll., 1944-68; exec. dir. Minn. Pvt. Coll. Council, 1968-75. Author: The Reinterpretation of Luther, 1948, The Church and the Public Conscience, 1956, The Classic Christian Faith, 1959, Church Sponsored Higher Education in Lutheran Church in America, 1967, Public Policy and Church-Related Higher Education, 1972. Mem. theol. commn. Luth. World Fedn., 1963-70; mem. bd. Found. Reformation Rsch.; mem. planning commn. World Council Chs. Gen. Assembly, 1953; rep. Lutheran World Fedn. Europe, summer 1951. Mem. Am. Ch. History Soc., Royal Order North Star, Pi Gamma Mu, Pi Kappa Delta, Rotarian. Home: Saint Paul Minn. Died Apr. 9, 1992.

CARLSON, EDWARD ELMER, holding company executive; b. Tacoma, June 4, 1911; s. Elmer E. and Lula (Powers) C.; m. Nell Hinckley Cox, June 26, 1936; children: Edward eugene, Jane Leslie. Student, U. Wash., 1928-32. Mgr. Pres. Hostel, Mt. vernon, Wash., 1936-37, Rainier Club, Seattle, 1937-42; with Western Internat. Hotels, inc., Seattle, 1946-70, exec. v.p., 1953-61, pres., 1961-69, chmn., 1969-70, dir., 1953-90; pres., CEO, dir. UAL, Inc., Chgo., 1970-74, CEO, 1975-90, chmn. bd. 1979-90; pres., CEO, dir. United Air Lines, 1970-74, chmn., CEO, 1975-76, also past dir.; past bd. dirs. 1st Nat. Bank of Chgo., Dart Industries Inc., Deere & Co., Univar Corp., 1st Chgo. Corp., Seafirst Corp., Seattle First Nat. Bank. Pres. Century 21 Expn. Inc., Seattle, 1957-59, chmn. bd., 1959-61; chmn. Wash. World's Fair Commn., 1955-63, Wash. Oceanographic Study commn.; mem. Pres. Johnson's Industry-Govt. Task Force, 1968, Navy Ship's Store Office adv. com. to undersec. navy, 1965-90; hon. chmn. Pacific Sci. Ctr. Found., 1967-68; past mem. Henry Kaiser Family Found.; past bd. dirs. Virginia Mason Hosp. and Found. Recipient Am. tourism award New Sch. Social Rsch., 1978; named 1st citizen of Seattle, 1966; Alumnus summa laude dignatus U. Wash., 1970. Mem. Cornell Soc. Hotelmen (hon.), Am. Soc. Order St. John of Jerusalem, Seattle Golf, Univ., Rainer (Seattle), Comml. (Chgo.), Bohemian (San Francisco). Home: Chicago Ill. Died Apr. 3, 1990.

CARLSON, JACK WILSON, corporate government specialist; b. Salt Lake City, Nov. 20, 1933; s. Oscar William and Gretta (Wilson) C.; m. Renée Pyott, Mar. 20, 1954; children: Catherine, Cristine, Steven, Diane, John, David, Paul. B.S., U. Utah, 1955, M.B.A., 1957; M.P.A., Harvard U., 1962, Ph.D. in Econs, 1963. Commd. 2d lt. USAF, 1955, advanced through grades to maj., 1966; air def. pilot, 1957-59; assoc. prof. USAF Acad., 1959-64; asst. to sec. of Air Force, 1964-66; ret., 1966, mem. Res., 1966-78; sr. staff economist Pres.'s Council Econ. Advisers, 1966-68; asst. dir. Office of Mgmt. and Budget, Washington, 1969-71, asst. to dir., 1971-74; chmn. sr. econ. advisers Econ. Commn. Europe of UN, 1970-72; asst. sec. Dept. Interior, 1974-76; v.p., chief economist U.S. C. of C., 1976-79; chief exec. officer Nat. Assn. Realtors, 1979-86, Am. Assn. Ret. Persons, 1987-88; chmn. bd. Ctr. Ednl. Competitiveness, 1988-92; mem. Nat. Commn. Employment and Unemployment Stats., 1977-79; cons., del. UN Commn. Human Settlements, 1982-83, 85; chmn. sr. econ. advisers, Econ. Commn. Europe, UN, 1970-72; cons. nat. security and fin., corp. bd. dirs. Am. Hotel & Realty Corp., Countrywide Mortgage Corp., N.Y. Stock Exch., Advantage and Ptnrs. Home Health Care and Providential Home Income, Philibus, 1988-92; mem. Bretton Woods Com., 1985-92. Author Knowledge Revolution for all Americans, 1992; contbr. articles to mags., books, jours., chpts. to books. Candidate for U.S. Senate, 1976. Mem. Internat. Real Estate Fedn. (vice chmn. 1980-86). Home: Rockville Md. Died Dec. 7, 1992. †

CARLSON, WILLIAM DONALD, education educator; b. Sandstone, Minn., Jan. 15, 1914; s. C. Oscar and Jennie A. (Bjorklund) C.; m. Marian A. Finseth, Feb. 15, 1942; children—John W., Marcia A., Audrey J., Meridee J. B.E. with high honors, St. Cloud State Teachers Coll., 1939; M.A., U. Minn., 1951, Ph.D., 1955. Tchr. elementary schs. Minn., 1932-36; tchr., prin., secondary schs., 1937-41; with U.S. Bur. Prisons, 1941-42, 46-47; research asst. bur. ednl. research U. Minn., 1947-48; dir. student personnel U. Minn. (Coll. Edn. High Sch.), 1948-52; dean student affairs U. Nev., Reno, 1952-57; dean so. regional div. U. Nev., Las Vegas, 1957-65, prof. edn., 1952-80, prof. emeritus, 1980-88, also grand marshal. Mem. adv. council U.S. Civil War Centennial Commn.; Member U.S. Regional Export Expansion Council. Served to capt. inf. AUS, 1942-46. Decorated Bronze Star with oak leaf cluster. Mem. Clark County Mental Health Assn. (pres.), Nev. Mental Health Assn. (v.p.), Nev. Psychol. Assn., Am. Personnel and Guidance Assn., Am. Coll. Personnel Assn., Higher Edn. Assn., Phi Delta Kappa, Psi Chi, Kappa Delta Pi, Phi Kappa Phi, Tau Kappa Alpha.; mem. Order Eastern Star, Vasa Order Am. Clubs: Mason (33 deg.), Rotarian. Home: Las Vegas Nev. Died Sept. 26, 1988; buried Bunkers Memory Gardens, Las Vegas, Nev.

CARLSON, WILLIAM HUGH, librarian; b. Waverly, Nebr., Sept. 5, 1898; s. Swan August and Christine (Johnson) C.; m. Claire Dyer, June 17, 1924; 1 child, Ruth Sherrill. AB, U. Nebr., 1924; cert., N.Y. State Libr. Sch., 1926; MA Sch. Librarianship, U. Calif., 1937. Farmer, 1919-22; asst. Nebr. Legis. Reference Bur. Libr., 1924-25; supr. dept. librs. U. Iowa, 1926-29; libr. U. N.D., 1929-35; vis. libr. Vanderbilt U., 1935-36; libr. U. Ariz., 1937-42; assoc. libr. U. Wash., 1942-45; dir. libr. Oreg. System Higher Edn., Corvallis, 1945-65, planning and rsch. assoc., from 1965. Author: Development and Financial Support of Seven Western and Northwestern State University Libraries, 1938; contbr. articles to profl. jours. Mem. ALA (libr. edn. div., pres. 1952-53), Assn. Coll. and Reference Librs. (pres. 1947-48), Bibliog. Soc. Am., Pacific N.W. Libr. Assn. (pres. 1952-53), Soc. Advancement Scandinavian Studies. *

CARNES, JAMES ROBERT, naval officer, trade association executive; b. Acworth, Ga., Oct. 23, 1909; s. James Erwin and Fannie (McDowell) C.; m. Virginia Richmond, Aug. 20, 1940; 1 son, Thomas Peter. B.S., Ga. Inst. Tech., 1930; J.D., Emory U., 1935; postgrad., George Washington U., 1962-63. Bar: Ga. bar 1935, D.C. bar 1962. Operating mgr. B.F. Goodrich Co., Johnson City, Tenn., 1930-33; practiced in Columbus, Ga., 1936-41, 46; served to comdr. USNR, 1941-46; commd. USN, 1946, advanced through grades to capt., 1954; asst. judge adv. gen. Navy, 1959-61; ret., 1961; dir. govt. relations Chem. Mfrs. Assn., Washington, 1962-67; sec.-treas. Chem. Mfrs. Assn., from 1967, v.p., 1972-73; ret., 1973. Decorated Bronze Star. Mem. Alpha Tau Omega, Phi Delta Phi, Phi Kappa Phi. Democrat. Clubs: Army Navy Country (Washington); Farmington Country (Charlottesville, Va.). Home: Bethesda Md. Died 1992. †

CARNEY, JAMES F., archbishop; b. Vancouver, B.C., Can., June 28, 1915; s. John and Ethel (Crook) C. Ed., Vancouver Coll., Jr. Sem. of Christ the King, 1930-38,

St. Joseph's Sem., Alta., Can., 1938-42. Ordained priest Roman Catholic Ch., 1942; pastor Corpus Christi Ch., Vancouver; later vicar gen., domestic prelate; consecrated bishop Corpus Christi Ch., 1966; ordained titular bishop of Obori and aux. bishop of Vancouver, 1966-69, installed as archbishop, 1969-90. Home: West Vancouver Can. Died Sept. 16, 1990.

CARNEY, ROBERT BOSTWICK, naval officer; b. Vallejo, Calif., Mar. 26, 1895; s. Robert E. and Bertha (Bostwick) C.; m. Grace Stone Craycroft, Sept. 7, 1918; children: Robert Bostwick Jr., Betty Bostwick Taussig. BS, U.S. Naval Acad., 1916; LLD (hon.), Loras Coll. Commd. ensign USN, 1916, advanced through grades to 4 star adm., 1950; chief staff to Adm. Halsey, 1943-45, dep. chief naval ops.,, 1946-50; comdr. 2d Fleet, 1950; comdr.-in-chief U.S. Naval Forces Ea. Atlantic and Mediteranean, 1950-52, Allied Forces So. Europe (NATO), 1951-53; mem. Joint Chiefs Staff, Chief Naval Ops., 1953-55; chmn. bd. Bath (Maine) Iron Works; bd. dirs. Nation-Wide Securities Co., Inc., Ryan Aircraft, Fairchild Aircraft; past pres. Naval Inst.; indsl. cons. Decorated Navy Cross, D.S.M. with 3 gold stars, Legion of Merit, Bronze Star, also various other Am. and fgn. decorations; recipient gold medal Am. Ordnance Assn. Mem. Brook Club (N.Y.C.), Met. Club, Chevy Chase Club, City Tavern Club, Alfalfa Club, Alibi Club. Home: Washington D.C. Died June 25, 1990; buried Arlington Nat. Cemetery, Washington, D.C.

CARNOVSKY, MORRIS, actor; b. St. Louis, Sept. 5, 1897; s. Isaac and Jennie (Stillman) C.; m. Phoebe Brand, Sept. 17, 1941; 1 child, Stephen Brand. AB, Washington U., St. Louis. Acting debut with Henry Jewitt Players, Boston; 1st N.Y. appearance with Provincetown Players in God of Vengence, 1922. Mem. Theatre Guild Acting Co., N.Y.C., 1924-30, prodns. include Men in White, Doctor's Dilemma, Awake and Sing, Golden Boy, on Broadway in An Enemy of the People, Uncle Vanya, Tiger at the Gates, Nude with Violin, A Family Affair, others; acotr, tchr. at the Am. Shakespeare Festival, Stratford, Conn., 1956-63, with repertory company in Hamlet, Midsummer Night's Dream; motion pictures include Cyrano de Bergerac, Dead Reckoning, Rhapsody in Blue; dir. Volpone, Monday's Heroes for Actor's Lab. *

CARPENTER, DAVID BAILEY, educator; b. Webster Groves, Mo., June 4, 1915; s. Fred Green and Mildred (Bailey) C.; m. Yoshi Horikawa, Aug. 6, 1946; children—Marie Yoshiko, Teresa Teiko, Gary Bailey, James Burton. B.A., Wash. U., 1937, M.A., 1938; M.A., Columbia U., 1944; Ph.D., U. Wash., 1951. Instr. sociology U. Wash., 1941-42; civilian chief of stats. div. MacArthur Hdqrs., Tokyo, 1946-48; instr. sociology U. Wash., 1948-49; asst. prof. sociology Wash. U., 1949-52, assoc. prof., 1952-63, prof., 1963-72; dean Wash. U. (Grad. Sch. Arts and Scis.), 1965-67; chief grad. acad. programs br. U.S. Office Edn., 1967-68; prof. U. Ill. at Chgo., 1972-83, prof. emeritus, from 1983, head dept. sociology, 1972-76. Author: (with Stuart A. Queen) The American City, 1953, The Social Life of a Modern Metropolis, 1954. Served with USNR, 1942-46. Mem. Ethical Soc. St. Louis (pres. 1969-71), Phi Beta Kappa. Home: Wilmette Ill. Died Nov. 24, 1988.

CARPENTER, JAMES MORTON, art educator, artist; b. Glens Falls, N.Y., Dec. 7, 1914; s. William Morton and Beulah (Mason) C.; m. Dorothy Neal Sauer, Nov. 4, 1939; children: William Morton, Stephen Sparrell, Elizabeth Ashley, Jane Mason. A.B., Harvard, 1937, Ph.D., 1943. Instr., then asst. prof. Harvard U., 1943-50; prof. art history Colby Coll., 1950-81, chmn. dept., from 1953; Jetté prof. art emeritus, dir. Colby Coll. Art Mus., 1959-65; organizer group show Maine and Its Artists, Boston Mus. of Fine Arts and Whitney Mus., N.Y.C., 1964. One-man retrospective show at Colby Coll. Mus. Art, 1980; Author: (with others) Maine and Its Role in American Art, 1963, (with Howard T. Fisher) Color in Art, a Tribute to Arthur Pope, 1974, Visual Art: A Critical Introduction, 1982. Home: Waterville Maine Died Feb. 11, 1992; buried Morningside Cemetery,Phippsburg, ME.

CARR, ARTHUR JAPHETH, English language educator; b. Bad Axe, Mich., Apr. 21, 1914; s. Arthur Wellesley and Margaret (McAuslan) C.; m. Penelope Gall, Feb. 1, 1964; children by previous marriage: Jennifer (Mrs. Rollis), Adam Fyfe, Daniel Arthur, Alice (Mrs. Jan A Van den Broek III). A.B., U. Mich., 1935; A.M., Syracuse U., 1937; Ph.D., U. Ill., 1947. Instr. English Syracuse U., 1937-40, U. Ill., 1947-49; mem. faculty U. Mich., 1949-67, prof. English, 1961-67; prof. English Williams Coll., Williamstown, Mass., 1967-83, Edward Dorr Griffin prof., 1970-82, prof. emeritus, 1983-91, chmn. dept., 1967-74; cons. U.S. Office Edn., 1965-69; Ednl. Testing Service, Coll. Entrance Exam. Bd., 1966-71; dir. NDEA Inst. U. Mich., 1965. Editor: Victorian Poetry; Clough to Kipling, 1959, 2d edit., 1972; co-editor: Norton Anthology of Poetry, 1970, 3d edit., 1983, Masterpieces of the Drama, 5th edit, 1986; Contbr. articles to profl. jours. Served with USNR, 1943-45, PTO. Mem. MLA, Nat. Council Tchrs. English, AAUP, Tennyson Soc., Phi Beta Kappa, Phi Eta Sigma, Phi Kappa Phi. Home: Lenox Mass. Died Dec. 4, 1991; buried Williams Coll. Cemetery, Williamstown, Mass.

CARR, ERNEST JAMES, railroad executive; b. Chgo., July 9, 1896; s. Ernest Fremyer and Mary Ann (Derby) C.; m. Pauline Eunice Dick, Jan. 1, 1925; children: Ernest James, Patricia Koontz, Madelyn Matthews. Student, Kent Coll. Law, 1915-17, DePaul U., 1919-20. From messenger to gen. traffic agt. Ill. Ctrl. Railroad, Chgo., from 1912; asst. traffic mgr. Ill. Ctrl. Railroad, St. Louis; gen. Ea. traffic mgr. Ill. Ctrl. Railroad, N.Y.; freight traffic mgr. Ill. Ctrl. Railroad, Chgo.; gen. freight traffic mgr. Ill. Ctrl. Railroad, 1912-53, asst. v.p., 1953-57, v.p. traffic, from 1957; dir. Chgo. & Ill. Western R.R., Peoria & Pekin Union Ry., Chgo. Produce Terminal, Paducah & Ill. Ry., Madison Coal Corp., Mississippi Valley Corp. Served with 13th Engrs., U.S. Army, 1917-19. Mem. Soc. Traffic and Transportation, Nat. Freight Traffic Assn., Am. Petroleum Inst., Mason, Clubs: Chicago, Chicago Athletic Assn., Flossmoor Country, Traffic (Chgo.), Boston (New Orleans), Missouri Athletic (St. Louis), Traffic (N.Y.C.). Republican. *

CARR, HAROLD JOHN, business executive; b. Williamson, N.Y., Apr. 4, 1895; s. Robert Stephenson and Anna L. (Nye) C.; m. Mary Catherine Shomier, June 4, 1932. BS, Colgate U., 1917. Sales mgr. Capstan Glass Co., Connellsville, Pa., 1920-23; v.p. Anchor Cap & Closure Corp., Long Island City, N.Y., 1923-40; gen. mgr. closure div. Anchor Hocking Glass Corp., Lancaster, Ohio, 1940-41; adminstrv. dir. Owens-Illinois Glass Co., 1942-43, 52-60, gen. mgr. closure and plastics div., 1943-52, v.p., from 1947, dir. of bus. rsch., 1952-59, sr. cons. in mktg., 1959-60; also cons. containers and packaging div. Nat. Prodn. Authority, 1950-53, bus. and def. svcs. adminstrn., 1953-62; mem. Packaging Industry Adv. Com. Munitions Bd., 1952-53, Dept. Def., 1953-54; mem. Glass Container Mfrs. Industry Adv. Com., W.P.B., 1944-46; chmn. N.R.A. Code Authority for Closure Mfg. Industry, 1933-34. Mem. survey and planning com. Hosp. Planning Assn., Greater Toledo area, from 1961.; mem. Nat. Def. Exec. Res. Served with U.S. Army, WWI, with U.S. Army Ambulance Svc. in Italy, France, Germany, 1917-19. Recipient Cert. of Svc., Dept. Commerce, 1952. Mem. Canning Machinery & Supplies Assn. (life, dir. 1929-37, pres. 1934-35), Clubs: Toledo, Toledo Country, Carranor Hunt, Polo (Perrysburg, Ohio), Beta Theta Pi. Republican. Methodist. *

CARR, HOBART CECIL, economist, educator; b. Hawkeye, Iowa, Jan. 27, 1912; s. Cecil Earl and Mary Eleanor (Carney) C.; m. Virginia Marilyn Eichler, Oct. 12, 1935; children: Gerald Lawrence, Valerie Catherine. BA, U. Iowa, 1937, MA, 1938; PhD, U. Ill., Urbana, 1941. Instr. Wayne State U., Detroit, 1941-42; economist, chief of divs. Fed. Reserve Bank of N.Y., N.Y.C., 1942-56; prof. banking NYU, 1956-77, chmn. banking and fin. dept. Sch. of Commerce, 1956-70, Gerstenberg prof. of fin., 1962-64, prof. emeritus, 1977; prof. banking Adelphi U., Garden City, N.Y., 1978-89; cons. Fed. Home Loan Bank Bd., Washington, 1961-64; vis. prof. Vargas Inst., Brazil, 1969; expert on Mission, U.N., Iran, 1971. Author: Early History of Iowa Railroads, 1981; contbr. articles to profl. jours. Commr. of Water, Police, Fire, trustee, Village of Garden City (N.Y.), 1963-70. Mem. Am. Econ. Assn., Am. Fin. Assn., Phi Beta Kappa, Phi Alpha Kappa, Beta Gamma Sigma. Club: University. Home: Garden City N.Y. Died Mar. 25, 1990; cremated.

CARROLL, J(EFFERSON) ROY, JR., architect; b. Phila., Sept. 25, 1904; s. J. Roy and Mary (Greenaway) C.; m. Doris Hansen Packard, Dec. 15th, 1945 (dec.); children: Spencer, Mary Margaret Morrison, Patricia.; m. Ann Darlington Haggerty, Oct. 11, 1981. B.Arch., U. Pa., 1926, M.Arch. (fellow), 1928; LHD (hon.), Spring Garden Coll., 1989. Registered architect, Pa. With J. Roy Carroll, Jr., FAIA (architect), 1935-46, 77-82; ptnr. Carroll, Grisdale & Van Alen, Architects,, Phila., 1946-77; asst. prof., exec. chmn. design staff U. Pa., 1945; vis. lectr. architecture Pa. State U., 1953-54; archtl. cons. Dept. Army, from 1964; mem. archtl. rev. bd. Dept. Navy, from 1965. Contbr. articles to profl. publs.; Bldgs. designed by firm include Phila. Internat. Airport Terminal Bldgs., Phila. State Office Bldg., nat. hdqrs. ASTM, Student Union bldg., dormitories La Salle Coll., Franklin Bldg., Physics Annex, Law Sch. Bldg., others U. Pa, all Phila., Student Union Bldg., Fine Arts Bldg. & Theatre, Maintenance Bldg. Lincoln U., other bldgs. Temple U., Grove City Coll., Haverford Coll., Pa. Mil. Colls., FAA Office Bldg., The Mall, NASA Bldg., both Washington, Lister Hill Nat. Center for Biomed. Communications, NIH, Bethesda, Md., U.S. Army Engrs. Topographic Research and Devel. Labs., Ft. Belvoir, Va., U.S. Courthouse and Fed. Office Bldg, Phila., numerous others. Chmn. Delaware County Adv. Com. on Housing and Planning, 1947-52; pres. Citizens Council Housing and Planning of Delaware County, 1953-56; mem. Swarthmore Borough Council, 1955-60; assoc. trustee, chmn. fine arts bd. U. Pa.; adv. bd. Temple U. Sch. Architecture. Recipient award Appomattox Monument competition, 1932; Woodman fellow U. Pa., 1940. Fellow AIA (Phila. pres. 1951-52, Gold medal Phila. chpt. 1963, regional dir. 1956, nat. sec. 1959-62, 1st v.p. 1962-63, nat. pres. 1963-64, pres. AIA Found. 1964-68, pres. Phila. architects charitable trust 1968-72, chancellor Coll. of Fellows 1971-72), Royal Soc. Arts London (Benjamin Franklin fellow 1975), Philippine Inst. Architects (hon.), Royal Archtl. Inst. Can. (hon.); mem. Colegio de Arquitectos de Mexico (hon.), Pa. Soc. Architects (Gold medal 1963, pres. 1945-46), Phila. Housing Assn. (dir.), Franklin Inst. of Phila. (chmn. Brown medal com.), Archtl. League N.Y., Phila. Numis. and Antiquarian Soc. (pres. 1984), Pa. Acad. Fine Arts, Gen. Alumni Soc. U. Pa. (pres. 1944-46, Alumni award of merit 1948), Sigma Xi, Tau Sigma Delta. Presbyterian (pres. bd. trustees 1952, elder, mem. session 1965-68), deacon 1984. Clubs: Cosmos (Washington); Carpenters Company Phila. (mng. com.). Home: Swarthmore Pa. Died July 17, 1990.

CARROLL, JOSEPH FRANCIS, management consultant, former air force officer; b. Chgo., Mar. 19, 1910; s. James Michael and Sara Kane C.; m. Mary Ann Morrissey, Aug. 21, 1937; children: Joseph Francis, James Michael, Brian Patrick, Dennis Thomas, Kevin Martin. AB, St. Mary.s, Mundelein, Ill., 1933; JD, Loyola U., Chgo., 1940. Bar: Ill. 1940. Spl. agt. various field offices FBI, 1940-44, chief gen. criminal sect., Washington asst. div. chief, 1944-45; dir. compliance enforcement div. Surplus Property Adminstrn., War Assets Adminstrn., 1945-47; insp. in charge fraud and acctg. matters FBI, 1948; commd. col. USAF, advanced through grades to maj. gen., 1948; dir. Def. Intelligence Agy., Washington, 1961-69; ret. USAF, 1969; exec. dir. Nat. Coun. Cath. Men, Washington, 1968-72; v.p. Grady Mgmt. Inc., Washington, 1972-91. Dir. Wackenhut Corp., Coral Gables, Fla. Decorated Legion of Merit, DSM with oak leaf clusters; recipient N.C.C.M. St. Thomas More award. Mem. Ill. Bar Assn. Roman Catholic. Home: Alexandria Va. Died Jan. 20, 1991.

CARROLL, WALLACE EDWARD, instruments and equipment manufacturing company executive; b. Taunton, Mass., Nov. 4, 1907; s. Patrick J. and Katherine (Feely) C.; m. Lelia Holden, Nov. 7, 1936; children: Wallace E. Jr., Denis H., Barry J., Lelia K.H. PhB, Boston Coll., 1928, LLD, 1957; postgrad., MIT, 1929; postgrad. in bus., Harvard U., 1930, NYU, 1933; postgrad., Northwestern U., 1936; LLD, DePaul U., 1966; HHD (hon.), St. Xavier Coll., 1986. With acctg. dept. N.Y. Telephone Co., 1930-33; indsl. engr. Reed & Barton, 1933-34; with sales dept. Fed. Products, 1934-40; chmn., bd. dirs. Wacker Sales, from 1940, Size Control Co., from 1941, Walsh Press & Die Co., from 1945; pres., chmn. bd. dirs. Am. Gage & Machine Co., Elgin, Ill., from 1948; chmn., bd. dirs. Simpson Electric Co., 1950-89; vice chmn. bd. dirs., chief exec. officer Katy Industries, Inc., Elgin, 1970-88, vice chmn., chmn. exec. com., 1988-90; vice chmn., dir. Ludlow Typograph Co.; vice chmn. bd. dirs. M-K-T R.R., Dallas; treas., dir. G.M. Diehl Machine Co., Champion Pneumatic Machinery Co., from 1957; bd. dirs. numerous cos. including Binks Mfg. Co., Franklin Park, Ill., OEA, Inc., Denver, CRL, Inc., Denver, British LaBour Pump Co., London, Ruttonsha-Simpson Pvt. Ltd., Bombay, Bush Universal, Inc., N.Y.C., Mercantile Nat. Bank Chgo.; dir. metal-working equipment div. BDSA, Dept. Commerce, Washington, 1957; with U.S. Trade Mission to India, 1958-59, UAR, 1960, Ireland and Portugal, 1966, U.S. Council Commerce and Industry, 1973, U.S. Bus. Trade Mission Korea, 1974, Trade and Investment Mission Rep. China, 1975. Chmn. fed. agys. Community Fund drive, 1959; mem. citizen's com. Loyola U.; bd. dirs. Cath. Charities, 1962, Chgo. Boys Club, Chgo. Girls Club, Gregorian U. Found., N.Y.; founding dir. Am. Irish Found. (now merged with Am. Leland Fund); past bd. regents Boston Coll.; trustee Christine and Alfred Sonntag Found. Cancer Research, U. Chgo. Cancer Rsch. Found.; past trustee DePaul U. Served with U.S. Army Air Corps, 1929, with N.G., 1930-33. Recipient Civic award Loyola U., 1965, Heinze/Winzeler award, 1982; named hon. mem. Chippewa Indian Tribe; Boston U. Sch. Mgmt. named in his honor, 1989. Mem. Tool and Die Inst. (pres. 1952-53), U.S. C. of C. (econ. policy com. 1959-62), Nat. Machine Tool Builders Assn. (pres. 1962-63). Roman Catholic. Clubs: Chgo. Athletic, Chgo., Mid-Am., MIT, Harvard, Harvard Bus., Boston Coll., NYU (Chgo.); Burning Tree (Bethesda, Md.); Exmoor Country (Highland Park, Ill.); East Chop Beach, Martha's Vineyard, Edgartown Yacht (Mass.); Everglades, Bath and Tennis (Palm Beach, Fla.); Univ. (N.Y.C.). Home: Lake Forest Ill. Died Sept. 29, 1990; buried Lake Forest (Ill.) Cemetery.

CARSON, ALLAN GRANT, lawyer; b. Salem, Oreg., Sept. 7, 1897; s. John A. and Helen (Fraser) C.; m. Merle Hamilton, Nov. 4, 1922; children: Allan Hamilton, Marian Andree Fager. Student, U. Oreg., 1919-20; LLB, Willamette U., 1922; LaSalle Extension U., 1935. Admitted to Oreg. bar, 1922, U.S. Dist. Ct., 1924, U.S. Supreme Ct., 1927. Gen. practice of law, specializing trial & appelate work, 1922-42, from 1946; dep. dist. atty. Marion County, Oreg., 1922-27; spl. legal counsel Gov. Oreg., 1927, 29; bd. dirs. Salem Fed. Savs. & Loan Assn., from 1934. Mem. Oreg. Ho. of Reps., 1940-42, Senate, 1942-46, 46-50; bd. control Salem Gen. Hosp., 1933-57, Salem Boxing Commn., from 1946; chmn. Oreg. Law Improvement Com., from 1963. Served as cpl., inf., Mexican Border Expdn., 1916; to 1st lt., inf., AEF, U.S. Army, WWI, France, Germany; to lt. col. USAAF, WWII, CBI. Decorated Air medal. Mem. Willamette Univ. Coll. Law Alumni Assn. (pres. 1947-49), Am. Judicature Soc., ABA, Oreg. Bar Assn. (pres. 1937-38), Marion County Bar Assn., VFW (post comdr.

1923), Am. Legion (post comdr. 1933), Kappa Sigma, Delta Theta Phi, Mason, Elk. Republican. Episcopalian. *

CARSON, CHARLES WILLIAM, banker; b. Bethany, N.Y., Dec. 23, 1897; s. Theodore W. and Eunice E. (Blood) C.; m. Dorothy B. Knight, Sept. 16, 1924; children: Charles William, Mary H. Student, U. Rochester, 1920-22. Sec. YMCA, Batavia, Buffalo, N.Y., 1915-35; treas. Colgate-Rochester Div. Sch., 1935-43; exec. v.p. Community Savs. Bank of Rochester, 1944-45, pres., from 1946; dir. N.Y. Bus. Devel. Corp.; pres. M.S.B. Fund, Rochester Mgmt. Inc. Pres. Highland Hosp.; dir., past pres. YMCA, Rochester, trustee, N.Y. exec. com.; bd. dirs. Rochester Hosp. Fund.; trustee Colgate-Rochester Div. Sch., Rochester Bur. Mcpl. Rsch. Mem. Savs. Bank Assn. N.Y. State (past. pres.), Nat. Assn. Mut. Savs. Banks (past chmn. com. edn. and mgmt. devel.), Rochester C. of C. (past pres.), City Club (past pres.), Genesee Valley Club, Univ. Club, Country Club (Rochester). *

CARSON, GERALD HEWES, author; b. Carrollton, Ill., July 6, 1899; s. James Anderson and Minnie (Hewes) C.; m. Lettie Gay, Nov. 28, 1923; children: Nancy Gay Carson Payne (dec.), Sara Ann Carson Forden. A.B., U. Ill., 1921, M.A., 1922. Reporter N.Y. Herald, 1922-23; copywriter Calkins & Holden, Inc., 1923-27; with J. Walter Thompson Co., 1928-29, Batton, Barton, Durstine & Osborn, 1929-32; v.p. William Esty & Co., 1933-40; v.p., copy dir. Benton & Bowles, Inc., 1940-47; v.p., dir. Kenyon & Eckhardt, Inc., 1947-51; contbg. editor Am. Heritage mag., 1964-76; mem. usage panel Am. Heritage Dictionary of English Lang., 1969-76. Author: The Old Country Store, 1954, Cornflake Crusade, 1957-76, The Roguish World of Doctor Brinkley, 1960, One for a Man, Two for a Horse, 1961, The Social History of Bourbon, 1963, The Polite Americans, 1966, Men, Beasts and Gods: A History of Cruelty and Kindness to Animals, 1972, The Golden Egg: The Personal Income Tax, Where It Came From, How It Grew, 1977, A Good Day at Saratoga, 1978, The Dentist and the Empress: The Adventures of Dr. Tom Evans in Gas-lit Paris, 1983 (spl. citation 1985); contbr. to Dictionary Am. Biography, Notable Am. Women; contbr. revs. to mags., jours. Chmn. Francis Parkman award, 1972, 74, com. mem., 1986. Recipient award of merit Am. Assn. State and Local History, 1954, Dunning prize Am. Hist. Assn., 1954. Fellow Soc. Am. Historians (exec. bd. 1974-86); mem. N.Y. Hist. Soc., Newtown Hist. Assn., S.R. Club: University (N.Y.C.). Home: Newtown Pa. Died Dec. 4, 1989; body donated to science.

CARSTENS, KARL WALTER, former president Federal Republic Germany; b. Bremen, Fed. Republic Germany, Dec. 14, 1914; s. Karl and Gertrud (Clausen) C.; m. Veronica Prior, 1944. Student various univs., 1933-35; Dr.jur, Hamburg U., 1936; LLM, Yale U., 1949. Pvt. practice Bremen, 1945-49; rep. Free City Bremen, Bonn, 1949-54; German rep. Coun. Europe, Stasbourg, France, 1954-55; sect. chief Fgn. Office, Bonn, 1955-60, state sec. dep. fgn. min., 1960-66, state sec. dept. def. min., 1967; chief Office Fed. Chancellor, Bonn, 1968-69; prof. internat. constl. law U. Cologne, Fed. Republic Germany, 1960-73; dir. Rsch. Inst., German Soc. for Fgn. Affairs, 1970-73; mem. German Bundestag (CDU), 1972-79. Author: Grundgedanken der Amerikanschen Verfassung, 1954, Das Recht des Europarats, 1956, Politische Fuhrung, 1971, Bundestagsreden und Zeitdokumente, 1978, Reden und Interviews, 1979-84, Deutsche Gedice, 1983, Wanderungen in Deutschland, 1985, Vom Geist der Freiheit, 1989. With German Army, 1939-45. Home: Meckenheim Germany Died May 30, 1992. †

CARTER, CURTIS HAROLD, physician, college dean; b. Scott, Ga., Oct. 1, 1915; s. Carr Richard and Mary Claudia (Cheek) C.; m. Sara Jones Milligan, June 21, 1938; children: Curtis Harold, Michael P., King R., Mary Carter Peel, Sara M. Student, Ala. Poly. Inst., 1931-32; MD, U. Ga., 1938, BS, 1939. Diplomate Am. Bd. Internal Medicine. Intern Univ. Hosp., Augusta, Ga., 1938-39, resident internal medicine, 1947-50; assoc. med. officer VA, Augusta, 1939-40; practice medicine specializing in internal medicine Augusta, 1951-55; chief pulmonary disease div. Eugene Talmadge Meml. Hosp., 1956-68; attending physician internal medicine, 1956-92; dir. med. edn. Meml. Hosp., Savannah, Ga., 1968; assoc. in medicine, instr. Postgrad. Sch. U. Tex. Sch. Medicine, M.D. Anderson Hosp., Houston, 1950-51; vis. assoc. prof. medicine U. Colo. Sch. Medicine, Denver, 1956; asst. prof. medicine Med. Coll. Ga., Augusta, 1951-55, assoc. prof., 1955-57, prof., 1957-76, prof. emeritus, 1976-92, assoc. dean clin. scis., 1968-71, acting dean, 1971-72, dean, med. dir., 1972-75, dean emeritus, 1977-82; cons. Milledgeville (Ga.) State Hosp., 1952-59, VA Hosp., 1956-67, Ga. State Tng. Sch., Gracewood, 1957-60. Contbr. articles to profl. jours. Comdr. USNR, 1940-47. Fellow A.C.P., Am. Coll. Chest Physicians (gov. Ga. chpt. 1960-67, sec.-treas. Ga. chpt. 1962-63, v.p. 1963-64); mem. Am. Ga. med. assns., Richmond County Med. Soc. (v.p. 1961-62), Am., Ga. (dir. 1954-57) heart assns., Nat., Ga. lung assns., Am. (counselor Ga. 1967-69), Ga. thoracic socs., AAAS, Assn. Am. Med. Colls., , Augusta Country Club, Alpha Omega Alpha, Alpha Kappa Kappa. Home: Augusta Ga. Died Feb. 3, 1992.

CARTER, DAVID CLIFFORD, association executive; b. Amarillo, Tex., Jan. 9, 1929; s. Clifford Marion and Jessie Elizabeth (Bryden) C.; m. Alice Elaine Tooke; children: Kathleen, Jennifer. BA, San Jose State U., 1958. Asst. to pres. Spreckels Sugar Co., San Francisco, 1962-69; v.p. U.S. Beet Sugar Assn., Washington, 1969-74, pres., 1974—; chmn. Sweetener Producers Group, Inc., Washington, 1983—; pres. N.Y. Sugar Club, 1990. Mem. Pub. Relations Soc. Am., Am. Soc. Assn. Execs., Nat. Press Club, Lakewood Country Club (bd. dirs. 1982—). Episcopalian.Deceased. Home: Rockville Md. †

CARTER, DUDLEY CHRISTOPHER, sculptor, forest engineer; b. New Westinster, B.C., Can., May 6, 1891; came to U.S., 1928; s. Foster Clyde and Sophia (Miller) C.; m. Teresa Williams Easthope, Dec. 19, 1919 (dec. 1975); 1 dau. Mavis Anne Carter Vaughan. Degree in Fine Arts, City Coll., San Francisco, 1983, degree in Fine Arts (hon.), 1985. Forester, construction Western Power Co. of Can., Stave Falls, B.C., 1909-1916; timber cruiser, forest engr. Clark & Lyford B.C.and Pacific N.W., 1919-1928; instr. sculpture U. Wash., Seattle, 1944-45; freelance forest engr., 1947-56; instr. U. Calif.-Santa Cruz, 1983. Exhibitor one man shows: Sunshine Coast Gallery, Sechelt, B.C., Carnegie Art Ctr., Vancouver, B.C., 1983; art in action, Golden Gate Internat. Expt., San Francisco, 1939-40, UN Habitat Forum, Vancouver, B.C. Recipient award HUD, 1973, Hall of Honor award Wash. State Centennial, 1983, Heroes award U.S. Congress, 1988, Wash. State Centennial award, 1989. Mem. B.C. Sculptors Soc. (hon. life pres.), Seattle Art Mus., Golden Gate Internat. Expn. Alumni. Home: Redmond Wash. Deceased. †

CARTER, GRANVILLE WELLINGTON, sculptor; b. Augusta, Maine, Nov. 18, 1920; s. Brooks Eaton and Araletta Tarr (Payne) C.; m. Senta Jacobshagen, Oct. 15, 1955; children: Juliana S., Richard S. Student, Coburn Classical Inst., 1938-39, Portland Sch. Fine and Applied Art, 1944-45, N.Y. Sch. Indsl. Art, 1945-49, N.A.D., 1945-48, Grand Chaumiere de Paris, 1954, Scuolo del Circolare Internazionale di Roma, 1955. Lectr. sculpture Washington Cathedral and Hofstra U., 1966-92; instr. Nat. Acad., Sch. Fine Arts, 1967-92. Exhibited in U.S., Paris, Rome, also collections; important works include Toro Malo Bronze Relief, Bullfighter fountain group, Neptune fountain urns, Gilded terra cotta capitals; limestone St. Augustine of Canterbury; heroic size limestone Archangels Michael and Gabriel at South Transept, Washington Cathedral; medals and also Stonewall Jackson portrait medal for Hall of Fame for Great Ams. at NYU, also George Washington, Thomas Edison, James Fenimore Cooper and Jane Addams portrait medals Nat. Commemorative Soc., Ofcl. Sesquicentennial medal for State of Maine, Francis Marion medal Brookgreen Gardens, S.C.; heroic size bust of Charles A. Lindbergh, Garden City Hist. Soc.; heroic size bronze bust Chaing Kai-Shek, St. John's U. and Chiang Kai-shek Meml. Hall, Taipei, Republic China, central tower dedication medal also figures depicting The Passion in central nave, Washington Cathedral, 2 bronze portrait placques for Edison Nat. Mus., West Orange, N.J.; monumental bronze portrait bust Alexander Stewart at, Garden City, N.Y.; 3-figure heroic-sized West Tex. Pioneer Family monument in bronze at, Lubbock, Tex., heroic sized equestrian monument of Gen. Casimir Pulaski in bronze, Hartford, Conn., Coach John Heisman bronze portrait plaque, Ga. Inst. Tech., Jay Panzirer monument, Orlando, Fla.; represented in permanent collections Smithsonian Instn., Hall of Fame for Gt. Ams., N.Y. U., Am. Numismatic Soc., Mus. for State of Maine, Thomas Edison Nat. Mus., NAD, Morristown Hist. Mus., Wroclaw (Poland) Mus. Medals, St. Pauls Sch., Garden City.; mem. editorial bd.: Nat. Sculpture Rev. Mem. adv. bd. Brookgreen Gardens, 1981-92. Recipient 1st prize N.A.D. Art Sch., 1946; Louis Comfort Tiffany fellow, 1954, 55; Lindsey Morris Meml. prize Nat. Sculpture Soc., 1966; Henry Hering Meml. medal for collaborative archtl. sculpture, 1968; Gold medal Am. Artists Profl. League, 1970, 78; J. Sanford Saltus award Am. Numismatic Soc., 1976; Therese and Edward H. Richard Meml. prize Nat. Sculpture Soc., 1980. Fellow Nat. Sculpture Soc. (dir., pres. 1979-81); mem. NAD (academician; Dessie Greer portrait prize 1980), Am. Artists Profl. League (dir.), Am. Numismatic Soc. (life), Council Am. Artist Socs. (pres. 1982-92). Home: Baldwin N.Y. Died Nov. 21, 1992. †

CARTER, GWENDOLEN MARGARET, political science educator, author; b. Hamilton, Ont., Can., July 17, 1906; came to U.S., 1935, naturalized, 1948; d. Charles and Nora (Ambrose) C. B.A., U. Toronto, 1929, Oxford (Eng.) U., 1931; M.A., Oxford (Eng.) U., 1936, Radcliffe Coll., 1936; Ph.D., Radcliffe Coll., 1938; D.H.L., Wheaton Coll., 1962, Russell Sage Coll., 1963, Northwestern U., 1977; LL.D., Western Coll. for Women, 1964, Goucher Coll., 1964, Carleton U., 1965, Boston U., 1966, McMaster U., 1966, Toronto U., 1970, Smith Coll., 1979, Stetson U., 1981, Dalhousie U., 1984, Ind. U., 1985. Instr. McMaster U., Hamilton, 1932-35, Wellesley Coll., 1938-41, Tufts U., 1942-43; asst. prof. Smith Coll., 1943-47, assoc. prof., 1947-52, prof. govt., 1952-64, Sophia Smith prof., 1961-64; Melville J. Herskovits prof. African affairs, dir. program of African studies, prof. polit. sci. Northwestern U., Evanston, Ill., 1964-74; prof. polit. sci. and African studies Ind. U., Bloomington, 1974-84, U. Fla., Gainesville, 1984-87; Mem. adv. council for Africa State Dept., 1962-67; Bd. trustees African-Am. Inst., from 1964; mem. joint com. Project 87, 1978-81. Author: British Commonwealth and International Security, 1947, (with John Herz) Major Foreign Powers, 1949, 52, 57, 62, 67, 72, The Politics of Inequality, 1958, 59, Independence for Africa, 1960, Government and Politics in the Twentieth Century, 1961, 66, 72, The Government of United Kingdom, 1964, 68, 72, The Government of Soviet Union, 1964, 68, 72, (with Thomas Karis and Newell Stultz) South Africa's Transkei: The Politics of Domestic Colonialism, 1967, The Government of France, 1968, 72, Which Way is South Africa Going?, 1980; Editor: (with W.O. Brown) Transition in Africa; Problems of Political Adaptation, 1959, African One-Party States, 1962, Five African States; Responses to Diversity, 1963, (with Alan Westin) Politics in Europe, 1965, Politics in Africa, 1966, National Unity and Regionalism, 1966, Africa in the Modern World series, 1968-72, (with Ann Paden) Expanding Horizons in African Studies, 1969, (with Louise Holborn and John Herz) German Constitutional Documents since 1871, 1970, (with Thomas Karis) From Protest to Challenge: A Documentary History of African Politics in South Africa, 1882-64, Vol. I, 1972, Vol. II, 1973, Vol. III, 1977, Vol. IV, 1977, (with Patrick O'Meara) Southern Africa in Crisis, 1977, Southern Africa: The Continuing Crisis, 1979, 2d edit., 1982, (with E. Philip Morgan) From the Front Line: Speeches of Sir Seretse Khama, 1980, (with Patrick O'Meara) International Politics in Southern Africa, 1982, African Independence: The First Twenty-Five Years, 1984, Continuity and Change in Southern Africa, 1985. Recipient George V medal pub. service, 1935, Achievement award Radcliffe Coll., 1962, Achievement award AAUW, 1962, Disting. Tchrs. award, 1962, Disting. Scholar award African Studies Assn., 1978; book of essays African Themes published in her honor by faculty African Studiesprogram Northwestern U., 1975. Fellow Am. Acad. Arts and Scis.; mem. Am. Polit. Sci. Assn. (council 1954-56, v.p. 1963-64), New Eng. Polit. Sci. Assn. (pres. 1959-60), Internat. Polit. Sci. Assn., Canadian Hist. and Polit. Sci. Assns., African Studies Assn. (v.p. 1957-58, pres. 1958-59, mem. policy and plans com. 1963-65), AAUW (internat. relations com. 1951-57, world problems rep., dir. 1967-69), African-Am. Inst. (dir. 1964—), Chgo. Council Fgn. Relations (dir. 1967-74). Home: Orange City Fla. Died Feb. 20, 1991.

CARTER, JOHN BERNARD, insurance company executive; b. Phila., Sept. 21, 1934; s. John Mein and Elise Hoban (Alexander) C.; m. Hope Elliot, Apr. 12, 1958; children: Hope, John, Helen, Charleds, Henry, George, Charlotte, Ann, Katherine, Elizabeth, Richard, Kerry. BA, Yale U., 1956; MBA, Harvard U., 1961; postgrad., Am. Coll., Bryn Mawr, Pa., 1967; LLD (hon.), Morehouse Coll., 1986. With Equitable Life Assurance Soc., N.Y.C., 1960-90, chief ins. officer, 1981-82, pres., chief operating officer, 1982-83, pres., chief exec. officer, 1983-90; dir. Colgate-Palmolive Corp., Westinghouse Electric Corp. Trustee Marymount Coll., Tarrytown, N.Y., from 1984, Morehouse Coll., Atlanta; bd. dirs. Diabetes Research Found., N.Y.C. Partnership Inc., from 1988, Inner City Scholarship Fund, Dole Found., Found. for Children with Learning Disabilities, Com. Econ. Devel.; commr. Statue of Liberty Ellis Island Found., United Way of Tri State. With USN, 1956-59. Mem. Health Ins. Assn. Am. (past chmn.), Life Ins. Coun. N.Y. (past chmn.), Nat. Alliance Bus. (bd. dirs., chmn. bd.), Assocs. Harvard Bus. Sch. (bd. dirs.). Home: New Canaan Conn. Died May 21, 1991.

CARTER, ROBERT WARREN, lawyer; b. Toronto, Ont., Can., Oct. 7, 1941; s. E. William and Phyllis M. (Deverill) C.; m. Alison Louise James, Dec. 13, 1969. B in Applied Sci., U. Toronto, 1966, LLM, 1972. Registered profl. engr., Ont. Rep. tech. service DuPont Canada, Inc., Kingston, Ont., 1966-69; barrister, solicitor Fasken & Calvin, Toronto, 1973-77; staff solicitor Ford Motor Co. Can., Ltd., Oakville, Ont., 1977-86, gen. counsel, sec., 1986-89; sec., bd. dirs. Ford New Holland Can., Ltd., Oakville. Chmn. campaign United Way Oakville, 1988. Mem. Can. Bar Assn., Law Soc. Upper Can., Assn. Profl. Engrs. Ont.; Royal Kingston Yacht Club, Bronte Harbour Yacht Club, Oakville Harbour Yacht Club. Home: Oakville Can. Died May 24, 1989; buried Woodland Cemetery, Hamilton, Ont., Can.

CARTER, WILLIAM LYNN, dancer, choreographer; b. Durant, Okla., Mar. 21, 1936; s. Noah Lee and Mae Belle (Lynn) C. Ed. pub. schs. Soloist Am. Ballet Theatre, N.Y.C., 1957-59; prin. dancer N.Y.C. Ballet Co., 1959-62, Martha Graham Dance Co., 1972-88, Pearl Lang Dance Co., 1973-88; founder, co-artistic dir. 1st Chamber Dance Quartet, N.Y.C., 1961-69; founder, artistic dir., prin. dancer Ballet Espanol Co., 1979-88, William Carter Dance Ensemble, N.Y.C., 1989-88; artist-in-residence U. Wis., Milw., 1979, Portland State U., 1976; choreographer-artist-in residence Ea. Ill. U., 1978-79; guest artist Maia Alba Spanish Dance Co., 1976; artistic dir., resident choreographer Chamber Dance Theatre, 1978; tchr. Am. Ballet Theatre Sch., 1980; concert soloist. Fellow Nat. Endowment for Arts, 1976, 77, 78. Mem. Am. Guild Mus. Artists. Home: New York N.Y. Died July 7, 1988; cremated.

CARTEY, WILFRED GEORGE ONSLOW, educator, author, poet; b. Port-of-Spain, Trinidad, July 19, 1931; came to U.S., 1955, naturalized, 1972; s. Samuel and Ada C. BA, U. W.I., 1955; MA, Columbia U., 1956, PhD, 1964. Mem. faculty Columbia U., 1957-69; prof. comparative lit. CCNY, 1969-72, disting. prof. dept. black studies, 1973-92; Martin Luther King prof. Bklyn. Coll., 1972; vis. scholar, lectr. U. P.R., summer 1959; vis. prof. U. Vt., summer 1964, U. W. Indies, Jamaica, summer 1965, U. Ghana, Legon, 1967-68; resident prof. extra mural dept. U. W. Indies, Nassau, summer 1973; vis. disting. prof. Romance langs. Howard U., 1976; vis. disting. prof. Afro-Am. studies U. Calif., Berkeley, spring 1979. Author: The West Indies, Islands in the Sun, 1967, Black Images, 1970, Palaver, 1970, Whispers from the Continent, 1971, (poems) The House of Blue Lightning, 1973, Waters of My Soul, 1975, Red Rain, 1977, Suns and Shadows, 1978, Fires in the Wind, 1980, Embryos, 1982, The Dawn, the Desert, the Sands, Kundiya, 1982, Black Velvet Time, 1984, Children of Lalibela, 1985, Potentialities, 1987, Choreographers of the Dawn, 1989, Whispers From the Caribbean, 1990, others; editor: (with Martin Kilson) Colonial Africa, 1971, Independent Africa, 1971; editor in chief Cimarron; collaborator: Human Uses of the University: Planning a Curriculum in Urban and Ethnic Affairs at Columbia University, 1970; mem. editorial bds. profl. jours.; contbr. articles to profl. jours. Bernard Van Leer Found. fellow, 1955-56; Fulbright grantee, 1955-59; grantee Urban Center, 1970; CUNY Research Found. fellow, 1985-86. Mem. MLA, PEN, AAUP, African Heritage Studies Assn., African Studies Assn., Fulbright Assn., Am. Friends Service Com., Assn. Black and P.R. Faculty, Black Acad. Arts and Letters, Columbia U. Seminars, Hispanic Inst. U.S., African Am. Heritage Assn., Am. Soc. African Culture, Inst. Caribbean Studies, Inst. Black World. Home: New York N.Y. Died Mar. 28, 1992.

CARTHY, MARGARET, college dean; b. N.Y.C., Oct. 15, 1911; d. Patrick and Ellen (Hosburg) C. A.B., Coll. of New Rochelle, 1933; postgrad., Columbia, 1934-36; M.A., Catholic U. Am., 1948, Ph.D., 1957. Asst. to bus. mgr. Tchrs. Coll., Columbia, 1933-37; asst. registrar Coll. of New Rochelle, 1941-49, dean, 1950-57, pres, 1957-61; staff editor New Cath. Ency., 1962-66; editor Corpus Instrumentorum, Inc., 1966-67; asso. prof., asst. dir. gen. edn. program U. Md., College Park, 1968-71; asst. dean undergrad. studies U. Md., 1971-75; dean Grad. Sch., Coll. of New Rochelle, 1975-79; archivist Ursulines of Eastern Province, 1984-86; lectr. Cath. U. Am., 1963-66. Mem. Am. Cath. Hist. Assn., Phi Kappa Phi. Home: New Rochelle N.Y. Died June 21, 1992. †

CARTOUN, MYER FRED, business executive; b. N.Y.C., Mar. 18, 1898; s. Saul and Ethel (Freeman) C.; m. Harriet Ethyl Sims, Feb. 24, 1921; 1 child, Alan Robert. BS in Ch.E., Poly. Inst. of Bklyn., 1919. Exec. asst. L. Heller and Son, Inc. (later Heller Deltah Co.), 1921-23, sales mgr., 1923-26, pres., 1926-35; exec. v.p., dir. Longines-Wittnauer Watch Co., 1935-45, chmn. bd., treas., CEO, from 1945, pres., until 1962. Served in Engrs. Res. Corps., U.S. Army, WWI. Mem. Poly. Alumni Assn., Phi Delta Pi, Tau Beta Pi, 24K Club, Columbia U. Club. *

CASAGRANDE, LEO, educator, foundation engineer; b. Haidenschaft, Austria, Sept. 17, 1903; came to U.S., 1950; s. Angelo and Anna (Nusssbaum) C.; m. Carla Maria Busch, May 6, 1939; children: Christian E., Dirk R., Raif R., Imogen R., Carl N. Diploma in engring., Tech. U. Vienna, Austria, 1928; D Engring., Tech. U. Vienna, 1933. Design engr., Augsburg, Germany, 1928-30; rsch. assst. in soil mechanics MIT, Cambridge, 1930-32; asst. to Prof. Karl Terzaghi, Tech. U. Vienna, 1932-33; in charge orgn. Soil Mechanics Inst., Tech. U. Berlin, 1933-34; in charge soil mechanics and found. div. Office Ins. Gen. for German Hyws., 1934-41; lectr. applied soil mechanics Tech. U. Braunschwig, Germany, 1940-45; cons. engr. earthworks, Germany, 1941-44; chief engr. Orgn. Todt, Berlin, 1944-45; dir. Hwy. Div., Luebeck, Germany, 1945-46; rsch. engr. bldg. rsch. sta. Brit. Dept. Sci. and Instnl. Rsch., Watford, Eng., 1946-50; cons. engr. founds., 1950-86; rsch. fellow Harvard U., Cambridge, 1953-57, vis. prof. practice found. engring., 1957-88, prof., 1959-72; hon. prof. Tech. U. Braunschweig, 1940. Mem. and fellow ASCE (citation for contbns. 1966), NAE, Boston Soc. Civil Engrs. (prize structural sect. 1952, 66-67), N.Y. Acad. Scis., Mass. Soc. Profl. Engrs., Sigma Xi. Home: Winchester Mass. Died Oct. 25, 1990; buried Mt. Auburn Cemetery, Cambridge, Mass.

CASASSA, CHARLES STEPHEN, university chancellor, clergyman; b. San Francisco, Sept. 23, 1910; s. Charles S. and Margaret G. (Power) C. Student, U. Santa Clara, 1930-32, LHD (hon.), 1973; BS, Gonzaga U., Spokane, Wash., 1934, MA, 1935; STL, Alma Coll., 1939; PhD, U. Toronto & Pontifical Inst. Mediaeval Studies, 1946; DD (hon.), U. Judaism, 1964; STD (hon.), U. So. Calif., 1965; LHD (hon.), Calif. Coll. Medicine, 1965, Loyola Marymount U., 1981; LLD (hon.), St. Mary's Coll., 1967, U. San Francisco, 1969; DHL (hon.), Marymount Coll., 1969. Joined S.J., 1928, ordained priest Roman Cath. Ch., 1938. Asst. prof. philosophy U. Santa Clara, Calif., 1946-49, dean Coll. Arts and Scis., 1948-49; instr. Loyola U. (now Loyola Marymount U.), L.A., 1939-41, pres., 1949-69, chancellor, 1969-89, trustee, 1973-89; mem., v.p. Senate of Priests, Archdiocese of L.A., 1964-75, chmn. social action com., 1970-72, mem. exec. com., 1973-75. Pres. Friendship Day Camp, 1953-89; mem. adv. bd. Jr. League L.A., 1978-81; mem. McCone Commn. (formed after Watts riots), 1965-66; v.p. So. Calif. Interfaith Coalition on Aging, 1974-80; mem. Am. Revolution Bicentennial Com., L.A., 1974-77; mem. West Coast study group Am. Immigration and Citizenship Conf., 1972-80, hon. mem., 1980-89; bd. dirs. Constnl. Rights Found., 1968-72, Knudsen Found., 1971-89, Western div. United Way, 1981-89; trustee U. San Francisco, 1973-81, Gonzaga U., 1977-89. Recipient Disting. Citizenship citation Los Angeles County Conf. on Community Rels., 1954, Judge Harry A. Hollzer Meml. award L.A. Jewish Community Coun., 1955, ann. award NCCJ, 1958, Prism award Pub. Rels. Soc. Am., 1973, Pub. Svc. award Jewish Chautauqua Soc., 1980. Mem. Assn. Ind. Calif. Colls. and Univs. (exec. com. 1955-74), Western Coll. Assn. (pres. 1965-67), Industry-Edn. Coun. Calif. (trustee 1973-89), Rotary (hon.). Republican. Home: Los Angeles Calif. Died July 12, 1989; buried Santa Claus (Calif.) Cemetery.

CASE, JOSEPHINE YOUNG (MRS. EVERETT CASE), poet, writer; b. Lexington, Mass., Feb. 16, 1907; d. Owen D. and Josephine (Edmonds) Young; m. Everett Case, June 27, 1931; children: Josephine, James Herbert III, Samuel, John Philip. BA, Bryn Mawr Coll., 1928; MA, Radcliffe Coll., 1934; LittD (hon.), Elmira Coll., 1946, Skidmore Coll., 1957, St. Lawrence U., 1959; LHD (hon.), Colgate U., 1962. Bd. dirs. RCA, 1961-72; mem. gen. adv. com. Fgn. Assistance Programs, 1965-69. Author: At Midnight on the 31st of March, 1938, Written in Sand, 1945, Freedom's Farm, 1946, This Very Tree, 1969, (with Everett N. Case) Owen D. Young and American Enterprise, 1982; contbr. to anthology American Remembers, 1956. Mem. nat. bd. dirs. Girl Scouts U.S.A., 1947-48; bd. dirs. Bryn Mawr Coll., 1935-55; trustee Skidmore Coll., 1938-72, chmn. bd. trustees, 1960-71; trustee Am. Assembly, 1966-73, Colgate U., 1969-72; bd. dirs. Overseas Devel. Coun., 1969-72, Fund for Advancement Edn., 1965-67, Nat. Merit Scholarship Corp., 1969-72. Mem. Colony Club (N.Y.C.). Democrat. Universalist. Home: Van Hornesville N.Y. Died Jan. 8, 1990; buried Van Hornesville, N.Y.

CASEY, WARREN PETER, playwright, composer, lyricist; b. N.Y.C., Apr. 20, 1935; s. Peter Leonard and Signe (Ginman) C. B.F.A., Syracuse U., 1957. Author: (with Jim Jacobs) Grease, 1971 (book, music, lyrics), Mudgett, 1976 (music and Lyrics), Island of Lost Coeds, 1981 (book, music and lyrics). Mem. Dramatists Guild, ASCAP, Joseph Jefferson Com., Sigma Nu. Home: Chicago Ill. Died Nov. 8, 1988.

CASHMAN, ROBERT J., physicist, educator; b. Wilmington, Ohio, Sept. 27, 1906; s. John and Corina (Smithson) C.; m. Agnes Jones, June 8, 1940; children—Linda Lloyd, John Elliott. A.B., Bethany Coll., 1928, D.Sc., 1953; A.M., Northwestern U., 1930, Ph.D., 1935; student, U. Mich., 1931. With Northwestern U., Evanston, Ill., from 1930, successively instr. physics, asst. prof., asso. prof., 1937-47, prof. physics, from 1947, govt. researcher, 1941-73. Contbr. articles to sci. and profl. jours., books. Recipient certificates of commendation U.S. Navy, Dept. Def., 1947. Fellow Am. Phys. Soc., Am. Optical Soc.; mem. AAUP, Sigma Xi, Kappa Alpha. Club: Mason. Home: Redmond Wash. Died Sept. 27, 1988.

CASNER, ANDREW JAMES, legal educator; b. Chgo., Feb. 7, 1907; s. Andrew James and Margaret Jane (Connell) C.; m. Margaret Snell, June 12, 1926; children—Andrew James, Truman Snell. A.B., U. Ill., 1930, LL.B., 1929; J.S.D., Columbia U., 1941; A.M. (hon.), Harvard U., 1942, LL.D., 1969; S.J.D. (hon.), Suffolk U., 1970. Bar: Ill. 1929, Md. 1934, Mass. 1940. Instr. law U. Ill., 1929-30, prof. law, 1936-38; prof. law U. Md., 1930-35; prof. law Harvard U., from 1938, Austin Wakeman Scott emeritus prof., assoc. dean sch., 1961, acting dean, 1967-68; assoc. Ropes, Gray, Best, Coolidge & Rugg, Boston, 1945-58; chmn. law editorial bd. Little, Brown & Co. Author: (with W.B. Leach) Cases and Text on Property, 1959, supplement, 1982, 3d edit., 1984, supplement, 1989, Estate Planning, 1953, 5th edit., 1985, ann. supplements; editor-in-chief: Am. Law of Property, 1951, supplement, 1976; reporter: Restatement of Property; contbr. to legal periodicals. Served as col. USAAF, 1942-45, ETO. Decorated Legion of Merit, Bronze Star. Mem. Am., Mass., Boston bar assns., Am. Law Inst. (advisor numerous projects from 1930), Order of Coif, Sigma Chi, Phi Delta Phi, Delta Sigma Rho. Republican. Episcopalian. Home: Cambridge Mass. Died Aug. 31, 1990; buried Mt. Auburn Cemetery, Cambridge, Mass.

CASPERSEN, O(LAUS) W(ESTBY), corporate official; b. Risor, Norway, June 15, 1896; s. John A. and Augusta (Bertelsen) C.; m. Freda R., Mar. 3, 1928; children: John W., Finn. Grad., Pace Inst., N.Y.C., 1923. With Beneficial Fin. Co., from 1920, successively auditor, v.p., pres., 1944-62, chmn. bd., 1956-62, chmn. emeritus, from 1962; chmn. bd. Beneficial Corp., from 1962; dir. Bankers Nat. Life Ins. Co., Peoples Bank and Trust Co.; pres., dir. Beneficial Found., Wilmington. Trustee S. Sarasota County Meml. Hosp., Venice, Fla.; bd. corporators Peddie Sch., Hightstown, N.J. Mem. Masons. *

CASSAT, DAVID BERRYHILL, finance company executive, religious assn. ofcl.; b. Vail, Iowa, Jan. 25, 1894; s. David Williams and Lillian (Berryhill) C.; m. Ruth Boleyn Lyon, Apr. 20, 1922; children: George Lyon, Jean Boleyn Christman. AB, Parsons Coll., 1916, LLD, 1955. With Interstate Fin. Corp., Dubuque, Iowa, from 1925; pres. Interstate Fin. Corp., Dubuque, from 1935, chmn., from 1961; chmn. bd., dir. Midwest Security Life Ins. Co., Henke Mfg. Co., Janesville, Iowa, Plantation Devel. Corp., Ft. Lauderdale, Fla., Sunrise Golf Devel. Corp., Ft. Lauderdale; v.p., dir. Presbyn. Life, Inc., Phila.; dir. Am. Trust & Savs. Bank, Dubuque. Mem. City Coun., Sunrise Golf Village; voting del. World Coun. Chs., Evanston Assembly, 1954; treas., mem. exec. com. Nat. Coun. Chs. U.S.A.; past pres. Dubuque Community Chest; chmn. Iowa Study Com. on Higher Edn., 1957-61; chmn. bd. dir. U. Dubuque. Served as 2d lt., inf., U.S. Army, WWI. Mem. Am. Fin. Conf. (pres. 1936-37, past chmn. exec., pub. rels. coms.), Am. Indsl. Bankers Assn. (dir. Washington), Nat. Coun. Presbyn. Men (pres. 1954-55), Rotarian (past pres. Dubuque). Presbyterian. (mem. bd. missions 1947-53). *

CASSIN, WILLIAM BOURKE, lawyer; b. Mexico City, Sept. 11, 1931; s. William Michael and Elouise (Hall) C.; m. Kristi Shipnes, July 15, 1961; children: Clay Brian, Michael Bourke, Macy Armstrong. AB, Princeton U., 1953; JD, U. Tex., 1959. Bar: Tex. 1959. Law clk. Judge Warren L. Jones, Fifth Circuit U.S., 1959-60; assoc. Baker & Botts, Houston, 1960-70; v.p., gen. atty. United Gas Pipe Line Co., Houston, 1970-73, sr. v.p., gen. atty., 1973, group v.p., gen. counsel, dir., mem. exec. com., 1974-76; exec. v.p., gen. counsel, mem. exec. com. United Energy Resources, Inc., Houston, 1976-84, dir., 1976-86; of counsel Mayer, Brown & Platt, Houston, 1985-87; chmn., pres., chief exec. officer D2 Software, Inc., Houston, 1984-89; mem. Pub. Utility Commn., Austin, Tex., 1988-89; pvt. practice, energy cons. Houston, 1989—; with ADR Group, 1991; gen. counsel Houston Grand Opera Assn., 1961-70, mem. governing coun., 1977-88 , also bd. dirs.; adj. prof. U. Houston Law Ctr., 1988. Contbr. articles to profl. jours.; editor-in-chief Tex. Law Rev, 1959. Gen. counsel Harris County Rep. Exec. Com., 1963-64, 67-68; exec. v.p. Tex. Bill Rights Found., 1967-68; mem. exec. com. Assoc. Reps. of Tex., 1976—, Landmark Legal Found., 1985-90, Armand Bayou Nature Ctr., 1986—; bd. dirs. Iowa State Utility Regulatory Conf., 1986-91, Legal Found. Am.; trustee Tex. Mil. Inst., 1984-90, Atwill Meml. Chapel, 1984-90; mem. vestry Christ Ch. Cathedral, 1970-72, 80-82, lay reader. Lt. Airborne Arty. AUS, 1953-57; capt. Res. ret. Fellow Tex. Bar Found. (life), Houston Bar Found.; mem. ABA, Tex. Bar Assn., Houston Bar Assn., Fed. Energy Bar Assn., Am. Arbitration Assn., Am. Judicature Soc., Fed. Bar Assn., Nat. Assn. Regulatory Utility Commrs., Houston Country Club, Bayou Club, Ramada Club, Allegro Club, Garwood Hunting Club, Argyle Club, Army and Navy Club, Northport Point Club, Princeton Club, princeton Terrace Club, Order of Coif, Phi Delta Phi. Episcopalian. Home: Houston Tex. Deceased. †

CASTAÑEDA, HECTOR-NERI, philosopher, educator; b. Zacapa, Guatemala, Dec. 13, 1924; came to U.S., 1956, naturalized, 1963; s. Ezequiel V. and Sara (Calderon) C.; m. Miriam Mendez, Dec. 24, 1946 (div. Feb. 1983); children: Xmucane (Mrs. Gerald Wiebeck), Kicab, Hector Neri, Omar Sigfrido, Quetzil Eugenio; m. Rhina Toruno, Apr. 24, 1987. B.A., U. Minn., 1950, M.A., 1952; Ph.D., 1954; Brit. Council fellow, Wadham Coll., Oxford, 1955-56; H.H.D., Governors State U., 1974, U. Francisco Marroquin, Guatemala, 1984. Instr. U. Minn., 1953-54; vis. asst. prof. Duke U., 1956-57; asst. prof. Wayne State U., 1957-61, assoc. prof., 1961-64, prof., 1964-69, acting chmn. philosophy dept., 1965-66, summer 1968, vis. prof. philosophy, 1970; prof. Ind. U., Bloomington, from 1969, Mahlon Powell prof. philosophy, from 1974, 1st dean Latino affairs, 1978-81; prof. U. San Carlos, Guatemala, 1954-55; vis. lectr. U. Tex., Austin, 1962-63, vis. prof., 1966; adj. vis. prof. U. Cin., 1970; vis. mem. U. Mexico Inst. Philosophy, summer 1970; adj. vis. prof. U. Pitts., 1972; dir. summer seminar Nat. Endowment for Humanities, 1974, 76, 78, 84, 86, year-long seminar, 1980-81; vis. prof. Univ. Venice, Italy, 1985, U. Heidelberg, Fed. Republic Germany, 1987, U. Freiburg, Fed. Republic Germany, fall 1987; Tinbergen prof. Erasmus U., Rotterdam, The Netherlands, fall 1989. Author: Fundamentos de la didáctica del lenguaje, 1948, La Dialectica de la Conciencia de Sí Mismo, 1960, The Structure of Morality, 1974, Thinking and Doing: The Philosophical Foundations of Institutions, 1975, La Teoria de Platon sobre las Formas, las Relaciones y los Particulares en el Fedon, 1976, On Philosophical Method, 1980, Sprache und Erfahrung: Texte zu einer neuen Ontologie, 1982, Thinking, Language and Experience, 1989; editor, contbr.: (with G. Nakhnikian) Morality and the Language of Conduct, 1963, Intentionality, Minds and Perception, 1967, Action, Knowledge and Reality, 1974, (with James E. Tomberlin) Agent, Language and Structure of the World: Essays presented to Hector-Neri Castaneda, with His Replies, 1983, (with James E. Tomberlin) Hector-Neri Castaneda (Profiles of Philosophers No. 6), 1986, (with Klaus Jacobi and

Helmut Pape) Das Denken und die Struktur der Welt: Castanedas epistenische Ontologie, Darstellung und Kritik, 1990; founding editor: Nous, from 1966; mem. editorial bd.: Critica, from 1966, Manuscrito, from 1977, Brain and Cognition, 1980-85, Revista Latinoamericana de Filosofía, from 1984, Theoria II, from 1985, Philosophical Perspectives, from 1986, Cambridge Dictionary of Philosophy, from 1989, Symposium on His Views at the U. Cincinnati, 1978 and the U. Freiburg, 1986; contbr. numerous articles to profl. jours. Recipient First award in humanities Wayne State Recognition Fund, 1961, Pres.'s medal Ind. U., 1990; Guggenheim fellow, 1967-68; NEH fellow, 1975-76, 81-82; Center for Advanced Study in Behavioral Scis. fellow, 1981-82. Fellow Am. Acad. Arts and Scis.; mem. Aristotelian Soc., Am. Philos. Assn. (v.p. Western div. 1978-79, pres. 1979-80), Internat. Assn. for Philosophy of Law and Social Philosophy, Am. Metaphysical Soc., Hegel Vereinigung, Soc. for Exact Philosophy (pres. 1971-74), InstitutoGuatemalteco de Investigaciones Filosoficas (hon.), So. Soc. for Philosophy and Psychology. Home: Bloomington Ind. Died Sept. 7, 1991; ashes to Guatemala City, Guatemala.

CASTELLANI, MARIA, educator; b. Milan, Italy, July 29, 1898; came to U.S., 1946, naturalized, 1953.; d. Paolo and Eloisa (Namias) C. PhD, U. Rome (Italy), 1919; fellow, Bryn Mawr Coll., 1923-24. Actuary Nat. Social Security Fund, Italy, 1921-30, ILO, Geneva, Switzerland, 1931-32; chief actuary ILO, 1933-46; pvt. docent U. Geneva, 1932, lectr. math., 1932-40; pvt. docent U. Rome, 1940, lectr. math., 1940-46; instr. USAAF, Rome, 1945; Lena Haag prof. math. U. Kansas City, 1946-59, chmn. dept., 1950-59; prof. math Fairleigh Dickinson U., from 1959, chmn. dept., 1959-63; v.p. Internat. Fedn. Bus. and Profl. Women, 1932-46, pres., 1930-40. Author: Sulla Frequenza della invalidita, 1925, La Teoria dei compioni statistici, 1946; also numerous articles, translations. Mem. Am. Math. Soc., Am. Math. Assn., Inst. Math. Statistics, Inst. Italiano degli Attuari. *

CASTLE, WILLIAM BOSWORTH, physician, educator; b. Cambridge, Mass., Oct. 21, 1897; s. William Ernest and Clara Sears (Bosworth) C.; m. Louise Muller, July 1, 1933; children—William Rogers, Anne Louise. Grad., Browne and Nichols Sch., Cambridge, 1914; student, Harvard, U., 1914-17; M.D., Harvard, 1921, D.Sc. (hon.), 1964; M.S., Yale, U., 1933; M.D. (hon.), U. Utrecht, Netherlands, 1936; D.Sc. (hon.), U. Chgo., 1952, U. Pa., 1966, Marquette U., 1969, Mt. Sinai Sch. Medicine, 1972; LL.D. (hon.), Jefferson Med. Coll., Phila., 1964; D.H.L. (hon.), Boston Coll., 1966. Intern Mass. Gen. Hosp., Boston, 1921-23; asst. physiology Harvard Sch. Pub. Health, 1923-25; asst. medicine Harvard Med. Sch., 1925-27, alumni asst., 1927-28, asst., 1928-29, instr. to assoc. prof., 1929-37, prof., 1937-57, George Richards Minot prof. medicine, 1957-63, Francis Weld Peabody faculty prof. medicine, 1963-68, emeritus prof., 1968-90; hon. curator Harvard Med. Sch. Archives, 1972-83; Disting. physician VA, 1968-72; sr. physician West Roxbury (Mass.) VA Hosp., 1972-74, cons., 1974-79; asso. physician Thorndike Meml. Lab., Boston City Hosp., 1929-48, dir., 1948-63, jr. vis. physician, 1933-48, asst. vis. physician, 1948-55, vis. physician, 1956-63; dir. II and IV Harvard Med. Services, 1940-63, cons. physician, 1963-73; dir. Rockefeller Found. Commn. for Study Anemia, P.R., 1931-32; sr. cons. hematology Lemuel Shattuck Hosp., 1955-60; cons. medicine Beth Israel Hosp., 1956-63. Recipient William Procter Jr. Internat. award for disting. service in scis. Phila. Coll. Pharmacy and Sci., 1935; Walter Reed medal Am. Soc. Tropical Medicine, 1939; Mead Johnson & Co. award for research on vitamin B complex, 1950; Gordon Wilson medal Am. Clin. and Climatol. Assn., 1961; John M. Russell award Markle Scholars, 1964; ann. hon. lecture award Albany Med. Coll., 1964; Disting. Lecture award Coll. Medicine U. Ky., 1965; Oscar B. Hunter Meml. award Am. Therapeutic Soc., 1965; Joseph Goldberger award AMA and Nutrition Found., 1966; Key to City San Juan, P.R., 1967; Ann. Am. Coll. Nutrition award for disting. service in field nutrition and metabolism, 1970; Meritorious Service award VA, 1972; Sheen award AMA, 1973; Disting. Chmn. award Assn. Profs. Medicine, 1978; named perpetual student Med. Coll. St. Bartholomew's Hosp., London, 1970; Am. Coll. Nutrition Fellow, 1973. Master ACP (John Phillips prize 1932, Disting. Tchr. award 1978); fellow emeritus Am. Acad. Arts and Scis.; hon. fellow Royal Coll. Physicians London, Royal Coll. Physicians and Surgeons Can., Royal Australasian Coll. Physicians, Royal Coll. Physicians Edinburgh; mem. Am. Acad. Tropical Medicine, AAAS, AMA, Am. Philos. Soc., Am. Soc. Clin. Investigation (pres. 1940-41, from emeritus 1943), Am. Soc. Exptl. Pathology, Am. Soc. Tropical Medicine and Hygiene, Am. Fedn. Clin. Research, Assn. Am. Physicians (George W. Kober medal 1962, pres. 1959-60, emeritus from 1960), Boston Soc. Biologists, Mass. Med. Soc., Nat. Acad. Scis. (emeritus from 1976); corr. mem. Société Internationale Europeene Hematologie, l'Academie royale de Medecine de Belgique; hon. mem. Am. Soc. Hematology, Am. Clin. and Climatological Assn., Societas Medicorum Finlandae, Brit. Med. Assn., Royal Soc. Medicine London; mem. Phi Beta Kappa, Alpha Omega Alpha. Home: Brookline Mass. Died Aug. 9, 1990; buried Walnut Hills Cemetery, Brookline, Mass.

CASTRO, ALBERT, medical educator, scientist; b. San Salvador, El Salvador, Nov. 15, 1933; came to U.S., 1952; s. Alberto Lemus and Maria Emma (de la Cotera) C.; m. Jeris Adelle Goldsmith, Oct. 19, 1956; children: Stewart, Sandra, Alberto, Juan, Richard. B.S., U. Houston, 1958; postgrad., Baylor U., 1958; Ph.D., U. El Salvador, 1962; M.D., Dominican Republic, 1982. Asst. prof. microbiology and biochemistry U. El Salvador, San Salvador, 1958-60, assoc. prof. Dental and Med. schs., 1960-63, bd. dirs. dental sch., 1961-66, mem. research and scholarship com., 1964-65, dir. rsearch in basic sci. Dental Sch., 1964-68, co-dir. grad. research, 1965-66, prof., head dept. basic sci., 1965-68; asst. prof. pediatrics, co-dir. pediatrics metabolic lab. U. Oreg., Portland, 1969-73; dir. endocrinol. dept. and research unit United Med. Lab., Portland, 1970-73; sr. scientist Papanicolauou Cancer Research Inst., Miami, Fla., 1973-75; assoc. prof. pathology and medicine U. Miami, 1973-77, dir. Hormone Research Lab., 1974-82, coordinator Inter Am. Tech. Transfer and Tng. Program, 1976-88, prof. pathology, medicine and microbiology, 1977-88. Contbr. over 200 publs. to nat. and internat. sci. jours. NIH postdoctoral fellow, 1966-70; Northwest Pediatric Research fellow, 1971; U. Oreg. Med. Sch. grantee, 1966-69. Fellow Am. Inst. Chemists, Royal Soc. Tropical Medicine and Hygiene; mem. Acad. Clin. Lab. Physicians and Scientists, N.Y. Acad. Scis., Am. Chem. Assn., Am. Assn. Microbiology, AAAS, Nat. Acad. Clin. Biochemists (charter), Tooth and Bone Research Soc., Acad. Sci. El Salvador. Roman Catholic. Home: Miami Fla. Died May 1988. †

CATE, WIRT ARMISTEAD, author; b. Hopkinsville, Ky., Nov. 16, 1900; s. James Henry and Mary Lou (Armistead) C. AB, Emory U., 1923, AM (fellow), 1925; postgrad. (Edward Austin fellow), Harvard, 1926-27, 28-29. Instr. Baylor Sch., Chattanooga, 1923-24, Ga. Sch. Tech., 1925-26, 27-28; lectr. English Emory U., summers 1926, 28; Julius Rosenwald fellow Am. history, 1937-38; fellow Colonial Williamsburg, Inc., 1940-43; now engaged in biog., hist. research, writing. Author: Lucius Q.C. Lamar, Secession and Reunion, 1935, 3d edit., 1978; (with Margaret R. Cate) The Armistead Family and Collaterals, 1971; History of Richmond Virginia: 1607-1861; editor: Two Soldiers, The Campaign Diaries of Thomas J. Key, C.S.A. and Robert J. Campbell, U.S.A, 1938; Contbr. to: hist., philol. and coll. jours. Ency. Brit. Mem. Modern Lang. Assn. Am., So. Hist. Assn., Phi Beta Kappa, Sigma Upsilon, Sigma Chi. Democrat. Methodist. Home: Nashville Tenn. Died June 24, 1991; buried Hopkinsville, Ky.

CATHERWOOD, CUMMINS, mineral company executive, philanthropist; b. Haverford, Pa., Jan. 30, 1910; s. Daniel B.C. and Jessica (Davis) C.; m. Ellengowen Hood, Feb. 3, 1942 (dec. Aug. 1970); children—Virginia Tucker, Cummins; m. Dorothy Smith Littler, Apr. 17, 1971. Prep. edn., St. Georges Sch., Newport, R.I.; student, U. Pa., 1931-33; L.H.D., Pa. Mil. Coll. Assoc. various banking firms in Phila.; ptnr. Roberts, Fleitas & Catherwood, Ins.; dir. Fidelity-Phila. Trust Co., 1933-39; co-owner Evening Pub. Ledger, Phila., v.p., purchasing agt. Fox Munitions Corp., 1940-52; ltd. ptnr. Jenks, Kirkland & Grubbs, Phila.; Hallowell, Sulzberger, Jenks, Kirkland & Co., Phila., Oil & Gas Co., Madison, 1946-57; dir. Bryn Mawr Trust Co.; pres., dir. Mineral Prodn. Corp., Bryn Mawr; chmn. Madeira Oil Corp., Bryn Mawr; dir. Mid-Am. Minerals, Inc., Oklahoma City; dir., mem. exec. com. Vision, Inc. Trustee Catherwood Estates; pres. Catherwood Found.; trustee exec. com. Pa. Mill. Coll.; trustee Acad. Music, Phila.; bd. govs. Phila. Mus. Art; bd. dirs. Phila. Orch. Assn., Saratoga Performing Arts Ctr. Served to capt. USAAF, 1942-45. Mem. Res. Officers Assn., Am. Ordnance Assn. Home: Bryn Mawr Pa. Died Feb. 3, 1990; buried Ch. of the Redeemer, Bryn Mawr, Pa.

CAUDILL, HARRY MONROE, history educator, lawyer, author, social activist, conservationist; b. Whitesburg, Ky., May 3, 1922; s. Cro Carr and Martha Victoria (Blair) C.; m. Anne Robertson Frye, Dec. 15, 1946; children: James Kenneth, Diana Ellen, Harry Frye. LLB, U. Ky., 1948, LLD (hon.), 1971; LLD (hon.), Tusculum Coll., 1968, Berea Coll., 1971; LHD (hon.), Transylvania U., 1989. Bar: Ky. 1948. Pvt. practice, Whitesburg, 1948-76; prof. history U. Ky., Lexington, 1977-86. Author: Night Comess to Cumberlands, 1963, Appalachia, also 9 others; contbr. numerous articles to mags. Mem. Ky. Ho. of Reps., 1954-60. With AUS, 1942-44, MTO. Decorated Purple Heart, Bronze Star. Mem. ABA, Ky. Bar Assn., Letcher County Bar Assn., ACLU, Alta. Fish and Game Asss. (hon.), Am. Soil Conservation Soc., Ky. Hist. Soc., Ky. Nature Conservancy, Sierra Club, Garden Club Ky., Masons. Home: Whitesburg Ky. Died Nov. 29, 1990; buried Battle Grove Cemetery, Cynthiana, Ky.

CAULFIELD, JOAN, actress; b. Orange, N.J., June 1, 1922; d. Henry R. Jr. and Beatrice Young C.; m. Frank Ross, Apr. 29, 1950 div. Apr. 1959 . Grad., Columbia U., 1943. Mem. Morningside Players, Columbia U., 1939-43; mem. cast Beat the Band, 1942; star Kiss and Tell, 1943, Paramount Pictures, 1944; star CBS TV weekly show My Favorite Husband, Hollywood, 1953-57; star Sally, NBC, 1957-58. Motion pictures include Susie Slagles, Blue Skies, Welcome Stranger, Dear Wife, Dear Ruth. Mem. SAG, Actors Equity, AFTRA. Home: Beverly Hills Calif. Died June 18, 1991.

CAVALLON, GIORGIO, artist; b. Italy, Mar. 3, 1904; came to U.S., 1920, naturalized, 1929; s. Augusto and Agnese (Scarsi) C.; m. Linda Lindberg, Mar. 25, 1954. Student, Nat. Acad. Design, 1926-30; pupil of Charles Hawthorne,, Hans Hofmann. Artist in resident U. N.C., Greensboro, 1964; vis. critic art Yale, 1967; painting workshop Columbia, summer 1969. One-man exhbns. include Bottege D'Art, Vicenza, Italy, 1932, Egan Gallery, N.Y.C., 1946-48, 51, 54, Stable Gallery, N.Y.C., 1957-59, Kootz Gallery, N.Y.C., 1961, 63, 65, A.M. Sachs Gallery, N.Y.C., 1969, 71, 74, retrospective exhgn. Neuberger Mus., SUNY, Purchase, 1977, prin. group shows incude Whitney Mus. ann., 1959, 61, 65, Mus. Modern Art, 1963, 69, Pa. Acad. Fine Arts, 1966, Yale U., 1967, Am. Geometric Abstraction/1930s, Labriskie Gallery-Am. Fedn. Arts, 1972; represented in permanent collections Mus. Modern Art, N.Y.C., U. N.C. at Greensboro, Whitney Mus., Albright Art Gallery, Guggenheim Mus., Union Carbide Corp., Continental Grain Corp., Tishman Collection, Michener Collection U. Tex. at Austin, Chase Manhattan Bank, Singer Mfg. Co., Geigy Chem. Corp., NYU, Univ. Art Mus., Berkeley, Calif., Marine Midland Trust Co., Buffalo, Avco Delta Corp., Cleve., Am. Republic Ins. Co., Des Moines, Rose Mus. of Brandeis U., Lavon Corp., N.Y.C. Guggenheim fellow, 1966-67; recipient award in painting Nat. Inst. Arts and Letters, 1970, New Eng. Art Paintings Sculpture Invitation Show, 1971. Home: New York N.Y. Died Dec. 22, 1989.

CAZAYOUX, LAWRENCE MARIUS, grocery chain executive; b. New Roads, La., May 28, 1897; s. Clair M. and Olivia Hortence (Vignes) C.; m. Mary Murphy, Sept. 25, 1953. Grad., Poydras Acad., New Roads, 1913. Various positions from clk. to v.p. N.E. div. Great Atlantic & Pacific Tea Co., 1913-48; pres. N.E. div. Great Atlantic & Pacific Tea Co., Boston, from 1948; also v.p. and dir. parent co. Mem. Boston C. of C., Beacon Soc., Mass. Hist. Soc., Clubs: Algonquin (dir.), Brae Burn (Boston). *

CECERE, GAETANO, sculptor; b. N.Y.C., Nov. 26, 1894; s. Ralph and Catherine (La Rocca) C.; m. Ada Rasario, 1924. Student, NAD, Beaux Arts Inst. Design, N.Y.C.; fellow, Am. Acad. in Rome, 1920-23. Sculpture dept. Beaux Arts Inst. Design; mem. faculty Mary Washington Coll., Fredericksburg, Va. One man show Mary Washington Coll., 1963; prin. works include medals, war memls., pediment groups, portrait monuments, etc. Served in AEF, 1916-18. Recipient numerous awards including $1,000 Lincoln Meml. prize, Milw., 1933, Am. Acad. in Rome Collaborative medal, hon. mention Art Inst. Chgo., 1927, Medal of Honor, Knickerbocker Artists, Sculpture award, Allied Artist Am., Audubon Artists, Inc., Forst Sculpture Prize, Audubon Artists, 1957, sculpture prize Knickerbocker Artists, 1963. Mem. Nat. Sculpture Soc., N.Y. Archtl. League. *

CERRONE, JEAN BAPTISTE, ballet company administrator; b. Montecarlo, Monaco, Mar. 8, 1912; came to U.S., 1938; s. Jean and Marie (Noe) C.; m. Ruth Jaros, Dec. 24, 1945 (div. 1965); children—Jean Charles, Laurent M.; m. Yvette Guicharnaud, Dec. 14, 1970. Student, pub. schs., Monaco. Mgr. Ballet Russe de Monte Carlo, N.Y., and Monaco, 1936-54; asst. dir. Am. Ballet Theatre, N.Y.C., 1954-59; gen. mgr. Ballet U.S.A., N.Y.C., 1960-61, Harkness Ballet, N.Y.C., 1961-73; mgr. Music Box Theater, N.Y.C., 1975-80, Md. Ballet, Balt., 1975-76; gen. mgr. Houston Ballet, 1980-87; mng. dir. Harid Conservatory Dance and Music, Boca Raton, Fla., 1987-91. Decorated Chevalier Order Arts and Letters (France); recipient Dance Mag. awards, 1983. Home: Deerfield Beach Fla. Died Apr. 24, 1991.

CESARI, LAMBERTO, mathematics educator; b. Bologna, Italy, Sept. 23, 1910; came to U.S., 1949; s. Cesare and Amelia (Giannizzeri) C.; m. Isotta Hornauer, Apr. 2, 1939. Ph.D. in Math, U. Pisa, Italy, 1933. Asst. Nat. Research Council Italy, 1935-39; asso. prof. U. Pisa, 1939-42; asso. prof. U. Bologna, 1942-47, prof. math., 1947-48; staff Inst. Advanced Study, Princeton, N.J., 1948; prof. math. U. Calif. at Berkeley, 1949, U. Wis., 1950, Purdue U., 1950-60, U. Mich., Ann Arbor, from 1960; R. L. Wilder prof. math. U. Mich., from 1976; Corr. mem. Accademie delle Scienze di Bologna, Modena, Milano, Accademia Nazionale Lincei, Rome. Author: Surface Area, 1955, Asymptotic Properties, 1959, Optimization, 1983; also articles on differential equations, calculus of variations, real analysis. Asymptotic Properties; Editorial bd.: Applicable Math. Jour, from 1970, Jour. Differential Equations, from 1973, Rendiconti Circolo Matematico di Palermo, from 1960. Mem. Math. Assn. Am., Am. Math. Soc. Home: Ann Arbor Mich. Died Mar. 12, 1990; buried Forest Hill Cemetery, Ann Arbor, Mich.

CHAFEE, FRANCIS H(ASSELTINE), allergist; b. Providence, Dec. 12, 1903; s. Zechariah and Mary Dexter (Sharpe) C.; Ph.B., Brown U., 1927; M.D., Harvard U., 1931; m. Jane Spofford, June 26, 1929; children: Richard S., Mary Deborah, Nathaniel. Intern, Presbyn. Hosp., N.Y.C., 1931-33; pvt. practice medicine, Providence, 1934-75; vis. physician R.I. Hosp., 1939-65, dir. Allergy Clinic, 1938-65, cons. staff, 1966-92; mem. div. univ. health Brown U., 1935-61, vis. lectr. medicine, 1973-92; cons. allergy Butler Health Center, Miriam Hosp. (all Providence). Served from capt. to maj., U.S. Army, 1942-46; ETO. Fellow ACP, Am. Acad. Allergy, (v.p. 1968), Am. Coll. Allergists (award of merit 1977), AMA; mem. Am. Fedn. Clin. Research, Providence Med. Assn. (pres. 1955), R.I. Med. Soc., Providence Athenaeun, R.I. Hist. Soc., New Eng. (pres. 1961), R.I. (pres. 1970-72) socs. allergy. Clubs: Providence Art, University (Man of Yr. award 1975), Hope. Deceased. Home: Providence R.I. †

CHAFFEE, EUGENE BERNARD, educator; b. Aurora, Nebr., Mar. 10, 1905; s. Elmer Spencer and Grace (Lyman) C.; m. Lois Barton, June 26, 1937; children: Lois Ann, Eugene Barton. BA, Occidental Coll., 1927; MA, U. Calif., 1931, postgrad., 1932; postgrad., George Washington U., 1933. Tchr., music supr. pub. schs. Meridian, Idaho, 1927; supt., prin. grade and high schs. Ustick, Idaho, 1928-30; tchr. Boise Jr. Coll., 1932-36, pres., 1936-39; pres. Boise Jr. Coll. Dist., 1939-64; pres. Boise Coll., 1964-67, chancellor, 1967-70, pres. emeritus, 1970-92; Past pres., bd. dirs. Am. Assn. Jr. Colls.; pres. N.W. Assn. Jrs. Colls., 1941-42, 46-47; mem. exec. com. Pacific N.W. Conf. on Higher Edn.; mem. exec. com. Nat. Com. Regional Accrediting Agys. U.S.; chmn. Liberal Arts Coll. of Idaho; mem. Idaho Manpower Devel. and Tng. and Area Redevel. Adv. Com.; 2d v.p. and chmn. of higher commn. N.W. Assn. of Secondary and Higher Schs., 1958-64; mem. Ednl. Adv. Coun., Nat. Assn. Mfrs., Nat. Commn. Accrediting (exec. com.). Author: An Idea Grows (A History of Boise College), 1970; contbr. articles on history to profl. jours. Dir. YMCA, United Fund, Boise; exec. com. ARC. Lt. comrd. USNR, WWII; mem. Enemy Alien Hearing Bd., Idaho, 1941-42. Mem. Fgn. Rels., Boise, Am. Legion, Knife and Fork Club, Exch. Club (Boise). Presbyterian. Home: Boise Idaho Died Feb. 5, 1992; interred Day Creek Cemetery, Boise, Idaho.

CHAFFEE, PAUL STANLEY, veterinarian, zoo administrator; b. Port Huron, Mich., Jan. 23, 1928; s. Walter Henry and Leland Elizabeth (Green) C.; children: David P., Daniel P., Richard P., Denise J. AS, Port Huron Jr. Coll., 1949; BS, DVM with honors, Mich. State U., 1953. Asst. veterinarian Peigh Animal Hosp., 1953-54; owner, veterinarian McKinley Pet Hosp., Fresno, Calif., 1955-65; veterinarian Fresno Zoo, from 1960, zoo dir., from 1965. Contbr. numerous articles to profl. publs. V.p. Am. Assn. Zool. Parks and Aquariums. Cpl. U.S. Army, 1946-48. Mem. Am. Assn. Zoo Veterinarians (pres. 1972), Zoo Act (pres.), Am. Assn. Zool. Parks and Aquariums (pres. 1980-81, past chmn. ethics com., current bd. dirs.), Fresno Zool. Soc., Calif. Acad. Vet. Medicine, Phi Zeta. Republican. Lodge: Rotary (pres. Fresno club 1978-79). Home: Fresno Calif. Died Oct. 20, 1990. †

CHAIKIN, SOL CHICK, trade union official; b. N.Y.C., Jan. 9, 1918; s. Sam and Beckie (Schechtman) C.; m. Rosalind Bryon, Aug. 31, 1940; children—Robert Evan, Eric Bryon, David Reed, Karen. Grad., City Coll. N.Y., 1938; LL.B., Bklyn. Law Sch., 1940; L.H.D., Rutgers U., 1980, Brandeis U., 1980. With Internat. Ladies Garment Workers Union, 1940-86, asst. dir. N.E. dept., 1959-65, v.p., 1965-73, gen. sec.-treas., 1973-77, pres., 1975-86; v.p., mem. exec. council AFL-CIO, from 1975; AFL-CIO del. to Egypt, Chile, Argentina, Brazil, Portugal, Spain, rep. at labor summits in London, 1977, Tokyo, 1979; mem. bd. Trilateral Commn., from 1977; Com. Present-Danger-Atlantic coun., del. ILO, 1976; nat. chmn. Trade Union Coun. for Histadrut, Nat. Urban Coalition, 1977, 80; planning com. dir. Sen. Jacob K. Javits Convention Ctr., chmn. ctr.'s Operating Corp., mid 1980's, acting pres., 1989-90, pres., 1990-91; U.S. del. Commn. for Security and Coop. in Europe, 1977, 80. Author: A Labor Viewpoint: Another Opinion by Sol Chick Chaikin, 1980, also articles for profl. jours. Trustee L.I. Jewish-Hillside Med. Center, from 1967, Fashion Inst. Tech., 1975; trustee Brandeis U., from 1980, chmn. overseers Florence Heller Grad. Sch. Advanced Studies in Social Welfare at Brandeis. Served with USAAF, 1943-46, CBI. Recipient Three Founders Award Am. Vets. Com., 1976; Parsons Award Parsons Sch. Design, 1977; Labor Human Rights award Jewish Labor Com., 1977. Democrat. Home: Great Neck N.Y. Died Apr. 1, 1991; interred Mount Ararat, Farmingdale, N.Y.

CHALKER, WILLIAM ROGERS, chemical company executive; b. Atlanta, Feb. 17, 1920; s. Elliott Lamar and Mildred Edna (Crum) C.; m. Joan Windsor King, Feb. 12, 1955; children—William Rogers, Scott King. A.B., U. S.C., 1942, B.S., 1943; diploma engring., U.S. Naval Acad. Postgrad. Sch., 1945; M.S., Mass. Inst. Tech., 1948, Profl. Engr., 1950. Registered profl. engr., Del. Observer U.S. Weather Bur., Petersburg, W.Va., 1946; research asst. Mass. Inst. Tech., 1946-50; cons. meteorologist A.H. Glenn & Assos., New Orleans, 1950-51; with E.I. duPont de Nemours & Co., Inc., 1951-85; atmospheric dispersion research E.I. duPont de Nemours & Co., Inc. (Savannah River Plant), 1951-53, engr., sr. cons., 1965-72, prin. cons., 1972-77, prin. div. cons., 1977-85; ret., 1985; pres. W.R. Chalker and Assocs., 1985-92; Mem. Del. Air Pollution Authority, 1957-66; mem. tech. adv. com. Del. Water and Air Resources Commn., 1967-70; mem. air quality com. Mfg. Chemists Assn., 1960-85, vice chmn., 1974-76, chmn., 1976-78; chmn. air control com. Chem. Industry Council N.J., 1964-66; mem. petrochem. industry adv. com. U.S. EPA, 1972-74. Contbr. articles to profl. jours. Served to lt. USNR, 1943-46, ETO. Mem. Am., Royal meteorol. socs., Air Pollution Control Assn. (chmn. mid-Atlantic states sect. 1964-65, nat. bd. 1966-69), Am. Acad. Environ. Engrs. (diplomate 1976), Sigma Xi, Omicron Delta Kappa, Sigma Nu, Kappa Sigma Kappa. Republican. Episcopalian. Home: Ocean City N.J. Died Apr. 9, 1992. †

CHALMERS, BRUCE, metallurgy educator; b. London, Oct. 15, 1907; came to U.S., 1953, naturalized, 1959; s. Stephen Drummond and Clara (Rosenhain) C.; m. Ema Arnouts, July 1, 1938; children: Stephen P., Carol A., Jane H., Alison F., Heather C. BSc, U. London, 1929, PhD, 1931, DSc, 1941; AM (hon.), Harvard U., 1953. Lectr. U. London, 1932-38; physicist Tin Rsch. Inst., London, 1938-44; head metall. div. Royal Aircraft Establishment, 1944-46, Atomic Energy Rsch. Establishment, Harwell, Eng., 1946-48; prof. phys. metallurgy U. Toronto, Ont., Can., 1948-53; Gordon McKay prof. metallurgy Harvard U., Cambridge, Mass., 1953-78, master John Winthrop House, 1964-74. Author: Physical Examination of Metal, Vol. 1, 1939, Vol. 2 (with A.G. Quarrell), 1941, Structure and Mechanical Properties of Metals, 1951, Physical Metallurgy, 1959, Energy, 1963, Principles of Solidification, 1964, (with J.G. Holland, K.A. Jackson and R.B. Williamson) Introduction to Crystallography, 1965; editor: Progress in Materials Science, 1949-79, Acta Metallurgica, Scripta Metallurgica. Recipient Klamer medal Franklin Inst., 1965, hon. award Hindu U. Benares, India, 1973, 1st recipient Bruce Chalmers award Minerals, Metals and Materials Soc. AIME, 1990. Fellow Inst. Physics, Inst. Metallurgists, Am. Acad. Arts and Sci.; mem. AIME, Inst. Metals (London), Iron and Steel Inst. (London), Am. Soc. Metals (Sauveur award 1960), French Soc. Metallurgy (hon.), Sigma Xi. Home: Cambridge Mass. Died May 25, 1990.

CHAMBERLIN, GERALD WILKINSON, business counsellor; b. Detroit, Mar. 6, 1897; s. George Edwin and Adeline (Cosford) C.; m. Myrtle Fruehauf, Apr. 23, 1920; children: Joy Chamberlin Burns, Donald Fruehauf. Student pub. schs. Bus. counsellor Detroit, from 1939; pres. Wire Assemblies Corp., Detroit, 1946-55, South Whitley Industries, 1952-55, Chamberlin Products Corp., 1955-60; gen. ptnr. Arbor Tool Co., from 1943; pres. Electronic Devices, Inc., from 1959; dir. Fruehauf Trailer Co., Michigan Bank, Troy Nat. Bank (Mich.), Clubs: Detroit Athletic, Grosse Pointe (Mich.), Yacht. *

CHAMBERS, DAVID SMITH, statistician educator; b. Clarksville, Tex., Jan. 26, 1917; s. Clifton A. and Eva Ellen (Smith) C.; m. Mary Othella Parsons, Feb. 22, 1941. B.A. in Math, U. Tex., 1939, M.B.A. in Stats., 1947; postgrad., U. Mich. Instr. aero. engring. U. Tex., 1941-42, applied math. and astronomy, 1942-46, bus. stats., 1946-47; asst. prof. stats. U. Tenn., 1947-48, asso. prof., 1948-58, prof., 1958-82; quality control cons. AID, Dept. State, from 1962; pres. Indsl. Controls, Inc. Author papers in field. Recipient E.L. Grant award for edn. in quality control, 1970. Fellow AAAS; Fellow Am. Soc. Quality Control (mem. from 1947, bd. dirs. 1953-56 and from 65, exec. sec. 1959-61, chmn. exec. bd. Inst. Edn. and Tng. 1960-63, chmn. exam. com. inst. Tenn. sect., from 1958, chmn. textile and needle trades div., 1967-68, chmn. chem. div., 1969-70, pres., 1971-72, chmn. bd. dirs., 1972-73, dir.-at-large, 1975-77, chmn. awards bd., 1976-78), mem. ASTM (com. E-11 1969-82), Am. Statis. Assn., Engrs. Joint Council (dir. 1971-75, mem. awards com. 1977-79), Internat. Acad. Quality, Phi Beta Kappa, Phi Kappa Phi, Phi Eta Sigma, Beta Gamma Sigma. Home: Knoxville Tenn. Died Sept. 19, 1989.

CHAMBERS, MAURICE RIPLEY, shoe manufacturing company executive; b. St. Louis, July 14, 1916; s. M.R. and Ruth E. (Brooks) C.; m. Mae Mildred Bartlett, June 30, 1937; 1 child, Cynthia Ruth. Salesman Tweedie Footwear Corp., Jefferson City, Mo., 1931-39; buyer, mdse. mgr. Montgomery Ward, N.Y.C., 1939-49; mdse. mgr. Internat. Shoe Co., St. Louis, 1956-62, pres., 1962-66; chmn. bd., chief exec. officer Interco, Inc., St. Louis, 1966-76; bd. dirs. Merc. Bancorp., Julius Marlow Holdings Ltd., Gen. Am. Life Ins. Co., Dillards Dept. Stores, Laclede Gas Co., Emerson Electric Co., Gen. Steel Industries, Inc., Anheuser-Busch, Inc., Nat. Steel Corp., Seven-Up Corp., Southwestern Bell Telephone Co. Vice chmn. Barnes Hosp., St. Louis; trustee Washington U., St. Louis, Ranken Tech. Inst. Home: Saint Louis Mo. Died Oct. 14, 1990; buried Riverview Cemetery, Jefferson City, Mo.

CHAMP, FRANK PERCIVAL, banker; b. Salt Lake City, June 4, 1896; s. George Herbert and Alla Dora (Cochran) C.; m. Frances Elizabeth Winton, Dec. 21, 1921; children: George Herbert, Mary Knox, Frederick Winton. Student, Utah State Agrl. Coll., 1911, St. Stephens Sch., 1912-15, Harvard U., 1915-17; LLD, Utah State Agrl. Coll., 1954. Pres. Cache Valley Banking Co., 1922-56; pres. Utah Mortgage Loan Corp., Champ Investment Co.; bd. dirs. Cache Valley Devel. Co., Pro-Utah, Inc.; v.p., chmn. adv. com. Cache Valley br. Walker Bank and Trust Co.; bd. dirs. Title Ins. Co., Boise, Idaho, Walker Bank and Trust Co., Salt Lake City, Investors Ctrl. Mgmt. Corp., N.Y.C.; Salt Lake Dist. Bd. U.S. RFC, 1933-40. Author articles on pub. lands and mortgage banking. State chmn. U.S. Treas. Dept. Savs. Bond Orgn.; pres. Cache Valley Coun., 1940-43; nat. coun., regional exec. com. Boy Scouts Am., from 1943, Silver Beaver award, 1943, Silver Antelope award, 1947; active Utah State Hwy. Patrol Civil Svc. Commn., from 1950; former trustee, pres. bd. trustees Utah State Agrl. Coll.; exec. com. Utah Found., Utah Legislative Conf. Mem. Mortgage Bankers Assn. Am. (gov., past pres.), Am. Bankers Assn., Utah Bankers Assn. (past pres.), Am. Forestry Assn. (past bd. dirs.), Nat. Probation and and Parole Assn. (past co-chmn. Utah), Soc. of Royal Rosarians, Newcomen Soc., Scabbard and Blade, Alpha Kappa Psi (hon. life), Alpha Delta Epsilon, Rotary (hon. past pres. Logan), Logan Golf Club, Flat Rock Club, Harvard Club (N.Y.), Alta (Salt Lake City), Weber (Ogden, Utah). *

CHANCELLOR, SIR CHRISTOPHER, industrialist; b. Cobham, Eng., Mar. 29, 1904; s. Lt. Col. Sir John and Elsie (Thompson) C.; m. Sylvia Paget, 1926; 2 sons, 2 daus. MA (1st in class in history), Trinity Coll., Cambridge. Gen. mgr. Reuters, Ltd., 1944-59; chmn. The Bowater Paper Corp., Ltd., London, 1960-89. Decorated Companion of Order of St. Michael and St. George. Mem. St. James Club, Garrick. Home: Somerset England Died Sept. 9, 1989.

CHANDLER, ALBERT BENJAMIN, lawyer, governor; b. Corydon, Ky., July 14, 1898; s. Joseph and Callie (Sanders) C.; m. Mildred Watkins, Nov. 12, 1925; children: Marcella (Mrs. Thomas D. Miller), Mildred (Mrs. James J. Lewis), Albert Benjamin, Joseph Daniel. A.B., Transylvania Coll., 1921, LL.D., 1936; student, Harvard, 1921-24; LL.B., U. Ky., 1924, LL.D., 1937. Football coach Centre Coll., Danville, Ky., 1922-24; began law practice Versailles, Ky., 1924; apptd. master commr. Circuit Ct., Woodford County, 1928; elected mem. Ky. Senate, from 22d Dist., 1929; lt. gov. Ky., 1931-35; gov., 1935-39, 55-59, resigned, 1939; apptd. U.S. senator (to fill vacancy caused by death of Marvell Mills Logan); elected, 1940, to fill remainder term, to Jan. 1943, re-elected for 6 year term, 1942; high commr. of baseball, 1945-51; pres. Internat. Baseball Congress, Wichita; commr. Continental Profl. Football League, from 1965, Global Internat. Baseball League; v.p., dir. First Flight Golf Co., Chattanooga; dir. Coastal States Life Ins. Co. Ga.; Receiver for Inter-So. Life Ins. Co., Louisville, 1932; an organizer Ky. Home Life. Ins. Co., Louisville, 1932. Mem. athletic com. U. Ky., from 1966, life trustee, 1981; chmn. Woodford County Democratic Exec. Com.; Dem. nat. committeeman for Ky.; trustee Ty Cobb Found.; chmn. bd. trustees and fund raising com. Transylvania Coll. Served with U.S. Army, 1918; capt. J.A.G. Dept. Res. (ret.). Named Kentuckian of Year, Ky. Press Assn. and Ky. Broadcasters Assn., Man of the Century, Ky. Broadcasters Assn., Man of Yr., Rural Electric Cooperative, 1986, Centennial Alumnus of Century, U. Ky., 1987; named to Ky. Sports Hall of Fame, 1957; recipient Bishop's medal Episcopal Ch., 1959; Cross of Mil. service U.D.C., 1959; Jefferson Davis medal, 1975; U. Ky. Med. Center named in his honor, 1959; honored at spl. lecture Transylvania U., 1980; named to Nat. Baseball Hall of Fame, 1982; recipient award NCCJ, 1983, Ben Gurion award Jewish Community of Lexington, 1986, DAR medal, 1987. Mem. Am. Legion, 40 and 8, Pi Kappa Alpha. Episcopalian. Clubs: Mason (32 deg., K.T., Shriner), Ky. Mountain (hon.), Lexington Country, Idle Hour Country (Lexington). Home: Versailles Ky. Died June 16, 1991; interred Pisgah Cemetery, Woodford County, Ky.

CHANDLER, MARGARET KUEFFNER, business educator; b. St. Paul, Sept. 30, 1922; d. Otto Carl and Marie (Schaedlich) Kueffner; m. Louis Chandler, Apr. 8, 1943. B.A. in Polit. Sci, U. Chgo., 1942, M.A. in Econs, 1944, Ph.D. in Sociology, 1948. Mem. faculty U. Ill. at Urbana, 1947-62, assoc. prof. sociology and indsl. relations, 1954-62; assoc. prof. sociology U. Ill. at Chgo., 1962-63, prof., 1963-65; prof. bus. Columbia U., 1965-91, prof., faculty advisor Police Mgmt. Inst., Grad. Sch. Bus., 1989-91, mem. pres.'s arbitration panel, 1977-91; Fulbright research prof. econs. Keio U., Tokyo, Japan, 1963-64; lectr. Rutgers U., 1958, McGill U., 1963, Emory U., 1966, Columbia, 1962; labor arbitrator nat. labor panel Am. Arbitration Assn., from 1965, mem. collective bargaining methods study group., from 1964; assoc. mem. Center Advanced Study, U. Ill. Grad. Coll., 1964-65; asso. dir. Program Mng. Complex

Techs., from 1967; mem. women's salary rev. bd., also Affirmative Action Commn. Columbia U., from 1976; dir. program for Study Collective Bargaining in Higher Edn., from 1975; mem. N.Y. Gov.'s Panel for Dispute Resolution, from 1977; arbitrator, fact-finder N.J. Pub. Employment Relations Commn., from 1975; adminstrv. bd. Bur. Applied Social Research, from 1975; mem. spl. panel interest arbitrators, State of N.J., from 1978; mem. nat. adv. com. Nat. Center Study of Collective Bargaining in Higher Edn., from 1978; mem. state adv. council Inst. Mgmt. and Labor Relations, Rutgers U., from 1982; mem. Nat. Task Force on Teaching of Alt. Dispute Resolution Methods in Law and Bus. Schs., from 1985. Author: Labor Management Relations in Illini City, vols. 1 and 2, 1953, 54, Management Rights and Union Interests, 1964 (McKinsey Found. book award 1965), Managing Large Systems, 1971 (McKinsey Found. book award 1972); editor-in-chief: Columbia Jour. World Business, 1972—; contbr. articles, monograph to profl. lit. Postdoctoral fellow statistics Yale, 1953-54; Ford Found. Faculty research fellow social sci. and bus. U. Chgo., 1960-61; Ford Found. grantee, 1967-91; Fulbright prof. Central U. Planning and Statistics, Warsaw, Poland, 1974; recipient Recognition award Ill. Nurses Assn., 1960. Fellow Am. Sociol. Assn., Soc. Applied Anthropology; mem. Am. Statis. Assn., Am. Econ. Assn., Indsl. Relations Research Assn. (editor research vol. 1960). Home: Piscataway N.J. Died Mar. 11, 1991; buried Mt. Lebanon Cemetery, Iselin, N.J.

CHANDLER, REUBEN CARL, packaging company executive; b. Lawrenceville, Ga., Oct. 25, 1917; s. Reuben C. and Florine (Doster) C.; m. Sarah Megee, Oct. 27, 1940; children: Carla Evalynee, Robert Megee, David Pratt, Craig D. Grad., Marist Coll., Atlanta, 1935; student, Ga. Inst. Tech., 1935-37; A.B., Emory U., 1941; student, Atlanta Law Sch., 1946-48; D.Sc. in Bus. Adminstrn. (hon.), Detroit Inst. Tech., 1960. Sales rep. Gen. Motors Acceptance Corp., Atlanta, 1941-42; asst. dir. tng. Southeastern Shipbldg. Corp., Savannah, Ga., 1942-43; prodn. mgr. Mead-Atlanta Paper Co., 1946-49; salesman Union Camp Corp. (formerly Union Bag & Paper Corp.), 1949-50; dist. sales mgr. Union Camp Corp. (formerly Union Bag & Camp Paper Corp.), Trenton, N.J., 1950-51; Eastern div. sales mgr. Union Camp Corp. (formerly Union Bag & Camp Paper Corp.), 1951-52; dir. corrugated container and bd. sales Union Camp Corp. (formerly Union Bag & Camp Paper Corp.), N.Y.C., 1952; v.p. sales Union Camp Corp. (formerly Union Bag & Camp Paper Corp.), 1952-55; chmn., chief exec. officer, chmn. exec., finance coms. Standard Packaging Co., N.Y.C., 1955-66; chmn. bd. Crowell-Collier Pub. Co., N.Y.C., 1957; ltd. partner Elliott & Co. (investment bankers), N.Y.C., 1960-62; chmn bd. J.D. Jewell, Inc., Gainesville, Ga., 1962-72, pres., from 1969; also chmn. exec. com., dir.; pres. Identiseal Systems, Atlanta, from 1972, Perkins-Goodwin Mgmt. Services Co., N.Y.C., from 1973, Am. Resources Corp., 1973-75; chmn. bd. Lanier Mortgage Corp., Gainesville, Ga., 1973-75; pres., chief exec. officer Duncan & Copeland, Inc., 1976-79, Va. Packaging Supply Co., McLean, 1979-84; dir. Am. Agy. Life Ins. Co., Atlanta, Berry Steel Corp., Edison, N.J., Jones & Presnell, Charlotte, N.C. Trustee Detroit Inst. Tech., from 1960, Christ Ch. Sch., Short Hills, N.J., from 1963, Brenau Coll., from 1968, Emory U., Atlanta, from 1972, Ga. Found. for Ind. Colls., from 1969; bd. dirs. Am. Soc. Indsl. Security Found. Served as lt. (s.g.) USNR, 1943-46; Lt. col. aide de camp Gov.'s staff Ga. 1951-52, 70-72. Recipient Man of Year award Am. Jewish Com., 1964; Horatio Alger award, 1965; Achievement award Delta Tau Delta, 1966; Disting. Alumni award Marist Coll., 1985. Mem. Savannah Jr. C. of C. (v.p. 1942-43), Gainesville C. of C., Navy League (life), Def. Orientation Conf. Assn., Am. Pulp and Paper Mill Supts. Assn. (life), Emory U. Alumni Assn. (pres. 1965, Honor award 1968), Ga. Tech. Nat. Alumni Assn. (nat. adv. bd. from 1964), Ga. Poultry Fedn. (mem. round table from 1970), Tenn. Wesleyan Coll. Parents Assn., U.S. Navy Supply Corps Assn. (trustee from 1972), Delta Tau Delta (life), Alpha Delta Sigma, Omicron Delta Kappa. Episcopalian. Clubs: Atlanta, Athletic (Atlanta); N.Y. Area Emory (pres. 1964), University, Economic (N.Y.C.). Home: Dunwoody Ga. Died Jan. 28, 1989; buried Arlington Nat. Cemetery.

CHANDLER, STEPHEN S., judge; b. Blount County, Tenn., Sept. 13, 1899; s. Stephen Sanders and Evelyn Amelia (Johnson) C.; m. Margaret Patterson, 1922 (dec.); children—Frances Patterson (Mrs. Sim K. Sims), Stephen Sanders III, Frank Patterson. Student, U. Tenn., 1917-18; J.D., U. Kans., 1922. Pvt. law practice in Oklahoma City, 1922-43; U.S. dist. judge for Fed. Dist. Ct., Western Okla., from 1943, chief judge, 1956-69, sr. judge, from 1975; Mem. law faculty Oklahoma City U., 1957-60. Recipient Hatton Sumners award, 1961; named to Okla. Hall of Fame, 1960. Mem. various bar and other legal assns., Sigma Alpha Epsilon, Phi Delta Phi, Order of Coif. Democrat. Methodist. Clubs: Mason (Shriner), Oklahoma City Golf, Lotus, Petroleum, Rotary (pres. 1940-41); Nat. Press (Washington). Home: Oklahoma City Okla. Died Apr. 27, 1989.

CHANG, MIN CHUEH, experimental biologist, educator; b. Taiyuan, Shansi, China, Oct. 10, 1908; came to U.S., 1945, naturalized, 1952; s. Gin Shu and Shih (Laing) C.; m. Isabelle C. Chin, May 28, 1948; children—Francis Hugh, Claudia, Pamela. B.Sc., Tsing Hua U., Peking, 1933; Ph.D., Cambridge (Eng.) U., 1941, Sc.D., 1969; D.Sc. h.c., Worcester Poly. Inst., 1982, U. Nottingham (Eng.), 1982; DSc (hon.), Worcester Found. Exptl. Biol., 1974, Worcester State Coll., 1990. Researcher Cambridge U. Sch. Agr., 1941-45; research asso. Worcester Found., Shrewsbury, Mass., 1945-50; sr. and prin. scientist Worcester Found., Shewsbury, Mass., 1954, 70-82, prin. scientist emeritus, 1982; mem. faculty Boston U., from 1951, prof. reproductive biology, from 1961; hon. prof. Shanghai Inst. Physiology (China), 1979. Author over 350 sci. studies. Recipient Ortho award Am. Soc. Study Sterility, 1950, Lasker Found. award, 1954, Research Career award USPHS, 1962, Hartman award Am. Soc. Study Reprodn., 1970, Pioneer award Internat. Embryo Transfer Soc., 1983, Italian Agrl. Acad. medal, 1978, Barren medal, 1983, Axel Munthe award, 1985, Ortho award 5th Internat. Congress of In Vitro Fertilization and Embryo Transfer, 1987, 1st Sci. award Am. Planned Parenthood Fedn., 1987. Fellow Third World Acad. Scis. (assoc.); mem. NAS, AAAS (Francis Amory prize 1975), Am. Phys. Soc., Am. Anat. Assn., Brit. Soc. Study Fertility (Marshall medal 1971), Am. Fertility Soc. (Ortho medal 1961). Home: Shrewsbury Mass. Died June 5, 1991; buried Mt. View Cemetary, Shrewsbury, Mass.

CHANT, SPERRIN NOAH FULTON, dean; b. Canada, Oct. 31, 1896; s. Sperrin and Olivia (Berryman) C.; m. Nellie I. Cooper, July 23, 1923; children: RObert, Donald John. BA, U. Toronto, 1922, MA, 1924; student, U. Chgo., summers 1926, 27; LLD, U. B.C., 1961. Prof. psychology U. Toronto, 1923-40; dir. gen. rehab. for Can., 1944-45; dean Faculty Arts and Scis., head dept. psychology U. B.C., 1945-65; chmn. Royal Commn. Edn. for B.C., Acad. Bd. for Higher Edn. for B.C.; pres. Vancouver Inst. Author: Mental Training, 1934, Interpretative Psychology, 1958; also articles. Can. Army, 1917-18; group capt. RCAF 1940-44. Decorated officer Order Brit. Empire. Mem. Can. Psychol. Assn. (past pres.), Can. Assn. U. Adv. Svcs. (past pres.). *

CHAPIN, FREDERIC LINCOLN, foreign service officer; b. N.Y.C., July 13, 1929; s. Selden and Mary Paul (Noyes) C.; m. Cornelia Bonner Clarke, Aug. 2, 1952; children—John Clarke Noyes, Anne Cornelia, Grace Selden, Edith Clarke. Grad., St. Paul's Sch., Concord, N.H., 1946; student, Stanford U., 1948-49; B.A., Harvard U., 1950. Econ. analyst ECA, Paris, 1950-52; joined U.S. Fgn. Service, 1952; assigned Vienna, Austria, 1952-55; assigned State Dept., 1956-59, Managua, Nicaragua, 1959-61; charge d'affaires Am. embassy Fort Lamy, Chad, 1961; assigned State Dept., 1962-63; spl. asst. to under-sec. for polit. affairs, 1963-65; exec. sec. AID, 1965-66; Fgn. Service examiner, 1966-67, Fgn. Service insp., 1967; country dir. for Bolivia and Chile, 1968-70; dep. asst. sec. for mgmt. for Latin Am., 1970-72; consul gen. São Paulo, Brazil, 1972-78; U.S. ambassador to Ethiopia, 1978-80; dep. asst. sec. Dept. Def., 1980-81; chargé d'affaires Am. Embassy, San Salvador, El Salvador, 1981; ambassador to Guatemala, 1981-84; sr. insp. Dept. State, 1984-88. Mem. editorial bd. Fgn. Service Jour., 1962-66. Recipient Dept. Def. D.S.M., 1981; Grand Cross Jose Mathias Delgado (El Salvador). Mem. Am. Fgn. Svc. Protective Assn. (sec.-treas. 1970-71), Phi Beta Kappa. Home: Washington D.C. Died Sept. 8, 1989.

CHAPMAN, GRAHAM, performer, writer; b. Leicester, Eng., Jan. 8, 1941; s. Walter and Edith (Towers) C.; 1 child. M.A., Emmanuel Coll., Cambridge U., 1962; M.B., B.Chir., St. Bartholomews Hosp. Med. Sch., 1966. Dir. Python (Monty) Pictures Ltd., Python Prodns., Ltd., Kay-Gee-Bee Music, Ltd., Sea Goat Prodns. Ltd., Oversea Goats, Ltd.; free-lance writer film and TV scripts, N.Y.C., L.A., 1983-89. Appeared in revue Cambridge Circus, Broadway, 1964, Ed Sullivan Show; TV series include At Last the 1948 Show, 1967, Monty Python's Flying Circus, 1969-74; films include Monty Python and the Holy Grail, 1978, Monty Pythons Life of Brian, 1980, Monty Python Live at the Hollywood Bowl, 1981, The Secret Policeman's Other Ball, 1982, Monty Python's The Meaning of Life, 1983. Author: Monty Python and the Holy Grail, 1978, Monty Python's Life of Brian, 1980; writer, star (film) Yellowbeard, 1983; author: A Liar's Autobiography, 1981. Fellow World Wildlife Trust. Mem. Gen. Med. Council, Brit. Actors Equity, AFTRA. Club: St. James. Home: London Eng. Died Oct. 4, 1989.

CHAPMAN, HOMER DWIGHT, soil scientist; b. Darlington, Wis., Oct. 4, 1898; s. Faithful William and Nettie (Merriam) C.; m. Daisy E. Ernst, Mar. 10, 1925. BS, U. Wis., 1923, MS, 1925, PhD, 1927. Asst. soils U. Wis., 1925-27; asst. chemist citrus exptl. sta. U. Calif., 1927, assoc. chemist, 1938, chemist, prof. soils and plant nutrition, 1944, chmn. divsn. soils and plant nutrition, 1938-61, acting dir. citrus exptl. sta., 1951-52; specialist in soils Internat. Coop. Adminstrn. program in Chile, 1956-57; spl. study citrus industry Mediterranean countries, 1952, in S. Africa and Japan, 1957; faculty rsch. lectr. U. Cal. Riverside, 1952; del. 13th Internat. Hort. Congress, London, 1952, 2d Pan-Am. Congress on Agronomy, 1954; vis. prof. Indian Agricultural Rsch. Inst., New Delhi, 1961-62, U. Alexandria, Egypt, 1964; hon. mem. faculty of agronomy, Cath. U., Chile. Author: (with Parker F. Pratte) Methods of Analysis for Soils, Plants and Waters; (manual) Citrus Leaf and Soil Analysis; also tech. papers; editor: Diagnostic Criteria for Determining Nutrient Status of Plants; rsch. on citrus problems in Australia, India, Egypt. Fellow AAAS, Am. Soc. Agronomy; mem. Internat. Soc. Soil Sci., Am. Chem. Soc., Soil Sci. Soc. Am., Am. Soc. Hort. Sci., Western Soc. Soil Sci. (pres. 1938-39), Sigma Xi, Phi Lambda Upsilon, Gamma Alpha, Phi Sigma, Alpha Gamma Rho, Kiwanis (pres. 1955), Present Day, Riverside, Calif. (pres. 1951-52). Presbyterian. *

CHAPMAN, MARY ILSLEY, author; b. Chattanooga, Sept. 10, 1895; d. John Henry and Mary (Hamilton) Ilsley; m. John Staton Higham Chapman, Feb. 26, 1917. Privately educated. Missionary, lectr., engring. tech., novelist, from 1928. Co-author (with John Stanton Higham Chapman) Trail of the Cheery Cows, 1958, Doubloons, 1959, The Helpful Treasure, 1959, Devorguilla: A 13th Century Chronicle, and numerous books including adventure books for young people, biographies, hist. novels, chronicles medieval times. Mem. PEN, Mediaeval Acad. of Am. Democrat. Episcopalian. *

CHAPPELL, WARREN, artist, writer; b. Richmond, Va., July 9, 1904; s. Samuel Michael and Mary Lillian (Hardie) C.; m. Lydia Anne Hatfield, Aug. 28, 1928. BA, U. Richmond, 1926, DFA (hon.), 1968; student, Art Students League, N.Y.C., 1926-30, Offenbacher Werkstatt, Ger., 1931-32. Tchr. Art Students League, 1932-35, mem. bd. control, 1927-30; instr. Colorado Springs Fine Arts Center, 1935-36; artist-in-residence U. Va., 1979-91. Typographic and decorative designer for mags., 1926-35, book designer and illustrator, from 1936; prin. works for publishing cos. as Alfred A. Knopf, Random House, Harper & Row, Doubleday, Little, Brown include editions of: Adventures of Don Quixote, 1939, The Temptation of St. Anthony, 1943, A History of Tom Jones, 1943, Shakespeare: Tragedies, 1944, The Complete Novels of Jane Austen, 1950, Moby Dick, 1976, Gulliver's Travels, 1977, The Complete Adventures of Tom Sawyer and Huckleberry Finn, 1979, The Magic Flute, 1962, Bottom's Dream, 1969, They Say Stories, 1960, Moby Dick, 1976, All The King's Men, 1981, Miracle at Philadelphia, 1986; designer of typefaces: Lydian, 1938, Trajanus, 1940; his own books include: The Anatomy of Lettering, 1935, A Short History of the Printed Word, 1970, The Living Alphabet, 1975. Recipient Goudy award Rochester Inst. Tech., N.Y., 1970. Mem. Master Drawings Assn., Lawn Soc. of U. Va., Chilmark Assos. (Mass.), Phi Beta Kappa. Home: Charlottesville Va. Died Mar. 26, 1991; buried U. Va.

CHAPPELL, WILLIAM VENROE, JR., congressman; b. Kendrick, Fla., Feb. 3, 1922; s. William Venroe and Laura (Kemp) C.; m. Jeane Chappell; children: Judith Jane Chappell Gadd, Deborah Kay Chappell Bond, William Venroe III, Christopher Clyde. B.A., U. Fla., 1947, LL.B., 1949, J.D., 1967. Bar: Fla. 1949. Mem. Sturgis and Chappell (and predecessors), Ocala, Fla., from 1949; prosecuting atty. Marion County, Fla., 1950-54; mem. Fla. Ho. of Reps., 1955-65, 67-68, speaker, 1961-63; mem. 91st-100th congresses from 4th Dist. Fla., 1969-89. Aviator USN, World War II; capt. USNR, ret. 1983. Named Most Valuable Mem. Fla. Ho. Reps., 1967, Most Effective in Debate, 1967, Minute Man of the Yr. Res. Officers Assn., 1987, Harry S. Truman award N.G. Assn., 1987. Mem. ABA, Fla. Bar Assn., Marion County Bar Assn., Inter-Am. Bar Assn., Am. Trial Lawyers Assn., Acad. Fla. Trial Lawyers, Am. Legion. Democrat. Methodist. Lodges: Masons; Shriners; Lions; Elks. Home: Washington D.C. Died Mar. 30, 1989.

CHAPPELLET, CYRIL, aerospace manufacturing company executive; b. Oakland, Calif., Jan. 10, 1906; s. Felix and Mabel C. Dimon C.; m. Sybil B. Kane, 1930. Student, Stanford U. Sr. adviser, dir. Lockheed Corp., Burbank, Calif. Hon. trustee Pomona Coll. Home: Pebble Beach Calif. Died Sept. 18, 1991.

CHARNLEY, MITCHELL VAUGHN, journalism educator; b. Goshen, Ind., Apr. 9, 1898; s. William Herbert and Louise Carmien C.; m. Margery A. Lindsay, Sept. 12, 1922 div. Feb. 1936 ; 1 child, Donn; m. Jean Clifford, July 24, 1937; children: Deborah, Blair. BA, Williams Coll., 1919; MA in Journalism, U. Wash., 1921. Reporter Honolulu Star-Bull., 1921; news editor Walla Walla Bull., 1922; reporter Detroit News, 1922-23; editorial asst. to asst. mng. editor The American Boy, Detroit, 1923-26, acting mng. editor, 1926; from asst. prof. journalism to assoc. prof. journalism Iowa State Coll., 1930-31; from asst. prof. journalism to assoc. prof. journalism U. Minn., 1934-40, prof., 1940-66, William J. Murphy prof. journalism, 1966-68, prof. emeritus, 1968-91; acting chmn. dept. journalism U. Minn., 1937-38, asst. dean Arts Coll., 197-77, assoc. dir. univ. rels., 1969, spl. asst. to dean Arts Coll., 1970-77, asst. to pres., 1974, Fulbright lectr. journalism and mass communications U. Florence, Italy, 1952-53; editorial cons. Mpls Tribune, 1969-72; editorial cons. to newspapers and mental health enterprises, 1968-70. Author: Jean Lafitte, 1934, News by Radio, 1948, Reporting, 1959, 4th edit., 1978; editor, compiler of various works; mng. editor Journalism Quar., 1935-45, acting editor,

1937-38; contbg. editor The Quill, 1928-50; contbr. articles, fiction, verse and book revs. to mags. Mem. Coun. Radio-TV Journalism, 1944-58, chmn., 1948-49. Recipient Tchr. of Yr. award Sigma Detla Chi, 1968. Mem. Radio-TV News Dirs. Assn. Disting. Achievement award 1963 , ACLU, Assn. for Edn. in Journalism pres. 1959 , Nat. dir. , Minn. pres. 1959-60 assns. mental health, Phi Gamma Delta, Sigma Delta Chi nat. historian 1924-26, alumni sec. 1933-35, v.p. 1935-37, chmn. rsch. com. 1937-42 . Home: Minneapolis Minn. Died Feb. 16, 1991.

CHARPENTIER, ARTHUR ALDRICH, law librarian; b. Waterbury, Conn., Aug. 13, 1919; s. Donat Arthur and Mary Belle (Aldrich) C.; m. Phyllis Eugenia Smith, May 29, 1943; children: Meredith J., Susan A., Peter A., Nancy D. BS, Springfield (Mass.) Coll., 1941; LLB, Boston U., 1948. Bar: Mass. 1948. Libr. Boston U. Sch. Law, 1948-50; asst. libr. Assn. Bar City N.Y., 1950-57, libr., 1957-67; law libr. Yale U. Law Sch., New Haven, 1967-70, assoc. dean, libr., 1970-81; mem. libr. svcs. com. Am. Bar Found.; mem. libr. adv. com. Am. Arbitration Assn. Capt. F.A., AUS, 1941-46. Mem. ABA, Am. Assn. Law Librs. (exec. bd. 1962-65, pres. 1965-66), Internat. Assn. Law Librs. (v.p. 1968-71), Law Libr. Assn. Greater N.Y. (pres. 1957-58), Kappa Delta Pi. Congregationalist. Home: Mount Desert Maine Died Mar. 19, 1989; buried Somesville, Mt. Desert Island, Maine.

CHASE, GILBERT, writer, educator; b. Havana, Cuba, Sept. 4, 1906; s. Gilbert P. and Edelmira (Culmell) C.; m. Kathleen Barentzen, Dec. 27, 1929; children—Paul, Peter John. Student, Columbia U., 1926; B.A., U. N.C., 1950; D.Litt. (hon.), U. Miami, 1955; pvt. study music with, Max Wald, Paris. Music critic Continental Daily Mail, Paris, 1929-35; asso. editor Internat. Cyclopedia of Music and Musicians, N.Y.C., 1936-38; editor G. Schirmer, Inc., N.Y.C., 1939-40; Latin Am. specialist music div. Library of Congress, 1940-43; music supr. NBC U. of the Air, 1943-48; mgr. edn. dept. RCA Victor, Camden, N.J., 1948-49; cultural attache Am. embassy, Lima, Peru, 1951-53, Buenos Aires, 1953-55; dir. Sch. Music U. Okla., 1955-56; acting dean U. Okla. (Coll. Fine Arts), 1956-57; cultural attaché Am. Embassy, Brussels, 1958-60; prof. music and Latin Am. studies Tulane U., 1960-66; dir. Inter-Am. Inst. for Musical Research, 1961-69; sr. research fellow Inst. Studies in Am. Music, Bklyn. Coll., City U. N.Y., 1972-73; Ziegele vis. prof. music State U. N.Y. at Buffalo, 1973-74; vis. prof. comparative studies, history and music U. Tex. at Austin, 1975-79; Paris corr. Mus. America, N.Y.C., 1930-35, Mus. Times, London, 1931-35; adviser, reviewer Book of Month Club, 1936-49; lectr. history Am. music Columbia, 1946-48; Mem. adv. com. on music U.S. Dept. of State, 1943-45; mus. cons. Pan Am. Union, 1943-45; cons. for music loan libraries in Latin Am. Library of Congress, 1944-46; mem. U.S. Adv. Com. on Cultural Info., 1957-58; mem. bicentennial com. Nat. Music Council, from 1974. Author: Cities and Souls: Poems of Spain, 1929, The Music of Spain, 1941, 2d rev. edit., 1959, A Guide to Latin American Music, 1945, 2d rev. edit., 1962, America's Music: From the Pilgrims to the Present, 1955, 2d rev. edit., 1966, 3d rev. edit., 1983, The American Composer Speaks, 1966; Transl.: A Concise History of Latin American Culture, 1966; Author: Contemporary Art in Latin America, 1970; Editor: Music in Radio Broadcasting, 1946; music editor: Handbook of Latin Am. Studies, 1963-67, Inter-Am. Mag, 1940-43; editor: yearbook for Inter-Am. Mus. Research, 1964-76; contbg. editor: Yearbook for Arts in Soc, 1965-75. Hon. prof. faculty philosophy, letters U. Buenos Aires. Mem. Am. Musicol. Soc., Soc. for Ethnomusicology (1st v.p. 1963-65), Inter-Am Music Coun. (pres. 1960-63), Latin Am. Studies Assn. (constituent mem.), Société Française de Musicologie, Instituto Español de Musicología, Music Library Assn., Am. Studies Assn. Home: Chapel Hill N.C. Died Feb. 22, 1992; cremated.

CHASIN, WERNER DAVID, otolaryngologist; b. Free City Danzig, Feb. 29, 1932; came to U.S., 1939; s. Bernard and Joan (Kornfeld) C.; m. Judith Gilden, Jan. 27, 1963; children: Noah, Jonah, Ezra. AB cum laude, Harvard U., 1954; MD, Tufts U., 1958. Diplomate Am. Bd. Otolaryngology. Intern Mt. Sinai Hosp., N.Y.C., 1958-59; resident in otolaryngology Mass. Eye and Ear Infirmary, Boston, 1959-62; chief otolaryngology Beth Israel Hosp., Boston, 1964-68; otolaryngologist-in-chief New Eng. Med. Ctr., Boston, 1968-92; chmn., prof. otolaryngology Tufts U. Sch. Medicine, Boston, 1968-92. Fellow ACS; mem. AMA, Am. Acad. Otolaryngology, New Eng. Otolaryngol. Soc. (pres. 1976-77), Alpha Omega Alpha. Home: Newton Mass. Died Aug. 2, 1992. †

CHASTAIN, ELIJAH DENTON, JR., economics educator; b. Pickens, S.C., Sept. 26, 1925; s. Elijah D. and Ida (Hendricks) C.; m. Dr. Marian B. Faulkner, Aug. 25, 1956; children—Gwen Caroline, Philip William. B.S., Clemson U., 1947; M.S., Cornell U., 1948; postgrad., Va. Poly. Inst., 1950, Duke, 1961, U. Chgo., 1964; Ph.D., Purdue U., 1956. Assoc. prof. Va. Poly. Inst., 1949-56; research asst. Purdue U., 1954-56; assoc. prof. econs. Auburn U., 1956-63, prof., from 1963, dir. grad. studies Sch. of Bus., 1967-70; chmn. Gen. Faculty and Univ. Senate, 1970-71; econ. and managerial cons. Editor: Jour. Ala. Acad. Sci, 1962-65; Contbr. articles to profl. and semi-popular jours. Served to capt. C.E. U.S. Army, 1944-46, 47, 50-52. Mem. Am., So. econs. assns., Am. Agrl. Econ. Assn., Ala. Acad. Sci. (v.p.), Sigma Xi, Omicron Delta Epsilon, Delta Sigma Pi, Gamma Sigma Delta, Phi Delta Kappa, Omicron Delta Kappa. Home: Auburn Ala. Died Mar. 24, 1989; buried Fairview Cemetery, Whitehall, Pa.

CHASTEL, ANDRÉ ADRIEN, art historian, educator; b. Paris, Nov. 15, 1912; s. Adrien Marie and Marie Isabelle (Morin) C. Student Ecole Normale Supé rieure, 1933; Agregation des lettres, 1937, Doctorat è s lettres, 1951; m. Paule-Marie Grand de Saint-Avit, 1942; children: Louis, Arnaud (dec.), Laurent. Prof., Lycée Rollin, Henry IV, Carnot; asst. Inst. Art and Archaeology, Paris, 1945-48; dir. d'Etudes, Ecole pratique des Haute Etudes (IV sect.), Paris, 1951-81; prof. Sorbonne, 1955-70; prof. College de France, Paris, 1970-84; art critic newspaper Le Monde, Paris, from 1950; v.p. Internat. Com. Art History, 1969-85; pres. French Com. Art History, 1970-77; Andrew Mellon lectr. Nat. Gallery, Washington, 1977. Served with French Army, 1939-40. Decorated Croix de Guerre, Légion d'Honneur, Palmes Acadé miques, Com. Repubblica Italiana. Mem. L'Institut Acadé mie des Inscriptions et Belles-Lettres, AAAS, Racing Club of France. Author: L'art italien, 1947, 83, English edit., 1963; Art et Humanisme à Florence, 1949, 82; Marsile Ficin et l'Art, 1954, 75; La Renaissance Méridionale, le Grand Atelier, 1965; La crise de la Renaissance, le mythe de la Renaissance, 1967, Fables, Formes Figures, 2 vols., 1978, Italian edit., 1988; L'Image dans le Miroir, 1980; The Sack of Rome, 1983, French edit.; Chronique de la peinture italienne, 1983; Musca Depicta, 1984; Cardinal Louis d'Aragon, 1986, Italian edit., 1987; L'illustre incomprise (Mona Lisa), 1988; La grotesque, 1988; editor Revue de l'Art, 1969-88. Died July 18, 1990; buried Paris. Home: Paris France

CHATMAN, ABRAHAM DAVID, labor union official; b. Russia, Feb. 16, 1896; came to U.S., 1914, naturalized, 1926.; s. David and Norene (Brightman) C.; m. Gertrude Kadish, Aug. 19, 1926; children: Norine Doris (Mrs. Bernard Selby), Arthur Sheldon. Tailor Hickey Freeman Co., 1916-24; mgr. Rochester joint bd. Amalgamated Clothing Workers Am., from 1924, v.p., from 1926, dir. Western N.Y., from 1933; also exec. com. of gen. exec. bd.; bd. dirs. Amalgamated Bank N.Y., Amalgamated Ins. Fund. Active N.Y. Apprenticeship Coun., pub. policy adv. com. Advt. Coun. Rochester, Inc., Rochester Regional Hosp. Planning Coun.; bd. dirs. Sidney Hillman Found., mem. fin. com.; bd. dirs. Community Chest, Jewish Home for Aged. With SSS, 1940-46. *

CHATMAN, PETER See MEMPHIS SLIM

CHENAULT, LAWRENCE ROYCE, economics educator; b. Hico, Tex., July 3, 1897; s. Stephen Allen an dBettie Hand C.; m. Minetta Littleton, Dec. 31, 1928; children: Laurel, Jeannie. BBA, U. Tex., 1920; AM, Wayne U., 1933; PhD, Columbia U., 1938. CPA, Tex. Staff acct. Ernst & Ernst, 1920-21; auditor U.S. Treasury Dept., 1922-26; office mgr., ptnr. Simpson & Chenault, 1926-28; investment acct. Socony Vacuum Co., 1929-32; asst. prof. econs. U. P.R., 1935-36; assoc. prof. Hunter Coll., 1936-54, prof. econs., 1955-67, chmn. dept., 1956-67; vis. prof. Coll. William and Mary, 1945; lectr. Columbia Sch. Bus., 1949-50. Author: The Puerto Rican Migrant in New York, 1938; contbr. articles to tech. jours. Mem. Am. Econs. Assn., Met. Econs. Assn. N.Y. pres. 1953-54 , Population Assn. Am., AAUP. Unitarian. Home: State College Pa. Died Apr. 16, 1990.

CHERBERG, JOHN ANDREW, former lieutenant governor; b. Pensacola, Fla., Oct. 17, 1910; s. Fortunato and Annie (R) C.; m. Elizabeth Anne Walker, Aug. 17, 1935; children—Kay Elizabeth (Mrs. Ray Cohrs), Barbara Jean (Mrs. Dean Tonkin), James Walker. B.A., U. Wash., 1933. Cert. tchr., Wash. High sch. tchr., athletic coach, 1934-46; football coach U. Wash., 1946-56; lt. gov. Wash., 1957-89; Chmn. Nat. Conf. Lt. Govs., 1968-69. Mem. NEA, AFTRA, Nat. Acad. TV Arts and Scis., Wash. State Assn. Broadcasters (hon. life), Sigma Nu. Club: Variety. Home: Seattle Wash. Deceased. †

CHERNIACK, NATHAN, transportation economist; b. Odessa, Russia, Dec. 12, 1897; came to U.S., 1906, naturalized, 1915.; s. Abraham (rabbi) and Jenny (Levine) C.; m. Claire I. Miller, July 31, 1931; children: Phyllis Joyce (dec.), Armand Earl. BSc, MIT, 1922; MBA, NYU, 1934. Staff Port of N.Y. Authority, from 1923; traffic cons. N.Y.C. Tunnel Authority, Queens Midtown & Battery, 1936-37; spl. cons. Balt. arterial routes N.Y.C. Tunnel Authority, 1944; spl. cons. Louisville Area Devel. Assn. on Union Motor Truck Terminal, 1946, Union Motor Truck Terminal, Atlanta, 1947; with Ammann & Whitney, 1952; spl. lectr. Yale, Rutgers U., Columbia; mem. adv. com. econ. rsch. Yale Bur. for Street Traffic Rsch. Author: Use of Motor Trucks in Transportation within Terminal Markets, 1933, Methods of Estimating Vehicular Traffic Volume with the Aid of Traffic Patterns, 1936, Highway Transport Systems for Metropolitan Districts of the Future, 1940, Measuring the Potential Traffic of a Proposed Vehicular Crossing, 1940, A Statement of the Parking Problem, 1946, others. Commd. aide Coast and Geodetic Survey, WWI. Recipient D.S.M., Commrs. of Port of N.Y. Authority, 1954, Howard S. Cullman Disting. Svc. medal, 1960, Theodore M. Matson Meml. award, 1963. Fellow Am. Soc. C.E.; mem. Soc. Terminal Engrs. (pres. 1940-41), Inst. Traffic Engrs. (pres. 1952), Am. Bar Assn. (adv. to nat. com. on urban transp.), Am. Statis. Assn. Republican. Jewish. *

CHERRY, HERMAN, poet, artist; b. Atlantic City, N.Y., Apr. 10, 1909; s. Israel and Rose (Rothkovitz) C.; m. Regina S. Schneider, Nov. 29, 1976. Student, Otis Art Inst., Los Angeles, 1927-28, Art Students League, N.Y.C., 1930, Students Art League, Los Angeles, 1928, 30-31. Prof. painting U. Calif.-Berkeley, 1959-65; prof. U. Minn., Mpls., 1969, U. Ky., 1966-67, U. Miss., 1957, New Paltz Coll., 1970. Author: Poems of Pain and Other Matters, 1976; contbr. numerous articles and essays to art jours.; exhibited one-man shows, Stanley Rose Galleries, Hollywood, Calif., 1942, Gastine Gallery, Los Angeles, 1943, Weyhe Gallery, N.Y.C., 1947, 48, Ganso Gallery, N.Y.C., 1951, Stable Gallery, N.Y.C., 1955, Poindexter Gallery, N.Y.C., 1959, 61, Tanager Gallery, N.Y.C., 1956, Oakland Art Mus., Calif., 1961, Pasadena Art Mus., 1961, U. Miss., 1958, So. Ill. U., 1959, 59, U. Ky., 1967, U. Oreg., 1969, Benson Gallery, Bridgehampton, N.Y., 1972, Kingsborough Community Coll., 1972, Nobe Gallery, N.Y.C., 1979, il Punto Blu Gallery, Southampton, N.Y., 1984, Luise Ross Gallery, N.Y.C., 1984, 87, CUNY Grad. Ctr., N.Y.C., 1985, Anita Shapolsky Gallery, 1989, Staller Ctr. for Arts, SUNY-Brook, 1989, Ball State U. Art Gallery, Muncie, Ind., 1990, Luise Ross Gallery, N.Y.C., 1990, 92; group shows maj. museums, including, Met. Mus., Mus. Modern Art, Weyhe Gallery, Kootz Gallery, Am. Acad. and Inst. Arts and Letters, Kenkeleba House, Johnson Mus., Ithaca, N.Y., Cornell U., Newberger Mus., Purchase, N.Y., Stable Gallery, N.Y.C., Landmark Gallery, N.Y.C., Robeson Ctr. Gallery, Rutgers U., N.J., Pa. Acad., Phila., Denver Art Mus., U. Ill., U. Nebr., Walker Art Ctr., Minn., Los Angeles Mus., Benson Gallery, Bridgehampton, N.Y., U. Tex., U. Sask., Wichita Mus., Colo. Coll., Corcoran Gallery, Washington, numerous others; represented in permanent collections, Bklyn. Mus., U. Calif.-Berkeley, U. Iowa Mus., U. Tex. Mus., So. Ill. Mus., Worcester Mus., Walker Art Mus., Santa Monica Library, Guild Hall Collection, Deloitte-Haskins-Sells, Geigy Collection, Western Electric Co., Union Carbide, Ciba Geigy, Best Products, Solomon Guggenheim Mus., GE, AT&T, Ball State Art Mus., numerous others. Recipient 4 Longview grants, Rothko Found. grant, 1972, Gottlieb Found. grant, 1978, AVA award, Winston-Salem, N.C., 1982, Am. Acad., Inst. Arts and Letters, 1983. Home: New York N.Y. Died Apr. 10, 1992.

CHERRY, WENDELL, health care company executive; b. Riverside, Ky.; s. Geneva Cherry; m. Dorothy O'Connell; children from previous marriage: Angela Cherry Gehegan, Alison Cherry Alvarez, Andrew, Hagen; stepchildren: Jennifer Morton, Jonathon Morton, Timothy Morton. BS, U. Ky., 1957, LLB, 1959. Bar: Ky., 1959. Practice law Louisville, 1959; instr. econs. U. Louisville, 1959-61; co-founder Humana Inc., Louisville, pres., chief operating officer, dir., 1969-91, vice chmn., 1991; chief oper. officer Edison Homes-S.E., Louisville, Community Hosps. Humana, Inc. Louisville, Gwinnett Community Hosp., Inc., Snellville, Ga., Med. Specialties Inc., Humhosco Inc., Brandon, Fla., Humedicenters, Inc., Richlands, Va., Beaumont Hosps. Inc., Tex., numerous others; owner Ky. Cols. basketball team; pres. former Am. Basktbell Assn. Active various fin. campaigns for civic projects including Ky. Ctr. for Arts, chmn. bd. of ctr. 1980-87. Named one of Outstanding Young Men Am. U.S. Jaycees, 1970. Home: Louisville Ky. Died July 16, 1991.

CHILD, CHARLES GARDNER, surgeon; b. N.Y.C., Feb. 1, 1908; s. Charles Gardner and Helen (Francis) C.; m. Margaret MacCrae Austin, June 14, 1941; children: Caroline Child Tucker, Helen C., Cleland, Charles, Elizabeth Child Avsharian. B.A., Yale U., 1930; M.D., Cornell U., 1934. Diplomate Am. Bd. Surgery (past chmn.). Intern in surgery N.Y. Hosp., N.Y.C., 1934-35; resident in surgery N.Y. Hosp., 1936-42; asst. prof. surgery Cornell U. Med. Sch., N.Y.C., 1942-43, assoc. prof., 1946-52; prof. surgery, chmn. dept. Tufts U. Med. Sch., Boston, 1952-58; prof., chmn. dept. surgery U. Mich., Ann Arbor, 1978; prof. emeritus U. Mich., 1978-83; clin. prof. surgery Emory U. Med. Sch., Atlanta, 1978-83; assoc. chief staff for edn. VA Med. Center, Atlanta, 1980-83; cons. to Fed. agys., NAS, Inst. Sci. Author: The Liver and Portal Hypertension, 1954, The Portal Circulation, 1965, Portal Hypertension, 1975; past editor Jour. Surg. Rsch.; contbr. numerous articles to profl. jours. Served with USNR, 1944-46. Mem. Soc. Univ. Surgeons, Am. Surg. Assn., Soc. Clin. Surgeons, Inst. Medicine. Home: Atlanta Ga. Died June 24, 1991; buried Woodlawn Cemetery, Bronx, N.Y.

CHILDS, JAMES BENNETT, librarian; b. Van Buren, Mo., June 2, 1896; s. Trall B. and Mary C. (Michener) C.; m. Eleanor Atala Pirkner, Nov. 20, 1927; seven sons. AB, U. Ill., 1918, BLS with final honors, 1921. Asst. U. Ill. Libr., 1918-21; cataloguer John Crerar Libr., Chgo., 1921-25; chief documents officer Libr. of Congress, 1925-30, from 1934, chief of catalog div., 1930-34; ofcl. del. World Congress of Librs., Rome and

Venice, 1929; del. 8th Am. Sci. Congress, Washington, 1940. Wrote Sixteenth Century Books, 1925, Account of Govt. Document Bibliography in U.S. and Elsewhere, 3d edit., 1942, Memorias of Republics of Central America and Antilles, 1932, German Fed. Republic Official Publications, 1959, Spanish Government Publications, from 1936, vol. I., 1965; editor guide ofcl. publs. other American Republics, 1944, Publs. Bibliog. Soc. of America, 1926-36; contbg. editor Handbook of Latin Am. Studies. Served in inf., Camp Grant, Ill., 1918. Mem. ALA, Bibliog. Soc. Am., Am. Econ. Assn., Am. Polit. Sci. Assn., Inter-Am. Bibliog. and Libr. Assn. (mem. coun.), SAR, Phi Beta Kappa, Clubs: Cliff Dwellers (Chgo.), Cosmos (Washington). *

CHILDS, MARQUIS WILLIAM, journalist; b. Clinton, Iowa, Mar. 17, 1903; s. William Henry and Lilian Malissa (Marquis) C.; m. Lue Prentiss, Aug. 26, 1926 (dec.); children: Prentiss, Malissa Elliott (dec.); m. Jane Neylan McBaine. A.B., U. Wis., 1923, Litt.D., 1966; A.M., U. Iowa, 1935, Litt.D., 1969; LL.D., Upsala Coll., 1943. With UPI, 1923, 25-26; with St. Louis Post-Dispatch, 1926-44, spl. corr., 1954-62; chief St. Louis Post-Dispatch (Washington corr.), 1962-68; columnist United Feature Syndicate, 1944-54; made 3 month tour battlefronts, 1943; lectr. Columbia Sch. Journalism; Eric W. Allen Meml. lectr. U. Oreg., 1950. Author: Sweden The Middle Way, 1936, They Hate Roosevelt, 1936, Washington Calling, 1937, This Is Democracy, 1938, This Is Your War, 1942, I Write From Washington, 1942, The Cabin, 1944; Editor, writer: evaluation new edit. Brooks Adams' America's Economic Supremacy, 1947, The Farmer Takes a Hand, 1952, Ethics in Business Society, (with Douglass Cater), 1954, The Ragged Edge, 1955, Eisenhower, Captive Hero, 1958, The Peacemakers, 1961, Taint of Innocence, 1967, Witness to Power, 1975, Sweden The Middle Way on Trial, 1980; Co-editor: Walter Lippmann and His Times, 1959, Mighty Mississippi: Biography of a River. Decorated Order of North Star Sweden; Order of Merit Fed. Republic of Germany; Order of Aztec Eagle Mex.; recipient Sigma Delta Chi award for best Washington corr., 1944; award for journalism U. Mo.; Pulitzer prize for commentary, 1969. Mem. Kappa Sigma, Sigma Delta Chi. Clubs: Overseas Writers (pres. 1943-45); Century (N.Y.C.); Washington Press (Washington), Gridiron (Washington) (pres. 1957), Metropolitan (Washington), Cosmos (Washington). Home: San Francisco Calif. Died June 30, 1990; buried Clinton, Iowa.

CHINN, ROBERT CARSON, computer company executive, lawyer; b. Biloxi, Miss., July 30, 1916; s. Roy and Lula (Carson) C.; m. Twila Thompson, Jan. 1, 1944 (div. 1955); children: Robert Carson, Bennett Thompson; m. Eleanor Wyatt Walker, Aug. 31, 1957; children: Elizabeth Wyatt, Meredith Walker. BA, La. State U., 1939, JD, 1942. Bar: La. 1942; cert. mfg. engr. Labor atty. Ford Motor Co., Dearborn, Mich., 1946-48; staff exec. Ford Motor Co., Atlanta, 1948-58; mgr. assembly ops. Ford Motor Co., various locations, 1959-68; v.p. mfg. and ops. Control Data Corp., Mpls., 1969-73, sr. v.p., group exec., 1974-75, sr. v.p., asst. to chief exec. officer, 1976-83; pres. Control Data of Caribbean Basin, 1984-87; chmn. bd. Control Data Netherlands B.V., Rijswijk, 1978-84, Elbit Computers Ltd., Haifa, Israel, 1973-81; chmn. exec. com. WTG Systems, Ltd., Kingston, 1981-87; chmn., chief exec. officer Communications Research Group, Inc., 1984-87; pres., chmn. Carson-Walker Corp., 1988-91; chief exec. officer, chmn. Robotic Displays Corp., 1988-91; bd. dirs. Elron Electronic Industries, Ltd., Haifa, Fibronics Internat., John E. Chance Assocs., Inc., Lafayette, La. Trustee Am. Farmland Trust, Washington, 1982—, Caribbean/ C.Am. Action, Washington, from 1983; dir. La. Partnership for Tech. and Innovation; chmn. La. Gov's. Com. on Advance-Rsch. Based Industries, 1990; mem. La. Gov.'s Econ. Devel. Commn., 1991; mem. La. Commn. on Ports and Infrastructure, 1990, Gov.'s Pan Am. Commn., 1991. Maj. AUS, 1942-46. Elected to Hall of Distinction, La. State U. Alumni, 1988. Mem. ABA, La. Bar Assn., Am. Soc. Mfg. Engrs (cert engr.), Soc. Automotive Engrs., Engring. Soc. Detroit, St. Paul Area C. of C. (chmn., pres. 1972-73), U.S.-Israel C. of C. (bd. dirs. N.Y.C. 1979-87). Presbyterian. Clubs: Minnesota, Baton Rouge Country. Lodges: Masons; Shriners, Rotary. Home: Baton Rouge La. Died June 20, 1991; buried Baton Rouge, La.

CHIPMAN, JOHN, university professor; b. Tallahassee, Fla., Apr. 25, 1897; s. John and Maria (Randolph) C.; m. Ruth Hayes, Aug. 11, 1923; children: David Randolph, Ruth Elizabeth. BS, U. of the South, 1920; MS, State U. Iowa, 1922; PhD, U. Calif., 1926; ScD, U. South, 1940, U. Pa., 1962. Asst. prof. chemistry Ga. Inst. Tech., 1926-29; rsch. engr. U. Mich., 1929-35; assoc. dir. Rsch. Lab., Am. Rolling Mill Co., 1935-37; prof. metallurgy MIT, 1937-62, prof. emeritus, lectr., from 1962, head metall. dept., 1946-62. Author sci. articles pub. in transactions of tech. socs. Recipient awards including Clamer medal Franklin Inst., 1951, Losana gold medal Associazione Intaliana di Metallurgia, 1952, Brinell gold medal Ingeniors Vetenskaps Akademien, 1954. Fellow Am. Inst. Mining Metall. and Petroleum Engrs. (pres. Metall. Soc. 1960, Benjamin F. Fairless award 1963, dir. 1958-61); mem. Am. Soc. for Metals (pres. 1951-52, gold medal 1957), Am. Acad. Arts and Scis., Nat. Acad. Sci., Swedish Royal Acad. (fgn.), Iron and Steel Inst. Gt. Brit. (Bessemer medal 1955). *

CHOPPIN, ARTHUR RICHARD, college dean; b. Alexandria, La., Dec. 13, 1897; s. Dr. Arthur R. and Margaret (Whittington) C.; m. Eunice D. Bolin, Mar. 29, 1919; children: Arthur Richard, George Purnell. BA, La. State U., 1918, MS, 1925; PhD, Ohio State U., 1929. Tchr. Rapides Parish (La.) Sch. Bd., 1919-20; asst. prin. Vermillion (La.) Sch. Bd., 1920-23; grad. asst. La. State U., 1924-25, asst. chemistry, 1925-26, instr., 1926-28, asst. prof., 1929-31, assoc. prof., 1931-36, prof., from 1936, prof. and mgr. lab. stores, 1939-43, asst. to dean of Coll. of Chemistry and Physics, 1944, dean of coll., prof. chem., since 1944. Patentee in field; contbr. articles to profl. jours. La. State Civilian Gas Cons.; mem. State Emergency Relief Bd.; dir. Pelican Boys' and Girls' States; past pres. Baton Rouge (La.) Rotary Internat. Club; adv. mem. Econ. Devel. Com. of La.; adjutant U. Post of Am. Legion; state comdr. Am. Legion of La., 1946; dir. radiol. and spl. weapons div. La. Civil Def.; vice chmn. Louisian bd. Nuclear Energy; chmn. Community Recreation Coun., Selective Svc. com. of La. State U.; sec. La. Wildlife Assn., 1932. Served as 2d lt. Machine Gun Corps, WWI. Fellow Am. Inst. Chemists, Am. Inst. Chem. Engrs.; mem. Am. Chem. Soc., Am. Men of Sci., AAAS, Phi Kappa Phi, Phi Lambda Upsilon, Sigma Xi, Alpha Chi Sigma, Omicron Delta Kappa. *

CHOUKAS, MICHAEL EUGENE, sociology educator; b. Samos Island, Greece, Nov. 16, 1901; came to U.S., 1916, naturalized, 1924; s. Nicholas and Callipe Doukas C.; m. Gertrude Spitz, June 20, 1927; 1 child, Michael E. Prof. sociology Dartmouth Coll., 1929-68, chmn. dept., 1949-60; prof. sociology Johns Hopkins U., summer 1950; provost Pierce Coll., Athens, Greece, 1969-75; prof. sociology Bates Coll., summers 1939-40. Author: Black Angels of Athos, 1934, Propaganda Comes of Age, 1965; contbr. articles to Sociol. Rev. and other jours. and periodicals. Mem. N.H. Com. on Morale, 1941, Office of Strategic Svcs., 1944-45; dir. survey on alcoholism in N.H., 1946. Mem. Am. Sociol. Soc., Byzantine Soc., Phi Beta Kappa, Alpha Tau Omega. Orthodox. Home: Hanover N.H. Died Oct. 2, 1989; cremated.

CHRISTENSEN, CHRIS LAURITHS, business executive; b. Minden, Nebr., Dec. 29, 1894; s. Christian Marius and Hilda (Ibsen) C.; m. Cora Wells March, Dec. 18, 1929; children: Christian Lauriths and Charles March (twins). Grad., Nebr. U. Sch. Agr., 1916; BSc in Agr., U. Nebr., 1920, DAgr., 1937; LLD, Knox Coll., 1949; fellow Am.-Scandanavian Found., U. Copenhagen and Royal Agrl. Coll., Denmark, 1921-22. Spl. investigator on coop. agr. USDA, Europe, 1922-23; chief div. coop. mktg. USDA, 1924-29; exec. sec. Federal Farm Bd., 1929-31; dean Coll. Agr., dir. Agrl. Expt. Sta. and extension svc. U. Wis., 1931-43; v.p., dir., chmn. exec. com. Celotex Corp., 1943-61; vice chmn., dir. South Coast Corp., 1943-61; dir. Brookside State Bank, Tulsa, Goff Oil Co.; dir., mem. exec. com. Internat. Harvester Co.; dir. Armour & Co.; dir., sec.-treas. Dairy Mktg. Corp., 1933-35. Author bulls. on agrl. coops.; co-author: Cooperative Principles and Practices, 1936, The Significance of the Folk School Type of Education, 1939. Mem. Gov.'s Exec. Coun., State of Wis., 1931-32; mem. bd. trustees, chmn. exec. com. Farm Found.; mem. adv. bd., chmn. farm bldg. com. Producers Coun.; mem. Nat. Com. on Pub. Edn.; mem. sponsoring com. World Congress on Edn. for Democracy, 1939; nat com. Midcentury White House Children and Youth Conf., 1949-50; trustee Rural Youth Found.; pres., dir., chmn. exec. com. Nat. Commn. on Boys and Girls 4-H Club Work; mem. Northwestern U. Assns.; pres. Country Life Assn., 1939; pres. Chgo. chpt. Am.-Scandinavian Found., 1946-48. Sgt. U.S. Army, 1918. Recipient 4-H Nat. citation, 1962. Mem. Gamma Sigma Delta, Alpha Zeta, Farm House; clubs: Garden of Gods (Colorado Springs, Colo.), Chgo., Boston (New Orleans), Petroleum (Tulsa). Lutheran. *

CHRISTGAU, VICTOR, social service administrator; b. Austin, Minn., Sept. 20, 1894; s. Fred and Adeline (Vanselow) C.; m. Muriel Josephine Doyle, July 30, 1931 (dec. Apr. 1987). BS, U. Minn, 1923; student agrl. econs., 1923-25. Ptnr. Christgau Bros. Farmers, Austin; mem. State Senate (Minn.), 1927-29; chmn. Senate Com. on Agr., 1929; mem. 71st, 72d Congresses, 1st Minn. Dist.; exec. asst. to dir. prodn. AAA U.S. Dept. of Agr., 1933; asst. adminstr. AAA, 1934; works progress adminstr. Minn., 1935-38; dir. Minn. Div. Employment and Security, 1939-53; commr. Minn. Dept. Employment Security, 1953; dir. Bur. Old Age and Survivors Ins., Social Security Adminstrn., Washington, 1954-91; exec. dir. Social Security Adminstrn., 1963-66; asst. to the commissioner, 1966-69. Served as sgt. 33d Engrs., U.S. Army, World War I, France. Mem. Interstate Conf. of Employment Security Agencies (pres. 1947-48), Am. Pub. Welfare Assn., Am. Soc. Pub. Adminstrn., Alumni Assn. U. Minn. (pres. 1952-53), Am. Farm Econ. Assn., Am. Legion, Vets. Fgn. Wars. Lutheran. Home: Washington D.C. Died Oct. 3, 1991; buried St. Thomas Aquinas Cemetery, St. Paul Park, Minn.

CHRISTIAN, PERCY WILLIS, academic administrator, history educator; b. Viborg, S.D., Jan. 8, 1907; s. John Willis and Tillie Victoria (Peterson) C.; m. Evelyn Anna deVries, June 25, 1931 (dec.); 1 child, John Willis.; m. Ellen Louise Gibson, Dec. 27, 1981. B.A., Broadview Coll., 1926; B.S., Lewis Inst., Chgo., 1928; M.A., Northwestern U., 1929, Ph.D., 1935; LL.D., Walla Walla Coll., 1967. Instr. history Chgo. Acad., 1926-28, Broadview Coll., 1931-33; asst. prof. history Walla Walla Coll., 1933-35, assoc. prof., 1935-38, prof., 1938-43, pres., 1955-64; dean Pacific Union Coll., Angwin, Cal., 1943-45, pres., 1945-50, prof. history, 1964-77, prof. emeritus, from 1977; pres. Emmanuel Missionary Coll., 1950-55; vis. prof. Eastern Wash. Coll. Edn., summer 1934, State Coll. Wash., summer 1942, Loma Linda U., summer 1962, Andrews U., summer 1966, Seminaire Adventiste, Collonges, France, 1968-69; dir. pub. relations Taiwan Adventist Hosp., Taipei. Mem. Am. Hist. Assn., Assn. Western Adventist Historians (pres. 1972), Orgn. Am. Historians. Home: Angwin Calif. Died Sept. 14, 1990; buried St. Helena, Calif.

CHRISTIANSEN, ERNEST BERT, chemical engineering educator; b. Richfield, Utah, July 31, 1910; s. Ernest C. and Sarah (Nielsen) C.; m. Susan Mann, Sept. 6, 1935; children—David Ernest, Susan Catherine, Gale Ann, Alan Grant, Philip Arne, Richard Lee, Lisa Beth. B.S., U. Utah, 1937; M.S., U. Mich., 1939, Ph.D., 1945. Registered profl. engr., Utah. Chem. engr. E.I. DuPont de Nemours Co., 1941-46; prof. chem. engring. U. Idaho, 1946-47; prof. chem. engring. U. Utah, from 1947, head dept., 1947-75, disting. research prof., 1977-78. Contbr. articles to profl. jours. Fellow Am. Inst. Chem. Engrs. (nat. dir. 1966-68, Founders award), Utah Acad. Sci., Arts and Letters; mem. Am. Chem. Soc., Am. Soc. Engring. Edn., Am. Soc. Rheology, Tau Beta Pi, Sigma Xi, Phi Kappa Phi. Home: Salt Lake City Utah Died July 9, 1988; buried Salt Lake City.

CHRISTIANSEN, ROBERT LESTER, advertising executive; b. Chgo., July 2, 1927; s. Clarence Martin and Leta (Covey) C.; m. Annemarie Gabor, Sept. 7, 1952 (dec.); children: Eric Robert, Clarence Martin II; m. Joy Flodin, Jan. 23, 1965. B.S., Northwestern U., 1949; student, Law Sch., 1949-50. Sec.-treas. C.M. Christiansen Co., Phelps, Wis., 1949-51, pres., from 1957; with Cramer-Krasselt Co. (advt.), Milw., Chgo. and Phoenix,, 1951-84, exec. v.p., 1961-68, pres., 1968-79, chief exec. officer, 1971-79, chmn. bd. and treas., 1979-84, also dir.; v.p. Sylvan Products Corp., Phelps, from 1959; dir. Smoky Lake Corp., Lake Shore Inc., Iron Mountain and Kingsford, Mich. Former mem. Nat. Advt. Review Bd.; Former trustee Milw. Art Center; mem. Greater Milw. Com.; past bd. dirs. St. Joseph's Hosp., St. Michael Hosp.; former v.p.; dir. Florentine Opera Co., Milw.; asso. chmn., 1966, Milw. United Fund; bd. corp. Citizens' Govtl. Research Bur., Milw. Boys Clubs, Milw. Symphony Orch., Wis. Coll.-Conservatory, Milw.; bd. dirs., past chmn. Better Bus. Bur.; former mem. bd. dirs. Council Better Bus. Burs., Inc., Wis. Soc. Prevention Blindness; bd. regents Northwestern U., 1971; bd. govs. Mt. Mary Coll. Named Communicator of Year Wis. Advt. and Graphic Arts Industry, 1975. Mem. Am. Assn. Advt. Agys. (sec.-treas. 1977-78, dir., trustee group ins. trust, past chmn. central region bd. govs.), U.S. Navy League (dir. Milw. council). Clubs: Milwaukee (Milw.) (pres. 1979), University (Milw.), Milwaukee Country (Milw.); Chippewa (Iron Mountain, Mich.); Confrerie des Chevaliers du Tastevin. (Grand Genechal sous-commanderie de Milwaukee 1982). Home: Whitefish Bay Wis. Died Mar. 11, 1992.

CHRISTOPHERSON, FRED CARL, editor; b. Toronto, S.D., May 13, 1896; s. Christian Theodore and Mathilda (Frankson) C.; m. Marie Cilley, Feb. 13, 1926. Student, Luther Coll., 1914-15, U. S.D., 1916-17. Reporter Sioux Falls (S.D.) Press, 1917, Kansas City Star, 1920-21; mng. editor Sioux Falls Press, 1922-26, pub., 1927; exec. editor Sioux Falls Argus-Leader, 1928-45, editor, 1945-61. Trustee, v.p. Sioux Valley Hosp., Mt. Rushmore Nat. Meml. Soc., Crazy Horse Meml. Found. Served to 2d lt. US Army Air Svc., 1917-18, US Army Air Svc. Res. Corps., 1919-24, lst lt. 1924-29. Awarded St. Olav medal by King Haakon of Norway, 1947. Mem. Am. Soc. Newspaper Editors (bd. dirs.), S.D. Press Assn. (pres. 1942), Am. Legion, Sioux Falls C. of C. (pres. 1950), Sigma Delta Chi, Minnehaha Country Club, Sious Falls Rotary (pres. 1938). *

CHURCH, BROOKS DAVIS, microbiologist; b. Youngstown, Ohio, May 6, 1918; s. Brooks Davis and Clara (Sartorius) C.; m. Jean Marie Church, Nov. 20, 1965; children: Elizabeth, Stephen, Heather, Heidi. BS, U. Mich., 1947, MS, 1953, PhD, 1956. Sr. research assoc. Warner-Lambert, Morris Plains, N.J., 1955-60; asst. prof. microbiology U. Wash., Seattle, 1960-63; assoc. prof. U. Minn., Mpls., 1963-67; sr. research assoc. North Star Research Ctr., Mpls., 1967-72; prof. U. Denver, 1972-77; pres. BioSearch Assocs., Littleton, Colo., from 1981; cons. WACON, Denver, from 1983, PennWalt, Phila., 1985, Allied Mills, Sydney, Australia, 1983-84, Marion Labs., Kansas City, Mo., 1982-83. Contbr. numerous articles to profl. jours.; patentee in field. Vol. Am. Heart Assn., Denver, from 1985. Served as staff sgt. U.S. Army, 1942-46. Fellow Am. Soc. Microbiology (pres. Rocky Mountain chpt. 1973); mem. AAAS, N.Y. Acad. Sci., Sigma Xi, Phi Sigma. Democrat. Methodist. Home: Littleton Colo. Deceased. †

CHURCH, ERNEST ELLIOTT, academic administrator; b. Rutan, Pa., Oct. 19, 1897; s. James and Jennie (Riley) C.; m. Katharine Moore, June 15, 1939. AB, Waynesburg Coll., 1918, LLD, 1940; AM, W.Va. U., 1926. Prin. Claysville (Pa.) High Sch., 1918-19; tchr. social studies Fairmont (W.Va.) High Sch., 1919-23; prin. Martinsburg (W.Va.) High Sch., 1923-30, Parkersburg High Sch., 1930-35; pres. Potomac State Coll. of W.Va. U., Keyser, 1936-64; exec. sec. W.Va. Commn. Higher Edn., from 1964. Mem. NEA, W.Va. Edn. Assn., W.Va. Assn. Secondary Sch. Prins. (pres. 1925-27), W.Va. Coun. State Coll. and U. Presidents (sec. 1945-56, pres. 1957), Elks, Masons, Shriners, Rotary. Presbyterian. *

CIRESI, ANTHONY DAVID, architect, engineer; b. Bridgeport, Conn., Feb. 24, 1907; s. Anthony A. and Mary G. (Raymond) C.; C.E., Rensselaer Poly. Inst., 1929; m. Astrid L. Bulow, Nov. 16, 1940. Structural draftsman Am. Bridge Co., Phila., 1930-31; civil engr., Bridgeport, 1932-33; city engrs. office, civil engr., chief engr. F.E.R.A. Planning Bd., 1933-37; instr. Bridgeport Engring. Inst., 1937-42; structural engr. Fletcher-Thompson, Inc., 1937-39, Gibbs & Hill, N.Y.C., 1939, State Dept. Pub. Works, Hartford, Conn., 1940; with Fletcher-Thompson, Inc., 1940—, chief structural engr., 1943-48, chief field engr., 1948-56, exec. v.p., dir., chief engr., 1956-76; cons., 1976—. Engring. mem. bridge commn., Bridgeport, 1937-39; mem. Bridgeport Housing Authority 1939-52, vice chmn., 1944-46, chmn., 1946-52; chmn. Redevel. Agy., 1950-52. Registered profl. engr., Conn., Ill., N.Y., N.J., Pa., Mass., N.H., Md., Kan., R.I.; registered architect, Conn., Mich. Mem. Am. Concrete Inst., Nat. Soc. Profl. Engrs., A.I.A., Internat. Assn. Shell Structures, Prestressed Concrete Inst., Conn. Soc. Profl. Engrs. Deceased. Home: Redding Ridge Conn.* †

CISLER, WALKER LEE, electric power industry executive; b. Marietta, Ohio, Oct. 8, 1897; s. Louis H. and Sara S. (Walker) C.; m. Gertrude Demuth Rippe, July 28, 1939; adopted children: Richard Rippe, Jane Rippe (Mrs. Albert J. Eckhardt, Jr.). ME, Cornell U., 1922; Engring. D., U. Mich., Stevens Inst. Tech., S.D. Sch. Mines and Tech.; LLd, U. Detroit, Wayne State U., Marietta Coll., U. Akron, No. Mich. U.; DSci, U. Toledo, Ind. Tech. Coll., Mich. Technol. Inst. Various engring. positions Pub. Svc. Elec. and Gas, Newark, 1922-41; with WPB, Washington, 1941-43; chief engr. power plants Detroit Edison Co., 1945-47, exec. v.p., 1948-51, pres., 1951-64, chmn. bd., chief exec. officer, from 1964; chmn. bd. Freuhof Corp.; pres. Power Reactor Devel. Co., Atomic Power Devel. Assocs., Inc.; bd. dirs. Holley Carburetor Co., Detroit Bank & Trust Co., Burroughs Corp., Am. Airlines, Brazilian Traction, Light and Power Co., Ltd., Eaton Mfg. Co., Equitable Life Assurance Soc. U.S., Nat. Steel Corp., Chem. Bank N.Y. Trust Co. Cons. to AID; pres. Fund for Peaceful Atomic Devel., Thomas Alva Edison Found.; mem. lay adv. bd. U. Detroit; trustee Cornell, Cranbrook Inst. Sci., com. econ. devel. Marietta Coll.; bd. dirs. Coun. Fin. Aid to Edn., Atomic Indsl. Forum, Inc., Cornell Aero. Lab.; chmn. Mayor's com. for econ. growth, Detroit; mem. bus. coun. Dept. of Commerce. Col. AUS, chief pub. utilities sect. SHAEF, later chief pub. utilities sect. Office Mil. Govt. for Germany, 1943-45. Decorated by several fgn. govts. Fellow IEEE (U.S. recipient Edison medal 1965), ASME (pres. 1960); mem. Assn. Edison Illuminating Cos. (exec. bd.), Reserve Officers Assn., Am. Ordnance Assn., Soc. Am. Mil. Engrs., Edison Elec. Inst. (pres. 1964, bd. dirs.), Engrs. Joint Coun. (pres.), Newcomen Soc. N.A., Detroit Econ. Club (chmn.), Country Club, Athletic Club (Detroit), Metropolitan (Washington), Engineers Club, University Club, Fifth Ave. Club, Cornell Club, Brook Club (N.Y.C.). *

CLAGETT, OSCAR THERON, surgeon; b. Jamesport, Mo., Oct. 19, 1908; s. Oscar Frederic and Effie (Stevens) C.; m. Alicia M. Eames, Nov. 3, 1934; children—Mary Alice, Nancy Jane, Barbara Joan, Martha Eleanor, James Stevens, Robert Scott. M.D., U. Colo., 1933, D.Sc., 1962; M.S., U. Minn., 1938, postgrad., 1935-40. Diplomate Am. Surgery, Am. Bd. Thoracic Surgery (past sec.-treas.). Intern Colo. Gen. Hosp., Denver, 1933-34; practice medicine Glenwood Springs, Colo., 1934-35; fellow in surgery Mayo Found. Grad. Sch., 1935-38; asst. surgeon Mayo Clinic, 1938-40, head sect., div. of surgery, 1940; prof. surgery Mayo Found. Grad. Sch. U. Minn., from 1951; vis. prof. surgery Johns Hopkins Hosp., 1957. Recipient Norlin medal U. Colo., 1947; Clement Price Thomas award Royal Coll. Surgeons Eng., 1968. Fellow A.C.S., Am. Assn. for Thoracic Surgery (past pres.), Am. Surg. Assn., Central Surg. Assn., Western Surg. Assn. (past pres.), Mexican Nat. Acad. Surgery, Royal Coll. Surgeons Eng. (hon.); hon. mem. Royal Australasian Coll. Surgeons, Royal College Surgeons in Ireland, Thoracic Soc. (Eng.), Soc. Thoracic Surgeons Gt. Britain and Ireland, Royal Coll. Surgeons Eng., Societa Italiana di Chirurgia (corr.). Home: Rochester Minn. Died Sept. 30, 1990; buried Redstone, Colo.

CLARK, ANN NOLAN, writer, education consultant; b. Las Vegas, N.Mex., 1898; d. Patrick Francis and Mary (Dunn) Nolan; m. Thomas Patrick Clark, Aug. 6, 1919 (dec.); 1 child, Thomas Patrick. Student, Highlands U., Las Vegas. Formerly asst. English tchr. Highlands U.; supr. No. Pueblos U.S. Indian Svc., head material preparation for southwestern spl. programs, textbook editor; materials specialist Inst. Inter-Am. Affairs; U.S. del. UNESCO Conf., Brazil; head preparation materials dept., adult edn. Bur. of Indian Affairs until 1962; ednl. cons. Latin Am. br. IKnternat. Coop. Adminstrn. Author: In My Mother's House (N.Y. Herald Tribune Spring Festival award), 1941, Little Navajo Bluebird, 1943, Magic Money, 1950, Looking for Something (N.Y. Herald Tribune Spring Festival award), 1952, Secret of the Andes (Newberry medal), 1952 (these five books all Jr. Lit. Guild selections); A Child's History of New Mexico, 1944 (with others); Buffalo Caller, 1942, Blue Canyon House, 1954, Santiago: Third Monkey, Santos for Pasqalita, 1959, World Song Desert People: Paco's Miracle, others. Recipient Distikng. Svc. award Dept. Interior, 1962; Regikna medal Cath. Libr. Assn., 1963. Mem. Benjamin Franklikn Soc. (hon.), Nat. Women's Coun., Internat. Women's Coun., PEN, Altrusa. *

CLARK, BIRGE MALCOLM, architect; b. Palo Alto, Calif., Apr. 16, 1893; s. Arthur B. and Grace (Birge) C.; m. Lucile Townley, June 15, 1922; children—Richard Townley, Dean Townley, Birge Gaylord, Malcolm Mallory. A.B., Stanford, 1914; M. Arch., Columbia, 1917. Practicing architect, from 1921; vice chmn. bd. No. Calif. Savs. & Loan Assn.; lectr. in architecture Stanford, 1950-71. Served to capt. USAAF, 1917-18; comdg. officer 3d Balloon Co. Decorated Silver Star; named Palo Alto Citizen of Yr., 1981. Fellow AIA. Club: Kiwanian. Home: Palo Alto Calif. Died Apr. 30, 1989.

CLARK, CLARENCE C., physics, chemistry educator; b. Owensboro, Ky., Aug. 1894; s. Lee and Eleanor (Johnson) C.;/ m. Berenice Bodenhofer Wheeler, Dec. 1924. BS, U. Ky., 1917; MS, U. Chgo., 1924; PhD, NYU, 1932; student, L.I. Biol. Lab., summer 1933. In charge physics/chemistry Owensboro High Sch., 1919-20; instr. physics Wash. Sq. Coll., NYU, 1926-29, instr. gen. sci. Sch. Commerce, 1929-32, asst. prof., 1932-36, assoc. prof., 1936-40, in charge sci. course, 1938-59, prof., 1940-59, chmn. Gen. Course Group, 1951-59; prof. sci., chmn. phys. sci. U. So. Fla., 1960-92; rsch. scientist E.E. Free Labs., 1930-39; chief biol. Rainbow Bridge Expdn., summer 1934-37; cons. on slot machine N.Y. Police Dept., 1936-37; cons. on pin game machines Teaneck (N.J.) Mcpl. Govt., 1940; cons. and TV programs artist NBC, 1938-39; presented sci. TV programs Du Mont TV, System, 1946-47. Author books; contbr. articles to profl. mags. Lt. F.A., U.S. Army, 1918-19; maj. USAAF, 1943-45; lt. col. USAFR, 1947-54. Fellow AAAS; mem. Am. Assn. Physics Tchrs., Armed Forces Comm. Assn., Fla. Acad. Scis. (mem. coun. 1962-92), Phi Delta Kappa (pres. Rho chpt. 1938-39), Alpha Phi Sigma, Beta Gamma Sigma. Presbyterian. *

CLARK, EARL WESLEY, maritime consultant, political scientist; b. Cadwell, Ill., Aug. 10, 1901; s. Charles Wesley and Mary Comfort (Harding) C.; m. Mary Eudora Bracken, June 28, 1922 (dec. 1972); 1 child, Mrs. Joan C. Hoover. A.B., Eureka Coll., 1928; A.M., U. Ill., 1931. Instr. high sch. El Paso, Ill., 1928-32; vocat. dir. Bur. Pub. Welfare, Chgo. and Cook County, Ill., 1933; dist. and later state rep. Ill. Emergency Relief Comm., 1934-35; Peoria dist. dir., regional exec. officer, dep. regional adminstr., regional adminstr. (covering Ill., Wis., Minn., Nebr., Iowa, S.D., N.D.) Chgo. OPA Region, 1943-46; asst. and later nat. commr. OPA, 1947; mem. War Contracts Price adjustment Bd., 1947; nat. liquidation officer Office of Temporary Controls (included OPA, Civilian Prodn. Adminstrn., Office War Moblzn. and Reconversion, Office Econ. Stablzn.), 1947; dir. div. of liquidation Dept. Commerce (included OPA, Civilian Prodn. Adminstrn., Office War Moblzn. and Reconversion, Office Econ. Stablzn., Office Temp. Controls, Fgn. Econ, 1947-48; chief deptl. moblzn. staff, later dir. Office of Industry Cooperation, 1948-49; chmn. bd. appeals-employee grievances Dept. Commerce; also pub. hearing officer Office of Industry Cooperation; spl. asst. to sec. of commerce, 1949-50; dep. maritime adminstr. Maritime Administrn., 1950-53; pres. N.Y. & Cuba Mail S.S. Co.; maritime cons. Mem. Nat. Cargo Bur., Inc., 1954; co-dir. Labor-Mgmt. Maritime Com., 1955-80; lectr. Fla. State U., 1952; mem. nat. adv. bd. Operation Ship Shape, Inc., 1968-71; mem. adv. com. on requirements Dept. Commerce, 1949; adv. com. on tech. assistance Dept. State, 1949-50; industry adviser Intergovtl. Maritime Consultatory Orgn. of UN, London, 1965; mem. Radio Tech. Commn. Maritime Services; co-chmn. spl. com. Bridge-to-Bridge Communication, 1958. Author: O.P.A. reports, Div. of Liquidation reports, Industry Voluntary Agreements Reports, 1949, Cathedral, 1952, Program Imperatives for Strengthening the U.S. Merchant Marine, 1965, Bread Upon the Waters, 1970, Reply to the Rockefeller Report, 1970, Merchant Marine March, 1978; co-author: State Pilotage in America, 1960, 2d edit., 1978, Medical and Hospital Care for Merchant Seamen, 1964, A Dialogue on Maritime Policy, 1966, The U.S. Merchant Marine Today, 1970, The American Passenger Ship Fleet, 1970, Dual U.S.-Foreign Flag Shipping Interests, 1970. Red Cross div. chmn., 1947, Com. Fund div. chmn., 1947; mem. Gt. Lakes Pilotage Adv. Com., 1960-70; past bd. dirs., chmn. fgn. relations com. United Seamans Service. Recipient Spl. award United Seamen's Service, 1969, Recognition plaque P.R. Propeller Club, 1970, Hall of Fame award Sullivan, Ill., 1974. Former mem. Soc. Naval Architects and Marine Engrs., Nat. Def. Transp. Assn., Navy League; mem. Pi Kappa Delta, Lambda Chi Alpha. Episcopalian. Club: Propeller (pres. Washington club, mem. nat. bd. dirs. 1964-66, chmn. positions and resolutions com. of U.S. 1964-74, vice chmn. 1974-79, mem. nat. exec. com. 1966-79, nat. finance com. 1971-76, mem. nat. constn. and by-laws com. 1966-74, nat. conf. com. 1966-80). Home: Pinehurst N.C. Died Aug. 2, 1990.

CLARK, ERNEST JOHN, civil engineer, consultant; b. Worcester, Mass., Sept. 5, 1905; s. William A. and Flora (Milton) C.; m. Ruth I. Bohlman, Sept. 21, 1929; 1 dau., Jeanne Clark Saulnier. C.E., Rensselaer Poly. Inst., 1928; M.C.E., Poly. Inst. N.Y., 1942. Estimator Habirshaw Electric Cable Co., 1922-24; engring. asst. Westchester County (N.Y.) Park Commn., 1924-25, asst. engr., 1928-30; park engr. L.I. (N.Y.) State Park Commn., 1930-34; structural engr. N.Y.C. Dept. Parks, 1934-36; bridge engr. N.Y. World's Fair, 1936-38; structural engr., chief engr. W. Earle Andrews (Engr.), N.Y.C., 1938-45; ptnr. Andrews & Clark (Cons. Engrs.), N.Y.C., 1945-89; cons. Triborough Bridge and Tunnel Authority, Jones Beach Authority, Port of N.Y. and N.J. Authority, N.Y. State Dept. Transp., N.Y. Thruway Authority, City of N.Y. Prin. works include UN Plaza along 1st Ave. and 42d St, N.Y.C., Flushing Meadows-Corona Park, Brooklyn Heights Pedestrian Promenade, Bklyn.-Queens Expressway, including Bklyn. Heights pedestrian promenade. Fellow ASCE, Am. Cons. Engrs. Council; mem. Nat. Soc. Profl. Engrs., N.Y. State Assn. Cons. Engrs., Rensselaer Alumni Assn., Delta Phi. Home: Somers N.Y. Died Mar. 25, 1992.

CLARK, FREDERICK R., banker; b. Rochester, N.Y., July 22, 1916; s. Roy M. and Laura (Gamble) C.; m. Anne M. Murray, Sept. 3, 1950; children: Paul, Douglas, Stephen, Mary A. Clark Crowley, Cynthia Clark Hessberg, Pamela Clark Clemente. M.B.A., Harvard U.; LL.B., Bklyn. Law Sch. Bar: N.Y. 1940. Practiced in Rochester; commr. taxation State of N.Y., Albany, 1957-60; spl. rep. IBM Corp., 1960-61; exec. v.p. State Bank Albany, 1961-72, Key Banks, Albany, 1972-82; chmn. N.Y. State Power Authority, 1977-79; dir. Key Life Ins. Ltd., Key Trust Co., Key Bank U.S.A. Served with AUS, 1940-45. Decorated Order Crown Italy; recipient Conspicuous Service medal State N.Y., 1945. Mem. Schuyler Meadows Club, Sky Top Club, Ft. Orange Club. Home: Loudonville N.Y. Died Mar. 19, 1990; buried St. Agnes Cemetery, Albany, N.Y.

CLARK, GRADY WILLIAM, investment company executive; b. Lewisburg, Tenn., Nov. 8, 1897; s. John Calvin and Hallie (Clayton) C.; m. Mary Frances Moore, July 2, 1934. Student, Vanderbilt U., 1924. Tchr. high sch. Tenn., 1922; engaged in real estate Sheffield, Ala., 1922-33; with Investors Diversified Svcs., Inc., Mpls., 1934-92, pres., 1960-63, chmn., 1963-92; pres. Investors Syndicate Am., Inc., 1960-63, chmn., 1963-92; pres. Investors Syndicate Life. Ins. and Annuity Co., 1960-63, dir., 1963-92; v.p. affiliated cos. Investors Stock Fund, Investors Mutual Investors Group Can. Fund, Investors Selective Fund, Investors Variable Payment Fund, Investors Syndicate Title & Guaranty Co. Author: Developing Your Sales Personality. Bd. dirs. United Fund Appeal for Hennepin County; v.p. Elizabeth Kenny Found., Mpls. Club, Minikahda Club (bd. govs.) (Mpls.). Methodist. Mem. Mpls. Club, Downtown Men's Club, Minnkada Club (Mpls.), Thunderbird Country Club (Palm Springs, Calif.), Delta Tau Delta. *

CLARK, JOHN CONRAD, investment consultant; b. N.Y.C., Feb. 19, 1913; s. John C. and Marie (Sparnect) C.; m. Lillian Fischer, Dec. 17, 1949; 1 child, Roger Scott. Student, NYU, 1930-33. Mcpl. bond trader Shields & Co., N.Y.C., 1935-40; pres. John C. Clark & Co., N.Y.C., 1946-47; asst. mgr. bond dept. Chase Manhattan Bank, N.Y.C., 1947-51; mgr. bond dept. Wachovia Bank, Winston-Salem, N.C., 1951-55, v.p., mgr., 1955-63, sr. v.p., mgr. bond dept., sr. v.p., mgr. pub. fin., 1967-69; dir. Export-Import Bank, Washington, 1969-76; mng. dir. Laidlaw-Coggeshall, Inc., Washington, 1976-77; investment banking cons., 1977—; sec. N.C. Securities Adv. Com. to Banks in N.C., 1962-67. Contbg. author: Bankers Handbook, 1966. Vice chmn. bd. N.C. Mcpl. Coun., 1961-67. Lt. col. AUS, 1941-46, ETO. Recipient cert. of award Compt. of Currency, 1963. Mem. Investment Bankers Assn. Am., Univ. Club (Washington), Rotarian. Presbyterian. Home: Hilton Head Island S.C. Died Apr. 27, 1990; cremated.

CLARK, JOSEPH S., former United States senator; b. Phila., Oct. 21, 1901; s. Joseph S. and Kate R. (Avery) C.; m. Iris Richey; children by previous marriages: Joseph S., Noel C. Miller. Student, Middlesex Sch., 1919; BS magna cum laude, Harvard U., 1923; LLB, U. Pa., 1926; LLD, Temple U., Harvard U., 1952, Drexel Inst., 1957, U. Pa., 1963, Haverford Coll., 1966, Franklin and Marshall Coll., 1967; DCL, Susquehanna U., 1961; LHD, Lincoln U., 1961. Bar: Pa. 1926. Practiced law in Phila., 1926-51; city controller City of Phila., 1949-51, mayor, 1952-56; U.S. senator from Pa.,

1957-68; founder, pres. Mems. of Congress for Peace through Law; pres. World Federalists U.S.A., 1969-71; chmn. Coalition on Nat. Priorities and Mil. Policy, 1969-73. Author: The Senate Establishment, 1963, Congress: The Sapless Branch, 1964, 66, Readings in Congressional Reform, 1966. Mem. bd. overseers Harvard, 1953-59; trustee Fund for Peace. Col. USAAF, 1941-45; CBI. Decorated Bronze Star, Legion Merit, U.S., Order Brit. Empire; recipient Bok award, Phila., 1956. Fellow Am. Acad. Arts and Scis.; mem. Am. Acad. Polit. and Social Scis. (v.p.), Am. Philos. Soc., Arms Control Assn. (bd. dirs.), Phi Beta Kappa. Home: Chestnut Hill Pa. Died Jan. 12, 1990.

CLARK, LEIGH MALLET, judge; b. Auburn, Ala., May 16, 1901; s. George Samuel and Willie Gertrude (Little) C.; m. Evelyn Staggers, Aug. 8, 1928; 1 dau., Eva Jean (Mrs. Frank C. Marshall, Jr.) Student, Ala. Poly. Inst., 1917-19; A.B., U. Ala., 1921, LL.B., 1923. Bar: Ala. bar 1923. Pvt. practice Tuscaloosa, 1923-25, Birmingham, 1925-43, from 1951; circuit judge 10th Jud. Circuit Ala., 1935-51; mem. firm Cabaniss, Johnston, Gardner & Clark (and predecessor), 1951-73; supernumerary circuit judge 10th Jud. Circuit Ala., Birmingham, from 1973; spl. chief justice Supreme Ct. Ala., 1976; instr. Birmingham Sch. Law, from 1927. Served to lt. col. AUS, 1943-45; col. Res. Fellow Am. Coll. Trial Lawyers; mem. ABA, Ala. Bar Assn., Birmingham Bar Assn. (Outstanding Lawyer of Year award 1974), Ala. Assn. Circuit Judges (past pres., hon. life), Phi Alpha Delta. Democrat. Mem. Ch. of Christ (elder). Club: Mason (Shriner). Home: Birmingham Ala. Deceased. †

CLARK, PENDLETON SCOTT, architect; b. Lynchburg, Va., Feb. 21, 1895; s. John Robert and Bessie P. (Scott) C.; m. Alice S. Fleming, Oct. 22, 1923; children: Pendleton Scott, Betty Clark Roberts, Katherine Sanders Clark Agnew. Student, Agusta Mil. Acad., 1911-12; grad., U. Pa., 1917. With various archtl. firms, 1912-14, 19-21, pvt. practice arch., 1920-92; ptnr. Clark & Crowe, Architects, 1923-34; pvt. practice Pendleton S. Clark, Architect, 1934-92; ptnr. Clark, Nexsen & Owen, Architects; engaged in collegiate, instl., sch., housing, banks, comml. arch. and def. work; dir. Lynchburg Broadcasting Corp., Imperial Colliery Co., Co-op Bldg. & Loan, Langhorne Road Apts., Inc.; mem. Clark & Buhr, architects and engrs. for Naval Def. Work, 1950-53; mem. Clark, Buhr & Nexsen, Lynchburg, architects and engrs. Contbr. articles to profl. jours. Mem. adv. coun. on naval affairs Fifth Naval Dist.; chmn. Lynchburg Planning Commn., 1934-38, Bldg. Code Com., 1930, 39, 48-49. Ensign USN, 1917-19; comdr. USNR, 1942-45. Decorated Victory medal with 1 star, WWI, European, Am., Pacific theatre ribbons, WW II Philippine Liberation, Bronze Star medal. Fellow AIA (chmn. legis. com. 1953, chmn. com. awards, scholarships and allied arts Va. chpt. 1957-60); mem. Va. Found. Archtl. Edn. (pres. 1959-60), Soc. Mil. Engrs., Mil. Order World Wars, C. of C. (dir. 1935-36, 53), Lynchburg Hist. Soc. (charter mem., dir. 1934), Kiwanis (Lynchburg chpt. pres. 1929), Va. Engrs. Club, Southeastern Va. Engrs. Club, Boonsboro County Club, James River Club, Bob White Club, Kappa Alpha Soc. Presbyterian. *

CLARK, WESLEY CLARKE, newspaper editor, educator; b. Cleve., Sept. 17, 1907; s. William Chester and Mabel Ruth (Clark) C.; m. Frances Grace Stiles, Oct. 9, 1931 (dec. Sept. 1969); children: Sally Lee (Judd), William Standish; m. Rhea Doyle Eckel, Feb. 9, 1974 (dec. Jan. 1985). A.B., Marietta Coll., 1930; M.A., U. Pa., 1937, Ph.D., 1942. Reporter Marietta Times, 1930, Phila. Evening Bull., 1930-41; instr. polit. sci. Wharton Sch. U. Pa., 1937-41; asst. prof. Syracuse U., 1941-43, prof., 1947-73; dean Sch. Journalism, 1952-71, John Ben Snow prof. newspaper research, 1972-73; pres. Syracuse U. Press, 1954-55; asst. to Sec. of Interior, 1943-46; research dir. H.L. Ickes, 1946-47; v.p., treas. Skaneateles Press, N.Y., 1963-69; asso. editor Skaneateles Press, from 1978; vis. prof. Am. U., Cairo, 1973-74, Sweetbriar Coll., 1981; cons. Caribbean Commn., 1950. Author: Some Economic Aspects of a President's Popularity, 1942, El Derecho a la Information, 1966; editor: Journalism Tomorrow, 1959. Mem. N.Y. State Soc. Newspaper Editors, N.Y. State Press Assn., Caribbean Conservation Corp., Delta Upsilon. Clubs: Cosmos (Washington). Home: Skaneateles N.Y. Died Dec. 18, 1990; buried Mentor. Ohio.

CLARKE, JOHN L., college president emeritus; b. American Fork, Utah, May 14, 1905; s. James Hill and Bertha Harrison (Jackson) C.; m. Fay Christensen, Dec. 9, 1931 (dec. Feb. 1970); children: Fay Renee, Richard Gordon Scott, Catherine Ann, Peter O. Thompson III, John Robert; m. LaRae Pickett King, Oct. 14, 1970; stepchildren: William Christopher, Laurel Lyn, Kay Tamara. AB, AM, Brigham Young U., 1932; D.Pub. Service (hon.), 1969; postgrad., U. Cal. (L.A.), 1937. Missionary Ch. of Jesus Christ of Latter-day Saints, Gt. Britain, 1928-30; instr. Am. Fork High Sch., 1933; head social sci. dept. Uintah (Utah) High Sch., 1933-35; prin. Lovell-Cowley (Wyo.) Sem., 1935-36; Moroni (Utah) Sem., 1936-38, Juab Sem., Nephi, Utah, 1938-39; dir. Latter-day Saints Inst. Religion, Thatcher, Ariz., 1939-42; St. George, Utah, 1942-44; pres. Ricks Coll., Rexburg, Idaho, 1944-71; pres. emeritus 1971—; pres. New Eng. Mission, Ch. of Jesus Christ of Latter-day

Saints, 1971-74; pres. Monarch Mining Co., Am. Fork, 1948—. Adv. bd. Targhee Nat. Forest, mem. Rexburg Planning Bd., 1950-58; hon. mem. nat. council Boy Scouts Am., 1960; trustee Idaho Falls Hosp. Recipient Disting. Svc. award Brigham Young U., 1952. Mem. C. of C. (dir.) Am., Western polit. sci. assns., Am. Acad. Polit. and Social Sci., NEA, Ida. Edn. Assn., Northwest Assn. Jr. Colls. (pres. 1965-66), Delta Phi, Lambda Delta Sigma, Rotarian (dir., pres. 1962-63). Democrat. Home: Rexburg Idaho Died Feb. 20, 1991; buried Rexburg Cemetery, Rexburg, Idaho.

CLARKE, J(OSEPH) HENRY, dental educator, dentist; b. Salt Lake City, July 19, 1930; s. Emanuel Henry and Bertha Clara (Langton) C.; m. Linda Louise Maxfield, Apr. 8, 1953; children: Linda, Candice, Susan. Student U. Utah, 1948-50; B.S., Portland State Coll., 1955-57; D.M.D., U. Oreg., 1961. Practice gen. dentistry, Portland, Oreg., 1961-71, part time 1971—; mem. med. staff Woodland Park Hosp., Portland, 1963-74, chief dental service, 1970-71; supervising dentist Dental Hygiene Clinic, Oreg. Health Scis. U., Portland, 1971—; dir. div. behavioral sci., 1973—. Author videocassette and workbook: Dental Treatment of Family Members, 1977; contbr. chpt. to book. Served with U.S. Army, 1953-55. Recipient Outstanding Instr. award Dental Hygiene Class, Oreg. Health Scis. U., 1974, Outstanding Achievement in Teaching award, sr. dental class, 1978, 86. Excellence in Teaching award, Oreg. Health Scis. U., 1984. Mem. Am. Acad. History of Dentistry (pres. 1974-75), ADA, Soc. Clin. and Exptl. Hypnosis (ADA liaison 1984—), Portland Acad. Hypnosis (pres. 1983-84), Omicron Kappa Upsilon. Mormon. Deceased. Home: Portland Oreg. †

CLARKE, ROBERT BRADSTREET, publishing company executive; b. Mountainside, N.J., Oct. 31, 1928; s. Bert and Antoinette (Bartlett) C.; m. Roberta Powell, Aug. 26, 1950; children—William, Cynthia Clarke Paolillo. Exec. v.p. Grolier Enterprises, Inc., 1960-67, pres., dir., 1967-89; pres., dir. Am. Peoples Press, Westmont, Ill., 1965-70; v.p. mail order, then exec. v.p. Grolier Inc., N.Y.C., 1974-76; pres., chief exec. officer Grolier Inc., 1976-78, chmn., pres., chief exec. officer, 1978-87, chmn., chief exec. officer, 1987-89, ret., 1989; mem. adv. bd. Union Trust Co., Stamford, Conn.; dir. Book Industry Study Group, 1985; mem. direct mktg. adv. bd. NYU, 1983-85. Trustee Danbury (Conn.) Hosp., 1974-78; vice chmn. Danbury United Way, 1972; bd. dirs. Western Conn. State U., Corp. Coll. Council, from 1978; trustee Direct Mktg. Assn. Ednl. Found., from 1981. Named Direct Mktg. Man of Year Direct Mktg. Day in N.Y., Inc., 1977; recipient Edward N. Mayer Jr. award Direct Mktg. Ednl. Found., 1988. Mem. Am. Mgmt. Assn. (trustee, v.p., chmn. gen. mgmt. council) Direct Selling Assn., Direct Mktg. Assn. (dir., past chmn.), Danbury C. of C. (past chmn.), Cousteau Soc (founding dir. from 1974), Assn. Am. Pubs. (from bd. dirs. 1987), Tower Fellows. Clubs: Saugatuck Harbor Yacht (past commodore), N.Y. Yacht, Pubs. Lunch. Home: New Canaan Conn. Died Nov. 2, 1990; buried Lake View Cemetery, New Canaan.

CLARKE, ROBERT WARNER, investment company executive; b. Utica, N.Y., Dec. 25, 1896; s. Charles Patrick and Agnes Sinclair (Warner) C.; m. Catherine B. Cartan, Aug. 27, 1927; children: Henry Cartan, Richard Warner, Michael (dec.). Student, Amherst Coll., 1919, U.S. Naval Acad. Pres. Richard W. Clark Corp., Investment Bankers, N.Y.C., 1924-92; sr. ptnr. Richard W. Clark & Co.; mem. N.Y. Stock Exchange; assoc. mem. Am. Exchange. With USN, 1917-19, to lt. comdr. USNR, 1941-45. Mem. Sons Revolution, Soc. Colonial Wars (counsel), The Pilgrims, The New Eng. Soc. (dir.) Knickerbocker Club, Downtown Assn., N.Y. Yacht Club, Racquet and Tennis Club (N.Y.C.), Alpha Delta Phi. *

CLAUSEN, DONALD NEATH, lawyer; b. Racine, Wis., Aug. 30, 1898; s. Christian F.W. and Josephine (Burkert) C.; m. Henrietta Underwood, Sept. 3, 1938; children: Catherine (dec.), Karen Neath, Henrietta Carol, Barbara Jean. Student, U. Ill., 1917-18, U. Chgo., 1919-20; LLB, Chgo. Kent Coll. Law, 1923. Bar: Ill. 1925. Engaged in gen. civil practice in trial cases; sr. ptnr. Clausen, Hirsh & Miller, 1936-58, Clausen, Hirsh, Miller & Gorman, Chgo., 1958-92; dir., v.p. Tablet & Ticket Co.; dir. Certain-Teed Products Corp. Fellow Internat. Acad. Trial Lawyers, Am. Coll. Trial Lawyers; mem. ABA, Ill. Bar Assn., Chgo. Bar Assn., Internat. Assn. Ins. Counsel, Bar Assn. of U.S. Ct. of Appeals of 7th Cir., Exec. Club, Skokie Country Club, Chgo. Athletic Club, Union League, Wind and Food Soc. Chgo., Humidor Club, Phi Delta Phi, Chi Psi. Episcopalian. *

CLAYTOR, ARTHUR ADAMS, physician; b. Copper Hills, Va., Dec. 2, 1893; s. William A. and Judith A. (Reynolds) C.; m. Marie V. Walden, Sept. 28, 1940;l children: Elinor Marie Claytor Cowan, Carol Ann. PhG, Temple U., 1923; student, Northwestern U., 1928-30; MD, Meharry Med. Coll., 1934; postgrad., U. Mich., 1942. Intern Providen Hosp., Chgo., 1934-35; resident Parkside Hosp., Detroit, 1935-36; pvt. practice medicine Saginaw, Mich., 1936-92; mem. staff St. Luke's Hosp., St. Mary's Hosp., Saginaw Gen. Hosp., 1958-63. Bd. dirs. 1st Ward Community Ctr., Saginaw, 1943-92,

pres., 1955-58; mem. Saginaw Housing Commn., 1947-59; vice chmn. Buena Vista Twp. Scholarship Commn. With U.S. Army, WW I; AEF in France. Recipient citation for outstanding svc. to community local Am. Legion post, 1955, Study Culture Club, Saginaw, 1950. Mem. AMA, Mich. Med. Soc. (named foremost family physician of yr. 1959), Saginaw County Med. Soc., Acad. Gen. Practitioners, Am. Legion, Northwestern U. Alumni Assn., Phi Beta Sigma, Flint (Mich.) Sportsman Club. *

CLEARY, JOHN VINCENT, electric utility executive; b. Liberty, N.Y., Oct. 15, 1901; s. John P. and Sarah Jane (Tracy) C.; m. Lilian Dacey, June 1, 1926; children: John V., Thomas J. Student, NYU, 1925-28. Asst. contr. Consol. Edison Co. N.Y., Inc., N.Y.C., 1936-46, sr. asst. contr., 1946-52, contr., 1952-57, v.p., chief acctg. officer, 1957-62, sr. v.p., 1962-65. Mem. Fin. Execs. Inst., Edison Electric Inst., Am. Gas Assn., Manhattan Club, Leewood Golf Club. Roman Catholic. Home: Bronxville N.Y.

CLEARY, THERESA ANNE, university administrator; b. Shanghai, China, Dec. 12, 1935; d. Frank C. and Janet E. (Sweeney) C. BS, Marquette U., 1958; MA, U. Minn., 1960; PhD, U. Ill., 1964. Assoc. rsch. psychologist Rsch. Psychologist Ednl. Testing Svc., Princeton, N.J., 1964-66; assst. prof. U. Wis., Madison, 1966-69, assoc. prof. pscyhology, 1969-72; exec. dir. examinations Coll. Bd., N.Y.C., 1971-72, chief program svcs. div., 1972-74, v.p. program planning and rsch., 1974-75, rsch. cons., 1976-78; acting dir. admissions U. Iowa, Iowa City, 1985-87, dir. evaluation and examination svc., 1979-89, assoc. v.p. acad. affairs, 1989-92. Contbr. numerous articles to profl. jours. and reviewer of jours. (Palmer O. Jounson Meml award 1971); book review editor Jour. Ednl. Measurment, 1980-83; editorial bd. Review of Rsch. in Edn., Ednl. Psychologist, Ednl. and Psychol. Measurement. Ad Hoc panel on career edn. U.S. Commr. Edn., 1972; planning adv. com. Nat. Longitudinal Study, 1973; planning conf. studies of teaching Nat. Inst. Edn., 1974; adv. com. Project DIS-COVER, 1974; mem. Nat. Adv. Panel Reading Achievement, N.Y., 1977—. Mem. Psychometric Soc. (trustee 1971-74), NIMH (review com. 1972-74), Iowa Ednl. Rsch. and Evaluation Assn. (bd. dirs. 1980-82), Am. Ednl. Resch. Assn. (v.p. div. D), Am. Psychol. Assn. (pres. div. 5 1984-85, div. 15 1986-87, coun. rep. 1987-89, pres. coalition acad., sci. and applied psychology 1989-91, Thorndike award com. 1990-92). Home: West Redding Conn. Died Nov. 1, 1992. †

CLEMMONS, SLATON, lawyer; b. Rome, Ga., July 19, 1909; s. Thomas Edmondson and Annie Ross (Slaton) C.; student Davidson Coll., 1926-27; J.D., U. Ga., 1929; postgrad. U. Pa., 1929-30; m. Starr Reynolds Quigg, 1939 (div. 1957); children: Diana Edmondson, Byard Quigg, Thomas Slaton; m. 2d, Frances Mansell Crowder, Nov. 1965. Admitted to Ga. bar, 1929, U.S. Supreme Ct. bar, 1937; practiced in Rome, 1930-35, 46-54; spl. atty. U.S. Dept. Justice, 1935-37, 42-46; spl. atty. gen. Ga., 1938-39; spl. asst. to atty. gen. U.S., 1940-41; asst. U.S. atty. No. dist. Ga., 1954-62; 1st asst. U.S. atty., 1962-70, ret., 1970. Served as lt. (j.g.) USNR, 1942. Mem. Ga. Rome (past pres.) bar assns., Am. Legion, Mil. Order World Wars, Phi Delta Phi, Sigma Alpha Epsilon. Democrat. Presbyn. Mason. Clubs: Coosa Country, Nine O'clock Cotillion (Rome, Ga.). Died June 1991. Home: Rome Ga. †

CLENDINEN, JAMES AUGUSTUS, newspaper editor; b. Eufaula, Ala., Dec. 1, 1910; s. Thomas A. and Katherine M. (Powell) C.; m. Barbara Harrison, May 22, 1943; children: James Dudley, Melissa Louise. Student, U. Fla., 1929-30. Reporter, then mng. editor Clearwater (Fla.) Evening Sun, 1930-35; mem. staff Tampa Tribune, Fla., 1935-42, 1946-85; editor Tampa Tribune, 1958-85, chmn. editorial bd., 1974-85; pres. Nat. Conf. Editorial Writers, 1966; mem. Pulitzer Prize Jury, 1967, 68. Mem. Fla. Gov.'s Commn. on Edn., 1971-73, Fla. Jud. Commn., 1975-88. With USAAF, 1942-45. Recipient 1st prize for editorial writing Fla. Daily Newspaper Assn., 1953, 57, 58, 60, 64, 66, 68, 70, 71, 76, 78, 83, 84; traveling fellow to study conditions in Spain So. Assn. Nieman Fellows, 1957; Freedoms Found. award for editorial writing, 1961, 62; Fla. Edn. Assn. award, 1963; Nat. Headliners Club award, 1964; Pub. Service award Fla. Bar, 1965; Distinguished Service award U. Fla. Coll. Journalism, 1974; Pub. Service award ABA, 1977; Pub. Service award Fla. Legislature, 1965; named Outstanding Citizen, Tampa Civitan Club, 1985. Mem. Am. Soc. Newspaper Editors (mem. del. to Red China 1972, dir.), Fla. Soc. Editors (founder, 1st pres. 1955), Sigma Delta Chi (award editorial writing 1962), Phi Kappa Tau. Episcopalian. Clubs: Tampa Yacht and Country, University, Exchange (Tampa); Gasparilla Krewe. Home: Tampa Fla. Died Jan. 18, 1981; buried Tampa, Fla.

CLEVELAND, JAMES, gospel singer, composer, minister; b. Chgo., Dec. 5, 1931. Hon. doctorate, Temple Bible Coll. Minister Los Angeles, from 1961; pastor New Greater Harvest Baptist Ch., Los Angeles; founder, pastor Cornerstone Instnl. Baptist Ch., Los Angeles; founder Gospel Music Workshop of Am., 1968; organizer So. Calif. Community Choir, 1969, Gospel Girls, 1969. Singer with various groups including: The Caravans, Gospelaires, Roberta Martin Singers, Mahalia Jackson, Meditation Singers of Detroit, Gospel Chimes; singer, former of group: Cleveland Singers; mem. James Cleveland Singers; actor: film Save The Children, 1973; composer hundreds of gospel songs including Grace is Sufficient, God Specializes, He's Using Me, The Man, Jesus; recorded over 70 albums including All You Need, At The Cross, Bread of Heaven, Christ Is The Answer, Down Memory Lane, Free At Last, Give Me My Flowers, Peace Be Still, I'll Do His Will, Lord, Do It, I Stood on the Banks, Lord Help Me, Jesus Is The Best Thing. Recipient Grammy awards; recipient numerous gold albums, Image award NAACP, 1976, award Nat. Assn. Negro Musicians, 1975, numerous musical awards. Home: Los Angeles Calif. Died Feb. 9, 1991.

CLIFTON, CHESTER VICTOR, JR., public relations executive, army officer; b. Edmonton, Alta., Can., Sept. 24, 1913; s. Chester Victor and Minnie (Corbett) C.; m. Anne Bodine, Oct. 16, 1937. Student, U. Wash., 1931-32; B.S., U.S. Mil. Acad., 1936; M.A., U. Wis., 1948; grad., Nat. War Coll., 1954. Newspaper reporter Seattle Post Intelligencer, 1930-32, N.Y. Herald Tribune, summer 1936; commd. 2d lt. U.S. Army, 1936, advanced through grades to maj. gen., 1961; ops. officer Hdqrs. 22d F.A. Group, Ft. Bragg, N.C., 1942-43; comdg. officer 193d F.A. Group, 1943; comdg. officer 698th F.A. bn., Ft. Bragg, also Italy, France, Germany, 1943-45; pub. relations officer Hdqrs. Army Ground Forces, Washington, 1945-47; asst. sec. gen. staff Office Chief of Staff, Washington, 1948-49; asst. to chmn. Joint Chiefs Staff, 1949-53; exec. officer Hdqrs. 2d Armored Div. Arty., Germany, 1954-55; chief joint plans J-3 Div., European Command, France, 1955-56; dep. chief, then chief of information Dept. Army, 1956-61; mil. aide to Pres. Kennedy, 1961-63, Pres. Johnson, 1963-65; pres. Thomas J. Deegan Co., Inc., 1965-67, Clifton-Raymond Assos., Inc., 1967-68, Clifton Counselors, Inc., Washington, 1968-91. Author: The Memories: JFK, 1961-1963; Contbr. articles to mags.; Korean War history in Ency. Brit. Devel. cons. John F. Kennedy Ctr. for Performing Arts, Washington. Decorated Legion of Merit, D.S.M., Croix de Guerre (France), Cross of Valor (Italy). Mem. Assn. Grads. U.S. Mil. Acad. (trustee 1975-89, emeritus), Sigma Delta Chi, Delta Upsilon. Clubs: Nat. Press (Washington), Federal City (Washington), Burning Tree (Washington). Home: Washington D.C. Died Dec. 23, 1991; buried Arlington Nat. Cemetery.

CLIVE, JOHN LEONARD, history and literature educator; b. Berlin, Sept. 25, 1924; came to U.S., 1940, naturalized, 1943; s. Bruno and Rose (Rosenfeld) C. Student, Buxton Coll., Derbyshire, Eng., 1937-40; A.B., U. N.C., 1943; M.A., Harvard, 1947, Ph.D., 1952. From teaching fellow to asst. prof. history Harvard U., 1948-60, prof. history and lit., 1965-75, prof. history, 1975-79, William R. Kenan, Jr. prof. history and lit., from 1979; Vernon vis. prof. biography Dartmouth Coll., 1979; asst. prof., then asso. prof. history U. Chgo., 1960-65; vis. fellow All Souls Coll.. Oxford, 1977-78; spl. Ford lectr. Oxford U., 1978. Author: Scotch Reviewers: The Edinburgh Review, 1802-1815, 1957, Macaulay: The Shaping of the Historian, 1973, Not by Fact Alone, 1989; Gen. editor: Classics of British Historical Literature. Served to 2d lt. AUS, 1943-46. Recipient Nat. Book award, 1974; Robert Livingston Schuyler prize Am. Hist. Assn., 1976. Fellow Royal Hist. Soc., Am. Acad. Arts and Scis., Australian Acad. Humanities (hon.); mem. Mass. Hist. Soc., Phi Beta Kappa. Club: Century Assn. Home: Cambridge Mass. Died Jan. 7, 1990. †

CLOOS, ERNST, geologist, educator; b. Saarbrucken, Germany, May 17, 1898; came to U.S. 1929, naturalized 1938; s. Ulrich and Elisabeth (Hockel) C.; m. Margaret Spemann, Dec. 27, 1923; children: Gisela, Veronica. Student, U. Freiburg, U. Göttingen; PhD, U. Breslau, 1923. Geologist Seismos Co., Hannover, Germany, 1924-29; in charge geophys. exploration Tex., 1924-26, Eng., 1937, Germany and Iraq, 1927-28; conductor investigations Sierra Nevada granites, 1929-30; lectr. Johns Hopkins U., Balt., 1931-37, assoc. prof., 1937-41, prof., 1941-92. Chmn. Commn. Md. Dept. Geology, Mines and Water Resources, 1962. Guggenheim fellow, 1956-57. Fellow Geol. Soc. London; mem. AAAS, Nat. Acad. Sci., Geol. Soc. Am., Geophys. Union, Am. Philos. Soc., Geol. Soc. London, Geol. Soc. Finland, Geologists Assn., Sigma Xi, Phi Beta Kappa. *

CLOSS, GERHARD LUDWIG, chemistry educator; b. Wuppertal, Fed. Republic Germany, May 1, 1928; came to U.S., 1955; s. Ludwig and Maria (Pfeiffer) C.; m. Liselotte Else Pohmer, Aug. 17, 1956. Diplom Chemiker, Universität Tübingen, Fed. Republic Germany, 1953, PhD in Chemistry, 1955. Asst. prof. U. Chgo., 1957-61, assoc. prof., 1961-63, prof. chemistry, 1963-74, A.A. Michelson Disting. Service prof. chemistry, 1974-92; vis. prof. U. Ill., Chgo., 1965, Yale U., New Haven, 1965, Universiteit Leiden, Netherlands, 1971-72; adj. fgn. prof. Inst. Molecular Sci., Okazaki, Japan, 1985; head chem. div. Argonne Nat. Lab., Ill., 1979-82, sr. scientist, 1984-92. Cons. editor Ency. Britannica, Chgo., 1968-71; mem. editorial bd. Chem. Revs., 1973-79; contbr. 130 articles to profl. jours. Recipient Jean Servais Stas medal Societe Chimique de Belgique, 1971, award I-APS, 1991. Fellow AAAS, Am. Acad. Arts and Scis.; mem. NAS, Am. Chem. Soc. (James Flack Norris award 1974, Arthur C. Cope award 1991). Home: Palos Park Ill. Died May 24, 1992. †

CLOUD, PRESTON, geologist, author, consultant; b. West Upton, Mass., Sept. 26, 1912; s. Preston E. and Pauline L. (Wiedemann) C.; m. Janice Gibson, 1972; children by previous marriage: Karen, Lisa, Kevin. B.S., George Washington U., 1938; Ph.D., Yale U., 1940. Instr. Mo. Sch. Mines and Metallurgy, 1940-41; research fellow Yale U., 1941-42; geologist U.S. Geol. Survey, 1942-46, 48-61, 74-79, chief paleontology and stratigraphy br., 1949-59; research geologist, 1959-61, 74-79; asst. prof., curator invertebrate paleontology Harvard U., 1946-48; prof. dept. geology and geophysics U. Minn., 1961-65, chmn., 1961-63; prof. geology UCLA, 1965-68; prof. biogeology and environ. studies dept. geol. scis. U. Calif., Santa Barbara, 1968-74, prof. emeritus, 1974; vis. prof. U. Tex., 1962, 78; H.R. Luce prof. cosmology Mt. Holyoke Coll., 1979-80; Sr. Queens fellow Baas-Becking Geobiology Lab., Canberra, Australia, 1981; internat exchange scholar Nat. Sci. and Engrng. Research Council Can., 1982; hon. vis. prof. U. Ottawa (Ont. Can.), 1982; Nat. Sigma Xi lectr., 1967; Emmons lectr. Colo. Sci. Soc.; Bownocker lectr. Ohio State U.; French lectr. Pomona Coll.; Dumaresq-Smith lectr. Acadia Coll., N.B., Can.; A.L. DuToit Meml. lectr. Royal Soc. and Geol. Soc. of South Africa; mem. governing bd. NRC, 1972-75; mem. Pacific Sci. Bd., 1952-56, 62-65; del. internat. sci. congresses; cons. to govt., industry, founds. and agys. Author: Terebratuloid Brachiopoda of the Silurian and Devonian, 1942; (with Virgil E. Barnes) The Ellenburger Group of Central Texas, 1948; (with others) Geology of Saipan, Mariana Islands, 1957; Environment of Calcium Carbonate Deposition West of Andros Island, Bahamas, 1962, Cosmos, Earth and Man, 1978, Oasis in Space, 1988; editor and co-author: (with others) Resources and Man, 1969, Adventures in Earth History, 1970; mem. editorial bds. 6 jours.; author articles. Recipient A. Cressey Morrison prize natural history, 1941, Rockefeller Pub. Service award, 1956, U.S. Dept. Interior Distinguished Service award and gold medal, 1959, Medal, Paleontol Soc. Am., 1971, Lucius W. Cross medal Yale U., 1973, Penrose medal Geol. Soc. Am., 1976, C.D. Walcott medal Nat. Acad. Scis., 1977, R.C. Moore medal Soc. Econ. Paleontologists and Mineralogists, 1986; J.S. Guggenheim fellow, 1982-83. Fellow AAAS (life, com. on meetings 1963-65), Am. Acad. Arts and Scis. (com. on membership 1978-80, coun. 1980-83); mem. NAS (com. on nominations 1965, chair, 1969, mem. coun. 1972-75, exec. com. 1973-75), Am. Philos. Soc. (com. on membership 1988—), Polish Acad. Scis. (fgn. assoc.), Geol. Soc. Am. (fellow, life, coun. 1972-75), Paleontol. Soc. Am., Paleontol. Soc. India (hon.), Geol. Soc. Belgium (hon. fgn. corr.), Paleontol. Soc. Deutschland (hon. corr. mem.), Phi Beta Kappa, Sigma Xi, Sigma Gamma Epsilon. Home: Santa Barbara Calif. Died Jan. 16, 1991, buried Santa Barbara.

CLOUGH, SHEPARD BANCROFT, European economics historian, educator; b. Bloomington, Ind., Dec. 6, 1901; s. Clarence Edward and Mary Ellen (Shepard) C.; m. Rose Trillo, Jan. 5, 1926 (div. 1974); children: Shepard Anthony, Peter Nelson; m. Marion Diana McGill, June 12, 1976. AB, Colgate U., 1923; postgrad., U. Sorbonne, 1923-24, U. Heidelberg, 1924; PhD, Columbia U., 1930. Instr. history Columbia U., N.Y.C., 1928-37, prof. history, mem. faculty polit. sci., 1937-70; rsch. staff Mut. Life Ins. Co., 1941-42; div. econ. studies U.S. Dept. State, 1942-43; lectr. Sch. Mil. Govt., Charlottesville, Va., 1942-43, Office Fgn. Relief and Rehab., 1943-44; vis. prof. U. Paris, 1952, U. Grenoble, 1952, U. Turin, 1955-56, U. Bari, Italy, Internat. U., Florence, Italy, 1978; vis. lectr. univs. Berlin, Turin, Genoa and Rome, 1952-53; NATO prof. to Italy, 1966-67; mem. hist. svc. bd. Adv. Coun. on War History, Social Sci. Rsch. Coun., 1943-52. Authjor: History of the Flemish Movement in Belgium, 1931, France, 1789-1939, 1939, A Century of American Life Insurance, 1946, Rise and Fall of Civilization, 1951, Basic Values in Western Civilization, 1960, The Economic History of Modern Italy, 1964, others; co-author: European Economic History, Documents and Readings, 1965, History of Italy, 1968, Economic History of Europe, 1968, Columbia History of the World, 1972, European History in a World Perspective, 1975, others. Armed Forces, NATO fellow, 1958, Rockefeller fellow, 1961-62; decorated officer knight Order of Merit of Italian Republic. Mem. Am. Hist. Assn., Storia del Risorgimento, Econ. History Assn., Internat. Econ. History Assn., Am. Econ. Assn., Soc. Modern History (France), English Econ. History Soc., Soc. French Hist. Studies, Soc. Italian Hist. Studies, Acad. Polit. Sci., Phi Beta Kappa, Delta Upsilon. Home: East Peacham Vt. Died June 7, 1990; interred Peacham, Vt.

CLOUGH, WILSON OBER, English language educator; b. New Brunswick, N.J., Jan. 7, 1894; s. Clinton Wilson and Mary Ober C.; m. Laura Lee Bowman, June 22, 1921; children: Mary Schmiedeskamp, Frank R., David V.W. AB, Union Coll., 1917, LittD, 1957; postgrad., U. Montpellier, France, 1919; AM, U. Colo., 1925. Head Latin, French, English high schs. Mason City, Ill., St. Joseph, Mo., 1917-24, Leadville, Colo., Boise, Idaho, 1917-24; instr. U. Wyo., 1924-26, asst. prof., 1926-31, assoc. prof., 1931-38, prof., 1938-90, William Robertson Coe prof. Am. studies, 1956-9, sec. faculty, 1939-46, chmn. dept. English, 1946-49; faculty U. N.Mex., summer 1926, Lehigh U., summer 1936, NYU, summer, 1949. Mem. editorial bd. Western Humanities Rev.; author: History of the University of Wyoming, 1887-1937, 1937, Grammar of English Communication, 1947, Brief Oasis, 1954, Our Long, Heritage, 1955; contbr. articles, short stories, poetry to profl. publs. With U.S. Army, 1918-19, AEF, France. Mem. MLA, Am. Studies Assn., AAUP, Phi Beta Kappa, Psi Chi, Phi Sigma Iota. Home: Laramie Wyo. Died Sept. 19, 1990.

CLYMER, JOHN FORD, artist; b. Ellensburg, Wash., Jan. 29, 1907; s. John Perkepin and Elmira Elizabeth (Ford) C.; m. Doris E. Schnebly, Mar. 4, 1932; children: David J., Jo Lorraine Clymer Tatum. Student, Vancouver Sch. Art, 1925-28, Ont. Coll. Art, 1930, Wilmington Acad. Art, 1931-32, Grand Central Sch. Art, 1936. Illustrator stories for numerous mags. in Can. and U.S., 1925-64; painted more than 80 covers for Saturday Evening Post, 1942-62; exhibited group shows, Nat. Acad. Western Art Cowboy Hall of Fame, Oklahoma City, 1972-81, Cowboy Artists Am. Ann. Show, Phoenix, 1969-83, Cowboy Artists Am. Mus., Kerrville, Tex., 1983; represented in permanent collections, Mont. Hist. Soc., Helena, Buffalo Bill Hist. Ctr., Cody, Wyo., Nat. Cowboy Hall of Fame, Oklahoma City, Rockwell Corning Mus., Corning, N.Y., The Glenbow Found., Calgary, Can., Grand Teton Nat. Park Vis. Ctr., Moose, Wyo., Wildlife of Am. West Mus., Jackson, Wyo.; appeared on NBC Today Show, Jan., 1988. Recipient Franklin Mint Gold medal for western art, 1973, Gold medal in oil Nat. Acad. Western Art, 1974, Pre de West award Nat. Cowboy Hall of Fame, 1976; featured in PBS Profiles in Am. Art, 1982, in PBS series The West of the Imagination, 1987; John F. Clymer Studio recreated in Wildlife of Am. West Art Mus., Jackson, Wyo.; The Clymer Mus., Ellensburg, Wash., named and created in his honor and has permanent exhibit. Mem. Cowboy Artistsof Am., Nat. Acad. Western Art, Soc. Animal Artists, Ont. Soc. Artists, Hudson Valley Art Assn. Home: Teton Village Wyo. Died Nov. 2, 1989; buried Ellensburg, Wash.

CLYNE, JOHN VALENTINE, lawyer, business executive; b. Vancouver, B.C., Can., Feb. 14, 1902; s. Henry and Martha A. (Dillon) C.; m. Betty V. A. Somerset, Dec. 14, 1927 (dec. Mar. 1990); children—Valentine, (Mrs. Anthony W. Gamage), J. Stuart. B.A., U. B.C., 1923, LL.D. (hon.), 1984; postgrad. student law, London Sch. Econs., King's Coll., London; LL.D. (hon.), McGill U., 1981, U. B.C., 1984. Bar: Can. 1927. With E.P. Davis & Co., Vancouver, 1923-25, 27, Blake & Redden, legal firm, London, 1925-27, Williams & Mason, lawyers, Prince Rupert, Can., 1928-29; ptnr. Macrae, Duncan & Clyne, Vancouver, 1929-46, Campney, Owen, Clyne & Murphy, Vancouver, 1947-50; pres. Park S.S. Co. (Crown Co.), 1945-50; chmn. Can. Maritime Commn., 1947-50; judge Supreme Ct., B.C., 1950-57; chmn. bd. MacMillan and Bloedel Ltd., 1957-60; now hon. dir.; chmn. bd. MacMillan, Bloedel and Powell River (now MacMillan Bloedel Ltd.), 1960-73, chief exec. officer, 1960-72; Royal commr. Land Expropriation in B.C., 1961; rep. Can. sub-coms. UN and NATO dealing with shipping; chmn. prep. com. inter-govtl. Maritime Consultative Orgn., Lake Success, 1948-50; royal commr. to investigate Whatshan Power House Disaster, 1954; royal commr. on Milk Inquiry, 1954-55; chmn. adv. group Exec. Compensation Pub. Service, 1968-71; past provincial pres. St. John Ambulance Assn.; bd. dirs. Nat. Indsl. Conf. Bd., Can., 1961-73, Nat. Indsl. Conf. U.S., 1962-73; chmn. selection com. Royal Bank Award, 1967-82; hon. patron Can. Inst for Advanced Legal Studies, from 1977; hon. mem. C. D. Howe Inst.; chmn. B.C. Heritage Trust, 1978-81; gov. Consortium for Atlantic-Pacific Affairs, from 1977; chancellor U B.C., 1978-84; chmn. Consultative Com. on Implications of Telecommunications for Can. Sovereignty, 1979-80; chmn. roundhouse adv. com., 1981-82; mem. fed. govt. Task Force on Deep Sea Shipping, 1984. Author: (memoirs) Jack of All Trades, 1985. Mem. Cultural Heritage Adv. Com., 1981-82. Decorated comdr. Order Knights St. John, companion Order of Can. Mem. Can. Bar Assn., Law Soc. B.C. Clubs: The Vancouver, University, The Shaughnessy Golf and Country (Vancouver); Union (Victoria, B.C.); Bohemian (San Francisco). Home: Vancouver Can. Died Aug. 22, 1989; buried Vancouver.

COADY, JOHN MARTIN, dental association executive; b. Minooka, Ill., Apr. 2, 1927; s. John Jay and Mildred Schuyler (Brinckerhoff) C. AS, Joliet (Ill.) Jr. Coll., 1949; DDS, Loyola U., Chgo., 1953, MS, 1960; DSc (hon.), Georgetown U., 1980. Mem. faculty Loyola U. Sch. Dentistry, 1954-63; gen. practice dentistry Morris, Ill., 1953-57, Chgo., 1957-63; mem. adminstrv. staff ADA, Chgo., 1963-85, asst. exec. dir. edn. and hosps., 1972-78, acting exec. dir. assns., 1978-79, exec. dir., 1979-85; asst. sec. Council on Dental Edn., 1963-70, sec., 1970-72; mem. adv. com. for hosp.-sponsored ambulatory dental services Robert Wood Johnson Found., task force on dental medicine Commn. on the Future of Washington U. Dental Sch., St. Louis. Author papers in field. Served with USNR, 1945-46. Recipient ann. Dental Alumni award Loyola U. Sch. Dentistry, 1982. Fellow Pierre Fauchard Acad. (Pierre Fauchard medal 1983), Internat. Coll. Dentists, Am.

Coll. Dentists; mem. ADA, Am. Assn. Dental Schs., Am. Assn. Oral and Maxillofacial Surgeons (hon.), Am. Acad. Oral Medicine (hon.), Ill. State Dental Soc., Chgo. Dental Soc., Acad. Gen. Dentistry (hon.), Blue Key, Omicron Kappa Upsilon, Delta Sigma Delta (meritorious award 1983). Republican. Episcopalian. Home: Naples Fla. Died Nov. 11, 1990; buried Saugatuck, Mich.

COATES, ROBERT MYRON, writer, art critic; b. New Haven, Conn., Apr. 6, 1897; s. Frederick and Harriet (Davidson) C.; m. Elsa Kirpal, Feb. 3, 1927 (div. 1946); m. Astrid Peters, June 14, 1946. BA, Yale U., 1919. Author: The Eater of Darkness, 1929, The Outlaw Years, 1930, Yesterday's Burdens, 1933, All the Year Round, 1943, The Bitter Season, 1946, Wisteria Cottage, 1948, The Farther Shore, 1955, The Hour After Westerly, 1957, The View From Here, 1960, Beyond the Alps, 1961, The Man Just Ahead of You, 1963; contbr. to Whither, Whither, a Symposium, 1930, The American Caravan IV, 1931; contbr. articles and fiction to The New Yorker, others. Mem. Internat. Art Critics Assn., Nat. Inst. Arts and Letters, PEN, Century Assn. *

COBB, WILLIAM MONTAGUE, anatomist, physical anthropologist, medical editor, educator, civil rights worker; b. Washington, Oct. 12, 1904; s. William Elmer and Alexzine E. (Montague) C.; m. Hilda B. Smith, June 26, 1929 (dec. June 1976); children: Carolyn Cobb Wilkinson, Hilda Amelia Cobb Gray. A.B. (Blodgett scholar), Amherst Coll., 1925, Sc.D. (hon.), 1955; M.D., Howard U., 1929, L.H.D. (hon.), 1980; Ph.D., Western Res. U., 1932; Sc.D. (hon.), Colby Coll., 1984; L.H.D. (hon.), Med. Coll. Pa., 1986; cert. in embryology, Marine Biol. Lab., Woods Hole, Mass.; student, U.S. Nat. Museum, Washington U.; LL.D., Morgan State Coll., 1964, U. Witwatersrand, South Africa, 1977; Sc.D., Georgetown U., 1978, Med. Coll. Wis., 1979, U. Ark., 1983; D.Med. Sci., Brown U., 1983. Intern Freedmen's Hosp., Washington, 1929-30; instr. embryology Howard U., 1928-29, asst. prof. anatomy, 1932-34, assoc. prof., 1934-42, prof. anatomy, 1942-69, head dept., 1947-69, distinguished prof. anatomy, 1969-73, prof. emeritus, 1973; vis. prof. anatomy Stanford U., 1972, U. Md., 1974, W.Va. U., 1980; Disting. Univ. prof. U. Ark. Med. Scis. Center, 1979; vis. prof., Danz lectr. U. Wash., 1978; vis. prof. orthopaedic surgery Harvard U., 1981; vis. prof. anatomy Med. Coll. Wis., 1982; dir. Disting. Sr. Scholars Lecture Series U. D.C., 1983; jr. med. officer U.S. Dept. Agr., 1935; mem. Pub. Health Advisory Council of D.C., 1953-61, chmn., 1956-58; chief med. examiner Freedmen's Hosp. Bd., D.C. SSS, 1941; civilian cons. to surgeon gen. U.S. Army, 1945; mem. exec. com. White House Conf. on Health, 1965; Fellow in anatomy Western Res. U., 1933-39, asso. anatomy, 1942-44. Founder: Bull. of Medico-Chirurg. Soc. D.C, 1941; editor, 1945-54, Jour. Nat. Med. Assn, 1949-77; author monographs, articles. Active NAACP, 30 yrs., bd. dirs., pres., 1976-82; mem. Friends of Nat. Zoo, Jr. Police and citizens Corp. Rosenwald fellow, 1941-42; recipient citations from Opportunity mag., 1947, citations from Chgo. Defender, 1948, citations from Washington Afro-Am., 1948; Distinguished Service award Medico-Chirurg. Soc. D.C., 1952; D.S.M. Nat. Med. Assn., 1955; Meritorious Service award Med. Soc. of D.C., 1968; Meritorious Pub. Service award Govt. of D.C., 1972; Disting. Public Service award U.S. Navy, 1978, 82; recognized with inaguration of W. Montague Cobb Collection Moorland-Springarn Research Ctr., Los Angeles, 1979, dedication of W. Montague Cobb Med. Edn. Bldg., King-Drew Med. Ctr., Los Angeles, 1984, dedication of A Century of Black Surgeons-The U.S.A. Experience (book) to W. Montague Cobb, Howard U. Hosp., 1987. Fellow Am. Anthrop. Assn., Gerontol. Soc., AAAS (mem. 1957-59), Assn. Anatomists (Henry Gray award 1980), Am. Assn. Phys. Anthropologists (v.p. 1948-50, pres. 1957-59), Am. Eugenics Soc. (dir. 1957-68), Anat. Soc. Gt. Brit. and Ireland, Nat. Med. Assn. (state v.p. 1943, editor 1949-77, chmn. coun. on med. edn. and hosps. 1949-63, nat. pres. 1964-65), Nat. Urban League (health specialist 1945-47), NAACP (chmn. nat. med. com. 1950, bd. dirs. 1949-82, pres. 1976-82), Am. Soc. Mammalogists, Am. Assn. History of Medicine, Washington Soc. History of Medicine (pres. 1972), Assn. Study of Negro Life and History, Anthrop. Soc. Washington (pres. 1949-51), Medica-Chirurgical Soc. D.C. (rec. sec. 1935-41, pres. 1945-47, 54-56), Omega Psi Phi (chmn. scholarship com. 1939-48), Sigma Xi, Alpha Omega Alpha. Presbyterian. Club: Cosmos (Washington). Home: Washington D.C. Died Nov. 20, 1990; buried Lincoln Meml. Cemetery.

COBBLEDICK, GORDON, newspaper sports editor; b. Cleve., Dec. 31, 1898; s. William James and Nina (Armstrong) C.; m. Doris V. Mathews, Julyh 7, 1923; children: William Gordon, Dorn Matthews. Student, Case Inst. Tech., 1919-1921. Reporter Cleve. Plain Dealer, 1923-26; editorial writer Cleve. Times, 1926; sports writer Cleve. Plain Dealer, 1927-44; war corr. P.T.O., 1945; editorial columnist, 1945-46, sports editor and columnish, 1946-92. Pres. Cuyahoga County unit Am. Cancer Soc. With USMC, 1918. Mem. Baseball Writers Assn. Am. (pres. 1949), Sigma Alpha Epsilon, Sigma Delta Chi, Cleve. Athletic Club. *

COBBS, JOHN LEWIS, magazine editor; b. Washington, Sept. 10, 1917; s. John Lewis and Jessie (Ware) C.; m. Phyllis Conway White, Dec. 27, 1941; children: John Lewis, Nicholas Hamner. Student, U. N.C., 1935-36; B.A. with great distinction, Stanford U., 1939, M.A., 1940; postgrad., Harvard U., 1940-41. Research asst. Nat. Indsl. Conf. Bd., 1941-42; finance editor Bus. Week mag., N.Y.C., 1942-43; Washington corr. Bus. Week mag., 1943-45, bus. policy editor, 1945-50, asst. mng. editor, 1950-63, mng. editor, 1963-66, editor, 1966-82; Mem. vis. com., econs. dept. Harvard, 1970-76. Contbr. articles mags. Mem. Chappaqua Bd. Edn., 1957-61; Trustee Chappaqua (N.Y.) Pub. Library, 1967-73, Joint Council Econ. Edn., 1972-82. Recipient school bell award N.E.A., 1958, distinguished service award Sigma Delta Chi, 1959; Reporting award Overseas Press Club, 1972; G.M. Loeb Achievement award, 1972. Mem. Phi Beta Kappa, Phi Gamma Delta. Republican. Episcopalian. Clubs: Harvard (N.Y.C.); Miles River Yacht (St. Michael's, Md.). Home: Saint Michaels Md. Died Oct. 13, 1991; inurned; Christ Ch. Columbarium, St. Michaels, Md.

COCHRAN, ALEXANDER SMITH, architect; b. Balt., Jan. 22, 1913; s. William Francis and Nina (Gill) C.; m. Caroline Sizer, June 5, 1937; children—Alexander Smith, Theodore Sizer, Gill, Caroline Foster. A.B., Princeton U., 1935; postgrad. Sch. Fine Arts, Yale U., 1935-37; M. Arch., Harvard U., 1939; D.F.A. (hon.), Md. Inst., 1971. Registered architect, Md. Draftsman archtl. firms, 1940-41; constrn. insp. E.I. duPont Co., Del., 1941; project planner U.S. Housing Authority, Washington, 1941-42; pvt. practice architecture Balt., from 1945; chmn. bd. emeritus Cochran, Stephenson & Donkervoet Inc., from 1954; v.p. Sherwood Forest Co., 1945-59; prof. architecture U. Md., 1968; Thomas Jefferson prof. architecture U. Va., 1975. Mem. Balt. Planning Commn., 1958-60, 63-70; mem. adv. council Princeton Sch. Architecture, 1974-76; trustee Peabody Inst., Balt. Mus. Art, Goucher Coll. Served to lt. USNR, 1942-45. Fellow AIA (pres. Balt. chpt. 1962, dir. Mid Atlantic region 1971-74, Cochran Residence award merit 1951). Episcopalian. Clubs: Century Assn.; Cosmos; 14 W Hamilton St. (Balt.). Home: Cockeysville Hunt Valley Md. Died Aug. 9, 1989.

CODDINGTON, EARL ALEXANDER, mathematician, educator; b. Washington, Dec. 16, 1920; s. Cyrus Alexander and Lillian (Dezarn) C.; m. Susan Klaber, Nov. 17, 1945; children: Alan Alexander, Robert Henry, Claire Helen. Ph.D., Johns Hopkins, 1948. Instr. Johns Hopkins, 1948-49; instr. MIT, 1949-50, C.L.E. Moore instr., 1950-52; mem. faculty UCLA, 1952-91, prof. math., 1959-91, chmn. math. dept., 1968-71; Fulbright lectr. U. Copenhagen, Denmark, 1955-56, vis. prof., 1963-64; vis. asso. prof. Princeton, 1957-58. Author: (with N. Levinson) Theory of Ordinary Differential Equations, 1955, An Introduction to Ordinary Differential Equations, 1961; cons. editor math., Holden-Day, Inc., 1960-91. Mem. Am. Math. Soc. (coop. editor procs. 1952-55, coop. editor trans. 1957-62), Math. Assn. Am., AAUP, Phi Beta Kappa, Sigma Xi. Home: Pacific Palisades Calif. Died Nov. 11, 1991.

COE, CHARLES NORTON, language professional, educator; b. Rahway, N.J., Apr. 29, 1915; s. Maxwell Alanson and Ethel May (Norton) C.; m. Elizabeth Brown, July 11, 1953; children—Timothy Maxwell, Dorothy Elizabeth. BA cum laude, Amherst Coll., 1937; MA, Trinity Coll., Conn., 1940, Yale U., 1943; PhD, Yale U., 1950. Instr. English and Latin Williston (Mass.) Acad., 1937-39; asst. English Trinity Coll., 1939-47; headmaster Williston Jr. Sch., 1947-48; asst. prof. English U. Idaho, 1948-51, assoc. prof., 1951-54, prof., head dept. humanities, 1954-59; prof. English, dean Grad. Sch., No. Ill. U., 1959-64; provost Monmouth Coll., West Long Branch, N.J., 1964-66, v.p. acad. affairs, 1966-73, dean grad. studies, 1973-77, prof. English, 1964-80, prof. English emeritus, 1980-91. Author: Wordsworth and the Literature of Travel, 1953, Shakespeare's Villains, 1957, Demi-devils: The Character of Shakespeare's Villains, 1963. Served with AUS, 1943-46. Mem. Nat., N.J. edn. assns., MLA, Nat. Coun. Tchrs. English, Coll. English Assn., Phi Beta Kappa, Alpha Phi Omega, Phi Kappa Psi, Phi Delta Kappa. Episcopalian. Home: Eatontown N.J. Died Oct. 1, 1991; buried Fairview Cemetery, New Britain, Conn.

COFFEE, JAMES FREDERICK, lawyer; b. Decatur, Ind., Mar. 6, 1918; s. Claude M. and Frances N. (Butler) C.; m. Jeanmarie Hackman, Dec. 29, 1945 (dec. 1978); children: James, Carolyn, Susan, Sheila, Kevin, Richard, Elizabeth, Thomas, Claudia; m. Marjorie E. Masterson, Oct. 4, 1980. B.C.E., Purdue U., 1939; J.D., Ind. U., 1947. Bar: Wis. 1947, Ill. 1952. Patent atty. Allis Chalmers Mfg. Co., Milw., 1947-51; mem. firm Anderson, Luedeka, Fitch, Even & Tabin (and predecessors), Chgo., 1951-64; partner Anderson, Luedeka, Fitch, Even & Tabin (and predecessors), 1956-64; individual practice law Chgo., 1964-71; partner law firm Coffee & Sweeney, Chgo., 1971-76; partner, gen. counsel design firm Marvin Glass & Assos., Chgo., from 1973. Capt. AUS, 1941-46, Japanese prisoner of war, 1942-45. Mem. ABA, Ill. Bar Assn., Chgo. Bar Assn. (chmn. com. patents, trademark and unfair trade practices 1967), Am. Patent Law Assn., Patent Law Assn. Chgo. (chmn. com. copyrights 1969), Am. Judicature Soc., Tower Club of Chgo. (bd. dirs. 1978—,v.p. 1988—). Home: West Chicago Ill. Died Oct. 26, 1989; buried Ft. Wayne, Ind.

COFFEY, HAROLD F., furniture manufacturing company executive; b. Junction City, Kans., Mar. 6, 1898; s. Finley H. and Rose (Freeze) C.; m. Annie Neely, July 25, 1923. Student, Davidson Coll., 1916-17. With Kent-Coffey Mfg. Co., Lenoir, N.C., 1917-92, successively clk., v.p., pres., 1943-64, chmn. bd., 1962-92; founder Union Mirror Co., 1922, sec.-treas., 1922-43, pres., 1943-92; pres. Nu-Woods, Inc., Lenoir, Furniture Mfrs., Inc., Lenoir; dir. Charlotte br. N.C. Nat. Bank, Nat. Veneer Co., Carolina & Northwestern Rwy. Co., Southeastern Adhesives Co., Am. Furniture Mart Bldg. Co., Carlhiem Hotel, So. Furniture Exposition Bldg., Inc., Blue Ridge Devel. Corp., Fidelity Bankers Life Ins. Corp., Rikchmond, Va.; bd. govs. Am. Furniture Mart, Chgo., 1933-92, chmn., 1942-43; bd. govs. Dallas Trade Mart; adv. bd. N.Y. Furniture Exch. Mem. Lenoir City Coun., 1922-27; bd. dirs. N.C. State Ports Authority, 1953-57; chmn. Coffee Found.; pres. N.C. Indsl. Coun., 1960-61; adv. com. N.C. Indsl. Commn.; exec. com. Carolinas United Fund; bd. govs. Shrine Bowl Charlotte; mem. Lenoir Community Found.; bd. dirs. Caldwell Meml. Hosp. Recipient Outstanding Svc. award Free Ent. Awards Assn., 1962, Meritorious Achievement award Nat. Conf. Christians and Jews, 1964; named Man of the Yr. Am. Furniture Mart, 1964. Mem. Furniture Factories Mktg. Assn. South (pres. 1957-59, dir.), Southwestern Furniture Mktg. Assn., So. Furniture Mfrs. Assn. (pres.), Lenoir C. of C., Am. Numismatic Assn., N.A.M., Newcomen Soc. N.Am., Navy League U.S. (Miami coun.), Furniture Club of Am., Red Fez Club, Golf City, City Club, Charlotte Country Club, Lake Hickory Country Club, Blowing Rock Country Club, Athletic Club, Marco Polo (N.Y.C.), Commer Club (Atlanta), Masons, Shriner, Jester, Pi Kappa Phi, many others. Presbyterian. *

COFFILL, WILLIAM CHARLES, lawyer; b. Sonora, Calif., Jan. 19, 1908; s. Harris James and Olive Moore (Hampton) C.; m. Marjorie Louise Segerstrom, Jan. 25, 1948; children—William James, Eric John. A.B., U. Calif.-Berkeley, 1933; J.D., Hastings Coll. Law, 1937. Bar: Calif. 1938, U.S. Dist. Ct. (no. dist.) Calif. 1938, U.S. Dist. Ct. (so. dist.) Calif. 1938, U.S. Ct. Appeals (9th cir.) 1938, U.S. Supreme Ct. 1941, U.S. Dist. Ct. (ea. dist.) 1967. Gen. mgr. Riverbank Water Co., Riverbank and Hughson, Calif., 1948-68; sole practice Riverbank Water Co., Sonora, Calif., 1938-41, 45-76; ptnr. Coffill & Coffill, Sonora, Calif., from 1976; city atty., City of Sonora, 1952-75. Past mem., chmn. Tuolumne County Republican Central Com., Calif. Served to lt. comdr. USNR, 1941-46. Mem. Tuolumne County Bar Assn. (past pres.), Am. Legion, VFW. Lodges: Lions, Masons (32 degree), Elks. Died May 10, 1989. Home: Sonora Calif. Died May 14, 1989; buried Masonic Cemetery, Sonora, Calif.

COFFMAN, RAMON PEYTON, writer; b. Indpls., July 24, 1896; s. Walter McDowell and Effie Virginia (Stringer) C.; m. Nelle Ruth Gratton, Dec. 14, 1929; children: Gratton Eugene, Peyton, Ramon Roger, Kathleen Eleanor. Student, U. Wis., 1914-15, Yale U., 1915-16, New Sch. Social Rsch., 1918-19; AB, U. Wis., 1926. Founder, editor Typical Boy Mag., 1912-14; instr. Newark Acad., 1918-19; copy reader and reporter Milw. Leader and Wis. News, 1920-21; children's editor Wis. News and Milw. Jour., 1921-22; founder Uncle Ray Syndicate, 1922; founder, writer, editor daily syndicated feature Uncle Ray's Corner, pub., to 1992. Author 16 books (juvenile), 1924-92, latest titles being: Famous Kings and Queens, Famous Authors, Famous Pioneers, others; contbr. How and Why Library, 1941; contbr. World Book Ency., 1946; contbr. newspapers various countries incl. Brazil, Mexico, Spain, Japan, 1952-92. Pres. Citizens Pub. Welfare Assn., 1946-52. Fellow Am. hist. Soc.; mem. Soc. Midland Authors, AAAS, University Club, Tech. Club (Madison), Sigma Delta Chi. *

COHEN, ALLAN RICHARD, lawyer; b. Chgo., Feb. 25, 1923; s. Louis and Ruth (Cohen) C.; m. Audrey Doris Levy, Oct. 14, 1960; children: Joseph, David, Gale. B.A., U. Wis., 1947, J.D., 1949; postgrad., Northwestern U., 1953-54. Bar: Ill. 1950. Assoc. Blum, Jacobsen & Shkoler, Chgo., 1950-53; ptnr. Cohen & Cohen, Chgo., 1953-89. Served with AUS, 1943-45. Decorated Presdl. citation with oak leaf cluster. Mem. Fed. Bar Assn., Ill. Bar Assn. (vice chmn. comml. banking and bankruptcy sect. from 1977), Chgo. Bar Assn. (vice chmn. com. bankruptcy 1972-73, chmn. 1973-74, panelist bankruptcy seminars 1968, 72, 74, 82, 83, 84, 85, 86), Zeta Beta Tau, Tau Epsilon Rho. Home: Highland Park Ill. Died Dec. 1, 1989; buried Rosehill Cemetery, Chgo.

COHEN, BENNETT JAY, veterinarian educator; b. Bklyn., Aug. 2, 1925. D.V.M., Cornell U., 1949; M.S., Northwestern U., 1951, Ph.D., 1953. Diplomate Am. Coll. Lab. Animal Medicine. Dir. dept. animal care Northwestern U. Med. Sch., Chgo., 1949-53; univ. veterinarian U. Calif.-Berkeley, 1953-54; dir. vivarium, asst. prof. UCLA, 1954-62; assoc. prof. to prof. lab. animal medicine U. Mich., Ann Arbor, 1962-85, research scientist Inst. of Gerontology, from 1986, founder Unit for Lab. Animal Medicine, 1962, unit dir., until 1985; mem. various adv. coms. NIH, Bethesda, Md., 1960—; cons. univs., pharm. cos. Assoc. editor: Biol. Sci. Jour. of Gerontology. Recipient Charles River prize Charles River Found., 1980. Fellow Gerontol. Soc. Am.; mem. AVMA, Am. Assn. for Lab Animal

Sci. (pres. 1958-60, Griffin award 1966), Am. Physiol. Soc., Am. Assn. Accreditation Lab. Animal Care, Inst. Lab. Animal Resources in NAS, Mich. Soc. for Med. Research (pres. 1980-84). Jewish. Home: Ann Arbor Mich. Died Aug. 23, 1990.

COHEN, GERSON DAVID, academic administrator, historian; b. N.Y.C., Aug. 26, 1924; s. Meyer and Nehama (Goldin) C.; m. Naomi Wiener, May 26, 1948; children: Jeremy, Judith. B.A., CCNY, 1944; B.H.L., Jewish Theol. Sem. Am., 1943, M.H.L., 1948; Ph.D., Columbia U., 1958; D.D. (hon.), Princeton U., 1976, Trinity Coll., 1983, Yale U., 1984; D.H.L. (hon.), NYU, 1978, CUNY, 1979, Hebrew Union Coll., 1985, Brandeis U., 1987. Ordained Rabbi Jewish Theol. Sem. Am., N.Y.C., 1948, librarian, 1950-57, asst. prof. Jewish lit and instns., 1953-63, prof. history, 1970-86, Disting. Service prof. history, from 1986, chancellor, 1972-86, chancellor emeritus, from 1986; Gustav Gottheil lectr. Semitic langs. Columbia U., 1950-60, asso. prof. history, 1963-67, prof. Jewish history, 1967-70; dir. Center Israel and Jewish Studies, 1968-70, adj. prof. history, seminar asso., from 1970; bd. visitors Harvard U. Divinity Sch., 1979-83; mem. acad. com. Annenberg Inst. for Judaic and Near Ea. Studies, Com. on Rev. Meml. Found. for Jewish Culture, Yale Judaica Series Publs. Com., adv. bd. Inst. on Am. Jewish-Israeli Rels. Author: Story of the Four Captives, 1961, Sefer ha Qabbalah, 1967, Reconstruction of Gaonic History, 1972; contbr. to Great Ages and Ideas of the Jewish People, 1956, Ency. Brit., 1968. Recipient Townsend Harris medal CCNY, 1975. Fellow Am. Acad. Jewish Research (editor proc. 1969-72); mem. Alliance Israelite Universelle (dir.), Conf. Jewish Social Studies (dir.), Leo Baeck Inst. (dir.), Jewish Publ. Soc. (dir., chmn. publ. com. 1970-72), Mekize Nirdamin. Home: Bronx N.Y. Died Aug. 15, 1991.

COHEN, HERMAN, race track executive; b. Balt., Nov. 27, 1894; s. Isaac Meyer and Rosa Marsha (Pondfield) C.; m. Rosa Lebovitz, Jan. 26, 1930 (dec. Apr. 1975); 1 son, Nathan L. (dec. Dec. 1988); m. Grace Rein, Feb. 11, 1981. Ed. pub. schs. Owner dept. stores, shoe stores and men's wear stores in Md., Del., W.Va. and N.C., 1912-30, J.G. Valiant Co. (interiors), Balt., 1931-32, Herzog's Men's Store, Washington, 1932-47, Balt. Clothes Mfg. Co. (men's clothes), 1936-38, Louis C. Tiffany Studios (stained glass windows), N.Y.C., 1936-37; engaged in devel. and constrn. on Eastern Seaboard, Fla. to N.J., from 1940; builder, operator, sec., treas. Sta. WAAM-TV, Balt., 1946-57; v.p. J.A. Maurer Co. (cameras and sound equipment), N.Y.C., 1948-63, Precision Film Labs., N.Y.C., 1948-63; pres. Fairmount Steel Corp., Phila., 1948-57, Md. Jockey Club; pres., owner, operator Pimlico Race Course, 1952-86; sec.-treas. Charlestown (W.Va.) Race Track, 1958-65; pres. Willow Grove (Pa.) Park, amusement center, 1955-65. Bd. dirs. Thoroughbred Racing Assn., 1964-87, dir. emeritus, from 1988; pres. Jewish Welfare Fund, Balt., 1962-63; life mem. bd. Asso. Jewish Charities and Welfare Fund; trustee Sinai Hosp., 1952-60; v.p. Balt. chpt. Am. Technion, 1969-78; v.p., treas. Herman and Ben Cohen Charitable Found., 1950-82; trustee Oheb Shalom Cong. Jewish (trustee congregation 1948-65, co-chmn. bldg. com. 1957-62). Home: Baltimore Md. Died May 17, 1990.

COHEN, LEON WARREN, mathematician; b. N.Y.C., Apr. 24, 1903; s. Joseph W. and Sarah (Warren) C.; m. Isabel Ackerman, June 18, 1927; 1 child, Amy Judith. AB, Columbia U., 1923, AM, 1925; PhD, U. mich., 1928. NRC fellow Princeton (N.J.) U., 1919-31; prof. U. Ky., 1931-47; lectr. U. Wis., 1942-44; rsch. mathematician Columbia U., 1944-45, Brown U., 1945; prof. Ohio State U., Wright-Patterson Field, 1946, Queens Coll., 1947-54; program dir. math. scis. NSF, 1953-58; mem. div. math. Nat. Acad. Sci.-NRC, 1954-58, exec. sec. div., 1966-72; head dept. math. U. Md., 1958-68, prof., 1958-73, prof. emeritus, 1973-92; mem. Inst. Advanced Study, fellow Fund for Advancement Edn., 1952-53; rep. region 5 Nat. Woodrow Wilson Fellowship Found., 1958-59; exec. dir. Conf. Bd. Math. Scis., 1962-66. Fellow AAAS; mem. Am. Math. Soc. (assoc. sec., mem. coun. 1951-54), Math. Assn. Am., AAUP (chpt. pres. 1940), Phi Beta Kappa, Sigma Xi. Home: Washington D.C. Died Feb. 21, 1992;.

COHEN, MITCHELL HARRY, federal judge; b. Phila., Sept. 11, 1904; s. Harry and Minnie (Rubin) C.; children: Margaret, Fredric. Student, Temple U., 1922-24; LL.B., Dickinson Law Sch., 1928; LLD (hon.), Dickinson Sch. Law, 1975. Bar: N.J. 1930. Practiced in Camden, 1930-58, city prosecutor, 1936-42; freeholder Camden County, 1940; judge Camden Mcpl. Ct., 1942-47; county prosecutor Camden County, 1948-58; county judge, 1958-61; judge Superior Ct. N.J., New Brunswick, 1961-62; judge U.S. Dist. Ct. N.J., Camden, 1962-73, chief judge, 1973-74, sr. judge., from 1974. Founder, co-producer Camden County Music Fair, 1955; chmn. Camden County chpt. Sister Kenny Found., Allied Jewish Appeal, Camden; leader Camden Republican Com., 1947-58. Served with AUS, World War II. Recipient Outstanding Alumni award Dickinson Coll., 1972, William J. Brennan Jr. award Assn. Fed. Bar N.J., 1988; Fed. Courthouse in Camden, N.J. named, in his honor, The Mitchell H. Cohen Courthouse. Mem. Am., N.J., Camden County bar assns., Am. Judicature Soc. Home: Philadelphia Pa. Died Jan. 7, 1991; buried Roosevelt Cemetery, Trevose, Pa.

COHEN, SAUL ZELMAN, investor; b. Rochester, N.Y., May 5, 1926; s. Max J. and Dora (Cohn) C.; m. Amy Scheuer, Aug. 26, 1956; children: Thomas, Helen, Daniel, Gail, David, Carolyn. B.A., U. Rochester, 1949; LL.B., Harvard U., 1952. Bar: N.Y. 1952. Atty. ABC, N.Y.C., 1952-54; mem. Kaye, Scholer, Fierman, Hays & Handler, N.Y.C., 1954-84, ptnr., 1959-84; ptnr. 61 Assocs., investments, 1984-92; mem. com. on labor law and social legislation Bar Assn. of the City of N.Y., 1970's. Pres. Jewish Bd. Family and Children's Svcs., Inc., N.Y.C., 1977-81, vice chmn. bd., 1981-83, chmn. exec. com., 1983-86; trustee Sarah Lawrence Coll., 1973-81, hon. trustee, 1981—; v.p. United Jewish Appeal Fedn. Jewish Philanthropies of Greater N.Y., 1988-91, chmn. domestic affairs div., 1986-88, chmn. governance com., 1990-91. Democrat. Clubs: Harvard, Harmonie (N.Y.C.); Beach Point (Mamaroneck). Home: Larchmont N.Y. Died Jan. 23, 1992.

COHN, AVERN LEVIN, judge; b. Detroit, July 23, 1924; s. Irwin I. and Sadie (Levin) C.; m. Joyce Hochman, Dec. 30, 1954 (dec. Dec. 1989); children: Sheldon, Leslie Cohn Magy, Thomas. Student, John Tarleton Agrl. Coll., 1943, Stanford U., 1944; J.D., U. Mich., 1949. Bar: Mich. 1949. Practiced in Detroit, 1949-79; mem. firm Honigman Miller Schwartz & Cohn, Detroit, 1961-79; U.S. dist. judge, from 1979. Mem. Mich. Civil Rights Commn., 1972-75, chmn., 1974-75; Mem. Detroit Bd. Police Commrs., 1975-79, chmn., 1979; bd. govs. Jewish Welfare Fedn., Detroit, 1972—. Served with AUS, 1943-46. Mem. ABA, Detroit Bar Assn., Mich. Bar Assn., Am. Law Inst. Home: Detroit Mich. Deceased. †

COHN, JUDITH R., lawyer; b. Phila., May 15, 1943; d. Mac and Evelyn (Greenbaum) Rutman; 1 son, Peter Lawrence. B.A., Barnard Coll., 1964; J.D. magna cum laude, U. Pa., 1969. Bar: Pa. 1970, U.S. Supreme Ct. 1974. Law clk. U.S. Ct. Appeals (3d cir.), Phila., 1969-70; assoc. firm Wolf Block Schorr & Solis-cohen, Phila., 1970-77; ptnr. Wolf Block Shorr & Solis-cohen, Phila., from 1977; instr. Law Sch., U. Pa.-Phila., 1978; lectr. Wharton Sch., U. Pa., 1978-83; arbitrator Am. Arbitration Assn., U.S. Dist. Ct. (ea. dist.) Pa.; lectr. in field. Editor U. Pa. Law Rev. Mem. ABA, Pa. Bar Assn., Phila. Bar Assn. Home: Philadelphia Pa. Deceased. †

COHN, NATHAN, engineer, consultant; b. Hartford, Conn., Jan. 2, 1907; s. Harris and Dora Leah (Levin) C.; m. Marjorie Kurtzon, June 30, 1940; children: Theodore Elliot, David Leslie, Anne Harris, Amy Elizabeth, Julie Archer. S.B., M.I.T., 1927; D.Eng. (hon.), Rennsalear Poly. Inst., 1976. With Leeds & Northrup Co., Phila., 1927-72, mgr. market devel. div., 1955-58, v.p. tech. affairs, 1958-65, sr. v.p. tech. affair, 1965-67, exec. v.p. research and corp. devel., 1967-72, dir., 1963-75; cons. mgmt. and tech. of measurement and control Jenkintown, Pa., 1972-88; gen. ptnr. Network Systems Devel. Assocs.; pres. Nat. Electronics Conf., 1950; mem. NRC; exec. bd. Found. Instrumentation, Edn. and Rsch., 1962-64; del. congress Internat. Fedn. Automatic Control, 1960, 63, 66, 69, 72, 75, 78, 81, 84, 87; chmn. tech. com. on applications, 1969-72, U.S. organizing com. 1975 World Congress, mem. tech. coms. on computers, systems, com. on social effects of automation, 1975-88, lifetime advisor, 1984-88; mem. vis. com. libraries MIT, 1964-69, philosophy, 1972-74. Contbr. articles to profl. jours., chpts. to books, textbook. Bd. dirs., v.p. Eagleville (Pa.) Hosp. and Rehab. Center. Fellow IEEE (life, Lamme medal 1968, Edison medal 1982, Centennial medal 1984 chmn. fellow com. 1974-76, chmn. awards bd. 1977-78, mem. Centennial com. 1979-84); chmn. Intersoc. Hoover Medal (Bd. of Award 1978-81); mem. Instrument Soc. Am. (v.p. industries and scis. 1960-61, sec. 1962, pres. 1963, Sperry medalist 1968, hon. mem. award 1976), AAAS, Franklin Inst. (life, Wetherill medalist 1968, mem. bd. mgrs. 1971—, chmn. bd. mgrs. 1971-75), Nat. Acad. Engring., Engrs. Joint Council (exec. bd. 1975-78, commn. on internat. relations 1978-79), Am. Assn. Engring. Socs. (council for internat. affairs 1980-81), Indsl. Research Inst., Engrs. Council Profl. Devel. (vis. com. curriculum accreditation), Sci. Apparatus Makers Assn. (exec. bd. 1961-62, 66-73, pres. 1969-71, SAMA award 1978), Nat. Soc. Profl. Engrs. (Engr. of Yr. Delaware Valley 1968, State of Pa. 1969), Sigma Xi, Tau Beta Pi, Eta Kappa Nu, Pi Lambda Phi. Jewish. Club: Rydal (Phila.). Home: Scottsdale Ariz. Died Nov. 16, 1989.

COHN, SIDNEY ELLIOTT, lawyer; b. N.Y.C., Feb. 22, 1908; s. Elias and Dora (Jaffe) C.; m. Vera Boudin, June 21, 1928 (dec.); m. Roberta Seidman Garfield, Sept. 30, 1954; 1 child, Janet (Mrs. Ronald Neschis); stepchildren: David Garfield, Julie Garfield. Student, U. Pa., 1925-27; LLB (mem. Law Rev.), St. John's U., 1931; LLD (hon.), CUNY, 1988. Bar: N.Y. 1933, U.S. Supreme Ct 1955. Practice in N.Y.C., 1933-91; sr. ptnr. Cohn, Glickstein, Lurie, and predecessor; prof. Grad. Ctr., CUNY, 1986; past gen. counsel various trade unions; pres. Highroad Prodns., Inc., Saugatuck Prodns. Enterprises, Inc.; dir. San Juan Racing Assn., Inc.; mem. adv. council CUNY Law Sch. at Queens Coll. Active United Jewish Appeal, Fedn. Jewish Philanthropies; mem. governing council Am. Jewish Congress; bd. visitors Grad. Sch., CUNY; mem. adv. council Tisch Sch. Arts, NYU, CUNY Law Sch. at Queens Campus; mem. Empire State Plaza Arts Commn. Recipient Justice award Am. Jewish Congress. Mem. ABA, N.Y. State Bar Assn., New York County Lawyers Assn., Bar Assn. City N.Y. Club: Harmonie (N.Y.C.). Home: New York N.Y. Died Aug. 25, 1991.

COHU, HENRY WALLACE, investment banker; b. N.Y.C., Feb. 18, 1897; s. Henry Moore and Annabell (Turck) C.; m. Kathryn Kimball, July 1, 1922. BA, Princeton U., 1917. With Cohu & Co. and predecessor firms, 1919-56; ltd. ptnr. Winslow, Cohu & Stetson, 1958-59; dir. Eastern Industries, Inc., Cohu Electronics, Inc., Century Investors, Inc., Angostura-Wuppermann, Inc. Mem. bd. mgrs. McBudney br. YMCA, N.Y.C. Ensign USN, 1917-19. Mem. Masons, Racquet and Tennis Club, Down Town Assn., Knickerbocker Club (bd. govs.) (N.Y.C.), Piping Rock (Locust Valley, L.I., N.Y.). *

COLADARCI, PETER PAUL, lawyer; b. Danbury, Conn., Oct. 24, 1927; s. Pietro and Catherine (Bisacca) C.; m. Margaret Alice Reynolds; children: Peter R., Anne M., John A., Thomas B. BA, U. Ill., 1950; LLB, Yale U., 1953. Bar: Ill. 1953. Assoc., then ptnr. Chapman and Cutler, Chgo., 1953-70, 73-91; ptnr. Frontenac Co., Chgo., 1971-73; dir. Fed. Res. Bank Chgo. Served with USMC, 1945-46. Founding fellow Am. Coll. Investment Counsel; mem. ABA, Ill. Bar Assn., Chgo. Bar Assn. Democrat. Home: Winnetka Ill. Died Sept. 18, 1991.

COLCLOUGH, OSWALD S., university president; b. Monroeton, Pa., Nov. 19, 1898; s. William Frederic and Sara Cooper (Guy) C.; m. Kathleen Bain, June 1, 1922; children: Eugenia Colclough Cooke, Dorothy Colclough Harris, Sara Kathleen Colclough Dolan. BS, U.S. Naval Acad., 1920; LLB, George Washington U., 1935, ScD, 1961; LLD, Muhlenberg Coll., 1945. Bar: D.C. Rear adm. USN, judge adv. gen., 1945-48, vice-adm.; prof. law George Washington U., Washington, 1949-64, prof. emeritus, 1964-92, acting dean law sch., 1956-58, acting pres., 1949-61, 64-92, provost, 1961-64; dir. Patent, Trademark and Copyright Rsch. Inst. Mem. Atomic Energy Labor-Mgmt. Rels. Panel, 1953-92; chmn. exec. com. Nat. Capital Downtown Com., 1959-92; mem. exec. com. Washington Ctr. Met. Studies, 1959-92; trustee Greater Washington Ednl. TV Assn., Fed. City Coun.; adv. coun. Korean Cultural and Freedom Found.; adv. bd. Nat. Fellowships in Edn. Program Fund for Advancement Edn. Decorated Legion of Merit with Gold Star, Chevalier Legion Honor, other mil. decorations; recipient Jefferson medal N.J. Patent Law Assn., 1959. Mem. ABA, D.C. Bar Assn., Fed. Bar Assn., Maritime Law Assn., U.S. Newcomen Soc., Nat. Security Indsl. Assn. (hon. life), U.S.S. N.C. Battleship Assn., Judge Adv. Assn., Order of the Coif, Army and Navy Club, Army-Navy Country Club, Phi Delta Phi. *

COLE, ALBERT, JR., magazine publisher; b. Chgo., Dec. 12, 1894; s. Albert Channing and Frances M. (Deininger) C.; m. Marguerite N. Haas, Dec. 10, 1921 (dec. July 1968); children: Jean Cole Van Buren, Margaret Cole Jennings, Robert Douglas; m. Margaret Winston, 1969. Student pub. schs., N.Y.C.; LLD, Macalester Coll., 1973. With Frank A. Munsey Publs., N.Y.C., 1910-15, Popular Sci. Pub. Co., 1915; pres., pub. Popular Sci. Monthly and Outdoor Life, 1929-39, dir., 1924-89; dir., gen. bus. mgr. Reader's Digest Assn., Inc., 1930-66, later v.p. Bd. dirs. Boys Clubs Am., Inc., 1947-89, chmn. exec. com., 1954, pres., 1954-69, chmn., 1969-81, chmn. emeritus, 1981-89. Ensign USNR, 1917-18. Mem. Links Club, Sky Club (N.Y.C.), Blind Brook Club (Port Chester, N.Y.), Round Hill Club (Greenwich, Conn.), Seminole Golf Club (Palm Beach, Fla.). Home: Greenwich Conn. Died Sept. 19, 1989.

COLE, ROBERT HUGH, chemistry educator; b. Oberlin, Ohio, Oct. 26, 1914; s. Charles Nelson and Mabel Stewart C.; m. Elizabeth French, Apr. 24, 1943. AB, Oberlin Coll., 1935; AM, Harvard U., 1936, PhD, 1940; AM, Brown U., 1952. Instr., tutor Harvard U., 1938-41; rsch. supr. Underwater Explosives Rsch. Lab., Woods Hole, Mass., 1941-46; assoc. prof. physics U. Mo., 1946-47; assoc. prof. chemistry Brown U., Providence, 1947-51, chmn. dept., 1948-85, prof. chemistry, 1951-85, Jesse H. and Louisa D. Sharpe Metcalf prof. chemistry; prof. assoc. Faculty Scis. d'Orsay, U. Paris, 1969-70. Author: Underwater Explosions, 1948; co-author: with J.S. Coles Physical Principles of Chemistry, 1964. Trustee Woods Hole Oceanographic Instn., 1968-91. Recipient Langmuir prize in chem. physics, 1975; Fulbright lectr., Guggenheim fellow U. Leiden, 1955-56, Oxford U., 1962, NSF Sr. postdoctoral fellow, 1961-62. Fellow Am. Phys. Soc.; mem. Am. Chem. Soc., Am. Acad. Arts and Sci., Sigma Xi, Phi Beta Kappa. Home: Providence R.I. Died Nov. 17, 1991.

COLE, ROBERT TAYLOR, political science educator; b. Bald Prairie, Tex., Sept. 3, 1905; s. Robert Wiles and Elizabeth Taylor C.; m. Anne C. Berton, 1935. AB, U. Tex., 1925, AM, 1927; PhD, Harvard U., 1936. Instr., asst. prof., assoc. prof. govt. La. State U., 1926-29, 31-33; instr. polit. sci. Harvard U., 1930-31, 34-35; asst. prof. polit. sci. Duke U., 1935-37, assoc. prof., 1937-45, prof., 1945-53, James B. Duke prof. polit. sci., 1953-75,

James B. Duke Rsch. prof. emeritus, 1975-91, provost, 1960-69, dir. grad. studies in polit. sci., 1947-49; Ford rsch. prof. govt. Harvard U., 1965; cons. to O.M.G.U.S., Germany, summers 1948, 49; mem. Social Sci. Rsch. Coun., 1952-58; rapporteur Internat. Polit. Sci. Assn. Meeting, Paris, 1953; chmn. com. on Brit. Commonwealth Studies, 1955-60; mem. Fulbright Com. on Internat. Exch. Persons; coun. Ahmadu Bello U., Nigeria, 1964-77; bd. dirs. Governmental Affairs Inst. Pub. Adminstrs. Svc., 1973-78. Author: The Canadian Bureaucracy, 1949; co-author: The Nigerian Political Scene, 1962; editor and contbr. European Political Systems, 1953, rev. edit., 1959; co-editor: Post-Primary Education and Political and Economic Development, 1964; editor Jour. Politics, 1945-49, Am. Polit. Sci. Rev., 1950-53; mem. editorial bd. South Atlantic Quar., 1945-60, 69-75, Jour. Commonwealth and Comparative Politics, 1973—, Can. Pub. Adminstrn., 1973-76; contbr. articles to profl. jours. Decorated Medal of Freedom; Guggenheim fellow, 1946-47, Fulbright Rsch. fellow, Italy, 1952-53. Mem. Am. Polit. Sci. Assn. pres. 1951-52 , Cosmos Club Washington , Phi Beta Kappa chmn. Emerson award com. 1975-76 . Democrat. Baptist. Home: Durham N.C. Died May 15, 1991.

COLE, W. STORRS, paleontologist, geomorphologist; b. Albany, N.Y., July 16, 1902; s. Frederick Willard and Edna (Storrs) C.; m. Gladys Florine Watt, June 3, 1926 (dec. 1979). B.S., Cornell U., 1925, M.S., 1928, Ph.D., 1930. Paleontologist Huasteca Petroleum Co., Tampico, Mex., 1926-27, Sun Oil Co., Dallas, 1930-31; research asso. in paleontology Scripps Inst. Oceanography, U. Calif., summers 1931, 35; cons. paleontologist Fla. Geol. Survey, 1929-47; instr. geomorphology Cornell U., 1928-30; instr. geomorphology Ohio State U., 1931-37, asst. prof., 1937-43, asso. prof., 1943-45, prof., 1945-46; geologist U.S. Geol. Survey, 1947-74; prof. Cornell U., 1946-68, prof. emeritus, from 1968, chmn. geol. dept., 1947-62; mem. geol. and geog. sect. NRC, 1944-47. Contbr. articles to sci. jours. Mem. N.Y. State Museum Adv. Council, 1958-63; bd. dirs. Cushman Found. for Foraminiferal Research, 1951-75, pres., 1953-54, hon. trustee, from 1975, recipient Cushman award, 1983. Fellow Geol. Soc. Am. (3d v.p. 1954), Am. Assn. Geographers, Paleontol. Soc. (pres. 1953), Paleontol. Research Inst., Ohio Acad. Sci. (v.p. 1939), Sigma Xi, Sigma Gamma Epsilon, Gamma Alpha (hon.), Acacia. Lodge: Masons. Home: Sun City Ariz. Died June 14, 1989; buried Mt. Albion, N.Y.

COLE, WARREN HENRY, surgeon; b. Clay Center, Kans., July 24, 1898; s. George and Mary (Tolin) C.; m. Clara Margaret Lund, June 13, 1942. BS, U. Kans., 1918; MD, Washington U., St. Louis, 1920, DSc (hon.), 1967. Diplomate Am. Bd. Surgery (founders group, chmn. 1951-53, exam. bd. 1947-67). Intern Balt. City Hosp., 1920-21; intern, asst. resident, resident in surgery Barnes Hosp., St. Louis, 1921-26; mem. dept. surgery Washington U. Sch. Medicine, 1926-36; prof. surgery, head dept. U. Ill. Coll. Medicine, Chgo., 1936-66, prof. emeritus, 1966-90; hon. cons. surgeon St. Vincent's Hosp., Australia, 1966; Frank Mann lectr., 1943; Arthur Hertzler lectr., 1945; Moynihan lectr., 1948; Straus lectr., 1952; Roswell Park lectr., 1953; Judd, Sir Thomas Dixon, Mayo lectr., 1954; project dir. standards in cancer NIH, 1967-68; pres. Interstate Postgrad. Assembly, 1953; mem. Joint Commn. Hosp. Accreditors, 1953; sec. com. surgery NRC, 1940-46; vice chmn. Adv. Bd. Med. Specialists, 1953; chmn. Conf. Com. Grad. Tng., 1957-59; mem. bd. sci. cons. Sloan-Kettering Inst., from 1957, chmn., 1968-69. Author: (with Graham, Moore and Copher) Diseases of the Gallbladder and Bile Ducts, 1928, (with Zollinger) Textbook of Surgery, 1936, 9th edit., 1969, (with Charles Puestow) First Aid, Diagnosis and Management, 6th edit., 1965; editor: Operating Technique, 2d edit., 1964, Chemotherapy of Cancer, 1969, (with T. Everson) Cancer of the Digestive Tract, 1969; mem. editorial bd. Annals Surgery, Jour. Trauma, Diseases Colon and Rectum, Jour. Am. Geriatric Soc.; assoc. editor Surgery; also articles. Co-recipient Leonard rsch. prize Am. Roentgen Ray Soc., 1926; recipient cert. of merit St. Louis Med. Soc., 1927, Disting. Svc. award U. Kans., 1949, Washington U., 1955, AMA, 1966, Edwin S. Hamilton Interstate Teaching award Ill. Med. Soc., 1966. Fellow ACS (treas. 1949-55, pres. 1955), Royal Coll. Surgeons (Edinburgh) (hon.), Royal Coll. Surgeons (Eng.); mem. AMA, Am. Geriatric Soc. (pres. 1958, sect. 1965, treas. 1966), Am. Assn. Colon Surgery (pres. 1960), Am. Surg. Assn. (pres. 1959), Soc. Univ. Surgeons (pres. 1940), Am. Assn. Surgery of Trauma (pres. 1955), Chgo. Surg. Soc. (pres. 1942), Soc. Clin. Surgery, Chgo. Med. Soc. (pres. North Side br. 1946, pres. 1950), Soc. Grad. Surgery, Chgo. Inst. Medicine (past bd. govs., pres. 1963), Western Surg. Assn. (sec. 1945-49, pres. 1950), Am. Goiter Assn. (pres. 1958), Cen. Soc. Clin. Rsch., Cen. Surg. Soc., Ill. Med. Soc., Am. Cancer Soc. (bd. dirs., pres. 1960, Nat. award 1967), Soc. Exptl. Biology & Medicine, Halsted Surgery Club (hon.), Detroit Acad. Surgery, Tacoma Surg. Soc. (hon.) Tex. Surg. Soc. (hon.), Minn. Surg. Soc. (hon.), B.C. Surg. Soc. (hon.), New Orleans Surg. Soc. (hon.), Buffalo Surg. Soc. (hon.), St. Louis Surg. Soc. (hon.), Argentine Surg. Soc. (hon.), Sigma Xi, Alpha Omega Alpha, Nu Sigma Nu. Home: Asheville N.C. Died May 25, 1990; buried Riverside Cemetery, Asheville, N.C.

COLEMAN, BEATRICE, intimate apparel company executive; b. Jersey City, 1916. Grad. Barnard Coll., 1938. Chmn., pres., chief exec. officer Maidenform, Inc., N.Y.C.; bd. dirs. Nat. Women's Law Ctr. Named to Working Woman mag. Hall of Fame, 1987. Mem. Internat. Ladies Garment Worker's Union (bd. dirs. retirement com.). Died June 12, 1990; buried Westchester, N.Y. Home: New York N.Y.

COLEMAN, CLARENCE J., lawyer; b. Everett, Wash., Dec. 6, 1897; s. Joseph and Winifred (Blair) C.; m. Margaret D. Gwin, Nov. 15, 1932. AB, U. Wash., 1919, LLB, 1922. Bar: Wash. 1922. Pvt. practice law Everett; pres. Bank of Everett. Nat. committeeman State of Wash., Dem. Nat. Com., 1944-48; state chmn. Dem. State Cen. Com., 1940-44; del. to Dem. Nat. Conv., Phila., 1948; chmn. Srohomish County Dem. Cen. Com., 1962-64; mem. com. on continuing legal edn. Am. Law Inst., 1951-54; mem. Pres.'s Adv. Com. Traffic Safety State of Wash., 1958-59; regent U. Wash., 1945-51, pres. bd. regents, 1946-47. Fellow Soc. Antiquaries Scotland, Royal Soc. Antiquaries Ireland, Am. Coll. Trial Lawyers; mem. Am. Coll. Probate Counsel (regent), Newcoment Soc. N.Am., Internat. Law Soc., ABA (mem. resolutions com. 1951), Wash. State Bar Assn. (bd. govs. 1947-50, chmn. com. on legal edn. 1950-58, Award of Merit 1958), Am. Polit. Sci. Assn., Coun. Fgn. Rels., Am. Cath. Hist. Soc., Am. Law Inst., Am. Soc. Internat. Law, Oval Club, College Club, Rainier Club (Seattle), Elks, Delta Kappa Epsilon. *

COLEMAN, JAMES PLEMON, lawyer, governor, judge; b. Ackerman, Miss., Jan. 9, 1914; s. Thomas A. and Jennie Essie (Worrell) C.; m. Margaret Janet Dennis, May 2, 1937; 1 child, Thomas Allen. Student, U. Miss., 1932-35; LL.B., George Washington U., 1939, LL.D., 1960. Bar: Miss. bar 1937. Sec. to Rep. Aaron Lane Ford, Washington, 1935-39; practiced in Ackerman, 1939-40, 1960-65, 1984-90; dist. atty. 5th circuit Ct., Dist. of Miss., 1940-46, circuit judge, 1946-50; commr. Supreme Ct. of Miss., Sept. 1 to Oct. 23, 1950; atty. gen. Miss., 1950-56, gov., 1956-60; mem. Miss. Ho. Reps. from Choctaw County, 1960-65; judge U.S. Ct. Appeals 5th Circuit, 1965-84, chief judge, 1979-81; publisher Choctaw Plaindealer, weekly, 1949-56. Trustee Miss. Coll., 1952-56. Democrat (presdl. elector 1944). Baptist. Club: Mason (Shriner). Home: Ackerman Miss. Died Sept. 28, 1991; buried Enon Cemetery, Ackerman, Miss.

COLEMAN, JOHN WINSTON, tobacco planter, author; b. Lexington, Ky., Nov. 5, 1898; s. John Winston and Mary (Payne) C.; m. Burnetta Z. Mullen, Oct. 15, 1930. BSME, U. Ky., 1920, ME, 1929; LittD, Lincoln Meml. U., Harrogate, Tenn., 1945; LittD (hon.), U. Ky., 1947. Engaged in engring. work N.Y., Ky., 1920-23; organizer, pres. Coleman & Davis, Inc., Lexington, 1924-36; owner, operator Winburn Farm, Lexington, 1936-92; pres. bd. Lexington Cemetary Co. Author: Masonry in the Bluegrass, 1933, Stage-Coach Days in the Bluegrass, 1935, The Court Houses of Lexington, 1937, Lexington During the Civil War, 1938, Slavery Times in Kentucky, 1940, A Bibliography of Kentucky History, 1949, The Beauchamp-Sharp Tragedy, 1950, Old Homes of the Blue Grass, 1950, Famous Kentucky Duels, 1953, The Springs of Kentucky, 1955; contbr. hist. articles to mags. Bd. mgrs. Henry Clay Meml. Found.; bd. dirs. George Rogers Clark Meml. Commn.; mem. Ky. Civil War Centennial Commn.; bd. trustees Lincoln Meml. U. With ROTC, U. Ky., WWI. Mem. John Bradford Hist. Soc. (pres.), Am. Antiquarian Soc., Miss. Valley Hist. Assn., So. Hist. LAssn., S.R. (pres. Ky.), Sigma Nu Phi, Alpha Theta, Masons, Shriner (32 deg.), Filson Club, Kiwanis. Presbyterian. *

COLLBOHM, FRANKLIN RUDOLF, engineer; b. N.Y.C., Jan. 31, 1907; s. Max Herman and Adelheid (michelson) C.; m. Kathryn Louise Pierce, Nov. 15, 1934; children: Carl Pierce, Robert Hamilton. Student, U. Wis., 1928. With Douglas Aircraft Co., Inc., Santa Monica, Calif., 1929-48, asst. to v.p. engring., 1942-48; cons. to Sec. of War Defense Dept., 1944-45; mem.-at-large Def. Sci. Bd., 1960-62; mem.-at-large Engring. OSRD, 1944-45; trustee, chmn. bd. System Devel. Corp., 1957-61, Analytic Svcs., Inc., 1958-61; pres. The Rand Corp., 1948-67. Fellow Inst. Aeronautical Scis.; mem. Tau Beta Pi, Eta Kappa Nu. Home: Palm Desert Calif. Died Feb. 12, 1990.

COLLENS, WILLIAM S., internist; b. N.Y.C., June 5, 1897; s. Jacob and Rebecca (Skolnick) C.; m. Clara Lerner, May 15, 1930; children: Joanna, Richard. BS, CCNY, 1917; MD, Cornell U., 1921. Diplomate Am. Bd. Internal Medicine. Intern Mt. Sinai Hosp., N.Y.C., 1921-23; vol. asst. in physiol. rsch. Cornell U. Med. Coll., 1923-25; guest investigator dept. physiology U. Rochester Med. Sch., 1928; asst. pediatric rsch. Jewish Hosp., Bklyn., 1925-30; chief diabetic clinic Maimonides Hosp., Bklyn., 1930-92, chief clinic for peripheral vascular diseases, 1930-92, attending physician, 1930-92; attending physician Jewish Chronic Disease Hosp.; cons. metabolic diseases Rockaway Beach Hosp., N.Y.; clin. asst. prof. medicine SUNY, N.Y.C. Author books including: Helpful Hints to the Diabetic, 1947, Peripheral Vascular Diseases; contbr. articles to profl. jours.; inventor of intermittent veneus occiasion apparatus for treatment of peripheral circulatory impairment, others. Fellow AMA, AAAS, ACP, N.Y. Acad. Medicine; mem. N.Y. State Med. Soc., Kings County Med. Soc., Am. Heart Assn., Am. Fedn. for Clin. Rsch., Soc. for Exptl. Biology and Medicine, Am. Diabetes Assn., Am. Soc. Study Internal Secretions, Am. Soc. Study Arteriosclerosis, Unity Club. *

COLLERY, ARNOLD, economics educator; b. Glen Cove, N.Y., Feb. 1, 1927; s. James Edward and Lillian (Froehlich) C.; m. Helen Odile Cassilly, Feb. 2, 1957; children: Peter Mitchell, Elizabeth Dorsey. B.A. magna cum laude, U. Buffalo, 1950; Ph.D., Princeton U., 1958; M.A. (hon.), Amherst Coll., 1964. Mem. faculty Amherst Coll., 1953-77, prof. econs., 1964-77, chmn. dept., 1957-58, 64-66, 72-73, Clarence Francis prof. social sci., 1974-77, acting dean faculty, 1975-76; prof. econs. Columbia U., N.Y.C., 1977-89, dean Columbia Coll., 1977-82; chmn. dept. econs. Columbia U., 1985-89; vis. prof. MIT, summers 1965, 68-74; mem. adv. council dept. econs. Princeton U., 1965-77, chmn., 1972-74; dir. Found. for Teaching Econs., 1979-85; cons. to industry; pres. Amherst Inn Co., 1972-74. Author: National Income and Employment Analysis, 1966, rev. edit., 1970, International Adjustment, Open Economies, and the Quantity Theory of Money, 1971; contbr. numerous articles to profl. publs. Asst. dir. for wage and price monitoring Council on Wage and Price Stability, Exec. Office of Pres., 1974-75. Served with AUS, 1945-47. NSF postdoctoral fellow, 1963-64. Mem. Am. Econ. Assn., Phi Beta Kappa. Home: New York N.Y. Died May 12, 1989; buried Amherst, Mass.

COLLETT, JOAN, librarian; b. St. Louis; d. Robert and Mary (Hoolan) C.; m. John E. Dustin, Nov. 19, 1983. B.A. magna cum laude, Maryville Coll., 1947; M.A., Washington U., St. Louis, 1950; M.S. in L.S, U. Ill., Urbana, 1954. Regional cons. W.Va. Libr. Commn., Spencer, W.Va., 1954-56; instr. Rosary Coll., River Forest, Ill., 1956-57; head extension dept. Gary (Ind.) Pub. Libr., 1957-64; libr. Grailville Libr., 1965; regional libr. USIA, Latin Am., Africa, 1966-78; exec. dir. libr. St. Louis Pub. Libr., 1978-86; libr. dir. Great Neck (N.Y.) Libr., 1986-87, CUNY Grad. Ctr. Mina Rees Libr., N.Y.C., 1988, St. John's U. Libr., Jamaica, N.Y., from 1988. Mem. ALA (councilor 1986—). Home: Saint Louis Mo. Deceased. †

COLLIE, MARVIN KEY, lawyer; b. San Antonio, July 16, 1918; s. Marvin K. and Gladys (Stanley) C.; m. Nancy Morriss, Nov. 21, 1942; children: Gwynne Collie Brooks, M. Key III, David Wade. BA, Washington & Lee U., 1939; LLB, U. Tex., 1941. Bar: Tex. 1941. From assoc. to ptnr. Vinson & Elkins, Houston. Home: Houston Tex. Died Jan. 2, 1989.

COLLIER, ALAN CASWELL, artist; b. Toronto, Mar. 19, 1911; s. Robert Victor and Eliza Frances (Caswell) C.; m. Ruth Isabella Brown, Apr. 7, 1941; 1 son, Ian Munro. Assoc., Ont. coll. Art, 1933; student, Art Students' League, 1937-39. Artist Charles Peters Studio, N.Y.C., 1939-42, various advt. studios, Toronto, 1946-55; trch. Ont. Coll. Art, Toronto, 1955-66. Artist one-man shows, Roberts Gallery, Toronto, 1956, Frye Mus., Seattle, 1964, KensingtonGallery, Calgary, Alta., 1968, Kitcherner-Waterloo Art Gallery, 1969, Culture and Art Ctr., Meml. U., 1970, retrospective exhbn. organized by, Robert McLaughlin Gallery, Oshawa, 1971, numerous Ont. galleries, 1971; group shows Biennial of Can. Art, Nat. Gallery, 1955, 61, Kitchener-Waterloo Gallery, 1956, Art Mus. London (Ont.), 1962, Faces of Can., Stratford, Ont., 1964, Can. Artists, 1968, Art Gallery Ont., 1968, permanent collections, Nat. Gallery Can., Art Gallery Ont., Art Mus. London, Hamilton Art Gallery, Frye Mus., Seattle, Can. Council Art Bank, others. Served with Can. Army 1943-46, ETO. Recipient Centennial medal Govt. Can., 1967, Queen's Jubilee medal Gov. Gen., 1977. Mem. Royal Can. Acad. Art (academician 1954), Ont. Soc. Artists (pres. 1958-61), Arts and Letters Club (Toronto). Mem. New Democratic Party. Mem. United Ch. Home: Toronto Can. Died Aug. 23, 1990; buried Toronto, Can.

COLLIER, EVERETT DOLTON, newspaper executive; b. Long Beach, Miss., Feb. 26, 1914; s. Thomas Lee and Elizabeth Naomi (Cruthirds) C.; m. Mary Margaret Chisholm, Mar. 26, 1950; 1 son, Ervin Cornell (dec.). B.A., Rice Inst., 1937. Mem. staff Houston Chronicle, 1934-87, polit. editor, 1946-52, editorial writer, 1952-57, asst. editor, 1957-59, mng. editor, 1959-65, v.p., editor, 1965-79, sr. v.p., 1979-87, also bd. dirs., 1965-87. Mem. Rice U. Alumni Assn. (pres. 1963), Tex. U.P.I. Editors Assn. (v.p. 1965), Houston C. of C. (dir. 1970), Sons Republic Tex. (hon.). Methodist. Club: Press (Houston). Home: Houston Tex. Died May 3, 1992.

COLLINS, CARVEL, literature educator; b. West Union, Ohio, June 14, 1912; s. John Edgar and Ina (Treber) C.; m. Mary Brewster, Nov. 17, 1939 (div. 1956); 1 child, Lucy Emerson; m. Ann Green, Oct. 1, 1960. BS, Miami U., 1933; MA, U. Chgo., 1937, PhD, 1944. Instr. English Colo. State Coll., 1938-39, Stephens Coll., 1939-40; instr. Harvard U., 1942-45, asst. dean, 1945, asst. prof., 1946-50; asst. prof. Swarthmore Coll., 1945-46; assoc. prof., then prof. English MIT, 1950-67; prof. English U. Notre Dame, 1967-90; vis. lectr. U. Calif., 1949, Salzburg Seminar, 1955, U. d'Aix-Marseille, 1955, U. Tokyo, 1961, U. Colo., 1962,

U. Miss., 1975. Author: The American Sporting Gallery, 1949, Literature in the Modern World (with others), 1954; editor: Sam Ward in the Gold Rush, 1949, William Faulkner's New Orleans Sketches, 1958, William Faulkner, The Unvanquished, 1959, Faulkner's University Pieces, 1961, Erskine Caldwell's Men and Women, 1961, William Faulkner: Early Prose and Poetry, 1962, William Faulkner's Mayday, 1976, Faulkner's Helen: A Courtship, 1981. Libr. of Congress fellow, 1946, Bollingen Found. fellow, 1964-65; grantee Am. Philos. Soc., 1963, Fidelis Found., 1963. Mem. Coll. English Assn., Nat. Coun. Tchrs. English, St. Botolph Club. Home: Notre Dame Ind. Died Apr. 10, 1990.

COLLINS, JAMES MITCHELL, congressman; b. Hallsville, Tex., Apr. 29, 1916; s. Carr P. and Ruth (Woodall) C.; m. Dorothy Dann, Sept. 16, 1942; children: Michael James, Dorothy Colville (Mrs. David R. Weaver), Nancy Miles (Mrs. Richard W. Fisher). B.S.C., So. Meth. U., 1937; M.A., Northwestern U., 1938; C.L.U., Am. U., 1940; M.B.A., Harvard U., 1943. Pres. Consol. Industries, Inc., from 1954, Internat. Industries, Inc., 1954-66, Fidelity Union Life Ins. Co., 1954-65, Pacific Industries, from 1972; mem. 90th-97th Congresses from 3d Dist. Tex., mem. Edn. and Labor com., 1967-70, Interstate and Fgn. Commerce com., 1970. Tex. chmn. White House Conf. Youth; bd. dirs. Greater Dallas Planning Council, Salvation Army (Pioneer award 1988), YMCA, Dallas Council, Big Bros., Dallas Assembly, United Fund, pres., Dallas Citizens Council World Affairs, Heart Assn.; chmn. Christmas Seal campaign; trustee So. Meth. U.; sr. vice chmn. Nat. Republican Congressional Com., from 1974; pres. Am. Enterprise Forum, 1987. Served to capt., C.E. AUS, World War II, ETO. Decorated Medal of Metz; named Man of Yr. Irving Jaycees, 1970, Distinguished Alumnus So. Meth. U., 1971, Man of Year Fedn. Ind. Bus., 1971; 1974 Legislator of Year Mexican-Am. C. of C.; Watchdog of Treasury Nat. Assn. Businessmen; recipeint Pioneer award Salvation Army, 1988. Mem. Am. Legion, Y.P.O., Cycen Fjodr, Mil. Order World Wars, VFW, Blue Key, Phi Delta Theta (Free Enterprise Entrepreneur USA award 1988), Alpha Kappa Psi, Psi Chi. Republican. Baptist. Lodges: Rotary, Elks. Home: Dallas Tex. Died July 21, 1989; buried Restland Meml., Dallas.

COLLINS, JOSEPH LAWTON, army officer; b. New Orleans, May 1, 1896; s. Jeremiah Bernard and Catherine (Lawton) C.; m. Gladys Esterbrook, July 15, 1921; children: Joseph Esterbrook, Gladys May Collins Stenger, Nancy Katherine Collins Rubino. Student, La. State U., 1912-13; BS, U.S. Mil. Acad., 1917; student, Command and Gen. Staff Sch., 1931-32; LLD, Tulane U., 1953. Commd. 2d lt. U.S. Army, 1917, advanced through grades to brig. gen., 1942, maj. gen., 1942, lt. gen., 1945, gen., 1948; with 22d Inf., N.Y.C., WW I, 1st Div. and Hdqrs. Am. Forces, Germany, 1919-21; instr. U.S. Mil. Acad., 1921-25, Inf. Sch., 1927-31, Army War Coll., 1938-40; asst. sec. War Dept. Gen. Staff, 1940-41; chief of staff VII Army Corps, Birmingham, 1941-42; Hawaiian Dept., 1941-42; comdr. 25th Div., 1942-44, VII Corps, 1944-45; dep. commd. gen. and chief of staff Army Ground Forces, Washington, 1945; chief of pub. info. War Dept., 1945-47; dep. and vice chief of staff U.S. Army, 1947-49, chief of staff, 1949-53; U.S. rep. on NATO's Mil. Com. and Standing Group, 1953-56; spl. rep. of U.S. in Vietnam, with personal rank of ambassador, 1954-55;. dir., vice chmn. Pres.'s Com. for Hungarian Refugee Relief, 1956-57; dir. Chas Pfizer & Co., Inc.; vice chmn. bd. dirs. Pfizer Internat. subsidiaries, 1957-92. Chmn. bd. dirs., Fgn. Student Svc. Coun. of Greater Washington, Inc., 1957-58, hon. chmn.; hon. trustee Inst. Internat. Edn., Inc., N.Y.C., 1965—, chmn. adv. com. to Washington officer, 1958-60. Decorated DSM with 3 oak leaf clusters, Army of Occupation Medal, Def. medal, Silver Star with oak leaf cluster, Victory medal, Asiatic Pacific medal, Legion of Merit with 2 oak leaf clusters, Europe-Africa-Middle East Campaign Ribbon; Companion Order of Bath (British), Order of Suvorov 2d Class (2 medals, Russian), Croix de Guerre Palm, Grand Officer Legion of Honor (French), Grand Officer Order of Leopold II, Croix de Guerre with Palm (Belgian), 1950 Laetare medal, Cartinal Gibbons medal, 1955. Mem. Army and Navy Club (Washington), Chevy Chase Club (Md.). *

COLLINS, LEROY, lawyer, governor; b. Tallahassee, Fla., Mar. 10, 1909; s. Marvin H. and Mattie Brandon C.; m Mary Call Darby, June 29, 1932; children: Leroy, Jane, Mary Call, Darby. LLB, Cumberland U., 1931. Bar: Fla. 1931, Ark. 1931, Tenn. 1931. Leon County rep. to Fla. Legislature, 1934-40; mem. Senate, 1940-54; gov. State of Fla., 1955-61; pres. Nat. Assn. Broadcasters, 1961-64; dir. Community Rels. Svc., 1964-65; undersec. U.S. Dept. Commerce, 1965-66; pvt. practice law Tampa, Fla., 1966-68; of counsel Ervin, Varn, Jacobs, Odom & Kitchen, Tallahassee, 1970-91; mem. Fla. Constn. Revision Commn., 1977-78, So. Legal Coun., 1977-91. Former chmn. Nat. Govs. Conf., So. Govs. Conf.; mem. nat. adv. coun. Peace Corps; mem. honor corps NCCJ; chmn. South Regional Edn. Bd., 1955-57; mem. Commn. on Goals for Higher Edn. in South, 1961-62, Commn. on Future of South, 1980-81; trustee Fla. Defenders of Environment, 1981—; bd. dirs. Com. on Constl. System, 1984—; chmn. Dem. Nat. Conv., 1960. Lt. USNR, World War II. Recipient Nelson Poynter Floridian award, 1981. Mem. ABA chmn. spl. com. legal edn. 1974 , Fla. History Assocs. Democrat. Episcopalian. Home: Tallahasse Fla. Died Mar. 12, 1991.

COLLINS, TRUMAN EDWARD, clergyman; b. Advance, Mo., Aug. 22, 1919; s. Edward and Pearl (Shell) C.; m. Dorothy Virginia Eaker, Dec. 23, 1939; 1 child, Edward Alan. Diploma, Calvary Bible Coll., Kansas City, Mo., 1952. Ordained to ministry Bapt. Ch., 1949. Pastor Mt. Zion Gen. Bapt. Ch., Granite City, Ill., 1950-64, First Gen. Bapt. Ch., Princeton, Ind., 1964-67, Dover Chapel Gen. Bapt. Ch., Louisville, 1967-69, Southland Gen. Bapt. Ch., Louisville, 1969-85, Lutesville (Mo.) Gen. Bapt. Ch., 1986-88; Pres. Nat. Sunday Sch. Bd. Gen. Bapt., 1956-63, moderator nat. conv., 1961-62; pres. Gen. Bapt. Publs. and Edn. Bd., Inc., 1964-66; mem. Liberty Presbyter Gen. Bapt. Assn., Ind., 1965-67, Christian Edn. and Publs. Bd., Inc. of Gen. Baptist Denomination, 1963-66, pres., 1964-65; pres. Illmo Assn. Endowment Corp., 1959-64; dir. Illmo Assn. Youth Camp of Gen. Bapt., 1954-64; mem. Hahn Chapel Gen, Bapt. Ch., 1987—; mem. Tri-City Ministerial Alliance, 1988. Author: Sun Rays In the Sickroom. Pres. Emerson Sch. PTA, 1962-63. Mem. Nat. Congress PTA, Quad City Ministerial Assn. (treas.), Kentuckana Assn. Gen. Bapts., S.E. Mo. Assn. Gen. Bapts., Greater Louisville Evang. Fellowship (v.p.), Old Liberty Assn. Gen. Bapts. Home: Marble Hill Mo. Deceased. †

COLLOFF, ROGER DAVID, broadcasting executive; b. Asbury Park, N.J., Feb. 1, 1946; s. Isadore and Shirley Edith (Dessen) C.; m. Margery Ann Bletcher, May 28, 1967; children: Pamela, David. AB summa cum laude, Brown U., 1967; MA (Woodrow Wilson fellow), Yale U., 1972, JD, 1972. Legis. asst. to Senator Walter Mondale, Washington, 1972-75; dir. govt. affairs CBS Inc., Washington, 1976; sr. staff mem. White House Office of Energy Policy and Planning, Washington, 1977; spl. asst. to sec. of energy Washington, 1977-78; v.p., asst. to pres. CBS News, N.Y.C., 1979-81; v.p., dir. public affairs broadcasts CBS News, 1981-82; v.p. policy and planning Broadcast Group CBS Inc., 1983-84; v.p., gen. mgr. Sta. WCBS-TV, N.Y.C., 1984-92. Mem. Nat. Acad. TV Arts and Scis. (bd. govs. 1986-92), Internat. Radio and TV Soc., Phi Beta Kappa. Home: New York N.Y. Died Feb. 6, 1992. †

COLON, DORIS E., genetics educator; b. Lares, P.R., Jan. 9, 1930; d. Vicente E. and Elmina (Gonzalez) C.; m. Walter Yudex, June 2, 1953; 1 child, Myra Yudex Fanning. BS, U. P.R., 1950; MS, U. Pa., 1953; PhD, Okla. State U., 1963. Rsch. asst. U. P.R. Sch. Medicine, Mayaguez, 1954-56, instr. genetics, 1956-64, asst. prof., 1964-65, assoc. prof., 1966-71, prof., 1971-88; cons. in field. Mem. AAUP, Am. Inst. Biol. Sci., Fedn. Am. Scientists, Senada Academico, Comite Curriculo de Biologia, Comite Asuntos Academicos, Comite Cursos Institucionales, Consejera de Sociedad Honoraria Estudiantil, Sigma Xi (v.p. 1974), Alpha Delta Kappa (pres. 1977-78), Beta Beta Beta. Democrat. Roman Catholic. Home: Mayaguez P.R. Died Dec. 9, 1988; buried Mayaguez, P.R.

COMAY, SHOLOM DAVID, corporation executive, lawyer; b. Pitts., Sept. 28, 1937; s. Amos and Ethel (Berez) C.; m. Estelle P. Fisher, Aug. 18, 1963; children: Laura Beth, Joseph Fisher. AB, Brandeis U., 1960; JD, U. Pitts., 1962. Bar: Pa. 1962. Ptnr. Kaufman & Harris, Pitts., 1963-75; housing court magistrate City of Pitts., 1967-71; corp. sec. Action Industries, Inc., Cheswick, Pa., from 1979, sec., gen. counsel, 1975-89, vice chmn., 1987-91, also bd. dirs. Nat. treas, Am. Jewish Com., N.Y.C., 1986-89, nat. pres., 1989-91; pres., chair Health and Welfare Planning Assn., Allegheny County, Pa., 1976-82; bd. dirs. Pitts. Ballet Theatre, from 1984, Pitts. Symphony, from 1989, Jewish Healthcare Found., from 1990, United Way of Allegheny County; mem. Pres.' Council Brandeis U., Waltham, Mass.; chmn. The Pitts. Found., from 1987; trustee Harmarville Rehab. Ctr., 1987-90; treas. United Jewish Fedn. of Greater Pitts., 1988-91, vice chmn., 1991. Recipient Nat. Brotherhood award NCCJ, Pitts., 1978. Mem. ABA, Pa. Bar Assn., Allegheny County Bar Assn., Am. Corp. Counsel Assn. Home: Pittsburgh Pa. Died May 18, 1991.

COMBS, BERT THOMAS, lawyer; b. Manchester, Ky., Aug. 13, 1911; s. Stephen Gibson and Martha (Jones) C.; m. Mabel Hall, June 15, 1937; children: Lois Ann Combs Weinbert, Thoms George; m. Helen C. Simons, Rechtin, Aug. 30, 1969; m. Sara Walter, Dec. 1988. Student, Cumberland Coll., 1929-31; LL.B., U. Ky., 1937. Bar: Ky. 1937. City atty. City of Prestonburg, Ky., 1950; commonwealth's atty. 31st Jud. Dist. Ky., 1950-51; judge Ct. Appeals of Ky., 1951-55; gov. Commonwealth of Ky., 1959-63; judg U.S. Ct. Appeals (6th cir.), 1967-70; ptnr. Wyatt, Tarrant & Combs, Louisville, from 1970; dir. Forum Group, Inc., Cin., New Orleans, and Tex., Pacific R.R. Co.; bd. dirs. Ky. Export Resources Authority; bd. dirs. Ky Funeral Dirs. Burial Assn., Inc.; mem. ACDA, 1978-80. Served to capt. AUS, 1941-46. Decorated Bronze Star; decorated Medal of Merit Philippines; recipient Joseph P. Kennedy Internat. award, 1963; named Ky.'s Outstanding Atty., 1964. Fellow Am. Bar Found.; mem. Ky. Council Higher Edn., Order of Coif, Phi Delta Phi. Democrat. Baptist. Lodge: Masons. Home: Louisville Ky. Died Dec. 3, 1991; buried Manchester, Ky.

COMPERE, CLINTON LEE, physician; b. Greenville, Tex., Feb. 17, 1911; s. Edward L. and Clara (Davison) C.; m. Katharine Gram, Mar. 31, 1949; children: Clinton Lee, Mary Katherine. B.S., U. Chgo., 1936, M.D., 1937. Diplomate: Am. Bd. Orthopaedic Surgery. Intern Henry Ford Hosp., Detroit, 1938-39; resident Blodgett Meml. Hosp., Grand Rapids, Mich., 1939-40; practice medicine specializing in orthopaedic surgery Chgo., from 1946; mem. sr. attending staff Chgo. Wesley Meml. Hosp., from 1949, chief staff, 1964-66; acad. dir. Prosthetic Rsch. Ctr., Chgo., from 1955, Prosthetic-Orthotic Edn., Chgo., from 1958; dir. Rehab. Engrng. Ctr., from 1972; cons. 5th Army Hdqrs., from 1947; cons. amputee clinics Regional Office VA, from 1947; assoc. prof. orthopaedic surgery Northwestern U. Med. Sch., 1954-65, prof., 1965-80, Edwin Ryerson prof., chmn. dept. orthopaedic surgery, 1978-80; prof. emeritus, from 1980; founding mem., Rehab. Inst., Chgo., vice chmn. bd. until 1980; mem. med. adv. com. Ill. Div. Vocational Rehab.; sec.-treas. Orthopedic Research and Edn. Found., 1972-78; med. dir. Ill. State Med. Drs. Svcs., from 1980; chmn. merit rev. bd. for rehab. R & D VA, from 1982; bd. dirs. Nat. Rehab. Hosp., Washington, from 1983. Co-author: Fracture Treatment, 1937, also articles. Served to lt. col., M.C. AUS, 1940-46. Recipient citation Pres.'s Com. Employment Physically Handicapped, 1959; Profl. Achievement award U. Chgo., 1979. Mem. Am. Acad. Orthopaedic Surgeons (sec. 1959-62, pres. 1963-64), Ill., Chgo. med. socs., A.M.A., A.C.S., Am., 20th Century Orthopaedic Assn. (founder, former pres.), Chgo. Orthopaedic Soc., Clin. Orthopaedic Soc., Ill. Soc. Med. Research, Internat. Soc. Orthopaedic Surgery and Traumatology, Alpha Omega Alpha. Home: Tucson Ariz. Died May 26, 1991; buried Oakwood Cemetery, Chgo.

CONANT, KENNETH JOHN, archaeologist, educator; b. Neenah, Wis., June 28, 1894; s. John Franklin and Lucie Ell (Micklesen) C.; m. Marie A. Schneider, Sept. 1, 1923; children: Kenneth John, John Simon; m. Isabel Pope, Jan. 14, 1956. AB, Harvard U., 1915, MArch, 1919, PhD, 1925; LittD (hon.), Lawrence Coll., 1933. Archtl. draftsman, instr. Harvard U., Cambridge, Mass., 1920-23, faculty, instr., later asst., assoc. prof., 1923-36, prof., 1936-569, prof. emeritus, 1956-92; George A. Miller exch. prof. U. Ill., 1955; exch. prof. The Sorbonne, Paris, 1935-36, 50, Nat. U. Mexico, 1942; hon. lectr. U. Buenos Aires, 1947; mem. Carnegie Instn. expdn. to Yucatan, 1926; also mem. Nat. Geog. expdn. to N.Mex., 1926; rsch. assoc. in archaeology excavating abbey of Cluny, France, for Medieval Acad. Am. Author books especially on Romanesque ch. architecture; adv. editor, contbr. articles on arch.; also sketching and designing including Harvard Tercentenary ware. Trustee Bur. of Univ. Travel, Newton, Mass. With C.E., U.S. Army; AEF. Guggenheim fellow, 1927, 53-58; recipient AIA sch. medal, Harvard, 1919, Congress medal Societe Francaise d'Archeologie, 1935, Chevalier of the Legion of Honor, 1936. Fellow Am. Acad. Arts and Scis. (former officer), Medieval Acad. Am., Archaeol. Inst. Am. (former pres., hon. pres.), Royal Soc. Arts, Soc. Antiquaries (hon.) of London, Chevalier du Tastevin; mem. Pilgrim Soc., Colonial Soc. Mass., Soc. Archtl. Historians (past pres., hon. pres.), Am. Philos. Soc., Boston Soc. Architects, AIA (hon.), Academie de Macon (hon.), Societe des Antiquaries de France (hon.), Academie de Dijon (non-resident mem.), Phi Beta Kappa, Gargoyle Club, Signet Club. Republican. Greek Orthodox Ch. *

CONAWAY, CHRISTINE YERGES, educator; b. Columbus, Ohio, Nov. 18, 1901; d. Frederick Joseph and Ada May (Crothers) Yerges; m. Samuel Steele Conaway, Aug. 29, 1924 (dec.); children: Patricia Ann Conaway Ruddell, Samuel Steele, Lawrence Yerges (dec. 1970). AB, Ohio State U., 1923, AM, 1942; LHD, Otterbein Coll., 1957. Tchr. Athens (Ohio) Pub. Schs., 1924; asst. to dean Coll. Arts and Scis. Ohio State U., Columbus, 1937-42, acting sec., 1942-44, dean of women, 1944-67, emeritus, 1967. Mem. Grandview Heights Sch. Bd. Edn., 1943-51, v.p., 1945-50; mem. Community Village Program Com., Continuing Edn. for Women Com.; chmn. Women's Juvenile Bd.; v.p. Childhood League; bd. dirs. Florence Crittendon Homes; bd. govs. Arrowmont Sch., Gatlinburg, Tenn. Mem. NEA, AAUW (past v.p. Columbus chpt.), Nat. Assn. Women Deans and Counselors (past officer), Ohio Assn. Women Deans, Adminstrs. and Counselors, Nat. Coun. Family Rels., Am. Coll. Pers. Assn., Am. Pers. and Guidance Assn., U.S. Nat. Student Assn., Cen. Ohio Guidance Assn., Nat. Vocat. Guidance Assn., Mortar Bd., Chimes, Delta Kappa Gamma, Theta Sigma Phi, Alpha Lambda Delta, Pi Beta Phi, Sigma Phi Alpha.. Home: Columbus Ohio Died Apr. 23, 1989.

CONCHON, GEORGES, author; b. Saint-Avit, France, May 9, 1925; s. Eugene and Marcelle (Gancille) C.; m. Yvonne Message, Aug. 8, 1946; 1 dau., Catherine. Licence de philosohie, Sorbonne, U. Paris, 1946, Diplom etudes superieures de philosophie, 1947. Div. head Assemblee de L'Union Francaise, Paris, 1947-58; sec.-gen. Assemblee Nationale Bangui, 1959; journalist France-Soir, Paris, 1960; div. head Senat, Paris, 1960-80;

producer Antenne 2, Paris, 1981-84; author novels, screenplays, 1953-90. Author: (novels) L'Etat Sauvage (Prix Goncourt 1964), 1964; Le Bel Avenir, 1984, Colette/Stern, 1987; (films) Black and White in Color (Oscar for best fgn. film 1978), 1977; La Banquiere, 1980; Mon Beau-frere a tué ma soeur, 1986. Named officer des Arts et Lettres, officier Ordre National du Merite; chevalier de la légion d'honneur. Died July 30, 1990. Home: Paris France

CONNAR, RICHARD GRIGSBY, surgeon; b. Zanesville, Ohio, Jan. 11, 1920; s. Virgil Norwood and Anna Margaret (Grigsby) C.; m. Elizabeth Dickens, May 18, 1946; children: Cathleen, Elizabeth Ann, Richard Grigsby. BA, Duke U., 1941, MD, 1944. Intern, then resident in internal medicine Duke U. Hosp., 1944-46, resident in gen. and thoracic surgery, 1948-53; asst. prof. surgery Duke U. Med. Sch., 1953-55, regional rep., 1956-87; practice medicine specializing in thoracic and cardiovascular surgery Tampa, Fla., from 1955; mem. staff Tampa Gen. Hosp., from 1955, chief surgery, 1962-66, from 72, chief sect. thoracic and cardiovascular surgery, 1969-88; clin. prof. surgery U. South Fla. Med. Sch., Tampa, 1972-82, prof., chmn. dept. surgery, from 1982, v.p. med. affairs, 1984-86, adv. com., 1972-77; cons. Fla. Crippled Children's Commn., MacDill AFB Hosp., S.W. Fla. Tb Sanitarium; chmn. med. adv. bd. Hillsborough County Hosp. and Welfare Bd., 1962-64; mem. Fla. Tb Bd., 1964-69; adv. com. U. Fla. Coll. Medicine, 1975, residency rev. com. for thoracic surgery, from 1987; bd. dirs. H. Lee Moffit Cancer Hosp., 1983-86. Contbr. articles to med. jours. Bd. dirs. U. South Fla. Found.; bd. counselors U. Tampa, 1965-70; chmn. Duke U. Nat. Council, 1970-71. Served to capt. M.C. USAAF, 1946-48. Fellow A.C.S. (pres. Fla. chpt. 1967-68, bd. govs. 1970-76); mem. AMA (ho. dels. 1971-88, council med. edn. 1974-82, vice chmn. 1981), Fla. Med. Assn., Hillsborough County Med. Assn. (pres. 1970-71), Fla. Heart Assn. (award 1967, dir. 1962-68), Hillsborough County Heart Assn. (dir. 1957-76, award 1960), So. Surg. Assn., Am. Assn. Thoracic Surgery, So. Thoracic Surg. Assn., Soc. Vascular Surgery, Fla. Thoracic Soc. (pres. 1971-72), Soc. Thoracic Surgeons (governing council 1981-85), Am. Coll. Chest Physicians, Internat. Cardiovascular Soc.), So. Assn. Vascular Surgery, Fla. Soc. Thoracic and Cardiovascular Surgeons (pres. 1978-79), Royal Soc. Medicine, Liaison Com. for Grad. Med. Edn., Liaison Com. for Med. Edn., Duke U. Gen. Alumni Assn. (pres. 1973-74), Phi Beta Kappa, Omicron Delta Kappa, Alpha Omega Alpha, Sigma Alpha Epsilon. Clubs: Explorers, University, Tampa Yacht and Country, Ye Mystic Krewe of Gasparilla, Palma Cela Golf and Country, Tampa; Athaneum (London). Home: Tampa Fla. Died June 14, 1990; buried Garden of Memories, Tampa.

CONNAWAY, JAY HALL, artist; b. Liberty, Ind., Nov. 27, 1893; s. Cass and May L. (Brown) C.; m. Flora Sherman, 1919; m. Louise Boehle, Feb. 14, 1928; 1 child, Leonebel Marie Frances. Student, John Herron Art Inst., Indpls., 1910-11, Art Students League, N.Y.C., 1912-14, Julian Acad., Paris, 1919-21. Owner, tchr. Connaway Art Sch., Dorset, until 1964; summer tchr., lectr. So. Vt. Art Ctr., 1962-92; dir., tchr. So. Vt. Art Ctr. Sch., 1962-64. Represented in permanent collectionsJohn Herren Art Inst., others; one man shiows annually MacBeth Gallery, N.Y.C., 1926-40, Kennedy Gallery (work on permanent exhbn.), 1957, 62, Long Galleries, Houston, Houston Galleries, Galaxy Gallery, Phoenix, Summer Gallery, Manchester, Vt., 1968, other mus. and galleries; represented in permanent exhbn. Deeley Gallery, Manchester. Trustee So. Vt. Art Ctr., Manchester, 1954-92. With U.S. Army, WWI. Awarded numerous prizes since 1912; later ones include New Haven Paint and Clay Club prize, 1944, Hans Hinrich prize, Allied Artis Am., 1945, Hossier Salon prize Indpls., Boothbay Harbor (Me.) Marine prize, 1947, Lucille Dingley best marine prize, 1949, Meriden (Conn.) Arts and Crafts Assn. Popular prize, 1950; best marine and landscape prize N. Shore Art Assn., Gloucester, Mass., 1959, 1st prize Rutland Art Assn., 1961, So. Vt. Art Ctr. prize, 1962; Cracker Barrel Bazaar 1st prize, 1964. Mem. Mem. Allied Artists Am. (nat. academician mem.), Audubon Artists, Art Students League N.Y., Salmagundi Club, Nat. Arts Club, Portland Soc. of Art, Meriden Arts and Crafts Soc., Masons, K.P. *

CONNELLY, JOHN FRANCIS, manufacturing company executive; b. Phila., Mar. 4, 1905; m. Josephine O'Neill, Apr. 1938; children: Josephine, Emily, John, Thomas, Judith, Christine. LLD (hon.), LaSalle Coll., Villanova U., 1958. Dir. Crown Cork & Seal Co., Phila., from 1956, pres., 1957-76, chmn. bd., from 1957, chief exec. officer, 1979-89; chmn. bd. Connelly Containers, Inc. Chmn. Archbishop's laity com. Home: Philadelphia Pa. Died July, 1990. †

CONNOLLY, JAMES LOUIS, bishop; b. Fall River, Mass., Nov. 15, 1894; s. Francis T. and Agnes (McBride) C. AB, AM, St. Mary's U., Balt., 1919, 1920; STB, Suipician Sem., Washington, 1923; AM, Cath. U. Am., 1924; PhD, Cath. U. Louvain, 1927. Ordained priest Roman Cath. Ch., 1923. Prof. history and philosophy St. Paul Sem., 1928-33, spiritual dir., 1933-40; prof. history and religion Diocesan Tchrs. Coll., St. Paul, 1929-43, dean of studies, 1939-45; rector Nazareth Hall Prep. Sem., 1940-43, The St. Paul Sem., 1943-46; apptd. coadjutor bishop Fall River, 1945; consecrated bishop St. Paul Cath. Ch., 1945; bishop Fall River, 1951-92. Author: John Gerson, Reformer and Mystic, 1928, Catholic Action Conferences, 1932. Bd. dirs. St. Thomas Coll., St. Paul, 1942-45, St. Paul Sem., 1943-45, Minn. Soc. for Control of Cancer, 1943-45, Our Lady of Good Counsel Free Cancer Home, 1941-46, Rose Hawthorne Lathrop Home, Fall River, 1945-46. Mem. Cath. Hist. Soc. of St. Paul (editorial bd. 1930-36), Minn. Hist. Soc. (exec. coun. 1938-48), Cath. Hist. Assn., Fall River Hist. Soc., Medieval Acad. Am. KC (chaplain), Mpls. Serra Club. *

CONNOLLY, THOMAS ARTHUR, archbishop; b. San Francisco, Oct. 5, 1899; s. Thomas and Catherine (Gilsenan) C. Ed., St. Patrick's Sem., Menlo Park, Calif., 1915-26, Cath. U., 1930-32; J.C.D. Ordained priest Roman Catholic Ch., 1926; asst. pastor, 1926-30, sec. to archbishop, 1934-39; chancellor Archdiocese San Francisco, 1935-48; named domestic prelate, 1936; pastor Mission Dolores Ch., San Francisco, 1939-48; consecrated bishop, 1939; apptd. aux. bishop of San Francisco and titular bishop Sila, 1939-48; apptd. vicar del. Cath. Chaplains U.S. Army and Navy, Pacific Coast, 1941; apptd. coadjutor bishop Seattle, 1948-50, bishop, 1950-51, archbishop, 1951-75; apptd. asst. at Pontifical Throne, 1959; chaplain del. Sub Vicariate VIII, Mil. Ordinariate. Author: Appeals in Canon Law, 1932. Home: Seattle Wash. Died Apr. 18, 1991.

CONNORS, CHUCK KEVIN JOSEPH, actor; b. Bklyn., Apr. 10, 1921; m. Betty Jane Riddle (div.); 4 children. Ed., Seton Hall U. Profl. basketball player with Boston Celtics, 1946, 47, 48; profl. baseball player with Bklyn. Dodgers, 1949, Chgo. Cubs, 1951; later on West Coast; instr. tank warfare U.S. Mil. Acad., World War II. TV appearances include: The Rifleman (series), 1957-61, Arrest and Trial, 1963, Branded, 1964-65, Cowboy in Africa, 1967, The Thrillseekers, 1972, Roots (miniseries), 1977, The Yellow Rose (series), 1983, Werewolf (series), 1987, Once Upon A Texas Train (TV film); films include: Pat and Mike, 1952, Dragonfly Squadron, 1953, The Human Jungle, 1954, Three Stripes in the Sun, 1955, Walk the Dark Street, 1956, Ola Yeller, 1957, Tomahawk Trail, 1957, Designing Woman, 1957, Geronimo, 1962, Move Over Darling, 1963, Synanon, 1965, Ride Beyond Vengeance, 1966, Captain Nemo and the Underwater City, 1969, Pancho Villa, 1971, Support Your Local Gunfighter, 1971, Soylent Green, 1972, Standing Tall, 1978, Tourist Trap, 1979, Airplane II: The Sequel, 1982, Capture of Grizzly Adams, 1982, Summer Camp Nightmare, 1987, others. Served with U.S. Army. Recipient TV Champion award, 1958; Golden Globe award, 1959. Home: Beverly Hills Calif. Died Nov. 10, 1992. †

CONNORS, STEPHEN WILFRED, lawyer; b. Monroe, Wis., Mar. 11, 1918; s. Patrick J. and Alice (Norder) C.; student U. Wis., 1937-41, U. Minn., 1951; B. Sci. Law, St. Paul Coll. Law, 1950, LL.B. cum laude, 1952; J.D., William Mitchell Coll. Law, 1969; m. Louise Pharr, Feb. 4, 1946; children: Maureen, Patricia, Constance, Mary, Michele, Kelly. Bar: Minn. 1952, Ariz. 1954, U.S. Dist. Ct., 1954, U.S. Ct. Appeals (9th cir.) 1963, U.S. Supreme Ct., 1960; practice Phoenix, 1953-91; pres. Olympia Realty, Inc.; dir. Truten Investment Corp. Mem. Ariz. State Athletic Commn., 1961; founding mem. Ariz. State U. Law Sch.; mem. adv. council Am. Security Council; precinct committeeman Democratic Party, 1954-59, 61-72, 84-91; mem. Dem. State Central Com., 1954-59, 61-72. Served as sr. pilot USAF, 1943-53, disch. capt. Decorated Chinese Air Force Wings, 1986. Mem. Am., Ariz., Maricopa County, Minn., Ramsey County bar assns., VFW (life), Am. Legion, Amvets, Hump Pilots Assn. (life), Mil. Flight Service (life dir., legal officer, past pres.), Air Force Assn., Fraternal Order of Police, Friendly Sons of St. Patrick, Am. Trial Lawyers Assn., Internat. Assn. Jewish Lawyers and Jurists, Internat. Acad. Law and Sci., Am. Judicature Soc., Academia Internationali Lex et Scientia. Roman Catholic. Moose. Clubs: Phoenix Execs., Prescott Mountain, Phoenix Press, Terrace, Arizona, Thunderbird Country (founding mem.), Statesman's, Westerner. Died Nov. 1991. Home: Scottsdale Ariz. †

CONRAD, LARRY ALLYN, lawyer, state government official; b. Laconia, Ind., Feb. 8, 1935; s. Marshall and Ruby (Rooksby) C.; m. Mary Lou Hoover, Dec. 28, 1957; children—Jeb Allyn, Amy Lou, Andrew Birch, Jody McDade. A.B., Ball State U., 1957; LL.B., Ind. U., 1961. Legis. asst. to Senator Birch Bayh of Ind., Washington, 1963-64; chief counsel U.S. Senate Subcom. on Constnl. Amendments, 1964-69; sec. state Ind., 1970-78; ptnr. firm Conrad & Hafsten, Indpls., 1978-83; v.p. corp. affairs Melvin Simon & Assocs., Inc., from 1983. Hon. chmn. Ind. March of Dimes, 1974; chmn. bd. dirs. Mus. of Indian Heritage, Indpls.; bd. dirs. Dance Kaleidscope, Commn. for Downtown, Inc., Indpls., Indpls. Zool. Soc.; pres. Hemophilia of Ind., 1979-83; vice chmn. membership Indpls. Urban League; bd. dirs. Ind. Resource Corp.; hon. chmn. crusade Ind. div. Am. Cancer Soc., 1983; bd. dirs., chmn. Downtown Promotion Council; mem. Greater Indpls. Progress Com.; mem. Mayor's Community Council; mem. Indpls. Project; Democratic candidate for gov. Ind.; nat. bd. dirs. U.S. Clay Ct. Championships, Inc., AAU Found.; nat. bd. dirs., Ptnrs. for Livable Places, del. to Strasbourg and Lyons, France; active Ind. State Mus., Ind. Repertory Theatre; mem. adv. bd. Winona Meml. Hosp. Found., Hist. Landmarks Found.; mem. United Way Centennial Commn.; assoc. dir. Ind. Basketball Hall of Fame; co-chmn. opening ceremonies Pan Am. Games, 1987; co-chmn. spl. events com. Nat. League of Cities; co-chmn. opening ceremonies Nat. Sports Festival IV, 1982. Recipient citation of merit Ind. Vocat. Rehab. Services, 1972; recipient Man of Yr. award Indpls. Press Club, 1983, Disting. Alumni award Ball State U. Mem. NAACP (life); mem. ABA, Ind. State Bar Assn., Indpls. C. of C., Ind. C. of C., Indpls. Conv. and Visitors Bur. (bd. dirs.). Home: Indianapolis Ind. Died July 7, 1990.

CONROY, JACK (JOHN WESLEY CONROY), author, editor; b. Moberly, Mo., Dec. 5, 1898; s. Thomas Edward and Eliza Jane (McCollough) C.; m. Elizabeth Gladys Kelly, June 30, 1922 (dec. Oct. 1982); children: Margaret Jean Swartz Tillery (dec.), Thomas Vernon (dec.), Jack (dec.). Student, U. Mo., 1920-21; L.H.D., U. Mo. at Kansas City, 1975. Editor The Rebel Poet, 1931-32, The Anvil, 1933-37, The New Anvil, 1939-41; assoc. editor Nelson's Ency. and Universal World Reference Ency., 1943-47; sr. editor New Standard Ency., Chgo., 1947-66; dir. Standard Information Service, 1949-55; lit. editor Chgo. Defender, 1946-47, Chgo. Globe, 1950; instr. fiction writing Columbia Coll., 1962-66. Author: The Disinherited, 1933, reissued 1963, new edit. with introduction by author, 1982, A World To Win, 1935, (with Arna Bontemps) The Fast Sooner Hound, 1942, They Seek A City, 1945, Slappy Hooper, The Wonderful Sign Painter, 1946, Sam Patch, The High, Wide and Handsome Jumper, 1951, Anyplace But Here, 1966, The Jack Conroy Reader, (edited by Jack Salzman and David Ray), 1980, The Weed King and Other Stories (edited by Douglas C. Wixson), 1985; editor: (with Ralph Cheyney) Unrest, 1929-31, Midland Humor: A Harvest of Fun and Folklore, 1947, (with Curt Johnson) Writers in Revolt: The Anvil Anthology, 1973. John Simon Guggenheim fellow for creative writing, 1935; recipient James L. Dow award Soc. Midland Authors, 1966; award Literary Times, 1967; Lit. award Mo. Library Assn., 1977; Mark Twain award Soc. for Study Midwestern Lit., 1980; Louis M. Rabinowitz Found. grantee, 1968; Nat. Endowment of Arts grantee, 1978. Mem. Soc. Midland Authors (v.p. Mo.), Chgo. Council Fgn. Relations, Internat. Platform Assn. Methodist. Home: Moberly Mo. Died Feb. 28, 1990; buried Sugar Creek Cemetery, Moberly, Mo.

CONTA, LEWIS DALCIN, mechanical engineer; b. Rochester, N.Y., Sept. 16, 1912; s. Joseph and Mary Elizabeth (Dalcin) C.; m. Hilda Agnes Bowen, Aug. 31, 1935 (div.); children: Jean Patricia Conta Holland, Barbara Ann Conta Boyer, Robert Lewis; m. Carolyn H. Conklin. B.S. with highest distinction, U. Rochester, 1934, M.S., 1935; Ph.D., Cornell U., 1942. Registered profl. engr., N.Y. Instr. U. Rochester, N.Y., 1935-37; prof. mech. engring., chmn. engring. div. U. Rochester, 1950-59, assoc. dean for grad. studies, 1959-64; on leave as program dir. spl. engring. programs engring. div. NSF, 1967-69; instr. Cornell U., Ithaca, N.Y., 1937-42; asst. prof. mech. engring. Cornell U., 1942-46; instr. diesel engine Naval Tng., 1941-42, asst. supr., 1942-45, supr., 1945-46; research engr. and sect. head Air Reduction Research Labs., Murray Hill, N.J., 1946-48; cons. Air Reduction Research Labs., 1948-60; dean engring., dir. div., also prof. U. R.I., Kingston, 1969-77; dir. Univ. Energy Ctr., dir. div. research and devel., prof. mech. engring., 1977-78, prof. emeritus, from 1980; resident engr. Engring. Socs. Commn. on Energy, Washington, 1978-80; engring. cons., from 1980; adj. prof. aerospace and mech. engring. U. Ariz., from 1980; cons. and research Crucible Steel Co., Marquette Metal Products Co., NRC, Thermoelectron Corp., A.D. Little, Inc., Brookhaven Nat. Lab., others; mem. com. to reorganize Navy Diesel Engine Schs., Washington, Feb.-Apr. 1943; mem. commn. on Edn. for Engring. Professions, Nat. Assn. State Univs. and Land Grant Colls., 1971-74. Author tech. papers and reports. Fellow ASME (v.p. 1966-68, v.p. for research 1981-83, chmn. Rochester sect. 1956-57, chmn. diesel and gas engine power div. 1973-74, mem. policy bd. research 1973-81); mem. Am. Soc. Engring. Edn. (chmn. New Eng. sect. 1970), Nat. Soc. Profl. Engrs., AAUP, Assn. Engring. Colls. N.Y. (pres. 1953-55), Phi Beta Kappa, Sigma Xi, Tau Beta Pi, Phi Kappa Phi, Pi Tau Sigma. Home: Green Valley Ariz. Deceased. †

CONTE, SILVIO OTTO, congressman; b. Pittsfield, Mass., Nov. 9, 1921; s. Ottavio and Lucia (Lora) C.; m. Corinne L. Duval, Nov. 11, 1947; children: Michelle, Sylvia, John, Gayle. LL.B., Boston Coll., 1949; hon. degrees, Williams Coll., 1970, Hampshire Coll., North Adams State Coll., 1972, U. Mass., 1974, Amherst Coll., Boston Coll., Georgetown U., Tufts U., Am. Internat. Coll., 1979, Curry Coll., 1979, Mt. Vernon Coll., 1979, Northeastern U., 1979, Boston U., 1983, Westfield State Coll., 1983, Lesley Coll., 1984, George Washington U., 1984, Emmanuel Coll., 1986, Mt. Holyoke Coll., 1987, Gallaudet U., 1987, Stonehill Coll., 1987, Our Lady of the Elms, 1987, Ohio Dominican Coll., 1987, Howard U., 1988; Mass. Maritime Acad., 1988, Albert Einstein Sch. Medicine, 1988, Rochester Inst. Tech., 1989. Bar: Mass. 1949. Since practiced in Pittsfield; mem. 86th-102d Congresses from 1st Mass. dist.; ranking mem. appropriations com., transp. subcom., house select com. on small bus., migratory bird conservation commn.; mem. Mass. Senate, 1950-58; chmn. coms. on ins., constl. law, jud., chmn. legis. research council, chmn. spl. coms. for investigation health and welfare trust funds; co-chmn. New Eng. Congressional Caucus, 1973-91. Bd. regents Smithsonian Instn. Named outstanding young man of year Mass. Jr. C. of C., 1954; recipient President Medal of Merit award Georgetown U., 1982, President award Berkely Community Coll., 1979, Leadership award Morehouse Schl Medicine, 1985, Bicentennial medal Georgetown U., 1989, St. Thomas Moore award Boston Coll. Law Sch., 1986. Republican. Home: Pittsfield Mass. Died Feb. 8, 1991; buried Pittsfield, Mass.

CONTINI, GIANFRANCO, critic, educator; b. Domodossola, Italy, Jan. 4, 1912; s. Riccardo and Maria (Cernuscoli) C.; m. Margaret Piller, Aug. 3, 1955; children: Riccardo, Roberto. PhD, U. Pavia, 1933; DSc (hon.), Oxford (Eng.) U., 1965; U. Brussels, 1975. Prof. romance philology U. Fribourg (Switzerland), 1938-53; U. Florence (Italy), 1953-75, Scuola Normale Superiore, Pisa, Italy, 1975-90. Contbr. to jours. in field. Mem. Accademia Nazionale dei Lincei, Accademia della Grusca, Societa Dantesca Italiana. Died Feb. 1, 1990.

CONVY, BERT, actor; b. St. Louis, July 23, 1933; s. Bert and Monica Convy; m. Anne Anderson (div.); children: Jennifer, Joshua, Jonah.; m. Catherine Hills, Feb. 14, 1991. BA, UCLA, 1955; studied acting with Jeff Corey. Stage debut in The Matchmaker, Players Ring, Hollywood, Calif., 1957; also appeared in A Tree Grows in Brooklyn and Liliom; N.Y.C. stage debut in The Billy Barnes Review, 1959; other N.Y.C. theater appearances include Vintage '60, 1960, Nowhere To Go But Up, 1962, The Fantasticks, 1963, Morning Sun, 1963, Love and Kisses, 1963, Fiddler on the Roof, 1964, The Impossible Years, 1965, Cabaret, 1966, The Front Page, 1969, Nine, 1983; dir. Do It Again, 1971; game show host, actor, singer; host: TV prodns. Tattletales, 1974, The Late Summer, Early Fall Bert Convy Show, 1976, Win, Lose or Draw (also co-exec. producer) until 1989; appeared in: motion pictures Gunmen's Walk (debut), 1958, Susan Slade, 1963, Act One, 1963, John Goldfarb, Please Come Home, 1964, Give Her the Moon, 1969, Semi-Tough, 1978, The Man in the Santa Claus Suit, 1979, The Dallas Cowboys Cheerleaders, 1979, Hero At Large, 1980, Help Wanted: Male, 1982, Love Thy Neighbor, 1984; dir., co-exec. producer film Weekend Warriors, 1986. Recipient Emmy award as best game show host Nat. Acad. TV Arts and Scis., 1977. Home: Brentwood Calif. Died July 15, 1991.

CONWILL, ALLAN FRANKLIN, lawyer; b. Hutchinson, Kans., Oct. 21, 1921; s. Joseph Dillard and Phyllis Ruth (Fuhr) C.; m. Arolyn Frances Hodgkins, Aug. 30, 1947; children—Joseph Dillard, Stephen Hodgkins, Michael Francis. A.A., Wentworth Mil. Acad., 1941; B.S., Northwestern U., 1943, J.D., 1949. Bar: N.Y. 1949. Assoc. editor The Free Press, Hutchinson, Kans., 1946; prof. law N.Y. Law Sch., N.Y.C., 1951-56; lectr. law Columbia U., N.Y.C., 1964-67; assoc. then ptnr. Willkie Farr & Gallagher, N.Y.C., 1949-61, 64-86; gen. counsel, dir. SEC Corp. Regulatory div., Washington, 1961-64. Contbr. articles to profl. jours. Lt. USN, 1941-49; ATO, ETO. Decorated Bronze Star with battle star. Democrat. Presbyterian. Home: Wyckoff N.J. Died Oct. 9, 1989; cremated.

COOGAN, THOMAS PHILLIPS, mortgage banker; b. Springfield, Mass., July 27, 1898; s. John Patrick and Helen (Phillips) C.; m. Helen Harrington Kennelly, June 24, 1922; 1 child, Jacqueline H. Coogan Beatty. Student, MIT, 1924. Pres. South Fla. Bldrs. Assn., 1945-46, Nat. Assn. Home Bldrs., 1950, Housing Credit Corp., N.Y.C., Housing Securities, Inc., N.Y.C., 1950-92; chmn. bd., dir. Community Fed. Savs. & Loan Assn., Hialeah, Fla.; housing cons. ICA, 1958-92; chmn. bd. Housing Investment Corp., San Juan, P.R.; bd. dirs. ACTION, Nat. Housing Ctr., Wasington; asst. to Sec. of Def., 1952-53; del. Am. Constrn. Indsl. Mission to Soviet Union, 1956; leader Housing Mission to Soviet Union, 1958. Author: (monthly) Mortgage Market Memo. Mayor City of Surfside, Fla., 1949-50. With A.S., USN, 1917-18. Mem. Boston Soc. Civil Engrs., Nat. Assn. Home Bldrs., Assn. Gen. Contrs., Oyster Harbors (Mass.) Club, Surf Club, Indian Creek Club, La Gorce Club, Bal Harbour Club (Miami Beach). *

COOK, DAVID CHARLES, III, publisher and editor; b. Elgin, Ill., June 11, 1912; s. David Charles, Jr. and Frances Lois (Kerr) C.; m. Nancy L. Nagel, Nov. 11, 1983; children: Margaret Anne, Martha L., Bruce L., Gregory D., Rebecca; 1 stepson: Todd Erin Cahill. Student, Occidental Coll., 1930-32; Ph.B., U. Chgo., 1934; Lit.D., Judson Coll., 1965. Chmn. bd. David C. Cook Pub. Co. (founded by grandfather 1875), Elgin, Ill., 1934; editor-in-chief of its 35 curriculum publs. David C. Cook Pub. Co. Author: Walk the High Places, 1964, Invisible Halos, 1975. Dir. youth study tour Cultural Travel Found., 1955; v.p. Elgin Council Chs., 1954, pres., 1956-57; governing bd. Elgin Community Chest; pres. David C. Cook Found.; trustee Conf. Point Camp, Judson Coll., Elgin, Laubach Literacy, Immanuel United Ch. of Christ. Mem. Phi Kappa Psi. Home: Elgin Ill. Died Apr. 6, 1990; buried Bluff City Cemetery, Elgin, Ill.

COOK, DAVID S., banker; b. Elyria, Ohio, Apr. 17, 1921; s. Don S. and Alfreda (Davis) C.; m. Peg Bernheisel, Feb. 26, 1949; children: Candice, David S. Jr., Nancy Cook Backner, Robert T. BBA, Ohio State U., 1949; grad., Am. Inst. Banking. Cert. mortgage banker. Pres. Galbreath Mortgage Co., Columbus, Ohio, 1964-75; chmn. Chem. Realty Corp., N.Y.C., 1974-75; asst. sec. U.S. Dept. HUD, Washington, 1975-76; pres. Buckeye Fed. Savs. & Loan, Columbus, 1977-85; chmn., chief exec. officer Buckeye Fin. Corp., Columbus, 1977-88, also bd. dirs., 1980-88, pres., from 1980, also dir.; trustee Monyre, N.Y.C., from 1976; bd. dirs. Midland Mut. Life Ins., Columbus, Fed. Home Loan Bank, Cin. Chmn. Citizens for Ohio, 1982, Ohioans for Fair Taxation, 1984; trustee Columbus Assn. Performing Arts, 1977-87, Capital South, Columbus, from 1979. Sgt. USAF, 1942-45, ETO. Named Outstanding Young Man, Cleve. Jr. C. of C., 1956, Outstanding Mortgage Banker, Mortgage Bankers Assn. Am., 1972, Outstanding Mortgage Banker, Ohio Mortgage Bankers Assn., 1985. Mem. Ohio C. of C. (bd. dirs. 1985-88), Ohio Savs. and Loan League (chmn. 1984-85), Columbus Club (bd. dirs. 1985-89), Scioto Country Club (bd. dirs. 1984-88, pres. 1986-87), Pinnacle Club, Capital Club. Republican. Home: Dublin Ohio Deceased. †

COOK, JAMES CURTIS, government official; b. Fulton, Ill., Sept. 5, 1896; s. William E. and Ruby (Smith) C.; m. Laurel Dana, June 27, 1922. LLB, Southeastern U., 1924, LLM, 1933. Bar: D.C. 1924. Govt. employee and ofcl. Dept. of the Army, 1917-1992; dep. adminstrv. asst. Office Sec. of Army, 1941-61, adminstrv. asst., 1961-92. With USMC, 1918-19. Recipient Medal for Exceptional Civilian Svc., Dept. of the Army, 1949. Mem. Am. Legion, D.C. Bar Assn., Masons. Presbyterian. *

COOK, ROBERT CARTER, editor; b. Washington, Apr. 9, 1898; s. O.F. and Alice (Carter) C.; m. Margaret Brown, Aug. 4, 1921; children: John Robert, Barbara Alice, Victoria Marian; m. Helen Hall Jennings, Feb. 28, 1944; m. Annabelle Deumond, Aug. 19, 1946. Student, George Washington U., 1917-19, U. Md., 1920-21. Sci. aid U.S. Bur. Standards, 1916-18; mgr., editor The Jour. of Heredity, 1922-52, editor, 1952-62; dir. Population Ref. Bur.; editor Population Bull., 1951-58, pres., editor, from 1959; prof. lectr. med. genetics Med. Sch. George Washington U., 1944-63, lectr. biology, 1946-63. Author: Human Fertility: The Modern Dilemma, 1951; contbr. articles to popular mags. and tech. jours. Mem. program com., organizer sect. I, Inter-Am. Conf. on Conservation, 1948; mem. adv. com. Conservation Found.; dir. Assn. for Rsch. in Human Heredity, 1947-50. Recipient Albert and Mary Lasker Found. award in planned parenthood, 1956. Fellow AAAS; mem. Am. Eugenics Soc. (editor Eugenical News 1942, dir.), Am. Genetic Assn., Genetics Soc. Am., Am. Soc. Human Genetics, Am. Acad. Polit. and Social Sci., Acad. Medicine Washington, Washington Acad. Sci., Nat. Parks Assn. (trustee), Nat. Assn. Sci. Writers, Cosmos Club (Washington), Nat. Press Club. *

COOK, WILLIAM SUTTON, transportation company executive; b. Duluth, Minn., Sept. 6, 1922; s. Ellis Ray and Marjorie Sutton C.; m. Jacqueline Chambers Simmons, Nov. 29, 1980; children by previous marriage: Virginia Ann, William Sutton, James J., Andrew J. B.B.A., U. Minn., 1948. Various fin. positions Gen. Electric Co., 1948-62; comptroller, then v.p., comptroller Pa. R.R./Pa. Central Co., 1962-68; v.p., comptroller Ebasco Industries, Inc., 1968-69; v.p. fin., then exec. v.p. Union Pacific Corp., N.Y.C., 1969-77, pres., 1977-87, chief exec. officer, 1983-87, chmn., 1985-87, chmn. exec. com., 1985-87, ret., 1987; dir. Aluminum Co. Am., Boise Cascade Corp., DCNY Corp. Served to capt. AUS, 1943-46. Mem. Fin. Execs. Inst., Am. Petroleum Inst., Council for Fin. Aid Edn., Conf. Bd., Bus. Roundtable. Clubs: Links, Brook, Econ., Board Room (N.Y.C.); Blind Brook (Purchase, N.Y.); Quail Creek Country (Naples, Fla.); Mid Ocean (Bermuda). Home: New York N.Y. Died July 30, 1992. †

COOKE, PAUL DENVIR, advertising agency executive; b. Phila., Jan. 26, 1920; s. Charles J. and Katharine (Freer) C.; m. Marian K. Spiegel, Oct. 17, 1943; 1 dau., Katharine M. B.A., Yale, 1942. Account exec. Compton Advt., Inc., N.Y.C., 1948; v.p. Compton Advt., Inc., 1953-63, sr. v.p., 1963-67, exec. v.p., 1967-70, vice chmn. bd., 1970-76. Served to lt. USNR, 1942-48. Mem. Newcomen Soc. N.Am., Navy League U.S. Clubs: Univ. (N.Y.C.), Yale (N.Y.C.); Hackensack Golf (Oradell, N.J.). Home: Teneck N.J. Deceased. †

COOKINGHAM, L. PERRY, city manager; b. Chgo., Oct. 23, 1896; s. Joseph Fitch and Ella (Gordinier) C.; m. Harriette West, Jan. 2, 1921. Student, Detroit Inst. Tech., 1933-35, MS (hon.), 1936; LLD, Park Coll., 1952. Began as rodman C.&E.I. R.R., 1915; with Engr. Corps, until 1920; staff Pub. Wks. Dept., Flint, Mich., 1920-27; city mgr. City of Clawson, Mich., 1927-31, City of Plymouth, Mich., 1931-36, City of Saginaw, Mich., 1936-40, City of Kansas City, Mo., 1940-59, City of Ft. Worth, 1959-63; exec. dir. People to People, Kansas City, Mo., 1963-92; mem. adv. com. on tng. in city mgmt. Kans. U.; mem. vis. com. Joint Ctr. for Urban Studies, Harvard and MIT, 1959-62. Author, lectr. on subjects in field of pub. adminstrn. Dep. adminstr. Wayne County Emergency Relief Adminstrn., 1933, 34; mem. commn. for state govt. reform Mich., 1938; mem. mcpl. adv. com. W.P.B., 1943-45; mem. com. on urban rsch. Hwy. Rsch. Bd., 1958; adv. coun. Yale U. Traffic Bur., 1955-61; mem. Urban Renewal Study Bd., Balt., 1956; bd. dirs. Am. Coun. to Improve Our Neighborhoods, 1956-92; bd. govs. Starlight Theatre Assn. Recipient La Guardia Meml. Assn. award, 1951; named Aviation Man of Yr. Kansas City, 1955. Mem. Am. Soc. Planning Ofcls. (pres. 1945-46), Internat. City Mgrs. Assn. (pres. 1939, chmn. com. on profl. tng. 1958-59), Michn. Mcpl. League (hon. life), Nat. Mcpl. League, Am. Soc. for Pub. Adminstrn., Pi Sigma Alpha, Saddle and Sirloin Club, Kansas City Club, Masons. Congregationalist. *

COOLEY, THOMAS MCINTYRE, II, lawyer, educator, arbitrator; b. Detroit, Mar. 5, 1910; s. Thomas Benton and Abigail (Hubbard) C.; m. Helen Stringham, June 24, 1938; children—Abigail Jane, Harriet Stringham, Hilary Elizabeth. Grad., Phillips Exeter Acad., 1928; A.B., U. Mich., 1932; LL.B., Harvard, 1935; LL.B. grad. fellow, 1935-36. Bar: Mich. bar 1936, D.C. bar, Va. bar 1947, Pa. bar 1958. Assoc. firms Dykema, Jones & Wheat, Detroit, 1937-38, Barbour, Garnett, Pickett, Keith & Glassie, Washington, 1948-50, Weaver & Glassie, Washington, 1950-58; instr., asst. prof. law Western Res. U., 1938-41; mem. Bd. Immigration Appeals, Dept. Justice, 1941, assoc. dir. alien enemy control, chief alien enemy litigation, 1941-44, 46-47; dep. dir. displaced persons UNRRA, 1944-45; counsel immigration com. U.S. Ho. of Reps., 1945-46, subcom. on labor mgmt. relations U.S. Senate, 1949-50; assoc. counsel com. on govt. ops. U.S. Ho. of Reps., 1950; prof. Ohio State U. Law Sch., summer 1949; dean U. Pitts. Law Sch., 1958-65, prof. law, 1966-80, prof. emeritus, from 1981, pres. univ. faculty senate, 1967, chief research div. Health Law Center, 1966-68; prof. law U. Ill. Law Sch., 1965-66; Counsel Citizens Com. on Displaced Persons, 1947-48; counsel Central Blood Bank Pitts., 1960-76; arbitrator numerous labor relations matters, 1960—. Contbr. articles and revs. to legal periodicals. Mem. Am. Arbitration Assn., Nat. Acad. Arbitrators. Home: Philomont Va. Died Dec. 10, 1990; buried Waterford, Va.

COONS, CLIFFORD VERNON, corporate consultant; b. St. Joseph, Mo., Nov. 13, 1911; s. Edwin and Carrie (Fairhurst) C.; m. Delma DeYoung, Aug. 9, 1941; 1 child, Robert. Student, St. Joseph Coll., 1930-32. With acctg. dept. Rheem Mfg. Co., N.Y.C., 1934, advanced to v.p., 1935-56, exec. v.p., 1956-67, pres., 1967-72, cons., 1972-90. Mem. Gas Appliance Mfrs. Assn., Westchester Country Club, Canadian Sky Club, Pine Valley Golf Club. Home: Rye N.Y. Died Jan. 22, 1990.

COOPER, DELMAR CLAIR, genetics educator; b. Sutherland, Iowa, Apr. 10, 1896; s. Henry Ernest and Alvaretta (Fresh) C.; m. Irene Chapin, Apr. 5, 1917 (dec.); 1 child, Delmer Chapin; m. Lillian Margaret Scheuber, Aug. 29, 1933; children: Elizabeth Jean, Robert Ernest. AB, Morningside Coll., 1916, DSc, 1948; MS, Purdue U., 1926; PhD, U. Wis., 1939. Instr. biology Morningside Coll., 1917-19; instr. botany Purdue U., West Lafayette, Ind., 1926-28; instr. botany U. Wis., 1928-30, rsch. assoc. genetics and biology, 1930-36, asst. prof. genetics, 1936-42, assoc. prof., 1942-47, prof. genetics, 1947-92. Contbr. articles to profl. jours. Mem. AAAS, AAUP, Bot. Soc. Am., Am. Soc. Naturalists, Genetics Soc. Am., Potato Assn. Am., Internat. Soc. Plant Morphologists, Wis. Acad. Sci., Arts and Letters, Genetics Soc. Can., Sigma Xi, Phi Sigma, Acadia, Masons. *

COOPER, GRANT BURR, lawyer; b. N.Y.C., Apr. 1, 1903; s. Louis Baxter and Josephine (Christensen) C.; m. Edna Reynolds, Nov. 21, 1929 (dec. 1934); children: Judith Ann (Mrs. James J. Tracy), Natalie Caroline (Mrs. Rollin D. Wallace); m. Phyllis A. Norton, Apr. 3, 1935; children—Meredith Jane (Mrs. Robert K. Worrell), Grant Burr, John Norton. Student, Pace Coll., N.Y.C., 1921; LL.B., Southwestern U., 1926. Bar: Calif. bar 1927. Dep. dist. atty. Office Dist. Atty., Los Angeles, 1929-35; chief dep. dist. atty. Los Angeles County Dist. Atty.'s Office, 1940-42; dep. city atty. City of Los Angeles, 1942-43; pvt. practice Los Angeles, 1946-90; spl. prosecutor, State of Hawaii, 1976-78, spl. dep. atty. gen., 1976-78, Chief asst. ins. commr., Calif., 1943; pres. Los Angeles Health Commn., 1944; Mem. bd. councilors U. So. Calif. Law Center, from 1969. Fellow Am. Bar Found., Am. Coll. Trial Lawyers (past bd. regents, pres. 1962-63); mem. Los Angeles County Bar Assn. (pres. 1960-61, trustee 1951-52, 56- 62), State Bar Calif. (bd. govs. 1953-56, v.p. 1956). Clubs: Mason (Los Angeles) (Shriner), Chancery (Los Angeles), Century City Rotary (Los Angeles), Legion Lex (Los Angeles); Tuna (Catalina, Calif.). Home: Studio City Calif. Died May 3, 1990.

COOPER, HENRY NOBLE, government official; b. LaGrange, Ill., July 27, 1896; s. Henry Noble and Julia Lupton (Pardee) C.; m. Elizabeth McNair, Sept. 25, 1920 (dec. 1949); children: Henry Noble III (dec. 1948), Kenneth McNair, Christopher Moore; m. Ila Spencer, Aug. 25, 1950. Student, U. Ill., 1914-17, Kent Coll. Law, Chgo., 1919-20. Officer, dir. FitzSimons & Connell Dredge & Deck Co., also other corps. in Chgo., 1919-41; organizer 1st coop. apt. bdlg. in, Ill., 1920;

engaged as aircraft seating mfr., 1941-49; mission controller AID and predecessors, from 1950; fin mgmt. officer 13 African countries, Washington Hdqrs., from 1964. Served with Am. Field Svc., 1917. With C.A. U.S. Army, 1918-19; AEF in France. Decorated comdr. Order White Elephant (Thailand), 1955. Mem. Delta Kappa Epsilon, Phi Delta Phi. *

COOPER, JAMES WAYNE, lawyer; b. New Britain, Conn., May 22, 1904; s. James E. and Elizabeth C. (Wayne) C.; m. Louise B. Field, June 26, 1929; children: Field McIntyre, James Nicoll, Peter Brintnall. Grad., Choate Sch., 1922; B.A., Yale, 1926, LL.B., 1929. Bar: Conn. 1929. Law clk. to Judges T.W. Swan, Learned Hand, N.Y.C., 1929-30; instr. Yale Law Sch., 1930-32; asso. Watrous, Hewitt, Gumbart & Corbin, New Haven, 1932-35; partner Tyler, Cooper & Alcorn (and predecessor firms), from 1935; Counsel Anna Fuller Fund, 1938-79. Pres. Foote Sch. Assn., Inc., 1947-49; sec. New Haven Found., 1947-67; mem. Yale Council, 1954-59, exec. com., 1956-59, pres., 1958-59. Fellow Saybrook Coll., Am. Bar Assn.; mem. Conn. Bar Assn. (pres. 1957-58), New Haven County Bar Assn. (pres. 1948-49), Conn. Bar Found. (pres. 1973-75). Clubs: Graduate (New Haven), Quinnipack (New Haven). Home: Woodbridge Conn. Died Jan. 16, 1989.

COOPER, JOHN SHERMAN, lawyer, diplomat; b. Somerset, Ky., Aug. 23, 1901; s. John Sherman and Helen Gertrude (Tartar) C.; m. Lorraine Rowan Shevlin, Mar. 17, 1955. Student, Centre Coll., Ky., 1918-19; A.B., Yale U., 1923; postgrad., Harvard Law Sch., 1923-25; postgrad. hon. degrees, U. Ky., U. Pitts., Yale U., Georgetown Coll., Berea Coll., Eastern Ky. State U., Lincoln Meml. U., Nasson Coll., Centre Coll., Thomas More Coll., Pikeville Coll., Morehead State U., Georgetown U., U. Louisville. Bar: Ky. 1928. Mem. lower ho. Ky. Legislature, 1928-30; judge Pulaski County, Ky., 1930-38; circuit judge 28th Jud. Dist. Ky., 1946; mem. U.S. Senate from Ky., 1947-1948, 52-55, 57-73; mem. com. fgn. relations, pub. works and environment, com. rules and adminstrn., mem. select com. on standards and conduct; apptd. adviser to Sec. State Acheson, NATO meetings, 1950-51; U.S. del. Gen. Assembly, UN, 1949-51, 68, 81; U.S. ambassador to India Nepal, 1955-56, German Democratic Republic, 1974-76; mem. law firm Gardner, Morrison & Rogers, Washington, 1949-51; of counsel Covington & Burling (attys.), Washington, 1973-74, from 1976; adj. prof. George Washington U., 1973-74; mem. Pres.'s Commn. to Investigate Assassination of Pres. Kennedy, 1964. Trustee Centre Coll., John F. Kennedy Sch. Govt., Harvard. Served from pvt. to capt. AUS, 1942-45, ETO. Decorated Bronze Star. Mem. Am., Ky., D.C. bar assns., Am. Acad. Polit. Sci., Am. Legion, VFW, Beta Theta Pi. Republican. Baptist. Club: Rotarian. Home: Washington D.C. Died Feb. 21, 1991; buried Arlington Nat. Cemetery.

COOPER, LOUISE FIELD, author; b. Hartford, Conn., Mar. 8, 1905; d. Francis Elliott and Anna (Dunning) Field; m. James Wayne Cooper, June 26, 1929; children: Field (Mrs. Colin McIntyre), James Nicoll, Peter Brintnal. Student, Miss Porter's Sch., Farmington, 1921-24. Author: The Lighted Box, 1942, The Deer on the Stairs, Love and Admiration, Summer Stranger, 1947, The Boys from Sharon, 1950, The Cheerful Captive, 1954, The Windfall Child, 1963, Widows and Admirals, 1964, A Week at the Most, 1967, One Dragon Too Many, 1971, large print edit., 1978, Breakaway, 1977, 5 pub. works issued in paperback 1973, also large print edit. 1978; Contbr. short stories to New Yorker mag. Home: New Haven Conn. Died Oct. 9, 1992. †

COOPER, ROBERT ARTHUR, JR., pathologist, educator; b. St. Paul, Aug. 27, 1932; s. Robert Arthur and Theodora (Yarborough) C.; m. Stephanie A. Coffey, Feb. 2, 1991; children from previous marriage: Robert Arthur, III, Timothy Rychener, Theodore Thomas. Student, Stanford U., 1950-52; A.B., U. Pa., 1954; M.D., Jefferson Med. Coll., Phila., 1958. Intern Moffitt Hosp., U. Calif., 1958-59, resident in pathology, 1959-62; chief resident in pathology Women's Free Hosp. and Boston Lying-in Hosp., Harvard, 1962-63; teaching fellow Harvard Med. Sch., 1962-63; from asst. prof. to prof. pathology U. Oreg. Med. Sch., 1963-69; mem. faculty U. Rochester (N.Y.) Med. Sch., 1969-92, assoc. dean curricular affairs, assoc. prof. pathology, 1969-72, prof. pathology, dir. surg. pathology, 1972-75, prof. oncology in pathology, dir. cancer center, 1974-92; cons. subcom. on comprehensive cancer ctrs. Nat. Cancer Adv. Bd., Nat. Cancer Inst., 1976-78, mem. breast cancer treatment com. (breast cancer task force), div. cancer biology, 1974-77, mem. cancer ctr. support grant rev. com., 1978-82, chmn., 1981-82; bd. sci. counsellors div. cancer prevention and control Nat. Cancer Inst., 1983-85; mem. spl. study sect. cancer epidemiology NIH, 1972; bd. dirs. United Cancer Council, Inc., v.p., 1981-90; bd. dirs. Monroe County unit Am. Cancer Soc., 1976-80, mem. profl. edn. com. N.Y. State div., 1974-78; cons. Population Council, Rockefeller U., 1972-82; mem. Lasker award jury Lasker Found., 1977. Author articles, chpts. in books; assoc. editor Internat. Jour. Radiation Oncology, Biology and Physics, 1974-81; mem. editorial bd. Cancer Clin. Trials, 1977-92. d. dirs. Brighton Little League, 1973-77, vice commnr., 1975-76; bd. dirs. Wilmot Found., 1981-92 . Recipient Allan J. Hill Teaching award U. Oreg. Med. Sch., 1966, 67, 69; named 2d Year Tchr. of Year U. Rochester Med. Sch., 1973; Lester P. Slade civic achievement award Real Estate Bd. of Rochester, 1980; research fellow Am. Cancer Soc., 1960-61; grantee Nat. Cancer Inst., 1975-92. Mem. Alpha Omega Alpha. Home: Pittsford N.Y. Died Mar. 19, 1992. †

COOTE, COLIN REITH, journalist; b. Fenstanton, Huntingdonshire, Eng., Oct. 19, 1893; s. Howard and Jean Reith (Gray) C.; m. Amalie Marinus, Mar. 29, 1946. Student, Rugby Sch., 1907-11; BA, Balliol Coll., Oxford, 1914. Mem. Paliament, 1917-22; Rome Correspondent The Times, 1922-25; Parliamentary sketch writer, 1927-30, Times leader-writer, 1930-42; dep. editor Daily Telegraph, 1942-50, mng. editor, 1950-64. Author: Italian Town and Country Life, 1924, In and About Rome, 1925, Maxims and Reflections of Winston Churchill, 1947, Through Five Generations, 1949, Sir Winston Churchill, A Self-Portrait, 1953, Companion of Honour- A Life of Walter elliot, 1965. Served with the Gloucester Regiment, 1914-18, the French 26th Inf. Divsn. France and Italy, 1917-18. Decorated Companion Disting. Svc. Order, 1918, Legion of Honor, 1956, Knight Batchelor, 1962. *

COPELAND, MORRIS ALBERT, economist; b. Rochester, N.Y., Aug. 6, 1895; s. Albert Edwards and Jenny (Morris) C.; m. Mary Phelps Enders, Dec. 21, 1929; children—Helen (Mrs. R.E. Grattidge), Robert Enders. A.B., Amherst Coll., 1917, L.H.D., 1957; Ph.D., U., Chgo., 1921. Instr. econs. Cornell U., 1921-25, asst. prof., 1925-28, prof., 1928-30, leave of absence, 1927-29; served successively with Brookings Grad. Sch., Nat. Bur. Econ. Research, U. Wis. Exptl. Coll. and; Fed. Res. Bd.; prof. econs. U. Mich., 1930-36, leave of absence, 1933-35; exec. sec. Central Statis. Bd., Washington, 1933-39; dir. research Bur. of Budget, Washington, 1939-40; chief munitions br. WPB, 1940-44; with Nat. Bur. Econ. Research, 1944-59; prof. econs. Cornell U., 1949-65, Robert J. Thorne prof. econs., 1957-65; vis. prof. econs. U. Mo., 1966-67, State U. N.Y. at Albany, 1967-71; Fulbright lectr. Delhi (India) Sch. Econs., 1950-51. Author: A Study of Moneyflows in the U.S, 1951, Fact and Theory in Economics, 1958, Trends in Government Financing, 1961, Our Free Enterprise Economy, 1964, Toward Full Employment, 1966, Essays in Socioeconomic Evolution, 1980; contbr. to econ. publs. Fellow Am. Statis. Assn. (past v.p.); mem. Am. Econ. Assn. (past pres.), Phi Beta Kappa, Phi Delta Theta. Home: Sarasota Fla. Died May 4, 1989; cremated.

COPLAND, AARON, composer; b. Bklyn., Nov. 14, 1900; s. Harris Morris and Sarah (Mittenthal) C. Grad., Boys High Sch., Bklyn., 1918; studied music privately; pupil piano, Victor Wittgenstein and Clarence Adler; composition, Rubin Goldmark and Nadia Boulanger; HHD (hon.), Brandeis U., 1957, Ill. Wesleyan U., 1958; MusD (hon.), Princeton U., 1956, Oberlin Coll., 1958, Temple U., 1959, U. Hartford, 1959, Harvard U., 1961, Syracuse U.; Mus. D., U. R.I., U. Mich., 1964, Kalamazoo Coll., 1965, U. Utah, 1966, Jacksonville U., 1967, Rutgers U., 1967, Fairfield U., 1968, Ohio State U., 1970, NYU, 1970, Columbia U., 1971, York U., Eng., 1971, U. Fla., 1972, L.I. U., 1974, Bklyn. Coll., 1975, U. Portland, Oreg., 1975, Ottawa (Kans.) U., 1976, U. Rochester, N.Y., 1976, U. Leeds, Eng., 1976, Tulane U., New Orleans, 1976. Lectr. music New Sch. for Social Research, N.Y.C., 1927-37, Harvard U., spring 1935, 44; instr., then asst. dir. Berkshire Music Center, 1940; Charles Eliot Norton prof. poetry Harvard U., 1951-52; dir. Am. Music Center; treas. Arrow Music Press.; dir. Koussevitsky Music Found.; v.p. Edward MacDowell Assn., Walter W. Naumberg Found. Founder (with Roger Sessions) Copland-Sessions Concerts, 1928-31, Am. Music Festivals at Yaddo, Saratoga Springs, N.Y., 1932; composer music, 1920—; works include Orchestral Variations, 1957, First Symphony, 1928, Music for the Theatre, 1925, A Dance Symphony, 1925, Concerto for Piano and Orchestra, 1926, Symphonic Ode, 1929, 55, Short Symphony, 1933, Statements, 1935, El Salon Mexico, 1936, Music for Radio, 1937, An Outdoor Overture, 1938, Quiet City, 1940, Lincoln Portrait, 1942; ballet Grohg, 1925, Hear Ye, Hear Ye, 1934, Billy the Kid, 1938, Rodeo, 1942, Appalachian Spring, 1944; opera for high schs. The Second Hurricane, 1937; music for motion pictures The City, 1939, Of Mice and Men, 1939, Our Town, 1940, North Star, 1943, The Red Pony, 1948, The Heiress, 1949, Something Wild, 1961; chamber music Two Pieces for String Quartet, 1928, Vitebsk, 1929, Piano Variations, 1930, Piano Sonata, 1941, Violin Sonata, 1943, Third Symphony, 1946, In the Beginning, mixed chorus, 1947, Clarinet Concerto, 1948, Twelve Poems of Emily Dickinson, 1950, Quartet for Piano and Strings, 1950, Music and Imagination, 1952, The Tender Land, opera, 1954, Piano Fantasy, 1957, Nonet for strings, 1960, Connotations for Orch., 1962, Music for a Great City, 1964, Emblems for Band, 1965, Inscape for orch., 1967, Duo for flute and piano, 1971, Three Latin America Sketches for orch, 1971, Night Thoughts for piano, 1972, Threnody I: Igor Stravinsky, In Memoriam, 1971, Threnody II: Beatrice Cunningham, In Memoriam; author: What to Listen For in Music, 1939, rev. ed., 1957, Our New Music, 1941, 1968, Copeland on Music, 1960; contbr. to: Modern Music; author: Copland 1900 Through 1942, 1987, (with Vivian Perlis) Copland: Since 1943, 1989. Guggenheim fellow, 1925-26; recipient RCA Victor award ($5,000), 1930, Pulitzer prize for music, 1944, N.Y. Music Critics Circle award for Appalachian Spring, 1945, Acad. Award for film score The Heiress, Acad. Motion Picture Arts and Sci., 1950, gold medal for music Am. Acad. Arts and Letters, 1956, Presdl. medal of Freedom, 1964, Howland Meml. prize Yale U., 1970, Nat. Medal of Arts, 1986; decorated comdr.'s cross Order Merit West Germany; hon. mem. Accademia Santa Cecilia, Rome, Academia Nacional de Bellas Arts, Buenos Aires, Argentina, Royal Philharmonic Soc., London, N.Y. Philharmonic Soc., Internat. Soc. for Contemporary Music, Royal Acad. Music, London. Mem. Am. Acad. Arts and Scis., League Composers (chmn. bd. dirs.), ASCAP, Nat. Inst. Arts and Letters, Am. Acad. Arts and Letters (past pres.), Royal Soc. Arts London, Academie de Beaux Arts of Academie Francaise. Home: North Tarrytown N.Y. Died Dec. 2, 1990.

COPPOLA, CARMINE, composer, conductor; b. N.Y.C., June 11, 1910; s. August and Maria (Zasa) C.; m. Italia Pennino, Apr. 30, 1934; children—August, Francis, Talia. Diploma, Juilliard Sch. Music, 1933; Mus.M., Manhattan Sch. Music, 1950. Mem. music staff Sta. WTIC, Hartford, Conn., Radio City Music Hall, 1st flutist, Detroit Symphony, NBC Orch., music dir., Merrick Prodns., Los Angeles Civic Opera; composer: numerous scores for film including Napoleon, The Godfather, Parts I and II, Apocalypse Now, The Black Stallion, Tonight for Sure, 1982, The Outsiders, 1983, Gardens of Stone, 1987; contributed music to Tucker: The Man and His Dream, 1988; opera Escorial, 1979; recipient Oscar for musical score The Godfather Part II, Acad. Motion Pictures Arts and Scis., Arts and Letters medal of France, 1985. Calif. Arts Coun. grantee. Mem. ASCAP, Acad. Motion Pictures Arts and Scis., Beta Gamma. Home: Los Angeles Calif. Died Apr. 26, 1991.

CORBETT, CLETUS JOHN, lawyer, shoe company executive; b. Columbus, Ohio, June 18, 1907; s. Patrick J. and Mary (Byrne) C.; m. Margaret P. Burns, Aug. 26, 1946 (dec.); 1 child, Margaret Corbett Lenzer. Student, Ohio State U., 1924-29; LL.B., Franklin U., 1941; J.D., Capital U., 1966. Bar: Ohio 1941. Acct. Proctor-Gamble Co., Jackson, Miss., Memphis, 1929-33; with SCOA Industries, Inc., Columbus, 1934-86; counsel, v.p. SCOA Industries, Inc., 1957-66, sec., 1966-72, dir., 1966-83, emeritus dir., 1983-85; practiced in Columbus; counsel firm Porter, Stanley, Platt & Arthur, Columbus, until 1976; with firm Iverson, Yoakum, Papiano & Hatch, Los Angeles, 1976; counsel firm Postlewaite, O'Brien & Mann, Columbus, 1976; individual practice law Columbus, from 1976. Served with USAAF, 1942-45. Decorated Air medal with nine oak leaf clusters, three bronze stars. Mem. Am., Ohio, Columbus bar assns., Am. Judicature Soc., Phi Kappa, Iota Lambda Pi. Clubs: Columbus Athletic, Univ. Home: Columbus Ohio Died Dec. 20, 1989; buried Resurrection Cemetery, Columbus.

CORBETT, J. RALPH, foundation executive; b. Flushing, L.I., N.Y., Dec. 5, 1900; s. Burnett Lewis and Pearl C.; m. Patricia Barry, July 23, 1930; children: Gail Barry, Thomas R. LL.B., N.Y. Law Sch., 1923; D.H.L., U. Cin., 1967; LL.D., Xavier U., 1974, Edgecliff Coll., 1975. Began career in N.Y.C., serving as marktg. cons. and adviser to Eastern mfg. and fin. orgns.; owner advt. agy.; cons. to early radio broadcasting stas.; adviser Sta. WLW, 1932-37; founder NuTone, Inc., Cin., 1936; pres., then chmn. bd. NuTone, Inc., until 1967; pres. Corbett Found., Cin., from 1967; Spl. adviser Coll.-Conservatory Music, U. Cin., 7 years; head publicity com., spl. adviser fund drive Cin. Inst. Fine Arts, 1973; cons. Nat. Endowment for Arts, Washington. Author: In Spite of All. Donated funds for constrn. Corbett Auditorium and Patricia Corbett Pavilion at Corbett Center for Performing Arts at U. Cin.; active (through found.) in support 7 Cin. hosps., 24 U.S. opera orgns., Royal Opera House, Covent Garden, Eng., Glyndebourne Opera, Cin. Symphony Orch., teaching studio for young Am. opera singers in, Zurich, Switzerland, Montessori Sch. at, Mercy Center, Cin.; apptd. 1st chmn. Ohio Arts Council, 1965; mem. U.S. Govt. businessmen's team conducting seminars in, Belgium, 1954, Jamaica, 1960; Pres. May Festival Assn., 1971, now mem. bd.; former chmn. bd. trustees Cin. Symphony Orch.; now mem. exec. com.; mem. bd. Cin. Opera Assn., Cin. Ballet Co., Cin. Inst. Fine Arts; chmn. bd. Cin. Music Hall Assn.; established Corbett Lecture Series at U. Cin. Recipient Great Living Cincinnatian award Cin. C. of C., 1970; (with wife) Ohio's first Cultural Honor award, 1971; recipient Founders of Chgo. Province of Soc. of Jesus award Jesuit Community of Xavier U.; inducted into Housing Hall of Fame, 1982. Mem. MacDowell Soc. Cin., Cin. Hist. Soc. Presbyn. Clubs: Commercial (Cin.), Queen City (Cin.), Bankers (Cin.). Home: Cincinnati Ohio Died Oct. 3, 1988; buried Spring Grove Cemetery & Arboretum, Cincinatti.

CORCORAN, HOWARD FRANCIS, federal judge; b. Pawtucket, R.I., Jan. 25, 1906; s. Thomas Patrick and Mary Josephine (O'Keefe) C.; m. Esther Pierce, May 31, 1952. Grad., Phillips Exeter Acad., 1924; A.B., Princeton, 1928; LL.B., Harvard, 1931. Bar: N.Y. bar 1935, D.C. bar 1956. With Dept. Agr., 1933-34, TVA,

1934-35; legal asso. SEC, 1935-38; asst. Office U.S. Atty. for So. Dist. of N.Y., 1938-43; U.S. atty. So. Dist. N.Y., 1943; partner firm Corcoran, Kostelanetz & Gladstone, N.Y.C., 1946-54, Corcoran, Foley, Youngman & Rowe, Washington, 1954-65; U.S. dist. judge for D.C. Washington, 1965-87. Served to lt. col. AUS, 1943-45. Decorated Bronze Star, Croix de Guerre with star France). Mem. Am., Fed. bar assns., Bar Assn. of D.C., Assn. Bar City N.Y., Phi Delta Phi. Roman Catholic. Clubs: Princeton (Washington and N.Y.C.), Army-Navy (Washington), Congressional Country (Washington). Home: Washington D.C. Died May 11, 1989; buried Arlington Nat. Cemetery.

CORDELL, JOE B., diversified corporation executive; b. Daytona Beach, Fla., Aug. 4, 1927; s. Joe Wynne and Ada Ruth (Wood) C.; m. Joyce Hinton, June 16, 1951; children: Joe B., Coleman Wynn, Lauren. Student, Yale U., 1945-46, Fla. So. Coll., 1946-47; BS in Bus. Adminstrn, U. Fla., 1949. C.P.A. Intern Price Waterhouse Corp., N.Y.C., 1948-49, staff acct., 1949-50; audit mgr. Price Waterhouse Corp., Atlanta, 1950-58; v.p. Jim Walter Corp., Tampa, Fla., 1958-70, sr. v.p., treas., 1970-74, pres., from 1974, chief oper. officer, from 1974; pres., chief exec. officer Walter Industries Inc. (formerly Jim Walter Corp.), Tampa, Fla., also bd. dirs.; bd. dirs. Barnett Banks of Fla., Inc., Jacksonville. Chmn. adv. bd. Tampa/Hillsborough County Area command The Salvation Army; trustee Palma Ceia United Meth. Ch.; mem. bus. adv. coun. U. Fla.; past pres. U. Fla. Found., also ex-officio mem. bd. trustees, mem. devel. com. With USN, 1945-46. Mem. Greater Tampa C. of C., Com. of 100, Tampa Yacht and Country Club, Palma Ceia Golf and Cuntry Club, Wildcat Cliffs Country Club, Avila Golf and Country Club, Univ. Club of Tampa, Ye Mystic Krewe of Gasparilla, Alpha Kappa Psi, Alpha Tau Omega. Methodist. Home: Tampa Fla. Deceased. †

CORNELIUS, EDWARD GORDON, marketing and management specialist; b. Berea, Ky., Feb. 13, 1896; s. Frank and Nancy (Edwards) C.; m. May Fischer, 1932. AB, Maryville (Tenn.) Coll., 1925; AM, Vanderbilt U., 1926, PhD, 1936; grad. study (summers), George Peabody Coll. for Teachers, 1926, U. N.C., 1927, U. Chgo., 1928, 29, U. Calif., 1932, U. Ky., 1937, Ind. Coll. Armed Forces, 1951-52. Head economics and bus. Southwestern Coll., Winfield, Kans., 1928, 33; assoc. prof. commerce and fin. Bucknell U., 1936-46; prof., chmn. mktg. and mgmt. La. Poly. Inst., 1947-51; prof. bus. adminstrn., head dept. bus. and ind. mgmt. Tenn. Tech., Cookeville, 1951-61; prof. bus. edn. Tenn. Tech., from 1961. Author books, numerous articles, pamphlets. Served as non-commd. officer U.S. Army, 1918-19. Mem. NEA, Am. Arbitration Assn., Soc. for Advancement Mgmt., Acad. Mgmt., Assn. Higher Edn., Sigma Iota Epsilon, Pi Gamma Mu, Kappa Alpha Order, Omicron Delta Gamma, Omicron Delta Kappa, Pi Kappa Delta, Tau Kappa Alpha. Presbyterian. *

CORNISH, GEORGE ANTHONY, editor; b. Demopolis, Ala., Sept. 22, 1901; s. Edward Seymour and Martha (Graves) C.; m. Constance Brown; children: Edward Seymour, Robert Mangum. AB, U. Ala., 1921. Reporter Birmingham (Ala.) Age-Herald, 1921-23; with N.Y. Herald Tribune, 1923-60, mng. editor, 1941-52, exec. editor, 1952-60; editor-in-chief Ency. Internat., 1960-65, Ency. Americana, 1965-70; mem. usage panel Am. Heritage Dictionay, 1968-89. Mem. Dutch Treat Club, Phi Beta Kappa, Pi Kappa Phi. Home: Saint Petersburg Fla. Died May 14, 1989.

CORREA, HENRY A., former manufacturing executive; b. N.Y.C., Mar. 9, 1917; s. Enrique A. and Maria (Helm) C.; m. Elizabeth Winchester, Dec. 9, 1944. B.S. in Bus. Adminstrn., St. Louis U., 1937. With Robertson Aircraft Corp., St. Louis, 1937-38; chief pilot, sales mgr. Atlantic Aviation Service, Wilmington, Del., 1938-41; fgn. sales mgr. Bendix Internat. div. Bendix Corp., 1945-57; v.p. fgn. ops. ACF Industries, Inc., N.Y.C., 1958; v.p. mktg. ACF Industries, Inc., 1959-63, v.p. exec. dept., 1964-65, exec. v.p., dir., 1965-67, pres., 1967-81, vice chmn., from 1981; dir. Petroleum & Resources Corp., Adams Express Co. Hon. trustee Children's Aid Soc. Served from 1st lt. to maj. AUS, 1943-45. Decorated Army Commendation medal; recipient hon. pilot wings Colombia Air Force, 1945; Andrew Wellington Cordier fellow Columbia U. Mem. Quiet Birdmen. Clubs: Sky, Union, N.Y. Yacht (N.Y.C.), John's Island, Riomar Bay Yacht (Vero Beach, Fla.), Vero Beach. home: Vero Beach Fla. Deceased. †

CORSON, JOHN JAY, consultant, trustee; b. Washington, Dec. 8, 1905; s. Eben White and Ellen (Pawling) C.; m. Mary Turner Tilman, Nov. 15, 1930 (dec. July 1975); children: John Jay, Nancy Tilman. B.S., U. Va., 1926, M.S., 1929, Ph.D., 1932. Editorial asso. Richmond (Va.) News Leader, 1929-33; prof. econs. U. Richmond, 1933-38; asst. exec. dir. Social Security Bd., 1936-38; dir. Bur. Old Age and Survivors Ins., 1938-41, 43-44, U.S. Employment Service, 1941-42; dep. dir. gen. UNRRA, 1944-45; exec. Washington Post, 1945-50; mgmt. cons. McKinsey & Co., 1951-66; prof. pub. internat. affairs Woodrow Wilson Sch., Princeton U., 1962-66; pres. Am. Blood Commn., 1975-78; cons. to dir. gen. UNESCO, 1963-64, OAS, 1960, ILO, 1962; cons. govts. of, Tanzania, 1974, San Salvador, 1975, Panama, 1976-78, Iran, 1976-77, Turkey, 1978, Argentina, 1979, Sri Lanka, 1980, Pakistan, 1980, Thailand, 1982, 83; Bd. overseers Sweet Briar Coll., 1960-70; trustee Marymount Coll. Va., 1970-85, Chgo. Med. Sch., 1971-75, George Mason U., 1972-80, Salzburg (Austria) Seminar Am. Studies, 1966-68, Ednl. Testing Service, 1964-68. Author: Manpower for Victory, 1943, Executives for the Federal Service, 1952, Economic Needs of Older People, (with John W. McConnell), 1955, The Governance of Colleges and Universities, 1960, rev. edit., 1975, (with Joseph P. Harris) Public Administration in Modern Society, 1964, (with Shale Paul) Men Near the Top, 1966, Business in the Humane Society, 1971, (with Harry V. Hodson) Philanthropy in the 70's, 1973, (with George A. Steiner) Measuring Business Social Performance: The Corporate Social Audit, 1974. Trustee numerous ednl. instns. including Chgo. Med. Coll., Sweet Briar Coll., Gerge Mason U. Mem. Am. Soc. Pub. Adminstrn. (pres. 1948-49), Phi Beta Kappa. Home: Fairfax Va. Died Sept. 2, 1990.

CORSON, PHILIP LANGDON, industrial executive; b. Plymouth Meeting, Pa., Oct. 31, 1898; s. Walter Harris and Katherine I. (Langdon) C.; m. Helen Thomas Payson, Jan. 30, 1930. Student, Haverford Coll., 1915-19; LLD (hon.), Ursinus Coll., 1959. Lime mfr. G. & W.H. Corson Inc., Plymouth Meeting, from 1919, plant mgr., 1923-28, v.p., mem. bd., 1928-39, pres., 1933-53, chmn., from 1953; dir. Baldwin-Ehret Hill Co., Hughes-Foulkrod Co., S.D.M.&R. Assocs., Taylor Corp., Williams & Marcus Co., Franklin Printing Co., Foote Mineral Co. Pres. Tri-County Mental Health Clinics, Inc., Norristown, Pa., 1949-57; mem. bd. Norristown State Hosp., 1942-46, pres. bd. 1946-56; bd. trustees Germantown Acad.; trustee, mem. exec. com. Ursinus Coll. Served as pvt. U.S. Army, 1918. Mem. Merion Cricket, Sunnybrook Golf, Mid-Ocean Club, Racquet Club, Pinehurst Country Club, Plymouth Country Club. *

COSSENTINE, ERWIN EARL, academic administrator; b. Eagle Bend, Minn., Aug. 23, 1896; s. George and Myrtle C.; m. Mildred Parker, Feb. 15, 1917; children: Robert Erwin, Ruth (wife of Joseph Maschmeyer), Verna Mildred (Mrs. Victor Barton). Student, Atlantic Union Coll., 1917-19; AB, Emmanuel Missionary Coll., 1922; AM, Claremont Coll., 1933; student, U. So. Calif., 1934-36. Preceptor East N.Y. Acad., Clinton, 1920-21; prin. Flat Rock (Ga.) Acad., 1922-23; ednl. supt. N.C., 1923-24; prin. New Zealand Missionary Coll., 1924-28; pres. Avondale Coll., Australia, 1928-30, So. Calif. Jr. Coll., 1930-40, La Sierra Coll., Calif., 1940-42, Union Coll., Lincoln, Nebr., 1942-46; sec. Dept. Edn., Gen. Conf. Seventh Day Adventists, from 1946; Bd. dirs. Seventh-Day Adventists Theol. Sem., chmn. bd. regents; chmn. bd. regents Seventh-Day Adventist Instns. Bd. dirs. Andrews U., Loma Linda U., Atlantic Union Coll. Mem. Gen. Conf. Com. Seventh-Day Adventists, pres.' adminstrv. coun. European rehabilitation, Review and Herald Book Com., Home Study Inst. (vice chmn.), Ministerial Assn., chmn. Commn. on Grad. Edn., Internat. Temperance Assn. *

COSTANTINO, MARK AMERICUS, federal judge; b. Staten Island, N.Y., Apr. 9, 1920; s. Anne Marie (Caruselle) C.; m. Dorothy Summers, July 28, 1944; children: Mark, Thomas, Dennis, Richard, Kathryn Ann. Student, Manhattan Coll., 1938-40; LL.B., Bklyn. Law Sch., 1947. Spl. dep. atty. gen. State of N.Y., N.Y.C., 1947-51; sole practice Staten Island, 1951-56; judge City Ct., N.Y.C., 1957-61, Civil Ct., N.Y.C., 1961-71; judge U.S. Dist. Ct. N.Y., Bklyn., 1971-87, sr. judge, 1987-89; acting judge N.Y. State Supreme Ct., 1958-71; nat. chmn. Am. Inns of Ct., Bklyn., 1984—; bd. dirs. Eden II Sch. for Autistic Children, Staten Island. Contbr. articles to profl. jours. Active Boy Scouts Am.; bd. dirs. Drs. Hosp., Staten Island; arranged and conducted naturalization proceedings for Chief Justice Warren E. Burger for July 3, 1987 Liberty Bicentennial, Constitutional Bicentennial celebration, Sept. 11, 1987, first En Banc hearing in Ea. Dist. of N.Y. to determine legal questions involving Grand Jury proceedings, Jan. 21, 1988; mem. Am. com. on Italian immigration. Served with U.S. Army, 1942-46. Recipient Alumnus of Yr. award Bklyn. Law Sch. Alumni Assn., 1978, 1st ann. Warren Burger award Bklyn. Trial Lawyers Assn., 1970, Man of Yr. award Amicus Curiae Columbia Assn., 1984, resolution DAR, 1984, Am. Legion award for Meritorious Svc., Disting. Svc. award Boy Scouts Am., Raoul Wallenberg's award. Mem. Fed. Bar Council, Richmond County Bar Assn., Columbian Lawyers, Am. Legion (citation 1982), Phi Delta Phi, Italian-Am. Assn. Republican. Roman Catholic. Home: Staten Island N.Y. Died June 17, 1990.

COSTIGAN, GIOVANNI, educator; b. Kingston-on-Thames, Eng., Feb. 15, 1905; s. John Francis and Helen Anne (Warren) C.; m. Amne MacMillan Johnson. B.A., U. Oxford, 1926, M.A., 1930, M.Litt., 1941; M.A., U. Wis., 1928, Ph.D., 1930; D.Litt., Lewis and Clark Coll., Portland, Oreg., 1967. Faculty dept. history U. Idaho, 1930-34; mem. faculty dept. history U. Wash., Seattle, 1934-75, prof., 1948-75, emeritus prof., from 1975; Mem. nat. com. ACLU; guest lectr., Seville, Spain, Mar. 1990. Author: Sir Robert Wilson: A Soldier of Fortune in the Napoleonic Wars, 1932, Life of Sigmund Freud, 1965, Makers of Modern England, 1967, History of Modern Ireland, 1969. Mem. Wash. State Centennial Hall of Honor, 1989. Capt. USAAF, 1943-45. Mem. Phi Beta Kappa. Home: Seattle Wash. Died Mar. 24, 1990.

COTTER, JOHN M., diversified company executive; b. 1904. With Dayton's Bluff Hardware Co., 1916-23; salesman Raymer Hardware Co., 1923-28; gen. ptnr. Kohloop Hardware, 1928-31; gen. mdse. mgr. Kelly-How-Thompson Co., 1933-42; v.p., gen. mgr. Oakes & Co., 1942-48; with Cotter & Co., Chgo., from 1948, chmn. bd., dir., from 1978. Home: Chicago Ill. Deceased. †

COTTER, MICHAEL DENNIS, advertising agency executive, consultant; b. New Rochelle, N.Y., June 7, 1939; s. Michael Joseph and Dorothy Mavis (Gardam) C. Student, NYU. Asst. art dir. Doherty, Clifford Steers Shenfield, N.Y.C., 1963; art dir. BBDO, N.Y.C., 1963-66; exec. art dir. Cunningham & Walsh, N.Y.C., 1966-74; exec. art dir., v.p. The C.T. Clyne Co., N.Y.C., 1974-79; exec. v.p. creative and prodn. Kornhauser & Calene, N.Y.C., 1978-87; with Cotter Concepts Inc., N.Y.C., 1987-89. Served with USAR, 1963-67. Recipient Gold Lion award 16th Cannes Film Festival, 1969; Effie award, 1983. Mem. Advt. Club N.Y., Art Students League N.Y. Republican. Roman Catholic. Home: New York N.Y. Died Apr. 15, 1989; buried Los Altos, Calif.

COTTON, WILLIAM DAVIS, lawyer, banker; b. Jonesville, La., Feb. 9, 1904; s. George Spencer and Lizzie (Davis) C.; m. Anna Mae Puddin Allen, Nov. 25, 1927; children—Carole, Jean Ann, Stephen Wayne. Student, La. State U., 1922-27, LL.B., 1927, J.D., 1968. Bar: La. bar 1928. Practice in Rayville, La., from 1929; sr. mem. firm Cotton, Bolton, Roberts & Hoychick, from 1946; chmn. bd. 1st Republic Bank Rayville, 1952-88, pres., 1952-68; mem. council La. Law Inst., from 1959. Del. gen. confs. Methodist Ch., 1960, 64, 66, 68, 72, 76, 80, chancellor La. conf., 1961-86; mem. La. Commn. on Constnl. Revision, 1970-72; Mem. La. Senate from 32d Dist., 1940-44; chmn. Richland Parish Democratic Exec. Com., 1961-76; Trustee Glenwood Hosp., West Monroe, La., 1962-78. Served to lt. col. AUS, 1941-46, ETO. Decorated Bronze Star; named Outstanding Layman La. Miss. W. Tenn. Dist. Kiwanis, 1970, Meth. Man of Yr., La., 1965. Fellow Am. Coll. Probate Counsel, Am. Bar Found.; mem. Am. Bar Assn., La. Bar Assn. (bd. govs. 1946-48, pres. 1965), Am. Judicature Soc. Clubs: Mason (32 deg.), Kiwanian (internat. trustee 1941-42, 46-48). Home: Rayville La. Died Dec. 23, 1989.

COULL, JAMES, chemical engineer, educator; b. Aberdeen, Scotland, Apr. 29, 1898; Came to U.S. 1924, naturalized 1933.; s. James F. and Elizabeth B. (Molyneaux) C.; m. Margaret A. MacLean, Feb. 8, 1933; children: James M., Margaret E., Bruce M. BSc, U. Aberdeen, 1924; Yuilli traveling scholar from, U. Aberdeen, to MIT, 1924-25; AM, Columbia U., 1928, PhD, 1934. Part-time analytical chemist with Dr. J.F. Tocher, 1919-24; rsch. chem. engr. Tide Water Oil Co., Bayonne, N.J., 1925-27; instr. chem. engring. Cooper Union, N.Y.C., 1927-33, asst. prof. chem. engring., 1933-39; prof. chem. engring., head dept. U. Pitts., from 1939; cons. chem. emgring. butadiene divsn. Koppers Co. from 1944; chmn. cooperating com. Western Pa. to advise Office Prodn., Rsch. and Devel., W.P.B.; adviser Smaller War Plants Corps. Contbr. articles to profl. jours. Mem. AICE (chmn. Pitts. 1946), Soc. Promotion Engring. Edn., Am. Chem. Soc., Sigma Xi. *

COUSINS, NORMAN, author, lecturer; b. Union Hill, N.J., June 24, 1915; s. Samuel and Sara (Miller) C.; m. Ellen Kopf, June 23, 1939; children: Andrea, Amy Loveman, Candis Hitzig, Sara Kit. LittD (hon.), Am. U., 1948, Denison U., 1954, Syracuse U., 1956, Newark State Coll., 1958, Mich. State U., U. N.C., 1969, Albion Coll., 1972, Incarnate Word Coll., 1980; DLitt (hon.), Boston U., 1951; LittD (hon.), Elmira Coll., 1951, Chapman Coll., 1953, Colby Coll., 1953, Ripon Coll., Wilmington Coll., 1957, R.I. Coll. Edn., 1958, Western Mich. U., 1960, Temple U., 1961, Maryville Coll., Southeastern Mass. U., 1976; HHD (hon.), Albright Coll., 1955, Manchester Coll., 1966, Lafayette Coll., 1967; LHD (hon.), U. Vt., 1957, Colgate U., 1959, Adelphi Coll., 1960, U. R.I., 1965, Creighton U., 1967, Chapman Coll., 1968, Brandeis U., 1969, Denver U., 1972, U. Ala., U. Ariz., 1973, St. Olaf Coll., Minn., 1976, U. Colo., Kalamazoo Coll., 1980, Occidental Coll., Hebrew Union Coll., Tex. Christian U., 1982, U. Santa Clara, 1984, Mass. Sch. Profl. Psychology, 1988; LLD (hon.), Washington & Jefferson U., 1956, U. Bridgeport, 1965, Aquinas Coll., 1969, George Washington U., 1982; D Social Sci. (hon.), Duquesne U., 1972; D Creative Sci. (hon.), Butler U., 1978; MD (hon.), New Haven County Med. Assn./Conn. State Med. Soc., 1984. Lit. editor, mng. editor Current History mag., 1935-40; editor Saturday Rev., 1940-71, 73-77, chmn. bd. editors, 1978, editor emeritus, 1980-82; adj. prof. Sch. Medicine, UCLA., 1978-90; Chmn. bd. dirs. Nat. Ednl. TV, 1969-70; chmn. Nat. Programming Council for Pub. TV, 1970-71; Editor U.S.A.; mem. editorial bd. Overseas bur. O.W.I., World War II; U.S. Govt. lectr. (Smith Mundt) in, India, Pakistan, Ceylon, 1951, Japan-Am. Exchange lectr., Japan, 1953; Chmn. Conn. Fact Finding Commn. on Edn., 1948-52; co-chmn. Citizens' Com. for Nuclear Test Ban Treaty;

mem. Commn. to Study Orgn. Peace; hon. pres. United World Federalists; chmn. Com. Culture and Intellectual Exchange, Internat. Cooperation Yr., 1965, Mayor's Task Force Air Pollution, N.Y.C., from 1966. Author: The Good Inheritance: The Democratic Chance, 1942, Modern Man Is Obsolete, 1946, Talks with Nehru, 1951, Who Speaks for Man? 1953, Dr. Schweitzer of Lambarene, 1960, In Place of Folly, 1961, Present Tense: An American Editor's Odyssey, 1967, The Improbable Triumvirate: An Asterisk to the History of a Hopeful Year, 1972, The Celebration of Life: A Dialogue on Immortality and Infinity, 1975, Anatomy of An Illness, 1979 (transl. 9 fgn. langs.), Human Options: An Autobiographical Notebook, 1981, The Healing Heart: Anicdotes to Panic and Helplessness, 1983, Albert Schweitzer's Mission: Healing and Peace, 1985, The Human Adventure; A Camera Chronicle, 1986, The Pathology of Power, 1987, Head First: The Biology of Hope, 1989; editor: A Treasury of Democracy, 1942, In God We Trust; The Religious Beliefs of the Founding Fathers, 1958, A Treasury of Democracy, 1941, (with William Rose Benét) Poetry of Freedom, 1948, Writing for Love or Money, 1949, The Physician in Literature, 1981, K. Jason Sitwells' Book of Spoofs, 1989, others; editorial supr.: (with William Rose Benét) March's Dictionary-Thesaurus, 1980. Mem. Hiroshima Peace Center Assos.; trustee Charles F. Kettering Found., Menninger Found., Ruth Mott Found. Recipient Thomas Jefferson award for Advancement of Democracy in Journalism, 1948; Tuition Plan award for outstanding service to Am. Edn., 1951; Benjamin Franklin citation in mag. journalism, 1956; Wayne U. award for nat. service to edn., 1956; Lane Bryant citation for pub. service, 1958; John Dewey award for service to edn., 1958; N.Y. State Citizens Edn. Commn. award, 1959; Publius award N.Y. met. com. United World Federalists, 1964; Eleanor Roosevelt Peace award, 1963; Overseas Press Club award, 1965; Distinguished Citizen award Conn. Bar Assn., 1965; N.Y. Acad. Pub. Edn. award, 1966; Family of Man award, 1968; Aquinas Coll. Ann. award, 1968; nat. mag. award Assn. Deans Journalism Schs., 1969; Peace medal UN, 1971; Carr Van Anda award for contbns. to journalism Ohio U., 1971; Gold medal for lit. Nat. Arts Club, 1972; Journalism Honor award U. Mo. Sch. Journalism, 1972; Irita Van Doren Book award, 1972; award for service to environment Govt. of Can.; Henry Johnson Fisher award as mag. pub. of yr. Mag. Pubs. Assn., 1973; Human Resources award, 1977; Convocation medal Am. Coll. Cardiology, 1978; Author of Yr. award Am. Soc. Journalists and Authors, 1981, Niwano Peace award, Japan, 1990, Physicians For Social Responsibility award, 1990, Albert Schweitzer Peace prize Johns Hopkins U., 1990. Mem. World Assn. World Federalists (pres.), P.E.N., UN Assn. (dir. U.S.), Council Fgn. Relations, Nat. Acad. Scis. (commn. on internat. relations). Clubs: Coffee House, Nat. Press, Overseas Press, Century Assn, Pilgrims Am. Home: Los Angeles Calif. Died Nov. 30, 1990.

COVINGTON, WILLIAM SLAUGHTER, executive consultant; b. Bowling Green, Ky., Oct. 4, 1897; s. Joseph Gilmore and Eleanor (Kennedy) C.; m. Elizabeth Morse, Oct. 4, 1924; children: William Slaughter, Lynn (Mrs. Stanley Adams Chrapkiewicz), Betsy (Mrs. C. Carter Smith Jr.), George. Student, Cornell U., 1916-20; LLB (hon.), John Marshall Law Sch, 1922. With E.H. Rollins & Sons, Chgo., 1920-26; mgr. Washington office Fairbanks, Morse & Co., 1931-32, mgr. Seattle br., 1932-36, mgr. Omaha br., 1936-40, dir., 1940-42, from 1956; stockbroker Jas. H. Oliphant & Co., Ritter & Co., Chgo., 1946-56; bd. dirs. Beverly Farms Found., Godfrey, Ill., from 1959, chmn. bd. dirs. 1962-63. Served as 2d lt., 17th Divsn., U.S. Army, 1918-19, lt. comdr. Bur. Ships, USNR, 1942-46. Recipient Naval citation. Mem. SCV, Sons Colonial Wars (gov. Ill. 1955-56), St. Andrews Soc., Chgo. Mus. Natural History (life), Sigma Phi, Masons (Shriner), University Club, Caxton Club (Chgo.), Onwentsix Club (Lake Forest, Ill.). *

COVINO, BENJAMIN GENE, anesthesiologist, educator; b. Lawrence, Mass., Sept. 12, 1930; s. Nicholas and Mary (Zannini) C.; m. Lorraine Gallagher, Aug. 22, 1953; children: Paul, Brian. A.B., Holy Cross Coll., 1951; M.S., Boston Coll. Grad. Sch., 1953; Ph.D. (Life Ins. fellow), Boston U. Grad. Sch., 1955; M.D., U. Buffalo, 1962. Teaching fellow Boston U., 1954-55; asst. prof. pharm. Tufts U. Sch. Med., Boston, 1957-59; asst. prof. physiology U. Buffalo Sch. Med., 1959-62; med. dir. Astra Pharm. Products, Worcester, 1962-66; v.p. sci. affairs Astra Pharm. Products, 1967-78; prof. anesthesiology U. Mass. Med. Sch., 1976-79; chmn. dept. anesthesia Brigham and Women's Hosp., Boston, 1979-91; prof. anesthesia Harvard U. Med. Sch., 1979-91; cons. physiologist St. Vincent's Hosp., Worcester, 1963-79. Contbr. articles to profl. jours. Bd. dirs. St. Vincent's Research Found.; trustee Assumption Coll., Worcester, Mass. Served to 1st lt. USAF, 1955-57. Mem. Am. Physiol. Soc., Am. Heart Assn., Am. Fedn. Clin. Research, Am. Soc. Pharmacology and Exptl. Therapeutics, Am. Soc. Anesthesiology, Alpha Omega Alpha. Home: Shrewsbury Mass. Died Apr. 4, 1991; buried Shrewsbury, Mass.

COWAP, CHARLES RICHARDSON, aluminum company executive; b. Orange, N.J., Nov. 2, 1931; s. Charles Richardson and Agnes Isabel (Pike) C.; m. Mildred Jeanne Weir, Aug. 18, 1962 (div. Dec. 1978); children: Heather Jeanne, Charles Richardson. AB magna cum laude, Dartmouth Coll., 1953; MBA, NYU, 1959. Security analyst, sr. security analyst Goodbody & Co., N.Y.C., 1957-59; sr. security analyst Shields & Co., N.Y.C., 1959-62; fin. analyst, asst. to treas., asst. treas. Amax Inc., Greenwich, Conn., 1962-74; treas. Alumax Inc., San Mateo, Calif., 1974-89; trustee, chmn. audit and fin. com. Health Systems Inst., Burlingame, Calif. Vestryman Christ Ch., Pelham, N.Y., 1969-74. Lt. (j.g.) USN, 1953-56. Mem. Fin. Analysts Fedn., N.Y. Soc. Security Analysts, Yale Club (N.Y.C.), Phi Beta Kappa, Beta Gamma Sigma. Republican. Home: Foster City Calif. Died Aug. 27, 1989; buried Lake Champlain, Vergennes, Vt.

COWEN, WILSON WALKER, publisher; b. Dalhart, Tex., June 5, 1934; s. Wilson and Florence Elizabeth (Walker) C.; m. Claudine LaHaye, Aug. 25, 1971; children: Charles Wilson, Francois. A.B., Harvard, 1956, Ph.D., 1965. Advt. and promotion Little Brown & Co., 1958-59; partner Walker-deBerry Pubs., Cambridge, Mass., 1959-64; with U. Press of Va., Charlottesville, 1965-87, asso. dir., 1968-69, dir., 1969-87; teaching fellow Harvard, 1959-64; lectr. English U. Va., 1965-71, prof., from 1971. Mem. bd.: Papers of George Washington. Woodrow Wilson fellow, 1960; Timothy Dexter fellow, 1964. Mem. Bibliog. Soc. U. Va. (dir.), Phi Beta Kappa. Democrat. Clubs: Cosmos (Washington); Farmington Hunt (Charlottesville). Home: Charlottesville Va. Died Feb. 22, 1987; buried Finistere, France.

COWLES, WILLIAM HUTCHINSON, III, newspaper publisher; b. Spokane, Wash., Mar. 4, 1932; s. William Hutchinson and Margaret (Paine) C.; m. Allison Stacey, Mar. 28, 1959; children: William Stacey, Elizabeth Allison. BA, Yale U., 1953; JD, Harvard U., 1959. Bar: Wash. 1959. Pres., pub. Cowles Pub. Co. (pubs. The Spokesman-Rev., Spokane Chronicle), N.W. Farmer-Stockman, Inc. (pubs. Wash. Farmer-Stockman, Oreg. Farmer-Stockman, Idaho Farmer-Stockman, Utah Farmer-Stockman), Spokane, 1970-92, Mont. Farmer-Stockman, Inc. (pubs. Mont. Farmer-Stockman), Billings, 1970-92; v.p., dir. Inland Empire Paper Co., Millwood, Wash., from 1964; dir. AP, 1974-83, 1st vice chmn., 1982-83, dir. Am. Newspaper Publs. Assn., 1980—, chmn., 1989-90, dir. Newspaper Advt. Bur., 1968—, chmn., 1978-80, dir. Allied Daily Newspapers, 1970-71, pres., 1972-74. Bd. dirs. Inland N.W. coun. Boy Scouts Am., from 1960, Spokane Symphony Soc., 1962-78, United Crusade Spokane County, 1963-74, pres., 1970; bd. overseers Whitman Coll., 1966-90; fellow Yale Corp., 1984-90. Lt. USNR, 1953-56. Mem. Am. Soc. Newspaper Editors, Spokane Area C. of C. (chmn. 1987-88), Spokane Club, Beta Theta Pi, Sigma Delta Chi. Home: Spokane Wash. Died Apr. 18, 1992.

COWLEY, MALCOLM, writer; b. Belsano, Pa., Aug. 24, 1898; s. William and Josephine (Hutmacher) C.; m. Muriel Maurer, June 18, 1932; 1 child, Robert William. A.B., Harvard, 1920; postgrad., U. Montpellier, France, 1921-22; Litt.D. (hon.), Franklin and Marshall Coll., 1961, Colby Coll., 1962, U. Warwick, Eng., 1975, U. New Haven, 1976, Monmouth Coll., 1978, U. Conn., 1983, Indiana U. of Pa., 1985. Free lance writer and translator, 1925-29; assoc. editor The New Republic, 1929-44; lit. adviser Viking Press, 1948-85; vis. prof. U. Wash., 1950, Stanford, 1956, 59, 60-61, 65, U. Mich., 1957, U. Calif., 1962, Cornell, 1964, U. Minn., 1971, U. Warwick, Eng., 1973; Lectr. Author: Blue Juniata, 1929, Exile's Return, 1934, rev. edit., 1951, (with others) After the Genteel Tradition, 1937, rev. edit., 1964, The Dry Season, 1941, The Literary Situation, 1954, (with Daniel P. Mannix) Black Cargoes, 1962, The Faulkner-Cowley File, 1966, Think Back on Us, 1967, Blue Juniata: Collected Poems, 1968, A Many Windowed House, 1970, (with Howard E. Hugo) The Lesson of the Masters, 1971, A Second Flowering: Works and Days of the Lost Generation, 1973, -And I Worked at the Writer's Trade, 1978, The Dream of the Golden Mountains, 1980, The View from 80, 1980, The Flower and the Leaf, 1985: A Contemporary Record of American Writing Since 1941; translator (from the French): Variety (Paul Valéry), 1926, The Sacred Hill (Maurice Barrés), 1929, Imaginary Interviews (André Gide), 1944, others; editor: Adventures of an African Slaver, Captain Canot, 1927, Books That Changed Our Minds, 1939, The Portable Hemingway, 1944, The Portable Faulkner, 1946, The Portable Hawthorne, 1948, The Complete Whitman, 1948, The Stories of F. Scott Fitzgerald, 1950, Writers at Work, 1958, Leaves of Grass: The First Edition, 1959, (with Robert Cowley) Fitzgerald and the Jazz Age, 1966; contbr. to mags. Recipient award Nat. Endowment for Arts, 1967; Signet Soc. medal, 1976; Hubbell medal MLA, 1979; Gold medal Am. Acad. and Inst., 1981. Mem. Nat. Inst. Arts and Letters (pres. 1956-59, 62-65), Am. Acad. Arts and Letters (chancellor 1967-77, Gold medal 1981), Phi Beta Kappa. Clubs: Harvard (N.Y.C.), Century (N.Y.C.); Bibliophages. Home: Sherman Conn. Died Mar. 27, 1989.

COWLEY, R. ADAMS, physician; b. Layton, Utah, July 25, 1917; s. William Wallace and Alta Louise (Adams) C.; m. Roberta S. Cowley; children: R. Adams II, Kaye Pace. Student, U. Utah, 1938-40; MD, U. Md., Balt., 1944. Intern U. Md. Hosp., 1944-45, resident in surgery, 1945-46, 48-49; jr. clin. instr., sr. clin. instr. thoracic surgery U. Mich. Hosp., Ann Arbor, 1949-51; fellow in exptl. surgery U. Md. Med. Sch., 1947-48, dir. cardiopulmonary lab., 1951-62, assoc. dept. surgery, 1953-55, mem. faculty, 1955-91, chmn. div. thoracic surgery, 1961-70, prof. thoracic and cardiovascular surgery, 1961-91; dir. Md. Inst. Emergency Med. Svcs. Systems, 1973-91; past mem. coms. NRC; mem. Nat. Hwy. Safety Adv. Com., 1978-81, Md. Hwy. Safety Coordinating Com., 1978-91; Md. gov.'s spl. advisor on trauma and emergency med. svcs., 1990; papers collected by U. Utah. Author books, contbr. over 400 articles to med. jours. Elder LDS Ch. Officer M.C., U.S. Army, 1946-47. Recipient Alumni award U. Utah, 1979, Balt.'s Best awardd, 1980, Congl. cert. of merit, 1980, Lifetime Achievement award Md. Hosp. Assn., 1991, also various svc. and appreciation awards. Fellow ACS; mem. AMA, AAAS, Am. Surg. Assn., So. Surg. Assn., Soc. Vascular Surggry, Am. Assn. Automotive Medicine, Am. Assn. Thoracic Surgery, Soc. Thoracic Surgeons (a founder), Balt. Med. Soc., Med. and Chirurg. Soc. Md., John Alexander Soc., Am. Trauma Soc. (a founder, William S. Stone lectr. 1978), Internat. Cardiovascular Soc., So. Thoracic Surg. Assn., Am. Assn. for Surgery Trauma, Shock Soc., Internat. Soc. Surgery, Soc. Med. Cons. Armed Forces, So. Surg. Congress, Soc. Critical Care. Home: Baltimore Md. Died Oct. 27, 1991; buried Arlington Nat. Cemetery, Washington, D.C.

COWNIE, JOHN BOWLER, economist, educator, former academic administrator; b. Des Moines, Iowa, Aug. 31, 1940; s. John Francis and Catherine (Bowler) C. B.S. cum laude in Physics, Loyola U., Los Angeles, 1961; M.A. in Physics, U. So. Calif., Los Angeles, 1964, M.A. in Econs., 1966, Ph.D. in Econs., 1967; M.B.A., U. Chgo., 1983. Mathematician Douglas Aircraft Co., Santa Monica and Long Beach, Calif., 1960-61, assoc. engr., 1961-62; teaching asst. dept. physics U. So. Calif., Los Angeles, 1961-63, rsch. asst. dept. econs., 1964-65, lectr. dept. econs., 1966-67; intern Office Program Coordination AID, Washington, 1965-66; systems analysis Office Asst. Sec. Defense, Washington, 1967; agrl. economist, cons. Consortium for Study of Nigerian Rural Devel., Lagos, 1968; econs. program convener Fed. City Coll.-U. D.C., Washington, 1968-69, asst. prof. econs., 1968-70, social sci. div. chmn., 1969-70, assoc. prof. econs., 1970-74, prof. econs., 1974-77, spl. asst. to v.p. acad. affairs and provost, 1975, assoc. provost, 1975-77; prof. econs. Northeastern Ill. U., Chgo., from 1977, provost, 1977-87; acting pres. Northeastern Ill. U., 1985-86; adj. prof. econs. U. Ill., Chgo., from 1990; faculty adv. com. Ill. Bd. Higher Edn., from 1988, chmn., 1990-91; resch. assoc. Food Rsch. Inst., Stanford U., Calif., 1967-68; vis. scholar, 1970, 72; vis. assoc. prof. social sci. SUNY-Old Westbury, 1970; rsch. assoc. AAAS, Washington, 1975-76; cons. and lectr. in field. Co-author: Commodity Exports and African Economic Development, 1974; Competing Economic Philosophies in Contemporary American Capitalism, 1975. contbr. chpts. to books, articles to profl. jours. Recipient Archdiocese of Los Angeles Math. award, 1957-61; Nat. Merit scholar, 1957-61; NSF fellow, 1965-67; Social Sci. Research Council, Am. Council Learned Socs. African Research Studies grantee, 1971-72. Mem. AAAS, Am. Assn. Higher Edn., Am. Econ. Assn., Assn. Advancement Agrl. Scis. in Africa, Beta Gamma Sigma, Sigma Pi Sigma, Omicron Delta Epsilon, Alpha Sigma Nu. Home: Chicago Ill. Deceased. †

COX, ALVIN JOSEPH, JR., pathologist, educator; b. Manila, P.I., Mar. 6, 1907; s. Alvin Joseph and Mary Amelia (Barnett) C.; m. Helen Files Pollard, Feb. 2, 1947; children: Roger Allen, Barbara Anna, Carolyn Frances. A.B., Stanford U., 1927, M.D., 1931. Instr. pathology Stanford U., 1933-35, asst. and assoc. prof. pathology, 1936-41, prof., from 1941, head dept., 1941-64, prof. pathology in dermatology, 1964-85, emeritus prof., 1972-85; exchange asst. Pathol. Inst., U. Freiburg, Germany, 1935-36. Mem. Am. Assn. Pathologists and Bacterologists, Soc. for Exptl. Biology and Medicine, A.M.A., Am. Soc. Exptl. Pathology, Internat. Acad. Pathology, Am. Acad. Dermatology, Soc. Investigative Dermatology, Am. Soc. Dermatopathology, Alpha Omega Alpha, Alpha Kappa Kappa. Home: San Francisco Calif. Died Dec. 6, 1990; buried San Francisco.

COX, CHARLES WESLEY, construction company executive; b. Chester, Pa., June 24, 1918; s. Wilmer and Sara Hopkins (Price) C.; m. Ellen Shrom, June 1939; children: Samuel, Charles; m. Helen Allison, May 7, 1948; children: Barry, Christina Cox Gray, Kelle Cox Webb; m. Margaret Jill Nicholls, Dec. 16, 1976. Student, Drexel Inst. Tech., Phila. Apprentice draftsman Am. Viscose Corp., Marcus Hook, Pa., 1935-38; constrn. engr. Nitro, W.Va., 1940-42, devel. mgr. staple mech. devel. dept., 1943-49; mgr. engring. machine design Nitro, Phila., 1949-51; field supt. constrn. Chemstrand Corp., Decatur, Ala., 1951-52, dir. engring., 1955-57; sr. project mgr. Daniel Constrn. Co., Greenville, S.C., 1957-58; sales mgr. Daniel Constrn. Co., N.Y.C., 1958-61, v.p., mgr. sales, 1961-68; v.p., gen. mgr. exec. offices Daniel Constrn. Co., Greenville, 1968-74, pres., COO, 1974-77, vice chmn., 1977-92; vice chmn. Daniel Internat. Corp.; dir. Fluor Corp., So. Bank & Trust Co. With USNR, 1944-46. Mem. Greenville Country Club, Poinsett Club (Greenville). Republican. Methodist. Home: Greer S.C. Died Jan. 9, 1992; buried Christ Episcopal Ch., Greenville, S.C.

COX, OWEN DEVOL, judge; b. Joplin, Mo., Mar. 20, 1910; s. George B. and Agnes (Swartz) C.; m. Geraldine Martin, Nov. 18, 1939; children: Cornelia Fay Cox Cole, Courney Quinn Cox Gibson, George Martin. BA, U. Kans., 1931, LLB, 1933. Bar: Kans. 1933, Tex. 1934. Asst. atty. gen. State of Tex., Austin, 1942; city atty. City of Corpus Christi, 1943-47; assoc. S.L. Gill Law Firm, Raymondville, Tex., 1934-37, Boone, Davis & Cox, Corpus Christi, Tex., 1948-52, Boone, Davis, Cox & Hale, Corpus Christi, 1952-70; judge U.S. Dist. Ct. (so. dist.) Tex., Corpus Christi, 1970-90. Mem. Corpus Christi Charter Commn., 1953; alt. del. Rep. Nat. Conv., 1964, del., 1968; mem. Tex. Rep. Exec. Com., 1966-70. Mem. ABA, Nueces County Bar Assn. (pres. 1948), State Bar Tex., Am. Judicature Soc., Kiwanis Club. Episcopalian. Home: Corpus Christi Tex.

CRABBE, JOHN ROTH, lawyer; b. London, Ohio, Mar. 29, 1906; s. Charles C. and Isa M. (Roth) C.; m. Eleanor S. Hommon, Dec. 20, 1933; children—Constance (Mrs. Michael A. Dehlendorf), Benjamin R. (dec.). B.A., Ohio State U., 1927, M.A., J.D., 1931; LL.M., Harvard, 1932. Bar: Ohio bar 1931. Asst. atty. gen. State of Ohio, 1933-37, dep. supt. ins., 1939-43, supt. ins., 1943-45; ptnr. Crabbe & Tootle, London, 1937-39; assoc. Ballard & Dresbach, Columbus, Ohio, 1945-51; ptnr. Crabbe, Brown, Jones, Potts & Schmidt (and predecessor firms), Columbus, 1951-78, of counsel, 1978-89. Pres. Bexley Area Art Guild, 1967; Mem. Bexley (Ohio) City Council, 1955-72, pres., 1966-72. Fellow ABA Found., Ohio Bar Assn. Found. (trustee 1970-76); mem. ABA (chmn. tort and ins. practice sect. 1962-63, chmn. standing com. unemployment and social security 1965-66), Ohio Bar Assn., Columbus Bar Assn., Am. Judicature Soc., Assn. Life Ins. Counsel, Pi Kappa Alpha, Phi Delta Phi. Republican. Methodist (past chmn. ofcl. bd., trustee). Clubs: Mason. (Columbus), Columbus Country (Columbus), University (Columbus), Crichton (Columbus). Home: Columbus Ohio Died Apr. 2, 1989; buried Greenlawn Cemetery, Columbus.

CRABTREE, AUBREY, manufacturing executive; b. Joliette, Que., Can., Apr. 1, 1898; s. David and Alice (Woods) C.; m. Dorothy Hall, June 12, 1931; children: Mary Diana (Mrs. Edward Tabor McFarlin), Jay Alan, Dennis Aubrey (dec.). Student, Stanstead Coll., Que., Burdett Coll., Boston; LLD (hon.), U. N.B., 1953. With Edwin Crabtree & Sons, Sunapee, N.H., Adams Paper Co., Wells River, Vt., Howard Smith Paper Mills, Ltd., Crabtree Mills and Beauharnois, Que., 1920-28; gen. supt. Can. Paper Co., Windsor Mills, Que., 1928, resident mgr., 1928-30; mill mgr. Fraser Paper, Ltd. subsidiary Fraser Cos., Ltd., 1930-35, gen mgr., 1935-40; v.p., gen mgr. Fraser Cos. Ltd. and subsidiaries Fraser Paper Ltd. and Restigouche Co. Ltd., 1940-41; pres., gen. mgr. Fraser Cos. Ltd. and subsidiaries, 1941-56; pres., chmn. Fraser Cos. Ltd. and subsidiary Fraser Paper Ltd., 1956-63, chmn., from 1963; bd. dirs. Wabasso Cotton Co., Ltd.; adv. com. Groundwood Paper Industry WPB. Served with the CEF, 1916-19. Mem. Can. Pulp and Paper Assn. (past chmn., mem. exec. bd.), Am. Pulp and Paper Mill Supts. Assn. *

CRADDOCK, MARIAM NARCISSA, librarian; b. McLoud, Okla., Apr. 5, 1897; d. John Edwin and Laura Louise (Claunts) Craddock. AB, U. Okla., 1918; BLS, Simmons Coll., 1922. With Okla. City Pub. Libr., from 1922, chief acquisition and processing divsn., 1948-61, dir. librs., from 1961. Mem. Women's com. Okla. City Symphony Soc., 1956-61, Community Coun. Okla. City, from 1961; bd. dirs. Okla. County Mental Health Assn., 1962-64. Recipient Salute to Women Who Work Week award, Woman of Yr. in Govt. award, Okla. City Downtown Assn, 1961. Mem. AAUW, ALA (chmn. membership com. Okla. 1958-60), Southwestern Libr. Assn. (Okla. rep. on bd. 1958-60), Okla. Libr. Assn. (sec.-treas. 1945-47, 2d v.p. 1956-57, chmn. pub. librs. sect. 1960-61), Oklahoma City C. of C., Pilot Club, Oklahoma City (treas. 1959-60, dir. 1960-62), Kappa Kappa Gamma. Baptist. *

CRAFTS, ALDEN SPRINGER, plant physiologist, educator; b. Ft. Collins, Colo., June 25, 1897; s. Henry Alonzo and Elizabeth Dunscomb (Bleakley) C.; m. Alice E. Hardisty, June 25, 1926; children: Harold S., Helen E. Crafts Hedges. BS, U. Calif., 1927, PhD, 1930; MA, Oxford U.; LLD, U. Calif., Davis, 1966. NRC fellow Cornell U., 1930-31; asst. botanist Calif. Agrl. Expt. Sta., Davis, 1931-36; asst. botanist, asst. prof. botany U. Calif., Davis, 1936-39, assoc. botanist, assoc. prof. botany, 1939-46, botanist, prof. botany, 1946-64, prof. emeritus, 1964-90, acting chmn., 1959-60, chmn. dept. botany, 1960-64; vis. prof. P.R. Agrl. Expt. Sta., 1947-48; del. to Bot. Congress, Paris, 1954; chmn. Calif. Weed Control Conf., Fresno, 1951; del., vice chmn. Gordon Rsch. Conf. on Biochemistry in Agr., 1955; hon. mem. Calif. Weed Conf., 1972. Author: (with H.B. Currier and C.R. Stocking) Water in the Physiology of Plants, 1949, (with W.W. Robbins and R.N. Raynor) Weed Control, 1942, revised edit., 1952, (with W.W. Robbins) revised edit., 1962, The Chemistry and Mode of Action of Herbicides, 1961, Translocation in Plants, 1961, (with S. Yamaguchi) The Autoradiography of Plant Materials, 1964, (with Carl E. Crisp) Phloem Transport in Plants, 1971, (with Floyd M. Ashton) The Mode of Action of Herbicides, 1973, Modern Weed Control, 1975; editor: Annual Review of Plant Physiology, 1956-58. Guggenhime fellow, 1938, 57; Fulbright grantee, 1957-58. Fellow AAAS; mem. Am. Soc. Plant Physiologists (chmn. we. sect. 1940-41, nat. pres. 1955-56, Charles Reid Barnes life membership award 1962), Weed Sci. Soc. Am. (hon. mem., pres. 1958-60), Zool.-Bot. Soc. Vienna (hon.), Bot. Soc. Am., PHi Beta Kappa, Sigma Xi, Phi Sigma, Gamma Alpha. Home: Woodland Calif. Died Feb. 9, 1990.

CRAIG, BEN TRUMAN, banker; b. Gastonia, N.C., Jan. 27, 1933; s. Ben Wesley and Lois (Sams) B.; m. Jane Cobb Smith, June 12, 1954; children: Cathryn Elizabeth Craig Coles, Sarah Jane, Ben Truman. B.S. in Econs., Davidson Coll. (N.C.), 1954. Various positions with Wachovia Bank & Trust Co., Winston-Salem, N.C., 1954-61; exec. v.p. Bank of Lancaster (S.C.), 1963-67; treas. Springs Mills, Inc., Lancaster, 1967-72; pres., chief exec. officer Am. Bank & Trust Co., Reading, Pa., 1972-77; chmn., chief exec. officer Northwestern Fin. Corp., Greensboro, N.C., from 1978; bd. dirs. Arrow Internat., Inc., Reading, Pa., from 1977. Chmn. bd. trustees Davidson Coll.; mem. Gov.'s Bus. Council on Arts and Humanities, North Wilkesboro, N.C.; bd. dirs. N.C. Textile Fedn., Charlotte Uptown Devel. Corp; chmn. U. N.C. Charlotte Univ. Bus. Incubator Ctr. Mem. N.C. Bankers Assn. (bd. dirs., past pres.), Am. Bankers Assn. (mem. council 1983-84), Assn. Bank Holding Cos. (bd. dirs., research com. 1983-84). Presbyterian. Died Oct., 1988. Home: Charlotte N.C.

CRAIG, GERALD SPELLMAN, natural science educator; b. DeGraff, Ohio, May 6, 1893; s. Lorain D. and Estelle (Spellman) C.; m. Prudence Bower, Dec. 27, 1915; children: Lawrence C. and Alice Estelle (Mrs. Richard A. Erney). BS, Baylor (Tex.) U., 1915; AM, Columbia U., 1917, PhD, 1927. Instr. phys. sci. Ballinger Tex. High Sch., 1915-16, Baylor U., summer 1916, State Normal Sch., Bloomsburg, Pa., 1921-23; instr. sci. edn. Pa. State Coll., summers 1923-24; cons. in elem. sci. Teachers Coll. Columbia U., N.Y.C., 1925, from assoc. prof. to prof. natural scis., 1927-56, prof. emeritus natural scis., from 1956; cons. elem. scis. pub. sch. systems from 1929; studied status of sci. in European schs., 1931; developed natural sci. field ctrs. Ala., Conn., N.H., P.R., 1934-50. Author: Horace Mann Course of Study in Elementary Science, 1927, sects. on Elementary Science in the Classroom Teacher, 1927, Pathways in Science, 1932, New Pathways in Science, 1940, Science for the Elementary School Teacher, 1940, Science in Childhood Education, 1944, Our World of Science, 1946, Science Today and Tomorrow (sr. with others), 1954-58, What Research Says to The Teacher About Teaching Science for A.E.R.A., 1957, (with others) Science for You, 1965; contbr. numerous articles in field. Mem. Elem. Sci. Syllabus Com. N.Y. State, 1926-31; pres. Nat. Coun. Suprs. of Elem Sci., 1930-31; pres. Nat. Assn. Rsch. in Sci. Teaching, 1935-36; sec. Conf. on Edn. of Teachers in Sci., 1936-40; pres. Sci. Edn. Inc., 1931-43. Served as 1st sgt. AEF in France, 1917-18. Recipient 1st Sci. Edn. Recognition award, 1956, citation disting. svc. in sci. edn. Fellow AAAS; mem. N.Y. Acad. Sci., Edn. Rsch. Assn., Philippine Sci. Teachers Assn. (cons. 1960), Nat. Soc. for Study of Edn.. *

CRAIG, MARY FRANCIS SHURA, writer, educator; b. Pratt, Kans., Feb. 27, 1923; d. Jack Fant and Mary Francis (Milstead) Young; m. Daniel Charles Shura, Oct. 24, 1943 (dec. 1959); children: Marianne Francis Shura Sprague, Daniel Charles Shura, Alice Barrett Craig Stout; m. Raymond C. Craig, Dec. 8, 1961 (div. Oct. 1984); 1 child, Mary Forsha Craig. Creative writing tchr., summer conf. U. Kans., Lawrence, from 1961; tchr. adult edn. Coll. St. Teresa's, Kansas City, Mo., 1960-61; tchr. creative writing Avila Coll., U. N.D., Calif. State U., U. Kans., Central Mo. State U., N.E. Mo. State U.; lectr. confs.; v.p., dir. Young Bros. Cattle Corp., from 1950. Writer adult and children's books (as Mary Francis Shura, Mary Craig, M.S. Craig): Simple Spigott, 1960 (on 100 Best list World Book Ency. 1960), Garrett of Greta McGraw, 1967, Mary's Marvelous Mouse, 1962, Nearsighted Knight, 1963 (on Best list NY. Times 1963), Run Away Home, 1964, Backwards for Luck, 1968, Shoeful of Shamrock, 1965, A Tale of Middle Length, 1967, Pornada, 1969, The Valley of the Frost Giants, 1971, Topcat of Tam, 1972, The Shop on Threnody Street, 1972, A Candle for the Dragon, 1973, Ten Thousand Several Doors, 1973, The Cranes of Ibycus, 1974, The Riddle of Ravens Gulch, 1975, The Season of Silence, 1976, Gray Ghosts of Taylor Ridge, 1978, Mister Wolf and Me, 1979, The Barkley Street Six-Pack, 1979, Chester, 1980 (Pinetree award 1983), Happles and Cinnamunger, 1981, Eleanor, 1983, The Chicagoans, Dust to Diamonds, 1981, Were He a Stranger, 1978, To Play the Fox, 1982, Lyon's Pride, 1983, Pirate's Landing, 1983, Gillian's Chain, 1983, The Third Blond, 1985, The Search for Grissi, 1985 (Carl Sandburg Lit. Arts award), The Josie Gambit, 1986 (Booklist Editor's Choice, ALA Notable Book, 1987), The Chicagoans: Fortune's Destiny, 1986, Flash Point, 1987, Don't Call Me Toad, 1987, The Sunday Doll, 1988, The Mystery at Wolf River, 1989, Darcy, 1989, Kate's Book, 1989, Polly Panic, 1990, Kate's House, 1990, Gentle Annie, 1991, The Super Christmas Romance, 1992; contbr. anthologies: Sisters In Crime, 1989, The Courage to Grow Old, 1989; contbr. fiction, poetry to popular mags.; weekly columnist: Scrapbook from Shura'nuh Farm, 1960-64. Recipient Creative Achievement award N.W. Mo. State U., 1989; fellow Northeastern Ill. U., 1989. Mem. Authors Guild, Authors League Am., Soc. Children's Bookwriters, Mystery Writers Am. (past regional pres., nat. dir. 1987-91, gen. awards chmn. 1988, nat. pres. 1990), Childrens Reading Round Table, Crime Writers Great Britain. Home: Hinsdale Ill. Died Jan. 12, 1991; buried B Bar Ranch, Ashland, Kans.

CRAMER, MAURICE BROWNING, language professional, educator; b. Camden, N.J., Apr. 24, 1910; s. Alfred and Anna Browning (Doughten) C.; m. Alice Carver, Aug. 24, 1935; children: Owen Carver, Maurice Browning. AB, Princeton U., 1931, MA, 1934, PhD, 1937. Instr. English dept. Mt. Holyoke Coll., 1934-40, asst. prof., 1940, reader entrance exam. bd., 1937, 38; assoc. prof. U. Tampa, Fla., 1940-41, prof., 1941-42, chmn. English dept., 1940-42; lectr. English dept. Princeton U., 1942-43; asst. prof. humanities U. Chgo., 1945-48, assoc. prof., 1948-53, prof., 1953-59, chmn. humanities staff, 1951-57; Fulbright prof. Am. life and civlization U. Athens, 1957-58; prof. English Pa. State U., University Park, 1959-72, prof. emeritus, from 1972; Thomas Shipley lectr. Haverford (Pa.) Coll., 1964; humanities cons., external examiner New Sch. Coll., N.Y.C., 1967-68. Author: Phoenix at East Hadley, 1941; contbr. articles to profl. jours. Recipient Quantrell award for excellence in undergrad. teaching, 1957; festschrift Aeolian Harps: Essays in Literature, 1976. Mem. MLA, ACLU, AAUP, Assn. Princeton Grad. Sch. Alumni (governing bd. 1964-68), Phi Beta Kappa. Home: Chapel Hill N.C. Deceased. †

CRANSTON, MILDRED WELCH, civic, educational volunteer; b. Adrian, Mich., Nov. 21, 1898; d. John Wesley and Edith Farwell (Dissette) Welch; m. Earl Cranston, Jan. 28, 1929; children: John, Margaret Brayton (Mrs. Thomas S. Parsons), Florence Pitkin. AB, U. Ill., 1921; MA, Boston U., 1922, PhD, 1930. Missionary Methodist Ch., Chengtu, West China, 1922-27; instr. Boston U., 1930, U. Redlands, 1936; mem., commr. health, police, charities City Coun., Redlands, Calif., 1936-38; pres. Redlands YWCA, 1935-37, mem. Nat. Bd., 1945-49, 52-64; mem. World Coun. Western Region Nat. YWCA, 1946-52, 55-64; chmn. Eastern Region Nat. YWCA, 1946-49; v.p., chmn. Western Region Nat. YWCA, 1955-58; v.p.-at-large YWCA of U.S., 1958, hon. mem. nat. bd., from 1965; mem. Bd. Edn., Pasadena, Calif., 1951-55. Mem. Calif. adv. com. Fair Employment Practices. Fellow Nat. Coun. Religion in Higher edn.; mem. LWV, United Coun. Ch. Women (Com. of 100), PEO, Phi Beta Kappa, Kappa Delta Pi, Delta Kappa Gamma. Methodist. *

CRAWFORD, ROBERT PLATT, writer, educator; b. Council Bluffs, Iowa, Dec. 7, 1893; s. Nelson Antrim and Fanny (Vandercook) C. AB, U. Nebr., 1917; AM, Columbia U., 1926. Reporter Nebr. State jour., Lincoln, 1914-16; agrl. editor U. Nebr., 1917-18; asst. editor U.S. Dept. Agr., Washington, 1918; assoc. editor Nebr. Farmer, Lincoln, 1919-21; hist. rsch. for U. Nebr., 1922, from asst. prof. to prof. journalism, 1923-59, emeritus prof. journalism, asst. to chancellor, 1928-38, est. course in creative thinking, 1931; sec. U. Nebr. Found., 1937-39; vis. prof. journalism U. Tex., 1940-41; sr. field rep. Office of War Info., 1944; specialist on bus. and fin., Washington, Overseas Br., O.W.I., 1945; mem. journalism faculty U.S. War Dept. U. Florence, Italy, 1945; sr. pubs. analyst (mag. analysis) Civil Info. and Edn., SCAP, Tokyo, Japan, 1946-47; chief neutral property Civil property custodian, 1947; hist. banking and fin. (SCAP, Tokyo), 1948. Author: These Fifty Years, 1925, The Magazine Article, 1931, Think For Yourself, 1937, How to Get Ideas, 1948, The Techniques of Creative Thinking, 1954 (in German, Swedish and Japanese), Direct Creativity With Attribute Listing, 1964; originated nat. syndicated daily feature Dollars and Sense, 1922; spl. writing for Barron's, 1924-26, Country Gentleman, 1926-31; econ. investigations for Barron's, 1942-44; Financial World (Realty series), 1952-60. Fellow Royal Econ. Soc.; mem. AAUP (sec. chpt. 1928-29), Am. Econ. Assn., Midland Authors (v.p.), New Writers' Guild (hon.), Am. Legion, Mil. Gov. Assn., London Authors Club. *

CREE, ALBERT ALEXANDER, public utilities executive; b. Spruce Creek, Pa., June 15, 1898; s. Harry C. and Minnie Louella (Irvin) C.; m. Marie Louise Coizet, July 3, 1920; children: Anne Marie (Mrs. Earl C. McGuire), Albert Alexander. AB, Columbia Coll., N.Y., 1919. With Lee, Higginson & Co., N.Y.C., 1919-32; asst. treas. Lee Higginson Corp., 1932-34; with N.E. Pub. Svc. Co., Augusta, Me., 1934-35, dir., 1943-53; v.p. Ctrl. Vt. Pub. Svc. Corp., Twin State Gas and Electric Co., Rutland, Vt., 1935-36; pres., dir. The Twin State Gas and Electric Co., 1936-43; dir. Ctrl. Vt. Pub. Svc. Corp. (merger Twin State Gas and Electric Co.), from 1936, pres., 1936-61, chmn., CEO, from 1961; pres., dir. Conn.Valley Electric Co., Inc., N.H., from 1949, Vt. Electric Power Co. Inc., from 1957; dir. Gen. Telephone Corp. of Vt., from 1948, Am. Woolen Co., 1954-55, Textron-Am. Inc., 1955, Yankee Atomic Electric Co., from from 1954; chmn. Electric Coord. Coun. of N.E., 1952-53, pres., from 1959. Dir. Civil Def., Vt., 1941-45; trustee Green Mtn. Coll. Served as aviator pilot U.S. A.S., 1917-19. Mem. Nat. Assn. Electric Cos. (dir. from 1955), Am. Legion (comdr. Vt., nat. vice comdr. 1947-48), Vt. C. of C. (pres. 1938-41), Vt. Electric Assn.

(pres. 1938), Vets Fgn. Wars, Phi Kappa Sigma, Masons, Elks. *

CREMIN, LAWRENCE ARTHUR, educator; b. N.Y.C., Oct. 31, 1925; s. Arthur T. and Theresa (Borowick) C.; m. Charlotte Raup, Sept. 19, 1956; children: Joanne Laura, David Lawrence. BS in Social Scis., CCNY, 1946, LHD, 1984; AM, Columbia U., 1947, PhD, 1949, LittD, 1975; LHD, Ohio State U., 1975, Kalamazoo Coll., 1976; LLD, U. Bridgeport, 1975, U. Rochester, 1980; LHD, Coll. William and Mary, 1984, SUNY, 1984, George Washington U., 1985, DePaul U., 1985, U. Wis., 1989. Mem. faculty Columbia Tchrs. Coll., N.Y.C., from 1948, Frederick A.P. Barnard prof. edn., from 1961; pres. Columbia Tchrs. Coll., 1974-84, Spencer Found., 1985-90; Guggenheim fellow, 1957-58; fellow Center for Advanced Study in Behavioral Scis., 1964-65, 71-72; vis. scholar Inst. Advanced Study, 1984-85. Author: The American Common School, 1951, The Transformation of the School (Bancroft prize Am. history), 1961, The Genius of American Education, 1965, The Wonderful World of Ellwood Patterson Cubberley, 1965, American Education: The Colonial Experience, 1970, Public Education, 1976, Traditions of American Education, 1977, American Education: The National Experience, 1783-1876, 1980 (Pulitzer prize), American Education: The Metropolitan Experience, 1988, Popular Education and Its Discontents, 1990; gen. editor: Classics in Education. With USAAF, 1944-45. Recipient Research award Am. Ednl. Research Assn., 1969; Butler medal Columbia U., 1972. Mem. Hist. Edn. Soc. (pres. 1959-60), Nat. Soc. Coll. Tchrs. Edn. (pres. 1961-62), Nat. Acad. Edn. (pres. 1969-73), Am. Philos. Soc., AAAS, Soc. Am. Historians, Council Fgn. Relations. Home: New York N.Y. Died Sept. 4, 1990; buried Beth Israel Cemetery, Woodbury, N.J.

CRILE, GEORGE, JR., surgeon; b. Cleve., Nov. 3, 1907; s. George and Grace (McBride) C.; m. Jane Halle, Dec. 5, 1935 (dec.); children—Ann, Joan, Susan, George; m. Helga Sandburg, Nov. 9, 1963. Ph.B., Yale, 1929; M.D., Harvard, 1933. Intern Barnes Hosp., 1933-34; resident surgeon Cleve. Clinic, 1934-37, mem. surg. staff, from 1937, head dept. gen. surgery, 1956-69, sr. cons. dept. surgery, 1969-72, emeritus cons., 1972; Hon. civilian cons. to surgeon gen. USN, 1951-55; appeared on Radio WERE, Cleve.program: 90 secs. with Dr. George Crile, Jr., 1988. Author: (with Frank Shively) Hospital Care of the Surgical Patient, 1943, Practical Aspects of Thyroid Disease, 1949, Cancer and Common Sense, 1955, (with Jane Crile) Treasure Diving Holidays, 1954, More than Booty, 1966, A Biological Consideration of the Treatment of Breast Cancer, 1967, A Naturalistic View of Man, 1969, To Act as a Unit (The Story of Cleveland Clinic with A.T. Bunts), 1970, (with H. Sandburg) Above and Below, 1970, What Women Should Know about the Breast Cancer Controversy, 1973, Surgery—Your Choices, Your Alternatives; The Crile Cornball Collection, 1979, The Way It Was 1907-1987—Sex, Surgery, Treasure and Travel, 1992. Served from 1st lt. to comdr. USNR, 1942-45. Fellow A.C.S., Royal Coll. Surgeons (hon.); mem. Am., Central, So. surg. assns., Am. Thyroid Assn. Home: Cleveland OH Deceased. †

CROCKER, LIONEL GEORGE, speech educator; b. Ann Arbor, Mich., Jan. 17, 1897; s. George and Jennie (Musson) C.; m. Geraldine Hamilton, Aug. 15, 1925; children: Joan Elizabeth, Laurence Gordon, Thomas Hamilton (dec.). AB, U. Mich., 1918, AM, 1921, PhD, 1933. Teacher of speech U. Minn., 1919, U. Mich., 1920-28, Waseda U., Tokyo, 1921-22, U. Colo., summer 1924, Floating U., 1926-27; head dept. speech Dennison U., Granville, Ohio, from 1928, sr.prof., from 1954; teacher of speech Mich. State Teacher's Coll., U, Mich., Mich. State Coll., Ind. State Teachers Coll., Univ.Me., Stanford, Coll. of Pacific, various summers from 1929; prof. in pub. utilities exec. program U. Mich. Author several books including: Augmentation and Debate, 1944, 3rd edit. 1955, Oral Reading, 1947, 56, Effective Speaking, 1948, rev. edit. 1959, Business and Professional Speech, 1951, Introduction to Interpretive Speech, 1952, Advice to Freshmen by Freshmen, 1952, Public Speaking for College Students, 1954, Effective Speaking, 1959, Effective Debating, 1961, (with Paul Carmack) Readings in Rhetoric; editor Ctrl. States Speech Jour., 1948-50; assoc. editor Quarterly Jour. Speech, 1937-44, Jour. of Communication, 1962-63. Mem. staff the Ministers Rsch. Found., Inc. Served as corporal Med. Corps, U.S. Army, 1918-19. Mem. AAUP (sec. local chpt.), Nat. Assn. Coll. Teachers of Speech (v.p. 1934, exec. coun. 1946), Ohio Assn. Coll. Teachers of Speech (pres. 1938), Speech Assn. Am. (1st v.p. 1951, pres. 1952), Tau Kappa Alpha (editor The Speaker 1938-48, sec. 1940-48, historian), Delta Sigma Rho (historian), Theta Chi, Omicron Delta Kappa, Pi Delta Epsilon, Phi Beta Kappa (pres. Denison chpt.), Rotarian. Republican. Baptist. *

CROMWELL, JAMES HENRY ROBERTS, corporate executive; b. N.Y.C., June 4, 1898; s. Oliver Eaton and Lucretia (Roberts) C.; m. Delphine Dodge, June 20, 1920 (div. 1928); 1 child, Christine; m. Doris Duke, Feb. 13, 1935 (div. 1948); m. Maxine MacFetridge, Apr. 1948; 1 child, Maxine Hope. Student, U. Pa.; LLD (hon.), John Marshall Coll., 1939, Bethany Coll., 1940. With Drexel & Co., Phila.; then pres. Cromwell, Dodge Corp.; pres. Am. Brit. Improvement Corp.; then v.p. Peerless Motor Car Corp.; ptnr. Cromwell's Co.; pres., dir. Bonnyville Oil & Refining Co., Ltd. (Can.), 1955-57; pres. Kardar Canadian Oils, Ltd., 1957-69; U.S. envoy to Can., 1940; Am. adviser Pres. Syngman Rhee, Korea, 1941-45; mem. N.J. Tax Law Revision Commn., 1938-39. Author: Voice Young America, 1933, In Defense of Capitalism, 1937, Pax Americana, 1941. Dem. candidate for U.S. senator from N.J., 1940. With USN, USMC, WWI; capt. USMC Res. to 1924. Mem. Marine Corps League, Mil. Order Fgn. Wars, Met. Club, St. Nicholas Co. Club (N.Y.C.). Home: Birmingham Ala. Died Mar. 19, 1990.

CROMWELL, JARVIS, corporate executive; b. N.Y.C., Nov. 5, 1896; s. Lincoln and Mabel Wheeler (Smith) C.; m. Barbara Mildred Kissel, June 21, 1924; children: David Everett, Patricia Mary Cromwell Miller, Roger James Kissel; m. Edith Ely Kirk, Apr. 9, 1969. AB, Princeton U., 1919. Dir. Mut. Benefit Life Ins. Co.; dir. emeritus Dan River, Inc. Chmn. Greater N.Y. Red Cross War Fund, 1945-46; trustee N.Y. Hist. Soc., Boys Club of N.Y., St. Luke's Hosp.; bd. dirs. John and Mary R. Markle Found. 1st lt. U.S. Army, 1917-18, maj. 17th regt. N.Y. Guard, 1940-45. Mem. Racquet and Tennis Club, Princeton Club, Century Club. Republican. Episcopalian. Home: Morristown N.J. Died Mar. 15, 1992.

CRONQUIST, ARTHUR JOHN (FRANKLIN ARTHUR BEERS), botanist; b. San Jose, Calif., Mar. 19, 1919; s. Frank and Edith Marguerite (Cronquist) Beers; m. Mabel Allred, Dec. 25, 1940; children: John, Elizabeth Lynne. Student, U. Idaho, 1934-36; BS, Utah State Coll., 1938, MS, 1940; PhD, U. Minn., 1944; hon. Doctorate, Utah State U., 1987. Mem. staff N.Y. Bot. Garden, 1943-46, 52-74, sr. scientist, 1974-92; asst. prof. U. Ga., 1946-48; asst. prof. State Coll. Wash., 1948-51, rsch. assoc., 1953-66; tech. adviser Belgian Govt., 1951-52. Author: Introductory Botany, 1961, 2d edit., 1971, The Evolution and Classification of Flowering Plants, 1968, 2d edit., 1988, Basic Botany, 1973, 2d edit., 1982, Asteraceae of Southeastern United States, 1980, An Integrated System of Classification of Flowering Plants, 1981; also numerous articles; co-author: Manual of the Vascular Plants of Northeastern U.S. and Adjacent Canada, 1963, 2d edit., 1991, Vascular Plants of the Pacific Northwest, 5 vols, 1955-69, Natural Geography of Plants, 1964, Intermountain Flora, 4 vols., 1972-88. Recipient Leidy medal Nat. Acad. Scis., Phila., Disting. Svc. award N.Y. Bot. Garden, 1981, Gleason award N.Y. Bot. Garden, 1982; named hon. v.p. XII Internat. Bot. Congress, Leningrad, 1975. Fellow Linnean Soc. London (Linnean medal for Botany 1986); mem. AAAS, Am. Soc. Plant Taxonomists (pres. 1962, Asa Gray award), Am. Inst. Biol. Scis., Interant. Assn. Plant Taxonomists, Bot. Soc. Am. (pres. 1973, Merit award 1974), Torrey Bot. Club, New Eng. Bot. Club, Calif. Bot. Soc. Home: White Plains N.Y. Died Mar. 22, 1992.

CROOK, THEO HELSEL, geologist; b. Groveton, Tex., Mar. 13, 1898; s. William McKissack and Jennie Maude (Helsel) C.; m. Alice Louise Thomas, Aug. 26, 1930. AB, U. Calif., Berkeley, 1919, MA, 1921. With geol. and land-lease divsn. Standard Oil Co. of Calif. and its fgn. subsidiaries, 1921-41; consulting geologist, conductor geol. rsch. on maganese U. Calif., 1941-43, lectr. geology, 1943-46, sr. mus. geologist, 1946-54; independent cons. geologist, pvt. practice, from 1954. Coauthor (with J.M. Kirby) paper The Capay Formation presented before Geol. Soc. AM., 1934; author paper Occurrence and Minerals of Maganese (State of Calif. Dept. Natural Resources), 1944. Voluteer in civic war activities, Berkeley, Calif., W.W.II; apptd. by Ecuadorian govt. mem. spl. commn. to investigate Ecuadorian earthquakes, 1938; apptd. by pres. of Ecuador as Geologo Ad Honorem del Estado, 1938. Fellow Geol. Soc. Am.; mem. Am. Assn. Petroleum Geologists, U. Calif. Alumni Assn. (life), Phi Delta Teta, Theta Tau, Masons, Faculty Club, Le Conte. Republican. Protestant. *

CROSBIE, STANLEY BLANDFORD, physician; b. Mpls., May 12, 1906; s. William and Eva (Blandford) C.; m. Helen Blair, Dec. 20, 1937; 1 dau., Joan. Student, Carleton Coll., 1924-26; B.A., U. Minn., 1936, M.D., 1941. Intern, Jersey City Med. Center, 1941-42; resident psychiatry Hudson River State Hosp., Poughkeepsie, N.Y., 1942-43; resident medicine VA Hosp., Mpls., 1946-47; practice medicine, specializing in gastroenterology Alburquerque, 1947- 49, Grand Junction, Colo., 1949-59, Mpls., 1959-62, Dearborn, Mich., 1962-65; chief gastro-intestinal service VA Hosp., Albuquerque, 1947-49; chief med. service VA Hosp., Grand Junction, 1949-59; dir. profl. services VA Hosp., Mpls., 1959-62; dir. VA Hosp., Dearborn, 1962-65, Denver, 1965-70, Phoenix, 1970-72; clinician Maricopa County Dept. Health Services, Phoenix, 1973-83; asst. prof. medicine U. Minn., 1959-62, asst. dean Med. Sch., 1979-62; asso. prof. Wayne State U., 1963-65; asso. prof. medicine U. Colo., 1966-70. Served to maj. M.C., AUS, 1943-46. Fellow ACP; mem. Am. Hosp. Assn., AMA, Chi Psi. Home: Phoenix Ariz. Died Dec. 22, 1989; cremated.

CROSBY, JOHN CAMPBELL, author; b. Milw., May 18, 1912; s. Fred G. and Edna (Campbell) C.; m. Mary B. Wolferth, Dec. 7, 1946 (div.); children: Michael Wolferth, Margaret Campbell; m. Katharine J. B. Wood, Dec. 1, 1964; children: Alexander, Victoria. Student, Yale U., 1931-33. Reporter Milw. Sentinel, 1933, N.Y. Herald Tribune, 1935-41; syndicated columnist, 1946-65; columnist The Observer, London, Eng., 1965-75. Author: Out of the Blue, 1952, With Love and Loathing, 1963, Sappho In Absence, 1969, The Literary Obsession, 1973, Contract on the President, 1973, An Affair of Strangers, 1975, Nightfall, 1976, Company of Friends, 1977, Dear Judgment, 1978, Party of the Year, 1979, Penelope Now, 1981, Men in Arms, 1983, Take No Prisoners, 1985, The Family Worth, 1987, Wingwalker, 1989. Served with AUS, 1941-46. Recipient George Foster Peabody award, George K. Polk meml award. Home: Esmont Va. Died Sept. 7, 1991.

CROSS, FRANK BRADLEY, manufacturing executive; b. Cin., Mar. 31, 1897; s. Frank B. and Camilia (Shinkle) C.; m. Mary Pounsford, June 30, 1919; 1 son, Frank B. Student, U. Cin., 1917. Agent Columbia Life Ins. Co., 1919, gen. agent, 1920, v.p., 1937, pres., 1938; sold co. to Ohio Nat. Life Ins. Co., Cin., 1940; v.p., dir., chmn. exec. com. The Black-Clawson Co., Hamilton, Ohio; pres., dir. The Kenton Realty Co., Covington, Ky.; v.p., dir. The Home Fed. Savings and Loan Assn., Cin., The Covington and Cin. Bridge Co., Covington, Ky.; dir., v.p., asst. sec., treas. The Cin. Tobacco Warehouse Co.; dir. The Dixie Terminal Co., Cin., The Ohio Nat. Life Ins. Co., Cin. chmn. com. mgmt. Williams YMCA (Cin.). Mem. Sigma Chi. Republican. Episcopalian. *

CROUCH, GEORGE SANFORD, bank executive; b. Morristown, Tenn., Aug. 23, 1896; s. George Sanford and Cordelia (Legg) C.; m. Katherine Harris, Nov. 2, 1929; children: George S., Jack S. Student, Davidson (N.C.) Coll., 1914-18. With Union Nat. Bank of Charlotte (N.C.) (name later changed to 1st Union Nat. Bank N.C.), from 1919, successively bookkeeper, asst. cashier, cashier, v.p., pres., 1947-52, chmn. bd. dirs., from 1952; dir. Fed. res. Bank of Richmond, Va. (Charlotte br.). Trustee Davidson Coll.; active ARC, Community Chest, others. Mem. C. of C., Charlotte Country Club (dir.), City Club (dir.), Quail Hollow Country Club. *

CROWE, VINCIL PENNY, lawyer; b. Braymer, Mo., July 7, 1897; s. Thomas William and Laura Belle (Penny) C.; m. Katherine Francis Latimer, Nov. 19, 1925. AB, Ctrl. Coll., Fayette, Mo., 1918; LLB (hon.), U. Mo., 1921. Bar: Mo. 1920, Okla., 1921. Mem. firm Crowe, Boxely, Dunlevy, Thweatt, Swinford & Johnson; co. atty. Garfield Co., 1923-24; asst. Atty. Gen. Okla., 1925-29; dir. Liberty Nat. Bank & Trust Co., Oklahoma City; chmn. Okla. Co. Ration Bd., 1942-46; pres. Sunbeam Home of Oklahoma City, 1948-49. Bd. dirs. Family and Children's Svc. of Oklahoma City, 1949-51; nominee for Congress, 8th Okla. Dist., 1924). Fellow Am. Coll. Trial Lawyers; mem. ABA (del.), Okla. Bar Assn. (pres. 1960), Oklahoma County Bar Assn., Oklahoma City C. of C., Phi Alpha Delta, Delta Sigma Rho, Oklahoma City Golf and Country Club, Men's Dinner Club. Methodist. *

CROWELL, GENTRY, state official; b. Chestnut Mound, Tenn., Dec. 10, 1932; m. Terrijean Crowell; children—Melissa, Brooks, Chris. Mem. 86th-89th Tenn. gen. assemblies, 1969-77; sec. state Tenn., 1977-89; past pres. Nat. Assn. Secs. State. Mem. Jaycees. Democrat. Methodist. Lodges: Masons; Lions. Home: Nashville Tenn. Died Dec. 20, 1989.

CROWL, PHILIP AXTELL, educator, historian; b. Dayton, Ohio, Dec. 17, 1914; s. Frank Denton and Clementine (Axtell) C.; m. Mary Ellen Wood, Sept. 9, 1943; children: Ellen Wood, Catherine Pauline, Margaret Axtell. A.B., Swarthmore Coll., 1936; postgrad., Yale Law Sch., 1936-37; M.A., U. Iowa, 1939; Ph.D., Johns Hopkins, 1942. Instr. Princeton, 1941-42, asst. prof. history, 1945-49, research asso., 1964; historian Dept. Army, 1949-55; intelligence officer State Dept., 1957-67; dir., cons. John Foster Dulles Oral History Project, Princeton, 1964-66; prof., chmn. dept. history U. Nebr., 1967-73; chmn. dept. strategy Naval War Coll., 1973-80, prof. emeritus, from 1980; Harmon meml. lectr. U.S. Air Force Acad., 1978; lectr. Nat. War Coll., 1981; pres. adv. bd. archival affairs Nat. Archives region 6, Kansas City, Mo., 1968-71; bd. dirs. Harry S. Truman Library Inst., 1968-73; mem. hist. adv. bd. USMC, 1969-71, USAF, 1983-86; mem. Nat. Hist. Publs. Commn., 1969-72. Author: Maryland During and After the American Revolution, 1943, (with J.A. Isely) The U.S. Marines and Amphibious War, 1951, (with E.G. Love) Seizure of the Gilberts and Marshalls, 1955, Campaign in the Mariannas, 1960, The Intelligent Traveller's Guide to Historic Britain, 1983, The Intelligent Traveller's Guide to Historic Scotland, 1986, The Intelligent Traveller's Guide to Historic Ireland, 1990; editor (with J. Smith) Prince George's County Maryland Court Records, 1696-1699, 1964; editorial bd. Mil. Affairs, 1970-73. Served to lt. comr. USNR, 1942-45. Decorated Silver Star medal. Mem. Am. Hist. Soc., Am. Mil. Inst. (trustee 1976-80), U.S. Naval Inst., Marine Corps History Found. (bd. dirs. 1982-86), Phi Beta Kappa, Delta Upsilon. Presbyn. Clubs: Cosmos (Washington); Nassau (Princeton, N.J.). Home: Annapolis Md. Died May 5, 1991; buried St. Ann's Cemetery, Annapolis.

CROWN, HENRY, business executive; b. Chgo., June 13, 1896; s. Arie and Ida (Gordon) C.; m. Rebecca Kranz, Aug. 12, 1920 (dec. Oct. 1943); children: Robert (dec. July 1969), Lester, John Jacob; m. Gladys Kay, Mar. 1946. Student public schs., Chgo.; LL.D. (hon.), Syracuse U., Barat Coll., DePaul U., DePauw U., Loras Coll., Brown U.; D.Engring. (hon.), Tri State Coll.; L.H.D. (hon.), Jewish Theol. Sem. Am., Northwestern U. Clk. Chgo. Fire Brick Co., 1910-12; traffic mgr. Union Drop Forge Co., 1912-16; partner S.R. Crown & Co., 1916-19; treas. Material Service Corp. (bldg. materials), 1919-21, pres., 1921-41, chmn. bd., 1941-59; dir., chmn. exec. com. Gen. Dynamics Corp., 1959-66, 70-86, hon. chmn. bd. dirs., from 1986; chmn. bd. Henry Crown & Co., 1967; past dir. Hilton Hotels, Waldorf Astoria Corp. Mem. Chgo. CD Corps.; trustee Chgo. Boys' Clubs; adv. mem. bd. trustees DePaul U.; mem. U. Ill. Citizens Com., Loyola U. Citizens Bd., Northwestern U. Assos.; fellow St. Joseph's Coll., Rensselaer, Ind.; asso., fellow Brandeis U.; hon. v.p. N.E. Ill. council Boy Scouts Am. Served as col., C.E. AUS, World War II. Decorated Legion of Merit U.S.; chevalier Legion d'Honneur France; Gold Cross Royal Order Phoenix Greece; Order Ruben Dario Nicaragua; recipient Horatio Alger award Am. Schs. and Colls. Assn., Damen award Loyola U., Chgo., Humanitarian Service award for industry Eleanor Roosevelt Cancer Research Found., Julius Rosenwald Meml. award Jewish Fedn. and Welfare Fund, Chgo., Edn. for Freedom award Roosevelt U., Chgo., Meritorious Public Service award U.S. Navy; named to Jr. Achievement's Chgo. Bus. Hall of Fame. Mem. Mil. Order World Wars. Clubs: Executives, Mid-Day, Standard, Tavern, Commercial (Chgo.); St. Louis; Tamarask (Palm Beach, Fla.); Hillcrest Country (Los Angeles). Lodges: Masons (33d deg.), Shriners. Home: Evanston Ill. Died Aug. 14, 1990; buried Rosehill Cemetery, Chgo.

CROXTON, FREDERICK EMORY, statistician, educator; b. Washington, May 23, 1899; s. Fred. C. and Mattie M. (Stocks) C.; m. Rosetta Ruth Harpster, Sept. 14, 1921; children: Frederick Emory, Rosetta Harpster Croxton Clark. AB, Ohio State U., 1920, MA, 1921; PhD, Columbia U., 1926. Asst. in econs. Ohio State U., 1919-21, instr. econs., 1921-26; lectr. stats. Ohio Wesleyan U., 1920-21; lectr. stats. Columbia U., N.Y.C., 1926-27, asst. prof., 1927-37, assoc. prof., 1937-44, prof., 1944-64, prof. emeritus, 1964-91, spl. asst. to v.p. and provost, 1951-53; interim dir. univ. admissions Columbia U., 1951-53; lectr. stats. U. Chgo., summer 1926, U. Colo., summer 1948; assoc. with U.S. Pers. Classification Bd., 1928; mem. rsch. staff Nat. Bur. Econ. Rsch., 1929-30; lectr. stats. N.Y. Sch. Social Work, 1930-32, 44; dir. div. stats. N.Y. State TERA, 1933-34. Author or joint author numerous books in field including Applied General Statistics, 3d edit., 1967, Workbook in Applied General Statistics, 5th edit., 1967, Elementary Statistics with Applications in Medicine and the Biological Sciences, 1959, Practical Business Statistics, 4th edit., 1969; books transl. into Spanish, Portuguese, Japanese and Hindu; also pamphlets and articles. With U.S. Army, 1918-19. Fellow AAAS, Am. Statis. Assn.; mem. Phi Beta Kappa, Phi Delta Kappa, Beta Gamma Sigma. Home: Lakeland Fla. Died Jan. 10, 1991; interred Rock Creek Cemetery, Washington.

CRUICKSHANK, WILLIAM MELLON, educator; b. Detroit, Mar. 25, 1915; s. Ward and Alice (Shanor) C.; m. Dorothy Jane Wager, Dec. 26, 1940; children: Penny Alice (Mrs. Michael Dorsey), Dorothy Patricia (Mrs. David Crosson), Carol Jean (Mrs. Frederick Adler). AB, Eastern Mich. U., 1936, ScD (hon.), 1962; MA, U. Chgo., 1938; PhD, U. Mich., 1945; DHL (hon.), Central Mich. U., 1982, SUNY, 1985; JD (hon.), Cardinal Stritch Coll., 1982; DPed (hon.), Syracuse U., 1982. Margaret O. Slocum disting. prof. edn., psychology; dir. divsn. spl. edn. and rehab. Syracuse U., 1946-67, dean summer sessions, 1953-66; prof. psychology, prof. edn., prof. child and family health U. Mich., Ann Arbor, 1966-85; prof emeritus child and family health, psychology, and edn. U. Mich., 1985-92, chmn. dept. spl. edn., hearing and speech scis., 1977-79; dir. Inst. for Study Mental Retardation and Related Disabilities, 1966-80, dir. emeritus, 1980-92; vis. scholar Duke U., 1986-87; Fulbright lectr., Peru, 1968; vis. disting. prof. U. New Orleans, 1982, 87-88; vis. prof. UCLA, 1983-84, Calif. State U., Los Angeles, 1983-84; prof.-in-residence Nat. Inst. Dyslexia, Chevy Chase, Md., 1988-89; vis. prof. U. So. Fla., 1990-92; cons. Rainbow Rehab. Ctrs., 1992; assoc. dir. Inst. San Gabriel Arcangel, Lima, Peru, 1962-63; author, lectr.; Priorsfield rsch. fellow U. Birmingham, Eng., 1973; sr. scholar U. S. Fla., 1989-91; mem. profl. adv. com. Assn. Crippled Children; mem. profl. adv. com. Nat. Soc. Crippled Children and Adults, Nat. Soc. for Prevention Blindness; sr. cons. Teaching Resources Corp., Boston, 1966-80; cons. health and ednl. instns., Japan, Eng., France, Netherlands, Denmark, Sweden, Peru, Fed. Republic Germany, India; former chmn. Canadian-U.S. Study Group on Mental Retardation, 1968-74; cons. Havern Sch., Colo., 1970-77, Neuro-Edn. Ctr., William Beaumont Hosp.; mem. bd. cons. Ctr. for Rsch. on Exceptional Children. U. N.C., 1969-75; mem. adv. com. dept. edn. Govt. Am. Samoa, 1969-71; past mem. profl. adv. bd. Pathway Sch., Norristown, Pa., 1966-70; cons. to study for Nat. Ctr. Sci. Studies, Ministry of Pub. Health, Havana, Cuba. Author, editor; co-editor books on cerebral palsy, learning disability, perception, exceptional children.; Editorial cons., Syracuse U. Press, 1966-80, editorial adviser, Prentice-Hall, Inc., 1966-78, mem. adv. bd. various jours. Cons. Durham County Bd. Edn. Pub. Schs., N.C., 1986-87; bd. dirs. Detroit League for Handicapped, Goodwill, Inc., 1978-80; former adviser Ednl. Policies Commn.; mem. N.Y. State Regents' Coun. Physically Handicapped; adv. com. tchr. edn. Am. Found. for Blind; ednl. adv. com. Fed. Epilepsy League, 1955-64, United Cerebral Palsy Assn.; mem. Mich. State Planning Adv. Com. on Devel. Disabilities and Constrn. Facilities, 1971-80; mem. tech. rsch. adv. com. Mich. Dept. Mental Health, 1975-79; mem. profl. adv. com. Detroit Orthopaedic Ctr., 1975-79, chmn., 1977-79; mem. profl. adv. com. Barkeley Sch., Atlanta, 1978-88; bd. dirs. Mich. Human Svcs., Inc., 1986-87; Past trustee Cove Schs., Racine, Wis., 1948-60. Capt., adj. gen. dept. AUS, 1942-45. Recipient Catedratico Honorario Universidad Nacional Mayor de San Marcos Lima, Peru, 1962; J.E. Wallace Wallin award Nat. Coun. for Exceptional Children, 1965; Outstanding Profl. award Assn. for Children with Learning Disabilities, 1970; Honor award Internat. Fedn. Learning Disabilities, 1976; Newell C. Kephart award Purdue U., 1977, Educator of Yr. award Durham Assn. Retarded Citizens and N.C. State Assn. Retarded Citizens, 1987; U. Fla. sr. scholar, 1989-90; others. Fellow APA (life, pres. Div. 22, psychol. aspects phys. disability 1969-70), Am. Assn. Mental Deficiency (Outstanding Educator award 1975), Am. Acad. Mental Retardation, Am. Acad. Cerebral Palsy; mem. Internat. Coun. Exceptional Children (pres. 1952-53, mem. adv. com. div. learning disabilities 1983-92), Internat. Neuropsychology Soc., Assn. for Children with Learning Disabilities (profl. adv. com. 1969-75), Internat. Acad. for Rsch. on Learning Disabilities (founder, pres. 1979-86, exec. dir. 1986-92), Mich. Assn. for Children with Learning Disabilities (profl. adv. com. 1969-74, 79-92), N.Y. State Psychol. Assn., Nat., Mich. Home: Ann Arbor Mich. Died Aug. 13, 1992. †

CSOKA, STEPHEN, painter, etcher; b. Gardony, Hungary, Jan. 2, 1897; came to U.S., 1934, naturalized, 1941; s. Istvan and Julianna (Nagy) C.; m. Margaret Muller, Mar. 18, 1934; children—Clara Eve, Frank Stephen. Student, Royal Acad. Art, Budapest, 1922-27. Author: Pastel Painting, 1962; Work shown at internat. exhbns., also, Corcoran Gallery, Washington, 1945, 47, one-man shows, Contemporary Arts, N.Y.C., 1940, 43, 45, 56, Phila. Art Alliance, 1943, Minn. State Fair, 1943, Merrill Gallery, N.Y.C., 1963, Galerie Paula Insel, N.Y.C., 1976, Ponce (P.R.) Mus. Art, 1976, one-man retrospective, Fashion Inst. Tech., N.Y.C., 1979, Odin Gallery, Port Washington, N.Y., 1981; represented in several museums, including, Library of Congress. Recipient numerous awards and prizes, the later of which are La Tausca Pearl Co. award, 1945; 1,000 purchase prize-etching nat. Print Competition Assn. Am. Artists, 1947; 1,000 Grant Am. Acad. of Arts and Letters, 1948; First in oil Bklyn. Artists, 1949; John Taylor Arms Prize, etching Soc. Am. Etchers, 1952; Gold Medal award Arpad Acad., 1972; 1st Prize Dr. Maury Leibvitz art awards program, 1986; several hon. mentions. Mem. Soc. Am. Graphic Artists, Pastel Soc. Am., NAD, Audubon Soc. Home: Kings Park N.Y. Died Jan. 5, 1989; buried Cypress Hills Cemetery, Queens, N.Y.

CUGAT, XAVIER, violinist, conductor; b. Barcelona, Spain, Jan. 1, 1900; s. Juan and Mingall de Bru C.; m. Carmen Castillo, Oct. 17, 1929; m. Lorraine Allen, 1947; m. Abbe Lane div. ; m. Charo, 1966. First appearance as guest artist Cuban Symphony at age 6; toured World with Enrico Caruso as assisting artist and accompanist at age of 16; gave concerts in Europe and U.S.; formed his own dance orch. and played in all the prominent hotels and night clubs; conducted many radio programs; recorded album, Spanish Eyes, 1972; caricatured prominent artists as a hobby; painted murals and theater curtains. Mem. ASCAP. Home: New York N.Y. Died Oct. 27, 1990.

CULBERTSON, JOHN HARRISON, engineer; b. Lansdowne, Pa., Dec. 3, 1905; s. Walter Edwards and Katherine (Evans) C.; m. Grace Jessie Kirby, Sept. 6, 1941; children: Marian Grace Culbertson Hvolbeck, Katherine Kirby Culbertson Prentice, John Harrison. Student, Lehigh U., 1924-28. Plant mgr. Schering Corp., Bloomfield, N.J., 1940-42, Heyden Pennicillin Plant, Princeton, N.J., 1946-47; prodn. mgr. Unexcelled Chem. Corp., N.Y.C., 1947-49; v.p. Drum Co., Bristol, Pa., 1949-50; project dir. Port of N.Y. Authority Harbor Radar Tests, N.Y.C., 1951-52; pres. Nat. Ceramic Co., Trenton, N.J., 1954-55, Culbertson Enterprises, Morristown, N.J., from 1956; also dir. Culbertson Enterprises; Ex-officio trustee Assn. N.J. Environ. Commns., from 1969, pres., 1969-73. Bd. mgrs. Morristown Neighborhood House, from 1960, pres., 1969-73; Formerly trustee Wilson Coll., Chambersburg, Pa.; trustee Kirby Episcopal Conf. Center, Glen Summit, Pa., pres., 1974-77; trustee Hist. Speedwell Village, from 1979. Served from lt. to comdr. USNR, 1942-45. Recipient Harding Township (N.J.) Outstanding Citizenship award, 1970. Mem. Psi Upsilon. Republican. Presbyn. Clubs: Morristown (N.J.) Field (N.Y.C.) (pres. 1959-65), Chemists (N.Y.C.). Home: Morristown N.J. Died Sept. 28, 1988; buried New Vernon, N.J.

CULLEN, BILL (WILLIAM LAWRENCE CULLEN), radio and television entertainer; b. Pitts., Feb. 18, 1920; m. Ann Roemheld. Student, U. Pitts. Announcer, then master of ceremonies radio sta. WWSW, Pitts., 1939-44; staff announcer CBS, 1944-46; master of ceremonies Winner Take All, 1946; TV debut I've Got a Secret, 1952; master of ceremonies $25,000 Pyramid, To Tell the Truth, Place the Face, Quick as a Flash, Hit the Jackpot, Give and Take, Down You Go, Price is Right, Eye Guess, Three on a Match, Blockbusters, Chain Reaction, NBC-TV, Emphasis, NBC radio. Home: Los Angeles Calif. Died July 7, 1990.

CULLITON, EDWARD MILTON, Canadian justice; b. Grand Forks, Minn., Apr. 9, 1906; s. John Joseph and Katherine M. (Kelly) C.; m. Katherine M. Hector, Sept. 9, 1939. B.A., U. Sask., 1926, LL.B., 1928, D.C.L., 1962. Bar: Sask. 1930. Practice in Gravelbourg, 1930-51; mem. Sask. Legislature, 1935-44, 48-51; provincial sec. Patterson Govt., 1938-41; minister without portfolio, 1941-44; judge Ct. Appeal Sask., 1951-62, chief justice, 1962-81; vice chmn. Can. Jud. Council, 1973-81; chancellor U. Sask., 1963-69. Served with Can. Army, 1941-46. Decorated knight comdr. Order of St. Gregory (Vatican), 1963, companion Order of Can., 1981, Sask. Order of Merit, 1987. Home: Regina, Sask. Can. Died Apr. 2, 1991; buried Regina, Sask.

CUMMING, JOSEPH BRYAN, lawyer; b. Augusta, Ga., Aug. 10, 1893; s. Bryan and Mary Gairdner (Smith) C.; m. Virginia Neville Burum, Nov. 15, 1922; children: Neville Cumming Riley, Joseph Bryan, Nancy C. Connolly. LittB, Princeton U., 1915; student, Harvard U., 1915-17. Bar: Ga. 1920. Mem. firm Cumming & Harper, now Cumming, Nixon, Eve, Waller & Capers; lectr. med. jurisprudence Med. Coll. Ga.; bd. dirs. Riverside Mills, Ga. R.R. Bank and Trust Co., 1st R.R. and Banking Co. Ga., Ga. R.R. and Banking Co. (Augusta). Mem. Gen. Assembly Ga., 1923-24; chmn. bd. trustees Summerville Cemetary; v. chmn. Acad. of Richmond County, Tubman Home; trustee Clinton Anderson Hosp., Augusta Mus., Herbert Meml. Inst. Art; pres. trustees Young Men's Libr. Assn.; chmn. Ga. Hist. Commn., Richmond County Dem. Party Hon. amb. Cherokee Nat. Entered 1st O.T.C. Ft. McPherson, Ga. 1917; commd. 1st lt. U.S. Army, assigned to 321st F.A., 82d Divsn.; with A.E.F. 1 yr. Fellow Am. Coll. Trial Lawyers; mem. ABA, Augusta Bar Assn. (pres. 1935-36), Ga. Bar Assn. (pres. 1938-39). Democrat. Episcopalian. *

CUMMING, WILLIAM PATTERSON, English language educator; b. Nagoya, Japan, Oct. 31, 1900; parents Am. citizens; s. Calvin Knox and Ona (Patterson) C.; m. Elizabeth Lathrop Chandler, Dec. 22, 1931; children: Edward Chandler (dec.), Robert Patterson. AB, Davidson Coll., 1921; MA, Princeton U., 1922. Mem. faculty Davidson (N.C.) Coll., 1927-89, prof. English, 1937-68, chmn. dept. English, 1964-68, Irvin prof. English, 1961-68, Irvin prof. emeritus, 1968-89; attache Dept. State, 1945-46; vis. prof. Annamalai U., India, 1963-64, Shikoku Christian Coll., Japan, 1964; cartographic cons. U.S. Dept. Justice, 1961, State of S.C., 1978. Author: The Southeast in Early Maps, 1958, Cartography of Colonial Carolina, 1961, North Carolina in Maps, 1966, Captain James Wimble, His Maps and the Colonial Cartography of the North Carolina Coast, 1969, British Maps of Colonial America, 1974; co-author: The Discovery of North America, 1971, The Exploration of North America 1630-1776, 1974, The Fate of a Nation: The American Revolution through Contemporary Eyes, 1975;. editor: The Revelations of St. Birgitta, 1929, The Discoveries of John Lederer, 1958; co-editor: A Map of the British Empire in America...by Henry Popple, 1972, North America at the Time of the Revolution: A Collection of Eighteenth Century Maps, 1975; contbr. articles to profl. jours. Chmn. Davidson-North Mecklenburg chpt. ARC, 1941-43. Grantee Social Sci. Rsch. Coun., 1938, Carnegie Found., 1946; R.D.W. Connor award Hist. Soc. N.C., 1969; Guggenheim fellow, 1958-59; Fulbright lectr., 1963-64; Nebenzahl lectr. history of cartography, fellow Newberry Libr., 1970. Mem. MLA, AAUP, So. Atlantic MLA (pres. 1957), Hist. Soc. N.C. (pres. 1955-56), Lions, Phi Beta Kappa, Omicron Delta Kappa. Presbyterian. Home: Davidson N.C. Died Aug. 16, 1989.

CUMMINGS, BOB (ROBERT ORVILLE CUMMINGS), motion picture, stage, television performer; b. Joplin, Mo., June 9, 1910; s. Charles C. and Ruth A. Kraft C.; m. Regina Young; children: Robert Richard, Mary Melinda, Sharon Patricia, Laurel Ann, Anthony Bob, Charles Clarence, Michelle Helene; m. Janie Cummings. Student, Drury Coll., Carnegie Inst. Tech., Am. Acad. Dramatic Arts. lectr. in field; comml. airplane pilot, instr. Actor in starring roles motion pictures, 1936-90, including, Kings Row, Princess O'Rourke, Saboteur, You Came Along, Lost Moment, Dial M for Murder, The Carpetbaggers, What a Way to Go, others; star, dir. TV series: on tour in My Daughter's Rated X, 1975-79, Harvey, Dad's Dilemma, Fun and Games, Marriage-Go-Round, Never Too Late, Love

Boat 79; author: Stay Young and Vital, 1960. Founding mem. Ecology Found. U.S., Washington. Recipient Emmy award as best actor, 12 Angry Men, 1954, award as best actor in comedy Billboard, 1955, best comedy series award for Bob Cummings Show, Billboard, 1955; Emmy nominations for dir. and actor, 1955-59. Home: Bellevue Wash. Died Dec. 2, 1990.

CUMMINS, ALFRED BYRON, management engineer, educator; b. Ute, Iowa, Mar. 19, 1905; s. Daniel Byron and Myrtle (Chase) C.; m. Maxine Ellen Price, Dec. 23, 1934; children: Mary Alice (Mrs. Wilson), Judith Maxine Cummins Morrison. BS cum laude, State U. Iowa, 1931, JD cum laude, 1936, MS, 1938; postgrad., Mass. Inst. Tech., 1931-32, U. Minn., 1938-41, U. Pa., 1941-42. Registered profl. mgmt. engr. Prodn. civilian specialist Armed Services, Phila., 1942- 46; chief indsl. engr. Wilkening Mfg. Co., Phila., 1943-46; cons. mgmt. engr., from 1946; prodn. cons. Armed Services, War Labor Bd., WPB, Engring. Sci. Mgmt. War Tng. Program, War Labor Bd., 1941-45; asst. prof. mgmt. Wharton Sch., U. Pa., 1941-47; prof. mgmt. dept. Case Western Res. U. Sch. Mgmt., 1947-91; organizer, dir. Hough Mfg. Co.; chmn. L-C-L, Inc., Cleve.; cons. OEEC-EPA, Paris; mgmt. cons. VA hosps.; dir. research pub. health mgmt. systems; mem. nat. panel arbitrators Fed. Mediation and Conciliation Service. Contbr. tech. articles to profl. jours.; mem. pioneer team Productivity Files Western Res. Hist. Soc. Mem. Iowa Bar, Soc. for Advancement Mgmt. (past pres. Phila.), Am. Arbitration Assn. (nat. panel arbitrators), Sigma Xi, Tau Beta Pi, Beta Gamma Sigma, Delta Sigma Pi. Home: Chagrin Falls Ohio Died Apr. 21, 1991; buried Evergreen Meml. Cemetery, Chagrin Falls.

CUNEO, ERNEST L., lawyer, journalist, author; m. Margaret Watson (dec. 1976); children: Sandra, Jonathan. B.A., Columbia U., LL.B., LL.D., D.H.L. Bar: N.Y., D.C., U.S. Supreme Ct. Past law sec. Fiorello H. La Guardia; past assoc. counsel Dem. Nat. Com.; past dir. Freedom House, Woodrow Wilson Inst. Internat. Scholars; past pres., chmn. bd. N.Am. Newspaper Alliance; former editor-at-large Saturday Evening Post. Author: Dynamics of World History. Served to maj. USMCR; ret. OSS liaison officer to White House, British Security, State Dept., FBI World War II. Decorated by Italy, Britain and City of Genoa. Clubs: Varsity, National Press, Overseas Press, Silurians, OSS Veterans. Home: Arlington Va. Deceased. †

CURRIE, LAUCHLIN MACLAURIN, chemical engineer; b. Chapel Hill, N.C., Aug. 13, 1898; s. Daniel Johnson and Stella Alston (Hogan) C.; m. Ethel Snyder Jopp, Aug. 11, 1921; children: Helen Catherine, Christian MacLaurin. BA, Davidson Coll., 1918, DSc, 1951; PhD, Cornell U., 1925; DSc, Clarkson Inst., 1950. With Union Carbide Corp., 1925-58, successively rsch. chemist, plant supt., dir. vinylite divsn., 1925-40; plant supt. Bakelite Co., 1940-42; v.p., dir. rsch. Nat. Carbon Co., 1945-55; v.p. Union Carbide Nuclear Co., 1955-58, Babcox & Wilson Co., N.Y.C., 1958-62; also dir. Babcox & Wilson Co.; dir. devel. Rsch. Triangle N.C., 1962-64; chmn. adv. com. isotopes and radiation AEC; assoc. dir. divsn. war rsch. Manhattan Engring. Dist., 1943-45; observer Bikini Bomb Tests, 1946; del. Orgn. European Econ. Conf., Nancy, France, 1954, Geneva Conf. U.N., 1955, 58, Calder Hall, London, 1956; chmn. N.Y. State adv. bd. atomic energy, 1957-58; chmn. nuclear energy commn. N.A.M., 1957-62, also dir. assn. Served from 1st lt. to major, AUS, 1942-45. Mem. AICE, Am. Chem. Soc., Soc. Chem. Industry, Am. Nuclear Soc. Atomic Indsl. Forum, Engrs. Joint Coun., Newcomen Soc., Sigma Xi, Phi Gamma Delta, Chemists Club, Rotary (N.Y.C.), Larchmont Club (N.Y.), Yacht Club. Republican. Presbyterian. *

CURTIS, LAURENCE, lawyer, state congressman; b. Boston, Sept. 3, 1893; s. Louis and Fanny Leland (Richardson) C.; m. Helen Schryver. Grad., Groton Sch., 1912; AB, Harvard U., 1916, LLB, 1921; JD (hon.), Calvin Coolidge Coll., 1960. Admitted to Mass. bar, 1921, practiced in Boston, 1922; sec. to Mr. Justice Holmes, 1921-22; asst. U.S. atty. Boston, 1923-25; mem. Boston City Council, 1930-33, Mass. Ho. of Reps., 1933-36, Mass. Senate, 1936-41; state treas. Mass., 1947-48; mem. 83d-87th Congresses 10th (Mass.) Dist., 1953-63. Del. Republican Nat. Conv., 1976; candidate for Republican nomination Gov. of Mass., 1952, Republican nomination for U.S. Senate from Mass., 1962, defeated in primary by George Cabot Lodge. Served as lt. AC, USNRF, 1917-20. Decorated Silver Star; decorated chevalier Legion of Honor. Past comdr. Mass. dept. DAV, 1944-45 (nat. sr. vice comdr. 1945-46). Mem. ABA, Mass. Bar Assn., Boston Bar Assn., Phi Beta Kappa. Clubs: Harvard (Boston); Somerset, Ancient and Honorable Artillery Co. Home: Boston Mass. Died July 11, 1989.

CURTIS, WILLIAM HALL, lawyer; b. Arkansas City, Kans., Oct. 9, 1915; s. John Warner and Addie (Thompson) C.; m. Vivian Swearingen, Apr. 2, 1947; children: Gregory, Ann, John, Carolyn. AB, U. Nebr., 1937; LLB, Harvard U., 1940. Bar: Mo., Kans. 1941. Ptnr. Morrison, Hecker, Curtis, Kuder & Parrish, Kansas City, 1950-89, ret., 1989; dir. New Eng. Ranch & Oil Corp. Hon. trustee Kansas City (Mo.) Research Hosp. Served to maj. AUS, 1941-46. Fellow Am. Coll. Trial Lawyers; mem. ABA, Kansas City Bar Assn., Lawyers Assn. Kansas City (pres. 1965-66), Assn. Life Ins. Counsel, Assn. R.R. Trial Counsel, Am. Royal Assn. (bd. govs.), Blue Hills Country Club (pres. 1960), Kansas City Club. Clubs: Blue Hills Country (pres. 1960), River, Kansas City. Home: Shawnee Mission Kans. Died Dec. 12, 1991. †

CUSHMAN, EDWARD L., arbitrator, consultant, former university administrator; b. Boston, Apr. 6, 1914; s. Robert and Sarah C.; m. Katherine Jean Moore, Nov. 18, 1938; children: Robert Moore, Elizabeth Ann. AB, U. Mich., 1937; LLD (hon.), Park Coll., St. Augustine's Coll. Successively economist, civil service dir., asst. to employment service dir. Mich. Unemployment Compensation Commn., 1937-42; dep. dir. for Mich., War Manpower Commn., 1942-43, dir., 1943-46; spl. asst. to sec. of labor, 1946; prof. public adminstrn. Wayne U., 1946-54; v.p. indsl. relations Am. Motors Corp., 1954-59, v.p., 1959-66; dir. Wayne State U., Detroit, 1961-85, exec. v.p., 1966-84, exec. v.p. emeritus, 1984-92, Clarence Hilberry U. prof., 1977-84, prof. emeritus, 1984-92. Mem. Nat. Acad. Arbitrators, Indsl. Relations Research Assn. Home: Detroit Mich. Died June 26, 1992. †

CUTLER, MAX, lawyer; b. Athens, Ga., July 21, 1912; s. Louis and Gertrude (Narinsky) C.; m. Claire R. Mintz, Oct. 8, 1944; children: William Louis, John Martin. BA, N.Y. U., 1934; JD, Harvard U., 1937. Bar: N.Y. 1938. Practiced in N.Y.C., 1938-88; mem. firm John H. Levy, 1937-39, Davis & Gilbert, 1942-44; sr. partner Cutler & Cutler, 1944-88; counsel to Mazur, Carp & Barnett P.C., from 1985; gen. counsel numerous bus., med. profl. corps.; sec., gen. counsel Gabriel Industries, 1956-78; sec., gen. counsel Ophthalmic Research Found., Inc., 1975-82, Inst. for Visual Scis., Inc., from 1982; dir., gen. counsel Sonocare Inc., from 1983; pres., dir. Vanderbilt Assocs., N.Y.C., 1944-55. Pres., founder Citizens Caucus for Stamford Bd. Edn.; bd. dirs. Citizens Sch. League, Stamford; founder, bd. dirs. N. Stamford Democratic Club; mem. legal com. Lexington Dem. Club, N.Y.C.; bd. visitors Washington Sq. Coll., 1957-60, NYU; pres., bd. dirs. Stamford Mid-Ridge Civic Assn., 1955-57; bd. dirs. Stamford Chamber Residences, 1956-60; bd. dirs., chmn. edn. com. Stamford Good Govt. Assn. Recipient N.Y. U. Alumni Gold medal, 1934; Meritorious Service award N.Y. U. Alumni Fedn., 1954; Crystal award N.Y. U. Alumni Fedn., 1982. Mem. Washington Sq. Coll. Alumni Assn. (dir., past pres.), N.Y. U. Alumni Fedn. (v.p., dir.), Am. Bar Assn., N.Y. County Lawyers Assn., Harvard Law Sch. Assn. (life), NYU Alumni Fedn. (bd. dirs. from 1940), Alpha Gamma. Jewish. Clubs: Harvard (N.Y.C.), N.Y. U. (N.Y.C.). Home: New York N.Y. Died Oct. 1, 1988.

CUTLER, RICHARD SCHUYLER, investment company executive; b. Pana, Ill., Jan. 26, 1898; s. Frank A. and Myrtle (Newcomb) C.; m. Dorothea Wales, Oct. 8, 1921; children: Richard Schuyler, Robert Bruce. Student, Northwestern U., 1920. Dept. mgr. Butler Bros., 1920-29; with Norris & Kenly, 1929-33, Security Suprs., Chgo., from 1933; ptnr. Security Suprs., from 1947; v.p. Selected Am. Shares, Inc., Chgo., from 1945. Trustee F. J. R. Mitchell Scroll Fund. Mem. Investment Analysts Soc. Chgo., Phi Delta Theta. *

DACHÉ, LILLY, hat designer; b. Beigles, France; came to U.S., 1924; m. Jean Despres, 1931. Student pub. schs., France. Apprentice in millinery Reboux's, Paris; millinery sales person R.H. Macy Co., N.Y.C.; designer hats Daché's, N.Y.C.; pres. Lilly Daché, N.Y.C.; mgr. activities also include dresses, accessories, jewelry. Author: Lilly Daché's Glamour Book: Talking Thru My Hat. Recipient Am. Design award for creation of half-hat Lord & Taylor, 1941, design award for creation Neiman Marcus, numerous awards from maj. firms. Home: Bedford Village N.Y. Died Jan., 1990.

DAGGETT, ALBERT H., business executive; b. Mile, Maine, July 25, 1898; s. Clinton Lowell and Amy Lois (Murray) D.; m. Ruth H. Sowle, Aug. 17, 1929; children: Ellen Nedred, Judith Kalafat, John C. Edn. pub. schs. With Stone & Webster, Inc., 1919-27, Ames Shovel & Tool Co., 1927-31; bus. adviser First Nat. Bank, St. Paul, Toro Mfg. Corp., Mpls., Mutual Boiler & Machinery Ins. Co., Waltham, Mass., N.C. Natural Gas Corp., Fayetteville, N.C., St. Paul Hilton Hotel, North Star Rsch. and Devel. Inst. of Minn. Dir. Children's Hosp.; trustee Macalester Coll. Mem. (clubs): Minnesota, Somerset Country, White Bear (Minn.) Yacht, Hole-in-the-Wall Golf (Naples, Fla.). Republican. Presbyterian. *

DAHL, GEORGE LEIGHTON, architect; b. Mpls., May 11, 1894; s. Olaf G. and Laura (Olson) D.; m. Lillie E. Olsen, Sept. 24, 1921 (dec. Apr. 1957); 1 child, Gloria Lille Akin. BArch, U. Minn., 1921; MArch, Harvard U., 1922; student, Am. Acad. in Rome, 1923; Nelson Robinson traveling fellow, Africa and Europe, 1922-24. Designer Myron Hunt & H. C. Chambers, L.A., 1925; designer, mem. firm Herbert M. Greene, Dallas, 1926-28; mem. firm Herbert M. Greene, LaRoche & Dahl, Dallas, 1928-33, LaRoche & Dahl, Dallas, 1933-35; propr. firm George L. Dahl, architects and engrs., Dallas, from 1935; tech. dir. Tex. Centennial Exposition, 1935-37; architect, engr. Dallas Meml. Auditorium, 1956; mem. Tex. Bd. Archtl. Examiners, 1951-63, chmn., from 1955. Author: (monograph) Portals, Doorways and Windows, 1925. Mem. Dallas City Planning Adv. Com., 1943-45, Greater Dallas Planning Coun., 1948-56; mem. Tex. Bd. Corrections, 1950-60; bd. dirs. Dallas Better Bus. Bur.; past chmn. exec. com. Dallas Nat. Conf. Christians and Jews, Dallas Community Chest, Dallas coun. Boy Scouts Am., Dallas chpt. ARC, Dallas Salvation Army, Tex. Soc. Crippled Children, Dallas City-County Boy's Indsl. Home, Dallas Civic Opera; bd. dirs. Dallas YMCA. 1st lt. U.S. Army, WWI. Fellow AIA (past pres. Dallas); mem. Tex. Soc. Architects (past pres.), Soc. Am. Mil. Engrs. (past v.p. Dallas, nat. dir.), Dallas C. of C., Dallas Symphony Assn., Harvard Archtl. Soc., Dallas Art Assn., Harvard Found. Advanced Study, Nat. Coun. Archtl. Registration Bds., Mason, Rotary (past pres.), Town and Gown Club, Dallas Athletic Club, Dallas Country Club, Downtown Club, Engrs. Club, Knife and Fork Club, Dallas Club, City Club, Harvard Club (Dallas), Brookhollow Club. *

DAHL, ROALD, writer; b. Llandaff, Wales, Sept. 13, 1916; s. Harold and Sofie (Hesselberg) D.; m. Patricia Neal (dissolved 1983), July 2, 1953; children: Olivia (dec.), Tessa, Theo, Ophelia, Lucy; m. Felicity Crosland. Student, Repton (Eng.) Sch., 1930-34. Author: (juvenile fiction) The Gremlins, 1943, James and the Giant Peach, 1962, Charlie and the Chocolate Factory, 1964, The Magic Finger, 1965, Fantastic Mr. Fox, 1970, Charlie and the Great Glass Elevator, 1972, Danny, the Champion of the World, 1975, The Enormous Crocodile, 1978, The Twits, 1981, George's Marvellous Medicine, 1981, Dirty Beasts, 1982, Revolting Rhymes, 1982, The BFG, 1983, The Witches, 1984, The Giraffe and The Pelly and Me, 1985, Matilda, 1988, Rhyme Stew, 1989, Esio Trol, 1990, The Minpins, 1990; (short story collections) Over to You, 1945, Someone Like You, 1953, Kiss Kiss, 1960, Switch Bitch, 1974, The Wonderful Story of Henry Sugar and Six More, 1977, Tales of the Unexpected, 1979, More Tales of the Unexpected, 1980, Roald Dahl's Book of Ghost Stories, 1984; (adult fiction) My Uncle Oswald, 1980; (fables) Sometime Never, 1948, Al Sweet Mystery of Life, 1990; (plays) The Honeys, 1953; (screenplays) You Only Live Twice, 1967, Chitty Chitty Bang Bang, 1968, Willy Wonka and the Chocolate Factory, 1971; (autobiographies) Boy, 1984, Going Solo, 1986. Wing comdr. RAF, 1939-45. Recipient Edgar Allen Poe award Mystery Writers Am. Soc., 1954, 59. Home: Buckinghamshire Eng. Died Nov. 23, 1990; buried Cemetery at Ch. of St. Peter & St. Paul, Great Missendon, Buckinghamshire, England.

DAHLGREN, JOHN ONSGARD, lawyer; b. Missoula, Mont., Sept. 7, 1913; s. John and Geneva (Newhouse) D.; children: John Robert, Robin Reed. B.A., George Washington U., 1936; J.D., Georgetown U., 1939. Bar: D.C. 1939, Md. 1961. Chief counsel requisitioning div. Bd. Econ. Warfare, Washington, 1941-42; ptnr. firm Dahlgren & Close, Washington, from 1946. Pres. Internat. Humanities, Inc., from 1960; bd. dirs. Inter-Am. Bar Found. Served to comdr. USNR, 1942-45. Mem. Inter-Am. (sec.-gen. from 1967), Am., D.C. bar assns., Bar Assn. D.C. Clubs: Univ. (Washington), Internat. (Washington). Home: Bethesda Md. Died Mar. 13, 1989; buried Arlington Nat. Cemetery, Washington.

DAILY, JAMES WALLACE, engineering educator, consultant; b. Columbia, Mo., Mar. 19, 1913; s. Wallace Edgar and Marjory Isabel (McGrath) D.; m. Sarah Vanderlip Atwood, Sept. 10, 1938; children: John Wallace, Sarah Anne Vanderlip (Mrs. Charles Rosenberg). AB, Stanford U., 1935; MS, Calif. Inst. Tech., 1937, PhD, 1945. Registered profl. engr. Test engr. Byron Jackson Co., Berkeley, Calif., 1935; research asst. hydraulics Calif. Inst. Tech., 1936-37, research fellow, mgr. hydraulic machinery lab., 1937-40, instr. mech. engring., 1940-46; hydraulic engr. OSRD, Navy Research Projects, 1941-46; asst. prof. hydraulics MIT, 1946-49, asso. prof., 1949-55, prof., 1955-64; prof. engring. mechanics, chmn. dept. U. Mich., 1964-72, prof. fluid mechanics and hydraulic engring., 1972-81, prof. emeritus, from 1981; vis. prof. Tech. U. of Delft, Netherlands, 1971; vis. scientist Electricite de France Centre de Recherches et d'Essais, Paris, 1971; mem. U.S. del. water resources specialists to, People's Republic of China, 1974; vis. prof. East China Coll. Hydraulic Engring., Nanking, 1979; domestic and internat. cons. various firms. Author: (with D.R.F. Harleman) Fluid Dynamics, (with R.T. Knapp and F.G. Hammitt) Cavitation; Contbr. tech. articles Am., fgn. jours. Mem. sch. com. Town of Arlington, Mass., 1959-65. Recipient Naval Ordnance Devel. award, 1945. Mem. Nat. Acad. Engring., Internat. Assn. Hydraulic Research (hon. mem., pres. 1967-71, mem. Council 1963-65, 71-77), ASCE (Rouse lectr. 1985), ASME (hon.), Japan Soc. C.E. (hon.), Sigma Xi, Tau Beta Pi, Chi Epsilon. Congregationalist. Clubs: Athenaeum (Pasadena), Cosmos (Washington). Home: Pasadena Calif. Deceased. †

DALLIS, NICHOLAS PETER, comic strip writer, physician; b. N.Y.C., Dec. 15, 1911; s. Peter Nicholas and Sophia (Alexandre) D.; m. Sara Louise Luddy, May 29, 1939; children: Peter, Sally Dallis Anderson, Carolyn Dallis Uchman. AB, Washington and Jefferson Coll., 1933; MD, Temple U., 1938. Intern Washington (Pa.) Hosp., 1938-39; resident in psychiatry Henry Ford

Hosp., Detroit, 1941-45; practice medicine specializing in psychiatry Toledo, 1945-59. Creator comic strip Rex Morgan M.D, from 1948, Judge Parker, from 1952, Apt. 3-G, from 1961. Trustee Camelback Hosp., Phoenix. Recipient Decency award Kiwanis Internat., 1973, award on pub. health edn. AMA, 1954, Disting. Svc. award Pres.'s Com. Employment of Handicapped, 1954, Print Media award Nat. Fedn. Parents for Drug Free Youth, 1985. Charter fellow Am. Coll. Psychiatrists (life); mem. Am. Psychiat. Assn. (life). Home: Scottsdale Ariz. Died July 6, 1991; buried Green Acres, Scottsdale.

DALMAU, EDWARD MARTINEZ, bishop; b. Havana, Cuba, June 29, 1893; s. Cecil Martinez and Sophie Dalmau. Ed. philosophy and theology, Rome, 1908-16. Ordained priest Roman Cath. Ch. Prof. history and canon law Rome, 1917-26; bishop of Cienfuegos Cuba, 1933-61; titular bishop Euzi, West Palm Beach, Fla., 1961-87. Decorated officer Legion of Honor; great cross Carlos M. Cespeo (Cuba). Home: West Palm Beach Fla. Died Nov. 19, 1987.

DALTON, HARRY LEE, business executive; b. Winston-Salem, N.C., June 13, 1895; s. Rufus I. and Cora (McCanless) D.; m. Mary Keesler, Apr. 28, 1928; children: David McRae, Mary Elizabeth. AB, Duke U.; postgrad., NYU Coll. Tech. Vice chmn. bd. Am. Viscose Corp., Phila., N.Y.C.; chmn. bd. Charlotte br. Wachovia Bank & Trust Co., Blue Ridge Ins. Co.; pres. Kartex Oil Co.; dir. B & D Corp., Filatex Corp., Microtron Corp., Shaw Mfg. Co., Gastonia Theater Corp., The Beach Corp., Home Fin. Group, Carlton Yarn Mills, Wachovis Bank & Trust Co., Chemstrand Corp., Pyramid Life Ins. Co., Burlington Industries; mem. adv. bd. 45th St Br. Chase Nat. Bank, So. Dyestuff Corp.; chmn. exec. com. Am. Credit Corp.; mem. Washington Bd. Trade; chief silk and nylon sect. WPB, Washington, 1941-44; cons. Nat. Distbn. Coun., U.S. Dept. Commerce. Former editor: So. Textile Bull. Dir. Mint Mus.; dir. and mem. adv. coun. So. Rsch. Inst.; mem. nat. panel arbitrators Am. Arbitration Assn., Charlotte Meml. Hosp.; trustee The Pa. Hosp, Queens Coll., Textile Rsch. Inst., Princeton, Phila., Textile Inst., Crozer Theol. Sem.; mem. libr. com. Duke U.; dir. A. J. Ginsberg Found., Ludington Libr.; chmn. bd. visitors Davidson Coll.; chmn. patrons Queens Coll. Mem. (Clubs) Links, Univ. (N.Y.C.), Charlotte Country, Execs., Good Fellows (dir.), Rotary, Metropolitan (Washington), Pine Valley Country, Rittenhouse, Merion Cricket, Acorn, Philadelphia Country, Orpheus (Phila.), Old Town (Winston-Salem, N.C.). Democrat. Presbyterian. *

DALTON, TED, judge; b. Carroll County, Va., July 3, 1901; s. Curell and Lodoska Vernon (Martin) D.; m. Mary Turner, Jan. 4, 1932; 1 child, John N. AB, Coll. William and Mary, 1924, LLB, 1926; LLD (hon.), Milligan Coll., 1966. Bar: Va. 1923. Commonwealth's atty., Radford, Va., 1928-36; judge U.S. Dist. Ct. (we. dist.) Va., Roanoke, 1959-60, chief judge, 1960-73. Mem. Rep. Nat. Com., 1952-59; Rep. candidate for gov. Va., 1953, 57; U.S. senator from Va., 1944-59; mem. Commn. on Va. Constl. Revision, 1969. Recipient Disting. Service award Va. Trial Lawyers Assn., 1971, Commonwealth award James Madison U., 1983. Mem. ABA, Va. Bar Assn. (v.p. 1944), Montgomery-Radford-Floyd Bar Assn. (pres. 1948-49), Order Coif, Phi Beta Kappa, Alpha Kappa Psi, Omicron Delta Kappa, Sigma Nu, Phi Delta Phi. Baptist. Club: Flat Hat. Died Oct. 30, 1989. Home: Radford Va.

DALY, JOHN CHARLES, JR., radio and television consultant; b. Johannesburg, South Africa, Feb. 20, 1914; came to U.S., 1923; s. John Charles and Helene Grant (Tennant) D.; m. Margaret Criswell Neal, Jan. 7, 1937 (dec.); children: John Neal, John Charles, Helene Grant; m. Virginia Warren, Dec. 22, 1960; children: John Warren, John Earl Jameson, Nina. Student, Marist Bros. Coll., Johannesburg, 1920-23; grad., Tilton (N.H.) Sch., 1930; student, Boston Coll., 1930-33; D.Litt. (hon.), St. Bonaventure U., 1959; D.H.L. (hon.), Am. Internat. Coll., 1963; LL.D. (hon.), Norwich U., 1964. Schedule engr. Capital Transit Co., Washington, 1935-37; corr. and news analyst CBS, U.S., Europe and S.Am., 1937-49, spl. events reporter and White House corr., 1937-41; war corr. London and Mid. East, Italy, 1942-44; corr. ABC, N.Y.C., 1949-53, v.p. in charge of news, spl. events and pub. affairs, 1953-60; dir. Voice of Am., 1967-68; forum moderator Sound of Economy for Citibank N.Y., 1971-86, Am. Enterprise Inst., 1971-86; corr. Modern Maturity program, Pub. Broadcasting Sta., Washington, 1984-89; lectr., mem. Water Pollution Control Adv. Bd., 1960-62. Corr.-analyst, ABC; moderator programs on all networks (programs include) We Take Your Word, What's My Line, March of Time Thru the Years, News of the Week, etc., N.Y.C., 1949-53; currently narrating ednl. TV and radio series Modern Maturity; contbr. articles in nat. mags. Moderator Nat. Town Meeting, 1974; pres. bd. trustees emeritus Tilton (N.H.) Sch.; trustee emeritus Norwich U.; mem. Nat. Digestive Diseases Adv. Bd., NIH, 1982-87. Mem. Artists and Writers Assn., Internat. Radio and TV Soc. (past pres.), Assn. Radio News Analysts, Radio Corr. Assn., Sigma Delta Chi. Episcopalian. Clubs: Burning Tree, Columbia Country (Washington), , Overseas Press of America (past pres.), Met. (N.Y.C.), San Francisco Golf, The Family (San Francisco). Home: Chevy Chase Md. Died Feb. 25, 1991, buried Washington.

DALY, LLOYD WILLIAM, classics educator; b. Plano, Ill., Oct. 6, 1910; s. William H. and Jessie H. (Fidlar) D.; m. Alice Bernadine Abell, Aug. 22, 1935; children: Caryl Abell Daly Johnson, Sara Sue Daly Rothenberger. A.B., Knox Coll., 1932, Litt.D., 1955; M.A., U. Ill., 1933, Ph.D., 1936. Research asst. in classics U. Ill., 1936; acting prof. Greek, Kenyon Coll., 1937; mem. Am. Sch. Classical Studies in Athens, 1937-38, mem. mng. com., from 1953; from instr. to asso. prof. classical langs. and lit. U. Okla., 1938-47; assoc. prof. classical studies U. Pa., 1947-54, prof., 1954-77, Allen Meml. prof. Greek, 1958-77, prof. emeritus, 1977-89; chmn. dept. classical studies U. Pa., 1960-67, vice dean Grad. Sch. Art and Scis., 1951-52, acting dean, 1966, dean of Coll., 1952-59. Author: (with W. Suchier) The Altercatio Hadriani Augusti et Epicteti Philosphi, 1939, History of Alphabetization, 1967, Brito Metricus, 1968, (with Bernadine A. Daly) Summa Britonis, 1975, Johannes Philoponus on the Accent of Homonyms, 1983; editor and author in part of Graeco-Roman articles in: Thesaurus of Book Digests, 1949; assoc. editor: Classical Philology, 1953-55; translator, editor: Aesop Without Morals, 1961; contbr. to: Am. Illustrated Med. Dictionary; contbr. articles to learned jours. Guggenheim fellow, 1959-60. Mem. Am. Philos. Soc., Mediaeval Acad. Am., Am. Philol. Assn., Archaeol. Inst. Am., Classical Assn. Atlantic States, Pa. State Assn. Classical Tchrs., Phi Beta Kappa, Phi Kappa Phi, Eta Sigma Phi. Home: Englewood N.J. Died Feb. 26, 1989.

DALY, THOMAS FRANCIS, lawyer; b. N.Y.C., Dec. 30, 1902; s. Thomas F. and Josephine (Walsh) D.; m. Isabel Hope, Apr. 12, 1933 (dec. 1964); m. Virginia Barrett Melniker, June 16, 1966 (dec. Feb. 1988). Bar: N.Y., 1928, N.J., 1947. Student William and Mary Coll.; LLB, Columbia U., 1927. Assoc., ptnr. firm Lord, Day & Lord, N.Y.C., 1927-75, now of counsel; practiced in N.J., 1947; mem. Atty. Gen.'s Nat. Com. To Study Antitrust Laws; mem. N.Y. Supreme Ct. Med. Malpractice Panel, 1971—. Bd. dirs. Monmouth County Soc. for Prevention Cruelty to Animals, 1955-69 , Monmouth County chpt. ARC; trustee Monmouth Mus., 1974-88; mem. Rumson (N.J.) Sch. Bd., 1960-69. Fellow Am. Bar Found., N.Y. Bar Found., Am. Coll. Trial Lawyers; mem. ABA, N.Y. Bar Assn., N.J. Bar Assn., Guild Catholic Lawyers (gov. 1969-71). Clubs: Rumson (N.J.) Country; Root Beer and Checker (Red Bank, N.J.). Died Apr. 2, 1990. Home: Rumson N.J.

DAMMANN, RICHARD WEIL, lawyer; b. N.Y.C., Oct. 23, 1911; s. Milton and Reta (Weil) D.; m. Marjorie Spiegel, Aug. 22, 1935; children: Debora, Pamela, Penelope. A.B., Princeton U., 1932; LL.B., Harvard U., 1935. Bar: N.Y. 1935. Practiced in N.Y.C.; ptnr. law firm Dammann & Engel, 1935-88. Home: Rye N.Y. Died Dec. 26, 1988.

DAMMIN, GUSTAVE JOHN, medical educator; b. N.Y.C., Sept. 17, 1911; s. Gustave Frank and Anna Barbara (Anselm) D.; m. Anita Coffin, July 19, 1941; children: Susan, Tristram, Abigail. A.B., Cornell U., 1934, M.D., 1938; certificate in parasitology and tropical medicine, U. Havana, 1937; M.A. (hon.), Harvard, 1953. Diplomate Am. Bd. Pathology, Nat. Bd. Med. Examiners. Intern medicine Johns Hopkins Hosp., 1938-39; asst. resident in medicine Peter Bent Brigham Hosp., Boston, 1939-40, pathologist in chief, 1952-74, cons., from 1974; mem. adv. med. bd. Leonard Wood Meml., from 1969; acting chief lab. service West Roxbury VA Hosp., 1976-77, assoc. chief lab. service, 1978-81, cons., from 1981; instr. Columbia Coll. Phys. and Surg., 1940-41; asst. prof. pathology, then assoc. prof. Washington U. Med. Sch., St. Louis, 1946-50, prof., chmn. bd., 1950-52; prof. pathology Harvard Med. Sch., 1952-62, Elsie T. Friedman prof. pathology, 1962-78, prof. emeritus, from 1978; lectr. tropical public health Harvard Sch. Public Health, from 1978; Niles lectr. Cornell Med. Coll., 1953; Phi Delta Epsilon lectr. Yale Sch. Medicine, 1956; I.W. Held lectr. Beth Israel Hosp., N.Y.C., 1963; Wadsworth lectr. N.Y. Lab Soc., Syracuse, 1970; cons. to surgeon gen. Dept. of Army, USPHS; nat. cons. global preventive medicine and epidemiology to surgeon gen. USAF; lab. cons. OCDM, 1950-60; pres. Armed Forces Epidemiological Bd., 1960-73; sci. adv. bd. Armed Forces Inst. Pathology, 1961-71; WHO expert adv. panel on enteric diseases, chmn. com., 1963; mem. subcom. geographic Pathology NRC, 1962-65; bd. dirs. Gorgas Meml. Inst., from 1967; nat. cons. to surgeon gen. USAF, 1968; mem. sci. adv. com. N.E. Regional Primate Research Center; mem. com. Yugoslavian Endemic Nephropathy, HEW, 1970-75; Kidney adv. com. Joint Commn. Accreditation Hosps., 1972-76; mem. Cholera adv. com. NIH, from 1965 ; mem. internat. Centers Com. NIH, 1972; del. U.S.-Japan Co-op. Med. Scis. Program, Dept. State, from 1972. Editorial com.: Ann. Rev. Medicine, 1957-60, Human Pathology, from 1969; Editorial bd.: Jour. Infectious Diseases. Served from 1st lt. to lt. col. M.C. AUS, 1941-46; dir. labs. div. Office Surgeon Gen. 1945-46; col. Res. ret. Decorated Legion of Merit with oak leaf cluster; recipient Walter Reed medallion, 1971, Distinguished Pub. Service medal Dept. Def., 1973, cert. of appreciation for cons. service Armed Forces Epidemiol. Bd., Dept. Def. and Surgeon Gen. Army, 1984; award of distinction Cornell U. Med. Coll. Alumni Assn., 1975; co-recipient Sci. achievement award Kidney Found. Mass., 1979; Organism (tick cause of Lyme disease and babesiosis) Ixodes dammini named in his honor. Mem. Nat. Acad. Sci. (mem. ad hoc coms. div. med. sci. 1970), N.Y. Acad. Scis., Am. Soc. Clin. Investigation, Am. Assn. Pathologists and Bacteriologists, Internat. Acad. Pathology (exec. council), AMA (vice chmn. sect. pathology and physiology), Transplantation Soc., Am. Soc. Tropical Medicine and Hygiene, Am. Soc. Exptl. Pathology, Assn. Am. Physicians, NIH (tropical medicine and parasitology study sect.), Soc. Med. Cons. to the Armed Forces (pres. 1963), Infectious Diseases Soc. Am., Assn. Mil. Surgeons, Assn. U.S. Army, Japanese-Am. Soc. Pathologists, Assn. Mexican Pathologists, Korean Med. Assn., 38th Parallel Med. Soc. Korea, AAUP, Sons and Daus. of Nantucket (pres. 1974-77), Sigma Xi, Alpha Omega Alpha. Home: Weston Mass. Died Oct. 11, 1991.

DAMON, RICHARD WINSLOW, physicist; b. Concord, Mass., May 14, 1923; s. Winslow Johnson and Florence Mabel (Smith) D.; m. Anna M. Trotter, Aug. 4, 1946; children: Laura, Louise, Paul Trotter. B.S., Harvard U., 1944, M.A., 1947, Ph.D., 1952. Teaching fellow Harvard U., Cambridge, Mass., 1946-48, 49-50; engr. Raytheon Co., Waltham, Mass., 1948-49; research assoc. Gen. Electric Research Lab., Schenectady, 1951-60; dept. mgr. Microwave Control Devices, Microwave Assocs., Burlington, Mass., 1960-62; dir. Applied Physics Lab. Sperry Research Center, Sudbury, Mass., 1962-83; dir. tech. Sperry Corp., Waltham, 1983-86; cons., 1986-88, Gordon Inst., Wakefield, Mass., 1986-88; adv. group mem. on electronic materials NASA, 1967-71, adv. mem. subcom. on electrophysics, 1966-71, chmn., 1969-71, adv. com. on basic research, 1969-71; mem. evaluation panel to electromagnetic div. Nat. Bur. Standards, Nat. Acad. Sci./NRC, 1969-74, chmn., 1971-73; mem. adv. panel to Nat. Bur. Standards Inst. Basic Standards, 1971-73; mem. electronics study group, 1972-74; adv. group on electron devices, working group A, under-sec. for research and engring. Dept. Def., 1973-80; mem. external adv. com. Lab. Surface Sci. and Tech., U. Maine, 1981-84; mem. United Engring. Trustees, 1982-86; treas., mem. exec. com. John Fritz Medal bd. of awards; mem. fellowship com. Marconi Internat., 1984-87; vis. lectr. in applied physics Harvard U., 1962; lectr. Contbr. articles to profl. jours. Mem. Concord (Mass.) Spl. Sch. Salary Practices Com., 1964, Concord Comprehensive Town Plans Com., 1974-76. Served to lt. (j.g.) USNR, 1943-46, PTO. Fellow Am. Phys. Soc., AAAS, IEEE (pres. 1981, bd. dirs. 1977-78, 81-83, Centennial medal 1984); mem. IEEE Electron Devices Soc., IEEE Microwave Theory and Techniques Soc., IEEE Magnetics Soc., IEEE Soc. on Ultrasonics, Ferroelectrics and Frequency Control, NAE, Acad. Electromagnetics (adv. group on Electron Devices cert. of honor 1980), Sigma Xi. Republican. Home: Concord Mass. Deceased. †

DANAHER, JOHN ANTHONY, judge; b. Meriden, Conn., Jan. 9, 1899; s. Cornelius J. and Ellen (Ryan) D.; m. Dorothy King, Feb. 3, 1921; children—John A., Robert Cornelius, Jeanne. A.B., Yale U., 1920; postgrad., Yale Law Sch., 1922; LL.D. (hon.), Georgetown U., 1979. Bar: Conn. 1922. Law clk. White & Case, N.Y.C., 1921-22; practiced Hartford, Conn., and Washington, 1922-53; ptnr. law firm Danaher, Fahey & Poole, Washington, 1944; asst. U.S. atty., 1922-34; sec. State of Conn., 1933-35; U.S. senator, 1939-45; counsel Rep. Senatorial Com., 1946-53; U.S. circuit judge U.S. Ct. of Appeals, Washington, 1953-69; sr. U.S. circuit judge Hartford, Conn., 1969-80. Del. Republican Nat. Conv., 1944; Congl. aide Rep. Nat. Com., 1945-46; exec. dir. U.S. Senatorial Campaign, 1948; mem. Pres.'s Commn. Internal Security and Individual Rights, 1951; mem. Pres.'s Conf. Adminstrv. Procedure, 1953-54; dir. div. spl. activities Eisenhower campaign, 1952. Served as 2d lt. F.A., U.S. Army, 1918. Mem. D.C., Conn., Hartford County bar assns., Beta Theta Pi, Elihu. Republican. Roman Catholic. Club: Metropolitan (Washington). Home: West Hartford Conn. Died Sept. 22, 1990; buried Meridian, Conn.

D'ANDREA, ALBERT PHILIP, artist, educator; b. Benevento, Italy, Oct. 27, 1897; came to U.S., 1901, naturalized, 1911; s. Gregory and Emilia (Mainella) d'A.; m. Rose Castaldo, July 5, 1924; children: Gilbert, Philip. AB, CCNY, 1918; student, U. Rome, 1922. Instr. art Townsend Harris High Sch., 1918-35; asst. prof. CCNY, 1935-40, assoc. prof., 1940-48, prof., chmn. dept. art, from 1948, dir. planning and design of coll., from 1945. Creator medals including Bernard M. Baruch, 1954, Jonas E. Salk medal, 1955, George William Eggers medal, 1959, Edison award, 1959, Buell G. Gallagher medallion, 1961, Dr. Robert Hofstadter medal, 1962, James K. Hackett medal, 1964; (bronze bas-reliefs), Dr. W. B. Guthrie, 1939, Dean E. R. Mosher, 1946 (oil paintings); exhibited N.A.D., 1944, Nat. Sculpture Soc., 1951, 52, 54, 55, 57, 59-61, Audubon Artists Annual, 1953-61, Martha's Vineyard Art Workers Guild, 1953-56; represented collections Libr. of Congress, Mus. City of N.Y., N.Y. Hist. Soc., Smithsonian Instn., Hyde Park Meml. Libr., Bibliothèque Nationale, Biblioteca Apostolica Vaticans, Jewish Mus., N.Y.C. Recipient Alumni Svc. medal CCNY, 1933, also Townsend Harris medal, medal Engrs. of France, 1954, hon. academician Academia di

Belle Arti, Perugia, 1952. Fellow Royal Soc. Arts (London); mem. Coll. Art Assn., Bklyn. Soc. Artists, Audubon Artists, AAUP, Nat. Sculpture Soc. (Lindsey Morris prize 1963, James K. Hackett medal 1964), Phi Beta Kappa (chpt. pres. 1965). Roman Catholic. *

DANFORTH, DAVID NEWTON, physician, educator; b. Evanston, Ill., Aug. 25, 1912; s. William Clark and Gertrude (MacLean) D.; m. Gladys Blaine, 1938; 1 son, David Newton. B.S., Northwestern U., 1934, M.S., 1936, Ph.D., 1938, M.D., 1939. Diplomate Am. Bd. Obstetrics and Gynecology (dir. 1966-73, v.p. 1970-72). Intern N.Y. Postgrad. Hosp., N.Y.C., 1938-39; resident Sloane Hosp. for Women, Columbia U., 1939-44; clin. asst. obstetrics and gynecology Northwestern U. Med. Sch., 1946-47, asst. prof. obstetrics and gynecology, 1947-52, assoc. prof., 1952-59, prof., 1959-80, Thomas J Watkins prof. emeritus, from 1980, chmn., 1965-72; asst. attending obstetrician and gynecologist Wesley Meml. Hosp., Chgo., 1946-47, chmn. dept. obstetrics and gynecology, 1965-71; chief dept. obstetrics and gynecology Evanston Hosp., 1947-65. Co-author: Pregnancy, 1975, The Complete Guide to Pregnancy, 1984; editor, contbr.: Textbook of Obstetrics and Gynecology, 1966, 5th edit., 1986; Danforth's Obstetrics and Gynecology, 6th edit., 1990; contbr. articles to profl. jours. Served to lt. (s.g.), M.C. USNR, 1944-46. Recipient Capps prize for med. research, 1939, Gold Medal award Barren Found., 1965, Merit award Northwestern U., 1966, Silver Medal award Columbia, 1967. Mem. Am. Fertility Soc. (pres. 1963), ACS (gov. 1959-61), Soc. Gynecol. Investigation, Am. Gynecol. Soc. (council 1962-64, pres. 1974), Chgo. Gynecol. Soc. (pres. 1961), Am. Coll. Obstetricians and Gynecologists (1st v. p. 1969), Am. Gynecol. Club (pres. 1974), Am. Gynecol. and Obstet. Soc., Inst. Medicine Chgo., Soc. Exptl. Biology and Medicine, AAAS, AMA, Central Assn. Obstetricians and Gynecologists, Central Travel Club (sec. 1953-59, pres. 1960), Alpha Omega Alpha, Sigma Xi, Pi Kappa Epsilon. Home: Evanston Ill. Died Jan. 22, 1990.

DANIEL, JAQUELIN JAMES, lawyer, corporate executive, newspaper publisher; b. Jacksonville, Fla., Sept. 22, 1916; s. Richard Potts and Mary Goff (Palmer) D.; m. Anne Page Coachman, Oct. 18, 1947; children: Eleanor Page Daniel McCranie, Jaquelin Daniel Cook. AB, Princeton U., 1939; LLB, U. Fla., 1942; LLD (hon.), Fla. State U., 1965, U. N.Fla., 1989. Bar: Fla. 1942. Mem. firm Daniel & Daniel, Jacksonville, 1942-60; pres., chmn. exec. com. Stockton, Whatley, Davin & Co., Jacksonville, 1960-76; chmn. exec. com. Ponte Vedra Co.; pub. Fla. Times Union and Jacksonville Jour., 1976-83; dir. First Union Bancorp., Am. Gen. Corp., Freeport McMoran, CSX Corp. Pres. United Way, 1955, 62; mem. bd. control Fla. Instns. Higher Learning, 1957-61, chmn., 1959-61; chmn. Duval County Local Govt. Study Commn., 1965-67; del. Democratic Nat. Conv., 1956; chmn. bd. visitors Davidson Coll., 1965; trustee Daniel Meml. Home for Children; chmn. bd. trustees George Peabody Coll., 1967-70; mem., chmn. bd. regents State Univ. System, 1971-82; pres. Evergreen Cemetery Assn., 1956; trustee Princeton U., 1972-76, Episcopal Ch. Found.; pres. Gator Bowl Assn.; pres. Community Council on Citizen Involvement. Served from ensign to lt. comdr. USNR, 1942-45. Decorated Bronze Star; recipient Disting. Service award U.S. Jaycees, 1950; Disting. Citizen award Nat. Mcpl. League, 1968; Brotherhood award NCCJ, 1970. Mem. Jacksonville Hist. Soc. Kappa Alpha. Democrat. Episcopalian. Clubs: Florida Yacht (Jacksonville) (commodore 1956), River (Jacksonville) (past pres.), Timuquana Country (Jacksonville), Ponte Vedra (Jacksonville); Princeton (N.Y.C.). Home: Jacksonville Fla. Died Aug. 7, 1990.

DANIEL, ROBERT EDWIN, investment banker; b. Joplin, Mo., Aug. 19, 1906; s. Robert Brown and Lilian (Boswell) D.; m. Margaret Moir, July 16, 1932; children: Robert William, Phillip Merrill, Linda Jane. A.B. magna cum laude, Ottawa U., 1927; LL.D., Whitworth Coll., 1971. With Blyth & Co., 1928-31, Pacific Northwest Co., Seattle, 1931-41, 46-66; pres. Pacific Northwest Co., 1959-66; v.p. United Pacific Corp.; ret., 1961; Chmn. regional bus. conduct com. Nat. Assn. Securities Dealers, 1959-60; gov. Midwest Stock Exchange, 1959-60. Trustee, treas. Wash.-Alaska Synod United Presbyn. Ch., dir. finance, 1966-72; trustee United Presbyn. Found., 1973-82. Served to maj. AUS, 1941-45. Republican. Presbyn. (elder). Home: Seattle Wash. Died, Sept. 2, 1992. †

DARBAKER, JAMES MATEER, steel executive; b. Vandergrift, Pa., Nov. 19, 1898; s. Isaac Kinnard and Elizabeth (Mateer) D.; m. Agnes Gibson, Oct. 22, 1923. BS in Mech. Engring., U. Mich., 1920. Master mechanic Am. Sheet & Tin Plate Co., 1926-36; gen. supt. Gary Sheet & Tin Mill, Carnegie Illinois Steel Corp., 1936-43; asst. mgr. to mgr. ops. Gary Sheet & Tin Mill, Carnegie Illinois Steel Corp., Chgo. dist., 1943-49, gen. mgr. sales, 1949-53; sr. v.p., dir. Copperweld Steel Co., Pitts., 1954-55, pres., dir., 1955-57, pres., CEO, 1957-64, chmn., from 1964. Mem. Sigma Xi, Tau Beta Pi. *

DARCY, THOMAS FRANCIS, JR., conductor; b. Vancouver, Wash., May 7, 1895; s. Thomas Francis and Jose Lea (Harrell) D.; m. Neyna Colomo, Jan. 20, 1948 (div.). Grad., Band Leaders & Musicians Sch., Chaumont, France, 1919; student, Inst. Musical Art, N.Y.C., 1922-23; grad. with highest honors, Army Music Sch., 1926. Pres. Somerset Music Press, from 1952; Pvt., 2d F.A. band U.S. Army, playing coronet, 1912; served 2 yrs. Philippines; sgt. 18th Inf., 1915; asst. band leader/ band leader; with 18th Inf. 1st Div. A.E.F., 1918-20 (wounded Nov. 1, 1918); cited for gallant conduct; designated rep. Am. band leader, conducted composite 1st Div. Band on concert tour; became asst. leader, The Army Band, 1926; promoted to capt. and leader, The Army Band, 1935; dean Army Music Sch., Washington; apptd. adviser to War Dept. on matters relative to bands, 1940. Author tng. manuals.; compiled and arranged Nat. Anthems of UN, adopted by U.S. Army as ofcl. Compositions, including: An American Overture, Legende, Vanguard of Victory, From Foreign Parts, With Flags Unfurled, Fantasy for 3 Trumpets, Fireflies, The Spirit of Freedom, Tripoli, Flashing Sabres, Battle Brigade, Range Riders, Blazing Guns, The Somerset Suite (3 parts), The Frosty Sons of Thunder, Nostalgia, Maple Festival. Decorated Silver Star, Purple Heart, Verdun medal, Victory medal with 5 stars, French Fourregere. Mem. Am. Bandmasters Assn., ASCAP, Kappa Kappa Psi. *

DARLEY, JOHN GORDON, psychologist, educational administrator; b. Pitts., Feb. 20, 1910; s. William Watson and Edith (Gordon) D.; m. Kathleen Berry McConnon, Aug. 15, 1936 (div. May 1975); children: John McConnon, Janet Berry Darley Griffith; m. Janet M. Hively, Nov. 26, 1976. BA, Wesleyan U., 1931; MA, U. Minn., 1932, PhD, 1937. Diplomate Am. Bd. Profl. Psychology; lic. consulting psychologist, Minn. Dir. student counseling bur. U. Minn., Mpls., 1935-43, 46-47, assoc. dean grad. sch., 1947-59, chmn. psychology dept., 1963-75, prof. psychology, 1975-78, prof. emeritus, from 1978. Author numerous monographs, books, tech. reports, articles to profl. and scholarly jours.; editor Jour. Applied Psychology, 1955-60, Am. Psychologist, 1959-62, Psychol. Documents, 1982-85. Lt. USNR, 1944-46. Decorated Strong Meml. medal for rsch. in interest measurement, 1966. Fellow Am. Psychol. Assn. (exec. officer, Washington 1959-62), Minn. Psychol. Assn. (award for disting. contbns. 1982), Phi Beta Kappa, Sigma Xi. Club: Cosmos (elected mem.). Home: Minneapolis Minn. Died Sept. 6, 1990; buried Mpls.

DARLING, STEPHEN FOSTER, chemistry educator; b. Desmet, S.D., May 1, 1901; s. Andrew Delos and Harriet Elizabeth (Sturgeon) D.; m. Delphine Deziel, Aug. 20, 1930; children: Stephen Deziel, Charlotte Elizabeth, Anne Marie, Andrew Delos. BS, U. Minn., 1922, MS, 1924; AM, Harvard U., 1926, PhD, 1928. Instr. Harvard U., 1926-28; Sheldon traveling fellow, 1928-29; assoc. prof. Lawrence Coll. (now Lawrence U.), Appleton, Wis., 1929-37, Robert McMillan prof., head dept. chemistry, 1937-66, prof. emeritus, 1966-91; rsch. assoc. Inst. Paper Chemistry, Appleton, 1930-70. Sec. Valley Coop. Svcs. 1st lt. C.W.S. Res., 1926-36. Fellow Am. Inst. Chemists; mem. Am. Chem. Soc., Photog.Soc. Am., Am. Philatelic Soc., Soc. Philatelic Ams., Wis. Acad. Arts, Scis. and Letters (pres. 1956), Sigma Xi, Alpha Chi Sigma, Gamma Alpha, Phi Lambda Upsilon. Home: Appleton Wis. Died Oct. 14, 1990; buried Appleton, Wis.

DAUTERMAN, CARL CHRISTIAN, museum curator; b. Newark, July 25, 1908; s. Charles and Emma Pauline (Reiff) D.; m. Felicia Marie Sterling, Feb. 12, 1942; children—Eunice Gay, Gail Dana, Merrill Edith. B.A., NYU, 1949; M.A. in Art History, Columbia U., 1960. First asst. sci. dept. Newark Mus., 1929-38; spl. exhbns. mgr. Cooper Hewitt Mus., N.Y.C., 1938-46; catalogue writer Parke-Bernet Galleries, N.Y.C., 1946-54; adj. prof. Columbia U., 1951-85; curator Western European Decorative Arts, Met. Mus. Art, N.Y.C., 1954-73, curator emeritus, 1973-89; cons. Campbell Mus., Camden, N.J., 1972-13 , trustee, from 1973, Krannert Art Mus., Champaign, Ill., from 1975; guest archaeologist Mexican Govt. Field Expedition, Monte Alban, 1936. Contbr. articles to profl. jours. Author: (with James Parker and Edith Standen) Decorative Art from the Samuel H. Kress Collection at the Met. Mus. of Art, 1964, Sèvres, 1968, The Wrightsman Collection, vols. III, IV, 1970, Sèvres Porcelain: Makers and Marks, XVIIIth Century, 1986. Served with U.S. Army, 1942-45. Mem. Am. Ceramic Circle (1st pres. 1970-72, founding trustee 1970—), Am. Soc. Eighteenth-Century Studies. Episcopal. Avocations: mineral collecting; nature studies. Died Nov. 22, 1989. Home: New York N.Y.

DAVID, DONALD KIRK, foundation executive; b. Moscow, Idaho, Feb. 15, 1896; s. Frank Alva and Ella (Jameson) B.; m. Elizabeth Souien, Aug. 30, 1917; children: Helen Jameson, Philip Kirk. AB, U. Idaho, 1916, LLD (hon.), 1941; MBA, Harvard U., 1919, LLD (hon.), 1948; LLD (hon.), St. Lawrence U., 1947, Washington & Lee U., 1949, Northeastern U., 1951, Carleton Coll., 1952, Colgate U., 1954, UCLA, 1964; LittD (hon.), U. Western Ontario, 1951, Ohio U., 1952. Instr. grad. sch. bus. adminstrn. Harvard U., 1919-21, asst. dean, 1920-27, asst. prof. mktg., 1921-26, assoc. prof., 1926-27, assoc. dean, 1942, dean, 1942-55; vice chmn. bd. The Ford Found.; exec. v.p. Royal Baking Powder Co., 1927-29, pres., 1929-30; v.p. Standard Brands, Inc., 1929-30, Gt. Island Corp., 1930-41; dir. City Investing Co., Gustin-Bacon Mfg. Co., R. H. Macy & Co., Pan Am. World Airways, Inc., Aluminium, Ltd., Ford Motor Co., The Great Atlantic & Pacific Tea Co., Sinclair Oil Corp. Author: Retail Store Management Problems, 1922, (with Malcolm P. McNair) Problems in Retailing, 1926. Mem. Bus. Coun.; chmn. bd. Com. Econ. Devel., 1957-62; mem. bd. trustees Rockefeller Inst., Ford Found. With USN, WWI. Decorated Order of Orange-Nassua. Mem. Phi Beta Kappa, Phi Delta Theta, Order of St. Olaf, Fifth Ave Club, Univ. Club, Links Club, Sky Club (N.Y.C.), Mill Reef Club, Wianne Club. Republican. Conglist. *

DAVIDSON, IAN DOUGLAS, bank executive; b. Isle of Man, U.K., Oct. 27, 1901; s. John and Elizabeth Whyte D.; m Eugenia Bermejillo, Aug. 6, 1938; children: Claire Peppiatt, Monica. Crad., King Williams Coll., 1920. With Royal Dutch Shell Group, 1921-61; pres. Mexican Eagle Oil Co., 1935-48, Cia Shell de Venezuela, 1953-57, Can. Shell Ltd., 1957-61. Trustee Toronto Ont., Can. Gen. Hosp., Ont. Mental Health Found., 1964—; founder chmn. Clarke Inst. Psychiatry, Toronto; gov. U. Toronto. Decorated comdr Order Brit. Empire, Orden del Libertador Venezuela , Order St. Mark Lebanon . Presbyterian. Home: Wimbledon Eng. Deceased.

DAVIDSON, JAMES JOSEPH, JR., lawyer; b. Lafayette, La., June 24, 1904; s. James Joseph and Lilla May (Kennedy) D.; m. Virginia L. Dunham, Aug. 6, 1930; 1 son, James Joseph III. Student, Southwestern La. Inst., 1919-22; A.B., Tulane U., 1925, J.D., 1927. Bar: La. bar 1927. Practiced in New Orleans, 1927-29, Lafayette, from 1929; mem. firm Davidson, Meaux, Sonnier, McElligott; Mem. La. Supreme Ct. Bar Examining Com., 1936-50. Vice pres. La. Civil Service League; mem. exec. com. Evangeline Area council Boy Scouts Am., pres., 1967-68; mem. La. Commn. on Human Relations Rights and Responsibilities, 1965-70; bd. dirs. Council for a Better La., Public Affairs Research Corp.; La. com. Pres.' Cabinet Com. on Edn. Fellow Am. Bar Found., Southwestern Legal Found.; mem. Assn. of Bar of City of N.Y., La. Judiciary Commn. (1970-74), Nat. Mcpl. League (mem. council 1969-73), Internat. Assn. Ins. Counsel, ABA (mem. ho. of dels. 1964-68, 73-75), La. Bar Assn. (pres. 1958), Lafayette Bar Assn., 15th Jud. Dist. Bar Assn., Am. Law Inst., La. Law Inst. Council (pres. 1973-77), Am. Counsel Assn., Am. Judicature Soc., Am. Coll. Trial Lawyers, Am. Coll. Probate Counsel, Lafayette C. of C. (past pres.), Lafayette Library Assn. (past pres.), Lafayette Community Concert Assn. (past pres.), Order Coif, Phi Alpha Delta, Phi Kappa Phi. Methodist. Clubs: Petroleum, City (Lafayette); Internat. House, Boston (New Orleans). Lodges: Masons, Rotary (past pres. Lafayette chpt.). Home: Lafayette La. Died May 22, 1990; buried Lafayette, La.

DAVIDSON, LEROY, grocery co-operative executive; b. 1920; married. Pres. Twin County Grocers, Inc., Edison, N.J., 1976-83, chmn., from 1983, also dir. Served with U.S. Army, 1942-45. Home: Edison N.J. Deceased. †

DAVIDSON, MARSHALL BOWMAN, magazine editor, author; b. N.Y.C., Apr. 26, 1907; s. Henry F. and Frances Aubrey (Holt) D.; m. Ruth H. Bradbury, Aug. 20, 1935 (dec. 1979). B.S., Princeton, 1928. Assoc. curator Am. wing Met. Mus. Art, N.Y.C., 1935-47, editor publs., 1947-61; mng. editor Horizon Books, 1961-63; editor Horizon mag., 1964-66, sr. editor, from 1966. Author: Life in America, 1951, The American Heritage History of Colonial Antiques, 1967, The American Heritage—History of American Antiques, 1784-1860, 1968, The American Heritage—History of Antiques, USA, 1865-1917, 1969, Bantam Book of Early American Furniture, 1980, The American Wing, A Guide, 1980, (with others) The History of the 20's and 30's, 1970, The American Heritage—History of Notable American Houses, 1971, A Concise History of France, 1971, The Artists' America, 1973, The Writers' America, 1973, Great Historic Places of Europe, 1974, The World in 1776, 1975, Fifty Early American Tools, 1975, The Drawing of America, 1983, 500 Years of Life in America, 1987, Treasures of the New York Public Library, 1988; contbg. author: The Romance of North America, 1958, America and Russia, 1962, ; contbr.: Dictionary American Biography; editor, commentator: A Pictorial History of Architecture in America, 2 vols., 1976, A Pictoral History of New York State, 1977; also articles in Am. decorative art jours., others.; adv. editor: Am. Heritage mag.; editor: The Original Water-color Paintings of John J. Audubon, 1966. Home: New York N.Y. Died Aug. 8, 1990; cremated.

DAVIES, JOHN SHERRARD, international trading company executive; b. Delphos, Ohio, Apr. 4, 1917; s. Homer M. and Elizabeth (Sherrard) D.; m. Marie Donat, July 8, 1940; children: John Morgan, Anne Donat Davies Hunter. B.A., Ohio Wesleyan U., 1939. Exec. Bell Telephone System, 1941-69; spl. asst. to Pres. Nixon and; dir. Office White House Visitors, 1969-71; dir. Hawaii-Pacific dist. office Industry and Trade Adminstrn., Dept. Commerce, 1971-79; pres. Davies & McMurtray, Ltd., Honolulu, 1979-83; mem. Nat. Visitor Facilities Adv. Commn., 1969-71; exec. sec. Hawaii Dist. Export Council; mem. policy com. Honolulu-

Pacific Fed. Exec. Bd.; Mem. Gov.'s Adv. Com. for Hawaii World Trade Center. Served to capt. USAAF, 1942-46. Decorated Bronze Star; Order Brit. Empire. Mem. Hawaii World Trade Assn., Hawaiian Businessmen's Assn., Air Force Assn., Navy League U.S., Sigma Chi, Omicron Delta Kappa, Gamma Phi. Lodge: Rotary (Honolulu). Home: Atascadero Calif. Died Feb. 1, 1990; buried Greentown, Ohio.

DAVIES, RALPH KENNETH, business executive; b. Cherrydale, Va., Sept. 9, 1897; s. Percival and Nellie (Waldron) D.; m. Louise Stivers, Aug. 29, 1927; children: Maryon Davies Lewis, Ellen Rush, Alice. Student, Fresno High Sch., 1909-12; spl. studies, U. Calif. Ext., Berkeley, San Francisco. With Standard Oil Co., Calif., 1912-46; dir. Standard Oil Co., 1930-42, sr. v.p., 1935-46; with Anglo Am. Oil Co., Eng., 1928-29; organizer and exec. v.p. Internat. Bitumen Emulsions Co., 1929, pres., 1938-41; exec. v.p. Standard Stations, Inc., 1930-38, pres., 1938-40; pres. Trunkline Gas Supply Co., 1947-49, dir., 1947-52; pres., dir. Am. Ind. Oil Co., 1947-58, Am. Ind. Oil de Mexico, S.A. de C.V., 1949-58, Am. Ind. Oil Co. Iran, 1955-58; dir., chmn. bd. Am. Ind. Oil Co., 1958-62; chmn. bd. dirs. Ind. Tankships Inc., 1948-57; dir. chmn. exec. com. Golden State Co. Ltd., 1948-54; bd. dirs. Am. Pres. Lines, from 1948, chmn. bd. from 1952; pres., dir. APL Assocs. Inc., 1952-56; chmn. bd., dir. Natomas Co., from 1956, Natomas Co. Peru, from 1961, St. Mary's Sq. Inc., from 1961; dir. Bank of Calif., from 1956, others. Trustee Franklin Hosp., San Francisco; chmn. FTC Code Com., 1936; pres. Fair Practices Assn. (Petroleum Products), 1937-39; dep. petroleum adminstr. Petroleum Adminstrn. for War, 1942-46; mem. Pres.'s Mission to London to negotiate Anglo-American oil treaty; spl. cons. to sec. of the interior, 1946-47. Awarded Presdl. Medal for Merit in recognition of disting. war svc., 1945. Mem. Calif. C. of C. (dir. 1935-41), Pacific Union Club, Menlo Country Club (San Francisco), Sulgrave Club (Washington). *

DAVIS, BETTE RUTH ELIZABETH, actress; b. Lowell, Mass., Apr. 5, 1908; d. Harlow Morrell and Ruth (Favor) D.; m. Harmon Oscar Nelson, Jr., Aug. 18, 1932 (div.); m. Arthur Farnsworth, Dec. 1940 (dec. Aug. 25, 1943); m. William Grant Sherry, Nov. 30, 1945; 1 child, Barbara Davis; m. Gary Merrill, Aug. 1950 (div.); adopted children: Margot, Michael. Ed., Cushing Acad., Ashburnham, Mass. Began as stage and motion picture actress 1931; pictures include Dangerous (Acad. award Best Actress 1935), The Petrified Forest, Jezebel (Acad. award Best Actress 1938), Dark Victory, Juarez, The Old Maid, The Private Lives of Elizabeth and Essex, The Great Lie, The Bride Came C.O.D, All About Eve, 1950, Payment on Demand, 1951, Phone Call from a Stranger, 1952, The Star, 1953, The Virgin Queen, 1955, Storm Center, The Catered Affair, 1956, John Paul Jones, 1959, The Scapegoat, 1959, What Ever Happened to Baby Jane, Dead Ringer, Painted Canvas, 1963, Where Love Has Gone, Hush, Hush, Sweet Charlotte, 1964, The Nanny, The Anniversary, 1967, Connecting Rooms, 1969, Bunny O'Hare, 1970, Madam Sin, 1971, The Game, 1972, Burnt Offerings, 1977, Death on the Nile, 1979, Watcher in the Woods, 1979, The Whales of August, 1987; TV movies Sister Aimee, 1977, The Dark Secret of Harvest Home, 1978, Strangers (Emmy award 1979), White Momma, 1980, Skyward, 1980, Family Reunion, 1981, A Piano for Mrs. Cimino, 1982, Little Gloria-Happy at Last, 1982, Right of Way, 1983 (pilot) Hotel, 1983, Murder with Mirrors, 1984, As Summers Die, 1985; appeared in play The Night of the Iguana, 1961; The Musical, Two's Company, 1952; and Miss Moffett, 1974. Author: The Lonely Life, 1962; (with Michael Herskowitz) This 'N That, 1987; co-author: Mother Goddam, 1974. Recipient Am. Film Inst. Life Achievement award, Rudolph Valentino Life Achievement award, 1982, Am. Acad. Arts award, 1983, Disting. Pub. Service medal Dept. Def., 1983, Crystal award Women in Films, 1983, Cesar award French Film Inst., 1986, Order Arts et Belles Lettres, French Ministry Culture, 1986, Legion of Honor French Ministry Culture, 1987, Kennedy Ctr. Honors medallion, 1987, Life Achievement award Film Soc. Lincoln Ctr., 1989, Acting Career award San Sebastian Film Festival, Spain, 1989. Home: West Hollywood Calif. Died Oct. 6, 1989; buried Forest Lawn Cemetery, Beverly Hills, Calif.

DAVIS, BRAD, actor; b. Fla., Nov. 16, 1949. Actor: (stage prodns.) The Elusive Angel, 1977, Entertaining Mr. Sloane, 1981, Metamorphosis, 1982, The Normal Heart, 1985, Crystal and Fox, (feature films) Midnight Express, 1978, A Small Circle of Friends, 1980, Chariots of Fire, 1981, Querelle, 1982, Cold Steel, 1987, (TV mini-series) Roots, 1977, Chiefs, 1983, Robert Kennedy and His Times, 1985, (TV movies) Sybil, 1976, A Rumor of War, 1980, Blood Ties, 1986, Vengeance, 1986, When the Time Comes, 1987. Home: Studio City Calif. Died Sept. 8, 1991. †

DAVIS, DEANE CHANDLER, former governor, lawyer; b. East Barre, Vt., Nov. 7, 1900; s. Earl Russell and Lois (Hillary) D.; m. Corinne Eastman, June 14, 1924 (dec. Mar. 9, 1951); children—Deane (dec.), Marian Davis Calcagni, Thomas C.; m. Marjorie Smith Conzelman, July 5, 1952. LL.B., Boston U., 1922, LL.D., 1969; LL.D., U. Vt., 1957, Middlebury Coll., 1964; Litt.D. (hon.), Norwich U., 1963, D.Pub.Service (hon.), 1976. Bar: Vt. 1922. Practiced law Barre, Vt., 1922-31, 36-40; city atty. Barre, 1924-26, 28-30; states atty. Washington County, Vt., 1926-28; superior judge State of Vt., 1931-36; mem. Wilson, Carver, Davis & Keyser, Barre and Chelsea, Vt., 1936-40; gen. counsel Nat. Life Ins. Co., 1940-50, v.p., 1943-50, pres., chief exec. officer, 1950-66, chmn. bd., chief exec. officer, 1966-67, chmn. bd., 1967-68, also dir., mem. adv. com.; gov. State of Vt., 1969-73; mem. Barre City Council, 1923-24; mem. adv. bd. Union Mut. Fire Ins. Co.; bd. dirs. Bertex, Inc., Swxnton and St. Albans, Vt. Author: Justice in the Mountains, 1980, Nothin' But The Truth, 1982, Deane C. Davis, An Autobiography, 1991. Pres. Vt. State C. of C., 1942-43; del. Republican Conv., 1948, 72, mem. resolutions com., 1948; pres. Calvin Coolidge Meml. Found.; bd. dirs. Life Ins. Med. Research Fund, 1955-57, Mary Fletcher Hosp., 1955-59; pres., mng. dir. Coop. Health Info. Center Vt., 1973-75, bd. dirs., 1973-77. Recipient Haugen award Vt. Soc. Public Adminstrs., 1980. Mem. ABA (gov. 1945-48, chmn. Vt. com. representing council on legal edn. and admissions to bar), Vt. Bar Assn. (pres. 1942), Life Ins. Assn. Am. (dir. 1953-63, pres. 1959-60), Am. Life Conv. (v.p.), Inst. Life Ins. (dir. 1961-64, chmn. bd. 1963), Am. Judicature Soc., Vt. Morgan Horse Assn. (chmn. bd.), Am. Morgan Horse Assn. (pres. 1963-64), Green Mountain Horse Assn. (v.p.), Delta Theta Phi. Methodist. Lodges: Masons, K.P. Home: Montpelier Vt. Died Dec. 8, 1990; buried Elmwood Cemetery, Barre, Vt.

DAVIS, FRANCIS A., business executive; b. Balt., July 25, 1893; s. E. Asbury and Jennie C. Davis; m. Antoinette Biggs, Oct. 10, 1916; children: Dorothy Peck, Antoinette Crocker, Margaret Stockbridge, Francis Jr. Student, Boys Latin Sch., Balt., 1901-10; AB, Johns Hopkins U., 1914. Bookkeeper to v.p. F.A. Davis and Sons, Balt.; dir. Balt. Transit Co., U.S. Fidelity and Guaranty Co., Sandura Co., Phila. Chmn. adv. com. Dept. Pub. Welfare; trustee Goucher Coll.; pres. bd. trustees Roland Park Country Sch. Mem. Delta Upsilon, Johns Hopkins Club, Merchants Club (Balt.). *

DAVIS, HARRY, engineer, consultant; b. N.Y.C., Dec. 2, 1909; s. Joseph and Annie (Goldner) D.; m. Fay Oxhorn, 1931. B.S., Coll. City N.Y., 1931, E.E., 1933; M.E.E., Poly. Inst. Bklyn., 1948, Sc.D., 1973. Project engr. design and devel. meteorol. direction finders Signal Corps, sect. chief in charge devel. nav. systems, 1940-45; in charge devel. nav. equipment Air Force Watson Lab., 1945-50; chief (Nav. Lab.), 1949-51; tech. and sci. dir. Rome Air Devel. Center, 1951-60; dep. for research asst. sec. Air Force, Washington, 1960-66; dep. asst. sec. research and devel. Air Force, 1966-68; dep. under sec. systems rev. Office Under Sec. Air Force, 1968-73; pres. Systems Rev. Assos., Inc., Arlington, Va., from 1973; Lectr. U. Cal. at Los Angeles, 1966-75; faculty elec. engring. staff Columbia, from 1956; mem. sci. adv. com. Harry Diamond Labs., US Army; mem., chmn. panels Def. Dept. Recipient George W. Goddard award Soc. Photog. Instrumentation Engrs., 1969; citation of honor Air Force Assn., 1969; named Man of Year award Hap Arnold chpt., 1970; Distinguished Alumni award Poly. Inst. Bklyn., 1973. Fellow IEEE (Harry Diamond Meml. award 1968, Man of Yr. award 1976), Am. Optical Soc., AAAS; mem. Am. Ordnance Assn., Am. Phys. Soc., Sigma Xi. Home: Falls Church Va. Deceased. †

DAVIS, JACQUELINE MARIE VINCENT (MRS. LOUIS REID DAVIS), child development educator, academic administrator; b. Birmingham, Ala.; d. Jud Fred and Marie (Yates) Vincent; m. Louis Reid Davis, July 17, 1943. A.B. cum laude, Birmingham So. Coll., 1943; M.A., Columbia, U., 1950; M.S., U. Ala., 1958, Ed.D., 1961; postgrad., U. Va., George Washington U. Tchr. Fork Union (Va.) Mil. Acad., 1943-46; tchr. Fork Union (Va.) Mil. Acad., Ft. Belvoir, Va., 1946-48; tchr., adminstrv. asst., supr. Quantica (Va.) Post schs., 1950-52; instr., prof. dept. child devel. and family life U. Ala. Sch. Home Econs., 1952-57, assoc. prof., 1957-67; prof. child devel., dir. U. Ala. Sch. Home Econs. (Child Devel. Ctr.), from 1967; mem. grad. council, adminstr. head start tng. program, dir. U. Ala. Sch. Home Econs. (Ala. Presch. Inst.), from 1964; mem. NASA scholarship selection bd. U. Ala., 1966; mem. Gov.'s Advisory Com. on Day Care, 1963-66, State Adv. Com. on Children and Youth, from 1960; coordinator Head Start supplementary tng. programs State of Ala. Contbr. articles to profl. jours. Adviser, mem. selection com. Tombigbee council Girl Scouts U.S.A., 1961-66; cons. Tuscaloosa Community Action Program, 1965-66; chmn. Ala. Advisory Com. Children and Youth, from 1978. Mem. Nat. Assn. for Edn. of Young Children (mem. planning bd. 1963-64), U.S. Nat. Com. for Early Childhood Edn., World Orgn. for Early Childhood Edn., Southeastern Council Family Relations, So. Assn. Children Under Six (pres. 1961, mem. exec. bd. from 1961, chmn. 19th ann. conf.), Ala. Assn. Children Under Six (pres. 1963-64), Ala. Home Econs. Assn. (chmn. profl. sect. family life and child devel. from 1963, v.p. mem. governing bd. 1969-70), Comparative Edn. Soc., NEA, Am. Home Econs. Assn., Phi Beta Kappa, Kappa Delta Pi, Kappa Delta Epsilon. Methodist. Home: Tuscaloosa Ala. Died Dec. 11, 1989; buried Birmingham, Ala.

DAVIS, JOHN EDWARD, government official, banker, rancher; b. Mpls., Apr. 18, 1913; s. James Ellsworth and Helen (Wilson) D.; m. Pauline Huntley, June 4, 1938 (div.Jan. 1978); children: John Edward, Richard James, Kathleen Anne (dec.); m. Marilyn Westlie, Dec. 13, 1980. BS, U. N.D., 1935. Farmer, rancher Wells & Sheridan Counties, N.D., from 1935; banker then chmn. bd. First Nat. Bank, McClusky, N.D., from 1935; mem. N.D. Senate, 1952-56; gov. State of N.D., 1956-60; bd. dirs. Provident Life Ins. Co., Bismarck, N.D., 1959; former dir. Fed. Civil Def. Mayor of McClusky, 1946-52. Decorated Silver Star, Bronze Star, Purple Heart; recipient Sioux award for Disting. Svc. and Outstanding Achievements, 1966, U.S. Dept. Defense Disting. Civilian Svc. medal, 1978, Greater N.D. Assn. Svc. award. Mem. Am. Legion (nat. comdr. 1967-68), DAV, Masons, Shriners, Elks. Republican. Lutheran. Home: Bismark N.D. Died May 12, 1990; interred Fairview Cemetery, Bismark, N.D.

DAVIS, JONATHAN FARR, advertising executive; b. Auburn Twp., Pa., Aug. 15, 1893; s. Clarke E. and Minnie (Farr) D.; m. Mae L. Clark, Jan. 22, 1925; children: Jean A. Lang, Nancy M. Nyhan. BS in Agr., U. Del., 1918. Ext. specialist agrl. econs. U. Del., 1919-20; country agrl. agt. U. Md., 1920-21; agrl. mktg. N.W. Ayer & Son., Phila., 1922-24; with Griswold Eshleman Co., Cleve., from 1924; chmn., treas. Griswold Eshleman Co., from 1957; pub. The Delaware Farmer; dir. Hillwood Mfg. Co., Euclid, Ohio. Mem. Euclid Bd. Edn.; chmn. bd. Euclid-Glenville Hosp., 1950-53, life trustee, from 1953; past pres. REp. Club, Euclid. Mem. Phi Kappa Phi, Kappa Alpha, Kiwanis, Mentor Harbor Yachting Club. Republican. *

DAVIS, MILES DEWEY, trumpeter; b. Alton, Ill., May 25, 1926; divorced. Student, Juilliard Sch. Formerly played with Eckstine Orch., Charlie Parker, Benny Carter, others; composer film soundtracks Elevator to the Gallows, 1957, Jack Johnson, 1970, You're Under Arrest, 1985, Siesta, 1988; numerous albums include Sketches of Spain (Grammy award 1960) Bitches Brew (Grammy award 1970), Jack Johnson, Kind Of Blue, Get Up With It, Tutu, (with John Coltrane) Miles And Coltrane, 1988, Pangaea, 1990; author (with Quincy Troupe) Miles: The Autobiography, 1989. Recipient Hall of Fame award Downbeat mag., Grande Medaille de Vermeil, 1989, Grammy award, 1990, reader's poll award Electric Jazz Group, 1989, Lifetime Achievment award. Home: New York N.Y. Died Sept. 28, 1991.

DAVIS, RALPH CURRIER, educator, management consultant; b. Mohawk, N.Y., Dec. 24, 1894; s. Frank Colin and Susie Helen (Greene) D.; m. Dorothy Rebecca O'Neil, Apr. 5, 1926; 1 child, Dannette Davis Palmer. ME, Cornell U., 1916; MA, Ohio State U., 1926; DSc, Wayne State U., 1964. Spl. machinists apprentice, 1913; jr. indsl. engr. Winchester Repeating Arms Co., 1916-18; indsl. engr. The Gleason Works, Rochester, 1919; asst. labor commr. Cleveland C. of C., 1919-23; asst. prof. Ohio State U., 1923-27; head mgmt. dept. Gen. Motors Inst., 1927-30; assoc. prof. Ohio State U., 1930-36; prof. bus. orgn., sr. prof. mgmt. Coll. of Commerce and Adminstrn., Ohio State U., from 1936; vis. prof. Ark. U., NYU, Columbia U., Ind. U., Stanford U.; cons. to mfrs. on orgn. and mgmt. Author: Principles of Factory Orgn. and Mgmt., 1928, Purchasing and Storing, 1931, Principles of Industrial Organization and Management, 1940, Shop Management for the Shop Supervisor, 1941, Fundamentals of Top Management, 1951, Industrial Organization and Management, 1957; contbr. articles and monographs in field. Pvt. Signal Corps, 1918, ensign USN, 1918-19, lt. col. USAF, 1942-46. Recipient Taylor Key, Soc. Advancement Mgmt., 1958. Mem. AIM (dir.), Acad. Mgmt. (pres. 1948), Soc. Advancement Mgmt. (v.p. 1942-43, 46-47, 53-58), Am. Mgmt. Assn., Sigma Iota Epsilon, Beta Gamma Sigma, Sigma Phi Epsilon, Torch Club, Faculty Club (Columbus). *

DAVIS, SAMMY, JR., entertainer; b. N.Y.C., Dec. 8, 1925; s. Sammy and Elvera (Sanchez) D.; m. Loray White, 1958 (div. 1959); m. May Britt, Nov. 13, 1961 (div.); children: Tracey, Mark, Jeff; m. Altovise Gore, May 11, 1970. V.p. Tropicana Hotel, Las Vegas, Nev. Vaudeville appearances, Will Mastin Trio, 1930-48; singer, dancer, impressionist hotel, nightclub shows; rec. songs, Decca Records, 20th Century Records, Warner Records, (others); albums include: At His Greatest, That Old Black Magic, Closest of Friends, Hello Detroit; Broadway shows Mr. Wonderful, 1956-57, Anna Lucasta, 1959, Porgy and Bess, 1959, Golden Boy, 1964; film appearances include The Benny Goodman Story, 1956, Anna Lucasta, 1958, Porgy and Bess, 1959, Ocean's 11, 1960, Pepe, 1960, Sergeants Three, 1962, Johnny Cool, 1963, Robin and the Seven Hoods, 1964, Sweet Charity, 1968, A Man Called Adam, 1966, Salt and Pepper, 1968, One More Time, 1970, The Pigeons, 1970, The Cannonball Run, 1981, Cannonball Run II, 1984, Tap, 1989, others; TV appearance Mod Squad, Name of the Game, Laugh-In, Lucy Show, All in the Family, Wednesday Night Mystery Movie Spl. Segment, 1973, Poor Devil, 1973, Sammy and Co., numerous spls.; producer: TV show The Trackers; author (with others) autobiography Yes I Can, 1965, Hollywood in a Suitcase, 1980, Why Me?, 1989. Served with AUS, 1943-45. Mem. Am. Soc. Mag. Photographers. Club:

Friars (N.Y.C.). Home: Beverly Hills Calif. Died May 16, 1990.

DAVIS, SAVILLE ROGERS, journalist; b. Watertown, Mass., Apr. 5, 1909; s. Francis Woodward and Esther (Saville) D.; m. Anita Pawolleck de Varon, Aug. 12, 1935; 1 dau., Julie Davis Jewett. A.B., Williams Coll., 1930; M.B.A., Harvard U., 1932. Reporter, Christian Sci. Monitor, Boston and N.Y.C., 1932-39, radio news writer, broadcaster, 1934-36; State Dept. corr. Christian Sci. Monitor, Washington, 1939; Mediterranean corr. Christian Sci. Monitor, Rome and Madrid, 1939-41, asst. to editor, 1941-45; chief London bur., roving corr. European internat. confs. Christian Sci. Monitor, 1945-47, Am. news editor, 1947-57, mng. editor, 1957-61, chief editorial writer, 1961-64, chief Washington news bur., White House corr., 1965-71, spl. corr., from 1971; BBC Washington corr., 1965-71; roving corr. South and East Asia, 1971-72; free lance journalist, from 1971; corr. in residence Fletcher Sch. Law and Diplomacy, 1974-76; seminar leader Brookings Instn., 1967-81; mem. adv. council NSF, 1976-80. Trustee, Wheelock Coll., chmn, 1963-65, hon. trustee, from 1980; pres. Christian Sci. Mother Ch., Boston, 1980-81; mem. U.S. Nat. Commn. for UNESCO, 1980-87. Fellow Am. Acad. Arts and Scis. (sec., mem. council and exec. bd. 1976-80); mem. Harvard Bus. Sch. Alumni Assn. (pres. 1960-61), Internat. Inst. for Girls in Spain (pres. 1949-69), Phi Beta Kappa. Clubs: National Press (Washington), Federal City (Washington); Harvard (Boston). Home: Lincoln Center Ma. Died Oct. 1, 1991; buried Newton Cemetery, Newton, Mass.

DAVIS, WATSON, editor; b. Washington, Apr. 29, 1896; s. Allan and Maud (Watson) D.; m. Helen Augusta Miles, Dec. 6, 1919 (dec.); children: Charlotte, Miles; m. Marion Shaw Mooney, Nov. 21, 1958. BSCE, George Washington U., 1918, Civil Engr., 1920, DSc, 1959. Registered profl. engr., D.C. Asst. engr. and physicist U.S. Bur. of Standards, 1917-21; sci. editor Washington Herald, 1920-22; mng. editor Sci. Svc., from 1921, dir., from 1933; editor Sci. News Letter, from 1922, THINGS of Sci., from 1940, Chemistry (mag.), 1944-62, Columbia Broadcasting System radio program, 1930-59; pres. Am. Documentation Inst., 1937-47; William L. Honnald lectr. Knox Coll., 1939; chmn. U.S. del. World Congress of Documentation, 1937; mem. Nat. Inventors Coun., from 1940; dir. Sci. Clubs Am., from 1941, Westinghouse Sci. Talent Search, from 1942, Nat. Sci. Fair Internat., from 1949; emeritus mem. exec. bd. Nat. Child Rsch. Ctr.; chmn. Sci. Clubs Com., UNESCO, 1949, Popularization Sci. Conf., Madrid, 1955; mem. Sec. Navy's Adv. Bd. Ednl. Requirements, 1959-61; mem., chmn. Sec. Commerce's Patent Office Adv. Com., 1960-62. Editor: Sci. Today, 1931, New World of Science Series, 1931, The Advance of Science, 1934, Atomic Bombing, 1950; author: The Story of Copner, 1924, Science Picture Parade, 1940, From Now On, 1950, The Century of Science, 1963; contbr. articles to mags. and engring. jours. Mem. Nat. Adv. Dental Rsch. Coun., 1949-53; trustee George Washington U., 1949-61, Jackson Lab., 1949; mem. vis. com. Harvard Obsevty., 1941-54. Recipient Syracuse U. Journalism medal, 1944, Westinghouse Sci. Writing award, 1946, War-Navy cert. appreciation, 1946, Phila. Sci. Coun. award, 1951, Thomas Alva Edison Found. award, 1955, 56, Pioneer medal Nat. Microfilm Assn., 1959, James T. Grady medal Am. Chem. Soc., 1960. Fellow Am. Inst., AAAS; mem. Overseas Writers, Congl. Press Gallery, White House Corr. Assn., Am. Soc. for Testing Materials, Am. Eugenics Soc., Am. Polar Soc., Am. Concrete Inst., Nat. Assn. Sci. Writers (founder mem.), Aviation Writer's Assn., Acad. Medicine Washington (pres. 1956-58), Population Soc. Am., Brit. Assn. Advancement Sci., Assn. Française pour l'avancement des scis., Hist. Sci. Soc., Newcomen Soc., Seismol. Soc. Am., Philos. Soc. Washington, Geol. Soc. Washington, Washington Soc. Engrs., Sigma Xi, Pi Delta Epsilon, Sigma Delta Chi, Cosmos Club, Nat. Press Club, Torch Club, Harvard Club. *

DAVIS, WILLIAM HOWARD, publishing company executive, free-lance writer; b. Chgo., Mar. 6, 1922; s. Philip D. and Anne Helen (Tripp) D.; m. Chermaine Ryser, Oct. 11, 1952; 1 dau., Susie. B.S., Northwestern U., 1943. News editor Printer's Ink mag., Chgo., 1946-49; founder Golf Digest, 1950; asst. to sales mgr. WGN-TV, Chgo., 1949-52; account exec. CBS-TV, Chgo. and N.Y.C., 1952-59; pres. Golf Digest/Tennis Inc., Norwalk, Conn., 1959-75; pres. mag. group N.Y. Times Co., 1975-87, chmn., 1985-87. Author: Great Courses of the World, 1974, Greatest Golf Courses and Then Some, 1982. Bd. dirs. Big Brothers, Inc., N.Y.C. Served to lt. comdr. USNR, 1943-46. Mem. Mag. Pubs. Assn. (exec. com., bd. dirs. 1975-87), Phi Kappa Sigma, Golf Found. (bd. dirs. 1980-91). Christian Scientist. Clubs: Milbrook (Greenwich, Conn.); Winged Foot Golf (Mamaroneck, N.Y.); Royal and Ancient Golf of St. Andrew (Scotland), Pine Valley Golf (Pine Valley, N.J.); Jupiter Hills (Fla.). Home: Jupiter Fla. Died Jan. 2, 1991; buried Greenwich, Conn.

DAWIDOWICZ, LUCY SCHILDKRET, historian, author; b. N.Y.C., June 16, 1915; d. Max and Dora (Ofnaem) Schildkret; m. Szymon M. Dawidowicz, Jan. 3, 1948. B.A., Hunter Coll., N.Y.C., 1936; postgrad. research fellow, Yivo Inst. Jewish Research, Vilna, Poland, 1938-39; M.A., Columbia U., 1961; L.H.D. (hon.), Kenyon Coll., 1978, Hebrew Union Coll.-Jewish Inst. Religion, 1978, Monmouth Coll., Yeshiva U.; D.H.L. (hon.), Spertus Coll., Jewish Theol. Sem. Am., 1987. Asst. to research dir. Yivo Inst. Jewish Research, N.Y.C., 1940-46; edn. officer displaced persons camps Am. Jewish Joint Distbn. Com., Germany, 1946-47; research analyst, then research dir. Am. Jewish Com., N.Y.C., 1948-69; mem. faculty Yeshiva U., N.Y.C., 1969-78, prof. social history, 1974-78, Paul and Leah Lewis prof. holocaust studies, 1970-75, Eli and Diana Zborowski prof. interdisciplinary holocaust studies, 1976-78; vis. prof. Jewish civilization Stanford U., 1981; vis. prof. SUNY-Albany, 1982; bd. dirs. Leo Baeck Inst., N.Y.C., Libr. Corp., Jewish Theol. Sem.; mem. Pres.'s Commn. on Holocaust, 1978-79; pres. Fund for Translation of Jewish Lit., N.Y.C. Author: (with L.J. Goldstein) Politics in a Pluralist Democracy, 1963, The Golden Tradition: Jewish Life and Thought in Eastern Europe, 1967, The War Against the Jews, 1933-1945, 1975, transl. into French, German, Japanese, Hebrew (Anisfield-Wolf prize 1976), 10th anniversary edit., 1986, A Holocaust Reader, 1976, The Jewish Presence: Essays on Identity and History, 1977, The Holocaust and the Historians, 1981, On Equal Terms: Jews in America 1881-1981, 1982, From That Place and Time: A Memoir 1938-47, 1989 (Nat. Jewish Book award 1990); editor: (with Joshua A. Fishman, others) For Max Weinreich: Studies in Jewish Languages, Literature and Society, 1964; contbr. articles to jours. and newspapers. Recipient award Nat. Found. Jewish Culture, 1965, award Meml. Found. Jewish Culture, 1968, 73, 74, 79, award Atran Found., 1971, award John Slawson Fund Research, Tng. and Edn., 1972, 79, award Lucius N. Littauer Found., 1972, 80, award Gustav Wurzweiler Found., 1974, 78; Outstanding Achievement award Hunter Coll., 1978; Guggenheim fellow, 1976. Mem. Am. Hist. Assn., Am. Jewish Hist. Soc., Conf. Jewish Social Studies., Nat. Assn. Scholars. Home: New York N.Y. Died Dec. 5, 1990.

DAWLEY, MELVIN EMERSON, retail store executive; b. Grand Rapids, Mich., Feb. 9, 1905; s. Albert Emerson and Mary (Vandenberg) D.; m. Dorothy Tisch, June 26, 1931; children: Donna Gayle, David Albert. BS, Northwestern U., 1927. Supr. stores Marks Stores, Inc., Grand Rapids, 1927-33; asst. to sales v.p. Montgomery Ward & Co., Chgo., 1933-35, dislay dir., 1935-36; buyer, mdse. mgr. Lord & Taylor, N.Y.C., 1936-46, v.p., 1946-59, pres., chief exec. officer, 1959-68, chmn., chief exec. officer, 1968-72, also bd. dirs. Pres. Fifth Avenue Assn., 1966-68, chmn., 1968-70; trustee Citizens Budget Commn. N.Y.; hon. chmn. bd. dirs. Ednl. Found. Apparel Industry; bd. dirs. Better Bus. Bur. Hon. life fellow Met. Mus. Art, N.Y.C. Mem. Field Club, Siwanoy Country Club (Bronxville, N.Y.), Univ. Club (N.Y.C.), Nat. Golf Links Club Am., Delta Tau Delta, Alpha Kappa Psi. Mem. Protestant Reformed Ch. Home: Lake Wales Fla. Died Dec. 21, 1989; buried Columbariam, Bronxville, N.Y.

DAWSON, HORACE, lawyer; b. Knoxville, Tenn., Nov. 18, 1897; s. William Robert and Elizabeth (Elmore) D.; m. Frances Ledlie, June 26, 1929; children: Jeanette Elizabeth, Margaret Lydia. Student, Maryville (Tenn.) Coll. Prep., until 1914; AB, Maryville Coll., 1918; studied chemistry, U. Chgo. Grad. Sch., 1919-21; JD, U. Chgo., 1923. Bar: Ill. 1923. Mem. of firm Dawson, Tilton, Fallon, Lungmus and Alexander, from 1923; bd. dirs. Fibro-felt Corp., Changewood Corp., Sylvan Engr. Co., Inc.; lectr. U. Chgo. Law Sch., 1933-38. Pres. Evanston Sch. World Affairs, 1952; dir. Christopher House. Comdr. USNR, WWII. Mem. ABA, Ill. Bar Assn., Chgo. Bar Assn., Patent Law Assn., Phi Alpha Delta, Clubs: Legal Law, National Republican, Chemists, Literary, Westmoreland Country, Highland Park Florida (Lake Wales, Fla.). Republican. Presbyterian. *

DAY, RICHARD LAWRENCE, pediatrician; b. N.Y.C., Mar. 28, 1905; s. William S. and Emily H. (Lawrence) D.; m. Ida Holt, Jan. 10, 1936; children: Sarah, Elizabeth, Kathleen. BS cum laude, Harvard U., 1927, MD, 1931. Intern to assoc. prof. Columbia U., 1933-53; instr. Cornell U., 1940-42; with SUNY Coll. Medicine, 1953; prof. pediatrics, chmn. dept. U. Pitts., 1960-65; dir. Children's Hosp., 1960-65; med. dir. Planned Parenthood-World Population, N.Y.C., 1965-68; prof. pediatrics Mt. Sinai Sch. Medicine, N.Y.C., 1968-72; researcher in neonatology, Heimlich maneuver, acupuncture Yale-New Haven Med. Sch. Editor-in-chief Am. Jour. Diseases of Children, 1957-59, mem. editorial bd., 1955-57, 64-72; contbr. articles to profl. jours. Richard L. Day lectureship established in his noor Babies Hosp., 1975. Mem. AMA, Am. Pediatric Soc., Soc. Pediatric Rsch. Home: New York N.Y. Died June 15, 1989; body donated to sci.

DEAN, DWIGHT GANTZ, sociology educator; b. McCluney, Ohio, Dec. 9, 1918; s. Edgar Brooke and Della May (Gantz) D.; m. Ruth Jean Fennell, Apr. 22, 1949; children: Philip Leslie, Robert Wesley. A.B., Capital U., 1943; M.Div., Garrett Sem., 1946; M.A., Northwestern U., 1947; Ph.D., Ohio State U., 1956. Instr. Wright Jr. Coll., Chgo., 1949-51; grad. asst. Ohio State U., 1951-53; instr. Capital U., 1953-56, asst. prof., 1956-59; asst. prof. Denison U., Granville, Ohio, 1959-63, assoc. prof., 1963-68, chmn. dept. sociology, 1965-68; prof. Iowa State U., Ames, from 1968. Author: Experiments in Sociology, 1963; Sociology in Use, 1965; Dynamic Social Psychology, 1969. Contbr. numerous articles to profl. jours. Fellow Am. Assn. for Middle East Studies, Ohio Acad. Sci. (v.p. 1962-63); mem. Am. Sociol. Assn., Nat. Council on Family Relations, North Central Sociol. Assn. (pres. 1969-70, mem. exec. council 1968-71), Iowa Council on Family Relations (pres. 1972-74), Midwest Sociol. Soc. (various coms.), Sigma Xi, Phi Kappa Phi, Alpha Kappa Delta. Home: Ames Iowa Deceased. †

DEAN, WALTER CLARK, manufacturing executive; b. Albion, Mich., Oct. 1, 1898; s. George E. and Belle A. (Clark) D.; m. Mate W. Wonsey, June 14, 1923; children: Ethel, Dagmar, Joanna, Jon. BA, Albion (Mich.) Coll., 1921, D of Bus. Adminstrn. (hon.), 1960; BS, U. Mich., 1922. With Westinghouse Electric & Mfg. Co., East Pittsburgh, Pa., 1922-24; with Union Steel Products Co., Albion, from 1924, v.p., gen. mgr., 1930, pres., gen. mgr., 1932-63, chmn. bd., from 1962; dir. Gen. Portland Cement Co. Mayor Albion, 1945-46; hon. mem. bd. trustees Albion Coll. Mem. Sigma Chi, Mason. Methodist. *

DEANE, HERBERT ANDREW, political philosophy educator; b. Bklyn., May 26, 1921; s. Andrew and Annette (Franzen) D. A.B., Columbia, 1942, Ph.D., 1953; postgrad., Harvard U., 1946-47. Mem. faculty Columbia U., 1948-84, prof. govt., 1961-84, vice provost acad. planning, 1968, Lieber prof. polit. philosophy, 1969-84, prof. emeritus, from 1984; cons. legal and polit. philosophy Rockefeller Found., 1952-53. Author: The Political Ideas of Harold J. Laski, 1955, The Political and Social Ideas of St. Augustine, 1963; editor Jour. History Ideas, from 1961, Polit. Theory, from 1972. Served with USNR, 1942-46. Rockefeller fellow, 1958-59; Guggenheim fellow, 1960-61; NEH sr. fellow, 1974-75. Mem. Am. Soc. Polit. and Legal Philosophy, Inst. Internat. de Philosophie Politique, Acad. Polit. Sci., Century Assn. (N.Y.C.), Phi Beta Kappa. Democrat. Home: New York N.Y. Died Feb. 14, 1991.

DEBEVOISE, ELI WHITNEY, lawyer; b. N.Y.C., Dec. 14, 1989; s. Thomas M. and Anne (Whitney) D.; m. Barbara Clay, June 23, 1923 (div.); children: Elizabeth Anne Healy, Thomas M. II; m. Agnes Holder Black Debevoise, Feb. 2, 1966. AB, Yale U., 1921; JD, Harvard U., 1925. Bar: N.Y. 1926. Master Hotchkiss Sch., Lakeville, Conn., 1921-22; assoc. Davis, Polk, Wardwell, Gardiner & Reed, N.Y.C., 1926-31; ptnr. Debevoise, Plimpton, Lyons & Gates, and predecessors, N.Y.C., 1931-90; gen. counsel Office U.S. High Commr. for Germany, 1951-53, acting dep. high commr., 1952-53; bd. dirs. Bank N.Y., Bank N.Y. Co.; Embree lectr. Yale U., 1953; lectr. on German postwar devel., 1953-56; chmn. Alien Enemy Hearing Bd., N.Y.C., 1942-45; mem. Nat. Appeal Bd., 1943-45; mem. N.Y. Spl. Legis. Com. on Integrity and Ethical Standards in Govt., 1954; chmn. N.Y. Gov.'s Com. To Rev. N.Y. Laws and Procedures in Human Rights Area, 1967-68; del. Conf. on Germany and Western Europe, Bruges, 1955, Internat. Commn. Jurists, 1955, 61, 62, 65, 66, 67, 67, 68, 71. Chmn. N.Y. State Task Force on Youth and Juvenile Delinquency, 1959-60; trustee Rockefeller U., 1954-75, trustee emeritus, 1975-90; trustee William Nelson Cromwell Found.; bd. dirs. N.J. Conservation Found.; bd. dirs. N.Y. Assn. Blind, pres., 1946-51. 2d lt. F.A., U.S. Army, 1918; mem. Squadron A, N.Y. Militia, 1927-29. Mem. ABA, N.Y. State Bar Assn., New York County Bar Assn., Internat. Bar Assn., Bar Assn. City N.Y., Am. Bar Found., Am. Law Inst., Internat. Commn. Jurists (bd. dirs., pres. Am. Assn.), Internat. Law Assn., Union Internat. Avocats, Coun. Fgn. Rels., Univ. Club (past pres.), Century Club, Econ. Club, Sky Club, Union Club, Yale Club, Met. Club (Washington), Pilgrims. Home: New York N.Y. Died June 30, 1990; buried Fair Mount Cemetery, Chatham, N.J.

DEBUSK, EDITH M., lawyer; b. Waco, Tex., Apr. 12, 1912; d. Otto Clifton and Margaret (Hatcher) Mann; m. Manuel C. DeBusk, June 13, 1941. LL.B., Dallas Sch. Law, 1941; Cert., So. Meth. U. Sch. Law, 1941. Atty. Regional Atty.'s Office (O.P.A.), Dallas, 1942; assoc. atty. Office of Karl F. Steinmann, Balt., 1943-46; mem. firm DeBusk & DeBusk, from 1946. Former mem. Gov.'s Com. on Aging; dir. Dallas Citizens Commn. on Action for Aging, Inc.; del. to White House Conf. Children and Youth, 1960, Conf. on Aging, 1961; mem. Dallas Bd. Adjustment, 1963-65; former bd. dirs. Dallas United Cerebral Palsy Assn., Tex. Soc. Aging, Dallas County Community Action Com., Inc.; trustee Nina Fay Calhoun Scholarship Fund Trust; former mem. adv. council Sr. Citizens Found., Inc.; former mem. div. aging Council of Social Agys., Citizens Traffic Commn.; former sec., legal adviser Tex. Fedn. Bus. and Profl. Women's Clubs; bd. visitors Freedoms Found. at Valley Forge. Named Woman of the Month Dallas Mag., 1948; Woman of Week Balt., 1945; recipient George Washington honor medal Freedoms Found., Eleanor Roosevelt Humanitarian award, 1989. Fellow Tex. Bar Found. (life); mem. ABA (chmn. com. state and local taxation 1979-81), State Bar Tex., Dallas Bar Assn. (numerous coms.), Women's Council of Dallas County (legis. com.), Bus. and Profl. Women's Club Dallas (past pres.), Nat. Assn. Women in Constrn. (hon.), Altrusa Internat. Inc. (mem. Dallas chpt., pres. internat. orgn. 1963-65, Community Svc. award 1989), Delta Kappa

Gamma (hon.), Kappa Beta Pi (past dean province IV). Presbyterian. Home: Dallas Tex. Deceased. †

DEBUTTS, HARRY ASHBY, railroad official; b. Delaplane, Va., Oct. 13, 1895; s. Dulany Forrest and Emma Virginia (Ashby) deB.; m. Margaret Ross Blair, June 7, 1922 (dec.); 1 child, Frances Van Meter Page; 2d m. Mary Moore Glascock, Mar. 7, 1956. BS, Va. Mil. Inst., Lexington, 1916. With So. R.R. System, from 1916; beginning as student apprentice became track supr. So. R.R. System, Strasburg, Va., 1919; trainmaster So. R.R. System, Sheffield, Ala., 1921; div. supt. So. R.R. System, Selma, Ala., 1924, Macon, Ga., 1924-29; gen. supt. So. R.R. System, Danville, Va., 1930; gen. mgr. So. R.R. System, Charlotte, N.C., 1934; v.p. in charge operation So. R.R. System, Washington, 1937, pres., dir., 1952-62, chmn. bd., 1962-63; dir. So. Rlwy., Woodward & Lothrop, Inc., Washington, Riggs Nat. Bank, Washington, Equitable Life Assurance Soc. U.S. Mem. exec. com. Stonewall Jackson Found., Geo. C. Marshall Rsch. Found. 1st lt. USMC, WW. Mem. Va. Hist. Soc. (exec. com.), Kappa Alpha, Mason, Chevy Chase Club, Met. Club (Washington). Episcopalian. *

DECKER, DAVID GARRISON, physician; b. Pittsford, N.Y., Sept. 14, 1917; s. Judson and Edith (Garrison) D.; m. Elizabeth Bavis, June 23, 1941; children: Margaret Louise, David Judson, Arthur Bavis, Ann Elizabeth. A.B., U. Rochester, 1939; M.D., Yale U., 1942; M.S., U. Minn., 1951. Diplomate: Am. Bd. Ob-Gyn. Intern Mary Imogene Bassett Hosp., Cooperstown, N.Y., 1942-43, asst. resident biochemistry and ob-gyn, 1946-47; resident ob-gyn Mayo Grad. Sch. Medicine, 1947-50, prof. ob-gyn, 1970-82, prof. emeritus, from 1982; mem. staff Mayo Clinic, Rochester, Minn., 1950-82; emeritus staff Mayo Clinic, from 1982, chmn. dept. ob-gyn, 1969-76, sr. cons. dept. ob-gyn, 1976-82. Contbr. articles profl. jours. Served to maj. M.C., AUS, 1942-46. Mem. Am. Assn. Obstetricians and Gynecologists, Am. Radium Soc., Am. Fertility Soc. (mem. exec. com. 1970-74), Am. Coll. Ob-Gyn, Central Assn. Obstetricians and Gynecologists (sec.-treas. 1968-71, pres. 1973), Assn. Profs. Ob-Gyn, Soc. Gynecol. Oncologists, Minn. Obstet. and Gynecol. Soc., Obstet. and Gynecol. Travel Club, Central Travel Club (pres. 1970), Minn. Med. Assn., Sigma Xi. Presbyterian. Club: Masons. Home: Rochester Minn. Died July 17, 1990; buried Grandview Meml. Gardens, Rochester.

DEDIJER, VLADIMIR, author; b. Belgrade, Feb. 4, 1914; m. Olga Popovic, 1943 (dec.); m. Vera Krizman, 1944; 5 children. Ph.D., Belgrad U. Lt. col. Army of Yugoslavia, World War II; Yugoslav del. UN Gen. Assemblies, 1945, 46, 48, 49, 51, 52; mem. Yugoslav del. to Peace Conf., Paris, 1946; mem. central com. League of Communists Yugoslavia, 1952-54; prof. modern history Belgrade U., 1954-55; defender right of M. Djilas to free speech, 1954, 56, 81, 85; expelled from Central Com., League of Communists, 1954; sentenced to 6 months on probation, 1955; Simon Sr. fellow Manchester U., 1960-62, hon. fellow; fellow St. Antony's Coll., Oxford, 1962-63; research assoc. Harvard Univ., 1963-64; vis. prof. Cornell Univ., 1964-65, MIT, 1969, Brandeis U., 1970-71, U. Mich., 1971, 74, 81, 83, 87; pres. Bertrand Russell's Internat. War Crimes Tribunal, from 1964; mem. Serbian Acad. Scis., 1968, pres. genocide com.; mem. Internet on the Holocaust and Genocide, Tel Aviv, 1989; mem. Order of Liberation of Yugoslavia; mem. Nuremberg Council for Publ. of Documents on Post-Nuremberg Trials, 1987, Russell Hist. Com. on Waldhem, 1987. Publs. include: Partisan Diary, 1945, English edit., 1990; Notes from the United States, 1945; Paris Peace Conf. 1948; Yugoslav-Albanian Relations, 1949; Tito, 1952; The Beloved Land, 1962; Sarajevo, 1965; The Battle Stalin Lost, 1969; History of Yugoslavia, 1973; New Documents for Tito's Biography, 1984, Vatikan and Jasenovack, 1987. Died Nov. 30, 1990; buried Ljubljana, Yugoslavia. Home: Ljubljana Yugoslavia

DEEVEY, EDWARD SMITH, JR., biologist; b. Albany, N.Y., Dec. 3, 1914; s. Edward Smith and Villa (Augur) D.; m. Georgiana Baxter, Dec. 24, 1938 (dec. Jan. 1982); children: Ruth (Mrs. Lehmann), Edward Brian, David Kevin.; m. Dian R. Hitchcock, Jan. 22, 1983. B.A., Yale, 1934, Ph.D., 1938. Instr. biology Rice Inst., Houston, 1939-43; research asso. biology Woods Hole Oceanographic Instn., 1943-46; asst. prof. biology Yale U., 1946-51, asso. prof., 1951-57, prof., 1957-68; Dir. Geochronometric Lab., 1951-62; Killam research prof. biology Dalhousie U., Halifax, N.S., Can., 1968-71; grad. research prof. U. Fla., Gainesville, from 1971; curator paleoecology Fla. State Mus., from 1971; sect. head environ. and systematic biology NSF, 1967-68; mem. Fisheries Research Bd., Canada, 1969-71, Nat. Acad. Scis. NSF sr. postdoctoral fellow; Fulbright travel grantee U. Canterbury, Christchurch, New Zealand, 1964-65; recipient Fulbright research award Denmark, 1953-54; Guggenheim fellow Denmark, 1953-54; Vis. Scholar award Com. on Scholarly Communications with People's Republic China, 1987. Fellow AAAS, Geol. Soc. Am.; mem. Am. Soc. Limnology and Oceanography (pres. 1974), Ecol. Soc. Am. (pres. 1970, Eminent Ecologist award 1982), Am. Anthrop. Assn., Soc. Am. Archaeology, Am. Soc. Naturalists. Home: Gainesville Fla. Died Nov. 29, 1988; buried Canaan, N.Y.

DE GAETANI, JAN, singer; b. Massillon, Ohio, July 10, 1933; m. Thomas De Gaetani (div.); m. Philip West, 1969; children: Mark, Francesca. B.S., Juillard Sch. Music, 1955. Mem. mus. group Gramercy Chamber Ensemble, later sang with, Contemporary Chamber Ensemble, performed at, Am. Music Festival, Washington, 1962, concert series at, Met. Mus. Art, 1976-77, 79-82, Kaufman Auditorium, N.Y.C., 1981; mem. faculty, Eastman Sch. Music, U. Rochester, N.Y., from 1972, Kilbourn prof., from 1976 , appeared with N.Y. Philharmonic, Boston Symphony, Berlin Philharmonic, BBC Orch., Chgo. Symphony, others; recs. for Nonesuch, Columbia, Decca, Vanguard, others; has recorded with Gilbert Kalish, pianist, Abbey Singers, Riverside Chamber Singers, N.Y. Pro Musica, Waverly Consort.; Recs. include Songs of Stephen Foster (Stereo Rev. Record of Yr. 1972), Ancient Voices of Children, Schoenberg Book of the Hanging Gardens and Pierrot Lunaire, Songs from the Spanisches Liederbuch songs of Schubert, Chausson and Rachmaninoff, duets of Schumann, Songs of America, 1988, Songs of Berlioz and Mahler, 1989. Recipient Koussevitsky award for rec. Punch and Judy 1981. Home: Rochester N.Y. Died Sept. 15, 1989; cremated.

DEGENKOLB, HENRY JOHN, engineering executive; b. Peoria, Ill., July 13, 1913; s. Gustav J. and Alice (Emmert) D.; m. Anna Alma Nygren, Sept. 9, 1939; children: Virginia A. Degenkolb Craik, Joan A. Degenkolb, Marion S. Degenkolb Hune, Patricia H. Degenkolb Blanton, Paul H. B.S. in Civil Engring., U. Calif., Berkeley, 1936. With various engring. firms, 1936-46; from chief engr. to partner John J. Gould & H.J. Degenkolb, engrs., San Francisco, 1946-61; pres. H.J. Degenkolb & Assocs., San Francisco, 1961-79, chmn. bd., 1980-85; lectr. U. Calif. extension, 1947-58; mem. Calif. Bldg. Standards Commn., 1971-85, Calif. Seismic Safety Commn., 1975-77, Presdl. Task Force Earthquake Hazard Reduction, 1970-71; mem. engring. criteria rev. bd. Bay Conservation and Devel. Commn., 1970-76; past trustee Cogswell Coll., San Francisco. Contbr. profl. publns. Mem. ASCE (structural research div. 1987, hon. mem., Moiseiff award 1953, Ernest E. Howard award 1967), Nat. Acad. Engrs., Am. Concrete Inst., Am. Cons. Engrs. Council, Cons. Engrs. Assn. Calif., Structural Engrs. Assn. Calif. (pres. 1958), Earthquake Engring. Research Inst. (pres. 1974-78), Forest Hills Assn. (pres. 1957). Club: San Francisco Engineers. Home: San Francisco Calif. Died Dec. 8, 1989.

DE GROOT, MORRIS HERMAN, statistician, educator; b. Scranton, Pa., June 8, 1931; s. Archibald L. and Florence (Dinner) DeGroot; m. Dolores Pine, Sept. 7, 1952 (dec. Sept. 1974); children: Jenny, Jeremy; m. Marilyn Dallolio Fischer, May 19, 1979. B.S., Roosevelt U., 1952; M.S., U. Chgo., 1954, Ph.D., 1958. Mem. faculty Carnegie-Mellon U., 1957-89, prof. math. statistics, 1966-77, prof. statistics and indsl. adminstrn., 1977-85, Univ. prof., 1985-89, head dept. statistics, 1966-72; adj. prof. psychiatry U. Pitts., from 1978; prof. European Inst. for Advanced Studies in Mgmt., Brussels, Belgium, 1971; Univ. disting. vis. prof. Ohio State U., 1986; mem. com. nat. statistics NRC, 1975-79, assoc. chmn., 1978-79, mem. Commn. on Behavioral and Social Scis. and Edn., 1980-86 , mem. numerical data adv. bd., 1984-87 , mem. math. scis. edn. bd., 1985-87 ; mem. commn. on Applied and Theoretical Statistics, from 1987, chmn., from 1988; mem. Bd. on Math. Scis., from 1988; mem. Spl. Task Group, Strategic Hwy. Rsch. Program, from 1988; mem. adv. com. div. math. scis. NSF, 1984-87. Author: Optimal Statistical Decisions, 1970, Probability and Statistics, 1975, 2d edit., 1986, Bayesian Analysis and Uncertainty in Economic Theory, 1987; editor: Bayesian Statistics, 1981, 85, 88, Statistics and the Law, 1986; exec. editor: Statis. Sci., from 1985; contbr. articles to profl. jours. Fellow Am. Statis. Assn. (asso. editor jour. 1970-74, book rev. editor 1971-75, editor 1976-78), Inst. Math. Stats. (assoc. editor Annals of Statistics 1974-75, council 1975-78, from 1981), Royal Statis. Soc., AAAS (mem.-at-large statistics sect. com. 1978-82), Econometric Soc.; mem. Internat. Statis. Inst. Home: Pittsburgh Pa. Died Nov. 2, 1989; buried Pitts.

DEHAAN, NORMAN RICHARD, architect; b. Chgo., July 8, 1927; s. Peter Arend and Clara Anna (Nordstrom) DeH.; m. Christopher Welles, Dec. 1957 (div. Jan. 1963). Student, Ill. Inst. Tech., 1944-45. Project dir. AID, Korea, 1958-61; established Norman DeHaan Assocs., Chgo., 1964, pres., 1967-90; regional rep. nat. accessions com. art in embassies program Dept. State, 1965-75; v.p. Bright New City Inc.; mem. Sculpture Chgo. Steering Com., from 1985; v.p. Chgo. Wildflower Works, 1986-88. Art dir., Country Life Ins. Co., Chgo., 1947-48, archtl. and interior designer, Sidney Morris & Assocs., Chgo., 1948-53, designer, architect, UN Korean Reconstrn. Agy., 1953-54, archtl. adviser, Office of Pres. Korea, 1953-55, asst. dir. design, Container Corp. of Am., Chgo., 1955-57. Dir. Lake Michigan Regional Planning Coun., 1963-76; trustee Columbia Coll., Chgo., 1976-84, Chgo. Sch. Architecture Found., 1966-71. With USNR, 1945-46; C.E. U.S. Army, 1950-52. Fellow AIA (nat. chmn. com. interior architecture 1976-78, bd. dirs. Chgo. chpt. 1981-87, pres. 1985-86, pres. Chgo. chpt. found. 1986-87, mem. Joint AIA/White Ho. Adv. Group 1990), Am. Soc. Interior Designers (nat. pres. 1974-75, chmn. Ednl. Found. 1976); mem. Internat. Fedn. Interior Architects and Designers (del. 1973-87, exec. bd. 1988-90, pres.-elect 1989-90), Cliff Dwellers Club, Arts Club, Casino Club. Home: Chicago Ill. Died Aug. 24, 1990; buried Chgo.

DE HOFFMANN, FREDERIC, nuclear physicist, research institute executive; b. Vienna, Austria, July 8, 1924; came to U.S., 1941, naturalized, 1946; s. Otto and Marianne (Halphen) de H.; m. Patricia Lynn Stewart, June 10, 1953. B.S., Harvard U., 1945, M.A., 1947, Ph.D. (fellow NRC, 1946-48), 1948. Staff mem. Los Alamos Sci. Lab., 1944-46, 48-55, alternate asst. dir., 1950-51; cons. AEC, 1947-48, com. sr. responsible reviewers, 1947-51; cons. Joint Congl. Com. Atomic Energy, 1954; asst. v.p. nuclear planning Convair div. Gen Dynamics Corp., San Diego, 1955; v.p. Gen. Dynamics Corp., San Diego, 1955-67, also gen. mgr. Gen. Atomic div., 1955-59, pres., 1959-67; pres. Gen. Atomic Europe, Zurich, Switzerland, 1960-67; v.p. Gulf Oil Corp.; also pres. Gulf Gen. Atomic and Gulf Gen. Atomic Europe, 1967-69; chancellor Salk Inst. Biol. Studies, 1970-71, pres., from 1972; chmn., pres. Salk Inst. Biotech./Indsl. Assocs. (SIBIA), from 1981; hon. prof. theoretical physics U. Vienna, from 1968; sci. sec. UN Internat. Conf. Peaceful Uses Atomic Energy, 1955; pres. Conf. Future Sci. and Tech., Austria, 1972; governing bd. Courant Inst. Math., N.Y. U., 1968-85; dir. Atomic Indsl. Forum, 1962-70; bd. dirs. Salzburg Sem. in Am. Studies, 1978-81; mem. Nat. Acad. Sci. subcom. mgmt. and tech. Internat. Inst. Applied Systems Analysis Vienna, 1978-82; chmn. internat. panel of advs. on biol. scis. for Sci. Council Singapore; chmn. Industrie 2000 Conf., Vienna, 1985; speaker First Internat. Symposium on New Chemistry, Tokyo, 1987. Author: (with K. M. Case and G. Placzek), Vol. 1) Introduction to the Theory of Neutron Diffusion, 1954, (with H. A. Bethe and S. S. Schweber) Vols. 1 and 2) Mesons and Fields, 1955. Trustee Salk Inst., 1970-89, Scripps Clinic and Research Found., 1956-66. Decorated Cross of Honour for Sci. and Arts, Decoration of Honour for Merit in Silver, Decoration of Honour in Gold Republic Austria, Decoration of Honour in Gold Province of Vienna, Austria. Fellow Am. Phys. Soc., Am. Nuclear Soc. (bd. dirs. 1964-67); mem. Harvard Alumni Assn. (dir. 1961-64), Sigma Xi. Clubs: Bohemian (San Francisco); Duquesne (Pitts.); Cosmos (Washington); Univ. (N.Y.C.); Atheneum (London). Home: La Jolla Calif. Died Oct. 4, 1989.

DE JONG, RUSSELL NELSON, neurologist; b. Orange City, Iowa, Mar. 12, 1907; s. Conrad De Jong and Cynthia J. Bursma; m. Madge Anna Brook, Apr. 23, 1938; children: Mary C. Obuchowski, Constance J. Armitage, Russell N. Jr. AB, U. Mich., 1929, MD, 1932, MS in Neurology, 1936. Diplomate Am. Bd. Psychiatry and Neurology. Intern in neurology U. Mich., Ann Arbor, 1932-33, resident, 1933-36, instr. neurology, 1936-37, asst. prof., 1937-41, assoc. prof., 1941-50, prof., chmn. dept., 1950-76, prof. emeritus, from 1977; mem. World Fedn. of Neurology research group on Headache, research group on Huntington's Chorea; cons. neurology and psychiatry Surgeon Gen. U.S. Army Far East Command, 1949; Stephen W. Ranson lectr. Northwestern U. Med. Sch., 1964; vis. prof. neurology U. Calif. Sch. Medicine, San Francisco, 1961, UCLA, 1966. Author: The Neurologic Examination, 1950, A History of American Neurology, 1982, numerous others; founding editor-in-chief Neurology, 1951-76; neurology editor Yearbook of Neurology and Neurosurgery, from 1969; contbr. articles to profl. jours. Mem. U.S. Pharmacopiea Adv. Panel on Neuropsychiatry, mem. med. adv. bd. Nat. Multiple Sclerosis Soc., from 1955, chmn. 1967-69. Mem. Deutsche Gesellschaft für Neurologie (hon.), Instituto Neurologico de Guatemala (hon.), AMA, Nat. Acad. Sci. (drug efficacy com., nat. research council), Am. Assn. for History of Medicine, Am. Acad. Neurology (hon., v.p. 1961-63), Am. Epilepsy Soc. (pres. 1955-56), Am. Med. Writers Assn. (bd. dirs. 1962-64), Am. Neurol. Assn. (hon., v.p. 1957-58, pres. 1964-65), Am. Psychiat. Assn. (chmn. sect. convulsive disorders 1950-52), Cen. Neuropsychiat. Assn., Mich. Neurol. Assn., Alpha Omega Alpha, Phi Kappa Psi, Sigma Xi. Home: Ann Arbor Mich. Died Aug. 20, 1990; interred Forest Hill Cemetery, Ann Arbor, Mich.

DELACORTE, GEORGE THOMAS, JR., publisher, philanthropist; b. N.Y.C., June 20, 1894; s. George T. and Cecilia Koeing D.; m Margarita von Doenhoff, Aug. 3, 1912 dec. ; children: Albert, Margarita, Malcolm, Consuelo, Marianne, Victoria; m. Valerie Hoecker, May 15, 1959. Student, Harvard U., 1910-11; AB, Columbia U., 1913. Chmn. bd. Dell Pub. Co., Inc.; pres. GTD Holdings, Inc. investments, N.Y.C. Mem. Lost Tree Club North Palm Beach, Fla. , Univ. Club N.Y.C. . Home: North Palm Beach Fla. Died May 4, 1991.

DELAPLAINE, EDWARD SCHLEY, author, jurist; b. Frederick, Md., Oct. 6, 1893; s. William T. and Fannie (Birely) D. BA, Washington and Lee U., Lexington, Va., 1913; postgrad., Washington and Lee U., 1913-14, U. Md. Law Sch., Balt., 1914-15. Bar: Md. 1915. Instr. Washington and Lee U., Va., 1913-14; atty. Frederick, 1915-38; mem. Md. Ho. of Dels., 1916-18; mem. state Coun. sect. Coun. of Nat. Defense, Washington, 1918; city atty. of Frederick, 1919-22; atty. Supreme Ct. U.S., 1932; U.S. Conciliation commr., 1934-38; counsel to Bd. of Suprs. of Elections County of Frederick, 1935-38, counsel to Bd. of County Commrs., 1935-38; chief judge 6th jud. cir., City of Md., 1938; assoc. judge Ct. of Appeals 6th jud. cir., 1938-57, 6th jud. cir. from 3rd Appellate Jud. Cir., 1945-56; v.p. Great So. Printing & Manufacturing Co., 1955-90; Mem. First Conf. Chief Justices, St. Louis, 1949; chmn. comm. on Amendments to Constitution of State Md. Ho. of Dels., 1918; codified Frederick City code, 1920. Author: Roger B. Taney: His Career as a Lawyer, 1918, Thomas Johnson, Maryland and the Constitution, 1925, The Life of Thomas Johnson, 1927, The Dred Scott Case, 1934, Francis Scott Key, Life and Times, 1937, Religious Liberty and the Courts, 1944, Francis Scott Key and the National Anthem, 1947, The Origin of Frederick County Maryland, 1949, Lincoln's Companions on the Trip to Antietam, 1954, Maryland in Law and History, 1964; contbr. Dictionary of American Biography, Dictionary of Am. History; pub. Frederick News, Frederick Post. Sec. Frederick County Chpt. ARC, 1921-38; treas. Frederick chpt. Wakefield Nat. Meml. Found., 1926-27; active Md. Tercentenary Commn., 1927-34; pres. Roger Brooke Taney Home Inc., 1929-46; treas. Roger Brooke Taney Nat. Meml. Found., 1933-46; active Bicentennial Comm. Frederick, 1944-45, United Citizens League, Balt., (war svc. coun. 1944-45, hon. pres. 1956-63), Md. and Va. Potomac River Commn., 1958; hon. mem. Lincoln Sesquicentennial Commn., 1959; vice chmn. Md. Civil War Centennial Commn.; v.p. Francis Scott Key Meml. Found., Inc.; active Govs'. Star Spangled Banner sesquicentennial Commn., 1963-64; trustee C. Burr Arts Libr. of Frederick, 1935-49. Recipient Disting. Svc. award U. Md., 1963. Mem. SAR (pres. Sgt. Lawrence Everhart chpt. 1926-28), ABA, Md. Bar Assn., Frederick County Bar Assn., Md. Hist. Soc., Columbia Hist. Soc., Frederick County Hist. Soc., Montgomery County Hist. Soc., Manuscript Soc., Lincoln Group of D.C., Star-Spangles Banner Flag House Assn., Balt. (life mem. 1929), Md. Soc. New York (hon. mem. 1945), Operation Town Affiliations (hon.), Phi Beta Kappa, Delta Sigma Rho, Omicron Delta Kappa (hon. 1939), Kiwanis. Republican. Episcopalian. *

DE LAUER, RICHARD D., aerospace consultant, government official, aerospace company executive; b. Oakland, Calif., Sept. 23, 1918; s. Michael and Matilda (Giambruno) DeL.; m. Ann Carmichael, Dec. 6, 1940; 1 child, Richard Daniel. A.B., Stanford U., 1940; B.S., U.S. Naval Postgrad. Sch., 1949; Aero. Engr., Calif. Inst. Tech., 1950, Ph.D., 1953. Structural designer Glenn L. Martin Co., Balt., 1940-42; design engr. Northrop Co., Hawthorne, Calif., 1942; commd. ensign USN, 1942, advanced through grades to comdr., 1958; assignments in U.S., 1943-58; ret., 1966; lab. dir. Space Tech. Labs., El Segundo, Calif., 1958-60, Titan Program dir., 1960-62, v.p., dir. ballistic missile program mgmt., 1962-66; v.p., gen. mgr. systems engring. and integration div. TRW Systems Group, Redondo Beach, Calif., 1966-68, v.p., gen. mgr., 1968-70; exec. v.p. TRW, Inc., Redondo Beach, 1970-81; also dir.; undersec. for research and engring. Dept. Def., Washington, 1981-84; chmn. The Orion Group Ltd., Arlington, Va., 1985-89; chmn., chief exec. officer Fairchild Space and Def. Corp., Germantown, Md., 1989-90; bd. dirs. GenCorp., McNeil-Schwendler Inc.; vis. lectr. UCLA; chmn. Nat. Alliance Businessman, 1968-69; chmn. Region IX, 1970; mem. Def.Sci. Bd., Dept. Def. Author: (with R.W. Bussard) Nuclear Rocket Propulsion, 1958, Fundamentals of Nuclear Flight, 1965. Former trustee U. Redlands. Decorated Dept. Def. medal for disting. pub. service; recipient Disting. Civilian Service award U.S. Army, Exceptional Civilian Service award U.S. Air Force, Disting. Service medal NASA. Fellow AIAA, Am. Astron. Soc.; mem. Nat. Acad. Engring., AAAS, Aerospace Industries Assn. (former gov.), Sigma Xi. Home: Los Angeles Calif. Died Apr. 22, 1990; buried Forest Lawn Cemetery, Glendale, Calif.

DELLIQUADRI, PARDO FREDERICK, university dean; b. Pueblo, Colo., Jan. 20, 1915; s. Colombo Frederick and Rose Marie (Russo) D.; m. Velma Lee Ingram, Sept. 9, 1939; children—Toni Cheryl, Lyn Christine, Geri Martha. B.A. cum laude, U. Colo., 1938; M.S. in Social Work, U. Nebr., 1941. WPA investigator in Wyo., 1938-39; research Brookings Instn., 1940; pub. welfare childrens worker Yakima, Wash., 1941; state statistician Wyo. Pub. Welfare Dept., 1942, dir. childrens div., 1946-48; supt. child welfare Ill. Dept. Pub. Welfare, 1948-50; dir. div. children and youth Wis. Dept. Pub. Welfare, 1950-60; dean N.Y. Sch. Social Work, Columbia, 1960-67, Sch. Social Work, U. Hawaii, 1967-68; chief U.S. Children's Bur., Washington, 1968-69; dean Sch. Social Welfare, U. Wis., Milw., 1969-72; dean Sch. Social Work, U. Ala., 1972-81, Univ. prof., 1981; Exec. sec. Ill. Com. Children and Youth, 1948, Wis. Com. Children and Youth, 1950-60; tech. adv. com. White House Conf. Children and Youth, 1950; adv. council child welfare U.S. Congress, 1958-59; UN social welfare adviser to, El Salvador, 1959; U.S. rep. Inter-Am. Children's Inst., Montevideo, Uruguay, 1958-61, v.p., 1959-61; vice chmn. U.S. delegation Pan Am. Child Congress, Bogata, Columbia, 1959; U.S. exec. bd. UNICEF, 1961-69; mem. of Mayor N.Y.C. Com. Pub. Welfare, 1961-67; mem. bd., exec. com. N.Y. Citizens Com. Children, 1961-67; ad hoc com. HEW, 1961; panel tng. grants Pres.'s Commn. Juvenile Delinquency, 1962-66, chmn., 1963-66; chmn. adv. group N.Y. State Legis. Com. on Child Care, 1965-67; chmn. N.Y. Adv. Welfare Study Com., 1965-66; del. White House Conf. on Children, 1970-71; exec. bd. Wis. Welfare Council, 1969; cons. Community Research Assos., N.Y.C., 1970-74; chmn. adv. com. Ala. Dept. Pensions and Security, from 1975; lectr. UCLA, 1981-82; cons. on volunteerism First Interstate Bank of Calif., from 1983; cons. Los Angeles County Dept. Mental Health, from 1985. Mem. task force on leisure Nat. Council Chs. U.S.A., 1965-67; U.S. del. UN Conf. for Internat. Ministers Social Welfare, 1968; nat. bd. dirs. Am. Humane Assn., from 1975, v.p. children's div., 1974, pres., from 1977. Served to lt. USNR, 1942-46. Recipient FONEME Internat. award on youth Milan, Italy, 1968; Norlin medal, 1969; Fulbright scholar fgn. exchange program to Taiwan, 1980-81. Mem. Am. Pub. Welfare Assn. (chmn. membership com. 1950-52, dir. 1952, 54, 57, chmn. self-study com. 1965), Child Welfare League Am., Am. Assn. Social Workers (chmn. nominating com. 1954-55), Council Social Work Edn. (chmn. career com. 1961-67, chmn. com. on adminstrn. 1968-69, chmn. dean's steering com. 1971, nat. nominating com. from 1975), Nat. Assn. Social Workers (chmn. Wis. 1957-59, nat. dir. from 1975), Am. Council Nationality Services, Nat. Conf. Social Work (v.p. 1960-61, chmn. program com. 1970-71), confs. social welfare Wyo., Ill., Wis., N.Y., Wis. PTA (life), Ala. Conf. Social Work (pres. 1976-77), Alumni Assn. U. Colo. (pres. Northeastern chpt.), Phi Beta Kappa, Phi Kappa Phi. Home: Los Angeles Calif. Died Dec. 14, 1989; cremated.

DE LUBAC, HENRI SONIER CARDINAL, theologian, writer; b. Cambrai Nord, France, Feb. 20, 1896; s. Maurice Sonier de Lubac and Gabrielle de Beaurepaire. Hon. degree, U. Notre Dame, South Bend, Ind., Cath. U. Chile, Univ. Innsbruck, Austria. Joined S.J., 1913; ordained priest Roman Cath. Ch., 1927. Prof. theology and History of religion Cath. U. of Lyon and Jesuit Faculty Fourviere, France, 1929-61; elevated to cardinal, 1983; Deacon St. Maria in Dominica, 1984-91. Author: Catholicisme, 1938, Corpus Mysticum, 1944, Proudhon et le Christianisme, 1945, Le Fondement Theologique des Missions, 1946, Surnaturel, 1946, Histoire et Esprit, 1950, Aspect du Bouddhisme, 2 vols., 1951, 55, Rencontre du Bouddhisme et de l'Occident, 1952, Meditation sur l'Eglise, 1953, Nouveau Paradoxes, 1955, Sur les Chemins de Dieu, 1956, Exégèse Médiévale, 4 vols., 1959-64, La Pensée Religieuse du Père Teilhard de Chardin, 1962, La Prière du Père Teilhard de Chardin, 1964, L'Eglise dans La Crise Actuelle, 1969, La Structure du Symbole des Apôtres, 1971, Teilhard et Notre Temps, 1971, Les Eglises Particulieres dans L'Eglise Universelle, 1972, Dieu Se Dit Dans L'Histoire, 1974, Pic de la Mirandole, 1975, Teilhard Posthume--Reflexions et Souvenirs, 1977, La Postérité Spirituelle de Joachim de Flore, 1979, La Revélation Divine, 1983, Théologie D'Occasion, 1984, Correspondance Commentée entre G. Marcel et G. Fessard, 1985, Entretien autour de Vatican II, 1985, Lettres de M. Etienne Gilson au P. de Lubac, 1986. Served with French Armed Forces, 1914-18. Decorated Légion d'Honneur, Croix d'Guerre. Mem. Acad. Moral Sci. and Politics. Home: Paris France Died Apr. 9, 1991; buried Vaugirard, Paris.

DEMBNER, S. ARTHUR, magazine publisher; b. N.Y.C., Oct. 7, 1920; s. Jack Dembner; married, Dec. 5, 1948; 3 children. A.B. (evenings), New Sch. Social Research, 1950; postgrad. Advanced Mgmt. Program, Harvard U., 1971. Account exec. Modern Mdse. Bur., 1945-47; circulation exec. Time, Inc., 1947-52; with Newsweek mag., 1952-73, circulation dir., 1961-62, v.p., 1962-73, mem. exec. com., 1969-73, dir., from 1969, also pub. book div.; sr. v.p. Newsweek, Inc., 1971-76; pres. Newsweek Books, 1973-76, Red Dembner Enterprises Corp., N.Y.C., 1976-90; pub. Dembner Books, N.Y.C., 1976-90; dir. Ptnrs. in Care; Chmn. bd. govs. Direct Mail Advt. Assn., 1959-60; chmn. com. advisers on direct mail Dept. Agr., 1956-58; adv. com. sales and subscriptions Com. Econ. Devel., 1960. Editor: Modern Circulation Methods. Bd. dirs., v.p. Vis. Nurse Service N.Y.; Chmn. Vols. in Politics, N.Y.C., 1953; Bd. dirs. Encampment for Citizenship. Served to capt. USAAF, World War II. Mem. Advt. Fedn. Am., Assn. Am. Pub. (gov.), Hundred Million Club (past pres.), Sales Promotion Execs. Assn., Mag. Pubs. Assn. (chmn. circulation com.). Clubs: Players, Dutch Treat. Home: New York N.Y. Died May 14, 1990; ashes to sea.

DEMPSEY, WILLIAM LAWRENCE, business executive; b. Newark, July 29, 1894; s. William A. and Ella (Conroy) D.; m. Mary Shanley, Apr. 26, 1923; children: William Lawrence, Bernard Shanley, Mary Catherine, Elizabeth Ann. BS, Princeton U., 1917. Gen. mgr. Ivy Lee, pub. rels. counsel, 1920-24; ptnr. Cowan, Dengler & Dempsey, advt. agy.; formerly pres. Sharp & Dohme, Inc.; ltd. ptnr. Drexel & Co., investment bankers; dir., mem. exec. com., mem. fin. com. Reliance Ins. Co., Phila.; mgr. Savs. Fund Soc. of Germantown and Its Vicinity. Former chmn. bd., dir., mem. exec. com. Health Info. Found., N.Y.; past dir. United Fund Bd.; mgr. Germantown Hosp.; former v.p., mem. exec. com. Am. Drug Mfrs. Assn. Mem. Cap and Gown Club, Sunday Breakfast Club, Sunnybrook Golf Club, Racquet Club, U. of N.Y. Club. Republican. Roman Catholic. *

DENBY, JAMES ORR, museum director; b. Am. Legation, Peking, China, Aug. 30, 1896; s. Charles and Martha (Orr) D.; m. Phyllis Douglas Cochran, Feb. 19, 1927; children: George Cochran, Douglas. AB, Princeton U., 1919; AM, George Washington U., 1921. Third sec. Embassy, Tokyo, 1921-23; 3d sec. Legation, Athens, Greece, 1923-27; 2d sec. Legation, Peiping, China, 1927-30; 1st sec. Legation, Dublin, Irish Free State, 1930-36; consul Capetown, South Africa, 1936-43; assigned to State Dept., Washington, 1943, 49-56; counselor Legation, Vienna, 1946; dir. Mus. of Soc. of Cincinnati, from 1954. Served in Intelligence Corps, U.S. Army, 1914-18. Decorated Chevalier of the French Legion of Honor. Mem. Met. Club (Washington), Quadrangle Club (Princeton), City Club (Capetown), Meath Hunt Club (Dublin). *

DEN HARTOG, JACOB PIETER, consulting mechanical engineer; b. Java, East Indies, July 23, 1901; came to U.S., 1924, naturalized, 1930; s. Marten and Elisabeth (Schol) Den H.; m. Elisabeth Stolker, July 29, 1926; children: Martin Dirk, Stephen Ludwig. EE, U. Delft, Holland, 1924, Dr. Tech. Sci. (hon.), 1967; PhD, U. Pitts., 1929; AM (hon.), Harvard U., 1942; D.Eng. (hon.), Carnegie Inst. Tech., 1962; DSc (hon.), U. Ghent, Belgium, 1966, Salford U., 1970, U. Newcastle on Tyne, 1975. Engr. Westinghouse Rsch. Labs., Pitts., 1924-32; asst. prof. mech. engring. Harvard U., 1932-36, assoc. prof., 1936-41; prof. MIT, Cambridge, 1945-67, prof. emeritus, 1967-89, head dept. mech. engring., 1954-58. Author: Mechanical Vibrations, 1934, 41, 46, 54, Mechanics, 1948, Strength of Materials, 1949, Advanced Strength of Materials, 1952. With USN, 1941-45, capt. USNR. Fellow AIAA, Am. Cons. Engrs. Coun., Brit. Inst. Mech. Engrs.; hon. mem. ASME, Japan Soc. Mech. Engrs.; mem. Nat. Acad. Sci., Nat. Acad. Engring., Dutch Acad. Arts and Scis. Home: Hanover N.H. Died Mar. 17, 1989.

DENISON, EDWARD FULTON, economist; b. Omaha, Dec. 18, 1915; s. Edward Fulton and Edith Barbara (Brown) D.; m. Elsie Lightbown, June 14, 1941; children: Janet Denison Howell, Edward. Student, Central YMCA Coll., Chgo., 1932-34, Loyola U., Chgo., 1935; A.B., Oberlin Coll., 1936; A.M., Brown U., 1938; Ph.D., 1941; Ph.D. fellow in econs., Brookings Instn., 1939-40; grad., Nat. War Coll., 1951. Instr. Brown U., 1940-41; economist., nat. income div. Office of Bus. Econs., U.S. Dept. Commerce, 1941-47, acting chief, nat. income div., 1948; asst. dir. Office of Bus. Econs., 1949-56; assoc. dir. Bur. Econ. Analysis, 1979-82; economist Com. Econ. Devel., 1956-62; sr. fellow Brookings Instn., 1962-78, sr. fellow emeritus, from 1978; vis. research prof. U. Calif. - Berkeley, 1966-67; chief aggregates unit U.S. Strategic Bombing Survey, Germany, 1945; lectr. Am. U., Washington, 1946. Author: The Sources of Economic Growth in the United States and the Alternatives Before Us, 1962, Why Growth Rates Differ, 1967, Accounting for United States Economic Growth, 1929-1969, 1974, (with William K. Chung) How Japan's Economy Grew So Fast, 1976, Accounting for Slower Economic Growth, 1979, Trends in American Economic Growth, 1929-82, 1985, Estimates of Productivity Change by Industry: An Evaluation and An Alternative, 1989. Recipient Woytinsky award, 1967; named Disting. Alumnus Brown U. Grad. Sch. Fellow Am. Acad. Arts and Scis., Am. Econ. Assn. (Disting. fellow; v.p. 1978), Am. Statis. Assn. (Disting. fellow); mem. Internat. Assn. Research in Income and Wealth, NAS, Conf. Research in Income and Wealth, Nat. Economists Club (bd. govs.). Club: Sherwood Forest (Md.). Home: Annapolis Md. Died Oct. 28, 1992. †

DENNARD, CLEVELAND LEON, business consultant, former university president; b. Sebring, Fla., Feb. 17, 1929; s. Nathaniel and Betsy Ann (Crocker) D.; m. Belle Brooks, Aug. 27, 1948; children: Judy, Sadie Jo, Beth Elaine, Ann. B.S., Fla. A&M U., 1948; M.S., Colo. State U., 1958; D.Ed., U. Tenn., 1964. Asso. prof. Ala. A&M U., 1957-60; prin. Carver Vocat. and Adult Sch., Atlanta, 1960-65; dep. commr. for manpower and program mgmt. City of N.Y., 1965-67; pres. Technol. Inst., Washington, 1967-77, Atlanta U., 1977-83, Dennard & Co., Atlanta, from 1983; dir. First Atlanta Corp., 1st Nat. Bank of Atlanta; chmn. So. Edn. Found., Atlanta; mem. Pres.'s Adv. Com. on Sci. and Tech. Policy, Sec. of Navy's Adv. Bd. on Edn. and Tng., Sec. of HEW adv. com. on accreditation and institutional eligibility, Nat. Acad. Sci.-Nat. Research Council Commn. on Human Resources. Trustee Robert F. Kennedy Meml. Found.; trustee Martin Luther King Jr. Ctr. for Social Change, Metro Atlanta YMCA; bd. dirs., v.p. Island Teleradio Services, Inc.; bd. dirs., chmn. Dist. Communications, Inc.; bd. dirs., fin. chmn. Ctr. for Community Change; dir. Cen. Atlanta Progress; bd. dirs. Nat. Manpower Inst.; bd. dirs., treas. African-Am. Scholars Council; bd. dirs. United Way, Atlanta; dir. Fed. City Council. Named Washingtonian of Year, 1972. Mem. Phi Kappa Phi, Iota Lambda Sigma, Omega Psi Phi, Kappa Boule. Democrat. Baptist. Clubs: Atlanta Guardsman, Masons. Home: Atlanta Ga. Died Oct. 10, 1992. †

DENNEN, DAVID WARREN, microbiologist; b. Clarks Summit, Pa., Mar. 20, 1932; s. William L. and Ruth L. (Lufkin) D.; m. Jane Dersheimer, Mar. 27, 1954; children: Laurie, Melinda, David H. B.S., MIT, 1954; M.S., Ind. U., 1964, Ph.D., 1966. With Eli Lilly & Co., from 1954, assoc. phys. chemist, 1954-56, phys.

chemist, 1959-64, sr. microbiologist, 1966-69, mgr. antiobiotic devel., 1969-71, dir. antibiotic devel., 1971-74; mng. dir. Lilly Pharmachemie GmbH, 1974-75; dir. antibiotic prodn. and tech. services Eli Lilly & Co., Indpls., 1975-80; mng. dir. Lilly Rsch. Centre, Ltd., Eng., 1980-82; exec. dir. Lilly Rsch. Labs., 1982-83, v.p. biochem. devel. and biosynthetic ops., 1983-86, v.p. labs., 1986-90; v.p. BIOGEN, Inc., Cambridge, Mass., 1990; dir. Lilly Industries, Ltd., Eli Lilly Group Pension Trustees, Ltd.; mem. research and tech. com. Confedn. Brit. Industry. Contbr. articles to profl. jours. Comdt. Ind. Mil. Acad.; dir. personnel Ind. Adj. Gen.'s Office; mem. dean's indsl. adv. com. Ind. U.-Purdue U., Indpls.; vice-chmn., chmn. Sci Edn. Found. Ind., Inc.; ednl. counselor MIT. Served with AUS, 1956-59; troop comdr. Ind. Army N.G. NIH fellow, 1965-66. Mem. Am. Chem. Soc., Am. Soc. Microbiology, Assn. Brit. Pharm. Industries (sci. com.), Theta Chi. Home: Indianapolis Ind. Died June 21, 1990; buried Indpls.

DENNING, JOSEPH P., bishop; b. Flushing, N.Y., Jan. 4, 1907; s. Philip and Bridget (Cunningham) D. Grad., Cathedral Coll., Bklyn., 1926; MA, St. Mary's Sem., Balt., 1932; D.D. (hon.), St. John's U.; Litt.D. (hon.), St. Francis Coll. Ordained priest Roman Cath. Ch. Tchr. Cathedral Coll., 1933-53; pastor Queen of Angeles Ch., Long Island City, N.Y., 1953-60, Queen of Martyrs Ch., 1960-90; aux. bishop Bklyn., 1959-90; titular bishop of Mallus; mem. all sessions Vatican II. Home: Forest Hills N.Y. Died Feb. 12, 1990.

DENNIS, LAWRENCE EDWARD, educational administrator; b. Virginia, Minn., Sept. 20, 1920; s. Walter P. and Loretta B. (Driscoll) D.; m. Lorraine M. Bradt, Nov. 24, 1943; children: Patrick, Brian, Deborah, Thomas. BA, Iowa State Tchrs. Coll., 1940; postgrad., State U. Iowa, 1946-48; MA, U. Minn., 1948. Visual aids field rep. Iowa Tb Assn., 1940-41; grad. counselor men's residence halls U. Minn., Mpls., 1941-42; instr. polit. sci. and journalism State U. Iowa, Iowa City, 1946-48; assoc. prof. journalism and citizenship Kans. State Coll., Manhattan, 1948-49; spl. asst. to U.S. commr. edn., Washington, 1950-51; editorial writer Des Moines Register and Tribune, 1951-53; adminstrv. asst. to pres. Pa. State U., University Park, 1954-55, provost, v.p. acad. affairs, 1956-61; assoc. dir. Peace Corps, Washington, 1961-62; dir. Commn. on Acad. Affairs, exec. assoc. Am. Coun. on Edn., Washington, 1962-65; cons. Ford Found., Caracas, Venezuela, 1965-67; coancelor higher edn. State of R.I., 1967-70; dir. Mass. State Colls., 1970-75; acting pres. Wilson Coll., 1976; pub. affairs columnist Daily Iowan, Iowa City, 1946-48, Manhattan Tribune-News, 1948-49; news commentator Sta. KSAC, Manhattan, 1948-49; lectr. social sci. and internat. affairs Drake U., Des Moines, 1951-53; chmn. Joint Coun. Ednl. Broadcasting, 1961-62; spl. asst. to dir. Servicemems. Opportunities Colls., 1980-83; spl. asst. to v.p. Am. Assn. State Colls. and Univs., 1984-86. Author: (with Stensland) Keeping Up with the News, 1951, How To Read the News, 1952; mem. bd. editors Jour. Gen. Edn.; editor The Ednl. Record. Vice chmn. Iowa Gov.'s Commn. on Higher Edn., 1955-59; mem. Iowa Citizens Com. on Ednl. TV, 1952-53; mem. edn. and projects com. People to People Program, 1957-60. Lt. (j.g.) USNR, 1943-45. Recipient citation for outstanding svc. to adult edn. Des Moines Adult Edn. Coun., 1953. Mem. NEA, AAUP, Assn. for Higher Edn. (exec. com. from 1960), Am. Coun. Edn. (chmn. com. on equality of opportunity in higher edn. 1959-60), Adult Edn. Assn. U.S., Am. Polit. Sci. Assn., Assn. Edn. in Journalism, Soc. Profl. Journalists, Blue Key, Phi Delta Kappa, Phi Mu Alpha, Delta Chi, Kappa Tau Alpha. Home: Portsmouth R.I. Died Nov. 11, 1990; cremated.

DENNIS, SANDY, actress; b. Hastings, Nebr., Apr. 27, 1937; d. Jack D.; m. Gerry Mulligan, June 1965. Student, Wesleyan U., Nebr., U. Nebr.; studied acting, Herber Berghof Studio, N.Y.C. Stage debut in Bus Stop, Palm Beach, Fla.; N.Y. debut, 1957; appeared on Broadway in Burning Bright, 1960, Face of a Hero, 1960, The Complaisant Lover, 1961, A Thousand Clowns, 1962 (Tony award), Any Wednesday, 1964 (Tony award); film debut in Splendor in the Grass, 1961; other films include: Who's Afraid of Virginia Woolf?, 1965 (Academy award), Up the Down Staircase, 1967 (Moscow Film Festival prize best actress), The Fox, 1967, Sweet November, Daphne in Cottage D, The Millstone, The Out of Towners, Nasty Habits, Same Time Next Year, The Four Seasons, 1981, Another Woman, 1988, Parents, 1989; plays: And Miss Reardon Drinks A Little; toured, 1971, 72, Let Me Hear You Smile, 1973, Streetcar Named Desire, 1974, Born Yesterday, 1974, Absurd Person Singular, 1975, Cat on a Hot Tin Roof, 1975, Come Back to the 5 & Dime, Jimmy Dean, Jimmy Dean, 1980 and 82, The Supporting Cast, 1981, Buried Inside Extra, 1983; appeared in TV films Something Evil, 1972, The Man Who Wanted To Live Forever, 1970, Perfect Gentlemen, 1978, The Execution, 1985. Recipient N.Y. Critics Poll award, Moscow Film Festival best-actress award for Up the Down Staircase 1967). Home: Westport Conn. Died Mar. 2, 1992.

DENNIS, WARD HALDAN, university dean; b. Boston, Jan. 8, 1938; s. George Harold and Amarie (Whitters) D.; m. Sandra H. Dennis; children—Ward Stuart, Heather Amarie, John Bradford. A.B., Middlebury (Vt.) Coll., 1960; M.A., Columbia U., 1961, Ph.D., 1965. Tng. officer Def. Lang. Inst., Monterey, Calif., 1965-67; asst. prof. Spanish Columbia U., 1967-69, asso. dean, then acting dean Sch. Gen. Studies,, 1969-76, dean, from 1977, dir. Latin Am. Inst.,, 1974-77, dean summer session, spl. programs and Reid Hall programs in Paris, from 1985, acting v.p. arts and scis., 1989; co-founder, mem. Univ. Seminar Latin Am.; cons. in field. Author: Pérez Galdós: A Study in Characterization, 1968; also articles, revs. Served with AUS, 1965-67. Recipient Joint Service Commendation medal; Fulbright-Hays grantee Quito, Ecuador, 1974. Mem. Sigma Delta Pi. Clubs: Niantic Bay Yacht, Nannahagan Swim. Home: Pleasantville N.Y. Died Oct. 16, 1992. †

DEN UYL, SIMON DANKER, business executive; b. Holland, Mich., Apr. 21, 1896; s. Teunis and Jennie (Leys) Den U.; m. Marjorie Dykema, Dec. 28, 1920; children: Robert Dykema, Richard Simon. LLD, Hope Coll., Holland; D. in Bus. Adminstrn. (hon.), Yankton Coll.; LLD (hon.), Aquinas Coll. Clk. acctg. dept. Bohn Aluminum & Brass Corp., 1919, asst. sec., 1928, sec., asst. treas., 1929, dir., from 1938, sec.-treas., 1940-49, pres., 1949-58, chmn. bd. dirs., from 1958; v.p., dir. Chas. B. Bohn Corp.; dir. Royton Corp. Trustee, mem. exec. com. Mich. Colls. Found. With U.S. Army, WWI. Mem. Aluminum Assn., Employers Assn. Detroit (past pres.), Am. Legion, VFW, Mil. Order World Wars, Greater Detroit Bd. Commerce (past pres.), Newcomen Soc., C. of C., Mason, Clubs: Detroit, Detroit Athletic, Detroit Country, Economic (Detroit), Macatawa Bay Yacht, Gulf Stream Bath and Tennis, The Seagate (Delray, Fla.). *

DE PRIMA, CHARLES RAYMOND, mathematics educator; b. Paterson, N.J., July 10, 1918; s. Mario and Louise (Ruggiero) DeP.; m. Annemarie Boerschmann, June 15, 1951 (dec. July 23, 1984); m. Margaret E. Thurmond, July 11, 1987. A.B., Washington Sq. Coll., 1940; Ph.D., N.Y. U., 1943. Lectr. N.Y. U., 1942-46, vis. prof., 1962-63; mem. faculty Calif. Inst. Tech., Pasadena, 1946-92; prof. math. Calif. Inst. Tech., 1956-86, prof. emeritus, 1986-92; Mem. applied math. panel OSRD, 1942-46; head math. div. (Office Naval Research), 1951-52; mem. (Com. Undergrad. Programs Math.), 1961-92. Editor: Pacific Jour. Math, 1973-86. Mem. Am. Math. Soc., Math. Assn. Am., Soc. Indsl. and Applied Math. (council 1961-64), Phi Beta Kappa. Home: Gualala Calif. Deceased. †

DERAMUS, WILLIAM NEAL, III, railroad executive; b. Pittsburg, Kans., Dec. 10, 1915; s. William Neal and Lucile Ione (Nicholas) D.; m. Patricia Howell Watson, Jan. 22, 1943; children: William Neal IV, Patricia Nicholas Fogel, Jean Deramus Wagner, Jill Watson Dean. AA, Kansas City Jr. Coll., 1934; AB, U. Mich., 1936; LLB, Harvard U., 1939. Transp. apprentice Wabash R.R. Co., St. Louis, 1939-41, asst. trainmaster, 1941-43; asst. to gen. mgr. K.C.S. Ry. Co., Kansas City, Mo., 1946-48; asst. to pres. C.G.W. Ry. Co., Chgo., 1948, pres., dir., 1949-57, chmn. exec. com., 1954-57; pres., dir. M.-K.-T. R.R., 1957-61; chmn. bd. MAPCO, Inc., Tulsa, 1960-73, chmn. exec. com., 1973-81, also dir.; pres., dir. Kansas City R.R. Co. and subs., Mo., 1961-73; chmn. bd. Kansas City So. Lines, 1966-80; pres. Kansas City Southern Industries, Inc., Mo., 1962-71, chmn. bd., 1966-89; bd. dirs. Kansas City Royals. Capt. to maj. Transp. Corps, Mil. Ry. Svc. AUS, 1943-46, overseas, India. Mem. Beta Theta Pi. Clubs: Chgo.; Kansas City (Mo.); River (Kansas City), Mission Hills Country (Kansas City), Mercury (Kansas City). Lodge: Rotary (Kansas City). Home: Kansas City MO Died Nov. 15, 1989; buried Mt. Moriah Cemetery, Kansas City, Mo.

DERHAM, JOHN P(ICKENS), rail road company executive; b. Green Sea, S.C., Apr. 27, 1896; s. John Pickens and Loula (McGougan) D.; m. Olga Jones, Dec. 23, 1925; 1 child, Mrs. Mary L. Roberts. BS, Clemson Coll., 1917. With S.A.L. Rail Road, from 1920, advanced through grades to asst. v.p., 1920-55, v.p., from 1955; v.p. freight traffic Tavares & Gulf R.R., Ga., Fla., & Ala. R.R.; v.p. Southeastern Investment Co., Gainesville Midland R.R. Co., Tampa & Gulf Coast R.R. Mem. Am. Soc. Traffic and Transp., Nat. Freight Traffic Assn., Traffic Clubs of Am. *

DE ROBURT, HAMMER, former president of Nauru; b. Nauru, Sept. 25, 1923; ed. Geelong Tech. Coll., Victoria, Australia. Tchr., 1940-42, 51-57; deported by Japanese, 1942-46; ednl. liaison officer Dept. Nauruan Affairs, 1947-51; mem. Nauru Local Govt. Council, 1955-68; pres. Republic of Nauru, 1968-76, 78-89, also minister comml. aviation, minister internat. affairs, minister island devel. and industry, minister external affairs, pub. service, leader of opposition, 1976-78. Died July 15, 1992. Home: Yaren Nauru †

DESKEY, DONALD, industrial designer; b. Blue Earth, Minn., Nov. 23, 1894; m. Mary Douthett, 1923 (div.); children: Michael Douthett, Stephen Donald; m. Katharine Godfrey Brennan, 1952. Student, U. Calif., 1915-19, Mark Hopkins Art Sch., San Francisco, Art Inst. Chgo., Ecole de la Grande Chaumiere, Paris. Artist, 1919-23; head art dept. Juniata Coll., 1923-25; indsl. designer, 1926-89; head indsl. design dept. NYU, 1939-40; pres. Shelter Industries, Inc.; design cons. numerous firms and orgns.; chmn. bd. Airport Industries Inc., Bohemia, N.Y.; pres. Donald Deskey Assocs., Inc., Spl. Projects, INc.; dir. Donald Deskey Assocs., Ltd., Eng., Sculley, Deskey & Scott, Inc.; mem. exec. com. Half Moon Bay Ltd., Jamaica, B.W.I. Author, lectr. indsl. design. With CAC, World War I. Recipient Grand Priz, Gold medal, Paris Expn., 1937. Fellow Am. Soc. Indsl. Designers; mem. Package Designers Coun. (dir.), Am. Inst. Graphic Arts, Soc. Plastic Engrs., Inc. U.S.A. (adv. bd. plastics), Royal Soc. Arts London (Benjamin Franklin fellow), Art Dirs. Club, Archtl. League, Beaux Arts Inst. Design, Archtl. League, Brit.-Am. C. of C., Swedish C. of C. U.S., Met. Club, Dutchess Valley (Pawling, N.Y.), Marco Polo Club (N.Y.C.), Lambda Chi Alpha. Home: Vero Beach Fla. Died Apr. 29, 1989.

DESMOND, ALICE CURTIS, writer; b. Southport, Conn., Sept. 19, 1897; d. Lewis Beers and Alice (Beardsley) Curtis; m. Thomas C. Desmond, Aug. 16, 1923; m. Hamilton Fish, Oct. 16, 1976 (div. 1984). Grad., Miss Porter's Sch., Farmington, Conn., 1916; student, Parson's Art Sch., N.Y.C., 1920; Litt.D., Russell Sage Coll., 1946, Suffolk U., 1975. Has made three world tours. Author: Far Horizons, 1931, South American Adventures, 1934 (both books endorsed by Carnegie Endowment for Internat. Peace), The Lucky Llama, 1939, Soldier of the Sun, 1939, Feathers, 1940, For Cross and King, 1941, Jorge's Journey, 1942 (translated into Portuguese, Swedish, German), Martha Washington, 1942, The Sea Cats, 1944, Glamorous Dolly Madison, 1946, The Talking Tree, 1949 (translated into Swedish 1956), Alexander Hamilton's Wife, 1952, Barnum Presents: General Tom Thumb, 1954 (translated into French, Dutch 1956), Bewitching Betsy Bonaparte, 1958, Your Flag and Mine, 1960, George Washington's Mother, 1961, Teddy Koala: Mascot of the Marines, 1962, Sword and Pen for George Washington, 1964, Marie Antoinette's Daughter, 1967, Cleopatra's Children, 1971, Titus of Rome, 1976, Yankees and Yorkers, 1985; contbr. to anthologies: Roads to Travel, 1936, Boys of the Andes, 1941, Wonder and Laughter, 1947, Adventures in Reading Exploration, 1947, People and Progress, 1947, Told Under Spacious Skies, 1952, A Book of Gladness, 1953, American Backgrounds, 1959, This is Our Land, 1965, Cavalcades, 1965; contbr. articles, fiction, verse to newspapers and mags. Rochester Mus. Arts and Scis. hon. fellow, 1946. Fellow Soc. Am. Historians; mem. Nat. League Pen Women (Juvenile award 1949), Am. Anthrop. Assn., Am. Folk Lore Soc., Nat. Assn. U. Women, Soc. Mayflower Descs., Colonial Dames Am., Daus. Founders and Patriots Am., N.Y. State Hist. Assn., Soc. Woman Geographers, Federated Garden Clubs N.Y. State (hon.), N.Y. Hist. Soc. (Pintard fellow), NAD, Am. Water Color Soc., Photog. Soc. Am., Royal Photog. Soc. Gt. Britain, Am. Numis. Assn., Am. Philatelic Soc., Nat. Assn. Women Artists, Print Club Albany, Authors League Am., Pen and Brush. Episcopalian. Clubs: Women's Nat. Republican, Colony, Junior League, Collectors (N.Y.C.); Garden of Am. Home: Newburgh N.Y. Deceased. †

DE URZAIZ, LUIS, engineering educator; b. Vigo, Spain, Sept. 1, 1896; came to U.S., 1925; naturalized, 1939; s. Gen. Luis and Filomena (Duran) de U.; m. Elizabeth Norcott, Sept. 12, 1929; 1 child, Louis C. Diploma in bus. econs., U. Neuchatel, 1916; guest, polit. sci., philos. and pure sci., Columbia U., 1925-26. Lic. aviation pilot. Prof. econs. and bus. Ctrl. Coll. of High Econ. Studies, Madrid, 1919; charge stock exchange dept., banking Credit Lyonnais, Madrid, 1918-23; asst. to Brocker Sangrador Stock Exchange of Madrid, 1923-25; commr. of Spainish Govt. in U.S., 1925-26; engr. Ford Motor Co., Detroit and Barcelona, 1927-29; pres. Nat. Tech. Inst., N.Y.C., from 1929; dir. Luis de Urzaiz Assocs.; pres. Midwestern Tech. Inst., Chgo., Natec Pub., Inc., from 1961; v.p. Spanish Inst., N.Y.C. Edited arctl. drafting jours. Mem. Am. Soc. Engring., Edn. Club, The Wings Club (N.Y.C.). *

DEUTSCH, GEORGE CARL, metallurgical engineer; b. Budapest, Hungary, Apr. 19, 1920; s. Frank and Jennie (Greenbaum) D.; m. Ruth Amster, Oct. 4, 1942; children—Fred, Harvey, Marilyn. B.S. in Phys. Metallurgy, Case Western Res. U., 1942. With Copperweld Steel Co., Warren, Ohio, 1942-44; with Nat. Adv. Com. for Aero., to 1969, chief high temperature materials br., to 1969; with NASA, 1960-81, dir. research and tech. div., to 1981, cons., 1981-87; cons. aerospace research and tech.; mem. adv. group for aerospace devel. NATO; mem. nat. materials adv. bd. Nat. Acad. Sci.; cons. aerospace research and devel. Contbr. articles to profl. jours. Served with U.S. Navy, 1944-46. Recipient Disting. medal NASA, 1980. Fellow Am. Soc. Metals. Home: Bethesda Md. Died Feb. 27, 1988; buried King David Meml. Cemetery, Fairfax, Va.

DEVINE, C. ROBERT, publishing company executive; b. Clarksburg, W.Va., June 13, 1917; s. James J. and Frances M. (Ryan) D.; m. Louise C. Williams, Mar. 27, 1943 (div.); children: Mallory C., Rodney W., Ian C.; m. Gisele Edenbourgh Lichine, Dec. 23, 1966. Grad., Princeton U., 1938; L.H.D., Fairleigh Dickinson U., 1976. Promotion, research dir. U.S. News Pub. Co., 1946-48, asst. advt. dir., 1948-55; exec. bus. dept. Reader's Digest, N.Y.C., 1955-58; advt. dir. internat. edits. Reader's Digest, 1958-60, pres. Latin Am. div., 1960, asst. gen. mgr., 1960-66, dep. gen. mgr. internat.

edits., 1966; v.p. dir. corp. and public affairs Reader's Digest Assn., Inc., 1970-82. Bd. dirs. Met. Opera Assn., 1973-83; bd. dirs. Am. Hosp. Istanbul; trustee Am. U. Cairo; bd. dirs. Gen. Douglas MacArthur Found., Vail-Deane Sch. Served from pvt. to maj. AUS, World War II. Decorated Bronze Star medal. Mem. Council on Fgn. Relations, Internat. Advt. Assn. (chmn., chief exec. officer 1976-80, pres. 1962-64), Assn. Ex-Mems. Squadron A, XIIIth Corps Assn., Mil. Order Fgn. Wars, Assn. U.S. Army (v.p. N.Y. chpt.), Fgn. Policy Assn., Internat. Fedn. Periodical Press (v.p. 1978-79, pres. 1979-81, chmn. 1981-83), English-Speaking Union, World Press Inst. (chmn. 1982-84), Nat. Inst. Social Scis., Nat. Found. for Facial Reconstruction (bd. dirs.), Pub. Relations Soc. Am. Clubs: Union (N.Y.C.), Squadron A (N.Y.C.), Dutch Treat (N.Y.C.), River (N.Y.C.); Pilgrims U.S; Travellers (Paris). Home: New York N.Y. Died Jan. 6, 1990; buried Clarksburg, W.Va.

DEVITT, EDWARD JAMES, federal judge; b. St. Paul, May 5, 1911; s. Thomas Phillip and Catherine Ethel (McGuire) D.; m. Marcelle M. LaRose, Apr. 22, 1939; children: Marcelle Terese, Timothy Patrick. LLB, U. N.D., 1935, BS, 1936; also LLD; LLD, William Mitchell Coll. Law, Hamline U. Bar: D.C., Minn., Ill., N.D. Practiced law East Grand Forks, Minn., 1935-39, St. Paul, 1946-92; mcpl. judge, 1935-39, asst. atty. gen. Minn., 1939-42; instr. law U. N.D., 1935-39, St. Paul Coll. Law, 1945-92; mem. 80th Congress from 4th Minn. Dist.; probate judge Ramsey County, St. Paul, 1950-54; judge U.S. Dist. Ct., 1954-92. Author: (with Blackmar) Federal Jury Practice and Instructions. Bd. dirs. Fed. Jud. Center. Served as intelligence officer USNR, 1942-46. Decorated Purple Heart. Fellow Am. Bar Found.; mem. Am., Minn., Ramsey County bar assns., Am. Judicature Soc., Am. Legion, VFW, DAV, Order of Coif, Blue Key, Phi Delta Phi, Beta Gamma Sigma, Delta Sigma Rho. Republican. Roman Catholic. Clubs: K.C. (St. Paul), Athletic (St. Paul). Home: Saint Paul Minn. Died Mar. 2, 1992. †

DEVLIN, PAUL, investment banker; b. Chgo., Jan. 5, 1903; s. John L. and Carmen (Blesch) D.; m. Mary L. Brinkmann, July 5, 1924; children: Mary Lou Devlin O'Rourke, Joann Roath Devlin. Student, U. Ill., 1926. With Blyth & Co., Inc., N.Y.C., 1924-89; chmn. bd., mem. exec. com., dir. Banque Blyth & Cie, Paris. Mem. N.Y. Stock Exch. Lunch Club, Bond Club, 29 Club (N.Y.C.), Apawamis Club (Rye, N.Y.), Ocean Club, Deray Yacht Club, Country Club of Fla. (Delray Beach, Fla.), Old Baldy Club (Saratoga, Wyo.), Blind Brook Club (Portchester, N.Y.). Home: Golf Fla. Died June 13, 1989.

DEWEESE, DAVID DOWNS, physician, surgeon, emeritus educator; b. Columbus, Ohio, Mar. 16, 1913; s. Bernard D. and Vilette Downs (Gilfillan) DeW.; m. Mary Dorothy Jones, June 24, 1938 (dec. Aug. 1974); adopted children: Diane Downs, Dana Evelyn; m. Edna Elaine Kuckenberg, July 19, 1975; stepchildren: Peter William, Karen Anna. A.B., U. Mich., 1934, M.D., 1938. Diplomate: Am. Bd. Otolaryngology (pres. 1972-76). Intern U. Hosp., Ann Arbor, Mich., 1938-39; resident otolaryngology U. Hosp., 1939-40; instr. otolaryngology U. Mich. Med. Sch., 1941-44; instr. otolaryngology U. Oreg. Med. Sch., 1944-45, clin. prof., 1951-61, chmn. dept. otolaryngology, 1958-79, prof., 1961-80, prof. emeritus, from 1980; trustee Health Scis. Center Found., 1975-78; otolaryngologist Portland (Oreg.) Clin., 1944-61; Bd. dirs. Portland Center for Hearing and Speech, from 1947, pres., 1949-59, med. dir., from 1958; chmn. communicative disorders research tng. com. NIH, 1965-66, mem. dirs. adv. com., 1982-85; mem. adv. council Nat. Inst. Neurol. Diseases and Stroke, 1968-70; Bd. dirs. U. Oreg. Med. Sch. Advancement Fund, v.p., 1971-75. Sr. author: Textbook of Otolaryngology, 1960, 7th edit., 1988 (title changed to Otolaryngology--Head and Neck Surgery); Editorial bd.: AMA Archives of Otolaryngology, 1961-64, Laryngoscope, 1972-83. Trustee Marylhurst Coll., 1965-74. Jr. fellow ACS; mem. AMA, Ore., Multnomah County med. socs., Oreg. Acad. Ophthalmology and Otolaryngology (pres. 1958), Pacific Coast Oto-Ophthal. Soc. (pres. 1964), Am. Laryngol., Rhinol., Otol. Soc. (pres. 1974-75), Am. Acad. Ophthalmology and Otolaryngology (2d v.p. 1957-58), Portland Acad. Medicine, Am. Otol. Soc., Am. Broncho-Esophageal Assn., Am. Laryngol. Assn., Soc. Univ. Otolaryngologists (pres. 1968), Am. Council Otolaryngology (dir. 1968-74), Soc. Acad. Chairmen Otolaryngology, Lang Syne Soc. (pres. 1986), Sigma Chi (Significant Sig 1979), Nu Sigma Nu (nat. pres. 1959- 60), Alpha Omega Alpha. Clubs: Waverly Country, Golf, Multnomah Athletic, Rotary, Arlington. Home: Portland Oreg. Deceased. †

DEWHURST, COLLEEN, actress; b. Montreal, Que., Can., June 3, 1926; m. James Vickery, 1947 (div. 1959); m. George C. Scott (div.); 2 sons. Student, Downer Coll., Milw., Am. Acad. Dramatic Art; pupil of Harold Clurman and Joseph Anthony. lectr. on theatre; spkr. on arts at Congl. hearings, other forums. First profl. appearance in The Royal Family, 1946; Broadway appearances include Desire Under the Elms, 1952, Tamberlain the Great, 1956, Camille, 1956, The Eagle Has Two Heads, 1957, The Country Wife, 1957, All the Way Home, 1960 (Tony award 1961), Great Day in the Morning, 1962, Ballad of the Sad Cafe, 1963, Taming of the Shrew, Macbeth, Hello and Goodbye, Good Woman of Setzuan, Children of Darkness, Moon for the Misbegotten, 1974 (Tony award 1974, Sarah Siddons award 1974), The Big Coca-Cola Swamp in the Sky, Mourning Becomes Electra, An Almost Perfect Person, The Queen and the Rebels, The Dance of Death, You Can't Take It With You, Who's Afraid of Virginia Woolf, 1977, Rainshakes, 1984, one woman show My Gene, N.Y., 1987, Real Estate, 1986, Long Day's Journey Into Night and Ah Wilderness in Repertory, New Haven and N.Y.C., 1988, Love Letters, 1989; appearances with N.Y. Shakespeare Festival include My Gene, 1985-86; films include The Nun's Story, 1959, The Cowboys, 1972, McQ, 1974, Annie Hall, 1977, Ice Castles, 1979, When a Stranger Calls, 1977, Final Assignment, 1980, Tribute, 1980, The Dead Zone, 1983, The Boy Who Could Fly, 1986; dir. Broadway play Ned and Jack, 1981; numerous TV appearances, 1957-90; appeared in TV films The Story of Jacob and Joseph, 1974, Silent Victory: The Kitty O'Neil Story, 1979, Studs Lonigan, 1979, And Baby Makes Six, 1979, Mary and Joseph: A Story of Faith, 1979, Death Penalty, 1980, Escape, 1980, Guyana Tragedy: The Story of Jim Jones, 1980, The Women's Room, 1980, A Perfect Match, 1980, Baby Comes Home, 1980, A Few Days in Weasel Creek, 1981, Johnny Bull, 1986, Sword of Gideon, Those She Left Behind (Emmy award 1989); appeared in TV miniseries The Blue and the Gray, 1982, A.D., 1985, Anne of Green Gables, 1986 (Gemini award 1987, ACE award), Anne of Avonlea, 1988. Vice-chair bd. dirs. Save the Theatres, Inc.; mem. exec. bd. Actors' Fund Am.; bd. dirs. Am. Coun. for the Arts, Theatre Communications Group, Theatre Devel. Fund, Westchester Coun. for the Arts; active Mayor's Shelters for Homeless Com., Lighthouse for the Blind, United Jewish Appeal; founding bd. mem. The Family; mem. policy overview panel & theatre program panel Nat. Endowment for the Arts. Recipient Obie award, 1957, 63, Lola D'Annunzio award, 1961, Sylvania award, 1960, Theatre World award; Emmy awards for Between Two Women, 1986, for Those She Left Behind (best supporting actress in a miniseries or special), 1989; inducted into Wis. Artists' Hall of Fame, 1985; named Woman of Yr. by Westchester Woman's Club; honored by Am. News Women's Club, Washington. Mem. Actors Equity Assn. (pres. 1985-91, Colleen Dewhurst AIDS Meml. Trust Fund in her name, co-founder Equity Fights AIDS). Home: South Salem N.Y. Died Aug. 22, 1991.

DEWIRE, JOHN W., physicist; b. Milton, Pa., June 12, 1916; s. John W. and Ella Mae Aunkst DeW.; m Ruth Hale, Mar. 2, 1943; children: Susan DeWire Hosek, William. BS, Ursinus Coll., 1938; PhD, Ohio State U., 1942. Physicist Manhattan Project, 1942-46; mem. faculty dept. physics Cornell U., Ithaca, N.Y., 1946-90, prof., 1968-90, assoc. dir. Lab. of Nuclear Studies, 1968-90. Trustee East Lawn Sch, 1952-53. NSF postdoctoral fellow, 1960-61; Fulbright scholar, 1968; recipient Humboldt award, 1974-75. Mem. Am. Phys. Soc., AAAS, Fedn. Am. Scientists, Assoc. Univs. trustee 1975-90 . Home: Ithaca N.Y. Died Sept. 17, 1990.

DE WITT, LEW CALVIN, song writer; b. Roanoke, Va., Mar. 12, 1938; s. L.C. and Rose E. (Hogan) De W.; m. Judy Wells, Feb. 16, 1980; children: Denver Dale, Donna Kay, Brain Zachary, Shannon Lee. With Statler Bros., Nashville, 1955-82, v.p. prodn., 1973-75; v.p. Am. Cowboy, Nashville, from 1973. Songs include Just in Time, 1965, Samson, 1971, Is That What You'd Have Me Do, 1969, Flowers on the Wall, 1963, So This Is Love, 1970, Pictures, 1970, Ten Commandments, 1967, The Strand, 1973, The Boy Inside of Me, 1972, The Kingdom of Heaven is at Hand, 1974, The Dreamer, 1974, The Teacher, 1975, The Song of Solomon, 1975, Things, 1972, Thank You World, The Movies, Quite a Long Long Time, others. Recipient Grammy and Country Music Assn. awards. Home: Waynesboro Va. Died Aug. 15, 1990.

DEWOLFE, JAMES PERNETTE, bishop; b. Kansas City, Kans., Apr. 7, 1895; s. George Edward and Caroline Evangeline (Gilges) DeW.; m. Elizabeth Spittler Owen, June 28, 1916 (dec. Jan., 1963); children: James Pernette Jr., Phillip, Elizabeth. BA, St. John's U., 1920; DD (hon.), Kenyon Coll., 1932; STD (hon.), Columbia U., 1941; LLD, Adelphi U., 1946. Rector various chs. Kans., Mo., 1919-40; dean The Cathedral Ch. St. John the Divine, N.Y.C., 1940-42; consecrated bishop Diocese of L.I., 1942; pres. Cathedral Sch. St. Mary, Cathedral Sch. St. Paul; pres. head. dept. practical theology L.I. Sch. Theology; pres. Provincial Synod Second Province Protestant Episc. Ch., 1952-55; numerous positions ch. affairs, from 1923. Author: The Churchman's Scrap Book, The Office and Work of the Holy Ghost, The Family Day Plan for the Pastoral Ministry, A Marriage Manual, Answers to Laymen's Questions; contbr. to profl. jours. Active Coun. Episc. Actors Guild of Am., Home for Old Men and Aged Couples, N.Y.C., 1940-42, Adelphi Coll., 1944-52, Gen. Theol. Sem., House of the Redeemer. Mem. Faculty Club of Columbia U., Cherry Valley Golf Club, Union Leage (N.Y.C), Meadowlands Country Club, Garden City Gold Club, Port Jefferson (L.I.) Club, Yacht Club, Sigma Xi. *

DEXTER, JOHN, opera, stage and film director; b. Derby, Eng., Aug. 2, 1925; s. Harry James and Rose D. Assoc. dir. English Stage Co., 7 yrs.; dir. plays Yes - and After, 1957, Each in His Wilderness, 1958, Chicken Soup with Barley, 1958, Roots, 1959, The Kitchen, 1959, This Year, Next Year, 1960, I'm Talking About Jerusalem, 1960, South, 1961, The Keep, 1961, England, Our England, 1962, The Blood of the Bambergs, 1962, Jackie the Jumper, 1963, Saint Joan, 1963, Hobson's Choice, Othello, Royal Hunt of the Sun, 1964, Armstrong's Last Goodnight, 1965, Black Comedy, 1965, The Storm, 1966, A Woman Killed with Kindness, 1971, Tyger, 1971, The Misanthrope, 1973, Equus, N.Y.C., 1973, 74, The Party, 1973, Phaedra Britannica, 1975, Do I Hear a Waltz?, N.Y.C., 1965, Benevenuto Cellini, 1966, Black Comedy and White Liars, N.Y.C., 1967, Wise Child, 1967, The Old Ones, 1972, In Praise of Love, 1973, Equus, N.Y.C., 1974 (Tony award best dir.), Pygmalion, 1974, M. Butterfly, N.Y.C., 1988 (Tony award best dir.); dir. prodns. of Un Ballo in Maschera, I Vespri Sicliani, From the House of the Dead, Hamburg State Opera, Boris Godurov, Billy Budd, all at Hamburg State Opera; dir. Sadler's Wells Opera prodn. The Devils of Loudon, Nat. Theatre prodn. Gallileo, 1980, Shoemaker's Holiday, 1981; ind. dir. on West End, London and Broadway including Jessica Tandy in The Glass Menagerie, 1983; dir. Paris Opera prodn. I Vespri Siciliani; dir. prodns. Met. Opera, N.Y.C., 1974-81, advisor, 1981-84, including Le Prophete, Dialogues of the Carmelites, Lulu, 1976-77, Rigoletto, 1977-78, Billy Budd, The Bartered Bride, Don Pasquale, Don Carlo, 1978-79, Die Entfuhrung aus dem Serail, 1979, The Rise and Fall of the City of Mahagonny, Don Carlo, 1979, Parade, 1981, Stravinsky, 1981, The Portage to San Cristobal, 1982, Gigi, The Cocktail Party, in London, from 1985; films The Virgin Soldiers, 1969, The Sidelong Glances of a Pigeon Kicker, 1970, I Want What I Want, 1972; assoc. dir. plays Nat Theatre, 1963-66, 71-75. Home: London England Died Mar. 23, 1990.

DEYOUNG, HERBERT CORNELL, lawyer; b. Harvey, Ill., Feb. 16, 1904; s. Frederic Robert and Miriam (Cornell) DeY.; m. Virginia Winston, Dec. 28, 1940; children: James Winston, Laura Cornell Morsman. AB, U. Chgo., 1925, JD, 1928. Bar: Ill. 1928. Assoc. Gorham, Adams, White & DeYoung and predecessors, Chgo., 1928-34, ptnr., 1934-89; mem. Ill. Commn. on Adoption Laws, 1957-59. Mem. Ill. Commn. on Higher Edn., 1959-61; bd. dirs. TB Inst. Chgo. and Cook County (now Chgo. Lung Assn.), 1936-89, mem. exec. com., 1937-89, pres., 1946-56; bd. dirs. Am. Lung Assn., 1947-89, mem. exec. com., 1956—, pres., 1961-62; bd. dirs. Welfare Coun. Met. Chgo., 1954-66, mem. exec. com., 1956, 59-61, treas., 1959-61. Recipient Dearholt and Ross medals Chgo. Lung Assn., Herbert C. DeYoung medal, 1985; elected citizen fellow Inst. Medicine, Chgo., 1950. Mem. Chgo. Law Inst. (bd. mgrs. 1940-47, sec. 1941-46, pres. 1947), Owl and Serpent, Phi Beta Kappa. Home: Kenilworth Ill. Died Dec. 6, 1989; buried Meml. Park Cemetery, Skokie, Ill.

DIAL, MORSE GRANT, business company exeuctive; b. Chgo., Aug. 29, 1895; s. Grant Dunnigan and Frances (Newman) D.; m. Ethelwyn Gamble, Sept. 20, 1924; 1 child, Morse G. ME, Cornell U., 1920; D. Eng. (hon), Stevens Inst. Tech., 1954; LLD, Holy Cross Coll., 1959, W.Va. U., 1960. Jr. sales mgr. Morse and Rogers, br. Internat. Shoe Co., St. Louis, 1920-27; v.p. Brownville Bd. Co., 1927-29; assoc. Union Carbide Corp. and divsns., N.Y.C., from 1929; treas. Union Carbide Corp. and divsns., 1945-52, v.p., 1949-52, dir., from 1949, exec. v.p., 1951-52, pres., 1952-58, mem. exec. com., from 1950, chmn. bd., CEO, 1958-63; bd. dirs. Continental Ins. Co., Prudential Ins. Co., Putnam Trust Co, Greenwich, Conn., Mfrs. Hanover Trust Co. Dir. Boys Club Am., Nat. Inst. Social Scis., Round Hill Club, Belle Haven Club, Hole in the Wall Golf Club, Greenwich, Conn., Port Royal Beach Club, Naples, Fla., Links Golf Club, Nat. Golf Links of Am., The Links, Rolling Rock Club, Blind Brook Club. *

DIAMOND, RICHARD JOHN, investment company executive; b. Phila., Aug. 6, 1941; s. Joseph John and Helen Rose D.; m. Doris Gruber, June 8, 1963; children: Laura Ann, Richard John. B.S., LaSalle Coll.; M.B.A., Temple U. Acctg. mgr. Campbell Soup Co., Camden, N.J.; controller Fed. Sweet & Biscuit Co., Clifton, N.J.; pres., chief operating officer Mickelberry Corp., N.Y.C.; pres., dir. Union Capital Corp. Served with U.S. Army, 1963-65. Decorated Army Commendation medal. Mem. Fin. Execs. Inst., Nat. Assn. Accts. Clubs: Montclair Golf (N.Y.C.), Univ. (N.Y.C.). Home: West Caldwell N.J. Died July 20, 1992. †

DIBNER, BERN, electrical engineer; b. Lisianka, Ukraine, Aug. 18, 1897; came to U.S., 1904; naturalized, 1913; s. David and Hannah (Goodman) D.; m. Barbara Druss, Apr. 15, 1923; 1 child, David. EE, Poly. Inst. Of Bklyn., 1921; student, U. Zurich, 1936-37, Columbia U., 1940-41; D.Eng., Poly. Inst. Of Bklyn., 1959. Profl. engr. N.Y., Conn. Engr. Adirondack Power & Light Corp., Schenectady, N.Y., 1921-23, Electric Bond & Share Co., N.Y.C., 1923-24; founder, chmn. bd. Burndy Corp., Norwalk, Conn., from 1924; cons. elec. equipment commn. Smithsonian Instn. Author: Leonardo da Vinci, Military Engineer, 1946, Moving the Obelisks, 1950, Heralds of Science, 1955, Agricola on Metals, 1958, The Atlantic Cable, 1959, Darwin of the Beagle,

1960, Oersted and the Discovery of Electromagnetism, 1961, The Victoria and the Triton, 1962, The New Rays of Prof. Rontgen, 1963, The Brundy Library, 1964, Alessandro Volta and the Electric Battery, 1965. Founder Burndy Libr., 1936; v.p. Fairfield Youth Sci. Mus.; trustee U. Bridgeport, Yale Med. Libr.; fellow Brandeis U., Pierpont Morgan Libr. With S.A.T.C, World War I.; lt. col. USAAF, 1942-45. Decorated Bronze Star medal. Fellow AIEE; mem. Coun. Hist. of Sci. Soc., Coun. Soc. Hist. Tech., Elec. Hist. Found. (chmn.), Am. Tech. Soc., Tau Beta Pi, Eta Kappa Nu. *

DICHTER, ERNEST, consulting psychologist, marketing educator; b. Vienna, Austria, Aug. 14, 1907; came to U.S., 1938; s. William and Mathilde (Schneider) D.; m. Hedy Langfelder, July 17, 1935; children—Thomas William, Susan Jane. PhD, U. Vienna, 1934; licenciés es lettres, Sorbonne, Paris, 1935. Cert. psychologist, N.Y. Dir. rsch. J. Stirling Getchell, Inc. (advt. agy.), N.Y.C., 1939-43; cons. psychologist on programs CBS, 1943-45; pres. Ernest Dichter Motivations, Inc., Peekskill, N.Y., 1945-91; cons. psychologist Dichter Inst. Internat., Ltd., 1990-91; prof. mktg. Nova U., Fort Lauderdale, Fla., 1972-73. Author: (chapter) Radio Research The Psychology of Radio Commercials, 1943-44, Television Research series of 9 articles in Tide mag., 1945, The Psychology of Everyday Living, 1946, Motivational and Market Behavior, chpt. on testing techniques, 1958, The Strategy of Desire, 1960, Handbook of Consumer Motivations, 1964, Motivating Human Behavior, 1971, The Naked Managers, 1974, The New World of Packaging, 1975, Why Not, Management Problems of the '70's, 1973, Sascha and the Onion, 1974, Sascha and the Suppose Store, 1974, Sascha is Not Afraid, 1974, Comment Vivrons Nous en L'An 2000, 1979, Getting Motivated, 1979, How Hot a Manager Are You?, 1987, New Thinking for New Markets, 1991; frequent speaker acad., bus. and advt. groups; contbr. articles on market rsch.; introduced depth interviewing into mktg. rsch., adapted numerous clin. techniques to gen. consumer testing. Named to Hall of Fame, Market Rsch. Coun., 1983. Mem. APA, Am. Mktg. Assn. (Hall of Fame 1985). Home: Cortland Manor N.Y. Died Nov. 21, 1991; buried Rose Hills Meml. Pk., Putnam Valley, N.Y.

DICK, ALBERT BLAKE, III, manufacturing company executive, corporate director; b. Chgo., Mar. 10, 1918; s. Albert Blake and Helen (Aldrich) D.; m. Elisabeth York, Sept. 14, 1940; children: Albert Blake IV, John Howard, Frederick Aldrich; m. Susan Drake Bent, Aug. 20, 1960. Student, Yale U., 1938-39. With A.B. Dick Co., 1939-82, holding various positions in purchasing, mfg., sales, and controllers divs., dir., 1946-82, treas., 1947-60, pres., 1947-61, chmn., 1961-82; dir. Northern Trust Bank/Lake Forest (Ill.). Life trustee Ill. Inst. Tech.; trustee, chmn. exec. bd. Rush-Presbyn.-St. Luke's Med. Center; dir. Lake Forest Hosp., former chmn.; chmn. Lake Forest Audit Com., 1989. Served with USN, 1942-45. Clubs: Economic, Chicago, Attic, Commercial, Metropolitan (Chgo.); Onwentsia (Lake Forest); Cotton Bay (Eleuthera, Bahamas); Old Elm (Ft. Sheridan, Ill.); Birnam Wood Golf, The Valley (Santa Barbara, Calif.), The Valley Montecito. Home: Lake Forest Ill. Died May 19, 1989; buried Lake Forest Cemetery.

DICK, WILLIAM A., banker. Former chmn., pres. Comml. & Indsl. Bank of Memphis; former exec. v.p. Gen. Bankshares; pres., also dir. First Nat. Bank & Trust Co. (dissolved), Oklahoma City, until 1985. Home: Oklahoma City Okla. Deceased. †

DICKERMAN, HERBERT WILLIAM, science administrator, molecular endocrinologist; b. N.Y.C., Aug. 3, 1928; s. Leopold and Bertha Lee Dickerman; m. Mary Elizabeth Cole, Feb. 3, 1963; children: Leah Anne, Samuel Cole, Sara Ruth; 1 child from previous marriage, Lisa Akchin. Student, U. Wis., 1945-47; MD, SUNY Downstate Med. Ctr., 1952; PhD in Biology, Johns Hopkins U., 1960. Intern Osler Med. Svc. Johns Hopkins U. Hosp., Balt., 1952-53; instr. medicine Johns Hopkins U. Sch. Medicine, Balt., 1960-63, assoc. prof., 1966-75; asst. resident internal medicine Stanford U. Hosp., 1953-54; investigator Nat. Heart Inst., Bethesda, Md., 1963-66; rsch. scientist labs and rsch. div. N.Y. State Dept. Health, Albany, 1975-82, dir. clin. scis. Wadsworth Ctr. for Labs. and Rsch., 1982-85, acting dir. Wadsworth Ctr. for Labs. and Rsch., 1985-86, dir. Wadsworth Ctr. for Labs. and Rsch., 1986-91. Lt. USNR, 1954-55. Mem. Am. Soc. Biochemistry and Molecular Biology, Endocrine Soc., John Hopkins U. Soc. Scholars. Democrat. Jewish. Home: Loudonville N.Y Died Dec. 23, 1991; buried Tampa, Fla.

DICKERSON, FREDERICK REED, lawyer, educator; b. Chgo., Nov. 11, 1909; s. Fred George and Rena (Reed) D.; m. Jane Morrison, June 14, 1939; children: Elizabeth Ann (Mrs. David D. Brown), John Scott, Martha Reed. Grad., Lake Forest Acad., 1927; AB, Williams Coll., 1931; LLB, Harvard U., 1934; LLM (Univ. fellow 1938-39), Columbia U., 1939, JSD, 1950; LLD (hon.), Ind. U., 1986. Bar: Mass. 1934, Ill. 1936, U.S. Supreme Ct. 1943. Assoc. Goodwin, Procter & Hoar, Boston, 1934-35, McNab, Holmes & Long, Chgo., 1936-38; asst. prof. law Washington U., St. Louis, 1939-40, U. Pitts., 1940-42; atty. OPA, 1942-47; asst. legis. counsel U.S. Ho. of Reps., 1947-49, Joint Army-Air Force Statutory Revision Group; chmn. com. on codification, dep. asst. gen. counsel U.S. Dept. Def., 1949-58; prof. law Ind. U., 1958-83, prof. emeritus, 1983-91, assoc. dean, 1971-75, founding dir. Inst. for Legal Drafting, 1988-91; disting. vis. prof. law So. Ill. U., 1976, 80; pres. F.G. Dickerson Co., Chgo., 1948-82; chmn. commn. on uniform laws State of Ind., 1969-81; mem. Ind. Statute Revision Commn., 1969-70, adv. bd. Ctr. Semiotic Research: Law, Govt.., Econs.; cons. Dept. Def., 1958-59, 66, FAA, 1960-65, Dept. Transp., 1967-69, Pres.'s Com. on Consumer Interests, 1967-68, Commn. on Govt. Procurement, 1971-72, Gen. Acctg. Office, 1973-76; lectr. Northwestern U., 1938, Am. U., 1956, 58, Practising Law Inst., 1961, 79, U.K. Govt. Legal Officers' Course, 1972, U.S. CSC, 1971-76, lectr. Center for Adminstrv. Justice, 1975-79. Author: Products Liability and the Food Consumer, 1951, Legislative Drafting, 1954, 2d edit., 1986, Fundamentals of Legal Drafting, 1965, 2d edit., 1986, Interpretation and Application of Statutes, 1975; editor: Legal Problems Affecting Private Swimming Pools, 1961, Product Safety in Household Goods, 1968, Professionalizing Legislative Drafting-The Federal Experience, 1973, Proc. International Seminar and Workshop on the Teaching of Legal Drafting, 1977, Cases and Materials on Legislation, 1978, Materials on Legal Drafting, 1981; mem. editorial bd. Jurimetrics Jour., 1962-85; bd. advisors Jour. of Legis., 1977-91; contbr.: articles to Harper's mag., Esquire, Ency. Americana. Mem. Arlington Civic Symphony, 1950-53; pres. Chevy Chase Citizens Assn., 1955-56, Friends of Music, Ind. U., 1972-73. Recipient Disting. Civilian Service Award, Dept. Def., 1957, award Assn. Am. Law Schs., 1983; Ford Found. law faculty fellow Harvard U., 1961-62; Am. Assembly fellow, 1968. Mem. Am. Law Inst., Nat. Conf. Commrs. on Uniform State Laws, ABA (chmn. standing com. law and tech. 1968-69, chmn. standing com. legis. drafting 1969-73, chmn. com. on lang. sci. and formal systems 1982-87), Ind. Bar Assn., Monroe County Bar Assn., Pierian Sodality of 1808, Order of Coif, Phi Alpha Delta, Phi Gamma Delta. Methodist. Home: Bloomington Ind. Died June, 1991; buried Bloomington, Ind.

DICKERSON, THOMAS MILTON, accountant, educator; b. Webster County, Ky., Feb. 2, 1898; s. Daniel Webster and Mina (Witherspoon) D.; m. Nelle Caldwell Vaughn, Nov. 28, 1922; 1 child, June Nelle (Mrs. John E. Sturgis). Student, U. Mich., 1919-21; BA, Bowling Green (Ky.) Coll. of Commerce, 1924; AB, Western Ky. State Tchrs. Coll., 1926; MBA, Northwestern U., 1929. CPA, Ky., Ohio. High sch. prin. Simpson County, Ky., 1921-23; asst. prof. acct. Bowling Green (Ky.) Coll. of Commerce, 1923-28, head dept. acct., 1929-30; teaching fellow Northwesten U., Chgo., 1928-29; asst. prof. econ. U. Louisville, Ky., 1930-31; asst. sec. Nat. Assn. Cost Accts., 1931-34; chief staff acct., Nat. Com. Municipal Acctg., 1934-35; chief staff acct., Nat. Com. Western Reserve U., 1935-63, assoc. prof. acctg., 1935-42, prof. acctg., 1942-63, head acctg. dept., 1936-62, dir. divsn. bus. adminstrn., 1943-48; lectr. acctg. Coll. Bus. Adminstrn. U. So. Fla., Tampa, Fla., from 1963; vis. prof. Grad. Bus. Sch. Stanford U., summer 1956. Contbr. articles to profl. jours. Mem. AICPAs, Am. Acctg. Assn. (v.p. 1952), Ohio CPA Soc., Nat. Assn. Accts. (mem. nat. bd., dir. 1939-46), Delta Sigma Pi, Beta Alpha Psi (past pres. grand coun.), Beta Gamma Sigma. Democrat. Baptist. *

DICKEY, JOHN MILLER, architect; b. Chgo., Jan. 9, 1911; s. Samuel and Louise (Atherton) D.; m. Harriet Marcy Hunt, Oct. 11, 1941; children: Samuel, Alice, John. A.B., Princeton U., 1933, M.F.A., 1935. Partner firm Price & Dickey, Media, Pa., 1947-62; propr. John M. Dickey (specializing in historic research and restoration), Media, Pa., 1962-90; mem. properties com. Nat. Trust Historic Preservation, 1973-80; mem. Pa. Rev. Bd., 1970-80, Valley Forge State Park Commn., 1972-77, Pa. Historic Preservation Bd., 1980-90. Author articles in field.; prin. restorations include Walnut St. Theatre, Phila., Athenaeum and City Tavern, Phila., Cliveden, Phila., Stenton, Phila., Andalusia, Phila., George Read, II House, New Castle, Del., Nat. Meml. Arch in Valley Forge (Pa.) Nat. Hist. Pk., Frelinghuysen House, Raritan, N.J., Morris Arboretum, Chestnut Hill, N.J. Recipient Nat. award Historic House Assn. Am., 1980. Fellow AIA (preservation coordinator Pa. 1972-76), Soc. Archtl. Historians (treas. 1962-66, dir. 1968-71), Assn. Preservation Tech. (v.p. 1973-75), Phila. Art Alliance. Democrat. Club: Princeton. Home: Westtown Pa. Died Sept. 19, 1990; buried Oxford, Pa. †

DICKEY, JOHN SLOAN, university president; b. Lock Haven, Pa., Nov. 4, 1907; s. John W. and Gretchen (Sloan) D.; m. Christina M. Gillespie, Nov. 26, 1932; children—Sylvia Alexander, Christina Louise (Mrs. Stewart P. Stearns, Jr.), John Sloan. A.B., Dartmouth Coll., 1929; J.D., Harvard U., 1932. Bar: Mass. bar 1932. Practiced in Boston, 1932; asst. to commr. Mass. Dept. Correction, 1933; asst. to asst. sec. of state and asst. to legal adviser U.S. Dept. State, 1934-36; law practice with Gaston, Snow, Hunt, Rice & Boyd, Boston, 1936-40; spl. asst. to sec. of state, 1940, spl. asst. to Coordinator of Inter-Am. Affairs, 1940-44; detailed to U.S. Dept. State as chief World Trade Intelligence div.; Dir. Office Pub. Affairs, Dept. State, 1944-45; pub. liaison officer U.S. delegation to UN Conf. on Internat. Orgn., San Francisco, 1945; lectr. in Am. fgn. policies Sch. Advanced Internat. Studies, Washington, 1944-45; pres. Dartmouth Coll., 1945-70, pres. emeritus, Bicentennial prof. pub. affairs, 1970; sr. vis. fellow Council on Fgn. Relations, 1971. Author: The Dartmouth Experience, Canada and the American Presence; Contbg. author: The Secretary of State; Editor: The United States and Canada; Contbr. law and fgn. affairs jours. Mem. Phi Beta Kappa. Home: Hanover N.H. Died Feb. 9, 1991.

DICKIE, HELEN AIRD, physician, educator; b. North Freedom, Wis., Feb. 19, 1913; d. Robert Bruce and Anna (Adams) D. BA with high honors, U. Wis., 1935, MD with high honors, 1937. Diplomate Am. Bd. Internal Medicine. Intern, chest resident Los Angeles County Hosp., 1937-40; resident medicine U. Wis. Med. Sch., Madison, 1940-42, staff instr. medicine, 1942-43, asst. prof., 1943-45, asso. prof., 1945-55, prof. medicine, 1955-83, prof. emeritus, from 1983; mem. dept. medicine and student health U. Wis. Hosps., 1942-44, mem. dept. pulmonary sect., 1944-73, head pulmonary sect., 1973-83, vice chief of staff , 1964-65, chief of staff, 1965-66; mem. U. Wis. Senate, 1970-78; cons. Middleton VA Hosp., Madison, 1942-88; mem. nat. task force rsch. on respiratory diseases NIH, 1972-74. Author numerous book chpts. and articles on diseases of the lung. Recipient Med. Woman of Yr. award Med. Coll. Physicians, 1975; J. Stephans Tripp scholar, 1936. Faculty Meml. Resolution for her work on Tb and edn. presented in her name. Master and Fellow ACP; mem. AMA, AAUP, AAUW (Woman of Distinction award), Wis. State Med. Soc., N.Y. Acad. Sci., Cen. Soc. Clin. Rsch., Am. Thoracic Soc., Am. Fedn. Clin. Research, Wis. Tb and Respiratory Diseases Assn. (pres. 1968, dir.), Am. Lung Assn. Wis. (dir., sr. coun. mem. 1986), Miss. Valley Thoracic Soc. (pres.), Wis. Acad. Sci., Ars and Letters, U. Wis. Med. Alumni Assn., U. Wis. Alumni Assn., Bascom Hill Soc., Nat. Trust Hist. Preservation, Friends U. Wis. Arboretum (life), Olbrich Bot. Soc. (life), Friends of WHA-TV, Wis. Wildlife Fedn., Sigma Delta Epsilon, Sigma Epsilon Sigma, Alpha Omega Alpha, Madison Civics Club, others civic orgns. Home: Madison Wis. Died Dec. 19, 1988; buried Oak Hill Cemetery, North Freedom, Wis.

DICKSON, CECIL B, journalist, newspaper editor; s. Joel Luther and Ida (Milam) D.; m. Daugherty Collins, Apr. 22, 1935; children: Cecile Beverly, Sarah Daugherty, Walter Milam. Student, A&M Coll., 1914-16, 20. Worked on Okla. ranch, in Tex. oil fields, lumber camps, gold mines (Colo.), shipyard (Mass.); sailed on tramp steamers; civil engr. A.T. & S.F. Railway; news reporter Quincy, Boston, Mass., New London, Conn.; editor Dennison (Tex.) Herald, Texarkanian, Ark.; corr. AP, Dallas, Austin, Tex., Washington; corr. Internat. News Svc. and King Features; chief corr. Chgo. Sun, 1941-43; chief Gannet Nat. Svc., Washington; assoc. editor Whaley Eaton News Letter Corp., 1943-48; war corr., 1945; coord. info. Ho. of Reps., Washington, 1949-51; asst. to pres. Motion Picture Assn. Am., 1951-59; legis. rep. AMA; sec. Congl. corr.'s com., 1943-44. Author: How to Write Your Congressman. Del. Dem. Nat. Conv., 1960, 64. With USMC, World War I. Mem. Overseas Writers, Am. Legion, Brotherhood of St. Andrews, Nat. Press Club, Sigma Delta Chi, Kappa Alpha. Episc. *

DIEDRICH, WILLIAM LAWLER, lawyer; b. De Kalb, Ill., Nov. 17, 1923; s. William Leo and Marie Antoinette (Lawler) D.; m. Margaret Lucille Benson, Aug. 6, 1949; children: Peter, Louise, Anne. B.A., St. Benedict's Coll., 1949; LL.B., Georgetown U., 1951. Bar: D.C. 1952, Calif. 1954, U.S. Supreme Ct. 1956. Assoc. Pillsbury, Madison & Sutro, San Francisco, 1952-63, ptnr., 1963-92; dir. San Francisco Com. Urban Affairs, 1972-74. Co-author: How to Defend an Employment Discrimination Case, 1982. Pres. bd. dirs. Catholic Social Service, San Francisco, 1980, 81; bd. dirs. Cath. Charities, 1982-87, Benedictine Coll., 1972-80; bd. dirs. San Francisco Bay Area Council Girl Scouts U.S., 1985-87, St. Anthony Found., from 1990. Served to sgt. U.S. Army, 1943-46, Burma, India. Recipient Kans. Monk award Benedictine Coll., Atchison, 1977, Cross of St. Benedict, 1987. Mem. State Bar Calif., Bar Assn. San Francisco (joint chmn. com. equal employment 1969-72, chmn. com. labor laws 1979-81), Bar Assn. D.C. Democrat. Roman Catholic. Home: San Francisco Calif. Died May 8th, 1992. †

DIEHL, WALTER FRANCIS, labor union official; b. Revere, Mass., Apr. 13, 1907; s. John H. and Mary J. (Levinus) D.; 3 children. Student, Northeastern U., 1925-27. Moving picture machine operator, 1927-46; with Internat. Alliance Theatrical Stage Employees and Moving Picture Machine Operators U.S. and Can., 1944-86; mem. exec. bd. Local 182, Boston, 1944-46, bus. agt., 1946-53, internat. rep., 1953-57, asst. internat. pres., 1957-74, internat. pres., 1974-86; mem. bd. Iatse (AFL-CIO affiliate). Mem. Catholic Actors Guild (v.p. 1964). Home: Hallendale Fla. Died Aug. 26, 1991.

DIERKS, HENRY ALFRED, mining engineer; b. Ribeauville, France, Jan. 7, 1894; s. John Jacob and Salome (Metzger) D.; m. Eva Humphries Le Sueur, June 5, 1926; children: John H., Kathleen (Mrs. Charles B. Gallagher, Jr.). Student, Sch. Mines, Bochum, France, 1912-14; Engr. of Mines, Mining Acad., Frieberg, France, 1920. Registered profl. engr., Pa. Asst. supt.

German Potash Corp., Bernterode, Germany, 1920-22; asst. to pres. Bavarian Lignite Mining Co., Frankfurt, Germany, 1922-24; gen. mgr. George F. Lee Coal Co., Wilkes-Barre, Pa., 1924-28; cons. engr. Stuart, James & Cooke Inc., N.Y.C., 1928-31, Pierce Mgmt., Scranton, Pa., 1931-43; chief mining engr. Glen Alden Coal Co., 1943-47, v.p., gen. mgr., 1948-56; pres. Assoc. Engrs. Inc.; cons. U.S. Bur. Mines for Pa. anthrocite, 1951-56; chief bur. of mine drainage U.S. Bur. of Mines, from 1956. Mem. AIME (chmn. Pa. anthracite sect. for 1950), Nat. Soc. Profl. Engrs., Mining and Metall. Soc. Am., U.S. and Pa. C. of C.'s, Pa. Soc. Profl. Engrs. (past pres., Luzerne), Mason. *

DIETRICH, MARLENE (MARIA MAGDALENA VON LOSCH), actress; b. Berlin, Germany; d. Edward and Josephine (Felsing) von Losch; ed. Augusta Victoria Sch., Berlin; m. Rudolf Siebet, May 13, 1924; 1 dau., Maria. Began as violinist; debut as actress in Broadway, Berlin; 4 years with Max Reinhardt; later in film The Blue Angel (German); came to U.S., 1930, and since starred in motion pictures, including: Martin Roumagnec (French), 1946, Golden Earrings, 1947, Foreign Affair, 1948, Stage Fright, 1950, No Highway in the Sky, 1951, Rancho Notorious, 1952, numerous others, the latest including The Monte Carlo Story, 1957, Around the World in 80 Days, 1956, Witness for the Prosecution, 1958, Judgment at Nuremberg, 1961, Just a Gigolo, 1978; also appearances in night clubs and theatres. Recipient Spl. Tony award, 1967-68. Author: Marlene Dietrich's ABC, 1962; My Life Story, 1979, autobiography Marlene, transl., 1989. Toured Army Service Camps, Europe, 1945; concert tour U.S., 1973. Decorated Comdr. Legion of Honor (France).Died May 6, 1992. Home: Paris France †

DIGGES, SAM COOK, broadcasting executive; b. Columbia, Mo., Jan. 8, 1916; s. Charles William and Frances (Cook) D.; m. Carol Jean Ellis, Dec. 16, 1961; 1 child by previous marriage, Sam Cook. B.A. in Journalism, U. Mo., 1937. Advt. salesman, columnist Washington Daily News, 1937-42; time salesman sta. WMAL/WMAL- TV, Washington, 1942-49; with CBS, Inc., 1949-81; gen. mgr. sta. WCBS-TV, N.Y.C., 1954-58; adminstrv. v.p. CBS Films Inc., N.Y.C., 1958-67; exec. v.p. CBS-owned AM stas. CBS Radio div., 1967-70; pres. CBS Radio div., 1970-81; commentator Sta WPTV, Palm Beach, 1982-87; bd. curators Stephens Coll., 1970-82; bd. dirs. Advt. Council, 1976-81, Radio Advt. Bur., 1969-81, New Eng. Patriots Football Club, 1981-89. Served with U.S. Mcht. Marine, 1944-45. Recipient medal of honor U. Mo. Sch. Journalism, 1973, Faculty-Alumni gold medal U. Mo.-Columbia Alumni Assn., 1974; Communicator of Year award Sales and Mktg. Execs. Internat., 1977; Maj. League Baseball Commr.'s award, 1980. Mem. Internat. Radio and TV Soc. (pres. 1963-65, bd. govs. 1959-67, gold medal 1981), Nat. Acad. TV Arts and Scis. (bd. trustees 1966-67, gov. N.Y.C. chpt. 1965-67), Phi Delta Theta. Republican. Lutheran. Clubs: Everglades, Beach (Palm Beach, Fla.). Home: Palm Beach Fla. Died Sept. 9, 1990; buried Palm Beach, Fla.

DI GIORGIO, ROBERT, consumer products executive; b. N.Y.C., Dec. 2, 1911; s. Salvatore and Marie (Meyer) Di G.; m. Eleanor Vollmann, Jan. 20, 1940 (div.); children: Ann, Barbara, Christine, Dorothy; m. Patricia Kuhrts Sharman, Aug. 7, 1964. A.B., Yale, 1933; B.L., Fordham U., 1936. Bar: N.Y. 1937. With Di Giorgio Corp., San Francisco, 1937-85, pres., 1962-71, chmn. bd., chief exec. officer, 1971-82, chmn. bd., 1982-86, chmn. exec. com., 1986-91. Clubs: Metropolitan (N.Y.C.); California (Los Angeles); Pacific-Union (San Francisco), Commonwealth (San Francisco), Bohemian (San Francisco). Home: San Francisco Calif. Died Feb. 13, 1991. †

DIKE, PHIL, artist, educator; b. Redlands, Calif., Apr. 6, 1906; s. Andrew Noble and Jennie E. (Twigg) D.; m. Betty Love Woodward, June 17, 1933; 1 son, Woodward Dike. Student, Chouinard Art Inst., 1924-28, Art Students League, 1928, Am. Acad., Fontainbleau, France, 1930. Color coord., story designer Walt Disney Studios, 1935-45; instr. figure painting Chouinard Art Inst., 1945- 50; instr. painting Scripps Coll., 1950, 70; prof. emeritus art Scripps Coll. and Clarmont CGrad. Sch. Recipient Dana Mention, Pa. Acad. Fine Arts 1947, Nat. Acad. Water Color prize 1950, 58, 1st prize Calif. Water Color Soc. 1931, 1st prize Watercolor Butler Inst. Am. Art 1959, Albert Dorne purchase prize Am. Water Color Soc. 1960, Grumbacher prize Calif. Water Color Soc. 1960, Paul B. Remmy Meml. award Am. Water Color Exhbn. 1962, purchase prize Springfield Nat. Watercolor Exhbn., 1967, Calif. Nat. Watercolor Exhbn. 1969, Water Color U.S.A. 1972, Watchung award Calif. Nat. Watercolor Exhbn. 1974, Richard S. Grant Meml. award Nat. Watercolor Exhbn. 1976), Exhbns., Carnegie, 1936, 37, 50, Chgo. Art Inst., Pa. Acad. Fine Arts, Salon, Paris, France, Met. Mus. Art, 1951, Nat. Acad.; Works in permanent collection, Met. Mus. Art, Wood Mus., Santa Barbara Mus. (Awarded 1st prize oil painting, Golden Gate Expn. 1940); Am. Watercolor Taipei Fine Arts Mus., Taiwan Republic of China, 1985, Springfield Art Mus., 1987, Calif. Romantics Pres.'s Show 1921-87, Nat. Watercolor Soc., Calif., 1987, Scripps Coll.; Claremont Grad. Sch. One Man Show, 1950-85, Los Angeles County Mus. Coll., Pasadena Art Mus. Coll., Scripps Coll., Claremont Calif., Coll.; exhibited in group shows at Santa Barbara Mus. Art, 1988; subject of artbook "Phil Dike" by Janice Loovos and Gordon McClellan, 1988. Recipient Achievement medal Pepsi Cola Co., 1946; Hatfield prize, 1946; Cole prize, 1952; Pottinger award, 1953; Brugger award, 1957, 66; John L. Ernst award, 1965; Phil Dike Meml. Scholarship established at Scripps Coll. Mem. Nat. Acad., Am. Watercolor Soc. (hon. v.p. 1954), Calif. Watercolor Soc. (past pres.), Nat. Watercolor Soc., West Coast Watercolor Soc. (v.p. 1964-65). Home: Claremont Calif. Died Feb. 24, 1990; buried Cambria, Calif.

DILLARD, DUDLEY, economist, educator; b. Ontario, Oreg., Oct. 18, 1913; s. John James and Frances (Cunning) D.; m. Louisa Gardner, August 22, 1939; children: Lorraine Gardner (Mrs. William C. Gray), Amber Frances (Mrs. Douglas G. Kelly). B.S., U. Calif., 1935, Ph.D., 1940; vis. scholar, Harvard, 1939, Columbia, 1940. Teaching asst. U. Calif., 1935-36, Flood fellow in econs., 1936-37, research asst., 1937-38, teaching asst., 1938-39; Newton Booth Travelling fellow, 1939-40; instr. econs. U. Colo., 1940-41, U. Del., 1941-42; asst. prof. to assoc. prof. U. Md., 1942-47, prof., 1947-84, prof. emeritus, 1984-91, chmn. dept. econs., 1951-75, acting provost div. behavioral and social scis., 1976-77; vis. asso. prof. econs. Columbia, 1948-50, vis. prof., summer, 1951, 55, 58; cons. U.S. Army, 1945-46. Author: The Economics of John Maynard Keynes, 1948 (translated 10 langs.); (with others) Post-Keynesian Economics, 1954; Economic Development of North Atlantic Community, 1967; (with others) The Policy Consequences of John Maynard Keynes, 1985, The Foundations of Keynesian Analysis, 1988; Editorial bd.: Jour. Econ. History, 1948-54; Contbr. profl. jours. Chmn. Gov.'s Com. on Employment in Md., 1962-64; mem. Gov.'s Adv. Com. on Manpower Devel. and Tng., 1962-67; Mem. U.S. exec. bd. Am. Coll. in Paris, 1966-86, chmn., 1979-81. Recipient Veblen-Commons award, 1986. Mem. Am. Econ. Assn., So. Econ. Assn. (pres. 1976-77), Eastern Econ. Assn. (exec. bd. 1982-85, pres. 1987-88), Assn. Evolutionary Econs. (pres. 1979), History Econs, Soc. (v.p. 1982-83, pres.-elect 1990), Econ. History Soc., AAUP, Phi Beta Kappa, Pi Gamma Mu, Beta Gamma Sigma, Beta Alpha Psi. Club: Cosmos (Washington). Home: University Park Md. Died Aug. 28, 1991; buried Ft. Lincoln Cemetery, Brentwood, Md.

DILLARD, WILLIAM ELBERT, rail road executive; b. Buena Vista, Ga., Feb. 13, 1898; s. Joseph Demps and Ella Jane (Mathis) D.; m. Elizabeth Pace, Jan 1, 1919; children: Jane (Mrs. B. Ellis deTreville), Sara (Mrs. T.F. Morrison, Jr.), William Elbert, James C. Student, Ga. Pub. Schs. With C. of Ga. Ry., from 1915, advances through levels to v.p., 1915-54; pres., dir., mem. exec. com. C. of Ga. Ry., Savannah, Ga., from 1954; pres., dir., mem. exec. com. Ocean S.S. Co. of Savannah, Southwestern R.R.; pres. dir. Albany Passenger Terminal Co., C. of Ga. Motor Transport Co., Chatham Terminal Co., Empire Land Co., Macon Terminal Co.; dir., mem. exec. com. Wrightsville & Tennville R.R., Savannah & Atlanta Ry., Fruit Growers Express Co.; v.p., dir. Atlanta Terminal Co.; dir. Augusta & Summerville R.R., Birmingham Terminal Co., Crossgate Homes, Port Wentworth Corp., Trailer Train Co., Savannah Bank & Trust Co. Dir. Savannah Children's Hosp.; trustee Shorter Coll., Rome, Ga. Mem. U.S. C of C., Ga. C. of C., So. States Indsl. Coun. (adv. bd.), Commerce Club (Savannah), Ogelthorpe Club, Rotary, Savannah Golf Club. Baptist. *

DILLON, W. MARTIN, steel and wire manufacturing executive; b. Sterling, Ill., Mar. 19, 1910; s. Paul Washington and Crete (Blackman) D.; m. Helene Reynolds, June 20, 1931 (dec. Jan. 1989); children: Peter W., Margo, Gale (Mrs. Philip Inglee). Grad., Culver Mil. Acad., 1929; student, Babson Inst., 1929-30; H.H.D., DePaul U., U. Chgo., U. Dubuque, Iowa. Asst. to pres. Northwestern Steel & Wire Co. (name formerly Northwestern Barb Wire Co.), 1939-48, pres., 1951-80, chmn. bd., 1980-86, chmn. emeritus, 1986-88. Bd. dirs. Sterling-Rock Falls Community Trust. Mem. Assn. Iron and Steel Engrs., Am. Iron and Steel Inst. (dir.), NAM, Cum Laude Soc. (Culver Mil. Acad.), Sterling C. of C. (pres. 1947, 48). Club: Union League (Chgo.). Home: Sterling Ill. Died Dec. 25, 1989; buried Riverside Cemetery, Sterling, Ill.

DIMITRIOS I, ECUMENICAL PATRIARCH See PAPADOPOULOS, DIMITRIOS

DIMMERLING, HAROLD J., bishop; b. Braddock, Pa., Sept. 23, 1914. Ed., St. Fidelis Prep. Sem., Herman, Pa., St. Charles Sem., Columbus, Ohio, St. Francis Sem., Loretto, Pa. Ordained priest Roman Catholic Ch., 1940; consecrated bishop, 1969; bishop Diocese of Rapid City, S.D., 1969-87. Home: Rapid City S.D. Died Dec. 13, 1987; buried Mt. Calvary Cemetery, Rapid City.

DIMOCK, MARSHALL EDWARD, political science educator; b. San Bernardino, Calif., Oct. 24, 1903; s. Milton Edward and Anne (Behrens) D.; m. Lucy Butler Stotesbury, Sept. 14, 1926 (dec.); children: Milton Marshall, Mark, Marianne; m. Gladys Gouverneur Ogden, June 29, 1940 (dec. July 1989); 1 child, Davis Ludlow. BA, Pomona Coll., Claremont, Calif., 1925; PhD, Johns Hopkins, 1928. Instr. polit. sci. UCLA, 1928-30, asst. prof., 1930-32; assoc. prof. pub. adminstrn. U. Chgo., 1932-41; lectr. Sch. Pub. Law and Administrn., NYU, 1941-44, prof., head govt. dept., 1955-62; 2d asst. sec. of labor, 1938-40; asso. commr. Immigration and Naturalization Service Dept. of Justice, 1940-42; dir. Recruitment and Manning Orgn. and asst. dept. war shipping adminstr., 1942-44; prof. polit. sci. Northwestern U., 1944-1948; rep. tech. assistance bd. UN, Turkey, 1953-54; co.-dir. Pub. Adminstrn. Inst. for Turkey and Middle East, 1953-54; cons. Adminstrv. Staff Coll., Eng., 1954; Ford vis. prof. pub. adminstrn. Internat. Christian U., Tokyo, 1966-67; vis. prof. U. Va., Mich., P.R., Carleton Coll., U. Ankara, Fla. State U., Adminstrv. Staff Coll., Eng., U. Colo.; vis. prof. Indian Inst. Pub. Adminstrn., U. Tex.; Fellow Social Sci. Research Council, 1932-33; Made studies for Sec. of War on Panama Canal enterprises and inland waterway transp., 1933-35; cons. Nat. Resources Com., 1935-39; chmn. Sec. of Labor's Commn. on Immigration Adminstrn., 1938-39; cons. War Dept., 1944, GAO, 1946-48; office of Sec. of Def., 1948-49; cons. Pres.'s Adv. Council Exec. Orgn., 1969-71; bd. dirs. Countryman Press, Woodstock, Vt. Author or co-author: numerous books including (textbook) Business and Government, 1949, American Government in Action, 1951, Free Enterprise and the Administrative State, 1951, Public Administration, 5th edit, 1983, A Philosophy of Administration, 1958, Administrative Vitality, 1959, The New American Political Economy, 1962, Creative Religion, 1963, The Japanese Technocracy, 1968, (autobiography) The Center of My World, 1980, Law and Dynamic Administration, 1980, (with Edgar N. Jackson) Doubting is not Enough, 1983, Crisis Management: Shoring Up America's Economy and Government, 1991; editor: Goals for Political Science, 1951; also author animal stories, 11 in book form; contbr. Internat. Jour. Pub. Adminstn. Bd. dir., mem. exec. com. United Seamen's Service, chmn. 1946-56; Pres. Shinner Found., 1947-50. Mem. Vt. State Legislature (1949-50), Fellow (council mem. 1955- 59), AAAS; mem. Internat. Inst. Adminstrv. Scis., Royal Inst. Pub. Adminstrn. (London), Internat., Am. polit. sci. assns., Nat. Acad. Pub., Unitarian Universalist Assn. (moderator 1961-64), Am. Soc. Pub. Adminstrn. (Dwight Waldo award), Soc. for Advancement of Mgmt. (pres. Washington Chapt. 1941-42, nat. dir. 1942-43, nat. v.p. 1945-46), Am. Econ. Assn., Rotary, Pi Sigma Alpha (nat. pres. 1962-64). Unitarian. Home: Bethel Vt. Died Nov. 14, 1991; buried Cherry Hill Cemetery, Bethel, Vt.

DINKELSPIEL, MARTIN J(ERROLD), lawyer; b. San Francisco, Nov. 30, 1898; s. Henry George Washington and Estelle (Jacobs) D.; m. Frances Delmore Lederman, June 20, 1929; children: Peter, Marcia. Student, U. Calif., 1916-19; LLB, Harvard U., 1922. Bar: Calif. 1921. Ptnr. Dinkelspiel& Dinkelspiel, San Francisco, from 1924; vice consul to Thailand U.S. Dept. of State, 1922-32, consul, 1932-41, consul gen., from 1947; mem. Calif. Commn. Uniform State Laws, 1944-59, chmn., 1949-59; mem. Calif. Commn. Interstate Cooperation, 1949-59; mem. bd. mgrs. Coun. State Govts. Laws, 1951-53, life mem., from 1961; mem. Govs. Adv. Com. on Children and Youth. Active Calif. Assn. Mental Health; chmn. Native Sons and Daughters Homeless Children com., 1931-36; mem. Calif. Citizens Com. Adoptions. Decorated Order of Crown of Thailand. Fellow ABA; mem. Calif. Bar Assn., San Francisco Bar Assn., Nat. Legal Aid Soc., Am. Law Inst., Am. Judicature Soc. (dir. 1957-61), Am. Arbitration Assn. (dir. from 1956), Harvard Law Sch. Assn. (pres. 1946-48), Mason. *

DINNING, JAMES SMITH, biochemist; b. Logan County, Ky., Sept. 28, 1922; s. James Starks and Fanny Blanche (Smith) D.; m. Sally Sue Hensley, Oct. 28, 1944; children: Katherine Sue, James Michael, Robin Joann, Randall Starks. B.S., U. Ky., 1946; M.S., Okla. State U., 1946, Ph.D., 1948; D.Sc. (hon.), Mahidol U., Bangkok, Thailand, 1974, U. Ark., 1984. Mem. faculty U. Ark. Med. Sch., Little Rock, 1948-63, prof. and chmn. dept. biochemistry, 1959-63, asst. dean Grad. Sch., 1959-63; dir. Rockefeller Found., Bangkok, 1963-75; research scientist U. Fla., Gainesville, 1975-85. Author research papers in field. Served with AUS, 1942-46. Recipient Lederle Med. Faculty award, 1954, Jordan Medal of Independence, 1963, Disting. Alumnus award U. Ky., 1986. Mem. Am. Inst. Nutrition (Meade-Johnson award 1964, Conrad Elvehjem award for pub. service 1984, editor jour. 1979-85), Soc. Exptl. Biology and Medicine, Am. Soc. Biol. Chemists, Sigma Xi. Home: Gainesville Fla. Deceased. †

DION, GERARD, social science educator; b. Ste. Cecile de Frontenac, Que., Can., Dec. 5, 1912; s. Albert and Georgianna (LeBlanc) D. B.A., Levis Coll., 1935; L.Th., Laval U., Quebec, Que., 1939, L.Ph., 1942, M.S.S., 1943; LL.D. (hon.), McGill U., Montreal, Que., 1975, U. B.C., Can.), Vancouver, 1976, U. Toronto, Ont., 1978, Concordia U., Montreal, 1980; D.Litt. (hon.), St. Francis Xavier U., Antigonish, N.S., 1977. Ordained priest Roman Catholic Ch., 1939; asst. prof. social sci. Laval U., 1944-49, prof. social sci., 1949-80, social sci. prof. emeritus, 1980-90, prof. indsl. relations, 1944-80, asst. dir. dept. indsl. relations, 1946-56, dir. dept. indsl. relations, 1956-63; mem. Can. Prime Minister's Task Force on Labor Relations, 1966-68; chmn. Can. Textile Labour-Mgmt. Com., 1967. Author: (with Louis O'Neill) The Christian and The Elections, Vocabulaire francais-anglais des relations professionnelles/Glossary of Terms Used in Industrial Relations, 1972, Dictionnaire canadien des relations du travail, 1976, 86; editor Relations industrielles/Indsl. Relations, from 1945; assoc. hon. editor Royal Soc. Can., from 1975. Mem. Econ. Council Can., 1976-80; mem. Acad. Panel Can. Council, 1976-78, Can. Social Scis. and Humanities Research Council, 1978-81. Decorated officer Order Can., Nat. Order Québec; Killam scholar, 1975-77; Dawson medal, 1987. Mem. Can. Indsl. Relations Assn., Assn. Internationale des relations professionnelles, Indsl. Relations Research Assn., Association internationale des sociologues de langue francaise, Association canadienne de sociologie et d'anthropologie, Association canadienne de theologie, Academie des lettres et des sciences humaines. Home: Quebec Can. Died Nov. 7, 1990.

DI PIETRO, ROBERT JOSEPH, linguist; b. Endicott, N.Y., July 18, 1932; s. Americo Dominick and Mary Agnes Di P.; m. Vincenzina Angela Giallo, Sept. 5, 1953; children: Angela Maria, Mark Andrew. B.A. cum laude, SUNY, Binghamton, 1954; M.A., Harvard U., 1955; Ph.D., Cornell U., 1960. Project linguist Center Applied Linguistics, Rome, 1960-61; mem. faculty Georgetown U., 1961-78, prof. linguistics, 1969-78, chmn. Italian dept., 1966-68; dir. Inter-Univ. English Program, Madrid, 1963-64; prof. linguistics and Italian, chmn. dept. lang., dir. inter-deptl. program in linguistics U. Del., Newark, 1978-85, prof. dept. linguistics, 1985-91; Fulbright lectr., Italy, 1960-61, Spain, 1963-64, Fed. Republic Germany, 1978; Andrew Mellon Disting. lectr. Georgetown U., 1975-78; lectr. Internat. Communications Agy., Yugoslavia, 1978-80, 86, Finland, 1981, Hungary, 1985, Argentina (USIA acad. specialist grants, 1986, 87, 88, 90), Brazil, 1990; Spanish lang. proficiency tester Dept. State, Venezuela, 1965; developer Strategic Interaction Methodology for Fgn. Lang. Instrn.; vis. fellow Australian Nat. U., Canberra, 1985, U. Va., 1987, 89; vis. prof. U. Mar del Plata, Argentina, 1988, Temple U., Tokyo and Osaka brs., 1988; cons. in bilingual edn. Regional Govt. of Alto Adige, Italy, 1989, 91. Author: Language Structures in Contrast, 2d edit., 1978, Japanese edit., 1974, Italian edit., 1978, Spanish edit., 1986, Language as Human Creation, 1978, Strategic Interaction Learning Languages through Scenarios, 1987; co-author: American Voices and Integrated Skills Reader, 1992; editor: Linguistics and the Professions, 1982, Ethnic Perspectives in America Literature, 1983; founder, editor: Interfaces, 1974-86, Second Language Learning, from 1988. Bd. dirs. Nat. Italian Am. Found., from 1979, Am. U. Rome, from 1983. Decorated Cavaliere Ufficiale Italy, 1977. Mem. MLA, AAAS, Linguistic Soc. Am., Linguistic Assn. Can. and U.S. (a founder, pres. 1989-90), Soc. Italiana di Linguistica, Am. Assn. Tchrs. Italian, Am. Anthrop. Assn. Club: Chesterbrook Swim (McLean). Home: McLean Va. Died Dec. 20, 1991; cremated.

DISHER, JOHN HOWARD, aerospace consultant; b. Olmstead, N.D., Dec. 23, 1921; s. Howard Merlin and Mary Christine (Johnston) D.; m. Lillian Helen Rusnak, Apr. 19, 1948; children—James Howard, John Thomas. B.M.E., U. N.D., 1943; grad., Advanced Mgmt. Program, Harvard U., 1969. With NASA, 1943-81; aero. research scientist Lewis Propulsion Lab., Cleve., 1943-51; head flight research sect. Lewis Propulsion Lab., 1951-58; project engr. Mercury, Langley Field, Va., 1959-60; head advanced manned systems Washington, 1960-61; asst. dir. Apollo spacecraft devel., 1961-63; dir. Apollo Test, 1963-65; dep. dir. Skylab program, 1965-74, dir. advanced programs manned spaceflight, 1974-80; aerospace cons., 1981-88; Mem. tech. com. Indpls. 500 Automobile Race, 1946-88; cons. Nat. Space Agy. of Italy, 1981-82. Author articles on hypersonic heat transfer, propulsion and aerodynamics. Mem. alumni adv. council U. N.D. Coll. Engring. Recipient Sustained Superior Performance award NASA, 1965, Exceptional Svc. medal, 1969, 80, Disting. Svc. medal, 1974, Disting. Alumni Sioux award U. N.D., 1974. Fellow AIAA, Brit. Interplanetary Soc.; mem. Internat. Acad. Astronautics, Harvard Alumni Assn., Explorers Club of N.Y.C., Corvair Soc. Am., U.S. Auto Club (tech. com.), Sigma Nu. Presbyterian. Home: Bethesda Md. Died Aug. 27, 1988; inurned; Columbarium Bradley Hills Presbyn. Ch., Bethesda, Md.

DISSTON, HARRY, author, business executive, horseman; b. Red Bank, N.J., Nov. 23, 1899; s. Eugene John Kauffmann and Frances Matilda Disston; A.B., Amherst Coll., 1921; m. Valerie Ivy Duval, Mar. 26, 1930 (dec. 1951); children: Robin John Duval, Geoffrey Whitmore (dec.); m. Catherine Sitler John, Aug. 26, 1960. With N.Y. Telephone Co., 1921-32, with AT&T, N.Y.C., 1932-60, exec. tng. student, dist. traffic supt., sales engr., dist. mgr., adv. staff engr., adv. staff exec. ind. co. relations, 1951-60; coordinator devel. activities, placement dir. Grad. Sch. Bus. Adminstrn., U. Va.; v.p. Equine Motion Analysis, Ltd., 1979-82; sr. v.p., dir. leasing Equivest Fin. Services Corp., Charlottesville, Va., 1986-88; pres. Harwood Corp., Ltd.; dir. AMVEST Horse Leasing Co., Charlottesville, Aide-de-camp to gov. Va.; chmn. Louisa County Electoral Bd.; mem. Va. Bd. Mil. Affairs; chmn. fin. com. Republican party Va.; chmn. Louisa County Rep. Com.; v.p. pres., dir. Park Ave. Assn.; mem. exec. com. Episcopal Diocese of Va., also pres. council, region 15; trustee Grant Monument Assn., Va. Outdoors Found.; bd. dirs. Atlantic Rural Expn.; bd. dirs., treas. Lee-Jackson Found.; chmn., bd. dirs. Charlottesville-Albemarle Clean Community Commn., 1978-84. Served from maj. to col., cav. and gen. staff corps, 1941-46; PTO; comdg. officer 107th Regtl. Combat Team, N.Y.N.G., 1947-57; brig. gen. ret. Awarded Legion of Merit, Bronze Star with oak leaf cluster; comdr. Order of Boliver; Philippine Liberation Medal; Medal of Merit with Swords, Free Poland. Mem. Am. Horse Shows Assn. (judge, steward, tech. del.), Vets. 7th Regt., N.Y. Soc. Mil. and Naval Officers World Wars (past pres.), Vet. Corps Arty., Mil. Order Fgn. Wars, Mil. Order World Wars, VFW, Ret. Officers Assn., Am. Legion, Res. Officers Assn. (chpt. pres.), St. Georges Soc., St. Andrews Soc., Va. Thoroughbred Assn., U.S. Pony Clubs (gov.), Phi Beta Kappa, Phi Kappa Psi. Clubs: Torch (past pres. Charlottesville-Albermarle); Union; Amherst; Church of New York; Farmington Country, Greencroft, Jack Jouett Bridle Trails (pres.) (Charlottesville, Va.); Pilgrims of U.S.; Keswick Hunt, Keswick of Va. Author: Equestionnaire, 1947; Riding Rhymes, 1951; Know About Horses, 1961; Young Horseman's Handbooks, 1962; Elementary Dressage, 1971; Beginning Polo, 1973; Beginning the Rest of Your Life, 1980; columnist Daily Progress, Cen. Virginian; several mag. articles on mil., equine and bus. subjects; contbr. to Ency. Brit. Deceased. Home: Keswick Va. †

DISTLER, THEODORE AUGUST, educational consultant; b. Bklyn., Nov. 22, 1898; s. Ernst Frederick and Marie Kossman D.; m. Alice Boxold, June 3, 1923; children: Theodore Alden, Paul Antonie, George Ernest. Student, Brown U., 1918-19; BS, NYU, 1922, MA, 1932; hon. degrees 37 colls. and univs. Mem. faculty NYU, 1922-25, sec. com. on admissions, 1925-26, 28-29, asst. dir. student welfare, 1926-28, dir. student welfare, 1928-29, dir. student pers., 1929-34; dean Lafayette Coll., Easton, Pa., 1934-41; pres. Franklin and Marshall Coll., 1941-54, pres. emeritus, 1965-91; pres. Assn. Am. Colls., 1954-65; instr. pers. adminstrn., summer 1932; adminstrv. cons. Svc. Assn. Am. Colls., 1968-7. Gen. chmn. Easton Community Chest, 1941; pres. Lancaster Community Chest, 1949; vice chmn. Lancaster Redevel. Authority, 1967; bd. dirs. Temple U., 1945-54; bd. regents Mercersburg Acad.; bd. visitors Davidson Coll.; mem. corp. Lancaster Theol. Sem.; mem. adv. coun. Nat. Merit Scholarship Sem. Corporator Presbyn. Ministers Fund, bd. dirs., 1945—; mem. adv. coun. Pa. Assn. Colls. and Univs., pres., 1946. Mem. Ea. Assn. Coll. Deans and Advisers of Men pres. 1933-34, mem. exec. com. 1929-36 , Soc. for Promotion Engring. Edn., Am. Acad. Polit. and Social Sci., Acad. Polit. Sci., Assn. Sch. and Coll. Placement v.p. 1941 , Hamilton Club Lancaster, Pa. , Century Club N.Y.C. , Scabbard and Blade, Phi Beta Kappa, Zeta Psi, Phi Delta Kappa, Tau Kappa Alpha. Home: Lancaster Pa. Died Apr. 7, 1991.

DITTMER, CLARENCE CHRISTIAN, publishing executive; b. Bklyn., Jan. 2, 1895; s. Joseph and Catherine Dorothy (Bauer) D; m. Marie Edith Hachtmann, June 15, 1921; children: Clarence Paul, Luther Albert. BCS, NYU, 1921. Asst. sec. Advt. Men's League of N.Y.C., 1914-15; purchasing and sales agent Student Vol. Movement for Fgn. Missions and Fgn. Missions Conf. of N.A., 1915-27; sales mgr. religious book dept. Doubleday Doran Co., 1927-31, Long and Smith, 1931-33; sales rep. Round Table Press, 1934-42, Augsburg Pub. House, 1934-44; pres., treas. Carroll Good, Inc., from 1936.; treas. Luth. League N.Y.; pres. Luth. League of Am.; bd. dirs. United Luth. Pub. House, Paradise Falls Luth. Assn.; treas., mgr. Paradise Falls Resort, 1949-51; treas. Missionary Edn. Movement for U.S. and Can., 1946-48. With U.S. Army, field clk. adj. gen. dept., World War I. *

DIXON, JOHN ALDOUS, surgeon; b. Provo, Utah, July 16, 1923; s. Henry Aldous and Lucille (Knowlden) D.; m. Karma Jeppsen, Sept. 28, 1944; children: Stephen, Kay, Lisa. Student, Weber Coll., Ogden, Utah, 1940-42, Idaho State U., 1942; BS, U. Wash., 1943; MD, U. Utah, 1947. Diplomate Am. Bd. Surgery. Surg. resident U. Rochester Med. Ctr., 1947-50; pvt. practice surgery Odgen, Utah, 1953-68; part-time tchr. U. Utah Med. Sch., 1953-68, assoc. clin. prof. surgery, 1965-68, assoc. prof. surgery, 1968-70, prof. surgery, 1970-90, prof. emeritus surgery, 1990-92, dir. endoscopic and laser surgery, 1978-84, dir. Laser Inst., 1985-88, sr. cons. Laser Inst., 1988-90, exec. v.p. of univ., 1970-72; dean U. Utah Med. Sch. (Med. Ctr.), 1972-76, v.p. for health scis., 1973-78; chief surgery McKay-Dee Hosp., 1965-67; mem. nat. adv. council on health professions edn., 1976-80. Contbr. to Am. Med. Jour. Chmn. Utah Bd. Health, 1960-63; bd. regents U. Utah, 1963-66; trustee Intermountain Health Care, 1974-78; mem. Ogden City Council, 1956. Served with USNR, 1943-46; served to capt. USAF, 1951-53. Fellow ACS; mem. AMA, Am. Gastroent. Assn., Soc. for Surgery Alimentary Tract, Am. Surg. Assn., Western Surg. Assn., Soc. Am. Gastroenterologic-Endoscopic Surgeons, Am. Soc. Gastrointestinal Endoscopy, Utah Med. Assn. (pres. 1980-81), Alpha Omega Alpha, Phi Kappa Phi. Home: Salt Lake City Utah Died Feb. 15, 1992; buried Ogden, Utah.

DIXON, WILLIE JAMES, musician; b. Vicksburg, Miss., July 1, 1915; s. Charlie and Daisey D. Founder Blues Heaven Found. Inc., Glendale, Calif. Composer (for groups) The Four Jumps of Jive, 1939, The Big Three Trio, 1940; producer, composer, rec. artist for groups Chess, rec. artist Columbia, 1969, Ovation Records, 1973, 76, Pausa Records, 1984, 86; long play record Hidden Charms; producer T Bone Burnett for Bug Records/Capitol, 1988, The Chess Box Set for MCA; compositions include I'm Your Hoochie Coochie Man, I'm Ready, I Ain't Superstitious, I Can't Quit You Baby, You Can't Judge a Book by Its Cover, You Shook Me, Built for Comfort, Wang Dang Doodle, Spoonful Seventh Son, Back Door Man, Little Red Rooster, My Babe, I Just Wanna Make Love to You; Ginger Ale Afternoon (soundtrack), 1989; rec. artist (album) Hidden Charms, 1988 (Grammy award, 1989); songs recorded by The Rolling Stones, Led Zeppelin, Hank Williams Jr., The Doors, Count Basie, Gil Evans, Robert Cray, Oingo Boingo, Elvis Presley, Muddy Waters, Howlin' Wolf, Eric Clapton, Bo Diddley, Rod Stewart, many others; (albums) The Big Three Trio, 1990, Boxcar Willie, 1986, Ginger Ale Afternoon, 1989, (with Memphis Slim) Willie's Blues, 1959, I Am The Blues; author: (with Don Snowden) I Am the Blues-The Willie Dixon Story, 1989. Six time Grammy nominee. Mem. Am. Fedn. Musicians, Nat. Acad. Rec. Arts and Scis. Home: Glendale Calif. Died Jan. 29, 1992; buried Burr Oaks Cemetery, Alsip, Ill.

DOAN, CHARLES AUSTIN, physician, educator; b. Nelsonville, Ohio, June 5, 1896; s. Robert Austin and Lella Minturn (Walch) D.; m. Margaret Dixon Riggs, May 28, 1926; children: Elizabeth, Ellen Virginia. BS, Hiram (Ohio) Coll., 1918; postgrad., U. Cin., 1919; MD, Johns Hopkins U., 1923; ScD (hon.), Ohio State U., 1964. Resident house officer Johns Hopkins Hosp., 1923; rsch. asst., asst. prof. Thorndike Meml. Labs., Harvard Med. Sch., 1924-25; assoc. Rockefeller Inst. Med. Rsch., 1925-30; prof. medicine, dir. dept. med. and surg. rsch. Ohio State U., Columbus, 1930-36, chmn. dept. medicine, dir. med. rsch., 1936-44, dean Coll. Medicine, prof. medicine, dir. Health Ctr., 1944-61, dir. div. hematology, 1961-66, dean and prof. medicine emeritus, 1961-90; tech. dir. Blood Donor Ctr. ARC, 1942-45, med. dir., 1947-57, past mem. sub-com. on blood and blood derivatives; chmn. Region 8 Grad. War Med. Meeting Commn.; chmn. Com. on Sci. Work, Ohio State Med. Assn., 1942-45; expert cons. Surgeon Gen., Dept. Army; mem. hematology study sect. NIH, USPHS; mem. com. on blood and blood-forming organs of panel on clin physiology NRC, also com. on growth; mem. panel on blood and blood-forming organs Med. Adv. Bd. Contbr. on sci. rsch. in hematology and tuberculosis. With M.C., U.S. Army, 1917-19, to lt. col. M.C. Res., AUS, 1940-42. Recipient Disting. Svc. award and Gold medal AMA, 1960, Ohioana Career medal, 1977. Mem. ACP, Am. Assn. Anatomists, Harvey Soc., Soc. Exptl. Biology and Medicine, Cen. Soc. Clin. Rsch., Am. Soc. Clin. Investigation, Am. Soc. Exptl. Pathology, Am. Soc. Clin. Pathology, Ohio Acad. Scis., Assn. Am. Physicians, Ohio Pub. Health Assn., Internat. R-E Soc., Am. Soc. Hematology, Masons (33d degree), Phi Beta Kappa, Sigma Xi, Phi Chi, Pi Kappa Delta, Alpha Omega Alpha. Mem. Disciples of Christ Ch. Home: Columbus Ohio Died Feb. 13, 1990.

DOANE, GILBERT H(ARRY), librarian, educator, clergyman; b. Fairfield, Vt., Jan. 28, 1897. AB, Colgate U., 1918; cert., N.Y. Libr. Sch., 1921; postgrad., U. Ariz., 1921-22, U. Mich., 1923-24; LLD, Nashotah House Sem., 1955. Ordained deacon P.E. Ch., 1943, priest, 1956. Asst. Springfield (Vt.) Libr., 1912-14, Colgate U. Libr., 1914-18; libr. "House-That-Jack-Built" U.S. Naval Tng. Sta., Newport, R.I., 1918-20; asst. N.Y. State Libr., 1920-21; asst. libr. U. Ariz., 1921-22, U. Mich., 1922-25; prof. bibliography U. Nebr., 1930-37, libr., 1925-37; dir. librs. U. Wis., 1937-56 (military leave 1943-45), archivist, 1957-62, prof. emeritus, from 1962; dir. Wis. Libr. Sch., 1938-41; active Nebr. Pub. Libr. Commn., 1925-33. Author: The Legend of the Book, 1924, Searching for Your Ancestors, 1937, Some Early Records of Fairfield, Vt., 1938, About Collecting Bookplates, 1941, History of Grace Ch., Madison, Wis., 1958; Contbr. Dictionary Am. Biography, Dictionary of Am. Hist.; editor: Nebr. and Midwest Geneal. Record, 1928-31, New England Hist. and Geneal. Register, from 1960; contbg. editor: The Prairie Schooner, 1927-37, The American Genealogist, 1932-43. Active Wis. Hist. Soc., Vt. Hist. Soc., Newport, R.I. Hist. Soc., Ch. Hist. Soc., Soc. of Genealogists, London, New Eng. Hist. Genealogy Soc. With USN, 1918-1919; capt. U.S. Army 1943-1945, retired major. Fellow Am. Soc. Genealogists; mem. Masons, Madison Literary Club. Republican. Episcopalian. *

DOBLIN, JAY, designer, educator; b. N.Y.C, Dec. 10, 1920; s. Frank C. and Evelyn (MacElroy) D.; m. Annette Woodward, Mar. 27, 1949. Grad., Pratt Inst., 1942. Indsl. designer, devel. work govt. projects, camouflage Raymond Loewy Assocs., N.Y.C., 1942-49, exec. designer, 1952-55; indsl. designer Singer Co., Frigidaire Co., SchicK Co., Coca Cola Co., Shell Oil Co., Nat. Biscuit Co.; dir. Inst. Design, Ill. Inst. Tech., 1955-69, prof., 1955-69; co-founder, sr. v.p., dir. Unimark Internat. Chgo. (design firm), 1965-1972; affiliated with Delta Planning Group, Chgo., until 1981; prin. Jay Doblin Assocs., Chgo., 1981-85; cons. J.C. Penney Co., Inc., Standard Oil Co., Ind., Am. Hosp. Assn., Xerox, Beatrice Corp., Borg-Warner; chmn. indsl.

design dept. night sch. Pratt Inst.; prof. Sch. Art Inst., Chgo., 1975-78; vis. prof. London Bus. Sch., 1979-80; lectr. Author: Perspective—A New System for Designers, 1955, 1OO Great Product Designs, 1970, also articles. Recipient honor student award Pratt Inst., 1942, Disting. Alumnus award, 1973; Kaufmann Internat. Design award Internat. Inst. Edn. Fellow Royal Soc. Arts (London), Indsl. Designers Soc. Am. (pres. 1956, dir., Outstanding Design Programs award 1974, Personal Recognition award 1982), Internat. Council Socs. Indsl. Design (v.p.), Internat. Design Conf. (dir.); mem. Indsl. Design Educators Assn. (past pres.). Home: Chicago Ill. Died May 11, 1989.

DODD, ED(WARD BENTON), cartoonist; b. La Fayette, Ga., Nov. 7, 1902; s. Jesse Mercer and Effie (Cooke) D.; m. Miriam Croft, Feb. 26, 1938 (dec. 1943); m. Rosemary Wood Johnston, Nov. 7, 1981. Student, Ga. Inst. Tech., 1921-22, N.Y. Art Students League, 1923-24; under, Daniel Beard. Instr., dir. Dan Beard Camp for Boys, 1920-38; instr. outdoor activities N.Y. Mil. Acad., Cornwall, N.Y., 1926-27; comml. artist N.Y.C., 1929-30. Drew: humor panel Back Home Again, United Feature Syndicate, 1930-45; cartoonist: Mark Trail, Field Syndicate, 1946—, N.Am. Syndicate; author: Mark Trail's Camping Tips; contbr. articles to popular publs. Recipient award for service to conservation Nat. Forestry Assn.; outstanding cartoon strip Sigma Delta Chi, 1948; for conservation wildlife Wis. Humane Soc.; for conservation edn. Detroit Sportsman's Congress; hon. chmn. Nat. Wildlife Week, 1952-53; Conservation award Nat. Wildlife Fedn., 1967. Mem. Outdoor Writers Am., Delta Tau Delta (Nat. Achievement award 1972). Episcopalian. Clubs: Homosassa (Atlanta);, Piedmont Driving (Atlanta); Chattahoochee Country (Gainesville, Ga.). Home: Gainesville Ga. Died May 27, 1991; buried Arlington Cemetery, Atlanta.

DODD, LESTER PAUL, lawyer; b. nr. Hayden, Ind., June 28, 1895; s. Samuel Joseph and Mary (VanRiper) D.; m. Edith Gillespie, Sept. 12, 1921; 1 child, James Stewart. Student, Franklin Coll., 1913; LLB, Detroit Coll. of Law, 1917, JD (hon.), 1962. Bar: Mich. 1917. Assoc. Kenna and Lightner (now Crawford, Sweeny & Dodd), from 1917, ptnr., from 1926. Active Mich. Fair Campaign Practices Commn. Fellow Am. Coll. Trial Lawyers; mem. ABA, Internat. Assn. Ins. Counsel (pres. 1954-55), Detroit Bar Assn., Am. Judicature Soc., State Bar Mich. (pres. 1951-52), Detroit Athletic Club, Detroit Golf Club, The Lawyers Club (U. Mich.), Phi Delta Theta, Delta Theta Phi. *

DODDS, JOHN WENDELL, English language educator; b. Grove City, Pa., July 20, 1902; s. Samuel and Alice (Dunn) D.; m. Jarjorie Jane Krantz, June 18, 1928; children: John Arthur, Christopher Deis. BA, Coll. of Wooster, 1924, Litt.D., 1945; MA, Yale U., 1927, PhD, 1932. Faculty dept. English U. Pitts., 1927-37; assoc. prof. English Stanford (Calif.) U., 1937-39, prof., 1939-67, dir. spl. programs in humanities, dean Sch. Humanities, 1942-48, Jackson Eli Reynolds prof. humanities, 1962-67, emeritus, 1967-89; vis. lectr., cons. humanities Emory U., 1953; vis. prof. U. Hawaii, 1953; sr. cons. humanities Ednl. Radio and TV Ctr., Ann Arbor, 1955-58; bd. dirs. Wenner-Gren Found., 1954-89, pres., 1965-77; editorial adv. bd. World Book Encyc., 1963-68. Author: Thomas Southerne, Dramatist, 1933, Thackeray: A Critical Portrait, 1941, The Age of Paradox: A Biography of England, 1841-1851, 1952, American Memoir, 1961, Everyday Life in Twentieth Century America, 1965, The Several Lives of Paul Fejos-A Hungarian-American Odyssey, 1973; co-editor: An Oxford Anthology of English Prose, 1935, Types of English Fiction, 1940, Modern British and American Plays, 1947; chmn. editorial bd. Pacific Spectator, 1946-56. Trustee Coll. of Wooster, Ohio, 1966-75, Mills Coll., Oakland, Calif., 1943-53, Pomona Coll., Claremont Coll., 1955-68. Fellow Guggenheim Found., 1947-48, Viking Fund, 1948. Mem. MLA, AAUP, Am. Coun. Learned Socs., Author's Club (London), Phi Beta Kappa, Delta Sigma Rho. Home: Stanford Calif. Died Mar. 31, 1989.

DODINGTON, SVEN H. M., electronics consultant; b. Vancouver, B.C., Can., May 22, 1912; came to U.S., 1927; s. Spencer Marriott and Martha Lise (Christoffersen) D.; m. Kathleen Loretta Dworak; children: Thomas, Susan, Peter. BA, Stanford U., 1934. Engr. Scophony Ltd., London, 1935-41; with ITT Labs., 1941-85, dept. head, N.Y.C. and Nutley, N.J., 1941-54, lab. dir., Nutley, 1954-58, v.p., 1958-69, asst. tech. dir., N.Y.C., 1969-85; cons. Mountain Lakes, N.J., from 1985; lectr. UCLA, 1967-69; mem. avionics panel Def. Sci. Bd., Washington, 1970-71; cons. NASA, 1971-76; tech. advisor Radio Tech. Commn. Aeros. Co-author: Avionics Navigation, 1969, Electronic Engineers Handbook, 1975; cons. editor: McGraw-Hill Ency., from 1984; holder 50 patents in TV, navigation. Inventor basic navigation system used to guide aircraft. Recipient Volare award Airline Avionics Inst., 1967, Inventor of Yr. award N.Y. Patent Law Assn., 1982, Achievement award Radio Tech. Commn. Aeros., Washington, 1984. Fellow IEEE (life, Pioneer award), AIAA; mem. Aerospace and Electronics System Soc. (pres. 1966-67), Inst. Navigation, Armed Forces Communications and Electronics Assn. (bd. dirs. N.Y. chpt.), Mountain Lakes Club (gov. 1967-70). Republican. Episcopalian. Home: Mountain Lakes N.J. Died Jan. 13, 1992; buried Marnhull, Eng.

DODSON, DANIEL BOONE, writer, educator; b. Portland, Oreg., Mar. 21, 1918; arrived in France, 1980; s. William Daniel Boone and Besse Ellen (Krumn) D.; divorced 1980; children: Dorian, Elizabeth. BA, Reed Coll., 1941; MA, Columbia U., 1947, PhD, 1952. Asst. prof. Columbia U., N.Y.C., 1952-54, assoc. prof., 1954-60, prof., 1960-80, prof. emeritus comparative lit., 1981-91. Author: The Man Who Ran Away, 1961, The Dance of Love, 1962, Scala Dei, 1964, On a Darkling Plain, 1964, Dancers in the Dark, 1968, Looking for Zo, 1970, The Drunken Boats, 1984, The Last Command, 1989. Capt. USAAF, 1941-46. Democrat. Home: Soliés-Ville France Died Jan. 7, 1991; buried Portland, Oreg.

DOKTOR, PAUL KARL, musician; b. Vienna, Austria, Mar. 28, 1919; came to U.S., 1947, naturalized, 1952; s. Karl and Georgine Stefanie (Engelmann) D.; m. Caryn G. Friedman, June 17, 1979; 1 child, Alexis-Karla. Diploma, Vienna State Acad. Music, 1938. Mem. viola and chamber music faculty U. Mich., co-founder, mem. Stanley Quartet, 1948-51; mem. viola and chamber music faculty Mannes Coll., from 1952, NYU, from 1965, The Juilliard Sch., from 1971; guest faculty mem. Mozarteum, Salzburg, Institut de Hautes Etudes Musicales, Montreux, Saratoga String Quartet Program, Bowdoin Coll. Summer Music Festival, 1977. Guest violist in Quintet series with Busch Quartet, Europe, 1936-38; mem. Lucerne String Quartet; viola prin. Lucerne Symphony and Paul Sacher's Collegium Musicum, Zurich, Switzerland, 1939-47; founder, mem. Rococo Ensemble, The Duo Doktor-Menuhin, N.Y. String Sextet, New String Trio of N.Y.; solo concert tours in Europe, Can., South Am., U.S., Mexico and Orient; contbr. articles to music jours. Recipient 1st prize Internat. Music Competition Geneva, 1942, Artist Tchr. of Year award Am. String Tchrs. Assn., 1977. Mem. Am. Viola Soc. (bd. dirs.), Am. String Tchrs. Assn. (hon. life), Internat. Viola Soc. (hon. life). Club: The Bohemians. Home: New York N.Y. Died June 21, 1989; cremated.

DOLAND, JACK VAN KIRK, university president, state senator; b. Lake Arthur, La., Mar. 3, 1928; s. Earl A. and Irma (Williams) D.; m. Nell Richardson, Oct. 17, 1952; children: Diane, Connie. BEd, Tulane U., 1950; MEd, La. State U., 1954, Ed.D., 1977. Tchr., coach Sulphur (La.) High Sch., 1950-66, Dequincy (La.) High Sch., 1953-57; asst. football coach La. State U., Baton Rouge, 1966-70; athletic dir. McNeese State U., Lake Charles, La., 1970-79, pres., 1980-87; senator from Dist. 26 State of La., 1988-91. Contbr. articles to profl. jours. Bd. dirs. So. Regional Edn. Bd., from 1980; mem. coun. Nat. Collegiate Athletic Assn. Bd., Kansas City; v.p. ARC, Lake Charles, 1982-91; dir. First Meth. Ch., 1970-91. Served with La. N.G., 1948-54. Mem. Am. Football Coaches Assn. Methodist. Home: Lake Charles La. Died Apr. 25, 1991; buried Lake Charles, La.

DOLE, MALCOLM, physical chemist; b. Melrose, Mass., Mar. 4, 1903; s. William Andrews and Grace Weld Soper D.; m. Frances Hibbard Page, Oct. 27, 1928; children: Priscilla Page, Malcolm. AB, AM, PhD, Harvard U., 1928. Rsch. phys. chemist Rockefeller Inst. Med. Rsch., 1928-30; instr. Northwestern U., 1930-35, asst. prof., 1935-38, assoc. prof., 1938-43, prof., 1945-69, prof. emeritus, 1969-90, chmn. Materials Rsch. Ctr., 1964-68; Robert A. Welch prof. chemistry Baylor U., Waco, Tex., 1969-82, prof. emeritus, 1982-90; dir. Nat. Def. Rsch. Com. Lab., Dugway Proving Ground, 1943-44; cons. Oak Ridge Nat. Lab., 1953-63, NSF, 1962-65; hon. mem. faculty U. San Marcos, Lima, Peru, U. Chile; mem. phys.-chemistry adv. panel Office Naval Rsch., 1948-5. Author: Experimental and Theoretical Electrochemistry, 1935, The Glass Electrode, 1941, Introduction to Statistical Thermodynamics, 1954; editor: The Radiation Chemistry Macromolecules, vols. I, II; assoc. editor Chem. Revs., 1956-59; contbr. sci. articles to profl. jours. Trustee Gordon Rsch. Conf., 1958-61. Named Most Outstanding Scholar, Baylor U., 1977; recipient Army-Navy cert. of appreciation, 1948, Alumnus Honoris Causa award Baylor U., 1982, SW regional award Am. Chem. Soc., 1979. Fellow Am. Phys. Soc., Electrochem. Soc. v.p. 1940 ; mem. Assn. Harvard Chemists pres. 1942-43 , Acad. Scis. Argentina fgn. mem. , Ridgewood Country Club, Sheridan Shore Yacht Club. Home: Waco Tex. Died Nov. 29, 1990.

DOLL, CHARLES GEORGE, geologist, educator; b. Providence, Aug. 22, 1898; s. Henry John and Hattie Anna (Otto) D.; m. Ruth Wells Bailey, June 29, 1940; children: Linda Beth, Charles George. PhB, Brown U., 1924, MA, 1926; MA, Harvard U., 1931; PhD, Columbia U., 1951. Asst. geologist Brown U., 1924-27; instr. U. Vt., 1927-32, asst., assoc. prof., 1932-51, prof., from 1952, chmn. dept. geology, from 1946; acting state geologist Vt., 1935, 39, state geologist from 1947. Author sci. papers. chmn. com. mineral resources N.Y.-Vt. Interstate Commn. on Champlain Basin; chmn. com. Vt. Project. Apprentice seaman USN, 1917-19. Fellow Geology Soc. Am.; mem. AAAS, Assn Geology Tchrs., Am. Assn. State Geologists, Seismoloy Soc. Am., Am. Geophys. Union, Sigma Xi. *

DOLSON, CHARLES HERBERT, airline company executive; b. St. Louis, May 13, 1906; s. Frank Edward and Hattie Mae (Harbison) D.; m. Bonnie Gooch, May 27, 1935 (dec.); m. Clara Allison, Aug. 30, 1962. B.S. in C.E, Washington U., St. Louis, 1928. Test pilot Curtiss Wright Airplane Co., St. Louis, 1930-31; pilot Am. Airlines, Inc., 1931-34, Delta Air Lines, Inc., Atlanta, 1934-40; chief pilot Delta Air Lines, Inc., 1940-42, 1945-47, operations mgr., 1947-48, v.p. operations, 1948-59, bd. dirs., 1955-87, exec. v.p., 1959-65, pres., 1965-70, chief exec. officer, 1966-71, chmn. bd., 1970-71, chmn. exec. com., 1971-87, hon. bd. dirs., from 1987; mem. adv. council Trust Co. Ga. Served as lt. comdr. USNRF, 1928-30, 42-45. Recipient Sec. Navy Commendation with ribbon, 1945; Alumni award Washington U., St. Louis, 1967; Gold medal for extraordinary service FAA, 1972. Mem. Alpha Tau Omega. Lodge: Elks. Home: Atlanta Ga. Died Sept. 4, 1992. †

DOMM, LINCOLN VALENTINE, anatomist, zoologist; b. nr. Ayton, Ont., Can., Oct. 22, 1896; came to U.S., 1917, naturalized, 1931; s. William Henry and Catherine Dorothy (Feick) D.; m. Hazel Marie Staufacher, Sept. 17, 1925; 1 child, William Alan. AB, North Cen. Coll., 1921; PhD, U. Chgo., 1926. Asst. in biology North Cen. Coll., Naperville, Ill., 1920-21; fellow in zoology U. Chgo., 1922-23, asst., 1923-35, rsch. assoc., 1930-46, asst. prof., 1938-46, assoc. prof., 1946-52; prof. anatomy, chmn. dept. Stritch Sch. Medicine, Loyola U., Chgo., 1952-89; guest Inst. Animal Genetics, Edinburgh, Inst. Animal Nutrition, Coll. Agr., Cambridge, 1935; prof. biology YMCA Coll. Liberal Arts, Chgo., 1928-34, chmn. dept., 1934-40; vis. prof. poultry rsch. ctr. and dept. anatomy U. Edinburgh, 1954; guest investigator sta. physiology Coll. of France, Paris, 1955; attendee World's Poultry Congress, Edinburgh, 1954, Internat. Anat. Congress, Paris, 1955, Internat. Zool. Congress, London, 1958. Co-author: Sex and Internal Secretions, 1932, 2d edit., 1939; contbr. articles to sci. jours. Mem. AAAS, Am. Soc. Naturalists, Am. Soc. Zoologists, Am. Assn. Anatomists, Assn. for Study Internal Secretions, Soc. Exptl. Biology and Medicine, Ill. Acad., Genetics Soc. Am., Wilson Ornithol. Club., Inst. Medicine Chgo., Quadrangle Club, Chaos Club, Sigma Xi, Gamma Alpha. Republican. Baptist. Home: Chicago Ill. Died Mar. 28, 1989.

DONAGAN, ALAN HARRY, philosophy educator; b. Melbourne, Victoria, Australia, Feb. 10, 1925; came to U.S., 1956, naturalized, 1983; s. Harry Cyril and Ruby Evelyn (Evans) D.; m. Barbara Lynn Galley, Aug. 18, 1951. BA, U. Melbourne, 1946, MA, 1951; PhB, Oxford (Eng.) U., 1954; DLitt (hon.), Ripon Coll., 1983. Sr. lectr. Univ. Coll., Canberra, Australia, 1954-56; asst. prof. philosophy U. Minn., Mpls., 1956-57, assoc. prof., chmn. philosophy dept., 1957-61; prof. philosophy, chmn. dept. Ind. U., Bloomington, 1961-64; prof. U. Ill., Urbana, 1965-69; prof. U. Chgo., 1970-84, Phyllis Fay Horton prof. humanities, 1977-84; prof. philosophy Calif. Inst. Tech., Pasadena, 1984-91, Doris and Henry Dreyfuss prof. philosophy, 1989-91; cons. Ency. Britannica., Chgo., from 1971. Author: The Later Philosophy of R.G. Collingwood, 1962, The Theory of Morality, 1977, Choice: The Essential Element in Human Action, 1987, Spinoza, 1989; contbr. articles to profl. jours. Fellow Am. Council Learned Socs., 1972-73, Guggenheim Meml. Found., 1976-77, Inst. for Advanced Study in Behavioral Scis., 1976-77, AAAS, 1986-91. Mem. Am. Philos. Assn. (pres. cen. div. 1980-81), Institut Internat. de Philosophie, Aristotelian Soc. Democrat. Episcopalian. Home: Pasadena Calif. Died May 29, 1991; buried Ch. of the Ascension, Sierra Madre, Calif.

DONALDSON, CHARLES RUSSELL, state justice; b. Helena, Mont., Feb. 2, 1919; s. Charles Mortimer and Mabel (King) D.; children: Karen, Holly, Jean, Laurel, Sarah, Charles. Student, Willamette U., 1937-38; B.A., U. Idaho, 1941, LL.B., 1948; postgrad., George Washington Law Sch., 1943-44. Bar: Idaho 1948. Practice law Boise, 1948-64; dist. judge, 1964-68; justice Idaho Supreme Ct., Boise, from 1969, chief justice, 1973, 79-80, 83-86; mem. Idaho Ho. of Reps., 1955-57; justice of peace, 1960-64. Mem. governing com. Idaho chpt. Arthritis and Rheumatism Found. Served with Signal Corps, AUS, World War II. Mem. Conf. Chief Justices (dep. chmn. 1980—). Methodist. Lodges: Kiwanis (past pres.), Masons, Shriners. Home: Boise Idaho

DONALDSON, FRANK ARTHUR, JR., manufacturing executive; b. Mpls., Aug. 19, 1919; s. Frank Arthur and Ruth (Chase) D.; m. Irene Elizabeth Sweeney, Mar. 1, 1954; children: Frank Arthur III, John Andrew. Engring. degree cum laude, Harvard U., 1942. Engr. Donaldson Co., Inc., Mpls., 1941-44; v.p. Donaldson Co., Inc., 1947-51, pres., gen. mgr., 1951-73, chmn. bd., chief exec. officer, 1973-82, chmn. bd., 1982-85; dir. Donaldson Co. Inc., ADC Telecommunications Inc., Graco, Inc. Served with USN, 1944-45. Mem. Soc. Automotive Engrs. Clubs: Desert Forest (Carefree, Ariz.); Minneapolis, Woodhill Country (Mpls.). Home: Excelsior Minn. Died Mar. 23, 1991; buried Mpls.

DONALDSON, WILLIAM V., zoo director; m. Ann Donaldson; children: John, David. City mgr. Scottsdale, Ariz., Cin.; Pres., exec. dir. Phila. Zool. Garden, Zool. Soc. Phila., 1979-91; pres. N.J. Acad. Aquatic

Scis., 1989-91; bd. dirs. CoreStates Fin. Corp., Phila. Nat. Bank, Phila Contributorship. Home: Philadelphia Pa. Died Nov. 26, 1991.

DONATELLI, AUGUST, professional baseball league umpire; b. Heilwood, Pa., Aug. 22, 1914; s. Antonio Joseph and Concetta Vincenza (DiSantis) D.; m. Marylouise Lamont, Oct. 12, 1946; children: Barbara Donatelli Rulek, Carol donatelli Holsonbeck, David, Patrick. Grad. high sch. Umpire minor league; umpire Nat. Laegue, 1966-90; umpire 5 World Series games, 4 All-Star games; umpiring instr. All Sommers Umpire Sch. With USAAF, World War II. Decorated Air medal with 3 oak leaf clusters. Mem. K.C. (3d degree), Am. Legion, Maj. League Umpires Assn. (founding). Home: Saint Petersburg Fla. Died May 24, 1990.

DONER, DEAN BENTON, English language educator, university official; b. Brookings, S.D., May 1, 1923; s. David Benton and Edna (Beals) D.; m. Lois Jacobsen, Dec. 23, 1944; children—Kalia Louise, Margaret, Lauren Elizabeth. B.S., S.D. State U., 1947, D.Litt. (hon.), 1985; M.F.A., U. Iowa, 1948, Ph.D., 1953. Instr. English U. Idaho, 1950-53; instr., prof. English, assoc. dean Sch. Humanities, Purdue U., 1953-67; dean Coll. Liberal Arts and Scis.; prof. English U. Ill., Chgo., 1967-73; v.p. prof. English Boston U., 1973-86; vis. prof. U. Hamburg, 1967; mem. faculty Salzburg Seminar in Am. Studies, 1967. Contbr. short stories, poems, article to mags. Served with USAAF, 1943-46. Democrat. Unitarian. Home: West Lebanon N.H. Deceased. †

DONER, WILFRED B., advertising agency executive; b. Detroit, Nov. 15, 1914; s. Nathan and Regina (Sobel) Silberstein; m. Rolla Friedman, Mar. 19, 1964; children (by previous marriage): Judith Anne, Frederick Nathan, Mary Alice. Pres. W. B. Doner & Co., Detroit, Balt. and Southfield, Mich., 1937-68, chmn. bd., 1968-73, chmn. exec. com., 1973-90. Recipient Dir.'s award Adcraft Club Detroit, 1987. Home: Birmingham Mich. Died Jan. 4, 1990.

DONNELLEY, GAYLORD, printing company executive; b. Chgo., May 19, 1910; s. Thomas E. and Laura L. (Gaylord) D.; AB, Yale U., 1931; postgrad. Cambridge U., 1931-32; LLD (hon.), Wabash Coll., 1965, Yale U., 1974, U. Chgo., 1976, U. S.C., Spartanburg, 1979; m. Dorothy Williams Ranney, May 4, 1935; children: Elliott R., Strachan, Laura. With R.R. Donnelley & Sons Co., Chgo., 1932-75, comptroller, office mgr., 1940-42, sec., 1945-47, exec. v.p., 1947-52, pres., 1952-64, chmn. bd., 1964-75, chmn. exec. com., 1975-83, hon. chmn. bd., 1983-92; chmn. Gaylord Lockport Co., from 1984; past dir. Borg-Warner Corp., Dun & Bradstreet Corp., Reuben H. Donnelley Corp., First Nat. Bank of Chgo., First Chgo. Corp., Lakeside Bank; chmn. Prairie Holdings Corp., 1987; adv. bd. Ill. Dept. Conservation, 1978-84; mem. Ill. Bd. Higher Edn., 1979-85; chmn. Nature of Ill. Found., from 1985; mem. Canal Corridor Assn., from 1982; pres. Community Fund Chgo., 1969-71, bd. dirs., 1964-73; vice chmn. exec. com. mem., 1978-79; mem. Ill. Nature Preserves Commn., 1968-74; trustee Savs. and Profit Sharing Fund of Sears Employees, 1976-81; trustee Newberry Library, 1953-72, life trustee, 1972-92, first v.p. of bd., 1970; trustee Sarah Lawrence Coll., 1965-73, hon. trustee, from 1973; mem. Com. for Corp. Support of Pvt. Univs., 1977-80; chmn. Am. Friends of Cambridge U., 1977-83, dir., from 1969 ; trustee U. Chgo., 1947-80, life trustee, 1980-92, chmn. bd. trustees, 1970-76; mem. devel. bd. Yale U., 1964-71; hon. bd. advisors Mercy Hosp., from 1971 , lay bd. trustees, 1965-71; chmn. bd. Beverly Farm Found., 1962-64; elder First Presbyn. Ch., Libertyville; dir. Protestant Found. of Greater Chgo., 1970-79; trustee United Presbyn. Found., 1963-75, 1st v.p., 1972-73; trustee Nat. Recreation Found., 1969-92, N.Am. Wildlife Found., 1980-89, Nat. Humanities Ctr., 1984-87, Waterfowl Rsch. Found., 1978-89, World Wildlife Fund/Conservation Found., 1982-89, Cambridge U. Found., 1989-91; mem. nat. com. Ams. for Coast, 1980; mem. nat. adv. bd. Center for Book in Library of Congress, 1980-90. Recipient Yale medal, 1972, The Lambs Good Shepherd award, 1978, Citations to Disting. Citizens award Protestant Found. Greater Chgo., 1977, Oak Leaf award The Nature Conservancy, 1976, Conservation Merit award Ill. Dept. Conservation, 1981, Lewis Meml. award Printing Industries Am., 1976, Philanthropist award Nat. Soc. Fundraising Execs., 1980, Charles H. Wacker award United Charities, 1980, Lifetime Achievement award Nature Preserves Commn., 1988, Spl. Recognition Svc. award Wildlife Soc., 1989; named to Chgo. Bus. Hall of Fame, 1987; numerous others; hon. Fellow Corpus Christi Coll., Cambridge U., 1979. Fellow Royal Soc. for Encouragement Arts, Mfg. and Commerce, Am. Acad. Arts and Scis., Smithsonian Assocs. (nat. dir. 1977-83); mem. Am. Antiquarian Soc., Ducks Unltd. (pres. 1975-77, trustee 1962-80, trustee emeritus 1980-92, chmn. exec. com. 1978-80, vice chmn. bd. 1977-78), Ducks Unltd. (Can.) (trustee 1968-80, hon. dir. 1980-92), Ducks Unltd. de Mexico (trustee 1976-79), Nat. Recreation and Parks Assn. (life trustee, Spl. Recognition award 1975). Clubs: Coleman Lake (Goodman, Wis.); Old Elm (Highland Park, Ill.); Onwentsia (Lake Forest, Ill.); Shoreacres Golf (Lake Bluff, Ill.); Links, Grolier (N.Y.C.); Casino, Caxton, Chgo., Chgo. Commonwealth, Comml., Econ., Execs., Quadrangle, Racquet, Univ., Wayfarers (Chgo.). Author: To Be A Good Printer, 1977. Died Apr. 19, 1992; buried Lake Forest, Ill. Home: Libertyville Ill.

DONNER, ARVIN NEHEMIAH, principal; b. Dayton, Wis., Mar. 25, 1898; s. Henry Albert and Carrie Belle (Burnham) D.; m. Florence Myrtle Graham, June 4, 1922; 1 child, Arvin Nehemiah. Student, Lawrence Coll., 1915-17, U. Minn., 1920-22, Columbia U., 1930; BS, State U. of Iowa, 1927, MA, 1928, PhD, 1937. High school tchr. Mason City, Iowa, 1920; elem. sch. prin. Ft. Madison, Iowa, 1920-23, jr. high sch. prin., 1923-27; platoon sch. prin. Port Arthur, Tex., 1928-32, jr. high sch. prin., 1932-36, sr. high sch. prin., 1937-39; assoc. prof. edn. U. Houston, 1939; asst. supt. schs. Houston, 1942; dir. Sch. Edn., Grad. Sch. U. Houston, 1945, dean, Coll. Edn., 1950; vis. summer prof. U. Iowa, 1937-38, U. Ark., 1929, Ind. State Tchrs. Coll., 1948, U. Tex., 1949. Contbr. to ednl. yearbooks, jours. Mem. NEA, Tex. State Tchrs. Assn., Nat. Soc. for Study of Edn., Am. Assn. Sch. Adm., Dept. of Supv. and Curriculum Devel., Phi Delta Kappa, Kappa Delta Phi. *

DONOVAN, HEDLEY WILLIAMS, journalist; b. Brainerd, Minn., May 24, 1914; s. Percy Williams and Alice (Dougan) D.; m. Dorothy Hannon, Oct. 18, 1941 (dec. 1978); children: Peter Williams, Helen Welles, Mark Vicars. A.B. magna cum laude, U. Minn., 1934; B.A. (Rhodes scholar), Oxford U., 1936; Litt.D. (hon.), Pomona Coll., Boston U., Mt. Holyoke Coll.; L.H.D. (hon.), Southwestern at Memphis, Rochester U., Transylvania U.; LL.D. (hon.), Carnegie-Mellon U., Lehigh U., Allegheny Coll. Reporter Washington Post, 1937-42; writer, editor Fortune mag., N.Y.C., 1945-51, assoc. mng. editor, 1951-53, mng. editor, 1953-59; editorial dir. Time Inc., 1959-64, editor-in-chief, 1964-79, dir., 1962-79; sr. advisor to Pres. of U.S., 1979-80; fellow faculty of govt. Harvard U., 1980-87; vis. research fellow Nuffield Coll. Oxford (Eng.) U., 1986. Author: Roosevelt to Reagan: A Reporter's Encounters with Nine Presidents, 1985, Right Places, Right Times: Forty Years in Journalism Not Counting My Paper Route, 1989. Served to lt. comdr. USNR, 1942-45. Recipient Outstanding Achievement award U. Minn. Alumni, 1956; Loeb Journalism award, 1978; Gallatin medal NYU, 1979; hon. fellow Hertford Coll. Oxford (Eng.) U.; Leslie Moeller Disting. Lectureship, U. Iowa, 1985. Fellow Am. Acad. Arts and Scis.; mem. Council Fgn. Relations (dir. 1969-79), Phi Beta Kappa, Delta Upsilon. Clubs: Univ., Manhasset Bay Yacht, Century; Met. (Washington); St. Botolph (Boston). Home: New York N.Y. Died Aug. 13, 1990.

DONOVAN, TIMOTHY PAUL, historian; b. Terre Haute, Ind., Dec. 25, 1927; s. Harry Thomas and Gretchen Alma (Stakeman) D.; m. Eugenia Matella Trapp, June 1, 1950; children: Kevin, Rebecca, David, Richard. B.A., U. Okla., 1949, M.A., 1950, Ph.D., 1960. Instr. Okla. Mil. Acad., 1950-52, chmn. humanities div., 1952-57; teaching asst. U. Okla., 1957-60; asst. prof. history Tex. Tech U., 1960-63, assoc. prof., 1963-68, prof., 1968-69; prof. U. Ark., Fayetteville, 1969-87, chmn. dept. history, 1976-86, univ. prof. history, 1987-90. Author: Henry Adams and Brooks Adams, 1961, Historical Thought in America: Postwar Patterns, 1973, The Governors of Arkansas, 1981. Recipient Disting Teaching award Standard Oil, 1968. Mem. Am. Hist. Assn., Orgn. Am. Historians, Popular Culture Assn., Ark. Hist. Assn., So. Hist. Assn., Phi Alpha Theta. Democrat. Roman Catholic. Home: Fayetteville Ark. Died May 5, 1990; buried Fayetteville, Ark.

DOOLITTLE, ARTHUR K(ING), chemical engineer; b. Oberlin, Ohio, Nov. 15, 1896; s. Frederick Giraud and Maud (Tucker) D.; m. Dortha Bailey, Aug. 8, 1923; children: Robert Frederick II, Elizabeth May (Mrs. Donald Charles Peckham). AB, Columbia U., 1919, BS, 1920, ChemE, 1923. Registered profl. engr., W.Va., N.Y., N.J. Rsch. engr. The Dorr Co., Westport, Conn., 1923-25; plant engr. Sherwin-Williams Co., Chgo., 1925-29; chief lacquer divsn. Sherwin-Williams Co., Newark, 1929-31; devel. engr. spray drying Bowen Rsch. Corp., N.Y.C., 1931; dir. lacquer rsch. Bradley Vrooman Co., Chgo., 1931-32; tech. head coatings rsch. Carbide and Carbon Chems. Co., South Charleston, W.Va., 1932-44, asst. dir. rsch., 1944-45, sr. scientist, 1955-61; pres., cons. Arcadia Inst. for Sci. Rsch., Charleston, W.Va., from 1959; ptnr. Dorr Consultants, N.Y.C., 1959-61; prof. chem. Drexel Inst. Tech., Phila., 1961-64; mem. adv. bd. chem. engring. dept. Princeton, 1955-58. Author: The Technology of Solvents and Plasticizers, 1954; also articles in sci. jours.; contbr. Ency. of Chem. Tech., 1954; patentee in field. From pvt. to 2d lt. A.S., AUS, 1917-19, acceptance test pilot, 1919. Mem. AAAS (chmn. mgmt. com. Gordon Confs., 1955-56, adv. bd. 1950-58), Am. Inst. Chem. Engrs. (dir. 1951-54, v.p. 1955, chmn. Charleston sect. 1943-44), Am. Chem. Soc. (chmn. paint plastics and printing ink divsn. 1952-53, divsn. coun. 1952-56, coun. com. on nat. meetings and divsnl. activities 1952-56, adv. bd. indsl. and engring. chem 1954-56), Phi Beta Kappa, Tau Beta Pi, Phi Lambda Upsilon, Chi Beta Phi, Alpha Chi, Sigma Xi Rho, Columbia U. Club (N.Y.C.), Quiet Birdmen, Cosmos (Washington). *

DORFMAN, JOSEPH, economist, educator; b. Ramanovska, Russia, Mar. 27, 1904; s. Mendel and Etta Dorfman; m. Susan Lois, Mark Harris. AB, Reed Coll., 1924; AM, Columbia U., 1925, PhD, 1935. Economist Nat. Indsl. Conf. Bd., 1927-29; assoc. dept. econs Columbia U., 1931-36, lectr., 1936-40, asst. prof., 1940-46, assoc. prof., 1946-48, prof., 1948-71, prof. emeritus, 1971-91; cons. August M. Kelley Publisher, 1966-75. Author: Thorstein Veblen and His America, 1934, Economic Mind in American Civilization 5 vols. , 1946-59, with R.G. Tugwell Early American Policy, 1960, with others Institutional Economics, 1963, New Light on Veblen, 1973; editor: Relation of the State to Industrial Action and Economics and Jurisprudence H.C. Adams , 1955, Types of Economic Theory: From Mercantilism to Institutionalism, Vol. 1, 1967, Vol. 2, 1969; contbr.: Chief Justice Marshall: A Reappraisal, 1956. Two-yr grantee Rockefeller Found. for study Devel. Am. Econ. Thought, 1945; Guggenheim fellow, 1953-54, Ford Faculty Rsch. fellow, 1959-60. Mem. Assn. Evolutionary Econs. exec. bd. 1965-66, pres. 1969, Veblen-Commons award 1974 , Am. Econs. Assn. supervising com. history assn. . Home: New York N.Y. Died July 21, 1991.

DORRANCE, JOHN THOMPSON, JR., food processing executive; b. Cinnaminson, N.J., Feb. 7, 1919; s. John Thompson and Ethel (Mallinckrodt) D.; m. Diana R. Dripps, Apr. 26, 1979; children: John Thompson, III, Bennett, Mary Alice Malone; stepchildren: Keith Bassett, Langdon Mannion, Robert D. Dripps, III, Susan Stauffer. Grad., St. George's School, Newport, R.I., 1937; A.B., Princeton, 1941. With Campbell Soup Co., from 1946, asst. treas., 1950, asst. to pres., 1955, chmn. bd., 1962-84, chmn. exec. com., 1984-89, also dir.; dir. Neiman Marcus Group, Morgan Guaranty Trust Co. of N.Y., J.P. Morgan & Co., Inc. Served as capt. U.S. Army, World War II. Mem. Soc. Cin. Republican. Clubs: Union (N.Y.C.); Philadelphia (Phila.), Rittenhouse (Phila.), Union League (Phila.), Racquet (Phila.); Gulph Mills (Pa.) Golf; Pine Valley (N.J.). Golf, Nat. Golf Links of Am. (Southampton, N.Y.). Home: Gladwyne Pa. Died Apr. 9, 1989; buried West Laurel Hill Cemetery, Pa.

DORRITIE, JOHN FRANCIS, pharmaceutical advertising agency executive; b. N.Y.C., Feb. 26, 1934; s. George D. and Mary C. (Pollock) D.; m. Carol Kelley, July 23, 1960; children: George, Teresa, John, Carol Jean. B.S., Iona Coll., 1955. Product mgr., asst. advt. mgr. Sandoz Pharms., 1957-65; v.p. account services Sudler & Hennessey, Inc., 1965-68; founder, pres. Stat-Kit, Inc., 1968-69; exec. dir. Council for Interdisciplinary Communications in Medicine, N.Y.C., 1970; sr. v.p. Sudler & Hennessey, N.Y.C., 1970-77; exec. v.p. Sudler & Hennessey, 1977-79; pres. Dorritie & Lyons Inc. (now Dorritie Lyons & Nickel), 1979-91—. Served with U.S. Army, 1955-57. Mem. Am. Mktg. Assn., Pharm. Advt. Club, Midwest Pharm. Advt. Club, Soc. Advanced Med. Systems., AAAS, N.Y. Acad. Scis. Roman Catholic. Home: New City N.Y. Died May 24, 1991; buried Ascension Cemetery, Monsey, N.Y.

DORST, STANLEY ELWOOD, physician, educator; b. Cin., July 20, 1897; s. John Louis and Florence May (Elwood) D.; m. Mary Conway, Oct. 1926; 1 child, John Phillips; m. Emma H. Prince, Apr. 11, 1935. AB, Wittenberg Coll., 1919, ScD, 1948; MD, U. Cin., 1923, LHD, 1962; LLD, Xavier U., 1963. Diplomate Am. Bd. Internal Medicine. Intern Lakeside Hosp., Cleve., 1923-24; resident physician Cleve. Clinic Hosp., 1924-26; from asst. prof. medicineto assoc. prof. medicine U. Cin., 1926-53, prof. medicine, from 1953, dean Coll. Medicine, 1940-63, dean emeritus, from 1963; asst. attending physician Cin. Gen. Hosp., 1926-30, attending physician, from 1930, chief physician to out-patient dispensary, 1930-41; dir. Louis Kuhn Meml. Lab., 1926-37; cons. internist Children's Hosp., 1935-61; chmn. directing med. staff Cin. Gen. Hosp., Christian R. Holmes Hosp., 1940-63; cons. med. edn., 5th Svc. Commd., 1942-46. Author Sect. Diseases of Hypersensitivity in Reimann's System of Treatment; sect. on Body Weight in Ency. of Medicine; contbr. numerous articles to sci. jours. 2d lt. Infantry, U.S. Army, 1918-19. Mem. AAAS, AMA, (commn. study Brit. Medicine, 1949-50), Am. Soc. for Clin. Investigation, Ctrl. Soc. of Clin. Rsch., Assn. Am. Med. Coll. (mem. exec. coun., pres.), Am. Splty. Bds. Medicine (adv. coun. 1949-60), Alpha Omega Alpha, Sigma Xi, Pi Kappa Epsilon, Alpha Kappa Kappa, Beta Theta Pi, University Club, Literary Club (Cin.). *

DOTTS, HAROLD WILLIAM, business executive; b. Corydon, Ia., May 7, 1904; s. William E. and Pauline (Goodell) D.; m. Evelyn Dosey, Oct. 10, 1931; children—Harold W., Robert D., Dorothy Catherine; m. Glady Carlisle, Dec. 26, 1965. A.B., Simpson Coll., 1926; postgrad., Harvard Bus. Sch., 1936. With Jewel Tea Co., Barrington, Ill., 1926-53, successively salesman, asst. mgr., br. and dist. mgr., asst. gen. sales mgr., gen. sales mgr. and v.p., 1942-53; pres. Stonegate China Co., 1953-62; exec. dir. Nat. Home Service Assn., 1962-68; with Knox Assocs., Oak Brook, Ill., 1968-70; pub. relations dir. Northwest Trust & Savs. Bank, Arlington Heights, Ill., 1970-78. Exec. dir. Northwest Community Hosp. Found., 1978-90; trustee Simpson Coll., Northwest Community Hosp.; past pres. Arlington Heights Police and Fire Commn. Mem. Am. Soc. Assn. Execs., Nat. Premium Sales Execs., Epsilon Sigma. Republican. Clubs: Chgo. Sales Executives (pres. 1948-49), Nat. Sales Executive (dir. 1950-54), Economic.

Home: Arlington Heights Ill. Died July 9, 1990; buried Memory Gardens, Arlington Heights. †

DOTY, ROBERT MCINTYRE, museum administrator; b. Rochester, N.Y., Dec. 23, 1933. A.B., Harvard U.; M.A., U. Rochester. Group shows include: Photo-Secession, 1960; Photography America, 1965, 74, Whitney Ann., 1966-71, Adolph Gottlieb, 1968, Human Concern/Personal Torment, 1969, Contemporary Black Artists Am., 1971, Lucas Samaras, 1972, Am. Folk Art in Ohio Collections, 1976; now dir. Currier Gallery Art, Manchester, N.H. Died Nov. 1992. Home: Manchester N.H. †

DOUGHTIE, VENTON LEVY, mechanical engineering educator; b. Montgomery County, Tex., Apr. 22, 1897; s. Sim Taylor and Cora (Leslie) D.; m. Norma Polliard, June 6, 1922; children: Darlyne Raynel, Venton Levy. Student, Rice U., 1916-18; BS, U. Tex., 1920, MS in Mech. Engring., 1940. Registered profl. engr., Tex. Tech. apprentice Westinghouse Mfg. Co., Phila., 1920-21; instr. Johns Hopkins U., 1921-25; adj. prof. mech. engring. U. Tex., 1929-30, assoc. prof. mech. engring., 1938-39, prof. mech. engring., since 1939, chmn. dept. mech. engring., 1949-51, 57-62; asst. prof. mech. engring. Tex. Tech Coll., Lubbock, 1930-33, assoc. prof. mech. engring., 1933-35, prof. mech. engring., 1935-38. Author: Fundamentals of Engineering Problems, 1938, (with A. Valiance) Design of Machine Members, 1943, rev. 1964, Caleulo de Elementos de Maguinus, 1959; (with W.H. James) Elements of Mechanism, 1954, Elementos de Mecanismos, 1962; (with others) Elements of Mechanism, 1947, Nociones de Mecanismos, 1954; contbr. Kent's Mech. Engr.'s Handbook, 1950, articles to profl. jours. Seaman USNRF, World War I; coord. pilot tng. U. Tex., World War II. Fellow ASME, AAAS; mem. Am. Soc. Engring. Edn., Tex. Acad. Sci., Nat., Tex. Socs. Profl. Engrs., Sigma Xi, Tau Beta Pi, Chi Phi, Pi Tau Sigma, Masons (K.T., Shriner), Rotary. Presbyterian. *

DOUGLAS, LEWIS WILLIAMS, government official, insurance company executive; b. Bisbee, Ariz., July 2, 1894; s. James Stuart and Josephine Leah (Williams) D.; m. Peggy Zinsser, June 19, 1921; children: James Stuart, Lewis W., Sharman. BA, Amherst Coll., 1916; student, MIT, 1916-17; LLD, Amherst Coll., 1933, Harvard U., 1933, Queens Coll., 1938, Princeton U., 1938, Brown U., 1938, NYU, 1938, Wesleyan U., 1938, U. Ariz., 1940, Leeds, Eng., 1948, U. Bristol, St. Andrews, London, 1949, Edinburgh, Birmingham, Glasgow, 1950, U. Calif., McGIll U., Columbia U., Dalhousie, 1951; DCL, Oxford U., 1948. Instr. Amherst Coll., 1920; min., genl. bus. Ariz., from 1921; mem. Ariz. Ho. of Reps., 1923-25, 70th-73d Congresses, 1927-33; at large Ariz.; dir. of budget, 1933-34; v.p., dir. Am. Cyanamid Co., 1934-38; prin., vice chancellor McGill U., Montreal, 1938-39; pres. Mutual Life Ins. Co. of N.Y., 1940-47; amb. to Great Britain London, 1947-50; chmn. bd. Mutual Life Ins. Co. of N.Y., 1947-59; chmn. bd. dirs. So. Ariz. Bank & Trust Co., Douglas Investment Co.; bd. dirs. Tech. Studies, Inc., Western Bancorp., Gen. Motors Corp., Empire Trust Co., Internat. Nickel Co., Newmont Mining Corp., Union Corp., Ltd., Nichols Engring. & Rsch. Corp.; chmn. U.S. investment com. No. Assurance Co., Employer's Liability Assurance Co. Dep. War Shipping Adminstr., 1942-44; spl. adv. Gen. Clay, German Control Coun., 1945. Chmn. Nat. Policy Bd.; pres., chmn. Am. Assembly, ALfred P. Sloan Found., Am. Mus. Nat. Hist.; trustee emeritus Amherst Coll.; pres., trustee Acad. Polit. Sci.; nat. chmn. Am. Shakespeare Festival Theatre and Acad.; hon. pres. Nat. Soc. for Prevention of Blindness; mem. adv. bd. Meml. Hosp. 1st lt. F.A., U.S. Army, World War I; AEF in France. Recipient citation from Gen. Pershing; decorated Croix de Guerre (Belgium), Grand Croix de la Legion d'Honneur (France), Grand Croix de l'Order de al Couronne (Belgium), hon. knight grand cross Order Brit. Empire. Mem. English-Speaking Union (hon. chmn.), Nat. Inst. Social Scis. (v.p.), Am. Philos. Soc. (trustee). Democrat. Episcopalian. *

DOW, JENNINGS BRYAN, electronics executive; b. Bowling Green, Ohio, Jan. 2, 1897; s. Cyrus Marion and Anna S. (Kahler) D.; m. Kathryn Pfister Burkhardt, Feb. 19, 1955; stepchildren: Edward Arnold Burkhardt, Douglas Carroll Burkhardt. BS, U.S. Naval Acad., 1919, postgrad. engring. sch., 1924-25; MS, Harvard U., 1926. Various positions in electronics; asst. chief, dir. electronics Bur. of Ships, 1941-47; retired, 1947; with Hazeltine Corp. and Hazeltine Electronics Divsn., from 1947; v.p., dir. Hazeltine Corp.; pres., dir. Hazeltine Rsch. Corp. Commd. 2 lt. USN, 1919, advanced to commodore 1947. Recipient Legion of Merit. Fellow Inst. Radio Engrs.; mem. N.Y. Yacht Club, Creek Club (Locust Valley, N.Y.), Army-Navy Club (Washington). *

DOW, WILBUR EGERTON, JR., lawyer; b. Bklyn., Aug. 5, 1906; s. Wilbur Egerton and Minnie Chloe (Oltman) D.; m. Ruth Elizabeth Paul, Sept. 2, 1931; children: William Paul, Lynn Elizabeth, Ruth Lee. Student, U. Wash., U. So. Calif.; LL.B., N.Y. U., 1934. Bar: N.Y. 1936. Pvt. practice law N.Y.C., from 1936; pres. Lake George (N.Y.) Steamboat Co.; admiralty lawyer; mcht. marine licensed unltd. master, 1st class pilot N.Y. Harbor, Hudson and East Rivers; officer, dir. s.s. cos.; leader Dow Expdn. to Magnetic North Pole, 1954; former chmn. New Orleans Steamboat Co. Mem. Soc. Naval Architects and Marine Engrs., Maritime Law Assn., Am. Bar Assn., Marine Soc. City N.Y., Delta Tau Delta. Clubs: Down Town Assn. (N.Y.C.); Glens Falls Country (N.Y.); Plimsoll (New Orleans). Home: Lake George N.Y. Died Nov. 14, 1991; buried Evergreen Cemerty, Lake George, N.Y.

DOWNEY, FAIRFAX DAVIS, writer; b. Salt Lake City, Nov. 28, 1893; s. Brig. Gen. George Faber and Mattie Louise (Davis) D.; m. Mildred Adams, Oct. 19, 1918; children: F. Davis (dec.), Marjorie Adams Downey Knowlton. Grad., The Hill Sch., Pa., 1912; AB, Yale, 1916; LhD (hon.), Keene State Coll., 1975. Mem. staff Kansas City Star newspaper, 1918-21, N.Y. Tribune and Hearld Tribune, 1921-27, N.Y. Sun, 1927. Author numerous books including When We Were Rather Older, 1926, Richard Harding Davis: His Day, 1933, Portrait of an Era as Drawn by C.D. Gibson, 1936, Disaster Fighters, 1938, Indian-Fighting Army, 1941, Our Lusty Forefathers, 1947, Horses of Desitny, 1949, Free and Easy, 1951, Mascots, 1954, The Shining Filly, 1954, Sound of the Guns, 1956, General Crook, Indian Fighter, 1957, The Guns at Gettysburg, 1958, Clash of Cavalry: The Battle of Brandy Station, 1959, The Red Bluecoats, 1973, others. Served to Capt. U.S. Army, 1918, maj., 1942-43; lt. col. F.A. Res., 1946. Decorated Silver Star citation. Fellow Co. Mil. Historians; mem. Ancient Order Artillerists, Am. Soc. Composers, Authors and Pubs., Authors League, Yale of N.H. Club, Univ. Club, Aztec Club (hon.), Elihu Club. Home: West Springfield N.H. Died May 31, 1990.

DOWNS, ROBERT BINGHAM, librarian; b. Lenoir, N.C., May 25, 1903; s. John McLeod and Clara Catherine (Hartley) D.; m. Elizabeth Crooks, Aug. 17, 1929 (dec. Sept. 13, 1982); children: Clara Downs Keller, Mary Roberta Downs Andre.; m. Jane Bliss Wilson, Sept. 16, 1983. A.B., U. N.C., 1926, LL.D., 1949; B.S., Columbia U., 1927, M.S., 1929; Litt.D., Colby Coll., 1944; D.L.S., U. Toledo, 1953; L.H.D., Ohio State U., 1963, So. Ill. U., 1970; Litt.D., U. Ill., 1973. Asst. U. N.C. Library, 1922-26, N.Y. Pub. Library, 1927-29; librarian Colby Coll., Waterville, Maine, 1929-31; asst. librarian U. N.C., 1931-32, librarian and assoc. prof. library sci., 1932-34, librarian, prof., 1934-38; dir. libraries N.Y. U., 1938-43; dir. Library and Library Sch.; prof. library sci. U. Ill., Urbana, 1943-58, dean library adminstrn., 1958-71, dean emeritus, 1971; assoc. Columbia Sch. Library Service, 1942-43; cons. Kabul U., Afghanistan, 1963; adviser U. Tunis, 1973; chmn. ALA Bd. on Resources Am. Libraries, 1939-42, 45-50; pres. Assn. Coll. and Reference Libraries, 1940-41; spl. cons. civil information and edn. sect. SCAP, Japan, 1948, 1950; vis. chief Union Catalog Div.; cons. in bibliography Library of Congress, 1949; adviser Nat. Library and Nat. U. Mexico, 1952; library adviser to Turkish Govt., 1955, 68, 71; vis. prof. U. Toronto, 1974. Author: The Story of Books, 1935, Resources of Southern Libraries, 1938, Resources of New York City Libraries, 1942, Am. Library Resources, 1951-81, Books that Changed the World, 1956, 2d edit., 1978 (translated into 17 langs.), Molders of the Modern Mind, 1961, Famous Books, Ancient and Medieval, 1964, Family Saga, 1958, Resources of North Carolina Libraries, 1965, How To Do Library Research, 1966, 2d edit. (with Clara D. Keller), 1975, Resources of Missouri Libraries, 1966, Resources of Canadian Academic and Research Libraries, 1967, Books That Changed America, 1970, Famous American Books, 1971, British Library Resources, 1973, Horace Mann, Champion of Public Schools, 1974, Books and History, 1974, Guide to Illinois Library Resources, 1974, Heinrich Pestalozzi, Father of Modern Pedagogy, 1975, Famous Books, 1975, Books That Changed the South, 1976, Henry Barnard, 1977, Friedrich Froebel, 1978, In Search of New Horizons, 1978, Australian and New Zealand Library Resources, 1979, British and Irish Library Resources, 1981, Landmarks in Science, 1982, Memorable Americans, 1983, Perspectives on the Past, an Autobiography, 1984; (with Ralph E. McCoy) The First Freedom Today, 1984; More Memorable Americans, 1985, Books In My Life, 1985, Images of America, 1987, Scientific Enigmas, 1988; editor: Library Specialization, 1941, Union Catalogs in the United States, 1942, Status of American College and University Librarians, 1958, The First Freedom, 1960, The Bear Went Over the Mountain, 1964, (with Frances B. Jenkins) Bibliography, Current State and Future Trends, 1967; Contbr. articles to library jours. Decorated Order of Sacred Treasure (Japan), 1983; recipient Clarence Day award, 1963, Joseph W. Lippincott award, 1964, Centennial medal Syracuse U., 1970, Life Long Achievement award Columbia U. Sch. Libr. Svc., 1988, Melvil Dewey award, 1974; hon. adm. Tex. Navy, 1971; Guggenheim fellow, 1971-72. Mem. ALA (1st v.p. 1951-52, pres. 1952-53), Ill. Library Assn. (pres. 1955-56), Southeastern Library Assn., AAUP, Authors League Am., Soc. Midland Authors, Phi Beta Kappa, Beta Phi Mu, Phi Kappa Phi. Democrat. Clubs: Dial (Urbana); Caxton (Chgo.). Lodge: Rotary. Home: Urbana Ill. Died Feb. 24, 1991; buried Woodlawn Cemetery, Urbana, Ill.

DOWNS, WILBUR GEORGE, physician, educator; b. Perth Amboy, N.J., Aug. 7, 1913; s. James Cloyd and Mabel Lulu (Lehman) D.; m. Helen Hartley Geer; children: Helen (Mrs. Christian J. Haller III), Anne (Mrs. James A. Carroll), William M., Isabel (Mrs. Robert Warner); m. Dorothy Gardner, Feb. 10, 1973. A.B., Cornell U., 1935, M.D., 1938; M.P.H., Johns Hopkins U., 1941; M.A. (hon.), Yale, 1964. Diplomate: Am. Bd. Preventive Medicine. Mem. staff Rockefeller Found., 1941-61, asso. dir., 1961-71, dir. virus program, div. biomed. scis., 1961-71; prof. epidemiology Yale Med. Sch., 1964-71, clin. prof. epidemiology and pub. health, 1973-91; founder (Rockefeller Found.) Trinidad Regional Virus Lab., now Caribbean Epidemiology Ctr., Port-of-Spain, 1952; mem. standing adv. com. Med. Research Brit. Caribbean, 1956-71; expert panel arthropod-borne viruses WHO, from 1956, chmn. various adv. coms.; commn. for malaria Armed Forces Epidemiological Bd., 1965-71; mem. adv. coms. USPHS, U.S. State Dept., U.S. Dept. Def., NAS. Bd. dirs. Hartley House, N.Y.C. Served with AUS, 1942-46. Decorated Bronze star; recipient presdl. and mil. citations for work with malaria and communicable diseases. Mem. Am. Soc. Tropical Medicine and Hygiene, Royal Soc. Tropical Medicine and Hygiene. Home: Branford Conn. Died Feb. 17, 1991.

DOYLE, JAMES EDWIN (NED), advertising executive; b. N.Y.C., Oct. 23, 1902; s. William Joseph and Josephine (Huttenbrauch) D.; m. Helen Aisley; 1 child, Anthony Edwin; m. Marion E. Lance, May 26, 1945 (div. 1966); children: Michael Varian, Ellin Downey; m. Margaret Rivelli, Aug. 14, 1967 (div. 1977). Student, Hamilton Coll., 1920-22, LLD, 1977; LLB, Fordham U., 1931. Advt. mgr. Look mag., 1937-42; account exec., v.p. GreyAdvt. Agy., 1945-49; exec. v.p. Doyle Dane Bernback advt. agy., N.Y.C., 1949-89; chmn. Simmons Market Rsch. Bur., 1978; owner Floridians basketball team, 1970-72; mem. bus. adv. com. on mgmt. improvement State of N.Y. Trustee Hamilton Coll. Capt. USMC, 1942-45. Mem. NFL Alumni Assn. (hon.), Farmington Country Club, Rockefeller Ctr. Luncheon Club, Princeton Club (N.Y.C.), Alpha Phi, Chi Psi. Home: New York N.Y. Died Mar. 5, 1989.

DOYLE, KENNETH JOSEPH, priest, lawyer, journalist; b. Troy, N.Y., Apr. 3, 1940; s. W. Kenneth and Sallie (Shea) D. B.A., Cath. U. Am., 1961, M.A., 1962; J.D., Albany Law Sch., 1978. Bar: N.Y.; ordained priest Roman Cath. Ch. Bur. chief Rome Office, Nat. Cath. News Service, 1981-84; info. officer Nat. Conf. Cath. Bishops, 1984-86; dir. govt. rels. N.Y. State Cath. Conf., 1986-89; dir. media rels. Nat. Conf. Cath. Bishops, from 1989. Recipient awards Nat. Cath. Press Assn., N.Y. State Press Assn. Home: Washington D.C. Deceased. †

DOYLE, MARION WADE (MRS. HENRY GRATTAN DOYLE), volunteer civic activities; b. Cambridge, Mass., Oct. 30, 1894; d. John F. and Joanna T. (Phelan) Sharkey; m. Henry Grattan Doyle, Sept. 15, 1917 (dec. 1964); children: Henry Grattan, Marion (Mrs. Charles Campbell, Jr.), Robert Carr. AB cum laude in Romance Langs., Radcliffe Coll., 1914; LHD, Am. U., 1955. Chief employee relations, personnel divsn. Dept. Treas., 1945-47. Contbr. to ednl. jours. Pres. Washington Bd. Edn. 1935-49, mem. 1929-49; regional dir. Nat. LWV, 1929-31, nat. exec. v.p. 1931-33; exec. dir. Washington Self-Help Exchange, 1939-45, pres.; mem. 4th Regional Loyalty Bd., Civil Svc. Commn., 1948-52; mem. Nat. Loyalty Rev. Bd., 1952-53; asst. to dir., rep. for orgns. White House Conf. on Edn., 1954-55, U.S. Office of Edn., 1955-57, chmn. Washington com. White House Conf. on Children and Youth, 1960; chmn. nat. capital area Ten Yr. Program for Radcliffe Coll; chmn. adv. com. Washington Juvenile Ct., 1951-53, 57-59; chmn. Washington Commrs.' Youth Coun., 1953-56, hon. chmn. from 1959; v.p., then pres. Washington Commrs.' War Hospitality Com., 1946-47, chmn. successor orgn. Washington Armed Svcs. Hospitality Com., 1950-54, also pres. Recreation Svcs. until 1954, then mem. com.; treas. Chevy Chase Civilian Def. Com.; past sec. Chevy Chase Women's Club; pres. Chevy Chase Community Coun.; active Visiting Nurse Assn; bd. dirs. Cath. Charities, Archdiocese Wash., from 1962. Recipient various awards and honors including certificate of merit Washington Commrs., 1954, citation disting. alumna Radcliffe Coll., 1954, John Benjamin Nichols award Washington Med. Soc., 1955, Achievement award Corrections divsn. United Community Svcs. Washington, 1956, Nat. Brotherhood award Nat. Conf. Christians and Jews, 1959, Cath. Youth Orgn., 1960. Mem. Radcliff Coll. Alumnae Assn. (bd. mgmt. from 1964), Columbian Women of George Washington U. (pres.), Kappa Delta Pi, Delta Kappa Gamma, Twentieth Century Club (hon.). *

DOZIER, WILLIAM, motion picture and television producer, executive; b. Omaha, Feb. 13, 1908; s. Robert C. and Emma (McElroy) D.; m. Katherine Foley, Sept. 14, 1929; 1 son, Robert J.; m. Joan Fontaine, May 2, 1946 (div. 1950); 1 dau., Deborah Leslie; m. Ann Rutherford, 1953. A.B., Creighton U., 1929. Rep. Berg-Allenberg Writers and Artists Agy., 1935; head story and writing dept. Paramount Studios, Hollywood, Calif., 1941-44; prodn. exec. RKO-Radio Pictures, 1944-51, v.p. charge prodn., 1955-56; v.p. Universal-Internat. Pictures; producer Columbia Pictures, 1949-51; program exec. CBS, N.Y.C., 1951-55; exec. producer dramatic programs CBS, 1955; v.p. charge programs Hollywood CBS-TV, 1957-59; v.p. charge prodn. Screen Gems,

1959-64; pres. Greenway Prodns., from 1964; prof. creative TV and drama Mt. St. Mary's Coll., West Los Angeles, Calif., 1972-78. Producer (TV series) Batman for ABC-TV. Home: Beverly Hills Calif. Died Apr. 23, 1991; buried Holy Cross Cemetery, L.A.

DRADDY, VINCENT DE PAUL, apparel company executive; b. N.Y.C., Jan. 31, 1907; s. William Gregory and Marg (Kearns) D.; m. Ruth H. Crystal, Sept. 26, 1932 (dec.); children: Vincent de Paul, Diane. BA, Manhattan Coll., 1930, LLD, 1961. With David Crystal, Inc., N.Y.C., 1934-90, chmn. bd., to 1990; v.p. Gen. Mills Corp., 1968-90; pres. Haymaker Co., Alligator Coats, Crystal Sunflowers. Chmn. Harrison (N.Y.) Planning Com., 1962-68; chmn. Westchester Classic Golf Tournament, 1966-78; chmn. bd. dirs. Manhattan Coll.; trustee United Hosp. Recipient Torch of Truth award Nat. Food Found., 1976, Gold Medal award Nat. Football and Hall of Fame, 1978. Mem. Westchester Country Club, Blind Brook Club, Nat. Golf Club, Everglades Club, Seminole Club, Bath and Tennis Club, Country Club Fla., Shawnee Country Club. Roman Catholic. Home: Rye N.Y. Died July 8, 1990.

DRAGOO, DONALD WAYNE, research administrator, anthropologist; b. Indpls., Nov. 4, 1925; s. Calvin Ellsworth and Josephine (Coy) D.; m. Christine Worthington, Aug. 23, 1971; 1 child, Stephen W. A.B., Ind. U., 1948, M.A., 1949; postgrad., U. N.Mex., 1949-50; Ph.D., Ind. U., 1957. Archeologist Am. Found. Arabian Expdn., 1950-51; biochemist antiobiotic research and devel. Eli Lilly and Co., Indpls., 1951-52; archeologist Upper Ohio Valley Archaeol. Survey, Carnegie Mus., Pitts., 1952-55, asst. curator sect. man, 1956-59, assoc. curator, 1959-63, curator, 1963-77; sr. curator, head Carnegie Mus. Anthropology Center, Butler, Pa., 1975-77; assoc. prof. anthropology U. Pitts., 1959-63, adj. research prof., 1971-77; pres. Auctor Research, Inc., Gloucester, Va., 1980-82, dir., from 1983; pres. Inst. for Human History, Gloucester, Va., 1982-88; prin. assoc. D&C Research Assocs., Gloucester, 1987-88; dir. anthropology Environment Cons., Dallas, 1977-79. Author: Archaic Hunters, 1957, Mounds for the Dead, 1962, Early Lithic Cultures of the New World, 1970, Wells Creek-An Early Man Site, 1973, Some Aspects of Eastern North American Prehistory, 1976, Palaeo-Indian Points and Tools, 1982; also numerous monographs, reports, and articles; editor: Carnegie Mus. Archeol. Newsletter, 1963-77, Pandemia, from 1982; assoc. editor: Ethnology, 1962-63, Pa. Archaeologist, 1963-77, Man in the Northeast, 1971-78; collaborator: Abstracts of New World Archaeology, 1965-67; editorial chmn. Annals of Carnegie Mus., 1967-68; mem. adv. bd. The Chesopiean, 1987-88. Served with USNR, 1944-46. Fellow AAAS, Am. Anthrop. Assn.; mem. Eastern States Archaeol. Fedn. (pres. 1970-72), Soc. for Am. Archaeology, Nat. Geog. Soc., Soc. Profl. Archaeologists, Am. Quaternary Assn. Home: Gloucester Va. Died Aug. 27, 1988; cremated.

DRAKE, PAUL W(OODHULL), architect; b. Morristown, N.J., July 31, 1897. BArch, Cornell U., 1921. With Ludlow & Peabody, 1922-24, Voorhees, Gmelin & Walker, 1924-25, McKim, Mead & White, 1925-26; ptnr. Drake, Tuthill, Convery & Cueman, and predecessor firms, Summit, N.J.; asst. prof. Drew U., 1942-43; lectr. high schs., service clubs; v.p. Nat. Coun. Archtl. Registration Bds. Prin. works include Masonic Temple, Morristown, 1930, Welfare Home, Morris County, N.J., 1953, (with Charles A. Scheuringer) Presbyn. Ch., 1954, First Nat. Iron Bank, Morristown, Sperry & Hutchinson Co., office and warehouse, Natick, Mass., 1959, Short Hills (N.J.) Country Day Sch., 1961. Mem. zoning bd., Madison, N.J., 1950-53. Recipient Award of Merit N.J. Soc. Architects, 1950. Fellow AIA (v.p. N.J. chpt. 1939-41, pres. 1941-43); mem. N.J. Bd. Architects. *

DREILING, DAVID A., surgeon; b. N.Y.C., June 5, 1918; s. Louis and Rosalia (Lustic) D.; m. Muriel A. Oppenheimer, June 25, 1946; 1 child, David Arne. B.A., Cornell U., 1938; M.D., NYU, 1942. Diplomate: Am. Bd. Surgery. Prof. surgery Mt. Sinai Med. Ctr., N.Y.C.; Alfred and Florence Gross prof. surgery Mt. Sinai Med. Ctr.; dir. Ctr. for Lab. Animal Sci., N.Y.C.; mem. staff Rockefeller Inst., Elmhurst Hosp.; mem. Bronx VA Hosp. Author: (with Janowitz and Perrier) Pancreatic Inflammatory Disease, 1964; editor: Am. Jour. Gastroenterology, Mt. Sinai Jour. Medicine; assoc. editor Internat. Jour. Pancreas. Recipient Jacobi medal; recipient Copernicus medal. Mem. Am. Surg. Assn. (sr.), ACS, Am. Gastroenterol. Assn., Am. Coll. Gastroenterology (disting. service award), N.Y. Surg. Soc. Democrat. Jewish. Home: Hollywood Fla. Died Sept. 24, 1991; buried Hollywood, Fla.

DRESSEL, PAUL LEROY, educator, academic administrator; b. Youngstown, Ohio, Nov. 29, 1910; s. David Calvin and Aura Olive (Jacobs) D.; m. Wilma Frances Sackett, Sept. 18, 1933; children—Carol Ann, Linda Kathleen, Jeana Lynn. A.B., Wittenberg Coll., 1931, LL.D. (hon.), 1966; A.M., Mich. State Coll., 1934; Ph.D., U. Mich., 1939. From instr. to dir. counseling and chmn. bd. examiners Mich. State Coll., 1934-54; dir. coop. study evaluation gen. edn. Am. Council Edn., 1949-53; prof. univ. research Mich. State U., East Lansing, from 1954; dir. Mich. State U. (Office Evaluation Services), East Lansing, 1954-59, dir. instl. research, asst. provost, 1959-76, prof. univ. research, 1976-81; chmn. evaluation com. Nat. Sci. Tchrs. Assn., 1956-58; cons. Bd. Higher Edn., Mo. Synod, Lutheran Ch., 1959-75; mem. exec. bd. commn. on instns. higher edn. N. Central Assn., 1966-70, mem. commn. on research and service, 1970-76; cons. chmn. commn. scholars Ill. Bd. Higher Edn., 1966-87; cons. Okla. Consortium on Research Devel., 1968-70; chmn. com. gen. edn. Am. Assn. Higher Edn., 1953-54, v.p., dir., 1969-70, pres., 1970-71; chmn. com. on nontraditional study Fedn. Regional Accrediting Assns., 1972; cons. to colls. and univs. on problems of research and curriculum devel. Author: Comprehensive Examinations in a Program of General Education, 1949, Evaluation in the Basic College at Michigan State University, 1958, Evaluation in Higher Education, 1961, The Undergraduate Curriculum in Higher Education, 1963, College and University Curriculum, 1968, The Confidence Crisis, 1970, The World of Higher Education, 1971, Institutional Research in the University: A Handbook, 1971, Blueprint for Change: Doctoral Programs for College Teachers, 1972, Return to Responsibility, i972, Independent Study, 1973, Handbook of Academic Evaluation, 1976; Editor: The New Colleges: Toward An Appraisal, 1971, The Autonomy of Public Colleges, 1980, Improving Degree Programs, 1980, Administrative Leadership, 1981, On Teaching and Learning in College, 1982, College to University, 1987; editorial bd.: Jour. Higher Edn, 1969-72, Internat. Ency. Higher Edn, 1972-77; publs. bd.: Assn. Instnl. Research, 1972-75; editorial cons. bd.: Research in Higher Edn, 1972-84; cons. editor: Jour. Exptl. Edn, 1972-84. Home: East Lansing Mich. Died Nov. 22, 1989; buried Jackson, Mich.

DRESSLER, ROBERT EUGENE, communications and education consultant; b. Evanston, Ill., Jan. 31, 1922; s. Eugene Francis and Hazel Margaret (Smith) D.; m. Marion E. Benken, Dec. 28, 1949 (div.); children—Heidi, Bruce, Wendy, Brian, Suzanne; m. Patricia P. Peden, May 28, 1976. B.A., Northwestern U., 1947, Mus.M., 1948. Faculty Shawnee Mission (Kans.) High Sch., 1948-49; free lance composer/arranger/condr. N.Y.C., 1949-50; faculty Jamestown (N.D.) Coll., 1950-53; faculty mem., dir. Glee Club U. Chgo., 1953-54; program mgr., producer/dir. WMAQ-TV (NBC), Chgo., 1954-61; dir. advt. and pub. relations Field Enterprises Ednl. Corp., Chgo., 1961-67; dir. Ampex Video Inst., Elk Grove, Ill., 1967-70; co-owner Dressler & Robinson, Chgo., 1970-72; gen. mgr. KOMU-TV; assoc. prof. U. Mo. Sch. Journalism, 1972-74; pres. So. Ednl. Communications Assn., Columbia, S.C., 1974-76; cons. communications and edn., 1976-90; Vis. prof. Northwestern U., 1955-56, Columbia Coll., Chgo., 1956. Bd. govs. Chgo. chpt. Acad. Television Arts and Scis., 1955-63. Served to lt. (j.g.) USNR, 1943-46. Mem. Phi Kappa Psi, Phi Mu Alpha Sinfonia. Presbyn. (dir. music 1966-72, 74—). Home: Columbia S.C. Died July 26, 1990; buried St. Martin's in the Fields Meml. Garden, Columbia, S.C.

DREWRY, GUY CARLETON, author; b. Stevensburg, Va., May 21, 1901; s. Rev. Samuel Richard and Julia Harriett (Pinckard) D.; student public schs. Va.; m. Margaret Elizabeth McDonald, Apr. 2, 1942; children: Barbara Louise, Guy Carleton. Statistician, Norfolk & Western Rwy., 44 yrs. Assoc. editor The Lyric, 1929-49; vis. lectr. English, Am. poetry Hollins Coll., 1952-53; instr. creative writing U. Va. Extension Div. Named Poet Laureate of Commonwealth of Va. for life, 1970. Contbr. poetry to The Dial, later The Nation, The New Republic, Poetry; A Magazine of Verse also Voices. Work appeared in N.Y. Times, N.Y. Herald Tribune, The Georgia Rev., Prairie Schooner, Sat. Rev., Queen's Quar., Va. Quar. Rev., Yale Rev.; included in following anthologies: American Writing, Lyric Virginia Today, Moult's Best Poems, Virginia Reader, Poetry Awards (1949, 51), Lyric Virginia Today, No. 2, The Best Poems of 1956. Author: (poetry) Proud Horns, 1933, The Sounding Summer, 1948; A Time for Turning, 1951 (Poetry Awards Found. prize 1952), The Writhen Wood, 1953, Cloud Above Clocktime, 1957, (lyrics) To Love that Well, 1975; editor Southern Issue of Voices. Winner The Voices award, 1940. Mem. Poetry Soc. Va. (pres. 1952-55), Poetry Soc. of Am. (regional v.p.). Died Aug. 3, 1991; buried Roanoke, Va. Home: Roanoke Va

DRIMMER, MELVIN, historian, educator; b. Bronx, N.Y., Nov. 2, 1934; s. Oscar and Natalie (Stessin) D.; m. Iris Alteres, June 26, 1959 (div. 1982); children: Alan Stessin, Barbara; m. Lillian Boehmer, 1985. BA, CCNY, 1956; postgrad., Oxford U., summer 1957; PhD, U. Rochester, 1965; Ford postdoctoral fellow, Sch. Oriental and African Studies, U. London, 1966-67. Lectr. Hunter Coll., 1960-63; asst. prof. to prof., chmn. history dept. Spelman Coll., Atlanta H. Center, 1963-72; prof. Cleve. State U., 1972-92, chmn. history dept., 1972-74; vis. asst. prof. NYU, summers 1965-66, vis. asso. prof., summer 1968; A. Lindsey O'Connor vis. prof. Am. instns. Colgate U., 1969-70; Lyceum vis. prof. Dillard U., 1977; research asso. DuBois Inst., Harvard U., 1981-83; exec. dir. Am. Forum Internat. Study; dir. numerous summer insts., Africa and Caribbean, 1968-92; dir. NDEA Insts. in Black History, Spelman Coll., 1966, 68-92 ; cons. Ford Found. Aspen Conf., 1970, Yale Danforth program, 1970, John Jay Coll., 1970, A. Philip Randolph Inst., 1970-72. Author: Black History, A Reappraisal, 1968, Issues in Black History, Reflections and Commentaries on The Black Historical Experience, 1986, 2d edit., 1990; contbr. articles to various periodicals. Bd. dirs. Karamu House, Cleve. Recipient Field Summer grants, 1964, 65, Atlanta U. research grant, 1966, Ford Humanities grant Colgate U., 1969-70; Dept. State grantee, 1975; Hayes-Fulbright grantee, 1976. Mem. Am. Hist. Assn., Assn. Study Afro-Am. Life and History, Phi Beta Kappa. Home: Cleveland Ohio Died June 17, 1992; Cleveland, OH. †

DRISCOLL, JOHN GERALD, JR., lawyer; b. Wadsworth, Nev., Sept. 5, 1897; s. John Gerald and Annie M. (Kearns) D.; m. Maybelle Branch, Jan. 6, 1917; children: Moyna, John Gerald, Harlan. AB, Stanford U., 1918, LLB, 1920. Bar: Calif. 1920, Wash. 1921, Wyo. 1923. Lectr. U. Wash., 1920-23; dean law sch. U. Wyo., 1923-26; pvt. practice law San Diego, from 1927; U.s. commr. Inter-Am. Tropical Tuna Commn. Mem. ABA, Internat. Assn. Ins. Counsel, Am. Soc. Internat. Law, Univ. Club, Yacht Club, Propellor Club (San Diego). *

DROZDA, HELEN DOROTHY, psychiatric social worker; b. Omaha, Mar. 21, 1924; d. Joseph J. and Mary E. (Sabatka) D.;. BS, U. Nebr., 1955; MS, So. Ill. U., 1965; postgrad., Tex. Tech U., 1969, Midwestern U., 1968-69; PhD, Colo. State Christian Coll., 1973. Diplomate Clin. Social Workers; cert. social worker, advanced clin. practitioner, Tex., rehab. counselor. Supervising group counselor San Diego Probation Dept., 1956-57; health edn. dir. YWCA, Omaha, 1954-56; Y-teen dir. YWCA, Alton, Bloomington and Peoria, Ill., 1958-62; guidance dir. Acad. of Our Lady, Peoria, 1962-64, St. Teresa Acad., East St. Louis, Ill., 1964-67, Knox County Pub. Schs., Benjamin, Tex., 1967-69, Wilbarger County Pub. Schs., Vernon, Tex., 1969-70; exec. dir. Burk Guidance and Counseling Services, Burkburnett, Tex., 1970-86; social service supr. Western unit Wichita Falls State Hosp., Burkburnett, Tex., 1970-86. Named Social Worker of Yr., 1984. Mem. Am. Legion, Air Force Assn., Am. Guidance and Personnel Assn., Nat. Assn. Social Workers (past chmn. Red River unit, diplomate), Midwest Soc. Individual Psychology, Tex. Pub. Employees Assn., Tex. Social Psychotherapy Assn., Acad. Certified Social Workers, Nat. Rifle Assn., Am. Assn. Ret. Persons. Home: Burkburnett Tex. Deceased. †

DRUMMOND, EDWARD JOSEPH, English language educator; b. East St. Louis, Ill., Apr. 6, 1906; s. William Riley and Mary Elizabeth (Streuber) D. AB, St. Louis U., 1928, AM, 1930, STL, 1938; PhD, U. Iowa, 1942. Mem. Soc. Jesus; ordained priest Roman Cath. Ch., 1937. Instr. English, Latin, Greek Creighton Prep. Sch., 1931-34; lectr. religion and ethics U. Iowa, 1942; instr. English Marquette U., 1942-44, assoc. prof., 1944-62, acting dir. dept. English, 1947-48, dean grad. sch., 1944-53, acting v.p., 1953-54, v.p. acad. affairs, 1954-62; v.p. Med. Ctr. St. Louis U., 1962-73, exec. v.p., 1973-75, exec. v.p. emeritus, 1975-91, also assoc. prof. English, 1962-70, prof. edn., 1970-75, prof. emeritus, 1975-91; Cath. chaplain and dir. Newman Club, U. Iowa, 1942; edn. asst. to provincial Mo. Province, 1975-91. Editor Mo. Province News-Letter, 1934-36; contbr. articles, revs. and books. Cons. task force orgnl. structure, bd. dirs. Nat. League Nursing, 1963-74; mem. long range planning com. Wis. State Coord. Com. for Higher Edn., 1960-62; mem. bd. commrs. Nat. Commn. on Accrediting, 1967-91. Recipient Fleur de Lis medal St. Louis U., 1975. Mem. North Cen. Assn. (commr., mem. exec. bd. commn. on colls. and univs. 1958-64, vice chmn. 1961-62, chmn. 1962-64, v.p. 1967-68, pres. 1968-69, dir. 1967-91), Nat. Cath. Ednl. Assn. (mem. commn. on grad. studies 1945-53, chmn. resolutions com. 1952 conv., chmn. plans and problems com. 1953-54, chmn. com. on faculty welfare coll. and univ. dept. 1958-62), Hosp. Assn. Met. St. Louis, Jesuit Edn. Assn. (chmn. commn. on grad. studies 1948-49), Fedn. Regional Accrediting Commns. Higher Edn. (vice chmn. exec. com. 1964-66, chmn. 1966-70), Am. Hosp. Assn. (mem. com. nursing edn. 1964-67, mem. coun. on manpower and edn. 1968-71), Sigma Tau Delta, Phi Alpha Theta. Home: Saint Louis Mo. Died July 23, 1991; buried Calvary Cemetery, St. Louis.

DRURY, CHARLES MILLS, Canadian offical; b. Westmount, Que., Can., May 17, 1912; s. Victor Montague and Pansy (Mills) D.; m. Jane Ferrier Counsell, Sept. 12, 1939 (dec.); children: Diana, Leith, Victor Montague, Charles Gibbons. Student, Bishop Coll., Royal Mil. Coll.; B.Civil Law, McGill U.; postgrad., U. Paris; D.Sc., N.S. Tech. Coll. Bar: Que. Chief UNRRA Mission Govt. Can., Poland, 1945-47; civil servant Govt. Can., Ottawa, 1947-55; pres. Provincial Transport Co., Montreal, Que., Can., 1955-60; cabinet minister Parliament Govt. Can., Ottawa, 1963-76; chmn. Nat. Capital Commn., Ottawa, 1978-84; spl. rep. constl. devel. Govt. Can., N.W. Territories, 1977-81. Pres. Bd. Trade, Montreal; pres. U.N. Assn. Can., Can. Centenary Council; chmn. Can. Inst. Internat. Affairs, Montreal; mem. Parliament Can., Ottawa, 1962-78. Brig. Gen., Can. Army, World War II. Decorated Order of Can. Club: St. James (Montreal). Home: Ottawa Can. Died Jan. 12, 1991. †

DRURY, CLIFFORD MERRILL, educator and author; b. Early, Iowa, Nov. 7, 1897; s. William and Mae (Dell) D.; m. Miriam Mayhew Leyrer, Nov. 17,

1922; children: Robert Merrill, Patricia, Philip Edward. AB, Buena Vista Coll., Sterm Lake, Iowa, 1918; BD, San Francisco Theol. Sem., San Anselmo, Calif., 1922; STM, San Francisco Theol. Sem., 1928; PhD, U. Edinburgh, 1932; DD, Buena Vista Coll., 1941; Litt.D., Whitworth Coll., 1955; DHL, Whitman Coll., 1964. Ordained to ministry Presbyn. Ch., 1922. Asst. pastor First Ch., Berkeley, Calif., 1921-23; pastor Community Ch. (Am.), Shanghai, China, 1923-27, First Presbyn. Ch., Moscow, Idaho, 1928-38; prof. ch. history San Francisco Theology Sem., 1938-63. Author: Henry Harmon Spalding, Pioneer of Old Oregon, 1936, Marcus Whitman, M.D., Pioneer and Martyr, 1937, Mary and Elkanah Walker, Pioneers Among the Spokanes, 1940, A Tepee in His Front Yard, 1949, Presbyterian Panorama, 1952, Diary of Titian Peale, 1956, History of Chaplains Corps, U.S. Navy, 2 vols., 1950-51, U.S. Navy Chaplains, 3 vols., 1949-57, The Diaries and Letters of Henry H. Spalding and Asa Bown Smith, 1958, The First White Woman Over the Rockies, 2 vols., 1963, San Francisco Y.M.C.A.; One Hundred Years by the Golden Gate, 1963; contbr. to religious and hist. jours. With ARC, Ft. Des Moines, Iowa, 1919. Served in Chem. Warfare Svc., U.S. Army at Yale U., 1918; chaplain, capt. USNR, 1933-58, active duty, 1941-46, historian Chaplain Corps., USN, 1944-56. Recipient award Presbyn. Hist. Soc., 1960. Mem. Am. Ch. History Soc., Phi Beta Kappa, Mason (K.T.). Republican. *

DRYFOOS, NANCY PROSKAUER, sculptor; b. New Rochelle, N.Y., Mar. 25; d. Richman and Edith (Harris) Proskauer; m. Donald Dryfoos (dec.). Cert. Sarah Lawrence Coll., 1939; postgrad. Columbia U. Extension Sch., 1945-46. One-person shows include: Contemporary Arts Gallery, N.Y.C., 1952, Silvermine Guild Gallery, 1954, Wellons Gallery, 1956, Bodley Gallery, 1958, Collectors Gallery, 1960, Dime Savs. Bank, Bklyn., 1969, Lincoln Savs. Bank, N.Y.C., 1975-76, 87, Donnell Libr., N.Y.C., 1987 (Pen and Brush solo show winner, 1989); group shows include: Lever Bros., Warner Communications Corcoran Gallery, Pa. Acad. Fine Arts, 1947, Syracuse Mus., 1948, Bklyn. Mus., 1952, Corcoran Gallery, 1954, Nat. Acad. Fine Arts, N.Y.C., 1952-76, Lincoln Savs. Bank, 1987, Donnell Libr. Ctr., 1987, others; work in permanent collections Columbia U., Brandeis U., NYU, Boca Raton (Fla.) Mus., Kean Coll., N.J., others; v.p. Fine Arts Fedn. of N.Y. Contbr. articles to profl. publs. Mem. Creative Arts Award Commn. Brandeis U. Fellow Nat. Sculpture Soc. (rec. sec. 1973, former officer); mem. Allied Artists America (Medal of Honor 1978, contest juror), Audubon Artists (exhbn. dir. 1983-84, asst. treas. 1987-88, prize), Am. Soc. Contemporary Artists (dir. 1970-72, exhbn. dir., prize), Contemporary Artists Guild (dir.), N.Y. Soc. Women Artists (dir.), Fine Arts Fedn. N.Y. (v.p.), Pen and Brush Club (Joyce and Eliot Listen award 1985, Bedy Marky Art Foundry award 1982, award of merit 1986, Emily Nichols Hatch award 1988), Nat. Trust for Hist. Preservation, Network Visual Arts Ctr. (dir.), Artists Equity Assn. (bd. dirs. 1978-80), Mcpl. Art Soc., Womens City Club N.Y. Avocations: printmaking, enameling. Died Oct. 13, 1991. Home: New York N.Y.

DUARTE, JOSÉ NAPOLEÓN, president of El Salvador; b. Nov. 23, 1925; m. Inés Duráan; children: Inés Guadalupe, José Alejandro, María Eugenia, Marí Elena, Lorena. M Engring., U. Notre Dame. Founder Christian Dem. Party, San Salvador, El Salvador, 1960; sec.-gen. Christian Dem. Party, San Salvador, 1960-64, 68-70, pres., 1972-90; civil engr., to 1964, mayor of San Salvador, 1964-70; pres. Republic of El Salvador, 1972, 84-90; imprisoned, then exiled to Venezuela, 1972-79, returned to El Salvador, 1979, after mil. coup served as mem. ruling juntsa, 1980-82. Home: San Salvador El Salvador Died Feb. 23, 1990.

DU BOIS, CORA, anthropologist, educator; b. N.Y.C., Oct. 26, 1903; d. Jean Jules and Mattie Schreiber Du B. BA, Barnard Coll., 1927; MA, Columbia U., 1928; PhD, U. Calif., Berkeley, 1932; ScD, Wilson Coll., 1958. Rsch. assoc. anthropology U. Calif., 1932-35, NRC fellow, 1935-36; tchr. Hunter Coll., 1936-37; social sci. rsch. fellow Columbia U., 1937-39; tchr. Sarah Lawrence Coll., 1939-42; br. chief OSS, also Dept. State, 1942-50; social sci. cons. WHO, UN, 1950-51; dir. rsch. Inst. Internat. Edn., 1951-54; Zemurray-Stone prof. Harvard U. and Radcliffe Coll., 1954-69, prof. emeritus, 1969-91; prof. at large Cornell U., Ithaca, N.Y., 1971-76; curator South Asian Ethnology, Peabody Mus., Harvard U., 1969; vis. prof. U. Calif., 1948, Colo., 1954, U. Calif., San Diego, 1974; Carnegie vis. prof. U. Hawaii, 1957; field rschr. in Am. Indians, Calif., 1929-36, Alor, Indonesia, 1937-39, Orissa, India, 1961-72. Author: People of Alor, 1944, Social Forces in Southeast Asia, 1949, Foreign Students and Higher Education in the United States, 1956; editor: Lowie's Selected Papers in Anthropology, 196, also various monographs; contbr. articles to profl. jours. Fellow Ctr. for Advanced Study Behavioral Scis., Palo Alto, Calif., 1958-59; recipient exceptional civilian svc. award U.S. Army, 1946, Achievement award AAUW, 1961; decorated Order of Crown of Thailand 3d class, 1949. Mem. Assn. Asian Studies pres. 1970-71 , Am. Acad. Arts and Scis., Am. Anthropol. Assn. pres. 1968-69 , AAAS sectional v.p. 1966-67 , Phi Beta Kappa, Sigma Xi. Home: Cambridge Mass. Died Apr. 7, 1991.

DUCHAC, KENNETH FARNHAM, librarian; b. Antigo, Wis., Jan. 8, 1923; s. Carl O. and Alice Alberta (Farnham) D.; m. Gretchen Nommensen, May 12, 1944; children—Frederic Carl, John Nommensen. A.B., Carroll Coll., Waukesha, Wis., 1947; B.L.S., U. Chgo., 1947, postgrad. history, 1947-49. With Detroit Pub. Library, 1949-50; asst. dir. Decatur (Ill.) Pub. Library, 1950-53; dir. Kingsport (Tenn.) Pub. Library, 1953-57; cons. Wis. Free Library Commn., 1957-60; cons., supr. pub. librs. Md. Dept. Pub. Edn., 1960-68; dep. dir. Bklyn. Pub. Library, 1969-70, dir., 1970-87; vis. prof. Pratt Inst., 1974-75; Dept. State spl. cons. in, Jordan, 1960; cons. Pahlavi Nat. Library, Tehran, Iran; mem. N.Y. Commr. Edn.'s Com. on Libraries; trustee N.Y. Met. Reference and Research Library Agy., pres., 1980-84. Bd. dirs. Bklyn. Arts Coun.; dir., chmn. bd. Bklyn. Ednl. and Cultural Alliance, 1981-85; commr. Bklyn. Bridge Centennial, 1983. Served with USNR, 1943-46. Mem. ALA, N.Y. State Library Assn., L.I. Hist. Soc., Internat. Assn. Met. City Libraries (sec.-treas. 1974-77). Home: Ellicott City Md. Died May 9, 1989; cremated.

DUDLEY, E. WALLER, lawyer; b. Alexandria, Va., Feb. 12, 1923; s. Luther H. and Katherine Carrol (Waller) D.; m. Letty Waugh; children: Carter, Waller, Luther. A.B., Washington and Lee U., 1943, LL.B., 1947. Bar: Va. 1947, D.C. 1982, U.S. Ct. Appeals (4th cir.) 1950, U.S. Supreme Ct. 1952. Sr. ptnr. Boothe, Prichard & Dudley, Alexandria, from 1947; dir. 1st Am. Bank Va. Trustee Washington and Lee U., Lexington, Va.; chmn. ARC, Alexandria, 1955-58, Alexandria Traffic Bd., 1954-57. Lt. j.g. USNR, 1943-46. Fellow Am. Coll. Trial Lawyers, Am. Bar Found.; mem. Va. Bar Assn. (past pres.), Alexandria Bar Assn. (past pres.), ABA. Episcopalian. Club: Kiwanis. Home: Alexandria Va. Deceased. †

DUDLEY, TILFORD E., public affairs counsellor; b. Charleston, Ill., Apr. 21, 1907; s. Gerry Brown and Esther Wilhoit (Shoot) D.; m. Martha Fairchild Ward, Aug. 28, 1937; children: Donica Ward, Gerric Ward, Martha Fairchild. Ph.B. cum laude, Wesleyan U., 1928; LL.B., Harvard U., 1931; LL.D. (hon.), Eastern Ill. U., 1979. Bar: Ill. bar 1931. Gen. practice law Aurora, Ill., 1931-34; chief legal sect. Land Program, Fed. Emergency Relief Adminstrn., 1934-35; chief land sect. Suburban Resettlement Adminstrn., 1935-37; chief land acquisition R.D.P., Nat. Parks Service, 1936-37; trial examiner NLRB, 1937-42; prin. mediation officer Nat. War Labor Bd., 1942-43; dir. disputes Nat. War Labor Bd. (Region VI), 1943-44, prin. adminstrv. officer, 1944; assoc. gen. counsel and Washington rep. United Packinghouse Workers Am., 1944-45; asst. to Sidney Hillman, chmn. CIO Polit. Action Com., 1945-46, asst. dir., 1946-55; asst. dir. AFL-CIO Com. on Polit. Edn., 1955-58; dir. AFL-CIO Speakers Bur., 1958-69; dir. Washington office Council for Christian Social Action, United Ch. of Christ, 1969-75, pres. property mgmt. and maintenance, 1975-85. Author: The Harvard Legal Aid Bureau, Its History and Purposes, 1930, Harvard Legal Aid Bureau, 1931, Digest of Decisions of National Labor Relations Board, Vol. 8, 1939, King for a Day, 1969, Poverty and Hunger, 1970, Need for a 30 Hour Week, 1975; editor: The Washington Report, 1969-75. Chmn. of Citizens Council for D.C., 1962-67; mem. exec. bd. div. Christian life and work and mem. gen. bd. Nat. Council Chs., 1954-57, 64, exec. bd. div. life and mission, 1965-70; cons. 2d Assembly World Council Chs., 1954; alt. mem. Dem. Nat. Com., 1948-68; del. Dem. Nat. Conv., 1948, 52, 60, 68; vice chmn. Dem. Central Com. for D.C., 1964-67, chmn., 1967-68; sec.-treas. Am. Com. on East-West Accord, 1983-85. Established Dudley Found. to fund social and environ. programs. Mem. NAACP, Ams. for Democratic Action, Sigma Chi, Delta Sigma Rho. Methodist and Congregationalist. Club: Harvard (Washington). Home: Charleston Ill. Died Jan. 18, 1990; buried Charleston, Ill.

DUFF, HOWARD, actor; b. Bremerton, Wash., Nov. 24, 1917; m. Ida Lupino. Student, Repertory Playhouse, Seattle. With Sta.-KOMO, 1935; originator role of Sam Spade; films include Brute Force, 1947, Naked City, 1948, Shakedown, 1950, While the City Sleeps, 1956, Boy's Night Out, 1962, The Late Show, 1977, A Wedding, 1978, Kramer vs. Kramer, 1980, Double Negative, 1980, Oh God!, Book II, 1980, East of Eden, 1981, Monster in the Closet, 1986, No Way Out, 1987; appeared in TV series Mr. Adams and Eve, 1956-57, Dante, 1960-61, Felony Squad, 1966-68, Flamingo Road, 1980, The Dream Merchants, 1980, This Girl for Hire, 1983; other TV appearances include Lou Grant, Combat, The Rogues, Name of the Game, Police Story, Medical Center, Kung Fu, Mannix; guest TV appearances The Golden Girls, Midnight Caller. Served with U.S. Army, 1941-45. Home: New York N.Y. Died July 8, 1990. †

DUGGAN, JEROME TIMOTHY, utilities executive; b. Kansas City, Mo., Oct. 30, 1914; s. Jerry F. and Claire (Aaron) D.; m. Dorothy Blanche Castle, May 4, 1940; children—Jerome Castle, Dorothy Lucinda Kobusch. A.B., U. Mo., 1936, LL.B., 1938. Bar: Mo. bar 1938. With Hook & Thomas, Kansas City, 1938-40; asst. city counselor Kansas City, 1940-42; regional rationing atty. OPA, 1942-43; mem. firm Gage, Hillix & Phelps, 1946-50; gen. counsel Gas Service Co. Kansas City, Mo., 1950-68; v.p., dir. Gas Service Co. Kansas City, 1956-64, exec. v.p., dir., gen. counsel, 1964-68, pres., dir., 1968-78, chmn. bd. dirs., 1978-79; dir. Commerce Bank, Kansas City; mem. Gov.'s Adv. Commn. on Indsl. Devel., from 1961; chmn. Kansas City Housing Authority, 1947-50; dir. Indsl. Coun. Kansas City, 1951-55; mem. Indsl. Devel. Commn., Kansas City, from 1959, Mcpl. Svc. Commn., 1955-56. Bd. dirs. Citizens Regional Planning Council, Downtown Inc., Kansas City Indsl. Found.; pres. bd. dirs. Asso. Inustries of Mo., 1970—; Trustee, pres. Research Hosp. and Med. Center, 1970-71; trustee Mo. Pub. Expenditure Survey, Midwest Research Inst., Jacob Loose Fund.; bd. regents Rockhurst Coll. Served as lt. USNR, World War II. Mem. Mo. Bar Assn., Am. Gas Assn. (dir.), Am. Royal Assn. (bd. govs.), Kans. Assn. Commerce and Industry (dir.), Sigma Nu, Phi Delta Phi. Clubs: Kansas City (pres. 1976-77), Mission Hills Country. Home: Kansas City Mo. Died Aug. 8, 1990; buried Mt. Olivet Cemetery, Kansas City.

DUKE, THOMAS WALTER DANIEL, lawyer; b. Richmond, Va., Dec. 13, 1896; s. T. Wiley and Mary Florence (Smith) D.; m. Dolores Carrillo de Albornoz, Jan. 8, 1925 (div. 1942); children: Renee Eckelberry, Diane Amussen; m. Penny Nichol, Jan. 29, 1946. Bar: Va. 1920, N.Y. 1923, D.C. 1942. Ptnr. Duke & Landis and predecessor firms, from 1926; co-founder S.W. Lumber Mills, Inc., Ariz.; dir. Venezuelan Devel. Corp., Paramount Motors Corp., Monorailway Corp.; dir., mem. exec. com. original Com. for Econ. Recovery. Author various reviews of books on legal and econ. subjects. Chmn. Enzyme Rsch. Found. Flight lt. USAC, WWI. Mem. Mason, Met. Club (Washington), Union Club. *

DUKES, HENRY HUGH, veterinary physiologist; b. St. George, S.C., Sept. 9, 1895; s. Oren Boswell and Angie Rebecca (Risher) D.; m. Mary Alice Kent, June 7, 1927. BS, Clemson Coll., 1915; DVM, Iowa State U., 1918, MS, 1923; D.Honoris Cause, Universidad Rural Brazil, 1953. Teaching fellow in vet. physiology Iowa State Coll., 1915-18; asst. prof. vet. sci. and asst. state veterinarian S.C. Clemson Coll., 1918-20; vet. practice and health officer Greer, S.C., 1920-21; instr., later asst. prof. vet. physiology Iowa State Coll., 1921-29, asst. prof. vet. investigation (physiology), 1929-32; prof. vet. physiology and head dept. physiology N.Y. State Vet. Coll., Cornell, 1932-60, prof. vet. physiology emeritus, 1960-92; sec. vet. faculty N.Y. State Vet. Coll., Cornell, 1945-48, prof. physiology Coll. Vet. Medicine, Iowa State U., 1961-92. Author: The Physiology of Domestic Animals, 1933, 7th edit., 1955; contbr. rsch. papers in field of animal physiology in profl. publs. With U.S. Army, 1918. Recipient Iowa State Coll. Alumni Merit award, 1953, Mich. State Coll. Centennial award, 1955, Borden award, 1960, XII Internat. Vet. Congress prize, 1963. Fellow AAAS, N.Y. Acad. Sci.; mem. Am. Vet. Med. Assn. (chmn. sect. on rsch. 1938-39, mem. rsch. coun. 1941-50, sec., 1941-47, rep. on div. biology and agr. NRC 1943-45), Conf. Rsch. Workers Animal Diseases N.Am., Am. Physiol. Soc., Soc. for Exptl. Biology and Medicine, AAUP, N.Y. State Vet. Med. Soc., Asociacion de Medicos Veterinarios del Peru (hon.), Sigma Xi, Phi Kappa Phi, Phi Zeta (nat. pres. 1940-46), Phi Lambda Upsilon, Alpha Psi. *

DU MAURIER, DAPHNE, author; b. London, May 13, 1907; d. Gerald and Muriel (Beaumont) du M.; m. Frederick Arthur Montague Browning, July 19, 1932; children: Tessa, Flavia, Christian. Ed., Camposena Meudon, Paris. Author: The Loving Spirit, 1931, I'll Never Be Young Again, 1932, The Progress of Julius, 1933, Gerals, A Portrait, 1935, Jamaica Inn, 1936, The Du Mauriers, 1937, Rebecca, 1938, Happy Christmas, 1940, Com Wind, Come Weather, 1941, Frenchman's Creek, 1941, Hungry Hill, 1943, The King's General, 1945, The Years Between, 1945, September Tide, 1948, Castle D'or, 1962, The Glass-blowers, 1963;. dramatic works include: The Parasites, 1949, My Cousin Rachel, 1952, Kis Me Again, Stranger, 1953, Mary Anne, 1954, The Scapegoat, 1957, The Breaking Point, 1958, The Infernal World of Branwell Bronte, 1961, The Flight of the Falcon, 1965, Vanishing Cornwall, 1967, The House on The Strand, 1969. Fellow Royal Soc. Lit. Home: Par England Died Apr. 19, 1989.

DUMKE, GLENN S., university and college chancellor; b. Green Bay, Wis., May 5, 1917; s. William F. and Marjorie S. (Schroeder) D.; m. Dorothy Deane Robison, Feb. 3, 1945. A.B., Occidental Coll., 1938, M.A., 1939, LL.D. (hon.), 1960; Ph.D., U. Calif., 1942; H.L.D. (hon.), U. Redlands, 1962, Hebrew Union Coll., 1968, Windham Coll., 1969; LL.D. (hon.), U. Bridgeport, 1963, Transylvania Coll., 1968, Pepperdine Coll., 1969, Our Lady of the Lake U., 1977, Dickinson State Coll., 1978, Calif. State U., 1982. Teaching asst. U. Calif. at Los Angeles, 1940-41; instr. history Occidental Coll., 1940-43, asst. prof., 1943-46, assoc. prof., 1947-50, prof. history, 1950, Norman Bridge prof. Hispanic Am. history, 1954, dean faculty, 1950-57; pres. San Francisco State Coll., 1957-61; vice chancellor acad. affairs Calif. State Colls., 1961-62; chancellor Calif. State Univ. and Colls., 1962-82, chancellor emeritus, 1982; pres. Inst. for Contemporary Studies, 1982-86, Found. 21st Century, 1986-89; bd. dirs. Farmers Ins. Group, Trust Services Am., Forest Lawn Co.; 1st chmn. Calif. Council Econ. Edn., 1968; past mem. exec. com., chmn. Western Interstate Commn. for Higher Edn.; Mem. founding bd.

Civilian/Mil. Inst., USAF Acad. Found.; former chmn. bd. Econ. Lit. Council Calif.; former mem. exec. com., chmn. fin. com. Council on Postsecondary Accreditation; former trustee Community TV So. Calif.-KCET; past mem. exec. com. Calif. Council for Humanities in Pub. Policy, 1974-77; chmn. Calif. Selection Com. for Rhodes Scholarships, 1966; former mem. com. on state relations Am. Assn. State Colls. and Univs.; past mem. bd. visitors USAF Acad., Am. U.; bd. commrs. Nat. Commn. on Accrediting, 1959-65, 70-74; bd. dirs. Am. Council Edn., 1967-68; former trustee Calif. Industry-Edn. Council. Author: The Boom of the Eighties in Southern California, 1944, Mexican Gold Trail, 1945, (with Dr. Osgood Hardy) A History of the Pacific Area in Modern Times, 1949 (under name of Glenn Pierce) The Tyrant of Bagdad, 1955, King's Ransom, 1986, (under name Jordan Allen) Cavern of Silver, 1982, The Condor, 1980, Texas Fever, 1980; co-author, editor: From Wilderness to Empire: A History of California, 1959; contbr. articles to profl. and popular publs. Alt. del. Republican nat. conv., 13th dist. Calif., 1948, 24th dist. Calif., 1952; trustee emeritus U. Redlands; trustee Pepperdine U. Haynes Found. grantee, 1943; named Kinght Commdr. of North Star King of Sweden; recipient Order of Merit Fed. Republic Germany, Taiwan. Mem. Los Angeles World Affairs Council (dir.), Calif. Hist. Soc., Joint Council Econ. Edn. (dir. from 1969), Western Coll. Assn. (past chmn. membership and standards com.), Am. Mgmt. Assn. (dir. 1970-73, 74-77, 79-82), Inst. Internat. Edn. (West Coast adv. bd. 1972-87), Calif. C. of C. (dir. 1980-88), Phi Beta Kappa. Methodist. Clubs: California, Bohemian, Town Hall, Regency. Home: Encino Calif. Died June 30, 1989; buried Meml. Ct. of Honor, Forest Lawn Cemetery, Glendale, Calif.

DUNCAN, ROBERT MICHAEL, lawyer; b. N.Y.C., May 23, 1931; s. John Collamer and Doris (Bullard) D.; m. Nancy Young, Mar. 23, 1958; children: Angus M., Diana G. BA, Yale U., 1953; LLB, Harvard U., 1958. Bar: D.C. 1958. Trial atty. tax div. U.S. Dept. Justice, Washington, 1958-62; assoc. Cleary, Gottlieb, Steen & Hamilton, Washington, 1962-68; ptnr. Cleary, Gorrlieb, Steen & Hamilton, Washington, 1968-91. Served to 1st lt. U.S. Army, 1953-55. Home: Washington D.C. Died July 20, 1991; buried West Charleton, N.Y.

DUNCAN, VIRGINIA BAUER, power corporation executive, television producer and director; b. Lansing, Mich., June 9, 1929; d. Theodore Irving and Maurine Virginia (Foote) Bauer; B.A., U. Mich., 1951; m. Bruce G. Duncan, Oct. 27, 1956; children: John C., Michael G., Timothy B. Producer, dir. KQED-TV, San Francisco, 1960-75; pres. Candide Prodns., Inc., San Francisco, 1966-91; corp. exec. Bechtel Power Corp.; dir. Corp. for Public Broadcasting, Washington, 1975-79, First Interstate Bank of Calif., 1979-91. Bd. dirs. Town Sch. for Boys, San Francisco, 1966-70; pres., Parents Assn. Marin Parents Assn. Marin County Day Sch., Corte Madera, Calif., 1971-72; mem. public media panel Nat. Endowment for Arts, Washington, 1973-79; chmn. bd. dirs. Yosemite Inst., 1974-84; trustee Katharine Branson/Mt. Tamalpais High Sch., Ross, Calif., 1975-82; assoc. council Mills Coll., Oakland, Calif., 1975-91; mem. Carnegie Commn. on Future of Public Broadcasting, 1977-79; mem. Council for Arts, M.I.T., 1977-80; bd. dirs. James Irvine Found., 1979-91. Recipient Edward W McQuade award for disting. programming in field of social justice, 1964; NET award for excellence for individual contbn. to outstanding television programming, 1966; Readers Digest Found. award, 1969; CINE Golden Eagle award, 1970; Emmy award Nat. Acad., TV Arts and Scis., 1971. Died Jan. 14, 1991. Home: San Francisco Calif. †

DUNDES, JULES, mass media communications educator; b. N.Y.C., Sept. 12, 1913; s. Leopold and Ida (August) D.; m. Frances Becker, July 31, 1937; children: Leslie Weir, Suresa. BS, Columbia U., 1933. Sports reporter N.Y. Post, 1929-34; copywriter Hallee Co., 1934-36; promotion copywriter CBS, 1936-40; advt. and sales promotion mgr. WCBS, N.Y.C., 1940-49; dir. sales and advt. KCBS, San Francisco, 1949-55; mgr. KCBS, 1955-56, gen. mgr., 1961-67; v.p. advt., sales promotion CBS Radio, 1956, v.p. charge sta. adminstrn., 1956-61; v.p., gen. mgr. KCBS, 1961-67; lectr. in communication Stanford U., 1967-92; dir. Stanford Mass Media Inst., 1972-92; prof. Fromm Inst. for Lifelong Learning U. San Francisco. Chmn. communications com. San Francisco Human Rights Commn.; chmn. bd. Cerebral Palsy Assn. Mem. San Francisco Radio Broadcasters Assn. (pres.), Cal. Broadcasters Assn. (chmn. bd.), Radio Pioneers, Sigma Delta Chi. Home: San Francisco Calif. Died Mar. 23, 1992. †

DUNHAM, AILEEN, history educator; b. Columbia, Mo., Nov. 29, 1897; d. Samuel S. and Frances (Walker) Dunham. BA, U. Alta., 1920; MA, U. Toronto, 1921; PhD, U. London, 1924. Faculty Coll. of Wooster (Ohio), 1924-92, prof. history, 1929-92, Michael O. Fisher prof., 1955-92, chmn. dept., 1946-92; vis. prof. U. Alta, summers 1946, 47. Author: Political Unrest in Upper Canada, 1815-1837, 1927; contbr. articles, reviews to profl. jours. Mem. Am. Hist. Assn., Ohio Acad. History, Renaissance Soc. Am., Fgn. Policy Assn., AAUW, AAUP, League Women Voters. Presbyterian. *

DUNN, HARRY LIPPINCOTT, lawyer; b. Santa Barbara, Calif., Feb. 24, 1894; s. Ebenezer Pedrick and Margaret Ann (Robinson) D.; m. Louise Dodge Reding, Feb. 7, 1925 (dec. 1952); children—Peter Reding, Priscilla (Mrs. Priscilla D. Flynn); m. Katharine Tilt McCay, Feb. 3, 1955 (dec. 1976). A.B., U. Calif., 1915; postgrad., Columbia Law Sch., 1915-16, Harvard, 1919-21. Bar: N.Y. State bar 1922, Calif. bar 1925. Assoc. firm Cravath, Henderson, Leffingwell & de Gersdorff, N.Y.C., 1921-24, O'Melveny & Myers, Los Angeles, 1924-27; ptnr. firm O'Melveny & Myers, 1927-68, counsel, from 1968. Trustee Claremont U. Center. Served Commn. for Relief in Belgium, 1916-17; with Am. Field Service, 1917, France; 1st lt., 6th F.A., 1st Div. AEF, 1917-19; with Am. Relief Adminstrn. in Poland, 1919. Mem. Am., Los Angeles bar assns., Am. Bar Found., Los Angeles C. of C., Harvard Law Sch. Assn. (past v.p.), Friends of Claremont Colls. (past pres.), Los Angeles World Affairs Council (past v.p., Phi Delta Theta.). Republican. Clubs: California (Los Angeles); Annandale Golf (Pasadena, Calif.), Harvard (Pasadena, Calif.), Zamorano (Pasadena, Calif.), Twilight (Pasadena, Calif.), Valley Hunt (Pasadena, Calif.). Home: Pasadena Calif. Died Nov. 13, 1988.

DUNNE, IRENE, actress; b. Louisville, Dec. 20, 1901; m. Francis D. Griffin, July 16, 1928 (dec. 1965); 1 child, Mary Frances Griffin Gage. Student, Chgo. Coll. Music. U.S. del. 12th Gen Assembly UN. Began career with tour mus. comedy Irene, 1920; starred in movies, including Joy of Living, 1938, Over 21, 1941, Penny Serenade, 1941, A Guy Named Joe, 1943, The White Cliffs of Dover, 1944, Anna and the King of Siam, 1946, Life with Father, 1947, The Mudlark, 1950, It Grows on Trees, 1952; also occasional TV appearances. Recipient Acad. award nominations for Cimarron, 1930, Theodora Goes Gild, 1936, The Awful Truth, 1937, Love Affair, 1939, I Remember Mama, 1948; Laetare medal U. Notre Dame, 1949; honored by Kennedy Ctr., 1985. Home: Los Angeles Calif. Died Aug. 28, 1990; buried Calvary Cemetery, Whittier, Calif.

DUNNE, PHILIP, screenwriter, director, playwright, essayist; b. N.Y.C., Feb. 11, 1908; s. Finley Peter and Margaret Ives (Abbott) D.; m. Amanda Duff, July 15, 1939; children: Miranda, Philippa, Jessica. Student, Harvard U., 1925-29. Reader Fox Film Corp., Los Angeles, 1930-31; screenwriter various studios, 1931-41; writer, producer, dir. 20th Century Fox, Los Angeles, 1945-65; writer, dir. Universal Studio, Universal City, Calif., 1965-70; columnist Words by Wire Syndicate, 1982-92, L.A. Times, 1988-92; radio commentator In the Public Interest, 1982-92; bd. govs. Motion Picture Acad. Arts and Scis., 1946-48; chief prodn. bur. motion pictures OWI (overseas br.), 1942-45. Author: Mr. Dooley Remembers, 1963, Take Two-A Life in Movies and Politics, 1980, rev. and expanded edit., 1992, (screenplay, essayist) How Green Was My Valley, 1990, (play) Mr. Dooley's America, 1991; contbr. short stories to New Yorker mag.; contbr. articles on sci. to Harvard mag.; essayist Time mag., 1990-92, Constitution mag.; writer (films) The Count of Monte Cristo, 1934, The Rains Came, 1939, Stanley and Livingstone, 1940, How Green Was My Valley, 1941, The Late George Apley, 1946, The Ghost and Mrs. Muir, 1947, Pinky, 1950, David and Bathsheba, 1951, The Agony and the Ecstasy, 1965; producer, dir. Prince of Players, 1955; writer, producer, dir. The View from Pompey's Head, 1956; writer, dir. Ten North Frederick, 1958, Blue Denim, 1959, Blindfold, 1965; dir. In Love and War, 1960, Wild in the Country, 1961, Lisa, 1963. Pres. Verde Valley Sch., Sedona, Ariz., 1965-70; vice chmn. Dem. State Cen. Com. Calif., 1937-41. Recipient 2 Oscar nominations Acad. Motion Picture Arts and Scis., Star on Hollywood Walk of Fame Hollywood C. of C., 1987; named Vol. of the Yr. Environment County L.A., 1986. Mem. Writers Guild Am. (Laurel award 1961, Valentine Davies award 1974), Dirs. Guild Am., Producers Guild Am., Screen Writers Guild (v.p. 1938-40), Dramatists Guild, Nat. Audubon Soc., Nature Conservancy Assn., ACLU. Home: Malibu Calif. Died June 2, 1992. †

DUNNIGAN, FRANK JOSEPH, publishing company executive; b. Westport, Conn., Dec. 15, 1914; s. Francis P. and Kathryn (Grossmann) D.; m. Teresa L. Razete, Aug. 13, 1966. AA, Jr. Coll. Conn., 1934; BS, NYU, 1940; LHD (hon.), U. Bridgeport, 1976. Acct. Consol. Edison Co., N.Y.C., 1934-37; with Prentice-Hall, Inc., Englewood Cliffs, N.J., 1937-86, exec. v.p., 1965-71, pres., chief exec. officer, 1971-80, chmn. bd., chief exec. officer, 1980-83, chmn. bd., 1983-85, also dir. Pres. Palisades Ednl. Found. Served to capt. AUS, 1941-46. Recipient Madden Meml. award NYU, 1980. Mem. Newcomen Soc., Phi Theta Kappa. Home: Fort Lee N.J. Died Nov. 4, 1990.

DUNNING, JAMES MORSE, dentist; b. N.Y.C., Oct. 16, 1904; s. William Bailey and Rose (Morse) D.; m. Mae Myrick Bradford, Aug. 24, 1935; (dec. Oct. 1972); children—Cornelia Dunning Hollister, Rose; m. Nora Gladwin Fairbank, Apr. 12, 1975. A.B., Harvard U., 1926, M.P.H., 1947; D.D.S., Columbia U., 1930; DSc (hon.), Tufts U., 1986. Summer dentist Grenfell Labrador Mission, 1930, 32; practice gen. dentistry N.Y.C., 1930-42, Boston, 1952-65; asst. operative dentistry Columbia U. Dental Sch., N.Y.C., 1930-35; dental dir. Met. Life Ins. Co., N.Y.C., 1935-45; attending dentist Heckscher Found. for Children, N.Y.C., 1932; dean Harvard U. Sch. Dental Medicine, Boston, 1947-52, dir. univ. dental health service, 1955-65, clin. asst. prof. pub. health dentistry, 1963-65, prof., 1965-72, prof. emeritus, from 1972; pres. Dental Health Service Inc., 1941-45. Author: Principles of Dental Public Health, 1962, 4th edit., 1986, Dental Care for Everyone, 1976, The Harvard School of Dental Medicine, Phase Two in the Development of a University Dental School, 1981; contbr. articles to profl. jours. Pres. Cambridge Mental Health Assn., 1960-65. Served as dental officer USNR, 1942-45. Recipient John W. Knutson award, 1983. Fellow Am. Coll. Dentists, Am. Acad. Dental Sci., Am. Pub. Health Assn.; mem. ADA, Inst. Medicine, Nat. Acad. Scis. (sr.), Omicron Kappa Upsilon. Unitarian. Home: Cambridge Mass. Died June 20, 1991; buried Mosswood Cemetery, Cohuit, Mass.

DUNNOCK, MILDRED, actress; b. Balt.. AB, Goucher Coll.; MA, Columbia U. Made profl. debut in Life Begins, N.Y.C., 1932; toured with Katharine Cornell in Herod and Marianne, 1938, with George M. Cohan in Madam, Will You Walk?, 1941; in: The Corn is Green, 1942; appeared in: Richard III, N.Y.C., 1943, Only the Heart, 1944, Foolish Notion, 1945, Another Part of the Forest, 1946, The Hallams, 1948, The Leading Lady, 1948, Death of a Salesman, 1949, Pride's Crossing, 1950; film version TheCorn is Green, 1945, Child of Fortune, Love Me Tender, 1956, many others. Home: New York N.Y. Died July 5, 1991.

DUPREE, LOUIS BENJAMIN, anthropologist; b. Greenville, N.C., Aug. 23, 1925; s. Chauncey Leary and Luna Emily (Tripp) D.; m. Nancy Marie Shakuntala Hatch, Feb. 20, 1966; children by previous marriage: Duggie, Louis F.R., Sally. A.B. cum laude, Harvard U., 1949, A.M., 1953, Ph.D., 1955. Asst. prof. Air U., Maxwell AFB, Ala., 1954-57, assoc. prof., 1957; assoc. prof. anthropology Pa. State U., University Park, 1957-66, adj. prof., 1966-83; dir. Archaeol. Mission in Afghanistan, 1959-78; rep. Am. univs. field staff Afghanistan, Pakistan, Soviet Central Asia, 1959-83; faculty assoc. Columbia U. Seminar in Archaeol. of Eastern Mediterranean, East Europe, Near East, 1967; vis. lectr. Kabul U., 1962, 64-66, U. Chgo., 1968; Disting. prof. U. Md., 1981, Mary Washington Coll., 1981, U. Nebr., 1980; vis. prof. Woodrow Wilson Sch., Princeton U., 1983-84, U.S. Mil Acad., 1984-85; prof., sr. research assoc. Islamic and Arabian Devel. Studies, Duke U., 1985-89; prof. U. N.C., Chapel Hill, 1987-89; mem. Near and Middle Eastern com. of Social Sci. Research Council, N.Y., 1958-59; mem. commn. of Govt. Afghanistan for Japanese Archaeology Exhbn., 1963; Archaeol. Inst. Am. rep., People's Republic of China, 1978; mem. Eisenhower Exchange Fellowship Com. for Afghanistan, 1971; cons. AID, 1963, 66, Internat. Rescue Com., 1980-89, UNESCO, 1977, World Bank, 1982, Nat. Security Council, 1986; mem. Internat. Parliamentary Group for Human Rights in the Soviet Union, Am. Inst. Pakistan Studies; mem. adv. bd. Afghanistan Freedom Orgn.; trustee Am. Friends of Afghanistan, Afghan Relief Com.; mem. adv. council Com. for a Free Afghanistan; bd. dirs. Afghan Freedom Orgn., Am. Aid for Afghans, Com. for a Free Afghanistan, Am. Inst. Archaeology in Pakistan, Internat. Med. Alliance, Free Afghanistan Alliance, Commn. Internat. d'Enquete Humanitaire sur les Personnes Deplacées en Afghanistan; advisor on Afghanistan to U.S. Amb. to Pakistan, 1988; mem. Agy. Coordinating Body for Afghan Relief. Author: 13 books including Afghanistan, 1973, 2d edit., 1978, paperback edit., 1980; editor: (with L. Albert) Afghanistan in the 1970's, 1974; G. S. Robertson's Kafirs of the Hindu Kush (1896), 1974; contbr. articles to profl. jours. Served with M.M.R., USNR, 1943-44; Served with AUS, 1944-47. Decorated Air Force Commendation medal for meritorious civilian service; Army Outstanding Civilian Service medal; recipient Bronze medal Internat. Rescue Com., 1987; fellow Am. Council Learned Socs., King's Coll., Cambridge, Eng., 1972-73; Fulbright Sr. Scholar (Pakistan/Afghanistan), 1988; Grantee Am. Philos. Soc., 1964-66, Social Sci. Research Council, 1964-65, NSF, 1969-70, Heinze Found., 1970-71, NEH, 1972-73, Wenner-Gren Found., 1959-60, 65, 78-80, Ford Found., 1982-83, 84-85, Duke U. Research Council. Fellow Am. Anthrop. Assn. (com. ethics 1966), AAAS, Soc. Applied Anthropology, Am. Oriental Soc., Am. Geog. Soc., Am. Ethnol. Soc., Soc. Am. Archaeology; mem. Soc. Afghan Studies (founding), Archaeol. Inst. Am., Royal Soc. Asian Affairs, N.C. Archaeol. Soc., Societe Prehistorique Française, Brit. Inst. Persian Studies, Soc. World War I Aero Historians, Explorers Club, Friends of Nat. Army Mus. (U.K.), Gamma Alpha, Phi Kappa Phi. Club: Harvard Travellers. Home: Durham N.C. Died Mar. 21, 1989; buried in Afghanistan.

DUPUIS, RENE, electrical engineer; b. Pike River, Que., Can., May 5, 1898; s. Phillias and Ernestine (Poisant) D.; m. Simoen Giroux, Sept. 17, 1931; children: Marthe Dupuis Durand, Yolande Dupuis Leblanc, Andree Dupuis Bellefeuille, Suzanne, Jacques, Helene. BA, Laval U., 1919, DSc (hon.), 1954; student, McGill U., 1921; Deg. in Elec. Engring., U. Nancy, France, 1924. Registered profl. engr., Que. Engr. Shawinigan Water & Power Co., Montreal, 1928-42; founder, 1st dir., prof. Sch. Elec. Engring., Laval U., 1942-47; supt. engr. Beauharnois Light, Heat & Power

Co., 1947-48, v.p., 1948-61; commr. Que. Hydro-Electric Commn., 1948-61; mem. Internat. Joint Commn., Ottawa-Washington, 1962-92. Author: De l'anglais au francais en electrotechnique, 4th edit., 1939; contbr. articles to profl. jours. Bd. dirs. Ste. Jeanne d'Arc Hosp., Montreal. Recipient 1956 medal Laval Alumni Assn.; decorated Palmes Academiques (France). Fellow IEEE (v.p. 1959-61), McGill Grad. Sch. Engring. Inst. Can., Internat. Assn. Hydraulic Engrs. *

DURBIN, JAMES HAROLD, company executive; b. Sharon, Pa., Mar. 17, 1898; s. Alfred and Mary (Dougherty) D.; m. Helen Frances Cleveland, Oct. 28, 1922; children: James Harold, Hugh Cleveland. LLB, Georgetown U., Washington, 1920. Bar: D.C. 1920. Stenographer Petroleum Iron Works Co., Sharon, 1914-17; clk. Hon. Newton D. Baker, sec. of war, Washington, 1917-20; sec., treas. Petroleum Supply Co., N.Y.C., 1920-23; treas. Am. Republics Corp., 1923-26, v.p., dir., 1926-50, treas., 1941-50, exec. v.p., 1950-55; v.p., dir. Barber Oil Corp., 1955-56, pres., 1956-92; also v.p., dir. Am. Gillsonite Co. With U.S. Army, 1918. Mem. ABA, Houston Country Club, Tejas Club (Houston), Sleepy Hollow Country Club (Scarborough on Hudson, N.Y.), Phi Alpha Delta. Roman Catholic. *

DURKEE, ARTHUR BOWMAN, investment securities company executive; b. Mpls., Sept. 28, 1928; s. Arthur Farrington and Marjorie (Langley) D.; m. Katherine Agee, Jan. 10, 1956; children: Katherine R., Arthur Bowman Jr., Rucker A. Student, U. Minn., 1946-48; BS, Macalester Coll., 1950. V.p. Durkee Atwood Co., Mpls., 1954-57, also bd. dirs.; with Sterne Agee & Leach, Inc., Birmingham, Ala., 1957-82; pres. Sterne Agee & Leach, Inc., Birmingham, 1969-82. Bd. dirs. Crippled Children's Clinic, Birmingham. Lt. USAF, 1950-52. Mem. Ala. Securities Dealers Assn. (pres. 1965-66), Investment Bankers Assn. (bd. govs. 1971-72), Mountain Brook Club, Birmingham Country Club, Redstone Club, Relay House Club, Downtown Club. Home: Birmingham Ala. Died Feb. 17, 1982; buried Elmwood Cemetery, Birmingham, Ala.

DUROCHER, LEO (THE LIP), baseball player, manager; b. West Springfield, Mass., July 27, 1905. Shortstop N.Y. Yankees, 1925-29, Cin. Reds, 1930-33, St. Louis Cardinals, 1933-37; shortstop Brooklyn Dodgers, 1938-45, mgr., 1939-48; mgr. N.Y. Giants, 1948-55, Chgo. Cubs, 1966-72, Houston Astros, 1972-73. Voted Nat. League All-Star 1936, 38, 40; Mgr. Nat. League Pennant winning Brooklyn Dodgers, 1941, N.Y. Giants, 1951, 1954, World Series Championship, N.Y. Giants, 1954. Mem. famed "Gas House Gang," St. Louis Cardinals, 1934. Died Oct.7, 1991. †

DURRELL, LAWRENCE GEORGE, author; b. Julundur, India, Feb. 27, 1912; s. Lawrence Samuel and Louise Florence (Dixie) D.; ed. Coll. of St. Joseph, Darjiling, India, also St. Edmund's Coll., Canterbury, Eng.; 2 daus. With Brit. fgn. service; press attache, Belgrade, Yugoslavia; dir. Brit. Inst., Cordoba, Argentina; dir. pub. relations, Dodecanese Islands; press attache, Alexandria, Egypt; sr. press officer Brit. embassy, Cairo; dir. Brit. Inst., Kalamata, Greece; sr. press officer, Athens, Greece; dir. pub. relations Govt. of Cyprus, 1954-56; spl. corr. for Economist in Cyprus, 1953; lectr. lit. for Brit. Council in Greece and Argentina. Fellow Royal Soc. Lit. Author: (novels) Panic Spring, 1937, The Black Book, 1938, Prospero's Cell, 1945, Cefalu, 1947, Reflections on a Marine Venus, 1953, Bitter Lemons, 1956, (the Alexandria quartet) Justine, 1956, Balthazar, 1958, Mountolive, 1958, Clea, 1960, Tunc, 1968, Nunquam, 1970, Livia, or Buried Alive, 1978, Constance, or Solitary Practices, 1982, Sebastian, or Ruling Passions. 1984, Quinx, 1985, Antrobus Complete, 1985, ; (humor) Stiff Upper Lip, 1958, Esprit de Corps, 1957; (verse) Private Country, 1943, Cities, Plains and Peoples, 1946, On Seeming to Presume, 1948, Tree of Idleness, 1955, Selected Poems, 1956, Sappho (play), 1950, Acte (play), 1962, An Irish Faustus (play), 1964; Collected Poems, 1960; Selected Poems, 1953-1963, 1964; The Ikons and Other Poems, 1967; Sauve Qui Peut, 1967; (criticism) A Key to Modern Poetry, 1952; (non-fiction) Caesar's Vast Ghost: A Portrait of Provence, 1990; (translation) Pope Joan, 1948; A Private Correspondence, 1963; Spirit of Place; letters and essays on travel, 1969; also articles mags., newspapers; editor: The Henry Miller Reader, 1959. Died Nov. 7, 1990; cremated. Home: Sommières France

DURRENMATT, FRIEDRICH, writer; b. Konolfingen, Switzerland, Jan. 5, 1921; s. Reinhold and Hulda (Zimmermann) D.; m. Lotti Geissler, 1946 (dec.); 3 children; m. Charlotte Kerr, 1984. Ed., U. Berne, 1941-42, U. Zurich, 1941. Author plays: Es steht geschrieben, Der Blinde, Romulus der Grosse, Die Ehe des Herrn Mississippi, Ein Engel kommt nach Babylon, Grieche sucht Griechin, Der Besuch der alten Dame, Frank V, Die Physiker, Herkules und der Stall des Augias, Der Meteor, Die Wiedertäufer, König Johann (after Shakespeare), Play Strindberg, Titus Andronicus (after Shakespeare), Porträt eines Planeten, Der Mitmacher, Die Frist, Die Panne, Achterloo, (with Charlotte Kerr) Rollenspiele; plays for radio: Der Doppelgänger, Der Prozess um des Esels Schatten, Nächtliches Gespräch mit einem verachteten Menschen, Stranitzky und der Nationalheld, Herkules und der Stall des Augias, Das Unternehmen der Wega, Abendstunde im Spätherbst; fiction: Der Richter und sein Henker, Der Verdacht, Das Versprechen, Justiz, Durcheinandertal; prose: Pilatus, Der Nihilist, Der Hund, Der Theater-direktor, Der Tunnel, Grieche sucht Griedhin, Im Coiffeurladen, Das Bild des Sisyphos, Deir Sturz, Dramaturgisches und Kritisches, Stoffe I-III (rev. edit. under title Labyrith 1990), Minotauras, Der Auftrag, Turmbau (Stoffe IV-IX), Theaterschriften und Reden, Gerechtigkeit und Recht, Zusammenhänge, Friedrich Schiller, Sätze aus Amerika, Gespräch mit Heinz Ludwig Arnold, Lesebuch, Einstein-Vortrag, Versuche; recipient N.Y. Critic's award for best fgn. play, The Visit (on Broadway), 1958. Died Dec. 14, 1990. Home: Neuchâtel Switzerland

DUTTON, LELAND SUMMERS, librarian; b. Lorain, Ohio, Mar. 9, 1905; s. Joseph and Evalena May (Summers) D.; m. Ruth Genevieve Clitty, Dec. 24, 1937; children: Lee Summers, Lynore Evalena. BA, Miami U., Oxford, Ohio, 1929; BS in Libr. Sci., Columbia U., 1932, psotgrad., summer 1939. Asst. loan dept. Miami U. Libr., Oxford, 1929-31; asst. genealogy and local history N.Y. Pub. Libr., 1931-34; loan libr. Miami U. Libr., Oxford, 1934-38, reference libr., 1939-56, dir. librs., chmn. dept. libr. sci., 1956-59, prof., 1961-91, rsch. resources libr., 1970-91. Contbr. articles, revs. to profl. jours. Elder Presbyn. Ch. Mem. ALA, Ohio Libr. Assn. (pres. 1941, exec. bd. 1942-45), Oxford Mus. Assn. (pres. 1954), Coll. and Rsch. Librs. Assn. Home: Oxford Ohio Died Oct. 2, 1991.

DUTY, TONY EDGAR, lawyer, judge; b. Golinda, Tex., May 14, 1928; s. Tony and Glennie Mae (Butler) D.; m. Kathleen Lou Lear (dec. 1988); children: Valerie Ann, Barbara Diane, Dan Richard; m. Peggy Arline Scott. Student, U. Colo., 1947-49; B.B.A., Baylor U., 1952, J.D., 1953. Bar: Tex. 1954, U.S. Dist. CT. (we. dist.) Tex. 1970, U.S. Ct. Appeals (5th cir.) 1978, U.S. Ct. Appeals (11th cir.) 1981, U.S. Supreme Ct. 1982, U.S. Dist. Ct. (no. dist.) Tex. 1983. Pvt. practice law Waco, Tex., 1954-56, 64-90; 1st asst. atty City of Waco, 1957-63; 1st asst. atty. City of Waco, 1957-63; mcpl. judge City of Woodway, Tex., 1963-80, City of Lacy-Lakeview, Tex., 1976-78, City of Beverly Hills, Tex., 1976-78, City of Waco, 1957-87, City of Bellmead, Tex., 1964-86; prof. bus. law, corps. and real estate Baylor U., 1976-78; ptnr. Indian Creek Estates; dir. Shannon Devel. Co., Telco Systems Inc., Sun Valley Water and Devel. Co., Inc., Hewitt Devel. Co. Author: The Coronado Expedition, 1540-1542, 1970, James Wilkinson: 1757-1825, 1971, Champ D'Asile, 1972, The Home Front: McLennan County in the Civil War, 1974; contbr. articles to hist. jours. Mem. Waco Plan Commn., 1966-69, Waco-McLennan County Library Commn., 1968-72, chmn., 1971-72; mem. Waco Fire and Police Civil Service Commn., 1975-81, chmn., 1980-81; mem. Waco Am. Revolution Bicentennial Commn., 1974-76; chmn. Waco Heritage '76, 1974-76; mem. McLennan County Hist. Survey Commn., 1970—; chmn. Ft. House Mus., Waco, 1968-72; bd. dirs. Waco Heritage Soc., 1960—. Served with USAF, 1946-49. Mem. State Bar Tex., Waco-McLennan County Bar Assn., Waco-McLennan County Def. Lawyers Assn. (v.p.), 5th Cir. Bar Assn., Delta Theta Phi. Democrat. Baptist. Lodges: Masons, K.P. Home: Waco Tex. Died 1990. †

DYCHE, DAVID BENNETT, pharmaceutical company executive; b. Evanston, Ill., Dec. 19, 1902; s. William Andrew and May Louise (Bennett) D.; m. Julia Hoyt, Sept. 22, 1928; 1 child, David Bennett. BS, Dartmouth Coll., 1924; postgrad., Northwestern U., 1927-28. With Ill. Steel Co., 1924-27, Arthur Andersen & Co. CPAs, 1927-31, Nat. City Co., N.Y.C., 1931-34, Lazard Freres & Co. investment bankers, 1934-42; fin. adviser, treas., v.p. and treas. Gen. Aniline & Film Corp., 1942-47; with CIBA Corp. and predecessor cos., 1947-67, v.p. fin., 1962-64, pres., 1964-67, bd. dirs., 1947-70; treas. Toms River Chem. Corp. and predecessor, 1948-55, pres., 1949-64, chmn. bd. dirs., 1962-64; pres., dir. CIBA States Export Corp., 1950-67; treas., dir. Supramar Chems., Inc., 1947-67; v.p., dir. Nat. Fund for Grad. Nursing Edn. Hon. trustee United Hosp., Port Chester, N.Y. Mem. Univ. Club, Anglers Club (N.Y.C.), Apawamis Club, Manursing Island Club (Rye, N.Y.). Republican. Home: Hanover N.H. Died Jan. 8, 1990.

DYE, MARVIN REED, lawyer, judge; b. Forestville, N.Y., July 12, 1895; s. Daniel A. and Virginia (Marvin) D.; m. Miriam Kelley, June 25, 1918; children: Stanley, Julianne, Emily. LLB, Cornell U., 1917; LLD, Syracuse U., 1964; postgrad., N.Y. Law Sch., 1965. Bar: N.Y. 1920. Assoc. Ernest Whitbeck, 1920-28, ptnr., 1928-40; atty. Monroe County, 1934-35; judge Ct. of Claims, N.Y. State, 1940-44, Ct. of Appeals, N.Y. State, 1945-92. Democrat. *

DYER, GEORGE CARROLL, naval officer; b. Mpls., Apr. 27, 1898; s. Harry Blair and Georgia (Mortimer) D.; m. Mary Adaline Shiek, Apr. 2, 1921; children: Mary Elizabeth, Georgia Mortimer, Virginia Ann. AB, U.S. Naval Acad., 1918. Commd. ensign USN, 1918, advanced through grades to vice adm., 1955; comdr. U.S. ships D-3, 1919-20, L-10, 1920-22, S-15, 1922-24, Widgeon, 1931-33, Gamble, 1933-34, Submarine Div. 8, 1939, U.S. Astoria, 1944-45; staff of comdr. Battlle Force, 1939; comdr. in chief Battl Force, 1940, comdr. in chief and chief naval ops., 1942, chief gen. planning group, naval ops., 1946; comdr. Cruiser Div. 10, 1946-48, dep. commandant Naval War Coll., 1949-51; comdr. U.N. Blockade and Escort Force, 1951-52, Tng. Command U.S. Pacific Fleet, 1952; commandant 11th Naval Dist. Author: Naval Logistics, 1960. Decorated Legion of Merit with 3 gold stars, Bronze Star, Purple Heart, D.S.M., Comdr. of Brit. Empire, French Legion of Honour, others. Mem. Soc. Philatelic Ams., Am. Philatelic Soc., Soc. of the Cincinnati, U.S. Naval Acad. Alumni Assn. (pres. 1959-61), Army and Navy Club (Washington), University (L.A.). *

DYER-BENNET, RICHARD, minstrel; b. Leicester, Eng., Oct. 6, 1913; came to U.S., 1925, naturalized, 1935; s. Richard Stewart and Miriam Wolcott (Clapp) D.-B.; m. Elizabeth Hoar Pepper, June 1936 (div.); children: Ellen, Eunice; m. Melvene Ipcar, June 1942; children: Bonnie, Brooke. Student, U. Calif., 1932-35; vocal studies with Gertrude Beckman, 1934-41, Cornelius L. Reid, from 1968; guitar instrn. with Jose Rey De La Torre, 1943-46. assoc. prof. theatre arts dept. SUNY, Stony Brook, 1970-83; managed by Hurok mgmt., from 1944, Tornay mgmt., 1964; ptnr. Dyer-Bennet Records, 1955-01. Appeared as 20th century minstrel Village Vanguard and other clubs, N.Y.C., early 1940's; composed and broadcast propaganda songs OWI, 1942-43; solo concert Town Hall, N.Y.C., 1944, Carnegie Hall, N.Y.C., 1944; had repertory of 600 songs; performed on radio; recorded almost 24 albums, including Schubert's The Lovely Milleress, 1968; studies, performed Robert Fitzgerald transl. Homer's Odyssey, 1981-91. Grantee NEH. Home: Monterey Mass. Died Dec. 14, 1991; buried Monterey, Mass.

DYKES, JEFFERSON CHENOWTH, author; b. Dallas, July 20, 1900; s. George Richard and Melrose (Chenowth) D.; m. Martha Lewin Read, Aug. 1, 1923 (dec. July 1989); 1 dau., Martha Ann Dykes Goldsmith. B.S., Tex. A&M Coll., 1921; postgrad., Colo. Agrl. Coll., 1924-29. Tchr. vocation agr. Stephenville and McAllen, Tex., 1921-29; prof. agrl. edn. Tex. A&M Coll., 1929-35; erosion specialist Soil Conservation Service, Dept. Agr., Lindale, Tex., 1935; chief erosion control practices div., asst. regional conservator Soil Conservation Service, Dept. Agr., Ft. Worth, 1936-42; asst. chief Soil Conservation Service, Dept. Agr., 1942-50, dept. chief, 1950-53, asst. adminstr. field services, 1953-63, dep. adminstr. field services, 1963-65; western Americana dealer, 1965—. Author: Billy the Kid: Bibliography Of a Legend, 1952, American Guide Series-A Bibliographic Check List, 1966, (with O.C. Fisher) King Fisher, 1966, Rangers All, 1969, Four Sheriffs of Lincoln County, 1969, My Dobie Collection, 1971, (with J. Frank Dobie) 44 Range Country Books, 1972, 44 More Range Country Books, 1972, Russell Roundup, 1972, Fifty Great Western Illustrators, 1975 (Western Heritage Wrangler award 1976); introduction Custer in Periodicals (John M. Carroll), 1975; Western High Spots, 1977, I Had All the Fun, 1978, The True Life of Billy the Kid, 1980, Collecting Range Life Literature, 1982, Rare Western Outlaw Books, 1985, The Ranger's Tour on the Prairie, 1989; also articles, chpts. in books, revs. in mags. and profl. jours.; editor: Great Western Indian Fights, 1960, On the Border with Mackenzie, 1962, The West of the Texas Kid, 1962, Trans-Missouri Stock Raising, 1962, Cow Dust and Saddle Leather, 1968; co-editor: Flat Top Ranch: A Grassland Venture, 1957; assoc. editor: Brand Book, from 1950; cons.: Cowboys and Cattle Country, 1962. Pres. Friends of Tex. A&M U. Library, 1979. Named Disting. Alumnus, Tex. A&M U., 1984. Fellow Soil Conservation Soc. Am. (council); mem. Western Writers Am., Range Soc. Am., Westerners Internat. (pres. 1980, 81), Antiquarian Booksellers Assn. Am. Home: College Park Md. Died Dec. 29, 1989; cremated.

DYKES, MICHAEL H. M., anesthesiologist; b. Bearsden, Scotland, U.K., July 17, 1931; came to U.S. 1957; s. John Morton and Agnes Catherine (Hume) D.; m. Marion Jane Hogarth, 1961 (dec. 1971); m. Emily E. Czapek, 1972 (div. 1985); children: Stephen H.M., Christopher M.C.; m. Karma Irene Rodholm, Feb. 1, 1986. BA, Cambridge U., Eng., 1953; MB, BChir, Cambridge U., 1956; MEd, Northwestern U., Evanston, Ill., 1959. Diplomate Am. Bd. Anesthesiology. Intern Ayr County Hospital, Scotland, 1956-57, St. Thomas Hosp., London, 1957, Newton-Wellesley Hosp., Mass., 1957-58; resident Mass. Gen. Hosp., Boston, 1959-60; instr. anesthesia U. Vt. Med. Sch., Burlington, 1961-62, Harvard Med. Sch., Boston, 1962-65; asst. prof. anesthesiology U. Rochester, N.Y., 1965-69, Harvard Med. Sch., 1969-72; assoc. prof. anesthesiology Northwestern U., Chgo., 1972-78, prof. clin. anesthesiology, 1978-90, assoc. chmn., 1978-90, dir. edn., 1990; cons. in field. Author/editor: Anesthesia and The Liver, 1970; contbr. articles to profl. jours., chpts. to books. Mem. Am. Soc. Anesthesiologists, Assn. of Univ. Anesthetists, Internat. Anesthesia Research Soc., Soc. for Edn. in Anesthesia, Prestwick Golf Club (Scotland). Home: LaGrange Ill. Died July 1, 1990; buried Oakridge Cemetery, Hillside, Ill.

EAGER, HENRY IDE, state judge; b. Hopkinsville, Ky., July 16, 1895; s. Ben F. and Carrie (Downer) E.; 1 child, Henry G. (dec.). Student, U. Wash., 1913-14; J.D., U. Mich., 1920. Bar: Mo. bar 1920. Mem. firm

Blackmar, Eager. Swanson, Midgley & Jones, Kansas City, 1920-55; judge Supreme Ct. Mo., 1955-68, spl. commr., 1969-89; Mem. Bd. Law Examiners., 1946-54. Served from 2d to 1st lt. 34th Inf., 7th Div. U.S. Army, 1917-19. Recipient Hon. Order of the Coif U. Mo., 1965, Bicentennial award St. Louis Bar Assn., 1965, Sesquicentennial award U. Mich., 1968. Mem. ABA, Mo. Bar Assn. (gov., chmn. appellate practice com.), Kansas City Bar Assn., Lawyers Assn. Kansas City, Delta Theta Phi. Baptist. Home: Jefferson City Mo. Died Feb. 10, 1989; buried Forest Hill Cemetery, Kansas City, Mo.

EAGLE, HARRY, cell biologist, science administrator; b. N.Y.C., July 13, 1905; married, 1928; 1 child. AB, Johns Hopkins U., 1923, MD, 1927, MS, 1948; DSc (hon.), Wayne State U., 1965, Duke U., 1981, Rockefeller U., 1982. Intern Johns Hopkins U., Balt., 1927-28, med. sch. asst., instr., 1929-32; asst. in bacteriology, then asst. prof. U. Pa. Med. Sch., Phila., 1933-36; with NIH, 1947-61, sci. dir. rsch. br. Nat. Cancer Inst., 1947-49, chief lab. exptl. therapeutics Microbiol. Inst., 1949-58, mem. staff, then chief lab. cell biology Nat. Inst. Allergy and Infectious Diseases, 1958-61; prof. cell biology Albert Einstein Coll. Medicine, Bronx, N.Y., from 1961, now prof. emeritus, chmn. dept. cell biology, 1961-70, dir. Cancer Rsch. Ctr., from 1975, now dir. emeritus. Recipient Louisa Gross Horwitz award, 1973, Sidney Farnber Med. Rsch. award, 1974, Waterford award Scripps Clin. and Rsch. Found., 1983, Nat. Medal of Sci., 1987. Mem. NAS, Am. Acad. Arts and Scis., Am. Soc. Biol. Chemists, Am. Soc. Clin. Investigation. Home: Bronx N.Y. Died June 12, 1992. †

EAGLETON, LEE CHANDLER, chemical engineer, educator; b. Vallejo, Calif., July 27, 1923; s. William L. and Mary Louise (Chandler) E.; m. Mary E. Stewart, Feb. 21, 1953; children: James C., William L., Elizabeth L. S.B., MIT, 1946, S.M., 1947; D.Eng., Yale U., 1950. Research assoc. Columbia U., 1950-51; devel. engr. Rohm & Haas Co., Phila., 1951-56; lectr. Drexel Inst. Tech., 1954, U. Pa., Phila., 1954-55; assoc. prof. U. Pa., 1956-65, prof., 1966-69; prof. Pa. State U., 1970-85, prof. emeritus, from 1985, head dept. chem. engring., 1970-83; cons. Rohm & Haas, 1956-74, Inst. for Def. Analyses, 1961-63, Martin Marietta Co., 1970-72, 74. Served with AUS, 1942-46. Fellow Am. Inst. Chem. Engrs. (bd. dirs. 1980-82, Founders award 1987), Am. Soc. Engring. Edn. (chmn. chem. engring. div. 1970-71); mem. Am. Chem. Soc., AAUP. Home: State College Pa. Died May 15, 1990; buried Center County Meml. Pk, State College, Pa.

EAKER, IRA C., manufacturing company executive; b. Llano County, Tex., Apr. 13, 1896; s. Y.Y. and Dona Lee (Graham) E.; m. Ruth Huff Apperson, Nov. 23, 1931. AB, Southeastern Normal Coll., Okla., 1917; student, Columbia U., 1923-24, George Washington U., 1924-26; AB in Journalism, U. So. Calif., 1933. Commd. 2d lt. Inf. U.S. Army, 1917; transferred to Air Corps, 1917; capt. Air Corps, 1920, advanced through grades to brig. gen., 1942, maj. gen., 1942, lt. gen., 1943; acting air officer Philippine Dept., 1921; adjutant Mitchel Field, 1922-24; asst. exec. Office Chief of Air Corps, 1924-26, exec., 1939-40; comdg. officer 20th Pursuit Group, 1941; comdg. gen. 8th Bomber Command, 1942, 8th Air Force, U.K., 1943; comdr.-in-chief Mediterranean Allied Air Forces, 1944; dep. comdr. AAF and chief of air staff, 1945-47; v.p. Hughes Tool Co., 1947-57; v.p. ea. office Douglas Aircraft Co., Inc., 1957; chmn. adv. bd. Hughes Aircraft Co., 1961-92. Author: (with Gen. H.H. Arnold) This Flying Game, 1936, Winged Warfre, 1940, Army Flyer, 1942. Decorated Disting. Svc. Medal, Legion of Merit, DFC with 2 oak leaf clusters, Silver Star (U.S.); knight of Brit. Empire, Order of Katusov, 2d degree (USSR), Order of the So. Cross (Brazil), Order of the Partisan Star, 1st class (Yugoslavia), Order of the Sun (Peru), Order of Liberator (Venezuela), Order of Condor of Andes (Bolivia), Order of Merit (Chile). Mem. Christian Ch. *

EARLES, WILLIAM EUGENE, corporation executive; b. New Orleans, May 9, 1928; s. John Henry and Beatrice (Hughes) E.; m. Joan Ann Sturdivant, Aug. 14, 1954 (div. 1976); children: William H., Glenn A., Janet L.; m. Kathleen Zoie Daigle, Feb. 17, 1976; 1 stepson, Jerry J. Rock III. Student, Southeastern La. Coll., 1948-49, Southwestern La. Inst., 1949-51. Draftsman Austin Co., Freeport, Tex., 1951-52, J.F. Pritchard & Co., New Orleans, 1952-54; sr. v.p. McDermott, Inc., New Orleans, 1954-85, dir., 1975-80, cons., 1988-89. Served with USMC, 1946-47. Mem. Am. Welding Soc. (dir. Morgan City chpt.), Am. Soc. Mill. Engrs. (adv. bd. Atchalafaya chpt. 1977-81), Am. Petroleum Inst., Morgan City C. of C. (dir. 1980-81). Club: Morgan City Petroleum (pres. 1975-76, dir. 1977-81). Lodge: Lions (past dir.). Home: Kenner La. Died Oct. 17, 1989.

EASTLICK, JOHN TAYLOR, library science educator; b. Norris, Mont., Apr. 28, 1912; s. Jack T. and Stella Mae (Tate) E. A.B., Ariz. State Tchrs. Coll., 1934; B.L.S., U. Denver, 1940; M.A., Colo. State Coll. Edn., 1939. Instr. English, speech dramatics Yuma (Ariz.) Union High Sch., 1934-38; librarian U. Wis., Wis. High Sch., Madison, 1940-42; instr. library sci. Mich. State Coll., East Lansing, summers 1940, 41, Wash. State Coll., Pullman, summer 1942; chief library div. VA, Denver, 1946-48; instr. hosp. and med. library coll. librarianship U. Denver, 1946-50; prof. librarianship U. Denver (Grad. Sch. Librarianship), 1969-76, assoc. dean, 1976-79, prof. emeritus, from 1979; cons. to Sec. of Army (instructing Japanese educators in reorgn. Japanese ednl. system), Japan, 1948-49; circulation dept. Denver Pub. Library, 1939-40, asst. to librarian, 1948-51, librarian, 1951-61, 62-69; asst. state supt. edn. for library services, State Hawaii, 1962; mem. U.S.A.-Mex. Bi-lateral Com. on Edn. and Tng., from 1976; Dir. Adult Edn. Council, Denver; chmn. finance com., asst. treas. Bibliog. Center for Research, Rocky Mountain Region, 1949-51, treas., 1951-65; Mem. adv. com. U.S. Office of Edn., 1956-57. Author: (with Robert Steuart) Library Management, 1976, 2d edit., 1981; Editor: (with Robert Steuart) Changing Environment in Libraries, 1971. Served as capt. USAAF, 1942- 46. Mem. A.L.A. (pres. pub. libraries div. 1956-57, com. architecture and bldgs. 1949-51, 2d v.p. 1959-60, mem. com. on accreditation 1971-76), Colo. Library Assn. (exec. bd.), Denver Dist. Library Assn. (pres. 1950-51), Ariz. State Library Assn. (pres. 1937), Alpha Psi Omega, Phi Delta Kappa. Club: City (Denver). Home: Denver Col. Died Jan. 18, 1990; cremated.

EASTMAN, DEAN HUNTLEY, lawyer; b. Hot Springs, S.D., Feb. 15, 1896; s. Charles Sumner and Agnes (Colgan) E.; m. Floreen Glover, Nov. 26, 1925. LLB, U. Nebr., 1923. Bar: S.D. 1924, Wash. 1929. Pvt. practice law Hot Springs, S.D., 1923-29, Seattle, 1929-36; atty. N.P. Ry., 1936-37, asst. western counsel, 1937-48, western counsel, 1948-92, asst. v.p., 1950-52, v.p., 1952-92; trustee Spokane, Portland & Seattle Ry. Co., Oreg. Electric Ry. Co., Oreg. Trunk Ry., Ruth Realty; dir. Nat. Bank of Commerce, Rainier Nat. Park Co.; state's atty. Fall River County, S.D., 1925-28. Trustee Mcpl. League, Seattle. Mem. C. of C. (past pres.), Rainier Club (past pres.), Seattle Golf Club. *

EATON, VERNET ELLER, physics educator; b. Castleton, Ind., Dec. 25, 1895; s. Frank Otis and Minnie Adel (Eller) E.; m. Annabel Glaze, Sept. 8, 1923; 1 child, David Warren. AB, Ind. U., 1921, AM, 1924, PhD, 1931. Tchr. Ind. pub. schs., 1913-17; instr. physics Williams Coll., Williamstown, Mass., 1921-25; instr. Wesleyan U., Middletown, Conn., 1925-27, asst. prof., 1927-45, assoc. prof., 1945-46, prof. physics, 1946-64, prof. emeritus, 1964-92; adv. com. NBC Continental Classroom, 1958-59. Author, co-author physics textbooks; editorial advisor Sci. and Math. Weekly, 1961-64. Mem. Middletown Water Commn., 1963-92. With U.S. Army, 1917-19. Fellow AAAS; mem. Am. Phys. Soc., Am. Assn. Physics Tchrs. (exec. com. 1951-60, pres. 1957, Oersted medalist 1954, dir. conf. on lecture demonstrations 1959), Am. Inst. Physics (ednl. adv. com. 1957-59, governing bd. 1958-61, vis. scientist 1964-92), AAUp, Phi Beta Kappa, Sigma Xi. *

EATON, WILLIAM MELLON, lawyer; b. N.Y.C., Oct. 5, 1924; s. Ernest Risley and Carolyn (Mellon) E.; m. Elizabeth Waring Witsell, Dec. 21, 1956; children: Carolyn Taylor, Alexander, Sarah, Lisa. B.S., Duke, 1945; J.D., Harvard, 1949. Bar: N.Y. 1949, U.S. Supreme Ct. 1961. Since practiced in N.Y.C.; asso. firm White & Case, 1949-60; mem. firm Hardy, Peal, Rawlings, Werner & Maxwell, 1960-65; sr. partner firm Eaton & Van Winkle, 1965-85, of counsel, from 1986; pres. BT Capital Corp., SBIC of Bankers Trust, N.Y. Corp., 1972-80, dir., 1972-83. asst. sec., ofcl. adviser U.S.-Japan Found., 1980-85; sec. Moroccan Am. Found., 1982-86. Served with USNR, 1943-46, PTO. Mem. ABA. (chmn. com. investment securities 1969-73, mem. 1973-83), N.Y. State Bar Assn. (chmn. investment com. 1974-81), N.Y. County Lawyers Assn., Soc. Colonial Wars (chancellor Gen. Soc. 1978-86), St. Nicholas Soc. (gov. 1965-68). Episcopalian. Home: New York N.Y. Died Oct. 2, 1992. †

EBAUGH, FRANKLIN GESSFORD, JR., physician, medical school dean; b. Phila., Dec. 25, 1921; s. Franklin G. and Dorothy (Reese) E.; children: Sandra D., Patricia S., Jeanette H. B.A. magna cum laude, Dartmouth Coll., 1944; M.D., Cornell U., 1946. Intern, then resident N.Y. Hosp., 1946-50; research fellow physiology Cornell U. Med. Coll., 1948; research fellow Evans Meml. Hosp., Boston U. Med. Sch., 1950-53; surgeon USPHS, 1953-55; asso. prof. clin. pathology, also asso. dir. labs. Dartmouth Med. Sch. and Mary Hitchcock Meml. Hosp., 1955-64; dean Boston U. Sch. Medicine, 1964-69; prof. medicine U. Utah, 1969-72; dean Sch. Medicine U. Utah, 1969-71; chief of staff VA Med. Ctr., Palo Alto, Calif., 1972-90; asso. dean, prof. medicine Stanford U. Med. Sch., 1972-90; mem. staff Evans Meml. Hosp., 1964-69; vis. physician Boston City Hosp., 1965-69; chmn. Boston VA Hosp. deans com., 1965-69, Salt Lake City VA deans com., 1969-71; cons. council health professions constrn. facilities USPHS, 1965-70; mem. study sect. tng. grants USPHS-NIH, 1960-64; mem. study sect. program projects grants NIH-Nat. Inst. Neurol. Diseases and Blindness, 1965-69. Author articles, contbr. to books in field. Col. USAR. Recipient Med. Dir. Commendation Dept. VA, Disting. Physician award Sec. Dept. VA. Fellow ACP, Am. Coll. Pathologists; mem. Am. Soc. Clin. Investigation, Am. Acad. Arts and Scis., Am. Soc. Hematology (exec. com. 1965-69), Am. Assn. Med. Coll. (exec. council 1967-69), Nat. Assn. VA Chiefs of Staff (pres. 1976), Phi Beta Kappa, Sigma Xi, Alpha Omega Alpha, Delta Tau Delta, Nu Sigma Nu. Home: Stanford Calif. Died July 7, 1990.

EBERLE, AUGUST WILLIAM, educator; b. Emporia, Kans., June 8, 1916; s. Carl and Minnie Ernestine (Merker) E.; m. Elizabeth Ann Bush, July 31, 1940 (dec. Oct. 1991). BS, Emporia State U., 1936, MS, 1940; PhD, U. Wis., 1953. Tchr. high sch., Pleasanton, Kans. 1936-40; prin. high sch., Dwight, Kans., 1940-41; tchr. Pratt High Sch. and Jr. Coll., 1941-42; asst. dean Pratt Jr. Coll., 1945-50; instr. U. Wis., 1950-52; asst. prof. Ind. U., Bloomington, 1952-55, assoc. prof., 1955-57, prof., 1966-81, prof. emeritus, from 1981, chmn. dept. higher edn., 1966-73; provost U. Chattanooga, 1957-65; chief ednl. svcs. Oak Ridge Associated Univs., 1965-66; dir., moderator weekly pub. affairs TV program, 1961-65. First chmn. Chattanooga-Hamilton County Health Dept. Adv. Com., 1964; 1st pres. Chattanooga-Hamilton County Community Action Program for Econ. Opportunity, 1965; mem. Nat. Commn. on United Meth. Higher Edn., 1975-77; charter mem. bd. Ind. Nurses' Found., from 1977. Served with USAAF, 1942-45. Recipient Disting. Alumnus award Emporia State U., 1972. Mem. NEA, Nat. Soc. Study Edn., Assn. Higher Edn., Blue Key, Kappa Delta Pi, Phi Delta Kappa (internat. commn. on higher edn. 1968-70), Alpha Phi Omega, Alpha Soc. Home: Bloomington Ind. Died Oct. 29, 1990; buried Bloomington, Ind.

ECHLIN, JOHN EDWARD, manufacturing company executive; b. Oakland, Calif., Feb. 28, 1897; s. Charles Claire and Madeline (Arndt) E.; m. Beryl Goldsworthy, Feb. 8, 1927; children: Margaret Jane Echlin Kammerer, John Edward. Student, Poly. Coll. Engring., Oakland, Alexander Hamilton Inst. With Safe-Lite Mfg. Co., San Francisco, 1918-24; v.p. J.J. Schnerr Co., San Francisco, 1924-26; pres. Echlin & Echlin, Inc., San Francisco, 1926-36; pres. Echlin Mfg. Co., New Haven, 1936-59, Branford, Conn., 1959-92; pres. Echlin United of Can., Ltd., Echlin Sales Co., United Parts Mfg. Co., Chgo.; dir. Plasticrete Corp., New Haven, John P. Smith Co., Inc., Branford; past mem. auto. replacement parts mfrs. industry adv. com. OPS and N.P.A., elec. contact industry adv. com.; mem. industry adv. U.S. Sec. Commerce. Mem. Nat. Metal Trades Assn. (dir.), New Haven County Mfrs. Assn. (past dir.), Nat. Auto. Parts Assn. (dir. mfrs. coun.), SAE, New Haven C. of C. (past dir.), Masons (32 degree), Shriner. *

ECKLER, A. ROSS, consultant; b. Van Hornesville, N.Y., May 22, 1901; s. Albert Henry and Mary Jane (Young) E.; m. Jennie Howe, Aug. 7, 1924; children: Albert Ross, Mary Lois Eckler Dennison. AB, Hamilton Coll., 1922, DSc, 1966; AM, Harvard U., 1928, PhD, 1934. Tchr. math. Tome Inst., Port Deposit, Md., 1922-24; statistician, dir. stats. lab. Harvard Econ. Soc., 1924-31; asst. libr., instr. pub. utility econs. Harvard U., 1931-35; chief spl. inquiries, asst. dir. rsch. WPA, Washington, 1935-39; chief eocn. stats., population div. Bur. Census, 1939-42, asst. chief population div., 1942-43, chief spl. surveys div., 1943-45, chief social sci. analyst, 1945-47; asst. dir. U.S. Bur. Census, 1947-49; dep. dir. Bur. Census, 1949-65, acting dir., 1965, dir., 1965-69; adviser 6th Internat. Conf. Labor Statisticians, ILO, 1947, alt. del. 8th, 9th Internat. Confs., Geneva, 1954, 57; U.S. del. 27th conf. Internat. Statis. Inst., New Delhi, 1951, 30th Conf., Stockholm, 1957, 32d Conf., Tokyo, 1960, 33d Conf., Paris, 1961, 34th Conf., Ottawa, Can., 1963, 35th Conf., Belgrade, Yugoslavia, 1965, 36th Conf., Australia, 1967, 37th Conf., London, 1969, 38th Conf., Vienna, 1973; U.S. alt. del. com. improvement nat. stats. Inter-Am. Statis. Inst., Buenos Aires, 1958. Author: The Bureau of the Census, 1972; contbr. articles to profl. jours. Recipient Gold medal award Dept. Commerce, 1961, Nat. Civil Svc. League award, 1962. Fellow Am. Statis. Assn. (v.p. 1967-69, pres. 1969), Royal Statis. Soc. (Eng.) (hon.); mem. Internat. Statis. Inst., Inter Am. Statis. Inst., Am. Econ. Assn., Kenwood Golf and Country Club, Cosmos Club (Washington), Masons, Kiwanis, Phi Beta Kappa. Congregationalist. Home: Silver Spring Md. Died Mar. 14, 1991; buried Springfield Center Cemetery, N.Y.

EDDY, WILLIAM CRAWFORD, broadcast executive, cartoonist; b. Saratoga Springs, N.Y., Aug. 28, 1902; s. William Daniel and Ethel (Thomas) E.; m. Christine Woolridge, July 11, 1927; children—Nancy Jane (Mrs. George McClure), William Crawford, Dianna Kay (Mrs. Lucas Schuyler Van Orden). Student, N.Y. Mil. Acad., 1917-21; B.S., U.S. Naval Acad., 1926. Registered profl. engr., Ind. Employed Farnsworth TV, Phila., 1934-36, NBC-TV, N.Y.C., 1936-49; dir. TV sta. WBKB, Chgo., 1940-48; former chmn. bd., pres. TV Assos. of Ind., Inc.; cartoonist Ann. Mpls.-Honeywell Calendar, from 1935; cons. TV sta. installation, microwave network planning, installation, design, devel. equipment for TV studios, design, devel. audio-visual equipment. Author: Television, the Eyes of Tomorrow, 1945, A Little Humor Now and Then, 1956, Back to the Drawing Board, 1962; co-author: Wartime Refresher in Mathematics, 1943. With USN, 1936-34; comdg. officer radar tng. USN Radio Chgo., 1942-45; ret. as capt. Decorated Legion of Merit Navy; Recipient Ann. Achievement award Nat. Assn. Radio and TV Broadcasters, 1947. Mem. Soc. Motion Picture and TV Engrs., Soc. Mil. Engrs., U.S. Naval Acad. Alumni Assn., Soc. TV Pioneers. Club: Army-Navy. Home:

Michigan City Mich. Died Sept. 16, 1989; buried Arlington Nat. Cemetery.

EDEN, CHARLES HENRY, lawyer; b. Boston, Apr. 14, 1895; s. Charles H. and Evelyn (MacLellan) E.; m. Harriet E. Carpenter, 1924 (div. 1949); children: Harriet E. Eden Barksdale, Charles H. Student, Brown U., 1914-17; LLB, Harvard U., 1922. Bar: R.I. 1923, Mass. 1927. Pvt. practice law Providence, 1923-92; town solicitor Coventry, R.I., 1928-30; asst. U.S. atty. Dist. of R.I., 1930-33; co-founder, dir., sec. Fram Corp., East Providence, 1932-43. Alderman City of Providence, 1939-40; mem. gov.'s commn. to revise election laws, 1939-40; chmn. Willkie for Pres. Com. of R.I., 1940; mem. Rep. State Cen. Com. R.I., 1942-52, 54-60, chmn., 1952-54; del. Rep. Nat. Conv., 1960; Rep. cand. U.S. Congress, 1942, for mayor of Providence, 1946; mem. Eisenhower for Pres. Club, 1952; mem. Rep. Nat. Com., 1952-54; chmn. R.I. Goldwater for Pres. Com., 1964. With R.I. N.G., 1916; AEF, 1917-19, U.S. Army, 1943-44. Mem. ABA, R.I. Bar Assn., Am. Judicature Soc., Young Reps. of R.I., Rep. Club of R.I. (pres. 1940-41). *

EDEY, MAITLAND ARMSTRONG, writer; b. N.Y.C., Feb. 13, 1910; s. Alfred and Marion H. (Armstrong) E.; m. Helen Winthrop Kellogg, Apr. 24, 1934; children: Maitland Armstrong, Winthrop K., Beatrice W., Marion B. A.B., Princeton U., 1932. Editorial assoc. various book pub. cos., 1933-41. Editor: Life mag, 1946-56; free-lance writer mag. articles, 1957-60; editor: Time-Life Books, N.Y.C., 1960-66; editor-in-chief, 1966-72; free-lance writer books and mag. articles, 1972-92; author: American Songbirds, 1941, American Waterbirds, 1942, (with F. Clark Howell) Early Man, 1965, The Cats of Africa, 1968, The Northeast Coast, 1972, The Missing Link, 1973, The Sea Traders, 1974, The Lost World of the Aegean, 1975, Great Photo Essays from Life, 1978, (with D.C. Johanson) Lucy: The Beginnings of Humankind, 1981 (Am. Book award for best book on sci. subject 1982), Blueprints: Solving the Mystery of Evolution, 1989; contbr. articles on wildlife, sea adventure and anthropology to popular mags. Mayor Village of Upper Brookville, N.Y., 1956-60; chmn. Council Old Westbury Coll., SUNY, 1968-73; bd. dirs. N.Y. Philharm. Symphony, 1952-75, Putney (Vt.) Sch., 1957-75, Conservation Found., Washington, 1966-86; hon. bd. dirs. Scudder Capital Growth Fund, 1983-92, Scudder Devel. Fund, 1983-92, Scudder Internat. Fund, 1983-92; Felix Neck Wildlife Sanctuary, Martha's Vineyard, Mass., 1975-92, Sheriff's Meadow Found., Martha's Vineyard, 1978-92. Served with USAAF, 1942-46. Decorated Legion of Merit; recipient Disting. Service medal Coll. Old Westbury, 1981. Mem. Am. Ornithologists Union. Clubs: Century Assn. (N.Y.), Coffee House (N.Y.). Home: Vineyard Haven Mass. Died May 9, 1992.

EDGELL, ROBERT LOUIS, publishing executive; b. Port Huron, Mich., Aug. 2, 1922; s. Carl Robert and Faye Alberta (Neikirk) E.; m. Yvonne de Clairmont Richardson, Nov. 10, 1981; children: Robin, Douglas, Sarah, Deborah, Jane. B.S., Mich. State U., 1944. With Young Am. Pub., N.Y.C., 1946-48; founder, prin. Robert Edgell & Assos. (merged with Davidson Pub. Co., 1951-62), N.Y.C., 1948-51; exec. v.p. Ojibway Press, Inc. (after merger with Davidson Pub. Co.), 1962-68; various positions Harcourt Brace Jovanovich (after merger with Ojibway Press, Inc.), 1968-76; pres. Harcourt Brace Jovanovich Publs., 1977, chmn., 1977-87, sr. v.p. bus. publs. and broadcasting group, 1977-78, exec. v.p., pres. and head gen. books, mags. and broadcasting group, 1978-87, also bd. dirs.; vice-chmn. Harcourt Brace Jovanovich, Inc., 1985-87; chmn. Edgell Communications, Inc., Cleve., 1987-90, cons., 1990; trustee The Advt. Coun.; two term chmn. Am. Bus. Press. Bd. dirs. Cleve. Ballet; trustee Cleve. Clinic. Mem. Assn. Bus. Pubs. (past chmn., mem. pub.'s adv. com.), Mfrs. Assn. Home: Longboat Key Fla. Died Jan. 1, 1991; buried St. Bart's Cathedral, N.Y.C.

EDGERTON, HAROLD EUGENE, electrical engineering educator; b. Fremont, Nebr., Apr. 6, 1903; s. Frank Eugene and Mary Nettie (Coe) C.; m. Esther May Garrett, Feb. 25, 1928; children—Mary Louise, William Eugene, Robert Frank. B.S., U. Nebr., 1925, D.Eng. (hon.), 1948; M.Sc., Mass. Inst. Tech., 1927, D.Sc., 1931; LL.D. (hon.), Doane Coll., 1969, U. S.C., 1969. Elec. engr. Nebr. Light & Power Co., 1920-25, Gen. Electric Co., 1925-26; asst. prof. MIT, 1932-38, assoc. prof., 1938-48, prof., 1948; ptnr. Edgerton and Germeshausen, 1931, Edgerton and Grier, 1934, EG&G Inc., 1947; pioneer in strobe and underwater photography. Author: (with James R. Killian Jr.) Moments of Vision, 1979, Electronic Flash, Strobe, 1979, Sonar Images, 1986, Stopping Time: The Photographs of Harold Edgerton, 1987, also numerous tech. articles. Trustee New Eng. Aquarium, Boston, 1965, Mus. Sci., Boston, 1967. Recipient medal Royal Photog. Soc., Gold medal Nat. Geog. Soc., Modern Pioneer award, Potts medal Franklin Inst., Albert A. Michelson medal, 1969, Nat. Medal Sci., 1973, Nat. Medal Tech., 1988. Fellow IEEE, Am. Inst. Elec. Engrs., Soc. Motion Pictures and TV Engrs., Royal Soc. Gt. Britain; mem. Nat. Acad. Scis., Nat. Acad. Engrs., Marine Tech. Soc., Sigma Xi, Eta Kappa Nu, Sigma Tau. Republican. Conglist. Club: Mason. Home: Cambridge Mass. Died Jan. 4, 1990; buried Mt. Auburn Cemetery, Cambridge, Mass.

EDQUIST, ERHART DAVID, food company executive; b. McKeesport, Pa., Apr. 24, 1898; s. Frederick and Marie (Carlson) E.; m. Marie Thomas, Dec. 25, 1920; children: Elnora Edquist Reimer, Thomas. Grad., Minnehaha Acad., 1916. With Fairmont Foods Co., Omaha, Nebr., 1917-92; successively mgr. Fairmont Foods Co., Concordia, Kans.; div. mgr. S.W. div., operating v.p. Fairmont Foods Co., 1917-59, pres., chief adminstrv. officer, 1959-63, chmn. bd., CEO, 1963-92; dir. Western Light & Telephone Co., Kansas City, Mo., Omaha Nat. Bank, Fidelity Title Ins. Co. Bd. dirs. Milk Industry Found. With U.S. Army, 1917-18. Mem. C. of C., Internat. Assn. Ice Cream Mfrs., Rotary. *

EDWARDS, DANIEL JAMES, economics consultant; b. Washington, Dec. 30, 1928; s. James Daniel and Anna (Lattin) E.; m. Ruth Knight, Oct. 7, 1952 (div. 1971); children—Richard Kenneth, Glenn Steven, Laura Jeanne, Deborah Suzanne, Donna Charlene, Patricia Ann. B.A. in Russian, U. Md., 1956, M.A. in Econs., 1958; Ph.D. in Econs., U. Va., 1961. Instr. USAF Security Svc. Hdqrs., 1953, Trailways, 1955-58; teaching asst. U. Md. Bur. Bus., Econ. Research, 1956-57; instr. U. Va., 1957-59; grad. asst. Bur. Population and Econ. Research, 1959-60; vis. lectr. internat. econs. Sweet Briar Coll., 1959; asst. prof. Western Md. Coll., 1960-61; economist Fed. Res. Bd., 1961-62, Housing and Home Fin. Adminstrn., 1964; chief economist for special studies Sec. of Treasury, 1964-67; presdl. adv. com. (SST) Office of Tax Analysis, 1964-67; assoc. prof. George Washington U., Washington, 1961-68; economist Bus. Def. Services Adminstrn. Dept. Commerce, 1962-64; assoc. lecturer Georgetown U., 1963; vis. lectr. U. Md., 1969; chief supply-demand group Bur. Mines, 1969-75, chief ecologic-econ. analysis, 1975-81; chief economist Presdl. Rev. Nonfuel Policy, 1978-79; sr. analyst Analytic Studies, 1979-81; sr. logistics engr., economist E-Systems, 1983-84; vis. prof. St. Mary's Coll., Md., 1986; econs. cons. Washington, from 1981; econ. advisor to commr. Andre ICC, from 1986; tax reform cons., 1985; econ. cons. sec. Treasury, 1967-68, Joint Econ. Com., 1967; chief economist Ho. Banking and Currency Com., 1967-69, numerous govtl. agys.; chief mineral economist Bailow Internat.; sr. cons. Energy Internat.; advisor Lykes Assocs., P.R. sec. Natural Resources. Contbr. articles to profl. jours. Mem. Mayor's Drug Adv. Com., Washington. Served with USAF, 1951-54. Earhart fellow, Relm fellow U. Va., Intergovt. Personnel Act fellow, 1974; recipient Disting. Service award Soc. Govt. Economists, 1982. Mem. Bd. Civil Service Examiners, Soc. Environ., Geochem. and Health, Internat. Soc. Tech. Assessment, World Future Soc., Assn. Comparative Econ. Studies, Am. Econ. Assn., So. Econ. Assn., Am. Humanist Assn., Am. Inst. Mining, Metall. and Petroleum Engring., Am. Soc. Dowsers, Royal Econ. Assn., Am. Statis. Assn., Arica Inst., Am. Fin. Assn., Assn. Study Soviet-Type Econs., Assn. Research and Enlightenment, Intercollegiate Soc. Individualists (adv. com. on narcotics addiction), Choice in Currency Commn. Ctr. Econ. Growth, Nat. Assn. Bus. Economists (pres. nat. capitol chpt.1988-89), Nat. Geog. Soc., Soc. Govt. Economists, Parents Without Partners, Spiritual Frontiers Fellowship, Potomac Rose Soc., Pi Gamma Mu. Home: Washington D.C. Deceased. †

EDWARDS, DOUGLAS, radio, television news reporter; b. Ada, Okla., July 14, 1917; s. Tony and Alice (Donaldson) E.; m. Sara Byrd, Aug. 29, 1939; children: Lynn Alice, Robert Anthony, Donna Claire; m. May H. Dunbar, May 10, 1966. Student, U. Ala., 1934-35, Emory U., 1936, U. Ga., 1937-38. Jr. announcer radio Sta. WHET, Troy, Ala., 1932-35; mem. radio news staff radio Sta. WSB, Atlanta and Atlanta Jour., 1935-38; news reporter radio sta. Sta. WXYZ, Detroit, 1938-42; with CBS-TV, 1942-88; fgn. corr. CBS-TV, Britain, France, Germany, Middle East, 1945-46; anchored 1st polit. conv. gavel-to-gavel coverage CBS-TV, 1948, anchor show Douglas Edwards with the News. Features included Report to the Nation, 1942-45, CBS Radio World News Round Up and TV News. Recipient George Foster Peabody award for best TV news, 1955. Mem. Radio-TV Corrs. Assn., Washington Assn. Radio and TV Analysts, Sigma Delta Chi. Clubs: Field (New Canaan, Conn.); Overseas Press (N.Y.C.). Home: Sarasota Fla. Died Oct. 13, 1990.

EDWARDS, FRANCIS HENRY, clergyman; b. Birmingham, Eng., Aug. 4, 1897; came to U.S. 1921, naturalized, 1938.; s. Francis Henry and Ellen (Smith) E.; m. Alice Myrmida Smith, June 27, 1924; children: Lyman Francis, Ruth Ellen, Paul Madison. Student, Graceland Coll., 1921-23, U. Kans., 1925, 28, Kansas City U., 1934, William Jewell Coll., 1942. Ordained to ministry Reorganized Ch. of Jesus Christ of Latter Day Saints, 1916. Mem., sec. Coun. of Twelve Reorganized Ch. of Jesus Christ of Latter Day Saints, 1922-46, counsellor in first presidency, 1946-92; served as first counsellor of the presiding coun. of Gen. Ch., which edits the Saints Herald, 1946-92. Author: Fundamentals, 1930, Life and Ministry of Jesus, 1933, Commentary on Doctrine and Covenants, 1938, Missionary Serman Studies, 1940, God Our Help, 1943, Authority and Spiritual Power, 1958, All Thy Mercies, 1961, For Such a Time, 1962, The Divine Purpose, 1964, others. Mem. Independence Civic Inst.; mem. bd. dirs. Civic Rsch. Inst. of Kansas City; trustee, v.p. Independence Sanatarium and Hosp. Mem. Utah Hist. Soc., Mo. Hist. Soc., Kiwanis. *

EDWARDS, LEVERETT, lawyer; b. Cordell, Okla., Jan. 21, 1902; s. Thomas Allison and Rose Catherine (Leverett) E.; m. Louise Replogle, Nov. 5, 1929; children: Jamie Louise, Katherine Allison. LLB, U. Okla., 1926. Bar: Okla. 1926. Asst. atty. gen. Okla., 1926-27; pvt. practice Oklahoma City, 1927-49; mem. State Indsl. Commn. Okla., 1949-50; mem., chmn. Rlwy. Emergency Bds. under Rlwy. Labor Act, 1946-49; mem. Nat. Mediation Bd., chmn., 1952; mem. industry adv. com. on aviation moblzn. Civil Aeros. Bd. Mem. ABA, Okla. State Bar Assn., County Bar Assn., Am. Law Inst., Nat. Acad. Arbitrators, Phi Delta Phi, Phi Delta Theta. Home: Fort Worth Tex. Died Apr. 2, 1989.

EDWARDS, PRENTICE DEARING, mathematics educator; b. Owensville, Ind., Dec. 21, 1895; s. James Robert and Rosalie (Green) E.; m. Katharine Gawne, June 10, 1921; 1 child, Jane Edwards McColm. BS, Oakland City Coll., 1915; MA, Ind. U., 1923, PhD, 1929; postgrad., U. Chgo., 1925-26. Prin. Zionsville (Ind.) High Sch., 1915-17; tchr. math. Cen. High Sch., Ft. Wayne, Ind., 1917-18, Tech. High Sch., Indpls., 1919-25; instr. Harvard U., 1924-25; faculty Ball State Tchrs. Coll., Muncie, Ind., 1926-92, successively asst. prof., assoc., prof., 1926-50, prof. math., head dept., 1950-62, prof. emeritus, 1962-92; vis., prof. math. Air Force Inst. Tech., Wright-Patterson AFB, Ohio, 1962-63; prof. math. Rose Poly. Inst., Terre Haute, 1963-92, chmn. dept. math., 1965-92. With U.S. Army, 1918-19. Fellow AAAS, Ind. acad. Sci. (pres., editor Proc.); mem. Math. Assn. Am. (bd. govs., pres., sec. Ind.), Exchange Club (past pres.), Torch Club (Muncie), Phi Beta Kappa, Sigma Xi. Presbyterian. *

EDWARDS, RICHARD AMBROSE, lawyer, business educator; b. Roachdale, Ind., May 10, 1922; s. Ralph A. and Bess May (McCampbell) E.; children: Craig Richard, Barbara F. A.B., Ind. U., 1947; LL.B. Harvard U, 1949; Ph.D. (Curtis fellow), Columbia U., 1952. Bar: Ind. 1949, U.S. Supreme Ct. 1954. Instr. Rutgers U., 1949-51; assoc. prof. pub. law and govt. Lafayette Coll., 1952-56; dir. rsch. U.S. Commn. on Govt. Security, Washington, 1956-57; assoc. dir. legis. drafting fund Columbia Law Sch., N.Y.C., 1957-58; assoc. gen. counsel Health Ins. Assn. Am., N.Y.C., 1958-66; v.p. head public relations dept. Assos. Investment Co., South Bend, Ind., 1966-68; sr. v.p., head govt. and industry rels. dept. Met. Life Inst. Co., N.Y.C., 1968-85; Frederick R. Kappel prof. bus.-govt. rels. U. Minn., 1985-88. Author: (with N.T. Dowling) American Constitutional Law, 1954; editor: Index Digest of State Constitutions, 1959. Trustee Nat. Mcpl. League. Capt. U.S. Army, World War II, Korea. Decorated Bronze Star; Curtis fellow, 1949. Mem. ABA, Am. Acad. Mgmt., Assn. Life Ins. Counsel, Phi Beta Kappa. Republican. Presbyterian. Home: Crawfordsville Ind. Died Sept. 8, 1992. †

EDWARDS, RUSSELL, newspaper editor; b. Bklyn., May 11, 1909; s. Cyrus George and Katherine Donaldson E.; m. Martha Joe Verrill, Apr. 5, 1934; children: Priscilla Browning, Constance Alden Ott; m. Willette Ockendon Brown, May 24, 1968; stephild, Alison Hamilton. Mem. staff N.Y. Times, 1929-76, asst. head desk, then head desk obituary, culture, soc. sect, 1939-54, soc. editor, 1954-76. Contbr. numerous feature articles on old N.Y. Mem. Andrew's Soc., Silurians N.Y.C. . Home: Newport R.I. Died Aug. 28, 1991.

EELLS, RICHARD, emeritus business educator, author; b. Cashmere, Wash., Aug. 5, 1917; s. Fred K. and Sophia (Fox) E. A.B., Whitman Coll., 1940, LL.D., 1982; M.A., Princeton, 1942. Fellow Library of Congress, 1945-46, chief div. aeros., 1946-50, Guggenheim chair aeros., 1949-50; field dir. Near East Coll. Assos., 1950-52; ednl. cons. Gen. Electric Co., N.Y.C., 1952-53; mgr. pub. relations research Gen. Electric Co., 1953-56, mgr. pub. policy research, 1956-60; founder, pres. Richard Eells and Assocs. Inc., 1961-92; sr. researcher Grad. Sch. Bus., Columbia U., N.Y.C., 1959-60; adj. prof. Grad. Sch. Bus., Columbia U., 1960-85, adj. prof. bus. emeritus, 1985-92; dir., editor Studies of the Modern Corp., 1964-85, mem. nat. devel. bd., 1974-92, counselor to dean, 1975-92, spl. adviser to pres., 1977-92, chmn., 1985-92; ct.-apptd. observer U.S. Ct., Berlin, 1979; John M. Olin Disting. Lectr. Berry Coll., 1980; cons., adviser IBM; cons., adviser Gen. Electric Co., Kaiser Cos., Rockefeller Bros. Fund, Com. for Econ. Devel., Continental Group, Ashland Oil Co.; Mem. adv. research bd. Nat. Merit Scholarship Corp., 1957-59; pres. Found. Study Human Orgn.; trustee Arkville Erpf Fund, 1962-82, also sec. and treas.; dir. Midgard Found., 1958-87. Author: Corporation Giving in a Free Society, 1956, The Meaning of Modern Business: An Introduction to the Philosophy of Large Corporate Enterprise, 1960, (with Clarence Walton) Conceptual Foundations of Business, 1961, 3d edit., 1974 (McKinsey Found. Acad. Mgmt. award), The Business System: Readings in Ideas and Concepts, 1967, Man in the City of the Future, 1968, The Government of Corporations, 1962, The Corporation and the Arts, 1967, (with Kenneth G. Patrick) Education and the Business Dollar, 1969, Global Corporations: The

Emerging System of World Economic Power, 2d edit, 1976, (with Neil H. Jacoby and Peter Nehemkis) Bribery and Extortion in World Business, 1977, International Business Philanthropy, 1979, The Political Crisis of the Enterprise System, 1980; author: (with Peter Nehemkis) Corporate Intelligence and Espionage, 1984. Trustee New Eng. Conservatory Music, 1974-78, Next Century Found., from 1970, Southeastern Coll., Athens, Greece, 1987-90, Biopolitics Internat. Orgn., Athens, from 1987; trustee, v.p., treas. Weatherhead Found., 1958-87; bd. overseers Whitman Coll.; bd. founders Acad. Gerontol. Edn. and Devel.; spl. advisor The N.Y. Bot. Garden, 1987-88; bd. dirs. Aging-in-Am. Served with USAAF, 1943-45. Named to Most Venerable Order of Hosp. of St. John of Jerusalem; Alfred P. Sloan Found. grantee, 1956; Rockefeller Found. grantee, 1963. Mem. Nat. Inst. Social Scis., The Pilgrims, Phi Beta Kappa. Episcopalian. Clubs: Metropolitan (N.Y.C.); Church; Cosmos (Washington). Home: New York N.Y. Died Oct. 5, 1992. †

EFFERSON, HENRY MANNING, university dean; b. Stateburg, S.C., Mar. 27, 1897; s. Charles and Elizabeth (Thompson) E.; m. Clara B. Moon, Dec. 24, 1925 (dec. 1957); 1 child, Victoria Elizabeth Efferson Warner; m. Verdelle T. McDuffie, Aug. 27, 1958. AB, Atlanta U., 1922; MA, Columbia Tchrs. Coll., 1928; postgrad., U. Minn., U. Iowa, Columbia U.; LLD, Edward Waters Coll., 1953. Head math. dept. Snow Hill (Ala.) Inst., 1922-23; instr., then prof. math., head dept. Fla. A&M Coll. (now univ.), 1923-46, dir. Summer Sch., 1934-92, dean div. arts and scis., 1946-48, adminstrv. asst., 1948-49, acting pres., 1949-50, dean adminstrn., 1950-57, dean univ., 1957-92. Bd. dirs. Fla. Conf. Social Welfare, Fla. Tb and Health Assn., Leon County Tb Assn. Mem. NEA, NAACP, Am. Assn. Sch. Adminstrs., Am. Tchrs. Assn., Assn. Higher Edn., K.P. (grand master exchequer), Omega Psi Phi, Alpha Phi Omega. Mem. AME Ch. *

EFFINGER, CECIL, educator, composer; b. Colorado Springs, Colo., July 22, 1914; s. Stanley Smith and Lucy (Graves) E.; m. Corinne Ann Lindberg, June 14, 1968; children (by previous marriage): Elizabeth Effinger (Mrs. Ted Baker), Gove Effinger. A.B. in Math, Colo. Coll., 1935, Mus.D. (hon.), 1959. Instr. math. Colorado Springs High Sch., 1936; instr. music Colo. Coll., 1936-41, asst. prof., 1946-48; instr. music Colo. Sch. for Blind, 1939-41; 1st oboist Denver Symphony, 1937-41; music editor Denver Post, 1946-48; asso. prof. music U. Colo., Boulder, 1948-56, prof., 1956-81, prof. emeritus and composer-in-residence, 1981-90, faculty research lectr., 1955, faculty fellow, 1969-70; pres. Music Print Corp. Composer numerous compositions, from 1937, including Little Symphony No. 1, 1945, Symphony No. 5, 1958, Cello Suite, 1945, Quartet No. 5, 1963, Symphony for Chorus and Orchestra, 1952, The Glorious Day is Here, 1955, Set of Three for Chorus and Brass, 1961, Four Pastorales for Oboe and Chorus, 1962, Cyrano de Bergerac; opera, 1965; The Invisible Fire, 1957, Paul of Tarsus, 1968, The St. Luke Christmas Story, 1953, A Cantata for Easter, 1971, Concerto for Violin and Chamber Orchestra, 1974, Capriccio for Orch, 1975, Fantasy for Piano and Voices, 1980, Ten Miniatures for Piano, 1982, Landscape II for Orchestra, 1983, cantata From Ancient Prophets, canticles Six Poems of E.E. Cummings, Sonata for flute and piano, Two Sonnets From the Portuguese, Quartet No. 6 (opus 118); inventor musicwriter, open-end Typewriter; designer tempowatch. Served with USAAF, 1941-46. Presser scholar, 1931; Cooke Daniel lectr. Denver Art Mus., 1957; recipient Stoval prize in composition Am. Conservatory, Fontainbleau, France, 1939, Naumburg Recording award, 1959; Gov.'s award in arts and humanities, 1971; U. Colo. medal, 1981; Cecil Effinger grad. fellow in composition established at U. Colo., 1983. Mem. A.S.C.A.P., Am. Fedn. Musicians, Sigma Chi, Tau Beta Sigma, Phi Mu Alpha, Pi Kappa Lambda, Delta Omicron. Home: Boulder Col. Died Dec. 22, 1990; cremated.

EFROYMSON, ROBERT ABRAHAM, investment company executive; b. Indpls., Sept. 27, 1905; s. Gustave Aaron and Mamie (Wallenstein) E.; m. Shirley Green, Mar. 20, 1977; children by previous marriage: Gustave A., Daniel R., Mary Ann Efroymson Stein. Student, Butler U., 1922-23, LL.B. (hon.), 1969; A.B., Harvard U., 1926, LL.B., 1929. Bar: Ind. bar 1930. Practiced law Indpls., 1929-42; pres. Real Silk Hosiery Mills, Inc., Indpls., from 1946; bd. dirs. Lincoln Nat. Life Ins. Co., Lincoln Nat. Corp. Trustee Indpls. Found., from 1946; dir. William E. English Found., Indpls., from 1959; bd. dirs. Jewish Welfare Fedn. Served to capt. USAAF, 1942-45. Mem. Ind. Acad. Jewish. Clubs: Indpls. Athletic, Broadmoor Country. Home: Indianapolis Ind. Died Dec. 30, 1988.

EGGAN, FRED RUSSELL, anthropology educator; b. Seattle, Sept. 12, 1906; s. Alfred Julius and Olive M. (Smith) E.; m. Dorothy Way, Aug. 9, 1938 (dec. 1965); m. Joan Rosenfels, June 29, 1969. Ph.B., U. Chgo., 1927, A.M., 1928, Ph.D., 1933; M.A., Oxford U., 1970. Research asso. in Philippine ethnology U. Chgo., 1934-35, instr. anthropology, 1935-40, asst. prof., 1940-42, asso. prof., 1942-48, prof., 1948-74, Harold H. Swift Disting. Service prof., 1963-74, prof. emeritus, 1974, chmn. dept., 1948-52, 61-63, dir. Philippine studies program, 1953-74; Morgan lectr. U. Rochester, 1964; Frazer lectr. Cambridge, 1971; vis. fellow All Souls Coll., Oxford U., 1970; vis. prof. U. Calif., Santa Cruz, winter 1976; Weatherhead research scholar Sch. Am. Research, Santa Fe, 1979-80; ofcl. U.S. del. 8th Pacific Sci. Congress, Manila, 1953, 9th, Bangkok, 1957, 10th, Honolulu, 1961, 11th, Tokyo, 1966, 13th, Vancouver, B.C., Can., 1975; mem. Pres.'s Com. on Scientists and Engrs., 1956-57; mem. bd. Human Relations Area Files, Inc., 1953-74; research asso. Lab. Anthropology, Santa Fe, from 1964; adv. com. social scis. NSF, 1961-62; hon. cons. Bernice P. Bishop Mus., Honolulu; mem. Commn. Coll. Geography, 1965-67; councillor Smithsonian Instn., 1966-78; mem. adv. bd. Desert Research Inst., U. Nev.; bd. dirs. Founds. Fund for Research Psychiatry, 1967-69; mem. Pacific Sci. Bd., from 1968. Author: Social Organization of the Western Pueblos, 1950, The American Indian, 1966; Editor: Social Anthropology of North American Tribes, 1937, enlarged edit., 1955; supr.: Handbook on the Philippines, 4 vols., 1956; Supr.: Essays in Social Anthropology and Ethnology, 1975; mem. sr. adv. com.: Ency. Brit., from 1953; editorial bd.: Science, 1968-70. Trustee Mus. of American Indian, Heye Found., 1981-90. Served as capt. AUS, 1943; dir. Civil Affairs Tng. Sch. for Far East, U. Chgo., 1943-45. Fulbright research scholar Philippines, 1949-50; Guggenheim fellow, 1953; fellow Center for Advanced Study in Behavioral Scis. Stanford, 1958-59; recipient Viking Fund medal and award, 1956; hon. curator Chgo. Natural History Mus., 1962-91. Fellow AAAS, Royal Anthrop. Inst. (hon.), Brit. Acad. (corr.), Human Relations Area Files (hon.); mem. Nat. Acad. Scis. (mem. com. on scis. and pub. policy 1965-67, mem. council 1967-70), Assn. Asian Studies (dir. 1966-68), Am. Anthrop. Assn. (pres. 1953, Memoirs editor 1960-64, Disting. Svc. award 1990), Am. Philos. Soc. (council 1983-91), Am. Acad. Arts and Scis. (council 1981-83), Am. Ethnol. Soc., NRC (chmn. com. Asian anthropology 1952-53), Social Sci. Research Council (chmn. bd. 1953-56), Phi Beta Kappa, Sigma Xi, Tau Kappa Epsilon. Club: Quadrangle. Home: Santa Fe N.Mex. Died May 7, 1991.

EHNI, BRUCE LOYAL, neurosurgeon; b. Temple, Tex., 1948. BS, U. Tex., 1971; MD, Baylor Coll. Medicine, 1976. Diplomate Am. Bd. Neurol. Surgery. Intern Northwestern U. Hosp., Chgo., 1976-77; resident neurosurgeon La. State U., New Orleans, 1977-82; fellow U. Western Ont., London, Ont., Can., 1981; staff neurosurgeon Meth. Hosp., Houston, 1982-86, Hermann Hosp., Houston, 1982-86; clin. instr. Baylor U. Med. Ctr., U. Tex. at Houston. Mem. AMA. Home: Houston Tex. Died Oct. 1986. †

EICHENBERG, FRITZ, artist, writer, educator; b. Cologne, Germany, Oct. 24, 1901; came to U.S., 1933, naturalized, 1941; s. Siegfried and Ida (Marcus) E.; m. Mary Altmann, 1926 (dec. 1937); 1 dau., Suzanne; m. Margaret Ladenburg, 1941 (div. 1965); 1 son, Timothy; m. Antonie Schulze-Forster, 1975. Student, Sch. Applied Arts, Cologne, 1916-20, State Acad. Graphic Arts, Leipzig, 1921-23; D.F.A., Southeastern Mass. U., 1972, U. R.I., 1974, Pratt Inst., Bklyn., 1976, Calif. Coll. Arts and Crafts, 1978; D.H.L., Marymount Coll., 1984, Stonehill Coll., 1985. With art dept. New Sch. for Social Research, 1935-41; mem. Pennell Fund com. Library of Congress, 1962-68; prof. art, chmn. dept. graphic art Pratt Inst., 1956-63; prof. U. R.I., 1966-71, chmn. dept. art, 1966-69; founder, dir. emeritus Pratt Graphic Art Center; mem. art faculty Albertus Magnus Coll., 1972-73; also lectr. Staff artist and illustrator for German mags. and newspapers, 1926-33; illustrator numerous book classics with wood engravings and lithographs, works in ann. print exhbns.; represented by prints and drawings in major collections in U.S. and abroad; exhibited numerous one man shows including AAA Galleries, N.Y., 1967, 77, Boston Public Library, Impressions Gallery, Boston, 1976, Yale U. Library, 1979-85; retrospective exhbns. Klingspor Mus., Offenbach am Main, Germany, 1974, Smithsonian Instn., 1976-78, Yale U., 1978 (established archives of his work 1978), and 85, Internat. Found., 1979-80, AAA Gallery, 1987, Traveling show through Europe, Asia and Australia, 1988—; author: Art and Faith, 1952, The Art of the Print, Masterpieces, History and Techniques, 1976, The Wood and the Engraver; author-illustrator: Ape in a Cape, 1952, Dancing in the Moon, 1955, Artist on the Witness Stand, 1985, Homage, 1986; illustrator-translator: Erasmus In Praise of Folly, 1972; author-illustrator: The Wood and the Graver, 1977, Endangered Species and other Fables with a Twist, 1979 (nominated for Nat. Book Award 1980), The Adventures of Simplicissimus, 1981, Dance of Death, 1983, Catalogue Raisonné of his Illustrated Books, 1988; editor, founder: Artist's Proof Ann., 1961-72; free-lance contbr. N.Y. Times. Recipient Silver medal Ltd. Editions Club, 1954, Purchase prizes Library of Congress Print Exhibit, 1943-54; S.F.B. Morse medal NAD, 1973; R.I. Gov.'s AA award, 1981; Pennell medal Pa. Acad., 1944; J.D.R. III Fund grantee, 1968; 1st prize Prints, NAD, 1946; named to R.I. Heritage Hall of Fame, 1987. Fellow Royal Soc. Arts Gt. Britain , Royal Soc. for Encouragement of Arts, Mfrs. and Commmerce (U.K., hon. corr.); mem. NAD, Soc. Am. Graphic Artists, NAD. Mem. Soc. of Friends. Home: Peace Dale R.I. Died Nov. 30, 1990.

EIGER, NORMAN NATHAN, circuit court judge; b. Chgo., Aug. 6, 1903; s. Isaac and Rachel (Brender) E.; m. Leona Wolan, Dec. 31, 1935; children: Lawrence H., Rodney I. J.D., De Paul U., 1924. Bar: Ill. 1924. Mem. exec. staff, capital stock tax assessor Ill. Tax Commn., 1932-36; asst. corp. counsel City Chgo., 1936-47; chmn. Ill. Bd. Rev., Dept. of Labor, 1948-52; judge Municipal Ct., Chgo., 1952-64, Circuit Ct., Cook County, Ill., Chgo., 1964-85; adj. clin. prof. DePaul U. Law Sch.; Past v.p. Coll. Jewish Studies; now hon. trustee; arbitrator, mem. panel Am. Assn. Arbitrators; mem. panel arbitrators Fed. Mediation and Conciliation Service; mem. panel of arbitrators Chgo. Transit Authority Amalgamated Transit Union Local #241, #308, Ill. State Labor Relations Bd.; lectr. groups; past v.p. Adult Edn. Council Met. Chgo.; exec. sec. Patriotic Found. Chgo. Past chmn. lawyers div. Chgo. Combined Jewish Appeal; past v.p. Bd. Jewish Edn., now hon. life trustee; hon. life trustee K.A.M. Isaiah Israel Congregation. Served with USCGR, World War II. Named to Chgo. Sr. Citizens Hall of Fame, City of Chgo., 1989. Mem. Ill. Bar Assn., Chgo. Bar Assn., Decalogue Soc. Lawyers (fin. sec.), Ill. Judges Assn. (past pres., chmn. ann. conv. 1972-77, chmn. emeritus 1977-87, bd. dirs. emeritus, chmn. emeritus ann. conv. 1988-89), Nu Beta Epsilon (past grand chancellor), Alpha Epsilon Pi (hon.). Mem. B'nai B'rith (past v.p. Chgo. Council, past pres. Jackson Park Lodge, former mem. awards com. Youth Orgn.). Home: Chicago Ill. Died May 2, 1990; buried Meml. Pk., Skokie, Ill.

EISENBIES, RAY FRED, manufacturing company executive; b. Marengo, Ill., Sept. 4, 1897; s. Charles Joseph and Grace Lee (Hale) E.; m. Nona Helen Tkach, May 20, 1947; children: Ray Paul, Nona Lee. With Roberts & Schaefer Co., Chgo., 1915-35, chief estimator, 1935; with Sawhill Tubular Products, Inc., Wheatland, Pa., 1935-92, pres., 1955, chmn. bd.; chmn. bd. Dietrich Industries, Pitts.; dir. Shenango Inn, Sharon, Pa. Past pres. United Fund Shenango Valley; bd. dirs. Sharon Gen. Hosp. mem. Am. Iron and Steel Inst., Duquesne Club (Pitts.), Sharon Country Club, Iroquois Club (Conneaut Lake, Pa.). *

EISZNER, JAMES RICHARD, food products company executive; b. Chgo., Aug. 12, 1927; s. William Henry and Gertrude (Peifer) E.; m. Joyce Carolyn Holland, Oct. 14, 1950; children: James Richard, Timothy John. Student, Drake U., 1945; B.S., U. Ill., 1950; Ph.D., U. Chgo., 1952. Chemist Standard Oil Co. (Ind.), Whiting, 1952-54; market analyst Indoil Chem. Co., Chgo., 1954-57; dir. market devel. Amoco Chems. Co., Chgo., 1957-63; v.p. mktg. Ott Chem. Co., Muskegon, Mich., 1963-65; exec. v.p. Ott Chem. Co., 1965-66, pres., 1967-70; also dir.; sr. v.p. indsl. div. CPC Internat. Inc., Englewood Cliffs, N.J., 1970-71, pres., 1971-76, v.p. parent co., 1971-76, also bd. dirs., exec. v.p., chief adminstrv. officer, 1977-79, pres., 1979-88, chief operating officer, 1979-84, chief exec. officer, 1984-90, chmn., 1987-90; bd. dirs. Grocery Mfrs. Am., Ams. Soc., Reader's Digest Assn.; mem. Chgo. Bd. Trade, 1971-80. Bd. dirs. Muskegon Area Econ. Planning and Devel. Assn., 1967-70. Served with AUS, 1946-47. Mem. Comml. Devel. Assn. (mem. conf. bd. 1988—), Corn Refiners Assn. (dir. 1971-83, chmn. bd. 1981-82). Republican. Presbyterian. Clubs: Econ. (N.Y.C.), Sky (N.Y.C.); Knickerbocker Country (Tenafly, N.J.). Home: Cresskill N.J. Died Sept. 11, 1990; cremated.

EKBLAW, GEORGE ELBERT, engineering geologist; b. Rantoul, Ill., June 1, 1895; s. Andrew and Ingrid (Johnson) E.; m. Emma Josephine Nyberg, May 14, 1931; 1 child, Andrew II. AB, U. Ill., 1922, AM, 1923; student, U. Chgo., 1920; PhD, Stanford U., 1927. Field asst. Ill. State Geol. Survey, summer 1920, asst. geologist, summers 1921-25, assoc. geologist, 1925-26, assoc. geologist engrng. geology, 1927-29, geologist, geologic editor, 1929-45, in charge engrng. geology sect., 1929-31, head engrng. and areal geology div., 1931-45, geologist, head div. engrng. geology, topographic mapping, 1945-57, geologist, head sect. engrng. geology. topographic mapping, 1957-92. Author ednl. bull. With U.S. Army, 1917-19. Fellow Geol. Soc. Am., AAAS; mem. NSPE, Ill. Soc. Profl. Engrs. (pres. 1950, recipient ann. Ill. award 1953), Western Soc. Engrs., Am. Soc. Photogrammetry, Am. Congress Surveying and Mapping, Ill. Acad. Sci. (pres. 1952-53), Am. Geog. Soc., Am. Ornithol. Union (assoc.), Wilson Ornithol. Club, Am. Legion, Acacia, Masons, Sigma Xi, Phi Beta Kappa, Gamma Alpha, Alpha Phi Omega. *

EL-ABIAD, AHMED HANAFY, electrical engineering educator; b. Mersa Matruh, Egypt, May 24, 1926; came to U.S., 1958, naturalized, 1963; s. Mohamed H. and Fatima (Abdel-Rahman) El-A.; m. Doha M. Gouda, Apr. 17, 1952; children: Amira, Omar A. BSc, Cairo U., 1948; MSEE, Purdue U., 1953, PhD, 1956. Asst. engr. Egyptian State Tel. & Tel. Co., Cairo, 1948-49; teaching asst. in elec. engrng. Cairo U., 1949-52, lectr., 1956-58; asst. prof. elec. engrng. Purdue U., West Lafayette, Ind., 1958-62, assoc. prof., 1962-65, prof., 1965-87; prof. U. Petroleum and Minerals, Dhahran, Saudi Arabia, 1981-87; vis. prof. MIT, 1961-62, Fed. U. Rio de Janeiro, summer 1971, Lund (Sweden) Inst. Tech., summer 1972, Kuwait U., 1979-80; co-founder, ptnr. Tech. Engrng. and Trading Office, Cairo, 1952-57; cons. to industry Mideastern countries, 1956-87. Author: (with G.W. Stagg) Computer Methods in Power System Analysis, 1968; also articles. Fulbright scholar Purdue U., 1952-53. Fellow IEEE; mem. Assn. Muslin Scientists and Engrs. (pres. 1976-80), Internat. Conf.

Large High Tension Electric Systems, Sigma Xi, Eta Kappa Nu. Home: West Lafayette Ind. Died, 1987.

ELATH, ELIAHU, author, former Israeli diplomat; b. Snowsk, Russia, July 20, 1903; naturalized Israeli citizen, 1929; s. Menahem and Rivka Elath; m. Zehava Zalel, Sept. 14, 1931. BA, Am. U., Beirut, 1934; MA, Hebrew U., Jerusalem, 1930; PhD, Hebrew U., 1945. Corr. Reuter's News Svc., Syria and Lebanon, 1931-34; head Middle-East div. polit. dept. Jewish Agy., Jerusalem, 1934-45; dir. polit. office Jewish Agy., Washington, 1945-49; spl. rep. Provincial Coun. Israeli Govt., Washington, 1948-49; amb. to U.S. Provincial Coun. Israeli Govt., 1949-50, amb. to Gt. Britain, 1950-59; pres. Hebrew U., 1962-68; hon. pres. Israeli Oriental Soc.; hon. chmn. Afro-Asian Inst., Truman Inst. Peace at Hebrew U.; v.p. Jewish Colonization Assn. Author: Bedouin, Life and Manners, 1931, Transjordan, 1934, Israel and Her Neighbors, 1957, Elath and Israel, 1966, San Francisco Diary, 1971, Britain and Her Routes to India, 1972, Zionism and the Arabs, 1973, Zionism at the UN, 1976, The Struggle for Statehood, 1979. PhD (hon.), Dropsy U., Phila., 1950, Brandeis U., 1955, Hebrew Union Coll., N.Y.C., 1962, Wayne State U., Detroit, 1964. Home: Jerusalem Israel Died June 21, 1990.

ELDREDGE, HANFORD WENTWORTH, urban planning educator; b. Bklyn., Oct. 16, 1909; s. Hanford W. and (Taylor) E.; m. Diana Younger, Apr. 21, 1947; children: James Wentworth, Alan Wentworth. A.B., Dartmouth Coll., 1931; Ph.D., Yale U., 1935. Instr. sociology Dartmouth Coll., 1935-39, asst. prof., 1939-49, prof., 1949-74, chmn. dept. sociology, 1953-57, 65-68, chmn. internat. relations program, 1959-62, chmn. city planning and urban studies program, 1959-65; guest lectr. Royal Archtl. Assn. London, Yale U., U. Pa., U. N.C., MIT, Cornell U.; vis. lectr. on city planning Harvard, 1963; vis. prof. city planning U. Calif.-Berkeley, 1967; vis. prof. city and regional planning Harvard U., 1974; orgns. analyst Dept. Justice, 1942; intelligence officer Dept. State, 1942; cons. Exec. Office of Pres., 1956; guest lectr. NATO Def. Coll., Paris, 1955-60, Institut des Hautes Etudes de Defense Nationale, Paris, 1960; Fuehrungs Akademie der Bundeswehr USAF Acad., 1961, Ecole de Guerre, Brussels, 1962; faculty Salzburg Seminar in Am. Studies, 1965. Author: (with F.E. Merrill) Culture and Society, 1952, The Second American Revolution, 1964; editor: Taming Megalopolis, 1967; Editor: World Capitals, 1975; contbr. to Studies in the Science of Society, 1937. Trustee Outboard Bound, Inc. Served with USAAF, 1942-45. Decorated Bronze Star medal; recipient cert. of appreciation CIA and U.S. Joint Chiefs of Staff, 1982. Mem. Am. Sociol. Soc., Am. Soc. Planning Ofcls., Am. Inst. Planners, AAUP, Beta Theta Pi. Clubs: Wianno, Brook; American (London). Home: Gaithersburg Md. Died Feb. 17, 1991; buried Norwich, Vt.

ELDRIDGE, JOSIAH BAKER, trucking company executive; b. Oxford, N.C., Apr. 2, 1927; s. James and Mary (Cheek) E.; m. Roxie Ann Walters, June 30, 1951; children: Jo Ann, Jeffery, Mark. BS in Commerce, U. N.C., 1950. Resident auditor State of N.C., Raleigh, 1950-52; with McLean Trucking Co., Winston-Salem, N.C., 1952-89, asst. compt., 1961-71, compt., 1971-72, v.p. acctg., 1972-73, treas., 1972-89, exec. v.p., bd. dirs., 1974-89. Contbr. articles on acctg. in motor carrier industry to tech. jours. With USN, 1944-46. Mem. Am. Trucking Assn. (pres. nat. acctg. and fin. coun. 1972-73, chmn. bd. 1973-74), Adminstrv. Mgmt. Soc. (merit award 1966), N.C. Motor Carriers Assn. (chmn. acctg. coun. 1961-62), Delta Sigma Pi. Home: Advance N.C. Died Feb. 19, 1989; buried Forsyth Meml. Park, Winston Salem, N.C.

ELFELT, JAMES SIDLE, naval officer; b. Mpls., Dec. 28, 1929; s. Lawrence DeHuff and Helen McGuire E.; m. Sally Dahm, Nov. 26, 1955; children: Elizabeth Ann, Helen Suzanne, James Sidle, Cordelia Ann. B.B.A., U. Minn., 1951; M.A., Stanford U., 1959, George Washington U., 1966. Commd. ensign USN, 1951, advanced through grades to rear admiral, 1979; 2d div. officer USS Rush, 1951; communications officer (USS Shannon), 1952-53; chief staff officer Mine Div. 2 USN, 1953-54; comdg. officer (USS Warbler), 1955-56; ADP officer Bur. Naval Personnel USN, 1956-58; missile officer (USS Helena), 1959-61; exec. officer (USS Preston), 1961-63; distbn. officer (Bur. Naval Personnel), 1963-65; comdg. officer (USS Henderson), 1966-67; exec. officer USS New Jersey USN, 1967-69; strategic plans officer (Chief Naval Ops.), 1970-73; comdg. officer (Naval Support Activity), Naples, Italy, 1973-75; internat. affairs officer (Chief Naval Ops.), 1975-76; Navy mem. (Chmn's. Staff Group, Joint Chiefs Staff), 1976-79; dep. chief of staff for plans, policy, and intelligence (Supreme Allied Comdr. Atlantic), 1979-81; comdr. (South Atlantic Force, U.S. Atlantic Fleet), 1981-82; dir. ops. Hdqrs. U.S. European Command, 1982-84; ret., 1984. Decorated Legion of Merit; Bronze Star. Republican. Roman Catholic. Home: Arlington Va. Deceased. †

ELFRED, FRANK STILLMAN, coal company executive; b. Denver, Dec. 12, 1893; s. Frank S. and Amelia (Miller) E.; m. Bernice Wynn, Nov. 25, 1915 (dec.); 1 child, Jane Elfred St. Clair; m. Julia Baroni Schlesinger, Dec. 21, 1954. Grad., Mo. Sch. Mines, Rolla, 1917, DEng (hon.), 1955. With Olin Industries, Inc. and successor, Olin Mathieson Chem., 1938-58, exec. v.p., 1951-58, dir., 1951-62; chmn. bd. Peabody Coal Co., 1958-92; dir. Chgo. Gt. Western Ry. Co. Mem. Am. Inst. Mining, Metall. and Petroleum Engrs., Nat. Coal Assn. (dir.), Metall. Soc. Am., Ordnance Assn., Metro. Club (N.Y.C.), University Club, Noonday Club, Racquet Club (St. Louis), Kappa Alpha Alpha. Republican. Roman Catholic. *

ELIAS, TASLIM OLAWALE, judge international court of justice; b. Nov. 11, 1914. Ed., Igbobi Coll., Lagos, Nigeria; B.A., U. London; LL.B., LL.M., Univ. Coll., London, Ph.D.; postgrad., Inst. Advanced Legal Studies, London; LL.D., U. London, Dakar; Yarborough Anderson scholar, Inner Temple, London, 1946-49; D.Litt., U. Ibadan, U. Lagos, U. Nsukka; LL.D., U. Ahmadu Bello, U. Ile-Ife, Howard U., U. Jodhpur, 1976, U. Hull, 1980, U. Dalhousie, U. Nairobi, 1983, U. Manchester, 1984, U. Buckingham, 1986; D.Sc. (Econ.), London, Lagos State U., U. Jos, Nigeria, 1987. Called to bar, 1947; created Queen's counsel, 1961. UNESCO fellow Africa, 1951; Simon research fellow U. Manchester (Eng.), 1951-53; Oppenheim research fellow Inst. Commonwealth Studies, Nuffield Coll. and Queen Elizabeth House, Oxford, Eng., 1954-60; vis. prof. polit. sci. Delhi (India) U., 1956; mem. del. Nigerian Constl. Conf., London, 1958; fed. atty.-gen., also minister justice Nigeria, 1960-66, atty.-gen., 1966-72, commr. for justice, 1967-72; prof. law, dean faculty law U. Lagos, 1966-72; chief justice of Nigeria, 1972-75; judge, v.p. Internat. Ct. Justice, The Hague, Netherlands, pres., 1981-85. Mem. Internat. Law Commn., UN, 1961-75, chmn. com. constl. experts to draft Congo Const. 1961-62; mem. governing council U. Nigeria, 1959-66; gov. Sch. Oriental and African Studies, London U., 1957-60; mem. Council Legal Edn., 1962-72, chmn., 1973; chmn. Adv. Jud. Com., 1972-75, Internat. Law Commn. UN, 1970, Drafting Com. Protocol, Mediation, Conciliation and Arbitration, 1964, UN Conf. Law of Treaties, 1968-69, 13th Session Asian-African Legal Consultative Com., 1972; exec. Council Internat. Commn. Jurists, from 1975. Author: Nigerian Land Law and Custom, 1951; Nigerian Legal System, 1954; Ghana and Sierra Leone: Development of their Laws and Constitutions, 1962; British Colonial Law: A Comparative Study, 1962; Government and Politics in Africa, 2d edit., 1963; Nature of African Customary Law, 2d edit., 1962; Nigeria: Development of its Laws and Constitution, 1965; Africa and Development of International Law, 1972; Modern Law of Treaties, 1974; New Horizons in International Law, 1979; The International Court of Justice and Some Contemporary Problems, 1983. Co-author: British Legal Papers, 1958; International Law in a Changing World, 1963; Sovereignty Within the Law, 1965; African Law: Adaptation and Development, 1965; Law, Justice and Equity, 1967; Nigerian Prison System, 1968; Nigerian Press Law, 1969; editor Nigerian Law Jour., 1968-73. Decorated comdr. Fed. Republic of Nigeria, 1963; recipient Nat. Merit award Fed. Republic of Nigeria, 1979. Fellow Delian Inst. Internat. Relations; mem. Nigerian Inst. Internat. Affairs (chmn.), Am. Soc. Internat. Law (hon.), Inst. Internat. Law (titular), Hague Acad. Internat. Law, Nigerian Soc. Internat. Law (pres. from 1968), Soc. Inner Temple (bencher), Curatorium Hague Acad. Internat. Law., World Assn. Internat. Relations., African Soc. Internat. and Comparative Law., African Assn. Internat. Law, Permanent Ct. Arbitration, Am. Acad. Arts and Scis., Internat. Acad. Comparative (assoc.), Soc. Pub. Tchrs. Law, Am. Soc. Internat. Law. Home: Victoria Island Lagos, Nigeria Died Aug. 14, 1991; buried Oke Suna Cemetery, Lagos.

ELIASON, NORMAN ELLSWORTH, language professional, educator; b. Glenwood, Minn., Mar. 12, 1907; s. Andrew and Marie (Sagvold) E.; m. Dorothy Haskins, Aug. 23, 1930. A.B., Luther Coll., Decorah, Ia., 1927; A.M., U. Ia., 1931; Ph.D., Johns Hopkins, 1936; Litt.D., Luther Coll., 1967. Prin. high sch. Charter Oak, Ia., 1927-28; instr. English Luther Coll., 1928-29, U. Neb., 1929-32; instr., asst. prof. Ind. U., 1932-37; prof. English U. Fla., 1937-46; prof. English U. N.C., Chapel Hill, 1946-66, Kenan prof., from 1966, then prof. emeritus; research at the Linguistic Inst., Mich., 1936, U. Oslo, summer 1939; vis. prof. U. Ia., summer 1952, U. Innsbruck, Austria, 1956, King's Coll., U. London, 1962, Columbia, summer 1964, U. Wash., 1965, Harvard, 1966, Stanford, 1968. Author: Tar Heel Talk: An Historical Study of the English Language in North Carolina to 1860, 1956, The Language of Chaucer's Poetry, 1972, English Essays Literary and Linquistic, 1975; Co-author: The Effect of Stress upon Vowel Quantity, 1939; Co-editor: Ideas and Models, 1935, Studies in Heroic Legend and Current Speech, 1959, Aelfric's First Series of Catholic Homilies, 1966; Asst. editor So. Folklore Quar., 1937-47; adv. editor Am. Speech, 1939-40, 60-61; co-editor: Anglistica, 1964-80; Contbr. articles and revs. to profl. jours. Served from lt. (j.g.) to lt. comdr. USNR, 1942-46. Guggenheim fellow, 1951-52; sr. fellow Southeastern Inst. Medieval and Renaissance Studies, 1969. Mem. Am. Dialect Soc. (exec. com. 1956-60), Acad. Literary Studies, Linguistic Soc. Am. (exec. com. 1940), MLA (chmn. practical phonetics group 1937-39, sec. exptl. phonetics group 1942-44, sec. Old English group 1954, chmn. 1955, sec. English sect. 1960, chmn. 1961), Medieval Acad. Am., Internat. Assn. U. Profs. English (mem. cons. com. 1956-71, v.p. 1971-74), N.C. Folklore Soc. Democrat. Episcopalian. Home: Chapel Hill N.C. Died Jan. 23, 1991; buried Ch. of the Holy Family, Chapel Hill.

ELICKER, PAUL EDGAR, educator; b. York, Pa., June 4, 1894; s. John Spangler and Elizabeth Ann (Kuhl) E.; m. Elsie Madeline Finkenor, Mar. 23, 1918; 1 child, Paul Hamilton. AB, LLD (hon.), Ursinus Coll., 1914, 1956; AM, Columbia U., 1921; EdM, Harvard U., 1931; ScD, Boston U., 1941. Asst. prin. Malverne High Sch., Lynbrook, N.Y., 1914-16; head dept. math. Franklin High Sch., Hasbrouck Heights, N.J., 1916-17, Franklin Sch., N.Y.C., 1917-18, Collegiate Sch., N.Y.C., 1919-23; instr. math. Newton High Sch., Newtonville, Mass., 1923-27; asst. prin. Newton High Sch., 1927-32, prin., 1932-40; lectr. edn. Harvard U., 1931, Boston U., 1937, 47, 48, Denver U., 1942; lectr. edn. UCLA, 1950; chmn. Zone Com., Coop. Study of Secondary Sch. Standards, 1936-37; cons. Pres. Roosevelt's Adv. Com. on Edn., 1937; mem. Radio Free Europe Tour, 1954; adv. coun. Nat. Merit Scholarships, 1956; mem. U.S. delegation on edn. NATO Conf., Paris, 1956, chmn., 1958; examiner in math. Coll. Entrance Exam. Bd., mem. exec. com. Author: The Administration of the Junior and Senior High School, 1963; co-author with coms.: Planning for American Youth, 1944, How Good Are Our Schools; editor: The Bulletin, 1940-60. Lt. U.S. Army, WW I. Mem. Nat. Assn. Secondary Sch. Prins. (pres. 1938-39), New Eng. Assn. Colls. and Secondary Schs. (chmn. secondary sch. com.), Nat. Conf. Mobilization of Edn. (exec. com.), Nat. Sch. Wk. Coun., Nat. Com. on Edn. and Def., Nat. Assn. Student Couns. (sec.), Mass. Schoolmasters Club (pres. 1937-38), Davis Club (pres.), Rotary (pres. 1938-39), Washington Roundtable, Harvard Alumni Assn., Boston U. Alumni Assn., Phi Delta Kappa, others. *

ELIOT, THOMAS HOPKINSON, educator; b. Cambridge, Mass., June 14, 1907; s. Samuel Atkins and Frances Stone Hopkinson E.; m. Lois A. Jamesson, Oct. 10, 1936; children: Samuel Atkins, Nancy Freeman. Bar: N.Y., Mass., U.S. Supreme Ct. Reporter Boston Globe, 1923-24; assoc. law Kenefick, Cooke, Mitchell, Bass & Letchworth, Buffalo, 1932-33; asst. solicitor Dept. Labor, 1933-35, regional dir. wage and hour div., 1939-40; lectr. govt. Harvard U., 1937-38, 48-51; ptnr. Foley, Hoag & Eliot, 1945-52; prof., chmn. dept. polit. sci. Washington U., St. Louis, 1952-61, chancellor, 1962-71; pres. Salzburg Seminar in Am. Studies, 1971-76; tchr. Buckingham Browne & Nichols Sch., 1977-91; mem. 77th Congress from 9th Mass. Dist.; mem. Spl. Commn. on Reorgn. Higher Edn. in Mass., 1977-79; vis. prof. Princeton U., 1958-59; exec. dir. Spl. Commn. on Structure of State Govt., 1950-52. Author: Basic Rules of Order, 1952, American Government Problems for Analysis, 1959, Governing America, 1960, Public and Personal,1 971; co-author: State Politis and the Public Schools, 1963; contbr. articles to profl. jours. Mem. nat. com. ACLU, 1942-67; vice chmn. U.S. Adv. Commn. Intergovtl. Rels., 1964-67; bd. overseers Harvard U., 1964-70; trustee Monticello Coll., 1958-6. Mem. Am. Polit. Sci. Assn. coun. 1956-58, book rev. editor 196-62 , Am. Acad. Arts and Scis. Democrat. Unitarian. Home: Cambridge Mass. Died Oct. 14, 1991.

ELKO, NICHOLAS THOMAS, clergyman; b. Donora, Pa., Dec. 14, 1909; s. John and Mary (Vazur) E. B.A., Duquesne U., 1931, LL.D., 1958; M.Theology, Byzantine Cath. Sem., Uzhorod, Czechoslovakia, 1935; L.H.D., Stuebenville Coll., 1960; Litt.D., St. Vincent Coll., Latrobe, Pa., 1962. Ordained priest Roman Cath. Ch., 1934; consecrated bishop, 1955; bishop Byzantine Cath. Diocese of Pitts., 1955-67; named archbishop Oriental Congregation, Rome, 1967; head liturgical commn., ordaining prelate Byzantine Rite Vatican, 1967-71; aux. archbishop of Cin., vicar gen., 1971-85; Bd. visitors Thomas Aquinas Coll., Ojai, Calif.; bd. dirs. Athenaeum of Ohio, Cin.; spiritual dir. Cath. Physicians Guild; chmn. Archbishop Elko Found., Dayton, Ohio; active orgn. More Agr. Prodn. Mem. Newcomen Soc., Veneration Soc. Sanctity (spiritual dir.), Internat. Orgn. More Agrl. Prodn. Home: Dayton Ohio Died May 18, 1991; buried Gate of Heaven Cemetery, Cin.

ELLER, CHARLES HOWE, physician; b. Bloomington, Ind., June 5, 1904; s. Charles Asbury and Alice Belle (Howe) E.; m. Jacqueline Marie Rousseau, Dec. 1933 (dec. Feb. 1982); children: Patricia Ann, Mary Jacqueline; m. Jeannette Hoffman, Nov. 26, 1983. A.B., Stanford U., 1927; M.D., U. Colo., 1930; Dr.P.H., John Hopkins U., 1934. Diplomate Am. Bd. Preventive Medicine and Pub. Health. Health officer Valencia and Bernalillo countries, N.M., 1931-34; health officer Charlottesville, Va., 1934-35; asso. prof. preventive medicine U. Va. Med. Sch., 1934-35; asst. dir., later dir. rural health Va. Health Dept., 1935-37; dir. Eastern health dist., Balt., 1937-46; asso. prof. pub. health adminstrn. Johns Hopkins Sch. Hygiene, 1937-46; dir. health Richmond, Va., 1946-49, Louisville, also Jefferson County, Ky., 1949-55; asso. prof. preventive medicine Med. Coll. Va., 1946-49; prof., chmn. dept. community health U. Louisville, 1949-59; commr. health St. Louis County, Mo., 1959-73; prof. pub. health Washington U. Sch. Medicine, 1959-75; ret., 1975; Bd. dirs. Louisville Rehab. Center.; Cons. NIH, 1951-55, 57-59; exec. dir. Health Delivery Systems, Inc., St. Louis, from 1973-75; spl. cons. commn. Research Assos.,

N.Y.C., from 1955; former asso. area med. dir. United Mine Workers's Welfare and Retirement Fund; cons. preventive medicine, Ft. Knox, 1958; mem. task force Nat. Commn. Community Health Services, 1963; mem. Mo. Adv. Council for Comprehensive Health Planning, from 1968. Fellow Am. Pub. Health Assn. (gov. 1962-65 67-70, exec. bd. 1970-73), Am. Coll. Preventative Medicine; mem. Am., Mo. med. assns., St. Louis County Med. Soc. (past pres.), Mo. Pub. Health Assn. (past pres.). Home: Santa Fe N.Mex. Died Jan. 26, 1992. †

ELLINGSON, STEVE, newspaper executive; b. Havana, N.D., Oct. 6, 1910; s. Stephen and Florence (Young) E.; m. Lois Lawson, Feb. 22, 1958. B.S., U. Minn., 1932. Credit mgr. Bullocks, Los Angeles, 1935-41; spl. investigator Western Def. Command, Fourth Army, 1941-42; syndicated newspaper columnist, from 1942; pres. U-B Newspaper Syndicate, Cathedral City, Calif., from 1947. Bd. dirs. Valley Youth Found. Mem. Los Angeles Press Club, Phi Sigma Kappa (U. Minn.). Club: Mason. Home: Cathedral City Calif. Died July 27, 1990; buried Forest Lawn, Hollywood Hills, Burbank, Calif.

ELLIOTT, ALBERT RANDLE, college president; b. St. Louis County, Mo., Jan. 10, 1914; s. Thomas Barrett and Olinda (Hoevel) E.; m. Gwendolyn Stager Crawford, Jan. 28, 1948; 1 dau., Dawn. A.B., Westminster Coll., 1935; LL.D., 1962; A.M., Harvard U., 1938, Ph.D., 1949. Teaching asst. depts. govt. Harvard U. and Radcliffe Coll., 1936-39; research assoc. Fgn. Policy Assn., 1939-41; adminstrv. assoc. Inst. Internat. Edn., N.Y.C., 1941-43; dir. Counsel and Guidance Center for Fgn. Students in U.S., Washington, 1943-45, administr. Washington Bur., 1946-47; econ. analyst U.S. Strategic Bombing Survey, Eng. and Germany, 1945; chief reports officer Office Mil. Govt. for Germany, Berlin, 1945-46; London corr. McGraw-Hill World News, 1947-48; exec. dir. Greer Sch., Hope Farm, Dutchess County, N.Y., 1949-61; pres. Hood Coll., 1961-71, Bay Path Jr. Coll. (name now Bay Path Coll.), Longmeadow, Mass., 1971-79; trustee Bay Path Coll., 1971-80, mem. adv. council, from 1980. Author: Spain After Civil War, 1940, The Resources and Trade of Central America, 1941, (with others) The United States at War, 1942, The Institute of International Education, 1919-44, 1944; editor (with others) numerous govt. reports; contbr. articles to periodicals. Exec. bd. Dutchess County council Boy Scouts Am., 1950-61, Pioneer Valley council, 1972-79; mem. nat. council Boy Scouts Am., 1953-58; mem. Md. State Com. for Fulbright Scholarships, 1967-71. Rockefeller Found. research fellow, 1939-41; recipient alumni achievement award Westminster Coll., 1980. Mem. Council World Affairs (vice chmn. Dutchess County 1955-61, dir. Conn. Valley 1972-79), Council Fgn. Relations, Am. Polit. Sci. Assn., Acad. Polit. Sci., Assn. Ind. Colls in Md. (dir. 1961-71, pres. 1964-66), Am. Acad. Polit. and Social Sci., Am. Mus. Nat. History, Md. Ind. Coll. and Univ. Assn. (sec.-treas. 1970-71), Nat. Council Ind. Jr. Colls. (dir. 1976-79), Springfield Adult Edn. Council (exec. com., v.p. 1976-79), Omicron Delta Kappa, Pi Kappa Delta, Beta Theta Pi. Republican. Episcopalian (vestryman). Clubs: Harvard (N.Y.C.); Millbrook Golf and Tennis (N.Y.); Colony, Rotary, Century (Springfield, Mass.); Pioneer Valley Racquet (Agawam, Mass.). Home: Millbrook N.Y. Died Dec. 1, 1990; buried Oak Grove Cemetery, St. Louis, Mo.

ELLIOTT, DENHOLM MITCHELL, actor; b. London, May 31, 1922; s. Myles Layman and Nina (Michell) E.; m. Virginia McKenna, Mar. 1, 1954; children: Jennifer, Mark. Stage tng., Royal Acad. Dramatic Art, 1939. Stage debut in The Drunkard, Amersahm, Eng., 1945; stage appearances include The Guinea Pig, London, 1946, Frenzy, 1948, The Green Cockatoo, 1948, Don't Listen, Ladies !, 1948, Horn of the Moon, 1949, John Keats Lives Here, 1949, Bouyant Billions, 1949, Ring Round the Moon, 1950, Venus Observed, 1950, A Sleep of Prisoners, 1951, Third Person, 1951-52, The Confidential Clerk, 1953, South, 1955, 61, The Long Echo, 1956, Who Cares?, 1956, Traveller Without Luggage, 1959, The Ark, 1959, The Games as Played, 1964, Come as You Are, 1970, Hedda Gabler, 1972, Mad Dog, 1973, Chez Nous, 1975, The Return of A.J. Raffles, 1975, Heaven and Hell, 1976, The Father, 1979. N.Y. appearances include The Green Bay Tree, 1951, Camino Real, 1957, Monique, 1957, Write me a Murder, 1961, The Seagull, 1864, The Crucible, 1964, The Imaginary Invalid, Still Life, A Touch of the Poet, 1967, The New York Idea, Tree Sisters, 1977. Other prin. stage appearances include A Fiddle At the Wedding, Brighton, Eng., 1952, The Delegate, Manchester, Eng., 1955, King of Hearts, Liverpool, Eng., 1958, The Merchant of Venice, Troilus and Cressida, The Two Gentlemen of Verona, 1960, Domino, Brighton, 1963, Design for Living, Los Angeles, 1971, Turn On, Windsor, Eng., 1973. Film debut Dear Mr. Prohack, 1948; prin. film appearances include: Breaking the Sound Barrier, 1951, The Ringer, 1952, The Holly and the Ivy, 1953, The Cruel Sea, 1953, Heart of the Matter, 1954, They Who Dare, 1955, The Man Who Loved Red Heads, 1955, The Night My Number Came Up, 1955, Lease of Life, 1956, Scent of Mystery, 1960, Marco Polo, 1962, Nothing But the Best, 1964, Station Six Sahara, 1964, King Rat, 1965, You Must Be Joking, 1965, Alfie, 1966, Here We Go Round the Mulberry Bush, 1968, The Night They Raided Minsky's, 1968, The Sea Gull, 1968, Too Late the Hero, 1970, The House That Dripped Blood, 1971, Percy's Progress, 1971, The Hero, 1972, Vault of Horror, 1973, A Doll's House, 1973, The Apprenticeship of Duddy Kravitz, 1974, Russian Roulette, 1975, To the Devil a Daughter, 1976, Voyage of the Damned, 1976, Partners, 1976, Robin and Marion, 1976, voice role Watership Down, 1978, Sweeney 2, 1978, The Boys from Brazil, 1978, Zulu Dawn, 1979, A Game for Vultures, 1979, Saint Jack, 1979, Bad Timing/A Sensual Obsession, 1980, Rising Damp, 1980, Raiders of the Lost Ark, 1981, Sunday Lovers, 1981, Brimstone and Treacle, 1982, The Missionary, 1982, The Wicked Lady, 1983, The Hound of the Baskervilles, 1983, Trading Places, 1983, Illusions, 1983, A Private Function, 1984, The Razor's Edge, 1984, Past Caring, 1985, A Room With A View, 1986, The Happy Valley, 1986, Whoopee Boys, 1986, Maurice, 1987, Over Indulgence, 1988, Stealing Heaven, 1988, Indiana Jones and the Last Crusade, 1989, Killing Dad, 1989, Return to the River Kwai, 1989, Toy Soldiers, 1991, Noises Off, 1992; TV film: Codename: Kyril, 1988, A Murder of Quality, 1991. Served with RAF, 1939-45. Mem. Actors' Equity Assn., SAG, Am. Fedn. TV and Radio Artists, British Acad. Film and TV Arts. Club: Garrick. Home: West Hollywood Calif. Died Oct. 6, 1992. †

ELLIOTT, ERROL THOMAS, clergyman; b. Carthage, Mo., Nov. 10, 1894; s. Elisha M. and Alice S. (Elleman) E.; m. Ruby M. Kelly, Dec. 25, 1916; children: Errol Thomas, Harriet Alice Elliott Combs, Paul Winston, Robert Kelly. AB, Friends U., 1927, LitD; student, Iliff Sch. Theology, Denver, 1928-29; AM, U. Colo., 1930. Student pastor Univ. Friends Ch., Wichita, Kans., 1926-28; pastor Friends Ch., Boulder, Colo., 1928-30; field sec. Five Years Meeting of Friends in Am., 1930-36; adminstrv. sec. Bd. Missions, 1932-34; pastor First Friends Ch., Indpls., 1936-42; pres. William Penn Coll., Oskaloosa, Iowa, 1942-44; gen. sec. Five Years Meeting of Friends, Richmond, Ind., 1944-57; editor The American Friend, Richmond, Ind., 1944-57; minister First Friends Ch., Indpls., 1957-65; rsch. assoc. Earlham Sch. Religion, Indpls., 1965-92; mem. Am. friends Svc. Com. Commn. to Europe, 1940, 46; rep. to Nat. Coun. Chs. of Christ in Am., 1944-57; mem. Am. Friends Svc. Com.; chmn. Friends World Com. for Consultation, 1952-58, vice chmn., 1958-64. *

ELLIOTT, MABEL AGNES, sociology educator; b. Liscomb, Iowa, May 13, 1898; d. William Lee and Nora Belle (Bash) Elliott. AB, Northwestern U., 1922, AM, 1923, PhD, 1929. Instr. sociology U. Minn., 1926-27, Stephens Coll., 1927-28; part-time instr. sociology Northwestern U., 1928-29; asst. prof. sociology U. Kans., 1929-37, assoc. prof., 1938-47; vis. prof. sociology U. Minn., 1936-37; cons. sociologist ARC, 1946-47; lectr. Am. U., 1947; chmn. dept., prof. sociology Chatham Coll., Pitts., 1947-92, Irene Heinz Given prof. sociology (hon.), 1962-92; mem. com. Fulbright and Mundl awards in sociology Fgn. Exchange Program; mem. Fulbright screening com., 1958-59. Author several books in sociology, 1926-47; also Coercion in Penal Treatment: Past and Present, 1947, Social Disorganization (with F.E. Merrill), 1950, 2d edit. 1961, Crime in Modern Society, 1952 (translated into Jugosilovenian 1962), Marriage and the Family (with others), 1955; asst. editor Am. Sociol. Rev., 1940-43, Dictionary of Sociology, 1944; contbr. articles, book revs. to profl. jours.; contbr. to Ency. Brit., 1961. Mem. Kans. Penal Affairs, Mayor's Civic Com., Pitts.; mem. adv. bd. Pitts. Community Coun.; adv. rsch. com. Mayor's Com. on Human Relations, 1959-92. Recipient Wieboldt rsch. fellow in sociology, 1924, Carola Woerischoffer Meml. fellow in social economy, 1924-26; Fulbright awardee U. Bonn, Germany, 1955-56; Pitts. Woman of Year award, 1957. Fellow Am. Sociol. Assn (nat. coun. 1955-58); mem. Internat. Platform Assn., Ea. Sociol Soc., Kan. Conf. Social Work (dir. 1930-36, exec. sec. 1933-34, treas. 1936-37), Internat. Sociol. Assn., Soc. Study Social Problems (exec. com. 1953-92, pres. 1956-57), AAUP, Am. Assn. Social Workers, Faculty Club, Univ. Women's Club, Phi Beta Kappa, Phi Beta Kappa Assocs., Alpha Kappa Delta, Alpha Pi Zeta. Democrat. Episcopalian. *

ELLIS, CHARLES CALVERT, corporate executive, educator; b. Balt., Feb. 2, 1919; s. Luke and Olivia (Kelley) E.; m. Jean Ella Good, Dec. 29, 1942; children: Charles Calvert III, Pauline Olivia, Nancy Ruth, Richard James. A.B., Juniata Coll., Huntingdon, Pa., 1940, LL.D., 1981; M.B.A., Harvard, 1942. With Armstrong Cork Co., 1946-52; plant controller Beaver Falls, Pa., 1949-52; with Ford Motor Co., 1952-59, regional fin. exec., internat. div., Latin Am., 1958-59; dir. Ford of Portugal, 1958-59; controller Kordite Corp., 1959-62; with Philco Ford Corp., 1962-65, controller consumer products div., 1964-65; with Irving Trust Co., N.Y.C., 1965-72, sr. v.p., comptroller, 1966-69, exec. v.p., 1969-72; asst. treas. Charter N.Y. Corp., 1966-69, sr. v.p., treas., 1969-72; sr. v.p. fin. RCA Corp., 1972-80, exec. v.p. long-range fin. planning, 1980-83; Disting. lectr. Georgetown U. Sch. Bus. Adminstrn., Washington, from 1983; chmn. RCA Internat. Ltd., RCA Internat. Devel. Corp.; pres. RCA Disc Corp.; dir. Random House, RCA Globcom, Hertz, RCA Ltd., U.K., Banquet Foods, RCA Americom, So. Gen. Internat. Fund, Coronet, USLIFE Income Fund, Optelicom, Inc., Fred F. French Investment Co.; tchr. extension U. Mich., 1956-59; Chmn. acctg. and fin. com. Nat. Flexible Packaging Assn., 1961-62; chmn. acctg. and tax com. N.Y. Clearing House, 1968-69; mem. Fin. Acctg. Standards Adv. Council, 1980-83. Trustee Juniata Coll., 1966-90, chmn. bd., 1990; former chmn. Pro Musicis Found. Served to lt. USNR, 1942-46. Home: Washington D.C. Died Sept. 26, 1990; cremated.

ELLIS, HOWARD SYLVESTER, economics educator; b. Denver, July 2, 1898; s. Sylvester Eldon and Nellie Blanche (Young) E.; m. Lilah Priscilla Whetstine, Jan. 1926; 1 child, Audrey Elinor; m. Hermine Johanna Hoerlesberger, July 1935; children: Dorothy Margaret, Martha Josephine. AB, State U. Iowa, 1920; AM, U. Mich., 1922, Harvard U., 1924; PhD, Harvard U., 1929. Instr. econs. U. Mich., Ann Arbor, 1920-22, 25-29, asst. prof., 1929-35, assoc. prof., 1935-37, prof., 1937-38; prof. econs. U. Calif., Berkeley, 1938-92; Flood prof. econs.; with Fed. Res. Bd., Washington, 1943-46, asst. dir. div. of rsch. and statistics, 1945-46; vis. prof. econs. Columbia U., 1944-45, 49, U. Tokyo, 1951, U. Bombay, 1958-59; UNESCO specialist Latin Am., 1960; dir. Marshall Aid Project, Coun. on Fgn. Relations, N.Y.C., 1949-50; econ. cons. U.S. Dept. State, 1952-53; rsch. prof. Ctr. Econ. Rsch., Athens, 1963. Author books including: Exchange Control in Central Europe, 1941; co-author: Approaches to Economic Development, 1955; contbr. articles to econ. jours.; co-editor: Readings in Theory of International Trade, 1949, Kyklos; editor: A Survey of Contemporary Economics, 1948, The Economics of Freedom, 1950, Economic Development for Latin America, 1961, The Teaching of Economics in Latin America, 1962, Industrial Capital in Greek Development, 1964. Fellow Social Sci. Rsch. Coun., Europe, 1933-35; Sheldon traveling fellow, Ricardo prize fellow, Wells award Harvard. Mem. Internat. Econ. Assn. (pres. 1953-56, exec. com. 1956-62, hon. pres.), Am. Econ. Assn. (pres. 1949), Royal Econ. Soc., Phi Beta Kappa. *

ELLIS, JOHN TRACY, clergyman, educator; b. Seneca, Ill., July 30, 1905; s. Elmer Lucian and Ida Cecilia (Murphy) E. A.B., St. Viator Coll., 1927; A.M., Cath. U. Am., 1928, Ph.D., 1930, Litt.D. (hon.), 1978; student, Sulpician Sem., Washington, 1934-38; D.H.L., Mt. Mary Coll., 1954; LL.D., U. Notre Dame, 1957, Belmont Abbey Coll., 1960, Fordham U., 1972, U. So. Calif., 1983, St. Anselm Coll., 1985, Manhattan Coll., 1985; Litt.D. (hon.), Loyola Coll., Balt., 1960, U. Portland, 1969, U. Fla., 1973, Marquette U., 1974, St. Vincent Coll., 1979; LHD (hon.), Mt. St. Mary's Coll., Emmitsburg, Md., 1989. Ordained priest Roman Catholic Ch., 1938; prof. history St. Viator Coll., 1930-32, Coll. St. Teresa, 1932-34; instr. history Cath. U. Am., 1938-41, asst. prof., 1941-43, asso. prof., 1943-47, prof. ch. history, 1947-64, vis. prof., from 1976; prof. ch. history U. San Francisco, 1964-76; professorial lectr. ch. history Cath. U. Am., from 1977; vis. prof. Brown U., 1967, U. Notre Dame, 1970, Grad. Theol. Union, Berkeley, Calif., 1970-71, Gregorian U., Rome, Italy, 1974-75, Angelicum U., Rome, 1976; cons. com. for observance bicentennial Nat. Conf. Cath. Bishops, 1973-76. Author: Anti-Papal Legislation in Mediaeval England, 1066-1377, 1930, Cardinal Consalvi and Anglo-Papal Relations, 1814-1824, 1942, The Formative Years of the Catholic University of America, 1946, The Life of James Cardinal Gibbons, Archbishop of Baltimore, 1834-1921, 2 vols, 1952, American Catholicism, 1956, rev. edit., 1969, Documents of American Catholic History, 1956, rev. edit., 1962, 67, American Catholics and the Intellectual Life, 1956, A Guide to American Catholic History, 1959, John Lancaster Spalding, First Bishop of Peoria, American Educator, 1962, Perspectives in American Catholicism, 1963, Catholics in Colonial America, 1965, A Committment to Truth, 1966, Essays in Seminary Education, 1967, Faith and Learning: A Church Historian's Story, 1988; editor, contbr.: The Catholic Priest in the United States: Historical Investigations, 1971, Catholic Bishops: A Memoir, 1983; mng. editor Cath. Hist. Rev., 1941-63; adv. editor, from 1963. Domestic prelate of Pope Pius XII, 1955; recipient John Gilmary Shea prize, 1956; Golden Jubilee medal St. Mary's Dominican Coll., New Orleans, 1960; Campion award Catholic Book Club, 1965; Bene Merenti medal Cath. U. Am., 1961; Research and Scholarship award Alumni Assn. Cath. U. Am., 1969; Laetare medal, 1978. Fellow Am. Benedictine Acad. (1969); Mem. Am. Cath. Hist. Assn. (pres. 1969), Am. Soc. Ch. History (pres. 1969), Phi Beta Kappa (hon.), Delta Epsilon Sigma (hon.), Phi Alpha Theta (hon.). Home: Washington D.C. Died Oct. 16, 1992. †

ELLIS, MARVIN EARL, newspaper publisher; b. Savannah, Ga., Oct. 27, 1934; s. Marvin Earl and Ruth (Harrell) E.; m. Shirley Calkins, Aug. 25, 1956; children: Stanley, Bradley, Wesley. B Chem. Engring., Ga. Inst. Tech., 1955; M Chem. Engring., Pa. State U., 1957. Asst. to pub. Bucks County Courier Times, Levittown, Pa., 1960-61; gen. mgr. South Dade News Leader, Homestead, Fla., 1961-67; pub. Burlington County Times, Willingboro, N.J., 1967-82; sec., bd. dirs. Calkins Newspapers. Pres. Burlington County United Way, 1976; v.p. Burlington County coun. Boy Scouts Am., 1973. 1st lt. U.S. Army, 1958-60. Mem. Am. Newspaper Pubs. Assn., N.J. Press Assn., Rotary, Beta Theta Pi.

Presbyterian. Home: Riverton N.J. Died Nov. 18, 1982; buried Lakeview Cemetery, Cinnaminson, N.J.

ELLIS, RICHARD HASTINGS, air force officer; b. Laurel, Del., July 19, 1919; s. Wilbur P. and Elsie C. (Hastings) E.; m. Margaret Parry Wolcott, Aug. 23, 1947; children: Richard Hastings, Mary Elsie; 1 adopted son, Josiah Wolcott. AB in History, Dickinson Coll., Carlisle, Pa., 1941, JD, 1949, LLD, 1974; LLD (hon.), U. Akron, 1979, U. Nebr., 1981. Commd. 2d lt. USAAF, 1942, advanced through grades to gen., 1973, assignments in U.S., Australia, New Guinea, Philippines,Eng., 1942-63; comdr. 315th Air Div., Tachikawa Air Base, Japan, 1963-65; dep. dir. J-5 Orgn. Joint Chiefs Staff, 1965-67; dir. plans, also asst. dept. cheif staff Plans and Ops. Hdqrs. USAF, 1967-69; comdr. 9th Air Force, Shaw AFB, S.C., 1969-70; vice comdr. in chief USAF Europe, Wiesbaden, Germany, 1970-71; comdr. 6th Allied Tactical Air Force, Izmir, Turkey, 1971-72, Airsouth, Naples, Italy, 1972-73; vice chief staff USAF, Washington, 1973-75; comdr. Allied Air Forces in Cen. Europe, comdr.-in-chief USAF in Europe Ramstein, Fed. Republic Germany, 1975-77; comdr.-in-chief SAC and dir. Joint Strategic Target Planning Staff Offutt AFB, Nebr., 1977-89. Bd. Trustees Dickinson Law Sch. Decorated D.S.C., D.S.M. with 4 oak leaf clusters, Silver Star, Legion of Merit with 2 oak leaf clusters, Air medal with 4 oak leaf clusters, Purple Heart; grand officer of Italian Republic; Korean Tong II Jang medal. Mem. Air Force Assn., Supreme Headquarters Allied Powers Europe Assn., Order Daedalians, Order Carabao, Order Freemasons, Military Order of the World Wars, Phi Kappa Sigma. Home: McLean Va. Died Mar. 28, 1989; buried Arlington Nat. Cemetary, Va.

ELLIS, WILLIAM LEIGH, government official, administrative law judge; b. Petoskey, Mich., Jan. 26, 1908; s. William E. and Gertrude May (Webb) E.; m. Norma Foster, Nov. 16, 1935; children—William L., Amy Foster. A.B., Hillsdale (Mich.) Coll., 1929; LL.B., George Washington U., 1933, LL.M., 1936. Bar: Mich. bar 1935. With State Dept., TVA, 1930-35; atty. GAO, 1935-45, asst. to comptroller gen., 1945-49, chief of investigations, 1949-55; trial atty. Fed. Energy Regulatory Commn., 1955-57, hearing examiner, adminstrv. law judge, 1960-80; dep. dir. Adminstrv. Office U.S. Cts., 1957-60; lectr. law George Washington U., 1942-52. Mem. Fed. Bar Assn. (pres. 1952-53), Mason. Club: Cosmos. Home: Arlington Va. Died Aug. 6, 1990; buried Greenwood Cemetery, Petoskey, Mich.

ELSASSER, WALTER MAURICE, physicist, educator; b. Mannheim, Fed. Republic Germany, Mar. 20, 1904; came to U.S., 1936, naturalized, 1940; s. Moritz and Johanna (Masius) E.; m. Margaret Trahey, July 17, 1937 (div.); children: Barbara, William; m. Suzanne Rosenfeld, June 24, 1964 (dec.). PhD, U. Goettingen, Fed. Republic Germany, 1927; PhD (hon.), U. Manchester, Eng., 1989. Instr. U. Frankfurt, Fed. Republic Germany, 1930-33; research fellow U. Paris-Sorbonne, 1933-36, Calif. Inst. Tech., 1936-41; staff war research on radar U.S. Signal Corps and RCA Labs., 1941-47; prof. physics U. Pa., 1947-50, U. Utah, 1950-56, U. Calif. at La Jolla, 1956-62; chmn. dept. physics U. N.Mex., Albuquerque, 1960-61; prof. geophysics, dept. geology Princeton U., 1962-68; research prof. U. Md., College Park, 1968-74; adj. prof. dept. earth and planetary sci. Johns Hopkins U., 1985-86; Homewood prof. Johns Hopkins U., Balt., 1987-89; pioneering researcher in planetary magnetism and plate techtonics. Author: The Physical Foundation of Biology, 1958, Atom and Organism, 1966, The Chief Abstractions of Biology, 1975, Memoirs of a Physicist in the Atomic Age, 1978, Reflections on a Theory of Organisms, 1987, Theory of Earth's Magnetic Field. Recipient U.S. Nat. Medal of Sci., 1987, Gauss medal Fed. Republic Germany, 1977. Fellow Am. Phys. Soc., Am. Geophys. Union (Bowie medal 1959, Fleming medal 1971); mem. Nat. Acad. Sci. Home: Baltimore Md. Died Oct. 14, 1991.

ELSBREE, WAYLAND HOYT, lawyer; b. Preston Hollow, N.Y., July 21, 1898; s. Willard Parker and Antoinette (Slingerland) E.; m. Miriam Atkinson Jenkins, June 27, 1925; children: Langdon Schuyler, Mary Elsbree Hoffman. AB, Swarthmore Coll., 1921; LLB, Harvard U., 1924. Bar: Pa. 1924. Since practiced in Phila.; assoc. White & Williams, 1948-92; regional counsel OPA, 1942; pres., editor Legal Intelligencer, 1948-92. Treas. Friends Cen. Sch., 1960-92; pres. trustees Phila. Yearly Meeting Friends, 1959-92; bd. dirs. Greater Phila. br. ACLU. Mem. ABA, Pa. Bar Assn., Phila. Bar Assn., Am. Judicature Soc., Harvard Club (Phila.), Phi Beta Kapopa, Delta Sigma Rho. *

ELSTAD, LEONARD M., college president; b. Ossee, Wis., Feb. 8, 1899; s. Ole Hagenstad and Mathilda (Jenson) E.; m. Margaret Wafter, June 16, 1924; children: Elizabeth Jane, Margaret Jean. AB, St. Olaf Coll., 1922, LLD, 1946; AM, Gallaudet Coll., 1923, LLD, 1952. Tchr. rural schs. Esmond, N.D., 1917-18; instr. Gallaudet Coll., Washington, 1923-24; prin. Kendall Sch., Columbia Inst. for Deaf, Washington, 1924-25; asst. prin. Wright Oral Sch., N.Y.C., 1925-26, prin., mgr., 1926-32; supt. Minn. Sch. for Deaf, Faribault, Minn., 1931-45; pres. Gallaudet Coll., Washington, 1945-90; pres. Conv. Am. Instrs. Deaf. Pvt. S.A.T.C., 1918. Recipient Silver Antelope award Boy Scouts Am. Mem. Washington Bd. Trade, Cosmos Club, Nat. Press Club, Fed. Schoolmen's Club (Washington), Univ. Club, Rotary Internat. (past dist. gov.). Home: Mauston Wis. Died June 27, 1990.

ELTON, WALLACE WESLEY, international service company executive; b. Dorchester, Mass., Dec. 15, 1907; s. Frederic and Ella Smith E.; m. Mary Helen Birchard, Aug. 15, 1934 dec. Aug. 1976 ; m. Jane Vrooman Rice, Sept. 29, 1977. PhB, Brown U., 1929. With N.W. Ayer, 1929-40; staff J. Walter Thompson Co., N.Y.C., 1940-41, v.p., dir., 1945-61, exec. v.p., 1961-66, mem. exec. com., 1960-66; v.p. U.S. ops., then v.p. devel. Internat. Exec. Svc. Corps, 1966-91; with firm Lennen & Mitchell, 1941-42. Author: Navy in the Sky, 1943, Guide to Naval Aviation, 1944, Responsibilities of Advertising Men, 1967; author, editor syndicated cartoon feature Zoologic, 1975-91. Lt. comdr. USNR, 1942-45. Mem. Assn. Am. Advt. Agys. chmn. Eastern region 1959 , Brown Alumni regional dir. 1967-91 , Nat. Soc. Art Dirs. pres. 1953-55 , Art Dirs. Club exec. bd. 195-52 , Soc. Illustrators, Coveleigh Club, Am. Yacht Club commodore 1973-74, Rye , Brown U. Club N.Y.C. , Westchester Country Club, Univ. N.Y. Club. Home: Rye N.Y. Died Feb. 14, 1991.

EMBRY, THOMAS ERIC, lawyer, state Supreme Court justice; b. Pell City, Ala., June 14, 1921; s. Frank Bernard and Isabella (Mungall) E.; m. Bedford Stall, Jan. 6, 1945 (dec. Sept. 1983); children—Corinne Embry, Vickers, Frances Alden Embry Burchfield. LL.B., U. Ala., 1947. Bar: Ala. 1947. Ptnr. Embry & Embry, Pell City, Ala., 1947-48; sole practice, 1949-55; ptnr. Beddow, Embry & Beddow, Birmingham, Ala., 1956-74; justice Supreme Ct. Ala., Montgomery, 1975-85; of counsel Emond & Vines, Birmingham, 1985-92; adj. mem. faculty dept. criminal justice U. Ala., Birmingham, 1975-85. Served to capt. U.S. Army, 1943-46. Mem. Ala. Bar Assn., Birmingham Bar Assn., Assn. Trial Lawyers Am., Ala. Trial Lawyers Assn., Internat. Soc. Barristers. Democrat. Roman Catholic. Home: Birmingham Ala. Died Jan. 12, 1992.

EMCH, ARNOLD FREDERICK, management consultant; b. Manhattan, Kans., Nov. 3, 1899; s. Arnold and Hilda (Walters) E.; m. Minna Libman, July 22, 1927 (dec. Sept. 1958); m. Eleanore Merckens, June 30, 1960; children: Arnold Devere, Frederick Bolebec. A.B., U. Ill., 1925, A.M., 1926; postgrad., U. Chgo., 1930; Ph.D., Harvard, 1934. Pres. Emch Constrn. Co., Wichita, Kans., 1920-22; regional dir. Tambly & Brown Co., Chgo., 1926-29; exec. dir. Chgo. Hosp. Council, 1936-39; assoc. dir. Am. Hosp. Assn., 1939-42, U. Chgo. Inst. for Hosp. Adminstrn., 1939-42; mgr. Booz, Allen & Hamilton, mgmt. consultants, Chgo., 1942-48, partner, 1948-60; cons. corp., from 1960, pvt. and personal mgmt. cons.; pres. North End Water Co., Colo., 1964-67; sec.-treas. North End Water Co., 1967-83; dir. mgmt. cons. Calif.-Time Petroleum Corp., 1967-70; pres. Glory Ranch Arabian Stables, 1966-85; sec.-treas. Eagle Rock Ranches, 1971-84. Author: Crowded Years, Uncommon Letters to a Son, Life, Love, and Logic; Contbr. articles to various jours. Trustee William Alanson White Psychiat. Found., Washington, 1945-46, v.p., 1947, pres., 1948-52; dir. Washington Sch. Psychiatry, 1946-56, Mental Health Soc. Greater Chgo., 1958-59, Council on Hosp. Planning and Resources Devel. State Colo., 1961-77. Served in AEF, 1918-19, France; comdr. USNR; mgmt. cons. to Navy Surg. Gen., 1942-45; hon. cons. Navy Surg. Gen., from 1945. Mem. Am. Philos. Assn., AAAS, Shakespearean Authorship Soc., English Cocker Spaniel Club Am., Chi Psi. Clubs: Harvard, University (Chgo.); Colo. Arabian Horse. Home: Estes Park Col. Died July 21, 1989.

EMERSON, ROBERT GREENOUGH, association executive; b. Haverhill, Mass., Jan. 17, 1897; s. Isaac Newton and Dorothy (Clarke) E.; m. Mary Ina Awtry, Apr. 26, 1924; 1 child, Robert G. BCS, NYU, 1917. Asst. sec. Fed. Res. Bd., Washington, 1919, asst. to gov., 1920-21; dep. gov. Fed. Res. Bank of Dallas, 1922-24; v.p. First Nat. Bank of Boston, 1924-47, sr. v.p., 1947-55, dir., 1942-56; dir. First Boston Corp., N.Y.C., Nev.-Mass. Co., Inc., Mill City, Nev., Stnadard Rwy. Fusee Corp., Balt., Sheraton Bldgs., Inc., Boston Tidewater Terminal, Baystate Corp., Avery & Saul Co., Newave Corp., Boston Gear Works, Inc., Quincy, Mass., Boston Gear Works of Can., Ltd., Toronto, Murray, S.A. de C.V., Monterey, Mex., Compressed Steel Shafting Co., Hyde Park, Mass.; dir., chmn. Murray Co. of Tex., Inc.; mem. adv. bd. Colonial Growth & Energy Shares, Inc.;. mem. exec. com., dir. Md. Casualty Co., Balt., Plymouth Rubber Co., Inc., Canton, Mass.; dir., fin. com. Commonwealth Oil Refining Co., Ponce, P.R.; trustee, bd. investment Suffolk Franklin Savs. Bank, Boston. Mem. exec. com., trustee Northeastern U. Mem. Algonquin Club, Down Town Club of Boston, Duxbury (Mass.) Yacht Club, Nat. Press Club, Metro. Club of Washington, Commonwealth Club (Richmond, Va.), Recess Club (N.Y.C., Md. Club (Balt.). Republican. Episcopalian. *

EMERSON, THOMAS IRWIN, law educator; b. Passaic, N.J., July 12, 1907; s. Luther Lee and Wilhelmina (Runft) E.; m. Bertha R. Paret, Oct. 9, 1934 (dec. 1958); Joan Paret, Robert Madden, Luther Lee; m. Ruth B. Calvin, May 27, 1960. A.B., Yale, 1928, LL.B., 1931, M.A., 1946; LL.D., U. Pa., 1976, Amherst Coll., 1976, Georgetown U., 1987. Bar: N.Y. bar 1932. Assoc. with law firm Engelhard, Pollak, Pitcher & Stern, N.Y.C., 1931-33; asst. counsel Nat. Recovery Adminstrn., 1933-34; prin. atty. NLRB, 1934-36, asst. gen. counsel, then assoc. gen. counsel, 1937-40; prin. atty. Social Security Bd., 1936-37; spl. asst. to atty. gen. U.S. Dept. Justice, 1940-41; assoc. gen. counsel OPA, 1941-43, dep. adminstr. for enforcement, 1943-45; gen. counsel Office of Econ. Stblzn., 1945, Office War Moblzn. and Reconversion, 1945-46; prof. law Yale U., 1946-76, Lines prof. law, 1955-76; vis. prof. London Sch. Econs. Polit. Sci., 1953-54, Brookings Instn., 1960-61. Author: (with David Haber and Norman Dorsen) Political and Civil Rights in the United States, 1952, 4th edit., 1976, Toward a General Theory of the First Amendment, 1966, The System of Freedom of Expression, 1970; Contbr. to profl. periodicals; editor-in-chief The Yale Law Jour., 1931. Recipient Medal of Liberty, ACLU, 1983; Guggenheim fellow, 1953, Fulbright fellow, Japan, 1974-75. Mem. Nat. Lawyers Guild (pres. 1950-51), Phi Beta Kappa. Home: New Haven Conn. Died June 19, 1991; cremated.

EMSHWILLER, ED, college dean, video artist; b. Lansing, Mich., Feb. 16, 1925; s. Errol Edmond and Susie B. (Maclellan) E.; m. Carol Fries, Aug. 30, 1949; children—Eve Ann, Susan Jenny, Peter Robert. B.Design, U. Mich., 1949; student, Ecole des Beaux Arts, Paris, 1949-50, Art Students League, N.Y.C., 1950-51. Self employed painter, illustrator N.Y.C., 1951-64, film maker, 1959-73; video artist TV Lab. WNET-Channel 13, N.Y.C., 1972-79; dean school film and video Calif. Inst. Arts, Valencia, from 1979, video artist, provost, 1981-86; cons., lectr. in field; bd. dirs. Ind. TV Svc., 1989-90. Contbr. articles to profl. jours.; producer, creator numerous films and videotapes including Thanatopsis , 1962 and most recently Passes, 1981, 83, Eclipse, 1982, Skin-Matrix, 1984, Vertigo, 1986, Hunger(s), 1987. Served to 2d lt. AUS, 1943-46. Grantee Ford Found., 1964; Guggenheim Found., 1973, 78; NEA, 1973, 75, 79, 86; Rockefeller Found., 1976, 86; Corp. Pub. Broadcasting , 1976; recipient numerous awards for excellence in film and video prodn. Mem. Am. Film Inst. (trustee 1969-75, Maya Deren award 1987), Filmmakers Coop. (bd. dirs. 1965-86), Assn. Ind. Video and Filmmakers (bd. dirs. 1973-75). Home: New York N.Y. Died July 29, 1990; cremated.

ENDICOTT, FRANK SIMPSON, education educator; b. Mankato, Minn., June 25, 1904; s. Ira L. and Lillie M. (Simpson) E.; m. Edith J. Franks, July 25, 1931; children: Robert Frank, Judith Louise Endicott Kuczek. AB, Cornell Coll., 1927; MA, Northwestern U., 1929, PhD, 1938. Tchr. high sch. Winnetka, Ill., 1929-30; dir. guidance Eveleth, Minn., 1930-35; mem. faculty Northwestern U., Evanston, Ill., 1935-72, dir. placement, 1942-72, prof. edn., 1960-72, prof. emeritus, 1972-90. Author: Annual Survey of Jobs for College Graduates, 1945-90, Guiding Superior and Talented High School Students, 1961, How 300 Companies Hire College Graduates, 1962, How to Plan for College, 1967, A College Student's Guide to Career Planning, 1967, Parents' Guide to College Planning, 1967, How to Get the Right Job and Keep It, 1969. Mem. Nat. Inst. Tchr. Placement Assn. (pres. 1937), N. Cen. Assn. Colls. and Secondary Schs. (pres. 1970), Ill. Assn. Sch., Coll. and Univ. Staffing (pres. 1966), Midwest Coll. Placement Assn. (pres. 1957, Disting. Svc. award 1977), Phi Delta Kappa. Presbyterian. Home: Evanston Ill. Died June 8, 1990.

ENGEL, ANTONIE JACOBUS, mechanical engineer; b. Oosthuizen, The Netherlands, Nov. 27, 1896; s. Frederik and Marie Antoinette (Allan) E.; m. Petronella Cornelia Gouldswaard, Aug. 16, 1922; children: Frederik, Cornelia Engel Block, Antonie Jacobus, Henri Pieter. Master deg. in Mech. Engring. with hons., Tech. U. Delft, The Netherlands, 1919. Mech. engr. state coal mines, Limberg, The Netherlands, 1919-24; with Algemene Kunstaijde Unrie N.V., Arnhem, 1924-92; mech. engr. to pres. Algemene Kunstaijde Unrie N.V., Arnhem, 1954-62, dep. chmn. supervisory coun., 1962-92; dir. Am. Enka Corp., N.V. Machinefabrick L. te Strake, Internationale Viscose Cie, N.V., La Seda de Barcelona S.A., Periofil S.A., Brit. Enkalon, Ltd., N.V. Rijnstaal, Arnhem, N.V. Ned Techn. Bur. v. Ontw. d. Industrie Tebodin. Chmn. bd. engring. Coll. Arnhem. Decorated Officer Order Orange Nassau, Knight Order of Netherlands Lion; recipient Peter Stuyvesant award, 1960. Mem. Royal Inst. Engrs. Holland. *

ENGELHARD, JOSEPH A., business executive; b. Owensboro, Ky., Oct. 15, 1898; s. John Cotten and Margaret (Hinsdale) E.; m. Cecile Sproul, Mar. 20, 1929; 1 child, John Cotten II. BS, Rose Poly. Inst., 1921. With U.S. Foil Co., 1921-26; pres., dir. Lima Ice & Coal Co., 1926-29; asst. treas. Reynolds Metals Co., 1929-33; pres., dir. Glenmore Distilleries Co., Louisville, 1933-92; dir. Citizens Fidelity Bank & Trust Co., Louisville, Bourbon Cooperage Co., Louisville Title Co., Gen. Plywood Co.; dir., mem. exec. com. Security Annuity Life Ins. Co. Dir., mem. exec. com. Distilled Spirits Inst. *

ENGLE, PAUL HAMILTON, writer, English language educator; b. Cedar Rapids, Iowa, Oct. 12, 1908; s. Hamilton Allen and Evelyn (Reinheimer) E.; m. Mary Nomine Nissen, July 3, 1936; children: Mary, Sara; m. Hualing Nieh, May 14, 1971. A.B., Coe Coll., 1931; A.M., State U. Iowa, 1932; postgrad., Columbia U., 1932-33; A.B., Merton Coll., Oxford (Eng.) U., A.M., 1939; Litt.D., Coe Coll., Monmouth Coll., Iowa Wesleyan U.; L.H.D. (hon.), U. Dubuque, 1981, U. Colo., 1981. Writer, prof. English, dir. program in creative writing U. Iowa, Iowa City, 1966-77; cons., co-founder univ. Internat. Writing Program U. Iowa, 1967-91. Librettist opera: produced TV Golden Child, 1960; (Recipient award for West of Midnight, Friends Am. Writers, Chgo. 1941), (with Hualing Nieh Engle) (Iowa award for disting. service to arts. Found. for Advancement Edn. fellow 1952-53); Author: books poetry including American Child, 1945, The Word of Love, 1951, Poems in Praise, 1959, A Prairie Christmas, 1960, Embrace, 1969, Images of China, 1981, A Woman Unashamed; Women in the American Revolution, 1976; Editor: anthology Midland, 1961, (with Joseph Langland) Poet's Choice,; Past editor: (with Joseph Langland) On Creative Writing, 1964, An Old Fashioned Christmas, 1964, Portrait of Iowa, 1974; co-editor: (with Joseph Langland) Reading Modern Poetry; Translator: (with Hualing Nich Engle) Poems of Mao Tse-Tung, 1972; Contbr. to popular mags.: (with Hualing Nich Engle) N.Y. Times. Pub. lectr. lit. at colls., Town Hall, N.Y.C., CBS-TV, others; participant Christmas Heritage Program, PBS, 1978; Mem. adv. com. John F. Kennedy Cultural Center, Washington; mem. nat. council on arts White House; judge Nat. Book Award, 1955, 70. Recipient Lamont award Acad. Am. Poets, 1958-61, Disting. Svc. to Arts award Am. Acad. and Inst. Arts and Letters, 1990, numerous other awards; Guggenheim Found. fellow, 1953-54; Rhodes scholar Merton Coll., Oxford; A Paul Engle Internat. Writing Fellowship established in his honor U. Iowa Found., 1991. Mem. Phi Kappa Phi, Phi Gamma Delta. Home: Iowa City Iowa Died Mar. 22, 1991.

ENGLE, ROBERT H., agronomist; b. Bainbridge, Pa., Feb. 5, 1895; s. Paris G. and Mattie Z (Hess) E.; m. Grace E. Riehl, Sept. 10, 1924; children: Ann Riehl Engle Spilman, Robert Riehl. Student, Millersville State Tchrs. Coll, Pa., 1914; BS, Pa. State U., 1919. County agrl. agt. Pa., 1921-28; agronomist Quality Lime Inst., 1928-38, Nat. Plant Food Coun., 1938-55; soils advisor ICA, Govt. of India, New Delhi, 1955-62; fertilizer advisor AID, Tunis, Tunisia, 1962-64; cons. agronomist Treasure Island, Fla., 1964-92; producer documentary motion pictures. Author: Soil Fertility Record Book; collaborator:L Hunger Signs in Crops, Care and Feeding of Garden Plants; contbr. articles to profl. jours., pamphlets. Chmn. civilian def. Washington; dir., pub. safety New Cumberland, Pa. With Armed Forces, WW I. Mem. Am. Soc. Agronomy, Indian Soc. Agronomy, Indian Soil Sci. Soc., Masons, Alpha Zeta, Gamma Sigma Delta, Acacia. Methodist. *

ENNALS, MARTIN FRANCIS ANTONY, human rights consultant; b. Walsall, Eng., July 27, 1927; s. Ford and Jessie Taylor E.; m. Jacqueline Morris, May 11, 1951; children: Marc, Kate. BSc in Internat. Rels., London Sch. Econs., 1948. Budget officer UNESCO, Paris and, Egypt, 1951-59; gen. sec. Nat. Coun. for Civil Liberties, U.K., 1959-66; info. officer Community Rels. Commn. U.K., 1966-68; sec. gen. Amnesty Internat., London, 1968-80; chmn./dir. Human Rights Internat. Documentation System, 1980-91; head police com. support unit Greater London Coun., 1982-91; cons. human rights program UNESCO; v.p. Campaign for Homosexual Equality; mem. U.K. Network of Human Rights Orgns., European Human Rights Found.; cons. non-govtl. orgns. UNICEF. Trustee Cobden Trust. Mem. UN Assn. exec. com., chmn. human rights com. . Home: London Eng. Died Oct. 5, 1991.

ENRIQUEZ, RENÉ, actor; b. Granada, Nicaragua, Nov. 24; s. Andres and Rosa Emilia (Castillo) E. A.A., San Francisco City Coll., 1955; B.A., San Francisco State U., 1958. Appeared in plays: Camino Real, 1959, Marco Millions, 1963, Diamond Orchid, 1964, The New Mount Olive Motel, 1973, Truck Load, 1975, The House of Blue Leaves; appeared in films: Bananas, 1970, Harry and Tonto, 1974, Under Fire, 1983, The Evil That Men Do, 1985, Bulletproof, 1987; appeared in TV movies: Choices of the Heart, Perry Mason; appeared in TV series: The Defenders, The Nurses, Hill Street Blues, Police Story, Quincy, Charlie's Angels, WKRP in Cincinnati, others, from 1974. Chmn., founder René Enrique Internat. Children's Fund, Inc. Served as sgt. USAF, 1951-55. Recipient Golden Eagle award. Mem. AFTRA, Screen Actors Guild (bd. dirs. 1984), TV Acad., Nat. Hispanic Arts Endowment (founder, pres.). Home: Tarzana Calif. Died Mar. 23, 1990; cremated.

ENTERS, ANGNA, dancer, playwright, artist, lecturer; b. N.Y.C., Apr. 28, 1907; d. Edward and Henriette (Gasseur-Styleau) E.; m. Louis Kalonyme. Self-educated in U.S., Europe, Near East. Artist-in-residence Baylor U.; play dir. Dallas Theatre Ctr.; fellow Ctr. for Advanced Studies, Wesleyan U., Conn., 1962. Creator 161 episodes and compositions in dance form in Theatre of Angna Enters, 1926-60; shown in many large cities, colls. of U.S., Can., London, Paris, Cuba, Hawaii, White House, Ringling Mus. Art, Sarasota, Fla., 1952; presented Greek Mime Pagan Greece (performing 12 characters with costumes and music of own creation), Met. Mus. Art, N.Y.C., 1943; originator phase dance mime; exhibited paintings Newhouse Galleries, N.Y.C. (12th exhbn. marked debut as sculptor, 18th exhbn. included 1st work in ceramics), other leading cities U.S., Eng., many mus.; also exhibited drawings of Greek Archaic forms Met. Mus. Art, 1943; 2 weeks repertory Mercury Theater, London (Arts Coun. Great Britain) for 10 seasons, including engagement at Cambridge U. Arts Theatre, 1952; mural painting Penthouse Theater, U. Wash., Seattle, 1950; represented Am. Theatre with week's solo performances Berlin Internat. Arts Festival, 1951; speaker on arts Cambridge U., 1951; creator Commedia dell'Arte sequence for film Scaramouche, 1952; dir., designer settings, costumes of Yerma, Denver U. Theatre Festival, Ithaca (N.Y.) Coll. Theatre, 1958; represented in Met. Mus. Art, Honolulu Mus. Art; author: First Person Plural, 1937, (play) Love Possessed Juana, 1939, (personal remembrance) Silly Girl, 1944, (screenplay) Mama's Angel, 1943, (novel) A Thing of Beauty, 1949, (screenplay) You Belong to Me, 1949, Among the Daughters, 1955, Artists Life, 1957, The Loved and the Unloved, 1961; contbr. articles Mime in Pulpit to Mag. of Art, 1943, essay to Nat. Theatre Conf. Bull., 1944, Pantomime, Ency. Brit.; author: Angna Enters on Mime, 1965. Guggenheim fellow, 1934, 35. Home: Tenafly N.J. Died Feb. 25, 1989.

EPSTEIN, ELENI SAKES (MRS. SIDNEY EPSTEIN), former newspaper editor; b. Washington, May 17, 1925; d. Constantine and Aspasia (Economon) Sakes; m. Sidney Epstein, Mar. 30, 1957. Student, George Washington U., 1943-45, Columbia U., 1947. Copygirl, women's staff writer Washington Star, 1945-46, fashion editor, 1946-81. Recipient J.C. Penney Fashion Writing award U. Mo., 1961; citation Nat. Women's party, 1966; N.Y. Fashion Reporters award, 1972; Frany award, 1973; Woman of Year award Am. Legion post Washington; Silver Cross Royal Order Benevolence Royal Greek embassy, 1973; decorated Order Al Merito (Italy). Mem. Washington Fashion Group. Greek Orthodox. Home: Washington D.C. Deceased. †

ERB, PAUL, editor, clergyman; b. Newton, Kans., Apr. 26, 1894; s. Tillman M. and Lizzie (Hess) E.; m. Alta M. Eby, May 27, 1917; children: Winifred (Mrs. Milford Paul), J. Delbert. Student, Hesston (Kans.) Coll., 1915-16, U. Chgo., 1939-42; BA, Bethel Coll., 1918; MA, State U. Iowa, 1923. Instr. English Hesston Coll., 1917-40, acting dean, 1924-29, registrar, 1929-33, dean, 1933-40; prof. English Goshen Coll., 1940-45; ordained to Ministry Mennonite Ch., 1919; editor Gospel Herald, Scottdale, Pa., 1944-62; book editor Herald Press, Scottdale, Pa., 1960-64; exec. sec. Mennonite Gen. Conf., 1954-61; chmn. pub. com. Mennonite Ency., 1946-59. Author: Old Testament Poetry and Prophecy, 2nd edit., 1956, The Alpha and the Omega, 1955, Don't Park Here, 1962, Our Neighbors South and North, 1965. Pres. Mennonite Community Assn., Mennonite Bd. Edn., 1963-65; field rep. Mennonite Bd. Missions and Charities, Elkhart, Ind., 1962-64. *

ERDMAN, WILLIAM JAMES, II, physician, educator; b. Phila., Apr. 8, 1921; s. Frederick and Mary (Hickok) E.; B.A. in Econs., Swarthmore Coll., 1943; M.D., U. Pa., 1950, M.S., 1954, M.A., 1971; m. Betty Jane Frick, June 30, 1956; children—Mary Belle, Jane Elizabeth. Intern Presbyn. Hosp., Phila., 1950-51; asst. instr. phys. medicine and rehab. U. Pa. Sch. Medicine, 1951-53, instr., 1953-54, asst. prof., chmn. dept., 1954-56, assoc. prof., chmn. dept., 1956-60, prof., chmn., 1960-87, prof. emeritus, 1987-89; also with Grad. Sch. Medicine, from 1951, asst. instr., 1951-53, instr., 1953-54, asso., 1954-55, asst. prof., 1955-56, asso. prof., 1956-60, prof., from 1960, chmn. dept., from 1955, asst. dean, 1968-74, dir. dept. phys. medicine and rehab. Hosp. U. Pa., chmn. med. staff, 1965-67, med. dir., 1968-78; nat. rehab. cons. Internat. Rehab. Assoc., 1971-89; mem. spl. med. adv. group VA, Washington; cons. Lebanon, Wilmington VA hosps.; chmn. dept. phys. medicine and rehab. Phila. Gen. Hosp.; cons. Presbyn. Hosp., Phila., VA Hosp. Vice pres., med. dir. Presbyn. Ministers Fund. Served with AUS, 1943-46. Decorated Bronze Star, Purple Heart. Diplomate Am. Bd. Phys. Medicine and Rehab. Fellow ACP; mem. AMA (chmn. sect. phys. medicine and rehab. 1967-68, del. 1978—), Am. Congress Phys. Medicine and Rehab. (pres. 1964-65, treas. from 1970), Internat. Fedn. Phys. Medicine and Rehab. (hon. treas. from 1980), Internat. Rehab. Medicine Assn. (treas. 1969-77), Am., Pa. (pres. 1958-59) acads. phys. medicine and rehab., Assn. Acad. Psychiatrists (pres. 1970), Coll. Physicians Phila., Gold Key. Presbyterian. (elder). Died Sept. 27, 1989; buried West Laurel Cemetery, Phila. Home: Philadelphia Pa.

ERICKSON, ROLF HERBERT, librarian, historian; b. Green Bay, Wis., Nov. 18, 1940; s. Herbert Stanley and Ethel Helena (Ramseth) E. BA, St. Olaf Coll., 1962; MA in Library Sci., U. Wis., 1966. Tchr., libr. Luth. Mission, Lae, Terr. of Papua, New Guinea, 1962-64; libr. Random Lake (Wis.) High Sch., 1964-65; asst. reference libr. Northwestern U. Libr., Evanston, Ill., 1966-67; adminstrv. asst. Northwestern U. Libr., Evanston, 1967-70, head circulation svcs. dept., 1970-92. Co-editor: From Fjord to Prairie, 1976, Our Norwegian Immigrants, 1978, Bridges to Norway, 1984, Bright Patches Growing up Norwegian in Shawano County Wisconsin, 1991. Chmn. Chgo. History Com., from 1981; trustee, mem. exec. com. Vesterheim Norwegian-Am. Mus., Decorah, Iowa, from 1977; mem. exec. com. Religion and Ethics Inst., Evanston, from 1984; bd. dirs. Ctr. for Scandinavian Studies, North Park Coll., Chgo., from 1987. Grantee U.S. Dept. State, 1984, Am. Scandinavian Found., 1986; recipient St. Olav medal H.M. King Olav V of Norway, 1985, Norway Am. Heritage Fund award, 1989; Royal Norwegian Ministry of Fgn. Affairs scholar, 1991. Mem. Norwegian-Am. Hist. Assn. (exec. com. from 1981, v.p. from 1984), Swedish Am. Hist. Soc. (bd. dirs. archives from 1983, exec. com. from 1987), Nordmanns Forbundet (pres. Chgo. chpt. 1984-86), Chgo. Caxton Club (editorial com. from 1983, centennial com. from 1989, v.p. from 1991), Chgo. Acad. Circulation Librs., Soc. Advancement Scandinavian Studies, Midwest Archives Conf., Northwestern U. Libr. Coun., Sons of Norway, Valdres Samband, Sigdalslag. Home: Evanston Ill. Died Nov. 2, 1992. †

ERIM, KENAN TEVFIK, classicist, educator; b. Istanbul, Turkey, Feb. 13, 1929; came to U.S., 1947; s. Kerim Tevfik and Fahime (Osan) E. Student, Coll. de Geneve, 1941-46; B.A., NYU, 1953; M.A., Princeton U., 1955, Ph.D., 1958; Vis. instr., Ind. U., 1957-58. Asst. prof. NYU, 1958-62, assoc. prof. classics, 1962-71, prof., 1971-90, field dir. research project, 1961, now dir. excavation archeol. discovery Aphrodisias in Turkey. Research and publs. in field. Recipient Franklin L. Burr prize Nat. Geog. Soc., 1973, Liberty medal Mayor Ed Koch of N.Y.C., 1986, Centennial award Nat. Geog. Soc., 1988; named Commendatore dell'Ordine al Merito, Italy, 1986; Guggenheim fellow, 1961-62; recipient Cultural Svcs. Citation, Ministry of Culture of Turkey, 1989. Mem. Archaeol. Inst. Am. (Charles Eliot Norton lectr. 1985-86), Royal Numis. Soc., Turk Tarih Kurumu (corr.), Phi Beta Kappa. Home: Princeton N.J. Died Nov. 3, 1990; interred Aphrodisias Excavation site, Karacasu, Aydin, Turkey.

ERSKINE, LAURIE YORK, author, educator; b. Kirkcudbright, Scotland, June 23, 1894; came to U.S., 1901; s. Wallace and Ada Margery (Bonney) E.; m. Doreene Joyce Pullinger, 1936 (div. 1947). Ed., Choir Sch. St. John the Divine, N.Y.C. Began writing stories for boys, 1921; editorial writer Detroit News, 1921-22; one of four organizers of Solebury Sch. for boys New Hope, Pa., 1925; staff writer Battle Creek (Mich.) Enquirer and News. Author book including: Valley of Wolves, 1940, Renfrew Flies Again, 1940; also plays for boys, and numerous short stories and texts; writer TV drama Renfrew of the Mounted; creator and narrator of radio program Adventure Stories. 1st lt. British Royal Flying Corps, 1916-18; commd.Capt. Coast Artillery Corps (anti-aircraft), U.S. Army, Sept. 11, 1942, advanced through grades to maj.; attached to 38th Brigade Anit Aircraft Artillery Command, Pacific Ocran Areas, 1944-45; and discharged, 1946. Decorated Bronze Star medal. Mem. Explorer's Club (N.Y.C.). *

ERTE, ROMAIN DE TIRTOFF, costume and theatrical designer; b. St. Petersburg, Russia, 1892; s. Peter and Nathalie Nikolenko de Tirtoff. Designer covers, fashion illustrations Harper's Bazaar, 1915-37; designer theatrical settings and costumes, 1913-90. Designer Chgo. Opera, Met. Opera, Ziegfield Follies, Winter Garden, George White Scandals, Folies-Bergère, Casino de Paris, Paris Opera, San Carlo Opera, Tabarin, Lido, London Palladium, London Coliseum, MGM Studios; one-man exhbns. of sculpture, paintings, illustrations and graphics including Paris, N.Y.C., Chgo., London, San Francisco, L.A., Tokyo, Madrid, Rome, others; represented in permanent collection Met. Mus. Art, N.Y.C.; author: Ertè's Fashions, 1973, Things I Remember, 1975. Decorated Officier des Arts et Lettres. Orthodox. Home: London Eng. Died Apr. 21, 1990.

ESTES, JOE EWING, federal judge; b. Commerce, Tex., Oct. 24, 1903; s. Joe Guinn and Della Marshall (Loy) E.; m. Carroll Virginia Cox, Dec. 1, 1931; children: Carl Lewis, Carroll. Student, E. Tex. State Tchrs. Coll., 1923-24; LL.B., U. Tex., 1927; LL.D., E. Tex. State U., 1974. Bar: Tex. 1927. Partner Crosby & Estes, Commerce, 1928-30, Phillips, Trammell, Estes, Edwards & Orn, Ft. Worth, 1930-45, Sanford, King, Estes & Cantwell, Dallas, 1946-52, Estes & Cantwell, 1952-55; U.S. dist. judge Dallas, 1955-60; chief judge U.S. Dist. Ct. No. Dist. Tex., Dallas, 1959-72; sr. judge U.S. Dist. Ct. No. Dist. Tex., from 1972; also judge Temp. Emergency Ct. Appeals U.S., from 1972; mem. adv. com. on rules evidence U.S. Supreme Ct. Contbr. articles to profl. jours.; also to: Handbook of Recommended Procedures for the Trial of Protracted Cases; co-author: Handbook for Newly Appointed U.S. District Judges; editorial bd.: Manual for Complex Litigation. Trustee, mem. exec. com. S.W. Legal Found.; Research fellow, mem. med.-legal com., chmn. Oil and Gas Inst. of S.W. Legal Found.; chmn. exec. com. bd. trustees St. Mark's Sch. of Tex., Dallas, 1951-55. Served as lt. comdr. USNR, 1942-45; mem. Res. Recipient Hatton W. Sumners award S.W. Legal Found., 1972, Citizen of Yr. award Kiwanis Club of Dallas, 1972. Fellow Am. Bar Found.; mem. Nat. Conf. Commrs. on Uniform State Laws, Am. Law Inst., Inter-Am., Fed., ABA (chmn. sect. jud. administrn. 1961-62, mem. ho.

dels.), Dallas Bar Assn. (past v.p.), Fort Worth Bar Assn. (past dir.), State Bar Tex., Am. Judicature Soc., Jud. Conf. U.S. (chmn. com. on trial practice and technique, mem. exec. com. 1969-71, dist. judge rep.), Nat. Lawyers Club, Inst. Jud. Adminstrn., Philos. Soc. Tex., Newcomen Soc., Am. Legion, Chancellors, Phi Delta Phi, Kappa Sigma, Order of Coif. Methodist. Clubs: Masons (33 deg.), Shriners (hon. insp. gen., Jester). Home: Dallas Tex. Deceased. †

ESTRICH, ROBERT MARK, English language educator; b. Mt Pleasant, Mich., Apr. 10, 1906; s. Charles Henry and Florence Adele (Moore) E.; m. Helen Elizabeth Watts, Aug. 9, 1932 (dec. Sept. 1944); m. Alice Elizabeth Heyes Olliffe, Dec. 24, 1947. BA, Ohio U., 1928; MA, Ohio State U., 1929, PhD, 1935. Instr. English Ohio State U., Columbus, 1929-37, asst. prof., 1937-45, assoc. prof., 1945-47, prof., 1947-69, prof. emeritus, 1969-89, chmn. dept., 1952-64. Author: (with Hans Sperber) Three Keys to Language, 1952; contbr. articles in field to profl. jours. Mem. MLA, Linguistic Soc. Am., Phi Beta Kappa. Home: Columbus Ohio Died Sept. 27, 1989; cremated.

ETHERINGTON, ROGER BENNETT, banker; b. Bayonne, N.J., Nov. 18, 1923; s. Charles K. and Ethel (Bennett) E.; m. Barbara H. Dean, Nov. 22, 1946; children—Sandra, Kim Anne, Caryn, R. Barrie. Student, Conn. Wesleyan U., Middletown, 1941-43, 47-48; A.B., Columbia U., 1950. With Am. Nat. Bank & Trust N.J., Morristown, N.J., 1950-89, pres., 1969-76, chmn. bd., chmn. exec. com., 1976-89; past chmn. bd., chmn. exec. com. Chem. Bank N.J., formerly Horizon Bancorp.; dir., chmn. Horizon Trust Co. N.A., 1981-89; dir. Care Dwellings, Inc.; bd. dirs. Chem. Bank N.J., Spartan Oil Co. 1st v.p., trustee Fairleigh Dickinson U., past bd. dirs.; 1st v.p., trustee Waterloo Found. for Arts, Mt. Hebron Cemetery Assn.; past bd. dirs., chmn. bd. Greer-Woodycrest Children's Svcs.; mem. bus. adv. bd. Community Coll. of Morris; trustee The Montclair Found. Officer AUS, 1943-46, 51-52, PTO. Recipient Peace medal, 1981. Mem. Morris County C. of C. (dir., past pres.), Nat. Alliance Bus. (bus. adv. bd.), Morgan Horse Club, N.J. Morgan Horse Assn. (pres. 1967). Congregationalist (trustee, treas. 1964-67). Clubs: Montclair Golf, Sky Top, Green Boundary (Aiken, S.C.), Morristown (N.J.). Home: Montclair N.J. Died Nov. 6, 1990; buried Mt. Hebron Cemetery, Montclair, N.J.

ETTER, BETTY, editor; b. Sigourney, Iowa, Aug. 3, 1911; d. William Luther and Flora Alice (Cotton) E. Student, Wilson Coll., 1927-29; B.J., U. Mo., 1931. Reporter Ponca City (Okla.) Daily News, 1931-32; society editor Cedar Rapids (Iowa) Gazette, 1932-34; assoc. editor Bankers mag., 1935-37, Am. Home, 1938-40; editor Ideal Pub. Co., 1941-51, Lady's Circle, N.Y.C., 1967-74; contbg. editor Lady's Circle, 1974-84; tchr. mag. editing CCNY. Club: Overseas Press of (N.Y.C.). Home: Venice Fla. Died Mar. 4, 1989.

EUCHARISTA, SISTER, history, political science educator; b. Waverly, Minn., Jan. 15, 1893; d. Thomas and Elizabeth (McCarthy) Galvin. AB, Coll. St. Catherine, St. Paul, 1924; student, Moorhead (Minn.) State Tchrs. Coll., summer 1920, U. Minn., 1924-25; AM, U. Chgo., 1925, PhD, 1929. Tchr. Westport, S.D., 1910-11, Waverly, Minn., 1911-14; entered novitiate, 1915; tchr. Jamestown, N.D., 1917, Grand Forks, N.D., 1917-18, Morris, Minn., 1918-20, LeSueur, Minn., 1920-23; registrar Coll. of St. Catherine, St. Paul, Minn., 1929-37, pres., 1937-43, prof. history and polit. sci., 1951-54; provincial superior St. Paul Province of the Sisters of St. Joseph of Carondelet, 1945-51, superior gen., from 1954. *

EVANS, EDWARD ARTHUR, engineer army officer; b. Muskogee, Okla., Sept. 17, 1895; s. Herbert J. and Jane L. (Berry) E.; m. Nancy Whittemore; 1 child, Jack Kenneth. Ed., Calif. schs. Lic. structural engr. and gen. contractor, Calif. Commd. 2nd lt. O.R.C., 1919, advanced through grades to brig. gen.; active duty in both World Wars; former exec. dir. Res. Officers Assn. of U.S. Former city mgr., Miami, Fla.; mng. dir. Oil Users Assn.; dir. United Nat. Bank, Miami; bd. dirs. United Fund of Dade County, Dade County chpt. ARC, Dade County Citizens Safety Coun., Lindsey Hopkins Edn. Ctr. of Dade County Pub. Schs. Decorated Legion of Merit, Croix Militaire de tēre classe (Belgium); Blue Dome fellow. Mem. Am. Legion, Am. Artists Profl. League, Res. Officers Assn. of U.S. (past exec. dir.), Mason (K.T., past commr.), Shriner, Jester, Rotary, Army-NavyCountry Club (Washinton), Miami Club, Kings Bay Yacht and Country Club (Miami). Democrat. *

EVANS, GERAINT LLEWELLYN, opera singer; b. Wales, Feb. 16, 1922; s. William John and Gladys May (Thomas) E.; m. Brenda Evans Davies, Mar. 27, 1948; children: Alun Grant, Huw Grant. Student, Guildhall Sch. Music; Mus.D. (hon.), U. Wales, 1965, U. Leicester, 1969, Council Nat. Acad. Awards, 1980, U. London, 1982, Oxford U., 1985. Prin. baritone, Royal Opera House, 1948-84, appearances include, Covent Garden, London, Glyndebourne Festival Opera, 1950—, also, Vienna State Opera, La Scala, Milan, Italy, Met. Opera, N.Y.C., San Francisco Opera, Lyric Opera, Chgo., Salzburg (Germany) Opera, Edinburgh Festival Opera, Paris Opera, Teatro Colon, Buenos Aires, Mexico, City Opera, Welsh Nat. Opera, Scottish Opera, Berlin Opera, Teatr Wielki, Warsaw, Poland; author: (with Noel Goodwin) Sir Geraint Evans: A Knight at the Opera. Decorated comdr. Brit. Empire, 1959, knight bachelor, 1969; officer Order St. John, 1986; recipient Sir Charles Santley Meml. award Worshipful Co. of Musicians, 1963, Harriet Cohen Internat. Music award, 1967, San Francisco Opera medal, 1980, Fidelio medal, 1980; fellow Guildhall Sch. Music, 1960, Royal No. Coll. Music, 1978, Univ. Coll., Cardiff, 1976, Jesus Coll., Oxford, 1979, Royal Coll. Music, 1981, Royal Soc. Arts, Trinity Coll. Music, London, 1987, Univ. Coll., Aberystwyth, 1987, Univ. Coll., Swansea, 1990.; hon. mem. Royal Acad. Music; Freeman of City of London, 1984. Mem. Royal Soc. Musicians, Gorsedd of Bards, Royal Nat. Eisteddfod Wales, Honourable Soc. Cymmrodorion (v.p.1984). Home: Dyfed Wales Died Sept. 19, 1992. †

EVANS, MAURICE, actor, manager; b. Dorchester, Dorset, Eng., June 3, 1901; came to U.S., naturalized, 1941; s. Albert Herbert and Laura (Turner) E. Student, Grocer's Co. Sch., London, 1912-18. Brought to U.S. by Katharine Cornell to play Romeo to her Juliet, 1936; later played the Dauplin in St. Joan and Napoleon in St. Helena; produced Richard II, which ran 171 consecutive performances on Broadway, 1937, Hamlet, 1938-39, Henry IV, 1939; appeared in Twelfth Night with Helen Hayes, 1940-41; produced and appeared in Macbeth, which ran 131 consecutive performances on Broadway, 1941-42, Hamlet (131 performances), 1945-47, also Man and Superman, 1947-49 (293 performances); roles also include The Browning Version, 1949, The Devil's Disciple, 1950, Richard II, 1951, Dial M for Murder, 1952-54, The Apple Cart, 1956-57, Heartbreak House, 1959-60, Tenderloin, 1960-61, The Aspern Papers, 1961-62, with Helen Hayes in Shakespeare Revisited, A Program for Two Players, 1962-63; prodr. Teahouse of the August Moon, 1953, No Time for Sergeants, 1955; prodr., actor TV prodns. of Hamlet, 1953, Richard II, Macbeth, 1954, Devil's Disciple, 1955, Taming of the Shrew, Man and Superman, 1956, Twelfth Night, 1957, Dial M for Murder, 1958, The Tempest, 1960; motion pictures include Kind Lady, 1950, Androcles and the Lion, 1951, Gilbert and Sullivan, 1952, Macbeth, 1960, Warlord, 1965, Jack of Diamonds, Planet of the Apes, 1967, Rosemary's Baby, Thin Air, 1968, Planet of the Apes Revisited, 1969; artistic supr. N.Y.C. Ctr. Theatre Co., 1949-50. Maj. AUS, 1942-45. Recipient Drama League medal, 1937. Home: Rottingdean England Died Mar. 12, 1989.

EVEREST, HARVEY PETTIT, banker; b. Hutchinson, Kans., Apr. 10, 1895; s. Claude Harrison and Martie (Pettit) E.; m. Ruth Whetstone, 1915; children: Jean I., Howard H. Student, U. Okla., 1914-17. With Mid-Continental News Co., Publ. News Co., Okla. City, mag. distbrs., from 1912, chmn.; v.p., treas. Darby-Everest Cadillac Inc., from 1955; dir. Liberty Nat. Bank & Trust Co., Oklahoma City, from 1946, exec. com., from 1947, pres., from 1955. Past pres. Community Chest, Oklahoma City; chmn. trustees Phillips Coll.; dir. United Community Funds and Councils Am., YMCA, ARC, Goodwill Industries, Family and Children's Svc., Okla. Med. Rsch. Found. Lt. (s.g.) USNR, World War II. Mem. Am. Bankers Assn., Oklahoma City C. of C. Mem. Christian Ch. (mem. bd., exec. com.). *

EVERETT, ARDELL TILLMAN, insurance executive; b. Littleton, Colo., Dec. 22, 1909; s. William Hume and Bessie (Shields) E.; m. Iva Lorene Ferrier, Aug. 3, 1935; 1 child, Ardell Gordon. BS in Commerce, U. Denver, 1932. Asst. atty. in fact Mfrs. & Wholesalers Indemnity Exchange, Denver, 1932-36; home office supr. Phoenix Mut. Life Ins., Hartford, Conn., 1936-38, Tex. mgr., Houston, 1938-46; mgr. Prudential Ins., Houston, 1946-48; exec. dir. agy. Los Angeles, 1948-51; v.p. Newark, 1951-62; chmn. N.Am. Co. for Life and Health Ins., Chgo., 1962-75, Service Ins. Co., N.Y.C., 1962-75; pres. Quality Adjustment Service, Inc., N.Y.C., 1970-72; dir. C.I.T. Fin. Corp. and subs., 1965-75; cons. to ins. cos.; founder Ins. Pub. Affairs Council, 1975; pres. Ardell T. Everett, Inc., from 1975; bd. dirs. Guarantee Res. Life Ins. Co., Calumet City, Ill. Mem. adv. bd. Bus. Industry Polit. Action Com., 1979. Served to lt. comdr. USNR. Recipient Edward H. O'Connor Disting. Service award, 1969, Harold R. Gordon Meml. award Internat. Assn. Health Underwriters, 1970. Mem. Health Ins. Assn. Am. (chmn. 1968-69), Health Ins. council (chmn. 1967-68), Ins. Econs. Soc. Am. (chmn. 1967-68), Am. Life Conv. (exec. com. 1968-72), Beta Theta Pi. Clubs: Union League (Chgo.); Pickwick Golf. Lodges: Masons, Shriners. Home: Arlington Heights Ill. Died Nov. 22, 1988.

EVERS, WALTER, management consultant; b. Englewood, N.J., May 9, 1914; s. Fritz Otto and Liesel Clara (Micho) E.; m. Emlen Davies Grosjean, Sept. 19, 1970; children by previous marriage: Sally Evers Everett, Ridgely Clyde. A.B., St. John's Coll., 1935; grad. student, Georgetown U. Sch. Fgn. Service, also Maxwell Sch. of Syracuse U. Pres., mgmt. cons. Walter Evers & Co., Cleve., 1960-84; dir. Medusa Corp., Cleve.; Dir. exec. recruitment WPB, 1941-42; exec. sec. def. mgmt. com. Office Sec. Def., 1949-50. Mem., past chmn. bd. visitors and govs. St. John's Coll., Annapolis, Md., Santa Fe, N.Mex., 1958-86, emeritus, 1986. Served to lt. USNR, 1942-47. Republican. Episcopalian. Clubs: University (N.Y.C.); Chagrin Valley Hunt (Gates Mills, Ohio). Home: Cleveland Ohio Died May 11, 1990; cremated.

EVES, JESSE PARVIN, publishing company executive; b. Springdale, Iowa, June 27, 1894; s. Joseph Walker and Amanda (Worthington) E.; m. Edna M. Johnson, Apr. 12, 1918; children: Wayne Parvin, Nelvyn (Mrs. Paul A. Mongerson). BS in Animal Husbandry, Iowa State U., 1916, M.Agr. (hon.), 1923. Sec. Iowa Dairy Assn., Waterloo, Iowa, 1916-23; with Meredith Pub. Co., Des Moines, from 1923, sales mgr., 1931-59, v.p., dir., from 1959. Sec.-treas., dir. Dairy Shrine Club, from 1949; chmn. type com. Brown Swiss Cattle Breeders Assn. Am., from 1948; judge all breeds dairy cattle, N. and S. Am., also Can. Recipient Centennial award Iowa State U., 1958, Guest of Honor, Dairy Shrine Club, 1954. Mem. Mason, Tavern Club, Detroit Athletic Club, Saddle and Sirloin Club (Chgo.), Alpha Zeta, Theta Delta Chi. *

EWING, GORDON A., government official; b. Newfane, N.Y., Nov. 1, 1912; s. Roy G. and Dorothy (Green) E.; m. Marjorie Edwards, June 29, 1946; 1 child, John Peter. Student, Stanford U., 1930-31, Kiel (Germany) U., 1931-32; BA, Wayne State U., 1935, MA, 1936. Dept. dir., then dir. Radio Sta. RIAS, Berlin, 1949-57; dep. dir. Voice of Am., USIA, 1957-59; counselor Embassy for Pub. Affairs, Bonn, Germany, 1967-90. Maj. AUS, 1941-45. Decorated Croix de Guerre; recipient Meritorious Svc. award Dept. State, 1952, USIA, 1959. Home: Fairhope Ala. Died July 24, 1990.

EWING, MEREDYTH HANWAY, lawyer; b. Uniontown, Pa., Nov. 13, 1895; s. John K. and Mary (Mitchell) E.; m. Betty Tinker, Nov. 1, 1933; children: Jane E. Moore, Ann E. Carrick, Meredyth H., Mitchell W. LittB, Princeton U., 1918; LLB cum laude, U. Pitts., 1923. Bar: Pa. 1923. Mem. firm Moorhead & Knox, from 1923, ptnr., from 1945. Dir. Sta. WRYT, Inc., Pitts., Rockwell Mfg. Co.; sec., dir. Television City, Inc. Lt. U.S. Army, 1917-18; AEF, France. Mem. ABA, Pa. Bar Assn., Allegheny County Bar Assn., HYP Club (Pitts.), Rolling Rock Club, Duquesne Club. Republican. Episc. *

EYDE, RICHARD HUSTED, curator, botanist; b. Lancaster, Pa., Dec. 23, 1928; s. Richard Husted and Thelma (Somers) E.; m. Lorraine Sylvia Dittrich, June 8, 1957; children: Douglas Alan, Dana Everest. B.S. in Biology, Franklin and Marshall Coll., 1956; M.S. in Botany, Ohio State U., 1957; Ph.D. in Biology, Harvard U., 1962. Research asst., then assoc. curator botany Mus. Nat. History, Smithsonian Instn., Washington, 1961-69, curator, 1969-90. Fulbright scholar India, 1960-61. Mem. AAAS, Am. Inst. Biol. Scis., Am. Soc. Plant Taxonomists, Bot. Soc. Am., Goethe Gesellschaft, Goethe Soc. N.Am., Internat. Assn. Plant Taxonomy, Internat. Soc. Plant Morphologists, Internat. Orgn. Palaeobotany, Soc. Systematic Zoology, Torrey Bot. Club. Home: Arlington Va. Died May 27, 1990; cremated, ashes scattered at Otter Creek, Pa.

EYEN, TOM, playwright, director; b. Cambridge, Ohio, Aug. 14, 1941; s. Abraham L. and Julia (Farhad) E. BA in English, Ohio State U., 1960. Dir.-in-residence repertory co., La Mama E.T.C., Theatre of the Eye, N.Y.C., from 1965; dir., writer repertory co. Theatre of Big Dreams, 1982-91; author: Frustrata, The Dirty Little Girl with the Red Paper Rose Stuck in Her Head, Is Demented!, 1963, White Whore and The Bit Player, 1964, Miss Nefertiti Regrets, 1965, Dirtiest Show in Town, 1970, 2008 1/2 (A Spaced Oddity), 1974, (with Gary William Friedman) Why Hanna's Skirt Won't Stay Down, 1964, Paris, 1974, Women Behind Bars, 1974, (with music by Henry Krieger) The Dirtiest Musical in Town, London, 1976, ; TV writer: Mary Hartman, Mary Hartman, 1976-77, Milliken Show, 1977, 78, Bette Midler TV Special, 1977, Neon Woman, 1979, Melody of the Glittering Parrot, 1980; writer, dir. (for Showtime TV) The Dirtiest Show in Town, 1980, (with music by Henry Krieger) (on Broadway) Dreamgirls, 1981 (Tony award 1982, Grammy award 1982, NAACP award 1982-83), Kicks: The Showgirl Musical, 1986, (with Alan Menken) Dangerous Music, 1988, (with Henry Krieger) Power, Greed & Self-Destruction in America, part 1 or Give My Regards to Off-Off Broadway, 1987. Rockefeller fellow, 1967, Guggenheim fellow, 1970. Home: New York NY Died May 26, 1991; buried Cambridge, Mass.

FABEL, DONALD CRISTON, mechanical engineer, educator, consultant; b. Conneaut, Ohio, Aug. 27, 1897; s. Frederick John and Jessie Bell (Ingersoll) F.; m. Sally-Jane Grim, Aug. 9, 1941. AB, Cornell U., 1921; BS, Case Inst. Tech., 1925, MS, 1926; grad. study, Yale U., 1939-40, D.Eng., 1947. Instr. metallurgy Case Inst. Tech., 1923-26; mech. engr. Cleve. Twist Drill Co., 1926-28; head dept. mech. engring. Fenn. Coll., Cleve., 1928-39, head dept. mech. and metall. engring., 1946-58, head dept. mech. engring., 1958-63, prof. mech. engring, 1963-65; prof. mech. engring., head dept. metall. The Cleveland State U., from 1965; cons. mech. and metall. engring. from 1932. Co-author: The Forging Handbook, Engineering Materials. Dir. S.J. Grim Co. Col. Ordinance Corps, U.S. Army, 1940-46; O.R.C., from 1918. Decorated Commendation medal. Mem. ASME, AIME, ASEE, SAR, NRA, Am. Philatelic Soc., Am. Soc. Engring. Edn., Nat. Geog. Soc., Soc. Mayflower Descendents (lt. gov.), English Speaking Union, Bristish Field Sports Soc., Mason (past master), Shriner, Cornell Club, Yale Club, Cheshire Cheese Club (Cleve.), Kappa Sigma, Tau Beta Phi. Episc. *

FABRICANT, SOLOMON, economics educator; b. Bklyn., Aug. 15, 1906; s. Samuel and Sarah (Plotkin) F.; m. Bessie Blacksin, Feb. 7, 1934 (dec. Sept. 1989); children: Ruth Fabricant Lowell, Peter, Sarah. BCS, NYU, 1926; BS, CCNY, 1929; MA, Columbia U., 1930, PhD, 1938. Pub. acct., 1925-29; mem. rsch. staff Nat. Bur. Econ. Rsch., 1930-53, 65-72, dir. rsch., 1953-65, rsch. assoc. emeritus, 1972-89; acing dir. requirements coordination div. European Regional Office UNRRA, 1944-45; lectr. econs. NYU, N.Y.C., 1946-47, assoc. prof., 1947-48, prof., 1948-73, prof. emeritus, lectr., 1973-89; vis. prof. econs. Columbia U., 1952; cons. U.S. Bur. Census, 1945-50, Bur. Budget, 1946-52, NSRB, 1948-49, N.Y. State Tax Commn., 1951-52, GAO, 1970-71, Nat. Com. on Productivity, 1974-78, U.S. Treasury Dept., 1976-77, Cost Acctg. Standards Bd., 1978; mem. econ. forum Nat. Indsl. Conf. Bd., 1946-72; mem. rsch. adv. bd. Com. Econ. Devel.; dir. dir. non-mil. div. program bur. WPB, 1942-44; mem. President's Task Force on Sci. Policy, 1969-70, President's Commn. on Fed. Stats., 1970-71. Author: Capital Consumption and Adjustment, 1938, Output of Manufacturing Industries, 1940, Employment in Manufacturing, 1942, Trend of Government Activity, 1952, Investing in Economic Knowledge, 1958, The Study of Economic Growth, 1959, An Economist's View of Philanthropy, 1961, Primer on Productivity, 1969, Productivity Growth: Purpose, Process, Prospects, Policy, 1978; (with others) Economic Principles and Problems, 1936, War and Defense Economics, 1952, Studies in Income and Wealth, 1958, Economic Consequences of the Size of Nations, 1960, 1, (with others) Labor Productivity, 1965, Business Problems of the Seventies, 1973, Capital for Productivity and Jobs, 1976, Economic Calculation Under Inflation, 1976, Business and the American Economy, 1776-2001. Fellow Am. Statis. Assn.; mem. Am. Econ. Assn. (exec. com.), Joint Coun. Econ. Edn. (trustee), Am. Fin. Assn., Am. Philos. Soc., Royal Econ. Soc., Econometric Soc., Econ. History Assn. (trustee), Internat. Assn. Rsch. Income and Wealth (coun.), Am. Acad. Arts and Scis. Home: South Salem N.Y. Died Sept. 20, 1989; cremated.

FADELEY, HERBERT JOHN, JR., banker, lawyer; b. Ambler, Pa., Feb. 14, 1922; s. Herbert John and Jennie Miller (Lewis) F.; m. Eleanor A. Battafarano, Feb. 8, 1947; children: Herbert John, Brett Duane, Theresa Jane, Scott Lewis. B.S. in Commerce, Drexel U., 1946; J.D., Temple U., 1953; postgrad., Stonier Sch. Banking, Rutgers U., 1957. Bar: U.S. Supreme Ct. 1957, U.S. Ct. Appeals, U.S. Dist. Ct., U.S. Tax Ct.; registered mortgage underwriter (RMU); cert. rev. appraiser (CRA). Asst. cashier First Nat. Bank, Media, Pa., 1951-57; v.p. Boardwalk Nat. Bank, Atlantic City, N.J., 1957-60, Indsl. Trust Co., Phila., 1960-62; v.p., trust officer County Trust Co., White Plains, N.Y., 1963-68; pres. Troy Savs. Bank, N.Y., 1969-82, chmn. bd., chief exec. officer, 1982-87, also trustee; pres., dir. 32 Second St. Inc., Realty Umbrella Ltd., Corhar Inc., Russtend Realty Corp.; lectr. banking and law Drexel U., 1962, Rockland Community Coll., Suffern, N.Y., 1964-68, Westchester County chpt. Am. Inst. Banking, 1965-68, Hudson Valley Community Coll., Troy, 1970; dir., past chmn. bd. Mut. Thrifts Service Ctr. Chmn. Rensselaer County Am. Cancer Fund Crusade, 1970-73; also v.p., dir. Cancer Soc., 1970-73, pres., 1975-76; bd. dirs. Troy Downtown Devel. Found.; mem. Troy Downtown Devel. Council, Tri-county Fifty Group; bd. dirs. Russell Sage Coll., chmn. fin. com., past treas., gen. chmn. 1972 fund drive; bd. dirs. United Community Services; bd. dirs. Soc. Friendly Sons St. Patrick, pres., 1976-77; bd. dirs. Mary Warren Free Inst., also v.p.; pres., bd. dirs. The Family Agy. Inc.; bd. dirs., v.p. Uncle Sam Mall, Inc., 1971-73. Served to lt. (j.g.) USNR, 1942-43, 48-59; maj. Old Guard City of Phila. Named Outstanding Alumnus Drexel U., 1961; recipient trust div. sch. awards N.Y. State Banker's Assn., 1967, 68. Mem. ABA, Am. Inst. Mgmt. (mem. pres.'s council), Am. Judicature Soc., Nat. Assn. Rev. Appraisers (sr.), Assn. U.S. Army, Lambda Chi Alpha, Phi Alpha Delta (named outstanding alumnus 1957, chief justice Dr. Elden S. Magaw Alumni chpt. 1955-56), Greater Troy C. of C. (dir. 1969-75, pres. 1973-74). Episcopalian. Club: Troy. Lodges: Shriners, Jesters, Masons (Troy). Home: Altamont NY Died Nov. 28, 1988; buried Albany Rural Cemetery.

FAHY, EDWARD JOSEPH, military officer. Rear adm. USN; formerly comdr. Mare Island Naval Shipyard, Vallejo, Calif.; row comdr. Naval Ship Systems Command/Navy Dept. Home: Washington D.C. Died Oct. 25, 1989.

FAIN, SAMMY, composer, singer, pianist; b. N.Y.C., June 17, 1902. Began career as mem. staff music pub. co.; composer: songs for films include Majorie Morningstar, Weekend at the Waldorf, Sweet Music, Anchors Aweigh; film scores include Just You and Me Kid, Alice in Wonderland, Peter Pan, Calamity Jane, Mardi Gras, Jazz Singer, Three Sailors and a Girl, April Love; Broadway stage scores include Something More, Hezapoppin, George White's Scandals, Flahooley, Around the World in Eighty Days, Ankles Aweigh, Christine; songs include Secret Love (Acad. award 1953), Love is a Many-Splendored Thing (Acad. award 1955), Let a Smile Be Your Umbrella, Wedding Bells Are Breaking Up That Old Gang of Mine, When I Take My Sugar To Tea, You Brought a New Kind of Love To Me, Was That the Human Thing to Do?, I Can Dream, Can't I?, Are You Havin' Any Fun?, I'm Late, Dickey Bird Song, Something I Dreamed Last Night, That Old Feeling, I'll Be Seeing You, Dear Hearts and Gentle People, A Very Precious Love, Tender Is the Night, A Certain Smile, By a Waterfall, April Love, Strange are the Ways of Love (Acad. award nomination), A World That Never Was (Acad. award nomination), If Every Day Were Valentine's Day, Someone's Waiting for You (Acad. award nomination), Katie. Recipient 10 Acad. award nominations, Nashville Country Music award, Diploma di Benemerenza Hall of Artists, Nice, France, Augusto Messinese Gold award Italy, 2 Laurel awards, Lifetime Achievement Spl. award ASCAP, 1989; named to Songwriters Hall of Fame. Home: Beverly Hills Calif. Died Dec. 6, 1989.

FAIRBANK, JOHN KING, historian, educator; b. Huron, S.D., May 24, 1907; s. Arthur Boyce and Lorena C.V. (King) F.; m. Wilma Cannon, June 29, 1932; children: Laura, Holly. BA summa cum laude, Harvard U., 1929, LLD (hon.), 1970; DPhil, Oxford (Eng.) U., 1936; LLD (hon.), Korea U., 1964, U. Toronto, Can., 1967, Swarthmore Coll., 1968, Oberlin Coll., 1971, U. Cin., 1973; LHD (hon.), U. Wis., 1969, U. Mass., 1974, Middlebury Coll., 1975, Northwestern U., Evanston, Ill., 1978, Brandeis U., 1979, Clark U., 1979, U. S.D., 1981, U. Mich., 1982, Johns Hopkins U., 1983, Tufts U., 1988, DaRTMOUTH Coll., 1988. Faculty dept. history Harvard U., Cambridge, Mass., 1936-77, Francis Lee Higginson prof. history, 1959-77, dir. East Asian Rsch. Ctr. (now renamed John King Fairbank Ctr. for East Asian Rsch.), 1955-73, chmn. Council East Asian Studies, 1973-77; coord. of info., OSS, Washington, 1941-42; spl. asst. to Am. amb., Chungking, Republic of China, 1942-43; with OWI, Washington, 1944-45; dir. USIS, China, 1945-46. Author numerous books including The United States and China, 1948, 4th rev. edit., 1979, enlarged edit., 1983, (with Conrad Brandt and Benjamin Schwartz) A Documentary History of Chinese Communism, 1921-50, 1951, Trade and Diplomacy on the China Coast, 1954; (with S.Y. Teng) China's Response to the West, 1954, (with E.O. Reischauer) East Asia: the Great Tradition, 1960, (with E.O. Reischauer and A. Craig) East Asia: The Modern Transformation, 1965, East Asia: Tradition and Transformation, 1972, China Perceived, 1974, (autobiography) Chinabound: A Fifty Year Memoir, 1982, The Great Chinese Revolution 1800-1985, 1986, Entering China's Service: Robert Hart's Journals, 1854-63, 1986, China Watch, 1987, A New History of China, 1992; author and gen. editor series: (with Dennis Twitchett) Cambridge History of China, editor, contbr. to vol. 10, 1978, vol. 11 (with K.C. Liu), 1980, vol. 12, 1983, vol. 13 (with A. Feuerwerker), 1985, vols. 14 (with R. MacFarquhar), 1987; editor, author intro. (with S.W. Barnett) Christianity in China: Protestant Missionary Writings in Chinese, 1985, (with E. May) America's China Trade in Historical Perspective: Chinese and American Performance, 1985, ; author (6 cassettes of lectures) China Talks, 1974, (15 filmstrips with commentaries) China Old and New, 1975; contbr. numerous articles to profl. jours., newspapers, mags.; numerous appearances on radio and TV shows; lectr. U.S. and abroad. Recipient Harvard medal for svc. to univ. Harvard Alumni Assn., 1986; Rhodes scholar, Peiping, China, 1932; Rockefeller Found. fellow, Peiping, 1933-35; Guggenheim Found. fellow, Japan, 1952-53, 1960; Am. Coun. Learned Socs. travel award, Japan, 1964. Mem. Far Eastern Assn. (v.p. 1950-51), Am. Inst. Pacific Relations (trustee 1947-51), Council on Fgn. Relations, Am. Hist. Assn. (pres. 1968, Centennial keynote speaker 1985), Assn. for Asian Studies (pres. 1959), Nat. Com. U.S.-China Relations, Am. Acad. Arts and Scis., Am. Philos. Soc., Signet Soc., Mass. Hist. Soc., Am. Council of Learned Socs. (Far Eastern Studies com.), Phi Beta Kappa, Beta Theta Pi. Home: Cambridge Mass. Died Sept. 14, 1991; cremated.

FAIRBANK, WILLIAM MARTIN, physicist, educator; b. Mpls., Feb. 24, 1917; s. Samuel Ballantine and Helen Leslie (Martin) F.; m. Jane Davenport, Aug. 16, 1941; children: William Martin, Robert Harold, Richard Dana. A.B., Whitman Coll., Walla Walla, Wash., 1939, D.Sc. (hon.), 1965; postgrad. fellow, U. Wash., 1940-42; M.S., Yale, 1947, Ph.D. (Sheffield fellow), 1948; D.Sc., Duke U., 1969, Amherst Coll., 1972. Instr., mem. staff Radiation Lab. MIT, 1942-45; asst. prof. physics Amherst Coll., 1947-52; asso. prof. Duke U., 1952-58, prof., 1958-59; prof. physics Stanford U., from 1959, Max H. Stein prof. physics, from 1985, prof. emeritus. Bd. overseers Whitman Coll. Named Calif. Scientist of Year Calif. Museum Sci. and Industry, 1961; recipient Fritz London award, 1968; Wilbur Lucius Cross medal Yale U., 1968; Guggenheim fellow, 1976-77. Fellow Am. Phys. Soc. (Oliver E. Buckley Solid State Physics prize 1963, Research Corp. award 1965); mem. AAAS (chmn. physics sect. 1980-81), Nat. Acad. Scis., Am. Acad. Arts and Scis., Am. Philos. Soc. Home: Menlo Park Calif. Died Sept. 30, 1989.

FALK, KARL L., savings and loan executive; b. Berkeley, Calif., Sept. 12, 1911; s. Henry and Helen S. (Ruecker) F.; m. Doris Finger, June 21, 1936. A.B., Stanford U., 1932; Ph.D., U. Berlin, 1936. Mem. faculty dept. fgn. lang. Fresno State Coll. (now Calif. State U. at Fresno), 1938-42, faculty div. soc. sci., 1946-68, head div. social sci., 1950-63, from prof. econs. to prof. econs. emeritus, from 1968, acting pres. coll., 1969-70; chem. economist Dept. Commerce, Washington, 1942; dean Sierra Summer Sch., 1948; Fulbright lectr. Technische Hochschule Stuttgart, Germany, 1954-55; pres. First Savs. & Loan Assn., 1957-75, chmn. bd., 1957-81; dir. Calif. State Internat. Programs, Germany and Sweden, 1963-64; dir. internat. affairs Calif. State Colls., 1965-66; lectr. U.S. Dept. State in, Germany, Austria, 1955, 56, 60, 64. Author articles on chem. developments, European problems, housing and urban renewal problems, others. Mem. U.S. Nat. Commn., UNESCO, 1957-59; Chmn. Fresno City Housing Authority, 1951-69; vice chmn. Fresno County Housing Authority, from 1981, chmn., from 1982 ; pres. Nat. Assn. Housing and Redevel. Ofcls., 1960-61; mem. Calif. Commn. for Housing and Community Devel., 1966-67; bd. dirs., vice chmn. Found. for Coop. Housing, 1965-80, chmn., 1981-88, emeritus chmn., hon. trustee, 1988; chmn. overseas cooperative devel. com., Washington, 1985-86. Served with AUS, 1943-46. Mem. Am. Econ. Assn., Phi Beta Kappa, Pi Gamma Mu, Beta Gamma Sigma. Home: Fresno Calif. Died Sept. 16, 1988; cremated.

FALLS, RAYMOND LEONARD, JR., lawyer; b. Youngstown, Ohio, Feb. 24, 1929; s. Raymond Leonard and Vernita Belle (Bowden) F.; m. Alice Van Fleet, June 22, 1952; children: Janette Rae, Nancy Margaret, Raymond Taylor, Thomas Alan, Lawrence David. B.A., Coll. of Wooster, 1950; LL.B., Harvard U., 1953. Bar: N.Y. 1957, U.S. Supreme Ct. 1961. Law clk. to judge U.S. Ct. Appeals 2d Cir., 1955-56; assoc. Cahill, Gordon & Reindel, N.Y.C., 1956-63, ptnr., 1963-90, sr. counsel, 1990-91; assoc. adj. prof. NYU Law Sch., 1967-73. Mem. Mayor's Task Force on Reorgn. Govt., N.Y.C, 1965-66. Mem. Am. Coll. Trial Lawyers, ABA, Assn. Bar City N.Y. Home: New York NY Died Nov. 10, 1991; buried Prospect Hill Cemetery, Nantucket, Mass.

FALSTEIN, EUGENE I., psychoanalyst, psychiatrist; b. Chgo., Oct. 29, 1908; s. Samuel and Pearl (Levin) F.; m. Charlotte Rosenfield, Dec. 25, 1932. B.S., U. Ill., 1928, M.D., 1930; Rockefeller fellow psychoanalytic tng., Chgo. Inst. Psychoanalysis, 1936-42. Diplomate: Am. Bd. Psychiatry and Neurology. Intern psychiatry Elgin State Hosp., 1930-31, psychiatrist, 1933-37; intern Michael Reese Hosp. and Med. Center, Chgo., 1931-33, psychiat. clinic staff, 1933-40; faculty Northwestern U. Med. Sch., 1933-37; child psychiatrist Inst. Juvenile Research, 1937-42; asst. prof. dept. criminology U. Ill., 1937-51; attending psychiatrist children's div. Ill. Neuropsychiat. Inst., 1940-51; clin. prof. emeritus in psychiatry Chgo. Med. Sch.; pvt. practice psychoanalysis and psychiatry, 1946-88; sr. attending psychiatrist dept. of psychiatry, former chief adolescent care Inst. Psychosomatic and Psychiat. Research and Tng., 1960-75; psychiat. cons., adv. bd. Jewish Children's Bur.; hon. cons. Nicholas Pritzker Children's Center. Author sci. articles, chpts. in books. Bd. dirs. Am. Friends of Hebrew U., founder med. sch.; bd. dirs. Jewish Fedn. Met. Chgo., Am. Jewish Physicians Com. Served as lt. comdr. USNR, 1942-46. Recipient Israel Scroll, 1957, Torch of Learning award Hebrew U., Jerusalem, 1976. Fellow Am. Psychiat. Assn. (life), Am. Orthopsychiat. Assn. (life), Am. Acad. Psychoanalysis (life), Am. Acad. Child Psychiatry (life), AMA; mem. Ill. Med. Soc. (life mem.; mem. 50 Yr. Club), Chgo. Psychoanalytic Soc. (life), Am. Psychoanalytic Assn., Internat. Psychoanalytic Assn., AAAS, Pan Am. Med. Assn. (life), Ill. Council Child Psychiatry (life mem., past pres.), Ill. Psychiat. Soc. (founding mem., past sec., life), Alpha Omega Alpha, Phi Delta Epsilon. Club: Ravisloe Country. Home: Chicago Ill. Died July 6, 1989; buried Westlawn Cemetery, Norridge, Ill.

FANNING, JOHN HAROLD, labor organization executive; b. Putnam, Conn., Sept. 19, 1916; s. John Joseph and Eva Marie (Dumas) F.; m. Eloise Marie Cooney, Dec. 5, 1942 (dec. 1982); children: Mary Ellen Fanning Dunn, John Michael, Ann Eloise Fanning Gallagher, Gaele Therese Fanning De Gross, Stephen Thomas. AB, Providence Coll., 1938, D of Pub. Adminstrn., 1969; LLB, Cath. U. Am., 1941. Bar: R.I. 1941. Pvt. practice R.I., 1941-42; with Dept. Labor, Washington, 1942-43; legal and indsl. rels. adviser depts. War, Army and Def., Washington, 1943-57; mem. NLRB, Washington, 1957-90, chmn., 1977-90. Contbr. articles to various publs. Mem. Cardinal O'Boyle's Com. of Laity for Washington, 1968-90; bd. dirs. Cath. Youth Orgn., Washington. Recipient Ann. Career award Nat. Civil Svc. League, 1957, Meritorious Civilian Svc. medal Dept. Def., 1958. Home: Washington D.C. Died July 21, 1990.

FANNING, WILLIAM LINCOLN, newspaper executive; b. Burlington, Vt., Feb. 12, 1893; s. William and Emile (DuMont) F.; m. Mercy Burgess Dawes, Apr. 11, 1917; children: William Lincoln, Katharine F. (Mrs. Robert S. Potter). Pres., dir. Westchester Rockland Newspapers Inc., White Plains, N.Y., from 1964; pub.

Herald Statesman (Yonkers, N.Y.), Daily Argus (Mt. Vernon, N.Y.), Standard-Star (New Rochelle, N.Y.), Daily Times (Mamaroneck, N.Y.), Daily Item (Port Chester, N.Y.), Reporter Dispatch (White Plains), Daily News (Tarrytown, N.Y.), Citizen Register (Ossining, N.Y.), Rockland Jour.-News (Nyack, N.Y.), Review Press & Reporter (Bronxville, N.Y.). Chmn. bd. commrs. N.Y. State Ins. Fund; bd. dirs. Am. Cancer Soc., Westchester chpt. With U.S. Army, 1918; capt. N.Y. NG, 1919-29, 40-43. Mem. Am. Newspaper Pubs. Assn. (past treas., dir.), N.Y. State Pubs. Assn. (past pres.), N.Y. State Assn. Dailies (past pres.), Sleepy Hollow Country Club, Lake Placid Club. Episc. *

FARIES, MCINTYRE, judge; b. Wei Hsien, Shantung, China, Apr. 17, 1896; s. William R. and Priscilla Ellen (Chittick) F.; m. Margaret Lois Shorten, Oct. 7, 1922 (dec.); children: Barbara Simpson, Marjorie Gaines. AB, Occidental Coll., 1920; student, So. Calif.; JD, Southwestern U., 1926. Bar: Calif. 1922. Assoc. counsel Auto Club of So. Calif., L.A., 1922-24; dep. L.A. Co. Pub. Defender, 1924-26, L.A. Co. Counsel, 1926-27; instr. in law Southwestern, 1927; assoc. Faries and Williamson, 1927; ptnr. Faries & McDowell; judge Superior Ct. Calif., 1953-63; counsel numerous corps., founds., assns., partnerships and individuals. Del. Rep. Nat. Convs., 1936, 40, 44, 48, 52; mem. Rep. Nat. Com., Calif.; also vice chmn., mem. exec. com.; past pres. Calif. Assembly; campaign chmn. So. Calif., 1938, 40, 42, 44; mem. S. Pasadena-San Marino High Sch. Bd., 1940-48, pres., 1948. Mem. Am. Law Inst., U.S. Bar Assn., Calif. Bar Assn., L.A. County Bar Assn., Calif. Water Assn. (past pres.), 6th Dist. Agrl. Assn. (pres.), Am. Acad. Polit. and Social Scis., Judicature Soc., Phi Beta Kappa, Phi Gamma Delta, Phi Delta Phi, Calif. Club, Lincoln Club, Oneonta Club. Republican. Presbyterian. *

FARINHOLT, LARKIN HUNDLEY, foundation executive; b. Balt., Sept. 24, 1905; s. Leroy Whiting and Elizabeth (Gwin) F.; m. Mary Kathryn Snyder, Dec. 26, 1947; children: Larkin Jr., Kathryn, Mary Victoria. BS in Chemistry, Johns Hopkins, 1927, grad. study, 1927-28; DPhil (Rhodes scholar), Oxford U., 1931; DSc (hon.), Clarkson Coll. of Tech., 1967. Asst. prof. chemistry Washington and Lee U., 1933-37, asso. prof., 1937-41; asso. prof. chemistry Columbia U., 1947-54, prof., 1954-60, dir. Chem. Labs, 1953-60; adminstr. program for basic research in phys. scis. Alfred P. Sloan Found., N.Y.C., 1960-73, v.p., 1962-70, trustee, 1962-69, cons., 1971-73; dept. sci. adviser State Dept., 1958-60; sci. attaché Am. Embassy, London, 1951-52; exec. officer Explosives Research Lab., NDRC, OSRD, 1941-45; spl. asst. to chmn. NDRC, 1945-46; mem. Com. Internat. Exchange of Persons, 1953-56. Recipient Presdl. Certificate of Merit. Mem. AAAS, Am. Chem. Soc., Phi Gamma Delta, Omicron Delta Kappa, Tau Beta Pi. Club: Cosmos (Washington). Home: Baltimore Md. Died July 12, 1990.

FARISS, JAMES LEE, JR., health care products and services executive; b. Austin, Tex., July 4, 1934; s. James Lee Sr. and Dolores (Hanson) F.; m. Mary Earl Adkins, Aug. 21, 1959; children: Joe Leslie, Jill Leigh. BBA in Acctg., U. Tex., 1961. CPA, Tex. Controller Brown Schs. subs. Healthcare Internat., Austin, from 1965; pres., chmn. Healthcare Internat., 1979-84; mem. Legis. Task Force on AIDS State of Tex., from 1987. Author: (with others) Hospital Management: Winning Strategies for the 80's, 1985. Precinct chmn. City of Austin; bd. visitors Univ. Cancer Found., U. Tex. M.D. Anderson Cancer Ctr. Served with USN, 1963. Mem. Fedn. Am. Health Systems (bd. dirs. from 1985), U. Texas Chancellor's Coun. Clubs: Capital, Headliners, Austin Country (Austin). Home: Austin Tex. Deceased. †

FARLEY, ROBERT JOSEPH, law educator; b. Hernando, Miss., Dec. 7, 1898; s. Leonard Jerome and Lilian (Lauderdale) F.; m. Alice Lockard, Sept. 7, 1928. AB, U. Miss., 1919, LLB, 1924; JSD, Yale U., 1932. Bar: Miss. 1924. Principal high sch. Canton, Miss., 1919-20, Natchez, Miss., 1920-21; mayor City of Oxford, Miss., 1923-25; mem. firm Somerville and Farley, Oxford, Miss., 1924-29; private practice, 1929-31; city atty. City of Oxford, Miss., 1926-31; asst. prof. law U. Miss., 1926-30, prof. law, 1932-35, dean and prof. law, 1946-63; prof. law Tulane U., 1935-46, dean pro tem, 1942-45; prof. law U. Fla., from 1963. Compiler: Miss. Annotations, Restatement of Law of Trusts, 1937, La. Annotations, Restatement of the Law of Trusts, 1941. With U.S. Army, 1918. Mem. Miss. Bar Assn. (pres. 1954-55), La. Bar Assn. (hon.), New Orleans Bar Assn., Am. Law Inst., La. Law Inst., Miss. Econ. Coun. (dir.), Order of Coif, Phi Delta Phi, Sigma Upsilon, Sigma Chi. *

FARLEY, WALTER LORIMER, author; b. N.Y.C., June 26, 1922; s. Walter Patrick and Isabelle (Vermilyea) F.; m. Rosemary Lutz, May 26, 1945; children: Pamela, Alice, Walter Steven, Timothy. Grad., Mercersburg (Pa.) Acad., 1936; also ed. at, Columbia U., 1941. Author: The Black Stallion, 1941, Black Stallion and Flame, 1960, Black Stallion and Satan, 1949, Black Stallion Challenged, 1964, Black Stallion Mystery, 1957, Black Stallion Returns, 1945, Black Stallion Revolts, 1953, Black Stallion's Courage, 1956, Black Stallion's Filly, 1952, Black Stallion's Sulky Colt, 1954, Blood Bay Colt, 1950, Great Dane Thor, 1968, Horse Tamer, 1958, Horse that Swam Away, 1965, Island Stallion, 1948, Island Stallion Races, 1955, Island Stallion's Fury, 1951, Little Black, a Pony; Little Black Goes to the Circus, 1963, Little Black Pony Races, 1968, Man O'War, 1962, Son of the Black Stallion, 1947, Big Black Horse, 1953, Black Stallion's Ghost, 1969, Black Stallion and the Girl, 1971, The Black Stallion Picture Book, 1979, The Black Stallion Returns Picture Book, 1983, The Black Stallion Comic Book, 1983, The Black Stallion Legend, 1983, The Black Stallion Beginner Book, 1986. Served with AUS, 1941-46. Home: Venice Fla. Died Oct. 16, 1989; cremated.

FARNAM, ANNE, museum executive; b. Chgo., Apr. 6, 1940; d. George B. and Mary E. (Forgan) F. BA, NYU, 1967; MA, U. Conn., 1970; postgrad., Boston U., 1971-77. Curatorial asst. Mus. Fine Arts, Boston, 1974-75; curator Essex Inst., Salem, Mass., 1975-84, pres., from 1984. Contbr. articles to profl. jours. Mem. Colonial Soc. Mass., Costume Soc. Am., Am. Assn. Mus. Home: Salem Mass. Deceased. †

FARNSLEY, CHARLES ROWLAND PEASLEE, publisher; b. Mar. 28, 1907; s. Burrel Hobson and Anna May (Peaslee) F.; m. Nancy Hall Carter, Feb. 27, 1937; children: Sally (Mrs. Robert S. Bird, Jr.), Ann, Alexander, Burrel Charles Peaslee, Douglass Charles Ellerbe. LL.B., U. Louisville, 1930, A.B., 1942, LL.D., 1950; postgrad., U. Ky., 1943-44; LL.D., Wesleyan U., Middletown, Conn., 1959. Practiced law, 1930-48, 54-64; mem. Ky. Ho. of Reps., 1936-40; mayor City of Louisville, 1948-53; mem. 89th Congress, 3d dist. of Ky., 1965-67; pres. Lost Cause Press. Trustee U. Louisville, 1946-48, sec., 1947-48, mem. bd. overseers, 1948-64; curator Transylvania U., Lexington, Ky., 1947-58; trustee Louisville Free Pub. Libr., 1945-48; bd. dirs. Louisville Philharmonic Soc., 1947-48, Louisville Orch. Mem. Soc. Colonial Wars, Delta Upsilon, Omicron Delta Kappa. Democrat. Episcopalian. Clubs: River Valley, Pendennis, Filson (pres. 1979-80) (Louisville); Century (N.Y.C.). Lodge: Masons (Louisville). Home: Louisville Ky. Died June 19, 1990; buried Cave Hill Cemetery, Louisville, Ky.

FARNSWORTH, HARRISON EDWARD, physicist; b. Green Lake, Wis., Mar. 24, 1896; s. Edward H. and Marion (Fortnum) F.; A.B., Ripon Coll., 1918, D.Sc., 1977; A.M., U. Wis., 1921, Ph.D., 1922; D.Sc., Fairfield U., 1971; m. Gertrude Roming, 1925 (dec.); children—Edward Allan, James Alden (dec.); m. Alice Schultze, 1960 (dec.); m. Margaret Bergeron, 1985. Physicist, Western Electric Research Lab., N.Y., 1918; instr. U. Pitts., 1918-19; Nat. Research fellow U. Wis., 1922-24; assoc. prof. physics U. Maine, 1924-26; asst. prof. physics Brown U., 1926-29, assoc. prof., 1929-46, prof., 1946-60, dir. Barus lab. surface physics, 1946-70, research prof., 1960-70, Annette L.R. Barstow Univ. prof., 1963-70, research prof. physics emeritus, 1970; vis. prof. dept. physics U. Ariz., from 1971; dir. Farnsworth Research Lab., Green Valley, Ariz., 1979-84; exec. sec. panel on electron tubes Research and Devel. Bd., dir. coordinating group on electron tube reliability, N.Y.C., 1952-53 (on leave from Brown U.); mem. Planning div. Office Naval Research, summer 1946; cons., 1946-47; cons. Philips Labs., Inc., 1947-49; research physicist on war project Radiation Lab., M.I.T. (leave of absence from Brown U.), 1941; ofcl. investigator N.D.R.C., on war project, Brown U., 1942-43; chmn. dept. physics Brown U., 1942-43, mem. exec. com. dept. physics, 1954-55, mem. Phys. Scis. Council, 1953-63; cons. Lawrence Radiation Lab., Livermore, Calif., 1962-68, Ultek div. Perkin-Elmer Corp., 1965-69, Yale U., 1966-67, Nat. Phys. Research Lab., Pretoria, South Africa, 1970-71; co-operating expert for Internat. Critical Tables; vis. research prof. Wash. State U., summer 1970. Recipient Alumni citation Ripon Coll., 1947, Medal of Merit, 1984 Medard W. Welch award Am. Vacuum Soc., 1981; past fellow Royal Soc. Arts. Fellow AAAS, Am. Phys. Soc., Am. Acad. Arts and Scis.; mem Am. Chem. Soc., Phi Beta Kappa, Sigma Xi, Gamma Alpha. Contbr. numerous sci. articles on electron emission, reflection and diffraction, atomically clean surfaces, reconstrn. of elemental semicondr. surfaces, surface migration, chemisorption, place exchange, oxidation and catalysis, and related subjects. Died Nov. 14, 1989. Home: Tucson Ariz.

FARNSWORTH, RICHARD ARMSTRONG, contractor; b. Henderson, Ky., June 17, 1898; s. Richard Prentiss and Ada (Sisk) F.; m. Dorothy Coyle, Aug. 24, 1921; children: Patricia Farnsworth Jones, Richard Armstrong, Alan Coyle. Student, Washington U., 1917-19, Tulane U., 1919-20. V.p. R.P. Farnsworth & Co., Inc., 1920-49; chmn. bd. Farnsworth & Chambers Co., Inc., 1949-63; chmn. F. & C. Engrng. Co., F. & C. Equip. Co., F. & C. Realty Co., So. Indsl. Piping Co., Farnsworth & Chambers Ltd. Bd. dirs. Stillman Coll., Tuscaloosa, Ala.; mem. internat. com. YMCA, 1943-53, vice chmn. World Svc. Com., 1944-55, bd. dirs., New Orleans, 1937-44; v.p., bd. Houston-Harris Co., 1945-57, pres. S.W. area, 1954; bd. dirs. Houston Symphony Soc., 1947-57, Nat. Recreation Assn.; v.p. Nat. Coun. Chs. of Christ in U.S.A., 1954-57, mem. bd., 1951-63; pres. Tex. Coun. Chs., 1956; mem. Com. Inter-Ch. Relations, Presbyn. Ch. U.S., 1945-53; trustee Tex. Presbyn. Found. Mem. Coun. Christian Relations. Presbyterian. *

FARQUHAR, NORMAN, banker; b. Olney, Md., May 10, 1921; s. Arthur Douglas and Helen (Thomas Nesbitt) F.; m. Ann Randolph Jennings, Oct. 4, 1947 (dec.); children: Katherine, Douglas Brooke, Edward Pleasants, William Thomas Nesbitt, Witt Jennings; m. Elinor Kenney Brown, Jan. 3, 1981; stepchildren: Elizabeth M. Brown, Sarah B. O'Hagan, Marcia B. Brown. BA, U. Va., 1943; LLB, Nat. U., 1954. Bar: D.C. 1954. Asst. sec. Savs. Instn. Sandy Spring, Md., 1946; rep. Alex Brown & Sons, Washington, 1948-58, gen. ptnr., 1958-87; pres. Chevy Chase (Md.) Fed. Savs. Bank, 1988-91; dir. Montgomery Mut. Ins. Co., Sandy Spring, Chevy Chase Savs. Bank. Served to capt. C.E., AUS, 1942-45. Mem. Securities Industry Assn. (past chmn. Mid-Atlantic div.), Delta Psi. Clubs: Metropolitan, Chevy Chase, Alibi. Home: Washington D.C. Died July 14, 1992. †

FARREL, GEORGE T., bank holding company executive; b. 1931; married. B.S., U. Notre Dame, 1953. With Mellon Bank (N.A.), 1955-89, asst. v.p. credit dept., 1962-64, asst. v.p. internat. dept., 1964, v.p. internat. dept., 1966-74, sr. v.p. internat. dept., 1974, exec. v.p., 1978-80, vice chmn., 1980-81, pres., dir., 1981-87, sr. vice chmn., 1987-89; also sr. vice chmn. Mellon Bank Corp.; dir. Banco Bozano, Network Fin. Ltd., First Boston (Europe) Ltd.; v.p. Mellon Nat. Corp. Served with U.S. Army. Mem. Bankers Assn. Fgn. Trade (dir.). Home: Pittsburgh Pa. Died July 7, 1989.

FARRELL, MARIE, university dean; b. West Pittsfield, Mass., July 4, 1897; d. Christopher and Katherine (Canning) Farrell. EdD, Tchrs. Coll., Columbia, 1948. Pvt. duty nurse, 1921-24; gen. staff nurse R.I. Hosp., 1924-25; operating rm. supr., instr. medicine and surg. nursing Homeopathic Hosp., R.I., 1925-30; asst. dir. nursing svcs., also asst. prin. Sch. Nursing, Elizabeth Gen. Hosp., 1932-33, Rochester Gen. Hosp., 1934-37; instr. nursing Tchrs. Coll., Columbia U., 1938-43; nurse edn. cons. div. nursing USPHS, 1943-47; prof. nursing Boston U. Sch. Nursing, 1947-92, acting dean, 1955-57, dean, 1957-64; dean emeritus Boston U. Sch. Nursing, 1964-92; hon. cons. Bur. Medicine and Surgery, USN, 1954-58; cons. tng. com. NIMH, 1954-59; cons. nursing VA Hosp., Brockton, Mass., 1954, 55, Boston, 1955-60, VA Hosp., Providence, 1961-92; bd. govs. Boston U. Human Relations Ctr., 1957-60; co-chmn. Mass. Am. Nurses Found., 1962-63. Exec. editorial bd. Nursing Rsch., 1951-58; contbr. Yearbook of Modern Nursing, 1956-57; contbr. articles to profl. jours. Mem. Com. on Edn. (nursing), State of N.H.; survey nursing edn. N.Y. State Commn. Higher Edn., 1947; mem. N.E. Conf. on Pub. Health Nursing Edn., 1947; adv. com. div. nursing W.K. Kellogg Found., 1950-54; exec. com. Nat. League Nursing Accreditation Svc., 1950-54; adv. com. dept. nursing Mass. State U., R.I. State U., 1953-57; mem. bd. Community Svcs. Orgn., Mass., mem. bd. nursing coun., Boston, 1954-58. Mem. ANA, Nat. League Nursing Edn. (adv. com. jour. 1952, vice chmn. steering com. 1957-60, chmn. subcom. grad. edn. 1958-59), AAUP, Mass. League Nursing (pres. 1953-56, dir.), Am. Pub. Health Assn., Conf. Nursing Rsch. (chmn. 1964), Sigma Theta Tau, Pi Lambda Theta, Kappa Delta Pi. *

FARRINGER, JOHN LEE, JR., surgeon, educator; b. Bowling Green, Ky., Sept. 4, 1920; s. John Lee and Zora (Lawson) F.; B.A., Vanderbilt U., 1942; M.D., U. Tenn., 1945, M.S., 1950; m. Mary Margaret Smith, Mar. 8, 1947; children: John Lee, III, Janice Ann, Mary Jill. Intern, Harris Meml. Meth. Hosp., Ft. Worth, 1946; resident John Gaston and U. Tenn. Hosp., Memphis, 1949-54; practice surgery, Nashville, 1954-90; asst. clin. prof. surgery Vanderbilt U. Sch. Medicine, 1956-84, assoc. clin. prof. surgery, 1984-89, clin. prof. surgery, 1989-90; chief surgery Baptist Hosp., Nashville, 1966-69, pres. staff, 1971, vice chief staff, 1973-75, chief of staff, 1976-78; assoc. clin. prof. Surgery U. Tenn., 1983-85. Coord. Battle Nashville Centennial Commemoration, 1964; chmn. Met. Hist. Commn., Nashville, 1966-73; exec. bd. Middle Tenn. council Boy Scouts Am., from 1961 (Disting. Eagle Scout award, 1986); pres. Davidson County Found. for Med. Care, 1973-75; mem. Statewide Health Coordinating Council, 1977-81. Col. Tenn. Def. Force, 1984-87, brig. gen., 1988-90; bd. dirs. Davidson County unit Am. Cancer Soc., Davidson County Council Retarded Children, Police Assistance League, Profl. Systems Nashville, Tenn., Middle Tenn. Health Systems Agy.; ms Agy.; trustee Parkview Hosp., 1970-73. Served with AUS, 1943-45. Diplomate Am. Bd. Surgery. Fellow Soc. for Surgery of Alimentary Tract, A.C.S. (pres. Tenn. chpt. 1983-84, gov. 1987-89), Southeastern Surg. Congress, Collegium Internationale Chirurgiae Digestivae, SociétéInternational de Chirurgie, So. Surg. Assn., Am. Geriatric Soc.; mem. Nashville Acad. Medicine (dir. 1970-73), Davidson County Med. Soc. (dir. 1970-73), So. Med. Assn., Nashville Surg. Soc. (pres. 1973), Harwell Wilson Surg. Soc. (pres. 1977-78), Co. Mil. Historians, Assn. Mil. Surgeons of U.S., Nashville Area C. of C., Alpha Kappa Kappa. Clubs: Richland Country, Nashville City, University (Nashville). Contbr. articles to surg. jours. Died Sept. 19, 1990; buried Mt. Olivet Cemetery, Nashville. Home: Nashville Tenn.

FARRIOR, JEWEL REX, lawyer; b. Chipley, Fla., Oct. 5, 1896; s. Joseph R. and Gussie (Brown) F.; m. Lera Spotswood Finley, Nov. 24, 1925; children: Jewel Rex, Anne Preston Farrior King Jr., Jennie Finley Farrior Cornelius Jr. AB, U. Fla., 1916, JD, 1924. Bar: Fla. 1924. Asst. football coach, tchr. history, algebra, Latin U. Fla., Gainesville, 1917-18; tchr. history, algebra, Latin, coach high schs. in Chipley, Pensacola, Gainesville, 1919-23; fresman football/basketball coach, varsity baseball coach U. Fla., 1923-24; ptnr. Shackieford, Farrior, Stallings, Glos & Evans, 1924-92; state atty. 13th Jud. Cir., Fla., 1933-53. With F.A., U.S. Army, 1918-19. Mem. ABA, Fla. Bar Assn., Tampa Bar Assn., Blue Key, Masons, Shriners, Jester, Elks, K.P., Palma Cela Golf and Country Club, Tampa Yacht and Country Club, Kiwanis, Kappa Alpha, Phi Kappa Phi, Phi Delta Phi. *

FARRIS, MILTON GLENN, oil company executive; b. Rockwood, Tenn., Oct. 13, 1906; s. Oscar Alexander and Myrtle Amy (Derrick) F.; LL.B., Atlanta Law Sch., 1935; m. Elizabeth Herzberg, Nov. 15, 1934; children—Sandra Glyn, Janet Gail, Milton Carl, William, Stuart. Admitted to Ga. Bar, 1935; practiced in Atlanta from 1935; asso. Atlanta div. Gulf Oil Corp., from 1927, mgr. bus analysis, market research, 1954-59, mgr. marketing services, 1960-62, mgr. Atlanta div., 1962-65, v.p., from 1965 . Alderman, City Council, Atlanta, 1952-69; county commr. Fulton County, from 1971. Pres. bd. trustees Atlanta Pub. Library, 1940-52, awarded Trustee Citation at ALA Chgo. Conf. 1951. Mem. Am. Bar Assn., Ga. Bar Assn., West End Business Men's Assn. (dir.). Methodist. Mason (past master), Lion (past pres.), Kiwanian. Clubs: Commerce, Capital City, Atlanta City (Atlanta). Died June 19, 1989; buried Arlington Cemetery, Sandy Springs, Ga. Home: Atlanta Ga.

FATEMI, NASROLLAH SAIFPOUR, social sciences educator; b. Nain, Iran, June 15, 1910; came to U.S., 1946, naturalized, 1960; s. Saifulolma and Tuba (Tabe Tabai) F.; m. Shayesteh Ostowar, May 10, 1932; children: Faramarz, Fariborz, Farivar. B.A. with honors, Stuart Meml. Coll., Isfahan, Iran, 1932; M.A., Columbia U., 1949; Ph.D., New Sch. Social Research, 1954; LL.D., Kyung Hee U., Korea, 1973, Fairleigh Dickinson U., 1979. Mem., v.p. legislative council Province Isfahan, Iran, 1936-39; mayor Shiraz, Iran, 1939-41; gov.-gen. Province Fars, Iran, 1941-43; mem. Iranian Parliament, 1943-47; rep. Iran UNESCO Conf., 1948, Internat. Congress Americanists, 1949; del. Iran to UN, 1952-53; mem. Iranian Mission presenting case of Iran to UN Security Council, 1951; econ., polit. adviser Permanent Delegation Iran to UN, 1952-53; lectr. Asia Inst., 1949; tchr. Oriental culture and civilization Princeton U., 1950-55; prof. social scis. Fairleigh Dickinson U., 1955-81, chmn. dept., 1960-65, disting. prof. internat. affairs, 1971-81, dean Grad. Sch., 1965-71, dir. Grad. Inst. for Internat. Studies,, 1971-81; chmn. exec. com. Inter-Univ. Centre Post-Grad. Studies, Dubrovnik, Yugoslavia, from 1972; dir. Midland Bank, N.J. Author: Diplomatic History of Persia, 1951, Oil Diplomacy, 1954, The Dollar Crisis, 1964, (with others) Humanities in the Age of Science, 1967, While the United States Slept, 1982, (autobiography in Farsi) Reflections on the Time of Illusion, 1990, also 5 books in Persian; editor: Problems of Balance of Payment and Trade, 1974, Multinational Corporations, 1975, Sufism, 1976, Love, Beauty, and Harmony in Sufism, 1978. Former mem. environmental com. Borough of Saddle River.; Bd. dirs. United Fund of Bergen County, Health and Welfare Council of Bergen County; trustee Jersey State Coll.; mem. Commn. for UN Yr. of Peace. Honored for contbns. to Iranian-Am. community by grads. of Shiraz Med. Coll., Iran, 1989. Fellow Royal Acad. Arts and Scis.; mem. Internat. Assn. Univ. Pres. (mem.-at-large governing bd.), Acad. Polit. Sci., Inst. Mediterranean Affairs (vice chmn.). Home: Saddle River NJ Died Mar. 23, 1990; buried Hackensack (N.J.) Cemetery.

FAUCHER, ALBERT, economic historian; b. Beauce, Que., Can., July 20, 1915; s. Joseph and Tardif Corinne F.; m. Louisette Couture, Aug. 10, 1946; children: Louis, Adele Faucher Mainguy, Antoine, Francois. B.A., U. Montreal (1938); licentiate social sci., Laval U., 1941; M.A., U. Toronto, 1945. Prof. econ. history U. Laval, from 1945, now prof. emeritus; vis. prof. McGill U., 1970-71. Author: Histoire economique et Unité Canadienne, 1970, Quebec en Amerique au XIXe Siècle, 1973. Nuffield fellow London Sch. Econs., 1953-54; Can. Council fellow, 1969-70; recipient Can. Gov. Gen.'s Lit. award, 1973; Leon-Gerin award for the social scis. Govt. of Que., 1985; Esdras-Minville medal St. John the Baptist Soc. Montreal, 1988. Mem. Royal Soc. Can. (Innis-Gerin medal 1989). Social Democrat. Roman Catholic. Home: Sillery Can. Deceased. †

FAULK, JOHN HENRY, author, humorist, lecturer; b. Austin, Tex., Aug. 21, 1913; s. John Henry and Martha Cynthia (Miner) F.; m. Elizabeth Peake, May 29, 1965; 1 son, John Henry III; children by previous marriage: Tannehill, Johanna, Evelyn, Frank Dobie. BA in English, U. Tex., 1936, MA, 1940. Fellow Julius Rosenwald Found., 1941-42; mem. faculty dept. English U. Tex., 1942; field dir. A.R.C., Cairo, Egypt, 1942-44; star radio programs CBS, N.Y.C., 1946-48; star John Henry Faulk Show sta. WCBS, 1951-57; star It's News to Me CBS-TV, 1953-55, star Leave it to the Girls, 1953-55, star Walk a Mile for a Camel, 1953-55; lectr. on humor and Am. heritage, 1949-65; appeared in movies All the Way Home, 1963, The Best Man, 1964. Author: Fear on Trial, 1964. Precinct chmn. Austin Dem. Com.; mem. Travis County Dem. Exec. Com. With AUS, 1944-46. Mem. AFTRA (past v.p.), SAG, Internat. Platform Assn. (bd. govs. 1967-90). Home: Madisonville Tex. Died Apr. 9, 1990.

FAULKNER, EDWIN JEROME, insurance company executive; b. Lincoln, Nebr., July 5, 1911; s. Edwin Jerome and Leah (Meyer) F.; m. Jean Rathburn, Sept. 27, 1933 (dec. Feb. 1991). B.A., U. Nebr., 1932; M.B.A., U. Pa., 1934. With Woodmen Accident & Life Co., Lincoln, 1934-92; successively claim auditor, v.p. Woodmen Accident & Life Co., 1934-38, pres., dir., 1938-77, chmn. bd., chief exec. officer, 1977-83, hon. chmn., exec. counsel, 1983-92; pres., dir. Comml. Mut. Surety Co., 1938-92; dir. Lincoln Telecomm., Inc.; chmn. Health Ins. Coun., 1959-60; mem. adv. coun. on social security HEW, 1974-75. Author: Accident and Health Insurance, 1940, Health Insurance, 1960; Editor: Man's Quest for Security, 1966. Chmn. Lincoln-Lancaster County Plan Commn., 1948-67; mem. medicare adv. com. Dept. Def., 1957-70; Neb. Republican State Finance chmn., 1968-73; past chmn., trustee Bryan Meml. Hosp.; past trustee Doane Coll., 1961-70, Lincoln Found., Am. Coll. Life Underwriters; trustee Cooper Found.; hon. trustee Newcomen Soc. N.Am.; past chmn. bd. trustees U. Nebr. Found.; past bd. dirs. Nebraskans for Pub. TV., Bus. Industry Polit. Action Com., Washington. Lt. col. USAAF, 1942-45. Decorated Legion of Merit; recipient Disting. Service award U. Nebr., 1957; Harold R. Gordon Meml. award Internat. Assn. Health Ins. Underwriters, 1955, Ins. Man of Year award Ins. Field, 1958; Dist. Service award Nebr. Council on Econ. Edn., 1986, Exec. of Yr. award Am. Coll. Hosp. Adminstrs., 1971; Nebr. Builders award, 1979; Disting. Service award Lincoln Kiwanis Club, 1980. Mem. Health Ins. Assn. Am. (1st pres. 1956), Am. Legion, Am. Life Conv. (exec. com. 1961-70, pres. 1966-67), Ins. Econs. Soc. (chmn. 1971-73), Nebr. Hist. Soc. (pres. 1982-84), Ins. Fedn. Nebr. (pres.), Masons, Elks, Phi Beta Kappa, Phi Kappa Psi, Alpha Kappa Psi (hon.). Republican. Presbyterian. Home: Lincoln Nebr. Died Oct. 9, 1992. †

FAULKNER, JAMES MORISON, internist; b. Keene, N.H., Dec. 16, 1898; s. Herbert K. and Emily (Morison) F.; m. Mary B. duPont, Sept. 1, 1928; children: H. Kimball, Elise, Emily M., Charles S., Rosemary, Henry B., Andrew G. AB, Harvard U., 1920, MD, 1924; ScD, Boston U., 1959. Diplomate Am. Bd. Internal Medicine. Intern Mass. Gen. Hosp., 1924-25, asst. to out patients, 1927-38; asst. resident physician Hosp. of Rockefeller Inst., 1926, Johns Hopkins Hosp., 1926-27; mem. vis. staff Boston City Hosp., 1928-47, dir. 1st and 3d med. svcs., 1945-47; physician Mass. Meml. Hosps., 1940-43; asst. and instr. Harvard Med. Sch., Boston, 1928-40; asst. prof. medicine Boston U. Sch. Medicine, 1940-43, prof. clin. medicine, 1947-58; dean Boston U. Sch. Medicine, 1947-55; dir. Boston U.-Mass. Meml. Hosps. Med. Ctr., 1961; med. dir. MIT, 1955-60, cons. in medicine, 1960-92; prof. medicine Tufts Coll. Med. Sch., 1943-47. Trustee Phillips Exeter Acad., 1954-60; mem. New Eng. Bd. Higher Edn., 1955-58, Nat. Bd. Med. Examiners, 1956-92; bd. overseers Harvard Coll., 1958-64; pres. Nat. Fund for Med. Edn., 1964-92; pres. Med. Found., Inc., 1957-60; mem. bd. dirs. United Health Found., Unitarian Svc. Com. With C.E. 1917-19; lt. comdr. M.C. USNR, 1935-42, capt. 1944. Decorated Croix de Guerre, 1918, Navy Commendation Ribbon, 1944. Fellow ACP, Royal Soc. Medicine; mem. Am. Acad. Arts and Scis., Mass. Med. Soc., AMA, Am. Heart Assn., Am. Soc. for Clin. Investigation, Am. Clin. and Climatol. Soc. Republican. *

FAUNTLEROY, JOHN DOUGLASS, SR., judge; b. Washington, Sept. 6, 1920; s. Frederick Douglass and Esther Mary (Webb) F.; m. Phyllis Elizabeth Gibbs, Sept. 21, 1946; children: Phylicia A., Jacqueline I. Fauntleroy Barber-Long, John Douglass, Frederick G. LL.B, Robert H. Terrell Law Sch., Washington, 1941; B.S. in Govt., Am. U., Washington, 1953; post-grad., Georgetown U., Nat. Coll. State Judiciary, U. Nev. Bar: D.C. 1942, U.S. Dist. Ct. D.C., U.S. Ct. Appeals (D.C. cir.), U.S. Supreme Ct. Adjudicator, reviewer, sr. adjudicator, supr., instr. Office Dependency Benefits, Newark, 1942-46; pvt. practice law Washington, 1947-67; law mem. Bd. of Appeals and Rev., Washington, 1960-67; mem. Spl. Police Trial Bd., Washington, 1966-67; assoc. judge Juvenile Ct. of D.C., Washington, 1967-71; assoc. judge Superior Ct. of D.C., Washington, 1971-83, sr. judge, 1983-85, 89; ct. monitor, spl. asst. to mayor to insure D.C. compliance with ct. orders City of Washington, 1986-89; spl. officer U.S. Dist. Ct. D.C., 1987-89; mem. Jud. Conf. D.C. Circuit, 1960-67, 1981, 1982; mem. adv. bd. Law Students in Court, Washington, from 1974; mem. vol. faculty continuing legal edn. program Georgetown U. Law Sch., 1978-81; bd. dirs. Potomac Sch. Law, Washington, 1976-78, 1979-81. Mem. D.C. Democratic Cen. Com., 1964-67; vice chmn. spl. com. on met. orgns. Inter-Fedn. Council of Greater Washington Met. Area, 1962-64; mem. panel on human relations Police Acad., Met. Police Dept., 1962-63; bd. dirs. Neighbors, Inc., 1962-65, United Planning Orgns, 1965-79; mem. Citizens Adv. Com. to Supt. of Schs., 1966-68; pres. United Planning Orgn., 1971-72; bd. dirs. Info. Ctr. for Handicapped Children, from 1971, Capitol View Devel. Corp., from 1967, past mem. bd. dirs. D.C. Soc. for Crippled Children, 1971-78; mem. adv. bd. Crime Stoppers Club, Inc., Continental Soc.; substitute trustee Marion P. Shadd Scholarship Fund for Needy Female Grads. of McKinley Tech. High Sch., 1956; consumer rep. Devel. Disabilities State Planning Council, 1979-84; trustee Tabor Presbyn. Ch. (name now Northeastern Presbyn. Ch.), 1942-57, pres. bd. trustees, 1947-56, ch. atty., 1947-66, elder, 1971-74 76-78; info. program officer U.S. Naval Acad., 1975, D.C. coordinator, from 1979; mem. recruiting dist. adv. com., U.S. Navy, from 1975, ; mem. vis. com. Sch. Social Work, Howard U., 1976-85; mem. adv. bd. Georgetown U. Child Devel. Ctr., from 1978; mem. genetics adv. panel Georgetown Hosp., George Washington Hosp., Howard U. Hosp., Children's Hosp., from 1980, Served to comdr. USNR, 1973-81. Recipient George W. Norris Civil Rights award Anti-Defamation League B'nai B'rith and Am. Vets. Com., 1965; plaque of appreciation for service D.C. Assn. for Retarded Citizens, Inc., 1977; Mayor of D.C. Proclamation Day in his honor, 1983; Meritorious Service award Am. Vets. Com., 1983; named Disting. Alumnus Am. U., 1984; plaque for outstanding service Washington Recruiting Dist. USN, 1984; numerous other honors and awards. Honored with Ceremonial Resolution in Coun of D.C. The D.C. Register, 1989. Mem. Bar Assn. D.C. (cert. of appreciation 1983), D.C. Bar, Washington Bar Assn. (pres. 1962-64, plaque 1968), ABA (del. jud. adminstrv. div. 1969-83, chmn. standing com. lawyers in armed forces 1982-85), Nat. Bar Assn. (chmn. jud. com. 1979-81), Judge Advs. Assn. (nat. pres. 1984-85),VFW, Nat. Naval Officers Assn. (disting. mem.; pres. 1980-82). Democrat. Presbyterian. Home: Washington DC Died Oct. 29, 1989; buried Arlington Nat. Cemetery.

FEDELI, FREDERICK, insurance company executive; b. 1931; married. AB, Dartmouth Coll., 1953, MBA, 1954. With State Mut. Life Assurance Co. Am., 1953-89, exec. v.p., 1972-80, pres., chief exec. officer, 1980-89, also bd. dirs. Served with AUS, 1955-57. Home: Worcester Mass. Died Mar. 21, 1989.

FEIN, MARVIN MICHAEL, chemical company executive; b. Bklyn., July 31, 1923; s. William and Shirley (Nathanson) F.; m. Bernice Lillian Leiderman, June 8, 1946; children: David Andrew, Carrie Susan. AB, Brooklyn Coll., 1943; MS, Purdue U., 1948, PhD, 1949. Research chemist Allied Chem. Nat. Aniline, Buffalo, 1949-55; research supr. Reaction Motors div. Thiokol Chem., Denville, N.J., 1955-64; tech. dir. GAF Corp., Linden, N.J., 1964-70; v.p. research Dart Industries, Paramus, N.J., 1970-73, v.p. research and devel., 1973-83, v.p. sales and market Dartco Mfg. div., 1983-85, sr. v.p. bus. devel. Dartco Mfg. div., 1985-88; pres., chief exec. officer Corp. for Application of Rutgers Rsch., Piscataway, N.J., 1988-90. Candidate Town Council Dem. Party, Westfield, N.J., 1959. Served with U.S. Army, 1943-46. Research fellow Westinghouse/Purdue U., 1947; free grant research fellow Purdue U., 1947-49. Mem. Am. Chem. Soc. (treas. 1947-48), Assn. Research Dirs. (bd. dirs. N.Y. area 1979-82, 83-86), Orgn. Assn. Research Dirs. (bd. dirs. 1980-82), Ind. Research Inst. (bd. dirs. 1982-85) Sigma Xi, Phi Lambda Upsilon. Home: Westfield NJ Died July 17. 1990.

FEINBERG, GERALD, physics educator; b. N.Y.C., May 27, 1933; s. Leon and Florence (Weingarten) F.; m. Barbara J. Silberdick, Aug. 9, 1968; children—Jeremy Russell, Douglas Loren. B.A., Columbia U., 1953, M.A., 1954, Ph.D., 1957. NSF postdoctoral fellow Inst. Advanced Study, Princeton, N.J., 1956-57; rsch. assoc. Brookhaven Nat. Lab., Upton, N.Y., 1957-59, cons., 1960-74; also rsch. assoc. Stanford (Calif.) Linear Accelerator; faculty physics dept. Columbia U., N.Y.C., 1959-92, prof., 1965-92, chmn. dept., 1980-82; vis. prof. Rockefeller U., 1966-67, 1986. Author: The Prometheus Project, 1969, What is the World Made Of?, 1977, Consequences of Growth, 1977, Life Beyond Earth, 1980, Solid Clues, 1985, Cosmological Constants, 1986, also several texts on physics and cosmology; div. assoc. editor: Phys. Rev. Letters, 1983-86; Contbr. numerous articles to profl. jours. Recipient Great Tchr. award Columbia U., 1987; fellow Sloan Found., 1960-64, Overseas fellow Churchill Coll., Cambridge, Eng., 1963-64, Guggenheim Found. fellow, 1973-74. Fellow Am. PHys. Soc.; mem. Columbia U. Grad Faculties Alumni Assn. (bd. dirs. 1981-82), Sigma Xi. Home: New York NY Died May 21, 1992; buried N.Y.C.

FELDER, JEROME SOLON See POMUS, DOC

FELDMAN, ARBRAHAM JEHIEL, rabbi; b. Kiev, Ukraine, June 28, 1893; s. Jehiel and Elka (Rubin) F.; m. Helen Bloch, June 2, 1918; children: Daniel Bloch, Joan Helen Feldman Necklenburger, Ella Feldman Norwood. B.Hebrew Lit., Hebrew Union Coll., Cin., 1913, DD, 1944; AB, U. Cin., 1917; STD, Trinity Coll., 1953. Rabbi, 1918. Rabbi Free Synagogue, N.Y.C., 1981-19, Congregation Children of Israel, Athens, Ga., 1919-20, Ref. Congregation Keneseth Israel, Phila., 1920-25, Congregation Beth Israel, Hartford, Conn., 1925-92; lectr. O.T. Hartford Theol. Sem., 1954-92; assoc. editor English Yiddish Ency. Dictionary, 1910-12, Jewish Ledger; dir. Jewish Social Svc., Mt. Sinai Hosp., Hartford Jewish Fedn., Julius Hartt Mus. Found., Hebrew Home for Aged. Author numerous books since 1920, latest being: Reform Judaism -- a Guide, 1953;

contbr. to Universal Jewish Ency., the 20th Century Ency. of Religious Knowledge. Incorporator United War and Community Funds of Conn.; mem. exec. bd. Union Am.-Hebrew Congregations, 1945-49, 58-92; trustee, nat. co-chmn. on religious groups People to People Fedn.; founder, regent U. Hartford; mem. bd. dirs. Hillyer Coll., Hartt Coll. of Music, Am. Bibl. Ency., Hartford Jewish Community Ctr.; nat. co-chmn. Consultative Coun. on Desegregation, 1957—; chmn. Conn. Adv. Com. to U.S. Commn. Civil Rights, 1958-92; bd. trustees Union Am. Hebrew Congregations, 1956-92, others. Recipient Americanism and Civic award Conn. Valley coun. B'nai B'rith, 1955, George Washington medal of honor Freedoms Found., 1958. Mem. Cen. Conf. Am. Rabbis (pres. 1947-49), Am. Jewish Hist. Soc., Masons (32 degree), B'nai B'rith, K.P., Phi Epsilon Pi (nat. chaplain 1938), Rotary (pres. 1957-58), Get-Together Club, Tumble Brook Country Club. *

FELDMANN, HENRY, electronics company executive; b. Bremerhafen, Germany, Dec. 12, 1896; came to U.S. 1927, naturalized, 1944; s. Heinrich and Dora (Seidensticker) F.; m. Elisabeth Boede, May 21, 1928. Plant mgr. indsl. corp. Germany, to 1927; supr. plant Westinghouse Elec. Corp., 1927-44; ptnr. F.R. Machine Works, Inc. and predecessor firms, Woodside, N.Y., 1944-52, pres., 1952-58; pres., gen. mgr. FXR, Inc., 1958-59, 61, chmn. bd., 1960-61; bd. dirs. Amphenol-Borg Electronics Corp.; chmn. FXR div., 1961-65. Mem. Inst. Radio Engrs. *

FENDER, CLARENCE LEO, guitar manufacturing company executive; b. Anaheim, Calif., Aug. 10, 1909; s. Clarence Montraville and Harriet Elvina (Wood) F.; m. Esther Marie Klotzly, Aug. 1, 1934 (dec. Aug., 1979); m. Phyllis Marie Dalton, Sept. 20, 1980. Jr. Acct., Fullerton Jr. Coll. Acct. Calif. Hwy. Dept., San Luis Obispo, 1931-35; owner, pres. radio repair shop Fullerton, Calif., 1935-44; owner, pres. Fender Instruments, Fullerton, 1944-65, C.L.F. Research, Inc., Fullerton, 1976-80, G & L Musical Products, Inc., Fullerton, from 1980; cons. CBS Musical Instruments, Fullerton, 1965-70. Patentee Broadcaster guitar, renamed Telecaster, 1948; inventor electric bass guitar, 1951. Recipient Pres.'s award Country Music Assn., Nashville, 1965; recipient Pioneer award Acad. Country Music, Hollywood, Calif., 1982; named to Country Music Hall of Fame. Republican. Club: Century (Fullerton). Home: Fullerton Calif. Died Mar. 21, 1991.

FENN, HENRY COURTENSY, foreign language educator; b. Peking, China, Feb. 26, 1894; s. Courtenay Hughes and Alice Holstein (May) F.; m. Constance Latimer Sargent, Jan. 27, 1925; children: Courtenay, Robert, David Donald. BA, Hamilton Coll., 1916; MA, Columbia U., 1929; student, tchrs. coll., 1936-40. Ednl. missionary China, 1920-27; faculty Oak Lane Country Day Sch. of Temple U., Phila., 1929-35, Lincoln Sch. of Tchrs. Coll., N.Y.C., 1935-41, Presidio Hill Sch., San Francisco, 1941-43; faculty dept. Oriental Studies Yale U., New Haven, 1943-46; faculty Inst. Far Eastern Langs. Yale U., 1949-63, dir., 1953-63, emeritus, 1963-92; mem. faculty Darmouth Coll., 1964-66; pres. Coll. Chinese Studies, Peiping, China, 1946-48; dir. Chinese Lang. Info. Ctr., MLA, 1963-92; cons. U.S. Office Edn., 1960-63, N.Y. State Dept. Edn., 1963, Dartmouth, 1963. Author: Syllabus of Chinese History and Culture (with Goodrich), 1951; A Sketchof Chinese History in Yale Romanization, 1952; contbr. articles to profl. jours. 2nd lt. F.A., U.S. Army, 1917-18. Mem. MLA, Chinese Lang. Tchrs. Assn., Assn. for Asian Studies, Rotary, Yale-in-China (bd. trustees), Phi Delta Kappa. *

FENTON, JOHN E., judge; b. Concord, N.H., Aug. 28, 1898; s. Eugene and Margaret (Holden) F.; m. Elizabeth A. McMahon, June 26, 1929; 1 child, John E. BA, Holy Cross Coll., 1920, LLD, 1956; LLB, Suffolk U., 1924, JSD, 1949. Bar: Mass. 1925. Tchr. Lawrence (Mass.) Continuation Sch., 1920-23; tchr. Lawrence High Sch., 1923-29, faculty mgr. athletics, 1924-29; registrar of deeds N. Dist. Essex County, 1929-37; judge Mass. Land Ct., 1937-92; trustee Community Savs. Bank, Lawrence; dir. Arlington Trust Co., Lawrence. Past pres. Lawrence Community Chest; v.p., trustee Suffolk U.; bd. dirs. Lawrence Boys Club, Lawrence United Fund, St. Ann's Orphanage and Home, Methuen, Mass; chmn. trustees Paul A. Dever State Sch., Taunton, Mass. With U.S. Army, WW I. Named knight Holy Sepulchre, 1951, knight Grand Cross Holy Sepulchre, 1958. Mem. ABA, Mass. Bar Assn., Mass. Jud. Coun., Elks (pres. Mass. 1948-49, mem. com. judiciary Grand Lodge 1950-60, chmn. com. 1957-60, grand exalted ruler 1960-61, sec. Elks Nat. Found. Trustees 1961-92). *

FENWICK, MILLICENT HAMMOND, diplomat, former congresswoman; b. N.Y.C., Feb. 25, 1910; d. Ogden Haggerty and Mary Picton (Stevens) Hammond; children: Mary Fenwick Reckford, Hugh. Student, Columbia Extension Sch., New Sch. for Social Research. Assoc. editor Conde Nast Publs., 1938-52; mem. N.J. Gen. Assembly, 1969-73; dir. div. consumer affairs N.J. Dept. Law and Pub. Safety, 1973-74; mem. 94th-97th Congresses from N.J. 5th Dist., 1975-83; U.S. amb. UN Food and Agr. Orgn., 1983-87. Author: Vogue's Book of Etiquette, 1948, Speaking Up, 1982. Vice chmn. N.J. advisory com. to U.S. Commn. on Civil Rights, 1958-72; mem. Bernardsville (N.J.) Bd. Edn., 1938-41; mem Bernardsville Borough Council, 1958-64. Republican. Home: Bernardsville N.J. Died Sept. 16, 1992. †

FERBER, HERBERT, artist; b. N.Y.C., Apr. 30, 1906; s. Louis and Hattie (Lebowitz) Silvers; m. Edith Popiel, Feb. 1967. Student, CCNY, 1927, Columbia U., 1930. Free-lance painter and sculptor, 1930-91; one-man shows include Andre Emmerich Gallery, N.Y.C., 1960-77, Kootz Gallery, N.Y.C., 1955, 57, Betty Parsons Gallery, 1947, 56, 57, Walker Art Ctr., Mpls., 1962, Whitney Mus. Am. Art, 1961, Knoedler & Co., N.Y.C., 1978-91, Houston Mus. Fine Arts, 1981, Lorenzelli Fine Arts, Milan, Italy, Adams Milleton Gallery, Dallas; group shows include Mus. Modern Art, N.Y.C., 1952, 68, Antwerp (Belgium) Biennale, 1971, Nat. Coll. Fine Arts, Washington, 1976; metal constrn. commn. (And The Bush Was Not Consumed) for facade B'nai Israel Synagogue, Milburn, N.J., 1952, also included in Fifteen Americans show Mus. Modern Art, 1952, other commns. include copper sculpture John F. Kennedy office bldg., Boston, steel sculpture ADA bldg., Chgo.; represented permanent collections mus. throughout U.S. and Europe including Nat. Gallery Fine Arts, Washington, Mus. Modern Art, N.Y.C., Met. Mus. Art, N.Y.C., Whitney Mus. Am. Art, N.Y.C., Houston Mus. Fine Arts, Norton Simon Mus., Pasadena, Calif., Princeton Art Gallery, N.J., Centre Georges Pompidou, Paris; subject of book by Eugene Goossen. Home: New York NY Died Aug. 20, 1991; buried North Egremont, Mass.

FERGUSON, ARDALE WESLEY, industrial supply executive; b. Cedar Springs, Mich., Aug. 6, 1908; s. George Ardale and Alice Lucina (Andrus) F.; student pub. schs.; m. Hazel Frances Lokker, Oct. 28, 1931; children: Constance Ann Ferguson Klaasen, Mary Alice Ferguson Ritsema, Judy Kaye Furguson Ruffino; m. 2d G. Dolores Laker, Aug. 1976. Sales exec. John Deere Plow Co., Lansing, Mich., 1935-50; exec.-treas., mgr. Ferguson Welding Supply Co., Benton Harbor, Mich., 1950-76; sec.-treas. Lape Steel Stores, Inc., Benton Harbor, 1955-85; dir. Modern Light Metals, Inc. Mem. Benton Twp. Bd. Rev., 1963, Mich. Econ. Advancement Council, 1963-64; chmn. Mich. Hwy. Commn., 1964-68; pres. Twin Cities Community Chest, 1956. Treas. Mich. Republican Central Com., 1957-61; del. to Rep. Nat. Conv., 1960. Recipient award of spl. merit, Twin Cities Community Chest, 1956; named to Mich. Transp. Hall of Honor, 1984. Methodist. Clubs: Mountain Shadows Country, Peninsular. Lodges: Rotary, Free and Associated Masons (master 1933). Died Mar. 25, 1990; buried Paradise Meml. Gardens, Scottsdale, Ariz. Home: Troy Mich.

FERGUSON, MALCOLM P., company executive; b. Elmira Heights, N.Y., June 20, 1896; s. John C. and Ina (Fisher) F.; m. Vera Kilmer, Nov. 17, 1923. ME, Syracuse U., 1918, DSc, 1956; student, Navy Steam Engring. Sch., 1918; LLD, Mich. State U., 1962. Field engr. Eclipse Machine Co., Elmira, N.Y., 1919, asst. gen. mgr., 1938; gen. mgr. Bendix Products div. Bendix Aviation Corp., 1938-41, v.p., 1941-42, group exec., 1942-46, pres., dir., 1946-65, chmn. fin. com. and dir., 1965-92; dir. U.S. Rubber Co., Mich. Bell Tel. Co., Nat. Bank of Detroit; mem. bd. govs., exec. com. Aerospace Industries Assn. Mem. Def. Industry Adv. Coun.; bd. devel. coun. U. Mich.; mem. exec. adv. coun. Mich. State U. Grad. Sch. Bus. Adminstrn. Ensign USNR, 1918-19. Decorated French Legion of Honor, 1958. Mem. SAE, Inst. Aero. Schs., Athletic Club, Econ. Club Detroit, Masons, K.T., Tau Beta Pi, Phi Kapopa Phi. Republican. Presbyterian. *

FERNALD, CHARLES EDWARD, transportation company executive; b. Downington, Pa., Sept. 28, 1902; s. Josiah Pennell and Sophia (Weltner) F.; m. Getrude Marie Connell, Oct. 17, 1936; 1 son, Charles Edward. Student mech. engring., Drexel Inst. Tech., 1921-24, Wharton Sch. U. Pa., 1926-30. C.P.A., Pa., N.J., N.Y., Ill. With credit dept. Notaseme Hosiery Co., 1919-22; purchasing agt. Haslett Chute & Conveyor Co., Oaks, Pa., 1922-24; sr. partner Fernald & Co., Phila., 1924-63; sec. emeritus Chem. Leaman Corp., Lionville, Pa. Active Rep. Party.; past pres. Credit Rsch. Found., Inc. Lt. (j.g.) USCGR, World War II. Mem. AICPA, Pa. Soc. CPAs, N.J. Soc. CPAs, N.Y. Soc. CPAs, Ill. Soc. CPAs, Nat. Assn. Credit Mgmt. (past nat. pres.), Union League Club (life mem. Phila. and Chgo. chpts.), JDM Country Club (Palm Beach Gardens, Fla.), Roof Gardens Club (West Palm Beach, Fla.). Home: West Palm Beach Fla. Died Aug. 2, 1990.

FERNALD, DAVID GORDON, foundation executive; b. Glen Ridge, N.J., Aug. 16, 1923; s. Charles Barker and Olga Elleda (Hoff) F.; m. Julia Ida Gregg, May 19, 1957; children: David Gordon, Julia Dana, John Gregg. A.B., Brown U., 1944; M.B.A., Harvard U., 1947; J.D., N.Y. U., 1956. Bar: N.Y. 1957; C.P.A., N.Y., N.J. Staff acct. Loomis, Suffern & Fernald, N.Y.C., 1947-57; staff acct., ptnr. Lybrand, Ross Bros. & Montgomery, N.Y.C., 1957-67; treas. Rockefeller Family & Assocs., N.Y.C., 1967-88; treas. Rockefeller Bros. Fund, N.Y.C., Rockefeller Family Fund, N.Y.C., JDR 3d Fund, from 1988; bd. dirs. Montclair (N.J.) Savs. Bank Inc., Greenacre Found., N.Y.C. Trustee emeritus Brown U.; trustee Mt. Hebron Cemetery Assn., Montclair, The Rowland Found., Montclair; chmn. bd. Meml. Home of Upper Montclair; chmn. bus. adv. coun. sch. mgmt. William Paterson Coll., Wayne, N.J. Served to lt. (j.g.) USNR, 1943-46. Mem. Am. Inst. CP.A.'s, N.Y. State Soc. C.P.A.'s, Tax Execs. Inst., Tax Mgmt. (adv. bd.), Phi Beta Kappa, Sigma Xi. Republican. Methodist. Clubs: Union League (past gov.), Rockefeller Center Luncheon (N.Y.C.); Montclair Golf (past treas.), Montclair Republican (past pres.), Cosmopolitan (past pres.) (Montclair), Palm-Aire Country (Sarasota, Fla.). Home: Upper Montclair NJ Died Apr. 30, 1990; buried Mt. Hebron Cemetery, Upper Montclair, N.J.

FERNOS-ISERN, ANTONIO, senator; b. San Lorenzo, P.R., May 10, 1895; s. Buenaventura and Dolores (Isern) F.-T.; m. Gertrudis Delgado, Apr. 24, 1920. MD, U. Md., 1915, LLD. Pvt. practice medicine Caguas, P.R., 1916; health officer City of San Juan, 1918; asst. commr. health for P.R., 1919; dir. med. sch. svc. San Juan, 1921, commr. health, 1931-33; pvt. practice cardiology, 1933-42; commr. health P.R., 1942-45; resident commr. of P.R. to U.S., 1946-65; senator Commonwealth of P.R., 1965-92; head Med. Relief Mission to Dominican Republic, 1930;; hon. chmn. P.R. ARC; pres. P.R. Constl. Assembly, 1951-52. Author: Puerto Rico Libre y Federado; also numerous papers on pub. health, econ. and politics. Mem. Am. Social Hygiene Assn. *

FERRER, JOSÉ VICENTE, actor, producer, director; b. Santurce, P.R., Jan. 8, 1912; s. Rafael and Mariá Providencia (Cintrón) F.; m. Uta Hagen, Dec. 8, 1938 (div. 1948); 1 dau., Leticia Thyra; m. Phyllis Hill, June 19, 1948 (div. 1953); m. Rosemary Clooney, July 13, 1953 (div. 1967); children: Miguel, Maria, Gabriel, Monsita, Rafael; m. Stella Daphne Magee. AB, Princeton U., 1933, MA (hon.), 1947; H.H.D. (hon), U. P.R., 1949. Asst. stage mgr., Suffern N.Y., 1935; appeared in Let's Face It, as Iago to Paul Robeson's Othello, 1943; producer, dir. Strange Fruit, 1945, Stalag 17, 1952 (Tony award for dir.), Anything Can Happen, 1951, The Fourposter (with Hume Cronyn and Jessica Tandy), 1952 (Tony award for dir.), The Chase, 1952; producer and actor Cyrano de Bergerac, 1946 (Tony award); appeared in (on Broadway) The Silver Whistle, 1948, 4 Chekov 1-act plays; produced and acted in The Insect Comedy, N.Y. City Theatre Co., (on Broadway) Twentieth Century, 1950, The Shrike, 1952 (Tony award for acting, Pulitzer prize play), Richard III, Charley's Aunt, all 1953-54, musical version Rhinoceros, 1990; dir. My Three Angels, 1953, The Dazzling Hour, 1953, Return to Peyton Place, 1961; gen. dir., N.Y. Theatre Co., acted in Whirlpool, 1949, Crisis, 1950, Cyrano de Bergerac, 1950; motion pictures include Joan of Arc, 1948 (Oscar nomination), Moulin Rouge, 1952, Miss Sadie Thompson, 1953, The Caine Mutiny, 1953, Deep in My Heart, 1954, The Shrike, 1954, The Cockleshell Heroes, 1955, The Great Man, 1956, I Accuse, 1957, The High Cost of Living, 1957, Nine Hours to Rama, 1963, Lawrence of Arabia, 1962, Ship of Fools, 1965, The Greatest Story Ever Told, 1965; producer, dir., star (theatre) Edwin Booth, 1959; dir., co-author: Oh Captain, 1958; dir. The Andersonville Trial, 1960; star (play) The Girl Who Came to Supper, 1963-64, The Man of La Mancha, Broadway, 1966-67, A Life in the Theatre, 1978, White Pelicans, 1979, Sunshine Boys, 1980, Ring Round the Moon (Chichester Theatre Festival, Eng.), 1988, Tete à Tete (world premiere) Berkshire Theatre Festival, 1989, Born Again (world premiere) Chichester Theatre Festival, 1990; appeared in films Enter Laughing, 1967, Cervantes, 1966, The Marcus-Nelson Murders, 1973, Crash, 1977, Forever Young, Forever Free, 1977, The Sentinel, 1977, The Swarm, 1978, Fedora, 1979, The 5th Musketeer, 1979, Natural Enemies, 1979, The Big Brawl, 1980, Midsummer Night's Sex Comedy, 1982, And They're Off, 1982, Blood Tide, 1982, To Be Or Not To Be, 1983, The Evil that Men Do, 1984, Dune, 1984, Bloody Birthday, 1986, Old Explorers, 1988; dir. 2 complete live TV prodns. What Makes Sammy Run, A Case of Libel; mini-series The French Atlantic Affair, 1979; documentaries and numerous guest appearances; appeared in TV movies The Missing Are Deadly, 1975, The Art of Crime, 1975, Exo-Man, 1977; TV dramatic spl. Truman at Potsdam, 1976; TV ltd. series The Rhinemann Exchange, 1977, Gideon's Trumpet, 1980, The Dream Merchants, 1980, The Pleasure Palace, 1980, Evita Peron, 1981, Blood Feud, 1983, This Girl for Hire, 1983, George Washington, 1984, Samson and Delilah, 1984, Strange Interlude, 1988, The Rope, 1989, The Perfect Tribute, 1990; TV series Quincy, 1982, Bridges to Cross, 1986, The Bob Newhart Show, 1986. Recipient Acad. award as best actor for Cyrano de Bergerac, 1950, Don Quixote award Hispanic Heritage Festival, Fla., 1984, Nat. Medal of Arts, 1985, Nat. Puerto Rican Coalition Lifetime Achievement award, 1987, Star award Mus. of City of N.Y., 1987, Fla. prize N.Y. Times, 1990; named to Theatre Hall of Fame, 1981, Amb. of the Arts, State of Fla., 1983. Mem. Players Club (pres. 1983), Acad. Arts and Scis. Puerto Rico. Home: Coconut Grove Calif. Died Jan. 26, 1992. †

FERREY, EDGAR EUGENE, association executive; b. Columbia City, Ind., May 22, 1920; s. Ralph Roy and Sarah Delilah (Dowell) F.; m. Claudia Sue Leininger, Jan. 29, 1944; 1 son, Steven Edgar. A.B., Ind. U., 1942. Mem. editorial staff Ft. Wayne (Ind.) News-Sentinel,

1942-43; news dir. Sta. WHAS, Louisville, 1943-46; pub. relations dir. Farnsworth TV and Radio Corp., Ft. Wayne, 1946-48; editor news bur. Ind. U., Bloomington, 1948-52; pub. relations dir. Lenkurt Electric Co., San Carlos, Calif., 1952-60; pres. and chief exec. officer Am. Electronics Assn. (formerly Western Electronic Mfrs. Assn.), Palo Alto, Calif., 1960-85; electronics industry cons., 1986-88; bd. dirs. Winkler McManus, Micropolis Corp.; mem. adv. bd. Export-Import Bank of U.S., 1985-86; bd. govs. El Camino Hosp. Found., 1986—. Bd. dirs. San Mateo County Devel. Assn., 1953-54, Golden Gate chpt. ARC, 1959-60, v.p. Sequoia chpt., 1958-60; v.p., dir. Sequoia YMCA, 1953-60; pres., bd. dirs. San Carlos C. of C., 1956; bd. dirs. Urban Coalition, 1970-73; mem. adv. bd. Leavey Sch. Bus. and Adminstrn., Santa Clara U., 1984-86. Recipient Medal of Achievement, Am. Electronics Assn., 1985, Distinguished Alumni Service award Ind. U., 1987. Mem. Am. Soc. Assn. Execs. (dir. 1982-84, chartered assn. exec., Key award 1986), Pub. Relations Soc. Am., Armed Forces Communications and Electronics Assn., Am. Mgmt. Assn., Ind. U. Alumni Assn. (Disting. Alumni Service award 1987), Ind. Sagamore of Wabash, Sigma Delta Chi, Sigma Alpha Epsilon. Republican. Presbyterian. Home: Los Altos Hills Calif. Died Sept. 19, 1988; cremated.

FERRIL, THOMAS HORNSBY, poet, editor; b. Denver, Feb. 25, 1896; s. Will C. and Alice Lawton (MacHarg) F.; m. Helen Drury Ray, Oct. 5, 1921; 1 child, Anne Milroy. A.B., Colo. Coll., 1918; hon. M.L., U. Colo., 1934, Litt.D., 1960; LL.D., U. Denver, Colo. Coll. Reporter and dramatic editor Denver Times, The Rocky Mountain News, 1919-21; engaged in motion picture advt. Denver, 1921-26; editor Through the Leaves and The Sugar Press (mags. of Great Western Sugar Co.), 1926-68; assoc. and contbg. editor Rocky Mountain Herald, since 1918; Lectr. and mem. Regional Authors' Council of Writers Conf. in The Rocky Mountains, U. of Colo.; lectr. on poetry and Western culture, various univs. Author: New and Selected Poems, 1952, Words for Denver and Other Poems, 1966, Anvil of Roses, 1983, (with Mrs. Ferril) The Rocky Mountain Herald Reader, 1966; also poetry, prose and book revs. in many newspapers and mags.; writer 9 verse texts used in connection with Boettcher murals, Colo. State Capitol; author: (poems) Trial by Time, 1944; Author: (prose) I Hate Thursday, 1946; contbr.: Harper's Mag.; author: (drama) And Perhaps Happiness, 1957 ($10,000 award 1958); Author: (dramatization of poems) Feril, Etc (produced PBS-TV 1975). Commd. 2d lt. Aviation sect. Signal Corps, 1918. Recipient prize Acad. Am. Poets, 1939; Ridgely Torrence Poetry prize Soc. Am., 1953; prize Denver Post, and Perhaps Happiness, 1958; Service to Mankind award Sertoma, 1958; Robert Frost poetry award Poetry Soc. Am. Contest, 1960; named Centennial-Bicentennial Poet for Colo., 1975; apptd. Poet Laureate of Colo., 1979; award Western Am. Lit. Assn., 1982; named to Cowboy Hall of Fame, 1983; award Denver Press Club, 1983; Helen Black Arts and Letters award, 1985. Mem. Am. Hist. Trails Assn. (hon.), The Westerners, Phi Beta Kappa, Phi Delta Theta, Sigma Delta Chi. Clubs: Cactus, Denver Press, Mile High (Denver). Home: Denver Colo. Deceased. †

FERRIS, GEORGE MALLETTE, investment banker; b. Newtown, Conn., Sept. 25, 1894; s. George B. and Bertha E. (Clark) F.; m. Charlotte Hamilton, Apr. 14, 1920; children: Gene, George M. A.B., Trinity Coll., 1916; LL.D.; LL.D., Gallaudet Coll. Engaged in investment banking, from 1920; sr. ptnr. Ferris Co., Washington, from 1946; pres. Ferris & Co., Inc., Washington, 1933-71, chmn. bd., from 1971, also bd. dirs.; dir. Perpetual Am. Fed. Savs. & Loan Assn. Former chmn. bd. govs. Chevy Chase Village; mem. N.Y. Stock Exchange; mem. bd. Sibley Hosp.; trustee, treas. emeritus Gallaudet Coll.; trustee emeritus Trinity Coll. Mem. Washington Bd. Trade, Alpha Chi Rho. Clubs: Mason, Rotary, Chevy Chase, Columbia; Metropolitan (Washington); Burning Tree. Home: Bethesda Md. Died Oct. 29, 1992. †

FERRIS, MELTON, marketing consultant; b. Modesto, Calif., June 25, 1916; s. Leslie Allen and Georgia (Melton) F.; m. Mary Jane Kirby, Oct. 9, 1947; children: Kirby, Leslie Allen II, Roxana Winifred Lee. A.A., Riverside Coll., 1935; student, U. Calif.-Berkeley, 1935-37, Calif. Sch. Fine Arts, 1951-52. Cert. assn. exec. Newspaper reporter, photographer San Jose (Calif.) Mercury Herald, 1937-40, Hilo Tribune Herald, Hawaii, 1940-41; polit. reporter Internat. News Service, Sacramento, 1941-42; account exec. Gardner Advt. Co., St. Louis, 1948-50; photography editor San Francisco Chronicle, 1951-53; exec. v.p. Calif. council AIA, San Francisco, 1954-78; ptnr. M. & M. Ferris, Corte Madera, Calif. Author articles on photography, sailing, knife making. Chmn. Marin Parks and Recreation Commn., 1963-69; dir. Calif. Roadside Council, 1967-68, Bolinas Community Inc., 1965-69. Served to maj. C.E., USAAF, 1942-48. Mem. AIA (hon.). Clubs: Bay of Islands Yacht, Kerikeri Cruising, Probus, Royal N.Z. Yacht Squadron. Home: Kerikeri NZ Died Sept. 5, 1988; buried Bay of Islands, N.Z.

FETRIDGE, WILLIAM HARRISON, publishing company executive; b. Chgo., Aug. 2, 1906; s. Matthew and Clara (Hall) F.; m. Bonnie-Jean Clark, June 27, 1941; children: Blakeley (Mrs. Harvey H. Bundy III), Clark Worthington. B.S., Northwestern U., 1929; LL.D., Central Mich. U., 1954. Asst. to dean Northwestern U., 1929-30; editor Trade Periodical Co., 1930-31, Chgo. Tribune, 1931-34, H. W. Kastor & Son, 1934-35, Roche, Williams & Cleary, Inc., 1935-42; mng. editor Republican mag., 1939-42; asst. to pres. Popular Mechanics mag., 1945-46, v.p., 1946, exec. v.p., 1953-59; v.p. Diamond T Motor Truck Co., Chgo., 1959-61; exec. v.p. Diamond T div. White Motor Co., 1961-65; pres. Dartnell Corp., Chgo., 1965-77, chmn. bd., 1977-89; dir. Bank of Ravenswood, Chgo. Author: With Warm Regards, 1976; editor: The Navy Reader, 1943, The Second Navy Reader, 1944, Abbot Hall, USNR, 1945, American Political Almanac, 1950, The Republican Precinct Workers Manual, 1968. Trustee Greater North Michigan Ave. Assn., 1949-58; chmn. Ill. Tollway Dedication com., 1958; pres. United Republican Fund of Ill., 1968-73, 79-80; fin. chmn. Ill. Rep. Party, 1968-73; alt. del.-at-large Rep. Nat. Conv., 1956, del.-at-large, 1968, hon. del.-at-large, 1972; mem. Rep. Nat. Finance Com.; chmn. Midwest Vols. Nixon, 1960, Rep. Forum, 1958-60, Nixon Recount Com.; trustee Jacques Holinger Meml. Assn., Am. Humanics Found.; mem. nat. exec. bd., nat. v.p. Boy Scouts Am., 1958-76, chmn. nat. adv. bd., 1976-77; vice chmn. World Scout Found., Geneva, 1977-88; trustee Lake Forest Coll., 1969-77; pres. U.S. Found. for Internat. Scouting, 1971-79, hon. chmn., 1979-89; past pres. trustees Latin Sch. Chgo.; chmn. bd. dirs. Johnston Scout Mus., North Brunswick, N.J.; elected lauriate Lincoln Acad. of Ill., 1985. Served as lt. comdr. USNR, 1942-45. Decorated chevalier Grand Priory of Malta, chevalier Order St. John of Jerusalem; recipient Abraham Lincoln award United Rep. Fund, 1980, Silver Antelope, Silver Beaver, Silver Buffalo Boy Scouts Am., 1956, Bronze Wolf award World Orgn. of Scout Movements, Geneva, 1973, Disting. EAgle award, 1976; Baden-Powell fellow. Mem. Olave Baden-Powell Soc., World Assn. Girl Guides and Girl Scouts, London, Navy League U.S. (past regional pres.), Ill. C. of C., Ill. St. Andrew Soc. (Disting. Citizen award 1980), Newcomen Soc., Soc. Midland Authors, Casino Club, Chgo Club, Union League, Saddle and Cycle Club, Racquet Club, Capitol Hill Club, Chikaming Country Club, Rotary, Beta Theta Pi. Home: Chicago Ill. Died July 13, 1989; buried Rosehill Cemetery, Chgo.

FETTER, FRANK WHITSON, economist; b. San Francisco, May 22, 1899; s. Frank Albert and Martha (Whitson) F.; m. Elizabeth Garrett Pollard, Jan. 14, 1929 (dec. 1977); children: Robert Pollard, Thomas Whitson, Ellen Cole Fetter Gille; m. Elizabeth Miller Stabler, Apr. 15, 1978 (dec. 1985). AB, Swarthmore Coll., 1920; AM, Princeton U., 1922, PhD, 1926; AM, Harvard U., 1924. Instr. econs. Princeton U., 1924-25, 27-28, asst. prof., 1928-34; assoc. prof. econs. Haverford Coll., 1934-36, prof., 1936-48; prof. econs. Northwestern U., 1948-67; vis. prof. Dartmouth Coll., 1967-68; lectr. Sch. Advanced Internat. Studies, 1945-47, Swarthmore Coll., 1946-47; with Office Lend-Lease Adminstrn., 1943-44, Dept. State, 1944-46; vis. prof. U. Wis., 1951-52; v.p. Nat. Bur. Econ. Rsch., 1963-65, chmn., 1965-67, dir., 1950-73; mem. adv. bd. History of Polit. Economy, 1969-91. Editorial writer St. Louis Post-Dispatch, 1930-34; author books including The Economist in Parliament, 1780-1868; co-author books in field; contbr. articles on econs. to profl. jours. Mem. Am. Commn. Fin. Advisers to Govts., 1925-29. Guggenheim fellow, 1937-38; decorated knight Order Polonia Restituta, Poland, 1927, Order of Merit First Class, Ecuador, 1927. Mem. Am. Econ. Assn. (exec. com. 1944-46), Midwest Econ. Assn. (pres. 1952), Academia de Ciencias Economicas (Chile), Phi Beta Kappa. Home: Hanover NH Died July 7, 1991; buried Hanover, N.H.

FETZER, JOHN EARL, broadcasting and professional baseball team executive; b. Decatur, Ind., Mar. 25, 1901; s. John Adam and Della Frances (Winger) F.; m. Rhea Maude Yeager, July 19, 1926. Student, Purdue U., 1921; AB, Andrews U., 1927; student, U. Mich., 1929; LLD, Western Mich. U., 1958, Kalamazoo Coll., 1972, Andrews U., 1980; LittD, Elizabethtown Coll., 1972; D.Eng., Lawrence Inst., 1972; LLD (hon.), Purdue U., 1986. Owner Fetzer Broadcasting Svc., Mich., 1970-85, chmn. bd., 1979-85; owner, chmn. bd. Cornhusker TV Corp., Lincoln, Nebr., 1953-85; owner Detroit Tigers Baseball Club, 1956-83, chmn. emeritus, 1990; chmn. John E. Fetzer, Inc., from 1968, Pro Am Sports Systems, Inc., 1983-89; food franchise executive; chmn. Maj. League TV Com., 1963-71; U.S. Censor of radio, 1944-45; reporting to Gen. Eisenhower (engaged in ETO radio studies in), Eng., France, Russia, Germany, Italy and other European countries, 1945; fgn. corr. radio-TV-newspaper mission, Europe and Middle East, 1952; mem. mission Radio Free Europe, Munich, Germany, and Austrian-Hungarian border, 1956; mem. Broadcasters Mission to Latin-Am., Dept. State, 1962; Detroit Tiger Baseball tour of Japan, Okinawa, Korea, under auspices Dept. State, 1962; mem. A.P. tour, Europe, 1966; Dept. State del. Japanese-U.S. TV Treaty, 1972; mem. adv. bd. N.Am. Svc., Radio Diffusion Française, Paris, 1946-47. Author: One Man's Family, 1964, The Men from Wengen and America's Agony, 1972; Contbr. Radio and Television Project, Columbia, 1953. Trustee Kalamazoo Coll., from 1954. Recipient Mich. Frontiersman award, 1969, Fourth Estate award Am. Legion, 1972, citation Mich. Legislature, 1972, Tiger 75th Anniv. award, 1976, Mich. Legis. citation, 1976, Nebr. Pub. TV citation, 1976, Abe Lincoln Railsplitter award, 1979, Pioneer award Sporting News, 1987. Fellow Royal Soc. Arts London; mem. Nat. Assn. Broadcasters (chmn. TV bd. 1952, Disting. Svc. award 1969), C. of C. (past pres., Summit award 1977), Nat. Geneal. Soc., Acad. Polit. Sci., Am. Soc. Mil. Engrs., IEEE (life mem.), Internat. Radio and TV Execs. Soc., Broadcast Pioneers (award 1968, 19th Mike award 1981), Park Club, Kalamazoo Country Club, Econ. Club, Detroit Athletic Club, Press Club, Detroit Club, Tucson Country Club, Masons, Elks, Alpha Kappa Psi. Presbyterian. Home: Kalamazoo Mich. Died Feb. 20, 1991; buried Kalamazoo.

FEW, BENJAMIN FERGUSON, tobacco company executive; b. Greer, S.C., Nov. 10, 1894; s. I. Pierce and Frances (Cannon) F.; m. Caroline Weston, June 19, 1920; children: Benjamin Ferguson, Elizabeth V. AB, Duke U., 1915, AM, 1916. With Liggett & Myers Tobacco Co., 1916-59, pres., 1951-59, v.p., dir., 1936-59; dir. Duke Power Co., Charlotte; trustee The Bank for Savs., N.Y.C.; advisor to Bd. Chem. Corn Exchange Bank, N.Y.C. Trustee Duke U., Duke Endowment, Converce Coll., Spartanburg, S.C.; vice chmn. Duke Endowment, head com. on ednl. instns. 1st lt. U.S. Army, 1917-19. Mem. Acad. Polit. Sci. N.Y.C. (life), Links Club, Union Club (N.Y.C.), Fairfield (Conn.) Country Club, Fairfield Hunt (Westport, Conn.), To Bac Club (Durham, N.C.). *

FEY, HAROLD EDWARD, editor, clergyman; b. Elwood, Ind., Oct. 10, 1898; s. Edward Henry and Eva (Gant) F.; m. Golda Esper Conwell, July 20, 1922 (dec.); children: Russell C., Gordon Edward (dec.), Constance Fey Thullen. A.B., Cotner Coll., 1922; B.D., Yale U., 1927; D.D. (hon.), Chgo. Theol. Sem., 1948; Litt.D., Park Coll., 1960; H.H.D., Culver Stockton Coll., 1963. Ordained to ministry Christian Ch. (Disciples of Christ), 1923; minister 1st Christian Ch., Hastings, Nebr., 1927-29; prof. Union Theol. Sem., Manila, 1929-32; editor World Call mag., Indpls., 1932-35, Fellowship mag.; also nat. exec. Fellowship Reconciliation, N.Y., 1935-40; field editor, then mng. editor Christian Century, Chgo., 1940-56; editor-in-chief Christian Century, 1956-64, contbg. editor, from 1964; prof. social ethics Christian Theol. Sem., Indpls., 1964-68, emeritus, from 1968; editor World Council Chs. ecumenical history com., from 1968; pres. Christian Century Found., 1956-64, Associated Ch. Press, 1951-52; editor In Common, newsletter; also book rev. editor World Call, from 1964. Author: The Lord's Supper: Seven Meanings, 1948, Cooperation in Compassion, 1966, Life-New Style, 1968, With Solemn Reverence, 1974, How I Read the Riddle (autobiography), 1982, (with D'Arcy McNickle) Indians and Other Americans, 1959; editor The Ecumenical Advance, vol. II, 1970, Kirby Page, Social Evangelist, 1975. Served with U.S. Army, 1918. Recipient Disting. Service award Nat. Congress Am. Indians, 1955, citation Ill. chpt. ACLU, 1964, Leadership in Christan Journalism award Christian Ch., 1969; Disciples Peace Fellowship award, 1981; Sutphin lectr. Ind. Central Coll., 1972; Oreon E. Scott lectr. Christian Theol. Sem., 1973. Mem. Council Christian Unity, Cons. on Ch. Union, Sigma Delta Chi. Home: Claremont Calif. Died Jan. 30, 1990; interred East Hill Shrine Mausoleum, Rushville, Ind.

FIGUHR, REUBEN RICHARD, clergyman; b. Superior, Wis., Oct. 20, 1896; s. Jacob Edward and Julia (Ferrus) F.; m. May-Belle Holt, July 4, 1918; children: Richard Allen, Wilma Jean Figuhr Appel. Student, Pacific Union Coll., Angwin, Calif., 1919-20; AB, Walla Walla Coll., 1922. Ordained to ministry, Seventh-day Adventist Ch., 1918. Missionary Philippine Islands, 1923-41; pres. S.A. div. Gen. Conf. Seventh-day Adventists, 1941-50, v.p. gen. conf., 1950-54, pres., 1954-92. *

FINCH, STUART MCINTYRE, child psychiatrist; b. Salt Lake City, Aug. 16, 1919; s. Elmer E. and Ann (McIntyre) F.; m. Dorothy Ellen Standish, Sept. 2, 1941; children: Craig Standish, Ellen Stuart. Premed. student, U. Utah, 1936-39; M.D., U. Colo., 1944. Diplomate: Am. Bd. Psychiat. and Neurology (mem. com. on certification in child psychiatry 1968). Intern Alameda County Hosp., Oakland, Calif., 1943-44; resident psychiatry Temple U. Hosp. and Sch. Medicine, 1946-49, Phila. Psychoanalytic Inst., 1947-53; instr. psychiatry Temple U. Sch. Medicine, 1949, asso. prof., 1954; attending psychiatrist St. Christopher's Hosp. Children, Phila., 1953-56; mem. faculty U. Mich. Med. Sch., 1956-73, prof. psychiatry, chief children's psychiat. service, 1960-73; lectr. U. Ariz. Sch. Medicine, 1973-83; practice medicine, specializing in child psychiatry Tucson, 1973-83; prof. dept. psychiatry Med. Coll. Ga., Augusta, 1983-89, clin. prof. dept. psychiatry, from 1989; Mem. adv. council Mich. Dept. Mental Health, 1968-73; Bd. dirs. Washtenaw County Community Mental Health Center, from 1965. Author: (with O.S. English) Introduction to psychiatry, 3d edit, 1964, Fundamentals of Child Psychiatry, 1960, (with J.F. McDermott) Psychiatry for Pediatricians, 1970. Mem. Am. Psychiat. Assn. (chmn. com. psychiatry childhood and adolescence 1964-70), Group Advancement Psychiatry, Am. Orthopsychiat. Assn., AMA, Am. Acad. Child Psychiatry, Am. Psychoanalytic Assn. Home: Green Valley Ariz. Deceased. †

FINCH, WILLIAM GEORGE HAROLD, radio engineer, telecommunications executive; b. Birmingham, Eng., June 28, 1897; came to U.S., 1906; s. William Joseph and Amelia (Skelding) F.; m. Elsie Grace George, Nov. 29, 1916 (dec. May 1967); 1 child, Eloise Grace Finch Tholen; m. Helen Stork Ambler, Feb. 1, 1969 (dec. Nov. 1989). Student, U. Cin., Norwood, Ohio, 1915; radio communication course, Marconi Inst., N.Y.C., 1917; completed spl. course radio engring. and patent law, Columbia U., 1923; D.Sc. (hon.), Fla. Inst. Tech., 1983. Registered profl. engr., N.Y. patent atty. Asst. engr. Cleve. Electric Illuminatiing Co., 1916-17; inspecting engr. Nat. Dist. Telegraph Co., N.Y.C., N.Y. Compensating Rating Bd., 1917-19; elec. engr. Royal Indemnity Co., 1919-21; radio engr. and editor Internat. News Service, 1921-28; chief engr. Hearst Radio, 1928-34; asst. chief engr. and chief telephone engring. div. FCC and chief engr. fed. investigation telephone cos., 1934-35; pres. Finch Telecommunications, Inc., N.Y.C., 1935-41, Conn. Indsl. Research Corp., Newtown, from 1956; founder, owner Sta. WGHF-FM, N.Y.C., 1946-49; v.p. Sta. WCAE, Pitts.; dir. communications Rowley Newspapers of Ohio, Ashtabula; dir. Telecommunication Cons. Internat. Inc., Washington; patent atty., U.S. and Can.; cons. profl. engr., electronic, facsimile communications and patent engring.; mem. Internat. Radio Consultive Com., U.S. Congrl. Adv. Bd.; mem. tech. com. on radio and cable communication Am. Newspaper Pubs. Assn., 1924; mem. com. allocation of frequency Fourth Nat. Radio Conf.; del. Internat. Telegraphic and Radio Telegraphic Conf., Madrid, 1932, N.Am. Radio Conf., Mexico City, 1933. Contbr. numerous articles to profl. jours. Holder numerous patents in radio communications. Mem. 1st F.A., NYNG, 1917-18; lt. (s.g.) USNR; exec. officer USN Communication Res., 3d Naval Dist., from 1929, N.Y.C.; comdr. USN, 1913-45; capt., asst. chief Office Naval Research, 1945-57. Decorated Legion of Merit; recipient Presdl. award; Disting. Alumnus award for outstanding achievement U. Cin. Coll. Engring., 1985; active U.S. Congl. Adv. Bd., from 1984. Fellow IEEE (award 1956, Centennial medal for extraordinary achievement 1984), Radio Club Am. (dir. emeritus, Armstrong medal 1976, Dr. Lee DeForest award 1984, Pioneer citation 1989); mem. AAAS, N.Y. Acad. Scis., Armed Forces Communications and Electronics Assn. (Disting. life mem.), Mil. Order World Wars, Am. Legion, Am. Phys. Soc., Franklin Inst. Episcopalian (vestryman). Clubs: Mason. (N.Y.), Bankers (N.Y.), Army and Navy (N.Y.); Masons (Buffalo); Army and Navy (Washington); Crown Point Country, N.Y. Yacht, N.Y. Athletic; Saint and Sinners Yacht (Port St. Lucie, Fla.) (sec. from 1965, commodore 1978-79); St. Lucie (Stuart, Fla.) (rear commodore); Anchor Line Yacht (Jensen Beach, Fla.). Home: Port Saint Lucie Fla. Died Nov. 13, 1990; buried Arlington Nat. Cemetery.

FINE, MAX, ophthalmologist; b. Poland, Feb. 28, 1908; s. Michael and Martha (Damesek) F.; m. Emily Wellman Huggins, Oct. 16, 1965; children: Thomas, Edward. BS, NYU, 1927; MD, U. Calif., 1933. Diplomate Am. Bd. Ophthalmology. Assoc. clin. prof. Stanford (Calif.) U. Med. Sch., 1952-60; chief ophthalmology Mt. Zion Med. Ctr., San Francisco, 1959-68; clin. prof. Pacific Med. Ctr., San Francisco, 1974-89; cons. surgeon gen. U.S. Army, surgeon gen. USN; bd. dirs. Stanford U. Eye Bank, 1950-59, No. Calif. Soc. Prevention Blindness, 1977-89. Contbr. articles to profl. jours., chpts. to books. Maj. M.C., AUS, 1942-46. Recipient Outstanding Civilian Svc. medal U.S. Army, 1966, Castroviejo medal, 1979. Mem. AMA, Am. Acad. Ophthalmology (honor award 1972), Assn. Rsch. Ophthalmology, Pacific Coast Oto-Ophthalmologic Assn., Pan Am. Ophthalmologic Soc., Pan Pacific Surg. Assn., Calif. Acad. Medicine, Castroviejo Soc., Frederic C. Cordes Eye Soc., San Francisco Round Table Ophthalmology, Sigma Xi, Alpha Omega Alpha. Home: San Francisco Calif. Died Mar. 29, 1989.

FINE, TIMOTHY HERBERT, lawyer; b. Washington, Oct. 11, 1937; s. Nathan and Emily Newhall (Brown) F.; m. Mary Ellen Fox, June 16, 1960; children: Margaret Carol, Susan Emily, Rachel Winslow. B.E.E., U. Va., 1959; M.S. in E.E., U. So. Calif., 1962; LL.B., U. Calif.-Berkeley, 1965. Bar: Calif. 1966, U.S. Dist. Ct. (no., ea., so. and cen. dists.) Calif. 1966, U.S. Ct. Appeals (9th cir.) 1966, U.S. Supreme Ct. 1971. Law clk. to Hon. William T. Sweigert, U.S. Dist. Judge, San Francisco, 1965-67; assoc. G. Joseph Bertain, Jr., San Francisco, 1967-77; prin. Law Offices of Timothy H. Fine, San Francisco, 1977-90; del. White House Conf. Small Bus., 1980, chmn. No. Calif. delegation, 1986; del. Calif. State Confs. Small Bus., 1980, 82, 84, 86, 1st v.p., 1984-86; chmn. San Francisco Bay Area Small Bus. Caucus, 1984, Small Bus. Legal Def. Com., 1982—; author, lectr., cons., trial atty. on antitrust, franchise and small bus. legal matters.; mem. nat. adv. council U.S. Senate Small Bus. Com., from 1983; mem. adv. bd. Calif. Senate Select Com. Small Bus. and Calif. Assembly Select Com. on Snall Bus., from 1983; mem. Calif. Bd. Registration Profl. Engrs., 1982-86. Bd. dirs. Boalt Hall Law Sch. Alumni Assn., 1983-86, 87-90; nat. advisor drafting com. Uniform Franchise and Bus. Oppurtunites Act, from 1985. Served to lt. USAF, 1959-62. Mem. ABA (mem. governing bd., forum com. on franchising 1977-84, chmn. forum on franchising 1977-84, mem. governing bd. standing com. on specialization 1986-89, author model standards for franchise law, mem. industry adv. coun. to NAASA franchise and bus. opportunities com. 1989-90), Fed. Bar Assn. (exec. com. San Francisco chpt.), Calif. Bar Assn., San Francisco Bar Assn., Lawyers Club of San Francisco. Clubs: Berkeley Tennis, Calif. Commonwealth. Home: Berkeley Calif. Died May 11, 1990; cremated.

FINEBERG, HERBERT, chemist; b. Portland, Maine, Jan. 16, 1915; s. Abraham and Esther M. (Differes) F.; m. Geraldine Shirley Morris, Dec. 25, 1941; children: Joan Susan Fineberg Latchaw, Sharon Rachael Fineberg Garber. BS, Trinity Coll., 1935; PhD, U. Ill., 1941. Rsch. chemist Eastman Kodak Co., 1935-38; rsch. mgr. Conn. Hard Rubber Co., 1941-45; pres. Geral Chem. Co., 1945-48; v.p. rsch. Glyco Chem., 1948-62; rsch. mgr. Archer-Daniels-Midland Co., 1962-67; rsch. mgr. Tech. Info. Ctr. Ashland (Ohio) Chem. Co., 1967-85. Contbr. articles to profl. jours.; patentee in field. Mem. Am. Oil Chem. Assn., Am. Chem. Soc., Chem. Mktg. Rsch. Assn., Am. Inst. Chem. Engrs., Lic. Exec. Soc., Slaty Hollow Trout Club. Home: Columbus Ohio Died Feb. 4, 1991; buried Columbus, Ohio.

FINEBERG, S(OLOMON) ANDHIL, human relations consultant; b. Pitts., Nov. 29, 1896; s. Nathan and Libbie (Landau) F.; m. Hilda Cohen, 1925. A.B., U. Cin., 1917; Rabbi, Hebrew Union Coll., 1920, D.D., 1958; Ph.D., Columbia U., 1932. Rabbi Niagara Falls, N.Y., 1920-24, Pitts., 1924-25, Mt. Vernon, N.Y., 1929-37; nat. community relations cons. Am. Jewish Com., 1939-64; cons. NCCJ, 1965-80; coordinator N.Y. Interracial Colloquoy, 1966-78; specialist in human relations U.S. State Dept. Internat. Exchange Program in Germany, 1954. Author: Overcoming Anti-Semitism; Punishment Without Crime, 1949 (Anisfield Wolf Lit. award), The Rosenberg Case, Report on Germany, Deflating the Professional Bigot, Religion Behind the Iron Curtain, Plight of Soviet Jews. Served with USMC, 1917-19. Recipient Am. Heritage Freedom award, 1959; Interreligious Leadership award NCCJ, 1978. Mem. Central Conf. Am. Rabbis, Nat. Assn. Inter-group Relations Ofcls. (dir. 1954-56), Jewish Community Relations Workers Assn. (pres. 1950-54), U.S. Jewish War Vets. (nat. chaplain 1932-36). Home: Pikesville Md. Died Feb. 24, 1990; buried Hartsdale, N.Y.

FINEMAN, IRVING, author; b. N.Y.C., Apr. 9, 1893; s. Joseph and Rebecca Rachel (Blane) F.; m. Helene Hughes, July 7, 1935 (div.); children: Joseph Clinton, Jonathan Peter. BS, MIT and Harvard U., 1917. Pvt. engring. practice, 1912-29; faculty engring. U. Ill., 1925-28; faculty lt. Bennington Coll., 1932-38; lectr. in field. Author: This Pure Young Man (Longmans Green prize), 1930, Hear Ye Sons, 1933, Doctor Addams, 1938, Akiba, A Child's Play, 1950, Fig Tree Madonna (Stevens award for drama Dramatists Alliance, Stanford U.), 1951, Woman of Valor: The Life of Henrietta Szoid, 1961, Lovers Must Learn (made into movie Rome Adventure); contbr. short stories, verse lit. criticism and articles to leading mags; motion picture stories, screenplasy for Metro-Goldwyn-Mayer, Warner Brothers, University, R.K., Columbia. With USN, 1917-22. *

FINK, RICHARD WALTER, nuclear physics educator; b. Detroit, Jan. 13, 1928; s. Bernard and Ann (Walter) F.; m. Gunilla Gustafsson, Oct. 4, 1960; children: Kerry Leif, Roger Gunnar. B.S. in Chemistry, U. Mich., 1948; M.S., U. Calif. at Berkeley, 1949; Ph.D., U. Rochester, 1953. Assoc. prof. U. Ark., Fayetteville, 1953-61; prof. dept. physics Marquette U., Milw., 1961-65; vis. prof. Werner Inst. for Nuclear Chemistry, U. Uppsala, Sweden, 1959-60, Inst. for Exptl. Physics, U. Hamburg, Fed. Republic of Germany, 1963-64; prof. Sch. Chemistry, Ga. Inst. Tech., Atlanta, 1965-88, prof. emeritus, 1988-89; research nuclear chemist Knolls Atomic Power Lab., Schenectady, 1949-50; Cons. Lawrence Radiation Lab., U. Calif., 1961-69, Phillips Petroleum Co., Bartlesville, Okla., 1957-65; cons. on natural radiocarbon counting Coca-Cola Co., Atlanta, 1972-73; chmn. Internat. Conf. on Inner Shell Ionization Phenomena, Atlanta, 1972; Fulbright Travel grantee, 1963-64, Fulbright lectr., Europe, 1964, Nat. Acad. Sci. exchange lectr., Yugoslavia, 1971, Poland, 1977; Internat. Atomic Energy Agy. cons. to Greek Atomic Energy Commn., Nuclear Research Center, Demokritos, Athens, 1975-76. Contbr. 265 articles to profl. jours. Fellow Am. Phys. Soc.; mem. Sigma Xi (Research prize 1971, 72, 77, 79, 83). Home: Atlanta Ga. Died Jan. 27, 1989.

FINKELSTEIN, LOUIS, seminary administrator, rabbi; b. Cin., June 14, 1895; s. Rabbi Simon J. and Hannah (Brager) F.; m. Carmel Bentwich, Mar. 5, 1922; children—Hadassah, Ezra, Faith. A.B., Coll. City of N.Y., 1915; Ph.D., Columbia, 1918; Rabbi, Jewish Theol. Sem. Am., 1919; S.T.D., Columbia, 1944; Litt.D., Boston U., 1950; D.H.L., Dropsie Coll., 1961, Hebrew Union Coll.-Jewish Inst. Religion, 1967, Woodstock Coll., 1972, Brandeis U., 1972; LL.D., Temple U., 1963, Manhattan Coll., 1965, Fordham U., 1966; L.H.D., S.E. Mass. Inst. Tech., 1966; S.T.D., N.Y.U., 1967; D.D., Yale, 1967. Rabbi Congregation Kehilath Israel, N.Y. C., 1919-31; instr. Talmud Jewish Theol. Sem., 1920-24, Solomon Schechter lectr. in theology, 1924-30, asso. prof. theology, 1930, Solomon Schechter prof. theology, from 1931, asst. to pres., 1934-37, provost, 1937-40, pres., 1940, chancellor, 1951-72, chancellor emeritus, 1972-91; pres. Inst. Religious and Social Studies; Ingersoll lectr. Harvard Div. Sch., 1944; Active in ednl. publs. and ednl. coms. and commns. for various gen. and spl. purposes. Ambassador of Pres. Kennedy to Papal Coronation, 1963; hon. chmn. bd. edn. for recruiting young people for preprofl. jobs in war on poverty, 1964; dir. Am. Friends of Hebrew U.; adv. bd. Inst. for Advancement of Cultural and Spiritual Values. Author or co-author several books from 1924 including: Abot of Rabbi Nathan, 1950, The Pharisees: The Sociological Background of Their Faith, 1962, New Light on the Prophets, 1969, The Jews: Their History, Culture and Religion, 3 vols., 1971, Pharisaism in the Making, 1972, Sifra (critical edit.), 1985; Editor commentaries, biographies; co-editor numerous symposia; contbr. review and jours.; Vice pres. and mem. editorial bd.: Universal Jewish Ency. Recipient Phi Epsilon Pi Fraternity Nat. Service award, 1952, Townsend Harris medal, 1940, 125th Anniversary medal Coll. City N.Y., 1972, Excellence award Alumni Assn. Combined Grad. Faculties Columbia U., 1975, Akiba award Am. Jewish Com., 1980, Solomon Schechter award United Synagogue Am., 1985, Kenneth B. Smilen Lit. award Jewish Mus., 1986. Fellow Am. Acad. of Arts and Scis., Acad. of Jewish Research, Jewish Acad. Arts and Scis.; past pres. Conf. Sci. Philosophy and Religion.; Mem. several assns. and orgns. Home: New York NY Died Nov. 19, 1991; buried N.Y.C.

FINLEY, ROBERT LAWRENCE, lawyer; b. Lawrence, L.I., N.Y., Dec. 4, 1899; s. John Huston and Martha (Boyden) F.; m. Sarah Barney Bartlett, Oct. 14, 1933; children: James, Alexander. Grad., Phillips Exeter Acad., 1917; AB, Harvard U., 1921, LLB, 1925. Bar: N.Y. 1926, N.J. 1947. Pvt. practice N.Y.C., 1926-41, 46-49; ptnr. Spence, Hotchkiss, Parker & Duryee and predecessor firms, 1927-90; legal div. WPB, 1942-43; cons. AEC, 1947; spl. asst. to under-sec. of army, 1949-52; spl. asst. to adminstr. DPA, 1952-53; dep. asst. dir. ODM, 1953-54, asst. dir., 1957-58; dep. asst. dir. Office Civil Def. Moblzn., 1958-61; adviser Office Emergency Planning, 1961-62, dep. treas., N.J., 1955, acting treas., 1956-57; dep. asst. dir. U.S. Arms Control and Disarmament Agy., 1963-90. 2d lt. inf. U.S. Army, 1918, lt. col. AUS, 1943-45. Decorated Legion of Merit, Bronze Star medal, Croix de Guerre. Mem. Century Assn. (N.Y.C.). Home: Tamworth NH Died Apr. 22, 1990.

FINLEY, STATES RIGHTS GIST, electrical, mechanical engineer; b. York, S.C., Aug. 30, 1898; s. David Edwad and Elizabeth Lewis (Gist) F.; m. Grace Isobel Snyder, June 7, 1924; children: States R. (dec.), Kathryn Jr. BSEE and BSME, Clemson A&M Coll., 1918. Jr. engr. Henry L. Doherty & Co., 1919-20; successively engr., dist. supt., v.p., div. mgr. Oohio Pub. Svc. Co., Massillon, Elyria, 1920-33; v.p. Faultless Rubber Co., Ashland, Ohio, 1933-35; chief engr. Rural Lines, Ohio Farm Bur., Columbus, 1936-37; chief engr. Tenn. Elec. Power Bd., Chattanooga, 1937-39, gen. supt., 1937-60, gen. mgr., 1960-63, chmn., 1963-92. Chmn. Ashland County Relief Com., 1930-34, Tenn. Indsl. Pers. Conf., 1945-46, Chattanooga chpt. ARC, 1942-46; pres. Chattanooga Indsl. YMCA, 1942-46, Chattanooga Family Svc. Agy.; bd. govs. ARC, 1947-50, nat. vice chmn. ARC Fund Campaign, 1956; pres. Chattanooga Area Heart Assn., 1957-58; dir., sec. Tenn. Heart Assn., 1958-59; chmn. bldg. com. Chattanooga-Hamilton County Health Ctr.; dir. Hamilton County Meml. Hosp. Assn.; chmn. adv. com. U. Tenn. Sch. Social Wk., Hamilton County Pub. Welfare. Mem. Am. Pub. Power Assn. (pres. 1950), Tenn. Valley Pub. Power Assn. (pres. 1947-48), Chattanooga Art Assn. (dir.), Masons, Kiwanis (pres. 1947, chmn. internat. com. edn. and fellowship 155), Chattanooga Auto. Club (pres.), Sigma Chi. Democrat. Presbyterian. *

FINNEGAN, THOMAS JOSEPH, lawyer; b. Chgo., Aug. 18, 1900; s. Thomas Harrison and Marie (Flanagan) F.; J.D., Chgo. Kent Coll. of Law, 1923; m. Hildreth Millslagel, July 1, 1933 (dec. Mar. 1977). Bar: Ill. 1923. Pvt. practice, Chgo.; mem. Fithian, Spengler & Finnegan, 1935-51; mem. firm Korshak, Oppenheim & Finnegan, 1951-89, ret., 1989. Mem. ABA, Fed. Bar Assn., Ill. Bar Assn., Chgo. Bar Assn., Chgo. Law Inst., Phi Alpha Delta. Died Oct. 20, 1989; cremated. Home: Chicago Ill.

FINUCANE, THOMAS GREGORY, lawyer; b. Washington, July 27, 1896; s. Daniel Francis and Norah (Moran) F.; m. Margaret Kirby, Oct. 30; children: Thomas Gregory, Patricia Ann. LLB, Georgetown U., 1920, LLM, 1921. Pvt. practice law, 1921-92; becamemem. Bd. Review, Dept. Labor, 1923; mem. successor bd. Bd. of Immigration Appeals, 1940, chmn., 1942-92; mem. Pres.'s Commn. on Immigration and Naturalization, 1952. *

FIRESTONE, BERNARD, holding company executive; b. N.Y.C., May 1, 1918; s. Martin and Kate (Chariton) F.; m. Sylvia Zussin, Dec. 24, 1939 (dec.); children: Frank Joseph, Frances Katherine, Bethann, Mellisa Jan, Wendy Elyse; m. Bettie Kaplan, Apr. 2, 1961. BS, Purdue U., 1939; MA, Loyola U., Chgo., 1948. With Chgo. & Northwestern R.R. Co., 1939-68, treas., 1962-68; v.p., treas. Northwest Industries, Inc., Chgo., 1968-89. With USN, 1944-46. Mem. Union League. Home: Highland Park Ill. Died July 11, 1989.

FISCHER, CARL CASTLE, pediatrician, educator; b. Phila., Oct. 13, 1902; s. John Adolph and Millie (Leupold) F.; m. Mae Adelaide Charles, Mar. 7, 1931; children—Elaine Lois (Mrs. Alexander Marshack), Charles Thomas, John William. B.S., Princeton U., 1924; M.D., Hahnemann Med. Coll. and Hosp., Phila., 1928, M.A. (hon.), 1938. Intern Hahnemann Hosp., Phila., 1928-29; pvt. practice pediatrics Phila., 1930-58; cons. pediatrician St. Vincent's Hosp., Misercordia Hosp., St. Lukes and Children's Hosps., Phila., Crozer Hosp., Chester, Pa., Meml. Hosp., Pottstown, Pa.; faculty Hahnemann U., 1930-67, prof. pediatrics, head dept., 1945-67, emeritus prof. pediatrics, 1967, assoc. dir. med. affairs, 1967-69; dir. health service Girard Coll., Phila., 1958-67. Author: The Role of the Physician in Environmental Pediatrics, 1960; editor: The Handicapped Child, 1958; cons. editor: Dorland's Med. Dictionary (Pediatrics), 1973. Vol. physician Project Hope, Natal, Brazil, 1972, vol. physician, Ganado, N.Mex., 1973; Chmn. Gov. Pa. Com. Children and Youth, 1956-59; mem. Gov. Pa. Com. Handicapped, 1959-60. Fellow AMA, A.C.P.; mem. Am. Acad. Pediatrics (pres. 1961-62), Pa. Heart Assn., Heart Assn. of Southeastern Pa. (dir., past pres.), Tropic Harbor Assn. (pres. 1982-83, dir.), Phi Chi, Alpha Omega Alpha. Unitarian. Lodge: Kiwanis (Delray Beach, Fla.). Home: Delray Beach Fla. Died Dec. 23, 1989.

FISCHER, CARL HAHN, actuary, educator; b. Newark, Aug. 22, 1903; s. Carl H.H. Fischer and Minnie (Hahn) F.; m. Kathleen Kirkpatrick, Sept. 25, 1925; children: Patrick Carl, Michael John. B.S., Washington U., St. Louis, 1923; M.S., U. Iowa, 1930, Ph.D., 1932. Spl. engr. Am. Steel Foundries, 1923-26; instr. math. Beloit (Wis.) Coll., 1926-29; asst. U. Iowa, 1929-32; instr. U. Minn., 1932-33; spl. research asst. Northwestern Nat. Life Ins. Co., 1933-34; mem. faculty Wayne U., 1934-41; mem. faculty U. Mich., 1941-74, prof. ins. and actuarial math., 1950-74, prof. emeritus, 1974; vis. prof. U. Calif., Berkeley, 1951; prof. U. Hawaii, 1955, Hebrew U., Jerusalem, 1965, 67, Netherlands Sch. Econs., Rotterdam, 1966; dir. summer actuarial program John Hancock Mut. Life Ins. Co., 1959, 61, Travelers Ins. Co., 1963; cons., actuary, from 1939. Author: (with P.R. Rider) Mathematics of Investment, 1951, (with W.O. Menge) Mathematics of Life Insurance, 1965, Vesting and Termination Provisions in Private Pension Plans, 1970; contbr. articles to profl. jours. Trustee Ann Arbor Employee Retirement System, 1948-73; actuary Tchrs. Retirement Fund, N.D., 1939-77; cons. Philippine Govt. Service Ins. System, 1956, Social Security System, Philippine Govt., 1956, 62, Nat. Social Security and Welfare Corp., Liberia, 1977; mem. Adv. Council Social Security Financing, 1957-58; chmn. study com. mil. retired pay U.S. Senate, 1960-61; mem. Ann Arbor Bd. Edn., 1957-60. Fellow Soc. Actuaries, Conf. Actuaries in Pub. Practice (v.p. 1970-75); mem. Am. Acad. Actuaries, Am. Risk and Ins. Assn., Am. Statis Assn., Math. Assn. Am.; ; mem. Acacia, Sigma Xi, Beta Gamma Sigma. Club: Mason. Home: Ann Arbor Mich. Died Dec. 21, 1988; buried Forest Hill Cemetery, Ann Arbor, Mich.

FISCHER, RAYMOND P., author, business consultant, lawyer; b. Wheaton, Ill., Oct. 15, 1900; s. Herman A. and Julia (Blanchard) F.; m. Marita McMillan, June 18, 1932; 1 child, Elizabeth Christine Fischer Lilly. A.B., Wheaton Coll., 1922, Pomona Coll., 1922; J.D., Harvard U., 1925. Bar: Ill. 1925. Practiced law in Chgo., 1925-41; v.p. to exec. v.p. Cuneo Press, Inc., Chgo., 1941-67; pres., chmn. Combined Locks Paper Co., Little Chute, Wis., 1945-69; bus. cons., investment advisor, prin. Associated Cons. of Wheaton (Ill.), from 1969. Author: (biography) Four Hazardous Journeys of the Reverend Jonathan Blanchard, Founder of Wheaton College, 1987, (poetry) An Aged Man Remembers April, 1985, also numerous poems pub. in Poetry mag., The Cresset, others. Lic. lay leader Episcopal Ch., vestry several chs.; mem. Diocesan Coun. Episcopal Diocese Chgo.; mem. Chgo. adv. bd. Salvation Army. Mem. Cypress Lake Country Club (Fort Myers, Fla.). Home: Wheaton Ill. Died Aug. 4, 1990.

FISH, HOWARD MACFARLAND, manufacturing company executive; b. Erie, Pa., Dec. 7, 1896; s. Henry Earl and Nellie (Slocum) F.; m. Dorothy Walrath Hall, Oct. 30, 1920; children: Douglas M., Henry E., Howard MacFarland, John H.; m. Marian W. Craig, Dec. 18, 1959. Litt.B, Princeton U., 1919. With Am. Sterilizer Co., 1919-92, successively factory apprentice, to sales mgr., chmn. bd., 1950-92; dir. Security-Peoples Bank & Trust Co., Erie, Pa.; chmn. Am. Sterilizer Co. of Can., Ltd.; v.p. Amsco-Europ (Bruges, Belgium). Mem. bd. Nat. Indsl. Conf.; bd. trusttesHosp. Assn. Pa.; bd. mgrs. Hamot Hosp.; vol. ambulance driver Am. Field Svc., French Army, 1917-19. Mem. Nat. Security Indsl. Assn. (trustee 1951-54), Masons (32 degree), Nassau Club, Elm Club (Princeton, N.J.), Princeton Club (N.Y.C.), Lake Placid Club, Erie Club (pres.). *

FISHBERG, ARTHUR MAURICE, physician; b. N.Y.C., June 17, 1898; s. Maurice and Bertha (Cantor) F.; m. Irene Levin, June 16, 1933 (dec.). A.B., Columbia U., 1919, M.D., 1921; D.Sc. (hon.), Mt. Sinai Sch. Medicine, 1979. Intern City Hosp., 1921-22; adj. and asso. physician Mt. Sinai Hosp., 1926-46; physician-in-chief Beth Israel Med. Ctr., N.Y.C., 1946-86; cons. physician St. Joseph's Hosp., from 1944; cons. Army Med. Center, Washington, from 1947; clin. prof. med. NYU, from 1947; cons. physician Mount Vernon Hosp., from 1957; clin. prof. medicine Mt. Sinai Sch. Medicine, from 1966; Pres. Dazian Found. for Med. Research, 1956. Author: Hypertension and Nephritis, 1930, Heart Failure, 1937; Contbr. numerous articles dealing with cardiovascular and renal disease. Mem. Am. Soc. for Clin. Investigation, AMA, Am. Heart Assn., N.Y. Acad. of Medicine; hon. mem. Buenos Aires Med. Soc., Brazilian Cardiological Soc. Jewish. Home: New York NY Died Jan. 20, 1992; buried Beth David Cemetery, Elmont, N.Y.

FISHER, ALTON KINDT, dentist, pathologist, educator; b. Abrams, Wis., Nov. 1, 1905; s. Fred Ward and Edith Bertha (Kindt) F.; m. Marcelia Coad Neff, Aug. 15, 1931. Student, U. Wis., 1925-32; D.D.S., Marquette U., 1935; B.S., Loyola U., 1948; grad. study, Tulane U., 1948-49. Asst. anthropology Milw. Pub. Mus., 1927-32; intern Milw. Children's Hosp., 1935-36; pvt. dental practice Milw., 1936-40; research asso. Milw. Pub. Mus., from 1937; instr. histology Marquette U., 1937-40; attending dentist St. Joseph's Hosp., 1937-40; asst. prof. pathology Loyola U., New Orleans, 1945-47; prof. Loyola U., 1947-49; prof., head dept. oral pathology U. Iowa, 1949-73, prof., head dept. stomatology, 1958-65, asst. dean for research, 1973-74, prof. emeritus, from 1974, adj. prof. anthropology, from 1976; phys. anthropologist Office of State Archeologist of Iowa, from 1976; vis. dental surgeon Charity Hosp. La., New Orleans, 1946-49; cons. VA Hosp., Des Moines, 1951-54, Iowa City, 1954-74. Author articles on pathology. Served to comdr. USN, 1940-46; rear adm. Res. ret. Recipient Lapham medal Wis. Archeol. Soc., 1946. Fellow Am. Coll. Dentists, Internat. Assn. Dental Research, Am. Acad. Oral Pathology, Am. Anthrop. Assn., AAAS, Explorers Club; mem. Internat. Acad. Pathology, ADA, Fedn. Dentaire Internationale, Am. Soc. Clin. Pathologists, Wis. Archeol. Soc., Archaeol. Inst. Am., Arctic Inst. N.Am., Am. Polar Soc., Am. Assn. Phys. Anthropologists, Sigma Xi, Omicron Kappa Upsilon. Episcopalian. Club: Mason. Home: Iowa City Iowa Died Oct. 9, 1991. †

FISHER, ERNEST MCKINLEY, economist; b. Macedonia, Ill., May 15, 1893; s. Marshall Duff and Ada Carey (Vise) F.; m. Ethel Moore, Aug. 9, 1922; 1 child, Robert Moore. AB, Coe Coll., 1914, LLD, 1950; AM, U. Wis., 1922; PhD, Northwestern U., 1930. Instr. Am. U., Beirut, Syria, 1914-17, U. Wis., 1919-23; dir. edn. and rsch. Nat. Assn. Real Estate Bds., 1923-26; assoc. prof. real estate mgmt. U. Mich., 1926-29, prof., 1930-36; dir. Div. of Econs. and Statistics and econ. advisor, FHA, 1934-40; dir. rsch. in mortgage and real estate fin. Am. Bankers Assn., 1940-45, dep. mgr., 1943-45; prof. unban land econs. Columbia U., 1945-61, emeritus prof. and spl. lectr. sch. arch., 1961-64; also chmn. adminstrv. bd., dir. Inst. for Urban Land Use and Housing Studies, 1947-55; staff Yale U. Calif. L.A., U. Hawaii, 1961-62; dep. advisor on liberated areas U.S. Dept. State, 1943; mem. bd. dirs., exec. com. Nat. Com. on Housing, Inc., 1946-48; cons. to subcom. on housing and urban re-devel. Senate Postwar Econ. Policy and Planning Com., 1944-55; chmn. adv. com. Bur. Census, 1941, 42; cons. Legis. Reference Svc., Libr. of Congress, 1947-49, Bur. of Budget, 1946-53, bd. govs. Fed. Res. Author books including: Home Mortgage Loan Manual, 1943, Urban Real Estate Markets: Characteristics and Financing, 1951, Urban Real Estate (with Robert Moore Fisher), 1954, The Mutual Mortgage Insurance Fund (with Chester Rapkin), 1956; editor Home Mortgage Lending; contbr. articles to profl. jours. Dir. First Fed. Savs. & Loan Assn. of N.Y., 1954-92. With Signal Corps, U.S. Army with A.E.F., 1918-19. Fellow AAAS, Am. Statis. Assn. (v.p. 1941); mem. Am. Econ. Assn., Beta Gamma Sigma, Alpha Kappa Psi, Lambda Alpha, Cosmos Club (Washington), Columbia Faculty Club. Presbyterian. *

FISHER, FREDERICK G., JR., lawyer; b. Brockton, Mass., Apr. 19, 1921; s. Frederick G. and Genevieve M. (Clark) F.; m. Talia Benz, Sept. 18, 1943; children: Frederick G. III, Genevieve, Hamilton. A.B. summa cum laude, Bowdoin Coll., 1942; LL.B., Harvard U., 1948. Bar: Mass. 1948, N.Y. 1983. Mem., chmn. comml. law dept. Hale and Dorr, Boston; lectr. on bankruptcy reorgn., ABA-Am. Law Inst., Am. Bar Inst., Mass. Continuing Legal Fedn., New Eng. Legal Inst.; participant London Times Conf. on Reorgn., 1981. Contbr. articles on bankruptcy reorgn. to profl. jours. Mem. Boston Bar Assn. (chmn. Conf. Personal Fin. Law 1980—), Mass. Bar Assn. (pres. 1975-76), ABA (chmn. gen. practice sect. 1974-75, ho. of dels. 1975-86, Mass. del. 1982-86, chmn. gen. com. Conf. on Consumer Fin. Law 1980-89, chmn. bankruptcy reorgn. subcom. fed. cts. com.), Am. Judicature Soc. (bd. dirs. 1983-89). Home: Boston Mass. Died May 25, 1989; buried Sagamore, Mass.

FISHER, JOSEPH LYMAN, economist, educator, congressman; b. Pawtucket, R.I., Jan. 11, 1914; s. Howard Colburn and Caroline (Nash) F.; m. Margaret Saunders Winslow, June 21, 1942; children: H. Benjamin, Caroline, Robert W., William B., Elizabeth, James H., Barbara W. B.S., Bowdoin Coll., 1935, D.Sc., 1965; postgrad., London Sch. Econs., 1935-36; M.A., Harvard U., 1938, Ph.D. in Econs. (teaching fellow 1946-47), 1947; M.A. in Edn, George Washington U., 1951; LL.D., Allegheny Coll., 1966; L.H.D., Starr King Sch. Ministry, 1971. Instr. econs. Allegheny Coll., 1938-40; planning technician Nat. Resources Planning Bd., 1939-43; economist Dept. State, 1943; economist, exec. officer Council Econ. Advisers, Washington, 1947-53; assoc. dir. Resources for the Future, Inc., Washington, 1953-59, pres., 1959-74; mem. 94th-96th Congresses from 10th Dist. Va.; dir. policy analysis The Wilderness Soc., 1981-82; sec. human resources Commonwealth of Va., 1982-86; prof. George Mason U., Fairfax, Va., from 1986; vis. prof. U. Colo., 1957, U. Calif., 1971, 76, Va. Commonwealth U., from 1984; staff dir. Cabinet Com. Energy Supplies and Policies, 1955; Population Reference Bur. (bd. dirs. from 1981, chmn. bd., 1987); cons. to govt. agys. Author: (with others) World Prospects for Natural Resources, Resources in America's Future; contbr. chpts. to books, articles to profl. jours. Mem. Arlington County Bd., 1964-74, chmn., 1965, 71; trustee Unitarian Universalist Assn., 1961-65, moderator, chmn. bd. trustees, 1965-77; trustee Tchrs. Ins. and Annuity Assn., 1966-74, United Planning Orgn., 1966-71, Chesapeake Bay Found., from 1987; bd. dirs. Met. Washington Council of Govts., 1966-74, pres., 1969, chmn., 1970; bd. dirs. Washington Met. Area Transit Authority, 1972-74, chmn., 1972; bd. overseers Bowdoin Coll.; adv. council Electric Power Research Inst., 1973-79, chmn., 1973-75. Served with inf. AUS, 1943-46. Mem. AAAS, Am. Forestry Assn. (dir. 1966-84), Wilderness Soc. (dir. 1983—), Am. Econ. Assn., Am. Soc. Pub. Adminstrn., Nat. Acad. Pub. Adminstrn. (chmn. bd. dirs. 1988—, trustee 1986—), Cosmos Club (Washington), Phi Beta Kappa, Phi Delta Kappa. Home: Arlington Va. Died Feb. 19, 1992.

FISHER, MORTON POE, lawyer, judge; b. Balt., Feb. 14, 1897; s. Abraham Henry and Bertha (Hamburger) F.; m. Adelaide Rose Block, May 28, 1928; children: Ann Fisher Bacharach, Morton Poe. AB, Johns Hopkins U., 1918; LLB, U. Md., 1920. Bar: Md. 1919. Pvt. practice law Balt., 1919-92; asst. U.S. atty. Md., 1923-25; spl. asst. to atty. gen. tax div. Dept. Justice, 1928-30; instr. fed. taxation U. Balt., 1940, instr. in pleading, 1948-54; mem. excess profits tax coun. IRS, 1946-47; judge Tax Ct. U.S., 1954-92. Author: Fisher on Maryland Pleading (with James P. Gorter), 2d edit., 1921. Lt. col. U.S. Army, 1943-46. Mem. ABA (vice chmn. sect. taxation 1948-50, chmn. 1950-52, ho. dels. 1952-54), Md. Bar Assn. (v.p. 1952-53), Balt. Bar Assn., Phi Beta Kappa. *

FISHER, PIETER ALRICKS, investment banker; b. Balt., Apr. 15, 1931; s. Louis Miller and Katharine Busteed (Streett) F.; m. Margaret Morgan, Jan. 2, 1971 (div. June 1979); m. M. Helen Anderson, Sept. 8, 1979; children from previous marriage: Pieter A., Ellen McCrea. B.A., Princeton U., 1953; M.B.A., U. Va., 1957. Research exec. Young & Rubicam, Inc., N.Y.C., 1957-59; v.p. Doherty, Clifford, Steers & Shenfield, Inc., N.Y.C., 1959-65; v.p. Goldman Sachs & Co., N.Y.C., 1965-74, gen. ptnr., 1974-86, ltd. ptnr., 1986-92. Chmn. David K.E. Bruce Found., Princeton, N.J., from 1979; trustee Que. Labrador Found., Ipswich, Mass., from 1964, Atlantic Ctr. for Environment, from 1980 ; dir. Vol. Cons. Group, N.Y.C., from 1975. Served as 1st lt. U.S. Army, 1953-55. Mem. Council Fgn. Relations, Fgn. Policy Assn., The Pilgrims, Newcomen Soc., Met. Mus. Art. Republican. Episcopalian. Clubs: River (N.Y.C.), Recess (N.Y.C.); Ivy (Princeton, N.J.); Duquesne (Pitts.). Home: Rutherford Calif. Died May 24, 1992.

FISHER, WALTER TAYLOR, lawyer; b. Chgo., Feb. 20, 1892; s. Walter Lowrie and Mabel (Taylor) F.; m. Katharine Dummer, Aug. 21, 1915 (dec. 1961); children—Walter, Ethel, John, Roger, Francis, Gerard Henderson; m. Margaret W. Rieser, Jan. 25, 1962 (dec. 1978); m. Laura K. Pollak, Nov. 2, 1979. Grad., Chgo. Latin Sch., 1909; A.B., Harvard, 1913; student law, U. Chgo., 1914-15; LL.B., Harvard, 1917. Bar: Ill. bar 1918. Law clk. with Matz, Fisher & Boyden, Chgo., 1917; with Bell, Boyd & Lloyd., Chgo., from 1918; Chmn. Ill. Commerce Commn., 1949-53; Asst. gen. counsel War Finance Corp., Washington, 1921-22; pres. Amalgamated Trust & Savs. Bank, Chgo., 1926-29; Counsel for Chgo. agy. RFC, 1932-33; alt. pub. mem. Nat. Def. Mediation Bd., 1941; mem. Pres.'s Emergency Bds. in nat. nonoperating railway employees case, 1943, and other cases; also mediator, arbitrator or permanent umpire for various labor disputes. Author: What Every Lawyer Knows, 1974, also articles in jours. Trustee U. Ill., 1929-31; Pres. Chgo. Council Fgn. Relations, 1944-46; lectr. Northwestern U. Law Sch., 1962. Mem. ABA (chmn. com. on lawyer referral service 1956-57), Ill. State Bar Assn., Chgo. Bar Assn. (chmn. com. initiating lawyer reference plan for low-cost legal service 1939-43). Clubs: Law, Legal (pres. 1936-37), City (pres. 1925-27), University, Attic. Home: Highland Park Ill. Died Aug. 28, 1991.

FISHKO, SOL, union executive; m. Bella Gold; children: Sara Fishko Gill, Robert. Pres. Internat. Pressmen's and Asst.'s Union N.Am. N.Y. Printing Specialties and Paper Products Union Local 447, 1939-64, internat. v.p., 1964-74; pres. Internat. Printing and Graphic Communications Union, Washington, 1974-89; bd. dirs. indsl. union dept. AFL-CIO; chmn. com. which negotiated merger of Internat. Printing Pressmen and

Asst.'s Union with Internat. Stereotyper's Electrotypers' and Platemakers Union, 1973. Home: New York NY Died Apr. 9, 1989.

FISHMAN, WILLIAM SAMUEL, business executive; b. Clinton, Ind., Jan. 26, 1916; s. Max and Fannie (Dumes) F.; student Sch. Internship Polit. Sci., Washington, 1934-35; BA with highest honors in Polit. Sci., U. Ill., 1936; postgrad. U. Chgo., 1936-37; DBus. Adminstrn., Bryant Coll., 1968; LLD, Lincoln Meml. U., 1969; m. Clara K. Silvian, June 28, 1936 (dec.); children: Alan F., Fred B., David J.; m. Selma Demchick Ellis, May 9, 1982; stepchildren: Joshua Ellis, Jill Ellis Feninger. Exec. v.p. Automatic Mdsg. Co., Inc., Chgo., 1942-56, pres. 1956-59; sr. v.p. ARA Services, Inc., Phila., 1959-63, exec. v.p., 1963-64, pres., 1964-77, chief exec. officer, 1975-83, chmn. bd., 1977-84; dir. VS Services, Ltd., Can., Fidelity Bank. Phila., Fidelcor, Phila. Past pres. Jewish Publ. Soc. Am.; fellow Brandeis U.; trustee Com. for Econ.; dir. Phila Mus. Art, Franklin Inst., Acad. Music. Devel. Mem. Nat. Restaurant Assn., Nat. Automatic Merchandising Assn. (dir., exec. com. pres. 1958-59), Standard Club (Chgo.), Palm Beach (Fla.) Country Club, Locust, Philmont Country, Union League (Phila.), Phi Beta Kappa, Phi Kappa Phi, Delta Sigma Rho. Jewish (past pres. synagogue). Died June 15, 1991. Home: Merion Pa.

FITCH, ELIOT G., banker; b. Milw., Mar. 12, 1896; s. Grant and Eliza (Eliot) F.; m. Janet Margaret Fell, July 15, 1922 (div. 1941); children: John Grant, Janet Margaret, Jared Eliot; m. Ruth Bartlett Jones, Sept. 10, 1943. BA, Yale U., 1918; MA in Econs., U. Wis., 1921. With The Nat. Exchange Bank of Milw. (now Marine Nat. Exch. Bank), 1923-92, pres., 1942-92, dir., 1925-92; chmn. bd. Marine Capital Corp.;/ pres., dir., chmn. bd. Marine Corp.; pres., dir. Poharis Corp.; dir. Jared Corp., Norway-Gravure, Inc., Braun-Hobar Co., Brownberry Ovens, Inc., Nordberg Mfg. Co., Northwestern Nat. Ins. Co. Dir., trustee, chmn. bd. govs. Menninger Found.; bd. dirs. Milw. Children's Hosp.; mem. adv. bd. Milw. Boys Club, Citizens Bur. Milw.; treas. Ole Evinrude Found. 1st lt. F.A., U.S. Army, WW I. Mem. Res. City Bankers Assn., Phi Upsilon, Milw. University Club, Country Club of Milw. *

FITCHEN, JOHN FREDERICK, III, fine arts educator, architect; b. Ithaca, N.Y., May 24, 1905; s. John Frederick Jr. and Ruth (Williams) F.; m. Mary Elizabeth Nelson, June 23, 1934; children: Allen Nelson, Leigh Williams, John Hardy. BA, Yale U., 1927; MArch, Harvard U., 1932. Mem. faculty dept. fine arts Colgate U., Hamilton, N.Y., 1934-71, prof. emeritus, 1971-90, chmn. dept., 1950-65; cons. architect N.Y. State Emergency Housing Project, 1946-47. Author, illustrator: The Construction of Gothic Cathedrals, 1961, The New World Dutch Barn, 1968, Building Construction before Mechanication, 1986; editor Philobiblon, 1962-65; contbr. articles to archtl. jours. Chmn. Friends Colgate U. Libr., 1962-65. Mem. AIA (citation of merit Cen. N.Y. chpt. for design Phi Kappa Tau frat. house Colgate U. 1951), Soc. Archtl. Historians, Cen. N.Y. Archtl. Historians (past pres.), Internat. Ctr. Medieval Art, Assn. for Preservation Tech. Home: Hamilton N.Y. Died June 3, 1990; buried Hamilton, N.Y.

FITT, ALFRED BRADLEY, lawyer; b. Highland Park, Ill., Apr. 12, 1923; s. Frank and Harriett (Bradley) F.; m. Lois D. Rice, Jan. 7, 1978. BA, Yale U., 1946; JD, U. Mich., 1948. Bar: D.C., Mich. With firm Lewis and Watkins, Detroit, 1948-54; ptnr. Lewis and Watkins, 1952-54; legal adviser to gov. Mich., 1954-60; assoc. counsel subcom. adminstrv. practice U.S. Senate Judiciary Com., 1960-61; chief counsel spl. com. FAA adminstrv. procedures, 1961; dep. under sec. manpower Dept. Army, 1961-63; dep. asst. sec. for civil rights Dept. Def., 1963-64; gen. counsel Dept. Army, 1964-67; asst. sec. for manpower Dept. Def., 1967-69; spl. adviser to the pres. Yale U., 1969-75; gen. counsel Congl. Budget Office U.S. Congress, Washington, 1975-92. Served with AUS, 1943-46. Home: Washington D.C. Died July 7, 1992. †

FITZGERALD, EDMOND JAMES, artist; b. Seattle, Aug. 19, 1912; s. Maurice F. and Elizabeth (Norton) F.; m. Mary Louise Streets, Sept. 7, 1940 (dec. Feb. 1977); children—Desmond, Ryder O'Bannon; m. Margaret Boyer Trent, Oct. 26, 1978. Student, Eustace P. Ziegler, Mark Tobey. lectr., tchr. (Recipient grand prize Art USA 1958, Am. Artists Profl. League prize 1955, anonymous watercolor prize 1959, gold medal of honor Hudson Valley Art Assn. 1952, 58, 60, also, Jane Peterson prize for oil painting 1962, Famous Artists' Sch. award 1969, Washington Sch. Art award 1970); Author: Painting and Drawing in Charcoal and Oil, 1959, Marine Painting in Watercolor, 1972; One-man shows include, Seattle Art Mus., 1941, Grand Central Gallery, 1946; murals include Trail to Oreg, Ontario, Oreg., 1937, Pathfinders, Colville, Wash., 1939, Battle of Bear River, Preston, Idaho, 1940, Normandy Invasion, Nat. Maritime Union's Curran Plaza Bldg., Man and the Land, Am. Mus. Nat. History, 1949, Pasteur, Kenilworth, N.J., murals for, Union First Nat. Bank, N.J., 1958, Cranford (N.J.) Jr. Coll., 1959, Jamaica (N.Y.) Savs. Bank, 1964, Chem. Constrn. Co., N.Y.C., 1961, Revlon, Inc., N.Y.C., 1976; represented in permanent collections, White House, George Washington U., Swope Mus., Terre Haute, Ind., New Britain (Conn.) Mus., Seattle Art Mus., Frye Mus., Seattle, Wash. State Coll., U.S. Naval War Coll., IBM, Nat. Cash Register Co. Served as officer USNR, 1942-46; comdr. Res.; ret. Ranger Fund purchase N.A.D., 1963; Club prize, 1961; Frank B. Williams prize, 1958; Frank B. Williams prize Salmagundi Club. Academician NAD; fellow Royal Soc. Art; mem. Allied Artists Am. (pres., Jane Peterson prize 1956, Robert S. Brush award 1959), Am. Watercolor Soc. (v.p., dir., hon. pres. from 1970, Herb Olsen prize 1961), Nat. Soc. Mural Painters (first prize 1946). Club: Salmagundi (N.Y.C.). Home: Cincinnati Ohio Died July 6, 1989; buried Oak Hill Cemetery, Cin.

FITZGERALD, JAMES EDWARD, obstetrician/gynecologist; b. Superior, Wis., July 1894; s. James Henry and Margaret (Kelly) F.; m. Dorothy Dow, Nov. 3, 1925. AB, U. Mich., 1916; MD, Northwestern U., 1921. Intern, resident Cook County Hosp., Chgo., 1920-23; pvt. practice Chgo.; attending obstetrician/gynecologist St. Luke's Hosp.; chmn. dept. gynecology Cook County Hosp., Chgo.; cons. obstetrician Chgo. Meml. Hosp.; prof. dept. ob/gyn. Northwestern U. Mem. Chgo. Gynecol. Soc. (pres. 1946), Cen. Soc. Obstetricians and Gynecologists (maternal welfare com.), University Club, Tavern Club. *

FITZPATRICK, PAUL EARLY, company executive; b. Buffalo, Sept. 25, 1897; s. William H. and Clara (Hillery) F.; m. Marion agnes Lenahan, Sept. 28, 1921; children: Clairose Fitzpatrick Magee, Ella Fitzpatrick Moloney. CE, Cornell U., 1921; LLD, Canisius Coll., 1956. Pres., dir. W.H. Fitzpatrick & Sons, Inc., Buffalo, 1925-92; pres. Am. Lubricants, Inc., 1935-55, past chmn.; pres. Fitzpatrick Donahy, Inc., 1938-92, El Clair, Inc., 1945-92; dir. First Nat. Bank of Ft. Lauderdale, Harkin, Inc., Ft. Lauderdale, El Clair Projects, Inc. Dir. Buffalo City Planning Assn.; past commr. State Ins. Fund N.Y.; past Dem. chmn. Erie County and N.Y. State; del. Dem. Nat. Conv., 1940, 44, 48, 52; trustee Cornell U.; bd. regents Canisius Coll. Mem. Cornell Engring. Soc., Knights of Malta, K.C., Cornell Club, Buffalo Country Club, Cherry Hill Country Club, Coral Hill Country Club (Ft. Lawderdale). *

FITZSIMONS, RUTH MARIE, speech, language pathologist, educator; b. Pawtucket, R.I.; d. Leo A. and Helena (Hollis) F. B.Ed., R.I. Coll., 1940; M.Ed., Boston U., 1949, D.Ed., 1955; postgrad., NYU, 1956, Brandeis U., summer 1958. Tchr., prin. Warwick (R.I.) Sch. Dept., 1940-49, speech and hearing therapy coordinator, 1949-68; prof. speech and lang. pathology U. R.I., Kingston, 1969-89; ednl. cons. Creative Services Source, Inc., 1985-89; lectr. Boston U., 1956, 58, 59, U. Maine, summer 1966; cons. speech and hearing therapy R.I. Dept. Edn., Providence, 1968-69; cons. editor T.J. Denison & Co., Mpls., from 1966. Author: Stuttering and Personality Dynamics, 1960, Christopher Listens, 1966, Make Believe with Mike, 1968; contbr. articles to profl. jours.; designer, author ednl. software for children and adolescents; designer, author ednl. VCR programs and complementary program books. Fellow Am. Speech and Hearing Assn.; mem. R.I. Speech and Hearing Assn. (pres. 1964-65), Am. Speech and Hearing Assn. (legislative councillor 1969-71), Am. Psychol. Assn., Am. Acad. Psychotherapists, Soc. for Research in Child Devel. Home: Warwick R.I. Died Dec. 11, 1989; buried Mt. St. Mary Cemetery, Pawtucket, R.I.

FLACK, JAMES MONROE, business executive; b. Baxterville, Miss., Aug. 29, 1913; s. Jesse James and Lenora (Lucas) F.; m. Hertha E. Eisenmenger, Aug. 30, 1941; children: James Monroe, Sonya Karen, Robert Frank, Suzanne Margaret. B.S., Delta State U., 1935; M.Div., Yale U., 1942; postgrad., Harvard U., 1952. Prin. Shaw (Miss.) High Sch., 1935-39; with employee relations dept. Standard Oil Co. of N.J., 1946; officer, dir. subs. Textron, Inc., 1946-53; v.p., dir. Indian Head, Inc., from 1953, vice chmn., 1972-74. Served as lt. comdr. USN, 1942-45. Clubs: N.Y. Athletic, Yale of N.Y.C, Red Fox Country, Tryon (N.C.) Country. Home: Tryon N.C. Died June 16, 1989; buried Tryon, N.C.

FLAHERTY, EUGENE DEWEY, ocean shipping company executive; b. N.Y.C., Apr. 9, 1898; s. William Patrick and Ella Barbara (Fisher) F.; m. Georgiana Boneau, July 16, 1923; children: Robert, Mary Eileen, William. Student, L.A. Coll. Law, 1927-31. Office mgr. Beh & Herter, N.Y.C., 1916-18; clk. U.S. ICC, Washington, 1918; sec. to dir. gen. U.S. R.R. Adminstrn., 1918-20; sec. W.G. McAdoo, N.Y.C., 1920-22; gen. office mgr. McAdoo, Neblett & O'Connor, L.A., 1923-31; dir., sec. Seaboard Devel. Co., Seaboard Realty Co., L.A., 1923-38; gen. office mgr., sec. Am. President Lines, 1938-46, v.p. ops., 1949-50, v.p. S.W. div., 1950-63; gen. mgr. Marine Exchange of L.A., Long Beach Harbor, Inc.; dir., sec. Jameson Petroleum Co., L.A., 1923-38; dir., pres. Culver City (Calif.) Airport, 1928-32; dir., sec. State Consol. Oil Co., 1932-34. Mem. L.A. World Affairs Coun.; mem. export expansion coun. U.S. Dept. Commerce. With USNR, 1935-92, capt. 1945-58. Recipient Sec. of Navy Commendation ribbon for svcs. in WW II. Mem. C. of C., Japan-Am. Soc. So. Calif., Nat. Def. Transp. Assn., Calif. Club, SKAL (L.A.), Army-Navy Club (Washington), Propeller Club (bd. govs.). Democrat. Roman Catholic. *

FLAHIFF, GEORGE BERNARD CARDINAL, archbishop; b. Paris, Ont., Can., Oct. 26, 1905; s. John James and Eleanor Rose (Fleming) F. B.A., St. Michael's Coll., U. Toronto, 1926; student, U. Strasbourg, France, 1930-31; Dipl. Archiviste-Paleographe, Ecole Nat. des Chartes, Paris, 1935; Hon. degrees, U. Seattle, 1965, U. Notre Dame, 1969, U. Man., 1969, U. Windsor, 1970, U. Winnipeg, 1972, U. Toronto, 1972, U. St. Francis Xavier, 1973, Laval U., 1974, St. Bonaventure U., 1975, U. St. Thomas, Houston, 1977. Ordained priest Roman Cath. Ch., 1930; prof. medieval history Pontifical Inst. Medieval Studies and U. Toronto, 1935-54, sec. inst., 1943-51; superior-gen. Basilian Fathers, 1954-61; consecrated archbishop of Winnipeg, Can., 1961-82; elevated to cardinal, 1969, served, 1969-82; pres. Can. Cath. Conf.; dir. Nat. Liturgical Conf. in U.S.; rep. from Can. to Second Vatican Coun. Mem. Sacred Congregation for Religious. Decorated companion Order of Can., 1974. Home: Winnipeg MB, Canada Died Aug. 21, 1989.

FLAMSON, RICHARD JOSEPH, III, banker; b. Los Angeles, Feb. 2, 1929; s. Richard J. and Mildred (Jones) F.; m. Arden Black, Oct. 5, 1951; children: Richard Joseph IV, Scott Arthur, Michael Jon, Leslie Arden. B.A., Claremont Men's Coll., 1951; cert. Pacific Coast Banking Sch., U. Wash., 1962. With Security Pacific Corp., Los Angeles, 1955-91; v.p. Security Pacific Nat. Bank, Los Angeles, 1962-69, sr. v.p., 1969-70, exec. v.p. corp. banking dept., 1970-73, vice-chmn., 1973-78, pres., chief exec. officer, 1978-81, chmn., chief exec. officer, 1981-87, dir., 1973-91; vice-chmn. Security Pacific Corp., 1973-78, pres., 1978-81, chief exec. officer, 1978-90, chmn., from 1981; bd. dirs. Northrop Corp., Allergan Inc. Trustee Claremont Men's Coll. 1st lt. AUS, 1951-53. Mem. World Affairs Coun., Town Hall, Calif., Balboa Bay (Newport Beach, Calif.) Club, Balboa Yacht (Newport Beach) Club, Big Canyon Country Club (Newport Beach). Home: Corona Del Mar Calif. Died Oct. 17, 1991.

FLECK, PAUL DUNCAN, continuing education center administrator; b. Montreal, Que., Can., Apr. 17, 1934; s. Robert Douglas and Norma Marie (Byrnes) F.; m. Margaret Louise Pollard, Sept. 1, 1956; children: John Christopher, Franklin Conor. B.A., U. Western Ont., 1955, M.A., 1958; Ph.D., Queen's U., Northern Ireland, 1961. Chmn. dept. English, U. Western Ont., London, Can., 1967-70, prof. English, 1970, chmn. dept. English, 1970-74; pres. Ont. Coll. Art, Toronto, Can., 1975-82, The Banff Centre, Alta., Can., 1982-92; dir. The Ency. of Music in Can., The Banff Television Found.; pres., chmn. bd. dirs. NDWT Theatre Co., Toronto, 1979-82; bd. dirs. Art mag., Toronto, 1980-82, Toronto Consort, 1981-82, Ballet Opera House, Toronto; mem. exec. bd. Council for Bus. and Arts in Can., 1982-88; mem. OCO '88 Arts Festival com.; lectr. in field. Contbr. articles to profl. jours. Imperial Oil fellow, 1958-61; Can. Council grantee, 1964, 75. Mem. Assn. Can. Univ. Tchrs. of English (pres. 1974-76), Byron Soc. (chmn. Can. com. 1974-92), Can. Assn. Fine Arts Deans (chmn. 1980-82), Internat. Council Fine Arts Deans (Can. exec. bd. 1980-83), Can. Soc. Decorative Arts (v.p. 1985-92), Ballet Opera House Toronto (bd. dirs. 1990-92) Died July 4, 1992. United Ch. of Can. Clubs: University, Arts and Letters (v.p. 1980-82) (Toronto). Home: Banff Can. †

FLEMING, BERRY, author; b. Augusta, Ga., Mar. 19, 1899; s. Porter and Daisy (Berry) F.; m. Anne Shirley Molloy, 1926; 1 child, Shirley Moragne. BS, Harvard U., 1922. Reporter, Augusta, 1922-23. Author 20 books, including The Conqueror's Stone, 1927, Colonel Effingham's Raid, 1943 (Book-of-Month Club section, made into movie), The Lightwood Tree, 1947, The Fortune Tellers, 1951 (Lit. Guild selection), Carnival, 1953, Autobiography of a Colony, 1957, The Winter Rider, 1960, (play) The Acrobats, 1961, Captain Bennett's Folly, 1990; compiler: 199 Years of Augusta's Library, 1948; contbr. to mags. Home: Augusta Ga. Died Sept. 15, 1989; buried Augusta, Ga.

FLEMING, NED NELSON, wholesale food distributor; b. Lyndon, Kans., Jan. 18, 1900; s. Oliver Albert and Edith May (Hollingsworth) F.; m. Marjorie Virginia Miller, Oct. 15, 1923 (dec. 1984); children: Marilyn Fleming Harrison, James B., Stephen M. Student, Washburn U., 1917-19, D.B.A. (hon.), 1963; B.S. in Econs, U. Pa., 1921. With Fleming Cos., Inc., Topeka, 1921-90, treas., gen. mgr., 1922-33, v.p., gen. mgr., 1933-45, pres., 1945-64, chmn. bd., chief exec. officer, 1964-66, chmn. bd., 1966-81, hon. chmn. bd., 1981-91; dir. Unitog Co., Kansas City, Mo.; former pres., chmn. bd. govs. Nat. Am. Wholesale Grocers' Assn.; former bd. dirs. Ind. Grocers Alliance. Adv. dir. Boys Clubs, Topeka, from 1969; trustee, mem. fin. com. Washburn Coll.; former mem. exec. com. Menninger Found., Topeka; mem. adv. com. U. Kans. Sch. Bus.; trustee Midwest Rsch. Inst. Recipient Herbert Hoover award Nat. Am. Wholesale Grocers Assn., 1964, Disting. Svc. citation U. Kans., 1971. Mem. Phi Delta Theta. Clubs: Topeka Country; Paradise Valley (Ariz.) Country. Home: Topeka Kans. Died Jan. 24, 1990.

FLENNIKEN, CECIL STEPHENSON, forest products company executive; b. Chickasaw, Ala., Aug. 11, 1925; s. Warren S. and Pearle M. (Stephenson) F.; m. Alyce Quince Parrish, June 15, 1948; 1 son, Bruce Phillips. BME, Ga. Inst. Tech., 1949. With Internat.

Paper Co., 1949-69; mgr. pulp and paper mill Internat. Paper Co., Pine Bluff, Ark. and Bastrop, La., 1965-69; with Can. Pacific Forest Products Ltd., Montreal, Que., from 1969, v.p., 1970, exec. v.p., 1971, chmn., pres., chief exec. officer, 1972-91; chmn. Can. Pacific Forest Products Ltd., Montreal, from 1991; bd. dirs. Toronto-Dominion Bank, Pulp and Paper Rsch. Inst. Can., The Conf. Bd. Can. With USN, 1943-45. Mem. Paper Industry Mgmt. Assn. (trustee emeritus), TAPPI, Can. Mfrs. Assn. (adv. bd.). Clubs: Mt. Royal, Le Club St. Denis, Toronto. Home: 1321 Sherbrooke St W E-50, Montreal, PQ Canada H3G 1J4 Died Aug. 25, 1991.* †

FLETCHER, GILBERT HUNGERFORD, radiotherapist, educator; b. Paris, Mar. 11, 1911; s. Walter Scott and Marie (Boudol) F.; m. Mary Critz, June 10, 1943; children: Walter Scott, Thomas. B.A., U. Paris, 1929; B.A. in Engring., U. Louvain, Belgium, 1932; M.S. in Math., U. Brussels, 1935, M.D., 1941. Diplomate: Am. Bd. Radiology. Rotating intern U. Brussels Hosp., 1939-41; intern obstetrics French Hosp., N.Y.C., 1942-43; asst. resident radiology N.Y. Hosp., 1942-43, resident radiology, 1943-44; fellow radiotherapy Royal Cancer Hosp., London, Eng., Curie Found., Paris, France, 1947-48; chmn. dept. radiotherapy M.D. Anderson Hosp., Houston, 1948-81, prof., from 1981; prof. radiotherapy U. Tex. Med. Sch., Houston, from 1965; cons. Baylor U. Coll. Medicine, Houston, Santa Rosa Med. Center, San Antonio; nat. cons. to surgeon gen. USAF, 1968-85; worked on first design cobalt-60 radiotherapy unit, helped develop high-voltage linear accelerations tool. Served from 1st lt. to capt. M.C. AUS, 1944-47. Recipient Medal of Honor Am. Cancer Soc. Fellow Am. Coll. Radiology; mem. Inter-Am. Coll. Radiology, Radiol. Soc. N.Am., Am. Soc. Therapeutic Radiologists (pres. 197-68), Am. Radium Soc. (treas. 1959-61, pres. 1962-63, Janeway lectr. 1970), Tex. Radiol. Soc., AMA, Harris County Med. Soc., Royal Soc. Medicine London, French Soc. Radiotherapists Paris. Home: Houston Tex. Died Jan. 11, 1992; buried Starkville, Miss.

FLETCHER, JAMES CHIPMAN, engineering educator, government official; b. Millburn, N.J., June 5, 1919; s. Harvey and Lorena (Chipman) F.; m. Fay Lee, Nov. 2, 1946; children: Virginia Lee, Mary Susan, James Stephen, Barbara Jo. AB, Columbia U., 1940; PhD, Calif. Inst. Tech., 1948; DSc (hon.), U. Utah, 1971, Brigham Young U., 1977, U. Colo., 1987; LLD (hon.), Lehigh U., 1978. Research physicist bur. ordnance Dept. Navy, 1940-41; spl. research assoc. Cruft Lab., Harvard U., 1941-42; instr. Princeton U., 1942-45; teaching fellow Calif. Inst. Tech., 1945-48; instr. UCLA, 1948-50; dir. theory and analysis lab. Hughes Aircraft Co., 1948-54; assoc. dir. guided missile lab., dir. electronics guided missile research div., later in space tech. labs. Ramo-Wooldridge Corp., 1954-58; pres., founder Space Electronics Corp., 1958; pres. Space-Gen. Corp. (merger between Space Electronics Corp. and Aerojet-Gen. Corp.), 1960; chmn. bd. Space-Gen. Corp., 1961-64; pres. U. Utah, 1964-71; adminstr. NASA, Washington, 1971-77, 86-89; Whiteford prof. U. Pitts., 1977-84, Disting. Pub. Svc. prof., 1984-86, 89-91; cons. engr. McLean, Va., 1977-86; mem. subcom. on stability and control NACA, 1950-54; asst. sec. USAF, 1961-64, to ACDA, 1962-63, Aerojet-Gen. and Space-Gen. Corps., 1964-71; cons., then mem. Pres.'s Sci. Adv. Com., 1958-70; chmn. com. rev. Minuteman Command and Control System, 1961; mem. Air Force Sci. Adv. Bd., 1962-67; chmn. physics panel rev. com. NIH, 1962-64; mem. strategic weapons panel, 1959-61, mil. aircraft panel, 1964-67, chmn. naval warfare panel, 1967-73; mem. Pres.'s Nat. Crime Commn., 1966; mem. tech. assessment adv. coun. Office of Tech. Assessment,1978-86, mem. def. sci bd., 1982-86; chmn. safety adv. bd. Three Mile Island No. 2, 1981-86; governing bd. NRC, 1978-82; trustee Nat. Space Soc., 1977-86; bd. dirs. Astrotech Internat. 1984-86, Fairchild Industries, 1985-86, 89-92, Amoco Corp., 1977-86, Burroughs Corp. 1977-86, Comarco, Inc., 1979-86, Raytheon Co., 1989-92, Structural Dynamics Rsch. Corp., 1989-92; internat. adv. bd. Pan Am. Airways, 1977-86. Author classified papers, sci. papers, chpts. in books; bd. editors, Addison-Wesley Pub. Co., 1958-64. Trustee Rockefeller Found., 1978-85, Theodore von Karman Meml. Found.; mem. governing bd. Univ. Corp. on Atmospheric Research, 1982-86, Argonne Nat. Lab., 1984-86; bd. regents Nat. Library Medicine, 1971; bd. visitors Def. Intelligence Sch., 1970-71; nat. adv. bd. Gas Research Inst., 1984-86. Recipient Disting. Svc. medal NASA, Exceptional Civilian Svc. award USAF, Dept. Energy award, 1982, John Jay award Columbia U., Strategic Def. award, Am. Def. Preparedness Assn., Willard F. Rockwell Excellence in Tech. medal Internat. Tech. Inst., Digital Discovery award Digital Equip. Corp., Disting. Svc. award Brigham Young U., Wm. P. Medcalf award, Western Pa., Sanger award, Berlin, 1988. Fellow IEEE (Centennial award), Am. Acad. Arts and Sci., AIAA (hon.), Am. Astron. Soc.; mem. NAE (governing coun. 1978-84, Arthur M. Bueche award, 1989), Am. Phys. Soc., Univ. Club (Pitts.), Alta Club (Salt Lake City), Cosmos Club, Sigma Xi. Club: Cosmos. Home: McLean Va. Died Feb. 22, 1991; buried Salt Lake City.

FLETCHER, JOEL LAFAYETTE, JR., college president; b. Grant Parish, La., Jan. 12, 1897; s. Joel Lafayette and Lela (Craig) F.; m. Frances McLees, Oct. 15, 1919; children: Ellen Craig, Lorraine Ruth, Florence Saucier, Joel Lafayette III. BI, La. Poly. Inst., 1914; BS, ScD (hon.), La. State U., 1918, 1964; MS, Iowa State Coll. Agr., 1926; DSc (hon), Southwestern U. Memphis. Tchr. agr. Ansley High Sch., 1917; county agt. Union Parish, La., 1919; assoc. U. Southwestern La., 1920-92, successively asst. prof. agr., assoc. prof., prof., 1940-92, dir. agr. and indsl. tng. and dean Coll. Agr., pres., 1940-92. Mem. state com. Nat. Youth Adminstrn., state com. Rural Rehab., Lafayette Parish Works Progress Adminstrn. com.; com. on leaders program Am. Coun. ELdn.; trustee U. South, Sewanee, Tenn. With USNRF, WW I. Decorated Legion of Honor (France); recipient civic cup Parish of Lafayette, 1938; named Man of the Yr. La. Agr. by Progressive Farmer Mag., 1948. Mem. La. Farm Bur. Fedn. (past v.p.), Commn. Higher Edn. for So. Assn. of Colls., Lafayette Libr. Commn., Blue Key (hon.), La. Jersey Cattle Club (past pres.), Rotary (past pres. Lafayette, internat. dist. gov. 1948-49), Alpha Zeta, Phi Kappa Phi, Kappa Delta Pi, Alpha Phi Omega, Theta Xi. *

FLETCHER, MRS. JOHN GOULD See SIMON, CHARLIE MAY

FLEXNER, STUART BERG, editor, publishing executive, educator; b. Jacksonville, Ill., Mar. 22, 1928; s. David and Gertrude (Berg) F.; m. Doris Louise Hurcomb, Nov. 21, 1967; children: Jennifer, Geoffrey. B.A., U. Louisville, 1948, M.A., 1949; postgrad., Cornell U., 1950-52. Exec. editor Verlan Books, Inc., N.Y.C., 1952-57; mng. editor coll. div. Macmillan Co., N.Y.C., 1957-58; pres. Jugetas, S.A., Mexico City, 1958-64; div. v.p. Random House, Inc., N.Y.C., 1964-72, editor-in-chief reference dept., 1980-89; v.p. The Hudson Group, Pleasantville, N.Y., 1972-80; pres. Stuart Flexner Assocs., Greenwich, Conn., 1989-90; tchr. Cornell U., Ithaca, N.Y., 1950-52. Author: (with Harold Wentworth) The Dictionary of American Slang, 1960, I Hear America Talking, 1976, Listening to America, 1982; chief lexicographer: The Oxford American Dictionary, 1980. Named Outstanding Alumni U. Louisville, 1977. Mem. MLA, Nat. Council Tchrs. English, Dictionary Soc. N. Am., Am. Hist. Assn. Home: Greenwich Conn. Died Dec. 3, 1990; cremated.

FLINN, EDWARD AMBROSE, III, geophysicist; b. Oklahoma City, Aug. 27, 1931; s. Edward Ambrose and Marion Catalina (Prater) F.; m. Jane Margaret Bott, Dec. 29, 1962; 1 dau., Susan Katherine. B.S. in Geophysics (William Barton Rogers scholar), Mass. Inst. Tech., 1953; Ph.D. in Geophysics (NSF fellow 1953-54), Calif. Inst. Tech., 1960; postgrad. (Fulbright scholar), Australian Nat. U., 1958-59; certificat, Le Cordon Bleu Ecole de Cuisine et de Patesserie, 1971. Seismologist United ElectroDynamics Inc., Pasadena, Calif., 1960-62; chief seismologist, lab. seismic data Teledyne Geotech, Alexandria, Va., 1962-64; dir. research Teledyne Geotech, 1964-68; assoc. dir. Alexandria labs., 1968-74; dir. lunar programs office space sci. NASA, Washington, 1975; dep. dir., chief scientist lunar and planetary programs NASA, 1976-77, chief scientist earth and ocean programs, 1977, chief scientist geodynamics program, 1978-85, acting chief solid earth scis. geodynamics program, 1985-89; mem. joint research panel AEC-U.K. Atomic Energy Authority, 1963-74; vis. research assoc. Calif. Inst. Tech., 1969, 78; vis. assoc. prof. geophysics Brown U., 1970; cons. subcom. planetology steering com. space sci. and applications NASA, 1969-70, Nat. Swedish Inst. Bldg. Research, Stockholm, 1970; participant sci. exchange Nat. Acad. Sci.-Acad. Scis. USSR, 1970; mem. com. lunar and planetary exploration Nat. Acad. Scis., 1973-75, mem. com. on seismology, 1973-75, mem. com. on internat. geology, from 1982; mem. adv. com. earthquake studies U.S. Geol. Survey, from 1975. Trans., editor two books; assoc. editor for gen. seismology: Geophysics, 1965-67; editor sect. earth and planetary surfaces and interiors: Jour. Geophys. Research, 1973-78. Mem. adv. bd. No. Va. br. Urban League, 1970-71; mem. Alexandria Council on Human Relations, 1970-82; mem. traffic bd., Alexandria, 1972-74; mem. Alexandria Democratic Com., 1970-74, exec. bd., 1971-73. Fellow Am. Geophys. Union (sec. sect. seismology 1970-74; mem. AAAS, Am. Astron. Soc., Royal Astron. Soc. (editorial bd. Geophys. Jour. 1969-74), Assn. Earth Sci. Editors, Internat. Union Geodesy and Geophysics (chmn. commn. planetary scis. 1976-83, sec. Commn. on Internat. Coordination of Space Techniques for Geodesy and Geodynamics, sec. Intern-Assn. Com. Math. Geophysics 1971-75), Seismol. Soc. Am., Soc. Exploration Geophysicists, Inter-Assn. Com. Math. Geophysics (sec. 1971-75), Internat. Council Sci. Unions (sec.-gen. Inter-Union Commn. on Lithosphere 1980-86, mem. com. on publs. and communications 1982-86), 89ers Soc., Sigma Xi, Beta Theta Pi. Club: Cosmos. Home: Alexandria Va. Died Aug. 13, 1989.

FLIPSE, MATHEW JAY, cardiologist; b. Passaic, N.J., Nov. 16, 1896; s. Martin and Maggie (Pfanstiehl) F.; m. Alice Rasp, Aug. 18, 1921; children: Thomas E., Robert Frank. AB, Hope Coll., 1917, MS (hon.), 1919; MD, U. Cin., 1921. Intern, resident Cin. Gen. Hosp., 1921-23; pvt. practice medicine Miami, Fla., 1923-92; mem. courtesy staff various hosps. in Miami and Miami Beach area; sr. cons. svc. chronic pulmonary diseases, past pres. staff Jackson Meml. Hosp., Miami, 1938, Kendall Hosp.; clin. assoc. prof. medicine U. Miami Sch. Medicine, 1960-92. Contbr. articles to profl. jours. Fellow AMA (past chmn. sect. diseases chest 1959), Am. Coll. Chest Physicians (pres. 1960-61), ACP (life), Am. Coll. Cardiology, Am. Heart Assn., Am. Geriatrics Soc., Am. Acad. Compensation Medicine, Am. Coll. Angiology, Am. Coll. Allergy, Acad. Internat. Medicine; mem. So. Med. Assn., Fla. Med. Assn., Dade County Med. Assn. (past pres.), Am. Thoracic Soc., Am. Therapeujtic Soc., Nat. Tb Assn. (dir. 1939-40), Am. Acad. Gen. Practice, Am. Diabetic Soc. *

FLOERSHEIMER, WALTER D., banker; b. Wehrheim, Germany, Mar. 11, 1900; s. David F. and Fanny (Rosenthal) F.; m. Charlotte Saloman, May 21, 1931; 1 child, Stephen F. Student, U. Frankfurt; PhD, U. Wurzburg. V.p. Dresdner Bank, Germany; ptnr. E.J. Meyer Banking House, Berlin; sr. ptnr. Sutro Bros. & Co. Mem. N.Y. Stock Exch., Bankers Club (N.Y.C.), North Shore Country Club (Glen Head, L.I.), Palm Beach (Fla.) Country Club. Home: Zurich FL Died Apr. 3, 1989.

FLORINSKY, MICHAEL, author, educator; b. Kieff, Russia, Dec. 27, 1894; s. Timothy and Vera (Florinsky-Kremkoff) F.; m. Louise Ligott Dear, Sept. 5, 1946. Student, U. Kieff Law Sch., 1913-14, 18-19, London Sch. Econs., 1920-21; MA, Columbia U., 1927, PhD, 1931. Assoc. editor Econ. and Social History of the World War, 1921-33; assoc. in econs. Columbia U., N.Y.C., 1931-36, lectr., 1936-46, asst. prof., 1947-53, assoc. prof., 1953-56, prof. econs., 1956-63, prof. emeritus, 1963-92. Author several books on Europe; also Russia: A History and an Interpretation, 1953, Integrated Europe, 1955, Russia: A Short History, 1964, Commercial and Tariff History, 1919-41, Ency. on Russia and the Soviet Union, 1960-61; editor paperback div. Crowell-Collier; contbr. articles to mags. Jr. officer 31st Regiment F.A., Russian Army, 1915-18. Decorated four Russian Army decorations. Mem. Coun. Fgn. Relations, Am. Hist. Assn., Author's Club (London). Russian Greek Ch. *

FLORY, PAUL JOHN, chemist; b. Sterling, Ill., June 19, 1910; s. Ezra and Martha (Brumbaugh) F.; m. Emily Catharine Tabor, Mar. 7, 1936; children—Susan, Melinda, Paul J. B.S., Manchester Coll., 1931, Sc.D. (hon.), 1950; M.S., Ohio State U., 1931, Ph.D., 1934, Sc.D., 1970. Engaged in research on synthetic fibers, synthetic rubber and other polymeric substances Dupont Exptl. Sta., Wilmington, Del., 1934-38, U. Cin., 1938-40, Standard Oil Devel. Co., Elizabeth, N.J., 1940-43; dir. fundamental research Goodyear Tire & Rubber Co., Akron, Ohio, 1943-48; prof. chemistry Cornell U., 1948-57; exec. dir. research Mellon Inst., Pitts., 1956-61; J.G. Jackson-C.J.Wood prof. chemistry Stanford, 1961-85. Author: Principles of Polymer Chemistry and of Statistical Mechanics of Chain Molecules; Contbr. to sci. publs. Recipient Sullivant medal Ohio State U., 1945; Baekeland award Am. Chem. Soc., 1947; George Fisher Baker non-resident lectureship in chemistry Cornell U., 1948; Peter Debye award in phys. chemistry Am. Chem. Soc., 1968; Gibbs medal, 1973; Priestley medal, 1974; Cresson medal Franklin Inst., 1971; Nobel prize for chemistry, 1974; Nat. medal of sci., 1974. Fellow AAAS; mem. Am. Chem. Soc., Nat. Acad. Scis., Am. Acad. Arts and Scis., Am. Phys. Soc., Am. Philos. Soc. Home: Portola Valley Calif. Died Sept. 9, 1985.

FLORY, WILLIAM R., hotel executive; b. Rockingham County, Va., Mar. 26, 1897; s. George William and Leila Abbie (McKinney) F. AB, Juniata Coll., Huntington, Pa., 1921. Pres., dir. Grenoble Hotels, Inc., Harrisburg, Pa., 1933-92, Chambersburg (Pa.) Hotel Corp., 1943-92, Va. Operating Co., Portsmouth, 1945-92, Tenn. Hotels, Inc., Cleve., 1954-92; dir. Am. Hotels Corp., N.Y.C., Richard McAllister Realty Corp., Hanover, Pa., Radford (Va.) Hotel Corp., Assoc. Hotels, Inc., Whiteville, N.C., Assoc. Va. Hotels, Inc., Wytheville, Va., Hotel Operaters, Inc., Radford. Trustee Juniata Coll. Mem. Am. Hotel Assn. (past nat. chmn. smaller hotels com.), Masons (32 degree), Shriner. *

FLOYD, EDWIN EARL, mathematics educator; b. Eufaula, Ala., May 8, 1924; s. John Quincy and Ludie (James) F.; m. Marguerite Stahl, May 11, 1945; children—Judith L., Sally J., William J. B.A., U. Ala., 1943; Ph.D., U. Va., 1948. Instr. math. Princeton U., 1948-49; mem. faculty U. Va., from 1949, prof. math., from 1956, Robert Taylor prof., from 1966, chmn., 1966-69; dean U. Va. (Faculty of Arts and Scis.), 1974-81, v.p., provost, 1981-86; mem. Inst. Advanced Study, 1958-59, 63-64. Author: (with P.E. Conner) Differentiable Periodic Maps, 1964; also articles. Sloan Research fellow, 1962-64; recipient Thomas Jefferson award U. Va., 1981. Home: Charlottesville Va. Died Dec. 9, 1990; buried U. Va. Cemetery.

FODOR, EUGENE, publishing executive, editor; b. Léva, Hungary, Oct. 14, 1905; came to U.S., 1938, naturalized, 1942; s. Gyula Mátyás and Malvin (Kürti) F.; m. Vlasta Maria Zobel, Dec. 4, 1948. Baccalaureat, Lucenec, Czechoslovakia, 1924; Licenciéés Econ. Politique, Faculté de Droit, U. Grenoble, France, 1927; postgrad., U. Hamburg, Germany. Travel corr. Prague Hungarian Jour., 1930-33; travel editor European Travel Guides, London, 1934-38; fgn. editor Query mag., London, 1937-38; editor, pub. Fodor's Modern Guides, Inc., Paris, France, 1949-64; pres. Fodor's Modern

Guides, Inc., Litchfield, Conn., 1964-81; chmn. bd. Fodor's Modern Guides, Ltd., London, 1964-81. Editor 86 travel books pub. annually, 1950, trans. French, German, Italian, Dutch, Spanish, Hungarian. Served to capt. AUS, 1942-47. Recipient Grand prix de Littérature de Tourisme, 1959; award Caribbean Tourist Assn., 1960; Spl. award Pacific Area Tourist Assn., Hong Kong, 1962; Austrian Govt. Honor medal, 1970; other recent awards England, Spain, Italy; Discover Am. Travel Orgn. award New Orleans, 1975; Travel Hall of Fame award, 1978; George Washington laureate, 1982. Mem. Nat. Assn. Travel Orgns. (award 1966), Soc. Am. Travel Writers (spl. award 1989), Internat. Union Ofcl. Travel Orgns., Fedn. Internat. des Journalistes et Ecrivains de Tourisme, Pacific Area Travel Assn., S.Am. Travel Orgn., Caribbean Tourist Assn. Home: Litchfield Conn. Died Feb. 18, 1991; buried East Litchfield Cemetery, Conn.

FOGERTY, THOMAS RICHARD, recording artist, songwriter; b. Berkeley, Calif., Nov. 9, 1941; s. Galen Robert Fogerty and Edith Lucile (Lytle) Loosli; m. Gail Skinner (div. 1977); children: Scott, Jeff, Kristine, Jill; m. Tricia Suzanne Clapper, Oct. 19, 1980; children: Ashley Suzanne, Nicole Elizabeth. Grad. high sch., Berkeley. Singer, songwriter Tommy Fogerty and the Blue Velvets, San Francisco, 1959-63; singer, songwriter, guitarist The Golliwogs, San Francisco, 1964-67, Creedence Clearwater Revival, San Francisco, 1967-71; ind. rec. artist San Francisco, 1971-80; leader TFRO, San Francisco, 1987-90; owner Wild Cherry Music, Scottsdale, Ariz., 1986-90. Rec. artist: (albums) CCR, Bayou Country, Green River, Willy and the Poor Boys, Cosmo's Factory, Pendulum, CCR: The Concert. Mem. AFTRA, Am. Fedn. Musicians. Home: Scottsdale Ariz. Died Sept. 6, 1990. †

FOLEY, DENNIS DONALD, metal processing executive; b. Bainville, Mont., Mar. 17, 1923; s. Louis J. and Alice (Gessner) F.; m. Mary Ann Brichler, Apr. 26, 1947; 1 child, Diane. B in Chem. Engring., Ohio State U., Columbus, 1947, MS in Physics, 1949, PhD in Chem. Engring., 1954. Registered profl. engr., Ohio, Calif., Conn. Asst. div. chief Battelle Meml. Inst., Columbus, 1954-61; gen. mgr., nuclear prodn. Am. Standard, Mountain View, Calif., 1961-63; mgr. materials and applied mechs. Ventura div. Northrop Aviation, Thousand Oaks, Calif., 1963-64; dir. engring. and lab. Neptune Internat., Wallingford, Conn., 1964-73; v.p. tech. Alcan Aluminum, Cambridge, Mass., 1973-88. Home: Warner NH Died Aug. 13, 1988.

FOLEY, DORANCE VINCENT, clergyman; b. Ryan, Iowa, Apr. 6, 1900; s. Frank M. and Lillian (Synan) F. A.B., Campion Coll., 1921; student priesthood, St. Paul Sem., Minn., to 1925; LL.D., Loras Coll., 1947, Clarke Coll., 1975. Ordained priest Roman Catholic Ch., 1925; curate Nativity Ch., Dubuque, Iowa, 1925-26; chancellor and sec. Archdiocese of Dubuque, 1926-51, vicar gen., 1944-52, officialis, 1950-51, prothonotary apostolic, 1952, papal chamberlain, 1934, domestic prelate, 1945; irremovable rector St. Patrick's Parish, Dubuque, 1952-56, pastor, 1966-72; dean Dubuque Roman Cath. Clergy, 1952-56; pres. Loras Coll., Dubuque, 1956-66, spl. asst. to pres. for devel., 1972-88; Chaplain Mercy Hosp., Dubuque, 1926-31, Mt. Loretto, Dubuque, 1931-52; Vice pres., treas. Archdiocese Dubuque, Inc., 1944-52, archdiocesan consultor, 1944-81; v.p. Cath. Charities, Archdiocese of Dubuque; dir. The Witness, Cath. Charities, Inc., 1944-52. Served Students Army Tng. Corps., World War I. Mem. Am. Legion (past chaplain Dubuque post), C.O.F., Delta Epsilon Sigma. Club: K.C. Home: Dubuque Iowa Died Oct. 12, 1988; buried Dubuque, Iowa.

FOLEY, JAMES THOMAS, federal judge; b. Troy, N.Y., July 9, 1910; s. Thomas David and Mary (Malone) F.; m. Eleanor Marie Anthony, July 16, 1953; 1 dau., Mary Jude Foley Mayoli. A.B., Fordham U., 1931; LL.B., Albany Law Sch., 1934. Bar: N.Y., 1934. Engaged in private practice law Troy, 1935-42; sec. to Supreme Ct. Justice William H. Murray, 1939-42, 46-49; judge U.S. Dist. Ct., No. Dist. N.Y., 1949-63, chief judge, 1963-80, sr. judge, 1980-90. Served as lt. USNR, 1942-45. Albany Courthouse renamed James T. Foley Fed. Courthouse in his honor, 1989. Mem. Am., N.Y. bar assns., VFW, Am. Legion. Clubs: K.C, Elk. Home: Rensselaer NY Died Aug. 17, 1990; buried St. Mary's Cemetery, Troy, N.Y.

FOLEY, WILLIAM EDWARD, federal courts administrator; b. Danbury, Conn., Feb. 7, 1911; s. Edward L. and Hertha (Braun) F.; m. Marguerite M. Pratt, June 6, 1951; children: William, Christopher, Anne, Richard, Jonathan, David, Carl. A.B., Harvard U., 1932, LL.B., 1935, A.M., 1939, Ph.D., 1940. Bar: Mass. 1935. Practiced in Boston, 1935-40; chief internal security fgn. agts. registration sect. Dept. Justice, 1948-54; exec. asst. internal security div. U.S. Dept. Justice, 1954-58, 1st asst. criminal div., 1958-64; dep. dir. Adminstrv. Office U.S. Cts., Washington, 1964-77, dir., 1977-85, sec. com. on rules of practice and procedure; chief adminstrv. officer, dir. Fed. Jud. Ctr., Washington, 1977-85. Served to lt. comdr. USNR, 1942-46; capt. Res. Mem. Am. Law Inst., Am., Fed. bar assns., Am. Judicature Soc. Home: Chevy Chase Md. Died Aug. 11, 1990.

FOLEY, WILLIAM THOMAS, physician, educator; b. N.Y.C., Oct. 30, 1911; s. Edmund Leo and Sarah (O'Loughlin) F.; m. Barbara Ball, June 29, 1946; children: Caroline Ball, Lucy L., Claire E., Laura D.; m. Regula von Muralt, Apr. 25, 1970; 1 child, Alix E. B.A., Columbia U., 1933; M.D., Cornell U., 1937. Diplomate Am. Bd. Internal Medicine. Instr. anatomy Hong Kong U., 1939-41; organizer Fong Pin Hosp., Canton, China, 1940; mem. pub. health survey Orient for Navy, 1941; research fellow Pekin Union Med. Coll., 1941; mem. staff N.Y. Hosp., 1946-92, asso. attending physician, 1960-85, attending physician, 1985-92, chief vascular clinic; clin. prof. medicine Cornell U. Med. Coll., 1984-92; cons. physician N.Y. Infirmary, Mary Walsh Home, Southampton, Beckman Downtown hosps., Community Hosp., Glen Cove, North Shore Univ. Hosp.; mem. med. bd. Doctors Hosp. Del. Internat. Cardiovascular Congress, Paris, 1950, Buenos Aires, 1952, Basel, 1954, Stockholm, 1956, Brussels, 1958, Mexico, 1962, Barcelona, 1967, London, 1970; del. European-Am. Symposium on Venous Disease, Zurich, 1978; mem. U.S. nat. commn. USPHS; mem. med. adv. bd. Am. Cancer Found. Author: Vascular Diseases, 1947, Colored Atlas and Management of Vascular Diseases, 1959; co-author: Diseases of the Heart and Blood Vessels, 1964; editor: Advances in the Management of Vascular Diseases, Vol. I, 1980, Vol. II, 1981, Vol. III, 1983, also 108 articles in med. jours. Served as lt. (j.g.) USN, 1937-38; comdr. 1941-46. Decorated D.S.M. Navy, Bronze Star, Purple Heart, China War medal, 1978; 9 named to Xavier Hall of Fame, 1973; established William T. Foley Endowed Disting. Prof. Medicine chair Cornell U. Med. Coll., 1988; named Hon. Alumnus Univ. Dublin, 1990. Fellow A.C.P. (life), N.Y. Acad. Medicine, Am. Coll. Cardiology; mem. Am. Fedn. Clin. Research, A.M.A. (cons. to council pharm. and chemistry), Am. Heart Assn. (circulation bd.), N.Y. Physicians Sci. (pres.), Internat. Council Health and Travel, Harvey Soc., Beta Theta Pi. Clubs: Dutch Treat, University (N.Y.C.); Piping Rock, Seawanhaka Yacht, Everglades, Palm Beach Bath and Tennis. Home: New York N.Y. Died Oct. 3, 1992. †

FOLK, ERNEST L., III, legal educator; b. Suffolk, Va., Apr. 18, 1930. A.B., Roanoke Coll., 1952; LL.B., U. Va., 1956, A.M., 1958. Bar: Va. 1956. Atty. U.S. Dept. Justice, 1956-59; assoc. prof. S.C., 1959-63; assoc. prof. U. N.C., Charlottesville, 1963-66, prof., 1966-68; prof. U. Va., Charlottesville, 1968-77, Charles O. Gregory prof. law, 1977-82, William S. Potter prof. law, 1982-90; vis. prof. Columbia, 1975-76. Editor: Securities Law Rev., 1970-75; author: The Delaware General Corporation Law, 1972, (with R. Ward and E. Welch) 2d edit., 1987. Home: Charlottesville NC Died Nov. 16, 1989.

FOLSOM, FRAN M., electronics company executive; b. Sprague, Wash., May 14, 1894; s. Edward Presley and Anna Maria (Wilson) F.; m. Gladys Mabel Jordan, Aug. 5, 1917 (dec.); children: Betty Marian Folsom Leslie Jr., Dorothy Gladys Folsom Macrae, Jeanne Frances Folsom Cook. LLD, U. San Francisco; postgrad., St. Joseph's Coll., Manhattan Coll., Fordham U. Several positions in merchandising field, 1910-32; with Montgomery Ward & Co., 1932-39, Goldblatt Bros., Chgo., 1940-41; asst. coord. purchases OPM, Washington, 1941-42; asst. chief in charge procurement, spl. asst. Under Sec. of Navy, Washington, 1942-43; exec. v.p., dir. RCA Victor div. RCA, 1944-49, pres., 1949-57, chmn. exec. com. bd., 1957-92; dir. Coca-Cola Bottling Co. of N.Y., Inc., John P. Maguire Co., 480 Park Ave. Corp., NBC, Gen. Cable Corp., RCA Comms., Crown Cork & Seal Co., RCA Victor Co., Ltd., Tishman Realty and Constrn. Co., Inc.; permanent rep. of Holy See, Internat. Agy. for Atomic Energy, 1957. Mem. adv. bd. N.Y. Foundling Hosp.; dir. Alfred E. Smith Meml. Found.; trustee Nat. Jewish Hosp., Denver, St. Mary-of-the-Woods Coll., Rosemont Coll., Cath. Charities (N.Y.), Samuel H. Kress Found., Nat. Cath. Community Svc.; adv. coun. on sci. and engring. U. Notre Dame. With U.S. Army, 1917-18. Recipient numerous honors and awards orgns., univs., chs. and states. Mem. Bohemian Club (San Francisco), Augusta (Ga.) Nat. Golf Club, Eureka Athletic Club (Phila.), Pilgrims of the U.S., Blind Brook Club (Port Chester, N.Y.), Everglades Club (Palm Beach, Fla.). *

FOLTS, FRANKLIN ERTES, business administration educator; b. Machias, N.Y., Mar. 10, 1893; s. Burdette and Frederica (Gee) F.; m. Eva A. Boyed, Sept. 21, 1920; children: Naomi Jane Folts Lewis Jr., Patricia Folts Dooley. Student, Cornell U., 1915-17; AB, U. Oreg., 1919, MBA, 1923; AM (hon.), Harvard U., 1940. Instr. bus. adminstrn. U. Oreg., asst. prof., asso. prof., prof., asst. dean, acting dean, 1920-28; assoc. prof. indsl. mgmt. Harvard Grad. Sch. Bus. Adminstrn., 1928-39, prof., 1939-64, prof. emeritus, from 1964; cons. Indian Inst. Mgmt., Ahmedabad, 1965, 66; faculty AMP in Far East, Taiwan, 1959, Hong Kong, 1960, 61, Bangalore, India, 1961, Advanced Mgmt. Seminar, Kelo U., Tokyo, 1959; cons. Brit. Colonial Govt., Hong Kong, 1961; dir. Breech Sch. Bus. Adminstrn., Drury Coll.; cons. sch. bus. adminstrn. Boston U. Author: (with A.B. Stillman) Interpretive Accounting, 1929; (with E.C. Robbins) Industrial Management, 1932; Introduction to Industrial Management, 1938. 1st lt. U.S. Army, WW I. Mem. Am. Econ. Assn., Soc. for Advancement Mgmt., Am. Acad. Mgmt. (nat. sec. 1945-47, v.p. 1952-53, pres. 1953-54). Republican. Presbyterian. *

FONTAINE, ATHANAS PAUL, aircraft executive; b. Ludlow, Mass., Aug. 1, 1905; s. Clovis and Oliva (Lavoie) F.; m. Arline McGrath, Oct. 20, 1930; children: John Clovis, Edward, Thomas, Anne. BS, NYU, 1930; DSc in Engring., Wayne State U., 1962; DBA (hon.), U. Mich., 1968. Aircraft designer Fairchild Aircraft Corp., Hagerstown, Md., 1935-36; project engr. Republic Aircraft Corp., Farmingdale, N.Y., 1936-39; chief engr. Convair's Stinson div. Vultee Aircraft, Inc., Wayne, Mich., 1938-40, Convair's Vultee field div., 1940-42; asst. dir. engring. Consol. Vultee Aircraft Corp., 1942-44, exec. v.p., 1951-52; dir. exptl. aircraft div. Bendix Aviation Corp., Detroit, 1944-45, staff exec. ea. group, 1952-54, dir. engring., 1954-55, v.p. engring., 1955-60; dir. Aero. Rsch. Ctr., U. Mich., 1945-51; bd. dirs. Rohr Corp., Nat. Bank Detroit, Uniroyal, Inc. Mem. Econ. Devel. Corp. Greater Detroit; Mich. chmn. U.S. Savs. Bond program, 1971-72; trustee Traffic Safety Coun. Mich., Citizens Rsch. Coun. Mich.; bd. dirs. U. Mich. Devel. Coun.; mem. corp. Merrill-Palmer Inst.; exec. com. Air Found. Recipient Disting. Alumnus award NYU, 1961, Mich. Wolverine award, 1961;named Alumknus of Yr., NYU Coll. Engring., 1962. Mem. NAM (bd. dirs.), Conf. Bd., Econ. Club Detroit (bd. dirs.). Home: Birmingham Mich. Died May 15, 1989.

FONTANA, MARS GUY, metallurgical engineer, educator; b. Iron Mountain, Mich., Apr. 6, 1910; s. Dominic and Rosalie (Amico) F.; m. Elizabeth Frances Carley, Aug. 21, 1937; children—Martha Jane, Mary Elizabeth, David Carley, Thomas Edward. B.S., U. Mich., 1931, M.S., 1932, Ph.D., 1935, D.Eng. (hon.), 1975. Research asst., dept. engring. research U. Mich., 1929-34; metall. engr., group supervisor engring. dept. duPont Co., Wilmington, Del., 1934-45; prof., chmn. dept. metall. engring. Ohio State U., 1945-75, prof. emeritus, 1976, Regents prof., 1967-70, Duriron prof., 1970-75; dir. Corrosion Center; supr. metall. research; dir. Worthington Industries, 1973-86, mem. audit com., 1975-80; research NASA, USN, USAF, Nat. Sci. Found., Alloy Casting Inst.; cons. engr. several pvt. and govtl. orgns. Author: Corrosion: A Compilation, 1957, Corrosion Engineering, 1967, 3d edit., 1986; contbr.: column Indsl. and Engring. Chemistry, 1947-56; also other tech. publs. Recipient distinguished alumnus citation U. Mich., 1953, Sesquicentennial award, 1967; Frank Newman Speller award in corrosion engring. Nat. Assn. Corrosion Engrs., 1956; Native Son award Iron Mountain (Mich.) Rotary Club, 1969; Neil Armstrong award Ohio Soc. Profl. Engrs., 1973; MacQuigg Teaching award Coll. Engring., Ohio State U., 1973; 1st Educator award Metall. Soc., 1986; Mars G. Fontana Labs. at Ohio State U. named in his honor, 1981. Fellow Am. Soc. Metals (hon.; Gold medal 1979), AIME, Am. Inst. Chem. Engrs.; mem. Nat. Assn. Corrosion Engrs. (pres. 1952, editor Jour. Corrosion 1962-74), Electrochem. Soc., Materials Tech. Inst. of Chem. Process Industries (exec. dir. from 1977), Nat. Acad. Engring., Nat. Soc. Profl. Engrs., Am. Soc. Engring. Edn. (award for excellence in engring. instruction 1969), Sphinx, Texnikoi, Sigma Xi, Tau Beta Pi, Alpha Chi Sigma, Iota Alpha, Phi Eta Sigma, Phi Lambda Upsilon. Clubs: Port au Villa (Naples, Fla.) (pres. 1967-70); Faculty, Univ. Golf. Home: Columbus OH Died Feb. 29, 1988; buried Greenlawn Cemetery, Columbus.

FONTEYN DE ARIAS, DAME MARGOT, ballerina; b. Reigate, Surrey, Eng., May 18, 1919; d. Felix J. Hookham; m. Roberto E. Arias, 1955. Hon. degrees; Litt.D., U. Leeds; D.Mus., U. London, Oxford U.; LL.D., U. Edinburgh; D.Litt., U. Manchester. Prima ballerina Royal Ballet Co., London; pres. Royal Acad. Dancing, London, from 1954; chancellor Durham U., from 1982. Author: Margot Fonteyn, 1975, A Dancer's World, 1978, The Magic of Dance (BBC series), 1979, 80, Pavlova Impressions, 1984; films include I am a Dancer, 1972. Recipient Benjamin Franklin medal Royal Soc. Arts, 1974; Internat. Artist award Philippines, 1976; Hamburg Internat. Shakespeare prize, 1977; award of merit Phila. Art Alliance, 1985; Decorated comdr. Order of Brit. Empire, 1951, dame , 1956, Order Finnish Lion, 1960, Order Estacio de Sa Brazil, 1973, chevalier Order Merit of Duarte, Sanchez and Mella Dominican Republic, 1975. Home: Panama City Panama Died Feb. 21, 1991; buried Panama.

FOOSHEE, MALCOLM, lawyer; b. Charleston, Tenn., Oct. 1, 1898; s. Joseph Crockett and Lillian (Powell) F.; A.B., U. South, 1918, D.C.L., 1983; J.D., Harvard, 1921; B.C.L., Christ Church, Oxford U. (Rhodes scholar), 1924; m. Clare Fraser Murray, 1930 (dec. 1951); children—Joan Murray (Mrs. Shepard A. Spunt) (dec.), Clare Fraser Childres; m. 2d, Wynne Byard Taylor, 1953. Admitted to N.Y. bar, 1922, since practiced in N.Y.C.; with Murray, Aldrich & Roberts, 1921-22, Davis, Polk, Wardwell, Gardiner & Reed, 1925-42; mem. Donovan, Leisure, Newton & Irvine, N.Y.C. and Washington, 1943-81, of counsel, from 1981; legal work, Europe and Japan. 1928, 35, 49, 50; barrister; mem. Inner Temple (Inns of Court), London, from 1922. Mem. legislative com. Citizens Union, N.Y.C., 1926-27; mem. Rye (N.Y.) Planning Commn., 1943-45, Rye Sch. Consolidation Commn., 1943-44; mem. Diocesan Commn. Coll. Work, N.Y.C., 1951-58. Pres. Rye Library, 1950-53, trustee, 1948-59; trustee Rye Country

Day Sch., 1947-51, trustee U. of South, 1953-56. Mem. Am. delegation to Atlantic Congress, London, 1959. Mem. Harvard Naval Unit, 1918; Squadron A Cav., N.Y. N.G., 1926-20. Assoc. Knight Order St. John Jerusalem. Mem. ABA (chmn. sect. corp., banking and bus. law 1951-52), Internat. Bar Assn., N.Y. State Bar Assn., Assn. of Bar of the City of N.Y., Am. Law Inst., Am. Judicature Soc., Assn. Am. Rhodes Scholars (bd. dirs. 1949-82), Huguenot Soc. Am. (chancellor 1976-79, dir.), S.R., Phi Beta Kappa, Kappa Sigma. Democrat. Episcopalian. Clubs: Century, Harvard, Church (N.Y.C.). Contbr. to legal publs. Died June 23, 1989; buried Christ Ch., Rye, N.Y. Home: New York NY

FOOTE, EMERSON, advertising corporation executive; b. Sheffield, Ala., Dec. 13, 1906; s. James Adonijah and Ruth (Penn) F.; m. Sabina Fromhold, Apr. 18, 1938 (dec. Oct. 1985); children: Florence Anne, Katherine Penn, James Adair, Jennifer Broughton. Student pub. schs.; D.Pub. Service, Brigham Young U., 1965. With bldg. and loan assn., automobile distbg. co., life ins. co., 1923-31, Leon Livingston Advt. Agy., San Francisco, 1931-35, Yeomans & Foote, 1935-36, J. Stirling Getchell, Inc., N.Y.C., 1936-38; with Lord & Thomas, 1938-42, exec. v.p., 1942; co-founder Foote, Cone & Belding, 1942, pres., 1942-50; with McCann-Erickson, Inc., 1951-64, pres., 1960-63, chmn. bd., 1962-64; 1st chmn. Nat. Interagy. Council on Smoking and Health, Washington, 1964-67; chmn. Campaign to Check Population Explosion, 1967-69; dir. Nat. Liberty Corp., Valley Forge, Pa., 1969-73; chmn. bd. DeMoss Assos., Inc. subsidiary, 1969-73. Mem. Pres. Johnson's Commn. on Heart Disease, Cancer and Stroke, 1964-65; adviser to Govt. India on Family Planning, 1969; mem. U.S. Senate Panel Consultants on Cancer, 1970-71, USPHS Cancer Control Adv. Com., from 1972; hon. dir. Non-Smokers' Rights Assn., Can., from 1979; Trustee or bd. dirs. numerous non-profit orgns. including Menninger Found., Am. Cancer Soc., AAPC, Inc., others; bd. dirs. Putnam Hosp. Ctr., 1975-82. Recipient Clement Cleveland medal for cancer work, 1953, Nat. Vol. Leadership award Am. Cancer Soc., 1974. Home: Lake Carmel N.Y. Deceased. †

FORBES, HARLAND C(LEMENT), utilities company executive; b. Colebrook, N.H., Feb. 21, 1898; s. Allen A. and Mary (Corcoran) F.; m. Frances I. Ransom, May 29, 1928 (dec. 1968); children: Howard R., Barton A.; m. Elizabeth S. Clay, April 1, 1969. BS, U. N.H., 1921, DE, 1960; SM, MIT, 1923. Instr. MIT, 1921-23; design and testing staff cen. office telephone apparatus Western Electric Co., N.Y.C., 1923-24; with N.Y. Edison Co. and successor co. Consol. Edison Co. N.Y., 1924-90, rsch. engr., 1928-32, system engr., 1932-40, asst. v.p., 1940-45, v.p., 1945-49, exec. v.p., 1949-55, pres., 1955-57, chmn. bd. dirs., 1957-66; trustee N.Y. Bank for Savs.; bd. dirs. Erie Lackawanna R.R. Fellow IEEE; mem. Soc. Gas Lighting, Pinnacle Club (N.Y.C.), Sarasota (Fla.) Yacht Club. Home: Sarasota Fla. Died May 15, 1990; buried Sarasota, Fla.

FORBES, MALCOLM STEVENSON, publisher, author, former state senator; b. N.Y.C., Aug. 19, 1919; s. Bertie Charles and Adelaide (Stevenson) F.; m. Roberta Remsen Laidlaw, Sept. 21, 1946 (div. 1985); children: Malcolm Stevenson Jr., Robert Laidlaw, Christopher Charles, Timothy Carter, Moira Hamilton Forbes Mumma. Grad. cum laude, Lawrenceville Acad., 1937; AB, Princeton U., 1941; LHD (hon.), Nasson Coll., 1966; LLD (hon.), Okla. Christian Coll., 1973; LittD (hon.), Milliken U., 1974, Ball State U., 1980; DFA (hon.), Franklin Pierce Coll., 1975; DSc of Bus. Adminstrn. (hon.), Bryant Coll., 1976; D of Journalism (hon.), Babson Coll., 1977, Central New Eng. Coll., 1981; LLD (hon.), Am. Grad. Sch. Internat. Mgmt., 1977, Pace U., 1979, Potomac Sch. Law, 1979, Kean Coll. N.J., 1981, Westminster Coll., 1981, Seton Hill Coll., 1981, U. Vt., 1982, U. No. Colo., 1983, E. Tex. State U., 1984, Lehigh U., 1984, Webster U., 1984, Wittenberg U., 1985; D of Econ. Journalism (hon.), Lakeland Coll., 1980; HHD (hon.), Hofstra U., 1981, Ohio U., 1981, Southwestern at Memphis, 1983; DBA (hon.), Bloomfield Coll., 1982, Husson Coll., 1983; LHD (hon.), Lincoln Coll., 1983, U. Denver, 1983, Hillsdale Coll., 1984, Johns Hopkins U., 1984, Pratt Inst., 1985, St. Peter's Coll., 1986, Hampden-Sydney Coll., 1986; LittD (hon.), Miami U., 1983, Franklin and Marshall Coll., 1984, Rider Coll., 1986; DCS (hon.), St. Bonaventure, 1986; LLD (hon.), U. Aberdeen, 1986, Lewis and Clark Coll., 1986; Degree in Internat. Entrepreneurship (hon.), Armand Hammer United World Coll. of Am. West; DCS (hon.), Suffolk U., 1987; LHD (hon.), Carnegie-Mellon U., 1987, Centenary Coll., 1987; LLD (hon.), U. Mo., 1987; D of Bus. Adminstrn., Johnson & Wales Coll., 1987; LLD (hon.), Southwestern Adventist Coll., 1987, Spring Garden Coll., 1987; LHD (hon.), U. Tampa, 1988, Loyola Coll., 1988, Wilkes Coll., 1988; LLD (hon.), Syracuse U., 1988, Trenton Coll., 1988; D of Pub. Svc. and Bus. Leadership, Adams State Coll., 1988. Owner, pub. Fairfield Times (weekly), Lancaster, Ohio, 1941; est. Lancaster Tribune (weekly), 1942; assoc. pub. Forbes Mag. Bus., N.Y.C., 1946-54, pub., editor-in-chief, 1957-90; v.p. Forbes Inc., N.Y.C., 1947-64, pres., 1964-80, chmn., chief exec. officer, 1980-90; chmn. bd. 60 Fifth Ave. Corp.; pres. Forbes Trinchera Inc.; chmn. Fiji Forbes; founder, pres., pub. Nations Heritage (bi-monthly), 1948-49; chmn. bd. Sangre de Cristo Ranches Inc.; 1st person to fly coast-to-coast in U.S. in hot air balloon; set 6 world records in hot air ballooning, 1973; founded the world's 1st balloon mus., Chateau de Balleroy in Normandy, France, 1973; made 1st free flight of hot air balloon over Beijing, also 1st motorcycle tour of People's Rep. of China, 1982. Author: Fact and Comment, 1974, The Sayings of Chairman Malcolm, 1978, Around the World on Hot Air and Two Wheels, 1985, The Further Sayings of Malcolm Forbes, 1986, They Went That-a-way, 1988, More Than I Dreamed: A Lifetime of Collecting, 1989. Campaign chmn. ARC, Somerset Hills, N.J., 1949; mem. Borough Council Bernardsville, N.J., state senator, 1952-58, Republican candidate for gov., N.J., 1957, N.J. del.-at-large Rep. Nat. Conv., 1960; bd. dirs., Naval War Coll., 1975-77; trustee St. Mark's Sch., 1976-80, Princeton U., 1982, charter trustee, 1986—; bd. dirs. Coast Guard Acad. Found.; chmn. N.J. Rhodes Scholarship Com., 1976, 78, 79; mem. Princeton Art Council, 1973-79. Served with inf. AUS, 1942-45. Decorated Bronze Star, Purple Heart, Order of Merit France, Order of Ouissam Alaoyite (Morocco), President's Medal of Achievement (Pakistan); assoc. officer Order of St. John; recipient Freedoms Found. Medal, 1949; named Young Man of Year N.J. Jr. C. of C., 1951; recipient Aeronauts trophy, Harmon award, 1975; named hon. paramount chief Nimba tribe, Liberia, Philanthropist of Yr. Greater N.Y. chpt. Nat. Soc. Fund Raising Execs., 1986, Grand Dad of Yr. Old Grand Dad Club, 1986; recipient Eaton Corp. award Internat. Platform Assn., 1979, Disting. Achieement award in Periodical Journalism U. So. Calif. Journalism Alumni Assn., 1979; Image award for bus. and industry Men's Fashion Assn. Am., 1979; Bus. Leadership award Columbia U. Sch. Bus., 1980; Man of Conscience award Appeal of Conscience Found., 1980; Franklin award for disting. service Printing Industries Met. N.Y., 1981; Sacred Cat award Milw. Press Club, 1981; award for entrepreneurial excellence Yale U. Mgmt. Sch., 1982; Superstar of Yr. award Police Athletic League, 1982; Manstyle award Gentlemen's Quar., 1983; Community Service award Greenwich Village C. of C., 1983; Communicator of Yr. award Bus. Profl. Advt. Assn., 1983; Communicator of Yr. award 33d Ann. Enterprise award, award Council for Econ. Edn., 1983, Pub. of Yr. award Mag. Pubs. Assn., 1983; Medal of Honor Culinary Inst. of Am., 1983; Henry Johnson Fisher award, 1984; Free Enterprise award Ins. Fedn. N.Y., 1984; Mr. N.Y.'s Finest Championship award Patrolmen's Benevolent Assn., 1984; Person of Yr. award French-Am. C. of C. in U.S., 1985; Ann. Citation of Merit, Salvation Army Assn., 1985; inducted into Aviation Hall of Fame of N.J., 1985; Am. Eagle award Invest in Am. Nat. Council, 1986, Hands in Applause award Sales Execs. Club of N.Y., 1986; recipient Diplome Montgolfier Fedn. Aeronautique for outstanding contrib. to devel. ballooning, 1986; named Philanthropist of Yr. Greater N.Y. chpt. Nat. Soc. Fund Raising Execs., 1986, Assoc. Comdr. Brother of the Most Venerable Order Hosp. St. John of Jerusalem, 1986; Honored by the Govs. Com. on Scholastic Achievement, 1986; Salmagundi Honor award and the Richard M. Cyert Medal for Profl. Excellence Carnegie-Mellon U., 1987; Motorcyclist of Yr. award Motorcyclist Mag., 1987; Internat. Motorcyclist of Yr. award Internat. World of Motorcycles, 1988; inducted into Hall of Fame of N.Y. Fin. Writers Assn., 1988; promoted to the rank of officer by the French Gov. Legion of Honor, 1988; apptd. Knight Grand Cross of the Most Noble Order of the Crown of Thailand, 1988. Mem. St. Andrew's Soc., 84th Inf. Div. Assn., Def. Orientation Conf. Assn., N.J. Hist. Soc., Nat. Aero. Assn. (dir., exec. v.p.), Internat. Balloonists Assn., Balloon Fedn. Am. (dir. 1974-76), Aircraft Owners and Pilots Assn., Lighter than Air Soc., Brit. Balloon and Airship Club, Internat. Soc. Balloonpost Specialists, Newcomen Soc., Confrerie des Chevaliers du Tastevin, Pilgrims of U.S., Asian Inst. Technology (trustee 1988). Episcopalian (vestryman). Clubs: Princeton, Essex Fox Hound, New York Racquet and Tennis, New York Yacht, Links, Explorers. Home: Far Hills NJ Died Feb. 24, 1990; cremated.

FORBES, THOMAS ROGERS, anatomist, medical historian and administrator; b. N.Y.C., Jan. 5, 1911; s. James Bruff and Stella (Rogers) F.; m. Helen Frances Allen, June 19, 1934; children—Thomas R., William M. B.A. cum laude, U. Rochester, 1933, Ph.D., 1937; M.A. (hon.), Yale U., 1962. Fellow anatomy U. Rochester, 1933-37; asst. anatomy Johns Hopkins U., 1937-38, instr., 1938-45; instr. anatomy Yale U., 1945-46, asst. prof., 1946-51, asso. prof., 1951-62, prof., 1962-79, E.K. Hunt prof. anatomy, 1977-79, E.K. Hunt prof. emeritus, from 1979, asst. dean, 1948-60; asso. dean Sch. Medicine, 1960-69, chief sect. gross anatomy dept. surgery, 1974-78, sr. research scholar in history of medicine, 1979-88, lectr. surgery, 1979-84; fellow Branford Coll., Yale U., from 1951; adviser on Yale med. memorabilia, from 1974; tech. aide, div. med. scis. NRC, OSRD, 1942-45; mem. spl. study sect. med. history NIH, 1977-78. Author: The Midwife and the Witch, 1966, Chronicle from Aldgate, 1971, Crowner's Quest, 1978, Surgeons at the Bailey, 1985; editor: Thomas Palmer's The Admirable Secrets of Physick and Chyrurgery, 1984; bd. editors Jour. History of Medicine, 1956-68, 83-86; bd. mgrs., 1951—, pres., 1958-74, acting editor, 1960-62, editor, 1962-63; contbr. research papers on endocrinology, history of medicine; producer films John Hunter, Enlightened Empiricist, 1972, Vesalius, Founder of Modern Anatomy, 1972, Ambroise Paré, Military Surgeon, 1974, The Resurrectionists, 1977. Guggenheim fellow, 1942. Fellow AAAS, Soc. Antiquaries London, Royal Hist. Soc. (London), Royal Soc. Medicine (London); mem. Am. Assn. Anatomists, Endocrine Soc., Am. Assn. History Medicine, Faculty Hist. and Philosophy Pharmacy and Med., Worshipful Soc. Apothecaries (London, Giedon de Laune lectr., medal 1975), Conn. Acad. Arts and Scis., Soc. Social History Medicine (London), Internat. Soc. History Medicine, Athenaeum Club, Beaumont Club, Phi Beta Kappa, Sigma Xi, Phi Upsilon. Club: Athenaeum. Home: Hamden Conn. Died Nov. 13, 1988; buried Grove St. Cemetery, New Haven.

FORBUS, WILEY DAVIS, pathologist; b. Zeiglerville, Miss., Mar. 14, 1894; s. William and Georg'ellen (Davis) F.; m. Elizabeth Knox Burger, Sept. 25, 1926; children: Georg'ellen Davis, Elizabeth Terry, Martha Carolina. AB, Washington and Lee U., 1916, DSc, 1956; MD, Johns Hopkins U., 1923. Asst. in chemistry Washingtona nd Lee U., 1915-16; instr. gen. sci. Nat. Cathedral Sch. for Boys, 1916-18; asst. instr. and assoc. in pathology Johns Hopkins U., Balt., 1923-30; asst. resident, resident and assoc. pathologist Johns Hopkins Hosp., Balt., 1923-36; guest asst. Pathologisches Institut der Ludwig Maximilians Universitat, Munich, 1928; prof. pathology, also chmn. dept. Duke U.; cons. pathologist many N.C. hosps., 1933-92; cons. Oliver Gen. Hosp., Augusta, Ga., 1949-50; br. sect. chief pathology VA, 1948, area cons. in pathology, 1949-92; cons. Walter Reed Hosp., 1952, AEC, div. biology and medicine, 1952-92, other govtl. agencies and Surgeon Gen. of the Army; hon. cons. Armed Forces Inst. of Pathology, 1963-92; chief party U. Calif.-Arlangga U. Affiliation in Med. Edn. Indonesia, 1961-62. Author: Reaction to Injury, vols. I and II, Pathology for Students of Disease, Granslomatous Inflammation, Tokyo Lectures; assoc. editor: Archives of Pathology; contbr. articles to med. and sci. jours. With U.S. Army, 1918, 1st lt. USAR, 1923-33. Mem. AAAS, Nat. Bd. Med. Examiners, Coll. Am. Pathologists, Am. Assn. Pathologists and Bacteriologists (pres. 1947), Phi Beta Kappa, Sigma Xi. *

FORD, JAMES DAYTON, lawyer, moving company executive; b. Harrisburg, Ill., May 31, 1924; s. J. Dayton and Anna (Dorris) F.; m. Alice Maria Evans, June 9, 1944; children—Lynn Alice (Mrs. G. Personius), Katherine Anne (Mrs. Wayne E. Graham), Anna Maria (Mrs. M.S. Rottenstein), Elizabeth Ellen (Mrs. James E. Flores), Jamie LaCene (Mrs. C.C. Carrier). B.B.A., U. Mich., 1948, M.B.A., 1948, J.D., 1951. Bar: Ill. bar 1952, Ariz. bar 1960. Tax. atty. U.S. Steel Corp. subsidiaries in, Duluth, Minn. and Pitts., 1951-54; tax mgr. M.W. Kellogg Co., N.Y.C., 1954-58, Comml. Solvents Corp., N.Y.C., 1958-59; partner firm Hull, Terry & Ford, Tucson, 1960-66; gen. counsel Allied Van Lines, Broadview, Ill., 1966-68; exec. v.p. Allied Van Lines, 1968-71, pres., 1971-75; practice law Tucson, 1976-88. Served with AUS, 1943-46. Mem. Ariz., Pima County bar assns., Nat. Def. Transp. Assn. (life), Nat. Rifle Assn. (life), Household Goods Carriers Bur. (v.p. 1974-76), Am. Movers Conf. (dir. 1973-76), Delta Sigma Pi. Republican. Presbyterian. Club: Tucson Rod and Gun. Lodges: Masons, Shriners, Elks. Home: Tucson Ariz. Died Nov. 7, 1988; buried Tucson.

FORD, NEWELL F., English language educator; b. Portland, Oreg., Mar. 10, 1912; s. Olin F. and Esma (Newell) F.; m. Alysoun Huntley, Mar. 21, 1941 (div. 1967). BA, Reed Coll., 1936; MA, Harvard U., 1938; PhD, U. Calif., Berkeley, 1945. Mem. faculty Stanford (Calif.) U., 1945-89, prof. English, 1963-77, prof. emeritus, 1977-89. Author: The Prefigurative Imagination of John Keats, 2d edit., 1966; editor: The Poetical Works of Shelley, 1975; contbr. articles to profl. jours. Home: Stanford Calif. Died Apr. 4, 1989.

FORD, TENNESSEE ERNIE (ERNEST JENNINGS FORD), entertainer; b. Bristol, Tenn., Feb. 13, 1919; s. Clarence and Maude (Long) F.; m. Betty Jean Heminger, Sept. 18, 1942 (dec. Feb. 1989); children: Jeffrey Buckner, Brion Leonard; m. Beverly Wood-Smith, June 1989. Student, Cin. Conservatory Music, 1939. Headliner London Palladium, from 1953. Host The Ford Show, NBC-TV, 1955-61, daytime TV show, ABC, 1962-65; headliner: 1st country music show to USSR, 1974; rec. artist Capitol Records, 1949-76; outstanding records include 16 Tons. Served to lt. USAAF, World War II. Recipient Presdl. medal of Freedom, 1984; inducted into Country Music Hall of Fame, 1990. Home: Portola Calif. Died Oct. 17, 1991.

FOREMAN, JAMES DAVIS, cement company executive; b. Barnesville, Ohio, Mar. 13, 1925; s. J. Harrison and Freda (Davis) F.; m. Helen Laura Bolon, Nov. 27, 1943; children: James Bolon, Barbara Jean, Helen Marie. BS magna cum laude, Syracuse U., 1949; MBA, U. Pa., 1956. CPA, Conn. With Arthur Young & Co. (C.P.A.'s), N.Y.C., 1945-51, Ernst & Ernst (C.P.A.'s), Hartford, Conn., 1951-55; mgr. accounting and adminstrn. Xerox Corp., 1955-60; v.p., controller, sec. Olivetti Corp., 1960-79; exec. v.p., dir. River Cement Co., St. Louis, 1980-86; pres. RC Cement Co. Inc., St. Louis, from 1987, also vice chmn. bd. Served with USAAF, 1943-46, PTO. Home: Ballwin Mo. Deceased. †

FORMAN, H(ENRY) CHANDLEE, art educator, architect; b. N.Y.C.; s. Horace Baker, Jr. and Elizabeth (Chandlee) F.; m. Caroline Biddle Lippincott, Sept. 28, 1929 (dec. June 5, 1975); children: Elizabeth (Mrs. Bryant Harrell, Jr.), Richard Townsend Turner, Lawrence Thorne; m. Rebecca Anthony Russell, May 26, 1978. A.B., Princeton U., 1926; M.Arch., U. Pa., 1931, Ph.D. in Fine Arts, 1942; Litt.D. St. Mary's Coll. of Md, 1981. Pvt. practice architecture as H. Chandlee Forman, Easton, Md.; specializing in residences, chs., hist. restorations, 1931-35, 52-78; chief architect Jamestown (Va.) Archaeol. Project, 1935-36; editor nat. records Historic Am. Bldgs. Survey, 1936-37; lectr. fine arts Haverford Coll., 1937-38; instr. art Rutgers U., 1939-40; lectr. history art U. Pa., 1940-41; Catherine L. Comer prof. fine arts Wesleyan Coll. of Ga., 1941-45; prof. art, head dept. Agnes Scott Coll., 1945-52; cons. architect Ga. Hist. Commn., 1952-60. Author: numerous books, including Early Manor and Plantation Houses of Maryland, 1934, 2d edit., 1982, Jamestown and St. Mary's, Buried Cities of Romance, 1938, The Architecture of the Old South, The Medieval Style, 1948, Virginia Architecture in the 17th Century, 1957, Early Nantucket and its Whale Houses, 1966, Old Buildings, Gardens and Furniture in Tidewater Maryland, 1967, The Virginia Eastern Shore and its British Origins, 1975, The Rolling Year on Maryland's Upper Eastern Shore, 1985, Early Buildings and Historic Artifacts in Tidewater Maryland: The Eastern Shore, 1989; Art work exhibited, Library Congress, Art Inst. Chgo., Balt. Mus. Art, U. Pa., others. Adviser Md. St. Mary's City Commn., 1965-69; mem. Md. Archeol. Commn., 1968-77, chmn., 1973; sec. bd. dirs. Soc. Preservation Md. Antiquities, 1952-54; mem. corp. bd. Haverford Coll., 1975-85; lectr. throughout world for State Dept., 1964; donor H. Chandlee Forman Nature Preserve to nantucket Maria Mitchell Assn., 1973, The Ending of Controversie mus. and collections to Hist. Soc. of Talbot County Md., 1984. Recipient George Barnard White prize Princeton, 1926, Calvert prize for historic preservation State of Md., 1976, Historic Preservation award Assn. Preservation Va. Antiquities, 1982, Gov.'s citation for history and archaeology State of Md., 1983, Cross Bottony Disting. Svc. to Md. award St. Mary City Commn., 1989, Presdl. Citation of AIA, 1989, Carnegie Found. fellow creative painting, 1947. Fellow AIA (exec. com. Balt. chpt., charter mem., v.p., historian Chesapeake Bay chpt.); mem. Talbot County (Md.) Hist. Soc. (bd. dirs., co-organizer, 1st curator, librarian), Nantucket Garden Club (hon.), Townsend Soc. Am. (hon.), Archeol. Soc. Md. (hon.), Soc. Colonial Wars, Princeton Alumni Assn. Eastern Shore (pres. 1960-61, 70-72, 77-79, sec.-treas. 1974-77), The Robert Gilmore Soc. Club: Explorers (fellow). Home: Easton Md. Died Mar. 18, 1991.

FORSGREN, JOHN H., JR., entertainment executive; b. Cleve., Aug. 31, 1946; s. John H. and Jeanne Marie (Sullivan) F. B.A., Georgetown U., 1967; M.B.A., Columbia U., 1969; M.S., U. Geneva, Switzerland, 1972. With Alcan, 1969-75; dir. internat. fin. Sperry Corp., N.Y.C., 1977-80, staff v.p., 1980-83, treas., 1983-86; v.p., treas. The Walt Disney Co., Burbank, 1986-90, sr. v.p., chief fin. officer Euro Disney, 1990-91. Trustee Georgetown U. Library, Washington, 1983. Republican. Roman Catholic. Clubs: N.Y. Athletic; Essex Yacht (Conn.); Cercle de l'Union Internalliee (Paris); Metropolitan (N.Y.C.). Home: Old Lyme Conn. Deceased. †

FORSYTH, GEORGE HOWARD, JR., art historian; b. Highland Park, Ill., Sept. 2, 1901; s. George Howard and Sarah (Brockunier) F.; m. Eleanor Marquand, Feb. 5, 1927 (dec. Feb. 1988); children: Eleanor, Mary Blaikie, George Allan; m. Mary Isom Hayes, Aug. 18, 1942 (dec. Nov. 1958); 1 child, Hope Gifford; m. Ilene Eleanor Haering, June 4, 1960. A.B., Princeton U., 1923, M.F.A., 1927, mem. Inst. Advanced Study, 1935-36, 45. Instr. and later asst. prof., dept. art and archaeology Princeton U., 1927-42; prof. history of art U. Mich., 1947-72, chmn. dept., 1947-61; dir. Kelsey Mus. Archaeology, 1961-69, research prof. archeology, 1969-72; dir. survey and excavation Ch. St. Martin, Angers, France; field dir. Mich., Princeton, Alexandria univs. archeol. expdn. to Mt. Sinai, excavation of St. Catherine's Monastery, Egypt, 1958, 60, 63, 65; bd. scholars Dumbarton Oaks Research Library and Collection, Harvard U., 1957-72, hon. asso., from 1972; research asso. Freer Gallery, Smithsonian Instn., 1954, 56, 60. Author: Church of St. Martin at Angers, 1953; (with Kurt Weitzmann) Monastery of St. Catherine at Mt. Sinai, 1973, The Church and Fortress of Justinian: Vol. 1: Plates, 1973; contbr. to art publs. Served as lt. USNR, 1942-45. Recipient traveling fellowship Mediaeval Acad. Am., 1924-25, Haskins medal, 1955; Rockefeller Found. research grantee, 1946; Guggenheim fellow, 1953. Life mem. Société française d'archéologie; mem. Coll. Art Assn. (dir. 1949, 54), Royal Soc. Arts (London), Phi Beta Kappa, Phi Kappa Phi. Clubs: Century Assn. (N.Y.C.); Cosmos (Washington). Home: Ann Arbor Mich. Died Jan. 26, 1991; cremated.

FORTUNE, PORTER LEE, JR., university chancellor emeritus; b. Old Fort, N.C., July, 1920; s. Porter and Eunice (Ross) F.; m. Mary Elizabeth Cummings, Oct. 15, 1944; children: Philip Lee, Peggy Jean, Janet Cummings, Carey Ross. B.A., U. N.C., 1941, Ph.D., 1949; M.A., Emory U., 1946. Instr. Emory U., 1946; teaching asst. U. N.C., 1946-47; faculty Miss. So. Coll., 1949-61; successively asst. prof. history, assoc. prof., dean Miss. So. Coll. (Basic Coll.), 1948-57; prof., dean Miss. So. Coll. (Coll. and Grad. Sch.), 1957-61; nat. exec. v.p. Nat. Exchange Club, 1961-68; chancellor U. Miss., 1968-84, chancellor emeritus, from 1984. Civilian aide to sec. army for Miss., 1971-79; founding chmn. Miss. Com. for Humanities; past pres. Southeastern Conf., So. Univ. Conf., Miss. Assn. Colls., So. Assn. Land-Grant Colls. and State Univs.; former chmn. awards jury Freedoms Found. Served as lt. (s.g.) USNR, 1942-46; advisory council Naval Affairs. Decorated Bronze Star, Navy Disting. Public Service award; recipient John R. Emens Nat. award for a Free Student Press; Gov.'s Outstanding Mississippian award; Freedoms Found. George Washington honor medal, 1966; Leadership award dist. 43 Toastmasters Club, 1974; Miss. Disting. Civilian Service medal, 1980; U.S. Disting. Civilian Service medal, 1980. Mem. Miss. Hist. Soc. (past pres.), Miss. Council Devel. Marine Resources, So. Regional Edn. Bd., So. Assn. Com. on Colls., So. Assn. Colls. and Schs. (nomination and assessment of planning com.), Miss. Art Assn. (trustee), Orgn. Am. Historians, So. Hist. Assn., C. of C., Miss. Humanities Commn. (past chmn.), Phi Alpha Theta, Pi Kappa Delta, Omicron Delta Kappa (disting.), Phi Kappa Phi (disting.), Pi Gamma Mu, Delta Theta Pi, Alpha Phi Omega, Delta Sigma Pi, Phi Delta Kappa, Pi Tau Chi, Kappa Alpha, Kappa Delta Pi, Delta Pi Epsilon. Methodist. Clubs: Masons (32 deg.), Shriners, Exchange (past pres. Hattiesburg, past pres. Miss. chpt., nat. regional v.p., chmn. nat. edn. com., nat. bd. control, past nat. pres., Golden award for service 1968), Nat. Ct. Honor. Home: University Miss. Deceased. †

FORWARD, DEWITT ARTHUR, banker; b. Shelbyville, Ky., Sept. 23, 1894; s. DeWitt Daniel and Grace Abbey (Harvey) F.; m. Alice Mason, June 30, 1920. AB, Colgate U., Hamilton, N.Y.; LLD, Colgate U., 1954. With Nat. City Bank of N.Y., 1916-20, asst. cashier, 1920-23, asst. v.p., 1923-27, v.p., 1927-45, sr. v.p., 1945-58, vice chmn., 1958-59, dir., 1954-59; dir. Am. nat. Gas Co., Fruehauf Trailer Co., Allis-Chalmers Mfg. Co.; trustee Dime Savs. Bank of Bklyn. Trustee Colgate U. Mem. University Club (N.Y.C.), Scarsdale Golf, Phi Beta Kappa, Delta Kappa Epsilon. Republican. *

FOSS, THOMAS E., economics laboratory executive; b. Litchfield, Minn., Nov. 20, 1934; s. Peter E. and Mary (Connole) F.; m. Joyce F. Hillman, Sept. 14, 1973; children: Theresa, Thomas J., Timothy. B.A., U. Minn., 1961. Acctg. trainee Economics Lab, Inc., St. Paul, 1961-63, accountant to sr. cost accountant, 1963-67, v.p. adminstrn. internat., 1967-73; v.p., treas. Economics Lab. Inc., St. Paul, 1973-76, v.p. corp. planning, 1976-80; sr. v.p. ops. Economics Lab, Inc., St. Paul, from 1980. Served with AUS, 1957-58. Republican. Roman Catholic. Home: Hastings Minn. Died 1989. †

FOSTER, FERN ALLEN (FERN ALLEN MERONEY), sex therapist, administrator, consultant; b. Ranger, Tex., Sept. 19, 1921; d. Jess and Grace (Bradley) Meroney; m. Austin Foster; children—Gayanne, Stuart, Ann, William, David. A.A., Ranger Coll., 1941; B.A., Newport U., 1981. Cert. social worker, Tex. Sex counselor Marriage Counseling Assocs., Fort Worth, 1964-69, The Edna Gladney Home, Fort Worth, 1971-83; psychotherapist VA Hosp. and Clinic, New Orleans, 1969-71; sex counselor Fort Worth Counseling Ctr., 1971-84, dir., 1984-91; fellow in human sexuality Tex. Sch. of Profl. Psychology, Fort Worth, 1985-88; cons. human sexuality Blackwell Counseling Ctr., Fort Worth, 1985-91. Mem. Am. Assn. Sex Educators, Counselors and Therapists (cert.), Sex Info. and Edn. Council of U.S., Nat. Council on Adoption, Am. Assn. Counseling and Devel., Am. Mental Health Counselors Assn. Club: Century II (Fort Worth). Died Mar. 12, 1991. Home: Fort Worth Tex.

FOSTER, JOHN MERRILL, glass company executive; b. Evanston, Ill., May 20, 1891; s. Adelbert M. and Lillian (Ragley) F.; m. Eleanora Lutz, Jan. 30, 1932; children: John Joseph, Robert Lutz. AB, Williams Coll., 1920. With Foster-Forbes Glass Co., Marion, Ind., from 1920, treas., 1929-35, pres., 1935-65, chmn. bd., CEO, from 1965; dir. First Nat. Bank, Marion. Active ARC; active fund drive Marion Gen. Hosp. Served with U.S. Navy, 1918. Mem. Glass Container Mfrs. Inst. (pres., trustee), Rotary, Zeta Psi. Republican. Congregationalist. *

FOWKES, FREDERICK MAYHEW, chemist; b. Chgo., Jan. 29, 1915; s. William Herbert and Eleanor (Seley) F.; m. Royce-Elisabeth Budge, 1937; children: Gordon Seley, Joan Berkeley Piper, Mary Elisabeth Tobin, Virginia Mayhew Clark. BS, U. Chgo., 1936, PhD, 1938. Rsch. supr. Shell Devel. Co., Emeryville, Calif., 1947-62; dir. rsch. Sprague Electric Co., North Adams, Mass., 1962-68; prof., chmn. chemistry dept. Lehigh U., Bethlehem, Pa., 1968-81; adj. prof. Rensselaer Poly. Inst., 1967-68; vis. scientist Wright-Patterson Air Force Base, Ohio. Editor: Contact Angle: Wettability and Adhesion, 1964, Hydrophobic Surfaces, 1969; contbr. articles to profl. jours.; patentee in field. Maj F.A., AUS, 1942-46, PTO. Decorated Silver Star medal. Mem. Am. Chem. Soc. past div. chmn. , Electrochem. Soc., Faraday Soc. Home: Bethlehem Pa. Died Oct. 18, 1991.

FOWLER, BEN B., lawyer; b. Hopkinsville, Ky., Mar. 9, 1916; s. William Thomas and Ila (Earle) F.; m. Eleanor Randolph, Oct. 19, 1940. B.S. in Commerce, U. Ky., 1937; LL.B., U. Va., 1940. Bar: Ky. bar 1940. Atty. firm Fowler & Fowler, Lexington, 1940-41; asst. atty. gen. Ky., 1945-47; mem. firm Dailey & Fowler, Frankfort, Ky., 1948-71, Stites, McElwain & Fowler, Frankfort and Louisville, 1972-83, Stites & Harbison, 1983-90; city solicitor, Frankfort, 1958-60; chief counsel Ky. Civil Code Com., 1953; chmn. Ct. Appeals Adv. Com. Civil Rules Procedure, 1953-73; Vice pres., gen. counsel, dir. Frankfort & Cin. R.R., 1963-86. Pres., dir. Community Service, Inc.; Adv. com. Ky. Ednl. TV; Served as 2d lt. AUS, 1941, ETO, to maj. inf., 1945, to lt. col. Ky. N.G., 1946-53. Decorated Bronze Star. Fellow Am. Coll. Trial Lawyers; mem. Am. Judicature Soc., ABA (ho. of dels. 1955-60), Ky. Bar Assn. (bd. bar commrs. 1953-60, pres. 1959-60, Outstanding Service award 1954), Franklin County Bar Assn. (pres. 1969), Frankfort C. of C. (pres. 1957-58, chmn. indsl. devel. 1958-59), Ky. C. of C. (bd. dirs.), Delta Tau Delta, Phi Alpha Delta. Presbyn. (deacon 1947-53, elder from 1953). Clubs: Rotary (pres. Frankfort 1952-53), Frankfort Country (dir. 1953-56, v.p. 1955). Home: Frankfort Ky. Died June 23, 1990; buried Frankfort, Ky.

FOWLER, JOSEPH WILLIAM, amusement park executive; b. Monmouth, Maine, July 9, 1894; s. William and Jennie (Larkin) F.; m. Marguerite Turner, Apr. 13, 1918; 1 son, Joseph William. Grad., Monmouth Acad., 1911; BS, U.S. Naval Acad., 1918; MS, MIT, 1921; grad., U.S. Naval War Coll., 1929. Commd. ensign U.S. Navy, 1917, advanced through grades to rear adm., 1946; prodn. officer Navy Yard, Mare Island, Calif., 1940-42; asst. indsl. mgr. (naval work in pvt. yards), San Francisco, 1942-45; became comdr. San Francisco Naval Shipyard, 1945; dir. indsl. survey Office Sec. of Navy, 1946-48; dir. Def. Supply Mgmt. Agy., 1952; v.p. Disneyland, Anaheim, Calif., Walt Disney Prodns., Burbank, Calif. Decorated World War I Victory medal and clasp, Yangtze Svc. medal; World War II Legion of Merit, Victory medal, Pre-Pearl Harbor ribbon; Order el Merito (Chile). Mem. Soc. Naval Engrs., Army Navy Country Club (Arlington, Va.), Army and Navy Club (Washington), Bohemian Club (San Francisco), Balboa Bay Club (Newport Beach, Calif.). *

FOWLKES, JOHN GUY, author, educator; b. Greenville, Mo., July 8, 1898; s. John Thomas and Lois (Burroughs) F.; m. Dec. 27, 1917 (dec. 1925); m. Helen Agatha Karlen, May 20, 1928; children: SWarah Anne, Nancy Lee. AB, Ouachita Coll., Ark., 1916; AM, Columbia U., 1921, PhD, 1922. Asst. in math. Ouachita Coll., 1914-16; tchr., high sch. prin., headmaster in Ark. and N.Y., 1916-22; asst. prof. edn. U. Wis., 1922-24, assoc. prof., 1924-26, prof., 1927-92, dir. summer session, 1942-54, dean sch. edn., 1947-54; vis. prof. U. Calif., Berkeley, 1926-27; ednl. advisor Ministry Edn. India, 1954-56; mem. Miss., Va., Nev. state ednl. survey staffs; dir. surveys including Pasadena, Ft. Worth, Flint, Kansas City. Author: School Bonds, Financial Accounting for Schools; several textbooks including Healthy Life Series; also series of charts Democracy at Work and bulls. of Bur. Ednl. Research, U. Wis.; (with Knezevich) Business Management of Local School Systems, 1960; mem. cons. editorial bd. The Nation's Schools; editorial adv. A.J. Nystrom & Co.; adv. editor Exploration Series in Edn., Harper & Row. Dir. Wis. Improvement Program, also tchr. edn. and local sch. systems, 1959-92. Fellow AAAS; mem. NEA, AAUP, Am. Assn. Sch. Adminstrs., Am. Ednl. Rsch. Assn., Maple Bluff Country Club, University, Phi Delta Kappa, Alpha Kappa Lambda, Masons. Congregationalist. *

FOX, HAZEL METZ (MRS. ALLAN E. FOX), nutrition educator; b. Barton, Md., July 2, 1921; d. Jefferson and Blanche (Inskeep) Metz; m. Allan E. Fox, Jan. 6, 1951; children—Jeff, Margaret, Allan, Robert, Frank. BA, Western Md. Coll., 1943, DSc, 1969; M.S., Iowa State U., 1947, Ph.D., 1954. Research assoc. Children's Fund Mich., 1947-50; grad. asst. Iowa State U., 1950-54, instr., 1954-55; mem. faculty dept. food and nutrition U. Nebr. at Lincoln, 1955-87, prof., 1962-87, George Holmes prof., 1968-87, prof. emeritus, from 1987, chmn. dept., 1963-87. Contbr. articles to profl. jours. Recipient Human Nutrition award Borden Co., 1969, Centennial award Iowa State U. Alumni Assn., 1971. Mem. Am. Inst. Nutrition, Am. Dietetic Assn., Am. Home Econs. Assn., AAAS, Sigma Xi, Sigma Delta Epsilon. Home: Lincoln NE Died Sept. 8, 1989; buried Wyuka Cemetery, Lincoln.

FOX, SIDNEY ALBERT, ophthalmologist; b. Russia, Jan. 30, 1898; brought to U.S., 1904, naturalized, 1912; s. Louis Asir and Rebecca (Albert) F.; m. Dorothea Doctors, 1931. AB, Brown U., 1919; MD, St. Louis U., 1931; SciM, U. Pa., 1935. Diplomate Am. Bd. Ophthalmology. Resident Bellevue Hosp., N.Y.C., 1934-35; practiced ophthalmology N.Y.C., from 1935; clin. prof. NYU Med. Sch.; assoc. attending ophthalmologist Univ. Hosp.; asst. attending ophthalmologist Bellevue Hosp.; cons. ophthalmologist Goldwater Meml. Hosp., VA Hosp., Hosp. for Joint

Diseases; mem. ophthal. adv. com. Commr. Health, N.Y.C., 1956-58. Author: Your Eyes, 1944; Ophthalmic Plastic Surgery, 1952; Affections of the Lids, 1964; contbr. articles to profl. jours. Lt. col. M.C., AUS, from 1943. Decorated Legion of Merit. Fellow ACS, N.Y. Acad. Medicine, Am. Acad. Ophthalmology and Otolaryngology, Pan-Pacific Surg. Assn.; mem. AMA, Alpha Omega Alpha. Jewish. *

FOXX, REDD (JOHN ELROY SANFORD), actor, comedian; b. St. Louis, Dec. 9, 1922; s. Fred Sanford; m. Evelyn Killibrew (div. 1951); m. Betty Jean Harris, 1955 (div.); 1 stepchild, Debraca; m. Kahoe Foxx. Ed. pub. schs., Chgo. Mem. amateur mus. group, Bon-Bons, 1939-41; performer numerous night clubs, N.Y.C., Balt., San Francisco, Los Angeles, Las Vegas, Honolulu, Miami Beach, Chgo., 1941-91; performed with Slappy White, 1947-51; film appearances include Cotton Comes To Harlem, 1970, Norman . . . Is That You?, 1976; TV appearances include Soul; series Sanford and Son, 1972-77, 80-81, The Redd Foxx Comedy Hour, 1977, The Redd Fox Show, ABC-TV, 1984-85, The Royal Family, 1991; rec. artist series, Dooto Records, Loma Records; recs. include Laff of the Party, 1956. Home: Los Angeles Calif. Died Oct. 12, 1991.

FRANCESCATTI, ZINO RENE, concert violinist; b. Marseille, France, Aug. 9, 1902; s. Fortuné and Ernesta-Feraud F.; m. Yoland de la Briere, Jan. 2, 1930. Violin tchr. Ecole Normale, 1920's; also asst. concertmaster Concerts Poulet Orch. Debut in concert Paris Opera; Appeared in concerts throughout Europe with leading condrs. and orchs., 1928-38, concert tour in, South Am., 1938, 47, 52, first tour in, U.S., 1939; appeared with leading orchs. tours of South Am. and Mexico, 1947, 52, Europe, yearly, concert performances in Israel, 1949-56, 58, 63, 66; 1st internat. violin competition Aix En Provence, 1987, 2d internat. violin competition, Marseille, France, 1989, Festivals De Violin Zino Francescatti Aix en Provence, 1988, 89, 91; sonata and concerti recs. with Robert Casadesus. Founded Zino Francescatti Found. to help young artists, 1986. Decorated commandeur De L'Ordre de la Légion d'Honneur, commandeur l'Ordre des Arts et Lettres; commandeur l'Ordre de Leopold (Belgium); Grand-Croix officier de l'Ordre National du Merite. Roman Catholic. Home: La Ciotat France 13600 Died Sept. 17, 1991.

FRANCIS, DALE LYMAN, publisher, columnist; b. Newark, Ohio, Mar. 8, 1917; s. Clarence Theodore and Florence (Day) F.; m. Barbara Hoole, Oct. 15, 1943 (dec. 1961); children: Guy Edward, Marianne Elizabeth; m. Margaret Alexander, Jan. 6, 1962; 1 dau., Rita Kathryn. B.A., Bluffton (Ohio) Coll., 1941; postgrad., U. Notre Dame, 1946-50; Litt.D. (hon.), St. Leo Coll., Fla., 1968. Sports writer Troy (Ohio) Daily News, 1932-35; reporter Lima (Ohio) News, 1935-36; reporter, columnist Dayton (Ohio) Jour.-Herald, 1936-38; founding editor N.C. Cath., Raleigh, 1946-47; dir. publs., founder U. Notre Dame Press, 1950-52; dir. bur. information Nat. Cath. Conf., Washington, 1952-55; dir. Def. of Faith, Matanzas, Cuba, 1955-56; founding editor Lone Star Cath., Austin, Tex., 1956-61; editor Troy Daily News, 1961-64; exec. editor Our Sunday Visitor, Huntington, Ind., 1964-68, 74-78; pub. Twin Circle, Los Angeles, 1968-70; editor, pub. Nat. Cath. Register, 1970-74; pres. Julian Press, 1974-83; editor Cath. Standard, Washington, 1978-83; columnist Huntington (Ind.) Herald-Press, from 1983; syndicated columnist 23 newspapers, from 1964; adminstr. Our Sunday Vis. Inst. Adv. Council, 1987. Books include Catholic Prayer Book, 1959, Kneeling in the Bean Patch, 1960, Caring Is Living, 1978. Bd. dirs. Citizens for Ednl. Freedom, 1968-86; founding bd. dirs. Cath. League for Religious and Civil Rights, 1973-86. Served with USAAF, 1941-46, PTO. Recipient Religious Communication award U. Dayton, 1989. Mem. Cath. Press Assn. (bd. dirs. 1970-74, St. Francis de Sales award 1959), Am. Newspaper Guild, Sigma Delta Chi. Club: Kiwanis. Home: Huntington Ind. Died Mar. 24, 1992.

FRANCISCUS, JAMES GROVER, actor; b. Clayton, Mo., Jan. 31, 1934; s. John Allen and Loraine (Grover) F.; m. Kathleen Kent Wellman, Mar. 28, 1960; children: Jamie, Kellie, Korie, Jolie. B.A., Yale U., 1957. V.p., producer Omnibus Prodns. Inc., Ltd., 1968. Star: TV series Naked City, 1958, Mr. Novak, 1963-65, Longstreet, 1971, Doc Elliot, 1973, Hunter, 1977; films include The Outsider, 1962, Youngblood Hawke, 1963, Hell Boats, 1968, Marooned, 1969, Beneath the Planet of the Apes, 1969, Cat and Nine Tails, 1970, The Amazing Dobermans, 1976, Puzzle, 1977, Good Guys Wear Black, 1977, The Greek Tycoon, 1977, Greed, 1978, The Concorde, 1978, City on Fire, 1978, Killer Fish, 1979, Nightkill, 1980, Butterfly, 1980, White Death, 1980, Jacqueline Bouvier Kennedy, 1981, The Courageous, 1982; producer TV shows Heidi, 1969, David Copperfield, 1970, Jane Eyre, 1971, Kidnapped, 1972, The Red Pony, 1973; regular guest actor TV shows The FBI, Combat, Father Knows Best, The Twilight Zone. Home: Los Angeles Calif. Died July 8, 1991.

FRANK, CURTISS E., lawyer, organization executive; b. N.Y.C., Nov. 13, 1904; s. Augustus A. and Mary (Fowler) F.; m. Grace Watkins, Oct. 11, 1929 (dec. Nov. 1957); children: Anne Fairfield Frank DuBois, Curtiss Ely; m. Lila Bonhus Shaw, Dec. 13, 1958 (dec. Jan. 1986). A.B., Colgate U., 1925, L.L.D., 1969; L.L.B., Columbia U., 1928. Bar: N.Y. 1928. Asso. Hughes, Schurman & Dwight, 1928-37; asst. U.S. atty. So. Dist. N.Y., 1931-32; partner firm Hughes, Hubbard & Ewing, 1937-49; v.p., gen. counsel Reuben H. Donnelley Corp., 1949-51, exec. v.p., 1952-55, pres., 1956-61, chmn. bd., chief exec. officer, 1961-66; pres. Dun & Bradstreet, Inc., 1966-67, vice chmn., 1968-69; pres. Council for Fin. Aid to Edn., N.Y.C., 1970-73; chmn. exec. com. Council for Fin. Aid to Edn., 1974-78, mem. adv. bd., from 1978; dir. Willcox & Gibbs, Inc., Shearson Mut. Funds, Brown Bros. Harriman Trust Co. Fla., Naples, Elderworks; pres. Nat. Exec. Service Corps, 1977-80, vice chmn. from 1981; mem. cons. panel to comptroller gen. U.S., 1967-69. Councilman City of Yonkers, 1942-43, mayor, 1944-49; chmn. bd. trustees Colgate U., 1969-75, trustee emeritus, from 1976; bd. visitors Columbia U. Law Sch., from 1976; bd. dirs. Marco Philharm. Mem. Phi Beta Kappa. Episcopalian. Clubs: Union League, Blind Brook, Round Hill (Conn.) Country; Port Royal, Naples Yacht, Hole-in-the-Wall Golf (Naples, Fla.). Home: Naples Fla. Died Feb. 3, 1990.

FRANK, ILYA MIKHAILOVICH, physicist; b. Leningrad, Oct. 23, 1908. Ed., Moscow U. Asst. to prof. S. I. Vavilov, 1928; with Leningrad Optical Inst., 1930-34, Lebedev Inst. Physics, USSR Acad. Scis., 1934-70; prof. physics Moscow U., from 1944; head lab. of neutron physics, Joint Inst. for Nuclear Research, from 1957; corr. mem. USSR Acad. Scis., 1946-48, academician, from 1968. Author: Function of Excitement and Curve of Absorption in Optic Dissociation of Tallium Ioclate, 1933; Coherent Radiation of Fast Electron in a Medium, 1937; Pare Formation in Krypton under Gamma Rays, 1938; Doppler Effect in Refracting Medium, 1942; Radiation of a Uniformly Moving Electron Due to Its Transition from One Medium into Another, 1945; Neutron Multiplication in Uranium-Graphite System, 1955; On Group Velocity of Light in Radiation in Refracting Medium, 1958; Optics of Light Sources Moving in Refracting Media, 1960; On Some Peculiarities of Vavilov-Cherenkov Radiation, 1986. Recipient Nobel prize for physics (with Tamm and Cherenkov), 1958; State Prize, 1946, 54, 71; Order of Lenin (3); Order of Red Banner of Labor; Order of October Revolution 1978; Varilov Gold medal, 1979. Home: Moscow Russia Died June 22, 1990.

FRANK, MORTON, newspaper executive; b. Pitcairn, Pa., June 14, 1912; s. Abraham and Goldie (Friedenberg) F.; m. Agnes Dodds, June 2, 1944 (div. 1957); children: Allan Dodds, Michael Robert, Marilyn Morton; m. Elizabeth Welt Pope, Dec. 31, 1963. A.B., U. Mich., 1933; postgrad., Carnegie Inst. Tech., U. Pitts., Duquesne U.; LL.D., Alfred U., 1979. Advt. mgr. Braddock (Pa.) Daily News-Herald, 1933-34; editor Braddock Free Press, 1934-35; advt. salesman, entertainment writer, 1935-37; rotogravure mgr. Pitts. Press, 1937-42; writer, commentator Pitts. radio stas., corr. trade mags., 1935-42; v.p., bus. mgr. Ariz. Times, Phoenix, 1946; editor, pub. Canton (Ohio) Economist, 1946-58, Lorain (Ohio) Sun News, 1949-50, Inter-County Gazette, Strasburg, Ohio, 1950, Stark County Times Canton, 1950-58, Farm and Dairy, Salem, Ohio, 1952-53; pres. Tri-Cities Telecasting, Canton, 1953-61, Printype, 1956-58, Property Devel. Corp., 1956-58; dir. publisher relations, v.p. Family Weekly and Suburbia Today, N.Y.C., 1958-65; pub., exec. v.p. Family Weekly, N.Y.C., 1966-71, pres., pub., 1971-75, 76-80, chmn., 1976, chmn., pub., 1980-82, chmn. emeritus, 1982-85; cons. CBS, 1982-88; cons. USA Weekend/Family Weekly, CBS, Gannett Co., 1985-88; chmn. emeritus USA Weekend, from 1985; dir. Horizon Communications, Inc., from 1984; dir. Am. Jour. of Nursing Co., 1984-88, chmn. fin. com., 1986-88; cons. Greenhow Newspapers, 1982-86. Chmn. Commn. Corr. Ind. Higher Edn. N.Y., 1976-79, exec. com., 1980-82; exec. com. Council Governing Bds., from 1982; trustee Alfred U., from 1968, Mus. Cartoon Art, from 1980; bd. dirs. Cancer Care/Nat. Cancer Found., from 1985, Canton Symphony Orch., 1950-56. Served to lt. USNR, 1942-45. Recipient 1st prize for feature writing N.E.A., 1954; community service award Accredited Hometown Newspapers Am., 1954. Mem. Tri-State Fedn. Non-Comml. Theatres (pres. 1936-38), Controlled Circulation Newspapers Am. (dir. 1948-56), Pitts. Fgn. Policy Assn. (dir. 1940-42), Newspaper Advt. Bur. (plans com. 1974-82), Am., So., Inland, Tex., Calif., N.Y. newspaper pubs. assns., Internat. Press Inst., Interam. Press Assn., Internat. Circulation Mgrs. Assn., Internat. Newspaper Promotion Assn., Internat. Newspaper Advt. Execs. Assn., Sigma Alpha Mu, Sigma Delta Chi. Clubs: Canton Advt, Players, N.Y.C. Sales Execs, Overseas Press (dir. 1983-87, found. trustee 1983—), Deadline (pres. 1974-75, chmn. 1975-76, bd. dirs. from 1977, N.Y. Journalism Hall of Fame 1985); Silurians (dir. 1985-86, v.p. 1986-87, pres. 1987-88). Home: New York N.Y. Died Dec. 7, 1989; buried Mt. Pleasant, N.Y.

FRANK, PAUL ADDISON, machinery manufacturing executive; b. Akron, Ohio, Oct. 22, 1895; s. John C. and Celia (Esselburn) F.; m. Frances Halbert, Jan. 22, 1921; children: Halbert, Paul Addison, Peter F., John V. Student, Butchtel Acad. With B.F. Goodrich Co., 1915-23; propr. machinery firm, 1923-40; pres. Nat. Rubber Machinery Co. (name changed to NRM Corp.), Akron, Ohio, 1940-65, chmn. bd. dirs., from 1965; dir. Cooper-Bessemer Corp., Gilbert Lumber Co. Trustee Oberlin Coll., Ohio Found. Ind. Colls., 1952-58; pres. Akron Community Trusts, 1959-60. Mem. Mayflower Club, Portage Country Club. Episcopalian (vestryman). *

FRANK, WILLIAM GEORGE, manufacturing company executive; b. Mainz, Germany, Mar. 28, 1898; came to U.S., 1923, naturalized, 1930; s. William and Louise (Bartz) F.; m. Helen Calhoun, Dec. 20, 1924; children: William G., Richard C. ME, Tech. U., Hanover, Germany, 1922. Chief engr. Nat. Air Filter Co., Chgo., 1923-29; dept. mgr. Am. Air Filter Co., Louisville, 1929-44, v.p., exec. v.p., dir., 1944-55, pres., dir., from 1955; dir. Louisville Trust Co., Reliance Varnish Co., Louisville. Trustee Air Filter Found. Mem. Louisville Boat Club, Pendennis Club (Louisville). Presbyterian. *

FRANKE, JOHN JACOB, JR., federal official; b. Tonkawa, Okla., June 28, 1930; s. John Jacob and Golda Elaine (Peace) F.; m. Melba Jean Graul, June 17, 1950; children: Michael D., John P., Robert K. Student, Kansas City Bus. Coll., Mo., 1947-48, U. Kansas City, Mo., 1951-52, LaSalle U., 1954-55. With Franke Barber Supply, Inc., Kansas City, Mo., 1952-72; councilman City of Merriam, Kans., 1965-70; mayor City of Merriam, 1970-72; mem. Johnson County Bd. Commrs., 1973-81; regional adminstr. EPA, 1981-82; asst. sec. U.S. Dept. Agr., Washington, 1982-89; dir. Fed. Quality Inst., Washington, from 1989; vice chmn. Pres. Council Mgmt. Improvement, Fed. Adv. Com. Occupational Safety and Helath; chmn. Human Relations Commn., Govtl. Ops. Com.; bd. dirs. Rural Telephone Bank Bd. Mem. Kans. Legis. Council League Municipalities, 1966-73, commr., 1973, chmn., 1974-77; mem. adv. bd. Nat. Park Service, 1973-76; mem. Kaw council Boy Scouts Am., 1962-76, Republican Central Com. Johnson County, 1972-81; chmn. Johnson County Library Bd., 1974-77; chmn. human resources policy com. Kans. Mcpl. League; bd. dirs., v.p. Mo.-Ark. Water Resources; bd. dirs. Greater Kansas City Resources Found.; chmn. labor mgmt. steering com. Nat. Assn. Counties. Served with USMC, 1948-52. Recipient Man of Yr. Exec. Excellence award IRM, 1986, Pub. Employees Roundtable award, 1987, Outstanding Pub. Service award Am. Soc. Pub. Adminstrn., 1987. Mem. Christian Ch. Lodges: Masons; Shriners. Home: Shawnee Mission Kans. Deceased. †

FRANKE, WILLIAM BIRRELL, secretary of the navy; b. Troy, N.Y., Apr. 15, 1894; s. William G. and Helena E. (Birrell) F.; m. Bertha Irene Reedy, June 28, 1919; children: Phyllis Birrell (Mrs. Harding Hall Fowler), Ann Tallmadge (Mrs. John Anthony Ulinski Jr.), Patricia Wendell (Mrs. W. Sherman Kouns). ScD, U. Louisville, 1948; DCL, Pace Coll., 1955. Pres. Securities Co.; spl. asst. to Sec. of Def., 1951-52; asst. sec. for fin. mgmt. Navy, 1954-57, under-sec., 1957-59, sec., 1959-60; bus. cons., from 1960; vice chmn. bd. Fram Corp.; pres., dir. Carolina, Clinchfield & Ohio R.R.; dir. Penn-Dixie Cement Corp., Rutland County Bank, Rutland, Vt. Recipient Patriotic Civilian Svc. commendation U.S. Army, 1951, Disting. Svc. award Dept. Def., 1951; Medal of Freedom, 1961. Mem. Union League Club (N.Y.C.), Army and Navy Club (Washington), Rutland Country Club. Republican. Presbyn. *

FRANKOVICH, MIKE J., film producer; b. Bisbee, Ariz., Sept. 29, 1910; m. Binnie Barnes. B.A., U. Calif. Producer, commentator on radio, 1934-38; mng. dir. Columbia Pictures Corp. Ltd., 1955-59, chmn., 1959-67; v.p. Columbia Pictures Internat. Corp., 1955-67; head Columbia Pictures Internat. Prodns., 1958-67, 1st v.p. charge world prodn., until 1967; dir. BLC Films; chmn. Screen Gems Ltd.; ind. producer, from 1967; founding mem. Am. Film Inst., mem. bd. and exec. com. Author screenplays for Universal Studios, 1938, Republic Pictures, 1940-49; producer for Columbia: (films) Cat Ballou, Look Who's Coming to Dinner, To Sir With Love, In Cold Blood, A Man for all Seasons, Bob & Carol & Ted & Alice, 1969, Marooned, 1969; ind. producer (films) Cactus Flower, 1969, The Looking Glass War, 1970, Doctor's Wives, 1971, There's a Girl in My Soup, 1970, The Love Machine, 1971, Dollars, 1971, Butterflies Are Free, 1972, Stand Up and Be Counted, 1972, Forty Carats, 1973, Report to the Commissioner, 1975, From Noon Till Three, 1976, The Shootist, 1976, also TV films. Pres. L.A. Coliseum Commn., early 1980's. Served with AUS, World War II. Recipient Jean Hirsholt Humanitarian award Acad. Motion Picture Arts and Scis., 1984. Mem. Variety Club (chief banker Tent 36). Home: Los Angeles Calif. Died Jan. 1, 1992.

FRAPPIER, ARMAND, microbiologist, educator; b. Salaberry-de-Valleyfield, Que., Can., Nov. 26, 1904; s. Arthur Alexis and Bernadette (Codebecq) F.; m. Therese Ostiguy, June 29, 1929; children—Lise Davignon, Monique Desrochers, Michelle Daignault, Paul. B.A., Seminary, Salaberry-de-Valleyfield, 1924; M.D., U. Montreal, 1930, Dr. honoris causa, 1976, L.Sc., 1931; Diploma, Trudeau Sch. Tb, 1932; Dr. (hon.), U. Paris, 1964, U. Laval, Can., 1971, U. Que., 1978, U. Cracovie, 1978, McGill U., 1989. Prof. medicine U. Montreal, Que., 1933-71, prof. emeritus, from 1971; founder, dean Sch. Hygiene U. Montreal, 1945-65; dir. clin. labs. St. Luke's Hosp., Montreal,

1927-43; founder, dir. Inst. Armand Frappier, U. Que., 1938-74; mem. adv. com. Med. Research Council, Can., 1952-55, Biol. Warfare Def. Research Can., Pub. Health Research Can., 1954-60; mem. experts com. on Tb WHO, 1953. Contbr. articles to profl. jours. Decorated officer Order Brit. Empire, companion Order du Can., grand officer Ordre National du Que.; recipient Jean Toy prize Acad. Sci., France, 1971, Prix Marie-Victorin, 1979, medal and prize Found. J.L. Levesque, 1983. Fellow Am. Pub. Health Assn. (v.p. 1965-66), Am. Soc. Microbiologists; mem. Corp. Profl. des Médecins and Chirurgiens, Coll. Royal des Médecins and Chirurgiens, Can. Soc. Microbiologists (pres. 1954), Royal Soc. Can., Acad. Nat. de Medicine (France). Roman Catholic. Club: LaRoue du Roy. Home: Montreal PQ, Canada Died Dec. 18, 1991; buried Salaberry de Valleyfield, Can.

FRASER, JOSEPH T., JR., fine arts academy administrator; b. Phila., Sept. 15, 1898; m. Mary Isabel Chism, Oct. 10, 1926; children: Joseph Thompson III, Sarah Ann. BS in Architecture, U. Pa., 1922. Registered architect, Pa. Practicing architect State of Pa., 1922-34; curator summer sch. Pa. Acad Fine Arts, Phila., 1934, curator winter and summer sch., 1935-38, sec., dir., from 1938. Dir. Phila. Art Alliance, Fairmount Park Art Assn., Woodmere Art Gallery. Recipient Gold medal of honor Pa. Acad. Fine Arts, 1955. Mem. Mus. Coun. Phila. (pres.), Am. Assn. Museums, Assn. Art Mus. Dirs., Am. Fedn. Arts, AIA, Met. Mus. Art, Phila. Mus. Art, Mus. Modern Art N.Y.C., U. Pa. Mus., Hist. Soc. Pa., Orpheus Club, Phi Delta Theta. Republican. Episc. *

FRASER, THOMAS AUGUSTUS, JR., bishop; b. Atlanta, Apr. 17, 1915; s. Thomas Augustus an dLena Lee Connell F.; m. Marjorie Louise Rimbach, May 29, 1943; children: Thomas Augustus III, Constance Louise. BA, Hobart Coll., 1938, STD, 1965; BD, Va. Theol. Sem., 1941, DD, 1960. Ordained to ministry Episcopal Ch. as deacon, 1941, priest, 1942, bishop, 1960. Missionary Diocese L.I., N.Y., 1941-42; sec., chaplain Bishop of L.I., 1942; sr. asst. N.Y.C., 1942-44; rector Alexandria, Va., 1944-51, Winston-Salem, N.C., 1951-60; bishop coadjutor Diocese of N.C., Raleigh, 196-65, bishop, 1965-89; mem. editorial com. Anglican Congress, Toronto, Can., 1963; chmn. Joint Commn. on Edn. Holy Orders Episcopal Ch., 1963-89. Mem. Community Nursing, Alexandria, 1944-5, Winston-Salem, 1951-60, Alcoholic Rehab., Winston-Salem, 1954-59, United Fund, Winston-Salem, 1957-60, Family and Child Welfare, Winston-Salem, 1955-57, Children's Psychol. Clinic, Winston-Salem, 1955-57; trustee U. of South, Va. Theol. Sem., St. Mary's Jr. Coll., Raleigh, St. Augustine's Coll.; mem. exec. com. Gov.'s Commn. on Piedmont Crescent, 1964-89, sec. Commn. Priesthood, 1968; Lambeth Conf., London. Mem. Tau Kappa Alpha, Sigma Chi. Home: Raleigh N.C. Died Oct. 20, 1989.

FRATCHER, WILLIAM FRANKLIN, lawyer, educator emeritus; b. Detroit, Apr. 4, 1913; s. Vernon Claude and Ethel Stuart (Thomas) F.; m. Elsie Florene Briscoe, Aug. 22, 1941; 1 child, Agnes Ann. AB with distinction, Wayne U., 1933, AM, 1938; JD with distinction, U. Mich., 1936, LLM, 1951, SJD, 1952; grad., Command and Gen. Staff Sch., U.S. Army, 1944; spl. study, U. Paris, 1945. Bar: Mich. 1936. Assoc., mem. Lewis & Watkins, 1936-41; assoc. prof. law U. Mo., 1947-49, prof., 1949-92, R.B. Price Disting. prof. law, 1971-83, prof. emeritus, 1983-92, sesquicentennial prof., 1989-92, chmn. civil def. com., 1957-63, chmn. faculty com. on tenure, 1970-83, chm. com. on hon. degrees, 1980; research dir. spl. com. model probate code sect. real property, probate and trust law ABA, 1962-63; research counsel N.Y. Temporary State Commn. Estates, 1963; vis. prof. law U. Mich., summer 1952, NYU, 1954-55, summer 1963, 65, U. Calif.-Hastings Coll. Law, 1976, U. Puget Sound, 1983-85, Western New Eng. Coll., 1986-87; Ford Found. Law Faculty fellow Inst. Advanced Legal Studies; also hon. mem. Faculty of Laws, King's Coll., U. London (Eng.), 1963-64; research asso. U. Mich., summer 1953; chmn. joint com. on cooperation between Assn. Am. Law Schs. and Am. Assn. Law Libraries, 1969; mem. adv. com. to Sec. of State on UNIDROIT Draft Conv. to Establish Internat. Form of Will. Author: The National Defense Act, 1945, Perpetuities and Other Restraints, 1954, (with Lewis M. Simes) Cases and Other Materials on Fiduciary Administration, 1956, Trusts and Estates in England, 1968, Cases and Materials on Veterinary Jurisprudence, 1968, (with others) Landmark Papers on Estate Planning, Wills, Estates and Trusts, 1968, Planning Large Estates, 1968, Uniform Probate Code, 1970, Uniform Probate Code Practice Manual, 1972, 2d edit., 1977, Fascicle on Trust, Internat. Ency. Comparative Law, 1974, (with others) Death, Taxes and Family Property, 1977, The Law Barn: A Brief History of The School of Law, University of Missouri-Columbia, 1978, 2d edit., 1988, The Luncheon Guest, 1979, (with others) Trusts and Trust-Like Devices, 1981, (with others) Equity, Fiduciaries and Trusts, 1989, Materials for a Course in English Legal History, 1990 (with others) Introduction to the Law of the United States, 1992; editor: (pocket parts) Simes and Smith, The Law of Future Interests, 1961, 65, 67, 69, 72, 73, 75, 77, 79, 81, 83, 85, 87, 89, 91, Supplements to Scott, The Law of Trusts, annually 1982-92, 4th edit. of Scott, The Law of Trusts, 1986-91 (12 vols.); gov. publs. on mil. law; mem. editorial bd.: Manual for Courts-Martial, U.S.A, 1949; reporter: Uniform Probate Code, 1963-70; gen. reporter: Internat. Ency. Comparative Law, 1966-74; reporter: Mo. Probate Laws Revision Project, 1973-80, Mo. Guardianship Laws Revision Project, 1975-83, Mo. Trust Laws Revision Project, 1980-83; contbr. to Ency. Brit., 1974; also articles to various publs. Mem. Gen. Assembly Permanent Jud. Commn. Presbyn. Ch. (U.S.A.), 1983-89. Served as 2d lt. cavalry Civilian Conservation Corps, 1934-35; commd. capt. JAGC U.S. Army, 1941; served as chief, control br., Office JAG, War Dept. 1942; exec. to asst. judge adv. gen. in charge civil matters 1943-44; chief, miscellaneous br., Mil. Justice div., Br. Office JAG 1945, ETO, Paris; chief war crimes br., legal div., Office Mil. Govt. U.S. 1945-46, Berlin; U.S. commr. and chmn. Internat. Commn. for Control of Central Registry of War Criminals and Security Suspects 1946; staff judge adv., Berlin Dist. and hdqrs. command U.S. Forces, European Theater, 1946; reviewed Kronberg Castle jewel theft cases lt. col. Res. 1947; col. 1957. Decorated Legion of Merit, Commendation medal; Acad. fellow Am. Coll. Probate Counsel, 1971; Loyd E. Roberts prize in adminstrn. of justice, 1982; Spurgeon Smithson award Mo. Bar Found., 1983; research grantee Nat. Conf. Commrs. on Uniform State Laws at U. Mich., summer 1966; research grantee Am. Bar Found. at U. Colo., summer 1967; research grantee Internat. Assn. Legal Sci. at U. Oxford, Eng., summer 1969. Mem. ABA (spl. com. mil. justice 1959-61, 64-71, vice chmn. 1970-71, chmn. com. real property lit. 1953-55, vice chmn. 1975-77, vice chmn. com. probate and trust lit. 1974-83), Mo. Bar (chmn. mil. law com. 1967-68, mem. council probate and trusts com. 1969-83, 85-86), Judge Advs. Assn., Am. Law Inst.(cons. Restatement Third, Trusts 1988-89, adviser 1989-92), Res. Officers Assn. U.S., Selden Soc. (Mo. corr.), Soc. Pub. Tchrs. Law (U.S. corr.), Am. Soc. Legal History, Pipe Roll Soc., Order of Coif. Presbyterian. Home: Columbia Mo. Died June 24, 1992. †

FRATT, CHARLES KENNEDY POE, management consultant; b. Seattle, Mar. 31, 1931; s. Norbert and Laura (Emory) F.; m. LouAnn Johnson, Sept. 6, 1958; children—Laura, C.K. Poe, William H.E. B.M.E., Cornell U., 1955; M.B.A., Stanford U., 1959. C.P.A., Calif. With John Fluke Mfg. Co., Seattle, 1959-61; cons. Mgmt. Systems Corp., Palo Alto, Calif., 1962-65; ptnr.-in-charge Peat, Marwick, Livingston & Co., Los Angeles, 1965-68; ptnr.-in-charge mgmt. cons. Peat, Marwick, Mitchell, San Francisco, 1969-78; ptnr.-in-charge mgmt. cons. Europe Peat, Marwick, Mitchell, Paris, 1978-81; ptnr. exec. office No. Calif. Peat, Marwick, Mitchell, N.Y.C., from 1981; bd. dirs. Continental European Partnership, 1978-81; dir. 151 E. 79th Corp.; vice chmn. Cornell U. Council; mem. Library Council, Ithaca, N.Y., from 1981; adv. council Grad. Sch. Mgmt. Cornell U., from 1980, chmn., founder strategic task force, 1982, audit com. bd. trustees, 1980-82, trustee, 1977-82. Nat. chmn. Keystone Program Stanford Centennial, 1987—; dir. Dem. Nat. Com., 1987—. Recipient Gold Spike, Stanford U., 1978. Mem. Am. Inst. CPA's, Calif. Soc. CPA's, Stanford Assocs. (outstanding achievement award 1985), Cornell U. Alumni Assn. (bd. dirs.), Phi Delta Theta. Clubs: Univ.-Seattle, Pacific-Union, Seattle Golf, Claremont Country, Seattle Tennis. Home: New York N.Y. Died Nov., 1988.

FRAZIER, THOMAS ALEXANDER, lawyer, army officer; b. Chattanooga, Oct. 31, 1894; s. James Beriah and Louise Douglas (Keith) F.; m. Margaret Dolan, Mar. 22, 1930; children: Frances, Thomas Alexander, Jr., Jane Louise. AB, Vanderbilt U., 1917; LLB, Chattanooga Coll. Law, 1920; mil. student law dept., U. Montpelier, France, 1919. Bar: Tenn. 1920, Miss. 1920. Attended Frist Officers' Tng. Camp, Ft. Oglethorpe, Ga.; commd. 2d lt. 11th U.S. Cavalry; 1st lt. U.S. Army, 1917; served with Hdqrs. Battery, Hdqrs. Army Arty. 1st Army, France, 1918; participated in Aisne-Marne defensive, St. Mihiel and Meuse-Argonne offensives; with 15th U.S. Cavalry, to 1919; mem. Frazier & Frazier, Chattanooga, 1920-22, 39; practiced at, Clarksdale, Miss., 1922-36; apptd. adj. gen. State of Tenn., 1939; organizing State Div. CD; apptd. state dir. Selective Svc., 1940, inducted into active duty ast brig. gen. U.S. Army; sec. maj. gen., comdg. 1st div. Tenn State Guard, 1942; ret. as brig. gen. U.S. Army, 1945. Author: Historical and Pictorial Review of Tennessee National Guard; From Peace to War: The Military March of Time in Tennessee. Mem. Tenn. Bar Assn., Hamilton County Bar Assn., Am. Legion, Mil. Order World War, VFW, Masons, Elks, Phi Delta Theta. Democrat. Methodist. *

FREDERICK, PAULINE, broadcast news analyst; b. Gallitzin, Pa.; d. Matthew Phillip and Susan (Stanley) F.; m. Charles Robbins. A.B., Am. U., Washington, also A.M.; numerous hon. degrees. State Dept. corr. U.S. Daily; radio editorial asst. H.R. Baukhage, Blue Network and ABC; free-lance Western Newspaper Union, N.Am. Newspaper Alliance; also news commentator ABC, 1946-53; news corr. NBC, 1953-74; also UN corr. ABC, NBC; radio anchor Dem. and Rep. Convs. NBC, 1956; internat. affairs analyst Nat. Public Radio; moderator 2d debate Pres. Ford-Gov. Carter, Oct. 6, 1976. Trustee Am. U.; mem. council Save the Children, UN Assn. U.S.A. Recipient Headliner award Theta Sigma Phi, Alfred I. duPont award, George Foster Peabody award for contbn. to internat. understanding, Golden Mike award for outstanding woman in radio-TV McCall's; Paul White award for contbn. to broadcast journalism Radio and TV News Dirs. Assn.; voted radio's woman of the year Radio-TV Daily poll; U. Mo. Sch. Journalism medal; spl. citation for UN coverage Nat. Fedn. Women's Clubs; East-West Center award; Journalism Achievment award U. So. Calif.; 1st Pa. Journalism Achievment award; Carr Van Anda award Ohio U. Sch. Journalism; named to N.Y. Profl. Journalists Soc. Hall of Fame. Fellow Soc. Profl. Journalists; mem. UN Corrs. Assn. (pres.), Assn. Radio and Television Analysts, Council on Fgn. Relations. Home: Sarasota Fla. Died May 9, 1990.

FREE, WILLIAM AUGUSTUS, SR., food canning executive, trade association exective; b. York, Pa., June 25, 1898; s. Harry Kister and Annie Margaret (Stallman) F.; m. Sarah Ruth Motter, Dec. 14, 1922 (dec. Jan. 1963); children: William Augustus, Robert K., Elizabeth (Mrs. Raymond Protheroe, Jr.); m. 2d, Janet S. Hutton, Feb. 14, 1964. Grad., York High Sch. Terr. salesman Niagara Sprayer Co., Middleport, N.Y., 1919-30; founder, pres. Hungerford (Pa.) Packing Co. Inc., from 1930; pres. Hungerford Fine Foods, Inc., Delta Canning Co., Inc., Deltaville, Va.; exec. sec. Pa. Canners Assn., 1934-51. Served with Mcht. Marine, 1917-19. Mem. Nat. Canners Assn. (bd. dirs. 1943-45, chmn. conv. com. 1947, chmn. regional adjustment com. 1952-59, v.p. 1962, pres. from 1963), Coun. Canning Assn. Execs. (pres., sec.), Young Guard Soc. (founder, adv. com., pres., sec.), Am. Inst. Food Distbn. (exec. coun.), Mfrs. Assn. York, Rotary, Lafayette Club, Country Club of York. *

FREELAND, EMILE CHARROPPIN, government official; b. Winnsboro, La., Sept. 29, 1896; s. Jesse Beaumont and Estelle (Lockwood) F.; m. Leonor E. Zalles, Feb. 22, 1931; children: George Lockwood, Consuelo Zalles, Christina Calderon. BS, La. State U., 1918. Lic. cons. engr., N.Y. Cons. chemist Audubon Park Sugar Expt. Sta., New Orleans, 1918-19; sugar and alcohol technician Booker Bros., McConnel & Co., Georgetown, Guiana, 1919-23; asst. supt. syrup and molasses canning plant Penick & Ford, Ltd., Inc., New Orleans, 1923-26; indsl. engr. W.R. Grace & Co., N.Y.C., 1926-53; cons. chem. engr., advisor Pakistan Nat. Planning Bd., Ford Bacon & Davis, N.Y.C., 1955-58; chem. engring. adviser U.S. Ops. Mission, Tel Aviv, Israel, 1958-61, AID, Taiwan, 1961-64; chem. engr. C.W. Robinson Co., AID contract, Pakistan, from 1964. Author: (autobiography) Tales of A Sugar Tramp; contbr. articles to profl. jours. Mem. ASME, Am. Inst. Chem. Engrs., Am. Chem. Soc., Explorers Club (N.Y.C.), Alpha Chi Sigma. *

FREELAND, T. PAUL, lawyer; b. Princeton, Ind., Sept. 26, 1916; s. Leander Theodore and Leona B. (Tryon) F.; m. Caroline Van Dyke Ransom, July 7, 1941; 1 child, Caroline Carr (Mrs. Torrance C. Raymond). A.B., DePauw U., 1937; LL.B., Columbia U., 1940. Bar: N.Y., D.C., Mass. Assoc. firms Cravath, de Gersdorff, Swaine & Wood, N.Y.C., summer 1939, Dunnington, Bartholow & Miller, 1940-42; atty. office chief counsel IRS, 1945-48; ptnr. firms Wenchel, Schulman & Manning, Washington, 1948-62, Sharp & Bogan, Washington, 1962-65, Bogan & Freeland, Washington, 1965-83, Sutherland, Asbill & Brennan, Washington, 1983-88; lectr. various tax insts. Trustee Embry-Riddle Aero. U., 1972-82. Served as lt. USCGR, 1942-45, ETO. Fellow Am. Bar Found.; mem. Am., Inter-Am., Fed., D.C. bar assns., Internat. Fiscal Assn., U.S. C. of C. (task force on internat. tax policy), Phi Delta Phi. Clubs: Met. (D.C.), Chevy Chase (Md.). Home: Bethesda Md. Died Aug. 28, 1988. †

FREEMAN, GAYLORD, bank executive; b. Chgo., Jan. 19, 1910; s. Gaylord A. and Pauline A. Miser F.; children: Nancy Lee Freeman Ellett dec. , Linda Jan Freeman Taylor, Clara Tollerton Freeman Farah. AB, Dartmouth Coll., 1931, LLD, 1962. Bar: Ill. 1934. Atty. First Nat. Bank of Chgo., 1940-50, v.p. corr. bank div., 1950-53, gen. v.p., 1953-60, pres., 1960-62, vice chmn. bd., 1962-69; chmn. bd., chmn. and dir. First Chgo. Corp., 1969-75; hon. chmn. bd., dir. First Nat. Bank of Chgo. and First Chgo. Corp., 1975-80. Trustee Aspen Colo. Inst. Humanistic Studies; life trustee Northwestern U.; hon. trustee Com. Econ. Devel., N.Y.C.; sr. mem. Conf. Bd., Inc., N.Y.C.; chmn. Nat. Commn. on Postal Svc., 1976-77, Gov. Ill. Cost Control Task Force, 1977-81; chmn. select task force on inflation Am. Bankers Assn., 1979-80. Mem. Casino Club, Chgo. Club, Comml. Club, Mid-Day Club, Dunham Woods Club. Congregationalist. Home: Wayne Ill. Died Mar. 7, 1991.

FREEMAN, HARRY BOIT, JR., financial executive; b. Providence, June 14, 1926; s. Harry Boit and Theodora (Hollander) F.; m. Leslie Stires, June 14, 1947; children: Tracy Clark Freeman Wells, Harry Boit III. Grad., Middlesex Sch., 1944; B.A., Yale U., 1949; M.B.A., N.Y.U., 1952. With City Bank Farmers Trust Co., N.Y.C., 1949-52; v.p. Tchrs. Ins. & Annuity Assn., also Coll. Retirement Equities Fund, N.Y.C., 1953-59; gen. partner Wood, Struthers & Winthrop (and predecessor), N.Y.C., 1959-67; v.p. Engelhard Hanovia,

Inc., Newark, N.J., 1967-70; pres., dir. Channing Mgmt. Corp., also The Channing Funds, N.Y.C., 1970-73; with Lord, Abbett & Co., N.Y.C., 1973-80; gen. partner Lord, Abbett & Co., 1974-80, asso mng. partner, 1977-78, mng. partner, 1978; dir. Lexington Group of Mut. Funds. Served with USMCR, 1944-45. Mem. Am. Finance Assn. Clubs: Knickerbocker (N.Y.C.); Rumson (N.J.). Home: New York N.Y. Died Aug. 16, 1990.

FREEMAN, HOVEY THOMAS, insurance company executive; b. Winchester, Mass., July 15, 1894; s. John Ripley and Elizabeth Farwell (Clark) F.; m. Marjorie E. Wellman, Nov. 24, 1917; children: Charles Wellman, Bertha Beth, Nancy Duxbury, Marjorie Ellen, Juliette Adams, Hovey Thomas. BS, MIT, 1916. Constrn. engr. Chase Cos., 1916; field engr. Mfrs. Mut. Fire Ins. Co., 1919-23, v.p., engr., 1923-32, pres., dir., treas., 1932-63, mem. exec. com., dir., chmn. bd., from 1963; dir. Am. Mut. Reins. Co., Eaton Paper Corp., Indsl. Nat. Bank, Am. Mut. Liability Ins. Co., Am. Mut. Ins. Co. Boston, Gorham Corp; asst. treas. John R. Freeman Trust Estate. Trustee Roger Williams Hosp. Capt., ordnance dept. AEF, World War I. Mem. ASME, Providence Engring. Soc., Art Club, Agawam Hunt Club, Turks Head Club, Union League (N.Y.C.), Delta Kappa Epsilon. Republican. Episc. *

FREEMAN, HOWARD EDGAR, sociology educator; b. N.Y.C., May 28, 1929; s. Herbert M. and Rose H. (Herman) F.; m. Sharon W. Kleban, Apr. 20, 1952 (div. 1977); children—Seth R., Lisa J.; m. Marian A. Solomon, Feb. 2, 1979. BA, NYU, 1948, MA, 1950, PhD, 1956. Asst. social scientist Rand Corp., Santa Monica, Calif., 1955-56; rsch. assoc. sch. pub. health Harvard U., Boston, 1956-62; Morse prof. urban studies Brandeis U., Waltham, Mass., 1960-72; social sci. advisor Ford Found., Mexico City, Mex., 1972-74; prof. sociology UCLA, 1974-92, chmn. dept. sociology, 1986-89; sociologist Russell Sage Found., N.Y.C., 1967-77; rsch. advisor Robert Wood Johnson Found., Princeton, N.J., 1976-88; advisor Inst. Nutrition Cen. Am. and Panama, 1965-92, U.S.-Mex. Border Health Assn., San Antonio, 1981-82; cons. NIMH, Washington, 1971-76; mem. panel on social indicators HEW, Washington, 1966-69. Author: (with others) The Mental Patient Comes Home, 1963 (Hofheimer prize, 1967), The Middle Income Negro Family Faces Urban Renewal, 1965, The Clinic Habit, 1967, Social Problems, 1957, 3rd edit., 1967, Academic and Entrepreneurial Research, 1975, Evaluation Research, 1971, 4th edit, 1989; editor Evaluation Review, Los Angeles, 1976—, Health and Social Behavior, Washington, 1969-72, Policy Studies Review Annual, 1987; (with others) Handbook of Medical Sociology, 1963, 4th edit., 1989, The Social Scene, 1972, America's Troubles, 1973, The Dying Patient, 1982, Applied Sociology, 1983, Collecting Evaluation Data, 1985, others; contbr. articles to profl. jours. Capt. USAF, 1952-53. Mem. Am. Sociol. Assn., Am. Psychol. Assn., Am. Assn. Pub. Opinion Rsch., Am. Pub. Health Assn., Nat. Acad. Scis. (Inst. Medicine). Home: West Hollywood Calif. Died Oct. 21, 1992. †

FREEMAN, KENNETH DAVID, musician; b. Chgo., Apr. 13, 1906; s. Louis Milton and Emily (Fernette) F. Edn. high sch., pvt. tutors. Tenor soloist with Tommy Dorsey, Benny Goodman and Eddie Condon, 1936-47; tenor saxaphonist; featured with World's Greatest Jazz Band. Winner jazz poll, Metronome and Downbeat mags., 1936; named Soloist of Yr., Life mag., 1938; author: You Don't Look Like a Musician; composer: The Eel. Mem. ASCAP, Fedn. Musicians. Home: Chicago Ill.

FREEMAN, RALPH MCKENZIE, judge; b. Flushing, Mich., May 5, 1902; s. Horace B. and Laura D. (McKenzie) F.; m. Emmalyn E. Ellis, Aug. 13, 1938. LL.B., U. Mich., 1926. Bar: Mich. bar 1926. Pvt. practice law Flint, 1926-27, 33-54; mem. Freeman, Bellairs & Dean, 1953-54; pros. atty. Genesee County, Mich., 1930-32; U.S. dist. judge Eastern Dist. Mich., 1954-67, chief judge, 1967-72, sr. judge, 1973-90. Mem. Flint (Mich.) Bd. Edn., 1933-49, pres., 1938-39, 48-49. Fellow Am. Bar Found.; mem. Am. Bar Assn., State Bar Mich., Phi Kappa Tau, Sigma Delta Kappa. Clubs: Circumnavigators; Economic (Detroit); Birmingham Country. Home: Birmingham Mich. Died Mar. 29, 1990; buried Sunset Hills, Flint, Mich.

FREEMAN, ROGER ADOLPH, research economist; b. Vienna, Austria, Sept. 2, 1904; came to U.S., 1940; s. Samuel and Emma (Ferber) Freimann; m. Emily Georgia Harpster, Aug. 10, 1944 (div. Nov. 1972); children: Mary Christine Freeman Pressfield, Roger Charles Montague. Diploma, Vienna Sch. Bus. Adminstrn., 1927; LLD, Brigham Young U., 1966. With mdse. dept. Delka Inc., Vienna, 1927-39; mdse. mgr. W.L. Douglas Shoe Co., N.Y.C. and Brockton, Mass., 1940-42; buyer, dept. mgr. L. Bamberger & Co., Newark, 1943-45; controller, asst. to pres. Shoe Corp. of Am., Seattle, 1945-49; spl. asst. to gov. State of Wash., Olympia, 1950-55; asst. in White House Office, Exec. Office of the Pres., Washington, 1955-56; fin. adviser to govt. of Bolivia, U.S. Treasury AID, La Paz, Bolivia, 1957; v.p. Inst. of Social Sci. Research, Washington, 1957-60; research dir. Inst. for Studies in Federalism, Claremont (Calif.) Mens' Coll., 1960-62; sr. fellow Hoover Instn., Stanford (Calif.) U., 1962-75, sr. fellow emeritus Hoover Instn., 1975-91; spl. asst. to U.S. Pres., White House, Washington, 1969-70; prof. econs., chmn. div. econs. and bus. Hillsdale (Mich.) Coll., 1977; sr. research assoc. Minority Conf., U.S. Senate, Washington, 1978; mem., co. chmn. state and local govt. adv. com. U.S. Bur. of Census, Washington, 1952-56; cons. on sch. fin. White House Conf. on Edn., Washington, 1955; chmn. task force on Fed. Revenue Sharing Republican Coordinating Com. Republican Nat. Com., 1967; chmn. Census adv. com. on Privacy and Confidentiality, Washington, 1974-75, Adv. Council on Fin. Aid to Students U.S. Office of Edn., Washington, 1974-75. Author: Federal Aid to Education: Boon or Bane?, 1955, School Needs in the Decade Ahead, 1958, Taxes for the Schools, 1960, Crisis in College Finance, 1965, Socialism and Private Enterprise in Equatorial Asia, 1968, Tax Loopholes: the Legend and the Reality, 1973, The Growth of American Government, A Morphology of the Welfare State, 1975, The Wayward Welfare State, 1981, Does America Neglect Its Poor ?, 1987, numerous articles in field. Recipient Disting. Research award Govt. Research Assn., 1959, Most Disting. Research award Govt. Research Assn., 1975, George Washington Honor Medal award Freedoms Found. at Valley Forge, 1967, 73; decorated Knight Grand Cross Equestrian Order of the Holy Sepulchre in Jerusalem, 1964. Home: Stanford Calif. Died Dec. 25, 1991; buried Holy Cross Cemetery, Menlo Pk., Calif.

FREIBERG, JOSEPH ALBERT, orthopedic surgeon; b. Cin., Oct. 3, 1898; s. Albert Henry and Jeannette (Freiberg) F.; m. Louise Rothenberg, Oct. 6, 1928 (dec. Jan. 1961); children: Richard Albert, Elinor (Mrs. Elliott Meyer). AB, Harvard U., 1920; AM, U. Cin., 1922, MD, 1923. Diplomate Am. Bd. Orthopedic Surgery. Intern Cin. Gen. Hosp., 1923-24, asst. surg. resident, 1924-25; grad. in orthopedic tng. Boston Children's Hosp. and Mass Gen. Hosp., 1925-27, Brit. and Continental orthopedic clinics, 1927; assoc. with Dr. Albert H. Freiberg in practice of orthopedic surgery, 1928-40, Dr. Richard A. Freiberg, from 1963; instr., asst. prof. orthopedic surgery Coll. Medicine, U. Cin., 1928-39, assoc. prof., dir. orthopedic div., 1939-62, prof. surgery, from 1962; area cons. orthopedic surgery VA; dir. orthopedic svc. Cin. Gen. Hosp., Holmes Hosp., Cin. Children's Hosp.; cons. in orthopedic surgery Jewish Hosp.; orthopedic cons. VA Hosp., Cin., Hamilton County Tb Sanatorium (Dunham Hosp.); orthopedic cons. Selective Svc. Bd. 1, Cin.; dir. Brace Shop, Inc.; mem. med. adv. com. Infantile Paralysis Com. of Hamilton County. Contbr. chpts. to Nelson's Looseleaf Surgery, Bancroft's Surgery; contbr. numerous articles to profl. jours. Served with S.A.T.C., U. Cin., 1918. Fellow ACS; mem. Am. Bd. Orthopedic Suragery, Am. Orthopedic Assn. (pres. 1962), Am. Acad. Orthopedic Surgeons (v.p. 1949), World Med. Assn. (U.S. com.), Am. Rheumatism Assn., Orthopedic Forum, Clin. Orthopedic Soc. (pres. 1945), AMA, Ohio Med. Assn., Cin. Acad. Medicine, Univ. Club, Harvard Club of Cin., Losantville Country Club, Sigma Xi, Alpha Omega Alpha. Jewish. *

FREINKEL, NORBERT, physician, educator, researcher; b. Mannheim, Germany, Jan. 26, 1926; s. Adolf and Veronika (Kahn) F.; m. Ruth Kimmelstiel, June 19, 1955; children: Susan Elizabeth, Andrew Jonathan, Lisa Ann. A.B., Princeton U., 1947; M.D., NYU, 1949; M.D. honoris causa, Uppsala U., Sweden, 1981, Umea U., Sweden, 1985. Postdoctoral tng. in medicine, endocrinology and metabolism Bellevue Hosp., N.Y.C., Boston City Hosp., Thorndike Meml. Lab., Harvard U. Med. Sch., ARC Inst. Animal Physiology, Cambridge, Eng., 1949-56; from research fellow to assoc. prof. medicine Harvard Med. Sch. and Thorndike Meml. Lab., Boston City Hosp., 1952-66, chief metabolism div., 1957-66; C.F. Kettering prof. medicine, chief sect. endocrinology, metabolism and nutrition, dir. Endocrine Clinics, Northwestern U. Med. Sch., 1966-89, prof. biochemistry, 1969-89, prof. molecular biology, 1981-89, dir. Center for Endocrinology, Metabolism and Nutrition, 1973-89; mem. metabolism study sect. NIH, 1967-69, chmn. designate, 1970; mem. adv. com. on alcoholism NIMH, 1967-70; mem. subcom. on diabetes Fogarty Internat. Center, NIH, 1972-76; mem. Space Flight Space Sci. Bd., Nat. Acad. Sci., 1973-74; cons. surg. gen. U.S. Army, 1962-79; mem. endocrinology and metabolism adv. com. Bur. Drugs, FDA, 1973-76, cons., from 1976; mem. career devel. com. VA, Washington, 1975-77; mem. spl. study sect. DRTC NIAMDD, 1976-77; mem. nutrition coordinating com. NIH, 1978-80; chmn. 1st and 2d Internat. Workshop-Conf. Gestational Diabetes, 1979, 84; bd. dirs. BioTechnica Internat. Inc., 1981-86; mem. nat. Diabetes adv. bd. HEW, 1986-89, dir. WHO Collagorating Ctr. Diabetes in Pregnancy, 1986-89; coconvener steering com. maternal and child, health, Internat. Diabetes Fedn., 1986. Co-editor: Handbook of Physiology Series, Am. Phys. Soc.; Editorial bd.: Endocrinology, Jour. Developmental Physiology, Ann. Rev. Medicine, Jour. Clin. Investigation, Jour. Clin. Endocrinology, Jour. Lab. Clin. Medicine, Bull. Internat. Diabetes Fedn. Hippocrates; editor-in-chief: The Year in Metabolism, 1975-79, Contemporary Metabolism, 1979-86; Contbr. articles to profl. jours., chpts. in textbooks. Served with USNR 1943-45; Served with USNR AUS, 1950-52. Recipient Lilly award and medal Am. Diabetes Assn., 1966; Woodyatt award No. Ill. Diabetes Assn., 1976; Mosenthal award N.Y. Diabetes Assn., 1978; Banting Meml. medal Am. Diabetes Assn., 1978, Banting Meml. award and Lectureship, Am. Diabetes Assn., 1980; Joslin medal New Eng. Diabetes Assn., 1978; Kellion medal Australian Diabetes Assn., 1981, First Priscilla White Lectr., Harvard Med. Sch., 1985, Solomon A. Berson Clin. Sci. award, NYU Med. Sch., 1986, McCollum award Am. Soc. Clin. Met., 1986; Agnes Higgins award March of Dimes Found., 1988. Fellow A.C.P., AAAS, Diabetes Assn. of India (hon.); mem. Assn. Am. Physicians, Am. Soc. Clin. Investigation (editorial com. 1971-76), Am. Physiol. Soc., World Med. Assn. (mem. med. bd. advisers from 1975), Endocrine Soc. (council 1969-72, chmn. meetings com. 1980-83, postgrad. program com. 1983-86), Am. Thyroid Assn. (chmn. Van Meter award com. 1977-78), Am. Diabetes Assn. (dir. 1968-79, chmn. com. sci. programs 1971-75, v.p. profl. sect. 1975-76, pres. 1977-78, exec. com. 1975-79), Am. Clin. and Climatol. Assn., Am. Soc. Clin. Nutrition (council 1984-87), Soc. Exptl. Biology and Medicine, AAAS (mem. at large, sect., med. scis.), Alpha Omega Alpha, Phi Beta Kappa, Sigma Xi; hon. mem. High Table, King's Coll., Cambridge, Eng. Home: Evanston Ill. Died Sept. 5, 1989; buried Shalom Meml. Pk., Palatine, Ill.

FREIRIA, EVARISTO, JR., business executive, consultant; b. San Juan, P.R., Jan. 4, 1929; s. Evaristo and Sara (Umpierre) F.; m. Maritza Villamil, Sept. 27, 1929; children: Maritza, Rosa, Evaristo, Sara Isabel. BBA, U. Conn., 1950. Salesman Freiría Hnos S. en C., San Juan, 1950-55; v.p. Freiría & Co. Inc., San Juan, 1955-74, pres., 1974-81; v.p. F. & J.M. Carrera Inc., San Juan, 1981-86, Recaíto Inc., San Juan, 1981-86; v.p., gen. mgr. Erick's Products Inc., Bayamón, P.R., 1986-89; exec. v.p., gen. mgr. Intermares Group Inc., Cataño, P.R.; cons. internat. affairs McCormick & Co. Inc., Balt., 1975-80; cons. F. & J.M. Carrera Inc., San Juan, 1984-89. V.p. P.R. Telephone Authority, 1979-84, now bd. dirs.; v.p. P.R. Communication Authority, 1979-84, now bd. dirs.; pres. Rotary Internat., Santurce, 1969, UN Day, San Juan, 1982. Recipient Pres.'s award McCormick Internat. div., Balt., 1961, Gov.'s award Rotary Internat., San Juan, 1977, Disting. Service award, UN, Washington, 1982. Mem. Wholesale C. ofC. (disting. citizen award 1973). Republican. Roman Catholic. Home: San Juan P.R. Died Jan. 2, 1989.

FRENCH, VICTOR, actor, director; b. Santa Barbara, Calif., Dec. 5; m. Julie Cobb; children: Victor A., Lee Kelly, Lee Tracy. Grad., L.A. State Coll.; student, Herbert Berghoff Studio, N.Y.C. Prin. character on TV series Little House on the Prairie, Carter Country, Highway to Heaven; stage appearances include: All the King's Men, Night of the Iguana, Of Mice and Men, Time of Your Life, After the Fall; TV appearances: Gunsmoke, Bonanza, Get Smart, Petrocelli; movie appearances: Flap, The Wild Rovers, The Other, The Nickel Ride; dir. TV episodes, theatrical prodns. Home: Beverly Hills CA Died June 15, 1989.

FRETTER, WILLIAM BACHE, physics educator; b. Pasadena, Calif., Sept. 28, 1916; s. William Albert and Dorothy (Bach) F.; m. Grace Powles, Jan. 1, 1939; children: Travis D., Gretchen, Richard Brian. A.B., U. Calif. at Berkeley, 1937, Ph.D., 1946. Research engr. radar counter-measures Westinghouse Electric Co., 1941-45; mem. faculty U. Calif. at Berkeley, 1946-78, prof. physics, 1955-78; dean U. Calif. at Berkeley (Coll. Letters and Sci.), 1962-67, v.p. system wide, 1978-83; chmn. internat. adv. panel World Bank Chinese U. Devel. Project II, Washington, 1984-87. Author: Introduction to Experimental Physics, 1955, (with David S. Saxon) Physics for the Liberal Arts Student, 1971. Fulbright scholar France, 1952-53, 60-61; Guggenheim fellow., 1960-61; decorated chevalier Legion of Honor France, 1964. Fellow Am. Phys. Soc. Home: Berkeley Calif. Died Mar. 24, 1991.

FREUD, ANNA, psychoanalyst; b. Vienna, Austria, Dec. 3, 1895; d. Sigmund and Martha (Bernays) Freud. Grad., Cottage Lyzeum, Vienna, 1912; LLD, Clark U., 1950; ScD, Jefferson Med. Coll., Phila., 1964. Chmn. Inst. Psycho-Analysis, Vienna, until 1938; organizer exptl. day nursery Jackson Nursery, Vienna, 1937-38; organizer residential war nursery for homeless children London, 1940-45, practicing psychoanalyst, from 1938; dir. Hampstead Child Therapy Course and Clinic, London, from 1953. Author numerous books; contbr. numerous articles to profl. jours. Mem. Brit. Psychoanalytical Soc. and Inst. *

FREUND, MORTON, advertising executive; b. N.Y.C., Sept. 17, 1900; s. Adolph and Mary (Strauss) F.; m. Elizabeth R. Ruben, Mar. 16, 1923. Student, Columbia U. Advt., sales mgr. various mfg. firms, 1921-27; officer Menken Advt., Inc., 1927-30; pres. Morton Freund Advt. Agy., 1930-52; merged with L.C. Gumbinner, 1953; exec. v.p. L.C. Gumbinner Advt. Agy., N.Y.C., 1953-90, also dir. Home: New York NY Died Feb. 6, 1990.

FREUND, PAUL ABRAHAM, law educator; b. St. Louis, Feb. 16, 1908; s. Charles and Hulda (Arenson) F. AB, Washington U., 1928, LLD, 1956; LLB, Harvard U., 1931, SJD, 1932; LLD (hon.), Columbia U., 1954, U. Louisville, 1956, U. Chgo., 1961, Boston U., 1964, Queens. U., Ont., 1970, Brown U., 1972, Yale U., 1972, Brandeis U., 1974, Williams Coll., 1974, Clark U., 1977, Harvard U., 1977, Georgetown U., 1983, U.

Bologna, 1981; LHD (hon.), Hebrew Union Coll., 1961; LittD (hon.), Cornell Coll., 1968, Bates Coll., 1973, Temple U., 1973, Yeshiva U., 1975; DCL (hon.), Union Coll., 1968; HHD (hon.), Stonehill Coll., 1978. Bar: D.C. 1935, Mass. 1947. Law clk. to Justice Louis Brandeis U.S. Supreme Ct., 1932-33; mem. legal staff U.S. Dept. Treasury, 1933-35; spl. asst. to atty. gen. Office of Solicitor Gen., U.S. Dept. Justice, 1935-39, 42-46; lectr. law Harvard U., Cambridge, Mass., 1939-40, prof. law, 1940-50, Charles Stebbins Fairchild prof., 1950-57, Royall prof., 1957-58, Carl M. Loeb U. prof., 1958-76, prof. emeritus, from 1976; Pitt prof. Am. history and instns. Cambridge (Eng.) U., 1957-58; Jefferson lectr. NEH, 1975; mem. Jud. Nominating Commn. 1st Cir. Author: On Understanding the Suprme Court, 1949, The Supreme Court of the U.S., 1961, On Law and Justice, 1968; editor: Experimentation with Human Subjects, 1970; co-editor: Cases on Constitutional Law, 1962, 4th revised edit., 1977; mem. editorial bd. Daedalus; contbr. articles to Ency. Brit., Ency. Social Sci., legal jours. Dir. Salzburg Sem. Am. Studies; trustee Washington U. Fellow Trinity Coll., Cambridge U., 1957-58, Ctr. for Advanced Study in Behavioral Scis., 1969-70; recipient Research award Am. Bar Found., 1973, Learned Hand award Fed. Bar Council, 1978, Law award Thomas Jefferson Meml. Found., 1979. Fellow Am. Acad. Arts and Scis. (past pres.) Brit. Acad. (corr.); mem. Am. Judicature Soc., Mass. Hist. Soc., Am. Philos. Soc., ABA, Am. Law Inst. (Henry J. Friendly award 1989), Harvard Soc. Fellows, Signet Soc., Phi Beta Kappa, Pi Sigma Alpha. Club: St. Botolph (Boston). Home: Cambridge Mass. Died Feb. 5, 1992; buried St. Louis.

FREY, ALBERT WESLEY, marketing educator, consultant; b. Lynn, Mass., Aug. 10, 1898; s. Fred James and Lena Mabel (Johnson) F.; m. Hope Lincoln, Sept. 3, 1961; 1 dau., Janet Wendell (Mrs. Edward H. Harte). AB, Dartmouth Coll., 1920, MA (hon.), 1937; MBA, Amos Tuck Sch. Bus. Adminstrn., 1921. Instr. econs. Dartmouth Coll., 1920-21; instr. mktg. Amos Tuck Sch. Bus. Adminstrn., 1921-27, asst. prof., 1927-37, prof., 1937-60, asst. dean, 1930-37; dep. dir. Office Surplus Property, U.S. Treasury Dept. and Dept. Commerce, 1944-45; chief tech. rsch. Office Surplus Proterty R.F. C., 1945; mktg. cons., 1960; prof. mktg. Grad. Sch. Bus. U. Pitts., 1961, dir. exec. devel. programs, from 1962; vis. prof. advt. UCLA, 1949. Author: Merchandise Control, 1927; Manufacturers' Product, Package and Price Policies, 1940; Advertising, 3d edit., 1961; How Many Dollars for Advertising, 1955; staff editor Mktg. Handbook, 1947, editor, 1965; mng. editor Jour. of Mktg., 1950-53, editor in chief, 1953-55. Trustee Mktg. Sci. Inst., from 1964, Distbn. Hall of Fame, 1963. Served as 2d lt. Coast Arty. Res. Corps, 1919. Mem. AAUP, ACLU, Am. Mktg. Assn. (dir. 1953-55, 56-57, pres. 1960-61), Phi Beta Kappa, Chi Phi. *

FREY, EDWARD JOHN, banker; b. Grand Rapids, Mich., July 3, 1910; s. John Edward and Stella (Reeves) F.; m. Frances Taliaferro, Nov. 7, 1936; children—Mary Caroline, John Monroe, David Gardner, Edward John. A.B., U. Mich., 1932; grad., Rutgers U. Grad. Sch. Banking, 1940; Litt.D. (hon.), Grand Valley State Coll., 1968; LL.D. (hon.), Olivet (Mich.) Coll., 1974. Pres., chmn. bd. Union Bank and Trust Co., N.A., Grand Rapids; chmn. bd., dir. Foremost Corp. Am., Foremost Ins. Co., Grand Rapids; pres. Gt. Lakes Fin. Corp., Grand Rapids; past mem. faculty Rutgers U. Grad. Sch. Banking; past mem. Downtown Devel. Com., Grand Rapids. Bd. dirs. United Community Services of Grand Rapids and Kent County; chmn. bd. trustees Grand Rapids Found.; trustee Little Traverse Hosp.; trustee, chmn. fin. com. Grand Valley Coll., Grand Rapids. Served to lt. comdr. USNR, 1943-46, PTO. Recipient Sesquicentennial Alumni award U. Mich., 1967. Mem. Am. Bankers Assn. (state legis. com.), Mich. Bankers Assn. (exec. council), U.S. (taxation and fin. com.), Mich. (past v.p. and dir.), Grand Rapids (dir., past pres.) chambers commerce.). Episcopalian (vestryman, sr. warden). Clubs: Rotary (past pres.), Peninsular (past pres.), Kent Country (Grand Rapids); River (N.Y.C.); Kinne Creek (Baldwin, Mich.). Home: Grand Rapids Mich. Died July 6, 1988.

FREY, JOSEPH RICHARD, banker; b. Secor, Ill., Jan. 2, 1897; s. Clarence W. and Geneva (Colburn) F.; m. Hilda Kohl, Nov. 5, 1921; 1 child, Richard Kohl. BS, U. Ill., 1919. State bank examiner Ill., 1923-29; v.p. Lake Shore Trust & Savs. Bank, 1929-33; pres., dir. Lake Shore Nat. Bank, 1933-52, pres., chmn., CEO, 1952-62, chmn., CEO, 1962-90; bd. dirs. C.W. Frey & Sons, Bloomington, Ill. Dir. emeritus Blue-Cross/Blue Shield; treas., dir. Rehab. Inst. Chgo.; past bd. dirs., exec. com. Chgo. chpt. ARC; mem. planning com. Northwestern U. Med. Ctr.; assoc. Northwestern U. Mem. Am. Bankerss Assn., Ill. Bankers Assn., Greater North Mich. Ave Assn. (past pres., bd. dirs.), Masons, Tau Kappa Epsilon. Home: Chicago Ill. Died Mar. 22, 1990.

FRICKER, PETER RACINE, composer, educator; b. London, Sept. 5, 1920; came to U.S., 1964; s. Edward Racine and Deborah (Parr) F.; m. Helen Clench, Apr. 17, 1943. Student, Royal Coll. Music, London, 1937-41; Mus.D. (hon.), U. Leeds, Eng., 1958. Dir. music Morley Coll., London, 1953-64; prof. music Royal Coll. Music, London, 1956-64; prof. music dept. U. Calif. at Santa Barbara, 1964-90, Corwin chair, 1987-90; condr., lectr., 1948-90; pres. Cheltenham Internat. Festival Music, 1983-86. Composer 5 symphonies, 2 oratorios, 2 violin concertos, 2 piano concertos, horn concerto, viola concerto, organ concerto, concerto for orch., chamber music, music for piano and 2 pianos, music for films and radio. Pres. emeritus Cheltenham Internat. Festival, 1987. Served to flight lt. RAF, 1941-46. Decorated Order of Merit (Fed. Republic Germany); recipient Freedom City of London, 1962. Fellow Royal Coll. Organists, asso. Royal Coll. Music; mem. Composer's Guild Gt. Britain (chmn. 1955, v.p. 1986), Royal Philharmonic Soc. London, Soc. Promotion New Music, Am. Music Ctr., AAUP, Am. Soc. Univ. Composers, Royal Acad. Music (hon.). Home: Santa Barbara Calif. Died Feb. 1, 1990. †

FRIEDENSOHN, ELIAS SOLOMON, artist, educator; b. N.Y.C., Dec. 12, 1924; s. Abraham and Celia Friedensohn; m. Doris Platzker, Feb. 1, 1969; children: Shola, Adam. A.B., Queens Coll., 1948. Mem. faculty Queens Coll., CUNY, 1951-87, prof. art dept., 1979-87, prof. emeritus, 1987. One-man shows include Hewitt Galleries, 1955, 57, Isaacson Galleries, N.Y.C., 1958, 59, 61, Vassar Coll., 1961, Feingarten Gallery, N.Y.C., 1962, 63, Terry Dintenfass Galleries, N.Y.C., 1967, 70, 73, 76, 80, 85, Moravian Coll., 1977, Magnes Mus., Berkeley, Calif., 1981, M.Pine Library, Fairlawn, N.J., 1986, Martin Sumers Graphics, N.Y.C., 1989, Jersey City State Coll., 1989, A.J. Lederman Gallery, Hoboken, N.J., 1991, Ryder Coll.,1991, others; group shows include Whitney Mus., N.Y.C., Art Inst. Chgo., Denver Art Mus., Dallas Mus. Art; represented in permanent collections Whitney Mus. Am. Art, N.Y.C., Art Inst. Chgo., Mpls. Mus. Art, L.A. County Mus., Walker Art Center, Mpls., Krannert Art Mus., Champaign, Ill., Magnes Mus., Berkeley, Jersey City State Coll., others; contbr. articles to profl. jours. Served with inf. U.S. Army, 1943-46. Guggenheim fellow, 1960; Fulbright grantee, 1957; PSC-BHE Univ. Found. for Research grantee, 1981, 85; N.J. Council on Arts grantee, 1981, 85; Magnes Mus. travel grantee, 1982. Home: Leonia N.J. Died Aug. 26, 1991; cremated.

FRIEDLAND, BERNICE UDELLE, psychologist, educator; b. Akron, Ohio, June 18, 1935; d. Hymen H. and Ida S.; B.Sc., Ohio State U., 1956; M.Ed., Frostburg State Coll., 1969; Ed.D., W.Va. U., 1972; children by previous marriage: Holli, David Michael. Assoc. prof. psychology Coppin State Coll., 1972-80; adj. prof. Bowie State Coll., Loyola Coll.; pvt. practice psychology, Balt., 1976-88; psychologist Spring Grove State Hosp., Balt., 1978-83; chief psychology and psychiat. services Md. Correctional Instn. for Women, from 1983; bd. dirs. Blind Industries and Services of Md.; bd. advisors rehab. div. Balt. Goodwill Industries, 1979-83; cons., inservice trainer ednl. and vocat. rehab. agys. Bd. dirs. Alfred Adler Inst., Washington, 1984-88. Mem. Am. Personnel and Guidance Assn., Am. Psychol. Assn., Nat. Rehab. Assn., N.Am. Soc. Adlerian Psychology. Author: (with W. McKelvie) Career Goal Counseling, 1978; editor Individual Psychologist, 1976-80; mem. editorial bd. Jour. Rehab., 1979-80; contbr. articles to profl. publs. Died July 12, 1988; buried Beth El Cemetery, Balt. Home: Baltimore Md.

FRIEDLICH, HERBERT AARON, lawyer; b. Rochester, N.Y., Dec. 21, 1893; s. Abraham and Nettie (Bloch) F.; m. Margaret H. Becker, Mar. 10, 1923; children: John, Mary. AB, Harvard U., 1915, LLB, 1917. Bar: Ill. 1919. Legal com. War Industries Bd., 1918; practice law Chgo., 1919-69; ptnr. Mayer, Friedlich, Spiess, Tierney, Brown and Platt, to 1969. Overseer Harvard Law Rev., 1966-72. With U.S. Army, 1918; spl. asst. to under sec. of war, 1942; commd. lt. col. U.S. Army, 1942; chief contracts and facilities div. Office of Under-Sec. of War, Washington, 1944; col. JAG dept. AUS, 1945. Decorated Legion of Merit, 1945; recipient Silver medal Carnegie Hero Fund, 1922. Mem. ABA, Am. Bar Found., Ill. Bar Assn., Chgo. Bar Assn., Mid-Day Club Chgo., Lake Shore Country Club (Glencoe, Ill.). Republican. Home: Highland Park Ill. Died Mar. 22, 1989.

FRIEDLUND, JOHN ARTHUR, lawyer; b. Chgo., July 1, 1898; s. John Peter and Hannah (Nelson) F.; m. Frances Garetson, Nov. 27, 1941; children: John E., Elizabeth C. (Mrs. John McCracken), Ann S. LLB, U. Mich., 1922. Bar: Ill. 1922. Practiced in Chgo., from 1922; sr. mem. firm Friedlund, Levin & Friedlund, and predecessor, from 1944; chmn. exec. com., dir., gen. counsel Automatic Canteen Co. Am., from 1937; gen. counsel N.Y. Yankees Baseball Club; dir. W.F. Hall Printing Co., Wirtz, Haynie & Ehrat, Inc., Forman Realty Corp., Am. Furniture Mart Corp., Bismarck Hotel Co., Franklin Savs. Assn., Casualty Mut. Ins. Co., Hubshman Factors Corp., Comml. Discount Corp. Treas., counsel, trustee endowment fund Swedish Retirement Assn., Evanston, Ill.; truste Folke Bernadotte Meml. Found., St. Peter, Minn. Served to 2d lt., inf. U.S. Army, World War I. Mem. Chgo. Bar Assn., Chgo. Athletic Club, Mid-Day Club, Tavern Club, Swedish Club, Saddle and Cycle Club, Phi Alpha Delta. *

FRIEDMAN, ARNOLD PHINEAS, neurologist; b. Portland, Oreg., Aug. 25, 1909; s. Carl and Lena (Levy) F.; m. Sara Fritz, July 10, 1939; 1 child, Carol Ludwig. BA, U. So. Calif., 1932, MA in Psychology, 1934; MD, U. Oreg., 1939. Diplomate Am. Bd. Psychiatry and Neurology (bd. dirs. from 1964, pres. 1971). Intern, then resident in neurology Los Angeles County Hosp., L.A., 1939-42; asst. in neurology U. So. Calif., L.A., 1941-42; asst. physician Boston Psychopathic Hosp., 1942-43; resident in charge head injury project, rsch. assoc. Boston City Hosp., 1943-44; fellow in neurology Harvard U. Med. Sch., Boston, 1943-44; pvt. practice, N.Y.C., 1946-73; physician-in-charge headache unit Montefiore Hosp., N.Y.C., 1947-73, attending physician div. neurology, 1949-73; prof. neurology U. Ariz. Med. Sch., Tucson, 1973-75; cons. Neurol. Assocs., Tucson, 1975-85; assoc. attending physician Presbyn. Hosp., N.Y.C., 1949-71, attending physician, 1971-73; instr. Columbia U., 1944-45, asst. clin. prof., 1950-54, assoc. clin. prof., 1954-67, clin. prof., 1967-73; spl. cons. NIH, 1961-73, chmn. panel on headache, 1960-67; chmn., sec. rsch. group on headache and migrane World Fedn. Neurology, 1967-73; mem. scope panel on neuropsychiatry U.S. Pharmacopeia, 1960-70, mem. adv. panel on neurol. disease therapy, 1970-85; hon. surgeon N.Y.C. Police Dept., 1961-73. Author: Modern Headache Therapy, 1951; co-author, editor: Headache: Diagnosis and Treatment, 1959, Headaches in Children, 1967, The Headache Book, 1973; editor-in-chief Rsch. and Clin. Studies in Headache: An Internat. Rev., 1963-73; also numerous articles, chpts. to books. Lt. (j.g.) USNR, 1941-42. Recipient award for AMA exhibit Am. Acad. Gen. Practice, 1968. Fellow ACP, Am. Acad. Neurology (trustee 1958-59), Am. Psychiat. Assn. (Rush silver medal 1969), N.Y. Acad. Medicine (chmn. sect. neurology and psychiatry 1966-68); mem. AMA (vice chmn. sect. nervous and mental diseases 1962-63, chmn. 1963-64, cons. new and non-ofcl. drugs 1960-85), Billings silver medal 1959, cert. of merit 1972), Am. Assn. Neuropathologists, Am. Neurol. Assn., Internat. Collegium Allergilocicum, Pan Am. Med. Assn., Assn. for Rsch. in Nervous and Mental Diseases, N.Y. State Med. Assn., N.Y. County Med. Assn., N.Y. Neurol. Soc., Psi Chi. Home: Tucson Ariz. Died Sept. 17, 1990; buried Falls Church, Va.

FRIEDMAN, HAROLD, investment company executive; b. Bklyn., Mar. 14, 1911; s. Max and Tillie Friedman; m. Sylvia Nirenberg; children: Lewis, Diane. Student, St. John's Coll., Bklyn., 1928-29, NYU, 1965-66. Mng. ptnr. Sutro Bros., brokerage, 1928-62, Abraham & Co., N.Y.C., 1969-92; pres. Edward A. Viner & Co., Inc., 1963-68; Pres. United HIAS Svc. Mem. N.Y. Soc. CPAs, AICPAs, K.P. Home: New York N.Y. Died Feb. 28, 1992.

FRIEDMAN, IRVING SIGMUND, international economist; b. N.Y.C., Jan. 31, 1915; s. Sigmund and Sara (Tobor) F.; m. Edna M. Edelman, Sept. 27, 1938; children: Barbara Ellen Friedman Chambers (dec.), Kenneth Sigmund, John Stephen. A.B., Columbia U., 1935, M.A., 1937, Ph.D. (Univ. fellow 1938-39), 1940; hon. degree, Oxford U., Am. Coll., Switzerland. Asst. to trade commr. Govt. of India, 1940-41; with div. monetary research U.S. Treasury, 1941-46, asst. dir., 1944, 46; acting fin. attache U.S. Embassy, Chungking, China; fin. adv. to U.S. Army Hdqrs., Chungking; also spl. missions to India and Egypt U.S. Army Hdqrs., 1944; chief U.S.-Can. div. IMF, 1946-48, policy asst. to dept. mng. dir., 1948-50, dir. exchange restriction dept., 1950-64, in charge of cons. with mem. counties, 1951-64; econ. adv. to pres. IBRD, 1964-72, chmn. econ. com., 1964-72, mem. pres.'s council, 1964-71; prof.-in-residence World Bank, 1971-74, adv. to pres., 1972-74; sr. adv. internat. ops., sr. v.p. Citibank, N.Y.C., 1974-80; sr. internat. advisor First Boston Corp., 1980-85; advisor, cons. Inter-Am. Devel. Bank, 1980-82, Bancade, Talca, Chile, 1980-82; advisor Asian Devel. Bank, 1981-84; advisor, cons. Security Pacific Bank, 1981-82; sr. advisor African Devel. Bank, 1982-87; advisor, cons. Nordic Devel. Bank, 1982-84, Am. Security Bank, 1982-86; head spl. missions to mem. countries IMF and World Bank; sr. ptnr. Washington Capital Markets Group; vis. faculty Yale U., 1970-71; vis. fellow All Soul's Coll., Oxford, Eng., 1970-71; guest lectr. Vatican univs., 1970, also numerous other univs. worldwide; vis. prof. U. Va., 1980, Fordham U., 1986; sr. fellow Centre for Internat. Banking Studies, U. Va.; mem. counsil SID, 1975-85; pres., treas. Soc. Internat. Devel., 1960-75; spl. responsibility for staff work Nat. Adv. Council Internat. Monetary and Fin. Problems; Chmn. Center of Concern, from 1971, Population Resource Ctr.; vice chmn. North South Round Table on Money and Fin.; bd. dirs. Internat. Resources Group, Resource Devel. Found., Agricare; spl. ptnr. Robert Weaver and Assocs. Author: (with M.G. deVries) Post-war U.S. Economic Policy, 1948, Foreign Exchange Controls, 1959, Inflation: A Worldwide Disaster, 1973 (transl. into German, Spanish, Japanese, Turkish and Finnish), 2d edit., 1980, Emerging Role of Private Banks in the Developing World, 1978, World Debt Dilemma: Managing Country Risk, 1983, Towards World Prosperity: Reshaping the Global Money System, 1987; contbr. articles on fin. and econs. and evolution of internat. payment systems to profl. jours., Ency. Brit., others U.S. and abroad. Chmn. Paul Hoffman Awards Found., 1975-86. Decorated Order of Sacred Treasure Japan, comdr.

Order of Falcon Iceland); recipient Medal of Honor World Bus. Council, 1983, numerous others. Mem. Am. Econ. Assn., Internat. Devel. Soc. (pres. 1974-75), Council on Fgn. Relations. Clubs: Metropolitan, International (Washington); Century (N.Y.). Home: Bethesda Md. Died Nov. 20, 1989; buried Parklawn Cemetery, Rockville, Md.

FRIEDMAN, RALPH, financial executive; b. N.Y.C., Jan. 11, 1904; s. Uri Mark and Mary (Behrman) F.; m. Ruth J. Ehrich, Feb. 11, 1933 (dec. July 1981); children: Peter R., Robert E. Student, CCNY, 1921, N.Y. U., 1922-24. Sr. gen. partner Friedman & Co.; mem. N.Y. Stock Exchange, 1933-46; chmn. bd. dirs. Met. Body Co., 1940-48, Standard Milling Co., Kansas City, Mo., 1951-63; dir. Bank Leumi Le Israel, Tel Aviv and N.Y., 1963-79; chmn. exec. com., dir. Bank Leumi Trust Co., N.Y., 1968-79; chmn. finance com., dir. Eastern Life Ins. Co., N.Y., until 1971. Trustee Friedman Found., N.Y.C.; mem. coun. com. Yale Sch. Forestry and Environ. Studies, 1971-83; mem. cave expdn. to Mex. for N.Y. Zool. Soc., 1940; mem. Friedman-Anthony Alaska Expdn. for Am., Mus. Natural History, U.S. Nat. Park Svc., 1948, Friedman-Mozambique Expdn. for Am. Mus. of Natural History, 1968, S.W. Africa Expdn. for Am. Mus. Natural History, 1970; chmn. Am. Jewish Com., 1964-66; dir. Nat. Park Found., 1968-70. Mem. N.Y. Acad. Scis., Linnean Soc., Am. Mus. of Natural History (patron), N.Y. Zool. Soc. (life), N.Y. State Forestry Assn., Am. Acad. Polit. Sci., Explorers Club, Met. Mus. Art (fellow in perpetuity), Pierpont Morgan Libr.(fellow). Home: New York N.Y. Deceased. †

FRIEDMAN, STANLEY JOSEPH, lawyer; b. N.Y.C., Feb. 26, 1928; s. Samuel J. and Gertrude (Rabinoff) F.; m. Shari Ostow, Mar. 17, 1957; children: Jessica R., Alexandra C., Sophia R. AB magna cum laude, Harvard U., 1948; LLB, Yale U., 1951. Bar: N.Y. 1951, U.S. Dist. Ct. (so. and ea. dists.) N.Y. 1961, U.S. Ct. Appeals (2d cir.) 1961, U.S. Supreme Ct. 1961. Assoc. Berlack, Israels & Liberman, 1953-59, ptnr., 1960-71; sr. ptnr. Shereff, Friedman, Hoffman & Goodman, N.Y.C., 1971-92. Bd. editors Yale Law Jour., 1950-51; contbr. articles on securities law to profl. publs. Counsel Rabbinical Assembly, 1962-92; dir. library corp., mem. chancellor's council Jewish Theol. Seminary Am., N.Y.C., 1983-92; bd. dirs. Schocken Inst. Jewish Research, N.Y., 1983-92; mem. bd. govs. Am. Jewish Com. Served with Signal Corps, AUS, 1951-53. Mem. ABA, Assn. Bar City N.Y., Phi Beta Kappa. Democrat. Club: Harvard (N.Y.C.). Died Dec. 9, 1992. Home: Bronx N.Y. †

FRIEND, WALTER WILLIAM, JR., investment banker; b. Allenhurst, N.J., June 25, 1920; s. Walter William and Helen E. (Butcher) F.; m. Doris Eleanor Schwanhausser, Dec. 20, 1947; children—Walter William III, Eleanor Provost. Grad., Polytech. Prep. Country Day Sch., 1938; B.A., Dartmouth, 1942; postgrad. in law, Yale, 1942, 46. With Pressprich Corp., N.Y.C., 1948-76, partner, 1962-68, exec. v.p., 1968-69, pres., 1969-76; 1st v.p. Blyth Eastman Dillon & Co., N.Y.C., 1976-80; sr. v.p. Blyth Eastman Paine Webber, Inc., N.Y.C., 1981-89; bd. dirs. Greater N.Y. Savs. Bank. Trustee Low-Haywood Sch., Stamford, Conn. Served to 1st lt. AUS, 1942-46. Mem. Mcpl. Fin. Officers Assn. U.S. and Can., Municipal Forum N.Y., Municipal Analysts N.Y. (pres. 1950-53). Home: Norwalk Conn. Died Aug. 29, 1989.

FRISCH, MAX RUDOLF, writer; b. Zurich, May 15, 1911; diploma in architecture ETH, 1941; Dr. h.c., Philipps U., Marburg, 1963, Bard Coll., N.Y.C., 1980, CUNY, 1982. Fgn. corr. for newspapers in Europe and Near East, 1931-33; practice architecture, Zurich, 1946-54; lived in Mexico, 1951-52, U.S., 1951-52, 73-74, Rome, 1966; plays and novels include: Blätter aus dem Brotsack, 1940, J'adore ce qui me brule oder Die Schwierigen, 1942, Santa Cruz, 1943, Bin oder Die Reise nach Peking, 1945, Nun singen sie wieder, 1945, Die chinesische Mauer, 1946, Tagebuch mit Marion, 1947, Als der Krieg zu Ende war, 1949, Graf Oederland, 1951, Don Juan oder Die Liebe zur Geometrie, 1953, Stiller, 1954, Homo Faber, 1957, Herr Biedermann und die Brandstifter, 1958, Die grosse Wut des Philipp Hotz, 1958, Andorra, 1961, Mein Name sei Gantenbein, 1964, Biografie: Ein Spiel, 1967, Öffentlichkeit als Partner, 1968, Wilhelm Tell für die Schule, 1971, Tagebuch 1966-71, 1972, Dienstbüchlein, 1974, Montauk, 1975, Werkausgabe, 1976, Triptychon-3 szenische Bilder, 1978, Der Mensch erscheint im Holozän, 1979, Blaubart, 1982. Rockefeller drama grantee, 1951; recipient Conrad Férdinand Meyer prize, 1951; Georg Büchner prize German Acad. Lang. and Poetry, 1958; Jerusalem prize, Literaturpreis der Stadt Zûrich, 1958, Schillergedâchtnispreises des Landes Baden-Württemberg, 1965, Grosser Schillerpreis, Zurich, 1975; Peace prize German Book Trade, 1976; decorated commandeur de l'Ordre des Arts et des Lettres (Paris), 1985; recipient Commonwealth award MLA; Neustadt prize for lit., 1986. Mem. Am. Acad. Arts and Letters, Akademie der Künste, Deutsche Akademie für Sprache und Dichtung. Archtl. design includes Zurich Recreation Park. Died Apr. 4, 1991. Home: Zärich Switzerland

FRISCH, SIDNEY, lawyer; b. Chgo., May 4, 1899; s. Morris and Pauline (Unger) F.; m. Helen Carroll Hunter, Sept. 1, 1934; 1 son: Sidney. Ph.B., U. Chgo., 1920, J.D., 1922. Bar: Ill. 1922. Ptnr. Frisch & Frisch, Chgo., 1922-87, sr. mem.; pres., dir. Rogers Park Apts., Inc., Chgo., from 1934. Bd. dirs. Highland Park (Ill.) Playground and Recreation Bd., 1954-58, Presbyterian Home, Evanston, Ill., 1965-69. Served with U.S. Army, 1918-20. Mem. Chgo. Bar Assn. (50 year mem., chmn. corp. law com. 1958-68), Ill. State Bar Assn. (chmn. real estate law sect. 1955-57, 50 year mem.), ABA (chmn. com. current lit. on real property law 1953-54). Republican. Presbyterian. Died Mar. 29, 1987. Home: Highland Park Ill.

FRITZSCHE, ALLAN W., industrial executive; b. Cleve., Apr. 28, 1895; s. Alfred L. and Clara (Neracher) F.; m. Josephine Burke, June 20, 1918; children: Mary Jo (Mrs. Foster), Allan W. (dec.). Student, Notre Dame U., 1912-15. Motor repair man, 1919-20; br. mgr. Gen. Phonograph Mfg. Co., Grand Rapids, Mich., 1921-23; salesman N.Y. territory Gen. Phonograph Mfg. Co., 1924-26; sales mgr., v.p. Okeh Record Co., 1927-29; pres. Gen. Phonograph Mfg. Co., N.Y.C., 1929-31; v.p., gen. mgr. Gen. Industries Co., Elyria, Ohio, 1932-43, pres., 1943, chmn., chief exec. officer, from 1957; dir. Troxel Mfg. Co., First Nat. Bank of Elyria, Gen. Industries Co., Elyria, Johnson Furnace Co., Bellvue, Ohio, Am. Dist. Telegraph Co., N.Y.C., Neracher Investment Co., Warren, Ohio, Grinnell Corp., Cleve. Indians, Inc. Mem. NAM, Radio Mfrs. Assn., Soc. Plastics Industry, C. of C., Elks, KC, Union Club of Cleve., Elyria Country Club. *

FROCK, EDMOND BURNELL, industrialist, banker, youth home executive; b. Hanover, Pa., Nov. 26, 1910; s. Edmond A. and Vivian (Huff) F.; m. Rebecca Black, Apr. 24, 1936; children: Edmond Burnell Jr., J. Daniel, Judith A., James W. (dec.). BA, Catawba Coll., 1933, LLD (hon.), 1986. Pres. Hanover Wire Cloth, 1933-81; v.p. CCX, Inc. (formerly Continental Copper & Steel Industries, Inc.), N.Y.C., 1948-74, exec. v.p., 1974-81; chmn. bd. Bank of Hanover & Trust Co., 1963-89, pres., 1970-77; past pres., bd. dir. Downtown Hanover, Inc.; past pres. Wire Weavers Assn., Indsl. Wire Cloth Inst., Hanover Pub. Library; pres., chief exec. officer Hanover Bancorp, Inc., 1983-88. Pres., mem. fin. com. Hoffman Homes for Youth, 1987-91; vice chmn. Christian Bus. Men Com.; past pres. Emmanuel U.C.C. Consistory Ch.; hon. chmn. and bd. dir. emeritus Hanover Bancorp Inc. and Bank of Hanover & Trust Co.; past pres. Hanover Dist. Sch. Bd.; bd. dirs. Hanover Gen. Hosp.; emeritus trustee Catawba Coll., Hanover YMCA; chmn. adv. com. York County Earn it Ct. Program; mem. York chpt. S.C.O.R.E.; pres., trustee Hoffman Home for Youth, Gettysburg, Pa., Hanover Area Rehab. Tng., Hart Ctr., New Oxford, Pa. Recipient O.B. Michael Disting. Alumnus award Catawba Coll., 1991; named Disting. Pennsylvanian Phila. C. of C., 1982. Mem. Hanover Area Indsl. Mgmt. Club (founder), Mfrs. Assn. S. Cen. Pa. (past pres., dir.), So. Hardware Assn. (mem. Old Guard), Hanover Area C. of C. (past pres.), Indsl. Mgmt. Club York County (past pres.), Christian Businessmen's Com. Hanover, Christian Businessmens Com. U.S.A., Pine Valley Golf Club, Masons, Shriners. Home: Hanover Pa. Died Sept. 3, 1991; interred Rest Haven Cemetery, Hanover, Pa.

FROMKES, SAUL, lawyer, insurance company executive. LL.B., St. Johns U. Sch. Law, 1928, LL.D. (hon.), 1968; D.C.S. (hon.), Pace U., 1973; L.H.D. (hon.), N.Y. Med. Coll., 1983. Bar: N.Y. 1930, U.S. Supreme Ct. 1964. Mem. firm Fromkes Brothers, N.Y.C., from 1930; founder, pres. City Title Ins. Co., N.Y.C., 1929-91; vice chmn. legis. com. Real Estate Bd. N.Y.; mem. Ins. Bd. State of N.Y., from 1980; arbitrator Small Claims Ct. Part, Civil Ct. City of New York, 1967-77; treas., dir. 1128 Park Ave. Corp.; dir., chmn. investment com. Empire Mut. Ins. Co.; guest lectr. Yale U. Law Sch., Cornell U. Law Sch., Harvard U. Law Sch., St. Johns U. Sch. of Law; Mem. N.Y. State Com. of Adv. Panel Experts on Real Estate and Condominiums, 1969, Task Force Health and Hosps., Diocese of New York, from 1974; com. on character and fitness Supreme Ct. Appellate Div., First Dept., 1977; chmn. seminars, moderator St. Johns U. Sch. Law Homecomings, from 1959, also chmn. alumni fund drive, chmn. law library fund campaign; chmn. bd. regents N.Y. State Adv. Com. on Higher Edn. Facilities Planning, 1968. Guest columnist: New York World Telegram; Hon. editor: St. Johns Law Rev., 1973. V.p., trustee Old Met. Opera House; vice chmn. bd. trustees St. Johns U.; founding trustee Inner-City Scholarship Fund, from 1972; trustee, mem. exec. com. N.Y. Med. Coll., from 1978, chmn. com. on affiliations; bd. govs. N.Y.C. Nat. Shrines Assn.; mem. adv. com. N.Y. State Commn. on Estates; mem. hon. adv. bd. Nat. Real Estate Show; mem. hon. com. March of Dimes Man of Year, 1964, N.Y.C. Baseball Fedn., Navy Yard Boys Club, Catholic Interracial Council; chmn. Columbus 92 com. for 500th anniv. discovery of Am., 1987-91. Recipient cert. of merit St. Johns Alumni Fedn., 1960-61, Pietas medal St. Johns U., 1961, also medal of honor, 1978, Pres.'s medal, 1970, Dean George W. Matheson Medal of Honor, 1990, certificate of merit SSS, 1947, certificate of recognition Bklyn. Acad. Music, 1967; named Hon. Brother Phi Delta Phi, 1970, Man of Year, 1971, Ky. Col.; decorated Order of Merit Republic of Italy, 1982. Mem. ABA (Merit award 1972), N.Y. State Bar Assn., Assn. Bar City N.Y., Am. Land Title Assn. (chmn. legis. com.), Pa. Land Title Assn., N.Y. State Land Title Assn. (chmn. com. to confer with N.Y. State Bar Assn., pres. 1967-68), Am. Land Title Ins. Assn., N.J. Land Title Ins. Assn. (dir.), St. Johns U. Sch. of Law Alumni Assn. (pres. 1957-58, dir.), Lawyers Club (v.p., bd. govs. from 1972), Bankers Club Am. Clubs: Circus Saints and Sinners, Metropolis Country, Golf Soc. Gt. Britain, Profl. Golfers Assn. Am, The Club at World Trade Center. Lodge: Knights of Malta. Home: New York N.Y. Died June 8, 1991.

FROMM, ARNO HENRY, physician; b. Elkhart Lake, Wis., May 5, 1902; s. Ferdinand F. and Adeline (Miller) F.; m. Emily A. Kramp, Jan. 26, 1934 (dec.); children: Barbara Gale, Kathleen Ann (Mrs. Philip Lane); m. Constance Crafts, Aug. 30, 1962. Student, U. Wis., 1920-24; M.D., Marquette U., 1929; postgrad., Columbia U., 1937, U. Minn., 1940, Cook County (Ill.) Postgrad. Sch. Medicine, 1944. Intern St. Mary's Hosp., Milw., 1928-29; resident Univ. Hosp., Madison, Wis., 1950-52; instr., research asst., dept. anatomy Marquette U., Milw., 1929-32, 33-36; practice medicine, 1932-50; resident instr. U. Wis., 1950-52; cons. Mendota (Wis.) State Hosp., 1954-56, internist, 1952-60; field rep. Joint Commn. on Accreditation of Hosps., from 1962, research dir., from 1966; asso. med. dir. Interstate Blood and Plasma Center, Milw., from 1974; staff Howard Young Med. Center, Inc., Woodruff, Wis.; cons. Eagle River (Wis.) Meml. Hosp.; Dir., trustee dept. hematology Ed K. Holz Research Fund, from 1957. Recipient citation Med. Coll. Wis., 1978. Fellow Royal Soc. Health; mem. AMA, Wis. Med. Soc., Civitan Club (charter). Clubs: Mason (32 deg.), Shriner. Home: Madison Wis. Died Dec. 23, 1991. †

FROSCH, AARON R., lawyer; b. N.Y.C., July 9, 1924 m. Marjorie MacMillan, Jan. 17, 1955; children: Juliana Phoebe, Suzanna. BA, Bklyn. Coll., 1944; LLB, Bklyn Law Sch., 1947. Bar: N.Y. 1948. Gen. counsel, dir Marilyn Monroe Prodns., 1962-72, Elizabeth Taylor Prodns., from 1964, Harkness Found., 1962-69, also Richard Buton Prodns., Rex Harrison Prodns. Ltd Chmn. Mayor's Com. for N.Y. Shakespeare Festival 1967, trustee, from 1963; founder Hardecker Lab. and Children's Clinic, Nassau, Bahamas. Mem. Am. Judicature Soc., ABA, N.Y. State Bar Assn., Assn. Bar of City of N.Y., N.Y. County Lawyers Assn. Democrat. Jewish. Home: Quogue NY Died Apr. 30, 1989.

FROST, DOUGLAS VAN ANDEN, nutritionist; b. Pitts., Oct. 31, 1910; s. Donald Karne and Amy (Craig) F.; m. Muriel Louise Newkirk, Aug. 10, 1940; children: Nancy Newkirk (Mrs. James Kroening), Melodie Louise (Mrs. Peter Cooey), Roy Craig, Constance Frost Petr. B.A. in Chemistry, U. Ill., 1933; M.A. in Biochemistry, U. Wis., 1938, Ph.D., 1940. Petr Analytical and research chemist Chappel Bros. Co. Pacini Labs., also Rival Packing Co., 1936; grad. asst U. Wis., 1936- 39, research and teaching asst., 1938-40 with Abbott Labs., 1940-66, head nutrition research 1946-59, research specialist nutrition, 1959-66; research assoc. Dartmouth Med. Sch. Trace Element Lab. a Brattleboro Hosp., 1966-69; cons. nutrition-biochemistry Selenium-Tellurium Devel. Assn.; Mem. com. on selenium in nutrition Nat. Acad. Sci.-NRC, 1968—chmn. Animal Nutrition Research Council, 1960; mem amino acids adv. com. U.S. Pharmacopeia XIV, 1950 cons. USPHS Drinking Water Standards Com., also Industry Task Force Agrl. Arsenical Pesticides, 1970 vice chmn. OST Subpanel on Arsenic, 1970-72; chmn EPA PAX Co. arsenic adv. com., 1973; mem. diet-nutrition-cancer workshop Nat. Cancer Inst., 1975-76. Recipient Friedrich Schiller U. medal and scroll for research on arsenic and selenium, 1983, Klaus Schwart Commemoration medal Internat. Assn. Bionorganic Scientists, 1989. Nominee for Nobel prize in chemistry. Fellow N.Y. Acad. Scis., AAAS; mem. Assn. Vitamin Chemists (pres. 1953), Am. Inst. Nutrition (treas. 1962-65), Agrl. Research Inst. (v.p. 1965-66), Metric Assn (pres. 1969-70), Poultry Sci. Assn., Soc. Animal Sci. Am. Feed Mfg. Assn. (nutrition council), Sigma Xi Gamma Alpha, Phi Eta Sigma, Alpha Chi Sigma, Delt Tau Delta. Presbyterian (elder). Home: Schenectady NY Died Aug. 8, 1989; body donated science.

FROST, FREDERICK GEORGE, JR., architect; b. N.Y.C., June 10, 1907; s. Frederick G. and Bessi (Wilcox) F.; m. Gwendolyn B. Corwin, May 13, 1933 children: Arthur Corwin, Claudia Elizabeth Frost Dole Freerick George III. AB, Princeton U., 1930, MFA 1932; postgrad., Yale U., 1930-31. Ptnr. Frederick G Frost, 1936-55, Frederick G. Frost Jr. and Assocs N.Y.C., 1955-68, Frost Assocs., 1968-78; mem. N.Y State Bd. Examiners of Architects, 1961-64; rep. Union Internat. des Architects to UN, 1964-76; archtl. cons rewriting N.Y.C. Bldg. Code, 1962-66. Dir. Citizen Housing and Planning Coun. N.Y., 1950-76, v.p., 1954-56, 60-65, pres., 1965-68; trustee N.Y. Sch. for Deaf 1950-76; bd. govs. Lawrence Hosp., Bronxville, 1947-58 pres., 1954-55; trustee mem. architecture vis. com. R.I Sch. Design. Fellow AIA (1st v.p., mem. exec. com N.Y. chpt. 1970-71, pres. 1971-72, nat. dir. 1973-75 mem. N.Y. Soc. Architects, N.Y. Bldg. Congress (dir. Century Assn. (N.Y.C.), Bronxville (N.Y.) Club, Fiel Club (pres. bd. govs. 1952), Princeton Club of N.Y. Home: Bronxville NY Died Oct. 27, 1991; buried Kensico Cemetery, Valhalla, N.Y.

FROST, HORACE WIER, investment banker; b. Chelsea, Mass., Jan. 25, 1893; s. Thomas Bell and Sarah Louise (Wier) F.; m. Mildred S. Kip, July 23, 1932; children: Thomas Bell, Peter Kip, Richard Van Houten, Ellen Louise. AB, Harvard U., 1914. Assoc. Tucker, Anthony & Co., Boston, from 1915, mem. firm, from 1935; trustee County Savs. Bank; dir. Thomas Stationery Mfg. Co., Springfield, Ohio; mem. bd. govs. N.Y. Stock Exch., 1957-60. Treas., Mass. Eye and Ear Infirmary. Served as 2d lt. A.S., U.S. Army, 1918. Mem. Assn. Stock Exch. Firms (pres. 1949-55), Harvard Clubs of N.Y.C. and Boston, Essex County Club (Manchester, Mass.), Union Club of Boston, Country Club of Brookline. Republican. *

FROST, JOHN KINGSBURY, pathologist, educator, author; b. Sioux Falls, S.D., Mar. 12, 1922; s. Roland Curtis and Madeleine (Veale) F.; m. Moira Anne Keane, Aug. 20, 1949; children: Moira Anne, Rosanne Grace, Noreen Anne Regina, Therese Anne Olivia, John Kingsbury, Sheila Anne Maureen, James Keane. B.A., U. Calif.-Berkeley, 1943; M.D., U. Calif.-San Francisco, 1946. Diplomate Am. Bd. Pathology. Intern-fellow U. Calif. Med. Sch., San Francisco, 1946-48; fellow Harvard U. Med. Sch., Cambridge, Mass., 1948; instr. pathology U. Calif. Sch. Medicine, San Francisco, 1953-56; assoc. prof. pathology U. Md. Sch. Medicine, Balt., 1956-59; asst. prof. ob-gyn Johns Hopkins U. Sch. Medicine, Balt., 1956-59, joint appointment with ob-gyn, assoc. prof. pathology, 1959-75, prof. pathology, 1975-89, dir. Sch. of Cytology and postgrad. Inst. for Pathologists, 1959-89; cons. U.S. Army, from 1955, USPHS, from 1959, WHO, from 1965, Armed Forces Inst. Pathology Registry of Cytopathology, Washington, from 1968. Author: The Cell in Health and Disease, 1969, 86, Concepts Basic to General Cytopathology, 1959, 61, 72, also in fgn. lang. edits.; med. dir., author: (films) Cytology I (Golden Eagle award CINE), 1962, Cytology II (Golden Eagle award CINE), 1962; contbr. over 350 articles to profl. jours. Served to lt. col. USAR, 1948-53, Korea. Fellow Coll. Am. Pathologists, Am. Soc. Clin. Pathologists (Disting. Achievement award 1977), Internat. Acad. Cytology (Goldblatt award and lectr. 1979); mem. Am. Soc. Cytology (pres. 1964-65, Papanicolaou award and lectr. 1972), Am. Cancer Soc. (Disting. Service award 1976), Phi Beta Kappa, Alpha Omega Alpha. Republican. Roman Catholic. Club: Serra Internat. Home: Brooklandville Md. Died Aug. 29, 1990.

FROWICK, ROY HALSTON See HALSTON

FRYE, (HERMAN) NORTHROP, English language educator, writer; b. Sherbrooke, Que., Can., July 14, 1912; s. Herman and Catharine and (Howard) F.; m. Helen Kemp, Aug. 24, 1937 (dec.); m. Elizabeth Brown, 1988. B.A., U. Toronto, 1933; MA, Oxford U., 1940; also 38 hon. degrees. Ordained to ministry United Ch. Can., 1936. Lectr. English Victoria Coll., U. Toronto, from 1939, prof., 1947-91, chmn. dept. English, 1952, prin. coll., 1959-67; Univ. prof. U. Toronto, 1967-91; chancellor Victoria U., from 1978; adviser curricular planning and English teaching, Can. and U.S.; mem. adv. com. Am. Council Learned Socs., 1965; adv. mem. Can. Radio and TV Commn., 1968-77. Author: Fearful Symmetry, 1947, Anatomy of Criticism, 1957, The Great Code: The Bible and Literature, 1982, Words With Power: Being a Second Study of 'The Bible and Literature', 1990; also 21 other books; editor Canadian Forum, 1948-52. Decorated companion Order Can.; Hon. fellow Merton Coll., Oxford, 1973. Fellow Brit. Acad. (corr.); mem. MLA (exec. council 1958-61, pres. 1976), Am. Acad. Arts and Scis. (hon. fgn.), Am. Acad. and Inst. Arts and Letters (hon.). Home: Toronto ON, Canada Died Jan. 23, 1991.

FUGATE, DOUGLAS BROWN, civil engineer; b. Reed Island, Va., Aug. 14, 1906; s. Jesse Honnaker and Elizabeth Gertrude (Brown) F.; m. Mary Addison Lathan, June 15, 1940 (dec.); 1 son, Douglas B.; m. Emma Stimson Reed, July 7, 1973. B.S. in Civil Engring., Va. Mil. Inst., 1927. Civil engr. Va. Dept. Hwys. and Transp., 1927-42, asst. chief engr., 1947-59, chief engr., 1959-60, asst. chief engr., 1961-64; commr. Va. State Hwys. and Transp., 1964-76; cons. engr., Richmond, Va., 1976-88; chmn. Elizabeth River Tunnel Commn., 1964-74; mem. Va. Gov.'s Council on Transp., 1976-80. Bd. dirs. Va. Outdoor Recreation Commn., 1964-76; bd. dirs. Keep Va. Beautiful, 1964-76. Served to lt. col. AUS, 1942-46. Mem. ASCE (hon., past pres. Va. sect.), Am. Assn. State Hwy. and Transp. Ofcls. (past pres.), Southeastern Assn. State Hwy. and Transp. Ofcls. (past pres.), Am. Rd. and Transp. Builders Assn. (past sr. v.p.), Hwy. and Transp. Research Bd. (past exec. com.), Automobile Club Va. (treas., dir. 1976-82, dir. emeritus 1982-88). Episcopalian. Home: Richmond Va. Died Dec. 11, 1988. †

FULDHEIM, DOROTHY, journalist, commentator; b. Paterson, N.J., June 26, 1893; d. Herman and Bertha (Wishner) Snell; m. Milton Fuldheim (dec.); 1 child, Dorothy Fuldheim Urman; m. W.L. Ulmer (dec.). Student, Milw. Coll., 1914; numerous hon. degrees. With Scripps-Howard, Inc., 1924-89; news analyst Sta. WEWS-TV, Cleve.; lectr., interviewer. Author: I Laughed, I Loved, I Cried, 1965, Where Were the Arabs, 1967, A Thousand Friends, 1974, Three and One-Half Husbands. Recipient Overseas Press Club award 1959, Ohio Firemen and Police award, 1955, 72, Israeli Freedom award, 1967 Theta Sigma Phi Ann. Nat. award, 1964, Ohio AFL-CIO award, 1973; first anchorwoman U.S. Home: Cleveland Ohio Died Nov. 3, 1989.

FULFORD, JOHN HURTMAN, manufacturing company executive; b. Clearfield, Pa., Dec. 18, 1895; s. George M. and Olive L. (Lemon) F.; m. Rebekah W. Smith, June 8, 1921. Student, Lebanon Valley Coll., 1915-17. With Jeffrey Mfg. Co., Columbus, Ohio, from 1931, salesman, dist. mgr., mgr. minig div., v.p., pres., dir., 1951-62; pres. Jeffrey Co., from 1963; pres., dir. Jeffrey Gallion Mfg. Co., 1963-65, chmn., from 1965; dir. Jeffrey-Galion (Pty.) Ltd., Johannesburg, South Africa, Jeffrey Mfg. Co., Ltd., Montreal, Jaeger Machine Co., Buckeye Steel Castings Co., Jeffrey Co., City Nat. Bank and Trust Co. (all Columbus), Brit. Jeffrey-Diamond, Ltd., Wakefield, Eng. Mem. exec. bd. Cen. Ohio coun. Boy Scouts Am.; trustee Children's Hosp. Served as 1st lt., aviation sect. Signal Corps, U.S. Army, 1917-19. Mem. Am. Mining Congress, Machinery and Allied Products Inst., Elec. Mfrs., Ohio C. of C., Columbus Country Club, Duquesne Club of Pitts. *

FULHAM, GERARD AQUINAS, business executive; b. Winthrop, Mass., Mar. 7, 1920; s. John N. and Mary E. (Maloney) F.; m. Barbara Ann McGoldrick, Feb. 22, 1944; children: John Bernard, Trudy Deane Fulham Sullivan, Gerarda Marie, Gerard Aquinas, Barbara Ann, Maura Jude. A.B., Harvard U., 1942. With Estabrook & Co., Boston, 1946-47; pres., treas. Fulham Bros., Inc., Boston, 1947-57; chief fin. officer, fin. v.p. Cleve. Pneumatic Tool, 1958-61; sr. v.p., dir. Pneumo Corp. (successor to Cleve. Pneumatic Tool), Boston, 1961-69, chmn. bd., chief exec. officer, 1969-85; pres. LaTouraine Coffee Co., Boston, from 1961, vice chmn. bd. dirs., 1963; dir. Aeronca, Inc., Pineville, N.C. Served to lt. (s.g.) USNR, 1942-46. Mem. Woods Hole Oceanographic Instn. Clubs: Union (Cleve.); Engrs. (Boston), Mchts. (Boston), Harvard (Boston); Oyster Harbors (Osterville, Mass.). Home: Oyster Harbors Mass. Died Aug. 19, 1990; buried Holyhood Cemetery, Brookline, Mass.

FULLER, CURTIS G., publisher; b. Necedah, Wis., Mar. 2, 1912; s. Clarence Curtis and Lyda (Gross) F.; m. Mary Margaret Stiehm, Sept. 24, 1938; children—Nancy Abigail, Michael Curtis. A.B., U. Wis., 1933; M.S., Northwestern U., 1937. Newspaper work, 1933-37; assoc. editor Nat. Almanac and Yr. Book, 1937-38; info. dir. State of Wis., 1938-39; assoc. editor Better Roads Mag., 1939-43; from asst. mng. editor to mng. editor Flying Mag., 1943-48, editor, 1948-51; founder Fate mag., 1948; editorial dir. Pubs. Devel. Corp., 1951-53; pres. Clark Pub. Co., 1952-77, chmn., 1977-88; editor Advt. Publs. Inc., 1953-55; mng. dir. Modern Castings Mag., 1955-56; v.p. Greenleaf Pub. Co., 1956-57; pres. Oak Ridge Atom Industries Sales Corp., 1960-62; pres. Woodall Pub. Co., 1965-77, chmn. bd., 1977-85. Winner 1st place indsl. mktg. competition for conceiving and executing best bus. mag. promotion of yr., 1941. Mem. Ill. Soc. for Psychic Research (pres. 1961-64), Spiritual Frontiers Fellowship (treas. 1962-69, v.p. 1970-72), Sigma Delta Chi, Theta Delta Chi, Phi Kappa Phi. Home: Lake Forest Ill. Died Apr. 29, 1961; buried Necedah, Wis.

FULLER, JOHN GRANT, author, columnist, playwright, documentary film producer-director; b. Phila., Nov. 30, 1913; s. John Grant and Alice (Jenkins) F.; m. Elizabeth Brancae, Nov. 17, 1976; children: (by previous marriage) Judd Wheatley, John Grant III, Geoffrey Tousley, (by present marriage) Christopher Lewis. A.B., Lafayette Coll., 1936. Engaged in pub. and industry, 1936-49; sales promotion mgr. NBC, 1949-53. Producer: TV series Road to Reality, 1960-61; writer, dir.: TV series Twentieth Century, 1958-59, Conquest, 1957, du Pont Show of the Week, 1962; writer: TV series Home Show, 1953-55, Garry Moore Show, 1956, Candid Camera staff, 1957, others; producer: Great Am. Dream Machine (Emmy award 1971), Nat. Ednl. TV, 1971; columnist: Trade Winds in Sat. Rev, 1957-67; contbr. to: Reader's Digest, Omni, Sci. Digest, various other mag.; also documentary film producer and dir.; producer, writer, dir. documentaries for, USIA, NBC-TV, ABC-TV, CBS-TV, Nat. Ednl. TV.; author: (plays) The Pink Elephant, 1953, Love Me Little, 1959; (books) Gentlemen Conspirators, 1962, The Money Changers, 1962, Incident at Exeter, 1966, Interrupted Journey, 1966, Games for Insomniacs, 1966, The Day of St. Anthony's Fire, 1968, Aliens in The Skies, 1969, The Great Soul Trial, 1969, 200,000,000 Guinea Pigs, 1972, Fever: The Hunt for a New Virus Killer, 1973 (N.Y. Acad. Scis. award), Arigo, 1974, We Almost Lost Detroit, 1975, We Almost Lost Detroit, 1975, The Ghost of Flight 401, 1976, The Poison That Fell From the Sky, 1977 (ALA award), The Airmen Who Would Not Die, 1979, Are the Kids All Right?, 1981, Armored Warfare, 1983, The Day We Bombed Utah, 1984, Tornado Watch No. Two Eleven, 1987; (novel) The Pack, 1989. Recipient award Nat. Assn. Improvement Mental Health, 1961, award Nat. Assn. Womens Clubs for Road to Reality, 1961; Sigma Delta Chi award for Light Across the Shadow (TV documentary), 1966; Distinguished Alumnus award Lafayette Coll., 1972. Mem. Author's League, Dramatist's Guild, WGA, Director's Guild Am., Delta Kappa Epsilon, Pi Delta Epsilon. Democrat. Mem. Soc. of Friends. Home: Westport Conn. Deceased. †

FULLER, JOHN JOSEPH, financial executive, consultant; b. N.Y.C., June 23, 1931; s. John and Elizabeth C. (Finn) F.; m. Patricia M. Costanzo, Oct. 30, 1970; children by previous marriage: Audrey M., Kathy A., John E., George A. B.B.A., Pace U., 1958, postgrad., 1959; postgrad., Wabash Coll., 1967-69. Asst. v.p. Equitable Life, N.Y.C., 1968-70, regional v.p., 1971-72, v.p., 1973-79, sr. v.p., 1980-83; pres. Fuller Assocs., Litchfield, Conn., from 1983. Chmn. bd. dirs. Palisades Gen. Hosp., North Bergen, N.J., 1981-86, Palisades Health Care Holdings, Palisades Mgmt. Enterprises, Palisades Gen. Care; mem. pres.'s adv. council Pace U., N.Y.C., from 1981; chmn., pres. coun., trustee Xavier High Sch.; bd. dirs. Nazareth Nursery, N.Y.C. Served with U.S. Army, 1951-53, Korea. Roman Catholic. Home: Litchfield Conn. Deceased. †

FULLER, JOHN LANGWORTHY, psychobiologist; b. Brandon, Vt., July 22, 1910; s. John H. and Joyce (Langworthy) F.; m. Ruth I. Parsons, Sept. 2, 1933 (dec. Dec. 1989); children: Mary Jean, Sarah Ann. B.S., Bates Coll., 1931; Ph.D., Mass. Inst. Tech., 1935. Instr. biology Sarah Lawrence Coll., 1935-36, Clark U., 1936-37; instr. zoology U. Maine, 1937-41, asst. prof., 1941-45, assoc. prof., 1945-47; staff scientist Jackson Lab., Bar Harbor, Maine, 1947-58; sr. staff scientist Jackson Lab., 1958-70, asst. dir. tng., 1958-63, assoc. dir., 1963-70; prof. psychology SUNY, Binghamton, 1970-78; emeritus SUNY, 1978-92; vis. lectr. Harvard U., 1964-65, AID-NSF India Program, 1968. Author: (with W.R. Thompson) Foundations of Behavior Genetics, 1978, Nature and Nurture, 1954, Motivation, 1962, (with J. P. Scott) Genetics and Social Behavior of the Dog, 1965; contbr. sci. articles to profl. jours. Guggenheim fellow, 1955-56. Fellow Am. Psychol. Assn.; mem. Behavior Genetics Soc. (pres. 1973-74, Dobzhansky award 1987), Soc. for Study Social Biology (pres. 1982-84), Phi Beta Kappa, Sigma Xi. Democrat. Episcopalian. Home: Cambridge Mass. Died June 8, 1992. †

FULTON, JAMES MURDOCK, lawyer; b. Cin., Jan. 2, 1914; s. Herbert F. and Marie Louise (Murdock) F.; m. Anne Hall O'Connor, Feb. 23, 1943; children: Pattison, Judith Hodd, Millicent Barnard, Joan Murdock, James Murdock Jr. BS with honors, Yale U., 1935, LLB, 1938. Bar: Ohio 1939, N.Y. 1940. Assoc. Tomkins, Boal & Tomkins, N.Y.C., 1939-41, 45-51; assoc. gen. atty. Merck & Co., Inc., Rahway, N.J., 1951-53, gen. atty., 1953-55; counsel Merck Sharp & Dohme Internat., 1955-61, gen. counsel, 1961-70, gen. counsel, sec., 1970-71, v.p., gen. counsel, sec., 1972-74, v.p. legal affairs, 1975-77, sec., 1975-76; chmn., bd. dirs. Tivoli Industries, Santa Ana, Calif., from 1976; bd. dirs. Red Devil, Inc., Union, N.J., Woodclins Designers Inc., Vineyard Haven, Mass. Chmn. fin. com. Martha's Vineyard Hosp. Mem. ABA, Assn. Bar City N.Y., West Chop Assn., Mink Meadows Assn., Vineyard Haven Yacht Club.. Home: Vineyard Haven Mass. Died Oct. 16, 1989; buried Vineyard Haven (Mass.) Cemetery.

FURBER, EDWARD PARKER, judge; b. Newton, Mass., Jan. 2, 1898; s. George Pope and Laura Mabel (Parker) F.; m. Ruth Haynes, Jan. 12, 1918; children: Barbara (Mrs. Robert Hovey Clapp), George Pope. AB cum laude, Harvard U., 1918, LLB, 1922. Bar: Mass. 1922. Tchr. Mill Brook Sch., Concord, Mass., 1918-19; asst. in govt. Harvard U., 1919-22; tchr. Camp Aloha Summer Sch., Holderness, N.H., 1919-22; with Warner Stackpole & Bradlee, Boston, 1922-24, Charles P. Howard, Boston, 1924-26; pvt. practice Boston, 1926-42; chief justice Trust Territory Pacific Islands, from 1948; assoc. atty. Watertown (Mass.) Savs. Bank, 1929-42, trustee, 1937-49; trustee New Eng. Gas & Electric Assn., 1937-46, also dir. prin. subsidiaries, 1940-42. Adviser U.S. delegation UN Trusteeship Coun., 1949-51; fund chmn. for Watertown, Greater Boston Community Fund, 1938-40, area vice chmn. charge Watertown, Waltham, Lexington and Belmont, 1941; chmn. selectmen, Watertown, 1930-32, moderator, 1935-37. Served from lt. (s.g.) to comdr. USNR, 1942-51. Mem. ABA, Am. Unitarian Assn. (dir.), Unitarian Laymen's League U.S. and Can. (pres.), Masons, Shriners. *

FURLONG, NADINE MARY, nursing administrator; b. Detroit, Mar. 7, 1945; d. William Garfield and Violet Melinda (Herford) F.; m. Jan Frederick Miller, Oct. 1980. R.N., Henry Ford Hosp., Detroit, 1966; B.S. in Nursing magna cum laude, U. Mich., 1976, M.S. in Psychiat. Nursing, 1978. Staff nurse William Beaumont Hosp., Royal Oak, Mich., 1966; spl. edn. nurse teaching asst. Hawthorn Children's Psychiat. Ctr., Northville, Mich., 1966-70; head nurse inpatient unit York Woods Children's Psychiat. Ctr., Ypsilanti, 1970-73; dir. Ann Arbor program Browndale Group Home, Mich., 1973; instr. inservice nursing edn., then nursing edn. dir. Ctr. Forensic Psychiatry, Ann Arbor, Mich., 1974-78; dir. nursing Met. Regional Psychiat. Hosp., Eloise, Mich., 1978-79; exec. dir. Mich. Nurses Assn., from 1979; treas. Washtenaw County Staff Devel. Com. in Nursing, 1977-78, chmn., 1978-79; cons. mental health tech. program Washtenaw Community Coll., 1976-77; adj. asst. prof. U. Mich. Sch. Nursing, 1979-80. Bd. dirs. ARC, from

1976, exec. bd., from 1977, 1st v.p., 1979-80, pres., 1981-82; instr., trainer CPR. James B. Angel scholar, 1976; recipient A.J. Brown Pub. Health Nursing award, 1976. Mem. Am. Nurses Assn. (adv. council), Mich. Nurses Assn., Sigma Theta Tau. Home: East Lansing Mich. Deceased.

FUSFELD, IRVING SIDNEY, special education educator; b. N.Y.C., Nov. 5, 1893; s. Jacob and Rose (Isaacson) F.; m. Cecile Leban, Dec. 28, 1919; children: Robert David, Daniel Roland. BS, Columbia U., 1915, MA, 1917; BPd, Gallaudet Coll., 1916, MA, 1921. Normal fellow Gallaudet Coll., 1915, instr., 1916-22, asst. prof., 1922-25, prof., 1925-56, dir. rsch. dept., 1938-56, dean, 1939-53, v.p. of coll., 1953-57; supr. counseling and child guidance Calif. Sch. Deaf, 1957-64; survey cons. for schs. for deaf in Ala., Ga., Idaho, Ill., Md., N.J., Tex. and Wash. Author: (with Day and Pintner) A Survey of American Schools for the Deaf, 1928; A Study of Teacher Certification Requirements Among Public Residential Schools for the Deaf, 1948; A Cross-Section Evaluation of the Academic Program of Schools for the Deaf, 1954; Counseling the Deafened, 1954; asst. editor Am. Annals of the Deaf, 1917-18, editor, 1920-43. Served with U.S. Army, 1918-19. Recipient Edward Allen Fay award, 1964. Mem. Conv. of Am. Instrs. of the Deaf, Am. Psychol. Assn., Pi Gamma Mu, Phi Delta Kappa. *

FUSSELL, PAUL, lawyer; b. Pasadena, Calif., Jan. 15, 1895; s. Edwin Neal and Sara Elizabeth (Haswell) F.; m. Wilhma Wilson Sill, Sept. 28, 1921; children: Edwin Sill, Paul, Florence Elizabeth (Mrs. Norman J. Lind.). AB, U. Calif., Berkeley, 1916, JD, 1920; Dr of Laws, Pomona Coll., Claremont, Calif., 1964. Bar: Calif. 1920. Practiced in L.A., from 1921; ptnr. O'Melveny & Myers and predecessors, 1925-64; dir. Title Ins. and Trust Co., Stae Mut. Savs. & Loan Assn., Pacific Mut. Life Ins. Co., Thrifty Drug Stores Co., Inc., L.A. Brush Mfg. Corp. Mem. exec. com., trustee Pomona Coll.; v.p. Haynes Found.; trustee Hollenbeck Home for Aged, Claremont Grad. Sch. Served as 2d lt. U.S. Army, 1918-19; AEF in France. Mem. ABA (ho. of dels. 1944-46), Calif. Bar Assn., L.A. Bar Assn. (pres. 1947), Friends of Colls. at Claremont (pres. 1952-54), L.A. Town Hall (pres. 1946), Univ. Club (pres. 1940), Calif. Club (pres. 1960-61), Sunset Club, Lincoln Club (pres. 1961-62), Newport Harbor Yacht Club, Twilight Club, Phi Beta Kappa, Alpha Sigma Phi. Republican. Presbyn. *

FYE, PAUL MCDONALD, oceanographer; b. Johnstown, Pa., Aug. 6, 1912; s. Orlando and Jennie (McDonald) F.; B.S., Albright Coll., 1935; Ph.D., Columbia U., 1939; Sc.D. (hon.), Albright Coll., 1955, Tufts U., 1970, S.E. Mass. U., 1970, Fla. Inst. Tech., 1973, L.I.U., 1978; LL.D. (hon.), Northeastern U., 1974; m. Ruth Elizabeth Heym, Apr. 26, 1942; children: Kenneth, Elizabeth. Asst. prof. Hofstra U., Hemstead, N.Y., 1939-41; research assoc. high explosives Nat. Def. Research Com., Carnegie Inst. Tech., Pitts., 1941-42; research supr. underwater explosives research lab. Woods Hole (Mass.), Oceanographic Inst., 1942-44, dep. research dir. to research dir., 1944-47; assoc. prof. chemistry U. Tenn., Knoxville, 1947-48; dep. chief Naval Ordnance Lab., White Oak, Md., 1948-51, chief explosives research dept., 1951-56, assoc. tech. dir. research, 1956-58; dir. Woods Hole Oceanographic Instn., 1958-77, pres., 1961-86, pres. emeritus, 1986-88; dir. Lord Abbett Funds, Devel. Sci., Inc.; trustee Bermuda Biol. Sta. Trustee Har Branch Found., 1975-81, Cape Cod Community Coll., 1961-80, Center for Oceans Law an Policy, U. Va., 1975-88, Internat. Atlantic Salmon Found., 1970; mem. adv. bd. Mass. Maritime Acad., 1973-80, trustee, 1980-88; mem. adv. bd. New Eng. Aquarium, from 1970. Recipient Bur. Ordnance Devel. award, 1946; Presdl. cert. of merit, 1948; Disting. Alumni award Albright Coll., 1951; Meritorious award U.S. Navy, 1951, cert. of commendation, 1960, 66, Disting. Pub. Service award, 1977; ann. Achievement award Assn. Govt. Accts., 1977. Mem. Am. Acad. Arts and Scis., AAAS, Am. Chem. Soc., Am. Geophys. Union, Am. Phys. Soc., Am. Soc. Limnology and Oceanography, Council Fgn. Relations, Marine Tech. Soc. (pres. 1968-69), U.S. Naval Inst., Boston Marine Soc. (hon.), Sigma Xi, Tau Beta Pi, Phi Lambda Upsilon, Epsilon Chi. Died Mar. 11, 1988; buried Woods Hole, Mass. Home: Falmouth Mass.

GACCIONE, ANTHONY SALVATORE, paper mill executive; b. Cosenza, Italy, May 13, 1898; s. Angelo and Christine (Pignataro) G.; m. Helen Frances Adams, Aug. 30, 1921 (dec. Apr. 1956); m. Marion Bunnell, May 4, 1957. Student, Cornell U., 1917-20. Ptnr. Gaccione Bros. and Co., Inc., N.Y.C., 1921-26; mgr. paper stock dept. Box Board & Lining Co., N.Y.C., 1926-31; mgr. Charles A. Mastronardi & Co., N.Y.C., 1931-36; pres. Toga Paper Stock Co., Inc., 1936-63, Toga Paper Stock Co., Inc. divsn. Fed. Paper Board Co., Inc., Bogota, N.J., from 1963; pres. Kingsland Paper Corp., N.Y.C., 1937-62, Seaboard Mill Supply, Inc., N.Y.C., 1948-63. Mem. Cornell U. Coun., from 1954; apptd. adminstrv. bd. Casa Italiana, Columbia U., from 1958. Decorated chevalier Ancient Order of St. Hubert (Europe); recipient Columbia U. Casa Italiana award, 1962. Mem. N.Y. State C. of C., U.S. C. of C., N.Y. Assn. Dealers in Paper Mills Supplies (pres. 1951-54), Nat. Assn. Waste Materials Dealers (dir. 1952-55), Italian Hist. Soc. Am. (hon.), Cornell Alumni Assn. (pres. N.Y.C. 1955), Saints and Sinners Club (hon. life; exec. dir.), Cornell Club, Lambs Club, Manhattan Club. *

GAERTNER, WOLFGANG WILHELM, physicist, research company executive; b. Vienna, Austria, July 5, 1929; came to U.S., 1953, naturalized, 1961; s. Wilhelm and Maria (Schuetz) G.; m. Marianne L. Weber, Feb. 22, 1955; children: Marianne P., Karin C., Christopher W. Ph.D. in Physics, U. Vienna, 1951; Dipl.Ing., Technische Hochschule, Vienna, 1955. Research physicist Siemens Halske, Vienna, 1951-53, U.S. Army Signal Research and Devel. Lab., Ft. Monmouth, N.J., 1953-60; v.p. CBS Labs., Stamford, Conn., 1960-65; pres. W.W. Gaertner Research, Inc., Norwalk, Conn., 1965-89; cons. NATO. Author: Transistors: Principles, Design and Applications, 1960, Adaptive Electronics, 1973; contbr. articles to profl. publs. Fellow IEEE; mem. Am. Phys. Soc. Home: Stamford Conn. Died Feb. 23, 1989; buried Stamford.

GAGE, ROBERT, banker; b. Chester, S.C., July 18, 1885; s. George Williams and Janie (Gaston) G.; m. Mary Smith, Dec. 18, 1906; 1 dau., Mrs. Alice Gage Davidson. Prep. edn., Kings Mountain Mil. Acad., York, S.C.; student, Wofford Coll., Spartanburg, S.C., 1901-03. With Comml. Bank, Chester, from 1903; v.p., cashier Comml. Bank, from 1906, pres., from 1941; pres. Chester Bldg. & Loan Assn.; dir. Fed. Res. Bank of Richmond, Charlotte (N.C.) br. Fed. Res. Bank of Richmond; fed. receiver Peoples State Bank of S.C.; chmn. bd. dirs. Aragon-Baldwin Mills, Whitmire, S.C.; mem. adv. coun. Charlotte Loan Agy., Reconstrn. Fin. Corp.; bd. dirs. J.P. Stevens & Co., Inc., N.Y.C. Mem. City Coun., Chester, 1914-17, from 1922; mem. Chester County Hwy. Commn., 1917-20; chmn. Pub. Works Dept. of Chester, builders of modern water system; mem. S.C. State Bd. Bank Control; chmn. Alien Enemy Hearing Bd. for Western Dist. of S.C.; chmn. Chester County War Fin. Com. of 5th Fed. Res. Dist. Recipient Alumni citation Wofford Coll.; citation for disting. svc. to ch. and state Columbia Coll. Mem. S.C. Bankers Assn. (pres. 1937), Rotary, Chi Psi. Methodist. *

GAINES, ALEXANDER PENDLETON, lawyer; b. Atlanta, May 27, 1910; s. Lewis M. and Virginia Ethel (Alexander) G.; m. Mary Delia Upchurch, Oct. 2, 1937 (dec. Nov. 1975); children: Mary (Mrs. William F. Ford), Alexander Pendleton, Delia (Mrs. Charles C. Thompson III); m. Mary Cobb Gardner, June 27, 1976. A.B., U. Ga., 1932; LL.B., Emory U., 1935. Bar: Admitted Ga. 1935, D.C. 1967. Assoc. Jones, Fuller and Clapp, 1935-41; asst. regional counsel OPA, 1942; partner Clapp and Gaines, 1945-50, Gaines, Simpson & Peabody, 1950-54, Hurt, Gaines and Baird, 1954-62; mem. firm Alston, Miller and Gaines, Atlanta, 1962-82, Alston and Bird, Atlanta, from 1982; sec., dir. George Muse Clothing Co., 1947-81; dir. Genuine Parts Co., 1950-81. Trustee Charles Loridans Found., Vassar Wooley Found., John Bulow Campbell Found., 1958-80; trustee U. Ga. Found., 1964-81, trustee emeritus, from 1982; trustee Berry Schs., 1964-81, trustee emeritus, from 1982; trustee J.M. Tull Found., 1964-81; trustee Agnes Scott Coll., 1959-84, trustee emeritus, from 1984; trustee Piedmont Hosp. Found., from 1971, So. Acad. Letters, Arts and Scis., 1971-83; mem. Ga. Post-Secondary Edn. Commn., 1977; co-chmn. Joint Tech. Ga. Devel. Fund., 1967-68. Served with USAAF, 1942-45. Recipient Pres.'s award Assn. Pvt. Colls. and Univs., 1977, Disting. Alumni Merit award U. Ga., 1978, Merit award , 1980. Fellow Am. Coll. Probate Counsel; mem. Am., D.C., Ga., Atlanta bar assns., Atlanta C. of C., Phi Delta Theta, Phi Delta Phi. Presbyterian (elder). Clubs: Commerce, Piedmont Driving. Home: Atlanta Ga. Deceased. †

GAINES, WILLIAM MAXWELL, publishing executive; b. N.Y.C., Mar. 1, 1922; s. Max C. and Jessie K. (Postlethwaite) G.; m. Hazel Grieb, Oct. 21, 1944 (div. Feb. 9, 1948); m. Nancy Siegel, Nov. 17, 1955 (div. Mar. 1, 1971); children: Cathy, Wendy, Chris; m. Anne Griffiths, Feb. 21, 1987. Student, Poly. Inst. Bklyn., 1939-42; B.S. in Edn, N.Y. U., 1948. Pres. E. C. Publs. Inc. (pub. MAD Mag.), N.Y.C., 1948-92. Served with AUS, 1942-46. Mem. Wine and Food Soc., In Search of Name Soc. (charter), Phi Alpha. Home: New York N.Y. Died June 3, 1992. †

GAINSBOURG, SERGE (LUCIEN GINSBURG), author, composer, actor, director; b. Paris, Apr. 2, 1928; s. Joseph Ginsburg and Goda (Besmann) G.; m. Francoise Pancrazzi (div.); 1 child with Jane Birkin, Charlotte, 1 child with Caroline von Paulus, Lucien. Attended Ecole nationale superieure des beaux-arts. Made show bus. debut as pianist and guitarist at Cabaret Milord l'Arsouille; films include: Voulez-vous danser avec moi, 1960, l'Inconnue de Hong Kong, 1963, le Jardinier d'Argenteuil, 1966, Ce sacre grand-pere, Vivre la nuit, le Pacha, 1968, Slogan, Paris n'existe pas, Mr. Freedom, Erotissimo, le Chemins de Katmandou, 1969, Cannabis, 1970, le Voleur de Cheveux, 1971, Trop jolies pour etre honnetes, 1972, Serieux comme le plaisir, 1975, Je vous aime, 1980; dir. film Je t'aime moi non plus, 1976, Charlotte Forever; screenwriter film Equateur, 1983; TV appearances include Les Cinq Dernieres Minutes, Les Dossiers de l'agence O, Vidocq, Anna; composer of music for films including: Les Loups dans la bergerie, l'Eau a la bouche, Le Jardinier d'Argenteuil, l'Espion, l'Horizon, Break Down, Toute Folles de lui, Paris n'existe pas, Ce sacre grand-pere, le Pacha, Manon, Sex-Shop, Trop jolies pour etre honnetes, la Horse, Un petit garcon nomme Charlie Brown Projection privee, Je t'aime moi non plus, Madame Claude, Charlotte for ever, 1986; composer of music for TV films: La Lettre dans un taxi, Vidocq, Anna; songwriter: Le Poinconneur des Lilas, La Chanson de Prevert, La Javanaise, Poupee de are, Poupee de son, Elisa, Harley Davidson, Comment te dire adieu, L'Eau a la Bouche, Manon, La Gadoue, Initials B.B., Histoire de Melody Nelson, La Nostalgie camarade, numerous others; author: Eugenie Sokolov, 1980; Albums include: Baby Alone in Babylone, Chio, 1983, Love on the Beat, 1984, You're Under Arrest, 1987; Recipient grand prize Acad. Charles-Cros, 1959; Soc. of Authors prize, 1963; Creators prize, 1964; Gold Leaf award, Canada, 1968; Platinum disc for album Aux armes et caetara, 1981; Gold disc for album Mauvaises nouvelles des etoiles, 1982; Nat. grand prize for song, Ministry of Culture, France, 1984. Died Mar. 2, 1991. Home: Paris France

GALKIN, ELLIOTT WASHINGTON, music educator; b. Bklyn., Feb. 22, 1921; s. Samuel and Ethel (Heifetz) G.; m. Ruth K. Inglefield, June 12, 1988. BA, Bklyn. Coll., 1943; diplôme direction d'orchestre, Conservatoire Nat. de Paris, 1948; certificate equivalentlà licence concert, L'Ecole-Normale de Musique de Paris, 1948; MA, Cornell U., 1955, Ph.D., 1960. Assoc. condr. L'Orch. Philharmonique internat., 1949; instr. music Saranac Lake Rehab. Guild, 1949-52; apprentice condr. Vienna (Austria) Staatsoper, 1955-56; faculty Goucher Coll., Balt., 1956-77, chmn. dept. music, 1960-77, prof., 1964-77; faculty Peabody Conservatory, 1957-90, condr. orch., 1957-64, chmn. music history and lit. dept., 1964-77, dir., 1977-82; dir. mus. activities, prof. Johns Hopkins U., 1968-90; dir. Peabody Inst., 1977-82, dir. grad. program in music criticism, from 1983; guest condr. Balt. Symphony Orch., from 1965; dir. Rockefeller Found.-Balt. Symphony Orch. Am. Composers Project at Goucher Coll., 1965, 66, 67; condr. Balt. Chamber Orch., from 1960; music editor, critic Balt. Sun, 1962-77; vis. lectr. Tanglewood Music Festival, 1965, 66, chmn. music critics projects, from 1968; dir. Fromm Found. fellowship program in music criticism, 1969, 70, Music Critics Insts., Aspen, Kennedy Ctr., Cin., Ravinia, U. Md., Santa Fe, from 1967. Author: A History of Orchestral Conducting in Theory and Practice; translator: Schule Fuer Viola d'Amore; contbr. articles to profl. jours. Mem. Md. Adv. Council Arts, 1966-70; mem. music adv. planning panel Nat. Endowment for Arts, 1977-80, mem. profl. tng. panel, from 1980. Served with USAAF, 1943-46. Recipient Deems Taylor award ASCAP, 1972, 75, George Peabody medal for outstanding contbns. to music in Am., 1982. Mem. Internat., Am. musicol. socs., Coll. Music Soc., Am. Fedn. Musicians, Music Critics Assn., Am. Newspaper Guild, Phi Beta Kappa. Club: Cosmos. Home: Timonium Md. Died May 24, 1990; buried Balt.

GALLAGHER, BERNARD PATRICK, editor, publisher; b. N.Y.C., Feb. 25, 1910; s. Bernard A. and Mary Helen (Fitzsimmons) G.; m. Harriet Denning, Oct. 17, 1942; 1 dau., Jill. Student, Columbia U., 1928-29, Akron U., 1941-44. Mgr. single-copy sales Crowell Pub. Co., 1932-34; sales mgr. charge sales tng. Stenotype Co., Inc., Chgo., 1934-39; pres. Stenotype Co. Ohio, Inc., Cleve., 1939-45, World Wide Publs. Inc., 1945-83, Gallagher Communications, Inc., 1974-89; editor-in-chief pub. The Gallagher Report, 1952-89, The Gallagher Presidents' Report, 1965-89, Gallagher Med. Report, 1983-89; pres. Gallagher Found., 1978-89. Served with AUS, 1944-45. Mem. Southampton Assocs. Clubs: Canadian, Met. Home: New York NY Died June 21, 1989.

GALLAGHER, JOHN BENTLEY, lawyer, banker; b. St. Paul, Nov. 9, 1894; s. Michael William and Julia (Bentley) G.; m. Anastasia Murphy, June 1, 1921. LLB, St. Paul Coll., 1916. Practiced law St. Paul, 1916-17; engaged in banking, 1917-18, 19-22; with War Fin. Corp., Washington, 1922-25; practiced law Mpls., 1925-28; pres. Chgo. Joint Stock Land Bank, agrl. loans, from 1928; chmn. exec. com. Western Power & Gas Co.; dir. Central Life Ins. Co., Mpls. Gas Co., Brinks, Inc., Chgo., Milw., St. Paul and Pacific R.R.; mem. adv. com. Chgo. Dist. of Reconstrn. Fin. Corp.; trustee Chgo., North Shore & Milw. R.R. Bd. dirs Arlington Park Jockey Club. Mem. Attic Club, Tavern Club, Everglades Club (Palm Beach, Fla.). Republican. Roman Catholic. *

GALLAGHER, RAYMOND JOSEPH, bishop; b. Cleve., Nov. 19, 1912; s. Hugh and Ella Reedy G. BA, John Carroll U., 1934; postgrad., St. Mary's Sem., Cleve., 1939; MSW, Loyola U., Chgo., 1948. Ordained priest Roman Cath. Ch., 1939. Asst. pastor St. Colman Ch., Cleve., 1939-44; dir. Cath. Youth Svc. Bur., Cleve., 1948-55, St. Anthony's Home for Boys, Cleve., 1949-61; sec. Nat. Conf. Cath. Charities, Washington, 1961-65; bishop Lafayette, Ind., 1965-83. Founder Cath. Big Bros., Cleve., 1951, Cath. Child Guidance Clinic, Cleve., 1953, Don Bosco Sch. for Boys, Cleve., 1957; vice chmn. White House Conf. Children and Youth, 1960; mem. exec. planning com. White House Conf. on Aging, 1961; vice chmn., mem. nat. exec. com. Citizens Crusade Against Poverty; bd. dirs.

Nat. Coun. Aging, United Community Funds and Couns. Am.; Nat. Social Welfare Assembly, Nat. Housing Conf.; trustee Nat. Coun. Crime and Delinquency. Lt. USNR, 1944-46. Recipient Alumni award Loyola U., Chgo., 1960. Mem. Nat. Cath. Edn. Assn. pres.-gen. 1968, chmn. bd. 1969-83 , Alpha Sigma Nu. Home: Lafayette N.C. Died Mar. 7, 1991.

GALLANT, WADE MILLER, JR., lawyer; b. Raleigh, N.C., Jan. 12, 1930; s. Wade Miller and Sallie Wesley (Jones) G.; m. Sandra Kirkham, Sept. 15, 1979. BA summa cum laude, Wake Forest U., 1952, JD cum laude, 1955. Bar: N.C. 1955. Pvt. practice Winston-Salem, N.C.; ptnr. Womble, Carlyle, Sandridge & Rice, 1963-88; bd. dirs. EuroCaribe Bank & Trust Co. Ltd., Brenner Cos., Inc., Piece Goods Shops Corp., Trinity Am. Corp.; lectr. continuing edn. N.C. Bar Found., 1966-88. Contbr. articles to legal publs. Pres. Forsyth County Legal Aid Soc., 1963-67; assoc. Family and Child Service Agy., Winston-Salem, 1962-65, Winston-Salem Symphony Assn., 1965-66, Forsyth Mental Health Assn., 1972-73, N.C. Mental Health Assn., 1974-75; dir.-at-large Nat. Mental Health Assn., 1978-84, v.p., 1981-82; bd. dirs., exec. com. Blumenthal Jewish Home for the Aged Inc. Fellow Am. Bar Found. (life); mem. Internat. Bar Assn., N.C. Bar Assn., Forsyth County Bar Assn., Am. Counsel Assn. (hon.), Am. Law Inst., Old Town Club, Twin City Club, Piedmont Club, Bald Head Island (N.C.) Club, Phi Beta Kappa, Omicron Delta Kappa, Phi Delta Phi. Democrat. Episcopalian. Home: Winston Salem N.C. Died Dec. 10, 1988. †

GALLOP, RICHARD CHARLES, lawyer, business executive; b. N.Y.C., Nov. 15, 1938; s. M. Robert and Sally G.; m. Ann McEldowney, Sept. 30, 1961; children: Jeffrey, James. BA cum laude, Williams Coll., 1960; JD, Harvard, 1963. Bar: N.Y. Partner firm Milbank, Tweed, Hadley & McCloy, N.Y.C., 1963-79; firm Caplin & Drysdale, Washington, 1979-81; sr. v.p., gen. counsel Columbia Pictures Industries, Inc., N.Y.C., 1981, pres., chief operating officer, 1983-86; mng. dir. Allen & Co. Inc., N.Y.C., 1986-89. Mem. fin. com. Williams Coll.; trustee Marymount Coll., Holderness Sch., Plymouth, N.H.; bd. overseers Pace U. Law Sch. Club: Sleepy Hollow Country. Home: Briarcliff Manor N.Y. Died Nov. 23, 1989.

GALLOWAY, PAUL VERNON, clergyman; b. Mountain Home, Ark., Apr. 5, 1904; s. James Jesse and Ella (Burkhead) G.; m. Elizabeth Boney, June 14, 1932; 1 child, Paul Vernon. AB, Henderson-Brown Coll., 1926; postgrad., So. Meth. U., 1926-27; BD, Yale U., 1929; postgrad., U. Chgo., 1933. Ordained to ministry Meth. Ch., 1929, consecrated bishop, 1960. Pastor Ark., 1925-50, Okla., 1950-60; bishop N.W. Tex. area San Antonio, 1960-64; bishop Ark. area Little Rock, 1964-72; bishop Houston area, Tex. conf., 1973-90; spl. missioner Bd. Evangelism, 1979-90; visitor mission fields abroad, 1947, 54, 58, 59, 61, 65; chmn. conf. hosp. and homes Meth. Ch., 1939-48, chmn. commn. world svc. and fin., 1952-60, program chmn., also chmn. commn. entertainment, 1952-60; Episcopal adviser, 1960; mem., v.p. nat. div. Bd. Missions, 1960-64, chmn. home sect., 1964-90, chmn. com. on Spanish-speaking work. Mem. gov. Ark. Com. to Study Vocat. Tng., 1939; rep. Ark. A&M Coll. on Ednl. Com. Colls. and Higher Edn., 1936-50; trustee Meth. Hosp., Memphis, Meth. Children's Home, Little Rock; bd. dirs. So. Meth. U., Lydia Petterson Inst., El Paso, McMurry Coll., Southwestern U., Ark. A&M Coll., Hendrix Coll., Lon Morris Coll., Wiley Coll., Tex. Meth. Found., Meth. Hosp. Houston; bd. mgrs. Ark. Indsl. Schs. Hon. degrees include DD, Hendrix Coll., 1951, LD, So. Meth. U., 1964, LLD, Ark. A&M Coll., 1947, LHD, Oklahoma City U., 1960, LittD, McMurray Coll. Mem. Masons (32d degree), Delta Chi, Pi Kappa Delta. Home: Houston Tex. Died Aug. 4, 1990.

GAMBLE, BERTIN CLYDE, business executive; b. Chgo., Mar. 1, 1891; s. William Clyde and Florence Mae (Moody) G.; m. Gladys Lucille Pearson, Nov. 24, 1927; children: Jerry (dec.), Karen, Rae. Ed. pub. schs. and high sch. Ptnr. automobile bus., from 1920; opened first Gamble Store, St. Cloud, Minn., 1925; inc. Gamble-Skogmo, Inc., which owned 55 stores, 1928; organized Gamble Stores, Inc., 1925; established Solar Corp., mfg. paints, batteries, washing machines, Milw., Cudahy, Wis., Webster City, Iowa, L.A., 1933; acquired Nasco, Inc., fin. co., Fargo, N.D., 1935, Western Auto Supply Co., L.A., 1939; following merger, chmn. bd. Gamble-Skogmo, Clark's Gamble Corp.; dir. Northwestern Nat. Bank, Aldens Inc., Cousins & Fearn Co., Inc., Gamble Macleod Ltd., Retailers Growth Fund, Inc. Mem. men's adv. com. Northwestern Hosp.; trustee Ripon (Wis.) Coll.; mem. gov.'s coun. YMCA; patron Mpls. Soc. Fine Arts. Mem. Mpls. Club, Minikahda Club, Mpls. Athletic Club, Hazeltine Country Club, Woodhill Country Club (Wayzata, Minn.), Eldorado (Calif.) Club. Methodist. *

GAMMIE, GEORGE, clay products manufacturing company executive; b. Glasgow, Scotland, Nov. 2, 1898; s. James Alexander and Jane (Leslie) G.; m. Rena Anys, June 8, 1923; children: Donald, James, Jane (Mrs. William G. Barnard). Mgr. Hydraulic Press Brick Co., 1936-40; sales mgr. Ill. Brick Co., 1940-47, v.p., gen. sales mgr., 1947-60, pres., dir., from 1960; pres., dir.

Poston-Herron Brick Co., Attica, Ind.; treas., dir. Structural Clay Products Inst., Washington. Mem. Builders Club, Rotary, La Grange Country Club. *

GAMORAN, ABRAHAM CARMI, management consultant, real estate broker; b. Cin., Mar. 15, 1926; s. Emanuel and Mamie (Goldsmith) G.; m. Ruth Kump, Apr. 14, 1973; children: Shirley, Mary, Samuel, Benjamin, Joseph. BBA, U. Cin., 1948; MBA, NYU, 1950. CPA, N.Y.; lic. real estate broker, N.Y., Ohio. Mem. staff Harris, Kerr Forster & Co., N.Y.C., 1949-52, supr. mgmt. services div., 1962-67; mgmt. cons. Burke, Landsberg & Gerber, Balt., 1953-54; v.p. Helmsley-Spear, Inc., N.Y.C., 1969-81; v.p. Helmsley-Spear, Inc., Cleve., 1981-90; lectr. Cornell U., Mich. State U., Okla. State U., Am. Hotel and Motel Assn., others; vis. prof. U. Nev., Las Vegas, Coll. Hotel Adminstrn., 1985-87. Author articles in field, also real estate rev. portfolios. Recipient medal Wall St. Jour., 1948; Benjamin Franklin award, 1982. Mem. AICPA, Am. Soc. Real Estate Counselors, N.Y. State Soc. CPAs. Democrat. Jewish. Died Sept. 23, 1991; interred Union Field Cemetery, Queens, N.Y. Home: Wooster Ohio

GANGER, ROBERT MONDELL, business executive; b. Greenville, Ohio, June 20, 1903; s. Ora Lynn and Della (Cox) G.; m. Jean Wyvle Ward, Dec. 25, 1933; 1 child, Robert Ward. AB, Ohio State U., 1926. V.p. Geyer, Cornell, Newell, Inc., N.Y.C., 1933-45; ptnr. Geyer, Newell & Ganger, Inc., 1945-50; exec. v.p. P. Lorillard & Co., 1950-52, pres., 1952-53, dir., mem. exec. com., 1950-53; chmn. bd., exec. com. D'Arcy Co., 1953-69. Bd. dirs., mem. exec. com. United Svc. Orgn.; Advt. Coun.; bd. dirs. Advt. Rsch. Found. Mem. Am. Assn. Advt. Agys. (past chmn. bd.), Ohio Soc. N.Y., Siwanoy Club, Univ. Club, Nat. Golf Links Club, Country Club of Fla., Mid Ocean Country Club (Bermuda), Gulf Stream Golf Club, Golf Stream Bath and Tennis Club. Republican. Mem. Reformed Ch. Home: Gulfstream Fla. Died Apr. 23, 1992.

GANN, ERNEST KELLOGG, author; b. Lincoln, Nebr., Oct. 13, 1910; s. George Kellogg and Caroline (Kupper) G.; m. Eleanor Michaud, Sept. 18, 1933 (div.); children: George Kellogg (dec.), Steven Anthony, Polly Wing; m. Dodie Post, May 20, 1966. Grad. magna cum laude, Culver (Ind.) Mil. Acad., 1930; student, Yale U.; HHD (hon.), U. Calif., 1979. Ind. writer, 1939-89. Author: Island in the Sky, 1944 (made into movie), Blaze of Noon, Fiddler's Green, Benjamin Lawless, The High and the Mighty (made into movie), Soldier of Fortune (made into movie), Twilight for the Gods, Trouble with Lazy Ethel, Fate is the Hunter (made into movie), Of Good and Evil, In the Company of Eagles, Song of the Sirens, The Antagonists, Band of Brothers, Flying Circus, Hostage to Fortune, A, Brain 2000, The Aviator, The Magistrate, Gentleman of Adventure, The Triumph, The Honey of Poisoned Flowers, The Bad Angel, The Black Watch, 1989; also many short stories; 4-part TV series, Masada, based on one of his books, 1981; painting exhbn. include 2 one man shows in Seattle, 1991. Served as capt. Air Transport Command AUS, 1942-46. Recipient Aviation Journalist of Yr. Flying and Comml. Aviation, 1975, Achievement award Nat. Aviation Club, 1983. Mem. Am. Fighter Pilots Assn., Daedalians, Black Birds. Republican. Presbyterian. Clubs: OX-5, Quiet Birdmen, Colgate President's, Washington Athletic, Grey Eagles. Home: San Juan Island Wash. Died Dec. 19, 1991.

GAPP, PAUL JOHN, journalist; b. Cleve., June 26, 1928; s. Bernard Leonard and Florence (Ganley) G.; m. Mary Joan Finch, May 16, 1970. B.S., Ohio U., 1950. Reporter, editor Columbus (Ohio) Dispatch, 1950-56; reporter, editorial page writer, feature editor Chgo. Daily News, 1956-66; exec. dir. Chgo. chpt. and Ill. council AIA, 1967; account exec. Dale O'Brien & Co., Chgo., 1968-69; dir. spl. projects, office of v.p. pub. affairs U. Chgo., 1969-72; architecture critic Chgo. Tribune, 1972-92; mem. communications com. Met. Housing and Planning Council, 1968-70; bd. dirs. Nat. Building Mus., 1980-83. Contbr. articles to U.S. and fgn. newspapers, mags., profl. publs. Co-recipient Ill. AP award for best news reporting, 1965, 77; recipient Pulitzer prize for criticism, 1979, Orchid award AIA, 1980; Disting. Alumnus medal Ohio U., 1980, L.J. Horton Disting. Alumnus award, 1988; award for feature writing UPI, 1981, award for disting. criticism Art World, 1983, Chgo. Architecture award Chgo. Architecture Found., 1987. Mem. AIA (hon.), Am. Philatelic Soc., South African Philatelic Frat. (hon.), S. Allan Taylor Soc. (founder 1963, pres. 1963-76), Architects Club Chgo. (hon.), Pi Kappa Alpha. Home: Chicago Ill. Died July 30, 1992. †

GARBO, GRETA, actress; b. Stockholm, Sweden, Sept. 18, 1905; came to U.S., 1925, naturalized, 1951; d. Sven and Louvisa Gustaffson. Ed. Royal Dramatic Acad., Stockholm. Won first film recognition in Goesta Berling, 1924, through work in Royal Acad.; came to U.S. and appeared in (silent movies) The Temptress, 1926, The Torrent, 1926, Love, 1927, Flesh and the Devil, 1927, (talking movies) Anna Christie, 1930, Susan Lenox, 1931, Mata Hari, 1931, Grand Hotel, 1932, As You Desire Me, 1932, Queen Christina, 1933, The Painted Veil, Anna Karenina, 1935, Camille, 1936, Conquest, 1937, Ninotchka, 1939, Two Faced Woman,

1941 (Recipient Spl. Acad. award 1954). Home: New York N.Y. Died Apr. 15, 1990.

GARDENIA, VINCENT, actor; b. Naples, Italy, Jan. 7, 1921. Actor appearances include (films) Bang the Drum Slowly (Oscar nomination 1973), Death Wish I and II, Front Page, Heaven Can Wait, Lucky Luciano, Cold Turkey, Where's Poppa, The Hustler, Little Shop of Horrors, Moonstruck, 1988 (Oscar nomination), Skin Deep, 1989, The Super, 1990, (Broadway plays) God's Favorite, Sly Fox, Ballroom, California Suite, Ballroom (Tony nomination 1979), Glengarry Glen Ross, Breaking Legs, 1991, and others, (TV) All in the Family, Mary Tyler Moore, Kennedy, Age Old Friends, 1989 (Emmy award 1989), (TV series) Breaking Away, 1980-81. Recipient Tony award for Prisoner of Second Avenue 1971, Obie awards for Machinal, Passing Through from Exotic Places; Oscar nominee, 1973. Home: New York N.Y. Died Dec. 9, 1992. †

GARDNER, AVA, actress; b. Smithfield, N.C., Dec. 24, 1922; d. Jonas B. and Mary Elizabeth G.; m. Mickey Rooney, Jan. 10, 1942 (div.); m. Artie Shaw, 1945 (div.); m. Frank Sinatra, 1951 (div. 1957). Student, Atlantic Christian Coll. Motion picture debut in We Were Dancing, 1942; other motion pictures include Three Men in White, 1944, Maisie Goes to Reno, 1944, She Went to the Races, 1946, Whistle Stop, 1946, The Killers, 1946, The Hucksters, 1947, Singapore, 1947, One Touch of Venus, 1948, The Bribe, 1949, The Great Sinner, 1949, East Side, West Side, 1949, My Forbidden Past, 1951, Show Boat, 1951, Pandora and the Flying Dutchman, 1951, Lone Star, 1952, The Snows of Kilimanjaro, 1952, Ride Vaquero, 1953, Mogambo, 1953 (Oscar nomination), Knights of the Round Table, 1954, The Barefoot Contessa, 1954, Bhowani Junction, 1956, The Little Hut, 1957, The Sun Also Rises, 1957, The Naked Maja, 1959, On the Beach, 1959, The Angel Wore Red, 1960, 55 Days at Peking, 1963, Seven Days in May, 1964, The Night of the Iguana, 1964, The Bible, 1966, Devil's Widow, 1971, Life and Times of Judge Roy Bean, 1972, Earthquake, 1974, The Sentinel, 1976, Permission to Kill, 1976, The Bluebird, 1976, The Cassandra Crossing, 1977, City on Fire, 1978, The Kidnapping of the President, 1979, Priest of Love, 1980, Regina, 1982; TV miniseries include A.D., 1984, The Long Hot Summer, 1985, Harem, 1985; recurring role on Knots Landing, 1984-85. Home: London England Died Jan. 25, 1990.

GARDNER, GEORGE HENRY, gynecologist; b. Osborn, Ohio, Aug. 18, 1897; s. Clarence E. and Ana Mae (Startzman) G.; m. Marion E. Nelson, May 31, 1924; children: George Henry (dec.), Elizabeth Ann, Mary Louise. Grad., Wittenberg Acad., Springfield, Ohio, 1913; AB, Wittenberg Coll., 1917; MD, Johns Hopkins U., 1921. Diplomate Am. Bd. Obstetrics and Gynecology. Intern, asst. resident, resident in gynecology Johns Hopkins Hosp., Balt., 1921-26; practiced in Chgo., specializing in gynecology, from 1926; from clin. asst. to prof. obstetrics and gynecology Northwestern U. Med. Sch., from 1927, chmn. dept. obstetrics and gynecology, from 1947, asst. dean, 1943-49; attending gynecologist Passavant Meml. Hosp., 1929-45; chmn. dept. obstetrics and gynecology Chgo. Wesley Meml. Hosp., from 1946. Served with U.S. Navy, 1918-19. Fellow ACS (life), Am. Gynecol. Soc. (pres. 1962-63); mem. AMA, Am. Coll. Obstetricians and Gynecologists, Inst. Medicine, Ill. State Med. Soc., Chgo. Med. Soc., Chgo. Gynecol. Soc., Johns Hopkins Surg. Soc., Am. Assn. Obstetricians and Gynecologists, Phi Gamma Delta. Republican. Lutheran. *

GARDNER, HY, columnist, television and radio performer, writer, producer; b. N.Y.C., Dec. 2, 1908; s. John Jacob and Sarah (Guilden) G.; m. Marilyn Boshnick, Apr. 1958; 1 child, Jeffrey Scott; 1 child by previous marriage, Ralph Richard. Student, Columbia U. Sch. Journalism. Syndicated Broadway columnist; with N.Y. Herald Tribune, 15 yrs.; editor Trib TV mag.; star TV and radio Broadway and Hollywood Hy Gardner's Celebrity Party, Miami, Fla.; producer, performer Miami TV-WCIX, nat. syndicate; formerly on NBC TV series; celebrity panelist To Tell the Truth; CBS-TV series Hy Gardner Calling; producer Hi-Yank; actor movie The Girl Hunters. Author: So What Else is New, 1960, Tales Out of Night School, Off-Beat Guide to New York, Glad You Asked That; column pub. News Am. Syndicate, formerly Field Syndicate. Capt. AUS, 1942-45, ret. maj. Res. Recipient Freedoms Found. award in journalism. Home: Miami Fla. Died June 17, 1989.

GARDNER, MARJORIE HYER, science association administrator; b. Logan, Utah, Apr. 25, 1923; d. Saul Edward and Gladys Ledingham (Christiansen) Hyer; B.S., Utah State U., 1946, Ph.D. (hon.), 1975; M.A., Ohio State U., 1958, Ph.D., 1960; cert. Ednl. Mgmt. Inst., Harvard U., 1975; m. Paul Leon Gardner, June 6, 1947; children: Pamela Jean, Mary Elizabeth. Tchr. sci., journalism and English high schs. Utah, Nev., Ohio, 1947-56; instr. Ohio State U., Columbus, 1957-60; asst. exec. dir. Nat. Sci. Tchrs. Assn., 1961-64; vis. prof. Australia, India, Yugoslavia, Nigeria, Thailand, Peoples Republic of China, 1965-82; assoc. dean, dir. Bur. Ednl. Rsch. and Field Svc., College Park, Md., 1975-76; dir. Sci. Teaching Ctr., U. Md., College Park, 1976-77, prof. chemistry, 1964-84; dir. Lawrence Hall Sci., U. Calif.-

Berkeley, 1984-89, rsch. assoc., 1989-91; div. dir. NSF, 1979-81; cons. UNESCO, from 1970; NSF grantee, from 1964; recipient Catalyst medal Chem. Mfrs. Assn., 1980, Nyholm medal Royal Soc. Can., 1987, U.S.U. Centennial award, 1987, ACS Chemical Edn. award, 1988. Fellow AAAS (coun.), Am. Inst. Chemistry; mem. Am. Chem. Soc., Chemistry Assn. Md. (pres.), Internat. Union of Pure and Applied Chemistry (exec. com.), Internat. Orgn. Chemistry in Devel. (edn. panel), Assn. Edn. of Tchrs. of Sci., Nat. Assn. Rsch. in Sci. Teaching, Nat. Sci. Tchrs. Assn., Am. Assn. Higher Edn., Soc. Coll. Sci. Tchrs. (pres.), Fulbright Alumni Assn. (pres., dir.), Phi Delta Kappa, Phi Kappa Phi. Author: Chemistry in the Space Age, 1965; editor: Theory in Action, 1964, Vistas of Sci. Series, 1961-63; Investigating the Earth, 1968, Interdisciplinary Approaches to Chemistry, 1973, 1978-79; Under Roof, Dome and Sky, 1974, Toward Continuous Professional Development: Designs and Directions, 1976; contbr. articles in on chemistry and sci. edn. to profl. jours. Died Apr. 19, 1991; buried Logan, Utah. Home: Berkeley Calif.

GARDNER, PETER D., chemistry educator, academic administrator; b. Salt Lake City, Jan. 17, 1927; s. Pete D. and Margaret (Rasmason) G.; m. Arlene Thomas, Aug. 6, 1950; children—Mark S., Connie J., Stephen P. B.S., U. Utah, 1949, M.S., 1950, Ph.D., 1953. Chemist Merck & Co., Rahway, N.J., 1951-52; faculty U. Tex., Austin, 1953-65, prof. chemistry, 1962-65; prof. chemistry U. Utah, Salt Lake City, 1965-89, prof. biology, 1977-85, dean sci., 1970-73, acad. v.p., 1973-77. Served with AUS, 1945. Home: Salt Lake City UT Died Feb. 4, 1989; buried Wasatch Lawn Mortuary, Salt Lake City.

GARDNER, WARNER WINSLOW, lawyer; b. Richmond, Ind., Sept. 25, 1909; s. Frank Karl and Camilla (Winslow) G.; m. Henrietta Gertrude Tucker, Sept. 10, 1940 (dec.); children: Hannah Winslow, William Tucker, Richard Randolph, Frances Winslow; m. Josephine P. McGowan, Oct. 28, 1989. A.B., Swarthmore Coll., 1930; M.A., Rutgers U., 1931; LL.B., Columbia U., 1934. Law clk. Justice Stone, U.S. Supreme Ct., 1934-35; atty. and spl. asst. to atty. gen. Office Solicitor Gen., Dept. Justice, 1935-41; solicitor U.S. Dept. Labor, 1941-42; solicitor U.S. Dept. Interior, 1942-46, asst. sec., 1946-47; mem. firm Shea & Gardner, Washington, from 1947; Dir. Natomas Co., 1971-76; Spl. counsel Fed. Maritime Bd., 1957; chmn. informal action com. Adminstrv. Conf. U.S., 1968-76. Author: Building and Loan Liquidity, 1931, Taxation of Government Bondholders and Employees, 1938; Contbr. articles to mags. Served with AUS, 1943-45. Decorated Legion of Merit; Croix de Guerre. Mem. Phi Beta Kappa. Mem. Soc. of Friends. Clubs: Metropolitan, Cosmos. Home: Washington D.C. Deceased. †

GARDNER, WARREN HENRY, speech pathologist, educator; b. Ottumwa, Iowa, Mar. 23, 1895; s. Alvah Thomas and Laura Jeannette (Klinker) G.; m. Dorothy D. Chase, June 12, 1942; children: Donald Hunt, Mary Ellen (adopted wife's children). AB, Harvard U., 1918; PhD, State U. Iowa, 1936. With import-export bus., N.Y.C., 1918-22; hearing and vision cons. Oreg. State Bd. Health, 1940-42; hearing conservation specialist Calif. State Bd. Health, 1942-45; prof. hearing and speech therapy Western Res. U., 1945-54; also chief, hearing and speech div. Cleve. Hearing and Speech Ctr., 1945-54; chief audiology and speech pathology dept. otolaryngology Cleve. Clinic, 1954-65; prof. audiology and speech pathology Cleve. Clinic Ednl. Inst., 1955-65; pvt. practice, from 1965; lectr. Am. Acad. Ophthalmology and Otolaryngology, 1957, 58, summer sch. U. So. Calif., 1943-45, UCLA, 1943, San Francisco State Coll., 1943-45; inst. lectr. colls. edn., Calif. and Oreg. Author various books; editor: A Child has Cleft Palate, 1947. contbr. articles to profl. jours. Served as ensign U.S. Navy, 1917-18, mem. USNR, 1917-22. Fellow Am. Speech and Hearing Assn.; mem. Internat. Coun. Exceptional Children, Am. Hearing Soc. (dir. 1940-46, pres. 1942-45, chmn. com. conservation of hearing 1938-53), Speech Assn. Am., Central States Speech Assn., Am. Assn. Instrs. of the Deaf, Volta Assn., Ohio Assn. Speech and Hearing Therapy (pres. 1950-51), Internat. Assn. Laryngectomees (founder, bd. dirs. 1952-56, from 1965), chmn. nat. adv. com. 1956-65, dir. admissions, lectr. voice inst. 1960-64). *

GARFINKEL, DAVID, biological science and computer science researcher, educator; b. N.Y.C., May 18, 1930; s. Louis and Leah (Markosfeldt) G.; m. Lillian Magid, June 26, 1960; children—Susan Laura, Beth Diane. A.B., U. Calif.-Berkeley, 1951; Ph.D., Harvard U., 1955; M.A. (hon.), U. Pa., 1972. Postdoctoral fellow in biophysics U. Pa., Phila., 1955-58, rsch. assoc., 1961-63, asst. prof., 1963-65, assoc. prof. biophysics, 1965-72, assoc. in clin. medicine, 1971-83, assoc. prof. computer sci., 1972-77, prof., from 1977; research biochemist N.Y. State Psychiat. Inst., Columbia U., N.Y.C., 1958-60; mem. adv. com. in computers in research, NIH, 1960-62, various other rev. groups; vis. prof. Rutgers U., New Brunswick, N.J., 1987-88; reviewer NIH, NSF, others. Mem. editorial bd.: Computers and Biomed. Research, Jour. Theoretical Biology, Am. Jour. Physiology, Annals of Biomed. Engring., Magnesium; reviewer for various jours.; contbr. articles to profl. jours. NIH research career devel. awardee, 1961-70; NIH research grantee, 1962—. Fellow IEEE; mem. Soc. Computer Simulation (sr.), Biomed. Engring. Soc. (bd. dirs. 1982-85), Am. Soc. for Biochemistry and Molecular Biology, Am. Physiol. Soc., Biochem. Soc., Internat. Soc. for Heart Research, Soc. for Math. Biology, Assn. for Computing Machinery, Am. Assn. for Artificial Intelligence, N.Y. Acad. Sci., Phi Beta Kappa. Home: Merion Station Pa. Deceased. †

GARFINKEL, PHILIP, engineering company executive; b. Bklyn., Mar. 11, 1926; s. Louis and Ida (Kotick) G.; m. Gladys Bean, July 31, 1945; children: David, Barbara, Howard. BEE, CUNY, 1949. Registered profl. engr., N.Y., Mass., Conn., W.Va. Elec. design engr. Baker & Spencer, Inc., N.Y.C., 1950-52, Ebasco Svcs., Inc., N.Y.C., 1952-54; elec. project engr. Loewy Hydropress, Inc., N.Y.C., 1954-56; chief elec. engr. Malco Designs, Inc., N.Y.C., 1956-57; sr. design engr. Singmaster & Breyer, N.Y.C., 1957-58; chief elec. engr. Stone & Webster Engring. Corp., Garden City, N.Y., 1958-65, dep. mgr., N.Y.C., 1969-84, pres., chief exec. officer, Boston, 1984-92; sr. elec. engr. Burns & Roe Inc., Oradell, N.J., 1965-69. Pres. Deer Run Shores Property Owners Assn., Sherman, Conn., 1983, 84; bd. dirs. United Way Mass. Bay, Boston, 1989. Petty officer USN, 1944-46, PTO, ATO. Mem. IEEE (sr.). Jewish. Home: Framingham Mass. Died Nov. 8, 1992. †

GARMS, WALTER IRVING, JR., education educator, consultant, researcher; b. Hayden, Ariz., Mar. 14, 1925; s. Walter Irving Sr. and Margaret (Dehm) G.; m. George Ann Walters, Nov. 21, 1950; children—Margaret, Walter Irving III. B.A. in Engring. Chemistry, Stanford U., 1945, M.B.A., 1948, Ph.D. in Gen. Ednl. Adminstrn., 1967. Cert. gen. elem. edn., gen. secondary edn. and gen. ednl. administrn, Calif. Chemist Fibreboard Products, Inc., Antioch, Calif., 1948-51; elem. tchr. Antioch Unified Sch. Dist., 1951-59, adminstrv. asst., 1959-60, asst. supt. for bus., 1960-64; asst. dir. Great Cities Research Project, Stanford U., Calif., 1964-65; adminstrv. officer Stanford Ctr. for Research and Devel. in Teaching, Stanford U., 1965-67; dir. joint degree program in higher edn. fin. and bus. adminstrn. Tchrs. Coll. and Columbia Grad. Sch. Bus., N.Y.C., 1969-72; asst. prof. higher edn. Tchrs. Coll., 1967-71, assoc. prof. higher edn., dept. higher and adult edn., 1971-72; assoc. prof. edn. Grad. Sch. Edn. and Human Devel. U. Rochester, N.Y., 1972-76, prof., 1976-87, prof. emeritus, 1987-89, dean Grad. Sch. Edn. and Human Devel., 1980-83; vis. prof. U. Calif., Berkeley, 1984-85; cons. state depts. of edn. and legislatures in 15 states, 1965-89; expert witness, from 1976; researcher many projects on ednl. fin., from 1968; mem. nat. adv. panel on study of community coll. tuition Edn. Commn. of States, 1980-82; mem. nat. adv. panel on study of community coll. fin. Brookings Instn., 1978-81; nat. fellow U. Chgo. Ednl. Fin. and Productivity Ctr., 1978-81; mem. Sch. Fin. Coop., 1977-81; mem. vis. com. Syracuse U. Sch. Edn., N.Y., 1982-87. Author: Financing Community Colleges, 1977, (with others) State School Finance Alternatives, 1975, (with others) School Finance, 1978, (with others) School Finance and Education Policy, 1988; contbr. articles to profl. jours. Pres. Community Concerts, Antioch. Served as seaman USN, 1945-46. Recipient award for outstanding contbn. to research NEA, 1968; cert. of appreciation State of Wash., 1965, cert. of appreciation State of Fla., 1973; named Irving R. Melbo Disting. prof. U. So. Calif., 1984. Mem. Am. Edn. Fin. Assn. (hon. life, pres. 1982-83), Cleve. Conf. Home: Berkeley Calif. Died Nov. 9, 1989; cremated.

GARRETT, GUY THOMAS, newspaper executive; b. Peekskill, N.Y., June 7, 1932; s. Guy Thomas Garrett and Anna Lee (Day) Garrett Williams; children from previous marriage: Lynn Allyson, Guy Thomas III; m. Constance Marie Sklias, June 14, 1981. B.A., Howard U., Washington, 1954; postgrad., CCNY, N.Y.C., 1961-62; A.M.P., Harvard Bus. Sch., Cambridge, 1977. Br. mgr. Household Fin., N.Y.C., 1957-62; tchr. N.Y.C. Bd. Edn., 1962-63; personnel mgr. LILCO, Hicksville, N.Y., 1963-74; dir. personnel New York Times, N.Y.C., 1974-76; v.p. personnel New York Times Co., N.Y.C., 1976-88; bd. dirs. Graham-Windham, N.Y.C. Bd. dirs. Greater N.Y. chpt. March of Dimes, N.Y.C. Served to 1st lt. U.S. Army, 1955-57. Mem. Personnel Round Table, Human Resources Planning Inst.-Boston U., Am. Newspaper Pub. Assn. (human resources com.). Home: Canaan N.Y. Died Sept. 8, 1988. †

GARRETT, PEARSON BEVERLY, lawyer, banker; b. Brenham, Tex., Aug. 22, 1895; s. William Beverly and Elizabeth Overton (Pearson) G.; m. Ruth Evens, 1919; children: Pearson Beverly, Richard Gordon. LLB, U. Tex., 1915. Bar: Tex. 1915. Ptnr. Garrett & Garrett, 1915-17, Breg, Garrett & Co., investment bankers, 1919-24; owner Garrett & Co., investment bankers, 1924-45; pres. Tex. Bank and Trust Co. of Dallas, 1945-58, vice chmn. bd., from 1958; dir. Equity Corp., Bell Aircraft Corp.; pres. Assn. of State Chartered Banks Tex., Inc., 1962-63. Served from 1st lt. to capt. U.S. Army, 1917-19, AEF. *

GARRISON, EDWIN RONALD, bishop; b. Clinton County, Ind., Dec. 26, 1897; s. R. Elliot and Susie (Enright) G.; m. Edith Heritage, Jan. 20, 1922; children: Helen Carolyn (Mrs. Lewis Kauffman), Marion Ann (Mrs. James H. LoPrete). AB, De Pauw U., 1921, DD, 1944; BD, Drew Theol. Sem., 1925. Ordained to ministry Methodist Ch., 1927, consecrated bishop, 1960. Pastor in Sheridan, Elkhart, Bluffton and Ft. Wayne, Ind., 1928-50; supt. Wabash Dist. Meth. Ch., 1942-47; adminstrv. asst. Ind. Area Meth. Ch., 1950-60; bishop Dakotas Area, from 1960. Mem. Masons, Lambda Chi Alpha. *

GARRISON, LLOYD KIRKHAM, lawyer; b. N.Y.C., Nov. 19, 1897; s. Lloyd McKim and Alice Kirkham G.; m. Ellen Jay, June 22, 1921; children: Clarinda Kirkham, Ellen Shaw, Lloyd McKim. AB, Harvard U., 1919, LLB, 1922; LLD, Lawrence Coll., 1942, U. Wis., 1964. Bar: N.Y. 1923. Assoc. Root, Clark, Buckner and Howland, N.Y.C., 1922-26, Parker & Garrison, 1926-32; dean, prof. law U. Wis. Law Sch., 1932-45; gen. counsel, exec. dir. Nat. War Labor Bd., 1942-43, pub. mem., 1944, chmn., 1945; mem. Paul Weiss, Rifkind, Wharton & Garrison, 1946-73; faculty law NYU, evenings 1947-51; spl. asst. U.S. atty. gen. in charge nat. bankruptcy investigation, 1930-31; chmn. NLRB, 1934; mem. Pres.'s Commn. on Labor Rels. in Gt. Britain and Sweden, 1938; labor adv. com. AEC, 1946-48; co-author with Solicitor Gen. Thacher of report to pres. on Bankruptcy Act and its adminstrn. in U.S. cts., 1931; with Willard Hurst The Legal Process; referee Nat. R.R. Adjustment Bd., intermittently 1936-64. Vice chmn. nat. com. ACLU, 1937-67; treas. Nat. Urban League, 1926-32, pres., 1947-52; exec. com. Nat. Lawyers Com. on Civil Rights, 1965—; mem. Bd. Edn. N.Y.C., 1961-68, pres., 1965-67; overseer Harvard U., 1938-44; bd. dirs. Field Found., 195-73; trustee Inst. for Advanced Study, 1952-67; trustee Sarah Lawrence Coll., 1946-6, chmn., 1956-6; trustee, treas. Potomac Inst., 1953—; trustee, v.p. Taconic Found, 1953—. With USN, 1917-19. Mem. Assn. of Bar of City of N.Y. exec. com. 1952-55 , Coun. on Fgn. Rels., Harvard Club N.Y.C. , Century Club. Home: New York N.Y. Deceased.

GARRY, CHARLES R., lawyer; b. Bridgewater, Mass., Mar. 17, 1909; s. Hagop T. and Rose (Banaian) Garabedian; m. Louise, Nov. 9, 1932. J.D., San Francisco Law Sch., 1938. Bar: Calif. 1938, U.S. Ct. Appeals (7th cir.) U.S. ct. appeals (9th cir.), U.S. Supreme Ct. Founding mem. Garry, Dreyfus & McTernan, Inc., San Francisco, 1957-91; lectr. criminal law. Author: Streetfighter in the Court Room; (with Ann Fagan Ginger) Minimizing Racism in Jury Selection. Contbr. articles to profl. publs. and tapes. Served with U.S. Army, 1943-45. Mem. Assn. Trial Lawyers Am. (past chmn. criminal law sect.), Nat. Lawyers Guild (past pres. Bay Area chpt.), Calif. Trial Lawyers Am., Calif. Attys. for Criminal Justice (founding, past pres.), San Francisco Bar Assn., San Francisco Lawyers Club. Died Aug. 16, 1991. Home: San Francisco Calif.

GARY, WYNDHAM LEWIS, textile company executive; b. N.Y.C., Feb. 29, 1916; s. Irving Curtis and Marguerite (Case) G.; m. Shirley Davis Spaulding, Aug. 6, 1948; 1 son, Wyndham Bradford. B.A., Yale U., 1938, LL.B., 1941. Bar: N.Y. 1941. Assoc. mem. firm Breed, Abbott & Morgan, 1941-42, 46-60; with alien enemy control unit Dept. Justice, Washington, 1942-43; asst. gen. counsel J.P. Stevens & Co., Inc., 1961-64, asst. treas., 1965-68, treas., 1969-81, dir., mem. exec. com., 1974-81, cons., 1981-89; adv. bd. Mfrs. Hanover Trust Co., N.Y.C. Mem. Rumson (N.J.) Boro Council, 1956-58; chmn. design com. Middletown (N.J.) Planning Bd., 1960-65; Bd. dirs., pres. J.P. Stevens & Co. Found. Served to capt. AUS, 1943-46. Mem. Am. Bar assn., Delta Kappa Epsilon, Phi Delta Phi. Episcopalian (sr. warden). Clubs: Rumson (N.J.) Country, Seabright (N.J.) Beach (bd. govs.); Princeton (N.Y.C.), Treasurers (N.Y.C.) (sec.-treas.); Seven Lakes Country (Palm Springs, Calif.). Home: Fair Haven N.J. Died June 10, 1989; buried Rumson, N.J.

GASIOROWSKA, XENIA, Slavic literature educator; b. Kiev, Russia; came to U.S., 1945, naturalized, 1964; d. Grzegorz and Magdalena (Olszewska) Zytomirski; m. Zygmunt J. Gasiorowski, Mar. 3; 1949. Ph.D. in Slavic Langs. and Lit, U. Calif.-Berkeley, 1949. Mem. faculty U. Wis., Madison, 1949-89, prof. Slavic lit., 1965-81, prof. emerita, 1981-89; Vis. asso. prof. Wellesley Coll., 1958-59. Author: Women in Soviet Fiction, 1917-1964, 1968, The Image of Peter the Great in Russian Fiction, 1979; also 3 vols. verse and a novel in Polish. Nat. Endowment for Humanities fellow, 1980-81. Mem. AAUP, Am. Assn. Tchrs. Slavic and E. European Langs., Polish Acad. Scis. in Am. Home: Madison Wis. Died July 30, 1989; buried Forest Hill Cemetery, Madison, Wis.

GASKILL, DAVID ABRAM, lawyer; b. Greenville, Ohio, May 26, 1894; s. David Lewis and Sarah (Meeker) G.; m. Virginia Wenner, Apr. 4, 1925; 1 dau., Emily Jane (Mrs. William F. Veenstra). Student, Miami U., Oxford, Ohio, 1912-13; LLB, Ohio State U., 1916. Bar: Ohio 1916. Practiced in Cleve., from 1916; mem. firm Thompson, Hine & Flory, from 1916, ptnr., from 1926; dir. Hobart Mfg. Co., Cowles Chem. Co.; sec., dir. Towmotor Corp. Served as ensign USNRF, 1917-18. Mem. ABA (chmn. fed. income tax, fed. estate tax and fed. excise tax coms. sect. taxation), Ohio Bar Assn. (past chmn. sect. taxation), Cleve. Bar Assn., Cleve. C. of C. (vice chmn. fed. income tax com.), Masons, Union

Club, Mayfield Country Club (Cleve.), Leland (Mich.) Country Club, Order of Coif, Phi Delta Theta, Phi Delta Phi. Republican. Presbyterian. *

GATLIN, JOHN C(HRISTIAN), government official; b. Chgo., Jan. 9, 1897; s. John Christian and Stella Frances (Earl) G.; m. Elizabeth Ann Hall, June 9, 1927; children: Elizabeth Ann (Mrs. Medary), John Christian III. Student, pub. schs., Magdalena and Las Cruces, N.Mex. Field position U.S. Fish and Wildlife Svc., Dept. Interior, 1917-28; dist. agt. for control predatory mammals U.S. Fish and Wildlife Svc., Dept. Interior, Okla. and N.Mex., 1928-39; regional dir. U.S. Fish and Wildlife Svc., Dept. Interior, Ariz., Colo., Kans., N.Mex., Okla., Tex., Utah and Wyo., from 1939. Served as pvt. Co. D, 1st N.Mex. Inf., Pershing's Expeditionary Force, 1916-17. Mem. Internat. Park Forestry and Wildlife Refuge Commn., Wildlife Soc., Optimist Internat., Am. Fisheries Soc., Masons. *

GAVIN, JAMES M., corporate consultant, military officer; b. N.Y.C., Mar. 22, 1907; s. Martin Thomas and Mary (Terrel) G.; m. Jean Emert Duncan, July 31, 1948; children—Caroline, Patricia, Aileen, Chloe; 1 dau. (by previous marriage), Barbara Margaret. B.S., U.S. Mil. Acad., 1929; grad., Inf. Sch., officers course, 1933, Command and Gen. Staff Sch. Parachute Sch. Enlisted as pvt. U. S. Army, 1924; commd. 2d lt. inf., 1929, advanced through grades to lt. gen., 1944; service included World War II in ETO; ret., 1958; chmn. bd. Arthur D. Little, Inc., 1964-77; U.S. ambassador to, France, 1961-62, 62-63. Author: Airborne Warfare, 1947, War and Peace in the Space Age, 1958, France and The Civil War in America, 1962, Crisis Now, 1968, On to Berlin, 1978. Trustee Mus. Fine Arts, Boston. Decorated grand officer Legion of Honor, Croix de Guerre with palm France; D.S.C. with oak leaf cluster; Purple Heart; Silver Star U.S.; Distinguished Service Order Eng.). Home: Winter Park Fla. Died Feb. 23, 1990; buried West Point, N.Y.

GAYLE, ADDISON, English language educator, writer, literary critic; b. Newport News, Va., June 2, 1932; s. Addison and Carrie (Holliman) G. Lectr. CCNY, 1966-69; prof. Baruch Coll. CUNY, 1969-79, Disting. prof., 1980-91; Disting. prof. Grad. Ctr. CUNY, 1990-91. Author: (essays) The Black Aesthetic, 1978, The Black Situation, 1978; (autobiog.) Wayward Child, 1979, (biog.) Richard Wright, 1984; cons. Black Books Bull., Chgo., 1966-91, Our World Communications, N.Y.C., 1986-91. Mem. Writers Guild, PEN. Home: East Orange N.Y. Died Oct. 3, 1991; buried Hampton (Va.) Meml. Gardens.

GEALY, FRED DANIEL, clergyman, religious educator; b. Oil City, Pa., May 13, 1894; s. William Jefferson and Emma Caroline (Baum) G.; m. Mildred Gladys Reader, June 26, 1923; children: William James, Fred Daniel, John Robert. AB, Allegheny Coll., 1916, DD, 1937; STB, Boston U., 1919, PhD, 1929. Frank D. Howard fellow to univs. Basel and Berlin, 1920-21; STM summa cum laude, Union Theol. Sem., N.Y.C., 1929; grad. rsch. U. Chgo. Div. Sch., 1937. Ordained to ministry M.E. Ch., 1917. Pastor M.E. Ch., Townville, Pa., 1921-23; prof. N.T. Aoyama Gaukin, Tokyo, 1923-36; vis. prof. missions, history of religions and N.T. Iliff Sch. Theology, Denver, 1937-39; vis. prof. N.T. Greek Drew Theol. Sem., 1938; vis. prof. polit. and cultural history of Far East U. Denver, 1939; vis. prof. missions and N.T. So. Meth. U., 1939, prof. missions/history of religions, N.T. Greek, ch. music, 1939-52; prof. N.T. Greek and ch. music Perkins Sch. Theology, 1952-60, organizer, dir. Sem. Sionger, 1940-59, book rev. editor Perkins Sch. Theology Jour., 1947-59; prof. N.T. Meth. Theol Sch., Delaware, Ohio, from 1960; vis. prof. missions Garrett Bibl. Inst., 1950. Author: Introduction and Exegesis of the Pastoral Epistles (Vol. XI, Interpreter's Bible), 1955; Let Us Break Bread Together, 1960; editor: The Japan Christian Yearbook, 1935, 36; contbr. articles to religious jours. Dir. Tokyo Oratorio Soc., 1924036; dir. choir, organist Univ. Park Meth. Ch., Dallas, 1939-56; minister music Casa View Meth. Ch., 1957-60. Recipient Faculty Achievement award So. Meth. U. Alumni Assn., 1959. Mem. Soc. Bibl. Lit. and Exegesis, Nat. Assn. Bibl. Instrs. (pres. 1962), AAUP, Dallas Athletic Club, Phi Mu Alpha, Sigma Alpha Epsilon. *

GEE, JAMES GILLIAM, university president; b. Union, S.C., Aug. 20, 1896; s. James Monroe and Bessie (Farrar) G.; m. Cecile Gibbs, Dec. 14, 1922; 1 child, Thomas Gibbs. BS, Clemson (S.C.) A&M Coll., 1917; PhD, Peabody Coll., 1933; postgrad., Cornell U., 1919-20, Harvard U., 1931-32. Assoc. prof. agrl. edn. Sam Houston State Tchrs. Coll., 1920-25, prof. vocat. and ednl. guidance, 1933-37, dean coll. and grad. sch., 1937-46, acting pres., 1940-41, dean, 1947; pres. East Tex. State U., 1947-92. Contbr. articles to profl. jours. With U.S. Army, 1917-19, 41-47. Decorated Bronze Star medal, Army Commendation medal. Mem. Kappa Delta Pi, Phi Delta Kappa. Episcopalian. *

GEEHAN, ROBERT WILLIAM, consulting mining engineer; b. Yakima, Wash., Dec. 12, 1909; s. Michael and Susan (Stratton) G.; m. Iria Alanne, June 11, 1932; children: Roberta (Mrs. Robert Horton), David, Patrick. E.M., U. Minn., 1932; student, Am. U., 1954, U. Colo., 1959. Mining engr. Winston Bros. Co., Helena, Mont., 1932-34, Cripple Creek Mining Co., Folger and Anchorage, Alaska, 1934-39; designing engr. Alaska R.R., Anchorage, 1939-42; with U.S. Bur. Mines, 1942-72; successively mining engr., Nev. and Va., commodity specialist tungsten and molybdenum, Washington, asst. chief ferrous metals and alloys br., asst. chief div. minerals, chief div. mineral tech., Rolla, Mo., 1956-59, chief div. resources, Denver, 1959, regional dir., 1960-63, area dir., then program mgr., 1964-72; then cons. mining engr.; U.S. rep. for tungsten and molybdenum Internat. Materials Conf., Washington, 1952-53; mem. manganese ore com. Am. Standards Assn.-Internat. Standards Orgn. (meetings in), Leningrad, USSR, 1954, 56; cons. tungsten and molybdenum NATO, Paris, 1954; mem. tungsten raw materials panel Nat. Acad. Scis.-NCR, 1958-60; vol. exec. Internat. Exec. Service Corps, Brazil, 1973, El Salvador, 1974, Colombia, 1977. Contbr. articles to profl. jours., bulls. Mem. AIME, Denver Mining Club, Sigma Xi, Tau Beta Pi. Unitarian. Home: Sun City Ariz. Died Mar. 18, 1990; cremated.

GEELAN, PETER BRIAN KENNETH, publisher; b. London, May 28, 1929; arrived in U.S., 1979; s. Michael John and Elsie Doreen (Bath) G.; m. Joan Norris, Apr. 2, 1953; children: Michael Anthony, Jeremy Paul, Christopher Patrick; m. Marjorie Wells, Apr. 20, 1980; 1 child, Jane Lesley. Grad., Kilburn Grammar, London. Advtg. mgr. Ward, Lock & Co., London, 1949-50; sales mgr. Staples Press, London, 1951-57; European mgr. Prentice-Hall Internat., N.Y.C. and London, 1958-60; v.p. European ops. CBS Holt Publishing Group, N.Y.C., London, 1961-70; dir. European ops. Litton Pub. Internat., N.Y.C., 1970; mng. dir. Eurospan Group of Pubs., London, 1971-79, chmn., 1980-92; pres. Peter Geelan, Inc., Las Vegas, 1980-92; chmn. Adamantine Press Ltd., London, 1980-92. Sgt. British Army, 1947-49. Home: Las Vegas Nev. Died Nov. 18, 1992. †

GEISEL, THEODOR SEUSS (DR. SEUSS), author, artist, television producer, publisher; b. Springfield, Mass., Mar. 2, 1904; s. Theodor Robert and Henrietta (Seuss) G.; m. Helen Marion Palmer, Nov. 29, 1927 (dec. Oct. 1967); m. Audrey Stone Dimond, Aug. 6, 1968. Grad., Dartmouth Coll., 1925; postgrad., Lincoln Coll., Oxford (Eng.) U., 1925-26; LHD (hon.), Dartmouth Coll., 1955, Am. Internat. Coll., 1968, Whittier Coll., Lake Forest Coll.; LittD (hon.), John F. Kennedy U.; DFA (hon.), Princeton U., 1985; LittD (hon.), U. Hartford, 1986; LHD (hon.), Brown U., 1987. Began career as humorist, illustrator for publs. including Liberty mags.; advt. illustrator publs. 15 yrs, creator of humorous advt. campaigns for Standard Oil of N.J., including Quick Henry the Flit! series; mural painter, author and illustrator of children's books; editorial cartoonist: PM newspaper, N.Y.C.; now pres., pub., editor-in-chief, Beginner Books, Inc. div. Random House, Inc. Author: If I Ran the Zoo, 1950, Scrambled Eggs Super, 1953, Horton Hears a Who, 1954, On Beyond Zebra, 1955, If I Ran the Circus, 1956, How the Grinch Stole Christmas, 1957, The Cat in the Hat, 1957, The Cat in the Hat Comes Back, 1958, Yertle the Turtle, 1958, Happy Birthday, 1959, One Fish Two Fish Red Fish Blue Fish, 1960, Green Eggs and Ham, 1960, The Sneetches and Other Stories, 1961, Dr. Seuss's Sleep Book, 1962, Hop on Pop, 1963, Dr. Seuss's ABC Book, 1963, Fox in Socks, 1965, I had Trouble in Getting to Solla Sellew, 1965, The Cat in the Hat Songbook, 1967, The Foot Book, 1968, I Can Lick 30 Tigers Today and Other Stories, 1969, My Book About Me, 1969, I Can Draw it Myself, 1970, Mr. Brown Can Moo! Can You?, 1970, And to Think That I Saw It on Mulberry Street, The 500 Hats of Bartholomew Cubbins, The Seven Lady Godivas, The King's Stilts, Horton Hatches the Egg, McElligot's Pool, Thidwick the Big-Hearted Moose, Bartholomew and the Oobleck, The Lorax, Marvin K. Mooney, Will You Please Go Now!, Did I Ever Tell You How Lucky You Are?, The Shape of Me and Other Stuff, There's a Rocket in my Pocket, Great Day for Up, Oh, The Thinks You Can Think!, The Cat's Quizzer, I Can Read With My Eyes Shut, Oh, Say Can You Say?, Hunches in Bunches, You're Only Old Once, I Am Not Going to Get Up Today, Oh, The Places You'll Go! Six By Seuss; motion pictures Hitler Lives (Acad. award documentary short 1946), Design for Death (Acad. award documentary feature 1947), (with Helen Palmer Geisel) Gerald McBoing Boing, (Acad. award cartoon 1951); designer, producer amimated cartoons for TV: How the Grinch Stole Christmas (Peabody award), Horton Hears a Who (Peabody award), The Cat in the Hat, The Lorax, (Critics' award Internat. Animated Festival, Zagreb), Dr. Seuss on the Loose, The Hoober Bloob Highway, Halloween is Grinch Night (Emmy award), Pontoffel Pock Where Are You?, The Butter Battle Book; animated cartoons for TV: The Grinch Grinches the Cat in the Hat (Emmy award). Served to lt. col. Signal Corps and Information and Edn. Div. AUS, 1943-46, ETO; lt. col. Res. Decorated Legion of Merit for edn. and information film work; recipient Laura Ingalls Wilder award ALA, 1980, Spl. Pulitzer Prize, 1984. Home: La Jolla Calif. Died Sept. 24, 1991; cremated.

GEISSINGER, JOHN BLANK, educational administrator, consultant; b. Bethlehem, Pa., Aug. 27, 1906; s. John Benner and Sadie (Blank) G.; m. Amy Helen Findon, June 21, 1928 (dec.); children: Amy Diane, John Brent (dec.); m. Eve C. Nevard, June 25, 1977. A.B., Muhlenberg Coll., 1927; M.A., U. Pa., 1929, Ph.D., 1945. Tchr. Jenkintown (Pa.) High Sch., 1927-30; prin. high sch., supervising prin. Springfield Twp., Bucks County, Pa., 1930-40; supervising prin. North Wales, Pa., 1940-46; supt. schs. Palmyra, N.J., 1946-52, Somerville, N.J., 1952-58, Tenafly, N.J., 1958-76; instr., lectr. Pa. State Coll., 1949, U. Del., 1950-51, Lehigh U., 1952-58; Temple U., 1957-58; cons. Overseas Schs., U.S. Dept. State; exec. sec. Nat. Assn. Sch. Affiliates, Alexandria, Va., 1977; cons. Robert Strauss Assocs., 1978-91; ednl. cons. New Horizons Corp., 1981-91, Better Homes and Gardens, 1984-91. Mem. editorial bd. The Clearing House, 1966-91; contbr. articles to profl. jours. Mem. N.J. Scholarship Commn., 1961-68; adv. bd. Channel 13 Ednl. TV; adv. com. N.J. Tercentary, 1961-64; mem. awards jury Am. Freedom Found., 1972; Trustee Tenafly Pub. Library, 1958-76, pres., 1977-84; trustee Center Urban Edn., N.Y.C.; Englewood (N.J.) Hosp. and Sch. of Nursing Com. Upsala Coll., East Orange, N.J.; N.J. bd. dirs. Save the Children Fedn., People to People Program, 1976-77. Mem. Am. Assn. Sch. Adminstrs. (mem. exec. com. 1965-71, pres. 1971-72), N.J. Sch. Supts. Assn. (pres. 1958-59), Nat. Council Accreditation Tchr. Edn. (evaluation com., appeal bd.), N.J. Sch. Devel. Council (pres. 1957-58), NEA (life, adv. coun. 1988-91), N.J. State Interscholastic Athletic Assn. (mem. exec. com. 1959), Am. Inst. Fgn. Study (adv. bd.), Bergen County Ret. Edn. Assocs. (pres. 1985-87), N.J. Ret. Educators Assn. (pres. from 1987), Academic Decathlon N.J. (dir. 1987-90), Alpha Tau Omega, Phi Delta Kappa, Kappa Phi Kappa. Republican. Lutheran. Clubs: Mason (Tenafly, N.J.) (Shriner), Knickerbocker Country (Tenafly, N.J.). Home: Tenafly N.J. Died Nov. 1, 1991; buried Saucon Mennonite Ch. Cemetery, Coopersburg, Pa.

GEIST, JACOB MYER, chemical engineer; b. Bridgeport, Conn., Feb. 2, 1921; s. David and Anne Rose (Steinschreiber) G.; m. Sandra Levy, Nov. 17, 1972; children by previous marriage—Eric D., Ellen A., David C. B.S. in Chem. Engring, Purdue U., 1940; M.S., Pa. State U., 1942; Ph.D., U. Mich., 1951; ScD (hon.), Israel Inst. Tech., 1987. Instr. Pa. State U., 1943-44; teaching fellow, part-time instr. U. Mich., 1946-48; instr., then asst. prof. MIT, 1950-52; sr. lectr. Technion, 1952-55; with Air Products and Chems., Inc., Allentown, Pa., 1955-82, assoc. dir. research and devel., 1961-63, assoc. chief engr., 1963-69, chief engr., 1969-82, cons., 1982-91; pres. Geist Tech. and Engring. Co., Allentown, 1982-91; lectr., adj. prof. Lehigh U., Bethlehem, Pa., 1960-91; cons. AT&T, Memtek Inc. Author. Served to 2d lt. AUS, 1944-46. Hon. fellow Indian Cryogenic Soc., 1975. Fellow Am. Inst. Chem. Engrs. (award chem. engring. practice 1976), AAAS, mem. Nat. Acad. Engring., Am. Chem. Soc., Internat. Inst. Refrigeration (laureate 1983; v.p.), Cryogenic Engring. Conf. (dir.), Nat. Soc. Profl. Engrs., Sigma Xi, Tau Beta Pi, Phi Lambda Upsilon. Home: Allentown Pa. Died Mar. 22, 1991; buried Allentown.

GELLMAN, JACOB See GILFORD, JACK

GELTZ, CHARLES GOTTLIEB, forester, educator; b. McKeesport, Pa., Feb. 21, 1896; s. William and Mary (Ditter) G.; m. Mildred Harry Julin, Aug. 18, 1930; children: Charles Gottlieb, Betty Anne; stepchildren: Helen Julin (Mrs. Ralph L. Bailey), Jane Julin (Mrs. William T. Keenen, Jr.). BS, Pa. State Forest Sch., 1924; MSF, U. Calif., 1927; postgrad., U. Fla. Registered forester, Ga., Fla. Forester Ala. Commn. of Forestry, 1924-25; instr. forestry, registrar N.Y. State Forest Ranger Sch., Coll. Forestry, SUNY, Wanakena, 1925-26; rsch. asst. div. forestry U. Calif., 1926-27; jr. forester U.S. Forest Svc., 1927-29; instr. forestry State Forest Sch., Pa. U., 1929-30; asst. prof. Purdue U., 1930-34, assoc. prof., 1934-46; dir. Purdue Forestry Summer Camp, 1930-42; prof. silviculture Sch. Forestry, U. Fla., from 1946; operator Charles G. Geltz Assocs., forestry and conservation cons.; cons. Forest Recreation and Family Camping, Fla. Family Camping Assns.; outdoor recreation cons. to dir. resources programs Dept. Interior; mem. Fla. Gov.'s Resource Use Edn. Commn. Neighborhood commr. Boy Scouts Am. Served with 13th U.S. Cav., Mex. Border Campaign and World War I, to 1919, U.S. Cav. Res., 1922-42; with Adj. Gen.'s Corps, 1942-46; maj. U.S. Army. Res. ret. Recipient unit citation award and plaque, commendation ribbon; Silver Beaver award Boy Scouts Am. Fellow Am. Geog. Soc.; mem. Soc. Am. Foresters (historian of Southeastern sect.), Am. Forestry Assn., Fla. Forestry Assn., Fla. C. of C. (forestry div.), Forest Farmers Assn., Fla. Forestry Coun. (sec.) Ret. Officers Assn., Scabbard and Blade, Masons (32 deg.), Shriners, Xi Sigma Phi, Phi Sigma, Phi Delta Kappa, Kappa Delta Pi, Alpha Phi Omega (hon.). Episcopalian (lay reader). *

GEMMILL, ROBERT ANDREW, lawyer; b. Marion, Ind., Sept. 12, 1911; s. Willard B. and Florence (Jones) G.; m. Lottie Wine Lugar, Apr. 25, 1970 (dec.); m. Joan Lea McTurnan, June 27, 1987 (dec.). A.B., Ind. U., 1932, J.D., 1934. Bar: Ind. bar 1934. Since practiced in Marion; sr. partner firm Gemmill Browne Torrance Spitzer & Herriman and predecessors, 1935-74; of counsel Browne, Spitzer, Herriman, Browne, Stephenson and Holderead, 1975-87; ret., 1987; Mem. bd. law examiners Ind. Supreme Ct., 1956-60, pres., 1958-59; mem. Gov. Ind. Probate Study Commn., 1956-64; vis. com.

Ind. U. Sch. Law, 1964-74; bd. dirs. Ind. Bar Found., 1961-75, pres., 1965-66. Served to lt. comdr. USNR, 1942-45; comdr. Res. (ret. 1967). Decorated Navy Commendation medal. Fellow Am. Bar Found., Ind. Bar Found. (charter); mem. ABA (life) (ho. dels. 1962-64), Ind. State Bar Assn. (bd. mgrs. 1954-56, bd. mgrs. 61-65, bd. mgrs. 69-70, pres. 1963-64, chmn. ho. of dels. 1969-70), Grant County Bar Assn. (pres. 1951-52), Fifth Dist. Bar Assn. (pres. 1935-36), Indpls. Bar Assn. (life), Nat. Conf. Bar Pres. (council 1964-65), Am. Judicature Soc. (bd. dirs. 1967-71), Am. Legion, Delta Upsilon, Phi Delta Phi. Republican. Episcopalian. Clubs: Mason (Marion) (33 deg., Shriner), Mecca (Marion), Meshingomesia Country (Marion); Columbia (Indpls.). Home: Marion Ind. Deceased. †

GEORGE, HAROLD LEE, career officer, business executive; b. Somerville, Mass., July 19, 1893; s. Horace and Susan Elizabeth (Lee) G.; m. Violette A. Houghlan, May 26, 1929; children: Mary Suzanne, Sidney Regina, Loretta Adrian. Student, George Washington U., 1914-15; LLB, Nat. U., 1917; grad., Air Corps Tactical Sch., 1932, Army Command & Gen. Staff Sch., 1937. Dr. Aero Scis., Pa. Mil. Coll., 1943; rated command pilot, combat and aircraft observer. Commd. 2d lt. USAF, 1917, advanced through grades to lt. gen., 1944, comdg. officer 2d Bombadier Group, 1939, dir. dept. tactics and strategy Air Corps Tactical Sch., 1932-35, asst. chief of staff for war plans, 1941, comdg. gen. Air Transport Command, 1942-46, ret., 1946; chmn. bd., pres. Peruvian Airways, Lima, 1947-48; v.p. Hughes Tool Co.; gen. mgr. Hughes Aircraft Co., Culver City, Calif., 1948-53; sr. v.p. Ramo-Wooldridge Corp., L.A. Mem. City Coun., mayor Beverly Hills, Calif. Decorated DFC, DSM, Air medal, Legion of Merit, Order of So. Cross; knight comdr. Brit. Empire; Order of the Banner (China); comdr. Legion of Honor (France); DFC (Peru). Mem. Order of Daedalians, Masons, Army and Navy Club (Washington), Nacional Club (Lima), Jonathan Club (L.A.), L.A. Country Club, Ft. Worth Club, Omicron Delta. *

GERBER, JOHN JAY, public relations executive; b. Morton, Ill., Nov. 26, 1914; s. John E. and Anna (Mosiman) G.; m. Gladys Eittreim, Sept. 20, 1941; children—Jay T., Julia Ann, Stephen E. A.B., U. Utah, 1935; student, Northwestern, 1937-39. Salesman Keystone Steel & Wire Co., Peoria, Ill., 1935-37; with pub. relations dept. Northwestern U., Evanston, Ill., 1937-42, 46-52, dir. new students, sec. Century Fund, 1947, v.p. pub. relations, 1949-52; partner Gonser-Gerber-Tinker-Stuhr, Chgo., 1952-80, cons., from 1980; spl. agt. FBI, 1942-46; former vice chmn., dir. Bank of Westmont, Ill.; former chmn. Bank of Naperville, Ill.; past dir. Bank Lisle, Ill.; former vice chmn. bd., dir. 1st Security Bank Glen Ellyn, Ill., Bank of Lockport, Ill.; former chmn. 1st Security Bank of Fox Valley, Aurora, Ill.; past alumni regent Northwestern U. Author: (with Thomas A. Gonser) Gonser and Gerber on College Development, 1961. Recipient Alumni Service award Northwestern U., 1961. Mem. Phi Beta Kappa, Beta Gamma Sigma. Republican. Home: Davis Calif. Died July 7, 1991; buried Davis Cemetery.

GERBER, THOMAS WILLIAM, newspaper editor; b. Portland, Oreg., May 2, 1921; s. Thomas W. and Mary Anne (Smith) G.; m. Gail L. Graham, Jan. 20, 1951 (div. Jan. 1970); children: Cheryl Ann, Linda Lee; m. Electra Bilmazes, Dec. 26, 1971. A.B., Dartmouth, 1948. Reporter U.P.I., Boston, 1948-51; mgr. Providence bur. U.P.I., 1952-53; rewriteman, spl. assignment reporter Boston Herald and Traveler, 1953-56; chief Boston Herald and Traveler (Washington bur.), 1956-61; gen. mgr. Concord (N.H.) Monitor, 1961-67, editor, asst. pub., 1967-83; dir., sec. Monitor Pub. Co., 1962-78; dir. TeleCable, Inc., Concord, 1968-73, Concord br. Bank of N.H., from 1962. Mem. adv. com. N.H. Tech. Inst., 1966-70; chmn. air quality com. N.H. Environmental Council, 1970; mem. Citizens Task Force, 1969, N.H. Jud. Council, 1972-74; vice chmn. N.H. Council for Humanities, 1972-74; Bd. dirs. Concord YMCA, 1962-71, N.H. Council World Affairs, N.H. Council Better Schs., 1965-72, Concord Hosp., 1962-73; adv. bd. Dartmouth Pub. Affairs Center, from 1974; pres. bd. Bishop Brady High Sch., Concord, 1969-73; vice chmn. N.H. Free Press-Fair Trail Com., 1976-85; mem. Pulitzer Prize Jury, 1978-79. Served with USAAF, 1942-45; Served with USAF, 1951-52. Decorated Air medal with two oak leaf clusters; recipient Heywood Broun award Am. Newspaper Guild, 1955, Dartmouth Alumni award, 1988. Mem. New Eng. Newspaper Assn., Am. Soc. Newspaper Editors, New Eng. Soc. Newspaper Editors (pres. 1967), Sigma Delta Chi (Yankee Quill award 1973). Home: Concord N.H. Died Feb. 22, 1991; buried Concord, N.H.

GERMESHAUSEN, KENNETH JOSEPH, management consultant; b. Woodland, Calif., May 12, 1907; s. William and Florence (Bomberg) G.; m. Pauline Seltzer, 1934; 1 child, Nancy. Student, Poly. Coll. Engring., 1927-29; BS, MIT, 1931. Rsch. assoc. elec. engring. MIT, 1932-90, staff mem. radiation lab., 1941-45; ptnr. Edgerton, Germeshausen & Grier (now EG&G, Inc.), 1934-58; v.p., treas. Edgerton, Germeshausen & Grier (now EG&G, Inc.), Bedford, Mass., 1947-54, pres., 1954-65, chmn. bd. dirs., dir. rsch., 1965-72, dir., cons., 1972-90. Inventor strobotraon and hydrogen-thyraton; patentee in field. Mem. corp. Boston Mus. Sci.; mem. coun. for arts, mem. corp. MIT; incorporator Scis. Scis., Found.; trustee New Eng. Aquarium. Recipient Holly medal ASME, 1973. Fellow IEEE, Am. Acad. Arts and Scis.; mem. Am. Mgmt. Assn., Boston Rsch. Dirs. Club, Soc. Profl. Engrs., Alumni Assn. MIT (v.p.) Western Conservation Com. Home: Weston Mass. Died Aug. 16, 1990.

GERSTENMAIER, JOHN HERBERT, rubber company executive; b. St. Paul, Aug. 24, 1916; s. Walter and Alma (Lindenberg) G.; m. Lois Rolfing, Dec. 28, 1939; children: John Herbert, Jan Lee McClennan. B.M.E., U. Minn., 1938; M.Indsl. Mgmt., MIT, 1952. With Goodyear Tire & Rubber Co., Akron, Ohio, 1938-63, 67—; plant mgr. Goodyear Tire & Rubber Co., Logan, Ohio, 1963; exec. v.p., dir. Goodyear Tire & Rubber Co., Akron, 1971-74, pres., 1974-78, chief operating officer, from 1974, vice chmn., from 1978; pres. Motor Wheel Corp., Lansing, Mich., 1964-67. Mem. Soc. Automotive Engrs., Sigma Nu. Lutheran. Club: Portage Country (Akron). Home: Menlo Park Calif. Died July 8, 1991; buried St. Paul.

GERVASI, FRANK, artist, painter; b. Palermo, Italy, Oct. 5, 1895; brought to U.S., 1908, naturalized, 1919; s. Angelo and Elizabeth (Bottone) G.; m. Leonilda Isabella Sansone, Dec. 23, 1933. Student, N.Y. Sch. Indsl. Design, Art Students League of N.Y. Works exhibited nat. exhbns., Nat. Acad. Design, Allied Artists Am., Audubon Artists, Am. Watercolor Soc., Albany Inst. History and Art, Balt. Watercolor Club, So. Vt. Artists; works in collections Brueckner Mus., Albion Mich., also pvt. collections. Served with U.S. Army, World War I. Recipient bronze medal for painting Allied Artists Am., 1st prize for painting Salmagundi Club, Hudson Valley Art Assn., Balt. Watercolor Club. Mem. Allied Artists Am. (pres.), Audubon Artists (v.p.), Am. Watercolor Soc., NAD, Art Students Legue N.Y., Balt. Club, Watercolor Club, Salmagundi Club (N.Y.C.). *

GETZ, GEORGE FULMER, JR., holding company executive; b. Chgo., Jan. 4, 1908; s. George Fulmer and Susan Daniel (Rankin) G.; m. Olive Cox Atwater, Jan. 17, 1933 (dec. Sept. 22, 1980); children: George Fulmer, III (dec.), Bert Atwater. Pres. Eureka Coal & Dock Co., 1935-45; chmn. bd., chief exec. officer Globe Corp.; chmn. bd. Getz Coal Co., 1939-48, pres., 1948-53; dir. Chgo. Nat. League Ball Club, 1940-72; mem. exec. com., dir. A.T. & S.F. Ry., 1955-80, Sante Fe Industries, Inc., 1968-80; dir. Upper Ave. Nat. Bank, Chgo., 1936-74, Chgo. Transit Authority, 1945-47. Mem. United Republican Fund Ill.; mem. citizens bd. U. Chgo., 1956-71; bd. dirs. Jr. Achievement Chgo., 1939-92, v.p., 1947-49; v.p. Met. Jr. Achievement, 1942-44; mem. Pres.'s Commn. White House Fellowships, 1982, 83; bd. dirs. Getz Found.; dir. emeritus Ind. U. Found.; pres., dir. Arthur R. Metz Found.; hon. trustee Chgo. Zool. Soc.; past v.p. finance, treas. Nat. Safety Council; pres. Geneva Lake Water Safety Com., Inc., 1949-54, bd. dirs., 1949-69, hon. dir., 1969-92; mem. Ill. Com. Crusade for Freedom, Inc., 1957, 58; pres., dir. Nat. Hist. Fire Found., Globe Found.; bd. dirs. Ariz. Zool. Soc., 1966-81, 84-88, emeritus, 1988; trustee emeritus Am. Grad. Sch. Internat. Mgmt., vice chmn. bd., 1976-78; mem. organizing com., mem. Chgo. Rotary Found., 1936-45; mem. Nat. Rep. Fin. Com., 1976-92; trustee Grand Cen. Art Galleries, N.Y.C., 1982-89 (mem. emeritus) ; emeritus bd. dirs. Scottsdale Meml. Health Found., 1984-88. Mem. Chgo. Assn. Commerce and Industry (com. mem. govtl. affairs coun.), Phoenix 40 (emeritus), Chgo. Club, Tavern Club, Chgo. Yacht Club, Econ. Club (Chgo.), Los Rancheros Visitadores (Santa Barbara, Calif.), Paradise Valley Country Club (Ariz.), Circumnavigators, Valley Field Riding and Polo (Ariz.), Balboa Club (Mazatlan, Mex.). Episcopalian. Home: Paradise Valley Ariz. Died Nov. 9, 1992. †

GETZ, STAN, saxophonist; b. Phila., Feb. 2, 1927; s. Alexander and Goldie G.; m. Monica Silfveskiold, 1956; children: Steven, David, Beverly, Pamela, Nicholas. Mem. bands led by Jack Teagarden, Stan Kenton, Jimmy Dorsey, Benny Goodman, Woody Herman; leader own group, from 1949; film appearances: The Benny Goodman Story, 1955, Get Yourself a College Girl, 1964, The Hanged Man, 1964, Mickey One, 1965; recordings include: Early Autumn, 1948, Jazz At The Opera House (live), 1957, Jazz Samba, 1962, Big Band Bossa Nova, 1962, Getz/Gilberto, 1964 (Grammy award), Mickey One, 1965, Sweet Rain, 1967, Stan Getz Gold, 1978, Anniversary, 1987 (Grammy award), numerous others; artist-in-residence Stanford U., from 1986. Recipient Grammy award for rec. Desafinado 1962, The Girl From Ipanema, 1964; numerous Down Beat, Metronome and Playboy Jazz polls and mag. awards; inducted into Down Beat Hall of Fame, 1986. Home: Malibu Calif. Died June 6, 1991.

GIAMATTI, A. BARTLETT, sports executive, former university president; b. Boston, Apr. 4, 1938; married; 3 children. BA, Yale U., 1960, PhD in Comparative Lit., 1964; LLD, Princeton U., 1978, Harvard U., 1978, Notre Dame U., 1982, Coll. of New Rochelle, 1982, Dartmouth Coll., 1982; LittD, Am. Internat. Coll., 1979, Jewish Theol. Sem. Am., 1980, Atlanta U., 1981; HHD, Oberlin Coll., 1983. Instr. Italian and comparative lit. Princeton (N.J.) U., 1964-65, asst. prof., 1965-66; asst. prof. English Yale U., New Haven, 1966-69, assoc. prof. English and comparative lit., 1969-71, prof. English and comparative lit., 1971-86, master Ezra Stiles Coll., 1970-72, Frederick Clifford Ford prof. English and comparative lit., 1976-77, John Hay Whitney prof. English and comparative lit., 1977-78, pres. univ., 1978-86; pres. Nat. League, N.Y.C., 1986-89, also treas.; commr. Major League Baseball, 1989; vis. prof. comparative lit. NYU, N.Y.C., summer 1966; mem. faculty Bread Loaf Sch. English, summers 1972-74. Author: The Earthly Paradise and the Renaissance Epic, 1966, Play of Double Senses: Spenser's Faerie Queene, 1975, History of Scroll and Key, 1942-1972, 1978, The University and the Public Interest, 1981, Exile and Change in Renaissance Literature, 1984; editor: (with others) The Songs of Bernart de Ventadorn, 1962, rev. edit., 1965, Ludovico Ariosto's Orlando Furioso, 1968, A, Variorum Commentary On the Poems of John Milton, Western Literature, 3 vols, 1971, 6 vols., 1972, Dante in America: The First Two Centuries, 1983, Take Time for Paradise: Americans and Thier Games, 1989. Trustee The Ford Found., Mt. Holyoke Coll.; bd. dirs. Baxter Travenol Labs. Inc., Coca-Cola Enterprises Inc. Decorated comdr. Order of Merit Italian Republic, 1979, comdr. Cross of Fed. Order Merit, Republic Germany, 1985, comdr. l'Ordre Nat. des Arts et des Lettres, Republic France, 1985; J.S. Guggenheim fellow, 1969-70; recipient Outstanding Contribution to Higher Edn. award Brown U., 1985, Liberty Bell award New Haven County Bar Assn., 1985; Americanism award Anti-Defamation League of B'nai B'rith, 1986, Ellis Island Medal of Honor, 1986, Leonardo da Vinci award, 1986. Fellow Am. Acad. Arts and Scis.; mem. Am. Philos. Soc., Council on Fgn. Relations. Home: Edgartown Mass. Died Sept. 1, 1989.

GIANNINI, GABRIEL MARIA, industrialist, physicist; b. Rome, Oct. 21, 1905; came to U.S., 1930, naturalized, 1938; s. Torquato and Maria (Caccetti) G.; m. Luise Casazza, July 18, 1931; children: Maria Laura Giannini Madigan, Valerio; m. Olga Harrington, Sept. 27, 1964; 1 child, Gabriella-Caria. D Physics, U. Rome, 1929. Acoustics researcher RCA, Curtis Inst. Music., Phila., 1931-35; acoustics and telephony researcher Transducer Corp., N.Y.C., 1936-40; mem. engring. mgmt. staff Lockheed Aircraft Co., 1941-44; founder Giannini Controls Corp., Pasadena, Calif., 1945, pres., 1945-57; pres. Giannini Inst., 1957-89; assoc. Calif. Inst. Tech. Fellow AIAA (assoc.), Royal Aero. Soc.; mem. IEEE (sr.), ASME, Societa Italiana Di Fisica, Instrument Soc. Am., Am. Phys. Soc., Am. Optical Soc., Acoustical Soc., Soc. Automotive Engrs., Assn. Computing Machinery, Solar Energy Soc., Marine Tech. Soc., Brit. Interplanetary Soc., U.S. Naval Inst., Calif. Club (L.A.), Brook Club (N.Y.C.), Cruising Am. Club, Sewanhaka Corinthian Yacht Club (Oyster Bay, N.Y.), Circolo della Vela Club (Rome), Parkinson Transatlantic Trophy Club. Home: Indio Calif. Died Sept. 20, 1989.

GIBBS, DELBRIDGE LINDLEY, lawyer; b. Jacksonville, Fla., Jan. 13, 1917; s. Elbridge Lindley and Myrtle Josephine (King) G.; m. Jane Phillips Reese, Nov. 23, 1947; children: Elizabeth (Mrs. Michael V. Milton), Joanne, Delbridge Lindley. B.S. in Bus. Adminstrn, U. Fla., 1939, LL.B., 1940. Bar: Fla. 1940. Practice in Jacksonville, 1946-92; partner firm Marks, Gray, Conroy & Gibbs, 1957-92; mem. 1st Appellate dist. Nominating Commn. State of Fla., 1973-76; co-chmn. Nat. Conf. Reps. Am. Bar Assn.-AMA, 1973-75, mem., 1978-82. Trustee U. Fla. Law Center Assn., 1973-80. Served with AUS, 1941-46; col. Res. ret. Fellow Am. Bar Found., Am. Coll. Trial Lawyers; mem. Am. Coll. Real Estate Lawyers, ABA (ho. dels. 1964-68), Fed. Bar Assn., Jacksonville Bar Assn. (pres. 1956), Fla. Bar (pres. 1963-64), Duval County Legal Aid Assn. (pres. 1952), Am. Judicature Soc., Judge Adv. Assn. Clubs: Rotarian. (Jacksonville), River, Timuquana Country (Jacksonville); Ponte Vedra (Ponte Vedra Beach, Fla.). Home: Jacksonville Fla. Died July 11, 1992. †

GIBBS, FEDERIC A., neurology educator, electroencephalography consultant; b. Balt., Feb. 9, 1903; s. Rufus McQueen and Cornelia (Andrews) G.; m. Erna Leonhardt (dec. 1987); children: Erich L., Frederic A. BA, Yale U., 1925; MD, Harvard U., 1929; PhD (hon.), U. Montpellier, France, 1965; DS (hon.), U. Ill., 1977. Instr. neurology Harvard Med. Sch., Boston, 1937-44; assoc. prof. psychiatry U. Ill., Chgo., 1944-51, prof. neurology, 1951-73, prof. emeritus, 1973-92; cons. to various hosps. Author: Atlas of Electroencephalography, 1941, 2d edit., 1950, Vol. I Normal Controls, 1950, Vol. II Epilepsy, 1952, Vol. III Neurological and Psychiatric Disorders, 1964, Vol. IV Normal and Abnormal Infants from Birth, 1978, Epilepsy Handbook, 1959, rev. edit., 1972, Molecules and Mental Health, 1959, Electroencephalagraphy, 1967; chief editor Clin. EEG, 1970—; contbr. 232 articles to profl. jours. Recipient Mead Johnson award Am. Acad. Pediatrics, 1938, St. Valentine's award Govt. of Denmark, 1971, Archibald I. Hoyne award Chgo. Pediatric Soc., 1979; Lasker award (with others), 1951; Brain Rsch. Found award (with Erna L. Gibbs), 1983. Mem. AMA, Ill. Med. Soc., Chgo. Med. Soc., Am. Neurol. Assn., Am. Acad. Neurology, Am. Acad. Cerebral Palsy, Am. Electroencephalography Soc. (pres. 1949), Am. Med. Electroenephalographic Assn. (pres. 1965-67, 78-79), Am. Physiology Soc., Chgo. Neurol. Soc., Am. Epilepsy Soc., Assn. for Rsch. in Nervous and Mental Disease,

Norwegian Acad. Sci. (hon.). Home: Valparaiso Ind. Died Oct. 18, 1992. †

GIBSON, JAMES, lawyer, judge; b. Salem, N.Y., Jan. 21, 1902; s. James and Caroline H. (MacCartee) G.; m. Judith Angell, June 11, 1929 (dec. Mar. 1956); children: Caroline (Mrs. Paul Fordham Nugent, Jr.), Judith (Mrs. E.J. Conklin). A.B., Princeton U., 1923; LL.B., Albany Law Sch., 1926; LL.D., Union Coll., 1970. Bar: N.Y. 1926. Asso. firm Rogers & Sawyer, Hudson Falls, N.Y., 1926-29; ptnr. firm Sawyer & Gibson, Hudson Falls, 1929-36; pvt. practice, 1936-53; dist. atty. Washington County, N.Y., 1936-53; justice N.Y. State Supreme Ct., 1953-69, designated appellate div., 1956, presiding justice appellate div., 1964-69, judge, 1973-79; judge Ct. Appeals N.Y., Albany, 1969-78; judge spl. assignments Ct. Appeals N.Y., 1978-84; sole practice law Glens Falls, N.Y., 1979-85; Mem. adminstrv. bd. Jud. Conf. State of N.Y., 1964-69. Trustee Albany Law Sch., Union U. Served with AUS, 1943-45, ETO. Mem. ABA, N.Y. State Bar Assn. (chmn. jud. sect. 1970-71, mem. exec com. 1970-71), Washington County Bar Assn. Clubs: Ft. Orange (Albany); Princeton (N.Y.C.). Home: Hudson Falls N.Y. Died May 29, 1992.

GIBSON, JOSEPH EDWARD, education consultant; b. West Point, Miss., Feb. 7, 1893; s. Robert Clayton and Temple (Alexander) G.; m. Eulalie Williford, Dec. 1, 1916; children: Joe Allen, William Edward; m. 2d, Elise M. Holman, Apr. 17, 1965. AB, U. Miss., 1913; AM, Columbia U., 1927. Tchr., prin. Miss. high schs., 1913-20; supt. schs. McComb, Miss., 1920-36; prof. edn. Tulane U., 1936-41, 46-47, dir. devel., 1949-53, dir. pre-admissions, 1953-58; dir. higher edn. for La., 1941-46; pres. Northwestern State Coll., La., 1947-49, Gulf Park Coll., Gulfport, Miss., 1958-61; chmn. Miss. Com. for Reorgn. of Adminstrn. Structure of Higher Edn., 1932; chmn. La. Com. for Tchr. Edn. and Certification, 1942; dir. Miss. Study Higher Edn., 1945, cons., 1954; cons. S.C. Survey Higher Edn., 1945; dir. Assoc. Cons. in Edn., from 1961, editor, from 1954; exec. cons. Edward G. Schlieder Ednl. Found. Author: (with Lida Meriweather) The Little Citizen, 1937, Safety for the Little Citizen, 1939; editor Miss. Ednl. Advance, 1925-36. Served with AUS, 1918. G.E.B. scholar, 1926-27, Columbia U. scholar, 1935-36. Mem. NEA, Miss. Edn. Assn. (v.p. 1932-33, pres. 1933-34), Nat. Soc. Study Edn., Masons, Shriners, Rotary. Democrat. Presbyterian (elder). *

GIBSON, ROBERT FISHER, bishop; b. Williamsport, Pa., Nov. 22, 1906; s. Robert F. and Harriet (McKenney) G.; m. Alison Morice, June 1, 1935; children Robert Fisher III, John V.M., Margaret Alison, Peter McKenney. AB, Trinity Coll., Hartford, Conn., 1928; AM, U. Va., 1932; BD, Va. Theol. Sem., Alexandria, 1940, DD, 1948. Ordained deacon and priest Protestant Episcopal Ch., 1940. Various bus. and teaching positions, Balt., N.Y.C., The Phillipines, Dutch East Indies, 1928-38; assoc. prof. ch. history Va. Theol. Sem., 1940-46; liaison officer Protestant Episcopal Ch. in Mex., 1946-49; dean U. South Sch. Theology, Sewanee, Tenn., 1947-49; suffragan bishop Diocese of Va., Protestant Episcopal Ch., Richmond, 1949-54, bishop coadjutor, 1954-61, diocesan bishop, 1961-74; chmn. Joint Commn. on Ecumenical Rels.; former mem. Ho. of Bishops. Home: Richmond Va. Died Sept. 21, 1990; buried Va. Theol. Sem., Alexandria, Va.

GIBSON, WILLIAM WILLARD, lawyer; b. Collin County, Tex., Aug. 15, 1897; s. Isaac Harrison and Florence (Boles) G.; m. Genelle Works, May 28, 1925; children: Mary Nell (Mrs. F. Blair Reeves), Joan (Mrs. Mark A. Taylor), William Willard. Student, West Tex. State Coll., 1915-18; LLB, U. Tex., 1922. Bar: Tex. 1922. Practiced Amarillo, Tex.; mem. firm Turner, Culton & Gibson and predecessor, 1923-30, Gibson & Sutton, 1930-40, Gibson, Ochsner, Harlan, Kinney & Morris, from 1940; rsch. fellow Southwestern Legal Found. Fellow Am. Bar Found.; mem. ABA, Amarillo Bar Assn. (pres.), Am. Counsel Assn. (pres. 1957-59), Internat. Assn. Ins. Counsel, State Bar Tex., Hole in One Club, Lions (pres.), Knife and Fork Club (pres.) (Amarillo). Methodist (trustee, steward). *

GIERSBACH, WALTER C., church official; b. Green Bay, Wis., Sept. 28, 1897; s. William and Eliese (Ochsenfeld) G.; m. Marion Fisk, June 28, 1927; children: Charles W., Walter Fisk, William Hastings. AB, Northland Coll., Ashland, Wis., 1924; DD, Northland Coll., 1942; student, Oberlin Grad. Sch. Theology, 1929-30; BD, Chgo. Theol. Sem., 1930. PhD, U. Chgo. Div. Sch., 1933; LL.D., Pacific U., Forest Grove, Oreg., 1963. Printer Milw., 1912-18; instr. South High Sch., Youngstown, Ohio; dir. religions edn. Cleve., 1927-29; pastor Millard Congl. Ch., Chgo., 1933-36; supt. Ill. Congl. Christian Chs., 1937-40; pres. Pacific U., Forest Grove, 1941-54; sec. missions coun. Congl. Christian Chs., 1954-62; sec. wills, trusts, estate planning, stewardship planning United Ch. of Christ, 1962-63; Eastern rep. Pacific U., from 1963; pres. Oreg. Coun. Chs.; coord. Protestant Coun. Chs., Cherry Hill, N.J., from 1964. Chmn. Washington County Rep. Cen. Com., 1952-54; Oreg. state senator, 1953-54; mem. exec. and fin. coms. Camden County Boy Scouts Am. Mem. Masons, Royal Rosarians (Portland). *

GIGLIOTTI, FRANK BRUNO, clergyman; b. Italy, Oct. 15, 1896; came to U.S., 1900; s. Carmen and Mary (Guzzo-Pane) G.; m. Mabelle Esther Pirazzini, 1922; children: Agide Pirazzini, Mary, John David. Student, Bibl. Sem., N.Y.; postgrad., U. Rome, 1925-28; student, Monet-Mario Coll., Rome. Lic. minister Presbyn. ch., 1913, ordained, 1921. Pastor Italian Presbyn. Ch., Schenectady, 1921-24, Terry (Mont.) Community Ch., 1928-30, First Presbyn. Ch., Baker, Oreg., 1930-33; moderator Presbytery of Yellowstone, Baker, 1929-30, Presbytery of Grande-Ronde, 103-=33; pastor counselor Oreg. Soc. Christian Endeavor, 1930-32; ret. from ministry, 1933; chaplain Calif. Assembly, 1934-35; mem. Calif. State Bd. Social Welfare; chief cons. Italian sect. OSS, 1941-45; chmn. com. on social welfare and relief Tax Reduction Conf., 1936; mem. Calif. Relief Commn., 1937-39; chmn. San Diego County com. Gov.'s Com. for Employment of Handicapped, 1956; pres. San Diego County Taxpayers Assn., 1953-55, 59, 62; mem. Nat. Adv. Rehab. Coun., U.S. Office of Rehab., 1941. Author: Religious Liberty in Italy. Chmn. Citizens Com. Morality and Integrity in Govt., Calif., 1948; pres. San Diego Race Rels. Soc., 1958-61; mem. commn. on religious and civil rights Nat. Assn. Evangel. Chs. U.S.; del. Internat. Assn. Evangelicals, 1950; active in community and vets. orgns.; organizer Am. Legion in Italy, 1925; nat. comdr. Regular Vets. Assn. U.S., 1951-52; del. Rep. State Conv., Mont., 1928; pres. Calif. Civic Fedn., 1938-39. Served as pvt. AUS, World War I, AEF. Decorated Croix de Guerre with palm (France); recipient Alfaro medal Alfaro Found., 1950. Mem. Men's Rep. League of San Diego (pres. 1959), Sons of Columbus (hon. nat. pres.), Order of DeMolay (life mem. Internat. Supreme Coun.), Masons (33 deg., hon. grand master for life, Grand Orient of Italy, mem. emeritus Supreme Coun., Scottish Rite of Italy; recipient nine gold medals for work done in Italy for Masonry). *

GILBERT, HELEN HOMANS, college trustee; b. Quincy, Mass., Oct. 29, 1913; d. Robert and Abigail (Adams) Homans; m. Carl J. Gilbert, June 27, 1936 (dec.); 1 child, Thomas T. AB, Radcliffe Coll., 1936. Acting pres. Radcliffe Coll., 1964. Mem. bd. overseers Harvard U., 1970-76, pres., 1975-76; mem. governing bd. Harvard Corp.; trustee Radcliffe Coll., 1950-77, chmn., 1955-72; vol. Schlesinger Libr., Radcliffe Coll., chmn. adv. com., 1981-86. Home: Dover Mass. Died Sept. 26, 1989; buried Highland Cemetery, Dover, Mass.

GILFORD, JACK (JACOB GELLMAN), actor, comedian; b. N.Y.C., July 25, 1908; s. Aaron and Sophie (Jackness) G.; m. Madeline Lee Lederman, Apr. 6, 1949; children: Joseph Edward, Lisa, Sam. Student, pub. schs., Bklyn.; Hon. doctorate, Niagara U., 1989. Began career as vaudeville comedian, 1934, toured 1934-39, appeared with Milton Berle Revue, 1935-39; Broadway debut in Meet the People, 1940; vaudeville and stage show comedian touring U.S. 1941-50, with USO in PTO, 1945; film debut in Hey Rookie, 1944, Reckless Age, 1944, other films include Main Street to Broadway, 1953, A Funny Thing Happened on the Way to the Forum, 1965, Enter Laughing, 1966, Who's Minding the Mint?, 1967, The Incident, 1967, Catch 22, 1969, Save the Tiger, 1972, Harry and Walter Go to New York, 1976, Cocoon I, 1985, Cocoon II, 1988; TV films include Happy, 1983, Hostage Flight, 1985; appeared as Frosch in Die Fledermaus, Met. Opera, 1950, 58-59, 62-63, 66-67, on tour 1951-52; appeared on radio Philip Morris Show, 1947; TV appearances include Arrow Show, 1948, Gary Moore Show, 1950, Milton Berle Show, 1951, Jack Carson Show, 1951, Frank Sinatra Show, 1951, The World of Sholem Aleichem, 1960, Cowboy and the Tiger, 1963, Once Upon a Mattress, 1964, Wholly Moses, 1979, Cheaper to Keep Her, 1979, Caveman, 1980, The Very Special Jack Gilford Special, CBS Cable, Happy, 1983, Hostage Flight, 1985; appeared on stage as Bontche Schweig in The World of Sholem Aleichem, 1953, 81, other stage shows include Alive and Kicking, 1950, Passion of Gross, 1955, Once Over Lightly, 1955, Diary of Anne Frank, 1955, Romanoff and Juliet, 1957, Drink to Me Only, 1958, Once Upon a Mattress, 1959, The Tenth Man, 1959, The Policeman, 1961, A Funny Thing Happened on the Way to the Forum, 1962, Cabaret, 1966, Three Men on a Horse, 1969, No No Nanette, 1971, The Sunshine Boys, 1972, Sly Fox, 1976, The Supporting Cast, 1981; star TV series Apple Pie, 1978; other TV appearances The Duck Factory, Taxi, The Golden Girls; appeared in Cracker Jack commls. Recipient numerous Emmy and Cleo awards; nominee 2 Tony awards, Acad. award; recipient Arnold Weissberger Lifetime Achievement award Hall of Fame, N.Y., 1990. Home: New York N.Y. Died June 4, 1990; buried Mt. Hebron Cemetery, N.Y.

GILL, ERNEST CLARK, insurance executive; b. Kingston, Ont., Can., Apr. 5, 1903; s. William and Mary (Spankie) G.; m. Mercedes Rae, Oct. 26, 1929; 1 child, Mary Byers. BA, Queen's U., 1923, LLD (hon.), 1957. Joined Can. Life Assurance Co., 1923, asst. actuary, 1927-30, asst. treas., 1930-38, treas., 1938-39, asst. gen. mgr. and treas., 1939-46, gen. mgr., 1946-47, v.p., gen. mgr., 1947-51, pres., 1951-64, vice chmn. bd., 1964-74; v.p. Canadian Imperial Bank of Commerce, 1962-71; Chmn. Com. Inquiry into Unemployment Ins. Act, 1961-62. Chmn. investment adv. com. Presbyn. Ch. in Can. Recipient Gold medal Queen's U., 1923. Fellow Canadian Inst. Actuaries, Soc. Actuaries, Am. Life Conv. (past mem. exec. com. Chgo., v.p. Ont.); mem. Toronto Club, Granite Club, Eastbourne Club, York Club. Presbyterian. Home: Toronto, Canada Died Jan. 21, 1992.

GILL, STANLEY JENSEN, chemist, educator; b. Salt Lake City, Aug. 21, 1929; s. Stanley Hewitt and Frances (Jensen) G.; m. Jane C. Pittenger, June 7, 1952; children: Elizabeth J., Stanley C. Student, Occidental Coll., 1947; AB magna cum laude, Harvard U., 1951; PhD in Chemistry, U. Ill., 1954. Research and teaching asst. U. Ill., 1951-53; research assoc. Cornell U., 1954; faculty U. Colo., Boulder, 1956-91; prof. chemistry U. Colo., 1964-91; cons. NIH, 1966-69; vis. prof. U. Rome, 1986. Served with AUS, 1954-56. Recipient Sr. U.S. Scientist award Alexander von Humboldt Found., 1990. Mem. Am., Brit. chem. socs., Sigma Xi, Phi Lambda Upsilon, Alpha Chi Sigma. Home: Boulder Colo. Died June 25, 1991. †

GILLAM, CLIFFORD RIGGS, hotel executive; b. Langhorne, Pa., May 23, 1897; s. William H. and Rachel (Kirk) G.; m. Cornelia Miller Stabler, Dec. 31, 1921; children: Clifford Riggs, Eleanor G. (dec.). AB in Mech. Engring., Swarthmore Coll., 1920. Sec.-treas., gen. mgr. Sharples Milker Co., West Chester, Pa., 1920-25; sec. Sharples Co., Phila., 1925-27; with Buck Hill Falls Co. (Pa.), 1927-92, sec., 1929-39, dir., 1939-92, gen. mgr., 1943-61, pres., 1949-64, chmn. bd., 1965-92; pres., dir. Buck Hill Water Co., 1949-92. Nat. bd. YMCA; county chmn. war fund campaigns ARC; gen. chmn. bldg. campaign Monroe County Gen. Hosp.; pres. Barrett Welfare Fund, 1941-51; active Monroe County Community Chest, 1942-43, 62; trustee Camp Weygadt Boy Scout Reservation. With Air Corps, USN, 1918. Recipient Rush award; named Pa. Ambassador in Residence. Mem. Am. Hotel Assn. (dir. 1955-56, v.p. 1959, chmn. rsch. com. 1953-55, chmn. allied membership 1946-62), Pa. Hotels Assn. (pres. 1954), Am. Standards Assn. (chmn. instl. textile standards), Rotary, Midday Club (Phila.), Delta Upsilon, Sigma Tau, Sigma Eta Alpha. Soc. of Friends. *

GILLARD, PETER MCCANN, librarian; b. Jamaica, N.Y., Sept. 13, 1941; s. William A. and Katherine (McCann) G.; m. Rose Marie Luchini, Sept. 12, 1964; children: Laura Katherine, Anne Christine, Marguerite, Peter Jerome. B.A., St. John's U., 1963, M.A. in Am. History, 1965, M.S.L.S., 1967. Librarian Queen's Borough Pub. Library, Jamaica, N.Y., 1965-68; br. librarian The Smithtown (N.Y.) Library, 1968-79, dir., 1979-88. Pres. Bellaire Civic Assn., N.Y., 1975-77. Mem. Suffolk County Library Assn. (pres. 1979), N.Y. Library Assn. (exhibits com. chmn. 1981-85), ALA. Republican. Roman Catholic. Lodge: Rotary (pres. 1973-74). Home: Smithtown N.Y. Died Jan. 6, 1988; buried Holy Sepulchre Cemetery, Coram, N.Y.

GILLENSON, LEWIS WILLIAM, publishing company executive, author; b. Bklyn., Feb. 18, 1918; s. Sol and Nellie (Marder) G.; m. Bernice Zaconick, Feb. 3, 1946 (div. 1982); children: Wendy Fay, Joshua R., Amy Jo; m. Rochelle Clayman, 1982. BA, NYU, 1939, postgrad. in edn., 1940. Assoc. editor Look Mag., 1946-52; writer Am. Mag., Harper's Bazaar, Sports Life, McCall's, Redbook, Esquire, Woman's Home Companion, Family Circle, others; mng. editor Cosmopolitan, 1952-54; editor-in-chief Coronet, 1955-61; editor, pub. Esquire Books, 1961-66; v.p. editorial Grosset & Dunlap, Inc., N.Y.C., 1966-72; pres. T.Y. Crowell Pub. Co., N.Y.C., 1972-92, Funk & Wagnalls Pub. Co., Ramsey, N.J., 1972-92; pres., pub. Everest House Pub., N.Y.C., 1978-81; pub. Quest Mag., N.Y.C., 1979-81; pres., pub. Dodd, Mead & Co., N.Y.C., 1982-92; prof. Columbia Sch. Journalism, N.Y.C., 1969-92. Author: Billy Graham, The Man and His Message: Fabulous Yesterday, 1961, Billy Graham and Seven Who Were Saved, 1967; editor and producer: Pursuit of Equality; contbr. articles to Saturday Rev., Good Housekeeping. Served to maj. AUS, 1943-46. Decorated Bronze Star medal; recipient Freedom Found. lit. award, 1950. Club: Friars. Home: New York N.Y. Died Sept. 4, 1992. †

GILLESPIE, DAVID ELLIS, distributing company executive; b. Chgo., Dec. 18, 1933; s. David Ellis and Helen Leota (Andrews) G. B.A., Wayne State U., 1955; postgrad., U. Tex. Market research mgr. Gen. Steel Wares, London, Ont., Can., 1955-58; market research mgr. KLM Royal Dutch Airlines, Montreal, Que., 1958-60; media dir. Comcore Communications Ltd., Toronto, Ont., 1960-61, v.p., 1961-62, exec. v.p., 1963-65, pres., chief exec. officer, 1965-73; chief exec. officer Core-Mark Distbrs. Inc. (formerly Glaser Bros.), L.A., from 1974, also chmn.; chmn., chief exec. officer Core Mark Internat., Inc., Vancouver, from 1983; dir. Core Mark Midcontinent Inc., Denver, CM Products Inc., Los Angeles, Bingo Cash'n Carry Inc., Los Angeles, SJL Products Inc., Los Angeles, Davlin Bus. Systems, Inc., Toronto, ASI Telesystems, Los Angeles, Sandy's Fast & Fresh Inc., Los Angeles. Bd. dirs. Pritiken Research Found., Santa Monica, Calif., Vancouver Symphony Orch. Mem. Nat. Assn. Tobacco Distbrs. (dir.), Calif. Assn. Tobacco and Candy Distbrs. (dir.). Republican. Episcopalian. Club: Ontario (Toronto). Home: Richmond, B.C. Can. Deceased.

GILLESPIE, DIZZY (JOHN BIRKS GILLESPIE), musician; b. Cheraw, S.C., Oct. 21, 1917; s. James and Lottie (Poe) G.; m. Lorraine Willis, May 9, 1940. Student, Laurinburg (N.C.) Inst., 1933-35; MusD (hon.), Rutgers U., 1970; hon. degree, New Sch. for Social Rsch., 1987. Jazz trumpet player, 1930-93; played with Frankie Fairfax Band Phila., 1935-37; Rep. culture tour to Iran, Pakistan, Lebanon, Syria, Turkey, Yugoslavia, Greece and S.Am. U.S. Dept. State, 1956-58. Toured with Teddy Hill Band, 1937-39, Elgar Hayes, Cab Calloway, Earl Hines, Billy Eckstine, others, 1939-44; led band, 1945-50, combo, 1950-56; leader quintet, 1958-93; toured Argentina, 1961; appearances at Jazz Workshop, San Francisco, Monterey (Calif.) Jazz Festival, Juan-les-Pins (France) Festival, 1962; toured in: Giants of Jazz, Europe, Japan, U.S., 1971-72, Musical Life of Charlie Parker, Eastern and Western Europe, 1974; appeared in: (concert) Tribute to Dizzy Gillespie, Avery Fisher Hall, N.Y.C., 1975; many other tours, festivals, night club, TV appearances; author: To Be or Not...to Bop, 1979; composer: Night in Tunisia, Blue 'n Boogie, Groovin' High, others; recent recs. include Trumpet Kings at Montreaux Jazz Festival, 1975, Trumpet Kings Meet Joe Turner, Giants of Jazz, Something Old, Something New, Party, Bahiana, At Village Vanguard, 1969, My Way, 1969, Greatest Jazz Concert Ever, Oscar Peterson and Dizzy Gillespie, Carter, Gillespie, Inc., Havin' a Good Time in Paris, (with Lalo Schifrin) Free Ride, New Faces, Closer to the Source, (with Max Roach) Max and Dizzy—Paris 1989; appeared in documentary film A Night in Havana: Dizzy Gillespie in Cuba, 1989. Recipient 1st prize for soundtrack Berlin Film Festival, 1962, award Downbeat Critics Poll, 1971-75, Handel medallion, 1972, Grammy awards, 1975, 80, Nat. Music award, 1976, Nat. Medal of Arts, 1990, Duke ASCAP award, 1990; named Musician of Yr., Inst. High Fidelity, 1975; honored by S.C. Legislature, 1976. Mem. Baha'i Faith. Home: Englewood N.J. Died Jan. 6, 1993. †

GILLESPIE, KINGSLEY, publisher; b. Stamford, Conn., Aug. 15, 1895; s. Richard H. and Sarah E. (Scofield) G.; m. Doris Kenyon, June 2, 1928; children: Kenyon, Joan (dec.). SB in Chem. Engring., MIT, 1917. Registered profl. engr., Conn. Tech. mgr., dir. rsch. Stamford Rubber Supply Co., 1919-41; pub. Stamford Advocate, 1942-92; treas. Gillespie Bros., Inc., 1942-92, v.p., 1922-49, pres., 1949-92; pres., exec. dir. Western Conn. Broadcasting Co., 1946-92; v.p. Stamford Rubber Supply Co., 1925-52, pres. 1952-92; v.p., dir. Fidelity Title & Trust Co.; pub. Greenwich Time, 1958-92; pres., treas. Fairview Ent., Inc., 1958-92, Greenwich Pub. Co., 1958-92; dir. Stamford Savs. Bank, Hartford Elec. Light Co. Sec. The Ferguson Libr., 1942-92, Town Zoning Comm., 1937-49; mem. Conn. Aeronautics Commn., 1960-92. Mem. Am. Inst. Chem. Engrs., Am. Chem. Soc., Rotary, Stamford Yacht Club, Old Field Club. Republican. Presbyterian. *

GILLIAM, JAMES FRANKLIN, historian, educator; b. Seattle, Mar. 14, 1915; s. Clinton Cailey and Hazel Elvira (Carr) G.; m. Elizabeth Holzworth, Sept. 6, 1941; children: Elizabeth, John Franklin, Anne. B.A., San Jose State Coll., 1935; M.A., Stanford U., 1936; Ph.D., Yale U., 1940. Instr. classics Yale U., 1940-41, 45-47; asst. prof. Wells Coll., 1947-49; from asst. prof. to prof. history and classics U. Iowa, 1949-61; prof. history U. Oreg., 1961-62; prof. Greek and Latin Columbia U., N.Y.C., 1962-65, curator Papyri, 1970-81, adj. prof., from 1970; vis. lectr. Princeton U., 1972-75, mem. Inst. Advanced Study, 1958-59, 63-64, prof. Sch. Hist. Studies, from 1965. Co-author: The Excavations at Dura-Europos, V, The Parchments and Papyri, 1959. Served to capt. AUS, 1941-45. Decorated Bronze Star; Guggenheim fellow, 1955-56; Sather lectr. U. Calif.-Berkeley, 1979. Mem. Am. Philol. Assn., Archaeol. Inst. Am., Soc. Promotion Roman Studies, German Archaeology Inst. (corr.), Internat. Assn. Papyrologists, Am. Soc. Papyrologists (pres. 1971-73). Home: Princeton N.J. Died Mar. 16, 1990; buried Princeton Cemetery.

GILMAN, HERBERT, department store executive; b. Hartford, Conn., Dec. 25, 1924; s. Nathan and Pauline (Lapuk) G.; m. Evelyn S. Simon, June 20, 1948; children: Barbara R., Randy A. BSEE, U. Conn., 1949. Project engr. Sperry Gyroscope Co., 1950-54; sales engr. Hewlett Packard Co., Palo Alto, Calif., 1954-58; exec. v.p. Ames Dept. Stores Inc., Rocky Hill, Conn., 1958-73; pres. Ames Dept. Stores Inc, Rocky Hills, Conn., 1976-82; chmn. bd., chief exec. officer Ames Dept. Stores Inc., Rocky Hill, Conn., 1982-87, also bd. dirs. Trustee Mt. Sinai Hosp., Hartford; bd. dirs Hartford Jewish Fedn. Served with U.S. Army, 1943-45. Named to Discount Hall of Fame, 1989. Mem. Nat. Mass Retailers Inst. (officer, bd. dirs. from 1970). Jewish. Home: West Hartford Conn. Died July 12, 1990.

GIMMA, JOSEPH ANTHONY, investment banker; b. Bari, Italy, Apr. 12, 1907; s. Giovanni Batiste and Maria (DiBenedetto) G.; came to U.S., 1913, naturalized, 1932; grad. high sch.; m. Licia Albanese, Apr. 7, 1945; 1 son, Joseph Anthony. Trader, Herrick, Berg & Co., N.Y.C., 1924-37, B. M-P Murphy & Co., N.Y.C., 1937-43; with Hornblower & Weeks-Hemphill, Noyes, N.Y.C., from 1942, ptnr., 1950, sr. mng. dir. Shearson-Loeb Rhoades (formerly Loeb Rhoades, Hornblower), 1978-79, sr. v.p. investments, 1979-90 (name Shearson/Am. Express, 1981); gov. Am. Stock Exch., 1952-58; dir. Lionel Corp. Mem. Cardinal's Com. of Laity Catholic Charities, from 1950; mem. N.Y. State Racing Commn., chmn., 1965-73; mem. joint legis. task force to study and evaluate pari-mutual racing and breeding industry; mem. Commn. on Rev. Nat. Policy Toward Gambling; chmn. N.Y. Republican County Com., 1962-63; mem. adv. bd. Marymount Coll., N.Y.C., 1967; appointee N.Y.C. liaison for econ. devel., from 1981; trustee Nat. Mus. Racing Saratoga, Loyola Sch., N.Y.C.; bd. dirs., pres. Bagby Found., Mus. Arts, N.Y.C.; bd. dirs. Eymard Found., St. Peter's Coll., Rome; pres. Puccini Found., N.Y.C. Decorated knight Grand Cross Holy Sepulchre. Mem. Nat. Hunts Racing Assn., Turf and Field, U.S. Navy League, Knights of Malta. Club: Met. Opera. Died May 31, 1990. Home: New York N.Y.

GINADER, GEORGE HALL, business executive; b. Buffalo, Apr. 5, 1933; s. George Edward and Meredith (Hall) G. B.A., Allegheny Coll., 1955; M.S. in Library Sci, Drexel U., 1964. Asst. Buyer Lord & Taylor, N.Y.C., 1957-59; job analyst Ins. Co. N.Am., Phila., 1959-60; asst. buyer John Wanamaker, Phila., 1960-61; acting curator Automobile Reference Collection, Free Library Phila., 1961-63; librarian N.Y. C. of C., N.Y.C., 1964-66; chief librarian N.Y. Stock Exchange, N.Y.C., 1966-67; exec. dir. Spl. Libraries Assn., N.Y.C., 1967-70, chmn. bus. and fin. div., 1974-75, pres., 1981-82; mgr. research library Morgan Stanley & Co., N.Y.C., 1970-79; cons. to spl. libraries and info. centers, 1979-82; dir. ops. Internat. Creative Mgmt., N.Y.C., 1982-86; pres. Info/Tech Planning Service, Inc., Cranbury, N.J., 1986. Mem. N.Y. Geneal. and Biog. Soc., Internat. Platform Assn., Am. Records Mgmt. Assn. (treas. N.Y. chpt. 1975-76), Adminstrv. Mgmt. Soc., Nat. Microfilm Assn., Nat. Trust for Historic Preservation, N.Y. C. of C., S.A.R., Phi Delta Theta (asst. sec. chpt. 1967-68, pres. N.Y. alumni club 1970). Republican. Episcopalian. Home: Cranbury N.J. Deceased.

GINSBERG, HAROLD LOUIS, religion educator; b. Montreal, Que., Can., Dec. 6, 1903; came to U.S., 1936, naturalized, 1942; s. Mendel and Golda Anna Levinson G.; m. Anne Gelrud, Nov. 7, 1937 dec. . BA, U. London, 1927, PhD, 1930. Auditor Hebrew U., Jerusalem, 1928-29; instr. Bible Jewish Theol. Sem. Am., N.Y.C., 1936-40, Sabato Morais prof. Bibl. history and lit., 1941-90; vis. prof. Hebrew U., Jerusalem, 1957, 62, U. Pa., 1957-58, 68-69, Yale U., spring 1967, Dropsie U., 1971-72, Columbia U., 1972-73, Inst. for Advanced Studies, Hebrew U. Jerusalem, 1979-80. Co-editor Jewish Publ. Soc. Bible Transl., 1956-62, editor-in-chief, 1962-77, mem. publ. com., 1958—; hon. resident mem. Acad. Hebrew Lang., Jerusalem; mem. coun. World Union of Jewish Studies; author: The Ugarit Texts, 1936, The Legend of King Keret, 1946, Studies in Daniel, 1948, Studies in Koheleth, 195, Commentary on Koheleth, 1961, 2d edit., 1977, The Israelian Heritage of Judaism, 1982; contbg. author: Ancient Near Eastern Texts Relating to the Old Testament, 195, 55, 69. Fellow Am. Acad. Jewish Rsch. v.p. ; mem. Soc. Bibl. Lit. and Exegesis hon. pres. , Am. Oriental Soc., Israel Exploration Soc., Am. Schs. Oriental Rsch. assoc. . Home: New York N.Y. Died Oct. 4, 1990.

GINSBURG, LUCIEN See GAINSBOURG, SERGE

GINSBURGH, ROBERT NEVILLE, financial consultant, retired air force officer; b. Ft. Sill, Okla., Nov. 19, 1923; s. A. Robert and Elsie (Pinney) G.; m. Nancy Brand, Dec. 28, 1948 (div. Feb. 1958); children: Robert Brand, Charles Lee; m. Gail H. Whitehead Winslow, Apr. 4, 1959; children: Carolyn, Anne; stepchildren: Alan F. Winslow III, William C. Winslow. Grad., Phillips Acad., Andover, 1940; B.S., U.S. Mil. Acad., 1944; M.P.A., Harvard, 1947, M.A., 1948; Ph.D., 1949; postgrad., Field Arty. Sch., 1944, Air Tactical Sch., 1950, Air Command and Staff Coll., 1953, Indsl. Coll., 1960, Air War Coll., 1961, Nat. War Coll., 1963. Commd. 2d lt. F.A., 1944; advanced through grades to maj. gen USAF, 1971; asst. prof. social scis. U.S. Mil. Acad., 1948-51; with Air Force Liaison, 1951-55, Allied Air Forces So. Europe, Naples, 1955-58, Air Proving Ground Center, 1958; pub. affairs Dept. Def., 1959; asst. exec. air force chief of staff, 1959-62; research fellow Council Fgn. Relations, 1963-64; with Policy Planning Council, State Dept., 1964-66; staff group Office of Chmn. JCS; sr. staff mem. Nat. Security Council, 1966-69; comdr. Aerospace Studies Inst., Air U., Maxwell AFB, Ala., 1969-71; chief Air Force History, 1971-72; dir. Air Force Info., 1972-74; dep. dir. joint staff Orgn. Joint Chiefs Staff, 1974-75; editor in chief Strategic Rev., 1975-76, Neville Assos., from 1977; bd. dirs. Air Force Hist. Found. Author: US Military Strategy in the Sixties, 1965, US Military Strategy in the Seventies, 1970, The Nixon Doctrine and Military Strategy, 1971; editor: Principles of Insurance, 1949-50; contbr. to Economics of National Security, 1950, also articles in profl. jours. Bd. regents Coll. for Fin. Planning. Decorated D.S.M., Silver Star, Legion of Merit with oak leaf cluster, Purple Heart Joint Services, Purple Heart Air Force, Army commendation medals. Mem. Coun. Fgn. Rels., Lotos Club, Internat. Club, Rehoboth Bay Sailing Assn., Naples Bath and Tennis Club. Home: Bethesda Md. Deceased. †

GINZBURG, NATALIA LEVI, author; b. Palermo, Italy, 1916; d. Giuseppe Verdi; m. Leone Ginzburg, 1938 (dec.); children: Carlo, Andrea, Alessandra; m. Gabriele Baldini (dec. 1969). Author: La Strada che va in Città, 1942, E'stato cosi, 1947, Tutti i nostri ieri, 1947, Valentino, 1957, Le Piccole Virtu, 1962, Lessico Famigliare, 1963, L"inserzione, 1968, Caro Michele, 1973, Vita Immaginaria, 1974, Famiglia, 1977, La Famiglia Manzoni, 1983, La città e la casa, 1985, Serena Cruz, Or Trus Justice, 1990. Mem. Italian Communist Party, from 1983; elected rep. Ind. Left party Parliament of Italy, 1983. Recipient Tempo award, 1947, Veillon award, 1952, Viareggio award, 1957, Strega prize, 1963, Marzotto prize, 1968, Milan Club degli Editori award, 1969, Bagutto award, 1984, Ernest Hemingway prize, 1985. Home: Rome Italy Died Oct. 7, 1991; buried Vereus, Rome.

GIPE, FLORENCE MEDA, nurse, university dean; b. York County, Pa., Sept. 10, 1896; d. John Wesley and Mary Ellen (Hake) Gipe. Grad., Sch. Nursing York Hosp.; BS, Cath. U. Am., 1937; MS, U. Pa., 1940; EdD, U. Md., 1952. Instr. York Hosp. Sch. Nursing, 1921, Providence Hosp., Cath. U. Am., Washington, 1921-28; dir. York Hosp., 1928-35; dir. nursing edn. Reading Hosp., Albright Coll., 1935-40; dir. sch. nursing Md. Gen. Hosp., Balt., 1940-46; dir. nursing and nursing edn. U. Hosp., Balt., 1946-52; dean, prof. Sch. Nursing, U. Md., 1952-92. Chmn. So. Regional Edn. Bd. Com. Nursing Edn., 1956-58; chmn. collegiate div. Md. State League Nursing, 1955-58. Mem. Nat. League Nursing, Am. Heart Assn. (chmn. nursing edn.), Phi Kappa Phi, Pi Lambda Theta, Phi Delta Gamma. *

GIRAULT, THOMAS LACKEY, investment trust executive; b. Lincoln County, Miss., Jan. 28, 1893; s. John M. and Emily (Smith) G.; m. Willa Stevens, Dec. 28, 1915 (dec. 1951); children: Emily Stevens, John Stevens; m. 2d Louise Mimma, June 30, 1953 (dec. 1959); m. Lucille Tully, Feb. 8, 1962; stepchildren: Cullen Tully, Avaril Ross Wedemeyer. Student, U. Miss., 1913-15; BA, U. Denver, 1917, MA, 1918; DHL, Colo. State Coll., 1958. Supt. schs. Long Beach, Miss., 1912-14; prof. history Wayland Coll., 1915-17; tchr. history and govt. Sterling (Colo.) High Sch., 1918-24, Denver Pub. Schs., 1924-34; dep. collector U.S. IRS, 1934-36; chief field div. for Colo. Treasury Dept., 1937-53; pub. rels. officer Colo. Edn. Assn., 1953-57; owner, mgr. pvt. investment trust, 1953-92; dir. Model Credit Corp. Contbr. articles to profl. jours. Trustee State Colls. in Colo., 1947-63, chmn. bd., 1949-63; bd. assocs. U. Denver, 1947-59; bd. commrs. Denver Housing Authority, 1954-59, chmn., 1958-59; bd. dirs. Nat. Housing Conf., 1958-60; mem. adv. coun. Pub. Housing, 1958-60; chmn. Denver area Woodrow Wilson Centennial Commn., 1956; pres. Denver Fed. Bus. Assn., 1941-42; mem. Colo. Fulbright Commn., 1950-92, chmn., 1956-57; del. Western Interstate Commn. Higher Edn., 1957; treas. UN Com. for Colo., 1953-92. Recipient spl. citation Sec. Treasury, 1941, Spl. Alumni award U. Denver, 1953, spl. award ARC, 1956, Thomas L. Girault Residence Hall established at Adams State Coll., 1958. Mem. NEA, Colo. Edn. Assn., Colo. Schoolmasters, Masons (32 degree), Phi Delta Kappa, Omicron Delta Kappa. Democrat. Methodist. *

GIUSTI, GEORGE, artist, designer, sculptor; b. Milano, Italy; came to U.S., 1938, naturalized, 1946; s. Emil and Edmeda (Giusti) Wuermli; m. Margot Louise Reiche Joachimsthal, July 11, 1936. Student, Reale Accademia Di Belle Arti Di Brera, Milano, 1923-27. Free-lance artist, cons. to industry, editorial and advt. designer, ffrom 1931, exhibited at maj. capitals of world; represented in collections: Time Mag., Mus. Modern Art, N.Y.C., Smithsonian Instn., Boehringer-Ingelheim, Japan Barmens Assn., also pvt. collections. Author: The Human Heart, 1961. Recipient Golden medals art dirs. clubs Chgo., 1951, 56, Phila., 1954, 58, N.Y.C., 1955, Milw., 1959, others; Golden T. Square award; named Art Dir. of Year, 1958, inducted to Hall of Fame, 1979. Mem. Am. Inst. Graphic Arts, Alliance Graphique Internationale, Internat. Center for Typog. Arts, Art Dirs. Club (N.Y.C.). Home: West Redding Conn. Deceased. †

GLADNEY, WILLIAM BECKETT, banker; b. Natenez, Miss., Jan. 30, 1896; s. Wallace Gardner and Mary Alice (Power) G.; m. Ruth A. Washburn, Sept. 20, 1924; children: William W., Charles Wallace. AB magna cum laude, Wake Forest Coll., 1918. Bookkeeper Ouachita Nat. Bank, Monroe, La., 1917, asst. cashier, 1921-28; teller, gen. bookkeeper Comml. Nat. Bank, Shreveport, La., summer 1918; asst. cashier Citizens Nat. Bank (now Ouachita Nat. Bank), Monroe, 1918-21; v.p. Bastrop (La.) Bank & Trust Co. (now Bastrop Nat. Bank), 1928-38; exec. v.p. Fidelity Bank & Trust Co., Baton Rouge, 1938-44, pres., 1944-54, dir., 1938-92, vice chmn., 1954-60, vice chmn. bd., chmn., exec. com., 1960-92. Mem. State Adv. Bd. La., 1937-91; chmn. 2d War Loan Dr., co-chmn. 3d Dr.; parish chmn. Baton Rouge Relief Fund, 1939; pres. Baton Rouge Community Chest, 1945; v.p. United Givers Fund of Baton Rouge; chmn. Bastrop chpt. ARC. With U.S. Army, 1918. Recipient Silver Svc. award La. Bankers, 1944. Mem. Am. Bankers Assn. (ins. and protective com. 1936, chmn. 1937-44, exec. coun. 1935-36, 44-47, mem. fed. legis., coun. and state legis. coun., exec. com., nat. bank div. 1946-49, chmn. exec. com. 1947, pres. 1949-50, treas. 1951-53), First Regional Clearing House Assn. La. (organizer 1927, pres. 1928), La. Bankers

Assn. (exec. com. 1932-35, pres. 1935-36), Bastrop C. of C. (past pres.), Baton Rouge C. of C. (past pres.), Baton Rouge Port Devel. Assn., Elks, Masons, Kiwanis, others. Methodist. *

GLADSTONE, MILTON, publishing company executive; b. N.Y.C., Nov. 11, 1914; s. Max H. and Rose (Ungar) G.; m. Selma D. Lowitz, Sept. 12, 1942; children: Robert, William, Margaret, Thomas. BS, CCNY, 1936; MS, Columbia U., 1937; ME, U. Vt., 1942. Founder Arco Pub. Co. Inc., N.Y.C., 1937, chief exec. officer, 1937-81; co-founder Investers Planning Corp., N.Y.C. Author: Gardner Encyclopedia, 1947. Active fundraising Anti-Defamation League, 1947-55; mem. devel. fund Andover Acad.; trustee Hackley Sch. Served with Signal Corps, U.S. Army, 1941-46, ETO. Mem. Am. Booksellers Assn., Am. Book Pubs. Assn., Book Pub. Coun. Home: Palm Beach Fla. Died Feb. 21, 1992.

GLANVILLE, JAMES WILLIAM, chemical company executive, investment banking executive; b. Cooper, Tex., July 19, 1923; s. James L. and Bertha (Bates) G.; m. Nancy Hart, Nov. 26, 1949; children: John, Charles, Thomas, Robert. BSChemE, Rice U., 1944; MSChemE, Calif. Inst. Tech., 1949; profl. degree chem. engring., 1948. With Humble Oil & Refining Co., Houston, 1945-59; assoc. Lehman Bros., New Haven, 1959-63, ptnr., 1963-79; gen. ptnr. Lazard Freres & Co., N.Y.C., from 1978; bd. dirs. Halliburton Co., Internat. Minerals and Chem. Corp., Sterling Chem. Co. Trustee Calif. Ints. Tech.; treas., v.p. fin. affairs Rice U., from 1986. Mem. Nat. Petroleum Coun., Soc. Petroleum Engrs, River Oaks C. of C., Castle Pines C. of C., N.Y. Yacht Club, Wee Burn Country Club, Blind Brook Club, Indian Creek Country Club, Economics Club, Brook Club. Home: Darien Conn. Died Sept. 16, 1992. †

GLANVILLE-HICKS, PEGGY, composer, music critic; b. Melbourne, Australia, Dec. 29, 1912; came to U.S., 1940, naturalized, 1948; d. Ernest and Myrtle (Bailey) Glanville-H.; m. Stanley Bate, 1938. Scholarship, Royal Coll. Music, London, 1932-36, Ecole Normale, Paris; pvt. student, Egon Wellesz, Nadia Boulanger. Co-founder Internat. Music Fund to assist European artists; music critic N.Y. Herald Tribune, 1948-58; Dir. Composers Forum, prod. concert series for young composers, Donnell Libr. Auditorium and Columbia U., 1950-60; with, Chandler Cowles; prod. Lou Harrison's opera Rapnuzel, under name of The Artists Co., N.Y.C., 1959; with Yehudi Menuhin, master of ceremonies for concerts of Indian music Mus. Modern Art, 1955; commd. to compose ballet score Masque of the Wild Man for 1st Spoletto (Italy) Festival, 1958, ballet Saul for CBS-TV, 1959, full-length opera Nausicaa, Athens Festival, Greece, 1961. Composer operas: Transposed Heads, 1954, The Glittering Gate, 1959, Navsikaa, 1961, Sappho; composer ballet scores for CBS-TV, film scores for UN; contbr. articles to popular mags., profl. periodicals. Grantee Ford Found., Rockefeller Found., Fulbright Found.; recipient award Am. Acad. Arts and Letters, 1953; Gugenheim fellow, 1956-57, 57-58. Mem. League Composers, Contemporary Music Soc., Jr. Coun. of Mus. Modern Art. Home: Sydney Australia Died June 25, 1990.

GLASSTONE, SAMUEL, consultant; b. London, May 3, 1897; came to U.S. 1939, naturalized 1944.; m. Violette F. Collingwood, July, 1929. BSc, U. London, 1916, MSc, 1920, PhD, 1922, DSc, 1926. Lectr. in phys. chemistry U. London, 1919-21, Univ. Coll. of S.W. (Eng.), 1921-28, U. Sheffield (Eng.), 1929-39; rsch. assoc. Princeton (N.J.) U., 1939-41; sci. editor Princeton U. Press, 1941-42; prof. chemistry U. Okla., 1942-43, Boston Coll., 1947-48; cons. AEC, 1948-92; cons. Armed Forces Spl. Weapons Project, 1950-51, Los Alamos (N.Mex.) Sci. Lab., 1952-92. Author numerous books, latest of which are: Elements of Physical Chemistry, 1946, rev. 1960, Thermodynamics for Chemists, 1947, Sourcebook on Atomic Energy, 1950, rev. edit. 1953, Elements of Nuclear Reactor theory (with Edlund), 1952, Principles of Nuclear Reactor Engineering, 1955, Controlled Thermonuclear Reactions (with R.H. Lowberg), 1960, (with A. Sesonake) Nuclear Reactor Engineering, 1963, Sourcebook on the Space Sciences, 1965; co-editor: A Tretise on Physical Chemistry, 3d edit. 1942. Recipient Worcester Reed Warner medal ASME, 1959. Mem. Chem. Soc. London, Sigma Xi. *

GLAVIANO, VINCENT VALENTINO, educator, physiologist; b. Frankford, N.Y., July 19, 1920; s. Salvatore and Josephine (Manzo) G.; m. Eleanor Spargimino, July 18, 1943; children: Joan J., Vincent S. B.S., CCNY, 1950; Ph.D., Columbia U., 1954; M.D., Chgo. Med. Sch., 1982. Faculty Columbia U., 1951-53; fellow Columbia, 1954-56; instr. Hunter Coll., N.Y.C., 1952-54; asst. prof. physiology U. Ill. Coll. Medicine, Chgo., 1956-60; assoc. prof. physiology Loyola U. Sch. Medicine, Chgo., 1960-64; prof. Loyola U. Sch. Medicine, 1964-70; prof., chmn. Chgo. Med. Sch., 1970-85; dir. Biotech. Research Assocs., Glen Ellyn, Ill., from 1986; cons. Cook County Hosp. Cardiopulmonary Lab., Abbot Labs.; cons./physicist in therapeutic radiobiology Hines (Ill.) VA Hosp. Editorial bd.: Circulatory Shock, 1975-85. Postdoctoral research fellow N.Y. Heart Assn., 1954-56; travel awards Nat. Acad. Scis., 1962, 65, 67, 77. Fellow AAAS, N.Y. Acad. Scis.; mem. Am. Physiol. Soc., Soc. Exptl. Biology and Medicine, Am., Chgo. heart assns., Harvey Soc., Am. Soc. Pharmacology and Exptl. therapeutics, Internat. Soc. Heart Research, Sigma Xi, Alpha Omega Alpha. Home: Glen Ellyn Ill. Deceased. †

GLINES, VICTOR LEROY, government official; b. Noble County, Okla., Dec. 29, 1895; s. James Edward and Emma Jane (McGovern) G.; m. Joy Erma Davis, Jan. 31, 1933; children: Barbara Louise Glines Standly, Stanley Davis. Student, Okla. U., 1915-17. Dist. supt. Continental Oil Co., Ponca City, Okla., 1930-31; gen. mgr. Sheridan Oil Refining Co., Wyo., 1931-32; dist. supt. Union Gas Co., Independence, Kans., 1932-34; gen. mgr., ptnr. Peoples Appliances Co., Pittsburg, Kans., 1934-36; dist. sales mgr. Servel, Inc., Evansville, Ind., 1936-40; econ. advisor, gen. hdqrs. Supreme Comdr. Allied Powers, Japan, 1950-51; dir. tech. and govt. svcs. div. Korea Civil Assistance Command, UN Civil Affairs Command, 1951-54, dep. dir., 1954-55; pub. adminstrv. advisor Office Econ. Coord. for Korea, 1955-57; UN Command sec.-gen. Combined Econ. Bd., Office Econ. Coord. for Korea, 1957-58; provincial dir. U.S. Ops. Mission, Shiraz, Iran, 1958-92. Col. U.S. Army, 1942-50. Mem. Iran-Am. Soc., Masons. *

GLOVER, CONRAD NATHAN, religious worker; b. Prattsville, Ark., Oct. 27, 1895; s. Robert Washington and Mary Ann (Young) G.; m. Gladys Rushing, May 3, 1928; 1 child, Mary Beth. ThB, Missionary Bapt. Coll., 1925, DD (hon.), 1931; DCM, BD, Missionary Bapt. Inst., 1941. Rural letter carrier Sheridan, Ark. Contbr. articles to profl. jours. Sec. bd. trustees Missionary Bapt. Coll.; moderator Pine Bluff Missionary Bapt. Assn.; moderator Ark. State Bapt. Assn. of Chs.; co-founder, v.p. Missionary Bapt. Inst., Little Rock, lectr. homiletics, systematic theology and ch. history, 1934-92; pres. Am. Bapt. Assn., 1941-92; supr. Grant County Soil Conservation Dist., 1945-92; pastor Bethan Missionary Bapt. Ch., Pine Bluff; advocate Christian edn. and missionary-evangelist Pine Bluff, Ark. Assn. Missionary Bapt. Chs. With U.S. Army, WW I. Recipient Rural Minister's award for Ark., 1952. Mem. Ark. Assn. Soil Conservation Dist. Suprs. (v.p. Cen. area), Internat. Platform Assn., Alumni Assn. Missionary Bapt. Inst. (pres.), Masons, Rotary. *

GOBEL, GEORGE LESLIE, entertainer; b. Chgo., May 20, 1919; s. Herman and Lillian (MacDonald) Goebel; m. Alice Rose Humecke, Dec. 13, 1942; children: Gregg, Georgia Bryan, Leslie McIntosh. Grad. high sch., Chgo. Performer Sta. WLS Barndance program, Tom Mix Radio Show, Chgo., early 1930s; actor, comedian, from 1937; star George Gobel Show, 1954-61. Regular appearances (TV series) Hollywood Squares, Harper Valley, also The Tonight Show; star appearances all the top hotels, nightclubs, Las Vegas, Nev.; appeared on Broadway stage in Three Men On a Horse, Let It Ride, others. Served to 1st lt. U.S. Army AC, 1941-45. Recipient Emmy award Acad. TV Arts and Scis., 1954, Peabody award U. Ga., 1954, Sylvania award, 1954, others. Mem. AFTRA, Screen Actors Guild, Am. Fedn. Musicians, Am. Guild Variety Artists. Republican. Episcopalian. Clubs: Indian Wells Country, La Costa Country (Calif.). Home: Encino Calif. Died Feb. 24, 1991; buried San Fernando Mission Cemetery.

GODBOLD, ALBERT, clergyman; b. Summit, Miss., July 25, 1895; s. Gabriel C. and Ella (Felder) G.; m. Anna Lucile Ayres, Feb. 2, 1924; children: Adah Lucile Godbold Phelps, Channing, Edmund, Margaret Godbold Briscoe Jr. BA, So. Meth. U., 1921, BD, 1923; MA, Yale U., 1926; PhD, Duke U., 1939. Ordained to ministry Conglist. Ch., 1924, Meth. Ch., 1926. With Dept. Interior, 1914-16, Dept. Labor, 1916-17, 19-20; pastor Conn., 1924-26, N.C., 1926-34, Ark., 1934-41, Tenn., 1941-42, Mo., 1942-58; dist. supt. Meth. Ch., St. Louis, 1958-63; exec. sec. Assn. Meth. Hist. Socs., 1963-92; vis. lectr. homiletics Perkins Sch. Theology, So. Meth. U., 1946-49; mem. gen. bd. edn. Meth. Ch., 1956-64, chmn. St. Louis Conf. Bd. Edn., 1948-58; chmn. bd. mgrs. Mo. Meth. Pastors Sch., 1948-56; chmn. Mo. Meth. Commn. Higher Edn., 1956-60; leader conf. delegation to Meth. Ch. Gen. Conf., 1956, 60; mem. Fedn. Coun. Chs. Christ Am., 1948-50; ofcl. visitor World Coun. Chs., 1954; mem. div. Christian edn. Nat. Coun. Chs., 1958-64; del. World Meth. Conf., 1956. Author: The Church College of the Old South, 1944. Trustee So. Meth. U., 1946-92, St. Paul Sch. Theology Meth., 1957-63, McKendree Coll., 1959-92. With U.S. Army, 1917-19; AEF in Frances. *

GODDARD, PAULETTE, actress; b. Whitestone, N.Y., June 3, 1915; m. Edgar James; m. Charles Chaplin; m. Burgess Meredith, June 21, 1944 (div.); m. Erich Maria Remarque, Feb. 25, 1958 (dec. 1971). Student pub. schs. Began on N.Y. Stage; went to Hollywood for small part in Kid From Spain; actress appearing in Modern Times, 1936, Duffy's Tavern, 1945, Kitty, 1945, Standing Room Only, 1944, Diary of a Chambermaid, 1946, Proudly We Hail, 1943, Unconquered, 1947, An Ideal Husband, 1947, Hazard, 1948, On Our Merry Way, 1948, Anna Lucasta, 1949, Woman of Venegeance, 1948, The Torch, 1949, Time of Indifference, 1966; TV movies include the Snoop Sisters, 1972. Home: Ronco Switzerland Died Apr. 23, 1990.

GODFREY, DARWIN FOOTE, business executive; b. Toledo, Nov. 18, 1898; s. William M. and Hattie (Valentine) G.; m. Dorothy Clark, Mar. 23, 1925; 1 child, William C. Student, Stanford U. With Standard Oil Co. Calif., 1919-63; pres. Signal Oil Co. div., 1947-61, v.p. corp., 1962-63. Mem. World Trade Club (San Francisco), Calif. Jonathan Club (L.A.). *

GODWIN, BLAKE MORE, museum executive; b. Clinton, Mo., Jan. 13, 1894; s. William Martin and Jean A. (Blakemore) G.; m. Molly Conant Ohl, June 30, 1926. AB, U. Mo., 1915, AFD (hon.), 1955; MA, Princeton U., 1916; AFD (hon.), U. Toledo, 1952. Asst. in classical archaeology and history of art U. Mo., 1912-15; fellow in art and archaeology Princeton U., 1915-16; curator Toledo Mus. Art, 1916-26, dir., 1927-59, v.p., 1959-92; hon. mem. faculty fine arts U. Chile, 1943. Contbr. biographies of Am. painters and sculptors in Allgemeines Kunatler Lexikon and articles on art for many periodicals; designer of Gothic Hall, Cloister, other features of Toledo Mus.; author: Catalog of European Paintings in the Toledo Museum, 1939. Trustee Charities Found., Toledo Mus. Art; chmn., mng. trustee Mus. Endowment Fund, estate of Edward Drummond Libbey and Florence Scott Libbey; pres., gen. mgr. Scott Properties Corp.; mem. commn. on ch. arch. Episcopal Diocese of Ohio; trustee Toledo U., 1919-30, Northwestern Ohio History Soc., 1930-40, Toledo C. of C., 1940-42, Tb Soc. Toledo and Lucas County, 1943-62, pres. 1953-55; pres. Toledo Citizens Plan Assn. 1936-44. Decorated comdr. Order of Merit, Chile, 1948, Chevalier, Legion of Honor, Officer Order of Orange Nassau, Netherlands. Fellow Mus. Assn. G.B.; mem. Royal Hort. Soc., Am. Assn. Mus., Mus. Dirs. Assn. (pres. 1940-41), Coll. Art Assn. (treas. 1933-38), Archaeol. Inst. Am. Medieval Acad., Conseil de Direction, Gazette des Beaux Arts, Phi Beta Kappa, Sigma Delta Pi, Phi Kappa Phi, Princeton Club (N.Y.C.), Toledo Club, Tile Club, Hermits Club, Minor Prophets Club, Rotary (pres. 1952-53), Travellers (London). *

GOESS, FREDERICK V., banker; b. Bklyn., Apr. 12, 1896; s. Andrew C. and Margaret (Kirchner) G.; m. Helen E. Ochs, June 30, 1920;l children: Helen E. Thran, Grace K. Donovan, Mary, Frederick, Doris Powers, Margaret Peguillan. Dr.Comml. Sci., St. John's U. With Mfrs. Trust Co., N.Y.C., 1912-41, v.p., 1932-41; receiver Harriman Nat. Bank & Trust Co.; pres. Prudential Savs. Bank, Bklyn., 1941-92; pres. Fleetwood Ent., Inc., Fleetwood Parking, Inc. Bd. dirs. Bklyn. chpt. ARC, St. Catharine's Hosp.; mem. coun. adminstrn. St. John's U. With AEF, U.S. Army, 1918-19. Decorated Knight of St. Gregory, Knight of Malta. Roman Catholic. *

GOHEEN, HARRY EARL, mathematics educator; b. Bellingham, Wash., July 19, 1915; s. Frank and Minnie (Clement) G.; m. Malchen Pearl, Jan. 20, 1940; children: David Element, Miriam, Mark Stewart. Student, Western Wash. Coll., 1932-35; B.A., Stanford U., 1936, M.A., 1938, Ph.D., 1940. Teaching fellow Reed Coll., Portland, Oreg., 1939-40; instr. U. Wis., Madison, 1940-42; mathematician Office Naval Research, 1946-47; asst. prof. U. Del., Newark, 1947-48, Syracuse (N.Y.) U., 1948-50, U. Pa., Phila., 1950-51; assoc. prof. Iowa State U., Ames, 1951-55, Oreg. State U., Corvallis, 1955-58; prof. math. Oreg. State U., 1958-81, prof. emeritus, 1981; vis. mem. Inst. Advanced Studies, Dublin, Ireland, 1967; vis. prof. Cork Coll., U. Ireland, 1975-76. Served with USNR, 1942-46. Mem. Assn. for Computing Machinery (founding mem.). Home: Corvallis Oreg. Died Nov. 5, 1989; buried Yachats, Oreg.

GOING, RICHARD FULLER, government offical; b. Winona, Minn., Jan. 1, 1896; s. George and Mary Roberta (Butchers) G.; m. Anita Charlotte Bransell (div. 1951); 1 child, Richard Fuller; m. Bernice Beulah Bolmer, Aug. 5, 1952. Student, Winona State Tchrs. Coll., 1916-17. CPA, Md., Tenn. Libr. aid U.S. Naval Acad., 1921-22; salesman Met. Life Ins. Co., Annapolis, Md., 1923; asst. comptroller U. Md., 1924-27; CPA Balt., 1928-35; CPA, cons. Washington, 1944-45; state procurement officer procurement div. U.S. Treas. Dept., Del., Ky., Ill., 1936-41; regional dir. procurement div. U.S. Treas. Dept., Chgo., 1943; dir. procurement Fed. Pub. Housing Authority, Washington, 1942; v.p., treas. Schenuit Rubber Co., Balt., 1946; assoc. zone adminstr. War Assets Adminstrn., Chgo., 1947-48; v.p., gen. mgr. Hunt Heater Corp., Nashville, 1949-52, also dir.; chief spl. audits div. USAF, Chgo., 1953-57; dep. controller, acting controller ICA, Seoul, Korea, 1958-59, European area controller ICA and attachee Am. Embassy, Bonn, Germany, 1960-92. Mem. Md. Assn. CPAs, Tenn. Assn. CPAs, Fed. Govt. Accts. Assn. *

GOINS, JOHN CLEMENT, judge; b. Apison, Tenn., Sept. 27, 1896; s. Daniel Alexander and Mary Alta (Johnson) G.; m. Wilda Swick, 1922 (dec.); 1 child, John Clement; m. Martha Raulston, 1926; children: Martha Caroline Goins Harber, Landon. Student, U. Chattanooga; LLB, Chattanooga Coll. Law, 1919, LLM, 1920. Bar: Tenn. 1919. Pvt. practice law Chattanooga; former sr. mem. Goins, Gammon, Baker & Robinson; spl. cir. judge 1st, 2d, 3d, 4th divs. Circuit Hamilton County, 1958-63; regular cir. judge 1st Div. Cir. Ct., Hamilton County, Tenn., 1963-92. Mem. ABA (ho. of dels. from Tenn. 1953-56), Tenn. Bar Assn. (pres. 1941-

42), Chattanooga Bar Assn. (pres. 1934), Elks, Delta Theta Phi. Presbyterian. *

GOLD, ARTHUR, pianist; b. Toronto, Ont., Can., Feb. 6, 1917. Student, Juilliard Sch., 1936-39. Mem. piano duo Gold and Fizdale, 1944-82. Performed concerts throughout U.S. and Europe, 1944-82; recorded albums for Columbia Records. Co-author: Misia, 1980, The Gold and Fizdale Cookbook, 1984; contbr. articles to Vogue mag.; contbg. editor Archtl. Digest. Home: Water Mill N.Y. Died Jan. 3, 1990.

GOLDBERG, ALBERT LEVI, journalist, music critic; b. Shenandoah, Iowa, June 2, 1898; s. A.W. and Minnie (Levi) G. Student, Chgo. Mus. Coll., 1920-22; MMus, Gunn Sch. Music, 1923; pvt. study, Chgo. Mus. Coll., 1924-26, Gunn Sch. Music, 1926-35. Music critic Chgo. Herald Examiner, 1925-36, Chgo. Tribune, 1943-47, L.A. Times, 1947-92; lectr. UCLA, 1948-92. Contbr. articles to mus. periodicals. *

GOLDBERG, ARTHUR JOSEPH, lawyer, supreme court justice; b. Chgo., Aug. 8, 1908; s. Joseph and Rebecca (Perlstein) G.; m. Dorothy Kurgans, July 18, 1931; children—Barbara L. Goldberg Cramer, Robert M. B.S.L., Northwestern U., 1929, J.D. summa cum laude, 1930. Bar: Ill. 1929, D.C., N.Y., Va., U.S. Supreme Ct. 1937. Practiced in Chgo., 1929-48; sr. partner firm Goldberg, Devoe, Shadur & Mikva, Chgo., 1945-61, Goldberg, Feller & Bredhoff, Washington, 1952-61; gen. counsel CIO, 1948-55, United Steelworkers Am., 1948-61; spl. counsel, gen. counsel indsl. union dept. AFL-CIO, 1955-61; spl. counsel indsl. union dept. also numerous other internat. unions; Sec. of Labor, 1961-62; asso. justice U.S. Supreme Ct., Washington, 1962-65; U.S. rep. to UN, 1965-68, ambassador-at-large, 1977-78; sr. partner Paul, Weiss, Goldberg, Rifkind, Wharton & Garrison, N.Y.C., 1968-71; practice law Washington, from 1971; Charles Evans Hughes prof. Princeton U., 1968-69; disting. prof. Columbia, 1969-70; prof. law and diplomacy Am. U., Washington, 1972-73; vis. disting. prof. Hastings Coll. Law, San Francisco, 1974, Santa Clara U., 1980, Nova Law Ctr., 1980, Ala. U., 1985, Okla. U., Boston U., Akron U., No. Ky. U., also several other univs.; chmn. Center for Law and Social Policy, 1968-78, hon. chmn., from 1978; former chmn. Pres.'s Com. on Migratory Labor, Pres.'s Missile Sites Labor Commn., Pres.'s Com. on Youth Employment, Pres.'s Temporary Com. on Implementation of Fed. Employee-Mgmt. Relations Program, Workers' Adv. Com. on U.S., Pres.'s Adv. Com. on Labor-Mgmt. Policy, Pres.'s Com. on Equal Employment Opportunity; former mem. numerous other Presdl. and federal coms. and councils, including SEC com. on tender offers, Commn. on Wartime Relocation and Internment of Civilians; former ex-officio mem. and ad hoc participant Nat. Security Council; former pres. Internat. Edn. Assn.; U.S. rep., chmn. U.S. del. Conf. on Security and Cooperation in Europe with rank amb.-at-large. Author: AFL-CIO; Labor United, 1956, Defenses of Freedom, 1966, Equal Justice: the Warren Era of the Supreme Court, 1972; editor-in-chief Ill. Law Rev, 1929-30; contbr. articles to profl. jours. and jours. of opinion. Past pres., then hon. chmn. Am. Jewish Com.; past chmn., pres. Synagogue Council of Am., Jewish Theol. Sem., Internat. Assn. Jewish Lawyers. Served as civilian, then from capt. to maj. OSS; Served from capt. to maj. U.S. Army, 1942-44, ETO; col. USAFR ret. Recipient numerous awards and hon. degrees; Medal of Freedom Pres. Carter, 1978; Order of Lincoln; Northwestern U. Alumnus medal. Mem. Am., Ill., Chgo., D.C. bar assns., Assn. Bar City N.Y., UN Assn. (hon. chmn.), Order of Coif. Home: Washington D.C. Deceased.

GOLDBERG, LEON ISADORE, clinical pharmacologist, educator; b. Charleston, S.C., Sept. 26, 1926; s. Harry and Goldy (Cohen) G.; m. Faye Joan Girsh, Feb. 2, 1958 (div.); children—Mark, Claudia; m. Susanne K. Glink, Aug. 9, 1987. B.S. Pharmacy, Med. U. S.C., 1946, M.S., 1951, Ph.D., 1952, hon. doctorate; M.D. cum laude, Harvard U., 1956, D.H.L., 1978. Intern, asst. resident in medicine Mass. Gen. Hosp., Boston, 1956-58, research fellow anesthesia, 1954-56; research asst. in pharmacology Med. Coll. S.C., 1949-52, research assoc., 1952-54; clin. assoc. Exptl. Therapeutics Br., NIH, 1958-61; prof. medicine, pharmacology, dir. clin. pharmacology program Emory U., Atlanta, 1961-74; prof. medicine, pharmacology, chmn. com. on clin. pharmacology U. Chgo., 1974-89; cons. NIH, VA, FDA, Nat. Acad. Scis. Editor: Jour. Cardiovascular Pharmacology; mem. editorial bds. several pharmacology jours., 1961-89; contbr. chpts. to books, numerous articles on clin. pharmacology, cardiovascular pharmacology to profl. jours. Served as surgeon USPHS, 1958-61. Burroughs Welcome Fund scholar in clin. pharmacology, 1961-66. Fellow Am. Coll. Cardiology; mem. Am. Soc. Clin. Investigation, Am. Soc. for Pharmacology and Exptl. Therapeutics (Exptrl. Therapeutics award), Am. Soc. for Clin. Pharmacology and Therapeutics, Am. Heart Assn., Council for High Blood Pressure Research, Assn. Am. Physicians. Home: Chicago Ill. Died May 8, 1989.

GOLDEN, JOHN MATTHEW, political organization worker; b. Old Saybrook, Conn., Nov. 4, 1895; s. Matthew J. and Alice P. (Strickland) G.; m. Margaret J. Stumpf, Apr. 7, 1920;l children: Margaret Golden Bergen, Frances A. Golden Krenisky. Supt. The Greist Mfg. Co., 1915-30; dir. pub. wks. City of New Haven, 1932-45; pres. Golden, O'Neill & Gebhardt, Inc. ins. agy., 1940; dir. Gen. Bank & Trust Co., Winthrop Bank & Trust Co. Dir. Cath. Diocesan Bur.; trustee Hosp. St. Raphael, Albertus Magnus Coll., Amherst (Mass.) Coll., New Haven Found.; mem. Dem. Nat. Com., 1952-92; pres. Camp Palmer for Boys. Mem. Knights St. Patrick, K.C., Hibernian Club, Eagles, Union League, Cath. of N.Y. Roman Catholic. *

GOLDENHERSH, JOSEPH HERMAN, state supreme court justice; b. East St. Louis, Ill., Nov. 2, 1914; s. Benjamin and Bertha (Goldenberg) G.; m. Maxyne Zelenka, June 18, 1939; children: Richard, Jerold. LL.B., Washington U., St. Louis, 1935; LL.D. (hon.), John Marshall Law Sch., Chgo., 1972. Bar: Ill. 1936. Pvt. practice law East St. Louis, 1936-64; judge Appellate Ct. Ill., 1964-70; justice Supreme Ct. Ill., 1970-78, 82-87, chief justice, 1979-82. Chmn. Initial Gifts United Fund East St. Louis, 1952-53; dir. Mississippi Valley council Boy Scouts Am., 1952-58; pres. Jewish Fedn. So. Ill., 1949-51; Trustee emeritus Christian Welfare Hosp., East St. Louis. Recipient Disting. Alumnus award Washington U. Law Sch., St. Louis, 1985. Mem. Appellate Judges Conf. (exec. com. 1969-70), East St. Louis Bar Assn. (pres. 1962-63), ABA, Ill. Bar Assn. Clubs: Mason (St. Louis) (33 deg., Shriner), Missouri Athletic (St. Louis). Home: Belleville Ill. Died Mar. 11, 1992.

GOLDING, STUART SAMUEL, real estate company executive; b. Boston, Apr. 1, 1917; s. Harry and Pauline (Simon) G.; m. Roberta Marks, June 13, 1943; children—Paul R., Kenneth A., Harriet S. B.A., Brown U., 1939; M.B.A., Harvard U., 1947. Asst. to pres. R.H. White Corp., Boston, 1947-50; mdse. mgr. Raymonds, Inc., Boston, 1950-52; pres. Stuart S. Golding, Inc. (shopping center developers), Tampa, Fla., 1952-71; sr. v.p. U.S. Home Corp., Clearwater, Fla., 1971-73; pres., chief ops. officer, dir. U.S. Home Corp., 1973-76; chmn. Stuart S. Golding Co.; dir. Southeast Bank of Fla.; adv. bd. New Eng. Life Ins. Co.; Trustee Internat. Council Shopping Centers.; mem. Tampa Bay Regional Planning Council, Tampa Bay Area Com. Fgn. Relations; mem. pres.'s council Brandeis U.; developer historic Willard Hotel restoration, Washington, 1980; Redeveloper historic Willard Hotel, Washington, 1979. Served to lt. comdr. USNR, 1941-45. Recipient hon. award Brown U., 1979. Clubs: Rotarian, Brown of West Coast Fla. (pres. 1964-66), West Coast Fla. Harvard (v.p. 1970-71), Boston Yacht. Home: Tampa Fla. Died Dec. 12, 1988.

GOLDMAN, HENRY MAURICE, periodontology educator; b. Boston, Dec. 9, 1911; s. Joseph and Rebecca (Levy) G.; m. Dorothy Alter, June 7, 1936; children: Richard, Gerald. Student, Brown U., 1929-31, D.Sc. (hon.), 1978; D.M.D., Harvard U., 1935; D.Sc. (hon.), Boston U., 1976, N.J. Coll. Medicine and Dentistry, 1977, U. Pa., 1978, Central U., Venezuela; Dr. honoris causa, U. Marseille, France, 1985. Diplomate: Am. Bd. Periodontology (dir. 1952-58), Am. Bd. Oral Pathology (pres. 1955-56, dir. 1948-55), Am. Bd. Oral Medicine. Research fellow oral pathology Harvard U., 1935-37, instr. oral pathology, 1938-46; chief stomatology and dental research, dir. Riesman Dental Clinic, Beth Israel Hosp., 1948; prof. periodontology, chmn. dept. Grad. Sch. Medicine U. Pa., 1955-64; prof., chmn. dept. stomatology Sch. Medicine, Boston U., 1958-64, mem. exec. com., from 1963, prof., chmn. dept. oral pathology, 1964-77; dean Sch. Medicine, Boston U. (Grad. Sch. Dentistry), 1963-77; dean emeritus, also chief stomalogical service, bd. incorporators, trustee Sch. Medicine, Boston U. (Univ. Hosp.), from 1977; assoc. dir. Boston U. Med. Center, 1972-78; Cons. dental and oral registry Army Inst. Pathology, Washington; subcom. periodontia, com. dentistry NRC, 1948-51; cons. to NIH, 1969, surgeon gen. U.S. Army, from 1965; mem. vis. com. Boston U. Sch. Medicine, 1983-91. Author: Periodontia, 4th rev. edit, 1959, Atlas of Dental and Oral Pathology, 3 rev. edit, 1944; co-author: Periodontal Therapy, 6th edit, 1979, Introduction to Periodontia, 6th edit, 1977, Treatment Planning in Practice of Dentistry, 1959, Thoma's Oral Pathology, 1970, 6th edit, Current Therapy in Dentistry, 6th edit, 1977, Oral Pathology Atlas, 1973, 2d edit., 1979, Biologic Basis of Orthodontics, 1971, Periodontal Pathology, Oral Pathology, Surgical Management of Periodontal Disease, 1981; editor: Jour. Periodontology, 1968-80; editor emeritus, 1980-91; contbr. numerous articles to profl. jours. Served as capt., chief dental pathologic sect. AUS, 1943-45; pathologist dental registry Army Inst. Pathology. Recipient Thomas P. Hinman award, 1952, 67; Gold medal Am. Acad. Periodontolgoy, 1968; Gies award, 1970; 70th Year Celebration award Sao Paulo, Brazil; Alpha Omega award; Orban prize, 1976; Internat. award Friends of U. Conn., 1977; Fones medal and award, 1978; Found. of Marseille medal, 1985; Leaders in Medicine award Harvard U. Sch. Medicine, 1986; Henry M. Goldman Sch. Grad. Dentistry, Boston U., named in his honor. Fellow Am. Acad. Oral Pathology (pres. 1952-53), Am. Acad. Periodontology, Am. Coll. Dentists, Royal Soc. Medicine, Internat. Coll. Dentists; mem. Am. Pub. Health Assn., AAAS (mem. Ivory Cross expdn. 1948), Am. Soc. Perodontists (pres. 1963-64, editor jour.), M. Dental Assn. (coun. on dental rsch. 1952-54, 58-92), Acad. Periodontology, New Eng. Pathologic Soc., Internat. Assn. Dental Rsch., Nat. Inst. Dental Rsch. (ad hoc com. periodontology 1972-75, cons. to dir. 1971-75), Harvard Odontological Soc., Sr. Soc. Harvard Sch. Dental Medicine, Brit. Periodontology Soc. (hon. mem.), Italian Periodontology Soc. (hon.), Sigma Xi, Pi Lambda Phi, Omicron Kappa Upsilon. Clubs: Harvard (Boston); Belmont (Mass.) Country. Home: Boca Raton Fla. Died July 23, 1991; buried Wakefield Cemetery, Wakefield, Mass.

GOLDMAN, RALPH, physician, educator; b. N.Y.C., June 11, 1919; s. Henry and May (Hoffman) G.; m. Helen C. Wolfson, Jan. 15, 1941; children—Paul, Richard, Elizabeth. A.B., U. Calif. at Berkeley, 1939; M.D., U. Calif. at San Francisco, 1942. Intern L.A. County Gen. Hosp., 1942-43, resident internal medicine, 1943-44; resident internal medicine VA Ctr. L.A., 1946-48, chief metabolic and renal disease sect., 1948-55; chief med. service VA Hosp., Sepulveda, Calif., 1955-58; prof. medicine UCLA Med. Sch., 1958-77, prof. medicine/geriatrics in residence, from 1980, asst. dean allied health Professions, 1971-75; chief intermediate care and geriatric med. sect. VA Ctr. L.A., 1975-77; asst. chief med. dir. for extended care VA Central Office, Washington, 1977-80; asso. chief staff for edn. VA Wadsworth Med. Ctr., L.A., from 1980; clin. prof. medicine George Washington U., 1979-80. Contbr. articles to profl. jours. Served to lt., M.C. USNR, 1944-46. Fellow A.C.P., Gerontol. Soc., Geriatrics Soc.; mem. Internat. Assn. Gerontology, Am. Geriatric Soc. (Willard O. Thompson award 1970), Internat., Am. socs. nephrology. Home: Los Angeles Calif. Died Sept. 2, 1977.

GOLDSMITH, ROBERT HILLIS, English language educator; b. East Lansing, Mich., Sept. 3, 1911; s. Robert and Edith (Darrow) G.; m. Mary Alice Glass, June 1, 1942; children: Alice Darrow, Robert Glass. BA, Pa. State U., 1936; MA, Columbia, 1943, PhD, 1952. Instr. dept. English Temple U., Phila., 1946-52, U. Md., College Park, 1952-55; assoc. prof. Emory and Henry Coll., Emory, Va., 1955-60; prof. Emory and Henry Coll., 1960-92, chmn. dept., 1971-92, Henry Carter Stuart prof. English, 1974-92; Reader Folger Library, Washington, 1959; intern Southeast Renaissance Inst., U. N.C., Chapel Hill, 1965; humanities fellow Duke, 1966-67. (Recipient 1st prize playwriting Cal. Western U., San Diego 1963); Author: Wise Fools in Shakespeare, 1955, Survey of English Literature, vol. I, 1976; Contbr. articles to profl. jours. Served with USAAF, 1942-46. Mem. AAUP (pres. chpt. 1964-65), MLA, Shakespeare Assn. Am., Southeastern Renaissance Conf. (pres. 1974), Charlotte Sr. Scholars (program dir. 1981-83, pres. 1984), Phi Kappa Phi. Home: Charlotte N.C. Died June 19, 1992. †

GOLDSMITH, WILLIAM WALLACE, lawyer, coal company executive; b. Newark, May 17, 1893; s. W. H. and Amelia (Hensley) G.; m. Mary Nan McGinnis, June 15, 1921; 1 child, Beth Goldsmith Childers Jr. LLB, U. Richmond, 1913. Bar: Va. 1914, W.Va. 1920. Pvt. practice Richmond, Va., 1914-20, Beckley, W.Va., 1920-37, Charleston, 1937-92; pres. Elk Horn Coal Corp., 1953-92; dir. Ky. River Coal Corp. Mem. ABA, W.Va. Bar Assn., Edgewood Country Club (Charleston). *

GOLDWATER, LEONARD JOHN, emeritus medical educator; b. N.Y.C., Jan. 15, 1903; s. Abraham Lincoln and Belle (Delmar) G.; m. Margaret F. Jones, 1978. A.B., U. Mich., 1924; M.D., NYU, 1928, D.M.S., 1936; M.S. in Pub. Health, Columbia U., 1941. Diplomate: Am. Bd. Internal Medicine, Am. Bd. Preventative Medicine. Intern and resident physician Bellevue Hosp., N.Y.C., 1929-32; instr. medicine N.Y. U. Coll. Medicine, 1932-36; sr. indsl. hygiene physicians N.Y. Dept. Labor, N.Y.C., 1936-38; instr. and asst. prof. preventive medicine N.Y. U. Coll. Medicine, 1938-41, assoc. prof., 1946; prof. indsl. hygiene Columbia U. Sch. Pub. Health, 1946-52, prof. occupational medicine, 1952-68, emeritus, from 1969, spl. lectr., from 1969; cons. Office Vocat. Rehab., Dept. Health, Edn. and Welfare, 1952-60; social and occupational health WHO, 1951-77, AEC, 1947-48; Harben lectr. Royal Inst. Pub. Health and Hygiene, London, 1964; dir. Interuniversity Consortium for Environmental Studies, from 1971; cons. indsl. hygiene physician N.Y. Dept. Labor, 1954-68; corr. com. on occupational health and safety ILO; vis. scholar Duke U. Med. Center, 1967-69, prof., 1970-72, prof. emeritus, from 1983, cons., from 1973; vis. prof. U. N.C. Sch. Pub. Health, 1970-72, adj. prof., 1973-88; Praelector St. Andrews U., Scotland, 1966; Mem. N.C. State Water Quality Council, 1975-78. Author: Mercury: A History of Quicksilver, 1972; Contbr. articles indsl. medicine profl. jours. Trustee Village of Irvington, N.Y., 1958 -60, 61-63. Served with M.C. USN, 1941-46, PTO. Recipient Award of Merit, Duke U. Med. Ctr., 1981; Endowed Goldwater Professorship in Occupational Medicine established Duke U. Med. Ctr., 1988. Fellow Am. Occupational Med. Assn. (William S. Knudsen award 1980), N.Y. Acad. Medicine, Am. Pub. Health Assn., Am. Acad. Occupational Medicine (pres. 1959, Robert A. Kehoe award of merit 1975), Royal Inst. Pub. Health and Hygiene (hon.); mem. Am. Indsl. Hygiene Assn., Sigma Xi, Nu Sigma Nu, Alpha Omega Alpha. Home: Chapel Hill N.C. Died July, 1992. †

GOLEMON, ALBERT SIDNEY, architect; b. Whistler, Ala., Sept. 19, 1904; s. James Oliver and Anna

Ruth (Abbott) G.; m. Frances Elizabeth Perkins, May 4, 1930; 1 dau., Anabeth (Mrs. George M. Boedeker, Jr.). B.S., Auburn U., 1924, H.H.D. (hon.), 1978; M.Arch., Mass. Inst. Tech., 1925; diploma, Ecole des Beaux Arts, Fontainebleau, France, 1927. Ptnr. Steinman & Golemon, 1931-42; founder, ptnr. Golemon & Rolfe Architects, Inc., Houston, from 1946; Pres. Nat. Archtl. Accrediting Bd., 1962. Outstanding works include F.B.I. Acad, Quantico, Va., Houston Intercontinental Airport, VA Hosp, San Antonio, Golemon & Rolfe Office Bldg, Houston, 1951, Med. Towers Office Bldg, Houston, 1955, Dominican Coll. Bldgs, Houston, 1954-60, Galveston-Houston Diocese Chancery, 1963, U. Houston Engring. Bldg, 1966, Union Carbide Corp. Bldg, Houston, St. Joseph's Hosp, Houston, (with others) FAA Air Route Traffic Control Center, Houston, 1965, River Oaks Country Club, Houston, One Woodway Office Complex, Houston, 1976, Meth. Neurosensory Hosp, Houston; cons. architect: (with others) outstanding works include Exxon Oil Co. office bldg, George W. Brown Convention Ctr., Houston. Pres. Tex. Archtl. Found., 1956; mem. City Houston Appeals Bd., 1963-65; participant Pres.'s White Ho. Conf. Natural Beauty, 1965; mem. Gen. Services Adminstrn. Archtl. Adv. Panel, 1966. Served as lt. col. C.E. AUS, 1943-45. Fellow AIA (nat. dir. 1954-57, chancellor coll. fellows 1973-74); mem. Tex. Soc. Architects (pres. 1953), Phi Kappa Theta. Clubs: Petroleum, Houston, M.I.T. Alumni of South Tex, Auburn Alumni, River Oaks Country, Fontainebleau Alumni; Eldorado Country (Calif.). Home: Houston Tex. Died Nov. 23, 1991.

GOLIGHTLY, TRUEMAN HARLAN, banker; b. Metropolis, Ill., Feb. 25, 1897; s. Leander H. and May (Hanna) G.; m. Gertrude MacDonald, Mar. 11, 1918 (dec. June 1955); 1 dau., Katherine Hanna Golightly Burks; m. Hazel Bullock, Nov. 22, 1956. Grad., Sch. Commerce, Northwestern U., 1936. Gen. acct., clk. Chgo. Savs. Bank & Trust Co., 1918-23; successively auditor, asst. v.p., v.p. Chgo. Trust Co., 1924-29; v.p. Nat. Bank of the Rep., Chgo., 1929-32; asst. gen. receiver Ill. state banks in liquidation, 1933-35; pres., chmn. bd. Nat. Bank of Commerce, Chgo., 1936-64; merged with Central Nat. Bank, 1964, vice chmn. bd., from 1964, mem. dirs. adv. com., from 1966. Mem. nat. council Boy Scouts Am., from 1946; Pres., chmn. finance com. Trustees of Endowment Fund of Episcopal Diocese of Chgo., 1968-76. Served with USN, World War I. Recipient citation Chgo. Financial Advertisers, 1967, Silver Beaver award Boy Scouts Am. Mem. Ill. Bankers Assn. (past pres. bd. govs.), Chgo. Fin. Advertisers (pres. 1942), Robert Morris Assos. (life), Financial Pub. Relations Assn., Am. Legion, Tau Delta Kappa. Clubs: Mason (Chgo.) (Shriner), Economic (Chgo.), University (Chgo.); Oak Park Country. Home: Elmhurst Ill. Died Feb. 16, 1988.

GOLINO, CARLO LUIGI, educator; b. Pescara, Italy, June 6, 1913; s. Vittore and Elisabetta (Petrucciani) G.; m. Anna Jean Martin, Dec. 14, 1940; children: Carlo M., Elizabeth, Bruce, Jean, Susan, Robert, Michael, Laura, John. BA, Coll. City N.Y., 1936; MA, Columbia U., 1937; student, U. Florence, Italy, 1937-39; PhD, U. Calif., Berkeley, 1948. Teaching asst. Italian U. Calif., Berkeley, 1939-42, 46-47; mem. faculty UCLA, 1947-65, prof. Italian, 1960-65, chmn. dept. Italian, 1956-62, dean humanities, 1961-65; prof. Italian and dean Coll. Letters and Sci. U. Calif., Riverside, 1965-69; vice chancellor univ. U. Calif., 1969-73; chancellor U. Mass., Boston, 1973-78, Commonwealth prof., 1978-91. Author: Contemporary Italian Poetry, 1962, Galileo Reappraised, 1966, also 2 vols. Italian Barogue lit., text books; editor Italian Quar., 1957-91. Lt. (j.g.) USNR, 1942-46. Fulbright rsch. scholar, Italy, 1960-61; decorated Star of Solidarieta, Italy; recipient Commenda Pres. of Italian Republic, 1978. Mem. MLA, Am. Assn. Tchrs. Italian, Dante Soc. Am. Home: La Selva Beach Calif. Died Feb. 14, 1991; buried Soquel Cemetery, Calif.

GOLLONG, PAUL BERNHARD WERNER, consulting engineer; b. Berlin, Germany, May 24, 1916; came to U.S., 1925, naturalized, 1938; s. Richard Julius and Margaret (Hietzig) G.; m. Mildred Brannan, May 13, 1944 (dec. 1978); m. Marianna Jennings Wofford, Nov. 2, 1978. I.E., B.S., U. Cin., 1941. Registered profl. engr., Wash., Ohio, Pa., Ill. Signaling systems engr. Holtzer-Cabot Co., Ill., 1941-42; research engr. Celotex Corp., Chgo., 1942-43; project engr. Armstrong Cork Co., Lancaster, Pa., 1943-46; cons. engr. Griffenhagen & Assos., Chgo., 1947-50; prin. asso. Griffenhagen & Assos., 1950-51; research engr. IIT Research Inst. (formerly Armour Research Found.), Chgo., 1951-52; chief Asia and Far East ops. IIT Research Inst., 1952-54, mgr. internat. dept., 1954-58, dir. internat. div., 1958-62; internat. adminstr. Boeing Asso. Products, The Boeing Co., 1961-63; spl. indsl. devel. adviser to UN, 1963-66; UN project mgr. Center Indsl. Research, Haifa, Israel, 1966-69; sr. sci. affairs officer Center Indsl. Research, 1970-77; internat. research and devel. cons., from 1977; cons. on research and devel. to govts., Syria, Turkey, Portugal, Nigeria, Cyprus, Trinidad & Tobago; dir. Applied Tech., Ltd., U.K.; mem. Internat. Exec. adv. Council; chmn. Archtl. Rev. Bd.; bd. dirs. Bayou Sound Assoc. Author papers, lectr. on tech. devel. Asian, African and Latin Am. countries. Mem. vestry All Angels Episcopal Ch., Longboat Key, Fla.; chmn. mcpl. archtl. rev. bd., Longboat Key; bd. dirs. Bayou Assn. Bd., Longboat Key. Mem. AAAS, Am. Inst. Indsl. Engrs., Am. Mgmt. Assn., U.S. C. of C., Nat., N.Y., Ill. socs. profl. engrs., Chgo. Hist. Soc., Asia Soc., Soc. Internat. Devel., Library Internat. Relations. Home: Longboat Key Fla. Deceased.

GOLUB, WILLIAM, food chain executive; b. Schenectady, June 30, 1904; s. Lewis and Matilda (Gurkin) G.; student Union Coll., 1922-24; B.A., U. Mich., 1924-26; m. Estelle Dolores Ginsburg, Apr. 6, 1930; children: Paul David, Neil Mark, Meta Jill. With Lewis Golub, wholesale grocer, 1926-30; v.p. Grosberg-Golub Co., Inc., 1930-43, Central Markets, Inc., 1933-43; dir., v.p. Central Market Operating Co., Inc., 1937-43, pres., 1943-72; v.p. Golub Corp., Schenectady, 1943-68, pres., 1968-76, chmn. bd., 1972-82, chmn. bd. emeritus, 1982-92; dir., officer, various subsidary cos.; pres. Price Chopper Supermarkets 1972-76, chmn., 1976-82, hon. chmn., 1982-83, chmn. emeritus, 1983-92; lectr. in field. Bd. dirs. mem. Jewish Community Center Bd. Trustees; former mem. bd. Capital Dist. Daus. of Sarah Jewish Home for Aged; mem. adv. bd. Schenectady Community Coll., Jr. Achievement; vice chmn. Schenectady Traffic Safety Commn.; former chmn. bd., former dir. Schenectady City Hosp. Found.; bd. dirs. Schnectady Found.; bd. dirs. Sunnyview Hosp., Schenectady Kiwanis Found. Recipient B'nai B'rith Man of Yr. award, 1962, 78; Seal of Israel award, 1967; Prime Ministers Club State of Israel, 1977; N.Y. State Govs. award, egg industry, 1969; N.Y. State Sammy award, 1975; Kiwanis awards, others; named hon. patroon, City of Schenectady, 1957, Man of Century, 1990. Mem. Food Mktg. Inst., C. of C., Nat. Rehab. Soc., Food Distbn. Research Soc., Am. Mgmt. Assn., Internat. Platform Assn., Super Market Inst. (dir.), Nat. Assn. Food Chains (dir.), Tau Epsilon Rho. Republican. Clubs: Kiwanis, YMCA, Mus. of Art, B'nai B'rith. Contbr. articles to profl. jours. Died Oct. 19, 1992. Home: Sarasota Fla. †

GONZALEZ, XAVIER, artist; b. Almeria, Spain, Feb. 15, 1898; came to U.S. 1921, naturalized 1931; s. Emilio and Gracia (Arpa) G.; m. Ethel Edvarde, Aug. 24, 1935. Student, Art Inst. Chgo., 1921-23. Tchr. San Antonio pub. schs., 1924; prof. art Newcomb Coll., Tulane U., New Orleans, 1930, Bklyn. Mus., 1945; lectr. Nat. Coll. Assn., 1946, Metro. Mus. N.Y., 1945; artist in resident Western Res. U., Cleve. Exhibited N.Y.C., 1943, 46, 48; represented in permanent collections Whitney Mus., Met. Mus., Wellesley Coll., Delgado Mus., New Orleans, Witte Mus., San Antonio, Mus. Fine Arts, Seattle, IBM, N.Y. Guggenheim fellow; recipient Nat. Arts Club gold medal, Aubudon Artist gold medal, Am. Acad. Arts and Letters awards; Ellen P. Speyer prize, 1958; Clara Obrig prize Nat. Acad., 1962. Mem. Am. Water Color Soc., Am. Nat. Acad., Artists Equity, Century Club (N.Y.C.). *

GOOD, CARTER VICTOR, university dean; b. Dayton, Va., Sept. 16, 1897; s. Jacob S. H. and Anna Victoria (Early) G.; m. Irene Cooper, Sept. 6, 1920; 1 child, Gene Ann. AB, Bridgewater (Va.) Coll., 1918; AM, U. Va., 1923; PhD, U. Chgo., 1925; LLD, Bridgewater Coll., 1950. Asst. prin. high sch. Shenandoah, Va., 1919-20; prin. high sch. New Hope, Va., 1920-21, Marshall, Va., 1921-22; supt. schs. Burnsville, W.Va., 1922-23; prof. edn. Miami U., Oxford, Ohio, 1925-30; prof. edn. U. Cin., 1930-92, dir. grad. study in Tchrs. Coll., 1944-59, acting dean Tchrs. Coll., 1944-47, dean, 1947-59, dean and dir. grad. studies Coll. Edn. and Home Econs., 1959-92; instr. edn. U. Chgo., summer 1925; prof. edn. summer sessions U. Mich., 1927, 28, U. Cin., 1929, U. Wis., 1938, 40. Author books; contbr. to ednl. jours. and yearbooks; editorial bd. Jour. Ednl. Rsch., 1930-46, Jour. Exptl. Edn., Ency. of Ednl. Rsch.; author: Methods of Research (with Scates), 1954, Introduction to Educational Research, 1959, rev. 1963; editor: Dictionary of Education, 1945, rev. 1959, Guide to Colleges, Universities and Professional Schools in United States, 1945. Chmn. mayor's Friendly Relations Com., 1957-58. Ensign USN, 1918-19. Fellow AAAS (v.p. 1955), APA; mem. NEA, Am. Ednl. Rsch. Assn. (pres. 1940-41), Nat. Soc. Study Edn., Nat. Soc. Coll. Tchrs. of Edn. (pres. 1947-48), Kappa delta Pi, Phi Delta Kappa (nat. historian 1946-48), Kappa Phi Kappa, Omicron Delta Kappa. Presbyterian. *

GOODALL, NEWMAN, clergyman; b. Birmingham, Eng., Aug. 30, 1896; s. Thomas and Amelia (Batts) G.; m. Doris E.F. Stanton, June 22, 1920; children: David S., Olive M. Goodall Carke, Peter. MA, Mansfield Coll., Oxford U., 1922, DPhil, 1954. Ordained to ministry Congl. Union Eng. and Wales, 1922. Pastor London, 1922-28, Hertsfordshire, 1928-36; fgn. sec. for India and So. Pacific London Missionary Soc., 1936-44; London sec. Internat. Missionary Coun.; editor Internat. Rev. Missions, 1944-55; sec. joint com. World Coun. Chs. and Internat. Missionary Coun., 1955-61; asst. gen. sec. World Coun. Chs., 1962-92; asst. editor Ecumenical Rev., 1962-92. Author: With All Thy Mind, 1935, Pacific Pilgrimage, 1942, One Man's Testimony, 1949, History of the London Missionary Society 1895-1945, 1954, The Ecumenical Movement: What it is and What it Does, 1961, Christian Ambassador, a Life of A. Livingston Warnabals, 1963. Mem. Authors Club (London). *

GOODBODY, JOHN COLLETT, communications consultant, church official; b. Omaha, May 15, 1915; s. Maurice Fitzgerald and Nellie Jane (Collett) G.; m. Harriet Tuthill Linen, Aug. 5, 1939; children: Margaretta Goodbody Niles, David Lister, Joan Tuthill. A.B., Williams Coll., 1937; postgrad., Harvard U., 1939-41, 46. Corr. UP, 1937; reporter Toledo News-Bee, 1938; assoc. editor School Exec. mag., 1938; asst. sec. to pres. Williams Coll., 1939; teaching fellow Harvard U., 1945-46; staff Colonial Williamsburg, 1946-61; spl. asst. to John D. Rockefeller III, 1949-50, v.p., 1957-61; pres. Seabury Press, N.Y.C., 1961-72; exec. for communication Episcopal Ch., 1971-80; cons. Trinity Parish, N.Y.C., from 1980; communications officer Episc. Diocese of S.C., from 1980. Served to lt. comdr. USNR, 1941-45. Mem. Gargoyle Assn., Chi Psi. Club: Seabrook Island (S.C.). Home: Johns Island S.C. Deceased. †

GOODMAN, DEWITT STETTEN, physician, scientist, educator; b. N.Y.C., July 18, 1930; s. Max and Jennie (Katz) G.; m. Ann Bregstein, July 7, 1957; children: Daniel W., Elizabeth. A.B., Harvard U., 1951, M.D., 1955; Dr. Medicinae (hon.), U. Oslo, Norway, 1986. Intern Presbyn. Hosp., N.Y.C., 1955-56, asst. resident, 1958-59; investigator Nat. Heart Inst., 1956-58, 60-62; vis. fellow Hammersmith Hosp., London, Eng., 1959-60; mem. faculty Columbia Coll. Physicians & Surgeons, 1962-91, prof. medicine, 1969-91, Tilden-Weger-Bieler prof., 1971-91, dir. div. metabolism and nutrition, dept. medicine, 1971-91; dir. Arteriosclerosis Rsch. Ctr., 1976-91, Inst. Human Nutrition, Columbia U., 1988-91; mem. staff Presbyn. Hosp., 1962-91, attending physician, 1971-91; vis. fellow Clare Hall, Cambridge (Eng.) U., 1972-73; adj. prof. Rockefeller U., N.Y.C., 1974-77; vis. prof. Hebrew U.-Hadassah Med. Sch., Jerusalem, 1981-82; mem. metabolism study sect. NIH, 1966-70; mem. arteriosclerosis, hypertension and lipid metabolism adv. com. Nat. Heart, Lung and Blood Inst., 1978-87, chmn., 1985-87; chmn. Gordon Research Confs. on Lipid Metabolism, 1968, on Arteriosclerosis, 1981; chmn. FASEB Summer Conf. on Retinoids, 1988; chmn. expert panel on treatment of adults, Nat. Cholesterol Edn. Program, 1986-88; vice chmn. com. on diet and health, NRC, 1986-89; mem. food and nutrition bd. Inst. Medicine, 1988-91, vice chmn., 1991, com. on nat. rsch. agenda on aging, 1988-91. Co-editor, assoc. editor: Jour. Clin. Investigation, 1967-71; editor, 1971-72; editorial bd. Jour. Lipid Research, 1965-70; adv. bd., 1974-90; editorial bd. Jour. Biol. Chemistry, 1979-85, Arteriosclerosis, from 1981. Career scientist Health Research Council, N.Y.C., 1964-74. Recipient Meltzer award Soc. Exptl. Biology and Medicine, 1963, Stevens Triennial award Columbia, 1971, Macy Faculty Scholar award, 1981-82, Bristol-Myers award for Disting. Achievement in Nutrition Research, 1987; Guggenheim fellow, 1972-73; Harvey lecture, 1986. Fellow AAAS; mem. Am. Soc. Clin. Investigation (councillor 1973-76, Herman award 1991), Assn. Am. Physicians, Am. Soc. Biochemistry and Molecular Biology, Council Arteriosclerosis Am. Heart Assn. (chmn. 1979-81, exec. com. 1969-72, 79-86, award of merit 1990), N.Y. Heart Assn. (exec. com. 1983-91, pres. elect 1989-91, pres. 1991), Endocrine Soc., Am. Inst. Nutrition (Osborne and Mendel award 1974), Am. Soc. Clin. Nutrition (Herman award 1991), Harvey Soc. (councillor 1978-81, v.p. 1981-82, pres. 1982-83), Am. Oil Chemists Soc., Inst. Medicine, Interurban Clin. Club (councillor 1982-84, pres. 1985-86), Lipid Rsch. Inc. (mem. editorial bd. Jour. Lipid Rsch. 1965-70, adv. bd. 1974-90), Phi Beta Kappa, Alpha Omega Alpha. Home: Tenafly N.J. Died Nov. 4, 1991.

GOODMAN, MICHAEL A., architect, educator; b. Lithuania, Jan. 7, 1903; came to U.S., 1921, naturalized, 1927; s. Agran and Yacha (Barger) Gutman; m. Mildred Jacobs, Mar. 9, 1935; children: Michael A., Jr., Louise M. Heidner. A.B., U. Calif. at Berkeley, 1925, M.A., 1927. Faculty U. Calif. at Berkeley, 1927-91, prof. architecture, 1945-70, emeritus, 1970-91; research architect for Inst. Transp. and Traffic Engring., U. Calif., 1971-74; propr. firm Michael A. Goodman; architect Michael A. Goodman, Berkeley, 1934-91; mgmt. cons.; mem. Exec. Service Corps, San Francisco; speaker on housing and bus. planning insts., Calif.; chmn. Berkeley City Planning Commn., 1954; pres. Bay Area Fedn. Planning Councils, 1964; chmn. Berkeley Housing Authority, Redevel. Agy. City of Berkeley. Recipient Gold medal San Francisco Art Assn. 1925, award Fifty Prints of Year, Am. Graphic Artists Soc. 1930, 4 prizes state-wide exhbn. Calif. artists 1929-34, Centennial Celebration medal U. Calif., 1968, Berkeley Citation for distinguished achievement and notable service to U. Calif. 1970, U. Calif. Alumni Citation, U. Calif. The Mens Faculty Club Citation; contbr. to archtl. publs.; prin. works include Bio-Chemistry and Virus Lab (AIA award 1954), Melvin Calvin Hall, all U. Calif. at Berkeley, U. Calif., San Francisco Golden Gate Internat. Exposition, ,County of San Mateo Hall of Justice and Records, Jail, East Bay Municipal Utility Dist. Adminstrn. Bldg, Berkeley Pub. Health Adminstrn. Bldg, First Savs. & Loan Office Bldg, Research Facility of Decombinant DNA Particles, Berkeley, numerous residential projects; one man exhbn., de Young Mus. and War Meml. Mus., San Francisco, 1934; participant annual shows, throughout U.S., 1929—; rep. museums, pvt. collections.; Sr. tech. def. planner, Fed. Office Civilian Def. for 8 Western States, 1941-43; contbr. to:

OWI and Inter-Am. programs, 1942-46. Fellow AIA; mem. Am. Inst. Planners, Am. Pub. Works Assn., Am. Planning and Civic Assn., San Francisco Art Assn., San Francisco, Berkeley chambers commerce, San Francisco Mus. Art. Democrat. Clubs: Commonwealth (San Francisco); U. Calif. (Berkeley). Home: Berkeley Calif. Died Apr. 12, 1991. †

GOODMAN, PERCIVAL, architect, educator; b. N.Y.C., Jan. 13, 1904; s. Barnet and Augusta (Goodman) G.; m. Naomi Ascher, Sept. 28, 1944; children—Rachel, Joel. Student, Beaux Arts Inst. Design, Ecole Nat. des Beaux Arts, Am. Sch. Fine Arts, all France. Ptnr. Whitman & Goodman, N.Y.C., 1930-33; prin. Percival Goodman, N.Y.C., from 1933; prof. Sch. Architecture and Planning, Columbia U., N.Y.C., 1945-72, prof. emeritus, 1972-89; lectr. numerous colls. and univs.; adj. prof. Schl. Architecture, N.Y.U., from 1930. Painter, sculptor, book illustrator; author: (with Paul Goodman) Communitas, 1947, rev. edit., 1960, 90, The Double E, 1977, Choisy's Rationale of Architecture, 1986; contbr. articles on art, architecture and city planning to encys. and mags.; works include over 50 religious and community bldgs. through U.S. for Jewish orgns., numerous bldgs. for city and state of N.Y., planning studies especially for riverfront improvements, N.Y.C.; archive at Avery Archtl. Libr., Columbia U. Fellow AIA. Jewish. Home: New York N.Y. Died Oct. 11, 1989; buried Salem Fields Cemetery, N.Y.C.

GOODRICH, DONALD WELLS, humanities educator; b. Bklyn., Jan. 20, 1898; s. Charles Howard and Matilda Antoinette (Brant) G.; m. Violet Elizabeth Walser, June 24, 1922; children: Donald Wells, Charles Howard, Alice Jacqueline. AB, Williams Coll., 1918; AM, Harvard U., 1920; postgrad., Columbia U., 1923, 24; LittD (hon.), Emerson Coll., 1958. Master in English Hoosac (N.Y.) Sch., 1921, Lawrenceville (N.J.) Sch., 1921-23; head master Great Neck (L.I.) Prep Sch., 1923-28; sr. master lower sch. Tamalpais Sch., San Rafael, Calif., 1928-32; head master Calvert Primary Sch., Balt., 1932-40; ednl. rschr. Harvard Grad. Sch. Edn., 1940-42; registrar, dir. admissions, prof. humanities Suffolk U., Boston, 1947-56, dean, registrar,, 1956-92; served S.A.T.C., Williams, 1918. Author textbooks; editor: G.I. Roundtable Discussion Pamphlets, U.S. Army, 1943-45. Mem. Ednl. Records Bur. N.Y., 1933-40. Lt. col. adj. gens. dept. U.S. Army, 1942-47. Mem. Pvt. Sch. Assn. Balt. (pres. 1937-38), Country Day Sch. Headmasters Assn., Am. Conf. Acad. Deans, NEA, Publicity Club, Mass. Schoolmasters Club, Phi Beta Kappa, Phi Delta Kappa. Congregationalist. *

GOODRICH, LELAND MATTHEW, international relations educator; b. Lewiston, Maine, Sept. 1, 1899; s. Fred Bartlett and Alice Mae Tibbetts G.; m. Eleanor Allen, June 30, 1928; children: Richard Allen, John Bradbury. AB, Bowdoin Coll., 1920, ScD, 1952; AM, Harvard U., 1921, PhD, 1925. Instr. polit. sci. Brown U., 1922-23, asst. prof. polit. sci., 1926-31, assoc. prof., 1931-46, prof., 1946-5; instr. govt. and law Lafayette Coll., 1925-26; prof. internat. orgn. and adminstrn. Columbia U., 1950-67, acting chmn. dept. pub. law and govt., 1965-66, James T. Shotwell prof. internat. rels., 1967-68, emeritus, 1968-90; vis. lectr. in govt. Harvard U., 1949-50; prof. internat. orgn. and adminstrn. Fletcher Sch. of Law and Diplomacy, 1944—; vis. prof. Sch. Internat. Affairs, Columbia U., 1948-49, U. Toronto, 1969-71; dir. World Peace Found., 1942-46, Belgian-Am. Ednl. Found., 1953—; mem. sec. gen.'s com. to review orgn. and activities UN Secretariat, 1961. Author: Korea: A Study of United States Policy in the United Nations, 1956, The United Nations, 1959, The United Nations in a Changing World, 1974; co-author: with Edvard Hambro Charter of the United Nations: Commentary and Documents, revised, 1949, 69, with Anne Simons The United Nations and the Maintenance of International Peace and Security, 1955; editor: (with S. Shepard Jones, Denys Myers Documents on American Foreign Relations, Vol. IV, 1942, with Marie J. Carroll , Vols. V-VII. Mem. Internat. Secretariat, UN Conf. on Internat. Orgn., 1945; chmn. bd. editors Internat. Orgn., 1947-54, emm., 1947-75; trustee World Peace Found.; trustee overseer Bowdoin Coll. Mem. Fgn. Policy Assn. chmn. R.I. 1928-35 , Coun. on Fgn. Rels. sec. Providence com. fgn. rels. 1942-48 , Am. Soc. Internat. Law exec. coun. 1940-43 , Am. Polit. Sci. Assn., Acad. Polit. Sci. dir. 1973— , Phi Beta Kappa, Psi Upsilon, Conglist. Home: New York N.Y. Died Nov. 16, 1990.

GOODWIN, ROBERT CABANISS, college president; b. Brownwood, Tex., Mar. 17, 1898; s. John W. and Kate (Cabaniss) G.; m. Constance Bishop, Oct. 3, 1929. BA, Howard Payne Coll., 1917; MA, U. Tex., 1923; PhD, Harvard U., 1928. Instr. chemistry Grand Rapids (Mich.) High Sch., 1919-21; grad. fellow in chemistry U. Tex., 1922-24; teaching fellow Harvard U., 1924-26; asst. prof. chemistry U. Fla., Gainesville, 1926-30, prof. chemistry, 1930-92, head dept. chemistry and chem. engring., 1930-50; dean grad. div. Tex. Tech. Coll., 1938-45, dean arts and sci. div., 1945-59, v.p., acting pres., 1959-61, pres., 1961-92. With U.S. Army. Mem. Am. Chem. Soc., Sigma Xi, Phi Lambda Upsilon, Alpha Chi Sigma, Gamma Sigma Epsilon, Delta Tau Delta, Masons, Rotary. Presbyterian. *

GOODWYN, KENDALL WIRT, magazine editor; b. Springfield, Mass., June 18, 1911; s. William Wirt and Mabel Alice (Trask) G.; m. Helen Janet Zeman, Nov. 9, 1940; children: Pamela Goodwyn-Wolk, Camilla Kendall. Student, NYU, 1946-48. With advt. agy., 1933-38; freelance mag. writer, 1938-40; assoc. editor Popular Publs., pubs. Argosy, Adventure and Railroad mags., 1940-43, 46-48, editor Adventure mag., 1948-51, copy dir. Popular Sci., 1951-56, asst. mng. editor, 1956-62, mng. editor, 1962-76; editorial cons. audio-visual div. Popular Sci. Pub. Co., 1960-66, mem. mgmt. adv. bd., 1965-67. With AUS, 1943-46, ETO, PTO. Mem. AAAS, Philipse Manor Club. Episcopalian. Home: North Tarrytown N.Y. Died Sept. 15, 1990; buried Sleepy Hollow Cemetery, North Tarrytown, N.Y.

GOODYKOONTZ, BESS, educator; b. Waukon, Iowa; d. E.W. and Lela (Sherman) G. AB, State U. Iowa, 1920, AM, 1922; D Pub. Edn., N.Y. State Coll. Tchrs., 1935; LLD (hon.), Parsons Coll., 1951. Tchr. pub. schs., 1912-16; tchr. exptl. sch. State U. Iowa, 1919-21, prin. exptl. sch., 1921-22; supr. pub. schs. Green Bay, Wis., 1922-24; asst. prof. edn. U. Pitts., 1924-29; asst. commr. edn. Office Edn., HEW, Washington, 1929-46, dir. elem. edn. div., 1946-49, assoc. commr. edn., 1949-51, dir. comparative edn. Internat. Edn. div., 1952, dir. internat. edn. rels. br., 1956-90; v.p. U.S. Nat. Com. Early Childhood Edn.; pres. World Orgn. Early Childhood Edn., 1958-60; mem. edn. mission to Germany, 1946; presdl. appointee U.S. alt. del. to Am. Inst. for Protection of Childhood in Uruguay, 1953; rep. U.S. Office Edn. at confs. UNESCO, Cultural Coun. Pan Am. Union; pres. Orgn. Mondine Edn. Prescholaire. Contbr. articles on elem., internat. edn. to profl. publs. Mem. ASCD (pres. 1946-47), Am. Ednl. Rsch. Assn. (pres. 1939-40), Nat. Soc. for Study Edn., Nat. Coun. Adminstrv. Women in Edn., Altrusa, Mortar Bd., Phi Beta Kappa, Pi Lambda Theta (nat. pres. 1933-37, v.p. 1937-41), Delta Zeta. Home: South Newfane Vt. Died July 29, 1990; interred South Newfane (Vt.) Cemetery.

GORALSKI, ROBERT, writer, lecturer; b. Chgo., Jan. 2, 1928; s. Stanley and Caroline (Bielas) G.; m. Margaret Anne Walton, Aug. 22, 1948; children: Douglas, Dorothy, Katherine. B.S., U. Ill., 1949; student, Sch. Advanced Internat. Studies, Johns Hopkins, 1960-61; Litt.D., William Jewell Coll., 1969. News announcer WDWS, Champaign, Ill., 1948-51; combat corr. U.S. Navy, Korea, 1951-53; prodn. supr. Radio Free Asia, Tokyo, Japan, 1953-54; asst. rep. Asia Found., Karachi and Dacca, Pakistan, 1954-56; editor, desk supr. Voice of Am., Washington, 1956-61; White House and State Dept. and Pentagon corr. NBC News, 1961-75; dir. pub. info. Gulf Oil Corp., Washington, 1975-83; writer, lectr., 1983-89; Nat. Security fellow Hoover Inst., 1972-73. Author: World War II Almanac, 1981, Press Follies, 1983; co-author: Oil and War, 1987. Served with USNR, 1945-46, PTO; Served with USNR, 1951-53, PTO; Served with USNR, Korea. Mass media fellow Ford Found. Fund Adult Edn., 1960-61. Mem. Sigma Alpha Epsilon. Home: McLean Va. Died Mar. 18, 1988; buried Arlington Nat. Cemetery, Va.

GORDIS, ROBERT, biblical scholar, rabbi, educator, author, editor; b. Bklyn., Feb. 6, 1908; s. Hyman and Lizzie (Engel) G.; m. Fannie Jacobson, Feb. 5, 1928; children: Enoch, Leon, David. A.B. cum laude, Coll. City N.Y., 1926; Ph.D., Dropsie Coll., 1929; rabbi (with distinction), Jewish Theol. Sem. Am., 1932, D.D., 1950; D.H.L. (hon.), Spertus Coll., Chgo., 1981, Gratz Coll., Phila., 1986. Ordained rabbi, 1932. Teacher Hebrew Tchrs. Tng. Sch. for Girls, 1926-28, Yeshiva Coll., 1929-30, Sem. Coll. of Jewish Studies, 1931; Teacher Jewish Theol. Sem., N.Y.C., 1937-40, prof. Bibl. exegesis, 1940-60, Sem. prof. Bible, 1961-69, prof. Bible, also Rapaport prof. philosophies of religion, 1974-81, prof. emeritus, 1981-92; rabbi Rockaway Park (N.Y.) Hebrew Congregation, 1931-69, rabbi emeritus, 1969-92; adj. prof. religion Columbia U., 1948-57; cons. and asso. Center for Study Dem. Instns., Santa Barbara, Calif., 1960-79; vis. prof. O.T. Union Theol. Sem., 1953-54; vis. prof. religion Temple U., 1967-68, prof., 1968-74; vis. prof. Bible Hebrew U., Jerusalem, 1970; Chmn. soc. justice com. Rabbinical Assembly Am., 1935-37, mem. exec. council, 1935; del. Synagogue Council of Am., 1937-40, pres., 1940-41; pres. Rabbinical Assembly, 1944-46; founder Beth-El (now Robert Gordis) Day Sch., Belle Harbor, L.I., N.Y., 1950; mem. council on religious freedom Nat. Conf. Christians and Jews; chmn. Commn. on Philosophy of Conservative Judaism, 1985-87; bd. dirs. Inst. Ch. and State, Villanova U.; Lectr. radio and TV, pub. forums speaker; pioneer in area of interfaith relations. Assoc. editor dept. of Bible: Universal Jewish Ency; Contbg. editor: Medical Aspects of Human Sexuality; bd. editors: Judaism (jour.), 1942-68; editor, from 1969; Contbr. to jours. and mags.; Author: over 20 books including Wisdom of Ecclesiastes, 1945, Conservative Judaism-An American Philosophy, 1945, Koheleth, The Man and His World, 1951, The Song of Songs, 1954, Judaism for the Modern Age, 1955, A Faith for Moderns, 1960, The Root and The Branch-Judaism and the Free Society, 1962, The Book of God and Man, A Study of Job, 1965, Judaism in A Christian World, 1966, Leave a Little to God, 1967, Sex and the Family in Jewish Tradtion, 1967, Poets, Prophets and Sages, Essays in Biblical Interpretation, 1970, The Biblical Text in the Making, augmented edit., 1971; Song of Songs-Lamentations, 1973, The Book of Esther, 1974, The Word and the Book: Studies in Biblical Language and Literature, 1976, The Book of Job: Commentary, New Translation and Special Studies, 1978, Love and Sex—A Modern Jewish Perspective, 1978, Understanding Conservative Judaism, 1978, Judaic Ethics for a Lawless World, 1986, The Dynamics of Judaism, 1990; editor: books including Rabbinical Assembly and United Synagogue Sabbath and Festival Prayer Book, 1946. Overseas mission War-Navy depts., investigating religious condition armed forces, Pacific, Asiatic theatres, 1946; Mem. exec. com. Nat. Hillel Commn., 1960-80; nat. adminstrv. council United Synagogue Am.; bd. govs. Nat. Acad. Adult Jewish Studies; mem. Nat. Com. on Scouting; pres. Synagogue Council of Am., 1948-49, Jewish Book Council Am., 1980-83; trustee Ch. Peace Union; cons. on religion Fund for Republic, 1957-60; assoc. trustee Am. Sch. Oriental Research, 1971-73. Recipient Nat. Jewish Book award, 1979; Guggenheim fellow, 1973. Fellow Am. Acad. Jewish Research (mem. exec. com.). Home: New York N.Y. Died Jan. 3, 1992; buired Montefiore Cemetery, St. Albans, N.Y.

GORDON, ARTHUR ERNEST, Latin epigraphist; b. Marlborough, Mass., Oct. 7, 1902; s. Arthur Ernest and Susan Esther (Porter) G.; m. Maddalena Belloni, Sept. 15, 1924; 1 child, Paola (Mrs. Paola Zinnecker); m. Joyce A. Stiefbold, June 11, 1937. A.B., Dartmouth Coll., 1923; student, Am. Acad. in Rome, 1923-25; Ph.D. in Latin (Johnston scholar), Johns Hopkins, 1929. Instr. Latin Dartmouth Coll., 1925-27; student asst. Johns Hopkins U., 1927-28; instr. Latin Western Res. U., summer 1928; asso. prof. Latin, ancient history U. Vt., 1929-30; asst. prof. to prof. Latin U. Calif. at Berkeley, 1930-70, prof. emeritus, 1970-89, chmn. dept. classics, 1953-59; prof. classical langs. Ashland (Ohio) Coll., 1970; prof. classics Ohio State U., 1971; sr. research fellow classical studies Am. Acad., Rome, 1948-49. Author: Epigraphica I-II, 1935-36, Supralineate Abbreviations in Latin Inscriptions, 1948, reprinted 1977, A New Fragment of the Laudatio Turiae, 1950, Q. Veranius, Consul A.D. 49, 1952, Potitus Valerius Messalla, 1954, Notes on the Res Gestae of Augustus, 1968, On the Origins of the Latin Alphabet, Modern Views, 1969, The Letter Names of the Latin Alphabet, 1973, The Fibula Praenestina, Problems of Authenticity, 1975, Notes on the Duenos-Vase Inscription in Berlin, 1976, Illustrated Introduction to Latin Epigraphy, 1983, (with Joyce S. Gordon) Contributions to the Palaeography of Latin Inscriptions, 1957, reprinted, 1977, Album of Dated Latin Inscriptions, Parts I-IV, 1958-65; also monographs, articles and revs. in field; compiler, preparer Corpus of Latin Inscriptions, Vol. 6, part 6, fascicle 7, 1986-88. Mem. 2d Internat. Congress Greek and Latin Epigraphy, Paris, 1952. Guggenheim fellow and Fulbright rsch. scholar, 1955-56; NEH sr. fellow, 1972-73, NEH grantee, 1986-88. Mem. Am. Philol. Assn., Philol. Assn. Pacific Coast (pres. 1952), Calif. Classical Assn., Internat. Assn. for Greek and Latin Epigraphy, Fondation Hardt pour L'étude de L'antiquité classique, Vandoeuvres/Geneva. Clubs: Faculty (Berkeley). Home: Oakland Calif. Died May 11, 1989; cremated.

GORDON, DEXTER KEITH, jazz musician; b. Los Angeles, Feb. 27, 1923; m. Maxine Gordon; children: Robin Gordon, Diedre Gordon, Mikael Solfors, Benjamin Gordon, Woody Louis Armstrong Shaw. P-layed tenor saxophone with Lionel Hampton, 1940, Louis Armstrong, Billy Eckstine, Charlie Parker, Wardell Gray; band leader; rec. artist for Blue Note label, 1961-65; appeared at Village Vanguard, N.Y.C., 1976; solo albums include: Bikini Blues, 1947, Doin Alright, One Flight Up, Manhattan Symphonie, Homecoming; star (film) 'Round Midnight, 1986 (Acad. award nomination for best actor), also appeared in film Awakenings. Winner Downbeat Hall of Fame award, 1980; recipient Grammy award for best solo jazz instrumental performance, 1987. Home: New York N.Y. Died Apr. 25, 1990.

GORDON, GLEN E., chemistry educator; b. Keokuk, Iowa, Oct. 13, 1935; s. Scott Robert and Sara Pauline (Perry) G.; m. Constance Christine Herreshoff, May 31, 1958; children: Karl, Christine. B.S., U. Ill., 1956; Ph.D., U. Calif.-Berkeley, 1960. Instr. chemistry MIT, Cambridge, 1960-61, asst. prof., 1961-64, assoc. prof., 1964-69; assoc. prof. chemistry U. Md., Coll. Park, 1969-73, prof., 1973-92; cons. Electric Power Research Inst. Palo Alto, Calif., 1976-87, Oak Ridge Nat. Lab., Tenn., 1976-82, 86-90, Lawrence Livermore Nat. Lab., Calif., 1978-82, Brookhaven Nat. Lab. , N.Y., 1991. Author: The Delicate Balance—An Environmental Chemistry Module, 1973; (with others) Chemistry in Modern Perspective; assoc. editor: Jour. Geophysical Research, 1985-86; contbr. numerous articles to profl. jours. Recipient Air Products and Chemicals Inc. award for creative advances in environ. sci. and tech., 1992. Mem. Am. Chem. Soc. (councillor 1976-79, G.D. Searle award for nuclear applications in chemistry 1977), AAAS Alpha Chi Sigma. Presbyn. Died Jan. 13, 1992; buried Christ Church Cemetery, Port Republic, Md. Home: Silver Spring Md.

GORDON, HAROLD JOHN, business executive; b. Chgo., Apr. 11, 1896; s. Daniel C.and Anna N. (Zeeveld) G.; m. Ethel Rycroft Byford, Jan. 28, 1922; children: Ethel Ann Gordon Michael, Harold Rycroft,

Frances Theresa Gordon Lee. PhB, U. Chgo., 1917. Salesman Halsey, Stuart & Co., Inc., Chgo., 1917-26, dist. sales mgr., 1926-42; Chgo. sales mgr. Halsey, Stuart & Co., Inc., 1942-92; v.p. Halsey, Stuart & Co., Inc., Chgo., 1947-92. Bd. govs. Internat. House (past pres.), U. Chgo. Alumni Found. (past pres.). lt. USNR, 1917-18. Mem. Univ. Club, Chikaming Country Club (past pres.), Delta Kappa Epsilon. Republican. Presbyterian. *

GORDON, JAMES FLEMING, federal judge; b. Madisonville, Ky., May 18, 1918; s. John F. and Ruby (James) G.; m. Iola Young, Sept. 1, 1942; children: Maurice K. II, James Fleming, Marianna. LL.B., U. Ky., 1941. Bar: Ky. 1941. Practice in Madisonville, 1941-65; judge U.S. Dist. Ct., Western Dist. Ky., Owensboro, 1965-84, chief judge, 1968-75, sr. judge, 1976-84; chmn. Ky. Pub. Service Commn., 1955-59; Speakers chmn. Ky. Democratic Party, 1955, campaign chmn., 1962. Bd. dirs. Clinic Found., Madisonville. Served to 1st lt., JAG, AUS, 1941-46, PTO. Mem. Am. Coll. Trial Lawyers, Am. Legion, VFW, Phi Delta Phi. Home: Venice Calif. Died Feb. 9, 1990; buried Madisonville, Ky.

GORDON, JAMES ROYCROFT, mining executive; b. Kingston, Ont., May 26, 1898; s. Byron and Edith Harriet (Leonard) G.; m. Margaret Arthur, June 7, 1922 (dec.); children: James, David, Shirley Gordon Harrison, Ruth Gordon Parrott;/ m. Joan Ehretia Windus, 1955; 1 stepchild, Brian. BSc in Chemistry, Queen's U., 1920. Rsch. metallurgist M.J. O'Brien, Ltd., 1920-29; rschr. Ont. Rsch. Found., 1929-36; dir. rsch. Internat. Nichel Co. of Can., Ltd., 1936-41, asst. to v.p., 1941-46, tech. asst. to v.p., 1946, asst. v.p., 1947-52, asst. gen. mgr., 1952, v.p., dir., gen. mgr. Can. ops., 1953, v.p. N.Y. office, 1953; exec. v.p., pres. Internat. Nicel Co. Can. Ltd. also U.S. subsidiary, 1957-60, 60-92; trustee Bank of N.Y.; dir. Brit. Am. Oil Co., Steel Co. of Can., Ltd., Borden Co., Can. Life Assurance Co., Babcock & Wilcox Co., N.Y., Toronto-Dominion Bank, Page-Hersey Tubes, Ltd. Trustee Queen's U.; bd. gov.'s Ont. Rsch. Found.; mem. Ont. Mining Commn., 1943-44. Recipient Platinum medal Can. Inst. Mining and Metallurgy for contbns. to process metallurgy in smelting and refining of nicel, and improvements in metall. nicel recovery, 1948, James Douglas gold medal AIME, 1957. Mem. Ont. Mining Assn. (pres. 1949-50), Can. Inst. Mining and Metallurgy, Internat. Copper Rsch. Assn. (dir.), AIME, ASM, Chem. Inst. Can., Mining Club, Masons, Toronto Club, York Club (Toronto), Mt. Royal Club (Montreal), 29 Club, City Midday Club, University Club, India House (N.Y.C.)./. Presbyterian. *

GORDON, MAX, night club executive; b. Lithuania, Mar. 12, 1903; came to U.S., 1908, naturalized, 1908; s. Reuben and Sarah Gordon; m. Lorraine Gordon, Apr. 20, 1946; children: Rebecca, Deborah. B.A., Reed Coll., 1924. Owner, operator Blue Angel night club, N.Y.C., 1943-64, Le Directoire, N.Y.C., 1948-49, Village Vanguard, N.Y.C., 1934-89. Author: Live At The Village Vanguard, 1980. Democrat. Jewish. Home: New York N.Y. Died May 11, 1989.

GORDON, MILTON A., manufacturing company executive; b. Chgo., Jan. 9, 1912; s. Julius H. and Diana (Edison) G.; m. Elinor Loeff, Oct. 20, 1937; children—Stephen, Leslie Susan. Ph.B., U. Chgo., 1933, J.D., 1935. Bar: Ill. bar 1935. Pvt. practice Chgo., 1935-43; pres. Morris, Mann & Reilly, Inc., Chgo., 1943-45; v.p., dir. Walter E. Heller & Co., Chgo., 1945-53; founder TV Programs Am., Inc., N.Y.C., pres., 1953-58; founder, pres., then chmn. bd. M.A. Gordon and Co., Inc., N.Y.C.; sr. partner Halle & Stieglitz, N.Y.C., 1969-71; chmn. bd. Halle & Stieglitz, Inc., N.Y.C., 1971-89, Cable Funding Corp., 1972-73, Halle Industries, Inc., 1975-89, Vincennes Steel Corp., from 1979; chmn. exec. com. Irvin Industries Inc., 1979-89. Mem. fiscal commn., N.Y.C., 1964-66; mem. Presdl. del. to independence celebration of Kenya, 1963. Home: New York N.Y. Died Jan. 31, 1990.

GORE, WILBERT LEE, business executive, chemist; b. Meridian, Idaho, Jan. 25, 1912; s. Roscoe Blaine and Dora (Clark) G.; m. Genevieve Walton, Jan. 1, 1935; children—Robert W., Susan W., Virginia W., David W., Elizabeth W. B.S. in Chem. Engring., U. Utah, 1933, M.S. in Phys. Chemistry, 1935; H.H.D. (hon.), Westminster Coll., Salt Lake City, 1971. Analyst, chem. engr. Am. Smelting & Refining Co., Garfield, Utah, 1936-41; engring. supr. Remington Arms Co., Ilion, N.Y., 1941-45; research supt. E.I. duPont de Nemours, Wilmington, Del., 1945-57; pres. W.L. Gore & Assocs., Newark, 1957-76, chmn. bd., 1976-86; dir. Blue Cross/Blue Shield of Del. Author: Statistical Methods for Chemical Experimentation, 1952; Theory of Extrusion, 1960. Bd. dirs. Community Services, Newark, Del., Ams. for Competitive Enterprise Systems, Inc., Wilmington. Recipient Medal of Distinction, U. Del., 1983, Excellence in Mgmt. award Industry Week Mag., 1983. Mem. Am. Chem. Soc., Soc. Plastic Engrs., IEEE. Home: Newark Del. Died July 26, 1986.

GOREN, CHARLES HENRY, contract bridge expert, columnist; b. Phila., Mar. 4, 1901; s. Jacob and Rebecca G. LL.B., McGill U., Can., 1922, LL.M., 1923, LL.D., 1973. Bar: Pa. bar 1923. Practiced in Phila., 1922-35; profl. bridge player, writer, from 1930's. Author: numerous books including Contract Bridge in a Nutshell, 1946, Point Count Bidding in Contract Bridge, 1950, Contract Bridge Complete, 1951 (12 edits.), The Italian Bridge System, 1958, New Contract Bridge in a Nutshell, 1959, An Evening of Bridge with Charles Goren, 1959, Goren's Hoyle, 1961, Goren's Bridge Complete, 1963, Bridge is My Game, 1965, Go With the Odds, 1969, Charles Goren Presents the Precision System, 1971, Goren on Play and Defense, 1974, Goren's Modern Backgammon Complete, 1974, Goren Settles the Bridge Arguments, 1974, Charles H. Goren's One Hundred Challenging Bridge Hands, 1976, Goren on Bridge; daily column syndicated by numerous newspapers including Chgo. Tribune, from 1944; weekly column Sports Illus. mag.; master ceremonies, commentator: TV program Championship Bridge, 1959-64. Named Player of Yr. Am. Contract Bridge League, 8 times, named "Mr. Bridge", 1969; winner one World Bridge championship. Home: Encino Calif. Died Apr. 3, 1991; buried Encino, Calif.

GORES, LANDIS, architect; b. Cin., Aug. 31, 1919; s. Guido and Paula Margaret (Landis) G.; m. Pamela Whitmarsh, Dec. 12, 1942; children: Catherine Gores Keefe, Ainslie Gores Gilligan, Valerie, Karl, Elizabeth Anne. AB summa cum laude, Princeton U., 1939; BArch, Harvard U., 1942. Assoc. with Philip C. Johnson, N.Y.C., 1945-51; individual archtl. practice New Canaan, Conn., from 1951; lectr. Pratt Inst., 1947-48, 52-53. Contbg. bd.: Jour. AIA, 1958-62; prin. works include custom residences in Conn., N.Y., Va., middle sch. and sci. bldgs, New Canaan Country Sch., North Fairfield Geriatric Ctr., Strathmoor Village, Fairfield, York Research Corp. Offices and Labs, Stamford. Served to maj. AUS, 1942-46. Decorated Legion of Merit, Order Brit. Empire; recipient Sch. medal AIA, 1942, nat. honor award AIA, 1955, Sao Paulo Bieniale award, 1955, Award Merit Boston Arts Festival, 1956, Award Merit New Haven Festival Arts, 1959, First Honor Awards Program Conn. AIA, 1964. Fellow AIA; mem. Phi Beta Kappa. Republican. Episcopalian. Home: New Canaan Conn. Died Mar. 18, 1991; buried Spring Grove Cemetery, Cin.

GORMAN, THOMAS FRANCIS (MIKE GORMAN), writer, association executive; b. N.Y.C., Dec. 7, 1913; s. Frank and Mary (Naughton) G.; m. Ernestine Brown, June 3, 1946 (dec. June 1958); children: Michael, Patricia; m. Patricia Lea Vierling, Nov. 30, 1979; 1 stepson, Douglas. A.B., NYU, 1934, postgrad., 1934-36. Freelance writer, 1936-41; reporter Daily Oklahoman, 1945; writer numerous news stories and editorials in mental hosp. campaign, pioneered establishment of mental hygiene clinic in Okla., also mental hygiene orgn.; chief writer, dir. pub. hearings Pres.'s Commn. on Health Needs of the Nation, 1950-53; exec. dir. Nat. Com. Against Mental Illness, Washington, from 1953; mem. Menninger Found.; mem. Joint Commn. Mental Health of Children, from 1966; mem. nat. adv. mental health council USPHS, from 1961; mem. 1st U.S. Mental Health Del. to USSR, 1967; mem. World Fedn. Mental Health; exec. dir. Citizens for Treatment High Blood Pressure, from 1977; mem. Citizens for Pub. Action on Cholesterol, 1985. Author: Oklahoma Attacks Its Snake Pits, 1948, Every Other Bed, 1956, Psychiatry in the Soviet Union, 1969, Community Mental Health: The Search for Identity, 1970; contbr. articles on psychiat. and med. subjects to mags. Exec. dir. Citizens for Pub. Action on Cholesterol, from 1985. Served with USAAF, 1942-45. Recipient Spl. Lasker award Nat. Com. Mental Hygiene, 1948; Edward A. Strecker Meml. award, 1962; William C. Menninger award, 1971; 1st Dr. Benjamin Rush award, 1976; 1st Disting. Service award Nat. Council Community Mental Health Ctrs., 1973, Mental Health Service medallion Nat. Mus. Am. History, 1986; named one of ten Outstanding Young Men in Am. U.S. Jaycees, 1949. Fellow Am. Pub. Health Assn., Am. Psychiat. Assn. (hon.), Royal Soc. Health (Eng.), N.Y. Acad. Scis.; mem. Nature Conservancy, Nat. Press Club (med. writing award 1972), Phi Beta Kappa. Clubs: Federal City, City Tavern (Washington). Home: Washington D.C. Deceased. †

GORNTO, ALBERT BROOKS, JR., banker; b. Norfolk, Va., Aug. 23, 1929; s. Albert Brooks and Oretha (Brinn) G.; m. Barbara Joan Lassiter, Sept. 26, 1953; children: Neil Brooks, Suzanne Gornto Parr, Lynanne. BSBA, Old Dominion U., 1956; diploma Comml. Bankers Sch., U. Va., 1958; diploma, NABAC Sch. U. Wis., 1961, Stoner Grad. Sch. Banking Rutgers U., 1970. With Nat. Bank Commerce Norfolk, 1957-63, asst. cashier, 1958-61, cashier, 1961-63; founder Va. Nat. Bank, Norfolk, 1963, v.p., cashier, 1968-70, sr. v.p., cashier, 1970, corp. exec. officer, cashier, 1970-72, corp. exec. officer, 1972-80, exec. v.p., 1980-92; founder Va. Nat. Bankshares Inc., Norfolk, 1972, asst. sec., asst. treas., 1972-80, exec. v.p., 1980-92; founder Va. Nat. Bldg. Corp., Norfolk, 1963, sec., treas., 1963-80, v.p., 1980-92, project mgr. hdqrs. bldg. and garage, 1963-68; founder Sovran Fin. Corp., Sovran Bank N.A., Norfolk, 1983, sr. exec. v.p., 1983, pres., 1988-89, pres., chief exec. officer, chmn. bd., 1989-90; chmn. exec. com. C&S/Sovran Corp., Norfolk, 1990-92. Bd. visitors Old Dominion U.; bd. dirs. Old Dominion U. Ednl. Found., Norfolk, 1964, Sentara Hosps., Norfolk, 1985, Chrysler Mus., Norfolk, 1983, Forward Hampton Rds., Norfolk, 1988, Med. Coll. Hampton Rds. Found., Norfolk, 1988; bd. dirs., trustee Sentara Health System, Norfolk, 1983. Named Disting. Alumni Old Dominion U., Norfolk, 1979, Outstanding Alumni Sch. Bus. Adminstrn. Old Dominion U., Norfolk, 1982. Mem. Assn. Bank Holding Cos., Assn. Res. City Bankers, Va. Bankers Assn., Princess Anne Country Club, Town Point Club. Presbyterian. Home: Virginia Beach Va. Died Aug. 30, 1992. †

GOSNELL, HAROLD FOOTE, political science educator; b. Lockport, N.Y., Dec. 24, 1896; s. James and Sylvia (Foote) G.; m. Florence Lucy Fake, June 30, 1928; children: David Foote, John Seammon. AB, U. Rochester, 1918; PhD, U. Chgo., 1922. Instr. polit. sci. U. Chgo., 1922-26, asst. prof., 1926-32, assoc. prof., 1932-43; adj. prof. Am. U., 1946-62; sr. rsch. scientist Spl. Ops. Rsch. Office, 1960-61; vis., prof. U. Wash., 1955; prof. dept. gove. Howard U., Washington, 1962-92; editorial staff Pres.'s Rsch. Com. on Social Trends, 1932; rsch. cons. Nat. Resources Bd., 1937, Bur. of Budget, 1940, Office of Price Adminstrn., 1941-42, Bur. of Budget, 1942-46, Dept. of State, 1946-50. Author books including: Democracy, 1948, Champion Campaigner: Franklin D. Roosevelt, 1952, also numerous articles; co-author publs. including: The American Party System, 1949. With U.S. Army, 1918-19. Social Sci. Rsch. Coun. fellow, 1925-26, Spelman Fund fellow, 1933; recipient John Asnfield award, 1935. Mem. Am. Polit. Sci. Assn. (exec. coun.), Edgemoor Club, Phi Delta Kappa. *

GOTFRYD, ALEXANDER, art executive, photographer; b. Warsaw, Poland, Apr. 26, 1931; came to U.S., 1946, naturalized, 1951; s. Bernard and Regina (Lurie) G. B.A., Queens Coll., Sorbonne, L'Ecole des Beaux Arts, 1954; postgrad., Yale, 1954-55. Free lance comml. artist, 1955-60; art dir., v.p. Doubleday & Co., N.Y.C., 1960-90, exec. art dir., v.p., 1981-90, exec. art dir. emeritus, 1990; freelance photographer. Exhibited at Bodley Gallery, N.Y.C., 1959; one man shows include Lieberman and Saul Gallery, N.Y.C., 1988; co-author: (plays) The Blasphemy of Arthur Rimbaud's Sister, 1973, An Absence of Heroes, 1974; photographer (book) Egypt-The Eternal Smile (text by Allen Drury), 1980; author, photographer (book) Appointment in Venice, 1988; designer numerous book jackets, including many best sellers. Recipient Designer of Yr. award Literary Market Pl., 1990. Home: New York N.Y. Died Mar. 30, 1991.

GOUBEAU, VINCENT DE PAUL, management consultant; b. N.Y.C., July 19, 1898; s. Henry Walter and Mary (McGinnis) G.; m. Mary Louise Field. Student, De la Salle Inst., N.Y.C. Buyer dept. purchasing United Fruit Co., N.Y.C., 1922-25; purchasing agt. United Fruit Co., Boston, 1925-42; procurement specialist Navy Dept., Washington, 1942-45; asst. chief in charge procurement Office Procurement and Materials, 1944-45; purchasing mgr. RCA-Victor div. Radio Corp. of Am., Camden, N.J., 1945, v.p., dir. materials, 1949-65. Bd. lay trustees Trinity Coll., Washington; trustee Salena Hosp. Mem. nat. Assn. Purchasing Agts. (past dir.), New Eng. Purchasing Agts. Assn. (past pres.), Am. Standards Assn. (gold medalist, Coonley award), Knight of Malta, Knight Grand Cross, Order of Holy Sepulchre, University Club (Washington), Phila. Country Club, Salem (Mass.) Country Club, Algonquin Club (Boston). Roman Catholic. *

GOULD, BERNARD ALBERT, lawyer, consultant; b. Chelsea, Mass., Jan. 30, 1912; s. Harry and Rebecca (LeVine) G.; m. Edith Solomon, June 16, 1936; children: Susan Deborah Brome, John Richard. B.C.S., NYU, 1936, J.D., 1941; postgrad., George Washington U., 1937-38. Bar: N.Y. 1942, D.C. 1979, U.S. Supreme Ct. 1960. With R.R. industry, N.Y.C., 1929-36; various positions in govt. service, 1936-88; dir. Bur. Enforcement, ICC, Washington, 1967-76, cons., 1976-88; instr. interstate commerce law and procedure NYU; lectr. transp. law to industry and legal groups and seminars. mem. Gov.'s Commn. to Revise Mental Retardation and Devel. Disability Law; past pres. Montgomery County Assn. for Retarded Citizens; bd. dirs., legis. chmn. Md. Assn. Retarded Citizens; mem. govt. affairs com. U.S. Assn. for Retarded Citizens. Recipient Disting. Service citation for war transp. activities, 1945. Mem. Fed. Bar Assn., D.C. Bar Assn., Am. Judicature Soc., Nat. Lawyers Club, Alpha Epsilon Pi. Club: Aspen Hill Racquet. Home: Silver Spring Md. Died Nov. 22, 1988.

GOULD, LAWRENCE MCKINLEY, educator; b. Lacota, Mich., Aug. 22, 1896; s. Herbert and Anna (Updike) G.; m. Margaret Rice, Aug. 2, 1930. BS magna cum laude, U. Mich., 1921, MA, ScD, 1923, 25, LLD, 1954; ScD (hon.), Poly. Inst. Bklyn., 1931. Instr. geology U. Mich., 1921-26, asst. prof., 1926-30, assoc. prof., 1930-31; prof. geology Carleton Coll., 1932-45, pres., 1945-63, pres. emeritus, 1963-92; prof. geology U. Ariz., Tucson, 1963-92; asst. dir., geologist U. Mich. Greenland Expdn., 1926; asst. dir. and geographer Putnam Raffin Island Expdn., 1927; 2d in commd. and geologist-geographer Byrd Antarctic Expdn., 1928-30; dir. Antarctica program U.S. Nat. Com. Internat. Geophys. Year, 1957-58; chmn. polar rsch. com. Nat. Acad. Scis.; U.S. rep. spl. com. on Antarctic rsch. Internat. Coun. Sci. Unions, 1963-66. Author: Cold - the

Record of an Antarctic Sledge Journey, 1931; also papers on geology Baffin Island and Antarctica and pleistocene geology of upper Mississippi Valley. Trustee Ford Found., Carnegie Found. for Advancement of Teaching, 1958-62; mem. nat. sci. bd. NSF, 1952-62. With U.S. Army, 1917-19; with Italian Army summer 1918. Awarded Congl. Gold Medal, 1931, Cross of St. Olaf, 1st Class, Royal Norwegian Order; recipient Navy Disting. Pub. Svc. award, 1959, Explorer's Club medal, 1957. Fellow Geol. Soc. Am., AAAS (past pres.), Am. Geog. Soc. (David Livingston medal 1930); mem. Assn. Am. Geographers, Minn. Acad. Sci. (pres. 1938-39), Arctic Inst. N.Am. (chmn. bd. govs. 1946), Am. Meteorol. Soc., Coun. on Fgn. Rels., Phi Beta Kappa (pres., senator-at-large, United chpts.), Sigma Xi, Pi Kappa Alpha, Sigma Gamma Epsilon, Nat. Geog. Soc. (life), Geog. Soc. Chgo. (life), Am. Legion, Rotary, Phila. Geog. Soc. (corres. mem.), Explorers Club, Mpls. Skylight Club, Old Pueblo Club, other. *

GOULD, WILLIAM DRUM, religious, philosophy educator; b. Phila., Aug. 1, 1897; s. William Henry Gulickand Edith Myrtle (Drum) G.; m. Evelyn Louise Davenport, Sept. 26, 1922; 1 child, William Harold. BA, Wesleyan U., Conn., 1919; BD, Garrett Theol. Sem., 1922; postgrad., Harvard U., 1925-27; PhD, Boston U., 1929. Ordained to ministry Meth. Ch., 1924. Pastor Hamburg, Pa., 1923-24; prof. history Iowa Wesleyan Coll., 1929-33, dean of coll., prof. history and polit. sci., 1933-37; assoc. prof. history and polit. sci. Dickiknson Coll., 1937-44, assoc. prof. philosophy and religion, 1944-46, prof. philosophy and religion, 1946-63, George Henry Ketterer and Bertha Curry Ketterer prof., 1953-63, chmn. dept. philosophy and religion, 1953-63; pres. commn. profs. of religion Meth. Conf. Christian Edn., 1950-51; mem. faculty com. Mikddle Atlantic regional coun. Student Christian Movement, 1949-58, faculty advisor, 1950-51; mem. Phila. Conf. of the Meth. Ch. Author: (with G.B. Arbaugh and R.F. Moore) Oriental Philosophies, 1951; contbr. articles to profl. jours. Mem. Am. Assn. Tchrs. Chinese Lang. and Culture, Am. Philos. Assn., nat. Assn. Bibl. IKnstrs., AAUP, Masons (K.T.), Phi Beta Kappa, Alpha Chi Rho. Republican. *

GOULDING, RAYMOND WALTER, actor; b. Lowell, Mass., Mar. 20, 1922; s. Thomas M. and Mary (Philbin) G.; m. Elizabeth Leader, May 18, 1945; children: Raymond, Thomas, Barbara, Bryant, Mark, Melissa. Pres. Goulding, Elliot, Greybar Prodns. Inc., N.Y.C., 1954-90. Actor numerous network radio and TV prodns., motion pictures; co-star: Bob and Ray Show, NBC, CBS, ABC, from 1951; film appearances in Cold Turkey, 1969, Author! Author!, 1982; Broadway play The Two and Only, 1970-71; author: (with Bob Elliot) book From Approximately Coast to Coast...It's the Bob and Ray Show, 1983. Served to 1st lt. AUS, 1942-46. Mem. Screen Actors Guild, AFTRA, Am. Guild Variety Artists. Home: Manhasset N.Y. Died Mar. 24, 1990.

GOWANS, MRS. WILLIAM RORY See REMICK, LEE

GOWETZ, IRENE, lawyer; b. Worcester, Mass., Aug. 28, 1907; d. Arthur E. and Alice (Hemenway) G.; m. Carl A. Remington, June 18, 1959. LL.B. cum laude, Northeastern U., 1929. Bar: Mass. 1929. Ptnr. firm Bowditch, Gowetz and Lane, Worcester, from 1950; Chmn. Mass. Ballot Law Commn., 1955-58. Bd. dirs. Girls Clubs Am., 1955-81. Republican. Home: Mount Dora Fla. Died Oct. 16, 1988.

GRACE, OLIVER RUSSELL, business executive; b. Great Neck, N.Y., Dec. 2, 1909; s. Morgan H. and Ruth (Eden) G.; m. Anne Chilton McDonnell, Nov. 29, 1934 (div. 1944); children: Helen Miller (Mrs. Helen Spencer), Ann Chilton (Mrs. Ratus Lee Kelly), Ruth Elizabeth (Mrs. Wayne Jervis); m. Lorraine Graves, Oct. 23, 1949; children: Lorraine (Mrs. Lorraine L. Grace), Gwendolyn (Mrs. Stephen Kull), Oliver Russell, John Sheffield. Ph.B., Yale, 1930. Statistician Grace Nat. Bank, N.Y.C., 1930-36; ptnr. Sterling, Grace & Co., 1936-69, chmn., 1969-87; gen. ptnr. Sterling Grace Capital Mgmt. L.P., 1986-92; chmn., founder Grace & White, investments, Grace Geothermal Corp.; chmn. bd. dirs. Andersen Group, Bloomfield, Conn., 1959-92; bd. dirs. Am. Distilling Co., Am.-Hawaiin Steamship Co., Foster Wheeler Corp., Gt. Neck Trust Co., Kennecott Corp., Reeves Telecom Corp., Rep. Automotive Parts, Slattery Group, United Chem., Universal Am. Corp., Va. Carolina Chem. Corp., Webb & Knapp. Co-founder Cancer Research Inst., Inc., pres., 1953-58, 66-73, chmn., 1974-92; bd. dirs., exec. com. Theodore Roosevelt Assn.; trustee, mem. exec. com., sec. Cold Spring Harbor Lab., L.I.; v.p. Nat. Instr. Social Scis., 1984-92; bd. dirs. Franklin Coll., Switzerland. Episcopalian. Clubs: University, India House (N.Y.C.); Piping Rock, Seawanaka Corinthian Yacht; Bath and Tennis. (Palm Beach, Fla.); Portland (London). Home: Oyster Bay N.Y. Died Jan. 16, 1992; buried St. John's Cemetery, Cold Spring Harbor, L.I., N.Y.

GRAHAM, BILL, theatrical producer; b. Berlin, Jan. 8, 1931; came to U.S., 1941, naturalized, 1953; s. Jacob and Frieda (Zess) Grajonca; m. Bonnie McLean, June 1967 (div. 1969); 1 child, David; m. Marcia Sult, 1975 (div. 1979); 1 child, Alex. BBA, CCNY. Statistician Pace Motor Trucking Co., from 1955; paymaster Guy F. Atkinson Constructors; office mgr. Allis-Chalmers Mfg. Co., to 1965. Concert promoter producer, mgr. maj. rock music artists, Eddie Money, The Neville Bros., Joe Satriani; creator Fillmore Auditoriums East, N.Y.C., 1968-71, and West, San Francisco, 1965-71, pres. FM Prodns., San Francisco, 1966-91; Bill Graham Presents, San Francisco, 1976-91, Bill Graham Mgmt., 1976-91, Wolfgang Records, San Francisco, 1976-82 ; producer outdoor musical events including Watkins Glen, N.Y., 1974; operator Shoreline Amphitheatre, 1986—; country-wide tours, Bob Dylan, Crosby, Stills, Nash and Young and George Harrison, Rolling Stones World Tour, 1981-82, Mick Jagger World Tour, 1988; 70 maj. outdoor concerts at Oakland (Calif.) Stadium, 1973-90; actor, producer concert for film A Star Is Born, 1976, Last Waltz, 1976; actor Apocalypse Now, Cotton Club, Gardens of Stone, Bugsy; concert prodn. cons.; organizer, producer maj. benefit concerts for causes including Center for Self-Determination, 1975, Save Our Cities, 1976, San Francisco Sch. Dist., 1976, Live Aid, 1985, Amnesty Internat., 1986, 88, Crack-Down, 1986, Soviet-Am. Peace Concert, Moscow, 1987, Earthquake Relief benefit 1989, Nelson Mandela/ANC benefit, 1990; exec. producer (film) The Doors, 1991. Served with U.S. Army, 1951-53. Decorated Bronze Star medal, Purple Heart.; recipient B'nai B'rith Lodge award, 1973, MTV Lifetime Achievement award, 1986, City of Hope Spirit of Life award, 1987, Commendation Excellence Broadcast Music Inc., 1975, St. Francis Assissi award City San Francisco, 1975, Am. Friends Hebrew U. Scopus Laureate award, 1990; named Billboard Promoter Yr., 1975, 76, 77, Pollstar Promoter Yr., 1989, 90, Performance Promoter Yr., 1981, 82, 86, 89; lauded in U.S. Congl. Records 1968, 85. Home: Corte Madera Calif. Died Oct. 25, 1991.

GRAHAM, CHALMERS GEORGE, lawyer; b. San Francisco, May 10, 1895; s. Chalmers A. and Catherine Florence (Stapleton) G.; m. Marie Luise Meyer, Nov. 24, 1925; 1 child, Marie Luise (dec.). AB, Leland Stanford U., 1918; student, Sorbonne, Paris, 1919, Harvard U., 1921-22; JD, Leland Stanford U., 1923. Bar: Calif. 1923. Mem. Graham, James & Rolph; admiralty lawyer, 1923-92; admiralty counsel War Shipping Adminstrn., 1942-44; chmn. bd. Cat/Ink Chem. Co., Laurentide Fin. Corp. of Calif.; dir. Tenneco Chems., Inc. Decorated Chevalier Legion d'Honneur (France); Order of Rising Sun 3d Class (Japan), Hon. Comdr. Brit. Empire. Mem. Brit.-Am. C. of C. and Trade Ctr. (past pres.), Japan Soc., Internat. C. of C. (trustee U.S. coun.), Calif. World Affairs Coun. (bd. trustees), Bohemian Club, Menlo Country Club, India House Club (N.Y.C.). *

GRAHAM, MARTHA, dancer, choreographer; b. Pitts., May 11, 1894. Studied with Ruth St. Denis and Ted Shawn; LL.D., Mills Coll., Brandeis U., Smith Coll., Harvard, 1966, also numerous others. Faculty Eastman Sch., 1925. Soloist Denishawn Co., 1920, Greenwich Village Follies, 1923, debut as choreographer-dancer, 48th St. Theatre, N.Y.C., 1926; founder, artistic dir., Martha Graham Dance Co., 1926-91, also Martha Graham Sch. Contemporary Dance; choreographer with music composed by Aaron Copland, Paul Hindemith, Carlos Chavez, Samuel Barber, Gian-Carlo Menotti, William Schuman, others of more than 170 works including Appalachian Spring, Cave of the Heart, Errand into the Maze, Clytemnestra, Frontier, Phaedra, Herodiade, Primitive Mysteries, Night Journey, Seraphic Dialogue, Lamentation, Acts of Light, Rite of Spring, Judith, Heretic, Diversion of Angels, Witch of Endor, Cortege of Eagles, A Time of Snow, Plain of Prayer, Lady of the House of Sleep, Archaic Hours, Mendicants of Evening, Myth of a Voyage, Holy Jungle, Dream, Chronique, Lucifer, Scarlet Letter, Adorations, Point of Crossing; guest soloist leading U.S. orchs. in solos Judith, Triumph of St. Joan; fgn. tours with Martha Graham Dance Co., 1950, 54, 55-56, 60, 62-63, 67, 68; some under auspices U.S. Dept State; collaborated in over 25 set designs with Isamu Naguchi, also Alexander Calder; also designed costumes for many of her dances; Author: Notebooks of Martha Graham, 1973. Recipient Aspen award 1965, Creative Arts award Brandeis U., 1968, Disting. Service to the Arts award, Nat. Inst. Arts and Letters, 1970, Handel medallion City of N.Y., 1970, N.Y. State Council on Arts award, 1973, Presdl. Medal of Freedom, 1976, Kennedy Center honor, 1979, Samuel H. Scripps Am. Dance Festival award, 1981, Meadows award So. Meth. U., 1982, Gold Florin City of Florence, 1983, Paris Medal of Honor, 1985, Arnold Gingrich Memorial award N.Y. Arts and Bus. Council, 1985, Nat. Medal for Arts, 1985, Decorated knight Legion of Honor (France), 1983; Guggenheim fellow, 1932. Home: New York N.Y. Died Apr. 1, 1991.

GRAHAM, ROBERT MONTROSE, physician; b. Eagle Grove, Iowa, June 19, 1895; s. Samuel C. and Helen (Baldwin) G.; m. Fanchon E. Bennett, May 22, 1925; children: Robert Bennett, John Russell. BS, U. Iowa, 1917, MD, 1920. Physician USPHS, 1920-21; extern Augustana Hosp., Chgo., 1923; attending physician Ill. Social Hygiene Dispensary, 1924-28, Postgrad. Dispensary, 1928-29; physician med. dept. Pullman Co., 1922-92, dir. medicine and sanitation, 1942-92. Contbr. articles to profl. jours. Fellow AMA, Am. Pub. Health Assn., Am. Coll. Preventive Medicine; mem. Indsl. Med. Assn., Chgo. Med. Soc., Inst. Med., Am. Assn. Ry. Surgeons, AAAS, Phi Rho Sigma. *

GRANGE, RED (HAROLD) EDWARD (THE GALLOPING GHOST), professional football player; b. Forksville, Pa., June 13, 1903; m. Margaret, 1942. Student, U. Ill., 1925. Chgo. Bears (NFL), 1925, 1929-34, N.Y. Yankees (AFL), 1926, 1927 (NFL); Asst. coach Chgo. Bears (NFL), 1936; radio, TV announcer NBC, 1947-61. Charter mem. Profl. Football Hall of Fame, 1963, mem. Nat. Football Found. Col. Football Hall of Fame. Died Jan. 28, 1991; Lake Wales, Fla.* †

GRANICK, DAVID, economist, educator; b. N.Y.C., Jan. 13, 1926; s. Harry and Ray (Weiss) G.; m. Kaete Loette Boenheim, Sept. 12, 1950; children: Steve, Barbara Liza, Jim Timothy. BSS, CCNY, 1944; MA, Columbia U., 1948, PhD, 1951; cert., Russian Inst., 1949. Asso. prof. econs. Fisk U., 1951-57; asst. prof. econs. Carnegie Inst. Tech., 1957-59; assoc. prof. U. Wis., Madison, 1959-62; prof. econs. U. Wis., 1962-90, prof. emeritus, from 1990, chmn. Russian area program, 1965-66; chmn. Western European area program, 1972-74; Econ. affairs officer UN Secretariat, summers 1951, 52; research asso. U. N.C., 1953-54, Russian Research Center, Harvard, 1956-57; sr. research scholar U. Glasgow, Scotland, 1959-60; dir. d'etudes Associe, Ecole Pratique des Hautes Etudes, U. Paris, 1963-64; vis. prof. U. Manchester, Eng., 1964, Ecole des Hautes Etudes Commerciales, U. Montreal, 1975, Nihon U., Tokyo, 1987; mem. exec. com. Council for European Studies, 1972-74; mem. acad. council Kennan Inst. Advanced Russian Studies, Woodrow Wilson Internat. Ctr. for Scholars, 1983-85; vis. scholar Hoover Instn. on War, Revolution and Peace, 1985-86. Author: Management of Industrial Firm in the USSR, 1954, The Red Executive, 1960, The European Executive, 1962, Soviet Metalfabricating and Economic Development, 1967, Managerial Comparisons of Four Developed Countries: France, Britain, United States, and Russia, 1972, Enterprise Guidance in Eastern Europe, 1976, Job Rights in the Soviet Union: Their Consequences, 1987, Chinese Industrial Enterprises: A Regional Property Rights Analysis, 1990; contbr. articles to profl. jours. Served with AUS, 1944-46. Social Sci. Research Council fellow, 1949-50; Guggenheim fellow, 1956-57; Fulbright fellow, 1959-60; sr. research fellow European Inst. Columbia U., 1966-67; Internat. Research and Exchanges Bd. fellow Rumania, Hungary, Poland, 1970-71; fellow Netherlands Inst. for Advanced Study, 1974-75; fellow Kennan Inst. Advanced Russian Study, Woodrow Wilson Center, 1978-79; fellow for Chinese studies of Am. Council Learned Socs./Social Sci. Research Council, 1985-86. Mem. Assn. for Comparative Econ. Studies, Phi Beta Kappa. Club: Rotarian. Home: Madison Wis. Deceased. †

GRANIT, RAGNAR ARTHUR, neurophysiologist; b. Finland, Oct. 30, 1900; m. Baroness Marguerite (Daisy) Bruun; 1 child, Michael. Grad., Swedish Normallyceum, Helsinki, Finland, 1919; Mag. phil., Helsinki U., MD, 1927, DSc (hon.); DSc (hon.), U. Oslo, U. Oxford, Loyola U.; MD (hon.), U. Pisa, U. Göttingen, others. Docent Helsinki U., 1932-37, prof. physiology, 1937-40; fellow med. physics Eldridge Reeves Johnson Research Found., U. Pa., 1929-31; mem. staff Royal Caroline Inst., Stockholm, 1940-67; prof. neurophysiology Royal Caroline Inst., 1946-67, emeritus mem., from 1967; Thomas Young orator Phys. Soc. London, Eng., 1945; Silliman lectr. Yale U., 1954; Sherrington lectr. London, 1967, Liverpool, 1970; Murlin lectr. Rochester, N.Y., 1973; Jackson lectr. McGill U., 1975; vis. prof. Rockefeller U., N.Y.C., 1956-66, St. Catherine's Coll., Oxford, 1967, Smith-Kettlewell Inst. Med. Sci., San Francisco, 1969, Fogarty Internat. Center, NIH, Bethesda, Md., 1971-72, 75, Düsseldorf U., 1974, Max-Planck Inst., Bad Nauheim, Fed. Republic Germany, 1976. Author: Ung Mans Vägtill Minerva, 1941, Sensory Mechanisms of the Retina, 1947, Receptors and Sensory Perception, 1955, Charles Scott Sherrington, An Appraisal, 1966, Basis of Motor Control, 1970, Regulation of the Discharge of Motoneurons, 1971, The Purposive Brain, 1977, Hur Det Kom Sig (autobiography), 1983. Co-recipient Nobel prize in physiology or medicine, 1967; recipient Donders, Retzius, Sherrington, Purkinje, Tigerstedt medals; 3d Internat. St. Vincent prize, 1961; Jahre prize Oslo U., 1961. Mem. Royal Swedish Acad. Sci. (pres. 1963-65, v.p. 1965-69), Royal Soc. London (fgn. mem.), Nat. Acad. Sci. (U.S.), Am. Philos. Soc., Indian Acad. Sci. (hon.), Acad. di Med. (hon.) (Turin), Acad. Nat. d. Lincei (Rome), Physiol. Soc. Eng. (hon.), Physiol. Soc. U.S. (hon.), Am. Acad. Arts and Scis. (hon.), Societas Scientiarum Fennicae (hon.), Royal Danish Acad., Acad. Finland (fgn. mem.). Home: Stockholm Sweden Died Mar. 12, 1991.

GRANRUD, CARL FRITHJOF, lawyer; b. Decorah, Iowa, Sept. 13, 1896; s. John E. and Amalie (Olsen) G.; m. Agnes Biorneby, Oct. 20, 1920; children: Robert, Marian, Carolyn. BA, St. Olaf Coll., 1918; LLB, Minn. Coll. Law, 1921; LLD, Carthage Coll., 1956. Bar: Minn. 1921. Pvt. practice law Mpls., 1921-92. Chmn. bd. Luth. Brotherhood; gen. counsel, trustee St. Olaf Coll.; pres. Ins.Fedn. Minn., 1963-92. Mem. Mpls. C. of C. (dir.), Minn. Bar Assn., Nat. Fraternal Congress Am. (exec. com.), Mpls. Athletic Club, Midland Hills Country Club. *

GRANT, ARCHIE C., insurance company executive; b. Ely, Minn., Mar. 9, 1894; s. John and Mary (Nolan) G.; m. Zora Faye, Aug. 8, 1921; 1 child, Mary Myrtle. Student, St. Thomas Coll., St. Paul, 1911-12. Propr. A.C. Grant Ford Agy., 1928-55; dir. Transwestern Life Ins. Co., Reno, Nev. Mem. Nev. Planning Bd., Nev. Bd. Edn.; bd. regents U. Nev., 1952-92, chmn., 1956-92; state dir. U.S. Bond sales; state senator, 1941; mem. Nev. Assembly, 1943. With inf. U.S. Army, WWI. Mem. Las Vegas C. of C. (pres. 1933-34, 52), Am. Legion (nat. committeeman), VFW. *

GRANT, EUGENE LODEWICK, civil, industrial engineer; b. Chgo., Feb. 15, 1897; s. Bertrand Eugene and Eva May (Lodewick) G.; m. Mildred Brooks Livingston, Sept. 4, 1923; 1 child, Nancy Livingston. BS, U. Wis., 1917, CE, 1928; AM, Columbia U., 1928. With Butler Bros., Chgo., 1913, C.&I.W. R.R., summer 1914, C.E., U.S. Army, summer 1916, N.Y. State Rys., 1917, water resources br. U.S. Geol. Survey, 1917-19, summer 1921-22; with Bynum (Mont.) Irrigation Dist., summer 1920; instr. civil engring., later prof. indsl. engring. Mont. State Coll., 1920-30; assoc. prof. civil engring., later prof. econ. engring. Stanford U., 1930-62, emeritus, 1962-92; dir. project on engring.-econ. planning, Stanford U., 1961-62, exec. head dept. civil engring., 1947-56; cons. econ. analysis Dept. Water Rersources, Calif., 1958-59; instn. rep. and dir. engring. sci. and mgmt. war tng., 1941-44, pioneered with Holbrook Working short courses in statis. quality control for key pers. of war industries, 1942-44, courses used as nationwide pattern by office prodn. rsch. and devel. Ward Prodn. Bd. and E.S.M.W.T., 1943-45. Author: Principles of Engineering Economy, 1930, 2d edit. (with W.G. Ireson), 1960; Statistical Quality Control, 1946; (with Paul T. Norton, Jr.) Depreciation, 1949; Basic Accounting and Cost Accounting, 1956, 2d edit. (with L.F. Bell), 1964; editor (with W.G. Ireson) Handbook of Industrial Engineering and Management, 1955; contbr. articles to profl. jours. Cons. War Dept., U.S. Engrs. Office, Seattle, 1944-47, secondary blenefits U.S. Bur. Reclamation, 1958; mem. Bd. Pub. Wks., City of Palo Alto, Calif., 1931-37. Recipient Thomas Fitch prize ASCE, 1944. Fellow Am. Soc. Quality Control (Shewhart medalist 1952), Am. Statis. Assn., AAAS; mem. ASCE, Am. Soc. Engring. Edn., Am. Soc. Quality Control, Econometric Soc., Inst. Math. Statistics, Palo Alto Community Players (mem. exec. bd. 1937, 38-40, 46-48), Sigma Xi, Tau Beta Pi, Pi Kappa Alpha. *

GRANVILLE, KEITH, airline executive; b. Faversham, Eng., Nov. 1, 1910; m. Patricia Capstick, 1933; m. Truda Belliss, 1946; 7 children. Ed., Tonbridge Sch. Served in Italy, Tanganyika, Rhodesia, Egypt and India Imperial Airways, 1929; mgr. African and Middle East div. Brit. Overseas Airways Corp. (B.O.A.C.), 1947, comml. dir., 1954, dep. mng. dir., 1958-60, mng. dir., 1969, chmn., 1971-90; dep. chmn. Brit. Airways bd., 1972-74. Decorated comdr. Order Brit. Empire; created knight, 1974. Mem. Inst. Transport, Internat. Air Transport Assn. (exec. com., pres. 1972-73). Home: Kent England Died Apr. 7, 1990.

GRAU, FREDERICK VAHLCAMP, agronomist; b. Bennington, Nebr., Feb. 28, 1902; s. Charles and Ella (Vahlcamp) G.; m. Anne Bourne Fagan, Dec. 21, 1938 (dec. 1968); children: Ellen, Fred, Barbara (dec.); m. 2d, Frances Holyoke McCoy, 1973 (dec. 1976). B.Sc., U. Nebr., 1931; M.S., U. Md., 1933, Ph.D., 1935. Pub. Bennington Herald, 1924; mem. staff green sect. U.S. Golf Assn., Midwest Turf Gardens, Chgo., 1931, Arlington Turf Gardens, Washington, 1931; extension agronomist Pa. State Coll., University Park, 1935-45; dir. U.S. Golf Assn. Green Sect., Beltsville, Md., 1945-53; pres. Grasslyn, Inc., College Park, Md., 1950-81; cons. West Point Products, 1954-56; mem. staff Nitroform Agr. Products Corp., U.S., Can., 1956-68; pres., organizer Musser Internat. Turfgrass Found., College Park, 1968; pres. Fred V. Grau Inc., College Park, 1982-90; adviser Md. Turfgrass Council; turf cons. to numerous govts.; del. to profl. confs. Co-author: (with H.B. Musser) Turf Management, 1950; major contbr. to USDA yearbook Grass, 1948; contbr. to monograph Turfgrass Science, 1968; contbr. articles to profl. jours, chpts. to books on agronomy; contbg. author, editor numerous books and profl. publs.; columnist "Column for Golfdom", Golfdom mag., 1945-75; lectr. to profl. confs.; featured in Nat. Geog. mag. as developer zoysia grass for turf, 1953; developer: first hydroseeder, 1939; first crownvetch for seed prodn., 1940; seed prodn. of zoysia grasses, 1950; discovered developer Penngift crownvetch (legume); research on so. turf. Developer nat. program for turf improvement on playgrounds and athletic fields for Nat. PTA, 1983—. Recipient numerous awards for excellence in agronomy; Man of Yr. award Las Vegas Weeds, Trees and Turf, 1984; grantee in agronomy. Fellow Am. Soc. Agronomy (life mem.; past chmn.; organizer turf sect.), AAAS (life mem.); mem. Internat. Turfgrass Soc., Am. Council for Turfgrass, Sports Turf Mgrs. Assn., Am. Council Turfgrass, Golf Course Supts. Assn. Am. (hon. life), Nat. Sports Turf Council (chmn. exec. com.), Va. Turfgrass Council (hon. life), Pa. Turfgrass Council (hon. life); hon. mem. Midwest Assn. Golf Course Supts., Pocono Turfgrass Assn., Tidewater Turfgrass Assn., Keystone Golf Course Supts. Assn., No. Ohio Golf Course Supts. Assn., numerous others; mem. Sigma Xi, Phi Kappa Phi, Gamma Sigma Delta. Republican. Episcopalian. Club: Pine Valley Golf. Lodge: Masons. Died Dec. 1, 1990. Home: College Park Md.

GRAVES, AUSTIN TAYLOR, watch company executive; b. Louisville, Sept. 19, 1908; s. W.J. and Eva S. Raplee G.; m Mary Hill Goodall, Oct. 27, 1935; children: Linda, Austin Taylor. BS, U. Ky., 1929. Assoc. Marshall Field & Co., Chgo., 1930, v.p., gen. operating mgr., 1946-53; pres. John Wanamaker, N.Y., 1953-55; pres., dir. Products of Asia, Inc., 1955-64, Products of India, Inc., 1959-64; exec. v.p. Gruen Industries Inc., N.Y.C., 1966-67, pres., 1967-73, chmn., 1973-74, vice chmn. bd., 1974-91. Former dir. Child Welfare League of Am. Inc.; former trustee, sec. Ill. Children's Home and Aid Soc.; former v.p. Chgo. Crime Commn.; former mem. bus. adv. com. U. Wis., Green Bay. Mem. Christian Ch. Club, Univ. Club, Phi Mu Alpha, Delta Sigma Pi, Beta Gamma Sigma. Home: Port Saint Lucie Fla. Died Sept. 10, 1991.

GRAVES, FRANK XAVIER, JR., state senator, mayor; b. Paterson, N.J.; s. Frank X. and Sadie (Meyerhoffer) G.; m. Ethel M. Kirsop, 1945; children—Karole, Nancy, Linda. Student, U. Va., 1944, William Paterson Coll., 1946. Alderman, City of Paterson, 1946, Mayor, 1961-67, 82-86, 86-90, pres. city council, 1974-78; mem. N.J. Senate, 1978-90; Passaic County Freeholder, 1955-60. Served with U.S. Army, 1943-46; ETO. Decorated Purple Heart. Roman Catholic. Lodge: Elks. Mem. DAV, Delta Upsilon. Died Mar. 4, 1990; buried Holy Sepulchre Cemetery, Patterson. Home: Paterson N.J.

GRAVES, LAWRENCE MURRAY, mathematician; b. Topeka, Aug. 7, 1896; s. William James and Sarah Prescott (Cowgill) G.; m. Josephine Mary Wells, Aug. 27, 1924; children: Robert Lawrence, John Lowell, Anne Lowell. AB, Washburn Coll., 1918, ScD, 1941; AM, U. Chgo., 1920, PhD, 1924. Instr. in math. Washington U., St. Louis, 1920-22; nat. rsch. fellow Harvard, 1924-26; asst. prof. math. U. Chgo., 1926-30, assoc. prof., 1930-39, prof., from 1939; vis. assoc. prof. U. Mich., 1930, Stanford, summer 1937; vis. prof. Ind. U., 1947-48, Ill. Inst. Tech., from 1961. Author: The Theory of Functions of Real Variables, 1946; mem. editorial com.: Am. Jour. of Maths., 1946-50; chmn. editorial com.: Internat. Congress of Mathematicians, Cambridge, Mass., 1950; contbr. articles on calculus of variations and functional analysis to math. jours. Mem. applied math. panel Nat. Def. Rsch. Com., 1944-46. With A.E.F., 1918-20. Fellow AAAS (v.p., chmn. of sect. A 1952); mem. Am. Math. Soc. (v.p. 1943-44, editoral com. Bulletin 1938-43), Math. Assn. Am. (v.p. 1950-51), Sigma Xi, Literary Club (v.p. 1950-51), The Quadrangle Club (Chgo.). Episcopalian. *

GRAVES, WILLIAM H(ORACE), professor engineering; b. Leslie, Mich., Apr. 30, 1898; s. William H. and Gertrude (Covert) G.; m. Esther Sherwood, June 23, 1926; children: William Horace, Nancy Sherwood. BS, U. Mich., 1919. With Packard Motor Car Co., from 1919, chief metallurgist, 1924-44, quality control mgr., 1944-45, exec. engr., 1945-49, v.p., dir. engring., 1949-50, v.p. in charge engring., 1950-54; v.p. Studebaker-Packard Corp., 1954-56; prof. automotive engring., dir. lab. U. Mich., from 1956; bd. dirs. Detroit Dura Corp. Contbr. articles on automobile constrn. Mem. mayor's com. on oil, Huntington Woods, 1927-50, city commr., 1937-47; mem. task force com. N.P.A. Mem. Soc. Automotive Engrs. (v.p. 1947), Am. Soc. Testing Materials (exec. com.), Am. Soc. for Metals, Detroit Engring. Soc. (pres. 1958), Detroit Bd. of Commerce, Army Ordnance Assn., Sigma Xi, Pi Lambda Upsilon, Tau Beta Pi, Detroit Yacht Club, Detroit Athletic Club, Barton Hills Country Club, Town Club (Ann Arbor), Rotary. Republican. *

GRAY, EDWARD C., consultant; b. Bklyn.; s. Edward and Mary (Kuhn) G.; m. Dorothea Baier, Mar. 25, 1944; 1 child by previous marriage, Dorothy Joan. BCS, NYU. Various positions with N.Y. Stock Exch., 1918-68, sec. bus. conduct com., dir. dept. mem. firms, exec. v.p., 1948-68; cons. Oppenheim, Appel, Dixon & Co., CPAs, N.Y.C., 1968-89. Home: Westfield NJ Died Apr. 20, 1989.

GRAY, FRANKLIN DINGWALL, lawyer; b. Mpls., July 19, 1904; s. William Irving and Isabelle Wenonah (Welles) G.; m. Laura Erf, June 18, 1932; 1 dau., Ellen Gray. B.A. magna cum laude, U. Minn., 1925; B.A. in Jurisprudence (Rhodes scholar), Oxford (Eng.) U., 1927, B.C.L., 1928, M.A., 1953. Bar: Minn. 1929. Ptnr. firm Gray, Plant, Mooty, Mooty & Bennett, and predecessors, Mpls., from 1942; lectr. bus. law Sch. Bus. Adminstrn., U. Minn., 1937-45. Fellow Am. Coll. Trial Lawyers; mem. ABA, Minn. Bar Assn., Am. Arbitration Assn. (Twin Cities council), U. Minn. Alumni Assn. (pres. 1963-64), Phi Beta Kappa, Theta Delta Chi, Phi Delta Phi. Club: Rotary (pres. Mpls. 1965-66). Home: Minneapolis Minn. Died July 31, 1990; buried Lakewood Cemetery, Mpls.

GRAY, HORACE MONTGOMERY, economist; b. Lerna, Ill., June 29, 1898; s. Charles James and Nellie (Montgomery) G.; m. Emmogene Doolen, Aug. 15, 1925; children: Charles Montgomery, Nancy Jean. Student, Ea. Ill. State Tchrs. Coll., 1914-18; BS, U. Ill., 1922, MS, 1933, PhD, 1926. Asst. in accountancy U. Ill., 1922-23, instr. econs., 1923-25, fellow, 1925-26, assoc., 1926-27, asst. prof., 1927-35, assoc. prof., 1935-41, McKinley prof. econs. of pub. utilities, 1941-45, prof. econs., from 1945, asst. dean Grad. Sch., 1938-45, assoc. dean, 1945-48; sec. Ill. State Fulbright com., 1950-54, adv. 1948-54, mem. nat. selection com., 1951; dir. Inst. Govt. and Pub. Affairs, 1947-48. Contbr. articles to numerous econs. and sci. publs. Mem. Social Security Bd. Regional Office, Chgo., 1939; spl. examiner Chgo. Bd. Edn., 1940-42; econ. expert Fed. Trade Commn., 1942; mem. edn. com. Ill. State Coun. of Def., 1942-45; pub. mem. and chmn. appeals com. Nat. War Labor Bd., Region VI, Chgo., 1943-45; mem. dept. econ. and adminstrn. Hwy. Rsch. Bd., Nat. Rsch. Coun., 1945; cons. Pres.'s Water Resources Policy Commn., 1950; mem. and sec. grad. work Coun. Assn. Land Grant Colls. and Univs., 1947-49; pres. Midwest Conf. on Grad. Study and Rsch., 1947-48; trustee Judson King Found., Inc., 1951. With USN, 1918-19. Mem. AAUP (mem. nat. coun. 1938-41, pres. U. Ill. chpt. 1937-38), Am. Econ. Assn., Am. Acad. Polit. and Social Sci., Mid-West Econ. Assn., Am. Soc. for Pub. Adminstrn., Univ. Club (Urbana). Presbyterian. *

GRAY, JOHN STEPHENS, physiologist; b. Chgo., Aug. 11, 1910; s. Joseph William and Carrie (Weston) G.; m. Elma Nash, June 15, 1935; children—Ann R., Virginia B. B.S., Knox Coll., Galesburg, Ill., 1932; M.S., Northwestern U., 1934, Ph.D., 1936, M.D., 1946. Instr. in physiology Northwestern U., 1936-40, asst. prof., 1940-45, asso. prof., 1946, Nathan Smith Davis prof., 1946-70, prof. emeritus, from 1974; research physiologist A.A.F. Sch. of Aviation Medicine, Randolph Field, Tex., 1942-45. Author: The Sioux War of 1876, 1976, Cavalry and Coaches: The Story of Camp and Fort Collins, 1978, Mitch Boyer and Custer's Last Campaign, 1991; contbr. research articles in physiology and in Am. frontier history to various publs. Mem. AAAS, Am. Physiol. Soc., Soc. Exptl. Biology and Medicine, Chgo. Westerners, Sigma Xi, Phi Gamma Delta. Home: Fort Collins Colo. Dec. Dec. 25, 1991. †

GRAY, TRUMAN STRETCHER, engineering educator; b. Spencer, Ind., May 3, 1906; s. Clarence Truman and Bessie Lee (Stretcher) G.; m. Isabel Gilliam Crockford, June 20, 1931. BSEE, U. Tex., 1926, BA, 1927; MS, MIT, 1929, ScD, 1930. Asst. physics U. Tex., 1924-27; rsch. asst. MIT, Cambridge, 1927-28, Coffin fellow, 1928-29, Saltonstall fellow, 1929-30, instr., 1930-35, mem. faculty, 1935-71, prof. elec. engring., 1960-71, prof. emeritus, sr. lectr., 1971-92; engr. Leeds and Northrup Co., summer 1929, GE, summer 1935, Naval Ordnance Lab., summer 1941; cons. indsl. firms., govt. labs., from 1942. Author: Applied Electronics, 2d edit., 1954; contbr. sci. periodicals, books, handbooks, reports. Fellow IEEE (chmn. instruments and measurements com. 1945-47, Centennial medal 1984); mem. Am. Soc. Engring. Edn., Phi Beta Kappa, Sigma Xi, Tau Beta Pi, Eta Kappa Nu, Phi Mu Alpha, Pi Kappa Alpha. Home: Lexington Mass. Died Nov. 7, 1992. †

GRAYDON, ALLAN, lawyer; b. Toronto, Can., Jan. 21, 1898; s. Richard Albert and Sarah Jane (Hughes) G.; m. Elizabeth Palmer, Sept. 20, 1934; children: Jane, Barbara. Student, Royal Mil. Coll. of Can., Kingston, 1915-17; AB, U. Toronto, 1921; student, Osgoode Hall Law Sch., 1921-24. Called to the bar, Ont., 1924. Sr. ptnr. Blake, Cassels & Graydon; chmn. Barcelona Traction, Light & Power Co., Ltd.; dir. Toronto Type Foundry Co., Ltd., Abitibi Power & Paper Co., Ltd., Can. Imperial Bank of Commerce, Interlink Investments, Ltd., Sofasco, Ltd., Transcontinental Timber Co., Ltd., Steel Co. Can., Ltd., others. Officer Royal Arty., British Army, 1917-19. Mem. Can. Bar Assn. *

GRECH, ANTHONY PAUL, law librarian; b. N.Y.C., July 16, 1930; s. Annibale H. and Anna Jane (Cassar) G. B.B.A., Manhattan Coll., 1952; M.L.S., Columbia U., 1961. Asst. reference librarian Assn. Bar City N.Y., 1958-65, reference librarian, 1965-67, librarian, 1967-84, librarian, curator, 1984-90; mem. library com. of Eastman Arbitration Library, Am. Arbitration Assn., 1984-85. Mem. Am. Assn. Law Librs. (Joseph L. Andrews Bibilog. award 1967, chmn. micro facsimiles com. 1965-67, chmn. publs. com. 1975-76, exec. bd. 1980-83), Assn. Law Librs. Upstate N.Y. (treas. 1976-77), Bibliog. Soc. Am., Spl. Librs. Assn., Law Libr. Assn. Greater N.Y. (pres. 1967-68), ALA, Bibliog. Soc. U. Va., Internat. Assn. Law Librs., Am. Printing History Assn., Nat. Micrographics Assn., Beta Phi Mu. Home: New York N.Y. Died Apr. 17, 1990; buried St. Raymond Cemetery, Bronx, N.Y.

GREDE, WILLIAM J., business executive; b. Milw., Feb. 24, 1897; s. Henry Lewis and Fannie (Runkle) G.; m. Margaret Weiss, Sept. 17, 1919; children: Janet Grede Jacobs, Betty Grede Davis. Student, U. Wis., Madison, 1915-17; LLD (hon.), George Williams Coll., 1952, Carroll Coll., 1952; DBA (hon.), Northland Coll., 1953. Owner Liberty Foundry, Milw., 1920-23; pres. sucessor co. Grede Foundries, Inc., Milw., 1940-60, chmn., 1960-73, sr. vice chmn., from 1973; bd. dirs., chmn. exec. com., pres. J.I. Case; bd. dirs. Thomas Industries; bd. dirs., founder Coatings, Inc.; co-founder, bd. dirs. Kingsford Co. Chmn. state fin. Rep. Party, 1956; past mem. nat. coun. YMCA. Lt. U.S. Army, 1917-18. Recipient award Freedom Found. Valley

Forge, Pa., 1953, Svc. award John Birch Soc., 1986. Mem. Gray Iron Research Inst., Wis. Mfrs. Assn. (pres.), Employers Assn. (pres.), Nat. Assn. Mfrs., Gray Iron Founders Assn., Steel Founders Soc. of Am., SAR (Gold Medal for Good Citizenship and Service to Industry 1953). Congregationalist. Lodge: Kiwanis. Home: Brookfield Wis. Died June 5, 1989.

GREEN, FITZHUGH, author, government agency administrator, consultant; b. Jenkintown, Pa., Sept. 12, 1917; s. Fitzhugh and Natalie W. (Elliot) G.; grad. St. Paul's Sch., 1936; student Princeton U., 1940; M.A., Boston U., 1963; 1 dau., Penelope. Fgn. sales and advt. exec. Vick Chem. Co., 1946-49; div. mgr., advt. sales promotion exec. Life mag., 1949-52; asst. to chmn. FTC, 1953-54; with USIA, 1954-66; dir. USIS, Laos, 1955-56, Israel, 1956-58, chief pvt. enterprise div., 1958-60, dir. USIS, Belgian Congo, 1960, Republic of Congo, Leopoldville, 1960-62, grad. Naval War Coll., 1963, USIA rep. U.S. Mission to UN, dir. Fgn. Corrs. Center, N.Y.C., 1964-65; dep. dir. personnel and tng. USIA, 1965-66; oceanography, fgn. affairs expert on staff U.S. Senator Claiborne Pell, 1966-68; dep. dir. Far East ops. USIA, 1968-70; assoc. adminstr. EPA, 1971-77, 83-87; v.p. William D. Ruckelshaus Assocs., 1987-89; psychol. warfare cons. Am. U., 1959; rep. UN Conf. on Human Environment, Stockholm, 1972. Dep. vice chmn. Nat. Citizens for Eisenhower, 1954; Republican candidate for Congress from R.I., 1970. Trustee, mem. exec. com. Washington chpt. Nat. Multiple Sclerosis Soc.; bd. dirs. Boys Harbor, Inc., N.Y.C., Nat. Conf. Citizenship, 1982, Charles A. Lindbergh Fund, from 1986; mem. Nat. Com. on Am. Fgn. Policy; mem. admissions com. Georgetown U. Grad. Fgn. Service Sch. Served from ensign to lt. USNR, 1942-46; PTO. Clubs: Met., Burning Tree, Federal City (Washington); Spouting Rock Beach Assn. (Newport, R.I.); Explorers (N.Y.C.). Author: Fitz Jr. with the Fleet, 1931; A Change in the Weather, 1977; American Propaganda Abroad, 1988, George Bush, An Intimate Portrait, 1989; also numerous articles; editorial bd. Atlantic Council Quar., 1986-89. Died Sept. 5, 1990. Home: Washington D.C.

GREEN, JOHN RAEBURN, lawyer; b. St. Louis, Mar. 30, 1894; s. John Findley and Eleanor Essie (Ibbotson) G.; m. Elisabeth Haskell Cox, Dec. 24, 1917; children: Richard Cox (dec.), Elisabeth Cox Hair, John Raeburn, Lewis Cox, Henry Ibbotson (dec.). AB, Westminster Coll., 1914, LLD, 1954; LLB, Harvard, 1917; LLD, Washington U., 1959. Bar: Mo. 1915, U.S. Supreme Ct. 1919. Legal drafting officer Dept. of State, 1918-19; mem. Legal Sec. Secretarist of League of Nations, 1920-21; ptnr. Judson, Green & Henry and predecessor firms, from 1919; apptd. by U.S. Supreme Ct. to represent habeas corpua petitioners, 1944-45; spl. master in Tex. vs. N.Mex. (Rio Grande litigation), 1952-57. Author: Liberty Under the Fourteenth Amendment, 1942; contbr. to law revs. Bd. trustees Westminster Coll., chmn. bd. 1953-55; dir., sec. St. Luke's Episcopal Presbyn. Hosp., 1947-53; mem. coun. Wash. U., from 1957; adv. coun. St. Louis U., Sch. of Law, from 1958; mem. bd. trustees, exec. com. Jefferson Nat. Expansion Meml. Assn.; dir. Better Bus. Bur. of St. Louis and various corps. 2d lt. U.S. Army, 1917-18. Recipient Newspaper Guild Civic award, 1955. Mem. ABA, Mo. Bar Assn., St. Louis Bar Assn., Am. Law Inst., Lawyers Assn. St. Louis, Assn. of Bar of City of N.Y., Am. Soc. Internat. Law, Internat. Law Assn. (Am. br.), Am. Judicature Soc., Harvard Law Sch. Assn. (mem. coun. 1948-61), Am. Soc. Legal History, S.R., Mo. Hist. Soc. (bd. trustees), Am. Legion, Order of Coif (hon.), Phi Delta Theta, Zeta Tau Delta, Phi Delta Phi, Noonday Club, Univ. Club (St. Louis), Army and Navy Club (Washington), Harvard Club (N.Y.C.), Automobile Club Mo. Democrat. Presbyterian. *

GREENAWAY, DONALD, hotel administration educator; b. Frankfort, Mich., Apr. 14, 1911; s. George Henry and Mary Elizabeth (Orr) G.; m. Louise Constance Wadsworth, June 27, 1936; 1 dau., Jeanne Elizabeth Greenaway Des Camp; m. Lorraine Katherine Muellenbach, July 6, 1958 (dec. Feb. 1983); 1 dau., Karen. B.A., Mich. State U., 1934; LL.D., Northwood Inst., 1970. Hotel adminstrn. and mgmt., 1934-41; food service exec. Trans World Airlines, 1946-47; prof. hotel adminstrn. Coll. Bus., Wash. State U., 1947-51; prof. adminstr.-dir. Sch. Hotel, Restaurant and Instl. Mgmt., Coll. Bus., Mich. State U., 1951-58; exec. v.p. Nat. Restaurant Assn., Chgo., 1958-70; asso. dean Sch. Hotel and Restaurant Mgmt., U. Houston, 1970-76; asst. to exec. v.p. Tex. Restaurant Assn., from 1976; Dir. Wilkensburg Hotel Co., Pa., Hotel Elkhart, Ind.; Mem. Gov.'s Com. for Devel. State Wash., 1950-51; pres., founder Nat. Council Hotel and Restaurant Edn., 1946; adviser to bd. dirs. Army and Air Force Exchange Service; adviser USPHS, USAF, World-Wide Food Service; mgmt. cons. Soc. Advancement Food Service Research; mem. 5th Internat. World Food Congress, U.S. Travel Service; also trade assn. adv. com. U.S. C. of C.; trade missions to Europe auspices Dept. Commerce.; Disting. vis. prof. Fla. Internat. U.; First Westin Hotels Disting. prof. Wash. State U. Author: Manual for Resort Operations, 1950, also monographs, papers, articles. Bd. dirs. Govs. Confs. Tourism Pacific N.W., 1947-49, Pacific N.W. Trade Assn., 1947-48. Served to capt. USAAF, 1942-46. Mem. AAUP, Am. Soc. Assn. Execs., Execs. Forum, Mich., Resort Assn., Mich. Pa. hotel assns., Am. Standards Assn. (com. standards for food service industry), Food Execs. Assn., Internat. Ho-Re-Ca, Confrerie de la Chaine des Rotisseurs, Theta Chi, Alpha Kappa Psi. Club: Rotarian. Home: Manistee Mich. Died Apr. 2, 1989.

GREENAWAY, EMERSON, librarian; b. Springfield, Mass., May 25, 1906; s. James and Sara Elizabeth (Lilley) G.; m. Helen Kidder, June 18, 1938 (dec. 1986); children: Ann (Mrs. Robert C. Pugh), Jane (Mrs. John G. Sampson). A.B. in L.S, U. N.C., 1935; B.S., U. Mass., 1927, L.H.D., 1952; Litt.D., Western Md. Coll., 1950, Drexel Inst. Tech., 1959, Wheaton Coll., 1973; LL.D., Temple U., 1958. Reference asst. City Library Assn., Springfield, Mass., 1928-30; supr. brs. and asst. librarian Pub. Library, Hartford, Conn., 1930-34, 36; spl. asst. Enoch Pratt Free Library, Balt., 1935; librarian Enoch Pratt Free Library, 1945-51, Pub. Library, Fitchburg, Mass., 1937-40, Free Pub. Library, Worcester, Mass., 1940-45; lectr. library adminstrn. Simmons Coll. Sch. Library Sci., Boston, 1942-45, Columbia U. Grad. Sch. Library Service, 1963-64, Drexel Inst. Library Sch., 1965, Library Sch., Kent State U., 1977; dir. Free Library of Phila., 1951-69; former dir. Forest Press, Inc.; cons. in pub. libraries for UNESCO, 1947-49; N.H. State Library Council, from 1985. Mem. Adult Ednl. Council, Mus. Council, Spl. Library Council, all Phila., Nat. Adv. Commn. Libraries, 1967; adv. com. U.S. Internat. Book and Library Programs, Pa. Adv. Council Library Devel., 1957-68; former mem. books across the sea com. English Speaking Union; chmn. library vis. com. Wheaton Coll., Norton, Mass., 1967-85; trustee, hon. chmn. Schuylkill Valley Nature Ctr., from 1970; former trustee Harcum Jr. Coll.; trustee Union Library Catalog, Phila., 1952-69, Phila. Art Alliance, Tracy Meml. Library, New London, N.H., 1979-85; mem. N.H. State Library Council, from 1985. Recipient 1954 Good Govt. award, 1955, Citation Phila. Jr. C. of C. and U.S. C. of C., Disting. Achievement award Drexel Inst., 1965, Merit award Phila. Art Alliance, 1969, Disting. Alumni award U. N.C. Sch. Libr. Sci., 1981, Dorothy M. Little award for outstanding libr. svc. N.H. Libr. Assn., 1989; 1st recipient Great Libr. medal New Eng. Libr. Assn., 1988. Mem. ALA (council 1954-70, exec. bd. 1954-60, pres. 1958-59, Lippincott award 1955, Centennial citation 1976), Mass. Libr. Assn. (life mem.), N.H. Libr. Trustees Assn. (former bd. dirs.), Pa. Libr. Assn., Md. Libr. Assn. (life mem.), Friends N.H. Libr. Assn. (dir. 1982-86), Am. Philos. Soc. (councilor, libr. com.), Internat. Fedn. Libr. Assns. Clubs: Franklin Inn, Philobiblon; Science and Arts (Germantown); Boy's (New London, N.H.); Balt. Bibliophiles, Appalachian Mountain. Home: New London N.H. Died Apr. 8, 1990; buried New London, N.H.

GREENBERG, BEN NORTON, surgeon; b. Omaha, May 30, 1903; s. Samuel and Rose (Coren) G. A.B., U. Nebr., 1925, B.Sc. in Medicine, 1926, M.D., 1928. Diplomate: Nat. Bd. Med. Examiners. Intern U. Nebr. Hosp., 1928-30; postgrad. Manhattan Eye and Ear Hosp., N.Y.C., 1930-32; resident Babies Hosp.-Columbia U. Med. Center, 1933; ship surgeon Am. Export and Grace Steamship Lines, 1934; practice medicine, specializing in eye, ear, nose and throat York, Nebr., from 1934; staff York Gen. Hosp.; cons. in ophthalmology student health U. Nebr. Chmn. Coordinating Council for Pub. Higher Edn. in Nebr.; mem. nat. adv. council Center Disease Control, Atlanta.; Bd. dirs. Nebr. div. Am. Cancer Soc.; trustee Nebr. Med. Found.; regent U. Nebr., 1953—, pres. bd., 1957, 63, 68, v.p., 1967-70; mem. adv. council Nebr. Center for Regional Progress.; Alt. del. Nat. Republican Conv., 1972. Recipient Distinguished Service award Nat. Assn. Governing Bds. State Univs., 1962, Service to Mankind award Sertoma Internat., 1964, Builders award U. Nebr., 1973, Distinguished Service award U. Nebr. Alumni Assn., 1974. Fellow A.M.A.; mem. A.C.S., Nebr. Med. Assn. (councilor 1955-61), Nat. Assn. Governing Bds. State Univs. and Allied Insts. (pres. 1961-62, pres. found. from 1961), York County Med. Soc. (past pres.). Clubs: Mason, Rotarian (Cadwallader award 1969). Home: York Nebr. Died Sept. 24, 1988. †

GREENE, ARTHUR DALE, consulting engineer; b. Celina, Ohio, Dec. 8, 1894; s. Daniel Elza and Emma Elizabeth (Wollam) G.; m. Anna Lucile Evans, June 8, 1918. Student, Miami U., 1912-13; BCE, Ohio State U., 1919. Registered profl. engr. La., Tex. Engr. Pure Oil Co., 1920-27, Columbia Engring. & Mgmt. Co., 1927-30; chief engr. United Gas Pipe Line Co., Shreveport, La., 1930-47; v.p. United Gas Pipe Line Co., Shreveport, 1947-56, exec. v.p., 1956, dir., 1937-56; v.p. United Gas Corp., 1953-56, cons. engr., from 1957. Contbr. articles to trade mags. Dir. of gas ops. Petroleum Adminstrn. for Def., 1951-52. 2d lt. U.S. Army, 1917-18. Mem. Am. Gas Assn., So. Gas Assn., Am. Petroleum Inst., Petroleum Club Shreveport, Shreveport Country Club, Shreveport Club, Petroleum Club, Ramada Club (Houston). *

GREENE, BALCOMB, artist; b. Millville, N.Y., May 22, 1904; s. Bert Stillman and Florence (Stover) G.; m. Gertrude Glass, 1926 (dec. 1956); m. Terry Trimpen, 1961. AB, Syracuse U., 1926; MA in Art History, NYU, 1940; postgrad., U. Vienna, 1926-28. Tchr. Dartmouth Coll., 1928-31; assoc. prof. esthetics, art history and philosophy Carnegie Inst. Tech., Pitts., 1942-59. Exhibited in one man shows, Gallery, Paris, J.B. Neumann's New Art Circle, N.Y.C., 1947, Arts and Crafts Center, Pitts., 1953, Bertha Schaefer Gallery, annually 1950-61, Am. U., Washington, 1957, Brookhaven Nat. Lab., 1959, Centre Culture American, Am. embassy, Paris, 1960, A.C.A. Gallery, N.Y.C., 1980; retrospective exhbn. Whitney Mus. Am. Art, N.Y.C., 1961; exhbns. include Carnegie Inst. Tech., 1961, Munson-Williams-Proctor Inst., Utica, N.Y., 1961, Saidenberg Gallery, N.Y.C., 1962-68, Feingarten Galleries, Los Angeles, 1963, 64, Chgo., 1963, La Jolla (Calif.) Art Center, 1964, Tampa (Fla.) Art Inst., 1965, James David Gallery, Coral Gabels, Fla., 1965-66, Santa Barbara (Calif.) Mus. Art, 1966, Phoenix Art Mus., 1966, Berenson Gallery, Bay Harbor Islands, Fla., 1968, 70, Fairweather-Hardin Gallery, Chgo., 1969, Adele Bednary Galleries, Los Angeles, 1966-73, Forum Gallery, N.Y.C., 1970-73, Harmon Gallery, Naples, Fla., 1974, 75, A.C.A. Gallery, N.Y.C., 1977, Guild Hall, Easthampton, L.I., N.Y., 1978, Yares Gallery, Scottsdale, Ariz., 1979, Rich Perlow Gallery, N.Y.C., 1990, others; exhbn. restored mural from WPA Williamsburg project at Bklyn. Mus., 1990; represented in permanent collections Mus. Modern Art, Whitney Mus. Am. Art, Solomon Guggenheim Mus., Met. Mus., all N.Y.C., Carnegie Inst., Pitts., Walker Art Center, Mpls., U. Nebr., Joselyn Mus., Omaha, Smithsonian Inst., Washington, U. Va., U. N.C., numerous others; also pvt. collections; represented by, ACA Gallery, N.Y.C., Harmon Gallery, Naples, Fla.; Editor: Art Front, 1935-36; Contbr. to profl. publs. works included in numerous art books. Recipient awards Art News Magazine. Mem. Am. Fedn. Arts, Am. Abstract Artists (chmn. 1936-67, 38-39, 40-41), Theta Beta Phi. Club: Cosmopolitan of Syracuse U. Home: Montauk N.Y. Died Nov. 12, 1990.

GREENE, DAVID GORHAM, physician; b. Buffalo, Feb. 5, 1915; s. Clayton W. and Emma (Walmsley) Otis) G.; m. Edith M. Albertson, Dec. 14, 1946; children: Amy A., Stephen G., Eleanor O., Constance G. Klocke. A.B., Princeton U., 1936; M.D., Harvard U., 1940. Fellow Banting Inst., Toronto, Ont., Can., 1940-41; intern, then asst. resident in medicine Presbyn. Hosp., N.Y.C., 1941-46; Fellow Columbia U. Coll. Physicians and Surgeons, 1945-48; mem. faculty SUNY Med. Sch.-Buffalo, 1948-91, prof. medicine, 1956-85, prof. medicine emeritus, 1985-91, assoc. prof. physiology, 1970-91; sr. physician Buffalo Gen. Hosp.; hon. prof. medicine Autonomous U., Puebla, Mex., 1961; Litchfield lectr. Oxford (Eng.) U., 1967; MacArthur lectr. U. Edinburgh (Scotland), 1967; lectr. Keio U., Tokyo, 1978. Contbr. articles to med. jours., chpts. to books. Served as officer M.C. AUS, 1942-45. Mem. ACP, Am. Coll. Cardiology, Am. Coll. Chest Physician, Am. Heart Assn., Am. Physiol. Soc., Am. Fedn. Clin. Research, Assn. Univ. Cardiologists, N.Am. Soc. Cardiac Radiology, Soc. Cardiac Angiography and Interventions (pres. 1983-84, trustee for life 1987—). Democrat. Home: Buffalo N.Y. Died Oct. 30, 1991. †

GREENE, GRAHAM, author; b. Berkhamsted, Hertfordshire, Eng., Oct. 2, 1904; s. Charles Henry and Marion (Raymond) G.; m. Vivien Dayrell-Browning, 1927; 1 son, 1 dau. Ed., Berkhamsted Sch., Balliol Coll., Oxford, Eng.; Litt.D. (hon.), Cambridge (Eng.) U., 1962, Edinburgh (Scotland) U., 1967; D.Litt. (hon.), Oxford U., 1979; D. (hon.), Moscow State U., 1988. Sub-editor London Times, 1926-30; lit. editor Spectator, 1940-41; with (Fgn. Office), 1941-44; dir. Eyre & Spottiswoode, Ltd., 1944-48, Bodley Head, London, 1958-68. Author: books Babbling April, 1925, The Man Within, 1929, The Name of Action, 1930, Rumour at Nightfall, 1932, Stamboul Train, 1932, It's a Battlefield, 1934, England Made Me, 1935, The Basement Room; short stories The Bear Fell Free, 1935; Journey Without Maps, 1936, A Gun for Sale, 1936, Brighton Rock, 1938, The Lawless Roads, 1939, The Confidential Agent, 1939, The Power and the Glory, 1940 (Hawthornden prize), British Dramatists, 1942, The Ministry of Fear, 1943; short stories Nineteen Stories, 1947; The Heart of the Matter, 1948, The Third Man, 1950, The Lost Childhood and Other Essays, 1951, The End of the Affair, 1951, Essais Catholiques, 1953; short stories Twenty-one Stories, 1954; Loser Takes All, 1955, The Quiet American, 1955, Our Man in Havana, 1958, A Burnt-Out Case, 1961, In Search of a Character, 1961, A Sense of Reality, 1963, The Comedians, 1966, A World of My Own, a Dream Diary, 1992; film 1967 May We Borrow Your Husband? and Other Comedies of the Sexual Life; Collected Essays, 1969, Travels with My Aunt, 1969, A Sort of Life, 1971, The Pleasure Dome: The Collected Film Criticism 1935-40; short stories Collected Stories, 1972; The Honorary Consul, 1973, Lord Rochester's Monkey, 1974, An Impossible Woman, 1975, The Human Factor, 1978, Dr. Fischer of Geneva or The Bomb Party, 1980, Ways of Escape, 1980, Monsignor Quixote, 1982, J'Accuse, the Darker Side of Nice, 1982, Getting to Know the General, 1984, The Tenth Man, 1985, The Captain and the Enemy, 1988; plays The Living Room, 1953, The Potting Shed, 1957, The Complaisant Lover, 1959, Carving a Statue, 1964, The Return of A.J. Raffles, 1975, For Whom the Bell Chimes and Yes and No, 1980; children's books The Little Train, 1947, The Little Fire Engine, 1950, The Little Horse Bus, 1952, The Little Steamroller, 1953 (Recipient Black Meml. prize 1949, Shakespeare prize, Hamburg 1968). Mem. Panamanian del. to Washington for signing of Canal Treaty, 1977. Decorated Companion of Honour, Companion of Lit., Order of Merit; chevalier Legion of Honor; Grand Cross Order Vasco Nunez de Balboa (Panama); Order of Ruben Dario, Nicaragua, 1979; commandeur des Arts et des Lettres (France); named hon. citizen Anacapri, 1978; hon. fellow Balliol Coll.; recipient Thomas More medal, 1973, John Dos Passos prize, 1980, medal City of Madrid, 1980, Jerusalem prize, 1981. Home: London Eng. Died Apr. 3, 1991; buried Corseaux, Switzerland.

GREENFIELD, TAYLOR HATTON, former government official; b. Balt., Dec. 17, 1905; s. Amos Hatton and Lillian Estelle (Taylor) G.; m. Mildred Sophia Albert, Sept. 15, 1928 (dec. June 1984); children: Lillian Greenfield Tilles, Millette Greenfield Barber. LL.B., U. Balt., 1940. Bar: Md. bar 1949. Exec. Glenn L. Martin Co., 1929-43, Gen. Motors, 1944-45; field dir. A.R.C., Germany, 1945-46; property and supply supr. War Assets Adminstrn., 1946-48; practice law Balt., 1949-51; with Hayes Aircraft Co., Birmingham, Ala., 1951-55; adviser to Govt. Vietnam, 1955-62; mem. tech. adv. staff AID, Far East Bur., 1962-67; dir. Far East Logistics Office, 1965-67; chief logistics USOM; supply mgmt. officer USOM, Bangkok, Thailand, 1969-72. Recipient Meritorious Honor award AID, 1966. Mem. Internat. Transactional Analysis Assn. Club: Civitan. Home: San Antonio Tex. Deceased. †

GREENLEAF, ROBERT KIEFNER, business executive; b. Terre Haute, Ind., July 14, 1904; s. George W. and burchie M. Kiefner G.; m. Esther E. Hargrave, Sept. 26, 1931; children: Newcomb, Elizabeth, Madeline. BA, Carleton Coll., 1926, DHL, 1969. With Ohio Bell Telephone Co., 1926-29; with AT&T, 1929-64, dir. mgmt. rsch., 1957-64; Elis and Signe Olsson prof. bus. adminstrn. U. Va., 1973; mem. faculty Dartmouth Grad. Sch. Fin. Mgmt., 195-58, Salzburg Seminar in Am. Studies, 1968; exec. in residence Fresno U., 1968; sr. Woodrow Wilson fellow Dickinson Coll., 1974; cons. Ford Found., 1962-71, R.K. Mellon Found., 1962-72, Giovanni Agnelli Found., 1968-69, Lilly Endowment, 1973—; vis. lectr. Harvard Bus. Sch., Sloan Sch. Mgmt., MIT, 1962-63. Author: Servant Leadership: Teacher as Servant--A Parable. Trustee Russell Sage Found., 1957-65; vis. com. mem. Harvard Div. Sch., 1966-72; founder Ctr. for Applied Ethics Inc. now Robert K. Greenleaf Ctr. , Indpls. Mem. Harvard Club N.Y.C. . Home: Kennett Square Pa. Died Oct. 13, 1990.

GREENOUGH, WILLIAM CROAN, economist, pension executive; b. Indpls., July 27, 1914; s. Walter Sidney and Katharine (Croan) G.; m. Doris Decker, Jan. 4, 1941; children: David William, Walter Croan, Martha Alice. A.B., Ind. U., 1935, LL.D., 1965; M.A., Harvard U., 1938, Ph.D., 1949. Asst. to dean, instr. Ind. U. Sch. Bus., 1937-38, asst. to pres., 1938-41; asst. to pres. Tchrs. Ins. and Annuity Assn. Am., 1941-43, 46-48, v.p., 1948-55, exec. v.p., 1955-57, pres., 1957-67, chmn., chief exec. officer, 1963-79, trustee, 1955-85, exec. v.p., then pres., 1952-67; chmn., chief exec. officer, trustee Coll. Retirement Equities Fund, 1963-79, chmn. fin. com., 1979-81, trustee, 1955-85; pub. dir. N.Y. Stock Exchange, 1972-81; trustee Dry Dock Savs. Bank, 1961-83; dir. Turner Constrn. Co.; mem. adv. bd. Atlantic Richfield Retirement Plans. Author: College Retirement and Insurance Plans, 1948, A New Approach to Retirement Income, 1951; (with F. P. King) Retirement and Insurance Plans in American Colleges, 1959, Benefit Plans in American Colleges, 1969, Pension Plans and Public Policy, 1976; Editor: Pension Planning in the U.S, 1952; also numerous articles in field. Mem. Pres.'s Commn. Pension Policy, Washington, 1979-81; mem. various commns. Am. Council Edn., Assn. Am. Colls., U.S. Office Edn., 1958-70; mem. council Rockefeller U., 1973-89; Trustee Com. for Econ. Devel., Russell Sage Found., 1967-77, Devereux Found., Ind. U. Found., The Aspen Inst., Carnegie Inst., Washington., Acad. for Ednl. Devel., RSVP Internat.; trustee Devereux Found., chmn., 1990; current adv. coms. Unitarian-Universalist Soc., Homer Hoyt Inst., Boettger Found. Served from ensign to lt. USNR, 1943-45. Decorated Bronze Star; recipient Disting. Alumni Service award Ind. U., 1960, Elizur Wright award for inventing variable annuity, 1961, Founder's Gold medal for excellence Internat. Ins. Soc., 1984. Mem. Regional Plan Assn. N.Y.C. (dir. 1967-76), Am. Pension Conf., Am. Econs. Assn., Am. Finance Assn., AAUP, Am. Risk and Ins. Assn., Council on Fgn. Relations, Phi Beta Kappa. Clubs: Harvard (N.Y.C.), Century Assn. (N.Y.C.). Home: New York N.Y. Died Dec. 20, 1980.

GREENSPUN, H. M. HANK, newspaper publisher; b. Bklyn., Aug. 27, 1909; s. Samuel J. and Anna (Fleischman) G.; m. Barbara Joan Ritchie, May 21, 1944; children: Susan Gail, Brian Lee, Jane Toni, Daniel Alan. Student, St. John's Coll., 1930-32; LL.B., St. John's Sch. Law, 1934; L.H.D. (hon.), U. Nev., Las Vegas, 1977. Bar: N.Y. 1936. Practice law N.Y.C., 1936-46; pub. mag. Las Vegas Life, 1946-47; owner, pub., editorial writer, columnist Las Vegas Sun, North Las Vegas Sun, 1950-61; pres. Las Vegas Sun, Inc., 1950-85; owner Colorado Springs Sun, 1970-75; pres. KLAS-TV, Las Vegas TV, Inc., 1954-68; owner Prime Cable, Las Vegas; former owner Sun Outdoor Advt. Co.; founder Am. Nev. Corp., Green Valley Planned Community. Author: (autobiography) Where I Stand; co-author: The Night the MGM Burned. Bd. dirs. Sun Youth Found. Served from pvt. to maj. AUS, 1941-46, ETO. Decorated Croix de Guerre with silver star; Conspicuous Service cross State N.Y.; recipient Outstanding Journalist award Jewish War Vets, 1957. Mem. Am. Newspaper Pubs. Assn., Am. Soc. Newspaper Editors, Fed. Bar Assn., Nev. Press Assn. (pres. 1957), Internat. Platform Assn., Calif. Newspaper Pubs. Assn., Am. Legion, VFW, DAV. Clubs: Nat. Press, Overseas Press, Variety, Friars; Las Vegas Country. Home: Las Vegas Nev. Died July 22, 1989; buried Las Vegas, Nev.

GREENSTONE, J(OHN) DAVID, political scientist, educator; b. Rochester, N.Y., Mar. 25, 1937; s. Elmer and Helen (Berman) G.; m. Joan Fromm, June 14, 1962; children: Michael Benjamin, Daniel Noah. AB, Harvard U., 1958; MA, U. Chgo., 1960, PhD, 1963. Vis. lectr. Makerere U., Kampala, Uganda, 1963-64; asst. to assoc. prof. polit. sci. U. Chgo., 1963-72, prof., 1972-90, chmn. dept. polit. sci., 1972-75, William M. Benton Disting. Service Prof., 1984-90; vis. assoc. prof. Columbia U., N.Y.C., 1970-71. Author: Labor in American Politics, 1969; co-author Race and Authority/ Urban Politics, 1973; editor, author Public Values and Private Power in American Politics, 1982. Del. to nat. conv. Ams. for Dem. Action Ind. Voters Ill., 1982. Grantee Russell Sage Found., 1965-69, NIMH, 1974-77. Mem. Am. Polit. Sci. Assn. (sect. chmn. ann. meeting 1969, 76). Jewish. Home: Chicago Ill. Died Feb. 21, 1990; buried Oak Woods Cemetery, Chgo.

GREENWALL, FRANK KOEHLER, manufacturing executive; b. N.Y.C., May 6, 1896; s. Henry and Hattie (Koehler) G.; m. Anna Alexander, Jan. 4, 1920; children: Susan (dec.), Nancy MacGrath. Student, pub. schs., N.Y.C. With Nat. Starch & Chem. Corp. and predecessor firms, from 1920, salesman to v.p. sales, 1920-38, pres., dir., 1938-58, chmn. bd., CEO, 1958-64, chmn. bd., from 1964; dir. Mayal Realty Co., Maine Products Co.; mem. Pres.'s Emergency Food Adv. Com., Food Industries Adv. Coun., Bus. and Def. Svcs. Adminstrn., U.S. Dept. Commerce. Trustee Corn Industries Rsch. Found., Susan Greenwall Found.; chmn. Keep Am. Beautiful; dir. Monmouth Med. Ctr. With USNRF, WWI. Mem. Adhesive Mfrs. Assn. Am., Pinnacle Club, Madison Square Garden Club (N.Y.C.), Ocean Beach Club (Elberon, N.J.). *

GRESSENS, O., business executive; b. Sterling, Ill., Dec. 2, 1897; s. Lewis and Anna (Knigg) G.; m. Marguerite Gregori, Sept. 11, 1923 (dec.); children: Robert James, Peter Joseph; m. Dulcie Griffiths, Oct. 11, 1944. PhD, U. Ill., 1926. Statistician, bur. econ. rsch. U. Ill., 1923-26; asst. to pres. Rapid Transit Co. and Pub. Svc. Co. of No. Ill., Chgo., 1927-34; v.p., comptr. Commonwealth Edison Co., Chgo., 1945-51, Pub. Svc. Co. of No. Ill., 1945-51; v.p. Peabody Coal Co., 1951, dir., 1952, pres., 1954-55, chmn. bd., 1955-56, chmn. fin. com., 1956-58, cons., dir., from 1958; chmn., dir. Horders, Inc., from 1958; pres., dir. Associated Stationers Supply Co., Inc.; v.p., dir. First Trust & Savs. Bank, Taylorville, Ill., 1951, pres., 1954-55; dir. Roberts & Shaefer Co., Chgo. Great Western R.R. Contbr. articles to profl. jours. V.p. charge of fin. Nat. Safety Coun., 1946-52. Mem. Nat. Coal Assn. (dir. 1956), Western Soc. Engrs., Exmoor Country Club, Chgo. Club, Execs. Club, Chgo. Curling Club, Mid Am. Club (Chgo.). *

GRIDER, GEORGE WILLIAM, lawyer; b. Memphis, Oct. 1, 1912; s. John McGavock and Marguerite (Samuels) G.; m. Ann Elizabeth Curlin, June 18, 1936; children: George William, Gail Ann (Mrs. James Gurley), Sally Elizabeth (Mrs. Morton Weiss), Wilson Northcross. Student, Southwestern at Memphis, 1931-32; B.S., U.S. Naval Acad., 1936; LL.B., U. Va., 1950. Bar: Tenn. 1949, N.Y., U.S. Supreme Ct. Commd. ensign USN, 1936, advanced through grades to capt., 1947; ret., 1947; practice in Memphis, 1950-64; v.p., sec., gen. counsel Carborundum Co., Niagara Falls, N.Y., 1967-75; pres. Niagara River White Waters Tours, 1972-75; partner firm Apperson, Crump, Duzane & Maxwell, Memphis, 1975-82; Mem. 89th Congress from Tenn. Author: (with Lydel Sims) War Fish, 1958. Chmn. Travelers Aid Soc., Memphis, 1950-52; mem. pres.'s adv. bd. Southwestern at Memphis, 1955-64; mem. Memphis and Shelby County Planning Commn., 1958-60, Shelby County Quar. Ct., 1960-64; chmn. Memphis and Shelby County chpt. ARC, 1960-62; chmn. USO, Memphis, 1952-58, nat. bd. dirs., 1956-66; trustee Memphis Acad. Arts, 1975-82; trustee LeMoyne-Owen Coll., Memphis, 1975-82, chmn., 1980-82; bd. visitors U.S. Naval Acad., 1967-82. Decorated Navy Cross, Silver Star medal, Bronze Star medal; recipient Citizen of Year award Memphis Newspaper Guild, 1962. Mem. Raven Soc., Phi Delta Phi, Omicron Delta Kappa. Democrat. Methodist. Clubs: Rotary (Memphis), Engrs. (Memphis). Home: Memphis Tenn. Deceased. †

GRIER, MAURICE EDWARD, physician, educator; b. McCool, Nebr., Feb. 12, 1895; s. James and Jane (Tannehill) G.; m. Olive Jenkins, June 1, 1921; children: Maurice R., Joseph H., Thomas E. MD, Creighton U., 1917; MS, U. Pa., 1929. Diplomate Am. Bd. Ob-gyn. Intern Kansas City (Mo.) Gen. Hosp., 1917-18; prof. gynecology-obstetrics Creighton U., from 1919, dir. dept., 1936-61; attending gynecologist and obstetrician Creighton Meml., St. Joseph's Hosp., Salvation Army Booth Meml. Hosp., St. Catherine's Hosp.; mem. courtesy staff Immanuel Deaconess Inst. With U.S. Army, 1918-19. Fellow ACS, Am. Coll. Ob-gyn.; mem. AMA, Ctrl. Assn. Ob-gyn. *

GRIFFETH, ROSS JOHN, educator; b. Centralia, Kans., Dec. 22, 1896; s. Arthur Preston and Lucy (Dobelbower) G.; m. Fern Estelle Harmon, Dec. 24, 1925; children: Marjorie Marie, Robert Ross. AB, Phillips U., Enid, Okla., 1923; AM, Phillips U., 1924, LLD, 1945; BD, PhD, Yale U., 1925, 1938. Ordained to ministry Ch. of Disciples of Christ. Asst. chemist Lanyon Zinc and Acid Co., 1914-16; chemist Quinton (Okla.) Spelter Co., 1916-18, 20-21; asst. prof. Old Testament Phillips U., Enid, 1925-31, assoc. prof., 1931-33; asst. prof. bibl. lit. Butler U., 1933-38, assoc. prof., 1938-42, prof., 1942-44; pres. Northwest Christian Coll., Eugene, Oreg., 1944-65; pres. emeritus Northwest Christian Coll., Eugene, from 1965; v.p. Christian Freedom Found. Author: Bible and Rural Life, 1937, It Began Thus, 1937, Building the Church of Christ, 1931, Intermediate Bible Teacher and Leader, 1949. Dir. Disciples Hist. Soc.; adv. mem. dept. town and country ch., Nat. Coun. of Chs. of Christ, U.S.A.; pres. Oreg. Coun. Chs., 1956-58. Sgt. U.S. Army, 1918-19. Mem. AAUP, Soc. Bibl. Lit. and Exegesis, Nat. Assn. Bible Instrs., Am. Oriental Soc., Am. Schs. Oriental Rsch. (assoc.), Rural Sociol. Soc., Theta Pi, Tau Kappa Alpha, Masons. *

GRIFFIN, WILLIAM THOMAS, lawyer; b. N.Y.C., Sept. 27, 1905; s. John and Alice (Doonan) G.; m. Joan Mannix, Jan. 10, 1934; children: Christine, William, Gabrielle, Peter. AB summa cum laude, Holy Cross Coll., 1927; LLB cum laude, Fordham U., 1930. Bar: N.Y. 1931. Practiced in N.Y.C.; former v.p. law N.Y., New Haven and Hartford Ry. Co. Corp.; dir. New Eng. Transp. Co., Am. Trust Co.; dir., v.p., gen. counsel Roper Realization Co., Inc., John L. Roper Lumber Co., Norfolk So. Land Co.; dir., v.p., atty. Providence Produce Warehouse Co. Mem. Am., Fed., Richmond County bar assns., Am. Judicature Soc., Nat. Lawyers Club, N.Y. Law Inst., N.Y. County Lawyers Assn., Assn. ICC Practitioners, Internat. Assn. Barristers. Clubs: New York Athletic (N.Y.C.); Quinipiack (New Haven); Richmond County Country (S.I., N.Y.); Princess Anne Country (Virginia Beach, Va.). Home: Staten Island N.Y. Died May 21, 1992. †

GRIGGS, JAMES HENRY, dean, education educator; b. New Monmouth, N.J., Oct. 21, 1912; s. James Edward and Deborah Ann (Roberts) G.; m. Anne Elizabeth Cameron, Sept. 1, 1936; children—Carol Ann, Nancy Jane. A.B., Harvard, 1932; M.A., Columbia Tchrs. Coll., 1933, Ed.D., 1940. High sch. tchr. Middletown (N.J.) Township High Sch., 1933-34; elementary sch. tchr. Des Moines, 1934-36; successively demonstration sch. tchr., asst. dir. demonstration sch., dean instrs. Nat. Coll. Edn., Evanston, Ill., 1936-48; dir. tchr. edn. Western Mich. U., Kalamazoo, 1948-56; dean Western Mich. U. (Sch. Edn.), 1956-70, prof. edn., 1970-79, prof. emeritus, from 1979. Contbg. author: Curriculum Readers, 1937-38. Served to 2d lt. AUS, 1944-46. Mem. Phi Delta Kappa, Kappa Delta Pi. Baptist. Home: Kalamazoo Mich. Died May 20, 1989.

GRINNELL, JOHN ERLE, university executive; b. Renville County, N.D., July 10, 1896; s. William Everet and Emily (Nestor) G.; m. Swanhild Fiswold, Aug. 10, 1927; children: Sheldon Wayne, Robin Roy, Alan Dale. BA, U. N.D., 1921; MA, U. Minn., 1925; PhD, Stanford U., 1934. High sch. prin., 1921-27, jr. coll. dean, 1927-30; acting asst. prof. Stanford U., 1931-32; dean liberal arts Stout Inst., Menominee, Wis., 1932-38; dean instrn. Ind. State Tchrs. Coll., 1938-55; dean Coll. Edn. So. Ill. U., 1955-60, exec. v.p., 1960-90; vis. prof. summer session U. Colo., 1938, 53, U. Tex., 1940, Johns Hopkins U., 1950; instr., chief liberal arts sect. Biarritz (France) Am. U., 1945-46; tech. cons. charge rural edn. project Inst. Inter-Am. affairs under Point IV, Panama, 1950-51. Author: Interpreting the Public Schools, 1937; (with Raymond Young) The School and the Community, 1955; (with Mable Bartlett) Illinois, 1959; editor The Tchrs. Coll. Jour., 1938-41; contbr. articles to profl. jours. and mags. Fellow Royal Soc. Arts; mem. Rotary Club, Iota Lambda Sigma, Kappa Delta Pi, Phi Delta Kappa, Sigma Nu, Tau Kappa Alpha. Methodist. Home: San Luis Obispo Calif. Died Feb. 2, 1990.

GRISMER, RAYMOND LEONARD, Spanish language educator, author; b. Schenectady, N.Y., Mar. 30, 1895; s. Charles Valentine and Luna M. (Leonard) G.; m. Mildred Best, Aug. 20, 1919; children: Jean, Raymond, William. AB, U. Vt., 1916; Rhodes Scholar, Oxford U., Eng., 1916-17; MA, Ohio State U., 1922; PhD, U. Calif., 1930. Tchr. Mercersburg Acad., Pa., 1917-18, The Hill Sch., Pottstown, Pa., 1919-20; instr. romance langs. Ohio State U., 1920-24; head modern lang. dept. Oklahoma City U., 1924-27; assoc. Spanish U. Calif., 1927-31; asst. prof. U. Minn., 1931-34, assoc. prof., 1934-49, prof. romance langs., from 1949. Author: (with D. K. Arjona) Pageant of Spain, 1939, Reference Index to Twelve Thousand Spanish-American Authors, 1939, Sailing the Spanish Main, 1940, (with M. B. Grismer, J. Magraw) New Bibliography of the Literatures of Spain and Spanish America, 7 vols., 1941-46, A Brief Spanish Grammar for Beginners, 1942, (with R. H. Olmsted) Spanish Short Stories, 1943, (with C. I.

Arroyo) Buenos Vecinos, Buenos Amigos, 1943, (with N. B. Adams) Tales of Spanish America, 1944, Influence of Plautus in Spain before Lope de Vega, 1944, (with M.W. Molinos and E.D. Corbett) Easy Spanish-American Reader, 1945, (with L.C. Keating) Elementary Spanish Conversation, 1946, Cervantes: A Bibliography, Vol. I, 1946, Vol. II, 1963, (with Roy and Margarita Mills) Liberatadores y Defensores, 1953, Bibliography of Lope de Vega Vols. I and II, 1964-65, and others; contbn. articles to profl. jours. Mem. Am. Assn. Tchrs. Spanish, Modern Lang. Assn. Am., Phi Beta Kappa, Tau Kappa Epsilon. *

GRISWOLD, FRANCIS HOPKINSON, air force officer; b. Erie, Pa., Nov. 5, 1904; m. Jeff Sutherland, 1933; children: Mary S., Claire Griswold Pollack. Student, Columbia U., Ohio State U.; grad., Air Corps Primary Flying Sch., 1929; LLD. (hon.), Gannon Coll. Commd. 2d lt. AC Res., AUS, 1930, advanced through grades to lt. gen., 1957; commdg. gen. 20th Air Force and Marianas-Bonin Command, Guam; comdr. 35th Pursuit Squadron, Langley Field, Va., 1940, 33d Pursuit Group, Mitchel Field, N.Y., 1940-41; exec. officer 4th Interceptor Command, Riverside, Calif., 1941; asst. to asst. chief of staff S-3, 10th Pursuit Wing, Alexandria, La., 1941, 4th Interceptor Command, Riverside, Calif., 1941-41; regional comdr. North Calif. region 4th Interceptor Command, San Francisco, 1942; chief tng. sect., fighter div. Hdqrs. Army Air Forces, Washington, 1942, chief fighter div., 1942-43; acting chief Eighth Fighter Command, ETO, 1943, later chief of staff of unit, comdg. gen., from 1944; asst. dep. chief of staff materiel hdqrs. USAF, 1948-50, mil. dir. munitions bd., 1950; comdr. 3d Air Force, U.K., 1952-54; vice comdr.-in-chief SAC, 1954-61; comdt. Nat. War Coll., 1961-89. Decorated D.S.M., Legion of Merit with oak leaf cluster, Air medal, Legion of Honor (French), Croix de Guerre (French), Order of Polonia Restituta (Polish), Most Excellent Order Brit. Empire. Home: Laguna Hills Calif. Died Apr. 11, 1989.

GRISWOLD, RALPH ESTY, landscape architect; b. Warren, Ohio, Aug. 22, 1894; s. William Tudor and Mabel (Hull) G.; m. Dorothy Elizabeth Griffith, July 14, 1920; 1 child, Romola Brady. BS, Cornell U., 1916, M in Landscape Design, 1917; student, Am. Art Tng. Ctr., Paris, 1919, Am. Acad., Rome, 1920-23. Landscape architect A. D. Taylor, Cleve., 1923-27, Nicolet & Griswold, Pitts., 1927-30; pvt. practice Pitts., from 1930; commissions include Longue Vue, Fox Chapel, Rolling Rock Country Club, Buhl Found., Chatham Village Housing, Aluminum Co. Am. Lab., Cyrus McCormick, Lessing Rosenwald, Mrs. Max Ascoll, Edgar Kaufman; cons. Pitts Housing Authority; supt. Bureau Parks, Pitts., 1934-35; cons. Federal Housing Authority, U. Pitts., Westminster Coll., Ga. Warm Springs Found., Pa., Coll. for Women, others; resident landscape architect Am. Mil. Acad., Rome, 1949-50; landscape architect Am. Mil. Cemetery, Anzio, Italy; architect landscape restoration Athenian Agora, Am. Sch. Classical Studies, Athens, Greece; hist. rsch. for Williamsburg on 18th Century gardens. Contbr. Garden Dictionary, Historic Architecture of Western Pa.; contbr. articles to profl. jours. Dir. Pa. Parks Assn., Western Pa. Conservancy; mem. sponsoring com. Allegheny Conference on Community Devel. 1st lt. A.E.F., 1917-19. Rsch. fellow landscape architecture Dumbarton Oaks Rsch. Libr. and Collection; recipient Sarah Gildersleeve Fife award Garden Club Am., also Gold medal of Honor, Gold Cross of Royal Order of George I, Paul King of Hellenes. Fellow Am. Soc. Landscape Architects; mem. AIA (hon.), Nat. Acad. Design (assoc.), Pitts. Archtl. Club (pres. 1930-31), Longue Vue Club, Century Assn. Club (N.Y.C.), Cosmos Club (Washington). *

GRODINS, FRED SHERMAN, physiology educator, biomedical engineer; b. Chgo., Nov. 18, 1915; s. Abe E. and Minnie (Levine) G.; m. Sylvia Johnson, Mar. 28, 1942. B.S., Northwestern U., 1937, M.S., 1940, M.D., 1942, Ph.D., 1944. Instr. Northwestern U., Chgo., 1942-44, assoc. prof., 1947-50, prof. physiology, 1950-67; asst. prof. U. Ill., Chgo., 1946, assoc. prof., 1947; prof. elec. engring. and physiology U. So. Calif., 1967-76, prof., chmn. dept. biomed. engring., 1976-86, Z.A. Kaprielian prof., 1982-86, emeritus prof. biomed. engring., elec. engring., physiology, 1986-89; Mem. physiology tng. com. NIH, 1964-68, biomed. engring. tng. com., 1968-72, mem. pulmonary diseases adv. com., 1973-77, mem. cardiovascular and pulmonary study sect., 1979-80; cons. Rand Corp., from 1964. Author: Control Theory and Biological Systems, 1963, Respiratory Function of the Lung and Its Control, 1978. Served to capt. USAAF, 1944-46. Mem. Am. Physiol. Soc., Biomed. Engring. Soc., Soc. Exptl. Biology and Medicine, AAAS, Sigma Xi, Phi Beta Kappa, Alpha Omega Alpha, Phi Lambda Upsilon. Home: Rolling Hills Calif. Died Sept. 21, 1989; buried DeKalb, Ill.

GROESCHEL, AUGUST HERMAN, hospital administrator, physician; b. Jersey City, May 31, 1908; s. August Herman and Margaret (Murphy) G.; m. Mary T. Molloy, Feb. 21, 1933 (dec. 1945); children—Peter, Moya, Noel; m. Eileen D. Bosquett, Jan. 3, 1946; children—Margaret, Catherine. A.B., Holy Cross Coll., 1927; M.D., Columbia, 1931, M.S., 1947. Intern French Hosp., N.Y.C., 1931-33, N.Y. Nursery and Child's Hosp., 1933-34; pvt. practice Sussex, N.J., 1934-40; asst. med. dir. Health Ins. Plan Greater N.Y., 1947-48; asst. dir. N.Y. Hosp., 1948-52, asso. dir., 1954-66, adminstr., 1967-69; exec. dir. Phila. Gen. Hosp., 1952-54; v.p. N.Y. Hosp.-Cornell Med. Center, 1970-73; dir. N.J. Blood Services, 1973-75; asst. prof. pub. health and preventive medicine Cornell U. Med. Coll., 1954-73; spl. cons. surgeon gen. USPHS, from 1959; surgeon gen. U.S. Army, from 1954; Pres. Community Blood Council Greater N.Y., 1959-73, pres. emeritus, 1973, exec. asso., 1975-79; bd. dirs. Group Health Ins., Inc., N.Y., 1961-80; med. control bd. Health Ins. Plan Greater N.Y., Inc., 1957-75, bd. dirs., 1963-75; treas. Career Center Social Services, 1966-70; mem. nat. health resources adv. com. Office Emergency Planning, Exec. Offices President, 1963-68, also chmn. com. blood, health adviser to dir., 1969-79, chmn. nat. health resources adv. com., 1969-79; chmn. nat. adv. com. on selection physicians, dentists and allied specialists SSS, 1969-73, chmn. adv. com. on selection of drs., dentists and allied specialists, 1973-76; bd. dirs. Am. Bur. Med. Aid to China, 1968-80, 1st v.p., 1969, pres., 1970, hon. pres., 1971; mem. Nat. Bd. Med. Examiners, 1970-74. Author: (with Emanuel Hayt and Lillian R. Hayt) Law of Hospital, Physician and Patient, 2d edit, 1972, (with Emanuel Hayt and Dorothy McMullan) Law of Hospital and Nurse, 1958. Trustee La Guardia Hosp., N.Y.C. Served to lt. col. AUS, 1941-45; brig. gen. Res., ret. 1967. Decorated Legion of Merit. Fellow AMA, N.Y. Acad. Medicine (Disting. Service in Pub. Health Plaque 1984), Am. Pub. Health Assn., Am. Coll. Hosp. Adminstrs.; mem. Am. Hosp. Assn. Home: Sea Girt N.J. Died Apr. 23, 1989; buried St. Catherine's Cemetery, Spring Lake, N.J.

GROMYKO, ANDREY ANDREYEVICH, president of USSR and minister foreign affairs; b. Starye Gromyky, Byelo-russia, July 6, 1909; m. Lydia D. Grinevich; children: Anatoli, Emilia. Ed., Minsk Agrl. Inst., Econ. Inst., Moscow, 1931-36, M.A., 1936. Sr. sci. worker Econ. Inst., Acad. Scis. USSR, 1936-39, also lectr. Moscow univs., 1936-39; chief div. Am. countries People's Commissariat Fgn. Affairs, 1939; counselor Russian Embassy, Washington, 1939-43; minister to Cuba; ambassador to U.S., 1943-46, to Gt. Brit., 1952-53; USSR rep. on UN Security Council, 1943-46; dep. minister for fgn. affairs, 1946-49, 1st dep. fgn. minister, 1949-57, fgn. minister, 1957-85, pres., 1985-88; 1st dep. chair Council of Ministers, 1983-85; mem. Politburo, 1973-88. Author: Memoirs, 1990 (published posthumously). Named Hero Socialist Labor (twice); recipient Order of Lenin (6) Hammer and Sickle gold medal (2), also others. Home: Moscow Russia Died July 2, 1989.

GRONQUIST, CARL HARRY, bridge engineer; b. N.Y.C., Oct. 17, 1903; s. Axel Theodore and Hilma Rosenquist G.; m. Marjorie Duncan Hahn, June 19, 1937; children: Carl Robert, Arthur Richard. BS, Rutgers U., 1925, MS, 1927, C.E., 1940, DSc hon. , 1958. Draftsman Am. Car and Foundry Co., N.Y.C., 1925, Post & McCord, N.Y.C., 1926; asst. engr., resident engr., assoc. engr. Robinson & Steinman, cons. engrs., 1927-45; faculty civil engring. dept. Rutgers U., 1941, Princeton U., 1941-42; assoc. engr. D.B. Steinman, 1945-6; ptnr. Steinman, Boynton, Gronquist & London, N.Y.C., 196-75; cons. Steinman, Boynton, Gronquist & Birdsall, N.Y.C., 1976-91. Contbr. tech. articles to profl. jours. Fellow Am. Cons. Engrs. Coun., ASCE J. James R. Croes medal 1943 ; mem. Engring. Inst. Can., Can. Soc. C.E., Phi Beta Kappa, Sigma Xi, Tau Beta Pi, Pi Epsilon. Home: Murray Hill N.J. Died June 16, 1991.

GROOMS, HARLAN HOBART, judge; b. Jeffersonville, Ky., Nov. 7, 1900; m. Angeline M. Grooms; children: Harlan Hobart, Ellen Elizabeth, John Franklin, Angeline. J.D., U. Ky.; LL.D. (hon.), Samford U. Bar: Ky., Ala. Practiced in Birmingham, Ala., 1926-53; mem. Spain, Gillon, Grooms & Young; U.S. dist. judge No. Dist. of Ala., from 1953. Trustee Samford U. Mem. ABA, Ala. Bar Assn., Phi Alpha Delta, Omicron Delta Kappa, Pi Kappa Alpha. Baptist. Club: Civitan. Home: Birmingham Ala. Died Aug. 23, 1991.

GROSS, CHAIM, sculptor, educator; b. Kolomea, Austria, Mar. 17, 1904; s. Moses and Leah (Sperber) G.; m. Renee Nechim, Dec. 13, 1932; children: Mimi, Yudi. Student, Kunstegewerbe Schulle Edn. Alliance, N.Y., Beaux-Arts Inst. Design Art Students League, 4 yrs.; DFA (hon.), Franklin and Marshall Coll., 1970; LHD (hon.), Yeshiva U., 1978, Adelphi U., 1980; DFA (hon.), Bklyn. Coll., 1986. Instr. sculpture Edn. Alliance Arts Sch., 68 yrs., New Sch. for Soc. Research, 40 yrs., Mus. Modern Art, N.Y.C., 1952-57. Master wood sculptor; also worked in marble and bronze; one-man shows include Greenwich Village gallery, N.Y.C., 1932, later Medici II Gallery, Miami Beach, Fla., 1971, New Sch. Gallery, N.Y.C., 1971, Nat. Collection Fine Arts, Washington, 1974, Leonard Hutton Gallery, N.Y.C., 1974; exhibited watercolors and drawings Forum Gallery, N.Y.C., 1980, others; sculptures exhibited in group shows at Mus. Modern Art, 1961-62, Smithsonian Instn., 1961-63, N.Y. World's Fair, 1964-65; represented in permanent collections Met. Mus. Art, Art Inst. Chgo., Bklyn. Mus., Jewish Mus., Worcester Art Mus.; commns. include Naomi (Italian marble sculpture of large head), Jewish Mus., 1978, two portfolios in 18 colors executed in Paris, theme of Isiah and Song of Songs for Ltd. Edit. Publ., 1979, Isiah, Holy Cross Coll., 1979, life size bronze sculpture for shopping ctr., Ft. Lauderdale, Fla., 1980, bronze sculpture Jewish Community Ctr., Tenafly, N.J., 1980, others; created design for stamps commemorating 38th and 40th anniv. Assn. World Fedn. of UN, design for coins and medals Israel Govt.; retrospective exhbns. sculpture and drawings Montclair Art Mus., Jewish Mus., Lowe Art Mus., Coral Gables, Fla.; donated larger than life size sculpture "The Family" to City of N.Y., to be mounted on Bleeker St. and 7th Ave.; designer Tapestry of Peace presented to Pres. Begin of Israel, Pres. Sadat pf Egypt and Pres. Carter of U.S.A.; subject 30 audiotape cassettes of oral history (by Rachel Chodorov); demonstration appearance on Sta. WCBS-TV Gateway program; contbr. articles to various publs. Recipient first prize Boston Arts Festival, 1963, citation proclaiming Chaim Gross Day Manhattan Borough Pres. Percy E Sutton, Ateret Tifereth award in Art Theol. Sem. Am., Disting. Extraordinary Work in sculpture citation New Sch. Social Rsch., other awards. Fellow Jewish Acad. Arts and Scis. (Joseph Handelman prize in art); mem. NAD (2 Gold medals), Am. Acad. and Inst. Arts and Letters (chair #44), Sculptors Guild (bd. dirs.), Edn. Alliance Alumni Assn., Fedn. Modern Painters and Sculptors, Nat. Inst. Arts and Letters (grantee 1956, Award of Merit medal 1963). Home: New York N.Y. Died May 5, 1991; buried Mt. Lebanon Cemetery, Queens, N.Y.

GROSS, JOHN OWEN, clergyman, educator; b. Grant County, Ky., July 9, 1894; s. William and Anna (Chrisman) G.; m. Harriet Bletzer, June 30, 1920; children: George Albert, John Birney, Harriet Lucille Gross Smith. AB, Asbury Coll., Wilmore, Ky., 1918; DD, Asbury Coll., 1930; postgrad., Lane Sem., Cin., Ohio, 1918-19; STB, Boston U., 1921; grad. student, U. Cin., U. Ky., 1929; LHD, Union Coll., 1938, Mt. Union Coll., 1946, DePauw U., 1952, Cornell Coll., 1953, Lycoming Coll., 1964; LLD, W.Va. Wesleyan Coll., 1946, Ky. Wesleyan Coll., 1949, U. Chattanooga, 1950, Iowa Wesleyan Coll., 1955, Wiley Coll., 1956, Ohio Wesleyan Coll., 1959, Hendrix Coll., 1964, Syracuse U., 1964; STD, Boston U., 1949; DScEd., Morningside Coll., 1950; LittD, Fla. So. Coll., 1947; JUD, Simpson Coll., 1954; DD, Ohio Northern, 1958, Clark Coll., 1959, McKendree Coll., 1963, Emory U., 1964; DRE, Southwestern Coll., 1960, U. of the Pacific, 1962; HHD, Bethune Cookman Coll., 1962. Entered ministry Meth. Episcopal Ch., 1916, ordained deacon, 1918, elder, 1921; pastor First M.E. Ch., Barbourville, Ky., 1921-25; dist. supt. Barbourville Dist., Ky. Conf. M.E. Ch., 1925-29; pres. Union Coll., Barbourville, 1929-38, Simpson Coll., Iowa, 1938-41; sec. Dept. Ednl. Instns., Bd. of Edn., Meth. Ch., 1941-48; gen. sec. Div. Higher Edn., Bd. of Edn., Meth. Ch., from 1948; mem. various Meth. ecumenical and jurisdictional confs., from 1931; Alexander Gustavus Brown lectr. Randolph Macon Coll., 1950; Willson lectr. McMurry Coll., 1958; mem. exec. com. World Meth. Coun. Author: History of Cokesbury College, (with Bovd M. McKeown) You and Your College, Education for Life, Martin Ruter: Pioneer in Methodist Education, John Westey: Christian Educator, Methodist Beginnings in Higher Education, The Beginnings of American Methodism; contbr. to religious publs. Trustee Dillard U., Rust Coll., Huston-Tillotson Coll., Am. U., Meharry Coll., Clark Coll., Bethune-Cookman Coll., Scarritt Coll., W.Va. Wesleyan Coll.; ex-officio bd. mem. Bennett. Recipient St. George's award for disting. svc. to Methodism, 1961, Order of Achievement, Lambda Chi Alpha, 1962. Mem. Assn. Colls. and Univs. of Ky., Upper Cumberland Ednl. Assn., Assn. Am. Colls., Lambda Chi, Alpha Epsilon Sigma, Phi Kappa Delta, Phi Beta Kappa, Mason, Old Oak Club. *

GROSS, ROBERT, advertising executive; b. Newark, Aug. 16, 1930; s. Henry William and Esta (Riker) G.; m. Marilyn Greta Heller, Apr. 27, 1958; children: Laura Danielle, Sarah Kate. BA, Tulane U., 1951. With Doyle, Dane & Bernbach, N.Y.C., 1955-57, Kenyon & Eckhardt, N.Y.C., 1957-59, Benton & Bowles, N.Y.C. and London, 1959-61, 61-64; co-founder, chmn., chief exec. officer Geers Gross Advt., N.Y.C. and London, 1964-91. Author: Boy & Girl, 1982. Served with USN, 1952-55, Korea. Clubs: Brooks (London); Lotos (N.Y.C.). Home: London Eng. Died Apr. 7, 1991.

GROSSMAN, BURTON JAY, pediatric rheumatologist, educator; b. Chgo., Nov. 27, 1924; s. Paul and Neva (Sonnenschein) G. B.S., U. Chgo., 1945, M.D., 1949. Diplomate Am. Bd. Pediatrics. Intern Billings Meml. Hosp., U. Chgo. (Clinics), 1949-50; resident Bobs Roberts Meml. Hosp., 1950-51, 53-54, attending physician, from 1955; med. dir. La Rabida Children's Hosp. and Research Center, Chgo., 1961-85, med. dir. emeritus, 1985-90, attending physician, 1957-90; instr. pediatrics U. Chgo. Med. Sch., 1954-57, asst. prof., 1957-61, assoc. prof., 1961-66, prof. pediatrics, 1966-85, prof. pediatrics emeritus, 1985-90; Co-chmn. rheumatic fever prevention com. Chgo. Heart Assn., 1962-72. Author 100 sci. papers. Served to capt. M.C. USAF, 1951-53. Recipient Joseph P. Brenneman award Chgo. Pediatric Soc., 1981, Disting. Service award Arthritis Found., 1985; Helen Hay Whitney rsch. fellow, Denmark, 1954. Fellow Am. Acad. Pediatrics; mem. Am. Pediatric Soc., Soc. for Pediatric Research,

Midwest Soc. Pediatric Research, Chgo. Rheumatism Soc. (pres. 1969-71), Arthritis Found. (med. sci. com. 1968-77, vice chmn. 1972-75). Home: Chicago Ill. Died May 6, 1990.

GROVE, JEAN DONNER (MRS. EDWARD R. GROVE), sculptor; b. Washington, May 15, 1912; d. Frederick Gregory and Georgia V. (Gartrell) Donner; m. Edward R. Grove, June 24, 1936; children: David Donner, Eric Donner. Student, Cornell U., 1932, Hill Sch. of Sculpture, 1934-35, Corcoran Sch. of Art, 1935-37, 42-44, Cath. U. Am., 1936-37, Phila. Mus. Art Sch., 1967; B.S., Wilson Tchrs. Coll., 1939. Exhibited one-man shows, Wilson Tchrs. Coll., Washington, 1939, Grove Family Exhbns., Cayuga Mus. History and Art, Auburn, N.Y., 1964, Episcopal Acad. Gallery, Phila., 1966, group shows, Pa. Acad. Fine Arts, Phila., 1947, 48, 51, 53, N.A.D., N.Y.C., 1949, 78, 81, 83, 85, 87, 89, Nat. Sculpture Soc. at Archtl. League, N.Y.C., Topeka, 1957, Lever House, N.Y.C., 1974, 75, 86, Port of History Mus., Phila., 1987, Grace Bldg. N.Y.C., 1988, Equitable Gallery, N.Y.C., 1976, 78, 83, Park Ave. Atrium, N.Y.C., 1985, Art U.S.A., Madison Sq. Garden, N.Y.C., 1958, Corcoran Gallery Art, Washington, 1943-47, Internat. Gallery, Washington, 1946, Phila. Mus. Art, 1955, 59, 62, Phila. Art Alliance, 1957, 60, 66, Phila. Civic Ctr., 1968, Flagler Art Ctr., West Palm Beach, Fla., 1972, Norton Gallery Art, West Palm Beach, 1974, 81, 83, Cathedral St. John the Divine, N.Y.C., 1990; represented in permanent collections, Rosenwald Collection, Phila., Ch. of Holy Comforter, Drexel Hill, Pa., Fine Arts Commn., City Hall, Phila., Palm Beach County Govt. Ctr., West Palm Beach, Fla., Port of History Mus., Philadelphia; sculptor numerous portrait commns., garden figures and fountains, from 1940; (with E.R. Grove) Am. Express Goldpiece, 1982, St. Francis Meml. Plaque, 1990. Mem. adv. coun. Nat. Biog. Centre, Cambridge, Eng., from 1989. Recipient 1st prize sculpture Nat. Mus. Washington, 1946, 1st prize Sculpture Arts Club, 1946, Portrait prize Sculpture Arts Club, 1947, Morris Goodman award John Herron Art Mus., Indpls., 1957, Competition prize for design and sculpture Artists Equity Phila., 1960, Humane award Animal Rescue League of Palm Beach, 1974, 80, 85, Tallix Foundry award NSS Bicentennial Exhbn. Equitable Gallery, N.Y.C., 1976, Gold medal Acad. of Italy, 1979, Golden Centaur award, 1982, Competition prize and commendation Palm Beach County Commn.'s Meml. Chambers portrait plaque, 1986. Fellow Nat. Sculpture Soc.; mem. Nat. Acad. Design (assoc.), Artists Equity Assn. (dir. Phila. chpt. 1964-66), Phila. Art Alliance, Soc. of Four Arts, Norton Gallery Art, Soc. Washington Artists, Am. Medallic Sculpture Assn. (edit. bd. jour.), Fedn. Internat. de Medaille, English Speaking Union, Animal Rescue League of Palm Beach (com. chmn. from 1972, dir. from 1975), St. Mary's Guild of Episcopal Ch. Women (v.p. 1974-76), Nat. Women's Bd. Northwood Inst. (exec. com.), Kappa Delta Pi. Home: West Palm Beach Fla. Died Feb. 9, 1992. †

GROVES, CHARLES BARNARD, orchestra conductor; b. London, Mar. 10, 1915; s. Frederick and Annie (Whitehead) G.; m. Hilary Hermione Barchard, June 5, 1948; children: Sally Hilary, Mary Hermione, Jonathan Charles. Student Royal Coll. Music, London, 1932-37; Mus.D. (hon.), Liverpool U., 1970; Dr. (hon.), Open U., Milton Keynes, Eng., 1978; Litt.D. (hon.), Salford U. (Eng.), 1980; Dr. U. Surrey, Eng., 1991. Chorus master BBC Opera Unit, London, 1938-44; condr., musical dir. BBC No. Symphony Orch., Manchester, Eng., 1944-51, Bournemouth Symphony Orch. (Eng.), 1951-61, Welsh Nat. Opera Co., Cardiff, 1961-63, English Nat. Opera Co., London, 1977-80, Royal Liverpool Philharm. Orch., 1963-77, condr. laureate for life, 1985-92; assoc. condr. Royal Philharmonic Orch., London, 1967-92; prin. condr. Guildford Philharm. Orch.; condr. regularly in Europe, Am. and Japan; records with all London Orchestras. Decorated comdr. and knight bachelor Order Brit. Empire; named Freeman, City of London, 1976; fellow Royal Coll. Music, London, 1956, Royal Acad. Music, London, 1963, No. Sch. Music, Manchester, 1972, Trinity Coll. Music, London, 1974, Guildhall Sch. Music and Drama, London, London Coll. Music, 1981, Manchester Poly.; companion Royal No. Coll. Music, Manchester, 1983. Mem. Inc. Soc. Musicians (pres. 1972, 82), Royal Philharm. Soc. (hon.). Club: Savage (London). Died June 20, 1992. Home: London Eng. †

GROVES, HAROLD MARTIN, economics educator; b. Lodi, Wis., Oct. 3, 1897; s. Frank William and Emma Amelia (Herr) G.; m. Helen Hoopes, July 14, 1930; children: Thomas, Steven, Roderic, Susan. Student, Harvard, 1919-20; PhB, U. Wis., 1919, AM, 1921, PhD, 1927. Prof. econs. U. Wis., from 1927; chmn. bd. dirs. Nat. Bur. Econ. Rsch. Author: Postware Taxation and Economic Progress, 1946, Trouble Spots in Taxation, 1946, Economic Study of Milwaukee, 1948, Financing Government, 1939, revised 1958, Education and Economic Growth, 1961; co-author: Wisconsin's State and Local Tax Burden, 1959; editor: Viewpoints in Public Finance, 1947. Mem. Wis. Assembly, 1930-31, Wis. Tax Commn., 1931-32, Wis. Senate, 1934-36; com. on intergovernmental fiscal rels. U.S. Treasury, 1941-42, rsch. staff com. for econ. devel., 1943-44. Mem. Tax Adminstrs. Assn., Am. Econ. Assn., Nat. Tax Assn., Tax Inst., Phi Beta Kappa. Unitarian. *

GROVES, WALLACE, financier; b. Norfolk, Va., Mar. 20, 1901; s. James S. and Lillie (Edwards) G.; m. Georgette Cusson (dec.); children: Gordon, Gene, Graham, Gary, Gayle. M.A., B.Sc., J.D., LL.M., Georgetown U., Washington, 1924, D.Hum. (hon.), 1981; LL.D. (hon.), Ursinus Coll., Collegeville, Pa. Bar: Md. 1925. Practiced law, until 1931; then went to N.Y. to engage in reorganization and mgmt. industrial and financial concerns; formerly pres. and chmn. bd. Phoenix Securities Corp.; chmn. bd. Grand Bahama Port Authority Ltd.; founder Freeport, Grand Bahama. Home: Coral Gables Fla. Died Jan. 30, 1988; buried Freeport, Bahamas.

GRUENBERG, ERNEST MATSNER, psychiatrist, epidemiologist; b. N.Y.C., Dec. 2, 1915; s. Benjamin Charles and Sidonie (Matsner) G.; m. Lillian Saastamoinen, 1943; children: Nicholas Benjamin, Ann Matsner, Matthew Alan; m. Judith S. Stainbrook. BA, Swarthmore Coll., 1937; MD, Johns Hopkins U., 1941; DPH, Yale U., 1955. Intern St. Elizabeth Hosp., Washington, 1941-42; resident psychiatry Bellevue Hosp., N.Y.C., 1946-48; exec. dir. N.Y. State Mental Health Commn., 1949-54; sr. mem. tech. staff Milbank Meml. Fund, N.Y.C., 1955-61; prof. psychiatry Columbia U., 1961-75, lectr. psychiatry, 1975-91; pvt. practice psychiatry Syracuse, N.Y., 1950-55, N.Y.C., 1955-75, Poughkeepsie, N.Y., 1967-75, Balt., 1976-91; lectr. depts. psychiatry and pub. health Yale U., 1952-66; dir. psychiat. epidemiology rsch. unit N.Y. State Dept. Mental Hygiene, 1968-75; prof., chmn. dept. mental hygiene Johns Hopkins U., Balt., 1975-91, prof. psychiatry Sch. Medicine, 1976-91; lectr. epidemiology Harvard Sch. Pub. Health, 1959-69, Columbia Sch. Pub. Health, 1953-72; attending psychiatrist Presbyn. Hosp., N.Y.C., 1966-75, Hudson River Psychiat. Ctr., Poughkeepsie, 1967-75; mem. tech. bd. Milbank Meml. Fund, N.Y.C., 1961-68, 75-91; mem. tech. adv. bd. Maurice M. Falk Med. Fund, Pitts., 1963-91; mem. Milbank Meml. Fund Commn. on Higher Edn. for Pub. Health, 1972-75. Organizer, editor: (with F.G. Boudreau)ú Roundtable on Epidemiology of Mental Disorders, 1949; editor: Evaluating the Effectiveness of Mental Health Services, 1966; contbr. chpts. to psychiat. texts and handbooks, articles to sci. and profl. jours. With M.C., AUS, 1942-46. Fellow APHA (gov. coun., chmn. com. mental health), Am. Psychiat. Assn. (chmn. com. nomenclature and stats. 1965-68). Home: Washington D.C. Died July 2, 1991.

GRUNAU, HERMAN CARL, clergyman; b. Cleve., Sept. 8, 1895; s. Gustave and Martha Evelyn (Stone) G.; m. Beatrice Engel Guebert, June 24, 1926; children: David Leonard, Dan Anthony. Diploma, Concordia Jr. Coll., Ft. Wayne, Ind., 1917, Concordia Sem., St. Louis, 1921; MA, Columbia, 1924, BS in LS, 1938. Ordained to ministry Luth. Ch., 1922. Vicar Fedor, Tex., 1918-19; instr. history Concordia Coll., St. Paul, 1921-22, 24-26; tchr. social sci. Cleveland High Sch., St. Paul, 1926-27; libr., prof. social scis. Concordia Inst., Bronxville, N.Y., 1927-50; pastor Holy Trinity Luth. Ch., Bronx, 1936-50; libr. Valparaiso U., 1950-64; asst. pastor Peace Luth. Ch., Mill Valley, Calif.; pastor Faith Meml. Luth. Ch., Valparaiso, 1956-57; lectr. Queens Bible Inst., 1932, Bronx Sunday Sch. Assn., 1935, Walther League Tng. Seminars, N.Y.C., 1936, No. Ill. Bible Inst., 1955; survey coll. librs. for bd. higher edn. Luth. Ch.-Mo. Synod, 1939-40. Mem. ALA. *

GRUNDER, PAUL EDWIN, food products company executive; b. Minerva, Ohio, Dec. 8, 1931; s. Edwin and Gladys Ruth (Foltz) G.; m. Lois Harriet Farnum, Feb. 17, 1957; children: Robin, Alyson, Gordon, Linen. BS ChemE, Grove City Coll., 1953; postgrad. in bus., Harvard U., 1965. Various positions Dow Corning Corp., Midland, Mich., 1953-71; v.p. sales and mktg. Indsl. div. CPC Internat. Inc., Englewood Cliffs, N.J., 1971-73, pres. Penick Corp. unit, 1974-75, group v.p. Indsl. div., gen. mgr. corn products, 1975-76, corp. v.p., 1977, pres. indsl. div., 1977-78; pres. corn products CPC N.Am., 1978-79, pres. indsl. diversified unit, 1979-81; v.p. corp. indsl. bus. support CPC Internat. Inc., Englewood Cliffs, N.J., 1981-84, pres. CPC Diversified div., 1984-87, v.p. corp. devel., 1987-88, pres. Corn Refining Bus., from 1988. Served to lt. (j.g.) USN, 1954-57. Home: Ridgewood N.J. Deceased. †

GUBELMANN, WALTER STANLEY, real estate company executive; b. N.Y., June 16, 1908; s. William S. and Juliette E. (Metz) G.; m. Barton Green, Nov. 1, 1941; children: William Samuel II, James Barton. Student, Philips Andover Acad.; A.B., Yale U., 1931; postgrad. bus. adminstrn, Columbia U., 1931-33. Pres. Realty & Indsl. Corp. (patents, investments and real estate.), Palm Beach, Fla., from 1935. Trustee, pres. Soc. Four Arts, Palm Beach, Fla. Served as capt. AUS, World War II. Mem. Palm Beach Civic Assn. (dir.). Clubs: Racquet and Tennis, N.Y. Yacht (organizer and mgr. Constellation syndicate, winner Am.'s cup 1964), Cruising of Am., Leash (all N.Y.C.); Seawanhaka Yacht (Oyster Bay, N.Y.); Pilgrims (N.Y.); ; Royal Swedish Yacht Club (Stockholm); Clambake , Bailey's Beach, Newport Country, Reading Room (all Newport, R.I.); Bar Harbor (Maine) Yacht; Everglades (gov., v.p.), Seminole, Bath and Tennis (all Palm Beach, Fla.). Home: Palm Beach Fla. Died July 28, 1988; buried Palm Beach.

GUCCI, ALDO, retail stores executive; b. Florence, Italy, May 26, 1909; s. Guccio G. Owner, prin. Gucci Shops Inc., N.Y.C., Chgo., Beverly Hills, Calif., Palm Beach, Fla., other locations, until 1988; chmn. bd. Guccio Gucci Soc. r.l, Florence, Rome, Milan, Montecatini, Italy; dir. Gucci Ltd., London, Gucci Soc. Resp. Ltd., Paris. Home: Rome Italy Died Jan. 19, 1990.

GUEDENS, EUNICE See ARDEN, EVE

GUERRERO, JOSÉ, artist; b. Granada, Spain, Oct. 27, 1914; s. Emilio Garcia López and Gracia (Padial) Guerrero; m. Roxane Whittier Pollock, Apr. 25, 1949; children: Elisabeth Garcia, José Antonio. Lic. prof. art, Escuela Superior de Bellas Artes, Madrid, 1945; student, Ecole de Beaux Arts, Paris, 1946-47; studied with Stanley William Hayter, Atelier 17, N.Y.C., 1950. Prof. art Lycée Française, Madrid, New Sch. for Social Research, N.Y.C., 1962-65; master class in painting Circle of Fine Arts, Madrid, 1984, 88; vis. artist Atlanta Coll. Art, Cleve. Art Inst., 1975, U. Iowa, 1978. One-man shows include Galeria Secolo, Rome, 1948, Karl Buchholz Gallery, Madrid, 1950, Betty Parsons Gallery, N.Y.C., 1954, 57, 58, 60, 63, Rose Fried Gallery, N.Y.C., 1964, French & Co., N.Y.C., 1969, Graham Gallery, N.Y.C., 1969, Wolfgang Ketterer Gallery, Munich, 1975, Hoover Gallery, San Francisco, 1976, Juana Aizpuru Gallery, Seville, Spain, 1976, retrospective Museo de Bilbao, Spain, 1976, Gruenebâum Gallery, N.Y.C., 1978, 80, Ditesheim Gallery Neuchatel, Switzerland, 1979, retrospective exhbn. Spanish Ministry Culture, Edificio Arbos, Madrid, 1980-81 and Fundación Miró, Barcelona, 1981, ARCO Internat. Art Fair, Madrid, 1978, 80, 88, Internat. Art Market, Cologne, Fed. Republic Germany, 1983, Basel, Switzerland, 1978, FIAC, Paris, 1984, 88, Carlos TACHÉ GAL, Barcelona, 1990, Palacio de Gabia. Granada, Spain, 1990, Museo de Arte Contemp., Seville, 1990; two-man show with Joan Miró, Arts Club Chgo., 1954; 3 man shows Di Laurenti Gallery, N.Y.C., 1987, Juana Mordó Gallery, Madrid, 1964, 67, 71, 75, 82, 86; exhibited in numerous group shows at Guggenheim Mus., N.Y.C., 1954, Galerie de France, Paris, 1956, Dallas Mus., 1958, Whitney Mus. biennials, Corcoran Mus. annuals, Carnegie Inst. biennials, Centro de Arte Reina Sofia, Madrid, 1988, Petit Palais, Paris, 1987-88, Biennale de Alexandria, 1987, Mus. Contemporary Art, Madrid, 1988, Krugler Gallery, Geneva, 1989; represented in permanent collections Albright-Knox Gallery, Buffalo, Art Inst. Chgo., Carnegie Inst., Pitts., Bank of Spain, Chase Manhattan Bank, N.Y.C., Guggenheim Mus., N.Y.C., Whitney Mus., N.Y.C., La. Mus., Denmark, Mus. Contemporary Art, Madrid, Mus. Spanish Abstract Art, Cuenca, Nat. Treasure of Spain, Nat. Treasure of Audalucia, Reina Sofia Mus., Madrid, Yale U. Mus., New Haven, various others. Decorated chevalier de l'ordre des Arts and des Lettres, French Ministry Culture, 1959, officier, 1983; Ofcl. Cross, Order Isabel of Spain, 1948; Medallo de Oro de Bellas Artes Govt. Spain, 1985, Medallo de Oro de la ciudad de Granada, 1986, Medallo de Oro Rodriguez Acosta, Granada, 1989; Audalucia prize Govt. Audalucia, 1989; named Adopted son of Granada, 1986; Graham Found. for Advanced Studies of Fine Arts grantee, 1958. Mem. Juana Mordo Gallery (Madrid). Home: New York N.Y. Died Dec. 23, 1991.

GUEST, MAURICE MASON, research unit director, emeritus physiology educator; b. Fredonia, N.Y., July 30, 1906; s. Maurice S. and Daisy (Mason) G.; m. Alice Rhoda Avery, Aug. 16, 1936; children: Avery Mason, John Andrew. A.B., U. Mich., 1930; Ph.D., Columbia, 1941. Field asst. U.S. Dept. Agr. Bur. of Entomology, 1930-31; sci. tchr. Sherman (N.Y.) High Sch., 1931-36; instr. physiology Columbia, 1936-40, research assoc., 1940-42; assoc. prof. physiology Wayne U. Coll. Medicine, 1946-51; prof., chmn. dept. physiology U. Tex. Med. Br., Galveston, 1951-73; Ashbel Smith prof. physiology U. Tex. Med. Br., 1973-87, Ashbel Smith prof. physiology emeritus, from 1987; chief hematology div. Shriner's Burn Inst., Galveston, Tex. Contbr. articles to profl. jours. Served to maj. USAAF, 1942-46. Mem. Am. Physiol. Soc., AAAS, Soc. for Exptl. Biology and Medicine, Internat. Hematol. Soc. Home: Seattle Wash. Deceased. †

GUEST, RAYMOND RICHARD, former United States ambassador, horse breeder; b. N.Y.C., Nov. 25, 1907; s. Frederic Edward and Amy (Phipps) G.; m. Elizabeth Polk, June 1935; children: Raymond Richard, Elizabeth Stevens, Virginia; m. Caroline Murat, June 1960; children: Achille Murat, Laetitia Amelia. Student, McGill U., Montreal, Que., Can., 1927-28; BA, Yale U., 1931. Horse breeder, cattle farmer, King George, Va., 1931-91; spl. asst. to sec. def. Dept. Def., Washington, 1945-47; dir. Bessemer Securities, Inc., 1947; commr. Va. Game and Inland Fisheries, 1960-65; U.S. amb. to Ireland, Dublin, 1965-68. Chmn. fund raising drive Front Royal Hosp., 1950; del. Nat. Dem. Convs., 1940, 48, 60; mem. Va. Senate, 1947-53; trustee Va. Mus. Fine Arts. Comdr. USNR, 1941-46. Decorated Legion of Merit, Bronze Star medal; Croix de Guerre (France), Order Brit. Empire, Danish Def. medal, Norwegian Cross. Mem. Racquet and Tennis Club (N.Y.C.), Jockey Club (N.Y.C.), Commonwealth Club, Masons (32d degree). Home: King George Va. Died Dec. 31, 1991; buried Powhatan Plantation, King George, Va.

GUGGENHIME, RICHARD ELIAS, lawyer; b. San Francisco, Sept. 19, 1908; s. David J. and Elsa (Triest) G.; m. Charlotte M. Johnson, Mar. 2, 1939 (dec. 1987); children: Richard J., David J. A.B., Stanford U., 1929; LL.B., Harvard U., 1932. Bar: Calif. 1932. Assoc. Heller, Ehrman, White & McAuliffe, San Francisco, 1932-33, 34-39, partner, 1939-41, 46-79, of counsel, 1980-88; mng. ptnr. Fresno-Kern Assocs.; past dir. Wells Fargo Bank, N.A., Sara Lee Corp., SMV Minerals, Inc. Pres. San Francisco Community Chest, 1952; pres. Rosenberg Found., 1954-57; Trustee Stanford U., 1958-78, pres. bd., 1964-67. Served from lt. (j.g.) to comdr. USNR, 1941-45. Decorated Bronze Star medal with gold star. Mem. ABA, San Francisco Bar Assn., Phi Beta Kappa. Home: San Francisco Calif. Died July, 1988.

GUILD, LURELLE VAN ARSDALE, industrial designer; b. N.Y.C., Aug. 19, 1898; s. Thomas Lurelle and Alice Taylor (Gumble) G.; m. A. Louise Eden, Nov. 31, 1929; 1 child, Cynthia Eden. Student, King Sch., Stamford, Conn., 1916; B of Painting, Syracuse Sch. Fine Arts, 1920. Mag. and advt. illustrator, indsl. designer N.Y.C., from 1927; pres., owner Lurelle Guild Assocs., N.Y.C., Dale Decorators, Milestone Village Mus., Noroton, Conn.; advisor Nat. Housing Authority; dir. Regional Planning Commn., N.Y.C. of Fairfield County.; chmn. Darien Town and Planning Commn. Works exhibited in Met. Mus., Mus. Modern Art, L.A. Mus., others; works pub. in Ladies Home Jour., House and Garden, House Beautiful, Better Home and Gardens; author: Geography of American Antiques, 1929, New Geography of American Antiques, 1947, Bluebook of Interior Decoration, 1938, A Course in Period Furniture, 1934; editor: Pictorial Review, Delineator. Recipient Art Dirs. Club medal for paintings and drawings in color done through J. Walter Thompson Advt. Agy., 1924; Arents medal Syracuse U., 1941, Jordan Marsh award, Modern Plastics award, Fashion Acad. award for household products, Westinghouse, 1951. Fellow Am. Soc. Indsl. Designers; mem. Am. Inst. Decorators, Art Dirs. Club, Soc. Indsl. Designers, Delta Kappa Epsilon, Am. Dutch Treat Club. Republican. Presbyterian. *

GUILFOYLE, GEORGE H., bishop; b. N.Y.C., Nov. 13, 1913; s. James J. and Johanna (McGrath) G. AB, Georgetown U., 1935; student, St. Joseph's Sem., 1939-44; JD, Fordham U., 1939; postgrad. in banking, NYU, 1945; LLM, Columbia U., 1946; LLD, St. Francis College, 1958, Manhattan Coll., 1962, Iona Coll., 1966; LittD, St. Joseph's Coll., Phila., 1968. Bar: N.Y. 1940; ordained priest Roman Cath. Ch., 1944. Named papal chamberlain Roman Cath. Ch., 1955, domestic prelate, 1958; asst. St. Patrick's Cathedral, 1944-45, St. Andrew's Ch., 1944-46; asst. chancellor, also asst. St. Elizabeth's Ch., N.Y.C., 1946-47; with Catholic Charities, N.Y.C., 1947-66, exec. dir., 1956-66; episcopal vicar Richmond County (S.I.), also; pastor St. Peter's Ch., 1966-68; bishop of Camden, N.J., 1968-89; Asso. moderator coordinating com. Cath. Lay Orgns. Archdiocese N.Y., 1954-57; archdiocesan consultor, 1960-68; nat. spiritual dir. Soc. St. Vincent de Paul, from 1966; Pres. Nat. Conf. Cath. Charities, 1959-61, bd. dirs., 1959-67; mem. N.Y.C. Adv. Bd. Pub. Welfare, 1960-66, Archdiocesan Commn. for Community Planning, 1964- 68. Bd. dirs. Nat. Shrine Immaculate Conception; trustee Seton Hall U. Recipient John Carroll award Georgetown U., 1963; Knight grand cross Equestrian Order Holy Sepulchre Jerusalem. Home: Cherry Hill N.J. Died June 11, 1991.

GUILFOYLE, JOHN W., communications company executive; b. Burbank, Calif., 1921; m. Shirley Ann Lumpp; 1 child: Patricia Ann Guilfoyle Goldstein. Attended, Wilson Jr. Coll., Glendale, Calif. With ITT, N.Y.C., 1951-86; v.p., indsl. relations dir., then v.p. ops. Fed. Electric Corp. subs. ITT Corp., 1956-59, pres., 1959-64; pres. Am. Cable and Radio Corp., 1964; group exec. ITT U.S. Def./Space Group, 1964-66, v.p., 1966-79, group exec. Far East and Pacific, 1966-68, group exec. Latin Am., 1968-78, group exec. Africa and Middle East, 1978-79; pres. ITT Europe, from 1979; corp. sr. v.p. ITT Corp., N.Y.C., 1979-80; exec. v.p. ITT Corp., 1980-86; pres., chief exec. officer ITT Telecommunication Corp., 1984-86, also bd. dirs. Chmn. bd. Molloy Coll., Rockville Centre, L.I. Capt. USAAF, World War II. Decorated, Silver Star, DFC, Air medal with 14 clusters. Mem. NAM (past vice chmn. nat. def. com.), Council of Americas (dir., exec. com.), Navy League, Air Force Assn., Nat. Aviation Club. Home: New York N.Y. Died July 30, 1989.

GUILLAUMAT, PIERRE, oil company executive; b. La Fliche, France, Aug. 5, 1909; s. Adolphe and Louise Bibent G.; m. Monique Villemain, Feb. 5, 1946; children: Anne, Jean, Francois. Grad., Ecole Poly., 1930, Ecole des Mines, 1933. Sr. warden mines French Indo-China, 1934-39; head mining svcs. Tunisia, 1939-44; chief oil svcs. Ministry Industry, France, 1944-51; pres. Atomic Energy France, 1951-58; chmn. Oil State Corp., 1962-77; chmn. jud. matters Counseil Gen. des Mines, 1977-78, minister for armies, 1958-60, minister for sci. and atomic energy, 1960-62, minister for edn., 1961; chmn. State Electricity Bd., 1964-65. With French Army, 1939-40, 43-44. Decorated Croix de Guerre, Legion of Honor, Bronze Star U.S. . Home: Neuilly France Died Aug. 28, 1991.

GUINIER, EWART, educator; b. Panama, C.Z., May 17, 1910; s. Howard Manoah and Marie Louise (Beresford) G.; m. Eugenia Paprin, Oct. 16, 1945; children: Clotilde Yvonne Stenson, Lani Carol, Sary Elisabeth, Marie Louise. BS cum laude, CCNY, 1935; MA, Columbia U., 1939; JD, NYU, 1959; MA (hon.), Harvard U., 1969. Asst. v.p. Haarlem Rsch. Lab., N.Y.C., 1933-35; dir. Intake Welfare Dept., N.Y.C., 1935-37; examiner, dir. Svc. Rating Bur., N.Y.C., 1937-42; internat. sec.-treas. CIO Pub. Workers, 1946-53; cons. Pensions, Newark, 1953-54, N.Y.C., 1954-90; cons. pensions Govt. Sierra Leone, 1961-62; assoc. dir. Urban Ctr. Columbia U., N.Y.C., 1968-69; dir. Douglass Urban Corp., 1969-90; chmn. Afro-Am. studies Harvard U., 1969-76; dir. W.E.B. DuBois Inst. Afro-Am. Rsch., 1969-75; founder, chmn. Jamaica Coord. Coun., 1962-65, Harlem Affairs Com., 1953-56; adv. bd. Black Heritage: A History of Afro-Americans. Contbr. articles to profl. jours. Chmn. Queens Urban League, 1962-68; Am. Labor party candidate for borough pres. of Manhattan, 1949; bd. dirs. Pub. Edn. Assn., N.Y. Urban League, Queens Coll. Speech and Hearing Ctr., Ctr. Urban Edn. With AUS, 1942-46. Urban fellow Columbia U., 1969; recipient award Black Studies Dirs. and Nat. Ctr. Afro-Am. Artists; Malcolm X scholar and Carter G. Woodson award N.Y. African Am. Life and History Assn. Mem. NAACP (life), African-Am. C. of C., Acad. Polit. Sci., Assn. Study Afro-Am. Life and History (life, nat. dir.), Orgn. Am. Historians. Home: Cambridge Mass. Died Feb. 4, 1990.

GUMPERT, EMIL, judge; b. Stockton, Calif., Jan. 14, 1895; s. William and Sarah (Gellert) G.; m. Ruth Kenner, July 19, 1925; 1 child, William Kenner. Student, Columbia U., 1919-20, Washington & Lee U., 1919. Bar: Calif. 1916. Trial and corp. lawyer Stockton, 1916-47; judge Superior Ct. of Calif., from 1956; mem. adv. panel State of Calif. Youth Authority, 1953. Bd. editors: Calif. Jury Instructions. Fellow Am. Coll. Trial Lawyers (founder, pres. 1950-51, chmn. bd. regents 1952-53, chancellor from 1953), Am. Bar Found.; mem. ABA, L.A. World Affairs Coun., State Bar Calif. (gov. 1950-53, pres. 1951-52), Am Judicature Soc., Selden Soc., Am. Legion, Mason, B'nai B'rith. *

GUNN, HENRY MARTIN, educator; b. Lexington, Ky., July 7, 1898; s. Henry Martin and Roberta (Marrs) G.; m. Thelma Eiler, Nov. 29, 1928; children: Jack, Mary Elizabeth, Ruth Anne. BS, U. Oreg., 1928, AM, 1931; EdD, Stanford U., 1940. Tchr., coach Umatilla, Oreg., 1923-25; elem. sch. prin. Portland, Oreg., 1925-32; high sch. prin. Portland, 1933-40, asst. supt. of schs., 1940-44; supt. Eugene, Oreg., 1945-46; prof. edn. U. So. Calif., 1946-47; pres. Oreg. Coll. Edn., 1947-50; supt. schs. Palo Alto, Calif., from 1950; vis. prof. U. So. Calif. and Stanford U., 1952-53, from 1954, U. Oreg., 1955, others; prof. San Jose State Coll., head dept. sch. adminstrn., from 1962. Author: (with Ivan Linder) Problems and Practices in School Administration. Mem. State Calif. Gifted Children Com., Gov.'s Com. for Children and Youth, Rose Festival Assn. Bd., Portland; exec. bd. Boy Scouts Regional Com.; trustee Lewis and Clark Coll. Mem. NEA (state chmn.), Oreg. Edn. Assn. (chmn.), YMCA (pres. Palo Alto), Calif. Assn. Sch. Adminstrs. (chmn. instrn. com.), Phi Delta Kappa, Am. Legion, Mason, City Club (Portland), Stanford Faculty Club, Rotary, Faculty Club. Republican. Methodist. *

GUNNARSON, ARTHUR BERNARD, accountant; b. Mpls., May 15, 1896; s. Gustaf Anders and Anna Adolphina (Shipp) G.; m. Lillian Eastman, June 21, 1924 (dec. Nov. 1962); children; John Allan, Barbara Louise Coloney. AB, U. Minn., 1920; MBA, Harvard U., 1924. Instr. acctg. U. Minn., 1920-22, Northeastern U., 1922-24; rsch. field agt. Bur. Bus. Rsch., Harvard, 1924; instr. acctg. Harvard Bus. Sch., 1924-25; auditor Washburn-Crosby Co., 1925-28; contr. Red Owl Stores, Inc., 1928-30; mgr. depts. mfr. and distbn. U.S. C. of C., 1930-45; asst. sec. Nat. Assn. Cost Accts., 1945-48, sec., 1948-61, cons. to bd. dirs., 1961-63; Nat. Luth. Coun. observer to UN, from 1964. Contbg. editor: Cost Accountants Handbook; contbr. articles to profl. jours. With U.S. Army, 1918-19. Mem. Am. Econ. Assn., Nat. Assn. Accts. (dir. 1934-40), Am. Mktg. Assn., Am. Soc. Assn. Execs., Chi Phi, Beta Alpha Psi, Acct. Club, Harvard Club (N.Y.C.), Scarsdale Golf Club. *

GUNNEMANN, LOUIS HERMAN, dean, religion educator; b. Indpls., Dec. 12, 1910; s. Louis and Lydia Amelia Amt G.; m Johanna Diedericke Menke, June 4, 1935; children: Judith Ann Pullen, Jon Peter, Joanne Ruth Dempsey. BA, Lakeland Coll., 1932; BD, Mission House Theol. Sem., 1935, DD, 1952; ThM, Princeton Theol. Sem., 1953. Ordained to ministry, United Ch. Christ, 1935. Pastor Tipton, Iowa, 1935-41, Immanuel United Ch. Christ, Lafayette, Ind., 1941-52; tchr., dean Mission House Theol. Sem., Plymouth, Wis., 1953-62; tchr., dean United Theol. Sem. Twin Cities, New Brighton, Minn., 1962-89, v.p. acad. affairs, 1972-89; scholar-in-residence Harvard U., 1968; chmn. commn. worship United Ch. Christ, 1961-73, corp. mem. bd. homeland ministries, 1961-89; vice-chmn. com. worship Consultation ch. union, 1970-73; asst. moderator Gen. Synod, 1973-89; sec. Am. Assn. Theol. Schs., 1964-89; mem. adminstrv. com. N.Am. area coun. Alliance Ref Chs., 1960-89. Author: The Life of Worship, 1967, The Shaping of the United Church of Christ, 1977; editor Theol. Markings, 1970-89; mem. editorial com. Theology and Life, 1959-89. Home: Peoria Ill. Died Oct. 31, 1989.

GUNTHER, JACK DISBROW, chemical company executive; b. Grand View-on-Hudson, N.Y., Feb. 25, 1908; s. Charles O. and Beatrice (Disbrow) G.; m. Geraldyne Beyea, Apr. 22, 1933; children: Nancy, Jack Disbrow. AB, Dartmouth Coll., 1929; LLB, Harvard U., 1932. Bar: N.Y. 1933. Assoc. Shearman & Sterling, N.Y.C., 1934-40; asst. gen. counsel Hercules Powder Co., Wilmington, Del., 1940-45; with Air Reduction Co., Inc., 1945-64; sec. Air Reduction Co., Inc., 1946-51, v.p., 1951-64. Co-author: Identification of Firearms from Ammunition Fired Therein, 1935. Founder New Canaan (Conn.) Land Conservation Trust; chmn. New Caanan Conservation Commn. Mem. Del. State Bar, Am. Soc. Corp. Secs. (pres. 1948-49, hon. mem. 1955-90), Del. Bar Assn., Casque and Gauntlet, Conn. Assn. Conservation Commns. (past chmn.), Union League, Dartmouth Club, Pinnacle Club, Links Club, Country Club New Caanan, Tokeneke Club, Phi Beta Kappa, Phi Kappa Psi. Home: Bloomfield Conn. Died Mar. 23, 1990.

GURIN, ARNOLD, social work educator; b. N.Y.C., Dec. 5, 1917; s. Morris and Sarah (Nimetz) G.; m. Helen Bass, Dec. 27, 1942; children: Nathaniel, Naomi. B.S., CCNY, 1937; M.S., Columbia U., 1943; Ph.D., U. Mich., 1965. Dir. budget research Council Jewish Fedns. and Welfare Funds, N.Y.C., 1945-53; dir. field service Council Jewish Fedns. and Welfare Funds, 1953-58; lectr. social work Mich. State U., 1958-62; assoc. prof. social welfare adminstrn. Brandeis U., Waltham, Mass., 1962-66, prof., 1966-71, Maurice B. Hexter chair in Am. Philanthropy, 1971-82; dean Florence Heller Grad. Sch., Brandeis U., 1971-76; cons. to various orgns. U.S.A., Eng., France and Israel, 1982-91; dir. community orgn. curriculum project Council Social Work Edn., 1965-68. Author: (with Robert Perlman) Community Organization and Social Planning, 1972, Community Organization Curriculum in Graduate Social Work Education: Report and Recommendations, 1970; Contbr. articles to profl. jours. Mem. tng. grants rev. panel Office Juvenile Delinquency, HEW, 1963-68; mem. task force on social services 1968; vis. prof. Hebrew U. Sch. Social Work, Jerusalem, 1980; chmn. Internat. Com. on Evaluation of Project Renewal in Israel, 1981-85. Mem. Nat. Conf. Social Welfare (nat. bd. 1972-75), Nat. Assn. Social Workers, Am. Sociol. Soc. Home: Boston Mass. Died Feb. 15, 1991.

GURR, LENA, artist; b. Bklyn., Oct. 27, 1897; d. Hyman and Ida (Gorodnick) G.; m. Joseph Biel, Nov. 24, 1931 (dec.). Student, Bklyn. Tng. Sch. for Tchrs.; student of art, Art Students League, N.Y.C., France. Art tchr. Jr. High Sch. System, N.Y.C., 1918-44; artist in oil, water color, lithography, serigraphy, wood cuts. Represented in permanent collections in Biro-Bidjan Mus., Russia, Libr. of Congress, Washington, Ain Harod Mus., Israel, Contemporary Art Mus., Atlanta, Brandeis U., Waltham, Mass., N.Y. Pub. Libr., State Libr. Calif., Kans. State Coll., U. Wis., Va. Mus. Fine Arts, Reading (Pa.) Mus., Howard U., Washington, Coll. Nat. Assn. U. Women, U. Syracuse, Safed Mus., Israel, Brasenose Coll., Oxford, Eng., Norfolk (Va.) Mus., City State Coll. N.J.; exhibited in one-woman shows Carnegie Inst., Corcoran Mus., Phila. Acad., Va. Mus., Met. Mus. Recipient numerous awards including prize Nat. Soc. of Painters in Casein, 1961, 2d prize for oil Cape Cod Art Assn., 1962, 63, Samuel Mann Meml. prize for casein Nat. Assn. Women Artists, 1963, Marion K. Haldenstein prize for oil, 1964, Grumbacher prize, 1964. Mem. Nat. Soc. Painters in Casein, Provincetown Art Assn. (dir.), Nat. Assn. Women Artists, Audubon Artists, Artists Equity (dir.), Am. Color Print Soc., Soc. Am. Graphic Artists, Painters and Sculptors Soc. N.J., Casein Soc. (dir.). *

GUSSOW, DON, publisher, author; b. Pumpyan, Lithuania, Dec. 7, 1907; came to U.S., 1920, naturalized, 1923; s. Samuel (Simche) and Anna (Chaia) Sonia (Luria) G.; m. Betty Gussow, Oct. 19, 1930 (dec. 1990); children: Alan, Mel, Paul. Student, CCNY, 1926-27, Maxwell Tng. Sch. Tchrs., Bklyn., 1927-28; tchr. tng. diploma, U. Vt., 1928-29; student, NYU, 1929-31, BA, 1977. Editor Butcher's Advt., N.Y.C., 1929-30, Confectionery-Ice Cream World, N.Y.C., 1930-34, 39-44, Internat. Confectioner, N.Y.C., 1935-39; founder Candy Industry mag., 1944; chmn., editor-in-chief, chief exec. officer Magazines for Industry, Inc., N.Y.C., until 1966, then sold to Cowles Communications; bd. dirs., pres. trade mag. div. Cowles Communications, 1966-70, bought back bus.; resold bus. to Harcourt Brace Jovanovich, Inc., N.Y.C., 1982, v.p., editor, 1982-85; pres., editor-in-chief PG Communications Inc., 1986-90; dir. Am. Bus. Press, 1968-71, 76-85. Author: Divorce Corporate Style, 1972, The New Merger Game, 1978, Chaia Sonia, A Family's Odyssey Russian Style, 1980, The New Business Journalism, 1983; contbg. editor: Ency. Brit, 1939-63. Founder Am. Assn. Candy Technologists, 1948, created Kettle award of candy industry, 1946. Recipient Pub. Service award Nat. Confectioners Assn., 1971; Pres.'s award Am. Coll. Legal Medicine, 1974; Honor scroll Am. Bus. Press, 1979; Gallatin fellow N.Y. U., 1980; Disting. Pub. Service award Anti-Defamation League, 1983; Cert. of Distinction NYU, 1983. Clubs: NYU, Overseas Press, Marco

Polo (N.Y.C.). Home: New York N.Y. Died Feb. 19, 1992.

GUSTIN, ARNO ANTHONY, clergyman, educational administrator; b. Flasher, N.D., June 18, 1906; s. John and Gertrude (Schmidt) G. BA with honors, St. John's U., Collegeville, Minn., 1929; MA, Cath. U. Am., 1934; PhD, U. Minn., 1945. Joined Order St. Benedict, 1972, ordained prist Roman Cath. Ch., 1933. Prin. St. John's Prep Sch., 1936-40; registrar St. John's U., Collegeville, Minn., 1944-52, acad. dean, 1952-58, pres., 1958-64, prof. edn., 1944-58, chmn. dept., 1954-58, prof. edn., assoc. in devel., 1964-65, dir. assoc., fellow programs, 1970-91; pres. Mary Coll., Bismarck, N.D., 1965-70; pastor Sacred Heart Ch. and St. Mary's Ch., Roseau and Badger, Minn., 1972-91; mem. Minn. Adv. Com. Tchr. Edn., 1947-52; pres. Minn. Pvt. Coll. Coun., 1958-59, Minn. Pvt. Coll. Fund, 1960-61; participant Minn. Assembly on Fed. Govt. and Higher Edn., 1961; organizer Tri-Coll. program of St. Cloud State Coll., Coll. St. Benedict, St. John's U., 1958; mem. exec. com. Dakota-Assoc. Colls. Consortium of Rsch. Devel. Contbr. articles, revs. to periodicals. Mem. NEA, Nat. Cath. Edn. Assn. (chmn. deans meeting 1954), Assn. Am. Colls., Assn. Minn. Colls., Am. Ednl. Rsch. Assn., N.D. Edn. Assn., Collegeville C. of C., Phi Delta Kappa. Home: Roseau Minn. Died July 28, 1991.

GUTHRIE, ALFRED BERTRAM, JR., author; b. Bedford, Ind., Jan. 13, 1901; s. Alfred Bertram and June (Thomas) G.; m. Harriet Larson, June 25, 1931 (dec.); children: Alfred Bertram III, Helen Larson; m. Carol B. Luthin, Apr. 3, 1969. Student, U. Wash., 1919-20; A.B., U. Mont., 1923, Litt.D., 1949; L.H.D., Ind. State U., 1975; Litt.D., Mont. State U., 1977; L.H.D., Coll. of Idaho, 1986. Reporter Lexington (Ky.) Leader, 1926-29, city editor, editorial writer, 1929-45, exec. editor, 1945-47; tchr. creative writing U. Ky., 1947-52. Author: The Big Sky, 1947, The Way West, 1949, These Thousand Hills, 1956, The Big It, 1960, The Blue Hen's Chick, 1965, Arfive, 1971, Wild Pitch, 1973, (juvenile) Once Upon a Pond, 1973, The Last Valley, 1975, The Genuine Article, 1977, No Second Wind, 1980, Fair Land, Fair Land, 1982, Playing Catch-Up, 1985, Four Miles From Ear Mountain, 1987, Big Sky, Fair Land (ed. David Petersen), 1988, Murder in the Cotswolds, 1989, A Field Guide to Writing and Fiction, 1991; contbr. stories, articles to mags.; also author of screen plays. Recipient Pulitzer prize for Disting. Fiction, 1950, Wrangler award Nat. Cowboy Hall of Fame, 1970; Disting. Achievement award Western Lit. Assn., 1972; Golden Saddleman award Western Writers Am., 1978, Disting. Contbn. award State of Ind., 1979, Commemorative award Commonwealth of Ky., 1979, Mont. Gov.'s award for disting. achievement in arts, 1982, Lit. Contbn. award No. Plains Libr. Assn., 1987, Conservation award, 1988, Audubon award Mont. Environ. Info. Ctr., 1988; Named to Ky. Journalism Hall of Fame, 1983; Nieman fellow Harvard U., 1944-45. Home: Choteau Mont. Died Apr. 26, 1991; cremated.

GUTHRIE, RANDOLPH HOBSON, lawyer; b. Richmond, Va., Nov. 5, 1905; s. Joseph Hobson and Thomasia Harris (Parkinson) G.; m. Mabel Edith Welton, Mar. 24, 1934; children: Randolph Hobson, Jo Carol, George Gordon. BS (first honor grad.), The Citadel, 1925, LLD (hon.), 1976; LLB magna cum laude, Harvard U., 1931. Bar: N.Y. 1932. Sr. ptnr. Mudge, Rose, Guthrie, Alexander and Ferdon, N.Y.C., from 1931; chmn. bd. Studebaker Corp., Studebaker-Worthington, Inc., 1963-71, chmn. exec. com., 1971-81; chmn. bd. UMC Industries, Inc., 1969-76, chmn. exec. com., 1976-81. Editor Harvard Law Rev., 1930-31. Mem. ABA, N.Y. Bar Assn., Assn. Bar City N.Y. Episcopalian. Clubs: Knickerbocker (N.Y.C.), Harvard (N.Y.C.). Home: Hilton Head Island S.C. Died Sept. 11, 1989.

HAAS, KENNETH B(ROOKS), marketing educator; b. Pitts., Jan. 24, 1898; s. John Louis and Mary Anne (Brooks) H.; m. Verna Viola Hoffman, Dec. 24, 1921; children: Kenneth Brooks, Noel Lee. BS, U. Pitts., 1924, MA, 1931; EdD, NYU, 1935; spl. student, Harvard U., 1929. Engaged pvt. commn. bus. Pitts., 1924-28; tchr., dept. head of high schs. N.J., 1928-34; mem. placement bur. N.Y.C., 1934-35; prof. mktg. Coll. of Commerce, Bowling Green, Ky., 1935-38; regional agt. and bus. specialist U.S. Office of Edn., 1938-46; retail tng. dir. Montgomery Ward, 1946-48; supr. ednl. devel. CCNY, 1948; prof. mktg. Hofstra U., Hempstead, N.Y., from 1958; vis. lectr. Ohio State U., Conn. State Tchrs. Coll., U. Pitts., Temple U., NYU, 1939-45; rsch. and writing in field of adult tng. methods, 1938-49; prodn. and direction of films for sales and indsl. tng., 1944-49; vis. prof. mktg. U. Wash., Seattle, from 1964; cons. Dept. Pub. Instrn., State N.C., from 1962. Author: Studies in Problems of the Consumer, 1938, Adventures in Buymanship, 1939, Distributive Edn., 1941, Better Retailing, 1941, Military Instructors Manual, 1942, How to Coordinate School-Work Experience, 1944, Creative Salesmanship, 1950, Techniques of Supervisory Leadership, 1950, How to Develop Successful Salesmen, 1959, Opportunities in Selling, 1960, Professional Salesmanship, 1963, Psychological Dynamics of Salesmanship, 1964; co-author: How to Establish and Operate A Retail Store, 1946, Preparation and Use of Visual Aids, 1946, Tested Training Techniques, 1949, Sales Horizons, 1957; collaborator: Films for Business, Industry and Education, 1949, Business Practice in Veterinary Medicine; editor: Handbook on Sales Training, 1949; writer of numerous training manuals and vocational bulletins for Montgomery Ward; contbr. articles to profl. jours. With USN, WWI, major U.S. Army, 1942-43, WWII. Mem. AAUP, VFW, Phi Delta Kappa, Eta Mu Pi, Delta Pi Epsilon, Gamma Rho Tau. Republican. *

HAAS, MARC, business executive, philatelist; b. Cin., Mar. 16, 1908; s. Marc and Alice (White) H.; m. Helen Hotze, Feb. 3, 1951. Grad., Horace Mann Sch., 1925, Princeton U., 1929. Ptnr. Emanuel & Co., mems. N.Y. Stock Exchange, 1933-42; dept. dir. Office Def. Transp., Washington, 1942-45; assoc. Allen & Co., N.Y.C., 1945-55; pres. Am. Diversified Enterprises, Inc. and subs., N.Y.C., from 1955; dir. Cave Laurent Perrier. Vestry St. Bartholemew's Episcopal Ch., N.Y.C., over 25 yrs., also sr. warden; served as Dollar-a-Yr. Man U.S. Dept. Transp., World War II. Named Knight Order of St. John of Jerusalem. Mem. Philatelic Found. (emeritus trustee 1990). Home: New York N.Y. Died July 8, 1990; interred Santa Barbara, Calif.

HABER, FRANCIS COLIN, history educator; b. Flint, Mich., Apr. 21, 1920; s. Arthur and Amelia (Glenfield) H.; m. Ruth E. Owens, 1943 (div.); 1 son, Robert O.; m. Margaret A. Wilson, 1987. Student, U. Iowa, 1940-41; B.A., U. Conn., 1948; M.A., Johns Hopkins, 1951, Ph.D., 1957. Asso. editor Md. Hist. Mag., 1952-53; reference librarian Peabody Inst. Library, 1953-55; editor Md. Hist. Mag.; librarian Md. Hist. Soc., Balt., 1955-58; asst. prof. U. Fla., 1958-63, asso. prof., 1963-66; prof. U. Md., College Park, from 1966, chmn. dept. history, 1968-71. Author: Age of the World: Moses to Darwin, 1959, (with others) Forerunners of Darwin, 1959; contbr. (with others) articles profl. jours. Served with U.S. Mcht. Marine, 1941-45. Am. Philos. Soc. grantee, 1958-64; Folger fellow, 1962. Fellow Royal Hist. Soc. (London); mem. Internat. Soc. for Study of Time. Club: Cosmos (Washington). Home: Washington D.C. Died Mar. 11, 1990; buried Oak Hill Cemetery, Washington.

HABIB, PHILIP CHARLES, foreign service officer; b. Bklyn., Feb. 25, 1920; s. Alex and Mary (Spiridon) H.; m. Marjorie W. Slightam, Aug. 27, 1942; children: Phyllis A., Susan W. B.S., U. Idaho, 1942, LL.D., 1974; Ph.D., U. Calif. at Berkeley, 1952. Fgn. service officer, 1949-80; 3d sec. Am. embassy Ottawa, Can., 1949-51; 2d sec. Am. embassy Wellington, N.Z., 1952-54; research specialist Dept of State, Washington, 1955-57; Am. consulate gen. Port of Spain, Trinidad, 1958-60; fgn. affairs officer Dept. State, 1960-61; counselor for polit. affairs Am. embassy Seoul, Korea, 1962-65, Saigon, Vietnam, 1965-67; personal rank of minister, 1966-67; dep. asst. sec. State for East Asian and Pacific affairs, 1967-69; mem. U.S. delegation to meetings on Vietnam, Paris, 1968-71; personal rank of ambassador, 1969-71; ambassador to Republic of Korea, Seoul, 1971-74; asst. sec. state for East Asian and Pacific affairs, 1974-76, undersec. of state for polit. affairs, 1976-78; diplomat-in-residence Stanford U., 1978-79; sr. advisor to Sec. of State, 1979-80; personal rep. of Pres. to Middle East, 1981-83; sr. research fellow Hoover Instn., 1980-92; presdl. envoy to Philippines, 1986, pres.' spl. envoy for Cen. Am., 1986-87; adv. bd. Pacific Forum, Honolulu, 1980-91; bd. dirs. Bank Audi, Calif. Chmn. Pacific Forum, Honolulu, 1980-91; trustee Am. Univ. Beirut, 1983-92. Served from pvt. to capt. AUS, 1942-46. Decorated comdr. Legion of Honor (France); recipient Rockefeller Pub. Service award, 1969; Nat. Civil Service League award, 1970; Dept. State Disting. Honor award, 1977; Pres.'s award for disting. fed. service, 1979; Presdl. Medal of Freedom, 1982; Lebanon's Order of Cedars, 1982. Roman Catholic. Home: Belmont Calif. Died May 25, 1992.

HABIF, DAVID VALENTINE, surgeon, educator; b. Cin.. M.D., Columbia, 1939. Diplomate: Am. Bd. Surgery (mem. bd. 1966-72, vice chmn. 1971-72). Successively intern, asst. resident surgery, resident surgery, attending surgery, cons. Presbyn. Hosp., N.Y.C., 1939-47; Morris and Rose Milstein prof. surgery Columbia Coll. Phys. and Surg., 1972-89, prof. emeritus, 1989; sr. rsch. scientist Columbia U., 1989. Served with AUS, 1942-45. Decorated Bronze Star, Presdl. Citation with 2 oak leaf clusters. Fellow A.C.S.; mem. A.M.A., Soc. Exptl. Biology and Medicine, Am. Surg. Assn. (former vice chmn.), Soc. Univ. Surgeons, Halsted Soc., Soc. Surgery Alimentary Tract, Allen O. Whipple Surg. Soc. (pres. 1968-70), N.Y. Surg. Soc. (pres. 1974-75). Home: Tenafly N.J. Died Jan. 17, 1992.

HACK, JOHN TILTON, geologist; b. Chgo., Dec. 3, 1913; m. Clare Ferriter, 1942; children: Katherine Ferriter, John Tilton. AB, Harvard U., 1935, MA, 1938; PhD in Geomorphology, Harvard, 1940. Geologist Awatovi Expdn., Peabody Mus. Harvard, 1937-39; instr. geology Hofstra Coll., 1940-42; geologist U.S. Geol. Survey, Interior Dept., Washington, 1942-85; asst. chief geologist for environ. geology U.S. Geol. Survey, Interior Dept., 1966-71, research geologist, 1971-85; professorial lectr. George Washington U., Washington, 1980-83. Contbr. articles to profl. jours. Recipient Disting. Svc. award Dept. Interior, 1972; G.K. Warren prize NAS, 1982. Fellow Geol. Soc. Am. (Kirk Bryan award 1961, Disting. Career award 1990); mem. AAAS, Cosmos Club. Home: Washington D.C. Deceased. †

HACKWORTH, WERTER SHIPP, banking executive; b. South Pittsburg, Tenn., July 14, 1895; s. Thomas Reed and Sarah Anne (Kelly) H.; m. Marguerite Adams, Nov. 17, 1931. BS in Civil Engring., Ala. Poly. Inst., Auburn, 1916. With engring. dept. N.C. & St. L. Ry., Nashville, 1916-17, asst. engr., chief engrs. office, 1922-26; asst. engr. Atlanta div. N.C. & St. L. Ry., Atlanta, 1926-31; supt. of dairies and sanitation State of Ga., Atlanta, 1932-33; asst. engr. real estate agts. office N.C. & St. L. Ry., Nashville, 1933-37, asst. real estate agt., 1937-39, asst. to pres., 1939-46, pres., 1946-56; pres., dir. Nashville Bank and Trust Co., 1956-64; vice chmn., dir. Third Nat. Bank, from 1964; pres. Nashville & Decatur R.R., from 1961. Trustee, chmn. fin. com. George Peabody Coll. Tchrs. With AEF, 1917-19. Mem. Tenn. Taxpayers Assn., Nashville C. of C. (pres. 1951), Kappa Sigma, Belle Meade County Club (v.p.) Cumberland Club (past pres.). Democrat. Presbyterian. Deceased.*

HADDEN, JOHN ALEXANDER, lawyer; b. Cleve., July 11, 1886; s. Alexander and Frances (Hawthorne) H.; m. Marianne Elisabeth Millikin, Jan. 7, 1922; children: John Alexander, Alexander Hawthorne, Elisabeth Severance Alexander. AB, Harvard U., 1908, LLB, 1910. Bar: Ohio 1910. Assoc. Arter, Hadden, Wykoff & Van Duzer; asst. dist. atty. No. Dist. Ohio, 1912-13; dir., mem. exec. com. Youngstown Steel Door Co., Erie R.R. Co.; dir. Union Bank of Commerce, Enos Coal Mining Co., Enoco Collieries, Inc. Dept. regional dir. War Prodn. Bd., 1942-43; trustee Elizabeth Severance Prentiss Found.; trustee, mem. exec. com. U. Hosp.; Ohio state chmn. Harvard Law Sch. Fund, 1944; mem. Ohio State Legislature, 1925-31. Sgt. Ohio Nat. Guard, 1916-17, capt. AUS, 1917-19, AEF, 1918-19. Mem. ABA, Ohio Bar Assn., Cleve. Bar Assn., Sigma Alpha Epsilon, Union Club, Tavern Club, Kirtland Club, 50 Club (Cleve.), Ottawa Club, Shooting Club (Fremont, Ohio). Republican. *

HADLEY, ROLLIN VAN NOSTRAND, museum executive; b. Westboro, Mass., Dec. 13, 1927; s. Rollin Van Nostrand and Arabelle (McKinstry) H.; m. Jane Olmstead Houghton, Nov. 1950 (div. 1960); m. Shelagh Grace Pratt, Sept. 23, 1961 (div. 1989); children: Susan Olmstead, Jane Houghton, Hope McKinstry, Peter Van Nostrand, James Broughton, Sarah Hamilton. Grad., St. Mark's Sch., 1945; A.B., Harvard U., 1950, M.A., 1981. Reporter Harrisburg (Pa.) newspapers, 1950-52; with Corning Glass Works, 1952-60, mgr. budgets, 1957-59, dir., 1957-60; treas., dir. Corning Glass Internat., 1959-60; faculty U. Bocconi, Milan, Italy, 1960-62; adminstr. Isabella Stewart Gardner Mus., Boston, 1963-70, dir., 1970-88; dir. Newington-Cropsey Found., Hastings-on-Hudson, N.Y., 1990-92; vis. scholar Harvard Ctr. for Italian Renaissance Studies, Florence, Italy, 1972. Author: Drawings: Isabella Stewart Gardner Museum, 1968, Sculpture in the Gardner Museum (Renaissance Section), 1977, Museums Discovered: Isabella Stewart Gardner Museum, 1981, The Letters of Bernard Berenson and Isabella Stewart Gardner, 1987. Trustee emeritus Corning Mus. Glass; pres. Save Venice, Inc., 1974-86, chmn. bd. dirs., 1986-88. Served with AUS, 1946-47. Decorated comdr. Order of Merit (Italy), cavaliere di San Marco, City of Venice. Episcopalian. Clubs: Grolier, Knickerbocker (N.Y.C.). Home: Fort Lauderdale Fla. Died Feb. 2, 1992.

HAEHNEL, WILLIAM OTTO, JR., telephone company executive; b. San Antonio, July 30, 1924; s. William Otto and Marie Helena (Fricke) H.; m. Mildred E. Engelken, June 25, 1947; children: William Haehnel III, Nancimarie. Student, Tulane U., 1944-47; BSBA, B in Bus. Mgmt, U. Tex., 1949. With Southwestern Bell Telephone Co., Austin, Tex., 1949-90, pub. info. mgr., 1969-90; lectr. bus. to colls. and univs. Active Boy Scouts Am., Boys Club of Austin and Travis County, Austin State Sch. Council, Travis State Sch. Vol. Council, Austin Council Retarded Children, United Fund., Tex. Youth Conf., P.T.A., Austin Aqua Festival, Austin Civic Club Council, YMCA, Travis County Jr. Coll. Bd., Travis County Grand Jury Assn.; bd. dirs., chmn. fund raising com. Internat. Spl. Olympics; chmn. Civitan Internat. Spl. Olympics Com.; chmn. fin. com., mem. ch. council, mem. membership and long range planning coms., pres. Luth. Ch. Served with AUS, 1943-45. Recipient Club Honor key, 1964, George Washington Honor medal Freedoms Found. at Valley Forge, 1973-74, 85, numerous other awards; named Austin Citizen of Yr., 1973. Mem. U. Tex. Ex-Students Assn., Austin C. of C., San Antonio C. of C. (red carpet com.). Republican. Lodge: Civitans (life; bd. dirs. Austin club 1960, pres. 1964-65, lt. gov. Tex. dist. 1965-66, gov. 1966-67, internat. chmn. 50th anniversary yr. extension com. 1968-69, chmn. internat. contest and awards com. 1969-70, v.p. 1970-72, sr. v.p. internat. exec. bd. 1971-72, internat. pres. 1972-73). Home: Austin Tex. Died Feb. 4, 1991; buried Assumption Cemetery, Austin.

HAFEN, LEROY R., historian; b. Bunkerville, Nev., Dec. 8, 1893; s. John George and Mary Ann (Stucki) H.; m. Ann Woodbury, Sept. 3, 1915; children: Norma (dec.), Karl LeRoy. AB, Brigham Young U., 1916;

MA, U. Utah, 1919; PhD, U. Calif., 1924; LittD, U. Colo., 1935. Tchr. high sch. Bunkerville, Nev., 1916-18; teaching fellow U. Calif., 1920-23; tchr. A to Zed Sch., Berkeley, Calif., 1923-24; exec. dir. and state historians State Hist. Soc., Colo., 1924-54; prof. history Brigham Young U., U. Denver; vis. prof. Am. History U., Glasgow, Scotland, 1947-48. Editor: Colorado Mag., 1925-54, (with J. H. Baker) History of Colorado, 3 vols., 1927, The Past and the Present of the Pike's Peak Gold Region, 1932; author: The Overland Mail, 1926, (with W. J. Ghent) Broken Hand-Life of Thomas Fitzpatrick, 1931, Colorado-The Story of a Western Commonwealth, 1933, (with F. M. Young) Fort Laramie and the Pageant of the West, 1834-1890, 1938, (with C. C. Rister) Western America, 1941, (with Ann Woodbury Hafen) Colorado, a Story of the State and Its People, 1943, Colorado and Its People (2 vols.), 1948, (with Ann Hafen) The Colorado Story, 1953; editor: Pike's Peak Gold Rush Guide Books of 1859, 1941, The Colorado Gold Rush of 1859, 1941, Diaries of the Gold Rush 1859, 1942, Ruxton of the Rockies, 1950, Life in the Far West, 1951, (with Ann Hafen) The Far West and the Rockies series comprising 15 vols., 1954-62, The Hafens of Utah, 1962, Mountain Men series, from 1964; contbn. to various revs., dictionaries and encyclopaedias. Mem. Am. Hist. Assn., Miss. Valley Hist. Assn., Newcomen Soc., Colo. Authors League, Denver Westerners. *

HAFNER, THEODORE, lawyer, physicist; b. Vienna, Austria, Oct. 4, 1901; s. Mathias and Rose (Kohl) H.; Ph.D. in Physics and Math., U. Vienna, 1926; J.D., Fordham U., 1946; m. Renee Schwarz, May 6, 1950 (dec.); 1 dau., Erika (Mrs. Marvin Kalisch). Came to U.S., 1941, naturalized, 1947. Research on sound and video AEG and Telefunken, Berlin, Germany, 1927-33; asst. to pres. Brit. Acoustic Films and Technicolor, London, Eng., 1933-37; mng. dir. Mole-Richardson, Paris, France, 1937-41; design engr. N.Y. Eagle Electric, N.Y.C.-Internat. Resistance, Phila., 1941-43; patent counsel Internat. Tel. & Tel. Co., N.Y.C., 1943-45; with internat. patent operations dept. RCA, N.Y.C., 1945-49; admitted to N.Y. bar, 1947, U.S. Patent Office bar, 1946; pvt. practice, N.Y.C., 1949-87; pres., Surface Conduction, Beam Guidance Inc., Guided Space Transmissions (all N.Y.C.). Mem. Fed. Bar Assn. (com. atomic energy), Assn. Bar City N.Y., Patent Law Assn. (com. profl. ethics), IEEE (sr. mem.), Carl Neuberg Soc. Internat. Sci. Relations. Contbr. lectrs. and articles to profl jours. Patentee single-wire transmission line, laser resonator-light transmission line. Died Mar. 26, 1990. Home: Media Pa.

HAGEN, JOHN P., astronomer; b. Amherst, N.S., Can., July 31, 1908; s. John T. and Ella Bertha Fisher H.; m. Edith W. Soderling, Oct. 12, 1935; children: J. Peter, E. Christopher. BS, Boston U., 1929, ScD, 1959; MA, Wesleyan U., 1931; PhD, Georgetown U., 1949. Rsch. assoc. Wesleyan U., 1931-35; supt. atmosphere and astrophysics div. Naval Rsch. Lab., Washington, 1935-58, devel. microwave radar, radio astronomer, 1935-58; asst. dir. space flight devel. NASA, 1958-60; dir. OUNC, 1960-62; prof. astronomy Pa. State U., University Park, 1962-76, prof. emeritus, 1976-90, head dept. astronomy, 1966-76; project dir. Earth Satellite Project; chmn. study group Comite Consulatit Internationale des Radio Communications, mem. U.S. exec. com.; chmn. Inter-Union Commn. on Frequency Allocations for Radio Astronomy and Space Sci.; mem. Frequency Mgmt. Adv. Com.; lectr. Georgetown U. Recipient Presdl. certificate of Merit; decorated Disting Svc. medal USN. Fellow Inst. Radio Engrs., Am. Acad. Arts and Scis., Roayl Astron. Soc. Eng. ; mem. Am. Astron. Soc., Internat. Astron. Union, Washington Acad. Scis., U.R.S.I. past chmn. nat. com. , Phi Beta Kappa, Sigma Xi. Died Aug. 26, 1990.

HAINES, LEWIS FRANCIS, humanities educator; b. Endicott, N.Y., Oct. 28, 1907; s. William Joseph and Teresa Irene (Lewis) H.; m. Helen Mary Steere, Sept 1, 1930; 1 son, James Lewis. A.B., U. Mich., 1930, A.M., 1932, Ph.D., 1941. Instr. English Boys' Tech. High Sch., Milw., 1930-34; teaching fellow English U. Mich., 1935-41, instr. English, summer 1941; acting instr. English U. Fla., 1941-42, asst. prof., 1942-46, prof. humanities, 1946-67, prof. humanities and comprehensive logic, 1967-73, prof. humanities and behavioral studies, 1973-77, prof. emeritus, 1977-91; editor U. Fla. Press, 1945-67, dir., 1949-67; cons. specialist New Century Cyclopedia of Names. Contbr. to: New Century Handbook of English Literature, World Book Ency., Collier's Ency.; Contbr. also to scholastic and lit. jours. Mem. Gov's Hwy. Safety Conf. Recipient Rockefeller research grant, summer 1962. Mem. MLA, South Atlantic MLA, AAUP, Nat. Council Tchrs. English, Fla. Hist. Soc., Newcomen Soc. N.A., Assn. Am. U. Presses, Am. Book Pubs. Council, Acad. Polit. Sci., Assn. for Latin Am. Studies, Phi Kappa Phi, Kappa Phi Sigma. Home: Gainesville Fla. Died Jan. 29, 1991.

HAINES, WILLIAM WISTER, author; b. Des Moines, Sept. 1908; s. Diedrich Jansen and Ella Eustis (Wister) H.; m. Frances Tuckerman, Sept., 1934; children William Wister, Laura Tuckerman (Mrs. Murray Belman). B.S., U. Pa., 1931. Author: Slim, 1934, High Tension, 1938, Command Decision, 1947, The Honorable Rocky Slade, 1957, The Winter War, 1961, Target, 1964, The Image, 1968, Ultra and the History of the U.S. Strategic Air Force vs. the German Air Force, 1986; also mag. stories, motion picture scripts, play Command Decision. Commd. 1st lt. AC AUS, 1942; relieved of active duty as lt. col. 1945. Home: Laguna Niguel Calif. Died Nov. 18, 1989; body donated to science.

HALASI-KUN, TIBOR, educator, Orientalist; b. Zagreb, Austria-Hungary, Jan. 19, 1914; came to U.S., 1952, naturalized, 1961; s. Tibor and Priscilla (Tholt) H.-K.; m. Eva Metzger, Jan. 5, 1942; children: Adam, Tibor. PhD, U. Budapest, Hungary, 1936. Rsch. assoc. Turkic studies, also Hungarian protohistory U. Budapest, 1936, adj. prof., 1937-42; dir., prof. Hungarian studies Ankara (Turkey) U., 1943-51; prof. Turkic studies Columbia U., N.Y.C., 1952-82, dir. Turkish Ctr., 1952-82, chmn. near and mid. ea. dept., 1959-66, prof. emeritus, 1982-91; vis. prof. Princeton U., 1956; founder, pres. Am. Rsch. Inst. in Turkey, 1963-68. Author: Turkish Confession in Gennadios, 1936, Language of the Kipchaks, 1942, Historical Texts of Kazan Turkic, 1949, The Caucasus: An Ethno-Historical Survey, 1962, Ottoman Elements in Syrian Dialects, 1969-82, Hungarian Antiquities 1940-87; Publs. in Near and Middle East Studies, 1960.; founder, editor-in-chief jour. Archive Ottoman Studies, Archive Medieval Eurasian Studies; editor-in-chief Macar Klassikler Serisi, 21 vols., 1941-57; numerous other publs. Recipient of commendation by Com. Turkish Govt., Am. Friends of Turkey, TUTAV. Hon. mem. Am. Ukrainian Acad. Arts and Scis., Körösi-Csoma Soc., Turkish Hist. Soc., Hungarian Acad. Scis. Home: New Milford Conn. Died Oct. 19, 1991; buried Upper Merryall Cemetery, New Milford, Conn.

HALE, ORON JAMES, historian, educator; b. Goldendale, Wash., July 29, 1902; s. William Robert and Frances Isabella (Putnam) H.; m. Annette Van Winkle, Aug. 7, 1929 (dec. 1968); m. Virginia S. Zehmer, July 9, 1970 (dec.). A.B., U. Wash., 1926; A.M., U. Pa., 1928, Ph.D. (George Leib Harrison fellow history 1928-29), 1930; studied in, France and Germany, summers 1927, 28; Social Sci. Research Council fellowship in, London and Berlin, 1932-33; Litt. D., Hampden-Sydney Coll., 1958. Instr. history U. Pa., 1926-28; asst. prof. European history U. Va., 1929-38, asso. prof., 1938-46, prof., 1946-65, Corcoran prof. history, 1965-72, chmn. dept., 1955-62, emeritus prof., from 1972; dir. Inst. Pub. Affairs, 1942, 53; acting chmn. Woodrow Wilson Sch. Fgn. Affairs, 1947-48; vis. prof. Duke, summers, 1934, 38, 39, U. Mo., 1937, U. N.C., 1946, Harvard, 1955; prof. Inst. Advanced Study, Princeton, 1963-64. Author: Germany and the Diplomatic Revolution, 1904-1906, 1931, Publicity and Diplomacy, 1890-1914, 1940, The Captive Press in the Third Reich, 1964 (spl. Polk award 1965), The Great Illusion, 1900-1914, 1971; Contbr. to hist., lit. and mil. periodicals. Served to col. AUS, 1942-46; served intelligence div. War Dept. Gen. Staff 1942-45; mem. War Dept. Gen. Staff Hist. Mission in 1945, Germany; hist. div. War Dept. spl. staff 1945-46; col., M.I. Res. 1946-62; mem. Sec. Army's Adv. Com. on Mil. History 1958-62; with U.S. High Commn. for Germany as dep. state commr. for Bavaria 1950-51; commr. 1951-52. Recipient George Louis Beer prize diplomatic history Am. Hist. Assn., 1931; comdr.'s cross Order of Merit Fed. Republic Germany, 1969; Thomas Jefferson award U. Va., 1969. Mem. Am., So. hist. assns., Soc. Am. Historians, Va. Soc. Sci. Assn., Phi Beta Kappa. Democrat. Presbyn. Club: Colonnade. Home: Richmond Va. Died July 18, 1991; buried U. Va. Cemetery, Charlottesville.

HALEY, ALEX PALMER, author; b. Ithaca, N.Y., Aug. 11, 1921; s. Simon Alexander and Bertha George (Palmer) H.; m. Nannie Branch, 1941 (div. 1964); children: Lydia Ann, William Alexander; m. Juliette Collins, 1964 (div. 1972); 1 child, Cynthia Gertrude; m. Myra Lewis. Student, Elizabeth City (N.C.) Tchrs. Coll., 1937-39; LittD (hon.), Simpson Coll., Indianola, Iowa, 1970. Enlisted USCG, 1939, advanced to rank chief journalist, 1952, served until, 1959; former adj. prof. journalism U. Tenn., Knoxville. Author: The Autobiography of Malcolm X, 1965, Roots, 1976, Roots: The Saga of an American Family, 1979, novella A Different Kind of Christmas, 1988; contbr. articles to Atlantic, Harper's, Readers Digest, N.Y. Times Mag., others. Founder, pres. Kinte Found., Washington, 1972-92. Recipient Spl. Pulitzer prize, 1977. Mem. Authors Guild, Soc. Mag. Writers. Home: Knoxville and Norris Tenn. Died Feb. 10, 1992.

HALL, BRINLEY MORGAN, investment company executive; b. Boston, Jan. 4, 1912; s. John Loomer and Dorothy Brinley (Morgan) H.; m. Elizabeth Jaques, June 10, 1939; children—Brinley Morgan, Dorothy B., Denison M., Robert T. Grad., St. Mark's Sch., 1930; B.A., Yale U., 1934; student, Corpus Christi Coll., Cambridge U., Eng., 1934-35, Harvard Law Sch., 1935-37; LL.B., Northeastern U., 1947. Bar: Mass. 1947. Investment banker Whiting Weeks & Stubbs, Inc., Boston, 1937-42; pvt. practice Boston, 1942-47; with Choate, Hall & Stewart, Boston, 1947-62, ptnr., 1951-62; asst. atty. gen. Commonwealth of Mass., 1948-49; exec. dir Com. Central Bus. Dist., 1962-70; trustee Hubbard Real Estate Investments, 1970-87. Served as maj. USAAF, 1942-46. Mem. Boston Bar Assn. Home: Beverly Farms Mass. Died May 19, 1991; buried Manchester, Mass.

HALL, CAMERON PARKER, clergyman; b. Pelham Manor, N.Y., Aug. 30, 1898; s. William Webster and Emily (Parker) H.; m. Margaret Conant, May 18, 1926; 1 child, Alan Conant. Grad., Hotchkiss Sch., Lakeville, Conn., 1917; BA, Williams Coll., Williamstown, Mass., 1921; grad. study, New Coll., Edinburgh, Scotland, 1921-22, Mansfield Coll., Oxford, Eng., 1922-23, Union Theol. Sem., N.Y.C., 1923-25; DD, Yale, Chgo. Theol. Sem., 1963, Williams Coll., 1964. Ordained to ministry Presbyn. Ch., 1925. Student asst. 1st Presbyn. Ch., N.Y.C., 1923-24; asst. pastor Broome St. Tabernacle, N.Y.C., 1924-26; pastor Christ Ch., N.Y.C., 1926-35, U. Ch., Madison, Wis., 1935-39; dir. dept. social edn. and action Bd. Christian Edn., Presbyn. Ch. U.S.A., 1939-46; dir. Social Edn. Internat. Coun. of Rel. Edn., 1943-46; exec. sec., dept. ch. and econ. life Fed. Coun. Chs. Christ in Am., 1946-50; exec. dir., dept. ch. and econ. life Nat. Coun. Chs. Christ U.S.A., from 1951; cons. World Coun. Chs. Assembly, Evanston, Ill., 1954; chmn. youth sect. World's Sunday Sch. Assn. Conv., Oslo, Norway, 1936; leader in the World Conf. of Christian Youth, Amsterdam, Holland, 1939. Author: Economic Life: A Christian Responsibility, 1947, The Christian at His Daily Work, 1951, Decision Making in Business, 1963; editor: On The Job Ethics, 1964. Mem. Sigma Phi, Delta Sigma Rho. *

HALL, CHARLES WASHINGTON, lawyer; b. Dallas, June 30, 1930; s. Albert Brown and Eleanor Pauline (Hopkins) H.; m. Mary Louise Watkins, Aug. 3, 1957; children—Kathryn Louise, Allison Ash, Charles Washington III. BA, U. of South, 1951; JD, So. Meth. U., 1954, LLM in Taxation, 1959. Bar: Tex. 1954. Ptnr. Storey, Armstrong & Steger, Dallas, 1954-57; sr. ptnr. Fulbright & Jaworski, Houston, from 1957; dir. Maxus Energy Corp., Friedman Ind., Inc., Tex. Med. Ctr., Inc. Houston; mem. adv. group Commr Internal Revenue, 1990-91; mem. adv. coun. U.S. Claims Ct., from 1988. Pres., trustee Sarah Campbell Blaffer Found., Houston; trustee M.D. Anderson Found., Houston, Southwestern Legal Found., Dallas, S.W. Rsch., Inst., San Antonio; bd. dirs. Goodwill Industry, Houston, 1977-84, Inst. Religion, Houston, Houston Child Guidance Ctr., 1984-86. Fellow Am. Bar Found.; mem. ABA (chmn. sect. taxation 1987-88, ho. dels. frp, 1991, nat. conf. lawyers and CPAs chmn. from 1991), Houston Bar Assn., Dallas Bar Assn., State Bar Tex. (chmn. sect. taxation 1970-71), Internat. Bar Assn.,Am. Coll. Tax Counsel (regent 1982-91), Am. Law Inst., River Oaks Country Club, Ramada Club, Coronado (pres. 1982-83), Houston City Club, Met. Club (Washington). Episcopalian. Home: Houston Tex. †

HALL, C(HARLES) WILLIAM, surgical researcher, educator; b. Gage, Okla., Feb. 8, 1922; s. Cecil A. and Helen (Greene) H.; m. Betty Woodring, June 6, 1943 (div.); children—Daniel C., Kendall W. (dec.) Gregory A., Patrick C., Conan L.; 1 stepchild, M'Lis Watkins Brewer; m. Shirley Thompson, Oct. 20, 1962 (dec. 1979); m. Sheila Ann Fowler, Dec. 3, 1979. B.A., Kans. U., 1951, M.A. in Comparative Anatomy, 1952, M.D., 1956; D.Eng. (hon.), Rose-Hulman Inst. Tech., 1985. Diplomate: Am. Bd. Surgery. Rotating intern Kans. U. Med. Center, 1956-57, resident surgery, 1957-62, fellow in medicine, 1959-60; fellow cardiovascular surgery Baylor U. Coll. Medicine, 1962-64; project dir. artificial heart program Nat. Heart Inst., 1964; project dir., artificial heart program Baylor U. Coll. Medicine, 1964-68, asst. prof. surgery, also asst. prof. physiology, 1964-69; cons. S.W. Research Inst., San Antonio, 1966-68; mgr. artificial organs research dept. bioengring. S.W. Research Inst., 1968-70, dir. dept. bioengring., 1970-75, inst. med. scientist, from 1975; clin. prof. surgery U. Tex. Med. Sch. at San Antonio, from 1969. Editorial bd.: Jour. Biomed. Materials Research, Artificial Organs; assoc. editor: Jour. Investigative Surgery; contbr. articles to profl. jours. Served to cpl. USAAF, 1942-46. Recipient Medalla de Oro Minister Bienestar Sociale, Argentina, 1975; prof. honoris causa Cath. U. Cordoba, Argentina, 1965. Fellow Am. Coll. Cardiology, Am. Coll. Chest Physicians, Acad. Surg. Research (cofounder 1984, pres. 1985, Markowitz award 1992), Am. Inst. for Med. and Biol. Engring. (founding); mem. Am. Soc. Artificial Internal Organs, Am. Heart Assn. (pres. San Antonio chpt. 1972-73), Tex. Heart Assn., Soc. For Biomaterials (founding pres., Clemson award), Internat. Cardiovascular Soc., Soc. Surg. Rosario (Argentine), Sigma Xi (pres. Alamo chpt. 1981), Phi Beta Pi, Phi Sigma, Delta Upsilon. Republican. Unitarian. Lodges: Masons (32 deg.), Shriners. Home: San Antonio Tex. Deceased. †

HALL, ERNEST E., government agency administrator; b. Dayton, Nov. 17, 1901; s. Ozni and Julia (Schlotterbeck) H.; m. Florence M. Byrnes, Oct. 29, 1948; children: Kendra Elizabeth, Kevin Ernest. With Ozni Hall and Co., 1917-22; jr. acct. George P. Jackson and Co., 1922-25; asst. sec., treas. Hyde Motor Sales Co., 1925-29; asst. to sec. U.S. Dept. Agr., Washington, 1929-33; asst. chief div. control U.S. Bur. Pub. Rds., 1933-42; exec. officer Fed. Works Agy., 1942-47; v.p. C.F. Lytle Co. (heavy constrn.), Sioux City, Iowa, 1947-52; asst. adminstr. for ops. control services FCDA, Battle Creek, Mich., 1952-55; chief industry asst. br. Office Indsl. Devel. AEC, 1956-59; chief reports and statistics br. Div. Reactor Devel., 1959-64; chief reports staff Office Asst. Gen. Mgr. Reactors, Germantown, Md., 1965-70; ret. Chmn. Washington Grove Planning

Commn., 1957-60, town treas., 1961-72. Mem. Am. Cheviot Sheep Soc. (dir. emeritus), Eastern Seaboard Sheep Council (pres. 1978-80), Natural Colored Wool Growers Assn. (pres. 1979-83). Home: Keymar Md. Deceased. †

HALL, HAROLD H., railroad company executive; b. 1926; m. Joretta Hall; children: Martha Hall O'Donnell, Gregory M. With So. Ry. Co., from 1947; supt. to gen. mgr. Eastern lines So. Ry. Co., Atlanta, 1961-68; gen. mgr. Western lines So. Ry. Co., 1968-70, v.p. transp., 1970-76, sr. v.p. ops., 1976-77, exec. v.p. ops., 1977-79, pres., 1979-80, chief exec. officer, 1980-82; pres., chief operating officer, dir. Norfolk (Va.) So. Corp. (merger So. Ry. Co. with Norfolk Western Ry. Co.), Atlanta, 1982-87, vice chmn., 1987; bd. dirs. Citizens & So. Ga., Corp., FEC Ry., RF&P Ry., Pa.-Va. Corp. Served with USN, 1944-46. Home: Virginia Beach Va. Died Jan. 19, 1991; buried Andrews, N.C.

HALL, JEROME, lawyer, educator, author; b. Chgo., Feb. 4, 1901; s. Herbert and Sarah (Rush) H.; m. Marianne Cowan, July 2, 1941; 1 dau., Heather Adele. Ph.B., U. Chgo., 1922, J.D., 1923; Jur.Sc.D., Columbia U., 1935; S.J.D., Harvard U., 1935; LL.D., U. N.D., 1958, U. Tübingen, Fed. Republic Germany, 1978. Bar: Ill. 1923. With firm Kixmiller & Baar, 1923-26; pvt. practice, 1926-29; lectr. Ind. U. Extension, Gary, 1924-29; prof. law U. N.D., 1929-32; asst. state's atty. Cook County, Ill., summer 1931; Spl. fellow Columbia Law Sch., 1932-34; Benjamin research fellow Harvard Law Sch., 1934-35; prof. criminal law and criminology La. State U., 1935-39; prof. law Ind. U., 1939-57, Disting. Svc. prof. law, 1957-70; prof. Sixty-Five Club (legal scholars) Hastings Coll. Law, U. Calif., San Francisco, 1970-86, prof. emeritus, 1986; Hillman lectr. Coll. Pacific, 1947; Mitchell lectr. U. Buffalo, 1958; Fulbright lectr., U.K., 1954-55, U. Freiburg, Germany, 1961; Ford Found. lectr., Mex. and S. Am., 1960; Edward Douglass White lectr. La. State U., 1962; Murray lectr. U. Iowa, 1963; U.S. specialist State Dept. program, Far East and India, summers 1954, 68. Author: Readings in Jurisprudence, 1938, many re-edits., General Principles of Criminal Law, 1947, 2d edit., 1960, Cases and Readings on Criminal Law and Procedure, 4th edit., 1983, Living Law of Democratic Society, 1949, Theft, Law and Society, 2d edit., 1952, Studies in Jurisprudence and Criminal Theory, 1958, Comparative Law and Social Theory, 1963, Foundations of Jurisprudence, 1973, Law, Social Science and Criminal Theory, latest edit., 1982; Editor: 20th Century Legal Philsophy Series, 8 vols.; Contbr. articles to profl. jours. Recipient Lieber award for distinguished teaching, 1956; Bruce Smith award Acad. Criminal Justice Scis., 1984. Mem. ABA, China Acad., Am. Fgn. Law Assn., Internat. Acad. Comparative Law, Societé Européenne de Culture, Soc. Pub. Tchrs. Law, Am. Soc. Polit. and Legal Philosophy (pres. 1967-69), Internat. Assn. Legal and Social Philosophy (hon. 1986) (pres. Am. sect. 1966-68), Latin-Am. Assn. Sociology (pres. 1960), Council on Religion and Law (dir. 1977—). Home: San Francisco Calif. Died Mar. 1, 1992.

HALL, MARSHALL, JR., mathematics educator; b. St. Louis, Sept. 17, 1910; s. Marshall and Inez (Bethune) H. BA, Yale U., 1932, PhD, 1936; postgrad., Cambridge (Eng.) U., 1932-33; DSc (hon.), Emory U., 1988, Ohio State U., 1988. Mem. Inst. Advanced Study, Princeton U., 1936-37; instr., then asst. prof. Yale U., 1937-46; assoc. prof., then prof. Ohio State U., 1946-59; prof. math. Calif. Inst. Tech., Pasadena, 1959-85, exec. officer for math., 1966-69, IBM prof. math., 1973-85; prof. Emory U., Atlanta, from 1985; vis. research fellow Merton Coll., Oxford, Eng., 1977; Lady Davis vis. prof. Technion-Israel Inst. Tech., Haifa, 1980; vis. Woodruff prof. Emory U., 1982; vis. prof. U. Calif., Santa Barbara, 1984; dir. Summer Inst. Finite Groups, Pasadena, 1960, also several symposia. Author: Theory of Groups, 1959, Combinatorial Theory, 1967, 2d edit., 1986. Served with USNR, 1943-46, 50-52. Recipient Wilbur Cross medal Yale, 1973; Henry fellow, 1932-33; Guggenheim fellow, 1955-56, 70-71. Fellow AAAS; mem. Am. Acad. Arts and Scis., Phi Beta Kappa, Sigma Xi. Clubs: Valley Hunt (Pasadena); Oriental (London). Home: Beverly Hills Calif. Died July 4, 1990.

HALL, ROBERT DAVIDSON, textile company executive; b. Belmont, N.C., July 3, 1897; s. Matthews Neagle and Annie (Denny) H.; m. Mary Howe, Dec. 27, 1935; 1 child, Robert Davidson. AB, Davidson Coll., 1919; LLD, Phila. Coll. Textiles & Scis., 1962, Belmont Abbey Coll., 1963. Pres. Belmont Knitting Mills, N.C., from 1948; chmn. bd. Belmont Hosiery Mills, from 1962, Climax Spinning Co., from 1960; sec.-treas. Majestic Mfg. Co.; pres. Sterling Spinning Co., Stowe Thread Co.; dir. Bank of Belmont, Am. & Efird Mills, Inc., R.S. Dickson & Co. Mem. N.C. Employment Security Commn., 1941-65; pres. N.C. Citizens Assn., 1965; trustee St. Andrews Presbyn. Coll.; adv. com. Belmont Abbey Coll. 2d lt. U.S. Army, WWI. Mem. Am. Cotton Mfrs. Inst. (pres. 1961-62), Am. Legion (comdr. N.C. 1940-41), Phi Gamma Delta. Presbyterian. *

HALL, ROBERT LEICESTER, aircraft manufacturing executive; b. Taunton, Mass., Aug. 22, 1905; s. Bicknell and Estelle B. (Lane) H.; m. Eugenie Zeller, Jan. 1, 1930 (div. Nov. 1937; 1 child, Robert Leicester; m. Rhoda Halvorsen, Jan. 27, 1938; children: Edward Christian, Eric Robert Dudley, Benjamin Staples. Student, Harvard U., 1922-24; BS, U. Mich., 1927. Chief engr. Granville Bros. Aircraft, Springfield, Mass., 1926-31; aero. engr. Stinson Aircraft Co., Wayne, Mich., 1931-36; engr., test pilot Grumman Aircraft Engring. Corp., 1936-70, chief engr., 1956, v.p., 1956-70; designer World War II planes F4F Wildcat, F5F Hellcat, TBF Avenger, others. Exec. dir. offshore activities N.Am. Yacht Racing Union, 1969-74. Lt. USNR, 1938-40. Named to Test Pilots Hall of Fame, 1990. Fellow AIAA, Soc. Exptl. Test Pilots (hon.); mem. Am. Soc. Naval Engrs., Inst. Nav. Quiet Birdmen, N.Am. Sta. Royal Scandinavian Yacht Club, N.Y. Yacht Club, Cruising Am. Club (ex-commodore), Huntington Yacht Club (ex-commodore), Storm Trysail Club (ex-commodore), Off Soundings (ex-commodore), Phi Gamma Delta. Home: Newport R.I. Died Feb. 25, 1991.

HALL, WALLACE CLARE, lawyer, educator; b. Harbor Beach, Mich., Apr. 12, 1894; s. Charles L. and Ellen Sophia (Greeley) H.; m. Hazel Harmon Forte, June 17, 1920; children: Ellen Lee (dec.), Wallace Greeley. Student, Mich. State Normal Coll., 1911-13; AB, U. Mich., 1916, LLB, LLM, 1921. Bar: Mich. 1920; life teaching cert. Mich. High sch. sci. tchr. Highland Park, Mich., 1916-17; instr. English dept. U. Mich., 1919-21; prof. law of wills, estates and equity Detroit Coll. Law, 1923-38; pres. emeritus, gen. counsel Patriotic Edn., Inc.; orginator radio program Think Every Day for teh U.S.A. Author: Course Outline and Reference Quiz on U.S. Constitution; editor: Citizen Builders U.S.A., from 1963. Past chmn. bd. Denton Sleeping Garment Mills. With U.S. Army, WWI. Named Hon. citizen State of Tex., City of New Orleans. Mem. Mich. Bar Assn., SAR (past pres. Gen. Nat. Soc., past pres. Detroit chpt. and Mich. soc. nat. life trustee), Delta Theta Phi. *

HALLEY, HARRY L(EE) S(TUART), judge; b. Antlers, Okla., Sept. 5, 1894; s. John Henry and Annie Howard (Stuart) H.; m. Fredrica Probst, Sept. 6, 1923; 1 child, Matilda Ann Rummage. AB, U. Okla., 1915, LLB, 1917. Bar: Okla. 1916. Asst. city atty. Tulsa, 1922-28; dist. judge Tulsa (Okla.) and Pawnee Counties, 1931-47; justice Supreme Ct. State Okla., from 1949, vice chief justice, 1952, 63-65, chief justice, 1953-55. Capt. U.S. Army, 1917-18, col., 1942-45. Mem. ABA, Okla. Bar Assn., Tulsa County Bar Assn., Am. Judicature Soc., Res. Officers Assn., Am. Legion, VFW, C. of C., YMCA, Phi Delta Phi, Sigma Chi, Mason, K.P., High Twelve Club. Democrat. Methodist. *

HALLIGAN, ROBERT F., electronics company executive; b. Chgo., Mar. 22, 1925; s. William J. and Katherine M. (Fletcher) H.; m. Marilyn Boland, June 14, 1947; children: Robert F., Judith Lynn, Thomas Michael, Margaret Alice. Student, Notre Dame U., 1942, Northwestern U., 1943-44; BS, U.S. Mil. Acad., 1947. With Hallicrafters Co., Chgo., 1950-89, exec. v.p., 1959-61, pres., 1961-89, now chmn. With AUS and USAF, 1947-50. Mem. AFCEA, Inst. Radio Engrs. (sr.), PGEM, Execs. Club (Chgo.), Phi Delta Theta. Home: Indian Wells Calif. Died June 13, 1989.

HALLOWELL, ROGER, manufacturing company executive; b. Milton, Mass., Dec. 7, 1910; s. John White and Marian Hathaway (Ladd) H.; m. Frances Lee Weeks, Feb. 12, 1938; children: Roger Haydock, Beatrice W., Christian; m. Barbara Warner Noble. Student, Milton (Mass.) Acad., 1920-28; AB, Harvard U., 1933. Instr., coach Brooks Sch., North Andover, Mass., 1933-36; with Inc. Investors, Boston, 1936-38; with Reed & Barton Corp., Taunton, Mass., 1938-86, personnel dir., 1940-42, v.p., 1947-49, exec. v.p., 1951-53, dir., 1951-89, pres., 1953-71; chmn. bd., 1971-86; dir. First Bristol County Nat. Bank, Arkwright-Boston Ins. Co., Ludlow Corp. Pres. Boston coun. Boy Scouts Am., 1941, v.p., 1946-66, dir. Annawon coun.; trustee Milton Acad. With USNR, 1942-46. Decorated Silver Star. Home: Manchester Mass. Died Dec. 20, 1989.

HALPERN, BENJAMIN, educator; b. Boston, Apr. 10, 1912; s. Solomon Leib and Fannie (Epstein) H.; m. Gertrude Elizabeth Gumner, Nov. 26, 1936; children: Elkan Frank, Joseph David. A.B., Harvard, 1932, Ph.D., 1936; B.J. Ed., Hebrew Tchrs. Coll., 1932, D.H.L. (hon.), 1988; D.H.L. (hon.), Gratz Coll., 1989; Ph.D. (hon.), Tel-Aviv U., 1989. Mng. editor Jewish Frontier, N.Y.C., 1943-49; mem. editorial bd. Jewish Frontier, 1943-72; asso. dir. edn. and culture Jewish Agy., N.Y.C., 1949-56; research asso. Harvard Center for Middle East Studies, Cambridge, Mass., 1956-72; asso. prof. Near Eastern studies Brandeis U., Waltham, Mass., 1961-66; prof. Brandeis U., 1966-81, prof. emeritus, from 1981. Author: The American Jew, A Zionist Analysis, 1956, 83, The Idea of the Jewish State, 1961, 69, Jews and Blacks, the Classic American Minorities, 1971, A Clash of Heroes: Brandeis, Weizmann, and American Zionism, 1987. Exec. Jewish Agy., 1968-72; Trustee Hebrew Tchrs. Coll.; bd. govs. Tel Aviv U. Sr. fellow Nat. Endowment for Humanities, 1970; Guggenheim fellow, 1961-62. Home: Brookline Mass. Deceased. †

HALSTED, JOHN MAC HARG, management consultant; b. Chgo., May 27, 1905; s. Joseph and Mary (Mac Harg) H.; m. Nancy Leahy, May 2, 1944; children: Joseph, Ellen, Henry, John Matthew; m. Dorothy Moore Benson, Dec. 8, 1962; stepchildren: Richard Benson, Virginia Benson, Lynda Benson, Diane Benson. B.A., U. Mich., 1927. With Colgate-Palmolive Co., 1927-69, dir. purchases, 1958-61, v.p. purchasing, 1961-69, cons., 1969; now mgmt. cons. N.Y.C. Pres. Alpine (N.J.) Bd. Edn., 1952, 53; mem. Alpine Town Council, commr. police, 1954-55. Mem. Oil Trades Assn. N.Y. (pres. 1970). Clubs: N.Y. Yacht, Cruising of Am. (rear commodore Fla. sta. 1987-88), Light House Point Yacht, Corinthian. Home: Pompano Beach Fla. Died May 6, 1990. †

HALSTON (ROY HALSTON FROWICK), fashion designer; b. Apr. 23, 1932. Student, Ind. U., Sch. Chgo. Art Inst. Designer custom millinery, 1958; fashion designer Bergdorf Goodman, N.Y.C., 1959-68; designer boutique Halston Ltd., 1968-76; designer, pres. dress mfg. firm Halston Originals, N.Y.C., 1972-75; pres. design firm Halston Enterprises, Inc., N.Y.C., from 1975. Costume designer Martha Graham ballets, Dance Theatre of Harlem, motion picture and theatre. (Recipient Coty award (4), named to Coty Hall of Fame 1974, Martha Graham award (3). Home: New York N.Y. Died Mar. 26, 1990.

HAMBURGER, JEAN, medical educator, nephrologist, writer; b. Paris, July 15, 1909; s. Alfred and Marguerite (Marix) H.; m. Catherine Deschamps, July 30, 1964; children: Bernard, Françoise, Michel. PhD, Sorbonne U., Paris, 1930; MD, U. Paris, 1936. Chief nephrology svc. Hosp. Necker, Paris, 1952-83; prof. medicine U. René Descartes, Paris, 1956-83; dir. renal rsch. Inst. Nat. de la Santé Et de la Recherche Médicale, Paris, 1951-83; dir. Ctr. Nat. de la Recherche Scientifique Lab. Graft Immunology, Paris, 1951-83; pioneer in field of kidney transplants, developer of one of first two artificial kidneys, physician for 1st successful renal transplant between non-twins in the world, 1962. Author: The Power and Frailty (transl. 11 langs.), numerous others. Capt. WWII. Named Grand Officier de la Légion d'Honneur, 1985, Grand-croix de l'Ordre Nat. du Mérite, 1991, Comdr. de l'Ordre des Arts et Lettres, 1983. Mem. French Acad. Scis. (pres. 1991), Acad. Nat. Medicine (Paris), Acad. Française, Coun. l'Ordre de la Légion d'Honneur, Found. pour la Recherche Med., Am. Coll. Physicians (hon.), Royal Coll. Physicians (hon., London, Edinburgh, Can.), Internat. Soc. Transplantation (past pres.). Home: Paris France Died Feb. 1, 1992; buried Montmarte Cemetery, Paris.

HAMER, JESSE DEWEY, physician; b. Lyndon, Ohio, Mar. 28, 1898; s. William Anderson and Belle Ada (Brown) H.; m. Clarice Mabel Hellie, Feb. 8, 1929. AB, Wittenberg Coll., 1922; MD, Western Res. U., 1926. Intern Cleveland City Hosp., 1926-27; resident Good Samaritan Hosp., Phoenix, 1927-28; pvt. practice medicine Phoenix, from 1928; med. cons. Ariz. Dept. Pub. Welfare, from 1958; chmn. med. adv. com. Gompers Rehab. Clinic, from 1961; mem. Gov.'s Com. on Aging, from 1960. Dir. Roosevelt coun. Boy Scouts Am., 1931-57; co-founder Ariz. div. Am. Cancer Soc.; chmn., past mem. bd. county chpt. ARC, Ariz. Heart Assn., Ariz. Blue Cross. Fellow ACP; mem. AMA (Ariz. del. from 1934, v.p. from 1957), Phoenix Med. Assn., Maricopa County Med. Assn., Endocrine Soc., Geriatric Soc., S.W. Med. Assn., Acad. Internat. Medicine. *

HAMILTON, ANTHONY ROBERT, electronics company executive; b. North Bergen, N.J., July 14, 1924. Mgr. purchasing dept. Lear Inc., 1947-56; mgr. Daystrom Pacific, 1956-57; salesman Hamilton Electronics Co., 1957-62; with Avnet, Inc., N.Y.C., from 1962, sr. v.p., 1966-68, exec. v.p. electronic mktg. div., 1968-76, exec. v.p., vice chmn., dir., 1976-80, chmn. bd., chief exec. officer, dir., from 1980. Home: New York N.Y. Died Dec. 22, 1988.

HAMILTON, EARL JEFFERSON, economist, educator; b. Houlka, Miss., May 17, 1899; s. Joseph William and Frances Regina Anne (Williams) H.; m. Gladys Olive Dallas, June 2, 1923 (dec. June 1987); 1 child, Sita (Mrs. Joseph Halperin). B.S. with honors, Miss. State U., 1920; student, U. Tex., summers 1922, 23, M.A., 1924; A.M., Harvard U., 1926, Ph.D., 1929; Dr. Honoris Causa, U. Paris, 1952, U. Madrid, 1967; LL.D., Duke, 1966. Athletic dir., football and track coach secondary schs., 1920-24; Thayer fellow econs. Harvard U., 1925-26, Frederick Sheldon traveling fellow, 1926-27; asst. prof. econs. Duke U., 1927-29, prof., 1929-44; dir. civilian staff Mil. Govt. Fiscal Sch., 1943-44; prof. econs. Northwestern U., 1944-47; prof. econs. U. Chgo., 1947-67, prof. emeritus, 1968; disting. prof. econ. history SUNY, Binghamton, 1966-69, prof. emeritus, 1970; Prof. Universidad Internacional, Santander, Spain, summer 1933, Colegio de Mexico, summer 1943; mem. com. on research in econ. history Social Sci. Research Council, 1941-54, rapporteur, com. world regions of; rapporteur, com. world regions of Am. Council Learned Socs. and NRC, 1943; rapporteur 11th Congress Hist. Scis., Stockholm, Sweden, 1960. Author: American Treasure and the Price Revolution in Spain, 1501-1650, 1934, Money, Prices and Wages in Valencia, Aragon and Navarre, 1351-1500, 1936, War and Prices in Spain, 1651-1800, 1947, El Florecimiento del Capitalismo y Otros Ensayos, 1948; contbg. author: First Images of America: What the New World Gave the

Economy of the Old, 1976; bd. editors: Jour. Modern History, 1941-43, Jour. Econ. History, 1941-52, Revista de Historia Económica, from 1983; editor Jour. Polit. Economy, 1948-54; co-editor Landmarks in Political Economy, 1962; contbr. to Am., English, Spanish and French jours. of econs. and history. Trustee Com. Research in Econ. History, Inc., 1956. Recipient Gold medal as world's greatest exhibitor N. Am. Gladiolus Council, 1978; Social Science Research fellow, 1929-30; Guggenheim Meml. fellow, 1937-38; faculty research fellow Ford Found., 1956-57. Fellow Royal Econ. Soc., AAAS, Am. Acad. Arts and Scis.; mem. Am. Econ. Assn. (v.p. 1955), Econ. Hist. Assn. (v.p. 1941-42, pres. 1951-52), Am. Hist. Assn., Hispanic Soc. Am. Home: Flossmoor Ill. Died May 7, 1989; buried Meml. Pk., Memphis, Tenn.

HAMILTON, EDWARD PIERPONT, manufacturing executive; b. Two Rivers, Wis., Feb. 5, 1897; s. Henry Pierpont and Jessie (Luse) H.; m. Katherine Fletcher, Aug. 25, 1923; children: Diantha McDowell, Jacqueline Shiller, Nancy Eglee, Edward Pierpont. Student, Culver Mil. Acad., 1914-15, Columbia U., 1915-18. Pres. Hamilton Mfg. Co., Two Rivers, 1941-63; chmn., CEO Hamilton Mfg. Co., from 1963; bd. dirs. Manitowoc Savs. Bank. Trustee Lawrence Coll. Mem. Wis. Mfrs. Assn. (dir.), Nat. Assn. Mfrs. (dir.) Psi Upsilon, Mason, Rotary. *

HAMILTON, GEORGE E., JR., lawyer; b. Washington, Mar. 29, 1895; s. George E. and Louise (Merrick) H.; m. Marian Hamilton, Oct. 4, 1922. Student, Carlton Acad., 1909-13; A.B., Georgetown U., 1917, LL.B., 1920, Sc.D., 1971. Bar: D.C. bar 1920. Assoc. Hamilton & Hamilton, Washington, 1920-23; mem. Hamilton & Hamilton, 1923-46, sr. mem., from 1946; dir. railroads; counsel Cath. Archdiocese of Washington.; Bd. dirs. Washington Terminal Co. Trustee Corcoran Gallery Art. Served as sgt. U.S. Army, 1917-18. Decorated Knight of St. Gregory. Fellow Am. Bar Found.; mem. Am., D.C. bar assns., Soc. of Cincinnati. Clubs: Lawyers, Barristers, Chevy Chase (past pres.), Metropolitan (past pres.), Alfalfa (Washington) (past pres.); Alibi. Home: Washington D.C. Died Oct. 11, 1990. †

HAMILTON, H(ENRY) G(LENN), economist; b. Humboldt, Tenn., Mar. 29, 1895; s. Millard Filmore and Addie (James) H.; m. Mildred McArthur, May 29, 1923; children: Addie Virginia Bell, Marguerite Preston, Harry Glenn. Student, U. Tenn., 1915-16; BS, U. Fla., 1921, MSA, 1923; PhD, Cornell U., 1928; student, Columbia U., 1928. Instr. farm mgmt. U. Fla., 1923-25, asst. prof. mktg., 1926-27, assoc. prof., 1928-33, prof., 1934-48, head dept. agrl. econ., from 1950; rschr. USDA, summers 1936, 38, 39, Columbia Bank for Cooperatives, Columbia, S.C., summer 1937; head citrus sect. Prodn. and Mktg. Adminstrn., USDA, 1943, 44. Author: Fla. Agrl. Expt. Sta. rsch. bulls., also articles in field; editorial coun.: Jour. Farm Econs., 1952-54. Mem. Am. Farm Econ. Assn., Fla. Acad. Sci., Fla. Blue Key, Pi Gamma Mu, Alpha Zeta, Alpha Gamma Rho, Gamma Sigma Delta, Clubs: Executive, Athenaeum, Rotary. Presbyterian. *

HAMILTON, LEICESTER FORSYTH, chemistry educator; b. Medford, Mass., Feb. 23, 1893; s. Frank Herbert and Janet (Hintze) H.; m. Mary Alma Nichols, Oct. 6, 1917; children: Jean Stevens, Helen Paulsen. BS, MIT, 1914. Instr. MIT, 1915-19, asst. prof. chemistry, 1919-25, assoc. prof., 1925-35, prof. field analytical chemistry, from 1935, in charge undergrad. chemistry, 1934-45, chmn. dormitory bd., 1925-50, acting head chem. dept., 1942-46, exec. officer chem., 1946-63, asst. sec. faculty, 1951-53, sec. faculty, 1953-58, emeritus lectr., 1958-63, hon. lectr., 1963-90. Author: Calculations of Quantitative Chemical Analysis, 1923, Quanitative Chemical Analysis, 1932. Mem. Am. Chem. Soc., Alpha Chi Sigma. Episcopalian. *

HAMILTON, PIERPONT MORGAN, United States Air Force officer; b. Tuxedo Park, N.Y., Aug. 3, 1898; s. William Pierson and Juliet Pierpont (Morgan) H.; m. Marie Louise Blair, 1919 (div. 1929); children: Philip Schuyler, David Blair, Ian Morgan, Harold Erhardt; m. Rebecca Stickney, 1930 (div.); m. Norah Goldsmith, Aug. 20, 1946. Student, St. Bernards Sch., N.Y.C., 1908-11, Groton (Mass.) Sch., 1911-16, Harvard U., 1916-17; AM, Harvard U., 1946. Cashier, fgn. exchange officer Morgan Harjes & Co., internat. banking, Paris, France, 1920-27; mem. Kelley Converse & Co., investment banking, N.Y.C., 1926-32; self employed in devel. and comml. exploitation of various inventions in color and sound motion picture photography, 1933-40; exec. dir. Can. Aviation Bur., 1940-42; Entered aviation sect. U.S. Signal Corps, 1917, commd. 2d lt., 1918, and advanced to maj. gen. USAFR, 1954, various field and combat assignments, 1918-43, on staff of asst. chief of staff, plans and ops., Hdqrs. USAAF, Washington, 1943-46; mem. plans and ops. div. U.S. Gen. Staff, 1946-47; chief policy div. Directorate of Plans and Ops., Hdqrs. USAF, 1947-54, ret.; dir. Siegler Corp., Royal Industries, Inc. Decorated Congl. Medal Honor, Legion Merit, Army Commendation with 4 clusters (U.S.), Officer Legion Honor (France), Officer Order Brit. Empire (Gt. Britain), Order Merito Cristo. Mem. SAR, Mil. Order World Wars, U.S. Legion of Valor, Clubs: Union, Racquet and Tennis, Harvard (N.Y.C.), Met. (Washington), Travelers (Paris). Republican. Episcopalian. *

HAMMER, ARMAND, petroleum company executive, art patron; b. N.Y.C., May 21, 1898; s. Julius and Rose (Robinson) H.; m. Olga von Root, Mar. 14, 1927; m. Angela Zevely, Dec. 19, 1943; m. Frances Barrett, Jan. 26, 1956 (dec. Dec. 1989); 1 child. BS, Columbia U., 1919, MD, 1921, LLD, 1978; LLD, Pepperdine U., 1978, Southeastern U., Washington, 1978, U. Aix-en-Provence, 1981; D in Pub. Service, Salem (W.Va.) Coll., 1979; HHD, U. Colo., Boulder, 1979; DSc (hon.), U. S.C., 1983; PhD (hon.), Tel Aviv U., 1986. Pres. Allied Am. Corp., N.Y.C., 1923-25, A. Hammer Pencil Co., N.Y.C., London and Moscow, 1925-30, Hammer Galleries, Inc., N.Y.C., from 1930, J. W. Dant Distilling Co., N.Y.C. and Dant, Ky., 1943-54; pres., chmn. bd. Mut. Broadcasting System, N.Y.C., 1957-58; chmn. bd., chief exec. officer Occidental Petroleum Corp., Los Angeles, 1957-90; chmn. M. Knoedler & Co., Inc., N.Y.C., from 1972, Knoedler-Modarco S.A., N.Y.C., from 1977; dir. Nat. State Bank, Perth Amboy, N.J., 1949-56, City Nat. Bank, Beverly Hills, Calif., 1962-71, Can. Occidental Petroleum Ltd., Calgary, Alta.; dir. Raffinerie Belge de Petroles, Antwerp, Belgium, 1968-79, Cities Service Co., Tulsa; hon. dir. Fla. Nat. Bank of Jacksonville, 1966-72; mem. Nat. Petroleum Council, 1968-90, Com. on Arctic Oil and Gas Resources, 1980-90. Author: The Quest of the Romanoff Treasure, 1936, autobiography (with Neil Lyndon) Hammer, 1987, (with Neil Lyndon) Hammer: Witness to History, 1987; subject of biography: The Remarkable Life of Dr. Armand Hammer (Robert Considine), 1975; Brit. edit. Larger than Life, 1976; The World of Armand Hammer (John Bryson), 1985. Pres. N.J. Aberdeen Angus Assn., 1948-49; Bd. govs. Monmouth County Orgn. Social Service, Red Bank, N.J., 1949-61, Monmouth Meml. Hosp., Long Branch, N.J., 1946-58, Eleanor Roosevelt Cancer Found., N.Y.C., 1960-90, Ford's Theatre Soc., 1970-90, UN Assn. U.S.A., 1976-90; bd. dirs., exec. com. Internat. Council United World Colls., 1983-90; mem. Royal Acad. Trust, Eng., 1980-90; mem., fellow Met. Mus. Art, 1985; trustee U. North Africa Assn., 1968-71, Los Angeles County Mus. Art, from 1968, UCLA Found., 1973-76, Nat. Symphony, 1977-90, United for Calif., from 1977, Capitol Children's Mus., from 1978; chmn. wine and spirits div. Vis. Nurse Service Greater N.Y., 1946, Am. Aid to France, 1947; mem. Citizens Food Com., 1946-47, Cardinal Spellman's Com. of Laity for Catholic Charities, 1946-48, Public Adv. Com. on U.S. Trade Policy, 1968-69, Am. Com. for Nat. Archives, 1974-76, Los Angeles County-U. So. Calif. Cancer Assos., 1975-90, George C. Marshall Assos., James Smithson Soc. of Smithsonian Nat. Assos., 1977-90, U. Okla. Assos., 1981-90, Bus. Adv. Commn. for 1984 Olympics, 1981-84, Los Angeles Olympic Citizens Adv. Commn., 1981-84; hon. trustee Denver Art Mus., 1980-90; mem. adv. bd. Inst. of Peace, 1950-54, Los Angeles Beautiful, Inc., 1969-75, Com. for a Greater Calif., 1969, Fogg Art Mus. and Fine Arts Library, Cambridge, Mass., 1977, The Friendship Force, 1977, Am. Longevity Assn., Inc., 1980, Center Strategic and Internat. Studies, Georgetown U., 1981-90; mem. fine arts com. U.S. Dept. State, 1981-90; chmn. Pres.'s Cancer Panel, 1981; mem. exec. com. Econ. Devel. Bd. City of Los Angeles, 1968-73; trustee, chmn. exec. com. Salk Inst. Biol. Studies, San Diego, 1969-90; bd. dirs. Los Angeles World Affairs Council, 1969-90, Planned Parenthood World Population/Los Angeles, 1970-90, U.S.-USSR Trade and Econ. Council, 1973-90, Assos. Harvard Bus. Sch., 1975-90, Calif. Roundtable, 1976-90, Century City Cultural Commn., 1977-90, Corcoran Gallery Art, Washington, 1978-90, Keep Am. Beautiful, Inc., 1979-90, Bus. Com. for Arts, N.Y.C., 1980-90; bd. visitors Grad. Sch. Mgmt., UCLA, 1957-90, UCLA Sch. Medicine Center for Health Scis., 1980-90; exec. mem. Energy Research and Edn. Found., 1978-90; charter mem. Nat. Vis. Council of Health Scis. Faculties, Columbia U., 1978-90; mem. univ. bd. Pepperdine U., 1979-90; mem. fellows for life New Orleans Mus. Art, 1980-90; bd. dirs. Nat. Coordinating Ctr. for Vol. Bone Marrow Donors, 1986; mem. nat. support council U.S. Com. for UNICEF, 1980-90; founder mem. Pepperdine Assos., 1976-90; pres. Found. of Internat. Inst. Human Rights, Geneva, 1977-90; mem. exec. bd. dirs. UN Assn. L.A.; mem. Bd. Mcpl. Arts Commrs. L.A., 1969-73; mem. budget and fin. com. of bd. trustees L.A. County Mus. Art, 1972-74; sponsor Internat. Inst. Human Rights Peace Conf., Oslo, 1978, Campobello Peace Park, 1979, Warsaw, 1980, Aix-en-Provence, France, 1981. Served with M.C. U.S. Army, 1918-19. Endowed Armand Hammer Center for Cancer Biology, Salk Inst., 1969; Armand Hammer prof. bus. and public policy UCLA, 1968; Frances and Armand Hammer wing Los Angeles County Mus. Art, 1969; Armand Hammer Animal Facility Salk Inst., 1976; Calif. Inst. Cancer Research UCLA, 1976; Ann. Armand Hammer Cancer Conf. and Fund Salk Inst., 1976; Harvard/Columbia Russian Study Fund, 1977; Julius and Armand Hammer Health Scis. Center Columbia U., 1977; Five-Yr. Funding Program UN Assn., 1978; Five-Yr. Funding Program Corcoran Gallery Art, 1979; Five-Yr. Funding Program Jacquemart-André Mus., Paris, 1979; Ann. Armand Hammer Award Luncheon Los Angeles, 1980; Los Angeles City Dept. Parks and Recreation, 1981, Armand Hammer Cancer Prize, 1982; Hammer-Rostropovich Cello Scholarship award U. So. Calif., 1982; Theatre du Gymnase, Marseille, France, 1983, Armand Hammer chair Leonardo Ctr., UCLA, 1985; Armand Hammer Ctr. for Advanced Studies in Nucelar Energy and Health, Los Angeles, 1986; recipient Humanitarian award Eleanor Roosevelt Cancer Found., 1962; city commendation Mayor of Los Angeles, 1968; decorated comdr. Order of Crown Belgium, 1962; comdr. Order of Andres Bellos Venezuela, 1975; Order of Aztec Eagle Mex., 1977; officer Legion of Honor France, 1978; Order of Friendship Among Peoples USSR, 1978; Royal Order of Polar Star Sweden, 1979; officer Grand Order of Merit Italy, 1981; Knight Comdr.'s Cross Austria, 1982; comdr. Nat. Order French Legion Honor, 1983; named Hon. Citizen and Seal Bearer of City of Vinci, Italy, 1982; Disting. Honoree of Yr. Nat. Art Assn., 1978; Golden Plate award Am. Acad. Achievement, 1978; Aztec award Mexican-Am. Opportunity Fond., 1978; Appeal of Conscience award N.Y.C., 1978; Spirit of Life award Oil Industry Council of City of Hope, 1979; award Antique Monthly, 1980; Entrepreneur of Yr. award U. So. Calif., 1980; Maimonides award Los Angeles Jewish Community, 1980; Golden Achievement award Andrus Gerontology Center, U. So. Calif., 1981; Ambassador of Arts award State of Fla., 1981; recipient John Jay award Columbia Coll., 1981, Disting. Citizen award Greater N.Y. Councils Boy Scouts Am., 1982, James Ewing Soc. Layman's award, Soc. Surgical Oncology, 1983, Medaille d'Or Mayor of Marseille and French Minister of Interior, 1983, Golda Meir award Israeli Prime Minister, 1984, Hilal-i-Quaid-i-Azam award Pres. Pakistan, 1985, Jubilee Medal Ambassador Zhulev of Bulgaria, 1985, Golden Archigymnaseum Decoration Mayor Renzo Imbeni of Bologna, 1985, Humanitarian award LWV, 1986, Human Achievement award Op. Calif., 1986, Nat. Recognition award Pres. United States Mexico, 1987, 1987 Humanitarian award Internat. Physicians for Prevention of Nuclear War, Inc., 1987, Emma Lazarus Statue Liberty award Nat. Jewish Hist. Soc., 1987, Nat. Arts Medal, 1987, Eleanor Roosevelt Humanitarian award United Nations Assn. San Francisco, 1987, Norman Vincent Peale award Insts. for Religion and Health, 1987, Spl. award Gen. Hosp. Mexico City, Ministry Health, 1987, Franklin and Eleanor Roosevelt Freedom from Fear award, 1988. Mem. Los Angeles Petroleum Club, Royal Acad. Arts (London), hon. corr., Am. Petroleum Inst. (dir. 1975-90), Navy League U.S. (Los Angeles council 1980-90), Fifty-Yr. Club Am. Medicine, Royal Scottish Acad. (hon.), AMA (life), N.Y. County Med. Assn., Internat. Inst. Human Rights, Alpha Omega Alpha, Mu Sigma, Phi Sigma Delta. Home: Los Angeles Calif. Died Dec. 10, 1990; buried Westwood Village Cemetery, Los Angeles.

HAMMER, SANFORD S., academic administrator, engineering educator; b. Bklyn., Aug. 21, 1935; s. Murray and Gertrude H.; m. Marcia Rainer, June 22, 1958; children: Kenneth, Michele. B.S. in Physics, Poly. Inst. Bklyn., 1956, M.M.E., 1959, Ph.D. in Mech. Engring., 1966. Asst. prof. mech. engring. Poly. Inst. Bklyn., Farmingdale, N.Y., 1956-62, sr. research assoc., 1962-66; prof. engring. sci. Hofstra U., Hempstead, N.Y., 1966-75, chmn. engring. and computer scis. dept., 1972-74, exec. dean student services, 1975-82, provost, dean faculty, 1982-90; engring. cons. various aerospace corps. and govt. agys., 1959-75. Home: Melville N.Y. Died Feb. 14, 1990.

HAMMER, THORVALD FREDERICK, manufacturer malleable iron and steel; b. Branford, Conn., Dec. 5, 1893; s. Alfred E. and Cornelia (Foster) H.; m. Lucy Taylor, Feb. 19, 1927; 1 child, Alexandra. Student, Yale U., 1918. Pres., gen. mgr. Malleable Iron Fittings Co., Branford, from 1935; chmn. bd. dirs.; bd. dirs. Branford Trust Co., New Haven Gas Co.; regional dir. Am. Mutual Ins. Co. Chmn. bd. trustees James Blackstone Meml. Libr., Branford; trustee Berkshire Sch., Sheffield, Mass. *

HAMMITT, FREDERICK GNICHTEL, nuclear engineer; b. Trenton, N.J., Sept. 25, 1923; s. Andrew Baker and Julia (Stevenson Gnichtel) H.; m. Barbara Ann Hill, June 11, 1949; children: Frederick, Harry, Jane. B.S. in Mech. Engring., Princeton U., 1944; M.S., U. Pa., 1949; M.S. in Applied Mechanics, Stevens Inst., 1956; Ph.D. in Nuclear Engring, U. Mich., 1958. Registered profl. engr., N.J., Mich. Engr. John A. Roebling Sons Co., Trenton, 1946-48, Power Generators Ltd., Trenton, 1948-50; project engr. Reaction Motors Inc., Rockaway, N.J., 1950-53, Worthington Corp., Harrison, N.J., 1953-55; research asso. U. Mich., Ann Arbor, 1955-57, assoc. research engr., 1957-59, assoc. prof., 1959-61, prof. nuclear engring., from 1961, mech. engring., from 1965, also prof. in charge Cavitation and Multiphase Flow Lab., from 1967; cons. govt. and industry; vis. scholar Electricité de France, Paris, 1967, Société Grenobloise Hydrauliques, Grenoble, France, 1971; Fulbright sr. lectr. French Nuclear Lab., Grenoble, 1974; Polish Acad. Sci. lectr. Inst. Fluid Mechanics, Gdansk, 1976; invited lectr. People's Republic China, Japan, 1982. Author: (with R.T. Knapp, J.W. Daily) Cavitation, 1970, Cavitation and Multiphase Flow Phenomena, 1980; contbr. 500 articles to profl. jours.; holder 5 patents in field. Served with USN, 1943-46. Fellow Inst. Mech. Engrs. (U.K.), ASME (past chmn. cavitation com. fluids div.), ASTM (past chmn. cavitation and liquid impingement); mem. Am. Nuclear Soc. (past chmn. S.E. Mich. sect.), Internat. Assn. Hydraulic Research (chmn. cavitation scale effects com.), Phi Beta Kappa, Sigma Xi, Tau Beta Pi. Republican. Presbyterian (elder). Home: Spring Lake N.J. Died June 29, 1989; buried Ewing (N.J.) Ch. Cemetery.

HAMMON, WILLIAM MCDOWELL, physician, educator; b. Columbus, Ohio, July 20, 1904; s. William Henry and Adaline (McDowell) H.; m. Helen Black, Aug. 3, 1926; children: William M., Barbara Helen. DSc (hon.), Allegheny Coll., 1959; MD, Harvard U., 1936, MPH, 1938, DPH, 1939. Diplomate Am. Bd. Preventive Medicine and Pub. Health. Dir. med. dispensary Shabunda, Belgian Congo, 1926-30; instr. epidemiology sch. pub. health Harvard U., Boston, 1939-40; mem. faculty Hooper Found. for Med. Rsch. U. Calif., 1940-50, lectr. medicine and neurology sch. medicine, 1942-50, mem. faculty sch. pub. health, 1944-50, prof. epidemiology, 1947-50; prof. U. Pitts., 1950-73, emeritus, 1973-89, head dept. epidemiology and microbiology sch. pub. health, 1950-70; cons. surgeon gen. U.S. Army, 1941-73; dir. virus infection communication Armed Forces Epidemiology Bd., 1956-65, dir. tropical medicine communication, 1946, mem. bd., 1965-73; cons. Communicable Disease Ctr. USPHS, 1948-60; mem. Nat. Adv. Cancer Coun., 1960-63; adv. com. live polio virus vaccine Surgeon Gen., 1959-66; mem. panel viruses and cancer Nat. Cancer Inst., 1959-62; mem. Pacific Sci. Bd. NRC, 1950-56. Recipient Medal of Freedom, 1946, Richard M. Taylor award in arbovirology, 1980, Outstanding Civilian Svc. award Surgeon Gen. U.S. Army, 1973. Fellow Am. Pub. Health Assn. (rsch. and standards com. 1949, chmn. 1950-55), AAAS, N.Y. Acad. Scis., Am. Acad. Microbiology (gov.); mem. Soc. Am. Bacteriologists (pres. 1949), Am. Assn. Immunology, Am. Soc. Tropical Medicine and Hygiene (editorial bd. 1951—, pres. 1967-68), Exptl. Biology and Medicine, Soc. Exptl. Pathology, Am. Assn. Physicians, Am. Epidemiol. Soc. (pres. 1962-63), Phi Beta Kappa, Sigma Xi, Alpha Omega Alpha, Delta Omega. Home: Saint Petersburg Fla. Died Sept. 19, 1989.

HAMMOND, WILLIAM ROGERS, business administration educator; b. Atlanta, Oct. 19, 1920; s. Charles C. and Edna (Rogers) H.; children: Charlotte Claren, Alexandra Merlyn. BS, Ga. State U., 1941; MBA, Harvard, 1943; DBA, Ind. U., 1954. Ptnr. Brenner & Co. (C.P.A.'s), Atlanta, 1946-48; prof. bus. adminstrn., assoc. dean Sch. Bus. Adminstrn., Ga. State U., Atlanta, 1948-75, dean grad. studies, 1958-73, Regents' prof. emeritus, 1982-90; Regents' prof. emeritus Sch. Bus. Adminstrn., Ga. State U., 1982-90; cons. Ga. State U. Found., 1982-90. Author accounting mgmt. and ins. books. Served to capt. AUS, 1943-46. Decorated Bronze Star medal. C.P.A., Ga. Mem. Am. Inst. C.P.A.'s, Acad. Mgmt., Am. Risk and Ins. Assn. Home: Atlanta GA. Died Aug. 11, 1990; buried Westview Cemetery, Atlanta.

HAMRICK, KENNETH EDISON, newspaper editor; b. Clarksburg, W.Va., June 27, 1923; s. Blaine and Samantha Adeline (Hamilton) H.; m. Evelyn Mae Kyer, May 22, 1948; children: Karen Lyn, Kimberly Anne, Kristin Patricia. B.S. in Journalism, W.Va. U., 1948. Reporter Clarksburg Exponent, W.Va., 1949-50, city editor, 1950-54; copy and travel editor Columbus Dispatch, Ohio, 1954-67, news editor, 1967-79, editorial page editor, 1979-87. Served with U.S. Army, 1942-46, ETO. Decorated Bronze Star. Mem. Nat. Conf. Editorial Writers, Soc. Profl. Journalists, Am. Legion, SAR, Kappa Sigma. Republican. Presbyterian. Home: Columbus OH Deceased. †

HANBURY, UNA, sculptor; b. Eng., Oct. 8, 1909; came to U.S., 1944; d. Noel Hardwick and Violet Hilton (Cutbill) Rawnsley; m. Anthony H.R.C. Hanbury, Jan. 1926; children: Diana Hanbury King, Jillian Hanbury Poole, Anna Larkin, Josephine Bennin. Grad., Royal Acad., Eng.; studied sculpture, Chelsea Poly., Eng.; studied painting and drawing, La Grande Chaumier L'Academie Julian, France; studied marble carving, Italy. Exhibited Royal Acad., London, Salon d'Automne, Paris, Nat. Sculpture Soc., Na.t Acad. Design, Nat. Arts Club, Mostra d'Arte Moderna, Camaiore, Italy, 1970, Corcoran Gallery Art, Cowboy Hall of Fame; retrospective of portraits in bronze, Folger Shakespearean Library, 1971, St. John's Coll., Santa Fe, 1973; important works include busts of Rachel Carson, Georgia O'Keefe, J. Robert Oppenheimer, R. Buckminster Fuller, (all in Nat. Portrait Gallery, Smithsonian Instn.), Enrico Fermi, Edward Teller, Hans Bethe, (Los Alamos, N.Mex.), Andres Segovia (Embassy of Spain, Washington), Laura Gilpin, Georgia O'Keefe, Jesus Rios, (Mus. Fine Arts, Santa Fe), Polingaysi (Mus. N. Ariz.), David Sung (Hong Kong), Dr. Hans Bethe (Cornell U. 1976), Dr. Leonard Carmichael, Dr. Dillon Ripley (Smithsonian Instn. 1977), Julius Rudel (J.F. Kennedy Ctr.), Faith and John Gaw Meem (St. John's Coll., Santa Fe), Hugh Dryden (Nat. Acad. Sci., Edwards' Air Force Base); large sculpures appear on Wilson Blvd., Washington, St. Marks Luth. Ch., Springfield, Va., Balt., Cin., Arandjelov Sculpture Pk., Yugoslavia, also numerous private gardens; portraits include Quarter Horse Tonto Bars Hank, Fine Arts Mus., Santa Fe; work included in books: Bronzes of the American West (Patricia Broder), The Outdoor Sculpture of Washington, D.C. (James M. Goode), 1% Art in Civic Architecture, Washington Artists Today, Fifty Faces; recent works: The Pet Show, 6' bronze sculpture at Children's Hosp. in Memphis, Lioness and Two Cubs, 8' bronze sculpture in Rio Grande Zoo, Albuquerque, Musk Oxen, Yellow Knife Mus., N.W. Ter., Can., Isadora Reflected, 4' bronze relief plaque at Albuquerque Mus. Art; also work at many schs. and hosps., nationwide. Home: Santa Fe N.M. Died Feb. 9, 1990.

HANCOCK, JOHN, actor; b. Hazen, Ark., Mar. 4; s. Charles Hancock and Mattie (Perry) McKenzie. Student, Wayne State U., 1959-60. Actor Am. Conservatory Theatre, San Francisco, 1968-71, 72-73, 1976-77; actor Milw. Repertory Theatre, 1971-72, 74-75, Actors Theatre of Louisville, 1975-76, Pacific Conservatory of Performing Arts, Santa Maria, Calif., 1975-80, Denver Centre Theatre Co., 1990. Appeared in over 20 films including '10', 1979, The Black Marble, 1980, All the Marbles, 1981, A Soldier's Story, 1984, The Bonfire of the Vanities, 1990, 62 TV programs including Roots: Next Generation, 1979, Scruples, 1980, Family Ties, 1984-89, L.A. Law, 1986—; co-star (TV series) Houston Knights, 1987-88, Pacific Station, 1991—; theatrical prodns. Othello, 1977, Death of a Salesman, 1980, Fences, 1990 (Best Actor nomination). With U.S. Army, 1964-67. Home: Los Angeles Calif. Died Oct. 13, 1992. †

HANDS, WILLIAM ARTHUR, executive, educator; b. Bklyn., July 24, 1917; s. Arthur and Ottilie (Muller) H.; m. Grace Rita DeLapp, Aug. 21, 1943; children: James Albert, William Arthur, Bruce Cyril, Brian Thomas, Brent Edward, Carolyn Elizabeth. B.A., Bklyn. Coll., 1947; M.B.A., Harvard U., 1949. Asst. to controller Berger Bros. Co., New Haven, 1950-52; supr. cost accounting and inventory Ford div. Ford Motor Co., Detroit, 1952-57; controller MicroWave and Power Tube div. Raytheon Co., Boston, 1957-61; v.p., treas., dir. Nat. Casket Co., Inc., Boston, 1961-69; with StanHome, Inc., Westfield, Mass., 1969-82; fin. v.p., treas., dir., mem. exec. com. StanHome, Inc., to 1982; prof. bus. adminstrn. Am. Internat. Coll., Springfield, Mass., 1983, Internat. Coll. of Naples, Fla., from 1989. Served with USAAF, 1942-46. Mem. Nat. Assn. Accountants, Fin. Execs. Inst. Home: Marco Island Fla. Deceased. †

HANES, DAVID GORDON, lawyer, publisher; b. N.Y.C., July 7, 1941; s. John Wesley and Hope (Yandell) H.; m. Ann Derby Gulliver, Sept. 10, 1966; children: Allison, Jonathan. BA magna cum laude with exceptional distinction, Yale U., 1966; JD cum laude, Columbia U., 1969. Bar: N.Y. 1970, D.C. 1971, U.S. Supreme Ct. 1981, U.S. Ct. Appeals (6th cir.) 1985. Law clk. to Justice Reed U.S. Supreme Ct., 1969, sr. law clk. to Chief Justice Burger, 1970; assoc. Wilmer, Cutler & Pickering, Washington, 1972-74; spl. asst. to John Doar Counsel to House Judiciary Com. for Impeachment Inquiry, 1974; exec. asst. to adminstr. FEA, Washington, 1975-77; founding ptnr. Colby, Miller & Hanes, Washington, 1977-79; ptnr. Reid & Priest, N.Y.C. and Washington, 1979-87; mem. Nat. Adv. Commn. on Criminal Justice Standards and Goals, Police Task Force, 1972-73; bd. dirs., v.p. DCI Pub. Inc. of Alexandria, 1986-91. Author: The First British Workmen's Compensation Act, 1897, 1968; bd. editors: Columbia Law Rev, 1968-69. Bd. dirs., sec. Hanes Found., 1975-91; bd. dirs. Family and Child Svcs., Washington, 1972-76, vice chmn., 1975-76; trustee Conn. Coll., 1973-83, chmn. audit and mgmt. com., 1978-83; trustee Sheridan Sch., 1983-88, chmn. investment com., 1984-88; trustee Salisbury Sch., 1990-91. Served with USMC, 1961-64. Mem. Phi Beta Kappa. Republican. Roman Catholic. Clubs: Links, Fishers Island Sportsmen's, (N.Y.C.); Capitol Hill (life), Met., Chevy Chase, Prospect Hall Shooting, Friends Creek Angler's Assn. (Washington). Home: Washington D.C. Died Feb. 24, 1991; cremated.

HANEY, FRED, professional baseball team executive; b. Albuquerque, Apr. 25, 1898; s. William John and Frances (Voorhees) H.; m. Florence Cohn, June 1, 1919; 1 child, Patricia Lorraine Franklin. Edn. pub. schs., L.A. Prof. baseball player Portland, Oreg., 1918-19, L.A., 1919-20, 29-32, Omaha, 1920-21, Detroit, 1921-25, Boston, 1926-27, Chgo., Indpls., 1927-28, Hollywood, Calif., 1933-34; mgr. profl. baseball team Toledo, 1935-38, 42, St. Louis Browns, 1939-41; radio sports announcer L.A., Hollywood, 1943-45, Hollywood Club, 1946-48; mgr. profl. baseball team Hollywood, 1949-52; mgr. Pitts Pirates, 1953-55, Milw. Braves, 1956-60; with NBC Game of Week, 1960-61; gen. mgr. L.A. Angels, from 1961; mgr. Milw. Braves, team won pennant and World Series, 1957, won pennant and lost World Series, 1958, tied for pennant and lost playoffs, 1959. With USNRF, 1918-19. Named Most Valuable Player of Yr., Indpls. Am. Assn., 1928, Hollywood Baseball Club, 1934, Most Valuable Mgr. of Yr., 1958, Exec. of Yr., 1962. Mem. Phi Kappa Psi, Mason. *

HANEY, PAUL DUNLAP, environmental engineer; b. Kansas City, Mo., Feb. 5, 1911; s. Wille Merrit and Mae (Dunlap) H.; m. Nell Cecilia Rezac, Feb. 2, 1935; 1 son, Paul Alan. B.S. in Chem. Engring, U. Kans., 1933; M.S. in San. Engring, Harvard U., 1937. Registered profl. engr., Kans., Mo., Ohio. With div. san. engring. Kans. State Dept. Health, Lawrence, 1934-47; assoc. prof. san. engring. Sch. Public Health, U. N.C., Chapel Hill, 1947-48; commd. engr. officer USPHS, Cin., 1948-54; partner, engring. cons. Black & Veatch (Engrs.-Architects), Kansas City, Mo., from 1954; cons. in field. Contbr. articles to profl. jours. Mem. Nat. Acad. Engring., Am. Water Works Assn. (hon. mem., Diven medal 1971), Water Pollution Control Fedn. (hon. mem.; past pres., Bedell award 1970, Emerson award 1975, Orchard medal 1979), Am. Acad. Environ. Engrs. (Cleary award 1977), ASCE, Am. Inst. Chem. Engrs., Am. Chem. Soc., AAAS, Am. Public Health Assn., APWA, Nat. Soc. Profl. Engrs., Kans. Engring. Soc., Sigma Xi. Club: Carriage (Kansas City). Home: Shawnee Mission Kans. Deceased.

HANIGAN, THOMAS EDWARD, JR., industrial executive; b. Schenectady, July 18, 1922; s. Thomas Edward and Jane M. (Fessette) H.; m. Olga Emervk, Oct. 19, 1946; children: Ian Thomas, Vitold Michel. B.A., Union Coll., Schenectady, 1946. With W.R. Grace & Co., N.Y.C., 1946-80, beginning as trainee, successively mgr. ins. dept., asst. treas., asst. v.p., 1946-58, v.p., mem. appropriations com., 1958-69, exec. v.p., dir., 1969-80, cons., 1980-91; chmn. T.E. Hanigan Co., Inc.; bd. dirs. CRM Inc., Grace Culinary Systems (China) Ltd. Trustee, Trustee Union Coll. Served with AUS, 1943-46. Mem. Nat. Assn. Accts., Lake George Club, Sky Club, Glen Falls Country Club, Lost Tree Club, Psi Upsilon. Home: Rye N.Y. Died Nov. 17, 1991; buried Greenwood Cemetery, Rye.

HANKS, BRYAN CAYCE, lawyer; b. Gatesville, Tex., May 23, 1896; s. William Henry and Lillian (Cayce) H.; m. Virginia Margaret Wooding, Sept. 20, 1921; children: Nancy, Larry (dec.). Grad., Wichita Falls (Tex.) High Sch., 1915; student, Rice Inst., Houston, Tex., 1915-16, Southwestern U., Georgetown, Tex., 1917; LLB, U. Colo., 1922. Bar: N.Y. 1924, Fla. 1929. Assoc. Hughes, Rounds, Schurman & Dwight, N.Y.C., 1922-24; legal dept. Electric Bond and Share Co., N.Y.C., 1924-25; head legal dept. Fla. Power & Light Co., Miami, 1925-36; pres. Miami Water Power Co., 1933-39; pres., also dir. Fla. Power & Light Co., Miami Beach Ry. Co. and Consumers Water Co., 1937-39; mem. law firm Hanks & Preston, 1939-42; pres. Southeastern Electric Exchange, 1938-39. Sgt. U.S. Army, 1917-19. Mem. ABA, Am. Legion, Fla. Audubon Soc., Fla. Hist. Soc., Kappa Alpha, Phi Alpha Delta, Clubs: Lawyers (N.Y.), Com. of 100 (Miami Beach), Ft. Worth, Knife and Fork, Met. (Ft. Worth), Kiwanis. Democrat. Methodist. *

HANLEY, ROBERT FRANCIS, trial lawyer, educator, author; b. Spokane, Wash., June 26, 1924; s. Richard E. and Ada E. (St. Peter) H.; m. Margaret Lungren, June 12, 1947 (div.); children: Kathleen Hanley Creore, Marcia Hanley Hoover, Elizabeth; m. Joan McLaughlin, Mar. 26, 1982. BS, Northwestern U., 1947, JD, 1950. Bar: Ill. 1950, Colo. 1983, D.C. 1991. Asst. atty. gen. State Ill., Chgo., 1952-55; ptnr. Isham Lincoln & Beale, Chgo., 1959-68, Jenner & Block, Chgo., 1968-82; ptnr. Morrison & Foerster, Denver, 1982-90, Washington, 1990-91; co-founder Hedlund & Hanley, Chgo., July, 1991; mem. faculty Northwestern U., Chgo., 1960-82, U. Colo., 1986-87; lectr. Oxford, Eng., 1982, 84, 86. Contbr. articles to profl. jours. Lt. col. USMC, 1942-64. Fellow Am. Coll. Trial Lawyers, Internat. Soc. Barristers; mem. ABA (chmn. sect. litigation 1975-76, ho. of dels. 1976-87, chmn. Mass. Torts Commn. 1987-90, Francis Rawle award with Am. Law Inst. 1986), Nat. Inst. Trial Advocacy (chmn. bd. 1981-82, Robert E. Oliphant Svc. award 1991), Saddle and Cycle Club (Chgo.). Democrat. Home: Chicago Ill. Died Sept. 15, 1991; buried Meml. Pk. Cemetery, Skokie, Ill.

HANLON, JOHN JOSEPH, public health administrator, educator; b. Boston, May 7, 1912; s. John Joseph and Florence (Livingston) H.; m. Frances E. Pizzo, June 24, 1939; children: Jon Jerrold, Donald Livingston. B.S., MIT, 1933, M.S., 1934; spl. student, Harvard Sch. Public Health, 1934; M.B., Wayne U., 1940, M.D., 1941; M.P.H., Johns Hopkins U., 1942. Diplomate Am. Bd. Preventive Medicine. Asst. san. engr. Eaton County, Mich., 1934; asst. epidemiologist, statistician Detroit Dept. Health, 1935-40; staff Harper Hosp., Detroit, 1940-41; health officer Bradley County, Tenn., 1941; dir. nutrition Tenn. Public Health, 1942-43; assoc. prof. public health adminstrn. U. N.C., 1943-44; lectr. preventive medicine Duke U., 1943-44; asso. prof. U. Mich., 1944-49, prof. public health, 1951-52; chief health Mission, Inst. Inter-Am. Affairs, Bolivia, 1949-51; med. dir. USPHS; chief public health div. U.S. Fgn. Aid Program, 1952-57; dir. public health services City of Phila., 1957-64; prof., chmn. dept. preventive medicine and public health Temple U. Sch. Medicine, 1957-64; commr. pub. health Detroit and Wayne County; adj. prof. public health adminstrn. U. Mich.; prof., chmn. dept. community medicine Wayne State U. Sch. Medicine, 1964-68; asst. surgeon gen. USPHS and rear adm. USN, Washington, 1968-76; prof. pub. health, health program coordinator San Diego State U., 1976-83; mem. U.S. del. to World Health Assembly, 1953, 54, 56; chmn. Detroit-Wayne County Community Mental Health Bd., 1964-67. Author: (with Beeuwkes) Nutrition and Public Health, 1945, 47, Principles of Public Health Adminstration, 1950, 55, 60, 64, 69, 74, (with George E. Pickett) Public Health—Administration and Practice, 1979, 8th edit., 1984, Principios de Salud Pública, 1956, 63, Design for Health, 1963, 71, Guías Para La Salud de la Comunidad, 1967, (with others) A

Strategy for a Livable Environment, 1967; also articles, bulls. Decorated Order of Condor Bolivia, 1951; named hon. alumnus Coll. Human Services, San Diego State U., 1979; recipient Disting. Alumnus award Wayne State U., 1968. Fellow Am. Public Health Assn. (pres. 1967-68, presdl. citation 1977, 1st ann. award for excellence in health adminstrn. 1981), San Diego State U. John J. Hanlon Chair in Health Services, Research and Policy, 1988; hon. fellow Royal Soc. Health, Coll. Medicine of Phila.; mem. Soc. Prospective Medicine (treas. 1976-80), Alpha Omega Alpha, Sigma Xi, Delta Omega; hon. mem. Sociedad Boliviana de Salud Pública, Hellenic Public Health Soc. Home: La Jolla Calif. Died Feb. 18, 1988.

HANMER, HIRAM R(UPERT), chemist; b. Lincoln, Vt., Sept. 6, 1896; s. George A. and Frances M. (Gove) H.; m. Sallie B. Roome, June 9, 1928. BS, U. Vt., 1918; DSc, Med. Coll. Va., 1963. Control and rsch. chemist E.I. duPont de Nemours & Co., Wilmington, Del., 1918-21; rsch. chemist The Am. Tobacco Co., Richmond, Va., 1921-32; dir. rsch. The Am. Tobacco Co., Richmond, from 1932, dir. co. from 1938, v.p. dept. rsch. and devel., 1959-64; mem. Va. Mus. Sci. Commn., chmn., 1946-50; pres. Va. Inst. for Sci. Rsch.; bd. dirs. Va. C. of C., 1950-53; adv. coun. Va. economy from 1947, Richmond Citizens Assn. Mem. bd. trustees Crippled Children's Hosp., Valentine Mus. Recipient Disting. Svc. award U. Vt., 1963. Fellow Am. Inst. Chemists, AAAS, Chem. Soc. of London; mem. Am. Chem. Soc. (councilor 1944-45, chmn. Va. sect. 1942-43), N.Y. Acad. Scis., Soc. Chem. Industry, So. Assn. Sci. and Industry (trustee from 1945), Tech. Assn. of Pulp and Paper Industry, Va. Acad. Sci. (past pres., Ivey F. Lewis disting. svc. award 1965), Va. Inst. Sci. Rsch. (pres.), Richmond C. of C. (past dir.), Clubs: Chemists (N.Y.), Torch (past pres.), Commonwealth (Richmond), Downtown. *

HANNING, MAURICE F(RANCIS), lawyer; b. Delaware, Ohio, Feb. 4, 1894; s. Jerry S. and Ellen A. (Kelly) H.; 1 dau. by previous marriage, Geraldine; m. Ruth Biddulph, Dec. 1951. Student, Ohio U.; AB, Ohio Wesleyan U., 1916; LLB, Western Res. U., 1919. Bar: Ohio 1918; practice of law Cleve., from 1919. Mem. firm McAfee, Hanning, Newcomer, Hazlett and Wheeler. Mem. Dem. County Exec. Com., from 1932; Ky. col. Mem. Am. Coll. Trial Lawyers, ABA, Ohio Bar Assn. (exec. com.), Cleve. Bar Assn., Cuyahoga County Bar Assn., Am. Judicature Soc., Internat. Acad. Law & Sci., A.I.M., Am. Petroleum Inst., Ohio C. of C., Cleve. C. of C., Ohio Mfrs. Assn., Delta Sigma Rho, Phi Delta Phi, K.C., Shaker Heights Country Club, Mid-Day Club, Alhambra. *

HANSEN, ARNE RAE, art gallery owner and director, museum administrator; b. Fergus Falls, Minn., Mar. 4, 1940; s. Arnold Rudolph and Elma Mildred (Tolliver) H.; stepson L. R. Hinzmann; m. Diane Cecelia Bowman, Jan. 29, 1966; children: Kyla Kristine, Gueran Wray. A.A., Black Hawk Coll., 1968; B.F.A. (Kennedy scholar), U. Tex., 1970; M.F.A., U. Okla., 1972. Asst. to dir. museums Ill. State U., Normal, 1972-73; acting dir. museums Ill. State U., 1973-74, dir. museums, 1974-75, asst. prof. art, 1973-75; dir. Colorado Springs (Colo.) Fine Arts Center, 1975-79, Rocky Mountain Regional Art Conservation Center, U. Denver, 1979-85; owner, dir. Arnesen Fine Art Ltd, Vail, Colo., from 1985; cons. curator Colo. Springs Fine Arts Ctr., 1988-92; adv. com. Colo. Mountain Coll., Vail. Artist; represented in permanent collections Art Mus. of U. Okla., Ardmore (Okla.) Art Ctr. Mem. Pub. Art Commn., Vail, Colo.; v.p., bd. dirs. Pub. Access TV, Vail; bd. dirs. El Paso County (Colo.) Park and Recreation Dist., Broadmoor Ski Racing Acad.; pres. Colo. Springs AAU Swim Team. Served with USAF, 1958-65. Mem. Internat. Coun. Mus., Art Mus. Am (treas.), Colo.-Wyo. Assn. Mus., Assn. Art Mus. Dirs., Mountain Plains Mus. Assn. (v.p.), Am. Assn. Museums (sr. examiner accreditation program), Western Assn. Art Museums (treas.), Vail Valley Gallery Assn. (chmn. bd.), Vail Valley Arts Coun. (hon. bd. dirs.), Colorado Springs C of C., Phi Theta Kappa, Phi Kappa Phi. Home: Vail Colo. Died Mar. 23, 1992. †

HANSEN, ZENON CLAYTON RAYMOND, truck manufacturing company executive; b. Hibbing, Minn., July 23, 1909; s. N.C.M. and Ivah Delle (Raymond) H.; m. Juanita Kellog, Dec. 2, 1954 (div. June 1973); m. Marilyn Benson, Dec. 22, 1973. Student pub. schs., Sioux City, Iowa; HHD (hon.), Salem (W.Va.) Coll., 1959; LLD (hon.), Linfield Coll., McMinnville, Oreg., PMC Colls., Chester, Pa., St. Michaels Coll., Winooskie, Vt., Gardner, Webb Coll., Boiling Springs, N.C., Ferris State Coll.; DCS, Hardin-Simmons U.; DH, Stonehill Coll. With Internat. Harvester Co. and Internat. Harvester Export Co., Europe and North Africa, 1927-44; asst. dist. mgr. Internat. Harvester Co., Portland, Oreg., 1941-44; v.p., bd. dirs., mgr. Automotive Equipment Co., Portland, 1944-53; v.p., dir. sales Diamond T Motor Co., Chgo., 1953-55, exec. v.p., 1955-56, pres., 1956-58; pres., bd. dirs. Diamond T Motor Truck Co.; exec. v.p., bd. dirs. White Motor Co., Cleve., 1958-65; pres., chief exec. officer, bd. dirs. Mack Trucks, Inc., 1965-67, chmn. bd., pres., 1967-72, chmn. bd., CEO, 1972-74; v.p., dir., mem. exec. com. Signal Cos., Inc., L.A., 1968-74; chmn., dir. Dartnell Corp., Am. Heritage Life Inst. Co., 1971-78; bd. dirs. Super Food

Svcs., Inc. Chmn. Gov.'s Com. of 100,000 Pennsylvanians for Econ. Growth, 1968-70; pres. Portland Area coun. Boy Scouts Am., 1949-51, vice chmn. region 11, 1952-53, mem. exec. com. region 7, 1956-65, hon. mem., from 1965, chmn., 1959-62, mem. nat. exec. bd., 1959-74, mem. exec. bd. Chgo. coun., 1957-60, adv. bd., 1960-74, chmn. nat. explorer com., 1962-63, chmn. nat. fin. com., nat. treas., 1967-70; pres. Am. Humanics Founds., 1956-58, chmn. adminstrv. com., 1959-69, patron, hon. life mem., chmn. bd. dirs., 1968-69. Recipient Silver Beaver, Silver Antelope, Silver Buffalo awards Boy Scouts Am., also Disting. Eagle Scout award, 1969; St. George award, 1969, Disting. Svc. award Latin Am. C. of C., Bus. Leader award Religious Heritage Am., 1972. Mem. Soc. Automotive Engrs. (chmn. Oreg. 1942-43), Am. Ordnance Assn. (life, v.p Chgo. 1956-63, Mich. 1963-64), Soc. Am. Mil. Engrs. (life), Navy League U.S. (life), Automotive Old Timers (life), Newcomen Soc. N.Am., Giant Schnauzer Club Am., Chgo. Club, Union League Club (Chgo.), Oreg. Boxer Club (pres. Portland 1948), Masons (33d degree), Shriners, Jesters, Moose, Elks, Order Ea. Star, Alpha Phi Omega (nat. exec. bd.). Presbyterian. Home: Sebring Fla. Died Oct. 19, 1990; buried Allentown, Pa.

HANSON, EUGENE BAIL, financial company executive; b. Winona, Minn., Sept. 1, 1895; s. Morris Peter and Mary (Ball) H.; m. Katherine Lord Brewster, Sept. 3, 1919; children: Brewster Bo, E. Ross, Caroline Rohrbach. BA, U. Minn., 1917. Pres., dir. No. Fin. Corp., Mpls., from 1949, No. Credit Plan, Inc., Mpls., from 1959; v.p. dir. Kapak Industries, Inc.; dir. Investors Variable Payment Fund, Inc., Investors Intercontinental Fund, Ltd. Pres., dir. Nat. Comml. Fin. Conf., 1962-64, chmn., dir. from 1964. Capt. USMC, 1917-19. Mem. Mpls. Club (treas. from 1963). *

HANSON, ROBERT PAUL, epidemiology educator, researcher; b. Sarona, Wis., May 14, 1918; s. Fred Elmer and Marion (Bergquist) H.; m. Martha Goodlet, Jan. 18, 1946; children—Allan Neil, Diane Gail Hanson Crossfield. B.A., Northland Coll., 1940; M.S., U. Wis.-Madison, 1947, Ph.D., 1949. Asst. prof. U. Wis.-Madison, 1949-52, assoc. prof., 1952-57, prof., 1957-72, Samuel H. McNutt prof., 1972-84, disting. sr. prof., 1984-87. Contbr. articles to profl. jours.; patentee in field. Mem. U.S.-Argentine Foot and Mouth Disease Commn., Washington, Buenos Aires, 1965-75; mem. adv. com. Pan Am. Health Orgn., Rio De Janiero, 1970-82, U.S. Dept. Agr., Washington, 1975-82. State of Wis. Sci. Policy, Madison, 1980-83. Named Honorary Mem., AVMA, 1968; recipient Upjohn Achievement award, 1979. Mem. Am. Soc. Microbiology, Am. Assn. Avian Pathologists (mem. editorial bd. 1968—), Am. Soc. Tropical Medicine, Wis. Acad. Sci., Arts and Letters (pres.). Home: Madison Wis. Died, 1987.

HANSTEEN, HENRY B., electrical engineering educator; b. Bklyn., Apr. 28, 1904; s. Henry and Elise (Baatz) H.; m. Emma Burkat, Dec. 29, 1930; children: Robert Henry, Beatrice Anna. EE, Polytech. Inst. Bklyn., 1924; AM, Columbia U., 1929, PhD, 1942. With Westinghouse Elec. Corp., 1924-26, Bklyn. Edison Co., 1926-28, Bell Telephone Lab., 1929-30; mem. faculty Poly. Inst. Bklyn., 1930-37, CCNY, 1937-46, Cornell U., 1946-50; prof. elec. engring. CUNY, 1950-67, prof. emeritus elec. engring., 1967-91, chmn. dept. elec. engring., 1952-55; sr. engr. Brookhaven Nat. Lab., 1967-91; ednl. cons. Internat. Atomic Energy Agy., Vienna, Austria, 1960-63. Fellow AIEE; mem. AAUP, Am. Phys. Soc., Am. Soc. Engring. Edn., Fedn. Am. Scientists, Sigma Xi, Eta Kappa Nu, Tau Beta Pi, Epsilon Chi. Home: Ithaca N.Y. Died Apr. 23, 1991; buried Ithaca, N.Y.

HAPPEL, HENRY WILLIAM, lawyer; b. Bklyn., Dec. 4, 1911; s. Henry W. and Ottilee (Kieselbach) H.; m. Alice M. Hicks, Sept. 14, 1935; 1 childre, Henry William III. AB magna cum laude, Williams Coll., 1933; LLB, Harvard U., 1936. Bar: N.Y. 1937. With Gen. Counsel's office USN, 1944-45; with Brown, Wood, Fuller, Caldwell & Ivey, N.Y.C., 1936-90, ptnr., 1943-90. Sec. Charles E. Merrill Trust; trustee Nichols Found., Yorkshire Fund; bd. dirs. Spence-Chapin Adoption Agy. Mem. ABA, N.Y. State Bar Assn., Bar Assn. of City of N.Y., West Side Tennis Club (bd. govs. 1942-44, 55-56, sec. 1959-61), Quogue Club, Field Club (bd. govs., sec. 1950-60, 73-90), Phi Beta Kappa. Home: Garden City N.Y. Died Mar. 25, 1990.

HARDIN, ADLAI STEVENSON, sculptor; b. Mpls., Sept. 23, 1901; s. Martin D. and Julia (Stevenson) H.; m. Carol Moore, Feb. 22, 1934; children: Carol J., Adlai Stevenson. AB, Princeton U., 1923. With Quaker Oats Co., 1923-25, Z.L. Potter Co., 1925-33; v.p. Wm. Esty Co., 1933-60; free-lance artist, 1960-89. Rep. permanent collections Brookgreen Gardens, S.C., Pa. Acad. Fine Arts, New Britain (Conn.) Mus. Am. Art, IBM Collection of Sculpture of Western Hemisphere, McMaster Div. Coll., McMaster U., Interchurch Center, N.Y.C., Seamen's Bank for Savs., N.Y.C., Princeton, Aid Assn. for Lutherans, Appleton, Wis.; prin. works include: life-sized bronze figures of St. Peter and St. Paul, St. Patrick's Cathedral, N.Y.C., 1983, Bronze figure of St. Jude, St. Patrick's Cathedral, 4 walnut panels, First Congl. Ch., Old Lyme, Conn. Recipient many art and numismatic awards including Avery prize Archtl. League, 1940, medallion for Brookgreen Gardens S.C.

N.A. Fellow Nat. Sculpture Soc. (pres. 1957-59, winner Ecclesiastical Competition 1950, Lindsey Morris Meml. prize 1956, Mrs. Louis Bennett prize 1965); mem. NAD (Saltus medal 1945, Daniel Chester French medal 1968, Gold medal for sculpture 1976). Club: Century Assn. (N.Y.C.). Home: Lyme Conn. Died Oct. 16, 1989.

HARDISON, OSBORNE BENNETT, JR., language professional, educator; b. San Diego, Oct. 22, 1928; s. Osborne Bennett and Ruth (Morgan) H.; m. Marifrancis Fitzgibbon, Dec. 23, 1950; children: Charity Ruth, Sarah Frances, Laura Fitzgibbon, Agnes Margaret, Osborne Bennett, Mathew Fitzgibbon. B.A., U. N.C., 1949, M.A. in English Lit., 1950; Ph.D., U. Wis., 1956; Litt.D., Rollins Coll., 1970, Kalamazoo Coll., 1975, Georgetown U., 1977, Amherst Coll., 1979. Teaching asst. U. Wis., 1950-53; instr. English U. Tenn., 1954-56, Princeton U., 1956-57; mem. faculty U. N.C. at Chapel Hill, 1957-69, prof. English and comparative lit., 1967-69; dir. Folger Shakespeare Library, Washington, 1969-83; Univ. prof. English Georgetown U., 1984-90. Author: Lyrics and Elegies, 1958, Modern Continental Literary Criticism, 1962, The Enduring Monument, 1962, English Literary Criticism: The Renaissance, 1964, Christain Rite and Christian Drama in the Middle Ages, 1965, Practical Rhetoric, 1966, (with Leon Golden) Aristotle's Poetics: A Translation and Commentary for Students of Literature, 1968, Toward Freedom and Dignity: The Humanities and the Idea of Humanity, 1973, Pro Musica Antiqua, 1977, Entering the Maze: Identity and Change in Modern Culture, 1981, Medieval Literary Criticism, 1982, Prosody and Purpose in the English Renaissance, 1989, Disappearing through the Skylight: Culture and Technology in the Twentieth Century, 1989, (with Leon Golden) Horace's Ars Poetica: A Translation and Commentary for Students of Literature, 1994; editor: (with others) The Encyclopedia of Poetry and Poetics, 1965 (rev. edit. 1974), Medieval and Renaissance Studies, 1966, The Quest for Imagination, 1971, Film Scripts I-IV, 1971, The Princeton Handbook of Poetry and Poetics, 1986, Disappearing Through the Skylight: Culture and Technology in the Twentieth Century, 1989 (L.A. Times Book award; co-author: (with Leon Golden) Classical and Medieval Criticism, 1974; adv. editor: Jour. Medieval and Renaissance Studies; also series editor for book pubs. Trustee U. Detroit, 1969-79. Decorated Cavaliere della Republic Italiana, Order Brit. Empire; Fulbright fellow Rome, Italy, 1953-54; Folger Library fellow, summer, 1958; Guggenheim fellow, 1963-64; recipient Haskins medal Medieval Acad. Am., 1967, U. N.C. Disting. Alumnus award, 1987. Mem. MLA (exec. coun. 1968-71), Renaissance Soc. Am. (v.p. 1987-88, pres. 1988-89), Shakespeare Assn. Am. (pres. 1984-85), Am. Assn. Higher Edn. (dir. 1980-85), Nat. Humanities Alliance (chmn. 1985-86), Phi Beta Kappa. Home: Washington D.C. Died Aug. 5, 1990; buried Hardison Farm, Syria, Va.

HARDY, GEORGE, labor union official; b. North Vancouver, Canada, Dec. 15, 1911; s. Charles and Bertha (Fitchett) H.; m. Florence Robinson, May 6, 1966; 1 child, JOan Hardy Twomey. Grad. high sch. Bus. agt. local 9 Svc. Employees Internat. Union, San Francisco, 1932-36, organizer local 87, 1936; organizer, pres. local 399 Svc. Employees Internat. Union, L.A., 1946; nat. v.p. Svc. Employees Internat. Union, Washington, 1948-71; pres. Svc. Employees Internat. Union, 1971-90; mem. exec. coun. AFL-CIO, 1972-90. With AUS, 1943-46, ETO. Mem. Am. Legion. Home: Washington D.C. Died Sept. 13, 1990.

HARGRAVE, HELEN, librarian, educator; b. Bay City, Mich., Nov. 7, 1894; d. Edward Carrollton and Victoria Regina (Holmes) Hargrave. LLB. U. Tex., 1926. Asst. law libr. U. Tex., 1930-39, law libr., from 1940, asst. prof. law, 1950-60, assoc. prof. law, from 1960, libr. emeritus, from 1965. Mem. City of Austin Libr. Commn. Mem. Am. Assn. Law Librs. (exec. bd. 1942-43, 51-54, pres. 1957-58), State Bar Tex., Pi Beta Phi, Kappa Beta Pi, Order of Coif. Episcopalian. *

HARKINS, GEORGE FREDERICK, clergyman; b. Phila., Feb. 28, 1913; s. John and Jennie (Waters) H.; m. Janet I. Earhart, June 18, 1940; children—John Edgar, Paul Frederick. A.B., Gettysburg Coll., 1937, L.H.D., 1969; B.D., Gettysburg Sem., 1940; D.D., Muhlenberg Coll., 1954; Th.D., Midland Lutheran Coll., 1967; S.T.D., Thiel Coll., 1970; LL.D., Susquehanna U., 1971. Ordained to ministry Luth. Ch., 1941; pastor in Penbrook-Harrisburg, Pa., 1941-49; asst. to pres. United Luth. Ch., 1949-60, sec., 1960-62; asst. to pres. Luth. Ch. in Am., 1962-68, sec., 1968-74; gen. sec. Luth. Council in U.S.A., 1974-79; asst. to bishop N.J. Synod, 1982-87; v.p. Nat. Luth. Council, 1962-65, pres., 1965-66; mem. Luth. Resettlement Com., 1951-54, chmn., 1953-54; mem. Joint Commn. on Luth. Unity; pres. U.S.A. nat. com. Luth. World Fedn., 1966-70; mem. commn. on world service, 1970-77; mem. gov. bd., exec. com. Nat. Council Chs. Christ U.S.A., 1961-75; v.p. Luth. Council in U.S.A., 1970-74; pres. Religion in Am. Life, 1973-78, sec., 1971-73. Author: The Church and Her Work, 1960, Handbook for Committees, 1966, Handbook on the Ordained Ministry, 1971; Contbr. to: religious periodicals. Luth. Ency. Trustee Wagner Coll., S.I., N.Y., 1972-76; v.p. Am. Immigration and Citizenship Assn., 1974-79. Named Young Man of Yr. Harrisburg, Pa., 1948; George Frederick Harkins ann. lectureship on Martin Luther established in his honor Luth. Theol. Sem., Gettysburg, Pa., 1991. Mem. Alpha Kappa Alpha, Kappa Phi Kappa, Kappa Delta Rho. Home: Wyckoff N.J. Died Dec. 3, 1991; cremated.

HARKNESS, EARL, banker; b. Danbury, Conn., May 21, 1898; s. Alexander Harkness and Alicia (Hughes) H.; m. Millicent Pierce, Feb. 11, 1937. BCS, NYU Sch. Commerce, 1924. Dep. supt. of banks N.Y. State Banking Dept., 1934-35; comptr., exec. v.p. Jamaica Savs. Bank, N.Y., 1935-43; chmn. bd., pres., trustee Greenwich Savs. Bank, N.Y., from 1943; v.p. 555 Park Ave. Corp.; dir. Savs. Bank Trust Co., Instnl. Investors Mut. Fund; trustee Savs. Banks Retirement System. Treas. Citizens Budget Commn.; dir. Soc. for Prevention of Crime, N.Y. Seaman USN, 1918. Recipient Madden Meml. award, 1957. Mem. Ave. of the Ams. (dir.), Nat. Assn. Mut. Savs. Bank (dir.), Newcomen Soc., New Eng. Soc., Clubs: Economic, Union League (N.Y.), Quaker Hill Golf & Country. *

HARLAN, JOHN GRAYDON, JR., metallurgical and chemical company executive; b. Pitts., Apr. 30, 1918; s. John Graydon and Anna M. (Durning) H.; m. Margaret Fenwick Wetmore, June 15, 1940. Student, George Washington U., 1936-41. With Fed. Govt., 1937-69, with Treasury Dept., 1937-48, in Fgn. Aid Program, 1948-57; chief indsl. productivity and exec. officer AID Mission to Austria, 1950-53; dep. dir. indsl. tech. assistance FOA, 1953-54; asst. dir. Office Indsl. Resources ICA, 1954-57; mgmt. officer Office Adminstr. GSA, 1957-58, dep. commr. Def. Materials Svc., 1958-66, commr., 1966, commr. Property Mgmt. and Disposal Svc., 1966-69; v.p. Engelhard Minerals & Chem. Corp., 1969-71, sr. v.p., 1971-73, exec. v.p., 1973-90; v.p. Engelhard Industries div., 1969-70, exec. v.p., 1970-71, pres., 1971-90. Rep., Pres. Com. on Econ. Impact Def. and Disarmament; project mgr. Pres.'s Spl. Task Force on Use Surplus Property to Meet Critical Urban Needs for Housing; mem. Ind. Study Bd. to examiner effects govt. policies on regional econ. levels. Lt. USCGR, 1942-45. Recipient Meritorious Svc. award FOA, 1955, Meritorious Svc. award, 1960, Disting. Svc. award GSA, 1965. Mem. Sigma Chi. Home: Gloucester Va. Died Mar. 5, 1990.

HARLAN, W. GLEN, lawyer; b. Stuart, Iowa, Oct. 14, 1912; s. Wilber George and Lillian (Russell) H.; m. Esther Wadleigh, Mar. 15, 1941; children: Michael Glen (dec.), Esther Elizabeth (Mrs. Richard Greb). A.B., Simpson Coll., 1936; J.D., State U. Iowa, 1939. Bar: Iowa 1939, Ga. 1942, N.Y. 1961. Law clk. to Wiley Rutledge, assoc. justice U.S. Ct. Appeals D.C., 1939-41; assoc. Gambrell & White, Atlanta, 1941-47; partner Gambrell, Harlan, Russell & Moye (and predecessors), 1948-67; v.p. legal affairs Eastern Air Lines, Inc., 1967-69, sr. v.p. legal affairs, 1969-77, mem. exec. com., dir., 1972-77; ptnr. firm Gambrell, Russell & Mobley (and predecessors), Atlanta, 1978-81; of counsel Smith, Gambrell & Russell (and predecessors), Atlanta, 1981-90. Former trustee Simpson Coll. Mem. ABA (ho. of dels. 1956-58), Fed. Bar Assn., Atlanta Bar Assn., N.Y. State Bar Assn., N.Y.C. Bar Assn., State Bar Ga., Am. Judicature Soc., Lawyers Club, Internat. Air Transport Assn. (chmn. legal com. 1975-76), Air Transport Assn. (chmn. law council 1976-77), Am. Cancer Soc., Legal Aid Soc., Newcomen Soc. N.Am., Order of Coif, Pi Kappa Delta, Phi Alpha Theta. Methodist. Clubs: Waukewan Golf (Meredith, N.H.). Home: Meredith N.H. Died Feb. 27, 1990; buried Meredith, N.H.

HARLOR, JOHN CLAYTON, lawyer; b. Worthington, Ohio, Aug. 27, 1898; s. John David and Alice (McLeod) H.; m. Inez J. Turner, Sept. 24, 1930; children: John T., Douglas M. AB, Ohio State U., 1920, LLB, 1922. Bar: Ohio 1922. Mem. firm Wright, Harlor, Purpus, Morris & Arnold, from 1926. Mem. city coun., Bexley, Ohio, 1936-56, pres. coun., 1953-56; chmn. adv. bd. Ohio State U. Alumni Assn. Mem. ABA, Ohio Bar Assn., Columbus Bar Assn. (past pres.), Am. Judicature Soc., Chi Phi, Phi Delta Phi, Clubs: Kit Kat, Wheaton (pres.), Univ., Rocky Fork Hunt and Country (past pres.), Rocky Fork Beagle (Columbus). *

HARMAN, AVRAHAM, university chancellor, diplomat; b. London, 1914; B.A., Oxford U., 1936; married; 3 children. With Zionist Fedn. S. Africa, 1939-40, Jewish Info. Dept. Agy., 1940-48; dep. dir. Israel Govt. Press Office, 1948-49; consul gen., Montreal, P.Q., 1949-50; dir. Israel Office Info., counselor Israel Del. UN, 1950-53; consul gen., N.Y.C., 1953-55; asst. dir. gen. Ministry Fgn. Affairs, Jerusalem, 1955-56; ambassador to U.S., 1959-68; pres. Hebrew U., Jerusalem, 1968-83, chancellor, 1983-92; mem. exec. Jewish Agy., 1956-59. Died Feb. 23, 1992. Home: Jerusalem Israel

HARMON, DANIEL L(EWIS), physics educator; b. Milltown, Pa., Aug. 6, 1895; s. John W. and Louisa (Esenwine) H.; m. Mary Malloy, Jan. 23, 1922; children: Mary Ellen, John Daniel (dec.), Anne Therese, David Patrick, Frances Jane, James Malloy, Josephine Cecilia. BS, Pa. State Coll., 1921, MS, 1923; PhD, Ind. U., 1933. Asst. in physics Pa. State Coll., 1919-21, instr. physics, 1921-23; prof. physics, chmn. maths. and sci. St. Mary-of-the-Woods Coll., 1923-43; prof. physics and dept. dir. U. Detroit, from 1943; spl. instr. radio, indsl. electronics, applied physics, Engring. Sci. Mgmt. War Tng. Program, U. Detroit, 1942-43; cons. With U.S. Army, 1917-19, lt. USAR, 1923-36. Mem. Am. Assn. Physics Tchrs., Am. Phys. Soc., Phys. Soc. Japan, Ind. Acad. Sci., Detroit Physics Club, Terre Haute (Ind.), Literary Club, Acoustical Soc. Am., Optical Soc. Am. (sec. Detroit sect.), Am. Legion, Sigma Xi, Alpha Phi Omega, Alpha Epsilon Delta, Phi Kappa Phi, Theta Kappa Phi (co-founder, 1st nat treas.), K.C. Roman Catholic. *

HARNISH, JAY DEWEY, architect; b. Lancaster, Pa., May 21, 1898; s. Jacob Martin and Emma (Herr) H.; m. Jerene C. Reaver, Feb. 1, 1938 (dec. July 1980). B.Arch., U. Calif. at Berkeley, 1924. With art dept. MGM, 1936-37; pvt. practice Ontario, Calif., 1940-60; pres. firm Harnish, Morgan & Causey, architects (name now HMC Architects, Inc.), Ontario, 1960-77, chmn. bd., 1977-87, cons., 1984-87; sec., dir. Ontario Savs. & Loan Assn., from 1960; Mem. Calif. Bd. Archtl. Examiners, 1962-70, pres., 1964. Projects include San Antonio Community Hosp, Upland (recipient Hosp. of Month award Modern Hosp. 1966), HMC Bldg, Ontario (award for creative use concrete Portland Cement Assn. 1969), Ontario High Sch, (Merit award A.I.A. 1969), Lockheed Engring. Bldg, Ontario (Merit award A.I.A. 1970), Ontario Internat. Airport. Served with C.E. U.S. Army, 1916-17. Fellow AIA. Club: Red Hill Country (Cugamonga, Calif.). Home: Rancho Cucamonga Calif. Died July 6, 1991; buried Bellevue Cemetery, Ontario, Calif.

HARPER, JENE, oil producer, oil equipment supply company executive; b. Sapulpa, Okla., Dec. 27, 1910; s. Jacob P. and Myrtle (Ham) H.; m. June Aleff, Apr. 16, 1955; children: Paul, Ronald, Teresa, Debra. Student, U. Nev., 1929-30. Purchasing agt. Roosevelt Oil Co., Mt. Pleasant, Mich., 1933; founder, pres. Franklin Supply Co., Chgo. and Denver, 1933-74; chmn. bd. Franklin Supply Co., 1962-74; pres., dir. Lark Oil Co., Denver, Harper Internat. Ltd., Denver; asst. regional adminstr. Region 6 support services Emergency Petroleum and Gas Adminstrn., Washington, from 1966; dir. Colo. Nat. Bank Denver), Red Top Valley Ditch Co., Granby, Colo., Mountain States Pipe & Supply Co., Colorado Springs, Colo., Mannesman-Export/Franklin Supply, London, Eng.; past pres., dir. Franklin Pipe & Supply. Bd. dirs. Nat. Western Stock Show, Denver, U. Colo. Found., Orme Sch., Mayer, Ariz.; past pres. bd. trustees Graland Country Day Sch. Mem. Rocky Mountain Oil and Gas Assn. (dir. from 1968), Petroleum Equipment Suppliers Assn. (dir. 1933-62), Ind. Petroleum Assn. Am. (dir. from 1965). Clubs: Denver (Denver) (past dir.), Flatirons (Denver) (dir.), Denver Country (Denver), Cherry Hills Country (Denver) (past dir., treas.); Chicago, Chicago Oil Men's; Castle Pines Golf (Castle Rock, Colo.). Home: Denver Colo. Died Apr. 26, 1990; buried Fairmont Cemetery.

HARPER, MARION, JR., advertising executive; b. Oklahoma City, May 14, 1916; s. Marion and Lotus Alexander H.; m. Virginia Epes, Apr. 4, 1942; children: Stephen Henry, Chilton Epes, Francis Marion, Reid M.; m. Valerie Feit, Nov. 8, 1963; 1 child, Victoria. AB, Yale U., 1938. Trainee McCann-Erickson, Inc., 1939, mgr. copy rsch., 1942-44, assoc. dir. rsch., 1944-45, v.p. in charge rsch. and merchandising, 1945-48, dir., 1946-89, asst. to pres., 1947-48, pres., 1948-69, chmn. bd., 1958-69; chmn. bd., pres. Interpublic Group of Cos., 1961-68; chmn. exec. com. Interpublic, Inc., 1968-71. Author: Getting Results from Advertising, 1948; contbg. author Public Relations Handbook, 1950; contbr. articles on radio-TV, copy rsch. to publs. Mem. alumni coun. Phillips Acad., Andover, Mass. Decorated Cruzeiro do Sul, 1955; recipient Disting. Svc. award Young Men's Bd. Trade Inc., Parlin Meml. award. Mem. Nat. Distbn. Coun., Nat. Outdoor Advt. Bur. dir. , Am. Assn. Advt. Agys. chmn. bd. 1961-62 , Lotos Club, Met. Club, Yale Club, Pinnacle Club N.Y.C. , Ardsley Country Club. Home: Oklahoma City Okla. Died Oct. 25, 1989.

HARPER, THOMAS, lawyer; b. Greenwood, Ark., Nov. 23, 1908; s. Robert Atlas and Merton (Othella) H.; m. Vivien W. Tatum, Jan. 16, 1939 (dec.); children: Thomas, Granville T., Blake, Kay Nelson. Student, U. Ill., 1927-28. Bar: Ark. 1930. Pvt. practice Greenwood, 1930-39, Ft. Smith, Ark., 1939-67; sr. ptnr. Harper, Young, Smith & Maurrar, Ft. Smith, from 1967; spl. assoc. justice Ark. Supreme Ct., 1975; mem. Ark. Statute Revision Commn., 1975-83. Chmn. Dem. Nat. Com. for Ark., 1954-64, mem., 1964-72; del. Dem. Nat. Conv., 1956, 60, 64, 68, chmn. del., 1960, 64. Served to lt. (j.g.) USNR, 1944-46. Mem. Am. Coll. Trial Lawyers, ABA, Ark., Sebastian County bar assns., Ft. Smith C. of C., Delta Upsilon, Phi Eta Sigma. Methodist. Clubs: Ft. Smith Town. Home: Fort Smith Ark. Died Mar. 7, 1989.

HARPER, WILLIAM TAYLOR, business executive; b. Balt., Jan. 31, 1893; s. William J. and Margaret V. (Taylor) H.; m. Grace E. Buchheimer, June 23, 1917; children: Margaret Powers, Mary Elizabeth Porth, William T., Carolyn G. Proom. Student, Baltimore City Coll., 1907-11. Underwriter Md. Casualty Co., Balt., 1911-34, agy. dir., 1934-35, v.p., 1935-44, dir., from 1943, sr. v.p., 1944-47, pres., 1947-61, chmn. bd., from 1954; dir. Md. Nat. Bank. Mem. Balt. Assn. Commerce, Md. Hist. Soc., Clubs: Maryland, Casualty and Surety, Baltimore Country (Balt.). Democrat. Episcopalian. *

HARRELL, CHARLES ADAIR, educator; b. Madison, Va., Aug. 1, 1893; s. Emett Eugene and Laura Burrows (Lewis) H.; m. Dorothy Marie Buckley, Apr. 7, 1928; 1 child, Elbrey Adair. AB, Randolph Macon Coll., 1914, LLD (hon.); MA, Columbia U., 1920; CE, U. Cin., 1924, LLD (hon.), 1963; MS in Pub. Adminstrn., Syracuse U., 1927. Exec. asst. to city mgr. Cin., 1928-29; city mgr. Portsmouth, Ohio, 1930-31, Binghamton, N.Y., 1932-37, Schenectady, N.Y., 1937-46, Norfolk, Va., 1946-51, San Antonio, 1952-53, Cin., 1954; vis. prof. of pub. adminstrn. U. Cin.; chmn. dept. indsl. econs. Southwest Rsch. Inst., 1953-54; engaged in ednl. admnstrn. C. of C. work govtl. rsch. and city planning, to 1928. Author papers and tracts. Del. Inter-Am. Congress of Municipalities, Cuba, 1938, Panama, 1956; cons. Nat. Def. Commn., 1941, W.P.B., 1942; in charge of courses in state and local govt. Union Coll., 1942-43, lectr. math., 1943-44; pres. Better Housing League of Cin., 1964-65. Pvt. WWI. Mem. Internat. City Mgrs. Assn. (past pres.), Am. Soc. C.E., Am. Soc. Planning Ofcls. Nat. Municipal League, Am. Soc. for Pub. Adminstrn. (mem. coun.), Govt. Rsch., Assn. Am. Acad. Polit. and Soc. Sci., Cin. Assn., Lambda Chi Alpha, Tau Beta Pi, Omicron Delta Kappa, Chi Epsilon, Phi Delta Epsilon, Tau Kappa Alpha, Mason. Episcopalian. *

HARRINGTON, BOB (ROBERT WILLIAM HARRINGTON), critic, social worker; b. Richmond Hill, N.Y., Oct. 2, 1950; s. Jean Alexander and Josephine (Borruso) H. BA, SUNY, Oneonta, 1972. Sr. caseworker Nassau County Dept. Soc. Services, Mineola, N.Y., 1977-85; probation officer Nassau County Dept. Probation, Mineola, 1985-92; theater and cabaret critic, theater editor L.I. and N.Y. Nightlife mags., Deer Park, N.Y., 1981-91; cabaret and music critic Back Stage, N.Y.C., 1984-92; cabaret and theater critic New York Post, N.Y.C., 1986-92. Columnist Agt. & Mgr. Mag., N.Y.C., 1991-92. Recipient Am. Legion Citizenship award Am. Legion, Oneonta, 1972. Mem. Manhattan Assn. of Cabaret (v.p. 1985-92, Spl. Outstanding Contbns. award, 1986), Outer Critics Circle (bd. dirs. 1984-92), Soc. of Singers (bd. dirs. 1987-91), Drama Desk, Am. Theater Wing Tony Voter, Hearts and Voices (adv. bd. 1992). Roman Catholic. Home: East Meadow N.Y. Died Oct. 19, 1992. †

HARRINGTON, MARION THOMAS, university administrator; b. Plano, Tex., Sept. 8, 1901; s. Edwin O. and Nannie Belle (Coleman) H.; m. Ruth NOrris, Feb. 4, 1933; 1 son, John N. BS, Tex. A&M Coll., 1922, MS, 1927; PhD, Iowa State Coll., 1941. Chemist Tex. Co., Port Arthur, 1922-23, Lone Star Gas Co., Petrolia, Tex., 1924; from instr. chemistry to prof. Tex. A&M Coll., 1924-49, asst. to dean, 1946, dean sch. arts and scis., 1947-49, dean coll., 1949, pres., 1950-53, chancellor coll. system, 1953-57; from pres. to chancellor Tex. A&M Univ. System, 1957-66, coord. programs office internat. programs, 1965-90. Mem. Am. Chem. Soc., Sigma Xi, Tau Beta Pi, Phi Kappa Phi, Phi Lambda Upsilon, Phi Eta Sigma. Home: Bryan Tex. Died May 14, 1990.

HARRINGTON, MICHAEL, author; b. St. Louis, Feb. 24, 1928; s. Edward Michael and Catherine (Fitzgibbon) H.; m. Stephanie Gervis, May 30, 1963. B.A., Holy Cross Coll., 1947; postgrad., Yale Law Sch., 1947-48; M.A., U. Chgo., 1949; D.H.L., Bard Coll., 1966. Asso. editor Catholic Worker, 1951-52; orgn. sec. Workers Def. League, 1953; cons. Fund for Republic, 1954-89; editor New Am., 1961-62; organizer March on Convs. Movement, 1960; prof. polit. sci. Queens Coll., City U. N.Y., 1972-89. Author: The Other America, 1963, The Retail Clerks, 1963, The Accidental Century, 1965, Toward a Democratic Left, 1968, Socialism, 1972, Fragments of The Century, 1974, Twilight of Capitalism, 1976, The Vast Majority: A Journey to the World's Poor, 1977, Decade of Decision: The Crisis of the American System, 1980, The Next America: The Decline and Rise of the U.S, 1981, The Politics at God's Funeral, 1983, The New American Poverty, 1984, Taking Sides: The Education of a Militant Mind, 1985, The Next Left, 1987, The Long Distance Runner, 1988, Socialism: Past and Future, 1989; editor: (with Paul Jacobs) Labor in a Free Society, 1959; Newsletter Democratic Left, 1973-89; mem. editorial bd. jour.: Dissent. Mem. nat. exec. com. Socialist Party, 1960-72, nat. chmn., 1968-72; chmn. organizing com. Dem. Socialists Am., 1973-82, co-chmn. of orgn., 1982-89; bd. dirs. Workers Def. League, ACLU. Recipient George Polk award, 1963, Sidney Hillman award, 1963, Riordan award D.C. Newspaper Guild, 1964; Eugene V. Debs award Eugene V. Debs Found., 1973. Home: New York N.Y. Died July 31, 1989. †

HARRIS, CHARLES OVERTON, engineering educator; b. Altamont, Ill., June 22, 1909; s. William and Laura Ann (Parks) H.; m. Mary Louise Henebry, Dec. 26, 1934; children: Judith Anne, William Overton, Carolyn Louise, Susan Ruth. Student, James Millikin U., 1926-28; SB, U. Ill., 1930, MS, 1932; DSc, U. Mich., 1941. Rsch. asst. U. Ill., 1930-32; instr., then prof. Ill. Inst. Tech., 1934-46; prof. engring. mechanics, head dept. U. Notre Dame, 1946-49; head dept. civil engring. Mich. State U., 1949-51, head dept. applied mechanics, 1951-62; dir. faculty devel. Gen. Motors Inst., Flint,

Mich., 1962-74. Author: Slide Rule Simplified, 1943, Elementary Engineering Mechanics, 1947, Strength of Materials, 1949, Introduction to Structural Design, 1951, Introduction to Stress Analysis, 1959; also tech. papers. Mem. Sigma Alpha Epsilon, Triangle, Sigma Xi, Tau Beta Pi, Sigma Tau, Pi Tau Sigma, Chi Epsilon, Tau Omega. Home: Gettysburg Pa. Died Mar. 3, 1990.

HARRIS, HAROLD ROSS, aviation executive; b. Chgo., Dec. 20, 1895; s. Ross Allen and Mae E. (Plumb) H.; m. Grace Clark, July 14, 1917; children: Harold Ross, Alta Mae. BS in Mech. Engring., Calif. Inst. Tech. Officer U.S. Army, 1917-26; chief of flight sect. U.S. Army Air Corps, 1920-25; pioneer in use of parachute after airplane collapse, 1922; v.p., gen. mgr. Huff-Daland Dusters, 1926-28, Peruvian Airways Corp., 1928-30; v.p., ops. mgr. Pan Am. Grace Airways, 1929-42; mil. svc., 1942-46; v.p., gen. mgr. Am. Overseas Airlines, 1945-50; v.p. Atlantic div. Pa Am. World Airways, 1950-52; pres., CEO Northwest Airlines, Inc., 1953-54; pres. Aviation Fin. Svcs. Inc., N.Y.C., from 1954; dir. Overseas Securities Co., Inc.; chmn. bd. Flight Safety Found. Brig. gen. U.S. Army, chief of staff, Air Transport Command, Washington, D.C. Decorated Disting. Svc. medal, Legion of Merit, Air medal (U.S.), Commander British Empire, Corona di Italia, Fatiche de Guerra (Italy), Abdon Calderon (Ecuador), Orden del Sol (Peru). Fellow Inst. Aero. Sci. (awarded 13 world flying records by 1926); mem. Soc. Automotive Engrs., Am. Legion, Clubs: Country (New Canaan), Wings (pres. 1958-59), University, Sky, India House (N.Y.C.). *

HARRIS, JESSE GRAHAM, JR., psychologist, educator; b. Jacksonville, Fla., Jan. 5, 1926; s. Jesse Graham and Mona (Woods) H.; m. Julia Patricia McNamee, Sept. 5, 1953; children: Julia Kathleen, Cecilia Anne. B.A., Harvard U., 1946; Ph.D., Duke U., 1955. Diplomate: Am. Bd. Examiners Profl. Psychology. Asst. prof. psychology U. Conn., 1958-60; assoc. prof., dir. psychology, dept. psychiatry U. Ky. Med. Center, 1960-63; prof. psychology U. Ky., 1963-88, chmn. dept., 1963-67, 80-88, dir. clin. tng., 1963-67, 69-75, chmn. faculty council Coll. Arts and Scis., 1978-79; vis. lectr. U. Hawaii, 1968; cons. USPHS Hosp., Lexington, 1961-72, VA hosps. in Ky., 1962—, Peace Corps, 1968-75; field selection officer, 1968-70, tng. devel. officer, 1970, cons. in research and placement, 1970-75; chmn. Ky. Mental Health Manpower Commn., 1971-74; mem. Council of Grad. Depts. Psychology, 1981-88, Ky. Bd. Examiners of Psychologists, 1966-75, chmn. bd., 1970-75; chmn. adv. tng. council for psychology for Midwestern region VA, 1972. Adv. editor: Jour. Cons. and Clin. Psychology, 1970-88; contbr. articles to profl. jours., chpts. to books. Bd. dirs., v.p., mem. artists com. Central Ky. Concert and Lecture Series, 1960-80; chmn. bd. dirs. Ky. Manpower Devel., Inc., 1974-78; leader forum, 1976; elder 2d Presbyn. Ch., Lexington. Served to lt. USNR, 1955-58; capt. Res. Ret. Sr. fellow Culture Learning Inst. East-West Center, Honolulu, 1975. Fellow Am. Psychol. Assn.; mem. Southeastern Psychol. Assn., Ky. Psychol. Assn. (pres. 1979-80, disting. service award 1983), Central Ky. Psychol. Assn. (pres. 1962), Western Fla. Psychol. Assn. (pres. 1957), Midwestern Psychol. Assn., Phi Beta Kappa (pres. U. Ky. chpt. 1972-73), Sigma Xi. Home: Lexington Ky. Died Nov. 22, 1988; buried Arlington Nat. Cemetery.

HARRIS, LEONARD RICHARD, publishing company executive; b. N.Y.C., Oct. 16, 1922; m. Barbara Fox, 1949; 1 child, Elizabeth V.A. Brown. Student, NYU, 1939-42; BA, McGill U., 1947. Dir. promotion, mem. editorial bd. Prentice Hall Inc.; dir. new products Bantam Books; officer Book Club Guild and Channel Press Inc.; cons. new pub. projects N.Y. Times; v.p. editorial and corp. devel. Ency. Britannica, Chgo., 1967-69; exec. v.p., pub. World Pub. Co., 1969-73; dir. projects and subs. N.Y. Times, 1973-77, dir. corp. devel., 1977-80, dir. corp. relations and pub. affairs, 1980-88, cons., from 1988; cons. John Wiley & Sons, N.Y.C. Contbr. to Ency. Britannica, numerous mags. Bd. dirs. City Ctr., 55th St. Dance Found., Mayor's Midtown Citizen's Com., N.Y. Newspapers Found.; pres., bd. dirs. Jesse Owens Found; vice chmn. Partnership for Homeless. Served as sgt. AUS, 1943-46. Democrat. Clubs: Lotos, Players. Home: New York N.Y. Died July 9, 1991.

HARRIS, MILTON, chemist; b. Los Angeles, Mar. 21, 1906; s. Louis and Naomi (Granish) H.; m. Carolyn Wolf, Mar. 30, 1934; children: Barney Dreyfuss (adopted), John. B.Sc., Oreg. State Coll., 1926; Ph.D., Yale U., 1929; Dr. Textile Sci., Phila. Textile Inst., 1955. Indsl. research on silk Cheney Bros., 1929-31; research assoc. Am. Assn. Textile Chemists and Colorists, Nat. Bur. Standards, 1931-39; dir. research Textile Found., 1939-45; pres. and founder Harris Research Labs., 1945-61; dir. research Gillette Co. (its subsidiaries), 1956-66, v.p. corp., 1957-66; dir., chmn. exec. com. Sealectro Corp., 1966-83; adv. bd. Jour. Polymer Sci.; asso. editor Textile Research Jour.; cons. Exec. Office of Pres., Office Sci. and Technology, 1962-65; Adv. bd., cons. O.Q.M.G., World War II; chmn. com. on textiles and cordage, tropical deterioration project Nat. Def. Research Com.; sec. com. on clothing NRC, World War II; chmn. Wool Conservation Bd., World War II; mem. panel on clothing Research and Devel. Bd., World War II; mem. Yale Council, 1964-69, Yale Devel. Bd., 1964-67; exec. bd. Yale Grad. Sch. Assn., from 1965; mem. adv. com. Nat. Bur. Standards, from 1971, chmn. vis. com., from 1973; mem. sub-com. Food and Agrl. Orgn. UN; mem. Utilization R&D adv. com. USDA, 1966; mem. adv. com. planning NSF, from 1968; mem. Pres.'s Sci. Adv. Com. Panel on Environment, 1968-72; observer-cons. Task Group Nat. Systems Sci. and Tech. Information, Fed. Coun. Sci. and Tech., 1968-71. Contbr. articles to tech. jours.; Editor: Chemistry in the U.S. Economy. Recipient award Wash. Acad. Sci., 1943, Olney medal for textile chemistry research, 1945, honor award Am. Inst. Chemists, 1957, Harold DeWitt Smith Meml. medal, 1966, Disting. Svc. award Oreg. State U., 1967, Perkin Medal award Soc. Chem. Industry, 1970, Wilbur Lucius Cross medal Yale U., 1974, award for meritorious service Yale Sci. and Engring. Assn., 1983, Yale U. medal, 1989. Fellow Textile Inst., N.Y. Acad. Sci.; mem. Am. Assn. Textile Tech., Yale Chemists Assn. (past pres.), Am. Soc. Biol. Chemists, Nat. Acad. Engring., Am. Inst. Chemists (pres. 1960-61 Gold medal), N.A.M., Textile Research Inst., Am. Assn. Textile Colorists and Chemists, Am. Oil Chemists Soc., Soc. Cosmetic Chemists, Fiber Soc. (hon.), Am. Chem. Soc. (chmn. bd. dirs. 1966-70, dir.-at-large, treas. from 1973, Priestley medal, 1980), AAAS (editorial bd. publ. Sci. 1968-70), Soc. Chem. Industry, Wash. Acad. Sci., Sigma Xi, Tau Beta Pi, Phi Lambda Upsilon, Phi Kappa Phi, Gamma Alpha. Clubs: Cosmos (Washington); Chemists (N.Y.C.). Home: Chevy Chase Md. Died Sept. 12, 1991; cremated.

HARRIS, MORGAN HOVEY, JR., executive recruiting consultant; b. Cambridge, Mass., Dec. 8, 1932; s. Morgan Hovey and Gladys N. (Nordstrom) H.; B.A., Yale, 1954; m. Elizabeth Colgate Cowles, June 21, 1962; children: Elizabeth Colgate, Jennifer Hovey, Stephanie Morgan. With White Weld & Co. Investment Bankers, N.Y.C., 1957-63; with White Weld & Co., Los Angeles, 1963-71, v.p., 1965-71, gen. partner in charge So. Calif. region, 1968-71; pres. William O'Neil & Co., Securities, Los Angeles, 1971-72; pres. Seidler, Arnett, Spillane & Harris, Los Angeles, 1972-74; sr. v.p., mgr. Los Angeles office Russell Reynolds Assos., 1974-80; sr. partner, mem. exec. com. Korn/Ferry Internat., 1980-84, mng. ptnr., 1984-90. Pres., Internat. Student Center, Los Angeles, 1968-72, chmn., 1973-75; mem. St. Matthews Parish Sch. Bd., 1970-71; trustee St. John's Hosp., 1970—, treas., 1977, v.p., sec. 1978; regional chmn. Yale Alumni Fund, 1964-70, bd. dirs., 1969-92. Mem. Calif. del. Democratic Nat. Conv., 1968; statewide finance chmn. Jess Unruh for Gov., 1970; div. chmn. United Way, Los Angeles, 1977-78; chmn. bd. trustees Loyola-Marymont U., Los Angeles, 1974-78; trustee John Thomas Dye Sch., Los Angeles, 1975-78, Brooks Sch., North Andover, Mass., 1969-78; trustee Calif. Mus. Found., 1983-92, vice-chmn. nominating com. 1985, treas., 1984, pres. 1986-88, chmn. 1989-90. Served with AUS, 1954-56. Mem. Calif. Exec. Recruiters Assn. (founding pres. 1980), Spring St. Forum of Los Angeles (pres. 1972). Clubs: Los Angeles Country, Calif. (Los Angeles), Regency; Links (N.Y.C.); Beach (Santa Monica, Calif.). Died Dec. 8, 1992. Home: Pacific Palisades Calif. †

HARRIS, S. HERSCHEL, business executive; b. Carroll, Ga., 1898. Grad., Ga. Inst. Tech., 1921. Chmn., dir. Standard-Coosa-Thatcher Co., Chattanooga. *

HARRIS, THOMAS CUNNINGHAM, editor; b. Parrott, Va., July 28, 1908; s. Thomas Cunningham and Wilhelmina Cassie H.; m. Patricia Brock, May 19, 1929; children: Margaret Virginia and Shirley Patricia Burgin twins , Sharon Anita. Grad. high sch. Reporter Times Pub. Co., St. Petersburg, Fla., 1923-26, city editor, 1927-30, mng. editor, 1931-41, exec. editor, 1941-62, gen. mgr., exec. v.p., 1962-67, assoc. editor, 1967-68; exec. editor El Mundo Spanish lang. newspaper , San Juan, P.R., 1968-75. Dir. Com. 100, Pinellas County, Fla., 1965-67. Mem. Inter Am. Press Assn. dir. 1961-7, chmn. com. freedom of press 1967-7 , AP Mng. Editors Assn. Fla. past pres. , Nat. Press Club, St. Petersburg C. of C. v.p. 1965 , St. Petersburg Yacht Club, Bankers Club San Juan , Sigma Delta Chi. Home: Saint Petersburg Fla. Deceased.

HARRISON, GREGORY ALEXANDER, lawyer; b. San Francisco, Sept. 9, 1896; s. Edward Charles and Mary Gertrude (Bodkin) H.; m. Barbara Beardsley, Sept. 9, 1924; children: Gregory Alexander, Patricia H. Brown, Michael B., Elisabeth R., Barbara Ann. BS, U. Calif., 1917; LLB, Hastings Coll. Law, 1921. Bar: Calif. 1920. Ptnr. Brobeck, Phleger & Harrison, from 1931; dir. Pacific Power & Light Co. Trustee War Meml. of San Francisco, Calif. Acad. Scis. Mem. Am. Coll. Trial Lawyers. *

HARRISON, HAROLD EDWARD, physician; b. New Haven, Conn., July 23, 1908; s. Abraham and Rose (Chaikind) H.; m. Helen Miriam Coplan, Aug. 2, 1936; children: Stephen Coplan, Richard Gerald. BS, Yale U., 1928, MD, 1931. Intern, resident in pediatrics New Haven Hosp., 1931-35; instr. pediatrics Yale Sch. Medicine, 1935-38, asst. prof. pathology, 1942-45; asst. prof. pediatrics Med. Coll. Cornell U., 1938-42; investigator com. war gas casualties OSRD, 1942-45; pediatrician-in-chief Balt. City Hosps., 1945-75; assoc. prof. pediatrics Sch. Medicine Johns Hopkins, Balt., 1945-65, prof., 1965; mem. food and nutrition bd. Nat. Acad. Sci., NRC. Mem. editorial bd. Clin. Pediatrics, 1962-89; contbr. articles to profl. jours. Recipient (with Helen C. Harrison) E. Mead Johnson award for rsch. in pediatrics, 1941, Borden award Am. Acad. Pediatrics, 1960. Mem. Soc. for Pediatric Rsch. (past pres.), Am. Pediatric Soc. (v.p. 1973-74), Soc. Clin. Investigation, Endocrine Soc., Am. Inst. Nutrition, Sigma Xi, Alpha Omega Alpha. Home: Baltimore Md. Died Oct. 2, 1989.

HARRISON, REX CAREY, actor; b. Huyton, Eng., Mar. 5, 1908; s. William Reginald and Edith (Carey) H.; m. Marjorie Noel Collette Thomas, 1934; 1 child, Noel; m. Lilli Palmer, 1943 (div. 1957); 1 child, Carey; m. Kay Kendall, 1957 (dec. Dec. 1959); m. Rachel Roberts, 1962 (div. 1971); m. Elizabeth Rees Harris (div. 1976); m. Mercia Mildred Tinker, 1978. Ed., Liverpool Coll.; hon. degree, Boston U. Author: Rex, 1974; If Love Be Love; Stage debut, Liverpool (Eng.) Repertory Theatre, 1924, with theatre, 1924-27; played Jack on tour with Charley's Aunt, 1927; London stage debut as Rankin in The Ninth Man, Prince of Wales Theatre, 1931; N.Y.C. stage debut as Tubbs Barrow in Sweet Aloes, Booth Theatre, 1936; appeared in French Without Tears, at Criterion, 1936-38; in Design For Living and No Time for Comedy, Haymarket Theatre, 1939-41, Anne of the Thousand Days, Schubert Theatre, N.Y.C., 1948-49 (Antoinette Perry award for best actor), The Cocktail Party, New Theatre, London, 1950, Venus Observed, Century Theatre, N.Y.C., 1952; as Henry Higgins in My Fair Lady, Mark Hellinger Theatre, N.Y.C., 1956-57 (Antoinette Perry award for best actor), and at Drury Ln. London, 1958-59; in touring co., 1981; in The Fighting Cock, Anta Theatre, N.Y.C., 1959 Platonov, Royal Ct., 1960 (Evening Standard award for best actor), August for the People, Edinburgh (Scotland) Festival, 1961 and Royal Ct. Theatre in the Lionele Touch, Lyric, 1969, Henry IV, Her Majesty's, 1974; in Perrichon's Travels, Chichester, 1976; Caesar and Cleopatro, N.Y.C., 1977, and others; played in and produced Bell, Book and Candle, Ethel Barrymore Theatre, N.Y.C., 1951, and Phoenix Theatre, London, 1954, Aren't We All, 1985; dir. and appeared in Love of Four Colonels, Schubert Theatre, N.Y.C., 1953; producer: Nina, Haymarket Theatre, London, 1955; appeared in films including Storm in a Teacup, 1936, St. Martin's Lane, 1937, Over the Moon, 1938, Night Train to Munich, Major Barbara, 1940-41, Blithe Spirit, 1944, Anna and the King of Siam, 1946, The Ghost and Mrs. Muir, 1947, The Foxes of Harrow, 1947, Escape, 1948, Unfaithfully Yours, 1948, The Long Dark Hall, 1951, King Richard and the Crusaders, 1954, The Constant Husband, 1955, The Reluctant Debutant, 1958, Midnight Lace, 1960, The Happy Thieves, 1961, Cleopatra (as Julius Caesar), 1962, My Fair Lady, 1964 (Acad. award as best actor), The Yellow Rolls Royce, 1965, The Agony and the Ecstasy, 1965, The Honey Pot, 1967, Doctor Doolittle, 1967, A Flea in her Ear, 1967, Staircase, 1968, The Prince and the Pauper, 1976, Man in the Iron Mask, 1977, Devils Disciple, Ashanti, 1978; TV appearance: Don Quixote, 1972, The Kingfisher, 1982, Heartbreak House, 1984, Aren't We All?, The Admirable Chrichton, miniseries Anastasia: The Mystery of Anna, 1986. Served with RAF Vol. Res., 1941-45. Decorated Knight of Brit. Empire, 1989, Order of Merit, Italy; recipient Golden Globe award, Film Critics award, Antointette Perry award for David di Do'onattella award, Triumph award, Paris, 1957. Clubs: Players; Garrick, Beefstead, Green Room (London); Travelors (Paris). Home: New York N.Y. Died June 2, 1990.

HARRISON, THOMAS GALBRAITH, grocery executive; b. Mpls., July 8, 1895; s. Perry and Miriam (Thomas) H.; m. Gladys Baldwin, June 23, 1920; children: Edith Herman, Thomas G., Miriam R. Sigrist. Student, Hotchkiss Prep. Sch., 1911-12, Blake Sch., Mpls., 1913-14. With Winston, Harper, Fisher Co. now Super Valu Stores, Inc., Mpls., from 1919, successively asst. sales mgr., asst. treas., exec. v.p., 1919-44, pres., 1944-58, chmn. bd., chmn. exec. com., from 1958; dir. No. States Power Co., Mpls., Fed. Res. Bank, 9th Dist. Mpls., Green Giant Co., Le Sueur, Minn. Capt. U.S. Army, 1918. *

HARRISON, WILLIAM HENRY, former congressman; b. Terre Haute, Ind., Aug. 10, 1896; s. Russell Benjamin and Mary A. (Saunders) H.; m. Mary E. Newton,, Oct. 19, 1920; children: Mary Elizabeth, William Henry Jr. Student, U. Nebr.; LLD (hon.), Vincennes U. Bar: Ind. 1925, Wyo. 1937. Pvt. practice, Indpls., Sheridan, Wyo.; mem.-at-large 82d-83d, 87th-88th and 90th congresses from Wyo., Washington. Mem. Ind. Ho. of Reps., 1927, Wyo. Ho. of Reps., 1945-51; mem. Renegotiation Bd., 1969-70; county chmn. Wyo. Rep. Com., 1948-50, state committeeman, 1946-48. Mem. U.S. Jaycees (past exec. v.p.), Sheridan C. of C. (past pres.), VFW, Am. Legion, Masons (33d degree), Shriners, Rotary, Sigma Delta Kapa, Sigma Chi. Home: Sheridan Wyo. Died Oct. 8, 1990; buried Sheridan, Wyo.

HART, FRANCIS J(OSEPH), lawyer, telephone company executive; b. Saxon, Wis., Aug. 26, 1898; s. Michael J. and Bridget (Lane) H.; m. Claire Ryan, July 22, 1933; children: Ellen, Mary, Susan, Michael. BS cum laude, Marquette U., 1924, JD, 1927. Bar: Wis.

1927. Mem. firm Wolfe & Hart, 1927-41; v.p., gen. counsel Wis. Telephone Co., from 1947. Bd. dirs., exec. com. St. Rosa's Orphan Soc. Mem. ABA, Wis. Bar Assn., Milwaukee County Bar Assn., K.C., Athletic Club, Ozaukee Country Club Madison (Milw.). Roman Catholic. *

HART, HARVEY, motion picture producer, director; b. Toronto, Can., Mar. 19, 1928; s. Benjamin and Anita (Jessel) Applebaum; m. Helena Esther Postell, Oct. 28, 1951 (div. May 1988); children: Patreena Edana Anne, Bethelene Ellen, Mathew David Harris; m. Katherine Ann Downey, June 26, 1988. Student U. Toronto, 1945-48, Dramatic Workshop, N.Y.C., 1949-50. TV producer, dir. CBC, Toronto, 1952-64; freelance motion picture producer and dir., pres. Rohar Productions Ltd., Toronto, 1964-89; co-founder Civic Square Theatre, Toronto, 1962. Theatrical movies include Utilities, The High Country, Shoot, Goldenrod, The Pyx, Fortune and Men's Eyes, The Sweet Ride, Bus Riley's Back in Town; Mini-series for TV include Passion and Paradise, Master of the Game, East of Eden; Pilots for TV films include The Yellow Rose, W.E.B., The Young Lawyers, Judd for the Defense; Specials and movies for TV films include Christine Cromwell, Easy Come, Easy Go, Blood Sport, Stone Fox, Murder Sees the Light, Beverly Hills Madam, Reckless Disregard, Born Beautiful, Murder or Mercy, The Prince of Central Park, Can Ellen Be Saved, Panic on the 5:22, Like Normal People, Captains Courageous, The Aliens, This is Kate Bennett, Street Killing, Standing Tall, The City, four episodes of Alfred Hitchcock Presents, two episodes of The Name of the Game, four episodes of Columbo. Producer, dir. for the Can. Broadcasting Corp.: The Dybbuk, The Crucible, Enemy of the People, The Lark, The Wild Duck, Ondine, Home of the Brave, The Luck of Ginger Coffey, The Blue Hotel, The Gambler, Queen and the Rebels, A Very Close Family, Mrs. Dally Has a Lover and To-Day is Independence Day, Ward Six, Gallows Humour, Roots, David Chapter II, David Chapter III, The Morning After Mr. Roberts, The Quare Fellow, The Police, Eli the Fanatic, Sun in My Eyes, Flipside, The Double Cure, The Littlest of Kings, Panic at Parth Bay, Mr. Arcularis. New York Videotape Production: He Who Gets Slapped. Recipient of Venice Film Festival Award for Fortune and Men's Eyes, Can. Film award for Goldenrod (named Best Dir. of Feature Film), Golden Globe award for East of Eden, Emmy for Columbo-By Dawn's Early Light, Can. Gemini award for Passion and Paradise Best Dir. for drama or mini series. Died Nov. 22, 1989; buried Toronto. Home: Toronto ON, Canada

HART, JAMES DAVID, library director, educator; b. San Francisco, Apr. 18, 1911; s. Julien and Helen Louise (Neustadter) H.; m. Ruth Arnstein, June 14, 1938 (dec. 1977); children: Carol Helen (Mrs. John L. Field), Peter David; m. Constance Crowley Bowles, Feb. 9, 1985. A.B., Stanford U., 1932; M.A., Harvard U., 1933, Ph.D., 1936; L.H.D., Mills Coll., 1978. Mem. faculty to prof. emeritus of English U. Calif.-Berkeley, from 1936, chmn. dept., 1955-57, 65-69, vice chancellor, 1957-60; acting dir. Bancroft Library, 1961-62, dir., 1969-90; vis. prof. Harvard U., 1964; Phi Beta Kappa vis. scholar, 1980-81; chmn. Marshall Scholarship Com. Western U.S., 1959-63, 79-86, adv. coun. Brit. Ambassador, 1986-89. Author: The Oxford Companion Am. Literature, 1941, rev. edits, The Popular Book, 1950, 61, America's Literature, (with C. Gohdes), 1955, American Images of Spanish California, 1960, The Private Press Ventures of Samuel Lloyd Osbourne and R.L.S, 1966, A Companion to California, 1978, rev. edit., 1987; New Englanders in Nova Albion, 1976, Fine Printing: The San Francisco Tradition, 1985; editor: My First Publication, 1961, The Oregon Trail (Francis Parkman), 1963, From Scotland to Silverado (Robert Louis Stevenson), 1966, A Novelist in the Making (Frank Norris), 1970; contbr. articles to mags., revs. Trustee Mills Coll., 1970-78, 79-86, pres. bd., 1973-76; trustee Fine Arts Mus. San Francisco, 1983-90. Decorated comdr. Order Brit. Empire. Fellow Am. Antiquarian Soc., Am. Acad. Arts and Scis., Calif. Hist. Soc.; mem. Modern Lang. Assn., Philol. Assn. Pacific Coast, Book Club of Calif. (pres. 1956-60). Clubs: Bohemian (San Francisco); Grolier (N.Y.C.); Century Assn., Faculty (Berkeley). Home: San Francisco Calif. Died July 23, 1990; buried San Francisco.

HARTER, ROBERT LAWRENCE, investment banker; b. Ogdensburg, N.Y., Aug. 29, 1898; s. Everett Monroe and Kathrine (McDonagh) H.; m. Dorothea Easton, Dec. 26, 1921; children: Roberta Jean Smith, Kimball E., Stanly E., Donn A.; 2d m. Jean Budge, Oct. 11, 1933. Student, Stevens Inst. Tech., 1916-17; BS, U. Calif., 1920. V.p. First Boston Corp., N.Y.C., 1944-49, 54-63; dir. First Boston Corp., 1957-64; gen. ptnr. Sutro & Co., San Francisco, 1949-54; fin. cons. N.Y.C., from 1963. Mem. Sigma Nu, Bohemian Club (San Francisco), Stock Exchange Lunch Club (N.Y.C.). *

HARTLEY, FRED LLOYD, oil company executive; b. Vancouver, B.C., Can., Jan. 16, 1917; came to U.S., 1939, naturalized, 1950; s. John William and Hannah (Mitchell) H.; m. Margaret Alice Murphy, Nov. 2; children: Margaret Ann, Fred Lloyd. BS in Applied Sci., U. B.C., 1939. Engring. supr. Union Oil Co. Calif., 1939-53, mgr. comml. devel., 1953-55, gen. mgr. rsch. dept., 1955-56, v.p. in charge rsch., 1956-60, sr. v.p., 1960-63, exec. v.p., 1963-64, pres., chief exec. officer, 1964-73, chmn. bd. dirs., pres., 1974-85, chief exec. officer, 1985-88, chmn. bd. dirs., 1985-89, chmn. emeritus, 1989-90. Bd. dirs. L.A. Philharm. Assn.; sr. trustee Calif. Inst. Tech.; amb., commr. gen. U.S. exhbn. EXPO 86. Mem. Am. Petroleum Inst. (bd. dirs., former chmn. bd. dirs., hon. dir.). Home: Palos Verdes Estates Calif. Died Oct. 19, 1990; cremated.

HARTMAN, GEORGE EDWARD, marketing scientist, lawyer, educator; b. Newton, Kans., Oct. 20, 1926; s. Albert J. and Ellen (Pawlick) H. B.S., Kans. U., 1950; M.B.A., Ind. U., 1951; Ph.D., U. Ill., 1958; J.D., U. Cin., 1964. Bar: Ohio bar 1964. Instr. in mktg. Tex. A. and M. U., 1951-52; asst. prof. U. N.D., Grand Forks, 1952-55; instr. U. Ill., Urbana, 1955-58; prof. U. Cin., from 1958; pvt. practice law Cin., from 1964; cons. mktg. Contbg. author: Handbook of Modern Marketing, 1970, 86, Business and Its Environment, 1974, Fundamentals of Management Finance, 1981, 84; bd. editors legal devel. sect. Jour. Mktg, 1965-83; columnist Mktg. News, 1965-83. Mem. regional export council Dept. Commerce, 1969-74; mem. bd. mgrs. U. Cin. YMCA; bd. dirs. U. Cin., 1978-80, S.W. Ohio Consumer Assn. Served with Adj.-Gen.'s Office AUS, 1945-46. Mem. World Trade Club (chmn. edn. com. 1974-75), Cin. C. of C., Am. Mktg. Assn., Am., Ohio bar assns., Acad. Internat. Bus., Am. Council Consumer Interests, AAUP, Beta Gamma Sigma, Delta Sigma Pi, Phi Delta Phi, Lambda Chi Alpha. Democrat. Presbyterian. Club: Masons. Home: Cincinnati OH Deceased. †

HARTMAN, GLEN WALTER, radiologist; b. Pepin, Wis., Nov. 14, 1936; s. Walter Edward and Marie Emma (Castleberg) H.; m. Dorothy Fredrickson, June 23, 1957; children: Thomas, Laura, Robert. B.S., U. Wis., Madison, 1958, M.D., 1961. Intern USPHS Hosp., Balt., 1961-62; physician Indian Health Service, USPHS, Browning, Mont., 1962-64; resident in radiology Mayo Grad. Sch. Medicine, Rochester, Minn., 1964-67; hon. clin. fellow X-ray diagnosis Univ. Coll. Hosp., London, 1967-68; cons. diagnostic radiology Mayo Clinic, from 1967; prof. radiology Mayo Med. Sch., from 1981; asso. dir. Sch. Health Related Scis., Mayo Found., 1980-84; pres. Mayo Clinic Staff, 1985; chmn. Mayo Med. Ventures, from 1985. Bd. dirs. Ability Bldg. Center, 1971-81. Recipient Disting. Alumnus award U. Wis.-River Falls, 1983. Mem. Uroradiology Soc. (pres. 1980), Am. Roentgen Ray Soc. (exec. com. from 1979, chmn. adv. com. edn. and research 1979-83, chmn. instrnl. courses 1984-86, sec. from 1986), Am. Coll. Radiology (mem. bd. chancellors 1987-89, chmn. intersoc. commn. 1987-89, pres. Radiology Centennial Inc., from 1988), Radiol. Soc. N.Am., AMA, Minn. Med. Assn., Minn. Radiol. Soc. (pres. 1983), Sigma Xi. Home: Rochester Minn. Deceased. †

HARTSING, RALPH H., SR., advertising executive; b. Waterville, Ohio, Aug. 31, 1896; s. John J. and Lucy (Lincoln) H.; m. Marie Pfelder, Aug. 30, 1919; children: Ralph N. Jr., Rodney K. Student, Tri-State Bus. U., Toledo, Ohio, 1912. With Ann Arbor R.R., Toledo, 1914-16; asst. to dir. traffic Willys-Overland Co., Toledo, Washington, 1916-21; pres. The Caples Co. Adv. Agy., Chgo., 1921-60; exec. v.p. Geyer, Morey & Ballard, Chgo., from 1960. Mem. Chgo. Federated Advt. Club (charter mem.), Chgo. Press Club, Masons, Union League Club, Traffic Club, Execs. Club, Western Advt. Golf Club (Chgo.), Traffic Club (N.Y.C.). *

HARTSTEIN, JACOB I., educator, academic administrator; b. Stary Sambor, Austria, Sept. 10, 1912; came to U.S., 1920, naturalized, 1922; s. Nathan B. and Lea (Harris) H.; m. Florence Waldman, Aug. 16, 1942; children: Kalman, Norman Bernard. Ed., Talmudical Acad.; A.B., Yeshiva Coll., 1932, L.H.D., 1962; M.S., N.Y. City Coll., 1933; M.A., Columbia, 1936; Ph.D., N.Y. U., 1945. Sec. Rabbi Elchanan Theol. Sem. Tchrs. Inst., 1929-37; instr. social scis. Talmudical Acad., 1932-36; acting registrar Yeshiva Coll., N.Y.C., 1935-36, registrar, 1936-44, sec. faculty, 1938-43, instr. edn., 1939-41, asst. prof. edn., 1941-44; dir., asst. prof. edn. Bernard Revel Grad. Sch., Yeshiva Coll., 1944-45; prof. edn., dir. Grad. Schs., Yeshiva U., 1945-50, dean, 1950-53, also dean Sch. Edn. and Community Adminstrn., 1948-53; lectr. edn. L.I. U., 1938-41, lectr. psychology, 1939-41, asst. prof. edn. and psychology, 1941-45, prof., 1945-64, acting head dept., 1944-45, head dept., 1945-60, chmn. grad. div., 1949-51, dir. Grad. Sch., 1951-52, dean, 1953-60; dean sch. edn. L.I. U. (Grad. Sch.), 1960-64; founding pres. Kingsborough Community Coll., 1964-69; prof. CUNY, 1964-83, prof. emeritus, 1983; Supt. of schs., bd. secular edn. The United Yeshivos, 1945-48; research cons. Human Engring. div. U.S. Navy; cons. U.S. Office Edn.; dir. ednl. survey Jewish Community, Portland, Me.; vice chmn. Mayor's Com. on Scholastic Achievement, N.Y.C., 1954-66, Gov.'s Com. on Scholastic Achievement, 1966-86; chmn. Acad. Coms., from 1966; mem. state, city, regional edn. coms.; mem., presiding officer Nat. Adv. Com. on Supplementary Ednl. Centers and Services, U.S. office Edn., 1965-68; bd. dirs., pres. Council Higher Ednl. Instns. in, N.Y.C. Author: State Regulatory and Supervisory Control of Higher Education in New York, Jewish Education in New York City; Co-author: A Model Program for the Talmud Torah; Editor: Jews in America: Heritage and History, Edn. Abstracts, The Jews in America, History: A Resource Book for Teachers, 2 edits., Guide to General Psychology, 3 edits.; bd. editors: Presdl. Studies Quar; Contbr. on ednl. history and problems and psychology of learning to tech. and trade jours. Bd. govs. Jewish Acad. Arts and Scis.; mem. acad. adv. council; trustee Bar-Ilan U., Israel; mem. Met. N.Y. Commn. Tchr. Edn. and Profl. Standards, Community Planning Bd. 4, Borough Bklyn.; Bklyn. citizens adv. bd. N.Y. State Constl. Conv.; mem. acad. adv. council Ferkauf Grad. Sch. Edn., Yeshiva U.; mem. Nat. Adv. Council Center for Study of Presidency; bd. dirs. Bd. Jewish Edn. N.Y.C.; trustee, v.p. Fifth Ave. Synagogue; chmn. presdl. planning com. Yeshiva U. Recipient Abraham Freeda award, Scroll appreciation Yeshiva of Flatbush, award Yeshiva Coll. Alumni Assn., Bernard Revel Meml. award in arts and scis., Chief Rabbi Isaac Halevi Herzog Fellowship Gold medal, 1965, Yeshiva U. Disting.Svc. award, 1970, N.Y. Gov.'s citation for ednl. leadership, 1972, 76, Alumni Svc. award CCNY, 1978, Outstanding Leadership and Svc. award Edn. Alumni Assn. CCNY, 1984. Fellow AAAS, Jewish Acad. Arts and Scis.; mem. NEA, AAUP, Nat. Assn. Jewish Day Sch. Prins. (pres.), N.Y. Acad. Pub. Edn., Am. Ednl. Research Assn., Am. Assn. Sch. Adminstrs., N.Y. Psychol. Assn., Am. Psychol. Assn., Eastern Psychol. Assn., Bklyn Psychol. Assn. (chmn. com. profl. ethics; exec. com.), Eastern Assn. Coll. Deans (exec. com., dir.), Council Jewish Edn., Nat. Soc. Coll. Tchrs. Edn., N.Y. Counsellors Assn., Religious Edn. Assn. U.S., Soc. Advancement Edn., CCNY Edn. Alumni Assn. (pres.), Phi Delta Kappa, Phi Alpha Theta, Kappa Delta Pi. Jewish Orthodox. Home: New York N.Y. Died Nov. 21, 1991; buried N.Y.C.

HARTT, FREDERICK, art historian; b. Boston, May 22, 1914; s. Rollin Lynde and Jessie Clark (Knight) H.; m. Margaret DeWitt Veeder, Mar. 11, 1943 (div. July 1960). BA, Columbia U., 1935; postgrad., Princeton U., 1935-36; MA, NYU, 1937, PhD, 1949. Asst. Yale Art Gallery, 1941-42; vis. lectr. art, acting dir. art mus. Smith Coll., 1946-47; lectr. fine arts NYU, 1948-49; asst. prof. history art to prof. Washington U., St. Louis, 1949-60; prof. history art U. Pa., 1960-67, chmn. dept. art, 1960-65; McIntire prof. history art U. Va., Charlottesville, 1967-84, prof. emeritus, from 1984, chmn. dept. art, 1967-76; dir. U. Art Mus., 1971-76; vis. prof. history art Harvard U., 1961, Franklin and Marshall Coll., 1966-67, Baylor U., 1985, Georgetown U., 1991; vis. art historian Harvard Renaissance Ctr., Florence, Italy, 1965-66; sr. rsch. fellow CTR. for Advanced Study in the Visual Arts, Nat. Gallery of Art, 1988-89. Author: Florentine Art Under Fire, 1949, Botticelli, 1952, Giulio Romano, 2 vols, 1958, (with Kennedy and Corti) The Chapel of the Cardinal of Portugal, 1964, Love in Baroque Art, 1964, The Paintings of Michelangelo, 1964, Michelangelo, the Complete Sculpture, 1969, History of Italian Renaissance Art, 1969, 2d rev. edit., 1979, 3rd rev. edit., 1987, 1 Michelangelo's Drawings, 1971, Donatello, Prophet of Modern Vision, 1973, Art, A History of Painting, Sculpture and Architecture, 2 vols, 1976, 2d. rev. edit., 1985, 3d rev. edit., 1988, Michelangelo's Three Pietàs, 1976, David by the Hand of Michelangelo, 1987, New Light on Michelangelo in the Sistine Chapel, 2 vols., 1989-91 (also in French, German, Italian), Michelangelo: Imprint and Image: A Study in Creative Psychology, 1991, Saint Antoine of Florence and His Influence on Florentine Art, 1991; also contbr. numerous articles to profl. publs. Mem. exec. com. Com. to Rescue Italian Art, 1966-91; Bd. dirs. Am. Com. Restoration Italian Monuments, 1946-49. Served to 1st lt. USAAF, 1942-46. Decorated Bronze Star medal; knight of Crown of Italy; knight officer Order Merit Italian Republic; hon. academician Acad. Arts Design, Florence, 1970; hon. alumnus Baylor U., 1981; named hon. citizen Florence, 1946; Guggenheim fellow, 1948-49, 54-55; Fulbright research grantee, 1954-55, 65-66; Am. Council Learned Socs. fellow, 1965-66. Mem. Coll. Art Assn. Am. (dir. 1959-62), Am. Assn. U. Profs., Renaissance Soc. Am. (coun. 1970), Soc. Archtl. Historians, Nat. Trust Hist. Preservation. Roman Catholic. Home: Washington D.C. Died Oct. 31, 1991; buried Ch. San Miniato, Florence, Italy.

HARTUNG, HANS HEINRICH ERNST, artist; b. Leipzig, Sept. 21, 1904; s. Curt and Margarete (Nakonz) H.; m. Anna-Eva Bergman, Feb. 20, 1957. Student, Lycee, Dresden, Acad. Beaux Arts Leipzig U. Abstract painter, 1922-89. Exhibited paintings in one man shows, Desden, 1931, Oslo, 1932, Paris, 1939, Basle, 1952, Brussels, 1954, Paris, 1956, 61, 62, 64, Germany, 1957, traveling exhbn., N.Y., 1957, internat. exhbns., Venice, Turin, Sao Paulo, Pitts., London, N.Y.C., Tokyo, Berlin, Zurich, Vienna, Dusseldorf, Brussels, Antwerp, Mus. Modern Art, Paris, Germany. With Fgn. Legion, 1939-41, 43-45. Decorated Legion of Honor, Croix de Guerre; recipient 1st Internat. Painting prize 30th Venise Biennale, 1960. Mem. Acad. Fine Arts Berlin, Acad. Fine Arts Munich. Home: Antibes France Died Dec. 7, 1989.

HARTWICK, ELBERT STUART, investor; b. Fargo, N.D., Dec. 7, 1903; s. Louis B. and Roberta Frances (Stuart) H.; m. Margaret Smith, Dec. 29, 1930 (dec. Jan. 1980); m. Joy Iverson, Sept. 26, 1981; 1 son, Ronald Stuart. A.B., U. Minn., 1930, J.D., 1930. Bar: Ill. bar 1931, Minn. bar 1931. Atty. Theodore, Gary & Co.,

Chgo., 1930-33; atty., sec. Carnation Co., Los Angeles, 1933-44; v.p., dir. Carnation Co., 1944-67, sr. v.p., 1967-70; past pres., dir. Dairy Foods, Inc., Carnaco Equipment Co.; pres., dir. Bus. Investments Co., Rialto Ctr. Co. Formerly mem. Calif. Republican State Central Com.; hon. trustee Republican Assn.; Trustee emeritus U. Redlands. Recipient Outstanding Achievement award U. Minn., 1974. Mem. Am., Ill., Minn. bar assns., Acacia, Gray Friar, Alpha Delta Sigma, Pi Delta Epsilon, Phi Alpha Delta. Republican. Episcopalian. Clubs: Mason (Shriner), Rotarian, Los Angeles Country, Thunderbird Country. Home: Los Angeles Calif. Died June 12, 1990; buried L.A.

HARVEY, LESTER SCHLEY, insurance company executive; b. Manchester, N.H., July 3, 1898; s. Frank H. and Anna E. (Power) H.; m. Harriet N. Jenkins, June 1, 1925; children: Phyllis A. Wood, Frank L. Ed. pub. schs. Pres., dir. N.H. Fire Ins. Co., Manchester, from 1950; bd. dirs. Granite State Fire Ins. Co., Am. Fidelity Co., Montpelier, Vt., Mchts. Nat. Bank; pres., dir. Mchts. Savs. Bank, Manchester; dir. Gen. Adjustment Bur., N.Y.C.; past trustee Underwriter Labs., Inc. Trustee Colby Jr. Coll. With U.S. Army, WWI. Mem. Mason, Kiwanis (past pres.), Manchester Country Club, Drug and Chem. Club (N.Y.C.). Republican. *

HARVIN, EDWIN LAWRENCE, history educator; b. Crockett, Tex., Mar. 27, 1898; s. Richard R. and Florence (Miller) H.; m. Mary Brown, June 5, 1923; children: Edwin L., Laurel Solley, Mary Weaver. Student, Tex. A&M Coll., 1919-20; AB, Baylor U., 1921, LLD, 1949; AM, U. Tex., 1926. Dean of men San Marcos Acad., 1921-27; assoc. dean Texarkana Coll., 1927-38; dean Del Mar Coll., 1938-46, pres., 1946-61, pres. emeritus, prof. history, from 1961; dir. Am. Assn. Jr. Colls., 1952-54; trustee S. Tex. Children's Home, from 1961—. Mem. Lions Club (past pres. Texarkana), Rotary (past pres. Corpus Christi). Baptist. *

HASKINS, GEORGE LEE, lawyer, educator; b. Cambridge, Mass., Feb. 13, 1915; s. Charles Homer and Clare (Allen) H.; m. Anstiss Crowninshield Boyden, July 15, 1944 (dec. 1978); m. Gertrude Eleanor Lounder, Oct. 23, 1989. Classical diploma, Phillips Exeter Acad., 1931; AB summa cum laude, Harvard U., 1935, JD, 1942; MA (hon.), U. Pa., 1971. Bar: Mass. 1943, ICC 1951, Pa. 1952, U.S. Supreme Ct. 1952, U.S. Ct. Appeals (3rd cir.) 1953, Maine 1968, U.S. Ct. Appeals (1st cir.) 1969. Jr. fellow Soc. of Fellows, Harvard U., 1936-42, lectr. dept. sociology, 1937-38; Lowell lectr. Boston, 1938; assoc. Herrick, Smith, Donald & Farley, Boston, 1942; with office of spl. asst. to sec. of state, 1946; asst. prof. law U. Pa., 1946-48, assoc. prof., 1948-49, prof., 1949-85, Algernon Sydney Biddle prof., 1974-85, Algernon Sydney Biddle prof. emeritus, from 1985, mem. faculty arts and scis., 1976-85; pvt. practice Pa., 1986-91; of counsel Curtis, Thaxter et al, Portland, Maine, from 1988; rep. U.S. del. to UN conf., San Francisco, 1945; spl. atty. legal dept. Pa. R.R., 1951-54, cons. counsel, 1954-70; apptd. by Pres. Eisenhower to permanent com. on Oliver Wendell Holmes Devise, 1956; dir., v.p. Pa. Mut. Fund, N.Y.C., 1961-68; asst. reporter for Supreme and Superior Cts. Pa., 1970-72; univ. seminar assoc. Columbia, 1971-73, from 77; U.S. Supreme Ct. Hist. Soc. lectr., 1981; vis. prof. law Rutgers U., Camden, N.J., 1987; Hostetler, Baker and Hostetler prof. law Cleve. State U., 1990; lectr. continuing legal edn. program Cleve. Bar Assn., 1991; permanent mem. Jud. Conf. U.S. 3rd Cir.; vice-chmn. com. on legal history fellowships Am. Bar Found., 1978-83; mem. nat. adv. com. U.S. Constn., N.Y. Pub. Libr., 1985-87; Ann. Baker-Hostetler lectr., Cleveland Bar, 1991. Author: The Statute of York and the Interest of the Commons, 1935, The Growth of English Representative Government, 1948, (with others) American Law of Property, 1952, A History of the U.S. Supreme Court, vol. 2, part 1: John Marshall Foundations of Power, 1981, (with M.P. Smith) Pennsylvania Fiduciary Guide, 1957, 2d edit., 1962, Law and Authority in Early Massachusetts, 1960, 2d edit., 1977, A History of the Town of Hancock, Maine, 1978; also numerous articles in U.S., fgn. periodicals; contbr. to Ency. Brit.; mem. panel of authors preparing: History of U.S. Supreme Ct. (authorized by Congress), 1958; editor: Death of a Republic (John Dickinson), 1963, Phi Beta Kappa series, 1934-37; adv. bd. editors Speculum, 1949-69; bd. editors William and Mary Quar., 1969-70, Papers of John Marshall, Williamsburg, Va., Justice Bradley papers, Studies in Legal History. Mem. Hancock (Maine) 1976 Bicentennial Commn., 1978, Sesquicentennial History Commn., Internat. Commn. for History of Rep. Instns.; mem. humanities coun. Sta. WHYY-TV, Phila., Wilmington, Del., from 1976. With CAC AUS, 1942-43; from 1st lt. to capt. War Dept. Gen. Staff, 1943-46; from 1st lt. to capt. Gen. Staff Corps, 1945; maj. Res., 1946-54. Decorated Army Commendation medal with oak leaf clusters, various merit citations U.S. Army and sec. of state, 1946; recipient Demobilization award Social Sci. Rsch. Coun., 1946; elected Consejero del Instituto Internacional para Unificacion del Derecho Publico, 1956; John Simon Guggenheim fellow, 1957, Henry Fellow Merton Coll., Oxford U., 1935-36; Am. Bar Found. affiliated scholar, 1985-87; rsch. grantee Am. Coun. Learned Socs., 1987-88. Fellow Royal Hist. Soc., Am. Soc. for Legal History (hon.), Medieval Acad. Ireland (hon.); mem. ABA, Mass. Bar Assn., Maine Bar Assn., Pa. Bar Assn., Phila. Bar Assn., Assn. of Bar of City of N.Y., Hancock County Bar Assn., Swedish Colonial Soc., Am. Judicature Soc., Am. Arbitration Assn. (nat. panel arbitrators 1968—), C.H. Haskins Soc. Anglo-Norman Studies (hon.), Soc. Internationale pour l'Histoire du Droit (bd. dirs. from 1975), Am. Soc. for Legal History (pres. 1970-74, bd. dirs. 1977-80), Am. Antiquarian Soc., Internat. Law Soc., Soc. Colonial Wars, Am. Acad. Polit. Sci. Am. Hist. Assn., Am. Law Inst. (hon. life mem.), Assn. ICC Practitioners, Juristic Soc., Brit. Records Assn., Mediaeval Acad. Am. (council 1958-60), Soc. Comparative Legis., Colonial Soc. Mass., Mass. Hist. Soc. (corr. mem.), Maine Hist. Soc., Va. Hist. Soc., Colonial Soc. Pa. (gov.'s coun. 1977), Selden Soc. (hon. life mem., corr. sec. Pa.), Am. Geneal. Soc., Geneal. Soc. Pa., Inst. Early Am. History and Culture (council, editorial bd.), Soc. Jean Bodin Pour l'Histoire Comparative des Institutions, Soc. Internationale pour l'Etude de Philosophie Mediévale (membre titulaire), Académie d'Histoire Européenne (hon. corr.), S.R., Mayflower Descs., Boston Athenaeum, Libr. Co. Phila., U.S. Ct. Tennis Assn., Am. Soc. Ancient Instruments, Am. Soc. 18th Century Studies, Internat. Soc. St. Thomas Aquinas, Mil. Order Fgn. Wars U.S. (companion), Soc. War 1812, New. Eng. Land Title Assn., Hancock Hist. Soc. (bd. dirs. 1979-80), Century Assn., Renaissance Soc. Am., Asociata de Istorie Comparativa a Institui et Dreptulii (bd. dirs.), Order of Coif (award for scholarly writing Pa. chpt. 1982), Phi Beta Kappa. Clubs: Somerset (Boston); Legal, Racquet, Harvard (Phila.); Met. (Washington); Brit. Schs. and Univs., Pilgrims of U.S., Century Assn. (N.Y.C.); Royal Automobile, Athenaeum (London). Home: Hancock Maine Died Oct. 4, 1991; buried Riverside Cemetery, Hancock.

HASKINS, SYLVIA SHAW JUDSON, sculptor; b. Chgo., June 30, 1897; d. Howard and Frances (Wells) Shaw; m. Clay Judson, Sept. 3, 1921; children: Alice Clay Ryerson, Clay; 2d m. Sidney Gatter Haskins, Dec. 1, 1963. Student, Sch. Art Inst., Chgo., 1916-20; studied in, Paris, 1920-21; D Sculpture (hon.), Lake Forest Coll., 1952. tchr. sculpture Am. U., Cairo, Egypt, 1963. One-man shows include Art Inst., Chgo., 1938, Arden Gallery, N.Y.C., 1940, Ill. State Mus., Springfield, 1948, Chgo. Pub. Libr., 1955, Sculpture Ctr., N.Y.C., 1957; exhibited Phila. Mus. Art, Whitney Mus. Art, Mus. Modern Art, Met. Mus., Century of Progress Exhbns. at Chgo., Art Inst., N.Y. and San Francisco World's Fairs; represented in mus. collections in Phila., Dayton, Ohio, Springfield, Ill., Davenport, Iowa; others; Mary Dyer Statue erected Boston, 1959, Phila., 1961; Stations of the Cross, Sacred Heart Ch., Winnetka, fountain in Morton Arboretum, 1963, Art Inst. Chgo., 1963; author: The Quiet Eye, 1954; tchr. sculpture Am. U. Cairo, Egypt, 1963. Recipient Logan prize, 1929, hon. mention, 1925, 35, 45, Clyde Carr prize, 1947, Art Inst. Chg., hon. award in fine arts Chgo. chpt. AIA, Chgo. Assn. Commerce and Industry, 1956, Mcpl. Art League prize Chgo. No. Jury Sow, 1957, Speyer prize Am. Acad. Design, 1957, medal Garden Club of Am., 1957. Fellow Nat. Sculpture Soc.; mem. NAD. Mem. Soc. of Friends. *

HASS, ANTHONY, investment banker; b. Vienna, Austria, Dec. 15, 1923; m. Patricia Cary Cecil, July 20, 1957; children: Anthony, Elizabeth, John. B.S.E. in Chem. Engring, Princeton U., 1944. Research chemist Hercules Powder Co., Wilmington, Del., 1944-46; sci. cons. U.S. Army Intelligence, 1946-47; dir., gen. mgr. Kilgore Chems., Inc., Washington, 1947-49; div. mgr. Atlantic Research Corp., Alexandria, Va., 1949-54; pres. Dryomatic Corp., Alexandria, 1954-62; v.p. LogEtronics, Inc., Alexandria, 1962-65; dir. adminstrn. internat. div. Schering Corp., Bloomfield, N.J., 1965-68; v.p. Mergers & Acquisition, Inc., Washington, 1968-69; v.p. external devel. Gen. Foods Corp., White Plains, N.Y., 1969-87; exec. dir. Samuel Montagu and Co., London, 1988-91; sr. advisor AgriCapital Corp., N.Y.C., from 1991. Mem. Newcomen Soc. N.Am., Am. Chem. Soc., Assn. Corp. Growth (dir., past pres.). Clubs: Met. (Washington); Princeton (N.Y.C.). Home: New York N.Y. Died July 13, 1992. †

HASSENFELD, STEPHEN DAVID, manufacturing company executive; b. Providence, R.I., Jan. 19, 1942; s. Merrill Lloyd and Sylvia Grace (Kay) H. Student, Johns Hopkins U., 1959-62; D. Pub. Service, R.I. Coll., 1984; HHD, Bryant Coll., 1985. With Hasbro Industries Inc., Pawtucket, R.I., 1963-89; v.p. mktg. Hasbro Industries, Inc., Pawtucket, R.I., 1967-68, exec. v.p., 1968-74, pres., 1974-80, chmn. bd., chief exec. officer, 1980-89, also dir.; dir. Am. Stock Exchange; bd. govs. Bank of Boston; bd. dirs. Johns Hopkins U. Past fellow Brandeis U., Waltham, Mass.; past trustee Temple Emanu-El, Providence, R.I., 1981-84, Found. for Repertory Theatre of R.I., 1978-84; bd. trustees R.I. Pub. Expenditures Council, bd. govs., 1986-89; bd. dirs. Jewish Fedn. R.I., 1976-89, United Way of Southeastern New Eng., Inc., 1985-89, Southeastern region NCCJ, 1976-89, John H. Chaffee Steering Com., 1975-82, Am. Jewish Joint Distbn. Com., N.Y.C., 1982-89; mem. Young Pres. Orgn., 1983-89, Am. Jewish Joint Distbn. Com., N.Y.C., R.I. Philharmonic Council, R.I. Commodores, from 1978, R.I. Council of Nat. Jewish Hosp.-Nat. Asthma Center, 1980-89, Corp. of R.I. Philharmonic Orch., 1981, Providence Coll. pres. council, 1985-89; mem. bus. adv. council U. R.I., 1976-78; bd. dirs. Children's Friend and Service, Providence, 1974-77, Fed. Hill House, 1973-76; mem. adv. com. R.I. Strategic Devel. Commn., 1982-84 ; mem. adv. council Sch. Continuing Studies, Johns Hopkins U., 1983-89, dir. advanced internat. studies. Mem. Toy Mfrs. Assn. (dir. 1974-76). Home: New York N.Y. Died June 25, 1989.

HASSOLD, ERNEST CHRISTOPHER, educator; b. Corunna, Ind., Jan. 21, 1896; s. Stefan and Margaret (Weber) H.; m. Rosalie Sutton Kerr, Sept. 29, 1928; children: Cristie, Stefan. Student, Concordia Coll., Fort Wayne, Ind., 1909-14, Concordia Sem., St. Louis, 1914-15, 16-18; PhD, U. Chgo., 1934. Instr. in German and Latin Concordia Coll., Ft. Wayne, 1918-20; instr. in charge English Concordia Collegiate Inst., Bronxville, N.Y., 1921-25; asst. U. Chgo., 1925-27; asst. prof. English U. Louisville Coll. Liberal Arts, 1927-35, prof., 1937, head, 1935-55, chmn. div. of humanities, 1939-63, disting. prof. humanities, 1960; univ. officer Office Mil. Govt., Hesse, Germany, 1948-49; edn. specialist High Commr. Germany, summers 1952, 53. Author: American Literary History Before the Civil War, 1936; contbr. Humanities in General Education (Earl McGrath), 1949; contbr. articles to profl. jours. Trustee Louisville Art Ctr. Assn., 1946-48. Mem. AAUP, Modern Lang. Assn. (sec., chmn. group on lit. and art 1947-48, group on Anglo-German rels. 1954-55), Nat. Coun. Tchrs. English (editorial bd. Coll. English 1942-45, co-chmn. com. comparative lit. 1954-55), Internat. Congress Comparative Lit., Am. Coun. Learned Socs. (regional assoc.), Am. Soc. for Aesthetics (trustee 1952-55). *

HATCH, SINCLAIR, lawyer; b. Chgo., Dec. 7, 1906; s. Samuel G. and Mattie (Sinclair) H.; adopted s. George A. and Lucy (Sinclair) Kingsley; m. Laura Lee Robertson, Feb. 11, 1933; children: Robertson, George Kingsley, Sinclair; m. Jean Lithgow Paul, Dec. 11, 1973; m. Mary Wendell Vander Poel Miller, May 14, 1977. AB, Princeton U., 1928; LLB, Harvard U., 1931. Bar: N.Y. 1932. Assoc. Davis, Polk, Wardwell, Gardiner & Reed, N.Y.C., 1931-34, 35-41, Hatch, McLean, Root & Hinch, N.Y.C., 1941-42, Hatch, Root & Barrett and successors, N.Y.C., 1946-55; mem. staff securities div. FTC and SEC, 1934-35; asst. indsl. readjustment br. in charge contract termination Dept. Navy, Washington, 1944-45; ptnr. Graustein, Hatch & Kormendi, N.Y.C., 1956, Pell, Butler, Hatch, Curtis & LeViness, N.Y.C., 1957-60; ptnr. Milbank, Tweed, Hadley & McCloy, N.Y.C., 1960-79, cons. ptnr., 1980-89; regional dir. OCD, 1943. Bd. dirs. Blue Hill Found., Inc., 1941-71; trustee Emma Clark Meml. Libr., Setauket, N.Y., 1948-68, pres., 1958-68. Lt comdr. USNR, 1944. Decorated Legion of Merit, assoc. officer Order St. John of Jerusalem; recipient Episcopal Layman award Bard Coll., 1978. Fellow Am. Bar Found.; mem. ABA, Fed. Bar Assn., N.Y. State Bar Assn., Am. Judicature Soc., Am. Law Inst., New York County Lawyers Assn., Assn. Bar City N.Y., Univ. Club, Century Club, Down Town Assn., Piping Rock Club, Church Club (trustee 1967-77, pres. 1974-76), Phi Beta Kappa Assocs. Home: Oyster Bay N.Y. Died July 13, 1989; buried Crane Neck Point, Oldfield, N.Y.

HATCHER, HARLAN HENTHORNE, author, university president; b. Ironton, Ohio, Sept. 9, 1898; s. Robert Elison and Linda (Lesley) H.; m. Frank Wilson Colfax, Dec. 29, 1922 (dec.); m. Anne Gregory Vance, Apr. 3, 1942; children: Robert Leslie, Anne Linda. AB, Ohio State U., 1922, AM, 1923, PhD, 1927, LLD, 1952; postgrad., U. Chgo., 1925, in Europe, 1928; LittD, Miami U., 1947, U. Toledo, 1952, Albion Coll., 1952, U. Ky., 1955, U. Pitts., 1955; LLD, Bowling Green State U., 1948, U. Mich., 1951, U. Cin., 1952, Ohio Wesleyan U., 1953, U. Akron, 1953, Mich. State Coll., 1955, Butler U., 1955, U. N.D., 1956, Northwestern U., 1956, Kalamazoo Coll., 1958; LHD, Coll. Wooster, 1954, NYU, 1956, Lawrence Inst. Tech., 1958; EdD, Hillsdale Coll., 1961; LittD, Waseda U., Tokyo, 1962, Pa. Mil. Coll., 1963, No. Mich. U., 1964. Instr. English Ohio State U., 1922-28, asst. prof., 1928-32, prof., 1932-44, dean Coll. Arts and Scis., 1944-48, v.p., 1948-51; pres. U. Mich., from 1951; lectr. U. So. Calif., summer 1951; dir. Ann Arbor Bank, Detroit Edison Co., Tecumseh Products Co. Author: The Versification of Robert Browning, 1928, Tunnel Hill, 1931, Patterns of Wolfpen, 1934, Creating the Modern American Novel, 1935, Central Standard Time, 1937, The Buckeye Country: A Pageant of Ohio, 1940, The History of Ohio, Vol. VI (with others), 1943, Modern Dramas, Shorter Edition, 1944, The Great Lakes, 1944, Lake Erie (Great Lakes Series), 1945, The Western Reserve: The Story of New Connecticut in Ohio, 1949, A Century of Iron and Men, 1950; editor: The Ohio Guide, 1940, others. Trustee Inst. Def. Analyses; mem. Ford Found. Fellowship Adv. Bd.; dir. Coun. for Fin. Aid to Edn. Coord. War Accelerated Program, Ohio State U., 1942; lectr. State U. Iowa, 1932. Pvt. U.S. Army, 1918, lt. USNR, 1942-44. Decorated Comdr. Netherlands Order of Orange-Nassua; Companion Most Exalted Order White Elephant, Thailand, Ky. Col., Star Italian Solidarity, 2d Order Merit swith Middle Cordon of Rising Sun (Japan), Wolverine Frontiersman award. Mem. Modern Lang. Assn., Assn. Am. Univs. (pres.), AAUP, Nat. Coun. Tchrs. English, The Great Lakes Hist. Soc., Am. Hist. Soc., Phi Beta Kappa, Clubs: Century (N.Y.C.),

Economic of Detroit (member bd. dirs.), Detroit, Detroit Athletic, Rotary, Newcomen Soc. *

HATCHER, JAMES DONALD, medical educator; b. St. Thomas, Ont., Can., June 22, 1923; s. Fred Thomas and Cora (Rooke) H.; m. Helen Edith Roberts, June 14, 1946; children: Janet Louise, Carolyn Elizabeth. M.D., U. Western Ont., London, Can., 1946, Ph.D., 1951; LL.D. (hon.), Queen's U., 1985, Meml. U. New Foundland, 1990. Intern Hamilton (Ont., Can.) Gen. Hosp., 1946-47; instr. medicine Sch. Medicine Boston U., 1950-52; asst. prof. dept. physiology Queen's U. Med. Sch., Kingston, Ont., Can., 1952-55, assoc. prof., 1955-59, prof., chmn. dept., 1959-76; assoc. dean Faculty Medicine, 1968-71; prof. physiology and biophysics Faculty Medicine, Dalhousie U., Halifax, N.S., Can., 1976-89, dean, 1976-85, adviser to pres. on research & tech. transfer, 1985-89, dean emeritus, 1989-91; attending physician Hypertensive and Cardiac Clinic, Mass. Meml. Hosp., Boston, 1950-52; research fellow Robert Dawson Evans Meml. Hosp., Boston, 1950-52; mem. arctic panel Def. Research Bd. Can., 1957, chmn., 1962-67, mem. adv. com. bd., 1962-67; mem. adv. com. Surgeon Gen., Dept. Nat. Def., 1964-68; mem. grant panel Med. Research Council Can., 1964-74, 78-81, 85-87, mem. council, 1967-70, 79-85; bd. dirs. Connaught Labs., 1981-87; sci. adv. com. Can. Life and Health Ins. Assn., 1983-89; chmn. tertiary care adv. com. Dept. Health, Province of N.B., 1982-85; mem. com. on genetic predisposition to disease Sci. Council Can., 1987-90. Mem. editorial bd. Innovations, 1987-89; contbr. articles to profl. jours. Mem. adv. com. Ont. Heart Found., 1966-71, bd. dirs., 1969-71; mem. health care forum Vol. Planning N.S., 1987-89, mem. R&D com., 1988-89; bd. dirs. Dalhousie Med. Research Found., 1980-91. Served to lt. M.C. Royal Canadian Army, 1944-50. Nat. Research Council grad. med. research fellow, 1947-50; Markle scholar, 1952-57; Nuffield traveling fellow, 1956; Ont. Heart Found. fellow, 1957-59; Nat. Heart Found. Can. sr. research fellow, 1959-60; recipient Med. Research Council sabbatical award U. Calif. Med. Center, San Francisco, 1971-72, 25th ann. medal Queen Brit. Empire, 1977, Dalhousie Med. Research Found. award, 1984. Fellow Royal Coll. Physicians and Surgeons (Can. 1977); mem. Canadian Physiol. Soc. (pres. 1970-71), Assn. Can. Med. Colls. (exec. 1981-85, treas. 1981-83, v.p. 1983-85), Can Assn. Lab. Animal Sci. (hon. life), Alpha Omega Alpha. Home: Kingston ON, Canada Died Feb. 2, 1991; buried Elmdale Meml. Pk. Cemetery, St. Thomas, Ont., Can.

HATFIELD, JOHN NYE, hospital consultant; b. Rutland, Pa., Jan. 14, 1897; s. William Henry and Harriet (Updyke) H.; m. Alfretta Morris, Nov. 10, 1924; children: John Nye II, David Morris. Student, Pa. State U., 1916-18. Storekeeper State Sanatorium, Hamburg, Pa., 1921-23; steward Reading (Pa.) Hosp., 1923-24; purchasing agt. Pa. Hosp., Phila., 1924-27; asst. adminstr. Pa. Hosp., 1927-31, adminstr., 1931-52; dir. Passavant Meml. Hosp., Chgo., 1952-61; hosp. cons.; mem. organizing com. Phila. Blue Cross, 1936-38, dir., 1938-41; lectr. hosp. adminstrn. U. Chgo., 1954-60, Northwestern U. Con. Office Emergency Mgmt., 1941-43; mem. Joint Commn. Hosp. Accreditation, 1951-55. Editorial bd.: The Modern Hosp., from 1948; editor: Hosp. Assn. Pa. Bull., 1934-39, 41-43. With USMC, 1918-19. Recipient Disting. Svc. award Am. Hosp. Assn., 1958. Mem. Royal Soc. Health (Brit.), Am. Hosp. Assn. (life, treas., trustee, past pres.), Pa. Hosp. Assn. (life, past pres., trustee, exec. sec. 1934-37), Am. Assn. Maternal and Child Health (bd. dirs.), Am. Assn. Hosp. Cons. (pres. 1959-61), Hosp. Bur. Standards and Supplies (dir. 1941-44), Internat. Hosp. Fedn., Coun. Clin. Tng. Theol. Students (gov. 1939-42), Fla. Hosp. Assn., Delta Tau Delta. *

HATFIELD, RICHARD BENNETT, senator; b. Hartland, N.B., Can., Apr. 9, 1931; s. Heber Harold and Dora Fern (Robinson) H. B.A., Acadia U., 1952; LL.B., Dalhousie U., 1956; LL.D., U. Moncton, 1971, U. N.B., 1972, St. Thomas U., 1973, Mt. Allison U., 1975; Dr. in Polit. Sci. (hon.), U. Ste. Anne, 1983. Bar: N.S. 1956. Exec. asst. to minister trade and commerce Ottawa, Ont., Can., 1957-58; sales mgr. Hatfield Industries Ltd., 1958-66; mem. N.B. Legis. Assembly, 1961-87; named leader Progressive-Conservative party, 1969-87; elected premier of N.B., 1970-87; chmn. Beaverbrook Art Gallery, Fredericton, N.B., 1988; M.P. Senate, 1990-91. Hon. Micmac-Màliseet Indian chief, 1970; hon. mem. Course XLI Nat. Def. Coll., Canada, 1988; recipient Can.-Israel Friendship award, 1973; mem. Queen's Privy Coun. of Can., 1982; named serving brother Order of St. John, 1988. Aboriginal Order Can., 1985. Home: Fredricton N.B., Canada Died Apr. 26, 1991; buried Hartland, N.B., Can.

HATHORN, RICHMOND YANCEY, classics educator; b. Alexandria, La., July 31, 1917; s. John Wesley and Aimee Aileen (Sleet) H.; m. Isabel Voelker, May 23, 1947; children—Isabel Voelker, Richmond Yancey, Emily Montgomery. B.A., La. Coll., 1937; M.A., La. State U., 1940; Ph.D., Columbia, 1950. Lectr. classics Columbia, 1947-53; prof. Northwestern State Coll. La., 1953-61; asso. prof. La. State U., 1961-62; prof. classics, chmn. dept. U. Ky., 1962-66; prof. European langs. and lit. Am. U. Beirut, 1966-69; prof., chmn. dept. classics SUNY, Stony Brook, from 1969; vis. prof. U. Mich., 1959. Author: Tragedy, Myth and Mystery, 1962, Handbook of Classical Drama, 1967, Greek Mythology, 1977. Mem. Am. Philol. Assn. Home: Middle Island N.Y. Died Dec. 22, 1987; buried Lake Providence, La.

HAUGE, PHILLIP ENOCH, educator; b. Canton, S.D., Sept. 19, 1898; s. Lars Johan and Emma Marie (Kittelson) H.; m. Margrethe Jessen, July 1, 1922; children: Janet Cecelia, Lawrence Jessen. AB, St. Olaf Coll., Minn., 1920; AM, U. Wash., 1924, PhD, 1942; LLD, Pacific Luth. U., 1960. Instr. Pacific Luth. U., Tacoma, 1920-21, registrar, 1921-60, dean jr. coll. div., 1924-39, dean coll., 1939-60, univ. dean, 1960-63, acad. v.p., dean coll. profl. grad. studies, 1963-65, prof. edn., from 1965; sec.-treas. Douglas Fisheries Co., Inc., 1934-41. Contbr. to Studies in Luth. Higher Edn. Dir. Parkland Sch. Dist., 1928-42. Pvt. S.A.T.C., 1918, 1st lt. to lt. col. U.S. Army AC, 1942-46. Mem. NEA, Nat. Rehab. Assn., World Affairs Coun., Phi Delta Kappa, Pi Kappa Delta, Alpha Phi Omega. Lutheran. *

HAURY, EMIL WALTER, anthropology educator; b. Newton, Kans., May 2, 1904; s. Gustav A. and Clara K. (Ruth) H.; m. Hulda E. Penner, June 7, 1928; children: Allan Gene, Loren Richard; m. Agnes N. Lindley, July 6, 1990. Student, Bethel Coll., Newton, Kans., 1923-25; AB, U. Ariz., 1927, MA, 1928; PhD, Harvard U., 1934; LLD, U. N.Mex., 1959. Instr. U. Ariz., 1928-29, rsch. asst. in dendrochronology, 1929-30; asst. dir. Gila Pueblo, Globe, Ariz., 1930-37; prof. anthropology U. Ariz., 1937-70, head dept., 1937-64, Fred A. Riecker Disting. prof. anthropology, 1970-80, emeritus, 1980-92; dir. Ariz. State Mus.; chmn. div. anthropology and psychology Nat. Acad. Scis.-NRC, 1960-62; mem. Adv. Bd. Nat. Parks, Historic Sites, Bldgs. and Monuments, 1964-70, chmn., 1968-70. Author: publs. including The Excavations of Los Muertos and Neighboring Ruins in the Salt River Valley, Southern Arizona, Peabody Museum Papers, Vol. XXIV; No. 1, 1945; (with others) The Stratigraphy and Archaeology of Ventana Cave, 1950; The Hohokam: Desert Farmers and Craftsmen, Excavations at Snaketown, 1964-65, 1976; Mogollon Culture in the Forestdale Valley, East Central Arizona, 1985; Emil W. Haury's Prehistory of the American Southwest (edited by J. Jefferson Reid and David E. Doyel 1986); contbr. articles. Guggenheim fellow, 1949-50; Viking Fund medalist in anthropology, 1950; recipient Alumni Achievement award U. Ariz., 1957, Salgo-Noren Found. award for teaching excellence, 1967, Conservation Svc. award Dept. Interior, 1976, Alfred V. Kidder medal for Am. archeology, 1977, Disting. Citizen award U. Ariz. Alumni Assn., 1980, award Am. Soc. Conservation, 1980; Al Merito award Ariz. Hist. Soc., 1981, Disting. Scholar award Southwestern Anthrop. Assn., 1982, Edward B. Danson Disting. Assoc. award Southwest Parks and Monuments Assn., 1987. Mem. AAAS, Nat. Coun. Humanities, Am. Philos. Soc., Am. Acad. Arts and Scis., Nat. Speleological Soc. (hon. life mem.), Soc. for Am. Archaeology (pres. 1943-44, disting. svc. award 1985), Am. Anthrop. Assn. (pres. 1956), Nat. Acad. Scis., Tree-Ring Soc., Sigma Xi, Phi Beta Kappa, Phi Kappa Phi. Home: Tucson Ariz. Died Dec. 5, 1992. †

HAUSEMAN, DAVID NATHANIEL, steel corporation executive; b. Pottstown, Pa., Mar. 4, 1895; s. Morris Edward and Sallie (Rudy) H.; m. Rosa Rowan Pegues, June 13, 1920; 1 child, David Pegues. BS, U. Pa., 1918; BS in Mech. Engring., MIT, 1928; MBS, Harvard, 1935; grad., F.A. Sch., Ft. Knox, 1922, Army Indsl. Coll., 1939; DSc, Temple U., 1944. Enlisted as pvt. Ordnance, U.S. Army, 1917, commd. 2d lt., 1918, advanced through grades to brig. gen., 1944, ret., 1946; v.p. Temple U., 1946-48; dir. Rsch. Inst. of Temple U., from 1946; pres., dir. Houdry Process Corp., 1948-52; chmn. bd. Catalytic Constrn. Co., 1948-52; v.p. Davison Chem. Corp., div. of W. R. Grace Co., 1952-62; pres. dir. North Am. Steel, Lakeland, Fla., from 1962, Fla. Phosphate Terminal Corp., from 1964; dir. Lakeland Fed. Savs. and Loan Assn., Oliver B. Cannon and Son, Inc., Phila. Trustee Temple U., 1949-52; chief Phila. Ordnance Dist., 1940-43; dir. readjustment div. hdqrs. Army Svc. Forces, Washington, 1943-46, in charge gen. staff supervision of surplus property for Army Svc. Forces and Army Air Forces. Decorated Legion of Merit, D.S.M., John C. Jones medal. Mem. Army Ordnance Assn., Mason, Racquet Club (Phila.), Army-Navy Club (Washington), Army Navy Country Club (Arlington, Va.), Harvard Club (N.Y.), Md. Club (Balt.), Lakeland Yacht Club, Cleveland Heights Golf Club (Lakeland, Fla.). Episcopalian. *

HAUSER, NANCY MCKNIGHT, dance educator, choreographer; b. Bayside, N.Y., Nov. 20, 1909; d. Edgar Scott and Adelaide Burton McKnight; m. Rudolph Alonzo Hauser, Jan. 1, 1934; children: Michael Scott, Heidi Hauser Jasmin, Anthony Paul. Dance tng. with, Louise Revere Morris, 1926-36, Doris Humphrey, 1926-36, Charles Weidman, 1926-36, Hanya Holm, 1926-36. Mem. Hanya Holm Dance Co., 1932-36; instr. Finch Jr. Coll., 1933-37, Milw. Dept. Recreation, 1938-43; instr. Carleton Coll., 1944-47, asst. prof., 1950-60; instr. Macalester Coll., 1946-49; founder Dance Guild Theatre and Sch., 1961; artistic dir. Guild Performing Arts and Nancy Hauser Dance Co., Mpls., 1968-90; instr. Hanya Holm Sch. Dance, Colo. Coll., Colorado Springs, 1978-90, U. Minn., 1981-90; cons. artists-in-schs. Nat. Endowment for Arts. Dancer in Lysistrata, 1930; choreographer: Visions, 1966, Saeta, 1967, Everyman Sonata, 1966, Counterpoint, 1970, Lyric Suite, 1970, No Comment, 1971, Parta Partita, 1970, Abstract Beginnings, 1972, Back to Bank, 1979, Getting Along, Getting Together, 1978, Recherche, 1976, Dream Cycle, 1977, Everness, 1978, Circle of the Sun, 1980, U.S., Inc., 1981, Wheeling, 1981, Romanza, 1981, Requiem, 1983, Twin City Met. Arts Alliance. Active Mpls. Arts Commn., 1976-79, Minn. Alliance Arts in Edn., 1978-80; vis. artists U. Wis., Madison, spring 1983. Minn. State Arts Bd. grantee, 1976, 77, 80; recipient Outstanding Achievement in Arts award YWCA. Home: Minneapolis Minn. Died Jan. 17, 1990.

HAUSMAN, SAMUEL, textiles executive; b. Austria, Nov. 14, 1897; s. Morris and Bertha (Hoffman) H.; m. Vera Kuttler, May 4, 1924; children—Bruce Alan, Merna (Mrs. Richard Miller), Alice (Mrs. Morton I. Davidson). Vice chmn. bd. and dir. Belding Hemingway Co., Inc. Hon. chmn. United Jewish Appeal; 1st v.p. bd. Beth Israel Hosp.; chmn. emeritus Beth Israel Med. Ctr.; trustee Fedn. Jewish Philanthropies; bd. dirs. Am. Jewish Com.; former trustee N.Y. State U.; bd. sponsors Met. Adv. Council Internat. Recreation, Culture and Lifelong Edn.; former mem. Commn. to Establish Human Rights N.Y., N.Y. State Manpower Advt. Council; chmn. legis. adv. com. N.Y. Bd. Rabbis; past mem. adv. council Urban Devel.; past mem. fin. agy. N.Y. State Med. Care Facilities; past chmn. N.Y. State Health and Hosp. Commn.; treas. Am. Jewish Conf. on Soviet Jewry. Mem. Am. Arbitration Assn. Clubs: City Athletic (N.Y.C.); Fresh Meadow Country (Great Neck, N.Y.); Capitol Hill (Washington); Palm Beach Country. Home: New York N.Y. Died Aug. 14, 1992. †

HAUSNER, GIDEON MAKS, lawyer; b. Lwow, Poland, Sept. 26, 1915; s. Bernard and Ema Lande H.; m. Yehudith Liphshitz, Dec. 19, 1944; children: Tamar, Amos-Dov. Advocate, Hebrew Coll., Tel Aviv, 1933; student, Hebrew U., Jerusalem, 1941; grad. govt. law classes, Jerusalem, 1943. Admitted to bar, 1943. Pvt. practice law Jerusalem, 1943-47, 49-60, 1963; atty. gen. Israel, 1960-63; chief prosecutor in Eichmann trial, 1961-62; lectr. Hebrew U., 1956-60; cabinet minister Govt. of Prime Minister Yitzhak Rabin, Israel; mem. Cen. Com. Bar Assn. and Law Coun., 1954-60; del. Zionist Congress, 1954, 56, 64; mem. Israeli Parliament, 1965—; chmn. Parliamentary group Ind. Liberal Party Israel, 1968-90; chmn. Yad Vashem, Nat. Authority to Commemorate Victims World War II, 1969-91. Author: Justice in Jerusalem; author papers; contbr. articles to profl. jours. Mem. Jewish def. orgn. Hapana, 1932-48. With Israeli Army, 1947-49. Mem. Polit. Sci. Assn., Israel Assn. for Human Rights chmn. , B'nai B'rith, Rotary. Home: Jerusalem Israel Died Nov. 15, 1990.

HAVEMEYER, HORACE, JR., sugar refining executive; b. Islip, N.Y., July 14, 1914; s. Horace and Doris (Dick) H.; m. Rosalind Everdell, Sept., 1939; children: Horace, Rosalind, William, Christian. Grad. high sch., 1932. Exec. v.p. Nat. Sugar Refining Co., N.Y.C., 1942-48, pres., 1948-66, chmn. bd., 1966-68, bd. dirs., 1943-68; bd. dirs. Amalgamated Sugar Co. Bd. dirs. Drew U., Huntington Hosp. Home: Dix Hills N.Y. Died June 11, 1990.

HAVENS, WALTER PAUL, JR., physician; b. Farmingdale, N.J., Dec. 20, 1911; s. Walter Paul and Jessie Florence (Crouse) H.; m. Ida Markle Hessenbruch, June 14, 1941; children: Dreer Havens Graburn, Timothy Markle, Michael Crouse, Peter Hessenbruch, John Paul. A.B., Harvard U., 1932, M.D., 1936; D.Sc. (hon.), Ursinus Coll., 1974, Thomas Jefferson U., 1985. Diplomate Am. Bd. Internal Medicine. Asst. prof. preventive medicine Yale U., New Haven, 1946; assoc. prof. preventive medicine Jefferson Med. Coll., Phila., 1946-56, prof. medicine, 1952-72, ret., 1972, hon. prof. medicine, from 1972; cons. infectious diseases and diseases of liver; mem. com. viral infections Army Epedmiol. Bd., 1944-69; mem. com. viral hepatitis WHO, 1952-67; cons. Office Surgeon Gen., Dept. Army, 1946-67, VA, 1947-76. Med. editor: History of Internal Medicine of World War II, 3 vols., 1961, 63, 68; contbr. numerous articles on infectious and liver diseases to profl. jours. Served to maj. AUS, 1942-46; Middle East. Named hon. prof. medicine U. Chile, Santiago, 1956; recipient Outstanding Civilian Service medal, surgeon gen., 1970. Mem. Phila. County Med. Soc., Soc. Med. Cons. to Armed Forces, Am. Soc. Clin. Investigation (emeritus). Republican. Episcopalian. Club: Merion Cricket (Haverford, Pa.). Home: Haverford Pa. Died Apr. 6, 1992. †

HAVERS, LORD MICHAEL (LORD ROBERT OLFIELD), government chancellor; b. London, Mar. 10, 1923; s. Cecil Robert Havers; m. Carol Elizabeth Snelling, Sept. 3, 1949; children: Philip, Nigel. MA, Cambridge U., 1948. Atty., 1948-87; Queen's counsel Brit. Govt., 1964-87, solicitor gen., 1972-74, atty. gen., 1979-87, lord chancellor, 1987-92; Mem. Parliament from Wimbledon, Eng., 1970-87. Served as lt. Royal Navy Vol. Res., 1941-46, ETO, NATOUSA, CBI, MTO, U.S.A. Conservative. Mem. Ch. of England. Home: London Eng. Died Apr. 1, 1992. †

HAVIGHURST, ALFRED FREEMAN, history educator; b. Mt. Pleasant, Iowa, Sept. 30, 1904; s. Freeman Alfred and Winifred Weter H.; m. Mildred Linscott Porter, Nov. 23, 1966. AB, Ohio Wesleyan U., 1925;

AM, U. Chgo., 1928; PhD, Harvard U., 1936; AM hon. , Amherst Coll., 1954. Instr. history Holmes High Sch., Covington, Ky., 1925-27; prof. history and polit. sci. Pacific U., 1928-29; asst. history Harvard U., 1930-31; mem. faculty Amherst Coll., 1931-91, prof. history, 1954-70, prof. emeritus, 1970-91; vis. asst. prof. Mt. Holyoke Coll., 1942. Author: Twentieth Century Britain, 2d edit., 1966, Radical Journalist: H.W. massingham 1860-1924 , 1974; editor: The Pirenne Thesis: Analysis, Criticism and Revision, 1958, 2d edit., 1969; contbr. World Book Ency., Ency. Britannica; contbr. articles to profl. jours. 2d lt. AUS, 1942-46, ETO. Fellow Royal Hist. Soc.; mem. AAUP, Am. Hist. Assn., Conf. Brit. Studies. Hist. Assn. Eng. , Brit. Records Assn., Phi Delta Theta. Methodist. Home: Amherst Mass. Died Feb. 27, 1991.

HAVIGHURST, HAROLD CANFIELD, law educator; b. Findlay, Ohio, Dec. 24, 1897; s. Christian Rudolph and Emilie (Canfield) H.; m. Marion Perryman, July 23, 1927; children: Clark Canfield, Virginia Morgan. AB, Ohio Wesleyan U., 1919, LLD, 1950; AM, Harvard, 1922, LLB, 1926. Lawyer Miller, Otis Farr, N.Y.C., 1926-28; assoc. prof. law W.Va. U., 1928-30; assoc. prof. law Northwestern U., 1930-32, prof., from 1932, dean, 1948-57; vis. prof. Cornell U., 1957-58; mem. Nat. Conf. of Commrs. on Uniform State Laws, v.p., 1959-63; legal cons. office Fgn. Relief and Rehab. Ops., Dept. of State, 1943; chmn. bd. mgrs. Ill. Law Rev., 1932-45; spl. asst. to atty gen. of the U.S., 1939-40. Author: Cases on Contracts, 1934, rev. edit., 1950, The Nature of Private Contract, 1961; contbr. various legal periodicals. Mem. ABA, Ill. State Bar Assn. (chmn. com. for drafting Ill. Ins. Code 1937), Chgo. Bar Assn., Phi Delta Theta, Phi Beta Kappa, Delta Sigma Rho, Pi Delta Epsilon, Order of Coif, Tavern Club (Chgo.). Democrat. Presbyterian. *

HAVIGHURST, ROBERT J., education educator, chemistry and physics educator; b. DePere, Wis., June 5, 1900; s. Freeman Alfred and Winifred (Weter) H.; m. Edythe McNeely, June 21, 1930 (dec. Mar. 1988); children: Helen S. Havighurst Berk, Ruth L. Havighurst Neff, Dorothy C. Havighurst Kucera, James P., Walter M. A.B., Ohio Wesleyan U., 1921; Ph.D., Ohio State U., 1924. NRC fellow in physics Harvard, 1924-26; asst. prof. chemistry Miami U., Oxford, Ohio, 1927-28; asst. prof. physics, adviser in exptl. coll. U. Wis., 1928-32; assoc. prof. sci. edn. Ohio State U., Columbus, 1932-34; asst. dir. for gen. edn. Gen. Edn. Bd., Rockefeller Found., 1934-37, dir. for gen. edn., 1937-41; prof. edn. U. Chgo., from 1941; Co-dir. Brazil Govt. Center Ednl. Research, 1956-58. Co-author: Who Shall be Educated, 1944, Father of the Man, 1947, Adolescent Character and Personality, 1949, Personal Adjustment in Old Age, 1949, Social History of a War Boom Community, 1951, The American Veteran Back Home, 1951, Intelligence and Cultural Differences, 1951, Older People, 1953, The Meaning of Work and Retirement, 1954, American Indian and White Children, 1954, Educating Gifted Children, 1957, Society and Education, 1979, 6th edit., 1984, Psychology of Moral Character, 1960, Growing Up in River City, 1962, Society and Education in Brazil, 1965, Brazilian Secondary Education and Socioeconomic Development, 1969, 400 Losers, 1971, Adjustment to Retirement, 1970, Farewell to Schools???, 1971, Cross-National Research: Social Psychological Methods and Problems, 1972, To Live on This Earth: American Indian Education, 1972, Character y Personalidad del Adolescente, 1962, Social Scientists and Educators: Lives After Sixty, 1976; author: Developmental Tasks and Education, 1972, Human Development and Education, 1953, American Higher Education in the 1960's, 1960, Sociedad y Educacion en America Latina, 1962, The Public Schools of Chicago, 1964, The Educational Mission of the Church, 1965, Education in Metropolitan Areas, 1971, Comparative Perspectives on Education, 1968, Optometry: Education for the Profession, 1973; Contbr. articles to profl. jours. Former pres. Hyde Pk. Community Coun.; frequent chair civic and polit. coms. Mem. Soc. Research in Child Devel., AAAS, Am. Psychol. Assn., Am. Sociol. Assn., Am. Ednl. Research Assn., AAUP, Nat. Acad. Edn., Gerontol. Soc. (Kleemeier award for research 1967, Brookdale award 1979), Nat. Soc. Study Edn., Phi Beta Kappa, Sigma Xi, Phi Delta Theta. Home: Evanston Ill. Died Jan. 31, 1991; buried Evanston, Ill.

HAWK, CARL CURTIS, transportation company executive; b. New Philadelphia, Ohio, Sept. 29, 1931; s. Raymond Carl and Freda Emily (Walters) H.; m. Nan Campbell Kernohan, Aug. 21, 1954; children: Barbara Ann, Beverly Sue, Cynthia Lynn, Jeffrey Carl. B.S., Bowling Green State U., 1953; M.B.A., Case-Western Res. U., 1959. Tax acct. Nat. City Bank Cleve., 1954-56; budget and internal audit supr. Ferro Corp., Cleve., 1956-60; with Chessie System/CSX Corp., Richmond, Va., 1960-88; sec., sr. asst. v.p. Chessie System/CSX Corp., Richmond, 1977-80, v.p., sec., 1980-88, v.p. adminstrn., corp. sec., 1988. Bd. dirs., treas. Sci. Mus. Va. Found.; former dir. Carpenter Ctr. Mem. Am. Soc. Corp. Secs., Metro Richmond C. of C. dir., treas.), Alpha Tau Omega, Beta Mu Epsilon, Kappa Mu Epsilon. Republican. Presbyterian. Home: Richmond Va. Died May 12, 1989; buried Greenwood Meml. Gardens, Richmond. †

HAWKINS, J(ESSE) MILLS, corporation official; b. Bellport, N.Y., Sept. 9, 1898; s. John F. and Kate M. (Hawkins) H.; m. Kathryn Scott Williams, Dec. 27, 1922; children: Robert Clarke, Jesse Mills. Student pub. schs., N.Y. With White Oil Corp., N.Y.C., Houston, 1921-22, Pogson, Peloubet & Co., CPA's, N.Y.C., 1923-31; asst. comptr. Phelps Dodge Corp., N.Y.C., 1931-42, comptr., from 1942, v.p., from 1954; comptr., dir. Phelps Dodge Refining Corp., Moctezuma Copper Co.; comptr. Phelps Dodge Copper Products Corp. Mem. Am. Inst. Mining, Metall. and Petroleum Engrs., Controllers Inst. Am., Econ. Club, Mining Club, Can. Club (N.Y.C.), Upper Montclair (N.J.) Country Club. Republican. Episcopalian. *

HAWKINS, WALTER LINCOLN, materials consultant, engineer; b. Washington, Mar. 21, 1911; s. William Langston and Maude (Johnson) H.; m. Lilyan Varina Bobo, Aug. 19, 1939; children: Walter Gordon, Philip Lincoln. BChE, Renssalaer Poly., 1932; MS, Howard U., 1934, DSci (hon.), 1984; PhD, McGill U., 1938; LLD (hon.), Montclair State Coll., 1978, Kean Coll., 1983; D Engring. (hon.), Stevens Inst., 1980. Lectr. McGill U., Montreal, Que., Can., 1934-36; mem. tech. staff AT&T Bell Labs., Murray Hill, N.J., 1942-63, supr., 1963-72, dept. head, 1972-76, asst. dir., 1974-76; research dir. Plastics Inst. Am., Hoboken, N.J., 1976-83; pvt. practice materials cons. Montclair, N.J., 1976—. Author: Polymer Degradation and Stabilization, 1985; editor: Polymer Stabilization, 1971; 14 patents. Bd. dirs. Nat. Action Council for Minorities in Engring., 1978—; former bd. trustees Montclair State Coll.; former cub master Boy Scouts Am., Montclair. Recipient Percy Julian award Nat. Orgn. Black Chemists an Chem. Engrs., 1977, Nat. medal of tech., 1992. Fellow N.Y. Acad. Sci., Am. Inst. Chemists (hon. scroll); mem. Nat. Acad. Engring., Soc. Plastic Engrs. (Internat. award 1984), Am. Chem. Soc. (councillor). Episcopalian. Home: San Marcos Calif. Died Aug. 20, 1992. †

HAY, ALEXANDRE, humanitarian organization executive; b. Berne, Switzerland, Oct. 29, 1919; s. Frederic and Lydia (Trachsler) H.; m. Helene Morin Pons, 1945 (dec. 1973); children: Isabelle, Frank-Olivier, Cedric, Beatrice; m. Verena Vogler, 1980. Student Mat. class, Geneva Coll., 1931-38; LL.B., U. Geneva, 1942, Lawyer's Cert., 1944, LL.D. (hon.), 1986; Ph.D. (hon.), U. St.-Gall. Sole practice, Geneva, 1942-45; with Fed. Polit. Dept., Berne, 1945-48, Swiss legation, Paris, 1948-53; div. dir. Swiss Nat. Bank, Zurich, 1953-55, dir., acting chief dept. II, Berne, 1955-61, gen. mgr., v.p., Berne, 1961-76; pres. bd. mgmt. European Monetary Agreement, Paris, 1961-66; pres. Internat. Com. Red Cross (ICRC), Geneva, 1976-87. Died Aug. 23, 1991; buried Chéne-Bougeries, Geneva. Home: Geneva Switzerland

HAYAKAWA, SAMUEL ICHIYE, senator, college president, writer; b. Vancouver, B.C., Can., July 18, 1906; s. Ichiro and Tora (Isono) H.; m. Margedant Peters, May 29, 1937; children: Alan Romer, Mark, Wynne. B.A., U. Man., 1927; M.A., McGill U., 1928; Ph.D., U. Wis., 1935; D.F.A. (hon.), Calif. Coll. Arts and Crafts, 1956; D.Litt. (honoris causa), Grinnell Coll., 1967; L.H.D., Pepperdine U., 1972; LL.D., The Citadel, 1972. Instr. English extension div. U. Wis., 1936-39; asst. prof. English Ill. Inst. Tech., 1940-42, assoc. prof., 1942-47; lectr. univ. coll. U. Chgo., 1950-55; prof. English San Francisco State Coll., 1955-68, acting pres., 1968-69, pres., 1969-73, pres. emeritus, from 1973; U.S. senator from Calif., 1977-82; spl. advisor to U.S. Sec. of State, from 1983; Alfred P. Sloan vis. prof. Menninger Sch. Psychiatry, 1961. Author: (with Howard M. Jones) Oliver Wendell Holmes, 1939, Language in Action, 1941 (Book-of- the-Month Club selection), Language in Thought and Action, 1949, Language, Meaning and Maturity, 1954, Our Language and Our World, 1959, Symbol, Status and Personality, 1963, Through the Communication Barrier, 1979; Columnist: Chgo. Defender, 1942-47, Register and Tribune Syndicate, 1970-76; Editor: ETC., A Review of General Semantics, 1943-70, Funk & Wagnalls Modern Guide to Synonyms, 1968; supr. editorial bd.: Funk & Wagnalls Standard Dicts; Contbr. to: Middle English Dict, U. Mich., 1933-38. Fellow AAAS, Am. Psychol. Assn., Am. Sociol. Assn.; mem. Modern Lang. Assn., Internat. Soc. for Gen. Semantics (pres. 1949-50), Consumers Union U.S. (dir. 1953-55), Inst. Jazz Studies (dir.). Clubs: Bohemian; Athenian Nile (Oakland). Home: Mill Valley Calif. Died Feb. 27, 1992.

HAYCRAFT, HOWARD, publisher, author; b. Madelia, Minn., July 24, 1905; s. Julius E. and Marie (Stelzer) H.; m. Molly Randolph Costain, Oct. 9, 1942. AB, U. Minn., 1928; LHD, Gustavus Adolphus Coll., 1975. Mem. staff U. Minn. Press, 1928; with H.W. Wilson Co., N.Y.C., 1929-91, v.p., 1940-52, pres., 1953-67, chmn. bd., 1967-91; dir. Forest Press, 1951-68, pres., 1961-62; specialist War Dept., 1942. Author, editor, joint editor: Authors Today and Yesterday, 1933, Junior Book of Authors, 1934, Boys' Sherlock Holmes, 1936, British Authors of the Nineteenth Century, 1936, Boys' Book of Great Detective Stories, 1938, American Author: 1600-1900, 1938, Boys' Second Book of Great Detective Stories, 1940, Murder for Pleasure: The Life and Times of the Detective Story, 1941, Crime Club Encore, 1942, Twnetieth Century Authors, 1942, Art of the Mystery Story, 1946, Fourteen Great Detective Stories, 1949, British Authors Before 1800, 1952, Treasury of Great Mysteries, 1957, Ten Great Mysteries, 195[illegible] Five Spy Novels, 1962, Three Times Three, Myste[illegible] Omnibus, 1964, Sherlock Holmes' Greatest Cases (larg[illegible] print), 1967, Books for the Blind: A Postscript and a[illegible] Appreciation, 1972; contbr. to lit. publs. Mem. Pres. Com. Employment of Handicapped, 1963-74; chmn[illegible] ALA Round Table Svcs. to Blind, 1968-69. Maj. U.S[illegible] Army Svc. Forces, 1942-46. Recipient Outstandin[illegible] Achievement award U. Minn., 1954, Campbell med[illegible] and citation ALA, 1966, Centennial citation, 1976. Mem. Mystery Writers Am. (pres. 1963), Players Club[illegible] Baker St. Irregulars (N.Y.C.), Kappa Sigma. Home[illegible] Highstown N.J. Died Nov. 12, 1991.

HAYDEN, MARTIN SCHOLL, public relations con[illegible] sultant, newswriter; b. Detroit, May 21, 1912; s. Jay G[illegible] and Marguerite (Scholl) H.; m. Elizabeth Dodds, Jul[illegible] 26, 1938; children: Jay G. II, John D., Marti[illegible] Scholl. Grad., Culver Mil. Acad., 1929; A.B., U. Mich. 1934; L.H.D., Detroit Coll. Law, 1967. Reporte[illegible] Kansas City (Mo.) Star, 1929-30; mem. staff Detroi[illegible] News, 1930-77, corr. Ann Arbor bur., 1930-34, gen[illegible] reporter, 1934-37, city and state polit. writer, 1938-47[illegible] corr. Washington bur., 1948-58; fgn. assignments in[illegible] clude Japan, China, Philippines, 1936, Berlin fgn. minis[illegible] ters meeting, 1954, Geneva Conf., 1955, Hungarian an[illegible] Polish uprising, 1956, Bermuda Conf., 1957; assoc[illegible] editor Detroit News, 1958, editor-in-chief, 1959-77 cons. pub. relations Ford Motor Co., from 1977; v.p[illegible] AP, 1971, vice chmn., 1973. Trustee Cranbrook Sch. bd. pres., 1963-67; trustee Harper-Grace Hosp.; pres[illegible] Leader Dogs for Blind; bd. dirs. Detroit Med. Center mem. Mich. Jud. Tenure Com., 1977-84, vice chmn. 1982. Served from 2d lt. to lt. col. AUS, D-Day, ETO. Decorated Normandy Beach arrowhead. Mem. New[illegible] spaper Editors; Sigma Chi. Clubs: Chevy Chase (Washington), Gridiron (Washington), Nat. Press (Washington), Overseas Writers (Washington); Detroit, Country of Detroit. Home: Grosse Pointe Mich. Died Sept. 15, 1991.

HAYDON, GLEN, musicologist, university professor; b. Infman, Kans., Dec. 9, 1896; s. William Leslie and Ursula Evelyn (Parker) H.; m. Helen Bergfried, Sept. 14, 1922; children: Glen Bergfried, Valeska Howell. AB, U. Calif., 1918, MA, 1921; PhD, U. Vienna, 1932; European study with Eugène Cools (composition) and Auguste Périer (clarinet), Paris, 1923-24; PhD, U. Vienna, 1932. Instr. of instrumental music Berkeley (Calif.) High Schs., 1920-25; prof. music, head dept. music U. N.C., 1934-51, Kenan prof. music, chmn. dept. music, from 1951, chmn. div. humanities, 1950-56; vis. prof. Harvard U., summer 1956. Author: Introduction to Musicology, 1941; articles and revs. in publs. Composer: The Druids Weed (ballet), 1929, Mass (for a cappella choir), 1930, incidental music to Lysistrata, 1936; editor: F. Corteccia Hinnario Secondo L'Vso Della Chiesa Romana et Fiorentina (Nos. 1-10), C. Festa, Hymni Per Totum Annum. Mem. AAUP, Am. Musicol. Soc. (pres. 1942-44), Nat. Assn. of Music in Liberal Arts Colls., Music Educators Nat. Conf. (nat. bd. 1937-41), Music Tchrs. Nat. Assn. (pres. 1940-42), N.C. State Music Tchrs. Assn. (pres. 1937-40), Nat. Assn. of Schs. of Music (mem. grad. com. 1942-47), Am. Coun. Learned Socs. (com. on musicology 1934-48, chmn. 1941-48), So. Humanities Conf. (del. from Ea. chpt. Am. Musicol. Soc. 1947), Internat. Musicol. Soc., Music Libr. Assn., Royal Musical Soc. (London), Am. Soc. for Aesthetics (trustee 1946-47), Mediaeval Acad. of Am., Phi Mu Alpha, Phi Delta Kappa, Pi Kappa Lambda. *

HAYEK, FRIEDRICH AUGUST (VON), economist, educator; b. Vienna, Austria, May 8, 1899; s. August and Felicitas (von Juraschek) von H.; children: Christine M. F., Lauence J. H.; m. 2d, Helene Bitterlich, 1950. Dr.jur., U. Vienna, 1921, Dr.re.pol., 1923; D.Sc. in Econs., U. London, 1941; Dr. (hon.), U. Rikkyo, Tokyo, 1964, U. Salzburg, 1974, U. Dallas, 1975, Marroquin U., Guatemala, 1977, U. Santa Maria, Valparaiso, 1977, U. Buenos Aires, 1977, U. Giessen, 1982. With Austrian Civil Service, 1921-26; dir. Austrian Inst. for Bus. Cycle Research, 1927-31; lectr. econs. and stats. U. Vienna, 1929-31; Tooke prof. econ. sci. and stats. U. London, London Sch. Econs., 1931-50; prof. social and moral sci. U. Chgo., 1950-62; prof. econs. U. Freiburg (Germany), 1962-70; vis. prof. U. Salzburg (Austria), 1970-74. Author: Prices and Production, 1931; Monetary Theory and the Trade Cycle, 1933; Monetary Nationalism and International Stability, 1937; Profits, Interest and Investment, 1939; The Pure Theory of Capital, 1941; The Road to Serfdom, 1944; Individualism and Economic Order, 1949; John Stuart Mill and Harriet Taylor, 1951; The Sensory Order, 1952; The Counter-Revolution of Science, 1952; The Constitution of Liberty, 1960; Studies in Philosophy, Politics and Economics, 1967; Freiburger Studien, 1969; Law, Legislation and Liberty, Vol. I, 1973, Vol. II, 1975, Vol. III, 1979; Denationalization of Money, 1976; Further Studies in Politics, 1978; also numerous articles; acting editor Economica, 1940-50. Arty. officer Austrian Army, World War I. Decorated Companion of Honor (Great Britain), Order Pour le Mérite (Germany); Austrian Distinction for Arts and Sci.; recipient Nobel Prize for Econs., 1974. Fellow Brit. Acad.; hon. fellow Austrian Acad. Sci. Home: Freiburg Germany Died Mar. 23, 1992; buried Neustift Cemetery, Vienna, Austria.

HAYES, ALFRED, banking executive; b. Ithaca, N.Y., July 4, 1910; s. Alfred and Christine Grace (Robertson) H.; m. Vilma F. Chalmers, Dec. 30, 1937; children: Anita Robertson Gratwick, Thomas Chalmers. BA, Yale U., 1930; BLitt, New Coll., Oxford, England, 1933. Investment analyst City Bank Farmers Trust Co., N.Y.C., 1933-40; with bond dept. Nat. City Bank N.Y., N.Y.C., 1940-42; asst. sec. investment div. N.Y. Trust Co., 1942-47, asst. v.p. fgn. div., 1947-49, v.p. fgn. div., 1949-56; pres. Fed. Res. Bank N.Y., 1956-75; vice chmn. Fed. Open Market Com., 1956-75; chmn. MOrgan Stanley Internat. Inc., 1975-81; adv. dir. Morgan Stanley Inc., 1975-89. Pres. bd. trustees Lingnan U., Canton, China, 1947-54; mem. coun. Yale U., 1961-68; pres. Howard Florey Biomed. Found., 1973-89. Lt. USNR, 1944-46. Decorated Order of Merit of Italian Republic; recipient C. Walter Nichols award NYU, 1967, Disting. Svc. award U.S. Treasury, 1969. Mem. Coun. Fgn. Rels., Pilgrims U.S., Can. Soc., Econ. Club (pres. 1965-66), Century Assn., River Club, Phi Beta Kappa, Sigma Xi, Phi Alpha Kappa, Beta Gamma Sigma, Alpha Delta Phi. Home: New Canaan Conn. Died Oct. 22, 1989.

HAYES, HAROLD THOMAS PACE, broadcasting executive; b. Elkin, N.C., Apr. 18, 1926; s. James M. and Aline (Pace) H.; m. Susan Meredith, Apr. 7, 1955 (div. 1983); children: Thomas Pace, Carrie Meredith; m. Judy Kessler, Mar. 4, 1983. BS, Wake Forest Coll., 1948. With So. Bell Telephone Co., Atlanta, 1948-49, UPI, Atlanta, 1949-50; asst. editor Pageant mag., N.Y.C., 1952, assoc. editor, 1953; assoc. editor Tempo mag., 1953; editor Picture Week mag., 1954; asst. to pub. Esquire mag., N.Y.C., 1955-59, articles editor, 1959-62, mng. editor, 1962-63, editor, 1963-73, asst. pub., 1973; freelance journalist, cons. editor, 1973—; instr. mag. journalism New Sch. Social Rsch., N.Y.C., 1961-63; mem. exec. com., dir. Sat. Rev., 1977—. Host nightly discussion show Roundtable, Channel 13, N.Y.C., 1974—; exec. producer TV spl. The Late Great, 1968; sr. editorial producer 20-20 ABC News, 1978; v.p. editorial planning CBS, 1980-89; author: The Last Place on Earth, 1977, Three Levels of Time, 1981; editor: Smiling Through the Apocalypse, 1970. Chmn. bd. visitors Wake Forest U., 1972-76. With USNR, 1943-45, 1st lt. USMCR, 1950-52. Nieman fellow Harvard U., 1958-59; recipient Disting. Alumni award Wake Forest U., 1968. Mem. Am. Soc. Mag. Editors (chmn. exec. com.). Home: Los Angeles Calif. Died Apr. 5, 1989.

HAYNER, J(OHN) CLIFFORD, physician; b. N.Y.C., June 11, 1893; s. George M. and E. Bessie (Mettler) H.; m. Mary Malloch, May 22, 1922. BS, Amherst Coll., 1915; MD, N.Y. Med. Coll., 1919. Intern Hahnemann Hosp., N.Y.C., 1919-20, resident, 1920-21; resident Flower Hosp., 1921-22; pvt. practice medicine N.Y.C., 1922-44; mem. faculty N.Y. Med. Coll., 1922-61, prof. anatomy and dir. dept., 1944-61; emeritus; asst. attending surgeon Flower Hosp-5th Ave. Hosp.; assoc. vis. surgeon Met. Hosp., 1931-49, cons. surgeon, from 1949; cons. surgeon Bird S. Coler Meml. Hosp. & Home. Author: Regional Anatomy, 1935; editor: Jour. Am. Inst. Homeopathy, 1934-37. Fellow ACS, N.Y. Acad. Medicine; mem. AMA, N.Y. State Med. Soc., Bronx County Med. Soc., AAAS, Theta Delta Chi, Alpha Kappa Kappa, Alpha Club, Dennys River Sportsmen's Club. *

HAYNES, DONALD, librarian; b. Fieldale, Va., Oct. 8, 1934; s. Thomas Bernard and Laura Jeannette (Richardson) H. B.A., U. Va., 1960; M.L.S., U. N.C., 1966. Tchr. Va. pub. schs., 1960-62; manuscripts and reference asst. U. Va. Library, Charlottesville, 1963-65; librarian, asst. prof. Eastern Shore br., U. Va., Wallops Island, 1966-69; dir. library services Va. State Library, Richmond, 1969-72, state librarian, 1972-86; dir. Va. Hist. Soc., Richmond, 1986-88. Editor: Virginiana in the Printed Book Collections of the Virginia State Library, 1975. Mem. Va. Historic Landmarks Commn., 1972-86; chmn. Va. Hist. Records Adv. Bd., 1976-86, Va. State Rev. Bd. for Landmarks, 1980-88; Statewide coordinator Va. United Way, 1976; bd. dirs. Central Va. Ednl. TV, 1972-82; mem. exec. bd. Edgar Allan Poe Found., 1982-88. Served with AUS, 1954-56. Mem. Am., Southeastern, Va. library assns., Va. Hist. Soc., So. Hist. Soc., Am. Hist. Assn., Soc. Am. Archivists, Beta Phi Mu. Home: Richmond Va. Died Jan. 30, 1988.

HAYNES, SHERWOOD KIMBALL, physics educator; b. Boston, Apr. 7, 1910; s. John and Jessie M. (Bailey) H.; m. Pauline J. McBride, 1943; children: Charles M., Margaret E., Sherwood K. II, J. Marie. A.B., Williams Coll., 1932; Ph.D., Calif. Inst. Tech., 1936. Instr. Williams Coll., 1936-39; asst. prof. Brown U., 1940-42; instr. elec. communications Radar Sch., Mass. Inst. Tech., 1942-44, assoc. dir., 1944-45; asso. prof. Vanderbilt U., 1945-51, prof., 1951-58; head dept. physics and astronomy Mich. State U., 1957-66, chmn. dept. physics, 1966-69, prof. physics, 1969-80, prof. emeritus, 1980-90; vis. scientist Am. Inst. Physics, 1963-72, mem. placement service adv. com., 1970-73, mem. manpower adv. com., 1973-79, bd. govs., 1974-77; Cons.-examiner North Central Assn. Colls. and Secondary Schs., 1964-81; vis. physicist IKO, Amsterdam, 1965; cons. Fulbright selection com., 1955, Midwest planning com., 1959. French sci. fellow Inst. Internat. Edn., France, 1939-40; Fulbright lectr. Paris U., France, 1954-55; Recipient Disting. faculty award Mich. State U., 1977. Am. Phys. Soc. (v.p. Southeastern sect. 1953-54); AAAS; mem. Am. Assn. Physics Tchrs. (v.p. 1972, pres. 1974), Sigma Pi Sigma. rsch. in field of electron spectroscopy. Home: Okemos Mich. Died Mar. 7, 1990; buried Evergreen Cemetery, Hyde Park, Mass.

HAYNSWORTH, CLEMENT FURMAN, JR., federal judge; b. Greenville, S.C., Oct. 30, 1912; s. Clement Furman and Elsie (Hall) H.; m. Dorothy Merry Barkley, 1946. Ed., Darlington Sch., Rome, Ga.; AB, Furman U., 1933; LLB, Harvard, 1936; LLD, Furman U., 1964. Bar: S.C. 1936. Mem. firm Haynsworth, Perry, Bryant, Marion & Jonstone, Greenville, until 1957; judge U.S. Ct. Appeals 4th Circuit, 1957-64, chief judge, 1964-81, sr. judge, 1981-89; chmn. standing com. to Review Circuit Council Conduct and Disability Orders of Jud. Conf. of U.S., 1982-89. Adv. council Furman U. Served as officer USNR, 1942-45. Mem. Am., S.C., Greenville bar assns., Am. Law Inst. (council, life mem.), Am. Judicature Soc. (dir. 1970-74), Inst. Ct. Mgmt. (dir.), Greenville County Hist. Soc. (dir.). Episcopalian. Home: Greenville S.C. Died Nov. 22, 1989; buried Springwood Cemetery, Greenville.

HAYS, MRS. GLENN G., organization executive; b. Ransom, Kans., Feb. 6, 1895; d. William O. and Florence (LaPlante) Dubbs; m. Glenn G. Hays, Nov. 30, 1917. Student, Kans. State Tchrs. Coll., 1914-16, U. Colo., 1930; BA, Ft. Hays State Coll., 1965. High sch. tchr. English and Latin, 1916-21, 29-32; pres. Kans. Woman's Christian Temperance Union, 1938-44, rec. sec. nat. orgn., 1944-50, v.p., 1950-53, pres., 1953-59; 1st v.p. World's WCTU, 1956-62; legis. rep. Nat. WCTU, 1959-62; chmn. adminstr. Rebecca Dubbs' Meml. Fund. Mem. Christian Women's Fellow, Kans. Fedn. Women's Clubs (chmn. dist. scholarship loan), Nat. Coun. Women (corr. sec. 1955), Nat. League Pen Women, Profl. Writers Club, DAR, Delta Kappa Gamma. Mem. Christian Ch. *

HAZEN, RICHARD, engineering consulting company executive; b. Dobbs Ferry, N.Y., Aug. 5, 1911; s. Allen and Elizabeth (McConway) H.; m. Elizabeth Shute, June 19, 1937 (dec.); children: Richard (dec.), Annah Putnam Hazen Gorman, Mary Vanderlyn Hazen Gillam. A.B., Dartmouth Coll., 1932; B.C.E., Columbia U., 1934; M.S. in San. Engring, Harvard U., 1937. Asst. engr. Westvaco Corp., 1934-36; asst. engr. Malcolm Pirnie (Engrs.), 1937-40, asso. engr., 1940-42, partner, 1946-51; co-founder, partner Hazen and Sawyer, N.Y.C., 1951-81; vis. prof. U. N.C., Chapel Hill, 1968; cons. planning and design of water supply and waste disposal to govt. and industry. Contbr. articles to profl. jours., also chpts. on water supply to encys. and engring. handbooks. Bd. dirs. Children's Village, Dobbs Ferry, N.Y., 1952; bd. dirs. Dobbs Ferry Bd. Edn., 1946-52, pres., 1948-51. Served with USNR, 1942-46. Mem. Nat. Acad. Engring., Am. Inst. Cons. Engrs. (pres. 1968), ASCE (dir. 1966-69, hon. mem. 1983), Am. Water Works Assn. (hon. mem., dir. 1951-56), Am. Acad. Environ. Engring., Water Pollution Control Fedn., TAPPI, New Eng. Water Works Assn., Phi Beta Kappa, Tau Beta Pi. Home: New York N.Y. Died Feb. 12, 1990.

HEAD, HOWARD, manufacturer and designer sporting goods; b. Phila., July 31, 1914; s. Joseph and Annie (Wilkinson) H.; m. Martha B. Fritzlen; 1 dau., Nancy Stratton Head Thode. Grad., William Penn Charter Sch., Phila., 1928-32; A.B. in Engring. Scis, Harvard U., 1936. Journalist, writer, motion picture editor, 1937-38; mem. engring. dept. Glenn L. Martin Co., Balt., 1939-47; cons., designer engring. and physics research depts. Johns Hopkins U., Balt., 1948-51; founder, pres., chmn. bd., treas. Head Ski Co., Inc., Timonium, Md., 1950-70; chmn. bd. Prince Mfg., Inc., Princeton, N.J., 1971-82; Chmn. industry fund raising U.S. Olympic Ski Team, 1961-62. Head Theater in Center Stage, Balt. named in his and wife's honor as tribute to their many years of support. Mem. Ski Industries Am. (founding mem., pres., dir. 1958-59). Democrat. Clubs: Harvard (Balt.), Baltimore Country (Balt.), Ski (Balt.). Home: Baltimore Md. Died Mar. 3, 1991; buried Phila.

HEADLEY, SHERMAN KNIGHT, art museum director, broadcasting consultant; b. St. Paul, Oct. 10, 1922; s. Louis Sherman and Sylvia (Knight) H.; m. Alta McDonald, June 5, 1943; children: Sherman (dec.), Timothy, James, Susan. Student, Carleton Coll., 1939-41, U. Wis., 1941-42, U. Iowa, summer 1943; B.S., U. Minn., 1948. Tech. dir. Belfry Theatre, Lake Geneva, Wis., summer 1942; Tech. dir. Youngstown (Ohio) Playhouse, 1942-43, Cleve. Play House, 1943-45, Chautauqua Theatre, summers 1944-45; dir. Kanawha Players, Charleston, W.Va., 1946-47, Belfry Theatre, summer 1947, Tucson Little Theatre, 1947-48; prodn. mgr. Sta. WCCO-TV, Mpls., 1948-52; asst. mgr. Sta. WCCO-TV, 1952-69, v.p., gen. mgr., 1969-77; exec. v.p., exec. dir. Minn. Mus. Art, St. Paul, 1977-78; Mem. journalism adv. bd. U. Minn. Pres. Guild of Performing Arts, 1962; bd. dirs. Mpls. Downtown Council, 1958-62, Minn. Ednl. TV, 1966-80, Minn. affiliate Am. Heart Assn., 1978; pres. Mpls. Aquatennial, 1964-65. Mem. Minn. Broadcasters Assn. (pres. 1960-63), Mpls. Advt. Club (pres. 1965-66), Am. Fedn. Advt. (past lt. gov., Silver Medal award 1977), Mpls. Better Bus. Bur., Mpls. C. of C. Home: San Diego Calif. Died Nov. 11, 1988; cremated.

HEAPS, WILSON A., banker, farmer; b. Pylesville, Md., Dec. 5, 1896; s. Isaac W. and Annie L. (Wilson) H.; m. Maria J. Stokes, Jan. 5, 1918; children: Ethel J. Crosley, Henry W., Jeanne L. Heaps, Ruth A. Burkins. Grad. high sch. Owner, operator farm Street, Md., from 1918; dir. Delta Nat. Bank, from 1918, pres., from 1943; dir. Chesapeake & Potomac Telephone Co., Mut. Fire Ins. Co., Montgomery County, Blue Ridge Flooring Co. Mem. Gov.'s Commn. on Aging; chmn. Met. Commn. of Harford County; pres. Harford County Farm Bur., 1945-50; dir. Md. Farm Bur., from 1945, Am. Farm Bur., 1950-58; bd. dirs. Md. Hosp. Svc. (Blue Cross), Harford coun. ARC. Recipient cert. of meritorious svc. to agr. U. Md., 1951; named Man of Yr. for outstanding svc. to Md. agr. Progressive Farmer, 1954. Mem. Md. Coun. Econ. Edn., Mason, Lion. Presbyterian. *

HEARD, MANNING WRIGHT, lawyer; b. Baton Rouge, Aug. 31, 1896; s. William Wright and Isabelle Elizabeth (Manning) H.; m. Renee Montagnet, Aug. 16, 1920; children: Manning Wright, June H. Wadsworth. LLB, Tulane U., 1920. Bar: La. 1920, Conn. 1936. Asst. dir. atty. Parish of Orleans, 1920-24; atty. Union Indemnity Co., 1924-33; atty. Hartford Accident & Indemnity Co., 1933-37, sec., 1937-39, v.p., 1939-61, v.p., gen. counsel, 1946-53, 1st v.p., gen. counsel, 1953-59, exec. v.p., 1959-61, pres., 1961-63, chmn. of the bd., from 1963. Mem. Am. Judicature Soc., ABA, Hartford County Bar Assn., Internat. Assn. Ins. Counsel. *

HEARD, MARSTRON, banker; b. Manchester, N.H., Dec. 2, 1897; s. Arthur M. and Ora B. (Farrar) H.; m. Doris F. Fellows, Apr. 30, 1924; children: Mary Johnson, Joan White, Arthur, Elizabeth Lufkin. Student, Phillips Andover Acad., 1916; AB, Harvard, 1920. Asst. Nat. Bank Examiner, 1922-24; asst. cashier Amoskeag Nat. Bank, Manchester, 1924-38, v.p., 1938-50, pres., from 1950, dir., from 1931; pres., dir. Amoskeag Trust Co., from 1931; dir. N.H. Ins. Co., Amoskeag Industries, Inc., N.H. Pub. Svc. Co.; trustee Amoskeag Savs. Bank, 1950. Trustee Currier Gallery of Art. *

HEARST, AUSTINE MCDONNELL, newspaper reporter, free-lance feature writer, columnist; b. Warrenton, Va., Nov. 22, 1928; d. Austin and Mary (Belt) McDonnell; m. William Randolph Hearst, Jr., 1948; children—William Randolph III, John Augustine Chilton. Ed. Warrenton County schs., Convent Notre Dame, Md., King-Smith Jr. Coll. Columnist Washington Times-Herald, 1946-56; syndicated columnist King Features Syndicate; radio commentator CBS, 1946-56. Writer soc. column: Under My Hat, syndicated column: From the Capital; author The Horses of San Simeon. Clubs: Nat. Press (Washington), Sulgrave (Washington); Cosmopolitan. Home: New York N.Y. Died June 23, 1991; buried Cypress Lawn, Colma, Calif.

HEATON, CLAUDE EDWIN, physician, educator; b. Peekskill, N.Y., Aug. 21, 1897; s. Reuben Fancer and Ida (Mosher) H.; m. Pauline Elizabeth Reid, June 2, 1923; children: Marion Ruth, Thomas Reid. MD, NYU Med. Coll., 1921. Diplomate Am. Bd. Ob-Gyn.; practiced in N.Y.C. from 1926, limited to ob-gyn. Instr. in gynecology NYU Med. Coll., 1926-32, assoc. clin. prof. ob-gyn., 1932-44, assoc. prof. ob-gyn., 1944-58, prof., from 1958; attending obstetrician and gynecologist Bellevue Hosp., U. Hosp., cons.; assoc. attending obstetrician and gynecologist Lennox Hill Hosp.; dir. obstetrics French Hosp., 1951, dir. emeritus; former attending obstetrician N.Y. Nursery and Child's Hosp.; adj. asst. attending obstetrician Manhattan Maternity Hosp.; cons. obstetrician and gynecologist French Hosp., from 1963. Author: Modern Motherhood, 1935. Fellow Am. Coll. Ob-Gyn., N.Y. Acad. Medicine, N.Y. Obstet. Soc.; mem. AMA, N.Y. Med. Soc., N.Y. County Med. Soc., Alpha Omega Alpha, Century Club. Presbyterian. *

HEBBLE, WILLIAM JOSEPH, utility executive; b. Indpls., Oct. 18, 1931; s. Edmond O. and Rose (French) H.; m. Virginia L. Reese, Aug. 11, 1950; 1 dau., Sharon I. With Public Service Co. of Ind., Inc., Plainfield, from 1949; v.p. fin. ops. Public Service Co. of Ind., Inc., from 1986. Mem. Danville (Ind.) Town Bd., 1966-71. Mem. Phi Delta Kappa. Republican. Roman Catholic. Club: Elks. Home: Danville Ind. Deceased. †

HECKERT, JOSIAH BROOKS, accountant, educator; b. Tescott, Kans., Jan. 22, 1893; s. Uriah E. and Nancy Jane (Roy) H.; m. Marie Hood, June 5, 1918. AB, Kans. Wesleyan U., 1916, DCS (hon.), 1941; postgrad., U. Kans., 1916-17; AM, U. Chgo., 1923; LLD (hon.), Simpson Coll., 1950. CPA, Ohio. Prof. econs. Simpson Coll., Indianola, Iowa, 1920-25; assoc. prof. acctg. Ohio State U., Columbus, 1925-45, prof. acctg., from 1945, prof. emeritus acctg. and MIS; pres. Columbus Blank Book Mfg. Co.; v.p. Dollar Fed. Savs. and Loan Assn., Avis Rent-A-Car System, Inc.; bd. dirs. indsl. and fin. corps. Author: Accounting Systems--Design and Installation, 1936, Distribution Costs--Analysis and Control, 1946; (with I.J. Stone) Wholesale Accounting and Control, 1935; (with W.E. Dickerson) Drugstore Accounting, 1943; (with J.D. Wilson) Controllership, 1952; contbg. editor to Accts. Handbook, 1943, Cost Acctg. Handbook, 1944. Mem. Am. Inst. Accts., Nat. Assn. Cost Accts. (past nat. dir., pres. 1952-53), Beta Gamma

Sigma, Beta Alpha Psi, Lambda Chi alpha. Home: Columbus Ohio Died Dec. 6, 1990.

HEDMEG, ANDREW, state official, educator; b. Bratislava, Czechoslovakia; came to U.S., 1912, naturalized, 1922; s. John and Susan (Hutnik) H.; m. Jennie Katonak, May 21, 1932; 1 dau., Andra (Mrs. Francis Ledet). A.B., Ohio State U., 1931, M.D., 1936; M.P.H., Johns Hopkins, 1941. Diplomate: Am. Bd. Preventive Medicine. County health officer Miss. Bd. Health, 1937-52; dir. preventive medicine div., local health services div. La. Bd. Health, 1952-66; pres. La. Bd. Health, state health officer, 1966-72; dir. div. health La. Health and Human Resources Adminstrn., 1973-74; Clin. prof. pub. health adminstrn. La. State U. Med. Center, from 1953, acting head dept. pub. health and preventive medicine, from 1975; adj. prof. Tulane U. Sch. Tropical Medicine and Pub. Health, New Orleans, from 1953. Served with AUS, 1942-46. Recipient C.B. White Meml. award La. Pub. Health Assn., 1964, Outstanding Service award So. br. Am. Pub. Health Assn., 1966; Outstanding Service award Am. Assn. Pub. Health Physicians, 1974; Gov.'s Outstanding Service award to citizen La., 1974. Life fellow Am. Pub. Health Assn.; mem. Am. Coll. Preventive Medicine, La. State, Orleans Parish med. socs. Home: New Orleans La. Died Sept. 4, 1988; buried Lake Lawn Pk. and Mausoleum, New Orleans.

HEFFELFINGER, FRANK PEAVEY, business executive; b. Mpls., Oct. 15, 1897; s. Frank T. and Lucia L. (Peavey) H.; m. Elizabeth E. Bradley, Jan. 1, 1921. Ed., Yale, 1920. Workman British Am. Elevator Co., McNutt, Sask., 1920, Port Arthur (Ont.) Elevator Co., 1921; sec. No. Elevator Co., Winnipeg, Man., 1921-25; v.p. Globe Elevator Co., Duluth, Minn., 1925-29; v.p., gen. mgr. Monarch Elevator Co., 1929-30; former pres. Peavey Co. formerly named F.H. Peavey & Co., Mpls.; chmn. dir. Peavey Co. formerly named F.H. Peavey & Co.; dir. N. Star Rsch. and Devel. Inst., Northwest Bancorp., Gt. No. Ry. Co., Northwestern Nat Bank, Mpls. Dir. Found. for Am. Agr., Nat. Grain Trade Coun.; trustee Tax Found., N.Y. Served as regional dir. (Minn., N.D., S.D.), W.P.B., Mpls.; chmn. fin. com. Rep. Nat. Com., 1953-55. Mem. Grain and Feed Dealers Nat. Assn. (chmn. legis. com.), Izaak Walton League, Mpls. Club, Manitoba (Winnipeg) Club, Kitchi Gami Club (Duluth), Union League Club (Chgo.). *

HEFFERNAN, JOHN BAPTIST, naval officer; b. Washington, Ind., Oct. 21, 1894; s. William and Ellen (Sullivan) H.; m. Patricia Grattan Esmonde (d. late Sir Thomas Grattan Esmonde, Bart., M.P., of Ballynastragh, Gorey, Co. Wexford, Ireland), Nov. 18, 1927; children: Patricia Grattan, Henry Grattan, Eithne Mary Grattan Hartnett, Kathleen Barbara Grattan Wach. BS, U.S. Naval Acad., Annapolis, 1917; student, Naval War Coll., Newport, R.I., Army-Navy Staff Coll., Washington. Instr. of history U.S. Naval Acad., 1932-35, 38-40; chief of staff 7th Naval Dist., 1946, dir. naval history, 1946-56. Naval editor Ency. Brit. Served in destroyers, Europe, 1917-18; comd. destroyer div., Atlantic, 1940-41, destroyer Squadron, Atlantic, 1942; comd. U.S.S. Tenn. in battle for Leyte Gulf, 1944, at Iwo Jima and Okinawa, 1945; retired with rank of rear adm. USN. Decorated Legion of Merit, Bronze Star Medal (4), Commendation Ribbon (2). Mem. Naval Hist. Found. (trustee and v.p., sec.), Naval Inst., Am. Hist. Assn., Am. Irish Hist. Assn., Am. Cath. Hist. Assn., Ind. Hist. Soc., Soc. Nautical Rsch. (London), Mil. Hist. Soc. Ireland, Army and Navy Club (Washington). Roman Catholic. *

HEIDELBERGER, MICHAEL, chemist, educator; b. N.Y.C., Apr. 29, 1888; s. David and Fannie (Campe) H.; m. Nina Tachau, 1916 (dec. 1946); m. Charlotte Rosen Salomonski, 1956 (dec. 1988). B.S., Columbia U., 1908, A.M., 1909, Ph.D., 1911; postgrad, Fed. Poly. Inst., Zurich; 16 hon. degrees. Asst. in chemistry summer sessions Columbia U., Stevens Inst., N.Y.C., 1909, 11; fellow, asst., assoc. and assoc. mem. Rockefeller Inst. Med. Rsch., 1912-27; chemist Mt. Sinai Hosp., 1927-28, Presbyn. Hosp. of N.Y., 1928-56; assoc. prof. medicine Columbia U., N.Y.C., 1928-29, prof. biol. chemistry, 1929-45, prof. biochemistry, 1945-48, prof. immuno-chemistry, 1948-56, prof. emeritus, from 1956; vis. prof. immuno-chemistry Rutgers U., 1955-64; adj. prof. pathology (immunology) NYU, from 1964; chmn. research council Pub. Health Research Inst. of N.Y.C., 1951-56; cons. to Sec. of War, 1942-46, WHO, 1965-76; hon. mem. faculty several univs.; mem. Grad. Faculty Alumni Assn. Columbia U., 1979. Author: Advanced Laboratory Manual of Organic Chemistry, 1923, Lectures in Immuno-Chemistry, 1956; contbr. over 380 articles to profl. jours. 1st lt. San. Corps., AUS, 1918-19. Decorated chevalier Légion d'honneur, 1949, officier, 1966, Ordre de Léopold II, 1953; recipient Ehrlich Silver medal, 1933, Lasker award, 1952, 78, von Behring prize, 1954, Louis Pasteur Gold medal, Swedish Med. Soc., 1960, T. Duckett Jones Meml. award, 1964, Nat. medal for Sci., 1967, N.Y. Acad. Medicine medal, 1968, von Pirquet Gold medal, 1971, Virchow Soc. Gold medal, 1973, (with others) Louisa Gross Horwitz prize, 1977, Claude Hudson award, 1978, Achievement medal, Columbia U., 1979, Dean's Disting. Svc. medal Columbia U. Coll. Physicians and Surgeons, 1986, N.Y.C. Mayor's award for Sci. and Tech., 1987, John Jay award Columbia Coll., 1988; known as the father of immunochemistry. Mem. NAS, Am. Philos. Soc., Am. Chem. Soc., Am. Soc. Biol. Chemists, Am. Acad. Microbiology, Am. Soc. Microbiologists, Harvey Soc. (twice pres.), Am. Assn. Immunologists (twice pres.), Royal Danish Acad. Scis. (fgn.), Accademia Nazionale dei Lincei, Royal Soc. London (fgn. mem.), French Nat. Acad. Medicine (fgn. mem.), French Soc. Immunologists (hon.), German Soc. Immunology (hon.), Brit. Soc. Immunology (hon.), Mex. Soc. Allergy and Immunology (hon.), Mex. Med. Assn., Chemists and Pharmacists Assn., N.Y. Acad. Scis. (hon. life), Am. Acad. Allergy (hon.). Home: New York N.Y. Died June 25, 1991.

HEIGES, DONALD RUSSEL, clergyman, theological education director; b. Biglerville, Pa., June 25, 1910; s. Edmund Dale and Elsie (Slaybaugh) H.; m. Mary Susannah Kump, June 1, 1935; children—Carol Sue (Mrs. Kenneth Reinhardt), Joan Christina (Mrs. David Blythe). B.A., Gettysburg Coll., 1931, D.D., 1955; B.D., Luth. Theol. Sem., Gettysburg, 1934; M.A., Union Theol. Sem. and Columbia, 1941; D.D., Concordia Coll., Moorhead, Minn., 1954. Ordained to ministry Luth. Ch., 1935; mem. faculty, chaplain Gettysburg Coll., 1934-44; Luth. pastor to students, counselor Columbia, 1944-50; exec. sec. div. coll. and univ. work Nat. Luth. Council, 1950-58; dean Chgo. Luth. Theol. Sem., 1958-62; pres. Luth. Theol. Sem. at Gettysburg, 1962-76, Luth. Theol. Sem. at Phila., 1964-70; exec. dir. Council for Luth. Theol. Edn. in NE, 1976-78; Bd. dirs. Nat. Luth. Campus Ministry; mem. directing com., div. ednl. services Luth. Council U.S. Author: The Christian's Calling, 1958. Mem. Phi Beta Kappa, Eta Sigma Phi, Phi Sigma Kappa. Republican. Home: Gettysburg Pa. Died Aug. 10, 1990; buried Biglerville Cemetery.

HEIGES, JESSE GIBSON, lawyer, business executive; b. nr. Shippensburg, Pa., Sept. 19, 1914; s. Jesse Shearer and Susan (Fickes) H.; m. Virginia M. Rodgers, Apr. 20, 1957. A.B., Ursinus Coll., 1935, LL.D., 1974; LL.B., U. Pa., 1938. Bar: N.Y. bar 1939. Atty. Mudge, Stern, Williams & Tucker, N.Y.C., 1939-43, 46-50; atty. Pfizer Inc., N.Y.C., 1950-56, sec., 1956-69, gen. counsel, 1956-79, v.p., 1967-79, dir., 1960-79, corp. adv. council, 1983-88. Served as lt. USNR, 1943-46. Mem. ABA, N.Y. Bar Assn., Assn. Bar City N.Y., Palm Beach Civic Assn. Clubs: River of New York, West Side Tennis of Forest Hills (gov. 1955-62); Maidstone (East Hampton) (gov. from 1982); Bath and Tennis (Palm Beach, Fla.), Everglades (Palm Beach, Fla.). Home: Palm Beach Fla. Died Nov. 16, 1991; buried Riverside Meml. Pk., Tequesta, Fla.

HEIM, LEO EDWARD, musician, conservatory administrator; b. Chandler, Ind., Sept. 22, 1913; s. Raymond Earl and Emily J. Heim; m. Margaret Brigetta Borchers, Feb. 14, 1942. Student, Northwestern U., 1931-32; BM, Am. Conservatory Music, 1935, MM, 1946, Dr. Musical Arts (hon.), 1987. Mem. piano faculty Am. Conservatory Music, Chgo., from 1935, asst. dean, 1956-57, dean, 1957-71, pres., 1971-81, pres. emeritus, 1981-92; pianist, accompanist, ensemble player; former examiner, mem. ind. schs. com. Nat. Assn. Schs. Music. Trustee Am. Conservatory Music; sec. Cliff Dwellers Arts Found., from 1985; organist 1st Ch. of Christ, Scientist, Wilmette, Ill. Served with USAAF, 1942-45. Decorated Bronze Star. Mem. Soc. Am. Musicians, Musicians Union, Phi Mu Alpha Sinfonia. Clubs: Cliff Dwellers (pres. 1978-80), University, Executives (Chgo.). Died Jan. 1, 1992.

HEIMANN, ROBERT KARL, tobacco company executive; b. N.Y.C., Sept. 22, 1918; s. Charles and Elizabeth Quinan H.; m. Charlotte Parker, Feb. 19, 1950; children: Mark, Karia. AB summa cum laude, Princeton U., 1948; MA, NYU, 1949, PhD, 1953. Editor Nation's Heritage, 1948-49; mng. and exec. editor Forbes mag., 1949-53; with Am. Brands (formerly Am. Tobacco Co.), from 1954, asst. to pres., 1961-64, v.p. mktg. and pub. rels., 1964-66, exec. v.p., 1966-69, pres., COO, 1969-72, chmn., 1973-80, CEO, 1977-78. Author: Tobacco and Americans, 1960; contbr. articles to profl. jours. Capt. AUS, 1942-46. Mem. N.Y. Security Analysts Soc., N.Y. Fin. Writers. Home: Portland Oreg. Died Feb. 11, 1990.

HEIMBERGER, WILLIAM WENGERD, steel castings company executive; b. Columbus, Ohio, July 20, 1894; s. Harry Jacob and Sarah Evelyn (Wengerd) H.; m. Helen Reese, Nov. 4, 1918; 1 child, Helen Jean Caldwell. BS in Mining Engring., Ohio State U., 1916. With Buckeye Steel Castings Co., Columbus, from 1916; v.p. ops. Buckeye Steel Castings Co., 1960-62, pres., gen. mgr., 1963-64, chmn. of the bd., 1964-65, dir.; v.p., dir. State Savs. Co., Columbus. Mem. ferrous metall. adv. bd. cast armor Ordnance Dept., WWII and Korea; bd. dirs. Jr. Achievement Columbus, Columbus Symphony Orch. Recipient Benjamin G. Lamme Gold medal for engring. achievement Ohio State U., 1964. Mem. Steel Founders Soc. Am. (Tech. and Operating medal 1963, chmn. 1960 handbook com.), N.A.M. (past dir.), Columbus Indsl. Assn. (past pres.), Ohio Mfrs. Assn., Ohio C. of C., Columbus C. of C., Am. Inst. Mining and Metall. Engrs., Masons, Rotary, Clubs: Scioto Country, Univ. (Columbus), Faculty (Ohio State U.), Zanesville (Ohio), Rod and Gun. Republican. Presbyterian. *

HEINEMANN, EDWARD H., engineering executive aircraft design engineer; b. Saginaw, Mich., Mar. 14, 1908; s. Gustav Christian and Margaret (Schust) H.; m. Zell Shewey, 1959; 1 dau. by previous marriage, Joan Heinemann Coffee. Ed. pub. schs., Mich., Calif.; DSc, Northrup U., 1976. Designer, project engr., chief engr. Moreland Aircraft Corp., Internat. Aircraft Corp., Northrop Aircraft Corp., 1931-36; chief engr. El Segundo (Calif.) div. Douglas Aircraft Co., Inc., 1936-58, corp. v.p. in charge combat aircraft engring, 1958-60; v.p. European sales Douglas Aircraft Co., 1960; exec. v.p. Summers Gyroscope Co., 1960-62; v.p. engring. and program devel. Gen. Dynamics Corp., N.Y.C., 1962-73; now with Heinemann Assocs., Rancho Santa Fe, Calif.; cons. to numerous govt. coms.; guest adv. and observer for first U.S. staffed space shots. Recipient Sylvanus Albert Reed award, 1952, Collier trophy for aviation design, 1953, So. Calif. Aviation Man of Yr. award, 1954, Paul Tissandier diploma Fedn. Aeronautique Internat., 1955, Nat. Medal Sci., 1983. Fellow AIAA, Soc. Aero. Weight Engrs. (hon.), Inst. Aero. Scis. (hon.), Royal Aero. Soc., Am. Astronautic Soc.; mem. Soc. Naval Architects and Marine Engrs., Am. Soc. Naval Engrs., Nat. Acad. Engring., Soc. Automotive Engrs., Tau Beta Pi (hon.). Home: Rancho Santa Fe Calif. Died Nov. 26, 1991; cremated.

HEINS, ALBERT EDWARD, mathematician; b. Boston, Sept. 7, 1912; s. Samuel and Rose Lily H.; m. Miriam Yaskin, Aug. 15, 1939; 1 dau., Ellen Ruth. BS, MIT, 1934, MS, 1935, PhD, 1936. Instr. math. Purdue U., 1935-40, asst. prof., 1940-42, 46; rsch. assoc. Radiation Lab. (N.D.R.C. Project), MIT, 1942-46; assoc. prof. math. Carnegie Inst. Tech., 1946-51, prof., 1951-59; prof. math. U. Mich., Ann Arbor, 1959-92; guest prof. Technische Hochschule, Darmstadt, Germany, 1980. Purdue Rsch. Found. fellow, 1941; John Simon Guggenheim Found. fellow, 1953-54; Horace Rackham grantee U. Mich., 1960. Mem. AAUP, Am. Math Soc. Home: Ann Arbor Mich. Died June 24, 1992. †

HEINZ, HENRY JOHN, III, senator; b. Pitts., Oct. 23, 1938; s. Henry John II and Joan (Diehl) H.; m. Teresa Simoes-Ferreira, 1966; children: Henry John IV, Andre, Christopher Drake. Grad., Phillips Exeter Acad., 1956; B.A., Yale U., 1960; M.B.A., Harvard U., 1963; Litt.D.(hon.), Wilkes Coll., 1979; LL.D.(hon.), Temple U., 1978. Gen. product mgr. marketing H.J. Heinz Co., Pitts., 1965-70; lectr. Carnegie-Mellon U. Grad. Sch. Indsl. Adminstrn., 1970-71; mem. 92d-94th congresses from 18th Dist. Pa., 1971-77; U.S. senator from Pa., 1977-91; chmn. Senate spl. com. on aging; Del. Republican Nat. Conv., 1968, 72, 76, 80; chmn. Pa. Rep. Platform Com., 1970. Trustee Howard Heinz Endowment, Childrens Hosp., Pitts., U. Pitts.; bd. overseers Grad. Sch. Bus., Harvard U.; chmn. H.J. Heinz II Charitable and Family Trust. Served with USAF, 1963. Recipient Nat. Americanism award Anti-Defamation League of B'nai B'rith, 1977. Mem. Am. Inst. Pub. Service. Home: Pittsburgh Pa. Died Apr. 4, 1991. †

HEINZ, HENRY JOHN, II, senator, food products manufacturing company executive; b. Sewickley, Pa., July 10, 1908; s. Howard and Elizabeth (Rust) H.; m. Joan Diehl, June 18, 1935 (div.); 1 child, Henry John III; m. Drue Maher, Aug. 22, 1953. Grad., Shadyside Acad., 1927; A.B., Yale, 1931; student, Trinity Coll., Cambridge, 1931-32. With H.J. Heinz Co., Pitts., 1932, asst. to pres., 1937-41, pres., 1941-59, chmn., from 1959; U.S. senator from Pa., 1976-91. Chmn. Sarah Heinz House, Pitts.; mem. Nat. Council of World Wildlife Fund-U.S.; mem. exec. com. Allegheny Conf. on Community Devel.; chmn. Yale Art Gallery; trustee U.S. council Internat. C. of C., Com. Econ. Devel.; v.p., dir. Pitts. Symphony Soc.; Bd. dirs. Bus. Com. for Arts, Inc., Pitts. Regional Planning Assn., Nat. Assos. Smithsonian Instn.; mem. Conservation Found.; trustee Carnegie Inst., Carnegie-Mellon U., Internat. Life Scis. Inst./Nutrition Found., World Affairs Council Pitts. Decorated cross of comdrs. Royal Order of Phoenix (Greece); chevalier Legion of Honor (France); Knight comdr. Brit. Empire; comdr. Order of Merit (Italy). Mem. Council on Fgn. Relations, Am. Ditchley Found., Brit. N.Am. Com. Republican. Presbyn. Clubs: Duquesne (Pitts), Allegheny Country (Pitts); Buck's and White's (London); River (N.Y.C.); Rolling Rock and Laurel Valley (Ligonier, Pa.); The Brook. Home: Pittsburgh Pa. Died Feb. 23, 1987; interred Homewood Cemetery, Pitts. †

HELCK, (CLARENCE) PETER, artist; b. N.Y.C., June 17, 1893; s. Henry Philip and Clara (Brandt) H.; m. Priscilla Smith, Sept. 30, 1922; 1 child, Jerry Peter. Edn. pub. sch. and, DeWitt Clinton High Sch., N.Y.C.; studied under, George Bridgeman, 1915, Sir Frank Brangwyn, 1920-23, Harry Wickey, 1923-28, Lewis Daniel, 1940-45; student, Art Students League, 1912, 1923. Adv. artist for maj. indsl. and transp. corps., from 1918, illustrator leading publs., 1925-60; founding faculty mem. Famous Artists Schs., Westport, Conn., from 1948. Represented in permanent collections Met. Mus. Art (N.Y.C.), Congl. Libr. (Washington), Mus. of Fine Arts (Phila.), also pvt. collections; author, illustrator: The Checkered Flag, 1961 (winner gold medals Salmagundi Club 1961, Soc. Illustrators, 1962, Thomas McKean Meml. trophy 1962, Byron Hull cup 1962). Recipient Harvard award, 1929, Art Dirs.

medal, 1931, 36, 41, 44, 51, Phila. Art Dirs. 1st awards, 1939, 40, Chgo. Art Dirs. medal, 1947, Detroit Art Dirs. 1st awards, 1950-52, medals, 1954, 56, Cleve. Art Dirs. medal, 1951. Mem. NAD, Allied Artists, Am. Watercolor Soc., Audubon Artists, Phila. Watercolor Club, Soc. Illustrators, N.Y. Art Dirs. Club, Vet. Motor Car Club Am. (hon. mem.), Antique Automobile Club Am., Automobilists Upper Hudson Valley, Conn. Automobile Hist. Soc., H. H. Franklin Club. Presbyterian. *

HELLER, ANN WILLIAMS, nutritionist, writer; b. Vienna, Austria, Aug. 25, 1904; came to U.S., 1938, naturalized, 1944; d. Friedrich C. and Elsa (Spitzer) Wilhelm; m. Walter L. Heller, Dec. 27, 1933 (dec. Sept. 1966). Student, U. Vienna, 1933-34, Columbia U., 1938-39. Food and equipment editor Everywomans Mag., N.Y.C., 1955-57. Writer: feature articles mags. including Reader's Digest; contbr.: articles to newspapers, trade jours. and syndicate features, including all major syndicates; writer consumer product books; books include Soybeans from Soup to Nuts, 1944, Cooked to Your Taste, 1945, It's a Sin to Be Fat, 1947, Reducers Cookbook, 1948, The Busy Woman's Cookbook, 1948, Thrifty Gourmet's Meat Cookbook, 1971, Eat and Get Slim Cookbook, 1973, Nature's Own Vegetables Cookbook, 1973. Mem. Am. Soc. Journalists and Authors. Home: New York N.Y. Died Oct. 3, 1988.

HELLER, ERICH, educator, author; b. Komotau, Bohemia, Mar. 27, 1911; came to the U.S., 1959; s. Alfred and Else (Hoenig) H. Doctorate in Law and German, U. Prague, Czechoslovakia, 1935; Ph.D., Cambridge (Eng.) U., 1948; Litt.D. (hon.), Emory U., 1965. Asst. lectr. German London Sch. Econs., 1943-45; lectr. German, dir. studies modern langs. Peterhouse Coll., Cambridge U., 1945-48; prof. German U. Wales, 1948-60; vis. prof. U. Hamburg, 1947, U. Göttingen, 1948, U. Bonn, 1948, Harvard U., 1953-54, Brandeis U., 1957-58; prof. German Northwestern U., Evanston, Ill., 1960-67, Avalon prof. humanities emeritus, 1968-90; vis. prof. German U. Heidelberg, summer 1963; Carnegie vis. prof. humanities Mass. Inst. Tech., fall 1963. Author: The Disinherited Mind, Essays in Modern German Literature and Thought, 1952, The Ironic German, a Study of Thomas Mann, 1958, The Artist's Journey into the Interior and Other Essays, 1965, Essays über Goethe, 1970, Franz Kafka, 1974-75, Versuche über Rilke, 1975, The Poet's Self and the Poem, 1976, Die Wiederkehr der Unschuld, 1977, In the Age of Prose, 1983, The Importance of Nietzsche, 1988; editor: Studies in Modern European Lit. and Thought, 1950-68, Kafka's Letter to Felice, 1967, 73; Contbr. profl. and lit. jours. Recipient Kulturkreis lit. prize German industry, 1958; Johann-Heinnich-Merck prize for essay and lit. criticism German Acad. Lang. and Lit., 1969; decorated Great Cross of Merit Fed. Republic Germany. Fellow Am. Acad. Arts and Letters; mem. Bayerische Akademie der Schönen Künste, Deutsche Akademie für Sprache und Dichtung, P.E.N. Club (Germany and Austria). Home: Evanston Ill. Died Nov. 4, 1990.

HELLER, JOHN RODERICK, JR., health science association administrator; b. Oconee County, S.C., Feb. 27, 1905; s. John R. and Elizabeth (Smith) H.; m. Susie May Ayres, Dec. 27, 1934; children: John Roderick III, Hanes Ayres, Winder McGavock. BS, Clemson Coll., 1925; MD, Emory U., 1929. Diplomate Am. Bd. Preventive Medicine. Intern So. Pacific Gen. Hosp., San Francisco, 1929-30; resident Mills Meml. Hosp., San Mateo, Calif., 1930; clinician Ga. Dept. Health, Brunswick, 1931; acting asst. surgeon USPHS, 1931-34, with regular commd. corps, 1934-60, asst. surgeon gen. with grade brig. gen., 1957-60, med. dir., chief div. venereal disease, 1943-48; dir. Nat. Cancer Inst., Bethesda, Md., 1948-60; pres., chief exec. officer Meml. Sloan-Kettering Cancer Ctr., N.Y.C., 1960-65; spl. asst. in internat. med. and sci. activities Am. Cancer Soc., N.Y.C., 1965-76; professorial lectr. George Washington U. Sch. Medicine, Washington, 1948-60; mem. N.Y.C. Bd. Health, 1962-65; cancer coord. regional med. program D.C. Med. Soc., 1967-73. Author: (with R.A. Vonderlehr) The Control of Venereal Disease; editor Jour. Venereal Disease Info., 1943-48, Jour. Nat. Cancer Inst.; also numerous articles. With inf. USAR, 1926-34. Mem. AMA, APHA, Am. Venereal Disease Assn. (pres. 1948-49), Am. Cancer Soc. (bd. dirs.-at-large), Cancer Pub. Health Assn. (pres. 1957), N.Y. Acad. Medicine, Cosmos Club (Washington), Univ. Club (N.Y.C.), Masons, Phi Chi, Sigma Nu. Presbyterian. Home: Bethesda Md. Died May 4, 1989; buried Franklin, Tenn.

HELLER, PHILIP HENRI, physician; b. Des Plaines, Ill., Feb. 6, 1919; s. William Frederick and Magdalene (Henschel) H.; m. Ruth Wark, Apr. 28, 1945; children: Jeanne, Philip Henri Jr., Nancy, Patricia, Mary. AB, U. Nebr., 1941; MD, Northwestern U., 1945. Diplomate Am. Bd. Family Practice. Intern St. Luke's Hosp., Chgo., 1944-45; assoc. staff St. Francis Hosp., Evanston, Ill., 1946-53; attending staff, staff officer Resurrection Hosp., Chgo., 1952-64, assoc. dir. family practice residency program, 1978-85; emeritus staff Resurrection Hosp., from 1985; attending staff Luth. Gen. Hosp., Park Ridge, Ill., 1959-78, hon. staff, from 1978, v.p., 1970-71, chmn. div. family practice and dir. Family Practice Ctr. and residency program, 1972-77; attending staff Holy Family Hosp., Des Plaines, 1960-74; asst. prof. U. Ill. Sch. Medicine, 1972-78. Pres. Des Plaines Bd. Health, 1949-63. Served to lt. comdr. USNR, 1945-46, 54-56. Regent scholar U. Nebr. Fellow Am. Acad. Family Physicians (charter); mem. Chgo. Med. Soc. (council mem. 1963-71, pres. Irving Park br. 1969-70), Ill. Acad. Family Physicians (pres. North Suburban br. 1959-60), Ill. Med. Soc., AMA, Soc. Tchrs. Family Medicine, Phi Rho Sigma. Mem. United Ch. Christ. Lodge: Masons. Home: Hilton Head Island S.C. Deceased. †

HELLMAN, LOUIS M., government official, physician, educator; b. St. Louis, Mar. 22, 1908; s. Max and Helen (Schwab) H.; m. Ernestine Crummel, Jan. 26, 1934; children: Michael Moore, Ann Harper. Ph.B., Yale U., 1930; M.D., Johns Hopkins U., 1934. Diplomate Am. Coll. Ob-Gyn (pres. 1974, Disting. Svc. award 1976). Instr., then asst. prof. Sch. Medicine, Johns Hopkins U., 1938-42, assoc. prof. obstetrics, 1945-51; assoc. obstetrician Johns Hopkins Hosp.; prof., chmn. dept. ob-gyn Coll. Medicine, SUNY and Kings County Hosp., N.Y.C., 1950-70; dep. asst. sec. population affairs HEW, 1970-77; adminstr. Health Services Adminstrn., 1976-77; dir. med. info. Population Reference Bur., Washington, 1977-83; Chmn. adv. com. obstetrics and gynecology FDA, 1965-69. Author: (with R.A. Hingson) Anesthesia for Obstetrics, (with J.A. Pritchard) Williams Obstetrics, 14th edit., (with M. Kobayashi) Sonographic Atlas of Obstetrics and Gynecology; Contbr. to med. jours. Served to lt. comdr. M.C. USNR, World War II. Mem. N.Y. Obstet. Soc. (pres. 1969), Assn. Profs. Gynecology and Obstet., Am. Assn. Obstetricians and Gynecologists, Am. Assn. Pathologists and Bacteriologists, Soc. Gynecologic Investigation (pres.), ACS, N.Y. Acad. Medicine (trustee), Royal Coll. Obstetricians and Gynecologists, Phi Beta Kappa, Alpha Omega Alpha. Home: Hydes Md. Died Aug. 22, 1990.

HELLRING, BERNARD, lawyer, state official; b. May 7, 1916. B.A., Lafayette Coll., 1936; J.D., Harvard U., 1939. Bar: N.J. 1941, N.Y. 1981, U.S. Dist. Ct. N.J. 1941, U.S. Dist. Ct. (so. and ea. dists.) N.Y. 1981, U.S. Ct. Claims 1951, U.S. Tax Ct. 1943, U.S. Ct. Appeals (4th cir.) 1945, U.S. Ct. Appeals (3d cir.) 1948, U.S. Ct. Appeals (2d cir.) 1962, U.S. Supreme Ct. 1953, U.S. Ct. for Berlin 1981. Ptnr. Hellring Lindeman Goldstein & Siegel, Newark; advisor Restatement of the Law of Trusts, Second, 1955-63; spl. counsel N.J. Commr. of Conservation and Econ. Devel., 1956-65; N.J. commr. Nat. Conf. Commrs. on Uniform State Laws, 1956, mem. exec. com., 1971-73; mem. spl. com. on Uniform Marriage and Divorce Act, 1965-75, chmn. com. on Uniorm Marriage and Divorce Act, 1965-68; mem. spl. com. on Uniform Rules of Criminal Procedure, 1971-77, co-chmn. spl. com., 1974-77, mem. spl. com. on med. malpractice, 1975-77, chmn. spl. com. on med. malpractice, 1975-77, mem. spl. com. on consent to med. treatment, 1977-79, chmn. spl. com. on consent to med. treatment, 1977-79; del. Fed. Jud. Conf. for 3d Cir., 1975-79; mem. Pres. U.S. Cir. Judge Nominating Commn., 1977-81. Served with Washington office Sci. Rsch. and Devel., World War II. Fellow Am. Bar Found., Am. Law Inst. (life mem.); mem. Essex County Bar Assn., N.J. State Bar Assn., ABA, Assn. Fed. Bar of State N.J., Am. Judicature Soc., N.Y. County Lawyers Assn., Harvard Law Sch. Assn. N.J. (pres. 1953-54), Harvard Law Sch. Assn. (nat. vice chmn. scholarship com. 1967-69, nat. sec. 1971-72). Home: South Orange N.J. Died Jan. 4, 1991.

HELM, MARGIE MAY, librarian; b. Auburn, Ky., Aug. 21, 1894; d. Thomas Oliver and Nellie (Blakey) Helm. AB, Randolph Macon Woman's Coll., 1916; grad., Pratt Inst., 1922; AM, U. Chgo., 1933. Tchr. high sch. Jarrett, Va., 1916-17, Bowling Green, Ky., 1917-19; asst. N.Y. Pub. Libr., 1919-20; asst. Western Ky. State Coll. Libr., 1920-23, libr., 1923-56, dir. libr. svcs., 1956-65. Mem. ALA, Southeastern Libr. Assn., Ky. Libr. Assn., Ky. Edn. Assn., Ky. Hist. Soc., others. *

HELMBOLD, F. WILBUR, publisher, clergyman; b. Fowlerville, Pa., May 13, 1917; s. Andrew K. and Emma L. (Hildebrand) H.; m. Neola E. Wood, June 10, 1942; children—Neola J. (Mrs. Robert N. Trapnell), Arthur J. (dec.), Martha W. (Mrs. James F. Evans), Dale Marjorie (Mrs. Terry H. Cutrer). A.B. with honors, Samford U., 1949; M.A., Duke, 1954. Newspaper reporter Wilkes-Barre (Pa.) Record, 1934-36; printer Dallas (Pa.) Post, also owner printing bus., 1936-42; ordained to ministry Baptist Ch., 1947; pastor Selma, Ala., 1947-49, Springville, Ala., 1949-50, Durham, N.C., 1951-54; supply pastor, 1954-82; librarian Barrington (R.I.) Coll., 1954-57, Samford U., Birmingham, Ala., 1957-84; dir. Inst. Genealogy and Hist. Research, 1965-84; curator Ala. Bapt. Hist. Commn., 1957-84; Library cons., 1958-84; founding chmn., adv. cons. Bapt. Info. Retrieval System, 1972-84. Author: Born of the Needs of the People, 1967, Tracing Your Ancestry and Logbook, 1976; Editor: Ala. Bapt. Historian, 1967-85; gen. editor: pubs. Banner Press, 1961-66; pres., 1966-89; Contbr. to religious and hist. jours. Served with USAAF, 1942-46, ETO. Mem. So. Bapt., Ala. Bapt., hist. socs., Nat. Geneal. Soc., Assn. Gen. Edn. (founding pres.). Home: Birmingham Ala. Died July 21, 1989; buried Birmingham, Ala.

HENDERSON, BRUCE DOOLIN, management executive, educator; b. Nashville, Apr. 30, 1915; s. John B. and Ceacy (Doolin) H.; m. Frances Fleming, Sept. 5, 1949; children: Asta, Bruce Balfour, Ceacy, Bruce Alexander.; m. Bess L. Wilson, Oct. 22, 1983. B.E., Vanderbilt U., 1937; postgrad., Harvard U. Bus. Sch., 1940-41; L.L.D. (hon.), Babson Coll., 1983. Trainee Frigidaire div. Gen. Motors Corp., 1937-38; sales Leland Electric Co., 1938-39; buyer Westinghouse Electric Corp., 1941; asst. purchasing agt. Westinghouse Electric Corp., Lima, Ohio, 1942; purchasing agt. Westinghouse Electric Corp., Newark, 1943-46; mgr. purchases, stores Westinghouse Electric Corp., Sharon, Pa., 1946-49; asst. to v.p. Westinghouse Electric Co., Pitts., 1950; gen. purchasing agt. Westinghouse Electric Co., 1951, gen. mgr. purchases and traffic, 1952, v.p. purchasing and traffic, 1953-55, v.p., mem. corp. mgmt. com., gen. mgr. air conditioning div., 1955-59; sr. v.p. in charge mgmt. services div. Arthur D. Little, Inc., 1959-60, sr. v.p. charge mgmt. cons. div., 1960-63; sr. v.p. Boston Safe Deposit & Trust Co., 1963-68; founder Boston Cons. Group, Inc., 1963, chief exec. officer, 1968-80, chmn., 1980-85, chmn. bd. emeritus, from 1985; prof. mgmt. Vanderbilt U. Grad. Sch. Mgmt., from 1985; bd. dirs. Boston Cons. Group Inc. Author: Henderson on Corporate Strategy, The Logic of Strategy. Mem. Beta Gamma Sigma. Clubs: Belle Meade Country (Nashville), University (Nashville); St. Croix (V.I.) Country. Home: Nashville Tenn. Deceased. †

HENDERSON, EVERETTE L(ON), chemist, educator; b. Rogers, Ark., Jan. 20, 1896; s. Everette C. and Olive Bell (Layman) H.; m. Katharine Evelyn Moore, Dec. 27, 1919; children: Everette Chester, Richard Moore. BS, U. Ark., 1919; MS, Iowa State Coll., 1923, PhD, 1931. Instr. analytical chemistry Iowa State Coll., 1920-21, instr. inorganic chemistry, 1929-32; asst. prof. U. Tenn., 1921-29; assoc. cons. cehmist Memphis Gen. Hosp., 1923-29; asst. prof. phys. chemistry U. Detroit, 1932-33, assoc. prof., div. divsn., 1933-39, prof., dir. phys. chemistry, 1939-41, prof., dir. divsn. inorganic chemistry, 1941-53, prof., vice chmn. dept. chemistry, 1953-57, prof., from 1957; asst. dean freshman studies, from 1965. Author textbooks in field. Mem. Chem. Soc. London, Soc. Chem. Industry, Electrochem. Soc., Nat. Assn. Std. Med. Vocabulary, Am. Chem. Soc., others. *

HENDERSON, HERSCHEL BRADFORD, publishing executive; b. Waltham, Mass., July 10, 1929; s. Herschel Clifford and Lucy E. (Sturtevant) H. BA, New Sch. Social Rsch., 1959. Reporter Am. Banker, N.Y.C., 1959-62, reporter, news editor, assoc. editor, 1963-64, mng. editor, 1964-73, v.p., 1973-76, editor, 1976-82, dir. product devel., 1982-83; reporter N.Y. Post, 1962-63. With USN, 1951-54. Mem. N.Y. Fin. Writers Assn. Democrat. Home: New York N.Y. Died, 1983.

HENDERSON, LUCILE KELLING, university dean; b. Alma City, Minn., Sept. 8, 1894; d. William Frederick and Ada Irene (Taylor) Kelling; m. Archibald Henderson, June 15, 1957. AB, Whitman Coll., 1917; BLS, N.Y. State Libr. Sch., 1921. Libr. Carnegie Pub. Libr., Centralia, Wash., 1918-20; asst. Newark Pub. Libr., 1921-26; acting reference libr. Mills. Coll., Calif., 1926; instr. libr. sch. L.A. Pub. Libr., 1926-31; lectr. sch. pub. adminstrn. U. So. Calif., 1929-31; asst. prof. U. N.C., Chapel Hill, 1932-39, assoc. prof., 1939-46, prof., 1946-90, acting dean, 1950-51, dean, 1954-90; instr. sch. libr. svc. Columbia U., summer 1930; acting reference libr. Hoyt Libr., Kingston, Pa., 1932; asst. Tchrs. Coll. Libr., Albany, N.Y., summers 1932-34. Author: Adventures Around the World, 1936, Contemporary Poetry, 1938, United States Mural, 1940, Pattern of America, 1946, These United States of America, 1949, (with Albert Suskin) Index Verborum Iuvenalis, 1951, Bernard Shaw Around the World, 1956. Mem. ALA, AAUP, Am. Philol. Assn., Am. Assn. Libr. Schs., Shaw Soc. Am., Phi Beta Kappa, Kappa Kappa Gamma. Home: Chapel Hill N.C. Died July 29, 1990; buried Salisbury, N.C.

HENDERSON, RALPH ERNEST, editor; b. Mongnai, Burma, June 4, 1899; (parents Am. citizens); s. Albert Haley and Cora May (Shinn) H.; m. Clifford West Sellers, May 30, 1927 (dec. Mar. 1971); children: Clifford Sellers, Lee West, Ralph Hale; m. Alexandra Kropotkin von Streer (div.). AB, Harvard U., 1921. Bus. mgr. The Reader's Digest, Pleasantville, N.Y., 1925-27; war corr. The Readers Digest, Pleasantville, N.Y., 1944-45; mng. editor The Reader's Digest, Pleasantville, N.Y., 1948-65; v.p., editor Reader's Digest Book Club, Pleasantville, 1950-65, editorial dir., 1965-70; contbr. oral history program Columbia U., N.Y.C. Mem. Coffee House (N.Y.C.), Harvard Club (N.Y.C.), Runway Bay Club (Jamaica), Golf Club, Sharon Country Club (Conn.). Home: South Kent Conn. Died Oct. 6, 1989; buried Lexington, Va.

HENDON, ROBERT RANDALL, lawyer; b. Earlsboro, Okla., Mar. 20, 1894; s. Robert Randall and Mary Belle (Neabors) H.; m. Kathlene Marie Grubaugh, Dec. 21, 1921 (dec. Oct. 6, 1956); children—Robert Randall, Owen William; m. Muriel Louise Mackenzie, Mar. 29, 1958. LL.B., U. Okla., 1916; grad., Command and Gen. Staff Sch., 1935, War Dept. Indsl. Coll., 1945. Bar: Okla. bar 1916, U.S. Supreme Ct. bar 1920, D.C.

bar 1933, U.S. Ct. Hawaii 1944, Md. bar 1954, ICC bar 1954, U.S. Ct. Claims 1956. Gen. law practice Wewoka, Okla., 1916-17; mem. law firm Shawnee, Okla., 1921-25; atty. Bd. Contract Adjustment, War Dept., 1919, asso. mem., legal advisor to sec. war, 1920-21; atty., sr. atty., adminstrv. law judge ICC, 1925-50; asso. counsel U.S. Senate Com. Investigating R.R. Financing, 1934-36; dir. tax ammortization and def. loan div. Def. Transport Adminstrn., 1950-54; gen. law practice, from 1954; chief contract termination div. Office Chief Engrs., Washington, 1945-46; spl. asst. to adminstr. War Assets Adminstrn., 1946-47, dir. property mgmt. div., Mar.-Dec. 1947, mem. gen. bd., Jan.-May 1948; chief spl. projects div. Munitions Bd., Office Sec. Def., 1948-49; pres. Army Phys. Review Council, Office Sec., Dept. Army, Jan.-Nov. 1950; dir. C. & G.S., Dept. Army (O.R.C. School), Washington, 1950-54. Served as 1st lt. A.E.F., 1918-19, France; col. Arty. A.U.S., 1940-50; comdr. 98th Anti-Aircraft Regt. and Searchlight-Radar Groupment 1942-45, P.T.O. Decorated Purple Heart, Bronze Star citation, Legion of Merit, Commendation from Sec. of War, Nat. Mil. Establishment badge; recipient posthumous Presdl. Citation, 1986. Mem. ICC Practitioners Assn., Internat. Platform Assn., Res. Officer Assn. of U.S., Nat. Assn. Ret. Civil Employees, Am. Legion, DAV, Am. Security Council (nat. adv. bd.), Ret. Mil. Officers Assn., Order of Lafayette. Democrat. Baptist (chmn. finance com., trustee 1970—). Clubs: Mason (Shriner; life), Army and Navy, Nat. Lawyers (founder, life mem.). Home: Washington D.C. Died Jan. 26, 1986; buried Arlington Nat. Cemetery.

HENDRICK, JAMES POMEROY, lawyer, government official; b. Wainscott, N.Y., July 31, 1901; s. Ellwood and Josephine (Pomeroy) H.; m. Elinor Sullivan, Nov. 21, 1927; children: Arthur Pomeroy, Alice (Mrs. James Hardigg), Robert. B.A., Yale, 1923; student, Corpus Christi Coll., Cambridge, Eng., 1924; LL.B., Yale, 1927. Bar: N.Y. bar 1929. Atty. Winthrop, Stimson, Putnam & Roberts, N.Y.C., 1928-41; asst. to under sec. war, later sec. war, 1941-46; adviser to U.S. rep. UN Commn. on Human Rights, 1946-48; asst. to adminstr. ECA, 1948-53; with U.S. Treasury Dept., 1953-62, dep. asst. sec., 1962-69; head V.I. Parole Bd., St. Croix, 1970-88; Vice pres. INTERPOL, 1968-69; mem. U.S. Dist. Ct. Commn. to investigate V.I. Prison System, 1976; mem. U.S. Dept. Justice Task Force to Study Corrections in V.I., 1976; V.I. rep. Nat. Parole Symposium, 1980. Contbr. articles to profl. publs. Served to col. AUS, 1942-46. Decorated Legion of Merit, 1945; Ordre Nationale de Viet Nam, 1953. Mem. Wolf's Head Soc., Alpha Delta Phi, Phi Delta Phi. Democrat. Episcopalian. Clubs: Century Assn, Dutch Treat, The Players, River, Metropolitan, Chevy Chase. Home: Saint Croix V.I. Died Aug. 1, 1990.

HENDRICKS, CALVIN, retail company executive; b. Centerville, Utah, Mar. 6, 1933; s. Milo Calvin and Linda Randall (Watkins) H.; m. Lona Clair Jones, Nov. 24, 1956; children: Dixie, Jana, Kent, Denise, Craig, Jill. Student, Boise Jr. Coll., 1954-55; BS, Brigham Young U., 1957. Staff acct. Price Waterhouse and Co., Seattle, 1957-62; vice chmn. bd. Pay'n Save Corp., Seattle, 1962-86; pres. Bill's Drugs of No. Calif., Benicia, from 1986. With USAF, 1951-54. Home: Federal Way Wash. Deceased. †

HENGSBACH, FRANZ CARDINAL, archbishop; b. Velmede, Paderborn, Germany, Sept. 10, 1910. Ordained priest Roman Cath. Ch., 1937. Elected to titular Ch. of Cantano, 1953; consecrated bishop, 1953; transferred to Essen, 1957; created cardinal, 1988, served, until 1990. Home: Essen Germany Died June 24, 1991.

HENKLE, ROGER BLACK, English language educator; b. Lincoln, Nebr., Dec. 15, 1935; s. Elmer E. and Helen (Black) H.; m. Carol Thompson, June 28, 1960; children: Timothy R., Jennifer K. BA, U. Nebr., 1956; LLB, Harvard U., 1959; PhD, Stanford U., 1968. Bar: Okla. 1961. Assoc. Kerr, Conn & Davis, Oklahoma City, 1960-64; mng. editor San Francisco Bay Guardian, 1966-68; asst. prof. Brown U., Providence, 1968-74, assoc. prof., 1974-80, prof., 1980-91, chmn. dept. English, 1981-84, co-dir. program modern lit. and society, 1984-91, Nicholas Brown prof. oratory and belles lettres, 1981-91; cons. U. Tulsa, 1982; mem. NEH rev. panel, 1972-76, 79-80. Author: Reading the Novel, 1977, Comedy and Culture, 1980 (named an Outstanding Book of 1980-81 Assn. Coll. and Research Libraries); mng. editor: Novel: A Forum on Fiction, 1970—. Brown U. Henry Merrit Wriston grantee, 1978, NEH grantee, 1982, 84, 89; Woodrow Wilson Found. fellow, 1964, J.S. Guggenheim Meml. fellow 1984-85. Mem. MLA (del. gen. assembly 1977-79). Democrat. Home: Providence R.I. Died Oct. 5, 1991.

HENLE, GUY, magazine editor, consultant; b. N.Y.C., Dec. 22, 1920; s. James and Marjorie (Jacobson) H.; m. Mary Ellen Bowlby, Jan. 5, 1947; children: Richard Flexner, Peter Bradley (dec. June 1973). AB, Swarthmore Coll., 1941; MS in Journalism, Columbia U., 1942. With Vanguard Press, Inc., N.Y.C., 1946-53; assoc. editor Vanguard Press, Inc., 1949-51, sales mgr., 1951-53; workshop editor Woman's Home Companion mag., 1953-56; exec. editor House Beautiful mag., N.Y.C., 1957-72; bldg. architecture editor Am. Home mag., N.Y.C., 1973; mng. editor Consumer Reports, 1974-79, exec. editor, 1979-84; editorial cons., from 1985. Author: How to Plan Your Attic and Basement, 1955, New Car Buying Guide, 1991, 92. Served to 1st lt. AUS, 1942-46; capt. Res. Home: Scarsdale N.Y. Died May 11, 1992. †

HENNESSY, JOHN FRANCIS, consulting engineer; b. N.Y.C., July 18, 1928; s. John F. and Dorothy (O'Grady) H.; m. Barbara McDonnell, Oct. 24, 1953; children—John, Kathleen, James, Kevin, Peter, David; m. Bruce Rial, Dec. 30, 1971. B.S. in Physics, Georgetown U., 1949; B.S. in Engring, Mass. Inst. Tech., 1951. Registered profl. engr., N.Y., Calif., Colo., Conn., Va., D.C., Ga., N.J., Ill., Ind., others. With Syska & Hennessy, Inc., N.Y.C., 1951-89, exec. v.p., 1955-66, pres., 1967-89, chmn., chief exec. officer, 1973-89; former dir. Franklin Soc. Fed. Savs. & Loan; chmn. pres. In The Pink, Inc., N.Y.C., WTB, Inc., N.Y.C. Mem. exec. bd. Greater N.Y. council Boy Scouts Am., from 1958; former chmn. bd. trustees Whitby Sch.; past trustee Clark Coll., Atlanta; former mem. bd. dirs. Catholic Interracial Council; bd. dirs. N.Y. Heart Assn., Battery Park City Authority; former mem. MIT Ednl. Council; mem. vis. com. Sloan Sch. Mgmt., MIT. Served with USAF, 1951-52. Fellow Am. Cons. Engrs. Council; mem. Nat., N.Y. State, Conn. socs. profl. engrs., N.Y. Assn. Cons. Engrs. (past pres.), N.Y. Bldg. Congress, Soc. Am. Mil. Engrs., ASME. Clubs: River (N.Y.C.), Links (N.Y.C.), Univ. (N.Y.C.); Capitol Hill (Washington), Fed. City (Washington), Met. (Washington); Annabels, Marks (London); Castells, Travellers (Paris). Home: New York N.Y. Died Jan. 9, 1989; buried Gates of Heaven Cemetery, Valhalla, N.Y.

HENNESSY, WESLEY JOSEPH, management consultant, academic administrator; b. Queens, N.Y., Aug. 17, 1914; s. Charles A. and Lydia (Schneider) H.; m. Virginia Pershing MacArthur, June 20, 1942 (dec. Aug. 1955); children: Heather Michele, David Charles, Holly MacArthur; m. Virginia Ann Campbell, Apr. 4, 1959; children: Mark Campbell, Kevin, Karen, Anne. Student, Syracuse U., 1934-37; B.S. cum laude, Columbia U., 1951; LL.D., Phila. Coll. Osteopathy, 1966; D.Sc., Bethany (W.Va.) Coll., 1966. Pres. World's Fair Employees Assn., 1939; dir. tng. Grumman Aircraft Engring. Corp., Bethpage, L.I., 1940-44; asst. to dean Columbia U., N.Y.C., 1944-48, asst. dean, 1948-53, assoc. dean, 1953-64, exec. dean, 1964-69, dean Sch. Engring. and Applied Sci., 1969-75, dean emeritus, mem. adv. coun. Sch. Gen. Studies, 1975; pres. Polychrome Corp., Yonkers, N.Y., 1975-77, also bd. dirs.; resident dir. Summer Sch. Engring., Lakeside, Conn., 1946-64; spl. lectr. world econ. geography; condr. seminar on human relations ICA, Guatemala, 1959; dir. Hazeltine Corp., Greenlawn, N.Y., 1973-86, Megadiamond Industries, N.Y.C., Combustion Equipment Assos.; bd. advisers Gulf & Western Invention Devel. Corp.; Mgmt. cons. research and devel. div. Am. Machine & Foundry, Reflectone Electronics, Unidynamics div. Universal Match Corp., 1960-64; dir. refugee scientists program Nat. Acad. Scis., 1961-64; cons. Pres. of Korea on Indsl. and Higher Edn. Programs, 1968-80; Mem. N.Y. Gov.'s Adv. Commn. Higher Edn., 1958, Pres.'s Adv. Panel Aid to Edn. for Latin Am., 1961, N.Y. State Bd. Regents Task Force on Profl. Edn., from 1971. Bd. dirs. Am. Council for Emigres in Professions, 1962-80; trustee St. Hilda's Sch., N.Y.C., 1952-55, Hudson River Mus., Yonkers, 1975-78; bd. dirs. Armstrong Meml. Research Found., from 1970, pres., 1973-80; mem. bd. Anglo-Am. Hellenic Bur. Edn., 1971-76; adv. council Manhattan Coll., 1976; mem. N.Y. State Task Force on Hudson River, 1980-85. Recipient Distinguished Pub. Service award Columbia U. Sch. Gen. Studies, 1967, Gt. Tchr. award Columbia U., 1975. Mem. Am. Soc. Engring. Edn., Columbia U. Engring. Sch. Alumni Assn. (asso.), Assn. Deans Engring. Colls. N.Y. State (v.p. 1972), Am. Geog. Soc. (council 1973, dir. from 1973, v.p. from 1978), Am. Arbitration Assn., Am. Birding Assn. (charter), Linnaean Soc. Clubs: Columbia (Columbia), Men's Faculty (Columbia), Faculty House (Columbia); Princeton (N.Y.C.). Home: Deerfield Beach Fla. Died Oct. 8, 1991.

HENNINGER, G(EORGE) ROSS, educator, electrical engineer; b. Hamilton, Ont., May 22, 1898; s. George Henry Thomas and Harriet (Ross) H.; m. Leah Katharine Craven, Nov. 16, 1923; children: Beverley Anne, Nancy Katharine. BSEE, U. So. Calif., 1922. Power sta. operator So. Calif. Edison Co., L.A., 1917-22; assoc. editor Am. Inst. Elec. Engring., 1930-33, editor, 1933-48; dir. publs. Illuminating Engring. Soc., 1948-50; prof., head engring. ext. Iowa State U., 1956-58; dir. Nat. Survey Tech. Inst. Edn., 1956-57; pres. Ohio Mechs. Inst. & Coll. Applied Sci., 1956-62; dir. instnl. rsch., also assoc. prof. Oreg. Tech. Inst., Klamath Falls, from 1962. Author: The Technical Institute in America, 1959; also articles. Col. USAF. Fellow Am. Inst. Elec. Engring.; mem. NSPE, Am. Soc. Engring. Edn., Illuminating Engring. Soc., others. *

HENREID, PAUL (PAUL GEORG JULIUS VON HERNRIED RITTER VON WASEL-WALDINGAU), actor, director, producer; b. Trieste, Austria; came to U.S., 1940; s. Carl Alphons Von and Maria Louise (Lendecke) von Hernreid; m. Elizabeth Glueck, 1936; children: Monika. Grad., Academie Graphic Arts, Vienna; also, Konservatorium Dramatic Arts, Vienna. Mem. Max Reinhardt's Vienna Theatre and others. Appeared in: (Austrian films) Hohe Schule, Nur Ein Komoediant; London plays: Cafe Chantant, Victoria Regina, 1937, The Jersey Lilly; N.Y.C. stage appearances in Flight to the West, 1941, Festival, 1955; Hollywood movies include: Night Train, (best fgn. actor in film N.Y.C. critics), Goodbye Mr. Chips, 1939, Hollywood, Joan of Paris, 1940, Casablanca (voted favorite all time film), Now Voyager, Of Human Bondage, Spanish Main, Deception, Between Two Worlds, Song of Love, others; producer and star film Hollow Triumph (The Scar); co-producer and star film So Young So Bad; producer, dir., star film For Men Only; dir. film Dead-Ringer (Dead Image) (outstanding award merit Motion Picture Council Cal.), Ballade in Blue, others; actor film The Heretic; actor, dir. numerous TV films; starred as Comdr. in Don Juan in Hell, Nat. tour, 1972-73. Decorated Hon. Maltese Knight Cross; recipient Cross of Honor for scis. and arts, 1st class Republic of Austria, 1980, Artistry in Cinema award Am. Classic Screen Awards, 1980, Nat. Film award, 1980, Yellow Rose award Tex. Film Soc., 1983, Eagle award Dept. Army, 1983, Golden Decoration Star award, 1988, Golden Honor-Medal Land, Vienna, 1988, The Golden Star award (for important merits about Land Vienna) State of Vienna, 1988; Stars of Honor, Hollywood C. of C., Silverscreen Legend award St. Mary Med. Ctr., 1984; Internat. Tribute award 1984; two stars dedicated in his name Hollywood Walk of Fame, 1960. Mem. Screen Actors Guild, AFTRA, Dirs. Guild Am., Actors Equity, Acad. Motion Picture Arts and Scis. Club: Vereinigung Ehemaliger Theresianisten (Vienna). Home: Pacific Palisades Calif. Died Apr. 5, 1992.

HENRY, JOHN A., management consultant, lawyer; b. Devils Lake, N.D., Mar. 23, 1904; s. John F. and Martha (Jossman) H. Student, Amherst Coll., Union U. Bar: N.Y. 1931, Ill. 1945. With Utica Mut. Ins. Co., 1938-44; pres., dir. Continental Casualty Co., 1946-69, Transp. Ins. Co., Can. Health & Accident Ins. Co.; past v.p., dir. CNA Fin. Corp.; past ins. operations officer, dir. Am. Casualty Co., Nat. Fire Ins. Co., Hartford Transcontinental Ins. Co., Valley Forge Ins. Co.; mgmt. cons. Chmn. Gov.'s Ins. Adv. Bd., 1968-69; bd. dirs. Ill. Ins. Info. Svc, pres., 1966-67; bd. dirs. Internat. Coll. Surgeons' Hall of Fame, 1964-69. Mem. ABA, N.Y. Bar Assn., Ill. Bar Assn., Chgo. Bar Assn., Chgo. Club. Home: Des Moines Iowa Died Oct. 30, 1991.

HENRY, WAIGHTS GIBBS, JR., college chancellor, clergyman; b. Tuscaloosa, Ala., Feb. 13, 1910; s. Waights Gibbs and Mary Eliza (Davis) H.; m. Mamie Lark Brown, Feb. 16, 1935; children: George Madison, Waights Gibbs III, Mary Ann (Mrs. Ed P. Kirven). Student, Emory U., 1927-28; A.B., Birmingham-So. Coll., 1930, D.D., 1947; B.D., Yale U., 1934. Asst. pastor Bunker Hill Congl. Ch., Waterbury, Conn., 1932-36; joined N. Ga. Conf. Meth. Ch., 1936; ordained to ministry Meth. Ch., 1938; pastor Hoschton, 1937-38, Clayton, 1939-42; pastor Epworth Ch., Atlanta, 1943-44; exec. sec. Bd. Edn., No. Ga. Conf., 1945-48; pres. LaGrange (Ga.) Coll., 1948-78, chancellor, 1978-89; mem. Pacific Rim. Seminar in, Clina, Korea, Japan, 1980; preacher Meth. Series of Protestant Hour (radio), 1960; Sunday columnist Columbus (Ga.) Ledger-Enquirer, 1950-89. Contbr. ch. publs. Del. to Gen. Confs., 1948-56, Jurisdictional Confs., 1948-64; Chmn. bd. Protestant Radio and TV Center, 1970-71; chmn. Meth. Joint Radio Com., 1952-56, Gen. Bd. Edn., 1948-52; pres. Ga. Found. Ind. Colls., 1959-60, 70-71, Ga. Meth. Colls. Assn., 1950-62, Ga. Assn. Colls., 1959-60; mem. Ga. Higher Edn. Facilities Commn.; mem. pres.'s adv. com. Med. Coll. Ga., chmn. admissions policies com.; commr. Roosevelt Little White House; bd. dirs. East-West Found., Pitts Found., 1948-78, Meth. Found. Ret. Ministers, 1960-78; former bd. mgrs. Camp Glisson. Recipient award Assn. Pvt. Colls. and Univs. in Ga., 1981; Paul Harris fellow. Mem. Chattahoochee Valley Art Assn., Newcomen Soc. N.Am., Lafayette Groupe (French Resistance Movement, Le Puy, France) (hon.), Omicron Delta Kappa, Pi Kappa Alpha, Pi Gamma Mu. Clubs: Mason (LaGrange), Rotarian (LaGrange) (dist. gov. 1974-75), Highland Country (LaGrange). Home: LaGrange Ga. Died May 29, 1989; buried Westview Cemetery, Atlanta.

HENSEL, H. STRUVE, lawyer; b. Hoboken, N.J., Aug. 22, 1901; s. Herman D. and Eliza (Struve) H.; m. Edith T. Wyckoff, Oct. 3, 1929 (div. 1948); m. Isabel S. Bower, June 9, 1948 (dec. Oct. 1987). A.B., Princeton U., 1922; LL.B., Columbia U., 1925. Bar: N.Y. 1925, D.C. 1943. Assoc. Cravath, deGersdorff, Swaine & Wood, N.Y.C., 1925-33; mem. Milbank, Tweed & Hope, N.Y.C., 1933-41; organizer and 1st chief procurement legal div. Navy Dept., Washington, 1941-44, gen. counsel, 1944-45; asst. Sec. of Navy, 1945-46; mem. Carter, Ledyard & Milburn, N.Y.C., 1946-53; cons., spl. adviser to Sec. Def., 1952; gen. counsel Dept. Def., 1953-54; asst. Sec. Def. for internat. security affairs, 1954-55; pvt. practice Washington, 1955-66; ptnr. Coudert Bros., Paris, London, Hong Kong, Tokyo, Singapore, Brussels, 1966-76; pres., mng. dir. Maritime Fruit Carriers Co. Ltd., London, 1976; of counsel Vorys, Sater, Seymour & Pease, Washington, 1983-91; bd. dirs. EDO Corp., A.A.I. Corp., Integrated Resources, Inc.; cons. Commn. on Orgn. Exec., 1948. Decorated D.S.M. USN; medal of Freedom, 1953.

Republican. Clubs: City Tavern Assn., Chevy Chase, Metropolitan (Washington); University, Princeton (N.Y.). Home: Deerfield Beach Fla. Died May 27, 1991.

HENSHAW, CLEMENT LONG, physicist, educator; b. Pittsfield, Mass., Dec. 18, 1906; s. Arthur Williston and Jessie (Darling) H.; m. Rosemary Forbes, June 25, 1938; children: Claire Mather Henshaw McNeill, Arthur Clement, Philip Forbes. BS in Physics, Union Coll., Schenectady, 1928; MA, U. Mich., 1929; PhD, Yale U., 1936. Instr. physics Lehigh U., 1929-31; instr. physics Yale U., 1931-33, 35-36, asst., 1934-35; mem. faculty Colgate U., Hamilton, N.Y., 1936-91, prof. physics, 1948-73, prof. emeritus, 1973-91, chmn. dept. physics and astronomy, 1958-70; vis. prof. U. Chgo., 1956-57; cons. Ednl. Testing Svc., Princeton; testing cons. Coll. Entrance Exam. Bd., 1949-61, 66-72. Author: Problems in Physical Science, 2d edit., 1956; co-author: Atoms, Rocks and Galaxies, 2d edit., 1942; editor: Science Reasoning and Understanding, 1954; contbr. articles to profl. jours. Yale U. fellow, 1933-34; fellow Fund Advancement Edn., 1952-53. Mem. AAUP (pres. Colgate chpt. 1958-59), Am. Phys. Soc., Am. Assn. Physics Tchrs., Am. Assn. Higher Edn., Assn. Gen. and Liberal Studies, Fedn. Am. Scientists, Sigma Xi. Home: Hamilton N.Y. Died Dec. 21, 1991.

HENSKE, JOHN M., chemical company executive; b. Omaha, 1923. B.S. in Chem. Engring. and Indsl. Adminstrn, Yale U., 1948. With Dow Chem. Co., 1948-69; v.p., group v.p. chems. Olin Corp., Stamford, Conn., 1969-71, sr. v.p., pres. chems group, 1971-73, pres., 1973-78, 83-87, chief exec. officer, 1978-87, chmn. bd., 1978-88; dir. Harvey Hubbell, Inc., 1987-90; dir. Sun Co., Am. Precision Industries, Inc., N.E. Bancorp, Inc., The Hydraulic Co., Sun Co. Bd. dirs. , chmn. United Negro Coll. Fund, United Way campaigns; trustee Stamford Hosp., Yale-New Haven Hosp. Served with U.S. Army, 1943-46. Mem. Conf. Bd. (dir.), Am. Mgmt. Assn. (dir.), Chem. Mfg. Assn. (chmn., dir. 1979-80). Home: Greens Farms Conn. Died Feb. 20, 1990.

HENSON, ALBERT LEE, lawyer, furniture manufacturing executive; b. Chgo., Aug. 30, 1910; s. A. Lee and Nelle (Smith) H.; m. Margaret Elizabeth Spray, Oct. 16, 1937; children: Albert Lee III, Judd W. BA, Grinnell Coll., 1931; JD with distinction, U. Mich., 1934. Bar: Mich. 1934, Ill. 1946. Assoc. Yerkes, Goddard & McClintock, Detroit, 1934-42; pvt. practice Detroit, 1942-46; indsl. rels. mgr. Koehler Mfg. Co., Naperville, Ill., 1946-74, v.p. legal indsl. rels. dir., 1951-74, sec., from 1970, gen. counsel, 1974-76, also bd. dirs.; mem. Ill. Pers. Adv. Bd., 1960-64, Ill. Commn. on Labor Laws, from 1969. Bd. dirs. Koehler Found.; bd. dirs. Family Svc. Assn. Dupage County, Ill. Mem. ABA, Ill. Bar Assn., Mich Bar Assn. Home: Lombard Ill. Died Oct. 28, 1984.

HENSON, JAMES MAURY, television director and producer, puppeteer; b. Greenville, Miss., Sept. 24, 1936; s. Paul Ransom and Elizabeth Marcella (Brown) H.; m. Jane Anne Nebel, May 28, 1959; children: Lisa Marie, Cheryl Lee, Brian David, John Paul, Heather Beth. B.A., U. Md., 1960. Pres. Jim Henson Prodns.; pres., bd. dirs. Am. Ctr. of Union Internationale de la Marionnette, from 1974. Creator: The Muppets, 1954; producer: Sam and Friends, Washington, 1955-61; puppeteer: Rowlf on Jimmy Dean Show, N.Y.C., 1963-66, numerous TV guest appearances; creator numerous TV commls.; Sesame Street Muppets, 1969-90, The Muppet Show, 1976-81 (Best TV Script of Yr. award 1979, 80), Sesame Street, Special, 1988; producer: films The Muppet Movie, 1979 (Film Adv. Bd. citation 1979), The Muppets Take Manhattan, 1984; producer album The Muppet Show (Grammy award 1979); dir.: films The Great Muppet Caper, 1981, Labyrinth, 1986; co-dir.: film The Dark Crystal, 1981; creator Fraggle Rock (HBO series), 1983-87 (Internat. Emmy award 1983, ACE award 1983, 86); exec. producer: Muppet Babies, CBS series, 1984-90 (Emmy award 1985, 86, 87, 88), The Storyteller, NBC series, 1987, The Jim Henson Hour, 1989, The Jim Henson Hour, NBC series, 1989 (TV Critics Assn. award); puppeteer film Follow That Bird, 1985, HBO series: Jim Henson's The Ghost of Faffner Hall, 1989. Recipient Emmy awards, 1958, 1973-74, 75-76, 89 (Outstanding Directing for Variety or Music program, Jim Henson Hour, Dog City), Entertainer of yr. award AGVA, TV Acad. award 1978, TV Critics Assn. Career Achievement Award, 1990, Nat. Acad. of TV Arts and Scis. Gov's. Award, 1991, Peabody award, 1979, 87, Grammy award, 1981, Internat. Monitor Pioneer Award, 1990, Nat. Edu. Assn. Lifetime Learning Achievement Award, 1992, President's Fellow award R.I. Sch. Design, 1982. Mem. Puppeteers of Am. (pres. 1962-63), AFTRA, Dirs. Guild Am., Writers Guild, Nat. Acad. TV Arts and Scis., Screen Actors Guild. Home: New York N.Y. Died May 16, 1990.

HEPNER, HARRY WALKER, educator, consultant; b. Pa., Feb. 1, 1893; s. William S. and Catherine (Schnee) H.; m. Edna Carnahan, Nov. 25, 1920; 1 child, Flora Alyse. Student, Allentown Prep. Sch.; AB, Muhlenberg Coll., 1916; student, Cornell U., Harvard U., Syracuse U. Pers. officer U.S. Army, 1917-18; pers. rschr. Kaufmann's Dept. Store, Pitts., 1918, Phila. Co. & Affiliated Corp., Pitts., 1919, Goodyear Tire & Rubber Co., Akron, Ohio, 1920; instr. psychology Syracuse U., 1921-24, asst., assoc. prof. psychology, 1924-35, prof., from 1935. Author: Psychology Applied to Life and Work, Modern Advertising. Fellow APA; mem. Am. Mktg. Assn., Phi Beta Kappa, Sigma Xi, others. *

HERBERT, DONALD ROY, lawyer, business executive; b. Mpls., Nov. 4, 1935; s. Roy Patrick and Bertha Lydia (Mathre) H.; m. Carol A. Elofson, June 28, 1958; children: Karen, James, Phillip. B.S.L., U. Minn., 1957, LL.B. cum laude, 1959. Mem. firm Dorsey, Owen, Barker, Scott & Barber, Mpls., 1959-62; corp. lawyer Peavey Co., Mpls., 1962-77, v.p., gen. counsel, sec., 1977-85; sr. v.p., gen. counsel, sec. Gelco Corp., Eden Prairie, Minn., from 1985. Mem. ABA, Minn. State Bar Assn. (bd. govs. 1976-77), Corp. Counsel Assn. Minn. (pres. 1975-76). Republican. Lutheran. Club: Mpls. Athletic. Home: Saint Paul Minn. Deceased. †

HERLIHY, DAVID JOSEPH, history educator; b. San Francisco, May 8, 1930; s. Maurice Peter and Irene (O'Connor) H.; m. Patricia McGahey, June 4, 1952; children: Maurice, Christopher, David, Felix, Gregory, Irene. B.A., U. San Francisco, 1952, H.H.D. (hon.), 1985; M.A., Cath. U. Am., 1953; Ph.D., Yale U., 1956. Asst. prof., then assoc. prof. history Bryn Mawr Coll., 1955-64; prof. history U. Wis., 1964-72; prof. Harvard U., 1972-86, Henry Charles Lea prof., 1979-86, master Mather House, 1976-86; Barnaby Conrad and Mary Critchfield Keeney prof. Brown U., 1986-91; lectr. other univs. Author: Medieval and Renaissance Pistoia, 1967, Pisa in the Early Renaissance, 1957, A Social History of Italy and Western Europe, 1978, Cities and Societies in Medieval Italy, 1980, (with Christiane Klapisch) The Truscans and Their Families, 1984, Medieval Households, 1985, Women and Work in Medieval Europe, 1989, Opera Muliebria, 1990; also articles. Fulbright fellow, 1954-55; Guggenheim fellow, 1961-62; fellow Am. Council Learned Socs., 1966-67, Center for Advanced Study in Behavorial Scis., 1972-73, NEH, 1977. Fellow Mediaeval Acad. Am. (pres. 1981-82); mem. Am. Hist. Assn. (pres. 1989-90), Am. Cath. Hist. Assn. (pres. 1971-72), Midwest Mediaeval Conf. (pres. 1971-72), Soc. Italian Hist. Studies (pres. 1981-83), Am. Acad. Arts and Scis., Am. Philos. Soc. Home: Providence R.I. Died Feb. 21, 1991; buried Cambridge, Mass.

HERLIHY, ERNEST HERBERT, lawyer; b. N.Y.C., Jan. 31, 1895; s. Theodore E. and Jenny M. (Schultz) H.; m. Elisabeth des Meloizes, July 3, 1922; children: Richard George, Patricia Stone. Student, Stanford U.; LLB, U. Ariz., 1926. Bar: Calif. 1926. Newspaper reporter Bklyn. Eagle, 1914-17; practiced law L.A., from 1926; sr. mem. Herlihy & Herlihy, from 1929. 1st lt. U.S. Army, 1917-19; lt. col. Calif. N.G. Mem. ABA, L.A. Bar Assn., Calif. State Bar. *

HERMAN, ROBERT DIXON, judge; b. Northumberland, Pa., Sept. 24, 1911; s. Chester B. and Esther (Maurer) H.; m. Lou C. Witmer (dec. Nov. 1959); m. Elizabeth Dunn DeWitt, Apr. 4, 1963; 4 children. A.B., Bucknell U., 1935; LL.B., Cornell U., 1938. Bar: Pa. bar 1938. Practiced law, 1938-58; asst. dist. atty. Dauphin County, Pa., 1942-44; mem. Pa. Gen. Assembly, 1948-50; Dauphin County solicitor, 1950-57; judge Dauphin County Cts. Common Pleas, 1958-70, Juvenile Ct., 1965-70; judge U.S. Dist. Ct. for Middle Pa., Harrisburg, 1970-81, sr. judge, 1981-90. Former bd. mgrs. Harrisburg Area YMCA, Harrisburg Hosp.; former bd. dirs. Am. Cancer Soc. Served to lt. USNR, World War II. Mem. Am. Legion, VFW, Navy League (pres. Harrisburg council 1967-68, dir.), Harrisburg C. of C., Pa., Dauphin County bar assns., Nat. Lawyers Club (hon.). Mem. United Ch. Christ (trustee). Club: Mason (33 deg.). Home: Harrisburg Pa. Died Apr. 5, 1990; buried Northumberland, Pa.

HERMANOVSKI, EGILS P., designer, artist; b. Latvia; came to the U.S., 1947, naturalized, 1952; s. Theodor H.; m. Ibolya. Ed., U. Latvia, Tech. U., Stuttgart, Germany. owner Studio H Gallery, N.Y.C.; chmn. bd. Internat. Bus. Designs, N.Y.C. Artist, designer one-man shows include Studio H Gallery, N.Y.C., ann. 1963-75, Manhasset, N.Y., 1981; exhbn. series The Endless Space; archtl. designs for residences, restaurants, offices, motels, clubs; designer furniture, built-ins, fabrics, lighting, also indsl. designs, recent projects include bus. bldgs., Wakyama City, Japan, hotel in Riga, Latvia, 1990; books include Compact and Vacation Homes; contbr. articles to popular mags., trade papers, U.S. and Europe. Recipient numerous awards including Nat. Award for best house of the year Am. Home mag.; Nat. Award for best design and use of materials U.S. Plywood Corp.; Design award for residences Today's Home mag.; 1st prize Bronze Plaque for excellence in design for office bldg. of yr. C. of C. Borough of Queens, 1st place Bronze Plaque for best house-residence design of yr.; prize for community center, hosp., chapel, theater, sr. citizen homes Toronto; painting selected for postage stamp issue by World Fedn. UN Assns., 1989. Mem. A.I.D., Latvian Inst. Architects. Home: Farmingdale N.Y. Died Aug. 7, 1992. †

HERR, DAN, association executive, editor; b. Huron, Ohio, Feb. 11, 1917; s. William Patrick and Wilhelmina Margaret (Slyker) H. B.A., Fordham U., 1938; postgrad., McGill U., 1938, Columbia U., 1939; LL.D. (hon.), Rosary Coll., 1967. Asst. to editor Inf. Jour., Washington, 1945-46; free lance writer, 1946-48; pres. Thomas More Assn., Chgo., 1948-85, chmn. bd., 1985-90; pub. The Critic, 1948-81, 85-90; editor Overview, 1967-73. Author: Stop Pushing, 1961, Start Digging, 1987; co-editor six anthologies. Pres. Nat. Catholic Reporter, 1968-71; trustee Rosary Coll., 1969-73, chmn. bd. trustees, 1970-72. Served to maj. inf. AUS, 1941-45. Decorated Purple Heart, Silver Star; recipient Pere Marquette award Marquette U., 1957; Assn. Chgo. Priests award, 1978. Home: Chicago Ill. Died Sept. 28, 1990.

HERRICK, ALAN ADAIR, lawyer; b. Humboldt, Iowa, Apr. 22, 1896; s. Fred Goodrich and Dora L. (O'Connor) H.; m. Margie Pinkham, June 30, 1920; children: Robert Allan, Margie May Dyson, Jane Kathleen Grothe. AB, U. Iowa, 1917, LLB, 1920. Bar: Iowa 1920. Practiced law Estherville, 1920-25; mem. Strock Sloan & Herrick, 1926-31, Herrick & Langdon, from 1935; judge 9th Jud. Dist. Iowa, 1931-35. With USN, 1917-18; sr. lt. USNRF, 1933-39. Mem. Iowa Bar Assn., others. *

HERRIOTT, FRANK WILBUR, religious educator; b. Winfield, Kans., June 27, 1893; s. Samuel L. and Pearl (Martin) H.; m. Alice Lake, June 9, 1918; 1 child, Elizabeth Browning Davis. AB, Ottawa U., 1915; BD, Union Theol. Sem., N.Y.C., 1926; PhD, Columbia U., 1933. Ordained to ministry No. Bapt. Ch., 1918. Pastor Winfield, 1921-22; min. religious edn. Cen. Presbyn. Ch., Montclair, N.J., 1926-29; asst. dept. religious edn. & psychology Union Theol. Sem., 1929-34, instr. to assoc. prof., 1934-50, prof., 1950-60, Skinner & McAlpin prof. practical theology, 1957-60; interim min. edn. Riverside Ch., N.Y.C., 1960-61; acting staff assoc. for wartime svcs. Internat. Coun. Religious Edn. Author: A Community Serves Its Youth, 1933, Christian Youth in Action, 1935. Chaplain U.S. Army, 1918. Mem. Religious Edn. Assn., Pi Kappa Delta. *

HERSCHLER, EDGAR J., governor, lawyer; b. Kemmerer, Wyo., Oct. 27, 1918; s. Edgar F. and Charlotte (Jenkins) H.; m. Kathleen Sue Colter, 1944; children: Kathleen Sue (Mrs. Jerry Hunt), James C. Student, U. Colo., 1936-41; LL.B., U. Wyo., 1949. Bar: Wyo. 1949. County and pros. atty. Lincoln County, Wyo., 1951-59; mem. Wyo. Ho. of Reps., 1961-71, Parole Bd., State of Wyo., 1971-73; gov. Wyo., 1975-86; mem. law firm Cheyenne, Wyo., 1988-90. Served with USMCR. Decorated Silver Star medal, Purple Heart. Mem. ABA, Wyo. State Bar Assn. (pres. 1968-69), Am. Judicature Soc., Am. Legion. Democrat. Episcopalian. Home: Cheyenne Wyo. Died Feb. 25, 1990.

HERSHMAN, MENDES, lawyer; b. Northampton, Pa., May 20, 1911; s. Joel and Rose (Grossman) H.; m. Frances Sybil Stackell, June 2, 1935; children: Jane, Martha. A.B., N.Y.U., 1929; LL.B., Harvard U., 1932. Bar: N.Y. 1933. With N.Y. Life Ins. Co., N.Y.C., 1932-77, spl. counsel for housing, 1946-62, asst. gen. counsel, 1962-64, assoc. gen. counsel, 1964-69, v.p., gen. counsel, 1969-72, sr. v.p., gen. counsel, 1972-77; sr. ptnr. Rosenman & Colin and predecessor firm Rosenman Colin Freund Lewis & Cohen, N.Y.C., 1977-90; of counsel Rosenman & Colin, N.Y.C., 1990-92; adj. prof. law Fordham U., 1988; lectr. joint com. on continuing legal edn. Am. Law Inst.-Am. Bar Assn., Practising Law Inst.; chmn. legal adv. com. to bd. dirs. N.Y. Stock Exchange, 1978-83, mem. ex officio, from 1983; vis. prof. Marshall-Wythe Law Sch., Coll. William and Mary, 1978-79; chmn. Mayor's Com. on Judiciary, 1972-77, N.Y. State Commn. on Jud. Nominations, from 1978, N.Y. State Commn. on Uniform State Laws. Bd. editors: N.Y. Law Jour., from 1969; Contbr. articles profl. jours. Bd. dirs. N.Y. Landmarks Conservancy, N.Y. Pub. Deveo. Corp., 1966-87; vice chmn. Citizens Union; former pres. NYU Washington Sq. Coll. Alumni Assn.; past bd. dirs. Bronx-Lebanon Hosp.; past pres. Bronx Bar Assn. Recipient N.Y. State award, certificate of Outstanding Pub. Service, 1960. Fellow Am. Bar Found.; mem. Assn. Bar City N.Y. (com. chmn., past v.p., chmn. exec. com.), ABA (mem. council, sect. officer, former chmn. bus. law sect., mem. ho. of dels.), Am. Law Inst. (chmn. com. on continuing legal edn.), N.Y. County Lawyers Assn., Harvard Law Sch. Assn. N.Y.C. (trustee, pres.), Phi Beta Kappa. Home: New York N.Y. Died Mar. 2, 1992; interred Riverside Cemetery, Lodi, N.J.

HERTIG, ARTHUR TREMAIN, physician; b. Mpls., May 12, 1904; s. Charles Marshall and Florence (Long) H.; m. Linda Woodworth, Dec. 22, 1932 (dec. July 1988); children: Helen (Mrs. T.G. Craig) (dec.) Andrew. B.S., U. Minn., 1928; M.D., Harvard U., 1930. Diplomate: Am. Bd. Obstetrics and Gynecology, Am. Bd. Pathology (trustee 1959-70, pres. 1969-70). Entomol. asst. Kala Azar Field Studies, Rockefeller Found., Peking, China, 1925-26; pathol. tng. Peter Bent Brigham Hosp., Boston, Lying-in-Hosp. and Children's Hosp., 1930-33; NRC fellow in embryology Carnegie Instn. of Washington, 1933-34; with Boston Lying-in Hosp. (now Brigham and Women's Hosp), from 1934, obstet. trainee, 1936-38, asst. pathologist, 1934-39, pathologist, 1939-52, cons. pathology, from 1952; pathologist Free Hosp. for Women (now Brigham and Women's Hosp.), Brookline, Mass., 1938-52; cons. pathologist Free Hosp. for Women (now Brigham and Women's Hosp.), from 1952; with Harvard Med. Sch., from 1931, prof. pathology, 1948-52, 70-74, Shattuck prof. path. anatomy, 1952-70, Shattuck prof. path. anatomy emeritus, 1974, chmn. dept. pathology, 1950-68; chief div. pathobiology New Eng. Regional Primate Research Center, Southboro, Mass., 1968-74, assoc. dir. for research, 1972-74; Shattuck prof. emeritus pathological anatomy Harvard Med. Sch.; cons. in pathology Armed Services Inst. Pathology, Washington, 1948-78, mem. sci. adv. bd. cons., 1970-74; cons. in obstet. and gynecol. pathology USN, Chelsea, Mass., 1947-67; former sr. cons. adminstrn., edn. pathology Lemuel Shattuck Hosp.; cons. pathologist Peter Bent Brigham, Beth Israel, Children's hosps., all Boston. Author articles (with John Rock) on early development of normal and abnormal human embryos to Contributions to Embryology, 1941-58; Ultrastructure of mammalian oocytes and human corpus luteum, 1960-68, anatomy and pathology female reprodn. in subhuman primates, 1968, numerous others. Trustee Boston Med. Library, 1945-48. Recipient Am. Gynecol. Soc. award (with John Rock) for fundamental research on human reprodn., 1949; Outstanding Achievement award Centennial Celebration U. Minn., 1951; Ward Burdick award Am. Soc. Clin. Pathologists, 1966; Disting. Service award Coll. Am. Pathologists-Am. Soc. Clin. Pathologists, 1972; Disting. Service award Am. Coll. Obstetricians and Gynecologists, 1975; Gold-Headed Cane Am. Soc. Pathology, 1979, Presdl. medal Brigham and Women's Hosp., 1989; named a Leader in Medicine Boston U. Sch. Medicine, 1980. Fellow Royal Coll. Obstetricians and Gynecologists (London); mem. Am. Soc. Clin. Pathologists (hon.), Soc. Exptl. Pathologists, Coll. Am. Pathologists (gov. 1959-62), Am. Coll. Obstetricians and Gynecologists (Hall of Fame 1983), Internat. Acad. Pathology, Can. Acad. Pathology (Disting. Pathologist award 1990), Am. Assn. Pathology and Bacteriology, Am. Gynecology Soc., AAAS, Am. Acad. Arts and Sci., Am. Assn. Anatomists, N.E. Obstet. and Gynecol. Soc. (pres. 1950-51), N.E. Soc. Pathology (past pres.), Mass. and Middlesex East med. socs., Obstet. Soc. of Boston (past pres.), Sigma Xi, Alpha Omega Alpha, Nu Sigma Nu (past exec. councilor). Clubs: Harvard (Boston); Country (Winchester). Home: Lexington Mass. Died July 20, 1990; buried Mt. Auburn Cemetery, Cambridge, Mass.

HESS, RICHARD CLETUS, graphic artist, painter; b. Royal Oak, Mich., May 27, 1934; s. Cletus Paul and Evelyn Agnus (Stanley) H.; m. Diana Woodard, 1954 (div. 1959); 1 child, Mark; m. Carol Dwight Woodward, 1961 (div. 1976); children—Adam, Sarah. Student, Mich. State U., 1952-53. Art dir. J. Walter Thompson, Detroit, 1955-57; art group dir. N. W. Ayer & Son, Phila., 1958-61, Benton & Bowles, N.Y.C., 1962-64; pres. Richard Hess Inc., N.Y.C., 1965-68, Hess and/Or Antupit Inc., N.Y.C., 1969-71; dir. Hess and Hess, Roxbury, Conn., 1975-91; vis. prof. Syracuse U., N.Y., from 1974, U. Mich., Ann Arbor, 1975-76; Carnegie prof. Cooper Union, N.Y.C., 1980-81. Author, editor, designer: The Dorfsman and CBS, 1986; author: The Illustrator's Workshop: Six Influential Artists, 1986; co-author: The Visual Experience, 1985 ; translator/illustrator: The Snow Queen—Hans Christian Anderson, 1985; co-author, editor/designer: The Portraits of Philippe Halsman, 1983; designer posters for N.Y. Opera and TV series The Way It Was; exhbns. of work held in Paris, Venice, Milan, Detroit; painting in permanant collections Smithsonian Instn., Nat. Portrait Gallery, Mus. Modern Art; contbr. articles on communication arts to mags., 1973-83. Recipient Gold and silver medal N.Y. Art Dirs. Clubs, 1960-82, posthumous induction to its Hall of Fame, 1991; recipient Gold and Silver medals Soc. Illustrators, 1960-80, Exhbn. award Venice Biannale, 1975. Mem. Illustrators Guild (founding), Alliance Graphique Internationale, Am. Inst. Graphic Arts (bd. dirs. 1970-75), Soc. Publs. Designers (bd. dirs. 1970-73, v.p. 1971-75, Gold and Silver medals 1971-75). Home: Roxbury Conn. Died Aug. 5, 1991.

HESS, ROBERT LEE, college president; b. Asbury Park, N.J., Dec. 18, 1932; s. Henry and Ada (Davis) H.; m. Frances H. Aaron, Apr. 9, 1960; children: Carl, Laura, Jonathan, Roger. BA, Yale U., 1954, MA, 1955, PhD, 1960; DHL (hon.), Spertus Coll. Judaica, 1978, Hebrew Union Coll., 1987, U. New Haven, 1988. Instr., then asst. prof. Carnegie Inst. Tech., 1958-61; asst. prof. Mt. Holyoke Coll., 1961-64, Northwestern U., 1964-65; assoc. prof., then prof. U. Ill., Chgo., 1966-79, assoc. dean liberal arts and scis., 1970-72, assoc. vice chancellor acad. affairs, 1972-79; pres. Bklyn. Coll., 1979-92, Coll. Community Svcs., Inc., 1979-92. Author: Italian Colonialism in Somalia, 1966, Ethiopia: The Modernization of Autocracy, 1970, Bibliography of Primary Sources for 19th Century Tropical Africa, 1972, Dictionary of African Biography: Ethiopia, 1977; editor proc.: 5th Internat. Conf. Ethiopian Studies, 1979. Mem. Glencoe (Ill.) Planning Commn., 1975-76; bd. dirs. Jewish Council Urban Affairs, Chgo., 1972-79, Bklyn. Econ. Devel. Corp., 1980-83; bd. dirs. N.Y.C. Holocaust Meml. Commn.; mem. exec. bd. Jr. League Bklyn.; mem. exec. com. Greater N.Y. Conf. on Soviet Jewry, Junction Coll. Devel. Corp., 1986-92; v.p., bd. dirs. research and devel. found. Maimonides Med. Ctr.; bd. govs. Bklyn. Mus., Union of Am. Hebrew Congregations, 1987-92, Rockefeller Inst. Govt., 1987-92; chmn. bd. Bklyn. Sports Found. Ltd., 1987-92; trustee Hist. House Trust N.Y.C., 1989-92. Decorated Officer de l'Ordre des Palmes Academiques (France); Fulbright fellow, 1956-58; summer travel grantee Ford Found., 1964; Guggenheim fellow, 1968-69. Mem. Am. Profs. for Peace in Mid. East (exec. com.), Interfuture Internat. Adv. Coun., Am. Coun. on Edn., Assn. Am. Colls. (com. on coherence in baccalaureate degree, bd. dirs.), Mory's Club, Elizabethan Club, Bklyn. Club, Yale Club, Univ. Club, Rembrandt Club. Jewish. Home: Brooklyn N.Y. Died Jan. 12, 1992; buried Pitts.

HESTER, CLINTON MONROE, lawyer; b. Des Moines, Apr. 16, 1895; s. John Kenton and Sarah Hannah (Hamilton) H.; m. Elizabeth Murvin, May 3, 1924; 1 child, Jean Hamilton. Grad., Phillips-Exeter Acad., 1916; AB, George Washington U., 1920; LLB, Georgetown U., 1922. Bar: D.C. 1922. Atty. Dept. Interior, 1922; asst. counsel U.S. Shipping Bd., U.S. Shipping Bd. Emergency Fleet Corp., 1922-27; counsel Office U.S. Alien Property Cust., spl. asst. to Atty. Gen., 1927; chief atty. U.S. Dept. Justice, 1927-34; chief atty. U.S. Dept. Treasury, 1934-35, asst. gen. counsel, 1935-38; adminstr. CAA, 1938-40; supervised constrn. of Washington Airport; pvt. practice law, from 1940. With AUS, 1918-19. Mem ABA, D.C. Bar Assn., others. *

HEWES, LAURENCE ILSLEY, JR., natural resources economist; b. Kingston, R.I., Apr. 17, 1902; s. Laurence Ilsley and Agnes Bancroft (Danforth) H.; m. Patricia Esther Jackson, Jan. 29, 1932 (dec. 1976); 1 son, Laurence Ilsley; m. Martha Odle Overholser, Aug. 1, 1979. B.Sc., Dartmouth Coll., 1924; Ph.D., George Washington U., 1946; M.P.A., Harvard U., 1956. Engaged in investment banking San Francisco, 1925-33; asst. to undersec. agr., 1935; asst. to adminstr. Farm Security Adminstrn., 1935-39; regional dir. Farm Security Adminstrn., San Francisco, 1939-44; West Coast dir. Am. Council Race Relations, San Francisco, 1944-47; land reform adviser Hdqrs. SCAP, Tokyo, Japan, 1947-49; chief land settlement and agrl. economist Bur. Reclamation, Denver, 1950-59; chief forecasts and econs. U.S. Outdoor Recreation Resources Rev. Commn., 1959-62; asst. to adminstr. Office Rural Areas Devel., USDA, 1962-63; rural devel. adviser AID mission to India, New Delhi, 1963-65; chief natural resources conservation Rural Community Devel. Service, USDA, Washington, 1965-68; Sr. cons. UN Devel. Program, World Bank, FAO, with assignment, Ethiopia, Panama, India, Pakistan, Ceylon, South Vietnam, Mexico, Brit. Honduras, Nicaragua, Tanzania, from 1968; vis. fellow Center for Study Democratic Instns., Santa Barbara, Calif., 1972, 73, assoc., 1976-77; Mem. U.S. Inter Agy. Com. Post Def. Planning, 1939-41, Dept. Agr., War Bd. Calif. and Ariz., 1941-43; U.S. rep. Mexican Labor Transp. Negotiations, 1942-43; exec. sec. land and water policy com. Dept. Agr., 1965-68. Author: Japanese Land Reform Program, 1950, Japan-Land and Men, 1955, Boxcar in the Sand, 1957, Rural Development: World Frontiers, 1974. Recipient Disting. Service award Dept. Agr., 1968. Mem. Artus, Sigma Nu. Presbyterian. Club: Cosmos (Washington). Home: Brentwood Tenn. Died Mar. 31, 1989; body donated science.

HEWITT, FRANK SEAVER, electronics executive, lawyer; b. Pitts., Mar. 5, 1941; s. Kenneth Chadbourne and Mary (Seaver) H. A.B., Harvard U., 1963, LL.B., 1966; LL.M. in Comparative Law, NYU, 1967; post-grad., U. Munich, W.Ger., 1967-68. Bar: N.Y. 1967. Asso. Shearman & Sterling, N.Y.C., 1968-71; atty. Mobil Oil Corp., N.Y.C., 1972-74; gen. counsel, sec. Siemens Capital Corp., N.Y.C., 1974-78; corp. counsel, sec. Siemens Corp., N.Y.C., 1978-79; asso. gen. counsel, sec. Siemens Corp., 1979-90. Mem. N.Y. State Bar Assn., Bar Assn. City N.Y. Club: N.Y. Athletic. Home: Brooklyn N.Y. Died May 17, 1990; buried Greenwood Cemetery, Bklyn.

HEXNER, ERVIN PAUL, political science and economics educator, lawyer; b. Czechoslovakia, Aug. 13, 1893; came to U.S., 1939; naturalizd, 1946; s. Julius and Irene (Teltsch) H.; m. Gertrud Stern, July 10, 1922; children: Peter Eugene, John Tomas. D in Polit. Sci., Royal State U., Hungary, 1918; LLD, Czechoslovak State U., Bratislava, 1919. Sec. gen. v.p. Slovak Fedn. Industries, 1920-35; various other governmental positions; lectr. on pub. adminstrn. & adminstrv. law State U. Bratislava, 1931-39; vis. prof. polit. sci. & econs. U. N.C., 1939-41, assoc. prof., 1941-45, prof., 1945-46; sr. counsellor IMF, 1946-49, asst. gen. counsel, 1949-58; prof. polit. sci., econs. U. Pa., 1958-64, prof. emeritus, from 1964. Author numerous publs. in field. Mem. Am. Econ. Assn., Am. Polit. Sci. Assn., Am. Assn. Internat. Law. *

HEXTER, MAURICE BECK, philanthropic association executive; b. Cin., June 30, 1891; s. Max and Sarah (Beck) H.; m. Marguerite Mock, Aug. 11, 1921 (dec. 1978); 1 dau., Marjorie M. (Mrs. Howard M. Cohen). B.A., U. Cin., 1912, L.H.D. (hon.), 1980; M.A., Harvard U., 1923, Ph.D. in Social Ethics, 1924; Ph.D. honoris causa, U. Dominican Republic, 1955; L.H.D., Brandeis U., 1961, Yeshiva U., 1961, Mt. Sinai Med. Sch., 1980, Hebrew Union Coll., 1987. Exec. dir. Milw. Fedn. Jewish Charities, 1915, other social agys. in, Cin., Boston; exec. mem. Jewish Agy., Jerusalem, in charge colonization project, 1935; With Fedn. Jewish Philanthropies of N.Y., 1938-67, exec. v.p., 1941-66, exec. cons., 1966-90; mem. adv. bd. to Commr. Welfare, N.Y.C.; mem. N.Y.C. Council Against Poverty, 1965. Mem. grants com. Lois and Samuel Silberman Found.; v.p., treas. Henry Kaufmann Found., N.Y.C.; trustee emeritus Brandeis U.; Am. mem. Jewish Colonization Assn., 1952; pres. Nat. Conf. Jewish Social Work, 1924, Dominican Republic Settlement Assn., 1941. Hexter award established at Hunter Coll. in his honor, 1974; recipient 2 Gold medals Nat. Sculpture Show, 1979. Mem. Nat. Assn. Social Workers. Home: New York N.Y. Died Oct. 28, 1990.

HIBBERT, DAVID WILSON, lawyer; b. Atlanta, Nov. 21, 1950; s. George Wilfred and Dorothy Marie (Woodall) H.; m. Mary Frances Disco, June 21, 1975; children: Hector, Norman, Floyd. BA, Mercer U., 1972; JD, Emory U., 1972. Bar: Ga. 1975, U.S. Dist. Ct. (no. dist.) Ga. 1975. Sole practice Atlanta, 1975-89. Mem. Ga. Bar Assn., Atlanta Bar Assn. (chmn. referral com. 1981-89). Democrat. Baptist. Club: Lawyers of Atlanta, Atlanta Radio, Atlanta Bonsai (treas. 1982). Home: Lilburn Ga. Died Feb. 29, 1989; buried Erewhon, Ga.

HICKAM, WILLIS, lawyer; b. Spencer, Ind., May 3, 1894; s. Willis and Sallie (Meek) H.; m. Ruth Elliott, Feb. 4, 1919; children: Elliott, Jane Gay Grizzell. LLB, Ind. U., 1918. Bar: Ind. 1918. Practiced in Spencer; part-time prof. law Ind. U., 1949; v.p., dir. Owen County State Bank, from 1952; dir. Owen County Savs. & Loan Assn. Trustee Ind. U., from 1953, pres. trustees, from 1959. With U.S. Army, 1918. Fellow Am. Coll. Trial Lawyers, Am. Bar Found.; mem. Am. Judicature Soc., ABA, others. *

HICKMAN, FRANCIS GOULD, realtor; b. Phila., Feb. 15, 1896; s. William Francis and Amelia S.M. (Gould) H. Student, Dartmouth Coll., 1917-18, Columbia U., 1919, U. Pa., 1919-20. Salesman Grolier Soc., 1919-22; lectr. Phila. Chatauqua, 1920-21; editor, pub. Cotton Trade Jour., Memphis, 1930-61; pres., operator Parkview Hotel, Memphis, 1942-47; pres. Mid-South Realty Co.; pres. Lincoln Furniture Realty Co., Phila. Decorated Knight of Orange Nassau (Netherlands). Mem. Memphis C. of C., Sigma Chi. *

HICKS, HENRY DAVIES, university president, Canadian legislator; b. Bridgetown, N.S., Can., Mar. 5, 1915; s. Henry Brandon and Annie May (Kinney) H.; m. Paulene Banks, Dec. 28, 1945 (dec. Feb. 1964); m. Margaret Gene Morison, Apr. 15, 1965 (dec. Jan. 1988); children: Catherine Kinney, Henry Randolph Harlow, John George Herbert, Paulene Jane Francess; m. Rosalie Marie Comeau, Jan. 12, 1990. B.A. With honours in Chemistry, Mt. Allison U., 1936; B.Sc., Dalhousie U., 1937, LL.D.; B.C.L., Oxford U., 1940, M.A. (Rhodes scholar), 1944; D.Ed., St. Anne's; LL.D., Mt. Allison U.; D.C.L., King's Coll., U. N.B.; D.Lit., Acadia U.; D.H.L., Mt. St. Vincent U. Bar: 1941, Apptd. Queen's counsel 1957. With Orlando & Hicks, Bridgetown, N.S., Can., 1946-50; dean arts and sci. Dalhousie U., Halifax, N.S., 1960-61, v.p., 1961-63, pres., vice chancellor, 1963-80. Mem. N.S. Legislature, 1945-60, minister edn., 1949-54, provincial sec., 1954, premier, 1954-56, leader Liberal Party in N.S., 1954, leader Her Majesty's Loyal Opposition, 1956-60, mem. Senate of Can., 1972-90; mem. Canada Council, 1963-69; bd. dirs. Assn. Univs. and Colls. Can., 1966-69, 70-72, 74-75; rep. on bd. govs. U. Guyana, 1970-75; pres. Assn. Atlantic Univs., 1968-72; Canadian del. 28th gen. assembly UN, 1973. Capt. Royal Canadian arty. Can. Army, 1941-45. Invested companion Order Can., 1970. Fellow Royal Philatelic Soc. London, Royal Philatelic Soc. Can.; mem. Aesculapius Fishing Assn. Clubs: Saraguay, Halifax. Home: Halifax NS, Canada Died Dec. 9, 1991.

HICKS, SIR JOHN RICHARD, economist; b. Warwick, U.K., Apr. 8, 1904; s. Edward H.; ed. Clifton Coll., also Balliol Coll., Oxford; m. Ursula Kathleen Webb, 1935 (dec. 1985). Prof. polit. economy U. Manchester, 1938-46; fellow Nuffield Coll., Oxford, 1946-52, univ. prof. polit. economy, 1952-65, research fellow All Souls Coll., from 1965. Created knight, 1964; recipient Nobel prize in econs., 1972. Author: Theory of Wages, 1932; Value and Capital, 1939; The Social Framework, 1942; Contribution to the Theory of the Trade Cycle, 1950; A Revision of Demand Theory, 1956; Essays in World Economics, 1959; Capital and Growth, 1965; Critical Essays in Monetary Theory, 1967; A Theory of Economic History, 1969; Capital and Time, 1973; The Crisis in Keynesian Economics, 1974; Economic Perspectives, 1977; Causality in Economics, 1979; Collected Essays on Economic Theory, 3 vols., 1981-83. Died May 20, 1989. Home: London England

HIDAYATULLAH, MOHAMMAD, vice-president of India; b. Betul, India, Dec. 17, 1905; s. Hafiz Mohammad Wilayatullah and Mohammadi Begum; B.A., U. Nagpur, 1926; M.A., Cambridge (Eng.) U., 1930; barrister-at-law, Lincoln's Inn, London; LL.D. (hon.), univs. Philippines, Ravishankar and Rajasthan, Benares Hindu U.; D.Litt. (hon.), U. Bhopal, U. Kaketrya; m. Pusha Shah, May 5, 1948; 1 son, 1 dau. (dec.). Lectr., Univ. Coll. Law, Nagpur, 1934-42; successively advocate, advocate gen., judge, chief justice Nagpar and M.P. High Cts., 1930-58; justice, chief justice Supreme Ct. India, 1958-70; acting pres. India, 1969; vice pres. India, 1979-92 ; past dean Faculty Law, Nagpur U.; chancellor Delhi, Punjab and Jamia Millia Islamia Univs. Decorated Order Brit. Empire; Order Yugoslav Flag with sash; knight of Mark Twain; Silver Elephant and Bronze medal for gallantry. Clubs: Willingdon Sports (Bombay); Delhi Gymkhana (New Delhi); Gondwana (Nagpur). Author: Democracy in India and the Judicial Process; The South-West Africa Case; A Judges Miscellany, 1st, 2d and 3d series, U.S.A. and India; 5th and 6th Schedules to the Constitution of India; Mulla's Mohamadan Law, 16th-18th edits.; Rights to Property and the Indian Constitution; (memoirs) My Own Boswell. Died Sept. 18, 1992. Home: New Delhi India †

HIGGINSON, THOMAS LEE, lawyer; b. N.Y.C., Jan. 2, 1920; s. James Jackson and Lucy Virginia (Mitchell) H.; m. Theodora Winthrop, Sept. 11, 1948 (div. 1984); children: Thomas Lee Jr., Elizabeth, Robert Winthrop; m. Shirley Foerderer Ames, June 30, 1984. Student, Groton Sch.; A.B., Harvard U., 1942, LL.B., 1949. Bar: N.Y. 1950. Mem. firm Shearman & Sterling, N.Y.C., 1949-90, ptnr., 1957-90; exec. com., bd. dirs. Fiduciary Trust Co. Internat. Trustee, sec. The Frick Collection, Percival E. and Ethel Brown Foerderer Found., A. R. Tinker Meml. Fund; trustee Greenvale (L.I.) Sch.; dir. Winthrop-Univ. Hosp., Mineola, N.Y. Served from 2d lt. to maj. AUS, 1942-46. Decorated Bronze Star. Mem. ABA, N.Y. State Bar Assn., Assn. Bar City N.Y. Republican. Episcopalian. Clubs: Brook, Knickerbocker, Links, Downtown Assn. (N.Y.C.); Piping Rock (L.I.). Home: Cold Spring Harbor N.Y. Died Apr. 13, 1990; buried St. John's Meml. Cemetery, Cold Spring Harbor.

HIGINBOTHAM, BETTY LOUISE WILSON, botanist, consultant; b. Louisville, July 5, 1910; d. Samuel Gould Wilson and Stella Jane (Robbins) McCracken; m. Noe Higinbotham, Apr. 3, 1937 (dec. Feb. 1980). BA, Butler U., 1932, MA, 1935. Soc. editor New Albany (Ind.) Daily Ledger, 1935-37; editor Williams & Wilkins, Pubs., Balt., 1937-38; botanical writer Columbia Ency., N.Y.C., 1938-41; editor Washington State Inst. of Tech., 1950; head editorial dept. Washington State U. Press, Pullman, 1951-52; assoc. editor N.W. Sci., Pullman, 1952-56; bryological cons. Northrup Space Labs., 1967, Battelle N.W., Richland, Wash., 1968-71; instr. plants Orcas Island U. Washington, Seattle, 1981; instr. plants San Juan Island U. Wash., Friday Harbor, 1982-84; instr. plants San Juan Islands Skagit Valley Coll., Friday Harbor, 1985-86; bot. writer Internat. Ency., N.Y.C., 1938-51, study program Ency. Brittanica, N.Y.C., 1938-41; cons. Nat. Park Svc., Friday Harbor, 1986-87; mem. adv. com. Parks and Recreation Bd. Thurston County, 1990—; cons. Thurston County Noxious Weed Control Agy. Discovered new species of moss; pub. description of species Latin and English (with Noe Higinbotham) in scientific jour.; freelance writer nature mags.; contbr. papers to sci. jours. Mem. Am. Bryological and Lichenological Soc. (v.p. 1960-61, pres. 1961-62), Am. Radio Relay League, Amateur Radio Emergency Svcs., Delta Zeta, Theta Sigma Phi (hon.), Phi Kappa Phi, Kappa Tau Alpha. Home: Olympia Wash. Died Oct. 13, 1992. †

HILBURN, EARL DRAYTON, communications executive, consultant; b. Mpls., Apr. 16, 1920; s. Earl D. and Jess U. (Neutson) H.; m. Charlotte B. Johnson, Sept. 16, 1940; children: Scott L., Bruce J. Student, U. Wis., 1938-40; Indpls. extension br., Purdue U., 1943-44. Communications dept. United Air Lines, 1940-42; sr. engr. test equipment dept. RCA, Indpls., 1942- 44; field engr. RCA, Camden, N.J., 1944-46; project engr. Melpar, Inc., Alexandria, Va., 1946-47, cons., 1947-50, asst. to exec. v.p., 1950-53; (became subsidiary Westinghouse Air Brake Co. 1953); v.p. govt. contracts Westinghouse Air Brake Co., 1953-56; v.p. Link Aviation Inc., Binghamton, N.Y., 1956-60; pres., dir. Burtek, Inc., Tulsa, 1960-62; v.p., gen. mgr. electronics div. Curtiss-Wright Corp., 1962-63; dep. to asso. adminstr. and gen. mgr. NASA, 1963-66; v.p., asst. to pres. Western Union Telegraph Co., N.Y.C., 1966-69, exec. v.p., 1969-70, pres., 1970-77; pres. Western Union Corp., 1977-81, cons., 1981-89; cons. NASA, 1981-89, SIAC, 1981-89, Nat. Acad. Pub. Adminstrn., 1985-89; dir. Hudson City Savs. Bank; bd. dirs. Nat. Space Inst.; chmn. adv. com. Internat. Assn. Satellite Users. Mem. Armed Forces Communications and Electronics Assn., U.S. C. of C. (chmn. communications com., dir. 1970-76), U.S. Power Squadron. Clubs: Skytop (Pa.); Starcom, Treasure Coast PC Users (Stuart, Fla.). Home: Stuart Fla. Died Jan. 10, 1989; buried Stuart, Fla.

HILDEBRAND, H(ENDRICK) EDWARD, engineer; b. Sandstedt, Germany, Jan. 25, 1895; came to U.S., 1904, naturalized, 1916; s. Edward Christian and Elise (Ratjen) H.; m. Mario B. Gross, Nov. 23, 1918; children: H. Edward, Ruth Elsa. ME, Columbia U., 1917. Asst. chief engr. Newburgh (N.Y.) shipyards, 1917-22; engr. Continental Baking Co., 1922-26, dir. engring., 1926-63, v.p., 1944-63; v.p. Morton Frozen Foods, Inc., 1956-63; cons. Continental Baking Co., from 1963, Office Def. Transp., 1942-43. Mem. ASME, Am. Soc. Bakery Engrs., Soc. Automotive Engrs. *

HILDESHEIMER, WOLFGANG, author, artist; b. Hamburg, Germany, Dec. 9, 1916; s. Arnold and Hanna Goldschmid H.; m. Silvia Dillmann, Oct. 19, 1953. Student, Cen. Sch. Arts and Crafts, London, 1937-39. Brit. info. officer Palestine, 1943-45; lectr. Brit. Inst., Tel-Aviv, 1945-46; interpreter War Crimes Trials, Nuremburg, Germany, 1947-49; freelance writer, 1949-91; guest lectr. poetry Frankfurt U., 1967. Author: Lieblose Legenden, 1952, Die Verspatung, 1962, Nachtstuck, 1963, Tynset, 1965, Rivalen, 1965, Masante, 1973, play Mary Stuart, biography Mozart, 1977, Marbot, 1981. Recipient prize for radio play awarded by war blinded, 1955, Lit. prize, Bremen, 1965, Georg Buchner prize German Acad. Lang. and Poetry, 1966; Dr. h.c., 1982; named hon. citizen, City of Poschiavo, Switzerland, 1982. Mem. Acad. of Arts, Berlin. Home: Poschiavo Switzerland Died Aug. 21, 1991; buried Poschiavo, Switzerland.

HILL, SIR AUSTIN BRADFORD, physician, epidemiologist; b. July 8, 1897; s. Sir Leonard Erskine Hill; ed. Univ. Coll. London; PhD, 1926; DSc, 1929; m. Florence Maud, 1923 (dec. 1980); 3 children. Staff Med. Rsch. Coun. and Indsl. Health Rsch. Bd., 1923-33; reader in epidemiology and vital stats. London Sch. Hygiene and Tropical Medicine, 1933-45, prof., prof. emeritus, dean, 1955-57; hon. dir. statis. rsch. unit Med. Rsch. Coun., 1955-57; lectr. in field. Served with Royal Naval Air Service, 1916-18; seconded to Dept. Ministry of Home Security, 1940-42, to med. directorate RAF, 1943-45, civilian cons., 1943-78. Fellow Royal Soc.; knighted, 1961; decorated comdr. Brit. Empire, 1951. Fellow Royal Coll. Physicians (hon.), FFCM, FRSM, FAPHA. Recipient Galen medal Soc. Apothecaries, 1959, Harben Gold medal, 1961, Herbenden Soc., 1965, numerous others. Author: Internal Migration and Its Effects upon the Death Rates, 1925; The Inheritance of Resistance to Bacterial Infection in Animal Species, 1934; Principles of Medicial Statistics, 1937, 11th edit., 1985. Died Apt. 18, 1991. Home: near Windermere Eng.

HILL, DANIEL A., engineer, government official; b. Wapwallopen, Pa., Dec. 26, 1898; s. Charles Wallace and Susan Alverta (Karehner) H.; m. Janet Garland Farrar, July 2, 1938. Student, Carnegie Inst. Tech., Western Res. U.; AB, Case Inst. Tech., 1929, MBA, 1936. Devel. engr. Baker Waechtler Co., Cleve., 1920-22; ptnr. Hill Brown Constrn. Co., Cleve., 1922-23; cons. engr. H.M. Henton & Co., 1923-24; with Ohio Pub. Svc. Co., 1924-50, asst. to pres., 1940-46, gen. rate & valuation engr., 1946-49; gen. rate & valuation engr. Ohio Edison Co., 1950-51; cons. various, 1950-54, cons. engr., 1955-56; v.p. dir. Stock Equipment Co., 1956-59; with ICA, AID, from 1959. Mem. NSPE, IEEE, Am. Acad. Polit. & Social Scis., numerous others. *

HILL, DEREK LEONARD, chemistry educator; b. Croydon, Eng., Dec. 6, 1930; came to U.S., 1957; s. Leonard David and Jessie (Hoare) H.; m. Sandra Hale Cloke, Aug. 23, 1958; children: Lauren, Brenda, Amanda, Sharon. B.Sc., U. London, 1953, Ph.D., 1957; D.I.C., Imperial Coll., 1957. Asst. exptl. officer AEC U.K., 1956-57; research asso. Rensselaer Poly. Inst., 1957-59, asst. prof. chemistry, 1959-61; sr. lectr. phys. chemistry U. Hong Kong, 1961-68; asso. prof. chemistry SUNY-Brockport, 1968-71, prof. chemistry, 1971-89, chmn. dept., 1970-79, dean faculty nat. math. sci., 1979-82. Mem. Am. Chem. Soc., Chem. Soc. (London), Sigma Xi. Home: Brockport N.Y. Died July 2, 1989.

HILL, DUMOND PECK, lawyer; b. Fayetteville, N.C., Jan. 10, 1923; s. William Edwin and Zaida (English) H.; m. Elizabeth Hutcheson Willis, July 21, 1950; children: Emma Willis, Julia Haywood, Alice Chamberlayne. BS, Davidson Coll., 1946; LLB, U. Va., 1948, LLM, 1950. Bar: Va., D.C. Mem. staff AEC, Washington, 1950-51; asst. counsel-internat. security affairs Dept. Def., Washington, 1951-53; assoc. counsel Dept. of Army, Washington, 1953-54; trial atty. U.S. Dept. Justice, Washington, 1954-56; staff counsel U.S. Ho. of Reps. Com. on Fgn. Affairs, Washington, 1956-59; mng. ptnr. Surrey, Karasik, Greene & Hill, Washington, 1959-71, Hill, Christopher & Phillips, Washington, 1971-81, Kirkpatrick & Lockhart, Washington, 1981-91; vis. lectr. U. Va. Law Sch., Charlottesville, 1963-65; gen. counsel Ptnrs. of Americas, Washington, 1971-91. Contbr. articles to legal jours. Served to sgt. U.S. Army, 1943-45, ETO. Mem. ABA, Am. Soc. Internat. Law, Am. Soc. Naval Architects, U. Va. Law Sch. Alumni Assn. (mem. council 1975-77; v.p. 1986-87, pres. 1989-91). Democrat. Club: Metropolitan (Washington). Home: Washington D.C. Died June 29, 1991; cremated.

HILL, HYACINTHE (VIRGINIA ANDERSON KAIN), poet; b. N.Y.C., May 24, 1920; d. Joseph Thomas and Angela Virginia (Bradley-Bruen) Cronin; m. Johan Anderson, July 15, 1940 (dec.); children: John Luke Anderson, Matthew Mark Anderson (dec.); m. John Kain, 1978. B.A. cum laude with honors in English, Bklyn Coll., 1961; M.A. in English and Comparative Lit., Hunter Coll., 1965; postgrad., Fordham U., 1965-69; Ph.D. (hon.), No. Pontifical Acad., Sweden, 1969; D.Arts and Letters (hon.), Gt. China Arts Coll., 1969; D.Hum., Coll. Alfred the Great, Hull, Eng., 1970; H.L.D. honoris cause, U. Asia, Pakistan. Tchr. English James Monroe High Sch., Bronx, 1969-82. Author: Shoots of a Vagrant Vine (Avalon Nat. Sonnets prize 1950), 1950; Promethea (Cameo Press book award 1957), 1957; Squaw, No More, 1975, Poetry and the Stars, 1986; also numerous individual poems. Co-editor Diamond Year Anthology, 1970. Editor North Atlantic edit. Great Am. World Poets Anthology, 1973. Named poet laureate internat., 1973, 74, 75; decorated dame Knights of Malta; recipient Poetry Soc. Am. prizes, from 1958, N.Am. Chapbook award, 1966, 1st prize Eleanor Otto award N.Y. Poetry Forum, 1969, 70, 1st prize Internat. Inst., 1970, Commemorative Medal Honor Am. Biog. Inst., 1987, numerous other awards. Mem. Acad. Am. Poets, Poetry Soc. Am., League Am. Pen-Women, Alpha Delta Kappa. Home: San Rafael Calif. Deceased. †

HILL, JIM DAN, educational administrator; b. Leon County, Tex., Feb. 4, 1897; s. Dan Chapman and Alma Amyria (Hill) H.; m. Christine W. Cantwell, May 31, 1925; 1 child, Dana Militia Budde. BA, Baylor U., 1922; MA, U. Colo., 1924; PhD, U. Minn., 1931; DLitt (hon.), Baylor U., 1948. Prin. Blooming Grove High Sch., 1921-22; asst. comdt. Gulf Coast Mil. Acad., 1922-23; prof. English N.Mex. Sch. Mines, Socorro, 1923-24; asst. prof. English & econs. Mich. Coll. Mines, Houghton, 1924-26, assoc. prof., 1026; chmn. dept. social scis. State Tchrs. Coll., River Falls, Wis., 1926-31; pres. Wis. State Coll., Superior, 1931-64, pres. emeritus, from 1964. Author: Sea Dogs of the Sixties, 1935, The Texas Navy, 1936, The Minute Man in Peace and War, 1963; also articles. With USN, World War I; comdr. 190th F.A. regt., 1942-45. Decorated European Theatre with 5 campaign stars, Arrowhead for Normandy Beach Assault, Air Medal, Bronze Star, Legion of Merit, Croix de Guerre with palm, Chevalier Legion d'Honneur. Mem. Am. Hist. Assn., Wis. Hist. Soc., Authors League Am., others. *

HILL, LUTHER LYONS, army officer, publisher; b. Montgomery, Ala., Dec. 9, 1896; s. Luther Leonidas and Lily (Lyons) H.; m. Mary Hippee, Oct. 26, 1921; children: Luther L., Mildred. AB, U. Ala., 1916; BS, U.S. Mil. Acad., 1919; LLD (hon.), Yankton Coll., 1951. Pres. McMurray Hill & Co., Des Moines, 1929-35; dir. Viking Pump Co., Knapp Monarch Co., St. Louis, 1928-33; fin. advisor Reconstrn. Fin. Corp., 1933; v.p., dir. Iowa Broadcasting Co., 1933-42, Register & Tribune Co., from 1946; v.p. Cowles Broadcasting Co., 1946-60; pres. broadcasting divsn. Cowles Mags. & Broadcasting, Inc., from 1960; chmn. bd. Universal Cable Vision of Fla.; pub. Des Moines Register and Tribune, 1950-60. Trustee Drake U. Brig. gen. U.S. Army, 1919-23, 42-45. Awarded Legion of Merit. Mem. Phi Beta Kappa, others. *

HILL, RICHARD JOHNSON, sociologist, educator, academic administrator; b. N.Y.C., Sept. 9, 1925; s. Archie S. and Esther (Johnson) H.; m. Barbara Joyce Beall, June 21, 1947; children: Suzan Elizabeth, Laura Kathryn. Student, Rutgers U., 1946-48; A.B., Stanford U., 1950, M.A., 1951; Ph.D., U. Wash., 1955. Mem. labs. staff Bell Telephone Labs., N.Y.C., 1955-56; asst. prof. sociology UCLA, 1956-60; assoc. prof. sociology U. Tex., Austin, 1960-62, prof., 1962-65; prof. sociology Purdue U., Lafayette, Ind., 1965-71; prof. sociology U. Oreg., 1971-89, head dept. sociology, 1972-75; dean U. Oreg. Sch. of Community Service and Public Affairs, 1978-80, acting v.p. for acad. affairs, provost, 1980-81, interim vice-chancellor acad. affairs, 1981-88; cons. NSF, NIMH, Western Interstate Commn. Higher Edn. Author: Public Leadership, 1961, Sociological Measurement, 1967; Asso. editor: Sociological Methodology, 1968-71; Editor: Sociometry, 1966-70; Contbr. articles to profl. jours. Bd. dirs. Purdue-Calument (Ind.) Devel. Found.; bd. dirs. Inst. for Policy Analysis, Eugene, Oreg. Served with USMC, 1942-46. Mem. Am. Sociol. Assn. (council 1977-79, v.p. elect 1986-87, v.p. 1987-88), Pacific Sociol. Assn. (pres. 1974-75), Am. Statis. Assn., Sociol. Research Assn., Phi Beta Kappa (pres. Alpha chpt. Oreg. 1989-90). Home: Eugene Oreg. Died Dec. 20, 1989.

HILLMAN, BILL (CLARENCE WILLIAM HILLMAN), labor union executive; b. Rexburg, Idaho, Dec. 10, 1922; s. Clarence Lynn and Reva (Baird) H.; m. Virginia Carney, June 1948 (div. 1950); 1 son, Robert W.; m. Martha Ruth Apollonio, Dec. 31, 1959; children: Kenneth W., Nancy A. A.A., Boise Jr. Coll., 1942; B.A., U. Calif. at Berkeley, 1949. Reporter Sta. KPIX, San Francisco, from 1949; corr. Voice of Am., San Francisco, 1956-72; 1st nat. v.p. AFTRA, 1976-79, nat. pres., 1979-84; trustee health and retirement funds AFTRA, N.Y.C., from 1977. Home: San Rafael Calif. Deceased. †

HILTABIDLE, WILLIAM ORME, JR., consulting engineer; b. Glyndon, Md., Nov. 2, 1896; s. William Orme and Ada Elizabeth (Gosnell) H.; m. Kathleen Mohan, June 29, 1922; children: Elizabeth Ann Hagerty, Marilyn Williams, Sarah Jane Sheeley. CE, Lafayette Coll., 1919, DSc, 1945; grad., Indsl. Coll. Armed Forces, 1933. Civil engr., 1919; field engr. Hughes-Foulkrod Co., Phila., 1919-20; design engr. Truscon Steel Co., N.Y.C., 1920-21; commd. 2d lt. Corps Civil

Engrs. USN, 1921, advanced through grades to vice adm., 1951, asst. civil engr., civil engr. numerous locations, comdr. in charge 5th Naval Constrn. Brigade, 1944-45, asst. chief Bur. Yarda, 1947-49, insp., 1949-50; v.p. Charles R. Tompkins Co., Washington, 1952-61; Washington mgr. DeLeuw, Cather & Co., then mgr. DeLeuw, Cather Internat., Washington. Trustee Lafayette Coll. Decorated Victory medal, Am. Def. medal with star, World War II medal, Bronze Star, Legion of Merit, Asiatic-Pacific medal with two stars. Fellow ASCE; mem. Soc. Mil. Engrs., NSPE, others. *

HILTNER, WILLIAM ALBERT, astronomy educator; b. Continental, Ohio, Aug. 27, 1914; s. John Nicholas and Ida Lavina (Schafer) H.; m. Ruth Moyer Kreider, Aug. 12, 1939; children—Phyllis Anne, Kathryn Jo, William Albert, Stephen Kreider. BS, U. Toledo, 1937, DSc (hon.), 1968; MS, U. Mich., 1938, PhD, 1942. Mem. faculty U. Chgo., 1943-70, prof. astronomy, 1955-70; dir. Yerkes Obs., 1963-66; acting dir. Cerro Tololo Inter-Am. Obs., 1966-67; prof. U. Mich., Ann Arbor, 1970-85; chmn. dept. astronomy U. Mich., 1970-82, prof. emeritus, 1985; mgr. Magellan Project, Mt. Wilson and Las Campanas Obs., 1986-91. Co-author: Photometric Atlas of Stellar Spectra, 1946; Editor: Astronomical Techniques, 1962. NRC fellow, 1942-43. Mem. AAAS, Astron. Soc. Pacific, Am. Astron. Soc. (councilor 1962-65), Assn. Univs. for Rsch. in Astronomy (bd. dirs. 1959-71, 74-85, pres. bd. dirs. 1968-71). Home: Ann Arbor Mich. Died Sept. 30, 1991; cremated.

HIMELICK, ALAN EDWARD, advertising agency executive; b. Lakewood, Ohio, May 27, 1929; s. Francis Herbert and Harriet Grace (Woodward) H. B.S. in Journalism, Ohio U., 1951, M.A., 1951. Advt. mgr. Tectum Corp., Newark, Ohio, 1954-56; account exec. Griswold-Eshelman Co., Cleve., 1956-57; copywriter J.M. Mathes Inc., N.Y.C., 1957-63; copywriter, creative supr. Young & Rubicam, Inc., N.Y.C., 1963-70, creative dir., 1970-74, sr. v.p., 1974. Trustee, bd. mgrs. New Milford Hosp., from 1982; vice chmn. Children's Ctr., New Milford, Conn., from 1982; v.p. Merryall Community Ctr., New Milford, from 1983. Served with USN, 1951-53. Mem. Sigma Delta Chi, Delta Tau Delta. Republican. Espicopalian. Home: Washington Depot Conn. Died Dec. 27, 1991.

HINES, VINCENT JOSEPH, clergyman; b. New Haven, Conn., Sept. 14, 1912. Student, St. Thomas Sem., Conn., 1930-32, St. Sulpice Sem., Paris, 1932-37; JCD, Lateran U., Rome, 1949. Ordained priest Roman Cath. Ch., 1937. Curate Manchester, Conn., 1937-43; chancellor Hartford (Conn.) Diocese, 1959; bishop Diocese of Norwich, Conn., 1959-90. Chaplain AUS, 1943-46. Home: Wilton Conn. Died Apr. 23, 1990.

HINKE, KARL, business consultant, banker; b. Phila., Jan. 11, 1906; s. William John and Bertha Agnes (Berleman) H.; m. E. Donne Zick, Dec. 27, 1947; 1 child, Frederick W. II. Grad., Mercersburg (Pa.) Acad., 1923; BA, Hamilton Coll., 1927. With Marshall, Meadows & Stewart, Inc., Auburn, N.Y., 1927-30; with Marine Trust Co., Buffalo, 1930-71, sr. v.p., 1930-71, 1961-71; v.p. Marine Midland Banks, Inc., Buffalo, 1961-71, exec. v.p., 1962-71, also dir., mem. adv. bd.; v.p. Marine Midland Trust Co. We. N.Y., Buffalo, 1961-71; chmn. emeritus Interbank Card; ptnr. Karl Hinke & Assocs., bus. cons.; dir. Rand Capital Corp., Buffalo China, Inc., Sierra Rsch. Corp., Auburn Plastics, Inc., Auburn Cablevision, Inc. Bd. dirs. Auburn Theol. Sem. Capt. USMCR, 1942-45. Mem. Buffalo Club (v.p., dir.). Home: East Aurora N.Y. Died Dec. 22, 1990; buried East Aurora, N.Y.

HINKS, KENNETT WEBB, government consultant; b. Mpls., Sept. 3, 1897; s. William Herbert and Florence Mary (Webb) H.; m. Elizabeth Porter Dial, Nov. 2, 1946; stepchildren: Nathaniel Victor, Diana. AB, U. Minn., 1920. With J. Walter Thompson Co., N.Y.C., 1921-64, Pacific Coast mgr., 1925-28, Cen. European mgr., 1929-32, v.p., 1936-61, sr. v.p., 1961-63, dir., 1949-64; dir. Caribbean & Can. subs. J. Walter Thompson Co.; cons. Agrl. Svc., U.S. Dept. Agr., from 1963. 2d lt. inf. U.S. Army, World War I; lt. comdr. USNR, World War II. Mem. Nat. Planning Assn., Phi Beta Kappa, others. *

HIPCHEN, DONALD EUGENE, construction materials company executive; b. Bradford, Pa., June 30, 1932; s. John Clarence and Ernestine Elizabeth (Osmann) H.; m. Martha Josephine Rich, Dec. 28, 1954; children: Karl Alan, Emily Ann, John Michael. BS ChemE, U. Pitts., 1954. Prodn. engr. Union Carbide Corp., Bound Brook, N.J., 1954-59; plant engr. Mich. Chem. Corp., St. Louis, 1959-60; plant chemist Armstrong Cork Co., Lancaster, Pa., 1960-62; research supr. Allied Chem. Corp., Buffalo, 1962-65; research supr. Jim Walter Research Corp., St. Petersburg, Fla., 1967-77, dir. devel., 1977-79, pres., from 1979; v.p. research Jim Walter Corp., St. Petersburg, from 1984; bd. dirs. Celotex Inoue Corp., Nagoya, Japan. 8 patents in foam plastics; contbr. articles to tech. jours. Mem. Am. Chem. Soc., Soc. Plastics Engrs. Home: Largo Fla. Deceased.

HIRSCH, HAROLD SELLER, manufacturing company executive; b. Portland, Oreg., Sept. 3, 1907; s. Max S. and Clementine (Seller) H.; m. Barbara Honeyman, May 25, 1934 (div.); children—Frederic S., Janet H.; m. Elizabeth Blair, Nov. 5, 1949. A.B., Dartmouth Coll., 1929. With White Stag Mfg. Co., Portland, Oreg., 1929-72; pres. White Stag Mfg. Co., 1954-64, chmn. bd., 1964-70, chmn. exec. com., 1970-86; dir. Liberty Communications Inc., to 1975; dir. Warnaco, Inc., 1966-78, hon. dir., 1978-80; dir. Warnaco Fund, Inc., 1974-80. Commr. Port of Portland, 1961-69, treas., 1962, sec., 1963, v.p., 1966, pres., 1967; mem. nat. adv. council Nature Conservancy; Portland met. chmn. Nat. Alliance Businessmen, 1970-71; pres. Oreg. Mental Health Assn.; treas. Boys and Girls Aid Soc. Oreg.; mem. Dartmouth Coll. Alumni Council, 1960-61; v.p. Dartmouth Alumni Assn., 1969; bd. dirs. Contemporary Crafts Oreg., Portland Civic Theatre, Council Social Agys.; bd dirs. Portland Youth Philharm. Assn., 1973-79, v.p., 1978-79, 80-86; bd. dirs. Oreg. chpt. Nature Conservancy Found., 1972-79, v.p., 1977-79; trustee Pacific Internat. Livestock Expn., 1974-86; mem. SSS Bd., Portland, 1942-43; spl. cons. O.Q.M.G., Research and Devel. Div., Washington, 1943-44; Pres., trustee Gabel Country Day Sch., Portland; trustee Reed Coll., sec., 1972-77; mem. adv. bd. U. Oreg. Bus. Sch.; pres. Hirsch Found., 1966-77; bd. dirs. Oreg. Ind. Colls. Found., 1980-88, Isam and Rose White Found., 1966-78, pres., 1971-77; bd. dirs., treas. Neskowin Coast Found., 1970-77; bd. dirs. Parry Center, 1970-76, World Affairs Council, 1975-79; bd. dirs., treas. Neskowin Community Assn., 1970-86; dir. Oreg. chpt. NCCJ, 1977-85, sec., 1980-85, nat. trustee, from 1985; bd. dirs. Contemporary Crafts, 1979-85; mem. St. Vincent Med. Found.; bd. overseers Oreg. Health Scis. U., 1981-89; bd. dirs. Friends of Timberline, from 1987. Named to Pacific Northwest Winter Sports Hall of Fame, 1987, U.S. Nat. Ski Hall of Fame, 1990; recipient Disting. Svc. award. Reed Coll., 1990. Mem. Oreg. Men's Apparel Assn. (pres.), Pacific N.W. Apparel Mfrs. Assn. (pres.), United World Federalists (nat. adv. bd.), Jewish Hist. Soc. Oreg. (dir. 1975-85, treas. 1975-79), Ski Industries Am. (pres. 1963-65, hon. chmn. 1965-69, hon. dir.), Nat. Ski Patrol (hon.), U.S. Ski Writers Assn. (hon.), Japanese Garden Soc. Oreg. (dir., fin. v.p. 1974-88, hon. dir. 1988), Pi Lambda Phi, Beta Gamma Sigma, Alpha Kappa Psi. Clubs: Multnomah Athletic, Lang Syne Soc. Home: Portland Oreg. Died July 4, 1990.

HIRSCH, HOWARD CARLYLE, investment banker, broker; b. N.Y.C., Sept. 10, 1896; s. Charles Sidney and Ida (Hesslein) H.; m. Suzanne Madeline Couton, Feb. 18, 1937. Student, Columbia U., 1916-17; LLD (hon.), Syracuse U., 1961. With Hirsch & Co., N.Y.C., from 1920, sr. ptnr., from 1938. With USN, 1918-20. Mem. Chgo. Bd. Trade, N.Y. Commodity Exch., Liverpool Cotton Exch. *

HIRSCH, JOHN STEPHEN, theater director, consultant; b. Siofok, Hungary, May 1, 1930; emigrated to Can., 1947; s. Joseph and Ilona (Horvath) H. Student, Israel Gymnasium in, Budapest; D.Litt. (hon.), U. Man., 1966; also hon. fellow, Univ. Coll.; LL.D. (hon.), U. Toronto, 1967. lectr. Columbia, N.Y. U.; theatre cons. Can. Council, Ont. Arts Council; cons. BBC/PBS Shakespeare Project for Children's TV, 1978; cons. artistic dir. Seattle Repertory Theatre, from 1979. Directed first play The Time of Your Life at Little Theatre, Winnipeg, Man., Can., 1951; dir. Stratford Shakespearean Festival, Ont., 1965, The Cherry Orchard, Henry VI, 1966, Richard III, The Tempest, 1982, A Midsummer Night's Dream, The Three Musketeers, 1968, Satyricon, 1969; dir. first play in New York Lorca's Yerma, Vivian Beaumont Repertory Theater of Lincoln Ctr., 1966; dir. Galileo, 1967, St. Joan, 1968, The Time of Your Life, 1969, Beggar on Horseback, 1970, Playboy of the Western World, Antigone, 1971; dir. Broadway prodn. of We Bombed in New Haven, 1968, AC/DC, for Chelsea Theater Ctr., 1970, for Theatre du Nouveau Monde, Mere Courage, 1964, for the Habimah, Tel Aviv, The Seagull, 1970; assoc. artistic dir., Stratford (Ont.) Shakespearean Festival, 1967-69, artistic dir., Stratford (Ont.) Shakespearean Festival from 1981; founder Rainbow Stage, Theatre 77, Man. Theatre Centre; entered film prodn. in Can. with In The Shadow of the City, 1955; first directed on TV in 1954, and has since directed The Three Musketeers; co-artistic dir. Stratford Festival Theatre, 1968-69; dir. Midsummer Nights Dream, Mpls. Theatre, 1972, The Dybbuk, Los Angeles prodn. Mark Taper Forum, 1975, Maggie Smith in The Three Sisters, Stratford Festival, 1976, The Tempest, Mark Taper Forum, 1979, Number Our Days, Mark Taper Forum, 1979; exec. producer Sarah, 1976; head TV drama, English service div. CBC, 1976-78; History of the American Film, Nat. Arts Centre, Ottawa, 1979; Author: children's plays Rupert the Great; New Translation and Adaptation of Ansky's The Dybbuk.; contbr. articles to profl. jours. Bd. dirs. Theatre Communications Group, Royal Winnipeg Ballet. Recipient Order of Can. medal, Outer Circle Critics award for St. Joan, Obie award for AC/DC, Canadian Authors Assn. award for transl. and adaptation The Dybbuk. Home: Toronto Can. Died Aug. 1, 1989.

HIRSCH, NATHANIEL DAVID M'TTRON, psychologist; b. Nashville, Oct. 13, 1897; s. Joseph and Carrie (Bamberger) H.; m. Nancy Maddy, June 16, 1934 (div. 1942); m. Lucille Frenza, Oct. 16, 1958. AB magna cum laude, Harvard U., 1917, PhD, 1924; AM, Columbia U., 1920; student, Sorbonne, Paris, 1922-23. Tchr. psychology Harvard U., 1924; rsch. fellow NRC, 1924-26, Nat. Coun. Religion in Higher Edn., 1926-27; instr. Duke U., 1927-28, rsch. fellow, 1928-29; chief psychologist Wayne County Clinic for Child Study, Mich., 1929-33, dir., 1933-35; state dir. Nat. Health Inventory, N.J., 1935-36; pvt. practice Washington, 1936-37; sr. social pathologist Social Security Bd., Washington, from 1937; psychotherapist USPHS, 1940-45; pvt. practice psychotherapy, from 1945. Author: A Study of Natio-Racial Mental Differences, 1926, An Experimental Study of East Kentucky Mountains, 1928, Twins-Heredity and Environment, 1930, An Experimental Study of 300 Children over a Six-Year Period, 1930, Genius and Creative Intelligence, 1931, Dynamic Causes of Juvenile Crime, 1937, Mental Deviants in the Population of the United States, 1941. With U.S. Army, 1918. Mem. APA, N.Y. Soc. Clin. Psychologists, Am. Population Assn., Soc. for Religion in Higher Edn. *

HIRSCHFELDER, JOSEPH OAKLAND, chemistry educator; b. Balt., May 27, 1911; s. Arthur Douglas and May Rosalie (Straus) H.; m. Elizabeth Stafford Sokolnikoff, Mar. 7, 1953. B.S., Yale U., 1931; Ph.D., Princeton U., 1936; DSc (hon.), Marquette U., 1977, U. So. Calif., 1980. Fellow Inst. Advanced Study, 1936; asst. Princeton U., 1936-37; research fellow U. Wis., Madison, 1937-39, instr. physics and chemistry, 1940, asst. prof. chemistry and physics, 1941-42, prof. chemistry, 1946-62, Homer Adkins prof., 1962-81, Homer Adkins prof. emeritus, 1981, dir. theoretical chemistry lab., 1946-62, dir. Theoretical Chemistry Inst., 1962-81; head interior ballistics groups, geophys. lab. and cons. rockets Nat. Def. Research Com., 1942-43; chief phenomenologist Bikini Bomb Test, 1946; group leader Los Alamos Sci. Lab., 1943-46; head theoretical physics Naval Ordnance Test Sta., China Lake, Calif., 1945-46; chmn. div. phys. chemistry NRC, 1958-61; mem. computer panel NSF, 1952-65; mem. policy adv. bd. Argonne Nat. Lab., 1962-66; adj. prof chemistry and physics U. Calif.-Santa Barbara, from 1971. Co-author: Molecular Theory of Gases, 1954, 64, Intermolecular Forces, 1967; sr. editor: Effects of Nuclear Weapons, 1957; co-editor: Reminiscences of Early Days of Los Alamos, 1980, Lasers, Molecules and Methods, vol. 173, Advances in Chemical Physics, 1989. Recipient Nat. Medal of Sci. award, 1975, medal of Free Univ. Brussels, 1954, others; Hirschfelder Professorship in Theoretical Physics eastablished in his name U. Wis., 1990. Hon. fellow Norwegian Royal Soc., Brit. Royal Soc. Chemistry, fellow Am. Phys. Soc.; mem. Am. Chem. Soc. (Debyue award 1966), Am. Acad. Arts and Sci., Internat. Combustion Inst. (Edgerton Gold medal 1966), ASME (hon., life), Internat. Acad. Quantum Molecular Sci., NAS, AAAS. Home: Madison Wis. Died Mar. 30, 1990; cremated.

HOBSON, JAMES RICHARD, school psychologist; b. Empire, Ohio, Aug. 1, 1897; s. Harry Zachariah and Jessie Belle (Hunter) H.; m. Mary Emily McPeek, Aug. 15, 1933. AB, Mt. Union Coll., 1920; EdM, Harvard U., 1930, EdD, 1934. Tchr. math. Cambridge (Ohio) High Sch., 1920-25; also acting treas. City of Cambridge, 1921-23; tchr. math. Lorain, Ohio, 1925-29; asst. in edn. Harvard Psycho-Ednl. Clinic, 1930-31, 32-33; dir. child placement pub. schs. Brookline, Mass., 1933-61, coord. guidance svcs., 1961-64, coord. spl. svcs., from 1964; vis. instr. psychology & edn. Fitchburg State Coll., 1937, Harvard Grad. Sch. Edn., 1939-42, 44, Boston U., 1945, 47, Springfield Coll., 1949. Fellow AAAS, APA; mem. Mass. Psychol. Assn., NEA, others. *

HOCHWALD, WERNER, educator, economist; b. Berlin, Germany, Jan. 21, 1910; s. Moritz and Elsa (Stahl) H.; m. Hilde Landenberger, Jan. 28, 1938 (dec. June 1958); children: Miriam Ruth, Eve Fay. Student, U. Freiburg, 1928-29; LL.B., U. Berlin, 1933; B.S., Washington U., St. Louis, 1940, A.M., 1942, Ph.D., 1944. Counsel Com. on Aid and Reconstrn., 1933-38; instr. ASTP, 1942-44; instr. to asso. prof. Washington U., St. Louis, 1944-49, prof., from 1950, chmn. dept. econs., 1955-63, Tileston prof. polit. economy, from 1958; Kennedy Disting. prof. econs. U. of the South, 1981; cons. Fed. Res Bank of St. Louis, 1947-58; mem. citizens budget com., St. Louis. Author: Local Impact of Foreign Trade, 1960, An Economist's Image of History, 1968, The Rationality Concept in Economic Analysis, 1971; Contbg. author: Twentieth Century Economic Thought, 1950, Studies in Income and Wealth, 1957, Local Economic Activity and Foreign Trade, 1958, Design of Regional Accounts, 1962, Southern Economic Development, 1964, The Idea of Progress, 1973, Encyclopedia of Economics, 1981. Mem. Am. Econ. Assn., So. Econ. Assn. (pres. 1966-67), Midwest Econ. Assn., Nat. Bur. Econ. Research, Am. Statis. Assn. (nat. council 1950-52), Econometric Soc., Econ. History Assn., Internat. Assn. for Research in Income and Wealth, Phi Beta Kappa (chpt. pres.). Home: Saint Louis Mo. Died Aug. 7, 1989; buried St. Louis.

HODDINOTT, IRA SEYMOUR, insurance executive; b. Medina, Ohio, July 11, 1897; s. Sidney Herbert and Marta Grace (Bennett) H.; m. Annabel Lois Cole, June 23, 1923; children: Herbert, Richard Lee. Student, Hiram Coll., 1920; BS, Ohio State U., 1922. Co. agrl. agt. Belmont Co., 1922-27, Franklin Co., Columbus, Ohio, 1928-29; asst. prof. agrl. econs., dair mktg. ext.

Ohio State U., Columbus, 1929-31; with Mut. Benefit Life Ins. Co., Newark, from 1931, v.p., from 1950; resident v.p. in charge Nat. Farm Loan Office, Ames, Iowa, from 1954. Mayor Borough of Chatham, N.J., 1945-49. 2d lt. inf. U.S. Army, WWI. Mem. Nat. Farm Chemurgic Coun., Am. Farm Econs. Assn., Nat. Agrl. Credit Com., Ohio State U. Assn., Ohio Soc. N.Y., Rotary, Alpha Zeta. Republican. Congregationalist. *

HODES, HORACE LOUIS, pediatrician, educator; b. Phila., Dec. 21, 1907; s. Morris and Anna (Jacobson) H.; m. Anne E. Reber, June 10, 1931; children—Ruth Anne, David Samuel. A.B., U. Pa., 1927, M.D., 1931; D.Sc. (hon.), CUNY, 1982. Intern, asst. resident Children's Hosp., Phila., 1931-33, chief resident, 1934-35; asst. resident pediatrics Johns Hopkins Hosp., 1933-34, dir. pediatric dispensary, 1935-36; asst. pathology and bacteriology Rockefeller Inst. Med. Research, 1936-38; lectr. epidemiology, sch. hygiene Johns Hopkins U., 1938-49, asst. prof. pediatrics, 1938-45, asso. prof., 1945-49; dir. Sydenham Hosp., Balt., 1938-49; dir. med. research Balt. Health Dept., 1938-49; dir. pediatrics dept. Mt. Sinai Hosp., N.Y.C., 1949-76; clin. prof. pediatrics Columbia U., 1949-70; prof., chmn. dept. pediatrics Mt. Sinai Med. Sch., 1964-76, Disting. Service prof. to prof. emeritus, from 1976; Advisory council N.Y. Pub. Health Research Inst.; med. adv. bd. Hebrew U.; Mem. commn. control measles and mumps U.S. Army, 1940-42; cons. sec. of war. Co-author: Common Contagious Diseases, 1956; Editorial bd.: Pediatrics; Contbr. to profl. jours. Served as lt. comdr. USNR, 1942-46; officer charge virus lab. Guam. Named to Johns Hopkins U. Soc. Scholars, 1985. Mem. Am. Pediatric Soc. (pres. 1974-75, Howland medal and award 1982), Soc. Pediatric Research (pres. 1951-52), Am. Acad. Pediatrics (Mead-Johnson award 1946), Infectious Diseases Soc. Am., Soc. Explt. Biology and Medicine, N.Y. Acad. Scis., N.Y. Acad. Medicine, Pediatric Travel Club, Alpha Omega Alpha. Home: Manhasset N.Y. Died Apr. 24, 1989; buried Mt. Hope Cemetery, Hastings-on-Hudson, N.Y.

HODGE, RAYMOND JOSEPH, engineer, architectural designer; b. N.Y.C., May 15, 1922; s. Christopher George and Lucy Agnes (Madden) H.; m. Lorraine Cecelia Remmert, Aug. 5, 1950; children—Christopher, Susan, Raymond, Patricia. B.C.E., Manhattan Coll., 1944; M.C.E., Cornell U., 1948. Diplomate Am. Acad. Environ. Engrs. With Tippetts-Abbett-McCarthy-Stratton (Cons. Engrs., Architects and Planners), 1953-90; partner Tippetts-Abbett-McCarthy-Stratton, 1968-90; asst. prof. Cornell U., 1948-51; pres. Am. Chamber El Salvador, 1963-65; dir. planning and design Dallas/Ft. Worth Internat. Airport, redvel. Pennsylvania Ave., Washington. Bd. advisers Coll. Engring., Cornell U.; bd. dirs. World Environment Ctr. Served to lt. comdr. USNR, 1943-46, 51-53. Recipient Engring. News-Record award for Dallas/Ft. Worth Airport, 1974, Civil Engring. award, 1974, James Laurie prize, 1969. Fellow ASCE, Am. Cons. Engrs. Council, Inst. Engrs. Australia; mem. Nat. Acad. Engring., Am. Rd. and Transp. Builders Assn. (pres. planning and design div. 1974), Am. Inst. Mining Engrs., Soc. Am. Mil. Engrs., Nat. Soc. Profl. Engrs. Roman Catholic. Club: Congressional Country. Home: Rockville Md. Died Oct. 27, 1990.

HODGSON, HUGH, music educator; b. Athens, Ga., Apr. 1, 1893; s. Joseph Marshall and Isabella (Turner) H.; m. Jessie McKee; children: Edith Frances, Daniel Blake. BS, U. Ga., 1915; postgrad., Columbia, Guilman Sch. Organ, 1915, U. So. Calif., 1936; MusD, Sewanee, 1953. Concert pianist debut N.Y.C.; organist, dir. ch. choirs Athens & Atlanta, Ga., from 1914; dir. mus. dept. Lucy Cobb Inst., 1925; founder, head dept. music U. Ga., 1928-60, prof. emeritus, from 1960, chmn. divsn. fine arts, from 1934, regents' prof., 1948; originator weekly art and music appreciation programs in Ga. coll. ctrs.; lectr. Agnes Scott Coll; vis. prof. Emory U.; vis. prof. music Westminster Schs., Atlanta; vis. recitalist Assn. Am. Coll., 1940-47; performances with Roth Quartet, N.Y.C. and Chgo., 1943-44. Composer (chamber music) Trio in G and Quintet in D; Piano Concerto and Soli; Songs; Ch. Choral Music; Oratorio. Carnegie grantee, 1938; recipient Outstanding Svc. award U. Ga., 1953. *

HODSON, DARREL LEROY, lawyer; b. Amboy, Ind., July 20, 1912; s. Charles John and Dora Ellen (Sharp) H.; m. Elaine Emeline Estrich, June 8, 1941; children—John D., James L. Student Purdue U., 1929-30; B.S., Ind. U., 1935; J.D., Ind. U., 1937. Bar: Ind., 1937, U.S. Supreme Ct., 1943, U.S. Ct. Mil. Appeals, 1953. Assoc. Overson & Manning, Kokomo, Ind., 1937-38; ptnr. Hodson, Lucas & Hillis, Kokomo, 1938-40, Winslow & Hodson, Kokomo, 1940-42; sole practice, Kokomo, 1948-61; ptnr. Hodson & Osborn, Kokomo, 1962-86; judge, Kokomo, 1938; pros. atty., Kokomo, 1941-42, 55-58; claims investigator Claims Commn., 1943-46; dir. U.S. Claims Commns. in Europe, dep. chief of claims European Command, 1946-47; county atty. Howard County, Ind., 1950-52. Served with U.S. Army, 1942-47. Decorated Bronze Star. Mem. ABA, Ind. Bar Assn., Howard County Bar Assn., JAG Assn. Methodist. Clubs: Kiwanis (Legion of Honor 1976, 84, Outstanding Mem. award 1983), Elks. Died Dec. 25, 1986; buried Amboy, Ind. Home: Kokomo Ind.

HOERNER, RICHARD NORRIS, box manufacturing executive; b. Eaton, Ohio, Nov. 5, 1896; s. Charlie and Eola (Oldfather) H.; m. Kathryn Marie Pontius, June 18, 1925; children: Suzanne, Richard Norris. AB, Earlham Coll., 1920, hon. degree, 1964; MEd, Harvard U., 1921; LLD, Parsons Coll., 1956. Chmn. bd. Hoerner Boxes, Inc., Keokuk, Iowa, from 1956; bd. dirs. Security State Bank, Steel Casting Co. Trustee, hon. chmn. bd. Parsons Coll.; trustee Earlham Coll. *

HOERR, STANLEY OBERMANN, surgeon; b. Chgo., Sept. 29, 1909; s. Charles Ferdinand and Lillie Sophia (Obermann) H.; m. Janet Urie, July 9, 1932; children: Mary Hoerr Meyer, Joan Hoerr Schilling, Stanley O. (dec.), Charls M., Mark R. A.B., Antioch Coll., 1932; M.D., Harvard U., 1936. Diplomate: Am. Bd. Surgery. Intern, resident Peter Bent Brigham Hosp., Boston, 1936-42; pathology resident Huntington Meml. Hosp., Boston, 1938-39; asso. in surgery Peter Bent Brigham Hosp., 1945-47; asso. prof. surgery Ohio State U. Sch. Medicine, 1947-50; surg. staff Cleve. Clinic Found., 1950-74, chmn. div. surgery, 1956-71, resident emeritus staff, 1979-90; chmn. dept. surgery Fairview Gen. Hosp., Cleve., 1974-79. Contbr. articles to profl. jours., textbooks. Served from capt. to maj. AUS, 1942-45, ETO. Fellow ACS (gov. 1963-72, 2d v.p. 1970-71, pres. Ohio chpt. 1963, Disting. Service award 1979); mem. AMA (sec. sect. gen. surgery 1965-68, chmn. sect. 1973-75), Am. Surg. Assn., Central Surg. Assn. (pres. 1970-71), Internat. Surg. Soc., Eastern Surg. Soc. (pres. 1975-76), Soc. Surgery Alimentary Tract (pres. 1971-72), Soc. Univ. Surgeons, Am. Gastroent. Assn., Cleve. Surg. Soc. (pres. 1958), Cleve. Med. Library Assn. (trustee 1973-83, pres. 1977-78, 80-81), Cleve. Acad. Med. (Disting. Service award 1974). Clubs: Pasteur, Rowfant (Cleve.). Home: Lyndhurst Ohio Died Mar. 14, 1990.

HOFACKER, ERICH PAUL, educator; b. St. Gail, Switzerland, Dec. 5, 1898; came to U.S., 1924; naturalized, 1936; s. Paul Rudolf Wilhelm and Frida (Ostertag) H.; m. Gertrude H. Krider, Dec. 27, 1926; children: Erich Paul, Constance Maia. Grad., Reformrealgymnasium, Stuttgart, 1918; student, Univs. Munich & Freiburg; PhD, U. Tuebingen, 1924. Instr. in German U. Pitts., 1924-26, Yale U., 1926-28, Rutgers U., 1928-29; asst. prof. Washington U., St. Louis, 1929-40, assoc. prof., 1940-48, prof. German, from 1948, acting head dept., 1950-52, head dept., from 1952. Author: German Literature as Reflected in the German Language, 1946, Martin Luther, 1959, Toward Fluency in Speaking and Writing German, 1963; editor: Regions of the United States, 1936; contbr. to dictionaries and mags. Mem. MLA, AAUP, Am. Assn. Tchrs. German, MLA of Mo., Delta Phi Delta. *

HOFFMAN, EDWARD FENNO, III, sculptor; b. Phila., Oct. 20, 1916; s. Edward Fenno and Elizabeth Rodman (Wright) H.; m. Nadine Kalpaschnikoff, June 8, 1946; children—Susan Rush Johns, David Fenno, Cynthia Logan Carosso. Student, Pa. Acad. Fine Arts, 1946-50. One-man shows include Grand Central Galleries, N.Y.C., 1956, 70, Galerie Internationale, N.Y.C., 1977, IMF, Washington, 1984; group shows include Nat. Sculpture Soc., N.Y.C., 1956, NAD, N.Y.C., 1957; represented in permanent collections Am. Cathedral, Rome, Italy, Weightlifters Hall of Fame, York, Pa., Phila. Mus. Art, Pa. Acad. Fine Arts, Garden of Coll. Physicians, Phila., Our Lady of Grace Ch., Greensboro, N.C., Am. Coll., Bryn Mawr, Pa., U. Richmond, Va., Cathedral of St. John the Divine, N.Y.C., Brookgreen Gardens Sculpture Collection, S.C., The Soc. of the Four Arts, Palm Beach, Fla., others; sculptor in residence, Henry Clews Meml. Art Found., France, 1952-55; subject of Reaching and other Sculptures, 1985. Served with U.S. Army, 1940-45. Tiffany Found. grantee, 1951; recipient Barnet prize,1951, Artists Fund prize, 1969, Speyer prize, 1973, Thomas R. Proctor prize, 1982, all from NAD, Watrous gold medal, 1972, Mrs. Newington award Hudson Valley Art Assn., 1983. Fellow Nat. Sculpture Soc. (1st v.p. 1973-76, 88-89, Silver medal 1973, Hexter prize 1979); mem. NAD, Allied Artists Am., Am. Artists Profl. League (prize 1981), Artists Equity, Am. Acad. Arts and Sci. Episcopalian. Home: Wayne Pa. Died Sept. 20, 1991; buried St. Martin's Ch., Radnor, Pa.

HOFFMAN, GEORGE W(ALTER), geography educator; b. Vienna, Austria, June 19, 1914; came to U.S., 1939, naturalized, 1943; s. Albert W(ilhelm) and Hedwig (Weihs) H.; m. Viola Smith, Sept. 30, 1944 (dec. 1984); children: Jeane Pendery, A. Michael. Student, U. Vienna, 1934-36; PhD, U. Mich., 1950; student, Harvard U., 1946-47. Asst. editor Wirtschaftlicher Beobachter, Vienna, 1935-38; instr. Ind. U., 1946-47; grad. asst. U. Mich., 1948-49; asst. prof. U. Tex., Austin, 1949-53; assoc. prof. U. Tex., 1953-60, prof., 1961-84, prof. emeritus, 1985-90, chmn. dept., 1978-82; acting sec. East European program Woodrow Wilson Internat. Ctr. for Scholars, Washington, 1985-86; vis. prof. U. Vt., summer 1948, U. Mich., Pa. State Coll., 1952, U. R.I., 1959, Ind. U., 1967, Kent State U., 1968, U. Wash., Portland State U., Ind. U., U. Nebr., U. Md.; Fulbright prof. U. Munich, 1962, U. Heidelberg, 1972; vis. lectr. numerous European countries, also Fgn. Svc. Inst., Dept. State, 1959-90, Nat. Def. U.; professorial lectr. and rsch. prof. Sino-Soviet Inst., George Washington U., Washington, 1986-90; exec. sec. Austin Com. Fgn. Rels., 1954-75, chmn. bd. dirs., 1975-84; mem. joint com. Ea. Europe, Social Sci. Rsch. Coun. and Am. Coun. Learned Socs., 1966-72; dir. Am. Assn. Geographers program, Yugoslavia, 1971; mem. com. on Soviet Union Social Sci. Rsch. Coun., 1971-73; mem. Nat. Citizens Commn. Internat. Cooperation, Commn. Rsch. Devel. Internat. Instns.; mem. acad. adv. bd. Kennan Inst. for Advanced Russian Studies, Woodrow Wilson Internat. Ctr. for Scholars, 1974-77; bd. dirs., mem. exec. com. RFE-RL, Inc., 1977-82; project dir. and coord. exch. and rsch. seminars for Am. Assn. Geographers in Hungary, Poland, Fed. Republic Germany, Bulgaria, Czechoslovakia. Author and/or editor of 18 books, and over 100 scholarly articles; mem. bd. editors The East European Quar., from 1967; editorial advisor F.A. Praeger, 1968-72, Standard Ednl. Corp, Chgo., 1966-80; co-editor: Searchlight Books, 1961-82; editorial bd. Comparative Communism, 1974-81, East European/Soviet Series; mem. adv. com. Polit. Geography Quar. Served with OSS, U.S. Army, 1942-45. Decorated Verdienstkreuz 1st Class (Fed. Republic Germany); Grosse Goldene Ehrenzeichen (Republic of Austria); Merit of the Yugoslav Flag on Necklace, 1988; recipient Polit. Geography Contbn. award Nat. Coun. Geog. Edn., 1953, 58, Internat. Rels. award St. Mary's U., 1962, Thomas Jefferson award, 1978; NSF-IREX Travel grants, 1973; Am. Coun. Learned Socs. Travel award, 1970; Rsch. award, 1972; Am. Philos. Soc. Rsch. awards, 1957, 62, 69; NSF Rsch. award, 1964-67, 67-69; NAS Travel award, 1964, 76, Jiricek Gold medal Südosteuropa Soc., Munich, 1986. Fellow Royal Geog. Soc. (London); mem. Am. Assn. Geographers (chmn. com. Eastern Europe, chmn. com. internat. action, chmn. Am.-German Project, award splty. group on Eastern Europe and Soviet Union 1984, AAG honors award 1985), Am. Geog. Soc., AAAS, Am. Assn. Advancement Slavic Studies (dir., chmn. rsch. and devel. com. 1972-76, coun. 1972-76, 80), Nat. Coun. Geog. Edn., Osterreichische Geographische Gesellschaft (Vienna), Südost Europa Gesellschaft (Munich), Tex. Assn. Coll. Teachers (pres. Austin chpt. 1969-70), AAUP (sec.-treas. U. Tex. chpt. 1969-70), Tex. Coun. Geography Tchrs. (pres. 1954-55, dir. 1955-58), Serbian Geog. Soc. (hon.), Phi Kappa Phi, Pi Kappa Alpha. Home: Washington D.C. Died Oct. 27, 1990. †

HOFSOOS, EMIL, advertising executive; b. Stevens Point, Wis., July 11, 1896; s. John Sivertson and Karine (Docka) H.; m. Ruth Kallgren, May 31, 1924; children: Mary Louise Ewing, John Erling, Nancy Kallgren. AB, U. Wis., 1921. Comm. rschr. Washburn-Crosby Co. (now Gen. Mills), Mpls., 1921-23; staff sales plans divsn. Pillsbury Flour Mills Co., Mpls., 1923-24; exec. MacManus, Inc. advt. agy., Detroit, 1924-31; v.p. Ketchum MacLeod & Grove, Inc., from 1931, also dir. Mem. Phi Beta Kappa, Beta Gamma Sigma. *

HOFSTADTER, ROBERT, physicist, educator; b. N.Y.C., Feb. 5, 1915; s. Louis and Henrietta (Koenigsberg) H.; m. Nancy Givan, May 9, 1942; children: Douglas Richard, Laura James, Mary Hinda. B.S. magna cum laude (Kenyon prize), Coll. City N.Y., 1935; M.A. (Procter fellow), Princeton U., 1938, Ph.D., 1938; LL.D., City U. N.Y., 1961; D.Sc., Gustavus Adolphus Coll., 1963; Laureate Honoris Causa, U. Padua, 1965; D.Sc. (hon.), Carleton U., Ottawa, Can., 1967, Seoul Nat. U., 1967; Honoris Causa, U. Clermont-Ferrand, 1967; D. Rerum Naturalium honoris causa, Julius Maximilians U., Würzburg, Fed. Republic Germany, 1982, Johannes Gutenberg U. Mainz, Fed. Republic Germany, 1983; D.Sc. (hon.), Israel Inst. Tech., 1985. Coffin fellow Gen. Electric Co., 1935-36; Harrison fellow U. Pa., 1939; instr. physics Princeton U., 1940-41, CCNY, 1941-42; physicist Norden Lab. Corp., 1943-46; asst. prof. physics Princeton U., 1946-50; assoc. prof. physics Stanford U., 1950-54, prof., 1954-85, Max H. Stein prof. physics, 1971-85, prof. emeritus, 1985-90, dir. high energy physics lab., 1967-74; dir. John Fluke Mfg. Co., 1979-88. Author: (with Robert Herman) High-Energy Electron Scattering Tables, 1960; editor: Investigations in Physics, 1958-65, Electron Scattering and Nucleon Structure, 1963; co-editor: Nucleon Structure, 1964; assoc. editor: Phys. Review, 1951-53; mem. editorial bd.: Review Sci. Instruments, 1953-55, Reviews of Modern Physics, 1958-61. Bd. govs. Technion, Israel Inst. Tech., Weizmann Inst. Sci. Calif. Scientist of Year, 1959; co-recipient of Nobel prize in physics, 1961; Townsend Harris medal Coll. City N.Y., 1961; Guggenheim fellow Geneva, Switzerland, 1958-59; Ford Found. fellow; recipient Röntgen medal, Wurzburg, Germany, 1985, U.S. Nat. Medal Sci., 1986, Prize of Cultural Found. of Fiuggi, Italy, 1986. Fellow Am. Phys. Soc., Phys. Soc. London; mem. Nat. Acad. Scis., Am. Acad. Arts and Scis., AAUP, Phi Beta Kappa, Sigma Xi. Home: Palo Alto Calif. Died Nov. 17, 1990.

HOGAN, DAVID EARL, telecommunications executive; b. Ruston, La., Oct. 5, 1949; s. Frank Earl and Roberta Ruth (Morgan) H.; m. Cathey Dee O'Donnell, Apr. 10, 1971; children: Grant, Todd. BSME, La. Tech. U., 1971, MBA, 1973. Mktg. rep. IBM Corp., Shreveport, La., 1976-78, regional mktg. rep., 1978-79; adv. regional mktg. rep. IBM Corp., Dallas, 1979; mktg. mgr. IBM Corp., Ft. Worth, 1980-82; adminstrv. asst. to v.p. plans and controls IBM Corp., White Plains, N.Y., 1982-83; v.p., gen. mgr. Mobilecom of Ill., Chgo., 1983-84; v.p. mktg. Mobile Communication Corp. of Am. (MCCA), Jackson, Miss., 1985-86; sr. v.p. Century Tel., Monroe, La., 1986-87; pres. bus. group Century

Telephone, Monroe, La., 1987-89; pres., CEO Sterling Cellular, Roswell, Ga., from 1989. Mem. Cellular Tel. Industry Assn. (bd. dirs. 1986-89). Republican. Baptist. Home: Woodstock Ga. Deceased. †

HOGG, ROBERT LYNN, lawyer; b. Point Pleasant, W.Va., Dec. 30, 1893; s. Charles Edgar and Nancy Berden (Hawkins) H.; m. Mary Louise Holliday, June 24, 1926; children: Mary Lynn Shackelford, Charles Edgar II. AB, W.Va. U., 1914, LLB, 1916; LLD, Morris Harvey Coll., 1956. Mem. Hogg & Hogg, from 1916; pros. atty. Mason County, Va., 1920-24; mem. W.Va. State Senate, 1924-28, 71st and 72d Congresses from 4th W.Va. dist.; asst. gen. counsel Life Ins. Assn. Am., 1935-43, assoc. gen. counsel, 1943-45; mgr., gen. counsel Am. Life Conv., Chgo., 1944-46; exec. v.p., gen. counsel Am. Life Conv., 1946-54; sr. v.p., adv. counsel Equitable Life Assurance Soc., 1954-56, dir., then vice chmn. bd., 1955-59; bd. dirs. Equitable Life Assurance Soc., from 1959; counsel Jackson, Kelley, Holt and O'Farrell, Charleston, W.Va., from 1960. Co-author: Hogg's Pleadings and Forms. With U.S. Army, 1917-19. Mem. ABA, W.Va. Bar Assn., Assn. Life Ins. Counsel, Ins. Soc. N.Y., Masons. Republican. Presbyterian. *

HOGG, TONY JEFFERSON, editor; b. London, Jan. 27, 1925; came to U.S., 1953; s. Richard Jefferson and Lilian (Currie) H.; m. Elizabeth Moroney Maxon, Aug. 25, 1957; 1 child, John Jefferson. Student, Brit. pvt. schs. Contbg. editor Road and Track, 1961-83, editor, 1975-79, editor-in-chief, 1979-83, tech. editor, 1963-65; automotive editor Esquire mag., 1970-83; editor, pub. Sci. and Mechs., N.Y.C., 1969-74. Writer and photographer; contbr. articles to numerous mags. Mem. Am. Soc. Mag. Editors, Soc. Automotive Engrs. Home: Newport Beach Calif. Died Aug. 4, 1983; buried Forest Home Cemetery, Milw., Wis.

HOGLUND, ELLIS S., corporate executive; b. Chgo., July 29, 1898; s. Gustave E. and Ida (Sterner) H.; m. Helen Klinger, June 21, 1924; children: Peter Klinger, Charlotte, Margaret Jane, William Ellis. PhB, U. Chgo., 1921. Asst. gen. mgr. Square D Co., 1922-27; various exec. positions GM Overseas Ops., Copenhagen, 1927-28; mng. dir. GM Nordiska, Stockholm, 1928-37; with Adam Opel, A.G., Russelsheim, Germany, 1937-41, regional mgr., 1945-47, asst. gen. mgr., 1947-59; v.p. GM Corp., 1949-63, gen. mgr. overseas ops. divsn., 1959-60, group exec. in charge Can. & overseas ops., mem. exec. com., 1961-63; chmn. Nat. Fgn. Trade Coun., N.Y.C., from 1963. Spl. cons. USN Dept., 1942-43, Office Mil. Govt., Germany, 1945. Mem. Sigma Nu. *

HOLBROOK, CLYDE AMOS, theologian; b. Greenfield, Mass., Mar. 20, 1911; s. Fred Earl and Adella (Caswell) H.; m. Dorothy Bush Wheeler, Dec. 27, 1937; children: Richard Clyde, Arthur Wheeler, Deborah. A.B., Bates Coll., 1934; B.D., Colgate-Rochester Div. Sch., 1937; Ph.D., Yale U., 1945; postgrad. univs., St. Andrews and Basel, 1956; S.T.D., Denison U., 1969; H.H.D., Oberlin Coll, 1982. Ordained to ministry Baptist Ch., 1937; pastor Weston, Conn., 1937-42, New Haven, 1942-45; dean of chapel, asso. prof. religion Colo. Coll., 1945-49; asso. prof. religion Denison U., 1949-51; prof. religion Oberlin Coll., 1951-77, chmn. dept., 1951-75; prof. Christian ethics Oberlin Coll. (Grad. Sch. Theology), 1951-56, Danforth chair of religion, 1957-77, Danforth prof. emeritus; prof. Union Theol. Sem., summer 1961; vis. prof. religion U. Va., spring 1980; disting. vis. prof. religion Oberlin Coll., 1980-81, 84-85, Mead-Swing lectr., 1986; Colgate-Rochester fellow Yale U., 1937-40; sr. fellow Council of Humanities, Princeton U., 1961-62; past mem. commn. on higher edn. Nat. Council of Chs. of Christ. Author: Faith and Community, 1959, Religion a Humanistic Field, 1963, reprint, 1978, Jonathan Edwards: Original Sin, 1970, The Ethics of Jonathan Edwards, 1973, The Iconoclastic Deity, 1984, Jonathan Edwards, The Valley and Nature, 1987; co-author: The Humanities at Oberlin, 1958, A Handbook of Christian Theologians, 1965, 84, A Heritage of Christian Thought, 1965, Black Theology II, 1978, Encyclopedic Dictionary of Religion, 1979, Crime, Values and Religion, 1987; editorial bd.: Jour. Bible and Religion, 1969. Trustee Oberlin Shansi Meml. Assn., 1956-77, v.p., 1960-68, pres., 1968-72. Recipient E. Harris Harbison award Danforth Found., 1966-67; fellow Acad. Sr. Profls., 1982. Mem. Soc. Christian Ethics, Am. Acad. Religion (pres. 1963), Soc. Values in Higher Edn., Am. Theol. Soc., Phi Beta Kappa. Mem. United Ch. of Christ. Home: Oberlin OH Died Mar. 16, 1989; buried Oberlin. †

HOLDEN, THOMAS, clergyman; b. Larne, Northern Ireland, Sept. 12, 1896; came to U.S., 1914; naturalized, 1919; s. John and Anna Maria (Arnold) H.; m. Katharine Evelyn McDonald, Nov. 11, 1924; children: Rosemary Alice Smith, John. AB, Occidental Coll., 1921, DD, 1936; BD, San Francisco Theol. Sem., 1924. Ordained to ministry by presbytery, 1924. Asst. pastor Highland Park Presbyn. Ch., L.A., 1924-25; pastor Tropico Presbyn. Ch., Glendale, Calif., 1926-27; asst. pastor Immanuel Presbyn. Ch., L.A., 1927, pastor, 1927-50; asst. stated clk. Synod of Calif. Presbyn. U.S.A., 1929, stated clk., from 1932; stated clk. Presbytery of L.A., United Presbyn. Ch. U.S.A., 1939-50, Synod of Calif., from 1950. Trustee Occidental Coll., 1939-41, San Francisco Theol. Sem., from 1932. *

HOLLAND, ARTHUR JOHN, mayor; b. Trenton, N.J., Oct. 24, 1918; s. Joseph F. and Helen M. (Groh) H.; m. Elizabeth Anne Jackson, July 28, 1962; children: Cynthia, Elise, Christopher, Timothy, Matthew. Grad., St. Francis Coll., S.I.; A.B. in Social Studies, Rutgers U., 1954, M.A. in Pub. Adminstrn, 1959. Research analyst Opinion Research Corp., Princeton, N.J., 1945-49; asso. dir. Princeton Research Service, 1949-51; dep. dir. Dept. Pub. Affairs, Trenton, 1951-52, Dept. Parks and Pub. Property, Trenton, 1952-55; dir. Dept. Pub. Affairs, Trenton, 1955-62; acting city mgr. Passaic, N.J., 1967; mayor City of Trenton, 1959-66, 70-89; pres. Mercer County League Municipalities, 1956-57, 76; pres. N.J. Conf. Mayors, 1977; pres. U.S. Conf. Mayors, 1988-89, mem. exec. com.; mem. exec. com. Nat. Conv. Dem. Mayors, 1980-89, sec., 1985-89; past cons. HUD; past cons. Nat. Inst. Pub. Affairs, Brookings Instn.; adj. rsch. prof. Urban Studies Ctr., Rutgers U., 1966-70, lectr. polit. sci., 1967-72; lectr. grad. program for adminstrs. Rider Coll., 1974-75. Author: The Adventures of Bernie Bean, 1984. Bd. govs. Del. Valley United Way, 1962-63, from 73, pub. div. chmn., 1954, 55, 63, 70-78, 80-86, trustee of hon.; bd. dirs. Del.-Raritan Lung Assn., 1969-73, Social Service Council Greater Trenton, 1960-66, local chpt. ARC, 1953-68, 81-89; bd. dirs. Trenton Social Service Exchange, 1951-66, chmn., 1959-62; hon. bd. mem. Mercer County Soc. Prevention Cruelty to Animals, 1950-62, publicity dir., 1952, bd. dirs., 1957-58, hon. bd. dirs., 1958-62; hon. mem. Trenton Assn. of Blind, 1957-89; bd. dirs. Mercer County Assn. Mental Health, 1960-66; del. White House Conf. To Fulfill These Rights, 1966; N.J. v.p. and bd. mem. Del. Valley Citizens Council for Clean Air; mem. bd. Del. Valley Citizens Transp. Com.; chmn., 1969-70, Human Relations Council Serving Greater Trenton Area, 1959-66, 70, Del. Valley Regional Planning Commn., chmn. 1975, 77; mem. Council for NE Econ. Action; mem. exec. com. Transp. Research Bd., Del.-Raritan Canal Commn.; founding mem. bd. dirs. Urban League Met. Trenton, Inc., N.J. Social Welfare Council; past mem. bd. dirs. Social Welfare Research Found. N.J. , 1976, 84, 88; del. Dem. Nat. Conv., 1976, 84; mem. Dem. Nat. Com., 1988-89. Decorated knight Order Star of Solidarity (Italy), Order of the Polar Star (Sweden); recipient Young Man of Year Jr. C. of C., 1954; J.J. Hoey award for Interracial Justice Cath. Interracial Council N.Y., 1964; N.J. Americanization Conf. Citizenship award, 1964; Commendation for Meritorious Achievement Town Affiliation program Pres.'s People-to-People program; Brotherhood award Mercer County chpt. NCCJ; Internat. Humanitarian award Boys and Girls Towns of Italy, 1985; Garden State Pub. Svc. award, 1989; Disting. Pub. Svc. award U.S. Conf. Mayors, 1989; named to Rutgers U. Hall of Disting. Alumni, 1990; Arthur J. HollandEthics in Gov. Program announces by Rutgers U., 1989; Arthur J. Holland Scholarship Mercer County C.C., 1989; Arthur J. Holland Middle Sch. named., 1990; Arthur J. Holland Fed. Post Office Bldg named in Trenton, 1992. Mem. Nat. League of Cities (chmn. community facilities com., mem. exec. com., adv. council), N.J. League Municipalities (3d v.p.), Trenton Hist. Soc., NAACP, Am.-Hungarian Civic Assn., Trenton Cath. Alumni Assn. (pres. 1938-39), Ancient Order Hibernians, 1st Cath. Slovak Union, Regional Conf. Elected ofcls. (past pres., mem. exec. com. 1961-66). Clubs: K.C. (N.J.), Rutgers of Mercer County (N.J.) (v.p. 1955-56); Mercer County Social Welfare (treas. 1956-57). Home: Trenton N.J. Died Nov. 9, 1989; buried Trenton, N.J.

HOLLAND, DANIEL MARK, economics educator; b. N.Y.C., July 7, 1920; s. Abraham and Anna (Nydorf) H.; m. Jeanne A. Ormont, June 3, 1942; children—Laura, Jonathan, Andrew. B.A., Columbia U., 1941, Ph.D. in Econs., 1951. Instr. Columbia U., 1946-51; staff mem. Nat. Bur. Econ. Research, 1951-72; assoc. prof. NYU, 1957-58; assoc. prof. Sloan Sch. Mgmt., Mass. Inst. Tech., Cambridge, 1958-62, prof., 1962-86, prof. emeritus, sr. lectr., 1986-91, asst. provost, 1986-90; cons. to various U.S. govt. agys., fgn. govts., pvt. cos. Author: Income Tax Burden on Stockholders, 1958, Dividends Under the Income Tax, 1962, Private Pension Funds; Projected Growth, 1966; editor: Nat. Tax Jour., 1966-86; editor, contbr.: Measuring Profitability and Capital Costs, 1984; contbr. to: The Nations Capital Needs: Three Studies, 1979; contbr. articles to profl. jours. Served with USNR, 1943-46. Mem. Am. Econ. Assn., Royal Econ. Soc., Nat. Tax Assn. (pres. 1988-89), Internat. Inst. Pub. Fin., Am. Fin. Assn. Home: Lexington Mass. Died Dec. 15, 1991.

HOLLE, CHARLES G(EORGE), army officer; b. Cin., Oct. 25, 1898; s. Charles and Nell Louise (Leppert) H.; m. Martha Flora Kendrick, Sept. 12, 1928 (dec. Apr. 1960); childrren: Kendrick, Bradford; m. Anne Carter Baldwin Allen, May 5, 1962. Student, U. Cin., 1917-18; BS, U.S. Mil. Acad., 1920; postgrad., Rensselaer Poly. Inst., 1921-22; grad., Command and Gen. Staff Sch., 1939. Registered profl. engr., D.C. Commd. 2d lt. U.S. Army, 1920, advanced through grades to maj. gen., 1955; officer-in-charge European Office, Am. Battle Monuments Commn., 1939-41; asst. engr. maintenance Panama Canal, 1942-45, engr., 1948-49; exec. Office Chief Engrs., Washington, 1945-48; dist. engr. New Orleans dist. C.E., 1949-53; div. engr. South Atlantic div. C.E., Atlanta, 1953-55; dep. chief engrs. U.S. Army, 1955-56; spl. asst. to chief engrs. for St. Lawrence matters; alt. mem. St. Lawrence River Joint Bd. Engrs.; pres. Beach Erosion Bd.; chmn. bd. engrs. Rivers and Harbors, 1956-58. Treas. Ebenezer Cemetery Assn., Inc., 1961-88; pres. 2450 Massachusetts Ave. N.W., Inc., Washington, 1959-74; pres. Am. Shore and Beach Preservation Assn., 1958-72. Decorated Legion of Merit with oak leaf cluster, D.S.M. Mem. ASCE, Soc. Am. Mil. Engrs., Permanent Internat. Assn., Navigation Congresses (life, de Jure mem., sec. gen. 1961), Army and Navy Club. Episcopalian. Home: Washington D.C. Died Apr. 17, 1989; buried Arlington Nat. Cemetery, Arlington, Va.

HOLLIES, NORMAN ROBERT STANLEY, textile chemist, educator; b. Edmonton, Alta., Can., Oct. 18, 1922; s. Robert Talbot and Jessie Sutherland (McArthur) H.; m. Sheila Margaret Brigit Mercer, May 31, 1947; children—Brian Christopher, Robert Mercer, Kenneth Norman, Richard Ernest, David Ian. B.Sc. with honors, U. Alta., 1944; Ph.D., McGill U., 1947. Research chemist NRC Can., 1946-47; research asso. Harvard Med. Sch., Boston, 1947-50; project mgr., group leader Harris Research Labs., Washington, 1951-76; prin. scientist Gillette Research Inst., Rockville, Md., 1977-80; prof. dept. textiles and consumer econs. U. Md., College Park, 1981-89; chmn. Gordon Conf. Fiber Sci., 1981. Author: (with L. Fourt) Clothing Comfort and Function, 1970, (with R. F. Goldman) Clothing Comfort, 1977. Served with Chem. Warfare Service, Can. Army, 1944-47. Canadian Industries Ltd. grad. fellow, 1944-47. Mem. Am. Phys. Soc., Am. Chem. Soc., Fiber Soc. (pres. 1980), Am. Vacuum Soc., Internat. Microscopical Soc., AAAS, Washington Acad. Sci., N.Y. Acad. Sci. Republican. Club: Cosmos. Home: Montross Va. Died Dec. 7, 1989; cremated.

HOLLINGSWORTH, ALAN MERRILL, educational administrator; b. Westwood, Calif., Aug. 3, 1920; s. Merrill Windsor and Amy Marie (Weldt) H.; m. Jeanne Marie Heimann, June 9, 1958; children: Jeffrey Alan, Amy Marie. AB, U. Calif., Berkeley, 1948, MA, 1949, PhD, 1956. Prof. English Ind. U., 1954-67; prof. English, chmn. dept. Mich. State U., East Lansing, 1967-91, dean Coll. Arts and Letters; cons. U.S. Office Edn., HEW, Assn. Depts. of English. With AUS, 1942-45. Recipient Ulysses G. Weatherly Disting. Teaching award, 1960. Mem. Midwest MLA (pres. 1969), Assn. Depts. English (pres. 1977). Home: Seattle Wash. Died July 23, 1991; buried Seattle.

HOLLOWAY, FRED GARRIGUS, bishop; b. Newark, Mar. 28, 1898; s. Frank DeMott and Alice (Garrigus) H.; m. Winifred Maxwell Jackson, Apr. 12, 1923; children: Fred Garrigus, William. AB, Western Md. Coll., 1918, DD, 1932; student, Westminster Theol. Sem., 1918-19; BD, Drew Theol. Sem., Madison, N.J., 1921; LLD, Dickenson Coll., Carlisle, Pa., 1936; LHD, Baldwin-Wallace Coll., 1947; LittD, Kan. Wesleyan U., 1957; LLD, Rider Coll., 1959; DD, Adrian Coll., 1959; LLD, Western Md. Coll., 1963. Ordained to ministry Meth. Ch., 1921. Pastor 1st Ch., Wilmington, Del., 1921-23, Wilton Heights Ch., Balt., 1923-26, Cherrydale, Va., 1926-29; prof. Bibl. langs. Westminster Theol. Sem., 1927-35, pres., 1932-35; pres. Western Md. Coll., 1935-47; dean Drew Theol. Sem., 1947-48; pres. Drew U., 1948-60; bishop Meth. Ch., Charleston, W.Va., from 1960. Contbr. articles on religion and edn. to jours. Trustee Wesley Theol. Sem., Washington, Morris Harvey Coll., Charleston., W.Va. Wesleyan Coll., Buckhannon. Mem. Rotary. *

HOLLOWAY, ROBERT JOHN, business educator; b. Walker, Iowa, Sept. 13, 1921; s. John Theron and Mabel Marie (Condon) H.; m. Lois Anita Ita, Jan. 13, 1945; children: Steven Robert, Ann Louise (dec.), Bruce Ita. B.S.C., U. Iowa, 1943; M.B.A., Stanford U., 1948, Ph.D., 1952. Prof. bus. environ. and mktg. U. Minn., Mpls., 1950-89; ret., chmn. dept. bus. adminstrn., 1957-59; vis. prof. U. Philippines, 1955-56, Doshisha U., Kyoto, Japan, 1978-79, 85, Keio U., Tokyo, 1979, 83, 85, 87. Co-author: Marketing in a Changing Environment; co-editor: The Environment of Marketing Behavior. Mem. Am. Mktg. Assn. (pres. 1967-68). Home: Saint Paul Minn. Deceased. †

HOLLOWAY, STERLING PRICE, actor, recording artist; b. Cedartown, Ga.; s. William Boothby and Rebecca (Boyce) H.; 1 adopted child, Richard. Student, Am. Acad. Dramatic Art, 1921-23. Appeared in numerous stage plays, motion pictures, radio and television programs, 1925-92 including (TV, radio series) Life of Riley; motion pictures include Won Ton Ton, Dog Who Saved Hollywood; radio and TV appearances include Baileys of Balboa; numerous others; voice of Winnie-the-Pooh for, Disney Prodns., 1971-92 ; voice documentary Jungle Book, 1983; voice numerous TV commercials including Angel Soft Bath Tissue, 1987, Julie Doll, 1987; rec. artist, art lectr.; artist-in-residence, U. Calif., Irvine, 1971-72. Bd. dirs. Art Mus. Served with AUS, World War II. Recipient Grammy award for best childrens record, 1975; nominee, 1976; Americana award Cyprus Coll., 1978; bronze award, 1981; Annie award Internat. Animated Film Soc., 1985. Mem. Nat. Acad. Rec. Arts and Scis. Home: Laguna Beach Calif. Died Nov. 22, 1992. †

HOLM, HANYA, choreographer, dancer, educator; b. Worms-am-Rhine, Germany; came to U.S., 1931, naturalized, 1939; d. Valentin and Marie (Moerschel) Eckert; divorced; 1 child, Klaus Holm. Ed. pvt. schs., Germany; student of music, Hoch Conservatory and Dalcroze Inst., Frankfurt-am- Main; grad., Dalcroze Inst., Hellerau; dance diploma, Mary Wigman Central Inst., Dresden, Germany; D.F.A. (hon.), Colo. Coll., 1960, Adelphi U., 1969. Chief instr., co-dir. Wigman Inst., Dresden, 10 yrs; dir. dance dept. Mus. Theatre Acad., N.Y.C., 1962-92; dir. own sch. N.Y.C., until 1968; dir. summer sessions in dance Colo. Coll., 1941-83; mem. staff Alwin Nikolais/Murray Louis Dance Theatre Lab., N.Y.C., 1972-92, Juilliard Sch., N.Y.C., 1975-92; tchr., lectr. Bretton Coll., Eng., 1979; pioneer Labanotation for copyright on dance scores musicals Kiss Me, Kate, 1948, My Darlin' Aida, 1952, My Fair Lady, 1956. Mem. original Wigman Co., performer, dance dir., choreographer, Europe, until 1931, under auspices Sol Hurok, founder, dir., N.Y. Wigman Sch. Dance, 1931, which later became Hanya Holm Sch. Dance; began Am. concert career, 1936; major prodns. Trend, 1937 (N.Y. Times award from John Martin as best dance composition of year), Metropolitan Daily, 1938, Tragic Exodus, 1938 (Dance Mag. award for best group choreography in modern dance); choreographer: Eccentricities of Davey Crockett, 1948, Kiss Me, Kate (Cole Porter), 1948 (best choreographer N.Y. Drama Critics award), Eng. prodn., 1951, Out of this World (C. Porter), 1950, My Darlin Aida, 1952; choreographer, dir.: The Golden Apple, 1954 (Critics Circle citation best musical); Reuben- Reuben, 1955; staged dances for re-make of film Vagabond King, 1956; choreography and mus. numbers My Fair Lady, 1955-56 (Tony nominee), Israeli prodn., 1964, Where's Charley, My Fair Lady; English prodns., 1958; choreography and mus. numbers Camelot, 1960; Christine, 1960-61, Anya, 1965; staged dances television show Pinocchio, 1957, Dinner with the President, 1963, Metropolitan Daily; 1st dance prodn. on TV, 1939; dir., choreographer world premiere opera The Ballad of Baby Doe, Central City, Colo. opera house, 1956; appeared on Am. Cancer Soc. series Tactic, NBC, 1959; dir., choreographer opera Orpheus and Euridice (Gluck), Vancouver Internat. Festival, 1959. Recipient Capezio award, 1978, award Fedn. Jewish Philanthropies, 1959, Colo. Centennial award and Gov.'s award, 1973, 74, Heritage Honor award Nat. Dance Assn., 1976, award and medal of distinction in fine arts City of Colorado Springs, 1978, Samuel H. Scripps Am. Dance Festival award, 1984; subject of film Hanya Holm, Portrait of an Artist/ Teacher, 1983; Samuel H. Scripps Am. Dance Festival award, 1984, Astaire award (spl. citation for lifetime achievement) 1987, Dance Mag. award 1990. Mem. Am. Arbitration Assn. (nat. panel arbitrators), Soc. Stage Dirs. and Choreographers (v.p.). Home: New York N.Y. Died Nov. 1992. †

HOLMBERG, RICHARD HJALMAR, electronics executive; b. Wethersfield, Conn., Oct. 19, 1925; s. Hjalmar Julius and Glenna Amy (Campbell) H.; m. Barbara Gertrude Wilber, June 2, 1951; children: Richard, Robert, Cheryl. BSEE, MIT, 1950; MSEE, Stevens Inst. Tech., 1957. Dept. mgr. Lockheed Elec. Co., Plainfield, N.J., 1951-63; div. mgr. Lockheed Missile and Space Co., Sunnyvale, Calif., 1963-73; pres. Internat. Signal and Control Group, Lancaster, Pa., 1973-82; corp. tech. dir. Internat. Signal and Control Group, P.L.C., Lancaster, Pa., 1982-84; pres., chief exec. officer Sechan Elec., Inc., Lititz, Pa., 1984-88, also bd. dirs. Patentee in field. Served with USN, 1944-46. Home: Landisville Pa. Died July 5, 1988.

HOLMBLAD, EDWARD CHARLES, physician; b. Aurora, Ill., Apr. 10, 1894; s. Charles and Christine (Shogren) H.; m. Lillian Weltin, Dec. 19, 1919; children: James E., Ann Marie Dunk. Student, Lake Forest Coll., 1912-14; MD, U. Chgo., 1918. Intern Cook County Hosp., Chgo., 1918-20; practicing physician and surgeon Chgo., from 1920; sr. attending surgeon St. Luke's Hosp.; regional chief surgeon Ry. Express Agy., 1921-45; surgeon Rock Island R.R., C&EI R.R., Santa Fe R.R.; mng. dir. Indsl. Med. Assn., 1941-59; med. dir. Chgo. divsns. Eastman Kodak Co., from 1941, others. Chmn., mem. adv. com. Pres.'s Com. Employment Physically Handicapped, from 1955; bd. dirs. Goodwill Industries Am., from 1963. Fellow ACS, Am. Assn. Occupational Medicine, Am. Coll. Preventive Medicine, Am. Pub. Health Assn.; mem. AMA, Ill. Med. Soc., Chgo. Med. Soc., Indsl. Med. Assn., Chgo. Natural History Mus., Rotary. *

HOLMES, ALLEN CORNELIUS, lawyer; b. Cin., May 27, 1920. A.B., U. Cin., 1941; J.D., U. Mich., 1944; LL.D., John Carroll U., 1985. Bar: Ohio 1944, U.S. Supreme Ct. 1964, D.C. 1967. Assoc. Jones, Day, Reavis & Pogue, Cleve., 1944-54, ptnr., 1954-86, mng. ptnr., 1975-85, nat. mng. ptnr., 1975-85; bd. dirs. Sherwin-Williams Co., Kaiser Found. Hosps., Maxus Energy Corp. Hon. trustee, past chmn. Case Western Res. U., Cleve.; trustee Univ. Circle Inc.; mem. exec. com. Greater Cleve. Growth Assn.; trustee emeritus United Way Svcs.; chmn. bd. trustees Sta. WVIZ-TV; trustee, vice chair Cleve. Inst. Art. Mem. ABA (past chmn. FTC com. antitrust sect., chmn. antitrust sect. council), Ohio Bar Assn., Cleve. Bar Assn., Am. Law Inst. Clubs: Union, 50; Chagrin Valley Hunt, Tavern; Metropolitan (Washington); Links (N.Y.C.). Home: Cleveland Ohio Died Nov. 1, 1990; buried Cleve.

HOLMES, THOMAS HALL, psychiatrist; b. Goldsboro, N.C., Sept. 20, 1918; s. Thomas Hall and Elizabeth (Stephenson) H.; m. Janet Lawrence, Dec. 29, 1942; children—Thomas Stephenson, Janet, Eleanor Scott, Elizabeth Lawrence. A.B., U. N.C., 1939; M.D., Cornell U., 1943. Intern in medicine N.Y. Hosp., N.Y.C., 1943-44; resident in psychiatry N.Y. Hosp., 1944; research in neurology Bellevue Hosp., N.Y.C., 1944; Hofheimer research fellow psychosomatic medicine N.Y. Hosp.-Cornell U. Med. Center, 1947-49; provisional asst. physician outpatient dept. N.Y. Hosp.; also clin. asst. vis. psychiatrist and neurologist Bellevue Hosp., 1948-49; mem. faculty U. Wash. Sch. Medicine, Seattle, 1949-85; prof. psychiatry U. Wash. Sch. Medicine, 1958-85; attending physician Harborview Med. Center, 1949-85, Univ. Hosp., 1959-85; attending staff Seattle VA Hosp., 1951-85; hon. cons. psychiatrist Royal Prince Alfred Hosp., Sydney, Australia, from 1971. Co-author: The Nose, 1950, Life Change Events Research, 1984; contbr. to med. jours. Served to maj. M.C. AUS, 1944-46. Mem. AAAS, Am. Psychiat. Assn., Am. Psychosomatic Soc., Am. Public Health Assn., Assn. Am. Med. Colls., N.Y. Acad. Scis., Wash. Med. Assn., King County Med. Soc., N. Pacific Soc. Neurology and Psychiatry, Am. Sociol. Soc., Assn. Research in Nervous and Mental Diseases, Psychiat. Research Soc., Western Soc. Clin. Research. Home: Bellevue Wash. Died Dec. 24, 1988; buried Acacia Cemetery, Seattle.

HOLMES, VERNON HARRISON, insurance company executive, economic development company executive; b. Milford, Ill., Dec. 21, 1920; s. Harry and Alma (Schiewe) H.; m. Ruth Dewey, Oct. 24, 1943; children: Sharon Klabon, Charisse Holmes. BEd, Western Ill. U., 1943; grad., Inst. Mgmt., Northwestern U., 1965, Advanced Mgmt. Program, Harvard U., 1977. With Sentry Ins. Co., Stevens Point, Wis., 1946-85; pres. Sentry Found., 1985, vice chmn. bd. dirs.; exec. dir. Portage Co. Econ. Devel. Corp., Stevens Point, Wis., 1986-92. Past chmn. bd. dirs. St. Michael's Hosp., Stevens Point; bd. dirs. Western Ill. U. Found., Cen. Wis. Area Symphony Orch.; adv. coun. Marshfield Med. Rsch. Found.; past pres. Trinity Luth. Ch., Stevens Point. Served with USAAF, 1943-46. Mem. Stevens Point Area C. of C. (pres., bd. dirs.), Soc. Preservation and Encouragement of Barber Shop Quartet Singing in Am. (past pres. Stevens Point chpt.), Stevens Point Country Club (past v.p., bd. dirs.). Home: Stevens Point Wis. Deceased. †

HOLMES À COURT, (MICHAEL) ROBERT (HAMILTON), oil company executive; b. July 27, 1937; s. Peter Worsley and Ethnée Celia Holmes à Court; m. Janet Lee Ranford, 1966; 4 children. Grad., U. West Australia. Barrister, solicitor Supreme Ct. Western Australia, 1965-82; chmn. Associated Communications Corp., Australia, 1982-90, Weeks Petroleum Co., Australia, 1984-90, Bell Group Ltd., Australia, 1970-88, The Bell Group Internat. Ltd., 1982-88, Bell Resources Ltd., Australia, from 1983; bd. dirs. Standard Chartered Bank, joint dep. chmn., 1987-90. Home: Perth Australia Died Sept. 2, 1990.

HOLT, THAD, management consultant; b. Sumterville, Ala., Sept. 23, 1898; s. LeRoy and Elizabeth Cunningham (Burwell) H.; m. Sarah Ames Oliver, Feb. 4, 1928; children: Thad, Samuel Clark Oliver. AB, Colo. Coll., 1920. In advt. & sales work, 24 yrs.; advt. & sales mgr. Wofford Oil Co., 1921-27; served as state dir. FERA, WPA, CWA, NYA, Montgomery, 1932-36; asst. nat. adminstr. WPA, Washington, 1936-37; v.p. Famous Features Syndicate, 1921-22; pres., treas. The Television Corp.-stas. WAPI, WAFM and WAFM-TV, 1937-53; then chmn. Am. Electronix, Inc.; cons. New Orleans Times-Picayune, Voice of Am. (TV), Ampex Corp., CBS, Royal Crown Cola Corp.; chmn. Metalplate & Coating Inc. Mem. Ala. Hist. Assn., Newcomen Soc., C. of C., Com. on Fgn. Rels., Am. Legion, Kiwanis, Phi Beta Kappa, Phi Gamma Delta. Democrat. *

HOLT, WILLIAM STULL, history educator; b. N.Y.C., Oct. 2, 1896; s. Byron W. and Elizabeth G. (Kinsella) H.; m. Lois Crump, Feb. 12, 1921; children: Jocelyn, Enid. AB, Cornell U., 1920; PhD, Johns Hopkins U., 1926. Mem. staff Brookings Instn., 1921-27; asst. prof. history George Washington U., 1927-30; asst., assoc. prof. Johns Hopkins U., 1930-40; prof. history, head dept. history U. Wash., 1940-42, 45-54, prof., 1954—. Author several books. 1st lt. USAF, 1917-19, lt. col. U.S. Army, 1942-45, ETO. Decorated Silver Star, Bronze Star, Officer Order of Brit. Empire, Croix de Guerre (French). Mem. Am. Hist. Assn. *

HOLTFRETER, JOHANNES FRIEDRICH KARL, zoologist, emeritus educator; b. Richtenberg, Germany, Jan. 9, 1901; came to U.S., 1946, naturalized, 1951; s. Johannes K. and Sabine (Peters) H.;. Student, U. Rostock, 1918-19, U. Leipzig, 1919-20; Ph.D., U. Freiburg, 1924; Dr. Rerum Naturalium honoris causa, 1975. Asst. Kaiser Wilhelm Inst. Biology, Berlin-Dahlem, Fed. Republic Germany, 1928-33; assoc. prof. Zool. Inst., U. Munich, Fed. Republic Germany, 1933-38; mem. research staff Zool. Inst., U. Cambridge, Eng., 1939-40; mem. zool. dept. McGill U., Montreal, Que., Can., 1942-46; prof. dept. biology U. Rochester, N.Y., 1946-66; Tracy H. Harris prof. zoology U. Rochester, 1966-69, Tracy H. Harris emeritus prof., 1969-92. Fellow AAAS, Am. Acad. Arts and Scis.; mem. Deutsche Akad. Leopoldina, Nat. Acad. Scis., Zool. Soc. India (hon.), Asociacion Venezolansa para la avance de la Ciencia, Soc. Developmental Biology, Internat. Soc. Differentiation, Internat. Soc. Developmental Biologists, Internat. Soc. Cell Biology, Am. Soc. Cell Biology, Am. Assn. Anatomists, Am. Soc. Zoologists, Royal Swedish Acad. Scis. Home: Rochester N.Y. Died Nov. 13, 1992. †

HOMANS, GEORGE CASPAR, sociology educator; b. Boston, Aug. 11, 1910; s. Robert and Abigail (Adams) H.; m. Nancy Parshall Cooper, June 28, 1941; children—Elizabeth, Susan, Peter. A.B., Harvard U., 1932; M.A., Cambridge U., Eng., 1955. Jr. fellow Harvard U., Cambridge, Mass., 1934-39, faculty instr., 1939-41, assoc. prof., 1946-53, prof., 1953-80, prof. sociology emeritus, 1980-89; mem. human relations panel Dept. Def., Washington, 1950-51, chmn. com. on psychol. warfare, 1951-52; Simon vis. prof. Manchester U., Eng., 1953; prof. social theory Cambridge U., Eng., 1955-56; vis. prof. U. Kent, Eng., 1967. Author: numerous books including The Human Group, 1950, Marriage, Authority and Final Causes, 1955; Social Behavior: Its Elementary Forms, 1961, rev. edit., 1974, Sentiments and Activities, 1962, The Nature of Social Science, 1967, Coming to My Senses: The Autobiography of a Sociologist, 1984, Certainties and Doubts, 1987, (poems) The Witch Hazel, 1988; also numerous articles. Served to lt. comdr. USN, 1941-45. Fellow Nat. Acad. Scis., Am. Philos. Soc., Am. Acad. Arts and Scis.; mem. Am. Sociol. Assn. (pres. 1963-64, Disting. Career of Scholarship award 1988), Eastern Sociol. Assn. (pres. 1963-64, Disting. Career award 1985), Soc. Cin. Republican. Episcopalian. Club: Tavern (Boston). Home: Cambridge Mass. Died May 29, 1989; buried Medfield, Mass.

HONDA, SOICHIRO, automobile company executive; b. Iwata-Gun, Shizuoka, Japan, Nov. 17, 1906; s. Gihei And Mika Matsui H.; m. Sachi Isobe, Nov. 20, 1935; children: Keiko, Chikako, Hirotoshi, Katsuhisa dec. . Student of Japanese schs.; D.Eng. hon. , Sophi aU., Tokyo, Mich. Tech. U.; LHD hon. , Ohio State U. With Art Shokai, Tokyo, 1922-28; founder br. Art Shokai, Hamamatsu, 1928-34, Tokai Seiki Co., Ltd., 1934-46, Honda Gijutsu Kenkyu Sho, 1946-48; founder, pres. Honda Motor Co., Ltd., 1948-73, supreme adviser, 1973-91. Author 10 books; inventor automobile and motorcycle parts. V.p. Japan Automobile Mfrs. Assn., 1967-8; dir. Japan Automobile Fedn., 1972-74; founder Honda Found. sponsoring DISCOVERIES activities, 1977-91. Decorated grande ufficiale dell Ordine al Merito Italy , commandeur de l'Ordre de la Couronne Belgium , knight comdr. Royal Order of Polar Star Sweden , officier l'Ordre des Arts et des Lettres France , 198; recipient Mercurio d'Oro Italy , 1971, Transp. Culture award Ministry Transp., 1973, Holley Medal award ASME, 1980, 1st Class Order of Sacred Treasure Japan , 1981. Mem. Am. Soc. Metals hon. , Tokyo C. of C. v.p. , Royal Swedish Acad. Engring. Scis. fgn. . Home: Tokyo Japan Died Aug. 5, 1991.

HONEYWELL, CHARLES F., corporate consultant; b. Santa Ana, Calif., June 7, 1898; s. Frank and Flora (Wilson) H.; children: Patricia Evers, Barbara Booth, Constance Peterson. AB, U. Calif., 1921. Bus. mgr. Pacific Rural Press, San Francisco, 1921-26; propr. C.F. Honeywell & Co., Oakland, Calif., 1926-33; dept. mgr. Honolulu Iron Works, 1933-35; various positions, later v.p. C. Brewer & Co., Ltd., Honolulu, 1935-49; pres. Hilo (Hawaii) Transp. & Terminal Co., Ltd., 1947-49; owner Gregorie Neck Plantation, Coosawhatchie, S.C., 1950-52; spl. asst. to sec. commerce, 1953; adminstr. bus. and def. svcs. Dept. Commerce, 1953-56; pres. Bus. Devel. & Rsch. Co., 1956-57; exec. sec., mgr. Newsprint Svc. Bur., Inc., 1957-60; ind. cons., from 1960. Trustee Queens Hosp., 1938-47; chmn. Hosp. Svc. Study Commn., 1946-47. 2nd lt. AUS, 1917-19. Mem. Alpha Delta Phi. *

HOOK, SIDNEY, philosopher, educator; b. N.Y.C., Dec. 20, 1902; s. Isaac and Jennie (Halpern) H.; m. Carrie Katz, Mar. 31, 1924; 1 son, John Bertrand; m. Ann Zinken, May 25, 1935; children: Ernest Benjamin, Susan Ann. B.S., CCNY, 1923; M.A., Columbia U., 1926, Ph.D., 1927, L.H.D., 1960; LL.D., univs. Maine, Calif., Fla., Hebrew Union, Utah, Vt., Rockford Coll. Tchr. N.Y.C. pub. schs., 1923-28; lectr. Columbia U., summer session, 1927, 30; instr. philosophy Washington Sq. Coll., N.Y. U., 1927-32, asst. prof., 1932-34, asso. prof., chmn. dept. philosophy, 1934-39, prof., 1939-69, emeritus, from 1969; head all-univ. dept. philosophy N.Y. U., 1948-69; chmn. Washington Sq. Coll. Arts and Scis., until 1969; sr. research fellow Hoover Instn. on War, Revolution and Peace, Stanford, Calif., 1973-89; vis. prof. Harvard U., 1961, U. Calif., San Diego, 1975; regents prof. U. Calif., Santa Barbara, 1966. Author: Toward the Understanding of Karl Marx: A Revolutionary Interpretation, 1933, From Hegel to Marx, 1936, The Hero in History, 1943, Education for Modern Man, 2d edit., 1963, Heresy, Yes-Conspiracy, No, 1953, The Ambiguous Legacy: Marx and the Marxists, 1955, Common Sense and the Fifth Amendment, 1957, Political Power and Personal Freedom, 1959, The Quest for

Being, 1961, The Paradoxes of Freedom, 1962, The Place of Religion in A Free Society, 1968, Academic Freedom and Academic Anarchy, 1970, Education and the Taming of Power, 1973, Pragmatism and the Tragic Senses of Life, 1974, Revolution, Reform and Social Justice, 1975, Philosophy and Public Policy, 1980, Marxism and Beyond, 1983, Out of Step: An Unquiet Life in the XXth Century, 1987; contbr. articles to philos. jours.; editor: American Philosophers at Work: The Current Philosophic Scene, 1956, Determinism and Freedom in An Age of Modern Science, The Idea of a Modern University; others.ersity; others. Organizer Conf. on Methods in Philosophy and Sci., Conf. on Sci. Spirit and Dem. Faith, Am. Com. for Cultural Freedom, Congress for Cultural Freedoms, Univ. Centers for Rational Alternatives, N.Y. U. Inst. Philosophy; treas. John Dewey Found. Guggenheim fellow, 1928-29, 61-62; Jefferson lectr. NEH, 1984; recipient Presdl. Medal of Freedom, 1985. Fellow Am. Acad. Arts and Scis., Am. Acad. Edn.; mem. Am. Philos. Assn. (pres. eastern div. 1959), Nat. Endowment for Humanities (council 1972-78), League for Indsl. Democracy (v.p.), John Dewey Soc. Home: Stanford Calif. Died July 12, 1989; buried South Wardston, Vt.

HOOK, WALTER, artist; b. Missoula, Mont., Apr. 25, 1919; s. Herman and Elvira (Puskala) H.; m. Margaret Eloise Thieme, June 5, 1943; children: Janet Gay, Colleen Beth. B.A., U. Mont., 1942; M.A., U. N.Mex., 1950. Tech. illustrator Sandia Base, Albuquerque, 1950-53, Gen. Electric, Richland, Wash., 1953-54; art. tchr. Missoula County High Sch., Mont., 1954-55; prof. art U. Mont., Missoula, 1955-77; freelance artist Missoula, 1977-89. Exhibited numerous one-man shows, 1979. Recipient Mont. Gov.'s visual arts award, 1985; Western State Arts Found. fellow, 1976. Mem. NAD (assoc.). Home: Missoula Mont. Deceased. †

HOOLE, WILLIAM STANLEY, librarian, author; b. Darlington, S.C., May 16, 1903; s. William Brunson and Mary Eva (Powers) H.; m. Martha Anne Sanders, Aug. 7, 1931 (dec. May 1960); children: Martha DuBose, Elizabeth Stanley; m. Addie Shirley Coleman, May 31, 1970. A.B., Wofford Coll., 1924, A.M., 1931, Litt.D., 1954; Ph.D., Duke U., 1934; B.S. in L.S, North Tex. U., 1943; student, Columbia U., 1927, U. S.C., 1929, U. Chgo. Grad. Library Sch., summers 1935, 36, 38, 39; LL.D., U. Ala., 1975; D.Hum., Francis Marion Coll., 1980. Tchr. Spartanburg (S.C.) High Sch., 1924-25, Darlington High Sch., 1927-31; teaching fellow Duke U., 1931-34; asst. prof. English Birmingham (Ala.) So. Coll., 1934-35, librarian, 1935-37; librarian Baylor U., Waco, Tex., 1937-39; dir. libraries North Tex. State U., 1939-44; dean libraries U. Ala., Tuscaloosa, 1944-71; prof. librarianship U. Ala., 1971-73, dean emeritus, 1973-90; library cons. So. Assn. Schs. and Colls., 1942-60, mem. commn. instns. higher learning, 1948-50; research cons. U.S. Ho. of Reps. subcom. on spl. edn., 1957-58; cons. U.S. Office Edn., 1959-60, Pres.'s Nat. Commn. on Libraries, 1967, U.S. Dept. Commerce, 1968, also various govt. agys., coms. Editor: North Texas Regional Union List of Serials, 1943, Classified List of Reference Books and Periodicals for the College Library, rev, 1957, Seven Months in the Rebel States, 1863, 1958, Reconstruction in West Alabama, 1959, A Visit to the Confederate States of America in 1863, 1962, And Still We Conquer, 1968, The Logs of the C.S.S. Alabama and C.SS. Tuscaloosa, 1972, (with Marie B. Bingham) Catalogue of Yucatan Collection in University of Alabama Libraries, 1973, (with Addie S. Hoole) A History of Madison County, Ala., 1732-1840, 1976, Confederate Foreign Agent: The European Diary of Major Edward C. Anderson, 1976, (with Addie S. Hoole) A History of Tuscaloosa, Ala., 1816-1880, 1977, Florida Territory in 1844: The Diary of Master Edward C. Anderson, USN, 1977, (with A. S. Hoole) Early History of N.E. Ala, 1979, Early History of Montgomery, 1979, History of Tuscaloosa, Ala., 1816-1949, 1980, Cherokee Indians of Georgia, 1980, A Rebel Spy in Yankeeland, 1981, History of the 14th Regiment Alabama Volunteers, 1983, History of the 47th Alabama Infantry Regiment, 1983, The Pee Dee Light Artillery, C.S.A., 1983, History of the 7th Alabama Cavalry, 1984, Confederate Norfolk, 1984, History of Barton's Georgia Brigade, 1984, Reminiscences of the Autauga Rifles, 1984, History of the 46th Alabama Regiment, 1985, History of the 48th Alabama Regiment, 1985, History of the 53d Alabama Regiment, 1985. Author: Charleston Periodicals, 1936, Sam Slick in Texas, 1945, The Ante-Bellum Charleston Theatre, 1946, Let the People Read, 1946, A Library for Lauderdale, Alias Simon Suggs: The Life and Times of Johnson Jones Hooper, 1952, The James Boys Rode South, 1955, Vizetelly Covers the Confederacy, 1957, The Alabama Tories, 1862-65, 1960, Four Years in the Confederate Navy, 1964, Lawley Covers the Confederacy, 1964, According to Hoole, 1973, Ode to a Druid Oak, 1979, The Birmingham Horrors, 1979, Peedee Epiphany, 1981, Saga of Rube Burrow, 1981, Margaret Ellen O'Brien, 1981, Martha Young: Alabama's Foremost Folklorist, 1982, Alabama's Golden Literary Era, 1983, John Witherspoon Du Bose: A Neglected Southern Historian, 1983, History of Shockley's Alabama Escort Company, 1983, History of the 5th Alabama Regiment, 1985, History of the 8th Alabama Regiment, 1985, Yankee Invasion of West Alabama, 1985, Alabama Boy Generals of the Confederacy, 1985, History of the 36th Alabama Regiment, 1986, Memoir of Catherine Brown, a Christian Indian, 1986, Spanish Explorers in the Southeastern United States, 1527-1561, 1987; co-author: Mississippi Study of Higher Education, 1945, Studies of Higher Education in the South, 1947, A Study of Stillman Institute, 1947; Editor: The Alabama Rev, 1948-67, The Southeastern Librarian, 1951-52; assoc. editor: South Atlantic MLA Bull., 1947-52, Confederate Centennial Studies, 1956-65; contbr. articles to scholarly, profl. and popular publs., including Grolier Ency. Recipient Lit. award Ala. Library Assn., 1958, Tuscaloosa Heritage award, 1989; Fulbright research fellow U.K., 1956-57. Mem. Ala. Acad. Disting. Authors, Ala. Hist. Assn., Phi Beta Kappa, Phi Alpha Theta, Pi Tau Chi, Kappa Phi Kappa, Omicron Delta Kappa, Pi Kappa Phi. Methodist. Home: Tuscaloosa Ala. Died Dec. 12, 1990; buried Darlington, S.C.

HOOPER, JOHN WILLIAM, economics educator; b. Laona, Wis., Nov. 6, 1926; s. Frank Arnold and Myldred (Barlement) H.; m. Eva Salmang, Aug. 14, 1959; children: Ellen Myldred, Carol Ann, Joan Claire. B.A. in Econs, Stanford, 1950, Ph.D., 1961; postgrad., U. Wash., 1950-51. Research economist Rand Corp., 1958-59; assoc. prof. econs. Yale U., 1959-66; prof. econs. U. Calif. at San Diego, 1966-89, chmn. dept., from 1967; vis. prof. indsl. mgmt. U. Petroleum and Minerals, Dhahran, Saudi Arabia, 1977-79; sr. fellow Nat. U. Singapore, 1982-83; asst. dir. Cowles Found. Research Econs., 1961-64. Served with USNR, 1944-46. Fulbright scholar, 1957-58; sr. fellow Social Sci. Research Council, 1964-65; Ford Found. faculty research fellow, 1971-72. Mem. Am. Econ. Assn., Econometric Soc., Royal Econ. Soc. Home: San Diego Calif. Died Mar. 16, 1989; cremated.

HOOPER, LUCIEN OBED, investment analyst; b. Biddeford, Maine, July 9, 1896; s. William Howard and Jennie Wait (McIntire) H.; m. Vivian Lois Cole, Sept. 6, 1919; children: Lois Gould, David. Student, Boston U., Harvard U., 1918. Assoc. editor Boston Comml., 1919-23; investment analyst E.A. Pierce & Co., 1923-27; head rsch. dept. Frazier Jelke & Co., 1927-38; market letter writer Shearson, Hammill & Co., 1928-41; dir. rsch. W.E. Hutton & Co., 1941-63, sr. analyst, from 1963. Contbr. articles to fin. & econ. jours.; signed column in Forbes mag. Mayor Westwood, N.J., 1934-37, mem. planning bd., 1945-48, chmn., 1945-48; trustee Cushing Acad. With USN, WWI. Mem. N.Y. Soc. Security Analysts, Analysts Club, Fin. Analysts Fedn., Sigma Alpha Epsilon. Democrat. Methodist. *

HOOVER, KENNETH H., chemist; b. Albia, Iowa, Dec. 18, 1896; s. Charles George and Olive Myrtle (Wright) H.; m. Helen Grace Hoover, May 6, 1922; children: Helen Jane Kistner, Robert Harry, Charles John. Student, Kenyon Coll., 1913-15; AB, U. Wis., 1921. Rsch. chemist Nat. Aniline and Chem. Co., 1921-25; sr. fellow Miner Labs., 1926-34; plant mgr. Ind. Wood Preserving Co., 1934-36; rsch. chemist Comml. Solvents Corp., 1936-39, mgr. R & D dept., 1940-42, v.p. in charge R & D, 1943-49; dir. R.J. Reynolds Tobacco Co., dir. rsch., v.p., 1959-65. Lt. inf. U.S. Army, WWI. Fellow AAAS, Am. Inst. Chemists; mem. Am. Chem. Soc., Am. Inst. Chem. Engrs., N.Y. Acad. Scis., Rotary, Alpha Chi Sigma, Beta Theta Pi. *

HOOVER, WALTER BOYD, physician; b. Jackson County, Mo., Jan. 4, 1898; s. Conrad A. and Mary (Allen) H.; m. Lorna Lelley, Oct. 3, 1923; children: Patricia Hoover Petot, Jr., Walter Boyd, Charles J., Lorna Hoover Scammell. Student, Drake U., 1915-18; MD, Washington U., 1922. Intern City Hosp., St. Louis, 1922-23; specialty tng. Washington U. Sch. Medicine, Barnes Hosp., 1923-28; oto-rhinolaryngologist, broncho-esophagologist Lahey Clinic, 1928-89. Mem. AMA, Am. Acad. Ophthalmology and Otolaryngology, Am. Broncho-esophagol. Assn. (v.p., past pres.), New Eng. Otolaryngol. Soc. (past pres.), Am. Laryngol., Rhinol. and Otological Soc. Home: Boynton Beach Fla. Died June 17, 1989.

HOPE, HENRY RADFORD, fine arts educator, editor, art historian; b. Chelsea, Mass., Dec. 15, 1905; s. Frank Radford and Blanche (Lovett) H.; m. Dorothy Weil, Apr. 11, 1927 (div. Apr. 1944); m. Sarahanne Adams, June 3, 1944; children: Adams McClennen, James McClennen, Helen McClennen, Sara Jane, Roy, Ray. Student, Columbia U., 1931; cert., U. Paris, 1937; MA, Harvard U., 1941, PhD, 1942; DFA (hon.), Ind. U., 1978. Grad. asst. dept. fine arts Harvard U., 1939-40; chmn. fine arts dept. Ind. U., Bloomington, 1941-67, founder, dir. Art Mus., 1961-70; mem. U.S. Nat. Commn. for UNESCO, 1951-63. Author: Catalogue of Exhibition of Work of George Braque, 1949, Catalogue of Exhibition of Sculpture of Jacques Lipchitz, 1954; editor Coll. Art Jour., 1942-49, 52-60; editor Art Jour., 1960-73, cons. editor, 1973-79. Trustee Ft. Lauderdale (Fla.) Mus. Arts. Benjamin Franklin fellow Royal Soc. Art. Mem. Coll. Art Assn. (pres. 1949-51, hon. bd. dirs. 1976-89), Am. Fedn. Art (trustee 1950-61). Home: Fort Lauderdale Fla. Died Apr. 27, 1989; buried at sea off coast of Ft. Lauderdale, Fla.

HOPKINS, BERT EARL, lawyer, educator; b. Bowdon, N.D., Nov. 16, 1902; s. William H. and Marie (Larson) H.; m. Marie Hayes, Aug. 22, 1931; 1 child, William Hayes. PhB, U. Wis., 1924; LLB, Yale U., 1927; LLM, Columbia U., 1939, JSD, 1944. Bar: Minn. 1927. Pvt. practice St. Paul, 1927-29; state investigator and examiner Travelers Ins. Co., 1927-29; prof. law U. Idaho, 1929-45, Ind. U., 1945-46; dean, prof. law U. Conn., 1946-66, univ. prof. law, 1966-72, dean emeritus, 1972-89. Author: (monograph) Conflict of Laws in Adminstration of Decendents' Estates, 1944; contbr. articles to profl. jours. Mem. ABA, Conn. Bar Assn. Home: West Hartford Conn. Died Aug. 20, 1989.

HOPKINS, JOHN ABEL, JR., economist; b. Newark, Del., Apr. 4, 1897; s. John Abel and Ellen (Walker) H.; m. Marguerite Stotts, Sept. 14, 1929. BS, U. Del., 1917; AM, Harvard U., 1921, PhD, 1924. Mem. faculty Iowa State Coll., 1921-44; in charge agrl. sec. Nat. Rsch. Project WPA, Phila., 1936-38; economist Armour Rsch. Found. indsl. survey of Argentina, 1942; agrl. adviser U.S. Fgn. Svc. Aux., Bogota, Colombia, 1944-45; in charge Latin Am. divsn. Office of Fgn. Agrl. Rels. U.S. Dept. Agr., 1945-47; fgn. svc. officer, 1947-57; agrl. attaché & 1st sec. Mexico City, 1947-50; agrl. attaché & 1st sec. U.S. Embassy, Rio de Janeiro, 1950-52, Buenos Aires, 1953; counsellor of embassy for econ. affairs Buenos Aires, 1953-56; with Office Regional Econ. Affairs Bur. Inter-Am. Affairs, Dept. State, 1956-57; econ. counselor internat. Sugar Coun., London, 1958-59; economist Internat. Fed. Agrl. Producers, from 1961. Author: Elements of Farm Management, 1936, Farm Records, 1936, Report of Agricultural Section, National Research Project: Changing Technology and Employment in Agriculture, 1941, Administracion Rural, 1951, Records for Farm Management, 1958; various agrl. bulls. at Iowa State Coll.; contbr. articles to Jour. Farm Econs. and Fgn. Agr. Project dir. Inventory Info. Basic to Planning Agrl. Devel. in Latin Am., from 1962. 2nd lt. U.S. Army, 1918-19. Mem. Am. Econ. Assn., Am. Farm Econ. Assn., Phi Kappa Phi, Theta Chi. *

HOPPER, GRACE M., mathematician; b. N.Y.C., Dec. 9, 1906; d. Walter Fletcher and Mary Campbell (Van Horne) Murray; m. Vincent Foster Hopper, June 15, 1930 (div. 1945). BA, Vassar Coll., 1928; MA (Vassar fellow, Sterling scholar), Yale U., 1930, PhD, 1934; postgrad. (Vassar faculty fellow), NYU, 1941-42; DEng (hon.), Newark Coll. Engring., 1972; DSc (hon.), C.W. Post Coll. L.I. U., 1973, Pratt Inst., 1976, Linkoping (Sweden) U., 1980, Bucknell U., 1980, Acadia (Can.) U., 1980, So. Ill. U., 1981, Loyola U., Chgo., 1981; LLD (hon.), U. Pa., 1974; D Pub. Service (hon.), George Washington U., 1981. From instr. to assoc. prof. math. Vassar Coll., Poughkeepsie, N.Y., 1931-44; asst. prof. math Barnard Coll., N.Y.C., summer 1943; research fellow engring. scis., Applied Physics Computation Lab. Harvard U., Cambridge, Mass., 1946-49; sr. mathematician Eckert-Mauchly Computer Corp., Phila., 1949-50; sr. programmer Eckert-Mauchly div. Remington Rand, 1950-59; systems engr., dir. automatic programming devel. UNIVAC div. Sperry Rand Corp., Phila., 1959-64, staff scientist systems programming, 1964-71; vis. lectr. Moore Sch. Elec. Engring., U. Pa., 1959-63, vis. assoc. prof. elec. engring., 1963-74, adj. prof., 1974; professorial lectr. George Washington U. from 1971; sr. cons. Digital Equipment Corp., 1986-92. Contbr. articles to profl. jours. Served to comdr. WAVES, 1944-46; with USNR, 1976-86, advanced to rank of rear adm.; served active duty NAVDAC. Decorated Legion of Merit, Meritorious Service award; recipient Naval Ordnance Devel. award, 1946, Connelly Meml. award, 1968, Wilbur L. Cross medal Yale U., 1972, Sci. Achievement award Am. Mother's Com., 1970, Nat. Medal of Technology, 1991, others. Fellow Brit. Computer Soc. (disting.), Assn. Computer Programmers and Analysts, IEEE (McDowell award 1979, Piore award 1988), AAAS; mem. Nat. Acad. Engring., Assn. Computing Machinery, Data Processing Mgmt. Assn. (Man of Yr. award 1969), Am. Fedn. Info. Processing Socs. (Harry Goode Meml. award 1970), Soc. Women Engrs (Achievement award 1964, Franklin Inst., U.S. Naval Inst., Internat. Oceanographic Found., DAR, Dames Loyal Legion, Hist. Soc. Pa., Geneal. Soc. Pa., N.H. Hist. Soc., New Eng. Hist. Geneal. Soc., Valley Forge Hist. Assn., Ret. Officers Assn., Huguenot Soc. Pa., Nat., N.Y. geneal. socs., Pechin Soc., Phi Beta Kappa, Sigma Xi. Home: Arlington Va. Died Jan. 1, 1992.

HOPPING, LOUIS MELBERT, lawyer; b. Havana, Ill., May 31, 1900; s. Oliver Perry and Nannie Elizabeth (Yates) H.; m. Helen Irene Boutwell, Nov. 27, 1924; children—Eleanor Jean Hopping MacDonald (dec.), Helen Irene Hopping Johnson (dec.), George Boutwell, William Yates. Pre-med. and pre-law student, U. Ill., 1919-23; A.B., George Washington U., 1925, LL.B., 1927. Bar: Mich. bar 1932, also U.S. Supreme Ct 1932. With various companies Ill.; also Washington, to 1924; sec. to mng. editor Washington Herald, 1924-26; sec. Congressman Clarence McLeod, 1926-31; asst. U.S. atty., 1931-45; with firm Fitsgerald, Walker, Conley & Hopping, Detroit, 1945-87; magistrate 35th Mich. Dist. Ct., from 1976; Pres. Identity Registry, Inc. Author: History of Hopping Family in England and Genealogy of John Hopping in America. Mem. Northville Library Commn.; dir. Detroit Amateur Baseball Fedn.; pres. Mackenzie Meml. Assn.; founder, pres. Fed. Grand Jurors Assn.; mem. nat. awards jury Freedoms Found., Valley Forge, 1963. Served with USNRF, 1918-22. Named Distinguished Alumnus George Washington U., 1965, Japanese-Am. Soc. award. Mem. Inter-Am. Bar Assn. (del. cons. from 1949), ABA, Fed. Bar Assn.

(chmn. ad hoc com. to make naturalization process more meaningful), Detroit Bar Assn., Detroit Bd. Commerce, State Bar Mich., George Washington Law Assn., Am. Soc. Internat. Law, Am. Judicature Soc., Mich. Hort. Soc. (trustee), Nat., Mich., Plymouth hist. socs., Plymouth Symphony Soc., Bradford Compact, Smithsonian Assos., Gen. Soc. Mayflower Descs. Republican. Christian Scientist. Club: Civitan (pres. Detroit 1946-47, lt. gov. Great Lakes dist. 1949-50, gov. 1950-51, internat. sgt.-at-arms 1950-51, internat. judge adv. 1951-52, trustee internat. found., internat. pres. 1963-64, exec. bd. 1964-65). Home: Northville Mich. Died Sept. 17, 1987.

HORNE, J(AMES) BRYANT, municipal official, club executive; b. Lake Charles, La., July 29, 1898; s. Waldter Eldridge and Ellen (Rhodriguez) H.; m. Lena James, June 2, 1929; 1 son, James Bryant. Student pub. schs., corr. courses. Advt. salesman Jackson (Miss.) Daily News, 1924-39; salesman, dist. mgr. Mut. Benefit Life Ins. Co., also Reliance Life Ins. Co., Jackson, 1939-42; employment counselor, tech. analyst USES, 1942-43; pres. dir. Stonewall Cotton Mills, Miss., 1943-45; pers. & safety dir. Stedman Co., Beaumont, Tex., 1945-46; pub. rels. dir., sec. to Civil Svc. Commn., asst. to mayor City of Jackson, from 1947. Mem. exec. com. Community Svc. Coun.; gov. Jackson Community Chest, from 1958, Jackson Symphony Orch., from 1958; mem. fin. com. Jackson Opera Guild, from 1950. Recipient bronze medal Men's Garden Club Jackson, 1956. Mem. Garden Writers Assn. Am., Men's Garden Clubs Am. (pres. 1962), Jackson Pers. Execs. Assn., Jackson C. of C., Nat. Soc. Pub. Adminstrn., Gov. Pub. Rels. Assn., Pub. Rels. Assn. Miss., Am. Advt. Club, Miss. Advt. Club, Jackson Advt. Club, others. Baptist. *

HORSTMAN, HERMAN GERHARD, management and engineering consultant; b. Lafayette, Ind., Dec. 8, 1898; s. Bernhard and Anna K. (Kamping) H.; m. Mildred E. Smith, Nov. 5, 1925. BSChemE, Purdue U., 1920. Profl. engr., Ind. Cadet engr., dist. mgr. No. Ind. Gas & Electric Co., 1920-29; gas engr., asst. to v.p. Pub. Svc. Co. Ind., 1929-45, pers. dir., 1945-50; dir. sales-customer rels., asst. to pres. Tex. Gas Transmission Corp., Owensboro, Ky., 1950-55; v.p. Ind. Gas & Water Co., Indpls., 1955-57, pres., 1957-60, chmn. bd., 1960-63; mgmt. & engring. cons., from 1963. Sec. bd. dirs. Indpls. Sch. & Engring. Found. Mem. Am. Gas Assn., Ind. Gas Assn., Ind. Soc. Chgo., Indpls. C. of C., Newcomen Soc., Masons, Ulen Country Club, Scientech Club, Columbia Club. *

HORTON, LEONARD MEAD, banker; b. Glen Ridge, N.J., Nov. 30, 1906; s. John Marcus and Florence (Crane) H.; m. Gladys M. Wester, May 20, 1932; children: Nancy, William. BS, Lehigh U., 1928, LLD, 1965. With Nat. City Co., 1928-30; with Chem. Bank & Trust Co., 1930-49, asst. sec., 1941, asst. v.p., 1943, v.p., 1947-49; v.p., treas., dir. Aubrey G. Langston & Co., Inc., 1949-50, pres., 1959-63, chmn. bd., 1963-70; dir. Trustee Lehigh U., chmn. fin. com., 1946. Mem. Univ. Club, Bond Club (N.Y.C.), Baltusrol Golf Club, Ocean Club (Ocean Ridge, Fla.), Gulf Stream Golf Club (Delray Beach, Fla.), Beta Gamma Sigma, Alpha Chi Rho, Alpha Kappa Psi. Republican. Methodist. Home: Delray Beach Fla. Died 1989.

HORVATH, IAN, ballet consultant, dancer, choreographer; b. Cleve., June 3, 1946; s. Ernie W. and Helen Elizabeth (Nagy) H. Student, Sch. Performing Arts, N.Y.C., 1963. guest tchr. Nat. Assn. Regional Ballet, Am. Ballet Theatre; adj. prof. Cleve. State U., 1976; assoc. dir. Carlisle Project (nat. devel. program for choreographers); dance panelist NEA; cons. City Ctr. N.Y.; organizer Dancing for Life fund raiser, 1987. Appeared in summer stock in Musicarnival, 1962; dancer Broadway musicals Here's Love, 1963, Sweet Charity, 1966; appearances on Ed Sullivan Show, 1963, Dean Martin Show, 1966; soloist Joffrey Ballet, N.Y.C., 1964-66; dancer, Am. Ballet Theatre Corps de Ballet, 1967-69, soloist, 1969-74; founder, Cleve. Dance Center, 1974; founding artistic dir., Cleve. Ballet, 1976-84; cons., Cleve. Ballet, 1984-90; pres. bd. dirs. Dance/U.S.A., bd. dirs., from 1987; prod. dir. Jose Limon Dance Found. Recipient Ohio Dance award Assn. Ohio Dance Cos. Mem. Actors Equity Assn., AFTRA, Am. Guild Musical Artists, Screen Actors Guild, Am. Assn. Dance Cos. Democrat. Home: New York N.Y. Died Jan. 5, 1990.

HOSBACH, HOWARD DANIEL, publishing company executive; b. North Bergen, N.J., Mar. 9, 1931; s. Howard D. and Marjorie V. (Hoffer) H.; m. Eugenia Elizabeth Paracka, Apr. 10, 1954; children: Susan Hosbach Murray, Cynthia Hosbach Miezeiewski, Beth Ann Hosbach Lowry, Alyssa. BS, Fairleigh Dickinson U., 1953, MBA, 1967. Advt. mgr. McGraw-Hill Book Co., N.Y.C., 1958-62, dir. mktg., 1962-66, gen. mgr. dealer and library sales, 1966-69; group v.p. Standard & Poor's Corp., N.Y.C., 1970-73, exec. v.p., chief operating officer, 1973-80, pres., chief exec. officer, 1981-84, chmn., chief exec. officer, 1985-88; exec. v.p. ops. McGraw-Hill, Inc., N.Y.C., 1985-88; ptnr. Thermo-Roll Window Corp., L.I., N.Y., 1989-90; bd. dirs. Interlake Co., Chgo., Harbinger Corp., Teaneck, N.J. Trustee Fairleigh Dickinson U., Peirce Jr. Coll.; mem. Governing Bds. of Univs. and Colls., 1983-90. With AUS, 1953-55. Recipient Alumni medal for disting. service Fairleigh Dickinson U. Mem. Pinnacle Soc. of Fairleigh Dickinson U. Roman Catholic. Home: Allendale N.J. Died May 25, 1990; buried George Washington Cemetery, Paramus, N.J.

HOSKINS, LOWELL, agricultural products executive; b. Trinidad, Tex., Sept. 17, 1927; s. Will W. and Essie (Morgan) H.; m. Margaret Mitchell, Jan. 27, 1948; children—Bonnie, David, Melissa, Laurel, Jill. B.A., U. Tex., 1948. Vice pres. Mex. br., exec. v.p. Brazilian br., pres. Peruvian br. Anderson, Clayton & Co., Houston, Mex., Brazil, Peru, 1948-72; pres. P.V.O. Internat., San Francisco, 1972-73; pres. Arbor Acres Farm, Inc., Glastonbury, Conn., 1974-90, also dir.; bd. dirs. Booker PLC, London. Lodge: Rotary. Home: Glastonbury Conn. Died Dec. 30, 1990.

HOSTETTER, GENE HUBER, electrical engineering educator; b. Spokane, Wash., Sept. 14, 1939; s. John Huber and Virginia Lane (Yancey) H.; m. Donna Rae Patterson, Nov. 30, 1967; children—Colleen Rae, Kristen Lane. B.S.E.E., U. Wash., 1962, M.S., 1963; Ph.D., U. Calif.-Irvine, 1973. Dir. engring. Sta. KOL, Seattle, 1965-67; asst. prof. elec. engring. Calif. State U.-Long Beach, 1967-70, assoc. prof., 1970-75, prof., 1975-81, chmn. dept. elec. engring., 1975-81; prof. elec. engring. U. Calif.-Irvine, 1981, chmn. dept., 1983-85, acting dean engring., 1985-86. Author: Fundamentals of Network Analysis, 1980; Design of Feedback Control Systems, 1982; Engineering Network Analysis, 1984, Digital Control System Design, 1987. Recipient Outstanding Faculty award Calif. State U., 1975, 77, Engr. Faculty of Yr. award U. Calif.-Irvine, 1982. Fellow IEEE, Internat. Acad. Scis.; mem. AAAS, Am. Soc. Engring. Edn., Internat. Fedn. Automatic Control, Sigma Xi. Episcopalian. Home: Huntington Beach Calif. Deceased.

HOTCHKIS, PRESTON, insurance executive; b. L.A., June 19, 1893; s. Finlay Montgomery and Flora Cornelia (Preston) H.; m. Katharine Bixby, Dec. 11, 1923; children: Katharine, Joan, Preston Bixby, John Finlay. AB, U. Calif., Berkeley, 1916; postgrad., U. So. Calif., 1916-17; LLD, Pepperdine Coll., 1955, Whittier Coll., 1957. Bar: Calif. 1920. Asst. sec., later sec. Calif. Delta Farms, Inc., L.A., 1919-25; assoc. in founding Pacific Fin. Corp., 1920, Pacific Indemnity Co., 1926; organized Founder's Ins. Co., 1946; pres., dir. Coll. Shopping Ctr., Fred H. Bixby Ranch Co.; dir. Green Valley, Inc., Wimbleton Corp.; dir., also mem. constrn. com. Pacific Telephone & Telegraph Co.; dir. Consol. Lumber Co., Pacific Mut. Life Ins., Yosemite Park & Curry Co.; mem. adv. bd. Am. Mut. Fund, Inc. Councilman city of San Marino, 1940-55; U.S. rep. Econ. & Social Coun. UN, 1954-55; grad. mem. Bus. Coun.; mem. Hoover Commn. Task Force on Fed. Lending Agys.; mem. nat. adv. coun. Girl Scouts U.S.; mem. war fin. com. U.S. Treas. Dept. for Calif., 1942-45; del. Rep. Nat. Conv., Phila., 1940, Chgo., 1944, San Francisco, 1964; trustee Mills Coll., Good Hope Med. Found., S.W. Mus., U.S. Com. Dag Hammarskjold Found.; regent U. Calif., 1935-36. With USN, 1917-18. Mem. Calif. Bar Assn., L.A. Bar Assn., Calif. Alumni Assn. (pres. 1935-36), Calif. State C. of C. (pres. 1942-43), Calif. Club, Univ. Club, Valley Hunt Club, Bohemian Club, Pacific Union Club, Sigma Nu, Phi Delta Phi. Presbyterian. *

HOU, CHI MING, economics educator; b. Hopei, China, Dec. 3, 1924; s. H.T. and S.C. (Tien) H.; m. Irene Liu, June 20, 1953; children-Donald, William, Victor. LL.B., Fu Jen U., 1945; M.A., U. Oreg., 1949; Ph.D., Columbia, 1954. Faculty Colgate U., Hamilton, N.Y., 1956-91, Charles A. Dana prof. econs., 1968-91, chmn. dept., 1972-80, dir. Div. Social Svcs., 1980-84; research prof. Brookings Instn., 1965-66; research fellow Chinese econ. studies Harvard, 1959-62; Fulbright lectr. econs., Taiwan, 1970-71; vis. sr. rsch. fellow Chung-Hua Instn. for Econ. Rsch., Taipei, Taiwan, from 1981. Author: Foreign Investment and Economic Development in China 1840-1937, 1965; Contbr. articles profl. jours. Mem. Am. Econ. Assn., Assn. Asian Studies. Home: Hamilton N.Y. Died Aug. 22, 1991; buried Ferncliff Cemetery, Hartsdale, N.Y.

HOUCK, CALVIN BRYAN, advertising executive; b. Todd, N.C., Apr. 13, 1896; s. Sylvester Lee and Roxie Ann (Walker) H.; m. Margaret Moore McGuire, Aug. 22, 1922; children: William Bryan, Margaret Ann Griffin. AB, Duke U., 1922. Prof. grad study Columbia U., N.Y.C., 1924-25; prof. English High Point (N.C.) Coll., 1925-26; newspaper feature writer, trade paper editor, 1927-28; established Houck & Co., Inc., Roanoke, Va., 1928, served as chmn., treas. & dir. Trustee Duke U., from 1951. Sgt. U.S. Army, WWI. Mem. Duke Alumni Assn. (pres. 1950-51), Shenandoah Valley Club, Commonwealth Club, Rotary, Advertising Club. Presbyterian. *

HOUGH, ELDRED WILSON, petroleum engineering educator; b. Carrollton, Ill., Jan. 26, 1916; s. Thomas Crispin and Jennie (Eldred) H.; m. Jane Ruth Elder, Dec. 28, 1948; children—Christine E. Hough Smith, Phyllis J. Wheeler, Roger E., Carl E. B.S. in Engring. Physics, U. Ill., 1939; M.S. in Physics, Calif. Inst. Tech., 1941, Ph.D., 1943. Registered profl. engr., Calif., Tex., Maine. Research asst. Calif. Inst. Tech., Pasadena, 1941-46; sr. research fellow Calif. Inst. Tech., 1946-49; sr. research engr. Stanolind Oil & Gas Co., 1949-52; grad. prof. petroleum engring. U. Tex., Austin, 1952-61; cons. Humble Oil & Refining Co., 1954-61; prof., head dept. petroleum engring. Miss. State U., Mississippi State, 1961-65; asst. dean Sch. Tech. So. Ill. U., Carbondale, 1965-69; dean Coll. Engring. and Sci., U. Maine, Orono, 1969-74; prof. chem. engring. Coll. Engring. and Sci., U. Maine, 1975-76; prof. petroleum engring., chmn. dept. Coll. Petroleum and Minerals, Dhahran, Saudi Arabia, 1974-75; prof. petroleum engring. Miss. State U., 1976-82, also head dept.; owner E.W. Hough, mgmt. and engring., 1984-90; mem. Tex. Petroleum Research Commn., 1952-56. Contbr. articles to profl. jours. Grantee Am. Petroleum Inst., 1957-60, Am. Chem. Soc., 1960-63, NSF, 1961-65, NASA, 1963-65, U.S. Army C.E., 1966-69. Mem. Am. Soc. Engring. Edn., Am. Chem. Soc., Am. Inst. Chem. Engrs., AIME, Am. Petroleum Inst. (dist. v.p. 1963-65), Sigma Xi, Tau Beta Pi, Sigma Gamma Epsilon, Phi Eta Sigma, Phi Kappa Phi. Lodge: Lions. Home: Carrollton Ill. Died May 16, 1990; buried Carrollton, Ill.

HOUGHTON, ARTHUR AMORY, JR., glassworks company executive; b. Corning, N.Y., Dec. 12, 1906; s. Arthur Amory and Mabel (Hollister) H.; m. Nina Rodale, May 22, 1973; children by previous marriages: Sylvia Bigelow (Mrs. Richard G. Garrett), Arthur Amory III, Hollister Douglas (Mrs. William D. Haggard III). Student, St. Paul's Sch., Concord, N.H., 1920-25, Harvard U., 1925-29; recipient of 20 hon. degrees, 1950-71. With mfg. dept. Corning Glass Works, 1929, treas. dept., 1929-30, asst. to pres., 1930-32, v.p., 1935-42, dir., 1935-90; pres. Steuben Glass, N.Y.C., 1933-72; chmn. Steuben Glass, 1972-78; former dir. N.Y. Life Ins. Co., U.S. Steel Corp., U.S. Trust Co., Lackawanna R.R., Erie R.R.; v.p. Corning Mus. of Glass, Pierpont Morgan Library. Trustee N.Y. Pub. Library, Baltimore Mus. of Art, Boston Inst. Contemporary Art, St. John's Coll., Annapolis, Rockellefer Found; chmn. Am. Trust Brit. Library, Inst. Internat. Edn., Wye Inst., N.Y. Philharmonic Symphony, Met. Mus. of Art, Cooper Union, Parsons Sch. Design; overseer Harvard U.; hon. curator Keats Collection, Harvard U.; vice chmn. Ford Found. for Advancement of Edn.; pres. Shakespeare Soc. of Am., Keats Shelly Soc., English Speaking Union of U.S. Served from capt. to lt. col. USAAF, 1942-45. Decorated officer Legion Honor France; knight Order St. John of Jeruselem; comdr. l'Ordre des Arts et des Lettres (France); recipient Michael Friedsam medal in indsl. art; Gertrude Vanderbilt Whitney award Skowhegan Sch. Fellow Royal Coll. Art (sr.), Royal Soc. Arts; mem. Council Fgn. Relations. Episcopalian. Clubs: Century, Union, Harvard, Knickerbocker, Grolier (N.Y.C.), Odd Volumes (Boston), Philobiblon (Phila.). Home: Queenstown Md. Died Apr. 3., 1990; buried Old Wye Ch., Wye Mills, Md.

HOUGHTON, WOODSON PLYER, lawyer; b. Washington, Apr. 19, 1893; s. Harry Sherman and Alice Virginia (Ballentine) H.; m. Geta Triester, July 21, 1933. B.A., Washington and Lee U., 1915; LL.B., Georgetown U., 1918. Bar: D.C. bar 1918. Asst. sec. 2d Pan Am. Sci. Congress, 1916-17; practice in Washington; mem. firm Ellis, Houghton and Ellis, 1919-68, sr. partner, 1948-68; prof. law Nat. U. Law Sch., 1923-26; formerly mem. bd. Mut. Protection Fire Ins. Co., Norfolk and Washington Steamboat Co. Pres. Family Service Assn. (Asso. Charities); mem. bd. Family Welfare Assn. Am., Council Social Agys., Community Chest, D.C.; bd. govs. Nantucket Boys Club. Served as 1st lt. judge adv. gen. corps. U.S. Army., 1918-19; asst. port judge adv. Port Embarkation, Newport News. Va. Mem. Am., D.C. bar assns., DuPont Circle Citizens Assn., Sheridan-Kalorama Neighborhood Council, S.A.R., Barristers, Sigma Chi, Phi Delta Phi, Omicron Delta Kappa. Clubs: Nantucket Yacht, Sankaty Head Golf, Metropolitan, Chevy Chase, 1925 F Street (gov.), Pacific, Wharf Rat. Home: Washington D.C. Died June 4, 1990; Rock Creek Cemetery, Washington.

HOUSE, FRANK OWEN, legal educator, air force officer; b. Birmingham, Ala., Sept. 15, 1927; s. Frank Macon and Irene (Love) H.; m. Joan Marie Zierak, June 14, 1952 (dec.); 1 son, John Macon; m. Edna Earl McCarroll, July 6, 1984. J.D. cum laude, St. Louis U., 1957; LL.M., George Washington U., 1964. Bar: Mo. 1957, Ala. 1985, U.S. Ct. Mil. Appeals 1957, U.S. Supreme Ct. 1962. Commd. 2d lt. USAAF, 1946; advanced through grades to brig. gen. USAF, 1972; dep. dir. civil law USAF, Europe, 1957-60; spl. asst. and exec. to judge adv. gen. USAF, 1960-65; staff judge adv. Randolph AFB, Tex., 1966-68, Alaskan Air Command and Alaskan Command, 1968-70; dir. civil law USAF, Washington, 1970-73; judge adv. gen. Pacific Air Forces, 1973-76; assoc. prof. law Cumberland Sch. Law, Samford U. Decorated DSM, Legion of Merit with oak leaf cluster; Bronze Star; Commendation medal with 3 oak leaf clusters. Home: Birmingham Ala. Died Nov. 26, 1989; buried Elmwood Cemetery, Birmingham, Ala.

HOUSMAN, ARTHUR LLOYD, theater arts educator; b. Missoula, Mont., June 8, 1928; s. Robert Lloyd and Mary Chaddock (Webster) H.; m. Cathryn Elizabeth Puckett, Feb. 28, 1953 (div.); children: Donna Lynn, Mary Cathryn, Lisa Ann; m. Cigdem Fatma Selisik, May 1, 1974. Student, Wesleyan U., 1946-47; BA, Depauw U., 1950; MA, Iowa State U., 1951, PhD, 1956.

Mem. faculty State Coll., St. Cloud, Minn., 1956-62, prof., chmn. dept. speech and dramatic art, 1959-62; prof., chmn. theatre dept. Ohio State U., Columbus, 1968-71; prof., chmn. dept. dramatic art U. N.C., Chapel Hill, 1971-90. 1st lt. AUS, 1951-54. Specialist grantee Dept. State, 1965, 69. Mem. N.C. Theatre Conf., Nat. Theatre Conf., Am. Theatre Assn. Home: Chapel Hill N.C. Died Nov. 13, 1990. †

HOUSTON, DONALD L., government official; b. East St. Louis, Ill., Sept. 14, 1934; s. Walter Russell and Veronica Ann (Langhauser) H.; m. Joan Patricia Keck, Aug. 6, 1959; 1 child, Russell Walter. B.S., U. Ill., 1957, D.V.M., 1959. Diplomate Am. Coll. Vet. Preventive Medicine. Vet. med. officer meat and poultry inspection program Dept. Agr., St. Louis, 1961-65; staff ofcl. meat and poultry inspection program Dept. Agr., Washington, 1965-78, various positions, 1979-82, adminstr. food safety and inspection service, 1982-88. Served to capt. U.S. Army, 1959-61. Named Meritorious Exec., White House, 1978, Disting. Exec., White House, 1984. Mem. AVMA. Home: Arlington Va. Died 1988.

HOVET, THOMAS, JR., educator, political scientist; b. Helena, Mont., Feb. 4, 1923; s. Thomas and Elizabeth (Strauss) H.; m. Erica Steinleitner, Sept. 6, 1957; children—Lisa, Heather. B.A., U. Wash., 1948; M.A., N.Y. U., 1949; Ph.D., Victoria Univ. Coll., U. New Zealand, 1954. Employment interviewer Wash. Dept. Employment Security, 1949; dist. crew leader Census Bur., 1950; research asso. Internat. Studies Group, Brookings Instn., 1951-53; instr. govt. N.Y. U., 1953-54; asst. prof. govt. Miami U., Oxford, Ohio, 1954-56; mem. faculty N.Y. U., 1956-66; prof., 1962-66; prof. polit. sci. U. Oreg., Eugene, 1966-89, head dept., 1968-7O; cons. State Dept., 1966. Author: Legislative History and Subject Analysis-Documents of the United Nations Conference on International Organization, Vol. XXI, in English, 1956, Vol. XXII, in French, 1956, (with Waldo Chamberlin and Richard H. Swift) Chronology of the United Nations, 1959, Bloc Politics in the United Nations, 1960, (with Waldo Chamberlin) A Chronology and Fact Book of the United Nations, 1941-1961, 1961, (with others) A Guide to the Use of United Nations Documents, 1962, Africa in the United Nations, 1963, (with Waldo Chamberlin and Erica Hovet) Chronology and Fact Book of the United Nations, (1941-64, 1964), (with others) Primacy of Politics in Africa, 1966, (with Waldo Chamberlin and Erica Hovet) Chronology and Fact Book of the United Nations, 1941-69, 1970, (with David J. Finlay) 7304: International Relations on the Planet Earth, 1975, (with Waldo Chamberlin and Erica Hovet) Chronology and Fact Book of the United Nations, 1941-76, 1976, (with Erica Hovet), 1941-85; Editor: (with Waldo Chamberlin and Richard N. Swift) Annual Review of the United Nations, 1959, 1960. Vice pres. UN Assn. Oreg., 1968-79; v.p. Taraknath Das Found., 1957-78, mem. adv. com., from 1978; rep. ACLU to UN, 1962-66; Chmn. Lane County (Oreg.) Democratic Party, 1968-69; chmn. 4th Congl. Dist. Dem. Party Oreg., 1968; Bd. dirs. Internat. League Rights of Man, 1964-66. Served with AUS, 1942-46. Fulbright scholar, 1950-51; recipient Ersted award distinguished teaching U. Oreg., 1968, Burlington No. Found. award, 1988; Danforth Asso., 1964-66. Mem. Western Am., Internat. polit. sci. assns., Am., Indian socs. internat. law, Internat. Studies Assn., African Studies assn., Internat. Food and Agrl. Devel. (editor jour.). Home: Eugene Oreg. Died Mar. 28, 1989; cremated.

HOVGARD, CARL, oil company executive, publisher; b. Parsons, Kans., Oct. 1, 1905; s. Christopher and Gyda (Holm) H.; m. Marjorie Goodbout, June 19, 1989. A.B., Coll. Emporia, 1928; LL.D., Parsons U., 1940. Founder Research Inst. Am., N.Y.C., 1935, pres., 1935-67; ptnr. Nat. Law Press, N.Y.C., 1940-67; engaged in oil exploration and prodn., hdqrs. Abilene, Tex.; ptnr. Hovgard-Johnson Oil Co., Abilene, Tex., 1953-89; owner Worthree Mines (tungsten), Kingman, Ariz., 1953-60, Nevins Shipyard, City Island, N.Y., 1954-59; chmn. bd. Carefree Founders, Inc., 1971-74; pres. Hovgard Trust Co., 1972-78. Trustee Parsons Coll., 1948-64; pres. Hovgard Oil Trust, 1980-89. Republican. Methodist. Clubs: Union League (N.Y.C.) (past pres.), N.Y. Yacht (N.Y.C.), Wings (N.Y.C.); Am. Yacht (Rye, N.Y.) (commodore 1957-58); Cruising of Am; Royal Swedish Yacht (Stockholm); Royal Ocean Racing (London, Eng.); Royal Norwegian Yacht (Oslo); Royal Danish Yacht. Home: Carmel Calif. Died Sept. 1, 1989.

HOVING, WALTER, retail executive; b. Stockholm, Dec. 2, 1897; s. Johannes and Helga (Adamsen) H.; m. Mary Osgood Field, Nov. 4, 1924; children: Petrea Field, Thomas Pearsall; m. Pauline V. Rogers, Apr. 30, 1937; m. Jane P. Langley, Sept. 30, 1977. PhB, Brown U., 1920, PhD, 1976; LHD, L.I.U., 1966; LLD, Pratt Inst., 1966. With R.H. Macy and Co., N.Y.C., 1924-32, v.p., 1928-32; v.p. Montgomery Ward & Co., 1932-36, dir., 1934-36; pres. Lord & Taylor, N.Y.C., 1936-45, Hoving Corp., 1946-60, Bonwit Teller Inc., 1950-60; chmn. bd. Tiffany & Co., N.Y.C., 1955-89. Author: Your Career in Business, 1940, The Distribution Revolution, 1960. Chmn. organizing com. USO, pres., 1940, chmn. bd., 1941-48; chmn. bd. USO Camp Shows, 1941-48; pres. Salvation Army Assn., N.Y., 1939-60; chmn. drive Salvation Army Citizens Appeal, 1939; nat. chmn. United Negro Coll. Fund, 1944; chmn. N.Y.C. Anti-Sales Tax Com., 1943, 63; asst. campaign mgr. nat. Rep. Presdl. Campaign, 1944. With USNR, 1918-19. Decorated DSC, Legion of Honor (France), Order of Merit (Italy); recipient M. Greedman Gold medal N.Y. Archtl. League, 1967, award Am. Assembly Collegiate Bus. Schs., 1974; named Churchman of Yr. Religious Heritage Am., 1974. Mem. Commerce and Industry Assn. N.Y. (pres. 1948-50), 5th Ave. Assn. (pres. 1939-45, chmn. bd. 1946-52), Nat. Inst. Social Scis. (pres. 1953-56), Assn. Alumni Brown U. (pres. 1939-40), Masons, Cammarian Club, Racquet and Tennis Club, River Club, Brook Club, Delta Kappa Epsilon. Episcopalian. Home: New York N.Y. Died Nov. 27, 1989.

HOWARD, CHARLES BEECHER, lawyer; b. Redfield, S.D., Dec. 15, 1897; s. Charles T. and Eugenia (Beecher) H.; m. Dorothy Lundsten, Nov. 22, 1926; children: Charles O., Alice Bagwill, Karen Taylor. BA, Carleton Coll., 1922; LLB, U. Minn., 1925. Bar: Minn. 1925. Pvt. practice law Pipestone, Minn., 1925-28; practiced law Mpls., from 1928. Contbr. articles on mcpl. financing, probate law to profl. jours. Pres. Family & Children Svc., 1955-57. Mem. ABA, Minn. Bar Assn., Phi Beta Kappa, Delta Sigma Rho, Order of Coif. *

HOWARD, DONALD ROY, English language educator, author; b. St. Louis, Sept. 18, 1927; s. Albert and Emily (Johnson) H. A.B. summa cum laude, Tufts U., 1950; M.A., Rutgers U., 1951; Ph.D., U. Fla., 1954. Mem. faculty Ohio State U., 1955-63, U. Calif., Riverside, 1963-66, UCLA, 1966-67; prof. English Johns Hopkins U., Balt., 1967-77, Caroline Donovan prof. English, 1974-77; prof. English Stanford U., from 1977, Olive H. Palmer prof. in the humanities, from 1985. Author: The Three Temptations: Medieval Man in Search of the World, 1966, (with C.K. Zacher) Critical Studies of Sir Gawain and the Green Knight, 1968, (with James Dean) Chaucer, Canterbury Tales, A Selection, 1969, Chaucer, Troilus and Criseyde and Selected Short Poems, 1976, The Idea of the Canterbury Tales, 1976, (with M. W. Bloomfield, B.-G. Guyot, T. Kabealo) Incipits of Latin Works on the Virtues and Vices, 1979, Writers and Pilgrims: Medieval Pilgrimage Narratives and Their Posterity, 1980; also articles.; Mem. editorial bd.: Speculum, 1969-77, ELH (English Literary History), Chaucer Bibliographies; mem. adv. bd. PMLA, 1973-78, Essays.Chaucer: His Life, His Works, His World, 1987; (recipient, National Book Critics Circle Award for Biography, 1988). Served with USNR, 1945-46. Recipient Melville Cain award, 1977; Fulbright research fellow Italy, 1959-60; Am. Council Learned Socs. fellow, 1963-64; Guggenheim fellow, 1969-70, 84-85; NEH fellow, 1978-79. Mem. New Chaucer Soc. (trustee 1980-84), MLA (del. assembly 1970-74), Medieval Acad. (councillor 1969-73, fellow 1985), Internat. Assn. Univ. Profs. English, AAUP, Phi Beta Kappa. Home: Stanford Calif. Deceased.

HOWARD, JOHN ZOLLIE, editor; b. Gainesboro, Tenn., Dec. 20, 1897; s. John W. and Lizzie (Van Hooser) H.; m. Jessie Magill, Oct. 28, 1920; children: Joseph E., William Edwin. BA, U. Tenn., 1924. Instr. U. Tenn., 1924-25; reporter, Sunday editor, city editor Knoxville News-Sentinel, 1925-40; mng. editor Memphis Press-Scimitar, 1940-64, assoc. editor, editor editorial page, from 1964. Dir. Memphis Pub. Affairs Forum; treas. Goodfellows of Memphis, Inc. *

HOWELL, ROGER, JR., history and humanities educator; b. Balt., July 3, 1936; s. Roger and Katherine (Clifford) H.; children—Tracy Walker, Ian Christopher. A.B. summa cum laude, Bowdoin Coll., Brunswick, Maine, 1958; B.A. (Rhodes scholar), St. Johns Coll., Oxford (Eng.) U., 1960, M.A., D.Phil., 1964; LL.D., Nasson Coll., Colby Coll., 1970; L.H.D., U. Maine, 1971; Litt.D., Bowdoin Coll., 1978. Jr. instr. history Johns Hopkins U., 1960-61; research fellow, tutor final honour sch. modern history St. John's Coll., Oxford U., 1961-64, jr. dean arts of coll., 1962-64; tutor history and polit. theory Oxford U. Internat. Grad. Summer Sch., 1962-63, W.E.A. lectr. delegacy extramural studies, 1963-64; mem. faculty Bowdoin Coll., 1964-89, prof. history, 1968-86, chmn. dept., 1967-68, 82-85, William R. Kenan prof. humanities, 1986-89, acting dean coll., 1968-69, pres., 1969-78; vis. prof. U. Maine, 1968-69, mem. higher edn. planning commn., 1969-72; pres. WCBB (Colby-Bates-Bowdoin Ednl. Telecasting Corp.), 1969-71, 75-77; mem. internat. adv. com. Univ. Coll. at Buckingham, from 1974; chmn. Maine Savs. Bond Com., 1972-78. Author: Newcastle upon Tyne and the Puritan Revolution, 1967, Sir Philip Sidney: The Shepherd Knight, 1968, The Constitutional and Intellectual Origins of the English Revolution, 1975, Cromwell, 1977, Monopoly on the Tyne, 1978, Puritans and Radicals in North England, 1984, Maine in the Age of Discovery, 1988; also articles.; editor: Prescott: The Conquest of Mexico, Etc, 1966, British Studies Monitor, 1969-81; co-editor: Lit. and History, 1989—; corr. editor: Erasmus, 1976-81; editorial bd. Maine Hist. Soc. Quar., 1982-89. Bd. dirs. Allagash Group, 1970-73, Coast Heritage Trust, 1970-73; bd. govs. Inst. European Studies, 1974-77; trustee Waynflete Sch., Portland, Maine, 1969-78, Regional Meml. Hosp., Brunswick, 1970-78, North Yarmouth Acad., 1981-83, Campion Sch., Athens, from 1983. Recipient Outstanding Young Man of Year award Maine Jaycees, 1970, Outstanding Young Man of Year award New Eng. Jaycees, 1970. Fellow Royal Anthrop. Inst. Gt. Britain and Ireland, Royal Hist. Soc., Royal Soc. Arts; mem. Hist. Assn. Gt. Britain, Am. Hist. Assn., Past and Present Soc., Econ. History Soc., Soc. Antiquaries Newcastle, Stubbs Soc. (Oxford U.), Scottish History Soc., Soc. d'Etude du XVIIe siecle, Maine Hist. Soc. (adv. com. 1980-82, trustee 1982-89, pres. 1987-89, List and Index Soc. Gt. Britain (council 1980—), New Eng. Hist. Assn. (v.p. 1987-88, pres. 1988-89, exec. com. 1981-83, 87-89), Conf. Brit. Studies (exec. com. 1967-69, from 78), New Eng. Conf. Brit. Studies (exec. sec. 1967-69, hon. pres. 1969-70), Anglo-Am. Assos. (exec. com.), Renaissance Soc. Am., Am. Assn. Advt. Agys. Ednl. Found. (chmn. acad. adv. com. 1970-78, trustee 1970-78), Phi Beta Kappa. Clubs: St. Botolph (Boston); Hamilton Street (Balt.); Cumberland (Portland); United Univ. (London), Royal Commonwealth Soc. (London); London Scottish Rugby, Oxford Union; Century (N.Y.). Home: Brunswick Maine Died Sept. 27, 1989; buried Brunswick, Maine.

HOWELL, WILBUR SAMUEL, rhetoric educator; b. Wayne, N.Y., Apr. 22, 1904; s. Wood Augustus and Edna (Hanmer) H.; m. Charlotte Coombe, June 26, 1928 (dec. April 5, 1956); 1 child, Samuel Coombe; m. Cecilia Jonkman van Eerden, June 27, 1962 (dec. Apr. 1990). AB, Cornell U., 1924, MA, 1928, PhD, 1931; postgrad., U. Paris, 1928-29. Instr. public speaking Iowa State Coll., 1924-25, Washington U., 1925-27, Cornell U., 1929-30, Harvard U., 1930-33; asst. prof. Dartmouth Coll., 1933-34; asst. prof. Princeton U., 1934-40, assoc. prof., 1940-55, prof. rhetoric and oratory, 1955-72, emeritus, 1972, acting chmn. dept. English Summer Sch., 1947, clerk univ. faculty, 1958-68; sr. fellow Council Humanities, 1966; vis. prof. Stanford U., 1958, U. Mo., 1978. Author: The Rhetoric of Alcuin and Charlemagne, 1941, Problems and Styles of Communication, 1945, Fenelon's Dialogues on Eloquence, 1951, Logic and Rhetoric in England: 1500-1700, 1956, Eighteenth-Century British Logic and Rhetoric, 1971 (James A. Winans Book prize, Golden Anniversary Book prize Speech Communication Assn. 1972), Poetics, Rhetoric and Logic, 1975 (Golden Anniversary Book Prize 1976); editor: Jefferson's Parliamentary Writing, 1988; also articles and reviews profl. jours.; editor-in-chief Quar. Jour. Speech, 1954-56; assoc. editor Papers of Thomas Jefferson, 1973-88; contbr. to Quar. Jour. Speech, Speech Monographs, William and Mary Quar., Philosophy and Rhetoric, Ency. Brit. Foreman Mercer County (N.J.) Grand Jury, 1944; mem. Princeton Police Res., 1941-45; instr. A.S.T.P., 1943-45. Guggenheim fellow, 1948-49, 57-58, Huntington Library fellow, 1951-52, 62-63. Mem. MLA, AAUP, Speech Communication Assn. (Disting. Service award 1985), Renaissance Soc. Am., N.J. Edn. Assn. (parliamentarian 1938, 41), Phi Beta Kappa, Delta Sigma Rho, Pi Kappa Phi. Democrat. Episcopalian. Club: Nassau. Home: Princeton N.J. Died Apr. 20, 1992.

HOWLAND, RICHARD HENRY, marketing educator; b. Grand Rapids, Mich., Mar. 27, 1925; s. Henry James and Wilma (Rauser) H.; m. Marilyn Ruth Michaels, June 14, 1957; children: Carol Dawn, Michael Richard, Richard James, Mark Richard, Douglas Richard, John Richard. A.B., U. Mich., 1949; M.S., Simmons Coll., 1950; Ph.D., U. Mich., 1964. Distributive edn. tchr. and coordinator Grand Rapids, 1950-55; assoc. prof., head mktg. dept. Ferris State Coll., Big Rapids, Mich., 1955-64; prof. mktg. dept. No. Ill. U., DeKalb, from 1964, chmn. dept.; founder, pres. MAP Retail Computer Systems, Inc.; mem. adv. bd. Vector Corp. Co-author: Principles of Marketing, 1961; author: Salesmanship, 1972, Merchandising Analysis and Planning, 1979. Served with USAAF, World War II. Decorated Presdl. citation, Air medal with 6 oak leaf clusters; recipient award for teaching excellence Coll. Bus., No. Ill. U., 1977, 79, 80, 83, 85; George Washington medal for excellence in econ. edn. Freedoms Found. at Valley Forge, 1985, 86, Pres.'s award No. Ill. U. Found., 1988. Mem. World Inst. Profl. Selling (founder, pres.), Am. Inst. Merchandising (founder, pres.), Am., So., Southwestern mktg. assns., Sales-Mktg. Execs. Internat., Midwest Bus. Adminstrn. Assn., Mich. Pine Growers Assn., Delta Sigma Pi (Delta Sig educator-of-year award 1970), Beta Gamma Sigma, Pi Sigma Epsilon. Republican. Congregationalist. Club: Toastmasters (past pres. Grand Rapids). Home: De Kalb Ill. Died Nov. 17, 1990; buried Geneva, Ill.

HOWLETT, ROBERT GLASGOW, lawyer; b. Bay City, Mich., Nov. 10, 1906; s. Lewis Glasgow and Anne Lucile (Hurst) H.; m. Barbara Withey, Sept. 19, 1936; children: Eleanor Howlett Burton, Craig G., Douglas W. BS, Northwestern U., 1929, JD, 1932. Bar: Ill. 1932, N.Y. 1940, D.C. 1945, Mich. 1947, Tenn. 1947. Ptnr. Varnum Riddering Schmidt & Howlett, Grand Rapids, Mich., 1949-83; of counsel Varnum Riddering, Schmidt & Howlett, Grand Rapids, Mich., 1983-88; mem. Mich. Employment Relations Commn., 1963-76, chmn., 1964-76; chmn. Fed. Service Impasses Panel, 1976-78, 82-84, mem., from 1984; sec., bd. dirs. Light Metals Corp., Elston Richards Inc.; mem. Fgn. Service Impasse Disputes Panel, 1976-78, from 1981; industry mem. shipbldg. commn. Nat. War Labor Bd., 1943-45; spl. asst. atty. gen., dept. aero. State of Mich., 1957-61; vis. prof. Mich. State U., East Lansing, 1972, 75.

Contbr. articles to profl. jours. Chmn. Kent County Republican Com., 1956-61; del. Rep. Nat. Conv., 1960. Mem. ABA, Grand Rapids Bar Assn. (pres. 1962-63), State Bar Mich., Nat. Acad. Arbitrators, Indsl. Relations Research Assn. (pres. Detroit chpt. 1978-79), Soc. Profls. in Dispute Resolution (pres. 1974-75), Assn. Labor Relations Agys. (pres. 1977-78), Am. Arbitration Assn. (bd. dirs. from 1975, Disting. Service award 1982, Whitney North Seymour Sr. award 1984), Soc. Labor Relations Profls. (Disting. Service award 1988). Clubs: Kent Country, Peninsular (Grand Rapids). Home: Grand Rapids Mich. Died June 3, 1988; cremated.

HOYT, HENRY HAMILTON, pharmaceutical company executive; b. N.Y.C., June 28, 1895; s. Frank A. and Susan (Gardiner) H.; m. Anna Orcutt, June 1925; children—Henry Hamilton, Charles O., Suzanne K. Litt.B., Princeton U., 1917. Partner A.D. Strauss & Co., 1925-30; with Carter-Wallace, Inc. (formerly Carter Products, Inc.), N.Y.C., 1930-86, dir., 1930-86, chmn., until 1972, chmn. exec. com., until 1986; hon. dir. Bank of N.Y. Hon. trustee Hosp. Center at Orange, N.J. Served as capt., 2d Div. U.S. Army, 1917-19, AEF. Clubs: University (N.Y.C.); Union League (N.Y.C.); Baltusrol Golf (Springfield, N.J.); Oyster Harbors (Osterville, Mass.); Lyford Cay (Nassau, Bahamas). Home: Short Hills N.J. Died Nov. 5, 1990.

HOYT, ROBERT JOSEPH, pharmaceutical company executive; b. Utica, N.Y., Jan. 21, 1934; s. Joseph Andrew and Helen (Burns) H.; m. Joan Beverly Farrell, 1957; children—Michelle, Michael, Lisa, Robert. B.S. in Indsl. and Labor Relations, Cornell U., 1958. With Ross Labs., Columbus, Ohio, 1958-71; sr. v.p. Ross Labs., 1968-71; dir. comml. devel. Latin Am. Abbott Internat., 1971-75; dir. mktg. Searle Labs., 1975-76; pres. Bio Products, Inc., N.Y.C., 1976-78; pres., chief operating officer Ketchum & Co., Inc., Westport, Conn., 1978-86; mng. dir. Dameon Ptnrs., Inc., Georgetown, Conn., 1986-88. Served with AUS, 1954-56. Mem. Nat. Assn. Wholesale Druggists, Nat. Assn. Pharm. Mfrs., Pi Kappa Alpha. Roman Catholic. Clubs: University (N.Y.C.); Brooklawn Country (Fairfield, Conn.). Home: Westport Conn. Died Dec. 14, 1988; buried Greens Farms Cemetery, Westport, Conn.

HUBAY, CHARLES ALFRED, surgeon, educator; b. Chagrin Falls, Ohio, Jan. 23, 1918; s. Stephan and Mary Elizbaeth (Szitar) H.; m. Gladyce E. Jones, Sept. 8, 1945; children: Charles Alfred, William C., Thomas A. A.B., Adelbert Coll., 1940; M.D., Western Res. U., 1943. Diplomate: Am. Bd. Surgery. Intern Univ. Hosps., Cleve., 1943-44; resident Univ. Hosps., 1946-50; practice medicine, specializing in surgery Cleve., from 1950; prof. surgery Western Res. U., 1965-85, emeritus prof. surgery, from 1985, dir. gen. surgery, 1965-80; assoc. surgeon Highland View Hosp. Contbr. articles to profl. jours. Served with AUS, 1944-46, ETO. Mem. ACS, Am., Central surg. assns., Soc. Univ. Surgeons. Home: Chagrin Falls OH Deceased. †

HUBBARD, ELIZABETH WRIGHT, physician; b. N.Y.C., Feb. 18, 1896; d. Merle St. Croix and Louise (Wilson) Wright; m. Benjamin Alldritt Hubbard, Sept. 6, 1930; children: Theodore Chickering, Elizabeth Wright II, Merle St. Croix Wright. Grad. summa cum laude, Horace Mann Sch., 1912; student, Bryn Mawr Coll., 1913-14; AB, Barnard Coll., 1917; MD, Columbia U., 1921. Intern Bellevue Hosp., N.Y.C., 1921-23; postgrad. study Vienna, Geneva, Tubingen, 1923-24; pvt. practice medicine Boston, 1924-30, N.Y.C., from 1930. Pres. bd. dirs. Rudolf Steiner Sch., N.Y.C. Mem. Internat. Hahnemannian Assn., Am. Inst. Homeopathy, Alumnae Assn. Barnard Coll., Internat. Homeopathic League, Anthroposophical Soc. Am., others. *

HUBBARD, JOHN PERRY, physician, educator; b. Phila., Oct. 26, 1903; s. Russell Sturgis and Elizabeth Russell Perry H.; m. Dorothy Allen, June 30, 1933; children: Elizabeth Edgerton, Florence Allen Lloyd. AB, Harvard U., 1925, MD, 1931; MD hon. , Upsalla U., 1977; DSc hon. , Med. Coll. Ohio, 1978. Intern Children's Hosp., Boston, 1931-34; Rockefeller traveling fellow, 1934-35; staff physician medicine and pediatrics St. Luke's Hosp., Tokyo, 1935; Commonwealth rsch. fellow, 1936-37; instr. med. sch. Harvard U., 1937-42; assoc. physician Children's Hosp. Boston, pvt. practice, 1937-42; dir. study of child health svcs. Am. Acad. Pediatrics, 1945-49; George S. Pepper prof. pub. health and preventive medicine U. Pa. Sch. Medicine, 1950-66, emeritus prof., 1966-90; exec. dir. Nat. Bd. Med. Examiners, 1950-67, pres., dir., 1967-74, pres. emeritus, 1974-90; pres. Am. Bd. Med. Specialties, 1970-72. Author: Early Detection and Prevention of Disease; Multiple Choice Examination in Medicine; Measuring Medical Education. Maj. Med. Corps, AUS, 1942-45. Decorated Order of Danneborg Denmark ; recipient award merit Am. Heart Assn., 1966, Duncan Graham award Royal Coll. Physicians Surgeons, Can., Disting. Physician award Pa. Med. Soc., 1976. Master ACP; fellow APHA, Am. Acad. Pediatrics; mem. AMA, Am. Heart Assn. bd. dirs. 1960-63 , Heart Assn. Southeastern Pa. pres. 1959-60 , Soc. Pediatric Rsch., Am. Pediatric Soc., Soc. Med. Consultants World War II, Coll. Physicians Phila. pres. 1973-78 . Home: Gladwyne Pa. Died Nov. 27, 1990.

HUBBARD, THOMAS FOY, educator; b. Balt., Sept. 14, 1898; s. Thomas Matthew and Mary Ann (Plummer) H.; m. Rose Elizabeth Hicks, Nov. 26, 1924; children: Thomas Hicks, John Gardner, James Hugh. Student, Balt. Poly. Inst., 1916; BE, Johns Hopkins U., 1921. Instr. various schs. Balt., 1917-24; asst. supr. indsl. arts dept. Balt. City Sch., 1925; mem. faculty Johns Hopkins U., from 1925, prof. civil engring., 1947-64, prof. emeritus, from 1964. Author: Capital Improvement Program for Maryland (9 vols.), 1941-56, Long-Range Capital Improvement Program for Baltimore (5 vols.), 1947-55; also reports, manuals, articles. Trustee Peale Mus. Mem. Am. Soc. Civil Engrs., Am. Soc. Pub. Adminstrn., Am. Soc. Promotion Engring. Edn., Johns Hopkins Alumni Assn., others. *

HUBBELL, GEORGE LORING, JR., lawyer; b. Garden City, N.Y., Apr. 20, 1984; s. George Loring and Eliza (Platt) H.; m. Sophie Milbank Young, Oct. 20, 1917; children: George Loring III, Elizabeth Platt Hubbell Parsons, Barbara Hubbell Field, Susan Grice Hubbell Wohlers, William Mather, Sophie Milbank Hubbell Collens (dec.). BA, Williams Coll., 1915; LLB, Columbia U., 1919; LLD (hon.), Hofstra Coll., 1957, Adelphi U., 1964; LittD (hon.), C.W. Post Coll., L.I. U., 1959. Bar: N.Y. 1919. Practiced in N.Y.C., from 1919; ptnr. Hubbell & Van de Walle, N.Y.C., from 1961, Cullen & Dykman, Garden City, until 1990; bd. dirs. L.I. Trust Co., Garden City; counsel Ind. Village of Garden City, from 1921. Mem. Nassau County Charter Revision Commn., from 1961; mem. N.Y. State Bd. Regents, 1955-65. Maj. inf. U.S. Army, 1917-18. Mem. ABA, N.Y. State Bar Assn., Assn. Bar City N.Y., New York County Lawyers Assn, Bar Assn. Nassau County, Nat. Inst. Mcpl. Law Officers, St. Nicholas Soc., Downtown Assn. (N.Y.C.), Williams Club (N.Y.C.), Garden City Golf Club, Ft. Orange Club (Albany, N.Y.), Lawrence Beach Club (Atlantic Beach, N.Y.). Republican. Episcopalian. Home: Garden City N.Y. Died Sept. 27, 1990; buried Champlain, N.Y.

HUBBELL, THEODORE HUNTINGTON, entomology educator; b. Detroit, July 4, 1897; s. Clarence William and Winifred (Waters) H.; m. Grace Griffin, June 23, 1927; children: Roger Gaige, Mary Joan, Stephen Philip. AB, U. Mich., 1920, PhD, 1934; postgrad., Harvard U., 1922-23. Mem. faculty U. Fla., 1923-46, bcame prof. biology and geology; vice chmn., chmn. war tng. courses in geography, 1943-44; assoc. curator Mus. Zoology, U. Mich., Ann Arbor, 1934-46, curator insects, from 1946, dir. Mus., from 1956, prof. zoology, from 1946; mem. numerous sci. expdns., from 1923; bd. dirs. Orgn. for Tropical Studies, from 1964; mem. adv. panel on spl. facilities and biol. scis. NSF, from 1962. Author: (with J.S. Rogers) Man and the Biological World, 1942, rev., 1952; sects. on Orthoptera in Ency. Brit.; also articles. With Signal Corps, U.S. Army, 1918. Fellow AAAS, Entomol. Soc. Am.; mem. Mexican Soc. Natural History (corr.), Sigma Xi, Phi Sigma (hon.), Phi Kappa Phi. Home: Ann Arbor Mich. Died Sept. 22, 1989; buried Forest Hill Cemetery, Ann Arbor, Mich.

HUBBERT, MARION KING, geologist, geophysicist; b. San Saba, Tex., Oct. 5, 1903; s. William Bee and Cora Virginia (Lee) H.; m. Miriam Graddy Berry, Nov. 11, 1938. Student, Weatherford Coll., 1921-23; B.S., U. Chgo., 1926, M.S., 1928, Ph.D., 1937; D.Sc. (hon.), Syracuse U., 1972, Ind. State U., 1980. Asst. geologist Amerada Petroleum Corp., Tulsa, summer 1926, 27-28; teaching asst. geology U. Chgo., 1928-30; instr. geophysics Columbia U., 1930-40; geophysicist Ill. Geol. Survey, summers 1931-32, 35-37; assoc. geologist U.S. Geol. Survey, summer 1934; pvt. research, writing, 1940-41; sr. analyst Bd. Econ. Warfare, Washington, 1942-43; research geophysicist Shell Oil Co., Houston, 1943-45, assoc. dir. research, 1945-51, chief cons. gen. geology, 1951-55; cons. gen. geology Shell Devel. Co., Houston, 1956-64; vis. prof. geology and geophysics Stanford U., 1962-63, prof., 1963-68, prof. emeritus, 1968-89; vis. prof. geography Johns Hopkins U., spring 1968; regents prof. U. Calif. at Berkeley, spring 1973; mem. adv. bd. U. Calif. at Berkeley (Coll. Engring.), 1974-77; research geophysicist U.S. Geol. Survey, 1964-76; cons., from 1976; mem. U.S. delegation UN Sci. Conf. Conservation and Utilization Resources, Lake Success, N.Y., 1949; mem. com. geophysics Nat. Research Council; adviser Office Naval Research, 1949-51; mem. com. Disposal Radioactive Waste Products, 1955-63; mem. Adv. Selection Com. for Allowing Grants under Fulbright Act, 1950-51; vis. lectr. Calif. Inst. Tech., 1953; mem. vis. com. earth scis. Mass. Inst. Tech., 1958-60; mem. earth scis. adv. panel NSF, 1953-57, chmn., 1954-57; vis. lectr. Stanford U., 1955, M.I.T., 1959; regents lectr. UCLA, 1960; mem. vis. com. inst. geophysics and planetary scis. U. Calif., 1961; mem. com. natural resources Nat. Acad. Scis., 1961-62; chmn. div. earth scis. Nat. Acad. Scis.-NRC, 1963-65; nat. adv. bd. U. Nev. Desert Research Inst., 1967-73; mem. com. resources and man NRC, 1966-70. Author: Energy Resources, The Theory of Groundwater Motion and Related Papers, U.S. Energy Resources, A Review as of 1972; co-author: Energy for Ourselves and Our Posterity, Resources and Man, Structural Geology; Editor: Geophysics, 1947-49; assoc. editor: Jour. Geology, 1958-82, Bull. Am. Assn. Petroleum Geologists, 1955-74; Contbr. articles to profl. jours. Trustee, sec. Population Reference Bur., 1966-72; lectr. exec. seminars U.S. Civil Service, Office of Personnel Mgmt., 1971-84, USIA lectr., Europe, 1975, 77. Recipient Lucas medal AIME, 1971, hon. mem. 1978; Rockefeller Pub. Service award, 1977; William Smith medal Geol. Soc. London, 1978; Elliott Cresson medal for outstanding work in field of geology Franklin Inst., Phila., 1981; Vetlesen prize gold medal and cash award Columbia U., 1981. Mem. Am. Acad. Arts and Scis. (life), AAAS (life), Nat. Acad. Scis., Geol. Soc. Am. (Day medal 1954, Penrose medal 1973, council 1947-49, pres. 1962), Internat. Union Geol. Scis. (U.S. nat. com. 1961-64, com. on geosci. and man 1972-76); mem. Am. Assn. Petroleum Geologists (hon., Distinguished lectr. U.S. and Can. 1945, 52, 73-74), Am. Geophys. Union (life), Soc. Petroleum Engrs. (hon., Distinguished lectr. 1963-64), Soc. Exploration Geophysicists (hon.), Canadian Soc. Petroleum Geologists (hon.), 28th Interat. Geol. Congress (hon.), Sigma Xi, Gamma Alpha. Club: Cosmos (Washington). Home: Bethesda Md. Died Oct. 18, 1989.

HUBER, FRED DALE, insurance company executive; b. Ellsworth, Wis., Dec. 3, 1898; m. Helen Hollingsworth, July 3, 1929; 1 child, Fred D. Student, Wis. State Tchrs. Coll.; LLB, U. Wis., 1926. Bar: Wis. 1926. Pvt. practice law Milw., 1926-31; with Northwestern Nat. Casualty Co., Northwestern Nat. Ins. Co., from 1931, exec. v.p., from 1957, also dir. *

HUCKER, GEORGE JAMES, bacteriologist; b. Cascade, Iowa, Aug. 19, 1893; s. James Burleigh and Esther (Pangburn) H.; m. Alice Mackenzie, Sept. 4, 1917. BS, Lenox Coll., 1915; AM, Columbia U., 1916; PhD, Yale U., 1924; DHL (hon.), Hobart & Wm. Smith Colls. Instr. Allegheny Coll., 1916-17, asst. prof., 1917-18; spl. agt. U.S. Dept. Agr., 1918; asst. bacteriologist N.Y. State Agrl. Expt. Sta., 1919-22, assoc. rsch. bacteriologist, 1922-29, chief in rsch., from 1929; asst. prof. Cornell U., 1922-29, prof. bacteriology, from 1929. Cutler fellow Yale U., 1923. Mem. Inst. Food Technologists, Soc. Am. Bacteriologists, Am. Pub. Health Assn., Internat. Milk Sanitarians. Republican. Presbyterian. *

HUDSON, G(EORGE) DONALD, geography educator; b. Osaka, Japan, Apr. 26, 1897; s. George Gary and Delia Anne (Herndon) H.; m. Nellie Ruckelshausen, Mar. 20, 1926; children: Donald Gylum, James Wallace, Glenn Gary. Student, James Millikin U., 1917-18; PhB, U. Chgo., 1925, AM, 1926, PhD, 1933. Dir. middle sch. Am. Univ. Beirut, 1926-29; geographer TVA, 1934-39; prof. geography Northwestern U., 1939-51, chmn. dept. geography, 1945-51; prof. geography U. Wash., 1951-63; land planning cons. Nat. Resources Planning Bd., 1939-43. Geog. editor Ency. Britannica, from 1942. With USN, 1918-19. Fellow Am. Geog. Soc.; mem. Assn. Am. Geographers, Chgo. Geog. Soc., others. *

HUDSON, JACK WILLIAM, JR., biology educator; b. Denver, Oct. 30, 1926; s. Jack William and Louise (Hibbs) H.; m. Virginia Clare Petersen, Mar. 30, 1947; children: Christine Ann Hudson Schroeder, Connie Lou Hudson Harrington. Student, Stanford U., 1943-45; B.A., Occidental Coll., 1948, M.A., 1950; Ph.D., UCLA, 1960. Instr. El Camino Coll., 1950-55; instr. Occidental Coll., 1955-59; vis. asst. prof. UCLA, 1961-62; asst. prof. Rice U., 1962-65, assoc. prof., 1965-67; assoc. prof. Cornell U., Ithaca, N.Y., 1967-70; prof. Cornell U., 1971-78, chmn. dept. ecology and systematics, 1969-74; prof. biology U. Ala., Birmingham, from 1978; chmn. dept. U. Ala., 1978-81; program dir. NSF, 1974-75; cons. NSF; vis. prof. Sch. Zoology, U. New South Wales, Australia, 1974, 78; NIH cardiovascular trainee, 1959-60. Contbr. articles to profl. jours. Served with AUS, 1945-46. Danforth Tchr. grantee, 1957-58; NSF and NIH grantee, from 1963; Allied Chem. & Dye fellow, 1953-54. Mem. Am. Physiol. Soc., Alpha Kappa Lambda. Home: Birmingham Ala. Deceased. †

HUFNAGEL, CHARLES ANTHONY, surgeon; b. Louisville, Aug. 15, 1916; s. Charles John and Lucina (Kirst) H.; B.S., U. Notre Dame, 1937; M.D., Harvard U., 1941; D.Sc. (hon.), Georgetown U., 1966, N.J. Coll. Medicine and Dentistry, 1975; children—Katherine Lucina, Judith Ann. Dir. lab. surg. research Georgetown U. Med. Sch., Washington, 1950-59, prof. surg., chmn. dept. Georgetown U. Med. Center, 1969-79, prof. surgery emeritus, 1981-89; clin. prof. surgery George Washington U. Sch. Medicine, 1983-89; prof. surgery Uniformed Services U. Health Scis., 1985-89; cons. in cardiovascular surgery VA Hosp., Washington, Clin. Center NIH, Bethesda, Md., Sibley Hosp., Washington D.C. Gen. Hosp., Doctor's Hosp., Washington; cons. thoracic surgery Providence Hosp., Washington, No. Va. Doctors Hosp., Arlington; cons. in vascular surgery Prince Georges Hosp., Cheverly, Md.; cons. in surgery and thoracic surgery Children's Hosp., Washington; cons. in thoracic and cardiovascular surgery Arlington Hosp. Recipient Disting. Service award U.S. Jaycees, 1949; named Notre Dame Man of Year, Boston, 1949, 53; Disting. Service award Ind. Jaycees, 1949; Disting. Service medal Washington Cosmopolitan Club, 1954; Modern Medicine award, 1961; T. and S. Cummings Humanitarian award, 1965, 67, 71; Mendel medal Villanova U., 1965; Disting. Service award Am. Heart Assn., 1969; James F. Mitchell Internat. award for heart and vascular research, 1970; Clarence J. Shaffrey S.J.

medal, 1975; John H. Gibbon medal, 1975; Patrick Healy award Georgetown U. Alumni Assn., Benefactor's medal Ecuadorian Med. Soc.; named Humanitarian of Yr., D.C. Dental Soc., 1975. Diplomate Am. Bd. Surgery, Am. Bd. Thoracic Surgery, Pan Am. Med. Assn. Fellow ACS; hon. fellow Buffalo Surg. Soc.; mem. Am. Coll. Angiology, Am. Assn. Thoracic Surgery, Am. Heart Assn., Soc. Univ. Surgeons, Am. Surg. Assn., AAUP, AMA, So. Surg. Assn., Internat. Cardiovascular Soc., Am. Soc. Nephrology, Soc. Thoracic Surgeons, Soc. Vascular Surgery, AAAS, Am. Fedn. Clin. Research, Am. Coll. Chest Physicians, So. Med. Assn., N.Y. Acad. Scis., Soc. Artificial Internal Organs, Eastern Surg. Assn., Am. Coll. Cardiology (bd. govs.), Internat. Soc. Surgery, Allen O. Whipple Surg. Soc., Am. Med. Writers Assn., Royal Acad. Medicine (Spain), Southeastern Surg. Assn., Soc. Cryobiology, Med. Soc. D.C., Pan Pacific Surg. Assn., Washington Soc. Medicine and Surgery, Washington Acad. Surgery, D.C. Thoracic Soc., Smithsonian Soc. Assos., Sociedad Colombiana de Cirujanos, Sociedad Nacional de Cirugía de Cuba, Sociedad Brazilianos, Sociedad Neurológica de Colombia, Sociedad Antioqueña de Cardiología, Benemérita Sociedad Médico Quirúrgica del Guayas, Sociedad Peruana de Cardiología, Assn. Advancement of Med. Instrumentation (pres. 1976), Phi Beta Kappa, Sigma Xi, Alpha Omega Alpha. Mem. editorial bd. Am. Jour. Surgery, Chest, Am. Coll. Chest Physicians; assoc. editor Angiology. Inventor plastic heart valve; contbr. devel. of modern heart-lung machine. Died May 31, 1989. Home: Washington D.C.

HUGGINS, CHARLES EDWARD, surgeon, cryobiologist; b. Chgo., May 7, 1929; s. Charles Brenton and Margaret (Wellman) H.; m. Gareth Whittier; children from previous marriage: Elizabeth Ann, Margaret Ruth, Nancy Wellman, Charles Edward, Gordon Spencer. Ph.B., U. Chgo., 1947; M.D. cum laude, Harvard U., 1952. Diplomate: Am. Bd. Surgery, Am. Bd. Pathology (in immunohematology and blood banking). Surg. intern Mass. Gen. Hosp., 1952-53, surg. resident, 1953-60, asst. surgery, 1960-64, asst. surgeon, also asst. dir. blood bank and transfusion svc., 1964-67, clin. dir. blood bank and transfusion svc., 1968-73, chief surg. low temperature unit, 1969-90, vis. surgeon, 1968-90, dir. blood transfusion svc., 1973-90; instr., then clin. asso. surgery Harvard Med. Sch., 1960-63, 64-68, asst. prof. surgery, 1968-69, asso. prof. surgery, 1969-90. Bd. dirs. N.E. region ARC Blood Services, from 1980. Served to lt., USN, 1954-56, comdr. Res. Moseley Traveling fellow, 1958-59; clin. fellow Am. Cancer Soc., 1959-60. Fellow ACS; mem. Soc. Cryobiology (gov. 1965-66, 77-78, pres. 1968), Internat. Soc. Blood Transfusion, Soc. Univ. Surgeons, AMA, Soc. Internat. de Chirurgie, Mass. Med. Soc., Am. Assn. Blood Banks (dir. 1976-78), Alpha Omega Alpha. Home: Boston Mass. Died 1990. †

HUGGINS, NATHAN IRVIN, historian; b. Chgo., Jan. 14, 1927; s. Winston J. and Marie (Warsaw) H.; m. Brenda C. Smith, July 18, 1971. AB, U. Calif., Berkeley, 1954; MA, U. Calif., 1955; AM, Harvard U., 1959, PhD, 1962. Asst. profl Calif. State Coll., Long Beach, 1962-64, Lake Forest (Ill). Coll., 1964-66; from asst. to assoc. prof. U. Mass., Boston, 1966-70; prof. history Columbia U., N.Y.C., 1970-80; W.E.B. DuBois prof. history and Afro-Am. studies, dir. W.E.B. DuBois Inst. Harvard U., Cambridge, Mass., 1980-89; vis. prof. U. Calif., Berkeley, 1969-70; vis. prof. Am. civilization Heidelberg U., 1979; Fulbright-Hayes sr. lectr., 1974-75, Douglas Southall Freeman lectr. U. Richmond, 1986, Rayford Logan lectr. Howard U., 1987, Erasmus lectr. Leiden U., 1988, John Hope Franklin Disting. lectr. Adelphi U., 1989; juror NEH, Nat. Humanities Ctr. Author: Protestants Against Poverty, 1971, Harlem Renaissance, 1971, Black Odyssey, 1977, Slave and Citizen, The Life of Frederick Douglass, 1980; editor: Voices From Harlem Renaissance, 1976, W.E.B. DuBois Writings, 1986; co-editor; Key Issues of the Afro-American Experience, 1971; mem. editorial bd. Am. Hist. Rev., Jour. Ethnic History, Jour. Am. History, 1986-89, Am. Nat. Biography, 1986—. Commr. Mass. Tchr. Corps com., 1968-69; pres. Mus. Afro-Am. History, Boston, 1967-69; bd. advisors Children's TV Workshop, from 1970, Bradley Commn. on Teaching History, 1987-88, pres.'s panel on internat. exch. scholars, 1985-86; v.p. Howard Thurman Ednl. Trust, from 1968; trustee Radcliffe Coll., 1984-89, Edward Haskins Charity, 1987-89, Boston Atheneum, 1989; mem. coun. Smithsonian Instn.; bd. dirs. Am. Coun. Learned Socs., 1985-89, N.Y. Coun. for Humanities, Mass. Coun. for Humanities, Literary Classics of U.S. With AUS, 1945-46. Guggenheim fellow, 1971-72, Ford Found. travel-study fellow, 1971-72, Ctr. Advanced Studies in Behavioral Scis. fellow, 1979-80, Rockefeller Found. Humanities fellow, 1983-84. Fellow Am. Acad. Arts and Scis.; mem. Authors Guild, PEN, Am. Hist. Assn., Orgn. Am. Historians (exec. coun.), Assn. Study Negro Life, Am. Antiquarian Soc., Coun. Fgn. Rels., Harvard Club N.Y.C., Signet Club. Home: Cambridge Mass. Died Dec. 5, 1989.

HUGHES, JONATHAN ROBERTS TYSON, economist, educator; b. Wenatchee, Wash., Apr. 23, 1928; s. Benjamin Bartholomew and Rachel Estella (Ward) H.; m. Mary Gray Stilwell, Dec. 19, 1953; children: Benjamin, Margaret, Charis. BS, Utah State U., Logan, 1950; D. Phil., Oxford U., Eng., 1955. Economist Fed. Res. Bank N.Y., N.Y.C., 1955-56; asst. prof. Purdue U., West Lafayette, Ind., 1956-57; assoc. prof. Purdue U., West Lafayette, 1958-60, prof., 1960-66; vis. asst. prof. Columbia U., N.Y.C., 1957-58; prof. econs. Northwestern U., Evanston, Ill., 1966. Author: The Vital Few, 1966, Social Control in the Colonial Economy, 1976, The Governmental Habit, 1977, American Economic History, 1983. Rhodes scholar, 1952; Guggenheim fellow, 1962; Ford Faculty fellow, 1971; vis. fellow All Souls Coll. Oxford U., 1971. Mem. Econ. History Assn. (pres. 1980-81), Halifax Hist. Soc. Democrat. Club: Codrington. Home: Evanston Ill. Died May 30, 1992. †

HULSE, FRANK WILSON, airline executive; b. North Augusta, S.C., Sept. 12, 1912; s. Frank Wilson and Vivian (Chastaine) H.; m. Mary Jemison Cobb, Apr. 11, 1940; children: Mary Cobb (Mrs. Frank M. Young), Frank Wilson IV. B.S., Ga. Inst. Tech., 1934. Comml. pilot Augusta, Ga., 1927-34; asst. airport mgr. Augusta, 1934-35; sta. mgr. Delta Airlines, 1935-36; pres. So. Airways of Ga., 1936-43; founder, chmn. bd. So. Airways, Inc., Atlanta, 1943-77, So. Airways, Inc. (providing local airline service in Eastern U.S.), 1949-79; vice chmn. Republic Airlines, Inc., Mpls., 1979-92; past chmn. asso., local transport airlines; dir. Fuqua Industries, Asso. Distbrs.; Mem. Ala. Aviation Commn., 1939-40; mem. Chief Execs. Forum. Mem. bd. nominations Aviation Hall Fame. Decorated by Brit. Govt. for tng. RAF pilots, World War II. Mem. Birmingham C. of C., Am. Helicopter Soc., Ga. Tech. Nat. Alumni Assn. (trustee). Episcopalian. Clubs: Rotarian. (N.Y.C.), Wings (N.Y.C.); Aviation (Washington). Home: Birmingham Ala. DIed Sept. 3, 1992. †

HULT, MILTON, former dairy organization executive; b. Rockford, Ill., 1897; s. Carl Albert and Mary Louise (Danielson) H.; m. Ruth Hitzhusen Buckner, Feb. 16, 1948 (dec. Aug. 1963); m. Alice Marian Cooley, Oct. 5, 1968. BS, Knox Coll., 1919; MBA, Harvard U., 1921. Pres. Superior Dairy Co., Davenport, Iowa, 1921-36, Internat. Assn. Milk Dirs., Chgo., 1934-36; pres. Nat. Dairy Coun., Rosemont, Ill., 1936-68, pres. emeritus, 1968-90; cons. USDA, Internat. Exec. Svc. Corps; with Food and Nutrition Commn.; chmn., pres., bd. dirs. Dairy Soc. Internat., 1950-68; del. Internat. Dairy Congress, The Hague, The Netherlands, 1953, Rome, 1956, London, 1959; mem. food industry adv. com. Nutrition Found. Author articles and bulls. on dairy industry and govt.-industry rels. Trustee Knox Coll., 1934-40; mem. President's Coun. Phys. Fitness. Recipient Goodrich award for contbn. to Am. agr. N.Y. World's Fair, 1940, achievement award Knox Coll., 1956, Disting. Svc. award Am. Dairy Sci. Assn., 1968. Mem. Soc. Profl. Journalists, Lake Shore Club, Masons (32d degree), Shriners, Phi Gamma Delta, Delta Sigma Rho. Home: Chicago Ill. Died May 7, 1990; buried Scandinavian Cemetery, Rockford, Ill.

HUME, DAVID LANG, international trade consultant; b. Brookings, S.D., May 21, 1914; s. Albert Nash and Ruth (Thomson) H.; m. Selina Best, Oct. 11, 1942. B.S., S.D. State U., 1936, D.Agr. (hon.), 1977; M.S., N.D. State U., 1940. Adminstrv. asst. to dean agr. and to dir. agrl. expt. sta. N.D. State U., Fargo, 1940-41; with Q.M. Market Center System, U.S. Armed Forces, Chgo., 1945-52; v.p., partner Frank A. Donnelly Corp. (food wholesalers), Chgo., 1952-55; with USDA, Washington, 1955-77, asst. adminstr. Fgn. Agrl. Service, 1962-67; adminstr. Fgn. Agrl. Service U.S. Dept Agr., Washington, 1973-77; agrl. attache Am. embassy, London, 1968-72, Tokyo, 1972-73; internat. trade cons., from 1977; cons. to Nat. Dairy Promotion and Research Bd., chmn. export and mil. adv. com.;, 1984-89; prin. cons. Great Plains Symposium on World Agrl. Trade N.D. State U., Fargo, 1984-86, 89; founder Soc. Agrl. Cons. Internat. Served to maj. AUS, 1941-45. Recipient Superior Service award USDA, 1971; Disting. Alumnus award S.D. State U., 1973; Disting. Service award Am. Agrl. Editors Assn., 1974. Mem. Palmbrook Country Club (Sun City, Ariz.), Tokyo Club, Army Navy Country Club (Arlington, Va.), Alpha Gamma Rho. Home: Peoria Ariz. Deceased.

HUME, JAMES PICKRELL, lawyer; b. Washington, June 4, 1901; s. Thomas L. and Laura Gertrude (Cox) H.; m. Marion McFadden, Mar. 17, 1933; children: Andrew, Anthony, Alexander. Student chem. engring., George Washington U., 1921-22, LLB, 1926. Bar: D.C. 1926, Ill. 1927. Asst. examiner U.S. Patent Office, 1922-26; assoc. Wilkinson, Huxley, Byron & Knight, 1926-30, ptnr., 1930-47; ptnr. Wilkinson, Huxley, Byron & Hume, Chgo., 1947-56, Hume, Groen, Clement & Hume, Chgo., 1956-91; chmn. bd. Hume, Clement, Brinks, William, Olds & Cook Ltd.; mem. faculty Lawyers Inst., John Marshall Law Sch. Mem. citizens bd. U. Chgo.; mem. Chgo. Crime Commn.; chmn. bd. dirs. Aspen Valley Improvement Assn.; pres. bd. Latin Sch. Chgo.; mem. bd. Chgo. Coun. on Fgn. Rels.; bd. dirs. Music Assocs. of Aspen, Aspen Hist. Soc.; pres. Chgo. Hearing Soc. Fellow Am. Bar Found., Am. Coll. Trial Lawyers; mem. ABA (del., chmn. sect. on patent, trademark and copyright law), Chgo. Bar Found. (mem. bd.), Chgo. Orchestral Assn., Chgo. Bar Assn. (mem. bd. mgrs., chmn. patents and trademarks, Am. Patent Law Assn. (chmn. nat. coun. patent law assns., pres.), Chgo. Bar Assn. (pres.), Bar Assn. 7th Fed. Cir. (mem. libr. com., bd. dirs.), Internat. Patent and Trademark Assn. (exec. com.), U.S. Trademark Assn., Law Club, Wayfarers Club, Tavern Club, Cliff Dwellers, Univ. Club, Met. Club. Home: Chicago Ill. Died May 8, 1991.

HUMENIK, MICHAEL, automobile company executive; b. Garfield, N.J., Nov. 10, 1924; s. Michael and Rose (Biliy) H.; m. Audrey Svahra, Sept. 5, 1948; children: Gwen, Michael, Edward. BS, Alfred U., 1949; ScD in Ceramics, MIT, 1952. Rsch. asst. MIT, Cambridge, 1949-52; rsch. engr. Ford Motor Co., Dearborn, Mich., 1952-54, supr. ceramic and powder metallurgy, 1954-62, mgr. ceramics and glass rsch., 1962-69, asst. dir. mfg. rsch., 1969-75, dir. plastics and surface processing lab., 1975-76, dir. mfg. processes lab. rsch., 1976-84. With USAAF, 1943-45. Fellow Am. Ceramic Soc. (Ferro Enamels award 1952); mem. AIME, Am. Soc. Metals, Soc. Mfg. Engrs. (Progress award 1980). Home: Allen Park Mich. Died July 15, 1984; buried St. Hedwig Cemetery, Dearborn, Mich.

HUNDLEY, JOHN WALKER, foundation executive; b. Highstown, N.J., July 4, 1899; s. H. Rhodes and Mabel Parker (Lewis) H.; m. Eleanor Rothschild, Mar. 24, 1932; 1 child, Sally Lewis (Mrs. Robert Alan Bear). Student, Cornell U., 1917-18; Ph.B., Denison U., 1919. Asst. service dir. Oneida Truck Co., Green Bay, Wis., 1919-21; salesman No. Bond & Mortgage Co., Green Bay, 1921-22; baritone with Am. Opera Co., 1922-23; featured in 12 Broadway mus. prodns., 1924-34; gen. mgr., advt. mgr. Secrets of Smartness-Corr. Sch. Course for Women, 1935-38; network announcer, producer-writer, asst. dir. broadcasts-short wave dept. CBS Radio, 1938-48; charge day-time programming, mgr. network program services, mgr. client relations-network operations, mgr. sales devel. prodn. sales, editor program p CBS-TV, 1948-65; pres., cons., adv., services John Walker Hundley Enterprises, N.Y.C., 1965-66; exec. dir. Belle W. Baruch Found., N.Y.C., 1966-69; v.p. Found. Adv. Services, Inc., from 1970; cons. Catalyst for Environmental Quality mag. Trustee Actors Fund Am. Recipient citations Nat. Assn. Mental Health, 1952, NCCJ, 1951, Crusade for Freedom, 1950, Community Chest Am., 1950, Muscular Dystrophy Assn. Am., 1959-61; Denison U. Alumni citation, 1955. Mem. Beta Theta Pi, Phi Mu Alpha, Sinfonia. Clubs: Lambs, Players. Home: New York N.Y. Died Apr. 17, 1990.

HUNNINGHER, BENJAMIN, theatre history educator; b. Vlissingen, The Netherlands, Apr. 15, 1903; s. Christiaan and Aleda G.J. (ten Cate) H.; m. Anna M.L. Korthals van Schooten, Dec. 30, 1932; children: Louise Victoire Hunningher North, Joannes George Christiaan, Reinout Eduard. PhD, U. Utrecht, The Netherlands, 1931. Instr. Dutch lit. and history City Coll., Amsterdam, The Hague, The Netherlands, 1932; theater and fine arts critic, Amsterdam, 1935; govt. adviser, head theater dept. Ministry Edn. and Arts, The Hague, 1945-48; Queen Wilhelmina prof. Columbia U., N.Y.C., 1948-64; prof. history theatre arts U. Amsterdam, 1964-73; Erasmus lectr. Harvard U., Cambridge, Mass., 1975-76. Author: Life and Work of Dutch Dramatist, H.J. Schimmel, 1931, Theater and Education, 1946, Theater and Realism, 1947, Dutch Theater, 1940, 1949, Medieval Liturgy and the Theater, 1954, The Origin of the Theater, 1955, The Theater of Dionysus Eleuthereus, 1956, The Amsterdam Theater of 1637, 1959, The Idea in American Drama, 1963, The Mirror of Baroque Theatre, 1964, The Rise of Modern Theatre, 1984, Shakespeare and the Theater of His Time, 1987; contbr. articles to theatrical and art jours. Decorated comdr. Order of Crown (Belgium), knight Order of Netherlands Lion, comdr. Order of Orange Nassau (The Netherlands); fellow Rockefeller Found., 1946, Guggenheim Found., 1961. Died Nov. 21, 1991; cremated.

HUNT, JOHN E., congressman; b. Lambertville, N.J., Nov. 25, 1908; m. Doris R. Foster; 1 child, Deborah V. Brown. Student, Newark Bus. Sch.; grad., N.J. State Police Acad., FBI, Harvard Sch. Police Sci., U.S. Army Intelligence Sch. Mem. N.J. State Police, 1930-59; sheriff County of Gloucester, N.J., 1959-63; mem. N.J. Senate, 1963-67, 90th-93d Congresses from 1st N.J. dist.; bd. dirs. Gloucester County Fed. Savs. and Loan Assn. Past pres. Gloucester County United Fund; advisor Boys Ranch Hope, N.J. Major AUS, 1942-46, ETO. Decorated Bronze Star, Air medal with two oak leaf clusters, Purple Heart; recipient Voice of Democracy award Am. Legion, Humanitarian and Civic award, 1966, award Pitman Citizens Assn., 1966. Mem. Bapt. Mens Fellowship (past pres.), Gloucester County Firemens Assn., NRA, Harvard Assocs. in Police Sci., Nat. Sheriffs Assn., Parent-Tchrs. Congress N.J., Am. Legion, VFW, Bapt. Mens Fellowship, Masons, Rotary. Republican. Home: Pitman N.J. Died Sept. 22, 1989.

HUNT, J(OSEPH) MCVICKER, psychologist, educator; b. Scottsbluff, Nebr., Mar. 19, 1906; s. Robert Sanford and Carrie Pearl (McVicker, nee Loughborough) H.; m. Esther Dahms, Dec. 25, 1929 (dec. 1985); children: Judith Ann, Carol Jean. A.B., U. Nebr., 1929, A.M., 1930, D.Sc. (hon.), 1967; Ph.D., Cornell U., 1933; Sc.D. (hon.), Brown U., 1958, Ohio State U., 1984. Diplomate (clin.) Am. Bd. Profl. Psychology. Tng. and research, 1929-36; from instr. to asso. prof. Brown U., 1936-46; research cons. Inst. Welfare Research, Community Service Soc. N.Y., 1944-46, dir., 1946-51; lectr. Columbia Tchrs. Coll., 1948-50;

adj. prof. Grad. Sch., NYU, 1950-51; prof. psychology U. Ill., 1951-67, prof. psychology and edn., 1967-74, prof. emeritus, 1974-91; Benedict disting. vis. prof. Carleton Coll., spring, 1982; cons. VA Hosp., Danville, Ill., 1953-74; dir. Coordination Center, Nat. Lab. Early Childhood Edn., 1967-68, mem. adv. bd., 1968-70; chmn. White House Task Force Child Devel., 1966-67; lectr. Internat. Congress on Early Edn., Tokyo and Kyoto, Japan, 1978, hon. chmn., Tel Aviv, 1980. Editor: Personality and the Behavior Disorders (2 vols.), 1944, Jour. Abnormal and Social Psychology, 1950-55, Human Intelligence, 1972; Author: (with L.S. Kogan) Measuring Results in Social Casework: A Manual on Judging Movement, 1950, (with Blenkner and Kogan) Testing Results in Social Casework: A Field Test of the Movement Scale, 1950, (with Kogan and Bartelme) A Follow-Up Study of the Results of Social Casework, 1953, Intelligence and Experience, 1961, The Challenge of Incompetence and Poverty, 1969, (with I.C. Uzgiris) Assessment in Infancy: Ordinal Scales of Psychological Development, 1975; editor: (with N.S. Endler) Personality and the Behavioral Disorders, 2d edit., 1984; (with I.C. Uzqiris) Infant Performance and Experience: New Findings with the Ordinal Scales, 1987; contbr. articles and papers to profl. lit. Trustee Am. Psychol. Found., 1952-59, pres., 1953-54, 58-59; trustee Elizabeth McCormick Meml. Fund, 1954-61; trustee Rocky Ridge Music Center Found., 1963-91, pres., 1977-84. Recipient awards Am. Personnel and Guidance Assn., 1950, 60, Research Career award NIMH, 1962-74, Disting. Scholar award Hofstra Coll., 1973, citation significant contbns. Am. Montessori Soc., 1974; Heinz Werner Meml. lectr. Clark U., 1976; M.E.M. O'Neal lecture award in developmental pediatrics U. Nebr. Med. Center, 1977; Gold Medal award Am. Psychol. Found., 1979. Fellow AAAS (mem. council 1968-70), Am. Acad. Psychotherapists, Am. Psychol. Assn. (mem. council 1946-54, 68-71, dir. 1949-53, 70-73, pres. 1951-52, pres. div. personality and social psychology 1950-51, pres. div. clin. psychology 1968-69, Disting. Contbns. award div. clin. psychology 1973, G. Stanley Hall award div. developmental psychology 1976); mem. AAUP, Am. Statis. Assn., Eastern Psychol. Assn. (pres. 1947-48), Midwestern Psychol. Assn., Am. Sociol. Assn., Soc. for Research in Child Devel., Sigma Xi, Psi Chi, Phi Kappa Psi. Unitarian. Home: Urbana Ill. Died Jan. 9, 1991.

HUNTER, (JAMES) GRAHAM, cartoonist, caricaturist, watercolorist, writer, advertising producer; b. LaGrange, Ill., Feb. 2, 1901; s. William Clarence and Rebecca (Faul) H.; m. Cornelia Isabel Seward. Student, Landon Sch. Cartooning, Cleve., Art Inst., Chgo., Art Instrn. Schs., Mpls. Formerly with Assoc. Editors' Syndicate, Chgo., Pub. Ledger Syndicate, Phila., McClure Syndicate, N.Y.C. Creator Jolly Jingles strip, Chgo. Sunday Tribune and McClure Newspaper Syndicate, Bob Hope Golf Classic souvenir cartoon series, 1980—, Christmas Corners full-page watercolor feature for ann. Christmas book Augsburg. Pub. House, Mpls., 1982—, Hometown America cartoon series in Good Old Days mag., Motor Laffs, Biceps Brothers, Getting the Business, Motor mag., full page color illustrations Charisma mag.; cartoon series for Custom Comic Services; Sycamore Center cartoon feature, So. Agriculturalist and Farmer Stockman; Rhubarb Ridge cartoon feature, Curtis Pub. Co.; full-page bus. cartoons, full color covers Am. Bankers Assn.; Hometown Am., Only Yesterday, The Office Cat, Indsl. Press Service, hometown Am. cartoon series for good old days mag.; cartoon strip Am. Farm Bur. Fedn.; watercolor covers Our Sunday Visitor; religious book illustrations David C. Cook Pub. Co., Elgin, Ill., sch. bag art Acme Brief Case Co.; full color Christmas covers, Christian Life mag.; editorial cartoons NAM newspaper service; cartoon strip Bessie's Barnyard Banter, Milk Marketer, Strongsville, Ohio; ann. calendar art for Winthrop-Atkins, Middleboro, Mass.; safety cartoons N.J. Bell Co., Newark; editorial cartoons for Tobacco Inst., from 1977; indsl. cartoons for BASF Wyandotte Corp.; children's monthly cartoon feature in Marvel Comics, Electric Co. mag.; illustrations for Hoard's Dairyman mag., sales cartoons Chock Full O'Nuts Corp., also advt. cartoons and copy, mag. cover drawings, light verse, prose humor,; specialist detailed busyscene drawings, automotive cartoons, humorous animal art caricatures; Work has appeared in numerous nat. mags., newspapers, and advt.; represented in permanent FBI Cartoon Collection, Washington, Freedoms Found. Cartoon Collection, Valley Forge, Pa., Wayne State U. Cartoon Exhbn., Detroit, Peter Mayo Editorial Cartoon Collection, State Hist. Soc., Columbia, Mo.; author: Cartoon Humor in Advertising, Doin's in Sycamore Center, Art Instr. Schs. Lesson: Creating the Busy Scene Cartoon. Recipient Distinguished Service citation U.S. Treasury Dept., George Washington Honor medal Freedoms Found., 1959, 62, Honor cert. Editorial Cartoon award, 1960, 61, 75, 76. Presbyterian. Home: West Orange N.J. Died Mar. 30, 1988; buried Siloam Cemetery, Vineland, N.J.

HUNTER, JOHN, JR., financial institution executive; b. Kelty, Fifeshire, Scotland, Feb. 11, 1925; came to U.S., 1931; s. John and Mary E. (Wallace) H.; m. Sylvia J. Wightman, June 30, 1951; children: James D., Nancy J. Hunter Campi, Judith L. Hunter Daley, Linda C. BS cum laude, Ithaca Coll., 1949; MS in Edn., St. Bonaventure U., 1954; postgrad., NYU Mgmt. Inst., 1955, Alfred U., Am. Inst. Banking. Tchr., dir. athletics various schs., N.Y., 1955-60; with exec. tng. program, then asst. treas. Chase Manhattan Bank, N.Y.C., 1960-65; asst. sec., asst. v.p. then v.p. Lincoln Rochester (N.Y.) Trust Co., 1965-66; exec. v.p., pres. 1st Nat. Bank of Rochester, 1966-87; pres., chief exec. officer Vt. Fin. Services Corp. (parent co. Vt. Nat. Bank), Brattleboro, from 1983; frequent speaker on econs., bank mgmt., bus. devel. various Vt. agys.; mem. adv. council Vt. Small Bus. Adminstrn., from 1987; chmn. bd., v.p. Hunter Broadcasting, Inc., Burlington, Vt., Fed. Res. Bank of Boston, 1977-80. Former dir. Associated Industries, Vt., Small Bus. Investment Corp. Vt.; former mem. Gov.'s Council Econ. Advisors; past pres., bd. dirs. Small Bus. Devel. Ctr.; bd. dirs. Stratton Mountain Sch., 1987-88; past master ceremonies Brattleboro Winter Carnival, Miss Vt. Pageants; former auctioneer Ednl. TV Fund Raising Campaign; former chmn. United Way Windham County, Vt.Served to staff sgt. USMC, 1942-45, PTO. Decorated Air medal with 2 gold stars; named Man of Yr., Brattleboro Area C. of C., 1987. Mem. Am. Bankers Assn. (past dir., banking advisor, communications council, govt. relations council, from 1987), Vt. Bankers Assn. (past pres., govt. relations com. from 1987, outstanding community service banker 1987), Assn. Bank Holding Cos. (bd. dirs. from 1987). Republican. Home: Brattleboro Vt. Deceased. †

HURD, CARL BENTLY, hotel executive; b. Cleve., Sept. 20, 1919; s. Carl Bently and Esther Louise (Waldron) H.; children: Richard, Carl. Student, Cleve. Coll., Western Res. U., 1937-42. Resident mgr. Marriott Motor Hotel, Washington, 1956-58; gen. mgr. George Washington Motor Lodges, Willow Grove, Pa., 1958-60, 62-63; v.p. Am. Motor Inns, Roanoke, Va., 1964-77; gen. mgr. Ramada O'Hare Inn, Des Plaines, Ill., 1977-84, Comfort Inn-O'Hare, Des Plaines, 1986-89. Chmn. bd. trustees Second Ch. of Christ, Scientist, Balt., 1971-72, first reader, 1976-77. Recipient Mayor's citation City of Balt., 1977. Mem. Ill. Hotel Assn. (dir. 1960-61, 77-84), Greater Chgo. Hotel and Motel Assn. (dir.), Hotel Sales Mgmt. Assn., Am. Philatelic Assn. Democrat. Home: Cincinnati OH Deceased. †

HURD, CHARLES DEWITT, chemist; b. Utica, N.Y., May 7, 1897; s. Charles John and Susan Adrienne (Perlet) H.; m. Mary Ormsby Nelson, Aug. 29, 1921; 1 child, Richard Nelson. BS, Syracuse U., 1918, ScD (hon.), 1943; DuPont fellow, U. Minn., 1919-20; PhD, Princeton U., 1921. Asst. in lab. Thomas A. Edison, 1917; instr. in chemistry U. Ill., 1921-24; asst. prof. chemistry Northwestern U., Evanston, Ill., 1924-28, assoc. prof., 1928-33, prof., 1933-92, Morrison prof. of chemistry, 1949-51, Clare Hall rsch. prof., 1951-92; dir. several rsch. projects in organic chemistry; lectr. in field. Contbr. various articles to profl. jours.; mem. editorial bd. Jour. of Organic Chemistry, 1935-56. Served in Rsch. Div. Chem. Warfare Svc. U.S. Army, 1918, Nat. Def. Rsch. Com., 1940-45; com. on Med. Rsch. OSRD, 1945. Recipient Midwest award Am. Chem. Soc., 1958. Fellow AAAS; mem. Am. Chem. Soc. (chmn. Chgo. sect. 1938-39, mem. nomenclature com.), AAUP, Sigma Xi, Phi Lambda Upsilon, Pi Mu Epsilon, Gamma Alpha, Alpha Chi Sigma, Theta Alpha, Chemists' (Chgo.) Club, Chaos Club, Univ. (Evanston) Club, Ephraim (Wis.) Yacht Club. *

HURWITZ, HENRY, JR., physicist; b. N.Y.C., Dec. 25, 1918; s. Henry and Ruth (Sapinsky) H.; m. Jean Klein, 1944 (div.); 1 child, Barry I.; m. Alma Rosenbaum, Apr. 15,1951; children: Robin Elaine, Julia Lea, Wayne Mark. AB, Cornell U., 1938; MA, Harvard U., 1939, PhD, 1941. Rsch. assoc. Los Alamos (N.Mex.) Sci. Lab., 1944-46; rsch. assoc. Knolls Atomic Power Lab., GE, 1946-56, cons. physicist in charge advanced nuclear analysis, 1956, mgr. nucleonics and radiation sect. rsch. lab., 1957-68, mgr. theory and systems br. R & D Ctr., 1968-72, physicist corp. R & D, 1972-84, ret., 1984. Recipient Ernest Orlando Lawrence award AEC, 1961; Coolidge R & D fellow GE, 1975. Fellow AAAS, Am. Phys. Soc., Am. Nuclear Soc. (Glenn Seaborg medal for rsch. on peaceful uses of nuclear energy 1989, chmn. N.E. N.Y. sect. 1974-75), N.Y. Acad. Scis.; mem. IEEE (sr.), Phi Beta Kappa, Sigma Xi, Tau Beta Pi, Alpha Nu Sigma. Address: Schenectady N.Y. Died Apr. 14, 1992.

HURWITZ, LEO, film producer, director, educator; b. N.Y.C., June 23, 1909; s. Solomon and Eva Riva (Katcher) H.; m. Jane Dudley, 1935 (div. 1962); 1 child, Thomas Dudley; m. Peggy Lawson, 1964 (dec. 1971). BA summa cum laude, Harvard U., 1930. Ind. filmmaker, 1930-91; editor New Theatre Mag., N.Y.C., 1933-34; founder, v.p. Frontier Films, N.Y.C., 1936-42; writer, dir. OWI, N.Y.C., 1942-43, David O. Selznick, Culver City, Calif., 1943-44; producer, dir., founder, chief TV News CBS-TV, 1944-47; dir. film prodn. UN, N.Y.C., 1949-50; dir. TV prodn. Souvaine Co., N.Y.C., 1950-52; free-lance, 1952-60; dir. videotape trial of Adolf Eichmann Jerusalem, 1960-61; producer, dir. Nat. Ednl. TV, N.Y.C., 1964-67; pres. Leo Hurwitz Prodns., N.Y.C., 1967-91; artist-in-residence U. Iowa, Kirkland Coll., SUNY-Buffalo, 1974-79; prof. film, chmn., head Grad. Inst. Film and TV, Sch. Arts, NYU, 1969-74; lectr. Sarah Lawrence Coll., Am. Theatre Wing, New Sch for Social Research, Sch. Radio and TV Technique, NYU, Oberlin Coll., SUNY, Buffalo, William James Coll., 1979; advisor to Am. Film Inst., 1972—; speaker Internat. Fedn. Film Archives, Varna, Bulgaria, 1977; leader seminars on filmmaking Swedish Dramatic Inst., Stockholm, 1986-87, Film Acad., West Berlin, 1987. Producer films including Plow That Broke the Plains, 1936, Heart of Spain, 1937, Native Land, 1941, Strange Victory, 1947, The Museum and the Fury, 1956, Here At the Waters' Edge, 1961, Essay on Death, 1964, The Sun and Richard Lippold, 1965, In Search of Hart Crane, 1966, Discovery in a Landscape, 1968, This Island, 1970, Dialogue With a Woman Departed, 1980 (Choice award London Film Festival, 1980, Internat. Critics prize Berlin Film Festival, 1981, 3 1st prizes Figuera Da Foz, 1981, citation Festival Dei Populi, 1981); exhibited TV tapes of Eichmann trial at Jewish Mus., N.Y.C., 1986; scriptwriter (film series) In Search of John Brown. Recipient awards Am. TV Soc., 1944, 45, 46, Karlovy-Vary, Venice, Edinburgh, Turin Festivals, Montevideo Grand Prix, Acad. TV Arts and Scis., 1961, 62, also Peabody awards, 1962, Cine Golden Eagle awards, 1962, Homage at Cinematheque Francaise; grantee Ford Found., Nat. Endowment of Arts, N.Y. Council Humanities, N.Y. State Council for Arts. Mem. Screen Dirs. Internat. Guild (exec. bd.), Motion Picture Film Editors, Internat. Assn. Theatrical and Stage Employees, Dirs. Guild Am. (exec. bd.), AAUP, Film and Photo League, NYKino, Internat. Assn. Documentary Filmmakers, Phi Beta Kappa. Home: New York N.Y. Died Jan. 18, 1991. †

HUSAK, GUSTAV, president of Czechoslovakia; b. Bratislava, Czechoslovakia, Jan. 10, 1913; m. Viera H. (dec. 1977). LL.D., Law Faculty Comenius U., 1937, C.Sc., 1965. Jr. lawyer Bratislava, 1938-42; office worker, 1943-44, commr. Interior, 1944-45, commr. Transport and Tech., 1945-46, chmn. bd. commrs., 1946-50, commr. Agr., 1948; head cen. com. Communist Party of Slovakia, 1948, 1st sec., 1968-69, 1st chmn., from 1969; sci. worker Inst. State and Law, Slovak Acad. Scis., 1963-68; dep. premier Czechoslovakia, 1968; mem. cen. com. Communist Party Czechoslovakia, 1945, 49-51, 68, mem. presidium, 1945-50, 68, exec. com. presidium, 1968-69, mem. secretariat, from 1969, 1st sec., 1969-71, gen. sec., 1971-87; dep. to Ho. of Nations, Fed. Assembly, 1968-71, mem. presidium, 1969-75; mem. presidium, gen. com. Nat. Front, from 1971, chmn. cen. com., from 1971; comdr.-in-chief People's Militia, 1969, Armed Forces, from 1975; pres. Czechoslovak Socialist Republic, 1975-89. Author: On the Agricultural Problem in Slovakia, 1948; The Struggle for Tomorrow, 1948; Testimony on the Slovak National Rising, 1964; contbr. articles to mags., newspapers. Decorated Disting. Order Slovak Rising, Mil. Cross, Mil. medal for Services, Order of Lenin, (3), Hero of Czechoslovak Socialist Republic (3); recipient Karl Marx Gold medal USSR Acad. Scis., 1981, other awards. Home: Bratislava Czechoslovakia Died Nov. 18, 1991.

HUTCHINS, ROBERT SENGER, architect; b. Oakland, Calif., Dec. 13, 1907; s. Thomas Boyd and Alice Louise (Senger) H.; m. Evelyn Reed (Brooks), Oct. 12, 1934; children: Robert Ayer, Elizabeth O. Hutchins Bronnert. A.B., U. Calif., 1928; B.Arch., U. Pa., 1929, M.Arch., 1930. Lic. architect, N.Y. Apprentice Delano & Aldrich, N.Y.C., 1930-33; pvt. practice architecture N.Y.C., 1933-37, Moore & Hutchins Partnership, 1937-72; ptnr. Hutchins, Evans & Lefferts, 1972-85; Dir. bldg. services USO, 1942-46; mem. Commn. on Ch. Bldg., Diocese N.Y., 1965-70. Works include campus plans and numerous bldgs., Goucher Coll., Balt., N.Y., specializing, SUNY, Harpur Coll., Binghamton; St. Lawrence U., Canton, N.Y., S.I. Community Coll., N.Y., St. Timothy's Sch., Balt., Cazenovia (N.Y.) Coll., also numerous other schs., colls., univs., chs., U.S. Battle Monuments Commn. permanent mil. cemetery, Carthage, North Africa, U.S. Ambassador's Residence, Dakar, Senegal, Village Hall, Garden City, N.Y., Community Ch., Glen Rock, N.J., Grad. Sch. Bus., Columbia U., supervising architect, Vassar Coll., 1960-85.. Trustee St. Timothy's Sch., 1953-67, pres., 1956-60; trustee Mary I. Bassett Hosp., Cooperstown, Barnard Coll., 1955-76, Cathedral St. John the Divine, N.Y.C., 1964-70, St. Hilda's and St. Hugh's Sch., 1976-90; bd. dirs. Farmers Mus., Cooperstown; hon. trustee Met. Mus., N.Y.C., 1977-90. Winner Goucher Coll. competition, 1938, Village Hall competition Garden City, N.Y., 1950. Fellow AIA (pres. N.Y. chpt. 1954-56, chmn. edn. com. 1966-68, chancellor coll. fellows 1974-75); mem. N.Y. State Hist. Assn. (trustee), NAD (mem. council 1974-77, pres. 1977-89), Soc. Mayflower Descendants, Order St. John of Jerusalem. Episcopalian. Club: Century Assn. (N.Y.C.). Home: New York N.Y.

HUTCHINSON, DAME EDITH MARGARET EMILY See ASHCROFT, DAME PEGGY

HUTCHINSON, EDWARD PRINCE, demographer, educator, author; b. Auburn, Me., Jan. 3, 1906; s. Frederick William and Agnes (Prince) H.; m. Louise Forbes, Jan. 6, 1940 (dec. 1962); children: Joan, John. A.B., Bowdoin Coll., 1927, L.H.D., 1982; Ph.D., MIT, 1933; postdoctoral student, U. Stockholm, 1933-35, London Sch. Econs., 1935. Asst., instr. Harvard Sch. Pub. Health, 1929-32; fellow Social Sci. Research Council, 1933-35; instr. sociology Harvard U., 1935-40; sr. research technician Nat. Resources Planning Bd., Exec. Office of Pres., 1942-43; supr. research Immigration and Naturalization Service, 1943-45; asso. prof., then prof. sociology U. Pa., 1945-76, prof. emeritus, 1976-90; cons. Dept. Agr., Census Bur., UN, Dept. Justice, Dept. State. Author: (with K. A. Edin) Studies of Differential Fertility in Sweden, 1935, Guide to the Official Population Data and Vital Statistics of Sweden, 1943, Current Problems of Immigration Policy, 1949, Immigrants and Their Children, 1850-1950, 1956, The Population Debate, 1967, Legislative History of American Immigration Policy, 1981. Trustee emeritus Balch Inst. Ethnic Studies. Fellow Library of Congress, 1940; Guggenheim fellow, 1941-42, 56-57; Fulbright fellowship screening com. Com. Internat. Exchange of Persons, 1958-62; NSF fellowship panel Nat. Acad. Scis., 1959-65; vis. fellow Australian Nat. U., 1971-72. Mem. Am. Immigration and Citizenship Conf. (dir., chmn. research com.; editor Immigration Research Digest 1960-68), AAAS (sec. sect. social and econ. scis. 1936-44), Population Assn. Am. (past dir., treas., v.p.), Union Internationale pour l'Etude Scientifique de la Population, Phi Beta Kappa, Delta Upsilon. Home: Stafford Pa. Died Dec. 16, 1990; buried Radnor Friends Meeting, Pa.

HUTHMACHER, JACOB JOSEPH, history educator; b. Trenton, N.J., Nov. 1, 1929; s. Jacob John and Matilda (Goehrig) H.; m. Marilyn Anne Catana, June 22, 1957; 1 child, David James. BA, Rutgers U., 1951; MA, Harvard U., 1952, PhD, 1957. Instr. Ohio State U., Columbus, 1956-57; from instr. to assoc. prof. Georgetown U., Washington, 1957-66; prof. Rutgers U., New Brunswick, N.J., 1966-70; Richards prof. history U. Del., Newark, 1970-81. Author: Massachusetts People and Politics, 1919-1933, 1959, A Nation of Newcomers: Ethnic Minority Groups in American History, 1967, Senator Robert F. Wagner and the Rise of Urban Liberalism, 1968, The Truman Years, 1972. mem. Am. Hist. Assn., So. Hist. Assn., Orgn. Am. Historians, Historians Film Com., Phi Beta Kappa, Phi Alpha Theta. Home: Newark Del. Died Dec. 19, 1981, buried Trenton, N.J.

HUTTER, DONALD STEPHEN, editor; b. London, Dec. 30, 1932; s. Stefan Severin and Catherine (Hutter) Fraenkel; m. Martha Corbett, Aug. 17, 1957; children: Anne Victoria, Stephanie Grace, Sarah Catherine. B.A., Princeton U., 1954. Editor Charles Scribner's Sons, N.Y.C., 1957-67; sr. editor Dial Press, N.Y.C., 1967-69, editor in chief, 1969-72; exec. editor Holt, Rinehart & Winston, N.Y.C., 1972-81, editor in chief, 1981-82; v.p., sr. editor Simon & Schuster, 1982-85; editor Donald Hutter Books Henry Holt and Co., 1987-90. Author: Abraham, 1947, Upright Hilda, 1967; contbr. short stories to Best Am. Short Stories, 1965, also mags. including Esquire, Yale Rev. Served with F.A. AUS, 1955-57. Home: New Canaan Conn. Died Mar. 1, 1990.

HYDE, G(EORGE) OSMOND, government official; b. Downey, Idaho, Dec. 17, 1898; s. George Tilton and Emma (Nibley) H.; m. Lona Stratford, July 8, 1924; children: Marian S. (Mrs. Garn Anderson Brady), Lona Mae S. (Mrs. Vaughn Kent Lauritzen), Joanne S. (wife of Dr. Kenneth Latimer Kuttler), Edna Lou S. (Mrs. Donald Charles Harper-Smith), George Osmond, Adele S. Student, Brigham Young U., 1920; LLB, George Washington U., 1926. Bar: D.C. 1926, U.S. Ct. Appeals (D.C. cir.), U.S. Supreme Ct., Idaho. Missionary LDS Ch., Gt. Britain, 1921-23; elevator condr. Ho. of Reps. Bldg., Washington, 1923; law clk. then atty. Office Alien Property Custodian, Washington, 1923-29; atty. Office Alien Property Custodian, 1929-33; sr. atty., ehtn prin. atty. Solicitor's Office, USDA, Washington, 1934-44; spl. asst. to U.S. Atty. Gen., trial atty. war frauds sect. criminal div. Dept. Justice, 1944-45, 45-57; assoc. pros. for U.S., mem. internat. pros. sect., major Japanese war criminals Supreme Command Allied Powers, Tokyo, 1945-46; chief counsel spl. com. to investigate food shortages U.S. Ho. of Reps., 1945; cons. to market adminstr. N.Y. Met. Milk Mktg. Area, 1947-53; hearing examiner USDA, Washington, 1953-56, chief hearing examiner, from 1956. Sgt. Q.M.C., U.S. Army, 1918-19, AEF in France. *

HYDE-WHITE, WILFRID, actor; b. Gloucestershire, Eng., May 12, 1903; s. William Edward and Ethel Adelaide (Drought) Hyde-W.; m. Blanche Aitken, 1925; m. Ethel Koreman, 1957; children—Michael, Alexander Punch, Juliet. Diploma, Marlborough Coll., Wiltshire. Actor in plays and films, Eng. and U.S., 1922-91; stage appearances include Beggar on Horseback, 1925, Rise Above It, It Depends What You Mean, Caesar and Cleopatra, Affairs of State, Hippo Dancing, The Reluctant Debutants, Not in the Book, Miss Pell is Missing, The Doctor's Dilemma, Lady Windermere's Fan, Meeting at Night, The Jockey Club Stakes, The Pleasure of His Company, Rolls Hyphen Royce, others; film appearances include Rembrandt (debut), Gaily, Gaily, Tarzan, the Ape Man, 1981, The Cat and the Canary, 1982, The Toy, 1982; also numerous others including My Fair Lady, The Third Man, Mr. Denning Drives North, Ten Little Indians; TV appearances include series The Associates, 1979; series Buck Rogers in the 25th Century, miniseries The Rebels; numerous TV movies latest including Damien: The Leper Priest, 1980, The Letter, 1982. Home: Woodland Hills Calif. Died May 6, 1991.

HYER, FRANK PERRY, engineer, utility executive; b. Rhinelander, Wis., Sept. 22, 1897; s. Frank S. and Hattie A. (Broche) H.; m. Lorena Bergquist, Sept. 15, 1930; children: Frank S., Jayne Allerton (Mrs. Wilbert T. Davidson Jr.). BS, U. Wis., 1923. Registered profl. engr., Pa. Cadet course West Penn Power Co., Pitts., 1923, asst. to gen. supt., 1924; staff engr. A. C. Nielson Co., Chgo., 1925-27; asst. gen. mgr. Wis. Hydro Electric Co., Amery, 1928-33; asst. chief rates and rsch. dept. Wis. Pub. Svc. Commn., Madison, 1934-40; cons. power br. TVA, 1939-43; ops. and engring. cons. Gen. Pub. Utilities Corp. and predecessor firms, N.Y.C., 1841-48; with Del. Power & Light Co., Wilmington, from 1948, v.p. ops. engring. and constrn., 1953-59, pres., from 1959, dir., and of subsidieries, from 1958, chmn., CEO, from 1960; bd. dirs. Bank of Del., Atomic Power Devel. Assocs., Inc., Power Reactor Devel. Co., High Temperature Reactor Devel. Assocs., Inc. Active Delmarva coun. Boy Scouts Am.; bd. dirs. mem. exec. com. United Community Fund, Greater Wilmington Devel. Coun., Inc.; vice chmn. State Bd. Registration for Profl. Engrs. and Land Surveyors. 1st lt. inf. U.S. Army, 1916-19, AEF in France. Mem. N.A.M., Del. Soc. Profl. Engrs. (pres. 1958-59), Del. C. of C. (legis. com. 1957), Univ. Club, Whist Club, Newark Country Club, Waupapa Club, Kiwanis, Eta Kappa Nu, Zeta Psi. *

HYLAND, LAWRENCE AVISON, aerospace transportation executive; b. Nova Scotia, Canada, Aug. 26, 1897; s. George F. and Harriette (Balcom) H.; m. Muriel Evans, May 7, 1943. DEng (hon.), Lawrence Inst. Tech., 1954. Asst. radio engr. Naval Rsch. Lab., Bellevue, D.C., 1926-32; v.p. Radio Rsch. Co., Washington, 1932-37; with Bendix Aviation Corp., 1937-54; chmn. exec. com. Hughes Aircraft Co., Culver City, Calif., 1954-89; cons. Pres.'s Sci. Adv. Commn.; cons. and mem. several adv. coms. to Dept. Def. Sgt. U.S. Army, 1917-19, USN, 1920-26. Recipient medal for distinctive pub. svc. USN, 1950, Robert J. Collier award NASA, 1968, Gold medal Armed Forces Communications and Electronics Assn., 1968, Howard Hughes Meml. award. Fellow IEEE (Pioneer award 1957, Founder's Gold medal 1974); mem. Sci. Rsch. Soc. Am., Am. Nuclear Soc., Cosmos Club, L.A. Country Club. Home: Lancaster Calif. Died Nov. 24, 1989.

HYLAND, ROBERT FRANCIS, JR., broadcasting executive; b. St. Louis; s. Robert Francis and Genevieve (Burks) H.; m. Martha A. Claiborne (dec.); m. Patricia Sowle; children: Robert Francis III, William Claiborne, Matthew, Mary Genevieve. AB, St. Louis U.; LLD (hon.), Lindenwood Colls. Regional v.p. CBS Radio; gen. mgr. Sta. KMOX and KHTR/FM, St. Louis, 1973-92; dir. Centerre Bancorp., St. Louis Nat. Baseball Club, Inc., Wetterau, Inc. Chmn. bd. Lindenwood Colls.; pres. St. Louis Zool. Commn., Civic Progress, Mo. Commn. on Retirement, Removal and Discipline of Judges, 1971-92; bd. dirs. Downtown St. Louis, Inc., chmn., 1980; chmn. bd. St. Anthony's Med. Ctr., St. Louis; past chmn. Regional Commerce and Growth Assn.; trustee St. Louis County Hist. Soc.; bd. dirs. CORO Found.; pres. St. Louis Sports Hall of Fame. Ensign USN, 1942-44. Decorated magistral knight Sovereign Mil. Order Malta, Vatican; recipient numerous awards including St. Louis award, 1975, Honor award U. Mo., 1975, Abe Lincoln award So. Bapt. Radio-TV Commn., 1976, Silver Beaver award Boy Scouts Am., 1976, Brotherhood Through Sports award B'nai B'rith, 1973, Community Svc. award Negro History Week, 1972, Churchman of Yr. award Religious Heritage Am., 1980; named Outstanding Young Man St. Louis C. of C., 1955, to 10th Ann. Class of Mo. Acad. Squires, 1969. Mem. NAACP (life), Advt. Club Greater St. Louis (pres. 1962), Broadcast Pioneers, Cath. Actors Guild, Internat. Radio and TV Soc., Journalism Found. Met. St. Louis (hon. exec. com. 1973), Mo. Broadcasters Assn. (pres. 1962-63), Nat. Assn. Broadcasters (co-chmn. Mo. legis. liaison com.), N.Am. Adv. for Vatican Radio, St. Louis Ednl. TV Commn., Unda-USA (Gabriel Personal Achievement award 1973), Variety Club St. Louis, Am. Mgmt. Assn., Am. Acad. Polit. Sci., Internat. Soc. Semantics, Bellerive Country Club, Bogey Golf Club, Log Cabin Club, Media Club (founder, pres.), Mo. Athletic Club, Noonday Club, Racquet Club, St. Louis Club, St. Louis Stadium Club (founder, pres.), Univ. Club (hon. life). Roman Catholic. Home: Saint Louis Mo. Died Mar. 5, 1992.

HYMOFF, EDWARD, editor, author, news broadcasting and publishing company executive, corporate and university public affairs officer; b. Boston, Oct. 12, 1924; s. Gustave and Gertrude E. (Kravetsky) H.; divorced; children: Jennifer, Yves K. BS in Journalism, Boston U., 1949; MA, Columbia U., 1950. Reporter, city desk asst. N.Y. World Telegram and Sun, 1951; bur. chief, sr. war corr. Internat. News Svc., Korea and Indochina, 1951-54; news editor, mgr. NBC News, N.Y.C., 1954-58; spl. corr. CBS News, USSR and Eastern Europe, 1958-59; dir. news and pub. affairs radio sta. WMGM, N.Y.C., 1959; aero. sci. tech. and pub. affairs/pub. policy accounts rep. Carl Byoir & Assos., N.Y.C., 1959-63; mng. dir. Vietnam Mil. Histories Pub. Co., Atlantic Highlands, N.J., Hong Kong, Vietnam, 1966-69; assoc. editor THINK, IBM Corp., Armonk, N.Y., 1969-71; exec. editor NBC-TV News, 1974-75; dir. communications/pub. affairs Corp. for Pub. Broadcasting, Washington, 1977-80; mgr. editorial services Arthur D. Little, Inc., Cambridge, Mass., 1981-86; v.p. corp. comm. and mktg. Nat. Security Inst., Westborough, Mass., 1986-92; assoc. adminstr. external affairs Internat. Space U., Boston, 1988-89; bd. dirs. Universal Satellite Corp., 1981-92; trustee Inst. Conflict Mgmt., 1983-89; cons. USIA, 1957-58, Dept. Def., 1964-66, LWV Edn. Fund for Presdl. debates, TV producer Nat. Sci. Bd., NSF, 1980; TV documentaries and pub. affairs producer Nat. Ednl. TV Network, 1964-66; pub. relations cons. aerospace industries, 1963-66. Author: (with Martin Caidin) The Mission, 1964; author: The Kennedy Courage, 1965, International Troubleshooter for Peace, 1965, Guidance and Control of Spacecraft, 1966, 1st Marine Division in Vietnam, 1967, 1st Air Cavalry Division in Vietnam, 1967, 1st Marine Aircraft Wing in Vietnam, 1968, 4th Infantry Division in Vietnam, 1968, The OSS in World War II, 1972, rev. edit. 1986; (with Bill Cantor) Fire: Prevention, Protection, Escape, 1984; author over 1000 mag. articles. Served with AUS, OSS,World War II. Recipient Non-Fiction Writing award Aviation/Space Writers Assn., 1965, 78, Distinguished Alumni Achievement award for journalism Boston U., 1966, Apollo Achievement award NASA, 1971. Mem. Internat. Inst. Strategic Studies, Co. Mil. Historians, Authors Guild, Writers Guild Am. East, Am. Soc. Journalists and Authors, Aviation/Space Writers Assn., Radio-TV News Dirs. Assn., Vets. of the OSS (asst. sec. 1978-81, mem. exec. com. 1981-92), Soc. Profl. Journalists, Overseas Press Club, Nat. Press Club. Home: Belmont Mass. Died July 8, 1992. †

HYNNING, CLIFFORD J(AMES), lawyer, legal historian; b. Chgo., July 7, 1913; s. Peter Olav and Kirsti Knutsdatter (Raugstad) H.; 1 dau., Carol Hynning Smith. A.B. in Sociology, U. Chgo., 1934, Ph.D. in Polit. Sci., 1938; J.D., Kent Law Sch., 1934. Bar: Ill. 1934, D.C 1952. Corp. tax analyst Temporary Nat. Econ. Com., 1938-40; fin. analyst, enforcement atty. Office Price Adminstrn., 1941-43; prin. atty. internat. fin. Dept. Treasury, Washington, 1943-54; assigned as expert, in charge fin. interrogations leading Nazis War Dept., SHAEF and U.S. Control Council, Germany, 1945; planner for Marshall Plan and NATO aid, 1948-54; treasury del. to secure exemptions from taxes for U.S. Mil. from NATO countries and Japan, 1952; individual practice law Washington, from 1954; sec.-treas. Dean Acheson Com. to Maintain a Prudent Def. Policy, 1968-69. Author: State Conservation of Resources, 1938, Taxation of Corporate Enterprise, 1941, Selected Financial Laws, Decrees and Regulations of Germany, 5 vols, 1945; founding editor in chief: ABA quar. Internat. Lawyer, 1965-68; contbr. articles to profl. jours. Mem. ABA (del. to sec. of state's com. on pvt. internat. law 1965-69), Am. Law Inst., Phi Beta Kappa. Clubs: Cosmos, University. Home: Clifton Va. Died Aug. 14, 1990; buried Meml. Park, Falls Ch. Va.

IGLESKI, THOMAS ROBERT, lawyer, insurance company executive; b. Chgo., June 16, 1934; s. William E. and Wanda M. I.; m. Arline Skowronski, Nov. 10, 1962; children: Mark, Laura. B.B.A., U. Notre Dame, 1955; J.D., De Paul U., 1962. Bar: Ill. 1962, U.S. Supreme Ct. 1968. Atty. CNA Ins. Cos., Chgo., 1962-68; corp. sec., asst. gen. counsel CNA Ins. Cos., 1972-92, v.p., 1977-92; corp. counsel CNA Fin. Corp. subs. CNA Ins. Cos., Chgo., 1968-72. Served with U.S. Army, 1956-58. Mem. Am., Ill., Chgo. bar assns., Am. Soc. Corp. Secs. Clubs: Calumet Country, Union League. Home: Homewood Ill. Died June 10, 1992. †

IGNATIEFF, GEORGE, association executive; b. St. Petersburg, Russia, Dec. 16, 1913; s. Count Paul and Princess Natalie (Mestchersky) I.; m. Alison Grant, Nov. 17, 1945; children: Michael Grant, Andrew Grant. B.A., U. Toronto, 1936; M.A. (Rhodes scholar), New Coll., Oxford, Eng., 1938; LL.D. (hon.), Brock U., 1967, U. Toronto, 1968, U. Guelph, 1969, U. Sask., 1973, York U., 1975, Mt. Allison U., 1978; D.C.L. (hon.), Bishop's U., 1973; D.Litt. (hon.), U. Victoria Coll., 1977; D.S.L. (hon.), U. St. Michael's Coll., 1986. Pvt. sec. to Rt. Hon. Vincent Massey High Commr. for Can., London, 1940-44; sec. Post Hostilities Planning Com., Ottawa, Ont., Can., 1944-45; diplomatic advisor to Gen. A.G.L. McNaughton UN AEC, 1945-46; advisor Can. Del. UN, 1946-47; alt. rep. UN Security Council, 1948-49; counsellor Can. embassy, Washington, 1949-53; head def. Liason Div. Can. Dept. External Affairs, 1955-56; Can. ambassador to Yugoslavia, 1956-58; dep. to Hon. George Drew High Commr. Can. to U.K., 1959-60; asst. under-sec. State External Affairs, 1960-62; permanent Can. rep. NATO, 1963-65, UN Security Council, 1965-68, Disarmament Com., Geneva, 1968-71, European Office of UN, Geneva, 1971-72; provost Trinity Coll., 1972-78; chmn. bd. trustees Nat. Mus. Can., 1973-78; gov. Heritage Can., 1978-80; pres. UN of Can., 1980-82; chancellor U. Toronto, 1980-86; pres. Sci. for Peace, 1986-88; mem. Pugwash Coun. Author: The Making of a Peacemonger, 1985. Recipient Pearson Peace prize, 1984. Fellow Royal Soc. Can. Home: Toronto ON, Canada Died Aug. 7, 1989.

IKARD, FRANK NEVILLE, lawyer; b. Henrietta, Tex., Jan. 30, 1913; s. Lewis and Ena (Neville) I.; m. Jean Hunter, Oct. 15, 1940 (dec. Apr. 1970); children—Frank Neville, William Forsyth; m. Jayne Brumley, July 22, 1972. A.B., U. Tex., 1936, LL.B., 1936. Bar: Tex. 1936. Mem. firm Bullington, Humphrey & Humphrey, Wichita Falls, 1937-47; judge 30th

Jud. Dist. Ct., Wichita Falls, 1947-52; mem. 82d to 87th Congresses from 13th Tex. dist.; exec. v.p. Am. Petroleum Inst., 1961-63, pres., 1963-79; ptnr., of counsel firm Danzansky, Dickey, Tydings, Quint & Gordon, 1980-82; ptnr., of counsel Finley, Kumble, Wagner, Heine, Underberg, Manley, Myerson & Casey, 1983-87; of counsel Laxalt, Washington, Perito and Dubuc, Washington, 1988-89; chmn. Instl. Communications Co., 1990; dir. Sheller-Globe Corp., Toledo, First Am. Bank, N.A., Washington, Consol. Petroleum Industries, Inc., Ind. Refinery Group, Inc.; Mem. natural gas adv. council Fed. Power Commn., 1964-70; mem. adv. bd. Center for Strategic Studies, Washington, 1966-69; mem. Nat. Petroleum Council, 1964-83, Pres.'s Nat. Adv. Com. on Hwy. Beautification, 1966-68, Pres.'s Nat. Citizens Commn. on Internat. Cooperation, 1965-68, Pres.'s Industry-Govt. Spl. Task Force on Travel, 1966-68; mem. U.S. nat. conf. World Energy Congress, 1967-69, World Petroleum Congresses, 1963-70. Sec., trustee John F. Kennedy Center for Performing Arts, Washington; chmn. Meridian House Internat.; vice chmn. bd. regents U. Tex. at Austin. Served with AUS, 1942-45. Mem. Am. Bar Assn., State Bar Tex., D.C. Bar, Ind. Petroleum Assn. Am., Japan-Am. Soc., The Economic Club of Washington. Episcopalian. Clubs: Masons; Burning Tree (Chevy Chase, Md.); Carlton, City Tavern Assn., Internat., Met. (Washington); Hemisphere, Univ. (N.Y.C.). Home: Washington D.C. Died May 1, 1991.

INDIK, BERNARD PAUL, social work educator; b. Phila., Apr. 30, 1932; s. Jacob Joseph and Ida F. (Kaplan) I.; m. Harriet Sandra Simberloff, June 26, 1955; children: Joyce Janet, Martin Karl, Jay Joseph, Debra Ruth, William Aaron. B.S., U. Pa., 1954, M.B.A., 1955; textile engring. cert., Phila. Textile Inst., 1955; A.M., U. Mich., 1959, Ph.D., 1961. Asst. mgr. Textured Yarn Co., Phila., 1955; asst. study dir. Survey Research Center, U. Mich., 1957-60, study dir., 1961; asst. research specialist Rutgers U., New Brunswick, N.J., 1961-65; asso. research specialist research program psychology dept. and Inst. Mgmt. Rutgers U., 1965-68, prof. social work, from 1968, Disting. prof. social work, from 1978; cons. Pres.'s Commn. on Civil Disorders, 1967-68, Gov.'s Commn. Report for Action, 1968, Dept. Labor and Industry N.J., 1965, 74-76; cons. task force for 21st Century N.J. Gen. Assembly, 1987-88. Author: (with G. Sternlieb) The Ecology of Welfare, 1973, (with R. Beauregard) A Human Service Labor Market: Developmental Disabilities, 1979; editor: (with F.K. Berrien) People, Groups and Organizations, 1968; contbr. articles and book revs. to profl. jours., chpts. to books. Mem. exec. bd. South Brunswick Community Council, 1967-68, exec. sec., 1968-69; mem. exec. bd. South Brunswick Citizens for Johnson, 1964; trustee South Brunswick Twp. Library, 1965-70, treas., 1970; mem. South Brunswick Twp. Planning Bd., 1976-85, chmn., 1979-82; mem. long range planning com. United Way of Central Jersey, from 1976, trustee, v.p., 1978-79, 85-86; South Brunswick Twp. rep. Middlesex County Housing and Community Devel. Com., from 1976; chmn. South Brunswick Twp. Affordable Housing Agy., from 1986. Served with U.S. Army, 1955-57. Recipient Community Appreciation award United Way Central Jersey, 1976, 82, 86, 87; Mayor's Appreciation award South Brunswick, 1976; Small Community Mayors of N.J. award, 1980. Fellow Am. Psychol. Assn., Soc. Psychol. Study Social Issues; mem. Council on Social Work Edn., Nat. Assn. Social Workers, Am. Acad. Polit. and Social Scis., Soc. Gen. Systems Research, Eastern Psychol. Assn. Democrat. Jewish. Club: Willows Swim (trustee 1976). Home: Monmouth Junction N.J. Deceased. †

INGRAHAM, JOE MCDONALD, federal judge; b. Pawnee County, Okla., July 5, 1903; s. Millard F. and Emma (Patton) I.; m. Laura Munson, Oct. 29, 1954. LL.B., Nat. U., 1927. Bar: Okla. and D.C. bars 1927, Tex. bar 1928. Practice in Stroud, Okla., 1927-28, Ft. Worth, 1928-35, Houston, 1935-54; judge U.S. Dist. Ct. So. Dist. Tex., 1954-69; judge U.S. Ct. Appeals for 5th Circuit, 1969-73, sr. judge, from 1973; judge Temporary Emergency Ct. Appeals of U.S., from 1976. Served as officer USAAF, 1942-46. Mem. Am. Bar Assn., Houston Bar Assn., Tex. State Bar, Am. Judicature Soc., S.A.R. (pres. Tex. Soc. 1937-38, Good Citizenship award Tex. Soc. 1958), Am. Legion. Republican. Presbyterian. Home: Houston Tex. Died May 27, 1990; body donated science.

INOUE, YASUSHI, poet, novelist; b. Shizuoka, Japan, May 6, 1907; s. Hayao and Yae I.; m. Fumi, Nov. 1935; children—Ikyuo, Shuichi, Takyua, Yoshiko. Author: novels Fighting Bull, 1949 (Akutagawa award 1950); The Roof Tile of Tempyo, 1957 (Culture Minister award 1958); Tun-Huang, 1959 (Art of Mainichi award 1960); Honkakubo's Note, 1981 (Shincho award 1981); author numerous poems; pres. Japan Modern Literature House, from 1981. Mem. Peace Com. of the World, from 1982; pres. Japan-China Cultural Exchange Assn., from 1980. Mem. Art Acad. Japan, Japan PEN Club, Japan Writers Assn. Died Jan. 29, 1991. Home: Tokyo Japan

IRANYI, LADISLAUS ANTHONY, bishop; b. Szeged, Hungary, Apr. 9, 1923; came to U.S., 1953, naturalized, 1959; s. Ladislaus I. and Elizabeth J. (Pocker) I. BA, Pazmany U., Budapest, 1944; STD, Gregorianum U., Rome, 1951; PhD, Angelicum U., Rome, 1952. Ordained priest Roman Cath. Ch., 1948, bishop, 1983. Co-founder Piarist Fathers in U.S.A., House of Studies, 1953, provincial, 1967-82, provincial asst., from 1982; titular bishop of Castel Mediana for Spiritual Assistance of all Hungarians Livine Outside of Hungary; cofounder 1st rector House of Studies, Washington, 1954. Religious broadcaster Voice of Am.; contbr. articles to New Cath. Ency., Cath. Hungarians Sunday, other religious jours. V.p. Hungarian Cultural Ctr.; nat. dir. Am. Hungarian Fedn., chaplain. Recipient Spl. award Am. Hungarian Ref. Fedn. for Ecumenical Cooperation, 1975. Mem. AAUP, Cath. Theol. Soc., Am. Coll. Theology Soc., Cath. Bibl. Assn., Mariological Assn., Cath. Philos. Assn., Philil. Assn. Am. Home: Washington D.C. Died Mar. 6, 1987.

IRELAND, RALPH LEONARD, dentist, educator; b. Rock Port, Mo., Aug. 3, 1901; s. Leonard Alvin and Clara Agusta (Broughton) I.; m. Marion Ione Becker, June 27, 1935 (dec. Jan. 1972); 1 son, Robert Michael; m. Kathleen T. Von Gillern, Aug. 24, 1973. D.D.S., U. Neb., 1927, B.S., 1929, M.S., 1944. Diplomate: Am. Bd. Pedodontics (sec.-treas.). Practice dentistry Lincoln, Neb., 1929-36; mem. faculty U. Neb. Coll. of Dentistry, 1936-58, prof. pedodontics, 1939-58, chmn. dept., 1939-58, dean, 1958-68, dean emeritus, 1968-90, dir. postgrad. and grad. courses, 1948-58; Cons. staff Children's Meml. Hosp. Omaha, from 1949; cons. VA Hosp., Omaha, Lincoln; spl. cons. USPHS, from 1946. Author: Dentistry for Children Lincoln State Dept. of Health, 1938, rev. edits., 1942, 48; Contbr. articles to profl. jours. Fellow Am. Coll. Dentists; mem. Lincoln Dist., ADA (chmn. nat. bd. dental examiners 1964-66), Neb. Dental Assn. (editor jour. 1972-84), Am. Assn. Dental Schs. (pres. 1966), Neb. Soc. Dentistry for Children (past pres.), Am. Acad. Pedodontics (past pres.), Internat. Assn. Dental Research, Sigma Xi, Omicron Kappa Upsilon, Sigma Chi, Xi Psi Phi. Republican. Episcopalian. Home: Council Bluffs Iowa Died May 3, 1990; buried Lincoln, Nebr.

IRESON, WILLIAM GRANT, industrial engineering educator, author; b. N. Tazewell, Va., Dec. 23, 1915; s. Henry Frank and Hattie Grimm (Smith) I.; m. Mamie Gillespie, Dec. 26, 1938; children: William Randall, Robert Grant. B.S. in Indsl. Engring, Va. Poly. Inst., 1937, M.S., 1943. Indsl. engr. Wayne Mfg. Corp., Waynesboro, Va., 1937-41; from instr. to acting prof., acting head dept. indsl. engring. Va. Poly. Inst., 1941-48; prof. Ill. Inst. Tech., 1948-51; prof. Stanford U., 1951-81, co-founder, chmn. dept. indsl. engring., 1952-75, prof. emeritus, 1981-89; cons. to govt. and industry. Author or co-author: Principles of Engineering Economy, 7th edit, 1983, Factory Planning and Plant Layout, 1952, Handbook of Industrial Engineering and Management, rev. edit, 1971, also tech. papers.; Editor: Handbook of Reliability Engineering and Management, 1988. Recipient Air Force scroll appreciation, 1958; Order of Civil Merit, Mongryeon medal for contbns. to higher edn. Govt. S. Korea, 1978. Fellow Am. Inst. Indsl. Engrs. (Frank and Lillian Gilbreth Indsl. Engring. award 1980), Am. Soc. Quality Control (editor Reliability Rev., Eugene L. Grant award for contbns. to quality control edn. 1976, Austin J. Bonis Edn. award 1987); mem. Am. Soc. Engring. Edn., Tau Beta Pi, Phi Kappa Phi, Alpha Pi Mu. Episcopalian. Home: Stanford Calif. Died June 14, 1989; buried The Sierras.

IRVINE, RALSTONE ROBERT, lawyer, partner; b. Provo, Utah, Mar. 31, 1898; s. Robert R. and Dora (Davis) I.; m. Mamie M. Miller, June 9, 1928; children: Dora Jean (Mrs. Herrick Jackson Young), Mary Ann (Mrs. H. Melvin Sartin), Barbara Lael. AB, Cornell U., 1923, LLB, 1926. Bar: D.C. 1928, N.Y. 1930. Editor in chief Cornell Law Quarterly, 1926; spl. asst. to atty. gen. in enforcement of anti-trust laws, 1926-29; mem. firm Donovan, Leisure, Newton & Irvine, N.Y.C., Washington, 1934-92; pres. Telluride Assn., Ithaca, N.Y., 1924-26; bd. dirs. Telluride Power Co., 1940-47, Am. Cyanamid Co. Contbr. articles to profl. jours. Mem. Cornell Law Assn. (past pres.), St. Andrew's Soc., ABA, N.Y. Bar Assn., Fed. Bar Assn., Bar Assn. of City of N.Y., Phi Beta Kappa, Delta Sigma Rho, Delta Theta Phi, Downtown Assn., Univ. Club, St. Andrew's Golf Club. *

IRVING, ROBERT AUGUSTINE, conductor, pianist; b. Winchester, Eng., Aug. 28, 1913; came to U.S., 1958; s. Robert Graham and Oriane (Tyndale) I. Scholar, Winchester (Eng.) Coll., 1926-32, Royal Coll. Music, 1934-36; B.A. (scholar), New Coll., Oxford (Eng.) U., 1935. Prof. piano Winchester Coll., 1936-40; assoc. condr. BBC Scottish Orch., 1945-48; mus. dir. Royal Ballet Eng., 1949-58, N.Y.C. Ballet, 1958-89; vis. condr. London Philharmonic, N.Y. Philharmonic, Phila. Orch., numerous others, U.S. and Eng., 1951-91. Rec. artist for, HMV, RCA Victor, EMI, Capitol, Angel, Kapp records.; Composer: (with K. Hepburn) As You Like It, 1949, Floodtide 1949, 1958; also scores for films. Served with Royal Arty., 1940-41; Served with RAF, 1941-45. Decorated D.F.C. with bar. Home: Winchester England Died Sept. 13, 1991.

IRWIN, GRAHAM WILKIE, history educator; b. Adelaide, Australia, Oct. 12, 1920; came to U.S., 1962; s. William Henry and Edith Nina (Morris) I.; m. Jane Nora Bayly, Sept. 20, 1956. B.A., U. Adelaide, 1946; Ph.D., U. Cambridge, Eng., 1953. Lectr. history U. Malaya, 1953-56, U. Sydney, 1956-57; sr. lectr. history Univ. Coll., Accra, Ghana, 1958-59, prof. history, head dept. history, 1960-63; assoc. prof. Columbia U., N.Y.C., 1963-65, prof., 1965-87, dir. Inst. African Studies, 1974-83, vice dean Sch. Internat. and Pub. Affairs, 1983-87. Author: Nineteenth-Century Borneo, 1955, Africans Abroad, 1977; editor: Harper Ency. of the Modern World, 1970. Served with Australian Army, 1940-46. Mem. African Studies Assn. (acting sec. 1965-66), Hist. Soc. Ghana (past pres.), African Studies Assn. U.K., Am. Hist. Assn. Episcopalian. Home: New York N.Y. Died Oct. 12, 1991.

IRWIN, JAMES BENSON, astronaut, foundation executive, aeronautical engineer; b. Pitts., Mar. 17, 1930; s. James and Elsie (Strebel) I.; m. Mary Ellen Monroe, Sept. 4, 1959; children: Joy Carmel, Jill Cherie, James Benson, Jan Caron, Joe Chau. B.S., U.S. Naval Acad., 1951; M.S. in Aero. Engring, U. Mich., 1957, D. Astronautical Sci., 1971; D.Sc., William Jewell Coll., 1971, Samford U., 1972. Commd. 2d lt. USAF, 1951, advanced through grades to col., 1971; project officer Wright Patterson AFB, 1957-60; test dir. ASG-18/AIM-47 armament system, Edwards AFB, Calif., 1961-63; test pilot F-12 Test Force, Edwards AFB, Calif., 1963-65; br. chief Advanced Systems Hdqrs. Air Def. Command, Colorado Springs, Colo., 1965-66; astronaut NASA, 1966-72, mem. support crew Apollo 10, backup lunar module pilot Apollo 12, lunar module pilot Apollo 15 moon landing crew, July 30, 1971.; founder, pres. evang. orgn. High Flight Found., Colorado Springs, Colo., from 1972. Author: To Rule the Night, 1973, rev. edit. 1982, More Than Earthlings, 1983, More Than an Ark on Ararat, 1985, Destination Moon, 1989. Decorated NASA Distinguished Service Medal, D.S.M. USAF, City N.Y. Gold Medal, UN Peace medal, City Chgo. Gold medal; order Leopold Belgium; recipient David C. Schilling trophy, 1971, Kitty Hawk meml. award, 1971, Haley Astronautics award AIAA, 1972, John F. Kennedy trophy Arnold Air Soc., 1972, Freedoms Found. Washington medal, 1976, Nat. Citizenship award Mil. Chaplains Assn., 1978, others. Mem. Air Force Assn., Soc. Exptl. Test Pilots. Baptist. Home: Colorado Springs Colo. Died Aug. 8, 1991; buried Arlington Nat. Cemetery.

IRWIN, LEON, insurance company executive; b. New Orleans, June 29, 1898; s. Leon and Ada Baker (Call) I.; m. Olivia Munson Barlett, Apr. 17, 1937; children: Leon, John Bartlett. Student, Tulane U. Pres. Leon Irwin & Co., Inc.; gen. ins., gen. agt. John Hahcock Mut. Life Ins. Co. of Boston; bd. dirs. New Orleans Pub. Svc., Inc., Interstate Hosts., Inc.; past pres. bd. commrs. Port of New Orleans. Nat. vice chmn. for La. ARC, past vice chmn. New Orleans chpt.; past chmn. com. large donors div. Community Chest; past mem. bd. Greater New Orleans, Inc.; mem. bd. adminstrs. Tulane U. Named Kind of Mardi Gras, 1954. Mem. New Orleans C. of C. (past bd.), S.A.R., Internat. House, Navy League, Delta Kappa Epsilon, New Orleans Club, Boston Club, New Orleans Country Club, Stratford Club (past v.p.), New Orleans Athletic Club, La. Athletic Club, So. Yacht (New Orleans) Club, N.Y. Racquet and Tennis Club. *

IRWIN, RICHARD DORSEY, publisher; b. St. Joseph, Mo., Nov. 2, 1905; s. William Herbert and Ida Ferrell (Dorsey) I.; m. Ellen J. Mersch, Nov. 9, 1988; children from previous marriage: Jacqueline Marie Irwin Pipher, Richard Dorsey, Jr. Student, U. Ill., 1924-27; LL.D. (hon.), Ball State U., 1970. Mgr. coll. dept. A.W. Shaw Co., 1928, McGraw-Hill Book Co., 1928-32; chmn., founder Richard D. Irwin, Inc., Homewood, Ill., 1933-75; chmn. emeritus Richard D. Irwin, Inc., Homewood, 1975; hon. chmn. Dorsey Press, Learning Systems Co., Bus. Publs., Inc., Irwin-Dorsey Internat., Dow Jones-Irwin, Inc.; dir. emeritus 1st Nat. Bank of Harvey; cons. O.P.A., 1943; owner, operator Lin-Drake Farms; pres. Irwin Porperties, Homewood, Irwin Jet Svcs., Irwin Enterprises. Mem. Dist. 161 Sch. Bd., Flossmoor, Ill., 1948-54; chmn. bd. Irwin Family Found.; trustee U. Ill. Found., Glenwood Sch. for Boys. Richard D. Irwin Grad. Sch. Mgmt. of Am. Coll., Bryn Mawr, Pa. named in his honor; recipient Solomon S. Huebner Gold medal, 1988, Community Svc. award Anti-Defamation League, 1988; 2d annual AAP HED Achievement award, 1989; Paul Harris fellow, 1988. Mem. Am. Assn. Collegiate Schs. Bus., Am. Acctg. Assn., Am., Midwest, So. econ. assns., Am. Mktg. Assn., Midwest Bus. Adminstrn. Assn., Am. Bus. Law Assn., Profl. Golfers Assn. (nat. adv. com.), Alpha Kappa Psi, Omicron Delta Epsilon, Beta Gamma Sigma (1st Presdl. award 1988). Clubs: Olympia Fields (Ill.) Country, Flossmoor Country, Chicago Athletic Assn. Home: Homewood Ill. Died Nov. 26, 1989; buried Chgo.

ISAAC, WALTER, psychologist, educator; b. Cleve., June 13, 1927; s. Walter Roy and Irene (Pillars) I.; m. Dorothy Jane Emerson, Oct. 14, 1949; children: Susan Irene, Walter Lon. B.S., Western Res. U., 1949; M.A., Ohio State U., 1950, Ph.D., 1953. Predoctoral fellow Sch. Aviation Medicine, U.S. Air Force, Austin, Tex., 1953; research instr. Sch. Medicine U. Wash., Seattle, 1954-56; asst. research psychologist Sch. Medicine UCLA, 1956-57; asst. prof. psychology Emory U., Atlanta, 1957-60; assoc. prof. Emory U., 1960-65, prof., 1965-68; prof. physiol. psychology U. Ga., Athens, 1968-89. Served with USNR, 1945-46. Mem. Fellow

AAAS, Nat. Acad. Neuropsychology (posthumous); mem. Psychonomic Soc., So. Soc. for Philosophy and Psychology, Southeastern Psychol. Assn., Am. Assn. Lab. Animal Sci., Soc. Behavioral Medicine, Nat. Acad. Neuropsychologists, Internat. Neuropsychol. Soc. Home: Athens Ga. Died June 6, 1989; buried Oconee Hill Cemetery, Athens, Ga.

ISAACS, KENNETH L., banker; b. Scranton, Pa., June 18, 1904; s. Albert George and Anna Carpenter (Richards) I.; m. Helen Coolidge Adams, Mar. 10, 1949; children: Kenneth C.A., Anne Carpenter Richards Merwin. M.E., Lehigh U., 1925, LL.D., 1965; M.B.A., Harvard U., 1927. Buying dept. Nat. City Co., 1927-30; pvt. investment work, 1930-32; asst. to comptroller Cornell U. (specializing on endowment fund investments), 1932-36; with Mass. Investors Trust, 1936-69; formerly chmn., mem. investment mgmt. com. Mass. Investors Trust, Mass. Investors Growth Stock Fund, Inc.; former partner Mass. Financial Services; hon. trustee Suffolk-Franklin Savs. Bank; hon. dir. So. Pacific Co., Phelps Dodge Corp., Gen. Pub. Utilities Corp. Hon. trustee Lehigh U. Republican. Episcopalian. Clubs: Somerset (Boston); Brook (N.Y.C.), Harvard (N.Y.C.), Knickerbocker (N.Y.C.). Home: Boston Mass. Died May 9, 1991; buried Vine Lake Cemetery, Medfield, Mass.

ISAACSON, THORPE BEAL, clergyman, business executive; b. Ephraim, Utah, Sept. 6, 1898; s. Martin and Mary J. (Beal) I.; m. Lula M. Jones, June 16, 1920; children; Joyce (Mrs. Tribe), Richard A. Student, Snow Normal Coll., Brigham Young U., U. Calif., Utah Agrl. Coll.; LLD (hon.), Utah Agrl. Coll., 1956. Prin. schs. Box Elder county, Utah; supt. schs. Idaho; life ins. agt. Bus. Men's Assurance Co.; gen. agt. Lincoln Nat. Life Ins. Co., Utah, Idaho, Nev., 1938; dir. Hotel Utah, Zion Securities Corp., Utah Apt. House Assn. Mem. First Coun. Presiding Bishopric, LDS, now asst. to Coun. of 12 Apostles; bd. dirs. U. Utah; pres. Utah Valley Hosp., Provo, Thomad D. Dee Meml. Hosp., Ogden, Utah; dir. Utah Symphony. Mem. Salt Lake City C. of C., Utah Life Mgrs. Assn., Booneville (Utah) Knife and Fork Club. *

ISBELL, HORACE SMITH, chemist; b. Denver, Nov. 13, 1898; s. Harvey G. and Mary E. (White) I.; m. May Davidson, June 26, 1930. B.S., U. Denver, 1920, M.S., 1923; Ph.D. (USPHS fellow), U. Md., 1926. Asst. chemist Am. Smelting & Refining Co., Pueblo, Colo., 1920-21, Bur. Animal Industry, Dept. Agr., Washington, 1923-25; research chemist, chief organic chemistry sect. Nat. Bur. Standards, Washington, 1927-68; senior research scientist Am. U., Washington, 1968-92. Recipient meritorious award Dept. Commerce, 1950; Distinguished Alumni award U. Denver, 1953; issue Carbohydrate Research mag. dedicated in his honor, 1974. Mem. Washington, N.Y. acads. sci., Am. Chem. Soc. (Hillebrand award Washington sect. 1951, Hudson Honor award div. carbohydrate chemistry 1954, councilor 1946, 63-66, chmn. div. carbohydrate chemistry 1938, chmn. Washington sect. 1945), Chem. Soc. London (W.N. Haworth medal 1973), Sigma Xi, Phi Lambda Upsilon, Alpha Chi Sigma. Club: Cosmos (Washington). Home: Washington D.C. Died July 1, 1992. †

ISLE, JOHN STANLEY, newspaper editor, columnist; b. Stanberry, Mo., July 29, 1923; s. Ira Oden and Daisy F. (Baker) I.; m. Irene Anne Hayob, Dec. 22, 1943; children—Vicki Anne, Constance Lynn, Anita Louise, Janice Marie, Mary Beth. A.A., Moberly Jr. Coll., 1942; postgrad., U. Mo., Columbia, 1942-43. Sports editor Monitor-Index, Moberly, Mo., 1946-61; sports editor Daily Tribune, Wisconsin Rapids, Wis., 1961-65; assoc. editor Sporting News, St. Louis, 1965-84, sr. editor, 1984-89; exec. dir. Mo. Sports Hall of Fame, 1981-89. Served with USAAF, 1943-46, U.S. Army, 1950-51. Recipient 1st and 2d place awards for news story and personal column Mo. Press Assn., 1959, Outstanding Alumnus award Moberly Jr. Coll., 1989. Mem. Baseball Writers Assn. Am. (chmn. St. Louis chpt. 1973-74), Sigma Delta Chi. Democrat. Roman Catholic. Home: Florissant Mo. Died Dec. 28, 1989; buried Moberly, Mo.

ISRAEL, ADRIAN CREMIEUX, investment banker; b. N.Y.C., Nov. 6, 1915; s. Adolph Cremieux and Babette (Bloch) I.; m. Virginia Joy Whitmore, June 25, 1971; children by previous marriage: Ellen I Rosen (dec.), Andrew C. (dec.), Thomas C., Nancy. B.S., Yale U., 1936. Chmn., pres. A.C. Israel Commodity Co., Inc., N.Y.C., 1936-71; ltd. ptnr. Bache & Co., N.Y.C., 1945-64, gen. ptnr., 1964-65, pres., dir., 1965-66; pres., chief exec. officer ACLI Internat., Inc., N.Y.C., 1971-81; chmn. bd. Peoples Drug Stores, Washington, 1976-84; chmn. bd., pres. A.C. Israel Enterprises, Inc., White Plains, N.Y., 1944-91; officer many leading commodity exchs. in N.Y. and Chgo. Trustee Montefiore Med. Ctr., N.Y.C., Eisenhower Med. Ctr., Rancho Mirage, Calif., bd. incorporators Stamford Hosp., Conn., 1960-91; mem. exec. com. Yale Devel. Bd., New Haven, 1964-91, Andover Devel. Bd., Mass., 1984-88. Served with War Prodn. Bd. and War Food Adminstrn., 1942-45. Mem. Coffee, Cocoa and Sugar Exchange, N.Y. Futures Exchange. Republican. Clubs: Sky, Yale, Bond, Links (N.Y.C.); Century Country (Purchase, N.Y.); Stanwich (Conn.); Mid Ocean (Bermuda); Metropolitan (Washington); La Quinta (Calif.). Home: Pound Ridge N.Y. Died Sept. 13, 1991; buried Woodlawn Cemetery, Bronx, N.Y.

JABLONSKI, WANDA MARY, publisher; b. Czechoslovakia; d. Eugene and Mary J.; came to U.S., 1938, naturalized, 1945; BA, Cornell U., 1942; postgrad. Columbia U., 1943; LHD (hon.), St. Lawrence U., 1978. Oil editor Jour. Commerce, N.Y.C., 1943-54; sr. editor Petroleum Week, McGraw-Hill, N.Y.C., 1954-61; founder, editor, pub. Petroleum Intelligence Weekly, N.Y.C., 1961-88; trustee Strang Cornell Cancer Prevention Ctr., N.Y.C., 1990-92, coord. Nat. High Risk Registry, 1988-92. Mem. Oxford Energy Policy Club, Council Fgn. Rels. Died Jan. 29, 1992. Home: New York N.Y.

JABLONSKY, HARVEY JULIUS, army officer; b. Clayton, Mo., Jan. 10, 1909; s. Arthur T. and Eugenia (Reeb) J.; m. Virgie Storch, Nov. 11, 1950; children: Jean, David, Lea, Alice. BS in Bus. Adminstrn., Washington U., St. Louis, 1930; BS, U.S. Mil. Acad., 1934; grad., Army War Coll., 1952. Commd. 2d lt. U.S. Army, 1934, advanced through grades to maj. gen., 1962; asst. football coach U.S. Mil. Acad., 1934-42; comdg. officer 515 Parachute Rgt., 1945; chief staff 11th Airborne Div., 1947-48; comdg. officer 187th Airborne Rgt., 1948-50; pres. Airborne and Electronics Bd., 1957-59; asst. div. comdr. 82d Airborne Div., 1959-60; chief inf., also dir. Office Pers., Dept. Army, 1961-63; comdg. gen. 1st Armored Div., Ft. Hood, Tex., 1963-65; chief ARMISH/MAAG, Iran, 1965. Decorated Legion of Merit, Bronze Star, Army Commendation medal. Mem. Masons. Home: San Antonio Tex. Died Apr. 4, 1989.

JACK, GLEN ROBERT, lawyer, partner; b. Mount Angel, Oreg., Sept. 16, 1895; s. Joel Lincoln and Ida E. (Simmons) J.; m. Vanessa Chisholm, Jan. 22, 1922; children: Patricia (Mrs. James Skene), Norma (Mrs. Phillip Sabag). AB, Pacific U., 1919; LB, Northwestern Coll. Law, Portland, 1923. Bar: Oreg. 1923. Practice of law Oregon City, Oreg., 1924-92; mem. firm Butler & Jack, Oregon City, Oreg., 1924-47, Butler, Jack, Beckett & Holman, Oregon City, 1947-50, Butler, Jack & Beckett, Oregon City, 1950-55, Jack, Goodwin & Annicker, Oregon City, 1955-92; trustee Pacific U. Served with USN, World War I. Fellow Am. Coll. Trial Lawyers, ABA (del. from Oreg. to Ho. Dels.), Am. Bar Found.; mem. Oreg. Bar Assn., Calif. Bar Assn., Am. Judicature Soc., Nat. Conf. Bar Pres. (chmn. 1957-58), Delta Theta Phi. *

JACKSON, HAZEL BRILL, sculptor; b. Phila.; d. William Henry and Lizabeth Lee (Stone) J. Student, Friends Select Sch., Phila., Boston Mus. Sch. Fine Arts, Scuola Rosatti, Florence, Italy; with, Angelo Zanelli, Rome, Italy. Exhibited Nat. Mus. Modern Art, Rome, Trieste and Florence, Royal Acad. Scotland, Nat. Acad. N.Y.C., Guild Boston Artists; represented museums and pvt. collections including Brookgreen Garden, S.C., Newburgh Pub. Library, bronzes at Wellesley Coll., Vassar Coll., Dartmouth Coll., Springfield (Mass.) Art Mus., many others. Recipient Altman prize, 1945, Ellen Spayer Meml. award NAD, 1949; Allied Artists prize Smithsonian Instn., 1963; other awards. Fellow Nat. Sculpture Soc.; mem. NAD (Young Meml. prize 1965), Guild Boston Artists, Soc. Animal Artists, Am. Artists Profl. League. Clubs: American Alpine, Italian Alpine. Home: Newburgh N.Y. Died May 17, 1991.

JACKSON, JOHN ELLETT, lawyer; b. Palestine, Tex., Aug. 3, 1892; s. Alexander Ellett and Abby Frederick (Watts) J.; m. Mary Louise Allen, Dec. 29, 1917; children: Mary Allen (Mrs. H. Robert Corder), John E. Jr. LL.B., Georgetown U., 1916. Bar: Tex. bar 1914, La. bar 1920, U.S. Supreme Ct. bar 1928. Pvt. practice law New Orleans, from 1921; Republican candidate for lt. gov. of La., 1928; chmn. Rep. State Central Com., La., 1929-34; Rep. nat. committeeman for La., 1934-52, mem. exec. com., 1951-52, sub-com. on South, 1950-52; chmn. La. delegation Rep. Nat. Convs., 1932, 36, 40, 44, 48. Former trustee Robert A. Taft Meml. Found., Inc. Decorated hon. officer and comdr. Order Brit. Empire. Mem. ABA, La. Bar Assn., New Orleans Bar Assn. (pres. 1936-37). Republican. Presbyn. Clubs: Mason (New Orleans) (K.T., Shriner), Pickwick, Stratford (New Orleans). Home: Metairie La. Died June 19, 1989; buried Metairie Cemetery, New Orleans.

JACKSON, LAURA (LAURA RIDING), writer; b. N.Y.C., Jan. 16, 1901; d. Nathaniel S. and Sarah (Edersheim) Reichenthal; m. Schuyler Brinckerhoff Jackson, June 20, 1941 (dec. 1968). Student, Cornell U., other univs. Mem. The Fugitives, mid 1920's; mng. partner Seizin Press, 1927-38. Collaborator, 1st author: A Survey of Modernist Poetry, 1927, A Pamphlet Against Anthologies, 1928; critical essays Contemporaries and Snobs, 1928, Anarchism Is Not Enough, 1928, Four Unposted Letters to Catherine, 1930; essays and poems Though Gently, 1930; essays and stories Experts Are Puzzled, 1930; under pseudonym Madeleine Vara: essays and stories Convalescent Conversations, 1935; collected stories Progress of Stories, 1935, new edit., 1982; hist. novel A Trojan Ending, 1937, new edit., 1984, transl. into Spanish, 1986; hist. stories Lives of Wives, 1939, new edit., 1988; (with Harry Kemp) The Left Heresy, 1939, Collected Poems from 9 preceding vols, 1938, Selected Poems: In Five Sets, 1973, The Telling, 1972, (with husband) Rational Meaning: A New Foundation for the Definition of Words, publ. delayed; also articles and pamphlets, from 1925; editor, contbr.: gen. criticism Epilogue, Vols. I-III, 1935-37; editor, commentator: gen. criticism The World and Ourselves, 1938; Selected Writings, Published, Unpublished, book issue, Chelsea 35, 1976, Collected Poems, new edit, 1980, Description of Life, 1980, Some Communications of Broad Reference, 1984, First Awakenings: The Early Poems of Laura Riding, 1992. Recipient Fugitive poetry prize, 1925, Bollingen prize Yale U., 1989-90; appreciation grantee Mark Rothko Found., 1971; Guggenheim fellow, 1973. Home: Sebastian Fla. Died Sept. 21, 1991; buried Wabasso, Fla.

JACKSON, ROBERT HENRY, physician, medical administrator; b. Norwalk, Ohio, Oct. 5, 1922; s. Samuel Lloyd and Mona Mae (Zuelch) J.; m. Ann Elisabeth Dornback, Sept. 20, 1958; 1 child, Ann Dornback. BS, Western Res. U., 1947; MD, U. Heidelberg, Fed. Republic of Germany, 1953. Rotating intern St. Luke's Hosp., Cleve., 1953-54; fellow in Urology Mayo Clinic, Rochester, Minn., 1954-55; asst. surg. resident Luth. Hosp., Cleve., 1955-56, Perusse Traumatic Surg. Clinic, Chgo., 1956-57; gen. chmn. Internat. Congress on Neoplastic Diseases, Heidelberg, Fed. Republic Germany, 1973. Author: Joseph Colt Bloodgood: Cancer Pioneer, 1971, The Viral Etiology, Immunology, Immunodiagnosis, Immunotherapy and Immunoprophylaxsis of Human Neoplastic Diseases, 1985. Trustee Presdl. Task Force, Washington, 1984-90; mem. Senatorial Com., Washington, 1984-90, Nat. Commn. on Health Manpower, Washington, 1965-90. Served to brig. gen. U.S. Army, ETO. Named hon. prof. internat. affairs, recipient Jacob Gould Schurman plaque Cornell U., 1961; U. Heidelberg New Univ. dedicated in his honor. Fellow Am. Soc. Abdominal Surgeons; mem. Mayo Clinic Alumni Assn., AMA (founder sect. neoplastic diseases 1971), Am. Assn. Study Neoplastic Diseases (exec. sec. 1960-73, pres. 1974), Mil. Order of the World Wars, Assn. U.S. Army, Res. Officers Assn. (honor roll 1955-90), Cleve. Grays, World Med. Assn., Deutsche Medizinische Gesellschaft Von Chgo., Ohio State Med. Assn., Cleve. Acad. Medicine, VFW, U. Heidelberg Med. Alumni in U.S.A., Am. Legion, Cercle D'Etudes sur la Bataille des Ardennes (maj. gen., chargé d'affaires U.S. group, operation France-Luxembourg, 1984-90). Avocations: military, woodworking, fishing, boating. Died 1990. Home: Cleveland Ohio †

JACKSON, SEYMOUR SCOTT, lawyer, sole practice; b. Colchester, Conn., Oct. 23, 1897; s. George O. and Hattie (Crocker) J.; m. Gratice Whiteis, Oct. 23, 1925; children: Jane (Mrs. William B. White), Sarah Jackson (Mrs. M. S. Chase). BS, Trinity Coll., 1920; LLB, N.Y. Law Sch., 1925. Bar: N.Y. 1926. Lawyer pvt. practice N.Y.C., 1926-46; with Kennecott Copper Corp., N.Y.C., 1946-62, gen. counsel, 1954-60, v.p. adminstrn., 1960-62, mining law cons., 1962-92. Served as 2d lt. U.S. Army, 1918. *

JACOB, CHARLES WALDEMAR, investment banker; b. Hamilton, Ohio, Sept. 22, 1943; s. Charles W. and Nancy (Egbert) J.; m. Patricia Suzanne Charlton, June 28, 1969; children: Charles Waldemar, III, Christopher Charlton. BA, Wesleyan U., Middletown, Conn., 1965; MBA, Harvard U., 1967. Mem. fin. staff Ford Motor Co., Dearborn, Mich., 1967-71; dir. fin. analysis corp. staff Rockwell Internat. Corp., El Segundo, Calif., 1971-72; asst. controller automotive ops. Rockwell Internat. Corp., Troy, Mich., 1972-74; corp. controller Chemetron Corp., Chgo., 1974-77; v.p. fin., treas., dir. Flying Tiger Line, Inc., 1977-81; pres. Cunningham, Jacob & Assocs. Inc., Redondo Beach, Calif., 1981-88, Seattle, from 1988; exec. v.p., dir. Prudential-Bache Trade Services, Seattle, 1984-88; chmn. econs. and fin. coun. Air Transp. Assn., 1980; chmn. Bache Pacific Trade Ltd., Hong Kong, Bache Trade Fin. Asia Ltd., Hong Kong, 1986-88; bd. dirs. PB Trade Fin., Ltd., London, Bache Pacific Trade Ltd., Hong Kong, Bache Trade Fin. Asia Ltd., Hong Kong, PB Internat. Bank, S.A., Luxemburg. Mem. Fin. Execs. Inst., Econ. Club Chgo. Episcopalian. Home: Seattle Wash. Deceased. †

JACOB, LEONARD, communications executive; b. New Rochelle, N.Y., June 12, 1894; s. William Hearn and Mary (Phelps) J.; m. Eleanora Winslow, Feb. 21, 1925 (div. 1950); children: Anita (Mrs. Albert Hilton), Leonard. AB, Williams Coll., 1916. V.p. Internat. Telephone & Telegraph Corp.; pres., dir. Leonard Jacob Corp.; dir. Internat. Telelphone & Telegraph Corp., S.A., Internat. Telephone Bldg. Corp., Fed. Telephone & Radio Corp., Internat. Standard Elec. Corp.; pres. Berwind-White Coal Mining Co. Pres. Argentine-Am. C. of C., 1955-61; dir. Cuban-Am. C. of C.; dir. Nat. Fgn. Trade Coun.; trustee U.S. Inter-Am. Coun. Commerce and Prodn.; bd. dirs. Greenwich Garden Ctr., 1964-65; pres. Greenwich Art Soc., 1964-65; v.p. Greenwich Hist. Soc., 1964-65. Served with O.T.S., 1915; lt. (j.G.) USN overseas destroyer svc., 1917-19; lt. to lt. comdr. USNRF, Spl. duty, 1938-40. Decorated Order Merit, rank Knight Comdr., Chile. Mem. Naval Order U.S., Armed Forces Comms. Assn., Navy League U.S., Telephone Pioneers Am., Pan Am. Soc., Chile Am. Assn., Am. Brazilian Assn. (dir.), Pub. Rels. Soc. Am., Sigma Phi, Army and Navy Club, Williams Club. *

JACOBS, AMOS See THOMAS, DANNY

JACOBS, CARL NICHOLAS, insurance executive; b. Stevens Point, Wis., June 30, 1895; s. Peter James and Josephine (Krembs) J.; m. Ella Meyer, Nov. 18, 1920; children: James Peter, Robert Carl. LLD, St. Anselm's Coll., 1958. Asst. cashier Soo Line R.R., Stevens Point, Wis., 1913-14; clk. Hardware Mut. Casualty Co., Stevens Point, Wis., 1914-18; asst. sec. Hardware Mut. Casualty Co., Stevens Point, 1918-27, sec.-treas., 1927-29, v.p., 1929-30, pres., 1930-60, chmn., 1960-92; chmn. Hardware Dealers Mut. Fire Inst. Co., 1937-45, pres., 1945-60, chmn. 1960-92; pres. Sentry Life Inst. Co., Stevens Point, 1958-60, chmn., 1960-92; past pres., now dir. Am. Mut. Ins. Alliance, Nat. Assn. Mut. Casualty Cos.; trustee Am. Inst. for Property and Liability Underwriters, Inc., Phila., 1959-92. Dir. C. of C. of U.S., 1941-55, v.p., 1951-54, treas., 1954; trustee Northwestern Mut. Life Ins. Co., 1946-58; bd. dirs. St. Norbert Coll., DePere, Wis.; trustee Inter-Am. Coun. Commerce and Prodn., N.Y.C., 1951-58, Am. Enterprise Inst., Washington. Recipient Nat. Office Mgmt. Assn. award, 1956. Mem. Newcomen Soc., Elk, Rotary (Stevens Point), Milw. Athletic Club, Union League (Chgo.). Roman Catholic. *

JACOBS, WOODROW COOPER, meteorologist, oceanographer; b. Pasadena, Calif., Sept. 11, 1908; s. William Rozel and Mabelle (Cooper) J.; m. Dorothy Cecelia Quinn, June 15, 1933; 1 child, Marilyn Rozel (Mrs. Wilbur M. Ott). Student, Va. Mil. Inst., 1926-27; A.B., UCLA, 1930; Ph.D. in Meteorology, 1948; M.S., U. So. Calif., 1934; Ph.D., Scripps Instn. Oceanography. With U.S. Weather Bur., San Diego, 1931-36; forecaster fruit-frost service U.S. Weather Bur., Pomona, Calif., 1936-41; research assoc. Scripps Instn. Oceanography, also Carnegie Inst., 1937; chief civilian meteorologist Hdqrs. USAAF, 1941-46; head climatological branch U.S. Weather Bur., Washington, 1946-48; dir. climatology USAF Air Weather Service, Washington, 1948-60; phys. sci. specialist Library of Congress, 1960-61; dir. Nat. Oceanographic Data Center, 1961-67, World Data Center A, Oceanography, 1962-67; dir. environ. data service Environ. Sci. Service Adminstrn., Silver Spring, Md., 1967-70; sr. scientist Ocean Data Systems, Inc., Rockville, Md., from 1971; vis. prof. Mass. Inst. Tech., 1950, U. Chgo., 1956; lectr. meteorology and oceanography Dept. Agr. Grad. Sch., 1942-58; professorial lectr. George Washington U., 1957; USAF mem. two panels Research and Devel. Bd., Dept. Def., 1948-52; com. climatology joint meteorol. com. Joint Chiefs Staff, 1948-58; U.S. del. Internat. Meteorol. Orgn., Toronto, Can., 1947, pres. subcom. agrl. forecasts, 1947-50; mem. commn. climatology World Meteorol. Orgn., 1950-62, chmn. internat. com. exchange data, 1953-60; U.S. del. of Nat. Acad. Scis. to assembly Internat. Union Geodesy and Geophysics, Brussels, 1951, Rome, 1954, Toronto, 1957, Lucerne, 1967; mem. coms. NRC-NSF, from 1948; chmn. interagy. atmospheric scis. oceanography com. on air-sea research, 1963-64; com. on oceanography Smithsonian Instn., 1962-67; working group Intergovtl. Oceanographic Commn., UNESCO, 1962-67; panel mem. Interagy. Com. on Oceanography, 1961-67; adv. council Oceanic Research Inst. of San Diego, 1964—; adv. panel on sea-air interaction program Dept. Commerce, 1964-67; chmn. working group on air-sea inter actions World Meteorol. Orgn., UN, 1964-68; U.S. del. 2d Oceanographic Congress, Moscow, 1966; U.S. mem. Intergovernmental Oceanographic Commn. Com. on Ocean Stas., Paris, 1966; mem. data adv. panel Pres.'s Council on Marine Resources and Engring. Devel., 1967-69; mem. com. on radio frequency requirements for sci. research Nat. Acad. Sci., 1969-70; mem. com. biog. classification Internat. Assn. Phys. and Sci. Oceanography, from 1968; Dept. Commerce mem. Pres.'s Commn. Food from the Sea, 1968-69; adv. bd. Office Critical Tables Fed. Council, 1968-69; U.S. del. planning com. Internat. Indian Ocean Expdn., Paris, 1964. Author: Energy Exchange Between Sea and Atmosphere, 1951, Meteorological Satellites, 1962; co-author: Arctic Meteorology, 1956; also numerous articles in field.; Editor: English edit. Oceanology, Acad. Sci. USSR for scripta technica, Inc, 1962-75; adv. bd.: English edit. Meteorol. and Geoastrophys. Abstracts, 1963—; asso. editor: four publs. Am. Meterol. Soc, 1946-70. Recipient Certificate of Appreciation USAAF, 1946; Distinguished Service award Dept. Commerce, 1970. Fellow Am. Geophys. Union (exec. com. 1947-61, council 1961, sec. sect. meteorology 1947-74, chmn. com. geophys. data), Am. Meterol. Soc. (council 1961-64, chmn. bd. certified cons. meteorologists 1960-62), Washington Acad. Sci.; mem. Internat. Platform Assn., Royal Meteorol. Soc., Md., N.Y. acads. scis., Marine Tech. Soc., Oceanographical Soc. Japan, AAAS, Am. Soc. Limnology and Oceanography, Archeol. Soc. Md., U.S. Navy League (Ormond Beach, Fla.), U.S. Naval Inst. (Annapolis, Md.), SAR, Blue Circle C (UCLA), Sigma Xi, Alpha Tau Omega, Alpha Kappa Psi, Blue Key. Methodist. Clubs: Shawnee Country (Winchester, Va.); Palm Coast Yacht (Fla.); Cosmos (Washington). Lodge: Lions. Home: Flagler Beach Fla. Died Jan. 10, 1990.

JACOBSEN, OSCAR THORKLID, manufacturing executive; b. Racine, Wis., Dec. 30, 1895; s. Knud Ferdinand and Ellen Sophia (Hansen) J.; m. LaDora Ruth Vaughan; children; Ellen Jean (Mrs. George Holcomb), John Knud. Student, U. Minn., 1916-17. Pres. Jacobsen Mfg. Co., Racine, Wis., 1929-58; chmn. Jacobsen Mfg. Co., Racine, 1959-92. Chmn. campaign Racine chpt. ARC, 1958; active cancer, community chest campaigns; dir. Racine YMCA. Served as sgt. USMC, 1917-18; AEF, lt. col. Wis. N.G. Decorated Knight of Dannebrog (Denmark). *

JACOBSON, ALMA FRANK, telecommunications executive; b. Omaha, Apr. 27, 1905; s. Alma Frank and Vilate (Angel) J.; m. Ruth Saalfeld, Nov. 14, 1925; children: Allen, Mary Johnson. Student, U. Nebr., 1922-25; LHD (hon.), Midland Coll., 1960, Hastings Coll., 1968; LLD (hon.), Creighton U., 1963. Clk. Northwestern Bell Telephone Co., Omaha, 1922-28, various positions, 1928-51, pres., dir., 1955-70; v.p. ops., dir. Ill. Bell Telephone Co., 1951-52; dir. ops. long lines dept. Am. Telephone and Telegraph Co., 1952-53, asst. v.p. ops. dept. engring., 1953; cons. Bozell and Jacobs Advt., Omaha; communications cons. Govt. of Italy, Rome; dir. U.S. Nat. Bank, Nebr. Savs. and Loan Assn., Omaha, Northwest Bancorp., Mpl.s Cen. Nat. Ins. Group Omaha. Trustee U. Nebr. Found., Omaha Indsl. Found.; dir. Meyer Therapy Ctr., Inc., Omaha, 1959-65; chmn. bd. dirs. Creighton U.; trustee Joslyn Ctr. Soc. Liberal Arts, Omaha; bd. govs. Knights Ak-Sar-Ben, Omaha, Father Flanagan's Boys Home, Omaha; chmn. bd. dirs. Girls Town, Omaha. Recipient Americanism citation for meritorious svc. B'nai B'rith, 1958; named Knight St. Gregory, Civil Class. Mem. C. of C. (pres. 1961-62), Telephone Pioneers Am. (pres. 1966-67), Masons, Omaha Club, Omaha Country Club, Mpls. Club, Alpha Kappa Psi, Beta Gamma Sigma, Alpha Sigma Nu. Home: Omaha Nebr. Died Feb. 7, 1990.

JACOBSON, JOEL ROSS, state official; b. Newark, July 30, 1918; s. Herman and Gussie (Ross) J.; m. Lucie Jacobson; children—Howard Michael, Monica. B.S., N.Y. U., 1941; Litt.D. (hon.), Montclair (N.J.) State Coll., 1959; LL.D. (hon.), Rutgers U., 1974. Exec. sec. Essex-W. Hudson (N.J.) CIO Council, 1949-54; exec. v.p. N.J. CIO Council, 1954-60, pres., 1960-61; 1st exec. v.p. N.J. AFL-CIO, 1961-64; pres. N.J. Indsl. Union Council, AFL-CIO, 1964-68; dir. community affairs Region 9, UAW, Cranford, N.J., 1968-74; commr. N.J. Bd. Pub. Utility Commrs., 1974-76, pres., 1976-77; N.J. commr. Dept. Energy, 1977-81; commr. N.J. Casino Control Commn., 1981-86; U.S. Dist Ct. appointed trustee Local 560 Internat. Brotherhood Teamsters, 1986-87, chmn. Trucking Employees N.J. and Pension Funds, 1986-87; adj. prof. labor studies Rutgers U., New Brunswick, N.J., 1988; del. to White House Conf. Edn., 1955; mem. N.J. adv. com. to U.S. Civil Rights Commn., from 1960; mem. N.J. Health Planning Council, from 1969; lectr. labor and politics univs. including Rutgers, Yale, Princeton, Bklyn. Poly. Inst. Vice chmn. New Democratic Coalition, 1968-69; del. Dem. Nat. Conv., 1972; bd. govs. Rutgers U., 1959-74. Served to 2d lt. AUS, World War II. Decorated Bronze Arrowhead. Home: South Orange N.J. Died Dec. 26, 1989; buried Menorah Cemetery, Clifton. N.J.

JACOBSON, LEON ORRIS, physician; b. Sims, N.D., Dec. 16, 1911; s. John and R. Patrine (Johnson) J.; m. Elizabeth Benton, Mar. 18, 1938 (dec.); children: Eric Paul, Judith Ann; m. Elise Torczynski, Jan. 20. 1990. B.S., N.D. State Coll., 1935, D.Sc. (hon.), 1966; M.D., U. Chgo., 1939; D.Sc., Acadia U., N.S., 1972. Intern U. Chgo., 1939-40, asst. resident medicine, 1940-41, asst. in medicine, 1941-42, instr., 1942-45, asst. prof., 1945-48, asso. dean, div. biol. scis., 1945-51, asso. prof., 1948-51, prof. medicine emeritus, 1951-92, Joseph Regenstein prof. biol. and medicine emeritus, 1965-92, chmn. dept. medicine, 1961-65, dean div. biol. scis., 1966-75; head hematology sect. U. Chgo. Clinics, 1951-61; mem. Inst. Radiobiology and Biophysics, 1949-54; dir. Franklin McLean Meml. Research Inst., 1974-77; assoc. dir. health Plutonium project Manhattan Dist., 1942-45, dir. health, 1945-46; dir. Argonne Cancer Research Hosp., U. Chgo., 1951-67; U.S. rep. 1st and 2d UN Conf. on Peaceful Uses Atomic Energy, Geneva, 1955, 58, WHO conf. Research Radiation Injury, Geneva, 1959; cons. biology div. Argonne Nat. Lab.; mem. adv. com. on isotope distbn. AEC, 1952-56; mem. nat. adv. com. radiation USPHS, 1961, mem. com. radiation studies, cons. hematology study sect.; mem. com. cancer diagnosis and therapy NRC, 1949-55; mem. bd. sci. counselor Nat. Cancer Inst., 1963-67; mem. nat. adv. cancer council, nat. cancer adv. bd. NIH, 1968-72; chmn. sci. adv. bd. Council for Tobacco Research; Kennecott lectr., 1963; lectr. Internat. Soc. Hematology and Internat. Congress Radiology, Eng., France, Norway, Sweden, 1950, 5th Internat. Cancer Congress, Paris, 1950, Internat. Soc. Hematology, Argentina, 1952, Paris, 1954, others. Author book on erythropoletin; contbr. chpts. on specialized items to various med. books, articles to med. jours.; Book editor: Perspectives in Biology and Medicine, 1979-83. Recipient Janeway medal, 1953, Robert Roesler de Villiers award Leukemia Soc., Borden award Med. Scis. Assn., Am. Med. Colls., 1962, Modern Med. and Am. Nuclear Soc. awards, 1963, John Phillips Meml. award, 1975, Theodore Roosevelt Rough Riders award State of N.D., 1977, Gold medal of merit, Lincoln Laureate, State of Ill., 1979, Norwegian medal of honor, knighthood King Olav V of Norway, 1990, Gold medal of merit U. Chgo. Alumni Assn., 1990. Fellow AAAS; mem. NAS, Inst. Medicine, Nat. Acad. Medicine (Argentina), ACP (master), AMA, Am. Soc. Clin. Investigation, Assn. Am. Physicians, Soc. Exptl. Biology and Medicine, Central Soc. Clin. Research, Am. Assn. Cancer Research, Internat. Soc. Hematology, Central Clin. Research Club, Radiation Research Soc., Am. Soc. Exptl. Pathology, Sigma Xi, Theta Chi, Nu Sigma Nu, Blue Key, Alpha Omega Alpha. Home: Chicago Ill. Died Sept. 20, 1992. †

JACOBY, GEORGE ALONZO, personnel executive; b. Pleasureville, Ky., May 13, 1904; s. George Alonzo and Sarah (Hieatt) J.; m. Ruth Burtner, Oct. 6, 1928; children: George Alonzo, John Burtner. A.B., Georgetown (Ky.) Coll., 1924, LL.D., 1958; M.S., Columbia, 1927. With Irving Trust Co., N.Y.C., 1925-40; asst. sec. Irving Trust Co., 1929-37, asst. v.p., 1937-40; asst. personnel dir. Buick Motor div. Gen. Motors Corp., Flint, Mich., 1941-45; mem. labor relations staff Gen. Motors Corp., Detroit, 1945-46; dir. personnel services Gen. Motors Corp., 1946-56, dir. personnel relations, 1956-69; Pres. Mich. Safety Conf., 1954; dir. Nat. Safety Council, 1947-66; mem. Mich. Employment Security Adv. Council, 1947-60, Fed. Adv. Council Employment Security, 1952-54; exec. dir. Gen. Motors Com. Ednl. Grants and Scholarships, 1955-69. Regent Gen. Motors Inst., 1957-69; trustee Alma Coll., 1956-70; bd. govs. Inst. Indsl. Health, U. Mich., 1957-69. Recipient achievement award Georgetown Coll., 1963. Mem. Pi Kappa Alpha, Alpha Kappa Psi, Beta Gamma Sigma. Presbyterian. Home: Williamsburg Va. Died Oct. 2, 1991.

JACOBY, SIDNEY BERNHARD, lawyer, educator; b. Berlin, Dec. 7, 1908; came to U.S., 1934; s. Siegfried and Amanda Jacoby; m. Elaine Heavenrich, Oct. 17, 1942; children: Evelyn, Anne Jacoby Atkins. JD, Friedrich Wilhelm U., 1933; LLB, Columbia U., 1939. Bar: N.Y. 1941, D.C. 1958, Ohio 1970. Atty. U.S. R.R. Retirement Bd., 1940-45, U.S. Dept. Interior, 1945-47, Office Chief of Counsel, Nuremberg, Germany, 1945-46, U.S. Dept. Justice, 1947-57; prof. law Georgetown U., Washington, 1957-68; prof. law Case Western Res. U., Cleve., 1968-76, John C. Hutchins prof. law, 1975; prof. law Cleveland-Marshall Coll. Law Cleve. State U., 1976-81; lectr. Western Ont. Law Sch., London, fall 1977; counsel in proc. before World Ct., 1957, 58; adj. prof. Antioch Sch. Law, 1981. Author: (with David Schwartz) Government Litigation, 1963, (with John Steadman and David Schwartz) Litigation with the Federal Government, 1970, 2d edit., 1983, Ohio Civil Practice Under the Rules, 2 vols. with ann. supplements, 1970; contbr. articles to legal publs. Recipient dedication Case Western Res. U. Law Rev., 1977. Mem. Am. Law Inst., Fed. Bar Assn. Jewish. Home: Falls Church Va. Died Jan. 1, 1990.

JAECKLE, EDWIN F., lawyer, corporate; b. Buffalo, Oct. 27, 1894; s. Jacob and Mary (Marx) J.; m. Grace Drechsel, Aug. 19, 1920. LLB, U. Buffalo, 1915; LLD, Canisius Coll., 1960. Bar: N.Y. 1916. Mem. firm Jaeckle, Fleischmann, Kelly, Swart & Augspurger, Buffalo, 1916; sec. gen. counsel, dir. Mchts. Mut. Casualty Co., Buffalo; dir. Liberty Bank & Trust, Buffalo, Monroe Abstract & Title Corp., Buffalo, Niagara Mohawk Power Corp., Buffalo, Buffalo Evening News, Inc., Niagara Frontier Transit System, Inc., Buffalo; gen. counsel, dir. Erie & Niagara Ins. Assn.; trustee U. Buffalo. Chmn. Erie County Rep. Com., 1935-48, N.Y. Rep. State Com., 1940-44; mem. bd. of regents Canisius Coll. Mem. ABA, N.Y. State Bar Assn., Erie County Bar Assn., C. of C. *

JAEGER, RICHARD L., clothing company executive; b. 1933; married. MBA, U. Minn., 1965. Spl. agt. IRS, 1961-64; tax mgr. Carlson Co., 1964-67; dir. taxes Bemis Co., Inc., 1967-73; mgr. personnel William W. Farah, 1973-77; with Farah Mfg. Co. (now named Farah, Inc.), El Paso, Tex., from 1978, treas., v.p., sr. v.p., 1970, vice chmn., dir. Served with USAF, 1954-58. Home: El Paso Tex. Deceased. †

JAFFE, DAVID, author, publisher; b. Slonim, Poland, Jan. 20, 1911; came to U.S., 1912, naturalized, 1921; s. Louis and Sadie (Arner) Jaffe'; m. Sylvia S. Turner, Nov. 8, 1942. B.A., Duke U., 1933, M.A., 1937. State editor Durham (N.C.) Morning Herald, 1938-41; mem. editorial staff U. N.C. Press, 1942-44; freelance editor N.Y.C., 1946-47; mem. editorial staff Ctr. for Mil. History, Washington, 1948-76, sr. editor, 1961-76; pub. Mardi Press, Arlington, Va., 1976-90. Author: The Stormy Petrel and the Whale: Some Origins of Moby-Dick, 1976, Bartleby the Scrivener and Bleak House: Melville's Debt to Dickens, 1981; contbr. articles to newspapers, profl. lit. jours.; discoverer two unpublished letters by Mrs. Herman Melville to artist Elihu Vedder, which were published in Extracts, Melville Soc. publ., 1990. Mem. Melville Soc., Phi Beta Kappa. Home: Arlington Va. Died May 26, 1990; buried King David Meml. Gardens, Falls Church, Va.

JAFFE, HANS H., chemistry educator; b. Marburg, Germany, Apr. 17, 1919; came to U.S., 1940, naturalized, 1946; s. Gunther and Hedwig (Schlesinger) J.; m. Martha Ledbetter, Mar. 1946 (div. Jan. 1959); children—Charles, Charlotte, John. B.S., State U. Iowa, 1941; M.S., Purdue U., 1943; Ph.D., U. N.C., 1952. Phys. chemist U.S. Health Service, Balt., Chapel Hill, N.C., 1946-54; asst. prof. U. Cin., 1954-59, asso. prof.,

1959-61, prof., 1961-89, head dept. chemistry, 1966-71, 75-76. Author: Theory and Applications of Ultraviolet Spectroscopy, 1962, Symmetry in Chemistry, 1965, The Importance of Antibonding Orbitals, 1967, Symmetry Orbitals and Spectra, 1971; Contbr. articles to profl. jours. Served with AUS, 1943-46. Recipient Rievschl award U. Cin., 1982; Named Cin. Scientist of Year. Mem. Am. Chem. Soc. (Eminent Chemist Cin. sect. 1961, Morley medal Cleve. sect.), Am. Phys. Soc., AAAS, Tech. and Sci. Socs. Council Cin., Sigma Xi (1st Ann. Distinguished Research award U. Cin. chpt. 1961), Phi Lambda Upsilon. Home: Morgantown W.Va. Died Sept. 19, 1989.

JAGGER, DEAN, actor; b. Columbus Grove, Ohio, Nov. 7, 1905; s. Albert and Lily Mayberry J.; m. Etta Norton, June 22, 1966; 1 child, Diane Marion. Student, Wabash Coll., 1923-24, Lyceum Arts Cons, Chgo., 1925. Appeared in plays Tobacco Road, 1933, They Shall Not Die, 1934, Missouri Legend, 1938; pictures include Brigham Young, 1940, Western Union, 1941, Yank in London, 1944, Sister Kenney, 1945, Pursued, 1947, 12 O'Clock High, 1949, My Son John, 1951, It Grows on Trees, 1952, The Robe, 1953, Executive Suite, 1954, White Christmas, 1954, Bad Day at Black Rock, 1954, Threshold of Space, The Three Brave Men, 1955, The Great Man, 1956, The Nun Story, 1959, Elmer Gantry, 1960, Jumbo, 1962, Fury at Fire Creek, 1967, The Evil Gun, 1967, Tiger by the Tail, 1970, The Kremlin Letter, 1970, Vanishing Point, 1971, Alligator, 1980; TV series Mr. Novak, 1963-65; TV films include The Glass House, 1972, The Lindbergh Kidnaping Case, 1976; TV drama I Heard the Owl Call My Name, 1973. Recipient AP poll. Look Achievement award, Acad. Award, for performance in 12 O'Clock High, 1949, Laurel award, 1952. Mem. N.Y. Athletic Club, Lambda Chi. Home: Beverly Hills Calif. Died Feb. 5, 1991.

JALVING, CLARENCE LOUIS, banker; b. Holland, Mich., Oct. 21, 1895; s. Louis and Gertie (Sjoerdsma) J.; m. Elsie Van Dyken, Nov. 13, 1915; children: Louis, Jacob, Gertrude (Mrs. Adrian Kammeraad), Howard A., Marvin J., Donald P., David L. Student, Hope Coll., Holland, 1913. Asst. cashier Belgrade State Bank, Mich., 1918-20; teller Holland (Mich.) City State Bank, 1920-26; asst. cashier State Comml. & Savs. Bank, Holland, 1926-28; asst. cashier First Nat. Bank, Buchanan, Mich., 1928-30, bank examiner, 1930-32; pres., cashier Peoples State Bank, Holland, 1932-92. Pres. SPEBSQSA, Inc., 1959-60, Holland Econ. Devel. Corp., bd. dirs. Holland Hosp. Mem. Mich. Bankers Assn. (legis. com.), Holland C. of C. (chmn. com. planning and econ. devel.), Exchange club, Macatawa Bay Yacht Club, Legion Country (Holland) Club. *

JAMES, JOHN V., diversifed manufacturing corporation executive; b. Plains Township, Pa., July 24, 1918; s. Stanley S. and Catherine N. (Jones) J.; m. Helen L. Brislin, June 25, 1949; 1 dau., Barbara Ann. Certificate in mgmt., U. Pa., 1948, B.S. in Econs, 1941; D. Bus. Adminstrn. (hon.), Hillsdale Coll., 1976; D. Commercial Sci. (hon.), St. Bonaventure U., 1976. Office mgr., controller Carr Consol. Biscuit Co., Wilkes Barre, Pa., 1941-42; div. controller Corning Glass Works, 1948-56, mgr. budgets and procedures, 1956-57; asst. controller Dresser Industries, Inc., Dallas, 1957-58; v.p. finance subsidiary Clark Bros. Co., Olean, N.Y., 1958-60, controller parent co., 1960-65, v.p., 1962-65, group v.p. machinery, 1965-68, exec. v.p., 1968-69, pres., chief exec. officer, 1970-81; pres., chief exec. officer Dresser Industries, Inc., Dallas, 1970-81, chmn. bd., chief exec. officer, 1976-83, dir. emeritus, 1983-89. Served to capt. AUS, 1942-46. Mem. Financial Execs. Inst., Nat. Assn. Accountants (dir. 1960-62), Beta Gamma Sigma. Congregationalist. Clubs: Mason, Rotarian (pres. Corning 1957). Home: Dallas Tex. Died June 1, 1989; buried Dallas.

JAMES, WILLIAM FLEMING, geologist, consultant; b. St. John, N.B., Can., Dec. 1, 1894; s. Patrick Maurice and Matilda (Regina (Mullin) J.; m. Lenore James (dec. 1975); children: William, Paul McEvoy. B.A, St. Francis Xavier U., Antigonish, N.S., 1918, D.Sc. (hon.); M.S., McGill U., 1921; Ph.D., Princeton U., 1923; LL.D. (hon.), Dalhousie U., Halifax, N.S., York U.; LL.D., U. Toronto. Registered profl. engr., Ont. Geologist Geol. Survey Ottawa, Can., 1923-29; cons. engring., ptnr. firms Toronto, 1929-91; ptnr. Denison Mines Ltd.; cons. Templeton Funds, Grafton Group; dir. emeritus Dome Mines Ltd.; bd. dirs. many large mining and fin. cos. in Can. and U.S. Mem. founding bd., trustee York U. Inducted Can. Mining Hall of Fame, 1989; named Knight Comdr. of St. Gregory. Roman Catholic. Home: Toronto Ont., Canada Died Nov. 26, 1991.

JANIS, IRVING LESTER, research psychologist, emeritus educator; b. Buffalo, May 26, 1918; s. M. Martin and Etta (Goldstein) J.; m. Marjorie Graham, Sept. 5, 1939; children: Cathy Wheeler, Charlotte. B.S., U. Chgo., 1939; Ph.D. in Psychology, Columbia U., 1948. Rsch. asst., exptl. div. study war time comm. Library of Congress, 1941; sr. social sci. analyst, spl. war policies unit Dept. Justice, 1941-43; rsch. assoc., spl. com. Social Sci. Rsch. Coun., 1945-46, rsch. fellow, 1946-47; mem. faculty Yale U., 1947-85, prof. psychology, 1960-85, prof. emeritus, from 1985; adj. prof. U. Calif.-Berkeley, from 1985; research cons. RAND Corp., 1948-74; mem. panel social psychol. research NSF, 1965-66; mem. com. disaster studies NRC-Nat. Acad. Scis., 1953-57; mem. Surgeon Gen.'s Sci. Adv. Com. on TV and Social Behavior, 1969-71. Author: Air War and Emotional Stress, 1951, (with Hovland and Kelley) Communication and Persuasion, 1953, Psychological Stress, 1958, (with others) Personality and Persuasibility, 1959, Stress and Frustration, 1971, Victims of Groupthink, 1972, (with L. Mann) Decision Making, 1977, (with D. Wheeler) A Practical Guide for Making Decisions, 1980, (with others) Counseling on Personal Decisions: Theory and Research on Short-term Helping Relationships, 1982, Short-term Counseling: Guidelines Based on Recent Research, 1983, Groupthink, 1983, Stress, Attitudes and Decisions: Selected Papers (Centennial Psychology Series), 1982, Crucial Decisions: Leadership in Policymaking and Crisis Management, 1989; also articles, chpts. in books.; editor: Current Trends in Psychology: Readings from American Scientist, 1977; contbg. editor: Jour. Abnormal and Social Psychology, 1955-65; mem. editorial bd.: Jour. Exptl. Social Psychology, 1966-70, Am. Scientist, 1970-79, Jour. Behavioral Medicine, from 1978, Brit. Jour. Social Psychology, from 1980 ; chmn. editorial bd.: Jour. Conflict Resolution, from 1972. Served with AUS, 1943-45. Recipient Hofheimer prize Am. Psychiat. Assn., 1959, Socio-Psychol. prize AAAS, 1967, Kurt Lewin Meml. award Soc. for Psychol. Study Social Issues, 1985, Sanford award Internat. Soc. Polit. Psychology, 1990; Fulbright rsch. fellow, 1957-58, sr. faculty fellow Yale U., 1961-62, 69-70, faculty rsch. fellow Social Sci. Rsch. Coun., 1961-62, 66-67, Guggenheim fellow, also fellow Ctr. Advanced Study Behavioral Scis., 1973-74, rsch. fellow The Netherlands Inst. Advanced Studies, 1981-82. Fellow Am. Acad. Arts and Scis., Am. Psychol. Assn. (Disting. Sci. Contbn. award 1981). Home: Santa Rosa Calif. Deceased. †

JANIS, JAY, savings and loan executive; b. L.A., Dec. 22, 1932; s. Ernest and Diana (Friedman) J.; m. Juel Mendelsohn, 1954; children: Laura, Jeffrey. AB with high honors, Yale U., 1954. Ptnr., community developer Janis Corp. (named changed to MGIC-Janis Properties 1970) and related cos. in pvt. bldg. industry), South Fla., 1956-64, 69-75; with Dept. Commerce, Washington, 1964-66; exec. dir. nat. citizens' com., community rels. svc. Dept. Commerce, 1964-65; dir. OEO, spl. asst. to under sec. Commerce, 1965-66; exec. asst. to sec. HUD, Washington, 1966-69; under sec. HUD, 1977-79; chmn. Fed. Home Loan Bank Bd., Washington, 1979-80; pres. Calif. Fed. Savs. and Loan Assn., Los Angeles, 1981-82; chmn. exec. com. Gibraltar Savs. Corp., Beverly Hills, Calif., 1983-88; chmn. bd. Gibraltar Savs., Beverly Hills, Calif., 1988; chmn. bd. Flagship Fed. Savs; bd. dirs. Mortgage Guaranty Ins. Corp., Coast Savs., L.A.; sr. v.p. for mgmt. and bus. affairs U. Mass., 1976-77; former prin. housing adviser to gov. Fla.; former bd. dirs. Nat. Assn. Home Builders, Nat. Com. against Discrimination in Housing; former mediator labor disputes in constrn. industry. Past pres. bd. trustees Fla. Internat. Univ. Found., Miami. Served with Intelligence Corps U.S. Army, 1954-56. Home: Los Angeles Calif. Died Oct. 26, 1992. †

JANIS, SIDNEY, art dealer, author; b. Buffalo, July 8, 1896; s. Isaac and Celia (Cohn) J.; m. Harriet Grossman, Sept. 2, 1925; children: Conrad, Carroll. Student pub., tech. and aero. schs. Engaged in mfg., 1924-39, collector modern art,, 1925-89; owner Sidney Janis Gallery, N.Y.C., 1948-89; mem. adv. com. Mus. Modern Art, N.Y.C., 1933-48, hon. trustee, 1983-89; mem. art panel IRS, Washington, 1975-76. Author: They Taught Themselves, 1942, Abstract and Surrealist Art in America, 1944, (with Harriet Janis) Picasso: Recent Years, 1946, also articles in art jours. Decorated comdr. Order Arts and Letters, Legion of Honor (France); recipient mayor's award for arts and culture City of N.Y., 1986; named Living Legend, NYU Sch. Social Work, 1979; donated Sidney and Harriet Janis collection 20th century art to Mus. Modern Art, 1967. Home: New York N.Y. Died Nov. 24, 1989; buried Mt. Hebron Cemetery, Queens, N.Y.

JANSSEN, WERNER, symphony conductor; b. N.Y.C., June 1, 1900; m. Ann Harding (div. Feb. 1963); m. Christina Heintzmann; children; Werner Jr., Alice Krelle, Jennifer. BA, Dartmouth U., 1921, MusD, 1935. Condr. almost every major orch. in Europe and U.S., debut under Arturo Toscanini with N.Y. Philharm., 1934; guest condr. Europe, U.S., 1934-37; music dir. Balt. Symphony, 1937-39; condr. Janssen Symphony, L.A., 1940-52; chief condr. Utah Symphony, Portland (Oreg.) Symphony, San Diego Philharm. Compositions include symphonic score for The General Died at Dawn, 1936 (Acad. award), New Year's Eve in New York (Prix de Rome), 1930, Louisiana Symphony, 1932, Dixie Fugue, 1932, Foster Suite, 1937, Kaleidoscope for string quartet, 1932, Fantasy, for string quartet, 1934, String Quartet No. 1, 1934, String Quartet No. 2, 1935, Obsequies of a Saxophone, for six wind instruments, snare drums, 1930; commd. Quintet for ten instruments Harvard Music Assn., 1967. U.S. fellow Juilliard; decorated knight Order of White Rose (Finland). Home: Stony Brook N.Y. Died Sept. 19, 1990.

JARCHOW, CHARLES CHRISTIAN, business executive; b. Chgo., Dec. 22, 1894; s. Charles and Sophie (Kath) J.; m. Lillie Schreyak, June 25, 1919; children: Robert B., Marjorie (Mrs. R. H. Wellington). Student, Northwestern U., 1913-16. CPA, Ill. With Am. Steel Foundries, Chgo., 1912-92, comptroller, 1924-43, v.p., comptroller, 1943-47, exec. v.p., 1947-49, pres., 1949-59, dir., 1943-63, chmn. of bd., 1959-61; dir. Ill. Bell Telephone Co., Pure Oil Co. Pres. Taxpayers Fedn. Ill.; dir. Ill. Inst. Tech. Mem. Chgo. Club, Comml. Club, Tavern (Chgo.) Club, Glen View Golf Club, Westmoreland Country Club, Three Lakes (Wis.) Rod and Gun Club. Republican. Mason. *

JARVIS, PORTER M., business executive; b. Clarksburg, W.Va., Nov. 6, 1902; s. Hugh and Harriet (Maxwell) J.; m. Elizabeth Hauck, Feb. 11, 1928 (dec.); children: Hugh, Elizabeth. BS, Iowa State Coll., 1924. With Swift & Co., Chgo., 1926-91, v.p., 1941-49, dir., 1949-91, exec. v.p., 1950-55, pres., 1955-64, chmn., chief exec. officer, 1964-91; dir. Internat. Harvester Co., Continental Ill. Nat. Bank, Ill. Cen. R.R., Am. Meat Inst., Internat. Livestock Expn. Trustee U. Chgo., Com. Econ. Devel., Mus. Sci. and Industry. Mem. Chgo. Assn. Commerce (dir.), Econ. Club, Exec. Club, Comml. Club. Methodist. Home: Tubac Ariz. Died Dec. 30, 1991.

JASLOW, ROBERT IRWIN, physician, hospital administrator; b. Reading, Pa., Apr. 27, 1923; s. Paul and Frances (Miller) J.; m. Edith Kay Supak, May 18, 1946; children—Ann Sharon, Alan Philip, Paula Sue. B.A., Lehigh U., 1943; M.D., Jefferson Med. Coll. Phila., 1947. Diplomate: Am. Bd. Pediatrics. Intern Jewish Hosp., Phila., 1947-48; resident Willard Parker Hosp. for Contagious Diseases, N.Y.C., 1948; pediatrics Jewish Hosp., Bklyn., 1949-50; practice medicine specializing in pediatrics Chambersburg, Pa., 1953-60; adminstr. medicine Northville, Mich., 1960-65, Washington, 1965-71, White Plains, N.Y., 1971-72, Fairfax, Va., 1972-74; clin. dir. Pennhurst State Sch. Annex No. 1 South Mountain, Pa., 1955-59; psychiat. clin. dir. Plymouth State Home and Tng. Sch., 1960-61, acting med. supt., 1961, med. supt., 1961-65; asso. pediatrician Children's Hosp., Detroit, 1964-65; chief Mental Retardation br. USPHS, Washington, 1965-67; dir. div. mental retardation Dept. Health, Edn. and Welfare, 1967-71; dir. Westchesster (N.Y.) State Sch., 1971-72, No. Va. Tng. Center for Mentally Retarded, Fairfax, 1972-74, Woodhaven Center, Phila., 1974-78; med. dir. New Lisbon (N.J.) State Sch., 1978-84, Letchworth Devel. Disabilities Services, Thiells, N.Y., 1984-90; instr. pediatrics Sch. Medicine, Wayne State U., 1961-64, clin. asst. prof., 1964-65; assoc. prof. clin. pediatrics Georgetown U., 1966-70, prof. clin. pediatrics, 1970-71, 72-74; clin. prof. pediatrics Temple U., 1975-78, Camden br. Rutgers Med. Sch., 1978-85; Faculty Sch. Edn. U. Mich., summer 1963; lectr. maternal and child health Sch. Edn. U. Mich. (Sch. Pub. Health), 1963-65; cons. Nat. Inst. Child Health and Human Devel., HEW, 1963-65. Contbr. articles to profl. jours. Served to capt. AUS, 1951-53. Fellow Am. Acad. Pediatrics (past chmn. juvenile delinquency com. Mich. chpt.), Am. Assn. Mental Deficiency, Am. Pub. Health Assn.; mem. N.Y. Acad. Scis. Home: Nanuet N.Y. Died Nov. 26, 1990.

JAY, ERIC GEORGE, theology educator; b. Colchester, Eng., Mar. 1, 1907; s. Henry and Maude (Lucking) J.; m. Margaret Webb, July 22, 1937; children—Christine, Susan, Peter. B.A., Leeds (Eng.) U., 1929, M.A., 1930; B.D., London (Eng.) U., 1937, M.Th., 1940, Ph.D., 1951; D.D. (hon.), Montreal Diocesan Theol. Coll., 1965, Trinity Coll., Toronto, 1975, United Theol. Coll., Montreal, 1976. Ordained to ministry Anglican Ch., 1931; asst. curate St. Augustine's Ch., Stockport, Cheshire, Eng., 1931-34; lectr. theology King's Coll., London, 1934-47; dean of Nassau Bahamas, 1948-51; sr. chaplain to Archbishop of Canterbury, 1951-58; prin. Montreal Diocesan Theol. Coll., 1958-63; prof. hist. theology McGill U., Montreal, Que., Can., 1958-75, emeritus prof., 1977-89, dean faculty div., 1963-70; canon Christ Ch., Montreal, from 1960. Author: The Existence of God, 1946, Origen's Treatise on Prayer, 1954, Friendship with God, 1958, New Testament Greek, An Introductory Grammar, 1958, Son of Man, Son of God, 1965, The Church: Its Changing Image Through Twenty Centuries, 1977. Served as chaplain RAF, 1940-45. Fellow King's Coll., 1949. Mem. Canadian Theol. Soc. (pres. 1965). Home: Montreal P.Q., Canada Died Feb. 7, 1989.

JEANNERET, MARSH, publisher; b. Toronto, Ont., Can., Feb. 9, 1917; s. Francois Charles Archile and Evelyn Frances (Geikie) J.; m. Beatrice Mellon, Dec. 31, 1938; children: David Kenneth, Keith Marsh (dec.). BA in Honour Law, U. Toronto, 1938; LLD (hon.), McGill U., Montreal, Que., Can., 1966; DLitt (hon.), Meml. U., St. John's, Nfld., Can., 1977; DU (hon.), Laval U., Que., 1978; LLD (hon.), U. Toronto, 1987. Editor Copp Clark Co., Ltd., Toronto, 1938-53, also bd. dirs.; dir. U. Toronto Press, 1953-77; pres. Can. Book Pubs'. Coun., 1968-69; mem. Ont. Royal Commn. on Book Pub., 1970-73. Author: The Story of Canada, 1946, Canada in North America, 1956, God and Mammon, 1989; contbr. articles to profl. jours.; chmn. editorial bd. Scholarly Publishing, 1976-80. Decorated officer Order of Can., 1978. Mem. Assn. Canadian

Pubs., Assn. Am. Univ. Presses (pres. 1970-71), Canadian Book Mfg. Assn., Graphic Arts Industries Assn. Can., Internat. Assn. Sch. Pubs. (pres. 1976-78), Canadian Copyright Inst. Mem. United Ch. Can. Club: Bd. of Trade (Toronto). Home: King City Ont., Canada Died Aug. 10, 1990; buried King City, Ont.

JEFFEE, SAUL, film and theater company executive; b. Elizabeth, N.J., Mar. 30, 1918; s. Michael and Frieda (Copeland) J.; m. Beatrice Ball Kahn, Oct. 26, 1952; 1 dau., Gail Susan. Student, NYU, Columbia U. Founder, pres., chmn. bd. Movielab, Inc., from 1934; pres., chmn. bd. Movielab-Hollywood, Inc.; chmn. bd., chief exec. officer Movielab Video Inc.; chmn. bd., pres. Movielab Theatre Service, Inc.; Founding vice chmn. Film Soc. Lincoln Center, 1969-87; patron Lincoln Center for Performing Arts.; Am. tech. rep. U.S.-U.S.S.R. Cultural and Sci. Exchange Agreement, Russia, 1965; mem. N.Y.C. Mayor's Adv. Council for Motion Pictures; adv. bd. Cinema lodge B'nai B'rith; mem. film acquisition com., pvt. sector com. USIA. Author: Narcotics-An American Plan, 1966; patentee motion picture equipment. Nat. adv. com. on scouting for handicapped Boy Scouts Am.; trustee United Jewish Appeal, Fedn. Jewish Philanthropies, Will Rogers Meml. Fund; chmn. bd. trustees Lorge Sch., 1968-81; bd. dirs. Am. Liver Found; leader Anti-Defamation League, 1950's; donated libr. of hist. motion picture inventions to Margaret Herrick Libr. of Acad. Motion Picture Arts and Scis. Life fellow Soc. Motion Picture and TV Engrs. (treas.); mem. Assn. Cinema Labs. (pres. 1963), Motion Picture Pioneers, Acad. Motion Picture Arts and Scis., Nat. Acad. TV Arts and Scis., Internat. Radio and TV Soc., Max Steiner Music Soc. (life; chmn. life patron program), Variety Clubs Internat. (dir. N.Y.), Jewish Chatauqua Soc. Clubs: City Athletic, Friars, Masons (Shriner, 32 deg.). Home: New York N.Y. Died June 11, 1991.

JEFFERDS, VINCENT HARRIS, film production company executive; b. Jersey City, Aug. 23, 1916; s. Jerome V. and Jenny J.; m. Jean Macbride, Dec. 8, 1946; children: Jean, Vincent, Jenny. B.A. in Journalism and Advt, Rutgers U., 1941. Asst. to pres., dir. Times Sq. Stores, N.Y.C., 1946-51; with Walt Disney Prodns., Burbank, Calif., 1951-83, v.p. sales promotion, 1961-71, v.p. consumer products div., 1975-79, sr. v.p. mktg., 1980-83. Served to capt. U.S. Army, 1942-46. Named World's Outstanding Licensing Marketer Nuremberg Toy Conf., 1968; recipient U.S. Licensing Mfrs. Assn. award, 1983; numerous awards for mktg. programs Procter & Gamble; others. Home: Brentwood Calif. Died Apr. 12, 1992.

JEFFORDS, WALTER M., JR., utilities executive; b. Glen Riddle, Pa., Nov. 16, 1915; s. Walter M. and Sarah (Fiske) J.; m. Kathleen McLaughlin, 1984; children: George Vincent, John Dobson, Sarah Dobson. AB, Yale U., 1938. Pres., chmn. Bklyn. Borough Gas Co., 1949-59; cons. Bklyn. Union Gas Co.; dir. The Equity Corp., Bell Intercontinental Corp., Fedn. Bank & Trust Co. Mem. adv. bd. Coney Island Hosp; trustee Bklyn. Inst. Arts and Sci. With AUS, 1941-45. Mem. Bklyn. C. of C. (dir.), Coney Island C. of C. (dir.), Soc. Gas Lighting, Bankers of Am. Club, Bklyn. Engrs. Club, Knickerbocker Club, Racquet Club (Phila.). Home: South Padre Island Tex. Died Feb. 24, 1990.

JEFFRIES, WILLIAM WORTHINGTON, museum director, archivist, historian; b. Mobile, Ala., July 23, 1914; s. Frank Mauzy and Gertrude (Worthington) J.; m. Mary Ruth Franklin, Aug. 31, 1940; children: John Worthington, Susan Jeffries Schwartz, Gertrude Jeffries Parker, Margaret Jeffries McKee., Virginia Jeffries Oxford. A.B., Birmingham-So. Coll., 1935; M.A., Vanderbilt U., 1936, Ph.D., 1941. Teaching fellow Vanderbilt U., 1936-38, 40-41; instr. Birmingham-So. Coll., 1938-40; asst. prof. history U. Miss., 1941-42; officer instr. U.S. Naval Acad., 1942-46, asst. prof., 1946-48, assoc. prof., 1948-55, prof., 1955-89, sr. prof. English, history and govt., 1955-70, archivist, 1970-89, dir. Acad. Mus., 1973-89. Co-author: American Sea Power since 1775, 1947, International Relations, 1955, 3d, rev. edit., 1960; editor, co-author: Geography and National Power, 1956, 4th, rev. edit., 1967; editor: Ann. Command History of U.S. Naval Acad, 1970-89. Served with USNR, 1942-46. Mem. So. Hist. Assn., Middle Atlantic Regional Archives Conf., U.S. Naval Acad. Alumni Assn. (asso.), Sigma Alpha Epsilon, Omicron Delta Kappa, Pi Gamma Mu, Kappa Phi Kappa, Delta Phi Alpha. Democrat. Methodist. Home: Annapolis Md. Died Dec. 17, 1989; buried Forest Hill Cemetery, Birmingham, Ala.

JELINEK, HANS, artist, educator; b. Vienna, Austria, Aug. 21, 1910; came to U.S., 1938, naturalized, 1943; s. Hermann and Paula (Stwertka) J.; m. Gertrude Stwertka. Grad., U. Vienna, 1933, Vienna Kunstgewerbeschule, 1933. Mem. art faculty New Sch. Social Research, 1945-57; asst. prof. art Coll. City N.Y., 1948-58, asso. prof., 1958-66, prof., 1966-79, prof. emeritus, 1979-92; mem. faculty Nat. Acad. Sch. Fine Arts, from 1973. Represented in permanent collections, Met. Mus., Library of Congress, Cooper Union, Dartmouth, N.Y. Pub. Library, Nelson A. Rockefeller collection, many others, work exhibited, throughout U.S., Europe, Asia, one man shows, Va. Mus. Art, Smithsonian Instn., others. Recipient numerous awards for woodcuts including 1st prize Artists for Victory Nat. Graphic Art Exhbn., 1943; Pennell prize Libr. of Congress 3d nat. print exhbn.; Tiffany award, others; Benjamin Franklin fellow Royal Soc. Arts, London. Mem. NAD (Academician), Soc. Graphic Artists. Home: New York N.Y. Died Mar. 13, 1992.

JENKINS, HAROLD RICHARD, indexing services and library consultant; b. Pottstown, Pa., Aug. 23, 1918; s. Stanley Frederick and Flora (High) J.; m. Margaret Houston Leech, Nov. 1, 1957; children: M. Elizabeth, Richard H. B.A., Ursinus Coll., 1953; M.A. in L.S, U. Mich., 1956. Catalog librarian Washington and Lee U., Lexington, Va., 1956-58; dir. Kingsport (Tenn.) Pub. Library, 1958-59, Wise County (Va.) Regional Library, 1959-61, Pottstown Pub. Library, 1961-63, Lancaster County (Pa.) Library, 1963-74, Kansas City (Mo.) Pub. Library, 1974-83; 2d v.p. Pa. Library Assn., 1968; state chmn. Nat. Library Week, 1967. Author: Management of a Public Library, 1981; contbr. articles to profl. jours. Bd. dirs. Lancaster County Hist. Soc., 1972-73. Served with C.E. AUS, 1941-52. Mem. ALA, Spl. Libraries Assn., Mo. Library Assn. (pres. 1977-78), Am. Soc. Indexers, Jackson County Hist. Soc., Beta Phi Mu, Pi Gamma Mu. Lodge: Rotary. Home: Kansas City Mo. Died June 29, 1989; cremated.

JENKINS, JOHN HENRY, government official; b. Malvern, Eng., Sept. 25, 1898; s. Henry Martyn and Anna (Hancock) J.; m. Margaret Gordon, Oct. 2, 1923; children: Elizabeth Ann, William John. BA in Forestry Engring., U. B.C., 1923; DSc in Forestry, Laval U., 1960; LLD, U. New Brunswick, 1964. Chief timber products div. Forest Products Labs. of Can., Vancouver, B.C., 1924-39; asst. supt. Forest Products Labs. of Can., Ottawa, Ontario, 1946-50; chief Forest Products Labs. of Can., 1950-60; dir. forest products rsch. Can. Dept. Forestry, 1960-65, forest products adviser, 1965-92. Contbr. articles to govt. publs. Served with the Canadian Army, 1939; served as dir. mil. ops. and planning, Nat. Defence Hdqrs., Ottawa, 1942-46; also connected with activities of Can.-U.S. Joint Defence Bd. Decorated Order of Brit. Empire (officer), U.S. Legion of Merit (officer), Czechoslovak Order of White Lion, Belgian Order of Leopold, Cross of Freedom of King Haakon VII (Norway). Mem. ASTM, Forest Products Rsch. Soc. (chmn. E. Can. sect.), Canadian Standards Assn. (v.p.), Canadian Inst. Forestry, Profl. Inst. Civil Svc., Mil. Engrs. Assn. Can. Anglican. *

JENKINS, ROBERT SPURGEON, management consultant; b. Wellston, Ohio, Oct. 24, 1921; s. Isaac Spurgeon and Carolyn (Burns) J.; m. Margaret Gene Kennard, Sept. 1, 1946; children: Deborah Gene and Priscilla Ann (twins), Roberta Kennard, Cynthia Carolyn. A.A., Rio Grande Coll., 1943; A.B., Denison U., 1946; M.A., Ohio State U., 1948, Ph.D., 1951; M.P.A. (hon.), Rio Grande Coll., 1981. Capital investment analysis supr. Ford div. Ford Motor Co., 1952-55, exec. to exec. v.p., 1956-57; asst. orgn. and systems mgr. L-M Div. Ford Motor Co., 1958-60, mktg. adminstrn. mgr., 1960-63, sales and mktg. mgmt. mgr., 1964-65; sr. dir. personnel Trans World Airlines, 1965-69; pres. R.S. Jenkins & Co. (Mgmt. Cons. and Exec. Search), 1970-71; sr. v.p., mng. partner, dir. Eastman & Beaudine, Inc. (Internat. Mgmt. Cons.), 1971-91; Asst. dir. research Ohio Tax and Revenue Study Commn., 1951; prof. indsl. mgmt. Henry Ford Coll., 1958-63; lectr. Am. Mgmt. Assn., 1968-69; personnel cons. Peace Corps, Washington, 1970. Author: Financing Public Education in Ohio, 1951. Mem. Livonia (Mich.) Sch. Bd., 1957, Plymouth (Mich.) Sch. Bd., 1965; mem. adv. bd. Ohio State U., 1986-90; pres. Plymouth Symphony Soc., 1960-62; mem. personnel bd. N.Y. Light House Assn., N.Y.C., 1968-70; trustee Rio Grande Coll., 1981-92. Served with USAAF, 1943-46. Recipient Outstanding Alumnus Achievement award Rio Grande Coll., 1981. Mem. Am. Econ. Assn., Am. Mgmt. Assn., Wee Burn Country Club, Univ. Club, Board Rm. Club, Wings Club, Landmark Club, Sigma Chi (life). Presbyterian (elder 1969-71, 88-91). Home: Salem S.C. Died Nov. 19, 1992. †

JENKINS, WILLIAM ROBERT, architect, university administrator; b. Des Moines; s. Frank Lafette and Gladys Adel (Reach) J.; m. Mary Lou Forrester, June 14, 1947; children: Melena, Cassandra. B.Arch., U. Houston, 1951; M.Arch., Tex. A. and M. U., 1966. Prin. William R. Jenkins Architects, Houston; asst. prof. architecture U. Houston, 1956-60, assoc. prof., from 1960, prof., 1960-68, dean Coll. Architecture, from 1968. Co-investigator NSF/Solar Energy Project. Served with USN, 1942-46. Recipient design awards Tex. Soc. Architects, design awards AIA, design awards Contemporary Arts Soc., design awards House and Home Mag., design awards Progressive Architecture, design awards Houston Ind. Sch. Dist., design awards Houston Home and Garden. Fellow AIA; mem. Nat. Council Archtl. Registration Bds., Assn. Collegiate Sch. Architecture, Tex. Soc. Architects, Tex. Archtl. Found. (past sec.). Home: Houston Tex. Deceased. †

JENNINGS, ALVIN R., accountant; b. Newark, 1905. Exec. ptnr. Lybrand, Ross Bros. & Montgomery, CPAs, N.Y.C.; Trustee Com. Econ Devel. Home: West Orange N.J. Died Mar. 14, 1990.

JENSEN, GEORGE ALBERT, lawyer; b. St. Louis, June 27, 1929; s. Albert Peter and Mary E. (Baker) J.; m. Martha Jean Collins, Sept. 10, 1949; children: Noncy, Georgia, Peter. AB, Washington U., St. Louis, 1952, JD, 1954. Bar: Mo. 1954. Assoc. Peper, Martin, Jensen, Maichel & Hetlage, St. Louis, 1954-58, ptnr., 1958-90; bd. dirs. A.G. Edwards, Inc. and various subs. Editor in chief Washington U. Law Quarterly, 1953-54; contbr. articles to profl. jours. Trustee St. Louis U., from 1983. Mem. Nat. Coun. for Sch. of Law Washington U. (founding mem.), Univ. Club, Media Club, Old Warson Country Club, Noonday Club. Mem. United Ch. of Christ. Home: Alton Ill. Died Dec. 1990. †

JENSON, SHERMAN MILTON, insurance company executive; b. Berthold, N.D., Jan. 15, 1920; s. Canute T. and Emma (Rohne) J.; m. Mary G. Blaul, Oct. 14, 1948; 1 child, Jennifer Ann. B.A., Luther Coll., 1941; diploma bus. adminstrn., LaSalle U., 1948. Chemist, Solvay Process Co., Hopewell, Va., 1941-43; pharm. salesman Lakeside Labs., St. Paul, 1946-47; regional group mgr. Minn. Mut. Life Ins. Co., Chgo., 1947-55; v.p. group Am. United Life Ins. Co., Indpls., 1955-69; gen. mgr. group div. Bankers Life & Casualty Co., Chgo., 1969-73; pres., chief exec. officer, chmn. exec. com. Nat. Investors Life Ins. Co., Little Rock, 1973-83, pres. emeritus, 1983-88; dir., chmn. bd., pres. NOR Securities Co., 1975-83; dir., chmn. bd., pres., mem. exec. com. Nat. Investors Pension Ins. Co., 1978-83. Served with USNR, 1943-46. Club: Pleasant Valley Country. Home: Memphis Tenn. Died Oct. 16, 1988; buried Clifton, Tex.

JETTON, CLYDE THOMAS, education educator; b. St. James, Ark., Oct. 23, 1918; s. William Thomas and Laura Ellen (Greenway) J.; m. Dorothy Marie Chasteen, Nov. 30, 1944; 1 son, Ronald Clyde. B.A., Northeastern State Coll., 1939; M.A., Okla. State U., 1940; Ph.D., Tex. Tech. Coll., 1955. Tchr. elementary sch. Locust Grove, Okla., 1940; psychometrist Hardin-Simmons U., 1947-49; counselor VA, 1949-51, Sweetwater (Tex.) pub. schs., 1951-54; prof. edn. Hardin-Simmons U., Abilene, Tex., 1955-80; grad. dean Hardin-Simmons U., 1965-80; vis. prof. Colo. State U., 1957-59, George Peabody Coll., 1963; cons. mental retardation, psychol. testing, counseling. Served to maj. AUS, 1940-47. Decorated Bronze Star, Purple Heart. Mem. Am. Personnel and Guidance Assn., NEA, Tex. Tchrs. Assn., So. Assn. Counselor Educators and Suprs., Nat. Vocat. Guidance Assn., Phi Delta Kappa. Baptist. Club: Civitan (sec. 1963, bd. dirs. from 1962). Home: Abilene Tex.

JEWELL, EDMUND FRANCIS, newspaperman; b. Danville, Ill., Mar. 12, 1896; s. Frank M. and Edna (Watkins) J.; m. Jeanette Lawson, Dec. 28, 1921; children: Jean, Frances Edna. Second Naval Dist. Tng. Sch., 1917-18; Student, Boston U., 1919-21. Advt. salesman Manchester Union, 1922-27; asst. bus. mgr. Boston Am., 1928; advt. dir. Washington Times & Herald, 1929; bus. mgr., advt. dir.%, 1930; gen. mgr. Washington Times Co., 1931-32; part owner, asst. treas., asst. pub. Manchester Union-Leader, 1933, 33-40, pub., 1940-45; advt. dir., spl. acct. exec. Washington Time-Herald, 1946-50, 50-54; dir. Amoskeag Indsl. Inc.; v.p. Farrington Mfg. Co. Boston; past dir. N.E. Coun., 1st v.p. Poughkeepsie Inn, Inc. Contbr. articles to profl. jours. Mem. N.H. State Rep. Commn.; Va. chmn. Nat. Found. for Infantile Paralysis, 1952-55; dir. Boys Club; state chmn., dir. funds N.H. Children's Aid. Commd. ensigh USNR, 1918; order to active duty, 1941; promoted capt., 1943; mem. staff commandant First Naval Dist., 1942-45; served as naval attache to Govts. in exile, London, Eng., 1944. Commendation by sec. of Navy Dir. New Eng. Daily Newspaper Assn. Mem. Ret. Officers Assn., Sigma Alpha Epsilon, Army and Navy Club, Yacht (Washington) Club, Union (Boston) Club, Ocean Reef Yacht Club, Coral Reef Yacht Club. *

JEWETT, HUGH JUDGE, surgeon; b. Balt., Sept. 26, 1903; s. Hugh Judge Jr. and Anne Van Lent (Ingraham) J.; m. Rosalind Huidekoper, Nov. 22, 1941 (div. Oct. 1971); 1 child, Rosalind Nelson; m. Margaret Moseley, Dec. 27, 1975. AB, Johns Hopkins U., 1926, MD, 1930. Diplomate Am. Bd. Urology (bd. govs. 1959-66). Intern John Hopkins Hosp., Balt., 1930-31, asst. in urology dept. pathology, 1932-33; asst. in urology Brady Urol. Inst., 1933-34, resident in urology, 1935-36; instr. in urology Johns Hopkins Sch. Medicine, 1935-38, from asst. prof. to prof. emeritus, 1938-90; asst. in urology St. Mary's Hosp., Pierre, S.D., 1931-32; resident urologist Ancker Hosp., St. Paul, 1934-35; urologist Ch. Home and Hosp., Balt., 1937—; cons. in urology Balt. City Hosps., Walter Reed Gen. Hosp., 1948-59; chmn. registry genito-urinary pathology Armed Forces Inst. Pathology, 1958-64. Contbr. chpts. to books; editor-in-chief Urol. Survey, 1951-90; mem. editorial bd. Rev. Surgery, Md. Med. Jour., 1952-60. Trustee Am. Urol. Rsch. Found., 1952; pres. Md. Med. Svc., Inc., 1950-54; councilor Med. and Chirurg. Faculty State Md., 1953-55. Lt. USMC, USNR, 1942. Fellow ACS (gov. 1958-64); mem. Am. Urol. Assn. (pres. 1965-66, pres. mid-Atlantic sect. 1956-57, Ramon Guiteras award 1963), Clin. Soc. Genito-Urinary Surgeons (pres. 1968-69), Am. Assn. Genito-Urinary Surgeons (pres. 1970-71), Soc. Univ. Urologists, Internat. Soc. Urology, Soc.

Venezloana de Urologia, Elkridge Club, Hamilton Street Club, Johns Hopkins Faculty Club, Chevy Chase Country Club, Phi Beta Kappa, Alpha Delta Pi. Episcopalian. Home: Baltimore Md. Died May 6, 1990.

JIMERSON, JAMES COMPERE, SR., toxicologist; b. Little Rock, Oct. 10, 1936; s. George Alexander and Lois (Compere) J.; m. Ina Sue Jones, Aug. 18, 1957; children—Martha LeAnn, James Compere. A.B., B.S., Ouachita Baptist Coll., 1958; postgrad., U. Ark., 1959; M.B.A., Ind. Central U., 1984. Lab. instr. Ouachita Bapt. Coll., Arkadelphia, Ark., 1957-58; teaching asst. U. Ark., Fayetteville, 1958-59; sr. chemist Allied Chem. Corp., Metropolis, Ill., 1959-62; analytical chemist Tech. Service Labs., P.R. Mallory & Co., Indpls., 1962-65; engring. research group leader Mallory Capacitor Co., Indpls., 1965-72; toxicologist, dept. pathology Wishard Meml. Hosp., Indpls., 1972-79, adminstrv. dir. dept. pathology, 1979-83, asst. hosp. adminstr., 1983-86; chmn. bd. Mgmt. Concepts, Inc., Indpls., 1986-87; asst. prof. bus. adminstrn. U. Indpls., 1987-90; affiliate instr. Ind. Vocat. Tech. Coll.; adj. faculty grad. sch. bus. U. Ind., Indpls., 1986-90. Patentee in field. Sr. staff/communication coord. Office Civil Def., Indpls. and Marion County, from 1965; bd. dirs. Crossroads of Am. coun. Boy Scouts Am., 1973-85, v.p., exec. com., 1975-80, commr., 1969-72, tng. chmn., 1972-73, dist. chmn., 1973-76; bd. dirs. Marion County unit Am. Cancer Soc. Recipient Silver Beaver award Boy Scouts Am., 1976; Pub. Service award Am. Radio Relay League, 1966, 74; named Man of Yr., Civil Def., 1976. Fellow Am. Inst. Chemists, Am. Acad. Forensic Scis.; mem. Am. Chem. Soc., Soc. for Applied Spectroscopy, Coblentz Soc., Central Ind. Clin. Biochem. Forum, Am. soc. Analytical Toxicologists, Nat. Eagle Scout Assn. (Silver Wreath award 1979), Central Ind. VHF/UHF Club. Republican. Baptist. Lodges: Masons, Scottish Rite. Home: Indianapolis Ind. Died June 2, 1990; buried Corning, Ark.

JOHNS, CYRUS N., business executive; b. Sedalla, Miss., July 29, 1894; s. William Minton and Alice (Newkirk) J.; m. Helen Steinert, Oct. 8, 1924 (dec. 1937); children: Margery Ann, Dorothy Helen. Student, U. Mo., 1916. Sales engr. Am. Chain & Cable Co., Inc., 1913-14, prodn. mgr., asst works mgr., works mgr., 1915-39, v.p. in charge ops., 1939-46, exec. v.p., 1946, dir., 1939, chmn. bd., CEO, 1939-92; dir. Md. Bolt & Nut Co., Domninion Chain Co., Ltd., Bristol Co., Parsons Chain Co., Ltd., Brit. Wire Products, Ltd., Univ. (Pitts.) Club, Union Club, Piping Rock Club, Rotary (Monessen, Pa.), Cornell Club (N.Y.C.). *

JOHNSEN, HARVEY M., judge; b. Hastings, Nebr., July 16, 1895; s. Peter C. and Mary (Jensen) J.; m. Helene M. Miles, Oct. 5, 1949 (dec. 1957). AB, U. Nebr., 1921, LLB, 1919, LLD (hon.), 1951; LLD (hon.), Creighton U., 1960. Bar: Nebr. 1919. Lawyer, assoc. Montgomery, Hall & Young, Omaha, 1920-25; ptnr. Montgomery, Hall, Young & Johnsen, Omaha, 1926-31; mem. faculty Creighton Law Sch., Omaha, 1922-26; gen. counsel Farm Credit Adminstrn., Omaha, 1931-33; ptnr. Johnsen, Gross & Crawford, Omaha, 1934-38; assoc. justice Supreme Ct. of Nebr., 1939-40; judge U.S. Cir. Ct. of Appeals (8th cir.), 1940-92, chief judge, 1959-65. Mem. ABA, Nebr. State Bar Assn. (pres. 1938), Am. Judicature Soc., Am. Law Inst., Rotary, Order of Coif, Phi Beta Kappa, Phi Delta Phi. Democrat. Episcopalian. *

JOHNSON, ARLIEN, social worker; b. Portland, Oreg., Oct. 31, 1893; d. Andrew Martin and Anna Gertrude (Folck) J. AB, Reed Coll., 1917; Grad., N.Y. Sch. Social Work, 1922. Spl. agt. Bur. Labor Statistics, U.S. Dept. Labor, 1918; assoc. sec. Seattle Community Fund, 1930-34; dir. Grad. Sch. Social Work, U. Wash., 1934-39; dean sch. social work U. So. Calif., 1939-59; freelance cons., 1959-92. Author: Public Policy and Private Charities, 1930, School Social Work, 1962; contbr. to Social Work Year Book, Nat. Conf. on Social Welfare, Ency. Social Work. Mem. survey Brit. Social Svcs. Fulbright Commn., 1954; pres. Nat. Conf. Social Work, 1947; mem. tng. com. NIMH. Mem. NASW, Am. Assn. Social Workers, Calif. Conf. Social Work, Coun. on Social Work Edn., Alpha Kappa Delta, Phi Kappa Phi. *

JOHNSON, BOB, professional hockey team coach; b. 1931. Coach U.S. Olympic Team, 1976, Calgary Flames, N.H.L., Alta., Can., 1982-87; exec. dir. U.S.A. Hockey/Amateur Hockey Assn. of the U.S., Colorado Springs, Colo., 1987-90; head coach Pitts. Penguins, NHL, 1990-91. Team winners of Stanley Cup, 1990. Home: Colorado Springs Colo. Died Nov. 26, 1991; buried Evergreen Cemetery, Colorado Springs.

JOHNSON, CARL WRIGHT, lawyer; b. Clarksville, Tex., Apr. 17, 1895; s. Walter Wright and Lida Eugenia (DeBerry) J.; m. Elma Boone Hall, Apr. 3, 1948. Student, Valparaiso U., 1912-14; LLB, Cumberland U., 1915. Bar: Tex. 1915. County atty. Red River County, Tex., 1916-20; mem. firm Chambers, Watson & Johnson, San Antonio, 1920-23, Chambers & Johnson, 1923-27; chief asst. dist. atty. Bexar County, Tex., 1925-27; pvt. practice law San Antonio, from 1927. Served in Cen. Inf., O.T.C., World War I. Mem. Masons, Kappa Sigma, Delta Theta Phi. Democrat. *

JOHNSON, CLARENCE LEONARD, aircraft company executive; b. Ishpeming, Mich., Feb. 27, 1910; s. Peter and Christine (Anderson) J.; m. Nancy Powers Harrigen, 1980. BS, U. Mich., 1932, MS, 1933, D. Engring. hon , 1964; DSc, U. So. Calif., 1964. With Lockheed Aircraft Corp., Burbank, Calif., 1933-90, chief rsch. engr., 1938-52, chief engr., 1952-56, v.p. charge R&D, 1956-58, v.p. advanced devel. projects, 1958-74, sr. v.p., 1974-90. Recipient Lawrence Sperry award Inst. Aero. Scis., 1937, Sylvanus A. Reed award, 1956, 66, Wright Bors. medal Soc. Automotive Engrs., 1941, Coller award for design of air frame, 1959, Disting. Alumnus award in engring. U. Mich., 1953, Gen. Hap Arnold gold medal award VFW, 1960, Collier trophy Nat. Aero. Assn., Look Mag., 1964, Theodore Von Karman award Air Force Assn., 1963, Presdl. Medal of Freedom, 1964, Nat. Medal of Sci., 1966, Thomas D. White Nat. Def. award USAF Acad., 1966. Fellow NAS, Inst. Aero. Scis. (chmn. West Coast sect. 1946-47, nat. v.p. 1948-53), Nat. Acad. Engring., Soc. Automotive Engrs., L.A. C. of C., Sigma Xi, Phi Kappa Phi, Tau Beta Pi (hon.). Home: Burbank Calif. Died Dec. 21, 1990; buried Forest Lawn, Hollywood Hills, Calif.

JOHNSON, CLAYTON ERROLD, poultry company executive; b. DeSota, Wis., Apr. 20, 1921; s. James and Louella (Goodin) J.; student U. Wis., 1940-41, Tex. A. and M. Coll., 1946; m. Betty E. Higenbotham, May 23, 1943; children: Roderick and Ronald (twins), Richard. Pres. Flavor Fresh Brand, Inc., 1949—; Calif. gen. bldg. contractor, 1947—. With USAAF, 1942-45. Died Aug. 30, 1992.Aug. 30, 1992. Home: Las Vegas Nev. †

JOHNSON, EDGAR FREDERICK, manufacturing company executive; b. Waseca, Minn., June 13, 1899; s. Charles John and Edna Sophia (Swanson) J.; m. Ethel Jones, July 28, 1923 (dec. 1991); children: Shirley Johnson Anderson, Lois Johnson Chaffin. B.S. in Elec. Engring., U. Minn., 1921. Founder E.F. Johnson Co., Waseca, Minn., 1923, gen. mgr., 1923-53, pres., 1953-68, chmn. bd. dirs., 1968-78, founder dir., 1978-83; dir. Research, Inc., Mpls., 1950's; dir., treas. Waseca Savs. and Loan Assn., 1963-82. Mem. Minn. Econ. Devel. Council, 1948; mem. nat. bd. advisors SBA, 1954, 60; trustee Gustavus Adolphus Coll., 1976-89, Midwest Research Inst., 1976-78, North Star Research Inst., 1967-78, Courage Found., 1976-85; trustee Johnson Found., 1964-83, pres., 1975-83; trustee Operation Bootstrap Tanzania, 1963-80, pres., 1969; trustee for 18 yrs. 1st Congl. Ch.; exec. council Minn. Hist. Soc., from 1970; mem. Bd. Edn. Waseca, 1932-50, pres., treas.; mem. Charter Commn. Waseca, 1963-71, pres., 1950-58. Served with U.S. Army, 1918. Recipient Outstanding Achievement award U. Minn., 1977, Bi-centennial gold medal King Karl Gustaf XVI of Sweden, 1976; named to Minn. Bus. Hall of Fame, 1977; E.F. Johnson Professorship of Electronic Comm. named in his honor, Inst. Tech., U. Minn. Fellow Radio Club Am. (Edgar F. Johnson Pioneer Citation award named in his honor, Sharnoff citation 1975); mem. IEEE (life). Republican. Clubs: Waseca Lions (pres. 1931), Waseca Lakeside (pres. 1948), Masons. Home: Waseca Minn. Died Feb. 11, 1991; buried Woodville Cemetery, Waseca, Minn.

JOHNSON, EDWARD CROSBY, II, investment executive; b. Boston, Jan. 19, 1898; s. Samuel and Josephine (Forbush) J.; m. Elsie Livingston Johnson, Oct. 18, 1924; children: Elsie Pierrepont (Mrs. John Mitchell), Edward Crosby. Student, Milton Acad., 1916; AB, Harvard U., 1920, LLB, 1924. Bar: Mass. 1924. Assoc. law firm Ropes & Gray, Boston, 1925-39; v.p., treas. Inc. Investors, Boston, 1939-45; pres., dir. Fidelity Fund, Inc., from 1943, Fidelity Capital Fund, Inc., from 1958, Fidelity Trend Fund, Inc., from 1958; v.p., trustee Milton Savs. Bank; v.p., dir. Crosby Corp., Boston; pres., dir. Fidelity Mgmt. & Rsch. Co., Congress St. Fund, Inc., from 1960, Essex Fund, Inc., from 1961, Dow Theory Investment Fund, Inc., from 1963, FMR Investment Mgmt. Svc. Inc., from 1964, 2d Congress St. Fund, Inc., from 1964; dir. Crosby Corp. Chmn. bd. appeals, bd. pub. welfare, Milton, Mass.; mem. investment com., trustee Children's Hosp.; mem. corp. Milton Hosp.; trustee Mary A. Cunningham Fund. Mem. Milton-Hoosic Club, Harvard Club, Union Club, Down Town Club. *

JOHNSON, FRANK HARRIS, cell physiologist, microbiologist; b. Raleigh, N.C., July 31, 1908; s. A.R.D. and Mary Victoria Harris J.; m. Mary Frances McGhee, June 11, 1933; children: Virginia Lane, Mary Frances, Charlotte Elizabeth. AB, Princeton U., 1931, PhD, 1936; MA, Duke U., 1934. Teaching fellow Vanderbilt U.; grad. rsch. fellow Woods Hole Oceanographic Inst.; Eli Elly & Co. rsch. fellow bilogy Princeton U., 1936-37, instr. biology, 1937-41, asst. prof., 1941-46, assoc. prof., 1946-56, prof., 1956-90, Edwin Grant Conklin prof. biology, 1969-9; vis. prof. U. Utah, 1950-51; program dir. devel., environ. and systematic biology NSF, 1952-53, cons., 1953-56; com. photobiology NRC, 1952-64. Author: with H. Eyring, M.J. Polissar , The Kinetic Basis of Molecular Biology, 1954, (with H. Eyring and Betsy J. Stover The Theory of Rate Processes in Biology adn Medicine, 1974; editor: The Luminescensce of Biological Systems, 1955, The Influence of Temperature on Biological Systems, 1957, with Y. Haneda Bioluminescence in Progress, 1966, A Letter to Three Daughters, 1984, Luminescence, Narcosis, and Life in The Deep Sea, 1988; mem. editorial bd. Am. Jour. Microbiology, 1953-57; hon. editor Photochemistry and Photobiology, 1961-66; fgn. editor Can. Jour. Microbiology, 1953-57. Rockefeller Found. fellow for biophysics and microbiol. rsch., the Netherlands, 1939, Guggenheim fellow, 1944-46, 50-51; recipient award with D.E. Brown, D.A. Marsland for rsch. basic mechanism in biol. effects of temperature, pressure and narcotics AAAS, 1942. Fellow Am. Acad. Microbiology; mem. Am. Soc. Zoology, Am. Phys. Soc., Am. Soc. for Microbiology, Soc. Exptl. Biology and Medicine, Soc. Gen. Physiology, AAAS, Art Students League N.Y. life , Princeton Club, Quadrangle Club Princeton, N.J. , Sigma Xi, Phi Beta Kappa. Home: Princeton N.J. Died Sept. 22, 1990; cremated, ashes to ocean.

JOHNSON, FRIDOLF LESTER, writer, graphic designer; b. Chgo., Feb. 24, 1905; s. Herman Oscar and Sophia Maria (Hanson) J.; m. Heidi Ruth Lenssen, July 19, 1958. Student, Sch. Art Inst., 1923-25. Art dir. Frankel-Rose Co., Chgo., 1925-34; owner Contempo Art Svc., Hollywood, Calif., 1948-50, Mermaid Press, N.Y.C., 1958-88. Exec. editor Am. Artist Mag., 1962-70; free lance designer, calligrapher, writer, book reviewer. Author: 200 Years of American Graphic Art, 1976; A Treasury of Bookplates, 1977; A Treasury of Pen and Ink Illustrations 1881-1938, 1982. Author/editor: Rockwell Kent, An Anthology of His Work, 1982, others. Recipient Merit award Art Dirs. Club, 1983. Home: Woodstock N.Y. Died July 21, 1988; buried Woodstock, N.Y.

JOHNSON, GUY BENTON, sociology and anthropology educator; b. Caddo Mills, Tex., Feb. 28, 1901; s. John Edward and Ora (Clark) J.; m. Guion Griffis, Sept. 3, 1923; children: Guy Benton, Edward Stokes. Student, Burleson Coll., Greenville, Tex., 1917-19; AB, Baylor U., 1921; AM, U. Chgo., 1922; PhD, U. N.C., 1927. Instr. sociology Ohio Wesleyan U., 1922-23; prof. Baylor Woman's Coll., 1923-24; rsch. asst. Inst. for Rsch., U. N.C., Chapel Hill, 1924-27, rsch. assoc., assoc. prof. sociology, 1927-41, prof., 1941-43, 47, prof. sociology and anthropology, from 1947, Kenan prof., from 1963; exec. dir. So. Regional Coun., 1944-47; fellow Social Sci. Rsch. Coun., 1936-37; mem. staff study Negro in Am., Carnegie Corp., 1939-40; vis. prof. social anthropology Rhodes U., South Africa, 1959-60; rep. U.S.-South Africa Leader Exch. Program, 1959-60. Author books on Negro folk culture, articles on Negro folk songs, dialect, mus. talent and race rels.; co-editor Social Forces, from 1961; contbr. articles to sociol. and psychol. jours. Trustee Howard U. Fellow Am. Anthrop. Assn., Am. Sociol. Assn.; mem. So. Sociol. Soc. (pres. 1953-54), Archaeol. Soc. N.C. (sec. 1933-39, pres. 1941), Alpha Psi Delta, Alpha Kappa Delta, Delta Upsilon. Democrat. Methodist. Home: Chapel Hill N.C. Died May 23, 1991; buried Chapel Hill, N.C.

JOHNSON, HERBERT CONRAD, gas and oil industry executive; b. Staten Island, Mar. 25, 1909; s. Conrad and Clara Marie (Olson) J.; m. May Helene Welzin, July 3, 1940; children: Keith Eldridge, Douglas Welzin. Various positions Standard Oil Co. (N.J.), 1927-43; asst. treas. Consol. Natural Gas Co., 1943-51, treas., 1951-58, dir., 1955-90, v.p., 1956-63, exec. v.p., 1963-66, pres., 1966-70, chmn., 1970-74; bd. dirs. Bklyn. Union Gas Co. Bd. dirs. Nat. Coun. on Crime and Delinquency. Mem. N.Y. C. of C., Newcomen Soc., Am. Gas Assn., Soc. Gas Lighting (past pres.), Richmond Country Club (pres.), Univ. Club, NYU Club, Eastwand Ho Country Club, Beta Gamma Sigma. Republican. Episcopalian. Home: Staten Island N.Y. Died Aug. 29, 1990; buried Christ Ch., Staten Island, N.Y.

JOHNSON, HOLLIS EUGENE, internist; b. Weakley County Tenn., Apr. 11, 1893; s. Hollis Eugene and Martha Reuben (Roach) J.; m. Frances Settle, Aug. 2, 1932; children: Hollis, Eugene III, John Settle, Robert Marshall. Student, Union U., Jackson, Tenn., 1915-16; MD, Vanderbilt U., 1921. Diplomate Am. Bd. Internal Medicine. Asst. anatomy, asst. med., asst. clin. medicine Vanderbilt U., Nashville, 1917-55, prof. clin.medicine, 1955-58, prof. emeritus, 1958-92; intern Davidson County TB Hosp., 1921-22; resident physician Vanderbilt U. Hosp., Nashville, 1922-23, vis. physician, dir. chest clinic, 1926-58; cons. Baptist Hosp., St. Thomas Hosp.; staff Nashville Gen. Hosp.; cons. chest diseases Thayer Gen. VA Hosp.; past lectr. on tuberculosis Meharry Med. Coll.; introduced collapse therapy by pneumothorax, 1922, bronchography, 1927. Past mem. adv. editorial bd. Diseases of the Chest; contbr. articles to med. jours. Bd. dirs. Nashville chpt. ARC, Bill Wilkerson Hearing and Speech Ctr.; past chmn. profl. exec. com. Tenn. div. Am. Cancer Soc.; chmn. adv. coun. Civil Def., Nashville-Davidson County; bd. trustees Belmont Coll. Fellow ACP, Am. Coll. Chest Physicians (bd. regents; sec.-treas., pres. So. chpt., nat. pres. 1961-62); mem. AMA (past ho. dels.), So. Tenn. Med. Assn., Mid. Tenn. Med. Assn., Vanderbilt Med. Assn., Am. Trudeau Soc., Am. Assn. Thoracic Surgery, Nat. TB Assn. (past mem., bd. dirs.), Tenn. Thoracic Soc., Nashville Thoracic Soc., Nashville-Davidson County Acad. Medicine, Nashville Soc. Internists (past pres.), Nashville C. of C., U.S. C. of C., Am. Legion, Sigma Alpha Epsilon, Alpha Kappa Kappa. *

JOHNSON, HUGH BAILEY, retired architect; b. South Bombay, N.Y., Mar. 12, 1904; s. Fenton Wesley and Florence Genevieve (Bailey) J.; m. Ida Rita Viale, Aug. 3, 1928; children: Hugh Bailey, David Wesley, Philip Anthony; m. Phyllis Walker Alexander, Jan. 12, 1968. B.Arch., Syracuse U., 1929. Mem. staff architect's office Bd. Edn. Rochester, N.Y., 1928-40; researcher and writer Am. Council Edn., Washington, 1940-42; mem. staff War Dept., 1942-45, Nat. Housing Agy., 1945-47; pres. Hugh Johnson Assocs., Inc., Architects, Washington, 1945-70, McGaughan & Johnson, Architects, 1951-78, McGaughan & Johnson P.C., Architects, 1978-86; ret., 1986. Bd. dirs. Arlington Symphony Assn., Va., 1956-90, pres., 1956-62; mem. Arlington County Adv. Com. on Alt. Growth Policy, 1974-76, successor com., 1977-78. Fellow AIA (nat. govt. liaison com. 1963-70, chmn. 1963-64, mem. nat. regional devel. and natural resources com. 1970-88, chmn. 1973-74); mem. Va. Soc. AIA (dir. 1976-77, chmn. land use and natural resources com. 1976-79). Democrat. Methodist. Home: Arlington Va. Died July 11, 1992; buried Columbia Gardens Cemetery, Arlington, Va. †

JOHNSON, JESSE CHARLES, mining engineer; b. Clallam, Wash., Feb. 22, 1894; s. Robert R. and Mary (Rosebrook) J.; m. Alice Frein, Nov. 14,1 925; 1 child, Mary Virginia. BS, U. Wash., 1919. Cons. mining engr. Seattle, 1919-26; securities bus., 1926-42; engr. R.F.C., Washington, 1943, chief engr., 1943-45, dep. dir. in charge domestic and fgn. metal procurement, 1946-47; dep. dir. div. raw materials A.E.C., Washington, 1948-49, dir., 1950-63; cons. Adviser U.S. del. Internat. Confs. Peaceful Uses Atomic Energy, Geneva, Switzerland, 1955, 58. Recipient Ambrose Morrell medal and prize, 1961. Mem. Am. Mining and Metall. Soc., Am. Inst. Mining and Metall. Engrs., Sigma Xi, Tau Beta Pi, Alpha Delta Phi, Cosmos Club. *

JOHNSON, JOSEPH ESREY, former foundation executive; b. Longdale, Va., Apr. 30, 1906; s. Joseph Esrey and Margaret Hill (Hilles) J.; m. Catherine D.W. Abbott, Dec. 31, 1930; children: Anne Johnson Stone, William R.A. SB, Harvard U., 1927, AM, 1932, PhD, 1943; LLD (hon.), Williams Coll., 1951, Bowdoin Coll., 1967, L.I. U., 1969. Instr. history Bowwdoin Coll., 1934-35; instr. history Williams Coll., 1936-38, asst. prof., 1938-47, on leave, 1942-47, prof., 1947-50; officer U.S. Dept. State, Washington, 1942-47, acting chief div. internat. security affairs, 1944-45, chief, 1945-47; pres., trustee Carnegie Endowment for Internat. Peace, N.Y.C., 1950-71, pres. emeritus, 1971-90; adviser U.S. del. Dumbarton Oaks Conf., 1944, Inter-Am. Conf. on Problems War and Peace, Mexico City, 1945; expert U.S. del. UN Conf. Internat. Orgn., San Francisco, 1945; adviser U.S. del. 1st session Gen. Assembly UN, London, N.Y.C., 1946; adviser, U.S. rep. UN Security Coun., London, N.Y.C., 1946; mem. police planning staff U.S. Dept. State, 1947; dep. U.S. rep. interim com. UN Gen. Assembly, 1948; advisor U.S. govt. dels. ILO, 1957, 58; spl. rep. UN Conciliation Commn. for Palestine, 1961-62; alt. U.S. rep. 24th UN Gen. Assembly, 1969. Trustee World Peace Found.; bd. dirs. Coun. Fgn. Rels., 1950-74, UN Assn. U.S.A. Fellow Am. Acad. Arts and Scis.; mem. Internat. Inst. Strategic Studies (London) (v.p.), Am. Alpine Club, Century Club (N.Y.C.), Cosmos Club (Washington), Alpine Club (London). Home: Lynchburg Va. Died Oct. 24, 1990; buried St. Stephen's Episcopal ch., Forest, Va.

JOHNSON, JOSEPH H., retail company executive; b. 1922; m. Gretchen Johnson; children: Joseph 3d, James. BS, U. Ala. With M. O'Neil Co. unit May Dept. Stores, Akron, Ohio, chief fin. officer, 1956-70; with Associated Dry Goods Corp., N.Y.C., 1970-86, v.p., treas. Lord & Taylor div., 1970-79, corp. chief fin. officer, 1979-84, chmn., chief exec. officer, dir., 1984-86. Mem. Pres.'s Cabinet U. Ala. Home: Greenwich Conn. Died Jan. 30, 1991.

JOHNSON, JOSEPH KELLY, sociologist, educator; b. Ralls County, Mo., Jan. 8, 1897; s. Joseph K. and Flora A. (Moore) J.; m. Virigina Tobin, Dec. 23, 1917; children: Joseph Kelly, Leonard T. (dec.), Kathryn (Mrs. Robert Coleman). AB, U. Tex., 1929, MA, 1930; PhD, Washington U., 1937. Pers. officer Office Adj. Gen. Tex., 1920-33; adj. prof. sociology U. Tex., 1934; instr. sociology Wash. State Coll., 1935-36; asst. prof., assoc. prof., prof. sociology East Tex. State Tchrs. Coll., 1936-42; prof. sociology So. Ill. U., 1947-92. Assoc. editor Sociological Quarterly, 1960-92. Served as 2d lt. U.S. A.S., 1918-19; capt. to lt. col. U.S. Army, 1942-47; lt. col. Adj. Gen. Corps, O.R.C., active duty as mem. staff and faculty Command and Gen. Staff Coll., Ft. Leavenworth, Kan., summers 1956-61. Mem. AAUP, Midwest Sociol. Soc., Am. Sociol. Soc., Phi Beta Kappa, Alpha Kappa Delta. *

JOHNSON, JOSEPHINE WINSLOW (MRS. GRANT G. CANNON), author; b. Kirkwood, Mo., June 20, 1910; d. Benjamin H. and Ethel (Franklin) J.; m. Grant G. Cannon, Apr. 5, 1942 (dec. 2969); children—Terence, Jane Ann, Carol Lynn. Student, Washington U., St. Louis, 1933, L.H.D. (hon.), 1970. Author: Now in November, 1934 (Pulitzer prize 1935), reprinted, 1987, Jordanstown, 1937, Wildwood, 1947; short stories Winter Orchard, 1936; poetry Years End, 1939; novel The Dark Traveler, 1963, The Sorcerer's Son; short stories, 1965, The Inland Island, 1969, reissue, 1987; autobiog. memoir Seven Houses, 1973, Circle of Seasons, (pictures by Dennis Stock), 1974; also numerous stories in Best Short Stories, other anthologies, 1944-46 (O. Henry Meml. award 1934, 35, 42-45); contbr. articles for Country Jour., McCall's mag. and Ohio mag. Recipient Alumnae citation Washington U., 1955; Cin. Inst. Fine Arts award, 1964; Ohioana Library citation, 1964; Sarah Chapman Francis medal Ganden Club Am., 1970; Am. Acad. Arts and Letters award, 1974. Mem. Authors Guild. Home: Mount Carmel OH Died Feb. 27, 1990; body donated to science.

JOHNSON, KARL RICHARD, emeritus academic administrator; b. Galesburg, Ill., Feb. 28, 1907; s. Charles Theodore Emanuel and Sigrid (Swanson) J.; m. Evelyn Jo Hilander, Aug. 7, 1943; children: Thomas Arthur, Anne Christine Johnson Gilford. BS, Knox Coll., 1929; MS, U. Colo., 1932, PhD, 1939, L.H.D., 1973. Instr. sci. and music Toluca (Ill.) High Sch., 1929-31, Abingdon (Ill.) High Sch., 1932-35; instr. sci. Thornton Twp. High Sch., Harvey, Ill., 1935-37; asst. in biology U. Colo., 1931-32, 37-39; instr. biology Knox Coll., 1939-40; head sci. dept. Nat. Coll. Edn., Evanston, Ill., 1940-48, vice chmn. adminstrv. coun., asst. to pres., 1945-48, pres., 1949-72, pres. emeritus, 1972-91; assoc. prof. biology Augustana Coll., 1948-49. Contbr. articles to publs. Vice pres. Fedn. Ill. Colls.; pres. Assocs. Colls. Ill; trustee Luth. Student Found.; active civilian def. work tng. instrnl. staff and operation of control ctr., Evanston, World War II; active Peninsula Music Festival, Sister Bay, Wis., 1972-90. Fellow AAAS, Ill. Acad. Sci., AAUP; mem. Nat. Intercollegiate Flying Assn. bd. dirs. , Nat. Aviation Edn. Coun. pres. , Nat. Aeros. Assn. bd. dirs. , Assocs. Colls. Ill. pres. , C. of C. bd. dirs. , Ecol. Soc. Am., Univ. Club, Econ. Club, Execs. Club, Rotary, Sigma Xi, Beta Beta Beta. Home: Evanston Ill. Died June 17, 1991.

JOHNSON, LOWELL REXFORD, gases and equipment manufacturer; b. Cooks Mills, Ill., Oct. 19, 1895; s. Dennis L. and Minnie (Hart) J.; m. Barbara Warren, Dec. 10, 1925; children: Dorothy Ann (Mrs. William H. Copher), Lowell W. LLB, U. Mo., 1923. Bar: Mo. 1923. Lawyer Kansas City, Mo., 1923-49; with Rosenberg & Reed, 1923-26; mem. Shugart & Johnson, 1926-39, Johnson & Davis, 1939-49; v.p., gen. counsel Puritan Compressed Gas Corp., Kansas City, 1943-49, exec. v.p., gen. mgr., dir., 1949-57, vice chmn. bd., gen. counsel, 1957-61, dir. corp. and subsidiaries, 1949-92; dir. Kansas City Nat. Bank & Trust Co., others. Mem. nat. exec. bd. Boy Scouts of Am., regional chmn., 1957-58; trustee Am. Humanics Found., Am. Legion Trust Assn.; pres. Liberty Meml. Assn. Candidate for Congress, 1936. 2d lt. Infantry, U.S. Army, World War I. Recipient Silver Beaver award, 1949, Silver Antelope award, 1954. Mem. C. of C., Phi Delta Phi, Acacia Conglist. Mason, Rotary, Kansas City Club. *

JOHNSON, MARTIN WIGGE, biologist; b. Chandler, S.D., Sept. 30, 1893; s. Christian Hans and Julia M. (Hansen) J.; m. Lelia T. Clutter, Apr. 16, 1924; children: Byron M., Phyllis T. BS, U. Wash., 1924, MS, 1930, PhD, 1931. Tchr. high schs. Seattle, 1924; curator Puget Sound (Wash.) Biol. Sta., 1924-29; biologist Internat. Passamaguoddy Fisheries Commn., 1932-33; rsch. assoc. U. Wash., 1933-34, assoc. prof. summers, 1941, 47, prof. summers, 1960, 62; faculty Scripps Inst. of Oceanography, U. Calif., La Jolla, 1934-92, asst. prof., assoc. prof. marine biology, 1934-49, prof. marine biology, 1949-62, prof. emeritus, rsch. marine biologist, 1962-92; marine biologist U. Calif. Div. War Rsch., 1942-46. Author: (with H. U. Sverdrup, R.H. Fleming) The Oceans, 1942; contbr. profl. papers to publs. Staff Operation Crossroads, USN, 1946; NRC co-chmn. com. on marine biology 6th Pacific Sci. Congress, 1939; del. NRC, also U. Cal., 7th and 8th Pacific Sci. Congresses, New Zealand, 1949, P.I., 1953; adv. com. Pacific Sci. Bd. NRC, 1946-92; UNESCO adv. com. for Biol. Ctr., India, 1962-92; rev. cons. for NSF and for AEC. Served as muscian with CAC, U.S. Army World War I. Recipient cert. commendation for outstanding rsch., World War II, USN, Agassiz medal for contbn. to field of oceanography Nat. Acad. Scis., 1959. Fellow Calif. Acad. scis., San Diego Soc. Naturalists (pres. 1949), AAAS; mem. Am. Soc. Limnology and Oceanography (pres. western sec. 1952), Western Soc. Naturalists (pres. 1953), Am. Micros. Soc., Soc. Systematic Zoology, Sigma Xi. *

JOHNSON, OGDEN CARL, food products company executive; b. Rockford, Ill., Aug. 15, 1929; s. Martin and Hildur Marie J.; m. Lucille Bruner, June 15, 1955; children: Timothy, Debra, Jonathan, Suzanne. B.S., U. Ill., 1951, M.S., 1952, Ph.D., 1956. Research chemist A.E. Staley Mfg. Co., 1957-60; asst. dir. dept. food and nutrition AMA, 1960-66; asst. dir. nutrition sect. USPHS, 1966-70; dir. Office Nutrition-FDA, 1970-74; v.p. sci. and tech. Hershey Foods Corp. (Pa.), 1974-87, sr. v.p., dir., 1987. Vol. facility for developmentally disabled persons. Served with AUS, 1952-54. Mem. Inst. Food Technologists, Am. Chem. Soc., Am. Pub. Health Assn., Am. Inst. Nutrition. Home: Palmyra Pa. Died Oct. 1, 1988; buried Hershey (Pa.) Cemetery.

JOHNSON, RICHARD WINSLOW **See WINSLOW, DICK**

JOHNSON, ROBERT ELLIOTT, airline executive; b. Granger, Wash., July 10, 1907; s. Ashby William and Katherine (Pence) J.; m. Rosalie Gimple, May 14, 1937. AB, U. Wash., 1929. Mgr. advt. and publicity Boeing Aircraft Co., Seattle, 1929-32; Pacific N.W. publicity rep. United Air Lines; asst. v.p. traffic United Air Lines, Chgo., 1932-38, dir. advt., 1938-50, asst. to pres., dir. pub. rels. and advt., 1950-51, v.p., asst. to pres. sales, pub. rels. and advt., 1951-58, sr. v.p. sales and advt., 1958-63, sr. v.p. mktg. and svcs., 1963-71, exec. v.p., 1971-89, dir., 1954-89. Author: Flight Seven, Pilot Jack Knight, Airway One. Lt. USNR, World War II. Mem. Sales and Mktg. Execs. Internat. (pres. 1962-63), Nat. Travelers Aid Soc. (dir.), Saddle and Cycle Club, Tavern Club, Thunderbird Country Club, Pi Sigma Epsilon, Chi Phi, Sigma Delta Chi. Home: Palm Desert Calif. Died May 22, 1989.

JOHNSON, ROBERT KELLOGG, librarian, educator; b. Grand Rapids, Mich., July 27, 1913; s. Maurice Flower and Hazel Jeannette (Kellogg) J.; m. Mary Loretta Franks, Aug. 22, 1950; children: Phillip, Emily (dec.), Peter, Sarah, Robert Kellogg. A.B., U. Mont., 1937; B.A. in Librarianship, U. Wash., 1938; M.S., U. Ill., 1946, Ph.D., 1957. Reference asst. Library Assn. Portland, Oreg., summer 1938; circulation and reference librarian, instr. French Pacific U., 1938-39, acting librarian, instr. library sci., 1939-40, head librarian, asso. prof. library sci., acting head audio-visual dept., 1946-48; head librarian, instr. library sci. Central Coll., Fayette, Mo., 1940-42; payroll auditor, spl. asst. to plant exec. central devel, and expt. unit Gen. Motors Corp., 1942-43; bibliographer U. Ill. Library, 1948-50, cataloger, 1950-52; mem. staff Air U. Library, Maxwell AFB, Ala., 1952-59; asst. dir. libraries Drexel U., 1959-62; prof. library sci. Grad. Sch. Library Sci., 1959-64, dir. libraries, 1962-64; prof. library sci. U. Ariz., 1964-83, univ. librarian, 1964-72, prof. Grad. Library Sch., 1972-83, individual studies dir., 1979-83; cons. Westerners Internat., 1968-83; Chmn. Library Council Met. Phila., 1963-64; mem. Ariz. Library Survey Adv. Com., 1966-68, Com. Jr. Colls. in Phila. Area, 1962-63, Media (Pa.) Free Library Bd., 1959-60; mem. exec. and editorial bds. Seminar Acquisition Latin Am. Library Materials, 1969-72; cons. in field. Contbr. numerous articles to profl. jours. Trustee Bibliog. Center for Research, Rocky Mountain Region, Inc., 1968-72, pres., 1970-71. Served with USNR, 1943-46. Recipient Distinguished Alumnus award U. Wash. Sch. Librarianship Alumni Assn., 1973. Mem A.L.A. (mem. council 1969-72), Ariz. State Library Assn. (exec. bd. 1965-69, v.p. 1967-68, pres. 1968-69), Assn. Coll. and Research Libraries (bd. dirs. 1969-72), Seminar on Acquisition of Latin Am. Library Materials-Assn. Research Libraries (chmn. joint Latin Am. Farmington Plan subcom. 1970-73), Western Writers Am. (bd. of judges for non-fiction awards 1971-82), Southwestern Library Assn. (chmn. awards com. 1976-77). Home: Tucson Ariz. Died Jan. 8, 1990.

JOHNSON, SEARCY LEE, lawyer; b. Dallas, Aug. 30, 1908; s. Jesse Lee and Annie Clyde (Searcy) J.; m. Lillian Cox; 1 child, Susan Lee (Mrs. Keyes). A.B., Williams Coll., 1929; LL.B., U. Tex., 1933. Bar: Tex. 1933. Practiced in Dallas; partner Lawther, Cramer, Perry & Johnson, 1941; ptnr. Johnson, Guthrie, White & Stanfield; sole practice, until 1991; legal adv. Gen. Hershey (on vets. reemployment), 1944-45; spl. asst. to U.S. Atty. Gen., organizer, chief Veterans Affairs sect. Dept. Justice, 1945-47. Author: Feast of Tabernacles; contbr. to: Hildebrand's Texas Corporations, 1942, also articles to legal jours.; composer: The Ballad of the Thresher. Served as lt. comdr. USNR, 1941-45. Decorated Army Commendation award. Mem. Washington Bar Assn., Tex. Bar Assn., Dallas Bar Assn. (spl. prosecutor 1938), Am. Legion, Amvets (charter mem.), ASCAP, Am. Authors and Composers, S.A.R., Am. Judicature Soc., Fellows Tex. Bar, Psi Upsilon. Clubs: Dallas, Dallas Country. Home: Dallas Tex. Died Oct. 26, 1991. †

JOHNSON, VIVIAN WELLS, banker; b. Hampton, Iowa, June 26, 1896; s. John and Christinia (Rasmussen) J.; m. Bernice McClain, May 16, 1918; children: Patricia Maurine, Sonya McClain. Student, Iowa State Tchrs. Coll., Cedar Falls, 1915-16, U. Minn., 1916-17. Clk., teller Citizens Savs. Bank, Cedar Falls, Iowa, 1919-23; asst. cashier Citizens Savs. Bank, Cedar Falls, 1923-27, cahsier, 1927-28; exec. v.p., dir. Citizens-Security Trust & Savs. Bank, 1928-34; exec. v.p., dir. Union Bank & Trust Co., 1934-36, pres., dir., 1936-39; pres. First Nat. Bank, Cedar Falls, 1939-92, dir., 1939-92; dir. Fed. Res. Bank, Chgo.; lectr. Ctrl. State Sch. Banking, U. Wis. Mem. U.S. Senate banking and currency com. adv. group; mem. Iowa Legis., Iowa bd. regents Citizens Com. on Capital Improvements; trustee Sartori Meml. Hosp. Served as 1st lt., inf. in U.S. Army, 1917-19; overseas 13 most.; serving as maj. Iowa State Guard, 1942-92. Mem. Nat. Planning Assn., Chgo. Civil War Round Table, Iowa Bankers Assn. (mem. adminstrv. coun., v.p, 1937-38, pres., 1943-44), Am. Bankers Assn. (mem. Iowa com.; chmn. rsch. coun.), Am. Legion, VFW, Am. Econs. Assn., Acad. Polit. Sci., U.S. C. of C. (fin. com., policy com., membership com.), Phi Delta Theta, Mason, Elk, Rotary, Union League (Chgo.). *

JOHNSON, WENTWORTH PAUL, banker; b. Nashville, May 29, 1897; s. Wentworth Paul and Nannie

(Williams) J.; m. Dorothy Elizabeth Leahey; children: Shelby Mackay, Hope, Elizabeth W., Wentworth Paul III, Melinda. Grad., Hotchkiss Sch.; PhB cum laude, Yale U., 1917; JD, NYU, 1936. Staff acct. Lybrand, Ross Bros. & Montgomery, 1919-23; v.p. Irving Trust Co., 1923-48; sr. v.p., dir. Fidelity-Phila. Trust Co., from 1949; bd. dirs. Glen Alden Corp., Wilkes-Barre, Pa., Phila. Suburban Water Co., Edo Corp., N.Y.C., Berman Leasing Corp., John B. Stetson Co., Phila., Murphy Oil Co., Okla., Murphy Oil Co., Pa., Water Treatment Co., Co. for Investing Abroad, Star Capital Corp., Ultronics Systems Co., Atlas Credit Corp., Jerrold Corp. Bd. dirs. Agnes-Irwin Sch.; mem. Phila. Com. of Fgn. Rels.; trustee Temple U. 1st lt. U.S. Army, 1917-19, AEF. Decorated Croix de Guerre. Mem. Am. Bankers Assn., Pa. Bankers Assn., Soc. Cin., Phila. C. of C. (bd. dirs.), Mil. Order Fgn. Wars, Soc. Colonial Wars, Merion Cricket Club, Racquet Club, Mid-Day Club, Univ. Club N.Y.C., Phi Delta Phi. *

JOHNSTON, BRUCE GILBERT, civil engineer; b. Detroit, Oct. 13, 1905; s. Sterling and Ida (Peake) J.; m. Ruth Elizabeth Barker, Aug. 5, 1939; children: Sterling, Carol Anne. Snow, David. B.S. in Civil Engring, U. Ill., 1930; M.S., Lehigh U., Bethlehem, Pa., 1934; Ph.D. in Sci, Columbia U., 1938. Engaged in engring. constrn. Coolidge Dam, Ariz., 1927-29; with design office Roberts & Schaefer Co., Chgo., 1930; instr. civil engring. Columbia U., 1934-38; charge structural research Fritz Engring. Lab., Lehigh U., 1938-50, asst. dir. lab., 1938-47; engr. Johns Hopkins Applied Physics Lab., Silver Spring, Md., 1942-45; dir. Fritz Engring. Lab., Lehigh U., 1947-50, mem. univ. faculty, 1938-50, prof. civil engring., 1945-50; prof. structural engring. U. Mich., 1950-68, emeritus, from 1968; chmn. Column Research Council, 1956-62; prof. civil engring. U. Ariz., Tucson, 1968-70. Author: Basic Steel Design, 3d edit, 1986, also tech. papers.; Editor: Column Research Council Design Guide, 3 edits, 1960-76. Recipient Alumni Honor award for disting. service in engring. U. Ill., 1981, Special Citation award Am. Inst. Steel Constrn., 1988. Hon. mem. ASCE (chmn. structural div. 1965-66, chmn. engring. mechanics div. 1961-62, J.J.R. Croes medal 1937, 54, Ernest E. Howard medal 1974, first Shortridge Hardesty award 1987); mem. Nat. Acad. Engring., Sigma Xi, Phi Kappa Phi, Tau Beta Pi, Chi Epsilon. Methodist. Home: Tucson Ariz. Deceased. †

JOHNSTON, GEORGE SIM, investment counsel; b. Memphis, Nov. 30, 1924; s. George Sim and Marguerite (Aden) J.; m. Cynthia M. Cogswell, Feb. 23, 1951; children: George Sim III, William C., Scott Christian, Bart Alexander. B.S., Yale U., 1948; postgrad., N.Y. U., 1949-51. With Scudder, Stevens & Clark, N.Y.C., 1948-91, pres., chief exec. officer, 1970-88, chmn., 1988-91; chmn. bd., dir. Korea Fund, Scudder New Asia Fund, Scudder Internat. Fund, Brazil Fund, Scudder New Europe Fund, Scudder Global Fund, Scudder Internat. Bond Fund; pres., trustee Scudder U.S. Govt. Zero Coupon Target Fund, Scudder Equity Income Fund, Scudder Capital Growth Fund Inc., Scudder Short Term Bond Fund; trustee Scudder Devel. Fund; bd. dirs. Japan Fund, Bessemer Securities Corp., N.Y.C., Fiduciary Co. Inc., Boston; chmn. bd. AARP Investment Funds; officer, dir. or trustee numerous other funds; pub. dir. N.Y. Stock Exchange; mem. U.S. adv. bd. Zurich Ins. Co.; chmn. adv. bd. Sovereign High Yield Investment Co.; rep. to UN Investments Com. Bd. dirs. N.Y. Soc. for Prevention Cruelty to Children, 23 yrs.; mem. fin. com. Southampton Fresh Air Home for Crippled Children; bd. dirs. Vis. Nurse Svc. N.Y., Boys Club N.Y., Southampton Hosp. Served to 1st lt. AUS, 1942-46, 51-52. Decorated Army Commendation medal; recipient Brotherhood award NCCJ, 1989, Man of Vision award Eye-Bank for Sight Restoration, 1990. Mem. Investment Counsel Assn. Am., Nat. Golf Links of Am. (dir. from 1959, pres. from 1978), Coun. Fgn. Rels. Clubs: Racquet and Tennis, Links, Sky (N.Y.C.). Home: New York N.Y. Died Feb. 12, 1991.

JOHNSTON, HOWARD ANDREWS, county official; b. Dover, Del., Mar. 25, 1895; s. John and Mary Catharine (Jones) J.; m. Dorothy Evelyn Perkins, Oct. 4, 1934; children; Catharine Howard (Mrs. Harry W. Morgan), Darwin Perkins. Student, Wharton Sch. Fin., Alexander Hamilton Inst. Employee cost dept. Standard Roller Bearing Co., div. Marlin-Rockwell Corp., Phila., 1911-14, sales order dept., 1914-19, various positions sales dept., 1919-27; sales mgr. Marlin-Rockwell Corp., Jamestown, 1927-43, gen. sales mgr., 1943-47, dir., 1946-64, v.p. in charge sales, 1947-54, pres., 1954-64; pres. Marlin-Rockwell Co. Div. Thompson Ramo Wooldridge, Inc., 1964-92; dir. Thompson Ramo Wooldridge, Inc., First Nat. Bank, Jamestown. Chmn. bd. trustees YMCA; trustee, former chmn. Jamestown Community Coll. Pvt. A.E.F., World War I. Mem. Anti-Friction Bearing Mfrs. Assn. (former chmn., treas.; exec. com., dir.). Presbyterian. *

JOHNSTON, JOHN MACLIN, newspaper columnist; b. Chattanooga, Tenn., Nov. 20, 1898; s. Charles Campbell and Katharine (Lemley) J.; m. Jeanne Kershaw, Mar. 1, 1924; 1 child, Roger Ballard; m. Helen F. Fleming, June 22, 1957. Student, Vanderbilt U., 1918-22. Reporter Whelling (W.Va.) Intelligencer, 1924-25; city editor Cin. Post, 1932-35; reporter, city editor, chief editorial writer Cleve. Press, 1935-44; asst. mng. editor Bus. Week, 1945-46; editorial writer Chgo. Daily News, 1946-60, assoc. editor, 1961-64, columnist, 1964-92. *

JOHNSTON, MEANS, JR., lawyer, military officer; b. Schlater, Miss., Dec. 5, 1916; s. Meansand Annie Cecil (Wilsford) J.; m. Hope Manning Larkin, June 29, 1946; children: Hope Johnston Brown, Means III. BS, U.S. Naval Acad., 1939; JD, Georgetown U., 1950; grad., Nat. War Coll., 1959. Commd. ensign USN, 1939, advanced through grades to admiral, 1973, ret., 1975; pvt. practice law Greenwood, Miss., 1975-89. Decorated DSM with 2 gold stars, Bronze Star with gold star and combat V, numerous unit and area ribbons. Home: McLean Va. Died July 14, 1989.

JOHNSTON, THOMAS MCELREE, lawyer; b. Ben Avon, Pa., Dec. 19, 1897; s. Samuel Lawrence and Eunice Isabel (McElree) J.; m. Lorine Davis, July 11, 1i33; children: Thomas McElree, Anne Lorine (Mrs. Fred W. Beesley Jr.), Mary Margaret (Mrs. Charles P. Monroe), Shepherd. BS, Westminster Coll., 1920; LLB, U. Pa., 1924. Bar: Pa. 1924, Fla. 1925. Practice law Miami, Fla., from 1925; assoc. Evans & Mershon, 1925-38; ptnr. Evans, Mershon, Sawyer, Johnston & Simmons, 1938-64, Mershon, Sawyer, Johnston, Dunwody, Mehrtens & Cole, from 1964; spl. asst. to atty. gen. U.S. to handle Okeechobee Flood Control Project, 1933-45; bd. dirs. L.B. Wilson, Inc. Mem. Welfare Planning Coun., Miami, 1952-53; mem. Govt. Rsch. Coun., from 1962; bd. dirs. Vis. Nurses Assn.; bd. dirs., mem. exec. com. Ednl. TV Found.; chmn. bd. dirs. Coral Gables (Fla.) YMCA; bd. dirs., v.p. bd. Met. YMCA, Miami; trustee local Presbyn. Ch. Recipient Spl. award for meritorious svc. to YMCA, 1951. Fellow Am. Bar Found.; mem. ABA, Fla. Bar Assn., Dade County Bar Assn. (bd. dirs.), Am. Law Inst., Biscayne Bay Yacht Club, Miami Club, Riviera Counry Club, Coral Gables Country Club. *

JOHNSTON, WILLIAM NORVILLE, marine engineer, shipping bureau executive; b. Mobile, Ala., July 11, 1922; s. William Norville and Catherine Mary (Murray) J.; m. Kathryn Pauline Solberg, June 14, 1952; children: Kathryn Mary Johnston, William Norville, Stephen Gregory, Paul Brady. B.S. in Mech. Engring., Auburn U., 1947; B.S. in Naval Arch. and Marine Engring., MIT, 1950. Engr. Gulf Shipbuilding Corp., Mobile, Ala., 1957, Ala. Drydock and Shipbuilding Co., Mobile, 1947-48; hull surveyor United Fruit Co., New Orleans, 1950-51; from surveyor to area prin. surveyor Am. Bur. Shipping, N.Y.C., 1951-72, asst. to chmn., 1974-76, v.p., 1976-77, sr. v.p., 1977-79, pres., chmn., 1979-87; chmn. ABS Worldwide Tech. Services, ABS Computers Inc., ABS Group of Cos. Inc., ABS Properties Inc., Exam Co., Abstech Assocs. Inc.; trustee Webb Inst. Naval Architecture. Served with C.E. U.S. Army, 1943-46. Fellow Royal Instn. Naval Architects and Marine Engrs.; mem. Soc. Naval Architects and Marine Engrs., Maritime Assn. of Port of N.Y., Am. Welding Soc., Am. Mcht. Marine Library Assn. Roman Catholic. Clubs: Union League (N.Y.C.), India House (N.Y.C.), N.Y. Yacht (N.Y.C.), Whitehall Lunch (N.Y.C.); Army and Navy (Washington). Home: Short Hills N.J. Died Sept. 7, 1989.

JONES, ALBERT PEARSON, lawyer, educator; b. Dallas, July 19, 1907; s. Bush and Ethel (Hatton) J.; m. Annette Lewis, Oct. 3, 1936; children: Dan Pearson, Lewis Avery. B.A., U. Tex.-Austin, M.A., 1927, LL.B., 1930. Bar: Tex. 1930, U.S. Ct. Appeals (5th cir.) 1935, U.S. Supreme Ct. 1950. Assoc. Baker & Botts, Houston, 1930-43; ptnr. Helm & Jones, 1943-62; Joseph C. Hutcheson prof. law U. Tex.-Austin, 1962-77, prof. emeritus, from 1977; adj. prof. law U. Houston, 1981; 1st asst. atty. gen. Tex., 1963. Editor-in-chief Tex. Law Rev., 1929-30; pres. Tex. Law Rev. Publs., 1971-74; co-author: Texas Trial and Appellate Procedure, 1974, The Judicial Process in Texas Prior to Trial, 2d edit., Cases and Materials on Employees' Rights, 1970; contbr. articles to profl. jours. Fellow Am. Coll. Trial Lawyers; mem. State Bar Tex. (pres. 1950-51), Houston Bar Assn., Am. Law Inst. (life), Am. Judicature Soc., Phi Beta Kappa, Order Coif, Phi Delta Phi. Democrat. Episcopalian. Club: Houston Country. Lodge: Masons. Home: Houston Tex. Deceased. †

JONES, ARTHUR CARHART, physician; b. Oberlin, Ohio, Sept. 4, 1896; s. Burton Howard and Angeline (Talimon) J.; m. Doris Winifred Wolcott, Sept. 18, 1924; children: Ardis Carolyn (Mrs. David G. Hitchcock), Irving Wolcott. BA, Pacific U., 1921, D of Humane Letters, 1963; MA, U. Oreg., 1925, MD, 1926. Diplomate Am. Bd. Phys. Medicine and Rehab. Intern St. Luke's Hosp., Chgo., 1926-27; faculty mem. U. Oreg. Med. Sch., 1927-92, prof. phys. medicine, 1957-92; dir. depts. phys. medicine Good Samaritan, U. Oreg. Hosps., 1929-57; cons. San Francisco area office VA, Madigan Army Hosp.; med. dir., co-founder Rehab. Inst. of Oreg., 1947-61; chief phys. medicine Letterman Gen. Hosp., Mitchell Convalescent Hosp., 1942-46. Contbr. articles to profl. jours. Mem. Govs. Com. Alcohol Edn. and Rehab.; dir., co-founder Oreg. chpt. Arthritis and Rheumatism Found.; mem. bd., found. com. Oreg. Mus. Found.; dir. Scientists of Tomorrow. Served with machine gun bn., U.S. Army, 1918-19. Fellow Am. Acad. Phys. Medicine; mem. AMA, Oreg. Med. Soc., Portland Acad. Medicine, Am. Rheumatism Assn., World Med. Assn., Internat. Soc. Welfare Cripples, Nat. Rehab. Assn., U. Oreg. Med. Sch. Alumni Assn. (past pres.), Geol. Soc. Oreg. (charter mem., past pres.), Soc. Mayflower Descs. (vice gov., counselor), Am. congress Phys. Medicine and Rehab. (pres. 1958-59), Alcohol Rehab. Assn. (co-founder). Republican. Unitarian. *

JONES, BELLING, JR., stove and range manufacturer; b. Bristol, Va., Mar. 16, 1897; s. Samuel Dews and Elizabeth (Harrison) J.; m. Dorothy Hodgson, Jan. 3, 1920; children: Bolling III, Saunders II. BS, U. Ga., 1916. With Atlanta Stove Works, Inc., 1917-92, pres., 1926-92; mem. exec. com., dir., pres. Birmingham Stove & Range Co. (Ala.), 1930-92; chmn. exec. com., mem. fin. com., dir. Fulton Nat. Bank, Atlanta; dir., mem. exec. com. Scripto, Inc., Atlanta. Trustee, past chmn. bd. trustees YWCA, Atlanta; past v.p. trustee Inst. Cooking and Heating, Washington; chmn. exec. com., dir. Atlanta Freight Bur. Ensign USN, 1917-18. Mem. Am. Stove Assn. (past pres.), So. Stove Assn., Sigma Alpha Epsilon, Piedmont Driving Club, Capital City (Atlanta) Club. *

JONES, CHARLES FRANKLIN, petroleum company executive; b. Bartlett, Tex., Nov. 23, 1911; s. Charles Edward and Pearl Lee (Keeton) J.; m. Edith Temple Houston, Apr. 1, 1938; children: Dianne (Mrs. Orson C. Clay), Kenneth Franklin. B.S. in Chem. Engring, U. Tex., 1933, M.S. in Chem. Engring, 1934, Ph.D. in Phys. Chemistry, 1937; LL.D., Austin Coll., 1965. Registered profl. engr., Tex. With Humble Oil and Refining Co., 1937-47, 49-63; mgr. econs. and planning dept. Humble Oil and Refining Co., Houston, 1960-62; gen. mgr. central region Humble Oil and Refining Co., Tulsa, 1962-63; asst. to mgr. coordination and econs. dept. Standard Oil Co., N.J., 1947-49; pres., dir. Esso Research and Engring. Co., Linden, N.J., 1963-64; exec. v.p. Humble Oil & Refining Co., Houston, 1964; pres. Humble Oil & Refining Co., 1964-70, vice chmn., 1970-72; also dir.; dean Coll. Bus. Adminstrn., U. Houston, 1972-74; mgmt. cons., 1974-90; dir. Howell Corp., Coastal Corp., Western Co. of N.Am., Mosher, Inc., AIM Mgmt. Investment Funds; chmn. bd. Fed. Res. Bank of Dallas, 1969-73. Mem. Nat. sci. bd. NSF, 1966-72; former mem. Nat. Indsl. Conf. Bd.; former vice chmn. Tex. Research League; pres. Houston Symphony Soc., 1970-75, chmn., 1975-80; chmn. bd. trustees Houston Pub. Library, 1975-86. Recipient Distinguished Engring. Grad. award U. Tex., 1964. Mem. AAAS, Am. Chem. Soc., Am. Inst. Chem. Engrs., Sigma Xi, Tau Beta Pi, Phi Lambda Upsilon, Beta Gamma Sigma, Omicron Delta Epsilon. Presbyterian (elder). Home: Houston Tex. Died Apr. 30, 1991.

JONES, CHARLES WILLIAMS, language professional, educator; b. Lincoln, Nebr., Sept. 23, 1905; s. Charles Williams and Grace Elizabeth (Cook) J.; m. Sarah Frances Bosworth, June 30, 1928; children—Frances Elizabeth, Charles Bosworth (dec.), Lawrence Wager, Gregory Hunt. A.B., Oberlin Coll., 1926; Litt.D. (hon.), 1951; A.M., Cornell U., 1930, Ph.D., 1932. Rep. Allyn and Bacon (ednl. pubs.), 1926-29; instr. English Oberlin Coll., 1932-35; instr. English Cornell U., 1936-38, asst. prof., 1938-41, assoc. prof., 1941-48, prof., 1948-54, dir. summer sessions, 1946-48, dean Grad. Sch., 1948-53; prof. English U. Calif., Berkeley, 1954-73, prof. emeritus, 1973-89; dir. U.S. Mil. Acad. Preparatory, 1943-45. Author: Bedae Pseudepigrapha, 1939, (with others) Writing and Speaking 1943, Bedae Opera de Temporibus, 1943, Saints' Lives and Chronicles in Early England, 1947, Medieval Literature in Translation, 1950, The St. Nicholas Liturgy, 1963, Bedae Opera Exegetica: in Genesim, 1967, Opera Didascalica, 1977, 79, 80, (with Horn and Crocker) Carolingian Aesthetics, 1976, St. Nicholas of Myra, Bari and Manhattan, 1978; editor or contbr. Dictionary Sci. Biography; Dictionary Middle Ages, others. Research fellow Am. Council Learned Socs., 1935-36; Guggenheim Meml. Found., 1939-40, 45-46; recipient Berkeley citation, 1973; Shea prize Am. Cath. Hist. Assn., 1978; nonfiction medal Commonwealth Club, 1979. Home: Oakland Calif. Died June 25, 1989; buried Oberlin, Ohio.

JONES, CRANSTON EDWARD, magazine editor, writer; b. Albany, N.Y., Mar. 12, 1918; s. Edward Thomas and Katharine Phoebe (Lamson) J.; m. Jean Campbell, Dec. 24, 1949; children: Abigail Ainsworth, Baird Campbell. Grad., Phillips Acad., Andover, Mass., 1936; B.S., Harvard, 1940. Corr. for Time-Life mag., San Francisco, London and Paris, 1946-52; bur. chief Time-Life mag., Rio de Janeiro, 1952-55; mem. staff Time mag., 1955-69, sr. editor, 1961-69; editor-in-chief Travel & Camera, 1969-70, Travel & Leisure, 1970-71; exec. v.p. U.S. Camera Pub. Corp., 1969-71; exec. dir. Atlas Mag., 1971-73, editor, 1973; sr. editor People mag., 1974-88; contbg. editor Constn. mag., 1988-91. Author: Architecture Today and Tomorrow, 1961, Homes of American Presidents, 1962, Marcel Breuer: Works and Projects, 1921-1961, 1963; editor: Walking Tours of New York, 1961, The Best of People: The First Decade, 1984; contbr. numerous articles to profl. jours. Served to lt. USNR, 1941-45. Recipient award for excellence in archtl. journalism A.I.A., 1956, 58, 59, 60. Mem. Municipal Art Soc., Soc. Mayflower Descs., Soc. Archtl. Historians. Clubs: Century, Edgartown Yacht. Home: New York N.Y. Died June 1, 1992; buried The Cath. Ch. of St. John the Divine, N.Y.C.

JONES, DOROTHY CAMERON, language professional, educator; b. Detroit, Feb. 5, 1922; d. Vinton Ernest and Beatrice Olive (Cameron) J. B.A., Wayne State U., 1943, M.A., 1944; Ph.D., U. Colo., 1965. Attendance officer Detroit Bd. Edn., 1943-44; tchr. English Denby High Sch., Detroit, 1946-56, 57-58; exchange tchr. Honolulu, 1956-57; instr., asst. prof. English Colo. Women's Coll., Denver, 1962-66; mem. faculty U. No. Colo., Greeley, 1966-89, prof. English, 1974-89. Contbr. articles to profl. lit. Served with WAVES USNR, 1944-46. Faculty research grantee, 1970, 76. Mem. Internat. Shakespeare Assn., Central States Renaissance Soc., Patristic, Medieval and Renaissance Conf., Rocky Mountain Medieval and Renaissance Soc., Rocky Mountain MLA, Delta Kappa Gamma, Pi Lambda Theta. Home: Greeley Colo. Died Oct. 19, 1989; buried White Chapel Cemetery, Troy, Mich.

JONES, ELIZABETH, physiologist, zoologist educator; b. Ottawa, Kans., Sept. 12, 1898; d. Edward Archbold and Mary (Redmond) J. AB, Radcliffe Coll., 1920, PhD, 1930; MA, U. Maine, 1924. Rsch. asst. Sta. for Exptl. Evolution, Cold Spring Harbor, 1920-22; instr. biology U. Maine, 1924-25; fellow dept. biophysics cancer commn. Radcliffe Coll., Harvard, 1925-26, rsch. asst., 1926-27, fellow for advanced study, 1927-28, rsch. fellow dept. comparative pathology, 1930-34; mem. faculty Wellesley Coll., 1934-92, instr. zoology, asst. prof., assoc. prof., 1934-49, prof. zoology, 1949-64, prof. zoology emeritus, 1964-92; Lewis Atterbury Stimson prof. zoology, 1961, dean of class, 1947, chmn. dept. zoology and physiology, 1949-55; instr. Simmons Coll., 1936-37; rsch. fellow Fearing Rsch. Lab., Free Hosp. for Women Brookline, Mass., 1934-38; part-time staff war project group, 1942-44; spl. cancer rsch. fellow Nat. Cancer Inst., 1947-48, 55-56; rsch. assoc. Children's Cancer Rsch. Found., 1964-92. Contbr. articles to profl. jours. Recipient Harbison award Wellesley Coll., 1956-57. Fellow AAAS; mem. N.Y. Acad. Sci., Soc. Study Devel. and Grown, Am. Assn. Cancer Rsch., Am. Soc. Exptl. Pathology, Phi Beta Kappa, Sigma Xi, Coll. of Boston Club. *

JONES, GEORGE E., business executive; b. Pocatello, Fla., Oct. 18, 1893; s. William H. and Sarah K. (Jones) J.; m. Frances P. Jones, Sept. 1, 1917; children; John F., Richard W., George E. BS, U. Calif., 1915. Ltd. ptnr. Firm of Mitchum, Jones & Templeton, 1920-92; mem. exec. com., dir. Gen. Telephone Co. of Calif. (formerly named Associated Telephone Co., Ltd.), Gen. Telephone Directory Co.; dir. Gen. Telephone & Electronics Corp. Mem. Annandale Golf Club, Balboa Yacht Club, Stock Exchange Club. *

JONES, GORDON MERRILL, publisher; b. Oak Park, Ill., Dec. 12, 1896; s. Nathaniel M. and Mary (Merrill) J.; m. Kathleen Row, May 24, 1922; children: Laura Row, Gordon Row. AB, Northwestern U., 1918, LLB, 1922. Sec.-treas. Row Peterson & Co., Evanston, Ill., 1924-42, pres., 1942-60, chmn. bd., 1960-62; chmn. bd. Harper & Row Publishers, 1962-92; mem. bd. dirs. Ill. Bell Telephon Co., State Bank & Trust Co., Evanston, Ill. Power Co. Mem. Evanston Zoning Bd. Appeals, 1953-65; pres. Evanston United Fund, 1959-60; dir. North Shore Jr. Achievement Bd.; trustee Nat. Coll. Edn. Capt. USNR. Mem. Am. Textbook Publishers Inst. (pres. 1948-49), Ill. C. of C. (pres. 1952-53, dir.), Evanston Hist. Soc. (dir. 1950-65), U.S. C. of C. (edn. com.), Beta Theta Pi, Phi Delta Phi. Methodist. *

JONES, HAZEL LUCILE JAMES, university administrator; b. Eckert, Colo., Feb. 3, 1915; d. Robert Phelps and Ethel (Hart) James; 1 child, Annette. B.A., Western State Coll., 1937; M.A., U. So. Calif., 1958, Ed.D., 1963. Tchr. English, high schs. Colo., 1938-50, Calif. high schs., 1950-59; prof. edn. Los Angeles State Coll., 1959-60; prof. English Calif. State U.-Fullerton, 1960-74, assoc. dean Sch. Letters, Arts and Scis., 1967-70, dean, 1970-72, dean Sch. Humanities and Social Scis., 1972-74; v.p. acad. affairs Calif. Poly. State U.-San Luis Obispo, 1974-82; Chmn. Calif. Com. Tchr. Preparation in English, 1969-70; Chmn. adv. com. on tchr. preparation Calif. State U., 1983-86; mem. sr. com. Western Accrediting Assn. Colls. and Univs., 1982-85. Mem. exec. bd. Whittier (Calif.) Library, 1956-59. Delta Kappa Gamma fellow, 1961-62. Mem. Calif. Assn. Tchrs. English (pres. 1965-66), Calif. Assn. Econ. Edn. (exec. bd. 1965-74), Nat. Council Tchrs. English, Coll. English Edn. Home: Arroyo Grande Calif. Died Nov. 4, 1989; buried Cedaredge, Colo.

JONES, HOWARD W., college president; b. Palmyra, Ohio, Sept. 27, 1895; s. Evan L. and Mary Ann (Jones) J.; m. Mabel Lucile Hurd, June 23, 1921; children: Blanche Carroll, Marilyn Lucile. AB, Hiram Coll., 1920; AM, Western Res. U., 1930; Ped.D., Westminster Coll., 1943. Prin. "Y" Prep Sch.; asst. to pres. Hiram Coll.; pres. Youngstown (Ohio) U. Dir. Mahoning County chpt. ARC, Jr. Achievement of Youngstown Area, Inc., Med. Svc. Found., Mahoning County, Reuben Macmillan Libr. Served in USN, 1917-19. Mem. C. of C., Ohio Coll. Assn., Masons, Rotary, Woodmont Rod & Gun Club. Republican. Disciples of Christ. *

JONES, JOSEPH MARION, JR., economist; b. Lockhart, Tex., Oct. 29, 1908; s. Joseph Marion and Helen (Davis) J.; m. Sarah Plant Harrison, Aug. 17, 1935; children; Clergue, Clarissa Harrison; m. Lillian Grosvenor Coville, Nov., 1956. AB, Baylor U., 1928, LittD, 1945; MA, U. Pa., 1929, PhD, 1935. Econ. U.S. Tariff Commn., Washington, 1933-37; divisional asst. U.S. Dept. State, 1937-43, spl. asst. to asst. sec. for pub. affairs, 1946-48; assoc. editor Fortune Mag., 1943-46; spl. asst. to adminstr. ECA, 1949-52; spl. asst. to U.S. rep. in Europe ECA, Paris, 1952-53; fellow Yale U., 1954; spl. asst. to gov. N.Y., 1955-59; cons. to rsch. and edn. com. Lasker Found., 1959-62; rsch. assoc. Fletcher Sch. Law adn Diplomacy, 1965-67; adj. prof. Ctr. for Advanced Internat. Studies U. Miami, 1968-75. Author: Tariff Retaliation, 1934, A Modern Foreign Policy for the United States, 1944, The Fifteen Weeks, 1955, Does Overpopulation Mean Poverty?, 1962, The United Nations at Work, 1965; contbr. articles to profl. and popular jours. Mem. Cosmos Club, Coral Reef Yacht Club. Home: Arlington Va. Died Aug. 9, 1990.

JONES, RALPH COUGHENOUR, economist, educator; b. Geff, Ill., Aug. 11, 1897; s. David William and Fannie Amelia (Coughenour) J.; m. Bess Virginia Thomas, Aug. 15, 1931; 1 child, Ralph Coughenour. BS, U. Ill., 1922, MS, 1923; PhD, Yale U., 1929. CPA, Ill. Instr. acctg. U. Ill., 1922-24; instr. Yale U., 1924-27, asst. prof., 1927-32, assoc. prof., 1932-38, assoc. prof. econs., 1938-52, prof., 1952-92; vis. prof. U. calif., 1950, U. Mich., summers 1959, 60, 61, 62. Author: Price Level Changes and Financial Statements: Case Studies of Four Companies, 1955, Effects of Price Level Changes on Business Income, Captial and Taxes, 1956; contbr. articles to profl. jours. Fellow of Silliman Coll. Mem. Am. Inst. Accts., Am. Econs. Assn., Am. Acctg. Assn. (dir. rsch. 1950-53, v.p. 1941), Controllers Inst. Am., Nat. Assn. Accts. (nat. bd. dirs. 1942-45; pres. New Haven chpt. 1937-38), Beta Gamma Sigma. *

JONES, WALLACE SYLVESTER, lawyer, mayor; b. N.Y.C., May 23, 1917; s. Adam Leroy and Lily Sylvester (Murray) J.; m. Barbara Hardenbergh Ostgren, June 7, 1941 (dec. Dec. 1964); children—Karen Ostgren (Mrs. John Gordon Fraser, Jr.), Ellen Wallace (Mrs. Robert Q. Barr), Mark Lawrence, Sara Sylvester (Mrs. Tim Kaylor), Caroline Murray (Mrs. Gary Gooden); m. Helen Marion Nelson Anderson, Jan. 7, 1967. A.B., Columbia U., 1938, J.D. (Kent Scholar 1941, editor Law Rev. 1939-41), 1941. Bar: N.Y. 1941, U.S. Supreme Ct. 1948. Assoc. firm Davis Polk & Wardwell, and (predecessors), N.Y.C., 1941-56, mem., 1957-82, sr. counsel, 1982-89; mayor of Essex Fells, N.J., 1974-81; Mem. Essex Fells Bd. Edn., 1955-58; commr. Essex County Ednl. Audio-Visual Aid Commn., 1955-58; pres. W. Essex Regional Sch. Dist., Essex County, 1957-60; moderator No. N.J. Assn., United Ch. Christ, 1966-67, Central Atlantic Conf., 1969-70. Trustee Barnard Coll., 1958-76, trustee emeritus, 1976-89, chmn. bd., 1967-73; trustee Seeing Eye, Inc., 1971-89, sec., 1973-81, chmn., 1981-87; trustee Internat. Found., 1972-89, v.p., 1977-85, pres., 1985-89; bd. dirs. Kimberly Sch., Montclair, N.J., 1968-70, United Ch. Homes N.J., 1967-75; sec. Scottish Heritage USA, Inc., 1969-74, v.p., 1974-77, pres., 1977-82, chmn., 1982-89; Lay reader Episcopal Ch., 1980-89; lay reader The Village Chapel, Pinehurst, N.C., 1984-89, bd. dirs., 1986-88, pres. 1987, exec. com. 1987-88. Served to lt. comdr. USNR, 1942-46, PTO. Mem. ABA, Assn. Bar City N.Y., Moore County chpt. N.C. Symphony Soc, Sandhills br. English Speaking Union, Kiwanis, Adirondack Mountain Club (chmn. Hurrican Mountain chpt. 1952-53), Downtown Club (N.Y.C.), Montclair (N.J.) Golf Club, Country Club of N.C. (Pinehurst), The Sandhills Club (Moore County, N.C.), Psi Upsilon, Phi Delta Phi. Home: Pinehurst N.C. Died Sept. 18, 1989; buried Pinehurst, N.C.

JONES, WALTER BEAMAN, congressman; b. Fayetteville, NC, Aug. 19, 1913; s. Walter George and Fannie (Anderson) J.; m. Doris Long, Apr. 26, 1934 (dec.); children: Mrs. Dotdee Slaughter, Walter Beaman II; m. Elizabeth Fischer. B.S., N.C. State U., 1934. Mem. N.C. Gen. Assembly, 1955-59; mem. N.C. Senate, 1965, 90th-102d Congresses from 1st Dist. N.C., 1967-92; Dir. Security Savs. & Loan Assn., Farmville, N.C.; Mayor Farmville, 1949-53. Recipient Watchdog of Treasury award Nat. Assn. Businessmen, 1966; named Farmville Man of Year, 1955. Democrat. Baptist (deacon). Clubs: Mason (32 deg., Shriner), Elk, Rotarian, Moose. Home: Farmville N.C. Died Sept. 15, 1992. †

JONES, WALTER BRYAN, geologist; b. Huntsville, Ala., Feb. 25, 1895; s. George Walter and Elva Lena (Moore) J.; m. Hazel Lucile Phelps, June 30, 1924; children: Nelson Bolling, Douglas Eppes, Warren Phelps. AB, U. Ala., 1918, AM, 1920; PhD, Johns Hopkins U., 1924. Field geologist Mexican Petroleum Co., Tampico, Mexico, 1920-22; asst. state geologist Geol. Survey Ala., 1922-24; state geologist Ala., 1927-61, geologist emeritus, 1961-92, state oil and gas supr., 1939-61; dir. Dept. of Conservation, Ala., 1939-40; cons. geologist Ala., 1961-92; dir. Ala. Mus. Natural History, 1927-61, dir. emeritus, 1961-92. Contbr. reports, bulls. and papers to profl. jours. Served from 2d lt. to 1st lt., C.E., U.S. Army, 1918-19; to col. AUS, 1940-45. Fellow AAAS, Geol. Soc. Am.; mem. Am. Inst. Mining Metall. and Petroleum Engrs. (past pres. S.E. sect.), Am. Assn. Petroleum Geologists, Soc. Econ. Geolgists, Soc. Am.Mil. Engrs. (charter), Nat. Speleological Soc., Ala. Speleological Soc., Am. Geophys. Union, Ala. Acad. Sci. (charter mem., past pres.), Res. OFficers Assn., Am. Wildlife Inst., Ala. Wildlife Fedns. (past pres.), Southeastern Geol. Soc., Miss. Geol. Soc., Ala. Geol. Soc., Am. Numismatic Assn., Ala. Numismatic Soc., Am. Legion. *

JORDAN, CLARENCE LEE, university dean; b. Mount Carmel, Ill., Sept. 24, 1897; s. Edwin Russell and Luella (Frost) J.; m. Florence Umbreit, June 16, 1926; 1 child, Susan Lee. BS, U. Ill., 1924; MA, U. Chgo., 1929. Tchr. high sch. Mt. Carmel, 1920-22; asst. supt. twp. secondary schs. Waukegan, Ill., 1923-30; supt. Waukegan, 1948-50; supt. twp. schs. Streator, Ill., 1931-34; prin. duPont Man. Tech. High Sch., Louisville, 1935-39; supt. twp. high sch., jr. coll. Joliet, Ill., 1940-41; dir. pers. Philip Carey Mfg. Co., Cin., 1947; supt. Morgan Park Mil. Acad., Chgo., 1950-57; dean of students U. Orlando, Fla., 1958-92. With Ill. N.G., 1916-17; served from pvt. to col. USMC, World War I and II; exec. officer procurement br. Hdqrs. Marine Corps, Washington, 1943-44. Mem. Nat. Assn. Mil. Schs., Nat. Ind. Schs. Assn., Pvt. Schs. Assn. Ctrl. States, Am. Numismatic Assn., Mil. Order World Wars, Marine Res. Officers Assn., NEA, S.A.R., Am. Legion, Marine Corps League, Phi Delta Kappa, Alpha Delta Phi, Epsilon Pi Tau, Sigma Delta Sigma, Mason, Union League, Illini Club, Rotary. Republican. Presbyterian. *

JORDAN, DONALD LEWIS, manufacturer; b. Halifax County, Va., Sept. 9, 1896; s. Charles Meigs and Maude Alice (Betts) J.; m. Mary Preston Hughson, Feb. 27, 1924; children: Don Lewis, Charles Frederick. Grad., Am. Inst. Banking. With First Nat. Bank, Roanoke, Va., 1913-24, First Nat. Exch. Bank, 1925-27; with Johnson-Carper Furniture Co., Roanoke, 1927-92, acct., asst. sec.-treas., sec.-treas., v.p., pres., mgr., 1937-64, chmn. bd. dirs., 1964-92; v.p., dir. Thaden-Jordan Furniture Corp., 1946-52; mem. exec. com. Colonial-Am. Nat. Bank, 1953-92, dir., 1945-92; mem. Va. adv. bd. Liberty Mut. Ins. Co., Richmond, Va., 1951-92; mem. bd. govs. Am. Furniture Mart Bldg., Chgo., 1949-92, nat. chmn., 1952-53; mem. bd. govs. Atlanta Mdse. Mart, 1961-92. Mem. exec. com. Boy Scouts Am., 1947, 49-92, mem. nat. coun., 1962-92, pres. Blue Ridge Coun., chmn. So. Svc. Area, 1963-92; bd. dirs., past pres. Roanoke Valley Industries; v.p., bd. dirs. Elbynne Gill Eye and Ear Found., 1956-92; former mem., officer in ednl. fund drives, health fund drives; mem. bd. trustees Va. Found. Ind. Colls., 1957-92. Recipient Silver Beaver award Boy Scouts of Am., 1959; named man of yr. in furniture industry, 1950. Mem. Furniture Factories Mktg. Assn. of South (v.p. 1965-92), Mason, Furniture Am. (dir. 1941-43, 49-50), Advt. Club (v.p. 1949), Sales Execs. Club (v.p. 1951), Rotary, Roanoke Country Club. *

JORDAN, JOSEPH, chemist, educator; b. Timisoara, Rumania, June 29, 1919; came to U.S., 1950, naturalized, 1959; s. Victor and Maria (Purjusz) J.; m. Colina L. Fischer, Nov. 26, 1952; children—Saskia Audrey, Sharon Leah, Naomi Esther, Adlai David. M.Sc., Hebrew U., Jerusalem, 1942, Ph.D., 1945. Faculty asst., instr. Hebrew U., 1945-49; research fellow Harvard, 1950; research fellow, instr. U. Minn., Mpls., 1951-54; asst. prof. Pa. State U., University Park, 1954-57; asso. prof. Pa. State U., 1957-60, prof. chemistry, 1960-90; research collaborator Brookhaven Nat. Lab., 1960-63; prof. emeritus of chemistry, 1991—; vis. prof. U. Calif. at Berkeley, 1959, Swiss Fed. Inst. Tech., 1961-62, Cornell U., 1965, Hebrew U., Jerusalem, 1972, 84-85, Centre National de Recherches Scientifiques, Paris, 1975-76, Ecole Supérieure de Physique et Chimie, Paris, 1975-76, 85, Pierre and Marie Curie U., Paris, 1976, 85; Fulbright exchange lectr. U. Paris, 1968-69, U. Jodhpur, India, 1986-87; Mem. com. on symbols, units and terminology, numerical data adv. bd. NRC-Nat. Acad. Scis., 1973—; mem. evaluation panel for phys. chemistry div. Nat. Bur. Standards, 1975-78. Editor-in-chief: Treatise on Titrimetry, 1971—; editor: New Developments in Titrimetry, 1974; co-editor: Standard Potentials in Aqueous Solution, 1985; mem. editorial bd. Analytical Letters, 1967—, Talanta, 1972-74; mem. editorial adv. bd. Jour. Analytical Chemistry, 1968-70; contbr. articles to profl. jours. and chpts. to books. Recipient Benedetti-Pichler award Am. Microchem. Soc., 1978; hon. fellow U. Minn., 1950; Frontier of Chemistry lectr. Wayne State U., 1958; Robert Guehm lectr. Swiss Fed. Inst. Tech., 1969; I.M. Kolthoff sr. fellow in analytic chemistry Hebrew U., Jerusalem, 1972, 84-85; Plenary lectr. 5th Congress of Analytical Chemistry, Paris, 1989. Fellow AAAS, Am. Inst. Chemists, Royal Soc. Chemistry; mem. Am. Chem. Soc., Bioelectrochem. Soc., Internat. Union Pure and Applied Chemistry (chmn. electrochemistry commn. 1967-71, titular mem. phys. chemistry div. com. 1969-73, commn. on electroanalytical chemistry 1971-87, sec. 1979-81, chmn. 1981-85, U.S.A. nat. rep. 1985-87, titular mem. analytical chemistry div. com., 1987-91, coopted mem 1991—), Com. on Teaching Chemistry, 1989—, Assn. Harvard Chemists, AAUP, Internat. Soc. Electrochemistry, Sigma Xi, Phi Lambda Upsilon. Home: State College Pa. Died Aug. 14, 1992. †

JOSEPH, EDWARD DAVID, psychiatrist; b. Pitts., Aug. 26, 1919; s. A. Pinto and Hortense (Ury) J.; m. Harriet Bloomfield, Aug. 16, 1942; children: Leila, Alan, Brian. B.Sc., McGill U., 1941, M.D., C.M., 1943; postgrad., N.Y. Psychoanalytic Inst., 1949-55. Intern

Montreal (Que., Can.) Gen. Hosp., 1943-44; resident, fellow in psychiatry Mt. Sinai Hosp., N.Y.C., 1947-49, coordinator in-patient psychiat. service, 1965-71, clin. dir. psychiatry, 1971-76, vice chmn., 1976-78, attending psychiatrist, from 1949; practice medicine, specializing in psychiatry and psychoanalysis N.Y.C., 1949-91; tng. analyst N.Y. Psychoanalytic Inst., from 1964, lectr., from 1962; prof. psychiatry Mt. Sinai Med. Sch., N.Y.C., from 1968. Editor: Kris Monograph Series, from 1965; asso. editor: Psychoanalytic Quar, 1965-77, Jour. Am. Psychoanalytic Assn, 1977-81; contbr. articles profl. jours. Served to capt., M.C. AUS, 1944-46. Mem. AAAS, Am. Psychoanalytic Assn. (exec. councilor 1962-67, treas. 1967-72, pres. 1972-73, 83-86), Internat. Psychoanalytic Assn. (treas. 1973-77, pres. 1977-81), N.Y. Psychoanalytic Soc. (sec. 1965-67, v.p. 1975-77, pres. 1988-90), Am. Psychiat. Assn., Westchester Mental Health Assn., Town Club (Scarsdale). Home: Scarsdale N.Y. Died Sept. 24, 1991; buried Sharon Gardens, Valhalla, N.Y.

JOSEPH, MARJORY L., home economics educator; b. Milan, Ohio, Oct. 10, 1917; d. Ernest J. and Bertha (Allyn) Lockwood; m. William D. Joseph, Aug. 11, 1941; 1 child, Nancy-Joyce. B.S., Ohio State U., 1939; M.S., 1952; Ph.D., Pa. State U., 1962. Supr. alteration dept. Collegienne Shop, Lazarus Dept. Store, Columbus, Ohio, 1939-41; ind. designing and constrn. original design clothing, 1941-44; supr. workrooms custom designing shop Ruth Harris, Inc., N.Y.C., 1944-46; mgr., co-owner MarJay Co., Milan, 1946-48; tchr. secondary schs. Ohio, 1948-51; teaching assoc. textile div. Ohio State U. Sch. Home Econs., 1951-52; instr. to asso. prof. Juniata Coll., Huntingdon, Pa., 1952-62; part-time instr. in clothing and textiles research Pa. State U., 1957-62; asso. prof. home econs. Calif. State U., Northridge, 1962-66, prof., 1966-88, chmn. home econs. dept., 1969-82; cons. textile fiber and fabric care Springs Mills, Inc., Ft. Mill, S.C., U.S. Borax Co., Los Angeles. Author: Introductory Textile Science, 1966, 5th edit., 1986, Illustrated Guide to Textiles, 1973, 4th edit., 1985, Essentials of Textiles, 4d edit., 1988, (with W.D. Joseph) Essentials of Research Methodology and Evaluation in Home Economics, 1975, Research Fundamentals in Home Economics, 1979, 3d edit., 1986; editor (jour.) Clothing and Textiles Research Jour., 1982-88; contr. articles to profl. jours. Recipient Disting. Alumni award Ohio State U., 1972. Mem. Am. Assn. Textile Chemists and Colorists, ASTM, Am. Home Econs. Assn., Elec. Women's Round Table, Omicron Nu, Sigma Delta Epsilon. Home: Granada Hills Calif. Died June 4, 1988.

JOSEY, CHARLES CONANT, university professor; b. Scotland Neck, N.C., Jan. 1, 1893; s. Napoleon Bonaparte and Lydia Bruce (Brewer) J.; m. Miller Jeannette Lynch, June 1923; children: Elizabeth Bruce (Mrs. Logan T. Johnston, Jr.), Charles Conant. AB, Wake Forest Coll., 1913; AM, Columbia U., 1918, PhD, 1921. Instr. in psychology Dartmouth, 1921-22, asst. prof., 1922-23; prof. philosophy U. S.D., 1923-32, head dept. philosophy and psychology, 1932-39; head dept. psychology Butler U., 1939-63, prof. emeritus, 1963-92. Author: The Role of Instinct in Social Philosophy, 1921, The Social Philosophy of Instinct, 1922, Race and National Solidarity, 1923, The Psychology of Religion, 1927, Psychology of Normal People (with Tiffin and Knight), 1940,The Psychological Battlefront of Democracy, 1944, Psychology and Successful Living, 1948; contbr. articles and revs. to profl. jours. *

JOSLIN, ALFRED HAHN, lawyer, state supreme court justice; b. Providence, Jan. 29, 1914; s. Philip C. and Dorothy (Aisenberg) J.; m. Roberta Grant, Mar. 9, 1941 (dec.); children: Andrew J. (dec.), Susan Joslin Leader, Elizabeth Joslin Poirer. A.B. magna cum laude, Brown U., 1935, LL.D. (hon.), 1980; LL.B. cum laude, Harvard U., 1938; L.H.D. (hon.), Bryant Coll.; D.J.S. (hon.), Roger Williams Coll., 1984. Bar: R.I. 1938. Pvt. practice Providence, 1938-63; assoc. justice Supreme Ct. R.I., 1963-79; of counsel Edwards & Angell, Providence, from 1979; Vice pres. R.I. Health Facilities Planning Council, 1965-72; v.p., budget chmn. United Fund R.I., 1955-57; mem. com. to revise corp. laws R.I., 1949-50, com. to revise election laws R.I., 1959-60; del. R.I. Constl. Conv., 1957; pres. Butler Hosp., 1957-65, emeritus, 1965-91; pres. Providence Community Fund, 1960-63; trustee Brown U., 1963-69, vice chancellor, 1968-69, fellow, 1969-85; fellow Sec. Corp., from 1972. Bd. dirs. R.I. Legal Aid Soc., 1940-65; bd. dirs. Greater Providence YMCA, 1955-60, Jewish Children's Home R.I.; bd. dirs. R.I. region NCCJ; bd. dirs., v.p. United Fund; hon. trustee, sec. Miriam Hosp.; chmn. Capital Ctr. Commn., from 1980 . Served from lt. (j.g.) to lt. comdr. USNR, 1942-45. Recipient Big Bro. of Yr. award in R.I., 1957, Outstanding Accomplishment citation Brown U., 1959, Outstanding Contbn. award Brown U., 1984; named to R.I. Heritage Hall of Fame, 1980; named Jewish Man of Yr., 1969, Univ. Club Man of Yr., 1974; cited for outstanding service Associated Alumni Harvard U. Mem. ABA (chmn. jr. bar conf. R.I. 1940-41), R.I. Bar Assn. (chmn. exec. com. 1962-63), Harvard U. Alumni Assn., Alumni Assn. Brown U. (dir.), Phi Beta Kappa, Phi Alpha Delta (hon.), Pi Lambda Phi. Jewish (hon. trustee temple). Clubs: University, Hope, Ledgemont Country. Home: Bristol R.I. Died Oct. 16, 1991.

JOYCE, EILEEN, pianist; b. Tasmania, Australia; m. Christopher Mann. Student, Loreto Convent, Australia, Leipzig Conservatoire, Germany; studied with, Teichmuller, Schnabel; D. Music hon. , Bainbridge U., Eng., 1971. Concert debut, London; numerous concert tours, radio performances, recordings; played in assn. with London Philharm. Orch., World War II; concerts with all prin. orchs. in U.K., Berlin Philharm. Orch., Conservatoire and Nat. Orchs., France, Concertgebouw Orch., Netherlands, La Scala Orch., Italy, Phila. Orch., Carnegie Hall, N.Y.C., Royal Philharm. Soc.; played in concert tours, Australia, 1948, South Africa, 195, Scandinavia and Finland, 1952, Yugoslavia, 1953, New Zealand, 1958, others. Named a Companion of the Order of St. Michael and St. George, Queen Elizabeth II of Eng., 1981. Home: Kent Eng. Died Mar. 25, 1991.

JOYCE, JOHN MICHAEL, beverage company executive; b. Grand Rapids, Mich., Sept. 18, 1908; s. John Michael and Mary Agnes (McCann) J.; m. Catherine Bernice Peet, Oct. 16, 1934; children: John Michael III, Thomas Patrick, Patricia Anne (Mrs. John K. Figge), Mary Catherine (Mrs. Robert H. McCooey), Anne Elizabeth (Mrs. Thomas G. Grace), Timothy Joseph, Cathleen (Mrs. Thomas F. Egan). B.C.S., St. Louis U., 1930; LL.D. (hon.), Iona Coll., 1962, Coll. of Holy Cross, 1979. With Travelers Ins. Co., 1930-37; with Joyce 7-Up, Chgo., 1937-39; pres. N.Y. Seven-Up Bottling Co., New Rochelle, 1939-65, chmn. bd., 1965-73; chmn. bd., dir. Joyce Beverages, Inc., New Rochelle, 1973-84; dir. Joyce Beverages subs. in N.Y., Ill., Wis., N.J., Washington, Conn. Former chmn. bd. govs. New Rochelle Hosp. Med. Center; past trustee, past chmn. bd. lay trustees Iona Coll., New Rochelle; past pres. New Rochelle C. of C.; former mem. pres.'s com. Notre Dame U.; trustee Alfred E. Smith Meml. Found., Inc., Cath. Charities of Archdiocese of N.Y., 1978-89; pres. John M. and Mary A. Joyce Found.; bd. dirs. N.Y. Med. Coll., Valhalla, N.Y. Decorated Knight of Malta, Knight of Holy Sepulchre.; recipient merit award St. Louis U., Brother William B. Cornelia Founders award, 1965; Ignatian award, 1984, Terence Cardinal Cooke medal for disting. service in health care, 1985; charter mem. St. Louis U. Sports Hall of Fame, 1976. Clubs: Westchester Country, Minocqua (Wis.) Country; Metropolitan (N.Y.C.); Winged Foot Country (Mamaroneck, N.Y); St. Louis. Home: New Rochelle N.Y. Died Apr. 23, 1989.

JOYCE, ROBERT FRANCIS, bishop; b. Proctor, Vt., Oct. 7, 1896; s. Patrick J. and Helen (Connor) J. STL summa cum laude, U. Montreal, 1923; LLD, St. Michael's Coll., 1956; LHD, Norwich U., 1957; LLD, Stonehill Coll., 1962. Ordained priest Roman Cath. Ch., 1923. Prin. Cath. High Sch., Burlington, Vt., 1927-32; pastor Northfield, Vt., 1932-43, Rutland, Vt., 1946-57; aux. bishop Diocese of Burlington, 1954-57, bishop, 1957-72; engaged in ministry, Vt., Fla. Dir. Holy Name Soc. Diocese Burlington, 1947-57, pro-Synodal judge, 1938-57; active Fulbright Scholarship Com. for Vt., 1952-58; trustee Vt. Cancer Soc., Vt. Arthritis and Rheumatism Found., Vt. Multiple Sclerosis Soc., Champlain Coll. Major AUS, 1943-46. Mem. Am. Legion, VFW, K.C. (4 deg.), Phi Beta Kappa. Home: Burlington Vt. Died Sept. 2, 1990.

JUDSON, MARGARET ATWOOD, history educator; b. Winsted, Conn., Nov. 5, 1899; d. George W. and Minnie (Atwood) J. BA, Mt. Holyoke Coll., 1922; MA, Radcliffe Coll., 1923, PhD, 1933. Instr. history Douglass Coll., Rutgers U., New Brunswick, N.J., 1928-33, asst. prof., 1933-42, assoc. prof., 1942-48, prof., 1948-91, chmn. history and polit. sci. dept., 1954-63, acting dean, 1966-67; Alice F. Palmer vis. prof. U. Mich., 1959. Author: The Crisis of the Constitution, 1949. Guggenheim fellow, 1954-55. Mem. AAUP, LWV, Am. Hist. Assn., Brit. Conf., Berkshire Hist. Conf. (pres. 1948-50), Am. Assn. UN, Phi Beta Kappa. Home: Highland Park N.J. Died Mar. 23, 1991.

JUERGENS, WILLIAM GEORGE, judge; b. Steeleville, Ill., Sept. 7, 1904; s. H.F. William and Mathilda (Nolte) J.; m. Helen A. Young, Dec. 14, 1929 (dec. Feb. 1966); children: Jane Juergens Hays, William G.; m. Charlotte Louise Mann, Mar. 18, 1967. A.B., Carthage Coll., 1925, LL.D., 1970; J.D., U. Mich., 1928; S.J.D. (hon.), William Woods Coll., 1977. Bar: Ill. bar 1928. County judge Randolph County, 1938-50; judge 3d Jud. Circuit Ct. Ill., 1951-56; judge U.S. Dist. Ct. So. Dist. Ill. (formerly Eastern Dist. Ill.), 1956-88, chief judge, 1965-72, U.S. sr. dist. judge, 1972-88; Adv. bd. Inst. Juvenile Research, Ill., 1945-56. Recipient 1st Ann. Honor Alumnus award Carthage Coll., 1961; George Washington Honor Medal award Freedoms Found. at Valley Forge, 1978. Mem. Fed., Ill., Randolph County bar assns., Bar Assn. 7th Fed. Circuit, Nat. Lawyers Club. Republican. Presbyn. Clubs: Masons (32 deg.), Shriners. Home: Chester Ill. Died Dec. 7, 1988; buried Evergreen Cemetery, Chester, Ill.

KACHLEIN, GEORGE FREDERICK, JR., lawyer, association executive; b. Tacoma, May 9, 1907; s. George Frederick and Edna June (Burt) K.; m. Retha Hicks, Aug. 30, 1930; 1 son, George Frederick. A.B., Stanford U., 1929; LL.B., Harvard U., 1932. Bar: Wash. 1933. Asso. firm Bogle, Bogle & Gates, Seattle, 1933-37, partner, 1937-42, 46-65; asst. gen. mgr., asst. sec. Seattle-Tacoma Shipbldg. Corp., 1942-46; sec. Greater Seattle, Inc., 1952-57, pres., 1958-59; pres. Am Automobile Assn., 1962-64, exec. v.p., 1965-70, cons internat. affairs, 1971-72, also trustee; mcpl. ct. judge City of Langley, Wash., 1974-78, dist. justice ct commr., Island County, Wash., 1974-78. Sec. Seattle King Neptune VI, 1955. Named Seattle's Man of Year 1963. Mem. Inter-Am. Fedn. Touring and Automobile Clubs, ABA, Wash. Bar Assn., Seattle-King County Bar Assn. Clubs: O'Donnel Golf, Seattle Golf, Wash. Athletic (sec. 1950-51), Broadmoor Golf (pres. 1950-51). Lodge: Rotary. Home: Seattle Wash. Died Apr. 1, 1989.

KADANE, DAVID KURZMAN, lawyer, law educator; b. N.Y.C., Apr. 9, 1914; s. Joseph Carlisle and Fannie (Kurzman) K.; m. Helene Born, Oct. 5, 1936; children—Joseph B., Kathryn Ann (Mrs. Garry Crane). B.S.S., Coll. City N.Y., 1933; LL.B., Harvard, 1936. Asst. counsel U.S. Senate com. on interstate commerce investigation r.r. finance, N.Y.C., 1936-38; atty. SEC, Washington and Phila., 1938-41, spl. counsel and asst. dir., 1942-46; asst. to fed. housing expediter and nat. housing adminstr. Washington, 1946; gen. counsel L.I. Lighting Co., 1949-70; on leave as vol. Peace Corps, 1964-66; from prof. law to Harry H. Rains Disting. prof. emeritus Hofstra Law Sch., 1970-91; first dir. Hofstra Neighborhood Law Office; prof. Queens Coll. Sch. Law. Chmn. Nassau County Youth Bd. Jewish. Home: Rockville Centre N.Y. Died Apr. 13, 1991; buried Mt. Hope Cemetery, Elmont, N.Y.

KADEL, WILLIAM HOWARD, seminary administrator, clergyman; b. Gettysburg, Pa., Dec. 12, 1913; m. Katharine Bender Naylor; 4 children. S.T.B., Western Theol. Sem., 1938, S.T.M., 1939; ThD, Union Theol. Sem., 1951; DD hon. , Davidson Coll., 1960. Ordained to ministry, Presbyn. Ch., 1938. Pastor three-ch. parish Amsterdam, Bergholz, Kilgore, Oreg., 1937-39; pastor First Presbyn. Ch., Trafford, Pa., 1939-42, Palma Ceia Presbyn. Ch., Tampa, Fla., 1953-58; sr. pastor First Presbyn. Ch., Orlando, Fla., 1953-58; founding pres. Fla. Presbyn. Coll., 1958-68; exec. sec. Presbyn. U.S. Bd. Christian Edn., 1968-71; pres. Pitts. Theol. Sem., 1971-90; pres. Fla. Coun. Chs.; moderator Synod of Fla.; chmn. various ad interim and standing coms. Gen. Assembly Presbyn. Ch. U.S.; speaker numerous civic and other groups. Author: Prayers for Every Need, 1957. Bd. dirs. Orlando and St. Petersburg Fla. chpts. ARC for 10 yrs; traveled to Europe and Holy Land, 1956; participant Ford Found. sponsored two-month trip visiting colls., univs. for discussion with pres.'s, deans and faculty on innovative and exptl. ideas in higher edn. Chaplain AC, AUS, 1942-45. Recipient Distinguished Alumni cert. Gettysburg Coll., 1965, Outstanding Citizen award St. Petersburg Jaycees, 1967. Mem. Fla. Coun. 10, Tampa Ministers Assn. pres. , St. Petersburg C. of C. chmn. com. edn. , Kiwanis, Rotary. Home: Sarver Pa. Died Oct. 14, 1990.

KADISON, ALEXANDER, editor, author; b. N.Y.C., Feb. 23, 1895; s. Bernard James and Ethel (Baszenska-Silverdicht) K.; m. Isabel; 1 child, James Dean. BA, CCNY, 1915; MA, Columbia U., 1916. Freelance writer N.Y.C., 1915; ofcl. translator U.S. Govt., Washington, N.Y.C., 1917-18; head editorial dept. J. J. Little & Ives Co., N.Y.C., 1921-23; with Alfred A. Knopf, Inc., 1923-26, cons. editor and lit. adviser to publishers, 1926-29; with P.F. Collier & Son Co., 1929-30; local rep. Brit. Rationalist Press, 1930-92; editor, pub. Kadison's News and View's Letter. Author: Through Agnostic Spectacles, 1919, Immortality, 1922; represented in New Larned History for Ready Reference, Biolgraphical Dictionary of Modern Rationalists (London); contbr. essays and poems to Am. and Brit. periodicals; con. on newspaper problems; originator, 1931, of editorial policy for more effective opposition by newspapers to spread of communism in U.S. Literary executor of late Annie S. Peck; lectr. on contemporary and social and polit. topics; owner large colletion letters and diaries dealing with Am. life before, during and after Civil War. Fellow Royal Geog. Soc.; mem. Sci. League of Am., Rationalist Press Assn. (London, Eng.), Rep. Club. *

KAEP, LOUIS JOSEPH, artist; b. Dubuque, Iowa, Mar. 19, 1903; s. Henry John and Mayme Eulberg K.; m. Marion Luey, Feb. 10, 1934; m. Myrthine Herndon Corley, Sept. 29, 1973. Grad., Loras Coll., 1921, Chgo. Art Inst., 1924; fgn. travel and study, Julien Acad., Paris, 1928-31. Art dir. J. Walter Thompson, Chgo., 1923-29, Montgomery Ward & Co., N.Y.C., 1942-54; exec. v.p., gen. mgr. Vogue Wright Studios, N.Y.C., 1954-68; pres. Electrographic Corp., N.Y.C., 1968-70, vice chmn., 1970-91. Exhibited at Met. Mus. Art, Chgo. Art Inst., Wadsworth Atheneum, Hartford, Conn., Nat. Acad., U.S. Nat. Mus., Washington, John Herron Art Inst., Indpls., Chgo. galleries, others; rep. in permanent collection U. Dubuque Iowa ; commd. by USN to execute series of paintings in Mediterranean Area, 1960, in Pacific and Far East, 1961; contbr. Am. Artist. Recipient gold medal Hudson Valley Assn. Artists, 1955, 70, 1st honor award Profl. Art League N.Y., 1956, award, 1965, Grand Nat. award Am. Artists Profl. League, 1956, Winsor Newton award, 1964, AIA award, 1958, 1st award Art League L.I., 1958, Katharine M. Howe Meml. Fund award Knickerbocker Artists, 1961, Jane Peterson award 33d Ann. Hudson Valley Art Assn., 1961, USN Meritorious Pub. Svc. citation, 1963, Sidney Taylor Meml. award, 1965,

Muriel Alvord award, 1966, other awards. Mem. Artists and Writers Assn., N.A.D., Am. Watercolor Soc. 1st v.p. 1962-66, citation for outstanding svc. 1965 , Knickerbocker Artists, London Soc. Royal Arts, Balt. Watercolor Club, Allied Artists Am Assoc. Mems. award , Greenwich Soc. Artists treas. 1953-57 , Springfield Mass. Art League, Chgo. Painters and Sculptors, Chgo. Galleries Assn., Westport artists assns., Soc. Illustrators, Salmagundi Club N.Y.C., Clark Boyson award 1958, award for best in show 1969 Home: Greenwich Conn. Died Oct. 5, 1991.

KAIN, RICHARD MORGAN, English language educator; b. York, Pa., Dec. 19, 1908; s. George Hay and Cara (Watt) K.; m. Louise Kinsey Yerkes, June 16, 1931; children: Richard Yerkes, David Hay, Constance Louise Kain Milner. AB with highest honors, Swarthmore Coll., 1930; MA, U. Chgo., 1931, PhD, 1934; postgrad., Harvard U., 1931-32. Assoc. prof. English, Augustana Coll., Sioux Falls, S.D., 1933-34; asst. prof. Ohio Wesleyan U., 1934-40; mem. faculty U. Louisville, 1940-75, prof., 1947-75, prof. emeritus, 1975-90, disting. faculty lectr., 1975, acting chmn. dept. English, spring 1953, chmn. div. humanities, 1963-69, bd. overseers, 1970-75; summer vis. prof. Northwestern U., 1948, Harvard U., 1950, U. Colo., 1959, Yeats Internat. Summer Sch., Sligo, Ireland, 1961, 67, NYU, 1963, U. Wash., 1966; Fulbright lectr. Univ. Inst., Venice, Italy, 1961-62, Am. Seminar, Rome, 1962; lectr. James Joyce Tower, Dublin, Ireland, 1962; Centennial lectr. U. Mass., spring 1963; Peters Rushton lectr. U. Va., 1964; vis. prof. Univ. Coll., Dublin, spring 1972; mem. James Joyce Tower Com., Dublin, 1960-62; mem. editorial bd. U. Press Ky., 1969-71. Author: Fabulous Voyager: James Joyce's Ulysses, 1947, 2d edit., 1959, Dublin in the Age of William Butler Yeats and James Joyce, 1962, Susan L. Mitchell, 1972, (with Marvin Magalaner) Joyce: The Man, The Work, The Reputation, 1956, 2d edit., 1962, (with Robert Scholes) The Workshop of Daedalus, 1965, (with James H. O'Brien) A.E.: George William Russell, 1975; mem. editorial bd. James Joyce Quar., from 1963; also articles, chpts. to books. Mem. secreening com. internat. exch. persons Conf. Bd.; assoc. Rsch. Couns., 1962-65; pres. Friends Ky. Librs., 1957-58; chmn. Save Our Parks Com., 1958-59; bd. dirs. Louisville Orch., 1951-65; trustee James Joyce Found., 1967—. Mem. MLA (chmn. comparative lit. discussion group I, 1963), AAUP, South Atlantic MLA, Modern Humanities Rsch. Assn., James Joyce Soc., Am. Com. Irish Studies, Phi Beta Kappa, Phi Delta Theta, Delta Sigma Rho, Pi Delta Epsilon, Phi Kappa Phi. Home: Louisville Ky. Died Apr. 5, 1990; buried Louisville, Ky.

KAIN, RONALD STUART, writer; b. Mont., Mar. 5, 1899; s. Henry and Fanny (Clift) K.; m. Olive McKay, June 29, 1929. B.A., Mont. State U., 1922; postgrad., Harvard, 1925-26; M.A., Columbia, 1936. Assoc. editor Mont. Banker, Great Falls, 1922; reporter Yakima (Wash.) Herald, 1923, Butte (Mont.) Miner, 1923-25, N.Y. Herald Tribune, 1926-29; editor Am. Biography (supplement New Internat. Ency.), 1929; assoc. editor New Internat. Year Book, 1929-44; fgn. news editor news and features div. Outpost Service Bur., OWI, N.Y.C., 1944; with Psychol. Warfare Dept., SHAEF, London, 1944-45; chief press sect. Netherlands Unit of OWI in, London, 1945, Brussels, 1945, The Hague, 1945; press officer to psychol. warfare consolidation team 11 Allied mil. mission to The Netherlands; chief press and photo sects. USIS, Am. embassy, The Hague, 1945-46; with State Dept., 1946; free-lance writer and editorial cons., 1946-49; chief rev. officer Dept. State, 1949-61; dir. Internat. Surveys Staff, Office Sec. HEW, 1961-66; freelance writer, from 1967. Author: Europe: Versailles to Warsaw, 1939; contbr. articles to mags. Visited The Netherlands and Indonesia to study Indonesian revolution, 1947. Club: Cosmos (Washington). Home: Washington D.C. Deceased. †

KAIN, VIRGINIA ANDERSON See HILL, HYACINTHE

KAIRAMO, KARI ANTERO OSWALD, diversified manufacturing company executive; b. Helsinki, Finland, Dec. 31, 1932; s. Aulis O. and Aino S. (Kulvik) K.; m. Arja Eeva Sohlberg, June 2, 1957; children: Kristina, Aino-Marja, Juhani. MS, Helsinki U. Tech., 1959. Supt., project engr. W. Rosenlew & Co., Pori, 1960-62; project mgr. tech. div. Metex Corp., Helsinki, 1962-64; pres. Finnmetex Ltd., Sao Paulo, S.Am., 1964-65; pres. Madden Machine Co., N.Y.C., 1968-70, v.p., 1965-67; dir. fgn. ops. Nokia Corp., Helsinki, 1970-72, v.p., 1972-77, pres., chief exec. officer, from 1977, chmn., 1986-88. Dir. Finnish sect. ICC, 1981-88. Decorated knight, also comdr. of the Order of White Rose (Finland), Order of the Rising Sun, Gold and Silver Star, Japan, 1986; commdr. of 1st class of the Order of the Star of Jordan (Al-Kawkab Al-Urduni), 1987. Mem. Confederation of Finnish Industries (exec. com. 1981-88, chmn. 1985-87), Finnish Am. C. of C. (dir. 1967-70, pres. 1969-70, Helsinki, 1972-88), Assn. for Finnish Cultural Found. (dir. from 1977), Finnish Fgn. Trade Assn. (chmn.), Finnish Soviet C. of C. (presidium, from 1981), mem. French Finnish C. of C. (adminstrv. coun., from 1976), Finnish Sect. of the European Cultural Found. Home: Espoo Finland Died Dec. 11, 1988; buried Espoo, Finland.

KALCKAR, HERMAN M., science educator, scientist; b. Copenhagen, Denmark, Mar. 26, 1908; came to U.S., 1953, naturalized, 1956; s. Ludvig and Bertha (Melchior) K.; m. Agnete Kalckar; children—Sonja, Nina, Niels. MD, U. Copenhagen, 1933, PhD, 1938; MA (hon.), Harvard U.; DSc (hon.), Washington U., St. Louis, U. Chgo., U. Copenhagen. Sci. asst., also instr. Inst. Med. Physiology, U. Copenhagen, 1934-37, asst. prof., 1937; Rockefeller research fellow biology Calif. Inst. Tech., Washington U. Sch. Medicine, 1939-42; research asso. Pub. Health Research Inst., N.Y.C., 1943-46; asso. prof. physiology U. Copenhagen, 1946-49; research prof., dir. Inst. for Cytophysiology, 1949-54; vis. scientist NIH, Bethesda, Md., 1953-56; chief sect. metabolic enzymes NIH, 1956-58; prof. biology and biochemistry, dept. biology Johns Hopkins U., 1958-61; prof. biol. chemistry Harvard Med. Sch., 1961-79, emeritus; Disting. Rsch. prof. dept. chemistry Boston U., 1979-91; chief biochemistry, biochem. research lab. Mass. Gen. Hosp., Boston, 1961-79, vis. biochemist Huntington Lab., from 1974. Author numerous articles, monographs on phosphorylation and galactose metabolism.; Asso. editor: Cellular Physiology, from 1976. Recipient Saunders award Phila., 1964. Fellow Am. Acad. Arts and Scis.; mem. Soc. Biol. Chemists, Harvey Soc. (hon.), Royal Danish Acad. (fgn.), Nat. Acad. Scis. Home: Cambridge Mass. Died May 17, 1991; buried Mt. Auburn Cemetery, Cambridge. †

KALIFF, JOSEPH ALFRED, artist, writer, publishing syndicate executive; b. Fall River, Mass., Apr. 3, 1922; s. George and Marie (Fata) K. Student, Pratt Inst., 1940-41, Brown U., 1942, N.Y. Sch. Indsl. Arts, 1950-51. Free-lance artist, writer, 1940-43, and free-lance caricaturist for newspapers and mags., 1945-50; pres. Republic Features Syndicate, N.Y.C., 1950-55, Amusement Features Syndicate, N.Y.C., 1979-92; entertainment editor Broadway columnist Bklyn. Daily, 1951-71; mem. bd. judges Miss Universe Contest, 1955, Mrs. Am. Contest, 1951-52, Coll. Queen Contest, 1951-55. Starred in 2 TV programs, Sta.-WPIX; author: nationally syndicated columns Did You Know That?, 1950-52, Magic Carpet Over Broadway, 1950-92, It's A Cockeyed World, 1953-79, Karikature Karnival, 1979-92, TV and Hollywood Chatter. Served with U.S. Army, 1943-45, ETO. Mem. Caricaturists Soc. Am. (founder, dir. 1950-92 , pres. 1979-92), N.Y. Press Club Assn., Am. Legion. Clubs: Odd Fellows, Circus Saints and Sinners. Home: Brooklyn N.Y. Died Nov. 13, 1992. †

KALIJARVI, THORSTEN VALENTINE, diplomat; b. Gardner, Mass., Dec. 22, 1897; s. Gustaf and Ida Christina (Kuniholm) K.; m. Dorothy Corbett Knight, Sept. 4, 1926; 1 child, June. AB, Clark U., 1920, AM, 1923; Carnegie Endowment fellow, Harvard U., 1920-22; PhD, U. Berlin, 1935. Head dept. polit sci. U. N.H., 1927, prof. govt., 1939-45; exec. dir. N.H. state Planning and Devel. Commn., 1942-47; prin. analyst European Affairs, Legis. Ref. Svc., Libr. of Congress, 1947; rsch. counsel in internat. rels., 1947-50; sr. specialist Fgn. Affairs, 1950-52; staff assoc., cons. Senate Fgn. Rels. Com., 1947-53, dep. asst. sec. state for econ. affairs, ast. sec. state, 1953-57, 57; U.S. ambassador to El Salvador, cons. Dept. of State, 1957-61, 61; dean of faculty Cape Cod Community Coll., 1964-92; lectr. history and govt. Am. U., 1947-53, dir. Inst. on Communism and Am. Constitutionalism, 1963; adj. prof., 1964-92; lectr. Johns Hopkins U., 1952-53; pub. panel mem. War Labor Bd., Region I; arbitrator labor disputes. Author: Recent American Foreign Policy, 1952, Modern World Politics, 1953, Soviet Power and Policy, 1954, Central America, Land of Lords and Lizards, 1962; editor: Fascism in Action, 1948; contbr. articles to profl. publs. Dir. Manchester Pub. Forum, 1937. Served in S.A.T.C., 1918. Fellow Am. Acad. Scis., AAAS; mem. Am. Soc. Internat. Law, Am. Polit. Sci. Assn., Am. Arbitration Assn., Nat. Acad. Econ. and Polit. Sci., Washington Inst. World Affairs, Am. Legion, Phi Kappa Phi, Pi Gamma Mu, Davor Club, Cosmos Club. *

KALKHOFF, RONALD KENNETH, internist, medical educator; b. Milw., Dec. 6, 1933; s. Glenn Charles and Theodora Mathilde (Peterson) K.; m. Rhea Lynn Widerborg, June 12, 1956; children: Stephanie Lynn, Cynthia Lee, Richard Graham, William Webster. B.A., Yale U., 1956; M.D., Washington U., St. Louis, 1960. Diplomate Am. Bd. Internal Medicine. Intern St. Louis City Hosp., 1960-61; resident in internal medicine Barnes Hosp., St. Louis, 1961-62, 64-65; fellow in endocrinology and metabolism Washington U., 1962-64; asst. prof. medicine Med. Coll. Wis., Milw., 1965-71; assoc. prof. Med. Coll. Wis., 1971-74, prof., chief endocrine-metabolic sect., 1974-90; sr. staff Milwaukee County Med. Complex and Froedert Hosp. Contbr. articles and revs. on diabetes mellitus, obesity and pancreatic islet physiology to sci. jours., chpts. to books. Fellow ACP; mem. AAAS, Am. Soc. Clin. Investigation, Am. Soc. Pharmacology and Exptl. Therapeutics, Am. Fedn. Clin. Rsch., Central Soc. Clin. Rsch. (metabolism and endocrinology sect. 1987-88), Endocrine Soc., Am. Diabetes Assn. (Wis. dir., mem. editorial bd. 1971-78, chmn. coun. diabetes in pregnancy, 1988-90). Home: Cedarburg Wis. Died Dec. 21, 1990. †

KAMIN, HENRY, biochemist; b. Warsaw, Poland, Oct. 24, 1920; came to U.S., 1926, naturalized, 1932; s. Benjamin and Paula (Mirkowicz) K.; m. Dorothy Lee Lingle, Oct. 30, 1943. B.S., CCNY, 1940; Ph.D., Duke U., 1948. Prin. scientist VA Hosp., Durham, N.C., 1953-68; instr., asso. biochemistry Duke U. Med. Center, 1950-55, asst. prof., 1955-59, asso. prof., 1959-65, prof., 1965-88; cons. in field; mem. various profl. coms. including food and nutrition bd. NRC-Nat. Acad. Scis., 1978-84, vice chmn., 1979-81, chmn. dietary allowances com., 1980-85. Editor: Flavins and Flavoproteins III, 1971; contbr. numerous articles to profl. jours.; editorial bd.: Jour. Biol. Chemistry, 1974-79, 82-87. Served to 1st lt. San Corps, U.S. Army, 1943-46. USPHS postdoctoral fellow, 1948-50; NIH grantee, from 1955; NSF grantee, 1966-69, from 80. Mem. Am. Soc. Biol. Chemists, Am. Inst. Nutrition, AAAS, Am. Chem. Soc., Am. Soc. Clin. Nutrition. Jewish. Home: Durham N.C. Died Sept. 15, 1988; inurned Columbarium Searle Ctr., Duke U., Durham, N.C.

KAMMHOLZ, THEOPHIL CARL, lawyer; b. Jefferson County, Wis., Mar. 23, 1909; s. Frederic Carl and Emma (Donner) K.; m. Lura Walker, Apr. 22, 1935 (dec.); children: Carolyn Kammholz Hudson, Robert (dec.). LL.B., U. Wis., 1932. Bar: Wis. 1932, Ill. 1945, D.C. 1964. Assoc. Stephens, Sletteland & Sutherland, Madison, Wis., 1932-34; asso. Bogue & Sanderson, Portage, Wis., 1934-35; ptnr. Bogue, Sanderson & Kammholz, Portage, 1935-42; regional counsel War Labor Bd., Chgo., 1943; ptnr. Pope and Ballard, Chgo., 1944-52, Vedder, Price, Kaufman & Kammholz, Chgo., 1952-55, and from 1957; exec. dir. Chgo. Foundrymen's Assn., 1952; gen. counsel NLRB, Washington, 1955-57; dir. Fosdick Enterprises, Inc.; mem. legal adv. coun. Mid-Am. Legal Found., 1977-89; trustee Lincoln Legal Found., from 1989. Co-author: Practice and Procedure Before the NLRB; Contbr. articles profl. jours. Adv. U.S. del. ILO Conf., Geneva, 1954. Mem. ABA, Ill., Wis., Chgo. bar assns., Internat. Soc. Labor Law (U.S. exec. com. from 1983), Am. Arbitration Assn. (adv. council 1982), Wis. Law Alumni Assn. (pres. Chgo. 1953-55), Chgo. Assn. Commerce and Industry (chmn. labor-mgmt. relations com. 1966-68, v.p. govtl. affairs 1968-70, dir., mem. policy com. 1968-78, sr. council from 1978), Order of Coif, Delta Sigma Rho, Lambda Chi Alpha. Clubs: North Shore Country (bd. govs. 1971-74), Monroe, Law (exec. com. 1976-80, pres. 1978-79), Metropolitan, University (Chgo.); Kenwood Country (Washington); Portage (Wis.) Country. Home: Winnetka Ill. Deceased. †

KAMPHOEFNER, HENRY LEVEKE, architect, educator; b. Des Moines, May 5, 1907; s. Charles Herman and Mary Amelia (Leveke) K.; m. Mabel C. Franchere, Jan. 5, 1937. Student, Morningside Coll., 1924-26; B.S. in Architecture, U. Ill., 1930; M.S. in Architecture, Columbia U., 1931; certificate in architecture, Beaux Arts Inst. of Design, 1932; D.F.A. (hon.), Morningside Coll., 1967; LL.D. (hon.), Ball State U., 1972. Pvt. practice architecture Sioux City, Iowa, 1932-36; asso. architect Rural Resettlement Adminstrn., Washington, 1936-37; asst. prof. architecture U. Okla., Norman, 1937-39; asso. prof. U. Okla., 1939-40, prof., 1940-48; dean N.C. State U. Sch. Design, Raleigh, 1948-73; dean emeritus, prof. emeritus N.C. State U. Sch. Design, 1973-90; disting. vis. prof. art Meredith Coll., Raleigh, 1979-81; cons. in field. Humanist-in-residence Nat. Endowment on Humanities, Cumberland County, N.C., 1977; participant Princeton U. Bicentennial Conf. on Planning Man's Phys. Environment, 1947. Author: (with others) Cities are Abnormal, 1946, Churches and Temples, 1954, The South Builds, 1960; Contbr. (with others) numerous articles in field to profl. jours. Recipient three medals Beaux Arts Inst. Design, 1929-32; Edward Langley Scholar AIA, 1940; recipient Lasting Achievement in Architecture Edn. joint award AIA/Assn. Collegiate Schs. of Architecture, 1977; Gov.'s Gold medal in the Fine Arts N.C., 1978. Fellow AIA; mem. Assn. of Collegiate Schs. Architecture (nat. pres. 1963-65, treas. 1959-63, dir. 1959-67), Raleigh Council Architects (pres. 1955-56), Raleigh Chamber Music Guild (pres. 1954-56). Democrat. Club: Carolina Country (Raleigh). Home: Raleigh N.C. Died Feb. 14, 1990.

KAMPMEIER, RUDOLPH HERMAN, physician; b. Butler County, Iowa, Jan. 15, 1898; s. August and Mary (Ehrlicher) K.; m. Blanch Davis, June 18, 1922; 1 child, Joan. AB, State U. of Iowa, 1920, MD, 1923. Cert. Bd. of Internal Medicine. Rsch. fellow U. Chgo. Med. Coll., 1925; asst. prof. medicine Vanderbilt U. Sch. of Medicine, Nashville, 1936-38, assoc. prof. medicine, 1938-53, prof. medicine, 1953-63, acting dir. dept. of medicine, 1944-46, dir. post grad. medicine, 1946-63, prof. emeritus, dir. continuing edn., 1963-92; prof. medicine, sch. medicine Vanderbilt U. Sch. of Medicine, 1953-63; dir. med. edn. St. Thomas Hosp., 1960-64; adv. com. cancer control program USPHS, 1963-92, cons. venereal disease br., 1964-92. Author: Essentials of Syphilology, 1943, Physical Examination in Health and Disease, 1950. Mem. exec. com. Nashville Met. Regional Health Planning Coun., 1964-92. Pvt., attended O.T.C., World War I; cons. to surg.-gen. U.S. Army, 1944-45; made nutrition surveys in civilian population Am. zone in Germany, including Berlin, summer of 1945. Fellow A.C.P (regent 1961-92); mem. AMA (sec. sect. internal medicine 1956-59, chmn. 1960), Nashville Acad. Medicine (pres. 1951), Tenn. Acad. Medicine (editor jour. 1950-92, trustee 1950-92, pres. 1964), So. Med. Assn. (editor jour. 1954-92, pres. 1954), Am. Clin. and Climatol. Assn., Assn. Am. Physicians, So. Soc. for

Clin. Rsch., Alpha Kappa Kappa, Alpha Omega Alpha, Sigma Xi. Unitarian. *

KANE, DAVID SCHILLING, lawyer; b. Far Rockway, N.Y., Jan. 20, 1907; s. David and Bertha Dorothy (Schilling) K.; m. Mildred Irene Thompson, Sept. 23, 1931 (dec. 1984); children—David H., T. Sheila, Kathleen. Student, NYU, 1924-26, LL.B., 1930. Bar: N.Y. State 1931. Assoc. Duell, Dunn & Anderson, N.Y.C., 1931-34; ptnr. Duell & Kane, 1934-52; sr. ptnr. Kane, Dalsimer, Kane, Sullivan & Kurucz (and predecessors), N.Y.C., 1952-88; pres. Camloc Fastener Corp., 1942-44; asst. sec., dir. Sci. Devel. Corp.; lectr. grad. div. N.Y. U. Sch. Law, 1946-59, adj. asso. prof. law, 1960-64, adj. prof., 1964-88. Contbg. author: Ann. Survey Am. Law, from 1945. Mem. sch. bd., Port Washington, N.Y., 1948-50, mem. bd. appeals, Village of Sands Point (N.Y.), 1948-63, trustee, 1963-65, mayor, 1965-69; bd. dirs. Vanderbilt Assocs. of NYU Law Sch., 1968-80, Fairleigh Dickinson Labs.; trustee NYU Law Center Found., from 1967, C. F. Mueller Scholarship Found. Recipient Cert. Meritorious Service, 1950; Albert Gallatin fellow NYU, 1982. Mem. Nat. Council Patent Law Assn. (chmn. 1963-64), Am. Patent Law Assn. (pres. 1962-63), N.Y. Patent Law Assn. (pres. 1958-59), NYU Law Alumni Assn. (bd. dirs.), Am. Bar Assn., N.Y. State Bar Assn., N.Y.C. Bar Assn., N.Y. County Lawyers Assn., Am. Judicature Soc., Fed. Bar Council, Nat. Lawyers Club, Phi Delta Phi. Clubs: Union League, NYU (N.Y.C.) (founder mem.); Naples (Fla.) Yacht, Masons. Home: Naples Fla. Died Jan. 30, 1988; buried Nassau Knolls Cemetery, Port Washington, N.Y.

KANGER, STIG GUSTAF, philosophy educator; b. China, July 10, 1924. Ph.D., U. Stockholm, 1957. Prof. philosophy U. Uppsala, Sweden, 1968-88. Author: Provability in Logic, 1957. Died Mar. 1988. Home: Uppsala Sweden

KANTOR, TADEUSZ, painter, theater founder, director; b. Wielopole, nr. Cracow, Poland, Apr. 6, 1915; s. Marian and Helena K.; m. Maria Stangret-Kantor, 1960. Ed., Cracow Acad. Fine Arts. Organized underground theatre, Cracow, during occupation; prof. Cracow Acad. Fine Arts, 1948, 69; founder Cricot 2 Theatre, Cracow, 1955, participant with theatre in festivals: Premio Roma, 1969, 74, Mondial du Theatre, Nancy, 1971-77, Edinburgh Festival, 1972, 73, 76, 80, 8th Arts Festival, Shiraz, 1974-77, Festival d'Automne, Paris, 1977. Dir. numerous plays, including: Cuttle Fish, 1956; In a Little Manor House, 1961; The Madman and The Nun, 1963; Happening-Cricotage, 1965; Waterhen, 1967; The Dead Class, 1975; Ou sont les neiges d'antan, 1978; Wielopole-Wielopole, 1980; exhbns. of paintings: 30th Biennale of Art, Venice, Italy, 1960; L'Art Theatre, Baden-Baden, 1965; São Paulo Biennale, 1967; Happening and Fluxus, Cologne and Stuttgart, 1970; Whitechapel Gallery, London, 1976; Documenta 6, Kassel, 1977; ROSC, 1977; Moderna Museet, Stockholm; Mus. Modern Art, N.Y.C.; Solomon R. Guggenheim Mus., N.Y.C., Foksal Gallery, Warsaw, 1965, 67, 68, 70, 71, 73, 77, Modern Art Gallery Warsaw, 1976, 78, 79; author: Teatr Smierci (Theatre of Death), 1976. Recipient Premio Marzotto, Rome, 1968; prize for painting, Sã o Paulo, 1967; prix Rembrandt, J.W. Goethe-Stiftung Basel, 1978; Grand pix le Theatre des Nations, Caracas, 1978; OBIE prize, 1979, 82; Diploma of Minister of Fgn. Affairs, 1982; 1st prize 20th Edinburgh Festival, 1976, Chevalier, Ordre de la Legion d' Honneur (France), 1986. Died Dec. 8, 1990. Home: Krakow Poland

KAPLAN, ALBERT SYDNEY, microbiology educator, researcher; b. Phila., Nov. 29, 1917; s. Harry and Rose K.; m. Tamar Ben-Porat, Feb. 14, 1959; children: Nira I., Daniel H. B.S., Phila. Coll. Pharmacy and Sci., 1941; M.S., Pa. State Coll., 1949; Ph.D., Yale U., 1952. Nat. Found. Infantile Paralysis fellow Pasteur Inst., Paris, 1952-53, 53-54; instr. preventive medicine Yale U., 1954-55; research assoc. dept. microbiology U. Ill., Urbana, 1955-58; mem., head dept. microbiology Albert Einstein Med. Center, Phila., 1958-71; research prof. Temple U. Sch. Medicine, Phila., 1963-71; prof., chmn. dept. microbiology Vanderbilt U. Sch. Medicine, Nashville, 1972-89; chmn. Am. Cancer Soc. Adv. Panel on Virology and Microbiology, 1980-82; mem. microbiology testing com. Nat. Bd. Med. Examiners, 1979-83; mem. cancer spl. program adv. com. Nat. Cancer Inst., 1981-85, mem. sci. rev. com. virus cancer program, 1976-80; mem. virology study sect. NIH, 1970-73, chmn., 1972-73, chmn. exptl. virology study sect., 1983-85. Editor: The Herpesviruses (Albert S. Kaplan), 1973; editorial bd.: Jour. Virology, 1967-73, Intervirology, 1972-86; asso. editor: Virology, 1966-69, 72-76, Cancer Research, 1971-81. Served with U.S. Army, 1943-46. Recipient Research Career Devel. award NIH, 1963-68, grantee NIH, from 1956, grantee NSF, 1966, grantee Nat. Found. March of Dimes, 1977-78. Fellow AAAS; mem. Am. Soc. Microbiology (div. chmn. 1979-80), Am. Assn. Immunologists (program com. 1973-75), Am. Assn. Cancer Research, Am. Soc. Virology, Sigma Xi. Home: Nashville Tenn. Died Aug. 11, 1989.

KAPLAN, IRVING M.J., steel company executive; b. Pitts., Sept. 5, 1919; s. Frank R.S. and Madeline (Roth) K.; m. Joan Marie Meyerhoff, Nov. 10, 1955; children: William A., Thomas R., Fred M. B.A., Princeton U., 1941. Vice pres., sec., dir. Copperweld Corp., Pitts., 1954-85. Republican ward committeeman 14th Ward, Pitts., 1964-74; mem. exec. bd. Rep. Fin. Com. Allegheny County, 1966-74; Rep. state committeeman 43d Dist., 1966-74; pres. Vocat. Rehab. Center, 1961-63, bd. dirs., 1955-74; bd. dirs. Planned Parenthood Center Pitts., 1968-74, Am. Lung Assn. Southwestern Pa.; trustee Alumni Council Shady Side Acad., 1960-63; mem. Union Am. Hebrew Congregations, 1975-78, Western Pa. Conservancy, 1979-83. Mem. Am. Iron and Steel Inst., Am. Soc. Corp. Secs., Am. Soc. Metals, Pitts. Athletic Assn. Jewish (trustee congregation). Clubs: Masons, Duquesne, Concordia, Harvard-Yale-Princeton. Home: Pittsburgh Pa. Died July 22, 1989; buried Pitts.

KAPLAN, JOHN, legal educator; b. N.Y.C., July 9, 1929; s. Edward I. and Dorothy (Saron) K.; m. Elizabeth Brown, Nov. 5, 1960; children: Carolyn, Jonathan, Jessica. A.B. in Physics, Harvard U., 1951, LL.B., 1954. Bar: N.Y., Calif., D.C. Law clk. to Supreme Ct. Justice Tom. C. Clark, 1954-55; spl. atty. Dept. Justice, 1957-58; asst. U.S. atty. No. Dist. Calif., 1958-61; assoc. prof. law Northwestern U., 1962-64; vis. assoc. prof. law U. Calif., Berkeley, 1964-65; Jackson Eli Reynolds prof. law Stanford (Calif.) U., 1965-89. Author: Marijuna-The New Prohibition, 1970, Criminal Justice: Introductory Cases and Materials, 1973; co-author: (with Jon R. Waltz) The Trial of Jack Ruby, 1965; author: (with David Louisell and Jon R. Waltz) Cases and Materials on Evidence, 1968, Principles of Evidence and Proof, 1968, (with William Cohen) The Bill of Rights, 1976, The Court-Martial of the Kaohsiung Defendants, 1981, The Hardest Drug: Heroin and Public Policy, 1983. Mem. nat. adv. com. on alcoholism and alcohol abuse HEW. Home: Stanford Calif. Died Nov. 23, 1989; buried Palo Alto, Calif.

KAPLAN, JOSEPH, physics educator; b. Tapolcza, Hungary, Sept. 8, 1902; brought to U.S., 1910; s. Henry and Rosa (Lowy) K.; m. Katherine E. Feraud, June 24, 1933 (dec. Jan. 1977); m. Frances I. Baum, Feb. 1984. BS, Johns Hopkins U., 1924, AM, 1926, PhD, 1927; DSc, U. Notre Dame, 1957, Carleton Coll., 1957; LHD, Hebrew Union Coll., Yeshiva U., 1958, U. Judaism. Rsch. fellow Princeton U., 1927; asst. prof. physics U. Calif., 1928-35, assoc. prof., 1935-40, prof., 1940-70, prof. emeritus, 1970-91, chmn. dept. physics and meteorology, 1938-44; dir. Inst. Geophysics, 1946-47; nat. Sigma Xi lectr., 1948-49; v.p. Internat. Geodesy and Geophysics, 1960-63, pres., 1963-67; rep. com. space rsch. Internat. Coun. Sci. Unions, 1958-67, also mem. exec. bd.; chmn. West L.A. Coord. Coun.; mem. Commn. 22, Internat. Astron. Union; mem. Internat. Conf. Sci. Advancement New States, Weizmann Inst., Israel, 1960, also gov. Weizmann Inst.; chmn. U.S. Nat. Com. Internat. Geophys. Yr., 1953-63; chmn. panel geophys. rsch. Sci. Adv. Bd. USAF, also chmn. sci. adv. group Office Aero-space Rsch., 1963-69. Co-author: Physics and Medicine of the Upper Atmosphere, 1951, Across the Space Frontier, 1951, Great Men of Physics, 1969; contbr. articles to Phys. Rev., other sci. publs. Past chmn. acad. coun. Am. Friends Hebrew U.; hon. mem. bd. govs. Hebrew U., Jerusalem; past bd. govs. Hebrew Union Coll.-Jewish Inst. Religion; past bd. dirs. Reiss-David Clinic Child Guidance; past mem. Calif. adminstrv. bd. Hebrew Union Coll.-Jewish Inst. Religion. With USAAF, 1943-45. Decorated for exceptional civilian svc. War Dept., 1947, USAF, 1960, 69; recipient Achievement award Tau Delta Phi, Disting. Svc. award Phi Delta Epsilon, 1956, Astronautics award Am. Rocket Soc, 1956, Fellowship award Inst. Aero. Scis.; recipient Hodgkins medal and award Smithsonian Instn., 1965. Fellow AIAA, Am. Phys. Soc., Am. Geophys. Union (John A. Fleming award 1969); mem. NAS, Am. Astron. Soc., Am. Meteorol. Soc. (hon.), West L.A. Rotary (hon., pres. 1938), Tau Beta Pi, Tau Delta Phi, Scabbard and Blade. Republican. Jewish. Died Oct. 3, 1991; buried Westwood Mortuary, L.A.

KAPP, RONALD ORMOND, science educator, academic administrator; b. nr. Ann Arbor, Mich., Mar. 10, 1935; s. Ormond Emanuel and Anna Louise (Heller) K.; m. Phyllis Isabel Moreen, Jan. 30, 1960; children: Lisa, Marda, Sara, Jon. BA, U. Mich., 1956, MS, 1957, PhD, 1963. Instr. Alma (Mich.) Coll., 1957-60, asst. prof., 1960-64, assoc. prof., 1964-69, prof., provost, 1969-90. Author: How to Know Pollen and Spores, 1969; Contbr. articles to profl. jours. Mem. Mich. Wilderness and Natural Areas Bd. Fellow AAAS; mem. Ecol. Soc. Am., Mich. Acad. Sci., Arts, and Letters (pres. 1989-90), Mich. Natural Areas Council, Nature Conservancy of Mich. (trustee), Phi Beta Kappa, Sigma Xi. Home: Alma Mich. Died Mar. 24, 1990; buried St. Johns Evangelical Lutheran Cemetery, Northfield Township, Mich.

KARCHER, JOHN CLARENCE, geophysicist; b. Dale, Ind., Apr. 15, 1894; s. Leo and Mary (Madlon) K.; m. Lydia Kilborn, Oct. 16, 1920 (div. June 6, 1952); children: Colleen M. (Mrs. David J. Stone), John Paul. BS, U. Okla., 1916; PhD, U. Pa., 1920. Attached U.S. Embassy, Paris, 1918; rsch. analysis M.-series x-ray spectra, physicist Bur. Standards, 1920-21, 22-23; devel. gauge for measurement pressure curves, 1920, devel. reflection seismograph for oilfield exploration, 1920-30; div. engr. Western Elec. Co., 1923-25; v.p. Geophys. Rsch. Corp., 1925-30; pres. Geophys. Svc., Inc., 1930-39, Coronado Exploration Corp., 1939-41, Comanche Corp., 1945-48; pres., dir. Concho Petroleum Corp. 1950-92; past pres., dir. Mid-Continent Oil and Gas Assn.; dir. Rep. Nat. Bank. Trustee Tex. Rsch. Found. Served with U.S. Army, 1917-18. Fellow AAAS, Am. Phys. Soc.; mem. Dallas Coun. World Affairs (dir.), Ind. Petroleum Assn. (dir.), Soc. Exploration Geophysicists (past pres.), Am. Assn. Petroleum Geologists, Am. Inst. Mining and Metall. Engrs., Phi Beta Kappa, Sigma Xi, Sigma Tau, Tau Beta Pi. *

KARE, MORLEY RICHARD, chemical senses center administrator, physiology educator; b. Winnipeg, Man., Can., Mar. 7, 1922; m. Carol Abramson; children: Susan Kare Tannenbaum, Jordin. BSA, U. Man., 1943, DSc, 1983; MSA, U. B.C., 1948; PhD, Cornell U., 1952; MA, U. Pa., 1974. From asst. prof. to prof. physiology Cornell U., Ithaca, N.Y., 1951-61; prof. physiology N.C. State U., Raleigh, 1962-67, U. Pa., Phila., 1968-90; dir. Monell Chem. Senses Ctr., Phila., 1968-90; cons. food, flavor and fragrance industries; mem. nat. task force program planning Nat. Inst. Deafness and Other Communication Disorders. Editor over 50 books; patentee in field; contbr. articles on chem. senses and nutrition to profl. jours. Mem. exec. com. Franklin Inst. Mus. and Planetarium, Phila., 1975-84; pub. mem. Nat. Advt. Rev. Bd., N.Y.C., 1984-87; pub. trustee Nutrition Found., 1976-82, Internat. Life Scis. Inst., 1983-90; gov. Acad. Scis. Phila. Served to lt. Can. Army, 1943-46. Recipient Borden award, 1962, Underwood Prescott award MIT, 1978; numerous grants. Fellow AAAS; mem. Am. Inst. Nutrition (chmn. long range planning com. 1981-86), Am. Physiol. Soc., Can. Physiol. Soc., Inst. Food Technologies (sci. lectr. 1972-76, 82-86), Univs. Space Research Assn. (trustee 1987-90), Am. Wine and Food Soc. (nat. bd. dirs.). Clubs: Sunday Breakfast (Phila.); Cosmos (Washington). Home: Narberth Pa. Died July 30, 1990; buried Winnipeg, Man., Can.

KARLOVITZ, LES ANDREW, academic administrator; b. Budapest, Hungary, July 31, 1936; came to U.S., 1947; s. Bela and Maria (Koenig) K.; m. Julie Mahoney, July 11, 1959; children: Max, Leslie, Jennifer. B.S., Yale U., 1959; Ph.D., Carnegie Inst. Tech., 1964. Mem. faculty Case Western Res. U., Cleve., 1963-66; mem. U. Md., College Park, 1966-78; research prof. Inst. Fluid Dynamics and Applied Math, U. Md., 1971-78; dir., prof. Sch Math. Ga. Inst. Tech., Atlanta, 1978-82, dean Coll. Scis. and Liberal Studies, 1982-89; provost, v.p. acad. affairs Western Washington U., Bellingham, 1989-90; vis. prof. Carnegie-Mellon U., Pitts., 1973-74, U. Brasilia, (Brazil), 1974; program dir. math. NSF, 1976-77. Contbr. articles to profl. jours.; mem. editorial bd.: Jour. Math Anaylsis, Soc. Indsl. and Applied Math, 1973-82. Mem. Am. Math. Soc., Soc. Indsl. and Applied Math. Home: Bellingham Wash. Died Apr. 2, 1990.

KARR, HERBERT WILLIAM, professional services company executive; b. Macomb, Ill., June 24, 1925; s. Herbert Eldon and Florence Marguerite (Sturgeon) K.; m. Ann Lawruk, Dec. 27, 1947 (div. 1966); children—Randall William, Barrett Kendal; m. Tove Marie Miller, July 2, 1966; children—Linda Marie, Karen Anita. Student, Southeast Mo. State U., 1943, U. So. Calif., Los Angeles, 1946-49; B.S. in Bus. Adminstrn., UCLA, 1952, M.B.A., 1954. Trumpet player numerous dance bands, Ariz., Calif., La., Mo., N.Mex., Tex., 1940-54; tech. analyst Rand Corp., Santa Monica, Calif., 1954-57; project mgr. Gen Electric TEMPO, Santa Barbara, Calif., 1957-58; dept. mgr. Planning Research Corp., Los Angeles, 1958-60; co-founder, pres. CACI, Inc. (formerly Calif. Analysis Ctr., Inc.), Arlington, Va., 1962-71; chmn. bd. CACI Internat. (formerly Calif. Analysis Ctr., Inc.), Arlington, Va., 1968-90; cons. Rand Corp., Santa Monica, 1960-63, Douglas Aircraft Corp., Santa Monica and Long Beach, Calif. Author: (with others) Simscript Simulation Programming Language, 1962; dir. tng. film "The Supply Manager's Dilemma," 1954 (N.Y. Festival award). Contbr. articles to profl. jours. Served with USAAF, 1943-46, PTO. Home: Avalon Calif. Died Apr. 25, 1990; buried Avalon, Calif.

KARR, LLOYD, lawyer; b. Monticello, Iowa, May 19, 1912; s. Charles L. and Margaret E. (Houston) K.; m. Margaret E. Phelan, May 14, 1938; children—Janet A., Richard L. Bar: Iowa 1937. Since practiced in Webster City; mem. firm Karr, Karr & Karr (P.C.); county atty. Hamilton County, 1940-48; Pub. Webster City Daily Freeman Jour., 1952-55, Winter Park (Fla.) Sun-Herald, 1959-65; mem. adv. council naval affairs 6th Naval Dist., 1959-62. Contbr. articles to profl. publs. Served with AUS, 1943-45. Recipient Award of Merit Iowa Bar Assn., 1968. Fellow Am. Coll. Probate Counsel (editorial bd. 1988-90); mem. ABA, Iowa State Bar Assn. (bd. govs. 1959-61, pres. 1962- 63), Iowa Acad. Trial Lawyers, DeMolay Legion of Honor, Sigma Delta Chi. Clubs: Mason, Elk. Died July 1, 1990; buried Webster City.

KASHA, LAWRENCE N., producer, director theatrical and film productions; b. Bklyn., Dec. 3, 1934; s. Irving and Rose (Katz) K. BA, NYU, 1954, MA, 1955. Dir., producer: (Broadway plays) L'il Abner, 1958, Camelot, 1963-64, Bajour, 1964, Funny Girl, 1965, Show Boat revival, 1966, Cactus Flower, 1968, Star Spangled Girl,

1968, Lovely Ladies, Kind Gentlemen, 1970, (off-Broadway) Anything Goes, 1962, (London shows) Funny Girl, 1966, Mame, 1969; producer: (Broadway plays) She Loves Me, 1963, Hadrian VII, 1969, Applause, 1970, Father's Day, 1971, Inner City, 1972, Seesaw, 1973, No Hard Feelings, 1973, Seven Brides for Seven Brothers, 1978, (off-Broadway) Parade, 1960, (Los Angeles show) Heaven Sent, 1978, (CBS-TV spls.) Applause, 1973, Another April, 1974, Rosenthal & Jones, 1975, (TV series) Busting Loose, 1977, Komedy Tonite, NBC, 1978 (Tony award 1970, Outer Critics Circle award 1973), Knots Landing (also writer, dir. various episodes); dir. touring co. Singin' in the Rain, 1986-87; playwright: (with Hayden Griffin) The Pirate, 1968, (with Lionel Wilson) Where Have You Been, Billy Boy?, 1969, (with David S. Landay) Heaven Sent, 1978, Seven Brides for Seven Brothers, 1978, Woman of The Year, 1981. Mem. Dirs. Guild Am., Actors Equity Assn., Writers Guild West. Home: Beverly Hills Calif. Died Sept. 29, 1990.

KASKE, ROBERT EARL, English language educator; b. Cin., June 1, 1921; s. Herman Charles and Ann (Laake) K.; 1 child, David Louis; m. Carol Margaret Vonckx, June 4, 1958; 1 child, Richard James. BA, Xavier U., Cin., 1942; MA, U. N.C., 1947, PhD, 1950. Instr., asst. prof. Washington U., St. Louis, 1950-57; asst. prof. Pa. State U., University Park, 1957-58; assoc. prof. U. N.C., Chapel Hill, 1958-61; prof. U. Ill., Urbana, 1961-64; prof. English, Cornell U., Ithaca, N.Y., 1964-89, Avalon Found. prof. humanities, 1975-89; mem. editorial adv. com. A Manual of the Writings in Middle English; mem. adv. bd. Speculum. Contbg. author: Medieval Literature and Folklore Studies: Essays in Honor of Francis Lee Utley, 1970, Chaucer the Love Poet, 1973, Chaucer and Middle English Studies in Honor of Rossell Hope Robbins, 1974, The Wisdom of Poetry: Essays in Early English Literature in Honor of Morton W. Bloomfield, 1982, Dante, Petrarch, Boccaccio: Studies in the Honor of Charles S. Singleton, 1983, Sources and Relations: Studies in Honour of J.E. Cross, 1985, A Volume of Essays in Memory of Judson Boyce Allen 1932-85, 1986, Medieval English Studies Presented to George Kane, 1988, Traditions and Innovations: Essays on British Literature of the Middle Ages and Renaissance, 1990; author: Medieval Christian Literary Imagery: A Guide to Interpretation, 1988; chief editor Traditio; also articles. 1st lt. AUS, 1942-46. Sr. fellow Am. Coun. Learned Socs., 1971-72, Cornell U. Soc. for Humanities, 1972-73, Southeastern Inst. Medieval and Renaissance Studies, 1979, Guggenheim fellow, 1962-63, 77-78; grantee NEH, 1977-78, 84-85, 86, Am. Philos. Soc., 1986. Fellow Mediaeval Acad. Am. (councillor 1975-78); mem. MLA, Dante Soc. Am., Internat. Assn. Univ. Profs. English, Acad. Lit. Studies (original). Home: Mrs Carol V Kaske, Ithaca N.Y. Died Aug. 8, 1989; cremated.

KASLER, RICHARD EUGENE JEFF, construction company executive; b. Athens, Ohio, Oct. 23, 1925; s. Clinton Eugene and Vivian Eleanor (Landis) K.; m. Elaine Eldridge, July 5, 1947; children: Judy, Jill, Steven. BS in Aero. Engring., Purdue U., 1946. Aero engr. Northrup Aircraft, L.A., 1946-47; asst. bridge engr. Calif. Div. Hwys., Sacramento, 1948-49; civil engr. Fredericksen & Kasler, Sacramento, 1949-55, asst. gen. mgr., 1955-61; pres., chief exec. officer Kasler Corp., San Bernardino, Calif., 1961-82, chmn., chief exec. officer, 1982-91; also bd. dirs. Kasler Corp., San Bernardino. Bd. dirs. Long Beach (Calif.) Community Hosp. Found., 1975-83. Served to lt. (j.g.) USNR, 1943-46. Recipient Disting. Engring. Alumnus award Purdue U., 1984, Roger H. Corbetta award Am. Concrete Inst., 1985; named Contractor of Yr. Am. Pub. Works Assn., 1985, Lifetime Achievement award Greater L.A. C. of C., 1989. Mem. Assn. Gen. Contractors of Calif. (bd. dirs. 1961-80, pres. 1979), The Beavers (bd. dirs. 1970-87, v.p. 1990). Republican. Clubs: Jonathan (Los Angeles); Va. Country (Long Beach); Arrowhead Country; 4th of July Yacht (comdr. 1979). Home: Long Beach Calif. Deceased.

KASS, EDWARD HAROLD, physician, epidemiologist; b. N.Y.C., Dec. 20, 1917; s. Hyman A. and Ann (Selvansky) K.; m. Fae Golden, 1943 (dec. 1973); children: Robert, James, Nancy; m. Amalie Moses Hecht, 1975; stepchildren: Anne, Robert, Thomas, Jonathan, Peter. AB with high distinction, U. Ky., 1939, MS, 1941; PhD, U. Wis., 1943; MD, U. Calif., 1947; MA (hon.), Harvard U., 1958; DSc (hon.), U. Ky., 1962; MD (honorus cause), U. Gothenburg, Sweden, 1989. Diplomate: Am. Bd. Pathology, Am. Bd. Microbiology, Am. Bd. Preventive Medicine. Grad. asst., instr. bacteriology U. Ky., 1939-41; research asst., instr. U. Wis. Med. Sch., 1941-43, immunologist dept. phys. chemistry, 1944, grad. asst. dept. pathology, 1944-45; intern Boston City Hosp., 1947-48, resident, 1948-49, dir. Channing lab., dept. med. microbiology, 1963-77; research fellow Thorndike Meml. Lab., 1949-52, asst. physician, 1951-58; sr. fellow in virus diseases NRC, 1949-52; instr. in medicine Harvard U. Med. Sch., Cambridge, Mass., 1951-52, assoc. in medicine, 1952-55, asst. prof., 1955-58, assoc. prof. bacteriology and immunology, 1958-62, assoc. prof., 1968-69, prof., 1969-73, William Ellery Channing prof. medicine, 1973-88, prof. emeritus, 1988; assoc. dir. bacteriology Mallory Inst. Pathology, 1957-63; dir. Channing lab. Brigham and Women's Hosp., Boston, 1977-88, sr. physician, 1988; vis. prof. Hebrew U.-Hadassah Med. Sch., Jerusalem, 1974; vis. prof. community medicine St. Thomas Hosp., London, 1982-83; vis. prof. med. microbiology Royal Free Hosp., London, 1982-83; lectr. London Sch. Hygiene and Tropical Medicine; chmn. com.to study effects of weightlessness on astronauts, NASA, 1970's; cons. in field. Author 12 books; editor: Jour. Infectious Diseases, 1968-79, Revs. Infectious Diseases, 1979-89; mem. editorial bd. various profl. jours.; contbr. articles to med. jours. Recipient Josiah Marvel Cup award, 1982. Fellow Am. Coll. Epidemiology, ACP (Rosenthal award), Coll. Am. Pathologists, Am. Heart Assn., N.Y. Acad. Scis., Am. Coll. Nutrition, Royal Soc. Medicine (London), Royal Coll. Physicians (London), Infectious Diseases Soc. Am. (founding mem., sec. 1963-67, pres. 1970-71, spl. citation 1977, Bristol award 1982); mem. Inst. Medicine (sr.), Internat. Epidemiol. Assn. (treas. 1977-81), Internat. Congress for Infectious Disease (pres. 1983-85), Mass. Infectious Diseases Soc. (pres. 1985-88), Mass. Soc. Pathologists, New England Soc. Pathologists, Soc. Exptl. Biology and Medicine, Am. Acad. Arts and Scis., AAAS, Am. Epidemiol. Soc., Am. Fedn. Clin. Research, German Soc. Internal Medicine (hon.), AMA, Am. Pub. Health Assn., Am. Soc. Clin. Investigation, Am. Soc. Microbiology, Soc. Epidemiol. Research, Am. Soc. Nephrology, Am. Thoracic Soc., Assn. Am. Physicians, Am. Physicians Fellowship (pres. 1985—), Infectious Disease Soc. Mex. (hon.), Pan Am. Infectious Diseases Soc. (hon.), Japanese Soc. for Infectious Diseases (hon.), Nat. Aeronauties and Space Admin., Natl. Heart, Lung and Blood Internat., Phi Beta Kappa, Sigma Xi, Alpha Omega Alpha. Jewish. Club: Harvard (Boston, N.Y.C.). Home: Lincoln Mass. Died Jan. 17, 1990; cremated.

KASSEBOHM, WALTER, mechanical engineer; b. Hamburg, Germany, July 16, 1898; came to U.S., 1925; s. Heinrich and Sophie (Schaefer) K.; m. Elvira Lindow, Sept. 1935 (dec. 1952); children: Katherine, Sylvia, Walther-Werner; m. Velma Sparkman, July 1955. ME, Hamburg Engring. Coll., 1924. Design engr., prodn. engr. auto industry Detroit, 1925-29; design engr., tool engr., div. mgr. Marchant Calculators, Inc., 1929-40; factory mgr., v.p. ops. Marchant Calculators, Inc., Oakland, Calif., 1949-57; exec. v.p., gen. mgr. Marchant Calculators, Inc., Oakland, 1958-63, pres., 1963-92; plant mgr., v.p., gen. mgr. Prodn. Engring. Co., Berkeley, Calif., 1940-48; gen. mgr. Moore Machinery Machine Took Distbrs., San Francisco, L.A., 1948-49; v.p. European ops. Smith Corona Marchant Corp., 1963-92; pres. Smith Corona Marchant Internat. S.A., Lausanne, Switzerland. Contbr. tech. articles to profl. jours. Mem. ASME, Calif. Soc. Mech. Engrs., Am. Ordnance Assn., Am. Soc. Advancement Mgmt., Am. Soc. Tool Engrs., Rotary. *

KASTNER, ELWOOD CURT, educational administrator; b. N.Y.C., Sept. 5, 1905; s. George Curt and Emma (Le Rocker) K.; m. Madeline de Rimsingeur, June 27, 1930 (dec. Oct. 1956); children: Elwood Curt (dec.), Robert Keith; m. Eunice R. Hart, May 3, 1957. BS, NYU, 1928, postgrad., 1929; LLD, St. Michael's Coll., 1950. Dir. residence bur. NYU, 1928-29, asst. to registrar, 1930-34, asst. registrar and univ. recorder, 1934-41, acting registrar and supr. of admissions, 1941-42, registrar and supr. admissions, 1942-52, dean admissions and registrar, 1952-57, dean registration and fin. aid, 1957-62, dean of fin. aid, 1962-92; lectr. in coll. adminstrn., 1954-56; cons. to Navy Officer Procurement, 1942-48; mem. exec. com. Coll. Entrance Examination Bd., 1948-50; sec. Middle State Assn. Colls. and Secondary Schs. Contbr. to Adminstrs. in Higher Edn. jours. Trustee Halsted Sch. Mem. Am. Assn. Collegiate Registrars and Admissions Officers (pres. 1950-51), Mid. States Assn. Collegiate Registrars and Officers Admission (pres. 1948-49), Am. Coun. Edn. (com. accreditation), Faculty NYU Club (pres. 1940-41), NYU Club, Delta Upsilon. Methodist. Home: Crestwood N.Y. Died Feb. 29, 1992.

KATELL, SIDNEY, consulting cost engineer, educator; b. N.Y.C., Feb. 2, 1915; s. Aaron and Gusta (Ornstein) K.; m. Elvie League, July 4, 1948; children: Alan David, Barry Steven. B.Chem. Engring., NYU, 1941. Chem. engr. design U.S. Bur. Mines, Louisiana, Mo., 1948-53; chem. engr. U.S. Bur. Mines, Morgantown, W.Va., 1954-55; chief gas treating and testing sect. U.S. Bur. Mines, 1955-57; chief process evaluation group U.S. Bur. Mines, Morgantown, 1957-76; prof. mineral resource econs. Coll. Mineral and Energy Resources, W.Va. U., 1976-82; pvt. cons., 1982-90; chem. engr. Westinghouse Electric Co., Pitts., 1953-54. Contbr. articles to profl., govtl. jours. Mem. Am. Assn. Cost Engrs. (pres. 1970-71, award merit 1973), Am. Chem. Soc., Am. Inst. Chem. Engrs., Am. Gas Assn. (Operating Sect. award merit 1955), Morgantown C. of C. (chmn. pollution control com.), B'nai B'rith. Jewish (pres. congregation). Home: Boca Raton Fla. Died May 19, 1990.

KATZ, DONALD LAVERNE, chemical engineering educator, consultant; b. nr. Jackson, Mich., Aug. 1, 1907; s. Gottlieb and Lucy (Schnackenberg) K.; m. Lila Maxine Crull, Sept. 17, 1932 (dec. 1965); children: Marvin LaVerne, Linda Maxine; m. Elizabeth Harwood Correll, Nov. 26, 1965; stepchildren: Richard, Steven, Jonathan H. B.S., U. Mich., 1931, M.S., 1932, Ph.D., 1933. Research engr. Phillips Petroleum Co., Bartlesville, Okla., 1933-36; asst. prof. chem. engring. U. Mich., Ann Arbor, 1936-42, assoc. prof., 1942-43, prof., 1943-66, Alfred H. White univ. prof. chem. engring., 1966-77, prof. emeritus, 1977-89, chmn. dept. chem. and metall. engring., 1951-62; cons. engr., from 1936; mem. sci. adv. bd. EPA, 1976-79. Author 10 books including The Handbook of Natural Gas Engineering, 1959; contbr. articles to profl. jours. Trustee Ann Arbor Pub. Schs., pres. bd. trustees, 1953-56; trustee Engring. Index, 1966-72. Recipient Hanlon award Natural Gasoline Assn. Am., 1950; named Mich. Engr. Yr. Mich. Soc. Profl. Engrs., 1959; recipient John Franklin Carll award Soc. Petroleum Engrs., 1964; Founders award Am. Inst. Chem. Engrs., 1964; Warren K. Lewis award, 1967; W.H. Walker award, 1968; Mineral Industry Edn. award AIME, 1970; Disting. Pub. Service award USCG, 1972; E.V. Murphree award Am. Chem. Soc., 1975; Nat. medal of Sci., 1983; Donald L. Katz award for excellence in research established in his honor Gas Processors Assn., 1985. Fellow AAAS, Am. Nuclear Soc., Am. Inst. Chem. Engrs. (dir. 1955-57, v.p. 1958, pres. 1959, sec. commn. engring. edn. 1962-64, Eminent Chem. Engr. 1983); mem. Am. Chem. Soc., AIME (hon. mem. 1986, Lucas medal 1979), ASME, Am. Soc. Engring. Edn., Am. Gas Assn. (Gas Industry Research award 1977), Am. Assn. Petroleum Geologists, Ann Arbor Council Chs. (pres. 1944-46), Nat. Soc. Profl. Engrs., Nat. Acad. Sci. (chmn. USCG com. on hazardous materials 1964-72, 77-79, mem. sci. and tech. communications com. 1967-69, chmn. com. air quality and power plant emissions 1974-75), Engrs. Council Profl. Devel. (dir., mem. exec. com. 1959-65), EDUCOM (chmn. bd. trustees 1969-72, chmn. council 1971-72), Nat. Acad. Engring., Sigma Xi, Tau Beta Pi, Phi Lambda Upsilon (hon.), Phi Kappa Phi, Alpha Chi Sigma. Methodist (life mem. 1st United Ch.). Home: Ann Arbor Mich. Died May 29, 1989; buried Ann Arbor, Mich.

KATZ, JOSEPH MORRIS, entrepreneur; b. Yampol, Russia, July 7, 1913; came to U.S., 1914; s. Samuel and Sarah (Averbach) K.; m. Agnes Roman, 1937 (dec. Sept. 1987); children—Marshall P., Andrea Katz McCutcheon; m. Thelma W. Wechsler, May 26, 1989. Student, U. Pitts., 1931-34. Founder, chmn. bd. Papercraft Corp., Pitts., 1945-83, chmn. exec. com., 1983-84; sr. chmn. Papercraft Corp., 1984-88; chmn. Cavendish Holdings, Pitts., from 1988. Mem. Gov.'s Fiscal Task Force, 1970-71; mem. Gov.'s Bus. Adv. Coun. Commonwealth Pa., State Planning Bd. Commonwealth Pa., 1973-78; trustee U. Pitts.; chmn. bd. visitors Faculty Arts and Scis., mem. bd. visitors Joseph M. Katz Grad. Sch. Bus.; trustee Katz Found., Montefiore Found.; bd. dirs. Pitts. Symphony Soc., Civic Light Opera; bd. dirs., pres. Allegheny Trails coun. Boy Scouts Am., 1988-89, City of Hope, Horatio Alger Assn. Disting. Ams., Pitts. Opera; trustee numerous others. Recipient Man of Yr. Herbert Lehman award, 1970, Human Rels. award Am. Jewish Com., 1972, Horatio Alger award, 1981, Spirit of Life award City of Hope, 1982; nat. honoree Jewish Nat. Fund, 1984; Joseph M. Katz Grad. Sch. of Bus., U. Pitts. named after him. Clubs: Duquesne (Pitts.), Westmoreland Country (Pitts.), Concordia (Pitts.), Pitts. Athletic Assn. (Pitts.); Harmonie (N.Y.C.). Home: Pittsburgh Pa. Died May 4, 1991.

KATZ, PAUL, conductor, educator; b. N.Y.C., Nov. 2, 1907; s. Nathan and Molly (Rothenberg) K.; m. Phyllis Margolis, July 29, 1934; 1 son, Nevin. Mus.B. in Theory, Cleve. Inst. Music, 1931; postgrad., Am. Conservatory of Music, Fountainbleau, France; student of, Sevcik, Ysaye, Auer, Boulanger; hon. degrees, U. Dayton, Central State U., Wright State U. Tchr., condr., chmn. orch. dept. Cin. Coll. Conservatory Music; lectr., tchr. U. Dayton, Wright State U.; mem. 1st violin sect. Cin. Symphony, 1924-27, Cleve. Symphony, 1927-33. Condr., Dayton Philharmonic Orch., from 1933, emeritus, from 1975. Composer. Mem. Audubon Soc. Jewish. Home: Dayton OH Deceased. †

KAUFERT, FRANK HENRY, university dean; b. Princeton, Minn., Dec. 2, 1905; s. FRank and Mary Amelia (Kraft) K.; m. Ione Elizabeth Mossman, Oct. 28, 1938; 1 child, Joseph Mossman. BS, U. Minn., 1928, MS, 1930, PhD, 1935; student, U. Halle, Halle A. Saale, Germany, 1931. Asst. prof. U. Minn., 1936, assoc. prof. forestry, 1940-42, prof., dir. Sch. Forestry, 1946-70, dean Coll. Forestry, 1970-74, dean emeritus, 1974-90; rsch. chemist E.I. du Pont de Nemours, Wilmington, Del., 1936-40; asst. adminstr. Coop. State Rsch. Svc., Dept. Agr., 1963-64; sr. wood technologist U.S. Forest Svc. Forest Products Lab., Madison, Wis., 1942-45; dir. forestry rsch. project Soc. Am. Foresters, 1954. Author: (with others) Wood Aircraft Fabrication and Inspection, 1944, Forestry and Related Research in North America, 1955. Pres. Keep Minn. Green, 1951-64. Mem. AAAS, Forest History Soc. (pres. 1956-57, 63-65, 73-75), Soc. Am. Foresters (coun. 1950, 53), Am. Wood Preservers Assn., Assn. State Coll. and Univ. Forestry Rsch. Orgns. (pres. 1957-58), Sigma Xi, Xi Sigma Pi, Gamma Sigma Delta, Alpha Zeta. Congregationalist. Home: Saint Anthony Park Minn. Died Feb. 17, 1990.

KAUFFMAN, IRVIN HARTMAN, economist; b. Berks County, Pa., July 28, 1897; s. James Grimes and Mary Ann (Hartman) K.; m. Carolyn Grace Robison, Dec. 29, 1925; children: Frank Hartman, Thomas Irvin,

Robert David. BS in Econs., U. Pa., 1921. Exec. sec. Detroit Dairy and Food Coun., 1925-27, Pitts. Dist. Dairy Coun., 1927-33; v.p. Balt. Bank for Cooepratives, 1933-54; agrl. credit adviser U.S. Ops. Mission to Pakistan, 1954-56, agrl. credit adviser to China, 1956-60, agrl. credit adviser to Liberia, 1961-62; coops. cons. to Nyasaland, 1963, coops. cons. to North Rhodesia and Malagasy Republic, 1964. Served to 2d lt., inf. U.S. Army, 1917-19; to lt. col., mil. govt., AUS, 1943-46. Mem. Acacia Club, Mason, Annapolis (Md.) Yacht Club. *

KAUFMAN, CHARLES RUDOLPH, lawyer; b. Chgo., Dec. 25, 1908; s. Aaron C. and and Miriam (Eisenstaedt) K.; m. Violet-Page Koteen, Feb. 20, 1936 (dec.); children: Thomas H. (dec.), Constance Page Kaufman Dickinson, Christopher Lee. A.B., U. Mich., 1930; J.D. magna cum laude (Fay diploma), Harvard U., 1933. Bar: D.C. 1935, Ill. 1938, U.S. Supreme Ct. 1947. Law clk. Judge Learned Hand, U.S. Ct. Appeals, 1933-34; supervising atty. SEC, Washington, 1934-37; pvt. practice Pope & Ballard, 1937-52, Vedder, Price, Kaufman & Kammholz, Chgo., 1952-90. Legis. editor: Harvard Law Rev., 1932-33. Former mem. New Trier Twp. High Sch. Bd. Edn.; active in various charitable, civic and law sch. programs.; trustee Hadley Sch. for Blind. Mem. ABA, Ill. Bar Assn., D.C. Bar Assn., Chgo. Bar Assn., Harvard Law Soc. Ill., Chgo. Law Club. Home: Winnetka Ill. Died Sept. 26, 1990; buried Skokie, Ill.

KAUFMAN, IRVING ROBERT, federal judge; b. N.Y.C., June 24, 1910; s. Herman and Rose (Spielberg) K.; m. Helen Ruth Rosenberg; children: James Michael, Robert Howard (dec.), Richard Kenneth (dec.). LLB, Fordham U., 1931; LLD (hon.), Jewish Theol. Sem. Am.; LLD, Fordham U., Oklahoma City U.; LittD (hon.), Dickinson Sch. Law; DCL (hon.), NYU. Bar: N.Y. 1932. Spl. asst. to U.S. Atty., So. Dist. N.Y., 1935; asst. U.S. Atty., 1936-40; spl. asst. to Atty. Gen. U.S. in charge of lobbying investigation; established permanent lobbying unit for U.S. Dept. Justice, 1948; pvt. practice N.Y.C.; ptnr. Noonan, Kaufman and Eagan; U.S. dist. judge So. Dist. N.Y., 1949-61; cir. judge U.S. Ct. Appeals (2d. cir.), from 1961, chief judge, 1973-80; U.S. del. to 2d UN Congress Prevention Crime and Treatment Offenders, 1961, Conf. Anglo-Am. Legal Exchange, Ditchley, Eng., 1969, 77, 80; mem. exec. com. U.S. Jud. Conf., 1975-80, mem. com. standards jud. conduct, chmn. com. operation jury system, 1966-73, chmn. com. jud. branch, 1979-83; chmn. Pres.'s Commn. on Organized Crime, 1983-86. Contbr. articles to profl. jours. Trustee Mt. Sinai Med. Center, Mt. Sinai Med. Sch., Mt. Sinai Hosp.; trustee emeritus Riverdale Country Sch. Recipient Achievement in Law award Fordham Coll. Alumni Assn., Encaenia award Fordham Coll., Chief Justice Harlan Fiske Stone award Assn. Trial Lawyers City N.Y., Presdl. Medal of Freedom awarded by Pres. Reagan, 1987, Presdl. citation NYU; subject 2d Cir. En Banc ceremony honoring 40 yrs. jud. svc., 1989; Judge Irving R. Kaufman Pub. Svc. Fellowship established in his honor Harvard Law Sch.; Walter Annenberg Irving R. Kaufman Scholarship established in his honor Fordham Law Sch. Fellow Inst. Jud. Adminstrn. (Silver Anniversary Vanderbilt award, pres. 1969-71, chmn. exec. com., chmn. juvenile justice standards project), Am. Coll. Trial Lawyers (honoris causa); mem. ABA, Fed. Bar Assn., N.Y. Bar Assn., Assn. of Bar of City of N.Y. (Cardozo lectr.), Fed. Bar Coun. (Learned Hand medal) Am. Judicature Soc. (Herbert Harley award 1980), Am. Law Inst., Fordham Law Alumni Assn. (bd. dirs.), Tau Epsilon Phi (Man of Year citation), Phi Alpha Delta. Home: New York N.Y. Died Feb. 1, 1992.

KAUFMAN, RICHARD, investment services executive; b. White Plains, N.Y., July 10, 1936; s. Max Kaufman and Anne Kaufman Kaplan; m. Joanne Marie Ippolito, Apr. 29, 1976; children: Shari Ellen, Kenneth Craig. B.A. in Econs., Brandeis U., 1958. Regional v.p. Dupont Walston, Boston, 1966-74; exec. v.p. Paine Webber, N.Y.C., 1974-84; mng. dir. investment services group Donaldson, Lufkin & Jenrette, N.Y.C., from 1984; dir. Empire State Coll. Found. Parent chmn. Skidmore Coll., Saratoga Springs, 1981-85; bd. dirs. 75th Street Tenants Assn., N.Y.C. Served with U.S. Army, 1960-66. Mem. Securities Industry Assn. (com. mem.). Club: Rolling Hills. Home: Stamford Conn. Died Apr. 23, 1991. †

KAYE, SYLVIA FINE, producer, lyricist, composer; b. N.Y.C.; d. Samuel and Bessie Fine; m. Danny Kaye, Jan. 3, 1940; 1 child, Dena. Adj. prof. U. So. Calif., Yale U. Broadway shows include Let's Face It, Straw Hat Revue; film scores include On the Riviera, Up in Arms, Wonder Man, Secret Life of Walter Mitty; co-producer: film scores Court Jester, General, Knock on Wood; producer, writer several TV spls.; popular songs include Moon is Blue, Man with the Golden Arm; spl. songs for Danny Kaye include Lullaby in Ragtime, Stanislavsky, Pavlova, Melody in 4f, Anatole of Paris, Eileen, Five Pennies; exec. producer: Danny Kaye's Look-In at the Met. Opera; writer, producer, host 3 part TV series Musical Comedy Tonight (Peabody award); author: (book) Fine and Danny. Recipient Emmy award for TV children's spl., 1976. Home: New York N.Y. Died Oct. 28, 1991.

KAYSER, ELMER LOUIS, historian; b. Washington, Aug. 27, 1896; s. Samuel Louis and Susie Bronw (Huddleston) K.; m. Margery Ludlow, Feb. 11, 1922; 1 child, Katherine Ludlow (Mrs. Arthur Hallett Page, III). BA, George Washington U., 1917, MA, 1918; PhD, Columbia U., 1932; LLD, George Washington U., 1948. Asst. in history George Washington U., 1914-17, instr., 1917-20, asst. prof., assoc. prof., 1920-24, 25-29, prof., 1932-92, asst. libr., 1917-18; recorder, sec., 1918, 18-29, dir. summer sch., 1925-29, dir. univ. students, dean, 1930-34, 34-62, univ. historian, 1962-92; assoc. chmn. sch. govt. George Washington U., 1957-58; radio commentator on world affairs, 1940-45. Author: The Grand Social Enterprise, 1932, A Manual of Ancient History, 1937; co-author: Contemporary Europe, 1941; mem. bd. editors World Affairs. Sec.-treas. Gen. Alumni Assn., George Washington U., 1918-24, pres., 1950-53; vice chmn. bd. trustees Mount Vernon Sem.; chmn. com. improvement Adminstrn. of Justice in D.C.; past bd. govs. Nat. Cathedral Sch.; mem. sec. Navy's adv. com. Naval History. Mem. Am. Peace Soc., Inst. Judicial Adminstrn., Am. Hist. Assn. (treas.), AAUP (mem. coun. 1953-54), Sigma Phi Epsilon, Pi Gamma Mu, Omicron Delta Kappa, Delta Phi Epsilon, Gate Club, Key Club. *

KAYSER, PAUL WILLIAM, manufacturing executive; b. N.Y.C., Feb. 28, 1918; s. Paul G. and Julia M. (Buttlar) K.; m. Mary Viola Snell, Feb. 21, 1942 (div.); 1 child, Craig; m. Jame M. Satter, Oct. 1, 1965. BA, Wesleyan U., 1940. With Walter Kidde & Co., Belleville, N.J., 1943-47; dir. personnel, dir. Permacel Tape Corp., New Brunswick, N.J., 1947-52; dir. indsl. rels. P. Lorillard Co., N.Y.C., 1952-55; v.p. personnel Am. Airlines, Inc., N.Y.C., 1955-62, Anderson, Clayton & Co., Houston, 1962-65; v.p., dir. indsl. rels. Pepsi Co. Inc., N.Y.C., 1965-70; adminstrv. v.p. King Resources Co., Denver, 1970-71; ptnr., exec. v.p. Golightly and Co. Internat. Inc., N.Y.C., 1971-74; v.p. indsl. rels. and personnel Am. Standard Inc., N.Y.C., 1974-78, v.p. human resources, from 1978. Mem. Nat. Alliance Businessmen (pres. 1969-90), Newcomen Soc., N.Y. Indsl. Rels. Assn., Am. Mgmt. Assn., Union League Club, River Club, Thunderbird Country Club, Alpha Delta Phi. Home: Rancho Mirage Calif. Died Apr. 21, 1990.

KAZARINOFF, NICHOLAS D., mathematics educator; b. Ann Arbor, Mich., Aug. 12, 1929; s. Donat Konstantinovich and Rosalind (Yeska) K.; m. Margaret Louise Koning, July 17, 1948; children—Michael N., Nicholas N., Katherine T., Paul Donat, Alexander N., Dimitri N. B.S., U. Mich., 1950, M.S., 1951; Ph.D., U. Wis., 1954. Instr. math. Purdue U., 1953-55, asst. prof., 1955-56; mem. faculty U. Mich., Ann Arbor, 1956-71, asso. prof., 1960-64, prof., 1964-71; prof., chmn. dept. SUNY at Buffalo, 1971-75, Martin prof. math., 1972-91; on leave, vis. prof. U. New Mex., Albuquerque, 1991; vis. mem. Army Research Center, U. Wis., Madison, 1959-60; exchange prof. Steklov Math. Inst., Moscow, USSR, 1960-61, 65; vis. prof. Center Nat. Research, Italy, 1978, 80; vis. research prof. U. N.Mex., 1985; exchange prof. Beijing Poly. U., 1987; mem.-at-large Conf. Bd. Math. Scis., 1972-75. Author 4 books; mng. editor Mich. Math. Jour., 1961-65; cons. editor Math. Revs., 1966-69; contbr. to profl. jours. Mem. city council, Ann Arbor, 1969-71. Recipient Disting. Undergrad. Teaching award, 1968; Alexander von Humboldt sr. fellowship to Germany awarded for 1992. Fellow AAAS; mem. Am. Math. Soc., Math. Assn. Am., Soc. Indsl. and Applied Math. (jour. book rev. editor 1990-91), Phi Beta Kappa, Sigma Xi, Pi Mu Epsilon. Democrat. Unitarian (past local pres.). Home: Pentwater Mich. Died Nov. 21, 1991; buried Ann Arbor, Mich.

KAZMAYER, ROBERT HENDERSON, business analyst, publisher; b. Rush, N.Y., 1908; s. Jacob and Viola (Darron) K.; m. Clara V. Rapp, July 29, 1936 (div.); 1 child, Robert L.; m. Ida L. Wright, Nov. 18, 1955 (dec. Nov. 1970); m. Doris McMichael Sanderson, Aug. 29, 1988. Student, U. Rochester, 1929-31, Colgate-Divinity Sch., 1931-34; LL.D., Salem Coll., Salem. W.Va., 1956. Ordained deacon M.E. Ch., 1932, ordained elder, 1934; held pastorates at Indian Falls, 1930-31, Lewiston M.E. Ch., Rochester, N.Y., 1931-34, Monroe Av M.E. Ch., 1934-38; left ministry to devote full time to writing, lecturing, 1939, travelled annually in Cen. and S.Am., Far Ea., Eng., continental Europe, 1929-41; in 22 months following Pearl Harbor, travelled numerous states addressing over 400 audiences, lecturing on Germany, Russia, Japan, internat. politics; Rochester Town Hall of the Air, WHEC; three years as radio ch. editor WSAY; originator of Kazmayer Seminar Tours; Lectured throughout, U.S., Can., Europe, the East;. Pub. newsletter for U.S., Brit. businessmen Things To Watch and Watch For; Author: Out of the Clouds, 1944, New Strength for America; speeches; contbr. to We Believe in Prayer; Conducted: Pastor's Exchange in Christian Advocate, 1935-36. Recipient L'Accueil De Paris Conseil Municipal Paris, 1956; George Washington Honor medal Freedoms Found., 1961. Life mem. Acad. Polit. Sci., 1952; charter mem. Anglo-Am. Goodwill Assn. (Brit.), Authors League; mem. Am. Acad. Polit. and Social Sci. Methodist. Clubs: Union League (Chgo.); Adventurers (Chgo., N.Y., London); Overseas Press (N.Y.C.). Lodges: Masons (33d degree), Rotary (Paul Harris fellow). Home: Mariposa Calif. Died Aug. 4, 1991; body donated to science.

KEADY, WILLIAM COLBERT, judge; b. Greenville, Miss., Apr. 2, 1913; m. Dorothy Clark Thompson, July 31, 1935; children: William Colbert, Peggy Anne. JD, Washington U., 1936. Bar: Miss. 1936. Pvt. practice Greenville, 1936-68; chief judge U.S. Dist. Ct. Miss. (no. dist.), Greenville, 1968-89. Mem. Miss. Ho. of Reps. 1940-43, Miss. Senate, 1940-45; mem. Delta Coun. Miss. Econ. Coun.; mem. Jud. Conf. U.S., 1977-80; trustee William Percy Meml. Libr., 1946-49, Greenville Pub. Schs., 1947-51; chmn. bd. Greenville Pub. Schs. 1950-51; pres. Greenville Indsl. Found.; bd. dirs. Kings Daus. Hosp., Washington County YMCA. Mem. ABA, Fed. Bar Assn., Washington County Bar Assn., Miss. State Bar (commr. for 4th cir. 1954-55, pres.-elect 1968), Am. Coll. Trial Lawyers, Am. Judicature Soc. Presbyterian. Home: Greenville Miss. Died June 16, 1989.

KEAN, NORMAN, producer, theater owner, manager; b. Colorado Springs, Colo., Oct. 14, 1934; s. Barney B. and Flora (Bienstock) K.; m. Gwyda DonHowe, Oct. 12, 1958; 1 child, David. Student, U. Denver, 1952-54. Pres. Norman Kean Prodns., Inc., from 1966, Edison Theatre, N.Y.C., from 1970, Edison Enterprises, Inc., from 1974; owner, mgr. E. 74th St. Theater, N.Y.C., 1966-69; lectr. NYU Sch. Continuing Edn., 1976-79, Alvin Ailey Am. Dance Ctr., N.Y.C., 1987-88; mem. faculty Practising Law Inst., N.Y.C., from 1985. Stage mgr. Johnny Johnson, N.Y.C., 1956, Orpheus Descending, 1957, The Waltz of the Toreadors, 1957-58, A Touch of the Poet, 1958-59, Camino Real, 1960, stage mgr., asst. gen. mgr. Laurette, 1960; gen. mgr.: The Pleasure of His Company, 1960, Bayanihan Philippine Dance, Co., 1961, General Seeger, 1961, The Matchmaker, 1962, Tiger, Tiger, Burning Bright, Royal Dramatic Theatre of Sweden, 1962, Phoenix Theatre, N.Y.C., 1962, Laterna Magika from Prague, 1963, Cages, The World of Ray Bradbury, 1965, APA-Phoenix, APA Repertory Company, N.Y.C., 1964-69, Oh! Calcutta!, 1969; producer: Max Morath at the Turn of the Century, N.Y., U.S., Can., 1969-70; assoc. producer Hogan's Goat, 1965, gen. mgr., assoc. producer: The Worlds of Shakespeare, 1963, The Bernard Shaw Story, 1965, Jean Cocteau's Opium, 1970, Happy Birthday, Wanda June, N.Y.C., 1970-71, Orlando Furioso from Rome, N.Y.C., 1970, Don't Bother Me, I Can't Cope, N.Y.C., Chgo., Los Angeles, 1972-74; producer: Hosanna, N.Y.C., 1974, Sizwe Banzi is Dead, 1974-75, The Island, 1974-75, Boccacio, 1975, Me and Bessie, 1975-78, Oh! Calcutta!, N.Y.C. and worldwide, from 1976, Caracas, Venezuela, 1984-85, Rio de Janeiro and São Paulo, Brazil, 1984-87, Norway, 1985-86, Israel, 1986, By Strouse, 1978-80, A Broadway Musical, 1978. Trustee South Fork-Shelter Island chpt. Nature Conservancy, L.I., from 1984; mem. Concerned Citizens of Montauk, L.I., from 1986, Theatreworks/USA, from 1987. Served with U.S. Army, 1954-55. Mem. Am. Acad. Dramatic Arts (trustee 1980-84), League Am. Theatres and Producers (officer, exec. com., bd. govs. from 1970), Suffolk County Motion Picture and TV Commn. Jewish. Home: New York N.Y. Deceased. †

KEARNEY, LESTER T., JR., banker and air force officer; b. Sweetwater, Tex., Jan. 9, 1924; s. Lester T. and Mildred (Hendricks) K.; m. Jonnie Mae King, Dec. 8, 1980; children: Kathleen Lynn, Jamie Kearney Endahl, Leslie Ann. Student, San Angelo Coll., 1942; grad., Air Command and Staff Coll., 1959, Nat. War Coll., 1966. Commd. 2d lt. USAAF, 1944; advanced through grades to maj. gen. USAF, 1973; assigned to ETO, Korea, Panama and U.S.; chief staff Mil. Airlift Command, Scott AFB, Ill., 1973; comdr. 21st Air Force, McGuire AFB, N.J., 1973-75; vice dir. J-5 plans and policy Office Joint Chiefs Staff, Washington, 1975-77; former v.p. S.W. Bank, San Angelo, Tex.; tech. cons. Lockheed-Ga. Mem. polit. affairs com. San Antelo Bd. City Devel.; mem. San Angelo Planning Commn. Decorated D.S.M. with oak leaf cluster, Legion of Merit with oak leaf cluster, Air medal with 5 oak leaff clusters. Mem. Daedalians (life), Rotary. Home: San Angelo Tex. Died Feb. 19, 1988; buried Lawnhaven Meml. Gardens, San Angelo, Tex.

KEARNS, FRANCIS EMNER, bishop; b. Bentleyville, Pa., Dec. 9, 1905; s. George Verlinda and Jennie Mae (McCleary) K.; m. Alice Margaret Thompson, Sept. 1, 1933; children: Rollin Thompson, Margaret (Mrs. Richard E. Baldwin), Francis Emner II. A.B., Ohio Wesleyan U., 1927, D.D., 1954; S.T.B., Boston U. Sch. Theology, 1930; postgrad., U. Berlin, Germany, U. Edinburgh, Scotland, 1930-31; Ph.D., U. Pitts., 1939; LL.D., Mt. Union Coll., 1965; L.H.D., Ohio No. U., 1965; Ph.D., Baldwin-Wallace Coll., 1966. Ordained to ministry Meth. Ch., 1931. Pastor Dravosburg, Pa., 1931-32; asso. pastor Christ Meth. Ch., Pitts., 1932-35; assoc. pastor Ben Avon Meth. Ch., 1935-40, Asbury Meth. Ch., Uniontown, Pa., 1940-45, Wauwatosa (Wis.) Meth. Ch., 1945-64; bishop United Meth. Ch., 1964-92; mem. gen. bd. evangelism, 1965-68, vice chmn. gen. bd. edn., 1968-72, chmn. div. curriculum resources, 1968-72, mem. program council, 1968-72; mem. Meth. Corp., 1968-72; mem. gen. assembly Nat. Council Chs.; pres. Ohio Council Chs., 1969-71; mem. gen. bd. Global Ministries of United Meth. Ch., 1972-76, vice-chmn. div. health and welfare ministries, 1972-76; mem. gen. bd.

Ch. and Soc. of United Meth. Ch., 1972-76; chmn. Meth. Interbd. Com. on Christian Vocations, 1964-68, Faith and Order Commn., Ohio Council Chs., 1965-69; mem. Meth. Interbd. Commn. on Town and Country, 1964-68, North Central Jurisdictional Council, 1972-76; vis. prof. Meth. Theol. Sch., Ohio, 1976-78. Author: The Church is Mine, 1962; Contbr. articles profl. jours. Trustee Baldwin-Wallace Coll., Mt. Union Coll., Ohio No. U., Ohio Wesleyan U., Meth. Theol. Sch. in Ohio, Otterbein Coll., United Theol. Sem. Mem. Phi Beta Kappa. Clubs: Mason (33 deg.), Rotarian. Home: Sebring OH Died Jan. 29, 1992. †

KEARY, WILLIAM J., business executive; b. County Mayo, Ireland, Jan. 1, 1897; came to U.S., 1915; s. William and Ellen (Heaney) K. Spl. courses, Coll., Dublin, Ireland, Columbia U. With Chas. D. Barney & Co., 1922-26, J. & W. Selingman & Co., 1926-38; v.p., dir. Union Securities Corp., 1938-42, 46-52; pres. Madison-State-Dearborn Bldg. Corp., Chgo., 1948-52, Empire State Bldg., N.Y.C., 1952-54; fin. cons. to corps., 1955-59; assoc. Eastman Dillon, Union Securities & Co., 1960-92; dir. Coastal Ship Corp. Dir. Met. Opera, Opera Guild. Served AUS, A.E.F. in France, 1918-19; with A.A. F., War Dept. and W.P.B., 1942-45. *

KEATINGE, RICHARD HARTE, lawyer; b. San Francisco, Dec. 4, 1919; m. Betty West, Apr. 20, 1944; children: Richard West, Daniel Wilson, Nancy Elizabeth. A.B. with honors, U. Calif., Berkeley, 1939; M.A., Harvard U., 1941; J.D., Georgetown U., 1944. Bar: D.C. 1944, N.Y. 1945, Calif. 1947, U.S. Supreme Ct. 1964. Sr. economist, sr. indsl. specialist WPB, Washington, 1941-44; practice law N.Y.C., 1944-45, Washington, 1945-47; pvt. practice L.A., 1947-92; sr. ptnr. Keatinge, Pastor & Mintz (and predecessor firms), 1948-79, Reavis & McGrath, 1979-88, Fulbright & Jaworski, 1989-91, Lewis, D'Amato et al., L.A., 1991-92; spl. asst. atty. gen., State of Calif., 1964-68; public mem. Adminstrv. Conf. of U.S., 1968-74. Mem.: Georgetown Law Jour, 1943-44. Mem. Calif. Law Revision Commn., 1961-68, chmn., 1965-67; trustee Coro Found., 1965-73; bd. trustees, mem. exec. com. U. Calif. Berkeley Found., 1973-87, chmn. bd. trustees, 1983-85, mem. The Berkeley Fellows, 1989-92. Fellow (life) Am. Bar Found., Am. Coll. Tax Counsel; mem. ABA (bd. govs. 1978-79, mem. ho. of dels. 1974-81, 82-91, mem. coun. 1961-64, 65-69, 74-78, 82-91, chmn. adminstrv. law sect. 1967-68, mem. standing com. on resolutions 1973-74, chmn. com. on sales, exchs. and basis taxation sect. 1963-65, mem. coun. econs. of law practice sect. 1974-75, mem. commn. on law and economy 1976-78, vice chmn. 1977-78, mem. spl. com. on housing and urban devel. law 1968-73, vice chmn. adv. commn. on housing and urban growth 1974-77, nat. sec. Jr. Bar Conf. 1949-50), State Bar Calif. (del. conf. of dels. 1966-67, 77-92, mem. exec. com. public law sect. 1976-78), L.A. County Bar Assn. (chmn. taxation sect. 1966-67, mem. fair jud. election practices com. 1978-79, mem. exec. com. law office mgmt. sect. 1977-85, mem. housing and urban devel. law com. 1971-80, mem. arbitration com. 1974-92, mem. new quarters com. 1979-80), Assn. Bus. Trial Lawyers (bd. govs. 1974-79, pres. 1978-79), Inter-Am. Bar Assn., Internat. Bar Assn., Western Justice Ctr. Fdn. (pres. 1989-92), Am. Judicature Soc., Am. Law Inst., Am. Arbitration Assn. (nat. panel of arbitrators 1950-92), Com. to Maintain Diversity Jurisdiction, Lawyers Club L.A., Phi Beta Kappa. Home: Pasadena Calif. Died July 25, 1992. †

KEE, JAMES, congressman; b. Bluefield, W.Va., Apr. 15, 1917; s. John and Elizabeth (Simpkins) K.; m. Helen Lee Chapman, Sept. 7, 1939; children: Kirsten Cook, Kathleen Reagle, Karen. Student, Southeastern U., Georgetown U. Mem. 89th-92d Congresses 5th dist. W.Va. Democrat. Home: Bluefield W.Va. Died Mar. 11, 1989.

KEEFE, ROGER MANTON, former banker, financial consultant; b. New London, Conn., Feb. 26, 1919; s. Arthur T. and Mabel (Foran) K.; m. Ann Hunter, June 4, 1949; children: Christopher Hunter, Matthew Foran, Michael Devereux, Susan Ann, Robin Mary, Victoria Morrill. Student, Coll. St. Gregory, Downside Abbey, Eng., 1936-37; BA in History and Internat. Rls., Yale U., 1941. With Chase Manhattan Bank, N.Y.C., 1945-71; sr. v.p. charge div. financing devel. and tech. services Chase Manhattan Bank, 1966-71; exec. v.p. Conn. Bank & Trust Co., Hartford, 1971-76; vice chmn. Conn. Bank & Trust Co., 1976-80, CBT Corp., Hartford, 1976-83; chmn. exec. com. CBT Corp., 1980-83, Conn. Bank & Trust Co., 1980-83; pres. R.M. Keefe Assocs., Inc., 1983-92; dir. Callahan Mining Co., Maritime Ctr. Mem. exec. coun. Yale Class of 1941, 1962-92, treas., 1966-71, mem. bd. edn., Norwalk, Conn.; mem. nat. Rep. Fin. Com., 1961-92, also treas. adv. fin. com.; mem. N.Y. State Rep. Fin. Com., 1961-69; trustee St. Thomas More Corp., 1962-92, treas., 1964-69; trustee Greens Farms Acad., 1978-88, Fiarfield U., 1982-88, Maritime Ctr. Norwalk, 1984-92; bd. dirs. St. Joseph's Med. Ctr., 1978-92. Maj. AUS, World War II, ETO. Decorated Silver Star, Bronze Star with cluster, Purple Heart., Knight of St. Gregory, Knight of Malta. Mem. Fin. Execs. Inst., Assn. Res. City Bankers, Am. Arbitration Assn., Southwestern Area Commerce and Industry Assn. (dir. 1978). Clubs: Yale (N.Y.C.); Wee Burn Country, Harbor, Norwalk Yacht; Internat. (Washington). Home: South Norwalk Conn. Died May 30, 1992. †

KEELE, HAROLD M., lawyer; b. Monticello, Ill., Aug. 26, 1901; s. Frederick W. and Delta (Parsons) K.; m. Caryl Dunham, 1960. A.B. cum laude, U. Ill., 1923, LL.B., 1927. Bar: Ill. bar 1928. Mem. English faculty U. Ill., 1924-25, U. Mont., 1925-26; pvt. practice Chgo.; asst. U.S. atty. No. Dist. Ill., 1928-29; asst. states atty. Cook County, Ill., 1929-32; ptnr. Greenberg, Keele, Lunn & Aronberg (and predecessors), Chgo., from 1938; gen. counsel Select Com. to Investigate Tax Exempt Founds., 82d Congress, 1952. Author: Jottings, 1987; co-editor: vol. on founds. in Greenwood Ency. of Am. Instns.; contbr. articles to profl. publs. Served to maj. USAAC, 1942-45. Mem. ABA, Ill. Bar Assn., Phi Beta Kappa, Phi Delta Phi, Zeta Psi, Alpha Alpha Alpha, Delta Sigma Rho. Republican. Presbyn. Clubs: Casino, Tavern. Home: Chicago Ill. Died Feb. 26, 1991.

KEELEY, JOHN LEMUEL, surgeon; b. Streator, Ill., Apr. 12, 1904; s. John William and Mary Catherine (Fife) K.; m. Mary Edith Schneider, Oct. 14, 1937; children: John Lemuel, George William, James Michael. B.S., Loyola U., Chgo., 1927, M.D., 1929. Diplomate: Am. Bd. Surgery, Am. Bd. Thoracic Surgery. Asst. physician dept. student health U. Wis., 1931-33; resident surgery Wis. Gen. Hosp., Madison, 1933-36; Arthur Tracy Cabot fellow in surgery Harvard, 1936-37; Harvey Cushing fellow surgery, research fellow surgery, acting resident urology Peter Bent Brigham Hosp., Boston, 1937-38; instr. surgery La. State U., 1938-40, asst. prof., 1940-41; vis. surgeon Charity Hosp., New Orleans, 1938-41; asst. clin. prof. surgery Loyola U. Sch. Medicine, Chgo., 1941-43; asso. clin. prof. Loyola U. Sch. Medicine, 1943-54, prof. surgery, 1954-92; asst. chmn. dept. Loyola U. Sch. Medicine (Stritch Sch. Medicine), 1954-92, chmn., 1958-69; asso. attending surgeon Cook County Hosp., Chgo., 1941-52; attending surgeon Cook County Hosp., 1952-92; sr. attending surgeon Mercy Hosp. Chgo., 1941-92, chmn. dept., 1958-67; chmn. dept. surgery Loyola U. Hosp., 1968-69; attending gen. and thoracic surgeon West Side VA Hosp., 1953-63; surg. cons. Hines VA Hosp., 1963-92, Little Company of Mary hosps. Author articles surg. subjects. Fellow A.C.S.; mem. Chgo. Med. Soc., Chgo. Surg. Soc., Am., Central, Western surg. assns., Am. Assn. for Thoracic Surgery, Am. Coll. Chest Physicians, Soc. for Vascular Surgery, Am. Acad. Pediatrics (surg. affiliate), Phi Chi, Alpha Omega Alpha. Roman Catholic. Home: Riverside Ill. Died Nov. 25, 1992. †

KEELING, JOHN HENRY, finance company executive; b. London, Aug. 18, 1895; s. John Henry and Mary (Allis) K.; m. Dorothy May Finucane, Oct. 26, 1921; children: John Arthur Bernard, Michael Edward Allis, Brian Patrick Morgan, Caroline Mary (Mrs. Herbert Seitz). Joint founder London and Yorkshire Trust Ltd., Eng., 1923, chmn., 1939-92; chmn. Nat. Film Fin. Corp. Ltd., 1954-55, Brit. Lion Films Ltd., 1954-55, Safeguard Indsl. Investments Ltd., 1953-92; chmn. West Riding Worsted and Woollen Mills, Ltd., 1943-62, now mem. bd. dirs.; vice chmn. Bowater Paper Corp., Ltd., 1947-92; dep. chmn. Brit. European Airways Corp., 1947-92. With Ministry Aircraft Prodn., 1940-45, dir. gen. aircraft distbn., 1943-45; chmn. Issuine Houses Assn., 1951-52. Served with Brit. Army, World War I. Created knight, 1952. Mem. White's (London) Club, Brook (N.Y.C.) Club, Mount Royal (Montreal) Club. *

KEENLEYSIDE, HUGH LIEWELLYN, government official; b. Toronto, Ontario, Can., July 7, 1898; s. Ellis William and Margaret Louise (Irvine) K.; m. Katherine Hall Pillsbury, Aug. 11, 1924; children: Mary (Mrs. Sydney Segal), Miles, Anne (Mrs. J. A. McCullum), Lynn (Mrs. Gordon C. Jackson). BA, LLD, U. B.C., 1920, 45; MA, PhD, Clark U., 1921, 23; LLD, Carleton Coll., 1947; DSc, New Sch. for Social Rsch., 1958. Lectr. history U. B.C., 1925-27; staff Dept. External Affairs, Ottawa, Can., 1928; 1st sec. Canadian Legation, Tokyo, Japan, 1929-36, counsellor, 1940-41, asst. under-sec. state for external affairs, 1941-44; ambassador of Can. to Mexico, 1944-47; del. gen. assembly, dep. minister resources U.N., 1946, 47-50, head Canadian delegation sci. conf., chief tech. assistance, 1949, 50, various positions, 1050-59; chmn. Hydro and Power Authority, B.C., Can., 1960-92; mem. Can.-U.S. Joint Bd. Def., 1940-45, War Tech. and Sci. Devel. Com., 1941-45; staff N.W. Territories Coun., 1941-45, commr., chmn. coun., 1947-50. Author: History of Japanese Education (with A. F. Thomas), 1937, Canada and the United States (last edit.), 1952. Gov. Carleton Coll.; trustee Clark U. Served 2d tank bn., Can. Army, World War I. Recipient Haldane Medal of Royal Inst. Pub. Adminstrn., 1954, Vanier medal Inst. Pub. Adminstrn., Can., 1962. Fellow Royal Geog. Soc. Gt. Britain, Royal Hist. Soc. Gt. Britain, Asiatic Soc. Japan; mem. Arctic Inst. N.A., Can. Inst. Pub. Adminstrn. (dir.), Can. Geog. Soc., Mason, Canadian Club of Ottawa (pres. 1944), Assn. Canadian Clubs. *

KEEZER, DEXTER MERRIAM, economist; b. Acton, Mass., Aug. 24, 1895; s. Frank Merriam and Martha Moulton (Whitemore) K.; m. Anne Mellett, June 22, 1927; children: Anne Lowell Keezer Read, Berthe Mellett Keezer Ladd. AB, Amherst Coll., 1920, LLD, 1938; student, U. Paris, 1919; AM, Cornell U., 1923; PhD, Brookings Grad. Sch. Econs. and Govt., 1925; LLD, Mills Coll., 1940, Macalester Coll., 1957, Elmira Coll., 1959, Miami U., Oxford, Ohio, 1959, Monmouth Coll., 1962; LHD, Clarkson Coll. Tech., 1955. Reporter Denver Times, 1920-21; instr. econs. Cornell U., 1922-23; asst. prof. econs. U. Colo., 1923-24; assoc. prof. econs. U. N.C., 1926-27; corr. Washington bur. Scripps-Howard Newspapers, 1927-28; vis. lectr. Dartmouth Coll., 1928-29; assoc. editor Balt. Sun, 1929-33; exec. dir. Consumers' Adv. Bd. NRA, 1933-34; pres. Reed Coll., Portland, Oreg., 1934-42; dep. adminstr. OPA, 1942-43; econ. adviser U.S. mission econ. affairs Am. Embassy, London, 1943; pub. mem. Nat. War Labor Bd., 1944-45; with McGraw-Hill, 1945-71, v.p., 1953-60, econ. adviser, 1960-71, dir., 1958-64; del. internat. econ. confs. Author: (with Stacy May) The Public Control of Business; (with Addison Cutler and Frank Garfield) Problem Economics, The Light That Flickers, 1947, Making Capitalism Work, 1950, New Forces in American Business, 1959, A Unique Contribution to International Relations: The Story of Wilton Park, 1973; editor: Financing Higher Education, 1960-70, 1959, The Performing Arts-Problems and Prospects, 1965; contbr. articles to profl. jours. Pres. Truro (Mass.) Civic Assn., 1968-70; trustee Elmira Coll., 1963-70; pres., bd. dirs. Assn. for Improving Med. Resources of Outer Cape Cod, 1972-75; mem. Cape Cod Nat. Seashore Adv. Commn., 1976—. With U.S. Army, 1917-19. Home: Truro Mass. Died June 24, 1991; buried Truro Congl. Ch. Graveyard.

KEISER, HENRY BRUCE, lawyer, publisher; b. N.Y.C., Oct. 26, 1927; s. Leo and Jessie (Liebeskind) K.; m. Jessie E. Weeks, July 12, 1953; children: Betsy Cordelia Keiser Smith, Matthew Roderick. BA with honors in Econs., U. Mich., 1947; JD cum laude, Harvard U., 1950. Bar: N.Y. 1950, D.C. 1955, Fla. 1956, U.S. Supreme Ct. 1954. Trial atty. CAB, Washington, 1950-51; head counsel alcoholic beverages sect. OPS, 1951-52; legal asst. to Judge Eugene Black U.S. Tax Ct., 1953-56; pvt. practice law Washington, 1956-92; founder, chmn. bd., pres. Fed. Pubs., Inc., 1959-85; chmn. bd. dirs. Gene Galasso Assocs., Inc., Washington, 1963-92, Empire Carriages, London, 1984-92, Lion Worldwide, London, 1985-92, U.S. Telemktg., Inc., Atlanta, 1986-92, The Arkhon Corp., Cherry Hill, N.J., 1983-92, pres., 1991-92; founder, chmn. bd. Crown Eagle Communications Ltd., London, 1978-84; chmn. bd., pres. Keiser Enterprises, Inc., Washington, 1985-92, Phila. Inst., 1986-92; chmn. sec. adv. com. on constrn. contract document reform HUD, 1983-85; bd. dirs. Nat. Bank Commerce, 1983-84; mem. adv. cabinet Southeastern U., 1965-75; judge, bd. contract appeals AEC, 1965-75; profl. lectr. Dept. Agr., 1960-77, George Washington U., 1961-79, U. San Francisco, 1965-82, Coll. William and Mary, 1966-75, Calif. Inst. Tech., 1967-72, U. So. Calif., 1973-74, U. Denver, 1975-85, Air Force Inst. Tech., 1975-76, U. Santa Clara, 1975-81. Trustee Touro Coll., 1979-92. 1st lt. Judge Adv. Gen. Corps, USAF, 1952-53; maj. Res. (ret.). Lord of Tuxford (hereditary), Nottinghamshire, Eng. Fellow ABA (pub. contracts sect., coun. 1972-75, Disting. Svc. award 1987), Am. Bar Found., Nat. Contract Mgmt. Assn.; mem. N.Y. Bar Assn., Fla. Bar Assn., D.C. Bar Assn. (bd. dirs. 1965-66, chmn. adminstrv. law sect. 1964-65), Cosmos Club, Nat. Press Club, Army-Navy Club, Crockford's Club (London). Jewish. Home: Bethesda Md. Died Nov. 16, 1992. †

KELL, JAMES H., transportation consulting firm executive, researcher, educator; b. Ft. Wayne, Ind., Feb. 25, 1930; s. Arthur H. and Elizabeth E. (Marquardt) K.; m. Sally A. Miller, June 1956 (div. 1970); children: David, Brian; m. Ann Powers, June 1974; children: Kelly, Kerri, Chris. BSCE, Purdue U., 1951, MSCE, 1952; postgrad., U. Calif., Berkeley, 1954-64. Rsch. engr., lectr. U. Calif., Berkeley, 1954-64; prin. traffic engr. Traffic Rsch. Corp., San Francisco, 1964-67; prin. Peat, Marwick, Mitchell, San Francisco, 1967-71; pres. JHK & Assocs., San Francisco, 1971-84, chmn., from 1971; lectr. U. Calif., various locations, from 1964, Nat. Hwy. Inst., from 1986. Co-author: Traffic Engineering Handbook, 1965, Traffic Control Device Handbook, 1979, Interim Highway Capacity Manual, 1980, Manual of Traffic Signal Design, 1983, 2d edit., 1990, Traffic Detector Handbook, 1990, Traffic Detector Field Manual, 1990. Active Mt. Diablo coun. Boy Scouts Am., San Francisco Bay coun. Girl Scouts U.S. A. With Transp. Corps, U.S. Army, 1952-54. Named Disting. Engring. Alumnus, Purdue U., 1987. Fellow Inst. Transp. Engrs. (pres. 1986, chair tech. com. 1981-84, Theodore M. Matson award 1981, Tech. Coun. Chair award 1985); mem. ASCE, Transp. Rsch. Bd. (assoc., chair hwy. capacity com. 1977-83). Home: El Cerrito Calif. Deceased. †

KELLER, CHARLES RAY, history educator; b. Phila., Sept. 9, 1901; s. Harry T. and Bessie (Halzell) K.; m. Helen E. Ramsayer, June 15, 1929; 1 child, Anne. AB, Yale U., 1932, PhD, 1934. Instr. Coll. of Yale in China, 1923-27; mem. faculty Williams Coll., Williamstown, Mass., 1929-58, J. Leland Miller prof. Am. history and lit. eloquence, 1945-57, Brown prof. history, 1957-58, chmn. dept., 1949-58; dir. advanced placement program Coll. Entrance Exam. Bd., from 1958; dir. John Hay fellows program Greenwood Fund, John Jay Whitney Found., from 1958. Author: The Second Great Awakening in Connecticut, 1942. Recipient award for disting. svc. to Am. secondary edn. at nat. leval Nat. Assn. Secondary Sch. Prins., 1971. Mem. Am. Hist. Assn., Rotary, Phi Beta Kappa. Home: Williamstown Mass. Died July 18, 1990; buried Williams Coll. Cemetery, Williamstown, Mass.

KELLER, DEANE, artist; b. New Haven, Dec. 14, 1901; s. Albert Galloway and Caroline Louise (Gussmann) K.; m. Katherine P. Hall, July 16, 1938; children: William Bradford, Deane Galloway. AB, Yale U., 1923, BFA, 1926, MA, 1948; student, Art Students' League, N.Y.C., 1922-23. Fellow Am. Acad. in Rome, 1926-29; portrait and landscape painter, sculptor, 1929-92; asst. prof. Yale Sch. Fine Arts, 1930-36, assoc. prof., 1936-48, prof., 1948-92. Prin. works include: mural (with Bancel La Farge) New Haven Pub. Libr. Valley Forge Nat. Mus., Washington, 1933, ofcl. portrait Conn. Gov. John Lodge, 1954, portrait Sen. Robert A. Taft, Taft Sch. and Senate Reception Chamber of Capitol Bldg., portrait Herbert Hoover for Boys' Club Am.; murals Shriver Hall, Johns Hopkins, 1958; rep. permanent collections Yale, Bishop Mus., Honolulu, Hosp. San Salvador, Santiago, Chile, Wayne County Med. Soc., Detroit, Boston State House, Nat. Aero. Mus., Dayton, Ohio, Capt. Colin P. Kelly, N.A.D., N.Y.C., U. N.C. Maj. U.S. Army, 1943-46. Decorated Legion of Merit; Order Brit. Empire, Crown of Italy, Partisan medal (Italy), Order St. John Lateran (Vatican); recipient Priz de Rome, 1926, figure painting prize New Haven Paint and Clay Club, 1926, 41, 47, portrait prize Conn. Acad. 1940. Mem. Grand Cen. Galleries N.Y., Alumni Assn. Am. Acad. Rome, Conn. Acad. Fine Arts, Fifth Army Assn., Portraits, Inc., Paint and Clay Club (past pres.), Grad. Club, Century Club. Home: Hamden Conn. Died Apr. 12, 1992.

KELLER, REED T., gastoenterologist, educator; b. Aberdeen, S.D., May 26, 1938; s. Emil T. and Maybelle K.; m. Mary Ann Larsen, June 14, 1959; children: Kristen, Laura, Julie. B.A., U. N.D., 1959, B.S., 1961; M.D., Harvard U., 1963. Diplomate Nat. Bd. Med. Examiners (mem. 1985-88). Asst. prof. Case Western Res. Sch. Medicine, 1970-73; chief medicine U. N.D., Rehab. Hosp., Grand Forks, from 1973; prof., chmn. dept. medicine U. N.D. Med. Sch., Grand Forks, from 1973. Contbr. articles to profl. jours. Served with USAF, 1968-70. Fellow Am. Coll. Gastroenterology (gov. N.D. chpt.), ACP (Laureate awardee); mem. AMA, Soc. Exptl. Biology and Medicine, N.D. Commn. on Med. Edn., Assn. Profs. Medicine, Am. Soc. Gastrointestinal Endoscopy, N.D. Bd. Med. Examiners (chmn. 1991), Phi Beta Kappa, Alpha Omega Alpha. Home: Grand Forks N.D. Deceased. †

KELLEY, JAMES E., lawyer, corporate; b. Pinnconning, Mich., Dec. 3, 1895; s. Joseph Samuel and Electa Alvina (Segur) K.; m. Margaret Louise Hammn, Sept. 19, 1923; 1 child, Cynthia Hampton (Mrs. James C. O'Neill). LLB, St. Paul Coll. Law, 1923. Bar: Minn. 1917. Mem. Bundlie, Kelley & Torrison; pres. Kelley Land Cattle Co., The Kelmar Corp.; bd. dirs. Northwestern Nat. Bank, St. Paul; v.p. St. Paul Bur. Mcpls. Rsch.; dir. Hamm Found., Inc.; mem. bd. trustees Northland Coll., Ashland, Wis., St. Luke's Hosp., St. Paul. Served in Chem. Warfare Svc., U.S. Army, 1918-19. Mem. ABA, Minn. State Bar Assn., St. Paul Bar Assn., Ramsey County Bar Assn., Mason, Minn. (St. Paul) Club. *

KELLEY, WILBUR EDRALD, nuclear engineer; b. Birmingham, Ala., Dec. 2, 1908; s. Wilbur Edrald and Madeleine (Whitfield) K.; m. Elizabeth Lindley Wells, June 18, 1932; children: Wilbur E., William L., Elizabeth Anne. BS, U. Louisville, 1931, CE, 1940, D in Engring. (hon.), 1950. With U.S. Engrs., Rock Island, Galveston, Ill., Tex., 1931-40; involved in bomb-proof structure design and constrn. U.S. Engrs., Panama, 1940-42; involved in design and constrn. atomic bomb project U.S. Engrs., 1942-46; U.S. rep. tech. staff UN AEC, 1946-47; mgr. N.Y. ops. office AEC, 1946-53; v.p. engring. Catalytic Constrn. Co., Phila., 1953-56; pres. Assn. Nucleonics formerly Walter Kidde Nuclear Labs., Inc., Garden City, N.Y., 1956-89; assoc. Engrs. and Cons., Inc., Garden City; v.p., mgr. Stone & Webster Engring. Corp., Garden City, 1966-70. Lt. col. AUS, 1943-46. Decorated Legion of Merit. Mem. Theta Tau. Home: New Hyde Park N.Y. Died Mar. 16, 1989.

KELLOCK, ALAN, publishing consultant; b. N.Y.C., June 22, 1914; s. Harold and Alberta (Thompson) K.; m. Ruth Louise Helman, Jan. 24, 1937; children: Alan C., Susan, Thomas C. BA, Antioch Coll., 1936; postgrad., Columbia U., 1969-72. With Union Carbide Corp., 1937-43; with McGraw-Hill Book Co., N.Y.C., 1946-79, gen. mgr. tech. and vocat. edn. div., 1966-69, gen. mgr. community coll. div., 1970-73, v.p., 1971-79, gen. mgr. films div., 1973-75, v.p. audio-visual devel., 1976-79, cons. audio-visual devel., 1979-92. Co-author: How to Develop, Print and Enlarge Your Pictures, 1952. Pres. S.W. Civic Assn., Freeport, N.Y., 1951; mem. Freeport Planning Commn., 1953, Freeport Electric Power and Water Commn., 1954-56, Freeport Zoning Bd. Appeals, 1958-61; co-founder, pres. Freeport Citizens Adv. Com. on Edn., 1962-64; pres. Freeport Unity party, 1961. With AUS, 1943-46. Mem. Alumni Assn. Antioch Coll. Home: Sun City Ariz. Died Feb. 29, 1992.

KELLOGG, MARION KNIGHT, lawyer, educator; b. Bowling Green, Ky., July 24, 1904; s. Robert Marion and Nelle (Willis) K.; m. Virginia Dryden, Oct. 3, 1931. B.A., Va. Mil. Inst., 1925; LL.B, Yale U., 1928. Bar: N.Y. bar 1929, Mich. bar 1932, Va. bar 1961. Practiced in N.Y.C., 1928-32, Detroit, 1932-56, Charlottesville, 1956-76; asso. firm Chadbourne, Hunt, Jaeckel & Brown, Cravath, de Gersdorf, Swaine & Wood, 1928-32; pvt. practice, 1932-56; mem. firm Kellogg, Fulton & Donovan, 1942-46; lectr. law Sch. U. Va., 1956-64, prof. law, 1964-75, emeritus, 1975; exec. dir. Law Sch. Found., 1964-73. Pres. Charlottesville-Albermarie United Givers Fund, 1964; mem. Charlottesville Community Relations Com., 1964-65; mem. steering com. United Negro Coll. Fund, Shenandoah Area, 1966—. Served to lt. col., Q.M.C. AUS, 1942-45. Mem. Am., N.Y., Mich., Va., Charlottesville-Albermarle, Detroit, Fed., Inter-Am. bar assns., Internat. Law Assn., Am. Law Inst., Charlottesville Com. Fgn. Relations (past pres.), Order of Coif (hon.), Phi Delta Phi. Presbyn. Clubs: Farmington Country, Farmington Hunt Torch (past pres.), Colonnade (Charlottesville); Commonwealth (Richmond, Va.); Nat. Lawyers (Washington); Yale (N.Y.C.); Graduate (New Haven). Home: Charlottesville Va. Died Aug. 25, 1989.

KELLSTADT, CHARLES H., merchant; b. Columbus, Ohio, Oct. 9, 1896; s. Charles Henry and Mary Cecilia (Lynch) K.; m. Marguerite Elizabeth Stewart, Nov. 30, 1916. Student, Ohio State U., 1915; LLD, Mundelein Coll.; BCS, Suffolk U.; LLD, Loyola U. Asst. display mgr. Union Co., Columbus, Ohio, 1913-17; advt. mgr. Frankenberger & Co., Charleston, W.Va., 1917-19; mgr. Kramer's, Akron, Ohio, 1919-20; v.p., gen. mgr. The Kinney & Levan Co., Cleve., 1921-32; gen. mgr. Cleve. stores of Sears, Roebuck & Co., 1932-46; gen. retail merchandiser mgr. Cleve. stores of Sears, Roebuck & Co., Chgo., 1946-49, dir., 1948-92, v.p. in charge of South, 1949-58; pres. of co., chmn. bd. chief exec. officer, 1958-60, 60-62; chmn. bd. trustees Savs. & Profit Sharing Pension Fund, 1962-92; chmn. bd., CEO Gen. Devel. Corp.; dir. All-state Ins. Co., Ford Motor Co., Chem. Bank N.Y. Trust Co., 1st Nat. Bank Miami, Continental Ill. Nat. Bank & Trust Co.; mem. adv. bd. Guaranty Bank of Phoenix. Mem. def. adv. coun. Dept. of Def. Trustee Cath. Charities; chmn. bd. trustees Logistics Mgmt. Inst.; trustee Eisenhower Exch. Fellowships, Inc., Am. Heritage Found., Freedoms Found. Valley Forge; lay trustee Mercy Hosp., Loyola U.; mem. Citizens Bd. U. Chgo. Mem. Canadian-Am. Com. Trustee Com. Econ. Devel., Nat. Assn. Better Bus. Burs. (chmn. bd. govs.), Union Club, Cleve. Advt. (Cleve.) Club, Capital city Club, Commerce (Atlanta) Club, Chgo. Club, Old Elm Club, Mid-Am. Club. *

KELLY, EDWARD JAMES, lawyer; b. Des Moines, Nov. 23, 1911; s. Edward J. and Mary Elizabeth (O'Donnell) K.; m. Mary Elizabeth Nolan, May 1, 1946; children—Edward James, Mary Elizabeth, Brian Francis, Anne Nolan. B.A., State U. Iowa, 1934, J.D., 1936. Bar: Iowa bar 1936. Partner Whitfield, Musgrave, Selvy, Kelly & Eddy, Des Moines, 1946-86. Pres. Des Moines Jr. C. of C., 1940-41; Chmn. bd. edn. St. Joseph Acad., Des Moines, 1970-72; chmn. hosp. com. Health Planning Assembly of Polk County, Iowa, 1971-72; mem. bd. edn. Dowling High Sch., Des Moines, 1971-72; Iowa del. Republican Nat. Conv., 1956; pres. Des Moines Health Center, Des Moines Soc. for Crippled Children and Adults; bd. dirs. Def. Research Inst., Inc., Polk County Legal Aid Soc., N.W. Community Hosp., Inc. Served to maj. USAAF, 1942-46, ETO. Decorated Bronze Star (U.S.); Croix de Guerre with silver star (France); Croix de Guerre with palm (Belgium). Mem. ABA, Iowa, Polk County bar assns., Iowa Def. Counsel Assn. (pres.), Internat. Assn. Ins. Counsel (pres. 1971-72), Des Moines C. of C., VFW, Am. Legion, Delta Upsilon, Phi Delta Phi. Roman Catholic. Clubs: K.C. (4 deg.), Des Moines, Pioneer of Iowa, Des Moines Optimist (past pres.); Union League (Chgo.). Home: Des Moines Iowa Died Nov. 24, 1986; buried Des Moines.

KELLY, PETRA KARIN, member West German Bundestag, political activist; b. Günzberg, Fed. Republic Germany, Nov. 29, 1947; came to U.S., 1960, returned to Europe, 1970; s. John E. Kelly (stepfather) and Marianne (Birle) Lehmann Kelly. B.A. cum laude, Sch. Internat. Service, Am. U., Washington, 1970; M.A., U. Amsterdam. Vol. Robert F. Kennedy presdl. campaign, 1968; then worked as vol. for Hubert H. Humphrey; research asst. Europa Inst., Netherlands, 1970-71; internship EEC Commn., Bourse de Recherche, Brussels, 1972, adminstrv. counsel secretariat, 1973-83; co-founder Die Grunen (Green Party), Fed. Republic Germany, 1979-92, mem. exec. bd., 1980-82, speaker, 1983; elected to Bundestag as rep. of Die Grunen, 1st team in Parliament, Fed. Republic Germany, 1983-87, 2d team in Parliament, 1987; speaker Green Fraction in Parliament, 1983-87; mem. fgn. relations com., 1987-92, disarmament com., subcom. on European questions; adminstr. social affairs and health at economic and social com., 1972-83. Author: (with Jo Leinen) Life Principles: Okopax-The New Strength, 1983; Um Hoffhung Kämpfen, 1983; Hiroshima, 1984; Liebe gegen Schmerzen, 1986, Tibet: Ein vergewaltigtes Land, 1988, MitdemHerzen denken, 1988; mem. editorial bd. Forum. Founder Grace P. Kelly Assn. for Promotion of Cancer Research for Children, Nuremberg, Fed. Republic Germany, 1973. Recipient Women Strike for Peace prize, 1983, Alternative Nobel prize, 1982; Woodrow Wilson fellow Am. U. Mem. Fed. Assn. Citizens for Environ. Protection, Darmstädter Signel and Humanistische Union, White Rose Found., Bertrand Russell Found., Elmwood Inst. Died Oct. 1, 1992. Home: Bonn Germany †

KELLY, RAYMOND BOONE, oil company executive; b. Chgo., Aug. 13, 1898; s. Rowan B. and Harriet A. (Cain) K.; m. Katherine M. Brooks, Nov. 23, 1921; children: Raymond, Gordon, Katherine (Mrs. E. S. Ryan). BS, Auburn U., 1919. Jr. engr. Cities Svc. Oil Co., 1919-22; assoc. engr. U.S. Bur. Mines, 1922-25; petroleum engr. Pure Oil Co., 1925-32, asst. mgr., 1932-35; mgr., v.p., 1935-92; mem. Petroleum Industry War Counsel, 1943, Petroleum Adminstrn. War, 1943-44. Bd. dirs. Goodwill Industries, Ft. Worth, United Fund Tarrant County; pres. Tarrant County Assn. Mental Health. Mem. Am. Petroleum Inst., Am. Inst. Mining and Metall. Engrs., Ky. Oil and Gas Assn., Ind. Petroleum Assn., Tex. Mid-Continent Oil And Gas Assn., Rocky Mountain Oil and Gas Assn., Ill. Oil and Gas Assn., N.Mex. Oil and Gas Assn., Sigma Nu, Exchange Club, Rover Crest Country Club. Episcopalian. *

KELMAN, WOLFE, rabbi; b. Vienna, Austria, Nov. 27, 1923; came to U.S., 1946, naturalized, 1962; s. Hersh Leib and Mirl (Fish) K.; m. Jacqueline Levy, Mar. 2, 1952; children: Levi Yehuda, Naamah Kathrine, Abigail Tobie. B.A., U. Toronto, Ont., Can., 1946; M.H.L., Jewish Theol. Sem. Am., 1950, D.D. (hon.), 1973. Rabbi various congregations; vis. rabbi West London Congregation Brit. Jews, London, Eng., 1957-58; exec. v.p. Rabbinical Assembly, United Synagogue Am. and Jewish Theol. Sem. Am., N.Y.C., 1951-89, dir. joint placement commn., 1951-66; vis. prof. homiletics Jewish Theol. Sem. Am., 1966-73, adj. asst. prof. history, 1973-88, dir. Louis Finkelstein Inst. of Religious and Social Studies, 1989-90; vis. prof. Hebrew U., Jerusalem, 1984-85. Mem. governing council World Jewish Congress, 1968-90 chmn. cultural commn., 1975-77, co-chmn. interreligious affairs, 1979-86, chmn. com. on small communities, 1986-90 chmn. Am. sect., 1986-90; Pres. Com. Neighbors Concerned for Elderly, Their Rights and Needs, from 1971; bd. dirs., exec. com. Hebrew Immigrant Aid Soc., 1974-90. Served with RCAF, 1943-45. Home: New York N.Y. Died June 26, 1990; buried Lodi, N.J.

KELSO, LOUIS ORTH, investment banker, economist; b. Denver, Dec. 4, 1913; s. Oren S. and Nettie (Wolfe) K.; m. Betty Hawley (div.); children: Martha Jennifer Kelso Brookman, Katherine Elizabeth Balestreri; m. Patricia Hetter. BS cum laude, U. Colo., 1937, LLB, 1938; DSc (hon.), Araneta U., Manila, 1962; LLD (hon.), Tusculum Coll., Tenn., 1986; PhD (hon.), U. of Ams., 1990. Bar: Colo. 1938, Calif. 1946. Assoc. Pershing Bosworth, Dick & Dawson, 1938-42; ptnr. Brobeck, Phleger & Harrison, 1946-58; sr. ptnr. Kelso, Cotton, Seligman & Ray, 1958-70; mng. dir. Louis O. Kelso, Inc., San Francisco, 1970-75; chmn., chmn. adv. com. Kelso & Co., Inc. (mcht. bankers), San Francisco, Newport Beach and N.Y.C., 1975-91; also dir. Kelso & Co., Inc. (mcht. bankers), N.Y.C.; assoc. prof. law U. Colo., 1946; pres. Kelso Inst. Study Econ. Systems, San Francisco; econ. policy advisor ESOP Assn. Am., Washington, from 1983. Author: (with Mortimer J. Adler) The Capitalist Manifesto, 1958, The New Capitalists, 1961 (with Patricia Hetter) Two-Factor Theory: The Economics of Reality, 1967, (with Patricia Hetter Kelso) Democracy and Economic Power: Extending the ESOP Revolution through Binary Economics, 1986, 2d edit., 1991; editor-in-chief Rocky Mountain Law Rev., 1938; contbr. articles to profl. jours. Bd. dirs. Inst. Philos. Research, Chgo.; founding trustee Crystal Springs and Uplands Sch., Hillsborough, Calif. Served to lt. USNR, 1942-46. Mem. ABA, Calif. Bar Assn., Pacific Union Club, Bohemian Club, Villa Taverna Club, Chicago Club. Home: San Francisco Calif. Died Feb. 17, 1991.

KEMBLE, JOHN HASKELL, educator, historian; b. Marshalltown, Iowa, June 17, 1912; s. Ira Oscar and Caroline (Haskell) K. BA, Stanford U., 1933; MA, U. Calif., Berkeley, 1934, PhD, 1937. Mem. faculty Pomona Coll., 1936-90, prof. history, 1951-77, prof. emeritus, 1977-90; vis. lectr. history UCLA, 1948-49; vis. prof. mil. history U.S. Naval War Coll., Newport, R.I., 1952-53; vis. prof. history U. Tex., 1967; sec. Navy Adv. Com. Naval History, 1961-90. Author: The Panama Route, 1848-1869, 1943, San Francisco Bay: A Pictorial Maritime History, 1957; editor: Journal of a Cruise to California and the Sandwich Islands, 1841-1844 (William D. Myers), 1955, Two Years Before the Mast (Richard Henry Dana Jr.), 1964, To California and the South Seas: The Diary of Albert G. Osbun, 1849-1851, 1966, Sketches of California and Hawaii, 1842-1843 (William H. Meyers), 1970, A Naval Campaign in the Californias, 1946-1849. Active Calif. Hist. Resources Commn., 1976-79. Lt. comdr. USNR, 1941-46, PTO. Rockefeller fellow, 1947-48, Guggenheim fellow, 1956-57. Fellow Calif. Hist. Soc.; mem. Am. Hist. Assn. (sec.-treas. Pacific Coast br. 1941-42, 45-49), Am. Antiquarian Soc., Soc. Nautical Rsch., S.S. Hist. Soc., Hist. Soc. So. Calif. (pres. 1967-70), N.Am. Soc. Oceanic History (v.p. 1976-90), Zamorano, Westerners, E. Clampus Vitus. Republican. Episcopalian. Home: Claremont Calif. Died Feb. 19, 1990.

KEMNITZER, WILLIAM JOHNSON, economist, geologist; b. Sacramento, Calif., Sept. 2, 1898; s. Louis Henry and Emma Charlotte (Johnson) K.; m. Jacqueline Thomas Baldwin, Nov. 20, 1954. AB, Stanford U., 1923. Geologist, engr. various mining and petroleum cos. U.S., Mexico, 1923-27, 31-37; expert on investigations and litigation petroleum lands Fed. and Calif. State Govts., 1937-41; mem. U.S.-Mexico Oil Commn., 1942, U.S. Indsl. Mission to Brazil, 1942-43; chief fuel specialist Fgn. econ. Adminstrn., 1943-45; ind. contractor negotiating devel. petroleum lands, 1945-51, engaged personal interests, 1952-92; rsch. Sch. Mineral Sci., Stanford, 1959-92; lectr. Hispanic Am. Studies, Stanford, 1960-92, Am. Inst. Fgn. Trade, Phoenix, 1962-63. Author: (with R. Arnold) Petroleum in the United States and Possessions, 1931, Rebirth of Monopoly, 1938; contbr. tech. articles to petroleum jours., newspapers, other publs. Served with USNR, 1918-22, lt. comdr., 1937-56. Recipient Order Condor de los Andes, Bolivia, 1944. Mem. Inst. Petroleum Technology (London), Delta Upsilon, Commonwealth (San Francisco) Club. *

KEMPER, HATHAWAY GASPER, insurance executive; b. Van Wert, Ohio, Feb. 10, 1893; s. Hathaway and Mary (Scott) K.; m. Grace Clark Stover, Feb. 4, 1928; 1 child, Hathaway Clark. Student, U. Wis. With Kemper orgn., from 1912; chmn. sr. coun., dir. Lumbermens Mut. Casualty Co., Am. Motorist Ins. Co.; chmn. sr. coun. Am. Mfgs. Mut. Ins. Co., N.Y.C., Fed. Mut. Ins. Co., Boston; dir. Kemper Found. for Northwestern U., Traffic Inst. Mem. Chgo. Crime Commn. Mem. 1st Officers Tng. Camp, Ft. Sheridan, Ill., 1915, served in Field Arty. until end of World War I. Mem. Nat. Assn. Mut. Casualty Cos. (bd. dirs.), Fedn. Mut. Fire Ins. Cos., Nat. Assn. Automotive Mut. Ins. Co., Committee of Twenty-Five Club, Tavern Club, Chgo. Club, Thunderbird Country Club, Racquet Club. Republican. Presbyterian. *

KEMPFF, WILHELM WALTER FRIEDRICH, pianist, composer; b. Berlin, Nov. 25, 1895; m. Helen Hiller Von Gaertringen, 1926 dec. ; 7 children. Student, Berlin U. and Conservatoire. Prof., dir. Stuttgart Staatliche Hochschule für Musik, 1924-29; concert tours as pianist throughout the world, 1929-91. Composer 2 symphonies, 4 operas, piano concertos, also chamber, vocal and choral music; author: Unter dem Zimbelstern, autobiography Das Werden eines Musikers. Recipient Mendelssohn prize, Artibus et Litteris medal, Sweden. Mem. Prussian Acad. Arts. Home: London Eng. Died May 23, 1991.

KEMPTON, GRETA M., artist; b. Vienna, Austria; d. H.K. and Josephine K.; student Nat. Acad. Design, Art Students League, N.Y.C., 1930; 1 child, Daisy Dickson. One woman shows include: Corcoran Gallery Art, Washington, 1949, Canton (Ohio) Art Inst., 1964, Coll. of Wooster, 1963, Akron Art League, 1962, Circle Gallery, Cleve., 1963, Truman Libr., Independence, Mo., 1987, Jones Meml. Libr. Exhbn., Lynchburg, Va., 1991, others; group shows: NAD, N.Y.C., Dowling Coll., Oakdale, N.Y., Human Resources Ctr., Albertson, N.Y., L.I. U.; represented in permanent collections: White House, Washington, Truman Library, Independence, Mo., U.S. Supreme Ct., Washington, Dept. Interior, Smithsonian Inst. Portrait Gallery, Treasury Dept., Washington, Pentagon, Valentine Mus., Richmond, Va., Georgetown U., Washington, Nat. Acad. Design, U.S. Capitol, Blair House, Washington, Lyndon Johnson Libr., Austin, Tex., Franklin D. Roosevelt Libr., Hyde Park, N.Y., Riggs Nat. Bank, Washington, Ark. State Capitol, Little Rock, Fed. Res., Washington, numerous others. Fellow Royal Soc. Arts (London); mem. Soc. Arts and Letters (life); Nat. Arts Club, Corcoran Gallery (life), European Acad. Arts, Scis. and Humanities (corr.), Accademia Italia, Salmagundi Club. Died Dec. 9, 1991. Home: New York N.Y.

KENDALL, GEORGE PRESTON, SR., insurance company executive; b. Seattle, Aug. 11, 1909; s. George R. and Edna (Woods) K.; m. Helen A. Hilliard, Sept. 30, 1933; children: George Preston, Thomas C., Helen R. BS, U. Ill., 1931. With Washington Nat. Ins. Co., Evanston, Ill., 1931-75, sec., 1950-56, exec. v.p., 1956-68, dir., 1948-91, pres., 1962-67, chmn. bd., chief exec. officer, 1968-82, hon. chmn., 1982-91; chmn. bd. Washington Nat. Corp., 1968-82, dir., from 1968; bd. dirs. NBD Bank Evanston. Past pres. United Community Svcs. Evanston. 1st lt., inf. AUS, 1942-45. Decorated Purple Heart; recipient Alumni Achievement award Coll. Commerce and Bus. Adminstrn. U. Ill. Mem. Westmoreland Country Club, Optimists (past pres.), Masons, K.T., Shriners, Theta Chi. Home: Winnetka Ill. Died Apr. 4, 1991; buried Meml. Pk., Skokie, Ill.

KENDRICK, HERBERT SPENCER, JR., lawyer; b. Brownfield, Tex., Nov. 16, 1934; s. Herbert Spencer and Elsie Kathryn (Woosley) K.; children: Herbert Spencer III, Kathryn Gene. B.B.A., So. Methodist U., 1957, LL.B., 1960; LL.M., Harvard, 1961. Bar: Tex. 1960. Trial atty. tax div. Justice Dept., 1961-65; pvt. practice Dallas, from 1965; sr. ptnr. firm Akin, Gump, Hauer & Feld; dir. Capital Bank, Dallas, Bowie State Bank, Bandera Bank; adj. prof. taxation So. Meth. U. Law Sch., from 1966. Co-author: Texas Transaction Guide, 14 vols., 1972, 73. Recipient Disting. Alumni award So. Meth. U. Law Sch., 1986. Mem. ABA, Tex. Bar Assn., Dallas Bar Assn., Sigma Alpha Epsilon, Phi Alpha Delta. Presbyterian. Clubs: Dallas, Salesmanship of Dallas, Masons, Shriners, Brook Hollow Golf. Home: Dallas Tex. Died Feb. 15, 1989.

KENDRICK, JAMES BLAIR, JR., university official, research scientist; b. Lafayette, Ind., Oct. 21, 1920; s. James Blair and Violet (McDonald) K.; m. Evelyn May Henle, May 17, 1942; children: Janet Blair, Douglas Henle. B.A., U. Calif. at Berkeley, 1942; Ph.D., U. Wis., 1947. Mem. staff, faculty U. Calif., Riverside, 1947-68, prof. plant pathology and plant pathologist, 1961-68; chmn. dept. U. Calif., 1963-68, v.p. agrl. scis., 1968-77, v.p. agr. and univ. services, 1977-82, v.p. agr. and natural resources, 1982-86, v.p. agr. and natural resources emeritus, prof. plant pathology emeritus, 1986-89; dir. agrl. expt. sta., 1973-80, dir. coop. extension, 1975-80; Participant 10th Internat. Bot. Congress, Edinburgh, Scotland, 1964; mem. Calif. Bd. Food and Agr., 1968-84, U.S. Agrl. Research Policy Adv. Com., 1976; Mem. governing bd. Agrl. Research Inst., 1974-76; chmn. sci. rev. panel Calif. Air Resources Bd., 1987-89. Contbr. articles to profl. jours. Bd. dirs. Guide Dogs for Blind, San Rafael, Calif., from 1983. Served with AUS, 1944-46. NSF sr. postdoctoral fellow U. Cambridge (Eng.) and Rothamsted (Eng.) Exptl. Sta., 1961-62; recipient Agrl. Sci. Leadership award & lectureship Nat. Assn. State Univs. and Land Grant Colls./USDA, 1986. Fellow AAAS (chmn. sect. O 1978); mem. Am. Phytopath. Soc. (editorial bd. jour. 1965-68, councilor at large 1968-70), Internat. Soc. Plant Pathology (council 1968-73), Am. Inst. Biol. Scis., Calif. C. of C. (agrl. com. from 1968), Nat. Assn. State Univs. and Land Grant Colls. (chmn. div. agr. 1972-73, exec. com. 1974-76), Western Assn. State Agrl. Expt. Sta. Dirs. (chmn. 1975), Phi Beta Kappa, Sigma Xi. Congregationalist. Home: Berkeley Calif. Died Feb. 15, 1989; buried Davis, Calif.

KENNEDY, BERNARD R., government official; b. New Haven, Nov. 5, 1895; s. James W. and Elizabeth J. (Reilly) K. Student, Yale U., 1913-14, U.S. Naval Acad., 1914-17; AB, LLB, Washington and Lee U., 1923. Instr. Fishburne Mil. Sch., 1923-24, Staunton Mil. Acad., 1924-26; atty. U.S. Bd. Tax Appeals, 1927-35, SEC, 1935; dir. Fed. Register, from 1935. 1st lt. U.S. Army, 1917, capt. 1918, jag., 1925. Mem. ABA, Fed. Bar Assn., Va. Bar, John Carrol Soc., Nat. Press Club, Univ. Club, Army-Navy Club, Army and Navy Country Club, Nat. Lawyers, KC, Phi Beta Kappa, Kappa Sigma, Phi Delta Phi. Democrat. *

KENNEDY, EDWARD EUGENE, economist, statistician; b. Grand Junction, Iowa, Apr. 12, 1894; s. James M. and Mary N. (Ryan) K.; m. Edna Mae Crandell, May 1, 1919 (dec. 1938); children: Gertrude Elizabeth (dec.), Regene Maxine (Mrs. Paul F. J. LePore), Edward Charles (dec.), Edward Louis (dec.), Paul Eugene, Mary Darlene (Mrs. William W. Schmidt); m. Marie C. Puncke, Oct. 3, 1939. Student, pub. and parochial schs., Iowa. Livestock and grain farmer Grand Junction, St. James, Minn., 1915-26; sec.-treas. Nat. Farmers Union, 1931-37, legis. agt., 1933-41; rsch. dir., economist dist. 50 United Mine Workers of Am., from 1942; mem. chems., paper and paperboard and coal tar labor adv. coms. W.P.B., World War II; mem. roster tech. reps. cons. with Office Spl. Rep. for Trade Negotiations, Exec. Office Pres. Democrat. Roman Catholic. *

KENNEDY, JOHN A., editor, publisher, radio and television executive; b. St. Paul, Dec. 21, 1898; s. Charles C. and Mary M. (Sullivan) K.; m. Viera Hines, Nov. 19, 1924 (div. 1932); 1 child, John Hines; m. Ellen Bruce Lee, Nov. 21, 1932; children: Patricia Henry (Mrs. David Allen Grimsted), Davis Lee. Grad., Trinity Coll., Sioux City, Iowa, 1918; BS, Coe Coll., 1922; BCL, Georgetown U., 1923. Mem. staff Sioux City Tribune, 1918, Cedar Rapids Rep. and Cedar Rapids Gazette, 1919-22, Washington Herald, 1922-35; purchased control Exponent, Clarksburg, W.Va., 1935, sold 1940; owner W.Va. Network Charleston, Clarksburg, Huntington,, Parkersburg, 1936-50; former chmn. bd. Kennedy Broadcasting Co. (KFMB-KFMB-TV), San Diego; chmn. bd. Kenco Enterprises, Inc., San Diego. Contbr. editor Sioux Falls Argus-Leader, Sioux Falls, S.D. With U.S. Army, World War I, capt. USNR, World War II. Recipient Pugsley prize for most noteworthy work by a Washington corr., 1929. Mem. Iowa Bar Assn., D.C. Bar Assn., Met. Club, Nat. Press Club, Chevy Chase Club, Racquet and Tennis Club, LaJolla Beach and Tennis Club. *

KENNEDY, JOHN FISHER, engineering educator; b. Farmington, N.Mex., Dec. 17, 1933; s. Angus John and Edith Wilma (Fisher) K.; m. Nancy Kay Grogan, Nov. 21, 1959; children: Suzanne Marie, Sean Grogan, Brian Matthew Fisher, Karen Lynn. BSCE, U. Notre Dame, 1955, hon. doctorate, 1989; MS, Calif. Inst. Tech., 1956, PhD, 1960. Rsch. fellow Calif. Inst. Tech., Pasadena, 1960-61; asst. prof. MIT, Cambridge, 1961-64; assoc. prof. MIT, 1964-66; dir. Iowa Inst. Hydraulic Research; prof. fluid mechanics U. Iowa, Iowa City, 1966-91; Carver disting. prof. U. Iowa, 1981-87, Hunter Rouse prof. hydraulics, 1987-91; chmn. divsn. energy engring. U. Iowa, 1974-76; Fulbright scholar, vis. prof. U. Karlsruhe, Germany, 1972-73; Erskine fellow U. Canterbury, Christchurch, N.Z., 1976; cons. to govt. agys., indsl. firms, engring. cons. offices, 1960-91; vis. assoc. in hydraulics Calif. Inst. Tech., 1977; ASCE Hunter Rouse lectr., 1981; Gastdozent ETH, Zurich, Switzerland, 1985. Served to 2d lt. C.E., U.S. Army, 1957. Corning Glass Works fellow, 1959-60; W.L. Huber Rsch. prize, 1964; Karl Emil Hilgard Hydraulic prize, 1974, 78; Engring. Honor award U. Notre Dame, 1978; Gov.'s medal for Sci. Application, State of Iowa, 1983; hon. fellow Inst. Water Conservancy and Hydroelectric Power Rsch., 1985; hon. prof. East China Tech. U. Water Resources, 1985. Mem. ASCE (J.C. Stevens award. 1959), ASME, NAE, Am. Soc. Engring. Edn., Internat. Assn. Hydraulic Rsch. (mem. coun. 1972-76, 84-88, v.p. 1976-80, pres. 1980-84, hon. 1990-91), Hungarian Hydrol. Soc. (hon.), Chinese Hydraulic Engring. Soc. (corr.), Sigma Xi, Chi Epsilon (hon.), Tau Beta Pi. Roman Catholic. Home: Iowa City Iowa Died Dec. 13, 1991. †

KENNEDY, KEITH FURNIVAL, packaging company executive, lawyer; b. New London, Conn., Nov. 1, 1925; s. Joseph Reilly and Madeleine (Mason) K.; m. Joan Ruth Canfield, Feb. 11, 1956; children: Joseph Keith, Austin Robert, Thomas Canfield, Richard Furnival. BS, Yale U., 1949; LLB, Harvard U., 1953. Bar: N.Y. 1955. Atty. Vick Chem. Co., 1953-54, 58-60; sec., dir. personnel J.T. Baker Chem. Co., 1955-58; with Riegel Paper Corp., 1960-71, sec., 1961-69, gen., atty., 1964-69, v.p. finance and law, counsel, 1969-71; sr. v.p. Rexham Corp., 1972-90, also dir.; sr. v.p., sec., gen. counsel Rexham Inc., 1990-92; bd. dirs. Laminex, Inc. Bd. dirs. Adoption service Westchester, pres., 1971-73; mem. pres.'s adv. council Coll. New Rochelle, 1973-77; bd. dirs. Calvary Hosp., N.Y.C., 1977-85, vice chmn., 1982-85; bd. visitors Mercy Hosp., Charlotte, N.C; bd. dirs. Mercy Hosp. Found. Served to 1st lt. AUS, 1943-46, 51-52. Mem. Assn. Bar City N.Y., Am. Soc. Corp. Secs., St. Andrews Soc. N.Y., Union League, Econ. of N.Y., Yale Club (N.Y.C.), Larchmont Club (N.Y.), Yacht, Niantic Bay Club (Conn.). Roman Catholic. Home: Charlotte N.C. Died May 24, 1992. †

KENNEDY, WILLIAM, newspaper editor; s. Richard and Pearl (Anderson) K.; married; 1 child, Victor; children by previous marriage: Patricia, Ross. A.A., U. Minn., 1947; B.A. in Journalism, U. Calif. at Berkeley, 1950. Columnist-reporter Times-Star, Alameda, Calif., 1950, News-Observer, San Leandro, Calif., 1950-51; patrolman Berkeley (Calif.) Police Dept., 1951; reporter Duluth (Minn.) Tribune, 1954-55, Watsonville (Calif.) Register-Parjaronian, 1955-60; editor Cupertino (Calif.) Courier, 1960-62; reporter Southwest Times Record, Ft. Smith, Ark., 1962-63; polit. editor Southwest Times Record, 1964-69, editor, 1971-75; editor Hawaii Tribune-Herald, Hilo, 1975-77, Vista (Calif.) Press, 1977-81; Washington bur. chief Donrey Media Group, 1969-71; tchr. article writing and short story Monterey Peninsula Coll., 1957-58, Foothills Coll., Los Altos Hill, Calif., 1959-60. Author novels, short stories, articles. Served with USMCR, 1943-46. Newspaper recipient Pulitizer Service award, 1956. Mem. Am. Soc. Newspaper Editors, White House Corrs. Assn., Sigma Delta Chi. Club: Nat. Press (Washington). Home: Marble City Okla. Died Sept. 16, 1988.

KENNEY, W. JOHN, lawyer; b. Oklahoma City, June 16, 1904; s. Franklin R. and Nelle (Torrence) K.; m. Elinor Craig, Jan. 17, 1931 (dec. 1991); children: Elinor Kenney Farquhar, John F., Priscilla Kenney Streator, David T. A.B., Stanford U., 1926; LL.B., Harvard U., 1929. Practiced law San Francisco, 1929-36; chief oil and gas unit SEC, 1936-38; practice law Los Angeles, 1938-41; spl. asst. to under sec. navy, gen. counsel and chmn. Price Adjustment Bd., Navy Dept., 1941-46; asst. sec. Dept. Navy, 1946-47, undersec., 1947-49; head ECA, Eng., 1949-50; dep. dir. for mut. security, 1952; mem. Sullivan, Shea & Kenney, Washington, 1950-70; ptnr. Cox, Langford & Brown, Washington, 1971-73, Squire Sanders & Dempsey, Washington, 1973-89; dir. Riggs Nat. Bank, 1958-81, Mchts. Fund Inc., both Washington. Chmn. Democratic Central Com. D.C., 1960-64; chmn. bd. D.C. chpt. ARC, 1968-71; trustee, mem. exec. com. George Marshall Ednl. Found.; adv. council Sch. Advanced Internat. Studies, Johns Hopkins Univ. Mem. ABA. Democrat. Clubs: Calif. (Los Angeles); Alibi (Washington), Met. (Washington), Chevy Chase (Washington). Home: Washington D.C. Died Jan. 16, 1992; buried Rock Creek Cemetery, Washington, D.C.

KENT, HARRY CHRISTISON, geologist, educator; b. Los Angeles, May 20, 1930; s. Harry and Florence (Christison) K.; m. Sheila Marie Kelly, Aug. 18, 1956; children: Colleen Marie, Bruce Kelly. Geol. Engr., Colo. Sch. Mines, 1952; M.S., Stanford, 1953; Ph.D., U. Colo., 1965. Geologist The California Co., Fla. and La., 1953-56; mem. faculty Colo. Sch. Mines, Golden, 1956-91, assoc. prof., 1967-69, prof., 1969-89, prof. emeritus, 1989-91, head geology dept., 1969-75; dir. Inst. Energy Resource Studies, 1976-91. Bd. mgrs. Jeffco br., N.W. br. YMCA, Denver. Fellow Geol. Soc. Am.; mem. Am. Assn. Petroleum Geologists, Soc. Petroleum Engrs., Sigma Xi. Democrat. Home: Arvada Colo. Died Apr. 16, 1991. †

KEOGH, EUGENE JAMES, former congressman; b. Bklyn., Aug. 30, 1907; s. James Preston and Elizabeth (Kehoe) K.; m. Virginia Fitzgerald; children: Susan Keogh Clarke, E. Preston. BCS, NYU, 1927; LLB, Fordham U., 1930. Bar: N.Y. 1932. Tchr. pub. schs., N.Y.C., 1927-28; clk. N.Y.C. Bd. Transp., 1928-30; practiced in N.Y.C., 1932-36; mem. 75th to 87th congress from 9th N.Y. Dist., Washington; mem. 88th to 89th congress from 11th N.Y. Dist., Washington, mem. ways and means com.; with Halpin, Keogh & St. John, N.Y.C., from 1966; counsel Abberley, Koolman, Marcellino & Clay, N.Y.C., until 1988; trustee East N.Y. Savs. Bank; bd. dirs. City Title Ins. Co., Am. Chemosol Corp., Athlone Industries, Inc. Mem. N.Y. State Assembly, 1936, N.Y. State Racingg and Wagering Bd., 1973-76; former chmn. Franklin Delano Roosevelt Meml. Commn. Mem. ABA, N.Y. State Bar Assn., Assn. Bar City N.Y., Bklyn. Bar Assn., Delta Theta Phi, Theta Chi. Democrat. Roman Catholic. Home: New York N.Y. Died May 26, 1989; buried Gate of Heaven Cemetery, N.Y.

KEPNER, WILLIAM E., air force officer, aircraft company executive; b. Miami, Ind., Jan. 6, 1893; s. George Harvey and Julia Ann (Dawson) K.; m. Jean Howell Wilcox, Nov. 15, 1920. Student, La Salle U. Law Sch.; grad., Army Balloon Sch., 1921, Army Airship Sch., 1922, Naval Rigid Airships Sch., 1925, Air Corps. Tactical Sch., 1936, Command and Gen. Staff Sch., 1937. Enlisted USMC, 1909-13; with Ind. Nat. Guard and 28th Inf., Mexican Border, 1916-17; commd. 2d lt., cav. U.S. Army, 1917, transferred to inf., advanced through grades to lt. gen., 1950, transferred to Air Svc., 1920; asst. comdt. Army Airship Sch., 1925; comd. semi-rigid airship RS-1, 1927-29; comdr. 2d Air Div. 8th Air Force, 1944-45; comd. 8th Air Force ETO, 1945; comdr. 9th Air Forces, 1945. Decorated DSC, DSM, Legion of Merit, DFC, Purple Heart, Legion of Honor, Croix de Guerre with palm (France), Comdr. Mil. Order of Bath (Gt. Britain), Order of Crown, Croix de Gureer (Belgium), Order of Polonia Restituta (Poland). Mem. Army-Navy Legion of alor, Ahtens Athletic Club, Mo. Athletic Club, Kisanis, Rotary, Explorers, Masons (3d deg.). Episcopalian. *

KEPPEL, FRANCIS, organization executive; b. N.Y.C., Apr. 16, 1916; s. Frederick Paul and Helen Tracy (Brown) K.; m. Edith Moulton Sawin, July 19, 1941; children: Edith Tracy, Susan Moulton. A.B., Harvard U., 1938; several hon. degrees. With Harvard Coll., 1939-41; sec. of Joint Army and Navy Com. on Welfare and Recreation, Washington, 1941-44; asst. to provost Harvard, 1946-48, dean faculty edn., 1948-62; U.S. commr. edn., 1962-65; asst. sec. edn. HEW, 1965-66; chmn. bd. Gen. Learning Corp., N.Y.C., 1966-74; sr. fellow Aspen Inst. for Humanistic Studies, N.Y.C., 1974-84; sr. lectr. Harvard U., 1977-90; chmn. Nat. Student Aid Coalition, 1980-85; Vice chmn. bd. higher edn. City U. N.Y., 1967-71; bd. overseers Harvard U., 1967-73. Author: The Necessary Revolution in American Education, 1966. Trustee Am. Trust for Brit. Library, 1981-90; trustee Carnegie Corp., 1970-79; vice chmn. Lincoln Center for Performing Arts, 1981-84; bd. govs. Internat. Devel. Research Centre in Ottawa, from 1980; mem. Nat. Commn. Libraries and Info. Sci., 1978-83. Served to 1st lt. AUS, 1944-46. Fellow Am. Acad. Arts and Scis.; mem. Phi Beta Kappa. Clubs: Cosmos (Washington); Century Assn. (N.Y.C.). Home: Cambridge Mass. Died Feb. 19, 1990; buried North Hatley, Que., Can.

KERBY, WILLIAM FREDERICK, business executive; b. Washington, July 28, 1908; s. Frederick Monroe and Helen Frances (Hunter) K.; m. Frances Justina Douglass, June 8, 1935; children: Jean Frances, Judith Ann. AB, U. Mich., 1930. Staff corr. UPI, Washington, 1930-32, Wall St. Jour., Washington, 1933-35; copy editor Wall St. Jour., N.Y.C., 1936, news editor, 1938-40, asst. mng. editor, 1941-42, mng. editor, 1943-44, exec. editor, 1945-51; v.p. Down Jones & Co., Inc., pubs. Wall St. Jour., 1951-60, exec. v.p., 1961-66, dir., 1965-89, pres., 1966-72, CEO, 1966-75, chmn. bd., 1972-89, editorial dir., 1958-66; trustee Williamsburgh Savs. Bank, Bklyn. Regent L.I. Coll. Hosp.; trustee New Coll. Found., Sarasota, Fla.; pres. The Newspaper Fund. Mem. Union Club (N.Y.C.), Rock Spring Club (West Orange, N.J.), Phi Beta Kappa, Sigma Delta Chi, Phi Kappa Tau. Episcopalian. Home: Bethlehem Pa. Died Mar. 20, 1989.

KERR, A(RTHUR) STEWART, lawyer; b. Knoxville, Tenn., Aug. 12, 1915; s. John Thomas and Eunice Miller (Bruner) K.; m. Katherine Broyles, Nov. 18, 1938 (div. 1960); children: Katherine (Mrs. Kerr Campbell), A. Stewart Jr., Bruce B.; m. Jennie Ilene Veen, Nov. 29, 1968. B.A., U. Tenn., Chattanooga, 1936; J.D., U. Va., 1938. Bar: D.C. 1939, Tenn. 1939, U.S. Dist. Ct. Ill. 1939, Wis. 1941, U.S. Dist. Mich. 1943, U.S. Ct. Appeals (6th cir.) 1945, U.S. Ct. Claims 1952, U.S. Supreme Ct. 1952. Spl. asst. to U.S. Atty. Gen., Washington, Chgo. and Detroit, 1938-47; ptnr. Kerr, Russell & Weber (and predecessors), Detroit, 1947-85, of counsel, from 1986; dir. various corps.; mem. Atty. Gen.'s Nat. Com. to Study Antitrust Laws, 1953-55, 68. Bd. cons. Antitrust Bull., 1971-86. Bd. dirs. Children's Aid Soc., from 1962, pres., 1972-84; bd. dirs. Met. Detroit Coun. Chs., from 1976, pres., 1981-82; bd. dirs. Children's Ctr., pres., 1990; bd. dirs. Grosse Pointe War Meml. Assn., chmn., 1989-90. Mem. ABA (past council antitrust sect. bd. dirs. 1963-68), Fed. Bar Assn., Mich. Bar Assn. (past chmn. antitrust sect. and adminstrv. law sect.), Detroit Bar Assn., Detroit Club. Baptist. Home: Grosse Pointe Mich. Deceased. †

KERR, EDMUND HUGH, lawyer; b. Pitts., Nov. 27, 1924; s. Edmund H. and F. Josephine (Collins) K.; m. Jane Richard, Oct. 30, 1954 (div. 1968); children: Susan J., Daniel R.; m. Loretta Silano, May 1, 1968 (div. June 1982); children: Richard, Jill, Susan M., Jennifer; m. Claire Succio, Feb., 1983. AB, Stanford U., 1949, LLB, 1951. Bar: N.Y. 1952, U.S. Dist. Ct. (so. dist.) N.Y. 1954, U.S. Dist. Ct. (ea. dist.) N.Y. 1955, U.S. Ct. Appeals (2d cir.) 1958, U.S. Supreme Ct. 1975, U.S. Ct. Appeals (4th cir.) 1979, U.S. Dist. Ct. (ea. dist.) Mich. 1982, U.S. Ct. Appeals (9th cir.) 1989. Assoc. Cleary, Gottlieb, Steen & Hamilton, N.Y.C., 1951-62, ptnr., from 1962; bd. dirs. Franklin Custodian Funds Inc., San Mateo, Calif., Franklin Calif. Tax-Free Fund, San Mateo, Franklin N.Y. Tax-Free Fund, San Mateo, Franklin Fed. Money-Fund, Franklin Tax-Exempt Money Fund, Franklin Federal Tax-Free Income Fund, Franklin Tax-Advantaged U.S. Govt. Securities Fund, Franklin Tax-Advantaged High Yield Securities Fund; trustee Franklin Universal Trust, Franklin Prin. Maturity Trust, Franklin Tax-Free Trust, Franklin Calif. Tax-Free Trust, Franklin N.Y. Tx-Exempt Money Fund, Franklin Investors Securities Trust, Instl. Fiduciary Trust, Franklin Investment Trust, Franklin Valuemark Funds, Franklin Government Securities Trust. Contbr. articles to profl. jours. Served as cpl. AUS, 1943-45, MTO. Decorated Purple Heart with oak leaf cluster. Fellow Am. Bar Found.; mem. ABA, Assn. of Bar of City of N.Y. (chmn. com. on securities regulation 1980-83, com. on fed. cts. 1984-88), Am. Law Inst., Fed. Bar Council, Supreme Ct. Hist. Soc. Home: Greenwich Conn. Died Sept. 1, 1992. †

KERR, EWING THOMAS, federal judge; b. Bowie, Tex., Jan. 21, 1900; s. George N. and Ellen H. (Wisdom) K.; m. Ellen Irene Peterson, Feb. 22, 1933; children: Hugh Neal, Judith Ann. B.A., U. Okla., 1923; B.S., Central Coll., Okla., 1923; postgrad., U. Colo., 1925; LLD (hon.), U. Wyo., 1987. Bar: Wyo. bar 1927. Prin. jr. high sch. Hominy, Okla., 1923-25, Cheyenne Pub. Schs., 1925-27; practice at Cheyenne, 1927-29; asst. U.S. dist. atty. for Wyo., 1930-33, atty. gen., 1939-43; atty. for Wyo. Senate, 1943; U.S. dist. judge Dist. Wyo., Cheyenne, from 1955. Served as maj. AUS; with Allied Commn. in Italy; head legal div. in area reorganized civilian cts. in 1945, Austria. Recipient Herbert Harley award, 1987. Mem. Wyo. Bar Assn., Cheyenne C. of C. Republican. Presbyn. Clubs: Mason (past master lodge, past grand master lodge, 33 deg.), Rotarian. Home: Cheyenne Wyo. Died July 1, 1992. †

KERR, HUGH THOMSON, editor, theology educator; b. Chgo., July 1, 1909; s. Hugh Thomson and Olive May (Boggs) K.; m. Dorothy DePree, Dec. 28, 1938; 1 child, Stephen T. A.B., Princeton U., 1931; B.D., Western Theol. Sem., Pitts., 1934; M.A., U. Pitts., 1934; Ph.D., U. Edinburgh, Scotland, 1936. Ordained to ministry Presbyn. Ch., 1934. From instr. to prof. doctrinal theology Louisville Presbyn. Theol. Sem., 1936-40; prof. systematic theology Princeton Theol. Sem., 1940-74, Benjamin B. Warfield prof. theology, 1950-74, Warfield prof. emeritus, 1974; mem. univ. chapel com., 1960-63, nat. council com. on ch. architecture, 1960-62; dir. Gallahue Conf. Quo Vadis, 1968, Westminster Found., 1954-65; Del. for N.Am., World Alliance Reformed Chs., 1945-60; mem. commn. on women World Council Chs., 1950-54, del. faith and order conf., 1957; chmn. com. curriculum Council Theol. Edn., 1949-53; mem. coms. marriage and divorce, ordination of women Presbyn. Ch., 1955-57. Editor: Theology Today quar., 1944-92, sr. editor. 1950; editor: Sons of the Prophets, 1963; author: A Compend of Calvin's Institutes, 1938 (in Japanese 1958), Compend of Luther's Theology, 1963, Positive Protestantism: An Interpretation of the Gospel, 1960 (in Japanese 1954), Mystery and Meaning in the Christian Faith, 1958, What Divides Protestants Today, 1958, By John Calvin, 1960, Readings in Christian Thought, 1966, rev. edit., 1990, Our Life in God's Life, 1979, Protestantism, 1979, (with J.M. Mulder) Conversion, 1983, Calvin's Institutes: A New Compend, 1989, The Simple Gospel, 1991; author: ann. devotion manual A Year With the Bible; multi-media presentations, articles, chpts. in books. Guggenheim fellow, 1960. Mem. Am. Acad. Religion. Home: Princeton N.J. Died Mar. 27, 1992; buried Princeton Cemetery, Princeton, N.J.

KERR, ROBERT D., banker; b. St. Louis, 1893. Grad., Benton Coll. Law, 1926. Vice chmn., dir. Tower Grove Bank & Trust Co., St. Louis. Mem. Masons. *

KERR-GREEN, GRETCHEN HODGSON, therapist, administrator; b. Clearwater, Fla., July 17, 1935; d. Kenneth Wilson and Marguerite (Hodgson) Kerr; m. Leland J. Green, Oct. 24, 1974. B.A., Fla. State U., 1957; M.A., U. Plano, Tex., 1972. Adminstrv. asst. Am. Friends Service Com., Phila., 1959-62; therapist Insts. for Achievement of Human Potential, Phila., 1962-68, dir. childrens ctr., 1968-74, vice dir., 1974-80, dir., 1980-82, dir. emeritus, from 1982. Recipient Brazilian Gold medal of honor and merit Centro de Rehabilitación Nossa Senhora de Gloria, 1966, Statuette with pedestal Internat. Forum for Human Devel., 1973, Brit. Star of Hope, 1976, Sakura Koro Sho (Japan), 1978, Australian medal, 1981. Mem. World Orgn. for Human Potential (U.S. v.p. from 1974), AAAS, Com. for Excellence (sec. from 1982, Leonardo award 1983). Democrat. Home: Philadelphia Pa. Deceased.

KERSHAW, JOSEPH ALEXANDER, economist, educator; b. Bala-Cynwyd, Pa., Apr. 21, 1913; s. Isaac and Caroline (Alexander) F.; m. Mary Anna Nettleton, Oct. 8, 1936; children: David N., Stephen A. A.B., Princeton, 1935; A.M., N.Y. U., 1938; Ph.D., Columbia, 1947. Asst. prof. econs. Hofstra Coll., 1936-42; dir. ration banking br. OPA, 1942-47; asst., also head econs. dept. Rand Corp., 1948-62; prof. econs., provost Williams Coll., Williamstown, Mass., 1962-68, prof. econs., 1970-76, provost, 1971-74, prof. emeritus, 1976-89, acting v.p. and treas., 1980-81; comptroller Sterling and Francine Clark Art Inst., 1976-80; asst. dir. Office Econ. Opportunity, 1965-66; program officer Ford Found., 1968-70; Bd. advisers Inst. for Research on Poverty, U. Wis., 1966-68; mem. acad. council Marlboro Coll., 1975-83; exec. dir. Temporary N.Y. State Commn. on Post-Secondary Edn., 1976-77. Author: History of Ration Banking, 1947, (with R. McKean) Teacher Shortages and Salary Schedules, 1962, Government Against Poverty, 1970, The Very Small College, 1976. Trustee So. Vt. Coll., 1978-84. Home: Lenox MAss. Died July 9, 1989.

KERSHNER, HOWARD ELDRED, author, foundation executive; b. Tescott, Kans., Nov. 17, 1891; s. Isaiah and Cora (Lett) K.; m. Gertrude Elizabeth Townsend, July 6, 1915 (dec. Sept. 1976); children: Wendell Townsend, Margaret Lynette (Mrs. Stephen C. Weber), Mary Linaford (Mrs. Glenn C. Bassett, Jr.); m. Lenore Bowers, Sept. 10, 1978 (dec. Feb. 1981); m. Mary Hagedorn DuVall, Feb. 14, 1982. Grad., Fowler (Kans.) Friends' Acad., 1910; A.B., Friends' U., Wichita, Kans., 1914, LL.D. (hon.), 1948; grad. student, Harvard, 1923-24; L.H.D. (hon.), Washington and Jefferson Coll., 1941; Litt.D., Grove City (Pa.) Coll., 1957; D.D., George Fox Coll., 1969; H.H.D., Northwood Inst., 1970. With Boston real estate office, 1914-16; editor pub. Dodge City (Kans.) Daily Jour., 1917-18; asst. to chief newspaper sect. War Industries Bd., Washington, 1918; real estate operator in Boston, Kans. and Fla., 1919-27; publisher Nat. Am. Soc., N.Y.C., 1927-38; dir. relief in Europe for American Friends Com., 1939-42; exec. vice pres., dir. Internat. Commn. Child Refugees, 1939-52; dir. child feeding (Spanish Civil War), 1939-40, (in unoccupied France), 1940-42, (obtained funds from grants by 24 govts.); mem. bd. Save the Children Fedn., 1950-65, vice chmn., 1945-50, sec., 1959-69; radio-TV commentator, 1952-68; vis. prof. current econ. problems Northwood Inst., 1974-82; prof. econs. Fuller Theol. Sem., Winona Lake, Ind., summers 1961-63; also editor newsletter Answers to Economic Problems. Author: The Menace of Roosevelt and his Policies, 1936, William Squire Kenyon, 1931, One Humanity, 1943, Brit. edit., 1944, Quaker Service in Modern War, 1950, God, Gold and Government, 1956, Diamonds, Persimmons and Stars, 1964, Dividing the Wealth-Are You Getting Your Share?, 1970, A Saga of America, 1976, How to Stay in Love with One Woman for 70 Years, 1977; also chpts. in books.; edited and arranged Air Pioneering in the Arctic, 1928, James W. Ellsworth, a biography, 1929, Lincoln Ellsworth, 1930; founder, editor-in-chief semimonthly jour. Christian Economics, 1950-72; founder, editor monthly newsletter Answers to Economic Problems, 1974-84; narrator for film Children of Tragedy, 1945, and Reconstruction Begins, 1946; Author 500 papers, 9000 editorials; syndicated column Its Up to You, Howard Kershner's Commentary on the News, 1952-79; sermonettes pub. semimonthly in Christian Economics and used in church calendars of 1600 chs. Mem. Am.-African Affairs assn., Nat. Tax Reform Com., Am. Emergency com. Panama Canal, Com. to Unite Am., council advisers, Com. to Restore Constn.; sponsoring com. For Am.; adv. bd. Supreme Ct. Amendment League; mem. Am. Conservative Union; nat. adv. bd. SCALE; sr. adv. bd. Youth for Decency; exec. com. Nat. Com. Food Small Democracies, 1942-49; former dir. CARE; founder, chmn. Temp. Council on Food for European Children, 1943-45; diplomatic mission to principal Latin-Am. capitals, seeking grants for Internat. Children's Fund of UN, 1947-48; one of founders Christian Freedom Found., Inc., pres., 1950-72, chmn. bd., 1972-74; mem. N.Y. bd. dirs. Community Devel. Found.; mem. com. for monetary research and edn. U. Oreg., Eugene.; Mem. Mont Pelerin Soc. Decorated chevalier Order of Leopold Belgium; Medaille d'Honneur d'Argent des Affaires Etrangers France; Ordre de Merit Union Internationale de Protection de l'Enfants, Geneva, Switzerland; chevalier Legion of Honor France; Freedoms found. medal, 1952-57, 59-61, 65, 67, 71-72; recipient citation City of Los Angeles, 1971, citation and State of Calif., 1973. Mem. Internat. Platform Assn. Republican. Mem. Soc. of Friends (clk. N.Y. yearly meeting of Friends 1945-51). Home: Norwalk Conn. Died Jan. 1, 1990.

KERSLAKE, JOHN FRANCIS, railroad official; b. Green Island, N.Y., June 6, 1898; s. James Albert and Margaret Mary (Davine) K.; m. Beatrice L. Haun, Oct.

22, 1928 (dec. Mar. 1948); children: Shirley Ann (Mrs. Alan J. Southmayd), Margery Jane; m. Marguerite J. Hickling, Aug. 20, 1953. BS in Econs., U. Pa., 1921. CPA, N.Y., Pa. Ptnr. Will A. Clader & Co., CPAs, Phila., 1921-36; asst. comptr. Consol. Coal Co., N.Y.C., 1936-45; mgr. Peat, Marwick, Mitchell & Co., CPAs, N.Y.C., 1945-47; asst. comptr. C & O RR Co., 1947-58, treas., 1958-61, asst. v.p. fin., 1961-63; v.p. fin., dir. Peading Co., from 1963; dir. Mut. Fire, Marine & Inland Ins. Co., Phila. With U.S. Amry, 1917-19, AEF in France. Mem. Pa. Inst. CPAs. *

KESSLER, HENRY H., physician; b. Newark, Apr. 10, 1896; s. Simon and Bertha (Portugese) K.; m. Jessie Winnick, Dec. 25, 1918; children: Sanford, Jerome, Joan. AB, Cornell U., 1916, MD, 1919; AM, Columbia U., 1932, PhD, 1934. Diplomate Am. Bd. Orthopedic Surgery. Practice as orthopedic surgeon Newark, from 1920; attending orthopedic surgeon Newark City Hosp., Newark Beth Israel, Hosp. for Crippled Children, Hasbrouck (N.J.) Hosp.; cons. to UN on rehab. facilities in Yugoslavia, 1951, Indonesia, 1954, Philippines, 1955-56; cons. to Internat. Soc. for Welfare of Cripples on rehab. facilities in S. Africa, 1955; survey on rehab. needs and facilities in fgn. countries, 1947-53; del. ty Pres. of U.S. to Internat. Congress of Indsl. Accidents in Budapest, 1928, Geneva, 1931, Brussels, 1935, Frankfort, 1938; mem. N.J. Rehab. Commn.; Hungarian lectr., London, 1935. Author: Accidental Injuries, 1931, Occupational Disability Legislation, 1932, The Crippled and Disabled, 1934, Cineplasty, 1947, Rehabilitation of the Physically Handicapped, 1947, The Principles and Practices of Rehabilitation, 1950, Low Back Pain in Industry, 1955, Peter Stuyvesant and His New York, 1959. Past pres. Internat. Soc. for Welfare of Cripples; dir. Kessler Inst. for Rehab. Lt. comdr. from 1936; on active duty from 1941, in South Pacific, 1943; formerly capt. USNR serving as chief, amputation ctr., U.S. Naval Hosp., Mare Island, Calif. Recipient gold medal Am. Acad. Orthopedic Surgeons, 1936, Am. Design award, 1944, Advt. Club award, Newark, 1945, E. J. Ill award, 1951, Physicians award Pres. Com. on Employment Physically Handicapped, 1952, award NCCJ, 1953, Lasker award, 1954, Gold medal award Holland Soc. of N.Y., 1956, World Vets. Fed. award, 1956, Philippine Legion of Honor, 1956, William Anderson award, 1956, Order Phoenix citation (Greece), 1962, Red Cross award (Madrid), 1964. Fellow ACS, APHA, Am. Acad. Orthopedic Surgeons, AMA, Internat. Coll. Surgeons (Speidel award 1956); mem. Masons. *

KETCHUM, GEORGE, public relations and advertising executive; b. Blair, Nebr., Aug. 19, 1893; s. r. Lester and Luna Louise (Beard) K.; m. Thelma June Patton, Dec. 7, 1920; children: Richard Malcolm, Janet (Mrs. William C. Grayson). Grad. pres. dept., Maryville (Tenn.) Coll., 1968; student, U. Pitts., 1913-16. Stenographer, bookkeeper, clk. various employers, 1905-12; sec. to chancellor U. Pitts., 1912-16; with Frederic Courtenay Barber & Assocs. dir. fin. campaigns, N.Y.C., 1916-19; pres. Ketchum, Inc. pub. rels. and instnl. fin. co., 1919-44, dir., 1919-49; pres., dir. Ketchum, MacLeod & Grove, Inc. advt. agy., Pitts., 1923-62, chmn. bd. dirs., from 1962; bd. dirs. Thorofare Markets, Inc. Trustee Shadyside Hosp.; adv. bd. Allegheny coun. Boy Scouts Am.; bd. dirs. Pitts. Regional Planning Assn., WQED (Pitts. Ednl. TV). With A.S., U.S. Army with A.E.F., 1917-19. Mem. Pitts. Athletic Assn., Duquesne Club, Rolling Rock Club, Fox Chapel Club, The Island Club, Masons, Omicron Delta Kappa. Republican. Presbyterian. *

KETCHUM, MARSHALL DANA, economics educator; b. Buffalo, Dec. 16, 1905; s. Dorr Mason and Maude (Moore) K.; m. Clara Louise Whitten, Sept. 1, 1931; children: Marshall Dorr, Richard Jennings. B.S., Syracuse U., 1928, M.S., 1929; Ph.D., U. Chgo., 1937. Registrar Syracuse U., 1929-30; instr. Duke U., 1931-32; asst. prof., then asso. prof., prof. Utah State U., 1932-38, U. Ky., 1938-46; professorial lectr. Grad. Sch. Bus., U. Chgo., 1945, mem. faculty, from 1946, asso. prof., 1946-51, prof., 1951-71, prof. emeritus, professorial lectr., 1971-89; lectr. exec. devel. program U. Mich., 1954-63; Dir., bd. regents Life Officers Investment Seminar, 1948-74, Fin. Analysts Seminar, 1956-81; dir., chmn. exec. com. Conf. Savs. and Residential Financing, 1958-67; editoral adv. in fin. Houghton Mifflin Co., 1960-71. Author: The Fixed Investment Trust, 1937, (with Ralph R. Pickett) Investment Principles and Policy, 1954; Co-editor: (with Leon Kendall) Readings in Financial Institutions, 1965; Contbr. articles to profl. jours. Mem. Am. Econ. Assn., Am. Fin. Assn. (past pres., editor Jour. Finance 1946-55, chmn. bd. dirs., chmn. adv. com., chmn. editorial bd., mem. adv. com. 1957-61), AAUP. Club: Quadrangle (Chgo.). Home: Chicago Ill. Died Nov. 12, 1989; buried East Venice, N.Y.

KETTEL, LOUIS JOHN, internist, academic affairs administrator, educator; b. Chgo., Nov. 4, 1929; s. Alfred C. and Elanora E. (Stroud) K.; m. Lois Mary Bornemeier, June 23, 1951; children: Linda Kettel Paris, Louis Michael, Laura Kettel Khan. B.S., Purdue U., 1951; M.D., Northwestern U., 1954, M.S. (USPHS fellow), 1958. Diplomate: Am. Bd. Internal Medicine. Intern Passavant Meml. Hosp., Chgo., 1954-55; resident Northwestern U. Hosps., Chgo., 1955-56, fellow in internal medicine, 1956-57; resident VA Hosp., Chgo., 1957-58; practice medicine specializing in internal medicine Tucson, 1968-87; mem. staff Univ. Med. Ctr.; with VA Med. Ctr., Phoenix, chmn. Dean's Com., 1977-87; with VA Med. Ctr., Tucson, chmn. Dean's Com., 1977-87; instr. dept. internal medicine Northwestern U., 1960-62, assoc., 1962-65, asst. prof., 1965-68; assoc. prof. U. Ariz. Coll. Medicine, Tucson, 1968-73, prof., 1973-87, asso. dean Coll. Medicine, 1974-77, dean Coll. Medicine, 1977-87; chmn. Joint Bd. on Regulation of Physician's Assts., Ariz., 1977-87; v.p. for acad. affairs Assn. Am. Med. Colls., 1988-91; clin. prof. Georgetown U. Sch. Medicine, 1989-91. Guest editor: Chest, 1968-78, Am. Rev. Respiratory Disease, 1974-78, The Med. Letter, 1974—; abstractor: Am. Rev. Respiratory Disease, 1969-73; contbr. chpts. to books, articles and revs. to med. jours. Gov.'s observer White House Conf. on Aging, 1981; mem. Ariz. Statewide Health Coordinating Council, 1982-87, Ariz. State Health Planning Adv. Council, 1982-87; chmn. working group on education Health Policy Agenda for the Am. People, mem. steering com., 1982-88; chmn. Calvary Lutheran Ch. Bd. Edn., 1969-72, ch. pres., 1975-77, 79-80; bd. dirs. Luth. Campus Bd., 1974-80; pres. Switchboard, Inc., 1976-78; mem. guidelines com. United Way of Tucson, 1974; bd. dirs. Univ. Med. Ctr. Corp., sec., 1986-87. Served to capt. M.C. U.S. Army, 1958-60. USPHS cardiovascular trainee, 1960-62; VA research grantee, 1975-79. Fellow Am. Coll. Chest Physicians, ACP; mem. AMA (alt. del. for med. sch. sect. 1985-86, chmn. sect. on med. schs. 1985-86), Am. Thoracic Soc. (chmn. Sci. Assembly on Clin. Problems in Respiratory Disease 1971-72, rep. councilor 1972-75), Am. Fedn. Clin. Research, Ariz. Med. Assn., Pima County Med. Soc. (dir. 1981-87), AAAS, Assn. Am. Med. Colls. (exec. council, mem. adminstrn. bd., council of Deans 1982-87, chmn. 1986-87), Ariz. Lung Assoc. (exec. com. 1973-85). Home: Chevy Chase Md. Died Nov. 5, 1991; buried Tucson.

KETTER, ROBERT LEWIS, engineering educator, academic administrator; b. Welch, W.Va., Dec. 7, 1928; s. E.F. and Ella Louise (Drummn) K.; m. Lorelei Zimmerman, Dec. 22, 1948; children: Katharyn K. Ross, Susannah K. White, Mary, Michael. B.S. in Civil Engring., U. Mo., 1950; M.S. in Civil Engring., Lehigh U., 1952, Ph.D., 1956, D.Eng., 1981, 83; D.Sc., Kyungpook Nat. U., Taegu, Korea, 1973. From research asst. to research asst. prof. civil engring. Lehigh U., 1950-58; prof. civil engring., chmn. dept. U. Buffalo, 1958; acting dean Grad Sch. SUNY, Buffalo, 1964-65, dean, 1965-66, v.p. univ., 1966-69, pres., 1970-82, leading prof. engring. and applied sci., 1982-88, Disting. Svc. prof., 1988-89; dir. Nat. Ctr. for Earthquake Engring., Buffalo, 1986-89; dir. Marine Midland Bank-Western, 1970-83. Author: (with G.C. Lee and S.P. Prawel Jr.) Structural Analysis and Design, 1979, (with G.C. Lee and L.T. Shu) The Design of Single Story Rigid Frames, 1981; also articles in field and in edn. Chmn. bd. trustees Western N.Y. Nuclear Research Center, Inc., 1970-76; chmn. bd. Comprehensive Health Planning Council of Western N.Y., Inc., 1970-71; mem. N.Y. State Com. Electric Power Research, 1973-78; Bd. mgrs. Buffalo and Erie County Hist. Soc.; bd. visitors Roswell Park Meml. Inst., 1970-80; bd. dirs. Greater Buffalo Devel. Found.; trustee Univs. Research Assn., 1977-83, chmn. pres.'s council, 1981-82; bd. dirs. Sierra Research Corp., 1978-82; mem. N.Y. State Commn. Jud. Nomination, 1978. Recipient Adams Meml. award Am. Welding Soc., 1968; Disting. Service in Engring. award U. Mo., 1971; named hon. prof. Beijing Poly. U., Rep. of China, 1986; China Acad. of Bldg. Research fellow, 1986. Mem. ASCE (dir. Niagara Frontier sect., chmn. several nat. coms.), Structural Stability Research Council Found. (chmn. tech. coms.), Internat. Inst. Welding (ofcl. expert rep. U.S. on commn. X), Internat. Assn. Bridge and Structural Engrs., Am. Welding Soc., Nat. Assn. State Univs. and Land Grant Colls. (legal affairs com. from 1978), Buffalo Fine Arts Acad., Buffalo Soc. Natural Scis., Sigma Xi, Tau Beta Pi, Phi Eta Sigma, Omicron Delta Kappa, Pi Mu Epsilon, Chi Epsilon. Home: Buffalo N.Y. Died Apr. 18, 1989.

KEULEGAN, GARBIS HOVANNES, physicist, hydrologist, engineer; b. Sebastia, July 12, 1890; s. Hovannes Garabed and Emma Marguerite (Klein) K.; m. Nellie Virginia Moore, Sept. 15, 1928; 1 dau., Emma Pauline. A.B., Anatolia Coll., 1910; B.A., Ohio State U., 1914, M.A. (Univ. fellow), 1915; Ph.D., Johns Hopkins U., 1928. Research engr. Westinghouse Electric & Mfg. Co., East Pittsburgh, Pa., 1919-21; physicist Nat. Bur. Standards, Washington, 1921-62; cons. in hydraulics U.S. Waterways Expt. Sta., Vicksburg, Miss., 1963-89. Contbr. articles on hydraulics to profl. jours. Served with inf. U.S. Army, 1918-19. Recipient Gold Medal award for exceptional service Dept. Commerce, 1962, Achievement award Dept. Army, 1969, Meritorious Civilian Service award Dept. Army, 1972. Mem. ASCE (hon.), Nat. Acad. Engring., Washington Acad. Scis., Sigma Xi. Democrat. Roman Catholic. Home: Vicksburg Miss. Died July 28, 1989; buried Green Acres, Vicksburg, Miss.

KEYES, BALDWIN LONGSTRETH, physician; b. Rio de Janeiro, Brazil, July 29, 1893; s. Charles and Emily (Longstreth) K.; m. Harriet Kift, Feb. 25, 1925 (dec. 1947); m. Margaret Robertson, 1949. MD, Jefferson Med. Coll., 1917. Diplomate Am. Bd. Psychiatry and Neurology. Prof. emeritus psychiatry Jefferson Med. Coll.; cons. psychiatrist Jefferson Med. Coll. Hosp., Phila. Gen. Hosp., Pa. Hosp. (hon.), Eastern State Psychiat. Inst., N.J. Neuropsychiat. Inst., N.J. State Hosp., Ancora, N.J., Malvern Inst. (hon.); sr. cons. in psychiatry VA; chmn. med. adv. bd. Mcpl. Ct. of Phila.; dir. Pa. Citizens Assn., Mental Health Assn., Med. Legal Inst., Assoc. Hosp. Svc. of Phila. Author: Treatment of Nervous Disorders (Davis' Ency. of Med.), also articles profl. jours.; co-author: Manual of Mental Disorders. Trustee Drexel Inst. Tech., Phila. Inst. for Rsch. in Nervous and Mental Diseases, Willard Found., Fairmount Farm Sanitarium. Col. Med. Res., U.A. Army. Fellow ACP, Am. Psychiat. Assn., Phila. Coll. Physicians; mem. Am. Neurol. Assn., Alpha Omega Alpha. Republican. *

KEYHOE, DONALD EDWARD, writer; b. Ottumwa, Iowa, June 20, 1897; s. Calvin Grant and May (Cherry) K.; m. Margaret T. Bishop, Oct. 10, 1923; 1 child, Joseph Grant; m. Helen Wood Gardner, Aug. 18, 1930; children: Caroline and Cathleen (twins). Student, U.S. Naval Acad. Prep. Sch., Marine Officers Sch., Quantico, Va., Naval Aviation Tng. Sch.; BS, U.S. Naval Acad., 1919. Chief info. aeros. Dept. Commerce; mgr. North Pole plane tour with Floyd Bennett, 1926; aide Col. Charles A. Lindbergh, 1927; dir. Nat. Investigations com. on Aerial Phenomena. Author: Flying with Lindbergh, 1928, M-Day, What Your Government Plans for You, 1940, The Flying Saucers are Real, 1950, Flying Saucers from Outer Space, 1953, The Flying Saucer Conspiracy, 1955, Flying Saucers: Top Secret, 1960; contbr. articles, stories to popular and nat. mags. 2d lt. USMC, 1922-25, maj., 1942-45. *

KIERNAN, PETER DELACY, bank holding company executive; b. Albany, N.Y., Aug. 15, 1923; s. Peter DeLacy and Carroll (Guerin) K.; m. Mary Agnes Reilly, Jan. 28, 1953; children—Peter DeLacy, John S., Mary Carroll, Gregory F., Michael J., Stephen P., Anne M. A.B., Williams Coll., 1944; L.H.D. (hon.), Siena Coll., 1970; LL.D., Allen U., 1972. Vice pres., gen. mgr. Rose & Kiernan Ins., Albany, 1946-73, pres., 1963-73; vice chmn. United Bank Corp. N.Y., Albany, 1973-74, pres., chief exec. officer, 1974-75, chmn., chief exec. officer, 1975-76; chmn., pres. Norstar Bancorp Inc., Albany, 1976-87; chmn., chief exec. officer Fleet/Norstar Fin. Group, Albany, 1988-89. Mem. univ. council and adv. council Sch. Bus. SUNY, Albany; trustee Rensselaer Poly Inst. and mem. bd. overseers Sch. Mgmt. Mem. N.Y. State Bankers Assn. (bd. dirs., pres.). Roman Catholic. Clubs: Fort Orange (Albany); Williams (N.Y.C.); Beach, Wianno (Mass.); Mill Reef (Antigua); Jupiter Island (Fla.). Home: Newtonville N.Y. Died Sept. 14, 1989; buried Albany, N.Y.

KIKER, DOUGLAS, correspondent, journalist; b. Griffin, Ga., Jan. 7, 1930; s. Ralph Douglas and Nora Ellen (Bunn) K.; m. Ruth Rusling, Dec. 14, 1954 (div. 1972); children: Ann, James; m. Diana Simpson, May 1974; children: Craig, Douglas, Patrick. AB in English, Presbyn. Coll., 1952, PhD in Humanities, 1974. News reporter Atlanta Jour., 1959-62; info. dir. U.S. Peace Corps, Washington, 1962-63; white house reporter N.Y. Herald Tribune, Washington, 1963-66; Washington editor Atlantic Monthly, Boston, 1965-67; news corr. NBC News, Washington, 1966-91. Author: (novels) The Southerner, 1957, Strangers on the Shore, 1969, Murder on Clam Pond, 1986, Death at the Cut, 1988. Lt. USNR, 1954-59. Recipient Peabody award U. Ga., 1970. Mem. AFTRA, Writers Guild. Home: Washington D.C. Died Aug. 14, 1991.

KILBY, OSCAR MARCHANT, steel company executive; b. Anniston, Ala., Jan. 1, 1897; s. Thomas Erby and Mary (Clark) K.; m. Mary Pope Maybank, June 1, 1922; 1 child, Thomas Erby III (dec. Korea 1951). Grad., St. George's Sch., Newport, R.I., 1915; AB, Princeton U., 1919. With Kilby Steel Co., Anniston, 1920-61; pres. Kilby Steel Co., 1943-61; bd. dirs. Woodward Iron Co. Served with French Army, World War I. Decorated Croix de Guerre (France). Mem. Univ. Cottage Club, Nassau Club, Mountain Brook Club. *

KILKER, CLARENCE CHRISTIAN, management consultant; b. Le Mars, Iowa, July 13, 1905; s. Chris A. and Lena (Hinz) K.; m. Edna D. Spiecker, July 10, 1932; children: Wallace Jay, Karen Kay (Mrs. Harold G. Brown). B.A., Westmar Coll., 1927; B.S., Morningside Coll., 1931; M.A., U. Nebr., 1938; postgrad., U. So. Calif., summer 1934, Columbia, 1941, U. Kans., 1942. Tchr. Onslow (Iowa) High Sch., 1927-28; prin. Newburg (Mo.) High Sch., 1928-30, South Sioux City (Nebr.) Jr. High Sch., 1931-37, South Sioux City High Sch., 1937-39, Manhattan (Kans.) Jr. High Sch., 1939-44; mgr. Manhattan C. of C. and Credit Bur., 1944-48; exec. v.p. Kans. C. of C., Topeka, 1949-70; registered rep. Seltsam, Hanni & Co., Topeka, 1970-76; pres. Lil' Duffer Restaurants of Nebr. and S.D., Inc., 1966-78; now ret.; summer instr. U. Kans., Lawrence, 1942, Kans. State U., 1943, S.W. Inst. Orgn. Mgmt., Dallas, 1947-48, U. Colo., 1959, 64; sec. Manhattan Viking Co., Inc., 1945-48; lectr. coll. and univ. workshops on econ. edn. for tchrs., summers 1959-71; profl. speaker on community devel., mgmt. and pvt. enterprise econs. Trustee Kans. Council Econ. Edn., 1973-76; former trustee and deacon. Recipient Disting. Alumnus award Westmar Coll., 1977, Winston Churchill Medal of Freedom, 1988. Mem. Council of State C. of C.'s (exec.

com. 1953, sec. 1961), Kans. Assn. Orgn. Mgrs. (pres. 1948), Assoc. Credit Burs. Kans. (pres. 1946-47), Alpha Kappa Psi (hon.), Phi Delta Kappa. Presbyterian (trustee, deacon). Home: Topeka Kans. Died Dec. 19, 1988; interred Mt. Hope Mausoleum, Topeka.

KIM, YONGJEUNG, business executive; b. Kum-san, Korea, Apr. 2, 1898; s. Iltak and Madam Park K.; m. Mary Ann Kim, July 2, 1934; children: Marilyn Annette, Diane Claire. Student, Harvard U., Columbia U., U. So. Calif., George Washington U. Mgr. K. & S. Jobbers, L.A., 1934-43; founder, pres. Korean Affiars Inst., Washington, 1943; former mem. Korean Nat. Assn. of N.Am., exec. mem., dir. pub. rels., 1939-43; mem. exec. com., dir. pub. rels. UNRRA Conf., Montreal, 1944; contbr. broadcasts to Office War Info. During World War II; made observation trip to South Korea, summer, 1947; observed 3d session UN Gen. Assembly, Paris, 1948. Former Eng. lang. editor The New Korea Weekly; pub. The Voice of Korea; contbr. feature articles to periodicals. *

KIMBALL, LINDSLEY FISKE, foundation executive; b. Bklyn., N.Y., Nov. 27, 1894; s. Francis Tappan and Susie (Williams) K.; m. Maude Ryder Kouwenhoven, Sept. 9, 1926; children: Richard T., Dean F. AB, Columbia U., 1917; PhD, N.Y. U., 1930; LLD, Hobart and William Smith Colls., 1959, Xavier U., 1968; DSc, Rockefeller U., 1976. Asst. to v.p. Underwood Typewriter, 1919-24, Boy Scouts Am., 1924-38; dir. corps and spl. gifts Greater N.Y. Fund, 1938-42; cons. to pres. United Service Orgn., 1942-43, adminstrv. v.p., 1943-45, pres., 1945-49, 51-52; v.p. Rockefeller Found., 1949-53, exec. v.p., 1953-60; trustee Rockefeller U., 1947-71, treas., 1959-65, asst. to chmn. bd., 1971-75; v.p., dir. Gen. Edn. Board, Bd., 1959-60; mem. distbn. com. N.Y. Community Trust.; Cons. Nat. Indsl. Conf. Bd.; Mem. Wartime Joint Army and Navy Com. on Welfare and Recreation. Assoc. Rockefeller Bros. Fund; trustee Nat. Urban League, Inc., 1959-68; pres. Nat. Urban League, 1964-68; trustee Sealantic Fund; mem. exec. bd. ARC Greater N.Y.; v.p., mem. exec. com. Community Blood Coun. of Greater N.Y.; chmn. devel. com. N.Y. Blood Center and Lindsley F. Kimball Rsch. Inst., vice chmn., 1964-87; dir., mem. exec. com. United Negro Coll. Fund; vice chmn. N.AM. adminstrv. com. World Coun. Christian Edn; bd. dirs. Vets. Hosp. Camp Shows; trustee Sleepy Hollow Restoration; chmn. civilian com. on welfare and recreation Dept. Def., 1948; vice chmn. dirs., fin. com. Coun. on Founds.; trustee, treas. States Urban Action Ctr.; mem. adv. com. Urban America; mem. Pres.'s Com. Religion Welfare in Armed Forces. Awarded Joint Army and Navy citation; Presdl. award of Medal for Merit, 1946. Republican. Conglist. Clubs: Century Association (N.Y.C.), Rockefeller Center Luncheon (N.Y.C.), Hemisphere (N.Y.C.); Sands Point Bath and Tennis. Home: Newton Pa. Died Aug. 16, 1992. †

KIMBROUGH, WILLIAM DUKE, horticulturist; b. Jonesboro, Tenn., Dec. 10, 1896; s. Isaac Newton and Mattie Gilmore (Morris) K.; m. Mary Andrews Parent, Aug. 20, 1930; children: William Duke Jr., Robert Walter. BS with highest honors, Ala. Poly. Inst., 1920; MS, U. Md., 1924, PhD, 1925. Instr. horticulture Auburn (Ala.) U., 1920-22; grad. asst. U. Md., 1922-25; asst. horticulturist Ala. Agrl. Expt. Sta., 1925-30; assoc. horticulturist La. State U., 1930-43, horticulturist and prof. horticulture, from 1943. Deacon local Bapt. Ch. Mem. AAAS, Am. Soc. for Horticultural Sci., Am. Soc. Plant Physiologists, Am. Camellia Soc., Am. Rose Soc. (cons. rosarian), Sigma Xi, Phi Kappa Phi, Gamma Sigma Delta. Democrat. *

KIMPLE, LOUIS T., packaging manufacturing company executive; b. Wichita Falls, Tex., 1922. BBA, U. Tex., 1943. With Dixico Inc., Dallas, 1947-87, purchasing agt., from 1952, pres. and chief exec. officer, from 1964, chmn. bd., pres., chief exec. officer, chief oper. officer, 1984-87, also bd. dirs.; pres. and dir. Dixie of Calif.; exec. v.p. and dir. Dixie Wax Paper Co.; chmn. Madison Ave. Mag., Inc.; bd. dirs. Oak Cliff Bank and Trust Co. Served with U.S. Army, 1944-46. Home: Dallas Tex. Died Jan. 7, 1988.

KINARD, JAMES CAMPSEN, state official; b. Newberry, S.C., Oct. 1, 1895; s. George Mauney and Rena DeSaussure (Campsen) K.; m. Katherine Efird, June 17, 1920; children: James Efird, Frank Efird. AB, Newberry Coll., 1916, AM, 1917, LHD, 1954; DLitt, Erskine Coll., 1928; LLD, U. S.C., 1931. Instr. in math. Newberry Coll., 1916, continued as head dept. natural scis., 1918-30, dean, 1924-30, dir. summer session, 1920-30, pres., 1930-54; adminstr. asst. State Dept. Pub. Welfare. Mem. Rotary (past gov. 190th dist.). Democrat. Lutheran. *

KINCHEN, ROBERT PRESTON, library director; b. New Orleans, Mar. 12, 1933; s. Edward Preston and Ann Lou (Sutton) K.; m. Christine Rogers, Nov. 19, 1973. B.A., Northwestern State Coll. La., 1956; M.S., La. State U., 1966. Public service librarian Enoch Pratt Free Library, Balt., 1960-69; asst. to asso. dir. Enoch Pratt Free Library, 1969-72; assoc. dir. Rochester (N.Y.) Public Library, 1972-76; dir. Onondaga Public Library, Syracuse, N.Y., from 1976. Trustee Laubach Literacy Internat.; bd. dirs. N.E. Community Ctr. 1st lt. U.S. Army, 1956-60. Mem. N.Y. Library Assn. (pres. public libraries sect. 1981), ALA, University Club of Syracuse. Home: Manlius N.Y. Deceased. †

KINDER, HAROLD M., import company executive, small business owner; b. Pitts., Feb. 22, 1911; s. O. W. and Mary (Parsons) K.; m. Eva C. Korocz, Apr. 3, 1948. Student public schs., Flint, Mich.; student, Northwestern Traffic Inst., 1940. Supt. transp. Kirby-Butler Co., Flint, 1928-36; police exec. City of Flint, 1936-42, traffic engr., 1946-47, police chief, 1947-48, mgr., 1948-52; bus. mgr. Mich. Liquor Control Commn., 1952-54; mgr. Nat. Distillers Products Co., Ohio, 1954-61, v.p., 1961-68; control states div. mgr., v.p., mgr. nat. brands div. Nat. Distillers Products Co., N.Y.C., 1968-77; owner, mgr. Kinder Importing Co., Ft. Lauderdale, from 1977; industry com. Nat. Alcoholic Beverage Control Assn. Author: Circumstantial Evidence-Bah. Mem. Red Feather Fund of Flint; pres. bd. govs. Marine Tower Condominium , Inc., Ft. Lauderdale, Fla., 1987-88, from 1990. Commd. 2d lt. U.S. Army; adv. to maj. 1946; service in North Africa, Italy, France, Germany, Greece; disch. as major, Corps. Mil. Police, O.R.C. 1946. Decorated Order Brit. Empire, 1945; Legion of Merit; Bronze Star; Army Commendation ribbon; Corono de Italy; Morocco-Sultan's medal; E.A.M.E. campaign ribbon with 5 battle stars; recipient Gold medal Nat. Distillers, 1962. Mem. Internat. Assn. Chiefs of Police, Fraternal Order Police, Nat. Safety Council (mem. program com.). Clubs: Marine Tower Yacht (Ft. Lauderdale, Fla.), Lago Mar (Ft. Lauderdale, Fla.); Univ. (Jackson, Miss.); 60 East (N.Y.C.); Elks; Capitol Hill (Washington). Home: Fort Lauderdale Fla. Deceased. †

KING, ANNA ELIZABETH, social science educator; b. Syracuse, N.Y., Apr. 10, 1897; d. John A. and Mary (Hopkins) King. AB, Syracuse U., 1919; MS, Western Res. U., 1926. Tchr. English and French Highland Falls (N.Y.) High Sch., 1919-20; with advt. dept. Billings Chapin Co., Cleve., 1920-23; case worker Convent of the Good Shepherd, Cleve., 1923-26; supr. Convent of the Good Shepherd, 1927-39; instr. child welfare Western Res. U. Sch. Applied Soc. Sci., 1930-34; assoc. prof., dir. field work Fordham U. Sch. Social Sci. Svc., N.Y.C., 1934-55; dean Fordham U. Sch. Social Sci. Svc., 1939-54, prof. internat. social work, from 1955; UN cons. in social welfare to Italian Govt., 1942-45; cons. Nat. Conf. of Cath. Charities; vice pres. Conf. Nongovtl. Agys. for UNICEF. Contbr. to profl. jours. Mem. AAUP, Am. Assn. Social Workers (1st v.p. 1945, chmn. N.Y.C. chpt. 1941-45), Am. Assn. Schs. Social Work (pres. 1945-47), Internat. Soc. Welfare Assn. (coun. social work edn. com.), Nat. Social Welfare Assn., Phi Beta Kappa, Eta Pi Upsilon, Phi Kappa Phi. Democrat. Roman Catholic. *

KING, ARNOLD KIMSEY, educator; b. Hendersonville, N.C., Dec. 3, 1901; s. William Fanning Pinckney and Julia (Anderson) K.; m. Edna Coates, Aug. 31, 1929 (dec. Mar. 1978); children: Arnold Kimsey, William Dennis, Mary Ann; m. Louise Tunstall, Apr. 7, 1979. AB, U. N.C., 1925; AM, U. Chgo., 1927, PhD, 1951; LLD (hon.), N.C. Cen. U., 1983, N.C. Wesleyan Coll., 1991; LHD (hon.), U. N.C., Asheville, 1990. Instr. edn. U. N.C., Chapel Hill, 1925-26, asst. prof. teaching history, 1927-39, assoc. prof. edn., 1939-43, prof. edn., 1943-91; adviser Gen. Coll., 1942-45, assoc. dean Grad. Sch., 1945-58, dir. summer session, 1958-64; v.p. inst. research Consol. U. N.C., 1964-72, spl. asst. to pres., 1972-86; mem. TVA panel on regional ednl. materials, 1937-42; chmn. ednl. adv. com. NASA Ednl. Programs Br., 1963-74; Local coordinator U. N.C. participation in Coop. Study Teacher Edn. of Commn. on Tchr. Edn., 1939-43; chmn. region 6 Woodrow Wilson fellowship program Assn. Am. Univs., 1952-55. Editor: (with W. Carson Ryan and J. Minor Gwynn) Secondary Education in the South, 1946, Research in Progress, vols. 27-35 in U. N.C. Record Series, 1949-57, Planning for the Future, 1958, Long Range Planning, 1969, The Multicampus University of North Carolina Comes of Age, 1956-86, 1987. Trustee N.C. Wesleyan Coll., 1957-86. Recipient Hugh McEniry award for contbns. to higher edn., 1972, William Richardson Davie award bd. trustees U. N.C.-Chapel Hill, 1987, Univ. award U. N.C. Bd. Govs., 1987; Gen. Edn. Bd. fellow U. Chgo., 1933-34; Henry Milton Wolf fellow history, 1935-36. Mem. NEA, Assn. for Instl. Rsch., Kiwanis, Phi Beta Kappa, Phi Delta Kappa, Lambda Chi Alpha. Democrat. Methodist (del. to gen. conf. Dallas 1968, St. Louis 1970, Atlanta 1972). Home: Chapel Hill N.C. Died Mar. 31, 1992. †

KING, AUGUST ALLEN, lawyer, educator; b. Trousdale, Okla., Aug. 8, 1910; s. Homer and May (Graham) K.; m. Lillian S. Knollenberg, Mar. 23, 1944; children: Ronald Allen, Virginia May. BS, U. Tulsa, 1934, JD, 1941; LLM, U. Mich., 1947. Bar: Okla. 1941. With Stanolind Oil and Gas Co., 1937-46; with legal dept. Pub. Svc. Co. Okla., 1947-48; instr. U. Tulsa Sch. Law, 1948-52, adminstrv. dean, 1949-58, dean, 1958-63, assoc. prof., 1952, prof., 1953-65; prof. law Am. U. Coll. Law, Washington, 1965-90, dir. admission, 1968-69, assoc. dean, 1969-70. Asst. treas., trustee Tulsa County Legal Aid Soc., 1954-55. With USAAF, 1942-44. Mem. Okla. Bar Assn., ABA, Nat. Lawyers Club, Delta Theta Phi, Lambda Chi Alpha, Phi Mu Alpha. Home: Chevy Chase Md. Died May 26, 1990.

KING, ELMER RICHARD, physician, educator; b. Logan County, Ohio, May 5, 1916; s. John Oliver and Clara (Yoder) K.; m. Marie Hutchings Pace, Mar. 29, 1941; children—Marsha Ann, John Michael, Suzanne. B.A., Ohio State U., 1939, M.D., 1941; AEC fellow, Duke, 1948-49; postgrad. tng., Oak Ridge Inst. Nuclear Studies, 1949-50, Mayo Found., 1953. Diplomate: Am. Bd. Radiology, Am. Bd. Nuclear Medicine (founder). Commd. lt. (j.g.), M.C. USN, 1941, advanced through grades to capt., 1961; intern U.S. Naval Hosp., Pensacola, Fla.; with atomic def. div. Bur. Medicine and Surgery, 1946-47; sr. scientist Operation Sandstone, Eniwetok Atoll, 1947; resident radiology U.S. Naval Hosp., Bethesda, Md., 1950-53; dir. div. nuclear medicine U.S. Naval Med. Center, Bethesda, 1954-61, chief radiology, 1958-61; mem. faculty Med. Coll. Va., from 1961, prof. radiology, from 1965, prof. emeritus, 1981-92, chmn. dept. radiology, 1965-73, chmn. div. radiation therapy and oncology, 1973-76; Mem. Am. Bd. Med. Specialists. Author: (with T. G. Mitchell) Laboratory Guide to Nuclear Medicine, 1960; also numerous papers.; Editor: (with Charles Behrens) Atomic Medicine, 1969. Recipient certificate of merit Sec. Navy, 1947, certificate of merit Surgeon Gen. U.S., 1961; Alumni Achievement award Ohio State U., 1966. Fellow Am. Coll. Radiology (Gold medal 1979, 81); mem. Radiol. Soc. N.Am., Am. Radium Soc., Am. Roentgen Ray Soc., Soc. Nuclear Medicine, Am. Soc. Therapy Radiology, AMA, Va Med. Soc., Va. Radiol. Soc., Nu Sigma Nu. Republican. Methodist. Clubs: Willow Oaks (Richmond). Home: Richmond Va. Died Apr. 5, 1992.

KING, GILBERT, investment banker; b. N.Y.C., Oct. 4, 1898; s. William Bruce and Edith Estelle (Gilbert) K.; m. Frances Hood, June 3, 1922; children: Gilbert, Arthur Hood, William Bruce, Richard Hood. BA, Princeton U., 1919; MBA, Harvard U., 1922. Mem. faculty Harvard Grad. Sch. Bus. Adminstrn., 1922-23; econ. statistician, then ptnr. William A. Russell & Bro., Boston, 1923-31; security analyst Hayden, Stone & Co., Boston, 1931-37, ptnr., 1938-61; v.p. Hayden, Stone & Co., from 1962. Village warden civil def., Newton, Mass., 1942-46; mem. vestry local Episcopalian Ch. Ens. USNRF, 1917-19. Mem. Country Club, Down Town Club, Phi Beta Kappa. *

KING, ROBERT FRANCIS, software engineer, educator; b. Rockville Centre, N.Y., Sept. 11, 1947; s. Francis Michael and Catherine Rose (Bahr) K.; m. Loretta Margaret Radosta, June 14, 1969; children: Robert Francis II, James William, Loretta Marie, Christopher John Phillip, Timothy Stephen. MS in Systems Mgmt., U. So. Calif., 1977; BA in Psychology, Marist Coll., 1969. Commd. 2d lt. USAF, 1969, advanced through grades to capt., 1972; electronic warfare officer USAF, Mather AFB, Calif., 1969-79; resigned USAF, 1979; system analyst System Integrators, Inc., Sacramento, 1979-80; sr. software engr. Gen. Dynamics Corp., Sacramento, 1980-85; programmer analyst GTE Sprint, Rancho Cordova, Calif., 1985-86; software engr. Allnet Communication Services, Sacramento, 1986-87; core faculty mem. Nat. U., from 1983. Author: (software) Regional Surveillance System, 1986. Team mem. Worldwide Marriage Encounter, Sacramento, 1979-87, zone coordinator, 1982-83; lectr. Holy Family Parish, Citrus Heights, Calif., 1982. Decorated D.F.C. Mem. Nat. Model Railroading Assn., Sacramento PC User's Group. Roman Catholic. Club: Nat. Model Railroading Assn., Canton, Ohio. Lodge: KC. Home: Citrus Heights Calif. Died July 29, 1987; buried Calvary Cemetery, Citrus Heights, Calif.

KINGDON, KENNETH MAY, physicist; b. Montego Bay, Jamaica, B.W.I., May 13, 1894; s. William L. and Mary E. (Randall) K.; m. Leah M. Aeh, Nov. 1, 1924; 1 child, Mary Elizabeth. BA, McMaster U., 1914; PhD, U. Toronto, 1920. Rsch. assoc. physics, rsch. labs. GE Co., Schenectady, N.Y., 1920-59, tech. mgr. Knolls Atomic Power lab., 1946-54, mgr. Nucleonics and Radiation rsch. Rsch. Lab., 1954-57, mgr. project analysis Rsch. Lab., 1957-59; tech. cons., from 1959. Contbr. to Phys. Rev. Fellow Am. PHys. Soc., Am. Nuclear Soc., Mohawk Club. Republican. Presbyterian. *

KINGSBURY, FREDERICK HUTCHINSON, JR., banker; b. Scranton, Pa., May 21, 1907; s. Frederick H. and Hope (MacIntosh) K.; m. Charlotte Meyer Beresford, Apr. 27, 1934 (div. May 1962); children: Hope MacIntosh Costikyan, Frederick H. III; m. Eleanor Bried O'Donnell, Oct. 3, 1962. Student, The Hill Sch., 1923-25; A.B., Princeton U., 1929. With Brown Bros. Harriman & Co., N.Y.C., 1929-89, partner, 1949-89; chmn. bd. Prudential Ins. Co. Gt. Britain, N.Y., 1957-73; dep. chmn. Brown Harriman & Internat. Banks Ltd., London, 1972-77; dir. Hudson Ins. Co., Skandia Am. Reins. Corp., Skandia Corp., 1964-82; chmn. Am. European Reins. Corp., 1974-82; dir. Interpace Corp., 1952-79, Bangor Punta Corp., 1956-79; Hudson Life Reassurance Corp., 1980-82; mem. internat. adv. com. Am. Bankers Assn., 1962-65. Mem. alumni council Princeton, 1949-54; trustee St. Barnabas Hosp., N.Y.C. Decorated Officer Order Oranje-Nassau Netherlands). Presbyterian (trustee 1968-71). Clubs: University, Links, India House (N.Y.C.); University Cottage (Princeton); Pine Valley Golf (Clementon, N.J.); Blooming Grove

Hunting and Fishing (Hawley, Pa.). Home: New York N.Y. Died Nov. 27, 1989.

KINGSBURY, SLOCUM, architect; b. Governor's Island, N.Y., Jan. 31, 1893; s. Henry P. and Florence (Slocum) K.; m. Marion Schell, June 2, 1923. BArch, Cornell U., 1915. Ptnr. archtl. firm Faulkner & Kingsbury, Washington, 1939-46, Faulkner, Kingsbury & Stenhouse, Washington, from 1946; cons. VA hosp. program, 1946, hosp. planning to surgeon gen. USAF, 1956-57; adv. com. archtl. study project Am. Psychiat. Assn., 1955-58. Contbr. articles to profl. publs.Pathology, Walter Reed Med. Ctr., numerous hosps., also sch. and coll. bldgs. and bldgs. for Brookings Instn., Am. Chem. Soc., AAAS. Mem. D.C. Hosp. Adv. Coun., from 1960, vice chmn., 1961. Capt. calvalry U.S. Army, World War I; AEF in France. Fellow AIA (chmn. com. hosps. 1948-53, pres. Washington-Met. chpt. 1948); mem. Am. Hosp. Assn., Chevy Chase Club, Cosmos Club, Century Assn. *

KINGSLEY, FRANCIS GERARD, merchant; b. St. Albans, Vt., Oct. 31, 1895; s. Edward C. and Mary E. Kingsley; m. Ora Rimes, Jan. 6, 1925; 1 child, Ora. AB, Syracuse U., 1919; postgrad., London Sch. Econs., 1919-20. Jr. officer fgn. svc. Nat. City Bank, N.Y.C., 1920-25; buyer John Wanamaker, N.Y.C., 1925-32; v.p. Mercantile Stores, Inc., N.Y.C., 1932-34, pres., 1934-41, chmn. bd. dirs., 1941-60, chmn. exec. com., from 1960; pres. bd. dirs. King Mill Oil Co., D.M. Trucking Co., Excelsior Housing Corp., Excelsior Merchandising Co., Johnston Housing Corp., McCormick Housing Corp.; v.p., dir. Milliken Automotive Fabrics, Inc., Milliken Woolens, Inc., Peach Queen Farms, Inc., Redlyn Corp., Ridgeview Realty Corp., 1041 Realty Corp., Kingstree Mfg. Co., Inc., Hatch Mills, Excelsior Mills, Abbeville Mills Corp., Johnston Mill Inc.; v.p. Milliken, Inc.; mem. fin. com., dir. Home Life Ins. Co.; dir. Grace Petroleum Corp., W.R. Grace and Co., Gaffney Mfg. Co., Gayley Mill Corp., Kingsley Mill Corp., Judson Corp., Lockhart Railroad Co., Machias Mill Inc., Grace Bank. Monarch Mills, Pacolet Mfg. Co., Drayton Mills, Hartsville Cotton Mill, Laurens Mills. Mem. New Eng. Soc., India House Club, Union League, Univ. Club, N.Y. Skating Club, New Canaan Country Club, Lake Placid Club. *

KINOSITA, RIOJUN, pathologist; b. Japan, Sept. 17, 1893; s. Yukimichi and Nui (Tanabe) K.; m. Florence M. Ritson, Nov. 6, 1925; 1 child, Akiko (Mrs. Denis Lotspeich). MD, Tokyo U., 1921; student, Frieburg U., Germany, 1922-24, Cambridge (Eng.) U., 1924-26; PhD, Kokkaido U., 1926. Prof. pathology Hokkaido U., 1922-32; prof. pathology, dir. cancer rsch. Osaka (Japan) U., 1932-52; pres. Osaka City U., 1946-48; vis. prof. pathology and infectious diseases UCLA, from 1949; rsch. dir., then chmn. dept. exptl. pathology City of Hope Med. Ctr., 1952-62, rsch. dir. emeritus, from 1962; spl. rsch. carcinogenesis, cell multiplication, differentiation. Recipient Outstanding Rsch. award City of Hops, 1962. *

KINSKI, KLAUS (NIKOLAUS GUNTHER NAKSZYNSKI), actor; b. Sopot, Poland, Oct. 8, 1926; m. Ruth Brigitte Tocki (div.); 1 child, Nastassja; m. Minhoi Kinski; 1 child: Nanhoi; child from previous marriage: Pola. Ind. film actor, 1948-91. Feature film debut in Morituri, 1948; 180 other film appearances including Decision Before Dawn, 1951, Ludwig II, 1954, Sarajewo, 1955, A Time to Love and a Time to Die, 1957, The Counterfeit Traitor, 1961, The Black Abbot, 1963, Last Stage to Santa Cruz, 1964, Doctor Zhivago, 1966, For a Few Dollars More, 1966, Venus in Furs, 1969, Aguirre, the Wrath of God, 1972, The Web, 1975, Jack the Ripper, 1976, Entebbe: Operation Thunderbolt, 1977, Nosferatu, the Vampire, 1979, Woyzeck, 1979, Buddy, Buddy, 1980, Fitzcarraldo, 1982, Venom, 1982, Fruits of Passion, 1982, Burden of Dreams, 1982, Android, 1983, Little Drummer Girl, 1984, Crawlspace, 1986. Served with German Army, 1943-45. Home: West Hollywood Calif. Died Nov. 23, 1991. †

KINTNER, EARL WILSON, lawyer; b. Corydon, Ind., Nov. 6, 1912; s. Lee and Lillie Florence (Chanley) K.; m. Valerie Patricia Wildy, May 28, 1948; 1 child, Christopher Earl Mackelcan; children by previous marriage: Anna Victoria, Jonathan M., Rosemary Jane (dec.). AB, De Pauw U., 1936, LLD (hon.), 1970; JD, Ind. U., 1938. Bar: Ind. 1938, U.S. Supreme Ct. 1945, D.C. 1953. Pvt. practice law Princeton, Ind., 1938-44; city atty. City of Princeton, 1939-42; pros. atty. 6th Ind. Jud. Ct. (6th cir.), 1943-48; atty. U.S. Dept. of State, 1946-48; dep. U.S. commr. UN War Crimes Commn., 1945-48; sr. trial atty. FTC, 1948-50, legal adviser, 1950-53, gen. counsel, 1953-59, chmn., 1959-61; del., chmn. com. hearing officers Pres.'s Conf. on Adminstrv. Procedure, 1953-54; mem. panel on invention and innovation U.S. Dept. Commerce, 1965-66; mem. U.S. Adminstrv. Conf., 1972-76, 78-82; mem. adv. com. on civil rules U.S. Jud. Conf., 1971-82; mem., ptnr. then of counsel law firm Arent Fox Kintner Plotkin & Kahn, Washington, 1961-91; adj. prof. sch. law NYU, 1958. Author: An Antitrust Primer, 1964, 73, Robinson-Patman Primer, 1970, 79, A Primer on the Law of Deceptive Practices, 1971, 78, A Merger Primer, 1973; co-author: An Intellectual Property Primer, 1975, An International Anti-trust Primer, 1975, Anti-trust Legislation, 11 vols., 1986, An Anti-trust Treatise, Vols. 1-10, 1990; editor: The United Nations War Crimes Commission and Development of the Laws of War, 1948, The Hadamar Trial, 1948, FTC staff legal manual, 1952. Bd. dirs. D.C. Legal Aid Soc., 1963-88, pres., 1973-76; bd. visitors Ind. U. La., 1964—, chmn., 1973. Lt. USN, 1944-46. Recipient Disting. Svc. award Ind. U., 1960, Disting. Alumni award DePauw U., 1965, 75. Mem. ABA (chmn. adminstrv. law sect. 1959-60, coun. antitrust law sect. 1958-61), Fed. Bar Assn. (pres. 1956-59), N.Y. Bar Assn. (exec. com antitrust sect.), Fed. Bar Found. (pres. from 1959), Fed. Bar Bldg. Corp. (pres. from 1959), Bar Assn. D.C. (bd. dir. 1972-74), Am. Judicature Soc. (bd. dir. 1961-64), Am. Legion, DAV, Sigma Delta Chi, Phi Delta Phi (pres. Province II 1962-67), Pi Sigma Alpha, Delta Sigma Rho, Lambda Chi Alpha. Republican. Episcopalian. Clubs: Cosmos (Washington), National Lawyers (Washington) (pres. from 1959), Capitol Hill (Washington); Union League (N.Y.) until 1991; Coral Beach and Tennis (Bermuda). Lodges: Masons, Shriners. Home: Washington D.C. Died Dec. 28, 1991; buried Arlington Nat. Cemetery.

KIRBY, JAMES CORDELL, JR., law educator; b. Macon County, Tenn., June 19, 1928; s. James Cordell and Beulah (Russell) K.; m. Barbara Glenn Eggleston, Mar. 22, 1955. B.A., Vanderbilt U., 1950; student Law Sch., 1950- 51; LL.B., LL.M., N.Y.U., 1954. Bar: Tenn. 1954, Ill. 1966, Ohio 1971, N.Y. 1975, U.S. Supreme Ct 1975. With firm Waller, Davis & Lansden, Nashville, 1954-55, 57-61; chief counsel judiciary subcom. constl. amendments, helped write the 25th Amendment to Constitution. U.S. Senate, 1961-63; assoc. prof., then prof. law Vanderbilt U. Law Sch., 1963-65; prof. law Northwestern U. Law Sch., 1965-68; prof. law NYU, 1968-70, 74-79, v.p., gen. counsel, sec., 1974-75; dir. Appellate Judges Seminar, 1975-77; dean coll. law Ohio State U., 1970-74; vis. prof. U. Tenn. Coll. Law, 1978-79, prof. law, 1979-89, acting dean, 1980, 81; research dir. spl. study congl. ethical standards Assn. Bar City N.Y., 1967-70; mem. Ohio Ethics Commn., 1973-74, chmn., 1974; panel mem. Am. Arbitration Assn., Fed. Mediation and Conciliation Svc. Author: Fumble: Bear Bryant, Wally Butts and the Great Football Scandal, 1986. Served as 1st lt. AUS, 1955-57. Mem. ABA (spl. commn. presdl. inability and vice presdl. vacancy 1964, spl. comm. electoral coll. reform 1966), Authors Guild, Order of Coif, Phi Beta Kappa, Phi Kappa Sigma, Omicron Delta Kappa. Democrat. Episcopalian. Home: Nashville Tenn. Died Oct. 14, 1989.

KIRBY, WILLIAM THOMAS, lawyer; b. Chgo., Jan. 2, 1911; s. William T. and Margaret (Durkin) K.; m. Evelyn McAdams, Apr. 6, 1940 (dec. May 1967); children: Catherine, James, Mary, Judith. AB, U. Notre Dame, 1932, JD, 1934. Bar: Ill. 1934, U.S. Supreme Ct. 1934. Pvt. practice Chgo., 1945; ptnr. Hubachek, Kelly, Rauch & Kirby, Chgo., 1965-90; gen. counsel Bankers Life & Casualty Co., Chgo., Citizens Bank & Trust Co., Park Ridge, Ill; asst. atty. gen. Ill., 1949-53; fed. referee in bankruptcy, 1936-40. Mem. Ill.-Ind. Bi-state Devel. and Study Commn., 1957-59; bd. dirs. Waukegan Port Dist., 1960-70; zone real estate dir. War Assets Adminstrn., 1946-47. Capt., C.E., AUS, World War II. Fellow Am. Coll. Trial Lawyers; mem. ABA, Soc. Trial Lawyers, Ill. Bar Assn., Chgo. Bar Assn., Lake County Bar Assn., 7th Cir. Bar Assn., Glen Flora Country Club (Waukegan, Ill.). Roman Catholic. Home: Chicago Ill. Died Oct. 1, 1990; buried Ascension Cemetery, Libertyville, Ill.

KIRK, RUDOLF, English language educator; b. Washington, Jan. 20, 1898; s. Charles Farquhar and Annie (Brooke) K.; m. Clara Marburg, Sept. 8, 1930 (dec. Oct. 1976); children: Frances Jeffries (dec.), Susanne, Geoffrey (dec.), Donald. AB with honors in English, Princeton U., 1922, AM, 1928, PhD, 1932; MA, U. Iowa, 1925. Instr. English, State U. Iowa, 1922-25; instr., asst. prof., assoc. prof. English, Rutgers U., 1928-45, prof., 1945-63, prof. emeritus, 1963-89, acting chmn. dept., 1956-57, chmn. dept., 1960-63; disting. prof. S.W. Tex. State U., San Marcos, 1963-67; vis. prof. U. Ill., Chgo., 1967-69; vis. prof. U. Wis., 1964, U. N.Mex., summer 1948, NYU, 1949, U. Mo., 1950, 53; Fulbright prof. Am. lit. and civilization U. Liege, Belgium, 1955-56; Fulbright lectr. U. Ghent, 1955, Rome, 1956; chmn. Coll. Conf. on English, Cen. Atlantic STates, 1933 co-founder English Inst., 1939, sec., 1939-45, chmn., 1949, editor ann., 1940-43. Author: Mr. Pepys upon the State of Christ Hospital, 1935, (with Clara M. Kirk) The Church of St. John the Evangelist: a Parish History, 1961, William Dean Howells, 1962; also articles and revs.; editor: The City-Madam (Philip Massinger), 1934, Heaven upon Earth and Characters of Vertues and Vices (Joseph Hall), 1948, Moral Philosophie of the Stoicks (G. DuVair), 1951, Animadversions (J. Milton), 1953, Rise of Silas Lapham (W.D. Howells), 1962; (with Clara M. Kirk) Types of English Poetry, 1840,. Bd. dirs. New Brunswick area Community Chest, 1942-45; trustee William Alexander Procter Found., 1951-63. With U.S. Army, 1918. Recipient medal U. Ghent, 1956, Silver medal U. Liege, 1956; named hon citizen State of Tex., 1967; Charles Scribner fellow Princeton U., 1927-28. Mem. MLA (chmn. 17th century group 1944, Howells group 1950), AAUP, Guild Scholars, Phi Beta Kappa (hon.). Episcopalian. Died Nov. 7, 1989 .

KIRKCONNELL, WATSON, university president; b. Port Hope, Ont., Can., May 16, 1895; s. Thomas and Bertha (Watson) K.; m. Isabel Peel, 1924 (dec. 1925; children: James, thomas; m. Hope Kitchener, Aug. 6, 1930; children: Helen, Janet, Susan. MA, Queen's U., 1916; student, Oxford (Eng.) U., 1921-22; PhD, Debrecen U., Hungary, 1938; LLD, U. Ottawa, 1944, U. N.B., 1949; Dr. Polit. Econ., Ukraine Free U., 1950; DLitt, McMaster U., 1953, Assumption U., 1955, U. Manitoba, 1957; LHD, Alliance Coll., 1958; D.ésL., Laval U., 1962; Litt.D., Acadia U., 1964; DCL, St. Mary's U., 1964. Lectr., asst. prof., assoc. prof., prof. English Wesley Coll., Winnipeg, Can., 1922-32; prof. Latin United Coll., Winnipeg, 1932-40; prof., head dept. English McMaster U., 1940-48; pres. Acadia U., Wolfville, 1948-64; pres. emeritus Acadia U., 1964, prof. English, from 1964; mem. fed. adv. com. fgn. lang. groups, 1940-45. Author: European Elegies, 1928, Icelandic Verse, 1930, The Magyar Muse, 1933, Golden Treasury of Polish Lyrics, 1936, The Flying Bull and Other Tales, 1940, Twilight of Liberty, 1941, Seven Pillars of Freedom, 1944, Little Treasury of Hungarian Verse, 1946, The Celestial Cycle, 1952, Pan Tadeusz in English Verse, 1960, (with C. H. Andrusyshen) The Ukranian Poets, 1963, Complete Works of Shevchenko, 1963, That Invincible Samson, 1964, Centennial Tales and Other Poems, 1965. Capt. Can. Army, 1916-19. Named laureate Polish Acad. letters; decorated Knight Order of Polonia Restituta, 1936, Pierce gold medal, Royal Soc. Can., 1941, knight comdr. Order of Falcon, Iceland, Schevchenko medal, 1964, Gold Medal Freedom, Hungary, 1964. Fellow Royal Soc. Can., Icelandic Soc. Letters, Petöfi Soc. Hungary, Kisfaludy Soc. Hungary; mem. Can. Authors' Assn. (nat. pres. 1942-44, 56-58), Writers' War Com. Can. (chmn. 1942-44), Humanities Rsch. Coun. Can. (chmn. 1944-47), Bapt. Union Western Can. (pres. 1938-40), Bapt. Fedn. Can. (nat. pres. 1953-56), Masons. *

KIRKWOOD, JAMES, author, playwright, actor; b. Los Angeles, Aug. 22, 1930; s. James and Lila (Lee) K.; m. Muriel Bentley, Feb. 26, 1949 (div. 1957). Grad. high sch. Appeared on Broadway plays Wonderful Town, Dallas, N.Y.C., Panama Hattie, Dallas, Welcome Darlings, on tour, Oh Men, Oh Women, Buck's County, Pa. and on summer tour, The Tender Trap, Buck's County and summer tour, The Rainmaker, summer tour, Never Too Late, on South African tour; movies include Mommie Dearest, Oh, God , Book II, The Supernaturals, Monkeyshines; appeared on numerous TV shows including as Mickey Emerson on Valiant Lady, CBS-TV, for 4 years, Garry Moore Show, CBS-TV, for 2 years; appeared with Jim Kirkwood and Lee Goodman comedy-satire team in nightclubs, Number One Fifth Avenue, Bon Soir, Le Ruban Bleu, Cafe Soc., Downtown, Blue Angel, Mocambo, Hollywood, Calif., Embassy Club, London, Eng., Tic-Toc, Montreal, Ont., Can.; radio performances include Kirkwood-Goodman Show, WOR, N.Y.C., 2 years, Teenagers Unlimited, Mut. Network, 26 weeks, Henry Aldrich, Theatre Guild of the Air.; Author: There Must Be A Pony!, 1961, (adapted for TV 1986), Good Times/Bad Times, 1968, American Grotesque, 1970, P.S. Your Cat Is Dead!, 1972, Some Kind of Hero, 1975, also screenplay, 1982, Hit Me with A Rainbow, 1980; playwright: Unhealthy To Be Unpleasant (prod. on Broadway), 1966, P.S. Your Cat Is Dead! (prod. on Broadway) Golden Theatre), 1975, off-Broadway revival, 1978; Author (with Nicholas Dante) musical, A Chorus Line, 1976 (Drama Critics Circle award 1974, 75, Tony award 1975, Pulitzer prize 1976, Drama Desk award 1976); opened Newman Theatre, 1975, then prod. at Shubert Theatre, N.Y.C. (Drama Critics award for Best Mus. 1975), Legends, 1986-87. Served with USCGR, 3 years. Mem. Screen Actors Guild, Actors Equity Assn., AFTRA, Dramatists Guild, Am. Guild Variety Artists., PEN. Democrat. Roman Catholic. Home: Key West Fla. Died Apr. 22, 1989; cremated.

KIRSTEN, DOROTHY, soprano; b. Montclair, N.J., July 6, 1910; d. George W. and Margaret (Beggs) K.; m. John D. French, July 18, 1955. Mus. tng., U.S., France and Italy; MusD, Ithaca Coll.; DFA, Santa Clara U.; DFA (hon.), Pepperdine U.; DHL, Loyola Marymount U., 1990. Debut as Musetta in: La Boheme, Chgo. Opera Co., Nov. 1940; Debut as Mimi Met. Opera Co., Dec., 1945; with Met. Opera Co., 1945-57, 60-75; has sung roles of Violetta, Cho Cho San, Juliet, Marguerite, Manon Lescaut, Nedda, Micaela, Louise, Fiora, Tosca, Mimi, Manon, Cressida; Girl of Golden West and many operettas; also appeared: films Mr. Music, The Great Caruso, 1950; author: A Time to Sing, 1982. Episcopalian. Home: New York N.Y. Died Nov. 18, 1992. †

KIRWAN, THOMAS M., insurance firm executive; b. Passaic, N.J., Feb. 22, 1940; s. Raymond F. and Gertrude (G.) K.; m. Gloria E. Schnabel, June 18, 1966; children: Gloria, Kristen, Thomas. BS, Providence Coll., 1962; MBA, Fairleigh Dickenson U., 1969. CPA, N.J. With Price Waterhouse & Co., N.Y.C., 1965-68; asst. to treas., controller Elgin Nat. Industries, N.Y.C., 1969-72, v.p. fin., 1972-74; v.p. fin. Holt Rinehart & Winston div. CBS, N.Y.C., 1974-76; pres. W.B. Saunders Co. div. CBS, Phila., 1976-78; v.p. fin., chief fin. officer CBS, Inc., N.Y.C., 1978-81, sr. v.p., 1981; pres. CBS Columbia Group, 1981-85; exec. v.p., chief fin. officer Equitable Investment Corp. subs. Equitable Life Assurance Soc., 1985-87; sr. v.p., chief fin. officer

Individual Fin. Mgmt. Group Equitable Life Ins. Co. subs. Equitable Life Assurance Soc., 1987-88; pres., chief operating officer Equitable Variable Life Ins. Co. subs. Equitable Life Assurance Soc., N.Y.C., 1987; exec. v.p., chief fin. officer Equitable Life Ins. Co., N.Y.C., 1987-90, Equitable Life Assurance Soc., N.Y.C., 1990-92. Lt. U.S. Army, 1962-64. Mem. Am. Inst. C.P.A.s, N.J. Soc. C.P.A.s. Republican. Roman Catholic. Home: Franklin Lakes N.J. Died Apr. 6, 1992.

KISELEWSKI, JOSEPH, sculptor; b. Browerville, Minn., Feb. 16, 1901; s. Blasius and Sophie (Wollney) K.; m. Adeline Peters, June 20, 1931. Ed., Mpls. Sch. Art, 1918-21, N.A.D., 1921-23, Beaux Arts Inst. Design, 1923-25. Works: statue of Gen. Pulaski, Milwa., fishery pediment for the U.S. Dept. of Commerce Bldg., Washington; exterior and interior work on George Rogers Clark Meml, Vincennes, Ind.; groups at entrance of Bronx County Courthouse, N.Y.C., figure of John Wesley, Winston-Salem, N.C., Katherine Ely Tiffany sun dial, Bryn Mawr (Pa.) Coll., Madonna and Child, Rosary Coll., River Forest, Ill., Sea horse fountain, Huntington Mus., Brookgreen, S.C., 3 medallions for Lyman Ellyn Mus., New London, Conn., meml. to Jessir L. Eddy, Tarrytown, N.Y., two life size statues for garden at St. Joseph's Ch., Browerville, Minn., giant sundial, Bus. Systems Bldg. and four fountains for RCA Bldg., New York World's Fair, 1939, 11 works for Met. Housing Project, N.Y.C.; heroic figure of Christ for Bishop's Monument, Fargo, N.D., Good Conduct Medal for U.S. War Dept., World Peace Medal for Soc. of Medalists, N.Y.C.; bronze statue of Our Lady of the Mountains, Covington, Ky.; 4 plaques for House Chamber of Capitol Bldg., 2 reliefs for Gen. Accounting Bldg., Washington, heroic statue of John Peter Zenger, Bronx, N.Y., World War II meml. Vets, Cemetary Holland, Justice; large limestone panel, N.Y.C. Cts. Bldg., Moses for, Syracuse U. Law Sch., 1966, Harold Vanderbilt bronze statue, U. Nashville, 1965, Sylvanus Thayer bronze bust for Hall of Fame for Great Ams., N.Y.U., 1966, Gilmore D. Clarke bust, NAD; medals John F. Kennedy, others. Awarded Prix de Rome 1926-29, Beaux Arts Paris prize 1925-26, Elizabeth N. Watrous gold medal 1937, silver medal, Archtl. League, N.Y.C.. Asso. fellow Am. Acad. in Rome.; Mem. NAD, Archtl. League of N.Y., Nat. Sculpture Soc. Roman Catholic. Club: Century Assn. Home: Bowerville Minn. Died 1988; interred Christ The King Cemetery, Browerville, Minn.

KISH, GEORGE, geographer, educator; b. Budapest, Hungary, Nov. 24, 1914; came to U.S., 1939; m. Elvina Anger, 1949; 1 child. A.B. cum laude, Ecole Libre des Scle. Politiques, Paris, 1935; M.A. in Geography and History, U. Paris, Sorbonne, 1937; M.S., U. Budapest, 1938, D.Sc., 1939; Ph.D., U. Mich., 1945. Vol. Hungarian Ctr. for Tariff Policy, 1933; asst. sec. Hungarian Assn. Textile Industries, 1936-39; asst. dept. geography U. Mich., Ann Arbor, 1939-40, teaching fellow, 1940-43, instr. dept. history, 1942, instr. dept. geography, 1943-46, asst. prof., 1946-50, assoc. prof., 1950-56, prof., 1956-85, William Herbert Hobbs prof., 1981-85, emeritus prof., 1985-89, curator maps Clements Library, 1945-46; vis. prof. Northwestern U., 1946; vis. assoc. prof. U. Minn., 1953, James Ford Bell lectr., 1966; Carnegie Disting. vis. prof. U. Hawaii, 1957; Eva Germaine Rivington Taylor Lectr. Royal Geog. Soc., London, 1968; Kenneth Nebenzahl lectr. Newberry Library, Chgo., 1980. Author: Le Probleme de la Population au Japon, 1936, Land Reform in Italy: Observations on the Changing Face of the Mediterranean, 1966, History of Cartography, 1973, A Source Book in Geography, 1978, Bibliography of International Geographical Congresses: 1871-1976, 1979, La Carte, Image des Civilisations, 1980, (12 books) Around the World Series, 1956-66, To the Heart of Asia: The Life of Sven Hedin, 1984; contbr. articles to encys. and profl. jours. Pres. Ann Arbor (Mich.) Symphony Orch., 1972-74; pres. Mich. Orch. Assn., 1977-79. Served with OSS, 1942-45. Recipient Andree plaque for Polar Studies Swedish Geog. Soc., 1973; recipient Greater Linnaeus Silver medal History of Scis. Royal Swedish Acad. Scis., 1973, Jomard prize Paris Geog. Soc., 1981, Honors award Assn. Am. Geographers, 1979. Mem. Hungarian Geog. Soc. (hon.), Paris Geog. Soc. (hon.), Italian Geog. Soc. (corr.), Royal Swedish Acad. Scis. (fgn.), Assn. Am. Geographers, Medieval Acad. Am., Am. Assn. Advancement of Slavic Studies (exec. bd. 1961-71), Internat. Geog. Union (chmn. U.S. nat. com. 1966-73, sec.-treas. Working Group on Old Maps 1964-89). Home: Ann Arbor Mich. Died July 11, 1989; buried Ann Arbor, Mich.

KISSANE, RAY WILLIAM, cardiologist; b. Galion, Ohio, Nov. 15, 1894; s. Richard Percifer and Metta (Remy) K.; m. Helen Harrod, May 5, 1919; children: Richard Litter (dec.), Ellen Harrod (Mrs. Stewart Rose). MD, Ohio State U., 1918; postgrad., Washington U., 1925. Diplomate Am. Bd. Internal Medicine and Cardiology. Chmn. cardiology dept., past dir. med. div. White Cross Hosp., Riverside Meth. Hosp.; past dir. cardiology dept. Children's Hosp., Columbus, Ohio; prof. medicine in cardiology Ohio State U. Fellow ACP, AAAS, Am. Coll. Cardiology, Am. Geriatrics Soc., Acad. Internat. Medicine, Am. Coll. Chest Physicians (gov.); mem. AMA, Ohio Med. Assn., Columbus Acad. Med., Am. Heart Assn. (bd. dirs., founders group Sci. Coun.), Am. Therapeutic Assn. (past v.p.), Soc. for Study Arteriosclerosis), Cen. Ohio Heart Assn. (past pres., chmn. bd. dirs.), Ohio Heart Assn. (past pres., mem. exec. com.), Ohio Soc. SAR, Univ. Club, Faculty Club, Med. Rev. Club, Rotary, Phi Rho Sigma. *

KISTLER, JOY WILLIAM, physical education educator; b. Sedalia, Mo., Jan. 5, 1898; s. John and Frances (Stuart) K.; m. Elizabeth Bothwell, Aug. 29, 1923; children: Jean Joy (Mrs. Phillip Kendall), Judith (Mrs. J. P. Callaghan), James B. Student, Cen. Coll., Fayette, Mo., 1916-19; AB, Culver-Stockton Coll., 1925; AM, U. Iowa, 1932, PhD, 1935. Dir. athletics Mo. Mil. Acad., Mexico, Mo., 1920-25, 28-31; dir. phys. edn. and athletics Culver-Stockton Coll., Canton, Mo., 1925-28; dir. phys. edn. Univ. High Sch., Iowa City, 1931-35; assoc. prof. phys. edn. State U. of Iowa, 1935-41; head dept. health and phys. edn. La. State U., from 1941. Mem. Am. Acad. Phys. Edn., N.E. A.; mem. AAPHERD (v.p. 1963-64, chmn. phys. edn. div. 1964-65, honor award 1954), So. Dist. Assn. for Health Phys. Edn. and Recreation (pres. 1947-48), Iowa Assn. for Health, Phys. Edn. and Recreation (pres. 1940-41), La. Assn. for Health, Phys. Edn. and Recreation (prs. 1944-45), Am. Coll. Phys. Edn. Assn. (pres. 1961). *

KITAGAWA, JOSEPH MITSUO, religion educator, university dean; b. Osaka, Japan, Mar. 8, 1915; s. Chiyokichi and Kumi (Nozaki) K.; m. Evelyn Mae Rose, July 22, 1946; 1 child, Anne Rose. BA, Rikkyo U., 1937; PhD, U. Chgo., 1951. Assoc. prof. history of religion U. Chgo., 1959-64, prof., 1964-92, dean Div. Sch., 1970-92. Author: Religions of the East, 1969, rev. edit. , 1968, Gibt es ein Verstehen fremder Religionen, 1963, Religion in Japanese History, 1965, Gendai-Sekai to Shukyo-gaku, 1985, On Understanding Japanese Religion, 1987, The Quest for Human Unity, 1990; co-editor: The History of Religions: Essays in Methodology, 1959, Folk Religion in Japan, 1968, Myths and Symbols: Studies in Honor of M. Eliade, 1969, Introduction to the History of Religions, 1987, Essays in the History of Religionss, 1987, Buddhism and Asian History, 1989, Gendai Meicho-Zenshue, 8 Vols., 1060-66, Ency. Religion, (16 vols.), 1987; translator: The Great Asian Religions; editor: The Comparative Study of Religions, 1858, Modern Trends in Worls Religions, 1959, The History of Religions: Essays on the Problem of Understanding, 1967, Understanding and Believing, 1968, Understanding Modern China, 1969, American Refugee Policy: Ethical and Religious Reflections, 1984, The History of Religions: Retrospect and Prospect, 1985, The Religious Traditions of Asia, 1989, Religious Studies, Theological Studies and the University-Divinity School, 1991. Mem. Am. Coun. Learned Socs., Am. Soc. Study Religions (pres. 1969-72), Am. Acad. Religion, Internat. Assn. History Religions (v.p. 1975—), Assn. Religious Studies in Japan, Fund for Theol. Edn. Home: Chicago Ill. Died Oct. 1992. †

KITCHEN, HYRAM, veterinarian educator, dean; b. Oakland, Calif., Sept. 24, 1932; s. Samuel Earl and Clara (Peak) Scribner; m. Yvonne Saasta, Feb. 2, 1958; children: Diane, Michael. B.S., U. Calif., Davis, 1954, D.V.M., 1956; Ph.D., U. Fla., 1965. Practice vet. medicine Los Altos, Calif., 1957-58; research assoc. Coll. Medicine, U. Fla., 1960-63, fellow in cardiology, 1963-65, instr. dept. biochemistry and medicine, 1965-66, asst. prof., 1966-69; assoc. prof. Coll. Vet. Medicine, Mich. State U., 1969-73, prof., 1973-74; acting dir. Center Lab. Animal Resources, 1974; prof., head dept. environ. practice Coll. Vet. Medicine, U. Tenn., Knoxville, 1974-80; dean Coll. Vet. Medicine, U. Tenn. (Coll. Vet. Medicine), Knoxville, 1980-90; bd. dirs. Knoxville Zoo. Contbr. articles to profl. jours. Served to capt. U.S. Army, 1958-60. Recipient Outstanding Faculty award Tenn. Vet. Med. Assn., 1982, Disting. Alumni award U. Calif. Sch. Vet. Medicine, 1990, John C. Hodges Libr. Plaque U. Tenn., 1992; Peter J. Shield scholar, 1951-52, Chancellor's rsch. scholar, 1982. Mem. AAAS, AVMA, Am. Soc. Biol. Chemists, Am. Assn. Zoo Vets., Am. Assn. Vet. Med. Colls., N.Y. Acad. Scis., Am. Assn. Zool. Pks. and Aquariums, Am. Hampshire Sheep Assn., Tenn. Arabian Horse Assn., Internat. Arabian Horse Assn., Tenn. Farm Bur., Tenn. Sheep Breeders Assn., Sigma Xi, Phi Zeta, Sigma Alpha Epsilon, Phi Kappa Phi, Gamma Sigma, Alpha Zeta. Lutheran. Home: Knoxville Tenn. Died Feb. 8, 1990; buried Sanctuary of Love, Woodlawn Cemetery, Colma, Calif.

KLASSEN, ELMER THEODORE, government official; b. Hillsboro, Kans., Nov. 6, 1908; m. Bessie Crooks, May 19, 1929; 1 child, Joan Marie; m. Marie Callahan, June 8, 1963. Student, Harvard U., 1952. With Am. Can Co., N.Y.C., 1925-68, gen. mgr. indsl. rels., 1955-58, v.p. indsl. rels., 1958-61, v.p., asst. gen. mgr. Canco div., 1961-62, v.p., gen. mgr., 1962-64; exec. v.p. div. ops. Am. Can Co., 1964, exec. v.p. corp. ops., 1964-65, pres., 1965-68; dep. postmaster gen. U.S. Dept. Post Office, Washington, 1969-71, postmaster gen., 1972-74; gov. U.S. Dept. Post Office, 1971-74. Mem. Sky Club, Econ. Club, Harvard Bus. Sch. Club, Capitol Hill Club, Elks. Republican. Methodist. Home: Palm Harbor Fla. Died Mar. 6, 1990.

KLAUSLER, ALFRED PAUL, journalist, clergyman; b. Hankinson, N.D., Feb. 22, 1910; s. Joseph Paul and Amanda (Hunziker) K.; m. Signe Fox, June 28, 1934 (dec. Mar. 1990); children—Peter M., Paula S., Thomas A. Diploma, Concordia Coll., St. Paul, 1929, Concordia Sem., St. Louis, 1932; student, Columbia, U. Chgo.; M.A., Loyola U., Chgo., 1961; Litt.D. Valparaiso U. Ordained to ministry Luth. Ch., 1934 pastor Our Savior's Luth. Ch., Glendive, Mont., 1934-42; exec. sec. dept. comnunications Walther League 1946-66; exec. sec. Associated Ch. Press, 1961-74; religion editor Westinghouse Broadcasting, 1969-79; instr Valparaiso (Ind.) U., 1950-52, Concordia Tchrs. Coll. River Forest, Ill., 1954; lectr. Wartburg Sem., Kent State U., Concordia Sem.; asst. pastor St. Philip Luth Ch. Author: (fiction)Midnight Lion, 1957, Growth in Worship, 1957, Christ, and Your Job, 1958, Meditations for Youth, 1959, Censorship and Obscenity, 1966; also mag. articles.; Co-editor: The Journalist's Prayer Book, 1972; editor-at-large: Christian Century, 1974-90; editorial cons.: Christian Ministry, 1974-90. Served as chaplain AUS, 1942-46; col. Res. staff command chaplain, 322d Logis. Command 1961-62, Fort Lee. Decorated Army Commendation medal with oak leaf cluster; recipient Lipphard award for disting. service in religious journalism, 1974. Mem. Nat. Religious Publicity Council (pres. Chgo. 1958-59), Chgo. Bible Soc. (bd. mgrs. 1961-74), Luth. Human Relations Assn. Am. (dir.), Alpha Lambda Phi, Pi Gamma Mu, Sigma Delta Chi. Clubs: Headline (Chgo.), Press (Chgo.). Home: Cicero Ill. Died Dec. 1, 1991.

KLEBAN, EDWARD LAWRENCE, composer, lyricist; b. N.Y.C., Apr. 30, 1939; s. Julian Milton and Sylvia K. B.A., Columbia Coll., 1960. Mem. BMI (Broadcast Music Inc.) Mus. Theater Workshop under Lehman Engel, from 1966, tchr. advanced workshop, also bd. dirs. Producer, CBS Records, Hollywood, Calif., 1961-65, N.Y.C., 1965-68; freelance composer lyricist for theater, TV, films and recordings, 1968-87. Recipient 3 Gold Records, Recording Industry Assn. Am. 1964, 65, 78; Grammy nominations Nat. Acad. Recording Arts Scis., 1967, 68, 75, 79; N.Y. Drama Critics award 1975; Antoinette Perry award 1976; Pulitzer prize for A Chorus Line, 1976; Drama Desk award, 1976; Obie award Theater World 1975-76; Wedgie award, London 1977; Los Angeles Drama Critics award, 1977. Composer and/or lyricist: A Little Bit Different, 1960, The Refrigerators, 1971, The Revue, 1972, Irene, 1973, The Desert Song, 1973, Free to Be You and Me (TV), 1974, Feelin' Good (TV), 1974, A Chorus Line (with Marvin Hamlisch), 1975, The Hindenberg (film), 1975, Gallery, 1981, Chorus Line (film) (nominee Acad. award Surprise Surprise, 1986), 1985, Columbia College at the Met: The Bicentennial Gala, 1987. Order of Arrow Boy Scouts Am., 1952. Mem. Dramatists Guild, Am. Fedn. Musicians, Broadcast Music, Inc. Home: New York N.Y. Died Dec. 27, 1987.

KLEBANOFF, PHILIP SAMUEL, physicist, researcher; b. N.Y.C., July 21, 1918; s. Morris and Celia (Solowey) K.; m. Angelyn Effie Calvo, Dec. 23, 1950; children: Steven Michael, Susan Marian, Leonard Elliott. B.S., Bklyn. Coll., 1939; postgrad., George Washington U., 1942-43, 44-45; D.Eng., Hokkaido U., Sapporo, Japan, 1979. Staff mem. Nat. Bur. Standards, Gaithersburg, Md., 1941-83, asst. chief mechanics div., 1969-78, chief aerodynamics sect., 1969-75, chief fluid mechanics sect., 1975-78, sr. scientist, 1978-83, cons., 1983-85, guest sci., from 1985; mem. com. for theoretical and applied mechanics NRC-Nat. Acad. Scis., 1970-74; mem. indsl. profl. adv. com. dept. aerospace Pa. State U., 1970-75, Naval Sea Systems Command Hydro Mechanics Com., 1974-81, Boundary Layer Transition Study Group, U.S. Air Force, 1970-82; mem. organizing com. and internat. adv. bd. Beer-Sheva Internat. Seminar on MHD Flows and Turbulence, from 1975. Contbr. articles to profl. jours.; mem. editorial bd. Physics of Fluids, 1970-73. Recipient Naval Ordnance Devel. award, 1945, Gold medal Dept. Commerce, 1975; commendation Nat. Bur. Standards, 1968. Fellow AIAA, AAAS, Washington Acad. Scis., Am. Phys. Soc. (chmn. exec. com. fluid dynamics div. 1969, Fluid Dynamics prize 1981); mem. Philos. Soc. Washington, Nat. Acad. Engring. Home: Bethesda Md. Deceased. †

KLEIN, NORMA, author; b. N.Y.C., May 13, 1938; d. Emanuel and Sadie (Frankel) K.; m. Erwin Fleissner, July 27, 1963; children: Jennifer, Katherine. B.A., Barnard Coll., 1960; M.A. in Slavic Langs., Columbia U., 1963. Author: (short stories) Love and Other Euphenisms, 1972, Sextet in A Minor, 1982; (novels) Give Me One Good Reason, 1973 (Book of Month Club alternate), Girls Turn Wives, 1976 (Lit. Guild alternate), It's Okay if You Don't Love Me, 1977, Love is One of the Choices, 1978, Domestic Arrangements, 1981, Wives and Other Women, 1982, Beginner's Love, 1983, The Swap, 1983, Lovers, 1984, American Dreams, 1987, Give and Take, 1985; (teenage fiction) Mom, the Wolf Man and Me, 1972, Confessions of an Only Child, 1973, It's Not What You Expect, 1973, Taking Sides, 1975, What It's All About, 1975, Hiding, 1976, Tomboy, 1978, French Postcards, 1979, A Honey of A Chimp, 1980, Breaking Up, 1980, Robbie and the Leap Year Blues, 1981, The Queen of the What Ifs, 1982, Bizou, 1983, Angel Face, 1984, The Cheerleader, 1985, Family Secrets, 1985, My Life as a Body, 1986, Going Backwards, 1986, Older Men, 1987; (juvenile fiction) Girls Can Be Anything, 1973 (Jr. Lit. Guild alternate), If I Had My Way, 1974, A Train for Jane, 1974, Dinosaur's Housewarming Party, 1974, Naomi in the Middle, 1974, Blue Trees, Red Sky, 1975, A Train for Jane, 1974,

Visiting Pamela, 1979. Home: New York N.Y. Died Apr. 25, 1989.

KLEISNER, GEORGE HARRY, former retail executive; b. Chgo., Apr. 20, 1909; s. John and Marie (Frey) K.; m. Mary Cecilia Wetzel, Aug. 28, 1937 (dec. 1967); children: Patricia, Pamela, Kerry, Kim; m. Catherine Orlando, Oct. 12, 1974; children: Geoffrey, Christopher. B.S., Northwestern U., 1930. Mng. editor W. L. Johnson Pub. Co., 1930-33; with Montgomery Ward & Co., 1933-64; beginning as mdse. trainee Montgomery Ward & Co., Chgo.; successively asst. div. mgr. Montgomery Ward & Co., N.Y.C.; buyer, div. mgr. hosiery and accessories, asst. soft lines mdse. mgr., soft lines mdse. mgr. Montgomery Ward & Co., 1943-52; charge Montgomery Ward & Co. (N.Y. office), 1952-58, v.p., 1955-57, mdse. mgr., 1958-64; assoc. mgmt. cons. Wendell C. Walker & Assos., 1964-65; v.p. charge N.Y. office Bear Brand Hosiery Co., 1965-80; cons. Americal Corp., Henderson, N.C., 1980-87. Served as 2d lt. Q.M.C. U.S. Army Res., 1938-43. Mem. Northwestern U. Alumni Assn. (dir. 1931-33), Holy Name Soc., Wool Club N.Y.C., Theta Xi, Sigma Delta Chi. Republican. Roman Catholic. Club: Scarsdale (N.Y.) Golf. Home: Scarsdale N.Y. Died Dec. 27, 1987. †

KLERMAN, GERALD LAWRENCE, psychiatrist; b. N.Y.C., Dec. 29, 1928; s. Philip and Rose (Duxon) K.; m. Myrna M. Weissman, Apr. 17, 1935; children: Jacob, Elizabeth, Karen, Daniel. BA, Cornell U., 1950, MD, 1954. Diplomate Nat. Bd. Examiners; lic. psychiatrist Mass. 1954, N.Y. 1959. Med. and neurology intern Columbia U., N.Y.C., 1955-56; med. intern Mass. Mental Health Ctr., Boston, 1956-57, resident psychiatrist, 1957-58, chief of svc., 1958-59, prin. rsch. scientist, 1961-65, asst. dir. psychiatry, 1962-65; dir. clin. svcs. Conn. Mental Health Ctr., New Haven, 1965-67, dir., 1967-69; supt. Erich Lindemann Mental Health Ctr., Boston, 1970-76; prof. psychiatry Mass. Gen. Hosp., Boston, 1977-85; adminstr. alcohol, drug abuse and mental health adminstrn. NIMH, Washington, 1977-80; assoc. chmn. rsch., prof. psychiatry Cornell U. Med. Coll., N.Y.C., 1985-92; mem. Psychopharmacology rev. com. NIMH, 1971-75; chmn. adv. com. neuropharmacology, FDA, 1974-76; bd. dirs. Founds. Fund for Rsch. in Psychiatry. Mem. Group for the Advancement of Psychiatry (rsch. com.), Collegium Internat. Neuro-Psychpharmacologicum, Am. Psychiatric Assn. (drug reaction commn., chmn. com. on rsch. aspects of community mental health ctrs.), Am. Psychopath. Assn. (v.p. 1974-75, pres. 1976-77), Mass. Psychiat. Soc., Inst. Soc. Ethics and the Life Scis. (v.p. 1976-77), ACNP (pres.-elect 1976-77), numerous other orgns.. Home: New York N.Y. Died Apr. 3, 1992.

KLIBAN, B(ERNARD), cartoonist; b. Jan. 1, 1935; divorced; 1 child. Ed., Pratt Inst., Cooper Union. Cartoonist: books Cat, 1975, Never Eat Anything Bigger Than Your Head and Other Drawings, 1976, Whack Your Porcupine and Other Drawings, 1977, Tiny Footprints and Other Drawings, 1978, Playboy's Kliban, 1979, Two Guys Fooling Around with the Moon and Other Drawings, 1982, Luminous Animals and Other Drawings, 1983, The Biggest Tongue in Tunisia and Other Drawings, 1986; artist and cartoonist for posters, calendars, greeting cards. Home: Corte Madera Calif. Died Aug. 12, 1990.

KLINE, MORRIS, mathematician, consultant, author; b. Bklyn., May 1, 1908; s. Bernard and Sarah (Spatt) K.; m. Helen Mann, Sept. 4, 1939; children: Elizabeth, Judith, Douglas. BA, NYU, 1930, PhD, 1936. Instr. NYU, N.Y.C., 1930-36; fellow Inst. for Advanced Study, Princeton, N.J., 1936-38; dir. div. electromagnetic rsch. Courant Inst., NYU, 1946-66, prof., 1952-75; Fulbright lectr., Guggenheim fellow Tech. Hochschule Aachen, 1958-59; vis. prof. Bklyn. Coll., 1974-76; cons. Americana & Britannica Encys.; lectr. in field of math. edn. Author: Mathematics in Western Culture, 1953, Mathematics and the Physical World, 1959, MATHEMATICS, A Cultural Approach, 1962, Electromagnetic Theory and Geometrical Optics, 1965, Calculus, An Intuitive and Physical Approach, 2 vols., 1967, 2d edit., 1977, Mathematics for Liberal Arts, 1967, Why Johnny Can't Add, 1973, Mathematical Thought from Ancient to Modern Times, 1972, 90, Mathematics: the Loss of Certainty, 1980, 1985. Civilian employee U.S. Army, World War II. Recipient Teaching awards NYU. Jewish. Home: Brooklyn N.Y. Died June 10, 1992; buried Montefiore Cemetery, Queens, N.Y.

KLINGMAN, DARWIN DEE, business, computer science educator, consultant; b. Dickinson, N.D., Feb. 5, 1944; s. Virgil Wayne and Ethel Louella (Foster) K.; m. Brenda Mabel Sargent, Aug. 29, 1964 (div. Mar. 1974); m. Nancy Valree Phillips, Dec. 6, 1988; 1 child, Loren Phillips. B.A. in Math., Wash. State U., 1966, M.A., 1967; Ph.D. interdisciplinary, U. Tex., 1969. Asst. prof. bus. and computer sci. U. Tex., Austin, 1969-71, assoc. prof., 1972-75, prof., 1976-89; dir. Ctr. Bus. Decision Analysis U. Tex, Austin, 1982-89; Bruton Centennial chair U. Tex., Austin, 1983-85, Cullen Centennial chair, 1985-89; vis. prof. computer sci. Free U., Berlin, 1975; vis. prof. math. Wash. State U., Pullman, 1977. Editor Network Models and Associated Applications, 1982; assoc. editor Naval Rsch. Logistics Quar., 1984-89; contbr. numerous articles to profl. jours., 1969-89. Recipient Outstanding Grad. Tchr. award U. Tex., 1983, Outstanding Research award Golden Key Nat. Honor Soc., 1983, Franz Edelman award for Mgmt. Sci. Achievement, 1986, Jack G. Taylor award for Excellence in Teaching U. Tex., 1987; Alexander von Humboldt fellow Bonn, Fed. Republic of Germany, 1974. Mem. Inst. Mgmt. Sci. (v.p. at large 1981-82), Math. Assn. Am. (1977-81), Assn. Computing Machinery, Math. Programming Soc. (charter), Ops. Rsch. Soc. Am. Home: Austin Tex. Died Oct. 27, 1989; cremated.

KLITGAARD, GEORGINA, artist; b. N.Y.C., July 3, 1893; d. John Austen and Georgina (Berrian) Berrain; m. Kaj Klitgaard, 1919; children: Peter, Wallace. BA, Barnard Coll., 1912. One-man shows at N.Y.C., 1927, Concoran Gallery, Washington, 1941, Rehn Galleries, 6 shows, 1930-91, St. Gaudens Meml., 1948, St. Gaudens Meml., Woodstock, N.Y., 1955, 64; prin. works exhibited View of Kingston, Pitts., Internat. Chgo., San Francisco and N.Y. World's Fairs, Corcoran Gallery, Washington; murals for Goshen, N.Y., Poughkeepsie, N.Y., Pelham, Ga.; represented in permanent collections at Met. Mus. Art, Whitney Mus. Am. Art, Newarrk Mus., Dayton Art Inst., New Brit. Art Inst., Bklyn. Recipient awards Carnegie Internat. Exhbn., Pa. Acad., Art Inst. Chgo., Pan Am. Exhbn., San Francisco, others; fellow Huntington Hartford Found., 1965, Guggenheim Found., Helene Wurlitzer Found. N.M. grantee, 1967-69. Mem. Am. Soc. Painters, Sculptors and Engravers, Audubon Artists, Am. Recorders Soc. Home: New York N.Y. Deceased.

KLONIS, STEWART, artist, educator; b. Naughatuck, Conn., Dec. 24, 1901; s. Michael and Constance (Wren) K.; m. Charlotte O. Leal, June 26, 1931 (div. 1959); m. Laura Palumbo, Oct. 1959; 1 dau., Laura Maddalena. Student, N.Y. U., 1924-26, Art Students League N.Y., 1927-31. Mem. of Artists Aid Com., 1932-36; acting treas. Artists Coop. Market, 1933; mem. bd. Art Students League N.Y., N.Y.C., 1934, treas., 1935-36, pres., 1937-45, exec. dir., 1946-80; hon. mem. Art Students League N.Y., 1952-89; v.p. Am. Fine Art Soc. N.Y., 1939-41, pres., 1941-82; trustee Edward MacDowell Traveling Scholarship Fund, 1934-45; instr. Queens Coll., 1940-45; dir.-at-large Artists Equity Assn., from 1952; mem. advisory council N.Y.C. Center Gallery, from 1954, chmn., 1954; mem. arts com. Fulbright Awards, 1949-57, chmn., 1953-55, 57; mem. advisory com. for arts Inst. Internat. Edn., from 1961. Bd. dirs. MacDowell Colony, 1970-79; trustee Nat. Arts Mus. of Sports, from 1963. Recipient Gari Melchers award Artists Fellowships, Inc., 1975; gold medal of honor Nat. Arts Club Art Student League N.Y., 1977; citation for outstanding contbn. to art edn. in U.S. Artists Equity of N.Y., 1977. Benjamin Franklin fellow Royal Soc. Arts (hon. corr. mem. for N.Y. State 1975-78, hon. sr. corr. mem. for U.S. 1979-89); mem. Mcpl. Art Soc., Nat. Acad. Design (assoc.). Democrat. Club: Century Association. Home: Brooklyn N.Y. Died Dec. 16, 1989.

KLOPPENBURG, RALPH HAASE, architect; b. Davenport, Iowa, Nov. 9, 1903; s. Louis and Alvina (Haase) K.; m. Bernice Schlichting, Aug. 30, 1926; children: Jack (dec. 1988), Robert K., Jerry K.; Sally (Mrs. David Conley). BArch, U. Ill. Registered architect, Wis. Instr. U. Ill., 1926-28; pvt. practice as Ralph Kloppenburg, 1931-59, Kloppenburg & Kloppenburg, Milw., from 1959. Prin. works include schs. Menominee Falls, Wis., 1948-68, St. Christopher's Episcopal Ch., River Hills, Wis., 1956, West Bend Mut. Ins. Co., Wis., Milw. Downer Sem., River Hills, 1961, Zoology Rsch. bldg. U. Wis., Madison, 1961, Badger Meter Mfg. Co., Milw., Phys. Edn. and Bus. Econs. bldgs, Whitewater U., 1966-67, Univ. Sch., Milw., 1970, Germantown (Wis.) Schs., 1969-71, New Berlin (Wis.) Schs., 1969-70, Grafton (Wis.) High Sch., 1973, Weyenberg Libr., Mequon, Wis., 1973, numerous others. Fellow AIA (pres. Wis. chpt. 1945-47), Milw. Club, Univ. Club, Milw. Country Club, Rotary. Home: Milwaukee Wis. Died Mar. 11, 1990; buried Meml. Garden, St. Christopher's Episcopal Ch., River Hills, Wis.

KLOSS, JOHN ANTHONY, fashion designer; b. Detroit, June 13, 1937; s. Frank Joseph and Lillian Joan (Ostrawski) Klosowski. Grad., Traphagen Sch. Fashion, 1958. Designer, pres. studio, Henri Bendel, N.Y.C., 1965-69, owner, John Kloss, Inc., N.Y.C., from 1965, designer, Cira, from 1965, Lily of France, from 1972, Butterick Fashion Mktg. Co., from 1972, John Kloss Sportswear, from 1977, exhibited, Met. Mus., Pratt Retrospective, Glamour Hours of Hollywood (Recipient Coty Am. Fashion Critic's award for lingerie 1971, 74, Fashion award for lingerie 1975). Crystal Ball award; Calla award, 1975. Home: Stamford Conn. Deceased. †

KLUSZEWSKI, THEODORE BERNARD, professional baseball coach; b. Argo, Ill., Sept. 10, 1924; s. John and Josephine (Guntarski) K.; m. Eleanor Rita Guckel, Feb. 9, 1946. Student, Ind. U., 1944-46. Profl. baseball player Cin. Reds, Pitts. Pirates, Chgo. White Sox, Calif. Angels, 1946-61; profl. baseball coach, 1961-88; coach Cin. Reds, 1969-88; v.p. United County Life Ins. Co. Ohio. Active Multiple Sclerosis Soc.; mem. Greater Cin. Safety Coun. Named to Cin. Reds Hall of Fame, 1962, Ohio Baseball Hall of Fame, 1977. Mem. Fraternal Order Police, Ind. U. Alumni Assn., Ballplayers of Yesterday, Ind. I Men's Assn., Harper's Point Racquet Club. Home: Maineville OH Died Mar. 29, 1988; buried Cincinnati, Ohio.

KNAGGS, NELSON STUART, chemical company executive; b. Hagerstown, Md., Mar. 31, 1907; s. John Nelson and Carolynn (Pagenheardt) K.; m. Esther Aneshansel, July 19, 1929 (dec. May 1964); children—Nelson S. (dec. Sept. 1987), James F., David R.; m. Marielle Seidel, Nov. 23, 1976 (dec. Sept. 1986); m. Shirley K. Krueger, Sept. 1988. Student, Davis and Elkins Coll., 1925-27, LL.D., 1956; student, U. Cin., 1928-29, 33-34, L.H.D., 1971. Research chemist Hilton-Davis Chem. Co., Cin., 1933-41, dir. fgn. div., 1941-48, v.p. marketing and advt., 1948-71, sr. v.p., 1971-72; pres. Knaggs/World Enterprises, Inc., Cin., from 1972; v.p. Thomassett Color Co., Cin., 1954-72; chmn. bd. Nikko Inn, Inc., Ohio, 1962-80; dir. Amar Dye-Chem, India, 1956-59, Spectrum Exploration & Mining Co., South Africa. Author: Adventures in Man's First Plastic, 1947, The Romance of Natural Waxes, 1947, Dyestuffs of the Ancients, 1953, Lost in the Amazon, 1965, Journey to Nepal, 1968, The Rediscovery of John J. Audubon's White Wolf, 1970, also articles profl. jours. Trustee Davis and Elkins Coll., 1970-76; bd. dirs. Cin. Mus. Natural History, v.p., from 1948; bd. dirs., v.p. Cin. Council World Affairs; v.p. Internat. Visitors Center, Cin.; expeditions to Amazon River Basin, Cen. Am., Mex., India, Nepal, Cambodia, Seychelles Islands, Diamond Exploration, South Africa. Mem. Am. Chem. Soc., Engring. Soc. Cin., Cin. Lit. Soc., Cin. C. of C. World Trade Club, (pres. 1945-47), Explorers Club (dir. 1959-61), Queen City Club (bd. govs. 1978-87). Clubs: Queen City (Cin.) (bd. govs. from 1978), Cin. Travel (Cin.) (dir. from 1947, pres. 1947-50, 73-77), Fgn. Trade (Cin.) (pres. 1943-45), Cin. Lit.; Explorers (N.Y.C.) (dir. 1959-61); World Trade. Home: Cincinnati OH Died June 18, 1992. †

KNAPP, DANIEL C., association executive; b. Peoria, Ill., June 19, 1915; s. Christian and Nina (Fernsler) K.; m. Ruth Weinberger, Dec. 18, 1948; children: Terry L., Karen D. B.A., Bradley U., 1937; M.A., U. Ill., 1938; postgrad., Ohio State U., 1944-45; grad., Advanced Mgmt. Program, Harvard U., 1962. Govt. intern Nat. Inst. Pub. Affairs, Washington, 1938-39; adminstrv. aide Social Security Bd., 1939-42; chief, dept. recruitment and placement VA, 1946-51; exec. officer Dept. Army, Washington and Okinawa, 1951-62; joined U.S. Fgn. Service, 1962; dep. chief career devel. staff State Dept., 1962-64, chief manpower resources staff, 1964-66; dir. manpower planning program, 1966-68; dir. personnel environmental health service HEW, Washington, 1968-70; chief personnel policy U.S. EPA, Washington, 1970-74; dir. operating programs Nat. Inst. for Automotive Service Excellence, Washington, 1974-82. Contbr. articles to profl. jours. Served to 1st lt. AUS, 1942-46. Mem. Am. Soc. Pub. Adminstrn., Internat. Personnel Mgmt. Assn., Pi Gamma Mu. Home: Rockville Md. Died Nov. 2, 1988; buried Rockville, Md.

KNAPP, PETER HOBART, psychiatrist; b. Syracuse, N.Y., June 30, 1916; s. Martin Hobart and Sally (Hazard) K.; m. Shelby Owen, June 19, 1942 (div. 1955); children: Penelope, Peter Hazard, Martin Sedgwick; m. Jean Wechsler; children: Andrew Gannett, Rebecca Sedgwick, Caroline Hazard. BA, Harvard U., 1937, MD, 1941. Diplomate Am. Bd. Psychiatry and Neurology. Intern and resident Boston City Hosp., 1941-43; resident in psychiatry Mass. Gen. Hosp., Boston, 1946-48; from asst. prof. to prof. Boston U. Sch. Medicine, 1948-91, prof. emeritus, 1991; pvt. practice psychiatry Cambridge, Mass., until 1991; cons. NIMH, Bethesda, Md., 1967-84. Editor, contbg. author 4 books including: Expression of the Emotions in Man, 1963; mem. editorial bd. 4 psychiat. jours.; contbr. articles to profl. jours. Maj. USMC, 1943-46. Fellow Ctr. for Advanced Study in Behavioral Scis., Palo Alto, Calif., 1964-65. Mem. Am. Psychoanalytic Assn., Am. Psychosomatic Soc. (pres. 1969-70), Am. Psychiat. Assn. (diplomate). Home: Cambridge Mass. Died Apr. 7, 1992.

KNEIP, FREDERICK EVOY, paper company executive; b. Washington, Apr. 17, 1914; s. Frederick E. and Anita (Dieterich) K.; m. Loraine Condit, May 4, 1940; children: Frederick C., Loraine DeRonde, Edward Arthur. AB, Dartmouth, 1936; Grad. Advanced Mgmt. Program, Harvard U., 1960. With E.A. Pierce & Co., N.Y.C., 1936-38; sales engr. Nichols Engring. and Rsch., N.Y.C., 1938-41; with Union-Camp Corp., Savannah, Ga. and, Trenton, N.J., 1941-57; gen. mgr. Union-Camp Corp., Lakeland, Fla., 1957-58; div. sales and gen. mgr. Union-Camp Corp., N.Y.C., 1958-65; sr. v.p., dir. Sone Container Corp., Chgo., 1965-90. With USMC, 1942-46. Home: Winnetka Ill. Died Mar. 6, 1990.

KNIGHT, JAMES L., newspaperman; b. Akron, Ohio, 1909; m. Barbara Knight; children: Barbara Knight Toomey, Marilyn Knight Nort, Marjorie Knight Crane, Beverly Knight Olson. Dir. Knight-Ridder Newspapers, Inc.; dir. Knight Pub. Co., Charlotte, N.C.; chmn. bd. emeritus Miami Herald Pub. Co., Fla.; dir. Beacon Jour. Pub. Co., Tallahasse Democrat, Macon Telegraph Pub. Co., Boca Raton News, Inc., Bradenton Herald, Inc., Detroit Free Press, Inc., Lexington Herald-

Leader Co., Phila. Newspapers, Inc., Ridder Publs., Inc., Twin Coast Newspapers, Inc., N.W. Publs., Inc., Knight-Ridder Broadcasting, Inc. Mem. So. Newspaper Pubs. Assn. (pres. 1957, chmn. bd. 1958), Am. Newspapers Pubs. Assn. Clubs: Portage Country (Akron); Bath, LaGorce, Indian Creek, Surf (Miami); Detroit, Key Largo Anglers, Chub Cay; Lyford Cay (New Providence, Bahamas); Ocean Reef (Key Largo, Fla.). Home: Miami Fla. Died Feb. 5, 1991.

KNIGHT, LESTER BENJAMIN, consulting engineer; b. Albany, N.Y., June 29, 1907; s. Lester B. and Louise Vaast K.; m. Elizabeth Anne Field, Mar. 5, 1935 dec. 1978 ; children: Charles Field, Leslie; m. Frances Talbert Edens, Mar. 22, 1980. M.E., Cornell U., 1929; postgrad., Chgo. Kent Coll. Law, 1932-34. Vice pres. Nat. Engring. Co., Chgo., 1930-43; chmn., chief exec. officer Lester B. Knight & Assocs., Inc. mgmt. and cons. engrs. , Chgo., 1945-89; chmn. Lester B. Knight Internat. Corp., Chgo., 1952-89, A.B. Knight, Karlstad, Sweden, 1962-89; spl. rsch. foundry mgmt., operation, design, automation and mechanization. Pres., adminstrv. dir. Travelers Aid Soc. Chgo., 1958-6, pres. sponsoring bd., exec. com., 196-89; mem. pres.'s coun. Cornell U., U. Ill; established and funded Knight Fellowship program Cornell U.; founder Charles G. Rummel fellowship U. Ill., Urbana. lt. comdr. USNR, 1943-45. Mem. Am Foundrymen's Soc., ASME, Am. Mgmt. Assn., Assn. Cons. Mgmt. Engrs., Chgo. C. of C. bd. dirs., v.p. indsl. devel. and policy com. , Ill. Engr Coun. 1st v.p., bd. dirs., exec. com. , Univ. Club, Mid-Am. Cub, Chgo. Club, Econ. Club Chgo. , Glenview Golf Club Golf, Ill. , Army-Navy Club Washington , Country of Fla. Club Golf, Fla. , Quail Ridge Golf and Country Club Boynton Beach, Fla. , Alpha Tau Omega. Home: Saint Louis Mo. Died June 22, 1989; buried Christ Ch., Winnetka, Ill.

KNIGHT, ROBERT PATRICK, journalism educator, academic administrator; b. Mexico City, Mexico, Mar. 17, 1935; came to U.S., 1941; s. John Montiel and Margaret Mary (Kenny) K.; m. Rose Eleanor Janda, July 21, 1956; children: Robert Patrick, Mary Kathleen, Timothy F., Rodney J., Caroline E. B.J. with honors, U. Tex., 1956, B.A. in English with honors, 1956, M.J., 1964; postgrad., U. Chile, Santigao, 1956-57; Ph.D., U. Mo., 1968. Reporter Austin Am.-Statesman, Tex., 1953-56, Midland Reporter-Telegram, Tex., 1958; research and publs. asst., tchr. English and journalism Midland Pub. Schs., 1958-63; instr. Tex. A&M U., College Station, 1963-65, acting head dept., 1964-65; from instr. to prof. journalism U. Mo., Columbia, 1965-92, O. O. McIntry prof. Sch. Journalism, 1991-92, dir. African-Am./Hispanic/Asian-Am./Native Am. Workshop, from 1971, dir. journalism extension, from 1976; dir. Mo. Interscholastic Press Assn., from 1965. Author: monographs Polls, Sampling and the Voter, 1966, Voters, Computers and TV Forecasts, 1966; co-author: Manual for News Writing, 1970; editor: tabloid Urban Pioneer, from 1971, Telling the Story of America: Minorities and Journalism, 1982; interviewer: video-audio tapes World Journalism Resources Unit, from 1977. Recipient Order of Golden Quill award Tex. Interscholastic League Press Conf., 1977, Gold Key award Columbia Scholastic Press Assn., 1980, James Frederick Paschal award Columbia Scholastic Press Assn., 1989, Pioneer award Nat. Scholastic Press Assn., 1983, Lester A. Walton award Greater St. Louis Assn. of Black Journalists, 1989, Lifetime Achievement awad Okla. Interscholastic Press Assn., 1990; Knight award created in his honor Mo. Journalism Edn. Assn., 1989; Adrian (Mo.) High Sch. named the Robert P. Knight in his honor. Mem. Assn. for Edn. in Journalism and Mass Communication (head div. secondary edn. 1971-72, div. Honors lectr. 1981, Minority Recruitment award 1990), Journalism Edn. Assn. (editorial bd. 1968-89, Carl Towley award 1970), Student Press Law Ctr. (bd. dirs. 1976-89), U. Mo. Alumni Assn. (Faculty award 1991), Kappa Tau Alpah (cert. for outstanding svc. 1986). Roman Catholic. Home: Columbia Mo. Died Feb. 9, 1992.

KNORR, KLAUS EUGENE, educator; b. Essen, Germany, May 16, 1911; came to U.S., 1937, naturalized, 1940; s. Eugene and Bertha (Brill) K.; m. Marianne Uhlman, July 6, 1937; children: Monica, Annette, Nicholas. LLB, U. Tuebingen, Germany, 1935; PhD, U. Chgo., 1941. Rsch. assoc. Food Rsch. Inst., Stanford, Calif., 1941-45; assoc. prof. Yale U., New Haven, 1942-52; prof. econs. Princeton (N.J.) U., 1952-68, prof. internat. affairs, 1968-79, prof. emeritus, 1979-90, dir. Ctr. Internat. Studies, 1961-68; mem. sr. rev. panel CIA, 1979-90; cons. The Rand Corp., Dept. State, Dept. Def., other govtl. depts. Author: British Colonial Theories, 1944, The War Potential of Nations, 1956, NATO and American Security, 1959, Limited Strategic War, 1962, On the Uses of Military Power in the Nuclear Age, 1966, Military Power and Potential, 1970, The Power of Nations, 1975, Historical Dimensions of National Security Problems, 1976, Economic Issues and National Security, 1977; editor: World Politics; contbr. articles to profl. jours. Mem. Am. Econ. Assn. Unitarian. Home: McLean Va. Died Mar. 25, 1990.

KNOWLES, ASA SMALLIDGE, university chancellor; b. Northeast Harbor, Maine, Jan. 15, 1909; s. Jerome and Lilla Belle (Smallidge) K.; m. Edna Worsnop; children—Asa W., Margaret Anne. Ed., Thayer Acad., South Braintree, Mass., 1925-26; A.B., Bowdoin Coll., 1930, LL.D. (hon.), 1951; postgrad., Harvard Bus. Sch., 1930-31; A.M., Boston U., 1935; LL.D. (hon.), Northeastern U., 1957, Emerson Coll., 1960, U. Toledo, 1960, Brandeis U., 1968; D. Ped. (hon.), North Adams State Coll., 1974, Franklin Pierce Coll., 1974; Litt.D. (hon.), Western New Eng. Coll., 1961; Sc.D. (hon.), New Eng. Coll. Pharmacy, 1962, Lowell Tech. Inst., 1966; D.B.A. (hon.), U. R.I., 1967; Sc.D. in Bus. Edn. (hon.), Bryant Coll., 1967; L.H.D. (hon.), Mass. Coll. Optometry, 1975; Sc.D. in Edn. (hon.), Boston Coll., 1976. Assoc. prof. indsl. engring., also head dept. Northeastern U., Boston, 1936-39, dean Coll. Bus. Adminstrn., 1939-42, also dir. Bur. Bus. Research, 1939-42, pres., 1959-75, chancellor, from 1975, also dean Sch. Bus. Adminstrn.; dir. Div. Gen. Coll. Extension, U. R.I., Kingston, 1942-46; first chancellor Associated Colls. Upper N.Y., 1946-48; v.p. devel. Cornell U., Ithaca, N.Y., 1948-51; pres. U. Toledo, 1951-58; dir. Shawmut Corp.; mem. Mass. Commn. Edn., 1963-65; mem. Mass. Higher Edn. Facilities Commn., 1964-69, chmn., 1968-69; chmn. New Eng. Assn. Schs. and Colls., 1967-69, v.p., 1970-71, pres., 1971-72; mem. council Fedn. Regional Accreditation Commns. Higher Edn., 1966-72, chmn., 1970-72; chmn. Army Adv. Panel on R.O.T.C. Affairs, 1967-68; vice chmn. Nat. Commn. for Coop. Edn., 1962-75, chmn., from 1975; vice chmn. Assn. Ind. Colls. and Univs. in Mass., 1973-74, chmn., 1974-75; chmn. Mass. Commn. on Postsecondary Edn., 1975-76. Co-author: Industrial Management, 1944; co-author and editor: Handbook of Cooperative Education, 1971; Editor: Handbook of College and University Administration, 2 vols., 1970; Editor-in-chief: Internat. Ency. of Higher Edn., 10 vols., 1977. Recipient Legion of Honor Internat. Order DeMolay, 1960; Outstanding Civilian Service medal U.S. Army, 1962; Distinguished Civilian Service medal and citation, 1966; Distinguished Educator award Bowdoin Coll., 1972; named Outstanding Son of Maine, 1970; Man of Year award Mass. Jewish War Vets., 1974; Distinguished Service to Higher Edn. award Am. Coll. Pub. Relations Assn., 1974; Alumni award Univ. Coll. Law Enforcement, 1974; citation Boston chpt. Am. Soc. Indsl. Security, 1974; citation Mass. Chiefs Police, 1974; certificate of merit Am. Soc. Indsl. Security, 1974; Outstanding Service to Journalism award New Eng. Press Assn., 1975; Distinguished Pub. Service award Boston U. Alumni Assn., 1975; Co-op. Edn. Assn. Herman Schneider award, 1977; Bowdoin prize for outstanding service to humanity, 1978; named fellow of Pacific Hawaii Pacific Coll., 1974. Fellow Am. Acad. Arts and Scis.; mem. Pershing Rifles (hon.), Blue Key, Phi Kappa Phi (disting. mem. award 1973), Pi Delta Phi, Kappa Delta Pi (Compatriot in Edn. 1977), Chi Psi (Albert S. Bard award 1964), Alpha Kappa Psi, Alpha Pi Mu (hon.), Beta Gamma Sigma, Tau Beta Pi, Delta Sigma Theta (hon.), Sigma Epsilon Rho (hon.). Republican. Episcopalian. Home: Boston Mass. Died Aug. 8, 1990.

KNOX, JOHN MARSHALL, medical educator; b. Dallas, Apr. 11, 1925; s. John Marshall and Katie (Dickie) K.; m. Lullene Powell, Dec. 18, 1948; children: Lynda Lee, Jane Ann, John Marshall, Byron Powell (dec.). B.S., Tex. A&M U., 1947; M.D., Baylor U., 1949. Diplomate: Am. Bd. Dermatology (dir. 1976-85, pres. 1985, mem. com. for dermatopathology 1980-85, chmn. 1984). Intern New Orleans Charity Hosp., 1949-50; resident Univ. Hosp., Ann Arbor, Mich., 1950, 54-55, U. Okla. Hosp., 1953-54; mem. faculty Baylor U. Coll. Medicine, 1955-81, prof., chmn. dept. dermatology and syphilology, 1963-81; chief dermatology VA Hosp., Houston, 1963-69; cons. VA Hosp., from 1969; chief dermatology Ben Taub Gen. Hosp., Houston, 1963-81, Tex. Children's Hosp., Houston, from 1967; sr. attending physician Meth. Hosp., Houston, 1964-75; chief service Meth. Hosp., 1976-81; mem. staff St. Joseph's Hosp., Houston, from 1981; mem. commn. cutaneous diseases Armed Forces Epidemiol. Bd., 1968-72; chmn., dir. council, dir. Nat. Program for Dermatology, 1969-72; mem. Nat. Commn. Venereal Disease, 1971; tech. counsellor, mem. exec. com. Internat. Union Against Venereal Diseases and the Treponematoses, 1973-80; asst. sec. gen. for N.Am.; mem. council Internat. Union against Venereal Diseases and Treponematoses, 1977-80. Mem. editorial bds. jours. in field.; contbr. numerous articles to profl. jours. Bd. dirs. Dermatology Found., 1972-76. Served as capt., M.C., USAF, 1951-52. Recipient Disting. Alumni award Tex. A&M U., 1971. Mem. Soc. Investigative Dermatology (bd. dirs. 1960-65), Am. Social Health Assn. (bd. dirs. 1962-75), Am. Dermatol. Assn. (bd. dirs. 1980-84), AMA (council rep. to residency rev. com. for dermatology 1974-75), Houston Dermatol. Soc. (pres. 1965-66), Tex. Dermatol. Soc. (v.p. 1965-66, pres. 1982-83), Am. Acad. Dermatology (bd. dirs. 1966-69), Am. Venereal Disease Assn. (pres. 1968-69), So. Med. Assn. (chmn. sect. dermatology 1965-66), South Central Dermatol. Congress (chief exec. officer 1969-71), Assn. Former Students Tex. A&M U. (v.p. 1974-76, pres. 1977), Alpha Omega Alpha. Home: Houston Tex. Died Feb. 28, 1987; buried Meml. Oaks Cemetery, Houston.

KNOX, SEYMOUR H., company director; b. Buffalo, Sept. 1, 1898; s. Seymour Horace and Grace (Millard) K.; m. Helen Northrup, Nov. 20, 1923; children: Seymour Horace III, Northrup. BA, Yale U., 1920. Banker, 1920; v.p. Marine Trust Co., 1927, chmn. bd., 1943-70; dir. Marine Midland Bank N.Y. Trustee Aiken Prep. Sch.,; pres., dir. Buffalo Fine Arts Acad.; chmn N.Y. State Coun. on Arts. Mem. Scroll and Key Soc. Buffalo Country Club, Saturn Club, Buffalo Tennis and Squash Club, Racquet and Tennis Club, River Club Bucks Club, Travellers Club, Delta Kappa Epsilon. Home: Buffalo N.Y. Died Sept. 26, 1990.

KNOX, SEYMOUR HORACE, III, investment banker, professional hockey team executive; b. Buffalo, Mar. 9, 1926; s. Seymour Horace and Helen Elizabeth (Northrup) K.; m. Jean Read, May 15, 1954; children: Seymour H. IV, W.A. Read, Avery F., Helen Edith. B.A., Yale U., 1949. With Marine Midland Bank, N.Y.C., 1949-52; staff Dominick & Dominick, N.Y.C., 1952-54; mgr. Buffalo br. Dominick & Dominick, 1954-56, gen. partner, 1956-64, v.p., 1964-70, regional v.p., 1970-73; v.p. Kidder, Peabody & Co., Inc., Buffalo, from 1973; chmn. bd., pres. Buffalo Sabres Hockey Club: bd. govs. NHL; dir. F.W. Woolworth Co., Pratt & Lambert, Inc.; mem. adv. council Marine Midland Bank, Inc. Bd. dirs., pres. Albright Knox Art Gallery; bd. dirs., v.p. Seymour H. Knox Found., Inc.; bd. dirs. Skillman Assocs. of Yale U.; trustee Buffalo Gen. Hosp.; mem., former chmn., bd. trustees YMCA of Buffalo and Erie County. Served with AUS, 1945-46. Recipient Exec. of Year award Nat. Hockey League, 1975, Outstanding Citizen award Buffalo Evening News, 1970; former nationally ranked squash racquets player singles and doubles; 3-time winner U.S. Ct. Tennis Doubles Championship. Mem. Buffalo C. of C. (bd. dirs.), Smithsonian Assocs. (nat. bd. dirs.), U.S. Squash Racquets Assn. (former pres.), Brook Club, Buffalo Club, Buffalo Tennis and Squash Club, Country Club Buffalo, Crag Burn Club, Mid-Day Club, Racquet and Tennis Club, Downtown Assn., Saturn Club. Home: Buffalo N.Y. Died Sept. 28, 1990. †

KOCH, CARL GALLAND, lawyer; b. Seattle, May 26, 1916; s. Samuel and Cora (Dinkelspiel) K.; m. Joan R. Smith, Nov. 26, 1944 (dec. Apr. 1971); children—Carlyn Joan, Robert B.; m. Joy Jacobs, June 15, 1973; m. Rachel Spack Levenson, Oct. 13, 1985. B.A., U. Wash., 1938, J.D., 1940. Bar: Wash. 1940. Ptnr. Karr, Tuttle, Koch, Campbell, Mawer, Morrow & Sax and predecessors, Seattle, from 1940; lectr. 7th Ann. Tax Forum, U. Puget Sound, 1961. Mem. candidates investigating com. Seattle Municipal League, 1958-70; mem. child study commn. Health and Welfare Council, Seattle, United Good Neighbors, 1951-52; chmn. Seattle chpt. Am. Jewish Com., 1954-55, mem. exec. com., from 1950, mem. Western regional adv. com., from 1964, co-chmn., 1984, mem. nat. exec. bd., from 1966, bd. govs., from 1977, chmn. nat. legal com., 1980-87; v.p. Federated Jewish Fund and Council Seattle, 1964, bd. dirs., 1950-75; mem. regional bd. NCCJ, from 1954; trustee Jewish Publ. Soc. Am., 1971-79. Served to 1st lt. AUS, 1942-46. Life master Am. Contract Bridge League; mem. Am., Wash., Seattle-King County bar assns., Am. Judicature Soc., Seattle Estate Planning Council, Western Pension Conf., Nat. Found. Health, Welfare and Pensions Plans, Zeta Beta Tau (pres. Alpha Mu chpt. 1937-38), Pi Tau (pres. Seattle 1935), Phi Alpha Delta. Clubs: College (Seattle); Glendale Country (Bellevue, Wash.) (pres. 1965, bd. dirs. 1957-60, 63-66). Home: Seattle Wash. Died 1986.

KOEHLER, JOHN THEODORE, lawyer; b. North Braddock, Pa., Mar. 14, 1904; s. William Ernest and Mathilde (Hackbart) K.; m. Eleanor Rust Peirce, 1949; children: JOhn T., Mathilde R., Elizabeth P. AB in Politics with highest honors, Princeton U., 1926; LLB, Harvard U., 1930. Spl. atty. U.S. Dept. Treasury, 1933-34; spl. asst. to atty. gen., 1934-35; tax counsel Md. Casualty Co., Balt., 1935-37; assoc. Semmes, Bowen & Semmes, Balt., 1937-41; counsel Bur. Ships Dept. Navy, 1946, asst. gen. counsel dept., 1947-49, asst. sec., 1949-51; chmn. Fed. Maritime Bd. Maritime Adminstrn., 1950, Renegotiation Bd., 1951-53; ptnr. Hudson, Creyke, Koehler, Brown & Tacke, Washington, 1970-89; dir. Woodward and Lothrop, Washington; lectr. corp. tax problems Practising Law Inst., various banking and ins. execs. assns.; organizer, trainer Navy Underwater Demolition Teams, World War II. Comdr. U.S. Army. Decorated Silver Star, 1944. Mem. ABA, Md. Bar Assn., D.C. Bar Assn., Met. Club, Chevy Chase Country Club, Phi Beta Kappa. Lutheran. Home: Chevy Chase Md. Died Sept. 23, 1989.

KOENIG, VIRGIL, biochemist, educator; b. Kansas City, Mo., Oct. 10, 1913; s. John William and Hilah Ethel (Ward) K.; m. Hildegard Zerne, Feb. 26, 1949; children: LeRoy William, Lawrence Nils, Cynthia Sonsie, Patrick Christopher. A.B., U. Mo.-Kansas City, 1936; M.S., Okla. State U., 1938; Ph.D., U. Colo., 1940; LL.B., LaSalle Extension U., Chgo., 1975; M.A., U. Houston-Clear Lake, 1984. With Armour & Co., Chgo., 1941-48; staff mem. Los Alamos Sci. Lab., 1948-54; prin. scientist VA Research Hosp., Chgo., 1954-56; asst. prof., then asso. prof. biochemistry Northwestern U., 1954-60; prin. scientist Gen. Mills Co., Mpls., 1960-63; prof. biochemistry U. Tex. Med. Br., Galveston, 1963-84; chmn. dept. U. Tex. Med. Br., 1963-71, prof. emeritus, 1984-89; vis. investigator Oak Ridge Nat. Lab., 1972-73. Author papers in field. Trustee, Village of Brookfield, Ill., 1957-60. Mem. Seventh Day Adventist Ch. Home: Texas City Tex. Died June 12, 1989. †

KOERNER, HENRY, painter; b. Vienna, Austria, Aug. 28, 1915; came to U.S., 1939, naturalized, 1944; s. Leo and Fanny Mager K.; m. Joan Frasher, Aug. 15, 1953; children: Stephanie Beth, Joseph Leo. Student, Acad. Applied Art, 1935-37. artist in residence Chatham Coll., 1952-53; vis. artist Calif. Coll Arts, Crafts, summer 1955; resident vis artist Munson-Williams-Procter Inst., 1956-57; instr Art Inst. Pitts. Works exhibited, Berlin, 1947, Midtown Galleries, N.Y.C., 1947, 48, ann exhbn. Whitney Mus., 1947; permanent mem Midtown Galleries group, 1947—; paintings include: Vanity Fair, The Skin of Our Teeth, The Prophet, My Parents, Monkey Bars, A Winter Journey, Life Guard, The Rose Arbor, The Beach, Subway, Fence Between Us, Frozen, Looking, June Night, The Lot, Barber Shop, The Bride, Fire on the Beach, also gouaches and drawings; cover portraits for Time mag. With U.S. Army, 1943-46. Home: Pittsburgh Pa. Died July 4, 1991.

KOGAN, HERMAN, author, consultant; b. Chgo., Nov. 6, 1914; s. Isaac and Ida (Perlman) K.; m. Alice Marie Schutt, Dec. 28, 1940 (div. 1946); m. Marilew Cavanagh Lowry, Oct. 1, 1950; children: Rick, Mark. Student, Crane Jr. Coll., 1932-33; A.B., U. Chgo., 1936, postgrad., 1936; student violin with, Isidor Braus; harmony and composition with, Walter Dellers, 1919-34. High school corr. Chgo. Daily News and Chgo. Eve. Post, 1930-32; reporter, rewrite man Chgo. City News Bur., 1935-37; reporter, feature writer, rewrite man Chgo. Tribune, 1937-42; with Chgo. Sun, 1942-47, editorial writer, 1943; feature writer, book editor, drama critic Chgo. Sun-Times, 1947-58; dir. co. relations Ency. Brit. Inc., 1958-61; asst. to exec. editor Chgo. Daily News, originator and editor Panorama, 1962-65; asst. gen. mgr. for news and newspapers Sta. WFLD-TV Field Communications Corp., 1965-68; editor Chgo. Sun Times Book Week, 1968-70, Chgo. Sun Times Showcase (later Show), 1970-77; historian Field Enterprises, 1977-89; lectr. Medill Sch. Journalism, 1947-49; juror Pulitzer Prize Com., 1970-76; panelist NEH, 1970-75; host Writing and Writers, WFMT, from 1973; cons. Writers in Chgo. Program, 1975-78. Author (with Lloyd Wendt): Lords of the Levee, 1943, Bet A Million, 1948, Give the Lady What She Wants, 1952, Big Bill of Chicago, 1953, Chicago: A Pictorial History, 1959; author (with others): Uncommon Valor, 1947, (with others) Semper Fidelis, 1947; author: The Great EB, 1958, The Long White Line, 1963, Lending is Our Business, 1966, (with Robert Cromie) The Great Fire: Chicago 1871, 1971; A Continuing Marvel, 1973, The First Century, 1974; (with Rick Kogan) Yesterday's Chicago, 1976; Traditions and Challenges, 1983, Proud of the Past...Committed to the Future, 1985; contbr. to: Dictionary Am. Biography, Ency. Brit.; contbr.: articles to Midwest, Chgo. History, Nation, New Republic, Chgo., Fortune, Firehouse, Catholic Digest, others. Served with USMC, 1943-46, PTO. Decorated Presdl. Unit citation; recipient pub. award Geog. Soc. Chgo., contbns. to journalism award Am. Newspaper Guild, Adult Edn. Council award for Panorama, Book Week award Soc. Midland Authors and Friends of Lit., 2 Emmy awards Chgo. chpt. TV Acad. Arts and Scis., Communicator of Yr. award U. Chgo. Alumni Assn. 1972, Vicky Penziner award, Press Vet. of Yr. award Chgo. Press Vets. Assn. 1976, Ann. Disting. Service award Phi Beta Kappa 1976, Chgo. Press Club Hall of Fame. Mem. P.E.N., Art Inst. Chgo. (life), Chgo. Hist. Soc. (life), Authors Guild, Soc. Midland Authors, Friends of Lit., Nat. Book Critics Circle, Phi Beta Kappa, Sigma Delta Chi. Jewish. Clubs: Chgo. Press (past pres.), Arts (Chgo.), Chgo. Headline, Chgo. Press Vets. (past chmn.). Home: New Buffalo Mich. Died Mar. 8, 1989; interred Chgo.

KOGEL, MARCUS DAVID, medical college dean; b. Austria, Sept. 28, 1903; came to U.S., 1913, naturalized, 1914; s. Abraham I. and Rose Jacobowitz K.; m. Fannie Irene Tomson, June 24, 1930 dec. Jan. 1976 ; children: Isobel Pollack, Joan Roskin; m. Dora Rebish, Sept. 29, 1976. Student, CCNY, 1921-22, Columbia U., 1922-23; MD, N.Y. Med Coll., 1927, LHD, 1953. Diplomate Am. Bd. Preventive Medicine. Intern, asst. resident, chief resident physician Met. Hosp., N.Y.C., 1927-29; from dep. med. supt. to med. supt. Cumberland Hosp., Bklyn., 1930-35; med. supt. Queens Gen. Hosp., N.Y.C., 1935-41; gen. med. supt., dir bur. medicine and hosp. svcs. Dept. Hosps., N.Y.C., 1946-49; commr. hosps. N.Y.C., 1949-54; dean Albert Einstein Coll. Medicine, Yeshiva U., 1954-67, dean emeritus, 1967-89, prof., chmn. dept. preventive and environ. medicine, 1954-60, Atran prof. social medicine, 1960-67, dean Sue Golding Grad. Div. Med. Sci., 1957-67; chief med. officer Civil Def., N.Y.C., 1949-53. Bd. dirs. Atran Found. Col. Med. Corps, AUS, 1941-46. Fellow APHA, N.Y. Acad. Medicine, Am. Acad. Preventive Medicine. Home: Croton on Hudson N.Y. Died Nov. 28, 1989.

KOGLER, JAMES FOLEY, lawyer, philosophy educator; b. Buffalo, Oct. 18, 1939; s. Carl Joseph and Clara Veronica (Foley) K.; m. Susan Ruth McAvoy, Mar. 24, 1972; children: James Edward, Alexandra Clare. B.A. magna cum laude, Niagara U., 1961; S.T.B. magna cum laude, Gregorian U., 1963, S.T.L. magna cum laude, 1965; J.D. cum laude, SUNY-Buffalo, 1974. Bar: N.Y. 1975, U.S. Dist. Ct. (we. dist.) N.Y. 1975, U.S. Ct. Appeals (2d cir.) 1983; ordained priest Roman Catholic Ch., 1964; priest Diocese of Buffalo, 1964-70, laicized, 1970; prof. philosophy Rockhurst Coll., Kansas City, Mo., 1970-71; mem. firm Mattar, D'Agostino et al, Buffalo, 1974-77, ptnr. Mattar, D'Agostino, Kogler, and Runfola, Buffalo, 1977-87; adj. prof. Canisius Coll., Buffalo, part time from 1974; lectr., U.S.A., Can., Europe. panel of arbitrators Am. Arbitration Assn., Syracuse, N.Y., from 1978; mem. instl. rev. bd. Sch. Medicine, SUNY-Buffalo, from 1980; mem. adv. rehab. bd. Buffalo Psychiat. Ctr., from 1982. Contbr. ethics, philosophy and legal articles to various publs., 1967-83. Mem. ABA, N.Y. State Bar Assn., Am. Philos. Soc., Cath. Theol. Soc., Erie County Bar Assn., N.Y. State Trial Lawyers Assn., Thomas More Guild (pres. 1983-84), Young Lawyers Club. Democrat. Died Jan. 5, 1987; buried St. Francis Cemetery, Buffalo. Home: Buffalo N.Y.

KOHLER, FOY DAVID, ambassador, educator; b. Oakwood, Ohio, Feb. 15, 1908; s. Leander David and Myrtle (McClure) K.; m. Phyllis Penn, Aug. 7, 1935. Student, Toledo U., 1924-27, LL.D., 1964; B.S., Ohio State U., 1931, L.H.D., 1962; LL.D., U. Akron, 1967, Findlay Coll, 1967. Fgn. service officer, from 1931; vice consul Windsor, Ont., Can., 1932, Bucharest, Rumania, 1933-35, Belgrade, 1935; legation sec. and vice consul Bucharest, 1935-36, Athens, Greece, 1936-41, Cairo, Egypt, 1941; country specialist Dept. State, Washington, 1941-44; asst. chief. div. of Near Eastern Affairs, 1944-45; with Am. embassy, London, 1944; polit. and liaison officer U.S. del. UN Conf. on Internat. Orgn., San Francisco, 1945; sec. gen. U.S. Mission to Observe Greek Elections, 1945-46; spl. studies Cornell U., 1946; student Nat. War Coll., 1946; 1st sec. Am. Embassy, Moscow, Jan. 1947, counsellor, June 1948, minister plenipotentiary, 1948; chief Internat. Broadcasting Div., Dept. State, 1949; dir. Voice of Am. broadcasts, 1949; asst. adminstr. Internat. Information Adminstrn., Feb. 1952; policy planning staff Dept. State, 1952; counselor of embassy Ankara, Turkey, 1953-56; detailed to ICA, 1956-58; dep. asst. sec. of state for European affairs, 1958-59, asst. sec. state for European affairs, 1959-62; ambassador to USSR, 1962-66; dep. under sec. of state for polit. affairs Dept. State, 1966-67; adj. prof. Center Advanced Internat. Studies U. Miami, 1978-82; sr. assoc. Advanced Internat. Studies Inst., Washington, 1978-85; cons. Dept. State, 1968-82; Mem. Bd. for Internat. Broadcasting, 1974-78, cons., 1978-82. Author: Understanding the Russians: A Citizens' Primer, 1970; co-author: Science and Technology as an Instrument of Soviet Policy, 1972, Soviet Strategy for the Seventies: From Cold War to Peaceful Coexistence, Convergence of Communism and Capitalism: The Soviet View, 1973, The Role of Nuclear Forces in Current Soviet Strategy, The Soviet Union and the 1973 Middle East War: The Implications for Detente, 1974, The Soviet Union: Yesterday, Today, Tomorrow, 1975; author: foreword to Custine's Eternal Russia, 1976, SALT II: How Not to Negotiate with the Russians, 1979; co-editor: monthly Soviet World Outlook, 1976-85. Mem. Phi Beta Kappa, Beta Gamma Sigma, Delta Upsilon. Home: Juno Beach Fla. Died Dec. 23, 1990.

KOHN, CLYDE FREDERICK, geographer, educator; b. Mohawk, Mich., Apr. 10, 1911; s. George Ferdinand and Cora Frances (Saam) K.; m. Doris Venton Merker, Jan. 17, 1942; children—Susan, George. A.B., No. Mich. U., 1936; A.M., U. Mich., 1936, Ph.D., 1940. Tchr. rural sch. Marquette County, Mich., 1929-30; pub. schs. Gwinn, Mich., 1930-34, Miss. State Coll. for Women, Columbus, 1940-42; instr., lectr. Harvard U., 1942-45; asst. prof. geography and edn. Northwestern U., 1945-47, assoc. prof., 1947-58; prof. geography U. Iowa, 1958-80, dept. chmn., 1966-77; cons. author Scott, Foresman & Co.; wine writer Ft. Lauderdale News/Sun Sentinel, 1985-89. Author: Cross Country, 1951; co-author: City Town and Country, 1959, In All Our States, 1960, In The Americas, 1962, Beyond The Americas, 1964, Family Studies, 1970, Local Studies, 1970, Metropolitan Studies, 1970, Regional Studies, 1970, United States and Canada, 1970, Inter-American Studies, 1970, McGraw-Hill Book. Pub. The World Today, also profl. papers in geographic and ednl. jours.; Editor: 19th yearbook of Nat. Council Social Studies, Pacesetter Series, Nat. Council Geog. Edn, 1978-82; co-editor: Readings in Urban Geography, 1959. Mem. U.S. Nat. Commn. for UNESCO, 1960-66. Mem. Assn. Am. Geographers (pres. 1967-68), Nat. Council Geographic Edn. (pres. 1951-53), Phi Beta Kappa, Phi Kappa Phi, Kappa Delta Pi, Phi Gamma Delta. Episcopalian. Home: Fort Lauderdale Fla. Died Nov. 22, 1989; cremated.

KOHN, MARTIN BENNE, department store executive; b. Balt., Aug. 28, 1898; s. Benno and Clara (Strauss) K.; m. Rosa Rosenthal, Aug. 14, 1925; children: Eleanor C., Elizabeth (Mrs. M. Peter Moser). BA, Johns Hopkins U., 1918. With Hochschild, Kohn & Co., Balt., from 1923, pres., 1945-65, chmn. bd., from 1965; pres. Frederick Atkins, Inc., N.Y.C., 1948-51; bd. dirs. Md. Trust Co., Md. Nat. Bank, Balt. Vice chmn. Lexington Market Commn., Balt., 1953-64; mem. Md. Commn. Govtl. Efficiency and Economy, 1948-51; pres. Jewish Welfare Fedn., Balt., 1943-45; bd. dirs. Md. Tb Assn., 1932-51; bd. dirs. Balt. Symphony, 1943-64, v.p., 1947-48, 49-50; bd. dirs. Children's Rehab. Inst., Balt., Assoc. Jewish Charities, Balt. With U.S. Army, 1917-19. Mem. Nat. Retail Mchts. Assn. (chmn. exec. com. from 1964), Balt. Assn. Commerce (pres. 1958-60). *

KOLLER, CHARLES WILLIAM, clergyman, educator; b. Waco, Tex., Mar. 11, 1896; s. John U. and Mary (Holst) K.; m. Selma Steinhaus, Sept. 9, 1924; children: Carolyn Marie, Evelyn Jean. AB, Baylor U., 1923; ThM, Southwestern Bapt. Theol. Sem., 1926, ThD, 1935; student, Drew Sem., 1931-32; DD, Eastern Bapt. Theol. Sem., 1944; LLD (hon.), Baylor U., 1955; DD, Northern Bapt. Theol. Sem., 1962. Ordained to ministry Bapt. Ch., 1922. Pvt. sec., later acct. and adminstr. of real estate Waco, 1912-20; held part-time pastorates Wellborn, Riesel, Hallsburg and Morgan, Tex.; pastor Clinton Hill Bapt. Ch., Newark, 1927-38; pres. No. Bapt. Theol. Sem., Chgo., 1938-62, emeritus, from 1962; dir. Chgo. Bapt. Assn., 1938-60; bd. mgrs. N.J. Bapt. Conv., 1936-37; dir. Chgo. Bible Soc., from 1939; mem. gen. coun. No. Bapt. Conv., 1941-48; mem. commn. on the ministry Am. Bapt. Conv., 1955-60. Author: Tents Toward the Sunrise; Expository Preaching Without Notes; The Living Plus Sign; Sermons Preached Without Notes; contbr. articles to religious jours. Served with U.S. Army, 1918-19. Mem. Am. Bapt. Fgn. Mission Soc. (bd. mgrs. 1952-61). *

KOLSKY, HERBERT, physics educator; b. London, Eng., Sept. 22, 1916; came to U.S., 1960; s. Suskind and Deborah (Halber) K.; m. Mary Grant Morton, Dec. 15, 1945; children: David John, Peter Jonathan, Allan Benjamin. B.Sc., Imperial Coll. Sci. and Tech., London, 1937, Ph.D., 1940; D.Sc., U. London, 1957; MA (hon.), Brown U., 1962; D.Sc. (hon.), ETH Zurich, 1984. Head physics dept. Akers Research Labs., Imperial Chem. Industries, Welwyn, Eng., 1946-55; sr. prin. sci. officer Ministry Supply, Eng., 1958-60; vis. prof. engring. Brown U., 1956-57, prof. applied physics, 1961-83; vis. prof. Imperial Coll., 1968, M.E.T.U., Ankara, Turkey, 1968, Oxford (Eng.) U., 1974, E.T.H., Zurich; Springer prof. U. Calif. Berkeley, 1978. Author: Stress Waves in Solids, 1953; editor: (with W. Prager) Stress Waves in Anelastic Solids, 1964; developer split-Hopkinson device. Fulbright scholar, 1956-58; recipient Worcester Reed Warner medal ASME, 1982. Fellow Inst. Physics, Am. Acad. Mechanics, Acoustical Soc.; mem. Brit. Soc. Rheology (past pres.), ASME, Sigma Xi. Club: University (Providence). Home: Providence R.I. Died May 9, 1992.

KOLTERJAHN, PAUL HENRY, banker, consultant; b. Hackensack, N.J., May 2, 1924; s. Paul Henry and Ida Linnea (Nelson) K.; m. Marilyn Jean Hammer, Sept. 3, 1949; children: Paul Howard, Donald Scott. B.B.A., Westminster Coll., 1949; postgrad. Progam for Mgmt. Devel., Harvard U., 1961. Asst. cashier Citibank, N.A., N.Y.C., 1949-59, v.p. R&D, 1959-66, v.p. met. div. ops., 1966-70, sr. v.p. N.Y. banking, 1970-83, dir., 1983-86; sr. v.p. sec. Citicorp, N.Y.C., 1983-87, cons., 1992; chmn. Citiflight, 1984-87. Trustee Westminster Coll., New Wilmington, Pa.; pres. bd. trustees Westfield Meml. Library, N.J. Served to capt. U.S. Army, 1942-46; ETO. Republican. Presbyn. Club: Latrobe Country, Pa. Home: Westfield N.J. Died Jan. 21, 1992. †

KONARSKI, FELIKS (REF-REN), author, actor, poet, songwriter; b. Kiev, Russia, Jan. 9, 1907; (parents of Polish nationality); s. Feliks Konarski and Wiktoria (Polecka) Konarska; m. Nina Olenska, Jan. 31, 1931 (dec. Jan. 1983). BA, U. Warsaw, Poland, 1928. Contbg. songwriter Qui Pro Quo Theater, Nowosci Theater, Warsaw, 1926-30; dir. Ref-Ren Theater, Warsaw, 1930-40; dir., pub. affairs officer Theater of 2d Polish Corps, Iraq, Iran, Palestine, Egypt, Italy, 1941-46; dir. Ref-Ren Polish Theater, London, 1947-65, Chgo., 1966-91; cons. Polish Nat. Alliance, Chgo., 1983-91. Guest author Polish Radio, Paris, 1952; contbg. author Radio Free Europe, Munich, 1960; adj. instr. Alliance Coll., Cambridge Springs, Pa., summers 1958-63; dir. Red Poppies Polish Radio Program, Chgo., from 1962; author: (books) Songs from Ellen's Knapsack (Piosenki z plecaka Helenki), 1952, Love in my Life (Milosc w moim zyciu), 1967, Elastic Faces (Twarze z gutaperki), 1978, (poetry) Poems Written by the Heart (Wiersze sercem pisane) vol. 1, 1972, 2d edit., 1988, vol. 2, 1992; also writer, composer numerous songs, musical comedies, and stage revues. Decorated Order of Merit, 1st and 3d class (Polish Govt.-in-Exile, London), Polonia Restituta Order; recipient Vets. Cross 1st class Polish Vets. Assn., Toronto, Ont., Can., 1967, Spl. Cultural award Polish Am. Congress, Chgo., 1982, Ariz. div., 1989. Mem. Union Polish Actors Abroad (hon. pres. 1962-91). Home: Chicago Ill. Died Sept. 12, 1991; buried Maryhill Cemetery, Niles, Ill.

KONOPINSKI, EMIL JAN, physicist; b. Michigan City, Ind., Dec. 25, 1911; s. Joseph and Sophia (Sniegowski) K. BA, U. Mich., 1933, MA, 1934, PhD, 1936. Nat. Rsch. fellow Cornell U., 1936-38; prof. physics Ind. U., 1938, Disting. Svc. prof. physics; mem. rsch. staff AEC Labs., Chgo., 1941, Berkeley, Calif., 1942, Los Alamos, Calif., 1943-46; cons. AEC, 1946-90. Contbr. articles to profl. jours.; mem. bd. editors: Phys. Rev., 1946-49. Active fellowship bd. Nat. Rsch. Coun., 1951. Guggenheim fellow, 1950. Mem. Am. Phys. Soc., Phi Beta Kappa. Home: Bloomington Ind. Died May 26, 1990; cremated.

KOOTZ, SAMUEL M(ELVIN), art dealer; b. Portsmouth, Va., Aug. 23, 1898; s. Louis and Ann (Persky) K.; m. Jane Ogden, Sept. 25, 1937. LLB, U. Va., 1921. Owner Kootz Gallery, specializing in modern Am. and European art, N.Y.C., from 1944. Author: Modern American Painters, 1928; New Frontiers in American Painting, 1944; Puzzle in Paint, 1943; Puzzle in Petticoats, 1944; (play) Home is the Hunter, 1946. *

KOPPES, WAYNE FARLAND, retired architectural consultant and writer; b. Sullivan, Ohio, July 11, 1902; s. Charles William and Mary Ellen (Scheib) K.; m. Alice L. Nelson, Sept. 25, 1926; children: Alan W., Donald L., David N. A.B. in Architecture, Carnegie Inst. Tech., 1925; M.Arch., MIT, 1929; diploma, Ecole des Beaux Arts, Fontainbleau, France, 1925. Archtl. designer Walker & Weeks, Cleve., 1926-32; from instr. to prof. archtl. constrn. Sch. Architecture, Rensselaer Poly. Inst., 1932-45, adj. prof. bldg. research, 1959-70; asso. Cutting & Ciresi, Cleve., 1945-47; head dept. archtl. design and housing research John B. Pierce Found., Raritan, N.J., 1947-53; chief research architect SW Research Inst., Princeton, N.J., 1953-55; archtl. cons. Basking Ridge, N.J., 1955-79; tech. dir. Nat. Assn. Archtl. Metal Mfrs., 1962-68. Author or co-author: New Spaces for Learning, 1966, Educational Facilities with New Media, 1965, Aluminum Curtain Walls, periodical, 1970-73; author-editor: Metal Curtain Wall Manual, 1961, Metal Finishes Manual, 1969, Metal Stair Manual, 1971, Metal Bar Grating Manual, 1974, Pipe Railing Manual, 1977, Hollow Metal Manual, 1977; co-author: Metal Flagpole Manual, 1981; also numerous rsch. and tech. reports. Mem. Bd. Edn., Bernards Twp., N.J., 1952-55; mem. Planning Bd., 1968-77. Fellow AIA, Am. Soc. Testing and Materials (award merit 1971, Walter Voss award 1976); mem. N.J. Soc. Architects. Home: Jamesburg N.J. Deceased. †

KORÉE, JEAN ULYXES, industrial engineer; b. Bucharest, Roumania, Mar. 12, 1894; came to U.S., 1919, naturalized, 1943; m. Helen Moycah Brandow, Aug. 25, 1922; 1 dau., Moycah Bronson (Mrs. Antonio Poggi Cavaletti). Ed. pvt. tutors, Bucharest and Berlin. Vice consul of Roumania, N.Y.C., 1919, consul, 1920, dep. high commr., 1921; pres. Glycerine Corp. Am., Devel. Fin. Corp. Inventor numerous improvements on automatic firearms, airplanes, airplane equipment, other mech. devices; more recently invented and patented therapeutic preparations for intramuscular or subcutaneous injection and methods of making same. Pres. Jacques Loewe Rsch. Found., 1945-59; co-founder Soc. of Friends of Roumania; founder Mus. of City of N.Y. Decorated Knight Crown of Roumania, Knight Grand Cross of Charlemagne, Knight Grand Cross of St. Constantin and St. George, Knight Grand Cross of the Holy Sepulchre; officer Carlos J. Finlay Nat. Order Merit (Cuba); mem. Order of Red Cross of Constantine. Fellow N.Y. Acad. Scis.; mem. Acad. Polit. Sci., Nat. Inst. Social Scis. (life), Pan-Am. Soc. of U.S., Pilgrims of United States, Cuban C. of C. (life), Church Club, Met. Club, Am. Club of Havana, Masons. *

KOREY, LOIS BALK, advertising executive; b. N.Y.C., May 19, 1933; d. Samuel and Lillian (Rosenblatt) Balk; m. Stanton Korey, Jan. 12, 1958 (div.); children—Susan, Christopher. Jr. partner Jack Tinker & Partners Advt. Co., N.Y.C., 1964-66; jr. partner, copywriter McCann Erickson Advt. Co., N.Y.C., 1967-69; creative dir. Revlon, N.Y.C., 1972; exec. v.p., creative dir. Needham, Harper & Steers Advt., Inc., N.Y.C., 1973-82; pres. Korey, Kay & Ptnrs., Advt., N.Y.C., 1982-90. Writer: TV shows including Sunday Night Comedy Hour, Ernie Kovacs Show, Andy Griffith Show, Steve Allen Tonight Show, George Gobel Show, Wide Wide World; (Recipient 18 Clios, Am. TV Comml. Festivals: 16 Andys, Advt. Club N.Y., Cannes Film Festival TV Comml. award 1973, 10 Hollywood Film Festival awards.); contbr. articles to mags. and profl. jours. Mem. NATAS, Writers Guild Am., Dramatists Guild. Home: New York N.Y. Died Aug. 9, 1990.

KORFF, SERGE ALEXANDER, educator, physicist; b. Helsingfors, Finland, June 5, 1906; came to U.S., 1917; s. Baron Serge A. and Alletta (Van Reypen) K.; m. Marcella Brett. A.B., Princeton U., 1928, A.M., 1929, Ph.D., 1931. Nat. Research fellow Mt. Wilson Obs. and Calif. Inst. Tech., 1931-33; research fellow Calif. Inst. Tech., 1934-35; fellow Bartol Research Found., Swarthmore, Pa., 1937-40; research asso. Carnegie Instn., Washington, 1936-46, U. P.R., 1949-50; asst. prof. physics NYU, 1941-44, asso. prof., 1944-46, prof., 1946-72, prof. emeritus, 1973-89; nat. lectr. Sigma Xi, 1957; hon. prof. in cosmic radiation Universidad de San Andres, Bolivia, 1958; cons. UN, AEC, 1950-53; sr. sci. adviser atomic energy div. UN, 1953-55; leader cosmic ray expdn., Mexico and Peru, 1934-36, P.R., 1948-50; asso. astronomer Eclipse expdn., Peru, 1937; adviser U.S. Antarctic Service expdn., 1939-41; wartime supr. physics research NYU; del. 5th S.Am. Congress of Chemistry, Lima, Peru, 1951, 6th Congress Chemistry, Caracas, Venezuela, 1955; vice chmn. Cosmic Ray Tech. Panel, U.S. Nat. Commn. for Internat. Geophys. Year, also U.S. del. to meetings, Rome, 1954, Mexico, 1955, Rio de Janeiro, 1956; mem. IUBS Com. on High Altitude Research Stas. and editor of reports. Author: Electron and Nuclear Counters, 1945, (with J.B. Hoag) Electron and Nuclear Physics, 1947; also numerous articles in tech. jours.; editorial bd.: Rev. Sci. Instruments, 1945-51, Explorers Jour., from 1946. Trustee, Embry-Riddle Aero. U., from 1975. Recipient OSRD citation; decorated chevalier Legion of Honor, 1952; commendatore Order of Cyprus and Jerusalem, 1952; hon. mem. faculty U. Chile, 1951; recipient Pregel prize N.Y. Acad. Scis., 1955; Curie medal Union Internat. Contre le Cancer, 1957; decorated comdr. Order of Merit for Research, 1957, grand officer, 1966; comdr. Order of St. Denis, 1968. Fellow Am. Phys. Soc., Royal Geog. Soc. (life), N.Y. Acad. Scis. (life; v.p. 1948-49, pres. 1972), AAAS (life), Am. Geog. Soc. (council, pres. 1967-71, chmn. council from 1972); mem. Lima Geog. Soc. (hon.), Am. Astron. Soc., Peruvian Chem. Soc. (corr.), Am. Geophys. Union (life), World Acad. Art and Scis. (pres. Am. div. from 1977), Explorers Club (pres. 1955-58, dir.), Phi Beta Kappa, Sigma Xi (pres., v.p. NYU chpt. 1946-50), Sigma Pi Sigma (hon. mem.). Clubs: Princeton (N.Y.C.), Century Assn. (N.Y.C.); Cosmos (Washington). Home: New York N.Y. Died Dec. 1, 1989.

KORN, JOHN CARSTEN, stock broker; b. N.Y.C., Sept. 12, 1897; s. John P. and Marie (Sudmann) K.; m. Eve K. Schumacher, Sept. 11, 1927; children: Audrey, Dorothy. Student, The Kimball Sch., N.Y.C., 1912-14. With Pitts. Plate Glass, N.Y.C., 1914-18; various positions N.Y. Stock Exch., 1918-40, sec., 1940-50, mem., from 1950; ptnr. Bioren & Co. Author: (family history) Echoes of Wooden Shoes, 1948. Bd. dirs. YMCA, Rutherford, N.J., Rutherford Bd. Edn., 1943-46; bd. dirs. Luth. Soc. N.Y., pres., 1930; mem. various bds. and commns. United Luth. Ch. in Am., 1938-62, mem. exec. coun., from 1962. Mem. Nat. Arbitration Assn. (nat. panel arbitrators), Masons. Republican. *

KORNBLITH, JOHN HOWARD, business executive; b. Chgo., Oct. 30, 1924; s. Howard and Babette (Straus) K.; m. Ina Jean Russell, June 8, 1944 (div. 1972); children: Cathy R., Gary J., Polly R.; m. 2d Dorothy Weber, Oct 13, 1972; 1 stepdau., Lisa Goldstein Kaminir. BS, U. Chgo., 1947, MBA, 1948; LHD (hon.), CUNY, 1988. Advt. mgr. Eversharp Inc., Chgo., 1948-50; pres. Cricketeer Inc., Chgo., 1950-58; exec. v.p. Joseph & Feiss, Cleve., 1958-61; pres. Fashion Park Inc., Rochester, N.Y., 1961-67; chmn., pres. Intercontinental Apparel Inc., N.Y.C., 1967-83, Twenty-First Century Corp., Englewood, N.J., 1959-92. Bd. dirs. Inst. for Responsive Edn., Boston; bd. visitors, former chmn., mem. exec. com. Grad. Sch. CUNY, N.Y.C.; mem. bus. coun. U. Chgo; bd. dirs. N.Y. Assn. Blind, N.Y.C., Lighthouse Industries, N.Y.C.; trustee Project Return Found., N.Y.C., Phipps Community Devel. Corp.; v.p., dir., mem. exec. com. Children's Oncology Soc. N.Y.; chmn. Ronald McDonald Children's Charities of N.Y. 1st lt. USAF, 1943-46. Recipient Pres.'s medal Grad. Sch. U. Ctr. of CUNY, 1977, Human Rels. award Am. Jewish Com., 1977, Ann. Achievement award Textile Vets. Assn., 1983. Mem. Coun. for Competitive Economy, Beta Gamma Sigma. Jewish. Clubs: N.Y. Athletic (N.Y.C.); East Hampton Tennis (N.Y.). Home: New York N.Y. Died July 27, 1992. †

KORSON, SELIG MORLEY, physician, medical educator, hospital administrator; b. Bklyn., Nov. 28, 1910; s. Joseph and Rose (Lieb) K.; m. Beatrice Gunner Goldman, Nov. 30, 1941; children—Eileen, Jane, Cathy. A.B., Cornell U., 1932; M.D., Eclectic Med. Coll., 1936. Diplomate: Am. Bd. Psychiatry and Neurology. Intern Mercy Hosp., Wilkes-Barre, Pa., 1936-37; gen. practice medicine Wilkes-Barre, 1937-42; asst. physician Grafton (Mass.) State Hosp., 1946, sr. physician, 1947, asst. supt., 1948; chief grade psychiatrist VA Hosp., Northampton, Mass., 1949-55, Bay Pines, Fla., 1955-58; supt. Mental Health Inst., Independence, Iowa, 1958-78; asst. clin. prof. psychiatry U. Iowa Med. Sch., 1971-88; chmn. Iowa Eugenics Bd. Contbr. articles on neurosis, psychiat. therapy and metabolism to med. jours. Pres. Buchanan County United Fund, 1963. Served to maj. AUS, 1942-46. Fellow Am. Psychiat. Assn. (certified mental hosp. adminstr., mem. task force in liaison with A.I.A. 1969-70, mem. assembly of dist. brs. 1975-88), Am. Geriatric Soc.; mem. Iowa Psychiat. Soc. (mem. exec. com., past pres.), Buchanan County Med. Soc. (past pres.), Iowa Mental Health Assn. (profl. adv. bd.), Iowa Med. Soc., AMA, Am. Assn. Med. Psychiat. Adminstrs. (sec. 1975-88), Am. Legion., B'nai B'rith. Jewish. Lodges: Masons, Shriners, Rotary (past pres.). Home: Peoria Ariz. Died Aug. 26, 1988; buried Sun City, Ariz.

KOSINSKI, JERZY NIKODEM, writer; b. Lodz, Poland, June 14, 1933; came to U.S., 1957, naturalized, 1965; s. Mieczyslaw and Elzbieta (Liniecka) K.; m. Mary H. Weir, Jan. 11, 1962 (dec. 1968); m. Katherina von Fraunhofer, Feb. 15, 1987. MA in Sociology and History, U. Lodz, 1953, MA in History, 1955; postgrad., Columbia U., 1958-65; LHD (hon.), Albion Coll., 1988, SUNY, 1989; PhD in Hebrew Letters (hon.), Spertus Coll. Judaica, 1982. Asst. prof. Inst. Sociology and Cultural History, Polish Acad. Scis., Warsaw, 1955-57; Guggenheim Lit. fellow, 1967; fellow Ctr. Advanced Studies, Wesleyan U., 1968-69; sr. fellow Coun. Humanities; vis. lectr. English Princeton U., 1969-70; vis. prof. English prose Yale U. Sch. Drama; also resident fellow Davenport Coll., 1970-73; fellow Timothy Dwight Coll. Yale U., from 1986. Author: (pseudonym Joseph Novak): The Future is Ours, Comrade, 1960, No Third Path, 1962, (novels) The Painted Bird, 1965 (Best Fgn. book award France), Steps, 1968 (Nat. Book award), Being There, 1971, screenplay, 1978; The Devil Tree, 1973, rev. edit., 1981, Cockpit, 1975, Blind Date, 1977, Passion Play, 1979, screenplay, 1987, Pinball, 1982, The Hermit of 69th Street, 1988, Passing By, Essays 1960-1991, 1992; actor in movie Reds. Hon. chmn. bd. Found. for Polish-Jewish Studies, 1987-91; pres., founder Jewish Presence Found., 1988; co-chmn. Found. for Ethnic Understanding, 1989-91; chmn. bd. Polish Am. Resources Corp., from 1988. Recipient award in Lit. Am. Acad. Arts and Letters, 1970, Brith Sholom Humanitarian Freedom award, 1974, Best Screenplay of Yr. award for Being There, Writers Guild Am., 1979, Best Screenplay of Yr. award, Brit. Acad. Film and TV Arts, 1981, Polonia Media Perspectives award, 1980, Internat. award Spertus Coll. Judaica, 1982, Harry Edmonds Life Achievement award Internat. House, 1990; Ford Found. fellow, 1958-60. Mem. PEN (exec. bd., pres. 1973-75), Nat. Writers Club (exec. bd.), Internat. League for Human Rights (dir.), ACLU (chmn. artists and writers com., mem. nat. adv. council, First Amendment award 1980), Authors Guild, Century Assn. Home: New York N.Y. Died May 3, 1991.

KOSKOFF, THEODORE IRVING, lawyer; b. New Haven, June 23, 1913; s. Israel and Hattie (Taks) K.; m. Dorothy Fuchs, Feb. 21, 1937; chidren: Susan Glazer, Michael P., Elizabeth. Student Wesleyan U.; LLB, Boston U., 1936; LLD (hon.), Suffolk U., 1980. Bar: Conn. 1937, U.S. Dist. Ct. Conn. 1949, U.S. Ct. Appeals (2d cir.) 1963, U.S. Supreme Ct. 1972. Sole practice, Bridgeport, Conn., 1937-74; sr. ptnr., chmn. bd. Koskoff, Koskoff & Bieder, P.C., 1974-89. Contbr. articles to profl. law jours. Theodore I. Koskoff fellow U. Bridgeport, 1985. Founder Roscoe Pound-Am. Trial Lawyers Found. Mem. Nat. Bd. Trial Advocacy (founder, chmn.), Nat. Assn. Criminal Def. Lawyers, Internat. Soc. Barristers, Assn. Trial Lawyers Am. (past pres.), Conn. Bar Assn., Conn. Trial Lawyers Assn., Bridgeport Bar Assn. Died Mar. 13, 1989. Home: Westport Conn.

KOSSA, FRANK RAYMOND, army officer; b. Schulenberg, Tex., Nov. 1, 1897; s. John F. and Amelia (Klecka) K.; m. Grace L. Lindley, Oct. 3, 1925; 1 son, David L. Brubeck. BA, U. Louisville, 1936. With U.S. Govt., 1919-27; engaged in bus., 1927-42; served with U.S. Army, 1917-19, rejoined, 1942-46, advanced through grades to col., 1963; dir. SSS, Ind., 1948-57; with nat. hdqrs. SSS, from 1957, asst. to dir., from 1961; chmn. bd. Lindley Realty Co., Jeffersonville, Ind., from 1948. Mem. Def. Supply Assn., Mil. Order World Wars, Heroes of '76, World War I Vets. Assn., 40 and 8, Am. Legion (past comdr. Ind., vice chmn. security commn. from 1946), VFW, AMVETS, DAV, Regular Vets. Assn., Res. Officers Assn. (com. staff asst.), Army, Navy and Air Force Vets. Can. (sec.-treas. U.S. unit), Army Assn., Jeffersonville C. of C., Lions, Elks, Masons, Shriners. Republican. *

KOTCHER, EZRA, aeronautical engineer; b. N.Y.C., Sept. 19, 1903; s. Samuel and Sima Riva (Katz) K.; m. Etta Jean Horwitz, June 18, 1929; children: Nina Kotcher Aoni, Linda Ann. BA, U. Calif., Berkeley, 1928; MS in Aero. Engring., U. Mich., 1937. From instr. higher math. to sr. prof. aeros. Air Corps Engring. Sch., Wright Field, Ohio, 1928-41; sr. aero. engr. Air Materiel Command, 1942; 1st dir. USAF Inst. Tech., 1946-51; tech. dir. Directorate Labs., Wright Air Devel. Div., Wright-Patterson AFB, Ohio, 1951-60; dir. area office Aerospace Corp., El Segundo, Calif., 1961-64; aerospace cons., Oakland, Calif., 1064-90; USAF mem. NACA Spl. Com. on Self-Propelled Guided Missiles and Turbine and Jet Propulsion, 1942-46; mem. rsch. adv. com. aircraft aerodyns. NASA, from 1959. Pioneer conception and direction of X series of rocket-powered rsch. aircraft which first penetrated sonic barrier. With USAAF, 1942-46, USAF, 1951-53, col. Res. Recipient career award Nat. Civil Svc. League, 1956, Disting. Civilian Svc. award Dept. Def., 1959. Fellow AIAA; mem. Jet Pioneer Assn. (disting.), Tau Beta Pi. Home: Oakland Calif. Died Nov. 8, 1990; buried Presidio Nat. Cemetery, San Francisco, Calif.

KOTTLER, HOWARD WILLIAM, artist, educator; b. Cleve., Mar. 5, 1930; s. Paul L. and Nellie (Novick) K. B.A., Ohio State U., 1952, M.A., 1956, Ph.D., 1964; M.F.A., Cranbrook Acad. Art, 1957. Instr. art Ohio State U., 1961-64; vis. asst. prof. art U. Wash., Seattle, 1964-65; asst. prof. U. Wash., 1965-67, asso. prof., 1967-72, prof., 1972-89. One-man exhbns. include, Mus. Contemporary Crafts, N.Y.C., 1967, Nordness Galleries, N.Y.C., 1969, Meml. Art Gallery, Rochester, N.Y., 1975, Tacoma Art Mus., 1976, 79, Bellevue Art Mus., 1987, Rena Branstein Gallery, San Francisco, 1987; represented in permanent collections, Victoria and Albert Mus., London, Nat. Mus. Modern Art, Kyoto, Japan, Detroit Inst. Art, Cleve. Mus. Art, Cooper-Hewitt Mus., Am. Craft. Mus., N.Y.C. Fulbright grantee, 1957; Nat. Endowment Arts grantee, 1975. Mem. Am. Crafts Council. Home: Mercer Island Wash. Died Jan. 24, 1989.

KOUWENHOVEN, JOHN ATLEE, English language educator, writer, magazine editor; b. Yonkers, N.Y., 1909; s. John Bennem and Grace (Atlee) K.; m. Eleanor

W. Hayden, June 22, 1935 (div. 1959); children: Ann (dec.), Gerrit Wolphertsen; m. Joan Vatsek Arthur, June 12, 1960. A.B., Wesleyan U., Middletown, Conn., 1931; A.M., Columbia U., 1933, Ph.D., 1948. Master in English, Harvey Sch., Hawthorne, N.Y., 1932-36; instr. English, Columbia U., 1936-38; mem. lit. faculty Bennington (Vt.) Coll., 1938-41; asst. editor Harper's mag., 1941-44, assoc. editor, 1944-46, contbg. editor, 1946-54; assoc. English and Am. studies Barnard Coll., Columbia U., 1946-48, assoc. prof. English, 1948-50, prof., 1950-75, prof. emeritus, 1975-90, chmn. dept., 1950-54; dir. hist. files Brown Bros. Harriman & Co., 1964-68; mem. vis. com. Costume Inst., Met. Mus. Art, 1971-72; mem. adv. com. Archives Am. Art, 1967-86, Hist. Commn. N.Y.C. Bicentennial Com., 1972-74; hist. advisor Children's TV Workshop, 1975-77. Actor: TV series The Best of Families, 1976; Author: Adventures of America 1857-1900, 1938, Made in America: The Arts in Modern Civilization, 1948, The Columbia Historical Portrait of New York, 1953, The Beer Can by the Highway, 1961, Partners in Banking, 1968, Half a Truth is Better than None, 1982; also articles in profl. jours. and popular mags.; co-author: Creating an Industrial Civilization, 1952, American Panorama, 1957, American Studies in Transition, 1965, The Shaping of Art and Architecture in 19th Century America, 1972, The Arts in a Democratic Society, 1977, Technology in America, 1981; editor: (with Janice Thaddeus) When Women Look at Men, 1963, New York Guide Book, 1964; mem. editorial bd. Am. Quar., 1954-66, Technology and Culture, 1958-85, N.Y. History, 1973-74. Trustee Merck Forest Found., 1950-70, past sec., hon. trustee, 1985—; trustee R.I. Sch. Design, 1961-67, 68-70, Jennie Clarkson Home for Children, 1964-68; trustee Vt. Council on Arts, 1968-72, 76-78, v.p., 1969-71; trustee Park-McCullough House Assn., 1971-78. Decorated officer's cross Order Orange-Nassau Netherlands, 1954; recipient citation for outstanding achievement Wesleyan U., 1961. Fellow Royal Soc. Arts (Great Britain) (hon. corr. mem.); mem. Am. Studies Assn., Soc. Archtl. Historians, Soc. Indsl. Archaeology, Soc. History Tech. (exec. council 1962-64, adv. council 1958-61, 65-69). Home: Dorset Vt. Died Nov. 3, 1990.

KOZIN, FRANK, system engineering educator; b. Chgo., Jan. 19, 1930; s. Melvin and Shirley Helen (Pearl) K.; m. Cynthia H.P. Hsiao, Mar. 30, 1958; 1 son, Daniel G. B.S. in Math, Ill. Inst. Tech., 1952, M.S., 1953, Ph.D., 1956. Prof. Purdue U., 1958-67; co-dir. Ctr. for Applied Stochastics, 1963-67; prof. system engrng. Poly. U. Bklyn., 1967-90; dir. research Midwest Applied Sci. Corp., Lafayette, Ind., 1965-67; vis. prof. Inst. Math., Kyoto U., 1964-65; guest USSR Acad. Sci., 1967, Yugoslav Acad. Sci., 1971, MInistry of Edn., People's Republic China, 1980-85. NSF Sci. Faculty fellow London U., 1961-62. Fellow ASME; mem. Am. Math. Soc., Math. Assn. Am., Soc. Indsl. and Applied Math., Internat. Soc. Terrain Vehicle Systems. Home: Huntington N.Y. Died Apr. 5, 1990; buried Pinelawn (N.Y.) Meml. Pk.

KRAKOWER, CECIL ALEXANDER, physician, pathologist; b. Montreal, Que., Can., Sept. 4, 1907; s. Harry and Clara (Roth) K.; m. Emma de la Rosa, Mar. 10, 1939; children: Daniel, Diana. BS, McGill U., 1928, MD, 1932. Instr. pathology Harvard U., 1934-36; assoc. pathology Sch. Tropical Medicine, Columbia U., 1936-39, asst. prof., 1939-43; assoc. prof. pathology U. Ill. Coll. Medicine, 1944-48, prof., 1948-73, head dept., 1955-73, disting. rsch. prof., 1973-77; prof. emeritus —, 1977-89; pathologist-in-chief U. Ill. Hosps., 1955-73. Mem. Am. Assn. Pathologists and Bacteriologists, Am. Soc. Exptl. Pathology, Soc. Exptl. Biology and Medicine, Am. Coll. Pathologists, Internat. Acad. Pathology, Sigma Xi. Home: Phoenix Ariz. Died May 1, 1989.

KRAMER, GEORGE NICHOLAS, history educator, columnist; b. St. Mary's, Kans., Mar. 24, 1896; s. Mathias and Eva (Seitz) K.; m. Justina M. Kramer, June 20, 1922; children: Justin Anthony, Dolores Georgene (Mrs. Robert L. Waggoner) Regis Francis, Remigius Thomas. AB, St. Mary's Coll. (Kans.), 1918; student, Marquette U., 1919-20, Cath. U. Am., 1920-21; PhD, U. So. Calif., 1936. Instr. history and polit. sci. U. Detroit, 1922-23; prof. history Regis Coll., Denver, 1925-28; with Loyola U. of L.A., 1932-54, became prof. history and dir. social studies, 1946; mem. editorial staff Daily Am. Tribune, Dubuque, Iowa, 1921-22; mgr. and editor Walsenburg (Colo.) Independent, 1928-29; freelance writer, 1923-25, 29-32; mem. editorial staff The Tidings, L.A., from 1955, news analyst and columnist, from 1957. Author: Fundamentals of American Politics, 1948. Mem. Phi Beta Kappa. *

KRAMER, MAGDALENE E., speech educator; b. Canton, Ohio, June 17, 1898; d. John G. and Katherine (Loftus) Kramer. AB cum laude, Trinity Coll., 1920; AM, Columbia U., 1930, PhD, 1936. Tchr. English Washington High Sch., Massillon, Ohio, 1921-25, tchr. oral English, dir. dramatics, 1925-29; asst., dept. speech Tchrs. Coll., Columbia U., 1930-33, instr., 1933-36, assoc., 1936-37, asst. prof., 1937-39, assoc. prof., 1939-45, prof., 1945-63, chmn. speech dept., 1941-63, prof. emeritus, from 1963. Author: Dramatic Tournaments in Secondary Schools, 1936; assoc. editor Quar. Jour. of Speech, from 1956. Mem. Speech Assn. Am. (pres. 1947), Speech Assn. Eastern States (pres. 1947), N.Y. Speech Assn., NEA, N.Y. Tchrs. Assn., Am. Ednl. Rsch. Assn., Am. Ednl. Theatre Assn., Am. Speech and Hearing Assn., Kappa Delta Pi, Pi Lambda Theta, Zeta Phi Eta. Roman Catholic. *

KRAMER, SAMUAL NOAH, curator; b. Russia, Sept. 28, 1897; came to U.S., 1906, naturalized, 1919; s. Benjamin and Yetta (Weinstein K.; m. Mildred Tokarsky, Oct. 9, 1933; children: Daniel, Judith. Student, Sch. Pedagogy, 1915-17; BS, Temple U., 1921; postgrad., Dropsie Coll., 1926-27; PhD, U. Pa., 1929. Tchr. pub., pvt. schs., 1919-29; mem. excavating expdns. U. Pa., Billah, Gawra, also Fara, Iraq, 1930-31; rsch. asst. specializing Sumerian lang. Oriental Inst. U. Chgo., 1932-35, rsch. assoc., 1936-42; Guggenheim fellow copied Sumerian lit. tablets Mus. Ancient Orient, Istanbul, Turkey, 1937-39; student, copier of Sumerian lit. tablets Mus. U. Pa., 1939-90, rsch. assoc., 1942-43, assoc. curator, 1943-49, curator tablet collections, Clark rsch. prof. Assyriology, 195-68, emeritus, 1968-9; ann. prof. Am. Schs. Oriental Rsch., travel to Istanbul, Bagdad, Iraq, for archeol. epigraphic rsch., 1946-47; Fulbright rsch. prof., Turkey, 1951-52; exch. prof. to Soviet Union, 1957; prof. Sorbonne, Paris, 1970-71. Author: Gilgamesh and the Huluppu Tree, 1938, Lamentation Over the Destruction of Ur, 194, with C.J. Gadd Ur: Literary and Religious Texts, part one, 1963, part two, 1966; editor: Sumerian Epics and Myths, and Sumerian Texts of Varied Contents, 1934, The Sumerian Mythology: A Study of Spiritual and Literary Achievement in the Third Millenium B.C.: Sumerian Literary Texts from Nippur, 1944, Biblical Parallels from Sumerian Literature, 1954, many more; contbr. articles to profl. jours. Mem. Am. Acad. Arts and Scis., Am. Philos. Soc. John Frederick Lewis prize , Am. Oriental Soc., Am Anthrop. Assn. AAAS, Archeol. Inst. Am., Soc. Bibl. Lit., Acad. Scis. in Finland, Academie des Inscriptions et Belles Lettres of Instit de France, Brit. Acad., Oriental Club Phila. . Home: Philadelphia Pa. Died Nov. 26, 1990.

KRANICH, WILMER LEROY, chemical engineering educator, university dean; b. Phila., Nov. 20, 1919; s. Jacob H. and Elsie (Ernst) K.; m. Margaret Mansley, July 1, 1950; children: Laurence Wilmer, Deborah M., Gary R. B.S., U. Pa., 1940; PhD (McMullen fellow 1940-41), Cornell U., 1944. Instr. chem. engrng. Cornell U., 1941-44; asst. prof. chem. engrng. Princeton U., 1946-48; assoc. prof. chem. engrng. Worcester Poly. Inst., 1948-49, prof., 1949-67, head chem. engrng. and chemistry, 1958-67, George C. Gordon prof., 1967-85, prof. emeritus, 1985-92, head dept. chem. engrng., 1967-75, dean Grad. Studies, 1974-85, dean emeritus, 1985-92; staff cons. Arthur D. Little, Inc., 1949-74; vis. research scientist Hungarian Acad. Scis., Budapest, 1983; adj. prof. environ. and biochem. engrng. Duke U., Durham, N.C., 1985-92. Served to lt. (j.g.) USNR, 1944-46. Mem. Am. Inst. Chem. Engrs., Am. Chem. Soc., Am. Soc. Engrng. Edn., Sigma Xi, Tau Beta Pi, Alpha Chi Sigma. Home: Shrewsbury Mass. Died Aug. 25, 1992. †

KRAUSHAAR, OTTO FREDERICK, educational consultant; b. Clinton, Iowa, Nov. 19, 1901; s. Otto Christian and Marie Elizabeth (Staehling) K.; m. Maxine McDonald, Nov. 28, 1926; 1 child, Joanne K. Adams. AB, U. Iowa, 1924, AM, 1927; PhD, Harvard U., 1933; holder many honorary degrees. Instr. U. Iowa, 1926-27; asst. and instr. Harvard U., 1927-28, 29-33; asst. prof. U. Kans, 1928-29; from asst. prof. to prof. Smith Coll., 1933-48; pres. Goucher Coll., 1948-67, pres. emeritus, 1967-89; vis. prof. Amherst Coll., 1936-37, 46-47, Mt. Holyoke Coll., 1948-49; vis. rsch. assoc. Harvard U., 1967-71; ednl. cons., 1971-89. Author: Lotze and James, 1940, Kierkegaard in English, 1942, (with Max Fisch) Classic American Philosophers, 1951, American Non-Public Schools, 1972, Private Schools, From the Puritans to the Present, 1976, Schools in a Changing City: An Overview of Baltimore's Private Schools, 1965; assoc. editor: Jour. of Philosophy; contbr. articles to profl. jours. Chmn. Ralph Waldo Emerson award com., 1961-64; mem. Md. Commn. on Interracial Problems, 1952-57, Md. Commn. on Higher Edn., 1956-58, Planning Coun. Greater Balt. Com., 1956-62; chmn. labor arbitration bd. Newspaper Guild vs. Sunpapers, 1964, Md. Com. to Study State Aid to Pvt. Edn., 1970-71, Balt. Symphony Orch. strike, 1972, Loyola-Notre Dame Libr. Corp., 1974-89; bd. dirs. ACTION, Inc.; trustee Chatham Coll., Md. Inst. and Coll. Art, Park Sch., Calver Sch., Samuel Ready Sch. Decorated Legion of Merit; recipient award Md. Civil Liberties Union, 1959, Laymans award AIA, 1963, Andrew White medal Loyola U., 1966, award for disting. svc. to Am. edn. Coun. Am. Pvt. Edn., 1977; named Towson's Man of Yr., 1963. Mem. AAUP, Am. Philos. Assn., Century Assn., Johns Hopkins Faculty Club, Phi Beta Kappa, Omicron Delta Kappa. Home: Baltimore Md. Died Sept. 23, 1989.

KRAVIS, IRVING BERNARD, economist, educator; b. Phila., Aug. 30, 1916; s. Nathan and Ethel (Gelgood) K.; m. Lillian Beatrice Panzer, June 22, 1941; children: Robert, Marcia, Ellen, Nathan. B.S., U. Pa., 1938, M.A., 1939, Ph.D., 1947. Instr. econs. Whitman Coll., 1941-42; economist Dept. Labor, 1946-48; assoc. prof. U. Mass., 1948-49; mem. faculty U. Pa., 1949-87, prof. econs., 1956-86, Univ. prof. econs., 1980-87, Univ. prof. econs. emeritus, 1987-92, chmn. dept., 1955-58, 62-67; assoc. dean Wharton Sch. Fin. and Commerce, U. Pa., 1958-60; cons. govtl. and internat. agys., 1949-92; mem. research staff Nat. Bur. Econ. Research, 1962-92; dir. UN Internat. Comparison Project, 1968-82. Co-author: Price Competitiveness in World Trade, 1971; co-author: World Product and Income, 1982; Contbr. articles to profl. jours. Served to 1st lt. USAAF, 1942-46. Decorated Bronze Star; Ford Found. fellow, 1960-61; Guggenheim fellow, 1966-67; recipient Julius Shiskin award for Econ. Stats., 1987. Fellow AAAS, Am. Acad. Arts and Scis., Econometric Soc., Am. Econ. Assn. (Disting. fellow award 1992); mem. Royal Econ. Soc. Home: Haverford PA. Died Jan. 3, 1992; buried Sharon Cemetery, Springfield, Pa.

KREEGER, DAVID LLOYD, lawyer and insurance company executive; b. N.Y.C., Jan. 4, 1909; s. Barnet and Laura (Bernen) K.; m. Carmen Matanzo y Jaramillo, Jan. 12, 1938; children: Carolita Joy, Peter Laurens Harris. A.B. magna cum laude, Rutgers U., 1929, L.H.D. (hon.), 1972; J.D. magna cum laude, Harvard U., 1932; Mus.D. (hon.), Peabody Inst., 1972; LL.D. (hon.), George Washington U., 1976; L.H.D. (hon.), Am. U., 1982. Bar: N.J. 1933, D.C. 1941, U.S. Supreme Ct. 1944. Pvt. practice in Newark, 1932-34; sr. atty. Dept. Agr., 1934-35; prin. atty. Dept. Interior, 1935-41; spl. asst. to atty. gen., also chief Supreme Ct. sect., claims div. Dept. Justice, 1941-46; pvt. practice Washington, 1946-57; with Govt. Employees Ins. Co. (and affilates), Washington, 1957-79, sr. v.p., gen. counsel, 1957-64, pres., 1964-68, chmn. bd., chief exec. officer, 1970-74, chmn. exec. com., 1974-79, hon. chmn. bd., 1979-90; dir. Crestar Bank, Washington; mem. Citizens Adv. Coun. D.C., 1961-64; spl. presdl. ambassador to inauguration Pres. Frei of Chile, 1964; U.S. del. to Econ. Coun. on Europe, 1967. Contbr. articles profl. jours.; Editor: Harvard Law Rev., 1930-32. Pres. Nat. Symphony Orch., 1970-78; chmn. 5th Interam. Music Festival, 1971; pres. Corcoran Gallery Art, Washington, 1974-88, chmn., 1988-90; pres. Washington Opera, 1980-85, chmn., from 1985; trustee emeritus Am. U., Washington; mem. com. to visit Harvard Law Sch., 1967-70; mem. exec. bd. Am. Jewish Com.; mem. U.S. Nat. Commn. for UNESCO, 1977-80; pres. David Lloyd Kreeger Found. Recipient Meritorious Pub. Service award Govt. D.C., 1961, Bronze medal appreciation Corcoran Gallery Art, 1965, cert. appreciation N.Y. U. Grad. Sch. Bus. Adminstrn. Alumni Assn., 1965, Outstanding Service award Washington Jr. C. of C., 1966. Mem. ABA, D.C. Bar Assn., Rutgers U. Alumni Assn., Harvard Law Sch. Alumni Assn., Phi Beta Kappa, Sigma Alpha Mu. Democrat. Jewish. Clubs: Metropolitan, Alfalfa, Cosmos, Harvard, F Street, International, National Lawyers (Washington). Home: Washington D.C. Died Nov. 18, 1990; buried King David Cemetery, Washington.

KREHBIEL, HARRY, chemical company executive; b. Germany, Dec. 27, 1897; Came to U.S., 1912, naturalized, 1922; s. John and Elixabetha (Kirch) K.; m. Sigrid Reising, Sept. 24, 1927; children: Peter W., Harry E. Bank clk., 1917; with Catalin Corp. Am., N.Y.C., from 1931; successively salesman, sales mgr., v.p. Catalin Corp. Am., 1931-44, pres., from 1944, chmn. bd., from 1960; also dir. Mem. Scarsdale Art Assn., Fed. Grand Jury Assn., Plastic Pioneers Assn., Mfg. Chemists Assn., Soc. Plastics Industry. Clubs: Union LEague (N.Y.C.), Westchester Country (Rye, N.Y.). *

KREIDLER, ROBERT NEIL, foundation executive; b. Detroit, Nov. 21, 1929. B.A., Dartmouth Coll., 1951; M.P.A., Harvard U., 1953, M.A., 1954. With U.S. Govt., 1958-62, White House staff, 1958-61, with Office Sci. and Tech., Exec. Office Pres., 1961-62; with Alfred P. Sloan Found., 1962-80, v.p., 1965-68, exec. v.p., 1968-80; v.p. Carnegie Inst. of Washington, 1980-82; pres. Charles A. Dana Found., N.Y.C., 1982-92;; mem. bd. sci. and tech. for devel. Nat. Acad. Scis., 1963-73; dir. Nat. Med. Fellowships, Inc., 1973-78. Bd. dirs. Found. for Rsch. into Origin of Man, 1978-82; trustee Barnard Coll., 1980-90. Served with USMCR, 1954-58. Fellow AAAS, Am. Acad. Arts and Scis.; mem. Council on Fgn. Relations, Phi Beta Kappa. Home: New York N.Y. Died Aug. 30, 1992. †

KREISEL, HENRY, university administrator; b. Vienna, Austria, June 5, 1922; s. David Leo and Helene (Schreier) K.; m. Esther Lazerson, June 22, 1947; 1 child, Philip. B.A., U. Toronto, 1946, M.A., 1947; Ph.D., U. London, 1954. With dept. English U. Alta., from 1947, prof., from 1959, head dept., 1961-67, asso. dean Grad. studies, 1967-69, acting dean grad. studies, 1969-70, acad. v.p., 1970-75, Univ. prof., 1975-87, Univ. prof. emeritus, 1987—, chmn. Can. studies program, 1979-82; vis. fellow Wolfson Coll., Cambridge U., 1975-76; Chmn. English lit. Can. Council Fellowship Com., 1963-65, Gov.-Gen.'s Jury for Lit., 1966-69, 90; v.p. Edmonton Art Gallery, 1969-70. Author: The Rich Man, 1948, The Betrayal, 1964, The Almost Meeting, 1981, Another Country, 1985, (play) The Rich Man, 1987. Contbr.: numerous short stories, anthologies to mags., books, including Best American Short Stories, 1966, A Book of Canadian Stories, 1962. Author: plays for radio and TV, including Bob Hope Theatre, 1965, The Rich Man, 1987. Bd. govs. U. Alta., 1966-69; v.p. Edmonton Chamber Music Soc., 1978-80, pres., 1980-83; advisor to Sec. of State for Multiculturalism, 1987. Recipient U. Western Ont. President's medal, 1960; J. I.

Segal Found. award lit., 1983; Rutherford award for excellence in teaching U. Alba., 1986, Sir Frederick Haultain prize Govt. Alta., 1986, Order of Can., 1988; Reuben Wells Leonard fellow U. Toronto, 1946-47; Royal Soc. Can. Travelling fellow, 1953-54. Fellow Royal Soc. Arts (London), Internat. Inst. Arts and Letters (Geneva); mem. Assn. Can. U. Tchrs. English (pres. 1962-63). Home: Edmonton Can. Deceased. †

KREISKY, BRUNO, federal chancellor of Austria; b. Vienna, Austria, Jan. 22, 1911; s. Max and Irene (Felix) K.; m. Vera Fuerth, Apr. 23, 1942 (dec. Dec. 1989); children: Peter Staffan, Suzanne Christine. LLD, U. Vienna, 1938. Active youth movement Social-Democratic Party, to 1934; underground movement, imprisoned, 1935-36, 38, escaped to Sweden; mem. sci. staff Stockholm Coop. Soc., 1939-46; with Austrian Fgn. Svc., Austrian Legation, Stockholm, 1946-51; asst. dir. Austrian Pres.'s Office, 1951-53; sec. state for fgn. affairs Fed. Chancellery, Fgn. Affairs Dept., 1953-59; mem. Parliament, 1956-90; chancellor of Austria, 1970-83; chief Austrian del. UN Gen. Assembly, 1959-65; fed. minister fgn. affairs, 1959-66; chmn. Socialist Party of Austria, 1967-90, hon. chmn.;. Author: The Challenge: Politics on the Threshhold of the Atomic Age, 1963, Aspects of Democratic Socialism, 1974, Neutrality and Co-existence, 1975, The Times We Live In: Reflections on International Politics, 1978, L'Autriche entre l'Est et l'Ouest, 1979, Between the Times: Memoirs from Five Centuries, 1986, In the Stream of Politics, Memoirs II, 1988, also speeches, articles on internat. econ. affairs. Pres. Vienna Inst. Devel.; v.p. Inst. Advanced Studies, Ford Found.; v.p. Theodor Koerner Fund Promotion Arts and Scis. Decorated Gold Grand Cross of Honor, Austria, also numerous fgn. decorations; recipient Jawaharlal Nehru award for Internat. Understanding, 1985, Martin Luther King Jr. Internat. Peace award, 1989. Home: Vienna Austria Died July 29, 1990; buried Vienna Ctrl. Cemetery.

KREITNER, JOHN, educator; b. Aussig, Bohemia, Feb. 6, 1897; Came to U.S., 1938, naturalized, 1946; s. Leopold and Mathilde (Thaussig) K.; m. MAria Eichhorn, July 1925 (dec. Mar. 1936); 1 child, Frederick J.; m. Renate Theresia Koegl, Jan. 1944. ScD in Engring. Scis. summa cum laude, Vienna Inst. Tech., 1922. With J.M. Voith, hydro-power and marine engring., 1921-38; head rsch. in Austria, 1921-33, Japan, 1933-37; cons. Maierform, naval architects, N.Y.C., 1938-41; pres., tech. div. Am. Hydromath Corp., N.Y.C., 1941-54; prof. math. Adelphi U., from 1954, chmn. undergrad. math., from 1955; v.p., dir. Myrin Inst. Adult Edn. at Waldorf Sch., from 1956. *

KRENEK, ERNST, composer, author; b. Vienna, Austria, Aug. 23, 1900; came to U.S., 1938, naturalized, 1945; s. Ernst and Emanuela (Cizek) K.; m. Gladys Nordenstrom, Aug. 8, 1950. Student, U. Vienna, Acad. Music, Vienna and Berlin; numerous hon. degrees. Prof. music Vassar Coll., 1939-42; prof. music, dean Sch. Fine Arts Hamline U., St. Paul, 1942-47. Composer 242 mus. works, including (operas) Jonny Spelt Auf, 1925-26, Met. Opera premier performance, 1929, Karl V, 1930-33; author 16 books. Served with Austro-Hungarian Army, 1918. NEA fellow, 1977, 80; decorated cross of mert, gold medals Austria, gold medals Ger., gold medals Vienna, gold medals Hamburg, gold medals others; named hon. citizen Vienna. Mem. Broadcast Music Inc., Conseil International de la Musique, Am. Acad. Arts; hon mem. acads. music Vienna, Graz, Salzburg, Stuttgart, Hamburg, others. Roman Catholic. Home: Palm Springs Calif. Died Dec. 22, 1991; buried Vienna, Austria.

KRIEGER, LEONARD, history educator; b. Newark, Aug. 28, 1918; s. Isidore and Jennie (Glinn) K.; m. Esther J. Smith, Aug. 13, 1949; children: Alan Davis, David Jonathan, Nathaniel Richard. BA, Rutgers U., 1938; MA, Yale U., 1942, PhD, 1949. Mem. faculty Yale U., New Haven, 1946-62, prof. history, 1961-62; vis. lectr. Columbia U., N.Y.C., 1960-61, prof., 1969-72; Univ. prof. history U. Chgo., 1962-69, 72-90; vis. lectr. Northwestern U., 1950, Brandeis U., 1958; vis. prof. Stanford U., summer 1968, Johns Hopkins U., 1971-72; chmn. internat. conf. travel-grant com. Social Sci. Rsch. Coun., 1961-63; mem. book prize com. Phi Beta Kappa, 1960-61, Ralph Waldo Emerson prize com., 1982; assoc. Princeton Coun. Hamanities for Ford Humanities Project, 1959-64; fellow Ctr. Advanced Study Behavioral Sci., 1956-57; mem. Inst. for Advanced Study, 1963, 69-70. Author: The German Idea of Freedom, 1957, 2d edit., 1973, Politics of Discretion, 1965, Kings and Philosophers, 1970, Easay on the Theory of Enlightened Despotism, 1975, Ranke: The Meaning of History, 1977, Time's Reasons: Philosophies of History Old and New, 1989; co-author: History, 1965; series editor: Classic European Historians, from 1967; co-editor: The Responsibility of Power, 1967, 69; editor: Friedrich Engels, The German Revolutions, 1967; bd. editors Jour. History Ideas, from 1963. Mem. coun. Yale U., from 1975, chmn. vis. com. grad. sch., from 1975. 1st lt. AUS, 1942-46. Mem. Am. Hist. Assn. (chmn. program com. 1960, exec. com. modern history sect. 1968-71, chmn. 1976, speaker 1979), Am. Acad. Arts and Scis. (coun. 1975-79, exec. bd. from 1977), Am. Philos. Soc., Am. Soc. Polit. and Legal Philosophy. Home: Chicago Ill. Died Oct. 12, 1990; buried St. Johnsbury, Vt.

KRIGBAUM, WILLIAM RICHARD, chemist, educator; b. Beardstown, Ill., Sept. 29, 1922; s. Daniel Dwight and Ella (Sutton) K.; m. Esther Jean Wolfe, July 7, 1945; children—Mary Kathryn, Janet Ann, Lynn Carol. B.S., James Millikin U., 1944, Sc.D., 1966; M.S., U. Ill., 1948, Ph.D., 1949. Postdoctoral scientist Cornell U., 1949-52; mem. faculty Duke U., Durham, N.C., 1952-89, prof., 1962-89, James B. Duke prof. chemistry, 1969-89, prof. emeritus, 1989-91, chmn. dept., 1976-79; mem. nat. adv. panel chemistry NSF, 1970-73. Contbr. chpts. to 12 books; editorial bd. Macromolecules, Jour. Polymer Sci., Texture. Alfred P. Sloan Research fellow, 1956-60; NSF Sr. Postdoctoral fellow Centre des Recherches sur les Macromolecules, Strasbourg, France, 1959-60; NSF Sr. Postdoctoral fellow Institute fur physikalische Chemie, Graz, Austria, 1966-67. Fellow Am. Phys. Soc.; mem. Am. Chem. Soc. (Mobil Chem. Co. award in polymer chemistry 1989), Am. Crystallographic Assn., Sigma Xi. Home: Durham N.C. Died May 14, 1991; cremated.

KRIMENDAHL, HERBERT FREDERICK, business executive; b. Celina, Oreg., 1896; s. Otto and Freda (Schanzlin) K.; m. Mary Bess Christian, Dec. 10, 1925; children: David Christian, Herbert Frederick II. Ed. in pub. schs. Began career with Crampton Canneries, Inc., Celina, Oreg., 1919, pres., 1923-44; chmn. of bd. W.R. Roach & Co., Grand Rapids, Mich., 1941-46; v.p. Stokely Foods Inc., Indpls., 1944-46; exec. v.p. Stokely-Van Camp Inc., Indpls., 1946-48, pres., 1948-60, dir., from 1946, vice chmn. bd. dirs., from 1956; pres. Nora Plaza, Inc.; dir. Merchants Nat. Bank & Trust Co., Chgo., Indpls. & Louisville Ry. Co., Capital City Products Co., Stokely-Van Camp Food Products Co. Served with O.T.S., WWI. Mem. Nat. Canners Assn. (pres. 1940), Masons (Shriner), Indpls. Athletic Club (dir.). *

KRISCH, ADOLPH OSCAR, hotel executive; b. N.Y.C., June 3, 1916; s. Samuel J. and Miriam (Weinstein) K.; m. Heidrun Ilsa Feller, June 16, 1956; children—Victoria (Mrs. James Mills), Juliana. Student, Roanoke Coll., 1933-37, U. Va., 1937-41. With various retail jewelers, 1936-57; started motel bus., 1956; chmn. bd. Am. Motor Inns Inc., Roanoke, Va., 1957-85; chmn. bd. emeritus Krisch Hotels, Inc., Roanoke, 1985-87. Served with U.S. Army, 1943-44. Mem. Internat. Assn. Holiday Inns (dir., pres. 1969). Died Jan. 11, 1990. Home: Roanoke Va.

KRISS, JOSEPH PINCUS, internist, educator; b. Phila., May 15, 1919; s. Max and Sima (Charny) K.; m. Regina Tarlow, June 5, 1948; children—Eric, Paul, Mark. B.S. cum laude, Pa. State Coll., 1939; M.D. cum laude, Yale U., 1943. Diplomate: Am. Bd. Internal Medicine, Am. Bd. Nuclear Medicine (a founder), Nat. Bd. Med. Examiners. Successively intern, asst. resident in medicine, asst. resident in metabolism, resident in medicine New Haven Hosp., 1943-45; asst. in medicine, then instr. Yale U. Med. Sch., 1943-44; research fellow metabolism Washington U. Med. Sch., St. Louis, 1946-48; research assoc. in endocrinology and metabolism Michael Reese Hosp., Chgo., 1949; teaching asst. Stanford U. Med. Sch., 1948-49, mem. faculty, 1949-89, prof. medicine and radiology, 1962-89, dir. div. nuclear medicine., 1958-89; Macfarlane prof. U. Glasgow, 1986. Recipient Disting. Alumnus award Pa. State U., 1978; Alumni fellow, 1979; Kaiser fellow Center Advanced Study Behavioral Scis., 1979-80. Fellow Royal Coll. Physicians; mem. Soc. Nuclear Medicine (Western Regional award 1978), Endocrine Soc., AAAS, Am. Fedn. Clin. Research, Am. Thyroid Assn., Assn. Am. Physicians, Western Soc. Clin. Research, Western Assn. Physicians. Home: Stanford Calif. Died Sept. 9, 1989; cremated.

KROMM, FRANKLIN HERBERT, JR., newspaper syndicate executive; b. Ft. Wayne, Ind., Sept. 12, 1910; s. Franklin H. and Lena Bee (McKenzie) K.; m. Mildred C. Hershberger, Aug. 28, 1930; 1 child, Donald Eugene. Grad., Central Cath. High, Internat. Accounting Sch. Telephone maintenance Dudio Mfg. Co., 1928-29; salesman, 1930-33; pres. Kromm Trucking Co., 1933-36; gen. mgr. Frosty Cove Ice Cream Co., 1937-39; accountant, office mgr. McKinley Trucking Co., 1939-46; gen. mgr. Hopkins Syndicate, Inc., 1946-89, ret., 1989. Vice pres., treas. Sci. Marriage Found., from 1956. Republican. Roman Catholic. Home: Frankfort Ind. Died Jan. 30, 1990. †

KRONSTEIN, MAX, chemist, researcher; b. Basle, Switzerland, Oct. 7, 1895; came to U.S., 1939, naturalized, 1944; s. Abraham and Sonja (Schur) K.; m. Marion Ward, Nov. 24, 1948; children: Marianne R., Elisabeth W. Dipl. chem. Coll. of Engring., Karlsruhe, Germany, 1914; postgrad. U. Freiburg, Germany, 1920; Ph.D., U. Leipzig, Germany, 1922. Devel. chemist Elektra Varnish Works, Karlsruhe, 1922-38; devel. engr. William Zinsser & Co., N.Y.C., 1939-43; chief chemist research div. Titeflex, Inc., Newark, 1943-46; research assoc., adj. prof. Coll. Engring., NYU, 1946-55; research scientist NYU, 1955-73; research assoc. chemistry dept. Manhattan Coll., 1973-92. Contbr. chpts. to books, articles to profl. jours. Patentee in field. Recipient Roy H. Kienle award N.Y. Soc. Paint Tech., 1960; named to Aerophilatelic Hall of Fame, 1990. Mem. Am. Inst. Chemists (emeritus fellow), Am. Chem. Soc., N.Y. Soc. Coatings Tech., Controlled Release Soc. Club: Am. Air Mail Soc. (assoc. editor Airpost Jour.), Sigma Xi. Died Nov. 22, 1992. Home: Bronx N.Y. †

KRUEGER, MAYNARD C., economics educator; b. nr. Alexandria, Mo., Jan. 16, 1906; s. Fred C. and Nelle C. (Hoewing) K.; m. Elsie C. Gasperik, Aug. 25, 1934; children—Karen (Mrs. Harold F. Finn), Linda (Mrs. Bruce B. MacLachlan), Susan (Mrs. Winston A. Salser). A.B., U. Mo., 1926, A.M., 1927; postgrad. other univs. in, U.S. and Europe, 1925-32. Instr. U. Pa., 1928-32; asst. prof. U. Chgo., 1932-47, asso. prof., 1947-65, prof., 1965-77, emeritus, 1977-91; exec. dir. Internat. House, Chgo., 1977-81; vis. prof. U. Vienna, Austria, 1959-60, U. Athens, Greece, 1963-64, SUNY, 1965-66; cons. ECA programs, 1951; v.p. Am. Fedn. Tchrs., 1934-36. Author Economics Question Book, 1934. Chmn. Ind. Voters Ill., 1957-59; candidate v.p. U.S. Socialist Party, 1940. Club: Quadrangle. Home: Pleasanton Calif. Died Dec. 20, 1991.

KRUGER, RUDOLF, opera manager; b. Berlin, Germany, Oct. 30, 1916; came to U.S., 1939, naturalized, 1944; s. Eduard and Julie Eva (Herz) K.; m. Ruth Elizabeth Scallan, Aug. 28, 1951; children: Karen Elizabeth, Philip Edward. Grad., Staatliches Kaiserin Augusta Gymnasium, Berlin, 1935; diploma, Staatsakademie fuer Musik und Darstellende Kunst, Vienna, Austria, 1938; D.F.A. (hon.), Tex. Wesleyan Coll., 1983. Asst. condr. So. Symphony Orch., Columbia Choral Soc., Columbia, S.C., 1939-42; asst. condr. New Orleans Symphony Orch., 1942-45, condr. young people's concerts, 1942-45; asst. condr. New Orleans Opera House Assn. Orch., 1942-45, condr. light opera div., 1943; condr. Mid-Western tour Chgo. Light Opera Co., 1946-47; mus. dir. Jackson (Miss.) Opera Guild, 1948-51, Mobile (Ala.) Opera Guild, 1949-55, New Orleans Light Opera Co., 1949-50; 1st condr. Crescent City Concerts Assn., New Orleans, 1954-55; mus. dir., condr. Ft. Worth Opera Assn., 1955-58, mus. dir., gen. mgr., from 1958; resident mus. dir. Ft. Worth Symphony Orch. Assn., 1963-65; mus. dir., condr. Ft. Worth Ballet Assn., 1965-66; gen. dir. Arlington, Tex., Opera Assn., from 1987; condr. weekly orch. program ABC, MBS, 1943-44; guest condr. Shreveport (La.) Civic Opera, 1962-63, 75, 76-79, Cin. Summer Opera, 1969, New Orleans Opera House Assn., 1969, Dallas Civic Ballet Assn., 1971, P.R. Opera, 1972, State Opera, Hannover, Germany, 1974, Teheran (Iran) Opera, 1976, Conn. Grand Opera, 1979, Philippine Philham. Orch., 1985; dir. opera workshop Tex. Christian U., 1955-58. Served with AUS, 1945-46. Recipient Cert. of Recognition Tex. Fedn. Music Clubs, 1967. Mem. Am. Fedn. Musicians, Rotary. Episcopalian. Home: Fort Worth Tex. Deceased. †

KRYNSKI, MAGNUS JAN, Slavic literatures educator, translator; b. Warsaw, Poland, May 15, 1922; came to U.S., 1948, naturalized, 1957; s. Simon and Stefania (Boraks) K.; m. Elizabeth Girardet, Apr. 12, 1952. B.A., U. Cin., 1952; M.A., Brown U., 1955; M.A. cert. Russian Inst., Columbia U., 1956, Ph.D., 1962. Instr. Duke U., Durham, N.C., 1959-60, prof. Slavic lits., 1966-87; asst. prof. U. Pitts., 1961-63; assoc. prof. Kenyon Coll., 1964-66; vis. assoc. prof. Ohio State U., 1964-66. Translator, editor: The Survivor and Other Poems (T. Rozewicz), 1976, Building the Barricade (A. Swirszczynska), 1979, Sounds, Feelings, Thoughts (W. Szymborska), 1981. Founder, bd. dirs. N.C. Com. for Solidarity with Solidarity, Durham, 1982-89; bd. dirs. Socio-polit. movement POMOST, Washington, 1983-89, Freedom Fedn., Washington, 1983-89; mem. N.C. Hist. Records Adv. Bd., 1985-89. Recipient award for poetry transl. ZAIKS (Polish Writers Assn.), 1981; fellow Ford Found., 1955-56, 57-58; Nat. Def. Fgn. Lang. fellow, 1960-61; grantee Internat. Research Exchange Bd. Eastern Europe Research Program, 1980. Mem. Polish Inst. Arts and Scis. (dir. 1978-84), MLA, Am. Assn. Advancement of Slavic Studies. Republican. Home: Durham N.C. Died June 22, 1989; cremated.

KUHN, SHERMAN MCALLISTER, English language educator, editor; b. Alexandria, S.D., Sept. 15, 1907; s. Detmer Thomas and Helen (Sherman) K.; m. Esther Lucille Bacon, Dec. 31, 1926 (div. Apr. 1931); 1 child, Evelyn; m. Eleanor Jordan, Dec. 28, 1935 (dec. June 1987); children: Eleanor Anne, Barbara Jean, Dorothy Ruth. Student, U. Dubuque, 1925-28; B.A., Park Coll., Parkville, Mo., 1929; M.A., U. Chgo., 1933, Ph.D., 1935. Tchr. English Lincoln Community High Sch., (Ill.), 1929-32; prof. English Okla. State U., Stillwater, 1935-48; prof. English U. Mich., Ann Arbor, 1948-83, prof. emeritus, 1984-91, assoc. editor Middle English Dictionary, 1948-61, editor Middle English Dictionary, 1961-83, editor emeritus, 1984-91; cons. Clarence L. Barnhart, Inc., N.Y.C. Author: A Grammar of the Mercian Dialect, 1938, A Functional Grammar, Form A, 1938, Form B, 1940, Studies in the Language and Poetics of Anglo-Saxon England, 1984, others; editor: The Vespasian Psalter, 1965; adv. editor Mich. Germanic Studies, from 1975; mem. editorial com. The Barnhart Dictionary of Etymology, 1982-88; contbr. articles to profl. jours. Served with U.S. Army, 1944-45. Recipient Best Book award U. Mich. Press., 1973; recipient Disting. Faculty Achievement award U. Mich., 1983; grantee Horace H. Rackham Found., 1958, 65. Fellow Medieval Acad. Am., Dictionary Soc. N.Am.; mem. New Chaucer Soc., Am. Dialect Soc., Internat. Assn. Univ. Profs. English, Am. Legion. Republican.

Presbyterian. Home: Bloomfield Hills Mich. Died Jan. 7, 1991; buried Concord Ch., Hooker, Pa.

KULLERUD, GUNNAR, geosciences educator; b. Odda, Norway, Nov. 12, 1921; came to U.S., 1948; s. Finn and Clara Sofie (Kindberg) K.; m. Arrilla Joan Reading, Mar. 29, 1947 (dec. Mar. 1981); children: Finn Jon, Björn Kent, Kari Lynn, Marit Sue, Ingrid Diana; m. Ruth E. Foster. Ph.D. in Mining, Tech. U. Norway, 1947; D.Sc. in Geochemistry, U. Oslo, 1954; D.Sc. (honoris causa), Norwegian Inst. Tech., 1982. Instr., then research assoc. U. Chgo., 1948-52; research assoc. U. Oslo, 1952-54; sr. staff mem. geochemistry Geophys. Lab., Carnegie Instn., 1954-71; prof. dept. geoscis. Purdue U., Lafayette, Ind., 1970-89, head dept., 1970-76; adj. prof. Lehigh (Pa.) U., 1962-71; vis. prof. U. Heidelberg, Germany, 1964-70, 85, Tech. U. Norway, 1972, 74, 83, Charles U., Prague, Czechoslovakia, 1973, U. Oslo, 1976, 78, Cheng Kung U., Taiwan, Republic of China, 1982-83; CSIRO vis. research fellow, Australia, 1974, 83; cons. Los Alamos (N.Mex.) Nat. Lab., 1983; cons. Geol. Survey Norway, 1984, 86, 87, 88; cons. prof. Tex. Tech U., 1968-71; hon. collaborator, div. meteorites Smithsonian Instn., 1964-71; bd. dirs. Earth Scis. Inc.; mem. com. chem. solar system Space Sci. Bd., 1964-70; mem. Argonne (Ill.) Nat. Lab. Adv. Bd., 1975. Co-editor: Mineralium Deposita, 1964-84; mem. editorial bd.: Chem. Geology, 1966-85; contbr. articles on sulfide phase equilibria, geothermometry, ore deposits, meteorites, fossil fuels and mineral separation to profl. jours. Served with Royal Norwegian Air Force, also RAF, 1943-45. Recipient A.H. Dumont award Belgian Geol. Soc., 1965. Fellow Geol. Soc. Am., Am. Mineral. Soc., Washington Acad. Scis.; mem. Nat. Acad. Sci. (Norway), Soc. Econ. Geologists, Geochem. Soc., Meteoritical Soc., Soc. Applied Geology, Am. Geophys. Union, Royal Soc. Norway, Geol. Soc. Norway, Geol. Soc. Finland, Cosmos Club. Home: West Lafayette Ind. Died Oct. 21, 1989; buried Lafayette, Ind.

KULP, NANCY JANE, actress, comedienne; b. Harrisburg, Pa., Aug. 28, 1921; d. Robert Tilden and Marjorie (Snyder) K.; m. Charles Malcolm Dacus, Apr. 1, 1951. B.A. in Journalism, Fla. State U., 1943; postgrad., U. Miami, 1950. Publicity dir. radio sta. WGBS, 1946-47; continuity dir. radio sta. WIOD, Miami, 1947-49; continuity dir.-performer TV Sta. WTVJ, Miami, 1949-50; prof. TV and motion picture history Juniata Coll., Huntingdon, Pa., 1985, artist in residence, 1985. Began acting career in Hollywood, Calif., 1952; motion pictures include Model and the Marriage Broker, 1952, A Star is Born, 1953, Sabrina, 1954, Three Faces of Eve, 1955, The Parent Trap, 1957, A Wilder Summer, 1983; appeared on: TV shows Playhouse 90, 1956, Lux Video, 1955, Lucy Show, 1956, Bob Cummings Show, 1955-60, Beverly Hillbillies, 1961-71 (Emmy nomination 1967), Brian Keith Show, 1973, Sanford and Son, Return of the Beverly Hillbillies, 1981, Scarecrow and Mrs. King, 1986, Simon and Simon, 1986, Quantum Leap, Arsenio Hall, 1989; Broadway play Mornings at Seven, 1982; play Accent on Youth, Long Wharf Theatre, 1983, appeared in Romeo and Juliet, Ga. Shakespeare Festival, 1987, also London retropsective Showboat, Carnegie Hall, Angel Records. Hon. chmn. Humane Soc., 1965-91; co-chmn. Roosevelt Coachella Valley March of Dimes, Valley March of Dimes; Dem. candidate for Congress, 9th dist. Pa., 1984. Served to lt. (j.g.) WAVES, USNR, 1943-45. Mem. Acad. Motion Pictures Arts and Scis., Actors and Others for Animals, LWV, Pi Beta Phi. Democrat. Home: Palm Desert Calif. Died Feb. 3, 1991.

KULSKI, WLADYSLAW WSZEBOR, political scientist, educator; b. Warsaw, Poland, July 27, 1903; came to U.S., 1946, naturalized, 1952; s. Julian and Antonina (Ostrowski) K.; m. Antonina Reutt, Oct. 28, 1938. LL.M., Warsaw Law Sch., 1925; LL.D., Paris (France) Law Sch., 1927. With Polish Diplomatic Service, 1928-45; head legal service Polish Diplomatic Service (Ministry Fgn. Affairs), 1936-40; counsellor, minister plenipotentiary Polish Diplomatic Service (Polish embassy), London, Eng., 1940-45; pub. lectr. in U.S., 1946-47; prof. polit. sci. U. Ala., 1947-51, Syracuse U., 1951-64; vis. prof. Duke U., 1963-64, James B. Duke prof. Russian affairs, 1964-73; lectr. Fgn. Service Inst., from 1957, Army Strategic Intelligence Sch., from 1957, Air. U., from 1963. Author numerous books, 1927—; latest being The Soviet Regime: Communism in Practice, 1954, 56, 59, 63, Peaceful Co-Existence: An Analysis of Soviet Foreign Policy, 1959, (with others) The Ethic of Power, 1961, (with others) Systems of Integrating the International Community, 1963, (with others) Western Policy and Eastern Europe, 1966, (with others) Aspects of Modern Communism, 1968, International Politics in a Revolutionary Age, 1964, DeGaulle and the World, 1966, The Soviet Union in World Affairs, 1973, Germany and Poland, 1976; Contbr. articles to profl. jours., also book revs. Fulbright and Guggenheim research fellows France, 1961-62; Guggenheim research fellow, 1970; research grantee Am. Council Learned Socs. and Am. Philos. Soc., 1972. Mem. Am. Polit. Sci. Assn., Am. Assn. Slavic Studies, A.A.U.P. Home: Durham N.C. Died May 16, 1989.

KUPLAN, LOUIS, consulting gerontologist; b. N.Y.C., Aug. 11, 1906; s. Abraham and Eva (Brodsky) K.; m. Katherine FitzGerald, Sept. 9, 1936. B.A., UCLA, 1929; postgrad., U. Calif. at Berkeley, 1935, 38. County dir. Calif. Relief Adminstrn., 1934-40; adminstrv. asst. Farm Security Adminstrn., San Francisco, 1940-43; sr. adminstrv. asst. Fed. Pub. Housing Authority, San Francisco, 1943-45; pub. assistance analyst Social Security Adminstrn., San Francisco, 1945-47; chief div. old age security Calif. Dept. Social Welfare, 1947-51; exec. sec. Calif. Interdeptl. Coordinating Com. Aging, 1950-55, Calif. Citizens Adv. Com. Aging, 1955-60; editor Maturity mag., 1954-60; editorial cons. Harvest Years Pub. Co., San Francisco, 1960-63; specialist retirement planning Mgmt. Devel. Center, U. San Francisco, 1960-61; lectr. U. Calif. Extensions, 1965-69, 70, 73, U. San Francisco, 1962-69; instr. Merritt Coll., Oakland, Calif., 1969-74, Contra Costa Coll., from 1972, Diablo Valley Coll., from 1972; dir. Center on Aging, Urban Life Inst., U. San Francisco, 1968-69; Mem. adv. bd. Retirement Advisers, Inc., N.Y.C., 1958-60; chmn. trustees Emeritus Edn., Inc., Palo Alto, Calif., 1971-75; nat. adv. com. White House Conf. Aging, 1961; mem. tech. adv. com. on edn. White House Conf. on Aging, 1970-72; mem. adv. com. on aging Calif. Dept. Mental Hygiene, 1969-73; sci. council Gerontol. Research Found., St. Louis, 1957-63; council geriatrics and gerontology Pan Am. Med. Assn., 1957-62; com. aging Am. Public Welfare Assn.; chmn. Atty. Gen. Calif. Adv. Com. Problems Aging, 1972-74; pres. 5th Internat. Congress Gerontology, 1960; v.p., vice chmn. bd. dirs. Longevity Found., 1960-70; moderator, producer TV program A Gift of Time, KRON-TV, 1969-78; bd. dirs. Food Adv. Service, from 1975, Optimum Achievers, Inc., from 1981, San Francisco Catholic Com. on Aging, from 1975. Recipient award for outstanding services and leadership in developing programs for older adults San Francisco Sr. Center; award Arthritis Found. No. Calif., 1971; citation Calif. State Assembly, 1971; award for pub. service Social Security Adminstrn., 1973; award San Francisco Cath. Com. on Aging, 1973; award for services in edn. for elderly U. Calif. Extension Center for Learning in Retirement, 1975; award for leadership in health edn. for elderly San Francisco Lung Assn., 1977; citation for Outstanding and Dedicated Service, Am. Soc. on Aging, 1987. Fellow Gerontol. Soc. U.S. (pres. 1958-59); mem. Internat. Assn. Gerontology (pres. 1960-63, citation 1960), Western Gerontology Soc. (now Am. Soc. on Aging) (founder, pres. 1955-56, named Gerontologist of Year 1957, award leadership 1975), Nat. Assn. Social Workers, Am. Pub. Welfare Assn., Am. Psychol. Assn.; hon. mem. geriatric and gerontol. socs. Argentina, Chile. Home: San Francisco Calif. Died Nov. 7, 1991. †

KUSHNER, ROSE, writer; b. Balt., June 22, 1929; d. Israel and Fannie (Gravitz) Rehert; m. Harvey D. Kushner, Jan. 14, 1951; children: Gantt A., Todd R., Lesley K. BS in Journalism summa cum laude, U. Md., 1972. Pres., exec. dir. Breast Cancer Adv. Ctr., Kensington, Md., 1975-90; guest numerous local and nat. radio and TV programs; cons., participant TV documentaries on breast cancer; lectr., speaker U.S., Can., Europe, Gt. Britain, People's Republic of China. Author: Breast Cancer: A Personal History and Investigative Report, 1975, Why Me? What Every Woman Should Know About Breast Cancer to Save Her Life, 1977, What to Do If You Find Something that Suggests Breast Cancer, 1979, If You've Thought About Breast Cancer, 1979, 6th edit., 1987, A Breast Cancer Manual Every Woman Should Have, 1980, 2d edit., 1981, Why Me? Rewritten and Updated for the Eighties, 1982, Alternatives: New Developments in the War on Breast Cancer, 1984, 2d edit., 1985. Mem. Nat. Cancer Adv. Bd., 1980-86; mem. task force on breast cancer control Am. Cancer Soc., 1989; mem. Montgomery County (Md.) Commn. on Health, 1989-90. Recipient Nat. Media award Am. Psychol. Assn., 1974, Activist award Nat. Consumer League, 1983, Medal of Courage, Am. Cancer Soc., 1987, Medal of Honor, Am. Cancer Soc., 1987, Pub. Spirit award Am. Legion Aux., 1988, Gov.'s Vol. award for Md., 1989, James Ewing Layman's award Soc. Surg. Oncology, 1990; named One of 100 Most Important Women in Am., Ladies Home Jour., 1988. Mem. Am. Med. Writers' Assn. (first award for disting med. writing 1980, award for excellence in biomed. writing 1985), Am. Soc. Profl. Journalists, Sigma Delta Chi, Kappa Tau Alpha, Phi Kappa Phi. Home: Kensington Md. Died Jan. 7, 1990. †

KUSS, HENRY JOHN, JR., international trade company executive; b. N.Y.C., Nov. 10, 1922; s. Henry John and Olga (Sidlo) K.; m. Johanna Meta Derouet, June 28, 1944; children—Linda Joy, Karen Lisa. Student, Coll. Holy Cross, 1943-44; B.A., St. John's U., 1947. Dir. supply system planning Bur. Ordnance, Dept. Navy, 1947-50; budget analyst Office Sec. Def., 1950-53; dir. Army/Navy Def. Econ. Planning, Paris Office, 1953-55; asst. to under sec. navy, 1955-57; dir. fgn. mil. resources planning Office Sec. Def., 1957-59, dir. fgn. mil. assistance planning, 1959-61, dep. asst. sec. def. for internat. security affairs, 1962-69; pres. Am. Trade and Fin. Co., Arlington, Va., 1969-85, 88-90, Re-Top U.S.A., McLean, Va., 1986-90; advisor DGA Internat., Washington, 1987-90; dir. Calcusearch, Inc., Tanner Resources Corp.; Def. mem. Presdl. Commn. on Study Korean Economy, 1953; U.S. rep. NATO Econ. Cost Com., 1954-55; def. mem. Spl. Internat. Econ. Requirements and capabilities Commn., Italy, Norway, Turkey, Greece, 1954; chmn. com. mil. exports Def. Industry Adv. Council, 1962-69; gen. assoc. DGA Internat., Inc. V.p. Howard Hughes Med. Inst., 1985-86; chmn. budget and taxation com. McLean Citizens' Assn.; former pres. Potomac Hills Citizens Assn. Served with USNR, 1944-47. Recipient Meritorious Civilian Service medal Sec. of Def., 1965. Mem. Soc. Logistics Engrs., Am. Inst. Indsl. Engrs., Georgetown Club. Lutheran. Home: McLean Va. Died July 6, 1990; buried Arlington Nat. Cemetery.

KUST, LEONARD EUGENE, lawyer; b. Luxemburg, Wis., Mar. 14, 1917; s. Joseph Andrew and Anna (Mleziva) K.; m. Henrietta Bryan Logan, Apr. 17, 1948; children: Alice Lyon Kust Harding, Andrea Logan Kust. PhB, U. Wis., Madison, 1939; JD magna cum laude, Harvard U., 1942. Bar: N.Y. 1946, Pa. 1957. Assoc. Cravath, Swaine & Moore, N.Y.C., 1946-55; gen. tax counsel Westinghouse Electric Corp., Pitts., 1955-65, v.p., gen. tax counsel, 1965-70; ptnr. Cadwalader, Wickersham & Taft, N.Y.C., 1970-88, of counsel, 1988-89; mem. adv. com. Commr. Internal Revenue, 1959-61; chmn. Pa. Gov's Com. on Tax Adminstrn., 1963-65; chmn. task forces Pa. Gov.'s Tax Rev. Com., 1967-68. Contbr. articles to profl. jours. Trustee Ch. of Heavenly Rest Day Sch., N.Y.C., 1978-82; mem. vestry, Ch. of Heavenly Rest, N.Y.C., 1975-80, warden, 1980-86; warden Calvary Protestant Episcopal Ch., Pitts., 1966-67. Served to lt. USNR, 1942-46. Mem. ABA, N.Y. State Bar Assn., Nat. Tax Assn., Tax Inst. Am. (pres. 1969-70), U.S. C of C. (dir. 1967-73), Tax Execs. Inst. (pres. 1961-62), Union Club, Down Town Assn., Harvard Club, The Church Club (trustee 1981-89, v.p. 1986-89). Home: New York N.Y. Died Sept. 21, 1989; inurned Ch. of the Heavenly Rest, N.Y.C.

LABAREE, LEONARD WOODS, historian, educator; b. Urumia, Persia, Aug. 26, 1897; parents U.S. citizens; s. Benjamin Woods and Mary Alice (Schauffler) L.; m. Elizabeth Mary Calkins, June 26, 1920; children: Arthur Calkins, Benjamin Woods. Prep. edn., Hotchkiss Sch., Lakeville, Conn., 1912-15; AB, Williams Coll., 1920, LittD, 1955; AM, Yale U., 1923, PhD, 1926; LittD, Bucknell U., 1955, Franklin Coll., 1956, Franklin and Marshall, 1956, Dickenson Coll., 1963. Instr. in history Milford (Conn.) Sch., 1920-22; instr. in history Yale U., New Haven, 1924-27, asst. prof., 1927-38, assoc. prof., 1938-42, prof., from 1942, Farnam prof. history fellow Davenport Coll., from 1934; Carnegie vis. prof. Armstrong Coll., U. of Durham, Eng., 19290-30; Anson G. Phelps lectr. NYU, 1947; state historian of Conn., 1941-51. Author: Royal Government in America, 1930 (Justin Winsor prize Am. Hist. Assn.), Conservatism in Early American History, 1948; editor: Essays in Colonial History, 1931, Royal Instructions to British Colonial Governors, 1670-1776 (2 vols.), 1935, Records of the State of Connecticut, IV-VIII, 1782-96, 1942-51, The Papers of Benjamin Franklin; gen. editor: Yale Hist. Publs. (40 vols.), 1933-46; joint editor: Mr. Franklin, 1956, Autobiography of Benjamin Franklin, 1964. With Air Svc., U.S. Army, 1917-19; commd. 2d lt. 28th Balloon Co. Mem. Am. Philos. Assn., Am. Hist. Soc., Am. Antiquarian Soc., Conn. Hist. Soc., Colonial Soc. Mass. (corr.),, Mass. Hist. Soc. (corr.), Phi Beta Kappa, Psi Upsilon. *

LABES, LEON MARTIN, lawyer; b. N.Y.C., Aug. 7, 1913; s. Hyman and Anna Ethel (Rubel) L.; m. Peggy Karr, June 15, 1938; children—Barbara (Mrs. Howard R. Harrison), Steven Hugh. B.A., Bklyn. Coll., 1933; LL.B., Bklyn. Law Sch., 1936, J.S.D. cum laude, 1937. Bar: N.Y. bar 1937. Mem. law firm Bainbridge Colby, Brown & Pollack, N.Y.C., 1938-42, Hartman, Sheridan, Tekulsky & Pecora, N.Y.C., 1942-52, Alderman & Labes, N.Y.C., 1952-55; pvt. practice N.Y.C., 1955-70; mem. firm Auerbach & Labes, N.Y.C., 1970-89; Cons. U.S. War Prodn. Bd., 1942-45; treas. dir. Lewisohn Copper Corp., 1959-66; exec. dir. Electronics Mfrs. Assn., N.Y.C., 1962-74; moderator Labor Relations Forum, Radio Sta. WEVD, N.Y.C., 1962-65; lectr. labor law Columbia, Coll. City N.Y., N.Y. U.; mem. Supreme Ct. Panel for Mediation of Med. Malpractice litigation; spl. master apptd. by appellate div. Supreme Ct., N.Y. County; arbitrator for Civil Ct., N.Y. County. Author: A Fresh Approach to the Problem of Strikes, 1967; Contbr. numerous articles to profl. jours. Bd. dirs. Manpower Edn. Inst., 1968-80. Mem. Am. Bar Assn. (labor arbitration com.), N.Y. County Lawyers Assn. (labor com.), N.Y. State Bar Assn., N.Y. State Trial Lawyers Assn., N.Y. Urban League (dir.). Home: New York N.Y. Died June 23, 1989; cremated.

LACEY, DANIEL DAMIAN, consultant, author on workplace issues; b. Wilkes-Barre, Pa., Apr. 30, 1950; s. Harold E. and Florence J. (Godlewski) L.; m. Margaret Mary Mulvey, Dec. 1, 1978. AS in Journalism, Luzerne County Community Coll., 1980; student, Wilkes Coll., Ohio U. Editor bus. sect. Scranton (Pa.) Times, 1979-81; editor Sunday bus. sect. Miami (Fla.) Herald, 1981; editor morning bus. sect Cleve. Press, 1982; assoc. editor Personnel Adminstr., Alexandria, Va., 1983; account exec. Dix and Eaton, Cleve., 1984-86; pres. Lacey and Co., Rocky River, Ohio, from 1986. Author: The Paycheck Disruption, 1988, The Essential Immigrant, 1990, Your Rights in the Workplace, 1991; editor: (with others) Work in the 21st Century, 1984, (newsletter) Workplace Trends, from 1989; contbr. articles to various mags. and newspapers including The Times of London, Chgo. Tribune, Pitts. Post-Gazette, Cleve. Plain Dealer, The Legal Reformer, San Francisco Chronicle, Human Resource Executive. Mem. Soc. Profl. Journalists,

Greater Cleve. Coun. Smaller Enterprises, Authors Guild, Sierra Club (exec. com. Pa. chpt. 1979-80). Roman Catholic. Died Sept. 21, 1992. †

LACHNER, MARSHALL SMITH, management service executive; b. Anna, Ill., May 15, 1914; adopted s. Henry and Anna L.; m. Eleanor Blochwitz, Dec. 30, 1935; children: Melody, Marshall, Geoffrey, Crispin, Brandon. Student, Northwestern U., 1933-34, Wharton Sch. Bus., U. Pa., 1935-36. With R.H. Macy & Co., 1936-38; with Colgate Palmolive Co., Jersey City, 1938-56; successively displayman, salesman, supr., sales mgr. Jersey City dist. and Chgo. dist., div. sales mgr. Colgate Palmolive Co., Berkeley, Calif., gen. sales mgr., v.p. soap sales, 1954-56; pres. Pabst Brewing Co., Chgo., 1956-57; chmn. bd., pres., chief exec. officer B.T. Babbitt, Inc., N.Y.C., 1957-60; sr. v.p. cosmetics Revlon, Inc., 1960-62; pres. Lachner Assocs., Inc., creative services to mgmt., Lodi, Wis., 1962-65; dir. C.W. Carnrick. Mem. exec. com. Nat. Football Found. and Hall of Fame; dir. Parkingston Found. Recipient award Poor Richard Club Phila., 1958; Applause award Sales Exec. Club N.Y., 1958; award Adcraft Club Detroit, 1958; named Man of Yr. Summit Ind. Press. Mem. Phi Kappa Psi. Presbyterian (elder). Home: Lodi Wis. Died Apr. 4, 1991; buried Randolph, Wis.

LACKAS, JOHN CHRISTOPHER, business educator; b. N.Y.C., Oct. 15, 1904; s. John William and Caroline (Mildenberger) L.; m. Genevieve Mary Meekins, June 29, 1935. B.S., N.Y.U., 1930, M.A., 1931, Ph.D., 1938; J.S.D., St. John's U., 1938; LL.B., Rutgers U., 1929, LL.M., 1935; M.S.S., New Sch. Social Research, 1936. Dir. Sch. Bus., Seton Hall U., 1938-42; commd. 1st lt. U.S. Army, 1942, advanced through grades to col., 1950; from asst. comdt. to comdt. U.S. Army Finance Sch., 1948-52; asst. comptroller for internat. affairs Army Gen. Staff, 1952-56; mem. faculty Indsl. Coll. Armed Forces, 1956-60; prof. bus. Queensborough Community Coll., 1960-74, prof. emeritus, 1974-90, dean adminstrn., 1960-68, acting pres., 1961-63; Coe fellow Inst. Am. Studies, 1960. Author: (with Col. Seeds) Military Supply Management, 1957; also articles. Pres. Queensboro Council Social Welfare Agys.; Bd. dirs. L.I. Ednl. TV Council. Decorated Legion of Merit; recipient Excellence in Teaching award Bd. Higher Edn., City U. N.Y. Mem. Acad. Polit. Sci., AAAS, Am. Econs. Assn., Am. Polit. and Social Sci. Assn., AAUP, Phi Delta Kappa. Home: Jamesburg N.J. Died Aug. 20, 1990; buried Arlington Nat. Cemetery.

LADAR, SAMUEL ABRAHAM, lawyer; b. Jackson, Calif., Oct. 4, 1903; s. Max and Dora (Axelrod) L.; m. Sylvia Favorman, Jan. 1, 1927; 1 son, Jerrold M. A.B., U. Calif. at, Berkeley, 1925; J.D., U. Calif., 1928. Bar: Calif. bar 1928. With Jesse H. Steinhart (lawyer), San Francisco, 1928-46; mem. firm Steinhart, Goldberg, Feigenbaum & Ladar, San Francisco, 1946-81; of counsel firm Steinhart & Falconer, from 1981; vis. lectr. Boalt Hall, U. Calif. Law Sch., from 1951. Pres. San Francisco Bd. Edn., 1962, San Francisco Police Commn., 1965, Jewish Welfare Fedn. San Francisco, Marin County and Peninsula, 1965-66; mem. San Francisco Crime Commn., 1970-71; Bd. dirs. Mt. Zion Hosp. and Med. Center, San Francisco, 1979, San Francisco chpt. Am. Jewish Com.; nat. bd. dels. Am. Jewish Com. Mem. Am. Bar Assn., State Bar Calif., Bar Assn. San Francisco, U. Calif. Law Sch. Alumni Assn. (pres. 1967-68). Home: San Francisco Calif. Deceased. †

LADD, MASON, law educator, dean; b. Sheldon, Iowa, Jan. 9, 1898; s. Scott Mason and Emma (Cromer) L.; m. Esther Victoria Swanson, Sept. 11, 1924; children: Carolyn Joan, Mary Esther, Margaret Ann. AB, Grinnell Coll., 1920, LLD (hon.), 1954; postgrad., Harvard U., 1920-21; JD, U. Iowa, 1923; SJD, Harvard U., 1935. Bar: Iowa, 1923. Practice law Des Moines, 1923-29; asst. county atty. Polk County, Iowa, 1927-29; ptnr. Ladd & Ladd, 1923-29; lectr. in law Drake U., 1925-29; prof. law State U. of Iowa, 1929-39, dean, prof. law, from 1939, mem. bd. Control of Athletics; teaching fellow Harvard Law Sch.; mem. adv. com. Fed. Jud. Conf.; commr. Nat. Conf. Uniform State Laws; chmn. Fed. Legal Civil Svc. Exam. Com. for Iowa; adviser on evidence Am. Law Inst. Author: (with Armistead Dobie) Federal Jurisdiction and Procedure, 1939, The Law of Evidence, 2d edit., 1955, (with Brown and Vestal) Pleadings and Procedure, 1953, Comparative Study Iowa Law and Uniform Rules of Evidence, 1959; compiler: Cases on Extraordinary Remedies, 1931, (with Boyd) Materials on Iowa Probate Praceice, 6th edit., 1956; contbr. to legal periodicals and books. Mem. S.A.T.C., World War I.; col., Judge Adv. Gen. Dept., with Legal Div. Surgeon Gen. Office, U.S. Army; dir. of div. ETO, World War II. Decorated Legion of Merit; recipient Outstanding Civilian Svc. medal Dept. Army. Mem. ABA (mem. com. on rsch. ABA Found., chmn. spl. com. on mil. justide), Iowa Bar Assn. (award of merit), Mont. State Bar Assn. (hon. life), Order of Coif, Kiwanis (pres. 1941), Triangle Club, Masons (32 deg.), Phi Beta Kappa, Omicron Delta Kappa (hon.). Republican. Methodist. *

LAFARGE, LOUIS BANCEL, architect; b. Boston, May 17, 1900; s. Bancel and Mabel (Hooper) LaF.; m. Hester Emmet, July 28, 1928 (div. 1962); children: Timothy, Benjamin, Celestine; m. Margaret Hockaday, Apr. 12, 1962. Grad., Choate Sch., 1918; A.B., Harvard, 1922; B.F.A., Yale, 1925. A.N.A. Apprentice Delano & Aldrich, Peabody, Wilson & Brown, N.Y.C., 1925-32; practice architecture N.Y.C., 1932-38; partner LaFarge & Knox, 1938-42, LaFarge, Knox & Murphy, N.Y.C., 1947-60, LaFarge and Morey, N.Y.C., 1961-66; Mem. N.Y.C. Landmarks Preservation Commn., 1965-70; chmn. Historic Dist. Commn. for Nantucket, Mass., 1971-76; mem. adv. council Cooper Union Sch. Art and Architecture, 1959-61. Designer residences in Charlestown, S.C., the Hamptons on L.I., the Hudson Valley, N.Y., New Haven area; also shaped the Caneel Bay resort in V.I. Served from capt. to maj. USAAF, 1942-45; Gen. Staff Corps., 1945-46; chief monuments, fine arts and archives Hdqrs. SHAEF, 1945; chief monuments, fine arts and archives Office Mil. Govt. for Germany, 1945-46. Decorated Legion of Merit, Bronze Star U.S.; chevalier Legion of Honor; Croix de Guerre Medaille de la Reconnaissance, France; officer Ordre de la Couronne, Belgium; officer Order Orange-Nassau, Netherlands; Order of Merit 1st class Czechoslovakia). Fellow AIA (pres. N.Y. 1958-60, sec., dir. 1952-54, 56-60, chmn. fine arts com. 1960-63); mem. Beaux Arts Inst. Design (past trustee), Municipal Art Soc. N.Y. (pres. 1954-56, dir. 1956-59), Yale Arts Assn. (exec. com. 1959-61), Liturgical Art Soc. (pres., dir. 1949-51), Am. Arbitration Assn. (dir., exec. com. 1961-69), Archtl. League N.Y. Club: Century Assn. (N.Y.C.). Home: Newtown Pa. Died July 2, 1989; buried St. Columba Cemetery,Middletown, R.I.

LAGERSTROM, PACO AXEL, mathematician, educator; b. Oskarshamn, Sweden, Feb. 24, 1914; s. Paco Harald and Karin (Wiedemann) L. Filosofie Kandidat, U. Stockholm, 1935, Filosofie Licenciat, 1939; postgrad., U. Munster, Germany, 1938; Ph.D. in Math, U. Princeton U., 1942. Instr. math. Princeton U., 1941-44; flight test engr. Bell Aircraft, 1944-45; aerodynamicist Douglas Aircraft, 1945-46, cons., 1946-66; research assoc. in aeros., staff engr. Calif. Inst. Tech., 1946-47, asst. prof. aeros., 1947-49, assoc. prof., 1949-52, prof., 1952-67, prof. applied math., 1967-81, prof. emeritus, 1981-89; cons. TRW, 1966-68; vis. prof. U. Paris, 1960-61, Rensselaer Poly. Inst., 1984, Clarkson U., 1986. Author: Matched Asympholic Expansions: Ideas and Techniques, 1988 (#76 series Applied Mathematical Sciences); contbr. articles to profl. jours. and handbooks. Mem. bd. Coleman Chamber Music, Pasadena, from 1950, pres., 1958-60. Decorated Palmes Académiques (France); recipient Patron of Arts award Pasadena Arts Council, 1973; Guggenheim fellow, 1960-61; Fondation des Treilles fellow, France, 1982. Mem. Am. Math. Soc. Clubs: The Travellers (Paris); Brook, Knickerbocker (N.Y.C.); Assocs. of Caltech (life, Pasadena). Home: Pasadena Calif. Died Feb. 16, 1989; cremated.

LAIRD, DONALD ANDERSON, psychologist; b. Steugen County, Ind., May 14, 1897; s. Rev. Allan Max and Grace (Anderson) L.; m. Hilda Drexel, Nov. 18, 1916 (dec. Jan. 1938); 1 child, David Dresel; m. Eleanor Childs Leonard, Apr. 1940. BA, U. Dubuque, 1919, ScD (hon.), 1927; PhD, State U. of Iowa, 1923. Diplomate in indsl. psychology Am. Bd. Examiners in Profl. Psychology. Tchr. of psychology State U. of Iowa, U. Wyo., Yale U., Northwestern U., Colgate U., 1925-39; dir. Ayer Found. for Consumer Analysis, Phila., 1939-40; psychol. examiner Great Lakes Naval Tng. Sta., World War; dir. demonstration Sleep and Fatigue Lab., Century of Progress Expn., Chgo., 1933. Author: (with Eleanor C. Laire) books in general field of psychology, several of them in indsl. psychology and inter-person rels., including Menchenführung in Betrieb, 1953, Aufstieg durch Willenskraft, 1955, Practical Business Psychooogy, erv. 1965, The New Psychology for Leadership, 1956, Techniques of Delegating, 1957, Sound Ways to Sound Sleep, 1959, Psicologia practica de los Negocios, 1959, As Technicas de Delegar, 1960, Techniques for Efficient Remembering, 1960, Tired Feelings and How to Master Them, 1961, Dynamics of Personal Efficient Remembering, 1961, Be Active and Feel Better, 1962, O Segredo da Eficiencia Pessoal, 1962, La Dinamica del la Eficiencia Personal, 1964, How to Get Along With Automation, 1964; writer of popular articles in field; contbr. to profl. jours. Mem. exec. coun. Acoustical Soc. Am., 1937-39. NRC fellow in biol. scis., 1923-24. Fellow AAAS; mem. APA, Writers Guild of Authors' League Am., Columbia Club, Parlor Club, Theta Chi, Pi Delta Epsilon (hon.), Pi Gamma Mu (hon.). *

LALANDE, GILLES, consultant, Canadian government official; b. Montreal, Que., Can., May 10, 1927; s. Ernest and Azilda (Charette) L.; m. Simone Lavigne, June 11, 1951; children—Michele, Pierre, Dominique. M.Com., U. Montreal, 1949; Docteur d'universite, Institut de Geographie Alpine, U. Grenoble, France, 1953; LL.D. (hon.), York U., 1982. Fgn. service officer Dept. External Affairs of Can., Ottawa, Ont., 1954-62; asst. prof. internat. relations U. Montreal, 1962-65, asso. prof., 1965-71, prof., 1971-76; v.p. multilateral programs Can. Internat. Devel. Agy., 1976-78; Can. ambassador to Ivory Coast, Mali, Upper Volta and Niger, Abidjan, Ivory Coast, 1978-80; dep. commr. ofcl. langs. Ottawa, 1980-86; co-sec. Royal Commn. on Bilinqualism and Biculturalism, 1966-70; chmn. Que. Govt. Working Group on Bill 101, 1986. Author: The Department of External Affairs and Biculturalism, 1970, In Defence of Federalism—The View from Quebec, 1978. Mem. Royal Soc. Can., Canadian Polit. Sci. Assn. (pres. 1970-71). Roman Catholic. Home: Montreal Que., Can. Died Sept. 4, 1988; buried Montreal.

LAMBERT, CHARLES FREDERIC, manufacturing executive; b. Ypsilanti, Mich., Dec. 23, 1896; s. Charles Rosseau and Elizabeth (Vliet) L.; m. Dorothy Millen, June 5, 1920 (dec. Dec. 1962); children: Dorothy Jeanne (Mrs. George M. Christensen), Joan (Mrs. Henry Roemer McPhee), Charles Frederic. BA, U. Mich., 1919. Pres., gen. mgr. Clayton & Lambert Mfg. Co., Buckner, Ky., from 1926. Ens. USN, World War I. Mem. Pendennis Club, Harmony Landing Country Club. *

LAMBERT, ROBERT JOE, retired mathematics educator; b. Dubuque, Iowa, Dec. 23, 1921; s. Joe Edwin and Mahala Pauline (Wirkler) L.; m. Marion Elizabeth Kochheiser, Dec. 20, 1942; children: Tracey Robert, Daniel Joe. B.A., Drake U., 1943; M.S., Iowa State U., 1948, Ph.D., 1951. Instr. Drake U., Des Moines, 1943-44; instr. Iowa State U., Ames, 1946-51, prof., 1953-88, assoc. dir. computation ctr., 1978-88, prof. emeritus, from 1988; rsch. mathematician Nat. Security Agy., Washington, 1951-53; sr. mathematician Ames Lab., 1966-78; cons. Office Naval Research, Washington, 1953-59, Zenith Radio, Chgo., 1959-60, Collins Radio, Cedar Rapids, Iowa, 1960-63. Editor Trans-Mississippian Philatelic Jour., from 1981; contbr. articles to profl. jours., chpts. to books. Served to lt. (j.g.) USN, 1944-46 PTO. Fellow Iowa Acad. Sci.; mem. Am. Math. Soc., Math. Assn. Am., Soc. for Indsl. and Applied Math. (pres. Iowa sect. 1969-70), Assn. for Computing Machinery, Des Moines Philatelic Soc., Trans-Miss. Philatelic Soc. (pres. 1985-89). Republican. Presbyterian. Lodge: Elks. Home: Ames Iowa Deceased. †

LAND, EDWIN HERBERT, physicist, inventor; b. Bridgeport, Conn., May 7, 1909; s. Harry M. and Matha F. L.; m. Helen Maislen, 1929; children: Jennifer, Valerie. Ed., Norwich Acad.; student, Harvard U., ScD (hon.), 1957; ScD (hon.), Tufts Coll., 1947, Poly. Inst. Bklyn., 1952, Colby Coll., 1955, Northeastern U., 1959, Carnegie Inst. Tech., 1964, Yale U., 1966, Columbia U., 1967, Loyola U., 1970, NYU, 1973; LLD (hon.), Bates Coll., 1953, Wash. U., 1966, U. Mass., 1967, Brandeis U., 1980; LHD (hon.), Williams Coll., 1968. Founder Polaroid Corp., Cambridge, Mass., 1937, pres., 1937-75, chmn. bd., 1937-82, CEO and dir. rsch., 1937-80; founder, pres., scientist, dir. rsch. Rowland Inst. for Sci., Cambridge, 1980-91; William James lectr. psychology Harvard, 1966-67, Morris Loeb lectr. physics, 1974; vis. Inst. prof. Mass. Inst. Tech., 1956-91; mem. Pres.'s Sci. Adv. Com., 1957-59, cons.-at-large, 1960-73; mem. Pres.'s Com. Nat. Medal of Sci., 1969-72, Carnegie Commn. on Ednl. TV, 1966-67, Nat. Commn. on Tech., Automation and Econ. Progress, 1964-66; fgn. mem. Royal Soc., 1986. Trustee Ford Found., 1967-75. Recipient Presdl. Medal of Freedom, 1963, Nat. Medal of Sci., 1967, Hood medal Royal Photog. Soc., 1935, Cresson medal, 1937, Potts medal, 1956, Vermilye medal Franklin Inst., Phila., 1974, John Scott medal and award, 1938, Rumford medal Am. Acad. Arts and Scis., 1945, Holley medal ASME, 1948, Duddell medal Brit. Phys. Soc., 1949, Progress medal Soc. Photog. Engrs., 1955, Albert A. Michelson award Case Inst. Tech., 1966, Kulturpreis Photog. Soc. Germany, 1967, Perkin medal Soc. Chem. Industry, 1974, Proctor award, 1963, Photog. Sci. and Engring. Jour. award, 1971, Progress medal Photog. Soc. Am., 1960, Kosar Meml. award, 1973, Golden Soc. medal Photog. Soc. Vienna, 1961, Interkamera award, 1973, Cosmos Club award, 1970, Nat. Modern Pioneer award NAM, 1940, 66, Jefferson medal N.J. Patent Law Assn., 1960, Indsl. Research Inst. medal, 1965, Diesel medal in gold, 1966, Dudley Wright prize and award, 1980, Nat. Medal of Tech., 1988; named Nat. Inventors Hall of Fame, 1977, Nat. Air and Space Mus. trophy, 1989, Lifetime Achievement award Photographic Soc. Japan, 1989, Third Century award Found. for Creative Am., U.S. Patents and Copyrights Bicentennial, 1990. Fellow NAS, Photog. Soc. Am., Am. Acad. Arts and Scis. (pres. 1951-53), Royal Photog. Soc. Gt. Britain (Progress medal 1957), Royal Micros. Soc. (hon.), Soc. Photog. Scientists and Engrs. (hon., Lieven-Gevaert medal 1976); mem. N.Y. Acad. Sci. (L.W. Frohlich award 1986), NAE (Founders medal 1972), Optical Soc. Am. (hon. mem. 1972, dir. 1950-51, Frederic Ives medal 1967), Royal Instn. Gt. Britain (hon.), Am. Philos. Soc., German Photog. Soc. (hon.), Soc. Photog. Sci. and Tech. Japan (hon.), IEEE (hon.), Sigma Xi. Home: Cambridge Mass. Died Mar. 1, 1991.

LANDA, LOUIS A., English language educator; b. Hallettsville, Tex., Nov. 6, 1901; s. Max and Bessie Fanny (Nathan) L.; m. Hazel Schaeffer, Sept. 10, 1928. BA, U. Tex., 1923; MA, Columbia U., 1926; PhD, U. Chgo., 1941. Oldright fellow in philosophy U. Tex., 1924, instr. English, 1926-28; instr. U. Chgo., 1932-41, asst. prof., 1941-45; assoc. prof. Princeton (N.J.) U., 1946-53, prof., 1954-70, prof. emeritus, 1970-89, sr. fellow coun. humanities, 1958-59; hon. lectr. U. London, 1952-53, Fulbright lectr. Trinity term Oxford (Eng.) U., 1953; adv. editor Augustan Reprint Soc., Wesleyan-Clarendon edit. Henry Fielding. Author: (with Herbert Davis) Swift: Sermons and Irish Tracts, 1948, Swift and the Church of Ireland, 1954; editor:

(with James Clifford) Pope and His Contemporaries, 1949, (with R.S. Crane and others) English Literature 1660-1880: A Bibliography, 2 vols., 1952; Annual Eighteenth Century Bibliography, 1942-54, Gulliver's Travels, 1960, Journal of the Plague Year (Defoe), 1969, Essays in Eigtheenth-Century English Literature, 1980; mem. editorial com. HLQ, from 1963; also articles. Recipient Disting. Visitor award Australian-Am. Ednl. Found., 1970; Guggenheim fellow, Ireland and Eng., 1947-48, 67-68, Fulbright fellow, London and Oxford, 1952-53. Fellow Royal Hist. Soc.; mem. MLA (editorial bd. 1963-68), Modern Humanities Rsch. Assn., Old Guard Princeton. Home: Princeton N.J. Died Mar. 17, 1989; buried Eagle Lake, Tex.

LANDERS, MARY KENNY, mathematics educator; b. Fall River, Mass., Feb. 5, 1905; d. Bernard Francis and Katherine (Connell) Kenny; m. Aubrey Wilfred Landers, July 30, 1932; children: Robert Kenny, Patricia Joan Landers Savage, Richard Bernard. AB, Brown U., 1926, MA, 1927; PhD, U. Chgo., 1939. Instr. Hunter Coll., N.Y.C., 1927-46, asst. prof. math., 1947-57, assoc. prof., 1958-63, prof., 1964-75, chmn. grievance com., 1969-72; sec. The Legislative Conf. CUNY, 1959-90. Trustee City U. Welfare Bd., 1967-81; chmn. Isabelle Scott Bollard Scholarship Com. Fellow AAAS, N.Y. Acad. Scis.; mem. AAUP, NEA, Am. Math. Soc., Math. Assn. Am., N.Y. State Tchrs. Assn., Phi Beta Kappa, Sigma Xi, Sigma Delta Epsilon, Pi Mu Epsilon. Home: Forest Hills N.Y. Died Nov. 18, 1990; buried Swan Point Cemetery, Providence.

LANDES, RUTH, anthropologist, educator; b. N.Y.C., Oct. 8, 1908; d. Joseph and Anna (Grossman) Schlossberg; m. June 14, 1928 (div. Sept. 1935). BS, NYU, 1928; MSW, N.Y. Sch. Social Work, 1929; PhD, Columbia U., 1935. Social worker N.Y.C., 1929-31; rsch. fellow dept anthropology Columbia U., 1933-40; instr. Fisk U., Nashville, 1937-38, Bklyn. Coll., 1937; researcher Carnegie Corp., N.Y.C., 1939; rsch. dir. Coord. Inter-Am. Affairs, Washington, 1941; rep. Fair Employment Practices Com., Washington, 1941-45; dir. pvt. interim com. on fair employment practices, 1945; researcher L.A. Met. Welfare Coun., 1946-47; study dir. Am. Jewish Com., 1948-51; Fulbright sr. rsch. scholar Edinburgh (Scotland) U., 1951-52; lectr. Wm. Alanson White Psychiat. Inst., N.Y.C., 1953-54, New Sch. Social Rsch., N.Y.C., 1953-55; dir. geriatrics L.A. City Health Dept., 1958-59; lectr., cons. UCLA, U. Calif., Berkeley, 1962, L.A. State Coll., 1963; cons. Calif. Social Work Dept. and Agys., Calif. Bur. Mental Hygiene, Calif. Dept. Edn., Calif. Pub. Health Dept., San Francisco Police Dept.; field rsch. in Americas, We. Europe, South Africa, 1929-31, 32-36, 38-39, 46, 66, 68-72; vis. prof. U. So. Calif. Sch. Social Work, 1957-58; vis. prof., also dir. anthropology and edn. program Claremont Grad. Sch., 1959-62; cons. IBM, 1963-66; vis. prof. Tulane U., 1964; prof. U. Kans., Lawrence, summer 1964, McMaster U., Hamilton, Ont., Can., 1965-91. Author: Ojibwa Sociology, 1937, 2d edit., 1969, The Ojibwa Woman, 1938, 3d edit., 1970, The City of Women, 1947, in Portuguese, 1967, Culture in American Education, 1965, The Latin-Americans of the Southwest, 1965, Ojibwa Religion and the Midewiwin, 1968, The Mystic Lake Sioux, 1969, The Prairie Potawatomi, 1970; contbr. articles to profl. jours., chpts. to books. Recipient fellowships and grante Social Sci. Rsch. Coun., Philos. Soc., Rockefeller Found., Rosenberg Found., Can. Coun. Mem. Am. Anthrop. Assn., Author's League. Home: Hamilton, ON Canada Died Feb. 11, 1991.

LANDIS, FREDERICK, federal judge; b. Logansport, Ind., Jan. 17, 1912; s. Frederick and Bessie (Baker) L.; m. E. Joyce Stevenson, July 4, 1945 (dec. 1986); children: Diana, Frederick, Susan, Gillian, Kenesaw Mountain; m. Irene Rhodes, July 13, 1987. Student, Wabash Coll., 1928-29; A.B., Ind. U., 1932, LL.B., 1934. Bar: Ind. bar 1934. Asso. Long and Yarlott, 1935-38; mem. Landis & Hanna, 1938-46, Landis & Landis, 1946-54, Landis & Michael, 1954-55; pros. atty. 29th Jud. Circuit, 1938-40; justice Supreme Ct. Ind., 1955-65; judge U.S. Customs Ct., 1965-81, U.S. Ct. Internat. Trade (formerly Customs Ct.), 1981-84; Mem. Ind. Ho. of Reps., 1950-52, Ind. Senate, 1952-55. Served from enlisted man to lt. USNR, 1942-46. Mem. Ind. Bar Assn., Cass County Bar Assn. (pres. 1948-51), ABA, Am. Legion, VFW, Phi Delta Phi, Delta Tau Delta. Clubs: Elks; Columbia (Indpls.), Press (Indpls.). Home: Indianapolis Ind. Died Mar. 1, 1990; buried Mt. Hope Cemetery, Logansport, Ind.

LANDON, MICHAEL (EUGENE MAURICE OROWITZ), actor; b. Forest Hills, N.Y., Oct. 31, 1936; s. Eli Maurice and Peggy (O'Neill) Orowitz; m. Cindy Landon; children: Mark, Josh, Cheryl, Michael, Leslie Ann, Shawna Leigh, Christopher Beau, Jennifer, Sean. Student, U. So. Calif. Movie appearances include I Was a Teenage Werewolf, 1957, God's Little Acre, 1958, The Legend of Tom Dooley, 1959, Maracaibo, 1958, The Errand Boy, 1961; TV films Little House on the Prairie, 1974, Where Pigeons Go To Die (2 Emmy Nominations); star, writer, dir., TV series Bonanza, 1959-73; star, dir., exec. producer, writer TV series Little House on the Prairie, 1974-82, Highway to Heaven; dir. TV series It's Good to Be Alive, G.E. Theatre, 1974; writer, dir. TV film The Loneliest Runner, 1976; other TV appearances include Playhouse 90. Home: Malibu Calif. Died July 1, 1991; buried Hillside Meml. Pk., Calif.

LANDRES, MORRIS M., motion picture company executive; m. Clara Pollock; 1 son, Peter David. Student civil engring.; degree, Bklyn. Poly. Inst.; postgrad. edn. and art, Carnegie Inst. Tech. Pres. Century Pictures Corp., Gen. Film Library Calif., Inc.; head Morris M. Landres Prodns., Morris M. Landres Enterprises (producers short subjects and features); v.p., assoc. producer adventure Pictures, Inc.; producer, co-owner, pres. Action Film Producers, Landres-Weiss Prodns.; also producer comml. films and exploitation features; studio cons., writer. Mem. Ind. Motion Picture Producers Assn. (pres.), Acad. Motion Picture Arts and Scis. Home: Los Angeles Calif. Deceased.

LANDRUM, PHILIP MITCHELL, former congressman, lawyer; b. Martin, Ga., Sept. 10, 1907; s. Phillip Davis and Blanche Mitchell L.; m. Laura Brown, July 31, 1933; children: Phillip Mitchell, Susan. AB, Piedmont Coll., 1939, LLD, 1958; LLB, Atlanta Law Sch., 1941; LLD, Brenau Coll., 1976. High sch. athletic dir., coach Bowman, Ga., 1932-35; athletic dir., coach Nelson, Ga., 1935-37, supt. pub. schs., 1937-41; pvt. practice law Jasper, Ga., 1949-90; mem. 83d to 94th Congresses, 9th Dist. Ga., 1952-77; co-author Landrum-Griffin Bill, 1959. Trustee Piedmont Coll., Demorest, Brenau Coll.; chmn. bd. trustees Richard B. Russell Found. With USAAF, 1942-45. Mem. Ga. Bar Assn., Ga. Bar Assn., Am. Legion, VFW, Masons, Elks. Democrat. Baptist. Home: Jasper GA. Died Nov. 19, 1990.

LANE, HOWARD RAYMOND, architect; b. Chgo., Oct. 13, 1922; s. Mose and Libbie (Sax) L.; m. Shirley Robbins, June 14, 1947; children: Rod, Laura, Barbara. Student, Carnegie Inst. Tech., 1943-44, Archtl. Assn. Sch., London, 1946; BArch, Ill. Inst. Tech., 1947. Assoc. Skidmore, Owings & Merrill, Chgo., 1947, Allison & Rible, Architects, L.A., 1948, A.C. Martin & Assocs., L.A., 1949, Robert Alexander, L.A., 1949, Pereira & Luckman, L.A., 1950-53; pres. Lane Archtl. Group, Woodland Hills, Calif., 1953-88. Prin. works include Beverly Med. Bldg., West Hollywood, Calif., Solar Dining Facility, Camp Pendleton, Calif. (Coalition Energy Profls. 1st award 1981), PermaByte Magnetics, Inc. bldg., Chatsworth, Calif., Fleet Computer Programming Operation Bldg., San Diego (excellence awards AIA 1985), Core Instrumentation Facility, Ft. Irwin, Calif. (Corps Engrs. Design award 1985), Faculty Office Bldg., Northridge, Calif., Bus. Edn. Bldg., Woodland Hills, Calif., Flight Simulator Bldg., El Toro, Calif. (excellence awards AIA 1986). Founder, co-chmn. Valley Round Table Council, 1968-69; chmn. San Fernando Valley Conv. Center Com., 1968-69; patron Los Angeles County Mus. Art; mem. Greater L.A. Zoo Assn. Served with U.S. Army, 1943-47. Recipient Pub. Service award Los Angeles County, 1970. Fellow AIA (pres. Calif. council 1977, pres. L.A. chpt. 1974, vice-chmn. nat. energy com. 1979, chmn. nat. energy com. 1980-81, chmn. Calif. council ins. trustees 1982, chmn. architecture for edn. com. L.A. chpt. 1985); mem. Nat. Council Archtl. Registration Bds., Encino C. of C. (past pres.), Soc. Am. Mil. Engrs. (sustaining), Associated Chambers of Commerce (pres. 1968), Tau Epsilon Phi. Home: Woodland Hills Calif. Died Nov. 3, 1988; buried Eden Meml. Pk., Calif.

LANE, MILLS B., JR., banker; b. Savannah, Ga., 1912; m. Anne Waring; children: Mills B. IV, Anita. BA, Yale U., 1934. Pres., vice chmn., chmn. Citizens & So. Nat. Bank, Savannah, 1946-73; bd. dirs. Bibb Mfg. Co., Magic Chef Inc., Ga. Power Co., Winn Dixie Stores, Savannah Foods and Industries. Chmn. bd. dirs. Reinhardt Coll. Mem. Young Pres. Orgn. (bd. dirs.). Home: Savannah Ga. Died May 7, 1989; buried Bonaventure Cemetery, Savannah, Ga.

LANG, WILLIAM HENRY, steel company executive; b. Pitts., June 2, 1911; s. Charles Edward and Anna L. (Heachenroether) L.; m. Lida Jones, June 23, 1938; children: Marjorie, Janet, Jean. AB, Darmouth Coll., 1933; ML, U. Pitts., 1938; grad. advanced mgmt. program, Harvard U., 1951. With Gulf Oil Corp., 1933-34; with U.S. Steel Corp. and prior subsidiaries, N.Y.C., 1934-76, asst. treas., 1952-59, treas., adminstrv. v.p., 1959-70, exec. v.p. realth and fin., 1970-76; pres. U.S. Steel Credit Corp., 1954-76; vice chmn. 1st Nat. State Bank, Newark, 1968-70; dir. Extel Corp., Northbrook, Ill. Trustee St. Barnabas Med. Ctr., N.J. Mem. Am. Iron and Steel Inst., Links Club, Baltusrol Country Club, Short Hills Country Club, Pine Valley Country Club. Home: Belleair Fla. Died Mar. 14, 1990.

LANGELL, JEROME EDWIN, writer, feature editor; b. Cleve., Nov. 14, 1910; s. Alexander Hector and Agnes Helen (Jones) L. B.S., Wharton Sch., U. Pa., 1933. Mdsg. and market research Cleve. Press, 1933-38; market research, radio sta. WHK, Cleve., 1941; compliance investigator WPB, 1942-44; insp. Fisher Aircraft, 1944; asst. editor employee publs. Standard Oil Co. (O.), 1945; owner Allied Feature Syndicate (specializing in preparation and sale of editorial features to newspapers), Cleve., from 1946. Home: Cleveland OH Deceased.

LANGERMAN, HAROLD ALBERT, advertising executive; b. Phila., Dec. 20, 1923; s. Charles and Ida (Sanderofsky) L.; m. Doris Jean Lorenz, Mar. 20, 1982; 1 child, Stephen C. BA in English, Gettysburg Coll., 1949. Copywriter J. Walter Thompson Co., Tokyo, 1953-54; advt. mgr. Safeway Stores, Dallas, 1954-55; v.p., creative dir. Lewis & Gilman, Inc., Phila., 1956-69; exec. v.p., creative dir. Spiro & Assocs., Phila., 1969-79, Smith-Langerman, Phila., 1979-81; pres. Hal Langerman Advt., Blue Bell, Pa., from 1980; lectr. in field. Served with U.S. Army, 1949-53, Korea. Decorated Bronze Star. Jewish. Home: Blue Bell Pa. Deceased. †

LANGSTON, HIRAM THOMAS, surgeon, educator; b. Rio de Janeiro, Brazil, Jan. 12, 1912; s. Alva B. and Louise F. (Diuguid) L.; m. Helen M. Orth, June 22, 1941; children: Paula F., Thomas O., Carol E. Student, Collegio Batista, Rio de Janeiro, 1926-28, Georgetown (Ky.) Coll., 1929; AB, U. Louisville, 1930, MD, 1934; MS in Surgery, U. Mich., 1941. Diplomate: Am. Bd. Surgery, Am. Bd. Thoracic Surgery (a founder). Intern Garfield Meml. Hosp., Washington, 1934-35, resident pathology, 1935-37; asst. resident surgery Univ. Hosp., Ann Arbor, Mich., 1937-38, resident surgery, 1938-39, resident thoracic surgery, 1939-40; instr. thoracic surgery Med. Sch., 1940-41; pvt. practice, also assoc. surgery Northwestern U., 1941-42, asst. prof. surgery, 1946-48; pvt. practice thoracic surgery Detroit; also clin. prof. surgery Wayne U., 1948-52; clin. assoc. prof. surgery U. Ill., Chgo., 1952-62, clin. prof. surgery, 1963-78; clin. prof. surgery Northwestern U., Chgo., 1978-81, prof. emeritus, 1981-92; chief surgeon Chgo. Tb Sanitarium, 1952-71; cons. thoracic surgery VA Hosp., Hines, Ill., 1952-74; mem. staff St. Joseph's Hosp., chmn. dept. surgery, 1978-82, mem. staff emeritus, 1982-92; mem. staff Grant Hosp. Author numerous articles, chpts. in books.; Mem. editorial bd. John Alexander Series, 1956-73; mem. adv. editorial bd. Jour. Thoracic and Cardiovascular Surgery, 1964-79. Served with M.C. AUS, 1942-46. Fellow ACS, Ill. Thoracic Surg. Soc. (hon.); mem. AMA, Ill. Med. Soc., Chgo. Med. Soc., Am. Surg. Assn., Ill. Surg. Soc., Chgo. Surg. Soc., Pan-Pacific Surg. Assn., Western Surg. Assn., Cen. Surg. Assn., Am. Assn. Thoracic Surgery (pres. 1969-70), Soc. Thoracic Surgeons, Western Thoracic Surg. Assn. (hon.), Am. Coll. Chest Physicians, Theta Kappa Psi, Alpha Omega Alpha. Home: Savannah Ga. Died May 15, 1992. †

LANSBURY, CORAL, English language educator, dean, author; b. Melbourne, Victoria, Australia; came to U.S., 1969; d. Oscar and May (Morle) L.; divorced; 1 child, Malcolm Turnbull. MA, Auckland, New Zealand, 1967, PhD, 1969. Drama and feature writer Australian Broadcasting Commn., BBC, 1954-64; assoc. prof. English Rutgers U., Camden, N.J., 1974-78, prof., 1978-80, Disting. prof., 1980-91, dean Grad. Sch., 1984-91. Author: Arcady in Australia, 1970, Elizabeth Gaskell, 1976, 84, The Reasonable Man, 1980, The Old Brown Dog, 1986, (novels) Ringarra, 1986, Felicity, 1987, Sweet Alice, 1988, The Grotto, 1989. NEH fellow, 1984; Guggenheim fellow, 1986. Mem. MLA, Northeast Victorian Studies, Victorian Soc. Home: Villanova Pa. Died Apr. 2, 1991.

LANTERMAN, JOSEPH BARNEY, industrial executive; b. Elkhart, Ill., Dec. 5, 1914; s. Fred J. and Bertha (Brown) L.; m. Marjorie Morton, June 7, 1947. B.S., U. Ill., 1936. CPA, Ill. With Amsted Industries, Inc., 1936-80, successively accountant, asst. to controller, asst. controller, controller, v.p., 1954-59, pres., chief exec. officer, 1959-69, chmn. bd., chief exec. officer, 1969-74, chmn., 1969-80, dir., 1956-80; past bd. dirs. Midwest Stock Exchange, Ill. Bell Telephone Co., Peoples Energy Co., Kemper Inc., A. E. Staley Mfg. Co., Harris Bancorp, Inc., Ill. Central Gulf R.R., Ill. Power Co., Internat. Harvester Co., Trans Union Corp., U.S. Gypsum Co. Past v.p. bd. govs.; mem. exec. com. United Republican Fund Ill.; bd. dirs. Inst. Gas Tech., 1965-74; past bd. dirs. Bus.-Industry Polit. Action Com., nat. chmn., 1967-69; bd. dirs. Met. Crusade of Mercy, 1961-69, pres., 1963-64; chmn. mid-Am. chpt. ARC, 1959-61, nat. bd. govs., 1964-70; trustee Better Govt. Assn., 1964-74; vice chmn., trustee, exec. com.; sec. Mus. Sci. and Industry, Chgo.; trustee, exec. com. Ill. Inst. Tech.; past mem. citizens bd. U. Chgo.; former trustee Loyola U., Chgo., chmn. bd. trustees, 1968-71, chmn. citizen's bd., 1973-75, mem. pres.'s com.; dir. Lyric Opera Chgo.; past bd. dirs. Chgo. Boys Clubs, Protestant Found. Greater Chgo. Recipient Illini Achievement award U. Ill. Alumni Assn., Father Damen award Loyola U., Chgo., Good Scout award Chgo. area coun. Boy Scouts Am., Community Svc. award Chgo. chpt. Pub. Rels. Soc. Am. Mem. Ill. Soc. C.P.A.'s, Ill. Mfrs. Assn. (dir. 1964-69), Ill. C. of C. (dir. 1957-63), The Conf. Bd., Northwestern U. Assos., Alpha Sigma Phi, Beta Alpha Psi. Clubs: Chicago (Chgo.), Economic (Chgo.) (past pres., dir.), Mid-Am. (Chgo.) (bd. govs., pres. 1968-70), Commercial (Chgo.); Glen View (Ill.); Garden of the Gods, Eldorado Country. Home: Chicago Ill. Died Aug. 25, 1991.

LAPPIN, ALBERT ABRAHAM, rubber manufacturing executive; b. Boston, Dec. 25, 1897; s. William and Ida (Rutman) L.; m. Emma Gloth, Apr. 2, 1922; 1 child, William Robert. BCS, Northeastern U., 1918. Dir., mgr. Gold Seal Rubber Co., Boston, 1921-40; treas. Goodyear Rubber Co., Middletown, Conn., 1941-45, pres., treas., gen. mgr., 1945-61, chmn., from 1961, treas., 1961-64; mem. assoc. bd. dirs. Conn. Bank &

Trust Co.; bd. dirs. York Realty Inc., Boston; corporator Middletown Savs. Bank, Middlesex Meml. Hosp.; trustee Abraham Shapiro Charity Trust, Boston. Mem. Conn. Bd. Edn.; v.p. Middletown Community Chest. Mem. Conn. C. of C. (bd. dirs.), Middletown C. of C. (v.p.), Rubber Mfrs. Assn. (rsch. com.), Masons, Shriners, Rotary. *

LARAMORE, DON NELSON, judge; b. Hamlet, Ind., Dec. 22, 1906; s. Louis Nelson and Pearl (Stephenson) L.; m. Charlotte Schminke, Dec. 29, 1938; 1 dau., Prudence Ann. Grad., Ind. Law Sch., 1927. Ofcl. reporter Starke Circuit of Ind., 1924-31; judge Stark Circuit Ct., 1942-54; judge or sr. judge U.S. Ct. Claims, Washington, from 1954; sr. judge U.S. Ct. Appeals (Fed. cir.)., until 1989. Mem. Ind. Republican State Fin. Com., 1942-44, county chmn., 1936-42. Mem. Am. Bar Assn., D.C. Bar Assn., Fed. Bar Assn., Gamma Eta Gamma. Clubs: Nat. Lawyers, Congressional Country, Masons, Shriners, Elks. Died Aug. 9, 1989; buried Knox, Ind.

LARKEY, SANFORD V(INCENT), librarian, medical historian; b. Oakland, Calif., May 11, 1898; s. Alonzo Sanford and Anne (Jefferson) L.; m. Geraldine B. Gannon, Sept. 14, 1928. AB, U. Calif., 1921, MD, 1925; BA, Oxford U., 1928, MA, 1931. Intern U. Calif. Hosp., 1924-25; asst. prof. history of medicine, libr. Med. Sch. U. Calif., 1930-35; libr., dir. emeritus Welch Med. Libr., lectr. history med. Johns Hopkins U., from 1935; adv. com. VA Libr. Svc., from 1956; chmn. Citizens Com. Pub. Welfare, Md., 1950-51; mem. Md. State Bd. Pub. Welfare, 1951-63; mem. exec. com. Chem.-Biol. Coord. Ctr. NRC, from 1953; tech. aide com. med. rsch. OSRD, 1941-42. Mem. editorial bd. War Medicine, 1941-42; contbr. articles to profl. publs. 2d lt. U.S. Army, 1918; col. Med. Corps, AUS, 1942-46; chief sch. br. tng. div. Surgeon Gen.'s Office, 1942-43; chief hist. div. Office Chief Surgeon, ETO, 1944-45. Decorated Bronze Star; Henry E. Huntington Libr. fellow, 1933-34. Fellow AAAS; mem. ALA, Coun. Nat. Libr. Assns. (chmn. 1950-52), Am. Assn. History of Medicine, History of Sci. Soc., Med. Libr. Assn. (pres. 1949-50), Soc. Med. Cons. to Armed Forces, Bohemian Club, 14 W Hamilton St. Club, Johns Hopkins Club, Charaka Club, Phi Kappa Sigma, Nu Sigma Nu, Alpha Omega Alpha. *

LARKIN, FELIX EDWARD, corporation executive; b. N.Y.C., Aug. 3, 1909; s. John A. and Maria C. (Henry) L.; m. Evelyn Wallace, Dec. 28, 1937 (dec. 1990); children: Nancy Larkin Carr, John, James. A.B., Fordham U., 1931, LL.D. (hon.), 1978; M.B.A., N.Y. U., 1933; J.D., St. John's U., 1942. Engaged security bus., 1933-37; lectr. Fordham U. Sch. Bus., 1937-42; law sec. Judge James Garrett Wallace (Ct. Gen. Sessions), N.Y.C., 1939-47; asst. gen. counsel Dept. Def., 1947, gen. counsel, 1949-51; v.p. charge indsl. relations W.R. Grace & Co., N.Y.C., 1951-58, exec. v.p. adminstrn., 1958-69, exec. v.p., sr. mem. office of pres., 1969-71, pres., 1971-74, chmn. corp., 1974-81, chmn. exec. com., 1981-86, dir. emeritus, 1986-91; chmn. dirs. adv. council Marine Midland Bank, 1981—; prof. mgmt. Grad. Sch. Bus. Fordham U., 1982. Trustee Fordham U., 1969-78, emeritus, 1978-91, chmn. bd. trustees, 1970-77; trustee Gregorian Found., chmn. bd. trustees, 1983; bd. govs. New Rochelle (N.Y.) Hosp. Med. Center Assn. Recipient highest civilian award Dept. Def., 1951; named Man of Year NYU Grad. Sch. Bus., 1963; named to Fordham U. Sports Hall of Fame, 1979; recipient Brotherhood award NCCJ, 1980. Mem. Friendly Sons St. Patrick, Am. Arbitration Assn. (dir. 1975-84), Conf. Bd. Clubs: Winged Foot Golf (Mamaroneck) (gov. 1967-72, 74-76, 80, pres. 1982-84); Larchmont (N.Y.) Yacht; N.Y. Univ., Pinnacle (N.Y.C.) (gov.); Delray Beach (Fla.); Pine Tree Golf (Boynton Beach, Fla.); Knights of Malta. Home: Larchmont N.Y. Died Nov. 10, 1991; buried Gates of Heaven, Valhalla, N.Y.

LARKINS, JOHN DAVIS, JR., federal judge; b. Morristown, Tenn., June 8, 1909; s. C.H. and Mamie (Dorset) Larkins; m. Pauline Murrill, Mar. 15, 1930 (dec. Sept. 1982); children: Emma Sue (Mrs. D.H. Loftin), Polly (Mrs. J.H. Bearden). B.A., Wake Forest Coll., 1929, law student, 1930; LL.D., Belin U., 1957, Wake Forest U., 1977. Bar: N.C. 1930. Practiced in Trenton, from 1930; U.S. dist. judge Eastern Dist. N.C., from 1961, chief judge, 1975-79, sr. judge, from 1979; Sec. Larkins Stores, Inc.; dir. Life Ins. Co. of N.C.; Del.-at-large Democratic Nat. Conv., 1940, 44, 48, 56, 60; sec. N.C. Dem. Exec. Com., 1952-54, chmn., 1954-58; mem. Dem. Nat. Com., 1958-60, N.C. Senate 7th dist., 1936-44, 48-54, pres. pro tem, 1941-42; Chmn. gov.'s adv. budget commn., 1951-53, liaison officer, legislative counsel, 1955. Author: memoirs Bar and Bench. Mem. nat. bd. dirs., vice chmn. Am. Cancer Soc.; trustee U. N.C., Bapt. Hosp., Wake Forest U. Served as pvt. AUS, 1945. Recipient Distinguished Service award Am. Cancer Soc., Distinguished Service award Wake Forest U. Sch. Law, 1968; John D. Larkin Jr. Fed. Bldg., Trenton, N.C., named in his honor. Mem. Am. Legion, 40 and 8, Woodmen of World, Am., Fed., N.C. bar assns., N.C. Bar, Inc., Phi Alpha Delta. Baptist (chmn. bd. deacons 1930-78, hon. deacon for life). Clubs: Masons, Shriners, Elks, Moose. Died Feb. 16, 1990; buried Trenton, N.C.

LARRABEE, ERIC, writer, educator; b. Melrose, Mass., Mar. 6, 1922; s. Harold Atkins and Doris (Kennard) L.; m. Eleanor Barrows Doermann, Apr. 4, 1944. A.B. cum laude, Harvard U., 1943; LL.D., Keuka Coll., 1961. Assoc. editor Harper's mag., 1946-58; exec. editor Am. Heritage, 1958-61, mng. editor, 1961-62; mng. editor Horizon, 1962-63; editorial cons. Doubleday & Co., N.Y.C., 1963-69; provost Arts and Letters SUNY, Buffalo, 1967-70, prof., 1967-72; exec. dir. N.Y. State Coun. on Arts, N.Y.C., 1970-75; pres. Nat. Rsch. Ctr. Arts, N.Y.C., 1976-78; adj. prof. Sch. Art, Columbia U., from 1980; Noble Found. prof. art and cultural history Sarah Lawrence Coll., 1986; dean Sch. Art and Design Pratt Inst., Bklyn., 1987-90, Faculty prof., 1990. Author: The Self-Conscious Society, 1960, The Benevolent and Necessary Institution, 1971, (with Massimo Vignelli) Knoll Design, 1981, Commander in Chief, 1987 (Francis Parkman prize 1988); Editor: American Panorama, 1957, (with Rolf Meyersohn) Mass Leisure, 1958, Museums and Education, 1968; Co-editor: (with Robert E. Spiller) American Perspectives, 1961; Contbr. articles nat. mags. Served to 1st lt. AUS, World War II. Decorated Bronze Star medal; recipient Gold medal of honor Nat. Arts Club, 1971; Guggenheim fellow, 1982-83. Mem. Am. Council Learned Socs. (mem.-at-large 1955-59), N.Y. State Hist. Assn. (trustee 1976—), Phi Beta Kappa (hon.). Home: New York N.Y. Died Dec. 4, 1990; buried Wyoming Cemetery, Melrose, Mass.

LARSEN, JOHN WALTER, banker; b. N.Y.C., Sept. 7, 1914; s. Carl and Ella (Olsen) L.; m. Eleanor Waterhouse, June 10, 1939; children: John Walter, Nancy Larsen Farrell, Gregory, Melissa. B.S., NYU, 1939; postgrad., Rutgers U., 1946-48, Columbia U., 1957. CPA, N.Y. State. Clk., auditor, asst. sec., treas., asst. v.p. North River Savs. Bank, 1933-49; v.p. Bowery Savs. Bank, N.Y.C., 1949-53; v.p., treas. Bowery Savs. Bank, 1953-59, exec. v.p., treas., 1959-61, pres., 1962-76, vice chmn. bd., 1976-79, trustee, 1962-79; dir. United Jersey Banks, Diebold Computer Leasing, Inc.; Pres. Citizens Budget Commn., N.Y.C., 1974-82. Trustee Nat. Jewish Hosp. at Denver, Mus. City of N.Y., Inner-City Scholarship Fund of Roman Cath. Archdiocese N.Y., Jewish Guild for Blind; mem. Region II exec. com. Boy Scouts Am.; former chmn. Haworth, N.J. Planning Bd. Recipient Silver Beaver, Silver Antelope, Good Scout awards Boy Scouts Am., Dean John T. Madden award N.Y. U., 1964, Meritorious Service award N.Y. U. Alumni, 1965, Nat. Jewish Hosp. at Denver award, 1973, Interfaith Achievement award, 1974, N.Y. U. Urban Leadership award, 1977. Mem. Phi Alpha Kappa. Presbyterian. Clubs: Union League, Arcola Country. Home: West New York N.J. Died Mar. 11, 1990.

LARSEN, JOSEPH REUBEN, entomologist, rehabilitation educator; b. Ogden, Utah, May 21, 1927; s. Joseph Reuben and Anna Charlotte (Anderson) L.; m. Shauna Stewart, Dec. 15, 1948; children: Pamela Larsen Bates, Deborah Larsen Swensen, Jennifer Larsen Taylor. B.S., U. Utah, 1950, M.S., 1952; Sc.D., Johns Hopkins U., 1958. Asst. prof. entomology U. Wyo., 1962-63; asst. prof. entomology U. Ill., Urbana, 1963-65, assoc. prof., 1965-67, prof., 1967-69, head dept. entomology, 1969-75, dir. Sch. Life Scis., 1973-84, 75-85; Emens disting. prof. Ball State U., 1980; disting. prof. Brigham Young U., from 1984, dir. div. rehab. edn., from 1985; invited participant symposia XVI Internat. Congress Zoology, 1963, Functional Orgn. of Compound Eye in Sweden, 1965, Entomol. Soc. Am., 1973, 16th Internat. Congress Entomology Orgn. of Insect Brain, 1984. Author: A Laboratory Manual in Biology, 1965-1979, (with others), 1980-89; author: (with others) Bionomics and Embryology of Aedes vexans, 1973. Served with M.C., AUS, 1944-47. Inducted into the Nat. Hall of Fame for Persons with Disabilities, 1987. Mem. Entomol. Soc. Am., Am. Physiol. Soc., Am. Soc. Zoologists, Electron Microscope Soc. Am., Sigma Xi. Home: Champaign Ill. Died Feb. 17, 1989.

LARSON, LAWRENCE JOHN, insurance company executive; b. Madison, Wis., Mar. 20, 1904; s. Lars Anton and Ellen Sophia (Nelson) L.; m. Ann Mathilda Furseth, Oct. 16, 1934; 1 son, John D. BA, U. Wis., 1932. Asst. cashier Nat. Guardian Life. Ins. Co., Madison, 1935-37, comptroller, 1937-41, sec.-treas., 1941-47, exec. v.p., 1947-57, pres., 1957-69, chmn. bd., CEO, 1969-89, chmn. bd., 1989-92, also bd. dirs.; bd. dirs. Midwest Realty & Investment Corp., Madison. Chmn. campaign YMCA, Madison, 1956; chmn. campaign United Way, 1961. Mem. Madison C. of C. (pres. 1954-55), Life Office Mgmt. Assn. (assoc.). Republican. Lutheran. Clubs: Maple Bluff Country (pres. 1951-53), Madison. Lodge: Rotary (pres. 1961-62), Masons. Home: Madison Wis. Died Apr. 20, 1992. †

LARWOOD, CHARLES (HOMER), pharmacy educator; b. Melbourne, Ark., Nov. 8, 1895; s. Charles Monroe and Sarah McKindrick (Brewer) L. PhG, Okla. U., 1922, BS, 1925; MS, Okla. A&M Coll., 1929; PhD, Mich. State Coll., 1939. Instr. in sci. Sand Springs (Okla.) High Sch., 1924-28; prof. pharmacy Ferris Inst., Mich., 1929-34; prof., dean pharmacy U. Grand Rapids, Mich., 1936-42, U. Toledo, Ohio, from 1946. With USN, 1917-19, U.S. Army, 1942-45. Mem. Am. Pharm. Assn., N.W. Ohio Assn. Pharm., Ohio Assn. Pharm., Kappa Psi, Rho Chi. Republican. Methodist. *

LASKY, VICTOR, news columnist, author; b. Liberty, N.Y., Jan. 7, 1918; s. Max and Bella (Polen) L.; m. Patricia Pratt, Sept. 6, 1952. B.A., Bklyn. Coll., 1940; D.Letters (hon.), Ashland Coll., 1983. Reporter Chgo. Sun, 1941-47; corr. Stars and Stripes, ETO, 1943-45; rewriteman-reporter N.Y. World-Telegram, 1947-50; screenwriter Metro-Goldwyn-Mayer, Culver City, Calif., 1951-52; writer RKO Gen.-Teleradio, 1955; pub. relations exec. Radio Liberty, N.Y.C., 1956-60; news columnist N.Am. Newspaper Alliance, 1962-80. Author: (with R. de Toledano) Seeds of Treason, 1950, J.F.K., The Man and The Myth, 1963, The Ugly Russian, 1965, Robert F. Kennedy, The Myth and the Man, 1968, (with George Murphy) Say, Didn't You Used to be George Murphy, 1970, Arthur J. Goldberg, The Old and the New, 1970, It Didn't Start with Watergate, 1977, Jimmy Carter: The Man and The Myth, 1979, Never Complain, Never Explain, The Story of Henry Ford II, 1981; also chpts. in books; editor: American Legion Reader, 1953; mem. editorial bd. Am. Politics mag., 1986-88. Clubs: Overseas Press (N.Y.C.); Nat. Press (Washington). Home: Washington D.C. Died Feb. 22, 1990; buried Arlington Nat. Cemetery.

LASSETER, DILLARD BROWN, lawyer; b. Vienna, Ga., June 23, 1894; s. Edward S. and Lou Anna (Brown) L.; m. Helen Smith, Nov. 8, 1920. BA, Emory U., 1913; MA, NYU, 1914; postgrad., Columbia U., 1914-15. Entered Am. Fgn. Svc., Peking, China, 1915; vice consul Am. Fgn. Svc., Tientsin, 1920; consul Am. Fgn. Svc., Antung, Manchuria, 1921-23, Hankow, China, 1923-24; in cotton bus. Greenville, S.C., N.Y.C. and Chgo., 1925-30; state dir. Ga. NRA, 1934-35, NYA, 1935-40; dep. adminstr. NYA, Washington, 1940-42; counsel House Civil Svc. Investigating Com., Washington, 1943; regional dir. War Manpower Commn., Ga., 1943-46; adminstr. Farm Sec. Adminstrn., Farmers Home Adminstrn., 1946; lawyer and legis. cons., from 1954. Officer B.E.F., France, 1917-18. Mem. Order World Wars (so. comdr. 1945), Am. Legion, 40 and 8, SAR, Atlanta Athletic Club, Chevy Chase Club, Pi Kappa Phi. *

LASSETTRE, EDWIN NICHOLS, physical chemist, educator; b. Monroe County, Ga., Oct. 26, 1911; s. Carlos E. and Jennie J. (Nichols) L.; m. Ilse R. Sturies, Dec. 22, 1951. BS, Mont. State Coll., 1933; PhD, Calif. Inst. Tech., 1938; DTech (hon.), Royal Inst. Tech., Stockholm, 1977. Mem. faculty Ohio State U., 1937-62, prof. chemistry, 1950-62, chmn. phys. chemistry sect., 1952-62; group leader, research scientist Manhattan Project, SAM Labs., Columbia U., 1944, Carbide and Carbon Chems. Corp., 1945; staff fellow, mem. adv. com. Mellon Inst., Pitts., 1962-67; staff fellow, prof. chem. physics Carnegie-Mellon U., 1967-74, Univ. prof. chem. physics, 1974-77, emeritus, 1977-90; dir. Center for Spl. Studies, 1971-73; cons. gaseous diffusion plant Oak Ridge Nat. Lab., 1954-67; rev. com. radiol. physics div. Argonne Nat. Lab., 1968-70; del. Argonne Univs. Assn., 1971-74. Mem. editorial bd. Jour. Chem. Physics, 1967-69, Jour. Electron Spectroscopy and Related Phenomena, 1971-75; contbr. articles in field. Fellow Am. Phys. Soc.; mem. Am. Chem. Soc., N.Y. Acad. Scis., Optical Soc. Am., Math. Assn. Am., Am. Math. Soc. Home: Pittsburgh Pa. Died Jan. 16, 1990; buried Allegheny Cemetery, Pitts.

LATHROP, GERTRUDE KATHERINE, sculptor; b. Albany, N.Y., Dec. 24, 1896; d. Cyrus Clark and Ida Frances (Pulis) Lathrop. Art edn., Art Students League, Sch. Am. Sculpture, N.Y.C.; pupil, Solon Borglum, Charles Grafly. Represented in collections of numerous public instns. Recipient of many notable prizes and awards. Mem. Albany Numismatic Soc., Nat. Sculpture Soc., Nat. Assn. Women Artists, Allied Artists Am., Hispanic Soc. Am., Am. Numis. Soc., Prine Club of Albany, Albany Inst. History and Art, Soc. Medalists. *

LATIMER, JOHN FRANCIS, classics educator; b. Clinton, Miss., May 16, 1903; s. Murray and Myrtle (Webb) L.; m. Helen Blundon, July 27, 1946. AB, Miss. Coll., 1922, DLitt (hon.), 1964; MA, U. Chgo., 1926; PhD, Yale U., 1929; LHD (hon.), George Washington U., 1987. Tchr., prin. Clinton High Sch., 1922-24; instr. classics Vanderbilt U., 1926-27; master in Greek Taft Sch., 1929-31; asst. prof. classics Knox Coll., 1931-33; chmn. dept. classics Drury Coll., 1933-36; prof. classical langs. George Washington U., from 1936, prof. emeritus, 1973-91, chmn. dept. classics, 1936-71, asst. dean Coll. Gen. Studies, 1951-56, asst. dean faculties, 1956-59, assoc. dean, 1959-64, dir. fgn. student affairs, 1964-66, univ. marshal, 1953-69; mem. Com. Internat. Exchange of Persons, 1959-71; treas., dir. Council Basic Edn., 1958-77. Author: What's Happened to Our High Schools?, 1958, The Oxford Conference and Related Activities, 1968; editor: (with introduction) A Life of George Washington in Latin Prose (Francis Glass), 1976, (with foreword) A Grammatical and Historical Supplement to the Glass Washington, 1976, A Composite Translation of the Glass Washington, 1976, Paul Shorey: A Bibliography of His Classical Writings, 1986; contbr. articles to profl. jours. Trustee St. John's Child Devel. Center, Washington, pres. bd. trustees, 1973-77; pres. Friends of Libraries, George Washington U., 1977-

78, Soc. of Emeriti, George Washington U., 1978-91. Served to comdr. USNR, 1942-47; capt. Res. (ret.). Mem. Am. Philol. Assn., Archeol Inst. Am., Classical Assn. Atlantic States (pres. 1955-57; award of merit 1986), Am. Sch. Classical Studies, Am. Classical League (pres. 1960-66, exec. sec. 1966-73), Omicron Delta Kappa. Club: Cosmos (Washington). Home: Washington D.C. Died Oct. 29, 1991.

LATIMER, JOHN LESLIE, investor, petroleum consultant; b. Olean, N.Y., May 11, 1897; s. Amos J. and Katharine (Grear) L.; m. Helen Leone Heins, Apr. 14, 1925; children: Elizabeth Jane (wife of Dr. Ronald F. Garvey), Margaret Jean (Mrs. Robert S. Begien Jr.). DSc (hon.), U. St. Bonaventure, N.Y., 1960. With Magnolia Petroleum Co., 1915-61, pres., dir., 1946-61; company merged with Mobil Oil Co., 1959, sr. v.p., 1959-61; chmn. bd. dirs. Magnolia Pipe Line Co., 1952-61; dir. Republic Nat. Bank, Dallas, from 1949, Southwestern Life Ins. Co., from 1951, Tex. Utilities Co., from 1947; mem. adv. com. Com. Oil Pipe Lines, from 1947. Mem. Greater Dallas Planning Coun., City Dallas Water Survey Com., Gov. Tex. Water Conservation Com., Dallas Air Power Coun.; chmn. adv. com. Dallas coun. Navy League; trustee, exec. com. Tex. Rsch. Found.; v.p., trustee, exec. com. Southwestern Med. Found.; trustee Southeastern Legal Found., Tex. Found.; voluntarily supported colls. and univs., Grad. Rsch. Ctr. of So. Meth. U., Presbyn. Hosp., Dallas; adv. bd. U. Dallas, Cath. Women's League, Da..as-Ft. Worth Diocesan Coun.; lay adv. bd. St Paul's Hosp., Dallas; bd. dirs. Dallas Grand Opera Assn., Trininty Improvement Assn., Dallas Citizens Interracial Assn.; exec. bd. Dallas Camp Fire Girls, Circle Ten coun. Boy Scouts Am.; diocesan adv. bd. govs. Cath. Charities Dallas. Recipient Golden Driller award, 1959, Ann. Brotherhood award Dallas chpt. NCCJ, 1957; named Chief Roughneck of Yr., 1959, hon. life mem. Roughneck's Club; decorated lt. Equestrian Order Holy Sepulchre of Jerusalem (Pope Puis). Mem. Tex. Oil and Gas Assn. (hon. dir., exec. com. Disting. Svc. award 1952), Gen. Oil and Gas Assn. (hon. dir., exec. com.), Mid-Continent Oil and Gas Assn., Dallas C. of C., Serra Club (past pres., trustee), Dallas Country Club, City Club, Petroleum Club, Chaparral Club, Pipe Liners Club (past pres., bd. govs.). *

LATT, SAMUEL ARCH, geneticist; b. Harrisburg, Pa., Dec. 19, 1938; s. Herman Samuel and Ricci (Buch) L.; m. Barbara Diane Slosberg, June 24, 1965; 1 dau., Allison Barbara. S.B., M.I.T., 1960; M.D., Harvard U., 1964, Ph.D., 1971. Intern in medicine Peter Bent Brigham Hosp., Boston, 1964-65; USPHS staff assoc. NIH, 1965-67; postdoctoral fellow biol. chemistry Harvard U. Med. Sch., 1967-71, mem. faculty, 1971-88; prof. dept. pediatrics Children's Hosp. Med. Center and Med. Sch., from 1980, prof. dept. genetics, 1983-88; investigator Howard Hughes Med. Inst., 1986-88; mem. ad hoc sci. adv. coms. NIH, 1977, 81, 83-87, Am. Cancer Soc., 1978-82. Mem. editorial bd., contbr. articles to biomed. research jours. Recipient Mead Johnson pediatric research award, 1978. Mem. Am. Soc. Human Genetics, Am. Cancer Soc. (Francis Stone Burns award Mass. chpt., 1975), Am. Soc. Cell Biology, Histochem. Soc., Environ. Mutagenesis Soc., Soc. Analytical Cytology, Soc. Pediatric Research. Home: Newton Highlands Mass. Died Aug. 28, 1988; buried Sharon Meml. Pk., Mass.

LATTIMORE, OWEN, author, historian; b. Washington, July 29, 1900; s. David and Margaret (Barnes) L.; m. Eleanor Holgate, Mar. 4, 1926 (dec. Mar. 1970); 1 child, David. Student, Coll. Classique Cantonal, Laussane, Switzerland, 1913-14, St. Bees Sch., Cumberland, Eng., 1915-19; postgrad., Harvard U., 1929; DLitt (hon.), Glasgow (Scotland) U., 1964; PhD (hon.), U. Copenhagen, 1972; LLD (hon.), Brown U., 1975. Engaged in bus. Shanghai, China, 1920; newspaper worker Tientsin, China, 1921; with Arnhold & Co., Ltd., Tientsin and Peking, China, 1922-26; rsch. in Manchuria under Social Sci. Rsch. Coun., 1929-30, in Peiping under Harvard Yenching Inst., 1930-31, under J.S. Guggenheim Meml. Found., 1931-33; field work in Mongolia and rsch. in Peiping under Inst. Pacific Rels., 1934-37; lectr. Johns Hopkins, 1938-63; dir. Walter Hines Page Sch. Internat. Rels., 193-53; prof. Chinese studies U. Leeds (Eng.), 1963-70; Chichele lectr. Oxford (Eng.) U., 1965; polit. adviser to Chiang Kai-shek, 1941-42; dep. dir. Pacific ops OWI, 1942-44; mem. Author: The Desert Road to Turkestan, 1928, High Tartary, 1930, Manchuria, Cradle of Conflict, 1932, The Mongols of Manchuria, 1934, Inner Asian Frontiers of China, 1940, Mongol Journeys, 1941; (with Eleanor Lattimore) China, A Short History, 1947, Solution in Asia, 1945, The Situation in Asia, 1949, Ordeal by Slande, 1950, Pivot of Asia, 1950, Nationalism and Revolution in Mongolia, 1955, Nomads and Commissars, 1962, Studies in Frontier History, 1963; (with Eleanor Lattimore) Silks, Spices and Empire, 1968, History and Revolution in China, 1974; contbr. articles to learned jours., encys., and mags. Recipient Cuthbert Peek award Royal Geog. Soc., 1929, Patron's medal, 1942, Gold medal Phila. Geog. Soc., 1933, U. Ind. medal, 1974. Mem. Assn. Asian Studies, Royal Asiatic Soc., Royal Geog. Soc. (mem. coun. 1965-66), Royal Cen. Asian Soc., Am. Geog. Soc. (hon.), Am. Philos. Soc., Am. Hist. Assn., Acad. Sics. Mongolian People's Republic (fgn. mem.), Czsoma Körösi Soc. (hon.), Phi Beta Kappa (hon.). Home: Providence R.I. Died May 31, 1989.

LAUGHLIN, REGINALD S., lawyer; b. Santa Barbara, Calif., Feb. 25, 1894; s. Berton E. and Dora V. (Short) L. AB, Stanford U., 1920, LLB, 1921. Bar: 1921. Practice law San Francisco, from 1921; ptnr. Treadwell, Van Fleet & Luaghlin, 1925-33; asst. gen. counsel R.F.C., Washington, 1934-36; spl. counsel U.S. Maritime Commn., San Francisco, 1937-38; counsel Wallace, Garrison, Norton & Ray, from 1955. With U.S. Army, 1917-20; 1st lt. AEF, Siberia, 1918-20. Mem. ABA, Calif. State Bar Assn., San Francisco Bar Assn., Assn. Interstate Commerce Commn. Practitioners, Maritime Law Assn. U.S., Pacific Union Club, Bohemian Club, Menlo Country Club, Commonwealth Club, Met. Club, Phi Kappa Psi, PHi Delta Phi. *

LAUSCHE, FRANK JOHN, United States senator; b. Cleve., Nov. 19, 1895; s. Louis and Frances L. (Milavec) L.; m. Jane O. Sheal, 1928. LLB, John Marshall Sch. Law, 1920, LLM, 1936; LLD, hon. degrees, various univs. and colls. Practiced law Cleve., 1920-32; judge Mcpl. Ct., Cleve., 1932-37, Common Pleas Ct., Cleve., 1937-41; mayor City of Cleve., 1941-44; gov. State of Ohio, 1945-46, 49-56; mem. U.S. Senate Ohio, 1956-64. Recipient Centennial award Northwestern U., 1958, Good Citizenship medal Soc. S.A.R., George Washington award Am. Good Govt. Soc., 1964, cert. of merit, Am. Vets. WWII. Mem. Delta Theta Phi, Phi Sigma Kappa, Omicron Delta Kappa. Home: Washington D.C. Died Apr. 21, 1990.

LAUTERBACH, ROBERT ALAN, accountant; b. Sac City, Iowa, Aug. 26, 1921; s. Paul A. and Ada (Johnson) L.; m. Sarah M. Messenger, Apr. 27, 1943; children: Marian, Michael, John. B.S.C., Iowa U., 1946; LL.B., Denver U., 1948. Bar: Colo. 1949; C.P.A. Practice in Denver, 1949-50; with Ernst & Whinney (C.P.A.s), Denver, 1950-77; partner Ernst & Whinney (C.P.A.s), 1961-77; partner-in charge Denver office Ernst & Whinney, 1964-76. Served with USAAF, 1943-45, ETO. Mem. Colo. Soc. C.P.A.s (past dir.), Sigma Alpha Epsilon. Clubs: University (Denver); Thunderbird Country (Rancho Mirage, Calif.); Cherry Hills Country (Denver) (past dir., treas.); Garden of the Gods (Colorado Springs). Home: Denver Colo. Died July 17, 1988; buried Denver.

LA VARRE, WILLIAM, economic geographer, writer; b. Richmond, Va., Aug. 4, 1898; s. William Johanne and Lelia Goddin (Haynes) La V.; m. Alice Lucille Elliott, July 27, 1927; 1 child, Yvette (Mrs. William Worth Graham III). Student, Townsend Harris Hall, N.Y., 1914-16; Columbua U. extension and spl. student, Harvard U. Econ. explorer of S.Am. for gold, diamonds, oil and minerals, 1920-27, pub. newspapers; pres. Piedmont Press Assn., 1928-30; various trips through Latin Am. for newspapers articles N.Am. Newspaper Alliance, Consol. News Features, others, 1933-38; mng. dir., pres. Pan Am. Press, from 1939; exec. Latim-Am. specialist, chief Am. Repubiucs unit, U.S. Dept. Commerce, 1941-43; dir. rsch. and info. Rubber Devel. Corp., Reconstrn. Fin. Corp., S.Am., 1943; dir. Am. Fgn. Svc. Coun., Washington, from 1944; cons. Econ. Coop. Adminstrn., from 1950. Author: Up the Mazaruni, 1919, Johnny Round the World, 1934, Gold, Diamonds and Orchids, 1935, Dry Guillotine, 1938, Southward Ho!, 1939, The 114 Markets of South America, 1941, The Colossus of the South, 1941; syndicated feature Seeing is Believing, to U.S., fgn. newspapers; contbr. to Readers Digest; editor: Am. Mercury Mag., 1957-58. FDellow Am. Geog. Soc., Royal Geog. Soc. (Eng.), Harvard Club, Univ. Club. *

LAWRENCE, FREDERIC CUNNINGHAM, bishop; b. Cambridge, Mass., May 22, 1899; s. William and Julia (Cunningham) L.; m. Katharine Virginia Wylie, Apr. 10, 1928; children: Katharine, Julia (dec.), Margaret Lawrence Drinker, Frederic Cunningham Jr., Peter, Marian Appleton. AB, Harvard U., 1920; postgrad., Cambridge (Eng.) U., 1920-21, Union Theol. Sem., N.Y.C., 1921-23; BD, Episcopal Theol. Sch., Cambridge, Mass., 1924. Ordained to ministry Episcopal Ch., 1924. Curate, Worcester, Mass., 1924-25; Episcopal chaplain Harvard U., 1925-27; assoc. St. Paul's Cathedral, Boston, 1925-27; rector St. Peter's Ch., Cambridge, 1927-41, St. Paul's Ch., Brookline, Mass., 1941-56; suffragan bishop Episcopal Diocese of Mass., Boston, 1956-68. Trustee Milton (Mass.) Acad., Am. U. Beirut. Home: Brookline Mass. Died Apr. 16, 1989; buried Cambridge, Mass.

LAWRENCE, JOHN HUNDALE, physician; b. Canton, S.D., Jan. 7, 1904; s. Carl Gustavus and Gunda (Jacobson) L.; m. Amy McNear Bowles, June 20, 1942; children: John Mark, Amy Sheldon, James Bowles, Steven Ernest. AB, U. S.D., 1926, DSc honoris causa, 1942; MD, Harvard U., 1930; D honoris causa, U. Bordeaux, France, 1958; DSc honris causa, Cath. U. Am., 1959. Intern Peter Bent Brigham Hosp., Boston, 1930-31; postdoctoral Strong Meml. Hosp., U. Rochester, 1931-32; postdoctoral Yale U., New Haven Hosp., 1932-34, assoc. physician, 1934-37; instr. medicine Yale U., 1934-37; prof. med. physics, physician-in-chief Donner Pavillion U. Calif., Berkeley, 1937-91, dir. emeritus Donner Lab., regent; William H. Welch lectr., Ludwig Kast meml. lectr., 1949, Stephen Walter Ranson meml. lectr., Von Hevesy meml. lectr., and others, 1949-73; AEC cons., vis. prof. AEE of India, U. Bombay, 1961; vis. prof. medicine Am. U., Beirut, Lebanon, 1963, Ohio State U., 1965; Richardson lectr. Harvard U., 1963; Pasteur Inst. lectr., 1963; mem. sci. and tech. adv. com. NASA, 1965-67; leader med. mission to USSR, 1974. Author: Polycythemia, 1955; co-author: Radioisotopes and Radiation, Recent Advances in Medicine, Agriculture and Industry, 1964; co-editor: Advances in Biological and Medical Physics; editor: Progress in Nuclear Medicine, 1965, 68, 71, 74; contbr. articles to profl. jours. Decorated Silver Cross Royal Order Phoenix; recipient Caldwell medal, Davidson medal, Eng., Cert. of Appreciation War and Navy Depts., 1947, medal U. Bordeaux, 1958, Pasteur medal Pasteur Inst., Paris, 1963, Nuclear Pioneer award Soc. Nuclear Medicine, 1970, first Marshall Brucer medal and lectr., 1972, Katharine Berkhan Judd award Sloan-Kettering Meml. Hosp., N.Y.C., 1975. Fellow ACP, Am. Nuclear Soc.; disting. fellow Am. Coll. Nuclear Medicine; mem. Am. Soc. Clin. Investigation, Am. Clin. and Climatol. Assn., Soc. Nuclear Medicine (hon. mem., pres. 1966), Am. Assn. Neurol. Surgeons, Endocrine Soc., La Soc. Francaise de Physique, Biologilue et Med. (hon.), We. Assn. Physicians, Am. Physiol. Soc., European Soc. Hematology (hon.), Harvard Med. Alumni Assn. (pres. 1945-46, 62-63), Pacific Interurban Clin. Club (hon.), Bohemian Club, Explorers Club, Faculty Club U. Calif., Alpha Omega Alpha, Sigma Xi, Phi Beta Kappa. Home: Berkeley Calif. Died Sept. 7, 1991; buried Cypress Lawn Meml. Pk., Colma, Calif.

LAWRENCE, JUSTUS BALDWIN, public relations executive; b. Cleve., Dec. 16, 1903; s. L. N. and Dorothy (Lyman) L.; m. Mary Peace (dec.); m. Carlene Roberts Teetor. Ph.B., Yale U., 1927. Newspaperman and mag. writer, 1928-33; advt. and publicity dir., asst. to Samuel Goldwyn (motion pictures), 1933- 39; pub. relations dir. Assn. Motion Picture Producers, Hollywood, Calif., 1939-41; exec. v.p. J. Arthur Rank Orgn., Inc., N.Y.C., 1945-51; now pres. J.B. Lawrence, Inc. (pub. relations and research), N.Y.C. Contbr. articles to popular mags. Dep. chief pub. information SHAPE, Paris, 1951-52; U.S. del. 10th UNESCO Conf., 1958; presdl. mem. U.S.O. Corp., 1960-62. Served as pub. relations aide to Lord Mountbatten, Commandos, attached to Brit. Army, 1942-43; col., gen. staff U.S. Army; chief pub. relations officer 1943-45, ETO. Decorated Legion of Merit, Bronze Star U.S.; Legion of Honor France; Order Brit. Empire. Clubs: Yale (N.Y.C.), Sky (N.Y.C.), Dutch Treat (N.Y.C.); Army and Navy (Washington), Nat. Press (Washington), 1925 F St. (Washington); The Travellers (Paris); Bucks (London); University (Mexico City); Pilgrims U.S. Home: New York N.Y. Died Apr. 21, 1987. †

LAWRENCE, W. VERNON, railroad executive; b. Portsmouth, Va., Mar. 29, 1898; s. Wiley M. and Lillian Estelle (Smith) L.; m. Mae Johnston, Feb. 24, 1923 (dec.); children; Marianne (Mrs. C. L. Saunders, Jr.), Robert Vernon. Ed. pub. schs., Va.; grad. advanced mgmt. program, Harvard U., 1952. With S.A.L. RR, from 1916, asst. comptr., 1951-58, comptr., from 1958, v.p., from 1961; v.p., comptr. Athens Terminal Co., Tavares and Gulf RR Co., Ga., Fla. & Ga. RR Co., Gainesville Midland RR Co.; contr., mem. bd. dirs. Duval Connecting RR Co.; mem. fin. com. Trailer Train Co., Norfolk and Portsmouth Belt Line RR Co.; alternate dir., mem. express acctg. com. Ry. Express Agy., Inc.; v.p., comptr., dir. Southeastern Investment Co., Tampa & Gulf Coast RR Co.; v.p., auditor Tampa Union Sta. Co. Mem. Assn. Am. RR's, Fin. Exec. Inst., Harvard Club of Va., Hermitage Country Club, Rotunda Club. Presbyterian. *

LAWS, ROBERT FRANKLIN, advertising agency executive; b. Oklahoma City, Sept. 15, 1914; s. James Roy and Zelinn Alberta (Norman) L.; m. Janet West Wood, Oct. 23, 1938; children: Judith Ann Nelson Sutherlin, Dean Robert. B.A., U. Calif.-Berkeley, 1937. Writer, reporter San Francisco News, 1937-41; dir. publs. U. Calif.-Berkeley, 1941-45; promotion dir. Radio Sta. KGO, San Francisco, 1945-48; western dir. TV Philco Corp., San Francisco, 1948-49; western div. sales mgr. Am. Broadcasting Co., Los Angeles, 1949-54; pres. Robert F. Laws & Assocs., Los Angeles, 1954-58; exec. v.p., chief oper. officer, co-founder Eisaman, Johns & Laws Advt., Inc., L.A., 1959-82, pres., chief exec. officer, 1982-90, cons., pres. emeritus, 1990. Mem. Alpha Delta Sigma, Sigma Delta Chi. Republican. Home: Glendale Calif. Died Sept. 16, 1991; buried Forest Lawn Cemetery, Glendale, Calif.

LAWSON, DONALD ELMER, publishing company executive, author; b. Chgo., May 20, 1917; s. Elmer Daniel and Christina (Grass) L.; m. Beatrice M. Yates, Mar. 30, 1945. B.A., Cornell Coll., Mt. Vernon, Iowa, 1939, Litt.D. (hon.), 1970; postgrad., U. Iowa Writers Workshop, 1939-40. Editor The Advertiser, Nora Springs, Iowa, 1940-41; with Compton's Ency., Chgo., 1946-73, mng. editor, 1960-65, editor-in-chief, 1965-73; v.p., editor-in-chief Compton's Ency.-Ency. Brit., Chgo., 1972-73; exec. editor Am. Educator Ency., Chgo., 1973-74; editor-in-chief Am. Educator Ency., from 1974. Author: A Brand for the Burning, 1961, Young People in the White House, 1961, rev. edit., 1970, The United States in World War I, 1963, The United States in

World War II, 1963, The United States in the Korean War, 1964, Famous American Political Families, 1965, The War of 1812, 1966, Frances Perkins First Lady of the Cabinet, 1967, Great Air Battles: World Wars I and II, 1968, The Lion and the Rock: The Story of the Rock of Gibraltar, 1969, Youth and War: From World War I to Vietnam, 1969, Ten Fighters for Peace, 1971, The Colonial Wars, 1972, The American Revolution, 1974, The United States in the Indian Wars, 1975, The United States in the Mexican War, 1976, The United States in the Spanish-American War, 1976, The United States in the Civil War, 1977, Education Careers, 1977, Democracy, 1978, THe Secret World War II, 1978, Morocco, Algeria, Tunisia, and Libya, 1978, The Changing Face of the Constitution, 1979, FDR's New Deal, 1979, World War II: Homefronts, 1980, A Picture Life of Ronald Reagan, 1981, rev. edit., 1985, The United States in the Vietnam War, 1981, The War in Vietnam, A First Book, 1981, Libya and Qaddafi, 1982, rev. edit. 1987, The Long March: Red China Under Chairman Mao, 1983, The Pacific States, 1984, The French Resistance, 1984, The KGB, 1984, Marcos and the Philippines, 1984, rev. edit. 1987, Geraldine Ferraro, 1985, The Eagle and the Dragon: The History of U.S.-China Relations, 1985, South Africa, 1986, A Picture Album of the Vietnam War, 1986, The CIA, 1986, Landmark Supreme Court Cases, 1987, The Abraham Lincoln Brigade, 1989, Famous Presidential Scandals, 1990. Bd. dirs. Marcy-Newberry Assn. Settlement Houses. Served with USAAF, 1941-45, ETO. Mem. Authors Guild, Chgo. Book Clinic. Internat. Platform Assn., Chgo. Lit. Club, Soc. Midland Authors, Phi Beta Kappa. Methodist. Clubs: Cliff Dwellers (Chgo.), Press (Chgo.). Home: Chicago Ill. Died Feb. 3, 1990.

LAWTON, SHAILER UPTON, physician; b. Brattleboro, Vt., Mar. 30, 1894; s. Shailer Emery and Mary Lillian (Upton) L.; m. Aristine Pamela Knapp, July 6, 1918; 1 child, Aristine Lawton Winslow. MD, Columbia U., 1919, ScB, 1924, AM, 1925. Intern Brattleboro Retreat, 1919-20; attending physician Vanderbilt Clinic, 1922-29; instr. medicine Columbia U., N.Y.C., 1923-24, instr. anatomy, histology, etc., 1924-27, lectr. on endocrinology, extension div., 1925; attending physician Met. Hosp., 1924-25; chief attending physician Maternal Cardiac Rsch. Clinic N.Y. Nursery and Child's Hosp., 1925-33; assoc. chief diagnostic clinic N.Y. Post-grad. Hosp., 1928-32; med. dir. Houst of Detention, N.Y.C., 1934-40; vis. physician Houst of Detention, from 1940; assoc. prof. edn. NYU, from 1928, med. dir. Sch. Edn. Health Svc., 1930-32, curriculum dir. physio-therapy, 1932-33; lectr. sci. Briarcliff Jr. Coll., 1931-34; sci. lectr. YWCA, N.Y.C.; chmn. dept. health, phys. edn. and recreation Queen's Coll., 1942-44; instr. dept. medicine, asst. physician N.Y. Med. Coll. Flower and Fifth Ave. Hosps., from 1944; vis. prof. Yeshiva U., from 1949; med. dir. B-R Analytical Labs., N.Y.C., from 1953, dir., 1956; 1st v.p. Belray Chem. Co., Inc., 1956. Contbr. articles to sci. publs., mags., newspapers; pub. monthly mag. Self. Pres. Shailer Emery Lawton Found., Inc., 1945. Fellow ACP; mem. AMA, AAAS, N.Y. County med. Soc., N.Y. Micros. Soc., N.Y. Acad. Scis., Am. Assn. Sch. Physicians, N.Y. State Dept. Sci. Svc., Philomathean Soc., Kappa Phi Kappa. *

LAZARUS, A(RNOLD) L(ESLIE), English language educator, writer; b. Revere, Mass., Feb. 20, 1914; s. Benjamin and Bessie (Winston) L.; m. Keo Smith Felker, July 24, 1938; children: Karie (Mrs. John Friedman), Dianne (Mrs. James Runnels), David, Peter. Student, Coll. William and Mary, 1931-32; B.A., U. Mich., 1935; M.A., UCLA, 1941, Ed.D., 1957. Tchr. Calif. pub. schs., 1945-53; instr. Latin and Greek, tech. dir. coll. theatre Santa Monica (Calif.) City Coll., 1953-58; lectr. L.A. State Coll., 1958-59; assoc. prof. U. Tex., 1959-62; prof. English, dir. tchr. edn. in English Purdue U., Lafayette, Ind., 1962-79; dir. English Curriculum Center, 1963-79; gen. editor Purdue Research Found. Project English Study Units, 1969-79; mem. bd. judges Book-of-the-Month Club Writing Fellowships, 1967-70. Author: Your English Helper, 1953, Adventures in Modern Literature, 1956, 62, 70, Harbrace English Language Series, 1963, Selected Objectives in the Language Arts, 1967, Entertainments and Valedictions, 1970; (with others) A Catalogue of Performance Objectives in English, 1971, The Grosset and Dunlap Glossary to Literature and Language, 1971, 72, 73, A Suit of Four, 1973; (with Victor Jones) Beyond Graustark, 1981; (with H. Wendell Smith) The NCTE Glossary of Literature and Composition, 1983; Some Light: New and Selected Verse, 1988; poems anthologized in Light Year 1984, 85, 86, 87; contbr. poems to lit. jours.; editor: The Indiana Experience, 1977, The Best of George Ade, 1985, The World of George Barr McCutcheon, 1987, A George Jean Nathan Reader, 1990; editor (with others) Quartet mag, 1962-68; poetry editor, 1968-73; contbg. author New Book of Knowledge, 1967, Foundations of Education, 1967, College English: The First Year, 1968, 73, 78; contbr. articles to profl. jours. Mem. English com. Coll. Entrance Examination Bd. Served with AUS, 1942-44. Recipient Best Tchr. award Purdue Sch. Humanities, 1974; Kemper McComb award, 1976; Ford Found. fellow, 1954. Mem. MLA, NEA, Nat. Coun. Tchrs. of English (exec. com. Conf. English Edn. 1966-72), Poetry Soc. Am., Acad. of Am. Poets, Am. Soc. for Theatre Rsch., Am. Comparative Lit. Assn., Coll. English Assn., Phi Beta Kappa. Home: Sunnyvale Calif. Died Apr. 30, 1992. †

LAZRUS, BENJAMIN, watch manufacturing executive; b. N.Y.C., Apr. 29, 1894; s. Israel and Ella (Cohn) L.; m. Bess Feldman, Feb. 24, 1924; children: Natalie Louise, Jonathan Ezra. Student, Columbia Coll., 1912-13. Founder Benrus Watch Co., 1923, chmn. bd. dirs. Trustee Congregation Emanu-El, N.Y., Jewish Community Ctr. of White Plains, Nat. Jewish Hosp., Denver; exec. com. Am. Jewish Com., Jewish Bd. Guardians; chmn. Jewish Big Bro. Movement of N.Y.; v.p. Coun. Jewish Fedns. and Welfare Funds, Inc.; chmn. nat. adv. coun. Synagogue Coun. Am.; bd. dirs. Nat. Jewish Welfare Bd., Nat. Refugee Svc.; trustee, v.p. Fedn. Jewish Philanthropies N.Y.; treas. Am. Tercentenary Com.; bd. dirs. USO Greater N.Y. Mem. Harmonie Club, Quaker Ridge Golf Club, Metropolis Country Club, Jewelers 24 Karat Club. *

LEACH, JULIAN GILBERT, scientist, educator; b. Somerville, Tenn., Nov. 16, 1894; s. William Harvey and Julia Ann (Covington) L.; m. Margaret Clare Conover, Sept. 15, 1921; children: Margaret Ann (Mrs. Sam J. San Filippo), Alice Clare (Mrs. Robert Swan), William Harvey. BSA, U. Tenn., 1917; MS, U. Minn., 1918, PhD, 1922; postgrad., Imperial Coll. Sci. and Tech., London, 1927. Mem. faculty U. Minn., 1917-19, prof. plant pathology, 1937-38; assoc. prof. botany Colo. Agrl. Coll., 1919-20; Internat. Edn. Bd. fellow for study in Europe, 1927-28; prof. W.Va. U., from 1938, head dept. plant pathology, bacteriology and entomology, 1938-60; mem. com. on plant protection NRC, 1942-45. Author: Insect Transimssion of Plant Diseases, 1940. Fellow AAAS; mem. Am. Phytopath. Soc. (chmn. war emergency com. 1941-45, pres. 1941), Am. Potato Soc., So. Appalachian Bot. Soc., W.Va., Acad. Sci., Sigma Xi, Phi Kappa Phi, Alpha Zeta. *

LEAHY, OSMUND A., military officer; b. Oswego, N.Y., Aug. 31, 1915; s. James J. and Marie (LeRoy) L.; m. Elizabeth Pennell, Dec. 19, 1941 (dec. Jan. 1970); children: Margaret P. Vastola, James R., Elizabeth C., Thomas A.; m. Patricia Strand Dorn, Dec. 3, 1971. BS, U.S. Mil. Acad., 1940; MS, George Washington U., 1964. Commd. 2d lt. U.S. Army, 1940, advanced through grades to maj. gen., 1967, co. comdr. 2d Inf. Div., 1940-42, bn. comdr. 82d Airborne Div., 1942-47, comdr. 505 Parachute Regt., 1956-58, comdr. 7th Inf. Div., 1968; chief staff hdqrs. 6th U.S. Army, Presidio San Francisco, 1970-72; comdg. gen. Army Disability Agy., 1972-89; dir. Army Coun. Rev. Bds., also chmn. Army-Air Force Clemency and Parole Bd., Washington, 1975-89. Decorated Silver Star medal with 2 oak leaf clusters, Dutch Bronze Lion. Mem. Internat. City Mgrs. Assn. Home: Chevy Chase Md. Died Dec. 9, 1989.

LEAN, SIR DAVID, film director; b. Mar. 25, 1908; s. Francis William le Blount Lean and Helena Annie (Tangye) L.; m. Ann Todd, 1949 (div. 1957); m. Leila Matkar, 1960 (div. 1978); m. Sandra Hotz, 1981 (div. 1985); m. Sandra Cooke, 1990. Ed., Leighton Park Sch., Reading. Numberboard boy Gaumont-British Co., 1928; editor Gaumont Sound News and British Movietone News. Editor Escape Me Never, Pygmalion, 49th Parallel; co-dir. (with Noel Coward) In Which We Serve, 1942; dir. This Happy Breed, 1943, Blithe Spirit, 1944, Brief Encounter 1945, Great Expectations, 1946, Oliver Twist, 1947, The Passionate Friends, 1948, Madeleine, 1949, The Sound Barrier (British Acad. Award), 1952, Hobson's Choice, 1953, Summer Madness (Am. title Summertime), 1955, The Bridge on the River Kwai (Acad. Awards for Best Dir., for Best Picture), 1957, Lawrence of Arabia (Acad. Award, Italian Silver award), 1962, Dr. Zhivago, 1965, Ryan's Daughter, 1970, A Passage to India, 1984; author screenplay A Passage to India. Decorated Officier de l'Ordre des Arts et des Lettres, Comdr. Order of the Brit. Empire; recipient Life Achievement award Am. Film Inst., 1990. Fellow British Film Inst. Home: Stoke-on-Trent Eng. Died Apr. 16, 1991; buried London.

LEAR, FLOYD SEYWARD, history educator; b. Corfu, N.Y., July 7, 1895; s. William Sewyard and Harriet Laura (Mann) L.; m. Elsie Laura Mann, Dec. 25, 1920. AB, U. Rochester, 1917; AM, Harvard U., 1920, PhD, 1925. Head history dept. DuPont Manual Tng. High Sch., Louisville, 1920-22; asst. history Harvard U., Cambridge, Mass., 1922-23, Austin teaching fellow history, 1923-24, instr. history, 1924-25; instr. history Rice U. (formerly Rice Inst.), Houston, 1925-27, asst. prof., 1927-45, prof., 1945-53, Harris Masterson Jr. prof. history, from 1953, chmn. dept. history, 1933-60. Author: Monograph on Treason in Roman and Germanic Law, 1955; mem. adv. bd. Speculum, 1937-40; cons. editor: Corpus Juris Romani; contbr. in field. Sgt. 285th Aero Squadron, U.S. Army, 1917-19. Fellow Am. Geog. Soc.; mem. AAUP, Am. Acad. Polit. Sci., Medieval Acad. Am. (coun. 1953-56), Am. Hist. Assn., Tex. Hist. Assn., So. Classical Assn., Am. Mil. Inst., U.S. Naval Inst., Renaissance Soc., Am. Philos. Soc., Houston Philos. Soc. (pres. 1949-50), Phi Beta Kappa. *

LEARNED, HENRY DEXTER, philologist; b. Balt., Mar. 17, 1893; s. Marion Dexter and Annie (Mosser) L.; desc. William Learned, Mass. Bay Colony, 1630; m. Theodora Gingras, Aug. 27, 1917 (div.); children: Eugenia Anne (Mrs. Clifford R. James), Marion (Mrs. Walton E. Grundy); m. Erma Renninger, Sept. 19, 1933; children: William Dexter, Susan Jane. AB, U. Pa., 1912, PhD, 1917. Instr. in German Dickinson Coll., 1912-13, U. Pa., 1913-18; instr. in French U. Mich., 1919-21; prof. French U. Chattanooga, 1921-22, prof. French George Peabocy Coll. summer sch., 1922; assoc. prof. Romance langs. U. N.C., 1922-28; organizer mcpl. coll. for city of Asheville N.C., 1928-29; prof., head dept. French Temple U., 1930-36, chmn. dept. modern langs., 1936-46, prof. modern langs., 1945-60. Author: Syntax of Brant's Narrenschiff, 1917, Modern Introductory French Book, 1932, 2d edit., 1960; asst. editor Studies in Philology, 1923-28, Webster's New International Dictionary, 2d edit., 1929-34; contbr. articles to profl. publs.; exhibitor paintings and linoleum prints. 2d lt. Corps of Interpreters, U.S. Army, 1918-19, 1st lt. Mil. Intelligence Res., 1920-30; lt. comdr. USNR, 1941-45; col. M.I., USAR, grad. Command and Gen. Staff Course (ret.). Rosengarten traveling scholar, 1914; spl. rsch. fellow Belgian-Am. Ednl. Found., 1938; rsch. grantee Am. Philos. Soc., 1939. Mem. MLA, AAUP, Medieval Acad. Am., Anglo-Norman Text. Soc., Linguistic Soc. Am., Order of Founders and Patriots of Am. (historian Pa. Soc. 1946-51, gov. 1951-57, registrar from 1961, genealogist from 1964, editor Gen. Ct. Bull. from 1965, life mem.), Cruiser Olympia Assn., Inc. (founder, past 1st pres., chmn. bd. dirs. 1957-63), S.R., Mil. Order World Wars, Phi Beta Kappa Assocs. (pres. Phila. chpt. 1952-54, life mem.). *

LEARY, LEWIS, writer, lecturer; b. Blauvelt, N.Y., Apr. 18, 1906; s. Lewis Gaston and Beatrice Emily (Knight) L.; m. Mary Warren Hudson, Mar. 7, 1932; children—Carolyn (Mrs. William Bartholet), Martha Hudson (Mrs. Theodore Allen). B.S., U. Vt., 1928, LL.D., 1963; A.M., Columbia, 1932, Ph.D., 1941. Instr. English Am. U., Beirut, 1928-31; faculty U. Miami, 1935-40, asso. prof. English, 1938-40; faculty Duke, 1941-52, prof. Am. lit., 1950-52; prof. English Columbia, 1952-68, chmn. dept., 1962-68; William Rand Kenan, Jr. prof. English U. N.C., 1968-76; asso. Nat. Humanities Center, 1978-79; Spl. asst. OSS, Washington, Cairo, 1942-45; Fulbright lectr. U. Amsterdam, 1957-58; vis. prof. U. Pa., 1958-59, Swarthmore Coll., 1959-60, Duke U., 1978. Author: Idiomatic Mistakes in English, 1932, That Rascal Freneau: A Study in Literary Failure, 1941, 60, 71, The Literary Career of Nathaniel Tucker, 1951, Mark Twain, 1960, Mark Twain's Letters to Mary, 1961, John Greenleaf Whittier, 1962, Washington Irving, 1963, Norman Douglas, 1967, Southern Excursions, 1971, William Faulkner of Yoknapatawpha County, 1973, Soundings: Some Early American Writers, 1975, American Literature: A Study and Research Guide, 1976, Ralph Waldo Emerson: An Interpretive Essay, 1980, The Book Peddling Parson, 1984. Editor: The Last Poems of Philip Freneau, 1945, 71, Articles on Am. Literature, 1947, rev. and extended, 1954, 70, 79, Method and Motive in the Cantos of Ezra Pound, 1954, The Unity of Knowledge, 1955, Mark Twain's Correspondence with Henry Huttleston Rogers, 1969, Criticism: Some Major American Writers, 1971; Contbr. articles to profl. periodicals. Recipient Jay B. Hubbell medallion for distinction in Am. lit., 1976. Mem. Modern Lang. Assn., Bibliog. Soc. Am., Am. Antiquarian Soc. Clubs: Grolier (N.Y.C.), Century (N.Y.C.). Home: Chapel Hill N.C. Died May 1, 1990; cremated.

LEAVITT, JOSEPH, producer, musician, arts administrator; b. Chelsea, Mass.; s. Abraham and Mildred (Leavitt) L.; m. Sally Elissa; children: Howard, Joan. Grad., New Eng. Conservatory Music; BA, Am. U., 1954; student seminars, Harvard Bus. Sch.; student, Boston U., Manhattan Sch. of Music. mem. faculty tympani percussion Peabody Conservatory, 1948-49; faculty arts mgmt. U. Md. summer sch., 1974-76; adj. prof. arts mgmt. Goucher Coll., 1977-84; cons. Joseph Meyerhoff Symphony Hall, 1975-81, Pier 6 Pavilion, 1980-81. Successively musician, pianist, prin. musician, dir. ops. and asst. mgr. Nat. Symphony Orch., Washington, 1949-69; gen. mgr. N.J. Symphony Orch., 1969-71; exec. dir., exec. producer all Wolf Trap prodns., Wolf Trap Found. Performing Arts, Vienna, Va., 1970-73; gen. mgr. Balt. Symphony Orch., 1973-81, exec. dir. 1981-84; exec. v.p. Philharm. Orch. of Fla., 1984-90; engagements with Boston Pops, Balt. Symphony Orch.; rec. artist: RCA Victor, Westminster, Columbia records; author: The Rhythms of Contemporary Music, 1963, Reading by Recognition, 1960. Mem. adv. com. Fairfax County Council Arts, 1971-73, Balt. Mayor's Com. on Art and Culture; bd. dirs., v.p. Md. Council for Dance, 1976-78; mem. exec. com. Regional Cultural Commn.; field reader Program for Gifted and Talented, HEW; vice-chmn. cultural execs. com. Palm Beach County; dir. Fla. Cultural Action and Ednl. Alliances; panelist cultural affairs com. Dade County; mem. cultural execs. com. Broward County; panelist Nat. Endowment for the Arts. Recipient Louis Sudler award Am. Symphony Orch. League, 1986. Mem. Internat. Assn. Performing Arts Adminstrs. (bd. dirs.). Clubs: University, Boca Pointe Country, Polo (Boca Raton). Home: Boca Raton Fla. Died Sept. 21, 1990.

LEBLANC, CAMILLE (ANDRE), bishop; b. Barachois, N.B., Can., Aug. 25, 1898; s. Alphee C. and Zélica (Légere) LeB. Ed., St. Anne's Coll., Church

Point, N.B., Holy Heart Sem., Halifax, N.S. Ordained priest, Roman Cath. Ch. Ordained curate Shediac, N.B., Can., 1924-28; parish priest Shemogue, N.B., Can., 1928-38; pastor cathedral, Moncton, N.B., Can., 1938-42; bishop Bathhurst, N.B., Can., from 1942. *

LE CLAIRE, HARRY WALTER, information systems executive; b. Coeur d'Alene, Idaho, Oct. 10, 1914; s. Francis and Alice (Simmons) Le C.; m. Norma Greene, Feb. 9, 1939; children: Edward, Donald. B.A., Stanford U., 1936. With IBM, 1939-43, 46-47; self-employed, 1947-50; founder Tab Products Co., Palo Alto, Calif., from 1950. Planning commr. Town of Atherton, Calif., 1968-80. Served with USN, 1943-46. Republican. Presbyterian. Clubs: Menlo Country, Palo Alto. Home: Menlo Park Calif. Died Aug. 1, 1991. †

LEDERER, FRANCIS LOEFFLER, surgeon; b. Chgo., Sept. 18, 1989; s. Jacob and Frances (Loeffler) L.; m. Anne Pollock, Mar. 4, 1925; 1 child, Francis II. SB, U. Chgo., 1918; MD, Rush Med. Coll., 1921; postgrad., U. Berlin, 1925, U. Vienna, 1925. Pvt. practice Chgo., from 1921; prof., head dept. otolaryngology U. Ill. Coll. Medicine; mem. sr. staff Michael Reese Hosp., Grant Hosp., Columbus Hosp., Chgo.; chief otolaryngol. svc. Rsch. and Ednl. Hosps.; dir. otolaryngol. svc. Ill. Eye and Ear Infirmary, Hines Hosp.; cons. Presbyn.-St. Luke's Hosp., cons. otolaryngologist, mem. spl. med. adv. group VA; nat. cons. surgeon gen. USAF; cons. otolaryngol. U.S. Naval Hosp. Great Lakes, Ill.; area cons. in audiology VA. Author: Diseases of the Ear, Nose and Throat, 6th edit., 1953; contbr. to jours. and books on subjects pertaining to ear, nose and throat specialty; chief assoc. editor (Otolaryntology) of Cyclopedia of Medicine, Surgery, Specialties. With USMC, World War I; capt. M.C. (S) USNR, World War II; chief eye, ear, nose ant throat svc., chief Aural Rehab., U.S. Naval Hosp., Phila., 1942-46. Fellow ACS, Internat. Coll. Surgeons (hon.); mem. AMA, Ill. State Med. Soc., Chgo. Med. Soc., Inst. Medicine, Chgo. Laryngol. and Otolaryngol. Soc., Am. Otol. Soc., Chgo. Pathol. Soc., Am. Acad. Ophthalmology and Otolaryngology, Am. Otol., Rhinol. and Laryngological Soc., Am. Laryngological Assn., Am. Bronchoesophagol Assn., Am. Coll. Chest Physicians, Am. Assn. Mil. Surgeons, Masons, Shriners, Sigma Xi, Alpha Omega Alpha, Phi Delta Epsilon, others. *

LEE, ALFRED MCCLUNG, social scientist, educator; b. Oakmont, Pa., Aug. 23, 1906; s. Alfred McClung and Edna (Hamor) L.; m. Elizabeth Riley Briant, Sept. 15, 1927; children: Alfred McClung 3d, Briant Hamor. A.B., U. Pitts., 1927, A.M., 1931; Ph.D., Yale U., 1933. Newspaper, civic experience Pitts., 1927-31, New Haven, 1931-34; Kennedy T. Friend fellow in sociology Yale U., 1931-33, Sterling postdoctoral fellow, 1933-34; asst. prof. Inst. Human Relations, 1937-38; asst. prof. U. Kans., 1934-35, asso. prof., 1935-38; pub. affairs specialist Twentieth Century Fund, 1935-37; lectr. sociology NYU, 1938-39, asst. prof., 1939-42, vis. grad. prof., 1951-55; prof. sociology, anthropology Wayne U., 1942-49, chmn. dept., 1942-47, research sociologist, 1948-49; prof. sociology, anthropology Bklyn. Coll. and Grad. Center, CUNY, 1949-71, prof. emeritus, 1971-92; vis. prof. U. Mich., 1948-49; UNESCO prof. sociology, Milan, Italy, 1957-58; exec. dir., treas. Inst. Propaganda Analysis, 1940-50; cons. FCC, 1941, U.S. Dept. Justice, 1943-44, U.S. Office Edn., 1947-49; rsch. cons. Met. Applied Rsch. Ctr., N.Y.C., 1968-76; vis. scholar Drew U., Madison, N.J., 1975-92; cons. to civic, edn. orgns. Pres., Friends of Danilo Dolci, 1971-73; mem. bd. Pub. Affairs Pamphlets, from 1950, vice chmn., 1970-85; bd. dirs. Sociol. Abstracts, from 1965. Author numerous books including: The Daily Newspaper in America, The Evolution of a Social Instrument, 1937 (Rsch. award Sigma Delta Chi), The Fine Art of Propoganda, 1940's, How to Understand Propaganda, 1952, Fraternities Without Brotherhood, 1955, La Sociologia delle Comunicazioni, 1960, Che Cos'E' la Propaganda, 1961, Multivalent Man, 1970, Toward Humanist Sociology, 1973, Sociology for Whom?, 1978, rev. edit., 1986, Human Rights in the Northern Ireland Conflict, 1968-1980, Terrorism in Northern Ireland, 1983; co-author: Marriage and the Family, rev. edit., 1967, Race Riot, 1968, The Participant Observer, 1970, Sociology for People, 1988, rev. edit., 1990; editor, co-author textbooks in sociology.; contbr. to mags., jours. Recipient Fulbright award U. Rome, 1960-61; Honor award Corriere della Sera Newspapers (Italy), 1967; Marshall Field research grantee, 1947-48; Am. specialist grantee U.S. State Dept., India, Pakistan, Middle East, Italy, Austria, Iceland, 1967; Am. Humanist Assn. fellow, 1977; Alfred McClung Lee and Elizabeth Briant Lee Award established by Soc. Study of Social Problems, 1981. Fellow AAAS, Am. Anthrop. Assn., Am. Sociol. Assn. (pres. 1975-76, Disting. Career award); mem. Assn. Italiana di Scienze Sociali, Internat. Sociol. Assn. (U.S. del. 1966-70), Inst. Internat. de Sociologie (Rome), Eastern Sociol. Soc. (pres. 1954-55, Ann. Merit award 1974), Soc. Study of Social Problems (founder 1950-51, pres. 1953-54), Soc. Psychol. Study of Social Issues (charter mem. award 1986), Assn. Humanist Sociology (founder, acting pres. 1975-76, pres. 1976-77), Sociol. Practice Assn. (Disting. Career award 1984, cert. recognition 1986), Am. Fedn. Tchrs., NEA, Irish Texts Soc. (Dublin), ACLU, NAACP (chmn. com. social sci. cons. legal def. and ednl. fund 1954-57), Am. Com. Irish Studies, Irish Sociol. Assn. (hon.), Deutsche Gesellschaft für Soziologie (corr.), Sigma Xi, Omicron Delta Kappa, Sigma Delta Chi (Nat. Research award 1937, cert. appreciation 1984). Alpha Kappa Delta, Sigma Chi. Home: Madison N.J. Died May 19, 1992; buried Plum Creek Cemetery, Plum Creek, Pa.

LEE, DWIGHT ERWIN, university dean; b. Arcadia, N.Y., June 3, 1898; s. Henry Austin and Eunice Mary (Cull) L.; m. Margaret Lucinda Shipley, June 30, 1928; 1 child, Cora Lucinda. AB, U. Rochester, 1921, AM, 1922; postgrad., U. Mich., 1922; PhD, Harvard U., 1928. Asst. in hsitory, editor Alumni News Sheet U. Rochester, N.Y., 1921-22, instr. in history, 1922-24; asst. prof. modern European history Clark U., 1927-30, assoc. prof., 1930-38, prof., 1938-62, Jacob and Frances Hiatt prof. European history, from 1962, dean grad. sch., from 1962; adminstrv. sec. World and Peace Studies Project, Coun. on Fgn. Rels., N.Y., 1942-43; mem. Internat. Secretariat, UN Conf. for Internat. Orgn., San Francisco, 1945. Spl. editorial writer Worcester Telegram and Gazette, 1929-30; author: Great Britain and the Cyprus Convention Policy of 1878, 1934, Ten Years: The World on the Way to War, 1930-40, 1942; editor: The Outbreak of the First World War, 1958; gen. editor: Problems in European Civilization, from 1961; co-editor: Essays in History and Internat. Rels. (with George McReynolds), 1949; contbr. to profl. periodicals; mem. editorial bd. Jour. Modern History, 1944-46, Internat. Orgn., 1946-55. Mem. Am. Hist. Assn., Phi Beta Kappa. Unitarian. *

LEE, LAWRENCE J., lawyer; b. St. Louis, Nov. 15, 1934; s. George E. and Jennie M. (Dondalski) L.; m. Carol Diane Portante, Nov. 28, 1975; children: Scott, Shannon, Erin, Colin; children from previous marriage: Leslie, Sean, Scott. BA, U. Ill., 1955; LLB, Cornell U., 1958; LLM, Georgetown U., 1961. Ptnr. Lee, Theisen & Eagle, Phoenix, 1981-87. Bd. editors The Practical Lawyer; contbr. numerous articles to profl. jours. Mem. Commrs. Tax Adv. Group, Washington, 1982, Police Rev. Bd., Phoenix, 1985-86; spl. counsel on taxes City of Phoenix, 1983. Served to lt. comdr. USN, 1975-80. Mem. ABA (chmn. com. personal service orgn. tax sect.), Ariz. Bar Assn. (outstanding achievement award 1977), Fed. Bar Assn. (spl. achievement award 1980), Am. Law Inst. (tax adv. com.). Republican. Roman Catholic. Club: University (Phoenix). Home: Phoenix Ariz. Died Nov. 5, 1987; buried Phoenix, Ariz.

LEE, MANNING DE VILLENEUVE, illustrator; b. Summerville, S.C., Mar. 15, 1894; s. Brig. Gen. Joseph and Gertrude Marie (Sweeny) L.; m. Eunice Celeste Sandoval, Apr. 8, 1922; 1 child, Richard Sandoval. Student, Porter Mil. Acad., Charleston, S.C., Pa. Acad. Fine Arts, 1914-15, 19-22; grad., F.A. Sch., Saumur, France, Heavy Arty. Tractor Sch., Vincennes. Prin. works include protrait of Freas Styer, U.S. Mint, Phila., 5 marine paintings, U.S. Naval Acad., Annapolis, Md.; illustrator of books and mags., including Blue Fairy Book and Red Fairy Book (by Lang), Historic Ships, Historic Airships and Historic Railroads (by Rupert Sargent Holland), Kidnapped (Robert Louis Stevenson), When You Grow Up to Vote (by Eleanor Roosevelt), What to do Now, Fun With Paper Dolls, Dolls and Doll Houses, Manners to Grow On, by Tina Lee (Eunice Lee); series commemorative postage stamps for Guniea, Liberia, Indonesia; also edn. film strips. Served 1st Va. F.A., Mexican border, 1916; 2d lt. F.A., U.S. Army, 1917-19. Recipient medal Charleston Exposition, 1901, 2d Toppan prize Pa. Acad. Fine Arts, 1922; Cresson traveling scholar Pa. Acad. Fine Arts, 1921. Fellow Royal Soc. Arts, London; mem. Phila. Art Alliance, Companion Mil. Order Fgn. Wars of U.S., Soc. Mayflower Descs. Democrat. Episcopalian. *

LEE, MERRILL CLIFFORD, architect; b. Hazleton, Pa., Dec. 13, 1893; m. Hope T. Gravely, Apr. 25, 1922; 1 child, Harry G. Engaged in practice of architecture, from 1920; architect Bell Telephone Co., Va., from 1931, Randolph Macon Coll., Med. Coll. Va., 1936-40. Mem. Richmond (Va.) City Planning Commn., 1936-40; chmn. Bldg. Code Appeals Bd.; chpt. v.p. Va. Assn. Workers for Blind; governing bd. United Givers Fund; pres. Va. Found. Archtl. Edn.; mem. architects adv. commn. Williamsburg (Va.) Restoration. 2d lt. 311th F.A., 79th div. U.S. Army, later with Adj. Gen.'s Dept., Port of Embarkation, Newport News, Va., during World War I; disch. with rank 1st lt., Adj. Gen.'s Dept. Fellow AIA (bd. dirs. 1936-38), Royal Soc. Arts, London; mem. Nat. Acad. Arts and Scis. (bd. dirs.), Phi Sigma Kappa. Methodist. *

LEE, SIDNEY SEYMOUR, physician, educator; b. New Haven, Dec. 5, 1921; s. Nathaniel and Alma (Dickstein) L.; m. Vera Cohen, June 23, 1946 (div.); 1 child, Amanda; m. Frances Zellick, Dec. 11, 1959 (div.); children: Civia, Jonathan, Michael; m. Karen P. Karsten, Jan. 2, 1986; 1 child, Rebecca. B.S., Yale U., 1942, M.D., 1950, M.P.H., 1952, Dr.P.H., 1953. Diplomate Nat. Bd. Med. Examiners, Am. Bd. Preventive Medicine. Sr. asst. surgeon USPHS, 1950-54; dir. Bur. Venereal Disease Control, W.Va. Health Dept., 1952-53; chief dept. Ohio Dept. Health, 1953-54; asst. dir. Beth Israel Hosp., Boston, 1954-57, head dept. preventive medicine, 1955-66, dir. clin. services, 1958-60, gen. dir., 1960-66; instr. pub. health practice Harvard U., 1955-58, assoc. pub. health practice, 1958-60, lectr., 1960-63, lectr. preventive medicine, 1963-67, assoc. dean faculty medicine for hosp. programs, 1966-72, clin. prof. hosp. and med. care adminstrn., 1967-72, cons. to dean, 1972-73; prof. social medicine McGill U., Montreal, Que., Can., 1972-81, assoc. dean faculty medicine, 1972-81; dir. Health Care Centre, 1972-81; v.p. ambulatory services Michael Reese Hosp. and Med. Ctr., Chgo., 1981-82, pres., 1982-84, trustee health plan, 1982-84; prof. medicine U. Chgo.; pres. Milbank Meml. Fund, N.Y.C., 1985-88, advisor to pres., 1988-91; adj. prof. pub. health Cornell U. Med. Coll., N.Y.C., 1984-88; lectr. pub. health Yale Sch. Medicine, 1987-92; vis. prof. health policy, dept. social medicine Harvard Med. Sch., 1988-92; cons. Royal Victoria Hosp., Montreal, Montreal Gen. Hosp., Montreal Children's Hosp., Jewish Gen. Hosp., Montreal, Montreal Chest Hosp., 1973-81; mem. Nat. Health Grants Com. Can., 1973-75; chmn. health adv. com. Office of Tech. Assessment, U.S. Congress, 1980-86; chmn. health services devel. grants Nat. Center for Health Svcs. Rsch., USPHS, 1979-82; exec. com., trustee Harvard Community Health Plan, 1968-85, physicians' coun., 1985-87. Trustee Dimock Community Health Ctr., 1968-72, Royal Victoria Hosp., 1979-81, Jewish Gen. Hosp., 1979-81; bd. mgrs. Vis. Nurse Assn. Boston, 1966-72, bd. dirs., 1989-92; cons. Exec. Svc. Corps of New Eng., 1991-92. With AUS, 1943-45, ETO; med. dir. USPHS (R), 1970-92. Decorated chevalier Ordre de Sante Publique France, 1954. Fellow Am. Pub. Health Assn. (governing council 1970-71, 73-74), N.Y. Acad. Medicine, AAAS, Royal Coll. Physicians and Surgeons Can.; mem. Internat. Hosp. Fedn., Assn. Tchrs. Preventive Medicine, Am. Coll. Preventive Medicine (regent 1976-78), Soc. Med. Adminstrs. (pres. 1974-76), Hermann Biggs Soc. Home: Boston Mass. Died Nov. 29, 1992. †

LEECE, GIFFORD VANNIN, manufacturing executive; b. Bishop, Calif., Apr. 26, 1898; s. Thomas Edward and Grace (Gifford) L.; m. Edith Hewitt Baker, June 25, 1924; children: William E., Helen (Mrs. Tom Weston Hoyer), Florence (Mrs. Robert O. Mullins). Student, U. So. Calif., 1917-18. With Gardner-Denver Co., Quincy, Ill., from 1922, salesman, then dist. mgr., Pacific Coast mgr., N.Y. mgr., gen. sales mgr., pres., chmn. bd., mem. exec. com.; exec. com. Ill. Com. Trade Expansion; past mem. several U.S. govt. adv. coms. Past pres., bd. dirs. Blessing Hosp.; adv. coun. U. Ill.; trustee Culver-Stockton Coll. Mem. NAM (bd. dirs.), Machinery and Allied Products Inst., Internat. Compressed Air and Allied Machinery Assn. (exec. com.), Compressed Air and Gas Inst. (v.p.), Am. Petroleum Inst., Assoc. Equipment Dealers, Hydraulic Inst., Ill. C. of C., Tri-State Sales Execs. (past pres.), Quincy Country Club (bd. dirs., past pres.), Masons. *

LEECH, MARGARET KERNOCHAN (MRS. RALPH PULITZER), author; b. Newburgh, N.Y., Nov. 7, 1893; d. William Kernochan and Rebecca (Taggart) Leech; m. Ralph Pullitzer, Aug. 1, 1928 (dec. June 1939). BA, Vassar Coll., 1915. Author: The Back of the Book, 1924, Tim Wedding, 1926, Anthony Comstock (with Heywood Broun), 1927, The Feathered Nest, 1928, Reveille in Washington (Pulitzer prize in history), 1941, In The Days of McKinley, 1959 (recipient 1960 Bancroft Prize, 1960 Pulitzer History Prize), also short stories in mags. *

LEEDS, ANTHONY, anthropologist, educator; b. N.Y.C., Jan. 26, 1925; s. Arthur S. and Polly (Cahn) L.; m. Jo Alice Lowrey, Nov. 28, 1948; m. Elizabeth Rachel Plotkin, Jan. 28, 1967; children: Madeleine, John Christopher, Anne Lowrey, Jeremy, Jared Martin. B.A. with honors in Anthropology, Columbia U., 1949, Ph.D. in Anthropology, 1957, postgrad., 1957-60. Teaching asst. anthropology dept. Columbia U., N.Y.C., 1952-53, adminstrv. asst., 1953-54, part time instr., 1953-54, 59-60; sci. instr. Baldwin Sch., N.Y.C., 1954-56; instr. dept. sociology and anthropology Hofstra U., Hempstead, N.Y., 1956-59; instr. dept. sociology and anthropology CUNY, part-time 1956-59, asst. prof., 1959-61; chief program urban devel., dept. social affairs Pan Am. Union, Washington, 1961-63; assoc. prof. U. Tex., Austin, 1963-67, prof., 1967-72; research assoc. Inst. Latin Am. Studies, 1963-72; prof. Boston U., 1972-89; research assoc. Center for Study of History and Philosophy of Sci., 1973-89, African Studies Center, 1977-89; lectr. Cath. U., Am. U., Washington, 1962-63, U.S. Fgn. Service Dept., 1961-62; vis. prof. Fed. U. Rio de Janeiro, Brazil, Museu Nacional, 1969; vis. lectr. Am. Anthrop. Assn., 1963-72; Fulbright vis. prof. Oxford and London univs., Eng., 1972-73; tech. cons., evaluator AID, Rio de Janeiro, Brazil, 1966; cons. Columbia U. Inst. Urban Environment, 1968, Southwest Ednl. Devel. Lab., Austin, 1970-72; Mem. Nat. Acad. Scis.-NRC-Conselho Nacional de Pesquisas Joint Brazilian-Am. Commn. on Indsl. Research Devel., 1966-68. Exhibited photographs Hobart Coll., 1976, Coll. Atlantic, 1977, Queluz, Portugal, 1977 (hon. mention), Bentley Coll., 1982, Rockefeller Library, Brown U., 1984, Manuel Rogers, Jr. Ctr. for Portuguese Culture, Field Br., Cambridge City Library, Mass., 1984; editor: (with A.P. Vayda) Man, Culture and Animals: The Role of Animals in Human Ecological Adjustments, 1965, Social Structure, Stratification, and Mobility, 1967, (with Val Dusek) Sociobiology: The Debate Evolves, 1981-82; author: (with Elizabeth Leeds) A Sociologia do Brasil Urbano, 1978; contbr. chpts. to books, articles to profl. publs. and encys., also poetry. Brazilian Govt. exchange scholar, 1951-52; grantee Social Sci. Research Council , 1958, Columbia U. Council for Social Sci. Research, 1959, Am. Philos. Soc., 1960, Wenner-Gren Found., 1962, 64, 65, 78-79, 82, 85, Instituto Nacional de Estudos Pedagógicos, 1962, U. Tex. Univ. Research Inst., 1964, 67-68, 68-69, Ford Found., 1965-66, Fulbright Commn., 1969-70, 87, U. Tex. Inst. Latin Am. Studies, 1967, 68, 71, Gulbenkian Found., 1977-79, 81, Anthrop. Assn., 1960, Human Sci. Research Council at Urban Found., Republic of South Africa, 1986, numerous other grants; Fulbright Commn. fellow, 1972-73. Fellow AAAS (sect. 4), Soc. Gen. Systems Research, Soc. Urban Anthropology (pres. 1981-82, coordinator 1982-83), Council European Studies, Phi Beta Kappa, Sigma Xi. Home: Dedham Mass. Died Feb. 20, 1989; cremated.

LEETE, EDWARD, chemistry educator; b. Leeds, Eng., Apr. 18, 1928; came to U.S., 1954, naturalized, 1961; s. Edward Cecil and Elsie (Griffith) L.; m. Sheila Anne Slattery, Dec. 4, 1976; children: Jennifer Anne, Carolyn Marie, Lorraine Margaret, Michael Edward, Nicholas Slattery; children by previous marriage: Peter Andrew, Allison Jane. B.Sc., U. Leeds, 1948, Ph.D., 1950, D.Sc., 1965. Postdoctoral fellow NRC Can., 1950-54; asst. prof. UCLA, 1954-58; faculty U. Minn., Mpls., from 1958; prof. chemistry U. Minn., from 1963; vis. prof. Kyoto U., Japan, 1990; cons. NIH, 1962-65, Philip Morris Tobacco Co., 1974-77. Mem. editorial bd. Phytochemistry, Jour. Natural Products. Alfred P. Sloan fellow, 1962-65; Guggenheim fellow U. Oxford, Eng., 1965; recipient Disting. Tchr. award U. Minn., 1976. Fellow AAAS, Chem. Soc. London; mem. Am. Chem. Soc. (Minn. award 1990, Phytochemistry prize and medal, 1990). Home: Saint Paul Minn. Died Feb. 8, 1992. †

LE GALLIENNE, EVA, actress; b. London, Jan. 11, 1899; d. Richard and Julie (Norregaard) Le G. Ed., Collège Sévigne, Paris; M.A. (hon.), Tufts Coll., 1927; L.H.D., Smith Coll., 1930, Ohio Wesleyan U., 1959, Goucher Coll., 1960, U. N.C., 1964, Bard Coll., 1965, Fairfield U., 1966; Litt.D., Russell Sage Coll., 1930, Brown U., 1933, Mount Holyoke Coll., 1937. Debut in: The Laughter of Fools, Prince of Wales Theatre, London, 1915; New York debut in: The Melody of Youth, 1916; appeared, in New York and on tour in Mr. Lazarus, 1916-17, (with Ethel Barrymore in) The Off Chance, 1917-18, Not So Long Ago, 1920-21, Liliom, 1921-22, The Swan, 1923; Hannele in: The Assumption of Hanele, by Hauptmann, 1923, Jeanne d'Arc, by Mercedes de Acosta, 1925, The Call of Life, by Schnitzler, 1925, The Master Builder, by Ibsen, 1925-26; co-founder, dir., Civic Repertory Theatre, N.Y.C., opening Oct. 25, 1926, presented over 30 plays in 7 yrs. including Allison's House (Pulitzer prize), Alice in Wonderland, others, Am. Repertory Theatre, which produced Henry VIII, Ibsens' John Gabriel Brokman; Ibsen's Hedda Gabler and Ghosts, 1948; toured in: The Corn Is Green, 1949-50; on Broadway in The Southwest Corner, 1955; as Queen Elizabeth in: on Broadway in Schiller's Mary Stuart, N.Y.C., 1957, on tour, 1959-60; in, Maxwell Anderson's Elizabeth the Queen, 1961-62; toured in: Sea Gull, Nat. Repertory Theatre, 1963-64; in: The Trojan Women; appeared with, APA Repertory Theatre, N.Y.C.; as Marguerite in: Exit The King; also directed: Chekov's The Cherry Orchard, 1967-68, Doll's House, Seattle Repertory, 1975; appeared as Countess in: All's Well That Ends Well, Shakespeare Festival Theatre, Stratford, Conn., 1970; in: Dream-Watcher, White Barn Theatre, 1975, The Royal Family, Helen Hayes Theatre, N.Y.C., 1976, nat. tour, 1976-77; To Grandmother's House We Go, Biltmore Theatre, N.Y.C., 1980-81; appeared: in movie The Resurrection, 1979; (Spl. Tony award Am. Theatre Wing 1964, Emmy award 1978); Author: autobiography At 33, 1934, Flossie and Bossie, 1949 (London edit. 1950), With a Quiet Heart, 1953, The Mystic in the Theatre, a study of Eleonora Duse, 1966; Translator many works of Henrik Ibsen, Hans Christian Andersen; dir. Alice in Wonderland, Virginia Theatre, N.Y.C., 1982-83. Recipient Brandeis U. award for drama, 1966; winner of Pictoral Rev. Achievement award, 1926; gold medal Soc. Arts and Town Hall Club award, 1934; Am. Acad. Arts and Letters medal for good diction on the stage, 1945; Outstanding Woman of Year award Women's Nat. Press Club, 1947; spl. award ANTA, 1964; award, 1977; Handel medallion City N.Y., 1976; Nat. Medal of Arts award, 1986; decorated cross Royal Order St. Olaf, 1961. Mem. Actors' Equity Assn., AFTRA, Screen Actors Guild, Dramatists Guild. Home: Westport Conn. Died June 4, 1991; buried Weston, Conn.

LÉGER, PAUL-EMILE CARDINAL, archbishop; b. Valleyfield, Que., Can., Apr. 26, 1904; s. Ernest and Alda (Beauvais) L. Student, Sem. St. Therese; L.Th., Grand Sem. Montreal; J.C.L., Inst. Catholique, Paris, France; S.T.D., Laval U., 1951, U. Ottawa, 1961; Litt.D., Assumption Coll., 1954; LL.D., McGill U., 1960, St. Francis Xavier U., 1961, U. Toronto, 1965, U. Alta., 1967; D.C.L. (hon.), Bishop's U., Lennoxville, Que., 1965; L.H.D., Waterloo Lutheran U., 1969; Dr. honoris causa, U. Montreal, 1974, U. Sherbrooke, 1974, U. Kingston, 1979. Ordained priest Roman Catholic Ch., 1929; consecrated bishop Roman Catholic Ch., Rome, 1950; elevated to Sacred Coll. Cardinals, 1953; with Inst. Catholique, Paris, 1930-31; prof. Issy-les-Moulineaux, 1931-32, asst. master novices, 1932-33; founder, superior Sem. of Fukuoka, Japan, 1933-39; vicar gen., pastor cathedral Diocese of Valleyfield, 1940-47; rector Canadian Coll., Rome, Italy, 1947-50; archbishop of Montreal, Can., 1950-67; resigned for mission fields Africa, 1967-79; archbishop emeritus of Montreal, 1979-91; chancellor U. Montreal, 1950; nominated as parish priest St. Madeleine Sophie Barat's Parish, 1974, resigned, 1975; Papal legate closing Marian Year, Lourdes, France, 1954, St. Joseph's Oratory, Montreal, 1955, Ste. Anne de Beaupré, Quebec, Can., 1958; Mem. Central Commn. preparatory to Vatican II, 1961; mem. Council Commn. on Sacred Theology, 1962, Sacred Consistorial Congregation Rome, 1963; mem. commn. canon law Council Vatican II, 1963; mem. del. Can. bishops Synod of Bishops, Rome, 1967; mem. Council Propagation of Faith, Rome, 1972, Pontifical Commn. Pastoral of Tourism, Rome, 1972; co-pres. Can. Found. for Refugees, from 1979. Decorated knight grand cross Equestrian of Holy Sepulchre of Jerusalem, 1950; bailiff grand cross of honour and devotion Sovereign Order of Malta, 1954; knight grand cross Legion Honour, France, 1958; grand cross de Benemerencia Portugal, 1965; Coeur d'or Milan, 1967; comdr. Order of Valor and Merit Cameroun Republic, 1969; Medal Chomedey de Maissonneuve, 1983; recipient award for service to humanity Royal Bank Can., 1969; Humanitarian award Variety Clubs Internat., 1976; Man of Yr. award Lester B. Pearson Peace Found., 1979; award for exceptional contbns. to human relations Can. Council for Christians and Jews, 1980. Home: Montreal Can. Died Nov. 13, 1991; buried Mary Queen of the World Cathedral, Montreal.

LEGG, ROBERT HENRY, real estate, financial consultant; b. Geneva, N.Y., Aug. 22, 1917; s. Charles Quested and Alice Burton (Fothergill) L.; m. Jane Elizabeth Morris, Feb. 7, 1942; children: Robert Austin, Judy Ann Legg. Student, Hobart Coll., Geneva, 1935-36; AB magna cum laude, Kenyon Coll., Gambier, Ohio, 1939; MS, MIT, 1942; LLB, Columbia U., 1946. Bar: N.Y. 1946. Assoc. Cravath, Swaine & Moore, N.Y.C., 1946-49; ptnr. Hammond, Kennedy & Legg Co., 1949-62; v.p. Uris Bldg. Corp., N.Y.C., 1962-71; dir. Uris Bldg. Corp., 1965-73, exec. v.p., 1971, chmn. bd., CEO, 1971-73; dir. Mountain Med. Equipment, 1983-92. Trustee Westchester County Savs. Bank, 1959-74, Mem. bus. adv. com., Briarcliff Manor, N.Y., 1958-62, mem. planning bd., 1962-66; Sec.-treas. Briarcliff Found., 1964-74; bd. dirs. Phelps Meml. Hosp., 1960-66; trustee Kenyon Coll., 1965-78. Served from 2d lt. to capt. USAAF, 1942-46. Recipient Gregg Cup award Kenyon Alumni Coun., 1966. Mem. Phi Beta Kappa, Alpha Delta Phi, Phi Delta Phi. Home: Sun City West Ariz. Died Aug. 11, 1992. †

LEGGO, CHRISTOPHER, industrial physicist; b. Ottawa, Ont., Can., Jan. 23, 1897; came to U.S., 1919, naturalized, 1928; s. William and C. Mary (Waugh) L.; m. Helen Elizabeth Thum, Mar. 4, 1926; children: Helen, Christopher. MD, CM, McGill U., 1919; post-grad., Peter Bent Brigham Hosp., 1936-37. Diplomate Am. Bd. Preventive Medicine and Occupational Health. Intern Alameda County Hosp., Oakland, Calif., 1919; resident in medicine Barlow Sanitarium, L.A., 1920, U. Calif. Hosp., San Francisco, 1921; surgeon Providence Hosp., Oakland, 1922; pvt. practice medicine Suisun-Fairfield, Calif., 1923-28; surgeon San Francisco Emergency Hosp. Svc., 1929; med. dir. Calif. and Hawaiian Sugar Refining Corp., Ltd., Crockett, Calif., 1930-54, Eastman Kodak Processing Lab., Palo Alto, Calif., 1954-58; med. officer Calif. State Pers. Bd., from 1958; assoc. clin. prof. preventive medicine Stanford U., 1954-58; dir. indsl. hygiene Ohio Dept. Health, 1943-45; med. dir. Tenn-Eastman Corp., Oak Ridge, Tenn., 1945-46; cons. occupational diseases, Calif. State Bd. Health, 1939-42. Assoc. editor Indsl. Medicine and Surgery, from 1939, Archives of Indsl. Health, 1953-58; contbr. articles to med. jours. Surg. (R.) USPHS, 1942-45. On staff joint task forces, radiol. safety sect., Bikini, 1946. Recipient Citation Meritorious Svc., Pres.'s Com. Employment Physically Handicapped, 1962. Fellow Indsl. Med. Assn. (past coun.), Am. Coll. Preventive Medicine; mem. Western Indsl. Med. Assn. (past pres.), Calif. Med. Assn. (past chmn. com. indsl. health), Sacramento Med. Soc., Ramazzini Soc., Delta Kappa Epsilon. *

LEHMANN-HAUPT, HELLMUT E., author, bibliographer; b. Berlin, Oct. 4, 1903; came to U.S., 1929; naturalized, 1936; s. Carl F. and Therese (Haupt) Lehmann-H.; m. Letitia Grieson, Aug. 19, 1933; children: Christopher, Carl Andrew, H. Alexander; m. Rosemarie Muller, Mar. 1, 1948; children: John Peter, Roxana; m. Ingeborg Kreck, June 4, 1965. Student univs., Frankfurt, Vienna and Berlin; PhD, U. Frankfurt, 1927. Jr. curator Gutenberg Mus., Mainz, Germany, 1927-29; curator rare books Columbia U., 1930-37, asst. prof. books arts, 1937-50; vis. lectr. Smith Coll., 1939-41; vis. prof. U. Ill., 1940; rsch. prin. (Rockefeller Found. grant) New Sch. Social Rsch., 1950-52; bibliog. lectr. Pratt Inst., 1954-55, rsch. prin. (Rockefeller grant) 1956; bibliog. cons. H.P. Kraus, rare books and mss., 1952-68; rsch. assoc. hist. sci. and and medicine Yale, 1965-67; prof. bibliography, cons. rare books U. Mo., 1969-74, prof. emeritus, 1974-92.; dep. chief German policy desk OWI, London, 1944-45; with info. control div. SHAEF, Germany, 1945. Author: (with Samuel Ives) An English 13th Century Bestiary, 1942, The Terrible Gustave Dore, 1943, One Hundred Books about Bookmaking, 1949, Peter Schoeffer of Gernsheim and Mainz, 1950, Art Under a Dictatorship, 1954; editor, author: (with Lawrence C. Wroth, Rollo G. Silver) The Book in America, 1952, The Life of the Book, 1957, Gutenberg and the Master of the Playing Cards, 1966; editor: Homage to a Bookman, 1967, The Goettingen Model Book, others. Home: Columbia Mo. Died Mar. 29, 1992.

LEIBER, FRITZ, JR., author; b. Chgo., Dec. 24, 1910; s. Fritz and Virginia (Bronson) L.; m. Jonguil Stephens, 1936 (dec. 1969); 1 child, Justin. BA, U. Chgo., 1932; student, Gen. Theol. Sem., N.Y.C. Former positions include: staff writer Standard Am. Ency., Chgo., instr. speech and drama Occidental Coll., L.A.; mem. editorial staff Sci. Digest, 1945-56. Author: (novels) Conjure Wife, 1953, Gather Darkness!, 1956, Destiny Times Three, 1957, The Big Time, 1961, The Wanderer, 1964, A Specter is Haunting Texas, 1969, Our Lady of Darkness, 1977, The Ship of Shadows, 1979, numerous others; (short stories) The Best of Fritz Leiber, 1974, The Worlds of Fritz Leiber, 1976; Knight and the Knave of Swords, 1988. Recipient Hugo award, 1958, 65, 68, 70, 71, 76, Nebula award, 1967, 70, 75, Gandalf award, 1975, August Derleth Fantasy award, 1976, World Fantasy award, 1976, 78, World Fantasy life award, 1976. Home: San Francisco Calif. Died Sept. 5, 1992. †

LEIBMAN, MORRIS IRWIN, lawyer; b. Chgo., Feb. 8, 1911; s. Isadore M. and Clara (Leibman) L.; m. Mary Wolf, Oct. 14, 1981. Ph.B., U. Chgo., 1931, J.D., 1933. Bar: Ill. bar 1933. Ptnr. Leibman, Williams, Bennett, Baird & Minow, Chgo., until 1972; ptnr., then sr. ptnr. Sidley & Austin (merger with Leibman, Williams, et al), Chgo., 1972-92; lectr. law schs. U. Chgo., U. Ill., DePaul U., Northwestern U. Chmn. Nat. Adv. Council Econ. Opportunity; mem. Sec. Def. Adv. Com. Non-Mil. Instn., President's Panel Cons. Internal Affairs and Nat. Security; bd. dirs. Nat. Strategy Information Center, U.S. Inst. Peace, 1986-87; mem. exec. bd. Ctr. for Strategic and Internat. Studies, from 1964; civilian aide emeritus to Sec. of Army for life; mem. adv. bd. Edn. for Freedom, Atlanta; exec. bd. Center Strategic Studies, Georgetown U.; Trustee Loyola U. Recipient Presdl. Medal of Freedom, 1981. Fellow ABA (chmn. law and nat. security); mem. Def. Orientation Conf. Assn., Ill. Bar Assn., Chgo. Bar Assn., N.Y. Bar Assn., Assn. of Bar of City of N.Y., Chgo. Law Inst., Am. Judicature Soc. Clubs: Law (Chgo.), MidDay (Chgo.), Standard (Chgo.), Carlton (Chgo.); Sky (N.Y.C.); Army and Navy (Washington). Home: Chicago Ill. Died Apr. 21, 1992.

LEICESTER, HENRY MARSHALL, chemist, educator; b. San Francisco, Dec. 22, 1906; s. John Ferard and Elsie (Allen) L.; m. Leonore Azevedo, Feb. 22, 1941; children: Henry Marshall, Martha Katherine, Margaret Anne. AB, Stanford U., 1927, MA, 1928, PhD, 1930. Instr. chemistry Oberlin Coll., 1930-31; chemist Carnegie Instn., Washington, 1932; rsch. assoc. Stanford U., 1933-34; chemist Midgeley Found., Ohio State U., 1935-38; mem. faculty Coll. Physicians and Surgs., San Francisco, 1938-48, prof. chemistry, 1948-62; prof. U. Pacific Dental Shc., San Francisco, 1962-91, chmn. dept. biochemistry, 1962-72. Author: Biochemistry of the Teeth, 1949, (with H.S. Klickstein) Source Book in Chemistry, 1940-1950, 1952, Historical Background of Chemistry, 1956, Source Book in Chemistry, 1900-1950, 1968, Mikhail Vasil'evich Lomonosov on the Corpuscular Theory, 1970, Development of Biochemical Concepts From Ancient to Modern Times, 1974; editor-in-chief Chymia, 1951-67; contbr. articles to profl. jours. Mem. AAAS, Am. Chem. Soc. (Dexter award in history of chemistry 1962), Internat. Assn. Dental Rsch., History Sci. Soc., Soc. for History Tech. Home: Menlo Park Calif. Died Apr. 29, 1991; buried Holy Cross Cemetery, Menlo Park, Calif.

LEIDESDORF, ARTHUR DAVID, accounting firm executive; b. N.Y.C., July 31, 1918; s. Samuel D. and Elsa (Grunwald) L.; m. Joan Rose Wheeler, June 1, 1939 (div.); children: Samuel David II, William Alfred; m. Tova Dryman, Apr. 10, 1966; children: Edmond Hugo, Nicole Elsa. B.S. in Acctg., NYU, 1941. CPA, N.Y. Vice pres., past dir. Murray Hill Operating Co., Inc., N.Y.C., 1946; pres. Murray Hill Operating Co., Inc., 1968; past chmn. bd. Rio Verde Energy Corp., Cin.; past pres., dir. Pershing Square Bldg. Corp., N.Y.C.; past chmn. bd., dir. 100 Park Ave., N.Y.C.; mng. partner S.D. Leidesdorf & Co. (now part of Ernst & Young), N.Y.C., until 1976; past sec.-treas. Harbor Universal, Inc.; past v.p., dir. Sherman-Taylor Corp., N.Y.C., Beaux Arts Properties, Inc.; past chmn. bd. Mid-Central Properties Ltd.; bd. dirs. Trivest Fin. Svcs. Corp., Sarasota, Fla.; mem. nat. panel arbitrators Am. Arbitration Assn., from 1955. Former positions include vice chmn., chmn. finance com., exec. com. trustee Citizens Budget Commn.; asst. sec., asst. treas. Inst. for Advanced Study; pres., treas., also dir., bd. dirs., pres. exec. com., chmn. bd. dirs. 92d St. YMHA-YWHA; past mem. instl. trustees council Fedn. Jewish Philanthropies N.Y.; mem. Fine Arts Commn., Dept-State; pres. Leidesdorf Found.; treas., bd. dirs., Ocean Beach Club, 1125 Park Ave. Assn.; bd. dirs. Assn. Nat. Treas. of Am. Jewish Com. Grad. Adj. Gen.'s Sch. Served to

1st lt. AUS, 1942-46. Recipient Silver Beaver award Boy Scouts Am. Mem. Acad. Polit. Sci. (life), Met. Mus. Art, Army Ordnance Assn., Nat. Geog. Soc., Nat. Rifle Assn. (life), U.S. Revolver Assn., AICPA, N.Y. State Soc. CPAs, Nat. Assn. Cost Accts., Am. Inst. Accts., Albert Gallatin Assocs., Harmonie Club (N.Y.C.), Lotos Club (N.Y.C.), Friars Club (N.Y.C.), Palm Beach Country Club, Poinciana Club, Club Colette, Govs. Club, Union League (Phila.), Sunningdale Country Club (Scarsdale, N.Y.). Clubs: Harmonie, Lotos, NYU, Fiars (all N.Y.C.); Palm Beach Country, Poinciana, Club Colette, Governor's (all Palm Beach, Fla.); Union League (Phila.); Sunningdale Country (Scarsdale, N.Y.). Home: Palm Beach Fla. Died Feb. 2, 1991; buried West Chester, N.Y.

LEIFERMAN, SILVIA WEINER (MRS. IRWIN H. LEIFERMAN), artist, civic worker, sculptor; b. Chgo.; d. Morris and Annah (Kaplan) Weiner; m. Irwin H. Leiferman, Apr. 20, 1947. Student, U. Chgo., 1960-61; studied design and painting, Provincetown, Mass. Organizer, charter mem. women's div. Hebrew U. Chgo., 1947; Head Pres. Accessories by Silvia, Chgo., 1964; organizer women's div. Edgewater Hosp., 1954; chmn. bd. Leiferman Investment Corp.; chairwoman spl. sales and spl. events greater Chgo. Com. for State of Israel; originator, organizer Ambassador's Ball, 1956, Presentation Ball, 1963; met. chmn. numerous spl. events Nat. Council Jewish Women, Nathan Goldblatt Soc. Cancer Research, Chgo.; now life mem., trustee; chmn. numerous spl. events North Shore (Ill.) Combined Jewish Appeal; chmn. women's com. Salute to Med. Research City of Hope, 1959; founder Ballet Soc. of Miami; Bd. dirs. Jewish Children's Bur., North Shore Women's Aux., Mt. Sinai Hosp., George and Ann Portes Cancer Prevention Center Chgo., Nat. Council Jewish Women, Fox River (Ill.) Sanitorium, Edgewater Hosp., Greater Chgo. Bonds for Israel, Orgn. of Rehab. and Tng. Exhibited one-woman shows, Schram Galleries, Ft. Lauderdale, Fla., 1966, 67, D'Arcy Galleries, N.Y.C., 1964, Stevens Annex Bldg., Chgo., 1965, Miami (Fla.) Mus. Modern Art, 1966, 72, Contemporary Gallery, Palm Beach, Fla., 1966, Westview Country Club, 1968, Gallery 99, 1969; exhibited group shows, Ricardo Restaurant Gallery, Chgo., 1961, 62, Bryn Mawr (Chgo.) Country Club, 1961, 62, Covenant Club Ill., Chgo., 1963, D'Arcy Galleries, 1965, Internat. Platform Assn., 1967, Miami Mus. Modern Art, 1967, Bacardi Gallery, 1967, Hollywood Mus. Art, 1968, Gallery 99, Miami, Lowe Art Mus., Crystal Ho. Gallery, Miami Beach, 1968; represented in numerous pvt. collections. Bd. dirs. Brandeis U., Art Inst. Chgo., Miami Mus. Modern Art; co-founder, v.p. Silvia and Irwin Leiferman Found.; donor Leiferman award auspices City of Hope; internat. co-chairwoman Ball Masque; mem. pacesetter/trustee com. Greater Miami Jewish Fedn., 1976-77; founder Mt. Sinai Hosp. Greater Miami, Fla.; donor Michael Reese Hosp., 1978; benefactress Miami Heart Inst., 1979, St. Joseph Hosp., 1979, Mt. Sinai Med. Center, 1979. Recipient citations for def. bond sales U.S. Govt., for Presentation Ball State of Israel, 1965; Pro Mundi Beneficio Gold medal Brazilian Acad. Humanities, 1976; numerous awards Bonds for Israel; numerous awards Combined Jewish Appeal North Shore Spl. Gifts; Keys to cities Met. Miami area; named Woman of Valor State of Israel, 1963; donor award Miami Heart Inst. Fellow Royal Soc. Arts and Scis.; mem. Internat. Council Mus., 1st Ann. Cultural Conf. Chgo., Am. Fedn. Arts, Artist's Equity Assn., Fla. Poetry Soc., Miami Art Center, Miami Beach Opera Guild Com., Greater Miami Cultural Art Center, Guild Com. Greater Miami Cultural Art Center, Sculptors of Fla., Royal Acad. Arts, Internat. Platform Assn., Lowe Art Mus., Am. Contract Bridge League, Friends of U. Haifa. Jewish (mem. bd.). Clubs: Standard, Bryn Mawr Country, Covenant, Green Acres, International, Boye, Whitehall, Key (Chgo.); Jockey, Westview Country, Tower (Miami Beach, Fla.); Brickell Bay. Home: Miami Fla. Deceased. †

LEIGHTON, CLARE, artist, writer; b. London, Apr. 12, 1901; came to U.S., 1939, naturalized, 1946.; d. Robert and Marie L. Leighton; m. Henry Brailsford. Student, Slade Sch., U. London, Eng., 1921-23; D.F.A. (hon.), Colby Coll., 1940. Exhibited group shows: Victoria and Albert Mus., London; Nat. Gallery, Stockholm; Nat. Gallery Can.; Met. Mus., N.Y.C.; numerous others; commd. 33 stained glass windows St. Paul's Cathedral, Worcester, Mass.; mosaic Convent Holy Family of Nazareth, Monroe, Conn.; windows Lutheran Ch., Waterbury, Conn.; windows Methodist Ch., Wellfleet, Mass.; commd. plates for Josiah Wedgewood & Sons; designs for Steuben Glass Co.; 1 Woman exhbn. Associated Am. Artists, N.Y.C., 1983; work represented in permanent collections: Victoria and Albert Mus.; The British Mus., London; The Nat. Gallery, Stockholm; Nat. Gallery of Can., Ottawa; Met. Mus. of Art, N.Y.C.; Boston Fine Arts Mus.; Author-illustrator: The Farmer's Year; Four Hedges; Country Matters; Southern Harvest; Where Land Meets Sea; others. Mem. Royal Soc. Painters, Etchers and Engravers (London), Nat. Inst. Arts and Letters. Home: New York N.Y. Died Nov. 4, 1989.

LEINBACH, FREDERICK SWAVELY, paper manufacturer; b. Jonestown, Pa., Mar. 28, 1910; s. Henry Jerome and Mary (Swavely) L.; m. Pauline V. Dotterer, Dec. 25, 1931; children: Linda Jay, Michael Swavely. B.S., Lafayette Coll., Easton, Pa., 1931; postgrad. edn., U. Pa., 1932-33. Instr. sci. Swavely Sch., Manassas, Va., 1931-34; with Riegel Paper Corp., 1934-71, asst. to sales mgr., 1948-50, sec., 1950-55, v.p., asst. gen. sales mgr., 1955-57, exec. v.p., 1957-59, pres., 1959-68, chief exec. officer, 1962-68, dir., 1952-71; mem. governing com. U.S. Philips Trust, 1974-82; dir. Rexham Corp., 1971-80, N.Am. Philips Corp., 1971-82; asst. dir. containers div. WPB, 1942-43. Mem. Am Paper and Pulp Assn. (exec. com. v.p. 1961-65), Am. Paper Inst., Pulp, Paper and Paperboard Export Assn. (bd. govs., pres. 1964-66), Packaging Inst. (pres., dir., gen. tech. chmn. 1951-53). Home: Ocean City N.J. Died Feb. 2, 1990; cremated.

LEISY, JAMES FRANKLIN, publisher; b. Normal, Ill., Mar. 21, 1927; s. Ernest Erwin and Elva (Krehbiel) L.; m. Emily Ruth McQueen, June 8, 1949; children: James Franklin, Scot, Rebecca. BBA, So. Meth. U., 1949. Field rep., then editor Prentice-Hall, Inc., N.Y.C., 1949-54; editor Allyn & Bacon, Inc., Boston, 1954-56; founder, exec. editor Wadsworth Pub. Co., Inc., San Francisco, 1956-59, v.p., 1959-60, pres., 1960-77, chmn., chief exec. officer, 1977-85; dep. chmn. Internat. Thomson Orgn., Inc., 1978-85; founder, chmn. Sci. Books Internat., Inc., 1981-83; founder, chmn. Linguistics Internat., Inc., 1983-85; bd. dirs. Mayfield Pub. Co., Inc., Franklin, Beedle and Assocs., Carroll Pub. Co., Scott/Jones, Inc. Author: Abingdon Song Kit, 1957, Let's All Sing, 1958, Songs for Swinging Housemothers, 1960, Songs for Singin', 1961, Songs for Pickin' and Singin', 1962, Beer Bust Song Book, 1963, Hootenanny Tonight, 1964, Folk Song Fest, 1964, Folk Song Abecedary, 1966, Alpha Kappa Psi Sings, 1967, The Good Times Songbook, 1974, Scrooge, The Christmas Musical, 1978, Alice, A Musical Comedy, 1980, Pinocchio, A Musical Play, 1981, Tiny Tim's Christmas Carol, A Musical Play, 1981, The Pied Piper, 1982, The Nutcracker and Princess Pirlipat, 1982, A Visit from St. Nicholas, 1983, Pandora, 1984, Talkin' 'bout America, 1986, Mouse Country, 1987, The Dingaling Circus Holiday, 1987; composer: songs including Keep a Little Christmas In Your Heart, A Little Old Lady in Tennis Shoes, A Personal Friend of Mine, Please Tell Me Why, An Old Beer Bottle. Bd. dirs. Bethel Coll., Ctr. Entrepreneurial Devel., U. Calif.-Santa Cruz; bd. dirs., mem. exec. com. Calif. Council for Econ. Edn., 1968-71; mem. deans council Sch. Bus. Calif. State U., San Jose; mem. Nat. UN Day Com., 1978. Served with USNR, 1945-46. Named to Career Hall of Fame So. Meth. U., 1968; recipient 1st ann. Higher Edn. Achievement award Assn. of Am. Pubs., 1988. Mem. Young Pres.'s Orgn. (bd. dirs. 1970-73), Assn. Am. Pubs. (bd. dirs. 1982-85), ASCAP, So. Meth. U. Alumni Assn. (bd. dirs. 1965-70), Chief Execs. Orgn., World Bus. Council, Bohemian Club, Phi Eta Sigma, Alpha Phi Omega, Alpha Kappa Psi (nat. chmn. song com. 1963-71), Kappa Alpha. Home: Menlo Park Calif. Died July 8, 1989.

LELAND, MICKEY (GEORGE THOMAS LELAND), congressman; b. Lubbock, Tex., Nov. 27, 1944; s. George Thomas and Alice Rains (Lewis) L.; m. Alison Walton, 1983. BS in Pharmacy, Tex. So. U., 1970. Instr. clin. pharmacy Tex. So. U., 1970-71; mem. Tex. Ho. of Reps., 1973-78, vice chmn. pub. welfare subcom., 1975-76, mem. appropriations com., legis. budget bd., 1977-78; mem. 96th-100th congresses from 18th dist. Tex., 1979-89; freshman whip, co-chmn. Nat. Black-Hispanic Dem. Coalition, from 1978; Del. Dem. Nat. Com., 1976-85, Tex. Dem. Black Caucus. Home: Houston Tex. Died Aug., 1989. †

LELAND, SIMEON ELBRIDGE, economist; b. Madison, Ind., Sept. 2, 1897; s. Simeon Elbridge and Elizabeth Wood (Stanley) L.; m. Carolyn Victoria Hargan, Sept. 2, 1921; children: Carolyn Victoria, Elizabeth Stanley, Frances Elbridge. AB, DePauw U., 1918, LLD, 1947; AM, U. Ky., 1919; postgrad., Harvard U., 1919-20. Asst. prof. econs. U. Ky., 1920-24, assoc. prof., 1924-26, prof., 1926-28; dir. Bur. Bus. Rsch., 1927-28; assoc. prof. econs. U. Chgo., 1928-31, prof. econs., 1931-38, prof. govt. fin., 1938-46, acting chmn. Dept. Econs., 1939-40, chmn. Dept. Econs., 1940-46; prof. econs., dean Coll. Arts and Scis. Northwestern U., from 1946; mem. Ill. Tax Commn., 1933-40, chmn., 1936-40; dir. Fed. Res. Bank Chgo., 1941-47, chmn. of bd., 1942-46; spl. adviser to U.S. Sec. of Treasury, 1934; cons. Nat. Resources Planning Bd., 1935-36, TVA, 1939, Bur. of Budget, 1940-48; chmn. Ill. Public Aid Commn., 1952-53; chmn. Ill. Revenue Commn., 1961; mem. UN Econ. Mission to Chile, 1950; chmn. Tech. Com. of Citizens Com. (Strawn Com.), Chgo., 1930, Ill. Govt. Reorgn. Com., 1941-43; fiscal advisor to Panama, 1946. Author: Taxation in Kentucky, 1920, The Classified Property Tax in the United States, 1928, The Revenue System of Panama, 1946, also numerous articles on government finance; editor, contbr. State-Local Fiscal Relations in Illinois, 1941; contbr. to Division of Costs and Responsibility for Public Works, 1938. Chmn. commn. on colls. and univs. N. Cen. Assn., 1959-60. Recipient Hart, Schaffner & Marx Econ. Prize (2d prize), 1926. Mem. Am. Econ. Assn. (v.p. 1948), Nat. Tax Assn. (pres. 1937-38), Fedn. Tax Adminstrs. (chmn. bd. dirs. 1937-40), Royal Econ. Soc., Tavern Club, Econ. Club, Wayfarers Club, Phi Beta Kappa, Delta Upsilon. *

LEMAY, CURTIS E., former air force officer; b. Ohio, Nov. 15, 1906; m. Helen Maitland, 1934; 1 child, Patricia. BCE, Ohio State U., 1932, DSc (hon.); LLD (hon.), John Carroll U., Kenyon Coll., U. So. Calif., U. Akron, Bradley U., C.W. Post Coll.; DSc (hon.), Tufts U., U. W.Va.; ED (hon.), Case Inst. Tech. Flying cadet AC, U.S. Army, 1928, commd. 2d lt., 1930; advanced through grades maj. gen. USAAF, 1943; temp. gen. USAF, 1951; chief staff AUS Stategic Air Forces, 1945; dep. chief Air Staff for R & D, Washington, 1945; comdg. gen. USAF in Europe, 1947; vice chief staff Hdqrs. USAF, Washington, 1957-61, chief staff, 1961-65; chmn. bd. Networks Electronic Corp., after 1965. Author: (with MacKinlay Kantor) Mission with LeMay, 1965. Trustee Nat. Geog. Soc. Decorated D.S.C., D.S.M. with 3 oak leaf clusters, Air medal with 3 clusters, DFC. with 2 clusters; comdr. Legion of Honor (France), MacKay Trophy; comdr. Order Ouissam Alaouite Chefifien (Morroco), Medal for Humane Action, Crois de Guerre with palm (Belgium), Silver Star medal, Order of So. Cross (Brazil), D.F.C. (Eng.), Order of Patriotic war (USSR), Order Svc. Merit 1st class (Korea), Most Exalted Order of White Elephant 1st class (Thailand), Cross of Phoenix (Greece); recipient Robert J. Collier Trophy. Mem. Masons (33d degree), Sigma Tau, Tau Beta Pi, Theta Tau. Home: Moreno Valley Calif. Died Oct. 1, 1990; buried USAF Acad., Colo.

LEMELIN, ROGER, newspaper publisher, novelist; b. Quebec, Que., Can., Apr. 7, 1919; s. Joseph and Florida (Dumontier) L.; hon. degree Laurentian U., Sudbury, Ont., 1976; m. Valeda Lavigueur, Oct. 27, 1945; children: Pierre, Jacques, Diane and Andre (twins), Sylvie. Journalist, Time and Fortune mags., from 1948; creator TV series The Plouffe Family, in Can.; pres. DuBuisson Prodns., from 1960; pres., pub. French daily La Presse, Montreal, 1972-82. Recipient Legion d'honneur, 1990; Guggenheim Found. fellow, Rockefeller Found. fellow. Mem. Royal Soc. Can., Acad. Goncourt, Can. News Hall Fame. Clubs: Mt. Royal, St. Denis (Montreal); Garrison (Quebec). Author: The Town Below, 1944, The Plouffe Family, 1949 (made into TV series 1950's), Fantaisies sur les peches capitaux, 1949, In Quest of Spendor, 1952; also articles, revs. Died Mar. 16, 1992; buried Quebec. Home: Cap Rouge Que., Can.

LENHER, IRENE K. (MRS. SAMUEL LENHER), artist; b. Rye, N.Y., Oct. 4, 1907; d. John Wilkinson and Elena (Hellmann) Kirkland; student Slade Sch. Art, U. Coll. (London), 1925-26, Grande Chaumiere, Paris, 1927-28; M.A. (hon.), U. Del., 1968; m. Samuel Lenher, Dec. 14, 1929; children—John K., Ann B., George V. Exhibited one-woman shows: Warehouse Gallery Arden, Decoy Gallery, Kennett Square, Pa., Hunter Gallery, 1965, Books, Inc., Wilmington, 1966, Grand Gallery, Wilmington, 1978; exhibited two and three man shows, also group shows: Wilmington (Del.) Soc. Fine Arts, Rehoboth (Del.) Art League, Cottage Tour Art, West Chester, Pa.; staff artist Cokesbury Courier; work represented in collections: Wilmington Trust Co., Hotel Du Pont, Del. Hosp. Sustaining mem. Everyman's Gallery; represented permanent collections: Wilmington Soc. Fine Arts, Copeland Purchase Fund, U. Del. Asso. mem. bd. Del. Hosp. Recipient 2d prize, best of show awards Nat. League Am. Pen Women shows, award of merit, 1962. Mem. Nat. League Am. Pen Women (state pres.), Colonial Dames Am., Am. Watercolor Soc. (asso.), Soc. Mayflower Descs. (past gov.), Wilmington Studio Group, Phila. Art Alliance. Episcopalian. Clubs: Greenville Country, Wilmington Country. Died Feb. 18, 1986; cremated. Home: Hockessin Del.

LEONARD, IRVING A(LBERT), Spanish language educator; b. New Haven, Dec. 1, 1896; s. Henry Austin and Lillian May (Phelps) L.; m. Dorothea Hope Taggart, June 5, 1921; children: David Phelps, Dorothea Irving. PhB, Yale U., 1918; AM, U. Calif., 1925, PhD, 1928. U.S. postal censor (Spanish), 1918; jr. exec. Pacific Comml. Co., N.Y.C., Manila Cebu, 1919-21; prof. U. Philippines, Los Baños, P.I., 1921-22; tchr. Spanish Petaluma (Calif.) High Sch., 1922-23; grad. asst., instr., asst. prof. Spanish U. Calif., 1923-37; asst. dir. humanities Rockefeller Found., 1937-40; prof. history and Spanish Brown U., 1940-42; prof. Spanish Am. Lit. U. Mich., from 1942, chmn. dept. Romance langs., 1945-51, prof. Spanish Am. lit. and history, 1949-62; Am. del. Inter-Am. Conf. Coms. on Intellectual Coop., Santiago, Chile, 1939; com. on Study of Teaching Materials on Inter-Am. Subjects, Am. Coun. on Edn., 1943; com. on fellowships and grants Am. Coun. of Learned Socs., Washington, 1944. Author of books, including: Books of the Brave, 1949, Baroque Times in Old Mexico (Herber E. Bolton Meml. award), 1959; editor and translator books in field of work; assoc. editor: Handbook of Latin American Studies, 1935—; Hispanic American Historical Review, 1941-47, from 1954; Revista Hispánica Moderna, from 1940, Revista de Filologiá, from 1940. Recipient Diploma de Honor, Academia Mexicana, Am. Coun. Learned Socs. traveling fellowship, 1930-31, Guggenheim fellowship, 1936. Fellow Hispanic Soc. Am.; mem. Am. Assn. Tchrs. Spahish, Rsch. Club U. Mich. *

LEONHARD, ERNEST RUDOLPH, parchment manufacturing company executive; b. Haledon, N.J., May 14, 1896; s. Albert F. and Elizabeth Anne (Hughes) L.; m. Alma Walton, Jan. 27, 1944; children:

Elizabeth Ann (Mrs. R. A. Miller), Suzanne (Mrs. J. J. McIlhenny). BS in Econs., Dartmouth U., 1919. With Paterson Parchment Paper Co., Bristol, Pa., from 1920, beginning in acctg. dept., successively traffic and svc. positions, staff sales, v.p. charge sales, 1920-53, pres., 1953-65, chmn. bd. dirs., from 1961, CEO, from 1965. Eng., aviation USN, 1917-18. Mem. Vegetable Parchment Mfgs. Assn. (chem.), Can. Club, Paper Club, Huntingdon Valley Country Club, Phi Delta Theta. *

LEPAWSKY, ALBERT, political scientist, educator; b. Chgo., Feb. 16, 1908; s. Morris and Rose (Devin) L.; m. Rosalind Almond, Apr. 17, 1935; children: Martha L. Barker, Michael, Susan L. Rosenstreich, Lucy L. Di Bianca. Ph.B., U. Chgo., 1927, Ph.D., 1931; European fellow, Social Sci. Research Council, 1933-34; vis. fellow, U. Hamburg (Ger.), 1933, London Sch. Econs. and Polit. Sci., 1933-34, U. Berlin, 1934. Successively instr., rsch. asst., rsch. asso., lectr. dept. polit. sci. U. Chgo., 1930-42; dir. Inst. Pub. Service, U. Chgo., 1941-42, 45-46; rsch. dir. law dept. City of Chgo., 1935-36; asst. dir. Pub. Adminstrn. Clearing House, 1936-38; dir. Fedn. Tax Adminstrs. U.S., Can., 1938-41; prof. pub. adminstrn. and polit. sci. U. Ala., U. Tenn., U. Ky.; also ednl. dir. So. Regional Tng. Program in Pub. Adminstrn. Ala., Tenn., Ky., 1946-52; prof. polit. sci. U. Calif., Berkeley, 1951-75, prof. emeritus, 1976-92; vis. prof. polit. sci. U. B.C., dir. UN Regional Tng. Ctr., Vancouver, 1960-62; vis. scholar Inst. War and Peace Studies, Columbia U., 1971; mem. NSF Commn. on Higher Edn., 1976; scholar-in-residence Rockefeller Found. European Study Center, 1977; vis. prof. social sci. Pitzer Coll., Claremont, Calif., 1980; vis. prof. pub. adminstrn. and pub. policy Golden Gate U., San Francisco; mem., acting chief UN Tech. Assistance Mission to Bolivia, 1950-51; cons. fed., state, regional, local and UN agys. Author: Intellectual Responsibility and Political Conduct, 1965; (with Rosiland Lepawsky) Coalition and Coalescence: Berkeley Links Ecology and Ethnicity, 1972; editor: The Prospect for Presidential-Congressional Government (Benjamin V. Cohen), 1977, (with others) The Search for World Order; Studies by Students and Colleagues of Quincy Wright, 1971. Mem. Chgo. Plan Commn., 1942-45. Served from capt. to lt. col. USAF, 1942-45. Mem. Am. Polit. Sci. Assn. (v.p. 1956-57), Western Polit. Sci. Assn. (pres. 1963-64), Calif. Conservation Council (pres. 1958-60), Phi Beta Kappa. Democrat. Jewish. Home: Berkeley Calif. Died June 2, 1992; buried Oakmont Meml. Pk., Lafeyette, Calif.

LEPORE, ALBERT RALPH, psychologist, educator; b. San Diego, Apr. 13, 1920; s. Louis and Jeanne (Robin) L.; m. Margaret Alice Ashby, Dec. 28, 1947; children—Jeanne Robin, Lawrence Raymond. B.A., San Diego State U., 1942; M.A., Columbia Tchrs. Coll., 1949; Ph.D., Columbia U., 1960. Tchr. San Diego pub. schs., 1946-48; mem. faculty San Francisco State U., 1951-59; Calif. State U. Calif. State Coll., Hayward, from 1959, dean instrn., dean faculty, 1962-69, prof. edn., 1969-85, emeritus prof. edn., dean coll., 1985-89. Pres. Alameda County Mental Health Assn.; mem. Comprehensive Health Planning Council Alameda County.; pres., trustee St. Rose Hosp., Shorelands Found.; pres. St. Rose Found.; mem. Alameda County Commn. on Aging; trustee Hayward Unified Sch. Dist. Served to capt. AUS, 1942-46, ETO. Decorated Silver Star. Mem. Am. Psychol. Assn., Piaget Soc., Phi Delta Kappa. Home: Hayward Calif. Died May 12, 1989; buried Golden Gate Nat. Cemetery, San Bruno, Calif.

LERNER, MAX, author, columnist; b. Minsk, Russia, Dec. 20, 1902; came to U.S., 1907; s. Benjamin and Bessie (Podel) L.; m. Anita Marburg, July 20, 1928 (div. 1940); children: Constance, Pamela (dec.), Joanna; m. Edna Albers, Aug. 16, 1941; children: Michael, Stephen, Adam. AB, Yale U., 1923, student law, 1923-24; AM, Washington U., St. Louis, 1925; PhD, Robert Brookings Grad. Sch. Econs. and Govt., Washington, 1927. Asst. editor Ency. Social Scis., 1927, later mng. editor; mem. social sci. faculty Sarah Lawrence Coll., 1932-35; chmn. faculty Wellesley Summer Inst., 1933-35; dir. consumers div. Nat. Emergency Council, 1934; lectr. govt. Harvard U., 1935-36, prof. govt. summer sch., 1939-41; editor The Nation, 1936-38; prof. polit. sci. Williams Coll., 1938-43; radio commentator; editorial dir. PM, 1943-48; columnist N.Y. Star, 1948-49; prof. Am. civilization Brandeis U., 1949-73, dean Grad. Sch., 1954-56; worldwide syndicated columnist N.Y. Post and Los Angeles Times Syndicate, from 1949; vis. prof. politics Pomona Coll., 1973-74; Ford Found prof. Am. civilization Sch. Internat. Studies, U. Delhi, India, 1959-60; prof. human behavior Grad. Sch. Human Behavior, U.S. Internat. U., San Diego, from 1974; Welch prof. Am. studies U. Notre Dame, 1982-84. Author: It Is Later Than You Think, rev. edit., 1943, new edit. with Afterward, 1989, revised edit., 1990, new edit., 1991, Ideas Are Weapons, 1939, Ideas for the Ice Age, 1941, The Mind and Faith of Justice Holmes, 1943, revised edit. with Afterward, 1988, Public Journal, 1945, The Portable Veblen, 1948, Actions and Passions, 1949, America as a Civilization, 1957, rev. edit., 1987, The Unfinished Country, 1959, The Essential Works of John Stuart Mill, 1961, The Age of Overkill, 1962, Education and a Radical Humanism, 1962, Tocqueville and American Civilzation, 1969, Values in Education, 1976, Ted and the Kennedy Legend: A Study in Character and Destiny, 1980, Wrestling with the Angel: A Memoir of my Triumph over Illness, 1990; co-editor: Tocqueville, Democracy in America, 1966. Ford Found. grantee European civilization study, 1962-63. Mem. NEA (ednl. policies commn.). Home: New York N.Y. Died June 5, 1992; buried Oakland Cemetery, Sag Harbor, N.Y.

LERRIGO, EDITH MARY, association executive; b. Lithia, Mass., Sept. 20, 1910; d. Peter Hugh James and Edith (Dowkontt) L. BA, Bates Coll., 1932, LHD (hon.), 1961; MA, Columbia U., 1933; LHD, Keuka (N.Y.) Coll., 1962. Dir. religious edn. First Bapt. Ch., East Orange, N.J., 1934-37; dir. work nat. student YWCA in N.E. colls., 1937-42; adv. staff Nat. YWCA of China, 1943-47; dir. work Pacific S.W. nat. student YWCA, 1947-54; dir. World YWCA Leadership Tng. Inst., Switzerland, 1949; exec. coll. and univ. div. nat. bd. YWCA, 1954-59; exec. dir. YWCA of U.S., N.Y.C., 1960-74. Home: Claremont Calif. Died June 24, 1989.

LESCAZE, WILLIAM, architect; b. Geneva, Mar. 27, 1896; came to U.S., 1920, naturalized, 1929; s. Alexandre and Marthe (Caux) L.; m. Mary Connick Hughes, Sept. 29, 1933; 1 child, Lee Adrien. Student, Coll. de Geneve, Geneva; MArch, École Polytechnique Federal, Zurich, Switzerland. Worked in devastated areas of France, 1919-20, worked in Cleve., 1920-23; established own bus. as architect N.Y.C., 1923; ptnr. Howe & Lescaze, N.Y.C. and Phila., 1929-34; own firm, from 1934. Recent prin. works include Phila Savs. Fund Soc. Bldg., 1932, Theater, studios and offices BCS, Hollywood, 1938, Longfellow Bldg., Washington, 1941, Spinney Hill Homes, Manhasset, L.I., dwelling units 106, 1950, 711 3d Ave., N.Y.C. 20 stories, 1956, Borg-Warner Bldg., Chgo., 1955, Chancellery Bldg., Embassy of Switzerland, Washington, 1959, Church Peace Ctr. Bldg., N.Y.C., 1962, many others. Commn. N.Y. State Bldg. Code Commn., 1949-50. Benjamin Franklin fellow Foyal Soc. Arts; recipient Silver medals, Internat. Exhbn. Paris, 1937, Pan Am. Congress ARchitects Monterido, others. Fellow AIA; mem. Nat. Coun. Arts and Govt. (bd. dirs.). *

LESLIE, JOHN ETHELBERT, investment banker; b. Vienna, Austria, Oct. 13, 1910; came to U.S., 1938, naturalized, 1944; s. Julius and Valerie (Lawetzky) L.; m. Evelyn Ottinger Goetz, Mar. 28, 1940 (dec.); m. Miriam Paul Emmet, June 26, 1986. Dr. Jur., U. Vienna, 1932; diploma, Consular Acad. Polit. Sci. and Econs., Vienna, 1934; M.S., Columbia U., 1942. Sec. to judges Fed. Law Cts. Austria, 1934-36; pvt. practice Vienna, 1936-38; sr. auditor Arthur Anderson & Co., CPA's, N.Y.C., 1941-46; prin. R.G. Rankin & Co., tax cons., N.Y.C., 1946-55; with Bache & Co., Inc. (name later Prudential-Bache Securities Inc.), N.Y.C., 1955-82; chmn. bd. Bache & Co., Inc. (name later Bache Halsey Stuart-Shields Inc.), N.Y.C., 1969-78; chmn. exec. com. Bache & Co., Inc. (name now Bache Halsey Stuart-Shields Inc.), N.Y.C., 1964-69, chief exec. officer, 1970-77; chmn. bd. Bache Group Inc., 1969-78; chmn. policy com. Bache Group and Bache Halsey Stuart Shields, 1978-79; dir. Bache Group, Inc., 1969-82, chmn. emeritus, 1980-91; dir. emeritus Prudential Bache Securities; dir. 920 Fifth Ave. Corp.; hon. consul gen. of Austria in N.Y., from 1965; mem. adv. com. on internat. capital markets N.Y. Stock Exchange, chmn., 1973-75; chmn. U.S. Nat. Mkt. Adv. Bd., 1975-76. Hon. trustee Inst. Internat. Edn., Am.-Austrian Found.; hon. bd. dirs. N.Y.C. Partnership, Inc., bd. dirs. Econ. Devel. Council N.Y.; pres. H.L. Bache Found.; mem. adv. council internat. affairs Sch. Internat. Affairs, Columbia U., 1985-89. Decorated Cruz Vermelha de Dedicacao Portugal; comdr. Golden Order of Merit; Gt. Silver Cross of Honor with star Austria; Golden Star of Merit Vienna; officer Nat. Order Merit France; officer's cross Order of Merit W. Ger.; officer Order of Crown Belgium; recipient cert. of appreciation City N.Y. Mem. Council Fgn. Relations, Soc. Fgn. Consuls in N.Y.C., Austria C. of C. (past chmn., dir.), France-Am. Soc. (v.p., dir.), Alumni Assn. Sch. Bus. Columbia U., Alumni Assn. Diplomatic Acad., Am. Fgn. Svc. Assn., Fgn. Policy Assn. (hon. dir.), UN Assn. U.S.A. (past vice chmn., gov.), Pilgrims of U.S., Am. Acad. Poets (bd. dirs.), Union Club, Piping Rock Club, Down Town Assn. Home: New York N.Y. Died Apr. 23, 1991; buried Ferncliff, Ardsley-on-Hudson, N.Y.

LESLIE, WILLIAM, JR., consulting actuary; b. Berkeley, Calif., Oct. 2, 1918; s. William Leslie and Rose (Barker) L.; m. Georgie Ann Burke, Apr. 29, 1942; children—Meredith (Mrs. Robert A. Welch), Karen (Mrs. Dean Brian McKay), William III, David. A.B., Princeton U., 1940. With actuarial div. Nat. Bur. Casualty Underwriters, N.Y.C., 1941-46; gen. mgr. Nat. Bur. Casualty Underwriters, 1958-64; supt. spl. risks dept. Royal-Globe Ins. Cos., N.Y.C., 1947-50; asst. mgr. Nat. Council Compensation Ins., 1950-55, gen. mgr., 1955-57; sec., actuary Continental Ins. Cos., 1957-58, v.p., actuary, 1964-78; exec. v.p., dir. subs. INSCO Systems Corp., 1978-79; v.p. parent co. Continental Corp.; v.p Tillinghast, Nelson & Warren, Inc., 1979-81; pres., chmn. William Leslie, Jr., Inc. (Actuaries and Cons.), 1981-85; dir. Indsl. Indemnity Co., subs. Crum & Forster. Bd. dirs. Community Welfare Fund of Bronxville, Inc., 1959-61, pres., 1960. Served from ensign to lt., aviator USNR, 1942-46. Fellow Casualty Actuarial Soc. (pres. 1960-61); mem. Am. Acad. Actuaries (v.p. 1965). Episcopalian (dept. finance Diocese N.Y. 1956-61). Home: San Diego Calif. Died Aug. 22, 1990; cremated.

LESTER, CHARLES WILLARD, surgeon; b. Saratoga Springs, N.Y., Sept. 14, 1892; s. James Westcott and Bertha North (Dowd) L.; m. Marianme G. Stebbins, June 5, 1920. BA, Williams Coll., 1914; MD, Columbia U., 1918. Diplomate Am. Bd. Surgery, Am. Bd. Thoracic Surgery. Intern Roosevelt Hosp., N.Y.C., 1918-19, mem. staff, 1920-29, assoc. attending surgeon, 1943-49, attending thoracic surgeon, 1949-58, cons. thoracic surgeon, from 1958; intern L.A. County Hosp., 1919-20; mem. staff Fifth Ave. Hosp., 1929-35, St. Mark's Hosp., 1929-31; attending thoracic surgeon Hosp. Spl. Surgery, N.Y.C., 1936-56, cons. surgeon, from 1956; assoc. vis. surgeon Bellevue Hoep., 1937-40, vis. surgeon, 1940-58, cons. surgeon, from 1958; assoc. surgeon Mcpl. Sanitorium, Orisville, N.Y., 1937-40, vis. surgeon, 1940-50, cons. surgeon, 1950-56; cons. surgeon King's park (N.Y.) State Hosp., 1937-56; asst. clin. prof. surgery NYU, 1937-40, assoc. prof., 1940-49; asst. surgeon Tribore Hosp., 1941-43, assoc. surgeon, 1943-46; cons. thoracic surgery VA Hosp., Castle Point, N.Y., from 1944. Author: Thoracic Surgery, 1941; contbr. articles on surgery to profl. publs. Pres. bd. trustees Nitchie Sch. Lip Reading, 1935-52. 1st lt. U.S. Army, World War I. Fellow ACS, Am. Coll. Chest Physicians; mem. AMA, N.Y. Soc. Cardiovascular Surgery, Am. Assn. Thoracic Surgery, N.Y. Acad. Medicine, N.Y. Surg. Soc., N.Y. Soc. Thoracic Surgery, Century Club, Williams Club, Phi Delta Theta, Alpha Omega Alpha. *

LESTER, GARNER MCCONNICO, utility executive; b. Jackson, Miss., June 17, 1897; s. John Wallace and Willie (Hoover); m. Elizabeth Wilkins, Mar. 10, 1926; children: Elizabeth McConnico (Mrs. Charles H. Foster Jr.), Garner Wallace. BS, Millsaps Coll., 1919. Auditor, treas. Haiwatha Mfg. Co., Jackson, 1919-30; sec., mgr. Miss. Ginning and Mfg. Co., Jackson, 1930-37; owner, mgr. G. M. Lester & Co., cotton products, Jackson, from 1937; bd. dirs. Deposit Guaranty Bank & Trust Co., Jackson; bd. dirs. Nat. Tax Equality Assn., 1934-38, pres., 1948-63, chmn. bd. dirs., from 1963; organizer, 1st pres. Nat. Cotton Ginners Assn., 1933; bd. dirs. Nat. Cotton Coun. Am., 1941-57. Pres. Jackson YMCA, 1928; exec. com. Andrew Jackson coun. Boy Scouts Am., from 1957. With U.S. Army, World War I. Mem. Am. Water Works Assn., Water Pollution Control Fedn. (bd. dirs.), Jackson C. of C. (bd. dirs.), Am. Legion, Capital City Club, Rotary (past pres.), Pi Kappa Alpha, Omicron Delta Kappa. Methodist. *

LESTER, JAMES GEORGE, geology educator; b. Covington, Ga., Oct. 16, 1897; s. Richard P. and Estelle (Rush) L.; m. Virginia Merritt, Apr. 17, 1920; children: Virginia (dec.), Mary Elizabeth. BS, Emory U., 1917, MS, 1923; MSCE, Ga. Inst. Tech., 1925; PhD, U. Colo., 1938. Tchr. Pelham (Ga.) High Sch., 1918; spl. dep. U.S. Revenue Div., 1919; instr. Emory U., Atlanta, 1919-23, asst. prof., 1923-36, assoc. prof., 1936-38, prof., chmn. dept. geology, from 1938; summer cons. work, 1921-25, dir. athletics, 1921-27; cons. thoracic surgeon Rockland State Hosp., Orangeburg, N.Y., since 1947; assoc. clin. prof. surgery N.Y. Med. Coll., 1948-57; assoc. surgery Columbia, 1951-56; asst. clin. prof. surgery, 1956-58. With USN, 1918. Awarded C. H. Candler meml. professorship, 1960. Fellow Geol. Soc. Am., Ga. Acad. Sci.; mem. Ga. Mineral Soc., Geophys. Union, Am. Assn. Petroleum Geologists, Am. Assn. Geology Tchrs., Phi Beta Kappa, Sigma Xi, Sigma Gamma Epsilon, Phi Sigma, Omicron Delta Kappa, Chi Pi. Democrat. Methodist. *

LE VANDER, HAROLD, lawyer, governor Minnesota; b. Swede Home, Nebr., Oct. 10, 1910; s. Peter Magni and Laura (Lovene) Le V.; m. Iantha Powrie, Sept. 15, 1938; children: Harold, Jean, Diane. BA, Gustavus Adolphus Coll., 1932; LLB, U. Minn., 1935. Bar: Minn. Asst. county atty. Dakota County, 1935-39; past prof. speech Macalester Coll.; gov. State of Minn., 1967-71; sr. mem. Le Vander, Gillen, Miller & Magnussen, South St. Paul, Minn.; bd. dirs. Am. Nat. Bank, St. Paul; pres., United Fed. Savs. and Loan Assn. Sec., Nat. Luth. Coun. Mem. Am., Minn. bar assns., South St. Paul C. of C. (pres. 1949-52), St. Paul Athletic Club, Univ. Club, Pi Kappa Delta, Gamma Eta Gamma. Home: Saint Paul Minn. Died Mar. 30, 1992.

LEVENSON, CARL, physician, educator; b. N.Y.C., Sept. 21, 1905; s. Aaron and Sarah Sonia (Asheron) L.; m. Beatrice Magill Levy, Nov. 29, 1976; 1 son, Donald S.; stepchildren: Margaret Levy Shapin, Richard M. Levy (dec.). B.A., Cornell U., 1927; M.D., SUNY, Bklyn., 1931. Diplomate Am. Bd. Phys. Medicine and Rehab. (a founder). Intern Beth Israel Med. Center, N.Y.C., 1932-34; engaged in public relations for med. socs. N.Y.C., 1934-38, gen. practice medicine, 1934-42; gen. practice medicine Chester, Pa., 1946-51; chief phys. medicine Chester Hosp., 1947-51; assoc. Grad. Med. Sch., U. Pa., 1947-51; fellow, resident in phys. medicine and rehab. U. Pa. Hosp., 1958-61; med. dir. Moss Rehab. Hosp., Phila., 1961-67; sr. attending physician, chmn. dept. phys. medicine and rehab. Albert Einstein Med. Center, Phila., 1961-71, emeritus, 1971; clin. prof. Temple U. Med. Coll., 1963-71; clin. prof. rehab. medicine, psychiatry and human behavior Jefferson Med. Coll., Phila., 1979-83, hon. clin. prof. rehab.

medicine, psychiatry and human behavior, 1983-90; chief rehab. medicine service VA Med. Center, Coatesville, Pa., 1971-83; cons. VA, Dept. Army, 1946-51; bd. govs. Eastern Pa. chpt. Arthritis Found., 1965-79, mem. medicine and sci. com., 1961-80; mem. Montgomery-Bucks County Profl. Standards Rev. Bd., 1974-80; rehab. com. Am. Heart Assn., 1967-70. Contbr. articles to profl. publs. Maj. M.C., AUS, 1942-46. Decorated Army Commendation medal; named to Legion of Honor Chapel of Four Chaplains, 1982; recipient Disting. Service award Arthritis Found., 1967; Mack tuition fellow SUNY, 1927-31; grantee U.S. Govt., 1964. Fellow ACP, Coll. Physicians, Am. Acad. Phys. Medicine and Rehab., Am. Heart Assn. (council cerebrovascular diseases), Am. Assn. Clin. Scientists, N.Y. Acad. Medicine, N.Y. Acad. Scis., Royal Soc. Health; mem. AAAS, AMA, Pa. Acad. Phys. Medicine and Rehab. (pres. 1968-69), Phila. Soc. Phys. Medicine and Rehab. (pres. 1964-65), Phila. County Med. Soc., Pa. Med. Soc., Am. Congress Rehab. Medicine, Am. Assn. Electrodiagnosis and Electromyography, Internat. Rehab, Medicine Assn., Nat. Assn. VA Physicians (cert. merit 1985), Am. Coll. Rheumatology (emeritus), Phi Delta Epsilon. Home: Wyncote Pa. Died Nov. 27, 1990.

LEVET, RICHARD HARRINGTON, judge; b. Geneva, N.Y., Jan. 24, 1894; s. Alfred Barlow and Jennie Alice (Harrington) L.; m. Ida C. Guldi, Aug. 21, 1918; 1 child, Eleanor Harrington (Mrs. Thomas J. Harriman). AB, Colgate U., 1916, AM, 1917; JD, NYU, 1925. Bar: N.Y. 1926. High sch. tchr., 1916-26; practice law White Plains, N.Y., 1926-56; judge U.S. Dist. Ct. (so. dist.) N.Y., from 1956; instr. law NYU Sch. Commerce, 1946-51. Mem. Westchester County Bd. Suprs., 1938-56, chmn., 1945-46. Mem. ABA, N.Y. State Bar Assn., Westchester County Bar Assn. (ex-counsel), White Plains Bar Assn., Phi Beta Kappa. Congregationalist. *

LEVI, ALBERT WILLIAM, humanities educator; b. Indpls., June 19, 1911; s. Albert William and Stella (Levi) L.; children by previous marriage—Estelle (Mrs. Sasha (Weitman), Michael, David; m. Ute Schweitzer, May 2, 1966; children: Laurence, Susannah. A.B., Dartmouth, 1932; M.A., U. Chgo., 1933, Ph.D., 1935. Mem. faculty Dartmouth Coll., 1935-41, U. Chgo., 1941-45, Black Mountain Coll., 1945-50, U. Graz, Austria, 1951, U. Vienna, Austria, 1952, U. Munich, 1961, U. Graz, 1964-65; mem. faculty Washington U., St. Louis, from 1952, David May Disting. Univ. prof. humanities, 1965-79, prof. emeritus, 1979-88; Mem. Nat. Council Humanities, 1966-72. Author: A Study in the Social Philosophy of John Stuart Mill, 1940, Rational Belief, 1941, General Education in the Social Studies, 1948, Varieties of Experience, 1957, Philosophy and the Modern World, 1959 (first Ralph Waldo Emerson award Phi Beta Kappa 1960), Literature, Philosophy and the Imagination, 1962, Humanism and Politics, 1969, The Humanities Today, 1970, Philosophy as Social Expression, 1974, Nature and Art, 1980. Andrew W. Mellon prof. humanities Tulane U., New Orleans, 1980. Mem. Phi Beta Kappa. Home: Saint Louis Mo. Died Oct. 31, 1988.

LEVIN, BENJAMIN, lawyer; b. Boston, Dec. 22, 1899; s. Harry and Anna (Mintz) L.; m. Charlotte I. Dane, Dec. 16, 1928 (dec.); children: Philip Dane, Ira D., Charles R.; m. Lillian H. Cohan, Nov. 15, 1973. A.B., Trinity Coll., 1920; LL.B., Harvard U., 1923. Bar: Mass. 1923, Conn. 1924. Practice in Boston, from 1923; partner firm Mintz, Levin, Cohn, Ferris, Glovsky and Popeo, and predecessors, 1965-82, counsel, from 1982; Mem. Mass. Commn. Adoption, 1946-48; mem. com. social services to families and individuals Boston United Community Services, 1959-69, mem. pub. relations com., 1959-83; mem. com. pub. welfare Combined Jewish Philanthropies, Boston, 1961-70, trustee, from 1952; chmn. Com. Services to Unmarried Parents and Children, Boston, 1960-70; mem. nat. adv. com. Nat. Council on Illegitimacy, 1967-70; mem. com. services to mil. families Met. Boston chpt. A.R.C., 1965-69; adv. com. Crittendon Hastings House, from 1969. Bd. dirs. Mass. Soc. Prevention Cruelty to Children, 1958-74; trustee Found. for Character Edn., 1955-76. Mem. Am., Mass., Boston bar assns., Phi Beta Kappa. Jewish (trustee temple 1958-61). Clubs: Mason. Club, Belmont (Mass.) Country, Harvard. Home: Chestnut Hill Mass. Deceased. †

LEVIN, HERMAN, theatrical producer; b. Phila., Dec. 1, 1907; s. Abraham and Jennie (Goldfin) L.; m. Dawn McInerney, Apr. 16, 1956 (div.); m. Victoria Steiner (div.); 1 dau. by previous marriage, Gabrielle. Student, U. Pa., 1925, Dickinson Sch. Law, Carlisle, Pa., 1926, St. John's U. Law Sch., 1931-35. Bar: N.Y. 1935. Various positions in adminstrn. N.Y.C., from 1935; dir. Bur. Licenses, Welfare Dept., N.Y.C., until 1946; dir. Bowline Corp., Bala-Cynwyd, Pa., Vesper Corp., Bala-Cynwyd. Theatrical producer, from 1946; producer: (with Melvyn Douglas) Call Me Mister, 1946, (with Oliver Smith) No Exit, 1947, Richard III, 1948, Gentlemen Prefer Blondes (starring Carol Channing), 1949, Bless You All, 1950, (both with Oliver Smith) My Fair Lady, 1956, The Girl Who Came to Supper, 1963, The Great White Hope, 1968, Lovely Ladies, Kind Gentlemen, 1970, Tricks, 1973, revival, My Fair Lady, 1975. Pres. League N.Y. Theatres, 1955-57, Ind. Booking Offices, Inc., 1957-58. Mem. Coffee House Club. Home: New York N.Y. Died Dec. 27, 1990.

LEVINE, CHARLES HOWARD, political science research scholar, educator; b. Hartford, Conn., July 13, 1939; s. Benjamin Levine and Elaine B. (Cohen) Levine Gipstein; m. Elaine S. Marcus, Sept. 11, 1966; 1 child, Jordan Benjamin. B.S., U. Conn., 1963; M.B.A., Ind. U., 1965, M.P.A., 1968, Ph.D, 1971. Assoc. prof. Syracuse U., N.Y., 1973-77; vis. research prof. Cornell U., Ithaca, N.Y., 1975-77; prof., dir. U. Md., College Park, 1977-81; disting. prof. polit. sci. U. Kans., Lawrence, 1981-83; sr. staff mem. Brookings Instn., Washington, 1983-84, cons., 1980-83; sr. specialist Library of Congress, Washington, 1984-87; Disting. prof. govt. and pub. adminstrn. The Am. U., Washington, 1987-88; cons. Rand Corp., Santa Monica, Calif., 1979-84, Battelle Meml. Inst., Columbus, Ohio, 1980-83, Abt Assocs., Cambridge, Mass., 1981-84; disting. lectr. U. Mo., 1983; dep. dir. Nat. Commn. on Pub. Service, 1987—. Author: Racial Conflict and the American Mayor, 1974; co-author: The Politics of Retrenchment, 1981, The Quiet Crisis of the Civil Service; editor: Managing Fiscal Stress, 1980; editor Adminstrn. and Soc., 1973-76. Ford Found. faculty fellow Fed. Exec. Inst., 1970. Mem. Am. Soc. Pub. Adminstrn. (nat. council 1985, nat. program chmn. 1982-83, William E. Mosher award 1979, Marshall E. Dimock award 1987), Am. Polit. Sci. Assn. (sect. chmn. 1980-81), Acad. Mgmt. (sect. chmn. 1977-78), Nat. Assn. schs. Pub. Affairs and Adminstrn. (nat. council 1982-84, Disting. Research award, 1986), Nat. Acad. Pub. Adminstrn. (trustee 1987-88), Pi Sigma Alpha (trustee 1987-88). Club: Cosmos (Washington). Home: Chevy Chase Md. Died Sept. 23, 1988; buried Mt. Lebanon Cemetery, Adelphi, Md.

LEVINE, HELEN SAXON (MRS. NORMAN D. LEVINE), medical technologist; b. San Francisco; d. Ernest M. Saxon and Ann S. Dippel; m. Norman D. Levine, Mar. 2, 1935. AB, U. Ill., 1939. Supr. lab. San Francisco Dept. Pub. Health Tb Sanatorium, 1944-46, U. Ill. Health Services, Urbana, 1952-65; research assoc. in immunobiology, zoology dept. U. Ill., Urbana, 1965-89. Mem. Pres.'s Council U. Ill. Krannert Art Mus., docent. Mem. AAUP, AAAS, Am. Heart Assn., Ill. Acad. Sci., Ill. Pub. Health Assn., Am. Soc. Med. Technologists, Am. Soc. Clin. Pathologists, Sigma Delta Epsilon. Home: Champaign Ill. Died Nov. 27, 1989; buried Woodlawn Cemetery, Urbana, Ill.

LEVITINE, GEORGE, art history educator; b. Kharkoff, Russia, Mar. 17, 1916; came to U.S., 1942, naturalized, 1943; s. Joseph J. and Maria (Arlozorof) L.; m. Eda Mezer, Dec. 2, 1944; children: Elizabeth (Mrs. Michael Bucuvalas), Annette (Mrs. Blair Woodside), Denise (Mrs. Pat Walsh). P.C.B., U. Paris, 1938; M.A., Boston U., 1946; Ph.D. (Edward R. Bacon scholar), Harvard, 1952. Instr. to prof. art Boston U., 1949-64; faculty Harvard U. Extension, 1959-64; prof. U. Md., College Park, 1964-86, prof. emeritus, 1986-89, chmn. art dept., 1964-78; mem. Gov.'s Coun. of Arts, 1967-77; mem. com. Balt. Mus. Art, 1968-78; dir. acad. program devel. with European Acad. Instns., U. Md., 1986-89. Author: The Sculpture of Falconet, 1972, The Dawn of Bohemianism: The "Barbu" Rebellion and Primitivism in Neoclassical France, 1978, Girodet-Trioson: An Iconographical Study, 1978, All Alba della Bohème, 1985; guest editor: Comparative Literature Studies, 1968; rev. editor: Art Jour, 1971-76; editor-in-chief publs. U. Md. Art Gallery, 1967-78; mem. editorial bd. Art Bull., 1979-85; contbr. articles to profl. jours. Served with French Army, 1939-41; to 2d lt. AUS, 1942-45. Named Chevalier de l'Ordre des Art et des Lettres, French Govt., 1987; grantee Am. Council Learned Socs., 1961, Am. Philos. Soc., 1974, 78; Nat. Endowment for Humanities fellow Inst. for Advanced Study Princeton, N.J., 1977-78. Mem. Coll. Art Assn., Am. Soc. for 18th Century Studies, Société de l'Histoire de l'Art Français, Phi Beta Kappa (hon.). Home: Silver Spring Md. Died Sept. 2, 1989; buried Mount Lebanon-George Washington Cemetery, Adelphi, Md.

LEVY, BENJAMIN HIRSCH, lawyer; b. Savannah, Ga., Aug. 24, 1912; s. Arthur B. and Regena (Waterman) L.; m. Marion C. Abrahams, Aug. 7, 1940; children: Joan (Mrs. Gary M. Levy), Benjamin Hirsch Jr. B.S., U. Va., 1932; J.D., Harvard U., 1935. Bar: Ga. 1935. Assoc. Bright & Brennen, Savannah, 1935-40, Abrahams, Bouhan, Atkinson & Lawrence, Savannah, 1945-49; ptnr. Bouhan, Williams & Levy, Savannah, 1949-88; bd. dirs. Solomons Co., Chatham, Fiduciary Services Corp. Pres. Chatham County Bd. Edn., 1951-52; chmn. Savannah chpt. Am. Council for Judaism, from 1954; mem. nat. exec. com. Am. Jewish Hist. Soc.; trustee U.S. Constn. Council of the Thirteen Original States Inc.; nat. v.p. Am. Jewish Philanthropic Fund, Inc.; pres. Ga. Hist. Soc., from 1980; state chmn. Ga. Semiquincentenary Commn. Served to lt. col. USAAF, 1940-45. Mem. Mil. Order World Wars (past chpt. comdr.). Jewish (pres. congregation 1958-60). Club: Rotarian (pres. 1962-63). Home: Savannah Ga. Died Aug. 4, 1988; buried Bonaventure Cemetery, Savannah.

LEVY, GILBERT JOSEPH, pediatrician; b. Memphis, Jan. 4, 1893; s. Joseph B. and Hannah (Adler) L.; m. Helen H. Hart, Oct. 15, 1930; children: Doris, Joan, Helen. MD, U. Tenn., 1915. Diplomate Am. Bd. Pediatrics. Intern Memphis City Hosp., 1915-16, N.Y. Nursery and Child Hosp., 1916, Sea Side Children's Hosp., New Dorp, S.I., N.Y., 1917; practice specializing in pediatrics, from 1920; assoc. prof. pediatrics U. Tenn. Coll. Medicine, from 1937; mem. governing bd. St. Jude Children's Hosp. Capt. Med. Corps, U.S. Army, 1917-19, France. Recipient Joseph Newberger Cup for outstanding med. work in Memphis, 1930. Fellow AMA (chmn. pediatric sect. 1946-47), Assn. Am. Physicians; mem. Memphis Med. Soc., Shelby County Med. Soc. (pres., Tenn. State Med. Soc., So. Med. Assn., Alpha Kappa Kappa, Alpha Omega Alpha. Jewish. *

LEWIS, ALLAN, theater director, writer; b. N.Y.C., June 30, 1905; s. Barnett and Rebecca (Ehrlich) L.; m. Matilda Ross (div.); 1 child, Anita; m. Brooke Waring, June 24, 1944; 1 child, Lanny. Student, Townsend Harris Hall, 1919-22; BA, CCNY, 1926; MA, Columbia U., 1929; postgrad., New Sch. Social Research, N.Y.C., 1936-39; PhD, Stanford U., 1940, U. Mexico, 1952. Actor Woodstock (N.Y.) Theater, 1926-27; exec. dir. New Dramatists Guild, N.Y.C., 1928-30; chmn. dept. theater New Sch. for Social Research, 1930-40, Bennington (Vt.) Coll., 1940-42; prof. Shakespearean studies U. Bridgeport (Conn.), 1942-60; chmn. dept. Nat. U. Mex., Mexico City, 1960-65; drama critic New Haven Register, 1965-75; dir. Shakespeare Theater, Stratford, Conn., from 1965; resource participant Aspen (Colo.) Inst. for Humanities. Author: El Teatro Moderno, 1964, The Contemporary Theatre, 1965, American Plays and Playwrights, 1967, Ionesco, 1971, The Contemporary Shakespeare, 1980; Trans. Five Mexican Painters, 1957; contbr. articles to lit. jours. Mem. Theater Workshop, Westport, Conn. Served to lt. USAAF, 1943-45, CBI. Mem. AAUP, MLA, Internat. Shakespeare Conf. (Eng.), Am. Theatre Assn., Internat. Assn. U. Profs. English, World Shakespeare Assn. Democrat. Club: Y's Men (Westport). Home: Westport Conn. Deceased. †

LEWIS, ARCHIBALD ROSS, historian, educator; b. Bronxville, N.Y., Aug. 25, 1914; s. Burdett Gibson and Pearl Merriam (Archibald) L.; m. Elizabeth Z. Cutler, Dec. 27, 1954; children—David Adelbert, Allyson Cutler. A.B., Princeton, 1936, M.A., 1939, Ph.D., 1940. Adj. prof. history U. S.C., 1940-42, asso. prof., 1947-48, prof., 1948-51; Fulbright research scholar in Belgium, 1950-51; asso. prof. history U. Tex., 1951-55, prof. history, chmn. dept., 1955-59, 63-69; prof. history U. Mass., Amherst, 1969-85, former chmn. dept.; co-dir. Munson-Maritime Inst., Mystic Seaport, 1959-61; Fulbright prof. UAR, 1964-65; vis. prof. U. Ariz.; sec.-gen. 2d Internat. Congress Historians U.S. and Mexico, 1958; v.p. Internat. Maritime Commn., 1985. Author: Naval Power and Trade in the Mediterranean, 1951, The Northern Seas, 1958, Beyond Cape Horn and the Cape of Good Hope, 1986; (with T. McGann) The New World Looks at its History, 1963, The Development of Southern French and Catalan Society, Emerging Medieval Europe; Aspects of Renaissance, 1967, The High Middle Ages, 1970, The Islamic World and the West, 1970, Knights and Samurai, 1974, The Sea and Medieval Civilizations, 1978, Medieval Society in Southern France and Catalonia, 1984; (with T. Runyan) European Naval and Maritime History 300-1500, 1985, Nomads and Crusaders 1000-1368, A War in the West, 1989; editor: The American Neptune, 1984-90. Served to maj. AUS, 1942-46. Decorated Bronze Star medal; Croix de Guerre France).; Ford Found. fellow in Europe, 1954-55; Am. Council Learned Socs. fellow, 1959-60. Fellow Middle East Studies Assn., Royal Hist. Soc., Mediaeval Acad. Am. (councillor 1970—, v.p. 1987, pres. 1988); mem. New Eng. Medieval Conf. (sec. 1974-86), Am. Hist. Assn., N. Am. Soc. Oceanic History (v.p. 1987), Phi Beta Kappa. Presbyn. Club: Town and Gown (Austin). Home: Marblehead Mass. Died Feb. 4, 1990; buried Mt. Hope Cemetery, West Acton, Mass.

LEWIS, CARY BLACKBURN, JR., lawyer, accountant, educator; b. Chgo., Sept. 13, 1921; s. Cary Blackburn and Bertha (Mosley) L.; m. Eleanor Taylor, Feb. 28, 1943; 1 child, Cheryl (Mrs. Walker Beverly IV); m. Mary Lewis, Dec., 1970; 1 child, Cary Blackburn III. A.B., U. Ill., 1942; M.B.A., U. Chgo., 1947; J.D., DePaul U., 1966; Advanced Mgmt. certificate, Harvard, 1971. CPA, Ill. Asst. prof. accounting Ky. State Coll., Frankfort, 1947-50; asso. prof. So. U., Baton Rouge, 1950-51; sr. auditor M.T. Washington (C.P.A.'s), Chgo., 1951-53; auditor Collier-Lewis Realty Co., 1953-65, A.A. Rayner & Sons, 1960-66; tchr. Chgo. Pub. Schs., 1951-57; asso. prof. law, accounting Chgo. Tchrs. Coll., 1957-65, budget coordinator, 1966-67; asso. prof. law, accounting Ill. Tchrs. Coll., 1965-67, Chgo. State Coll., 1967-70; prof. Chgo. State U., from 1970, spl. asst. to v.p., from 1976; C.P.A. Chgo., from 1950, lawyer, from 1966; Budgetary cons. Office Econ. Opportunity; ednl. cons. to HEW; auditing cons. to Dept. Labor; mgmt. cons. to Black Econ. Union, from 1969; chmn. edn. adv. com. NAACP, from 1966. Author: How to Take an Inventory, 1948, Directory of Negro Business of Baton Rouge, La, 1950; Contbr.: Bus. Men's Guide, 1951. Served to 2d lt. AC AUS, 1942-54. Recipient Wisdom award of Honor, 1971; Enos Perry trophy for outstanding bus. educator of yr. Chgo. Bus. Edn. Assn., 1986. Mem. Am., Ill., Chgo. bar assns., Am. Assn. Accountants, AAUP, Am. Bus. Law Assn., Am. Judicature Soc., World Wide Acad. Scholars, Am. Inst. C.P.A.s. Clubs: Chicago, City. Home: Chicago Ill. Dweceased. †

LEWIS, C(HARLES) HYDE, mining engineer; b. San Francisco, Oct. 7, 1894; s. Charles Francisco and Abbie (Hyde) L.; m. Dorothy May Hess, Jan. 18, 1923; children: Charles Hyde, Abigail Lewis (Mrs. T. Clifford Melim Jr.). BS in Mining Engring., U. Calif., Berkeley, 1922. With Phelps-Dodge, Bisbee, Ariz., 1923-28, H. W. Gould & Co., San Francisco, 1928-32; cons. engr. Fredericksburg, Va., 1932-36; with Getchel Mining Co., Nev., 1936-37; gen. supt. New Idria (Calif.) Mining & Chem. Co., 1937-45, gen. mgr., 1945-55, v.p., 1955-56, pres., bd. dirs., from 1956. Ens. USNR, World War I. Mem. AIME, Dallas Petroleum Club, San Francisco Engr.'s Club, Olympic Club, Masons, Psi Upsilon. Episcopalian. *

LEWIS, CHESTER MILTON, publishing company executive, librarian; b. Oyster Bay, L.I., N.Y., Jan. 12, 1914; s. Harry Scudder and Mabel Cornelia (Hauser) L.; m. Isabelle Joan Finch, June 2, 1945 (dec. 1988); 1 dau., Holly Finch. Student, Columbia Coll., 1934. With N.Y. Times Library, N.Y.C., 1933-79, asst. mgr. morgue, 1945-46, library supr., 1946-47, chief librarian, 1947-64, gen. services mgr., 1964-69, dir. archives, 1969-79, dir. oral history programs, 1970-79, med. adminstr., 1972-79, Idea award program adminstr., 1976-79; curator Mus. of Printed Word, 1976-79; cons., historian emeritus, 1979-90; lectr. Grad. Sch. Library Sci., Pratt Inst., N.Y.C., 1956-58; vis. lectr. Grad. Sch. Bus. Adminstrn., Cornell U., 1959-60; cons. microphotography and library operations; dir. Microfilming Corp. Am., 1962-72; Mem. info. services com. Welfare Council, N.Y.C., 1950-53; v.p., treas. Rolling Wood Assn., 1950-51; Chmn. adv. council Grad Sch. Library Sci. C.W. Post Coll., 1966-69; mem. adv. com. Edward R. Murrow Meml. Library, 1966-70; mem. N.Y. State Adv. Com. on Newspaper Preservation, 1974-76. Co-author: Microrecording-Industrial and Library Applications, 1956; Editor: Special Libraries—How to Plan and Equip Them; mem. editorial bd.: Am. Documentation, 1962-71; contbr. bus. and profl. periodicals. Recipient Jack K. Burness Meml. award for distinguished librarianship, 1965; named Hon. Alumnus Alumni Assn. Sch. Library Sci. Columbia, 1956. Fellow Nat. Microfilm Assn.; mem. Spl. Libraries Assn. (chmn. newspaper div. 1964, award merit 1972, 2d v.p. 1952-53, 1st v.p. 1954-55, pres. 1955-56, chmn. hdqrs. salary rev. com. 1956-57, chmn. promotion techniques com. 1956-59, exec. bd. 1956-57, chmn. awards com. 1957-68, rep. Am. Standard Assn. com. on photo duplicating documents 1960-66, chmn. copyright law revision com. 1960-71, rep. joint libraries com. on copyright 1960-69, internat. mgmt. congress com. 1962-64, profl. cons. from 1960, Hall of Fame award 1978, Joseph Kwapil award 1981), A.L.A. (com. library standards microfilm 1961-64), Council Nat. Library Assns., Oral History Assn. (mem. com. on evaluation 1976-77, adviser oral history programs 1977, mem. nominating com. 1977-79, com. on copyright and legal agreements 1978-80, com. on evaluations and standards 1978-80, cons. 1978-80), New Eng. Oral History Assn., Oral History in the Mid-Atlantic Region, Cedar Swamp Hist. Soc. (v.p. 1980—), Beta Phi Mu. Home: Port Washington N.Y. Died Apr. 30, 1990.

LEWIS, EDWARD VAN VLIET, naval architect; b. East Hampton, N.Y., Jan. 6, 1914; s. Edward R. and Susan C. (Van Vliet) L.; m. Adelyn C. Sar, Sept. 9, 1939; children: Edward A., Pamela F. BA, Nebr. Wesleyan U., 1935; student, U. Glasgow, Scotland, 1935-36; MS, Stevens Inst. Tech., 1955. From jr. architect to asst. head design George G. Sharp, naval architect, N.Y.C., 1936-51; head ship div. Davidson Lab., Stevens Inst. Tech., Hoboken, N.J., 1951-61, research prof., 1959-61; research prof. naval architecture, dir. research Webb Inst. Naval Architecture, Glen Cove, N.Y., 1961-78; dir. Center Maritime Studies, 1967-78; vis. research prof. U.S. Naval Acad., Annapolis, 1979; tech. adviser Am. Bur. Shipping, 1970-78. Co-author: Ships, 1965; editor rev. edit.: Principles of Naval Architecture, 1988-89; contbr. articles to profl. jours., chpts. to books. Fellow Soc. Naval Architects and Marine Engrs. (hon. v.p., Linnard prize 1955, Davidson medal 1966), Sigma Xi, Phi Kappa Phi. Unitarian. Home: Largo Fla. Died Aug. 7, 1992. †

LEWIS, GAYLE F., clergyman; b. Elgin, Pa., Nov. 14, 1898; s. Charles A. and Nettie N. (Stillson) L.; m. Mary E. Stevenson, May 31, 1917; children: Mary Virginia, Olive Roberta, Gayle F. Ordained to Ministry Assembly of God, 1923. Dist. sec.-treas. cen. dist. Assembly of God, 1927-31, dist. supt., 1931-46, asst. gen. supt. nat. orgn., 1946-52, dir. publs. and adminstrn. Gospel Pub. House, 1946-52, gen. supt. nat. orgn., 1952-53, asst. supt. nat. orgn., exec. dir. nat. home missions dept., from 1954. Bd. dirs., adminstrn. Cen. Bible Inst. Mem. C. of C. *

LEWIS, HAROLD GREGG, economist, educator; b. Homer, Mich., May 9, 1914; s. Clayton Arthur and Florence (Gregg) L.; m. Julia Catherine Elliott, Dec. 14, 1938; children: Peter Elliott, John Gregg, Scott Porter. Student, Port Huron Jr. Coll., 1932-34; AB, U. Chgo., 1936, PhD, 1947. Instr. econs. U. Chgo., 1939-43, asst. prof., 1945-49, assoc. prof., 1949-57, prof., 1957-75; prof. econs. Duke U., Durham, N.C., 1975-84, prof. emeritus, 1984-92; asst. dir. wage stblzn. WLB, 1943-45. Author: Unionism and Relative Wages in the United States, 1963; Union Relative Wage Effects: A Survey, 1986. Contbr. articles to profl. jours. Served with USAAF, 1945. Disting. Fellow Am. Econ. Assn.; fellow Am. Acad. Arts and Scis.; mem. Phi Beta Kappa. Home: Chapel Hill N.C. Died Jan. 25, 1992.

LEWIS, JOSEPH HILLIARD, manufacturing executive; b. Elmira, N.Y., Nov. 30, 1896; s. Ransom T. and Ella (Hilliard) L.; m. Florence C. Meyers, Aug. 20, 1918; children: Polly Ann (Mrs. Earl S. Eichin, Jr.), Jane Meyers (Mrs. William Freehoff). BSChemE, Purdue U., 1918. Engr. Corning Glass Works, 1919-23, Proctor & Gamble Co., 1924, Dwight P. Robinson & Co., 1925-26; with Blue Ridge Glass Corp., 1926-58, pres., 1948-58; v.p. Blue Ridge div. Am.-St. Gobain Corp., N.Y.C., 1958-60, pres. corp., 1961-92; dir. First Nat. Bank, Kingsport, Tenn. Alderman City of Kingsport, 1965-69. Served on the Mexican Border, 1916; as 2d lt., F.A., U.S. Army, World War I. Mem. Am. Soc. Testing Materials, Ceramic Engring. Soc. Scabbard and Blade, Rotary. *

LEWIS, L(EO) RHODES, music educator; b. Emporia, Kans., Nov. 27, 1919; s. Edwin James and Mabel (Rhodes) L.; m. Roberta Palmquist, Dec. 25, 1942; children—Gavin Rhodes, Trevor Robert, Scott Rhys, Lisa Ellen. MusB, Baker U., 1941; MS, Kans. State U., 1949; PhD, Iowa U., 1956. Supr. music Swink (Colo.) pub. schs., 1948; instr. Kans. State U., Manhattan, 1948-49; prof. Eastern Oreg. Coll., LaGrande, 1949-63; prof. U. Wis., Eau Claire, 1963-83, chmn. dept. music, 1963-73. Mus. dir., condr., Am. Community Symphony Orch., European and Far East concert tours, 1961, 63, 65, 68, 69, 71, mus. dir., 1st Luth. Ch., Eau Claire, 1964-76. Mem. exec. com. Wis. Arts Council, 1966-73. Served with USN, 1941-48. Decorated Croix de Commandeur French Legion Honor, 1961; Melvin Jones fellow Lions, 1988. Mem. Young Audiences Wis. (v.p. 1967-75, exec. dir. 1975-78), Wis. Symphony Orch. Assn. (pres. 1966-68), Am. Symphony Orch. League (dir. 1956-59), Music Educators Nat. Conf., Nat. Assn. Am. Composers and Condrs., Wis. Music Educators Assn., Am. Fedn. Musicians, Phi Mu Alpha Sinfonia, Phi Delta Kappa, Delta Tau Delta. Presbyyerian (elder). Lodges: Lions (dist. gov. 1972-73, dir. Wis. Lions found. 1974-79), Elk. Home: Eau Claire Wis. Died Jan. 24, 1989; buried Emporia, Kans.

LEWIS, MEL (MELVIN SOKOLOFF), musician; b. Buffalo, May 10, 1929; s. Samuel and Mildred (Brown) S.; m. Doris J. Sutphin, Dec. 25, 1952; children—Anita Lynn, Lori Ellen, Donna Jeanne. Student pub. schs., Buffalo. Bandleader, tchr. New Eng. Conservatory-William Patterson State Coll.; mem. faculty NYU, from 1981. Drummer with orchs. of, Boyd Raeburn, 1948, Alvino Ray, 1948, Ray Anthony, 1949, 53-54, Tex Beneke, 1950-53, Stan Kenton, 1954-57, freelance recording, Hollywood, Calif., 1957-59; albums include Make Me Smile, Soft Lights, Hot Music, 1988; appeared with, ABC Studios, Hollywood, 1959-60, Gerry Mulligan Orch., 1960, Dizzy Gillespie, 1961, NBC Studios, Hollywood, 1961-62, Benny Goodman, 1962, with Thad Jones-Mel Lewis Orch., 1965-88, leader, 1979-88, named changed to Mel Lewis Jazz Orch. Recipient Russian Allstars Jazz Poll award as best drummer 1962, Downbeat Critics Best Drummer award 1963, Downbeat awards as best band 1966, 72, Readers Poll awards 1973, Jazz Forum awards 1975, Swing Jour. awards 1975, 76, Playboy Allstars Poll award 1975, Grammy awards 1977, 78. Recipient Grammy Nominations, 1979, 80, 82, 86. Mem. Am. Fedn. Musicians, Nat. Acad. Rec. Arts and Scis. Democrat. Jewish. Home: Yorktown Heights N.Y. Died Feb. 2, 1990; buried Mt. Hope Cemetery, Hastings-on-Hudson, N.Y.

LEWIS, ORME, lawyer; b. Phoenix, Jan. 7, 1903; s. Ernest W. and Ethel (Orme) L.; m. Margarethe H.T. Greene; 1 son, Orme. Ed., Stanford, 1920-21; LL.B., George Washington U., 1926. Bar: Ariz. 1926, Calif. 1931, U.S. Supreme Ct. 1955, D.C. 1969. Practice in Phoenix, from 1926; mem. Lewis and Roca, from 1950; asst. sec. Dept. Interior, 1953-55; mem. 9th Ariz. State Legislature; U.S. rep. GATT, 1955. Fellow ABA. Clubs: Ariz.; Phoenix; Metropolitan, Capitol Hill (Washington). Home: Phoenix Ariz. Died June 29, 1991; buried Phoenix. †

LEWIS, PRESTON W(ILHELM), dry goods company executive; b. LaGrange, Mo., Nov. 26, 1896; s. Samuel G. and Elizabeth (Wilhelm) L.; m. Edith W. Greaves, Oct. 15, 1927; children: Frances Joyce, Howard Preston (dec.). AM, Brown U., 1917. Instr. high schs. Okla. and Ill., 1919-22; asst. dept. mgr. Carleton Dry Goods Co., 1922-25; joined Ely & Walker Dry Goods Co., St. Louis, 1925, dir., from 1936, pres., until 1964. With U.S. Army, 1917-19. Mem. Algonquin Country Club, Univ. Club. St. Louis Club, Lambs Club, St. Louis Bath and Tennis Club. Republican. Presbyterian. *

LEWIS, R(OBERT) DONALD, agronomist; b. Wyalusing, Pa., Nov. 4, 1897; s. Edgar Darwin and Harriet Augusta (Smith) L.; m. Adelaide Florence Mason, Sept. 2, 1922; children: Charles Milton, William Mason. BS, Pa. State Coll., 1919; PhD, Cornell U., 1926. Instr. agronomy Pa. State Coll., 1919-22; fellow agr. Cornell U., 1922-23, asst. plant breeding, 1923-24, instr., 1924-26, asst. prof. extension div., 1926-30; prof. agronomy extension Ohio State U., 1930-39, resident tchr., 1933-39, prof., vice chmn. dept. agronomy, 1939-40, chmn., 1940-46, assoc. agronomy rsch. Ohio Agrl. Expt. Sta., 1939-46; co-operative agt. divsn. cereal crops and diseases Bur. Plant Industry Dept. Agriculture, 1936-46; dir. Tex. Agrl. Expt. Sta., 1946-62; sr. cons. Ford Found. Faculty Agr. U. Aleppo, Syria, 1962-1990; chmn. So. Agr. Expt. Sta. Dirs., 1955-57; chmn. task group on New and Spl. Crops Pres.' Commn. on Indsl. Use Agrl. Products, 1956-57; sec.-treas. Ohio Seed Improvement Assn., 1930-39; adv. trustee Ohio Hybrid Seed Corn Producers, 1937-46; mem. Agr. Expt. Sta. Com. on Orgn. and Policy, 1946-50; chmn. Nat. Adv. and Coord. Com. on New Plants, 1952-55; mem. Agrl. Rsch. Svc. Com. of Nine, 1953-55; A.R.A. Rice adv. com., 1952-62. Served in S.A.T.C., 1918. Fellow AAAS, Am. Soc. Agronomy (chmn. crops sect. 1935), Tex. Acad. Sci.; mem. Genetics Soc. Am., Assn. Land Grant Colls. and Univs (chmn. exptl. sta. sect. 1959), Am. Soc. Range Mgmt., Internat. Crop Improvement Assn., Corn Improvement Conf., Masons, Kiwanis, Sigma Xi, Alpha Zeta, Phi Kappa Phi, Gamma Sigma Delta. *

LEWIS, SIR WILLIAM ARTHUR, economist, educator; b. St. Lucia, W.I., Jan. 23, 1915; s. George and Ida (Barton) L.; m. Gladys Isabel Jacobs, May 5, 1947; children: Elizabeth Anne, Barbara Jean. Student, St. Mary's Coll., St. Lucia, 1924-29; B.Com., London Sch. Econs., 1937, Ph.D., 1940; M.A. (hon.), Manchester U., 1951, D.Sc., 1973; L.H.D., Columbia U., 1954, Boston Coll., 1972, Coll. of Wooster, 1980, DePaul U., 1981; LL.D., U. Toronto, 1959, Williams Coll., 1959, U. Wales, 1960, U. Bristol, 1961, U. Dakar, 1962, U. Leicester, 1964, Rutgers U., 1965, U. Brussels, 1968, The Open U., 1974, Atlanta U., 1980, U. Hartford, 1981, York U., 1981, Howard U., 1984, Harvard U., 1984; Litt.D., U. West Indies, 1966, U. Lagos, 1974, Northwestern U., 1979; D.Sc., U. London, 1982; D.Social Sci, Yale U., 1983; hon. fellow, London Sch. Econs., 1959, Weizmann Inst., 1962. Asst. lectr., then lectr., reader London Sch. Econs., 1938-48; Stanley Jevons prof. polit. economy U. Manchester, 1948-59; prin., vice chancelor U. West Indies, 1959-63; prof. econs., internat. affairs Princeton U., 1963-83, James Madison prof. polit. economy, until 1983, prof. emeritus, 1983-91; prin. Bd. Trade, then Colonial Office U.K., 1943-44; mem. Colonial Econ. Adv. Council U.K., 1945-49; dir. Colonial Devel. Corp. U.K., 1950-52; mem. Deptl. Com. on Fuel and Power U.K., 1951-52; econ. adviser Prime Minister of Ghana, 1957-58; dep. mng. dir. UN Spl. Fund, 1959-60; spl. adviser Prime Minister West Indies, 1961-62; dir. Indsl. Devel. Corp., Jamaica, 1962-63, Central Bank of Jamaica, 1961-62; pres. Caribbean Devel. Bank, 1970-73; chancellor U. Guyana, 1967-73; Mem. econ. adv. coun. NAACP, 1978-80; pres. Caribbean Devel. Bank, 1970-73. Author: Economic Problems of Today, 1940, The Principles of Economic Planning, 1949, The Economics of Overhead Costs, 1949, Economic Survey, 1919-39, 1950, The Theory of Economic Growth, 1955, Politics in West Africa, 1965, Development Planning, 1966, Reflections on the Economic Growth of Nigeria, 1967, Some Aspects of Economic Development, 1969, The Evolution of the International Economic Order, 1978, Growth and Fluctuations 1870-1913, 1978, Racial Conflict and Economic Development; editor: Tropical Development, 1970. Decorated Knight Bachelor, 1963; co-recipient Nobel prize in econs., 1979; Corr. fellow Brit. Acad. Mem. Am. Philos. Soc., Royal Econ. Soc. (council 1949-58), Manchester Statis. Soc. (pres. 1956), Econ. Soc. Ghana (pres. 1958), Am. Econ. Assn. (v.p. 1965, Distinguished fellow 1969, pres. 1983); hon. fgn. mem. Am. Acad. Arts and Scis. Home: Saint Michael Barbados Died June 15, 1991; buried Morne Fortune Castries, St. Lucia, W.I.

LIBERTE, JEAN, artist; b. Italy, Mar. 20, 1896; came to U.S., 1990; naturalized, 1932.; s. Salvatore and Carmelo (Russo) L. Student, Cooper Union, Art Students League. tchr. Art Students League N.Y., 1944. One-man shows, N.Y.C.; works exhibited Met. Mus., Modern Mus. Art, Whitney Mus. Art, Carnegie Inst., also Israel, Europe, Johannesburg, South Africa. Recipient Corcoran award, Washington, bronze medal, purchase prize Pepsi Cola, Obriz prize Nat. Acad., others. Mem. Audubon Soc., Nat. Acad., Am. Fedn. Painters and Sculptors, Casein Painters Am., Nat. Soc. Painters Casein, Inc. (bd. dirs.). *

LICHSTEIN, JACOB, physician; b. Phila., July 4, 1908; s. Solomon and Clara (Barmash) L.; m. Lilyan Cohen, Dec. 1939 (div. 1966); children: Henry Alan, Gabrielle; m. Mary McDonnell, Feb. 5, 1975 (div. 1976). Grad., Phila. Sch. Indsl. Art, 1921; student, U. Pa.; student (Mayor's competitive scholar), 1925-28; M.D., Jefferson Med. Coll., 1932. Diplomate: Am. Bd. Internal Medicine (sub-specialty gastroenterology). Rotating resident Albert Einstein Med. Center, Phila., 1932-34; attending staff med. div. Albert Einstein Med. Center, 1936-42, attending gastrointestinal clinic, 1936-41; contract surgeon Civilian Conservation Corps, Galeton, Pa., 1934-35; pvt. practice medicine Phila., 1935-42; specializing in internal medicine and gastroenterology Los Angeles, from 1946; demonstrator pathology Jefferson Med. Coll., Phila., 1936-40; examining physician Nat. Selective Svc., 1945; attending staff Cedars of Lebanon Hosp., 1947-76, supr. G.I. clinic, 1958-61; staff Los Angeles County Hosp., 1946-66, emeritus, from 1966; mem. staff Los Angeles County Hosp. Unit II, 1964-67, Temple Hosp., 1948-75, Union Health Center, 1956-58, Mt. Sinai Hosp., from 1966; attending specialist gastroenterology Wadsworth VA Gen. Hosp., 1963-70; cons. Midway Hosp., Los Angeles, 1970-75, Westside Hosp., Los Angeles, 1970-75; emeritus physician Cedars-Sinai Med. Center, Los Angeles, from 1976; instr. medicine U. So. Calif. Med. Sch., 1946-52, asst. prof. clin. medicine, 1952-64, post-grad. lectr. gastroenterology, 1947-53; asst. clin. prof. medicine Calif. Coll. Medicine, Irvine, 1964-67; assoc. clin. prof. medicine UCLA Sch. Medicine, 1975-77; asst. clin. prof. U. Calif. at Los Angeles Center for Health Scis., 1967-75; med. dir. Gay-Henry Gastrointestinal Research Found., Los Angeles, 1957-71; med. cons. county, state and fed. agencies; ind. med. examiner, State of Calif.; mem. Pan-Am. Cytology Union, 1952-61; named Citizen Ambassador, People to People Program, 1985, Citizen Ambassador to Europe, 1985, to China, 1986. Author memoir, 1935; contbr. numerous articles to profl. and popular jours.; pvt. book, art collector. Vice pres. bd. Players Prodn. Co., Inc., Los Angeles; producer-dir. Beards and Belles, 1937-40; bd. dirs. Kensington Synagogue and Community Center, Phila., 1935-40, ANTA Acad. Performing Arts, 1964; mem. Am. Jewish Com., from 1981. Served to 1st lt., M.C. Civilian Conservation Corps, 1934-35; to maj. AUS, 1942-46, ETO. Recipient 40 Yr. Disting. Service award Cedars Sinai Med. Ctr., 1986, grants clin. research gastroenterology, from 1952. Fellow ACP, Am. Coll. Gastroenterology (1st prize sci. exhibit 1959), Am. Geriatrics Soc; mem. Fellows Menninger Found., Am. Gastroent. Assn. (sr.), AMA, Calif., Los Angeles Bowling Green Assn., Los Angeles County med. socs., So. Calif. Soc. Gastroenterology (charter mem., pres. 1965), Am. Fedn. Clin. Research (sr.), Am., Calif., Los Angeles socs. internal medicine, AAAS, So. Calif. Soc. Gastrointestinal Endoscopy, Western Gut Club (founding mem.), N.Y. Acad. Scis., Internat. Platform Assn., ANTA (pres. So. Calif. chpt. 1967, prodn. head Free Shakespeare in the Parks program Los Angeles). Democrat. Clubs: Hollywood Comedy, 50-Yr. of Am. Medicine. Lodge: Masons (32d degree). Home: Los Angeles Calif. Deceased. †

LICHTMANN, SAMUEL ARTHUR, architect; b. N.Y.C., Feb. 27, 1898; s. Joseph and Esther (Lichtmann) L.; m. Molly Rosenberg, May 20, 1951. BS in Archtl. Engring., U. Ill., 1921. Chief draftsman, architect and designer Holabird & Root, Chgo., 1921-31; v.p. Charles E. Fox & Co., Chgo., 1932-36; sr. ptnr. Lichtmann & Bach, Chgo., 1936-42; pvt. practice Chgo., from 1948; vice chmn. Chgo. Commn. Preservation Archtl. Landmarks, from 1957; mem. Mayor Chgo. Com. to Amend Chgo. Bldg. Code, 1957-61, Greater Housing Conf. Chgo., 1948-50. 1st lt. F.A., U.S. Army, 1918. Fellow AIA (pres. Chgo. chpt. 1955-57, chmn. com. low income housing study, mem. nat. coms., pres. Chgo. chpt. Found.). *

LIEB, IRWIN CHESTER, philosophy educator, university official; b. Newark, Nov. 9, 1925; s. Moses Lewis and Gussie (Krytzer) L.; m. Martha Isabel Simonson, Aug. 23, 1960 (div.); children: Michael Adam, Gordon Nichols. A.B., Princeton U., 1947; A.M., Cornell U., Ithaca, N.Y., 1949; Ph.D., Yale U., 1953. From instr. to asst. prof. philosophy Yale U., 1953-59; prof. philosophy Conn. Coll., 1959-63; prof. philosophy U. Tex., Austin, 1963-81, assoc. grad. dean, 1973-75, v.p., dean grad. studies, 1975-79; prof. philosophy U. So. Calif., L.A., 1981-92, v.p., dean Coll. Letters, Arts and Scis., 1981-86; Mem. exec. com. Assn. Grad. Schs., Council Grad. Schs., Nat. Commn. on Research. Author: Peirce's Letters, 1953, Experience, Existence and the Good, 1961, The Four Faces of Man, 1973, Past, Present and Future, 1991; also monographs, articles. Bd. govs. U. of Judaism. With USN, 1943-45. Morse traveling fellow, 1956; fellow Am. Council Learned Socs., 1964. Mem. Am. Philos. Assn., Metaphys. Soc. (councillor 1968-70), Philosophy Edn. Soc. (dir.), Nat. Humanities Faculty (bd. trustees). Home: Pasadena Calif. Died May 23, 1992.

LIFSON, NATHAN, physiology educator; b. Mpls., Jan. 30, 1911; s. Benjamin and Sophie (Paley) L.; m. Helen Millman, July 27, 1939; children: Benjamin M., Matti P. BA, U. Minn., 1931, PhD, 1943; MD, Columbia U., 1937. Intern San Diego County Hosp., 1937-38; instr. physiology U. Minn. Med. Sch., Mpls., 1941-44, asst. prof., 1944-46, assoc. prof., 1946-49, prof., 1949-80, prof. emeritus, 1981-89. Mem. Am. Physiol. Soc., Soc. for Exptl. Biology and Medicine, Phi Beta Kappa, Sigma Xi, Alpha Omega Alpha. Home: Minneapolis Minn. Died Dec. 31, 1989; cremated.

LIGHTNER, EDWIN ALLAN, JR., foreign service officer; b. N.Y.C., Dec. 8, 1907; Edwin Allan and Helen Cleveland (Chute) L.; m. Dorothy M. Boyce, 1953; children: Edwin Allan III, John Boyce, Mary Elizabeth. AB, Princeton U., 1930; grad., Nat. War Coll., 1949. Joined Fgn. Svc., U.S. Dept. State, Washington, 1930; assigned to Venezuela, Chile, Brazil,, 1930-35, Argentina, Latvia, Oslo, 1935-40, Moscow, Stockholm, 1942-43; asst. polit. adviser, U.S. mem. European Adv. Commn., London, 1944-45; asst. chief, then assoc. chief Cen. European affairs U.S. Dept. State, 1945-48; dep. dir. Office Polit. Affairs U.S. High Commn., Frankfurt, Germany, 1949-51; dep. chief mission, counselor Am. Embassy, Seoul, 1951-53; U.S. land commr. for Bavaria Munich, 1953-56; dep. asst. sec. state for pub. affairs U.S. Dept. State, 1956-59; asst. chief of mission and U.S. minister Berlin, 1959-63; U.S. amb. to Kingdom of Libya, 1963-65; State Dept. rep. Water Resources Task Force, 1965-66; dep. comdt. fgn. affairs Nat. War Coll., 1966-69; amb.-in-residence Dayton Miami Valley Consortium, 1969-70. Co-author: The Department of State, 1976. Woodrow Wilson sr. fellow, 1973. Mem. Met. Club (Washington). Home: Belfast Maine Died Sept. 15, 1990; buried Rock Creek Cemetery.

LILLY, DORIS, author; b. Los Angeles, Dec. 26, 1921; d. Otto William and Edith Marie (Humphries) L. Grad. high sch., Santa Monica, Calif. Soc. columnist N.Y. Post, 1958-68; gossip columnist WPIX, N.Y.C., 1974-77, syndicated gossip columnist McNaught Syndicate, 1977-80; monthly social columnist Good Housekeeping mag., 1980-87; Author: How to Marry A Millionaire, 1951, How to Make Love in Five Languages, 1964, Those Fabulous Greeks: Onassis, Niarchos and Livanos, 1970, Glamour Girl, 1977, How To Meet A Billionaire, 1984; contbr. to maj. nat. mags. Home: New York N.Y. Died Oct. 9, 1991; buried N.Y.C.

LIM, ROBERT KHO-SENG, physiologist; b. Singapore, Oct. 15, 1897; came to U.S., 1949; naturalized, 1955; s. Boon-Keng and Margaret (Huang) L.; m. Margaret Torrance, July 10, 1920 (dec.); children: Effie (Mrs. O. Philip Edwards), James T.; m. Tsing-Ying Tsang. MB, ChB, U. Edinburgh, 1918, PhD, 1920, DSc, 1924; DSc, U. Hong Kong, 1961. Lectr. physiology U. Edinburgh, Scotland, 1919-23; Rockefeller Found. fellow U. Chgo., 1923-24; prof., head dept. physiology Peking Union Med. Coll., 1924-37; vis. rsch. prof. clin. sci. U. Ill., 1949-50; prof., head dept. physiology and pharmacology Creighton U., 1950-51; head physiology and pharmacology Miles-Ames Rsch. Lab., from 1951, dir. Med. Scis. Rsch. Lab., from 1960. Mng. editor Chinese Jour. Physiology, 1927-41; contbr. sci. papers Am., Brit., German, Belgian jours. physiology and parhmacology; contbr. A Stereotaxic Atlas of the Dog's Brain (C.C. Thomas), 1960. With Brit. Army, IVAC, 1914-16; lt. Royal Army Med. Corps., 1919; dir. Chinese Red Cross Med. Relief Corps, 1937-42; dir. Emergency med. Svc. Tng. Sch., 1939-41; insp. gen. med. svc. Chinese Army, 1942-44, surgeon gen., 1944-49. Decorated Legion of Merit, Medal of Freedom with silver palms, Order of Yun Hui. Fellow ACS (hon.), Royal Soc. Edinburgh, Academia Sinica; mem. Am. Gastroenterol Assn. (hon.), Assn. Mil. Surgeons (hon.), Deutschen Akademie der Naturfeorscher, Halle (hon.), Brit. Physiol. Soc., Am. Physiol. Soc., Chinese Physiol. Soc., Chinese Med. Assn. (pres. 1928-30), Royal Acad. Scis., Bologna (corr.), Nat. Acad. Scis. (fgn. assoc.). *

LINDAHL, LEON KENNETH (LINDY LINDAHL), business executive; b. Chgo., Dec. 1, 1897; s. Emil Frederick and Ida (Colson) L.; m. Mary Thomas, June 18, 1921; 1 child, Leon Thomas. Student, U. Ill., 1917, 19-20. With The Udylite Corp., from 1925, from sales rep. to gen. mgr., chmn. bd. dirs., pres., from 1953; pres. Udylite Rsch. Cor., from 1939; chmn. bd. dirs. Frederick B. Stevens Inc., from 1950; chmn. bd. dirs., pres. L.H. Butcher Co. of L.A., 1952-63; owner Muleshoe and SH Ranches, HIllside, Hi-Low Ranch, Cornville; pres. MTL Cattle Co., Bagdad, Ariz. 1st lt. USMC, 1918-19. Mem. Am. Electroplaters Soc., Am. Ordnance Assn., Ariz. Cattle Growers Assn., Masons, Detroit Club, Detroit Athletic Club, Univ. Club, The Recess Club (past pres., hon. life mem.), Econ. Club, Sigma Chi. *

LINDENBLAD, NILS E., research physicist; b. Norrkoping, Sweden, Oct. 30, 1895; s. Enoch and Hulda (Werner)L.; m. Elsie Christine Lawson, Sept. 14, 1926; children: Gordon, Irving. ME, Norrkoping Poly. Inst., 1915; EE, Royal Inst. Tech., Stockholm, 1919. With RCA, Princeton, N.J., from 1920, charge antenna rsch. and devel., 1920-29, charge ultra high frequency rsch., 1929-35, later rsch. physicist; fellow tech. staff RCA Labs., 1959-60, cons., from 1960; cons. to sec. of war, 1943-44. Inventor of travelling wave tube, 1939, TV broad band antenna, 1935-38, first electronic refrigerator, 1954, first electronic air conditioner, 1956. Recipient Modern Pioneer award, 1940, cert. of appreciation U.S. War Dept., 1947, award for outstanding rsch., RCA Lab., 1947, 54, David Sarnoff outstanding achievement award, 1959. Fellow IEEE (life); mem. Am. Bapt. Conv., Sigma Xi. *

LINDER, FORREST EDWARD, biostatistics educator; b. Waltham, Mass., Nov. 21, 1906; s. Gustaf Ferdinand and Lillian (Domville) L.; m. Gretchen Alma Otto, Dec. 21, 1931 (dec. Apr. 1984); children—Gordon Forrest, Louise Alma; m. Agnes Mary Whitfield, Nov. 1984. B.A., State U. Iowa, 1930, M.A., 1931, Ph.D., 1932. Asso. biostatistician Worcester (Mass.) State Hosp., 1932-35; asst. chief div. vital statistics Bur. Census, 1935-44; chief demographic and social statistics UN, 1946-56; dir. Nat. Center Health Statistics, 1956-67; vis. prof. U. N.C., 1966, prof. biostatistics Sch. Pub. Health, 1967-77; cons. Ford Found., 1962-88; adviser WHO, 1957-88; pres. Internat. Inst. for Vital Registration and Statistics, 1974-86. Author: Manual de Estadistica Vital, 1942, Vital Statistics Rate in the United States, 1900-1940, 1943, Improving Civil Registration, 1985, also articles. Served to comdr. USNR, 1944-46. Recipient Distinguished Service award HEW, 1966; Bronfman prize Am. Pub. Health Assn., 1967. Mem. Am. Statis. Assn., Internat. Statis. Inst., Internat. Assn. for Ofcl. Stats., Am. Population Assn., Internat. Union for Sci. Study Population, Sigma Xi. Club: Cosmos (Washington). Home: Silver Spring Md. Died Aug. 18, 1988; buried Arlington Nat. Cemetery.

LINDQUIST, EMORY KEMPTON, educator; b. Lindsborg, Kans., Feb. 29, 1908; s. Harry Theodore and Augusta Amelia (Peterson) L; m. Irma Lann, June 17, 1942; children: Elizabeth Ann Marie, Kempton Theodore. AB, Bethany Coll., 1930, LHD, 1964; BA, MA, Oxford (Eng.) U., 1930-33; PhD, U. Colo., 1941; LLD, Augustana Coll., 1952; LittD, Friends U., 1972. Prof. history and polit. sci. Bethany Coll., 1933-38, v.p., 1938-41, acting pres., 1941-43, pres., 1943-53; prof. Wichita State U., 1953-55; dean faculties, dean Fairmount Coll. Liberal Arts and Scis., 1955-57, dean faculties, 1957-61, Univ. prof., 1961-63, pres., 1963-68, interdeptl. prof., 1969-92; vis. scholar consortium four Iowa colls., 1968-69. Author: Smoky Valley People, 1953, Vision for a Valley, 1970, Drommen om en dal, 1970, An Immigrant's Two Worlds, 1972, An Immigrant's American Odyssey: A Biography of Ernst Skarstedt, 1974, Bethany in Kansas: The History of a College, 1975; contbr. to Kans. Hist. Quar., Mo. Hist. Rev. Decorated comdr. Royal Order North Star (Swden). Mem. NEA, Am. Hist. Assn., Kans. Hist. Soc. (pres. 1962), Phi Beta Kappa, Pi Kappa Delta. Home: Wichita Kans. Died Jan. 27, 1992.

LINDQUIST, JOHN ROBERT, lawyer; b. Rockford, Ill., Nov. 14, 1921; s. Axel Theodore and Augusta Fredericka (Kempe) L.; m. Lois Marie Mueller, Feb. 28, 1945; children: John R., James T., David L. B.S., Northwestern U., 1943, J.D., 1948. Bar: Ill. 1948, U.S. Ct. Claims 1953, U.S. Dist. Ct. 1961. Assoc. McDermott, Will & Emery, Chgo., 1948-54; ptnr. McDermott, Will & Emery, 1954-83, mem. mgmt. com., 1972-83. Pub. mem. Ill. Pub. Employees' Pension Laws Commn., 1978-84. Served to lt. (j.g.) USN, 1943-46. Mem. Chgo. Bar Assn. (chmn. employee benefits com. 1970-71), Am. Bar Retirement Assn. (dir., trustee 1982-86), Ill. State Bar Assn., ABA (mem. council real property, probate and trust law sect. 1977-83), Midwest Pension Conf. (chmn. 1976). Republican. Presbyterian. Club: Sunset Ridge Country. Home: Deerfield Ill. Died Apr. 28, 1989; buried Lake Forest (Ill.) Cemetery.

LINDSAY, RICHARD CLARK, air force officer; b. Minn., Oct. 31, 1905; s. Edwin Henry and MaBelle (Clark) L.; m. Margaret Eloise Ball, Sept. 13, 1930; children: Raylyn, Richard Ball. Student, Carleton Coll., 1924-26, U. Minn., 1926-28; grad. primary and basic flying sch., Kelly Field, Tex., 1929, Air Corps Tech. Sch., Chanute Field, Ill., 1931, Air Corps Navigation Sch., Rockwell Field, Coronado, Calif., 1934, Air Corps Tactical Sch., Maxwell Field, Ala., 1940. Commd. 2d lt. Air Corps U.S. Army, 1929, advanced through grades to lt. gen., 1957; various assignments U.S., 1929-43; mem. Joint War Plans Com. of Joint Chiefs Staff, Washington, 1943-44, AAF Joint Staff Planners of Joint Chiefs Staff Orgn., Washington, 1944-45; asst. chief staff Plans (A-5) Hdqrs. U.S. Army Strategic Air Forces, Guam, 1945, Pacific Air Command, Ft. McKinley, Manila, 1946, 8th Air Force, 316th Bombardment Wing, Okinawa; asst. chief staff A-2 Hdqrs. F.E.A.F., 1947; chief policy div. Directorate of Plans and Ops. and Air Planner, 1947-48; dep. dir. plans & ops. Office of DCS/O, 1948-49; dep. dir. for strategic plans Joint Chiefs of Staff, Washington; standing group liaison officer to Coun. Deps. NATO, Washington, London, Paris, 1951-52; comdg. gen. 3650th AF Indoctrination Wing, Sampson AFB, N.Y., 1952-54; dir. plans hdqrs. USAF, 1954-57, asst. chief of staff ops. for hqrs., 1957; asst. DCSO in the Pentagon, 1957; comdr. Allied Forces in So. Europe, 1957-90. Decorated Commendation Ribbon, Disting. Svc. medal, Legion of Merit with oak leaf cluster, Bronze Star, various area medals, Most Excellent Order of the Brit. Empire. Mem. Scabbard and Blade, Army and Navy Club (Washington), Army-Navy Country Club (Arlington, Va.), Phi Kappa Sigma. Home: Glendale Calif. Died Nov. 3, 1990.

LINDSEY, HENRY CARLTON, communications educator, college dean; b. Coushatta, La., Jan. 3, 1918; s. Benjamin Dennis and Vallie (Snead) L.; m. Evelyn Natille Pierce, Dec. 27, 1947; children: John Bryan, Lovie Denise, Mark Pierce. B.A., Ouachita Coll., 1948; M.A., La. State U., 1951; Ph.D., U. Denver, 1962. Instr. Ouachita U., Arkadelphia, Ark., 1952-53; chmn. drama dept. Howard Coll., Birmingham, Ala., 1953-56; edn. specialist USAF Air U., 1956-58; chmn. speech dept. Georgetown (Ky.) Coll., 1958-61; dir. extension Kans. State Coll., Emporia, 1961-63; chmn. drama dept. Baylor U., 1963-64; acad. v.p. Ouachita U., 1964-69; chmn. speech dept. Miss. State Coll. Women, 1969-70; acad. v.p. Howard Payne Coll., Brownwood, Tex., 1970-74; chmn. fine arts div. Howard Payne U., Brownwood, Tex., 1980-81, dean Coll. Arts and Scis., from 1982; ednl. specialist Community Coll. of Air Force, 1974-80;

prof. communication U. Tex., San Antonio, from 1980; ednl. cons. Kans. State Coll., 1968, 69, Western Ky. State U., 1975. Author: plays The Inner Light, 1947, Grey Harvest, 1951, Call Me Penny, 1952, Forever Judy, 1953, Mr. Sweeney's Conversion, 1954, Curfew, 1956, Trilogy in Red, 1981; asso. editor: plays Players Mag, 1953-56; Drama, book reviewer plays, Birmingham (Ala.) News. Served with AUS, 1942-45, ETO; lt. col. USAF; Res. (ret.). Decorated Bronze Star with oak leaf cluster. Fellow Internat. Inst. Arts and Letters; mem. Speech Assn. Am., Theta Xi, Theta Alpha Phi. Club: Rotary. Home: Atlanta Tex. Deceased. †

LINDVALL, FREDERICK CHARLES, manufacturing executive; b. Moline, Ill., May 29, 1903; s. Gustav and Alma (Freeberg) L.; m. Janet Smith, Aug. 27, 1928; children: Charles Eric, Martha Joan, John Robert. Student, U. Calif., 1920-22; BS, U. Ill., 1924; PhD, Calif. Inst. Tech., 1928. Registered profl. engr., Calif. Elec. inspector L.A. Ry., 1924-25; teaching fellow Calif. Inst. Tech., 1925-28, instr., 1930-31, asst. prof. elec. engring., 1931-37, assoc. prof. elec. and mech. engring., 1937-42, prof., 1942-69, chmn. div. engring., 1945-69; engr. Gen. Electric Co., 1928-30; v.p. engring. Deere Co., 1969-72; bd. dirs. Bell and Howell Co., Royal Industries. Bd. dirs. Stanford Rsch. Inst. Lt. USNR, 1935-53. Recipient Presdl. Cert. of Merit. Fellow ASME, IEEE; mem. AAUP, Am. Soc. Engring. Edn. (Lamme medal 1966, pres. 1957-58), Nat. Acad. Engring., Tau Beta Pi, Sigma Xi (pres. 1968-70), Masons, Twilight Club. Home: Pasadena Calif. Died Jan. 17, 1989.

LINEN, JAMES ALEXANDER, IV, communications company executive; b. Scranton, Pa., May 15, 1938; s. James Alexander and Sally (Scranton) L.; m. Diane Blumenthal, Sept. 28, 1985; children by previous marriage—James Alexander V, Barry Wilson, Stephen Spencer. B.A. magna cum laude, Yale U., 1960. Exec. trainee Field Enterprises, Chgo., 1963-65; founder, owner/chmn. Calumet Pub. Co., suburban Chgo., 1965-75; exec. v.p. Nat. Enquirer, Lantana, Fla., 1976-77; owner/chmn. Des Plaines Pub. Co., Ill., 1977; v.p. Media Gen. Inc., Richmond, Va., 1977-81, sr. v.p., 1981-85, exec. v.p. in charge broadcast ops., 1985-89; chmn. Media Gen. Broadcast Services, Inc., Richmond, 1983-89; chmn. bd. Am. Thai Corp., 1968-72; dir. TV Advt. Bur., 1985-89. Trustee Roycemoor Sch., 1965; bd. dirs. South Chgo. YMCA, 1966-70; advisor Chgo. Sch. Bd. Dist. 22, 1966-69; mem. adv. council on consumer affairs Ill. Dept. Agr., 1972-73; commr. Chgo. Regional Port Dist., 1971-76, mem. exec. com., sec., 1975-76; trustee Glenwood Sch. for Boys, 1968-76, Morgan Park Acad., 1973-76; gov. Mercy Hosp., 1968-76; bd. advisors Woodberry Forest Sch., 1986. Served to 1st lt. U.S. Army, 1960-63. Decorated Army Commendation medal. Mem. Ill. Press Assn. (dir. 1973-76). Clubs: Economic; Racquet of Chgo. (gov. 1974-76); Round Hill (Greenwich Conn.); Country of Va.; Commonwealth (Richmond); Yale, Brook (N.Y.C.). Home: Richmond Va. Died July 2, 1989.

LINSLEY, RAY KEYES, civil engineering educator; b. Hartford, Conn., Jan. 13, 1917; s. Ray Keyes and Flora Madelaine (Ladd) L.; m. Anne Virginia Cutler, Nov. 26, 1937; children: Dianne, Stephen, Alan, Brian. B.S., Worcester Poly. Inst., 1937, D.Engring. (hon.), 1979; D.Sc. (hon.), U. Pacific, 1973. Engr. TVA, 1937-40; engr. U.S. Weather Bur., Washington, 1941, Sacramento, 1942-44; chief hydrology U.S. Weather Bur., Washington, 1945-50; assoc. prof. Stanford U., 1950-55, prof., head dept. civil engring., 1956-67, prof. emeritus, 1975-90, assoc. dean School Engring., 1956-58, dir. project engring.-econ. planning School Engring., 1962-71; Fulbright prof. Imperial Coll., London, 1957-58; v.p. Carroll Bradberry & Assocs., 1959-67; pres. Hydrocomp Internat., 1967-78; chmn. Hydrocomp, Inc., 1972-78; pres. Linsley Kraeger Assocs. Ltd., Santa Cruz, Calif., 1979-85, chmn., from 1988; internat. hydrological cons. engr.; with Office Sci. and Tech., Washington, 1964-65. Author: Applied Hydrology, 1949, Elements of Hydraulic Engineering, 1955, Hydrology for Engineers, 1958, 3d edit., 1982, Water-Resources Engineering, 3d edit., 1979. Commr. U.S. Nat. Water Commn., 1968-73. Recipient Meritorious Service award Dept. Commerce, 1949. Fellow Am. Geophys. Union (pres. hydrology sect. 1956-59), ASCE (hon., Collingwood prize 1943, Julian Hinds award 1978, hon. mem. 1986); mem. Nat. Acad. Engring., Am. Meteorol. Soc., Nat. Soc. Profl. Engrs., Venezuelan Soc. Hydraulic Engrs. (hon.), Am. Inst. Hydrology (sr. v.p. 1983-88, hon. pres. 1988), Japan Soc. Civil Engrs. (hon.), Sigma Xi, Tau Beta Pi. Home: Novato Calif. Died Nov. 6, 1990.

LIONE, HENRY VINCENT, fundraiser; b. Queens, N.Y., Nov. 19, 1928; s. James Vincent and Erma (Biondi) L.; m. Margaret McNulty, Jan. 6, 1951; children: Debra Jayne, David Scott. A.B., NYU, 1948; M.A. in Edn., 1966; postgrad., Inst. Fine Arts, 1949. Mem. staff YMCA, N.Y.C., 1952-61, Community Service Soc., N.Y.C., 1961-64, Children's Aid Soc., N.Y.C., 1964-66, YMCA Greater N.Y., 1966-69; exec. dir. N.Y. chpt. Arthritis Found., 1969-70; dir. fin. devel. Valley Hosp., Ridgewood, N.J., 1970-77; nat. dir. Cystis Fibrosis Found., Rockville, Md., 1977-81; exec. dir. Pacific Med. Found., San Francisco, 1981-84; asst. v.p. Office Med. Devel. U. Miami Sch. Medicine, Fla., from 1984; pres. Henry V. Lione Enterprises, Ltd., Advent Corp., (fund raising cons.), Gaithersburg, Md., from 1984; founder, past pres. N.J. Soc. Fund Raisers; v.p. YMCA Bergen County (N.J.), 1973; bd. dirs. Fund Raising Inst., Plymouth, Pa., 1981; ordained to ministry United Methodist Ch., 1965. Served with U.S. Army, 1951-52. Recipient cert. of merit Acad. Hosps. Public Relations, 1974. Fellow Nat. Assn. Hosp. Devel. (Seymour award 1975, Silver award 1975); mem. Nat. Soc. Fund Raisers. Republican. Home: Cincinnati Ohio Died Mar. 30, 1988; buried Spring Grove Cemetery, Cin. †

LIPPERT, JACK KISSANE, editor, publisher; b. Allegheny, Pa., Nov. 14, 1902; s. Harry C. and Isabelle (Kissane) L.; m. Katherine Churchill, July 14, 1945; 1 stepchild, Dwight W. Tracy. Student, U. Pitts., 1924-25; grad. in journalism, Columbia U., 1928. Reporter Pitts. Press., 1923-26, N.Y. World, 1927-31; v.p. Scholastic, Inc., N.Y.C., 1953-62, exec. editor, 1951-65, bd. dirs., 1957-74, sr. v.p., 1962-74, pub., 1967-72, vice chmn. bd. dirs., 1970-73, cons., 1974-89, editor-in-chief emeritus, 1975-89. Chmn. Maurice R. Robinson Fund, 1982-89. Mem. Soc. Profl. Journalists, N.Y. Acad. Pub. Edn., Princeton Club. Home: Norwalk Conn. Died Nov. 9, 1989; cremated.

LIPTON, MORRIS ABRAHAM, research psychiatrist; b. N.Y.C., Dec. 27, 1915; s. Theodore and Rose (Latt) Lipschitz; m. Barbara Steiner, Dec. 28, 1940; children—Judith Eve, Susan Victoria, David Mark. B.S., City Coll. N.Y., 1935; Ph.M., U. Wis., 1937, Ph.D., 1939; M.D. with high honors, U. Chgo., 1948. Diplomate: Am. Bd. Psychiatry and Neurology, Am. Bd. Internal Medicine. Research asst. U. Wis., Madison, 1937-39; research fellow biochemistry U. Wis., 1939-40; research asso., instr. U. Chgo., 1940-41, instr. dept. physiology, 1941-45, sr. research chemist, 1941-45, research assoc., instr. dept. medicine, 1945-46; intern Michael Reese Hosp., Chgo., 1948-49; resident and fellow in psychiatry U. Chgo., 1949-51, part-time resident in medicine and instr. psychiatry, 1951-52, instr. and resident in medicine, 1952-53, asst. prof. medicine and psychiatry, 1953-54; asst. prof. medicine Northwestern U., Evanston, Ill., 1954-59; chief investigative medicine service and chief psychosomatic service VA Research Hosp., Chgo., 1954-56, asst. dir. profl. services for research, 1956-59; research assoc. Chgo. Inst. Psychoanalysis, 1954-59; vis. prof. U. Buenos Aires, 1958; asso. prof. psychiatry and dir. research devel. U. N.C., Chapel Hill, 1959-63, prof. psychiatry and dir. research devel., 1963-70, chmn. dept. psychiatry, 1970-73, prof. dept. biochemistry, 1973-86, Kenan prof. psychiatry and biochemistry, 1963-86, Sarah Graham Kenan Distinguished prof. of psychiatry, 1972-86, prof. emeritus, 1986-89; vis. scientist Nat. Heart Inst., Lab. of Clin. Biochemistry, Bethesda, Md., 1965-66; dir. Biol. Sci. Rsch. Ctr. U. N.C. Child Devel. Research Inst., 1965-86 ; cons. NIH, 1965-69, FDA, Bur. of Drugs, from 1973, NIMH, from 1972, VA Med. Rsch. Career Devel. Com., from 1975; sci. cons. N.C. Alcoholism Research Authority, from 1974; mem. N.C. Multi-university Task Force on univ.-state dept. of mental health resources, needs and collaborative opportunities, from 1972; mem. N.C. Found. for Mental Health Rsch.; chmn. Nat. Advisory Com. on Hyperkinesis and Food Additives, from 1975; mem. Presdl. Commn. on Obscenity and Pornography, 1968-70, many others. Cons. editor: Neuropharmacology and Psychopharmacology, 1969-70; editorial bd.: Am. Jour. Psychiatry, 1970-80; dep. editor, 1980-89; editorial bd.: Psychopharmacology Communications, from 1974, Neuropsychobiology, from 1974; editorial advisory bd.: N.C. Jour. Mental Health, from 1975, Ann. Rev. Psychiat. Drug Treatment, from 1973; contbr. numerous articles in field to profl. jours. Recipient NIMH Rsch. Career Devel. Award, Grade II, 1962-67. Fellow Am. Coll. Neuropsychopharmacology, Am. Coll. Psychiatrists, A.C.P., Am. Psychiat. Assn.; mem. AAUP, Soc. for Exptl. Biology and Medicine, Am. Soc. Biol. Chemists, Am. Psychosomatic Soc., Am. Fedn. for Clin. Research, N.Y. Acad. Sci., Soc. for Psychiat. Research, Soc. for Exptl. Biology and Medicine, So. Soc. for Clin. Investigation, Am. Psychopath. Assn., Soc. for Neurosci., Am. Assn. of Med. Colls., Sigma Xi, Phi Lambda Upsilon, Alpha Omega Alpha. Home: Chapel Hill N.C. Died Mar. 15, 1989; buried Chapel Hill.

LISTER, ROBERT HILL, archeologist, educator; b. Las Vegas, N.Mex., Aug. 7, 1915; s. Frank Hiram and Bye (Hill) L.; m. Florence Ellen Cline, July 24, 1942; children: Frank Cline, Gary Givhan. BA, U. N.Mex., 1937, MA, 1938; MA, Harvard U., 1947, PhD, 1950. Prof. Am. archeology U. Colo., 1947-70; with dept. anthropology U. N.Mex., Albuquerque; also with Nat. Park Service, 1971-79; research assoc. Ariz. State Mus., U. Ariz., Tucson, 1980-88; archaeol. excavations in Am. S.W., Mexico and, Nubia. Served to maj. AUS, 1941-46. Mem. Am. Anthrop. Assn., Soc. Am. Archaeology, Soc. Hist. Archaeology. Home: Mancos Colo. Died May 17, 1990.

LISTON, ROBERT TODD LAPSLEY, college president, clergyman; b. Oxford, Ala., Dec. 10, 1898; s. Robert Todd and Isabel Pratt (Lapsley) L.; m. Maria Preston Holman, June 25, 1929 (dec. 1957); children: Robert Holman, Jonathan Miller; m. Jane Leighton Richards, Aug. 7, 1959. AB, Davidson Coll., 1920, LLD, 1955; BDiv, Union Theol. Sem., 1924; ThM, Union Sem., 1925; student, U. Marburg, 1927; PhD, U. Edinburgh, 1930. Asst. prof. Hebrew Union Theol. Sem., 1927-28; pastor Richlands, Va., 1928-37; assoc. prof. Bible Southwestern Coll., Memphis, 1937-40; pres. Davis and Elkins Coll., 1940-43, King Coll., from 1943; Smythe lectr. Columbia Theol. Sem., 1952. Author: The Neglected Educational Heritage of Southern Presbyterians, 1956. Charles D. Larus fellow, 1925. Democrat. Presbyterian. *

LITTLE, CLEAVON JAKE, actor; b. Chickasha, Okla., June 1, 1939; s. Malchi and de Etta (Jones) L. B.A., San Diego Coll., 1965; postgrad., Am. Acad. Dramatic Arts, 1965-67. Actor, appeared in plays MacBird, 1967, Hamlet, 1967, Scuba Duba, 1967-68, Jimmy Shine, 1968-69, Someone's Comin' Hungry, 1969, Ofay Watcher, 1969, Purlie, 1970, Narrow Road To The Deep North, 1972, The Charlatan, 1974, All Over Town, 1974, The Poison Tree, 1976, Same Time Next Year, 1977, Sly Fox, 1978, Two Fish in the Sky, 1982, I'm Not Rappaport, Seattle, 1984-85, N.Y.C., 1985; TV appearance in Temperature's Rising, 1972-73, Felony Squad, All in The Family, The Homecoming, The Day The Earth Moved, Bros. Grimm, 1977, Don't Look Back, 1981, Now We're Cookin', Gore Vidal's Lincoln, All God's Dangers, 1990; appeared in films What's So Bad About Feeling Good, 1968, Cotton Comes to Harlem, 1970, Vanishing Point, 1971, Blazing Saddles, 1974, Greased Lightning, 1977, FM, 1978, Scavenger Hunt, 1979, High Risk, 1981, Jimmy the Kid, 1982, Double Exposure, 1983, The Salamander, 1983, Surf II, 1984, Toy Soldiers, 1984, Gig, Once Bitten, Fletch Lives, 1989. Recipient Tony award for best actor in a musical, 1969-70; N.Y. Critic Poll award, 1970; Drama Desk Award, 1970; F. and M. Schaefer Brewing Co. award, 1970; NAACP Image award, 1976. Home: New York N.Y. Died Oct. 22, 1992. †

LITTLE, JOSEPH CLYDE, lawyer; b. Liberty, Ind., Feb. 16, 1895; s. Joseph C. and Julia (Cully) L.; m. Zola Clark, Aug. 21, 1924; children: Zoann Dusenbury, Josephine Wettach, Robert E. C., John G. C. AB, Earlham Coll., 1917; BA, Oxford (Eng.) U., 1921, BCL, 1922. Bar: Ohio 1923. Mem. law firm Jones, Day, Cockley & Reavis, Cleve., from 1930. Mem. ABA, Ohio Bar Assn., Cleve. Bar Assn. *

LITTLE, NOEL CHARLTON, physics educator; b. Brunswick, Maine, Dec. 25, 1895; s. George Thomas and Lilly Thayer Wright (Lane) L; m. Marguerite Dorothy Tschaler, Sept. 8, 1923; children: Mary Thayer (Mrs. Richard Huggins), Clifford Carlton, Dana Anton. AB, Bowdoin Coll., 1917; AM, Harvard U., 1919, PhD, 1923. Mem. faculty Bowdoin Coll., from 1919, prof. physics, from 1927, chmn. dept. physics, 1952-64, Joshua Little prof. natural sci., from 1954; instr. Harvare U., summer 1925, vis. lectr., summer 1947; fgn. study, rsch. U. Tubingen, Germany, 1928, U. Geneva, 1937, Royal Inst. Tech., Stockholm, 1956; Maine coord. Atomic Devel. Activities. Author: College Physics, 1928, Physics, 1953. Ens. USN, 1917-19, comdr. USNR, 1941-46. Fellow Am. Phys. Soc.; mem. AAAS, IRE, Am. Assn. Physics Tchrs. *

LITTLE, RICHARD, publisher; b. Scranton, Pa., July 17, 1898; s. Richard and Jean (Niven) L.; m. Lois M. Thomas, Sept. 11, 1924; children: Richard, Jean (Mrs. William F. Hallstead III), Mary (Mrs. Richard B. Robb). Student, Bucknell U., 1921. Began career as printer's apprentice Scranton Pub. Co., 1916-18, newswriter, 1921-23, adr. mgr., 1923-26; pres. Scrantonian Pub. Co., Scranton, from 1926; dir. Scranton Rep. Pub. Co., Scranton Plain Corp. Trustee Scranton Keystone Coll. Mem. Waverly Country Club, Masons, Shriners. Republican. Episcopalian. *

LIUM, ELDER LEONARD, civil engineer; b. Christine, N.D., Sept. 23, 1896; s. John J. and Oline (Branno) L.; m. Margarete Marry MacLachlan, July 7, 1929; children: James Elder, Lesley Ann. BS, U. N.C., 1921, C.E., 1944. Registered profl. engr., Minn., N.D. Asst. city engr. Wahpeton, N.D., 1921-23, Breckenridge, Minn., 1921-23; gen. contractor Grants Pass, Oreg., 1923-24; constrn. engr. Carr & McFadden, West palm Beach, Fla., 1924-27; resident engr. on constrn. Oreg. Hwy. Dept., Grants Pass, 1927-28; city engr. Grand Forks, N.D., 1928-36; mem. firm Lium & Burdick cons. engrs., from 1938; mem. faculty U. N.D., from 1935, asst. prof. civil engring., 1935-39, assoc. prof. civil engring., head dept. civil engring., 1939-46, prof. civil engring., from 1946, dean engring., from 1951. 2d lt. Air Corps, U.S. Army, World War I. Mem. ASCE, Am. Soc. Engring. Edn., Fedn. Sewage Works Assn., Am. Assn. State Hsy. Ofcls., N.D. Sewage and Waterworks Conf., N.D. Soc. Profl. Engrs. (v.p.), Nat. Soc. Profl. Engrs., Elks, Sigma Xi. Democrat. Congretationalist. *

LIVI, YVO See MONTAND, YVES

LIVINGSTON, J. A., economics columnist; b. N.Y.C., Feb. 10, 1905; s. Solomon Joseph and Maud (Stern) L.; m. Rosalie L. Frenger, Sept. 16, 1927; 1 child, Patricia (Mrs. Matthew Herban III). BA, U. Mich., 1925; LLD, Temple U., 1966; LHD, Phila. Coll. Textiles and Sci., 1988. Newspaper reporter, 1925-30; exec. editor N.Y. Daily Investment News, 1931-34; pub. utility editor Fin. World, 1935; economist Bus. Week, 1935-42, W.P.B.

and Office War Moblzn. and Reconversion, 1942-45; began bi-weekly econs. columnist Business Outlook, 1945; fin. editor Phila. Record, 1946; bus. columnist Washington Post, 1947; fin. editor Phila. Bull, 1948-67, econs. columnist, 1968-72; econs. columnist The Phila. Inquirer, 1972-89; prof. econs. Temple U., 1971-72. Author: Reconversion-The Job Ahead, 1944, The American Stockholder, 1958, rev. edit., 1963; newspaper series: America's Stake in the British Crisis, 1949, The Soviet Challenge, 1956, The Kennedy Crash, 1962, The Common Market, 1962, The Powerful Pull of the Dollar, 1964, Gold and Dollar, 1966, The Great Society and the Stock Market, 1966, Economic Consequences of Vietnam, 1968, Gold vs. the Dollar, 1968, Money-A New Epoch, 1969, The British Economy-Human Race Against Ruin, 1974, The Second Battle of Britain, 1975, Great Britain in Adversity, 1977, The Decline of the Dollar: An American Tragedy, 1978, South Africa: In the Throes of Change, 1978, English Lessons for America, 1981, The 80s: The Dangerous Decade, 1983; contbr. to Ency. Social Scis., Compton's Ency., also nat. publs. and learned jours.; originator, condr. Livingston Survey, 1946-78, continued by Phila. Fed. Res. Mem. intensive rev. com. sec. commerce to analyze program U.S. Bur. Census. Recipient Loeb Mag. award, 1958, Loeb Newspaper award, 1960, 71, 76, citation for excellence in journalism Temple U., 1960, best bus. reporting from abroad award Overseas Press Club, 1962, 65, 75, Pulitzer prize for internat. reporting, 1965, Merit award Poor Richard Club, 1965, INGAA-U Mo. Journalism awards, 1966, 67, 68, Outstanding Achievement award U. Mich., 1964, Sesquicentennial award, 1967, Disting. Service award, 1976, Heroism award Phila. Police Dept., 1967, 1st Hentz award for fin. journalism, 1967, three John Hancock awards for excellence for syndicated and news service writers, 1967, 68, 74, Nat. Assn. Investment Clubs award, 1970, 1st Gerald Loeb Meml. award U. Calif at Los Angeles, 1974, 1st John Hancock Permanent Recognition award for excellence in fin. journalism, 1974, 1st pl. media award Amos Tuck Sch. Dartmouth Coll., 1978, 79, 80, 81, Nat. Headliners award, 1980, Disting. Alumnus in Econs. award U. Mich., 1980, Disting. Philadelphian-in-Residence Community Coll. of Phila., 1987. Fellow Nat. Assn. Bus. Economists; mem. Am. Econ. Assn., Am. Statis. Assn., Fin. Analysis Phila., Art Alliance, Sigma Delta Chi. Clubs: Cosmos (Washington); Sunday Breakfast, Union League (Phila.). Home: Philadelphia Pa. Died Dec. 25, 1989.

LIVINGSTON, MOLLIE PARNIS, designer; b. N.Y.C.; d. Abraham and Sarah Parnis; m. Leon Jay Livingston; 1 son, Robert Lewis. Sec.-treas. Parnis Livingston, Inc.; pres. Mollie Parnis Co.; founder Mollie Parnis Sch. Program for Keeping Surroundings Clean, from 1975; overseer Parsons Sch. Design, from 1983; pres. Mollie Parnis at Home.; Designer cadet nurses uniform. Founder Dress Up Your Neighborhood awards, N.Y.C., from 1972, Jerusalem, from 1967, Livingston awards for Young Journalists, from 1980; named Woman of Yr., Einstein Coll. Medicine, 1985. Home: New York N.Y. Died July 18, 1992. †

LI XIANNIAN, foreign government official; b. 1909, Huangan, Hubei; m. Lin Jiamei; 3 daus., 1 son. Joined Chinese Communist Party, 1927; polit. commissar 30th Army, 4th Front Red Army, 1935; Comdr. 5th Column, New 4th Army, 1938, Cen. China Mil. Region, 1944; mem. 7th Cen. Com., Chinese Communist Party, 1945; chmn. Provincial Govt. of Hubei, 1949; Comdr. polit. commissar Hubei Mil. Dist., People's Liberation Army, 1949; mayor Wuhan, 1952-54; vice premier State Council, 1954-80; mem. Nat. Def. Council, 1954; dep. 1st Nat. People's Congress, Hubei Province, 1954, 5th Nat. People's Congress, 1978; appointed army gen., 1954; minister of fin., 1957-75; mem. Politburo, 8th Congress, Chinese Communist Party, 1956, mem. secretariat of Cen. Com., 1958-66; dir. Fin. Econ. Affairs Com. Bur., State Council, 1959; vice chmn. State Planning Comm., 1962-72; mem. Politburo and Cen. Com., 9th Congress, Chinese Communist Party, 1969, 10th Cen. Com. Congress, 1973, vice chmn. Cen. Com., 11th Congress, 1977-82, mem. Standing Com., 1977; vice chmn. State Fin. Econ. Commn., 1979-81; del. head 6th Congress Workers' Party of North Korea, 1980; mem. Presidium 12th Congress, 1982; pres. People's Republic of China, 1983-88; chmn. 7th nat. com. Chinese People's Polit. Consultative Conf., 1988-92. Chmn. Cen. Patriotic Health Campaign Com., 1978-83. Decorated Star Socialist Republic Romania, 1984. Avocation: jogging. Died June 2, 1992. Home: Beijing People's Republic of China

LLAND, MICHAEL, ballet master. Attended, U. S.C.; studied ballet with, Igor Schwezoff, Margaret Craske, George Balanchine. Profl. debut on Broadway in Song of Norway; former prin. dancer Teatro Municipal, Rio de Janeiro, Brazil; joined Am. Ballet Theatre, N.Y.C., 1949; soloist Am. Ballet Theatre, 1949-56, prin., 1956-71, ballet master, from 1971. Home: New York N.Y. Deceased. †

LLOYD, DAVID PIERCE CARADOC, physiologist; b. Auburn, Ala., Sept. 22, 1911; s. Francis Ernest and Mary Elizabeth Hart L.; m. Kathleen Mansfield Elliott, Mar. 3, 1937; children: Marion Gwenellen, Owen H.T., Evan E.M.; m. Cynthia Meynell, Nov. 17, 1957. BSc, McGill U., 1932; BA, Oxford U., Eng., 1936; PhD, Oxford U., 1938, DSc, 1961. Deptl. demonstrator physiology Oxford U., 1935-36; from asst. to assoc. dept. med. rsch. U. Toronto, 1936-39; with Rockefeller U. Med. Rsch., 1939-43, 46, mem., 1949-71, prof., 1957-71; asst. prof. physiology Yale U., 1943-45; Johnston lectr. U. Minn., 1948; James Arthur lectr. Am. Mus. Natural History, 1958; hon. rsch. fellow U. Coll. London, 1958; mem. study sect. and coms. Nat. Inst. Neurol. Diseases and Blindness; mem. adv. com. Nat. Found. Infantile Paralysis, 1947-59. Contbg. author: Howell's Textbook of Physiology, revised edit., 1946, 49, 55, Annotations Reflex Activity of the Spinal Cord, 1972; contbr. articles on neurophysiology to profl. jours. Trustee Internat. Poliomyelitis Congress, 1948—. Recipient Reeve prize medicine U. Toronto, 1939. Mem. NAS, Am. Physiol. Soc., Physiol. Soc. Gt. Britain, AAAS, Assn. Rsch. Nervous and Mental Diseases, Harvey Soc. Home: San Jose Calif. Deceased.

LLOYD, FREDRIC REYNOLDS, former pharmaceutical company executive; b. Wilkes Barre, Pa., Sept. 25, 1923; s. John Stanley and Edith May (Reynolds) L.; m. Beverly Jeanne Brand, May 19, 1945; children: Beverly Christine, Carolyn Reynolds. B.S., Purdue U., 1944, Ph.D., 1949. With Eli Lilly & Co., Indpls., 1949-64; asst. dir. chem. mfg. Eli Lilly & Co., 1956-64; v.p. European ops. Eli Lilly Internat., 1965-72; v.p. production ops. div. Eli Lilly & Co., Indpls., 1973-84; bd. dirs. Fluid Mechanics Corp., Lafayette. Mem. Ind. Lt. Gov.'s Sci. Adv. Com., from 1973; trustee Westminster Village, 1987 . Served with USNR, 1943-45. Recipient Distinguished Engring. Alumnus award Purdue U., 1973, Shreve Disting. Indsl. fellow, 1984-85. Mem. Am. Inst. Chem. Engrs., Am. Chem. Soc., Nat. Assn. Profl. Engrs., Sigma Xi, Phi Kappa Psi. Episcopalian. Club: Woodstock. Home: Indianapolis Ind. Deceased. †

LOBB, JOHN CUNNINGHAM, telecommunications executive; b. Mpls., May 31, 1913; s. Albert James and Mary Florence (Cunningham) L.; m. Mary Dudley Montgomery, Sept. 12, 1936; children: Josephine Lobb Adamson, Carol Lobb Kimball. Grad., Phillips Exeter Acad., 1931; BA, U. Minn., 1934; LLB, U. Wis., 1937. Bar: Wis. 1937. Exec. v.p. Marine Corp., 1955-60; v.p. corp. planning A.O. Smith Corp., Milw., 1960-62; pres. H.M. Byllesby & Co., Chgo., 1962-63; exec.v.p. Internat. Tel. & Tel., N.Y.C., 1963-67; pres., chief exec. officer Crucible Steel Co., Pitts., 1967-70; chmn., dir. No. Elec. Co., Ltd., Montreal, Que., Can., 1972-90. Ensign USNR, 1942-43. Mem. Laurel Valley Golf Club, Rolling Rock Club (Ligonier, Pa.), Country Club of Fla. (Delray Beach), Mt. Bruno Golf Club, Mt. Royal Club, St. James Club (Montreal), Jupiter (Fla.) Hills Club. Home: Ligonier Pa. Died Mar. 7, 1990.

LOBSENZ, AMELIA, public relations executive; b. Greensboro, N.C.; d. Leo and Florence (Scheer) Freitag; m. Harry Abrahams, Aug. 17, 1957; children: Michael, Kay. BA, Agnes Scott Coll., 1944. Dir. mag. dept. Edward Gottlieb & Assocs., N.Y.C., 1952-56; pres. Lobsenz Pub. Rels. Co., N.Y.C., 1956-75; chmn. bd., chief exec. officer Lobsenz-Stevens Inc., N.Y.C., 1975-92; pres. Pinnacle Group Cos., 1983-84, chmn., 1985-86, chmn. internat. affairs, 1986-92; mem. bd. advisors, bd. dirs. Mercomm Inc.; lectr. in field. Author: Kay Everett Calls CQ, 1951 (Jr. Lit. Guild Selection), Kay Everett Works DX, 1952; contbr. 300 articles to profl. mags. Bd. govs. Nat. Women's Econ. Alliance. Recipient award for best article on ins. Mag. Writers, 1974; named to Acad. Women Achievers YWCA, 1978. Fellow Pub. Rels. Soc. Am. (accredited, bd. dirs. N.Y. chpt. 1971-79, chmn. nat. com. pub. rels. 1977-79, nat. bd. dirs. 1980-81, pres.' adv. com. 1988, Pres. awards for outstanding svc. 1975-79); mem. Am. Soc. Journalists and Authors, Am. Med. Writers Assn., Am. Women in Radio and TV, Nat. Assn. Sci. Writers, Internat. Pub. Rels. Assn. (bd. mgmt. 1984-85, pres. 1986), Nat. Women's Econ. Alliance (bd. dirs.), Overseas Press Club, Racquet Club Old Westbury, Cornell Club (spl. events com. 1991). Home: Old Brookville N.Y. Died Sept. 1, 1992. †

LOCHBILER, MARSHALL LEO, clergyman; b. Detroit, June 23, 1895; s. Leo and Elizabeth (Schulte) L. AB, U. Detroit, 1918; MA, St. Louis U., 1925; postgrad., U. Mich., 1935-36. Joined Soc. of Jesus, 1918, ordained priest Roman Cath. Ch., 1929. Chmn. dept. English U. Detroit, 1936-40, libr., 1940-43, rector, chmn. bd. trustees, 1956-64; rector-pres. St. Xavier High Sch., Cin., 1943-50; rector Jesuit House of Studies, Cleve., 1950-56; pres. Columbiere Coll., Clarkston, Mich., from 1964. Mem. Jesuit Ednl. Assn. *

LOCKHART, WILFRED CORNETT, former university administrator, consultant; b. Dundalk, Ont., Can., Oct. 17, 1906; s. Thomas Fraser and Frances Cornett L.; m. Margaret Eileen Armstrong, Sept. 20, 1933; children: Wendy Susan Sutherland, David Campbell. BA, U. Toronto, 1929, MA, 1932; DD in Theology, Emmanuel Coll., Toronto, 1933; PhD, U. Edinburgh, 1935. Ordained to ministry, Untied Ch. Can., 1933. Asst. toll engr. Bell Telephone Co. Can., London, Hamilton, Ont., 1933; asst. minister Edinburgh, 1934-35; gen. sec. Student Christian Movement, U. Toronto, 1935-40; chaplain Can. Officer Tng. Corps, 1939-46; 1st sec. Can. com. World Coun. Chs., 1937-40; minister Kingsway-Lambton Ch., Toronto, 1942-55; chmn. bd. govs. Balmoral Hall Sch. Girls, Winnipeg, 1957-58; prin. United Coll. Winnipeg, 1955-67; pres. U. Winnipeg, 1967-71, pres. emeritus, 1971-90. Author: John Fletcher Evangelist, 1939, In Such an Age, 1951, Bethlehem, 1955. Mem. Man. Coun. Higher Learning, 1965-67; chmn. Winnipeg Presbytery, United Ch. Can., 1962-63; moderator United Ch. Can., 1966-68; mem. Man. Local Boundaries Commn., 1966-71; bd. regents Victoria U., Toronto, 1950-55; chmn. bd. coll. and secondary schs. United Ch. Can., 1946-55. Recipient Can. medal. Mem. Rotary pres. Winnipeg 1965-66 . Home: Islington Can. Deceased.

LOCKRIDGE, RICHARD (ORSON), author; b. St. Joseph, Mo., Sept. 26, 1898; s. Ralph David and Mary Olive (Notson) L.; m. Frances Davis, Mar. 4, 1922 (dec.); m. Hildegarde Dolson, May 26, 1965. Student, Kansas City Jr. Coll., 1916-18, U. Mo., 1920. Reporter Kansas City Kansan, 1921-22, Kansas City Star, 1922; reporter N.Y. Sun, 1923-28, drama critic, from 1928. Author: Darling of Misfortune Edwin Booth, 1932, (with Frances Lockridge) Mr. and Mrs. North, 1936, The Norths Meet Murder, 1940, Murder Out of Turn, 1941, A Pinch of Poison, 1941, Death on the Aisle, 1942, Hanged for a Sheep, 1942, Killing the Goose, 1944, Payoff for the Banker, 1945, Cats and People, 1950, The Faceless Adversary, 1956, Show Red for Danger, 1960, The Empty Day, 1965, (with G. H. Estabrooks), Death in the Mind, 1945, others. With USNR, 1918, lt., 1942-45. Mem. PEN, Authors League Am. (mem. coun.), Mystery Writers Am., Inc. (co-pres. from 1960). *

LOEB, JAMES ISAAC, ambassador; b. Chgo., Aug. 18, 1908; s. James Isaac and Viola (Klein) L.; m. Ellen Katz, Nov. 23, 1932; children: Peter, Susan. AB, Dartmouth Coll., 1929; MA, Northwestern U., 1931, PhD, 1936. Tchr. romance langs. Northwestern U., 1930-36, Townsend Harris High Sch., N.Y.C., 1937-41; nat. dir. Union for Democratic Action, 1945-47, Americans for Dem. Action, 1947-51; cons. to Pres. Truman's Spl. Counsel, 1951-52; exec. asst. to W. Averell Harriman, 1952; co-publisher, editor Adirondack Daily Enterprise, Saranac Lake, N.Y., 1953-92; co-pub. Lake Placid News, 1960-92; U.S. ambassador to Peru, 1961-62, U.S. ambassador to Guinea, 1963-92. Contbr. articles to mags. Mem. Ams. for Democratic Action, Saranac Lake C. of C., Rotary, Phi Beta Kappa. Democrat. Home: Conakry Guinea Died Jan. 10, 1992.

LOEW, ARTHUR M., motion picture executive; b. N.Y.C., Oct. 5, 1897; s. Marcus and Caroline (Rosenheim) L.; m. Mildred Zukor, Jan. 6, 1920; children: Jane Constance, Arthur M.; m. Melita J. Schmitt, July 6, 1936; m. Jacqueline Gebhard Tull, Nov. 23, 1963. Student, Alexander Hamilton Inst.; BA, NYU, 1918. 1st v.p. Loew's Inc., 1928, pres., 1955, chmn. bd. dirs., 1956; pres. Loew's Internat. Corp., 1955-58. Chief machinist's mate USN, World War; commd. maj. Signal Corps, U.S. Army, 1942. Officer French Legion of Honor. Mem. City Athletic Club, Montauk Yacht Club, Turf and Field Club, Pi Lambda Phi. *

LOEWI, JACOB VICTOR, investment banker; b. Beloit, Wis., Sept. 9, 1898; s. Adolph and Sarah (Kohn) L.; m. Beatrice Marshall, Jan. 2, 1926; children: Marshall, Mary Jane. Student, Marquette U., 1917-20. Reporter, 1920; fin. editor Milw. Sentinel, 1923-28; pres. Loewi & Co., Inc. investment bankers, Milw., from 1929, N.W. Capital Corp., from 1962; treas., dir. Safway Steel Products, Inc., Milw., 1941-63; chmn. bd. com., dir. Compo Shoe Machinery Co., also Realist, Inc., Milw.; exec. com., dir. Basic Products Corp., Sta-Rite Products, Inc.; dir. Compo Chem. Co., Koehring Co., Universal Foods Corp., Aqua Chem. Inc., Waukesha, Webster Electric Co., Racine, U.S. Vitamin and Pharma. Co., N.Y. Pres. Village of Bayside, Wis., 1953-58; chmn. Met. Milw. area campaign, mem. exec. com., mem. bd. regents Marquette U., chmn. devel. program, 1962-64; dir. Greater Milw. Com. Community Devel., State YMCA Camp Manitowish. Mem. Milw. Assn. Commerce, Am. Legion, Investment Bankers Assn. Am. (chmn. indsl. securities com. 1961), N.Y. Stock Exch., Midwest Stock Exch., English Speaking Union, Milw. Athletic Club, Wis. Club, Bankers Club, Stock Exch. Luncheon Club. *

LOFTON, JOHN MARION, retired newspaper editor; b. McClellanville, S.C., Apr. 11, 1919; s. John Marion and Harriett (Lucas) L.; m. Anne O'Neil Watson, Dec. 27, 1954 (dec. 1968); children: John Marion, Charles Lewis; m. Priscilla Alvarado, 1969 (div. 1975); m. Joanne B. Lyon, 1981. B.S., Coll. of Charleston, 1940; J.D., Duke U., 1942; M.A., U. Pitts., 1956; postgrad., Stanford U., 1960-61. Bar: S.C. 1942. Reporter Spartanburg (S.C.) Herald, 1945-47; sci. editor, editorial writer Seattle Star, 1947; state news editor Orangeburg (S.C.) Times and Democrat, 1947-48; asso. editor Ark. Gazette, Little Rock, 1948-52; editorial writer Pitts. Post-Gazette, 1952-70, assoc. editor, editor editorial page, 1966-70; editorial bd. St. Louis Post-Dispatch, 1971-85; Lectr. U. Pitts., 1971, Washington U., 1972, Webster U., 1982. Author: Insurrection in South Carolina-The Turbulent World of Denmark Vesey, 1964, rev. edit., 1983, Justice and the Press, 1966, The Press as Guardian of the First Amendment, 1980; Contbr. articles profl. jours. Mem. nat. council ACLU. Served with AUS, 1942-45. Recipient Gavel award ABA, 1960;

Mass Media fellow Fund for Adult Edn., 1960-61. Mem. Nat. Conf. Editorial Writers, Sigma Delta Chi (disting. service award for research in journalism 1981, 88). Democrat. Unitarian. Home: Grantville Kans. Deceased. †

LOFTUS, JOSEPH ANTHONY, newspaper reporter; b. Scranton, Pa., June 1, 1907; s. George J. and Bridget (Duffy) L.; m. Mary Frances Schoeps, July 13, 1956; children: JoAnne Young, Marianne Cummings. AB, U. Scranton, 1928; MS in Journalism, Columbia U., 1931. Reporter, asst. city editor Scranton Tribune, 1926-30; bur. mgr. I.N.S., Harrisburg, Pa., 1931-32; state mgr. I.N.S., Pitts., 1933; with A.P., Harrisburg, Washington, 1933-44; labor and polit. corr. N.Y. Times, 1944-69; spl. asst. for communications U.S. Sec. Labor, 1969-73; spl. asst. U.S. Sec. Treasury, 1973-74; cons. labor-mgmt. rels., pub. rels., 1974-90. Mem. Nat. Press Club, Federal City Club. Home: Sarasota Fla. Died Jan. 3, 1990.

LOGAN, MILAN A(LEXANDER), chemistry educator; b. Brockton, Mass., July 15, 1897; s. William Robert and Margaret Annabelle (MacIntosh) L.; m. Queenie Mae Wilson, July 10, 1921. BS, Harvard U., 1919, PhD, 1928. Asst. prof. Harvard Med. Sch., 1928-38, assoc. prof., 1938-41; Andrew Carnegie Found. prof., chmn. dept. biol. chemistry U. Cin. Coll. Medicine, from 1941. Mem. AAAS, Am. Soc. Biol. Chemistry, Am. Chem. Soc., Soc. Exptl. Biology and Medicine. *

LOMAN, HARRY JAMES, insurance educator; b. North Wales, Pa., Mar. 19, 1896; s. Augustus Homer and Estelle (Christman) L.; m. Blanche Bernd, July 1, 1918; children: Janet Marie, James Gilbert. BS in Econs., u. Pa., 1918, MA, 1921, PhD, 1923. Expert in ins. U.S. Bur. of War Risk Ins., Washington, 1919; instr. in ins. U. Pa., 1919-21, asst. prof., 1921-25, prof., 1926-65, prof. emeritus, from 1965, vice dean Wharton Sch., 1933-39, assoc. dean, 1939-42, dir. gradn. div. in bus. adminstrn., 1938-42; dean, vice chmn. bd. trustees Am. Inst. for Property & Liability Underwriters, Inc., 1942-61, pres., from 1961; exec. v.p. Inst. Inst. Am., Inc., 1952-62, pres., from 1962; ins. cons. assoc. chmn. adminstrv. bd. Fels Inst. Local and State Govt.; chmn. adminstrv. bd. S.S. Huebner Found. for Ins. Edn. Author: Insurance of Foreign Credits, 1923, Taxation in Its Relation to Life Insurance, 1928; co-author: (with Robert Riegel) Insurance Principles and Practices, 1921); spl. editor Webster's New Internat. Dictionary; contbr. Ency. Britannica; various articles on ins. Trustee Thomas Skelton Harrison Found., also vice chmn. With USN, 1917-19. Mem. AAUP, Am. Assn. Univ. Tchrs. Ins. (pres. 1936-38), Am. Econ. Assn., Am. Fin. Assn., Masons, Lambda Chi Alpha, Beta Gamma Sigma, Pi Gamma Mu. Mem. United Ch. Christ. *

LOMBARDI, JOHN, educational administrator; b. Bklyn., Feb. 18, 1904; s. John and Maria (DePetrillo) L.; m. Maryellen Maher, Aug. 11, 1934 (dec. 1947); children: Mary, John; m. Janice Pidduck, June 22, 1948. BS in Social Scis., CCNY, 1929; MA, Columbia U., 1935, PhD, 1942. Project supt. Survey Fed. Archives, 1935-36; from instr., counselor, dean evening div. to dean instrn. L.A. City Coll., 1936-55, pres., 1955-66; asst. supt. L.A. Jr. Coll. Dist., 1966-69; rsch. educationalist, cons. jr. coll. adminstrn. UCLA, from 1969; dean L.A. State Coll., summer 1948; mem. L.A. Com. on All-Yr. Schs., 1954. Active Boy Scouts Am. Capt. USAAF, 1942-45. Mem. Am. Assn. Jr. Colls. (bd. dirs.), Calif. Tchrs. Assn., Calif. Jr. Coll. Assn., Los Angeles County Mus. Assocs., Am. Mus. Natural History, Phi Beta Kappa, Phi Delta Kappa. Home: Los Angeles Calif. Died Feb. 28, 1989; cremated.

LONDON, JACK, sociologist, adult educator; b. Duluth, Minn., Oct. 10, 1915; s. Hyman and Dora (Sanders) L.; m. Ethel Robbins, Nov. 22, 1947; children—Jack Murray, Daniel Gary; 1 stepdau., Robin Gail. A.B., Central YMCA Coll., 1939; Ph.D., U. Chgo., 1952. Lithographer Chgo., 1931-41; tng. specialist on-the-job tng. VA, 1946-48; asst. prof., research sociologist U. Chgo., 1948-53; tchr. in workers edn. Roosevelt U., Chgo., 1949-53; asst. prof. U. Calif., Berkeley, 1953-57, assoc. prof., 1957-64, prof., 1964-88; vis. prof., Can., Nigeria, Tanzania, Kenya, Hong Kong; cons. UNESCO, World Bank, Vista, and numerous other govtl. and pvt. orgns. Author: (with Joel Seidman, others) A Worker Views His Union, 1958, (with Robert Wenkert) Adult Education and Social Class, 1964; also chpts. in other books. Served with U.S. Army, 1942-45. Grantee Office Edn., 1960-64; recipient Distinguished Teaching citation U. Calif., 1972. Mem. Am. Sociol. Assn., Adult Edn. Assn. U.S.A. (award for outstanding service 1978). Home: Emeryville Calif. Died Jan. 13, 1988; buried Berkeley, Calif.

LONG, FORREST EDWIN, publisher, author, educator; b. Sweet Springs, Mo., Sept. 29, 1895; s. James K. and Dora B. (Robinson) L.; m. Hazel Tutt, Aug. 20, 1917; 1 child, Edwin Tutt; m. Helen I. Halter, June 22, 1944. A.B., William Jewell Coll., Liberty, Mo., 1917; Edn.M., Harvard U., 1923; Ph.D., NYU, 1928; LittD, William Jewell Coll., 1988. Tchr. math. William Jewell High Sch., 1915-17; tchr. sci. Leavenworth (Kans.) High Sch., 1917; prin. Jr. Sr. High Sch., Atchison, Kans., 1919-22; head dept. secondary edn. Sch. Edn., U. Tenn., 1923-24; asso. prof. edn. Washington U., St. Louis, 1924-28; asso. prof. edn. N.Y.U., 1928-30, prof., 1930-60, prof. emeritus, 1960-88; pres. Roxbury Press, from 1928; v.p., dir. research Inst. Instrl. Improvement, from 1960; pres. Mailings Clearing House, Inc., from 1967; dir. Chem. Bank; chmn. bd. Roxbury Press, Inc.; Mem. adv. council Pub. Edn. Assn., 1942-60; mem. U.S. Treasury Com. Tax Edn., 1942-43; mem. com. on ednl. policies NCCJ, 1940-44; exec. mgr. Nat. Safety Council, 1944-45; mem. adv. council Center for Safety Edn., 1942-60; mem. secondary edn. commn. President's Hwy. Safety Conf., 1946, chmn., 1947-50; hon. pres. Nat. Council for Jr. High Sch. Adminstrn., 1974-85. Author: (with P. W. L. Cox) Principles of Secondary Education, 1932, Problems of the Teacher in the New Secondary School, (with Wm. Newsom), 1937, Social Studies Skills, (with Helen I. Halter), rev. edit. 1978.); editor The Clearing House, 1929-76. Trustee Mo. Valley Coll., Marshall; mem. pres. coun. NYU, 1969-75; bd. dirs. Mo. Safety Coun., 1973-87; mem. No. Am. Revolution Bicentennial Hon. Commn., 1976. With U.S. Army, World War, 1917-19, AEF. First ann. Forrest E. Long lecture established in his honor Nat. Assn. Secondary Sch. Prins., 1986. Mem. Progressive Edn. Assn. (bd. dirs. 1933-38, treas. 1935-38), AAUP, Nat. Com. Advancement Secondary Edn. (sec.), Phi Gamma Delta, Phi Delta Kappa, Kappa Delta Pi. Clubs: Mason, Tri City Country (pres. 1968), Kansas City, NYU. Home: Sweet Springs Mo. Died Aug. 27, 1988; buried Sweet Springs, Mo.

LONG, JOSEPH M., retail drug company executive; b. Covelo, Calif., 1912; m. Tina deBoer. Ed., U. Calif., 1933. Asst. to city mgr. City of Berkeley, Calif., 1933-36; with Safeway Stores Inc., 1936-37; co-founder Longs Drug Stores Inc., Walnut Creek, Calif., 1938, pres., chief exec. officer, 1946-75, chmn. bd., chief exec. officer, 1975-77, chmn. bd., dir., 1977-90. Patron , active numerous civic and ednl. orgns., including U. Calif. at San Francisco Med. Ctr.; established Found. for Excellence Sch. Pharmacy U. Calif. at San Francisco, marine ctr. U. Calif. at Santa Cruz; co-founder, chmn. Calif. State Pks. Found.; co-founder, pres. Calif. Waterfowl Assn. Home: Danville Calif. Died Dec. 27, 1990.

LONGFELLOW, DON, hospital administrator; b. Hobbs, Ind., Mar. 29, 1898; s. Thomas William and Jeannette (Hobbs) L.; m. Helen Woodward, June 2, 1923; 1 child, Don. BS, Ind. U., 1923, MD, 1925; MPH, Yale U., 1947. Diplomate Am. Bd. Preventive Medicine. Commd. 2d lt. U.S. Army, 1916, advanced through grades to brig. gen., 1951; intern Walter Reed Hosp., 1926-27, chief typhoid rsch., 1939-43, chmn. med. rsch. and devel. bd., 1947-48, health dir. C.Z. Govt., 1952-55; chmn. U.S. Army Phys. Rev. Coun., Washington, 1955-57; med. dir. Charles H. Miner State Hosp., Hamburg, Pa., 1957-59; supt. Hamburg State Sch. and Hosp., 1960-64. Contbr. articles on typhoid to med. jours. Decorated Legion of Merit, Bronze Star. Fellow ACP, APHA, Am. Coll. Preventive Medicine; mem. Masons, Phi Kappa Psi, Phi Rho Sigma, Alpha Omega Alpha. *

LOOMIS, WALTER EARL, plant physiologist; b. Makanda, Ill., June 12, 1898; s. Walter Scott and Mary (Anderson) L.; m. Helen Parke, Oct. 9, 1924; children: Walter David, Robert Simpson. BS, U. Ill., 1921; MS, Cornell U., 1922, PhD, 1924. Asst. U. Ill., 1920-21; grad. asst. Cornell U., 1921-24; NRC fellow in botany, 1924-25; asst. prof. U. Ark., 1925-27; assoc. prof. and prof. plant physiology Iowa State U., from 1927; rsch. prof. Iowa Agrl. Exptl. Sta., 1943-; agt. U.S. Dept. Agr., B.P.I., 1938, Bur. Econs., 1941; spl. sci. aid Rockefeller Found., Mex., 1954; vis. prof. Cornell U., 1955, Duke U., 1962, U. N.C., 1964-65; agrl. adviser Egypt and Italy, 1956, Iran, 1957; vice chmn. com. on agrl. pests NRCA 1954-56. Author: (with Dr. C. L. Wilson) Botany, 1957, also author books and articles on plant physiology; editor: Growth and Differentiations in Plants, 1953; assoc. editor: Plant Physiology, 1953-59; mem. editorial staff Biol. Abstracts. Mem. subcom., div. sci. pers. War Manpower Commn. Fellow AAAS, Iowa Acad. Sci. (chmn. bot. sect. 1942-44); mem. Am. Soc. Naturalists, Bot. Soc. Am., Am. Soc. Plant Physiology (sec.-treas. 1939-41, v.p. 1942, pres. 1943, Charles Reid Barnes award 1957), Am. Soc. Hort. Sci., Am. Soc. Agronomy, Scandinavian Soc. Plant Physiology, Sigma Xi, Gamma Sigma Delta, Phi Kappa Phi. *

LOONEY, JOSEPH MICHAEL, physician; b. Somerville, Mass., Apr. 3, 1896; s. Michael and Mary (Breen) L.; m. Mildred Elizabeth Walsh, Aug. 7, 1922; children: Joseph M., Richard John, William Robert, James Arthur, Mildred Elizabeth, Anne Marie. AB cum laude, Harvard U., 1917, MD, 1920. Diplomate Am. Bd. Pathology. Intern Peter Bent Brigham Hosp., 1919; instr. dept. biochemistey Harvard Med. Sch., 1920-22; dir. lab. Sheppard Enoch Pratt Hosp., Towson, Md., 1922-26; asst. prof. physiol. chemistry Jefferson Med. Coll., 1926-30, prof., head dept., 1930-31; chem. pathologist Jefferson Hosp., Phila., 1926-31; dir. rsch. lab. Meml. Found. Neuro Endocrine Rsch., Worcester, Mass., 1931-42; cons. endicrinology Worcester, 1931-42; dir. clin. labs., endocrinologist VA Hosp., West Roxbury, Mass., 1946-49; chief clin. and rsch. labs., chief endocrine clinic VA Outpatient Clinic, Boston, from 1949; cons. endocrinology St. Elizabeth's Hosp., Boston, from 1947, Holy Ghost Hosp., Cambridge, from 1947; rsch. prof. biochem. Boston U. Sch. Medicine, 1951; clin. instr. medicine Sch. Medicine Tufts U., from 1957. Author: (with Morse Saunders) Applied Biochemistry, 1927; contbr. numerous articles in biochem. and med. jours. Served in med. reserve corps, asst. pharmacologist Chem. Warfare Svc., U.S.A., Oct. 1979-Dec. 1918; lt. col. U.S. Army Med. Corps, 1942-46, ETO, 1944-45; chief of lab. 199th gen. hosp.; chief spl. svcs. sta. hosp., Ft. Custer, 1942-44, col. USAR ret. Fellow AAAS, AMA, N.Y. Acad. Sci.; mem. Mass. Med. Soc. (alt. exec. councilor), Norfolk County Med. Soc. (prs. 1960-61), Am. Soc. Biol. Chemists, Am. Chem. Soc., Soc. Exptl. Biol. and Med., N.E. Rheumatism Soc., Boston Soc. Biology, N.E. Diabetes Assn. (dir.), Am. Diabetes Assn., Assn. Mil. Surgeons U.S., Endocrine Soc., Arthritis and Rheumatism Found., Am. Legion, K.C., Nat. Councilman, Daus of Mary of Sick, Chesterton Club (dir. 1935-38, pres. 1938), Harvard Club (Somerville, sec., treas. 1917-22), St. Luke's Guild, Sigma Xi. Roman Catholic. *

LOOS, A(MANDUS) WILLIAM, college president; b. Davenport, Iowa, Feb. 16, 1908; s. William and Bertha (Scheurman) L.; m. Dorothy Lucile Scott, July 29, 1943; 1 child, William Duncan Bradley. A.B., Carleton Coll., 1930; B.D., Andover Newton Theol. Sch., 1933; Ph.D., U. Edinburgh, Scotland, 1939; postgrad., U. Tuebingen, Germany, 1938, Harvard, 1940, U. Minn., 1942. Ordained to ministry Congrl. Ch., 1933. Pastor Congrl. Ch., Waltham, Mass., 1933-37; prof. religion and philosophy Spelman Coll., 1939-43; sec. dept. ministry to servicemen Ch. Fedn. Chgo., 1943-46; edn. sec. Council Religion and Internat. Affairs, N.Y.C., 1946-56, exec. dir., 1956-63, pres., 1963-74; acad. dean Mark Hopkins Coll., Brattleboro, Vt., 1975-76, pres., 1976-89. Author: Two Giants and One World, 1948; Editor: Religious Faith and World Culture, 2d edit, 1970, The Nature of Man, 2d edit, 1969, (with R.S Wright) Asking Why, 1939; translator: The Divine-Human Encounter, 1943. Chmn. bd. Council Christian Social Action, United Ch. Christ, 1963-67. Mem. Council Fgn. Relations, Fgn. Policy Assn. (bd. dirs. 1960-74, chmn. exec. com. 1971-74), Nat. Council Chs., Am. Polit. Sci. Assn., Soc. Internat. Devel., Adult Edn. Assn., Internat. Studies Assn., Internat. Study and Research Inst., Phi Beta Kappa, Pi Delta Epsilon. Home: Brattleboro Vt. Deceased. †

LORCH, EDGAR RAYMOND, mathematician, educator; b. Nyo, Switzerland, July 22, 1907; came to U.S., 1917; s. Henry John and Marthe (Racine) L.; m. Else B., July 31, 1937 (div. 1955); children: Edwin Duncan, Madeleine Louise, Ingrid Jacqueline; m. Maristella de Panizza Bové, Mar. 25, 1956; children: Lavinia Edgarda, Donatella Livia. B.A. summa cum laude, Columbia U., 1928, Ph.D., 1933. Instr. math. Columbia U., 1935-41, asst. prof., 1941-44, assoc. prof., 1944-48, prof., 1948-74, Adrain prof. math., 1974-76, prof. emeritus, 1976-90, chmn. dept. math., 1968-72, co-chmn. univ. seminar Computers, Man and Society, 1982-90; chmn. dept. Barnard Coll., 1948-63, chmn. com. on instrn., 1961; vis. prof. Carnegie Inst. Tech., 1949, U. Rome, 1953-54, 82, U. Florence, 1953-54, 75, Coll. de France, 1958, Stanford U., 1963, Middle East Tech. U., Ankara, 1965; vis. lectr., France, Germany, Scandinavia, Switzerland, Italy; univ. lectr. Fordham U., 1966-72; mem. secondary sch. Math. Curriculum Improvement Study, 1966-72; conseiller Scientifique du President Lycée, Francais de N.Y., 1977-88; exec. com. Ctr. Internat. Scholarly Exch. Author: Spectral Theory, 1962, Precalculus, 1973, Analisis Funcional, 1977, Mathematics at Columbia, 1990; editor: University Texts in Math. Sciences, La Qualità, Seminari Interdisciplinari di Venezia, 1974; mem. editorial bd.: Indiana Math. Jour, 1966-74; contbr. articles to math. jours. Sci. advisor to chief staff U.S. Army, 1948. NRC fellow Harvard U., 1933-34, Cutting Travel fellow Europe, 1934-35; rsch. mathematician NDRC, 1944-45; Fulbright lectr. Italy, 1953-54; Fulbright lectr. Colombia, 1977; Columbia U. fellow, 1932-33; recipient Albert Ascher Green prize, 1928. Mem. Am. Math. Soc. (coun. 1952-55, chmn. com. on nominations 1958, mem. editorial bd. 1945-50), Math. Assn. Am. (vis. mathematician 1961-63), Société Mathématique de France, Oesterreichische Mathematische Gesellschaft, Unione Matematica Italiana, Zürcher Gespräche, Sierra Club, Wilderness Soc., Catskill Center, Environ. Def. Fund, Nature Conservancy, Friends of Riverside Park (v.p. 1982-84), Phi Beta Kappa, Sigma Xi. Home: New York N.Y. Died Mar. 5, 1990; buried Napanoch, N.Y.

LORCH, FRED W., English language educator; b. Elberfeld, Germany, Oct. 29, 1893; came to U.S., 1895; s. Ferdinand and Katherine (Lenz) L.; m. Ruth Mary Raper, Dec. 23, 1922; children: Ruth Jean (Mrs. Glen R. Gerhardt), Robert Stuart. AB, Knox Coll., 1918; AM, U. Iowa, 1928, PhD, 1936. Tchr. English Mapleton (Iowa) High Sch., 1920; tchr. English Iowa State Coll., from 1921, from instr. to prof., head dept. English and speech, 1942-59, prof. English, asst. Office Dean Scis. and Humanities, from 1959, chmn. fgn. student com., from 1945; Fulbright lectr. Gittingen U., Germany, 1954-55; adviser to coll. English, 1938. Co-editor: Ideas and Backgrounds, 1964; contbr. articles to lit. hist., polit. jours. Mem. Nat. Coun. Tchrs. of English (dir. coll. sect.), Mark Twain Assn. of Am. (charter mem.), Iowa Colls. Conf. on English, Nat. English Assn., Speech Assn. Am., Phi Kappa Phi, Sigma Pi. *

LORD, ALBERT BATES, literature educator, curator; b. Boston, Sept. 15, 1912; s. Robert Whiting and Corinne Adeline (Bates) L.; m. Mary Louise Carlson, Aug. 24, 1950; children: Nathan Eliot, Mark Edwards. AB, Harvard U., 1934, AM, 1936, PhD, 1949. Lectr. Slavic Harvard U., Cambridge, Mass., 1950-52, assoc. prof. Slavic langs. and lit., 1952-58, prof. Slavic and comparative lit., 1958-91, Arthur Kingsley Porter prof., 1972-91; hon. curator Milman Parry Collection, Harvard Libr., 1959-91. Collection rsch. folk poetry, Yugoslavia, 1934-35, 37, 50-51, 61-64, 66-67, Albania, 1937, Bulgaria, 1958, 59; author: (with Bela Bartok) Serbo-Croatian Folk Songs, 1951, Serbo-Croatian Heroic Songs, 2 vols., 1952-54, (with David E Bynum) Vols. 3 and 4, 1975; Beginning Serbocroatian, 1958, The Singer of Tales, 1960, Beginning Bulgarian, 1962; (with David E. Bynum) A Bulgarian Literary Reader, 1968; Epic Singers and Oral Tradition, 1991. Decorated Order St. Sava, Yugoslavia, Order of Yugoslav Flag with Golden Wreath, 1988; jr. fellow Soc. Fellows, Harvard U., 1937-40; Guggenheim fellow, 1949-50. Home: Cambridge Mass. Died July 29, 1991; buried Mt. Auburn Cemetery, Cambridge, Mass.

LORD, JOHN WESLEY, bishop; b. Paterson, N.J., Aug. 23, 1902; s. John James and Catherine (Carmichael) L.; m. Margaret Farrington Ratcliffe, Apr. 29, 1931; 1 dau., Jean Phillips (Mrs. Arnold C. Cooper). Grad., Montclair (N.J.) State Normal Sch., 1922; BA, Dickinson Coll., 1927; BD, Drew Theol. Sem., 1930; postgrad. in philosophy, U. Edinburgh, Scotland, 1930-31, Rutgers U., 1931-34; DD, Dickinson Coll., 1943, LLD, 1949; STD, Boston U., 1949, Morgan State Coll., 1966; LHD, Western Md. Coll., 1963, Del. State Coll., 1971; LLD, Montclair State Coll., 1975. Tchr., prin. N.J. pub. schs., 1922-24; asst. pastor Emory Meth. Ch., Jersey City, 1927-30; pastor during constrn. with vol. labor Union (N.J.) Community Ch., 1931-34; pastor 1st Meth. Ch., Arlington, N.J., 1935-38, Westfield, N.J., 1938-48; elected bishop Meth. Ch., 1948; consecrated bishop Trinity Meth. Ch., Albany, 1948; assigned Boston area, 1948-60, Washington area, 1960, 64, 68; exec. coordinator The Bishop's Call for Peace and Self Devel. of People, Washington, from 1972; Del. to Gen Conf. The Meth. Ch., 1944-48; mem. Commn. Ecumenical Affairs; pres. Gen. Bd. Pensions; pres. council bishops United Meth. Ch., from 1970; pres. Mass. Council Chs., 1943-55, Meth. Corp., Washington; mem. bd. lay activities N.E. Jurisdiction; mem. gen. bd. Nat. Coun. Chs. of Christ in USA; corporator New Eng. Deaconess Assn. Trustee Claflin Coll., Orangeburg, S.C., Sibley Meml. Hosp., Washington, Am. U., Western Md. Coll., Dickinson Coll., Carlisle, Pa., Morgan Christian Ctr., Morgan State cOll., Balt.; chmn. bd. govs. Wesley Theol. Sem.; mem. and vice chmn. visitors com. Harvard Div. Sch.; mem. Nat. Coun. for Responsible Firearms Policy; chmn. Interreligious Com. on Race; trustee New Eng. Deaconess Hosp., pres., 1950-56; hon. chmn. Com. of Responsibility (for Vietnamese children); mem. U.S. Intereligious Com. on Peace; mem. Clergy and Laymen Concerned about Vietnam. Mem. Phi Kappa Sigma, Tau Kappa Alpha, Masons (33 deg.). Republican. Home: Wolfeboro N.H. Died Oct. 7, 1989; buried Wolfeboro, N.H.

LORD, JOSEPH SIMON, III, federal judge; b. Phila., May 21, 1912; s. Joseph Simon and Irene (Hicks) L.; m. Marie Catherine McCrudden, Nov. 25, 1936; 1 child, Mary Frances; m. Helen H. Kaltenbacher, Aug. 12, 1989. AB with honors, U. Pa., 1933, LLB with honors, 1936; LLD (hon.), Suffolk U., 1975. Bar: Pa. 1937. Assoc. Schnader & Lewis, 1937-42, Schnader, Kenworthy, Segal & Lewis, 1945-46; mem. Richter, Lord & Levy (and predecessor firm), Phila., 1946-61; U.S. atty. Eastern Dist. Pa., 1961; judge U.S. Dist. Ct., Eastern Dist. Pa., 1961-90, chief judge, 1971-82; Lectr. Am. Law Inst.; commr. Delaware River Port Authority. Asso. editor: The Shingle, 1946-54; editor in chief, 1954; editorial bd.: The Practical Lawyer, 1954-76. Served from lt. (j.g.) to lt. comdr. USNR, 1942-45. Mem. Law Alumni Assn. U. Pa. (sec. 1939-42), Order of Coif. Home: Philadelphia Pa. Died Apr. 23, 1991; buried Holy Sepulchre Cemetery, Phila.

LORD, RICHARD COLLINS, chemistry educator; b. Louisville, Oct. 10, 1910; s. Richard and Katherine (Trimble) L.; m. Wilhelmina Van Dyke, June 5, 1943; children: Diana Van Dyke Adam, Susan Trimble Fowlkes, Margaret Collins Adamowicz, Catherine Lewis. BS, Kenyon Coll., 1931, DSc (hon.), 1957; PhD, Johns Hopkins U., 1936. Teaching fellow, rsch. asst. in chemistry Johns Hopkins U., Balt., 1933-36, asst. prof., then assoc. prof., 1938-46; NRC fellow in chemistry U. Mich., Ann Arbor, 1936-37, U. Copenhagen, 1937-38; assoc. prof. MIT, Cambridge, 1946-54, prof., 1954-76, dir. Spectroscopy Lab., 1946-76, prof. emeritus, 1976-89; Reilly prof. chemistry U. Notre Dame, 1958; vis. prof. U. Ga., 1971; tech. aide optics div. NDRC, 1943-46; mem. panel infrared R & D bd. Dept. Def., 1974-52, chmn., 1952-53; cons. Du Pont Co., from 1948; rep. Triple Commn. on Spectroscopy, 1960-65. Author: (with G.R. Harrison and J.R. Loofbourow) Practical Spectroscopy, 1948. Trustee Kenyon Coll., 1960-66, Curry Coll., 1969-89. Recipient Presdl. Cert. of Merit, 1948, Pitts. Spectroscopy awarrd, 1966, Lippincott medal, 1976; Guggenheim fellow, 1959-60. Fellow Am. Acad. Arts and Scis.; mem. Internat. Union Pure and Applied Chemistry (chmn. commn. molecular spectroscopy 1960-67), Soc. Applied Spectroscopy (hon.), Coblentz Soc. (hon.), Am. Chem. Soc., Optical Soc. Am. (pres. 1964), Phi Bet Kappa, Sigma Xi, Psi Upsilon. Home: Milton Mass. Died Apr. 29, 1989; buried Spring Grove Cemetery, Cin.

LORENTE DE NO, RAFAEL, physiologist; b. Zaragoza, Spain, Apr. 8, 1902; came to U.S., 1931, naturalized, 1944; s. Francisco Lorente and Maria de No (de Lorente); m. Hede Birfeld, Mar. 21, 1931; 1 child, Edith. MD, U. madrid, 1923; MD honoris causa, Uppsala U., 1953. Asst. Inst. Cajal, Madrid, 1921-29; head dept. otolaryngology Valdecilla Hosp., Santander, 1929-31; neuro-anatomist Cen. Inst. Deaf, St. Louis, 1931-36; assoc. physiologist Rockefeller Inst., N.Y.C., 1936-38, assoc. mem., 1938-41, mem., 1941-90. Author: A Study of Nerve Physiology, Studies from The Rockefeller Inst., 1947; contbr. articles to profl. jours. Mem. Am. Physiol. Soc., Am. Assn. Anatomists, Am. Neurol. Soc., Nat. Acad. Scis., Am. Acad. Arts and Scis. Home: Los Angeles Calif. Died Apr. 2, 1990.

LORIMER, FRANK, sociologist; b. Bradley, Maine, July 1, 1894; s. Addison Benjamin and Florence Olive (Livermore) L.; m. Faith Moors Williams, Aug. 21, 1i22 (dec. Sept. 1958); children (adopted): Luba Joyce (Mrs. William C. Hill), David (dec.), Thomas; m. E. Peart Barris, Aug. 19, 1962; 1 child, Francine. AB, Yale U., 1916; AM, U. Chgo., 1921; BD, Union Theol. Sem., 1923; PhD, Columbia U., 1929. Assoc. dir. Abraham Lincoln Ctr., Chgo., 1920-21; minister N.Y.C. Bapt. Mission Soc., 1922-25; asst. prof. philosophy Wells Coll., Aurora, N.Y., 1927-28; lectr. in social theory Wellesley (Mass.) Coll., 1928-29; rsch. dir. Bklyn. Conf. in Adult Edn., 1929-30; rsch. fellow Eugenics Rsch. Assn., 1930-34; sec. Population Assn. Am., 1934-39, pres., 1946-47; prof. sociology Grad. Sch. Am. U., 1938-64, prof. emeritus, from 1964; tech. sec. com. population problems of Nat. Resources Com., 1936-37; cons. Nat. Resources Planning Bd., 1938-42, Va. Population Study, 1940-43, Office Strategic Svcs., 1942-43, Fgn. Econ. Adm., 1944-45; chief Population and Employment Br., R.S.D., E.S.S., Hdqr., Tokyo, 1946; adminstrv. dir. Internat. Population Union, 1948-56; rsch. assoc. Princeton U. Office Population Rsch., 1961-64; vis. prof. demography U. Philippines, 1964-66. Author: The Growth of Reason: A Study of the Role of Verbal Activity in the Growth of the Structure of the Human Mind, 1929, The Making of Adult Minds in a Metropolitan Area, 1931, Dynamics of Population; Social and Biological Signifigance of Changing Birth Rates in the United States (with F. Osborn), 1934, Foundations of American Population Policy (with E. Winston and L. Kiser), 1940, Population of the Soviet Union: History and Prospects, 1946, Culture and Human Fertility, 1954, Demographic Information on Tropical Africa, 1961. Served as pvt. Am. Expeditionary Forces World War I. Mem. Internat. Union for Sci. Study of Population (past pres.), Am. Statis. Assn., Am Sociol. Soc. *

LORMAN, WILLIAM RUDOLPH, civil engineer, naval officer; b. Cleve., Sept. 26, 1910; s. Rudolph Calman and Theresa Mary (Pollock) L.; m. Hulda Wanita Babel, May 2, 1936 (dec. May 26, 1980); children: Jonathan, Timothy. BS, Case Western Res. U., 1933; MS, U. Colo., 1939, profl. degree CE, 1956. Asst. dep. engr. Cuyahoga County Engr., Cleve., 1935-36; asst. engr. U.S. Bur. Reclamation, Denver and Redding, Calif., 1936-42; commd. lt. (j.g.) USNR, 1942, advanced through grades to lt. comdr., 1948, ret., 1970; spl. projects officer Air Ctr. Command USN, Vanuatu, 1943-44; helium officer USN, Moffett Field Air Station, Calif., 1944; staff officer Fleet Aircraft Command, Alameda, Calif., 1945-46; civil engr. USN, San Francisco, 1946-48; materials research engr. USN, Solomons, Md., Port Hueneme, Calif., 1948-82; cons. USN liaison DuBridge Oil Lease Panel, Exec. Office of Pres., Office Sci. and Tech., L.A., 1969, Com. Status of Cement and Concrete Rsch. in U.S., Nat. Materials Adv. Bd., Nat. Rsch. Coun., NAS, Washington, 1979-81. Contbr. over 80 articles to profl. jours. Fellow ASCE, Am. Concrete Inst. (com. 115 current rsch. 1955-76, com. 116 nomenclature and terminology 1961-92, com. 209 creep and shrinkage of concrete 1952-92, chmn. 1958-61); mem. ASTM (sr., rep. com. C-1, E-8 terminology 1956-77, subcom. C-1.31 volume change of Portland cement 1952-92, com. C-9 concrete and concrete aggregates 1956-92, subcom. C-9.2.2 chem. reactions of aggregates in concrete 1956-57, subcom. C-9.2.3. Elastic and Inelastic properties of concrete 1956-92, subcom. C-9.3.2. methods of testing for volume changes of concrete and concrete aggregates 1956-92), TROA, Ret. Officers Assn. (sec. Ventura County, Calif. chpt. 1983-87), Nat. Assn. Retired Fed. Employees, Masons (Calif.), Sigma Xi (emeritus). Home: Oxnard Calif. Died July 25, 1992. †

LOURIE, DONALD BRADFORD, former corporation executive; b. Decatur, Ala., Aug. 22, 1899; m. Mary King, Aug. 25, 1923; children: Donald K., Nancy B., Ann Z. Grad., Phillips Exeter Acad.; AB, Princeton U., 1922; LLD, Lincoln Coll., 1956, Cornell U., 1958, Lawrence U., 1965, U. Chattanooga, 1965. With Quaker Oats Co., 1922-90, mem. exec. com., dir., 1945-90, pres., 1947-53, 54-62, CEO, 1956-66, chmn. bd., 1962-70, under-sec. state for adminstrn., 1953-54; dir. No. Trust Co., I.C.R.R., Internat. Paper Co., Internat. Harvester Co. Charter trustee, Princeton, 1948—; mem. corp. Cardigan Mountain Sch., Retina Found. With Central Officers Tng. Corps, U.S. Army, 1918. Recipient Gold medal award Nat. Football Found. and Hall of Fame, 1964. Mem. Comml. Club, Commonwealth Club, Univ. Club, Indian Hill Club, Old Elm Club, Econ. River Club. Home: Longwood Fla. Died Jan. 15, 1990.

LOVE, GEORGE HUTCHINSON, coal company executive, automobile executive; b. Johnstown, Pa.; 3 children. Hon. chmn. bd. Consolidation Coal Co., 1956-72; chmn. Chrysler Corp., 1961-66. Bd. dirs. Gen. Adjustment Bur.; trustee U. Pitts. Mem. Laurel Valley Golf Club pres. . Home: Pittsburgh Pa. Died July 25, 1991.

LOVE, JOHN, JR., mechanical engineering educator; b. Paris, Tex., Jan. 26, 1916; s. John and Stella Maude (Reynolds) L.; m. Marjorie O. Zoeller, May 18, 1942. A.B., U. Mo., 1939; B.Mech. Engring., 1951, M.Mech. Engring., 1953; Ph.D., Okla. State U., 1966. Registered profl. engr., Mo. Condr. Mo.Kans. Tex. R.R., Parsons, Kans., 1939-49; asst. prof. mech. and aero. engring. U. Mo., Columbia, 1951-54; assoc. prof. mech. engring. U. Mo., 1958-78, prof., 1978-84, prof. emeritus, 1984; mgr. requistion engring. Gen. Electric Co., Norwood, Ohio, 1954-58; engring. cons. Black & Veatch (Cons. Engrs.), 1973-84. Mem. editorial bd. Elsevier Sci. Pub. Co., 1974-84. NSF sci. faculty fellow, 1962-63; recipient cert. of appreciation USAF Inst. Tech., 1967. Fellow ASTM (chmn. energy com. 1973-84, com. E-38 on resource recovery 1980, award of merit 1982); mem. Columbia Audubon Soc. (bd. dirs. 1966-68), Sigma Xi, Tau Beta Pi, Pi Tau Sigma, Alpha Chi Sigma. Home: Columbia Mo. Died Apr. 4, 1991; buried Garden of Resurrection, Meml. Pk. Cemetery, Columbia, Mo.

LOVE, MALCOLM A., academic administrator; b. Des Moines, Mar. 10, 1904; s. Forest Andrews and Leona (McGavran) L.; m. Maude Hale, June 9, 1927; 1 child, Joan Evangeline. AB, Simpson Coll., 1927, LLD, 1952; AM, State U. Iowa, 1933, PhD, 1937. Prin. jr. high sch. Marshalltown, Iowa, 1927-29; supt. schs. Monroe, Iowa, 1929-34, Toledo, Iowa, 1934-35; prof. edn. U. Toledo, 1937-38; dean adminstrn. Ill. Wesleyan U., Bloomington, 1938-48, 45-48; dean coll. arts and scis. Denver U., 1948-50; pres. U. Nev., 1950-52, San Diego State U., 1952-71. Lt. USNR. Mem. Masons, Lambda Chi Alpha, Pi Kappa Delta, Phi Kappa Phi. Home: San Diego Calif. Died May 12, 1990.

LOVEJOY, DONALD MESTON, broker; b. New Rochelle, N.Y., Feb. 22, 1897; s. John Francis and Abbie (Babson) L.; m. Winifred Walker, June 6, 1930; children: Donald Walker, Robert Meston, Thomas Babson. Grad., Dartmouth Coll., 1919. Ptnr. Prudential-Bache Securites (formerly Bache & Co.), N.Y.C., 1936-78; pres., co-founder Minent Ltd., 1954-84. Lt. USNR, WWI. Mem. N.Y. Stock Exch. Home: Greenwich Conn. Died July 23, 1990.

LOVELESS, HERSCHEL CELLEL, former governor of Iowa, corporation executive; b. Hedrick, Iowa, May 5, 1911; s. David H. and Ethel (Beaver) L.; m. Amelia R. Howard, Oct. 1, 1933; children: Alan K., Sandi A. Loveless Yates. Grad. high sch. With Chgo., Milw., St. Paul & Pacific Ry., 1927-39, 44-47, John Morrell & Co., Ottumwa, Iowa, 1939-44; supt. streets City of Ottumwa, 1947-49, mayor, 1949-53; owner, mgr. Mcpl. Equipment Co., Ottumwa, 1953-56; gov. State of Iowa, Des Moines, 1957-60; apptd. to Fed. Renegotiation Bd., Washington, 1961-69; v.p. Chromalloy Am. Corp., Washington, 1969-78; vice chmn. bd. E. Bruce Harrison Co., from 1978; bd. dirs. Inter Tech./Solar Corp. Chmn. Coun. Former Govs.; candidate for gov. of Iowa, 1952, for U.S. Senate, 1960. Democrat. Methodist. Home: Winchester Va. Died May 4, 1989; buried Ottumwa Cemetery, Iowa.

LOVESTONE, JAY, union official. BA, CCNY, 1918. Dir. internat. affairs AFL-CIO, until 1974, cons. dept. internat. affairs, from 1974; cons. dept. internat. affairs Internat. Ladies Garment Workers Union; Bd. dirs. Atlantic Council, Council on Fgn. Relations, Com. on Present Danger.; Mem. Pres. Labor Adv. Com., Nat. Planning Assn. (internat. com.). Decorated Grand Cross of Merit Republic of Germany; comdr. Order of Merit Republic of Italy. Mem. U.S. Startegic Inst., Am. Fgn. Service Assn., Nat. Council Sr. Citizens. Home: New York N.Y. Died Mar. 7, 1990.

LOW, ETHELBERT HERRICK, bank executive; s. Ethelbert Ide and Gertrude (Herrick) L.; m. Adelaide Low; children: E. Holland, Elizabeth Stewart. Sr. v.p. United Calif. Bank, San Francisco, 1961-63, execs. v.p., 1963-68, vice chmn. bd., 1968-72, hon. vice chmn., 1972; hon. dir. St. Louis, Continental Ins. Cos., Continental Corp., N.Y.C., Vancouver; dir. Pacific Ins. Co., San Francisco, Pan Am. Bancshares, Inc., Miami, Fla., Consol. Oil and Gas Co., McRae Oil Co.-Petrofund Inc., Houston, Hosp. Affiliates, Inc., Nashville; trustee Atico Mortgage Investors, Inc., Miami, Mills Meml. Hosp. Found., San Mateo; nat. trustee Ducks Unltd.

Maj. USAAF, WWII. Mem. S.R., San Francisco C. of C., River Club, Links Club (N.Y.C.), Pacific Union, Bankers Club (San Francisco), Burlingame County Club (Hillsborough, Calif.). Home: Hillsborough Calif. Died Feb. 14, 1990.

LOWENBERG, MIRIAM ELIZABETH, nutritionist, author; b. Ottumwa, Iowa, July 22, 1897; d. J. A. and Nettie (Cunningham) Lowenberg. PhB, U. Chgo., 1918; postgrad., U. Calif., 1923, student, 1923; student, Washington Med. Sch., 1934; MS, Iowa State Coll., 1929; PhD, State U. Iowa, 1943; DSc. (hon.), Hood Coll., 1960. Tchr. home econs. high schs., Ill. and Mich., 1918-22; head dept. econs. small colls., 1922-27; grad. asst. foods and nutrition Iowa State Coll., 1927-29, asst. prof. foods and nutrition, child devel., 1929-41; chief nutritionist Kaiser child svc. dept. Kaiser Co., Portland, Oreg., 1943-45; nutritional supr. Rochester Child Health Inst., 1946-52; head dept. foods and nutrition Pa. State U., 1952-63; vis. prof. dept. pediatrics and home econs. U. Wash., Seattle, from 1963. Author: Food for the Young Child, 1939, Your Child's Food, 1951, (with Dr. B. J. Spock) Feeding Your Baby and Child, 1955; contbr. articles to profl. publs., nat. mags. Recipient award of merit Iowa State Coll. Alumni, 1958, disting. citizen award Alpha Gamma Delta, 1959; Omicron Nu rsch. fellow, 1943. Mem. AAUW, APHA, P.E.O., Eugene Field Soc. Writers, Am. Dietetic Assn., Pa. Dietetic Assn. (pres. 1957-58), Am. Home Econs. Assn., Pa. Home Econs. Assn., Am. Sch. Food Svc. Assn., Pa. Health Coun., Sigma Xi, Omicron Nu (pres. 1950-52), Phi Gamma Mu, Sigma Delta Epsilon, Phi Kappa Phi, Alpha Gamma Delta. *

LOWY, LOUIS, educator, gerontologist, social worker; b. Prague, Czechoslovakia, June 14, 1920; came to U.S., 1946, naturalized, 1952; s. Max and Anna (Bolz) L.; m. Ditta Jedlinsky, Dec. 2, 1946; children: Susan, Peter. B.S., Boston U., 1949, MSW, 1951; PhD, Harvard U., 1966; PhD (hon.), Wheelock Coll., 1988. Dir. adult and older adult activities Bridgeport Community Ctr, Inc., Conn., 1951-53, asst. exec. dir., dir. older adult program, 1953-55; instr. Sch. of Social Work Boston U., 1955-57, asst. prof. social work, 1957-62, assoc. prof., 1962-66, prof., 1966-85, co-founder, co-dir. Ctr. for Gerontology, 1974-78, assoc. dean for curriculum, 1977-84, dir. joint doctoral program in sociolgy and social work, 1980-85, prof. Grad. Sch. Arts and Scis., 1981-91, prof. emeritus, 1985-91; vis. prof. Ruhr U., Bochum, W.Ger., 1972, U. Pa., 1977; vis. prof. Norfolk Sate U., 1981, 82, 83, 85, 86, U. Essen (W.Ger.), 1982-87; prof. social gerontology Bosotn U. Med. Sch., 1982-91; U.S. and abroad, condr. gerontology seminars, Lucerne, Switzerland, 1977-84, other conf.; mem. Mass. Gov.'s Commn. on Aging, 1970-91; chmn. profl. adv. com. Mass. Exec. Office Elder Affairs, 1971, 81; chmn. steering com. for Mass., White House Conf. on Aging, 1980-81; cons. social policy and social work. Author: (with others) Integrative Teaching and Learning, 1971, Adult Education and Group Work, 1955, Function of Social Work in a Changing Society, 1974, Lehrplanentwicklung, 1974, Social Work with the Aging, 1979, 2d rev. edit., 1985, Kooperation Freitatiger und Beruflicher, 1979, Social Policies and Programs on Aging, 1980, 6th printing, 1985, Sozialarbeit als Wissenschaft, 1983, Comparison of Social Work Methodologies Internationally, 1988; assoc. editor, contbr.: Handbook on Mental Health and Aging, 1977-79; contbg. author: Handbook of Gerontol. Services, 1985; sr. author (with O'Connor) Why Education in the Later Years?, 1986; contbr. over 100 articles and chpts. to profl. jours. and books. Recipient Disting. Alumni award Boston U., 1966, Metcalf award for excellence in teaching and scholarship, 1979; Gerontology Ctr. Library at Boston U. dedicated to Louis Lowy, 1984; Louis Lowy Cert. in Gerontological Studies Boston U. established in his honor, 1978; Disting. award Mass. chpt. Nat. Assn. Social Workers, 1963, 73; Lorenz Werthmann medal for outstanding services W.Ger., 1980; Ollie Randall award Northeastern Gerontol. Soc., 1985; Louis Lowy Fund in gerontology and social welfare established in his honor Boston U., 1989, 70th Birthday Pary Given in his honor, 1990. Fellow Gerontology Soc.; mem. Mass. Gerontol. Assn. (founder, pres. 1975), Nat. Assn. Social Workers (pres. Mass. chpt. 1961-63, Outstanding Lifetime Achievement award Mass. chpt. 1990), Council on Social Work Edn., Am. Sociol. Assn., Internat. Council Social Welfare, Internat. Assn. Schs. Social Work (project dir.), Am.-Swiss Com. for Social Work (pres., founder 1978-85, organizer conf. and symposia). Home: Newton Mass. Died May 22, 1991. †

LUCAS, JOHN H(AROLD), banker; b. Baxter, Pa., Oct. 28, 1984; s. John Simpson and Margaret (Magill) L.; m. Christine Miller; children: John Harold, David Miller. Student, Westminster Coll., 1915-17, Dr. Fin. (hon.), 1940; BS, U. Pitts., 1921. Organizer credit dept. Peoples Savs. & Trust Co., 1925-29, asst. to pres., 1929-37; asst. v.p. Peoples-Pitts. Trust Co., 1937-40, v.p., 1940-52; sr. v.p., dir. Peoples First Nat. Bank & Trust Co., 1952-54, pres., 1954-55, chmn. bd. dirs., 1955-59; vice chmn. bd. Pitts. Nat. Bank, 1959-61, then dir.; bd. dirs. Copperweld Steel Co., Yellow Cab Co., Sawhill Tubular Products, Inc., United Engring. & Foundry Co. Bd. dirs. Jr. Achievement, Better Bus. Bur., Pitts., Pitts. C. of C.; trustee Devereux Found.; treas. Pitts. dist. United Cerebral Palsy Assn. Mem. Robert Morris Assocs., Bankers Club, Econ. Club, Duquesne U. Club, Masons (K.T.), Shriners, Alpha Kappa Psi, Delta Mu Delta, Tau Kappa Alpha. *

LUCKEY, E. HUGH, physician, educator; b. Jackson, Tenn., Jan. 1, 1920; s. David William and Ethel May (Freeman) L.; m. Betty Ann Black, Dec. 25, 1942 (div. 1967); children: Linda Ann, John William, James Hugh, Robert Powers; m. Veronica Kusmin, Dec. 10, 1970. BS, Union U., 1941, ScD, 1954; MD, Vanderbilt U., 1944. Diplomate Am. Bd. Internal Medicine. Intern then asst. resident N.Y. Hosp., 1944-45, 45-46, 1948-49; vis. physician, dir. 2d Cornell Med. div. Bellevue Hosp., N.Y.C., 1950-54; assoc. prof. medicine Cornell U. Med. Sch., 1953-57, prof. medicine, 1957-89; dean Med. Coll., 1954-57; assoc. dean Grad. Sch., 1954-57; pres. N.Y. Hosp.-Cornell Med. Ctr., 1966-77; v.p. med. affairs Cornell U., 1966-77; v.p. Soc. N.Y. Hosp., 1966-77; attending physician N.Y. Hosp., 1955-57, 66-89, trustee Russell Sage Inst. Pathology, 1958-89; mem. cardiovascular study sect. USPHS, 1960-63; spl. med. adv. group to adminstr. VA, 1964-69; past trustee Meml. Sloan-Kettering Cancer Ctr.; past v.p. bd. trustees Vanderbilt U.; past pres. bd. dirs. Assn. Acad. Health Ctrs.; past mem. com. on medicine W.K. Kellogg Found. Capt. USAF, 1946-48. Named hon. prof. Nat. U. Childe, Faculty Medicine, U. Bahia, Brazil; recipient Disting. Alumni award Union U., 1975. Mem. Assn. Am. Physicians, Am. Fedn. Clin. Rsch. Practitioners Soc., Coun. Fgn. Rels., ACP (master, govs. Ea. N.Y. 1959-62, bd. regents 1965-68). Home: New York N.Y. Died Aug. 6, 1989.

LUDLOW, JOHN ALFRED, stock broker; b. East Orange, N.J., Dec. 24, 1894; s. John D. and Eugenie H. (Stubbs) L.; m. Elizabeth Laugher Stockbridge, Sept. 19, 1925 (div.); children: John Afred, Betty Jean (Mrs. B.C. Vautier), Charles Stockbridge; m. Louise Schlachter. With Erie R.R. Co., 1912-18; ptnr. Progressive Die Cutting Co., N.Y.C., 1919; cash grain broker, 1919-29; ptnr. Charles E. Grim Co., N.Y.C., 1930-34, 41-70, Peter R. Lawson & Co., N.Y.C., 1934-41; v.p. Herold Kastor & Gerald, N.Y.C., 1970-75; ltd. ptrn. Moore & Schleye Cameron & Co., N.Y.C., 1975-90. Trustee Village of Saltaire, N.Y., 1950-54, mayor 1954-62; past sr. warden, past vestryman Epsicopalian Ch.. With U.S. Army, 1918-19. Mem. Am. Stoc. Exch. (bd. govs. 1945-48, 62-66), Am. Stock Exch. Mems. Employers Assn. (pres. 1950-70), Am. Stock Exch. Realty Corp. (past chmn.), Saltaire Yacht Club (commodore 1946-48). Home: Upper Montclair N.J. Died July 4, 1990.

LUDWIG, DANIEL K., shipbuilder; b. South Haven, Mich., June 24, 1897. Student, pub. schs. Various positions shipbuilding firms; founder Welding Shipyards, Inc., Norfolk, Va., 1941; owner, operator Welding Shipyards, Inc., N.Y.C., 1936; pres. Sea Tankers, inc., Universe Tankships, Inc.; with Kure Shipyard Div., Japan, Bahama Shipyards, Ltd., Grand Bahama Island; organizer Panama Refining, Inc., Colon, Panama, Exportada de Sal, Baja California, Mex.; owner Hato Vergarena Ranch, Venezuela; bd. dirs. McLean Industries, Inc., Avco Corp.; adviser U.S. maritime policies, oil problems; mem. mil. petroleum adv. bd. Dept. Def.; adv. bd. Nat. Petroleum Coun.; mem. com. Am. Merchant Inst., Inc. Developer welding process to replace riveting in ship building, pioneered technique for side launching newly build ships; improved tanker design to increase payload. *

LUECK, JAMES FERGUSON, JR., publishing company executive; b. Chgo., Nov. 19, 1934; s. James Ferguson and Myrtle Marie (Seiler) L.; m. Carolyn Ann Beduhn, May 23, 1959; children: Steven (dec.), Scott. Student, U. Ill., 1952-55; B.Sc. in Accounting, Loyola U., Chgo., 1957. Mktg. dir. Banker's Life & Casualty Co., Chgo., 1957-73; pres. Fuller & Dees Mktg. Group, Inc., Montgomery, Ala., 1973-77; pres., owner Ess-Jay Ltd. Inc., Montgomery, from 1977. Served with AUS, 1957. Mem. Assn. Third Class Mail Users (dir. 1972-77), Chgo. Mail Advt. Club (dir. 1972-73), Direct Mail Mktg. Assn., Delta Sigma Phi. Lutheran. Lodge: Kiwanis. Home: Montgomery Ala. Deceased.

LUKE, DAVID LINCOLN, III, paper company executive; b. Tyrone, Pa., July 25, 1923; s. David Lincoln and Priscilla Warren (Silver) L.; m. Fanny R. Curtis, June 11, 1955. AB, Yale U., 1945; LLD (hon.), Juniata Coll., 1967, Lawrence U., 1976, Salem Coll., 1983, W. Va. U., 1984. V.p., dir. Westvaco Corp., N.Y.C., 1953-57, exec. v.p., dir., 1957-62, pres., bd. dirs., 1962-80, chief exec. officer, 1963-88, chmn. bd. dirs., from 1980; bd. dirs. Clupak, Inc., McGraw Hill Inc., N.Y. Stock Exch. Trustee Cold Spring Harbor Lab.; bd. dirs. Josiah Macy Jr. Found.; past chmn., trustee emeritus Hotchkiss Sch. Served from aviation cadet to capt. USMCR., 1942-45. Mem. Am. Paper Inst. (past chmn.), Inst. Paper Sci. and Tech. (trustee, past chmn.). Clubs: Links, The River (N.Y.C.); Piping Rock, Megantic Fish and Game Corp. Home: New York N.Y. Deceased. †

LUKE, HUGH J., English language educator; b. Kilgore, Tex., Feb. 26, 1932; s. Hugh J. and Stella Avis (Hamon) L.; m. Joyce McCain, Feb. 22, 1954 (div. 1969); 2 children—Karin Luke Kuhl, Richard; m. Virginia Carol Pavelka, Aug 15, 1969; 1 child, Katherine Pavelka. Student, Baylor U., 1949-51; B.A., U. Tex., 1956, M.A., 1957, Ph.D., 1963. Instr. English San Antonio Coll., Tex., 1957-58; asst. prof. English Tex. A&M Coll., College Station, Tex., 1961-63, U. Nebr., Lincoln, 1963-66, 1966-71, prof. English, 1971-88. Editor: The Last Man (Mary Shelley), 1965; William Blake, A Critical Essay (Swinburne), 1971; contbr. articles to profl. jours., literary revs.; assoc. editor Prairie Schooner, 1968-79, editor, 1980-87, sr. editor fiction, 1987-88; author: Gestures of Shape, Motions of Form in Modern Critical Views. Marched for Civil Rights with Martin Luther King, Selma, Ala., 1965; dir. research for Phillip Sorensen, Democratic candidate for gov. Nebr., 1966, Nebr. campaign for Robert Kennedy Presdl. Campaign, 1968; Nebr. sgt.-at-arms Dem. Nat. Conv., 1968, Chgo.; mem. steering com. Nebr. for Edward Kennedy, 1980. Served to sgt. U.S. Army, 1951-53. Fellow U. Tex., Austin, 1958-59, 59-60. Unitarian. Club: Torch. Home: Lincoln Neb. Died Nov. 23, 1988; body donated to science.

LUKIN, PHILIP, publisher, business consultant; b. N.Y.C., June 26, 1903; s. Nicholas and Sonya (Kranz) L.; m. May Harriet Shatt, 1926 (div. 1929); m. Cecil Schultz, Dec. 12, 1933 (dec. Sept. 1953); children: Richard, Alexandra (dec.); m. Vera Racolin Fadiman Cameo, May 23, 1957. Student, N.Y. U., 1921-22; Ph.B., Brown U., 1924. Copywriter, mag. salesman Robbins Pub. Co., N.Y.C., 1924-26; v.p., gen. mgr. Charles Austin Bates, Inc., N.Y.C., 1926-33; v.p. Lawrence Fertig & Co., Inc., N.Y.C., 1933-60, pres., 1960-61; sr. v.p., gen. mgr. wine and spirits div. Lennen & Newell, Inc. (advt.), N.Y.C., 1961-67, chmn. exec. com., 1966-67, cons., 1967-70; pres. Bolte, Lukin & Assocs., Inc. (bus. cons.), Palm Beach, Fla., 1969-74; chmn. The Bio-Virological Labs., West Palm Beach, Fla., 1972-76, Edgar D. Mitchell Corp., Palm Beach, 1975-76; prin. Philip Lukin, Bus. Cons., Palm Beach, 1977-90; chmn., editorial dir. Palm Beach Social Pictorial, Inc., 1978-88; editor, co-publisher Palm Beach Social Observer, 1988-90. Chmn. info. com. Unitarian Laymen's League, Boston, 1957-61, ch. lay leader, trustee; fellow Met. Mus. Art; alumni adv. council Brown U., 1934-50. Decorated knight comdr. Order St. John Jerusalem (Knights of Malta U.S.). Mem. N.Y. Acad. Polit. Sci. Clubs: Brown U. (N.Y.C.) (bd. govs. 1930-45), Lotos (N.Y.C.), Poinciana (Palm Beach, Fla.), Palm Beach Polo and Country (Palm Beach, Fla.), Tavern (Chgo.), Hurlingham (London), Royal Automobile (London). Home: Palm Beach Fla. Died Oct. 28, 1990.

LUMPKIN, GEORGE THOMAS, JR., financial planner, banker; b. Suffolk, Va., Nov. 30, 1919; s. George Thomas and Kate (Bagley) L.; m. Thelma Lydia Santoro, Nov. 10, 1966; children: Kathryn Love, George Thomas III. B.S., Wake Forest Coll., 1940; M.A., U. Mich., 1946; certificate, Grad. Sch. Banking, Rutgers U., 1951. Asst. actuary Integon Ins. Co., Winston-Salem, N.C., 1940-43; v.p., actuary Pension Service Co., Winston-Salem, 1946-47; v.p., trust officer Wachovia Bank & Trust Co., Winston-Salem, 1948-64; sr. v.p., trust officer Citytrust, Bridgeport, Conn., 1964-84; prin. G. Thomas Lumpkin Assocs., specializing in personal fin. planning, Bethany, Conn., 1984-89; guest lectr. on trust U. N.C., 1954-59, U. Va., 1957, U. Conn., 1965. Served with USAAF, 1943. Mem. Omicron Delta Kappa, Alpha Sigma Phi. Mem. Ch. of Christ. Club: Waterbury Rotary. Home: Bethany Conn. Died Apr. 25, 1989; buried Calvary Cemetery, Waterbury, Conn.

LUND, ARTHUR EARL, actor, entertainer; b. Salt Lake City, Apr. 1, 1915; s. Arthur Earl and Lillie Alma (Gotberg) L.; m. Kathleen Virginia Bolanz (dec.); children: Kathleen Ann, Arthur Earl III; m. Janet B. Chytraus, May 1, 1989. Grad., Westminster Jr. Coll., Salt Lake City, 1935, HHD (hon.), 1977; BS, East Ky. State U., 1937; MA, U.S. Naval Acad., Annapolis, Md., 1943. Baritone singer Benny Goodman Band, N.Y.C., 1941-42, 46-47, night clubs, TV shows, 1947-67; rec. artist Metro-Goldwyn-Mayer, 1947-56, Broadway cast albums, 1956-76; actor Broadway mus., N.Y.C. and London, 1957-67; film actor Hollywood, Calif., 1957-67; actor guest spots various TV shows, 1962-87; singer Billy May Orch., Australian tour, 1986-87. Creator role of Joey in Broadway musical The Most Happy Fella, 1956, other Broadway show Donneybrook!; appeared in off-Broadway prodn. Of Mice and Men, 1958; in touring cos. Fiorello!, No Strings, Destry Rides Again; films include The Molly Maguires, 1968, The Last American Hero, 1973; TV appearances include Gunsmoke, The Rockford Files, Little House on the Prairie, The Winds of War. Served to lt. comdr. USN, 1942-46, PTO. Recipient Star in Hollywood Walk of Fame, 1951; named Best Band Singer Metronome mag., 1947; Five Gold records for songs that include Blue Skies, My Blue Heaven, Mam'selle. Mem. Screen Actors Guild, AFTRA, Actors Equity Assn. Mem. LSD Ch. Home: Holliday Utah Died May 31, 1990; buried Forest Lawn Meml. Pk., L.A.

LUNDEEN, MALVIN HJALMAR, clergyman; b. Chgo., May 29, 1901; s. Hjalmar K. and Malvina Zetterlund L.; m. Anna Lorraine Sellin, Sept. 16, 1925; children: Richard, John, David, James. AB, Augustana Coll., 1925, BD, 1927, LLD, 1962; DD, Muhlenberg Coll., 1962. Ordained to ministry, Luth. Ch., 1927. Pastor Grace Ch., Des Moines, 1927-35, First Ch., Ottumwa, Iowa, 1935-54, Grace Ch., LaGrange, Ill., 1954-59; pres. Iowa Conf. Augustana Luth. Ch., 1946-52; v.p. Augustana Evang. Luth. Ch., 1951-59, pres., 1959-62; chmn. Joint Commn. on Luth. Unity, 1956-62; sec. Luth. Ch. in Am., 1962-68; asst. to pres. Minn. Synod Luth. Ch. Am., 1968-72; pres. Luth. Coun. in U.S.A., 1967-70; chmn. bd. dirs. Religion in Am. Life, 1965-67; mem. bd. mgrs. Am. Bible Soc., 1967-69. Contbr. articles to Church Press. Decorated comdr. Royal Order of North Star Sweden . Mem. Rotary. Home: Sun City Ariz. Died May 25, 1991.

LUNDQUIST, CARL HAROLD, college president, minister; b. Elgin, Ill., Nov. 16, 1916; s. Henry and Esther (Gustafson) L.; m. Nancy Mae Zimmerman, Sept. 15, 1942; children: Carole Lundquist Spickelmier, Eugene, Jill Lundquist Anderson, Susan Lundquist Robinson. B.A., Sioux Falls Coll., 1939; B.D., Bethel Theol. Sem., 1943; Th.M., Eastern Bapt. Theol. Sem., 1946; D.D. No. Bapt. Theol. Sem, 1957; Th.D., No. Bapt. Theol. Sem., 1960; LL.D., Houghton Coll., 1982. Ordained to ministry Baptist Ch., 1944; pastor Elim Bapt. Ch., Chgo., 1943-53; pres. Bethel Coll., St. Paul, 1954-82, Bethel Sem., St. Paul, 1954-82, Christian Coll. Consortium, 1982-91; chmn. com. on devel. Bapt. World Alliance; chmn. Evangel. Sem. Pres.'s Fellowship. Trustee Bapt. Hosp. Fund, St. Paul, Internat. Grad. Sch. Theology, San Bernadino, Calif.; mem. adv. bd. Discovery Network, Worldwide Friendship, Youth Investment Inc.; bd. dirs. World Relief Corp., Evang. Order of Burning Heart. Mem. NEA, Nat. Assn. Evangs. (bd. adminstrn.), Sem. Profs. in Practical Fields, Speech Assn. Club: Minnesota. Lodge: Rotary. Home: Saint Paul Minn. Died Feb. 27, 1991; buried Hillside Cemetery, Mpls.

LUNN, JOHN ALECK, manufacturing executive; b. Ft. Colorado, Colo., Sept. 6, 1894; s. John Gordon and Kate Eugenia (Wentz) L.; m. Susan Elizabeth Williams, Feb. 4, 1926; children: Jean Williams, John Gordon. BS, Colo. A & M Coll., 1915, MS, 1921, DSc (hon.), 1936; BS, Harvard Engring. Sch., 1917; SB, MIT, 1917. Rsch. in refrigeration Cambridge, Mass., 1919-23; factory mgr. Nat. Refrigerating Co., Boston, 1923-26; sales engr. Winchester Repeating Arms Co., 1926-29; with Dewey & Almy Chem. Co., Cambridge, 1929-50, v.p., 1950; v.p., dir. mfg. and dir. The Kendall Co., Boston, 1950-60, cons., dir., from 1960; dir. Lab. for Electronics, United Rsch., Inc., Foursquare Fund, Trans-Sonics, Inc., Jamesbury Corp., Am. Rsch. & Devel. Corp., Spencer Kennedy Labs., Mass. Small Bus. Investment Co., Baystate Corp., Adage, Inc.; trustee North Ave. Savs. Bank; mem. corp. Cambridge Savs. Bank; chmn. Cambridge Redevel. Authority, from 1960. Contbr. articles to trade and tech. publs. Mem. corp. Browne & Nichols Sch., MIT; pres. trustees Franklin Found. and Inst.; dir. Civic Assn., C. of C. 2d lt. Corps Engrs., 1st lt. and capt. C.W.S., A.E.F., 1917-19; group leader with FIAT investigation, German Chem. Industry, 1946. Mem. ASME (life), Alumni Assn. MIT (prs. 1950-51), Brookline Country Club, MIT Faculty Club, Harvard Club, Cambridge Club, Cambridge Boat Club, Army and Navy Club, Masons, Mass. Iota Tau Assn. (bd. dirs.), Sigma Alpha Epsilon, Theta Tau. *

LURIA, SALVADOR EDWARD, biology educator; b. Turin, Italy, Aug. 13, 1912; came to U.S., 1940, naturalized, 1947; s. David and Ester (Sacerdote) L.; m. Zella Hurwitz, Apr. 18, 1945; 1 son, Daniel. MD, U. Turin, 1935. Research fellow Curie Lab., Inst. of Radium, Paris, 1938-40; research asst. surg. bacteriology Columbia U., 1940-42; successively instr., asst. prof., asso. prof. bacteriology Ind. U., 1943-50; prof. bacteriology U. Ill., 1950-59; prof. microbiology MIT, 1959-64, Sedgwick prof. biology, 1964, Inst. prof., 1970-72, Inst. prof. emeritus, 1972-91; founder, dir. Ctr. for Cancer Rsch., MIT, 1972-85; non-resident fellow Salk Inst. Biol. Studies, from 1965; lectr. biophysics U. Colo., 1950; Jesup lectr. zoology Columbia U., 1950; Nieuwland lectr. biology U. Notre Dame, 1959; Dyer lectr. NIH, 1963; with OSRD, Carnegie Instn., Washington, 1945-46. Assoc. editor: Jour. Bacteriology, 1950-55; editor: Virology, 1955—; sect. editor: Biol. Abstracts, 1958-62; editorial bd.: Exptl. Cell Research Jour, 1948—; adv. bd.: Jour. Molecular Biology, 1958-64; hon. editorial adv. bd.: Jour. Photochemistry and Photobiology, from 1961. Co-recipient Nobel prize for medicine and physiology, 1969; Guggenheim fellow Vanderbilt U. and Princeton U., 1942-43, Pasteur Inst., Paris, 1963-64. Mem. Am. Philos. Soc., Am. Soc. Microbiology (pres. 1967-68), Nat. Acad. Scis., Am. Acad. Arts and Scis., AAAS, Soc. Gen. Microbiology, Genetics Soc. Am., AAUP, Sigma Xi. Home: Lexington Mass. Died Feb. 6, 1991.

LUSH, GERSON HARRISON, consultant; b. Phila., May 2, 1912; s. Max and Anna Leah (Harrison) L.; m. Claire Werchow, Nov. 25, 1937; children—Lee M., Anne, Susan. Student, George Washington U., U. Md. Reporter, newswriter Phila. Inquirer, 1933-40; chief Harrisburg (Pa.) bur., 1940-50; corr., contbr. N.Y. Times, Life and Time mags., Pitts. Press, Erie (Pa.) Times, 1940-50; adminstrv. asst. to U.S. Senator Duff, 1951-57; Washington dir. Office U.S. Commr. Gen., Brussels World's Fair, 1957-59; U.S. fgn. service res. officer, 1959-77, spl. asst. to dep. asst. sec. state for budget and finance, 1959-60, spl. asst. to asst. sec. state for adminstrn., 1960-65; dir. policy and pub. info. affairs program Office Dep. Under Sec. State for Adminstrn., Dept. State, 1965-72; dir. newsletter and info. Office Dir. Gen., U.S. Fgn. Service, 1972-77; govt. cons., 1977-78, 83-84; pub. affairs cons., adviser state and nat. polit. campaigns, 1952, 54, 56; pres. Pa. Legis. Corrs. Assn., 1949-50. Editor: Dept. State Newsletter, 1961-77; contbr. to Ency. Brit. Yearbook, 1959; contbr.-vol. Clearinghouse Newsletter, D.C. Mem. U.S. Senate Assn. Adminstrv. Assts. and Secs. Club: Nat. Press (Washington). Home: Washington D.C. Died Sept. 26, 1989; buried Judean Meml. Gardens, Olney, Md.

LUSK, HAROLD F., law educator; b. Owosso, Mich., Oct. 25, 1893; s. Walter Scott and Elizabeth Alma (Faver) L.; m. Vera Miller Ricker, June 3, 1922; children: Betty Jane (Mrs. Guy William Leonard Jr.), Barbara Jean (Mrs. Richard H. Buskirk). Life cert., Cen. Mich. Normal Coll., 1914; AB, U. Mich., 1921, JD, 1925, SJD, 1941. Bar: Mich. 1925. Practice law Grand Rapids, Mich., 1925-31; asst. prof. bus. law Ind. U., 1921-26, assoc. prof., 1936-39, prof., 1939-64, prof. emeritus, from 1964; vis. prof. bus. law CCNY, summer 1936; teaching fellow Law Sch., U. Mich., 1938-39; vis. prof. bus. law Ohio U., summer 1939. Author: Business Law, Principles and Cases, 7th edit., 1963, Legal Aspects of Business, 1949, Law of Real Estate Business, 1958, Indiana Supplement to Law of Real Estate Business, 1961; contbr. to Nat. Ency., 1957 edit., also legal periodicals. Ens. USN, 1917-18; dir. Office Mil. Info., Ind. U., 1943-45. Mem. Bus. Law Assn. (pres. 1940-41), Rotary (pres. Bloomington chpt. 1958-59), Masons, Acacia, Beta Gamma Sigma, Sigma Delta Kappa, Delta Sigma Pi. Republican. *

LUTNICKI, VICTOR A., insurance company executive; b. Chgo., Dec. 20, 1914; s. Anthony E. and Anna (Angel) L.; m. Harriet Howe, Feb. 4, 1940; children—Anne, Robert, William. B.A., Northwestern U., 1936, J.D., 1939; grad., Advanced Mgmt. Program, Harvard U., 1953. Bar: Ill. bar 1939, Mass. bar 1946. Asst. counsel Am. Life Conv., 1938- 42, 46; counsel, officer John Hancock Mut. Life Ins. Co., Boston, 1946-55, v.p., gen. solicitor, 1956-57, v.p. in charge group ins. ops., mem. exec. com., 1957-61, sr. v.p., 1961-67, exec. v.p., 1967-80; dir. John Hancock Mut. Life Ins. Co., 1966-80; chmn. bd. Windsor Life Ins. Co. Am., 1981-88, John Hancock Internat. Services (S.A.); pvt. practice law, 1980—; dir. mem. exec. and fin. com. Maritime Life (Caribbean) Ltd.; dir. Arthur D. Little Mgmt. Edn. Inst., Inc., Maritime Life Ins. Co., Halifax, N.S., Can., Flagstaff Corp.; Participant Aspen (Colo.) Inst. Humanistic Studies, 1960, moderator, 1961; corporator Mus. of Sci., Boston; bd. dirs. Am. Mgmt. Assn.; pres. bd. DeCordova and Dana Mus.; alumni regent Northwestern U. Contbr. articles to profl. publs. Chmn. bd. trustees Andover Newton Theol. Sch. Served to lt. comdr., aviation USNR, 1942-46. Decorated Air medal. Mem. Am. Bar Assn. (ho. dels.), Assn. Life Ins. Counsel, Phi Beta Kappa. Mem. United Ch. Christ (moderator). Clubs: Univ. (N.Y.C.). Home: Lincoln Center Mass. Died Nov. 2, 1988; buried Lincoln Ctr., Mass.

LUXON, NORVAL NELL, journalism educator; b. New London, Ohio, May 16, 1989; s. Jesse E. and Edna (Walker) L.; m. Ermina Cornelia Munn, Sept. 22, 1928; 1 child, Norval Neil. BS, Ohio State U., 1923, MA, 1931; PhD, U. Calif., Berkeley, 1940. Asst. city editor Columbus (Ohio) Citizen, 1923-25; city editor Canton (Ohio) Daily News, 1925; editor Oteen (N.C.) Skylight, 1926-27; asst. news editor El Paso (Tex.) Herald, 1927-28; instr., asst. prof., assoc. prof. journalism Ohio State U., Columbus, 1928-42, prof., 1942-53, asst. to pres., 1946-53; dean U. N.C. Sch. Journalism, Chapel Hill, 1953-64, prof., 1964-66, Alumni disting. prof., from 1966; chmn. accrediting com. Am. Coun. on Edu. for Journalism, 1946-53; del. internat. expert meeting on profl. tng. in journalism UNESCO, Paris, 1956. Author books, including Niles' Weekly Register: News Magazine of the Nineteenth Century, 1947, (with Philip W. Porter) The Reporter and the News, 1935, (with others) New Survey of Journalism, rev. edit., 1958, Education for the Professions, 1955, The Training of Journalists, 1958; also articles. With USN, 1917-19. Mem. AAUP, Assn. for Edn. in Journalism (pres. 1957), Am. Soc. Newspaper Editors, Am. Assn. Schs. and Depts. Journalism (pres. 1948), Soc. Profl. Journalists (Disting. Svc. award for rsch. in journalism 1939), Am. Legion, Rotarian, Sigma Nu. Home: Chapel Hill N.C. Died Sept. 4, 1989; buried Chapel of the Cross, Chapel Hill, N.C.

LYFORD, FREDERIC E(UGENE), consulting engineer; b. Waverly, N.Y., Jan. 20, 1895; s. Frederic Eugene and Jane Elizabeth (Lemon) L.; m. Eleanor Cabot, Oct. 30, 1920 (dec.); children: Nancy (Mrs. Robert Kiley), Frederic, Geoffrey, Sylvia (Mrs. R. B. Morgan); m. Walmy Dösvig Kleivdal, Dec. 16, 1957. M Engring., Cornell U., 1916. Shipfitter Bethlehem Steel Co., Sparrows Point, Md., 1916-17; insp. machine tool factories Allied Machinery Co. of Am., N.Y.C., 1917, fgn. sales agt., 1919-20; mgr. sales promotion Tioga Mills, Waverly, N.Y., 1920-23; with Lihigh Valley R.R., 1923-33, spl. engr. to exec. v.p., 1929-33; examiner R.R. div. Reconstrn. Fin. Corp., Washington, 1934-36; asst. to v.p. in charge of sales Baldwin Locomotive Works, Phila., 1936-37; trustee N.Y., Ohio & Western Ry., N.Y.C., 1937-44; asst. to chmn. bd. dirs. Merritt-Chapman & Scott Corp., N.Y.C., 1944-46, pres., dir., 1946-49; ptnr. Lyford and Eberle, 1949-52, cons. engr., from 1953; cons. harbors, heavy transp. various steel cos., railroads; exec. dir. Coun. Engring. Laws, from 1954. 1st lt. F.A., attached to air svc. as aerial observer, France, 1917-19; served as chief of Am. R.R. Mission to Portuguese r.r.s in their African Colonies of Angola and Mozambique for Office of Econ. Warfare, June-Nov. 1943. Mem. ASME (chmn. several coms. from 1941), Newcomen Soc. Eng., The Moles, Engrs. Club, India House Club, Shenorock Shore Club. Republican. Presbyterian. *

LYFORD, JOSEPH PHILIP, former journalism educator; b. Chgo., Aug. 4, 1918; s. Philip and Ruth (Pray) L.; m. Margaretta Jean Thomas, Feb. 16, 1963; children: Amy Jean, Joseph Philip. Grad., Phillips Acad., Andover, Mass., 1937; A.B. with honors, Harvard, 1941. Reporter Boston Post, 1938-41, Internat. News Service, 1946-47; asst. editor New Republic, 1947-48; press sec. to Gov. Bowles of Conn., 1949-50; exec. sec. to Senator Benton of Conn., 1950; European corr. Hartford (Conn.) Times, 1951; dir. staff Pub. Edn. Assn., N.Y.C., 1953-55; exec. Fund for Republic, 1955-66; prof. journalism U. Calif.-Berkeley, from 1966, now prof. emeritus; cons. Center Study Democratic Instns., Santa Barbara, Calif., 1966-92, Pub. Broadcast Lab., N.Y.C., 1968, subcom. exec. reorgn. U.S. Senate, 1966. Author: Candidate, The Agreeable Autocracies, 1961, The Talk in Vandalia, 1963, The Airtight Cage, 1966, The Berkeley Archipelago, 1981; also articles. Mem. bd. edn. Dist. 5, N.Y.C., 1964-66; chmn. Democratic Town Com., Westport, Conn., 1950-52; Dem. candidate for Congress, 1952, 54; pres. Fund For Peace, N.Y.C., 1969-71, trustee, 1969-92. Served to lt. USNR, 1941-46. Decorated for outstanding performance of duty during Okinawa invasion, 1947; recipient Sidney Hillman Found. award in lit., 1967. Mem. Council Fgn. Relations. Conglist. Home: Orinda Calif. Died Dec. 2, 1992. †

LYLE, MARY STEWART, home economics educator; b. Sibley, Ill., Sept. 12, 1897; d. Albert Francis and Rebecca (Stewart) L. Diploma, Ea. Ill. State Tchrs. Coll., 1917; BS, Purdue U., 1921; MS, Iowa State Coll., 1924; PhD, Ohio State U., 1942. High sch. tchr. Ill., 1917-19; head dept. home econs. Hardin Jr. Coll., Mexico, Mo., 1921-23; grad. asst. Iowa State U., 1923-24, asst. prof. home econs. edn., 1930-38, assoc. prof., 1938-42, prof., from 1943; critic tchr., home econs. tchr. gnr. Oreg. State Agrl. Coll., 1924-26; state supr. home econs. edn. Wyo., 1926-30; asst. prof. home econs. edn. U. Wyo., 1926-29; chmn. home sci. project, vis. prof. home sci. edn. and ext. Baroda (India) U., 1961-63. Author: Adult Education for Democracy in Family Life, 1944, (with Maude Williamson) Homemaking Education in High School, 1961, Homemaking Education for Adults, 1949. Elder local Presbyn. ch. Mem. NEA, AAUP, AAUW, Am. Vocat. Assn., Adult Edn. Assn., Am. Home Econs. Assn., Am. Ednl. Rsch. Assn., Bus. and Profl. Women's Club, Phi Kappa Phi, Pi Lambda Theta, Kappa Delta Pi, Omicron Nu, Delta Kappa Gamma, Chi Omega. *

LYMAN, RONALD THEODORE, JR., investment counsel; b. Waltham, Mass., Aug. 12, 1905; s. Ronald Theodore and Eliabeth Van Cortlandt (Parker) L.; m. Olivia L. Morgan Hallowell, June 14, 1941 (div.); children: Elizabeth P., Jennifer Lyman Littlefield, Mabel Lowell Lyman Whiteside; m. Susan Jameson Storey Shaw, Dec. 30, 1950; 1 child, Ronald Theodore III. AB magna cum laude, Harvard U., 1928. With Southwestern Stores, Tulsa, 1929-30; joined Scudder, Stevens & Clark, Boston, 1930, ptnr., 1940-70; pres. Scudder, Stevens & Clark Balanced Fund, Inc., Boston, Scudder, Stevens & Clark Common Stock Fund; pres., bd. dirs. Scudder Fund Distbrs., Inc.; vice chmn. bd. dirs. Waltham (Mass.) Fed. Savs. & Loan Assn.; bd. dirs. Fiduciary Trust Co. Trustee, asst. treas. Peter Bent Brigham Hosp., Boston. Comdr. USNR, 1941-45. Mem. Somerset Club, Union Boat Club, Phi Beta Kappa. Home: Boston Mass. Died Mar. 19, 1990; buried Mt. Auburn Cemetery, Cambridge, Mass.

LYNCH, EDWARD MICHAEL, labor union official; b. Brockport, N.Y., Oct. 1, 1920; s. Joseph R. and Ida M. (Ritchlin) L.; m. Gloria Jeanne Mangano, Nov. 25, 1978. Student parochial and pub. schs., Rochester, N.Y. Broadcast technician Sta. WHEC, Rochester, 1946-52; local pres. Nat. Assn. Broadcast Employees and Technicians, Rochester, 1947-52; regional dir. Nat. Assn. Broadcast Employees and Technicians, Buffalo, 1952-68; network coord. Nat. Assn. Broadcast Employees and Technicians, Bethesda, Md., 1968-86, internat. pres., 1971-86. Sgt. Signal Corps, AUS, 1943-46. Home: Gaithersburg Md. Died Nov. 22, 1991; buried Holy Sepulchre Cemetery, Rochester, N.Y.

LYNCH, ROBERT JOSEPH, foreign trade industry executive; b. N.Y.C., May 31, 1901; s. Patrick S. and Bridget A. (Feeney) L.; m. Mary Louise Farraher, July 21, 1929; children: Robert J., Richard T., Ronald P., Ralph D., Roger M., Rosemary Louise, Raymond E., Russell A., Rita Ann. Student, Fordham U., 1919-20, CCNY, 1921-22. Various positions GMC, 1927-30, 31-32; asst. aviation mgr. Gen. Motors Export Corp., 1930-31; supr. svcs. stas. Tex. Oil Corp., 1932-34; sec. to chmn. bd. U.S. Steel Corp., 1934-40; asst. to chmn. War

Resources Bd., Washington, 1939; asst. to commr. Coun. Nat. Def., 1940-41; exec. asst. to dir. priorities OPM, 1941; asst. adminstr. and exec. asst. to adminstr. Office Lend-Lease Adminstrn., 1941-43; spl. asst. to undersec. state Washington, 1943-44; spl. asst. to sec. state, 1944; spl. asst. to U.S. rep. UN and Security Coun. UN, 1945; pres. Lynch, Wilde & Co., Inc., 1946; pres., dir. Culpeper Corp., Richmond, 1947; pres. Am. and Fgn. Enterprises, Inc., 1947; v.p. Ingenieria y Construcciones Sala Amat. S.A., Madrid, Spain; gen. ptnr. Lynch Farm Enterprises, Centreville, Md. Spl. asst. to chmn. Am. delegation Inter-Am. Conf. on Problems of War and Peace, Mexico City, 1945, to chmn. and pres. UN Conf. on Internat. Orgn., San Francisco, 1945; dir. mem. exec. com. Internat. Rgn. Adminstrn; mem. nat. adv. bd. Am. Security Coun., Washington. Mem. Soc. Advancement Mgmt., Am. Arbitration Assn. (dir.), Pan-Am. Soc., English Speaking Union, Larchmont Yacht Club, Rockefeller Ctr. Luncheon Club (N.Y.C.), Met. Club (Washington), Clipper Club, Heritage Village Country Club (Southbury, Conn.). Home: Fairfield Conn. Died Feb. 9, 1989.

LYNCH-STAUNTON, FRANK C., Canadian provincial official; b. Pincher Creek, Alta., Can., Mar. 8, 1905; m. Monica Adams, Sept. 21, 1929 dec. Sept. 1976 ; children: Betty Lowe, Marina Field, Hugh.; m. Muriel Shaw, 1983. Student, U. Alta., 1923-27. With Imperial Oil Co.; founding mem. and dir. Community Auction Sales; councillor Mcpl. Dist., Pincher Creek; lt. gov. Province of Alta., Edmonton, 1979-85; mem. Govt. House Bd., 1978-79. Senator U. Lethbridge; mem. Can. Coun., 1959-65; bd. dirs. Glenbow Found., 1974-79. Maj. Can. Militia and Army Res., 1934-42. Home: Edmonton Can. Died Sept. 25, 1990.

LYNES, (JOSEPH) RUSSELL, JR., editor, author; b. Great Barrington, Mass., Dec. 2, 1910; s. Joseph Russell and Adelaide (Sparkman) L.; m. Mildred Akin, May 30, 1934; children—George Platt II, Elizabeth Russell. Student, Cathedral Choir Sch., N.Y., 1920-25, Berkshire Sch., Sheffield, Mass., 1925-28; B.A., Yale U., 1932; D.F.A. (hon.), Union Coll., Schenectady; L.H.D., Md. Inst., 1973, CUNY, 1980; Litt.D., North Adam State Coll., 1977. With Harper & Bros. (pubs.), 1932-36; dir. publs. Vassar Coll., Poughkeepsie, N.Y., 1936-37; asst. prin. Shipley Sch., Bryn Mawr, Pa., 1937-40, prin., 1940-44; asst. chief, civilian tng. br. Army Service Forces, War Dept., Washington, 1942-44; asst. editor Harper's Mag., 1944-47, mng. editor, 1947-67, contbg. editor, 1967-82. Author: Highbrow, Lowbrow, Middlebrow, 1949, Snobs, 1950, Guests, 1951, The Tastemakers, 1954, A Surfeit of Honey, 1957, Cadwallader, 1959, The Domesticated Americans, 1963, Confessions of a Dilettante, 1966, The Art-Makers of 19th Century America, 1970, Good Old Modern, 1973, More Than Meets the Eye, 1981, The Lively Audience, 1985, Life in the Slow Lane,1991; contbg. editor: Art in Am., 1969-71; Contbr. articles, stories, essays to mags. Mem. Landmarks Preservation Commn., N.Y.C., 1962-68, Art Commn., 1971-73; asso. fellow Berkeley Coll., Yale U.; mem. Humanities Com., Whitney Found.; trustee emeritus N.Y. Hist. Soc., Am. Acad. in Rome; pres. bd. trustees Archives of Am. Art, 1966-71, McDowell Colony, 1969-73; hon. trustee Cooper-Hewitt Mus.; mem. vis. com. for Am. art Met. Mus. Fellow Soc. Am. Historians; Benjamin Franklin fellow Royal Soc. Arts; mem. Authors League Am., P.E.N., Soc. Archtl. Historians, Zeta Psi. Episcopalian. Club: Century (N.Y.C.). Home: New York N.Y. Died Sept. 15, 1991; buried North Egremont, Mass.

LYNN, HENRY SHARPE, investment banker; b. Pitts., July 16, 1907; s. Albert Maxfield and Ethel Hansell (Sharpe) L.; m. Fariss Gambrill, Feb. 4, 1942; children: Henry Sharpe, George Gambrill. AB, Princeton U., 1928; MBA, Harvard U., 1930. Clk., salesman Sterne, Agee & Leach, Inc., Birmingham, 1930-40, ptnr., 1951-63, v.p., treas., 1963-67, pres., 1967-76, chmn. exec. com., 1976-82, vice chmn. bd., 1982-89, also bd. dirs.; asst. v.p., then v.p. Birmingham Trust Nat. Bank, 1940-51. Past bd. dirs., v.p. Jefferson County (Ala.) Coordinating Council; vice chmn. Jefferson County Health Council; bd. dirs. Jefferson Family Counseling Assn.; pres., trustee Jefferson Tb Sanatorium. Served to lt. comdr. USNR, 1942-45. Mem. N.Y. Stock Exchange, Soc. of Cin., SCW, SR, SAR, Soc. War 1812. Republican. Episcopalian. Clubs: Mountain Brook, Birmingham Country, Shoal Creek, Redstone, Downtown, Relay House (Birmingham); Boston (New Orleans); Princeton, Racquet and Tennis (N.Y.C.). Lodges: Order St. John of Jerusalem, Order of First Families of Va. Died Apr. 2, 1989; buried Elmwood Cemetery, Birmingham, Ala. Home: Birmingham Ala.

LYNN, KLONDA, educator; b. Linton, N.D., June 21, 1898; d. George Wellington and Mary (Barton) L. BA, U. N.C., 1920; BLI, Emerson Coll., 1922; MA, Boston U., 1925; PhD, La. State U. Tchr. Emerson Coll., 1922-25, Ariz. State Coll., Flagstaff, 1928-45; mem. faculty U. Ariz., Tucson, from 1945, prof., past head dept. Mem. AAUW, Speech Assn. Am., Am. Speech and Hearning Assn. *

LYNN, ROBERT T., information technology executive; b. Hazleton, Pa., May 8, 1937; s. Joseph P. and May E. (Roth) L.; m. Theresa R. Lesko, Aug. 26, 1961; children: Robert J., Diane L., Sharon E. B.S. in Elec. Engring., Pa. State U., 1961. Engring. supr. Gen. Electric, Valley Forge, Pa., 1961, mgr. ops., Phila., 1962; process engr., mgr. Tung-Sol, Weatherly, Pa., 1963, plant mgr., Hazleton, Pa., 1964; with IBM, 1965—, internat. assignments, Amsterdam, 1975-76, Paris, 1976-77, dir. info. system Info. Systems and Communications Group, IBM, White Plains, N.Y., 1980-85; sr. v.p. info. tech. Meml. Sloan-Kettering Cancer Ctr., N.Y.C., 1985-87; exec v.p., chief info. officer, CM Alliance, Hartford, Conn., from 1987; sr. v.p., chief info. officer, head Ind. Life Ins. Author 2 books; contbr. articles to profl. jours. Served with USMC, 1953-57. Mem. IEEE (exec. com., chmn. PAC), Am. Mgmt. Assn., Assn. Computing Machinery, Indsl. Mgmt. Club, Soc. Advancement of Mgmt., Internat. Execs. Assn., Pa. State U. Alumni, Americans in Paris, Am. Legion, Sigma Tau, Eta Kappa Nu. Republican. Clubs: Sands Golf & Tennis, 4 Seasons Tennis, Fairfield Beach and Yacht. Deceased. Home: Wilton Conn. †

LYNN, WILLIAM HARCOURT, beverage company executive; b. N.Y.C., Feb. 17, 1931; s. William Harcourt and Helen (Martin) L.; m. Gay Stirling, July 30, 1960; children: William Harcourt III, Margaret Stirling. BA, U. Toronto, 1953. Media planner Young & Rubicam, N.Y.C., 1953-55; dir. TV programs McCann-Erickson, N.Y.C., 1955-59; dir. TV devel. ABC, Los Angeles, 1960-62; v.p. Young & Rubicam, N.Y.C., 1962-65; sr. v.p. BBDO Inc., N.Y.C., 1965-69; sr. v.p. media and TV programming Ketchum Advt., N.Y.C., 1970-83; corp. v.p., dir. world-wide media The Coca-Cola Co., Atlanta, 1983-90; bd. dirs. Ga. Pub. TV, Atlanta, from 1988. Bd. dels. U.S. Olympic Com., Colorado Springs, 1981-84; pres. U.S. Yacht Racing Union, Newport, R.I., 1986-88; com. vice chmn. Internat. Yacht Racing Union, London, from 1987; trustee, pres. U.S. Sailing Found., Newport, 1980-85. Mem. Internat. Advt. Assn. (media com. from 1984), Assn. Nat. Advertisers (TV advt./policy com. from 1983). Clubs: Am. Yacht (Rye, N.Y.); Atlanta Yacht; Capital City; Hopetown Sailing (Bahamas); N.Y. Yacht; Royal Western Yacht (Glasgow, Scotland); Ft. Worth Boat; Ida Lewis Yacht (Newport) (hon.). Home: Atlanta Ga. Died Nov. 20, 1990.

LYON, CHARLES STUART, lawyer, law educator; b. Atlanta, N.Y., Nov. 24, 1916; s. Hyatt H. and Laura B. (Cotton) L.; m. Isabel Logan, Nov. 27, 1943; children—Charles Brooks, Jonathan Winslow, Emily Morgan. A.B., Swarthmore Coll., 1937; LL.B., Columbia U., 1941. Bar: Pa., 1942, N.Y., 1943, U.S. Supreme Ct., 1952. Assoc. firm Morgan, Lewis & Bockius, Phila., 1941-42, Alvord & Alvord, N.Y.C., 1942-46; trial atty., dep. chief counsel prosecution of war crimes Nuremberg, 1946-48; founding ptnr. Skadden, Arps, Slate & Lyon (now Skadden, Arps, Slate, Meagher & Flom), N.Y.C., 1948-51; asst. counsel, chief counsel King subcom. Ways and Means Com., Ho. of Reps., 1951-52; asst. atty. gen. tax div. Dept. Justice, 1952-53; ptnr. Spence & Hotchkiss, N.Y.C., 1953-54; practice in N.Y.C., from 1954; lectr. fed. taxation NYU, 1955-56, prof. law to prof. emeritus, from 1956. Contbr. articles to profl. jours. Mem. ABA. Presbyterian. Home: New York N.Y. Died Aug. 11, 1989.

LYON, ELIJAH WILSON, college president, historian; b. Heidelberg, Miss., June 6, 1904; s. Rufus and Willia (Wilson) L.; m. Carolyn M. Bartel, Aug. 26, 1933; children: Elizabeth (Mrs. Julian Pierce Webb), John Wilson. B.A., U. Miss., 1925; B.A. (Rhodes scholar), Oxford (Eng.) U., 1927, B. Litt. (Rhodes scholar), 1928; Ph.D., U. Chgo., 1932; LL.D., Colgate U., 1945, U. Calif., 1958, Grinnell Coll., 1966, Clarement Men's Coll., 1967, Coll. Idaho, 1967; D.Litt., Occidental Coll., 1947, U. Redlands, 1968; L.H.D., Trinity Coll., 1955, Claremont Grad. Sch., 1968, Hamilton Coll., 1974, Pomona Coll., 1974. Asst. prof. La. Poly. Inst., 1928-29; from asst. prof. to prof. history Colgate U., 1929-41; pres. Pomona Coll., Claremont, Calif., 1941-69, pres. emeritus, 1969-89; hon. dir. Adam H. Bartel Co., Richmond, Ind.; Tchr. summer sch. Syracuse U., 1935-36, U. Rochester, 1940, U. Mo., 1941; chmn. commn. on coll. students Am. Council Edn., 1957-58, chmn. commn. on lang. and area centers, 1960-61, mem. commn. on fed. relations, 1960-63, mem. overseas liaison com., 1962-68; mem. Nat. Commn. on Accrediting, 1957-60, Pacific Regional Com. for Marshall scholarships, 1960-66. Author: Louisiana in French Diplomacy (1759-1804), 1934, rev. edit., 74, The Man Who Sold Louisiana, The Life of François Barbé-Marbois, 1942, revised edit., 74, The History of Pomona College, 1977; editor: The History of Louisiana by François Barbé-Marbois, 1977; bd. editors: Jour. Modern History, 1943-46, The Am. Oxonian, 1956-62; contbr essays and critical revs. to hist. and coll. jours. Mem. Calif. Spl. Crime Study Commn. on Organized Crime, 1951-52; trustee Pacific Sch. Religion, 1969-85, Pomona Coll. (hon.), Latin Am. scholarship program of Am. Univs., 1968-71, John Randolph Haynes and Dora Haynes Found., 1968-83; hon. trustee Inst. Internat. Edn.; trustee emeritus Claremont U. Ctr. Recipient Alumni medal U. Chgo., 1967, award Am. Acad. Achievement, 1968; named to Hall of Fame U. Miss., 1975; decorated hon. comdr. Order Brit. Empire.; Grantee Social Sci. Research Council, 1937. Mem. Western Coll. Assn. (pres. 1943-44), Am. Council Learned Socs. (Pacific Coast com. on humanities 1947-58), Am., So. hist. assns., Orgn. Am. Historians, La., Miss., So. Calif. hist. socs., Council Fgn. Relations, Town Hall, Phi Beta Kappa, Beta Theta Pi. Conglist. Clubs: University (Los Angeles); University (Pasadena). Home: Claremont Calif. Died Mar. 3, 1989; buried Claremont, Calif.

LYON, GEORGE ROBERT, advertising executive; b. N.Y.C., Feb. 13, 1923; s. Gordon and Gladys (Dempsey) L.; m. Jacqueline Jacobson, Apr. 27, 1950; children: Maureen, Patrice, Dana Jean. Student, CCNY, 1943, Syracuse U., 1943. With advt. dept. Sterling Drug Co., 1939-43; from staff to v.p., gen. mgr. Fuller & Smith & Ross, 1947-65; owner, founder, pres., chmn. Conahay & Lyon, Inc., N.Y.C., 1965-80; chmn. Grey Conahay & Lyon (merger with Grey/2), N.Y.C., 1980-85; pres. GRL Devel. Inc., 1985-90. Chmn. Rigel Communications. Served with AUS, 1943-46. Mem. Am. Assn. Advt. Agys. (gov. Eastern region). Congregationalist. Club: Scarsdale Golf. Home: Scarsdale N.Y. Died Mar. 14, 1990.

LYON, QUINTER M(ARCELLUS), philosophy educator; b. Washington, June 10, 1898; s. William Marcellus and Fannie Susan (Stoner) L.; m. Ruth Rebecca Beekley, Sept. 2, 1925; children: Donna Marie (Mrs. Gilbert Lloyd Keck), David Beekley. AB, George Washington U., 1920; ThB, Princeton U., 1923, MA, 1923; PhD, Ohio State U., 1933. Editor in chief ch.-schs. pub.s Brethren Pub. Co., Ashland, Ohio, 1923-30; part time instr. in philosophy Ohio State U., Columbus, 1930-34; acting prof. philosophy and religion MacMurray Coll. for Women, Jacksonville, Ill., 1934-35; prof. philosophy and govt. State Coll., Minot, N.D., 1935-47, head social sci. div., 1938-47, dean sr. coll., 1945-47; chmn. dept. philosophy U. Miss., from 1946, assoc. prof., 1946-47, prof., 1947-63, prof. emeritus, from 1963; prof. philosophy, chmn. dept. Chico (Calif.) State Coll., from 1963; Smith-Mundt lectr. U. Panama, 1959-60; vis. lectr., cons. in philosophy program Chico State Coll., 1962-63. Author: Three Typical Views of Progress, 1933, The Great Religions, 1957, Quiet Strength from World Religions, 1960, Ensayos sobre la Filosofia Social, 1960, Meditations from World Religions, 1966, also articles profl. jours. Eng., Portuguese and Spanish. Organist Brethren Ch., Washington, 1914-20, Princeton Miller Chapel, 1921-23, Brethren Ch. and Meth. Ch., Ashland, 1924-30; minister of music Meth. Ch., Minot, 1937-46, Oxford Univ. Meth. Ch., 1947-63; condr. ednl. tours to Washington, 1941, 42, 46; jr. examiner U.S. Civil Svc. Commn., Washington, 1917-1, chmn. Minot, 1938-46; chmn. conf. on Victory through Edn., State Coll., Minot, 1944; chmn. Centennial Philosophy Conf., U. Miss., 1949. Mem. NEA, AAUP, Am. Philos. Assn. (del. to Inter-Am. Congress of Philosophy, San Jose, Costa Rica 1961), Miss. Philos. Assn. (pres. 1949-51), So. Soc. Philosophy and Psychology, So. Soc. Philosophy of Religion, Archaeol. Inst. Am., Miss. Edn. Assn., Metaphys. Soc. Am., Internat. Platform Assn., Masons (32 deg.), Shriners, Rotary, Phi Delta Kappa, Alpha Phi Omega, Phi Sigma Tau (nat. bd. dirs., bd. editors Dialogue). *

LYONS, CLIFFORD PIERSON, educator; b. Chgo., Oct. 5, 1904; s. Charles and Ina (Pierson) L.; m. Gladys M. Hart, Sept. 4, 1928. AB, Cornell Coll., Mt. Vernon, Iowa, 1925, Litt.D., 1953; postgrad., U. Chgo., 1927-29; PhD, Johns Hopkins U., 1932. Instr. English, speech, athletics, secondary schs. Berea (Ky.) Coll., 1925-28; prin. acad. Lincoln Meml. U. Harrogate, Tenn., 1928-29; instr. English Johns Hopkins U., 1930-36; prof. English, head dept. U. Fla., 1936-46, chmn. div. lang. and lit., 1939-46; prof. English U.N.C., 1946-61, Kenan prof. English, 1961-74, prof. emeritus, 1974-92, head dept. English, 1946-52; dean Coll. Arts and Scis., 1951-54; sec. faculty Coll. Arts and Scis., 1966-69; mem. English lit. com. Selection Fulbright Fellowships, 1954-57. Cofounder, assoc. editor ELH, Jour. English Literary History, 1934-54; assoc. editor South Atlantic Bull., 1939-50; editorial bd. Studies in Philology, 1950-73; contbr. articles, revs. to profl. jours. Lt. comdr. USNR, 1942-45. Mem. Modern Lang. Assn. Am. (exec. coun. 1953-56), Southeastern Renaissance Conf. (pres. 1964), Coll. English Assn., AAUP, Assn. U. Profs., South Atlantic Modern Lang. Assn. (pres. 1939), Tudor and Stuart Club (Johns Hopkins), Chapel Hill Golf and Country Club, Phi Beta Kappa, Phi Gamma Delta. Democrat. Episcopalian. Home: Chapel Hill N.C. Died Feb. 11, 1992.

LYONS, RICHARD JOSEPH, investment company executive; b. N.Y.C., Sept. 5, 1923; s. James Austin and Virginia (Malia) L.; m. Mary Josephine Sullivan, Aug. 9, 1944; children: Mary Josephine, Patricia Ann, Denise, Kathleen, Richard Joseph, Deirdre. B.B.A., Pace Coll., 1952. C.P.A., N.J. Jr. acct. Harris Kerr Forster, N.Y.C., 1946-47; staff acct. Sparrow Weymouth & Co., N.Y.C., 1947-50; sr. acct. Price Waterhouse & Co., N.Y.C., 1950-52; sec. treas. U.S. and Fgn. Securities Corp., N.Y.C., 1952-84; treas. ASA Ltd., Johannesburg, South Africa, 1973-85; prin. Richard J. Lyons, CPA, until 1989. Mem. Bd. Alderman, Morristown, N.J., 1964-65; mem. Morristown Airport Commn., 1967. Served to 2d lt. USAAF, 1943-46, PTO. Mem. AICPA, Am. Soc. Corp. Secs. Republican. Roman Catholic. Lodge: K.C. Home: Mendham N.J. Died Aug. 6, 1989.

MABRY, GEORGE LAFAYETTE, JR., army officer; b. Stateburg, S.C., Sept. 14, 1917; s. George Lafayette and Alberta (Stuckey) M.; m. Eulena Myers, Oct. 16, 1941; children: Abigail Eulena Mabry Ferrick, George Lafayette III, Benjamin Myers. BA, Presbyn. Coll., Clinton, S.C., 1940; grad., Command and Gen. Staff Coll., 1950, Nat. War Coll., 1958; postgrad., U. Pitts., 1960. Commd. 2d lt. U.S. Army, 1940, advanced through grades to maj. gen., 1971; chief collateral activities br. J-3, also dir. J-3 Hdqrs. U.S. Command, C.Z., 1962-65; asst. div. comdr., comdr. 1st Armored Div., 1965-66; head evaluation team Republic of Vietnam, 1966; comdr. U.S. Army Combat Devels. Command Experimentation Command, Ft. Ord, Calif., 1966-67, 8th Inf. Div., Bad Kreuznach, Germany, 1968; chief staff U.S. Army, Vietnam, 1969-70; comdr. U.S. Army Forces So. Command, C.Z., 1971-75, U.S. Army Readiness Region, Ft. Sheridan, Ill., 1975. Active local Boy Scouts Am., Girl Scouts U.S.A. Decorated Congl. Medal of Honor, D.S.C., D.S.M. with oak leaf cluster, Legion of Merit with 2 oak leaf clusters, Silver Star, Bronze Star with V, Purple Heart; Belgian Fourragere, Disting. Svc. Order (Eng.), Nat. Order 5th class (Vietnam), Vietnamese Cross of Gallantry with gold palm. Mem. Medal of Honor Soc., VFW, Am. Legion (hon.). Home: Columbia S.C. Died July 13, 1990; buried Holy Cross Episcopal Ch. Cemetery, Stateburg, S.C.

MACARTHUR, DONALD, insurance and mail order executive; b. Antigo, Wis., Dec. 17, 1901; s. William B. and Anna M. (Jeffers) MacA.; m. Margaret D. Dreiske, June 10, 1936; children: Donald, David, William, Robert, Bruce, Gordon, Mary, Carol, Andrew. BS, U. Wis., 1925. Securities salesman E.H. Rollins & Sons, 1925-34, Birger Asland & Co., 1934-40, Doyle O'Connor & Co., 1940-44, F.S. Moseley & Co., 1944-47; v.p., treas. Allstate Ins. Co., 1947-54, dir., 1953-90; treas. Sears, Roebuck & Co., Chgo., 1954-90; pres. Sears Roebuck Acceptance Corp., Chgo., 1956-60, dir., 1956-90; dir. Sears Bank & Trust Co., Chgo., Helene Curtis Industries, Inc. Mem. Univ. Club. Home: Sarasota Fla. Died May 3, 1990.

MAC ARTHUR, DONALD MALCOLM, business executive; b. Detroit, Jan. 7, 1931; s. Donald J. and Margaret (MacAulay) MacArthur; m. Diana Taylor, Mar. 31, 1962; children: Elizabeth, Alexander. B.Sc. with honors, St. Andrews (Scotland) U., 1954; Ph.D., Edinburgh (Scotland) U., 1957. Mem. faculty U. Conn., 1957-58; with Melpar Inc., 1958-66, mgr. chemistry and biology research center, 1964-66; dep. asst. sec. for research and advanced tech. Office Sec., Dept. Def., 1966-70, cons., 1970-72; pres., chief exec. officer Enviro Control Inc., 1970-80, also dir.; pres., chief exec. officer Dynamac Corp., 1975-85, chmn. 1985-88; chmn. bd. Borriston Research Labs., Inc., 1978-84, Consumer Dynamics, Inc., 1976-81; cons. water pollution U.S. Dept. Interior, 1965; U.S. Gaelic commentator BBC, 1985-88. Author tech. articles. Trustee Nat. Grad. U., 1970-72; mem. principal's council U. St. Andrews, Scotland, 1988. Fellow Am. Inst. Chemists; mem. Am. Chem. Soc., AAAS., Nat. Assn. Life Sci. Industries (dir. 1979-84, pres. 1981-84, bd. dirs. Profl. Services Council 1986-88), St. Andrew's Soc. Washington (chmn. charity and edn. com. 1984-87, sec. 1987-88). Home: Bethesda Md. Died Nov. 27, 1988; buried Dalmore, Isle of Lewis, Scotland.

MACBAIN, RICHARD NORMAN, osteopathic physician; b. Mildmay, Ont., Can., Jan. 29, 1897; came to U.S., 1920; naturalized, 1944; s. James Henry and Isabelle (McKnight) MacB.; m. Alice Peterman, Mar. 20, 1937; children: John, Judith Anne. DO, Chgo. Coll. Osteopathy, 1924; DSc (hon.), Coll. Osteopathic Phys & Surg., 1949. Mem. faculty Chgo. Coll. Osteopathy, from 1924, dean, 1930-37, pres., from 1937; practice osteo. medicine Chgo., from 1927. Contbr. articles to profl. jours. Trustee local Meth. ch. With C.E.F., 1916-19. Mem. Am. Assn. Osteo. Colls. (pres. 1931-34, 37-38, 44-45, 49-50, 55-56), Am. Coun. Osteo. Edn., Am. Osteo. Assn. (nat. bd. osteo. examiners, bur. profl. edn.), Ill. Osteo. Assn., Atlas Club, Masons, Sigma Sigma Phi. *

MAC DONALD, JOHN (HASKELL), educator; b. Brunswick, Maine, Sept. 1, 1896; s. William and Harriet (Haskell) Mac D.; m. Victoria Zukowsky, Sept. 20, 1921; children: Jeanette (Mrs. James Fifield), Helene. BCS, NYU, 1922, MCS, 1923. From instr. to asst. prof. bus. mgmt. NYU Sch. Commerce, 1922-28; asst. sec. McGraw-Hill Pub. Co., N.Y.C., 1928-29; contr. A. I. Namm and Sons, Bklyn., 1929-30, Walker Heisler and Sons, N.Y.C., 1931-33; sec. Trade Ways, Inc., N.Y.C., 1933-35; budget officer NBC, 1936-39, bus. mgr. rec. dept., 1939-40, adminstrv. v.p., 1947-50, asst. treas., 1941, v.p., 1942-47, adminstrv. v.p., 1947-50, v.p., treas., 1950-51; assoc. mgmt. cons. Rogers, Slade & Hill, 1951-52, ptnr., 1952-54; prof. mgmt. Sch. Bus. Adminstrn. U. S.C., from 1956. Author: (with W. B. Cornell) Business Organization and Management, 1927 (rev. 1936), Office Management, 1927 (rev. 1937, 47), Practical Budget Procedure, 1939, Controllership, Its Functions and Techniques, 1940. Mem. Contrs. Inst. Am. (pres. N.Y.C. Control 1938-39, nat. bd. dirs. 1939-42, 46-49, nat. pres. 1946-47, chmn. bd. dirs. 1947-48), Am. Mgmt. Assn., Lake Placid Club, Delta Sigma Pi, Beta Alpha Psi. Republican. *

MACDONALD, MARY ELIZABETH, social worker, educator; b. Laurium, Mich., Oct. 31, 1910; d. Norman and Minnie (King) MacD. BA, Wellesley Coll., 1922; AM, U. Chgo., 1939, PhD, 1943. Mem. faculty U. Chgo., from 1943, from rsch. assoc. to prof. social svc. adminstrn., 1943-57, Samuel Deutsch prof. social svc. adminstrn., from 1957. Author: Federal Grants for Vocational Rehabilitation, 1944. Mem. NASW. *

MACDONALD, NESTOR JOSEPH, electrical components company executive; b. N.Y.C., Dec. 15, 1895; s. Noble and Nellie (Cottrel) MacD.; m. Helen E. Johnson, Aug. 23, 1927; children: Sheila, Glenna. Corr. student, Columbia U., Alexander Hamilton Inst., Internat. Corr. Schs. V.p., pres., chmn. bd., dir. Thomas & Betts Co., Elizabeth, N.J., 1921-91; pres. Grandfather Mountain Highland Games, Linville, N.C. Trustee, v.p. Kessler Inst. Rehab., West Orange, N.J., Lees-McRae Coll., Banner Elk, N.C.; bd. dirs. Yard Sch. Art, Montclair, N.J.; dep. high commr. Clan Donald U.S.; pres. bd. dirs. Scottish Am. Heritage. Mem. St. Andrews Soc. (past pres. N.Y.), Union League, Canadian Club (N.Y.C.), Rock Spring Club (West Orange, N.J.), Baltusrol Golf Club (Springfield, N.J.), Royal Poinciana Golf Club (Naples, Fla.), Grandfather Golf and Country Club, Linville (N.C.) Golf Club, Hound Ears Club (Blowing Rock, N.Y.), Short Hills (N.J.) Club, Royal and Ancient Golf St. Andrews Club (Fife, Scotland). Home: Short Hills N.C. Died Oct. 17, 1991; buried Montclair, N.J.

MACE, DAVID ROBERT, family specialist, author; b. Scotland, June 21, 1907; s. Joseph and Josephine (Reid) M.; m. Vera Chapman, July 26, 1933; children: Sheila (Mrs. Jagan M. Rao), Fiona (Mrs. John S. Patterson). B.Sc., U. London, Eng., 1928; B.A., Cambridge (Eng.) U., 1930, M.A., 1933; Ph.D., U. Manchester, Eng., 1942; L.H.D., Alma Coll., 1977; D.S.S., Brigham Young U., 1977. Ordained minister Meth. Ch., 1933. Minister in Eng., 1930-44; marriage counselor, 1944-90; founding mem. Nat. Marriage Guidance Council, Gt. Britain, 1938, exec. dir., 1942-49, v.p., 1949; prof. human relations Drew U., 1949-59; assoc. prof. family study U. Pa. Sch. Medicine; staff cons. Marriage Council Phila., 1959-60; exec. dir. Am. Assn. Marriage Counselors, 1960-67; prof. family sociology Bowman Gray Sch. Medicine, Wake Forest U., Winston-Salem, N.C., 1967-77; field work in marriage guidance and family welfare in, Africa, Asia, 1954, 58, 68, Australia, New Zealand and, Asia, 1956, 67, Caribbean, S.Am., 1960, 61, Soviet Union, 1960; Pres. Nat. Council Family Relations, 1961-62; v.p. Internat. Union Family Orgns., 1961-70, chmn. internat. commn. marriage and marriage guidance, 1953-70; family life cons. World Council Chs., 1958-72; pres. Sex Info. and Edn. Council U.S., 1965-66, Assn. Couples for Marriage Enrichment, 1973-88; sec. Groves Conf. on Marriage and Family, 1968-71. Author: Does Sex Morality Matter?, 1942, Marriage Counselling, 1948, Marriage Crisis, 1948, Marriage, The Art of Lasting Love, 1952, Hebrew Marriage, 1953, Whom God Hath Joined, 1953, Success in Marriage, 1958, Youth Looks Toward Marriage, 1957, (with Vera Mace) Marriage East and West, 1960, The Soviet Family, 1962, The Christian Response to the Sexual Revolution, 1970, Getting Ready for Marriage, 1972, Abortion: The Agonizing Decision, 1972, Sexual Difficulties in Marriage, 1972, (with Vera Mace) We Can Have Better Marriages-If We Really Want Them, 1974, Men, Women, and God, 1976, Marriage Enrichment in the Church, 1976, Towards Better Marriages, 1976, How to Have a Happy Marriage, 1976, What's Happening to Clergy Marriages, 1980, Love and Anger in Marriage, 1982, Close Companions: The Marriage Enrichment Handbook, 1982, Prevention in Family Services, 1983, Letters to a Retired Couple, 1985, The Sacred Fire-Christian Marriage Through the Ages, 1986, (with Vera Nace) When The Honeymoon's Over, 1988; also numerous articles. Recipient numerous awards including Disting. Contbn. award Am. Assn. Marriage and Family Counselors, 1975, citation N.C. Family Life Council, 1975, Disting. Svc. to Families award Nat. Council Family Relations, 1975, Man of Year award Forsyth County Mental Health Assn., 1975, award Assn. Couples Marriage Enrichment, 1976, award Nebr. Family Strengths Symposium, 1983, Sperry award State of N.C., 1983, Disting. Svc. award Bapt. Christian Life Commn., 1983, award Nat. Assn. Cath. Diocesan Family Life Ministries, 1987, (posthumously) Pioneer award N.C. Assn. Marriage and Family Therapy, 1991. Mem. Soc. of Friends. Home: Black Mountain N.C. Died Dec. 1, 1990; cremated.

MACFADDEN, WILLIAM SEMPLE, investment banker; b. Fargo, N.D., Dec. 13, 1895; s. William Clifton and Jane (Semple) M.; m. Dorothy E. Sharp, Sept. 14, 1922. BS, U. Wis., 1917. Ptnr. Piper, Jaffray & Hopewood, from 1942; vice chmn. Midwest Stock Exch. Trustee St. Barnabas Hosp. Mem. Mpls. C. of C. (bd. dirs.), Mpls. Club, Phi Delta Theta. *

MACGREGOR, JOHN MURDOCH, lawyer, educator; b. Minneauwakan, N.D., Oct. 9, 1897; s. Alexander and Annie (Currie) MacG. AB, U. Oreg., 1923; JD, NYU, 1927; LLD (hon.), Gettysburg Coll., 1950. Bar: N.Y. 1927, U.S. Supreme Ct., U.S. Dist. Ct. N.Y. Practice law N.Y.C., from 1928; mem. faculty NYU, from 1928, prof. law of commerce, chmn. dept., from 1941. Trustee Internat. House, N.Y.C. Wireless operator USN, World War I; col. U.S. Army, World War II. Mem. ABA, Assn. of Bar of City of N.Y., Nat. Interfraternity Conf. (past pres.), Internat. House of N.Y.C. (trustee), Am. Legion, Century Assn., Pilgrims of U.S. St. Andrews Soc. of N.Y. (pres. 1953-55), Century Club, Phi Delta Phi, Alpha Tau Omega (nat. pres. 1946-50), Beta Gamma Sigma. *

MACHADO, ALFREDO C., publisher; b. Rio de Janeiro, Brazil, May 10, 1922; s. Raphael da Cruz and Isabel (Sapia) M.; m. Maria da Gloria Abreu, July 28, 1946; children—Sergio, Alfredo, Sonia. Student in law Fed. U., Rio de Janeiro, 1940-45. Translator, o Globo, Rio de Janeiro, 1937-46; co-founder, chief exec. officer Distribuidora Record, Rio de Janeiro, 1941-89. Roman Catholic. Clubs: Rio de Janeiro Country, Rio de Janeiro Iate. Died Feb. 8, 1991. Home: Rio de Janeiro Brazil

MACHT, STUART MARTIN, defense contractor executive; b. Balt., June 18, 1930; s. Louis Ephraim and Nettie (Harris) M.; m. Ann Custis Boyd, Nov. 12, 1951; children: Steven Craig, Linda Lee, Andrew Parks. BSME, Duke U., 1951. Registered profl. engr. Md. Exptl. test engr. Pratt & Whitney Aircraft, East Hartford, Conn., 1951-52; mech. engr. Indsl. Research Lab., Balt., 1952; pres., chief exec. officer AAI Corp., Balt., 1953-90; mem. Balt. County Fin. Adv. Group, from 1987. Author numerous tech. handbooks for company design use, 1956-79. Bd. dirs. Goodwill Industries, Balt., 1988-90, Balt. Mus. Industry; pres. Montview Community Assn., 1987-88; mem. Exec. Adv. Bd. on Higher Edn., Balt. County, 1989—; chmn. bldg. fund, hon. mem. Cockeysville Vol. Fire Co., 1989-90; mem. Balt. County Econ. Devel. Commn., Greater Balt. Community Econ. Devel. Coun. anbd High Tech Forum. Mem. Am. Def. Preparedness Assn., Nat. Security & Indsl. Assn. (bd. trustees), Am. Mgmt. Assn., ASME, Balt. County C. of C. (sr. v.p., bd. dirs. 1984-85, pres. 1986), Towson State U. Industry Club (chmn. bd. dirs. from 1985, mem. exec. coun. 1988-90), Towson State U. Alumni Assn. (pres. adv. coun. 1989-90), Towson State U. Alumni Assn. (pres. adv. coun. 1989-90), Pi Mu Epsilon, Tau Beta Pi, Pi Tau Sigma, Phi Beta Kappa. Home: Hunt Valley Md. Died May 5, 1990; buried Dulaney Valley Meml. Gardens, Timonium, Md.

MACINTOSH, FRANK CAMPBELL, physiologist; b. Baddeck, N.S., Can., Dec. 24, 1909; s. Charles Campbell and Beenie Annabel (Matheson) MacI.; m. Mary MacLachlan MacKay, Dec. 14, 1938; children—M. Christine, Barbara, Andrew, Janet, Roderick. B.A., Dalhousie U., Halifax, N.S., 1930, M.A., 1932, LL.D., 1976; Ph.D., McGill U., Montreal, Que., Can., 1937, D.Sc. (hon.), 1980; LL.D., U. Alta., Edmonton, Can., 1964, Queen's U., Kingston, Ont., Can., 1965, St. Francis Xavier U., Antigonish, N.S., 1985; M.D. (hon.), U. Ottawa, Ont., 1974. Mem. research staff Med. Research Council, London, 1938-49; Drake prof. physiology McGill U., Montreal, 1949-78, chmn. dept., 1949-65, prof., 1978-80, prof. emeritus, 1980-92; vis. prof. numerous univs., U.S., Can., France, Sweden, Hungary, Venezuela, Eng.; mem. Sci. Council Can., Ottawa, 1966-71; pres. XXX Internat. Conf. Physiol. Scis., Vancouver, B.C., Can., 1986. Editor Can. Jour. Physiology and Pharmacology, 1969-72; contbr. articles to profl. jours. Chmn. Fiddle Head Assn., Big Harbour Island, N.S., from 1983. Recipient Silver Jubilee medal Govt. of Can., 1978. Fellow Royal Soc. London, Royal Soc. Can., N.Y. Acad. Scis.; mem. Can. Physiol. Soc. (pres. 1960-61, Sarrazin lectr. 1979). Home: Montreal West Can. Died Sept. 11, 1992. †

MACINTOSH, WILLIAM JAMES, lawyer; b. Glens Falls, N.Y., May 12, 1901; s. Gershom Banker and Mattie May (Hood) MacI.; m. Elise Robinson McIlvaine, May 11, 1974. B.S., U. Pa., 1922, J.D., 1926. Bar: Pa. 1926. Instr. Wharton Sch., U. Pa., 1923-24, Law Sch. U. Pa., 1927-29; from assoc. to sr. ptnr. firm Morgan, Lewis & Bockius, Phila., 1926-79, of counsel, 1979-89; Dir., mem. exec. com. Phila. Suburban Water Co., 1945-80; dir. emeritus Am. Water Works Co.; dir. Better Materials Corp., Inc.; gen. counsel, renegotiation div. War Dept., U.S. Govt., 1943-44; gen. counsel War Contracts Price Adjustment Bd., 1944; Counsel Rep. State Com. Pa., from 1967; pres. Pa. Electoral Coll., 1972, mem., 1980. Chmn. bd. trustees Grundy Found. Mem. Am. Bar Assn. (ho. of dels. 1946, chmn. adminstrv. law sect. 1948, chmn. pub. utility law sect. 1964-65), Nat. Assn. Water Cos. (dir.), Fed. Power Bar Assn. (pres. 1951), Fed. Bar Assn., Am. Judicature Soc., Phi Gamma Delta, Beta Gamma Sigma, Order of the Coif. Republican. Home: Bryn Mawr Pa. Died May 15, 1989.

MACINTYRE, MALCOLM AMES, lawyer; b. Boston, Jan. 28, 1908; s. Charles H. and Martha Eloise (Alden) MacI.; m. Clare Bishop, Dec. 1, 1933; children: Bruce Bishop, Clare Alden, Pamela Ames. B.A., Yale U., 1929, J.S.D. (Sterling fellow), 1933; B.A. (Rhodes scholar), Oxford U., 1931, B.C.L., 1932. Bar: N.Y. 1934, Va. 1946, D.C. 1946. Assoc. Sullivan & Cromwell, 1934-42; ptnr. Douglas, Proctor, MacIntyre & Gates, Washington, 1946-48, Debevoise, Plimpton & McLean, N.Y.C., 1948-57; under-sec. Dept. Air Force, 1957-59; pres. Eastern Air Lines, Inc., 1959-63; chmn. Bunker Ramo Corp., 1969-71; pres. Chem. div. Martin Marietta Corp., N.Y.C., 1964-72; of counsel firm Winthrop,

Stimson, Putnam & Roberts, N.Y.C., Washington, Hale, Russell & Gray, N.Y.C., Washington, 1973-85. Author: Competitive Private Enterprise Under Government Regulation; contbr. articles to legal jours. Trustee Village of Scarsdale, N.Y., 1965-66, mayor, 1966-69; mem. N.Y. State Law Revision Commn., 1973-76. Served from 1st lt. to col., Air Transport Command USAAF, 1942-46. Decorated Legion of Merit.; Named to Lacrosse Hall of Fame. Mem. Am. Bar Assn., N.Y. State Bar Assn., D.C. Bar Assn., Va. Bar Assn. Republican. Presbyterian. Clubs: Scarsdale Town (pres. 1956-57); Chevy Chase (Washington), Metropolitan (Washington). Home: McLean Va. Died May 6, 1992.

MACINTYRE, W(ILLIAM) RALPH, textile business executive; b. Wilmington, Del., June 22, 1897; s. William Franklin and Emma (Wells) M.; m. Marie Louise Cella, Oct. 9, 1922; 1 child, William Ralph. Student, Phila. Textile Sch., 1917. Joined Eddystone Mfg. Co., 1918, pres., from 1943; v.p., gen. mgr. Joseph Bancroft & Sons Co., 1930, pres., from 1947; chmn. bd. dirs. Albert D. Smith & Co.; chmn. bd. dirs. Banco, Inc., William Sampson Sons & Co., Inc., Joseph Bancroft & Sons of N.Y., Inc.; bd. dirs. Cotton Inst., Inc., N.Y.; v.p., bd. dirs. Joseph Bancroft & Sons Co. of Pa., Reading; bd. dirs. Josephs Bancroft & Sons Co. Ltd., Eng., Joseph Bancroft & Sons de Mex. S.A. de C.V., Bancroft Brillotex Internat. S.A., V.P., Del. Importers, Wilmington, Bank of Del., Wilmington, Aponang Co., Indian Head Mills, Inc., Brandywine Bldg. and Loan Assn. Mem. W.P.B. adv. com. of cotton and rayon finishers' industry, office of prodn., rsch. and devel.; mem. Wilmington Mgmt.-Labor War Manpower Com.; mem. rationing com. OPA; asst. to pres. Nat. Cotton Coun. Am.; mem. Del. State Bd. Edn., chmn. vocat. rehab. com.. With U.S. Merchant Marine, World War I. Mem. Wilmington C. of C. (pub. rels. and post war planning com.), Nat. Assn. Finishers Textile Fabrics (chmn. task com.), Textile Color Card Assn. U.S., Inc. (bd. dirs.), Am. Standards Assn. (com. L-14), Am. Arbitration Assn. (nat. panel of arbitrators), Nat. Fedn. Commerce and Industry of France (hon.), Merchants Club, Bankers Club, Manhattan Club, N.Y. Athletic Club, The Lambs Club, Union League, Weavers Club, Wilmington Club, Wilmington Yacht Club, Cornithian Yacht Club, Phi Psi. *

MACIOCE, THOMAS MATTHEW, lawyer; b. N.Y.C., Jan. 2, 1919; s. Anthony and Angelina (Vodola) M.; m. Francesca Paula Spinelli, June 25, 1944; 1 dau., Francesca Lee. B.A., Columbia U., 1939, LL.B., 1942; student, NYU Sch. Finance, 1946-49. Bar: N.Y. 1946, U.S. Supreme Ct. 1966. Asst. sec. Flintkote Mines, Ltd., 1948; v.p., dir. Bloomsburg Mills, Inc., 1952-57; pres., dir. L.F. Dommerich & Co., 1957-60; corp. v.p. Allied Stores Corp., N.Y.C., 1960-69, sr. v.p., 1969-70, pres., 1970-72, chief exec. officer, 1972-81, chmn., 1981-86; sr. ptnr. law firm Shea & Gould, N.Y.C., from 1987; bd. dirs. Mfrs. Hanover Trust Co., Capital Cities/ABC Inc., Grossman's Inc.; fin. cons. Vatican; mem. supervisory bd. Vatican Bank. Pres. Inner-City Scholarship Fund of N.Y. Archdiocese; trustee emeritus Columbia U.; trustee St. John's U., Adelphi U. Served to lt. comdr. USNR, World War II. Recipient Theodore Roosevelt Assn. Meml. award; Brainard Meml. prize, 1939; Brotherhood award NCCJ, 1971; Silver Jubilee award Nat. Jewish Hosp. of Denver; Fund for Higher Edn. award, 1977; Israel Prime Minister's award, 1977; Alexander Hamilton medal Columbia U., 1984; decorated Legion of Order of Merit award (Italy), knight of Equestrian Order of Holy Sepulchre. Mem. Young Pres. Orgn., Acad. Polit. Sci. (dir.). Club: Knight of Malta. Home: Glen Head N.Y. Died Aug. 3, 1990.

MACK, MARION, actress, writer; b. Mammoth, Utah, Apr. 9, 1902; d. Robert D. and Anna Nesbit McCreery; m. Louis Lewyn, July 22, 1923; 1 child, Lanny Lewyn. Student, Los Angeles City Coll.; student, Orange Coast Coll., 1970-72. Actress Mary of Movies, 1922, The General, 1926; writer MGM studios, Culver City, Calif., 1937-41. Home: Costa Mesa Calif. Died, 1989. †

MACK, RUSSELL HERBERT, economist; b. Fulton, Kans., Sept. 21, 1897; s. Fred and Stella (Benham) M.; m. Blanche Case, June 26, 1925; 1 child, Russell Eugene. AB, Baker U., 1920; AM, Columbia U., 1924; PhD, U. Pa., 1933. High sch. social sci. tchr. Chanute, Kans., 1920-23, Stamford, Conn., 1924-25; mem. faculty dept. econs. Temple U., Phila., from 1925, prof. econs., chmn. dept. econs., from 1941, asst. dean Sch. Bus., from 1959; tax cons. Phila. C. of C., 1945-59. Co-editor: Business Forecasting in Practice, 1956. Mem. Phila. Milk Price com., 1949-50. Mem. AAUP, Am. Econ. Assn., Tax Inst., Zeta Chi, Beta Gamma Sigma, Pi Gamma Mu. Methodist. *

MACK, WALTER STAUNTON, corporate executive; b. N.Y.C., Oct. 19, 1895; s. Walter Staunton and Alice (Ranger) M.; m. Ruth J. Watkins, 1942 (dec. 1986); children: Walter III, Alice Ruth; children by previous marriage: Anthony Reckford, Florence Ann. A.B., Harvard, 1917. Salesman Bedford Mills, Inc., 1919, became pres., 1926; later v.p. Wm. B. Nichols & Co.; then v.p. Equity Corp.; chmn. bd., dir. United Cigar-Whelan Stores Corp.; v.p. Phoenix Securities Corp., 1934, pres., 1938-51; chmn. bd., pres. Pepsi-Cola Co., 1934-56; pres., chmn. bd. Nedicks, Inc., 1951; pres. C & C Super Corp. (parent co. B/G Foods, Inc.), Cantrell & Cochrane Corp. (mfr. several soft drinks, including Super Cola); former chmn. bd., chief exec. officer Gt. Am. Industries, Inc.; pres., chmn. Rubatex Corp.; pres. Gt. Am. Minerals Corp.; chmn. Aminex Resources Corp., from 1970, Aminex Petroleum Ltd.; chmn. bd. King Cola Corp., Compass Internat., N.Y.C., Horizon Coal Co., Beach City, Ohio; v.p., treas., dir. Polls Creek Coal Co., Leslie County, Ky., from 1977, Indian Head Mining Co., River Coal Co., Knott County, Ky., from 1977; dir. N.Y. Bd. Trade. Republican candidate N.Y. State Senate, 1932; treas. Rep. co. com. N.Y. State Senate, 1932, Rep. co. com., N.Y.C., 1934-36, Fusion Co. Com. for election Mayor La Guardia, 1937; chmn. Nat. Com. Reps. and Inds. for Johnson, 1964; Mem. Mayor's Adv. and Def. Coms.; vice chmn. Greater N.Y. Fund, 1941; dir. Queens C. of C., N.Y. World's Fair Com.; Manhattan counsel, mem. State Commn. Human Rights; dir. City Center Music and Drama; hon. chmn. Queens County Cancer Com., 1946, Queens Greater N.Y. Fund Com., 1946; chmn. Dewey-Warren Citizens Com., 1948; mem. Fiorello LaGuardia Found., treas. centennial com.; Trustee French and Polyclinic Hosp. Served as ensign USN, 1917-19. Mem. Litchfield Hunter Breeders Soc. (treas.). Jewish (trustee, treas. Temple Emoree El, N.Y.C.). Clubs: Jefferson Island (N.Y.C.), Harvard (N.Y.C.); Harvard (Boston); Sky, Ocean Country, Ariz. Country. Home: New York N.Y. Died Mar. 18, 1990; buried Litchfield, Conn.

MACKENZIE, ERIC FRANCIS, bishop; b. Boston, Dec. 6, 1893; s. Alexander and Angelina (Hogan) MacK. AB, Boston Coll., 1914, AM, 1919, LLD (hon.), 1951; DCL (hon.), Suffolk U., 1950. Ordained priest Roman Cath. Ch., 1918. Prof. St. John's Sem., Brighton, Mass., 1920-43; pastor St. Paul's Ch., Wellesley, Mass., 1943, Sacred Heart Ch., Newton Centre, Mass., from 1945; domestic prelate, 1945; consecrated bishop Boston, 1950; diocesan consultor, from 1945; defensor vinculi Tribunal of Archdiocese of Boston, 1932, vice-officialis, 1941, officialis, from 1945. Bd. dirs. Boston Legal Aid Soc., from 1946, United Community Svcs., Boston, from 1952. Fellow Am. Acad. Arts and Scis.; mem. Survey of Am. Bar (mem. lay adv. com. from 1948), Inter-profl. Commn. Divorce, Canon Law Soc. of U.S. (pres. 1945). *

MACKINNON, ALEXANDER DONALD, lawyer; b. Bushkill, Pa., Oct. 15, 1895; s. Alexander and Mary (Kennedy) MacK.; m. Helen Richadson Smith, Sept. 10, 1924; children: Nancy Jean London, Donna Flom. Student, Pa. State Coll., 1915-18, U. Mich., 1919-20; LLB, Columbia, 1922. Bar: N.Y. Ptnr. Milbank, Tweed, Hadley and McCloy, 1934-90; pres. James Founds., N.Y.C.; bd. visitors Columbia Law Sch. Mem. ABA, N.Y. State Bar Assn., Assn. Bar of City of N.Y., Am. Coll. Trial Lawyers, Columbia Law Sch. Alumni Assn. (pres. 1959-60), N.Y. County Lawyers Assn., Union Club, St. Andrew's Soc., Wall St. Club (N.Y.C.), Rock Spring Club (West Orange, N.J.), Morristown Club (N.J.). Home: West Orange N.J. Died June 21, 1990.

MACKRELL, FRANKLIN CUNNINGHAM, consulting executive; b. Port Jervis, N.Y., Dec. 31, 1895; s. Henry and Gertrude (Cunningham) MacK.; m. Olive Mesick Bostwick, May 18, 1922; 1 child, Barbara June. With Erie R.R., N.Y. Cen. R.R.; mem. engring. dept. Stone & Webster, Inc., Boston, 1922-24; asst. div. mgr. electric and gas refrigeration Servel Corp., 1924-27; staff engr. Johns-Manville Corp., 1928-29; steam and diesel-electric indsl. and marine devel. staff Am. Locomotive Co., 1930-39; steam turbine engr. Allis-Chalmers Mfg. Co., 1939-40; dist. mgr. Stone & Webster Engring. Corp., Washington; dir. purchasing Stone & Webster Engring. Corp., Boston; v.p., dir., midwest mgr. Stone & Webster Engring. Corp., Chgo., 1940-61; v.p. Lester Knight and Assoc., mgmt. cons., cons. engrs., N.Y.C.; adviser U.S. depts. War, State, Navy, 1945-48, to rubber dir. RFC; cons. Bur. Internat. Bus. Ops., Dept. Commerce. With U.S. Army, 1917-22, AEF. Mem. AIME, Assn. Cons. Mgmt. Engrs. N.Y., Com. Econ. Devel., U.S. Naval Inst., Am. Petroleum Inst., Newcomen Soc. Eng., Am. Ordnance Assn., Am. Soc. Naval Engrs., Harvard Musical Assn., Chgo. Club, Mid-Day Club, Chgo. Golf Club, Met. Club, Burning Tree Club, Dequesne Club, Army Athletic Assn., Engrs. Club, Downtown Club. *

MACLACHLAN, JAMES MORRILL, management educator; b. Geneva, Ill., Mar. 21, 1934; s. John Andrew and Gladys (Morrill) MacL.; m. Sally Gerig, Oct. 21, 1978; children: Sheila, Carolyn, Laura. BS, Carnegie Inst. Tech., 1956; MBA, Harvard U., 1971; PhD, U. Calif., Berkeley, 1975. Publ. The Tri-Town News, Sidney, N.Y., 1958-69; asst. prof. NYU, N.Y.C., 1975-79; assoc. prof. Columbia U., N.Y.C., 1980; assoc. prof. time mgmt. Rensselaer Poly. Inst., Troy, N.Y., 1981-91; pres. Timely Decisions, Inc., Delmar, N.Y., 1978-91, Biblical Films, Inc., Delmar, 1981-91. Author: Response latency: New Measure of Advertising, 1977; Co-author: Marketing in the Year 2000 and Beyond, 1990. Mem. Delmar (N.Y.) Full Gospel Fellowship. With U.S. Army, 1956-58. Mem. Soc. Motion Picture and TV Editors, Harvard Club. Pioneered time compression of audio-visual products. Died Aug. 18, 1991; buried Sidney, N.Y. Home: Delmar N.Y.

MACLEAN, CHARLES WALDO, bishop; b. Lincoln, N.H., June 28, 1903; s. Howard Douglas and Ethel Holmes MacL.; m. Grace Elizabeth Mentzer, May 31, 1928; children: Peter Duncan, Judith Ann Webber. BA, St. Stephens Coll., 1925; STD, Gen. Theol. Sem., 1928; DD, Bard Coll., 1962. Ordained priest Episcopal Ch., 1929. Curate Ch. of Epiphany, N.Y.C., 1928-30; vicar St. John's Chapel, Dunton, N.Y., 1930-33; rector Grace Ch., Riverhead, N.Y., 1933-49; archdeacon Suffolk, Diocese L.I., 1942-50; hon. canon Cathedral of Incarnation, Garden City, N.Y., 1947; adminstr. Diocese of L.I., 1950-62; asst. treas., trustee Estate Belongings to Diocese of L.I.; suffragan bishop L.I., 1962-76; sub-prelate, chaplain Order St. John of Jerusalem, 1972-85; dir. Diocesan dept. promotion; treas., instr., v.p. George Mercer Jr. Meml. Sch. Theology, exec. adminstr. scholarship fund; deployment officer Diocese of L.I.; v.p. Diocesan Coun. Pres. Suffolk County Social Agys., 1937-43, Anglican Found.; v.p. Suffolk Cen. Hosp., 1944-50, St. Mary's Hosp., Bayside, N.Y.; dir. Episcopal Charities, 1951-85; trustee Ch. Army, Am. Ch. Bldg. Fund. Mem. St. Andrews Soc. N.Y. chaplain , New Eng. Soc. N.Y., Bklyn. Club, Garden City Golf Club. Home: Garden City N.Y. Died Mar. 22, 1985.

MACLEAN, DONALD ISIDORE, university president, clergyman; b. Norwalk, Conn., Nov. 25, 1929; s. Chester M. and Irene A. (Paquette) MacL. A.B., Boston Coll., 1953, M.A., 1959; Ph.L., Weston Coll., 1954; Ph.D., Catholic U. Am., 1958; postgrad., U. Innsbruck, Austria, 1958-62. Ordained priest Roman Catholic Ch., 1961; Alexander von Humboldt fellow, research asso. Inst. Phys. Chemistry, U. Goettingen, Germany, 1962-65; asst. prof. Boston Coll., 1966-70, assoc. prof., 1970-73, dir. labs. dept. chemistry, 1967-71; prin. investigator Air Force Office Sci. Research, 1968-73; tech. dir., prin. investigator Boston Coll. Themis Program, Office Naval Research, 1969-74; v.p. acad. affairs, dean faculties Creighton U., Omaha, 1973-76; pres. St. Joseph's U., Phila., 1976-86, Spring Hill Coll., Mobile, Ala., 1989. Bd. dirs. St. Louis U., 1975-82, Phila. Urban Coalition, 1976-84; trustee Canisius Coll., 1982-88, Valley Forge Mil. Acad. and Jr. Coll., 1983-88, United Way of S.E. Pa., 1982-86. Mem. Am. Council Edn. (dir. 1978-83), Assn. Jesuit Colls. and Univs. (dir. 1976-86), Area Council for Econ. Edn. (dir. 1980-84), Union League, Compact for Lifelong Edn. Opportunity, Acad. Scis. Phila. (dir. 1977-89), Sigma Xi, Alpha Sigma Nu. Home: Mobile Ala. Died Nov. 13, 1989; buried Weston, Mass.

MACLEAN, NORMAN FITZROY, English literature educator, author; b. Clarinda, Iowa, Dec. 23, 1902; s. John Norman and Clara (Davidson) M.; m. Jessie Burns, Sept. 24, 1931 (dec. 1968); children—Jean Burns, John Norman. A.B., Dartmouth Coll., 1924; Ph.D., U. Chgo., 1940; Litt. D. (hon.), Mont. State U., 1980, U. Mont., 1981, Dartmouth Coll., 1987. Instr. English Dartmouth Coll., Hanover, N.H., 1924-26; instr. to prof. English Lit. U. Chgo., 1930-73, William Rainey Harper prof. English lit., 1963-73; dean students U. Chgo., 1942-45, acting dir. Inst. Mil. Studies, 1943-45, chmn. com. gen. studies humanities, 1952-66. Author: Manual of Instruction in Military Maps and Aerial Photographs (with Everett C. Olson), 1943, Critics and Criticism, Ancient and Modern (with others), 1952, The Theory of Lyric Poetry from the Renaissance to Coleridge; (semi-autobiography-2 novellas, 1 short story) A River Runs Through It and Other Stories, 1976 (Pulitzer prize nomination), Young Men and Fire, 1992. Recipient Quantrell prizes for Excellence in Undergrad. Teaching U. Chgo., 1932, 41, 73. Mem. MLA, Mont. Hist. Soc., Beta Theta Pi. Democrat. Club: Quadrangle. Home: Chicago Ill. Died Aug. 2, 1990.

MACLEAN, WILLIAM, insurance executive; b. Manchester, Eng., Dec. 27, 1908; came to U.S., 1921, naturalized, 1926; s. Robert and Eva (Epplestone) MacL.; m. Shirley A. Durring, Sept. 12, 1932 (dec. died 1949); 1 dau., Janet; m. Margaret Strickland, Aug. 20, 1953 (dec. 1984) 1 son, William; m. Barbara Anne McKinney, Dec. 28, 1984. Student pub. schs. of, Eng. With Joseph Froggatt & Co., Inc. (pub. accountants), N.Y.C., 1929-47; with Nat. Union Fire Ins. Co. of Pitts., 1947-69, dir., from 1949, v.p., 1951-56, pres., 1956-69. Clubs: University, Royal Poinciana Golf. Home: Naples Fla. Deceased. †

MACLENNAN, HUGH, writer; b. Glace Bay, N.S., Can., Mar. 20, 1907; s. Samuel J. and Katherine (McQuarrie) M.; m. Dorothy MacLennan, June 22, 1936 (div. 1957); m. Frances Aline, 1959. BA, Dalhousie U., 1928; BA, MA, Oxford U., 1932; MA, PhD, Princeton U., 1935; LLD, Dalhousie U., 1955, Sask. U., 1959, U. Toronto, 1965, Laurentian U., 1966, Carleton U., 1967; LittD, Western Ont. U., 1952, U. Man., 1953, Waterloo Luth., 1961, McMaster U., 1965, Sherbrooke U., 1967, U. B.C., 1968; LittD (hon.), St. Mary's U., 1970, Mt. Alison U., 1970, Laval U., 1973, Windsor U., 1976, Waterloo U., 1977, Université de Montréal, 1983. Prof. emeritus dept. English McGill U., 1979-90; vis. prof. Can. U., Montreal, Que. Author: Oxyrhynchus, 1935, Barometer Rising, 1941, Two Solitudes, 1945, The Precipice, 1948, Each Man's Son, 1951, Cross Country, 1954, Thirty and Three, 1954, The Watch That Ends the Night, 1959 (Gov. Gen. award for English fiction 1959), Scotchman's Return and Other Essays, 1960, Seven Rivers of Canada, 1961, The Colour of Canada, 1974,

Voices in Time, 1980; contbr. articles to numerous lit. jours. Recipient Gov.-Gen.'s award for Fiction, 1945, 48, 59, and Non-Fiction, 1949, 54, Lorne Pierce Gold medal for lit. Royal Soc. Can., 1952, Royal Bank award 1984, James Madison medal Princeton U., 1987. Fellow Royal Soc. Can. (assoc. 1953). Clubs: Montreal Amateur Athletic Assn.; North Hatley; McGill Faculty. Home: Montreal Can. Died Nov. 7, 1990. †

MACMAHON, LLOYD FRANCIS, judge; b. Elmira, N.Y., Aug. 12, 1912; s. Frank A. and Edith (Newton) MacM.; m. Margaret A. Daly, July 9, 1938; children: Patricia MacMahon Milano, Kathleen MacMahon Taylor, John, Theresa MacMahon Finneran. Student, Syracuse U., 1932-34; A.B., Cornell U., 1936, LL.B., 1938. Bar: N.Y. 1939. Assoc. Donovan, Leisure, Newton, Lumbard & Irvine, N.Y.C, 1942-53; chief asst. U.S. atty. So Dist. N.Y., 1953-55, U.S. atty., 1955; ptnr. Kramer, Marx, Greenlee, Backus & MacMahon, N.Y.C., 1955-57; individual practice N.Y.C., 1958-59; judge U.S. Dist. Ct. So. Dist. N.Y., 1959-89, chief judge, 1980-82, sr. judge, 1982-89; judge U.S. Fgn. Intelligence Surveillance Ct., Washington, from 1985. Served as lt. (j.g.) USNR, 1944-45. Mem. ABA, Fed. Bar Assn., Phi Delta Phi. Home: White Plains N.Y. Died Apr. 8, 1989; buried White Plains, N.Y.

MACMILLAN, HAROLD (EARL OF STOCKTON), former British prime minister; b. 1894; s. Maurice Crawford and Helen (Belles) M.; ed. Eton and Oxford U.; D.C.L. (hon.), Oxford U., 1958; LL.D., Cambridge U., 1961; m. Dorothy Evelyn Cavendish (dec. 1966); 1 son, 3 daus. (1 dec. 1970). Conservative M.P. from Stockton-on-Tees, 1924-29, 31-45, Bromley, 1945-64; parliamentary sec. Ministry of Supply, 1940-42; parliamentary under sec. of state for colonies, 1942; minister resident North West Africa and North Central Mediterranean, 1942-45; sec. of state for air, May-July 1945; minister of housing and local govt., 1951-54, minister of def., 1954-55, sec. of state for fgn. affairs, 1955, chancellor of Exchequer, 1955-57, Prime Minister, First Lord of Treasury, 1957-63; chmn. Macmillan Holdings, from 1963; dir. Pan Books, Ltd.; chancellor Oxford U., from 1960. Served with Grenadier Guards, World War I. Author: Memoirs, Vols. I-VI, 1966-73; War Diaries, 1984, others. Created 1st Earl of Stockton, 1984. Died Dec. 29, 1986. Home: Hayward's Heath, Sussex Eng. †

MACMILLAN, SIR KENNETH, choreographer, ballet director; b. Dumfermline, Scotland, Dec. 11, 1929; s. William and Edith (Shreeve) Mc.M.; m. Deborah Williams, Mar. 22, 1974; 1 dau., Charlotte. Dance tng. received at Sadler's Wells Sch., London; D (hon.), U. Edinburgh, 1976. Founding mem., dancer Sadler's Wells Theatre Ballet, London, 1946; dancer, then choreographer Sadler's Wells Ballet, London, 1952-66; dir. Deutsche Oper Ballet, Berlin, 1966-69; resident choreographer, dir. The Royal Ballet, London, 1970-77, prin. choreographer, 1977-92; artistic assoc. Am. Ballet Theatre, N.Y.C., 1984-92. Ballets choreographed include: Somnambulism, 1953, Laiderette, Dances Concertantes, Noctambules, 1956, The Burrow, 1958, Le Baiser de la Fee, 1960, The Invitation, 1960, The Rite of Spring, 1962, Romeo and Juliet, 1965, Das Lied von der Erde, 1965, Anastasia, Manon, 1974, Elite Syncopations, Requiem, 1976, My Brother, My Sisters, 1978, Mayerling, 1978, La Fin du Jour, Gloria, Isadora, 1981, The Wild Boy, 1981, Quartet, 1982, Orpheus, 1982, Valley of the Shadows, 1982, Different Drummer, Solitaire, Agon, and others. Knighted (Eng.) 1983; recipient Evening Standard Ballet award, 1979. Home: New York N.Y. Died Oct. 29, 1992. †

MACMURRAY, FREDERICK MARTIN, actor; b. Kankakee, Ill., Aug. 30, 1908; s. Frederick and Maleta (Martin) MacM.; m. Lillian Lamont, June 20, 1936; m. June Haver, June 28, 1954; 3 children. Student, Carroll Coll., Waukesha, Wis., 1925-26. Played in orchs. Chgo. and L.A., 1925-29; appeared in vaudeville, 1929-34; Broadway debut in Three's a Crowd, 1930; other stage appearances include Roberta, N.Y.C., 1934; motion pictures include The Egg and I, 1947, Miracle of the Bells, 1948, Don't Trust Your Husband, 1949, Family Honeymoon, 1949, The Caine Mutiny, 1953, The Far Horizons, 1954, Woman's World, 1954, Rains of Ranchipur, 1955, The Shaggy Dog, 1959, The Apartment, 1960, The Absent Minded Professor, 1961, Bon Voyage, 1962, Son of Flubber, 1963, Kisses for My President, 1964, Follow Me Boys, 1966, The Happiest Millionaire, 1967, The Swarm, 1978; star TV show My Three Sons, 1960-72; appeared in TV films The Chadwick Family, 1974 Beyond the Bermuda Triangle, 1975. Home: Los Angeles Calif. Died Nov. 5, 1991.

MACNAMARA, G. ALLAN, railroad executive; b. Winnipeg, Manitoba, Can., Feb. 4, 1894; came to U.S., 1925, naturalized, 1938; s. William B. and Constance (lePage) MacN.; m. Margaret Simpson, July 10, 1926; 1 child, Robert Simpson. Ed., pub. grade and high schs., Winnipeg. Sec. freight graffic dept. Can. No. Ry., 1912-14, rate clk., 1919-20; mem. staff freight traffic dept., tarris bur. Can. Pacific R.R. Co., Winnipeg, 1920-22, rate clk., asst. chief clk., travelling freight agt., 1922-25; traveling freight agt. Can. Pacific R.R. Co., Mpls., 1925-28; dist. freight agt. Can. Pacific R.R.-Soo Line, Indpls., 1928-34; div. freight agt. Can. Pacific R.R.-Soo Line, Detroit, 1934-36, gen. freight agt., 1936-40; gen. traffic mgr. Soo Line, Mpls., 1944-47; v.p. traffic Can. Pacific Ry., 1948-50; bd. dirs. 1st Nat. Bank of Mpls. Trustee Dunwoody Indsl. Inst.. With Can. Army, France, 1915-19. Mem. Nat. Freight Traffic Assn., Chgo. Club, Union League, Traffic Club, N.Y. Traffic Club, Mpls. Club, Minikahda Club, Athletic Club, Mpls. Traffic Club, Minn. Club. *

MACNEILL, EARL S(CHWORM), banker, lawyer; b. Garfield, N.J., Oct. 2, 1893; s. Quentin Stevenson and Ida (Schworm) MacN.; m. Marie Kelly, July 16, 1922; 1 child, Frank Kelly. LLB, Cornell U., 1915. Trust officer Continental Bank & Trust Co., N.Y., 1929-48; v.p. Irving Trust Co., N.Y.C., 1948-58, Merrill Anderson Co., from 1959; lectr. Practing Law Inst. N.Y., Grad. Sch. of Banking, Rutgers U.; bd. dirs. Flakice Corp. Author: The Man on Salary and His Estate, 1957, What Women Want to Know about Wills, 1959. Capt. Inf., U.S. Army, World War I. Mem. ABA (chmn. real property, probate and trust law sect. 1952-53), N.Y. Fin. Advertisers (pres. 1948), Fin. Pub. Rels. Assn. Republican. Methodist. *

MACNUTT, GLENN GORDON, painter, illustrator; b. London, Ont., Can., Jan. 21, 1906; came to U.S., 1922, naturalized, 1931; s. Gordon Ross and Ann Mary (Amirault) MacN.; m. Evelyn Louise Simpson, Oct. 12, 1935; children: Jean Ann, Glenn Stephen, Karen Louise. Student, Sch. Mus. Fine Arts, Boston, 1930-32, Mass. Sch. Art, Boston, 1924-28. Exhibited Bklyn. Mus., 1939-41, Art Inst. Chgo., 1939-41, 42, Met. Mus., 1941-42, Pa. Acad. Fine Arts, 1942-52, Los Angeles Pub. Library, 1954; one man shows include Guild Boston Artists, 1940-41, 43, Whistler House, 1942, Wellesley Coll., Doll and Richards Gallery, 1947, Salem (Mass.) State Coll.; represented in permanent collections Boston Mus. Fine Arts, New Britain (Conn.) Art Inst., Farnsworth Mus., Maine, Harvard U., Wheaton Coll., Mass., Mather Sch., Boston, Frye Mus., Seattle, Tufts U., Boston. Recipient award Concord Art Assn., 1953; Dolphin fellow Am. Watercolor Soc., 1981. Mem. NAD (Adolph and Clara Obrig prize 1963), Boston Soc. Watercolor Painters (v.p., sec.-treas. 1945-48, awards 1954-56), Guild Boston Artists (bd. mgrs.), Am. Watercolor Soc. (Richard Mitton award 1942, 55, 57, Herbert L. Pratt award 1956, Grumbacher award 1965, E. Heiland award 1971, Ford Times award 1972), NAD, Allied Artists Am. (Emily Lowe award 1960, Frank Liljegren award 1972). Home: Dorchester Mass. Died Oct. 16, 1987; buried Cedar Grove Cemetery, Boston.

MACRIDIS, ROY CONSTANTINE, political science educator, writer; b. Istanbul, Turkey, Dec. 25, 1918; s. Constantine and Maria M.; m. Jacklyn Williams, Aug. 28, 1946; children: Kathleen, Stephen. B.A., Athens Coll. (Greece), 1936; Lic.-en-Dr., U. Paris, 1941; M.A., Harvard U., 1943, Ph.D., 1947; Doct.-es-Lettres, Claremont-Ferrand (France), 1965. Asst. prof. Northwestern U., Evanston, Ill., 1949-52, assoc. prof., 1952-56; prof. Washington U., St. Louis, 1956-64; prof. polit. sci. SUNY, Buffalo, 1964-65; prof. polit. sci. Brandeis U., Waltham, Mass., 1965-89, Lawrence Wien prof. internat. cooperation emeritus, 1989, former head dept., Soc. Sci. Coun., Faculty Senate. Author 9 books including: Contemporary Political Ideologies, 1983, 5th edit., 1992, Modern Political Systems, 1985, Contemporary Political Regimes, 1986, French Politics in Transition, 1976, also numerous articles. Guggenheim fellow, 1972; Fulbright fellow, 1972,, 1978. Home: Belmont Mass. Died Dec. 20, 1991.

MAC VICAR, MARGARET LOVE AGNES, materials physicist, educator; b. Hamilton, Ont., Can., Nov. 20, 1943; came to U.S., 1946, naturalized, 1953; d. George Francis and Elizabeth Margaret (Thompson) MacV. SB in Physics, MIT, 1964, DSc in Metallurgy and Materials Sci, 1967; DSc (hon.), Clarkson U., 1985. Postdoctoral fellow NATO, Marie Curie fellow Cavendish Lab., U. Cambridge, Eng., 1967-69; instr. physics MIT, Cambridge, Mass., 1969-70, asst. prof., 1970-74, assoc. prof. physics, 1974-79, Class of 1922 Career Devel. prof., 1973-75, assoc. prof. phys. sci., 1979-83, prof. phys. sci., from 1983, Cecil and Ida Green prof. edn., from 1980, dean undergrad. edn., 1985-91; v.p. Carnegie Instn., Washington, 1983-87; Chancellor's Disting. prof. U. Calif., Berkeley, 1979; cons. to univs., industry, nonprofit orgns.; mem. corp. C.S. Draper Lab., Cambridge; dir. W.H. Brady Co., Exxon Corp., Harvard Coop. Soc.; past co-chair Project 2061 AAAS; vice chmn. adv. com. to directorat of sci. and engring. edn. NSF; mem. Adv. Council on Edn., Sci., Tech., and the Economy, Carnegie Corp.; mem. corp. Woods Hole Oceanographic Inst. Mem. editorial adv. bd. World Book Sci. Yr.; patentee in field. Past trustee Carnegie Found. for Advancement Teaching; trustee Boston Mus. Sci.; past mem. Carnegie Council on Policy Studies in Higher Edn. Recipient Most Significant Contribution to Edn. award MIT, 1977, Charles A. Dana awards for Pioneering Achievements in Higher Edn., 1986; Young Faculty Research award Gen. Electric Found., 1976-79; Danforth Found. assoc. 1972-91. Fellow Am. Phys. Soc.; mem. Am. Women in Sci., Am. Assn. of Higher Edn. Club: Boston Women's City. Home: Cambridge Mass. Died Sept. 30, 1991.

MADDEN, JOHN T., banker; b. N.Y.C., May 14, 1896; s. John and Ellen M. (Bodkin) M.; m. Gladys Wells, 1923. Student, Fordham U. Sch. of Law, NYU Sch. Commerce and Fin. With Nat. City Bank of N.Y., from 1925, asst. sec., v.p., 1925, sr. v.p., 1929, chmn. all adv. bds., 1930-44; CEO, chmn. bd. dirs. Emigrant Indsl. Savs. Bank, N.Y.C.; bd. dirs. Diamond Nat. Corp., Mfrs. Hanover Trust Co., J. P. Maguire and Co., Inc., W. R. Grace & Co. Mem. exec. com. N.Y. State adv. com. of U.S. Savs. Bonds div. of Treasury Dept.; mem. adv. coun. N.Y. chpt. Am. Inst. Banking. *

MADEIRA, CRAWFORD CLARK, fuel company executive; b. Phila., Feb. 23, 1894; s. Louis C. and Marion (Clark) M.; m. Sarah C. Neilson, Jan. 18, 1918; children: Crawford Clark, Lewis N., Harry R. Grad., Middlesex Sch., Concord, Mass., 1912; BS, U. Pa., 1916. V.p. Dickson Fuel Corp., Phila., from 1956, also dir. Served on Mex. Border, 1916, 1st lt., cav., U.S. Army, 1917-19, lt. col., cav., AUS, 1941-46. Mem. Gen. Alumni Soc. U. Pa. (pres. 1959-63), Merion Cricket Club, St. anthony Club, Racquet Club, Germantown Cricket Club, Univ. Barge Club, Bachelors Barge Club, Faculty Club. *

MADSEN, CHARLES CLIFFORD, retired college president, consultant; b. Luck, Wis., Feb. 13, 1908; s. Mads Peter and Ella (Johnson) M.; m. Esther Johnson, June 12, 1934; children: Carol Sonya (Mrs. Ray Lee Dickson), Maurice Lowell. A.B., U. Minn., 1931; B.D., Trinity Theol. Sem., 1934; Th.D., Central Bapt. Theol. Sem., Kansas City, Kan., 1949; D.D. (hon.), Midland Lutheran Coll., 1965; L.D.H. (hon.), Dana Coll., 1971. Ordained to ministry Luth. Ch., 1934; pastor Our Savior's Ch., Kansas City, Kan., 1934-42; prof. practical theol. Trinity Sem., Blair, Neb., 1946-56; dir. Christian activities Dana Coll., Blair, from 1946; chmn. Christianity dept. Christian activities Dana Coll., 1946-56, acting pres., 1956-57, pres., 1957-71, pres. emeritus, from 1971, cons., from 1971. Contbr. articles profl. jours. Mem. Neb. Higher Edn. Facilities Commn.; mem. Neb. Supreme Ct. Nominating Commn.; Past pres. Neb. Ind. Coll. Found., Tri-State Coll. Conf. Served to lt. comdr. Chaplains Corps USNR, World War II; capt., chaplain Res. (ret.). Decorated Knight Order of Dannebrog (Denmark). Mem. V.F.W., Neb. Assn. Colls. and Univs. (past pres.). Club: Rotarian. Home: Blair Nebr. Deceased. †

MAES, ROBERT ADAMSON, financial foundation executive; b. New Orleans, Jan. 31, 1910; s. Urban and Sabina Gertrude (Adamson) M.; m. Susan Brady, July 7, 1987; children by previous marriage: Robert Adamson, Nancy Maes Aherne; stepchildren: Kelley Shawn Buchanan, Matthew Grayson Buchanan. BS, Yale U., 1931; postgrad., Harvard U. Sch. Bus., 1931-32. CPA, Pa. With Union Transfer Co., Phila., 1932-33; overseer United Fruit Co., Guatemala, 1933-35; acct. Price Waterhouse & Co., CPAs, Phila., 1936-41; fin. cons., 1945-50; pres. Independence Found., Phila., 1950-91; also dir.; dir. Discount Corp. N.Y. Lt. USNR, 1942-45. Mem. Racquet Club (Phila.). Republican. Episcopalian. Home: Glenmoore Pa. Died July 9, 1991; buried Glenmoore, Pa.

MAGEE, FRANK LYNN, metal products company executive; b. Shamokin, Pa., Apr. 13, 1896; s. William F. and Ida L. (Boyer) M.; m. Marie Janet Weston, June 11, 1921 (dec.); 1 child, Curtis Weston; m. Dorothy C. Hurlock, June 10, 1938; stepchildren: George L. Hoffman Jr., William H. Hoffman. BSEE, Lehigh U., 1917, D Engring.; LLD (hon.), Maryville Coll. With Aluminum Co. Am., from 1917, mgr. sheet sales, 1937-43, gen. prodn. mgr., 1943-46, v.p., gen. prodn. mgr., 1946-55, exec. v.p., 1955-57, pres., 1957-60, chmn. bd. dirs., CEO, 1960-63, chmn. exec. com., 1963-65, also bd. dirs.; officer, dir. various Aluminum Co. of Am. subsidiaries; dir. Mellon Nat. Bank & Trust Co., Westinghouse Airbrake Co., Mohawk Airlines, Inc., SCM, Inc. Exec. com. Allegheny County Conf. Community Devel.; chmn. Hosp. Planning Assn., Allegheny County; bd. dirs. United Fund, Allegheny Co. Corp.; trustee Lehigh U., U. Pitts.; mem. Com. Econ. Devel.; dir. Presbyn. U. Hosp. With U.S. Army Signal Corps, 1917-19. Mem. AIEE, Western Pa. Engrs. Soc., Duquesne Club, Univ Club, Rolling Rock Club, Rox Chapel Golf Club, Laurel Valley Golf Club, Alpha Chi Rho. Episcopalian. *

MAGILL, JAMES MARION, music educator; b. Due West, S.C., Dec. 12, 1921; s. John Thomas and Zula Lee (Presnell) M.; m. Nell Kirk Hunter, Mar. 31, 1943; children: James Marion Jr. (dec.), Jane Hunter. BA, Erskine Coll., 1942; MA, Columbia U., 1952, EdD, 1957. Tchr. Ware Shoals (S.C.) Pub. Schs., 1942-44; dir. instrn. music Greenville (S.C.) City Schs., 1944-51; county supr. music Anderson (S.C.) Pub. Schs., 1951-55; dir. music Sch. Dist. Greenville County, 1955-63, Balt. Pub. Schs., 1963-70; prof., chmn. music dept. Columbia U., N.Y.C., 1970-74, prof. music, 1974-81, prof. emeritus, 1981-91; vis. prof. Hart Coll., Hartford, Conn., 1971-72; chmn. music dept. S.C. Gov.'s Sch. of Arts, Greenville, 1982-85. Author (listening guide) Music of the World's Great Composers, 1960; music condr. film strips Patriotic Series, 1967, 68; guest condr. State Choruses, various eastern states, 1960-80, Ch. Choir Festivals, various states, 1958-74; condr. Anderson Civic Oratorio and Orch., 1962-73. Deacon Greer (S.C.) Presbyn. Ch., 1948, elder Towson (Md.) Presbyn. Ch., 1968-70. Recipient Scroll of Honor Anderson Ind. and Daily Mail-Pubs., 1963, 71, Pres.'s award in Arts Balt. Arts Council, 1968, Outstanding Service Plaque A.R.

Presbyn. Synod, 1981. Mem. Music Educators Nat. Conf., Am. Choral Dirs. Assn., Phi Mu Alpha Sinfonia, Phi Delta Kappa, Kappa Delta Pi. Lodges: Torch Internat., Kiwanis. Home: Greenville S.C. Died June 2, 1991; buried WoodLawn Cemetery, Greenville, S.C.

MAGNUS, WILHELM, mathematician; b. Berlin, Germany, Feb. 5, 1907; came to U.S., 1948, naturalized, 1955; s. Alfred and Paula (Kalkbrenner) M.; m. Gertrud Remy, Aug. 5, 1939; children—Jutta, Bettina, Alfred. Ph.D., U. Frankfurt, Germany, 1931; D.Sc. (hon.), Poly. Inst. N.Y., 1980. Lectr. U. Frankfurt, 1933-38; prof. U. Goettingen, 1947-48; research asso. Calif. Inst. Tech., 1948-50; prof. math. NYU, 1950-73, prof. emeritus, 1973-90; spl. research group theory, spl. functions math. physics, diffraction problems, differential equations. Author books, articles in field. Rockefeller fellow, 1934; Guggenheim fellow, 1969; Fulbright-Hays sr. research scholar, 1973-74. Mem. Goettingen Acad. Scis., Am. Math. Soc. Home: New Rochelle N.Y. Died Oct. 15, 1990; nuried Prattsville, N.Y.

MAGNUSON, WARREN GRANT, United States senator; b. Moorhead, Minn., Apr. 12, 1950; m. Jermaine Elliott Peralta, Oct. 4, 1964. Student, U. N.D., N.D. State U., 1923-24; LLB, U. Wash., 1929. Bar: Wash. 1929. Pvt. practice Wash., 1929; spl. prosecutor King County, 1931; mem. Wash. State Legislature, 1933-34; asst. U.S. dist. atty., 1934; pros. atty. King County, 1934-36; mem. 75th to 78th Congresses from 1st Wash. Dist.; mem. U.S. Senate, 1944-81; pres. pro tem., chmn. com. on appropriations. Del. from Seattle to State Constl. Conv., 1933; sec. Seattle Mcpl. League, 1930-31. Lt. comdr. USNR. Mem. VFW, Am. Legion, Washington Athletic Club of Seattle, Burning Tree Club (Washington), Theta Chi. Democrat. Lutheran. Home: Seattle Wash. Died May 20, 1989.

MAGUIRE, BASSETT, botany educator, curator; b. Alabama City, Ala., Aug. 4, 1904; s. Charles T. and Rose (Bassett) M.; m. Ruth Richards, 1926; children: Bassett, Grace (Mrs. Daniel N. MacLemore, Jr.); m. Celia Kramer, Mar. 25, 1951. B.S., U. Ga., 1926; grad. student, U. Pitts., 1926; Ph.D., Cornell U., 1938. High sch. tchr. sci. and biology Athens, Ga., 1926-27; instr. botany U. Ga., 1927-29, Cornell U., 1929-31, 37-38; prof. Utah State U., 1931-43; curator, head curator N.Y. Bot. Garden, 1943-78, Nathaniel Lord Britton distinguished sr. curator, 1961-78, asst. dir., 1968-69, dir. botany, 1969-71, 73-75, dir. emeritus, sr. scientist, mem. bd. mgrs., 1971-91; dir. botany Jardin Botánico Nacional, Santo Domingo, Dominican Republic; exec. dir. Orgn. for Flora Neotropica, 1964-75; aquatic botanist N.Y. State Conservation Dept., 1930-31, U.S. Bur. Fisheries, 1932, 34; ecologist, spl. agt. U.S. Conservation Service, Dept. Agr., 1934-35; adj. prof. botany Columbia, N.Y.C., 1961-91, CUNY; non-resident prof. Utah State U.; Del. UNESCO, 1947, 64, FAO, 1961; dir. sci. N.Y. Bot. Garden, 1974-91; also mem. corp.; founder, exec. dir. Orgn. for Flora Neotropica, 1964-76; cons. Eli Lilly, Warner-Lambert, Tex. Instrument, Nat. Bulk Carriers; discoverer (with John J. Wurdack) Serrania de la Neblina, mountain complex on Venezuelan-Brazilian frontier, 1953, bot. exploration Neblina, 1953-54, 57-58, 64-65; bot. exploration N.Am., especially Rocky Mountains and Intermountain U.S., 1923-55; mem., leader, dir. numerous expdns. to tropical S.Am., including Roraima Formation (Lost Worlds) and Amazon Basin. Mem. editorial bd. Flora of Ecuador, Moscosoa, Santo Domingo; author articles, treatises on Western Am. botany, Neotropics vegetation and geography. Trustee Mary Cary Arboretum. Recipient Sarah Gildersleeve Fife Meml. award Hort Soc., 1952; David Livingstone centenary medal Am. Geog. Soc., 1965; grantee NSF, Am. Philos. Soc., Guggenheim Found., Explorers Club; herbarium of the Jardīn Botānico Nacional in Santo Domingo was named Herbario Dr. Bassett Maguire in his honor. Corr. mem. Royal Netherlands Bot. Soc. (hon.); hon. fellow Assn. for Tropical Biology (founder; pres. 1964-65); mem. AAAS, Orgn. Tropical Studies (founder), Torrey Bot. Club (pres. 1963-64), N.Y. Acad. Scis., Sociedad Venezolana de Ciencias Naturales (hon.), Bot. Soc. Am. (Cert. of Merit for Disting. Achievement and Contbns.1990), Internat. Soc. Plant Taxonomy, Am. Soc. Plant Taxonomists, Orgn. Flora Neotropica (commn.), Soc. Bot. Dominicana (hon.), Am. Geog. Soc. (hon.), Newcomen Soc. (life), Academia de Ciencias de la Républica Dominicana (founder, mem. biology com.), El Patronato Jardín Botánico Nacional (Santo Domingo, Dominican Republic). Home: Bronx N.Y. Died Feb. 6, 1991; buried Woodlawn Cemetery, Bronx, N.Y.

MAHER, LEO THOMAS, bishop; b. Mt. Union, Iowa, July 1, 1915; s. Thomas and Mary (Teberg) M. Ed., St. Joseph's Coll., Mountain View, Calif., St. Patrick's Sem., Menlo Park, Calif.; LHD, U. San Diego, 1986. Ordained priest Roman Catholic Ch.; asst. pastor in San Francisco, 1944-47, sec. archbishop of, 1947-61; chancellor Archdiocese San Francisco, 1956-62, dir. vocations, 1957-62, archdiocesan consultor, 1959-62; apptd. domestic prelate, 1954; bishop Santa Rosa, Calif., 1962-69; 3d bishop of San Diego, 1969-90; prior Western Lieutenancy of Knights and Ladies of Holy Sepulchre. Bd. dirs. Soc. Propagation of Faith, Youth's Director, Cath. Youth Orgn.; chmn. bd. trustees U. San Diego.; Del. Ecumenical Council, Rome, Italy, 1962, 63, 64, 65. Home: San Diego Calif. Died Feb. 23, 1991; buried Holy Cross Mausoleum, San Diego.

MAHER, PHILIP BROOKS, architect; b. Kenilworth, Ill., Oct. 21, 1894; s. George W. and Elizabeth (Brooks) M.; m. Madeleine Michelson, Dec. 22, 1921 (div. 1940); children: Philip Brooks, Hilary, Colin; m. Barbara Atwater, Mar. 14, 1946. Student architecture, U. Mich. Mem. firm George W. Maher, architect, Chgo., from 1914, George W. Maher & Son, 1921-26; established firm Philip B. Maher, from 1926. Prin works include Woman's Athletic Club, Farwell Office Bldg., 1301 Astor St. and 1260 Astor St., 2909 Sheridan Rd., 1445 N. State Pkwy., 1340 Astor St. (apt. bldgs.), Gary (Ind.) City Hall, Chgo. San. Dist. Adminstrn. Bldg. Mem. govt. adv. com. on design, 5 yrs.; mem. Am. commn. to negotiate peace, Paris. Ens. USN, World War I. Fellow AIA; mem. Arts Club, Tavern Club, Delta Kappa Epsilon. Presbyterian. *

MAHON, MARGARET MARY, manufacturing company executive; b. Crossmolina, Ireland, Nov. 19, 1928; came to U.S., 1951, naturalized, 1970; d. Patrick John and Mary Christina (McNamara) M.; B.S., Fordham U., 1974, M.B.A., 1977. Sec., NCR Corp., N.Y.C., 1951-54, 63-74, adminstrv. specialist, 1974-77, dist. sect. mgr., 1977-78, N.Y. dist. adminstrv. mgr., 1978-89; mgr. family bus., 1954-63. Mem. Assn. M.B.A. Execs., Grad. Bus. Alumni Assn. Fordham U., N.Y. C. of C. and Industry. Roman Catholic. Club: Lake Isle Country. Deceased. Home: Tuckahoe N.Y. †

MAI, LUDWIG HUBERT, university dean; b. Mannheim, Germany, Mar. 27, 1898; came to U.S., 1950; s. Hubert Chrysant and Anna Maria (Specht) M.; m. Ilse Behrend, Feb. 12, 1927; children: Veronica (Mrs. J. Ray Reynolds), Klaus L., Ursula (Mrs. Gordon A. White). BBA, Coll. Econs. & Bus. Adminstrn., Mannheim, 1920. Instr. Coll. Bus. Adminstrn., Augsburg, Germany, 1921; mgr. DEFAG, China, 1923-45; lectr. Jr. Coll. Tientsin, China, 1923-45; mem. faculty St. Mary's U., San Antonio, from 1950, prof. econs., dean Grad. Sch., from 1959; internat. trade cons. S.W. Rsch. Inst.; dir. Inst. Internat. Rels., San Antonio; ednl. dir. Tex. Internat. Trade Assn. Author: The Southwest Import and Export, 1956, Approach to Economics, 1960. Mem. Am. Econ. Assn., Southwestern Social Sci. Assn., San Antonio C. of C., Pi Gamma Mu, Omicron Delta Epsilon. Roman Catholic. *

MALAMUD, WILLIAM, psychiatrist; b. Kishinev, Russia, May 5, 1896; s. Ichael and Rita (Makler) M.; m. Irene B. Titus, Aug. 5, 1927; children: William, Michael H., Thomas J. MD, CM, McGill U., Montreal, Que., Can., 1921; DSc, Boston U., 1960. Prof. psychiatry U. Iowa, 1929-39; prof. psychiatry Boston U., 1939-58, head dept., 1946-58; prof. and rsch. dir. Nat. Assn. Mental Health, from 1958; cons. St. Vincents Hosp., N.Y.C., from 1959. Author: Outlines of General Psychopathology (publ. W. W. Norton), 1935, Tice Practice of Medicine-Psychoneuroses, 1938; contbr. sci. to med. jours. Mem. AMA, Mass. Med. Soc., Am. Psychiat. Assn. (pres. 1959-60), Am. Neurological Soc., Am. Acad. Arts and Scis. Democrat. Jewish. *

MALLENDER, MILTON FRED, lawyer; b. Birmingham, Mich., Nov. 6, 1905; s. Fred and Sarah Ann (Riley) M.; m. Eleanor M. Rainey, Aug. 3, 1929 (dec. Apr. 21, 1973); children: Fred II, William Harry. Student, Albion (Mich.) Coll., 1923-24; A.B., U. Mich., 1927; J.D., Wayne State U., 1929. Bar: Mich. 1929. Practiced in Detroit; partner Lewis & Watkins, 1936-67; partner Dahlberg, Mallender & Gawne, 1967-85, of counsel, 1985-89; dir. various corps. Commr., Birmingham, 1943-52, mayor, 1946-49. Bd. dirs. Children's Aid Soc. Detroit, 1950-74, Birmingham Community House Assn., 1952-60. Mem. ABA, State Bar Mich., Sigma Nu, Sigma Delta Kappa. Republican. Presbyterian. Home: Birmingham Mich. Died Sept. 28, 1989; buried Greenwood Cemetery, Birmingham, Mich.

MALLEY, JOHN WALLACE, lawyer; b. Parkersburg, W.Va., Feb. 17, 1906; s. Robert J. and Adelia (Carney) M.; m. Kathleen Pendleton, June 20, 1936; children—Kathleen Montague, John Wallace. B.S., U.S. Naval Acad., 1927; LL.B., George Washington U., 1934; grad., Indsl. Coll. Armed Forces, 1941. Bar: D.C. bar 1934. Counsel firm Cushman, Darby & Cushman (specializing patent, trademark and anti-trust law), Washington, from 1934; professorial lectr. patent law George Washington U., 1964-65; Area chmn. Patent, Trademark and Copyright Research Inst., 1954. Served from ensign to lt. (j.g.) U.S. Navy, 1927-31; from lt. to comdr. USNR, 1941-45. Recipient Profl. Achievement award George Washington U., 1981. Mem. Phi Delta Phi. Democrat. Clubs: Chevy Chase (Md.); Army and Navy (Washington). Home: Bethesda Md. Died Nov. 5, 1988; interred Arlington Nat. Cemetery.

MALULA, JOSEPH CARDINAL, archbishop of Kinshasa; d. Kinshasa, Zaire, Dec. 12, 1917. Ordained priest Roman Cath. Ch., 1946; titular bishop of Attanaso, also aux. bishop of Kinshana, 1959; archbishop of Kinshasa, 1964-89; elevated to Sacred Coll. Cardinals, 1969; titular ch. Ss. Protomartyrs (Via Aurelia Antica); mem. Congregation Evangelization of Peoples. Died June 19, 1989. Home: Kinsasha Zaire

MANCHESTER, HUGH WALLACE, lawyer; b. Youngstown, Ohio, Mar. 25, 1905; s. Curtis A. and Leona (Eckis) M.; m. Helen L. Tinney, May 31, 1930; children: Jane Manchester Wheeler, Hugh Wallace, Virginia Manchester Sanborn, Elizabeth Manchester Gilpatric, Gilbert Mott. A.B., Cornell U., 1926; LL.B., Harvard U., 1929; LL.D., Youngstown State U., 1983. Bar: Ohio 1930. Partner, dir. Manchester, Bennett, Powers & Ullman Co. (L.P.A.), Youngstowm, 1944-86, of counsel, 1986-88. Commr. Boardman Twp. Park Dist., 1947-69; trustee, sec. Youngstown U., 1930-67; sec. to trustees Youngstown State U., 1968-83; trustee Youngstown YMCA, from 1930; pres. Belmont Park Cemetery Assn., 1940-78. Mem. ABA, Ohio Bar Assn., Mahoning County Bar Assn., Beta Theta Pi. Republican. Presbyterian (elder 1945-65). Club: Youngstown. Home: Youngstown Ohio Died Dec. 22, 1988; buried Belmont Pk. Cemetery, Youngstown, Ohio.

MANGELSDORF, PAUL CHRISTOPH, agronomist, botany educator, natural history educator; b. Atchison, Kans., July 20, 1899; s. August and Mary (Brune) M.; m. Helen Parker, June 27, 1923 (dec. May 1979); children: Paul Christoph, Clark Parker. BS, Kans. State Coll., 1921, LLD (hon.), 1961; MS, DSc, Harvard Coll., 1925; DSc (hon.), Park Coll., 1960, St. Benedict's Coll., 1965, U. N.C., Chapel Hill, 1975, Harvard U., 1977. Asst. geneticist Conn. Agrl. Expt. Sta., 1921-27; agronomist Tex. Agrl. Expt. Sta., 1927-40, asst. dir., 1936-40; vice dir., 1940; prof. botany Harvard U., Cambridge, 1940-62, Fisher prof. natural history, 1962-68, prof. emeritus, 1968-89; asst. dir. Bot. Mus. Harvard, 1940-45, dir., 1945-68; vis. prof. biology Crown Coll., U. Calif. Santa Cruz, 1968; lectr. botany U. N.C., 1968; cons. Rockefeller Found., from 1949, chmn. bd. cons., 1956; hon. prof. U. San Carlos, Guatemala, 1956, Nat. Sch. Agr., Peru, 1959; mem. Rockefeller Found. Agrl. Commn. Mex., 1941. Co-author: (with R.G. Reeves) The Origin of Indian Corn and its Relatives, 1939, (with others) Races of Maize in Mexico, 1962, Races of Maize in Columbia, 1957, Races of Maize in Central America, 1957, The Origin of Corn, 1959, Races of Maize in Peru, 1962, (with E.C. Stakman and R. Bradfield) Campaigns Against Hunger, 1967, Corn, Its Origin, Evolution and Improvement, 1974, numerous articles on genetics, plant breeding, agr. Fellow Am. Soc. Agronomy; mem. Am. Soc. Naturalists (pres. 1951), AAAS, Am. Bot. Soc., NE Bot. Soc., Genetics Soc. Am. (pres. 1955), Am. Philos. Soc., Am. Acad. Arts and Scis., Linnean Soc. London, Soc. Econ. Botany (pres. 1962), Sigma Xi, Sigma Nu, Alpha Zeta, Gamma Sigma Delta. Club: Faculty. Home: Chapel Hill N.C. Died July 22, 1989.

MANGRAVITE, PEPPINO, artist; b. Italy, June 28, 1896; came to U.S., 1912, naturalized, 1924; s. John and Concetta (Bicchieri) M.; m. Frances Teall, Sept. 4, 1926; children: Nina, Denise. Student, Scuole Tecniche, Italy, 1903-12, Cooper Union, 1913-16, Art Students League, 1917-20. Art instr. Potomac Sch., Washington, 1924-26; head art dept. Ethical Culture Schs., N.Y.C., 1927-31, Sarah Lawrence Coll., 1932-34; acting head art dept. Colorado Springs Fine Arts Ctr., 1936-37; painting instr. Cooper Union, N.Y.C., 1939-43; prof. painting and departmental rep. Sch. Painting and Sculpture, Columbia U., 1940-54, prof. painting, from 1954; instr. mural painting Art Inst. Chgo., 1940-42. Represented in large museums and galleries throughout U.S. Trustee Am. Fedn. of Art, 1940-42, Am. Acad. in Rome, to 1949. Recipient many prizes and awards including Silver medal Arthcl. League, 1955. Mem. Century Assn. *

MANHEIMER, IRVING S(AMPSON), publisher; b. Bklyn., Mar. 15, 1895; s. Emanuel and Betsy (Schwartzbaum) M.; m. Ruth Bayer, Mar. 18, 1939; children: Lawrence H., Emanuel B., Raymond B. Student, Cornell U. Pres. Pubs. Surplus Corp., 1928-39; pres. Pubs. Distbg. Corp., 1939-55, chmn. bd. dirs., from 1961; pres. Mcfadden Publs. Internat. Corp., 1951-61, chmn. bd. dirs., from 1961. Pres. Spl. Social Svcs. Mem. Kiwanis, City Club, Masons, Shriners. *

MANLEY, JOHN H., physicist; b. Harvard, Ill., July 21, 1907; s. Benjamin F. and Effie (Justice) M.; m. Kathleen Porter Baird, Sept. 4, 1935; children: Kathleen Elizabeth, Harriet Jeanne. BS, U. Ill., 1929; PhD, U. Mich., 1934. Lectr. Columbia U., N.Y.C., 1934-37; assoc. U. Ill., 1937-42; rsch. assoc. metall. lab. U. Chgo., 1942; scientist Los Alamos (N.Mex.) Nat. Lab., 1942-46, assoc. dir., 1946-51, rsch. advisor, 1957-72, cons., from 1972; assoc. prof. Washington U., St. Louis, 1946; dep. dir. div. rsch., then sec. gen. adv. com. AEC, Washington, 1947-51; prof., exec. officer dept. physics U. Wash., Seattle, 1951-57; cons. AEC, 1972-74; sr. scientist U.S. mission to IAEA, Vienna, Austria, 1957; vis. prof. U. Wash., 1973. Guggenheim fellow, 1954. Fellow AAAS, Am. Phys. Soc.; mem. Sigma Xi, Tau Beta Pi. Home: Los Alamos N.Mex. Died June 11, 1990; cremated.

MANN, DANIEL, film director; b. N.Y.C., Aug. 8, 1912. Career began as musician in resort hotels; dir.: (Broadway prodns.) Come Back Little Sheba, Rose Tattoo, Street Car Named Desire, Paint Your Wagon, (films) Come Back Little Sheba, 1952, About Mrs. Leslie, 1954, The Rose Tattoo, 1955, I'll Cry Tomorrow, 1955, Teahouse of the August Moon, 1956, Hot Spell, 1958, The Last Angry Man, 1959, The Mountain Road,

1960, Butterfield 8, 1960, Ada, 1961, Five Finger Exercise, 1962, Who's Got the Action?, 1962, Who's Been Sleeping in My Bed, 1963, Judith, 1965, Our Man Flint, 1966, For Love of Ivy, 1968, A Dream of Kings, 1969, Willard, 1971, The Revengers, 1972, Interval, 1973, Maurie, 1973, Lost in the Stars, 1974, Journey into Fear, 1976, Matilda, 1978, (TV miniseries) How the West Was Won, 1974, (TV films) Playing for Time, 1980, The Day the Loving Stopped, 1981. Served with U.S. Army, World War II. Mem. Dirs. Guild Am. Home: Malibu Calif. Died Nov. 21, 1991. †

MANN, EDWARD BEVERLY, author; b. Hollis, Kans., Jan. 31, 1902; s. Grant and Mattie (Hill) M.; m. Helen Frazier Cubberly, Oct. 18, 1928 (div. 1939); m. Elizabeth Goodell Parkhurst, July 2, 1942. A.B., U. Fla., 1927. With Willard Price & Co. (advt.), N.Y.C., 1927-29; free-lance writer fiction and articles, from 1928; dir. U. N.Mex. Press, 1949-56; editor Guns mag., Guns Ann., The Shooting Industry, Pubs. Devel. Corp., 1956-68, contbg. editor, 1968—. Author: The Man from Texas, 1931, The Blue-Eyed Kid, 1932, The Valley of Wanted Men, 1932, Killers Range, 1933, Stampede, 1934, Gamblin' Man, 1934, Rustlers' Round-up, 1935, Thirsty Range, 1935, El Sombra, 1936, Boss of the Lazy Nine, 1936, Comanche Kid, 1936, With Spurs, 1937, Shootin' Melody, 1938, Gun Feud, 1940, The Mesa Gang, 1940, Troubled Range, 1940, Gunsmoke Trail, 1941, The Whistler, 1953, New Mexico: Land of Enchantment, (with others), 1955; mng. editor: American Rifleman, 1943-45; assoc. editor: Mil. Service Pub. Co, 1945-48; guns and gunning editor: Sun Trails, 1946-56; guns editor: Field and Stream, 1975-84. Mem. Nat. Rifle Assn. (life). Republican. Club: Bird Key Yacht (Sarasota, Fla.). Home: Sarasota Fla. Died Aug. 23, 1989; buried Washington, D.C.

MANN, GERALD C., lawyer, business executive; b. Sulphur Springs, Tex., Jan. 13, 1907; s. Grover Clevel and Edna Lenora (McClimons) M.; m. Anna Mary Mars, June 23, 1929; children—Gerald C., Lola Ann, Robert Mars. B.A., So. Meth. U., 1928; LL.B., Harvard Law Sch., 1933. Bar: Tex. bar 1933. Pvt. practice Dallas, 1933-35, 36-39, 72-82; sec. state Tex., 1935; Washington rep. Tex. Planning Bd., 1935-36; atty. gen Tex., 1939-44; asst. dist. atty. Dallas County, Tex., 1982-90. Bd. govs. V.I. active numerous civic orgns. Named Disting. Alumnus So. Meth. U.; mem. Nat. Football Hall of Fame, Tex. Sports Hall of Fame. Mem. Tex. Philos. Soc. Club: Salesmanship (Dallas). Home: Dallas Tex. Died Jan. 6, 1990; buried Hillcrest Meml. Pk., Dallas.

MANN, PEGGY, author; b. N.Y.C.; d. Edna Brand and Harvey Theordore M.; m. William Horlton; children: Jennifer, Betsy. BA, U. Wis. Author: A Room in Paris, 1959, Golda: The Life Of Israel's Prime Minister, 1971, (with r. Kluger) The Last Escape: The Launching of the Largest Secret Rescue Movement of All Time, 1973, Ralph Bunche: UN Peacemaker, 1975, The Telltale Line: the Secrets of Handwriting Analysis, 1976, Luis Munoz Marin: The Man Who Remade Puerto Rico, 1976, (with Nina Brodsky) Israel in Pictures, 1979, Gizelle, Save the Children!, 1981, Marijuana Alert!, 1984, The Street of the Flower Boxes, 1966, That New Baby, 1967, The Boy with the Billion Pets, 1968, Clara Barton: Battlefield Nurse, 1969, When Carlos Closed the Street, 1969, The Clubhouse, 1969, Amelia Earhart: Pioneer of the Skies, 1970, The Twenty-five-Cent Frien, 1970, How Juan Got Home, 1972, The Lost Doll, 1972, William the Watchcat, 1972, Whitney Young, Jr.: Crusader for Freedom, 1972, The Secret Dog of Little Luis, 1973, My Dad Lives in a Downtown Hotel, 1973, Now Is Now, 1974, Last Road to Safety, 1975, (with J. Houlton) Ghost Boy, 1975, Handwriting: A Secret Way to Look Inside, 1975, (with V. Siegal) The Man Who Bought Himself: The Story of Peter Still, 1975, A Present for Yanya, 1975, There Are Two Kinds of Terrible, 1976, Lonely Girl, 1976, The Secret Ship, 1977, Twelve Is Too Old, 1981; contbr. to mags. Men. PEN, Am. Soc. of Journalist, Am. Soc. Med. Writers. Home: New York N.Y. Died July 17, 1990. †

MANN, SEYMOUR, chemical company executive, chemical engineer; b. N.Y.C., Jan. 11, 1923; s. Abraham and Rose Mann; m. Claire G. Kessler, Nov. 7, 1950; children: Lisa F., Jonathan G. BS in Chem. Engring., CCNY, 1942; MS, NYU, 1947; postgrad., U. Pa., Columbia U., New Sch. Social Research. Founder, pres. Aceto Chem. Co., Inc., Flushing, N.Y., 1947-89; v.p. Pfaltz & Bauer, from 1965; founder, v.p. Alembic Ins. Co., Ltd., 1978-89; dir. various corps.; vis. lectr. Baruch Coll., New Sch. Social Research, CCNY; arbitrator Am. Arbitration Assn., from 1980; chmn. Jump St. Records. Author: (with others) Solvents Guide, 1964; contbr. numerous articles to profl. jours.; patentee in field. Recipient Alumni Service award CCNY. Mem. CCNY Alumni Assn. (pres. 1978-80, chmn. City Coll. Fund), CCNY Chemistry Alumni Assn. (pres. 1974-80), Chemists Club (trustee 1989). Home: New York N.Y. Died Dec. 9, 1989.

MANNES, MARYA, author, journalist, social critic, satirist; b. N.Y.C., Nov. 14, 1904; d. David and Clara (Damrosch) M.; m. Jo Mielziner, 1926 (div.); m. Richard Blow, Feb. 1937 (div.); 1 child, David J.; m. Christopher Clarkson, Apr. 2, 1948 (div.). Grad., Miss Veltin Sch. for Girls, N.Y.C.; DHL (hon.), Hood Coll., 1961. Feature editor Vogue mag., N.Y.C., 1933-36, Glamour mag., N.Y.C., 1946; intelligence analyst U.S. Govt., 1942-45; freelance journalist, 1947-52; staff writer Reporter mag., N.Y.C., 1952-63; numerous TV network appearances, from 1958; lectr. univs. and nat. assns., from 1960. Author: (autobiography) Message from a Stranger, 1948, (essays) More in Anger: Some Opinions, Uncensored and Unteleprompted, 1958, Who Owns the Air?, 1960, But Will It Sell?, 1964, They, 1968, (satiric verse) Subverse: Rhymes for Our Times, 1959, The New York I Know, 1961, Out of My Time, 1971, (nonfiction) Last Rights, 1974; co-author: Uncoupling: The Art of Coming Apart, 1972. Trustee Mannes Sch. Music, N.Y.C. Recipient George Polk Meml. award for mag. writing L.I. U., 1958, award of honor Phila. chpt. Theta Sigma Phi, 1962. Mem. AFTRA, PEN, Author's League. Home: San Francisco Calif. Died Sept. 13, 1990; buried San Francisco.

MANNING, RICHARD, economics educator; b. Dunedin, New Zealand, May 24, 1943; came to U.S., 1987; Arthur and Constance May (Morgan) M.; m. Janice Susan Taylor, Dec. 28, 1965; children: Julian, Kirsten. BA, U. Otago, Dunedin, 1965; MA with honors, U. Canterbury, Christchurch, New Zealand, 1968; PhD, La Trobe U., Melbourne, Australia, 1973. From lectr. to sr. lectr. U. Canterbury, 1972-74, prof. econs., 1979-86; from sr. lectr. to assoc. prof. U. New South Wales, Sydney, Australia, 1974-79; prof. SUNY, Buffalo, 1987-89, chmn. dept. econs., 1987-89; dir. Res. Bank of New Zealand, 1985-86; research dir. New Zealand Ctr. for Ind. Studies, Auckland, 1986. Co-author: The Logic of Markets, 1983; editorial advisor New Zealand Centre Ind. Studies; referee Am. Econ. Rev., Australian Econ. Papers, Bull. Econ. Rsch., Can. Jour. Econs., European Econ. Rev., others; contbr. numerous articles to profl. jours. Appeared in plays Shakespeare Soc. and Dunedin Repertory Soc., New Zealand. Grantee New Zealand Social Scis. Rsch. Fund Com., 1985. Mem. New Zealand Assn. of Economists (v.p. 1985-86), Am. Econ. Assn., Econometric Soc. Home: Getzville N.Y. Died Nov. 25, 1989; buried Christchurch, New Zealand.

MANNING, TIMOTHY CARDINAL, former archbishop; b. Cork, Ireland, Nov. 15, 1909; came to U.S., 1928, naturalized, 1944; s. Cornelius and Margaret (Cronin) M. Student, St. Patrick's Sem., Menlo Park, Calif., 1928-34; D.C.L., Gregorian U., Rome, 1938. Ordained priest Roman Cath. Ch., 1934; asst. pastor Immaculate Conception Ch., Los Angeles, 1934-35; consecrated bishop, 1946; appt. titular bishop of Lesvi and chancellor Roman Cath. Archdiocese of Los Angeles, 1946-67; first bishop of Fresno, 1967-69, titular archbishop of Capri and coadjutor archbishop of Los Angeles, 1969-70, archbishop of Los Angeles, 1970-85, created cardinal, 1973. Home: South Pasadena Calif. Died June 23, 1989. †

MANSHEL, WARREN DEMIAN, investment banker, publisher, ambassador; b. Jan. 6, 1924; m. Anita Coleman (dec. 1986) children: Liane Catherine, Michael Demian. B.A., M.A., Harvard U., 1949, Ph.D., 1952. Pub., editor Pub. Interest mag., 1969-90; founder, pub., editor Fgn. Policy mag., 1970-78; Am. amb. to Denmark, 1978-81; bus. cons. Manshel Consulting Svc., N.Y., 1981-90; co-chair leadership coun. N.Y. Internat. Festival of Arts; dir. Internat. U. Found., Art Mus. Aalborg, Denmark; bd. dirs. various mut. funds, other fin. instns. Trustee Scandinavian Found.; vis. com. Harvard Ctr. Internat. Affairs; mem. internat. adv. bd. Columbia U. Sch. Internat. and Pub. Affairs; mem. Am. Com. on Fgn. Policy. With U.S. Army, World War II. Teaching fellow Harvard U., 1949, recipient Chase Prize in Internat. Rels., 1952; Decorated Gt. Cross of Denmark, Copenhagen, 1981. Mem. Bus. Exec. Nat. Security, Coun. on Fgn. Rels., Century Club (N.Y.). Home: New York N.Y. Died Feb. 25, 1990; buried Sharon Gardens Cemetery, Valhalla, N.Y.

MANSURE, EDMUND F., manufacturing executive; b. Chgo., Mar. 14, 1901; s. Edmund L. and Nellie (Forsman) M.; m. Julia Carroll, Dec. 24, 1938. Student, Dartmouth Coll., 1924; LLB, Kent Coll. Law; student grad. sch., Northwestern U. Bar: Ill. 1927, Fed. 1928. With E.L. Mansure Co., 1922-92, v.p., 1925-35, pres., 1935-51, chmn. bd., 1952-92; also dir., adminstr. Gen. Svcs. Adminstrn., 1953-56, Def. Materials Procurement Agy., 1953-92; dir. Value Line Mut. Funds, Value Line Fund, Inc., Income Fund, Spl. Situations Fund, Leveraged Growth Investors Money Market Fund, Bond Fund. Mem. adv. bd. Chgo. Planning Commn., 1938-43; dir. Chgo. Crime Commn., 1933-34; pres. Crime Prevention, Inc. of Cook County; mem. Ill. Revenue Laws Commn., 1947-49, Ill. State Pension Commn., 1945-51, Nat. Capital Planning Commn., 1953, Pres.'s Com. on Govt. Contracts, 1953; chmn. Ill. State Bd. Unemployment Compensation and Free Employment Advisors; mem. exec. com. Citizen's Subway Com., 1938-43, South Side Planning Bd.; chmn. Chgo. div. Red Cross War Fund drive, 1945; mem. adv. com. Civic Fedn., chmn. citizens waterway com., 1937; chmn. Community Chest campaign, govt. div., 1954; co-chmn. Washington Community Chest, 1955; bd. dirs. Travelers Aid, 1933-35; pres. U. Ill.-Cook County Sch. Nursing, 1948-51, Cook County Hosp., 1948-51; dir. Rsch. Round. elected to Wisdom Hall of Fame, 1973; recipient Winston Churchill medal of Wisdom, 1975. Mem. Ill. Frs. Assn. (dr. 1939-40, treas. 1941-46, v.p. 1947-48, pres. 1949, chmn. bd. 1950), Chgo. Drapery Mfrs. Assn. (pres. 1933-47), Chgo. Assn. Commerce, South Central Assn. (pres.), Chgo. Athletic Club, Comml. Club, Delta Kappa Epsilon. Home: La Honda Calif. Died Jan. 25, 1992; cremated.

MANTELL, CHARLES L., chemical engineer; b. Bklyn., Dec. 9, 1897; s. John Henry and Emma (Smith) M.; m. Adelaide M. Smithenner, 1926; children: Cunthia Adelaide, Keith Charles. Student, McGill U., Montreal, Que., Can., 1914-16; AB, CCNY, 1918, BS, 1918; AM, Columbia U., 1924, ChemE, 1924, PhD, 1927. Chem. engr. Aluminum Co. of Am., 1918-21, Celluloid Corp., 1921-22; prof. chem. engring. Pratt Inst., Bklyn., 1922-37; cons. engr., from 1924; dir. rsch. Am. Bum Importers Assn., 1934-39; tech. adviser Netherlands Indies Govt., 1934-50; tech. dir. W. B. Driver Co., Newark, 1934-39, United Merchants and Mfrs. Corp., 1940-47; v.p. United Merchants, Labs., Inc., 1945; prof., chmn. dept. chem. engring. Newark Coll. Engring., from 1948; cons. to various govts. and their agys. Author: Industrial Carbon, 1928, 46, Tin, 1929, 49, Industrial Electrochemistry, 1931, 40, 50, Sparks from Electrode, 1932, Technology of Natural Resins, 1942, Adsorption, 1945, 51, Calcium Metallurgy and Technology, 1945, Water Soluble Gums, 1947, Electrochemical Engineering, 1960; editor-in-chief Engring. Materials Handbook, 1958; contbr. to Chem. Engr.'s Handbook, 1935, 40, 50; contbr. numerous articles to tech. jours. Trustee Newark Coll. Engring. Rsch. Found. Lt. Royal Flying Corps, Brit. Army, 1917-18. Mem. AIME, Am. Chem. Soc., Am. Inst. Chem. Engrs., Electro-chem. Soc., Am. Soc. Metals, Masons, Sigma Xi, Phi Lambda Upsilon, Epsilon Chi, Tau Beta Pi. Republican. Episcopalian. *

MANVILLE, ALFRED R., construction company executive; b. N.J., 1917; s. Keith Rollin and Kirsten (Tonning) M.; m. Michael Burdett, Jan. 28, 1969; children—Florence, Suzanne, David, Richard, Catherine, Peggy Jane, Elizabeth. B.S. in Elec. Engring, Rutgers U., 1938. Vice pres. J. Livingston & Co., N.Y.C., 1938-64; exec. v.p. L.K. Comstock Co., N.Y.C., 1964-70; pres., chief exec. officer Fischbach Corp., N.Y.C., 1970-89. Served with AUS, 1942-46. Decorated Legion of Merit. Home: Red Bank N.J. Died Mar., 1989.

MANWELL, REGINALD DICKINSON, malariologist, educator; b. Harford, Pa., Dec. 24, 1897; s. John P(arker) and Stella F(lorine) (Dickinson) M.; m. Elizabeth Skelding Moore, Aug. 6, 1930; children: John Parker, Henry Dickinson. Grad., Deerfield Acad., 1914; AB, Amherst Coll., 1919, AM, 1926; ScD, Johns Hopkins U., 1928; ScD (hon.), Syracuse U., 1963. Tchr., prin. St. Charles, Mich., 1920-21, Waterport Union High Sch., 1920-24; head biology dept. W.Va. Wesleyan Coll., Buckhannon, 1929-30; instr. in protozoology ad interim sch. hygiene/pub. health Johns Hopkins U., 1929-30; prof. zoology Syracuse (N.Y.) U., 1930-63, prof. emeritus zoology, from 1963; mem. faculty Mointain Lake Biol. Sta., U. Va., summer 1962; trustee, pres. Rocky Mountain Biol. Lab., Crested Butte, Colo. Author: (with Paul F. Russell and Luther West) Practical Malariology, (with Sophia Lyon Fahs) Chruch Across the Street, Protozoology; contbr. many articles on malaria, free-living protozoa, ornithology to profl. publs.; mem. editorial bd. Jour. Parasitology, Jour. Protozoology, Rivista di Malariologia, Rome (hon.). Capt. Sanitary Corps, U.S. Army, 1943-45; chief protozoology sect., div. tropical med. and parasitology Army Med. Sch., Washington, 1944-45. Grants-in-aid for rsch. in malaria and toxoplasmosis from NRC, AAAS, Sigma Xi, NIH, Am. Philos. Soc. Fellow AAAS, N.Y. Acad. Scis.; mem. Soc. Protozoologists (pres. 1962—), Am. Soc. Parasitologists, Am. Soc. Tropical Medicine and Hygiene, Am. Soc. Zool., Soc. Exptl. Biology and Medicine, Am. Soc. Naturalists, Sigma Xi, Delta Tau Delta, Kappa Delta. Democrat. Unitarian. *

MAPPLETHORPE, ROBERT, photographer; b. Floral Park, N.Y., Nov. 4, 1946; s. Harry Irving and Joan Dorothy (Maxey) M. Student, Pratt Inst., 1963-70. Exhibited solo exhbns. of photography, Light Gallery, N.Y.C., 1976, Holly Solomon Gallery, N.Y.C., 1977, La. Remise du Parc Gallery, Paris, 1978, Robert Miller Gallery, N.Y.C., 1978, Chrysler Mus., Norfolk, Va., 1978, Corcoran Gallery, Washington, 1978, Tex. Gallery, Houston, 1979, Vision Gallery, Boston, 1980, Gallerie Jurka, Amsterdam, Holland, 1980, Fraenkel Gallery, San Francisco, 1981, Lunn Gallery, Washington, 1981, Frankfurter Kunstverein (Germany), 1981, Fay Gold Gallery, Atlanta, 1982, Gagosian Gallery, Los Angeles, 1982, Leo Castelli Gallery, N.Y.C., 1983, Jane Corkin Gallery, Toronto, Ont., Can., 1983, Inst. Contemporary Art, London, 1983, group exhbns.of photography, Corcoran Gallery, Washington, 1977, 78, group exhbns., Mus. Modern Art, N.Y.C., 1979, Santa Barbara Mus. Art (Calif.), 1979, solo exhbns. of photography, Carson-Sapiro Gallery, Denver, 1980, Islip Town Art Ctr., N.Y., 1980, group exhbns., Mus. of Art, Norman, Okla., 1981, 82, solo exhbns. of photography: Nordiska Kompaniet, Sweden, 1981, 82, Taft Mus., Cin., 1983, Wadsworth Atheneum, Hartford, 1984. Home: New York N.Y. Died Mar. 9, 1989. †

MARAZITI, JOSEPH J., lawyer, congressman; b. Boonton, N.J., June 15, 1912; m. Margaret Eileen Hopkins, 1939; children: Joseph J., Mary Ellen Baldwin, Margaret Patterson, Charles, Maria Wilhelm, Catherine, Eileen. LLB, Fordham U., 1937. Legis. sec. N.. Senate, 1931-34; legis. sec. to N.J. Assembly, 1936-37; sr. ptnr. law Maraziti, Maraziti & Cerra, and predecessor firm; mem. 93d Congress from N.J., 1973-75; judge Boonton Mcpl. Ct., 1940-47; 1st asst. prosecutor Morris County, 195-53; chmn. Boonton Charter Commn. Study Group, 1955; legis. legal adviser Morris County Bd. Chosen Freeholders, 1956-57; mem. N.J. Assembly, 1958-67; mem. N.. Senate, 1968-72, majority whip, 1972. Mem. Morris County Bar Assn., KC, Elks. Republican. Home: Booton N.J. Died May 20, 1991.

MARBLE, SAMUEL DAVEY, college president, author; b. Mitchell, S.D., Nov. 15, 1915; s. Samuel William and Elsie Naomi (Davey) M.; m. Rebecca Sturtevant, Feb. 15, 1947; children: Mary, Anne, Rebecca; m. Gladys Kearns, Jan. 13, 1978. A.B., U. N.Mex., 1937; M.A., Syracuse U., 1939, Ph.D., 1941; Certificate in Internat. Adminstrn, Columbia, 1943; LL.D., Cedarville Coll., 1951; L.H.D., Wilmington Coll., 1969. Resident adviser Syracuse U., 1937-39; fellow and instr. Maxwell Sch. Citizenship and Pub. Affairs, 1939-41; procedure analyst Office of Civilian Supply, 1941-42; asso. sec. Am. Friends Service Com., 1943-46; chmn. Licensed Agys. for Relief in Asia, 1946; chmn. com. on Japan and com. on Korea Am. Council of Vol. Agys., 1946; prof. polit. sci. W.Va. Wesleyan Coll., 1946-47; pres. Wilmington Coll., 1947-58; dir. Clinton County Red Cross and Community Chest, 1958-61; pres. Delta Coll., Saginaw, Mich., 1961-64, Saginaw Valley State U., University Center, 1964-74; prof. polit. sci. John Wesley Coll., Owosso, Mich., 1975-77, pres., 1977-79; exec. Family Service Agy., Port Huron, Mich., 1979-82; exec. dir. Sound Mind Fedn., 1983-88; pres. Internat. Study Ctr., 1989-90; Dir. Midstate Broadcasting Corp., Wickes Corp.; Mem. commn. on internat. aspects tchr. edn. Am. Assn. Colls. for Tchr. Edn., 1948. Author: (with C. R. Read) Guide to Public Affairs Organizations, 1946, Glimpses of Africa, 1973, Before Columbus, 1980; Regular contbr. to various mags. and papers. Rep. Friend's World Com. to UN, 1956; candidate for Congress, 10th Dist. Mich., 1974, 76; Bd. dirs. Saginaw County United Appeal, Community Service, Inc., Saginaw Symphony Orch., Internat. Symphony Orch., Multiple Sclerosis Soc. Mich., Nat. Council for Prevention of War; bd. mgrs. Pendle Hill; trustee Seasongood Good Govt. Fund. Recipient citation of merit DAV; Paul Harris fellow. Mem. Am. Polit. Sci. Assn., Am. Acad. Social and Polit. Sci., Nat. Mental Health Found., Soc. Advancement Edn., Quaker Coll. Assn. (pres. 1951-53), Mich. Biofeedback Soc., Green Key, Mich. farm bur. fedns., Phi Alpha Theta, Kappa Alpha, Phi Kappa Phi, Pi Sigma Alpha and, Alpha Phi Gamma. Mem. Soc. of Friends. Clubs: Saltans, Rotary (pres.-elect 1988-89), Black River Country. Home: Harbor Springs Mich. Died Mar. 7, 1990.

MARCHESE DI BARSENTO See PUCCI, EMILIO

MARCOS, FERDINAND E., president of The Philippines; b. Laoag, Ilocos Norte, Philippines, Sept. 11, 1917; grad. in law, U. Philippines; m. Imelda Romualdez; 3 children. Spl. asst. to Philippine Pres. Roxas after World War II; mem. Philippine Ho. of Reps., 1949-59; mem. Senate, 1959-66, pres. of Senate, 1963-65; pres. of the Philippines, 1966-86, prime minister, 1973-81; leader Kilusan Bagong Lipunan, 1981-89. Served with Philippine Army and guerilla forces, World War II. Decorated 28 medals including D.S.C. (U.S.). Mem. Liberal Party until 1964, Nationalist Party, 1964-89.Died Sept. 28, 1989. Home: Manila Philippines †

MARCY, CARL MILTON, government official; b. Falls City, Oreg., June 11, 1913; s. Milton A. and Nellie (Rickson) M.; m. Mildred Kester, Dec. 21, 1934; children: Karen Christine, Eric Bruce. B.A., Willamette U., 1934; M.A., Columbia U., 1936, LL.B., 1939, Ph.D., 1942. Bar: N.Y. 1941, D.C. 1975. Instr. Columbia U., 1935-39, CCNY, 1939-42; officer Dept. State, Washington, 1942-49, legis. counsel, 1949-50; cons. Senate Com. on Fgn. Relations, 1950-55, chief staff, 1955-74; pvt. practice law Washington, 1974-90; co-dir. Am. Com. on East-West Accord, 1977-84; appointed to Gen. Adv. Com. on Arms Control and Disarmament. Author: Presidential Commissions, 1945, Proposals for Changes in UN Charter, 1955. Recipient Rockefeller Pub. Service award, 1963, fellow Inst. on Current Affairs, 1963. Mem. Am. Soc. Internat. Law. Club: Nat. Lawyers (Washington). Home: Annapolis Md. Died Sept. 19, 1990; cremated.

MARGULIES, JOSEPH, artist; b. Austria, July 7, 1896; s. Elias and Mary (Schachter) M.; m. Mary Polisuk, Nov. 22, 1921; 1 child, Herbert Felix. Student, Cooper Union, Arts High Sch., Ethical Culture Sch., Art Students League. Prin. works include portraits of many famous Americans; represented in the collections of numerous large galleries and msueums throughout the U.S.; contbr. articles to profl. publs. Recipient Chandler 1st prize in black and white at Salmangundi, in oil, North Shore Art Assn., for best portrait, Rockport Art Assn., Louis E. Seley pruchase prize Salmagundi Club. Mem. North Shore Art Assn., Rockport Art Assn., Soc. Am. Etchers, Chgo. Soc. Etchers, Art Students League, Louis C. Tiffany Guild, Audubon Soc., So. Print makers, Provincetown Art Assn., Am. Water Color Soc., Cape Anne Soc. Modern Art, Allied Artists Am., Am. Artists Profl. League (award), Soc. Western Artists, Salmagundi Club. *

MARK, HERMAN FRANCIS, dean; b. Vienna, Austria, May 3, 1895; came to U.S., 1940; s. Herman Carl and Lili (Mueller) M.; m. Mary Schramek, 1922 (dec.); children: Hans, Peter (dec.). PhD summa cum laude, U. Vienna, 1921; numerous hon. degrees. Rsch. assoc. Kaiser Wilhelm Inst. for Fiber Rsch., Berlin-Dahlem, 1922-26; rsch. chemist, to group leader, to asst. rsch. dir. I.G. Farben Industry, Ludwigshafen, Germany, 1927-32; prof. of chemistry, dir. Chem. Inst. Univ. Vienna, Austria, 1932-38; mgr. Cellulose Rsch. Lab. Can. Internat. Paper Co., Hawkesbury, Ont., 1938-40; adj. prof., organic chemistry Poly. Inst. of Bklyn., now Poly. U., 1940-42, prof., from 1942, dir. Polymer Rsch. Inst., 1946-64, dean of faculty, 1961-65, dean emeritus, 1965-92; assoc. prof. phys. chemistry Tech. Univ. Karlsruhe, 1927-30; mem. bd. edn. Vienna, govt. adviser in indsl. affairs; pres. com. wood utilization, Austrian Dept. Commerce, 1932-38; tchr. cons. USN, U.S. Army Quartermaster Corps, NSF; chmn. com. on fire safety aspects of polymer materials Nat. Rsch. Coun. of the Nat. Acad. Scis.; hon. chmn. sci. adv. coun. Weizmann Inst. Sci.; chmn. tech. com. Wood Chemistry in the Food and Agrl. Orgn. UN, many others. Editor: Jour. Polymer Sci., Jour. Applied Polymer Sci., Encyclopedia Polymer Sci. and Tech.; assoc. editor: Textile Rsch. Jour., Jour. Applied Physics, Jour. Chem. Physics; adv. bd. Chem. and Engring. News, Zeitschrift fuer Physikalische Chemie; author of 20 books; contbr. over 600 articles to profl. jours. Lt. Imperial Austrian Army, 1913-18 (decorated 15 medals). Fellow Am. Phys. Soc., Textile Inst. of Great Britain, N.Y. Acad. Scis., Am. Acad. Arts and Scis.; mem. Nat. Acad. Scis., Am. Chem. Soc., Am. Soc. European Chemists and Pharmacists, Am. Inst. Chemists, Am. Soc. for X-ray and Electron Diffraction, Soc. Rheology, AAAS, Tech. Assn. of the Pulp and Paper Industry, Am. Fiber Soc., Faraday Soc., Bunsen Gesellschaft, Chem. Inst. Can., Austrian Forum, Soc. Plastics Engrs., Royal Inst. Great Britian. Home: Austin Tex. Died Apr. 6, 1992; buried Vienna, Austria.

MARK, JULIUS, rabbi; b. Dec. 25, 1898; s. David and Ida (Tanur) M.; m. Margaret Corinne Baer, June 30, 1924; children: James Berthold David, Peggy. MHL, Hebrew Union Coll., 1917, Rabbi, 1922, DD, 1949; AB, U. Cin., 1921; postgrad., U. Chgo.; LLD, Cumberland U., 1936; HHD, U. Tampa; STD, NYU, 1959. Ordained rabbi, 1922. Rabbi South Bend, Ind., 1922-26, Vine St Temple, Nashville, 1926-48; sr. rabbi Congregation Emanu-El, N.Y.C., from 1948; prof. homiletics and practical theology Hebrew Union Coll., from 1949; bd. dirs. N.Y. World Fair 1964-65 Corp. Author: Behaviorism and Religion, 1930, The Rabbi Meets Some Big Dilemmas, 1956, Reading for the Moon, 1959; contbg. editor Observer; contbr. Universal Jewish Ency., also articles to profl. publs. Trustee Fedn. Jewish Philanthropies, N.Y.C., Hebrew Union Sch. Edn. and Sacred Music; bd. dirs. Housing and Planning Coun. N.Y., Hillel Found. Bldg. Corp., Welfare and Health Coun. N.Y., N.Y.C. chpg. ARC; mem. Mayor's Com. for Better Pub. Housing, Mayor's Com. of Citizens of Juvenile Delinquency Evaluation Project of N.Y.C.; conducted preaching missions for U.S. Armed Forces in Hawaii, Johnson Island, Guam, Japan, 1956; adv. com. on chaplains svc. N.Y. State Civil Def. Commn.; adv. com. Armed Forces N.E. area; bd. of chaplains, mem. Interfaith Com. NYU; co-convenor Nat. Conf. Religion and Race, Chgo., 1963; trustee Nat. Conf. Christians and Jews; bd. govs. Hebrew Union Coll., 1946-54; chmn. alumni bd. overseers Jewish Inst. Religion; trustee Union Am. Hebrew Congregations, 1958-62; mem. clerical adv. com. N.A.M.; chmn. Chgo. Inst. on Judaism, Mgmt., Labor, 1947, St. Louis Inst. Judaism, Civil Rights, 1948; mem. Eastern bd. dirs. Anti-Defamation League of B'nai B'rith; exec. com. N.Y. chpt. Am. Jewish Com., exec. and adminstrv. bds. from 1962; col. staff of govs. Tenn., Ky. Served to lt. USNR, 1942-45, promoted to lt. comdr., served as Jewish chaplain U.S. Pacific Fleet, staff of Adm. Chester Nimitz. Mem. Nat. Econ. Coun., Cen. Conf. Am. Rabbis (exec. com. 1938-42, chmn. commn. Justice and Peace 1946-49), Alumni Assn. Hebrew Union Coll. (exec. com. from 1946, pres. 1948-50), World Union for Progressive Judaism (mem. Am. bd. and governing bd.), Am. Jewish Ency. Soc. (hon. v.p.), Synagogue Coun. Am. (pres. 1961-63), Fgn. Policy Assn., Jewish Conciliation Bd. Am. (v.p.), Assn. Reform Rabbis N.Y. and Vicinity, N.Y. Assn. for New Ams. (bd. dirs.), Army and Navy Chaplains Assn., Harmonie Club, Shamus Club, Woodmont Country Club. *

MARKHAM, JAMES MORRIS, journalist; b. Washington, Mar. 7, 1943; s. James Morris and Mary Paul (Rix) M.; m. Stephanie Reed; children: Katherine Rix, Samuel Reed. BA, Princeton U., 1965; Rhodes scholar, Oxford U., 1965-67. Stringer Time Mag., New Delhi, 1966-67; reporter AP, New Delhi, 1968-69, Lagos, Nigeria, 1969-70; reporter N.Y. Times, 1971-73; bur. chief N.Y. Times, Saigon, Vietnam, 1973-75, Beirut, 1975-76, Madrid, 1976-82, Bonn, Fed. Republic Germany, 1982-87; bur. chief, dep. fgn. editor N.Y. Times, Paris, 1987-89. Home: Paris France Died Aug. 9, 1989.

MARKLEY, KLARE S(TEPHEN), chemist; b. Phila. Dec. 16, 1895; s. Jonah Jacob and Mabel (Montague) M.; m. Calla Inez Lepper, Dec. 24, 1921 (dec. Dec 1954); m. Carmen Nogueira de Mello, Mar. 14, 1955. BSChemE, George Washington U., 1924, MS, 1925; PhD, Johns Hopkins U., 1929. Asst., assoc. biochemist USDA, 1927-37; chief oil sect. Regional Soybean Lab. USDA, Urbana, Ill., 1937-39; chief oil and oilseed div. So. Regional Lab. USDA, New Orleans, 1939-52; mem. staff U.S. ops. mission USDA, Brazil, 1954-60; indsl. cons. Rio de Janeiro, Brazil, from 1960; with ICA, 12-60, successivley assigned to Paraguay, Brazil, Nicaragua, FAO in Venezuela, Guatemala.; sci. cons. tech. intelligence com. Joint Chiefs Staff, 1945. Author: (with W. H. Goss) Soybean Chemistry and Technology, 1944, Fatty Acids, 1947, Soybeans and Soubean Products, 2 vols., 1950, 51, Fatty Acids and Derivatives, 4 vols., also numerous sci. publs. Recipient superior svc. award USDA, 1950, group superior svc. award, 1952. Fellow AAAS; mem. Am. Chem. Soc. (past sec. Washington sect., S.W. regional award 1951), Am. Soybean Assn., Palm Soc., Fgn. Svcs. Assn., Cosmos Club, Sigma Xi, Phi Lambda Upsilon. *

MARKS, HENRY THOMAS, chemical and plastics company executive; b. Ottawa, Ont., Can., Sept. 11, 1908; came to U.S., 1936, naturalized, 1948; s. Edward and Emma (Foster) M.; m. Marcelle Snedecor, Oct. 14, 1937; children—Ronald H., Kenneth E. Student, Harvard U. Bus. Sch.; LL.D. (hon.), Baldwin-Wallace Coll., 1984. With Ferro Corp., Cleve., 1933-75, v.p. fgn. ops., 1950-55, exec. v.p., 1955-58, dir., 1954-78, pres., 1958-72, chief exec. officer, 1963-75, chmn. bd., 1972-75, cons., 1975-78, hon. dir., 1978-91. Trustee Baldwin-Wallace Coll., from 1967; trustee Cleve. Clinic Found., 1972, pres., 1975-81, emeritus trustee, 1981-91; trustee Bluecoats, Inc., from 1974; trustee Cleve. Zool. Soc., Cleve. Playhouse, Gt. Lakes Shakespeare Festival; mem., also chmn. Cleve. Council World Affairs, 1977-82, hon. trustee. Clubs: Union, Westwood Country, Fifty (Cleve.). Home: Cleveland Ohio Died Oct. 9, 1991.

MARKS, LAWRENCE IRWIN, consumer products company executive; b. Bklyn., May 7, 1925; s. Nathan and Sadie (Myers) M.; m. Barbara Etta Katzman, Sept. 1, 1946; children—Sheila Jay, Nancy Sharman. A.B., Harvard U., 1946, M.B.A., 1948. Office methods specialist Johns Manville Corp., N.Y.C., 1948-51; sr. acct. Touche Niven, N.Y.C., 1951-53; v.p., treas. Adler Electronics, New Rochelle, N.Y., 1956-63; group v.p. Litton Industries, New Rochelle, 1963-65; exec. v.p. for fin. Culbro Corp., N.Y.C., 1965-88, also dir. Interviewer Harvard Schs. Com., N.Y.C., from 1971; mem. mgmt. adv. bd. Poly. Inst. Bklyn. Served as lt. USNR, 1944-46, 51-53. Mem. AICPA. Democrat. Jewish. Home: Forest Hills N.Y. Died Sept. 16, 1989; cremated.

MARKS, MEYER BENJAMIN, pediatric allergist; b. Chgo., Feb. 16, 1907; s. Simon and Rose (Block) M.; m. Golda A. Nathan, Sept. 27, 1932; children: Linda, Stephen. B.S., U. Ill., 1929, M.D., 1933, M.S., 1934. Diplomate: Am. Bd. Pediatrics, Am. Bd. Allergy and Immunology. Intern Cook County Hosp., Chgo., 1934-35; resident Cook County Hosp., 1935-36; practice medicine, specializing in pediatrics Miami Beach, Fla., 1937-57; specializing in pediatric allergy and gen. allergy, 1957-91; founding mem. Mt. Sinai Hosp. (now Mt. Sinai Med. Ctr.), Miami Beach, Fla., 1947; mem. staff Jackson Meml. Hosp.; chief med. officer, v.p. Asthmatic Children's Residential Treatment Ctr., North Miami Beach, Fla., 1970-80; clin. prof. pediatrics, div. allergy and immunology U. Miami, 1980-91, chief div. pediatric allergy, 1955-80; founder, dir. 1st So. pediatric allergy clinic, 1955-80; v.p., sec. Asthmatic Children's Found. Fla., 1964-91; bd. dirs. Asthma Care Assn. Am., 1976-91. Author: Physical Signs of Allergy in the Respiratory Tract in Children, 1967, Stigmata of Respiratory Tract Allergies, 1972, rev. edit., 1978, Italian transl., 1976; contbg. author: The Allergic Child, 1963, Allergy and Immunology in Childhood, 1973; guest essayist, Am. Assn. Orthodontists, 1979; contbg. editor: Ear, Nose and Throat Jour., 1970-78; contbr. articles to profl. jours. Hon. pres. med. div. Southeastern div. Am. Friends Hebrew U., 1958-68; pres. Assn. Convalescent Homes and Hosp. for Asthmatic Children, 1971; established Cobra art collection Mus. Art, Ft. Lauderdale, Fla., 1978; donor with wife contemporary art collection Mayo Clinic, Rochester, Minn., 1982-91. Recipient Bela Schick Meml. Lecture award in pediatric allergy Paris, 1974, Bronze award Am. Acad. Pediatrics, 1977, Upjohn Med. Achievement award, 1980, numerous others. Fellow Am. Acad. Pediatrics (Silver award 1975, 1st recipient Jerome Glaser Disting. Service award sect. on allergy 1985), Am. Coll. Allergists (Fellow Disting. award 1979, chmn. com. problems in pediatric allergy 1982-85), Am. Acad. Allergy; mem. Fla., Dade County (Fla.) med. assns., AMA, Fla. Pediatric Soc., Miami Pediatric Soc. (pres. 1954-55), Am. Assn. Cert. Allergists, Internat. Assn. Asthmology, Internat. Assn. Allergology, Am. Med. Writers Assn., Fla. Acad. Scis., Fla. Allergy Soc. (pres. 1970), Sigma Xi. Jewish. Home: Miami Fla. Died Sept. 7, 1991. †

MARKUS, FRANK H., art history educator; b. Highland Park, Mich., May 8, 1898; s. Walter Franklin and Estelle H. (singer) M.; m. Claudia Nadra Kingston, Aug., 1925; children: Meryl Lynn, Charles Walter. BA, NYU, 1922; student, Parsons Sch. Design, 1923; MFA, NYU, 1927. Adjunct prof. art history Brooklyn Coll., 1923, asst. prof. art history, 1925; professor art history NYU, 1926, prof. emeritus, from 1970; Instr. Bklyn. Mus. Art Sch., noted lecturer in field, developed after school program for children Bklyn Mus. (Mayor's Golden Apple Award). Guggenheim Fellowship grantee. Salmagundi Club, Bklyn Mus., Met. Mus. Art, MOMA, Mus. Nat. History. Home: Brooklyn N.Y. Died Aug. 8, 1992.* †

MARKWARDT, L(ORRAINE) J(OSEPH), consulting engineer; b. Lansing, Iowa, Nov. 26, 1889; s. Joseph F. and Louisa (Besch) M.; B.S., U. Wis., 1912, C.E., 1922; m. Lula May Starks, June 21, 1917 (dec. 1974). Asst. city engr., Madison, Wis., 1912; instr. drawing, descriptive geometry, engring. coll. U. Wis., 1915-17; research engr. U.S. Forest Products Lab., Madison, 1912-14, asst. chief div. timber mechanics, 1917-39, chief, 1939-43, asst. dir., 1943-59, cons. engr., from 1959. Del. timber research conf. Internat. Union Forest Research Orgns., Princes Risborough, Eng., 1937, 39; U.S. del. internat. confs. mech. wood tech. FAO, UN, Geneva, Switzerland, 1948, 49, Igls, Austria, 1951, Paris, France, 1954, Madrid, , 1958; chmn. program com. Forest Products sect. 5th World Forestry Congress, 1958-59; mem. subcom. wood and plastics for aircraft NACA, 1944-47, aircraft structural materials, 1947-49. Dep. mem. materials com. Resources and Devel. Bd., Dept. Def., 1952-53; mem. materials adv. bd. and bldg. research adv. bd. Nat. Acad. Scis., NRC, 1954-59. Recipient hon. citation for engring. achievement U. Wis., 1950, Superior Service award USDA 1957; Hitchcock award for outstanding research accomplishments in wood industry Hitchcock Pub. Co. and Forest Products Research Soc., 1963; Friend of Edn. award Allamakee Sch. Dist., 1982; Disting. Contbr. to Wood Engring. and Research award U.S. Forest Service, 1985; Hist. Preservation award State Hist. Soc. Wis., 1985; ann. L.J. Markwardt Wood Engring. Research award established by ASTM and Forest Products Research Soc., 1970; awards given in his name to sr. boy and girl for outstanding merit Kee High Sch., Lansing, from 1982. Mem. ASTM (Edgar Marburg lectr. award 1943, Walter C. Voss award 1965, dir. 1944-54, v.p. 1948-50, pres. 1950-51, chmn. com. wood 1948-64; hon.), Am. Standards Assn. (chmn. sect. com. methods testing wood, 1922, sect. com. safety code constrn., care, use of ladders 1950, mem. constrn. standards bd., 1943, sect. com. specifications wood poles, 1946), Am. Wood Preservers Assn., Am. Ry. Engring. Assn. (com. wood bridges and trestles since 1944), ASCE, Nat. Soc. Profl. Engrs., Soc. Am. Foresters, AAAS, Forest Products Research Soc., Internat. Wood Research Soc. (v.p.), Am. Inst. Timber Constrn. (chmn. tech. rev. bd. 1960-75, profl. life mem.), Sigma Xi, Tau Beta Pi, Chi Epsilon. Presbyn. Mason, Rotarian (pres. Madison 1950-51). Club: Black Hawk Country (Madison). Author: Descriptive Geometry (with Millar and Maclin), 1919, also subsequent revisions; The Blackhawk Country Club and its Historic Indian Heritage, 1976; sect. on Blackhawk Indian Mounds, Nat. Registry of Historic Places, 1979; The Mosquito Bomber, 1986; sects. on timber several engring. handbooks; govt. bulls., tech., sci. papers. Dieceased. Home: Madison Wis.

MARLAND, SIDNEY PERCY, JR., educational company executive; b. Danielson, Conn., Sept. 19, 1914; s. Sidney Percy and Ruth (Johnson) M.; m. Virginia Partridge, June 29, 1940; children: Sidney Percy III, Pamela, Judith. AB, U. Conn., 1936, MA, 1950; PhD, N.Y.U., 1955; LLD (hon.), U. Pitts., 1967, N.Y.U., 1971, Northwestern U., 1971; DHL, Ripon Coll., 1972, Denison U., 1972, Bishop Coll., 1973, R.I. Coll., 1973, Fairfield U., 1973, U. Akron, 1973. Tchr. English W. Hartford (Conn.) High Sch., 1938-41; supt. schs. Darien (Conn.) Sch. Dist., 1948-56, Winnetka (Ill.) Pub. Schs., 1956-63, Pitts. Pub. Schs., 1963-68; pres. Inst. Ednl. Devel., Pitts., 1968-70; U.S. commr. edn. Washington, 1970-72; asst. sec. for edn. HEW, Washington, 1972-73; pres. Coll. Entrance Exam Bd., N.Y.C., 1973-79; chmn. edit. bd. Scholastic, Inc., Hampton, Conn., from 1979; bd. dirs. Altantic Mutual Cos., Mutual of N.Y., Scholastic, Inc., ; adj. prof. Columbia U.; vice chmn. White House Conf. on Edn., 1965; chmn. bd. dirs. Merit Scholarship, 1968; lectr. Harvard U., Northwestern U., Nat. Coll. Edn., U. Mont. Author: Career Education: A Proposal on Reform, 1975, (co-author) The Unfinished Journey, 1968, Religion in the Public Schools, 1963, Winnetka: The History and Significance of an Educational Experiment, 1963; editor: Essays on Career Education, 1972. Asst. dir. YMCA Camp, Hartford, Conn., 1937-40; pres. bd. Darien Library Assn., 1949-56, Isaac Walton League, Winnetka, 1957-61; mem. commn. Ch.-State Relations, nat. adv. council office Econ. Opportunity, 1960-68, Edn. Disadvantaged Children, 1964-68; trustee John F. Kennedy Ctr. for Performing Arts, 1970-74; pres. Great Cities Sch. Improvement Council, 1967-68, Nat. Ednl. TV, 1962-70; bd. trustees U. Pitts., 1965-68, Am. Coll., 1975—; bd. dirs. Joint Council on Econ. Edn., Urban League Pitts., 1963-68; bd. govs. Conn. Higher Edn., from 1984; warden, vestryman Episcopalian Ch., 1948-56, 57-63. Served to Col. AUS, 1941-47. Decorated D.S.M., Legion of Merit, Bronze star. Mem. VFW, NEA, Am. Assn. Sch. Adminstrs., Am. Legion, Rotary. Home: Hampton Conn. Died May 25, 1992.

MAROTTA, NICHOLAS G(ENE), specialty chemicals company executive; b. Conflenti, Italy, 1929; married. BS, Long Island U., 1952. With Nat. Starch & Chem. Corp., Bridgewater, N.J., from 1959, v.p. mktg. Starch div., 1972-73, corp. asst. v.p., 1973-76, corp. v.p., 1976-77, group v.p. Starch div., 1977-84, pres., chief operating officer, 1984-85, pres., chief exec. officer, 1985-91; ret., dir. Home: Bridgewater N.J. Died Apr. 8, 1991. †

MARSCHALK, WILLIAM JOHN, lawyer, savings and loan association executive; b. Passaic, N.J., Sept. 30, 1944; s. Frederick Paul and Irene Dolores (Bizub) M.; BA, U. Bridgeport, 1966; JD, Rutgers U., 1969; m. Jeanne Lynne Hendrickson, May 17, 1974; children—Cory L., Heather Helene. Bar: D.C. 1969, Calif. 1977. Trial atty. FTC, Washington, 1969-71; legis. counsel Nat. Assn. Realtors, Washington, 1971-72; v.p., legis. counsel Nat. Forest Products Assn., Washington, 1972-74; dir. House and Senate liaison, HUD, Washington, 1974-76; sr. v.p., legis. dir. Calif. Savs. and Loan League, Sacramento, 1976-77; sr. v.p. Gt. Western Fin. Corp., Beverly Hills, Calif., 1977-78, gen. counsel, 1978-87, exec. v.p. adminstn. svcs. div., mem. office of the pres., 1986-91. Republican. Roman Catholic. Died July 12, 1991; cremated. Home: Calabasas Calif.

MARSH, DOROTHY MARIE See WEST, DOTTIE

MARSH, R. BRUCE, advertising agency executive; b. Milw., Aug. 31, 1929; s. Lester B. and Margaret (Hermsen) M.; BA in Econs., State U. Iowa, 1951; m. Margaret Ross, Oct. 11, 1952; children: Marilyn Elaine, Robert Ross, Gregory Bruce; m. Gayle Johnson, June 14, 1981. Profl. baseball pitcher, 1951-52; indsl. sales rep. 3M Co., 1952-55; advt. sales rep. Curtis Publishing Co., 1955-56; advt. sales rep., then nat. sporting goods sales mgr. Sports Illus. Mag., Chgo., 1956-64; v.p., account supr. Campbell Mithun Inc., Chgo., 1964-67; pres. R. Bruce Marsh, Inc., pubs. reps., Chgo., 1967-70, R. Bruce Marsh, Inc., real estate, Chgo., 1970-71; v.p. mktg. Johnson & Quin, Inc., printers, Chgo., 1971-72; Midwest mktg. mgr. Project Health div. G.D. Searle & Co., Chgo., 1972-73; v.p., account supr. Fuller, Smith & Ross Advt., Chgo., 1974-75; v.p. account supr. exec., Frank C. Nahser, Inc. (advt.), Chgo., 1975-83, sr. v.p., mgmt. supr., 1983-85; exec. v.p., 1985-92, acting pres., fall 1988. Bd. dirs. GolfPro, Inc., 1989. Coach Northfield (Ill.) Boys Baseball Assn., 1970-85, pres., 1972-76, bd. dirs., 1968-85; chmn. North Suburban chpt. Fellowship Christian Athletes, 1980-83; area chmn. United Fund Northfield, 1963-65; speaker Ill. Prison Ministries. Recipient spl. recognition award contbn. to youth Community of Northfield. Mem. Sunset Ridge Country Club (Northbrook, Ill.), Univ. Club (Chgo.), Chgo. Soc. of Clubs. Died Jan. 13, 1992. Home: Lake Forest Ill.

MARSHALL, JAMES (EDWARD), author; b. 1942. Tchr. French and Spanish Cathedral High Sch., Boston, 1968-70; freelance writer, illustrator, 1970—. Author: George and Martha series, 6 vols., 1972-84, 1972, What's The Matter with Carruthers?, 1972, Yummers, 1972, Miss Dog's Christmas Treat, 1973, Willis, 1974, The Guest, 1975, Eugene, 1975, Sing Out, Irene, 1975, A Summer in the South, 1977, Portly McSwine, 1979, Taking Care of Carruthers, 1981, Rapscallion Jones, 1983, The Cut Ups, 1984, Three Up a Tree, 1986, Merry Christmas, Space Case, 1986, Wings, 1986, Yummers Too, 1986, The Cut-Ups Cut Loose, 1987, George and Martha Round and Round, 1988, Fox on the Job, 1988, The Cut-Ups At Camp Custer, 1989; (as Edward Marshall) Troll Country, 1980, Space Case, 1980, Three by Sea, 1981, Fox series, 6 vols., 1982-85; (with Harry Allard) The Stupids series, 3 vols., 1974-81, Miss Nelson series, 3 vols., 1977-85. Home: New York N.Y. Died Oct. 13, 1992. †

MARSHALL, JOHN, JR., lawyer; b. Anchorage, Ky., Sept. 14, 1894; s. John and Mary Craig (Barret) M. Grad., St. Paul's Sch., 1912; AB, Williams Coll., 1916; LLB, Harvard U., 1922. Bar: Ky. 1922. Practiced in Louisville; mem. firm Marshall, Cochran, Heyburn & Wells and predecessor firms, Louisville, from 1941; judge chancery br., 1st div. Jerrerson County Circuit Ct., 1931-34; standing master in chancery U.S. Dist. Ct. for Western Dist. Ky., 1934-38; spl. jduge Ky. Ct. Appeals, 1945-47; bd. dirs. Liberty Nat. Bank & Trust Co., from 1937, Continental Air Filers, Inc., from 1946, Puritan Cordage Mills, from 1935; chmn. bd. dirs. Blue Ridge Cord Co., from 1957, Majestic Theatre Co. Treas. of women's field army Soc. Cancer Control, from 1951; trustee John Norton Meml. Infirmary, 1934-39; pres. Louisville Law Libr., 1955-57. 2d lt. U.S. Army, 1917-19. Mem. ABA, Tri-State Bar Assn. (v.p., bd. dirs. 1951), Ky. Bar Assn. (pres., bd. dirs. 1940-51, exec. sec., bd. dirs. from 1951), Intercollegiate Bar Assn. (sec. 1913-15), Louisville Bridge Assn. (sec.-treas. 1936-40), Shelbyville Golf and Fishing Club, Oldham Country Club, Idle Hour Country Club. *

MARSHALL, MAX S(KIDMORE), microbiologist; b. Lansing, Mich., Dec. 20, 1897; s. Charles Edward and Maud Alice (Skidmore) M.; m. Constance Hopkin, June 21, 1922 (dec.); children: Craig Hopkin, Joan Karen (Mrs. Paul Ton), Margaret Taylor (Mrs. William James Micka); m. Barbara G. Trask, June 22, 1957. BS, U. Mass., 1918; AM, U. Mich., 1922, PhD, 1925. Rsch. on microbial assn. in milk U. Mass., 1919-20; researcher, tchr. U. Mich., 1920-23; rsch. bacteriologist Mich. Dept. Health, 1923-27; mem. faculty sch. medicine U. Calif., from 1928, prof. microbiology, 1943-65, prof. emeritus microbiology, from 1965, chmn. dept., also sch. dentistry, sch. pharmacy, 1948-62; cons. labs. San Francisco Dept. Pub. Health, 1936-52; disting. vis. prof. Mich. State U., 1958. Author: Laboratory Guide in Elementary Microbiology, 1941, Two Sides to a Teacher's Desk, 1951, Crusader Undaunted, 1958, (with others), Applied Medical Bacteriology, 1947; editorial aide, dir. manuals San Francisco Dept. Pub. Health; contbr. articles to ednl., med. jours. 2d lt. U.S. Army, 1917-19. Mem. AAAS, Soc. Microbiologists, Sigma Xi, Phi Kappa Phi, Delta Omega, Kappa Sigma. *

MARSHMAN, HOMER HENRY, lawyer; b. Jackson, Ohio, Aug. 3, 1898; s. Frank White and Letha (Radcliffe) M.; m. Ina Mae Foster Stouffer, Oct. 3, 1941; 1 child, Homer Henry. BA, Ohio U., 1920; LLB, Harvard U., 1923. Bar: Ohio, 1924. Practice law Cleve., from 1927; sr. ptnr. Marshman, Hornbeck, Hollington, Steadman & McLaughlin, from 1948; spl. counsel to atty. gen. Ohio, 1934-47; chmn. bd. dirs. Mut. Fin. Co., Painesville, Ohio; pres. Hommel Champagne Co., Candusky, Ohio, Painesville Raceway, Inc., Cleve.; co-owner Oates Motors, Inc., Erie, Pa.; owner Cleve. Rams, 1936-37; co-owner Cleve. Browns, 1953-60. Treas. Rep. Exec. Com. Cuyahoga County, 1936, chmn., 1950-51. With USN, 1918. Mem. ABA, Ohio Bar Assn., Cleve. Bar Assn., Country Club, Hermit Club, Everglades Club, Bath and Tennis Club, Seminole Country Club, Beta Theta Pi. *

MARTIN, ALBERTUS (JOSEPH ALBERT MARTIN), bishop; b. Southbridge, Mass., Oct. 4, 1913; s. Arthur and Parmelie (Beaudoin) M. BA, Nicolet Coll., 1935; STD, Laval U., 1941. Ordained priest Roman Cath. Ch., 1939; prof. philosophy Nicolet Coll., 1939-46, dir., 1946-49; vicar gen. Diocese Nicolet, 1949-50, ord. titular bishop of Oassiana and coadjutor bishop of Nicolet, 1950, bishop, 1950-89, bishop emeritus, from 1989; Mem. commn. for liturgy Council Vatican II. Home: Nicolet Can. Deceased. †

MARTIN, BILLY (ALFRED MANUEL MARTIN), professional baseball manager; b. Berkeley, Calif., May 16, 1928; s. Alfred M. Martin and Joan (Salvini) Downey; m. Lois E. Berndt, Oct. 4, 1950 (div. Oct. 1953); 1 dau., Kelly Ann; m. Gretchen Winkler, Oct. 7, 1959 (div. June 1982); 1 son, Billy Joe; m. Jill Guiver, Jan. 25, 1988. Grad., Berkeley High Sch., 1946. With Oakland (Calif.) Oaks, 1947-50; 2d baseman N.Y. Yankees, 1950-57, Kansas City Athletics, 1957; short stop Detroit Tigers, 1957-58; infielder Cleve. Indians, 1959; 2d baseman Cin. Reds, 1960, Milw. Braves, 1961; with Minn. Twins, 1961-69, coach, scout, 1965-68; mgr. Denver Bears, 1968-69, Minn. Twins, 1969-70, Detroit Tigers, 1970-73, Tex. Rangers, 1973-75; mgr. N.Y. Yankees, 1975-79, 83, 85, 88-89, spl. scout, 1985-86, 88-89, v.p., 1989; mgr. Oakland A's, 1980-82. Served with AUS, 1950-51, 53-55. Clubs: Moose, Elks. Home: Port Crane N.Y. Died Dec. 25, 1989; buried Gates of Heaven Cemetery, Hawthorne, N.Y.

MARTIN, DAVID STONE, artist; b. Chgo., June 13, 1913; s. Francis James and Grace Danforth (Hedges) M.; m. Thelma Durkin, June 10, 1934 (div. 1954); children—Stefan, Anthony; m. Gloria Sokol, July 10, 1955 (div. 1961); 1 child, Rio; m. Cheri Landry, Sept. 25, 1965. Student, Art Inst. of Chgo. Supr. mural project Western Ill. Fed. Arts. Program, Elgin, 1934-35; graphic arts dir TVA, Knoxville, 1936-41; art dir., graphic artist OSS, Washington, 1941-45, Office War Info., N.Y.C., 1941-45; art dir. Disc Records, N.Y.C., 1943-46, Verve Records, Los Angeles, 1947-55; cover artist Time mag., 1965-72; instr. Arts Students League & Parsons Sch. of Design, N.Y.C., 1972-79. Works include record album designs almost all covers for Asch, Clef and Jazz, Philharm. Orch. labels, 1940's,50's, numerous book illustrations, posters, billboards, advts. for film including Paint Your Wagon, Paramount Pictures, 1969, TV, theater including Lincoln Theater prodns., 1960's and 70's; artist cover portraits for Time mag.; artist war corr. WWII Life mag., Abbot Lab., 1943-45; works in collections of Art Inst. Chgo., Mus. Modern Art, N.Y.C., Met. Mus. Art, N.Y.C., Smithsonian Instn. Recipient Art Dirs.' medal Art Dirs.' Club, N.Y.C., 1948, 49; winner: Mural Competition U.S. P.O., Sweetwater, Tenn., 1941, Dayton, Tenn., 1942 Mural Competition Court House, Mobile, Ala., 1942. Home: New London Conn. Died Mar. 6, 1992, cremated.

MARTIN, EDWIN WEBB, diplomacy educator; b. Madura, India, Aug. 31, 1917; parents Am. citizens ; s. Azel Anson and Emma Webb M.; m. Emma-Rose Hubbard, Aug. 17, 1940; children: Marguerite L. Cairns, Sylvia M. Lindsay, Edwin H., David W. Vice consul Hamilton, Bermuda, 1941-44, Leopoldville, Belgian Congo, 1944, Beijing, China, 1946-48, Hankow, China, 1948-49; consul Republic of China, Taipei, 1949-50; with Dept. State, 1952-56; polit. adviser with personal rank minister to comdr in chief Pacific, Hawaii, 1961-64; consul gen. with personal rank minister Hong

Kong, 1967-70; ambassador to Burma, 1971-73; disting. prof. diplomacy Hiram Ohio Coll., 1976-91. Author: Southeast Asia and China: The End of Containment. With AUS, 1945. Mem. Internat. Studies Assn., Assn. Asian Studies, Asia Soc., Am. Fgn. Svc. Assn., Phi Beta Kappa. Congregationalist. Home: Hiram Ohio Died Oct. 5, 1991.

MARTIN, FRANK E(DWARD), railroad executive; b. Newton, Ill., May 7, 1895; s. Edward Truman and Catherine (Mason) M.; m. Ruth Ames, May 30, 1917; 1 child, Hariett (Mrs. William S. Propper). Grad. pub. high sch., Newton. Sta. clk. I.C. R.R., 1914, various clerical, acctg., valuation, engring. positions, 1914-35, asst. to auditor disbursements, 1935-38, auditor disbursements, 1938-41, gen. auditor, 1941-45, comptr., 1945-50, comptr. with jurisdiction over acctg. dept., 1950, v.p., comptr., from 1950. Mem. Union League, Chgo. Athletic Assn., Chgo. Club, Masons. *

MARTIN, GRAHAM ANDERSON, ambassador; b. Mars Hill, N.C., Sept. 22, 1912; s. Gustav Alexander and H. Hildreth (Marshbanks) M.; m. Dorothy Wallace; children: Janet Ann, Nancy Lane, David. AB, Wake Forest U., 1932, LLD, 1969; DHL, Campbell Coll., 1968. Washington newspaper corr., 1932-33; aide to dep. adminstr. NRA, 1933-36; asst. to chmn. Social Security Bd., 1936-37, dirst. mgr., 1937-41; regional dir. FSA, 1941-42, chief field ops., 1946; br. chief War Assets Adminstrn., 1946-47; with U.S. Fgn. Svc., 1947-73; attache Am. Embassy, Paris, 1947-50, counselor, 1951, asst. chief of mission, 1953-55, coord. European regional adminstrv. affairs, 1950; dept. state adviser Air War Coll., 1955-57; spl. asst. under sec. state for econ. affairs, 1957-59, spl. asst. under sec. state, 1959-60; consul gen. Geneva, Switzerland, 1960-61; ambassador to European office UN, 1960-62; dep. U.S. coord. Alliance for Progress, 1962-63, U.S. ambassador to Thailand, Bangkok, 1963-67; U.S. permanent rep. ECAFE, 1963-67; U.S. rep. 16th session Econ. Commn. Europe, 1961; U.S. coun. rep. SEATO, 1963-67; spl. asst. to sec. of state for refugee and migration affairs, 1967-69; U.S. amb. to Italy, 1969-73, to Vietnam, 1973-75. Col. USAAF, 1942-46. Decorated Legion of Merit, Bronze Star medal; recipient Disting. Honor award Dept. State, 1967, plaque for humanitarian Svc. Nat. Conf. on World Refugee Problems, 1969. Mem. Am. Fgn. Svc. Assn. (v.p. 1962-63), Am. Acad. Polit. and Social Sci., Univ. Club (Washington). Home: Winston-Salem N.C. Died Mar. 13, 1990.

MARTIN, JAMES ARTHUR, lawyer, educator; b. 1944. B.S., U. Ill., 1965; M.S., 1966; J.D., U. Mich., 1969. Bar: Mich. 1972. Law clk. U.S. Ct. Appeals (D.C. Cir.), 1969-70; asst. prof. U. Mich. Law Sch., 1970-73, assoc. prof., 1973-75, prof., 1975-85; mem. Com. to Revise and Consolidate Mich. Ct. Rules; chmn. Mich. Ct. Rules Adv. Com.; reporter com. to revise uniform statute of limitations on fgn. claims act Commrs. on Uniform State Laws. Mem. Stilyagi Air Corps, Order of Coif. Author: (with Epstein) Basic Uniform Commercial Code Teaching Materials, 1977, 2d edit., 1983; (with Honigman and Hawkins) Michigan Court Rules Annotated, Ann. Supplement; Conflict of Laws, 1978, 2d edit., 1984; Perspectives on Conflict of Laws: Choice of Law, 1980; (with Landers) Civil Procedure, 1981; (with Dean and Webster) Michigan Court Rules Practice, 1985; past exec. editor Mich. Law Rev. Died Dec. 10, 1985; buried Ann Arbor, Mich. Home: Ann Arbor Mich.

MARTIN, JAMES W(ALTER), economist; b. Muskogee, Indian Terr., Sept. 11, 1893; s. Luther Valentine and Mattie (Hancock) M.; m. Pearl Palmer, May 20, 1920; children: James Mayo, Lula Boyd; m. Dorothy Velander, June 13, 1925; 1 child, Charles Douglas. AB, East Tex. State Tchrs. Coll., 1920; postgrad., U. Chgo., 1922-24; LLD (hon.), U. Ky., 1965. Tchr. in pvt. and pub. schs. Tex., 1914-18; lectr. Northwestern U., Evanston, Ill., 1923; assoc. prof. econs., chmn. univ. rsch. com. Emory U., 1924-28; dir. Bur. Bus. Rsch., prof. econs. U. Ky., 1928-48, disting. prof., from 1948; cons. on fin. support, Ky. Ednl. Commn.; rsch. dir. Interstate Commn. on Conflicting Taxation, 1934-35; chief of staff Ky. REorgn. Commn., 1935-36; chmn. Tax Commn. of Ky., 1936; commr. of revenue of Ky., 1936-39; Ky. commr. of fin., 1955-57, commr. hwys., 1957-58, exec. dir. Property and Bldgs. Commn.; cons. in pub. fin. adminstrn.; past cons. on taxation or fin. adminstrn. to states, cities, countries, corps., U.S. Bur. Census, U.S. Treasury Dept., Civil Aeronautics Bd. of Dept. Commerce, Ky. Mcpl. League. Author monographs on taxation and fin. mgmt.; author or joint author publs. including Rsch. Report to Va. Pub. Svc. Tax Study Com., 1947, Safeguarding Kentucky's Natural Resources, 1948, Taxation of Manufacturing in the South, 1948, Administration of the Turkish Ministry of Finance, 1951, Kentucky Income Payments by Counties, 1953; contbr. to profl. jours. Mem. Pres. Roosevelt's Com. on Fiscal Rels. between U.S. and D.C., 1936-37; dir. hwy. fin. project Ky. Dept. Hwys.; mem. com. fiscal problems U.S. Commn. Intergovtl. Rels.; chmn. div. fin., taxation and cost studies Hwy. Rsch. Bd. of NAS-NRC, 1959. Mem. ASPA, AAUP, Tax Rsch. Found. (past pres.), So. Econ. Assn., Ky. Acad. Social Scis., Tax Inst., Inc., Nat. Tax Assn. (hon. life), Assoc. Burs. Bus. and Econ. Rsch., Nat. Assn. Tax Adminstrs. (past mem. governing bd.), Am. Econ. Assn., Nat. Assn. Assessing Officer (chmn. com. which prepared assessment orgn. and pers.), Am. Assn. Pub. Adminstrn., U. Ky. Club, Omicron Delta Kappa, Phi Eta, Beta Gamma Sigma. *

MARTIN, KIEL, actor; b. Pitts., July 26; 1 child, Jesse. Student, Trinity U., Tex.; student, U. Miami, Coral Gables, Fla. Ptnr. Mt. Jackson Cellars, Sonoma County, Calif., from 1982. Appeared in repertory theatre, Miami, Fla., Nat. Shakespeare Theatre at Old Globe, San Francisco, 1966, in repertory, New Orleans, N.Y.C.; movies: The Undefeated, 1969, The Panic in Needle Park, 1971, Lolly Madonna, 1973, others; appeared as regular on TV series: The Edge of Night, 1977-78; in TV shows: Delvecchio, Harry O, The Bold Ones, Ironside, Kung Fu, Murder She Wrote; TV feature film: The Child Bride of Short Creek, others; starred in U. Ala. prodn. of Bent, 1984; appeared as Detective Johnny La Rue on TV series Hill Street Blues, 1981-87, also short series Second Chance; actor TV movie Convicted: A Mother's Story. Served with U.S. Army, 1962-64. Home: Riverside County Calif. Died Dec. 28, 1990.

MARTIN, MARY, actress, singer; b. Weatherford, Tex., Dec. 1, 1913; d. Preston and Junita (Pressly) M.; m. Benjamin Hagman; 1 son, Larry; m. Richard Halliday, May 5, 1940 (dec. 1973); 1 dau., Mary Heller. Ed., Ward-Belmont Sch., Nashville, Tenn. Profl. debut in Hollywood nightclub; singer in mus. comedy Leave It to Me, N.Y.C., 1938; with Paramount Pictures, Inc., Hollywood, Calif., 1939-43; films include The Great Victor Herbert, Rhythm on the River, Kiss the Boys Goodbye, Love Thy Neighbors, Birth of the Blues, Star Spangled Rhythm, One Touch of Venus, Happy Go Lucky, True to Life, Lute Song; stage Night and Day; starred in Eng., 1946-47, Noel Coward's musical, Pacific 1860, 1947-48; star in tour of U.S. in musical Annie Get Your Gun, 1948, South Pacific; stage, N.Y. and London, 1949-52, Kind Sir, 1953-54, Peter Pan, 1954-55, The Skin of our Teeth; play The Sound of Music, 1959-61, Jennie, 1963; on tour, U.S., Japan, Vietnam, London, Hello Dolly, 1965, I Do, I Do; N.Y. stage and on tour, 1968-70, A Celebration of Richard Rogers, 1972; stage Do You Turn Somersaults, 1977; on tour, U.S., Legends, 1986-87; appeared in: TV film Valentine, 1979; co-host: TV series Over Easy, PBS, 1981-83; author: Needlepoint, 1969; autobiography My Heart Belongs, 1976, 84. Recipient numerous awards including Tony 1948, 55, 60, Emmy 1955, winner N.Y. Drama Critics Poll 1944, 49, 60, Kennedy Ctr. Honors award, 1989. Episcopalian. Home: Rancho Mirage Calif. Died Nov. 3, 1990.

MARTIN, PAUL ELLIOTT, bishop; b. Blossom, Tex., Dec. 31, 1897; s. Charles E. and Willie (Black) M.; m. Mildred Helen Fryar, June 29, 1920. AB, So. Meth. U., 1919, LLD, 1945; DD, Southwestern U., 1938, Hendrix Coll., 1945. Ordained as deacon Meth. Ch., 1924, elder, 1926. Prin. Blossom High Sch., 1919, supt. pub. sch., 1920-22; pastor Cedar Hill, 1922-24, Maple Ave Ch., Dallas, 1924-27; pastor Henrietta, 1927-29, Iowa Park, 1929-30, Kavanaugh-Greenville, 1930-35; dist. supt. Wichita Falls Dist., 1935-38; pastor First Ch., Wichita Falls, 1938-44; bishop Meth. Ch. (elected at South Cen. Jurisdictional Conf.), from 1944, assigned to Ark.-La. area, Little Rock, La. and North Ark. Confs., 1944-60, Houston area, Tex. and Rio Grande Confs., from 1960; del. to Gen. Conf. M.E. Ch., South, 1938, to Uniting Conf. of Meth. Ch., 1939, to Gen. Conf., Meth. Ch., 1940, 44; pres. coun. world svc. and fin. bishops of Meth. Ch., 1961-62; chmn. U.S. sect. World Meth. Coun. Trustee So. Meth. U., Southwestern U., Lon Morris Coll., Am. U., Tex. Meth. Children's Home, Lydia Patterson Inst., Scaritt Coll., Western Meth. Assembly, Meth. Hosp. Lt. inf. U.S. Army, World War I. Mem. Nat. Coun. Chs., Christ Am., Masons (33d deg.), Sigma Alpha Epsilon, Tau Kappa Alpha, Theta Phi. *

MARTIN, THOMAS BALDWIN, lawyer; b. Madison, Ga., Mar. 14, 1893; s. Frederick Robinson and Minnie (Baldwin) M.; m. Mary Benn Mathias, July 30, 1919; children: Rose Erdelle, Thomas Baldwin. LLB, Mercer U., 1914. Bar: Ga. 1914. Ptnr. Martin & Martin, 1914-25, Martin, Martin & Snow (now Martin, Snow, Grant and Napier), from 1925; bd. dirs. Home Fed. Savs. and Loan Assn. of Macon. Chmn. bd. trustees Mercer U., Southeastern Law Ctr. Found., Inc.; chmn. adv. coun. Walter F. George Sch. Law; pres., commr. Cen. Ga. coun. Boy Scouts Am.; mem. Bibb County coun. Girl Scouts U.S.A.; chmn. budget com. Macon Community Chest, 3 yrs. 1st lt. Infantry, 4th div. U.S. Army, with AEF, World War I. Mem. Alumni Assn. Mercer U. (pres. 1941), N.Y. So. Soc., Newcomen Soc. in N.Am., Nat. Assn. Coll. and Univ. Attys., Odd Fellows, Satilla River Fishing Club (pres.), Lions (pres. 1928), Masons, Shriners, Kappa Alpha. Baptist. *

MARTIN, WILLIAM C., bishop; b. Randolph, Tenn., July 28, 1893; s. John Harmon and Leila (Ballard) M.; m. Sally Katherine Beene, July 1, 1918; children: Donald Hankey, Mary Catharine, John Lee. Student, U. Ark., 1913-14; AB, Hendrix Coll., 1918, DD, 1929; postgrad., U. Aberdeen, 1919; BD, So. Meth. U., 1921, LLD, 1957; LLD, Nebr. Wesleyan U., 1940, Baker U., 1944; DD, Central Coll., 1947, Tex. Christian U., 1963. Ordained to ministry, M.E. Ch., 1921. Pastor Grace Ch., Houston, 1921-25; pastor First Ch., Port Arthur, Tex., 1925-28, Little Rock, 1928-31, Dallas, 1931-38; elected to Episcopacy M.E. Ch., South at Gen. Conf. Birmingham, Ala., 1938; bishop Pacific Area (Ariz. Northwest, Pacific, Western Mex. conf.), 1938-39; resident bishop Kans.-Nebr. Area Meth. Ch., 1939-48; resident bishop Dallas-Ft. Worth Area, 1948-64; lectr. ch. adminstrn. Perkins Sch. Theology So. Meth. U., Dallas, from 1964; pres. Coun. Bishops of Meth. Ch. 1952-53, Nat. Coun. Chs. in U.S.A., 1952-54; pres. Div of World Missions, 1960-64; chmn. Commn. on Promotion and Cultivation, 1948-64; del. World Coun. of Chs., 1948, 61, mem. cen. com., 1954-61; mem. World Coun. Gen. Assembly, 1952, 61; del. assembly World Coun. Chs., 1954, mem. cen. com. Author: To Fulfill This Ministry, 1949, Proclaiming The Good News, 1954. With Hosp. Corps, U.S. Army, with A.E.F., 1917-19. Mem. Masons (32d deg.), Chi Alpha, Theta Phi. *

MARTINO, ANTONIO P., painter; b. Phila., Apr. 13, 1902; s. Carmen M. (Clemntina) and Barrenello (Martino); m. Mary J. Hoffstetter, June 22, 1927; children: Anthony C., Marie C. Martino Manos. Retrospective show Woodmere Mus. Art., Chestnut Hill, Pa., 1982. Mem. NAD, Nat. Arts Club, Am. Watercolor Soc. Home: Thousand Oaks Calif. Died Sept. 3, 1988.

MARVEL, WILLIAM, state judicial official; b. Wilmington, Del., Sept. 29, 1909; s. Josiah and Mary Belle Jackson M.; m. Peggy Potter, Dec. 22, 1934; m. Laura Blair, Aug. 1, 1964. BA, Yale U., 1932, Cambridge, 1934; MA, Cambridge, 1944. Bar: Del. 1936. Assoc. law Marvel & Morford, Wilmington, 1936-42, ptnr., 1946-54; asst. U.S. atty., 1941-42, U.S. atty. dist. Del., 1948-53; vice chancellor State of Del., 1954-76, chancellor, 1976-82. Capt. AUS, 1942-45, NATOUSE, ETO. Recipient Josiah Marvel Cup award, 1982. Mem. ABA, Del. Bar Assn., Hist. Soc. Del. dir , Soc. Colonial Wars, Wilmington Club, County Club. Democrat. Episcopalian. Home: Greenville Del. Died June 28, 1991; buried Brandywine, Greenville, Del.

MARVIN, HAROLD MYERS, physician, educator; b. Jacksonville, Fla., Aug. 11, 1893; s. William and Gertrude Parthenia (Stoughton) M.; m. Elizabeth Turnbull, June 2, 1924; 1 child, John Turnbull. AB, Davidson Coll., 1914; MD, Harvard U., 1918; DSc (hon.), Davidson Coll., 1950. Med. house officer Peter Bent Brigham Hosp., Boston, 1918-19; dist. med. officer Near East Relief, Alexandropol, Armenia, 1919-20; asst. in medicine Harvard Med. Sch. and Mass. Gen. Hosp., 1920-21; instr. in medicine Yale U., New Haven, 1921-23, asst. prof., 1923-28, asst. clin. prof. medicine, 1928-33, assoc. clin. prof. medicine, 1933-62, prof. emeritus, from 1962; cons. cardiologist Meriden, Middlesex, Norwalk, Charlotte Hungerford (Torrington), New Britain, New Milford and Greenwich Hosps.; attending physician Grace-New Haven Community Hosp. Author of sect. on heart disease in several text books; Your Heart--Handbook For Laymen, 1960; editor, co-author: You and Your Heart, 1950; contbr. numerous articles on heart disease to non-med. jours. and sci. jours. in U.S. and Eng. Trustee Helen Hay Whitney Found., N.Y.C.; mem. nat. adv. heart coun. Nat. Heart Inst., USPHS, 1949-53. With Med. R.C., AUS, 1917-19. Mem. AMA, Am. Heart Assn. (dir. 1928-57, chmn. exec. com. 1931-46, acting exec. sec. 1932-48, pres. 1949-50, mem. editorial bd. Am. Heart Jour. 1933-50, Circulation 1950-58, from 1959), Assn. Am. Physicians, Am. Soc. Clin. Investigation, Conn. State Med. Soc. (pres. 1954-55), New Haven County Med. Assn., New Haven City Med. Assn. *

MARX, GROUCHO (JULIUS MARX), film and television comedian; b. N.Y.C., Oct. 2, 1895; m. Catharine Marvis; 1 child, Melinda; m. Eden Hartford; children: Arthur, Miriam. Began in vaudeville with mother, aunt and three brothers as "Six Musical Mascots"; later with three brothers as "Four Nightingales", then "The Four Marx Brothers"; has appeared on stage, screen and radio. Appeared with brothers in musical comedies The Cocoanuts, Animal Crackers, others, in motion pictures The Cocoanuts, Animal Crackers, Monkey Business, Horsefeathers, Duck Soup, A Night at the Opera, A Day at the Races, A Day at the Circus, Go West, The Big Store, others; collaborated on scenario of The King and the Chorus Girl, also scripts of many of own pictures, quiz master of TV program You Bet Your Life; author: Many Happy Returns, 1942, Groucho and Me, 1959. Recipient Emmy award NATAS. Mem. Am. Fedn. TV and Radio Artists, Acad. Motion Picture Arts and Sci. *

MARX, OTTO, JR., investment banker; b. Birmingham, Ala., Nov. 26, 1909; s. Otto and Agnes (Mosler) M.; m. Harriott P. Maxfield, Nov. 8, 1937; 1 stepchild: John V. Summerlin. B.S., U. Va., 1932. Ptnr. Ladenburg Thalmann & Co., N.Y.C., 1954-61; pres. Marx & Co., N.Y.C., 1961-65, 69-91, also bd. dirs., mem. exec. com.; pres., then chmn. Paribas Corp., N.Y.C., 1965-69; bd. dirs. Ohio Hotel Corp., Westover Travel Corp., Otmar Real Estate Corp., Birmingham Corp., The Lehman Capital Fund, Bremar Systems, Inc. Former trustee, adviser N.Y. Zool. Soc.; mem. Psychiatry and Neuroscis Devel. Council; vice chmn. nat. council Johns Hopkins U. Sch. Medicine, Balt. Served to lt. comdr. USNR, 1941-45. Clubs: N.Y. Yacht; Royal Bermuda Yacht, Coral Beach (Bermuda); Knickerbocker (N.Y.C.). Home: New York N.Y. Died June 8, 1991.

MASON, ALPHEUS THOMAS, political science, law educator, author, lecturer; b. Snow Hill, Md., Sept. 18, 1899; s. Herbert William and Emma Leslie (Hancock) M.; m. Christine Este Gibbons, June 12, 1934; 1 dau., Louise Este Mason Bachelder. A.B., Dickinson Coll., 1920, Litt.D., 1947, LL.D., 1963; A.M., Princeton U., 1921, Ph.D., 1923, LL.D., 1974; D.Litt., U. Louisville, 1957, Centre Coll. Ky., 1977; L.H.D., Washington Coll., 1969, Brandeis U., 1973; Sc.D., Utah State U., 1976; LL.D., Franklin and Marshall Coll., 1981. Proctor fellow Princeton U., 1922-23; asst. prof. polit. sci. Trinity Coll. (now Duke U.), 1923-25; asst. prof. politics Princeton U., 1925-30, assoc. prof., 1930-36, prof., 1936-47, McCormick prof. jurisprudence, 1947-68, McCormick prof. jurisprudence emeritus, 1968-89; Doherty prof. govt. and law U. Va., 1968-70; lectr. constl. law Mercer Beasley Sch. Law, Newark, 1928-32; lectr. Liberal Summer Sch., Cambridge, Eng., 1935; mem. Inst. Advanced Study, Princeton, N.J., 1938; acting prof. polit. sci. Stanford U., summer 1947; lectr. Conn. Coll., 1947, Syracuse U., 1948; Messenger lectr. Cornell U., Ithaca, N.Y., 1955; Edward Douglass White lectr. La. State U., 1957; Ford research prof., 1960; William W. Cook lectr. U. Mich., 1962; lectr. Hebrew U., Jerusalem, 1967; Henry L. and Grace Dougherty Found. prof. U. Va., 1968-70; vis. prof. govt. Harvard U., 1970-71, U. Calif. at Santa Barbara, 1971, Dartmouth Coll., 1971; Hill Found. vis. prof. U. Minn., 1971, U. Mich., 1972; Robb vis. prof. Barnard Coll., 1972, Johns Hopkins U., 1973; William A. Johnson Meml. distinguished vis. prof. Pomona Coll., 1974; Milton R. Merrill vis. prof. Utah State U., 1975; vis. prof. Claremont Men's Coll., 1976, Centre Coll. Ky., 1977, Humboldt State U., 1978, Yale U., 1979; Walter E. Edge lectr. Princeton U., 1979; bd. editors Am. Polit. Sci. Rev., 1936-40; mem. com. of experts to make survey of adminstrn. and expenditures of N.J. state govt., 1932; dir. Nat. Endowment for Humanities Summer Seminar, 1979. Author or co-author numerous books, from 1925; author: Brandeis: A Free Man's Life, 1946 (Best Seller List), American Constitutional Law, 1954, 8th edit., 1986, Security Through Freedom, 1955, Harlan Fiske Stone: Pillar of the Law, 1956 Liberty and Justice award ALA, Francis Parkman prize in history), The Supreme Court from Taft to Burger, rev. edit, 1979, In Quest of Freedom, 1959, 3d edit., 1981, The Supreme Court: Palladium of Freedom, 1962, The States Rights Debate: Antifederalism and the Constitution, 1964, 2d edit., 1972, Free Government in the Making, 1965, 4th edit. (Bicentennial), 1985, William Howard Taft: Chief Justice, 1965, The Supreme Court in a Free Society, 1969, Conversations on the Character of Princeton; editorial adv. bd.: Polit. Sci. Quar., from 1972, Univ. Press, from 1981; contbr. articles to profl. jours. Recipient grants-in-aid Social Sci. Research Council for study of Mr. Justice Brandeis, 1933, for study of trade unions and the state in London, 1935; Guggenheim fellow for biography of Harlan Fiske Stone, 1950; Northwestern U. Centennial lectr., 1951; Guggenheim fellow, 1952; Gasper G. Bacon lectr. Boston U., 1953; mem. Am. Studies Seminars, Tokyo U., 1953, Yugoslav-Am. Seminars, 1962, 63; 5,000 prize in history and biography ALA, 1957; Rockefeller Found. study award, 1960-63; McCosh Faculty fellow, 1963-64. Fellow Am. Acad. Arts and Scis.; mem. Am. Polit. Sci. Assn. (v.p.), Phi Beta Kappa, Sigma Alpha Epsilon. Presbyterian. Clubs: Nassau (Princeton); Princeton (N.Y.C.); Authors (London). Home: Princeton N.J. Died Oct. 31, 1989; cremated.

MASON, EDWARD SAGENDORPH, economist, educator; b. Clinton, Iowa, Feb. 22, 1899; s. Edward Luther and Kate (Sagendorph) M.; m. Marguerite Sisson La Monte, Apr. 4, 1930; children: Robert La Monte (stepson), Jane Carroll Mason Manasse, Edward H.L. AB, U. Kans., 1919; AM, Harvard U., 1920, PhD, 1925, LLD, 1956; BLitt, Oxford U., 1923; LittD (hon.), Williams Coll., 1948; LLD (hon.), Yale U., 1964, Concord Coll., 1971. Instr. Harvard U., Cambridge, Mass., 1923-27, asst. prof. econs., 1927-32, assoc. prof., 1932-37, prof. econs., 1937-92, George F. Baker prof. econs., 1958-61, Thomas W. Lamont Univ. prof., 1961-69, Lamont prof. emeritus, dean Grad. Sch. Pub. Adminstrn., 1947-58; econ. cons. Dept. Labor, 1938-39, Def. Commn., 1940-41, OSS, Washington, 1941-45; dep. to asst. sec. state charge econ. affairs, 1945; econ. cons. Dept. State, 1946-47; chief econ. adviser Moscow Conf., 1947; mem. Adv. Com. on Mgmt. Improvement to Assist in Improving Govt. Orgn.; mem. materials Policy Commn., 1951-52; chmn. adv. com. econ. devel. AID; cons. World Bank; chmn. Sloan Found. commn. on cable comms. Bd. dirs. Internat. Coun. for Ednl. Devel., Resources for the Future, Asian Devel. Corp. Recipient medal of Freedom, 1946, Star of Pakistan, 1967, Disting. Alumni award U. Kans.; hon. fellow Lincoln Coll., Oxford. Mem. Am. Philos. Soc., Am. Econ. Assn. (past pres.), Royal Econ. Soc. London, Am. Acad. Arts and Scis., The Saturday Club, Phi Beta Kappa, Delta Sigma Rho. Unitarian. Home: Cambridge Mass. Died Feb. 29, 1992.

MASON, FRANK EARL, public relations executive, publisher; b. Milw., Feb. 8, 1893; s. George F. and Cora Lee (Tussing) M.; m. Ellen Speltan-Thomsen, Jan. 15, 1920. AB, Ohio State U., 1915; Assoc. in Journalism, Columbia U., 1934. Asst. editor Am. Boy, 1915-16; asst. mil. attaché Am. Legation, The Hague; mil. attaché Am. Embassy, Berlin, 1919; Berlin corr. Internat. News Svc., 1920-21, London mgr., 1921, Paris mgr., 1922-26; bus. mgr. Internat. News Svc., N.Y., 1927; gen. mgr., pres. Internat. News Svc., 1928-31; v.p. NBC, 1931-45; dir. Loudoun Times-Mirror; pres. Loudon Press Inc.; spl. asst. to Sec. Navy, 1941-44; Mem. Hoover's Worldwide Food Survey of 38 Countries, 1946; mem. Hoover European Mission, 1947. Active History Fund, Inc., Authors Fund, Inc.; mem. adv. bd. Hoover Instn., Stanford U. Intelligence officer 9th Inf., U.S. Army, 1918; instr. Army Intelligence Sch., Langres, France, 1918; chief censor advanced G.H.Q., Gen. Staff, German occupied area, 1919; mil. observer, Berlin, 1919; col. AUS. Decorated Purple Heart, Croix de Guerre, France, Officer of the Crown, Rumania. Mem. 2d Civ. Assn. (pres. 1935), Soc. Silurians, N.Y. Soc. Mil. and Naval Officers of the World War, Ends of the Earty, Players Club, Dutch Treat Club, Coffee House Club, Army and Navy Club, Nat. Press Club, Circumnavigators Club, Univ. Club, Phi Beta Kappa, Sigma Delta Chi (hon. nat. pres. 1930), Delta Chi. *

MASON, HAROLD JESSE, communications executive, consultant; b. Bklyn., Dec. 13, 1926; s. Irving and Belle (Solomon) M.; m. Selma Ruth Werner, May 22, 1947; children: Lori Karen Reisman, Dione Ellen Katz. B.A., Emory U., 1952, M.A., 1954; Ph.D., Columbia U., 1966. Serials Librarian Ga. Inst. Tech., 1953-54; asst. mgr. Kraus Reprint Corp., N.Y.C., 1954-66; pres., co-founder Greenwood Press Inc., Westport, Conn., 1967-72; pres., founder Harold J. Mason, Inc., Phoenix and Norwalk, Conn., 1973-90, cons., from 1990. Contbr. articles to profl. publs. Mem. Phi Beta Kappa. Republican. Jewish. Home: Phoenix Ariz. Deceased. †

MASON, JERRY, publisher; b. Balt., Apr. 6, 1913; s. Daniel A. and Esther (Schapira) Myerberg; m. Clarise Finger, Nov. 26, 1936; children: Michael Maury, Judy Ann Mason Underhill. A.B., Johns Hopkins U., 1933; M.S. in Journalism, Columbia U., 1934. Writer for magazines, also engaged in pub. relations, 1934-41; mem. staff This Week mag., N.Y.C., 1941-49; asso. editor This Week mag., 1945-49; editor-in-chief Argosy mag., 1949-53; also editorial dir. Popular Publs. Co.; pres., founder Maco Mag. Corp., N.Y.C., 1953-57; founder Ridge Press, N.Y.C., 1957, Pound Press, 1981; pub. VBI, N.Y.C., 1979. Author: I Find Treason, 1939; editor, pub.: Family of Man, 1955, Private World of Pablo Picasso, 1958, The World's Family, 1983, The ICP Encyclopedia of Photography, 1984. Advisory council Internat. Center Photography; pres. Hiram Halle Meml. Library, Pound Ridge, N.Y. Mem. Phi Beta Kappa. Club: Book Table. Home: Pound Ridge N.Y. Died Feb. 20, 1991.

MASON, J(OHN) ALDEN, anthropologist; b. Phila., Jan. 14, 1885; s. William Albert and Ellen Louise (Shaw) M.; m. Florence Roberts, Dec. 23, 1921; 1 child, John Alden. AB, Cen. High Sch., Phila., 1903, U. Pa., 1907; postgrad., U. Pa., 1907-10; PhD, U. Calif., 1911; LittD, Franklin and Marshall, 1958. Rsch. fellow U. Calif., 1916; asst. curator Mex. and S. Am. archeology Field Mus. Natural History, Chgo., 1917-24; curator Mex. archeology Am. Mus. Natural History, N.Y., 1924-25; curator sect. Am. archeology and ethnology Univ. Mus., Phila., 1926-55; curator emeritus Am. sect. Univ. Mus., from 1955; editor, field adviser New World Archaeol. Found., from 1958; del. from U. Pa. to Internat. Sch. Mex. Archeology and Ethnology, 1911-13; mem. Puerto Rican Insular Survey, 1914-15; mem. ethnol. and archeol. expdn. to Utah, Calif., Mex., Can., P.R., Ariz., Colombia, Tex., Guatemala, Panama. Author: The Ethnology of the Salinan Indians, 1912, The Mutsun Dialect of Costanoan, 1916, The Language of the Salinan Indians, 1917, Tepecano, a Language of Western Mexico, 1918, Archeology of Santa Marta, Colombia, 1931, 26, 40, The Laugnage of the Papago of Arizona, 1950, The Ancient Civilizations of Peru, 1957, Las Antiguas Culturas del Peru, 1962, also anthrop. revs., articles to profl. publs. Mem. AAAS (v.p. 1944), Am. Anthrop. Assn. (v.p. 1944, editor 1945-48), Soc. Am. Archaeology (pres. 1944), Eastern States Archaeol. Fedn. (pres. 1942-46), Am. Ethnol. Assn. (treas. 1925), Am. Folk-Lore Soc. (coun.), Pa. Folklore Soc. (pres. 1963-65), Soc. Pa. Archeology (pre. 1929-30), Archeol. Soc. Del., Phila. Anthrop. Soc. (pres. 1927-54), Pan Am. Assn. Phila. (pres. 1948), Am. Mus. Nat. History, Sociedad de Geograifa e Historia de Guatemala (hon.), N.J. Archeol. Soc. (hon., editor), Sigma Xi. Unitarian. *

MASON, NORMAN PIERCE, housing consultant; b. Willsboro, N.Y., Dec. 24, 1896; s. Robert Lew Preston and Anne (Bebb) M.; m. Helen C. Proctor, Aug. 25, 1920; children: David H., Nancy (Mrs. Charles Svenson). Grad., high sch. Joined William P. Proctor Co., 1923, pres., 1925-36, treas., exec. officer, 1937-54; co-organizer Coop. Res. Supply, Inc., Cambridge, Mass., 1950, pres., chmn. bd. dirs., 1950-54; commr. FHA, Washington, 1954-59; adminstr. U.S. Housing and Home Fin. Agy., 1959-61; chmn. bd. dirs. Am. Internat. Housing Corp., 1961-64; cons. retirement housing projects, from 1964. Past v.p. Lowell (Mass.) Community Chest, Battles Home, Lowell; past mem. N.E. Coun. Adv. NPA, OPS, 1950-51, OPA during World War II; chmn. local Selective Svc. Bd., 1940-54; mem. Pres. Eisenhower's Adv. Com. Housing, 1953; dir. U.S. C. of C., 1949-54.. Radio operator USN, 1918-19. Mem. NAS, Nat. Retail Lumber Dealers Assn. (pres. 1947-48), Bldg. Rsch. Adv. Bd. Inst. (past pres. bd. govs., bd. dirs., exec. com.). *

MASON, RALPH SCHWEIZER, lawyer, association executive; b. Trenton, N.J., May 18, 1913; s. Ralph Silas and Emilia (Schweizer) C.; m. Jean Louise Harris, Sept. 23, 1950; children: Ralph Schweizer III, Karen A., Thomas S. A.B., Princeton U., 1936; LL.B., U. Pa., 1939; D.H.L. (hon.), George Williams Coll., 1976. Bar: N.J. 1939. Asst. counsel Commn. Statutes of State of N.J., 1940, 42, 46; individual practice law Trenton, N.J., 1940-46, Princeton, N.J., 1951-55; partner firm Montgomery & Mason, 1946-51, Mason, Griffin & Pierson (and precessors), Princeton, 1955-90; past sec.-treas., dir. Nassau Broadcasting Co.; mem. exec. com. of bd. Princeton Savs. & Loan Assn. (merged with Security Savs. and Loan). Pres. Nat. Council YMCA's of U.S.A., 1975-77, mem. nat. bd. and exec. com.; cons. and mem. to exec. com., mem. World Alliance YMCA's, 1961-85; chmn. bd. trustees Med. Ctr., Princeton, 1967-76; trustee, vice chmn. Med. Ctr. Princeton Found., from 1976; trustee, former pres. Princeton United Community Fund; former sec.-treas., trustee Hun Sch., Princeton; elder, former chmn. bd. trustees Nassau Presbyterian Ch.; former trustee New Brunswick (N.J.) Presbytery; incorporator Nat. USO, 1967-73; mayor Princeton Twp., 1956-57; chmn. Princeton Twp. Planning Bd., 1959-60. Served with U.S. Army, 1942-46. Decorated Bronze Star Medal; recipient Gerard B. Lambert award Princeton United Community Fund, 1961, Nat. Treasure award YMCA of USA, Francis G. Clark award Princeton YMCA. Fellow Am. Coll. Probate Counsel; mem. Greater Princeton C. of C. (bd. dirs., past pres., Man of Yr. 1972), ABA, N.J. Bar Assn., Mercer County Bar Assn. (past pres.), Princeton Bar Assn. (past pres.). Republican. Club: Nassau. Lodge: Rotary (past trustee, Paul Harris fellow). Home: Princeton N.J. Died Nov. 26, 1988; cremated.

MASON, STANLEY GEORGE, physical chemist, educator, consultant; b. Montreal, Que., Can., Mar. 20, 1914; s. David MacCallum and Margaret (Fraser) M.; m. Renata Vincenzi, June 14, 1969; children—Cheryl, Andrea. B.Eng. in Chem. Engring., McGill U., Montreal, 1936; Ph.D. in Phys. Chemistry, McGill U., 1939. Lectr. phys. chemistry Trinity Coll., Hartford, Conn., 1939-41; dept. head Suffield Exptl. Sta., Dept. Nat. Defence, Ralston, Alta., Can., 1941-45; assoc. research chemist atomic energy div. Nat. Research Council, Montreal, 1945-46; head phys. chemistry sect., dir. applied chemistry div. Pulp and Paper Research Inst. Can., Montreal, 1946-79, cons., from 1979; prof. dept. chemistry McGill U., 1946-85, Otto Maaas prof. chemistry, 1979-85, prof. emeritus, 1985-87; mem. adv. com. NRC, Defence Research Bd., Can.; lectr. Recipient Bingham medal Soc. Rheology, 1969; Dunlop award, 1975; Howard N. Potts medal The Franklin Inst., 1980, Prix Marie-Victorian, State of Que., 1986. Fellow Royal Soc. Can., Chem. Inst. Can. (medal 1973), TAPPI; mem. Can. Pulp and Paper Assn. (active, sometime officer tech. sect.), Am. Chem. Soc. (Kendall Co. award in colloid chemistry 1967, Anselme Payen award in cellulose chemistry 1969), Brit. Soc. Rheology, Soc. Rheology (U.S.A.), Internat. Soc. Biorheology (disting.), Nat. Acad. Engring. (fgn. assoc.). Home: Westmount Can. Died Apr. 22, 1987.

MASSENGALE, JOHN EDWARD, III, lawyer; b. Kansas City, Mo., Nov. 18, 1921; s. John Edward, Jr. and Frances (Haig) M.; m. Jean Mitchell Montague, Dec. 8, 1942; children: Sarah Choate Massengale Gregg, John Edward IV, Thomas Haig. A.B., Harvard U., 1942, LL.B., 1948. Bar: N.Y. 1949, D.C. 1971. Practice law N.Y.C., 1948-88; ptnr. Paul, Weiss, Rifkind, Wharton & Garrison, 1958-88. Rep. town meeting, Darien, Conn., 1955-61, 63-70; mem. Zoning Bd. Appeals, 1985-86, Darien Planning and Zoning Commn., 1986-88. Served to lt. USNR, 1942-45. Mem. Assn. Bar City N.Y., N.Y. State Bar Assn., ABA. Club: Noroton Yacht. Home: Noroton Conn. Died Dec. 21, 1988.

MASTON, THOMAS BUFFORD, educator, author; b. Jefferson County, Tenn., Nov. 26, 1897; s. Samuel Houston and Sarah Roselie (Sellers) M.; m. Essie Mae McDonald, June 11, 1921; children: Thomas McDonald, Harold Eugene. AB, Carson-Newman Coll., 1920, LittD, 1958; MA, Tex. Christian U., 1927; MRE, Southwestern Bapt. Theol. Sem., 1923, DRE, 1925; postgrad., U. N.C., 1928, U. Chgo., 1929, Yale U., 1932-33, 36-37; PhD, Yale U., 1939. Tchr. Southwestern Bapt. Theol. Sem., Ft. Worth, 1922-63; prof. Christian ethics Sch. of Theology, 1937-63. Author: Handbook for Church Recreation Leaders, 1937, of One, 1946, The Christian in the Modern World, 1952, A World in Travail, 1954, Right or Wrong, 1955, rev. edit., 1971, Christianity and World Issues, 1957, The Bible and Race, 1959, Segregation and Desegregation, 1959, Isaac Backus: Pioneer of Religious Liberty, 1962, God's Will and Your Life, 1964, Biblical Ethics, 1967, Suffering: A Personal Perspective, 1967, The Christian, The Church and Contemporary Problems, 1968, The Conscience of a Christian, 1971, Real Life in Christ, 1974, Why Live the Christian Life, 1974. Home: Fort Worth Tex. Died May 2, 1988.

MASURSKY, HAROLD, geologist; b. Fort Wayne, Ind., Dec. 23, 1923; s. Louis and Celia (Ochstein) M.; m. LesLee Masursky; 4 children. B.S. in Geology, Yale U., 1943, M.S., 1951; D.Sc. (hon.), No. Ariz. U., 1981. With U.S. Geol. Survey, 1951-90, chief astrogeologic studies br., 1967-71; chief scientist Ctr. Astrogeology, U.S. Geol. Survey, Flagstaff, Ariz., 1971-75, sr. scientist, 1975-89, sr. scientist emeritus, 1990; lunar orbiter Surveyor Missions, 1965-67; team leader, prin. investigator TV experiment Mariner Mars, 1971; co-investigator Apollo field geol. team Apollo 16 and 17, also mem. Apollo orbital sci. photog. team, Apollo site selection group; leader Viking Mars Missions Site Selection and cert. team, 1975; mem. imaging teams Voyager (Jupiter, Saturn, Uranus, Neptune), 1977; chmn. mission ops. group Venus Pioneer Mission, 1978, co-chmn. mission operational group Galileo Mission, 1981, mission ops. leader, radar team Magellan mission Magellan Mission, from 1981; mem. camera team Mars observer, 1986; mem. Space Sci. Adv. Com., 1978-81, solar system exploration com., 1980-86; mem. Space Sci. Bd., 1982-85; pres. intedisc com. B, COSPAR; sec. Coordinating Com. of Moon and Planets. Assoc. editor: Icarus, Geophys. Rev. Letters, Geodynamics. Served with AUS, 1943-46. Fellow Geol. Soc. Am. (assoc. editor bull., pres. planetary geol. div.), AAAS, Am. Geophys. Union (pres. nomenclature workgroup), Internat. Astron. Union, Am. Astron. Assn. (dir. planet studies, mem. exec. com. 1987). Home: Flagstaff Ariz. Died Aug. 24, 1990; buried Jewish Cemetery, Flagstaff, Ariz.

MATHER, KATHARINE, geologist; b. Ithaca, N.Y., Oct. 21, 1916; d. Walter Hamlin and Katharine Emily (Selden) Kniskern; m. Bryant Mather, Mar. 27, 1940. A.B. in Geology, Bryn Mawr Coll., 1937; student, Sch. Higher Studies, Johns Hopkins, 1937-40; D.Sc. (hon.), Clarkson Coll., 1978. Research asst. Johns Hopkins, 1939; research asso. Field Mus. Natural History, Chgo., 1940-41; geologist Corps Engrs., U.S. Army, 1942-82; assigned Waterways Expt. Sta., Vicksburg, Miss., 1946-82; chief petrography and X-ray br., engring. scis. div., concrete lab. Waterways Expt. Sta., 1947-76, chief engring. scis. div., 1976-80, spl. tech. asst., structures lab., 1980-82; mem. Internat. Symposia Chemistry Cement, 1960, 68, 80, 86, 4th and 5th Internat. Congresses Non-Destructive Testing, 1963, 64; mem., chmn. tech. coms. Transp. Research Bd. of Nat. Acad. Scis.-NRC; former mem. U.S. panel Tech. Coop. Program. Co-author: Butterflies of Mississippi, 1958; bd. dirs., editor: Jour. Miss. Acad. Scis, 1960-66. Recipient Exceptional Service award Sec. Army, 1962, Fed. Woman's award, 1963, Disting. Civilian Service award Sec. Def., 1964, award for contbns. to sci. Miss. Acad. Scis., 1986. Fellow Mineral. Soc. Am., Am. Concrete Inst. (hon. mem.; co-recipient Wason Research medal 1955, dir. 1968-71); life mem. Mineral. Soc. London; mem. ASTM (Sanford E. Thompson award 1952, various coms., hon. mem. com. C-1 on cement 1989), Clay Minerals Soc. (sec. 1964-67, pres. 1973), Alumnae Assn. Bryn Mawr Coll. (past dist. councillor), Sigma Xi. Home: Clinton Miss. Died Feb. 4, 1991; cremated.

MATHER, NORMAN WELLS, electrical engineering educator; b. Upland, Calif., Apr. 29, 1914; s. Wiley Wells and Glenn (Shaw) M.; m. Mary Adele Clark, June 10, 1939; children: John Norman, Margaret Ann. Student, Chaffey Jr. Coll., 1932-33; B.S. in Elec. Engring, U. Calif. at Berkeley, 1936; M.S. in Engring, Princeton U., 1947. Engr. Otis Elevator Co., San Francisco, Los Angeles, also Yonkers, N.Y., 1936-42; mem. faculty Princeton U., 1946-82, asso. prof. elec. engring., 1947-58, prof., 1958-82, prof. emeritus, 1982-90; asso. Project Matterhorn, 1952-61, Princeton Plasma Physics Lab., 1961-71. Served from ensign to lt. USNR, 1942-46. Mem. IEEE, Assn. Princeton Grad. Alumni (sec.-treas. 1963-71), The Old Guard of Princeton Club, Sigma Xi, Eta Kappa Nu. Home: Princeton N.J. Died July 3, 1990.

MATHER, PHILIP R., industrialist; b. Cleve., May 19, 1894; s. Samuel and Flora Amelia (Stone) M.; m. Madeleine Almy, Aug. 17, 1917; children: Constance (Mrs. John L. Price Jr.), Anne (Mrs. Frank C. Montero), Madeleine (Mrs. David L. Anderson), Phyllis (Mrs. Thornton Stearns). Student, U. Sch., 1903-12; BA, Yale U., 1916; psotgrad., Harvard U., 1919-20; LLD, Kenyon Coll., 1956. With Pickands, Mather & Co., Cleve., 1920-26, 30-36; dir. Riley Stoker Corp., Worcester, Mass., Cleve. Cliffs Iron Co. Editor: History of 322d Field Artillery, 1920. Past dir. United Community Funds and Couns. Am.; hon. trustee Goodrich Social Settlement, Hiram Ho., Cleve.; trustee Kenyon Coll., Gambier, Ohio; mem. Am. com. St. Luke's Internat. Hosp., Tokyo. Capt. 322d F.A., 1917-19, AEF, 1918-19. Mem. Am. Social Hygiene Assn. (bd. dirs., chmn. bd. dirs., mem. exec. com.), Nat. Health Coun. (pres. 1946-50, treas. 1950-60), World Affairs Coun. of Boston (past bd. dirs.), Lake Placid Club, Chagrin Valley Hunt Club, Union Club, Brookline Country Club, St. Botolph Club, Phi Beta Kappa, Beta Theta Pi. *

MATHESON, SCOTT MILNE, lawyer, governor of Utah; b. Chgo., Jan. 8, 1929; s. Scott Milne and Adele (Adams) M.; m. Norma Warenski, Aug. 25, 1951; children: Scott Milne, Mary Lee, James David, Thomas Douglas. B.S. in Polit. Sci., U. Utah, 1950; J.D., Stanford U., 1952. Bar: Utah 1953. Practice in Iron County Utah, 1953-54; atty. Parowan City, Utah, 1953-54; dep. atty. Iron County, 1953-54; law clk. to U.S. dist. judge, 1954-56; pvt. practice Salt Lake City, 1956-58; dep. atty. Salt Lake County, 1956-57; asst. gen. atty., then gen. atty. Union Pacific R.R., 1958-69, counsel, 1969-70, gen. solicitor, 1972-76; asst. gen. counsel Anaconda Co., 1970-72; gov. Utah, 1977-85; ptnr. Parsons Behle & Latimer, Salt Lake City, 1985-90; mem. Intergovtl. Task Force on Water Policy, from 1978, Pres.'s Commn. on Federalism; chmn. Four Corners Regional Commn., 1979-80, Western Govs. Policy Office, 1978-80; lectr. Coll. So. Utah, 1953-54; chmn. Utah R.R. Assn., 1972-76; mem. Adv. Commn. Intergovtl. Relations, 1983. Pres. Utah Young Democrats, U. Utah, 1948; mem. Utah Water Pollution Com., 1970-76. Mem. ABA (chmn. spl. com. youth edn. for citizenship), Am. Judicature Soc. (dir.), Utah State Bar (pres. 1968-69, trustee from 1971, del. 1973-76), Nat. Govs. Assn. (chmn. subcom. water mgmt. from 1977, chmn. 1982-83), Utah Tennis Assn. Mem. LDS Ch. Clubs: Rotary, Alta, Ft. Douglas Hidden Valley, Salt Lake Swimming and Tennis. Home: Salt Lake City Utah Died Oct. 7, 1990; buried Parowan, Utah.

MATHIAS, WILLIAM J., composer, educator; b. Whitland, Dyfed, Wales, Nov. 1, 1934; s. James Hughes and Marian (Evans) M.; m. Margaret Yvonne Collins, 1959; 1 child, Rhiannon. Ed. Univ. Coll. Wales; D.Mus., 1966; MusD (hon.), Westminster Choir Coll., Princeton, 1987. Lectr., Univ. Coll. North Wales, 1959-68, prof. music, head dept., 1970-88; sr. lectr. U. Edinburgh (Scotland), 1968-69; mem. Welsh Arts Council, 1974-88, chmn. music com., 1982-88; bd. govs. Nat. Mus. Wales, 1973-78; mem. music adv. com. Brit. Coun., 1974-83, mem. Welsh adv. com. 1979-88; mem. Cen. Music Adv. Com., BBC, 1979-86; artistic dir. North Wales Music Festival, 1972-92; gov. Nat. Youth Orch. Gt. Britain, 1985-92; v.p. Royal Coll. Organists, 1985; pres. Inc. Soc. Musicians, 1989-90. Composer orchestral pieces: Symphony #1, 1969, Piano Concerto No. 2, 1964, Piano Concerto No. 3, 1970, Harp Concerto, 1973, Clarinet Concerto, 1976, Organ Concerto, 1984, Celtic Dances, 1974, Divertimento for Strings, 1961, Serenade, 1963, Prelude Aria and Finale, 1966, Vistas, 1977, Laudi, 1978, Helios, 1978, Requiescat, 1978, (for brass band) Vivat Regina , 1978, Dance Variations, 1979, Investiture Anniversary Fanfare, 1979, Reflections on a Theme by Tomkins, 1981, (summer music) Symphony #2, 1983, Anniversary Dances, 1985, Symphony No. 3, 1991, Violin Concerto, 1992, Flute Concerto, 1992, In Arcadia, 1992; Chamber Music: Violin Sonata #1, 1963, Piano Sonata No. 1, 1965, String Quartet No. 1, 1970, String Quartet No. 2, 1981, No. 3, 1986, Wind Quintet, 1976, Zodiac Trio, 1977, Clarinet Sonatina, 1978, Concertino, 1977, Violin Sonata #2, 1984; Choral and Vocal: Wassail Carol, 1965, Three Medieval Lyrics, 1966, Ave Rex, 1970, A Babe is Born, 1971, A Vision of Time and Eternity (for contralto and piano), 1974, Ceremony after a Fire Raid, 1975, This Worlde's Joie (for solo, chorus and orchestra), 1975, Elegy for a Prince (for baritone and orch.), 1976, The Fields of Praise (for tenor and piano), 1977, A Royal Garland, 1978, A May Magnificent, 1980, Shakespeare Songs, 1980, Songs of William Blake (for mezzo and orch.), 1980, Rex Gloriae, 1982, Te Deum (for soli, chorus and orch.), 1982, Lux Aeterna, 1982, Riddles, 1987, Jonah, 1988, World's Fire, 1989; organ: Variations in a Hymn Tune, 1963, Partita, 1963, Postlude, 1964, Processional, 1965, Chorale, 1967, Toccata Giocosa, 1968, Jubilate, 1975, Fantasy, 1978, Canzonetta, 1978, Antiphonies, 1982, Organ Concerto, 1984, Berceuse, 1985, Recessional, 1986, A Mathias Organ Album, 1986, Fanfare for Organ, 1987, Fenestra, 1989, Carillon (for organ), 1990; Anthems and Ch. Music: O Sing unto the Lord, 1965, Make a Joyful Noise, 1965, Festival Te Deum, 1965, Communion Service in C, 1968, Psalm 150, 1969, Lift up your heads, 1970, O Salutaris Hostia, 1972, Gloria, 1972, Magnificat and Nunc Dimittis, 1973, Missa Brevis, 1974, Communion Service (Series III), 1976, Arise, shine, 1978, Let the People Praise Thee, O God (for marriage of Prince and Princess of Wales), 1981, Praise ye the Lord, 1982, All Wisdom is from the Lord, 1982, Except the Lord Build the House, 1983, A Grace, 1983, Jubilate Deo, 1983, O How Amiable, 1983, Tantum Ergo, 1984, Let Us Now Praise Famous Men, 1984, Alleluia! Christ is Risen, 1984, Missa Aedis Christi-in Memoriam William Walton, 1984, Salve Regina, 1986, O Clap Your Hands, 1986, Let All the World in Every Corner Sing, 1987, Rejoice in the Lord, 1987, I Will Lift Up Mine Eyes unto the Hills, 1987, Cantate Domino, 1987, Thus Saith God the Lord-An Orkney Anthem, 1987, O Lord our Lord, 1987, As Truly as God is our Father, 1987, St. David's Service, 1992; Opera: (libretto by Iris Murdoch) The Servants, 1980. Recipient Arnold Bax Soc. prize, 1968, John Edwards Meml. award, 1982; Univ. Coll. Wales fellow, 1990. Fellow Royal Acad. Music. Died July 29, 1992. Home: Anglesey, Gwynedd Wales †

MATHIS, BYRON CLAUDE, psychologist, educator; b. Longview, Tex., Mar. 10, 1927; s. Byron Claude and Pearl (Livsey) M.; m. Patricia Ann Purtell, June 7, 1958; children—Byron Claude III, Deborah Ann. B.A., Tex. Christian U., 1949, M.A., 1950; Ph.D., U. Tex., 1956. Asst. prof. ednl. psychology U. Tex., 1955-56; asst. prof. edn. Northwestern U., Evanston, Ill., 1956-60, assoc. prof., 1960-64, assoc. prof. edn. and psychology, 1964-65, prof., 1965-89, asst. dean Grad. Sch., 1964-65, assoc. dean, 1966-69, assoc. dean Sch. Edn., 1969-78, assoc. dean Sch. Edn. and Social Policy, 1989-90, dir. Ctr. for the Teaching Professions, 1969-90; cons. faculty devel. Bush Found., St. Paul. Author: (with John Cotton and Lee Sechrest) Psychological Foundations of Education-Learning and Teaching, 1970, (with Robert Menges) Key Resources on Teaching, Learning, Curriculum and Faculty Development, 1988; assoc. editor: Psychology In The Schools, 1964-70, editor, 1970-71; exec. editor (with William McGaghie): Profiles in College Teaching, 1972, (with Stephen Holbrook) Teaching: A Force for Change in Higher Education; contbr. articles to profl. jours. Bd. dirs. Family Counseling Service Evanston and Skokie Valley, 1971-77, pres., 1974-77; trustee Roycemore Sch., 1978-83. Served with USNR, 1944-46. Fellow Am. Psychol. Assn., AAAS; mem. Am. Ednl. Research Assn., AAUP. Home: Morton Grove Ill. Died Dec. 20, 1989; buried Morton Grove, Ill.

MATISSE, PIERRE, art dealer; b. Bohain, Alsace, France, June 13, 1900; s. Henri and Amelie Noelie (Parayre) M.; came to U.S., 1924 naturalized, 1942; educated privately; m. Alexina Sattler, Dec. 29, 1929; children: Jacqueline Matisse Monnier, Paul, Peter. Founder, 1931, since pres. Pierre Matisse Gallery, N.Y.C. Decorated knight Arts and Letters, Merite Nat., chevalier de la Légion d'Honneur (France). Mem. Am. Art Dealers Assn. (pres. 1964-66). Clubs: N.Y. Yacht, N.Y. Athletic; Yacht (France).Died Aug. 9, 1989. Home: New York N.Y. †

MATSUNAGA, SPARK MASAYUKI, senator; b. Kauai, Hawaii, Oct. 8, 1916; s. Kingoro and Chiyono (Fukushima) M.; m. Helene Hatsumi Tokunaga, Aug. 6, 1948; children: Karen (Mrs. Hardman), Keene, Diane, Merle, Matthew. Ed.B. with honors, U. Hawaii, 1941; J.D., Harvard U., 1951; LL.D. (hon.), Soochow U., 1973, St. John's U., 1977, Eastern Ill. U., 1978, U. Md., 1979; H.L.D., Lincoln U., 1979. Bar: Hawaii 1952. Vets. counsellor U.S. Dept. Interior, 1945-47; chief priority claimants div. War Assets Adminstrn., 1947-48; asst. pub. pros. City and County of Honolulu, 1952-54; practice law Honolulu, 1954-62; mem. Hawaii Ho. of Reps., 1954-59, majority leader, 1959; mem. U.S. Ho. Reps. 88th-94th Congresses; mem. Rules, Aging, Steering and Policy coms.; dep. majority whip; U.S. senator from Hawaii, 1976-90; mem. Fin., Energy and Natural Resources, Vets.' Affairs coms., chief dep. whip.; Mem. Hawaii statehood delegations to Congress, 1950, 54, Pacific War Meml. Commn., 1959-62; adv. com. Honolulu Redevel. Agy., 1953-54. Author: Rulemakers of The House, 1976. Chmn. bd. Kaimuki YMCA; pres. Naturalization Encouragement Assn. Honolulu.; Bd. dirs. World Brotherhood. Soc. Crippled Children and Adults, Honolulu Council Social Agys. Served from 2d lt. to capt., inf. AUS, 1941-45; ret. lt. col. JAGC 1969. Decorated Bronze Star with valor clasp, Purple Heart with oak leaf cluster. Mem. ABA, Hawaii Bar Assn., DAV, VFW, Japan-Am. Soc., U. Hawaii Alumni Assn. Democrat. Episcopalian. Clubs: Lions (Honolulu), 100 (Honolulu). Home: Kensington Md. Died Apr. 16, 1990; buried Punchbowl Nat. Cemetery, Honolulu.

MATTHEWS, LEMUEL HATCH, lawyer; b. Chgo., June 5, 1909; s. Avery Putnam and Fannie (Hatch) M.; m. Gwen Turner Matthews, Feb. 14, 1947 (dec. Feb. 1985); 1 son, George Putnam; m. Eve Maschal August, 1987. A.B., U. Calif.-Berkeley, 1931, LL.B., 1934. Bar: Calif. 1948, U.S. Supreme Ct. 1935. Advt. mgr. Salinas Index Jour., 1931; asso. firm Sterling Carr, San Francisco, 1935-51; with CIA, Washington, 1951-52; ptnr. Jonas and Matthews, San Francisco, from 1952; Lectr. Calif. Continuing Edn. of Bar, from 1955; dir. Overseas Central, Inc., Tropicraft Corp., Chan Nat., Inc. Pres. San Francisco Legal Aid Soc., 1968; Bd. dirs. Calif. Roadside Council, 1954-58, San Francisco Planning and Housing Assn., 1956-59; trustee Calif. Rural Legal Assistance Program, 1968, San Francisco Ladies Protection and Relief Soc., from 1970; trustee San Francisco Bar Found., 1972-73, pres., from 1974. Served to lt. col. AUS, 1941-47, ETO. Fellow Am. Bar Found., Am. Coll. Probate Counsel; mem. ABA, San Francisco Bar Assn. (pres. 1965, dir. 1962-66), State Bar Calif. (del. 1958-69, exec. com. 1970-72), UN Assn. Calif. (pres. 1960), UN Assn. (hon.). Clubs: Bohemian (San Francisco), World Trade (San Francisco), Commonwealth (San Francisco). Home: San Francisco Calif. Deceased. †

MATTHEWS, THOMAS STANLEY, author, editor; b. Cin., Jan. 16, 1901; s. Paul and Elsie (Procter) M.; m. Juliana S. Cuyler, May 16, 1925 (dec.); children: Thomas Stanley, John Potter Cuyler, Paul Clement, William Alexander Procter; m. Martha Gellhorn, 1953 (div.); m. Pamela Peniakoff, Oct. 8, 1964. AB, Princeton U., 1922; BA, Oxford U., Eng., 1924, MA, 1967. With New Republic, 1925-28, asst. editor, 1928, assoc. editor, 1929; books editor Time, Inc., 1929-37, asst. mng. editor, 1937-42, exec. editor, 1942; mng. editor Time, 1943-49, editor, 1949-53. Author: To the Gallows I Must Go, 1931, The Sugar Pill, 1958, Name and Address, 1960, O My America, 1962, The Worst Unsaid (verse), 1962, Why So Gloomy? (verse), 1966, Great Tom: Notes toward the Definition of T.S. Eliot, 1974, Jacks or Better, 1977, Angels Unawares: Twentieth Century Portraits, 1985. Mem. Bucks Club, Garrick Club, The Athenaeum Club, Brook's Club (London), Coffee House Club, Century Assn. (N.Y.C.), Reading Room Club (Newport, R.I.). Home: Cavendish Eng. Died Jan. 4, 1991; interred Princeton, N.J.

MATUSZAK, JOHN DANIEL, actor, sportscaster; b. Milw., Oct. 25, 1950; s. Marvin Francis and Audrey Catherine (Dugan) M. BS, U. Tampa, 1973. Profl. football player Houston Oilers, 1973-74, Kansas City (Kans.) Chiefs, 1974-75, Oakland (Calif.) Raiders, 1975-83; ind. actor, sportscaster Hollywood, Calif., 1979-89. Author: Cruisin' With the Tooz, 1987. Hon. chmn. United Stroke Found., Los Angeles; fundraiser Cystic Fibrosis Found., Los Angeles; bd. dirs. Athletes for Kids, Los Angeles. Recipient World Championship Super Bowl Ring NFL, 1977, 81. Mem. Screen Actors Guild, AFTRA, NFL Players Assn. Democrat. Roman Catholic. Home: Los Angeles Calif. Died June 17, 1989. †

MAUCK, ELWYN ARTHUR, educator, administrator; b. Toledo, Iowa, May 5, 1910; s. Garfield Arthur and Elsie Caroline (Buck) M.; m. Mary Frank Helms, June 4, 1948. A.B., Cornell Coll., Iowa, 1932, LL.D., 1973; A.M. (Roberts fellow 1932-36), Columbia U., 1933, Ph.D., 1937. Staff mem. Inst. Pub. Adminstrn., N.Y.C., 1935, Inst. Pub. Adminstrn. (N.Y. Commn. for Rev. of Tax Laws), 1935-37; asst. prof. polit. sci. U. N.C., 1937-45, asso. prof., 1945-47; on leave, 1942-47; chief reports and awards div. Office Civilian Def., Washington, 1942-45; teaching staff Dept. Agr. Grad. Sch., Washington; vis. prof. pub. adminstrn. U. P.R., Rio Piedras, 1945-46; chief orgn. and methods div. War Assets Adminstrn. (Nashville region), 1946-47; prof. govt. and politics U. Md., 1947-49; dir. Md. Fiscal Research Bur., Balt., 1948-53; lectr. McCoy Coll., Johns Hopkins U., 1949-53; vis. lectr. Goucher Coll., 1951, 52; pub. adminstrn. adviser Inst. Inter-Am. affairs, 1953-57; chief pub. and bus. adminstrn. div. USOM, Brazil, 1954-57; prof. pub. adminstrn. N.Y. U. in, Ankara, Turkey, 1958-59; prof. U. Minn. Project in, Seoul, Korea, 1959-62; prof. pub. adminstrn. U. Pitts., 1962-75, prof. emeritus, 1975-90; chief party U. Mich. Project in, Taipei, Taiwan, 1963-64, U. Pitts. Project in, Zaria, Nigeria, 1965-67; dean Faculty of Adminstrn., Ahmadu Bello U., Nigeria, 1967; coordinator of GSPIA Doctoral Study, 1968-73; dir. GSPIA Nigeria program, 1968-73; mem. Md. Commn. on Pub. Welfare, 1948; exec. sec. Md. Joint Legis. Com. to Study State Mental Hosps., 1949, 51; cons. Md. Tax Survey Commn., 1949-51; staff dir. Md. Commn. on Adminstrv. Orgn. of State, 1951-53. Author: Financial Control in the Suburban Areas of N.Y. State, 1937; contbg. author: Public Administration in Puerto Rico, 1948, Outside Readings in American Government, 1949, County Government Across the Nation, 1951; editor: County and Twp. Sect., Nat. Municipal Rev, 1940-53; contbr. numerous articles to profl. mags., other publs. Vol. info. specialist Smithsonian Instn., Washington, 1976-90; vol. tax cons. for elderly, 1986-90. Mem. Am. Polit. Sci. Assn. (sec. D.C. home rule com. Washington chpt. 1947-48, exec. council 1948-50), Am. Soc. Pub. Adminstrn. (charter mem., pres. Md. chpt. 1949-50), Phi Beta Kappa, Pi Sigma Alpha (nat. sec., treas. 1949-52, nat. pres. 1952-54), Tau Kappa Alpha. Home: Indian Head Md. Died Feb. 10, 1990; buried in Iowa.

MAUDLIN, C(ECIL) V(EARL), economist; b. Jacksonburg, Ind., July 14, 1895; s. Alonzo and Ida (Shiebla) M.; m. Eva Jane Wright, Aug. 20, 1919; children; Mary Jane (Mrs. Ziba Bennitt Ogden), Robert Vearl. BSCE, Purdue U., 1917. Designer of reinforced concrete structures, 1917; mgr. inspection of wooden parts of airplanes Signal Corps U.S. Army, Chgo., 1918-19; mgr. coord. and ops. U.S. Forest Products Lab., 1919-22; bus. mgr. Am. Forestry Assn. and Am. Forests and Forest Life Mag., 1922-28; mng. dir., treas. Bur. Applied Econs., 1928-38; cons. economist, 1938-52; ptnr. C.V. & R.V. Maudlin, from 1952; in charge U.S. Senate Investigation of Food Products, 1931; spl. expert Anthracite Coal Industry Commn., Commonwealth of Pa., 1937. Writer of many engring. and econ. bulls. and pamphlets. Active various civic orgns. Mem. Triangle (nat. treas. 1921), Masons, Sigma Xi. Republican. Mem. Christian Ch. (Disciples of Christ). *

MAUN, JOSEPH ANGUS, lawyer; b. Laurel, Nebr., June 24, 1909; s. Angus E. and Rosa (Gallagher) M.; m. Lucille McDermott, July 31, 1937; children: Lawrence, Sheila, Janis, Jeanne, James, Thomas. B.A. cum laude, U. Minn., 1932, LL.B., 1935. Bar: Minn. bar 1935. Pvt. practice law St. Paul, from 1935; ptnr. Maun, Hayes, Simon, Johanneson Brehl and Odlang and predecessor firms, St. Paul, from 1943; dir. Northland Co., Northland Mortgage Co., Northland Fin. Corp., Aslesen Co., Bayard Realty Co., Uptown Mgmt. Co., Anchor Paper Co., C.,M.,St.P.&P. R.R., Chgo. Milw. Corp., Vulcan-Hart Corp., Universal Title Co., St. Paul.; Former mem. Met. Planning Commn., 1965-67; Met. Airports Council St. Paul-Mpls.; mem. Met. Improvement Commn. St. Paul-Mpls. Bd. dirs. United Fund St. Paul. Served as pvt. AUS, 1944-45. Mem. Am., Minn. bar assns., St. Paul Area C. of C. (past pres.), St. Paul Winter Carnival Assn. (past. pres.), Am. Legion, St. Paul Jr. Assn. Commerce (past. pres.), Am. Mgmt. Assn., Phi Beta Kappa. Clubs: Kiwanian (dir. St. Paul), Town and Country (pres., dir.), Minn. Home: Saint Paul Minn. Deceased. †

MAURO, ALEXANDER, biophysics educator, researcher; b. New Haven, Conn., Aug. 14, 1921; s. John and Maria Grazia (Rapuano) M.; m. Jean Gilpatrick, Nov. 27, 1955. B.Elec. Engring., Yale U., 1942, Ph.D. in Biophysics, 1950. Electronics engr. Gen. Electric Co., 1942-45; asst. prof. dept. physiology Yale U. Med. Sch., 1951-59; asst. prof. biophysics Rockefeller U., N.Y.C., 1959-62, asso. prof., 1963-71, prof., 1971-89; vis. prof. U. Geneva, 1972-73; Rockefeller Found. fellow U. Copenhagen, Denmark, 1950-51. Editor: Regeneration of Striated Muscle and Myogenesis, 1970, Muscle Regeneration, 1979; co-editor: The Development and Regenerative Potential of Cardiac Muscle, 1992. Mem. fellowship com. Muscle Dystrophy Assn., 1974-81. Mem. Am. Physiol. Soc., Biophysics Soc., Sigma Xi. Home: New York N.Y. Died Oct. 6, 1989; buried New Haven, Conn.

MAXWELL, (IAN) ROBERT, publisher, film producer; b. Selo Slatina, Czechoslovakia, June 10, 1923; naturalized, 1945; s. Michael and Ann Hoch; m. Elisabeth Meynard, Mar. 15, 1945; children: Anne, Philip, Christine, Isabel, Ian, Kevin, Ghislaine. DSc (hon.), Moscow State U., 1983, Poly. Inst. N.Y., 1985; LLD (hon.), U. Aberdeen, 1988, Temple U., 1989, Washington U., St. Louis, 1990; Dr. honoris causa, U. Adama Mickiewicza, Poland, 1989, De l'Univ. du Que. a Trois-Riveres, 1989; hon. doctorate, Bar-Ilan U., Israel, 1989. Head press and publs. div. German sect. British Fgn. Office, 1945-47; founder, chmn., pub., dir. Pergamon Press Ltd., Oxford, Eng., N.Y.C. and Paris, from 1949; chmn. bd., pres. Pergamon Press Inc., N.Y.C., 1950-91; chmn., chief exec. officer Maxwell Communication Corp. plc (formerly British Printing & Communications Corp. Ltd.), 1981-91, Central TV plc., from 1983; chmn. Mirror Group Newspapers Ltd., pub. Daily Mirror, Daily Record, Sunday Mail, Sunday Mirror, The People, Sporting Life, Sporting Life Weekender, from 1984, Brit. Cable Services Ltd. (Rediffusion Cablevision), from 1984; chmn., chief exec. officer The Solicitors' Law Stationery Soc. plc, from 1985; chmn. Mirrorvision, from 1985, Robert Maxwell and Co. Ltd., 1948-86; chmn., chief exec. officer Clyde Cablevision Ltd., from 1985, Premier, from 1986, Maxwell Pergamon Pub. Corp. plc. (formerly Pergamon BPCC Pub. Corp. plc.), 1986-89, BPCC plc (formerly BPCC Printing Corp. plc.), from 1986, MTV Europe, from 1987, Maxwell Communication Corp. Inc., N.Y., from 1987, Macmillan Inc., N.Y.C., from 1988; pub. China Daily in Europe, from 1986, The London Daily News, 1987; pub. English edition Moscow News, from 1988; pub., editor-in-chief The European, from 1988; pub., owner The Daily News, N.Y.C., 1991; bd. dirs. Pergamon AGB plc (formerly Hollis plc), chmn., from 1988; bd. dirs. Selec TV plc, Central TV plc, Reuters Holdings plc, TF1, Agence Centrale de Presse, Maxwell Media, Paris, Solicitors' Law Stationery Soc. plc, Philip Hill Investment Trust; pres. European Satellite TV Broadcasting Consortium, from 1986; chmn. Gt. Britain-Sasakawa Found., from 1985; mem. internat. coun. USIA, from 1987. Co-producer films: Mozart's Don Giovanni, Salzburg Festival, Bolshoi Ballet, 1957, Swan Lake, 1968; producer children's TV series DODO the Kid from Outer Space, 1968; author: Public Sector Purchasing, 1968; editor: Progress in Nuclear Energy: The Economics of Nuclear Power, 1963; Gen. editor: Leaders of the World series, from 1980, The Econs. of Nuclear Power, 1965, Pub. Sector Purchasing, 1968; co-author: Man Alive, 1968. Labour mem. Parliament for Buckingham, 1964-70; chmn. Labour Fund Raising Found., 1960-69; chmn. labour working party on sci., govt. and industry, 1963-64; mem. Council of Europe, vice-chmn. com. on sci. and tech., 1968; treas. Round House Trust Ltd., 1965-83; chmn. Commonwealth Games (Scotland 1986), Ltd., 1966; chmn. Nat. Aids Trust fundraising group, from 1987; trustee Internat. Centre for Child Studies; mem. senate U. Leeds, from 1986; trustee Poly. Univ. N.Y.; pres. State of Israel Bonds, U.K., 1988; dir. Bishopsgate Trust Ltd., 1984; chmn. media com. NSPCC Centenary Appeal, 1984; chmn. United Oxford Football Club plc, 1982-87; chmn. Derby County Football Club, from 1987. Decorated Mil. Cross U.K., 1945, Officer 1st class Order Stara Planina, Bulgaria, 1983, Office 1st cl. Swedish Royal Order of Polar Star, 1984, Comdr. Order of Merit with Star, Poland, 1986, Comdr. 1st class Order of the White Rose, Finland, 1988, Officier de l'Ordre des Arts et des Lettres, France, 1989; recipient Prism award NYU Centre for Graphic Arts Mmgt. and Tech., 1989, World of Difference award Anti-Defamation League, N.Y., 1989. Fellow Imperial Coll. of London; mem. Newspaper Pubs. Assn. (council from 1984), Human Factors Soc., Fabian Soc. Gt. Brit., Internat. Acad. Astronautics (hon.), Club of Rome (exec. dir. Brit. Group). Home: Oxford Eng. Died Nov. 6, 1991.

MAYER, GEORGE B(AKER), architect; b. Cleve., Aug. 23, 1895; s. Jacob and Clara (Baker) M. BA in Arch., U. Pa., 1916. With Cleve. office C. R. Greco, Architect, Boston, 1919-32; propr. George B. Mayer, Architect, Cleve., from 1932; chief architect Assoc. Architects of Cleve., 1941-45; ptnr. Project Architects & Engrs., 1951-56; cons. to Ohio on mental hosp. program, 1957-58. Mem. Cleve. City Planning Commn., from 1942; mem. Cuyahoga County Regional Planning Commn., 1948-52, from 1957; trustee Jewish Community Ctr., Cleve., from 1922, pres. 1938-41; co-founder Jewish Vocat. Svc. and Jewish Young Adult Bur., Cleve., 1939; trustee Jewish Community Fedn., Cleve., Goodrich Social Settlement, Cleve.; bd. dirs. Nat. Jewish Welfare Bd., from 1945, founder, chmn. J.W.B. Bldg. Bur., from 1944, mem. Jewish Community Ctr. div., from 1945. With Air Svc. U.S. Army, 1917-19; with AEF in France. Decorated Purple Heart, Croix de Guerre, France. Fellow AIA (bd. dirs. 1961-64, pres. Cleve. chpt. 1948-49, sec.-treas. AIA Found. 1961-64); mem. Architects Soc. Ohio (pres. 1940-41), City Club (v.p.1957), Commerce Club. *

MAYFIELD, FRANK HENDERSON, surgeon; b. Garnett, S.C., June 23, 1908; s. John Weldon and Panthea Boyd White M.; m. Queenee Victoria Jones, Aug. 21, 1936; children: Sara, Frank Henderson, Richard Glen, Jeanne Victoria. Student, U. N.C., 1925-27; MD, Med. Coll. Va., 1931, postgrad., 1931-35. Diplomate Am. Bd. Neurol. Surgery. Intern hosp. div. Med. Coll. Va., 1931-32, resident hosp. div., 1932-35; instr. neurosurgery U. Louisville, 1935-37, pvt. practice neurosurgery, 1937-91; asst. prof. clin. surgery U. Cin. Coll. Medicine, 1947-51, prof., 1967-91; dir. dept. neurosurgery and grad. tng. program Christ Hosp. and Good Samaritan Hosp., Cin.; chief neurosurg. svc. Percy Jones Gen. Hosp., World War II. Contbr. articles to med., sci. jours. Lt. col. Med. Corps, AUS, World War II. Fellow ACS, Am. Assn. Surgery of Trauma; mem. Soc. Neurol. Surgeons, Am. Assn. neurol. Surgeons, Am. Acad. Neurol. Surgery past pres. , Cin. Soc. Neurology an d Med. Assn. past pres. , Ohio State Neurosurg. Assn. pres. 1955-56 , AMA, Literary Club Cin. , Alpha Omega Alpha, Phi Rho Sigma. Home: Cincinnati Ohio Died Jan. 2, 1991.

MAYNARD, ALLEGRA, educational administrator; b. East Weymouth, Mass., June 15, 1897; d. Laurens and Gertrude (Cain) Maynard. AB, Wheaton Coll., 1919, MA, 1953. With Madeira Sch., Greenway, Va., 1931-62; acad. sec., treas., v.p., assoc. headmistress Madeira Sch., 1933-57, headmistress, 1957-62; mem. coll. entrance examination bd. Treas. Fairfax County chpt. ARC; trustee Masters Sch. Mem. Nat. Coun. Ind. Schs., Headmistress Assn. East (exec. com., past pres.). Episcopalian. Home: Dedham Mass. Died Dec. 18, 1991.

MAYO, FRANK REA, chemist; b. Chgo., June 23, 1908; s. Frank and Clara (Rea) M.; m. Eleanor Louise Pope, Dec. 25, 1933; children: Carolyn (Mrs. Roger Mansell), Jean Louise (Mrs. John L. Howell). B.S., U. Chgo., 1929, Ph.D., 1931. Research chemist DuPont Co., Deepwater Point, N.J., 1933-35; instr. U. Chgo., 1936-42; research chemist U.S. Rubber Co., Passaic, N.J., 1942-50; research asso. Gen. Electric Research Lab., Schenectady, 1950-56; sci. fellow SRI Internat. (formerly Stanford Research Inst.), Menlo Park, Calif., from 1956; lectr. Stanford U., 1957-65. Mem. editorial bd.: Jour. Am. Chem. Soc, 1951-60, Jour. Organic Chemistry, 1964-68, Jour. Polymer Sci, 1967-83, Macromolecules, 1981-83. Eli Lilly fellow U. Chgo., 1931-32; Recipient Am. Chem. Soc. award in polymer chemistry, 1967. Mem. Am. Chem. Soc. (div. and sect. chmn.), Royal Soc. Chemistry (London), Phi Beta Kappa. Home: Atherton Calif. Died Oct. 30, 1987.

MAYROSE, HERMAN EVERETT, consulting engineer; b. Terre Haute, Ind., Feb. 18, 1893; s. Henry David and Myra Louise (Killion) M.; m. Ina Maud Smith, Sept. 14, 1915 (dec. Oct. 1915); m. Hazel Ursula Guirl, June 19, 1919 (dec. June 1962; m. Mabel Agnes Guirl, July 18, 1963. BS, Rose Poly. Inst., Terre Haute, 1915; M Engring., Rose Poly. Inst., 1935; MS in Engring., U. Mich., 1932. Engring. apprentice, tool designer Ingersoll Milling Machine Co., Rockford, Ill., 1915-17, 19-22; dir. dept. engring. drawing U. Detroit, 1921-40, prof., chmn. dept. engring. mech., 1927-64; cons. engr. exptl. stress analysis, from 1964. Author: Engineering Mechanics Laboratories, 1950; contbr. Design Data Sheets, ASME, from 1937. Cpl. 129th U.S. Inf., U.S. Army, A.E.F., 1917-19. Mem. ASME, Engring. Soc. Detroit. Methodist. *

MAZAN, WALTER LAWRENCE, former government official; b. Center Rutland, Vt., June 5, 1921; s. Lawrence Walter and Henrietta (Mazur) M.; m. Lee Duffy, July 14, 1956; children: Walter Lawrence II, Lorilee, Michelle, Michael. Student, Norwich U., 1941; B.S. in Commerce, U. Vt., 1949; LL.D., So. Colo. State Coll., 1971. With investigations dept. Gen. Adjustment Bur., N.Y.C., 1949-52; dir. civil def. for Vt., also asst. to gov., 1951-57; with Office Emergency Preparedness, Exec. Office Pres., 1957-69; dir. Office Liaison, 1969; asst. sec. of transp. for pub. affairs, 1969-70; dir. intergovtl. affairs White House Conf. on Children and Youth, 1970-71, exec. dir., 1971-72; spl. programs adviser to Sec. Transp., 1972-73; mng. dir. WLM Assos., Washington, 1973-74; staff asst. Com. Pub. Works, U.S. Ho. of Reps., 1974-85; lectr. in field, from 1963. Author reports. Vice pres. Nat. Conf. State Socs., 1967; pres. Office Emergency Preparedness Credit Union, 1965-66. Served with USAAF, 1942-46. Recipient Outstanding Performance award Office Emergency Preparedness, Sustained Superior Performance award, 1967; Merit certificate Nat. Jr. Achievers, 1970; Recognition award U. Tenn., 1969; Appreciation certificate U. Fla., 1970.

Mem. Nat. Geog. Soc., Arlington County Civic Assn., Vt. State Soc., Nat. Platform Assn. Roman Catholic. Home: Falls Church Va. Deceased. †

MCADAM, CHARLES VINCENT, SR., newspaper syndicate executive; b. N.Y.C., May 28, 1892; s. John and Mary (Barrett) Mc A.; m. Marguerite Wimbey, Sept. 28, 1920 (dec. Jan. 1965); children—Patricia Thom, Charles Vincent, Marguerite Lois Cook; m. Joanne Farris, Nov. 27, 1965; m. Sybil S. Speiller, June 15, 1979; stepchildren—Paul B. Speiller, Joyce Speiller-Morris. With McClure Newspaper Syndicate, 1914-17, Internat. and King Features Syndicate, 1917-19; v.p. McNaught Syndicate Inc., 1922, chmn. bd., from 1930; dir. emeritus Storer Broadcasting Co., Miami; v.p. Calder Race Course, Miami. Named Ky. Col. Mem. Soc. Magicians. Roman Catholic. Clubs: Westchester Country (Rye, N.Y.); Artists and Writers, Blind Brook, Indian Creek, Bal Harbour Beach; LaGorce Country (Miami Beach, Fla.). Home: North Miami Beach Fla. Died June 15, 1985; buried So. Meml. Pk., Fla.

MC ADOO, DONALD ELDRIDGE, artist; b. Chgo., Feb. 8, 1929; s. Frank Joseph and Marion Louise (Weigler) Kovarik; m. Carolyn Westbrook, Oct. 20, 1970. tutor, lectr., instr. to art groups, from 1972, judge art exhibits, from 1968. Exhibited 30 one-man shows, retrospective exhibit A Brush with Realism toured: La. Art Commn. Gallery, Columbus (Ga.) Mus., Columbia (S.C.) Mus., Mint Mus., Charlotte, N.C., Birmingham (Ala.) Mus., Rogers (Miss.) Mus., Telfair Mus., Savannah, Mobile (Ala.) Mus., Macon (Ga.) Mus., 1972-74; exhibited in 59 group shows including: Springfield (Mass.) Mus., 1966, Hudson Valley Art Assn. (N.Y.), 1966, Va. Mus., 1967, Norfolk (Va.) Mus., 1967, Chrysler Mus., Va., 1967, S.E. Center Contemporary Art, 1969-72, Nat. Acad. Galleries, N.Y.C., 1970, High Mus., Atlanta, 1971, Springfield (Mo.) Mus., 1971-72, El Paso (Tex.) Mus., 1972, Greenwich (Conn.) Workshop, 1979; represented in permanent collections: Va. Mus. Fine Arts, Richmond, Ga. Mus. Art, Athens, Springfield (Mo.) Mus., Birmingham Mus. Art, Columbia Mus., Wake Forest U., Columbus Mus., Mint Mus., Mus. of South Mobile, Ala., Mus. Art and Sci., Macon, Chrysler Mus., N.C. Mus. Art, Hunter Mus. Art, Tenn. Author: (with Carol McAdoo) Reflections of the Outer Banks, 1976. Recipient numerous awards for paintings and graphics, recognition for trompe l'oiel work. Mem. La. Watercolor Soc., Ala. Watercolor Soc., Southeastern Center for Contemporary Arts, Nat. Audubon Soc. Roman Catholic. Home: Marietta Ga. Died Aug. 17, 1987.

MCALPIN, DAVID H(UNTER), philanthropist, investment banker, lawyer; b. Mt. Pleasant, N.Y., May 21, 1897; s. David Hunter and Emma (Rockefeller) McA.; m. Nina Walter Underwood, June 10, 1924; children: Lorna U. McAlpin Hauslohner, David Hunter Jr., Esther Mead McAlpin Brownell; m. Sarah Sage Stewart, Jan. 3, 1942. AB, Princeton U., 1920, AM, 1921; LLB, Harvard U., 1924. Bar: N.Y. 1924. Law clk. Sherman & Sterling, N.Y.C., 1924-27; spl. asst. to dist. atty. 2d Fed. Dist., 1925-26; ptnr. Clark, Dodge & Co., N.Y.C., 1929-39, ltd. ptnr., 1939-60; then Inc. and non-voting stockholder; ptnr. Fraser, Burr & McAlpin, Dallas, 1937-48; bd. dirs. Tricontinental Corp., Tricontinental Fin. Corp., Broad Street Investing, Nat. Investors Corp., Whitehall Fund, Inc., United Svc. Corp.; mem. Navy Price Adjustment Bd., 1944-45. A founder, trustee Conservation Found., Washington; trustee Princeton U., 1945-49, N.Y. Zool. Soc.; former trustee and bd. dirs. N.Y. Philharm. Soc.; former bd. dirs. Nat. Orchestral Assn.; former treas. Met. Opera Club; past vice chmn. bd. Union Theol. Sem.; elder Nassau Presbyn. Ch., Princeton, N.J. Comdr. USNR, 1942-46. Recipient gold medal N.Y. Zool. Soc. Mem. Century Assn., Grolier Club, Univ. Club, Downtown Assn., Links Club, Brook Club. Home: Princeton N.J. Died June 1, 1989; buried Sleepy Hollow Cemetery, N.J.

MCANDREW, GORDON LESLIE, educational administrator; b. Oakland, Calif., Aug. 29, 1926; s. James and Margaret (Watts) McA.; m. Doris McGarry, Sept. 12, 1948; children: Kevin, Regan. A.B., U. Calif. at Berkeley, 1948, M.A., 1952, Ph.D., 1962. Tchr., adminstr. pub. schs. Oakland, 1949-64; dir. N.C. Advancement Sch. and Learning Inst., Durham, 1964-68; supt. Gary (Ind.) Pub. Schs., 1968-79, Richland County Sch. Dist., Columbia, S.C., 1979-86; sr. rsch. fellow U.S. Dept. Edn., 1986-88; spl. asst. to chancellor U. S.C., Columbia, from 1988; cons. Nat. Inst. Edn., U.S. Office Edn., from 1965, Robert Wood Johnson Found., from 1985; lectr. Sch. Mgmt., Nova U., Coll. Edn., U. S.C. Served with USAAF, 1944-45. Home: Columbia S.C. Deceased. †

MC BATH, JAMES HARVEY, speech educator; b. Watertown, S.D., Oct. 24, 1922; s. Earl A. and Edna (Harvey) McB.; m. Jean Bloomquist, July 6, 1963 (dec. Oct. 1979); children: Margot, Douglas, Janet. B.S., Northwestern U., 1947, M.A., 1948, Ph.D., 1950; fellow, Inst. Hist. Research, U. London, 1952-53. Asst. prof. speech U. N.Mex., 1950-52, U. Iowa, 1953-54, U. Md. European Program, 1954-56; mem. faculty U. So. Calif., from 1956, prof. speech communication, from 1963, chmn. dept., 1965-78, pres. faculty senate, 1977-78, vice chmn. pres.'s adv. council, 1978-80; cons. Am. Student Found., 1961-64, Calif. Office Econ. Opportunity, 1972, City of Hope, 1973, RAND Corp., 1973-78, Nat. Endowment for Humanities, 1973-75, Tokyo Inst. English Lang., from 1977, Nat. Center Ednl. Stats., 1975-78; mem. U.S. Dist. Ct. Com. Sch. Integration, 1978-79; cons. Calif. Curriculum Project, from 1989. Co-author: Guidebook for Speech Practice, 1961, British Public Addresses, 1828-1960, 1971, Guidebook for Speech Communication, 1973, Communication Education For Careers, 1975. Editor: Essays in Forensics, 1970, Forensics as Communication: The Argumentative Perspective, 1975, Argumentation and Debate, 1963, Jour. Am. Forensic Assn, 1966-68; assoc. editor: Quar. Jour. Speech, 1967-69; contbr.: Ency. of Edn, 1971; mem. editorial bd.: The Rhetoric of Protest and Reform, 1980. Trustee Pasadena Methodist Found., from 1985; mem. bd. edn. Pasadena Unified Sch. Dist., 1985-87, pres., 1987-89; mem. adv. coun. L.A. County High Sch. for the Arts, from 1987; chmn. bd. trustees 1st United Meth. ch., from 1991. With Psychol. Rsch. Unit USAAF, 1943-46. Mem. Speech Communication Assn. (exec. council 1966-70, chmn. bicentennial coordinating com. 1971-76, legis. council 1977-79, chmn. Winans-Wichelns award com. 1978-79, dissertation awards com. 1983, nominating com. 1983, adminstrv. com., 1983-87, chmn. fin. bd. 1986-87), Am. Forensic Assn. (pres. 1960-62), Western Speech Assn. (pres. 1968-69, Disting Svc.award 1991), Calif. Speech Communication Assn. (pres. 1987-89), Assn. Communication Adminstrn. (pres. 1975-76), World Communication Assn., Am. Inst. Parliamentarians, English-Speaking Union, Brit. Hist. Assn., AAUP, Am. Assn. Higher Edn., Assn. Coll. Honor Socs. (nat. council from 1975), Communication Assn. Pacific (adv. bd. 1972-86), Phi Kappa Phi, Phi Delta Kappa, Delta Sigma Rho-Tau Kappa Alpha (pres. 1969-72, disting. alumni award 1983). Methodist. Home: Pasadena Calif. Deceased. †

MC BURNEY, ANDREW MARVELL, paper manufacturing company executive; b. Phila., July 25, 1913; s. Andrew M. and Dorothy Irwin (Buck) McB.; m. Lidie Lane Sloan, Feb. 26, 1938; children: A. Sloan, F. Lane. Student, Germantown Acad., 1930; grad., Hill Sch., Pottstown, Pa., 1932; B.A., Yale U., 1936. With Oxford Paper Co. (became div. Ethyl Corp. 1967), N.Y.C., 1936-43, 46-76, various positions West Carrollton and Rumford Mills, successively mem. sales orgn. N.Y.C., asst. to exec. v.p., eastern sales mgr., sales mgr. gen. sales mgr., 1936-58, v.p., 1953-66, exec. v.p., 1966-76, also bd. dirs., until 1989; sr. adviser Boise Cascade (purchaser Ethyl Corp.), from 1976; bd. dirs. Lake Placid Co., Thomas Jefferson Life Ins. Co., Iroquois Brands Ltd., Mohasco Corp.; mem. Exec. Office of Pres. Office Emergency Preparedness, from 1968; chief pulp, paper and paperboard br., forest products div. OPS, Wash., 1951-52. Trustee, mem. exec. com. Lake Placid Edn. Found.; trustee Hill Sch., Pottstown, Pa., from 1965. Served to capt. USMCR, 1943-46; comdg. officer aircraft detachment. Mem. Salesmen's Assn. Paper Industry, Boston Paper Trade Assn., Printing Paper Mfrs. Assn. (chmn. 1962, 63). Republican. Presbyterian. Clubs: Sales Executives (N.Y.C.), Paper (N.Y.C.). Home: New York N.Y. Died Mar. 30, 1991; buried Lake Placid, N.Y.

MC CARTER, FRANCIS E. P., lawyer; b. New Brunswick, N.J., Sept. 10, 1917; s. George W.C. and Dorothy (Parker) McC.; m. Marna Kuelthau, June 19, 1948; children: George W.C., Robert Y., Lisa. Grad., Taft Sch., 1935; A.B., Princeton U., 1939; J.D., Harvard U., 1947. Bar: N.J. 1948. Assoc. McCarter & English, Newark, 1948-50, ptnr., 1950-88. Contbr. articles to legal periodicals. Councilman borough of Rumson, N.J., 1963-80, pres. of council, 1975-80. Served to lt. col., F.A. AUS, 1940-46. Decorated Medalia Merito Di Guerra Italy). Mem. ABA, N.J. Bar Assn. (chmn. com. on conservation and ecology 1970-73), Essex County Bar Assn. Home: Rumson N.J. Died Mar. 17, 1988.

MCCARTHY, DANIEL FENDRICH, business executive; b. Evansville, Ind., Aug. 5, 1895; s. Daniel Edward and Laura Gertrude (Fendrich) McC.; m. Eleanor Fenelon Burkley, Nov. 22, 1928; children: Daniel Fendrich, Burkley Francis. Student, Creighton Acad., Omaha; grad., Loyola Acad., Chgo., 1913, Georgetown U., Washington, 1917. With H. Fendrich, Inc., Evansville, from 1916; pres. Reitz Real Estate Co., Inc., Evansville, from 1947; v.p. Citizens Nat. Bank, Evansville; bd. dirs. Tampa Cigar Co. Bd. dirs. Found. for Evansville's Future Inc.; mem. adv. bd. St. Mary's Hosp.; trustee Francis J. Haney Scholarship Fund, Willard Libr. Lt. 12th Cav., U.S. Army, World War I. Decorated Knight of St. Gregory. Mem. Cigar Mfgs. Assn. Am. (bd. dirs.), Irish Am. Hist. Soc. (v.p.), Met. Club, Biltmore Forest Country Club, Evansville Country Club. *

MC CARTHY, EDWARD JAMES (ED MC CARTHY), publisher, writer; b. Newark, Jan. 5, 1914; s. F. Sanford and Ellen Mary (Mottley) McC.; m. Virginia Patterson Drace, Sept. 19, 1943; children: Eric Drace, Sean Sanford. Student, Essex County Jr. Coll., 1933-35. Reporter, feature writer N.Y. Mirror, 1937-41; mng. editor Tune In (radio mag.), 1945; picture editor newspaper PM, 1946-47, Sunday editor, 1947-48; editor This Week, N.Y. Herald Tribune edit., 1949-55, asst. mng. editor nat. edit., 1955-56, mng. editor, 1956-64; founder, pub. Graphophile Assos., 1962; v.p., partner Mayo-Infurna Design, Inc., 1969-79. Editor service mags.; Author: (with Bud Finger) Little Mr. Tootle, 1937, (with Ginny McCarthy) Fruits of the Hudson Valley, 1974; contbr. to periodicals. Served with USCGR, 1941-45. Home: Tappan N.Y. Deceased. †

MCCARTHY, GERALD T., consulting engineer; b. Dover, N.J., May 5, 1909; s. Daniel and Florence Bill McC.; m. Grace Baskerville, June 1, 1935; children: George, Susan. BS magna cum laude, Pa. State U., 1930. Diplomate Am. Acad. Environ. Engrs. Student engr., constrn. insp. Standard Oil Co., Elizabeth, N.J., 1930-31; engr. U.S. Corp. Engrs., St. Louis, 1931-34; assoc. engr. U.S. Corp. Engrs., Zanesville, Ohio, 1934-35; engr. U.S. Corp. Engrs., Eastport, Maine, 1935-36; sr. engr. U.S. Corp. Engrs., Providence, 1936-38; spl. ptnr. for L.Am. Parsons, Klapp, Brinckerhoff and Douglas, N.Y.C., 1938-47; ptnr. Tippetts-Abbett-McCarthy-Stratton, N.Y.C., 1947-75, ret. ptnr., cons., 1975-77. Contbr. articles on flood control engrng. to profl. jours. Pres. Internat. Commn. Large Dams, 1967-70; past chmn. U.S. Com. Large Dams. Mem. Nat. Acad. Engrng., ASCE hon. mem. , Am. Road Builders Assn. past dir., mem. exec. com. , Engrs.' Club, Canoe Brook Country Club, Phi Kappa Phi, Phi Mu Alpha, Kappa Gamma Psi, Tau Beta Pi, Chi Epsilon. Home: Summit N.J. Died Oct. 31, 1990.

MC CARTHY, JOHN FRANCIS, JR., aerospace executive; b. Boston, Aug. 28, 1925; s. John Francis and Margaret Josephine (Bartwood) McC.; m. Camille Dian Martinez, May 4, 1968; children: Margaret I., Megan, Jamie M., Nicole E., John F. S.B., M.I.T., 1950, S.M. in Aero. Engring, 1951; Ph.D. in Aeros. and Physics, Calif. Inst. Tech., 1962. Supr. air/ground communications TWA, Rome, 1946-47; project mgr. aeroelastic and structures research lab. M.I.T., 1951-55, prof. aeros. and astronautics, 1971-78; ops. analyst Hdqrs. SAC, Offutt AFB, Nebr., 1955-59; dir., asst. chief engr. Apollo, Space div. N.Am. Aviation, Inc., Downey, Calif., 1961-66; v.p. Los Angeles div./Space div., Rockwell Internat. Corp., 1966-71; dir. and prof. M.I.T. Center for Space Research, 1974-78; dir. NASA Lewis Research Center, Cleve., 1978-82; v.p., gen. mgr. Electromech. div. Northrop Corp., from 1982; dir. ENSCO, Inc., Springfield, Va., MacNeal-Schwendler Corp., Los Angeles; mem. Internat. Council Aero. Scis., Cologne, Germany, from 1978, USAF Sci. Adv. Bd., Washington, 1970-82; mem. sci. adv. group Joint Chiefs of Staff, Joint Strategic Target Planning Staff, Offutt AFB, 1976-81; com. mem. Energy Engring. Bd., Assembly Engring., NRC, 1979, Aeros. and Space Engring Bd., NRC., from 1984; cons. in field.; cons. Office of Undersec. Def. for Research and Engring. Author numerous tech. reports. Campaign chmn. Downey Community Hosp., 1968-69; bd. govs. Nat. Space Club, Washington, 1978-82; chmn. Fed. Exec. Bd., Cleve., 1979-80; mem. adv. bd. for dept. mech. engring., aero. engring. and mechanics Rensselaer Poly. Inst., from 1981; chmn. bd. Tech. Exchange Ctr., Orange County, Calif., from 1982; bus. bd. govs. The Register, Orange County, Calif., from 1984. Served with USAAF, 1944-46. Recipient Apollo Achievement award NASA, 1969, Meritorious Civilian Service medal USAF, 1973, Exceptional Civilian Service medal, 1978, Disting. Service medal NASA, 1982. Fellow Am. Astronautical Soc., AIAA (dir. 1975-76), Royal Aero. Soc. (London); mem. Nat. Acad. Engring., Am. Soc. Engring. Edn. (exec. com. aerospace div. 1969-72), Am. Mgmt. Assn. (pres.'s council from 1978), Sigma Xi, Sigma Gamma Tau. Unitarian. Clubs: Cosmos, 50 of Cleve. Home: Yorba Linda Calif. Deceased. †

MCCARTHY, JOSEPH DANIEL, physician; b. Lawrence, Mass., Oct. 1, 1893; s. Daniel Augustine and Brigid Adelaide (O'Brien) McC.; m. Maybelle L. Donohoe, Dec. 22, 1917 (dec. 1951); children: Joseph Daniel, Mary Jean (Mrs. Richard W. Hildebrand), John Augustine; m. Irene Rau, July 14, 1953. Student, Georgetown U., 1919-11, Med. Sch., 1911-14; MD, St. Louis U., 1916; postgrad., U. Vienna, 1927-28, Banhaus Clinic, Amsterdam, The Netherlands, 1928, U. Pa., 1938, 42. Diplomate Am. Bd. Internal Medicine. Extern Providence Hosp., Washington, 1914; intern Jewish Hosp., St. Louis, 1916-17; mem. staff Creighton U. Sch. Medicine, 1917; med. supr. Creighton Meml. St. Joseph's Hosp., dir. interns, instr. clin. microscopy and bedside medicine, attending physician; gen. practice medicine Elgin, Negr., 1920-27; practice medicine specializing in internal medicine Omaha, from 1928; mem. staff dept. clin. rsch. U. Nebr. Coll. Medicine, 1928-35, instr. medicine, 1928-36, asst. prof. medicine, 1937-47, assoc. prof. internal medicine, 1948-55, prof., 1956-60, sr. cons., 1960-63, emeritus prof. internal medicine, from 1963; mem. staff U. Nebr. Hosp., from 1928, instr. Sch. Nursing, 1928-31, chmn. Gastroenterol. Clinic, 1930-41; instr. Sch. Nursing Bishop Clarkson Meml. Hosp., 1928-30, staff physician, from 1928; br. sect. chief gastroenterology VA, 1946-48; area cons., 1948-55; con. Omaha VA Hosp., from 1951; staff physician Booth Meml. Hosp.; pres. Nat. Conf. on Med. Svc., 1942, exec. com., 1942-52; exec. com. North Ctrl. Med.Conf., 1944-47, pres. 1946; mem. Nebr. Bd. Med. Examiners, from 1953, mem. exec. com., from 1961, v.p., 1965; mem. Nat. Com. Aging; chmn. Gov. Com. Aging, White House Conf., 1961. Editor Jour. Omaha Med-West Clin. Soc., 1939-44; contbr. med. articles to profl. jours., editorials pres.'s page Nebr. State Med. Jour. Capt. Med. Corps, U.S. Army, 1917-19; spl. rsch. typhoid fever Walter Reed Hosp., Washington. Fellow

ACP (gov. for Nebr. 1946-55, bd. regents 1955-62, 1st v.p. 1961-62, exec. com. 1958-62); mem. AMA (ho. of dels. 1946-65, chmn. coun. on med. svc. 1948-60, counselor 1960-61), Nebr. Med. Assn. (trustee Nebr. Med. Found. 1948-62, trustee 1943-48, pres. 1949), Omaha-Douglas County Med. Soc. (chmn. legis. com. 1944-47, 54), Madison-Six County Med. Soc. (past sec., past pres.), Am. Geriatrics Soc., Am. Heart Assn., Nebr. Heart Assn., Am. Rheumatism Assn., World Med. Assn. (U.S. com. 1949), Omaha Mid-West Clin Soc. (founder, exec. com. 1932-54, pres. 1946), U.S. Omaha (chmn. health com. 1936-40, dir. 1937-43), C. of C., Internat., Am., Nebr. Socs. internal medicine, Assn. Am. Med. Colls., Fedn. of State Med. Bds. of U.S. (v.p. 1953), Phi Beta Phi. *

MC CARTHY, MARY, author; b. Seattle, June 21, 1912; d. Roy Winfield and Therese (Preston) McC.; 1 son, Reuel K. Wilson; m. James Raymond West, Apr. 15, 1961. AB, Vassar Coll., 1933; AB (hon.), Syracuse U., 1973, U. Hull, Eng., 1974, Bard Coll., 1976, U. Aberdeen, Scotland, 1979; DDL (hon.), Bowdoin Coll., 1981; LittD (hon.), U. Maine, Orono, 1982; DHL (hon.), Smith Coll., 1988, Tulane U., 1989, Colby Coll., 1989. Editor Covici Friede, 1936-37; editor Partisan Rev., 1937-38, drama critic, 1937-48; instr. lit. Bard Coll., 1945-46, Charles Stevenson chair of lit., 1986-89; instr. English Sarah Lawrence Coll., 1948; Northcliffe lectr. Univ. Coll., London, 1980. Author: The Company She Keeps, 1942, The Oasis, 1949, Cast a Cold Eye, 1950, The Groves of Academe, 1952, A Charmed Life, 1955, Sights and Spectacles, 1956, Venice Observed, 1956, Memories of a Catholic Girlhood, 1957, The Stones of Florence, 1959, On the Contrary, 1961, The Group, 1963, Mary McCarthy's Theatre Chronicles, 1963, Vietnam, 1967, Hanoi, 1968, The Writing on the Wall, 1970, Birds of America, 1971, Medina, 1972, The Seventeenth Degree, 1974, The Mask of State, 1974, Cannibals and Missionaries, 1979, Ideas and the Novel, 1980, Occasional Prose: Essays, 1985, How I Grew, 1987; contbr. articles to nat. mags. Recipient Horizon prize, 1949, Pres.' Disting. Visitor award Vassar Coll., 1982, McDowell award, 1984, Nat. Medal for Lit., 1984; named officier de l'ordre des arts et lettres, France, 1983; Guggenheim fellow, 1949-50, 1959-60; Nat. Inst. grantee, 1957. Mem. Nat. Inst. Arts and Letters, Am. Acad. Arts and Letters, Phi Beta Kappa. Home: Castine Maine Died Oct. 25, 1989; buried Castine, Maine.

MCCARTHY, RAYMOND MALCOLM, finance company executive; b. Chgo., Feb. 27, 1927; s. Raymond Jerome and Margaret V. (Deady) McC.; m. Mary C. Burns, Oct. 27, 1948; children: Raymond J., John T., Sheila M., Michael J., Timothy P., Kevin P., Kathleen M., Anne T. BBA, Loyola U., Chgo., 1950; AMP, Harvard U., 1980. With GMAC, N.Y.C., 1949-89, exec. v.p. ops., 1980-85; pres. GMAC, Detroit, 1986-89, also dir. Served with USMC, 1944-46. Club: Harvard (N.Y.C.). Home: Detroit Mich. Died Nov. 13, 1989.

MC CARTHY, STEPHEN ANTHONY, consultant, librarian; b. Eden Valley, Minn., Oct. 7, 1908; s. Stephen Joseph and Mary Agnes (Graham) McC.; m. Mary Louise Wedemeyer, Aug. 27, 1936 (dec. June 1971); children—Stephen Graham, Louise Bert (Mrs. Xerxes J. Mehta), Kathleen Marie, David John (dec. Apr. 1970); m. Dorothy E. Ryan, July 8, 1972 (dec. July 1979). BA, Gonzaga U., 1929, MA, 1930; BLS, McGill U., 1932, LittD (hon.), 1969; PhD, U. Chgo., 1941. Tchr. Gonzaga High Sch., Spokane, Wash., 1929-31; asst. librarian and cataloger St. John's U., Collegeville, Minn., 1933-34; reference asst. Chgo. American (newspaper), 1934-35; librarian Univ. Coll., Northwestern U., Chgo., 1935-37; asst. dir. libraries U. Nebr., 1937-41, asso. dir., 1941-42, dir., 1942-44; asst. dir. libraries Columbia U., 1944-46; dir. Cornell U. Library, 1946-67, dir. libraries, 1960-67; exec. sec. Assn. Research Libraries, Washington, 1960-62; exec. dir. Assn. Research Libraries, 1967-74; Fulbright lectr. in Egypt, 1953-54, Inst. U.S. Studies, U. London, 1967; vis. prof. U. Ill. Library Sch., summer 1943; Condr. surveys univ. libraries; library bldg. cons. Recipient Cornell medal, 1967. Mem. ALA, Assn. Coll. and Rch. Libraries (chmn. univ. libraries 1948-49), Nebr. Library Assn. (pres. 1940), N.Y. Library Assn. (pres. 1951-52), Phi Beta Kappa (hon.). Democrat. Roman Catholic. Home: Annapolis Md. Died Mar. 18, 1990; buried Hillcrest Meml. Gardens, Annapolis, Md.

MCCAULEY, JOHN CORRAN, JR., orthopedic surgeon, educator; b. Rochester, Pa., Feb. 25, 1901; s. John Corran and Jennie Campbell (Parks) McC.; m. Mildred Catherine Steil, Sept. 30, 1939; children: Ann Hamilton (Mrs. Robert Renfrew Trostle), Marcia Miller (Mrs. Robert J. Jordan). B.S., Hahnemann Coll. Sci., 1923; M.D., U. Colo., 1927. Diplomate: Am. Bd. Orthopedic Surgery. Intern Genesee Hosp., Rochester, N.Y., 1927-28; surg. resident Genesee Hosp., 1928-29; orthopedic resident Hosp. for Ruptured and Crippled, N.Y.C., 1929-30; practice medicine, specializing in orthopedic surgery N.Y.C., from 1930; asst. vis. orthopedic surgeon Bellevue Hosp., 1930-35, asso. vis. orthopedic surgeon, 1935-41, vis. orthopedic surgeon, from 1941; attending orthopedic surgeon U. Hosp., from 1941; asst. attending orthopedic surgeon N.Y. State Rehab. Hosp., Haverstraw, 1941-42; attending orthopedic surgeon N.Y. State Rehab. Hosp., 1942-43, sr. orthopedic surgeon, 1943-47, surgeon-in-chief, 1947-67; mem. staff Neponsit Beach Hosp., 1936, Seaside Hosp. St. John's Guild, 1937, N.Y. Orthopedic Hosp., 1941, Vanderbilt Clinic Presbyn. Hosp., 1950; instr. orthopedic surgery Med. Sch. N.Y. U., 1930-39, asst. prof., 1939-44, asso. prof. clin. orthopedic surgery, 1944-47, asso. prof. orthopedic surgery, 1947-56, prof., 1956-78, prof. emeritus, from 1978; cons. orthopedic surgeon Flushing (N.Y.) Hosp., Nyack (N.Y.) Hosp., Lawrence Hosp., Bronxville, N.Y., St. Agnes Hosp., White Plains, N.Y.; spl. cons. USPHS; impartial orthopedist N.Y. State Workmens Compensation Bd., Police Dept. N.Y.C., Fire Dept. N.Y.C. Contbr. articles med. jours. Mem. Med. Milk Commn.; Mem. adv. bd. Selective Service; mem. med. adv. bd. St. Johnsland. Recipient Presidential citation Internat. Poliomyelitis Congress, 1949. Mem. Am. Orthopedic Assn., A.C.S., Am. Acad. Orthopedic Surgeons, Internat. Soc. Orthopedic Surgery and Traumatology, N.Y. Acad. Medicine (past sect. chmn.), A.M.A., N.Y. State, County med. socs., Fla. Orthopaedic Soc. (hon.), Am. Assn. Med. Milk Commns. (past pres.). Presbyn. Club: Hospital Graduates. Home: Cleveland Ohio Deceased. †

MCCHESNEY, WILLIAM S., aluminum company executive; b. St. Louis, Feb. 4, 1909; s. Samuel P. and Methilde C. (Ferguson) McC.; m. Ruth Balmer, Feb. 22, 1941; children: William Samuel, Thomas Balmer. BS, Princeton U., 1930. With Aluminium Co. Am., 1930-70, gen. mgr. market rsch. and planning, 1960-61, v.p. charge market planning, 1961-64, v.p. mktg. svcs., 1964-70. Nat. bd. dirs. Boys Clubs Am.; bd. dirs. Boys Clubs Western Pa.; vestryman Episcopalian Ch. Home: Delray Beach Fla. Died June 30, 1990.

MCCLATCHY, CHARLES KENNY, editor; b. Fresno, Calif., Mar. 25, 1927; s. Carlos Kelly and Phebe (Briggs) McC.; m. Grace Kennan, Mar. 1, 1958 (div. 1968); children—Charles, Adair, Kevin. Grad., Deerfield Acad., Mass., 1945; B.A., Stanford, 1950. Reporter Washington Post, 1953-55, Washington news bur. ABC-TV, 1957-58; reporter Sacramento Bee Sacramento Bee, 1958-63; assoc. editor McClatchy Newspapers (pubs. include Sacramento Bee, Fresno Bee, Morning News Tribune in Tacoma, Wash., Tri-City Herald, Wash, Anchorage (Alaska) Daily News, 7 other West Coast papers, 3 S.C. papers), Sacramento, 1963-68, exec. editor, 1968-74, editor, 1974-89, corp. v.p., 1969-78, pres., 1978-87, chmn. bd., 1987-89; mem. Pulitzer Prize Bd.; trustee Washington Journalism Ctr. Asst. press sec. Adlai Stevenson Presdl. campaign, 1956. 1st lt. AUS, 1951-53. Mem. Am. Press Inst. (bd. dirs.). Clubs: Bohemian (San Francisco). Home: Sacramento Calif. Died Apr. 16, 1989; buried East Lawn Meml. Pk., Sacramento.

MCCLENDON, ERNESTINE EPPS, actress, drama coach; b. Norfolk, Va.; d. Edward and Lillie (Warren) Epps; m. George Wiltshire, Aug. 20, 1946 (dec.); 1 child, Phyllis Davis. Artists rep., owner Ernestine McClendon Enterprises, Inc., N.Y.C., 1960-74, Hollywood, Calif., 1972-80; pres. MC Prodns., L.A., from 1980. Actress, Woodstock Playhouse, N.Y.C., 1958, Casino Theatre, Newport, R.I., 1959, North Jersey, Playhouse, 1959, Jan Hus House, N.Y.C., 1959, Lenox Hill Playhouse, 1959-60, 60-61; toured summer theatres as Lena in: A Raisin in the Sun, 1961; appeared in numerous films including A Face in the Crowd, 1957, The Last Angry Man, 1959, The Apartment, 1960, The Rat Race, 1960, The Young Doctors, The World by Night, 1961, The Young Savages, 1961; TV appearances include Ed Sullivan Show, 1950; comedienne, drama coach; writer, producer, dir., actress: Heartbreak at Midnight, 1980; actress cable TV Homer and Eddie; writer, producer, actress one woman show: Twilight Memories, 1982; composer songs, 1966-86; producer, star Mulatto (tribute to Langston Hughes), 1986. Mem. Actors Equity, Screen Actors Guild, AFTRA, NAACP (life mem.; past v.p. Beverly Hills-Hollywood br.). Home: Los Angeles Calif. Died Sept. 23, 1991, cremated.

MCCLENDON, SIDNEY SMITH, JR., lawyer; b. Tyler, Tex., June 15, 1894; s. Sidney Smith and Annie (Bonner) McC.; m. Marie Dancy, Sept. 4, 1926; 1 child, Sidney Smith III. LLB, U. Tex., 1919. Bar: Tex. Ptnr. Vinson, Elkins, Weems & Searls, Houston; bd. dirs. Great So. Life Ins. Co., East End State Bank. Chancellor Episcopal Diocese Tex. Capt. U.S. Army, World War I. Mem. Houston Club. *

MCCLINTOCK, BARBARA, geneticist, educator; b. June 16, 1902. Ph.D. in Botany, Cornell U., 1927; D.Sc. (hon.), U. Rochester, U. Mo., Smith Coll., Williams Coll., Western Coll. for Women. Instr. botany Cornell U., Ithaca, N.Y., 1927-31, research assoc., 1934-36, former Andrew D. White prof.-at-large, from 1965; asst. prof. U. Mo., 1936-41; mem. staff Carnegie Instn. of Washington, Cold Spring Harbor, N.Y., 1941-47, Disting. Service mem., 1967—; cons. agrl. sci. program Rockefeller Found., 1962-69. NRC fellow, 1931-33; Guggenheim Found. fellow, 1933-34; recipient Achievement award AAUW, 1947; Nat. medal of Sci., 1970; MacArthur Found. prize; Rosenstiel award, 1978; Nobel prize, 1983. Mem. Nat. Acad. Scis. (Kimber genetics award 1967), Am. Philos. Soc., Am. Acad. Arts and Scis., Genetics Soc. Am. (pres. 1945), Bot. Soc. Am. (award of merit 1957), AAAS, Am. Inst. Biol. Sci., Am. Soc. Naturalists. Home: Cold Spring Harbor N.Y. Died Sept. 2, 1992. †

MC CLOY, JOHN JAY, lawyer, government official; b. Phila., Mar. 31, 1895; s. John Jay and Anna May (Snader) McC.; m. Ellen Zinsser, Apr. 25, 1930; children: John Jay, Ellen. A.B. cum laude, Amherst Coll., 1916; LL.B., Harvard U., 1921; LL.D. (hon.), Amherst Coll., Syracuse U., Colby Coll., U. Md., U. Pa., Yale U., Princeton U., U. Notre Dame, Swarthmore Coll., Wilmington Coll., Washington U., Harvard, Columbia U., Dartmouth Coll., Doshisha U., Tokyo U., NYU, Trinity Coll., Brown U., Williams Coll., Middlebury Coll., Boston U., Haverford Coll., Lehigh U., Franklin and Marshall Coll.; D.C.L. (hon.), Washington Coll.; Dr. Ing. (hon.), Tech. U. Berlin, Charlottenberg. Bar: N.Y. 1921. With Cadwalader, Wickersham & Taft, 1921-25; with Cravath, de Gersdorff, Swaine & Wood, 1925-40, mem. firm, 1929-40, became expert cons. to Sec. of War, Oct. 1940, asst. Sec. of War, Apr. 1941-Nov. 1945; mem. Milbank, Tweed, Hope, Hadley & McCloy, 1946-47; pres. World Bank, 1947-49; U.S. Mil. Gov. and High Commr. for Germany, 1949-52; chmn. bd. Chase Nat. Bank, N.Y.C., 1953, Chase Manhattan Bank; (merger Chase Nat. Bank and Bank of Manhattan Co.), 1955-60; co-ordinator U.S. disarmanent activities U.S. Govt., 1961-63; mem. Milbank, Tweed, Hadley, and McCloy, 1962-89; bd. dirs. emeritus Dreyfus Corp., Mercedes Benz N.Am.; chmn. emeritus Squibb Corp. Chmn. Pres.'s Gen. Adv. Com. on Arms Control and Disarmament, 1961-74; chmn. Am. Council on Germany.; Hon. trustee Lenox Hill Hosp.; trustee John M. Olin Found.; hon. chmn. bd., trustee emeritus Amherst Coll.; hon. chmn. bd. Council Fgn. Relations, Inc., Internat. House-N.Y.; hon. chmn. Atlantic Inst., Paris; chmn. Ford Found., 1953-65; mem. exec. com. Salk Inst. Served as capt., field arty. AEF, World War I. Decorated D.S.M., Presdl. Medal of Freedom, Grand Officer Legion of Honor France; Grand Ofcl. Order of Merit Italy; Grand Cross Order of Merit Germany). Mem. ABA, Assn. Bar City N.Y., Am. Inst. C.P.A.s (chmn. public oversight bd.), Bond Club of N.Y., Order of Coif. Republican. Presbyn. Clubs: Century, Clove Valley Rod and Gun, Links, Recess, University, Anglers (N.Y.C.); Metropolitan (Washington). Home: New York N.Y. Died Mar. 11, 1989; buried Lancaster, Pa.

MCCLOY, SHELBY THOMAS, history educator; b. Monticello, Ark., Jan. 27, 1989; s. AB, Davidson Coll., 1918, Davidson Coll., 1919; student, Union Theol. Sem. of Va., 1919-20, 1922-23; BLitt., U. Oxford, 1922, BA, 1924; PhD, Columbia U., 1933. YMCA sec., instr. in Bible Robert Coll., Constantinople, 1924-25; Jacob H. Schiff fellow Columbia U., 1929-30; instr. Duke U., 1927-41, asst. prof. history, 1941-45; vis. prof. U. Ky., 1944-45, prof. history, from 1945, Hallam chair of history, 1959-61, disting. prof. Coll. Arts and Scis., 1960-61. Author: Gibbon's Antagonism to Christianity, 1933, Government Assistance in Eighteenth Century France, 1952, The Humanitarian Movement in Eighteenth Century France, 1957, The Negro in France, 1961; contbr. articles to profl. jours. With S.A.T.C., 1918. Grantee Social Sci. Rsch. Coun., 1937, 39, 46; recipient Rhodes scholar U. Oxford, 1920-22, 23-24, Fulbright rsch. award, 1956-57, faculty sabbatical leave award for rsch. in France, Ky. Rsch. Found., 1963-64. Mem. AAUP, Soc. French Hist. Studies, Am. Hist. Assn., So. Hist. Assn., Masons, Phi Beta Kappa. Democrat. Presbyterian. *

MCCLUER, FRANC LEWIS, college president; b. O'Fallon, Mo., Mar. 27, 1896; s. Clarence Eugene and Martha Virginia (Savage) M.; m. Ida Belle Richmond, Sept. 2, 1920; 1 child, Richmond Harold. BA, Westminster Coll., Fulton, Mo., 1916, MA, 1920; PhD, U. Chgo., 1928; LLD, Westminster Coll., Washington U., Waynesburg Coll., U. Mo. Tchr. Fulton (Mo.) High Sch., 1916-18; asst. dept. history and econs. Westminster Coll., 1918-20, John J. Rice prof. sociology and econs., 1920-33, pres., 1933-47; pres. Lindenwood Coll., from 1947; instr. sociology U. Chgo., 1923-24, 25-26; vis. prof. sociology S.E. Mo. State Tchrs. Coll., summer 1927, U. Mo., summer 1929. Dem. presdl. elector, 1932; mem. Mo. State Constitutional Convention, 1943; exec. dir. Mo. Com. for the New Constitution; del. Del. Conf. on Basis of Just and Durable Peace; bd. dirs. Assn. Am. Colls., 1943-46, Louisville Presbyn. Sem., 1939-47; pres. bd. curators Lincoln U., Mo., 1939-43; pres. Mo. Coll. Joint Fund Com., Inc., from 1952; pres. Presbyn. Coll. Union, 1941; mem. Fed. Coun. Chs. Christ Am. State Children's Code Commn., 1946; mem. Mo. Commn. on Human Rights; bd. dirs. Christian Edn. Presbyn. Ch. USA, 1951-54; moderator Synod of Mo., Presbyn. Ch. USA, 1939-40, commr. to gen. assembly of Presbyn. Ch., 1942; chmn. coun. Nat. Presbyn. Ch. and Ctr., from 1961. Mem. Am. Sociol. Soc., Round Table Club, Univ Club, Kiwanis (pres. Fulton chpt. 1933), Masons, Pi Kappa Delta, Kappa Alpha, Zeta Phi, Pi Gamma Mu, Omicron Delta Kappa. Democrat. *

MCCLURE, JOHN ELMER, lawyer; b. Lincoln County, W.Va., Nov. 27, 1893; s. John W. and Lucy (Vickers) McC.; m. Helen Pendleton, Aug. 25, 1920; children: John Pendleton, William Pendleton; m. Helen Muller, Jan. 1, 1944; children: Joan Vickers, Arthur Acklin, John Elmer. Bar: D.C., 1923, Ill., 1940, U.S.

Claims Ct., 1924, U.S. Supreme Ct., 1926, U.S. Ct. Appeals, 1933. Practice law Washington; bd. dirs. Wilcox Oil Co. Spl. ambassador to Mex., 1960. Mem. ABA, D.C. Bar Assn., Ill. Bar Assn., Chgo. Bar Assn., Am. Judicature Soc., Ponte Vedra (Fla.) Club, Burning Tree Club, Nat. Press Club, Congl. Club, Met. Club, Masons. Baptist. *

MCCLURE, JOHN QUAYLE, insurance executive; b. L.A., Feb. 22, 1895; s. John and Nellie M. (Qualye) McC.; m. Lillian Jean Weir, Nov. 20, 1920; children: Beverly Jean (Mrs. Robert Errett), Barbara Alice (Mrs. William Newell West), John Quayle. Student, L.A. Coll., 1914-16. V.p. Nat. Aubomobile & Casualty Ins. Co., L.A., 1920-27; pres. Nat. Aubomobile & Casualty Ins. Co., 1927-56, Estate Ins. Co., L.A., from 1950; pres. Citizens Life & Casualty Ins. Co., from 1953, also chmn. bd. dirs. Mem. U.S. C. of C., L.A. C. of C., Masons, Shriners. Presbyterian. *

MCCOLLOUGH, WALTER, bishop; b. Great Falls, S.C., May 22, 1915; s. Robert and Missy (Tillman) McC.; m. Clara Price, Sept. 28, 1935; children: Walter, Charles L., James E., Regina B. Jr. DD (posthumously), Livingstone Col., Salisbury, N.C., 1991; elder, asst. minister United House of Prayer for All People, Charlotte Mission, Washington, 1939-41, sr. elder, 1941-60, minister Anacostia Mission, Washington, 1941-56, pastor Nat. Hdqrs., chmn. D.C.-Md. dist., 1956-60, bishop, trustee United House of Prayer for All People, Washington, 1960-91, founder/exec. dir. Coll. Scholarship Fund, 1971-91; founder, coordinator nationwide mortgage free bldg. program, from 1960; goodwill ambassador to Israel, 1967. Author: The Truth and Facts of the United House of Prayer, 1968; My Pilgrimage to the Holy land, 1969; Sixteen Dynamic Years, 1977. Initiator nationwide voters league. Recipient Presdl. Commendation, Gerald R. Ford, 1976, Jimmy E. Carter, 1980; Congl. testimonal Walter E. Fauntroy, 1976, Gov. tribute Richard Thornburg, 1980; Disting. Community Service award Nat. Urban Coalition, 1985. Died Mar. 21, 1991; buried Ft. Lincoln Cemetery, Brentwood, Md. Home: Washington D.C.

MCCOMB, JOHN HESS, clergyman; b. Phila., Aug. 7, 1898; s. George Shields and Laura (Hess) McC.; m. Mary E. King, Aug. 1942 (dec.); children: Mary King, John King; m. Helen Ann Riach, May 1945. AB, U. Pa., 1923; ThB, Princeton Theol. Sem., MA, 1927; DD, Dallas Theol. Sem., 1937. Ordained to ministry Presbyn. Ch., 1927. Newspaper reporter, 1919; rewrite man Phila. N. Am., 1920-23; with Phila. bur. AP, 1923-24; pastor Calvary Ch., Newark, 1927-29, Forest Park Ch., Balt., 1929-35, Broadway Ch., N.Y.C., 1935-59, N.W. Presbyn. Ch., Dallas, 1959-65; organizer, pastor Dallas Ind. Presbyn. Ch., from 1965; lectr. homiletics Westminster Theol. Sem., PHila., 1931-32, also trustee until 1936; conducted radio broadcast N.Y.C., 1951-59; lectr. Dallas Bible Inst., 1962-63. Author: Until the Flood, 1936, An Exposition of Ephesians, 1938, The Jew, the Gentile and the Church of God, 1939, God's Purpose in This Age, 1941, Wondrous Truths from the Word, 1943, The Faithful Word, 1945, The Faith Once Delivered, 1949, Things to Come, 1950, God's Prophetic Plan, 1952, Sermons on Bible Themes, 1955. With O.T.C., Ft. Monroe, Va., 1918. Mem. Presbyn. League of Faith (ex-pres.), Phi Beta Kappa, Sigma Nu. Republican. *

MCCONE, JOHN A., business executive; b. San Francisco, Jan. 4, 1902; s. Alexander J. and Margaret Enright McC.; m. Rosemary Cooper, June 21, 1938 dec. Dec. 1961 ; m. Theiline Pigott, Aug. 29, 1962. Student, U. Calif. Constrn. engr. Llewellyn Iron Works; supt. Consol. Steel Corp., 1929, exec. v.p., dir., 1933-37; pres., organizer Rechtel-McCone Corp., engrs., L.A., 1937-45; pres., dir. Calif. Shipbldg. Corp., 1941-46; pres., dir. Joshua Hendy Corp., 1945-58, chmn., 1958-69; dir. CIA, 1961-65; chmn. Hendy Internat. Co., 1968-71; pres., dir. Joshua Hendy Iron Works, 1945-58; dep. to Sec. of Def., 1948; under sec. USAF, 195-51; chmn. U.S. AEC, 1958-60. Mem. President's Air Policy Commn., 1947-48. Mem. Calif. Club, L.A. Country Club, Pacific Union Club, Bohemian Club San Francisco , Burning Tree Club, Met. Club, Chevy Chase Country Club Washington , The Links, Blind Brook Club N.Y.C. , Cypress Point Club Pebble Beach , Phi Kappa Sigma. Home: San Marino Calif. Died Feb. 14, 1991.

MCCONNELL, JAMES HOGE TYLER, businessman, lawyer, banker; b. Richmond, Va., Nov. 23, 1914; s. Frank Percy and Belle Norwood (Tyler) McC.; m. Jean Ellen duPont, Sept. 23, 1944 (div. 1972); children: Marion, Susan, James, William (dec.); m. Margaret Mahler, Apr. 25, 1973. B.A., Va. Mil. Inst., 1936; LL.B., U. Va., 1939, J.D., 1970. Bar: Va. 1938, Mo. 1942, Del. 1944. Vice pres., dir. Peoples Bank, Radford, Va., 1939-40; ptnr. Tyler, McConnell & Goldsmith, Radford, 1938-41; judge Civil Ct., Radford, 1940-41; asst. leader Inst. Pub. Affairs U. Va., Charlottesville, 1939; counsel Hercules, Inc., Wilmington, Del.; plant mgr., asst. gen. counsel, asst. to pres., corp. sec. Hercules Inc., Wilmington, Del., 1944-66; dir. fin. com. Hercules, Inc., Wilmington, Del., 1959-66, pres., 1966-79, chmn., 1966-85; chief exec. officer, chmn. exec. com., dir. Del. Trust Co., Wilmington, 1966-85; bd. govs. U.S. Postal Svc., 1985-88; dir., exec. com. Sta. WHYY-TV, from 1964; dir. Del. Dept. Health and Social Services, 1967-69, Del. Indsl. Fin., 1973-75; pres. Wilmington Clearing House, 1968-69, 79-80. Parent chmn. Bennett Coll., N.Y., 1965-66; bd. overseers, chmn. fin. com. Sweet Briar Coll., 1959-71; trustee Va. Mil. Inst., 1953-86; commr., chmn. Del. State Hwy. Dept., 1949-53; 1st chmn. Del. River Bay Authority, 1963-65; founder, mem. exec. com., dir. Greater Wilmington Devel. Council, 1960-85, pres., 1960-63; mem. Del. Roundtable Inc., 1980-86, mem. exec. com., 1983-87; mem. Del. Com. Organized Crime, 1966-67; chmn. Fair Hill Races, 1966-75; pres. Cecil County Breeders Fair, Inc., 1966-75; mem. nat. adv. com. Camp Fire Girls, 1971-72; bd. dirs. Del. chpt. ARC, 1948-88; campaign chmn. Nat. Safety Council, 1952, exec. com., chmn., 1969-71, trustee, 1972-80; mem. Del. Safety Council, from 1950, pres., 1960-63; mem. Block Blight, Inc., 1968-69; bd. dirs. Urban Coalition, 1977-79; mem. Del. Dept. Indsl. Fin., 1973-75; trustee Lawrenceville Sch., N.J., 1963-71; bd. dirs. Grand Opera House, Inc., 1981-88; founder, bd. dirs., mem. exec. com. Del. Mus. Natural History, 1958-81; life mem., dir., chmn., fin. com., treas. Soc. of The Four Arts, Palm Beach, Fla., 1987; Dem. nominee Gov. Del., 1956; chmn. Del. Dems. for Reagan-Bush, 1980; mem. exec. com. Pres.'s Private Sector Survey, 1982-88; bd. dirs. New Castle County Econ. Devel. Corp., 1981-88. Served as 1st lt. USAR, 1939-42; civilian aide to Sec. Army, 1968-70. Bridge across Brandywine River named for him; recipient NSC Flame of Life award,1971; Outstanding Civilian Service Medal Dept. Army, 1971, award Inst. Human Relations, 1982. Mem. ABA, Va. Bar Assn., Del. Bar Assn., Mo. Bar Assn., Am. Judicature Soc., Del. Bankers Assn. (exec. com. 1966-73, pres. 1972-73), Nat. Steeplechase, Hunt Assn. (steward 1964-76, v.p. 1971-76), Del. Racing Assn. (dir. 1948-82, v.p.), Am. Bankers Assn. (governing council 1974-76, chief exec. officer com. 1979-81), Soc. for Four Arts Palm Beach (bd. dirs., treas., chmn. fin. com. 1987—), Raven Soc., Phi Alpha Delta, Kappa Alpha. Episcopalian. Clubs: Wilmington, Wilmington Country; River (N.Y.); Farmington Country (Va.); Rehoboth Beach Country, Vicmead Hunt; Bath and Tennis (Palm Beach), Everglades (Palm Beach). Home: Wilmington Del. Died Mar. 13, 1989; buried Lower Brandywine Cemetery, Wilmington, Del.

MC CONNELL, JAMES VERNON, educator, psychologist; b. Okmulgee, Okla., Oct. 26, 1925; s. James V. and Helen (Stokes) McC. B.A. in Psychology, La. State U., 1947; M.A., U. Tex., 1954, Ph.D., 1956; student, U. Oslo, 1954-55. Mem. faculty U. Mich., Ann Arbor, 1956-88, prof. psychology, 1963-88, prof. emeritus, 1988-90; rsch. psychologist Mental Heath Rsch. Inst., U. Mich., 1963-80; pres. Planarian Press, Ann Arbor, Mich., from 1964; editor, pub. Worm Runner's Digest, Internat. Jour. Comparative Psychology, 1959-79; editor Jour. Biol. Psychology, 1966-79. Author: (with others) Psychology, 1961, (textbook) Understanding Human Behavior, 1974, 6th edit., 1989; also numerous articles, chpts. in books.; editor: The Worm Re-Turns, 1965; editor: (with Marlys Schutjer) Science, Sex and Sacred Cows, 1971, (with Robert Trotter) Psychology: The Human Science, 1978, (with Daniel Gorenflo) Classic Reading in Psychology, 1989. Served to ensign USNR, 1944-46. Recipient Disting. Teaching award Am. Psychol. Found., 1976; Fulbright scholar, 1954-55. Fellow AAAS, Am. Psychol. Assn.; mem. Psychonomic Soc., Animal Behavior Soc., Midwestern Psychol. Assn. Home: Ann Arbor Mich. Died Apr. 9, 1990; cremated.

MC CORD, JAMES ILEY, chancellor; b. Rusk, Tex., Nov. 24, 1919; s. Marshal Edward and Jimmie Oleta (Decherd) McC.; m. Hazel Thompson, Aug. 29, 1939; children—Vincent, Alison McCord Zimmerman, Marcia McCord Verville. B.A., Austin Coll., 1938, D.D., 1949; student, Union Theol. Sem., 1938-39; B.D., Austin Presbyn. Theol. Sem., 1942; M.A., U. Tex., 1942; student, Harvard, 1942-43, U. Edinburgh, 1950-51; Th.D., U. Geneva, 1958; S.T.D., Knox Coll., Toronto, Can., 1958; D.D., Princeton, 1960, Victoria U., Toronto, 1963, Westminster Coll., New Wilmington, Pa., 1969, U. Edinburgh, 1970, Presbyn. Coll., U. Montreal, 1975, Hamilton Coll., 1981; LL.D., Maryville Coll., 1959, Lafayette Coll., 1962, Tusculum Coll., 1964, Bloomfield Coll., 1966; Litt.D., Davidson Coll., 1959, Washington and Jefferson Coll., 1970, Rider Coll., 1977, Keimyung U., Taegu, Korea, 1979; L.H.D., Ursinus Coll., 1962; Th.D., Debrecen (Hungary) Ref. Theol. Faculty, 1967, United Protestant Theol. Coll., Cluj, Romania, 1974; LL.D., Park Coll., 1969; D.D., Davis and Elkins Coll., 1983, Taiwan Theol. Coll. & Sem., 1986, Alma (Mich.) Coll., 1986, Muskingum (Ohio) Coll., 1987, Yale U., 1987. Ordained min. Presbyterian Ch., 1942. Instr. U. Tex., 1940-42; adj. prof. Austin Presbyn. Theol. Sem., 1944-45, dean, prof. systematic theology, 1945-59; pres. Princeton (N.J.) Theol. Sem., 1959-83; founder, chancellor Center Theol. Inquiry, Princeton, 1983-89; Vis. prof. Presbyn. Theol. Sem. of South, Campinas, Brazil, 1956; chmn. North Am. Area Council World Alliance Ref. Chs., 1958-60, N. Am. sec. alliance, 1959-77, also chmn. theol. dept., 1956-70; past chmn. faith and order com., past chmn. nat. faith and order colloquium Nat. Council Chs.; former mem. commn. faith and order World Council of Chs.; chmn. council theol. edn. U.P. Ch., 1964-67, chmn. council theol. sems., 1978-81, chmn. consultation on ch. union, 1961-63; past chmn. commn. on accrediting Assn. Theol. Schs. U.S. and Can.; pres. World Alliance Ref. Chs., 1977-82; pres. United Bd. for Christian Higher Edn. in Asia, 1983-86, chmn., from 1986. Chmn. Christian Ministry in the Nat. Parks, from 1987. Mem. Assn. Theol. Schs. in U.S. and Can. (pres. 1978-80). Home: Princeton N.J. Died Feb. 19, 1990.

MCCORMICK, JAMES BYRON, lawyer, educator; b. Emden, Ill., Feb. 28, 1895; s. William and Flora Amanda (Ogden) McC.; m. Rachel Lee Staten, May 1, 1915; 1 child, Nancy Lee (Mrs. R. S. Clark). LLB, Ill. Wesleyan U., 1915, LLD, 1948; LLM, U. So. Calif., 1930; SJD, Duke U., 1933. Bar: Ill. 1916, Colo. 1926, Ariz. 1934. Practice law Ill., 1916-26; asst. prof., assoc. prof., then prof. law U. Ariz., 1926-38, dean Coll. of Law, 1938-47, pres., 1947-51, prof. of law, 1951-56; advisor to Bd. Regents U. and State Coll. of Ariz., from 1956. Contbr. to legal periodicals. Mem. Ariz. Interstate Stream Commn., 1956-61; sec. nat. convention ARC, 1948; bd. govs. Am. Nat. Red Cross, 1950-56. Fellow Am. Bar Found. (at-large); mem. ABA (mem. ho. of dels. 1945-47), State Bar of Ariz., Old Pueblo Club, Kiwanis, Masons (33 deg.), Phi Kappa PHi, PHi Alpha Delta. *

MCCORMICK, WILLARD F., management consultant; b. Tonawanda, N.Y., Feb. 18, 1904; m. Phyllis Webb, Sept. 23, 1950; children: Willard F., Anne E., Cathleen D., Thomas L., Margaret H., John C. With Remington Rand Co., 1920-38; mgmt. analyst U.S. Steel Corp., Pitts., 1938-42; a founder, sr. ptnr. Cresap, McCormick & Paget (Inc. 1969), N.Y.C., 1946-69, chmn., 1969-87; bd. dirs. Carborundum Co., Chgo. Pneumatic Tool Co., Schering-Plough Corp., Farrell Lines, Inc., N.Y.C., Midland Capital Corp. Mem. Cardinal's Com. for Laity, N.Y.C.; trustee, mem. exec. and fin. coms. Thomas Alva Edison Found. Lt. Comdr. USNR, 1942-46. Mem. N.Y. Fgn. Policy Assn. (former bd. govs.), Sky Club, Union League Club, Wee Burn Country Club. Home: Darien Conn. Died Apr. 8, 1989; buried Darien, Conn.

MCCOY, RALPH RICHARD, foundation executive; b. Richland, Ind., Oct. 14, 1909; s. L. Lyman and Louise (Link) McC.; m. Elizabeth Bacon, Apr. 23, 1936; children: Sankey McCoy Blondin, Elizabeth Noel. Student, George Washington U., 1930-35; LLB, Nat. U., 1938. Salesman svc. sta. Standard Oil Co., Washington, 1929-30; asst. purchasing agt. So. Dairies, Inc., Washington, 1930-32; with acctg., sales and fgn. svc. depts. Standard Oil Co. N.J., 1932-56; pres. Pate Oil Co., Milw., 1956-60, Okla. Oil Co. Chgo., 1956-60; pres. Okla.-Pate div. Humble Oil & Refining Co., Houston, 1960-61, regional mktg. mgr., 1961-65; mktg. coord. Esso Standard Ea., Inc., 1965-69; v.p. Teagle Found., N.Y.C., 1969-79. Mem. Wee Burn Country Club, Delta Phi Epsilon. Home: Darien Conn. Died Mar. 31, 1989; buried Noroton Presbyn. Ch., Darien, Conn.

MCCOY, WHITLEY PETERSON, arbitrator; b. Washington, Oct. 26, 1894; s. Joseph Melville and Ellen (Peterson) M.; m. Dorothy Dawson McConnell, Apr. 16, 1936; 1 child, Juliet Granville. AB, DArtmouth Coll., 1916; LLB, George Washington U., 1921. Bar: D.C. 1921. Assoc. prof. law U. Ala., 1921-22; asst. prof. law U. S.D., 1922-23, George Washington U., 1923-24; ptnr. Chilton & McCoy, Montgomery, Ala., 1924-26; assoc. Shackelford & Brown, Tampa, Fla., 1926-27; prof. law U. Ala., 1927-53; arbitrator U.S. Conciliation Svc., Nat. War Labor Bd., from 1941, Am. Arbitration Assn., from 1941; vis. prof. law George Washington U., 1945; trial examiner Nat. Labor Rels. Bd., summers, 1938-39; dir. Fed. Mediation & Conciliation Svc., Washington, 1953-54. Author: (brochure) Judicial Procedure in Alabama, 1935, (with Clarence M. Updegraff) Arbitration of Labor Disputes, 1946; editor: Cases and Statutes on Trial and Appellate Practice in Alabama, 1932, 2d edit., 1948; contbr. articles to law jours. Mem. exec. com. Assn. Am. Law Schs., 1945; v.p. Nat. Acad. Arbitrators, 1947, 48. Lt. (j.g.) USN, 1917-19. Mem. ABA, Ala. State Bar Assn., Labor Rels. Rsch. Assn., Order of Coif, Delta Tau Delta, Phi Alpha Delta. Democrat. Episcopalian. *

MC CRAKEN, ROBERT STANTON, newspaper and broadcasting executive; b. Washington, June 1, 1924; s. Tracy Stephenson and Lillian G. (Davis) McC.; m. A. Anne Wright, May 6, 1960; children—Michael, Cindy. Student, Washington and Lee U., 1945, U. Denver, 1946; B.A., U. Wyo., 1948. Reporter Rawlins (Wyo.) Daily Times, 1948-50; promotion mgr. Cheyenne (Wyo.) Newspapers, Inc.; pubs. Wyo. Eagle, Wyo. State Tribune, Wyo. Tribune Eagle, 1950-54, asso. pub., 1955-58, pres., pub., 1958-89; chmn. bd. Laramie Newspapers, Inc., Rawlins Newspapers, Inc., Rock Springs Newspapers, Inc., Big Horn Basin Newspapers, Inc.; dir. Wyo. Broadcasting Co., Cheyenne Nat. Bank. Trustee U. Wyo., 1961-67. Served with AUS, World War II. Mem. Cheyenne C. of C., Kappa Sigma, Kiwanis. Presbyterian. Home: Cheyenne Wyo. Died Aug. 21, 1989; buried Bethel Cemetery, Cheyenne, Wyo.

MCCRILLIS, JOHN WILMARTH, insurance executive, county official; b. Newport, N.H., Jan. 11, 1897; s. John and Mary (Wilmarth) McC.; m. Hester L. Cooper, Oct. 16, 1924; children: Sally Evelyn (Mrs. H. Nerwcomb Eldredge), John Cooper. AB, Dartmouth Coll., 1919. Tchr. Moran Sch., Seattle, 1920-24; propr.

McCrillis Ins. Agy., Newport, from 1924; dir., treas., clk. Brampton Woolen Co.; dep. clk. Superior Ct. of N.H., Sullivan County, 1925-35, clk., from 1935; dir. N.H. Ins. Co. Author: (with Otto Schniebs) Modern Ski Technique, 1932. Trustee, treas., clk. Newport Charitable Assn.; treas., trustee Richards Free Libr., 1930-63. Mem. Rotary, Masons, Sigma Alpha Epsilon. *

MCCRON, RAYMOND CHARLES, insurance company executive; b. Flushing, N.Y., Feb. 26, 1921; s. James Robert and Pauline (Meyer) McC.; m. Corinne H. Mathews, June 30, 1946; children—Linda Catharine, James Robert, II, John Howard, Trudy Jane. B.S. in Econs, Wharton Sch., U. Pa., 1943. Asst. sec.-asst. treas. D.&R. G.W. R.R., 1952-56; asst. to v.p. fin. N.Y.C. R.R., 1956-61, treas., 1961-68; also treas. subsidiary cos., treas. Penn Central, 1968-69; ind. fin. cons., 1969-70; v.p. Equitable Life Assurance Soc., N.Y.C., 1971-73, v.p., treas., 1973-78, sr. v.p., treas., 1978-86; ind. fin. cons., 1986-90. Served with AUS, 1943-46, 50-52, Korea. Mem. Sigma Phi Epsilon. Clubs: Larchmont (N.Y.) Yacht, Masons. Home: Scarsdale N.Y. Died Mar. 10, 1990.

MC CUNE, EMMETT LEE, avian pathologist; b. Cuba, Mo., Jan. 2, 1927; s. Roy Earl and Rhoda Angeletta (Houseright) McC.; m. Mable June Rector, June 8, 1952; children: Martha Grace, Roy Allen, Gordon Norman. B.S., U. Mo., 1956, D.V.M., 1956, M.S., 1961; Ph.D., U. Minn., 1968. Instr. U. Mo., Columbia, 1956-61; asst. prof. U. Mo., 1962-68, assoc. prof., 1969-78, prof. vet. microbiology, from 1978. Contbr. articles to profl. jours.; editor: Avian Diseases, 1977. Cubmaster Boy Scouts Am., Columbia, 1968-72; pres. High St. Neighborhood Assn., 1972. Served with U.S. Army, 1945-46, PTO. NIH fellow, 1963-64. Mem. Am. Coll. Vet. Microbiologists, AVMA, Am. Soc. Microbiology, Am. Assn. Avian Pathologists, N.Y. Acad. Sci., U. Mo. Alumni Assn. (pres. 1982-83), Sigma Xi. Home: Hallsville Mo. Deceased. †

MC CUNE, GEORGE DAVID, publisher; b. Cedar Rapids, Iowa, Oct. 18, 1924; s. James and Mary Esther (Vanous) McC.; m. Sara Joy Miller, Oct. 16, 1966; children: Cathy Jane, David Franklin, Keith Robert, Susan Marie. B.A., Butler U., 1948; M.A., U. Pa., 1950. With Macmillan Co., N.Y.C., 1950-66; v.p., dir. div. Free Press, 1964-65; div. Glencoe Press, 1965-66; chmn. bd., pub., treas. Sage Publs., Inc., Beverly Hills, Calif., 1966-85; dep. chmn., pub., treas. Sage Publs., Inc., Beverly Hills, 1985-90; chmn. bd. Sage Publs., Ltd., London, 1971-90; dir. Sage Publs. India Pvt. Ltd. Served with USAAF, 1943-46. Home: Los Angeles Calif. Died May 19, 1990.

MC CURRY, PAUL D., architect; b. Chgo., Dec. 3, 1903; s. Daniel J. and Ella (Crissinger) McC.; m. Irene Tipler, Aug. 30, 1935; children: Margaret, Marian, Alan. B.S., Armour Inst. Tech., 1926; M.Ed., U. Chgo., 1937. With Talmadge & Watson, Chgo., 1926-28, Rebori, Dewey, Wentworth & Smith, Chgo., 1929-30, Holibird & Root, Architects, Chgo., 1930, D.H. Burnham Architects, 1930-31; architect State of Ill., Chgo., 1931-33; tchr. Tilden High Sch., Chgo., 1934-46; staff then ptnr. Schmidt, Garden & Erikson (architects-engrs.), Chgo., from 1946. Prin. works include VA Research Hosp., Chgo., Schs. of Health Professions, U. Pitts, Amos Alonzo Stagg High Sch., Palos Hills, Ill., Marian Coll. of Fond du Lac, Wis., John Hancock Elementary Sch., Chgo., Mary C. Terrell Elementary Sch., Chgo., Deerpath Elementary Sch., Lake Forest, Marillac High Sch., Northfield, Ill., Kenwood High Sch., Chgo., Copley Hosp, Aurora, Ill., Lake Forest Club, Lake Forest, Ill., U. Ill. Hosp., Chgo., Doctor's Office Bldg. at Resurrection Hosp., Chgo., Passive Solar Residence, Fairbanks, Alaska; worked on restoration of New Salem Village, Ill and dome of Capitol bldg., Springfield, Ill. Chmn. Mayor's Archtl. Com., Lake Forest, Ill.; chmn. archtl. licensing com. Ill. Dept. Registration and Edn., 1971-81; mem. Lake Forest Plan Commn., 1970-75. Fellow AIA (pres. Chgo. chpt. 1968, Disting. Svc. award 1988); mem. Deerpath Art League (pres.). Clubs: Lake Forest (Ill.); Arts (Chgo.), Cliff Dwellers (Chgo.) (pres. 1961-61). Home: Lake Forest Ill. Died July 11, 1991; inurned; Columbarium Ch. of the Holy Spirit, Lake Forest, Ill.

MCDANEL, RALPH CLIPMAN, history educator; b. Phila., Nov. 17, 1893; s. Robert B. and Laura (Steelman) McD.; m. Mildred Lewis, Dec. 25, 1919; 1 child, Robert Lewis. BA, Richmond Coll., 1916; MA, Columbia U., 1925; PhD, Johns Hopkins U., 1926; grad., Inst. Internat. Studies, Geneva, Switzerland, 1935-36; LLD, Georgetown Coll., 1951. High sch. tchr., prin., 1916, 19-24; mem. faculty U. Richmond, Va., from 1926, prof. history, from 1930, chmn. dept. history and polit. sci., from 1941, William Binford Vest prof., from 1959. Mem. Richmond Citizens Assn.; pres. Bapt. Gen. Assn. Va., 1949-50; v.p. Bapt. Minister's Relief Fund of Va.; trustee Crozer Theol. Sem., 1949-59, Religious Herald, from 1950. 1st lt., inf., U.S. Army, 1917-19. Mem. Am. Hist. Assn., So. Hist. Assn., Am. Soc. Internat. Law, Va. Bapt. Hist. Soc. (pres.), Torch of Richmond Club (pres. 1943-44), Masons, Phi Beta Kappa, Omicron Delta Kappa (nat. pres. 1947-49), Phi Alpha Theta, Tau Kappa Alpha, Pi Sigma Alpha, Pi Delta Epsilon, Kappa Sigma. *

MCDANIEL, CHARLIE HOMER, government official; b. Talbotton, Ga., Feb. 6, 1895; s. Henry Patrick and Emma (Williams) McD.; m. Emily Pou Heath, Aug. 11, 1932. Grad. bus. coll., Macon, Ga., 1915; student, Pace Inst., 1919-20, Tulane U., 1921. Asst. auditor Hotel Dempsy, Macon, 1915-16; bookkeeper, asst. credit mgr. W. A. Doody Dept. Store, 1916-17; acct., auditor U.S. Shipping Bd., Merchant Fleet Corp., Washington, 1919-20; chief acct. U.S. Shipping Bd., Merchant Fleet Corp., New Orleans, 1921-22; supervising auditor U.S. Shipping Bd., Merchant Fleet Corp., 1919-23, dist. disbursing officer, dist. comptr., 1924-30; traveling auditor U.S. Shipping Bd., Merchant Fleet Corp., Washington, 1931-32, asst. gen. comptr., 1933-36, mem. spl. Senate com. investigating ocean and mail contracts, 1933-36; supervising acct. Reconstrn. Fin. Corp., 1932-33; acting asst. to dir., divsn. of fin. U.S. Maritime Commn., 1936-39, sr. fin. examiner, 1939-40, asst. to commr., office of commr., 1940-41, examiner, construction cost audit sect., 1941-44, chief of sect., procurement divsn., price revision sect., 1944-46, dir. divsn. of govt. aids, 1946-48; chief, divsn. of subsidy contracts Bur. of Govt. Aids, 1948-50; chief, divsn. subsidy contracts Office of Govt. Aid, 1959-64. With U.S. Army, 1917-18. Mem. Am. LEgion (past comdr.), Idle Hour Golf and Country Club, Lions, Masons, Shriners. *

MCDANIEL, JOHN S., JR., lawyer; b. Detroit, May 8, 1916; s. John S. and Helen Philippine (Strassel) McD.; m. Emily Kent Platt, Oct. 20, 1956; children: Emily Kent McDaniel Marget, John S. III, Mary Perine. BA, Amherst Coll., 1937; LLB, Yale U., 1940. Bar: Md. 1940. Assoc. Office Karl F. Steinmann, Balt., 1940-46, ptnr., 1946-54; ptnr. Cable & McDaniel, Balt., 1954-68, Cable, McDaniel, Bowie & Bond, Balt., 1968-91, McGuire, Woods, Battle & Boothe, Balt., 1991-92; bd. dirs. Am. Trading & Prodn. Corp., Balt.; adv. bd. dirs. Crown Cen. Petroleum Corp., Balt. Sgt. USAAF, 1942-43. Mem. ABA, Balt. City Bar Assn., Ctr. Club. Republican. Episcopalian. Home: Baltimore Md. Died Aug. 27, 1992. †

MCDERMIT, ROBERT EDWARD, health services executive, consultant, educator; b. Moose Jaw, Sask., Can., Nov. 16, 1932; a. John and Barbara (Melvin) McD.; m. Ruth Elsie Erickson, May 17, 1955; children: Dale Robert, Mary Lyn, Leslie Ann. BS in Pharmacy, U. Sask., Saskatoon, 1957; Pharma. chemist, Sask. Pharmaceutical Assn., Regina, 1957; Cert. Hosp. Orgn. Mgmt., Can. Hosp. Assn., 1965; Licentiate in Health Adminstrn., Inst. Health Service Adminstrs., London, 1976. Cert. health exec. Can. Coll. Health Service Execs., Ottawa, Can., 1984. Instr. pharmacy U. Sask. Coll. Pharmacy, Saskatoon, Can., 1957-58; pharmacy cons., N.W. Regional Hosp. Council North Battleford, Sask., Can., 1958-61; chief pharmacist Notre Dame Hosp., North Battlefield, Sask., Can., 1958-61; dir. pharmacy Regina Grey Nuns' Hosp., Sask., Can., 1961-63, adminstrv. asst., 1963-65, asst. gen. adminstr., 1965-67; adminstr. Wascana Hosp., Regina, Sask., Can., 1967-68; asst. exec. dir. S. Sask. Hosp. Centre, Regina, Sask., Can., 1968-69, adminstr. Wascana div., 1968-69; dir. edn. Sask. Hosp. Assn., Regina, Sask., Can., 1969-71; gen. mgr., v.p. Gordon A. Friesen Can., Ltd., Calgary, Alta., Can., 1971-74; chief, health care plan Dept. Social Devel., Govt. N.W. Ters., Yellowknife, N.W.T., Can., 1974-77; asst. dir. dept. health and social services Govt. N.W. Terrs., Yellowknife, N.W.T., Can., 1977-78; dir. Dept. Health, Yellowknife, N.W.T., Can., 1978-79; sr. asst. dep. minister Profl. and Instl. Services, Ministry Health, Govt. B.C., Victoria, Can., 1979-81; adminstr. U. B.C. Health Scis. Centre Hosp., Vancouver, 1981-82; pres. U. B.C. Health Scis. Centre Hosp., Vancouver, Can., 1983-87; exec. dir., chief exec. officer St. John Ambulance B.C., Vancouver, from 1987; pres. Futuristic Health Concepts, Richmond, B.C., from 1987; clin. lectr. U. B.C., Vancouver, from 1981; lectr. faculty health info. scis. U. Victoria, B.C., Can., from 1982. Contbr. articles to profl. jours. Bd. dirs. Regina Boys' Pipe Band, 1967-69, 70-71; mem. Vancouver Bd. Trade. Recipient Merck prize in Chemistry, Frank W. Horner Meml. prize in Pharmacology, Gold medal Sask. Pharm. Assn.; scholar F.J. Fear, Robert Martin, Can. Found. for Advancement Pharmacy, Burroughs Welcome. Fellow Am. Coll. Hosp. Adminstrs., Can. Coll. Health Service Execs., (cert.) Bd. and Coms.; mem. Can. Pub. Health Assn. (pres. N.W.T. br. 1975-76), B.C. Health Assn., Bd. and Coms., Sask. Hosp. Assn. (bd. dirs. 1967-69). Sask. Assn. Hosp. Adminstrs. (pres. 1966-68), Sask. Pharm. Assn., Can. Soc. Hosp. Pharmacists (pres. 1963-64, v.p. 1962-63). Club: Vancouver Can. Home: Richmond Can. Deceased. †

MCDERMOTT, JAMES T., state supreme court justice; b. Sept. 22, 1926; m. Mary Theresa McDermott; children: James, Thomas, Suzanne, Michael, John, Matthew. B.S., St. Joseph's Coll., 1947; LL.B., Temple U., 1950. Bar: Pa. Judge Pa. Ct. Common Pleas 1st Jud. Dist., 1965-82; justice Supreme Ct. Pa., Phila., from 1982. Chmn. Criminal Justice Com.; chmn. City Charter Revision Commn. Mem. Phila. Bar Assn., Pa. Bar Assn. Home: Philadelphia Pa. Deceased. †

MCDONALD, LLOYD PAUL, clergyman, educator; b. Seward, Ill., May 17, 1896; s. Edward and Alice Frances (Dooley) McD. AB, Loras Coll., Dubuque, Iowa, 1917; PhD, Cath. U. Am., 1928. Joined Soc. of St. Sulpice, 1922; ordained priest, Roman Cath. Ch., 1921. Instr. in English St. Charles Coll., Catonsville, Md., 1921-24; pres. Basselin Cath. U. of Am., 1930-33; rector Theol. Coll. Cath. U. Am., 1944-48; rector sch. philosophy St. Mary's Sem., Balt., 1933-44, pres., from 1948; provincial Soc. of St. Sulpice in U.S., from 1948. *

MC DONALD, MILES FRANCIS, lawyer, judge; b. Bklyn., May 24, 1905; s. John R. and Lucy (Malone) McD.; m. Alice Shelare, Dec. 27, 1933; children—John R., Joanne Mc Donald Roddy, Miles F. Jr., Alan Shelare. A.B. cum laude, Holy Cross Coll., Worcester, Mass., 1926, LL.D., 1951; J.D., Fordham U., 1929; LL.D., St. John's U., 1946. Bar: N.Y. 1929. Atty. Wingate & Cullen, Bklyn., 1929-40; asst. dist. atty. Kings County, N.Y., 1940-45; U.S. atty. Eastern Dist. N.Y., 1945; dist. atty. Kings County, 1946-54; justice Supreme Ct. of N.Y. State, 1953-71; presiding justice appellate term 2d and 11th Jud. Dists., 1968; adminstrv. Judge 2d Jud. Dist., 1968-71; counsel Shea & Gould, N.Y.C., 1971-90; dir. Butte Copper and Zinc Co., 1934-37, dir., sec., 1937-42, v.p., treas., 1942-60; dir. Jonathan Logan. Past chmn. bd. trustees Nat. Conf. on Crime and Delinquency. Mem. Am., N.Y. State, Bklyn. bar assns., Bklyn. Manhattan Trial Counsel Assn. (past pres.), Nat. Conf. State Trial Judges (past chmn.), Assn. Supreme Ct. Justices N.Y. (past chmn.), N.Y. State Dist. Attys. Assn. (past pres.), Nat. Assn. Dist. Attys. (past pres.), Turtle Creek Country Club, Knights of Malta. Democrat. Home: Tequesta Fla. Died Apr. 3, 1991.

MC DONALD, ROY, newspaper publisher; b. Graysville, Tenn., Nov. 25, 1901; s. Frank Jones and Nannie (Ketner) McD.; m. Elizabeth Williams, Dec. 8, 1923. Founder, publisher, later chmn. bd. Chattanooga News-Free Press Co. (pub. Chattanooga News-Free Press), from 1933. Chmn. bd. Blue Cross-Blue Shield of Tenn. Home: Chattanooga Tenn. Died June 19, 1990.

MCDONNELL, EVERETT NICHOLAS, business executive; b. Des Moines, June 25, 1893; s. John E. and Zoe (Wallace) McD.; m. Esther Sanders Raplee, Oct. 9, 1925; 1 child, Eileen. Student, Iowa State Coll., 1913-15, Cornell U., 1915-16. V.p. Harrison Constrn. Co., Des Moines, 1919-25; sec., bd. dirs. McAlear Mfg. Co., Chgo., 1919-25; ptnr. McDonnell & Miller mfrs. boiler controls and water-feeders, Chgo., 1925-29, chmn., from 1929. 1st lt. 301st Heavy Tank Corps A.E.F., 1917-19. Mem. Am. Soc. Heating and Ventilating Engrs., Iowa State Engrs.' Soc., Tavern Club, Athletic Club, Evanston Golf Club, Lake Geneva Country Club, Masons (32d deg.), Snriners, Beta Theta Pi. *

MCELLROY, WILLIAM SWINDLER, dean; b. Edgewood, pa., Sept. 26, 1893; s. John Moss and Ida May (Scheffler) McE.; m. Ellenore Hambly, June 10, 1917 (dec. Mar. 1941). BS, U. Pitts., 1916, MD, 1917; postgrad., Harvard Med. Sch., 1917; DSc (hn.), Waynesburg Coll., 1950; LLD (hon.), Temple U., 1951. Student asst. in physiology U. Pitts., 1915-17, instr. in phys. chemistry, 1917-19, asst. prof. phys. chemistry, 1919-20, prof. phys. chemistry, from 1920, asst. dean Sch. Medicine, 1921-38, acting dean Sch. Medicine, 1938, dean Sch. Medicine, 1939-58, dean emeritus Sch. Medicine, from 1958; chemist Elizabeth Steel Magee Hosp., also Children's Hosp., Pitts., from 1925, Presbyn. Hosp., Pitts., from 1925, St. Francis Hosp., Pitts., from 1920. Lt. (j.g.) Med. Corps, USNRF. Fellow ACP; mem. Am. Soc. for Exptl. Biology and Medicine, Am. Soc. for Biol. Chemists, Am. Chem. Soc., Pitts. Acad. Medicine, Assn. Am. Med. Colls. (pre. 1946-47), Allegheny County Med. Soc., Pitts. Athletic Assn., Faculty Club, Rolling Rock Club, Chesapeake Yacht Club, Miles River Yacht Club, Masons, Sigma Xi, Alpha Omega Alpha, Sigma Chi. Republican. Presbyterian. *

MC ENTYRE, PETER MICHAEL, investment company executive; b. Westmount, Que., Can., Aug. 15, 1917; s. John and May (Gear) McE.; m. Katharine Creelman, Mar. 15, 1941 (dec. 1983); children: David, Nancy Wright. Student, Bishop's Coll. Sch., 1928-35; B.Com., McGill U., 1939, C.A., 1941, C.F.A., 1963. Partner Creak Cushing & Hodgson, Montreal, 1939-48; sec.-treas. St. Lawrence Sugar Refineries Ltd., Montreal, 1948-63; pres., dir. Comml. Trust Co. Ltd., Montreal, 1963-79, Comtrust Holdings Inc., Toronto, 1979-83, Ashburton Investments Ltd., Montreal; bd. dirs. Cheni Gold Mines, Lafarge Can. Inc., Can., Internat. Atlantins Ltd. Bermuda. Alderman City of Westmount, 1962-69; commr. finance City Westmount, 1962-69; mayor, 1969-71; chmn. Boys' and Girls' Clubs of Can. Endowment Fund.; vice chmn. bd. dirs. Montreal Neurol. Hosp. Served with Royal Canadian Navy, 1941-46. Clubs: University, St. James's, Montreal Badminton and Squash, Royal Montreal Curling. Home: Montreal Can. Died Mar. 6, 1989; buried Montreal.

MC EVERS, ROBERT DARWIN, banker, business executive; b. Washington, May 18, 1930; s. John Henry and Beatrice (Holton) McE.; m. Joan Manning, Mar. 29, 1954; children: Robert Darwin, Allison Holton. B.S. with distinction, U.S. Naval Acad., 1952; M.B.A. with distinction, Harvard U., 1958. With First Nat. Bank of Chgo., 1958-61, 73-82, sr. v.p., 1973-76, head trust dept., 1974-77, exec. v.p., 1976-81, head exec. dept., 1977-82; spl. asst., exec. offices Trans Union Corp. (formerly Union Tank Car Co.), Chgo., 1961-64;

gen. mgr. Trans Union Corp. (Canadian subs.), Toronto, Ont., 1964; asst. to pres. Trans Union Corp., Chgo., 1964-65; v.p., gen. mgr. Trans Union Corp. (Tank Car div.), 1965-70, pres., 1970-73; v.p., dir. Trans Union Corp., 1966-73; pres. Ft. Dearborn Income Securities, Inc., 1973-77; pres., sec. Reading Industries Inc. (Pa.), 1982-83; vice chmn. Auerbach Med. Corp., 1982-87. Former bd. dirs. Chgo. YMCA Coll., Mather Home. 1st lt. USAF, 1952-56. Mem. Beta Theta Pi. Clubs: Univ. (Chgo.), Mid-Day (Chgo.); Kenilworth (Ill.); Indian Hill (Winnetka, Ill.). Home: Kenilworth Ill. Died Nov. 18, 1991.

MCEWEN, WILLIAM PETER, university administrator; b. Earl Park, Ind., Mar. 21, 1912; s. Peter and Ethel (Jones) McE.; m. Marjorie Susan Postle, Oct. 25, 1946; children: Susan Ellen, Priscilla Jean, Peter Stewart, William Byron. BA, Depauw U., 1934; MA, Boston U., 1936, PhD, 1940; postgrad., Harvard U., 1941-42. Student pastor Presbyn. Ch., Acton and Marshfield, Ind., 1930-35; lectr. philosophy Boston U., 1941-42; exec. dir. ARC, Middle East, North Africa, 1942-46; mem. faculty Hofstra U., 1946-78, prof. philosophy, chmn. dept. philosophy, 1959-61, chmn. social sci. div., 1959-61, dean faculty, 1961-66, provost, dean faculties, 1966-74, 1st Disting. Svc. prof., 1975-78. Author: Enduring Satisfaction, 1949, The Problem of Social-Scientific Knowledge, 1963; contbr. chpts. to books and articles to profl. jours. Mediator Hempstead Pub. Employment Rels. Bd.; pres. Fulton Sch. PTA, 1959-60; membership chmn. Friends of Hempstead Pub. Libr., 1961-63; elder Presbyn. Ch. Recipient Disting. Alumnus Citiation DePauw U., 1971. Mem. Am. Philos. Assn., Am. Conf. Acad. Deans, Nassau Forum, Phi Beta Kappa, Delta Tau Delta. Home: Garden City N.Y. Died Jan. 17, 1990.

MC FADDEN, FRANK WILLIAM, public relations company executive; b. San Diego, June 3, 1914; s. Clarence Ray and Mabel Mary (Hyde) McF.; m. Marion Pauline Story, Aug. 31, 1935 (dec.); children: Michael Frank, Judith Ann (dec.). Student, Southwestern U. Bus., 1933-34. Asst. publicity dir. Universal Pictures, Los Angeles, 1937-52; nat. publicity dir. Panoramic Prodns., Culver City, Calif., 1953; pres. Frank McFadden & Assocs., Los Angeles, 1954; partner McFadden & Eddy, Assocs., Los Angeles, 1955-66, McFadden, Strauss & Irwin, Los Angeles, 1966-76, ICPR Public Relations, Los Angeles, 1976-85. Recipient Les Mason award Publicists Guild Am., 1977. Home: Newport Beach Calif. Died Feb. 8, 1990; cremated.

MCFALL, KENNETH HELICER, college official; b. Cleve., Oct. 21, 1906; s. Frank H. and Mary Ella (Porter) McF.; m. Dorothy E. Vernon, Sept. 2, 1930; 1 dau., Mary Jane. B.S., Mt. Union Coll., 1929, LL.D., 1969; M.A., Western Res. U., 1941, Ph.D., 1947. Prin. Hanoverton (Ohio) High Sch., 1929-30, Franklin Sch., Kent, Ohio, 1930-32; exec. head Randolph (Ohio) Schs., 1932-34; dir. admissions Mt. Union Coll., Alliance, Ohio, 1934-43; dean freshman Bowling Green (Ohio) State U., 1943-45, dir. guidance services, 1945-47, asst. dean liberal arts, 1947-48; dean Bowling Green (Ohio) State U. (Coll. Liberal Arts), 1948-55, prof. psychology, from 1948, provost, 1955-60, v.p., 1960-72, v.p. emeritus, from 1972, sec. bd. trustees, 1972-76; fellow higher edn. Western Res. U., 1943-45; Dir. Indsl. Devel. Corp.; Mem. commn. on higher edn. Midwest Program Airborne TV. Contbr. articles to edn. publs.; Co-editor: Looking Toward College, 1942-48, To College in Ohio, 1944. Trustee Mt. Union Coll.; bd. dirs. Wood County chpt. Am. Cancer Soc. McFall Ctr., Western Res. U. named in his honor, 1976. Fellow AAAS; mem. Coll. Pub. Relations Assns. (pres. 1942-43), Ohio Assn. Coll. Admission Officers (pres. 1943-44), Ohio Coll. Assn. (treas. 1963-72, chmn. com. on inspection and membership 1957-63), C. of C., Mid Am. Athletic Conf. (pres. 1962), Am. Assn. Acad. Deans, North Central Assn. Acad. Deans (v.p. 1951-52, pres. 1952-53), Ohio Assn. Acad. Deans, Ohio Assn. Coll. Presidents and Deans (pres. 1953-54), Am. Ednl. Research Assn., NEA, Arnold Air Soc., Alpha Phi Omega, Omicron Delta Kappa, Alpha Tau Omega (nat. vocat. adv. bd. 1947-57), Pi Gamma Mu, Tau Kappa Alpha, Book and Mortar, Alpha Epsilon Delta. Presbyn. (elder). Lodges: Masons, Elks, Kiwanis. Home: Bowling Green Ohio Died Aug. 27, 1991; interred Oak Grove Cemetery, Bowling Green, Ohio.

MCFARLAN, ARTHUR CRANE, geologist; b. Mansfield, Ohio, May 7, 1897; s. Frank Gressinger and Mary Ella (Henninger) McF.; m. Gail Parker, Sept. 21; children: Arthur C. (dec.), Mary Beth. AB, U. Cin., 1919; PhD, U. Chgo., 1923. Asst. geologist Tenn. Geol. Survey, summers 1918; geologist South Penn Oil Co., Dallas, summer 1920, Bowling Green/Westchester, Ky., 1922-23; geologist Ky. State Geol., 1932-34; dir. Ky. Geol. Survey, 1948-58; assoc. prof. U. Ky., 1923-27, prof. geol., from 1927, head dept. geology, from 1928; cons. Ky. for Progress Commn., 1934-36; chmn. com. for Ky. Commn. on Natural Resources, 1946-50. Author: Geology of Kentucky, 1943; contbr. articles on Ordovician stratigraphy. Ordovician and Miss. paleontology and stratigraphy and Ky. geol. to various publs., misc. county geol. maps, Ky. Fellow AAAS, Geol. Soc. Am., Paleontol. Soc. Am.; mem. AAUP, Am. Assn. Petroleum Geologists, Appalachian Geol. Soc., Ky. Geol. Soc., Sigma Xi, Gamma Alpha. *

MCGEE, DEAN ANDERSON, petroleum company executive; b. Humboldt, Kans., Mar. 20, 1904; s. George Gentry and Gertrude Hattie (Sayre) McG.; m. Dorothea Antoinette Swain, June 28, 1938 (dec. Dec. 1988); children: Marcia Ann, Patricia Dean. BS in Mining Engring., Kans. U., 1926; LLD (hon.), Oklahoma City U., 1957; DSc (hon.), Bethany Nazarene Coll., 1967; D. Eng (hon.), Colo. Sch. Mines, 1968; LHD (hon.), Okla. Christian Coll., 1975. Geology instr. Kans. U., 1926-27; petroleum geologist Phillips Petroleum Co., Bartlesville, Okla., 1927, chief geologist, 1935-37; v.p. charge prodn., exploration Kerr-McGee Corp. (formerly Kerr-McGee Oil Industries), Oklahoma City, 1937-42, exec. v.p., 1942-54, pres., 1954-67, chmn. bd., chief exec. officer, 1963-83, hon. chmn. and dir., 1983-89; bd. dirs. Kerr-McGee Bldg. Corp.; owner McGee Keesee Angus Ranch. Contbr. articles to profl. jours. Trustee Okla. Zool. Soc., Presbyn. Hosp. (hon.), Calif. Inst. Tech., Oklahoma City Indsl. & Cultural Facilities Trust, Southwest Research Inst., San Antonio, Midwest Research Inst., Kansas City, Mo., Oklahoma City U., Kans. U. Endowment Assn., Okla. Eye Found., Scis. and Natural Resources Found.; pres., dir. Kerr-McGee Found., Inc., McGee Found. Inc.; mem. Okla.'s Future, Inc., Oklahoma City Arts Council; bd. trustees Myriad Gardens Trust Authority Oklahoma City; bd. dirs. Oklahoma City U. Found., Okla. Med. Research Found., Allied Arts Found., Com. of 100, Oklahoma City Symphony Soc., Ark. Basin Devel. Assn., NCCJ Oklahoma City; dir. Okla. State Fair and Expn.; chmn. exec. com. Okla. Health Scis. Found; trustee, mem. exec. com., hon. life mem. bd. dirs. Nat. Cowboy Hall of Fame; adv. bd. Coll. Bus. Adminstrn. U. Okla., 1975; chmn. gulf states dist. Rhodes Scholarship Selection Com., 1968-74. Recipient numerous honors and awards including Erasmus Haworth Disting. Alumni award in geology U. Kans., 1951, Kans. U. Alumni Disting. Service Citation, 1951, Outstanding Civilian Service award Dept. Army, 1965, Nat. Brotherhood award NCCJ, 1961, Headliner of Yr. award, 1968, Golden Plate award Am. Acad. Achievement, 1969, Oustanding Oil Man award Okla. Oil Council, 1970, Henry Bennett Disting. Service award Okla. State U., 1974, Disting. Service citation U. Okla. Regents and Alumni Assn., 1966, Disting. Service award Oklahoma City U., 1980, Disting. Service award U. Kans. Sch. Engring., 1981, Bronze award for distinction in oil industry Wall St. Transcript, 1981, Cert. Distinction in Petroleum Industry Fin. World, 1982, Outstanding Layman award Okla. State Med. Assn., others; elected Okla. Hall of Fame , 1958, U. Okla. Med. Scis. Hall of Fame, 1958, U. Tulsa Coll. Engring and Phys. Scis. Hall of Fame, 1976, U. Okla. Acad. Fellows, 1970. Fellow AAAS, Okla. Acad. Scis.; mem. Oklahoma City Geol. Soc. (hon. life), Nat. Petroleum Council, Am. Assn. Petroleum Geologists (hon. life mem., Pub. Service award 1974, Sidney Powers award 1975, Human Needs award 1984), Am. Petroleum Inst. (hon. life, bd. dirs. exec. com., Gold medal for Disting. Achievement 1981), Am. Inst. Profl. Geologists, Ind. Petroleum Assn. (bd.dirs.), NSPE, Okla. Soc. Profl. Engrs., Am. Mining Congress, Tex. Mid-Continent Oil and Gas Assn. (bd. dirs., Disitng. Service award 1975), Mid-Continent Oil & Gas Assn. (exec. com.), AIA (hon. life), Soc. Econ. Paleontologists and Mineralogists, U. Okla. Assocs. (founding chmn. 1979), Okla. Heritage Assn., Oklahoma City C. of C. (bd. dirs.), Okla.. Hist. Soc. (life), AIME (hon.), Okla. Bus. Edn. Assn. (adv. bd. to exec. bd.), Newcomen Soc. N.Am. (award 1970), Sigma Xi, Pi Epsilon Tau, Acacia, Tau Beta Pi, Delta Sigma Pi, Theta Tau, Beta Gamma Sigma (hon.), Sachem. Democrat. Presbyterian. Clubs: Oklahoma City Golf and Country, Oklahoma City Press, Oklahoma City Petroleum; Men's Dinner; Sirloin (bd. dirs.); Beacon; Touchdown; All-Am. Wildcatters. Lodges: Masons, Shriners, Jesters. Home: Oklahoma City Okla. Died Sept. 15, 1989; buried Okla. City.

MC GEE, GALE, business executive, ambassador, United States senator; b. Lincoln, Nebr., Mar. 17, 1915; s. Garton W. and Frances (McCoy) McG.; m. Loraine Baker, June 11, 1939; children: David, Robert, Mary Gale, Lori Ann. A.B., Nebr. State Tchrs. Coll., 1936; M.A., U. Colo., 1939; Ph.D., U. Chgo., 1947; LL.D., U. Wyo., 1965, Eastern Ky. U., 1967, Am. U., 1967, Allegheny Coll., 1969; L.H.D., Seton Hall U., 1969. Tchr. high sch., 1936-40; instr. history Nebr. Wesleyan U., Iowa State Coll., U. Notre Dame, U. Chgo., 1940-46; prof. history, dir. Inst. Internat. Affairs U. Wyo., 1946-58; legis. asst. Sen. Joseph O'Mahoney, 1955-56; mem. U.S. Senate from Wyo., 1958-77, chmn. Western Hemisphere affairs of senate fgn. relations com., chmn. subcom. on agr., environ. and consumer protection of senate appropriations com.; amb. to OAS, 1977-81; ptnr. Moss, McGee, Bradley, Kelly & Foley, from 1977; pres. McGee Assocs. Inc., 1981-92; mem. U.S. del. 27th Gen. Assembly UN, 1972; pres. Am. League for Exports and Security Assistance, 1986-87; profl. lectr. fgn. policy, from 1947, Internat. Knife and Fork lectr.; sr. cons. Hill & Knowlton, Inc., from 1987. Author: The Responsibilities of World Power, 1968. Wyo. dir. Crusade for Freedom; N.W. dir. Theodore Roosevelt Centennial Observance; dir. tour to Russia, 1956; pres. Am. League for Export and Security Assistance, 1986-87; study of Soviet intentions Council Fgn. Relations, N.Y.C., 1952-53; mem. Sec. State Indochinese Refugee Panel, 1985-86. Mem. AAUP, Am., Miss. Valley hist. assns., Theodore Roosevelt Assn., Izaak Walton League, Wyo. Edn. Assn. Club: Eagles. Home: Bethesda Md. Died Apr. 9, 1992; interred Oakhill Cemetery, Washington.

MCGILLICUDDY, LILLIAN GRACE, political organization official; b. Chgo., May 12, 1893; d. Gustave and Louise (Peters) Flumey; m. Shelby Martin Boorhem, Apr. 5, 1916; children: Shelby Martin (dec.), William; m. Frank McGillicuddy, Jan. 22, 1938. Degree in household arts and home econs., Chgo. Tchrs. Coll., 1912. Tchr. Chgo. pub. schs., 1912-16; chmn. Hot Spring County (Ark.) Rep. Com., 1952-56; vice chmn. Ark. Rep. Cen. Com., 1942-64; co-chmn. for Ark. Eisenhower Presdl. Campaigns, 1952; mem. Rep. Nat. Com. for Ark., from 1964; del. Rep. Nat. Conv., 1940, 44, 48, 52. Author column W R Campaigner, 1963-64; contbr. to Ark. Outlook, from 1965. Chmn. Hot Springs County chpt. ARC, 1942-48; pres. Little Rock Rep. Women's Club, 1964-65, Pulaski County Rep. Women's Club, 1958-60; active Ark. Art Ctr, from 1960. Mem. Nat. Soc. Arts and Letters (pres. Little Rock chpt. 1964-66), Nat. League Am. Pen Women, Fine Arts Club, Order Eastern Star. *

MCGOLDRICK, JAMES B., priest, dean; b. County Sligo, Ireland, Aug. 15, 1895; naturalized, 1930; s. Anthony and Catherine (McNulty) M. Student, Mungret Coll., Ireland, 1914-18, St. Stanislaus Coll., King's County, Ireland; Jesuit Novitiate, Ireland, 1918-20; student, U. Santa Clara, 1920-21; AB, Gonzaga U., 1923, AM, 1924; STD, Gregorian U., Rome, 1931; PhD, U. Wash., 1935, Weston Coll. Joined Soc. of Jesus, 1930; ordained priest, Roman Cath. Ch.; cert. psychologist. Lectr., tchr. Greek, Roman history, English, Latin, edn. Gonzaga U., 1924-26, head dept. edn., 1926-27; dean Seattle Coll., 1933-43; dean dept. psychology Seattle U., from 1944; mem. examining bd. psychologists State of Wash.; mem. Gov.'s Com. on Nature and Use of Alcohol, Wash., 1954-55. Author: (with John R. Cavanagh) Fundamental Psychiatry, 1953. Mem. APA, Nat. Cath. Edn. Assn. (chmn. western unit 1942-43), Nat. Wash. Edn. Assn., Wash. Psychol. Assn. Am. Cath. Psychol. Assn., Puget Sound Psychol. Assn., Phi Delta Kappa. *

MC GOWAN, WILLIAM GEORGE, telecommunications company executive; b. Ashley, Pa., 1927; married. BA, King's Coll., 1952; MBA, Harvard U., 1954. Bus. cons., 1954-68; with MCI Comm. Corp., Washington, 1968-92, founder, chmn., 1968-92. Home: Washington D.C. Died June 8, 1992. †

MCGRATH, FRANK JOSEPH, rubber manufacturing company executive; b. Phila., Dec. 23, 1900; s. John J. and Ann Marie McNamara McG.; m. Frances Mildred O'Donnell, June 19, 1929; 1 child, F. Gerard. Student, U. Pa., 1928. Cost clk. Baldwin Locomotive Works, Eddystone, Pa., 1917-20; br. office mgr. Warner Bros. Pictures, Phila., 1920-23; pub. acct. Price Waterhouse & Co., Phila., 1928-40; with U.S. Rubber Co., N.Y.C., 1940-66, asst. treas., 1942-55, treas. charge accounts and fin., 1956-66, fin. v.p., 1961-66. Mem. Pa. Soc. of N.Y., Philepatrian Lit. Inst. Phila., Contrs. Inst. Am., N.A.M., Town Club Scarsdale, N.Y. , Scarsdale Golf Club Hartsdale, N.Y. . Home: Scarsdale N.Y. Died June 6, 1989.

MCGRATH, THOMAS AUGUSTINE, priest, psychologist, educator; b. Quincy, Mass., May 4, 1919; s. Thomas Martin and Anna (Cronin) McG.; BA, Boston Coll., 1943, MA, 1944; MA, Cath. U. Am., 1948; Ph.D., Fordham U., 1960. Lic. psychologist, Conn. Joined Soc. of Jesus, 1937; ordained priest Roman Cath. Ch., 1950; dir. psychol. services Fairfield (Conn.) U., 1957-68, chmn. dept., 1962-70, 73-76; prof. psychology, 1969-1989; cons. to industry. Mem. Am. Psychol. Assn., Am. Mgmt. Assn. Died May 31, 1992. Home: Fairfield Conn.

MCGRATH, WILLIAM LOUGHNEY, business executive, research engineer, inventor; b. Duluth, Minn., Feb. 17, 1911; s. Augustus Henry and Anna (Barrington) McG.; m. Elizabeth Grobe, Sept. 17, 1934; children: Patricia (Mrs. Charles V. O'Connor), Nancy, Kathleen (Mrs. James F. Kelly), William Loughney. BS in Archtl. Engring, U. Minn., 1932. Registered profl. engr., N.Y. Assistant manager air conditioning control div. Honeywell, Inc., Minneapolis, 1934-39; air conditioning controls manager Honeywell, Inc., Phila., 1934-43; with Carrier Corp., Syracuse, N.Y., from 1943; executive vice president Carrier Air Conditioning Co. subsidiary, 1970-72; exec. asst. to chmn. Carrier Corp., 1970-72, from 1975; president Caricor Ltd., London, Eng., 1972-74; vice chairman building research advisory board Nat. Acad. Scis.-Acad. Engring.-NRC, 1968-71; chairman Fed. Constrn. Agy., NRC, 1969-71; vice president Am. Nat. Standards Inst., 1967-68. Contbr. numerous articles to tech. jours. U.S., fgn.; holder over 250 patents related to heating and air-conditioning field. Past chmn. Collier County (Fla.) Planning Commn.; mem. Internat. Exec. Svc. Corps., served in Brazil and Taiwan. Named Modern Pioneer N.A.M., 1965, numerous other awards. Fellow ASHRAE (nat. pres. 1966-67), Inst. Heating and Ventilating Engrs. (U.K.), Chartered Inst. Bldg. Services (U.K.); mem. ASME, ASTM, Tau Beta Pi, Alpha Delta Phi. Roman

Catholic. Clubs: Naples Country. Home: Naples Fla. Died Feb. 9, 1988; buried Naples (Fla.) Meml. Gardens.

MCGRATH, WILLIAM LYNN, company executive; b. Cin., May 1, 1894; s. John Edward and Margaret (Miller) McG.; m. Elsie G. Rademacher, June 1, 1918; children: Mary Margaret (Mrs. J. H. Linnenberg), Betty Mary (Mrs. Robert S. Brown), Robert Lynn, Carol Ann (Mrs. B. D. Tucker). With Williamson Co., Cin., from 1920, pres., from 1943, chmn. bd. dirs., 1959-64; bd. dirs. Cin. Gas & Electric Co., Fifth Third Union Trust Co., Cambridge Tile Mfg. Co., The Cin. Enquirer, Am. Tool Works; mem. adv. coun. McCormick & Co., Balt. Lectr., author articles on problems of sci. mgmt. and internat. treaties. Mem. governing body ILO; mem. U.S. Employer delegation to 1949-52 Confs.; U.S. Employer del. 1954, 55, confs. ILO (UN affiliate), Geneva; chmn. Found. for Study Treaty Law, Washington. Recipient Guidepost award, 1957. Mem. Cin C. of C. (past pres.), Soc. Advancement Mgmt. (past pres., nat. bd. dirs.), Nat. Warm Air Heating and Air Conditioning Assn. (past pres. Cleve.), Cin. Indsl. Assn. (past pres.), Comml. Club, Optimists, Queen City Club. *

MC GREGOR, MALCOLM FRANCIS, classics educator; b. London, Eng., May 19, 1910; s. Walter Malcolm and Alice Mary (Francklin) McG.; m. Marguerite Blanche Guinn, June 8, 1938 (dec. 1989); children: Heather Mary, Malcolm Rob Roy. B.A., U. B.C., 1930, M.A., 1931; postgrad., U. Mich., 1931-33; Ph.D., U. Cin., 1937; D.C.L., Bishop's U., 1970; D.Litt., Acadia U., 1971, Meml. U., 1982; LL.D., U. B.C., 1983. From teaching fellow to prof. classics and ancient history U. Cin., 1933-54; acting dean Grad. Sch. Arts and Scis., 1941-42; mem. Inst. Advanced Study, Princeton U., 1937-38, 48; vis. prof. classics U. B.C., 1952, prof. classics, 1954-77, prof. emeritus, 1977-89, head dept., 1954-75, asst. to dean faculty arts and sci., 1957-64, mem. univ. senate, 1963-66, 69-77, dir. residences, 1966-68, dir. ceremonies, 1968-77, master tchr., 1974; vis. prof. ancient history U. Wash., 1953, 76, 77; vis. prof. Oxford and Cambridge univs., Am. Sch. Classical Studies, Athens, 1961, 67-68, U. Cin., 1966, Ohio State U., 1975, Gettysburg Coll., 1976, 79, Simon Fraser U., 1978, SUNY-Albany, 1982; sr. fellow Can. Council, 1967-68; mgmt. com. Am. Sch. Classical Studies, Athens; Mary White lectr. U. Toronto, 1983; instr. Vancouver Community Coll., 1977-88; hon. prof. humanities U. Calgary, Alta. Author: (with B.D. Meritt, H.T. Wade-Gery) The Athenian Tribute Lists, 4 vols., 1929-53, (with D.W. Bradeen) Studies in Fifth Century Attic Epigraphy, 1973; Editor: (with D.W. Bradeen) Phoros: Tribute to Benjamin Dean Meritt, 1974, The Athenians and Their Empire, 1987; Contbr. articles to profl. publs. Dir. centennial com. B.C., 1955-60. John Simon Guggenheim Meml. fellow, 1948; decorated comdr. Order of Phoenix Greece; Queen's Jubilee medal, 1977. Fellow Royal Soc. Can.; mem. Am. Philol. Assn. (Merit award 1954, v.p. 1968-69, pres. 1969-70), Archaeol. Inst. Am., Hellenic Soc. Gt. Britain, Classical Assn. Can. (pres. 1968-70), Classical Assn. Pacific N.W. (pres. 1972-73), Ohio Classical Conf. (sec.-treas. 1949-54), B.C. Mainland Cricket League (sec. 1954-61, v.p. from 1968), B.C. Cricket Assn. (sec. 1961-67, v.p. from 1969), Assn. Cricket Umpires, Canadian Field Hockey Assn. (pres. 1969-71). Club: Literary (Cin.). Home: Vancouver Can. Died Nov. 15, 1989.

MC GUIRE, WILLIAM LAWRENCE, lawyer, sporting goods executive; b. Bklyn., May 24, 1926; s. William Lawrence and Catherine Elizabeth (Ellis) McG.; m. Gloria E. Corse, Sept. 10, 1949; children—William Lawrence, Brian James, Sharon, Mark, Susan. AB, Fordham U., 1950; JD cum laude, St. John's U., 1954. Bar: N.Y. 1954, U.S. Supreme Ct. 1954. Terminal renting agt. Port of N.Y. Authority, 1950-54; ptnr. firm Rogers, Hoge & Hills, 1954-65; ptnr. Graham, McGuire & Campaign, 1965-73; v.p., exec. counsel, sec. The Garcia Corp., Teaneck, N.J., 1973-78; pres., chief exec. officer The Garcia Corp., 1978-79; ptnr. firm Graham Campaign & McCarthy, P.C., N.Y.C., from 1980; lectr. trade regulation Seton Hall U., 1972-89. Trustee Village of Asharoken, N.Y., 1964, village justice, 1964-68; chmn. Huntington (N.Y.) Zoning Bd. Appeals, 1968-71. Served with USCGR, 1943-46, PTO. Mem. N.Y. State Bar Assn., Assn. of Bar of City of N.Y., N.Y. State Magistrates Assn. Democrat. Roman Catholic. Home: Northport N.Y. Died Oct. 3, 1992. †

MCHUGH, GLENN, business executive, lawyer; b. Baraboo, Wis., May 15, 1894; s. Michael LaValle and Amelia Hannah (Elier) McH.; m. Alice Arnold Peek, Sept. 6, 1928; children: Burton Peek, Kathleen. AB, U. Wis., 1916; student, Leland Stanford, 1919-20; LLB, Columbia U., 1921. Bar: N.Y. 1921, U.S. Supreme Ct. 1926. In legis. drafting rsch. bur. Columbia U., N.Y., 1920-21; asst. counsel, office of legis. counsel U.S. Senate, Washington, 1921-26; spl. asst. agrl. adjustment adminstrn. Export-Import Bank, 1933-34; office of spl. adviser to pres. on fgn. trade, 1933-34; with Equitable Life Assurance Soc. of U.S., N.Y., 1926-92, 2d v.p., 1936, v.p., 1944-60; ret., 1960, investment counsel real estate matters, 1960-92. Mem. Real Estate Task Force, Hoover Commn. on Reorgn. Exec. Br. of Govt., Indsl. Coun., Urban Land Inst., Phi Delta Phi, Union League Club, Pinnace Club (N.Y.C.), Siwanoy Golf Club (Bronxville, N.Y.0, Royal and Ancient (St. Andrews, Scotland), Mid-Ocean Club (Bermuda). Republican. Mason (32). *

MCINTYRE, JAMES CHARLES, life insurance company executive; b. St. Louis, June 5, 1922; s. James Francis and Ida Mae (Colestock) McI.; m. June Margaret Trider, Oct. 30, 1943; children: Pamela Ann, Sandra Lee (Mrs. Richard John Foshage), Janice Marie (Mrs. Gregory Hale Godfrey). B.S. in Math., St. Louis U., 1943. With Gen. Am. Life Ins. Co., St. Louis, 1946-87; 2d v.p. Gen. Am. Life Ins. Co., 1966-74, actuary, 1972-87, v.p., 1974-79, exec. v.p.-individual, 1979-87. Served to 2d lt. USAAF, 1943-46. Fellow Soc. Actuaries; mem. Am. Acad. Actuaries (charter), St. Louis Actuaries Club (sec.-treas. 1958-59, chmn. 1961). Home: Saint Louis Mo. Deceased. †

MCKAIG, DIANNE L., lawyer, soft drink company executive; b. Massillon, Ohio, Nov. 17, 1930; d. Sherman J. and Kathryn (Shaidnagle) McK. B.A., U. Ky., 1952, J.D., 1954; LL.M., Harvard U., 1955. Bar: Ky. 1954, Mass. 1956, D.C. 1984. Law clk. Ky. Ct. Appeals, Frankfort, 1954; mem. firm Palmer, Dodge, Gardner & Bradford, Boston, 1955-56; individual practice law Boston, 1956-58; atty. adviser Dept. Labor, Washington, 1958-62; regional dir. Office of Solicitor, Dept. Labor (Women's Bur.), Atlanta, 1963-66; chief div. legis. and standards Office of Solicitor, Dept. Labor (Women's Bur.), Washington, 1966-68; dir. Office Consumer Services, 1968-69; spl. asst. for consumer interests to sec. HEW, Washington, 1968; exec. dir. Mich. Consumers Council, 1969-72; asst. v.p. consumer affairs Coca-Cola Co., Atlanta, 1972-74; v.p. Coca-Cola Co., 1976-83; with Jones and McKaig, Washington; v.p. Coca-Cola U.S.A., 1974-76; dir. Fleet Fin. Group; mem. Maj. Appliance Consumer Action Panel, 1970-72; spl. lectr. Coll. Indsl. Mgmt., Ga. Inst. Tech., 1974; vis. com. U. Ky. Law Sch., 1981-84. Assoc. editor: Ky. Law Jour, 1953. Bd. dirs. Nat. Council Family Fin. Edn., 1970-72, Nat. Council Better Bus. Burs., 1971-72, Girl Scouts U.S., 1982-87, Met. Atlanta chpt. ARC, 1982-83; chmn. pub. affairs com. Food Safety Council, 1977; trustee Pace Acad., Atlanta, 1981-83; bd. govs. ARC, from 1985. Mem. Ky. Fed., Mass., D.C. bar assns., Soc. Consumer Affairs Profls. (dir. 1973-77, pres. 1975-76), Soc. Consumer Affairs Profls. Found. (chmn. 1984-85), U.S. C. of C. (consumer affairs com.), U. Ky. Alumni Assn. (pres. Washington 1962), Bus. and Profl. Women's Clubs, Order of Coif, Mortar Bd., Alpha Delta Pi (chpt. outstanding alumna 1965), Eta Sigma Phi, Phi Beta. Home: Arlington Va. Deceased.

MC KAY, CHARLES ALAN, manufacturing company executive; b. Timmonsville, S.C., Oct. 1, 1931; s. James Fairley and Stella Mae (Jones) McK.; m. Shirley Ann Robbins; children: Charles Alan, Sherrill Lynn, Sandra Kay, Sheila Gayle. B.S., UCLA, 1965; M.B.A., Boston U., 1974. Registered profl. engr., Mass. With Foxboro Co., 1956-85; dir. corp. devel. and engring., then v.p. Foxboro Co., Foxboro, Mass., 1966-74; exec. v.p. Foxboro Co., 1978-85, dir., from 1981; pres. McKay Assocs. Co., from 1985; bd. dirs. Mass. High Tech. Council, 1980-85, Inst. Guilfoyle, Intermetrics Inc. Trustee Gordon Coll., Wenham, Mass., 1981-85. Served with USN, 1949-55. Mem. Sci. Apparatus Makers Assn. (dir., chmn. standards com. 1979-85), Instrument Soc. Am. (chmn. president's industry adv. com. 1981), Am. Nat. Standards Inst. (internat. standards council 1980-82). Home: Aguila Ariz. Deceased. †

MC KAY, ROBERT BUDGE, law educator, dean; b. Wichita, Kans., Aug. 11, 1919; s. John Budge and Ruth Irene (Gelsthorpe) McK.; m. Sara Kate Warmack, Nov. 20, 1954 (dec. Oct. 1986); children: Kathryn Lee, Sara Margaret. BS, U. Kans., 1940; JD, Yale U., 1947; LLD (hon.), Emory U., 1973, Seton Hall U., 1975, U. Tulsa, 1981, John Jay Coll. Criminal Justice, 1983, Pace U., 1981, U. San Diego, 1982, N.Y. Law Sch., 1985, Villanova U., 1989; LHD (hon.), Mt. St. Mary Coll., 1973. Bar: Kans. 1948, D.C. 1948, U.S. Supreme Ct. 1953, N.Y. 1973. With Dept. Justice, 1947-50; asst., then assoc. prof. law Emory U., 1950-53; prof. law NYU, 1953-75, dean, 1967-75; dir. program on justice, soc. and the individual Aspen (Colo.) Inst. Humanistic Studies, 1075-80, sr. fellow, 1980-90; mem. exec. com. Assn. Am. Law Schs., 1964-65; mem. exec. com. Lawyers Com. for Civil Rights Under Law; chmn. N.Y. State Spl. Commn. on Attica (known as Mc Kay Commn.), 1971-72, N.Y.C. Bd. Correction, 1973-74; bd. dirs. Loews Corp. Author: Reapportionment: The Law and Politics of Equal Representation, 1965; editor: Annual Survey of American Law, 1953-56, An American Constitutional Law Reader, 1958, Time-Life Family Legal Guide, 1971. Chmn. bd. dirs. Citizens Union, 1971-77; pres. Legal Aid Soc. of N.Y.C., 1975-77; vice-chmn. Nat. News Coun., 1973-80; dir., bd. dirs. Inst. Jud. Adminstrn., 1980-83; bd. dirs. Am. Arbitration Assn., Mexican-Am. Legal Def. Fund, Revson Found., Vera Inst. of Justice; former chmn. bd. N.Y. Civil Liberties Union. Recipient award Am. Friends Hebrew U., 1972, William Nelson Cromwell medal New York County Lawyers Assn., 1973, Disting. Svc. medal U. Kans., 1983, Servant of Justice award Legal Aid Soc. N.Y.C., 1990, Whitney North Seymour award Fed. Bar Coun., 1990. Mem. ABA (chmn. commn. on correctional facilities and svcs. 1974-78, sect. legal edn. and admissions to bar 1983-84, action commn. to improve tort liability system 1985-86, bd. govs. 1986-89, ho. of dels. 1985-90), N.Y. State Bar Assn. (Gold Medal award 1987), Assn. of Bar of City of N.Y. (chmn. exec. com. 1975-76, v.p. 1976-77, pres. 1984-86, chmn. coun. criminal justice 1982-84), Am. Judicare Soc. (v.p. 1980-85, Justice award 1986), Delta Upsilon. Presbyterian. Home: New York N.Y. Died July 13, 1990.

MCKEE, EDWIN DINWIDDIE, geologist; b. Washington, Sept. 24, 1906; s. Edwin Jones and Ethel (Swope) McK.; m. Barbara Hastings, Dec. 31, 1929; children: William Dinwiddie, Barbara McKee Lajoie, Edwin Hastings. Student, U.S. Naval Acad., 1924-27; AB, Cornell U., 1929; postgrad., U. Ariz., 1930-31, U. Calif., Berkeley, 1933-34, Yale U., 1939-40; ScD (hon.), No. Ariz. U., 1957. Park naturalist Grand Canyon Nat. Park, 1929-40; asst. dir. charge rsch. Mus. No. Ariz., 1941-42, 42-53; mem. faculty U. Ariz., 1942-53, prof. geology, 1950-53, chmn. dept., 1951-53; chief paleotectonic map sect. U.S. Geol. Survey, Denver, 1953-61, rsch. geologist, 1962-84; dir. expdn. Pacific Sci. Bd., Kapingamaringa Atoll, 1954; rsch. investigator in field; vis. prof., participant numerous symposia, 1931-84; instr. astronaut tng. in stratigraphy for moon trip, 1965-66; mem. U.S. Nat. Com. on Geology, 1968-72; vis. lectr. NRC of Brazil, 1970, USSR Acad. Scis., 1970; prin. investigator desert sand seas of world Earth Resources Tech. Satellite, 1972-73; discipline expert (deserts) sci. support team Skylab IV, 1973-74; leader expdn. to Namib Desert, 1977; geologist Nepal Inst. Ecotechnics, Kathmandu; cons. Rsch. Inst., U. Petroleum and Minerals, Dhahran, Saudi Arabia, 1978-79; demonstrator dune structure investigation Soc. Brazileiro Geologia. Author books, monographs, articles in field. Commr., Bow Mar, Colo., 1962-63; trustee Mus. No. Ariz., 1953-84; bd. dirs. S.W. Parks and Monuments Assn., 1985-84. Recipient Disting. Svc. award Dept. Interior, 1962, Cert. of Achievement Cornell U., 1982, John Wesley Powell Centennial Guidebook of Four Corners Geol. Soc. dedicated to him, 1969; Symposium on Eolian Sediments and Processess, 11th Internat. Congress on Sedimentology dedicated in his honor, 1982; nine fossil species (3 trilobites, 1 nautiloid, 2 brachiopods, 1 reptile, 1 foraminifer, 1 ammonoid) Named mckeei in his honor. Mem. AAAS (Powell lectr. 1950), Grand Canyon Natural History Assn. (exec. sec. 1937-39), Tucson Natural History Assn. (pres. 1944), Ariz. Geol. Soc. (pres. 1952-53), Geol. Soc. Am. (councilor 1953-55), Am. Commn. Stratigraphic Nomenclature (chmn. 1957), Am. Assn. Petroleum Geologists (disting. lectr. 1957), Rocky Mountain Assn. Geologists (hon.), Soc. Econ. Paleontologists and Mineralogists (hon., pres. 1967-68, Twenhofel award 1975), Sigma Xi (pres. Ariz. chpt. 1950). Home: Littleton Colo. Died July 23, 1984; buried Grand Canyon, Ariz.

MCKEE, HAROLD EARL, lawyer; b. Chgo., July 8, 1937; s. Harold Earl and Ellen Theresa (Moran) McKee; m. Suzanne Catharine Wedemeyer, Sept. 5, 1959; children: Harold E. III, Theodore P., Catharine S. Czerwien, Mary Patricia, Ellen A. AB, U. Notre Dame, 1959, BSChemE, 1960, LLB, 1963. Bar: Ill. 1963, U.S. Supreme Ct. 1967. Law clk. to presiding judge U.S. Ct. Appeals (7th circuit), Chgo., 1963-64; assoc. Mayer, Brown & Platt, Chgo., 1964-70, ptnr., 1971-92, mem. policy and plannning com., 1988-91, ptnr.-in-charge L.A. office, 1988-90. Editor Notre Dame U. Law Rev. Named to Hall of Fame Fenwick High Sch., Oak Pk., Ill. Mem. ABA, Chgo. Bar Assn., Ill. Assn. Hosp. Attys., Nat. Assn. Bond Lawyers, Chicago Club, Oak Park (Ill.) Country Club, Union League Club (Chgo.), Dairymen's Country Club (Boulder Junction, Wis.). Roman Catholic. Home: River Forest Ill. Died Mar. 12, 1992.

MCKEE, WILLIAM, economist; b. Freeport, Kans., Apr. 29, 1895; s. Benjamin Prentice and Nettie (Cooper) McK.; m. Florence C. Pollar, June 18, 1929; children: William Pollard, Robert Cooper, Thomas Benjamin. Student, Southwestern Coll., 1914-15, U. Colo., 1919; AB, Ottawa U., 1920; AM, U. Chgo., 1924. Chmn. dept. econs. and bus. adminstrn. Westminster Coll., 1924-59, chmn. div. social sci., 1945-48; lectr. edn. U. Pitts., 1963-92; tchr. Youngstown Coll. Night Sch., 1927-33; mem. bd. dirs. McDowell Nat. Bank, Sharon, Pa.; pres. bd. trustees The Econ. and Bus. Found.; dir. indsl. survey New Castle, Pa., 1939,Sharon, Pa., 1941; dir. econ. forums. Author: Economic and Business Activities in the Shenango and mahoning Valleys, 1940, Uses and Users of Bank Loans in Industrial Communities, 1941, Size, Security, Interest Rates, Maturities, Renewals, and Turnover of Bank Loans in Industrial Communities, 1941; author: (with others) A Survey of Economic Education, 1951, Workbook in Economics, 1952; editor: Lectures for Bankers and Business Executives, 1940, The What, Why, and How of American Free Enterprise, 1941, American Economic Policies. Candidate Ctrl. Machine gun O.T.S., 1918. Mem. Am. Econ. Assn., Am. Polit. Sci. Assn., Am. Sociol. Soc., Mason, Youngstown (Ohio) Club, New Castle (Pa.) Country Club, Sharon (Pa.) Country Club. *

MCKEEVER, PORTER, organization executive; b. Lenox, S.D., Nov. 8, 1915; s. George L. and Maye M. (McIlvenna) McK.; m. Susan Clark Lobenstine, Aug. 10, 1946; children: James Edwin, William Kevin, Mary Karen; 1 foster child, Cho-Liang Lin. Student, New Coll., Columbia, 1933-37; LL.D., Springfield Coll.,

1973. Washington newspaper and radio corr., 1937-42; dir. OWI, Reykjavik, Iceland, 1942-44; chief Am. Psychol. Warfare Ops., N. Burma; chief Am. psychol. warfare S.E. Asia Command Hdqrs., 1944-45; press rels. officer Dept. State, 1945-46; press officer U.S. Mission to UN, 1946-47, dir. info., 1947-52; exec. dir. Chgo. Coun. Fgn. Relations, 1952-53; nat. dir. publicity Vols. for Adlai Stevenson Campaign; dir. pub. reports Ford Found., 1953-56; dir. info. Com. for Econ. Devel., 1956-65; founding pres. UN Assn. of U.S., 1965-73; sr. assoc. to the late John D. Rockefeller 3; v.p. JDR 3d Fund, 1973-79; cons. Rockefeller Family and Assocs., 1979-83; devel. dir. Julliard Sch., 1984-85; dir. UN Devel. Corp.; bd. dirs. Columbia U. Ctr. for U.S.-China Arts Exch., Yale-China Assn.; chmn. Am. Friends of Internat. House Japan. Author: Adlai Stevenson: His Life and Legacy, 1989; assisted former Sec. State James F. Byrnes in writing book Speaking Frankly, 1946. Bd. dirs. Franklin and Eleanor Roosevelt Inst. Mem. Coun. Fgn. Rels., Asia Soc. (hon. life trustee), Japan Soc. (hon. bd. dirs.). Club: Century Assn. (N.Y.C.). Home: Pelham N.Y. Died Mar. 3, 1992.

MCKELVEY, LOUIS WILLIAM, education educator; b. Alexis, Ill., Aug. 12, 1898; s. William S. and Louise (Murphy) McK.; m. Ruth Chandler, Aug. 16, 1926; children: Louis Chandler, James Lee. AB, Knox Coll., 1920; AM, U. Ill., 1927. Tchr. high sch. Alexis, Ill., 1920-24, Philippine Islands, 1922-24; tchr. high sch. Muskegon (Mich.) High Sch., 1924-25; instr., sch. of commerce U. Ill., 1925-30; asst. prof. English sch. of commerce Northwestern U., Evanston, Ill., 1930-37, assoc. prof., 1937-48, acting chmn. bus. writing, 1949-92; emeritus prof. bus. writing, chmn. dept. 1947-57; cons. in bus. writing. Author: Business Letters (with W. K. Smart), 1933, 4th edit. (with R. C. Gerfen), 1957; contbr. articles to juvenlie fiction to mags. Fellow Am. Bus. Writing Assn.; mem. AAUP, Sigma Delta Chi, Delta Sigma Pi, Beta Theta Pi. Republican. Methodist. *

MC KENZIE, HAROLD JACKSON, transportation executive; b. Houston, Oct. 11, 1904; s. Phillip Alexander and Alice Julia (Hannon) McK.; m. Ina Jewel Gatlin, Dec. 22, 1929; children: James Garrett, Marcella Ann. B.S., Tex. A&M Coll., 1927; postgrad., Houston Engring. Coll., 1929-32, Advanced Mgmt. Course, Harvard U., 1950; LL.D., Shurtleff Coll., 1953. Engring. dept. S.P. Co., Tex., La., summer 1926; draftsman, constrn. insp., chief draftsman, asst. to chief engr., asst. chief engr., chief engr. S.P. Co., 1927-45; exec. v.p. St. Louis Southwestern Ry. Co. (Cotton Belt), 1951, pres., 1951-69; former chmn. Southwestern Transp. Co., So. Pacific Transport Co., Houston; former pres. Bravo Oil Co., Houston; v.p. So. Pacific Co., Houston; transp. and mgmt. cons., Tyler, Tex., 1969-91. Author: Keeping on the Right Track, 1985, The Little Railroad That Could...and Did, 1985, Do Something Don't Just Sit There, 1992; contbr. articles to profl. jours. Mem. numerous civic orgns. including Retina Rsch. Found., Mental Health Assn. Tyler, U. Tex. Health Ctr.; pres. Tyler Area C. of C. Recipient numerous community awards including T.B. BUtler award and Outstanding Svc. award Smith County Bar Assn., 1954, East Texan of Month award East Tex. C. of C., 1972, Patriot of Yr. award U. Tex., Tyler, 1991. Mem. ASCE, Tex. Soc. Profl. Engrs. (past v.p.), Houston C. of C. (mem. ednl. com.), Tyler C. of C. (pres.), Am. Ry. Engring. Soc., Newcomen Soc., Tau Beta Phi. Republican. Baptist. Clubs: Masons, Shriners, Tyler, Tyler Petroleum (Tyler); Engineers (Houston). Home: Tyler Tex. Died Sept. 26, 1991; buried Resthaven Cemetery, Houston.

MCKEON, NEWTON FELCH, educator, library director; b. Paterson, N.J., Dec. 21, 1904; s. Newton Felch and Edith (King) McK.; m. Mary Maury Fitzgerald, July 27, 1935; children: Maury, Edith King, Lewis Herndon, James Rhodes. Student, Emmanuel Coll., Cambridge U., Eng., 1933-34. Master Lawrenceville (N.J.) Sch., 1926-27; with various cos., 1927-31; instr. English Amherst Coll., 1931-37, asst. prof. English, 1937-41, assoc. prof., 1941-48, prof., 1948-70, prof. emeritus, 1970; asst. to dir. Amherst Coll. Libr., 1935-37, asst. dir., 1937-39, dir., 1939-70; bd. dirs. Hampshire Inter-Libr. Ctr., 1951-70, sec., 1952-53, 55-57, treas., 1958-59, 60-70. Mem. ALA (coun. 1958-62), Assn. Coll. and Rsch. Librs. (dir. 1958-62), Bibliog. Soc. Am., Chi Phi, Phi Beta Kappa. Presbyterian. Home: Conway Mass. Died June 28, 1990.

MCKIBBEN, EUGENE GEORGE, government official; b. Almyra, Ark., Dec. 17, 1895; s. Frank and Dora (Collins) McK.; m. Ethel Marie Moorhead, July 27, 1922; children: Victoria Jean (Mrs. Hamilton), Dora Frances (Mrs. Williams), Mateal Browning (Mrs. Kiley). BS, Iowa State Coll., 1922, PhD, 1936; MS, U. Calif., 1927; student, Ala. Poly. Inst., 1935. Asst. U. Calif., 1922-24, instr., 1924-27, asst. prof., 1927-28; assoc. prof. Iowa State Coll., 1928-35, 37-40, prof. agrl. engring. dept., 1940-42; assoc. prof. agrl. engring. dept. Pa. State Coll., 1930; agrl. engr. for nat. rsch. project Works Progress Adminstrn., 1936-37; prof., head dept. agrl. engring. Mich. State Coll., 1942-45; head agrl. engring dept. Pineapple Rsch. Inst., Honolulu, 1945-50; various positions including chief agrl. engring. br. USDA, Auburn, Ala., 1950-56, 57-92. Contbr. articles to profl. jours. Mem. Am. Soc. Agrl. Engrs. (Cyrus Hall McCormick medalist 1949), Soc. Automotive Engrs., Am. Soc. Engring. Edn., Soil Conservation Soc. Am., Royal Swedish Acad. Agriculture and Forestry, Sigma Xi, Alpha Zeta, Tau Beta Pi, Phi Kappa Phi, Gamma Sigma Delta. *

MC KINNEY, FRANK EDWARD, JR., banker, private investor; b. Indpls., Nov. 3, 1938; s. Frank Edward and Margaret (Warner) McK.; m. Marianne Williams, June 2, 1989; children by previous marriage: Frank Edward III, Katherine Marie, Margaret Leonard, Madeleine Warner, Robert Warner, Heather Claire. B.S., Ind. U., 1961, M.B.A., 1962; LL.D. (hon.), Butler U., Indpls., 1975. Asst. cashier First Nat. Bank, Chgo., 1964-67; with Am. Fletcher Nat. Bank, Indpls., from 1967; exec. v.p., then pres. Am. Fletcher Nat. Bank, 1970-73; chmn. bd. Am. Fletcher Nat. Bank (now Banc One Corp.), from 1973, Bank One Corp., from 1974; bd. dirs. Am. United Life Ins. Co.; bd. dirs., mem. exec. com. Indpls. Power & Light Co., IPALCO Enterprises, Inc. Bd. dirs. Indpls. Mus. Art, Exec. Council on Fgn. Diplomats; adv. council Coll. Bus., U. Notre Dame; mem. Ind. State Olympic Com. Served to 1st. lt. AUS, 1962-64. Named to Internat. Swimming Hall Fame, 1975, Ind. U. Acad. Alumni Fellows, 1973, Ind. U. Intercollegiate Athletics Hall of Fame, 1982; recipient Disting. Service award Indpls. Jaycees, 1974. Mem. Assn. Res. City Bankers, Assn. Bank Holding Cos. (dir., vice chmn., exec. com.), Am., Ind. bankers assns., Ind. Soc. Chgo., Internat. Monetary Conf., Penrod Soc., Newcomen Soc. N.Am., Indpls. C. of C., Ind. C. of C., 500 Festival Assocs., Econ. Club Indpls. (pres. 1977), Am. Legion, Sigma Alpha Epsilon. Democrat. Roman Catholic. Clubs: Meridian Hill Country, Indpls. Athletic, Skyline, Notre Dame of Indpls. (Indpls.). Home: Columbus Ohio Died Sept. 11, 1992. †

MCKINNEY, WALTER BYRES, business executive; b. McKinney, Tex., May 2, 1894; s. John S. and Lura Belle (Morrow) McK.; m. Mary V. Miller, June 14, 1922; children; Lura Anne, Mary Lee, Nancy Miller, Ruth Frances, Walter B., Joan Morrow. MD, U. Tex., 1918. Engaged in practice of medicine, 1918-24; asst. to Harvey C. Miller; pres. various steamship and terminal cos., became pres. of cos. following his death, 1936; pres., mem. bd. dirs. Keystone Warehouse Co., Buffalo, Merchants Warehouse Co., Norfolk Tidewater Terminals, Newark Tidewater Terminals, Inc., Tidewater Assocs., Inc., 1936-92, Merrimac Trading Corp., 1936-92. Mem. Soc. Nav. Architects, Phila. Med. Soc., AMA, Phila. Cricket Club, Union League (Phila.), Saturn Club (Buffalo), Algonquin Club (Boston). Republican. Episcopalian. *

MCKINNON, ALLAN BRUCE, Canadian government official; b. Canora, Sask., Can., Jan. 11, 1917; s. Peter MacDonald and Belle Stewart McK.; m. Joan Elizabeth Menzies, Oct. 2, 1947; children: Ian Bruce, Peter Menzies. Student, U. Victoria. Sch. tchr., 1965-72; trustee Greater Victoria Sch. Bd., 1968-70, chmn., 1970-72; mem., opposition def. critic Parliament, Can., 1972-88, minister nat. def. and vets. affairs, 1979-8. Served with Can. Army, ret., 1965. Decorated Mil. Cross. Mem. United Svcs. Inst., Can. Legion. Progressive Conservative. Mem. United Ch. Can. Home: Ottawa Can. Died Sept. 19, 1990.

MCKISSICK, FLOYD BIXLER, lawyer, organization executive; b. Asheville, N.C., Mar. 9, 1922; s. Ernest Boyce and Magnolia Ester (Thompson) McK.; m. Evelyn Williams, Sept. 1, 1942; children: Joycelyn D., Andree Y., Floyd Bixler. Student, Morehouse Coll., 1949, U. N.C., 1951; AB, N.C. Coll., 1951, LLB, 1952. Bar: N.C. 1952, D.C. 1966, U.S. Supreme Ct. 1966. Gen. practice law; sr. ptnr. McKissick & Burt, Durham, N.C.; lectr., pub. speaker race rels., counsel Congress Racial Equality, 1960-68, nat. chmn., 1963-66, nat. dir., 1966-68, rep. March on Washington, 1963; pres. Floyd B. McKissick Enterprises, Inc., 1968-91, The Soul City Co., 1974-91; counsel Durham Bus. Coll., Durham East End Betterment League, local 208 Tobacco Workers Internat. Union AFL-CIO; v.p. Urban & Suburban Assocs., 1962-91; developer new town Soul City, N.C., 1969; vis. prof. SUNY, Binghamton, 1970; co-chmn. Nat. Conf. Black Lawyers, 1969. Columnist N.Y. Amsterdam Newspaper, 1965; author: Three-Fifths of a Man, 1968. Chmn. Nat. Com. for a Two-Party System. Recipient Man of Yr. award Durham Bus. and Profl. Chain, Housewives League Am., 1959, 60, 61, Ike Small's Civil Rights award NAACP, 1962, Conf. award for Civil Rights AME Ch., 1964. Mem. Nat. Bar Assn., Southestern Bar Assn. (mem. bd.), N.C. Coll. Alumni Assn., Durham Bus. and Profl. Chain (mem. bd.), Am. Vets. (mem. bd.), Elks, Alpha Phi Alpha. Home: Soul City N.C. Died Apr. 2, 1991; buried Soul City, N.C.

MCKNEW, THOMAS WILLSON, association executive; b. Washington, July 6, 1896; s. Thomas Willson and Bertha Virginia (Fisher) McK.; m. Virginia Chauncey Paff, Jan. 15, 1921 (dec. Sept. 1976); m. Lenore Knight Williams, Nov. 23, 1977. D.Eng. (hon.); S.D., Sch. Mines and Tech., 1935. With George A Fuller Constrn. Co., Washington, 1915-25; v.p. James Baird Constrn. Co., 1925-31; asso. with Nat. Geog. Soc., Washington, 1931-87, asst. sec., 1932-45, sec., 1945, life trustee, 1949, v.p., sec., 1955, exec. v.p., sec., 1958-62, vice chmn. bd., 1962-66, chmn. bd., 1966-67, adv. chmn. bd., 1967-87, chmn. emeritus, 1987-90. Constrn. engr. James Baird Co., Inc., Washington, notable bldgs. include, U.S. Internal Revenue Bldg., Washington, Folger Shakespeare Library, Washington, State Office Bldg., Charleston, W.Va., Harrisburg, Pa., R.J. Reynolds Tobacco Co. Office Bldg., Winston-Salem, N.C., Corcoran Gallery of Art, Washington, 1924-31. Recipient Distinguished Pub. Service awards U.S. Navy, 1957, 78; Exceptional Service award USAF, 1965. Episcopalian. Clubs: Chevy Chase Country (Washington), Alfalfa (Washington), Metropolitan (Washington), Alibi (Washington); Bohemian (San Francisco). Home: McLean Va. Died Sept. 24, 1990; buried Mt. St. Albans Cemetery.

MC KNIGHT, ROBERT KELLOGG, anthropology educator; b. Sendai, Japan, Jan. 10, 1924; s. William Quay and Mary (Kellogg) McKnight (parents Am. citizens); m. Veronica Margaret Schwartz, Nov. 7, 1947; children: William K., Victoria McKnight Labarge. B.A. cum laude in Psychology, Miami U., Oxford, Ohio, 1951; M.A. in Social Psychology, Ohio State U., 1954, Ph.D. in Anthropology, 1960. Dist. anthropologist Trust Ter. Govt., Palau, Micronesia, 1958-63; community devel. officer Trust Ter. Govt., Saipan, Micronesia, 1963-65; assoc. prof. anthropology U. Wis.-Milw., 1965-66; prof. anthropology Calif. State U., Hayward, 1966-87; chmn. dept. Calif. State U., 1969-74, prof. emeritus, from 1987. Author: (with J. Bennett and H. Passin) In Search of Identity, 1960; contbr. profl. jours. Served with AUS, 1943-46, 51-52. Mem. Am. Anthrop. Assn., AAAS, Am. Ethnol. Soc. Home: Hayward Calif. Deceased. †

MCLAGAN, THOMAS RODGLE, industrialist; b. Westmount, Quebec, Can., Jan. 22, 1897; s. Peter William and Effie (Westgate) McL.; m. Doris Baillie, June 27, 1927; 1 child, Peter William. Student, Lower Can. Coll., Montreal, 1915; BS, McGill U., Montreal, 1923. Employment supr. Laurentide Co., Grand Mere, P.Q., Can., 1924-32; ptnr., indsl. cons. Dufresne, McLagan Assoc., 1932-39; v.p., dir. and gen. mgr. Canadian Vickers, Ltd., Montreal, 1939-48; exec. v.p., gen. mgr. Canadian Vickers, Ltd., 1948-50, pres., gen. mgr., 1950-51; pres., gen. mgr. Can. Steamship Lines, Ltd., 1951-63, pres., chmn. bd., 1963-92; mem. bd. dirs. Canadair, Ltd., Can. Liquid Air Co., Ltd., Royal Bank of Can., Hilton of Can., Ltd., Nat. Drug & Chem. Co., Ltd., Algoma Steel Corp., Ltd., The Sherwin-Williams Co. Can., Ltd., The Royal Trust Co., Found. Co. of Can., Brit. Petroleum Co. of Can., ABitibi Power & Paper Co., Ltd., Toronto, Can. and Sperry Gyroscope Co. of Can., Ltd., Can. Power & Paper Securities, Ltd. Gov. McGill U., Lower Can. Coll., past chmn. Served in Canadian Army, 1914-18. Decorated Order of Brit. Empire, 1946. Mem. Montreal Bd. of Trade, Canadian Jfrs. Assn. (past pres., past chmn. Quebec div.), Profl. Engrs. P.Q., Phi Delta Theta, St. James's U., Royal Montreal Golf Club, Laval-surie-Lac Golf Club, Canadian Club, Montreal Club, Mt. Royal Club. Presbyterian. *

MCLAUGHLIN, FRANK, public utilities executive; b. Hingham, Mass., Jan. 24, 1895; s. Patrick Henry and Mary Elizabeth (Fee) McL.; m. Jean Gilchrist, Sept. 19, 1923. Grad. high sch., Hingham, Mass. Sec., asst. to mgr. Blackstone Valley Gas & Electric Co., 1912-16; asst. to mgr. Beaumont (Tex.) Electric Co., 1916-17; asst. to dist. mgr., rate case and appraisal Southwestern Dist., Stone & Webster, Boston, 1919-20, 20-21; supt. lighting and power El Paso (Tex.) Elec. Co., 1921-24; mgr. Baton Rouge (La.) Elec. Co., 1924-25; v.p. in charge ops., pres. Va. Electric and Power Co., Richmond, Norfolk, Va., 1925-29, 30; dist. mgr. Southwestern Dist., Stone & Webster, Boston, 1929-30; operating exec. Stone & Webster Svc. Corp., 1930-31; pres., chmn. Puget Sound Power & Light Co., Seattle, 1931-59, 59-60, cons., 1960-92. Contbr. articles to profl. jours. Dir., regional v.p. Navy League of U.S., 1940-42 (Navy Day chmn. State of Wash., 1933-40); mem. Wash. com. Nat. Jewish Hosp., Greater Am., Inc.; chmn. bd. dirs. King County Sci. Fair, 1959-62; dir., v.p. Seattle Community Fund, 1933-41, campaign chmn., 1933-34; mem. adv. bd. exec. com. devel. bd. Salvation Army, Seattle; dir. Jr. Achievement of Seattle; pres. Seattle Camp Fire Girls, 1936-41; Pacific N.W. sect. Amateur Athletic Union of U.S., 1937-40. Capt. U.S. Army, 1917-19. Mem. Seattle C. of C. (v.p. 1938-39, trustee 1931-40, mem. sr. coun.), N.W. Sci. Assn. (hon. trustee), Rainier Clubs, Seattle Golf Club, Overlake Golf Club, Washington Athletic Club (v.p. 1940, bd. govs. 1939-40). *

MCLAUGHLIN, ROBERT WILLIAM, architect; b. Kalamazoo, June 24, 1900; s. Robert William and Anna (Oggel) McL.; m. Katherine Thurber, Oct. 21, 1933; children—Meredith (Mrs. Marcus P. Knowlton III), Robert. A.B., Princeton U., 1921, M.F.A., 1926; Procter traveling fellow in, Italy, France and England, 1926. Architect H. Van Buren Magonigle; assoc. Charles Over Cornelius (in archaeol. and restoration work), 1928-30; ptnr. Holden, McLaughlin and Assos., 1930-53; pvt. practice as architect, from 1953; profl. adviser N.J. State Capitol Commn., 1964; founded Am. Houses, Inc. (for mfr. of prefabricated houses), 1932, chmn. bd., until 1945; established research lab. Bedford Village, N.Y., (for study of bldg. technique), 1940; prof. architecture, dir. Sch. Architecture, Princeton U., 1952-65, prof. emeritus, 1965-89; cons. architect Bahai World

Centre, Mount Carmel, Haifa, Israel; profl. adviser Dept. of State, London embassy, Port of N.Y. Authority. Author: Architect, 1962, These Perspicuous Verses, 1981; co-author: Curtain Walls, 1955, also archtl. monographs on brick architecture of Sweden and on San Gimignano.; Editor: Architecture and the University, 1954. Served as apprentice seaman USN, 1918. Fellow AIA; mem. Nat. Inst. for Archtl. Edn. (hon.), Soc. for Am. Archaeology, Archtl. League N.Y. (hon.), Soc. Preservation Historic Landmarks. Home: Princeton N.J. Died Nov. 30, 1989.

MC LAUGHLIN, WILLIAM EARLE, banker; b. Oshawa, Ont., Can., Sept. 16, 1915; s. Frank and Frankie L. (Houlden) McL.; m. Ethel Wattie, July 20, 1940; children: William, Mary. B.A., Queen's U., Kingston, Ont., 1936. With Royal Bank of Can., 1936-80; mgr. Royal Bank of Can. (Montreal br.), 1951-53, asst. gen. mgr., 1953-59, asst. to pres., 1959-60, gen. mgr., 1960-62, pres., 1960-62, chmn., pres., 1962-77, chief exec. officer, 1977-79, chmn. bd., 1977-80; chmn. bd. Sun Alliance Ins. Co.; trustee Can. Staff Pension Plan; bd. dirs. Nabisco Brands, Ltd., Royal Bank of Can., Textron Can. Ltd., mem. bd. dirs. adv. council Met. Life Ins. Co.; mem. corp. adv. council Gen. Motors Corp. Bd. govs. Royal Victoria Hosp. Clubs: Mount Royal, Forest and Stream, St. James's, Montreal; Seigniory (Montebello); Mt. Bruno Golf; Mid-Ocean (Bermuda). Home: Montreal Can. Died Oct. 30, 1991.

MCLEAN, HELEN VINCENT, psychiatrist; b. Sandusky, Ohio, May 27, 1894; d. Clarence Augustus and Lucy Seymour (Hall) Vincent; m. Franklin Chambers McLean, June 11, 1923; 1 child, Franklin Vincent (dec.). AB, Mt. Holyoke Coll., 1915; MD, Johns Hopkins U., 1921. Resident Peking Union Med. Coll., China, 1922-23; lectr. social hygiene Social Hygiene Coun., Chgo., 1925-30; pvt. practice Chgo., 1930-92; cons. psychiatrist nursing sch. Michael Reese Hosp., Chgo., 1941-48; assoc. attending physician Cook County Hosp., Chgo., 1942-46; staff mem. Inst. for Psychoanalysis, Chgo., 1932-92; trustee Mount Holyoke Coll., 1948-52. Recipient Elizabeth Blackwell Centennial Citation, 1949. Mem. Group for the Advancement for Psychiatry, AMA, Am. Psychiat. Assn., Am. Psychoanalytic Assn., Chgo. Inst. Medicine, Phi Beta Kappa. *

MCLINTOCK, (GEORGE) GORDON, maritime service officer; b. Sunderland, Eng., Feb. 10, 1903; s. William and Beatrice Reevel (Maddison) McL.; m. Winifred Russell Kidner, Aug. 8, 1929 (dec.); 1 child, Irene (dec.); m. Muriel Thomas Bristow; stepchildren: Elinor Schillberg, Allison Bristow, John Bristow. LLD, Adelphi U., 1954. Cadet Brit. Mcht. Navy, 1918-20; q.m. U.S. Mcht. Svc., 1920; 3d officer Std. Oil Co., 1922; 2d officer, chief officer, master, 1927; s.s. insp. Port of N.Y., 1930; head exams. div. Washington, 1937; head Casualty Investigation Div., 1940; chief inspection office Bur. Tng., U.S. Maritime Commn., 1941-46; lt. comdr. to capt., commodore, 1946, rear adm., 1948; supt. U.S. Mcht. Marine Acad., Kings Point, N.Y., 1948-70; mem. exec. com. Radio Tech. Commn. for Marine Svcs.; chmn. Mcht. Marine medal awards com.; pres. Inst. of Nav., 1946-48, hon. life mem., U.S. del. Internat. Conf. on Radio Aids to Marine Nav., London, 1946, N.Y.C., New London, 1947; U.S. del. ILO Conf., Seattle, 1946, Internat. Conf. on Radio Aids to Air Nav., Montreal, Que., Can., 1946, Internat. Meeting on Loran, Geneva, Switzerland, 1949; mem. Congl. panel to evaluate U.S. Svc. Acad., 1973-75; mem. Middles State Accreditation Evaluation Team. Recipient Disting. Svc. medal Am. Legion, 1951, Legion of Honor medal Philippine Govt., 1954, comdr. Order Maritime Merit of France; U.S. Presdl. Letter Commendation, 1970; Benjamin Franklin fellow. Fellow Royal Inst. Nav.; mem. Internat. Cargo Handling Coordination Assn. (pres.), St. Andrews Scottish Soc. (Washington), Soc. Naval Architects and Marine Engrs., Master Mariners Coun. Am. (hon. life), Def. Supply Assn. U.S. (pres. N.Y. chpt. 1969-70), Army and Navy Club, Princeton Club, India Ho. Club, Whitehall Club, Lotus Club. Home: Chevy Chase Md. Died Apr. 23, 1990; buried Arlington Nat. Cemetary, Va.

MC LOUGHLIN, ELLEN VERONICA, communications executive; b. Utica, N.Y.; d. James Henry and Mary Frances (Riley) McL. Student, Utica Free Acad.; A.B., Smith Coll., 1915; postgrad., Radcliffe Coll., 1921-22; L.H.D. (hon.), Lincoln Coll., 1949. Asst. editor woman's page Country Gentleman, 1915-17; circulation promoter Crowell Pub. Co., 1922-24; asst. advt. mgr. Grolier Soc., 1924-34, advt. mgr., 1934-41, editorial dir., 1947-59, v.p., 1956-64; mng. editor Book of Knowledge, Children's Ency., 1936-42; editor Book of Knowledge Annuals, 1940-53, Book of Knowledge, 1942-60, Story of Our Time, 1947-53, L'Encyclopédie de la Jeunesse, 1948-60, Le Livre de l'Année, 1950-61, La Science Pour Tous, 1960-64; pres. Cragsmoor Free Library Assn., 1965-69. Author: (with Lucile Rathbun, Anetia McLoughlin) The Murder of Doctor Casenova, 1934; contbr. verse to mags. Roman Catholic. Home: New Hartford Conn. Died May 31, 1989.

MCMAHON, ERNEST EDWARD, educational consultant; b. Elizabeth, N.J., Aug. 30, 1910; s. Edward Charles and Edith Allene (Dunn) McM; m. Warranita Peacher, June 14, 1932; 1 child, Audrey McMahon Stahl. BSc, Rutgers U., 1930, MEd, 1932; PhD, Columbia U., 1959; LLD, Rider Coll., 1971. Asst. dir. pub. info. Rutgers U., 1930-33, acting dir., 1935, alumni sec., 1933-40, asst. to pres., 1940-41, assoc. dean univ. coll., 1946-48, dir. alumni rels., 1948-51, dean univ. coll., 1951-65; dean extension div., assoc. dir. Stonier Grad. Sch. Banking, 1951-70, dean emeritus, 1970-90; dir., prof. adult edn. Inst. Mgmt. and Labor Rels., 1959-70, 70-90; cons. in continuing and higher edn., 1970-90; mayor Metuchen, N.J., 1960-61. Author: The Emerging Evening College, 1959, New Directions for Alumni: Continuing Education for the College Graduate, 1960, Needs of People and Their Communities and the Adult Educator, 1970; co-author: Speech is Easy, Chronicles of Colonel Henry. Mem. Metuchen Bd. Edn., 1947-48. Col. U.S. Army, 1941-46. Decorated Legion of Merit, Star Italian Solidarity, 1953. Mem. S.A.R., Res. Officers Assn., Ret. Officers Assn., Assn. Univ. Evening Colls. (pres. 1966-67), Nat. Univ. Extension Assn. (pres. 1957-58), Edge Creek Boat Club (commodore 1976-77), Phi Beta Kappa, Phi Delta Kappa, Theta Chi. Home: Royal Oak Md. Died Mar. 8, 1990.

MCMAHON, HOWARD OLDFORD, physicist, chemist; b. Killam, Alta., Can., Sept. 16, 1914; came to U.S., 1941, naturalized, 1948; s. Thomas Alexander and Tryphina (Oldford) McM.; m. Edna Lucile Nelson, July 9, 1941; childrne: Thomas, Arthur, Elizabeth Jean, Lucile Nancy. BA, U. B.C., 1935, MA, 1937; PhD, MIT, 1941. Rschr. MIT, 1941-43; rschr. Arthur D. Little, Inc., Cambridge, 1943-52, sci. dir., 1952-77, v.p., 1956-60, sr. v.p., 1960-63, head R&D div., 1962-63, exec. v.p., 1963-64, pres., 1964-74; founder Helix Tech. Corp., Waltham, Mass.; also bd. dirs. Helix Tech. Corp., Waltham, 1977-90. Patentee in field. Recipient Edward Longstreth medal Franklin Inst., 1951, Frank Forrest award Am. Ceramics Soc., 1952. Fellow AAAS, Am. Acad. Arts and Scis.; mem. Am. Phys. Soc., Am. Chem. Soc., Sigma Xi. Home: Lincoln Mass. Died Aug. 5, 1990.

MCMILLAN, EDWIN MATTISON, physicist, educator; b. Redondo Beach, Calif., Sept. 18, 1907; s. Edwin Harbaugh and Anna Marie (Mattison) McM.; m. Elsie Walford Blumer, June 7, 1941; children—Ann B., David M., Stephen W. B.S., Calif. Inst. Tech., 1928, M.S., 1929; Ph.D., Princeton U., 1932; D.Sc., Rensselaer Poly. Inst., 1961, Gustavus Adolphus Coll., 1963. Nat. research fellow U. Calif. at Berkeley, 1932-34, research asso., 1934-35, instr. in physics, 1935-36, asst. prof. physics, 1936-41, asso. prof., 1941-46, prof. physics, 1946-73, emeritus, 1973-91; mem. staff Lawrence Radiation Lab., 1934-73, asso. dir., 1954-58, dir., 1958-73; on leave for def. research at Mass. Inst. Tech. Radiation Lab., U.S. Navy Radio and Sound Lab., San Diego, and Los Alamos Sci. Lab., 1940-45; mem. gen. adv. com. AEC, 1954-58; mem. commn. high energy physics Internat. Union Pure and Applied Physics, 1960-67; mem. sci. policy com. Stanford Linear Accelerator Center, 1962-66; mem. physics adv. com. Nat. Accelerator Lab., 1967-69; chmn. 13th Internat. Conf. on High Energy Physics, 1966; guest prof. CERN, Geneva, 1974. Trustee Rand Corp., 1959-69; Bd. dirs. San Francisco Palace Arts and Scis. Found., from 1968; trustee Univs. Research Assn., 1969-74. Recipient Rsch. Corp. Sci. award, 1951, (with Glenn T. Seaborg) Nobel prize in chemistry, 1951, (with Vladimir I. Veksler) Atoms for Peace award, 1963, Alumni Disting. Svc. award Calif. Inst. Tech., 1966, Centennial citation U. Calif.-Berkeley, 1968, Nat. award of Sci., Pres. U.S., 1991; Faculty Rsch. lectr. U. Calif.-Berkeley, 1955. Fellow Am. Acad. Arts and Scis., Am. Phys. Soc.; mem. NAS (chmn. class I 1968-71), Am. Philos. Soc., Sigma Xi, Tau Beta Pi. Home: El Cerrito Calif. Died Sept. 7, 1991; buried Sunset View Cemetery, Calif.

MCMILLAN, MALCOLM COOK, history and political science educator; b. Stockton, Ala., Aug. 22, 1910; s. Malcolm and Carolyn Kolb (Cook) McM.; m. Dorothy Dismukes, Apr. 6, 1939; children: Carolyn Beverly, Dorothy Suzanne. Student, Southwestern Coll., Memphis, 1928-31; AB, U. Ala., 1935, MA, 1939; PhD, U. N.C., 1949. Mem. faculty Auburn (Ala.) U., 1948-89, rsch. prof., 1954-63, head prof. history and polit. sci., 1964-89. Author: Constitutional Development in Alabama: A Study in Politics, the Negro and Sectionalism, 1798-1901, 1955, The Alabama Confederate Reader, 1963, The Land Called Alabama, 1968, The Southern States Since the Ware, 1870-71 (Robert Somers), 1965, Auburn University Through the Years, 1856-1973, 1973, Yesterday's Birmingham, 1975; mem. bd. editors Ala. Rev., 1951-53, editor, 1968-76; contbr. articles to hist. publs.; condr. weekly TV program Civil War Ala., 1960-61. Mem. Ala. Civil War Centennial Commn., 1960-65, Ala. Hist. Commn., 1968. Guggenheim fellow, 1963-64. Mem. Ala. Hist. Assn. (pres. 1966-67), So. Miss. Valley Hist. Assn., Ala. Edn. Assn. (pres. local coll. chpt.), Phi Alpha Theta, Phi Kappa Phi, Omicron Delta Kappa. Home: Opelika Ala. Died July 1, 1989.

MC MILLEN, WHEELER, author; b. nr. Ada, Ohio, Jan. 27, 1893; s. Lewis D. and Ella (Wheeler) McM.; m. Edna Doane, May 28, 1915; 1 child, Robert Doane. Student, Ohio No. U., LL.D. (hon.), 1940; D.Litt., Parsons Coll., 1953. Reporter Cin. Post, 1912; owner Covington (Ind.) Republican, 1914-18; farmer Hardin County, Ohio, 1918-22; assoc. editor Country Home (formerly Farm & Fireside), 1922-34, editor, 1934-37, editorial dir., 1937-39; editor-in-chief Farm Jour., 1939-55; v.p., dir. Farm Jour., Inc., 1955-63; dir. N.J. Bell Telephone Co., 1948-65, Bankers Nat. Life Ins. Co., 1955-71; pres., chmn. Nat. Farm Chemurgic Council, 1937-62, Am. Assn. Agrl. Editors, 1934-38. Author: The Farming Fever, 1924, The Young Collector, 1928, Too Many Farmers, 1929, New Riches from the Soil, 1946, Land of Plenty, 1961, Why the United States is Rich, 1963, Possums, Politicians and People, 1964, Bugs or People?, 1965, Fifty Useful Americans, 1965, Farmers in the United States, 1966, The Green Frontier, 1968, Weekly on the Wabash, 1969, Ohio Farmer, 1974, Feeding Multitudes: A History of What Made the United States Rich, 1981, books transl. 13 langs.; editor: Harvest: An Anthology of Farm Writing, 1964. Mem. nat. exec. bd. Boy Scouts Am., 1938-63, v.p. nat. orgn., 1959-63; chmn. N.J. Pub. Health Council, 1947-49; bd. dirs. Nat. Audubon Soc., 1948-54; mem. adv. com. Pres.'s Council on Youth Fitness, 1957-58; exec. dir. Pres.'s Commn. on Increased Indsl. Use Agrl. Products, 1956-57. Recipient Silver Buffalo, Antelope awards Boy Scouts Am.; Hon. Am. Farmer award Future Farmers Am.; citation Nat. 4-H Clubs; Louis Bromfield gold medal Malabar Farm Found., 1965; numerous Freedoms Found. awards for editorials, speeches. U.S. del. Internat. Congress Indsl. Chemistry, Milan, 1950, Presdl. award, 1984, Ohio Farm Bur. award, 1985. Mem. Phila. Soc. Promoting Agr. (pres. 1960-62). Republican. Club: Cosmos (Washington). Home: Lovettsville Va. Died Mar. 4, 1992.

MCMURTREY, JAMES EDWARD, JR., plant physiologist; b. Burkesville, Ky., June 24, 1893; s. James Edward and Nannie Susan (Alexander) McM.; m. Sue Elizabeth Defibaugh, Feb. 1, 1923 (dec.); 1 child, Eleanor Ruth; m. Beulah Beall, Feb. 23, 1946 (dec.); children: James Edward III, John Josephus; m. Charlotte Brumgart, Aug. 24, 1958. BS in Agriculture, U. Ky., 1917; postgrad., USDA; MS, U. Md., 1928, PhD, 1931. Field asst. tobacco insect investigation Bur. Entomology, USDA, 1914-16; asst. in tobacco investigation Bur. of Plant Industry, USDA, 1917-22, jr. physiologist tobacco and plant nutrition, 1922-23, asst. physiologist, 1923-28, assoc. physiologist, 1928-35, sr. physiologist, 1935-45, prin. physiologist, 1945-57, head sect., 1957-59, leader tobacco investigator, 1959-92. Author chpt. in the two books Hunger Signs in Crops, Diagnostic Techniques for Soils and Crops; author and joint author of numerous tech. and practical papers on tobacco culture. Fellow AAAS, Am. Soc. Agronomy; mem. Am. Soc. Plant Physiologists, Washington Bot Soc. (past pres.), Alpha Zeta, Sigma Xi, Mason (K.T.). *

MC NEE, ROBERT BRUCE, geographer, educator; b. Big Timber, Mont., Aug. 20, 1922; s. William Wooldridge and Nina Lucy (Gates) McN.; m. Gilberta Lyons, Sept. 20, 1949 (annulled Sept. 1954); 1 son, Robert Andrew; m. Doris Smithers, Dec. 11, 1954 (separated 1980); children—Margaret Ann, William Smithers. B.A. with high honors, Wayne U., 1949; M.A., Syracuse U., 1950, Ph.D., 1953. From lectr. to assoc. prof. City Coll. N.Y., 1952-63; prof. geography U. Cin., 1963-73, 76-87, prof. emeritus, 1987, chmn. dept., 1963-69; dir. Am. Geog. Soc., N.Y.C., 1973-76; summer tchr. St. Lawrence U., Wayne State U., So. Ill. U.; cons. Ford Found., 1962-63; pioneered in fields of econ. geography relative to multinationa. corps., the geography of the lesbian/gay community. Author: A Primer on Economic Geography, 1971, also articles in field. Mem. Assn. Am. Geographers (chmn. N.Y.-N.J. div. 1960-62, regional councilor), Am. Geog. Soc., Nat. Council Geog. Edn. Unitarian. Home: Los Angeles Calif. Died Jan. 8, 1992; cremated.

MC NEELY, E. L., manufacturing company executive; b. Pattonsburg, Mo., Oct. 5, 1918; s. Ralph H. and Viola (Vogel) McN.; m. Alice Elaine Hall, Sept. 18, 1948; children: Sandra (Mrs. Ronald Gessl), Gregory, Mark, Kevin. Student, Central Bus. Coll., Kansas City, Mo., 1935-36, U. Mo., 1936-37; A.B., No. Mo. State U., Kirksville, 1940; student, Rockhurst Coll., Kansas City, Mo., 1942. With Montgomery Ward & Co., 1940-64, divisional mdse. mgr., 1961-64; dir. marketing Wickes Corp., Saginaw, Mich., 1964-65, sr. v.p., 1965-69, pres., 1969-74, chief exec. officer, chmn., 1974-80; chmn. bd., chief exec. officer Wickes Cos., Inc., 1980-82, 83-89; chmn., chief exec. officer Oak Industries Inc.; bd. dirs. Pacific Telesis Group, Transam. Corp., Dayco Corp., Fed. Mogul Corp. Served as officer USNR, 1942-46, PTO. Mem. Beta Gamma Sigma, Alpha Phi Omega. Republican. Presbyterian. Clubs: Union League, Metropolitan (Chgo.); La Jolla Country; Fairbanks Ranch Country, Cuyamaca (San Diego); San Francisco Golf; Deepdale Golf (N.Y.). Home: La Jolla Calif. Died May 12, 1991.

MC NEESE, AYLMER GREEN, JR., banker; b. Hubbard, Tex., June 4, 1911; s. Aylmer G. and Maude (Carter) McN.; m. Catherine Elsbury, Sept. 19, 1938; children: Thomas Dwyer, Margaret Carter. BA, U. Tex., 1933, LLB, 1937. Bar: Tex. 1937. With Fulbright, Crooker & Jaworski, 1939-43; v.p., gen. counsel McCarthy Oil & Gas Corp., 1943-51; adminstrv. asst. to pres. Houston Oil Co. of Tex., 1951-53; asst. pres. Second Nat. Bank of Houston, 1953-56; pres., chief exec. officer Bank of Southwest, Houston, 1956-67; chmn. bd. Bank of Southwest, 1967-82; pres., chief exec. officer SW Bancshares, Inc. (now merged with MCORP), 1970-76, chmn. exec. com., 1976-82; cons. MCORP, from 1987. Bd. dirs. Tex. Med. Center, Inc., from 1964; bd. regents U. Tex., 1956-62, 71-76, chmn., 1973-74; trustee M.D. Anderson Found. Decorated knight's cross Order of Crown (Belgium), Order of San Martin (Argentina). Mem. State Bar Assn. Tex., Army Athletic Assn., Sons Republic Tex., SAR. Episc. Clubs: Ramada, Houston Country, Coronado, Forest, Houston, Masons, Shriners; Metropolitan (N.Y.C.); Balboa (Matzalan, Mexico). Home: Houston Tex. Deceased. †

MCNELLY, WALTER C., educator; b. Brookville, Ohio, Mar. 2, 1898; s. Andrew Jackson and Viola (Heeter) McN.; m. Freda Mae Rasor, June 17, 1926; children: Joan Marilyn (Mrs. C.E. Teckman), Nancy Jane. BS, Miami U., Oxford, Ohio, 1921; MS, Ohio State U., 1928, PhD, 1934. Tchr. math. Miamisburg (Ohio) High Sch., 1921-23; critic tchr. sci. and math. McGuffrey High Sch., Oxford, Ohio, 1923-24; instr. biology Miami U., 1925-27, asst. prof. physiology, 1928-29, assoc. prof., 1930-36, acting head dept., 1937-39, prof., head dept., 1940-59, prof., chmn. dept. zoology and physiology, 1960-92. Served as pvt., S.A.T.C., 1918. Fellow Ohio Acad. Sci., AAAS; mem. Am. Physiol. Soc., Phi Beta Kappa, Sigma Xi, Sigma Alpha Epsilon. Presbyterian. *

MC NULTY, KNEELAND, former museum curator; b. Soochow, China, Oct. 25, 1921; s. Henry Augustus and Edith Clara (Piper) McN.; m. Anne Louise Rissmann, June 3, 1946 (div. 1980); children: David Kneeland, Claudia Marshall. A.B., Princeton U., 1943; postgrad., Harvard U., 1946-47; M.L.S., Columbia U., 1952. Asst. librarian N.Y. Pub. Library, 1949-52; mem. staff Phila. Mus. Art, 1952-80, curator prints, drawings and photographs, 1964-80; rep. Christie, Manson & Woods Internat., Inc., 1980-85; disting. vis. prof. U. Tex. at Austin, spring 1978. Author: The Collected Prints of Ben Shahn, 1967, Foreigners in Japan, Yokohama and Related Woodcuts, 1972, Peter Milton/Complete Etchings 1960-76, 1977; Contbg. editor: Artist's Proof, 1963-71; editor: The Lithographs of Jean Dubuffet, 1964, Alfred Bendiner: Lithographs, 1965, Marino Marini: Graphics and Related Works, 1965, The Art of Philadelphia Medicine, 1965, Eugene Feldman: Prints, 1965, Joan Miro: Prints and Books, 1966, Mauricio Lasansky: The Nazi Drawings, 1967, Master E.S.: Five Hundreth Anniversary, 1967, Suzuki Harunobu: Two Hundreth Anniversary, 1970, The Theatrical World of Osaka Prints, 1973. Bd. govs. Print Council Am., 1960-90. Served to 1st lt. USAAF, World War II. Decorated D.F.C., Air medal (3), Purple Heart. Mem. Drawing Soc. (nat. com. 1964-80), Print Club Phila. (bd. govs. 1955-86). Home: Albuquerque N.Mex. Deceased. †

MC QUILKIN, WILLIAM WINTER, corporation executive; b. San Jose, Calif., Apr. 5, 1907; s. Harmon Hudson and Elizabeth (Rhinehart) McQ.; m. Eleanor Godwin Atterbury, Sept. 15, 1934; children: Robert Rennie, William Winters, John Atterbury, Michael Godwin. BA, Princeton U., 1928, MA, 1929; BA, Balliol Coll., Oxford U., 1931, BCL, 1932. Bar: N.Y. 1933. Atty. Rushmore, Bisbee & Stern, N.Y.C., 1932-38; sec.-treas., v.p. Bausch & Lomb, Inc., Rochester, N.Y., 1938-57; dir. Bausch & Lomb, Inc., Rochester, 1943-79, exec. v.p., 1957-59, pres., CEO, 1959-71, chmn. bd., 1969-71, chmn. exec. com., 1971-79; dir. Security N.Y. State Corp.; trustee Monroe Savs. Bank. Trustee Rochester Sch. for Deaf, David Hochstein Sch. Music, U. Rochester, Monroe Community Coll., Indsl. Mgmt. Coun. Mem. Rochester C. of C., Am. Assn. Rhodes Scholars, Country Club of Rochester, Phi Beta Kappa. Home: Rochester N.Y. Died Feb. 6, 1992.

MCRAE, HAMILTON EUGENE, JR., lawyer; b. Arkadelphia, Ark., Feb. 9, 1905; s. Hamilton Eugene and Katherine (Old) McR.; m. Adrian Hagaman, Dec. 1, 1933; children: Mary Ann McRae Sloan, Hamilton Eugene III. Student, U. Ark., 1922-24; LL.B., U. Tex., 1928. Bar: Tex. 1928. Practice in Eastland, 1928-36, Midland, from 1936; mem. firm Conner & McRae, 1928-32, McRae & McRae, 1932-36, Stubbeman, McRae & Sealy, 1936-57, Stubbeman, McRae, Sealy & Laughlin, 1957-70, Stubbeman, McRae, Sealy, Laughlin & Browder, from 1970; dir. Midland Southwest Corp.; former dir. Depco, Inc. subs. DeKalb AgResearch, Inc., Santander Oil Co., Guanipa Oil Co. Pres. Midland Bd. Edn., 1943-44; Former trustee Austin (Tex.) Presbyn. Theol. Sem., Tex. Presbyn. Found.; past bd. dirs. Mus. of S.W., Permian Basin Petroleum Mus. Library and Hall of Fame, Midland Coll. Found.; formerly mem. fin. adv. com. United Way; active Jr. League. Mem. Am., Tex., Midland bar assns., Midland C. of C., Sigma Chi, Phi Delta Phi. Democrat. Presbyn. (elder). Clubs: Petroleum (past dir.), Midland Country (past pres., dir.), Racquet, Plaza. Home: Midland Tex. Died, 1991. †

MCRAE, JOHN FINLEY, banker; b. Montgomery, Ala., June 20, 1896; s. George W. and Fannie (Wilkes) McR.; m. Lucille Thompson, Mar. 8, 1934; children; John Finley, Mary Duncan (Mrs. Plumer B. Tonsmeire), Cynthia Jean (Mrs. James Bailey). Student, Howard Coll., Birmingham. With Mchts. Nat. Bank of Mobile, Ala., 1915-92, asst. cashier, 1919-27, v.p., 1927-37, exec. v.p., 1937-41; pres. Mchts. Nat. Bank of Mobile, 1941-92, chmn. bd., 1963-92; CEO, dir. Southern Industries Corp., Gulf Mobile & Ohio R.R. Co., Ala. Power Co., Internat. Paper Co., Am. Liberty Ins. Co., Ala. Drydock & Shipbuilding Co., Mobile, United Gas Corp. *

MCROBERTS, ROBERT M., lawyer; b. Middlesboro, Ky., Aug. 7, 1895; s. John Thompson and Lula K. (Sandifer) McR.; m. Helen M. Banister, Nov. 17, 1920; children: Robert H. Joyce E., Eve B. Student, U. Cin., 1912-13; AB, Washington U., 1917, LLB, 1919. Bar: Mo. 1919. With Bryan, Cave, McPheeters & McRoberts; pres., dir. Citizens Gas Co., Hannibal, Mo.; vice chmn. Stix, Baer & Fuller Co.; dir. Am. Ins. Co., Newark, Emerson Electric Mfg. Co., James R. KEarney Corp., Nursala Shoe Co., Inc., Day-Brite Lighting Inc. Mem. ABA, Mo. Bar Assn., St. Louis Bar Assn., Order of Coif, Phi Delta Theta, Phi Delta Phi. Clubs: Noonday, Mo. Athletic, Bellerive Country (St. Louis). *

MCROY, PAUL FURGESON, broadcasting executive; b. Carbondale, Ill., June 24, 1912; s. Robert D. and Ann Elizabeth (Furgeson) McR.; m. Mary Eleanor Helm, June 12, 1937; children—Paul, Ann McRoy Meyer. B.Ed., So. Ill. U., 1934; M.Philosophy, U. Wis., 1939. Tchr., dir. audio-visual edn. Houston public schs., 1934-43; instr. U. Houston, 1940-43; owner, mgr. sta. WCIL-WCIL-FM, Carbondale, 1946-88; devel. Bonnie Brae Subdiv., Carbondale, 1964-88; builder-owner Southgate Shopping Center, Carbondale, 1964; dir. Carbondale Savs. & Loan Assn., 1947-81, pres., 1962-81; bd. dirs. Carbondale Indsl. Corp., 1967-73, pres., 1968-73. Chmn. Carbondale United Fund, 1952; bd. dirs. Holden Hosp., Carbondale, 1949-55, So. Ill. U. Alumni Found., 1959-65; mem. Carbondale Grade Sch. Bd., 1949-55; pianist men's Bible class First Methodist Ch., Carbondale, 1984-88; scoutmaster local Boy Scouts Am., 1952-53; adv. Explorer troop, 1953-54; mem. Pres.'s Council, So. Ill. U. Found. Served to lt. comdr. USNR, 1943-46. Cum Laude fellow So. Ill. U. Found., 1974; Rotary Internat. Paul Harris fellow, 1979; recipient We All Made It award Boy Scout Philmont Sky Ranch, 1954. Mem. So. Ill. U. Alumni Assn. (pres. 1958), Carbondale C. of C. (pres. 1956, Man of Year award 1973). Methodist. Clubs: Flying Scot Sailing Assn. (dist. gov. 1967), So. Ill. Golf Assn, U.S. Golf Assn, N.Am. Yachting Union, Shriners, Rotary (past pres. Carbondale, pianist 1948-88), Crab Orchard Lake Sailing (commodore 1957), Jackson Country. Home: Carbondale Ill. Died Oct. 20, 1988; buried Oakland Cemetery, Carbondale, Ill.

MCSHAIN, JOHN, contractor; b. Phila., Dec. 21, 1898; s. John and Catherine (Malloy) McS.; m. Mary Horstmann, May 28, 1927; 1 child, Pauline Mary. LLD, Georgetown U., 1943; DSc, LaSalle Coll., 1943. Pres. John McShain, Inc., builders, Pa., Del., Md. and N.J. corps., Atlantic City Transp. Co., Barclay Hotel; mem. bd. Pa. Co. for Banking & Trusts. Builder Pentagon, Jefferson Meml., reconstrn. White House and Nat. Shrine of Immaculate Conception (all Washington). Mem. bd. LaSalle Coll., Rosemont Coll., Misericordia Hosp., Beneficial Saving Fund; mem. adv. bd. Villanova Coll. Decorated Knight Comdr. of St. Gregory the Great, 1950, Papal Chamberlain, 1951. Home: Killarney Ireland Died Sept. 9, 1989.

MCSHANE, EDWARD JAMES, mathematics educator; b. New Orleans, May 10, 1904; s. Augustus and Harriet Kenner (Butler) McS.; m. Virginia Haun, Sept. 10, 1931; children: Neill (dec.), Jennifer McShane Ward, Virginia McShane Warfield. BE, BS, Tulane U., 1925, MS, 1927, ScD (hon.), 1947; PhD, U. Chgo., 1930. Asst. prof. math. U. Wichita, Kans., 1928-29; instr. Princeton (N.J.) U., 1933-34, asst. prof., 1934-35; prof. U. Va., Charlottesville, 1935-57, Alumni prof., 1957-74, Alumni prof. emeritus, 1974-89; mathematician Ballistic Rsch. Lab., Aberdeen Groving Ground, Md., 1942-45. Author: Integration, 1944, Exterior Ballistics, 1953, Stochastic Calculus and Stochastic Models, 1974, (with J.L. Kelley and F.V. Reno) Order-Preserving Maps and Integration Processes, 1954, (with T.A. Botts) Real Analysis, 1959; also articles. Fellow NRC, 1930-32, U. Göttingen, 1932-33. Mem. NAS, Am. Math. Soc., Math. Assn. Am., Am. Philos. Soc. Home: Charlottesville Va. Died June 1, 1989; buried Charlottesville, Va.

MCSHEA, JOSEPH, bishop; b. Lattimer, Pa., Feb. 22, 1907; s. Roger Aloysius and Jeanette (Beach) McS. Student, St. Charles Sem., 1923-26; Ph.D., Pontifical Roman Sem., 1928, S.T.D., 1932. Ordained priest Roman Cath. Ch., 1931; prof. St. Charles Sem., Overbrook, Phila., 1932-35; ofcl. Sacred Congregation for Oriental Chs., Vatican City, 1935-38; sec. Apostolic Delegation, Washington, 1938-52; apptd. auxiliary bishop of Phila., 1952; 1st bishop Allentown Diocese, 1961-83. Home: Allentown Pa. Died Nov. 28, 1991.

MCSWAIN, ELDRIDGE TRACY, educator; b. Old Town, S.C., Oct. 3, 1898; s. William A. and Carrie Lee McS.; m. Mary Caughman, Aug. 29, 1922; 1 child, Rachel Ann. AB, Newberry Coll., 1919; AM, Columbia, 1928, EdD, 1935. Pub. sch. adminstr. Conway, S.C., Spencer, N.C., Greensboro, N.C., 1919-33; asst. instr. Columbia Tchrs. Coll., 1933-35; mem. faculty Northwestern, 1935-65, summer 1945-48, dean univ. coll., 1948-51, dean sch. edn., 1951-63, prof. edn., 1963-65; vis. prof. U. N.C., Greensboro, from 1965. Author: (with Harold G. Shane) Evaluation and The Elementary Curriculum, 1951. (with Ralph Cooke) Understanding and Teaching Arithametic, 1958; contbr. chpts. ednl. yearbooks, articles to profl. jours. Mem. edn. com. NAt. Conf. Christians and Jews. Mem. NEA, AAUP, Am. Childhood Assn., Am. Assn. Sch. Adminstrs., Elem. Prins. Assn., Am. Assn. Colls. of Tchr. Edn., Phi Delta Kappa. *

MC SWAIN, WILLIAM ADNEY, lawyer; b. Winston Salem, N.C., June 7, 1904; s. William A. and Caroline Thompson (Lee) McS.; m. Marian Hartig, Oct. 4, 1941; children—Barbara Ann, Marian, Jane, Nan, Betty Lee. B.S., U. S.C., 1925; LL.B., George Washington U., 1927. Bar: D.C. 1927, Ill., 1931. With Eckhart, McSwain, Silliman & Sears, and predecessors, Chgo., 1931-88; dir. De Soto Securities Co. Life trustee Art Inst. Chgo. Mem. ABA, Ill. Bar Assn., Chgo. Bar Assn. (pres. 1966), 7th Fed. Circuit Ct. Bar Assn. (pres. 1965). Presbyterian. Clubs: Union League (Chgo.); Glenview (Ill.). Home: Winnetka Ill. Died Apr. 8, 1989; buried Winnetka Congl. Churchyard.

MCVITTIE, GEORGE CUNLIFFE, educator, astronomer; b. Izmir, Turkey, June 5, 1904; s. Francis Skinner and Emily Caroline (Weber) McV.; m. Mildred Bond Strong, Sept. 3, 1934. MA, U. Edinburgh, Scotland, 1927; PhD, U. Cambridge, Eng., 1930. Asst. lectr. math. Leeds (Eng.) U., 1930-33; lectr. Edinburgh U., 1933-34, Liverpool (Eng.) U., 1934-36; reader math. Kings Coll., U. London, 1936-48; prof. math. Queen Mary Coll., 1948-52; prof. astronomy U. Ill., Urbana, 1952-72, head dept., 1952-70; hon. prof. theoretical astronomy U. Kent, Eng., 1972; vis. prof. U. Kent, 1971; mem. Meteorol. Office of Air Ministry and Fgn. Office, 1939-45; mem. Brit. Meteorol. Rsch. Com., 1948-52. Author: Cosmological Theory, 1937, Fact and Theory in Cosmology, 1961, General Relativity and Cosmology, 1965; editor: Problems of Extra-galactic Research, 1962; join editor Obs., 1938-48, Quar. Jour. Mechanics and Applied Math., 1948-52. Decorated officer Order Brit. Empire, 1946. Fellow Royal Soc. Edinburgh, Royal Astron. Soc.; mem. Am. Astron. Soc. (sec. 1961-69), Internat. Astron. Union (sec. commn. 28, 1958-64, pres. 1967-70), Athenaeum Club (London). Home: Kent England Died Mar. 8, 1988.

MEAD, STANTON WITTER, paper company executive; b. Rockford, Ill., Sept. 2, 1900; s. George W. and Ruth E. (Witter) M.; m. Dorothy E. Williams, Sept. 1, 1926 (dec); children: George W. II, Gilbert D., Mary M. Price; m. Elvira Jens Schulz, Oct. 1968 (dec.). A.B., Yale U., 1922. Pres. Consol. Papers, Inc., Wisconsin Rapids, Wis., 1950-66, also bd. dirs.; dir. Consol. Water Power Co., Wisconsin First Nat. Bank, Wisconsin Rapids. Home: Wisconsin Rapids Wis. Died Nov. 11, 1988; buried Forest Hill Cemetery, Wis. Rapids, Wis.

MEADE, RICHARD HARDAWAY, physician, surgeon; b. Richmond, Va., May 10, 1897; s. Richard H. and Nellie Prior (Atkins) M.; m. Mary Frazier, June 14, 1924; children: Richard Hardaway III, Charles H. Frazier, James Gardiner, David Everard; m. Mary A. Martin, Nov. 20, 1946. Student, Va. Mil. Inst., 1913-14, Richmond Coll., 1915; BS, U. Va., 1917, MD, Harvard U., 1921. Med. missionary China, 1924-27; asst. prof. surgery, gynecology U. Va., 1927-31; assoc. surgery U. Pa., 1931-42, Northwestern U., Evanston, Ill., 1946-48; attending chest surgeon VA Hosp., Hines, Ill., 1946-48; hon. cons. thoracic surgeon Blodgett Meml. Hosp.; cons., thoracic surgery VA Hosp., 1946-92. Author: A History of Thoracic Surgery, 1961; contbr. articles to profl. jours. Served from maj. to lt. col., M.C., AUS, 1942-45. Decorated Legion of Merit. Fellow A.C.S.; mem. Internat. Soc. Surgery, Am. Assn. Thoracic Surgery (sec. 1935-47, pres. 1956), Raven Soc., Delta Psi, Episcopalian. Clubs: Torch, Rotary, Kent Country. *

MEANEY, SIR PATRICK MICHAEL, business executive; b. London, May 6, 1925; s. Joseph and Ethel Meaney; m. Mary June Kearney, 1967; 1 child. Student Wimbledon Coll., No. Poly. With Thomas Tilling Plc, 1951, dir., 1961, group mng. dir. and chief exec., 1973-83; dir. Cable and Wirelss Ltd., 1970-84; dir. Rank Orgn. Plc, 1979-92, chmn., 1983-92; chmn. A. Kershaw and Sons Plc, 1983, Mecca Leisure Group Plc, 1990-92; dir. Midland Bank Plc, 1980-92, dep. chmn., 1984-92; dir. I.C.I. Plc, 1981-92, MEPC, Plc, 1986-92, Tarmac, Plc, 1990-92; dep. chmn. Horserace, Levy, Roard, 1985-92; head govt. rev. into Harland and Wolff, 1981; mem. Coun. Brit. N. Am. Com., 1979-91, CBI, 1979-91. Mem. adv. bd. World Econ. Forum, 1979-92, conf. bd., 1982-92; mem. adv. bd. CRH Plc, 1985-92, Brit. Exec. Svc. Overseas, 1987-92; mem. adv. com. Internat. Stock Exch. Listed Cos., 1987-92. Fellow Chartered Inst. of Mktg. (pres. 1981-91); mem. Brit. Inst. Mgmt., Royal Soc. Arts. Avocations: sport, music, travel.Died July 16, 1992. Home: London England †

MEANS, CYRIL CHESNUT, JR., lawyer, educator; b. Phila., Dec. 21, 1918; s. Cyril Chesnut and Annette Thayer (Handley) M.; A.B., Harvard U., 1938, LL.M., 1948; J.D., Wayne State U., 1941; m. Rosaline S. Linn, Nov. 8, 1958; children—Elizabeth Rose Thayer, Annette Thayer, Cyril Chesnut III. Admitted to Mich. bar, 1941; law sec. to Justice Henry M. Butzel, Mich. Supreme Ct., 1941-42; assoc. prof.

law Detroit Coll. Law, 1946-47; asst. prof. law Stanford U., 1948-50; legal adviser Office of U.S. High Commr. for Germany, 1950-54; arbitration dir. N.Y. Stock Exchange, 1955-56; exec. v.p., dir. Tech. Studies, Inc., 1957-86, sr. v.p., 1986—; chmn. bd. trustees Trent Sch., N.Y.C., 1963-64, dean, 1964-65; projects coordinator Western Australia Devel. Corp., 1965-66; asst. prof. N.Y. Law Sch., 1969-70, assoc. prof., 1970-73, prof., 1973-89, prof. emeritus, 1989—; fellow-in-residence Sch. Theology, U. South, Sewanee, Tenn., 1990. Am. co-founder Channel Tunnel Study Group; mem. N.Y. State Gov.'s Commn. to Review N.Y. State's Abortion Law, 1968. Chmn. legal com. Nat. Abortion Rights Action League, 1970-79; mem. adv. com. population affairs, sec. HEW, 1973-77; mem. Anglican Ch.; legal adviser Am. Ch. Union, 1962-65; chmn. N.Y. Met. Regional Br., 1963-64, lay canon Perth, Western Australia, 1966-67; vestryman Ch. of Resurrection, N.Y.C., 1975-78, 88-92, warden, 1978-80; counsel on canon law to the vestry, Trinity Cathedral, Newark, St. George's Ch., Flushing, N.Y., and to other ecclesiastical persons and corps., 1989-92. Lt. USNR, 1942-46. Mem. Am. Soc. Internat. Law, Assn. Bar City N.Y., Mich. State Bar, Am. Bar Assn., Selden Soc., Am. Soc. Legal History. Republican. Author: The Law of New York Concerning Abortion and the Status of the Foetus, 1664-1968; A Case of Cessation of Constitutionality, 1968; The Phoenix of Abortional Freedom, 1971; Surrogacy vs. The Thirteenth Amendment, 1987. Died Oct. 5, 1992. Home: Great Neck N.Y. †

MEANS, PAUL BANWELL, education educator; b. Orleans, Nebr., Jan. 5, 1894; s. Edgar L. and Jessie L. (Banwell) M.; m. Nathalie Alberta Toms, July 21, 1926; children: Gordon Paul, Mariel Janet (Mrs. E. T. Ames), Virginia Claire (Mrs. Lyle G. Rowe), Charlotte Louise (Mrs. Delbert Jones). AB, Yale U., 1915; B.Litt. (Rhodes scholar), Oxford, 1923; PhD, Columbia U., 1934. Ordained to ministry of the Meth. Ch., 1928. Prof. philosophy Berea (Ky.) Coll., 1923-24; asst. prof. psychology Oberlin (Ohio) Coll., 1925-27; commd. missionary Bd. Fgn. Missions, 1927; prin. Meth. Boys Sch., Medan, Sumatra, 1927-29; editor Malaysia Message, 1929-39; prof., head dept. religion U. Oreg., 1941-59; advisor mass edn. Ministry Edn., Govt. Malaya, 1959-60; literacy advisor Meth. Ch., Sarawak, Borneo, 1960-61; prof. Jamestown Coll., 1961-63; asst. prof. philosophy and religion Morningside Coll., 1964-65; Fulbright rsch. fellow S.E. Asia, 1950-51; sec. com. of selection Rhodes scholarships, State of Oreg., 1945-49. Author: Things That Are Cesar's, 1943; contbr. articles to religious publs. Mem. Religious Edn. Assn., Am. Assn. Rhodes Scholars, Atlantic Union, Fed. Union (mem. nat. com.), Rotary. *

MEDINA, HAROLD R., judge, author; b. Bklyn., Feb. 16, 1888; s. Joaquin A. and Elizabeth (Fash) M.; m. Ethel Forde Hillyer, June 6, 1911 (dec.); children: Harold Raymond, Standish Forde. A.B. (highest honors in French), Princeton U., 1909; LL.B., Columbia U., 1912, LL.B. (Ordronaux Prize); hon. degrees from 25 colls. and univs. Bar: N.Y. 1912. Practiced law N.Y.C.; prof. law Columbia U., 1915-40; apptd. judge U.S. Dist. Ct., So. Dist. N.Y., 1947-51; U.S. circuit judge Ct. Appeals for 2d Circuit, 1951-58, sr. circuit judge, 1958-80. Author numerous legal books, from 1922, including Judge Medina Speaks, 1954, The Anatomy of Freedom, 1959; Contbr. to legal reviews. Charter trustee emeritus Princeton U.; life trustee emeritus Tchrs. Coll., Columbia U. Recipient awards and medals Freedom Found., Holland Soc., N.Y. Bd. of Trade, Nat. Inst. of Social Sci.; recipient Eleanor Van Rensselaer medal Nat. Soc. Colonial Dames, Am. Edn. award N.E.A., Am. Edn. award Bklyn. Coll., Am. Edn. award Nat. Soc. New Eng. Women, Am. Edn. award S.A.R., Am. Edn. award, and Justice award Am. Judicature Soc., Justice award Texas Bill of Rights Found., James Madison award Nat. Broadcast Editorial Assn., 1976, Disting. Pub. Svc. award Ohio Newspaper Assn., others; Harold R. Medina Professorship of Procedural Jurisprudence established Columbia Law Sch., 1973; Harold R. Medina Courtroom dedicated Columbia Law Sch., 1981. Fellow Am. Acad. Arts and Scis.; mem., officer, chmn. coms. several profl. assns. and orgns.; hon. mem. several state bars. Episcopalian. Clubs: University, Princeton U., Westhampton Country, Century, Church. Home: New York N.Y. Died Mar. 11, 1990.

MEDUNA, LADISLAS JOSEPH, physician, psychiatrist; b. Budapest, Hungary, Mar. 27, 1896; s. Francis M. and Gisela (Eissler) M.; m. Clara Varga, 1934. MD, Royal U. of Sci., Budapest, Hungary, 1921. Asst. prof. Budapest Interacad. Inst. Brain Rsch., 1924-27; assoc. prof. U. Clinic for Mental and Nervous Diseases, 1927-33; dir. neuro-histology lab., head dept. male svcs. Leopold Field State Hosp. for Insane, Budapest, 1933-34, 34-38; head dept. male svcs. Nagel Field State Hosp., 1938-39; assoc. prof. psychiatry and neurology Loyola U., Chgo., 1939-43; assoc. prof. psychiatry U. Ill., Neuropsychiat. Inst., Chgo., 1943-50, prof., 1950-92; cons. psychiatry state Dept. of Pub. Welfare, Ill., 1954-92; hon. staff mem. Ridgeway Hosp., Chgo. Discovered Metrazol convulsive treatment; application of carbon dioxide therapy to neuroses; established presence of anti-insulinic factor in blood of schizophrenics; editor-in-chief: Jour. Neuropsychiatry. Recipient Guggenheim Found. fellowship, 1955. Hon. mem. Royal Medico-Psychol. Assn. (London), Sociedade Medicina de Pernambuco, Sociedad Brazileira, Asssociacao Paulists, Roman Acad. Medicine, Sociedade Cubana de Nurol. y Psiquiatria, Electro-Shock Rsch. Assn., Blue Key; mem. Chgo. Neurol. Soc. Am. Medieval Acad., Ill. Chgo. Med Socs., Milw. Neuropsychiat. Soc., Am. Psychiat. Assn., N.Y. Acad. Sci., AMA, Am. Soc. Med. Psychiatry (past pres.), Soc. Biol. Psychiatry (past pres.), AAAS, Phi Beta Pi, Sigma Xi, Blue Key. *

MEEK, PETER GRAY, health agency executive; b. Bellefonte, Pa., Apr. 15, 1911; s. George Reuben and Ellen Downing (Valentine) M.; m. Lucile Rasin, Oct. 4, 1941; children: Susan Gray Meek Landess, Katharine Rasin Meek Jones, Ellen Downing Meek Vaut. AB, Pa. State U., 1932, MA, 1933; postgrad., Carnegie Inst. Tech., 1934-35. With Bur. Pub. Assistance, FSA, 1938-49; asst. dir. Commn. Chronic Illness, Chgo. and Balt., 1949-56; regional dir. Nat. Soc. Crippled Children and Adults, N.Y.C., 1956-61; exec. dir. Nat. Health Coun., N.Y.C., 1961-73; lectr. Johns Hopkins Sch. Hygiene and Pub. Health, 1952-56, Columbia Sch. Pub. Health, 1962-70; mem. Nat. Commn. Community Health Svcs., 1962-66; participant guest program Parliament Fed. Republic Germany, 1963; v.p. Nat. Coun. Homemaker-Home Health Aide Svcs., 1967-92; adviser Nat. Com. on Pvt. Philanthrophy and Pub. Needs, 1974. Author: (play) The Fourth Generation, 1935, Self-Regulation in Philanthropy, 1974; author, editor: (with others) Chronic Illness in the United States, 1957. Bd. dirs. Pub. Affairs Com., Nat. Coun. on Aging; chmn. Nat. Vol. Orgns. for Ind. Living of the Aging, 1975-80. Lt. (sr. grade) USNR, 1943-46. Fellow APHA; mem. Am. Assn. World Health (v.p. 1968-74), Phi Gamma Delta. Episcopalian. Home: Wyckoff N.J. Died Jan. 7, 1992.

MEGEE, VERNON EDGAR, marine corps officer; b. Tulsa, June 5, 1900; s. George Daniel and Alice (Ford) M.; m. Nell Nemeyer, June 9, 1923; 1 child, Nell LaverneMegee Broad. BS, Okla. A&M Coll.; MA, U. Tex.; grad., Marine Corps Schs., Nat. War Coll., 1946. Enlisted USMC, 1919, commd. 2d lt., 1922, advanced through grades to lt. gen., 1956, qualified as naval aviator, 1931; instr. Marine Corps Schs., 1937-39; fgn. svc. U.S. Naval Air Mission, Haiti, China, P.I., Peru, 1940-43; air support comdr. Palau, Iwo Jima, Okinawa; chief staff Fleet Marine Force, Atlantic Fleet, 1947-49; asst. dir. Marine Corps Aviation, 1949-50; dir. intelligence Joint Staff, 1950-51; comdr. aircraft Fleet Marine Force Atlantic Fleet, Pacific, 1952; comdr. First Marine Air Wing, Korea, 1953; dep. comdr. Fleet Marine Air Force, Pacific, 1958-59; ret. as gen., 1959; chmn. bd. trustees Marine Mil. Acad., Harlingen, Tex. Contbr. articles on firearms and hunting to sportmen's mags. Chmn. bd. trustees Marine Mil. Acad., Harlingen, Tex. Decorated Legion of Merit (Iwo Jima), Navy-Marine Corps medal (Nicaragua), 1930, Bronze star (Okinawa), Cruz de Aviacion, 1st cl. (Peru), 1943, D.S.M., Mil. Order Taikuk with Silver Star (Korea). Mem. Army and Navy Club (Washington). Republican. Presbyterian. Home: Albuquerque N.Mex. Died Jan. 16, 1992.

MEGOWN, JOHN WILLIAM, marketing and technical consultant, educator; b. New London, Mo., Apr. 27, 1931; s. William P. and Fannie (Palmer) M.; m. Dorothy Astrid Wiebust, Apr. 6, 1957; 1 child, Jeffrey William. Assoc. Sci., Hannibal-LaGrange Coll., 1951; AB, U. Mo., 1953, MS, 1955; MS, Chgo. Grain Exchange Inst., 1956; postgrad., Northwestern U., 1957. Animal nutritionist Moorman Mfg. Co., Quincy, Ill., 1955; assoc. biologist Hales & Hunter Co., Chgo., 1955-56; asst. coord. rsch. and sales Peter Hand Found., Chgo., 1956-59; mgr. nutritional svcs. Morton Salt Co., Chgo., 1959-67, product mgr. custom and pvt. agrl. salt and mineral products, 1963-67, dir. agrl. coll. rels. program, 1964-67; mgr. rsch. comm. Allied Mills, Inc., Chgo., 1967-68; asst. v.p., pub. rels. dir. Vigortone Ag Products div. Beatrice Foods Co., Cedar Rapids, Iowa, 1968-70, v.p., dir. comm., 1970-72, v.p., dir. mktg. and pub. affairs, 1972-77, v.p. public affairs and govtl. rels., 1977-80, also bd. dirs.; sec., dir. resources devel., dir. Agrl. Fuel Devel. Corp., Milw., 1981-83; pres., CEO Possibilities Inc., Davenport, Iowa, 1980-81; gen. mgr. Farm Fuel and Feed div. McCrabb Mfg., Inc., West Liberty, Iowa, 1981-82; corp. mktg. advisor S.A. Clarke & Assocs. div. Clyde Industries, Ltd., 1981; pres. Megown & Assocs., Marion, Iowa, 1980-88, 90-92; dir. mktg. Nelson Mfg. Co., Cedar Rapids, 1983-85; asst. to pres. Vigortone Products, Inc., Cedar Rapids, 1985-86; exec. v.p. Profl. Bus. Svcs. Corp., Cedar Rapids, 1987-88; supr. telemktg. sales Iowa Farmer Today, Cedar Rapids, 1988; faculty mem. Mt. Mercy Coll., Cedar Rapids, 1988-92; TV newscast analyst Frank N. Magid Assocs., Cedar Rapids, 1989-90; radio commentator Food for Thought, 1978-80, Speaking Out, 1980-81; exec. v.p. Farm Care U.S.A., 1986-88; vice chmn. Nat. Agrl. Comm. Bd., 1972-73; nat. coord. Pub. Affairs Coun. for Am. Agr., 1969-70; chmn. Cedar Rapids Agrl. Exec.'s Forum, 1969-70; mem. Agribus, Coordinating Group, USDA, 1969-71, Gov. Iowa Agr. Promotion Bd., 1970-81, chmn., 1971-81; mem. agr.-tech. adv. com. for trade in grain and feed USDA, 1983-86; vis. prof. agri-bus. Coe Coll., 1980; mem. Curtis-Mahon Congl. Study Com., 1971-72; mem. nat. cattle industry adv. com. USDA, 1976-77; mem. agr. bus. adv. com. Joliet Jr. Coll., 1966-70; mem. Coun. Agr. and Sci. Tech., 1973-90; mem. adv. com. Ctr. for Vet. Medicine, FDA, 1984-86; spl. cons. HHS, 1984-87. Co-author: Beef Science Handbook, Vol. 4, 1967; author: Twenty-Four Turbulent Months, 1980; contbr. articles to tech. jours.; editorial adv. com.: Animal Health Inst, 1967-73; editorial adv. bd.: Agri Mktg. mag, 1978. Active Cedar Rapids YMCA; mem.-at-large Hawkeye Area coun. Boy Scouts Am., 1969-72, mem. dist. com., 1983-89; mem. Linn County Rural Devel. Com., 1971-85; chmn. parents adv. coun. Mt. Mercy Coll., 1981-83; Iowa chmn. Nat. Future Farmers Am. Found., 1970; hon. chpt. farmer Linn-Mar chpt., 1980; mem. Rep. Nat. Agr. and Food Com., 1968; bd. dirs. Rolling Meadows (Ill.) Community Chest, 1968, Cedar Rapids Jr. Achievement, 1972-73, Self Help Inc., Waverly, Iowa, 1976-77; trustee Livestock Industry Inst., 1977-88; mem. tech. adv. com. Landmark Legal Found., 1979-88; mem. Iowa Gov.'s Com. for Employment of the Handicapped. Col. Iowa N.G.; aide Gov. Iowa mil. staff. Recipient award for filmstrip Nat. Agrl. Advt. and Marketing Assn., 1968, Best Pub. Rels. Performance of Year award Midwest Feed Mfrs. Assn., 1974, hon. Am. farmer degree Future Farmers Am., 1973; Boss of Year award Marabwa chpt. Am. Bus. Women's Assn., 1975; Advt. Person of Yr. award Cedar Rapids Advt. Fedn., 1977; Faculty-Alumni award U. Mo., Columbia, 1978; Outstanding Svc. to Agr. award Linn County Farm Bur., 1979; Gov.'s Cert. of Recognition State of Iowa, 1981; Friend of Agr. award Iowa Dept. Agr., 1984; Disting. Alumnus award Hannibal-La Grange Coll., 1984; Rotarian of Yr. award, 1973. Mem. Nat. Feed Ingredients Assn. (dir. 1966-72, pub. rels. dir. 1966-69, 1st v.p. 1969-70, pres., CEO 1970-71, Essential Ingredient award 1978), Future Farmers Am. Alumni Assn., Animal Nutrition Rsch. Coun., Agrl. Rels. Coun., Nat. Agrl.-Mktg. Assn. (Iowa Farm Mktg. Man of Year 1975, spl. citation for radio commentaries Iowa chpt. 1979), Iowa Corn Growers Assn., Cedar Rapids C. of C. (exec. com. agr. bur. 1969-86, congl. action com. 1972-76), Nat. Eagle Scout Assn., Phi Theta Kappa, Alpha Phi Omega. Clubs: Ea. Iowa Advt. Fedn., Cedar Rapids Grain and Feed, Elmcrest Country; Capitol Hill (Washington). Lodges: Rotary (past pres.), Elks. Home: Marion Iowa Died Apr. 13, 1992. †

MEHREN, GEORGE LOUIS, business executive, government official, economist; b. Sacramento, July 6, 1913; s. Gale Thomas and Faye Laura (Swain) M.; m. Jean Dorothy McMurchy, June 26, 1938; children: Peter William, Elizabeth Jean; m. Ingeborg E. Hitchcock, 1968; 1 son, George Louis. Student, Coll. Pacific, 1937; A.A., Sacramento Jr. Coll., 1931; A.B. with honors, U. Calif., 1938, Ph.D., 1942. Research asso. Giannini Found. Agrl. Econs., Agrl. Expt. Sta., U. Calif., 1942, dir., 1957-62, instr. to asso. prof., 1946-51, prof. agrl. econs., 1951-71, prof. emeritus, 1971; chmn. dept. agrl. econs., chmn. dept. agrl. bus., dir. Giannini Found. Agrl. Econs., Agrl. Expt. Sta., U. Calif., Berkeley, Davis and Los Angeles, 1957-62; exec., adv., coordinating coms. Wild Lands Research Center, Water Resources Center Giannini Found. Agrl. Econs., Agrl. Expt. Sta., U. Calif., 1957-62, chmn. statewide curriculum agrl. bus. mgmt., 1957-62, exec. coms. Sch. Bus. Adminstrn., Inst. Internat. Studies, Inst. Indsl. Relations, 1958-62, mem. Legislative Assembly, 1960-62; asst. sec. U.S. Dept. Agr., Washington, 1963-68; dir. sci. and edn. U.S. Dept. Agr., 1965-68; spl. U.S. ambassador (spl.) to Panama, 1968; pres. Agribus. Council Inc., 1968-71; gen. mgr. Associated Milk Producers, Inc., 1972-76; exec. cons., 1976-78; v.p. Hitchcock GmbH, W.Ger., from 1976, San Antonio-Chgo. Investment, from 1973, Overseas Mktg., Inc., from 1977, Select Wines, Inc., from 1982, I. Mehren of Tex., Inc., from 1978, Mehren Hills, from 1983; mem. Fed. Council on Sci. and Tech., 1965-68, Fed. Interagy. Com. on Edn., 1966-68, Nat. Adv. Council on Extension and Continuing Edn., 1966-68, Pres.'s Com. on Consumer Interests, 1964-67; bd. dirs. Commodity Credit Corp., 1963-68; mem. adv. panel AEC, 1966-68; mem. adminstrv. com. Center for Specialization and Research in Agrl. Econs. and Stats., U. Naples, Portici, Italy, 1956-59; dir. food and restaurant div. OPS, Washington, 1951, acting dir. price ops., 1952, cons. to dir., 1952-53; cons. Mut. Security Agy., Fgn. Ops. Adminstrn., 1952-53; adviser Brit. minister agr. and fisheries and sec. of state for Scotland, London, 1952-53; cons. Ministry of Agr. Venezuela, Caracas, 1952-53, 70, Consejo de Bienestar Rural, Venezuela, 1953-54, OCDM, 1956-58, USOM to Korea, Republic of Korea, Seoul, U.S. Office Emergency Planning, AID, to govts., Pakistan, Iran, Mexico, Morocco, Indonesia, 1968-71; Egypt, 1968-78, Argentina, Greece, Turkey, India, Thailand, Philippines, 1979; adviser Ministry Agr. and Forestry for Italy, Rome, 1956; cons. div. econs. FAO, Rome, 1956-57; dean, vis. prof. Internat. Center for Tng. Agrl. Econs. and Statistics, Govt. Republic of Italy, U. of Rome, FAO, 1956; contract collaborator U.S. and Calif. depts. agr. for appraisal European promotion programs, 1962; mem. gen. editorial bd. Jour. Marketing, Am. Marketing Assn., 1952-55, mng. editor, 1955-57, editor-in-chief, 1957-58. Contbr. to profl. jours. Chmn. Calif. exec. com. U.S. Food for Peace Program, 1961. Served to lt. USNR, 1942-45. Fellow Internat. Biographic Assn.; mem. Western Agrl. Econs. Research Council, Am. Farm Econs. Assn., Am. Marketing Assn., Western Farm Econs. Assn., Alpha Zeta. Home: San Antonio Tex. Deceased. †

MEI, ALEXIS ITALE, university executive; b. San Francisco, Aug. 8, 1898; s. Valentino and Faustina (Milani) M. AB, Gonzaga U., Spokane, Wash., 1922; AM, Gonzaga U., 1923; S.T.D., Gregorian U., Rome, Italy, 1930; PhD, U. Calif., 1941. Entered Jesuit order, 1916; chmn. dept. physics U. San Francisco, 1942-50, prof. physics, 1942-46, dean, coll. of sci., 1947-92; mem. bd. trustees, 1950-56; acad. v.p. U. Santa Clara, 1956-92, mem. bd. trustees, 1958-92. Fellow Calif. Acad. Scis.; mem. Am. Phys. soc., Am. Assn. Physics, Nat. Geophys. Union, Am. Seismol. Soc., Sigma Xi. Roman Catholic. *

MEIKLEJOHN, DAVID SHIRRA, financial executive; b. N.Y.C., Oct. 4, 1908; s. David and Florence (Pickens) M.; 1 child, Shirra Belvoir. BA, Williams Coll., 1931. Wilson clk. Emigrant Savs. Bank, 1932-33; credit analyst Bankers Trust Co., 1933-36; asst. to pres. Dorr Co., 1936-40; dir. dept. commerce N.Y.C., 1940-42; exec. sec. Mayor Fiorello H. LaGuardia, 1945-46; asst. treas. Am. Machine & Foundry Co., 1946-51, treas., exec. v.p., 1951-70; exec. v.p. fin., CFO, dir. Integrated Resources, Inc., N.Y.C., 1970-82; bd. dirs. Am. Machine & Foundry Co., 1954-70, v.p., 1958-70; bd. dirs. Putnam Trust Co., W.J. Voit Rubber Corp. Lt. comdr. USNR, 1942-45. Mem. St. Andrews Soc., Williams Club, Union League (N.Y.C.), Stanwich Golf Club, Belle Haven Beach Club (Greenwich, Conn.). Home: Greenwich Conn. Died Mar. 18, 1989.

MELLIN, OSCAR ALVIN, patent lawyer; b. San Francisco, May 26, 1898; s. kCharles W. and Nell (Fearson) M.; m. Catherine L. Shultis, Nov. 24, 1917 (dec.); children: Alvin, Lois, (Mrs. Harold J. Truett, Jr.); m. 2d, Mabel G. DeLonais, 1953. Bar: Calif. 1933, U.S. Supreme Ct. 1947. Admitted to practice before U.S. Patent Office, 1922; assoc. Dewey, STrong, Townsend & Loftus, San Francisco, 1921-33; trial work in patent causes, 1933-35; pvt. practice patent law San Francisco, 1935-45; sr. ptnr. Mellin, Hanscom & Hursti, San Francisco, 1945-92. Mem. Elk, K.P., Jonathan Club (L.S.), Merchants Exch. (San Francisco). *

MELLON, ELEANOR MARY, sculptor; b. Narberth, Pa., Aug. 18, 1894; d. Charles Henry and Loraine W. (Roberts) Mellon. Studied with, Victor Salvatore, A.A. Weinman, Robert Aiken, N.Y.C., Harriet Frishmuth, E. McCartan. Exhibited 1921-92 with Nat. Sculpture Soc., N.Y.C., San Francisco, Nat. Acad. Design, N.Y.C., Pa. Acad. of Fine Arts, Phila., Allied Artists of Am., Soc. Washington Artists, Nat. Assn. Women Artists, N.Y.C., N.Y. World;s Fair, Art Inst. Chgo., Bklyn. Mus., Nat. Arts Club, N.Y.C., North Shore Art Assn., Gloucester, Mass., Archtl. League N.Y.C., Artists for Victory Exhbn. Met. Mus., N.Y.C., 1942. Received Helen Foster Barnet prize Nat. Acad. Design, 1927, bronze medal Soc. Washington Artists, 1931, hon. mention Nat. Assn. Women Painters and Sculptors, 1932, profl. prize N.Y. Jr. League, 1942, 2d silver medal Am. Artists Profl. League, 1944, gold medal from N.Y. Chpt., 1958, cash prize Pen and Brush Club, 1947, also silver medal for Sports in Sculpture, 1963, cash prize Brick Store Mus., Kennebunk, Maine, 1947. Fellow Nat. Sculpture Soc. (sec. 1936-40, 1945); mem. Pen and Brush, Am. Artists Profl. League (mem. bd. 1959—), Allied Artists, Mcpl. Art Soc., North Shore Art Assn., Colony Club, Cosmopolitan Club, Nat. Arts Club (N.Y.C.), Acorn Club (Phila.). Republican. Episcopalian. *

MELZAR, FREDERIC PRESTON, former holding company executive; b. Winchester, Mass., Dec. 6, 1920; s. Harold Eber and Edna Frances (McKusick) M.; m. Jean Jolly, Aug. 5, 1950; children: Victoria, Steven Parker, Alexandra, Frederica, Jonathan Preston, Jocelyn. Grad., Mass. Maritime Acad., Boston, 1938-40; student, Harvard U., 1945-46, M.B.A., 1948. Security analyst Nat. Shawmut Bank, Boston, 1948-52; security analyst Amoskeag Co., Boston, 1952-58, asst. sec., 1960-63, sec., 1963-78, v.p., sec., 1978-87; controller, dir. Avis, Inc., Boston, 1958-60; bd. dirs. Arthur T. Walker Estate Corp., Kittaning, Pa., 1983-88; trustee Clovely Fund, from 1955, Dumaines, from 1986. Trustee Wilmington Pub. Library, (Mass.), 1948-50; mem. Wilmington Bd. Selectman, 1950-53; mem. sch. com. Wilmington Pub. Schs., 1959-60; mem. Boxford Bd. Appeals, (Mass.), from 1980. Served to comdr. USNR, 1941-45. Decorated Bronze Star; decorated Silver Star. Republican. Congregationalist. Home: Boxford Mass. Deceased. †

MEMORY, JASPER LIVINGSTON, education educator; b. Whiteville, N.C., Mar. 2, 1901; s. Jasper Lutterloh and Mary Catherine McNeill M.; m. Margaret Durham, Dec. 27, 1935; 1 child, Jasper Durham. AB, Wake Forest Coll., 1921; AM, Columbia U., 1925. State inspector N.C. high schs., 1925-29; prof. edn., dir. placement bur. Wake Forest Coll., 1929-91, acting dir. summer sch., dean of coll., 1946-55, dir. of summer sessions, 1955-61, chmn. of the dept. edn., 1957-66, dir. pub. rels., 1929-46; gen. edn. bd. fellow, mem. Columbia Sch. Survey Staff, 1927-28; lectr. med. stats. Bowman Gray Sch. Medicine, 1950. Co-author: with J. Henry Highsmith High School Manual and Reorganization Program of North Carolina, 1927; author: Introduction to Educational Measurement and Guidance, 1953; editor: Select Prose of John Charles McNeill; editor Alumni News, 1941-47, sec. alumni, 1941-47. Chmn. Merit System Coun. N.C., 1943-53; panel arbitrators N.C. Dept. Labor, Fed. Mediation and Conciliation Svc., Bur. Nat. Affairs. Mem. Am. Arbitration Assn. panel arbitrators , AAUP, Phi Delta Kappa, Omicron Delta Delta Kappa. Democrat. Baptist. Home: Winston-Salem N.C. Died Mar. 19, 1991.

MEMPHIS SLIM (PETER CHATMAN), blues performer; b. Memphis, 1915. Blues artist, composer, from 1934. Mem. Big Bill Broonzy's band, 1940-44; performed with many blues greats including Sonny Boy Williamson, Washboard Sam, Willie Dixon; albums include Memphis Slim, Traveling With the Blues, Bad Luck & Troubles, The Real Boogie Woogie, The Blues Every Which Way, 'Frisco Bay Blues, All Them Blues, The Legacy of the Blues, Vol. 7, Raining the Blues, Chicago Boogie, Rock Me Baby, No Strain, Memphis Slim and the Real Honky Tonk, (with Big Bill Broonzy) Big Bill's Blues, (with Matt Murphy) Memphis Slim-Matt Murphy; compositions include Every Day I Have the Blues, Grinder Man Blues, You Didn't Mean Me No Good, Maybe I'll Lend You a Dime, Two of a Kind, I Believe I'll Settle Down; rec. artist for Folkways, Prestige Vee, Chess, Verve, United Artists. Home: Chicago Ill. Deceased.

MENDEL, WERNER MAX, psychiatrist, educator, publisher, sailor; b. Hamburg, Germany, June 11, 1927; came to U.S., 1939, naturalized, 1944; s. Herbert I. and Edith (Fraenkel) M.; m. Doris Richards; children: Carl, Dirk, Karin, Charles, Darryl. B.A., UCLA, 1948; M.A., Stanford U., 1949, M.D., 1953. Intern Los Angeles County Gen. Hosp., 1953-54; resident Menninger Sch. Psychiatry, Topeka, and St. Elizabeth's Hosp., Washington, 1954-57; practice medicine specializing in psychiatry and psychoanalysis Los Angeles, 1957-82; dir. outpatient services Met. State Hosp., Norwalk, Calif., 1958-60; chief, sr. clerkship in psychiatry U. So. Calif., 1961-62; chief teaching service psychiat. unit Los Angeles County-U. So. Calif. Med. Center, 1962-65, clin. dir. adult inpatient services, 1965-67; prof. psychiatry U. So. Calif., 1960-86, emeritus prof. psychiatry and behavioral scis., 1986-90, dir. div. profl. and staff devel., 1967-82; clin. prof. psychiatry and behavioral scis. Creighton U. Sch. Medicine, Omaha, 1987-90; clin. prof. psychiatry U. Nebr. Sch. Medicine, 1986-90; clin. dir. Hastings (Nebr.) Regional Ctr., 1986-90; cons. Calif. Dept. Mental Hygiene. Author: (with G.A. Green) The Therapeutic Management of Psychological Illness, 1967, A Celebration of Laughter, 1970, (with P. Solomon) Psychiatric Consultation, 1967, Supportive Care, Theory and Technique, 1975, Schizophrenia, 1976, Treatment of Schizophrenia, 1989, Profiles of Survivors, 1990; editor-in-chief Mara Books, Inc., 1969-82; contbr. over 100 articles to profl. jours. Recipient Bronze medal, U. Helsinki, Finland, Disting. Service award, Los Angeles County, Alumni Sci. Writing award Menninger Alumni Assn., 1990; scholar in residence Rockefeller Inst., Belagio, Italy. Mem. Am. Assn. Psychiat. Adminstrs., Dept. Pub. Instns. Med. Assn. (pres.). Home: Hastings Nebr. Died Aug. 6, 1990; cremated.

MENGEL, ROBERT MORROW, ornithologist, educator, curator, artist; b. Glenview, Ky., Aug. 19, 1921; s. Charles C. and Mary A. (Kelly) M.; m. Marion Anne Jenkinson, Dec. 21, 1963; 1 child, Tracy Lynn. B.S., Cornell U., 1947; M.A., U. Mich., 1950, Ph.D., 1958. Research assoc. U. Kans., Lawrence, 1953-62, mem. faculty, 1962-90, assoc. prof., 1967-71, prof. systematics and ecology, 1972-90; curator Mus. Natural History U. Kans., 1972-90. Author, illustrator: The Birds of Kentucky, 1965; author: The Ellis Collection of Ornithological Books in the University of Kansas Libraries, vol. 1, 1972, vol. 2, 1983; illustrator: Handbook of North American Birds, vol. 1, 1962, vols. 2 and 3, 1976, vols. 4 and 5, 1988, A Guide to Bird Finding in Kansas and Western Missouri, 1988; contbg. illustrator: The Birds of Colorado, 1965, Twentieth Century Wildlife Artists, 1986; editor: Spl. Publ. #9, Carnegie Mus. Natural History, 1984; one-man and group exhbns. of paintings and watercolors: Lawrence, 1973, 76, 77, Norman, Okla., 1974, Wichita, 1978, 81, Ithaca, N.Y., 1978, Wausau, Wis., 1979, 80, 81, Cleve., 1980, Edinburgh, Scotland, 1981, London, 1981, Pitts., 1981. Served with USAAF, 1942-46. Fellow Am. Ornithologists Union (editor jour. 1963-67, editor monograph series 1970-74, councillor 1968-70, 72-74); mem. Cooper Ornithol. Soc. (councillor 1966-68), Wilson Ornithol. Soc. (assoc. editor Bull. 1953-54), Kans. Ornithol. Soc., Ky. Ornithol. Soc., Soc. Study of Evolution, Am. Soc. Systematic Zoologists, Soc. Am. Naturalists, Brit. Ornithologists Union, Kans. Watercolor Soc., Sigma Xi. Home: Lawrence Kans. Died Jan. 15, 1990; buried Pioneer Cemetery, Lawrence, Kans.

MENIHAN, JOHN CONWAY, artist, designer; b. Rochester, N.Y., Feb. 14, 1908; s. Jeremiah G. and May Louise (Conway) M.; m. Margaret Teresa Hickey, Sept. 26, 1936; children: Mary, John Conway, Tom, Pete. Student, Phillips Exeter Acad., 1922-25; B.S. in Econs, U. Pa., 1930; LL.D. (hon.), St. John Fisher Coll., 1983. Mem. faculty U. Rochester, 1946-65; Bd. dirs. Rochester Meml. Art Gallery, 1968-73; Arts Council of Rochester, 1976. Oil painter, water colorist, printmaker of portraits, landscapes, genre; represented in permanent collections Carnegie Inst., Library Congress, Rochester Meml. Art Gallery, Print Club of Rochester, St. John Fisher Coll., Rochester, Columbia Banking, Rochester, Keuka Coll., Pennyan, N.Y.; retrospective exhbn. Nazareth Coll., Rochester, N.Y., 1983, lithographs Meml. Art Gallery, Rochester, 1988; watercolors Rochester Inst. Tech., 1989; designer mural window of Nazarath Coll. Library, convent chapel of St. John Evangelist, enamel tryptich for St. Thomas Convent, Stations of the Cross and altar crucifix for Our Lady of Lourdes Roman Cath. Ch. (all Rochester), St. Anthony Shrine; side altars for St. Ambrose Ch., baptismal font and candle stand for St. Mary's Ch., Scottsville, N.Y., ceremonial mace for St. John Fisher Coll., Rochester, D'Youville Coll., Buffalo, Community Coll. of Air Force; triptych Life of St. Elizabeth Seton for St. Thomas the Apostle Ch., Rochester; murals designed and executed for Xerox Corp., Webster, N.Y., Rochester Tel. Co., Security Trust Co., R.T. French Co., Rochester, N.Y. and Fresno, Calif., mural for, Lowenthal-Tenn., Columbia, Tenn.; enamel shrine St. Joseph, Pittsford, N.Y.; shrine Our Lady of Grapes, St. Januarius Ch., Naples, N.Y.; mural, St. John Fisher Library; designed and executed windows, wall hangings, furnishings, Notre Dame High Sch. Chapel, Elmira, N.Y., 6 liturgical wall hangings, St. Louis Ch.; wallhanging at Woodcliff Lodge, Victor, N.Y. (1st prize oil, watercolor drawing and print, Finger Lakes Show, Rochester 1947); illustrator: How Scientists Find Out, Hist. St. Mary's Ch.; designer, illustrator: St. Ann's of Hornell. Recipient Lillian Fairchild award; Marion Stratton Gould award, 1946. Fellow Rochester Museum and Sci. Center; Assoc. NAD; mem. Am. Soc. Graphic Artists, Am. Watercolor Soc., Friends Rochester Pub. Library, Sigma Nu. Roman Catholic. Clubs: Mask and Wig (Phila.); The Group, Art, Print (Rochester). Home: Rochester N.Y. Died Sept. 4, 1992. †

MENKES, SIGMUND JOSEF, artist; b. Lwow, Poland, May 6, 1896; came to U.S., 1935, naturalized, 1948; s. Marcus and Rose (Elb) M.; m. Stasia Theodora Weiss, Dec. 1928. Grad., Higher Inst. Art Decorations, 1914, Acad. Fine Art, 1919. Restoration of murals, chs. of Poland, 1912-14; one-man exhbns., Paris, Berlin, Brussels, Vienna, 1921-35; paintings exhibited permanent collections Met. Mus. Art, Wichita, Kans., Mus. Art, Murdock Collections, Mus. Fine Arts, Cranbrook, Bloomfield, Mich., Mus. Jeu de Paume, Paris, NAt. Mus., Warsaw, Plians, Nat. Mus., Belgrade, NAt. Mus., Tel-Aviv, Pa. Acad. Fine Arts, Bklyn. Mus., Brit., Abbott Labs., Whitney Mus. Am. Art, other pvt. collections U.S, Europe. Recipient Clark prize for landscape, honorable mention Corcoran ARt Gallery, Wash., 1941, also prize and golf medal, 1947, Cpl. H. Beck prize (golf medal) for portrait, Pa. Acad. Fine Arts, 1945, Thomas B. Clarke prize NAt. Acad., 1953, grand prize Art U.S.A., N.Y., 1958. Fellow Internat. Inst. ARts and Letters (life); mem. Salon D'Automne, Salon De Tuilleries, Salon Independent (Paris), Fedn. Modern Painters and Sculptors (pres. 1942-43). *

MENNINGER, KARL AUGUSTUS, psychiatrist; b. Topeka, July 22, 1893; s. Charles Frederick (M.D.) and Flora (Knisely) M.; m. Grace Gaines, Sept. 1916 (div. Feb. 1941); children: Julia Menninger Gottesman, Robert Gaines, Martha Menninger Nichols; m. Jeanetta Lyle, Sept. 1941; 1 dau., Rosemary Jeanetta Karla. Student, Washburn Coll., 1910-12, Ind. U., summer 1910; A.B., U. Wis., 1914, M.S., 1915, D.Sc. (hon.), 1965; M.D. cum laude, Harvard U., 1917; L.H.D. (hon.), Park Coll., 1955, St. Benedict's Coll., 1963, Loyola U., 1972, DePaul U., 1974; LL.D., Jefferson Med. Coll., 1956, Parsons Coll., 1960, Kans. State U., 1962, Baker U., 1965, Pepperdine U., 1973, John Jay Coll. Criminal Justice, N.Y., 1978; D.Sc., Washburn U., 1949, Oklahoma City U., 1966. Mem. Menninger Clinic, Topeka; chmn. bd. trustees Menninger Found., Topeka, until 1990; prof. at large U. Kans.; disting. prof. psychiatry Chgo. Med. Sch.; prof. Loyola U., Chgo., U. Cin.; vis. prof. U. Chgo.; cons. Ill. Dept. Mental Health, Ill. State Psychiat. Inst., 1967-73; founder Menninger Sch. Psychiatry, 1946, dean, 1946-69; cons. Topeka VA Hosp., Topeka State Hosp., Stormont-Vail Hosp., Kans. Reception and Diagnostic Center, Kans. Neurol. Inst., Fed. Bur. Prisons, Office Vocat. Rehab., HEW, President's Task Force on Prisoner Rehab., 1969, Mt. Sinai Med. Center, Chgo., Am. Bar Assn. com. on correctional facilities and services, 1970-76, Com. on Penal Reform, Kans. Assn. Mental Health; mem. spl. com. on psychiatry, OSRD, ETO, adv. to surgeon gen. U.S. Army, 1945; adviser on penology to Gov. Kans., 1966-75; mem. Nat. Council on Crime and Delinquency, Open Lands Project; mem. adv. bd. Adult div. Ill. Dept. Corrections, Ill. State Psychiat. Inst.; med. adv. council Gov. Ill.; mem. adv. coms. many other civic, govtl. orgns. Author: (with others) Why Men Fail, 1918, The Human Mind, 1930, rev., 1945, The Healthy-Minded Child, 1930, Man Against Himself, 1938, America Now, 1938, (with Mrs. Menninger) Love Against Hate, 1942, (with Devereux) A Guide to Psychiatric Books, 1950, 2d rev. edit., 1958, 3d rev. edit., 1972, Manual for Psychiatric Case Study, 1952, Theory of Psychoanalytic Technique, 1958, rev. edit, (with Holzman), 1973; selected papers A Psychiatrist's World, 1959, The Vital Balance, 1963, The Crime of Punishment, 1968, (with Lucy Freeman) Sparks, 1973, Whatever Became of Sin, 1974; also articles.; Editorial bd.: (with Lucy Freeman) Bull. Menninger Clinic. Bd. overseers Lemberg Center for Study Violence, Brandeis U.; bd. dirs. Chgo. Boys Club, John

Howard Assn. Chgo., W. Clement and Jessie V. Stone Found., Chgo.; founder, chmn. bd. dirs. the Villages, Inc., Topeka. Commd. lt. (j.g.) U.S. Naval Res. Force, 1918-21. Recipient T.W. Salmon award N.Y. Acad. Medicine, 1967, Good Samaritan award Eagles Lodge, 1968, 69, Ann. Service award John Howard Assn., 1969, Good Shepherd award The Lambs, Chgo., 1969, award Am. Acad. Psychiatry and Law, 1974, Roscoe Pound award Nat. Council Crime and Delinquency, 1975, Spl. award Kans. Dept. Corrections, 1976, Sheen award AMA, 1978, Presdl. Medal of Freedom, 1981, numerous others. Life fellow Am. Psychiat. Assn. (Isaac Ray award 1962, 1st distinguished service award 1965, 1st Founders award 1977), ACP (life master), ACLU, NAACP, Am. Coll. Psychiatrists, Am. Med. Writers Assn.; hon. fellow Royal Coll. Psychiatrists; life mem. AMA, Am. Psychol. Assn., Chgo. Psychoanalytic Soc., Am. Orthopsychiat. Assn., Am. Psychoanalytic Assn. (founder; pres. 1941-43); hon. mem. Am. Assn. Suicidology, Internat. Assn. for Suicide Prevention, Sigmund Freud Archives; joint founder, charter mem. Central Neuropsychiat. Assn., Central Psychiat. Hosp. Assn., Med. Assn. for Research Nervous and Mental Diseases; mem. Am. Assn. for Child Psychoanalysis, Am. Soc. Criminology, Ill. Acad. Criminology, Assn. for Psychiat. Treatment Offenders, Am. Acad. Psychiatry and Law, Am. Justice Inst. (adv. com. sponsors), Assn. Clin. Pastoral Edn., Ill. Com. on Family Law, Internat. Psychoanalytic Assn., Kans. Med. Soc., Sigmund Freud Soc. Vienna, World Soc. Ekistics, Nat. Congress Am. Indians, Am. Hort. Council, AAAS, ACLU (nat. adv. council), NAACP, Sierra Club, Chgo. Orchestral Assn. (gov.), Am. Assn. Bot. Gardens and Arboreta, Friends of the Earth, Am. Indian Center (Chgo. Grand Council), Am. Hort. Coun., Aspen Inst. for Humanistic Studies (former trustee, now hon. trustee), Am. Humanics Found., Nat. Commn. for Prevention of Child Abuse (co-chmn. hon. bd.), Save the Tallgrass Prairie Inc. (chmn. nat. hon. bd.), Topeka C. of C., Am. Legion, Phi Beta Pi. Democrat. Presbyterian. Clubs: University (Chgo.); Country. Lodge: Masons. Home: Topeka Kans. Died July 18, 1990; buried Hope Cemetery, Topeka.

MENNINGER, KARL AUGUSTUS, psychiatrist; b. Topeka, July 22, 1893; s. Charles Frederick and Flora (Knisely) M.; m. Grace Gaines, Sept. 9, 1916 (div. Feb. 1941); children: Julia, Robert Gaines, Martha; m. Jeanetta Lyle, Sept. 8, 1941; 1 child, Rosemary Karla Jeanetta. Student, Washburn Coll., 1910-12, Ind. U., 1910; AR, U. Wis., 1914, MS, 1915. Chmn. of bd. trustees, dir. ednl. dept. Menninger Found.; clin. prof. psychiatry U. Kans.; neuropsychiatrist Stormont-Vail Hosp., Topeka; chief staff Menninger Clinic; dean Menninger Sch. Psychiatry; mem. edn. com., sr. cons. Fed. Bur. Prisons, Forbes AFB Hosp.; cons. Office Vocat. Rehab., Dept. Health Edn. and Welfare. Author: Why Men Fail, 1918, The Human Mind, 1930 (rev. 1945), The Healthy-Minded Child, 1930, Man Against Himself, 1938, America Now, 1938, (with Mrs. Menninger) Love Against Hate, 1942: A Guide to Psychiatric Books, 1950, Manual for Psychiatric Case Study, 1952, Theory of Psychoanalytic Technique, 1958; contbr. numerous articles to profl. jours. Mem. spl. commn. on psychiatry, OSRD, ETO, adv. to surgeon gen. U.S. Army, 1945, lt. USNRF, 1918-21. *

MERCER, ELWYN JARVIS, manufacturing company executive; b. Bone Gap, Ill., Apr. 4, 1911; s. Charles Lawrence and Chloe Alice (Hocking) M.; m. Ione McPherson, Dec. 31, 1936. B.M.E., U. Idaho, 1936. With Allis-Chalmers Mfg. Co., 1937-68; mng. dir. Allis-Chalmers Mfg. Co., Eng., 1951-56; gen. mgr. constrn. machine div. Allis-Chalmers Mfg. Co., 1956-57, v.p., gen., 1957-62, v.p., mng. dir. internat. div., 1962-68; gen. mgr.-owner Mercer Enterprises, Protem, Mo., from 1968; Staff WPB, Washington, 1942-43. Served to lt. USNR, 1943-45. Clubs: Masons (32 deg.), Shriners. Home: Protem Mo. Deceased. †

MERCER, HENRY DICKSON, shippping executive; b. Lodi, N.J., Mar. 26, 1893; s. Andrew John and Sarah (Dickson) M.; m. Catherine Schroeder, June 2, 1920; children: Millicent Alva (Mrs. Neils W. Johnsen), Henry Dickson, Douglas Demarest. Pub. shc., Lodi and Passaic, N.J. Stenographer Erie R.R., Paterson, N.J., 1910-13; stenographer, clk. Great Nor. Ry., N.Y.C., 1913-15, comml. agt., 1916-17, gen. agt., 1920-22; pres. Dyson Shipping Co., Inc., N.Y.C., 1923-30; organizer States Marine Corp., 1931, pres., dir., 1931-53, chmn. bd., 1953-92; owner, operator Hominy Hill Farms, Monmouth County, N.J.; organizer Freighting, Inc.; bd. dirs. Global Bulk Transport, Inc., Chase Manhattan Bank, Republic Steel Corp., Magnavox Corp. Trustee Am. Sch. Classical Studies at Athens, Greece, Downtown Lower Manhattan Assn., N.Y.C. Served as gunner's mate USNRF, 1917-19. Mem. N.J. Guernsey Breeders Assn., Eastern Guernsey Breeders Assn., Nat. Golf Club, Links Recess, India House, Pinnacle, N.Y. Yacht Club, Links (N.Y.C.) Club, Rumson (N.J.) Country Club, Upper Montclair (N.Y.) Country Club, Manhasset Bay Yacht (L.I.) Club, Cat Key, Lyford Cay Club, Porcupine (Nassau) Club. *

MERGEN, FRANCOIS, forestry educator, dean; b. Grand Duchy of Luxembourg, May 1, 1925; s. Aloyse and Marie (Arens) M.; m. Andreé Bodson, Aug. 2, 1947; 1 son, John Francis. Certificat de fin d'etudes, Luxembourg Coll., 1946; student, Laval U., 1947; B.S., U. N.B., 1950; M.F. cum laude, Yale U., 1951; Ph.D., Yale, 1954. Mem. faculty Yale U., 1954-89, prof. forestry, 1963-89, dean Sch. Forestry and Environ. Studies, 1965-75, also Pinchot prof. forestry.; Hon. consul Grand Duchy of Luxembourg, from 1974. Contbr. numerous articles to profl. jours. Mem. underground resistance Luxembourg, World War II, later liason officer to Gen. Eisenhower, ETO. Mem. Soc. Am. Foresters (participant Vis. Scientist Program 1961-65, Barrington Moore award for outstanding achievement in biol. rsch. 1966), Sigma Xi. Home: Homosassa Fla. Died June 26, 1989.

MERONEY, FERN ALLEN See FOSTER, FERN ALLEN

MERRIAM, EVE, poet, author; b. Phila.; Children: Guy Michel, Dee Michel. Tchr. CCNY, NYU, 1966-89; lectr. on sexism in edn., from 1974. Author: Real Book About Franklin D. Roosevelt, 1952, The Voice of Liberty, 1959, Figleaf, 1960, Basics, 1962, After Nora Slammed the Door, 1964, A Gaggle of Geese, 1960, Mommies at Work, 1961, Growing Up Female in America, 1971, Boys and Girls, Girls and Boys, 1973, Unhurry Harry, 1978, Ab to Zog, 1978 ; author poems: Family Circle, 1946, Tomorrow Morning, 1951, Montgomery, Alabama, Money, Mississippi and Other Places, 1956, The Double Bed from the Feminine Side, 1958, The Trouble with Love, 1961, There is No Rhyme for Silver, 1962, It Doesn't Always Have to Rhyme, 1964, Catch A Little Rhyme, 1965, Independent Voices, 1968, The Inner City Mother Goose, 1969, The Nixon Poems, 1970, Finding A Poem, 1970, Out Loud, 1973, A Husband's Notes About Her, 1976, Rainbow Writing, 1976, The Birthday Cow, 1978, If Only I Could Tell You, 1984, Blackberry Ink, 1985, Fresh Paint, 1986, Halloween ABC, 1986; author plays: Inner City, 1971, The Club, 1976 , Dialogue for Lovers, 1980, And I Ain't Finished Yet, 1982, Plagues for Our Time, 1983; co-editor: Male and Female Under 18, 1973; Contbr. to numerous mags., anthologies. Recipient Yale Younger Poets prize, 1946, Collier's Star Fiction award, 1949, Obie award, 1977, Nat. Coun. Tchrs. of English award for Excellence in Poetry for Children, 1984. Mem. Dramatists Guild Council. Home: New York N.Y. Died Apr. 11, 1992.

MERRILL, AMBROSE POND, JR., physician, health services consultant; b. Provo, Utah, Dec. 14, 1909; s. Ambrose Pond and Lydia (Stephens) M.; m. Elizabeth Call, Apr. 7, 1931. A.B., Stanford, 1932, M.D., 1935; M.H.A. with distinction, Northwestern U., 1948. Intern San Francisco County Hosp., 1934-35; surg. house officer Stanford U. Hosps., 1935-36; gen. practice medicine and surgery, 1936-40; surgeon San Francisco Emergency Hosp. Service, Dept. Pub. Health, 1936-38; asst. supt. San Francisco County Hosp., 1938-40; asst. dir. St. Luke's Hosp., Chgo., 1940-42, med. dir., 1942-45; exec. dir. St. Barnabas Hosp., N.Y.C., 1945-67; asst. dir. bur. hosp. certification N.Y. State Dept. Health, 1967-68; pres. A.P. Merrill, M.D. & Assos. (Hosp. and Health Services Consultants), Delmar, N.Y., from 1968; asst. clin. prof. phys. medicine and rehab. N.Y. U., 1955-60; lectr. Sch. Hosp. Adminstrn., Columbia, 1946-53, preceptor, 1946-67; Pres. Middle Atlantic Hosp. Assembly, 1958-59, Hosp. Assn. N.Y. State, 1956-57, Greater N.Y. Hosp. Assn., 1953-54; mem. N.Y.C. Mayor's Adv. Com. for the Aged, 1955-60; del. Nat. Health Assembly, 1948, Nat. Conf. on Aging, 1950, Internat. Gerontological Congress, 1951, Nat. Conf. on Care of Long-Term Patient, 1954, White House Conf. on Aging, 1961; chmn. com. on chronic illness Welfare and Health Council of N.Y.C., 1949-55; chmn. med. adv. com. Fedn. of Protestant Welfare Agys., N.Y.C., 1956-59; mem. subcom. on aging and chronic illness Interdepartmental Health Council, N.Y.C., 1957-60. Contbr.: chpt. to Functional Planning of Gen. Hospitals, 1969; also articles to hosp. and med. jours. Bd. dirs. Bronx Bd. Trade, 1955-67; bd. mgrs. Bronx YMCA, 1955-67, Bronx div. Protestant Council N.Y.C., 1950-65; donor student loan fund Stanford U., 1965. Recipient Brotherhood award NCCJ, 1967; Modern Hosp. award and medal, 1945; numerous others. Fellow N.Y. Acad. Medicine, Am. Coll. Hosp. Adminstrs., Am. Coll. Preventive Medicine; mem. N.Y. State Med. Soc., Bronx County Med. Soc., Greater N.Y. Hosp. Assn. (pres. 1953, 54), N.Y. State Hosp. Assn. (pres. 1956, 57), Am. Hosp. Assn. (life), Am. Pub. Health Assn., AAAS, Am. Geriatric Soc., N.Y. Acad. Scis., Am. Assn. Health Care Consultants, Internat. Hosp. Fedn., World Med. Assn., AMA., Alpha Kappa Kappa. Republican. Mem. Ch. of Jesus Christ of Latter-day Saints (high council N.Y. stake 1961-67, Hudson River stake 1969-72). Club: University (N.Y.C.). Home: Delmar N.Y. Died Feb. 23, 1991.

MERRILL, MARUICE HITCHCOCK, lawyer, teacher; b. Washington, Oct. 3, 1897; s. George Waite and Mary Lavinia (Hitchcok) M.; m. Orpha Roberts, June 4, 1922; 1 child, Marilyn Jean. AB, U. Okla., 1919, LLB, 1922; SJD, Harvard U., 1925. Bar: Okla. 1922. Lawyer Tulsa, 1922-24; asst., spl. instr., instr. in govt. U. Okla., 1919-22; assoc. prof. law U. Idaho, 1925-26; asst. prof. law, prof. U. Nebr., 1926-28, 28-36; prof. law, acting dean U. Okla., 1936-50, 45-46, rsch. prof. law, 1950-92; atty. U. Okla. Rsch. Inst., 1941-92; vis. tchr. law summer sessions U. Calif., 1927, Cornell U., 1928, U. Iowa, 1931, U. Kans., 1934, U. Tex., 1937, U. Chgo., 1938, U. N.C., 1958, 63-92, U. Mich., 1960, 62. Author or co-author several books; latest publ.: Cases and Materials on Administrative Law, 1950, Law of Notice, 3 Vols., 1952, and supplements, 1957, Administrative Law, 1954, Covenants Implied in Oil and Gas Leases Supplement, 1964. Counsel, draftsman Tulsa Charter Revision Com., 1939; mem. Norman Charter Revision Com., 1940-45; chmn. local examining bds. for Okla., under U.S. Bd. Legal Examiners and Civil Svc. Commn., 1942-44; pub. panel mem. Eighth Regional War Labor Bd., 1943-45; chmn. permanent trucking panel, 1943-45; mem. labor panel Am. Arbitration Assn., 1944-92; mem. from Okla., Nat. Conf. of Commrs. on Uniform State Laws, 1944-92, v.p. 1964; mem. sec. Jud. Coun. Okla., 1945-46. Recipient Hatton W. Summers award, 1964. Fellow Inst. Jud. ADminstrn., ABA; mem. Nat. Adac. of Arbitrators (chmn. for Okla. pub. info. program 1942-44), Cleveland County Bar Assn., Okla. Bar Assn., Southwestern Soc. Sci. Assn., Am. Acad. Polit. and Social Sci., Acad. Polit. Sci., Indsl. Rels. Rsch. Assn., Okla. Hist. Soc., Am. Judicature Soc., Am. Rose Soc., Phi Beta Kappa, Alpha Kappa Psi, Phi Delta Phi, Order of Coif. *

MESSIAEN, OLIVIER, composer, educator; b. Avignon, France, Dec. 10, 1908; s. Pierre and Cecile (Sauvage) M.; student Etudes classiques au Conservatoire de Paris, 1919, Etudes de la rhythmique hindoue, 1935, Etudes d'ornithologie, 1943; Dr.h.c., Cath. U. Am., 1972; m. 2d, Yvonne Loriod, July 1, 1961; 1 son by previous marriage, Pascal. Prof. harmony Conservatory Paris, from 1942, prof. rhythmic and analysis, from 1947, prof. of composition, from 1966; organist Trinité, Paris, 1931; concert tours throughout Europe, S.Am., Japan, U.S.; cours de compositions, Budapest, Darmstadt, Buenos Aires, Tanglewood, Mass. Decorated grand cross Legion d'Honneur; grand cross Order of Merit; comdr. Arts and Letters of France; comdr. Mérite fédéral Allemagne; recipient Erasme prize, 1971. Sibelius prize, 1971; Von Siemens prize, 1975; Leonie Sonning prize, 1977; Liebermann prize, 1983; Wolf Found. prize, 1983; grandprize Académie Berlin, 1984; Prix Inamori de Kyoto, 1985; grand prize Ville de Paris, 1985, Inst. Paolo VI, Italy, 1988, L. Spohr Allemagne, 1990. Mem. acads. Baviere, Berlin, Rome, Hamburg, London, Stockholm, Madrid, Nat. Acad. Arts and Letters. Composer: L'Asension (orch.), 1933; Nativité du Seigneur (organ), 1935; Poèmes pour Mi, 1936; Quatuor pour la fin du Temps, 1941; Visions de l'Amen (2 pianos), 1943; Vingt Regards (piano), 1944; Trois petites Liturgies, 1943; Turangalîla-Symphonie, 1948; Livre d'Orgue, 1952; Catalogue d'Oiseaux, for piano, 1958; Chronochromie for orch., 1960; Sept Haï-Kaï for piano and small orch., 1963; Et exspecto resurrectionem mortuorum, pour cuivres, bois, percussions métalliques, 1964; Meditations sur le Mystère de la Sainte Trinité, pour orgue, 1969; Transfiguration de N.S. Jesus Christ (choir, 7 solos and grand orch.), 1969; La Fauvette des jardins, for piano, 1970; Des Canyons aux Étoiles, piano and orch., 1970-74; Saint François d'Assise (opera), 1975-83, Livre du Saint Sacrement, pour orgue, 1985, Petites Esquisses D'Oiseaux, for piano, 1986, Un Vitrail et des Oiseaux for piano and small orch., 1987, La Ville D'En-Haut for piano and orch., 1988, Un Sourire orch., 1990. Died Apr. 27, 1992. Home: Paris France

MESSICK, JOHN DECATUR, college official; b. South Creek, N.C., Nov. 9, 1897; s. Jesse M. and Mary Z. (Flowers) M.; m. Magdalene E. Robinson, Jan. 8, 1924; children: Helen Margaret, Mary Rosalyn, Norval Robinson, John Albert. PhB, Elon Coll., 1922; student, U. N.C., 1922-25; PhD, NYU, 1934; LittD, Elon Coll., 1948. Prin. consol. schs., 1922-29; supt. Spencer (N.Y.) Schs., 1929-35; prof. Asheville Coll., 1934-35; dean, head edn. dept. Elon Coll., 1935-44; dean Montclair State Tchrs. Coll., 1944-47; pres. East Carolina Coll., 1947-60; fed. investigations on spl. edn. and rehab. U.S. Ho. of Reps. Com. on Edn. and Labor, 1960-61; dean Lyndon State Coll., 1961-63; exec. v.p. Oral Roberts U., Tulsa, 1963-92; cons. higher edn.; dir. Wachovia Bank & Trust Co.; v.p., dir. So. Heritage Life Ins. Co. Author: Personality and Character Development, 1939, Discretionary Powers of Boards of School Control, 1949; contbr. articles to profl. jours. Mem. N.C. Commn. on Atomic Energy; dir. N.C. Cerebral Palsy Hosp.; county chmn. N.C. United Fund Drive, 1958; past pres. N.C. League Crippled Children and Adults; chmn. East Carolina Coun. Boy Scouts Am.; v.p. exec. com. N.C. Coll. Conf., 1938; state adviser Future Tchrs. Assn.; chmn. Montclair Vet. Svc. Com., 1941-47; planning com. U.S. Higher Edn. Conf., 1949; chmn. accrediting com. of A.A.C.T.E., 1953-54, pres., 1953. Mem. NEA, N.C. Edn. Assn., N.J. Coun. on Adminstrs., N.Y. Sch. Masters Club, PTA, Eugene Field Soc., Nat. Inst. Arts & Letters, Phi Delta Kappa, Kappa Delta Pi, N.C. Coll. Athletic Assn., N.C. Girls Athletic Assn., Pitt County Execs. Club (pres 1949-52). *

MEYER, AUGUST CHRISTOPHER, lawyer, television executive; b. Brookport, Ill., Oct. 28, 1900; s. Gus and Ida (Pierce) M.; m. Clara Rocke, Feb. 2, 1929; 1 child, August Christopher. Grad., So. Ill. U., 1922; J.D., U. Ill., Urbana, 1928. Bar: Ill. 1928. Banker Brookport, 1917-24; practice law Champaign, from 1928; mem. firm Leonard & Meyer, 1928-34, Meyer & Franklin, 1934-54, Meyer & Capel, 1954-65; atty. Ill.

Press Assn., 1946-54; founder Midwest TV, Inc., Champaign, Ill., 1952, pres., 1952-76, chmn. bd., 1976-91; chmn. bd. dirs. Bank of Ill. (formerly Trevett-Mattis Banking Co.), Champaign, 1962-91; Mem. CBS-TV affiliates adv. bd., 1960-63, 66-69; State of Ill. rep. in negotiations for procurement airport for U. Ill., 1943-45, mem. com. to study future devel. Sch. of Aeros. and devel. of aviation. Past pres., bd. dirs. Burnham City Hosp., Champaign; former trustee Lincoln Acad. Ill. Mem. Nat. Assn. Broadcasters, Assn. of Maximum Service Telecasters (dir.), Ill., Champaign County bar assns., Phi Alpha Delta, Alpha Kappa Psi. Republican. Presbyn. Clubs: President's (U. Ill.), Burning Tree (Bethesda, Md.); Champaign Country, La Jolla (Calif.) Country. Home: Champaign Ill. Died Dec. 16, 1991; buried Champaign, Ill.

MEYER, KARL, biochemistry educator; b. Kerpen, Cologne, Germany, Sept. 4, 1899; came to U.S., 1930, naturalized, 1937; s. Ludwig and Ida (Aaron) M.; m. Marthe M. Ehrlich, Apr. 15, 1930; children: Robert F., Janet R. Meyer Levy. MD, U. Cologne, 1924; PhD in Chemistry, U. Berlin, 1927; MD (hon.), U. Uppsala, 1977; DSc (hon.), Columbia U., 1986. Asst. to Prof. O. Meyerhof, Berlin-Dahlem, 1927-28; asst. prof. U. Calif., Berkeley, 1930-32; asst. prof. biochemistry Columbia U., N.Y.C., 1933-42, assoc. prof., 1942-54, prof., 1954-67, prof. emeritus, spl. lectr. medicine, 1967-90; prof. Belfer Grad. Sch. Sci., Yeshiva U., N.Y.C., 1967-77, prof. emeritus, spl. lectr., 1977-90. Recipient Claude Bernard medal U. Montreal, 1952, Lasker award, 1956, T. Duckett-Jones Meml. award, 1959, award Gairdner Found., 1960, Disting. Svc. medal Columbia U., 1983. Fellow Am. Acad. Arts and Scis.; mem. NAS, Am. Soc. Biol. Chemists, Am. Chem. Soc., Am. Rheumatism Assn., Harvey Soc., Acad. Medicine N.Y. Home: Teaneck N.J.

MEYER, RICHARD E(DWARD), music, film and video producer and executive, former advertising and cosmetics executive; b. Cin., May 8, 1939; s. Joseph H. and Dolores C. (Daley) M.; m. Julia I. Kallish; children: Donna, Valerie. AB in Journalism, Advt. and Mktg. with honors, U. Mich., 1961. Mgr. auto staff advt. dept. Chgo. Tribune, 1961-63; account supr., v.p. London & Assos., Chgo., 1963-64; founder, pres., chmn. bd. Meyer & Rosenthal, Inc. (formerly Richard E. Meyer, Inc.), Chgo., 1965-74; exec. v.p., gen. mgr. Jovan Inc., Chgo., 1974-75; pres., chief operating officer Jovan Inc., 1975-79, pres., chief exec. officer, 1980-85; pres., chief exec. officer Yardley of London, Lancaster, 1980-85, Beecham Cosmetics, 1980-85, Omni Cosmetics, 1980-85, Parfums Hermes U.S.A., 1980-85; pres., chmn. bd. Red Entertainment Inc., Chgo., 1983-86, Red Label Records Inc., Chgo., 1983-86; past pres. Fragrance Found., 1985. Writer, producer various feature videos/films including Super Bowl Shuffle (RIAA Gold and Platinum awards 1986, Grammy nominee 1986,87), Mike Ditka's Grabowski Shuffle (RIAA Gold and Platinum video awards, 1987); patentee various product designs. Recipient numerous awards N.Y. Advt. Club, Chgo. Advt. Club, Designers and Art Dirs., TV commls., Print Casebook, First Advt. Agy. Network; recipient Communication Arts awards Printing Industry Am., Mktg. Achievement award Am. Mktg. Assn., Chgo. Mem. NARAS, Am. Film Inst., Acad. Motion Picture Arts and Scis., U. Mich. Club of Chgo., Delta Upsilon (trustee from 1961, alumni corp. pres. 1965-68, pres., vice chmn., dir. internat. fraternity 1990-91). Home: Chicago Ill. Deceased. †

MEYER, SAMUEL JAMES, educator, ophthalmologist; b. Centralia, Ill., Dec. 3, 1896; s. Peter and Rose (Born) M.; m. Dorothy W. Asher, Oct. 14, 1938; 1 child, Patricia Meyer Livingston. B.S., U. Chgo., 1917; M.D., Rush Med. Coll., Chgo., 1923. Diplomate: Am. Bd. Ophthalmology. Intern Cook County Hosp., Chgo., 1923-24, resident ophthalmology, 1925, attending physician, from 1952; asst. German U. Eye Clinic, Prague, 1925-26; extern Allgemeines Krankenhaus, Vienna, 1927; attending opthalmologist Michael Reese Hosp., Chgo., from 1928, chmn. dept., 1938-50; attending physician Ill. Eye and Ear Infirmary, Chgo., 1933-52; prof. ophthalmology, chmn. dept. Chgo. Med. Sch., from 1952; cons. Highland Park (Ill.) Hosp., from 1945, Weiss Meml. Hosp., Chgo., from 1955. Author: Glaucoma Manual, 1964; Contbr. articles to profl. jours. Served as ensign USN, 1917-19. Fellow ACS, Am. Acad. Ophthalmology (hon. key 1950); mem. Assn. Research Ophthalmology, Ill. Med. Soc. (chmn. eye sect. 1936), Soc. Eye Surgeons, Assn. U. Profs. Ophthalmology, Chgo. Ophthal. Soc. (chmn. 1944), Phi Beta Kappa, Sigma Xi, Alpha Omega Alpha, Phi Delta Epsilon. Republican. Clubs: Standard (Chgo.); Northmoor Country (Highland Park). Home: Highland Park Ill. Died Apr. 5, 1992.

MEYER, WALTER, energy engineer; b. Chgo., Jan. 19, 1932; s. Walter and Ruth (Killoran) M.; m. Jacqueline Miscall, May 8, 1953; children: Kim, Holt, Eric, Leah, Suzannah. B.Chem. Engring., Syracuse U., 1956, M.Chem. Engring., 1957; postgrad. (NSF Sci. Faculty fellow), MIT, 1962; Ph.D. (NSF Sci. Faculty fellow), Oreg. State U., 1964. Registered nuclear engr., Calif. Prin. chem. engr. Battelle Meml. Inst., Columbus, Ohio, 1957-58; instr., then asst. prof. Oreg. State U., 1958-64; rsch. engr. Hanford Atomic Labs., Richland, Wash., 1959-60, Lawrence Radiation Lab., Livermore, Calif., 1964; from asst. prof. to prof. nuclear engring. Kans. State U., Manhattan, 1964-72; prof., chmn. nuclear engring. U. Mo., Columbia, 1972-82; Robert Lee Tatum prof. engring. U. Mo., 1974-82, co-dir. energy systems and resources program, 1974-82; co-founder Energy and Pub. Policy Ctr., 1981-82; 1st holder Niagara Mohawk Energy professorship Syracuse U., 1982-92, dir. Inst. for Energy Research, 1984-92, prof. pub. adminstrn. Maxwell Sch. Citizenship and Pub. Affairs, 1985-92, exec. dir. Indsl. Innovation Extension Svc., Cen. N.Y. Pilot Project, 1988-90, tech. dir. Electric Power Rsch. Inst. Knowledge Based Tech. Application Ctr., 1989-92, exec. dir. Mfrs. Assistance Ctr., 1990-92; dir. summer insts. NSF-AEC, 1969, NSF, 1972; co-dir. summer instr. AEC, 1972, dir. workshop, 1973; dir. (ERDA workshops), 1975-79; mem. Columbia Coal Gasification Task Force, 1977, Gov. Kans. Nuclear Energy Coun., 1971-72; cons. to govt. and industry; exec. dir. Indsl. Innovation Extension Svc. for Cen. N.Y., 1988-90. Author; patentee in field. Mem. Manhattan Human Relations Orgn., 1966-72; active local Boy Scouts Am.; co-chmn. No on 11 Com., 1980. Grantee NSF, 1965-67, 73-75, 77-80, AEC, 1969-71, 73-74, Dept. Def., 1969-72, ERDA, 1975, 77—, NRC, 1977-80, Dept. Energy, 1985, Army Rsch. Office, 1987-91. Fellow Am. Nuclear Soc. (chmn. pub. info. com. 1975-79, nat. spl. award 1974, outstanding service award 1980, bd. dirs. 1981-84, chmn. univ./industry relations subcom. edn. div. 1980—, exec. com. edn. div. 1989—); mem. Am. Inst. Chem. Engrs. (chmn. nuclear engring. div. 1977-78), Am. Chem. Soc. (touring lectr. 1976-83), Am. Soc. Engring. Edn. (chmn. nuclear div. 1976-77), Am. Wind Soc., N.Y. Acad. Scis., Sigma Xi (v.p., pres. Syracuse sect. 1984-86), Tau Beta Pi. Presbyterian. Home: Chittenango N.Y. Died Mar. 17, 1992.

MEYNER, ROBERT BAUMLE, lawyer, former governor; b. Easton, Pa., July 3, 1908; s. Gustave Herman and Mary Sophia (Baumle) M.; m. Helen Stevenson, Jan. 19, 1957. AB, Lafayette Coll., 1930, LLD, 1954; LLB, Columbia, 1933; LLD, Rutgers U., 1954, Princeton U., 1956, L.I. U., 1958, Fairleigh Dickinson U., 1959, Syracuse U., 1960, Lincoln U., 1960, Colo. Coll., 1961. Bar: N.J. 1934, U.S. Supreme Ct. Pvt. practice Pohatcong Twp., N.J.; county lawyer Warren County, 1942; mem. N.J. State Senate, 1947, minority leader, 1950; gov. State of N.J., 1954-62; ptnr. Meyner, Landis, Newark; dir. Engelhard Corp., Phillipsburg Nat. Bank & Trust Co., N.J., First Nat. state Bancorp., Newark, Del. & Bound Brook R.R.; civilian aide for N.J. to sec. army; co-chmn. Interracial Coun. Bus. Opportunity, Newark; turstee Ednl. Broadcasting Corp., 1962-86. Comdr. USNR, 1942-45. Mem. ABA, Lafayette Coll. Alumni Assn., N.J. Bar Assn., Hudson County Bar Assn., Essex County Bar Assn., Warren County Bar Assn., Phillipsubrg (past pres.), Greater Newark C. of C., Grange, Columbia U. Law Sch. Alumni Assn., Elk, Eagle, Odd Fellow, Moose, Rotary, Essex Club (Newark), River Club (N.Y.C.), Pomfret Club, alpha Chi Rho. Democrat. Home: Phillipsburg N.J. Died May 27, 1990.

MICHELIS, JAY, broadcaster, educator; b. Livermore, Calif., Oct. 24, 1937; s. John Robert and Eileen Mary (Scullion) M. B.A. in Humanities, San Jose State U., 1959; postgrad. Stanford U., 1959. Page, NBC, Hollywood, Calif., 1959-61, page supr., 1961-63, mgr. guest relations, 1963-64, coordinator promotion, 1964, adminstr. promotion, 1964-66, mgr. promotion, 1966-70, dir. nat. promotion, 1970-72, exec. dir. nat. promotion, N.Y.C., 1972-78, v.p. talent relations, 1978-79, v.p. creative services, 1979-81, v.p. talent relations and creative services, 1981-83, v.p. corp. creative services, Burbank, Calif., 1983-86, v.p. corp. and media relations, from 1986; lectr. in field; bd. dirs. NBC Employees Fed. Credit Union. Mem. Acad. TV Arts and Scis., Pasadena Hist. Soc., Big Sur Hist. Soc., Monterey Bay Aquarium Found. Democrat. Roman Catholic. Club: Am. Surfing Assn. Deceased. Home: Big Sur Calif. †

MICHELSON, MAX, JR., former publisher; b. N.Y.C., June 7, 1921; s. Max and Ida Rose (Landau) M.; m. Virginia Seames, Oct. 22, 1950; children: Gail Ida, Eric Seames, Bradley Maxwell. B.A., Lafayette Coll., Easton, Pa., 1941. Advt. bus. mgr. R.K.O. Radio Pictures, N.Y.C., 1946-57; maj. nat. account mgr. Reuben H. Donnelley Corp., N.Y.C., 1958-65; Eastern dist. sales mgr. Sch. Products News, N.Y.C., 1965-69; publisher Am. Sch. and Univ., N.Y.C., 1970-85; pres. ednl. div. N.Am. Pub. Co., 1979-86, pres. emeritus, from 1986; mem. adv. council Ednl. Facilities Planners. Served with AUS, 1943-46. Mem. Am. Mktg. Assn., Assn. Sch. Bus. Ofcls., Am. Assn. Sch. Adminstrs., Assn. Ednl. Communications Technology, Assn. Phys. Plant Adminstrs., Ednl. Industries Assn., Am. Mgmt. Assn., Assn. Curriculum Devel., Assn. Media Producers, Nat. Sch. Supply and Equipment Edn. Exhibitors (dir. 1982-86). Lodge: Masons. Home: Washingtonville N.Y. Deceased. †

MICHENER, DANIEL ROLAND, lawyer, Canadian governor general; b. Lacombe, Alta., Can., Apr. 19, 1900; s. Edward and Mary Edith (Roland) M.; m. Norah Evangeline Willis, Feb. 26, 1927; children: Joan (Mrs. Donald Rohr), Diana (Mrs. Roy Edward Schatz), Wendy (Mrs. Leslie G. Lawrence, dec.). B.A. (Rhodes scholar), U. Alta., 1920; B.A., Oxford U., 1922, B.C.L., 1923, M.A., 1929; LL.D., U. Ottawa, 1948, Queen's U., 1959, U. Laval, 1960, U. Alta., 1967, St. Mary's U., Halifax, U. Toronto, 1968, Royal Mil. Coll. Can., Mt. Allison U., U. Alta, 1967, Brock U., 1969, U. Man., McGill U., York U., 1970, U. B.C., 1971, Jewish Theol. Sem. Am., U. N.B., 1972, Dalhousie U., 1974; D.C.L., Bishop's U., Lennoxville, 1968, U. Windsor, 1969, Oxford U., 1970. Called to bar, Toronto, 1924, created King's counsel 1943. Barrister Middle Temple, Eng., 1923, Ont., 1924; private practice Toronto, 1924-57; mem. Lang, Michener Lawrence & Shaw and predecessor firms, Ont. Legislature for St. David, Toronto, 1945-48; provincial sec. Drew Adminstrn., Ont., 1946-48; mem. for St. Paul, Toronto Ho. of Commons, 1953-62, speaker, 1957-62, sworn Privy Council, 1962; Canadian high commr. to India, 1964-67, also ambassador to Nepal, gov. gen., comdr.-in-chief of Can., 1967-74; chancellor Queen's U., 1974-80; chmn. bd. Met. Trust Co., 1974-76, hon. chmn. bd., 1976-80; hon. chmn. bd. Nat. Trust Co., 1980-91; chmn. Teck Corp., 1974-81, hon. chmn., 1981-91; pub. gov. Toronto Stock Exchange, 1974-76; assoc. counsel Lang Michener Lawrence & Shaw, from 1974. Past pres. Bd. Trade Club.; Gen. sec. for Can. Rhodes Scholarships, 1936-64; Past hon. counsel Ont. div. Red Cross; past gov. Toronto Western Hosp. Served with RAF, 1918. Chancellor prin. companion Order of Can., 1967; chancellor, comdr. Order Mil. Merit, 1972; prior for Can., knight justice Most Venerable Order Hosp. St. John of Jerusalem, 1967; hon. fellow Hertford Coll., Oxford, 1961; hon. fellow Trinity Coll., Toronto, 1968; hon. fellow Frontier Coll., Toronto, 1972. Hon. fellow Royal Archtl. Inst. Can., Royal Coll. Physicians and Surgeons Can., Acad. Medicine Toronto, Royal Soc. Can., Royal Can. Mil. Inst., Heraldry Soc. Can.; mem. Can. Inst. Internat. Affairs (past pres.), Can. Assn. Adult Edn. (past chmn. exec. com.), Can. Med. Assn. (hon. mem.), Law Soc. Upper Can. (hon. bencher, life mem.), Lawyers Club (past pres.), Empire Club (past pres.). Home: Toronto Can. Died Aug. 6, 1991; interred St. Bartholomew's Anglican Ch., Ottawa.

MICHL, JOSEF, chemistry educator; b. Prague, Czechoslovakia, Mar. 12, 1939; came to U.S., 1969; s. Josef and Vera (Polakova) M.; m. Sara Margaret Allensworth, Mar. 14, 1969; children: Georgina Frances, John Allensworth. MS, Charles U., Prague, 1961; PhD, Czechoslovakia Acad. Sci., Prague, 1965. Postdoctoral U. Houston, 1965-66, U. Tex., Austin, 1966-67; research scientist Czechoslovak Acad. Sci., 1967-68; amanuensis Aarhus (Denmark) U., 1968-69; postdoctoral researcher U. Utah, Salt Lake City, 1969-70, rsch. assoc. prof. chemistry, 1970-71, assoc. prof., 1971-75, prof., 1975-86, chmn. dept., 1979-84; M.K. Collie-Welch Regents prof. chemistry U. Tex., Austin, 1986; chmn. commn. photochemistry Internat. Union Pure Applied Chemistry, 1985-89. Editor Chem. Revs., from 1984; mem. editorial adv. bd., Accounts of Chem. Research, from 1984, Jour. Physics and Chemistry Reference Data, 1985-88; assoc. editor Theoretica Chim. Acta, from 1985; contbr. numerous sci. papers. Recipient Alexander von Humboldt Sr. U.S. Scientist award, 1980, disting. research award U. Utah, 1978-79; Alfred P. Sloan fellow, 1971-75, Guggenheim fellow. Mem. Nat. Acad. Scis., Internat. Acad. Quantum Molecular Sci., Am. Chem. Soc. (exec. com. div. phys. chemistry, 1982-86, Utah sect. award 1986), Interam. Photochem. Soc. (exec. com. 1977-80), Chem. Soc., Am. Soc. Mass Spectroscopy. Roman Catholic. Home: Austin Tex. Deceased. †

MICKEN, RALPH ARLINGTON, educator; b. Mpls., Jan. 26, 1907; s. Hiram and Lillian (Hiller) M.; m. Lavina Morken, June 10, 1931 (dec. May 1964); children—Marguerite, Patrick H.; m. Doris Meagher, Aug. 28, 1965. B.A., Intermountain Union Coll., Helena, Mont., 1929; postgrad., U. N.D., 1931; M.A., Mont. State U., 1936; Ph.D., Northwestern U., 1947. Prin. Cut Bank (Mont.) High Sch., 1931-36; dir. forensics Gt. Falls (Mont.) High Sch., 1936-39; instr., then asst. prof. Mont. Sch. Mines, 1939-44; asst. prof., then asso. prof. Iowa State U., 1944-47, chmn. speech staff, 1948-49; grad. lectr. Northwestern U., 1947-48; sales speech counselor Banker's Life Ins. Co., 1947-49; prof. speech, dir. forensics Ill. State Normal U., 1949-57; chmn. speech dept. So. Ill. U., Carbondale, from 1957; Moderator World Affairs Forum, Bloominton, Ill., 1952-57. Author: Speaking for Results, 1958, America in Controversy, 1973, Where a Man Is, 1973; Editor: Cicero on Oratory and Orators, 1969; editorial bd.: Landmarks in Rhetoric Series, 1962. Mem. Central States Speech Assn. (adv. council 1961-62), Ill. Speech Assn. (pres. 1960-61), Speech Communication Assn. Am. (legislative council 1961-63), Pi Kappa Delta (gov. Ill. province 1954-55), Delta Sigma Rho. Home: Saint Annes on Sea Eng. Died Sept. 15, 1989; buried Lythem, St. Annes On Sea, Eng.

MIDDLETON, DREW, author; b. N.Y.C., Oct. 14, 1913; s. Elmer Thomas and Jean (Drew) M.; m. Estelle Mansel-Edwards, Mar. 31, 1943; 1 dau., Judith Mary. B.S. in Journalism, Syracuse U., 1935, LL.D. (hon.), 1963. Sports editor Poughkeepsie (N.Y.) Eagle News, 1936; reporter Poughkeepsie Evening Star, 1936-37; sports writer N.Y.C. office AP, 1939; war corr. attached to Brit. Expeditionary Force in France and Belgium, 1939-40; war corr. attached to RAF, Brit. Home Army, 1940-41, U.S. Army and Navy corr. in Iceland, 1941-42; Allied Forces London, 1942; mem.

staff N.Y. Times, London, 1942; corr. in Tunisia, Algeria and Mediterranean area and Allied Hdqrs., Algiers, 1942-43; with U.S. 8th Air Force and Bomber Command, RAF, 1943-44; accredited U.S. First Army and Supreme Hdqrs. Allied Expeditionary Force, 1944-45; at Frankfurt, Berlin and at Internat. Mil. Tribunal trials, Nuremberg, Germany, 1945-46; chief corr. N.Y. Times, to USSR, 1946-47, to Germany, 1947-53, London, 1953-63, PAris, 1963-65, UN, 1965-68; European affairs corr. N.Y. Times, 1968-70, mil. corr., 1970-84; columnist N.Y. Times Syndicate, N.Y.C., 1984-90. Author: Our Share of Night, 1946, The Struggle for Germany, 1949, The Defense of Western Europe, 1952, These Are the British, 1957, The Sky Suspended, 1960, The Supreme Choice, 1963, The Atlantic Community, 1965, Retreat From Victory, 1973, Where Has Last July Gone?, 1974, Can America Win The Next War, 1975, Submarine, 1976, The Duel of the Giants: China and Russia in Asia, 1978, Crossroads of Modern Warfare, 1983, Invasion of the United States, 1985, (with Gene Brown) Southeast Asia, 1985. Recipient Headliners Club award fgn. corr., 1943; Internat. News Service medal for Dieppe coverage, 1942; U.S. Navy Certificate of Merit, 1945; U.S. Medal of Freedom, 1948; Comdr. Order Brit. Empire (mil. div.), 1947. Mem. Delta Upsilon, Phi Kappa Alpha. Clubs: Garrick (London), Beefsteak (London); Brook (N.Y.C.), Century (N.Y.C.); Travellers (Paris). Home: New York N.Y. Died Jan. 10, 1990; cremated.

MIEDEL, RUSSELL J., manufacturing executive; b. Wheeling, W.Va., Mar. 18, 1895; s. Julius B. and Zetta (Halsey) M.; m. Sallie A. Love, June 20, 1917; children: S. Margaret (Mrs. George H. Reimer), Patricia E. (Mrs. John S. Tate). Stenographer Pa. R.R., 1914-16; traffic mgr., gen. traffic mgr. Hazel-Atlas Glass Co. of Cal., Wheeling, W.Va., 1925-29; v.p. Hazel-Atlas Glass Co. of Cal., Wheeling, 1929-36; dir. sales Pacific Coast div., Oakland, 1936-45; dir. Sierra Capital Co., Lyons-Magnus, Inc., Hunt Foods and Industries, Inc., Am. Distilling Co., Alameda County Industries, Inc.; pres. Alvarado Farms. Chmn. bd. Cosmos Found. Served with U.S. Army, World War I. Mem. Calif. Mfrs. Assn. (dir.), St. Francis Yacht (San Francisco), Marsh (Alvarado, Calif.), Cosmos (pres.). *

MILANOV, ZINKA, soprano; b. Zagreb, Yugoslavia, May 17; d. Rudolf and Ljubica (Smiciklas) Kunc. Grad., Girl's Evangel. Sch., Zagreb; diploma, Zagreb Acad. Music; pupil, Maria Kostrencic-Milka Ternina, Prof. Stueckgold, Prof. Bozidar Kunc. European operatic debut, Yugoslavia, as Leonora in II Trovatore, Met. Opera debut, same role, 1937; leading dramatic soprano roles Met. Opera, Chgo., Civic Opera, San Francisco Opera, Cin. Summer Opera, also in Buenos Aires, Rio de Janeiro, Sao Paulo, Vienna, Salzburg Festival, La Scala, Covent Garden, Lucerne Festival, others; opened Met. season four times, 1940-46; lead roles in Aida, L'Amore dei Tre Re, Un Ballo in Maschera, Madam Butterfly, Cavalleria Rusticana, Don Giovanni, Ernani, Faust, La Gioconda, La Juive, Fidelio, Mefistofole, Norma Otello, Pigue Dame, Der Rosenkavalier, Simon Boccanegra, Il Tabarro, Tannhäuser, Tosca, Il Trovatore, Turandot, Die Walkurè, William Tell, Andrea Chenier, Forza del Destino, Girl of the Golden West, Louise, Manon Lescaut; concert tours U.S., Can., Mex., Cen. Am., S.A., Europe; TV and radio artist; recs. with RCA Victor. Home: New York N.Y. Died May 30, 1989.

MILES, BERNARD, actor, director; b. Sept. 27, 1907; s. Edwin James and Barbara (Fletcher) Miles; m. Josephine Wilson 1931; 3 children. Student, Uxbridge County Sch., Pembroke Coll.; Hon. DLitt, City U., 1974. First stage appearance, 1930; writer, dir., actor films, 1937-91; West End stage appearances, 1938-91, music-hall stage appearances, 1950-91; founder Mermaid Theatre, North London, 1950; formed Mermaid Theatre Trust; opened Mermaid Theatre in City of London, 1959; author: The British Theatre, 1947, God's Brainwave, 1972, Favourite Tales From Shakespeare, 1976. Mem. Com. of Mgrs., Royal Inst. Gt. Britain. Home: Knaresborough England Deceased.

MILEY, WILLIAM MAYNADLER, army officer; b. Ft. Mason, Calif., Dec. 26, 1987; s. John D. and Sara Hayes (Mordecai) M.; m. Julia Athene Sudduth, Apr. 20, 1921; children: William M., John D. BS, U.S. Mil. Acad., 1918; grad., Air Corps Tactical Sch., 1930. Served with U.S. Army Ft. Houston, Tex., 1924-26; P.I., 1926-28, Ft. Benning, Ga., 1928-29; athletic officer, 1938-92; R.O.T.C. duty Miss. State Coll., 1920-24; comdr. 501st Parachute Bn., 1940-42; advanced through grades to maj. gen., Mar. 1943; instr. dept. tactics U.S. Mil. Acad., 1930-34; instr. dept. tactics Panama, 1934-36, Ft. Leavenworth, Kans., 1937-38. *

MILIVOJEVICM, DIENISIJE, bishop; b. Rabrovac, Serbia, Jugoslavia, July 26, 1898; s. Zivota and Stamenija (Jankovich) M. Ed. pub. sch., Rabrovac; gymnasium, Kragujevac; student, U. Belgrade, 1920-24; spl. course in lang. acad., Constantinople, 1930-32. came to U.S., 1940;. Tchr. gymnasium Kragujevac, 1925-30; in seminary, 1932; elected superior father Monastery of Vicoki Dechani, 1933; bishop vicar, 1938-40; bishop of Serbian Ch. U.S.A., Can., 1940-92; main superior St. Sava Serbian Monastery, Libertyville, Ill.; authorized by Holy Synod of Belgrade to take spiritual care over Serbian displaced persons and clery; pres. Am. Serbian Com. on Displaced Persons. Co-author: Martyrdom of the Serbs, 1943; author: The Persecution of the Serbian Orthodox Church in Yugoslavia, 1945; also several books on religion published in Europe. *

MILLAR, RICHARD WILLIAM, business executive; b. Denver, Jan. 8, 1899; s. Edward Richard and Marguerite Manitou (Atcheson) M.; m. Catherine Claiborne Armes, Feb. 25, 1934; children—Richard W. Jr., Roger James. Student, Occidental Coll., Los Angeles, 1917-18; B.A., U. Calif., 1921. Student security salesman Blair & Co., 1922; advancing to v.p., later v.p. successor Bancamerica-Blair Corp.; pres. Bankamerica Co., 1930-32, Vultee Aircraft, 1939-43; chmn. Avion, Inc.; mem. bd., also vice chmn. bd. Northrop Corp., from 1947, chmn. bd., 1947-49, 75-76; past vice chmn. Glore, Forgan, William R. Staats, Inc.; dir. Quotron Systems, Inc. Hon. trustee Occidental Coll., Webb Sch. Calif. mil. instr., later Central Inf., Officers Tng. Camp World War I, Waco, Tex. Mem. Owl and Key (Occidental Coll.), Phi Kappa Psi. Episcopalian. Clubs: Calif. (Los Angeles); Valley Hunt (Pasadena); Bohemian (San Francisco). Home: Pasadena Calif. Died June 1, 1990.

MILLER, A. EDWARD, publishing and communications consultant; b. N.Y.C., Aug. 28, 1918; s. Joseph and Sara (Miller) M.; m. Mary-Susan Morris, Nov. 19, 1949; children: Christopher, Eric Booth, Amy Katherine. B.B.A., Coll. City N.Y., 1939, M.B.A., 1942. C.P.A. Accountant Ernst & Ernst, 1945-47; dir. research Life mag., Time Inc., N.Y.C., 1947-54, asst. to pub., 1955-59; pub. McCall's mag., 1959-64; pres. Alfred Politz Research, Inc., subsidiary of Computer Sciences Corp., 1964-68; also dir.; pres., chief exec. officer, dir. World Pub. Co., subsidiary Times-Mirror Corp., 1968-70; v.p., dir. McCall Corp.; pres., dir. Berlitz Schs. of Langs. (subsidiary Crowell Collier and MacMillan, Inc.), 1970-72; pres. Berlitz Travel Services, Inc., 1970-72; exec. v.p., dir. Downe Publishing, Inc. subs. Charter Co., 1972-74, pres., chief operating officer, dir., 1974-79; pres. Downe Publishing, Inc. subs. Charter Co. (Downe Communications, Inc. div.), 1972-74; chmn. bd. Miller & Kops Inc., N.Y.C., 1982-87; pres. A. Edward Miller Assocs., N.Y.C., 1987-91, editorial advisor research alert; adj. prof. psychology Baruch Sch., CCNY, part-time from 1953; adj. prof. pub. NYU Sch. Continuing Edn., part-time from 1979; dir. U/Stat, Inc., Community Nat. Bank, Technology, Inc., Rising Star Assocs Inc.; cons. in communications to U.S. and internat. cos., from 1979; adv. com. Center for Advancement Human Communication, Fairfield U.; adv. bd. manpower research study U.S. Office of Edn., NSF; mem. exec. com., treas., sec. Nat. Book Com.; chmn. Nat. Library Week Steering Com.; mem. Nat. Marketing Adv. Com. to Sec. of Commerce. Mem. bd. editors: Jour. Mktg. Chmn. Mayor's Com. Indsl. Leaders Youth, N.Y.C.; mem. citizens adv. com. N.Y. Pub. Library; pres., dir. N.Y.C. Youth Bd. Research Inst.; trustee Center for Urban Edn.; bd. dirs., vice chmn. Advt. Research Found., 1974; head. fin. Nat. Book Com.; advisor Sch. Communications, Fairfield U. Recipient Alumni award U. City N.Y., 1969. Mem. Market Research Council, Am. Mktg. Assn. (dir.), Grad. Bus. Alumni N.Y.U. (v.p.), Am. Statis. Assn., Am. Econ. Assn., Am. Sociol. Assn., Am. Assn. Pub. Opinion Research, Alpha Delta Sigma. Club: New York University. Home: New York N.Y. Died Dec. 24, 1991.

MILLER, CARL PATTERSON, SR., newspaper publisher; b. Riley, Kans., Oct. 30, 1897; s. Alexander Quintella and Martha Lavina (Patterson) M.; m. Marvel Mona Merillat, Sept. 24, 1920 (dec. Oct. 28, 1948); children: Carl Patterson, Martha Iene (Mrs. W. G. Kerchoff); m. Ruth Bohe, June 5, 1950. Student, Kans. State Coll., 1916-20. Gen. mgr. Belleville (Kans.) Telescope, 1920-25; asst. fin. editor L.A. Times, 1925-27; sec., mgr. L.A. Stock Exch., 1927-29; exec. dir. Pacific Coast div. Dow, Jones & Co., Inc., 1929-64; pres., dir. San Gabriel Valley Newspapers, Inc., 1945-60; dir. Gen. Telelphone Co. Calif., 1955-59, Calif. Bldg. & Loan Assn., 1955-59, San Gabriel Valley Tribune, Inc., 1955-59; past chmn. Fed. Home Loan Bank of San Francisco, 1955-59, dir., 1958-62; dir. L.A. Fair Assn.; vice chmn. L.A. Community Chest, 1954. Mem. Calif. Newspaper Pubs. Assn., L.A. C. of C. (pres. 1955), L.A. Trade Fairs, Inc. (pres. 1954), Pomona Coll. Assocs., Sigma Delta Chi (nat. pres. 1935), Sigma Nu, Masons, Rotary (pres. 1945-46, gov. 160th dist. internat. 1951-52, dir. internat. 1957-59, 3d v.p. 1958-59, pres. internat. 1963-64), L.A. Country Club, Balboa Bay Club. *

MILLER, DAVID PHILIP, publishing executive; b. Warwick, N.Y., Nov. 29, 1921; s. Howard Pierson and Katherine M. (Avery) M.; m. Carol A. Lovell, May 10, 1952; children: Dean, Mark, Keith, Kevin, Alan. B.S., Rutgers U., 1949. With McGraw-Hill Co., N.Y.C., 1950-52; asst. v.p. W.B. Saunders Co., Phila., 1952-69; pub. med. dept. Harper-Row, Pubs., Hagerstown, Md., from 1969; v.p. Harper-Row, Pubs., 1976-81; sr. editor Univ. Park Press, Balt., 1981-83. Served with USAAF, 1942-46. Ky. Col. Mem. Rutgers Rowing Assn., Nat. Rifle Assn., Delta Kappa Epsilon. Home: Williamsport Md. Deceased. †

MILLER, DONALD RICHARD, sculptor, educator; b. Erie, Pa., June 30, 1925; s. Ira Russell and Laura Belle (Wise) M.; m. Harriet Elizabeth Phillips, Nov. 18, 1961; children: Russell Scott, Melanie Ann. B.F.A., Dayton Art Inst., 1952; postgrad., Pratt Inst., 1955-57; postgrad, Art Students League, N.Y.C., 1958-61; apprentice, Ulysses A. Ricci, N.Y.C., 1956-60. Studio asst. to William Zorach, Bath, Maine and Bklyn., 1952, Marshall Fredericks, S.I., N.Y., 1956-63, Joseph Kiselewski, N.Y.C., 1961, Wheeler Williams, Madison, Conn., 1961, Julian Harris, Perth Amboy, N.J., 1964; asst. prof. sculpture fine arts dept. Fashion Inst. Tech. SUNY, from 1972; works include animal sculpture, N.Y.C. and Warwick, N.Y., 4 gargoyles, Washington Cathedral, 1960-76, Nocturnus (animal relief), Phila. Zoo, 1973, The Pond The Sea (reliefs), Cin. Zoo, 1975, The Ridge Raccoons (Ridge Sch.), Ridgewood, N.J., 1979. Served with U.S. Army, 1943-45. Recipient Dr. Maurice B. Hexter prize Nat. Sculpture Soc., 1983; recipient Lindsey Morris Meml. prize, 1982, Tallix Foundry prize, 1980, Sculpture Assn. award Allied Artists Am., 1977. Fellow Nat. Sculpture Soc. (sec. 1983 exbhn.); assoc. NAD (Ellen P. Speyer prize 1987, Elliot Liskin Meml. prize, 1988); mem. Soc. Animal Artists (v.p. from 1979), Audubon Artists (exhbn. chmn. 1979-80), Allied Artists Am. Presbyterian. Home: Warwick N.Y. Died Aug. 21, 1989; cremated.

MILLER, DONALD SIDNEY, physician, educator, author; b. Maywood, Ill., Dec. 9, 1908; s. Harry and Sarah (Cohen) M.; m. children: Harvey D., Rollie Am. Grason, Alice J. Breakstone. BS, U. Ill., 1930, MS, 1932, MD, 1932, PhD, 1940. Intern Cook County Hosp., Chgo., 1933-34, attending orthopedic surgeon, 1948-89; attending orthopedic surgeon Oak Park (Ill.) Hosp., 1948-89, Mt. Sinai Hosp., Chgo., 1948-89; pvt. practice Chgo., 1946. Author 2 med. books; contbr. 74 articles to profl. jours. Active Combined Jewish Appeal. Lt. col. USMC, WWII. Mem. ACS, AMA, Ill. Med. Soc., Chgo. Med. Soc., Internat. Coll. Surgeons (v.p.), Sigma Xi, Alpha Omega Alpha. Home: Lincolnwood Ill. Died June 8, 1989.

MILLER, EDWARD WILLIAM, banker; b. Buffalo, Feb. 3, 1897; s. Eberhardt and Louise (Schaeffner) M.; m. Lilliam B. Briggs, Oct. 11, 1923; children: Edward William, Nan. B., Sally I. (Mrs. Don Marasi). Student pub. schs., Buffalo. With Fidelity Trust Co., Buffalo, 1913-92; merged with Manufacturers & Traders Trust Co., 1925, asst. sec., asst. treas., asst. to pres., 1925-29, v.p., 1929-58, exec. v.p., 1958-92; dir. M & T Discount Corp., N.Y.C. Served with U.S. Army World War I. Mem. Erie County Rep. Fin. Com., Buffalo C. of C., Mason, Buffalo Club, Park Club, Buffalo Athletic Club, Pytonga Fish and Game Club. *

MILLER, GEORGE ROLAND, state official; b. Easton, Pa., Jan. 3, 1894; s. George R. and Emily Alice (Sandt) M.; m. Lillian Lewis Postles, Dec. 19, 1925; 1 child, Mary Emily. AB, Lafayette Coll., 1915; MA, Tchrs. Coll., Columbia U., 1922; EdD, NYU, 1943. Prin. Martin's Creek, Pa., 1916-18; tchr. math. and Latin Casper, Wyo., 1919-21; tchr. math. N.Y. Mil. Acad., Cornwall on Hudson, 1922-23; supervising prin. Mt. Lakes, N.J., 1923-27; tchr. lang. and psychology Asheville Jr. Coll., 1927-30; co. supr. State Dept., Dover, Del., 1930-37; supt. Smyrna, Del., 1937-44, Salem City, N.J., 1944-46; supt. pub. instrn. Del., 1946-92. Dir. Del. Anti-TB Assn., Del. Safety Coun., Mental Health Assn.; trustee Wesley Jr. Coll., Dover. Served as ensign USNRF, 1918-19. Mem. NEA, Am. Assn. Sch. Adminstrn., Del. Assn. Sch. Adminstrn., Nat. Coun. Chief State Sch. Officers, Del. State Edn. Assn., Am. Legion, S.A.R., Phi Beta Kappa, Sigma Alpha Epsilon, Phi Delta Kappa, Mason (Shriner), Rotary. Methodist. *

MILLER, GLADYS, decorating expert; b. Franklin, Nebr., Apr. 10, 1896; d. George Owen and Carrie Lou (Graves) M. BS, Oreg. State Coll.; MA, NYU, 1957; AFD, Moore Inst. Art Sci. Industry, 1957. Instr. interior decorating Phoenix High Sch. and Jr. Coll.; decorator Frederick & Nelson, Seattle; study abroad; asst. mdse. mgr. Gimbel, Pitts.; in field promotion work F. Schumacher & Co.; instr. NYU; decorating editor Mademoiselle, 1938-42; decorating cons. Pub. Bldgs. Adminstrn., 1941-45; decorator diplomatic guest houses Blair House and Blair Lee, 1937-58; decorating editor Family Circle Mag., 1946-55; weekly columns on decorating syndicated by N.A. Newspaper Alliance, 1946-53; decorating cons. lamp div. G.E., 1952-57; cons. U.S. Army, Q.M.G., and Rsch. and Devel. Command, 1946-58; editor New Homes Guide and Home Modernizing Guide, 1955-63; assoc. pub. Bldg. Products Guide, 1964; now environ. cons. to builders; tchr. interior design seminar Oreg. State U., summer 1963. Author: Decoratively Speaking, 1939, Room Make-up, 1941, reprint, Your Home Decorating Guide, 1947, Your Decorating A-B-C, 1946, Furniture for Your Home, 1946. Fellow Am. Inst. Interior Designers; mem. Nat. Home Fashions League, The Fashion Group, Illumniating Engring. Soc., Phi Kappa Phi, Kappa Kappa Gamma, Eta Mu Pi, Theta Sigma Phi. Democrat. *

MILLER, HAROLD F., store executive; b. Balt., Aug. 7, 1897; s. S. F. and Minnie (Kaufman) M.; m. Sue Harris, Sept. 23, 1924; children: Janice Sue (Mrs. James

Douglas Freeman), Helen Sue (Mrs. John E. Dunn, 3d), Harold F. Student, Balt. Poly. Inst., Cornell U. Assoc. The Hub, Balt., 1919; merchandise mgr. Kaufman's, Harrisburg, Pa., 1923-26; div. mdse. mgr. Gilchrists, Boston, 1927-29, Gimbel Bros., N.Y.C., 1930-32; asst. gen. mdse. mgr. Lerner Stores Corp., 1933, gen. mdse. mgr., 1946, dir., v.p., 1947-56, sr. v.p., 1956-92. Served with Md. Nat. Guard, 1917, transferred to 117th Trench Mortar Battery, 42d Div.; commd. 2d lt. and assigned to 15th F.A., 2d Div., 1918-19. Awarded unit citation, French Fourragere, 1918. Mem. Manhattan Club, Bonnie Briar Country Club. *

MILLER, HERBERT JOHN, federal affairs counselor; b. Heron Lake, Minn., Nov. 17, 1894; s. Charles and Bertha (Behrenfield) M.; m. Catherine Johnson, Apr. 1, 1921; 1 child, Herbert J. Student, U. Minn., 1917, Sorbonne, 1918. Bus. mgr. U. Minn. Daily, 1916; sec. Voter Info. Club, Mpls., 1918-21, Mpls. Real Estate Bd., 1921-24; mgr. Mpls. Taxpayers Assn., 1924-35; exec. sec. Minn. Taxpayers Assn., 1927-30; pres. Mpls. Civic and Commerce Assn., 1935-39; exec. dir. Minn. Resources Com., 1939-42; commr. Iron Range Resources and Rehab., St. Paul, 1940-42; rsch., assoc. dir. Citizens Nat. Com., Washington, 1943-47; rsch. dir. Commn. on Orgn. of Exec. Br. of Govt., 1948-49. Served as sgt. 1/c, Base Hosp. 26, A.E.F., 1917-18; vice chmn. Minn. War Bd., 1940-41. Mem. Govtl. Rsch. Assn., Nat. Tax Assn., Coun. Basic Edn., Sigma Alpha Epsilon, Phi Delta Phi. Methodist. *

MILLER, JULIAN CREIGHTON, horticulturist; b. Lexington, S.C., Nov. 29, 1895; s. Simeon Jeremiah and Plumie Elizabeth (Shull) M.; m. Caroline Stone Leichliter, Dec. 26, 1923; children: Rodman B., Julian Creighton. BS, Clemson Coll., 1921, LLD, 1961; MS, Cornell U., 1926, PhD, 1928. Instr. horticulture N.C. State Coll., 1921-23; county agrl. agy. S.C., 1923-25; asst. Cornell U., 1925-28; assoc. prof. horticulture and rsch. Okla. A&M Coll., 1928-29; prof. horticulture, head dept. La. State U., from 1929; developed techniques for breeding vegetable crops; agr. advisor to P.R. and C.Am.; plant exploration for Ipomea species, econ. medicinal plants in W.I. in cooperation with USDA, 1953; U.S. del. to Internat. Hort. Congress, 1955. Author numerous expt. sta. bulls., spl. feature articles on rsch.; contbr. to sci. jours. Served with U.S. Navy, 1917-19, seaman, line officer as ensign and lt. (j.g.); developed process for dehydrating sweet potatoes for Army, World War II. Named Progressive Farmer's Man. of Yr., 1940 for La., Man of South, 1947; recipient Wilder medal for breeding and introdn. of Klonmore strawberry, also plaques for svcs. rendered in hort. field; named Vegetable Man of Yr., Vegetable Growers Assn. Am. Fellow AAAS; mem. Soc. Hort. Sci. (pres. 1942, chmn. So. sect. 1948), Am. Genetic Assn., Potato Assn. Am. (pres. 1938), Assn So. Agr. Workers, So. Assn. Sci. and Industry, Am. Inst. Biol. Scis., La. Farm Bur. Fedn. (hon. life mem.), So. Seedsmen's Assn. (hon. life mem.), Masons, Kiwanis, Sigma Xi, Phi Kappa Phi (provincial sec. so. sect. 1935-52, nat. regent), Omicron Delta Kappa, Alpha Gamma Rho, Alpha Gamma Delta, Alpha Zeta (Centennial hon. mem.). Democrat. Presbyterian (ruling elder). *

MILLER, LESLIE HAYNES, mathematics educator; b. Ironton, Ohio, Mar. 21, 1914; s. Thomas Jefferson and Mattie (Haynes) M.; m. Ethyl Rose, June 10, 1937; children: Joanne Miller Stichweh, Marilyn (Mrs. John Rehm). B.S. in Edn, Ohio U., 1935, M.A., 1938; Ph.D., Ohio State U., 1943. Tchr. pub. schs. Ironton, 1935-37; instr. Cedarville Coll., 1938-40; from instr. to assoc. prof. math. Ohio State U., 1943-57, prof., 1957-79, prof. emeritus, 1979-89, also mem. computer graphics research group.; artist in residence Otterbein Coll., 1985-88. Author: College Geometry, 1957, Fundamental Mathematics, 1957, Understanding Basic Mathematics, 1961; contbr. articles to profl. jours. Served with USNR, 1943-44. Recipient awards for artistic carved gourds. Fellow AAAS; mem. Math. Assn. Am., Ohio Ret. Tchrs. Assn. (life), Am. Gourd Soc. (dir., editor The Gourd jour.), N.Y. Acad. Sci., Sigma Xi, Pi Mu Epsilon. Home: Columbus Ohio Died Feb. 18, 1989; buried Kingwood Meml. Pk., Del. County, Ohio.

MILLER, LLOYD IVAN, manufacturing company executive; b. Cin., May 1, 1924; s. Lloyd Ivan and Louise (Ruscher) M.; m. Catherine Marie Crider, Jan. 5, 1952; children: Lloyd Ivan III, Martin Gregg. Student, U. Chgo., 1943-44; LL.B., U. Cin., 1948. Bar: Ohio 1948. Practice in Cin., 1948; stock broker, 1948-58; dir. Cin. Transit Co., 1950-73, chmn., 1956-72, pres., 1972-73; U.S. ambassador to Trinidad and Tobago, 1974-75; chmn. bd. LIMCO, Inc., Valley Industries, Inc., 1975-86; chmn., chief exec. officer Vulcan Corp., from 1975; pres. Am. Controlled Industries, 1975-86; bd. dirs. Super Food Services Inc., Central Trust Co., Eagle Picher Industries, Cin. Gas & Electric Co., PNC Fin. Comair, Inc.; mem. adv. com. internat. bus. problems State Dept., 1970-74; mem. U.S. Trade Mission, Yugoslavia and Poland, 1971, Regional Export Expansion Council, 1971-74, Adv. Commn. on Trade Negotiations, 1982-86; dir. Council Am. Ambassadors, 1984-90; former part owner Cin. Reds. Pres. U. Cin. Found., 1980-82. Served with inf. AUS, 1943-46. Mem. C. of C., Newcomen Soc. N.Am., Cin. Bar Assn. Clubs: University, Queen City, Cincinnati Country, Quail Creek Country, Hole in the Wall Golf. Lodges: Masons (33 deg.), Shriners. Home: Naples Fla. Died Apr. 22, 1990; buried Naples, Fla. †

MILLER, M. HUGHES, publisher; b. Phila., July 3, 1913; s. Samuel Maximillian and Sarah (Hughes) M.; m. Doris Gloria Ross, Jan. 1, 1936 (div.); children: Bruce Hyatt, Stephen Hughes; m. Mala Powers, May 17, 1970. A.B., Muhlenberg Coll., 1931; M.A., U. Pa., 1932. Editorial writer Phila. Pub. Ledger, 1929-32; editor Lehigh Valley Review, 1933; mgr. Nat. Advt. Service, 1933-36; mgr. coll. pub. Prentice-Hall, 1936-37; staff pub. relations Earl Newsom & Co., 1937-39; gen. mgr. book pub. Am. Edn. Press, publs. dir. Current Sci. and Aviation, v.p., gen. mgr. Charles E. Merrill, also Wesleyan U. Press, 1939-56; v.p. new pub. Am. Book-Stratford Press, Inc., 1956-58; pres. Bobbs Merrill Co., Inc. (pub. The Joy of Cooking), 1959-63, Book Pubs. Project, Inc., N.Y.C., 1963-86, Book Pubs. Enterprises, Inc., N.Y.C., 1986-89; pub. The New Lexicon Dictionary of Basic Words; editorial dir. Child's First Ency.; editor Dictionary of Basic Words, Am. edit. Blyton Secret Seven Series; mem. edn. bd. Education mag.; governing editorial bd. Mil. Pub. Inst.; pres. Hughes Miller Pubs. Projects, Inc., Four Seasons Estates Inc., Lake Tahoe, Calif.; chmn. bd. Inter-Assoc. Book Pub. Cons., 1966—; exec. com., dir. Devon Group, Inc. (formerly Gen. Edn. Services corp.); dir., chmn. acquisition com. Am. Book-Stratford Press, Inc.; founder Weekly Reader Children's Book Club, 1953; pres. Lottery Info. Services, Inc., Calif., from 1985; with prodn. Dial-a-Children's Story Svc. Mem. Am. Film Inst. (charter), Am. Childhood Assn. Nat. Council Social Studies, Profl. Bookmen Am. (past pres., founder mem.), Assn. Childhood Edn. Internat. (dir.), Am. Inst. Graphic Arts (chmn. textbook clinic), Am. Textbook Pub. Inst. (chmn. plans and program 1954-56, dir.), Am. Assn. Sch. Adminstrs., Assn. Supervision and Curriculum Devel., NEA (life), PEN London and Los Angeles (exec. com.), Am. Nat. Theatre Assn. (dir. 1973—), Ohio Soc. of N.Y., Internat. Reading Assn., Newcomen Soc. N.Am., Phi Beta Alpha, Kappa Beta Phi. Episcopalian. Clubs: University, Columbus Country (Ohio); Dutch Treat, Metropolitan, Canadian, Players (N.Y.C.); Siwanoy Country (Bronxville); Authors (London) Lodge: Masons. Home: North Hollywood Calif. Died Nov. 28, 1989; buried Forest Lawn, Hollywood Hills, Calif.

MILLER, MAX ARNOLD, utilities executive; b. Beatrice, Nebr., Feb. 1, 1896; s. Edwin S. and Ida (Arnold) M.; m. Phebe Folsom, Oct. 17, 1917; children: Morris F., Edwin Stanton II. Student, U. Nebr., 1914-17. With Miller Cereal Mills, 1917-43, exec. v.p., 1938-43; rancher, from 1943; vice chmn. bd., dir. No. Natural Gas Co., Omaha; chmn. exec. com., dir. Fairmont Foods Co., Omaha. Active Boy Scouts Am.; chmn. Jr. Achievement of Omaha, Inc.; trustee Hattie B. Munroe Home for Crippled Children. Served from pvt. to sgt. F.A., U.S. Army, World War I. Mem. Masons, Phi Kappa Psi. *

MILLER, OLIVER CHESTER, trading stamp company executive; b. McCune, Kans., Feb. 11, 1898; s. Turner J. and Permelia Jane (Lauck) M.; m. Mariam Seymour, Jan. 31, 1925; 1 dau., Barbara Ann (Mrs. Albert B. Long). Student, U. Nebr., 1922-24. Mdse. exec. Nebr. Buick Auto Co., Lincoln, 1919-22; with Sperry & Hutchinson Co., from 1924; purchasing agt., 1956-63, v.p., from 1956. Served with U.S. Navy, 1917-18. Mem. Masons, Maplewood (N.J.) Country Club. *

MILLER, PAUL, publisher, journalist; b. Diamond, Mo., Sept. 28, 1906; s. James and Clara (Ranne) M.; m. Louise Johnson, Oct. 19, 1932; children: Ranne Johnson, Jean Louise, Paul Talford, Kenper Wright. Student, U. Okla., 1929-30; BS, Okla. State U., 1931; DSc, Clarkson Coll., 1956; LLD, Ursinus Coll., 1959; DCL, Union Coll., 1965; LittD, Westminster Coll., Niagara U., 1968; DHL, Transylvania U., 1974, U. Mo., 1981; DL, Hobart and William Smith Coll., 1978. Reporter, editor various Okla. newspapers, including Pawhuska, Stillwater, Guthrie, Okemah and Oklahoma City, 1923-30; asst. dir. Bur. Info. and Service, Okla. State U., 1930-32; with AP, 1932-78; cable and gen. desk editor AP, N.Y.C.; night news editor AP, Kansas City; chief bur. AP, Salt Lake City, 1936; chief Pa. bur. AP, Harrisburg and Phila., 1937-41; exec. asst. to gen. mgr. AP, N.Y.C., 1941; chief Washington bur. AP, 1942-47, asst. gen. mgr., 1943-47, dir., 1950-58, 1960-78, pres., 1963-72, chmn., 1972-77; mem. exec. staff Gannett Newspapers, Rochester, N.Y., 1947-57; dir. Gannett Co., Inc., 1948-81, dir. emeritus, 1981-91, pres., chief exec. officer, 1957-70, chmn., chief exec. officer, 1970-73, chmn. bd., 1973-79; Mem. Pulitzer Prize Com., 9 yrs. Pres., chmn. Frank E. Gannett Newspaper Found. (name now Freed Forum), 1957-81; adv. bd. Am. Press Inst., 1953-63, chmn., 1958-63; dir. N.Y. World's Fair Corp., 1961; former trustee N.Y. Racing Assn.; hon. trustee Rochester Inst. Tech.; chmn. Rochester chpt. ARC, 1958; former bd. dirs. Boys' Clubs Am.; mem. Pres.'s Commn. for Observance of 25th Anniversary UN. Recipient William Allen White Found. award, 1963, NCCJ Brotherhood award, 1965, Hall of Fame award Okla. Heritage Assn., 1973, Journalism award Ohio U., 1979, Civic medal Rochester C. of C., 1979, Am. Eagle award Senate Chambers, 1980; Paul Miller Journalism Bldg. at Okla. State U. named in his honor and contains all his columns and papers. Fellow Sigma Delta Chi (hon. pres. 1962); mem. Inter Am. Press Assn., N.Y. State Pubs. Assn. (pres. 1954), Am. Soc. Newspaper Editors (del. Internat. Fedn. Editors and Pubs., Amsterdam 1949), Rochester Automobile Club (dir.), Gridiron Club, Nat. Press Club, Genesee Valley Club, Oak Hill Country Club, Augusta Nat. Club, Everglades, Kappa Sigma. Presbyterian. Home: Palm Beach Fla. Died Aug. 21, 1991; inurned Columbarium Third Presbn. Ch., Pochester, N.Y.

MILLER, PETER PAUL, financial company executive; b. Duluth, Minn., Nov. 20, 1895; s. Peter P. and Isabella (Bohnert) M.; m. Sara Speer, Oct. 22, 1921; children: Peter Paul, Richard S., Elizabeth (Mrs. John Francis). BA, Cornell U., 1918. With Nat. Dairy Products Corp., and predecessors, 1920-60, dir., 1935-60, v.p., 1950-60, pres. Sealtest div., 1958-60; pres., dir. Channing Fin. Corp., from 1960; dir. Agrl. Ins. Co., Brownville Paper Co. Trustee, Bronxville, N.Y., 1955-57, mayor, 1957-59; bd. dirs. Lawrence Hosp., Bronxville, Bronxville Community Fund. Served as 1st lt., inf. U.S. Army, World War I. Decorated Silver Star. Mem. Univ. Club of N.Y.C., Cornell Club of N.Y.C., Am. Yacht Club (Rye, N.Y.), Siwanoy Country Club (Bronxville), Chi Psi. Mem. Dutch Reformed Ch. (elder). *

MILLER, RAYMOND WILEY, public relations and legal trade consultant lecturer; b. San Jose, Calif., Jan. 21, 1895; s. David Wiley and Jennie Goodell (Pound) M.; m. Florence Estelle Burk, May 8, 1919; children: Ruth Genevieve (Mrs. William H. Powell, Jr.), Robert Wiley. Student, Coll. of Pacific Acad., 1909-13, San Jose State Coll., 1914-16, U. Calif., 1915; LLB, LaSalle Extension U., 1943. LLD, St. John's U., Collegeville, Minn., 1942. Prin. elem. sch., Colfax, Calif., 1916-17; developed and operated Walnut Grove, Linden, Calif., from 1919; pres. Pub. Rels. Rsch. Assocs., Inc., World Trade Rels. Ltd.; pres., gen. counsel Am. Inst. of Cooperation, 1945-48, trustee, from 1949; pub. rels. cons. to numerous N.Am. businesses, from 1930; lectr. pub. rels., from 1935; vis. lectr. Harvard Grad. Sch. Bus. Adminstrn., 1948-64; lectr. Grad. Sch. Pub. and Internat. Affairs, U. Pitts.; cons. fed. govt. agys., internat. econs., internat. trade, internat. aid. Author several books including: Can Capitalism Compete, 1959; A Conservative Looks at Cooperatives, 1964; contbr. to agrl., ednl., legal, econs., religious pub. rels. and mktg. jours. Mem. dept. ch. and econ. life Nat. Coun. Chs. of Christ in Am., from 1947; mem. nat. pub. rel. com. Boy Scouts Am., from 1945, Silver Buffalo award, 1951; mem. several nat. confs. Served at sgt. U.S. Army, World War I. Recipient Disting. Svc. award Nat. Cath. Rural Life Conf., 1949. Mem. ABA, Calif. Bar Assn., Transp. Assn. Am. (trustee), other profl. and tech. assns. and orgns., Masons (33 deg., KT), Canadian Club of N.Y., Commonwealth Club of San Francisco, Nat. Press Club, Cosmos Club. Methodist. *

MILLER, RICHARD ARTHUR, architect, educator; b. Sheboygan, Wis., June 27, 1925; s. Arthur Herbert and Evangeline Ruth (Hilpertshauser) M. A.B. magna cum laude, Harvard U., 1949, M.Arch., 1953. Lic. architect, N.Y., Ohio, others. Prin. Richard Miller, Architect, Elyria, Ohio, 1953-56; assoc. sr. editor Archtl. Forum Mag., N.Y.C., 1957-63; chmn. firm Westermann, Miller & Assocs., P.C., Architects, N.Y.C., 1962-78; prin. Richard Miller, F.A.I.A., Architect, Columbus, Ohio, from 1979; vis. lectr. Ohio State U., Columbus, 1960-61, prof. architecture, from 1978; assoc. prof. Columbia U., N.Y.C., 1961-63, adj. prof., 1976-78; profl. adviser Ohio State Univ. Visual Arts Ctr. Competition, 1983. Prin. works include Yale U. Health Ctr., Silverstein Pavillion, Hosp. of U. Pa., Smith Coll. Ctr. for Performing Arts. Editor: Four Great Makers Papers, 1962. Served with U.S. Army, 1943-45, ETO. Fellow AIA. Club: Harvard (N.Y.C.). Home: Columbus Ohio Died Oct. 19, 1988. †

MILLER, ROGER DEAN, entertainer; b. Fort Worth, Jan. 2, 1936; s. Laudene Burdine; raised by E.D. and Armelia M.; m. Mary Margaret Arnold, Feb. 14, 1978; children: Margaret Taylor, Adam Gray, Dean, Shannon, Alan, Rhonda, Shari. Student pub. schs., Erick. Pres. Roger Miller, Inc. Composer, rec. artist songs including: King of the Road, Dang Me, Chug-a-lug, England Swings; Composer, rec. artist: albums include Roger Miller-Off the Wall; TV program Roger Miller Show; personal appearances in, U.S., Eng., Japan, Australia, New Zealand; Composer: music Broadway play Big River; character voice for: movie cartoon Robin Hood, 1973. Served with AUS, Korean conflict. Recipient 5 awards Nat. Assn. Rec. Arts and Scis., 1965, 6 awards, 1966; Tony award, 1986; Drama Desk awards (2); Country Music Assn. Pioneer award, 1988. Home: Tesuque N.Mex. Died Oct. 26, 1992. †

MILLER, STEWART EDWARD, electrical engineer, consultant; b. Milw., Sept. 1, 1918; s. Walter C. and Martha L. (Ferguson) M.; m. Helen Jeanette Stroebel, Sept. 27, 1940; children—Jonathan James, Stewart Ferguson, Chris Richard. Student, U. Wis., 1936-39; BS, MIT, 1941, MS, 1941. With Bell Labs., N.Y.C., 1941-49; With Bell Labs., Holmdel, N.J., 1949-83, dir. guided wave research, 1958-80, dir. Lightwave Telecommunications Rsch. Lab., Crawford Hill, 1980-83; cons., researcher Bell Communications Rsch., Inc. (Bellcore), Red Bank, N.J., 1984-90; organizer first

IEEE-Optical Soc. Am. internat. Optical Fiber Communications Conf., 1975. Co-editor Optical Fiber Telecommunications, Vols. I and II, 1979. Recipient Ballantine medal Franklin Inst., 1977. Fellow IEEE (Liebmann award 1972, Baker prize 1975), Optical Soc. Am. (John Tyndall award 1989), AAAS; mem. NAE. Home: Toms River N.J. Died Feb. 27, 1990.

MILLER, WALTHER MARTIN, German language educator, clergyman; b. St. Paul, Nov. 3, 1895; s. Jacob William and Clara (Schachameyer) M.; m. Helen Brockman, Aug. 28, 1926; children: Helen (Mrs. Milton Heyne), Marion, Lois Jane (Mrs. Howard Heckner). Grad., Corcordia Sem., St. Louis, 1919; MA, Harvard U., 1922; student, U. Chgo., 1943-45; LittD honoris cause, Valparaiso U., 1965. Ordained to ministry Lutheran Ch., 1924. Instr. German Harvard U., 1920-23, 31, Concordia Coll., Ft. Wayne, 1923-26; asst. pastor St. Paul Luth. Ch., Ft. Wayne, 1924-26; mem. faculty Valparaiso U., from 1926, head dept. fgn. langs., from 1933, Friedricks Meml. prof. German, from 1951. Translator some of Luther's works. Mem. MLA, Am. Assn. Tchrs. German, Ind. Fgn. Lang. Tchrs. Assn. (pres. 1950). *

MILLER, WILLIAM MCKINLEY, trucking company executive; b. Louisville, Oct. 29, 1896; s. William H. and Christine (Florer) M.; m. Adelaide C. Kemper, July 23, 1918; children: Margaret, Dorothy C., Verna (Mrs. Robert C. Berthelsen), Mildred (Mrs. Richard V. Gadd, Sr.), Janey (Mrs. William C. Stoddard). Ed., night and corr. schs. With L.&N. R.R., 1915-17, Transp. Dept., Q.M. Depot, U.S. Govt., Jeffersonville, Ind., 1917-19, Louisville Freight Bur., 1919-31, So. Freight Traffic Bur., 1931-35; with So. Motors Carriers Rate Conf., Atlanta, from 1936, gen. mgr., from 1945, exec. v.p., from 1952; an organizer, charter mem. So. Shipper and Motor Carrier Coun., 1959; mem. traffic and transp. adv. coun. LaSalle Extension U., from 1940. Author traffic practice book for students. Chmn. motor carrier div. bus. unit Greater Atlanta United Appeal, 1960-63l bd. dirs. Warren Meml. Boys Club, Atlanta; mem. com. edn. Ga. State Coll. Mem. Am. Soc. Traffic and Transp. (bd. dirs.), ICC Practitioners Assn. (pres. 1963, exec. com. from 1959). Baptist (tchr., mem. fin. com.). *

MILLICAN, GEORGE EVERETT, oil company executive; b. Harriman, Tenn., Aug. 31, 1897; s. George Washington and Mary Emma (Cooper) M.; m. Beatrice Jones, May 25, 1927; children: Emily Clare (Mrs. C.H. Cowan), Mary Elizabeth (Mrs. E.S. Robinson III), George Everett. Ed. pub. schs., Atlanta; grad. Advanced Mgmt. Program, Harvard U., 1952; LLD, Atlanta Law Sch., 1952. With Gulf Oil Corp., from 1912; regional v.p. Gulf Oil Corp., Atlanta, 1960-62, v.p. domestic mktg., from 1962; chmn. Ga. Tax Rsch. Found., from 1959. Alderman, City of Atlanta, 1927-34, 60-62, mayor pro tem, 1932; mem. Ga. Senate from Fulton County, 1935-40, 43-48, 51-56, pres. pro tem, 1955-56. Recipient Statesmanship awrd Active Voters Ga., 1954. Mem. Am. Petroleum Inst., Am. Legion, Masons, Shriners, Kiwanis (dist. gov.), Capital City Club, Commerce Club, Ansley Golf Club of Atlanta, Houston Club, Petroleum Club of Houston. Democrat. Baptist (deacon, chmn. bd. trustees, chmn. bd. deacons). *

MILLIKEN, FRANK ROSCOE, mining company executive; b. Malden, Mass., Jan. 25, 1914; s. Frank R. and Alice (Gould) M.; m. Barbara Kingsbury, Sept. 14, 1935; children—Frank R., David C. B.S. in Mining Engring., MIT, 1934. Chief metallurgist Gen. Engring. Co., Salt Lake City, 1936-41; asst. mgr. Titanium div. Nat. Lead Co., 1941-52; v.p. charge mining ops. Kennecott Copper Corp., N.Y.C., 1952-58, exec. v.p., 1958-61, also bd. dirs., pres., chief exec. officer, 1961-78, chmn., chief exec. officer, 1978-79; chmn. Fed. Res. Bank N.Y., 1976, 77; bd. dirs. Proctor & Gamble. Life mem. corp. M.I.T.; head United Fund Greater N.Y., 1970. Named Copper Man of Yr. Am. Mining Congress, 1973; recipient 1st Disting. Svc. award U.S. Treasury, 1965, 68. Mem. Nat. Acad. Engring., Mining and Metall. Soc. Am., Am. Inst. Mining Metall. and Petroleum Engrs. (Robert H. Richards award of minerals beneficiation div. 1951), The Bus. Council. Clubs: River (N.Y.C.); Wee Burn Country (Darien, Conn.). Home: Darien Conn. Died Dec. 4, 1991.

MILLIKIN, SEVERANCE ALLEN, business executive; b. Cleve., July 13, 1895; s. Dr. Benjamin Love and Julia (Severance) M.; m. Marguerite Manville, May 5, 1952. Student, Univ. Sch.; LittB, Princeton U., 1916. With fgn. dept. Cleve. Tractor Co., 1919-22; pres., dir. 1310 Huron Co.; dir. Cleve. Trust Co., Interlake Iron Corp., Cleve. Electric Illuminating Co. Mem. Union Club, Tavern Club, Chagrin Valley Hunt Club, Kirtland Club, Union Club of N.Y.C., Recess Club of N.Y.C. *

MILLION, ELMER MAYSE, legal educator; b. Pond Creek, Okla., Dec. 10, 1912; s. Elmer Joseph and Jozie May (Mayse) M.; m. Zenna Belle Clark, Sept. 7, 1937 (div. 1956); children: Elmer Zen, Kenneth Mayse, Earl Clark, Tedder Riley; m. Angela Carman de Carteret, Sept. 27, 1958; children: Heather Carteret, Stephen Murray. A.B. magna cum laude, Southwestern Okla. State Coll., 1936; LL.B., U. Okla., 1935; J.S.D., Yale U., 1938. Bar: Okla. 1935. Pvt. practice law Weatherford and Norman, Okla., 1935-36; instr. law So. Meth. U., 1937-38; asst. prof. U. Idaho, 1938-44, assoc. prof., 1944-46; sr. atty. U.S. Dept. Justice, Washington, 1943-46; on leave from U. Idaho; assoc. prof. W.Va. U., 1946-47; asst. prof. NYU, 1947-48, assoc. prof., 1948-53, prof., 1953-70; prof. law U. Okla., 1970-83, prof. emeritus, 1983-90; vis. prof. U. Mich., 1964-65; mem. faculty Inter-Am. Law Inst. of N.Y. U., 1948-68, Comparative Law Inst., N.Y. U., 1955-68. Author: (with R.D. Niles) Walsh, Niles and Million Cases on Property, 3 vols, 1951, 54, 57; contbr. to: Landmarks of Law, 1960, Open Occupancy vs. Forced Housing Under 14th Amendment, 1963, Annual Survey of American Law, 1947-69; gen. editor: Okla. Practice Methods, 1970-82. Pres. Fairlington Civic Assn., Va., 1944-45; bd. dirs. Maternity Consultation Service, N.Y.C., 1949-55, Greenwich Village Montessori Sch., 1966-69, Burgundy Farms Country Day Sch., Va., 1945-46; judge Ecclesiastical Ct. of Episcopal Diocese of Okla.; ombudsman vol. Okla. Nursing Home, 1985-86; bd. dirs. Canterbury Living Ctr., 1983-90. Sterling fellow Yale U., 1936-37. Mem. Okla. Bar Assn., Phi Alpha Delta, Order of Coif. Democrat. Episcopalian. Home: Norman Okla. Died May 12, 1990.

MILLMAN, JACOB, electrical engineering educator, author, consultant; b. Russia, May 17, 1911; came to U.S., 1913, naturalized, 1917; s. Philip and Gertrude (Nachschen) M.; m. Sally Dublin, Oct. 11, 1936; children—Richard S., Jeffrey T. Student, U. Munich, Fed. Republic Germany, 1932-33; B.S. in Physics, MIT, 1932, Ph.D., 1935. From instr. to assoc. prof. elec. engring. CCNY, 1936-42, 45-52; mem. staff Radiation Lab. MIT, Cambridge, 1942-45; prof. elec. engring. Columbia U., N.Y.C., 1952-75, Charles Batchelor prof. emeritus, 1975-91, chmn. dept. elec. engring., 1965; Fulbright lectr., Italy, 1959-60, Montevideo, Uruguay, 1968; cons. to industry, 1946-75. Author: (with S. Seely) Electronics, 1941, rev. edit., 1952, (with H. Taub) Pulse Digital Circuits, 1956, Vacuum-Tube and Semiconductor Electronics, 1958, (with H. Taub) Pulse, Digital and Switching Waveforms, 1965, (with C. Halkias) Electronic Devices and Circuits, 1967, (with C.C. Halkias) Integrated Electronics, Analog and Digital Circuits and Systems, 1972, Electronic Fundamentals and Applications, 1975, Microelectronics, 1979, (with A. Grabel) rev. edit. 1987; patentee in field. Recipient citation OSRD, 1947, Great Tchrs. award Columbia U. Sch. Engring., 1967. Fellow Am. Phys. Soc., IEEE (life mem., Edn. medal 1970, named to Centennial Hall of Fame for Elect. Engring. Educators 1984). Home: Longboat Key Fla. Died May 22, 1991; buried Sarasota, Fla.

MILLMAN, PETER MACKENZIE, astrophysicist; b. Toronto, Ont., Can., Aug. 10, 1906; s. Robert Malcolm and Edith Ethelwyn (Middleton) M.; m. Margaret Bowness Gray, July 10, 1931; children: Barry Mackenzie, Cynthia Gray Millman Floyd. B.A., U. Toronto, 1929; A.M. in Astronomy, Harvard U., 1931, Ph.D., 1932. Asst. Dominion Astrophys. Obs., Victoria, B.C., Can., summers 1927-29; asst. in astronomy Harvard U., 1929-31; Agassiz scholar in astronomy Harvard U. (Harvard Coll. Obs.), 1932-33; assoc. Harvard Coll. Obs. Harvard U., 1955-75; lectr. in astronomy U. Toronto, 1933-45; chief stellar physics div. Dominion Obs., Ottawa, Ont., 1946-55; head upper atmosphere research Nat. Research Council Can., Ottawa, 1955-71; guest scientist Herzberg Inst. Astrophysics, 1971-86, researcher emeritus, 1986-90; counsellor Smithsonian Inst., Washington, 1966-72. Author: This Universe of Space, 1961; editor: (with L. Kresak) Physics and Dynamics of Meteors, 1968, Meteorite Research, 1969, (with C.L. Hemenway and A.F. Cook) Evolutionary and Physical Properties of Meteoroids, 1973. Fin. v.p. Ottawa Music Festival Assn., 1962-67; bd. dirs. Youth Sci. Found. Can., 1966-71. Served to squadron leader RCAF, 1941-46. Decorated U.K. Def. medal, Can. Vol. Service medal and clasp, War medal, Kings Commendation, Centennial medal, Queen's Silver Jubilee medal; recipient J. Lawrence Smith medal Nat. Acad. Scis., 1954; Gold medal in phys. scis. Czechoslovak Acad. Scis., 1980; minor planet 2904 named in his honor, 1984. Fellow Royal Soc. Can., Can. Aeros. and Space Inst.; mem. Royal Astron. Soc. Can. (nat. pres. 1960-62, nat. hon. pres. 1981-85), Can. Astron. Soc. (sec. 1971-77), AIAA, Can. Assn. Physicists, Meteoritical Soc. (pres. 1962-66), Internat. Astron. Union (pres. working group for planetary system nomenclature 1973-82), Planetary Soc., Gamma Alpha. Anglican. Home: Ottawa ON, Can. Died Dec. 11, 1990; buried Stewart Meml. Cemetery, Dwight, Ont., Can.

MILLMAN, RONALD BURTON, public relations executive; b. Chgo., Oct. 21, 1934; s. Boris I. and Pearl (Schwartz) M.; m. Marlee Karpel, Aug. 27, 1978; 1 son, Neil Roger. B.A., Roosevelt U., Chgo., 1959. Publicity writer Victor Adding Machine Co., Chgo., 1959-60; asst. public relations mgr. Brunswick Corp., Chgo., 1960-63; public relations mgr. Bastian-Blessing Corp., Chgo., 1963-66, Nat. Video Corp., Chgo., 1966-67; sr. v.p. Harshe, Rotman & Druck, Chgo., 1967-80; v.p., gen. mgr. Doremus & Co., Chgo., 1980-84; owner, pres. The Millman Group, Chgo., 1985-86; ptnr. The Fin. Relations Bd., Chgo., from 1986. Co-chmn. Chgo. Communications Scholarship Program. Served with AUS, 1954-57. Recipient Best-in-Industry award Fin. World Ann. Report Survey, 1967, 68, 87, 89; cert. of merit Chgo. Publicity Club, 1971; Golden Trumpet award, 1973, 74, 75, 79, 80; Addy award Am. Advt. Fedn., 1974; award Chgo. Fin. Advertisers, 1980. Mem. Public Relations Soc. Am. (pres., bd. dirs. Chgo. chpt.), Publicity Club Chgo., Roosevelt U. Alumni Assn. (bd. govs.). Home: Chicago Ill. Deceased. †

MILLS, CHARLES BRIGHT, seed company executive; b. Marysville, Ohio, May 14, 1896; s. Dr. Charles Drake and Ella Ann (Stewart) M.; m. Rachel Long, June 25, 1924; children: Rachel, Mary, Charles. AB, Ohio Wesleyan U., 1920. Chmn. bd. O.M. Scott & Sons Co., Marysville; pres. Scott Farm Seed Co.; dir. First Nat. Bank, Marysville, Transcontinental Investing Corp. County chmn. war fund ARC, 1942-44; chmn. Cen. Ohio Heart Assn.; chmn. pub. rels. commn. Ohio area. Meth. Ch.; alternate del. Rep. Nat. Conv., 1936; pres. bd. trustees Ohio Wesleyan U., Lakeside Assn.; trustee Ohio Meth. Theol. Sem.; bd. dirs. Am. Seed Rsch. Found. Mem. Third Class Mail Users Assn. (pres.), Am. Seed Trade Assn. (pres.), Nat. Coun. Bus. Mail Users (dir.), Am. Legion, Ohio Soc. N.Y., Am. Newcomen Soc., Ohio C. of C. (dir.), Masons (33 deg.), Shriner, Kiwanis, Marysville Golf Club, Univ. Club, Pi Delta Epsilon, Phi Gamma Delta, Omicron Delta Kappa. Methodist (trustee). *

MILLS, DUDLEY HOLBROOK, business executive; b. N.Y.C., Feb. 25, 1894; s. John Tyler and Harriett A. (Robinson) M.; m. Louise Morris, Nov. 8, 1922; children: Louise, Bradford, Harriett Lee, Gordon Lawrence. Student, Lawrenceville Prep. Sch., 1911; AB, Princeton, 1915; MBA, Harvard, 1917. With Discount Corp. of N.Y., 1918-58, became pres., 1934, chmn. bd. dirs., 1944-58, ret.; dir. Underwood Olivetti, Allied Concord Fin. Corp., Lincoln Nat. Life Ins. Co. N.Y.; mem. adv. bd. French Am. Banking Corp.; alternate dir. 1st Ins. Co. Hawaii; fin. adviser to HArkness Founds. Trustee Millbrook Sch. for Boys. Mem. Nat. Audubon Soc. (dir., chmn. investment com.). Clubs: Creek, Inc., Down Town Assn., Clove Valley Rod and Gun, Links Golf, Recess, Anglers, Links (N.Y.C.). *

MILLS, GLEN EARL, speech educator; b. Mpls., May 10, 1908; s. Albert William and Bertha (Erickson) M.; m. Ruth Arlene Pence, May 28, 1937; 1 son, Richard Pence. B.S., Eastern S.D. Tchrs. Coll., 1930; M.A., U. Mich., 1935, Ph.D., 1941. Instr. speech Tyndall (S.D.) High Sch., 1930-34, Yankton (S.D.) High Sch., 1934-35, Ann Arbor (Mich.) High Sch., 1935-40; teaching fellow U. Mich., 1940-41, instr. speech, 1941-42; instr. speech Northwestern U., Evanston, Ill., 1942; asst. dean Northwestern U. (Sch. Speech), 1956-64, prof. speech, 1957-68, asso. dean, 1964-68, coordinator grad. studies, 1965-68; prof. speech U. Calif. at Santa Barbara, from 1968, dept. chmn., 1971-75, emeritus, recalled, 1975-78; Cons. AMA, GM Electron.; past pres. Emeriti Assn. Author: (with McBurney) Argumentation and Debate, 1951, rev., 1964, Composing the Speech, 1952, Reason In Controversy, 1964, rev., 1968, (with Bauer) Guidebook for Student Speakers, 1966, Speech Preparation, Analysis and Structure, 1966, Putting a Message Together, 1972, Legal Argumentation, 1976; former editor: Jour. Am. Forensic Assn and Western Speech; contbr. articles to profl. jours. Past mem. county grand jury; pres. resident assn. Valle Verde Community, 1986-88. Recipient Outstanding Alumnus award Dakota State Coll., 1967. Mem. Speech Communication Assn., Am. Forensic Assn., Rhetoric Soc. Am., Calif. Speech Assn., Western States Speech Assn. (pres. Execs. Club 1981), Pi Kappa Delta, Delta Psi Omega, Phi Sigma Pi, Delta Sigma Rho (Disting. Alumni award 1980). Home: Santa Barbara Calif. Deceased. †

MILLS, SUMNER AMOS, insurance company executive, church official; b. West Newton, Ind., Oct. 20, 1895; s. Edwin S. and Margaret (Carter) M.; m. Lela Weatherly, Nov. 6, 1920; children: John E., Eugene S., Paul G. Student, Prudue U., 1915-16; AB, Earlham Coll., 1920. Tchr. West Newton High Sch., 1921-26, prin., 1923-26; a founder Maplehurst Farms, Inc., dairy bus., Indpls., 1926, pres., 1932-58; with Meridian Mut. Ins. Co. (formerly Farmers Mut. Liability Co.), from 1942, v.p., 1952-65, chmn. bd., from 1965; v.p., dir. Meridian Life Ins. Co.; dir. Farmers Mut. Ins. Co., Friends Extension Corp.; presiding clk. Five Yrs. Meeting of Friends, 1955-60; nat. chmn. Friends Com. Nat. Legislation; trustee, dir., treas. Friends of Fiduciary Corp.; vice chmn. bd. Am. Friends Svc. Com., Phila.; chmn. bd. fin. trustees Western Yearly Meeting of Friends, also presiding clk. permanent bd.; del. World Conf. Friends, Oxford, Eng., 1952; chmn. bd. Am. Friends Bd. of Missions, from 1960. Trustee Wilmington Coll.; chmn. bd. Flanner House, Indpls., 1948-50. Served with Am. Friends Svc. Com. and ARC, France, 1918-19. Mem. Indpls. C. of C., Assn. for Merit Employment (life dir.). *

MILLS, WILBUR DAIGH, lawyer, congressman; b. Kensett, Ark., May 24, 1909; s. Ardra Pickens and Abbie Lois (Daigh) M.; m. Clarine Billingsley, May 27, 1934; children—Martha Sue, Rebecca Ann. Student, Hendrix Coll., 1926-30, Harvard Law Sch., 1930-33. Bar: Ark. 1933, D.C. 1977. Began practice in Searcy; county and probate judge White County, 1934-38; cashier Bank of Kensett, 1934-35; mem. 76th-94th Congresses from 2d Ark. Dist., 1935-73, mem. Banking and Currency Com., 1939-42, mem. Ways and Means Com., from 1942, chmn., 1957; tax counsel firm Shea &

Gould, Washington, 1977-91. Mem. ABA. Democrat. Methodist. Club: Mason (33 deg.). Home: Kensett Ark. Died May 2, 1992; buried Kensett, Ark.

MILLSAPS, KNOX, aerospace engineer, educator; b. Birmingham, Ala., Sept. 10, 1921; s. Knox Taylor and Millie Mae (Joyce) M.; m. Lorraine Marie Hartle, June 12, 1956 (div. Nov. 1980); children: Melinda Marie, Mary Charmaine, Catherine Marie, Knox Taylor. B.A., Auburn U., 1940; Ph.D., Calif. Inst. Tech., 1943. Asso. prof. aero. engring. Ohio State U., Columbus, 1946-48; mathematician Office Air Research, 1948-49; prof. physics Auburn (Ala.) U., 1949-50, 51-52; research physicist Flight Research Lab., Wright Air Development Center, 1950-51; chief mathematician Aero. Research Lab., 1952-55; prof. mech. engring. Mass. Inst. Tech., Cambridge, 1955-56; chief sci. Air Force Missile Devel. Center, 1955-60; exec. dir. Air Force Office Sci. Research, 1960-63; research prof. aerospace engring. U. Fla., Gainesville, 1963-68, chmn. dept. engring. sci., 1973-86, prof. engring. sci., from 1986; head prof. mech. engring. Colo. State U., Fort Collins, 1968-73. Mem. Am. Phys. Soc., Am. Math. Soc., Math. Assn. Am., Soc. Indsl. and Applied Math., Soc. Engring. Sci., Am. Inst. Aeros. and Astronautics, Sigma Xi. Clubs: Cosmos, Gainesville Golf and Country. Home: Gainesville Fla. Deceased. †

MILNE, WILLIAM GORDON, educator; b. Haverhill, Mass., Mar. 17, 1921; s. Morton Russell and Lulu (Smith) M. A.B., Brown U., 1941, A.M., 1947; Ph.D., Harvard, 1951. Instr. English U. Kansas City, Mo., 1947-48; lectr. Mass. Inst. Tech., 1951, Tufts U., summers 1951, 52; mem. faculty Lake Forest (Ill.) Coll., from 1951, prof., from 1958; Fulbright guest prof. U. Würzburg, Germany, 1958-59, U. Canterbury, N.Z., 1987. Author: George William Curtis and the Genteel Tradition, 1956, The American Political Novel, 1966, The Sense of Society: A History of the American Novel of Manners, 1977, Stephen Crane at Brede: An Anglo-American Literary Circle of the 1890's, 1980, Ports of Call: A Study of the American Nautical Novel, 1986. Served to lt. comdr. USNR, 1942-46. Mem. AAUP, Modern Lang. Assn., Phi Beta Kappa. Home: Rye Beach N.H. Died July 17, 1989.

MILNER, JEAN SHEPARD, clergyman; b. Atlanta, Nov. 18, 1893; s. Benjamin Charles and Mary Ann (Whitner) M.; m. Sue Swigert Lyne, June 23. 1915; children: Jean S., Susannah Lyne, Mary Jean. Student, Ga. Sch. Tech., 1911-12, Purdue U., 1912-13; BS, U. Louisville, 1915; DD, Butler U., 1929. Ordained to ministry Presbyn. Ch., 1917. Pastor Edinburg, Ind., 1915-18; fin. agt. U. of South, 1919-20; asst. pastor Ashland, Ky., 1920-21; pastor 2d Presbyn. Ch., Indpls., 1921-60; minister emeritus 2d Presbyn. Ch.; past dir. Belt R.R. and Stockyards. Author: The Sky is Red, 1935. Pres. bd. Nat. Missions Presbyn. Ch. U.S., from 1941; pres. bd. trustees Peabody Meml. Home, Synod of Ind.; v.p., bd. trustees Meth. Hosp. Indpls.; trustee McCormick Theol. Sem., Chgo., Presbyn. Found. Synod of Ind., Hanover Coll. With ARC, WWI. Mem. Baronial Order Runnemede, SAR, Am. Hist. Assn., Phi Delta Theta, Mason (Scottish Rite 83). Clubs: Wranglers, Woodstock Country, Indpls. Lit. *

MINKOWSKI, JAN MICHAEL, physics educator, researcher; b. Zurich, Switzerland, Mar. 7, 1916; s. Anatol Witold and Anna Jadwiga (Zand) M.; m. Zofia Frankowski, Jan. 7, 1939 (div. 1943); 1 son, Andrew Jan; m. Anne Hastings Shreve, Jan. 20, 1951; children: John Shreve, Christopher Zand, Mark Hastings. BS, Swiss Fed. Inst. Tech., Zurich, 1948, MS, 1950; PhD, Johns Hopkins U., 1963. Rsch. assoc. Inst. Theoretical Physics, Zurich, 1949-50; rsch. physicist Erie (Pa.) Resistor Corp., 1950-52; rsch. scientist Radiation Lab., Balt., 1952-60; rsch. scientist Carlyle Barton Labs., Johns Hopkins U., Balt., 1960-70, assoc. prof. physics, 1963-80, prof., 1980-86, prof. emeritus, 1986-91; cons. in field. Patentee in field. V.p. Polish Heritage Assn., Balt., 1973-75. Lt. Polish Army, 1938-45. Recipient Incentive awards Dept. Army, 1975, 76. Mem. Am. Phys. Soc., Polish Inst. Arts and Scis. in Am., Johns Hopkins Club (Balt.), Phi Beta Kappa, Sigma Xi, Eta Kappa Nu, Tau Beta Pi. Republican. Roman Catholic. Home: Baltimore Md. Died Feb. 5, 1991; buried St. Mary of the Assumption Cemetery, Balt.

MINNE, NELS, college administrator; b. Catawba, Wis., Dec. 6, 1901; s. N.M. and Bertha S. Monson M.; m. Lenore C. Coborn, Sept. 3, 1931. Student, U. Chgo., 1923; AB, St. Olaf Coll., 1924; MS, U. Wis., 1930, PhD, 1932. Tchr. high schs. Minn., Ind, 1924-26; chemistry and math. tchr. St. Olaf Coll., 1926-30; instr., dept. head Winona Minn. State Coll., 1932-44, pres., 1944-91; mem. Minn. Commn. on Higher and Vocat. Edn., 1949-53. Author: Outlines of Physical Science, 1942; contbr. tech. and ednl. articles to profl. jours. Fulbright rsch. grantee in Norway, 1950; rsch. fellow U. Wis., 1930-32. Mem. Am. Chem. Soc., AAAS, Am. Assn. Sch. Adminstrs., NEA, Minn. Edn. Assn. ednl. policy commn. 1963-91 , Mason, Kiwanis, Sigma Xi, Pi Kappa Delta. Lutheran. Home: Winona Minn. Died June 2, 1991.

MINSHALL, WILLIAM EDWIN, JR., former congressman; b. Cleve., Oct. 24, 1911; s. William E. and Mable Rice M.; m. Frances Smith, Nov. 3, 1946; children: William E. III, Werner Ellis, Peter Charles. Student, U. Va., 1932-34; LLB, Cleve. Law Sch., 1940. Bar: Ohio 1940. Pvt. practice law Cleve.; gen. counsel Fed. Maritime Bd.; mem. 84th-93d Congresses from 23d Ohio dist., 1955-74. Lt. col. AUS, World War II. Decorated Bronze Star. Mem. ABA, Ohio Bar Assn., Cleve. Bar Assn., Rotary. Home: Lakewood Ohio Died Oct. 15, 1990.

MINTON, JOHN PETER, surgeon, educator; b. Columbus, Ohio, Nov. 29, 1934; s. Harvey Allen and Elsie (Steiger) M.; m. Janice Arlene Gurney, Aug. 29, 1958; children—Cathryn Anne, Elizabeth Ellen, Cynthia Jane, Christina Lynn. B.Sc., Ohio State U., 1956, M.D., 1960, M.Med. Sci., 1966, Ph.D. in Microbiology, 1969. Intern Ohio State U., 1960-61; clin. assoc. surgery Nat. Cancer Inst., Bethesda, Md., 1962-65; resident in surgery Univ. Hosp., Ohio State U., Columbus, until 1969; asst. prof. surgery Ohio State U., Columbus, 1969-73, assoc. prof. surgery, 1973-77, prof. surgery, 1977-90, Am. Cancer Soc. prof. clin. oncology, 1979-89; mem. grant rev. com. Nat. Cancer Inst., Am. Cancer Soc. Contbr. articles to med. jours. Served with USPHS, 1962-65. Mem. ACS (Ohio State U. field liaison chmn.), Ohio State Med. Soc., Columbus Surg. Soc., Soc. Univ. Surgeons, Am. Assn. Acad. Surgeons, Am. Assn. Cancer Edn., Am. Soc. Clin. Oncology, Internat. Fedn. Surgeons, Columbus Rose Club (pres. 1979), Central Ohio Rose Soc., Am. Rose Soc., Lido Soc. Republican. Presbyterian. Home: Columbus Ohio Died Dec. 1, 1990; buried Union Cemetery, Columbus, Ohio.

MINZ, ALEXANDER, ballet master; b. Minsk, Byelorussia. Grad, Vaganova Sch., Leningrad, USSR, 1960. Dancer Petrozovodsk Ballet Co., Leningrad, 1960-62, Maly Theatre, Leningrad, 1960-62, Kirov Ballet, Leningrad, 1962-72; ballet instr. Ctr. of Dance, Rome, 1972-73, La Scala, Milan, 1972-73; ballet instr., dancer Am. Ballet Theatre Sch., N.Y.C., 1973-80, ballet master, 1988-92; ballet instr. Berlin Opera House, Munich Opera House, La Scala, Teatro Colon, Buenos Aires, Bat Dor, Israel, San Francisco Ballet, 1980-88. Guest appearance on TV show Hart to Hart. Home: New York N.Y. Died Apr. 30, 1992.

MIRABITO, PAUL S., computer and office equipment manufacturing company executive; b. N.Y.C., June 7, 1915; s. Salvatore and Virginia (Marra) M.; m. Virginia Ellen Woodstock, May 25, 1940; children: Terrence, Maureen Mirabito Catanese, Kent, Lynn. BA, CCNY, 1935; postgrad., Columbia U., 1935-37; MBA, NYU, 1938. Acct., contr. N.Y.C., 1936-39; acct. contrs. div. Haskins & Sells (CPA's), N.Y.C., 1939-42; contr., dir. contracts Control Instrument Co., Inc. (subsidiary Burroughs Corp.), 1942-51; asst. contr. Burroughs Corp., Detroit, 1951-55, gen. mgr. def. contracts orgn. (Gemini space project NASA. Atlas Missile Guidance System), 1955-60, v.p., 1960-62, v.p. adminstrv., 1962-65, v.p., group exec. fed. and spl. systems group, 1965-68, exec. v.p., dir., 1968-73, pres., chief operating officer, 1973-77, chmn. bd., chief exec. officer, 1978-80. Bd. dirs., v.p. Detroit Symphony Orch., United Found. Met. Detroit; bd. dirs. The Conf. Bd., Detroit Econ. Growth Council, Detroit Renaissance. CPA, N.Y. Mem. Computer Bus. Equipment Mfrs. Assn. Club: Econ. Detroit. Home: North Palm Beach Fla. Died Mar. 6, 1991.

MISCH, ROBERT JAY, columnist, author; b. N.Y.C., Nov. 19, 1905; s. Moses and Jennie (Reshower) M.; m. Janet Wolff, June 23, 1938; children: Mary Misch Newmann Smith, Katherine Wolff Misch Koritzinsky. Grad., Dartmouth Coll., 1925. Numerous positions with advt. agys. N.Y.C., 1925-68; mag. writer, columnist, from 1925; Wine Wise columnist Newark Star-Ledger. Writer weekly syndicated newspaper column: Eat, Drink and Be Merry; author (books) including: At Daddy's Office, 1947, Quick Guide to Wine, 1965, Quick Guide to Cheese, 1969, Quick Guide to Spirits, 1970, Quick Guide to Wines of all the Americas, 1977, Wine Mixers Manual, Wine Course, NYU, 1987; articles appeared in The New Yorker, Esquire, Saturday Rev., other mags. Decorated officer L'Ordre de Mérite Agricole (France). Mem. Wine Writers Circle (exec. com.), Overseas Press Club, Chevaliers du Tastevin (officer), N.Y. Wine and Food Soc. (founder, past chmn.). Clubs: Dutch Treat, Dartmouth Coll. Home: New York N.Y. Died Nov. 11, 1990.

MITCHELL, JOAN, abstract expressionist painter; b. Chgo., 1926; d. James Herbert and Marion (Strobel) M. Student, Smith Coll., 1942-44; BFA, Art Inst. Chgo., 1947, MFA, 1950; hon. degree, Miami U., Oxford, Ohio, 1972. One-person shows, Stable Gallery, N.Y.C., 1953-65, Galerie Fournier, Paris, 1967-87, Everson Mus., Syracuse, N.Y., 1972, Whitney Mus., N.Y., 1974, Art Club, Chgo., 1974, Musee d'Art Moderne de la Ville de Paris, 1982, Herbert F. Johnson Mus. of Art, Cornell U., Ithaca, N.Y., Xavier Fourcade Gallery, N.Y.C., 1981, 83, 85, 86, 87, Manny Silverman Gallery, L.A., Robert Miller Gallery, N.Y., 1989, others; travelling retrospective Corcoran Gallery Art, Washington, San Francisco Mus. Art, Albright-Knox Art Gallery, La Jolla Mus.; group shows include Whitney Mus. of Arts, 1966, Kranner Art Mus., U. Ill., 1967, Jewish Mus., N.Y.C., 1967, Mass. Inst. Tech., bienniale Corcoran Gallery Art, 1975, 81, Haus der Kunst, Munich, 1981-82, Xavier Fourcade Gallery, N.Y.C., 1982, Hirshhorn Mus. and Scultpure Garden, 1980; biennial Whitney Mus., 1983; Mus. of Art, Ft. Lauderdale, 1986; represented in permanent collections, including Basel (Switzerland) Mus., Albright-Knox Art Gallery, Buffalo, Art Inst. Chgo., Mus. Modern Art, Phillips Collection, Washington, Whitney Mus. Am. Art, Musee National d'Art Moderne, Paris, Corcoran Gallery of Art, Washington, Solomon R. Guggenheim Mus., N.Y., Fogg Art Mus., Mass. Recipient creative arts citation Brandeis U., 1973, Disting. Artist award Coll. Art Assn., 1989, Painter of Yr. citation French Ministry Culture, 1989; Art Inst. Chgo. traveling fellow, 1947. Home: Vetheuil France Died Oct. 30, 1992. †

MITCHELL, JOEL STEPHENSON, food corporation executive; b. Birmingham, Ala., Dec. 23, 1898; s. George Brantley and Leila Malone M.; m. Gertrude Isabelle Mitchell, Sept. 22, 1928; children: Ruth Isabelle, Joel Stephenson. First v.p. Kellogg Co., 1939-44; v.p., dir. Standard Brands, Inc., 1944, exec. v.p., 1947, pres., 1947-60, chmn., CEO, 1960-63. Died Oct. 2, 1989.

MITCHELL, JOHN MURRAY, JR., climatologist; b. N.Y.C., Sept. 17, 1928; s. John Murray and Lanier (Comly) M.; m. Pollyanne Bryant, May 5, 1956; children: John Murray III, Brian Harrison, Katherine Comly Abib, Anne Stuart. B.S., MIT, 1951, M.S., 1952; Ph.D., Pa. State U., 1960; postgrad., Nat. War Coll., 1970-71. Research meteorologist Weather Bur., Commerce Dept., Suitland, Md., 1955-65; project scientist environ. data service NOAA, Silver Spring, Md., 1965-74; sr. research climatologist NOAA, 1974-86, sci. advisor, 1980-86; cons., 1986-90; mem. various coms. and panels Nat. Acad. Scis., NRC; vis. lectr., prof. U. Calif., U. Wash. Contbr. numerous articles to books, encys., tech. jours.; editor: Meteorol. Monographs, 1965-73; exec. editor Weatherwise mag., 1978-90. Mem. Fairfax County Air Pollution Control Bd. Served with USAF, 1952-55. Recipient Silver and Gold medals U.S. Commerce Dept., Adminstrs. award Climate Inst., 1988. Fellow AAAS, Am. Meteorol. Soc. (2d Half Century award), Am. Geophys. Union; mem. Royal Meteorol. Soc., Sigma Xi. Home: McLean Va. Died Oct. 5, 1990; buried St. John's Episcopal Ch., McLean, Va.

MITCHELL, OLIN JACKSON, architect, educator; b. Little Rock, Ark., Sept. 19, 1931; s. Olin and Florence (Jackson) M.; m. Carolyn Jean Edrington, Oct. 20, 1962; children: James Jackson, Mark Taylor. B.Arch., Washington U., St. Louis, 1954; M.Arch., U. Pa., 1961, M.City Planning, 1961. Registered architect, Tex. With Wittenberg, Delony & Davidson, Little Rock, Ark., 1954-56, 61-66, ptnr. in charge design, 1961-66; with Hellmuth, Obata & Kassabaum, St. Louis, 1956-57; with Caudill, Rowlett & Scott, Houston, 1957-58, 66-67, project designer, 1966-67; assoc. prof. Rice U. Sch. Architecture, Houston, 1966-67; asst. prof. Sch. Architecture, Tex. A&M U., College Station, 1957-59; prof. Rice U. Sch. Architecture, Houston, 1969-92, assoc. dir. of sch., dean, 1967-69; instr. Tex. A&M U.; vis. lectr. MIT, U. Tex.; mem. vis. team Nat. Arch. Accrediting Bd., 1982-83; frequent lectr. in field. Contbr. articles to profl. pubs. including Progressive Architecture and Archl. Record. Fellow AIA; mem. Assn. Collegiate Schs. Architecture (pres. 1982-83)., Sigma Alpha Epsilon. Home: Houston Tex. Died Feb. 18, 1992.

MITCHELL, PETER DENNIS, biochemist; b. Mitcham, Surrey, Eng., Sept. 29, 1920; s. Christopher Gibbs and Kate Beatrice Dorothy (Taplin) M.; m. Patricia Helen Mary French, Nov. 1, 1958; children: Julia, Jeremy, Vanessa, Daniel, Jason, Gideon. B.A., Jesus Coll., Cambridge U., 1943, Ph.D., 1950, Sc.D. (hon.), 1985; Dr.rer.nat. (hon.), Tech. U. Berlin, 1976; D.Sc. (hon.), U. Exeter, 1977, U. Chgo., 1978, U. Liverpool, 1979, U. Bristol, 1980, U. Edinburgh, 1980, U. Hull, 1980, U. East Anglia, 1981, U. York, 1982; hon. fellowship, U. Aberdeen, 1990. With dept. biochemistry Cambridge U., Eng., 1943-55, demonstrator, 1950-55; dir. chem. biology unit, dept. zoology U. Edinburgh, Scotland, 1955-63, sr. lectr., then reader, 1961-63, James Rennie Bequest lectr., 1980; dir. research Glynn Research Inst., Bodmin, Cornwall, 1964-87; chmn., hon. dir. Glynn Research Found., 1987-92; Sir Hans Krebs lectr. Fedn. European Biochem. Socs., 1978; Fritz Lipmann lectr. German Soc. Biol. Chemistry, 1978; Humphry Davy meml. lectr. Royal Inst. Chemistry and The Chilterns and Middlesex sect. of Chem. Soc., 1980; Croonian lectr. The Royal Soc., 1987. Author: Chemiosmotic Coupling in Oxidative and Photosynthetic Phosphorylation, 1966, Chemiosmotic Coupling and Energy Transduction, 1968; also papers. Hon. adv. editor Biosci. Reports. Recipient Louis and Bert Freedman Found. award N.Y. Acad. Scis., 1974; Wilhelm Feldberg prize Feldberg Found. Anglo/German Sci. Exchange, 1976; Lewis S. Rosenstiel award Brandeis U., 1977; Nobel Prize in chemistry, 1978; Medal of Honor, Athens (Greece) Mcpl. Council; co-recipient Warren Triennial prize Mass. Gen. Hosp., Boston, 1974; fellow Jesus Coll., Cambridge. Fellow Royal Soc. (Copley medal 1981), Royal Soc. Edinburgh (hon.); mem. Biochem. Soc. (CIBA medal 1973), Econ. Rsch. Coun., European Molecular Biology Orgn., U.S. Nat. Acad. Scis. (fgn. assoc.), French Acad. Scis. (fgn.), Soc. Gen. Microbiology (hon.), Am. Soc. Biol. Chemists, Am. Acad. Arts and Scis., Japanese Biochem. Soc., Biochem. Soc. USSR. Home: Bodmin Eng. Died Apr. 10, 1992.

MITCHELL, RICHARD SCOTT, mineralogist educator; b. Longmont, Colo., Jan. 28, 1929; s. Clarence Floyd and Margaret May (Hartman) M. Student, Scottsbluff Jr. Coll., 1946-47, U. Nebr., 1947-48; B.S., U. Mich., 1950, M.S., 1951, Ph.D., 1956. Mem. faculty U. Va., Charlottesville, 1953-88, acting chmn. dept. geology, 1964-69, prof. environ. scis., 1969-88; Sesquicentennial assoc. U. Ill., 1973. Author: Mineral Names: What Do They Mean?, 1979, Russian transl., 1982; Dictionary of Rocks, 1985; contbr. articles to profl. jours.; exec. editor: Rocks and Minerals Mag. Fellow Geol. Soc. Am., Mineral. Soc. Am.; mem. Am. Crystallographic Assn., AAAS, Mineral Assn. Can., Sigma Xi, Sigma Gamma Epsilon. Home: Charlottesville Va. Died Aug. 31, 1988; buried Mountain View Cemetery, Longmont, Colo.

MITCHELL, RONALD WARREN, association executive; b. St. Paul, Jan. 25, 1935; s. Warren Benjamin and Marion Lois (Hagerty) M.; m. Marlene Ann Haggenmiller, June 28, 1958; children: Stephen Patrick, Thomas Michael, Margaret Ann, James Francis. BS, U. Minn., 1961, MA in Edn. Psychology, 1965, PhD in Edn. Psychology, 1967. Elem. tchr. St. Paul Pub. Schs., 1960-61; instr. U. Minn., Mpls., 1961-66; asst. exec. sec. Internat. Reading Assn., Newark, Del., 1966-74, dir. confs., 1974-84, exec. dir., 1984-89; mem. steering com. World Conf. on Edn. for All sponsored by World Bank, UNESCO, UNICEF and UN devel. program; mem. adv. bd. Clearing House on Reading and Comminication Skills, Edn. Resources Info. Ctr.; mem. nat. adv. bd. Muscular Dystrophy Assn. of Del.; nat. adv. bd. Ctr. for the Book, Libr. of Congress, Washington, 1984-89; mem. read-a-thon Del. chpt. Multiple Sclerosis Soc., Wilmington, 1983-89. Contbr. articles to profl. jours. Served as corp. USMC, 1953-56. Mem. Am. Soc. Assn. Execs. (key profl. assns. com.), Internat. Reading Assn. Club: University (Washington). Home: Newark Del. Died Nov. 17, 1989; buried Newark, Del.

MITCHELL, WILLIAM LEROY, design consultant; b. Cleve., July 2, 1912; s. Guy S. and Hazel R. (Mann) M.; m. Marian Crocker, Sept. 14, 1963; children—Nancy Lynne, Wendelin L., Penelope. Student, Carnegie Inst. Tech., 1930, Art Student's League, N.Y., 1931-32. Comml. illustrator Barron G. Collier, 1931-35; With Gen. Motors Corp., 1935-77, successively auto designer, chief auto designer, chief designer Cadillac, 1935-58, v.p. in charge design, 1958-77, also bd. dirs.; v.p., dir. design Harley Earl Assos., 1949-53. Served from lt. (j.g.) to lt. USNR, 1942-45. Clubs: Bloomfield Hills (Mich.) Country, Bloomfield Open Hunt; Lost Tree, Old Port Yacht (Palm Beach, Fla.). Home: North Palm Beach Fla. Died Sept. 12, 1988; buried White Chapel Cemetery, Mich.

MITCHELL, WILLIAM REYNOLDS KEENEY, banker; b. Phila., Dec. 16, 1893; s. George Lippincott and Mary Ella (Keeney) M.; m. Blanche Curet, Feb. 21, 1928; 1 dau., June (Mrs. Ferdinand LaMotte 3d). Grad., Friends Central Sch., 1910; BS, U. Pa., 1914. Clk. Provident Life and Trust Co. of Phila. and successor Provident Trust Co. of Phila., 1914, asst. sec., 1923, asst. treas., 1924, treas., 1928, v.p., 1932; pres., dir. Provident Trust Co. Phila., 1947-52, chmn. bd. dirs., 1952-57; vice chmn. bd., chmn. exec. com., dir. Provident Tradesmens Bank & Trust Co., 1957-62; mem. exec. com., dir. fed. adv. coun. Republican Third Fed. Res. Dist., 1955-57; dir., chmn. exec. com. Commonwealth Land Title INs. Co.; dir., mem. exec. com. Provident Tradesments Bank & Trust Co., Provident Mut. Life Ins. Co. Trustee Friends Central Sch.; trustee, chmn. bd. Ellis Coll. for Girls. Served from 1st lt. to capt. Inf., U.S. Army, 1917-18; res. officer in France, 1918. Mem. Franklin Inst., Phla. Acad. Natural Scis., Merion Cricket Club, Merion Golf Club, Racquet Club of Phila., Skytop Club. Republican. Quaker (trustee, chmn. fin. com. Yearly Meeting of Friends). *

MITTON, EDWARD R(ICHARDSON), apparel executive; b. Brookline, Mass., 1896; s. George W. and Anne M. (Richardson) M.; m. Marie F. Taff; 1 son, Edward J. Student, Milton Acad., Harvard U. With Jordan Marsh Co., Boston, from 1917, pres., from 1937, also chmn. bd., dir.; dir. Allied Stores Corp. Overseer, Boys' Clubs of Boston; mem. corp. Northeastern U.; assoc. Harvard Bus. Sch. Mem. Boston Better Bus. Bur. (v.p., dir.), Beacon Soc., Algonquin Club, Harvard Club of Boston, Eastern Yacht Club. *

MIWA, RALPH MAKOTO, college administrator; b. Honolulu, Jan. 4, 1925; s. Nobuichi and Fuyu (Hashimoto) M.; m. Hilda Odan, June 23, 1951; children: Colin, Lani, Marie. B.A., U. Hawaii, 1948, M.A., 1950; Ph.D. (Laucheimer fellow 1951-52), Johns Hopkins U., 1953. Ford Found. fellow St. Johns Coll., 1953-54, U.S. Govt., 1954-57; asso. prof. polit. sci. U. Mo., Columbia, 1957-61; legis. asst. to Senator Inouye of Hawaii, Washington, 1963-64, adminstrv. asst., 1964-66; prof. polit. sci. U. Hawaii, Honolulu, from 1961, dean Coll. Continuing Edn. and Community Service, 1968-72; provost Leeward Community Coll., Pearl City, Hawaii, 1972-75; chancellor West Oahu Coll., 1975-86; acting chancellor U. Hawaii, Hilo, 1984-86; spl. asst. to pres. U. Hawaii, (statewide), 1986-89; dir. Bank of Honolulu.; mem. Hawaii Edn. Commn., 1970-76. Contbr. profl. jours. Vice chmn. Democratic Party Hawaii, 1968-70; del. Nat. Dem. Conv., 1968; bd. dirs. Kukui Gardens Corp., Honolulu; trustee Clarence T.C. Ching Found., Honolulu. Served with AUS, 1944-46, PTO. Mem. Phi Beta Kappa, Pi Sigma Alpha. Home: Honolulu Hawaii Died Oct. 25, 1989.

MIXON, FOREST ORION, JR., research institute executive, chemical engineer; b. Anderson, S.C., Dec. 4, 1931; s. Forest Orion and Daisy Lou (Major) M.; m. Sandra Kay Smith, Aug. 9, 1957 (dec. 1989); children: Forest Orion, III, Debra Lynn. B.S., N.C. State U., 1952, M.S., 1954; Ph.D., U. Del., 1958. Registered profl. engr., N.C. Research engr. E.I. DuPont Co., Wilmington, Del., 1958-62; engr., mgr., v.p. Research Triangle Inst., Research Triangle Park, N.C., 1962-89; adj. prof. U. N.C., Chapel Hill, 1972-89, N.C. State U., Raleigh, 1976-89; adj. assoc. prof. Duke U., Durham, N.C., 1968-72; mem. adv. bd. N.C. Bd. Sci. and Tech., 1983-89, N.C. Wastewater Research Ctr., 1968-72. Contbr. articles to profl. jours.; patentee in field. Mem. Am. Inst. Chem. Engrs. (sec. local sect. 1983, treas. 1984, vice chmn. 1985, chmn. 1986). Club: Chapel Hill Flying (pres. 1982). Home: Chapel Hill N.C. Died July 19, 1989.

MOCKLER, COLMAN MICHAEL, JR., manufacturing company executive; b. St. Louis, Dec. 29, 1929; s. Colman Michael and Veronica (McKenna) M.; m. Joanna Lois Sperry, Dec. 28, 1957; children: Colman Michael III, Joanna Lois, Emily McKenna, Andrew Sperry. A.B., Harvard U., 1952, M.B.A., 1954. With Gen. Electric Co., 1954-55; mem. faculty Harvard Grad. Sch. Bus., 1955-57; staff asst. to contr. Gillette Co., Boston, 1957-65, treas., 1965-68, v.p., 1967-68, sr. v.p., 1968-70, exec. v.p., 1970-71, also bd. dirs., vice chmn. bd., 1971-74, pres., chief operating officer, 1974-76, chief exec. officer, 1975-91, chmn. bd., 1976-91; dir. Bank of Boston Corp., First Nat. Bank Boston, Fabreeka Products Co., John Hancock Mutual Life Ins. Co., Raytheon Co. Chmn. corp. Simmons Coll.; mem. corp. Mus. Sci., Mass. Gen. Hosp. Served with AUS, 1948-49. Fellow Harvard Coll. Club: Harvard (N.Y.C.). Home: Wayland Mass. Died Jan. 25, 1991; buried Wayland, Mass.

MOE, GORDON KENNETH, physiology educator; b. Fairchild, Wis., May 30, 1915; s. Sylvester and Ellen Mae (Hanson) M.; m. Janet Woodruff Foster, Aug. 6, 1938; children—Christopher, Melanie, Jonathan, Bruce, Sally, Eric. Student, Virginia (Minn.) Jr. Coll., 1932-34; B.S., U. Minn., 1937, M.S., 1939, Ph.D., 1940; M.D., Harvard U., 1943; Sc.D. (hon.), SUNY Health Scis. Ctr., Syracuse, 1988. Instr. Physiology U. Minn., 1939-40; instr. pharmacology Harvard Med. Sch., 1941-44; asst. prof. pharmacology U. Mich. Med. Sch., 1944-46, assoc. prof., 1946-50; prof. physiology, chmn. dept. Coll. Medicine, SUNY, Syracuse, 1950-60; dir. Masonic Med. Research Lab., Utica, N.Y., 1960-84; Chmn. physiol. test com. Nat. Bd. Med. Examiners, 1956-57; mem. WHO (vis. scientists), Israel, Iran, 1951; cons. Walter Reed Army Med. Center.; mem. adv. council Nat. Heart and Lung Inst. Recipient travel award Internat. Physiol. Congress Oxford, 1947; Outstanding Achievement award U. Minn., 1958; Merit award Am. Heart Assn., 1968; Disting. Achievement award N.Y. State Masons, 1984; Am. Physiol. Soc. fellow Western Res. U., 1940-41; USPHS fellow Instituto Nacional de Cardiologia, Mexico City, 1948. Fellow AAAS (chmn. sect. 1958), Am. Coll. Cardiology (hon.); mem. Am. Physiol. Soc., N.Y. Soc. Med. Research, Am. Heart Assn. (chmn. basic sci. council 1962-63, chmn. research com. 1959-60), Mexican Acad. Medicine (hon.), Mexican Soc. Cardiology (hon.), Sigma Xi, Alpha Omega Alpha. Lodge: Masons (33 deg.). Home: Barneveld N.Y. Died Oct. 27, 1989.

MOFSKY, JAMES STEFFAN, lawyer, educator, consultant; b. Rochester, N.Y., May 16, 1935; s. Michael and Myna (Goldman) M.; m. Barbara Kaplan, Aug. 19, 1977; children: Russell David, Michael Benjamin, Jonathan Marshall, Allison Brooke. B.A., Wesleyan U., 1956; J.D., Cornell U., 1959; LL.M., U. Miami, Fla., 1968; J.S.D., George Washington U., 1971. Bar: N.Y. 1959, Fla. 1959, D.C. 1967. Sole practice Miami, 1960-66; asst. prof. U. Miami, 1968-70, assoc. prof., 1970-72, prof., from 1972; vis. assoc. prof. Ind. U., 1971; vis. prof. So. Meth. U., 1972; mem. securities law adv. council to state comptroller Fla., 1978-82, comptroller's task force on securities regulation 1985-86; cons. Nat. Assn. Realtors, 1972-75. Author: Blue Sky Restrictions on New Business Promotions, 1971; contbr. articles to legal jours. Earhart fellow, 1967-68. Mem. ABA, Am. Law Inst., Fla. Bar (exec. council sect. corp., banking and bus. law 1979-81), Assn. Am. Law Schs. (exec. council sect. bus. assns. 1973-80, chmn. 1973-75), Mont Pelerin Soc. Home: Miami Fla. Deceased. †

MOGENSON, GORDON JAMES, physiology educator; b. Delisle, Sask., Can., Jan. 24, 1931; s. Albert and Mildred Olive (Gilbertson) M.; m. Mary Ruth Wensley, June 26, 1954; children—Leslie Ruth, Gregory James. B.A. with honors, U. Sask., 1955, M.A., 1956; Ph.D., McGill U., 1959. Asst. prof. physiology U. Sask., Saskatoon, Can., 1958-64, assoc. prof. physiology, 1964-65; assoc. prof. physiology U. Western Ont., London, Can., 1965-68, prof. physiology, 1968-86, chmn. dept. physiology, 1976-84, dean grad. studies, 1986-91; rsch. prof. Med. Research Council Can., Ottawa, 1981-82, v.p., 1985-87. Author: The Neurobiology of Behavior, 1977; editor: Neural Integration of Physiological Mechanisms and Behavior, 1975; contbr. 180 rsch. papers in field, 21 chpts., revs. for various publs. Fellow Royal Soc. Can.; mem. Can. Physiol. Soc. (pres. 1981-82), Am. Physiol. Soc., Soc. for Neurosci. Mem. Ch. of Can. Home: London Ont., Can. Died Nov. 5, 1991; buried Mt. Pleasant Cemetery, London, Ont., Can.

MOHNEY, FRANKLIN WALTER, manufacturing company executive; b. Scranton, Pa., Feb. 18, 1927; s. Paul Ruben and Marguerite Mae (Palmer) M.; m. Patricia E. Main, Aug. 10, 1981; children—Geneve Lynn, Deborah Susan; stepchildren—Lisa Nicole, Susan Jennifer and Jacqueline Eve Singer. B.S. in Forestry, Pa. State U., 1949; S.M. (Sloan fellow 1960-61), M.I.T., 1961; postgrad., Sloan Sch. Indsl. Mgmt., 1961. With Singer Co., N.Y.C., 1949-67, gen. mgr. power tool div., 1964-67; v.p. Black & Decker Mfg. Co., Towson, Md., 1967-72; v.p. Chgo. Pneumatic Tool Co., also pres. components group, 1972-80; pres. Gen. Battery Corp., Reading, Pa., 1980-83; owner Venture Components Corp., N.Y.C., 1983-91; assoc. Gilbert C. Osnos & Co., Inc., 1984-91. Served with USNR, 1945-46. Home: New York N.Y. Died May 2, 1991; cremated.

MOHR, CHARLES, journalist; b. Loup City, Nebr., June 18, 1929; s. Clarence and Helen (Richardson) M.; m. Norma Foust, Mar. 27, 1952; children: Gretchen, Ned, Julie-Hguyen. BA, U. Nebr., 1951. Reporter Lincoln (Nebr.) Star, 1950-51, UPI, Chgo., 1951-54, Time mag., 1954-63; mem. staff N.Y. Times, 1963-89, chief corr. Vietnam bur., chief S.E. Asian corr., 1966-89. Mem. Phi Beta Kappa. Home: Bethesda Md. Address: For Estate of Mr. C. Mohr Mrs. Norma Mohr 229 W 43d St New York NY 10036 Died June 16, 1989.

MOKRZYCKI, ANDREW GUSTAV, aerospace scientist; b. Lwow, Poland, Oct. 1, 1899; came to U.S., 1944, naturalized, 1949; s. Andrew and Mary (Quel) M.; m. Lydia Picca-Senatori, June 1956. M.Mech. Eng., Inst. Tech., Lwow, 1918, Ph.D., 1925; M.Aero. Eng., Ecole Nat. Superieur d'Aeronautique, Paris, France, 1920. Dir. Samolot Aircraft Co., Poznan, Poland, 1922-27; prof. aeronautics Inst. Tech., Warsaw, Poland, 1927-39; chmn. Aero. Research Inst., Warsaw, 1929-36; prof. U. Montreal, Que., Can., 1942-44; sr. scientist Gen. Dynamics Corp., San Diego, 1944-46; chief aerodynamicist Ryan Aircraft Co., San Diego, 1946-50; dir. flight research dept. USAF Flight Test Center, Edwards AFB, Calif., 1950-52; sr. scientist missile div. N.Am. Aviation Co., Los Angeles, 1952-62; sr. research specialist aircraft div. Northrop Corp., Hawthorne, Calif., 1962-75; pres. Sci. Research Found. (studies nuclear fusion), Fullerton, Calif., from 1975. Author over 100 sci. publs. Served to capt. Polish Air Force, 1939; Served to capt. French Air Force, 1939-40; Served to capt. RAF, 1941-42. Fellow Am. Inst. Aeros. and Astronautics, Royal Aero. Soc., Polish. Inst. Art and Sci. Am. Home: Fullerton Calif. Deceased. †

MOLESE, MICHELE, tenor; b. N.Y.C., Aug. 29, 1936; s. Robert and Louise M.; m. Zoe Papadakis, Aug., 1971. Student, Conservatory Milan, Italy, Scuolo di Perfezionamento La Scala, Milan. Appeared with various opera cos. including La Scala, Vienna Opera, Berlin Opera; joined N.Y.C. Opera, from 1964; leading tenor Belgrade Opera, Yugoslavia six seasons; appeared in TV opera prodns., including Tales of Hoffman, BBC; rec. artist. Home: Broni Italy Died July 5, 1989.

MOLLENHOFF, CLARK RAYMOND, journalist, educator, writer, legal consultant; b. Burnside, Iowa, Apr. 16, 1921; s. Raymond Eldon and Margaret Pearl (Clark) M.; m. Georgia Giles Osmundson, Oct. 13, 1939 (div. Jan. 1978); children: Gjore Jean, Jacquelin Sue Mollenhoff Montgomery, Clark Raymond; m. Jane Cook Schurz, July 12, 1981. Student, Webster City Jr. Coll., 1938-41; LLB, Drake U., 1944; Nieman fellow, Harvard U., 1949-50; LLD, Colby Coll., 1959; LHD, Cornell Coll., 1960; LittD, Drake U., 1961, Iowa Wesleyan Coll., 1966, Simpson Coll., 1974. Bar: Iowa 1944, D.C. 1970, U.S. Supreme Ct. 1970, Fed. Ct. 1944. Reporter, Des Moines Register and Tribune, 1941-50; with Washington bur. Cowles Publs., 1950-69; spl. counsel to Pres. U.S., 1969-70; bur. chief Des Moines Register, Washington, 1970-77; prof. journalism and law Washington and Lee U., Lexington, Va., 1976-91; legal cons., author Lexington, Va., from 1979; Oxford exch. fellow Univ. Coll., 1980, 85; dir. Inst. on Polit. Journalism, Georgetown U.; Milward Simpson lectr. U. Wyo., 1990. Author: Washington Cover-Up, 1962, Tentacles of Power, 1965, Despoilers of Democracy, 1965, The Pentagon, 1967, George Romney Mormon in Politics, 1968, Strike Force, 1972, Game Plan for Disaster, 1976, The Man Who Pardoned Nixon, 1976, The President Who Failed, 1980, Investigative Reporting: From Courthouse to White House, 1981, Atanasoff: Forgotten Father of the Computer, 1988. Served to lt. (j.g.) USNR, 1944-46. Recipient Pulitzer prize for nat. reporting, 1958, numerous other awards. Mem. ABA, Iowa Bar Assn., Investigative Reporters and Editors, Inc. (bd. dirs. 1979-84), Nat. Press Club, (bd. govs. Washiington chpt. 1956-64, Gridiron Club, Omicron Delta Kappa, Sigma Delta Chi. Roman Catholic. Club: Nat. Press (Washington, bd. govs. 1956-64). Home:

Lexington Va. Died Mar. 3, 1991; buried Lohrville, Iowa.

MOLSTAD, MELVIN CARL, chemical engineer, educator; b. Spring Valley, Minn., Nov. 18, 1898; s. Kleber Guttorm and Josephine (Sorenson) M.; m. Barbara Van Tuyl, Dec. 27, 1924; 1 dau., Katharine Joan (Mrs. Samuel M. Harbison, Jr.). BA, Carleton Coll., 1920; BS, MIT, 1923; PhD, Yale U., 1930. Chem. engr. USDA, 1920-21, 23-26; instr. Yale U., 1926-29; chem. engr. E.I. duPont de Nemours & Co., 1929-31; asst. prof. Yale U., 1931-39; successively assoc. prof., prof., head dept. U. Pa., from 1939, dir. Sch. Chem. Engring., 1954-61; cons. chem. engr. Davison Chem. Co. dir. W.R. Grace & Co., from 1941; Fulbright lectr. Norwegian Tech. U., Trondheim, Norway, 1954-55, U. Tokyo, 1961-62. Mem. Am. Inst. Chem. Engrs., Am. Chem. Soc., Am. Soc. Engring. Edn., Sigma Xi, Phi Beta Kappa, Gamma Alpha, Alpha Chi Sigma. Democrat. Unitarian. *

MONAS, SIDNEY, history educator; b. N.Y.C., Sept. 15, 1924; s. David Joseph and Eva (Kiener) M.; m. Carolyn Babcock Munro, Sept. 5, 1948 (dec. Dec. 1985); children: Erica Beecher Monas Clements, Deborah Gardner Monas Werdmuller, Stephen Sidney; m. Claire Anderson, Nov. 1, 1987. A.B., Princeton U., 1948; A.M., Harvard U., 1951, Ph.D., 1955. Instr. history Amherst (Mass.) Coll., 1955-57; asst. prof. history Smith Coll., 1957-62; prof. history and lit., dir. Russian Studies Ctr., U. Rochester, N.Y., 1962-69; prof. Slavic lang. and history U. Tex., Austin, from 1969; chmn. dept. Slavic langs. U. Tex., 1969-75; Fulbright prof. Russian history Hebrew U., Jerusalem, 1966-67; sr. assoc. St. Antony's Coll., Oxford, 1984-85. Author: The Third Section, 1961; editor: Selected Works of N. Gumilev, 1972, Complete Poems of Osip Mandelstam, 1973; editorial bd. Jour. Modern History, 1967-70, Soviet Studies in Literature, from 1968, Am. Hist. Rev, 1980-83, PMLA, 1980-83; editor Slavic Rev., 1985-91; translator: Scenes from the Bathhouse, 1961, Crime and Punishment, 1968; editor, translator: Selected Essays of Osip Mandelstam, 1977. With AUS, 1943-45. Ford fellow, 1954-55, NEH fellow, 1973-74, fellow Humanities Rsch. Centre Australian Nat. U., 1977, Nat. Inst. Humanities U. Chgo., 1977-78, Rockefeller Humanities fellow, 1984-85. Mem. MLA, Am. Hist. Assn., Am. Assn. Advancement Slavic Studies. Home: Austin Tex. Deceased. †

MONTAND, YVES (YVO LIVI), actor, singer; b. Oct. 13, 1921; m. Simone Signoret, 1951 (dec. Sept. 1985); 1 son (with Carole Amiel) Valentin Giovanni Jacques Livi. Ed. primary sch., Marseilles, France. Interpreter of numerous famous songs including Autumn Leaves, The Urchins of Paris; first singing tour U.S., 1959; stage performances in straight plays and variety; films include: Les portes de la nuit, 1946, Wages of Fear, 1953, Les Sorcières de Salem, 1957, Aimez-vous Brahms, 1961, My Geisha, 1962, Is Paris Burning, 1966, Grand Prix, 1967, Let's Make Love, 1960, Compartiments Tueurs, 1964, La Guerre est Finie, 1966, Z, 1969, The Confession, 1970, On a Clear Day You Can See Forever, 1970, Tout va bien, 1972, Cesar et Rosalie, 1972, Etat de Siège, Le fils, 1973, Le hasard et la violence; Vincent, François, Paul et les autres, 1974, Le Sauvage, 1975, Le grand escogriffe, 1976, La Menace, 1977, I comme I care, 1979, Clair de femme, 1979, Le choix des armes, 1981, Tout feu tout flamme, 1981, Garçon, 1983, Jean De Florette, 1986, Manon Des Sources, 1986, 3 Pl. pour le 26, 1988, IP 5, 1992; author memoirs: Du soleil plein la tete, 1955, La Vie Continue, You See I haven't Forgotten, 1990. Pres. Cannes Film Festival, 1987; Recipient Spl. Tribute Film Soc. Lincoln Ctr. Died Nov. 9, 1991, interred Père Lachaise Cemetery, Paris. Home: Paris France

MONTGOMERY, DEANE, mathematician, educator; b. Weaver, Minn., Sept. 2, 1909; s. Richard and Florence (Hitchcock) M.; m. Katherine Fulton, July 14, 1933; children—Mary, Richard. A.B., Hamline U., 1929; M.S., U. Iowa, 1930; Ph.D., 1933; Ph.D. hon. doctorate, Hamline U., 1954, Yeshiva U., 1961, Tulane U., 1967, U. Ill., 1977, U. Mich., 1986. NRC fellow Harvard U., 1933-34; NRC fellow Princeton U., 1934-35, vis. assoc. prof., 1943-45; NRC fellow Inst. for Advanced Study, Princeton, 1934-35, Guggenheim fellow, 1941-42, mem., 1945-46, permanent mem., 1948-51, prof. math, 1951-80, prof. emeritus, 1980-92; asst. prof., prof. Smith Coll., 1935-41, 42-43; assoc. prof. Yale U., 1946-48; adj. prof. U. N.C., 1989. Mem. Am. Math. Soc. (pres. 1961-62, Steele award 1988), Nat. Acad. Sci., Math. Assn. Am., Am. Philos. Soc., Am. Acad. Arts and Scis., Internat. Math. Union (pres. 1975-78). Home: Chapel Hill N.C. Died Mar. 15, 1992.

MONTGOMERY, HARRY THOMAS, news service executive; b. Flint, Mich., July 30, 1909; s. Henry Arthur and Bessie (Henderson) M.; m. Emily Ruth Eaman, Oct. 9, 1931; children: Thomas E., Beth M. Montgomery Heath, Emily E. Montgomery Scandale, Henry A. Reporter Detroit Times, 1927-28, Detroit Free Press, 1929; night editor Internat. News Svc., N.Y.C., 1930-33, day cable editor, 1933-37; asst. city editor, cable editor AP, N.Y.C., 1937-45, charge fgn. and war report for morning newspapers, 1941-45; chief bur. AP, Ottawa, 1945-47, gen. bus. editor, 1947-50, asst. gen. mgr., 1951-54, asst. sec., 1953-61, sec., 1961-74, asst. gen. mgr., 1954-62; dep. gen. mgr. AP, N.Y.C., 1962-74, v.p., 1972-74. Nieman fellow Harvard U., 1940-41. Mem. Silurians Club, Dutch Treat Club, Harvard Club (N.Y.C.), Innis Arden Golf Club (past pres.) (Old Greenwich, Conn.). Home: Greenwich Conn. Died Apr. 5, 1991; cremated.

MONTGOMERY, ROYAL EWERT, economics educator; b. Moline, Ill., May 6, 1896; s. Robert John and Lillie (Matthews) M. PhB, U. Chgo., 1921, MA, 1923, PhD, 1925. Instr. U. Mo., 1921-22; asst. and instr. U. Chgo., 1922-27; assoc. prof. U. Tex., 1927-29; asst. prof. econs. Cornell U., 1929-37, prof., 1937-64, prof. econs. emeritus, from 1964, acting chmn. dept., 1952; staff Brookings Inst., 1938; mem. editorial bd. Am. Econ. Rev., 1938-41; artibtator Fed. Mediation and Conciliation Svc., from 1947; arbitrator, pub. panel mem. Nat. War Labor Bd., 1942-45; pub. rep., chmn. various industry coms. Wage and Hour div. U.S. Dept. Labor, 1940-45; rep. Am. Econ. Assn. on Social Sci. Rsch. Coun., 1941-44; mem. corp. Social Sci. Rsch. Coun., from 1946. Author: Industrial Relations in the Building Trades, 1927; (with H.A. Millis) Labor's Progress and Problems, 1938, Labor's Risks and Social Insurance, 1938, Organized Labor, 1945; contbr. chpts. to books, articles to profl. jours. Served in Mil. Intelligence div. U.S. Army, 1918-19. Mem. Am. Econ. Assn., Am. Statis. Assn., Am. Arbitration Assn., AAUP, Indsl. Rels. Rsch. Assn., Am. Acad. Polit. and Social Sci., Acad. Polit. Sci., Phi Kappa Sigma, Delta Sigma Rho. Democrat. *

MONTGOMERY, RUTHERFORD GEORGE, writer; b. N.D., Apr. 12, 1896; s. George and Matilda (Proctor) M.; m. Eunice Opal Kirks, Feb. 14, 1930; children: Earl, Pauline, Marilyn. Student, Western State Coll., Gunniston, Colo. Tchr. schs. Colo., 1921-27; county judge Ct. of Record, Gunnison County, Colo., 1930-36; budget and efficiency commr. for Colo., 1936-39, writer, from 1939; stories and adaptations for Walt Disney Prodns., from 1961. Author: (pseudonym Al Avery) A Yankee Flier in the RAF, 1940, A Yankee Flier in the Far East, 1941; (under own name) Carcajou, 1936, Iceblink, 1940, Big Brownie, 1945, Mystery of the Turquise Frog, 1946, Kildee House, 1950, Mystery of Crystal Canyon, 1951, Wapiti, 1952, Golden Stallion's Revenge, 1953; Golden Stallion to the Rescue, 1954, Black Powder Empire, Amikuk, Seecatch, 1955, Tim's Mountain, 1958, Kent Barstow, Special Agent, 1958, Klepty King of the Castle, 1961, others. Contbr. fiction to boys and girls mags.; author screenplays. Recipient Children's Spring Book Festival awrad N.Y. Herald Tribune, 1956. Mem. Masons, Kiwanis. Democrat. Episcopalian. *

MOON, MARJORIE RUTH, state treasurer, newspaper executive; b. Pocatello, Idaho, June 16, 1926; d. Clark Blakeley and Ruth Eleanor (Gerhart) M. Student, Pacific U., 1944-46; A.B. in Journalism cum laude, U. Wash., 1948. Reporter Pocatello Tribune, 1944, Caldwell (Idaho) News-Tribune, 1948-50; Salt Lake City bur. chief Deseret News, Boise, Idaho, 1950-52; owner, operator Idaho Pioneer Statewide (weekly newspaper), Boise, 1952-55; founder, pub. Garden City (Idaho) Gazette, 1954-68; ptnr. Sawtooth Lodge, Grandjean, Idaho, 1958-60, Modern Press, Boise, 1958-61; treas. State of Idaho, Boise, 1963-86; owner, pub. Kuna-Melba News, from 1987, Valley News, Meridian, Idaho, from 1988. Chmn. Idaho Commn. on Women's Programs, 1971-74; del. Dem. Nat. Nominating Conv., 1972, 76, 80, 84; Dem. candidate Lt. Gov., Idaho, 1986; mem. Idaho Commn. for the Blind, 1987-90, chmn., 1989-90. Named Idaho Statesman of Yr. Pi Sigma Alpha of Idaho State U., 1989. Mem. Nat. Assn. State Treas. (sec.-treas. 1976-78, regional v.p. 1978-79, 84-85), Nat. Fedn. Press Women, Idaho Press Women (past pres.), Kuna C. of C. (sec. treas. 1987-88-89), Soroptimists (pres. club 1971-73). Congregationalist. Home: Boise Idaho Died Mar. 1, 1991.

MOON, WARREN G., art historian, educator, appraisal company executive; b. Westfield, Mass., Mar. 2, 1945; s. G.F.W. and N.E. (Noblecourt-Richaud) M. BA, Tufts U., 1967; MBA, U. Chgo., 1969, PhD, 1975. Instr. art history U. Wis., Madison, 1970-73, asst. prof., 1973-75, assoc. prof. art history and classics, 1975-80, prof. art history and classics, 1980-92, research curator Elvehjem Mus. Art, 1975-85, chmn. Dept. Art History, 1990-92; guest curator Art Inst. of Chgo., 1975-80; pres. Warren G. Moon & Assocs. Aprraisers and Brokers, 1985-92; vis. prof. U. Mich. program in Florence, Italy, NEH Inst. Ctr. for Judaic Studies, Brown University, 1988. Author, editor: Ancient Greek Art and Iconography, 1983, Greek Vase Painting in Midwestern Collections, 1980; author intro.: Greek Monuments To Make, 1990; founder, co-gen. editor Wisconsin Studies in Classics, 1982-92; contbr. World Book Ency., 1985-86, Macmillan Dictionary of Art; mem. editorial bd.: Wis. Acad. Rev., 1983-88; book rev. editor Am. Jour. Archaeology, 1983-86. Chmn. bd. dirs. Center Gallery, Madison, 1982-83; bd. dirs. Creative Arts Over Sixty, Wis., 1981-90. Ryerson fellow, 1969-70; Fulbright fellow, 1969; Inst. for Research in Humanities vis. fellow, 1975. Mem. Archaeol. Inst. Am., Am. Philol. Assn., Am. Numis. Soc. (grad. fellow 1969), Coll. Art Assn., Midwest Soc. Art Historians, Wis. Acad. Scis., Arts and Letters. Home: Middleton Wis. Died June 23, 1992; buried Forest Hills Cemetary Madison, Wis. †

MOONEYHAM, WALTER STANLEY, clergyman, consultant; b. Houston, Miss., Jan. 14, 1926; s. Walter Scott and Mary Adeline (Sullivan) M.; m. LaVerda Mae Green, Dec. 13, 1946; children: Carol Gwen, Eric Scott, Robin Anne, Mark Randall; m. Nancy Nita Callaway, June 1, 1984. B.S., Okla. Bapt. U., 1950; Litt.D., Houghton Coll., 1964; D.H.L., Taylor U., 1977; LL.D., Seattle Pacific U., 1978. Ordained to ministry Bapt. Ch., 1947; minister in Tecumseh, Okla., 1948-49, Sulphur, Okla., 1949-52; exec. sec. Okla. Free Will Bapt. Conv., 1952-53, Nat. Assn. Free Will Baptists, Nashville, 1953-59; editor United Evangelical Action, 1959-64; spl. asst. to Billy Graham (coordinating dir. World Congress on Evangelism), Berlin, Germany, 1964-67; v.p. internat. relations Billy Graham Evangelistic Assn. (coordinating dir. Asia-S. Pacific Congress on Evangelism), Singapore, 1967-69; pres. World Vision Internat., Monrovia, Calif., 1969-82; internat. cons., 1982-91. Author: China, the Puzzle, 1972, What Do You Say to a Hungry World?, 1975, Come Walk the World, 1978, China, A New Day, 1979, Sea of Heartbreak, 1980, Traveling Hopefully, 1984, Is There Life Before Death?, 1985, Dancing on the Strait and Narrow, 1989; editor: The Dynamics of Christian Unity, 1963, Christ Seeks Asia, 1968; co-editor: One Race, One Gospel, One Task, 1967. Home: Rancho Mirage Calif. Died June 3, 1991; buried Desert Meml. Pk., Cathedral City, Calif.

MOORE, EDWARD FREDERICK, investor; b. Detroit, Feb. 1, 1900; s. George F. and Walfrid Louisa (Brudin) M. B.S. in Mech. Engring., U. Mich., 1922; B.A. U. Mich. with distinction, 1923; M.S. in Mech. Engring., U. Mich., 1923; postgrad., Columbia U., 1935-37, Union Theol. Sem., 1936-37. Mech. engr. Gen. Motors Corp., Detroit, 1923-26; fin. engr. natural gas pipeline financing P.W. Chapman & Co., N.Y.C., 1926-28, W. Va., Ohio, Ky., Tex., 1928-33; ind. investor N.Y.C., from 1933; assoc. with Doctor Alexis Carrel, N.Y.C., 1937-41; founder, pres. Found. for the Future of Man, Inc., N.Y.C., from 1972. Author-designer: Deep Water Salvage, 1923, Ency. of the Unknown, 1973, 77; author: Charting the Future, 1978. Mem. ASME, Phi Beta Kappa, Sigma Xi, Tau Beta Pi. Republican. Home: Englewood N.J. Deceased.

MOORE, FRANK CHARLES, state legislator; b. Toronto, Mar. 23, 1896; came to U.S., 1896, naturalized, 1904; s. James Frederick and Lillian Maude (Hewson) M.; m. Velma E. Kennedy, Mar. 19, 1920 (dec. 1961); children: Earle Kennedy, Joan Elizabeth (Mrs. Arthur T. von Mehren), Patricia Anne (Mrs. Robert J. Patterson); m. Rosalind G. Baldwin, Aug. 4, 1964. LLB, U. Buffalo, 1921; LLD, Hobart Coll., 1941, Syracuse U., 1948, Elmira Coll., 1953. LLD, Adelphi Coll., 1956; DHL, Alfred U., 1951. Counsel N.Y. State Legis. Com. to Recodify Town Law, 1927-32; mem. Legis. Commn. for Revision Tax Laws, 1934-39, Gov. Lehman's Commn. to Prepare for Constl. Conv., 1937; del. N.Y. State Constl. Conv., 1938; mem. N.Y. State Legis. Commn. on Extension Civil Svc., 1939-41, N.Y. State Legis. Commn. on Mcpl. Fin., 1939-47, N.Y. State Postwar Planning Commn., 1943-47; chmn. N.Y. State Legis. Commn. on Mcpl. Revenues, 1944-46, Com. on Constl. Debt, Tax Limits, City-Sch. Fiscal Rels., 1947-53, Com. on Tchrs. Salaries, 1950-51; mem. N.Y. State Bd. equalization and assessment, from 1949, also chmn.; chmn. Comptroller's Com. Local Non-Property Taxes, 1949-50; chmn. temporary legis. commn. on sch. bldgs., 1950-54, commn. on state-local fiscal rels., from 1962, local govt. adv. bd. State N.Y.. Pres. Govt. Affairs Found.; chmn. bd. trustees SUNY; bd. overseers Albert Einstein Coll. Medicine; hon. trustee Hobart and William Smith Coll.; exec. sec. Assn. of Towns, 1933-43, hon. pres., from 1943; trustee town and county officers tng. sch. State of N.Y.; state comptroller, N.Y. State, 1943-50; lt. gov. N.Y., 1951-53. Served with U.S. Army, 1917, discharged for phys. disability; enlisted Royal Flying Corps., Can., 1917; 2d lt. RAF, 1918. Mem. N.Y. State Bar Assn., Erie County Bar Assn., Am. Legion, Rotary, Kiwanis., Masons. Republican. Presbyterian. *

MOORE, FRONTIS H., lawyer; b. Suffolk, Va., July 27, 1894; s. Henry Coles and Ida (Johnston) M.; m. Gertrude Anderson,. Aug. 25, 1931. Student, Ala. Presbyn. Coll., 1910-11; AB, U. Ala., 1914; spl. law student, U. Mich., 1914. Bar: Ala. County solicitor Elmore County, Ala., 1919-21; city atty. Lanett, Ala., 1922-24; mem. Ala. Tax Commn., 1927-31; asst. atty. gen., 1931-35, 1st asst. atty. gen., 1935-36; mem. firm Benner Burr McKanny & Forman; mem. successor firm Burr, McKanny, Moore & Thomas, Birmingham, from 1936; mem. firm Moore, Thomas, Taliaferro, Forman & Burr. Mem. Soc. Colonial Wars, Rotary, Sigma Chi. Presbyterian. Democrat. *

MOORE, H(ENRY) COLEMAN, JR., utility company executive; b. Marion, Ky., June 22, 1893; s. Henry Coleman and Nannie Edna (Hodge) M.; m. Ruth Fritz, June 21, 1916; children: John Coleman, Marianna (Mrs. Theodore J. West). Student, Centre Coll., 1914. Audit clk. Ky. Pub. Svc. Co., 1913-15; chief clk., later acct. Richmond Light & R.R. Co., S.I., N.Y., 1915-18; asst. to chief div. auditor Western Union Telegraph Co.,

1918-23; comptroller S.I. Edison Corp., 1923-29; asst. comptroller A.G. & E. System, 1930; sec.-treas. N.E. Gas & Electric Assn., Cambridge, Mass., 1931-58, trustee, from 1939, v.p., 1951-58, vice chmn. bd., from 1958; dir., chmn. fin. com. Western Union Telegraph Co.; trustee U.S. Leather Co., N. Boston Lighting Properties, Worcester Transp. Assocs. Contbr. to bus. publs. Mem. Cambridge C. of C. (treas. 1947-48, clk. 1946-47), Am. Gas Assn., N.E. Gas Assn., Fin. Execs. Inst., Masons, Republican Club of Mass., Downtown Club of Boston, Kiwanis, Beta Theta Pi. *

MOORE, JEAN OLIVER, lawyer; b. Wichita, Kans., July 25, 1925; s. Jesse Lee and Olive F. (Bryant) M.; m. Arline Louise Watkins, June 9, 1947 (div.); children: Susan Moore Jackson, Rossanne Moore Thomson, Colin B.; m. Helen Leota Fritz, Aug. 21, 1979. BA, U. Kans., 1957, LLB, 1949, JD, 1968. Bar: Kans. 1949, U.S. Ct. Appeals (10th cir.) 1954, U.S. Supreme Ct. 1972. Practice in Wichita, 1949-92; sr. mem. Jean Oliver Moore, Wichita, 1961-92; lectr. Wichita State U., 1951-71; instr. U. Kans. Extension Div., 1951-52, Am. Inst. Banking, 1954-92; pres. Great Western Trading Corp., Wichita, 1972-92; dir. Karefree Nursing Ctrs., Inc., numerous other corps. Sub-local chmn. March of Dimes, 1967, 69. Mem. Assn. Trial Lawyers Am., Fed. Bar Assn., Kans. Bar Assn., Wichita Bar Assn. (chmn. criminal law com. 1982-85), Nat. Assn. Criminal Def. Lawyers (Kans. chmn. 1977-78, pres.; Pres.'s award 1977), Wis. Criminal Defense Lawyers Assn. (life), Am. Judicature Soc., Okla. Kans. Assn. Criminal Def. Lawyers (first time recipient outstanding practitioner Jean Oliver Moore award named after him on behalf of his membership), Criminal Def. Lawyers Assn., Masons, Albert Pike Lodge. Recipient Wisdom award of Honor Wisdom Soc., 1971. Republican. Methodist. Author: The Ancient Law, 1954; contbr. articles to legal jours. Avocations: reading, history. Died May 9, 1992. Home: Wichita Kans.

MOORE, JOHN DENIS JOSEPH, ambassador, lawyer; b. N.Y.C., Nov. 10, 1910; s. John D. and Julia Frances (Leader) M.; m. Mary Foote, July 28, 1936 (dec. 1975); children: John Denis, Margaret Foote (dec.), Anne (Mrs. Arnold L. Lisio), Julia (Mrs. Richard Bartholomew), Mary Faith, Martha (Mrs. Robert Battles). A.B., Yale U., 1932, LL.B., 1935; LL.D., Suffolk U., 1972, Nat. U. Ireland, 1976. Reporter, corr. Boston Evening Transcript, various newspapers, N.Y.C., 1927-35; assoc. law firm White & Case, N.Y.C.; asst. corp. counsel City N.Y.; asst. dist. atty. N.Y. County; with W.R. Grace & Co., 1946-69; U.S. ambassador to Ireland, 1969-75; dir. W.R. Grace & Co., 1976-84, dir. emeritus, 1984-88. Founder, pres. Family Care Found. for Mentally Ill, from 1961; vice chmn. Council Ams., 1964-69; chmn. U.S. Inter-Am. Council, 1960-64, Ireland-U.S. Council, 1966-69; trustee St. Thomas More House, Yale U., from 1969; bd. dirs., v.p. Council Am. Ambassadors; bd. dirs. Am. Ireland Fund. Mem. 51st regt. N.Y. N.G., World War II. Decorated Order of Merit Ecuador; comdr. Order of the Sun Peru; Order of Leopold II Belgium; recipient U. Louvain medal and honors of City of Geel (Belgium) for activities on behalf of family care for mentally ill, 1975. Mem. Pan Am. Soc. (Gold insignia 1972), Washington Assn. N.J., Am. Irish Hist. Soc. (gold medal 1966), Eire Soc. Boston (gold medal 1976), Lexington (Mass.) Hist. Soc., N.Y. Hist. Soc., Am. Assn. Knights of Malta (chancellor 1976-86), Alpha Delta Phi. Clubs: Nacional (Lima); Yale, India House, Links (N.Y.C.); Elihu (Yale); Metropolitan (Washington); Portmarnock (Ireland) Golf; Royal and Ancient Golf (St. Andrews, Scotland). Died Sept. 12, 1988.

MOORE, LAURENCE, publisher; b. Union City, Ga., Jan. 23, 1919; s. Laurence Pratt and Leila Camilla (Johnson) M.; m. Katharine Joanne Stevens, Apr. 1938; children: Karl Laurence, Alan Stevens, Kathleen Louise. B.S.E.E., Stanford U., 1953. Project engr. Levinthal Electronics Co., Palo Alto, Calif., 1954-57; founder, v.p. Moore Assos., Inc. (remote control and telemetry systems), San Carlos, Calif., 1957-63, Data Measurement Inc. (electronic instrumentation), Palo Alto, 1963-68; pres. Ramparts Press, Inc., Forestville, Calif., from 1968, chmn. bd., from 1969; bd. dirs. Pacific Studies Center, Palo Alto. Served as navigator USAAF, 1942-48, ETO. Decorated D.F.C., Air medal with 4 oak leaf clusters. Mem. IEEE, Audio Engring. Soc. Home: Forestville Calif. Deceased. †

MOORE, O. OTTO, judge; b. Floyd's Knobs, Ind., May 14, 1896; s. David Burke and Charlotte (Scott) M.; m. Ruth Naomi Dye, Apr. 12, 1919; 1 dau., Loahna Lou (Mrs. Warren L. Chandler). LLB, U. Denver, 1922. Bar: Colo. 1922. Practiced in Denver, 1922-49, practiced individually, 1939-49, dep. dist. atty., 1924-27, 37-39; justice Supreme Ct., State of Colo., from 1948, chief justice, from 1957. Author: Mile High Harbor, 1947. Served with U.S. Army, World War I, overseas. Mem. ABA, Colo. Bar Assn., Am. Legion, VFW, Masons (33 deg.), Shriners, Sigma Alpha Epsilon, Phi Delta Phi. Democrat. (candidate for dist. atty. 1940). *

MOORE, RICHARD ALBERT, lawyer; b. St. Paul, Aug. 11, 1915; s. Harry Albert and Mary (Lawless) M.; m. Elizabeth Donnelly Kennedy, Feb. 28, 1942 (dec. June 1989); children: Elizabeth (Mrs. Bruce Edmund Kiernat), Richard Albert. BA magna cum laude, U. Minn., 1936, JD, 1938. Bar: Minn. 1938. Practiced in St. Paul; assoc. Bundlie, Kelley & Finley, St. Paul, 1938-41, Covington, Burling, Rublee, Acheson & Shorb, Washington, 1941-47; ptnr. Moore, Costello & Hart (and predecessor firms), St. Paul, 1947-91, sr. ptnr., 1962-91; past dir. Norwest Bank of St. Paul, N.A., Maxson Steel Co., Inc., Bayport-St. Croix Co., Maxson Corp., Nobles Industries, Inc., First Midwest Corp., Villaume Industries Inc., First Midwest Capital Corp. Mem. Gov.'s Adv. Commn. on Securities, 1969-70; chmn. adv. com. med. edn. programs St. Paul-Ramsey Hosp., 1971-72; v.p. St. Paul Ramsey Med. Ctr. Commn., 1973-84, mem. joint study com., 1982-84; chmn. Ramsey County Med. Health Svcs. Com., 1974-84; mem. City of St. Paul Citizens Task Force for Library, 1980-86; mem. nominating com. St. Paul Arts and Sci. Coun., 1980-85; mem. adv. com. St. Paul YWCA, 1982-85; past pres., past bd. dirs. Family Svc., St. Paul, Capitol Community Svcs., Inc.; past bd. dirs. Greater St. Paul United Fund and Coun., St. Paul-Ramsey Hosp. Med. Edn. and Rsch. Found., St. Paul Met. Improvement Com., St. Paul Urban Coalition, Community Planning Orgn. Inc., Better Bus. Bur. St. Paul, St. Paul Winter Carnival Assn.; bd. dirs., v.p. St. Paul area C. of C. Found. 1979-82; bd. dirs., sec., v.p. Mary Livingston Griggs and Mary Griggs Burke Found.; bd. dirs. Mary and Jackson Burke Found., Minn. Found., 1984-91, J. Paper Found., 1984-91, L. & A.F. Paper Found., 1984-91; bd. dirs. Saint Paul Found., pres., 1973-82, chmn. distbn. com., 1972-86, hon. dir., 1988-91; trustee James Daniel Humphrey Found.; past assoc. Macalester Coll.; past trustee William Mitchell Coll. Law; bd. dirs., v.p. Como Conservatory Restoration Fund, 1986-91; vice chair Blomquist Family Found.; bd. dirs. Mounds Midway Hosp. Found., 1982-90, Healtheast Found., 1988-90. Mem. ABA, Ramsey County Bar Assn., Minn. State Bar (past sect. chmn.), Minn. Law Alumni Assn. (past dir.), U.S. Supreme Ct. Hist. Soc. (trustee, mem. nominating com. 1975-78), St. Paul area C. of C. (pres. 1971, chmn. bd. 1972, past dir., Great Living St. Paulite award), Order of Coif, Phi Beta Kappa, Phi Delta Phi, Delta Kappa Epsilon. Episcopalian. Clubs: Kiwanian. (St. Paul), St. Paul Athletic (past dir.), Gyro (St. Paul, past dir.), Minnesota (St. Paul, past dir.), University (St. Paul, past dir., past pres.). Home: Saint Paul Minn. Died Sept. 30, 1991. †

MOORE, ROGER ALLAN, lawyer; b. Framingham, Mass., Aug. 8, 1931; s. Ralph Chester and Mabelle (Taft) M. AB cum laude, Harvard U., 1953, JD, 1956; m. Barbara Lee Wildman, July 4, 1955; children: Marshall Christian, Elizabeth Lee, Taft Hayden Davis, Allan Baron. Bar: Mass. 1956. Assoc. firm, Ropes & Gray, 1956-66, ptnr., 1967-90. Chmn. bd. Nat. Rev., Inc.; gen. counsel Rep. Nat. Com., 1981-89; gen. counsel Rep. Nat. Conv., 1984, 88; del. Rep. Nat. Conv., 1964, 84, 88; mem. Electoral Coll., 1984; spl. parliamentarian Adminstrv. Conf. of U.S., 1981-88; gen. counsel Pres.'s Reelection Com., 1984; sec. Harvard Med. Ctr.; chmn. U.S. presdl. del. to Haiti's 1987 elections; clk. L.S. Starrett Co., Wrentham Steel Products Co.; pres. Harvard Young Rep. Club, 1953-54; former chmn. bd. dirs. Beacon Hill Civic Assn.; former mem. Bd. Fgn. Scholarships, Dept. State; bd. dirs. Historic Boston, Salzburg Sem. in Am. Studies, Austria, 1954-66; bd. dirs., clk. Corp. Maintaining Editorial Diversity in Am., 1989—; sec. Harvard Med. Ctr.; bd. dirs., clk. Bostonian Soc. Recipient Endicott Peabody Saltonstall prize Harvard U., 1953, Boylston prize, 1952. Mem. ABA (adv. commn. standing com. on law and the electoral process), D.C. Bar Assn., Mass. Bar Assn., Boston Bar Assn., Mass. Hist. Soc., Commanderie de Bordeaux, Somerset Club, Harvard Club (Boston and N.Y.C.), Country Club (Brookline, Mass.), Met. Club (Washington), Harvard Faculty Club. Episcopalian (sr. warden). Died June 4, 1990; buried Ch. of the Advent, Boston. Home: Boston Mass.

MOORE, WARD FREDERICK, chemical company executive; b. Tonawanda, N.Y., Mar. 24, 1922; s. Howard Frederick and Doris Agnes (Dicks) M.; m. Suzanne Forsey, Jan. 31, 1944; children: Leigh Carol Moore Del Vesco, Peter Michael, Jeffree Stephen, Jillann Katherine. B.S. in Chem. Engring, Cornell U., 1943; M.B.A., U. Buffalo, 1957. Div. v.p. Union Carbide Corp., N.Y.C., 1957-71; cons. W.F. Moore Assos., La Jolla, Calif., 1971-72; pres., dir. Filtrol Corp., Los Angeles, 1972-81; pres. Columbia Cement Corp., Columbus, Ohio, 1973-81, Horizon Coal Corp., Zanesville, Ohio, 1977-81, MBA, Inc., 1982-87; dir. Kawecki Berylco Inc, Material Scis. Inc., Atec Inc., Exotic Materials Inc., Electro-Metals Corp., Crested Corp., Phoenix Data Inc. Served as officer AUS, 1943-46. Mem. Am. Inst. Chem. Engrs., Chem. Mktg. Research Inst., Comml. Devel. Assn., Am. Petroleum Inst. Clubs: Desert Horizons Country (Indian Wells, Calif.); San Diego Yacht, La Jolla Beach and Tennis, La Jolla Country. Home: La Jolla Calif. Died July 16, 1989; cremated.

MORAVIA, ALBERTO (PINCHERLE), author; b. Rome, Nov. 28, 1907; s. Carlo and Teresa de (Marsanich) M.; m. Elsa Morante, Apr. 21, 1941 (dec. 1985); m. Carmen Lelera, 1986. Author: (novels) Gli indifferenti (The Indifferent Ones), 1929, Le Ambizioni Sbagliate (Mistaken Ambitions), 1935, La Mascherara (The Fancy Dress Party), 1941, Agostino (Corriere Lombardo prize 1945), 1944, La Romana (The Woman of Rome), 1947, La Disubbidienza, 1948, L'Amore Coniugale (Conjugal Love), 1949, Il Conformista (The Conformist), 1951, Il disprezzo (A Ghost at Noon), 1954, La Ciociara (Two Women), 1957, La noia (The Empty Canvas) Viareggio prize 1961), 1961 L'Attenzione (The Lie), 1965, Io e Lui (Two: The Phallis Novel), 1970, La Vita Interiore, 1978; (plays) Teatro, 1958, Beatrice Cenci, 1965, Il mondo e quello che e (The World As It Is), 1966, Il dio Kurt, 1967, La Vita e Gioco, 1970; (short stories) La bella vita, 1935, L'Imbroglio, 1937, I Sogni del Pigro, 1940, L'Amante infelice, 1943, L'Epidemia, 1945, Due Cortigiane, 1945, Racconti Romani (Roman Tales), 1945, I Racconti, 1954, Nuovi Racconti Romani (More Roman Tales), 1959, L'Automa (The Fetish), 1963, L'Uomo come fine, e altri saggi (Man as an End: A Defense of Humanism), 1965, Una cos e una cosa, 1966, Il Paradiso (Paradise and Other Stories), 1970, Un' altra Vita, 1973, A quale tribu appartieni, 1974, Boh, 1975, Impegno Controvoglia, 1980; (travel) La revoluzione culturale in Cina, 1967, The Voyeur, 1987, The Viaggi a Roma, 1988; Italian Ind. Party rep. to European Parliament, 1984; film critic L'Espresso, 1965—; editor for publishing house; guest Dept. State, U.S., 1955; lectr. Queens Coll., CUNY and other schs., 1964, 68; visited China, 1967. Decorated chevalier Legion d'Honneur (France); recipient Strega Lit. prize, 1952, Marzotto award for fiction, 1954. Mem. PEN, Am. Acad. Arts and Letters (hon.), Nat. Inst. Arts and Letters (hon.). Died Sept. 26, 1990; buried Verano Cemetery, Rome. Home: Rome Italy

MORECOCK, EARLE MONROE, college dean; b. Richmond, Va., Sept. 11, 1898; s. William Thomas and Florence (Simmons) M. BS in Elec. Engring., Clemson Coll., 1919, ME, 1939, EE, 1941; MA, U. Rochester, 1945. Registered profl. engr., N.Y. Student engr. Gen. Electric Co., Schenectady, 1919-20; engr. W. Va. Engring. Co., Charleston, 1920-24; with Rochester Inst. Tech., from 1924, from instr. to prof., 1924-30, head elec. dept., 1930-35, dean Coll. Applied Sci., from 1953. Author: Alternating Current Circuits, 1949, Direct Current Circuits, 1953. With USNR, 1918-22. Fellow IEEE; mem. Am. Soc. Engring. Edn., Rochester Engring. Soc. *

MORELAND, JESSE EARL, college president; b. Commerce, Tex., Oct. 2, 1897; s. Royal Bert and Mary Emma (Long) M.; m. Helen Elizabeth Hardy, Nov. 18, 1924; children: Jane Long (Mrs. Ben Vaughan Branscomb), Helen (Mrs. Clare Cotton Jr.), Mary (Mrs. Thomas Ellison Smith), Frances (Mrs. Lawrence Fossett). Student, Austin Coll., 1914; AB, So. Meth. U., 1918, AM, 1921; student, Peabody Coll., 1927; LLD (hon.), Morris Harvey Coll., 1941, Emory and Henry Coll., 1942, U. Chattanooga, 1955, U. Richmond, 1964; Dr. Humanidades (Hon.), Porto Allegre Coll., Brazil, 1948; LHD (hon.), So. Meth. U., 1950. Ednl. missionary Porto Alegre Coll., Brazil, 1921-22; prof., v.p. Brazil, 1922-26, pres., 1927-34; v.p. Scarritt Coll., Nashville, 1936-39; pres. Randolph-Macon Coll., Ashland, Va., from 1939; mem. Conselho Rio Grandense dos professors, Porto Alegre, 1931-34; Clapp lectr. Martin Coll., 1949; trustee Philander Smith Coll., Bennett Coll., The Penington Sch.; pres. Nat. Assn. Schs. and Colls. of Meth. Ch., 1952. Contbr. articles to profl. jours. v.p. State YMCA Tenn., 1937-38, pres., 1938-39; mem. Southeastern conf. Meth. Ch., 1940, 44, 48, 52, 56, 60, 64, mem. gen. bd. edn., also mem. gen. conf., 1944, 52, 56, 60, 64; mem. 1st assembly World Coun. Chs., Amsterdam, 1948, 2d, Evanston, Ill., 1954, 3d, New Delhi, 1962, mem. cen. com., chmn. joint commn. on crusade scholarships, 1946-48; mem. exec. com. Fed. Coun. Chs. of Christ in Am., 1940-50, mem. 1st orgnl. meeting Nat. Coun. Chs. of Christ in U.S.; chmn. NCCJ, from 1952. Mem. Va. Acad. Sci., Va. Social Sci. Assn., Newcomen Soc., The Club, Hermitage Club, Kiwanis, Phi Beta Kappa, Omicron Delta Kappa, Theta Phi, Pi Gamma Mu. *

MORETZ, WILLIAM HENRY, surgeon, college president; b. Hickory, N.C., Oct. 23, 1914; s. Joseph Alfred and Elizabeth (Leonard) M.; m. Laura Thelma Schlums, Dec. 5, 1947; children: William Henry, John D., Robert L., Richard E., Elizabeth L., David L. B.S., Lenoir Rhyne Coll., 1935, D.Sc. (hon.), 1960; postgrad. in medicine, U. N.C., 1935-37; M.D., Harvard U., 1939. Intern Strong Meml. Hosp., Rochester, N.Y., 1939-40, asst. resident, then resident surgery, 1940-43; instr. surgery U. Rochester Sch. Medicine, 1944-47; asst. prof. surgery Coll. Medicine, U. Utah, 1947-49, assoc. prof., 1949-55; prof., chmn. dept. surgery Med. Coll. Ga., Augusta, 1955-72, prof. surgery emeritus, 1983-90, pres. coll., 1972-83, pres. emeritus, 1983-90. Contbr. articles to surg. lit. Served from lt. to capt. M.C. AUS, 1944-47. Fellow A.C.S.; mem. Soc. Univ. Surgeons, Am., So., Western surg. assns., Soc. Surgery Alimentary Tract, AMA, Internat. Soc. Surgery, Internat. Cardiovascular Soc., Ga. Surg. Soc., Richmond County Med. Soc. Home: Augusta Ga. Died Dec. 27, 1989.

MOREY, ALBERT ANDERSON, industrial engineer; b. Belfast, Maine, Dec. 19, 1903; s. Herbert S. and Susan Anderson M.; m. Margaret D. Ice, Feb. 15, 1930; 1 child, Albert A. BBA, Boston U., 1925, LHD, 1969. Registered profl. engr., Ill., Mo. With Employer's Liability Assurance Corp., Boston, 1925-29;

with Marsh & McLennan Inc., Chgo., 1929-74, pntr., 1946, asst. v.p., 1938-47, v.p., 1947-59, sr. v.p., 1959-62, exec. v.p., 1962-66, chmn., 1966-69, mem. exec. com., 1961-70, chmn. exec. com., 1969-70. Contbr. articles to engring. mags. Mem. Chgo. Com.; mem. citizens bd. U Chgo.; mem. safety code, chem. welfare div. AUS, World War II; U.S. Civil Svc. chief insp. DPPS; chmn. Cook County March of Dimes, 1949; elector Ins. Hall Fame; bd. fellow Boston U., 1970—; bd. dirs. Rehab. Inst. Chgo. Recipient Outstanding Pub. Svc. award Boston U., 1963, Golden Plate award Am. Acad. Achievement, 197. Mem. ASME life, ASCE life, Am. Soc. Heating and Ventilating Engrs., AIME, Am. Soc. Mil. Engrs., Am. Soc. Safety Engrs., Soc. Automotive Engrs., Western Soc. Engrs., Vets. of Safety, NSPE, Ill. Soc. Profl. Engrs., Instn. Mech. Engrs. Eng., Lloyd's of London, Navy League U.S., Brit.-Am. C. ofC., Chgo. Assn. Commerce and Industry dir., v.p. pub. safety, Verein Deutscher Ingenieure Germany, Soc. des Ingénieurs Civils de France, Newcomen Soc., Coun. Fgn. Rels., many others. Home: Winetka Ill. Died June 10, 1991.

MOREY, WALTER NELSON, author; b. Hoquiam, Wash., Feb. 3, 1907; s. Arthur Nelson and Gertrude Regina (Stover) M.; m. Rosalind Alice Ogden, July 8, 1934 (dec. Feb. 1977); m. Peggy Kilburn, June 26, 1978. Student, Benkhe Walter Bus. Coll., 1927. Constrn. worker, Portland, Oreg., 1930; burner foreman, supt. Kaiser Shipyards, Vancouver, Wash., 1940-45; filbert farmer, from 1937; bd. dirs. Oreg. Nut Coop., Newberg, 1960-61. Author: No Cheers No Glory, 1945, North to Danger, 1954, 69, Gentle Ben, 1965, Home Is the North, 1967, Kävik the Wolf Dog, 1968, Angry Waters, 1969, Gloomy Gus, 1970, Deep Trouble, 1971, Scrub Dog of Alaska, 1971, Canyon Winter, 1972, Runaway Stallion, 1973, Run Far Run Fast, 1974, Operation Blue Bear, 1975, Year of the Black Pony, 1976, Sand and the Rock Star, 1979, The Lemon Meringue Dog, 1980, Death Walk, 1991. Recipient Dutton Jr. Animal Book award, 1965, 68, Sequoyah award, 1968, Dorothy Canfield Fisher award, 1970, William Allen White award, 1971, Pacific N.W. Booksellers award, 1974, award Portland coun. Internat. Reading Assn., 1984, achievement award Pacific N.W. Writers, Charles Erskine Wood retrospective award Oreg. Inst. Lit. Arts, 1991, award Oreg. Edn. Media Assn., 1991. Home: Wilsonville Oreg. Died Jan. 12, 1992; cremated.

MORGAN, CLINTON GERARD, JR., investment banker; b. Balt., July 31, 1897; s. Clinton Gerard and Emma E. (Roane) M.; m. Genevieve Carroll, Oct. 11, 1928; children: Carroll (Mrs. H. Allan Legge), Eugenia B. In investment banking, from 1917; with Legg & Co., Balt., from 1932, ptnr., from 1944. With U.S. Navy, World War I. Mem. Elkridge Club, Md. Club, Mchts. Club, Annapolis Yacht Club. *

MORGAN, PAUL WINTHROP, chemist; b. West Chesterfield, N.H., Aug. 30, 1911; s. Herbert and Olive (Lermond) M.; m. Elsie Louise Bridges, Aug. 27, 1939; children: Dennis Lee, Patricia Morgan Harding. B.S. in Chemistry, U. Maine, 1937; Ph.D. in Organic Chemistry, Ohio State U., 1940. Postdoctoral fellow Ohio State U., Columbus, 1940-41; with E.I. duPont de Nemours & Co., Wilmington, Del., 1941-76; research fellow E.I. duPont de Nemours & Co., 1957-73, sr. research fellow, 1973-76; chem. cons. West Chester, Pa., 1976-92; G.S. Whitby lectr. U. Akron, 1987; cons., lectr. in field; chmn. Gordon Research Conf. on Polymers, 1974. Author: Condensation Polymers, 1965; contbr. articles to profl. jours. Asst. dist. commr. Minquas Trail dist. Chester County council Boy Scouts Am., 1956-61; asst. scoutmaster Chester County council, 1961-76, chmn. troop com., 1976-88. Recipient Silver Beaver award Boy Scouts Am., 1967, Swinburne award Plastics and Rubber Inst., London, 1978, Engring. Materials Achievement award Am. Soc. Metals, 1978, award World Materials Congress 1988, Lavoisier medal, DuPont, 1991. Mem. NAE, Am. Chem. Soc. (Best Publ. of Yr. award Del. chpt. 1959, 78, nat. Polymer Chem. award 1976, Midgley award Detroit chpt. 1979, Del. chpt. award 1986, Carothers award 1988), Internat. Union Pure and Applied Chemistry, Franklin Inst. (Howard N. Potts medal 1976), Mineral. Soc. Pa., Sierra Club, Appalachian Trail Conf., Wilderness Soc., Audubon Soc., Nat. Wildlife Assn., Early Am. Industries Assn., Chester County (Pa.) Hist. Soc., Fiber Soc. (hon.). Home: West Chester Pa. Died May 28, 1992. †

MORIAL, ERNEST NATHAN, mayor; b. New Orleans, Oct. 9, 1929; s. Walter Etienne and Leonie Viola (Moore) M.; m. Sybil Gayle Haydel, Feb. 18, 1955; children: Julie Claire, Marc Haydel, Jacques Etienne, Cheri Michele, Monique Gayle. BS, Xavier U. of La., 1951; JD, La. State U., 1954. Bar: La. 1954. Auditor Keystone Life INs. Co., New Orleans, 1951; ptnr. Tureaud, Trudeau & Morial, New Orleans, 1954-60; gen. counsel Std. Life Ins. Co. of La., 1960-70; asst. U.S. atty. New Orleans, 1974-77; juvenile ct. judge, 1970-74; judge La. Ct. of appeal, New Orleans, 1974-77; fellow Inst. of Politics, Harvard U., 1978; mayor City of New Orleans, 1978-86; dir. Liberty Bank & Trust Co., Gourmet Svcs., Inc.; prof. law Tulane U. Law Sch., 1973-89; mem. La. Ho. Reps., 1968-70; bd. govs. Tulane U. Med. Ctr., bd. dirs. Loyola U.; trustee Xavier U. La. With AUS, 1954-56. Named one of 100 Most Influential Blacks Ebony mag., 197, 72, 73, 78, 79; recipient cert. for Disting. Svc. Links, Inc., 1972, Disting. Alumni award Xavier U., 1979. Mem. ABA, Nat. Bar Assn. (founder jud. coun.), La. Bar Assn., Am. Judicature Soc., New Orleans Mid-Winter Sports Assn. (exec. com.), La. Mcpl. Assn. (dir.), Alpha Phi Alpha (gen. pres. 1968-72), Knights of Peter Claver. Home: New Orleans La. Died Dec. 24, 1989.

MORKOVSKY, JOHN LOUIS, bishop; b. Moulton, Tex., Aug. 16, 1909; s. Alois Joseph and Marie (Raska) M. Grad., St. John's Sem., San Antonio, 1930; student, N.Am. Coll., Rome, Italy, 1930-36; attended lectures, Pontifical Univ. of Propagation of Faith, 1930-32; S.T.D., Pontifical Gregorian U., 1936; A.M., Cath. U. Am., 1943; LL.D. (hon.), St. Edward's U., 1958. Ordained priest Roman Catholic Ch., 1933; asst. pastor St. Michael's Ch., Weimar, Tex., 1936-39, St. Ann's Ch., San Antonio, 1940; prof. canon law St. John's Sem., San Antonio, 1940-41; archdiocesan supt. of schs., 1941-56; pastor St. Leo's parish, San Antonio, 1945-54, St. Mary Magdalen parish, 1954-56; titular bishop Hieron and aux. bishop Amarillo, 1956-58; vicar gen., chancellor Amarillo Diocese, 1957-58, bishop, 1958-63; coadjutor bishop, apostolic administrator Galveston-Houston, 1963-74, bishop, 1975-85, bishop emeritus, 1985-90; Judge on Archiocesan Tribunal, 1946-56; mem. Archdiocesan Bd. Consultors, 1947-56; pres. Tex. Conf. Christian Chs., 1971-72. Papal chamberlain with title very reverend monsignor, 1944; domestic prelate with title right rev. monsignor, 1954. Club: K.C. (4 deg.). Home: Houston Tex. Died Mar. 24, 1990.

MORRIS, BREWSTER HILLARD, former foreign service officer; b. Bryn Mawr, Pa., Feb. 7, 1909; s. George L. and Fanny S. (Hillard) M.; m. Ellen Downes, April 26, 1948 (dec. 1985). BS, Haverford Coll., 1930; BA, Oxford (Eng.) U., 1932, BLitt, 1933. Investment analyst Provident Trust Co., Phila., 1934-36; appointed fgn. svc. officer Dept. of State, 1936; vice consul Montreal, Can., 1936-38, Vienna, 1938-39, Dresden, 1939-40; 3d sec. of embassy Berlin, 1940-41; 2d sec. Stockholm, 1942-44; staff polit. adviser to U.S. Mil. Govt. Fed. Republic Germany, 1944-48; 1st sec. and counsellor Moscow, 1948-50; polit. officer Office U.S. High Commr. in Germany, 1950-51; Bd. dirs. Internat. Hospitality Ctr. Bd., San Francisco; trustee World Affairs Coun. No. Calif. Mem. Phi Beta Kappa. Home: Tiburon Calif. Died Sept. 3, 1990.

MORRIS, CHARLES ROBERT, dental educator; b. Houston, Nov. 21, 1924; s. Earl Luckett and Hazel (Hemphill) M.; m. Evelyn Barbee Williams, Sept. 13, 1947; children: Charles Robert, Jane Morris Longmire, Margaret Ann Morris Huff, Claire C. Morris Zively, Amy Frances (dec.), Earl Leslie. Student, Southwestern U., Georgetown, Tex., 1942-44, 46, Columbia U., 1944; D.D.S., U. Tex., 1950, postgrad. cert. oral surgery, 1960. Diplomate Am. Bd. Oral Surgery, Am. Bd. Oral and Maxillofacial Radiology. Commd. ensign U.S. Navy, World War II; commd. 2d lt. U.S. Air Force, 1949, advanced through grades to col., 1968; chief oral surgery (Air Force Hosp.), Wiesbaden, Germany, 1962-66; chief outpatient surgery (Willford Hall Air Force Hosp.), Lackland AFB, Tex., 1966-67; chief inpatient oral surgery (Willford Hall Air Force Hosp.), 1967-68; chief div. dentistry br. dental scis. div. (Sch. Aerospace Medicine), Brooks AFB, Tex., 1968-71; dep. chief dental scis. div. (Sch. Aerospace Medicine), 1969-71; ret., 1971; mem. faculty Dental Sch. U. Tx., Houston, 1966-71; mem. faculty Dental Sch. U. Tx., San Antonio, 1968-86, clin. prof. dept. diagnosis and radiology, 1970-71, prof., chmn. dept., 1971-86, prof. surgery Med. Sch., 1973-86; prof. pathology Health Sci. Ctr., U. Tex, 1974-76; v.p. ITM, Inc.; cons. various depts. U.S. Air Force, from 1960; mem. med. radiology adv. com. Ctr. for Devices and Radiol. Health, FDA, Health and Human Services, 1982-86, dental radiology cons., 1986; bd. dirs. Denex Corp. Contbr. articles to profl. jours. Active Boy Scouts Am., from 1959; pres. N.D. chpt. PTA, 1961-62, hon. life mem., 1962-86. Decorated Legion of Merit; recipient certificate of achievement Surgeon Gen. Air Force, 1970. Fellow Internat. Assn. Oral Surgeons, Am. Coll. Dentists; mem. ADA, Tex. Dental Assn., Western Germany Armed Forces, Orgn. Tchrs. Oral Diagnosis, San Antonio Dist. Dental Soc., Am. Acad. Dental Radiology (pres.), Am. Assn. Dental Schs., Internat. Assn. Dento-Maxillofacial Radiologists (pres.-elect 1983-85, pres. 1985-86), Kappa Sigma, Psi Omega, Omicron Kappa Upsilon (pres. 1986). Baptist (deacon). Home: San Antonio Tex. Died Nov. 16, 1986; buried Mission Pk. North, San Antonio, Tex.

MORRIS, E(LLIS) THEODORE, advertising executive; b. Cleve., Oct. 23, 1898; s. Thomas Silas and Jessie Caldwell (Ellis) M.; m. Mildred E. Hickman, Apr. 22, 1941; 1 child, Patricia Ann (Mrs. George A. Wells, II). AB, Western Res. U., 1920. Dist. sales and advt. mgr. B.F. Goodrich, Phila., 1923-25; advt. mgr. B.F. Goodrich, Akron, 1929-32, Pacific Goodrich Co., L.A., 1926-29; account exec. Meldrum & Fewsmith, Inc., Cleve., 1932-38, v.p., 1938-48, exec. v.p., 1948-54, pres., from 1955. Trustee Inner City Protestant Parish, Cleve. Playhouse; mem. sponsors com. Karamu Theatre. With USAAC, 1917-18,. Mem. Am. Assn. Advt. Agys., Hermit Club (dir., supr. drama sect.), Cleve. Athletic Club, Cleve. Country Club, Union Club of Cleve., Sigma Chi. Congregationalist. *

MORRIS, ERNEST BROUGHAM, lawyer, harness racing executive; b. Rensselaer, N.Y., May 11, 1908; s. John W. and Minnie (Brougham) M.; children: Alice (Mrs. Karl H. Schrade), Robert, David; m. Barbara Middaugh, Aug. 26, 1961. A.B., Union Coll., 1928; J.D., Albany Law Sch., 1931, LL.D., 1971. Bar: N.Y. 1932. Practiced in Albany, 1932-65; spl. counsel N.Y. State Tax Commn., 1943-45; dep. atty. gen. N.Y., 1944; dist. atty. Albany County, 1944; dir. Adirondack Trust Co.; owner Saratoga Raceway, Saratoga Springs, N.Y. 1963-87; former pres. Harness Tracks of Am. Trustee Saratoga Performing Arts Center, Albany Law Sch. (pres. 1965-70), Union U. (past pres. bd. govs.), Grayson Found.; counsel Hambletonian Soc.; v.p. Grand Circuit; trustee emeritus Albany Med. Coll. Inducted into Hall of Fame, Trotting Horse Mus., Goshen, N.Y. Mem. Saratoga County Bar Assn., Am. Horse Council, U.S. Trotting Assn. (bd. dirs., counsel), Internat. Trotting Assn. (pres. 1977-78), Saratoga Harness Racing Assn.(chmn. bd. dirs.). Republican. Presbyterian. Club: Fort Orange. Home: Saratoga Springs N.Y. Died Dec. 25, 1991.

MORRIS, GLORY HUCKINS, artist; b. Texarkana, Ark., Aug. 15; d. Joseph and Olive (Mills) Huckins; div. Student Smith Coll. Grad. Sch. Architecture, 1936-39, also Ecole des Beaux Arts, Fontainebleau, France, Art Students League, N.Y.C., Mus. Fine Arts Sch., Houston. One woman shows English Speaking Union, Houston, 1967, fine arts dept. Houston Pub. Library, 1970, Gallery Am. Art, Shreveport, 1971, River Oaks Garden Forum, Houston, 1976, Fidelity Bank, Oklahoma City, 1979, Town House, Houston, 1984, Palmer Fine Arts, Houston 1985; exhibited in group shows museums fine arts Dallas and Houston, Okla. Art Ctr., Okla. Mus. Art, Jr. League Gallery, Oklahoma City, McNey Mus., San Antonio; represented in permanent collections Okla. Art Ctr., Smith Coll. Recipient Ellen Goins Art award Children's Lit. Assn., Houston, 1982. Mem. Am. Watercolor Soc. (assoc.), Watercolor Art Soc., Tex. Watercolor Soc. Republican. Episcopalian. Died June 22, 1987; buried Rose Hill Burial Pk., Oklahoma City. Home: Houston Tex.

MORRIS, JOE ALEX, editor; b. Lancaster, Mo., Mar. 5, 1904; s. Alexander D. and Lillian Clare (Rippey) M.; m. Maxine Pooler, Oct. 3, 1926; children: Joe Alex, Clare Rippey. BJ, U. Mo., 1926. Reporter U.S. Daily and Washington Daily News, 1926, Tulsa Tribune, 1927; telegraph editor Denver Post, 1927; fgn. editor United Press Assn., 1928-43; with Office Censorship, Washington, 1943; fgn. editor N.Y. Herald Tribune, 1944; mng. editor Collier's Weekly, 1944-48. Mem. Nat. Press Club (Washington), Alpha Tau Omega, Sigma Delta Chi. Home: White Plains N.Y. Died Jan. 16, 1990.

MORRIS, JOHN JAMES, JR., lawyer; b. Georgetown, Del., Aug. 24, 1896; s. John Johnson and Belle (Donovan) M.; m. Marceline L. Kaiser, Sept. 9, 1939; 1 child, John James. Student, Occidental Coll., 1917-18; LLB, U. Va., 1922. Bar: Del. 1923. Assoc. U.S. Senator Daniel O. Hastings, 1923; ptnr. Hastings, Stockley, Southerland & Morris, Wilmington, Del., 1928-31, Hering, Morris, James & Hitchens, Wilmington, 1931-53, Morris, James, Hitchens & Williams, Wilmington, from 1954; U.S. atty. for Del., 1935-39; U.S. referee in bankruptcy for Dist. of Del., 1942-44; U.S. atty. Dist. of Del., 1944-48; bd. dirs. Bank of Del.; chmn. Del. Bar Examiners. Served as 2d lt. U.S. Army, World War I. Mem. ABA, Del. Bar Assn. (pres. 1946-48), Wilmington Country Club, Wilmington Club, Sigma Nu, Delta Theta Phi. *

MORRIS, LAWRENCE, animal husbandry educator; b. Mesa, Ariz., Jan. 4, 1896; s. Hyrum Bowles and Eliza (Smith) M.; m. Ada Fransworth, Sept. 10, 1917; children: Ezma (Mrs. W.D. Pew), Muriel (Mrs. Dale R. Curtis), Lawrence Wilford. Student, Brigham Young U., 1915-16; BS, U. Ariz., 1925; MS, Tex. A&M Coll., 1928; PhD, La. State U., 1938. Rschr., tchr. poultry dept. Okla. A&M Coll., 1928-44, U. Ark., 1944; chmn. poultry dept. U. Wyo., 1944-47, Utah State U., 1947-48; dir. field rsch. Dawes Labs., Chgo., 1948-49; dir. field rsch. and pers. Utah Poultry & Farmers Coop., Salt Lake City, 1949-52; chmn., prof. dept. animal husbandry Brigham Young U., from 1952; spl. rsch. on protein meat quality, high fiber poultry feeds, use of oxygen hatching chicken and turkey eggs at high elevations. With U.S. Army, 1917-18. Mem. Wyo. Feed Dealers Assn. (bd. dirs., sec.-treas.), Utah Feed Mfg. and Dealers Assn. (bd. dirs., sec.-treas.), Am. Poultry Assn. (life), Poultry Sci. Assn., World Poultry Sci. Assn., Sigma Xi, Alpha Zeta. *

MORRIS, MARY ELIZABETH, author, editor, columnist; b. Ironton, Ohio, Mar. 2, 1913; d. J. Boyd and Elizabeth (Jones) Davis; m. Donald McLeod Pond, Dec. 10, 1934; m. William Morris, Feb. 8, 1947; children: Ann Elizabeth (Mrs. Paul S. Downie), Susan Jane, John Boyd, William Frazer, Mary Elizabeth, Evan Nathanael. Student, Ohio State U., 1930-34. Editor No. Star, Columbus, Ohio, summers 1930-31; editor Ohio Republican Woman, 1930-32; reporter Columbus Citizen, 1931-34; free lance writer, editor, 1934-41; founder labor sect. A.R.C., Washington, 1941; chief A.R.C., 1941-45. Co-author: syndicated daily newspaper column Words, Wit and Wisdom, Morris Asocs., 1953-86; exec. editor: Xerox Intermediate Dictionary, also Xerox Beginning Dictionary, 1973, Ginn Intermediate Dictionary, 1974, Weekly Reader Beginning Dictionary, 1974, Ginn Beginning Dictionary, 1974; Author: (with William Morris) The Word Game Book, 1959, 2d edit., 1975, Dictionary of Word and Phrase Origins, Vol. I, 1962, Vol. II, 1967, Vol. III, 1971, Harper Dictionary Contemporary Usage, 1975, 2d edit., 1984, The Morris Dictionary of Word and Phrase Origins, 1977, 2d edit., 1987, Words, Wit and Wisdom, 1978, also Japanese edit.; contbr. articles to encys. and dictionaries. Mem. Theta Sigma Phi. Democrat. Episcopalian. Home: Old Greenwich Conn. Died Nov. 20, 1986; buried Rio Grande, Ohio.

MORRIS, RAYMOND PHILIP, librarian; b. Garnett, Kans., Mar. 16, 1904; s. Charles Elmer and Margaret Ann (Riley) M.; m. Jean Louise Kelly, May 1928; children: Thelma Jean, Marcia Morris Johnston, R. Philip. AB, Baker U., 1926, LittD (hon.), 1952; BD, Garrett Bibl. Inst., 1929; BS, Columbia U., 1930, MLS, 1932; MS (hon.), Yale U., 1951; DD (hon.), Drake U., 1965. Garrett Bible Inst.; Libr. Yale Div. Sch., 1931-32; asst. libr. Yale Div. Sch., 1932-34, libr., 1934-72, also prof. religious lit., libr. emeritus, 1972-90; cons. libr. programs World Coun. Chs., Geneva, 1956, Nat. Coun. Chs. and inter-Ch. Ctr., 1958, Nanking Bd. Founders, 1959, Nat. Coun. YMCA, Presbyn. Ch. Ecumenical missions; bd. dirs. Inst. for Ecumenical and Cultural Rsch., chmn. bd., 1971-76. Author: Libraries of Theological Seminaries, 1934, A Theological Book List, 1960, Aids to Theological Libraries, 1970; contrb. articles to periodicals; developer China Records Collection at Yale Div. Sch. Chmn. fin. N.Y. ea. conf. United Meth. Ch., 1945-54. Mem. Am. Theol. Libr. Assn. (pres. 1951-53, chmn. bd. microtext 1957-72, chmn. libr. devel. program 1961-67). Democrat. Home: Cleveland Ohio Died Oct. 21, 1990; buried Garnett (Kans.) Cemetery.

MORRIS, RICHARD BRANDON, colonial history educator; b. N.Y.C., July 24, 1904; s. Jacob and Tillie (Rosenberg) M.; m. Berenice Robinson, June 12, 1932; children: Jeffrey Brandon, Donald Robinson. BA cum laude, CCNY, 1924; AM, Columbia U., 1925, PhD, 1930, LittD (hon.), 1976; LittD (hon.), Rutgers U., 1976; LHD, Hebrew Union Coll., 1963. Instr., asst. prof., assoc. prof. CCNY, 1927-47, prof., 1947-49; vis. prof. Columbia U., N.Y.C., 1946-49, prof., 1949-59, Gouverneur Morris prof. history, 1959-73, Gourverneur Morris prof. emeritus, 1973-89, chmn. dept., 1959-61, spl. lectr., 1973-76; Fulbright rsch. scholar U. Paris, 1961-62; mem. Inst. for Advanced Study, 1948; vis. prof. Princeton U., 1948-49, U. Hawaii, 1957; Bacon lectr. Boston U., 1965-66; Anson G. Phelps lectr. NYU, 1965-66; disting. prof. Free U. Berlin, 1969; Paley lectr. Hebrew U., Jerusalem, 1969; lectr. Truman Found., 1970; John A Burns prof. U. Hawaii, 1976; regional dir. Survey Fed. Archives, 1936-37; mem. coun. Inst. Early Am. History and Culture, 1959-61, 65-67. Author: Fair Trial, 1952, The American Revolution: A Brief History, 1955, The Basic Ideas of Alexander Hamilton, 1957, Hamilton and the Founding of the Nation, 1957, Great Presidential Decisions, 1960, The New World, 1963, A Nation Is Born, 1963, The Life History of the United States, 1963, The Peacemakers, 1965 (Bancroft prize), The American Revolution Reconsidered, 1967, John Jay, the Nation and the Court, 1967, The Emergening Nations and the American Revolution, 1969, Seven Who Shaped Our Destiny, 1973; editor: Ency. Am. History, 1953, rev. edits., 1961, 65, 70, 76, 82, (with H.S. Commager) New American Nation series, from 1953, Documentary History of U.S., 1968-73, Harper Ency. of Modern World, 1969, Significant Documents in U.S. History, 2 vols., 1969, Labor and Management, 1973, John Jay: The Making of a Revolutionary, 1745-1780, Unpub. Papers, 1975, John Jay: The Winning of the Peace, Unpub. Papers, 1780-84, 1980, The U.S. Dept. Labor Bicentennial History of the American Worker, 1976, Dissertations in American Biography, from 1981; mem. editorial bd. Am. Jour. Legal History; chmn. editorial bd. Labor History, to 1976, N.Y. History, from 1978. dir. CD coun. CCNY, 1941-45; pub. panel mem. Regional War Labor Bd., 1945; chmn. N.Y.C. Mayor's Task force Mcpl. Archives, 1966-73, Am. Revolution Bicentennial Commn., 1967-69; chmn. N.Y. State Bicentennial Coordinating Coun., 1975-76; vice chmn. N.Y. State Bicentennial Commn., 1977-78; del. U.S.-Mex. Joint Commn. on Cultural Cooperation, 1973-75; pres. bd. trustees John Jay Homestead, 1977-89; co-founder, co-chmn. Project '87, 1977-87. Recipient joint award for best contbn. to Am. history by citizen N.Y. in 5 yrs. previous to 1930, Colonial Dames Am. and Nat. Soc. Colonial Dames, Townsend Harris medal CCNY, 1959; Univ. fellow Columbia U., 1930, Guggenheim fellow, 1947-48, 61-62. Fellow Royal Hist. Soc., Am. Acad. Arts and Scis.; mem. Am. Hist. Assn. (pres. 1976), Labor Historians (past pres.), Orgn. Am. Historians, Soc. Am. Historians (v.p. 1981), Mass. Hist. Soc. (corr.), Am. Antiquarian Soc. (corr.), Century Assn., Phi Beta Kappa. Home: Mount Vernon N.Y. Died Mar. 3, 1989; cremated.

MORRIS, SAMUEL SOLOMON, JR., bishop; b. Norfolk, Va., Nov. 1, 1916; s. Samuel Solomon and Mayme (Lawson) M.; m. Ermine Smith, Nov. 30, 1942; children—Joyce Green, Ermine, Samuel Solomon, III. BS, Wilberforce U., 1937; MDiv, Yale U., 1940; DD (hon.), Payne Sem., 1964; LLD (hon.), Kittrell Coll., 1963. Ordained to ministry A.M.E. Ch., 1940; pastor St. Luke A.M.E. Ch., Gallatin, Tenn. and St. John A.M.E. Ch., Springfield, Tenn., 1940-41, St. Paul A.M.E. Ch., Nashville, 1943-46, 1st A.M.E. Ch., Gary, Ind., 1949-56, Coppin A.M.E. Ch., Chgo., 1956-72; prof. Payne Sem. and Wilberforce U., 1941-43; pres. Shorter Coll., 1946-48, chmn. bd. trustees, 1972-76; bishop A.M.E. Ch., Little Rock, 1972-76, Jacksonville, Fla., 1976-84; bishop A.M.E. Ch. 4th Episcopal Dist., Chgo., 1984-89. Author: An African Methodist Primer, 1962. Pres. South Side br. NAACP, 1960-62; trustee Nat. Urban League. Recipient Silver Beaver award Boy Scouts Am., 1966. Mem. Alpha Phi Alpha. Home: Chicago Ill. Died Mar. 26, 1989.

MORRISON, DONALD MACKAY, business executive; b. Londonderry, N.S., Can., May 29, 1897; s. Kenneth John and Jeanette (Mackay) M.; m. Irene Elaine York, July 29, 1931; children: Donald, David, Anthony. BASc, U. B.C., 1921; PhD, McGill U., 1924, Cambridge U., 1927. Various positions Shell Oil Cos., U.S. and Can., 1928-55; v.p. mfg. Shell Oil Co. of Can., Ltd., Toronto, 1952-55; pres., dir. Trans Mountain Oil Pipe Line Co., Vancouver, 1955-60, Trans Mountain Oil Pipe Line Corp., Trans Mountain Housing, Alpac Constrn. & Surveys, Ltd.; bd. dirs. Clayburn-Harbison, Ltd.; mem. bd. mgmt. B.C. Rsch. Coun. Mem. Can. Govt. Svc., 1942-44, 51-52. Mem. Chem. Inst. Can., Am. Chem. Soc., Com. Oil Pipe Line Cos., Capilano Golf Club, Vancouver Club, Sigma Xi, Phi Kappa Phi. Mem. United Ch. Can. *

MORRISON, PAUL LESLIE, corporate administrator, educator; b. Hartsville, Ind., Nov. 25, 1899; s. James H. and Effie (Mahaffey) M.; BA, Depauw U., 1921, LL.D., 1949; PhD, Northwestern U., 1927, MBA, 1922; CPA, Ill., 1923; m. Carolyn L. Rosemeier, Dec. 31, 1924; children—Paul Leslie, James Frederick. Partner, Kohler, Pettengill & Co., accts., Chgo., 1925-27; founding partner Sheridan, Farwell & Morrison, Inc., investment counsellors, Chgo., 1933-40; mgr. investment dept., bus. office Northwestern U., 1941-42; mem. faculty Northwestern U., 1923-58, prof. finance, chmn. finance dept., dir. grad. div. Sch. Commerce, adminstrv. head of sch., also mgr. investment dept. univ. bus. office; dir., past chmn. exec. com. Calif. Cold Storage & Distbg. Co.; former dir. Harris Trust & Savs. Bank, Chgo.; former mem. Am. adv. bd. (dir., exec. com. Am. subs.) Zurich Ins. Co. (Switzerland); dir., chmn. exec. com. Gen. Fin. Corp; dir. Chgo. Nat. Bank, Harris Trust and Savs. Bank; Mem. diplomatic missions on German and Japanese peace treaties, 1951-52; spl. asst. to Pres. U.S., also mem. planning bd. Nat. Security Coun., 1953-54; asst. dir. Bur. Budget, 1953-54. Life trustee DePauw U.; past pres., dir. Owen L. Conn Found. Served as pvt., inf., U.S. Army, 1918; commd. capt., finance dept., 1942, disch. lt. col., 1946; chief cen. fiscal office China Theater, 1944-45; recalled to active duty, 1950 as col., gen. staff, serving as asst. comptroller army internat. affairs, 1950-52. Decorated Legion of Merit; recipient commendation sec. army. Mem. Am. Econ. Assn., Phi Beta Kappa, Alpha Tau Omega, Beta Gamma Sigma. Methodist. Clubs: University, Investment Analysts (past pres.) (Chgo.); Lauderdale Yacht, Tower (Ft. Lauderdale, Fla.); Westmoreland Country (Wilmette). Author: (with E.L. Kohler) Principles of Accounting, 2d edit., 1931. Author profl. articles. Died Jan. 24, 1991; buried Meml. Pk. Cemetery, Evanston, Ill. Home: Evanston Ill.

MORROW, HUGH, public relations executive; b. Williamsburg, Pa., Sept. 29, 1915; s. Hugh and Marjorie Stuart (Vickers) M.; m. Elise Vickers, Jan. 20, 1937 (div.); children: Hugh, Lance, Patrick, Michael (dec.), Christina, Cathleen; m. Carolyn Davison Hayden, May 7, 1957 (dec.); children: Davison, Carolyn; stepchildren—Hugh Hayden, Donald Hayden; m. Sally Shroyer, Jan. 7, 1978. Student, Bucknell U., 1933-35. Reporter Centre Daily Times, State College, Pa., 1935-37; reporter various newspapers and wire services Lewisburg, Pa., 1937-39; reporter, Washington corr. Phila. Inquirer, 1939-46; asso. editor Saturday Evening Post, Washington, 1946-57; press sec. to U.S. Senator Irving M. Ives, 1957-58, U.S. Senator Kenneth B. Keating, 1959; speech writer for Nelson A. Rockefeller, 1959-60; spl. asst. to Gov. Nelson A. Rockefeller, N.Y., 1960-69; dir. communications gov.'s office Gov. Nelson A. Rockefeller, 1969-73; press sec. to Vice-Pres. Nelson Rockefeller, Washington, 1974-76; public relations adviser to Nelson A. Rockefeller, 1976-78, Rockefeller family, others, 1978-1982. Served with USNR, World War II. Home: Chestnut Ridge N.Y. Died Sept. 25, 1991; buried Gate of Heaven Cemetery, Hawthorne, N.Y.

MORROW, JOHN CHARLES, III, chemistry educator; b. Hendersonville, N.C., Sept. 20, 1924; s. John Charles, Jr. and Marguerite (Jenkins) M.; m. Mary Frances Nunn, Dec. 20, 1950; children—Marguerite, William, Charles. Student, Mars Hill (N.C.) Coll., 1940-41; B.S. in Chemistry, U. N.C., 1944; Ph.D., Mass. Inst. Tech., 1949. Mem. faculty U. N.C., Chapel Hill, 1949-89, prof. chemistry, 1959-89, dean arts and scis., 1966-68, provost, 1968-84. Served to lt. (j.g.) USNR, 1944-46. Mem. Am. Chem. Soc., Am. Phys. Soc., Am. Crystallographic Assn., Am. Soc. Mass Spectometry, Phi Beta Kappa, Sigma Xi. Home: Chapel Hill N.C. Died July 21, 1989; buried Chapel Hill, N.C.

MORROW, ROBERT DOWDEN, state official; b. Amory, Miss., Dec. 31, 1896; s. David Nathaniel and Bessie Geraldine (Rogers) M.; m. Louise May, Dec. 25, 1922; children: Robert Dowden, David Louis. BSc, Miss. State U., 1922, MSc, 1925. Instr. agronomy Miss. State U., 1922-24; agrl. supr. U.S., 1924-26; state svc. commr. State of Miss., 1926-28, state athletic commr., then chmn. athletic commn., 1928-60, state treas., 1956-60, state bank comptroller, 1960; chmn. bd. Rankin County Bank; pres., gen. mgr. 1st Security Life Ins. Co., Forest Owners, Inc.; bd. dirs. Miss. Chem. Corp., Coastal Chem. Corp., Southeastern Life Ins. Corp., First Security Life Ins. Corp., First Miss. Corp., Morrow Realty & Ins. Corp., R.D. Morrow & Sons. Pres. State Citizens Coun. on Edn.; chmn. bd. trustees Instns. Higher Learning, State of Miss. From pvt. to lt. U.S. Army, World War I; from maj. to col., inf. AUS, World War II. Recipient Disting. Svc. award Am. Legion, also Miss. Farm Bur. Mem. Am. Legion (state comdr., chmn. nat. agrl. and conservation com. 1947, mem. nat. exec. com. 1950-56), VFW, DAV, Miss. Econ. Coun., Lions, Omicron Delta Kappa. *

MORSE, ADRIAN OSBORN, provost, educator; b. New Haven, Mar. 3, 1895; s. Clayton William and Jennie Thompson (Osborn) M.; m. Barbara Morse Paine, June 15, 1918; children: Jananne (Mrs. Edward W. McNitt), Content Douglas. AB, Yale U., 1918; AM (hon.), U. N.H., 1928; LLD, Temple U., Lebanon Valley Coll., 1956. Asst. edn. dir. Nat. City Bank, N.Y.C., 1919-21; instr. English U. N.H., 1922-23, exec. sec., 1923-28, dean of men, 1926-28; asst. to U.S. Sec. of Agr., 1928-29; exec. sec. Pa. State U., 1929-35, asst. to pres. in charge resident instrn., 1935-51, provost, 1951-56, provost emeritus, from 1956; cultural attaché Am. Embassy, New Delhi, India, 1956-59; lectr. humanities New Eng. Coll., Henniker, N.J., 1961-62, assoc. prof., 1962-63, spl. cons., from 1961; justice Durham (N.H.) Mcpl. Ct., 1926-28. Served ast 1st lt. F.A., U.S. Army, AEF, 1917-19. Mem. Phi Beta Kappa, Phi Upsilon. *

MORSE, DAVID A., lawyer; b. N.Y.C., May 31, 1907; s. Morris Moscovitch and Sara (Werblin) M.; m. Mildred Edna Hockstader, May 13, 1937. Litt.B., Rutgers U., 1929, LL.D., 1957; LL.B., Harvard U., 1932; LL.D., U. Geneva, 1962, U. Strasbourg, France, 1968; Sc.D., Laval U., Que., 1969; H.H.D., Brandeis U., 1971. Bar: N.J., N.Y., D.C. bars. Mem. solicitors staff U.S. Dept. Interior, Washington, 1933-34; chief counsel Petroleum Labor Policy Bd., Dept. Interior, 1934-35; spl. asst. U.S. atty. gen., 1934-35; regional atty. 2d region N.Y. NLRB, 1935-38; asst. sec. of labor U.S. Dept. Labor, 1945-47, under-sec. of labor, 1947-48, acting sec., June 9-Aug. 2, 1948; U.S. Govt. mem. ILO, Geneva, 1946-48; dir. gen. ILO, 1948-70; accepter Nobel Peace prize for ILO (UN affiliate); impartial chmn. milk industry met. area N.Y.C., 1940-42; gen. counsel NLRB, 1945-46; impartial chmn. ladies garment industry area N.Y.C., 1970—; sr. cons. UN Devel. Program, 1970; ptnr., to sr. ptnr. Jones, Day, Reavis & Pogue (and Surrey & Morse predecessors), 1970-90. Bd. dirs. World Rehab. Fund, N.Y. Found., Albert & Mary Lasker Found., Am.-European Community Found. Commd. 1st lt. AC, 1942-45, advanced to lt. col. assigned chief of labor div. Allied Mil. Govt. in charge labor policy Sicily and Italy; chief labor sect. U.S. group Control Council for Germany, preparing labor program and policy for Germany; dir. labor Mil. Govt. Group working with Brit., French and Russians to establish uniform labor policy for all occupied Germany. Decorated Bronze Star with 2 oak leaf clusters, Legion of Merit; Order of Merit of Labour Brazil; comdr. Order Equatorial Star Gabon; grand officer Fed. Republic of Cameroon; grand officer Nat. Order of Lion Senegal; grand officer French Legion of Honour; grand officer Republic of Italy, 1970; grand officer Republic of Colombia, 1969; Spl. Gold medal award UNESCO; Human Rights award Internat. League Rights of Man, 1970. Mem. ABA, Am. Arbitration Assn. (bd. dirs.), UN Assn. U.S.A. (bd. dirs.), N.Y. Soc. Internat. Affairs, Inc. (chair), Coun. on Fgn. Rels., Internat. Law Assn., Am. Legion. Clubs: Century Assn. (N.Y.); Metropolitan (Washington); Cercle Interallié (Paris). Home: New York N.Y. Died Dec. 1, 1990; cremated.

MORTENSEN, WILLIAM HENRY, foundation executive, state senator, mayor; b. Hartford, Conn., July 15, 1903; s. John L. and Karen (Petersen) M.; m. Trice Driver, Aug. 22, 1983. Student, Antioch Coll., 1921-23; A.F.D., U. Hartford, 1956; LL.D., Trinity Coll., Hartford, 1984. Mng. dir. Horace Bushnell Meml. Hall, Hartford, Conn., 1929-68; dir. Conn. Nat. Trust Co. of Fla.; former dir. Heublein, Inc., Nat. Fire Ins. Co., Transcontinental Ins. Co., Conn. Bank and Trust Co., 1937-74. Senator Conn. Legislature, 1942-44; mayor of Hartford, 1943-45, founder council-mgr. govt., 1947; chmn. State Development Commn., 1953-54; commr. Met. Dist. Commn., 1954- 60; vice chmn. Conn. Jud. Rev. Council, 1969-76; mem. Conn. Commn. for Higher Edn., 1968-71; trustee, former pres. Hartford Pub. Library, 1943-72; corporator Hartford Hosp., St. Francis Hosp., Inst. Living; hon. trustee Bushnell Meml.; trustee Heublein Med. Found.; hon. regent U. Hartford. Mem. Conn. Opera Assn. (hon. v.p.). Republican. Congregationalist. Clubs: Univ, Hartford, Hartford Golf, Hundred of Conn, Wampanoag Golf; Mariner Sands (Fla.) Country. Home: Stuart Fla. Died

Oct. 6, 1990; buried Fairview Cemetery, West Hartford, Conn.

MORTON, HAROLD COLEMAN, lawyer; b. L.A., May 17, 1895; s. John and Lillian (Bowers) M.; m. Dorothy F. Smith, Dec. 23, 1916; children: Barbara (Mrs. Joseph C. Shell), Betty (Mrs. Richard K. Jamison), Lynn, Dorothy (Mrs. Richard W. Wheaton). LLB, U. So. Calif., 1916. Bar: Calif. 1916. Ptnr. firm Hanna and Morton, L.A., from 1919; ind. oil operator, from 1934; bd. dirs. Western Oil and Gas Assn. Trustee U. So. Calif. Fellow Am. Coll. Trial Lawyers; mem. ABA, State Bar Calif., Los Angeles County Bar Assn., Am. Inst. Mining and Metall. Engrs., L.A. Club. *

MORTON, JAY ROBERT, transportation executive; b. Tarrytown, N.Y., July 24, 1914; s. Jay Daniel and Sara (Skerritt) M.; m. Barbara Louise Tyler, Feb. 8, 1941; children: Jay Robert II, Wellington Charles, Linda Joy. A.B., Syracuse U., 1936; M.S., advanced mgmt. course Am. Mgmt. Assn., 1967. With Vega Industries, Inc., Syracuse, N.Y., 1937-60; gen. traffic mgr. Vega Industries, Inc., 1946-58, asst. to pres., 1958-60; traffic mgr. Combustion Engring., Inc., Windsor, Conn., 1960-66; dir. corporate transp. and distbn. Combustion Engring., Inc., 1966-70, v.p. corporate transp. and distbn., from 1970. Past pres. Myasthenia Gravis Found., Inc., now chmn.; vestryman Episcopal Ch. Named Conn. Transp. Man of Yr. Traffic Assns. Conn., 1977; recipient Harry E Salzberg Meml. award and lectr. Syracuse U., 1980, Big Wheel award Myasthenia Gravis Found., 1983. Mem. Am. Boiler Mfrs. Assn., Am. Mgmt. Assn., Am. Soc. Traffic and Transp. (past regional v.p., Joseph E. Schleen award 1980), Central Conn. Transp. Assn., Nat. Def. Transp. Assn. (past regional v.p.), Conn. Quarter Century Traffic, Nat. Com. on Internat. Trade Documentation (dir.), Nat. Freight Traffic Assn. (v.p.), Nat. Indsl. Traffic League (past pres., chmn. exec. com., Outstanding Achievement award 1980), Newcomen Soc. N.Am., Stamford Area Commerce and Industry Assn., Traffic Club N.Y., Delta Nu Alpha (Spl. Plaque award 1949, past regional v.p.), Sigma Phi Epsilon. Clubs: Masons, City; Wampanoag Country (West Hartford, Conn.). Home: Naples Fla. Deceased. †

MORTON, ROY JAY, sanitary engineer; b. Jacksonville, N.C., May 4, 1897; s. Erasmus Mack and Elizabeth (Walton) M.; m. Will Hall Gillespie, Sept. 22, 1932 (dec. July 1959); children: Roy Jay, John; m. 2d. Margaret McNutt Hicks, Sept. 17, 1960. BA, Elon Coll., 1920; BS and MS in Civil Engring., U. N.C., 1923; MS, Harvard U., 1926. Asst. san. engr. Tenn. Dept. Pub. Health, Nashville, 1923-28, dir. div. san. engring., 1928-36; assoc. prof. san. engring. and pub. health Vanderbilt U. Sch. Medicine, 1936-48; leader radioactive waste R&D sect. Oak Ridge Nat. Lab., 1948-54; assoc. chief waste disposal rsch. and engring. sect., 1954-62; san engr. AEC, from 1962; spl. cons. div. radiol. health USPHS, from 1963; cons. san engring. projects Tenn. Dept. Pub. Health, 1936-48, health and safety div. TVA, 1940-48, Tenn. Stream Pollution Control Bd., 1945-48. Fellow APHA (exec. bd. from 1951, chmn. exec. bd. 1952-56, pres. 1957-58); mem. ASCE (exec. com. san. engring. div. 1952-57, chmn. 1955-56, pres. Tenn. Valley sect. 1955), Am. Water Works Assn., Fedn. Sewage and Indsl. Wastes Assn., Tenn. Acad. Sci., Engring. Assn. Nashville, Acacia, Rotary Club, Sigma Xi, Tau Beta Pi, Delta Omega. *

MOSCOW, WARREN, columnist, author; b. in Bklyn., Mar. 15, 1908; s. Jacob H. and Stella (Klaas) M.; m. Esther Loeb, Oct. 15, 1934 (div. 1944); 1 dau., Judith; m. Jean Shalen, Jan. 10, 1946; children: John W. and Katherine A. (twins). Student, Columbia U., 1925-26, Bklyn. Law Sch., 1926-27. City hall reporter Bklyn. Citizen, 1926-28, N.Y. Am., 1928-30; polit. reporter N.Y. Times, 1930-52, chief Albany corr., 1938-44; war corr. N.Y. Times, Pacific Ocean Area, 1945; commr. borough works Borough of Manhattan, 1952-53; asst. to mayor City of N.Y., 1954-55; exec. dir. N.Y.C. Housing Authority, 1955-57; pub. relations cons., 1957-58; exec. asst. to Mayor of N.Y.C., 1958-61; cons. to N.Y.C. on intergovtl. affairs, 1962-63; editor-in-chief N.Y. Law Jour., N.Y.C., 1963-66; columnist The Chief, 1982-92; dir. Pub. Service Awards Program, Fund for City of N.Y., 1973-81. Author: Politics in the Empire State, 1948, What Have You Done for Me Lately, 1967, Roosevelt and Wilkie, 1968, The Last of the Big-Time Bosses, 1971. Mem. Mayor's adminstrv. cabinet, 1954-61; mem. Am. assembly Arden House, 1955. Mem. N.Y. State Legislative Corrs. Assn. Home: New York N.Y. Died Sept. 20, 1992. †

MOSER, PAUL, church official; b. Meriden, Kans., May 1, 1895; s. John William and Jennie (Honsaker) M.; m. Ruth Inez McLucas, June 14, 1916; children: Ulista Jean (Mrs. Dean K. Brooks), Paul, Mary Margaret (Mrs. Carl Wasson). BA, Kans. U., 1918; LHD, Missouri Valley Coll., 1950; LLD, Parsons Coll., 1955. Sec. Hi Y dept. State Assn. YMCAs of Kans., 1920-21; asst. to minister First Presbyn. Ch., Topeka, 1922-23; asst. gen. mgr. Warren M. Crosby Drygoods Co., 1923-28; dist. mgr. for Kans., Mo. and Okla. Montgomery Ward & Co., 1928-31; gen. mgr., v.p. Arnold Drygoods Co., 1931-34, Paul Moser Food Stores, Topeka, 1934-47; sec. for laymen Bd. Fgn. Missions, Presbyn. Ch. U.S.A., 1946-47, acting sec. lay com. Gen. Assembly, 1947-48, exec. sec. nat. coun. of United Presbyn. Men, 1948-65, cons., from 1965; chmn. laymen's com. Restoration Fund. Kans. Synod; bd. mgrs. adminstrv. com. Dept. United Ch. Men., Nat. Coun. Chs.; mem. gen. coun. United Presbyn. Ch. U.S. A.; del. Presbyn. Ch. U.S.A. to World Coun. Chs. Assembly, Amsterdam, 1948. Author pamphlets. Trustee Missouri Valley Coll., Warren Wilson Coll. Republican. *

MOSES, WALTER, lawyer; b. New Orleans, Aug. 25, 1898; s. Joseph W. and Irma (Moses)M.; m. Helen Watson, Nov. 1921; 1 son, John Watson; m. 2d, Eleanor Plummer, 1930; 1 son, Walter Harper. BA, Harvard U., 1918, LLB cum laude, 1921. Bar: Ill. 1921, Calif. 1930, U.S. Supreme Ct. 1927. Mem. firm Moses, Bachrach & Kennedy, and predecessors, Chgo., 1925-30, 39-59, Beilenson & Moses, L.A., 1930-31; sr. mem. firm McKay, Moses, McGarr, Solum & Gibbons, Chgo., from 1960.; pub. mem. regional WLB, World War II; Ill. Supreme Ct. mem. character and fitness com. 1st Appellate Dist., 1957-60; mem. citizens com. Family Ct. Cook County, from 1963. Author: Stock Brokerage Law for Stockholders and Their Employees, 1937; mem. bd. editors Harvard Law Rev., 1920-21. Mem. sch. bd. nominating com., Chgo., from 1963; mem. Chgo. Crime Commn., from 1964; bd. dirs. Ill. Humane Soc. Fellow Am. Bar Found.; mem. ABA, Ill. Bar Assn., Calif. Bar Assn., Chgo. Bar Assn. (bd. mgrs. from 1958, 2d v.p. 1960, 1st v.p. 1961, pres. 1962), Bar Assn. U.S. Ct. Appeals, Chgo. Law Inst., Harvard Law Sch. Assn., Harvard Club, Execs. Club, Mid-Day Club, Law Club of Chgo. *

MOSHER, FREDERICK CAMP, political science educator, government administrator; b. Oberlin, Ohio, July 5, 1913; s. William Eugene and Laura May (Camp) M.; m. Edith Kern, Nov. 25, 1940; children—Alice C., James F., David F. A.B. magna cum laude, Dartmouth Coll., 1934; M.S., Syracuse U., 1939; D.P.A., Harvard U., 1953. With TVA, 1934-36, Pub. Adminstrn. Clearing House, Chgo., 1938-39, City of Los Angeles, 1939-41, War Dept., 1941-42, UNRRA, 1946-47, State Dept., 1947-49; mem. faculty Syracuse U., 1949-57, U. Bologna, Italy, 1957-59, U. Calif. at Berkeley, 1959-68; prof. govt. and fgn. affairs Miller Ctr., U. Va., 1968-80, rsch. scholar, 1980-90; cons. in budgeting and pers. affairs. Author: Program Budgeting: Theory and Practice, 1954, (with S. Cimmino) Elementi di Scienza dell'Amministrazione, 1959, (with Orville F. Poland) The Costs of American Governments, 1964, Democracy and The Public Service, 1968, revised edit., 1982, (with John Harr) Programming Systems and Foreign Affairs Leadership, 1970, The GAO: The Quest for Accountability in American Government, 1979, A Tale of Two Agencies: A Comparative Analysis of the General Accounting Office and the Office of Management and Budget, 1984, (with David Clinton and Daniel Lang) Presidential Transitions and Foreign Affairs, 1987, also monographs, articles; editor: Governmental Reorganizations: Cases and Commentary, 1967, Watergate: Implications for Responsible Government, 1974, American Public Adminstration: Past, Present, Future, 1975, Basic Documents of American Public Administration, 1776-1950, 1976, Basic Literature of American Public Administration, 1787-1950, 1981, (with Richard J. Stillman II) Professions in Government, 1982, The President Needs Help, 1987 ; editor-in-chief Pub. Adminstn. Rev., 1951-54. Served to maj. USAAF, 1942-45. Decorated Legion of Merit; recipient Maxwell Sch. Pub. Service award, 1968, Louis Brownlow Meml. Book prize, 1969, John Gaus award, 1990. Mem. Am. Soc. Pub. Adminstrn. (Dwight Waldo award 1981), Nat. Acad. Pub. Adminstrn., Phi Beta Kappa. Home: Charlottesville Va. Died May 21, 1990.

MOSS, ARNOLD, actor, producer, writer, director; b. Bklyn., Jan. 28, 1910; s. Jack and Essie (Joseph) M.; m. Stella Reynolds, June 3, 1933; chidren: Jeffrey Arnold, Andrea. AB cum laude, CCNY, 1928; AM, Columbia U., 1934; PhD, NYU, 1973. Tng. with Eva LeGallienne's Civic Repertory Theatre, 1928-30; instr. speech and theatre dept. Bklyn. Coll., 1933-40; vis. prof. dramatic arts U. Conn., 1973-74; vis. prof. Pace U., 1975, Purdue U., 1977; vis. prof. in eminent scholar program Coll. William and Mary, 1976; spl. lectr. Neighborhood Playhouse, 1974-76; Am. specialist U.S. Dept. State, Latin-Am., 1961, Africa and Far East, 1964; mem. adv. council Empire State chpt. Nat. Soc. Arts and Letters. Appeared in Broadway plays including The Fifth Column, Hold on to Your Hats, Journey to Jerusalem, Flight to the West, The Land is Bright, The Tempest, Front Page, Twelfth Night, King Lear, The Dark is Light Enough, Measure for Measure, Back to Methuselah, Follies; ann. appearances in various Shakespeare plays and other programs at Library of Congress, Washington, 1955-74; appeared in Medea in Paris, 1957, Time of Your Life at Brussels' World Fair, 1958, King John, Measure for Measure, Am. Shakespeare Festival, 1958; founder, dir., star Shakespeare Festival Players, 1959; title role in King Lear, U. Hawaii, 1966, U. Ky., 1968, Trenton State Coll., 1969, U. Conn., 1974, Coll. William and Mary, 1976; appeared as Willy Loman in Death of a Salesman, Kent (Ohio) State U., 1968; on tour in Whose Life Is It Anyway, 1980; motion pictures include The Fool Killer, Temptation, Loves of Carmen, Border Incident, Kim, Mask of the Avenger, My Favorite Spy, Viva Zapata!, Salome, Gambit, Casanova's Big Night, Bengal Brigade; TV shows include Star Trek, Bonanza, Alfred Hitchcock, Hallmark Hall of Fame; writer-actor: CBS Radio Mystery Theatre; narrator-soloist with Boston, Milw., Detroit Symphony Orchs.; speaking soloist at world premiere Paradise Lost, Chgo. Lyric Opera, 1978, European premiere at La Scala, Milan, 1979, command performance for Pope John Paul II, 1979; numerous radio broadcasts major networks and programs including staff announcer CBS Radio, N.Y.C.; reader talking books for Am. Found. for Blind, from 1959; contbr. crossword puzzles to N.Y. Times and other publs. Recipient James K. Hackett medal CCNY, 1968, Townsend Harris medal, 1978, Founders Day award NYU, 1973, cert. of appreciation Layman's Nat. Bible Com., 1977; Celebrity Path named in his honor Bklyn. Botanic Garden. Mem. AFTRA (v.p. N.Y. chpt.), Players, Am. Theatre Assn., Acad. Motion Picture Arts and Scis. (nat. vis. scholar 1983-84), Phi Beta Kappa (pres. CCNY Gamma chpt. 1955-56, pres. Middle Atlantic Dist. 1988-89). Home: New York N.Y. Died Dec. 15, 1989.

MOSS, JOSEPH S., JR., banker; b. Aug. 24, 1898; s. Joseph S. and Fanny (Frazier) M.; m. Helen Yantis, July 2, 1932. BBA, U. Tex., 1920. Trainee Nat. City Bank of N.Y., 1920-25; v.p. First Nat. Bank, Miami, 1925-30; v.p. Irving Trust Co., N.Y.C., 1930-59, sr. v.p., officer in charge nat. div., 1959; pres., dir. Pan Am. Bank of Miami, 1959-61; vice chmn. Miami Beach First Nat. Bank, 1961-64, chmn., from 1964. Lt. col. Ordnance, U.S. Army, 1942-46; with SHAEF-G5, 12th Army Group and 21st Army Group (Brit.), 1944. Mem. Univ. Club of N.Y.C., La Gorce Club of Miami Beach, Phi Kappa Psi, Alpha Kappa Psi. *

MOSTOFI, KHOSROW, political scientist, educator; b. Tehran, Iran, July 8, 1921; came to U.S., 1949; s. Mostafa and Nasrin (Djam) M.; m. Nesrin Imamverdi, Aug. 18, 1960; 1 dau., Simin S. (dec.). BA, U. Tehran, 1944; MA, U. Utah, 1957, PhD, 1958, grad. cert. in public adminstrn., 1965. Instr. langs. Ministry Edn., Tehran, 1944-49; asst. U. Utah Inst. Govt., Salt Lake City, 1956-58; mem. faculty Dept. Polit. Sci. U. Utah, Salt Lake City, 1960-92, prof. polit. sci., 1970-92, prof. emeritus, 1987-92, chmn. polit. sci., 1967, acting dir. Inst. Internat. Studies, 1961-62, dir. Middle East Ctr., 1967-83, staff specialist Middle East Ctr., 1987-91, coord. Arab Devel. Program, 1976-81; pres. Western Asian Trade and Investment Corp., 1983-87, Am. Found. for Islamic Studies, 1978-89; dir. Am. Ctr. Iranian Studies, Tehran, summer 1970; instr. polit. sci. Portland (Oreg.) State U., 1958-59, asst. prof., 1959-60; vis. prof. polit. sci. U. B.C., Vancouver, Can., summer 1962; cons. div. of higher edn. U.S. Dept. Edn., 1968-70, 76; co-sponsor, organizer Internat. Conf. on Islam, Iran, and Pakistan, 1975, Internat. Conf. on Higher Edn. and Devel. in Arab World, 1978; sponsor, organizer Internat. Conf. on Comparative Law, 1977. Author: Parsee Nameh, rev. edit, 1969, Aspects of Nationalism: A Sociology of Colonial Revolt, 1964; contbr. to: Ency. Britannica, 1974, 83, 87, Studies in Art and Literature of the Near East, 1974. Trustee Internat. Visitors-Utah Coun., 1984-87. Recipient disting. svc. award Utah Acad. Scis., Arts and Letters, 1983, Svc. award World Trade Assn. of Utah, 1981. Fulbright-Hayes fellow, 1965-66; mem. AAUP, Am. Inst. Iranian Studies (trustee), Western Polit. Sci. Assn., Middle East Inst., Middle East Studies Assn., Ctr. Arabic Studies Abroad (bd. dirs. 1970-83), Pi Sigma Alpha, Phi Kappa Phi. Moslem. Home: Salt Lake City Utah Died, Aug. 3, 1992. †

MOTHERSHEAD, JOHN LELAND, JR., philosophy educator; b. Indpls., Nov. 18, 1908; s. John Lel and Ethel (Warner) M.; m. Elisabeth Ashley Crossett, Aug. 9, 1932 (dec. Feb. 1976); children: John Leland, Ann Ashley; m. Diane Frazier Heffner, Jan. 21, 1978. A.B., Stanford U., 1930, M.A., 1933; Ph.D., Harvard U., 1938. Instr. philosophy Syracuse U., 1939-41; mem. faculty Stanford U., from 1941, successively asst. prof., asso. prof. philosophy, 1941-55, prof., 1955-74, prof. emeritus, from 1974. Author: Ethics: Modern Conceptions of the Principles of Right, 1955; editor: (with John D. Goheen) Collected Papers of Clarence Irving Lewis, 1970. Recipient Lloyd W. Dinkelspiel award outstanding service to undergrad. edn., 1964. Mem. Am. Philos. Assn., AAAS, AAUP. Home: Palo Alto Calif. Died Jan. 30, 1991.

MOTHERWELL, ROBERT, artist; b. Aberdeen, Wash., Jan. 24, 1915; s. Robert Burns and Margaret (Hogan) M.; m. Renate Motherwell; 2 children. AB, Stanford U., 1937; postgrad., Harvard U., 1937-38, Columbia U., 1940-41; hon. doctorate, Southeastern Mass. U., 1974, Mary. Inst. Art, 1974, U. Conn., 1979, R.I. Sch. Design, 1980, Otis Art Inst./New Sch. Social Research, 1985, Brown U., 1985, Hunter Coll., 1985. Lectr. numerous colls., insts., mus.; tchr. Black Mountain (N.C.) Coll., summers 1945, 51; vis. artist, prof. Oberlin (Ohio) Coll., 1952; assoc. prof. Hunter Coll., N.Y.C., 1952-59; disting. prof. Hunter Coll., 1972-73; vis. artist, prof. U. Pa., Phila., Bard Coll., Annadale-on-Hudson, N.Y., Brown U., Providence, R.I., Harvard U., Cambridge, Mass., Columbia U., N.Y.C., Internat. U., Miami, Fla.; lectr. Mt. Holyoke Coll., South Hadley, Mass., Mus. Modern Art, N.Y.C., 1951, Am. Acad. Psychotherapists, N.Y.C., 1963, Yale U.,

New Haven, Conn., 1982, Met. Mus. Art, N.Y.C., Art Inst. Chgo., lectr. various colls. and mus. Abstract expressionist artist; first exhibited in Paris, 1939; exhibited throughout U.S., Can. and Europe in major museums, exhbns. internat. art, 1944-91; represented in collections Mus. Modern Art, N.Y.C., Rio de Janeiro, Balt. Mus., Brown U. Mus. Art, Dallas Mus. Fine Art, Ft. Worth Art Mus., Peggy Guggenheim Found. Venice, Italy, Houston Mus. Fine Arts, Los Angeles County Mus. Art, Nat. Gallery Art, Washington, Pasadena Art Mus., Smithsonian Inst. Washington, San Francisco Mus. Modern Art, Bavarian State Mus. Modern Art, Munich, and numerous pvt. and fgn. collections; one-man shows Art of This Century, 1944, Sao Paulo Biennale, Brazil, 1961, Phillips Collection, Washington, 1965, Whitechapel Art Gallery, London, Museum Folkswang, Essen, Federal Republic of Germany, Mus. Civico, Turin, Italy, Wadsworth Atheneum, Hartford, 1973, Museo de Arte Moderna, Mexico City, 1975, Albright-Knox Art Gallery, Buffalo, N.Y., 1983, Los Angeles County Mus. Art, 1984, San Francisco Mus. Modern Art, 1984, Seattle Art Mus., 1984, Corcoran Gallery Art, Washington, 1984, Guggenheim Mus., N.Y.C., 1985, Bavarian State Mus. Modern Art, Munich, 1983; one of 14 Americans, Museum Modern Art, 1946 one of 6 Americans, Galerie Maeght, Paris, 1946, one of 4 Ams., Contemporary Arts Soc., Houston, 1953; exhibited Sidney Janis Gallery, 1957, 59, 61, Bennington Coll., 1959, only Am. Succession, Dusseldorf, Germany, 1954, Coll. exhbn., Palais des Beaux-Arts, Brussels, 1954; in addition to other works renowned for series painting Elegies to the Spanish Republic, 1945-75; Gen. editor: The Documents of Modern Art, 1944-55, Possibilities: An Occasional Review, 1951, Modern Artist in America, 1951, Documents of Twentieth Century Art, 1968-80; commissions include Nat. Gallery Art, Washington, John F. Kennedy Fed. Bldg., Boston, Art Mus. Iowa U.; his work subject of monographs and other publs. in field. Mem. corp. vis. com. on arts Tufts U., Medford, Mass., from 1976; trustee Am. Acad. Rome, 1979-80. Recipient IV Guggenheim Internat. award Guggenheim Mus., 1964, Spirit of Achievement award Yeshiva U., 1970, La Grande Medaille de Vermeil de la Ville de Paris, 1977, Pa. Acad. Fine Arts Gold Medal of Honor, 1979, U. Salamanca Medal of Merit, 1980, Skowhegan Printmaking award, 1981, Mayor's award of Honor Arts and Culture N.Y., 1981, N.Y. Nat. Arts Club Gold Medal of Honor, 1983, Great Artist Series award NYU/Guggenheim Mus., 1985, Macdowell Colony Medal of Honor, 1985, Medalla d'Oro de Bellas Artes, 1986, Nat. Medal of Arts, 1990. Fellow Royal Soc. Art (London); mem. Am. Acad. Arts and Letters, Am. Acad. Arts and Scis. Club: Century (N.Y.C.). Home: Greenwich Conn. Died July 16, 1991.

MOTT, CHARLES STEWART HARDING, charitable foundation executive; b. Utica, N.Y., Nov. 4, 1906; s. Charles Stewart and Ethel Culbert (Harding) M.; m. Isabel Specht, Nov. 5, 1932; children: Charles Stewart Harding, Claire Isabel. BS, Yale U., 1931; LLD (hon.), Olivet Coll., 1969, Eastern Mich. U., 1970, U. Mich., 1974, Ball State Coll., 1976; HHD (hon.), Fla. Atlantic U., 1973. With Chevrolet Motor Div., 1932-38; v.p., trustee Mott Found., Flint, Mich., 1944-65, pres., 1965-76, chmn., chief exec. officer, 1976-87, chmn. emeritus, 1988-89; dir. Realty and Equipment Corp., MFO Mgmt. Co., Gary Hobart Water Corp., L.I. Water Co., Nat. Can Corp., until 1982, No. Ill. Water Co., St. Louis County Water Co.; chmn. bd. U.S. Sugar Corp. Served with USAAF, 1942-44. Recipient ann. humanitarian award Nat. Soc. Autistic Children, 1972; named Citizen of Year Flint C. of C., 1970, Citizen of Year Flint Area Conf. Inc., 1974. Mem. Detroit Club, Flint City Club, Flint Golf Club, Royal Bermuda Yacht Club, Coral Beach and Tennis Club, Palm Beach Bath and Tennis Club, Everglades Club, Little Club, St. Andrews Club. Home: Flint Mich. Died May 10, 1989; buried Flint, Mich.

MOULTON, HORACE PLATT, lawyer; b. Burlington, Vt., Dec. 8, 1907; s. Sherman R. and Stella A. (Platt) M.; m. Gretta P. Sumner, Jan. 1, 1934 (dec. Nov. 1971); children: Sherman R. II, Desier Anne; m. Elizabeth H. Munson, Mar. 14, 1973. AB, Dartmouth Coll., 1928; LLB, Harvard U., 1931. Bar: Mass. 1931, N.Y. 1952. Assoc. Brown, Field & McCarthy, Boston, 1931-49; counsel New Eng. Tel. & Tel. Co., Boston, 1949-51; atty., gen. atty., assoc. gen. counsel AT&T, N.Y.C., 1951-55, v.p., gen. counsel, 1955-72; ptnr. Cadwalader, Wickersham & Taft, N.Y.C., 1973-78; bd. dirs. Goodspeed's Book Shop, Boston; trustee U.S. Trust Co., N.Y.C. Mem. Downtown Assn., Lawyers Club, Century Club, Richmond County Country Club (S.I., N.Y.), Gulf Stream Country Club (Del Rey, Fla.). Home: Hockessin Del. Died June 16, 1991; buried Bethel Cemetery, Md.

MOUNTAIN, WORRALL FREDERICK, lawyer, former state justice; b. East Orange, N.J., June 28, 1909; s. Worrall Frederick and Ethel Marian (Spohr) M.; m. Grace Dewes, May 4, 1960; children by previous marriage: Beverley (Mrs. Leandro S. Galban), John Anthony. A.B. cum laude, Princeton, 1931; LL.B., Harvard U., 1934. Bar: N.J. 1935. Assoc. firm Pitney, Hardin & Skinner, Newark, 1935-40; ptnr. firm Dillon, Bitar & Luther (and predecessors), Morristown, N.J., 1940-66; of counsel Dillon, Bitar & Luther (and predecessors), from 1979; judge N.J. Superior Ct. law div. and chancery div., 1966-70, appellate div. N.J. Superior Ct., 1970-71; justice N.J. Supreme Ct., 1971-79. Served to lt. USNR, 1943-45. Fellow Am. Bar Found., Am. Coll. Probate Counsel; mem. Am., N.J. State, Morris County, Passaic County, Essex County bar assns. Republican. Episcopalian. Clubs: Morristown (Morristown), Morris County Golf (Morristown); Nassau (Princeton, N.J.); Princeton (N.Y.C.). Home: Hightstown N.J. Died Aug. 24, 1992. †

MOZDZER, HENRY ANTHONY, editor; b. Manchester, Conn., Oct. 28, 1924; s. Sylvester and Maria (Obuchowska) M.; m. Irene Madelaine Dzurek, July 2, 1955; children—Carol, Robert, John. B.A. in Journalism, U. Bridgeport, Conn., 1950. Asst. to pub. Globe Feature Syndicate, Westport, Conn., 1951; reporter Bridgeport Sunday Herald, 1952-53; with R.H. Donnelley Corp., N.Y.C., 1955-88; editor Laundry Jour., Nat. Cleaner and Dyer, Bus. Abroad, Constructor publs., 1955-65; exec. editor World Constrn., 1965-82; invitee to inspect hwy. system Saudi Arabian Ministry of Communications., Nigeria's Fed. Ministry Works and Surveys. Served with USMC, 1942-46. Recipient Jesse Neal award A.P., 1962. Mem. World Trade Writers, N.Y. Bus. Press Editors (dir.), Conn. Press Club. Home: Stamford Conn. Died Apr. 18, 1988; buried Queen of Peace Cemetery, Stamford, Conn.

MRAZEK, ROBERT VERNON, chemical engineering educator; b. Chgo., Jan. 15, 1936; s. Vernon Elmer and Marjorie (Saxon) M.; m. Joyce Ann Freeman, June 6, 1959; children—Ellen Marie, Steven James, Karen Louise. BS, Purdue U., 1957; PhD, Rensselaer Poly. Inst., 1960. Registered profl. engr., Oreg. Chem. engr. Knolls Atomic Power Lab., Schenectady, 1960; mem. faculty dept. chem. engring. Oreg. State U., Corvallis, 1960-90, prof., 1967-90, head chem. engring. dept., 1988-90; Tech. adviser Omark Industries, Portland, Oreg., 1962, U.S. Bur. Mines, Albany, Oreg., from 1963; research asso. Rensselaer Poly. Inst., 1962. Contbr. articles to profl. jours. Recipient Carter award outstanding teaching Sch. Engring., 1965, 79, 90, Mosser award for teaching excellence, 1966, Elizabeth P. Ritchie Disting. Prof. award, 1978, all Oreg. State U.; NSF fellow, 1957-60. Mem. Oreg. chpt. Am. Inst. Chem. Engrs. (chmn. 1974-75), Am. Inst. Chem. Engrs. (mem. profl. exams. adv. com.), Blue Key (hon. faculty), Sigma Xi, Phi Eta Sigma, Omega Chi Epsilon, Tau Beta Pi. Home: Corvallis Oreg. Died May 1, 1990; buried St. Mary's Cemetery, Corvallis, Oreg.

MUAN, ARNULF, geochemistry educator; b. Lökken Verk, Norway, Apr. 19, 1923; came to U.S., 1952, naturalized, 1962; s. Anders O. and Ingeborg (Engen) M.; m. Hildegard Hoss, Jan. 29, 1960; children: Michael, Ingrid. Diploma in chemistry, Tech. U. Norway, 1948; Ph.D. in Geochemistry, Pa. State U., 1955. Asst. prof. metallurgy Pa. State U., University Park, 1955-57; assoc. prof. Pa. State U., 1957-62, prof., 1962-66, prof. mineral scis., from 1966, head dept. geochemistry and mineralology, 1966-71, head dept. geoscis., 1971-73, assoc. dean research, 1976-86, acting dean, 1985-86. Author: (with E.F. Osborn) Phase Equilibria Among Oxides in Steelmaking, 1965. Sr. NSF fellow, 1962; Fulbright-Hays lectr. USSR, 1973-74, Japan Soc. for the Promotion of Sci. lectr., 1976; recipient Alexander von Humboldt Sr. Disting. U.S. Scientist award, Fed. Rep. Germany, 1989-90. Fellow Am. Ceramic Soc. (Ross Coffin Purdy award 1958, John Jeppson gold medal 1978), Mineral. Soc. Am. (v.p. 1973-74, pres. 1974-75), Geol. Soc. Am.; mem. Am. Inst. Metall. Engrs., A.A.A.S., Geochem. Soc., Norwegian Chem. Soc., Sigma Xi. Home: State College Pa. Died Dec. 1990. †

MUCCIO, JOHN JOSEPH, foreign service officer; b. Agricola, Italy, Mar. 19, 1900; came to U.S., 1921; s. John Anthony and Filomena (Muccio) M.; m. Sheila McCullough, Oct. 19, 1953. PhB, Brown U., 1923, LLD, 1952; MA, George Washington U., 1923; LLD, Seoul Nat. U., Korea, 1952. Vice consul Hamburg, 1924, Hong Kong, 1926; consul Yunnanfu, 1928, Hong Kong, 1928, Foochow, 1939, Sahnghai, 1931; consul and 2d sec. LaPaz, Bolivia, 1935; 2d sec. Panama, 1938; 1st sec., 1939; cons. and 1st sec. Managua, 1940; counselor Panama, 1943; counsellor Am. Embassy, Havana, 1943-44; mem. American Mission to Germany, 1945-47, spl. rep. of Pres. of U.S. to Korea, 1948, apptd. 1st U.S. amb. to Korea, 1949; U.S. del. UN Trusteeship Coun., 1952; envoy extraordinaire to Iceland, 1954, AE & P, 1956-59; amb. to Guatemala, 1960-61. With U.S. Army, 1918. Recipient of Medal of Merit, Pres. Truman, 1950. Mem. Shanghai Club, Union Club, Panama Golf Club, Met. Club (Washington). Home: Providence R.I. Died May 19, 1989.

MUEHLENTHAL, CLARICE KELMAN, travel consultant; b. Cleve., Nov. 16, 1924; d. William and Ann (Teitel) Kelman; m. Arnold G. Muehlenthal, Dec. 17, 1950 (dec. Sept. 1980); children—Shelley Muehlenthal Mitchell, David M.; Cert., Draughons Bus. Coll., 1945; cert. travel counselor, Inst. Cert. Travel Agts., 1980. Owner, Cee-Jay Bus. Service, Riverhead, N.Y., 1952-55; travel cons. Journey House Travel, Dallas, 1967-73; ptnr. Alpha Travel, Dallas, 1973-76; owner World Wide Travel Service, Dallas, 1976-89. Round Table chmn. Dallas North dist. Boy Scouts Am., 1971-73; charter mem. Tex. Cultural Alliance, 1975-89; courier Hands Around the World, Tex., from 1975. Recipient Disting. Award of Merit Boy Scouts Am., Circle Ten award, Dallas, 1973, Internat. Fellowship Tex. Cultural Alliance, Dallas, 1982; named Ambassador of Goodwill, State Tex., 1975. Mem. The 3020 Soc. (sec.-treas. from 1982), Inst. Cert. Travel Agts. (study group leader 1983, life 1982). Died Nov., 1989. Home: Dallas Tex.

MUELLER, JOSEPH M., bishop; b. St. Louis, Dec. 1, 1894; s. George Fritz and Barbara N. (Ziegler) M. Grad., Sts. Paul and Peter Sch., St. Louis, 1907; DD, LittD, Pontifical Coll. Josephinum, Worthington, Ohio, 1919. Ordained priest Roman Cath. Ch., 1919, domestic prelate, 1939. Curate Carlyle, Mt. Carmel, East St. Louis, and Belleville, Ill., 1919-26; organizer Blessed Sacrament Parish, Belleville, 1926, pastor, 1926-30; pastor St. Peters Cathedral, 1930-47; consecrated bishop of Sinda and coadjutor of Sioux City, 1947; bishop of Sioux City Iowa, from 1948; asst. at Pontifical Throne, 1957. *

MUGAVERO, FRANCIS J., bishop; b. Bklyn., June 8, 1914. Ed., Cathedral Coll., Bklyn., Immaculate Conception Sem., Huntington, N.Y.; MSW, Fordham U. Ordained priest Roman Catholic Ch., 1940; head Cath. Charities, Bklyn., prior to 1968; consecrated bishop, 1968, bishop of Bklyn., 1968-90. Recipient La Guardia medal N.Y.C. Home: Brooklyn N.Y. Died July 12, 1991; buried Episcopal Crypt, Immaculate Conception Ctr., Douglaston, N.Y.

MUGGERIDGE, MALCOLM, editor, writer; b. Sanderstead, Surrey, Eng., Mar. 24, 1903; s. Henry Thomas and Annie (Booler) M.; m. Katherine Dobbs, Sept. 1927; 4 children. Student, Selwyn Coll., Cambridge. Lectr. Egyptian U., Cairo, 1927-30; editorial staff Manchester Guardian, Eng., 1930-32, Moscow corr., 1932-33; asst. editor Calcutta Statesman, 1934-35; editorial staff Evening Standard, 1935-36; Washington corr. Daily Telegraph, 1946-47, dep. editor, 1950-52; editor Punch, 1953-57; rector Edinburgh U., 1967-68. Author: Three Flats (production Stage Soc.), 1931, Autumnal Face, 1931, Winter in Moscow, 1933, The Earnest Atheist, a Life of Samuel Butler, 1936, In a Valley of this Restless Mind, 1938, The Thirties, 1940, Ciano's Papers, 1948, Affairs of the Heart, 1949, (with Paul Hogarth) London à la Mode, 1966, Tread Softly for You Tread on my Jokes, 1966, Jesus Rediscovered, 1969, Something Beautiful for God, 1971, (with Alec Vidler) Paul-Envoy Extraordinary, 1972, Chronicles of Wasted Time, Vol. I-The Green Stick, 1972, Vol. II-The Infernal Grove, 1973, Jesus-The Man Who Lives, 1975, The Third Testament, 1976, Christ and the Media, 1977, The End of Christendom, 1980, My Life in Pictures, 1987, (essays) Conversion: A Spiritual Journey, 1988; editor: (with Alec Vidler) English edit. Ciano's Diary, 1947. Served as maj. intelligence corps. Brit. Army, 1939-45. Decorated Legion of Honor, Croix de Guerre with Palm, Medaille de la Reconnaissance France). Home: East Sussex, Robertsbridge Eng. Died Nov. 14, 1990.

MULDER, BERNARD J., church official; b. nr. Holland, Mich., Jan. 25, 1896; s. John B. and Katherine (Bouma) M.; m. Louise Ella Weaver, May 31, 1921; children: Betty June, Dona Louise, Judith Ellen. AB, Hope Coll., Holland, 1919; BD, Western Sem., Holland, 1922; DD, Ctrl. Coll., Pella, Iowa, 1931. Ordained to ministry Reformed Ch. in Am., 1922. Pastor Covenant Ch., Muskegon, Mich., 1922-25, First Ch., Pella, 1926-31, Bethel Ch., Grand Rapids, Mich., 1932-36; editor Religious Digest, 1935-45, Ch. Herald, 1937-45, Christian Edn., 1947-53; gen. sec. bd. edn. Reformed Ch. in Am., from 1945, editor in chief Sunday Sch. Lit., from 1950; mem. pres.'s cabinet Reformed Ch. in Am., 1937, 38, also mem. staff conf.; mem. exec. com. Nat. Coun. Chs. of Christ in U.S.A.; spl. cons. to Nr. East Christian Coun. in curriculum devel.; mem. Gen. Commn. of Army and Navy Chaplains; pres. Nat. Protestant Coun. Higher Edn., 1947; dir. pub. rels. Reformed Ch. in Am., 1942-56. Author: The King Came Riding, 1943. Bd. dirs. New Brunswick Theol. Sem.; trustee Internat. Soc. Christian Endeavor, from 1939; pres. Mich. Coun. Chs.and Christian Edn., 1940-43; trustee Ctrl. Coll., Pella, Hope Coll.; pres. bd. trustees Western Theol. Sem., 1945-46. With U.S. Army, 1917-18. Mem. Am. Legion, Assoc. Ch. Press (pres. 1943-44), Pi Kappa Delta. *

MULDOON, ROBERT DAVID, former prime minister New Zealand; b. Auckland, Sept. 21, 1921; s. James H. and Amie R. Muldoon; Grad. Univ., London, 1946, Auckland, New Zealand, 1948; m. Thea Dale Flyger, 1951; 3 children. Ptnr. KPMG Chartered Accts., Auckland, 1947-88; lectr. in auditing Auckland Tech. Inst., 1948-54; mem. New Zealand Parliament for Tamaki, 1960-92 ; undersec. to minister finance, 1964-66; minister of tourism and publicity, 1967, of fin., 1967-72, 75-84; dep. prime minister, 1972; dep. leader opposition, 1973-74, leader, 1974-75, 84; prime minister, 1975-84; chmn. Public Expenditure Com., 1963-66; privy councillor, 1976. Pres. Auckland Hort. Council, 1959-60; dominion councillor New Zealand Nat. Party, 1960-84; chmn. Global Econ. Action Inst., 1988-89. Served with New Zealand Army, 1941-46. Decorated Companion of Honour, 1977; knight grand cross Order St. Michael and St. George, 1983. Fellow New Zealand

Inst. Cost Accts. (pres. 1956, Maxwell award 1956), New Zealand Soc. Accts., Inst. Cost and Mgmt. Accts., Inst. Cost and Works Accts. (Leverhulme prize 1946), Royal Hort. Soc. Author: The Rise and Fall of a Young Turk, 1974; Muldoon, 1977; My Way, 1981, The New Zealand Economy -A Personal View, 1985, 86. Avocation: horticulture. Angelican. Died Aug. 5, 1992. Home: Birkenhead, Auckland New Zealand †

MULFORD, DONALD LEWIS, publisher; b. Montclair, N.J., Apr. 22, 1918; s. Vincent S. and Madeleine (Day) M.; A.B., Princeton, 1940; m. Frances Root, Aug. 9, 1940 (div. Apr. 1954); children: Marcia M., Sally E., Sandra D. (dec.); m. Josephine M. Abbott Davisson, Apr. 23, 1954 (dec. Mar. 1956); stepchildren: Lee, Joanne, Sue; m. Emily L. Enbysk, Dec. 29, 1958. With Montclair Times Co., 1940-89, exec. v.p., 1950-89, asso. pub., 1956-71, pres., co-pub., 1971-79, pres., pub., 1979-89, pub. emeritus, 1989; pres., pub. Verona-Cedar Grove Times, 1979-89. Mem. N.J. Press Assn. (pres. 1980-81, chmn. bd. 1981-82), Phi Beta Kappa. Rotarian. Clubs: Princeton, Montclair Golf; Nat. Press (Washington); Nassau (Princeton, N.J.). Died June 3, 1990. Home: Montclair N.J.

MULLEN, JAMES HANNA, economics educator; b. Phila., Nov. 29, 1924; s. Joseph Aloysius and Marion (Tyre) M.; m. Irene Quinlan, Oct. 15, 1948; children: James Michael, Patrick Mark, Maria Regina, Christopher Anthony, Megal Frances. AB in English Lit., U. Pa., 1944, MBA, 1948, PhD in Econs., 1955. Asst. to dean admissions U. Pa., Phila., 1946-48, instr. Wharton Sch. Fin., 1947-49; instr. Temple U. Sch. Bus., Phila., 1949-55, asst. prof. mgmt., 1955-58, assoc. prof., 1959-61, prof., 1961-66; v.p. acad. affairs Rider Coll., Trenton, N.J., 1966-68; pres. Jersey City State Coll., 1968-73, Northeastern Ill. U., 1973-76; dean acad. affairs Phila. Coll. Textiles and Sci., 1976-89; prof. LaSalle Coll., 1979; ednl. cons. State Farm Mut. Ins. Co., Bloomington, Ill., 1958-73; vis. prof. econs., cons. Naval War Coll., Newport, R.I., 1960-61; mem. adv. coun. Phila. Health and Welfare Coun., 1956-63; mem. N.J. Bd. Mediators, 1966-73; mem. ad hoc adv. com. dist. V, U.S. Office Edn., 1973-89; mem. exec. bd. Union for Experimenting Colls. and Univs., 1973; chmn. N.J. Coun. State Colls., 1969-70, N.J. Bd. Examiners, 1969-73. Author: Against the Goad, 1961, Personality and Productivity in Management, 1966. Bd. dirs. Citizens Com. Pub. Edn., Phila., 1956-66, N.J. Citizens Transp. Coun., 1966-68, N.J. Coun. Econ. Edn., 1967-73, Ednl. Info. Svcs. Inc., 1972-73, Ill. Ednl. Consortium for Computer Svcs., 1974-89. Lt. (j.g.) USNR, 1943-46, PTO. Ford fellow Harvard Bus. Sch., 1958, U. Chgo., 1964. Fellow AAAS, Soc. Applied Anthropology; mem. AAUP, Am. Econ. Assn., Am. Arbitration Assn. (nat. panel), Joint Coun. on Higher Edn. (chmn. ad hoc com. on collective bargaining 1973-77), Acad. Mgmt., Indsl. Rels. Rsch. Assn., C. of C. (bd. dirs. 1969-73), Beta Gamma Sigma. Home: Jamaica Plain Mass. Died July 8, 1989; buried Holy Sepulchre, Phila.

MULLEN, JOHN WILFRED, professional athletics manager; b. Calais, Maine, Sept. 30, 1924; s. Wilfred Leo and Katherine (Murphy) M.; m. Claire Elaine Babineau, May 4, 1946; children: Kathleen C., Christopher J., Richard A. Grad. high sch. Sec.-stenographer Boston Braves Baseball Club, 1946-53; with Milw. Braves, 1953-66, scouting dir., to 1966; asst. gen. mgr. Houston Astros Baseball Club, 1966-79; v.p., gen. mgr. Atlanta Braves, 1979-85, v.p., asst. gen. mgr., 1985-91, also dir. Served with USCG, 1942-46. Roman Catholic. Home: Atlanta Ga. Died Apr. 3, 1991.

MULLENBACH, PHILIP, economist, investment adviser; b. Chgo., Oct. 26, 1912; s. James and Annie Louise (Towns) M.; m. Muriel Fullerton Moore, June 22, 1935; children: Andrea Wessel, Guy Towns, Hugh James. Student, Carleton Coll., 1930-32; PhB in Econs., U. Chgo., 1934; postgrad., Columbia U., 1936-38. Economist Harland Allen Assos. (investment mgrs.), Chgo., 1934-37, U.S. Tariff Commn., 1938-41, War Dept., 1941-44; dir. econ. and market research Surplus Property Bd. (and successors), 1944-47; economist AEC, 1947-54; research dir. productive uses of nuclear energy Nat. Planning Assn., 1954-57; dir. nuclear energy study Twentieth Century Fund, 1957-62; v.p., dir. Growth Research, Inc. (investment mgrs.), 1959-69; v.p., dir. Growth Industry Shares, Inc., 1958-61, pres., 1961-69, v.p., 1969-77; dir.; economist, investment mgr. William Blair & Co. (merger with Grwoth Industry Shares, Inc.), Chgo., 1969-77; investment adviser, 1978-89; lectr. econs. Roosevelt U., 1977-79; Vis. fellow Adlai Stevenson Inst., 1971-72. Co-author: The Foreign Trade of Latin America, 1942, Productive Uses of Nuclear Energy, Summary of Findings—Policy Suggestions for the Future, 1957; Author: Civilian Nuclear Power: Economic Issues and Policy Formation, 1963. Trustee Roosevelt U.; bd. dirs. Georgetown Day Sch., Washington, Meadville Theol. Sem.; bd. dirs. Ill. br. UCLA, 1960's. Mem. Am. Econ. Assn., Am. Nuclear Soc. Unitarian. Clubs: Cosmos (Washington); Michigan Shores (Wilmette). Home: Wilmette Ill. Died Mar. 5, 1989.

MULLENDORE, JAMES MYERS, health sciences educator; b. Ft. Wayne, Ind., Aug. 15, 1919; s. Harvey and Edith Aileen (Myers) M.; m. Elaine Gregg, June 6, 1942; children: Lauren G., James Myers, Richard H., Nancy E. BS, Northwestern U., 1941, MA, 1942, PhD, 1948. Instr. speech pathology Northwestern U., Evanston, Ill., 1944-45; asst. prof., then asso. prof. U. Va., Charlottesville, 1945-61, founder, dir. Speech and Hearing Ctr., 1945-61; prof., chmn. div. audiology and speech pathology Vanderbilt U. Med. Sch., 1961-63, also dir. Bill Wilkerson Hearing and Speech Ctr.; prof., coordinator speech pathology and audiology W.Va. U., Morgantown, 1963-67; prof., dir. Sch. Speech and Hearing Scis., Bradley U., Peoria, Ill., 1967-77, founding dean Coll. Health Scis., 1978-85, dean, prof. emeritus, 1985-89; ednl. cons. State Farm Mut. Ins. Co., Charlottesville, 1956-61. Contbr. articles to profl. jours., chpts. to books. Bd. dirs. Va. chpt. Easter Seal Soc., 1959-61, W.Va. chpt., 1965-67; pres. Peoria, Ill. chpt., 1982-85; founder Camp Woodrow Wilson Speech Camp, Fishersville, Va., 1949, Camp Easter Seal, Morgantown, 1964; co-founder Va. Hearing and Speech Found., 1958; Chmn. Republican city com., Charlottesville, 1946-49; pres. Va. Jr. C. of C., 1952-53. Fellow Am. Speech, Lang. and Hearing Assn. (legis. council 1960-61,70, 72-73, mem. ethical practices bd. 1974-78), Speech, Language and Hearing Assn. Va. (life mem., co-founder 1959, 1st pres. 1959-60, founder, 1st editor Jour. 1959-61); mem. Internat. Assn. Logopedics and Phoniatrics, W.Va. Speech, Language and Hearing Assn. (pres. 1965-66), Ill. Speech, Language and Hearing Assn. (life mem.; pres. 1973-74), Speech Assn. Eastern States (exec. council 1955-57), Va. Jaycees (Disting. Svc. award 1952, elected life mem. internat. senate 1989), Sigma Alpha Epsilon, Phi Kappa Phi. Club: Rotary. Home: Peoria Ill. Died Mar. 10, 1989; cremated.

MULLIGAN, WILLIAM G(EORGE), lawyer; b. N.Y.C., July 16, 1906; s. William George and Agnes (Murphy) M.; m. Dorothy K. Zimmer, Jan. 27, 1928 (dec.); 1 dau., Maura Elaine; m. Mary Luciel McGookey, Sept. 6, 1942 (dec.); children: Don John (dec.), Luciel Laurene; m. Elinor Patterson O'Connor, Dec. 6, 1975. A.B., Hamilton Coll., 1927; LL.B., Harvard U., 1930. Bar: N.Y. 1931, N.J. 1976. Asst. Wickersham Crime Commn., 1929-30; asst. to Hon. Hiram C. Todd, spl. dep. N.Y. atty. gen. pros. jud. frauds, 1930-31; asst. Hon. Samuel Seabury in proceedings before N.Y. State Gov. Franklin D. Roosevelt to remove James J. Walker as mayor of N.Y. City, 1931-32; assoc. White & Case, 1932-34; asst. corp. counsel City N.Y., 1934-38, chief div. transit, 1936, chief div. franchises, 1938; assoc. counsel Bd. Transportation, City N.Y., 1939-40; gen. counsel War Materials, Inc. (fed. material procurement agy.), Pitts., 1942-43; sr. ptnr. various law firms since, 1940; of counsel Grier H. Raggio Jr. P.C., N.Y.C., until 1991; ptnr. Mulligan and Mulligan, until 1991.; trial counsel N.Y. Curb Exch. in all litigations brought against it, 1943-50. Author: Expert Witnesses: Direct and Cross-examination, 1987; lectr. on legal topics; contbg. editor Edn. Fairshare, Nat. Family Law Rev. Mem. Assn. of Bar of City of N.Y., Am. Coll. Trial Lawyers, N.Y. County Lawyers Assn., Am., N.Y. State, N.J. bar assns., SAR (chancellor N.Y. chpt.), Law Soc. (London, hon.), Theta Delta Chi (grad. treas. grand lodge 1964-66). Roman Catholic. Clubs: Union League (N.Y.C.), Harvard (N.Y.C.); Panther Valley Golf and Country (Allamuchy, N.J.); Baltusrol Golf (Springfield, N.J.). Home: Hackettstown N.J. Died Nov. 21, 1991; buried Union Cemetery, Hackettstown, N.J.

MULLINS, MICHAEL GORDON, agricultural sciences educator, research scientist; b. Ipswich, Suffolk, U.K., June 9, 1937; came to U.S., 1987; s. Gordon Edwin and Rena Ellen (Murphy) M.; m. Ulla Torborg Borin, Dec. 31, 1960; children: Eva Borin, Lena Ellen. BSc, U. Reading, U.K., 1959; Diploma in Agr., U. Cambridge, U.K., 1960; PhD, U. London, 1964. Rsch. scientist hort. rsch. div. Commonwealth Sci. and Indsl. Rsch. Organisation, Adelaide, Australia, 1964-71; prof., head dept. U. Sydney, Australia, 1971-87, prof. emeritus, 1988-90, dean faculty agr., 1986-87; Amerine prof. viticulture and enology, chmn. dept. U. Calif., Davis, 1987-90; professeur associe U. Dijon, France, 1980. Contbr. 100 articles on plant physiology and hort. sci. to profl. jours. Mem. Am. Soc. Plant Physiologists, Am. Soc. Viticulture and Enology, Internat. Soc. Hort. Sci., Australian Inst. for Agrl. Sci., Chaine des Rotisseurs Club (Sacramento), Knights of the Vine Club (Sacramento). Home: Davis Calif. Died Nov. 13, 1990.

MULLINS, ROYAL LEEMAN, banker; b. Temple, Tex., Sept. 15, 1898; s. Lee and Ida (Jackson) M.; m. Nola Hallmark, Mar. 24, 1920; children: Jack R., H. Neill, Hal. Student, Simmons U., Tex. Christian U.; grad., Grad. Sch. Banking, Rutgers U., 1938. In banking in Knox City, Tex., Houston, Ft. Worth and Dallas, 1917-28; with Wolfe City (Tex.) Nat. Bank, from 1928, pres., from 1931; pres. Ind. Bankers Assn., 1957, nat. legis. chmn., 1959-62. Columnist, Bankers Digest, Dalls. Pres. Wolfe City Housing Authority, 1951-62, Hunt County Bankers Soil Conservation Assn., from 1952; pres. Bapt. Men's Bible Class). With U.S. Army, World War I. Mem. Am. Numis. Assn., Nat. Philatelic Soc., Bur. Issues Assn., East Tex. C. of C. (Man of Month 1957), Progressive Club (pres. 1937), Knife and Fork (Greenville, Tex.). *

MULLINS, WILLIAM HARVEY LOWE, aerospace executive; b. Independence, Mo., Feb. 9, 1935; s. Arlie Truman and Sudie (Lowe) M.; m. Florine Lucy Magnani; children: Todd, Daniel. BS, U.S. Mil. Acad., 1957; MBA, U. Ariz., 1966; grad., Air Command & Staff Coll., 1967, Nat. War Coll., 1972. Commd. lt. USAF, 1957, advanced through grades to brig. gen., 1977; F-100 Squadron pilot USAF, Japan, 1959-61; F-4 instr. pilot USAF, Fla., Ariz., 1963-66; F-4 pilot, chief tactics USAF, Thailand, 1967-68; action officer air staff, Pentagon, ops. and budget USAF, 1968-71, asst. dir. ops. 4th Tactical Fighter Wing, 1972-74, mem. chief of staff 6-man group., 1974-75, house liaison officer, then dep. dir. Sec. of Air Force legis. liaison, 1975-79, ret., 1979; dep. dir. legis. affairs Gen. Dynamics Corp., Washington, 1979-80, dir., 1980-84, staff v.p. legis. affairs, 1984-86, corp. v.p. govt. affairs, from 1986. Decorated D.F.C. with 4 oak leaf clusters, Bronze Star, Air medal with 12 oak leaf clusters. Mem. Nat. Security Indsl. Assn. (bd. dirs. from 1986). Clubs: Nat. Dem., Capitol Hill (Washington); Burning Tree (Bethesda, Md.); Belle Haven Country (Alexandria, Va.). Home: Alexandria Va. Deceased. †

MULROY, THOMAS ROBERT, SR., lawyer; b. Moline, Ill., Mar. 14, 1905; s. James Robert and Mary (Maley) M.; m. Dorothy Reiner, Aug. 12, 1933; children: Dee Mulroy King, Joan Mulroy Lifvendahl, Thomas Robert Jr. Ph.B., U. Chgo., 1926, J.D., 1928. Bar: Ill. 1931. Asst. legis. counsel U.S. Senate, 1928-31; atty. Defrees Buckingham, Jones & Hoffman, Chgo., 1931-40; atty., partner Jones, Mulroy & Staub, Chgo., 1940-44; sr. partner Hopkins & Sutter (previously Hopkins, Sutter, Mulroy, Davis & Cromartie), Chgo., 1944-80, sr. counsel, 1981-89; chmn. bd. Evanston (Ill.) Hosp. Corp., 1978-81, hon. chmn. bd., 1981-85, hon. life dir., 1985-89. Author: As Luck Would Have It: Memoirs of Thomas R. Mulroy, 1984. Pres. Chgo. Crime Commn., 1963; chmn. Motion Picture Appeal Bd., Chgo., 1962-64, Chgo. Citizens' Com. Study Police-Community Relations (Mulroy Report), 1966-67; chancellor Lincoln Acad. Ill., 1974-79; bd. dirs. Lyric Opera of Chgo., 1963-84, hon. life trustee, 1984-89; pres. U. Chgo. Alumni Assn., 1959; bd. dirs. Cath. Charities. Recipient (with Dorothy Mulroy) Bravo award Outstanding Svc. to Fine Arts, Rosary Coll., 1986, Useful Citizen in Pub. Service citation U. Chgo. Alumni Assn., 1962, Citizen Fellow for Health Care award Med. Inst. Chgo., 1984; Laureate and recipient Order of Lincoln for distinction in govt. and law, Gov. of Ill., 1982. Fellow ABA, Internat. Acad. Trial Lawyers (bd. govs. 1970-76), Am. Coll. Trial Lawyers; mem. Council Fgn. Relations (Chgo. com.), ABA, Ill.Bar Assn., Chgo. Bar Assn. (bd. mgrs., producer, author 4 ann. musical prodns.), Bar Assn. 7th Fed. Circuit (pres. 1970-71), Alpha Delta Phi. Clubs: Execs. (pres. 1943-44), Univ., Mid-Am., (charter, dir.), Law (pres. 1962-63), Legal, Commercial (Chgo.); Exmoor Country (Highland Park, Ill.); Met. (N.Y.C.); Bay Hill Country (Fla.); Abbey Springs Country (Wis.). Home: Winnetka Ill. Died Sept. 25, 1989.

MUMFORD, EMILY HAMILTON, medical sociologist, educator; b. Cape Girardeau, Mo., Dec. 19, 1922; d. Barney A. and Dola (Stolzer) Hamilton. A.B., U. Tulsa, 1941; M.A., Columbia U., 1958, Ph.D., 1963. Research asst. Bur. Applied Social Research, Columbia U., N.Y.C., 1958-59; instr., major adv. Hunter Coll., N.Y.C., 1960-64; vis. prof. behavioral and social scis. New Coll., Sarasota, Fla., 1965-66; asst. prof. sociology in psychiatry Mt. Sinai Sch. Medicine, N.Y.C., 1966-68; asso. prof. Mt. Sinai Sch. Medicine, 1968-73, cons. dept. psychiatry, 1969-71; asso. prof. sociology Grad. Center, CUNY, N.Y.C., 1968-73; prof. sociology grad. program in med. sociology Lehman Coll., 1973-74; prof. psychiatry Downstate Med. Center, SUNY, Bklyn., 1973-77; spl. asst. to dean Downstate Med. Center, SUNY, 1976-77, cons. nat. survey renal patients, 1972, cons. med. edn., 1977, cons. edn. in ethics, 1978; prof. psychiatry and preventive medicine Med. Center U. Colo., Denver, from 1977; asso. cons. in sociology to sci. adv. staff St. Luke's Hosp., N.Y.C., 1961; task force on studies devel. United Hosp. Fund N.Y., 1969-71; cons. Inst. for Study of Health and Soc., Georgetown, Md., 1972; co-chmn. panel, conf. on cancer rehab. Nat. Cancer Inst., Washington, 1972; mem. colloquium Am. Assn. Med. Colls., Washington, 1974; cons. on evaluation, dept. medicine Montefiore Hosp., N.Y.C., 1977; cons. Random House, 1978; cons., site visitor psychiat. edn. br. NIMH, 1978, mem. adv. council, 1979-82; bd. dirs. Davis Inst. for Care and Study of Aging, from 1980; project dir. HEW, 1978. Author: Interns: From Students to Physicians, 1970, (with J. Skipper, Jr.) Sociology in Hospital Care, 1967, Health, Sickness and Disease in Social Science Perspective, 1982, Medical Sociology: Patients, Providers and Policies, 1983; editor: (with J. Skipper, Jr.) Academic Guide, 1976-77; assoc. editor: (with J. Skipper, Jr.) Jour. Health and Social Behavior, 1976-79; cons. TV health series, 1976; contbr. invited book rev. to profl. publs.; reviewer manuscripts for publs.; contbr. (with J. Skipper, Jr.) articles to profl. publs. Travel grantee Milbank Meml. Fund, 1969; grantee Commonwealth Fund, 1968-70; grantee NIMH, 1975-76, 77. Fellow Am. Public Health Assn., Am. Sociol. Assn. (med. sociology sect.), Am. Psychiat. Assn. (hon.); mem. Sigma Xi. Home: Denver Colo. Deceased. †

MUMFORD, LEWIS, author, social philosopher; b. Flushing, L.I., N.Y., Oct. 19, 1895; s. Lewis and Elvina Conradina (Baron) M.; m. Sophia Wittenberg, 1921; children: Geddes (killed in action 1944), Alison. Student, CCNY, Columbia U., NYU, New Sch. for Social Research; LLD, Edinburgh U., 1965; D. Architecture, U. Rome, 1967. Prof. humanities Stanford U., 1942-44; prof. city and regional planning U. Pa., 1951-59, research prof., 1959-61; vis. prof. MIT, 1957-60, 73-75; research prof. U. Calif., Berkeley, 1961-62; sr. fellow Ctr. for Advanced Studies, Wesleyan U., 1963-64. Author: The Story of Utopias, 1922, Sticks and Stones, 1924, The Golden Day, 1926, Herman Melville, 1929, rev., 1963, The Brown Decades, 1931, Technics and Civilization, 1934, The Culture of Cities, 1938, Men Must Act, 1939, Faith for Living, 1940, The South in Architecture, 1941, The Condition of Man, 1944, City Development, 1945, Values for Survival, 1946, Green Memories: The Story of Geddes, 1947, The Conduct of Life, 1951, Art and Technics, 1952, In the Name of Sanity, 1954, The Human Prospect, 1955, From the Ground Up, 1956, The Transformations of Man, 1956, The City in History, 1961 (Nat. Book award), The Highway and the City, 1963, The Myth of the Machine, vol. I, Technics and Human Development, 1967, vol. II, The Pentagon of Power, 1970, The Urban Prospect, 1968, Interpretations and Forecasts-1922-1972, 1972, Findings and Keepings-Analects for an Autobiography, 1975, Architecture as the Home of Man, 1975, My Works and Days: A Personal Chronicle, 1979, Sketches from Life: The Autobiography of Lewis Mumford—The Early Years, 1982; Editor: American Caravan, 1927-36 (year book), Documentary films for, Nat. Film Bd. Can., 1964, 8 interviews for, BBC, 1976. Mem. Bd. Higher Edn. N.Y.C., 1935-37. Decorated knight Order Brit. Empire; recipient Townsend Harris medal, 1939, Howard Meml. medal, 1946, gold medal Town Plan Inst., 1957, Royal Gold medal R.I.B.A., 1961, Nat. Book award, 1962, U.S. Medal of Freedom, 1964, Silver medal Am. Soc. Planning Ofcls., 1965, Emerson Thoreau medal Am. Acad. Arts and Scis., 1965, Leonardo da Vinci medal Soc. Hist. Tech., Hodgkins Gold medal Smithsonian Inst., 1971, Gold medal Belles Lettres Nat. Inst. Arts and Letters, 1970, Nat. Medal for Lit., 1972, Thomas Jefferson Meml. medal, 1972, prix Mondial del Duca, 1976, award Lincoln Inst. Land Policy, 1979, Nat. Medal of Arts, 1986; Guggenheim fellow, 1932, 38, 56; hon. fellow Stanford U., 1941. Fellow Am. Acad. Arts and Scis., Royal Inst. Brit. Architects (hon.); mem. A.I.A. (hon.), Nat. Inst. Arts and Letters, Am. Philos. Soc., Am. Acad. Arts and Letters (pres. 1962-65), Am. Inst. Planners (hon.), Royal Town Planning Inst. London (hon.), Phi Beta Kappa (hon.). Home: Amenia N.Y. Died Jan. 26, 1990; buried Amenia, N.Y.

MUNRO, DANA GARDNER, Latin American history educator, researcher, writer; b. July 18, 1892; s. Dana Carlton and Alice Gardner (Beecher) M.; m. Margaret Bennett Wiley, June 1, 1920; children—Margaret Alice Munro Dayton, Carolyn Babcock Munro Monas, Gardner Wiley. A.B., Brown U., 1911, LL.D. (hon.), 1940; A.B., U. Wis., 1912; postgrad., U. Munich, Fed. Republic Germany, 1912-13; Ph.D., U. Pa., 1917. Carnegie Peace Endowment grantee Central Am., 1914-16; regional economist for Mex. and Caribbean region, fgn. trade adviser's Office Dept. State, Washington, 1919-20; economist cons. Valparaiso, Chile, 1920-21; detailed to Latin Am. div. Dept. State, 1921-30, asst. chief Latin Am. div., 1923-25; 1st sec. legation Panama, 1925-27, Managua, Nicaragua, 1927-29; chief Latin Am. div. Dept. State, 1929-30; envoy extraordinary minister plenipotentiary to Haiti, 1930-32; prof. Latin Am. history Princeton (N.J.) U., 1932-61, William Stewart Tod prof. pub. affairs, 1939-61; dir. Woodrow Wilson Sch. Pub. and Internat. Affairs, Princeton U., 1939-58; Carnegie vis. prof., Latin Am., 1935; v.p. Bondholders Protective Council, 1938-42, pres., 1942-44, 58. Author: Five Republics of Central America, 1918, The U.S. and the Caribbean Area, 1933, The Latin American Republics, A History, 1942, Refugee Settlement in Dominican Republic, 1942, Intervention and Dollar Diplomacy in the Caribbean 1911-21, 1964, A Student in Central America 1914-16, 1983. Trustee Doherty Charitable Found. Served to 2d lt. USAAF, 1917-18. Mem. Council Fgn. Relations, Phi Beta Kappa, Delta Phi, Phi Eta. Home: Princeton N.J. Died June 16, 1990; buried Waquoit, Mass.

MUNTER, GODFREY L(EON), lawyer; b. Berne, Switzerland, Apr. 15, 1897; m. Katherine Lannon, Sept. 6, 1924; children: Katherine Marie (Mrs. Phaon B. Derr, Jr.), Godfrey Leon, Frederick Alexander, Theodore Albert, Gloria Jane (Mrs. Richard A. Gustavson). AB, George Washington U., 1917; LLB, Nat. U., 1920, LLD, 1948. Bar: D.C. 1920, Calif. 1924, Va. 1929. Practice law Washington, 1919-56; judge Ct. Gen. Sessions, Washington, 1956-50; mem. Munter, Adams, Thomson & Bastian, from 1960; part-time prof. law, sales, evidence, wills and procedure Nat. U. (now merged with George Washington U.), 1923-56. Trustee Legal Aid Soc. D.C., George Washington U.; D.C. commr. Nat. Conf. Uniform State Laws, from 1948. Recipient Americanism medal DAR, 1964. Mem. ABA (ho. of dels.), D.C. Bar Assn. (pres. 1938), Univ. Club, Columbia Country Club (pres. 1959-61), Kiwanis, Sigma Nu Phi (nat. pres. 1938). *

MURNAGHAN, FRANCIS D., mathematics educator; b. Omagh, County Tyrone, Ireland, Aug. 4, 1893; came to U.S., 1914, naturalized, 1928; s. George and Angela (Mooney) M.; m. Ada May Kimbell, June 23, 1919; children: Francis D., Mary Patricia. BA, Nat. U. Ireland, 1913, MA, 1914, DSc honoris causa, 1940; PhD, Johns Hopkins U., 1916. Instr. math. Rice Inst., Houston, 1916-18; assoc. Johns Hopkins U., Balt., 1918-21, assoc. prof. applied math., 1921-28, prof., 1928-48; prof. math. Instituto Tecnico de Aeronautica, Sao Jose dos Campos, 1949-59; cons. U.S. Navy, 1955-63; dir. Math. Inst. Rutgers U., 1926; vis. prof. U. Chgo., 1928, 30, U. Pa., 1929, Duke U., 1941, Brown U., 1943-44, Dublin Inst. Advanced Studies, 1948, Carnegie Inst. Tech., 1948. Author: Vector Analysis and the Theory of Relativity, 1922; (with Joseph S. Ames) Theoretical Mechanics, 1929; (with H. Bateman and H.L. Dryden) Hydrodynamics, 1932; Theory of Group Representations, 1938; Analytical Geometry, 1946; Differential and Integral Calculus, 1947; Applied Mathematics, 1948; Finite Deformation of an Elastic Solid, 1951; Algebra elementar e Trigonometrica, 1955; The Laplace Transformation, 1962, The Calculus of Variations, 1962; The Unitary and Rotation Groups, 1962. Mem. AAAS (v.p. and chmn. Sect. A. 1943), Royal Irish Acad., Am. Phys. Soc., Nat. Acad. Scis., Am. Philos. Soc., Am. Math. Soc., Math. Assn. Am., London Math. Soc., Edinburgh Math. Soc., Acad. Bras das Cienciais, Acad. Nac. de Cien. de Lima, Phi Beta Kappa, Sigma Xi, Gamma Alpha. *

MURPHY, ANNE MARIE, library system director; b. N.Y.C., July 24, 1926; d. Timothy D. and Mary A. Murphy. AB, Coll. Mt. St. Vincent, 1948; BLS, Pratt Inst., 1950. Profl. asst. N.Y. Pub. Library, N.Y.C., 1950-51, asst. br. librarian, 1951-54; asst. dir. for pub. services Fordham U., Bronx, 1954-56, assoc. librarian, 1956-70, dir. libraries, 1970-89; trustee N.Y. Met. Reference and Research Library Agy., 1983—. Mem. ALA, Cath. Library Assn. Home: Ridgewood N.J. Died May 17, 1989; buried Hawthorne, N.Y.

MURPHY, C(HARLES) THORNE, steel company executive; b. New Haven, Nov. 10, 1895; s. Michael C. and Nora B. (Long) M.; m. Elise J. Vhay, May 30, 1925; children: Charles Thorne, William V., Michael C. Student, George Sch., 1911-13, Peddie Sch., 1913-16; BS, Yale U., 1921. Ptnr. John W. Gillette & Co., Detroit, 1926-29; with Sutro Bros. & Co., N.Y.C., 1929-42; v.p. McLouth Steel Corp., Detroit, from 1942. 1st lt. USAC, 1917-19. Mem. Hidden Valley Club (pres., dir.), Otsego Ski Club (pres., dir.). *

MURPHY, GERALDINE JOANNE, English language educator; b. Cambridge, Mass., Apr. 13, 1920; d. Timothy Francis and Mary Louise (Murphy) M. AB, Regis Coll., 1941; MA, Radcliffe Coll., 1942, PhD (James Bryant Conant fellow, Rockefeller grantee), 1960. Asst .prof. in MA teaching program Wesleyan U., Middletown, Conn., 1957-64, assoc. prof. English, 1964-70, prof. English, 1970-90; Cons. English studies Xerox Corp., 1969-73. Author: The Study of Literature, 1968, A Momentary Stay, 1972; Contbr. articles to profl. jours. Mem. AAUP. Home: New Haven Conn. Died Apr. 20, 1990.

MURPHY, RAYMOND E., geographer, educator; b. Apple River, Ill., July 24, 1898; s. Edward and Ellen (Bermingham) M.; m. Marion M. Fisher, May 22, 1926; 1 child, Patrick Alan. BS, Mo. Sch. Mines and Metallurgy, Rolla, 1923; MS in Geology, U. Wis., 1926, PhD in Geography, 1930. Asst. engr. Roxana Petroleum Corp., Okla., 1923-24; instr. geology U. Ky., 1926-28; prof. geography Concord State Tchrs. Coll., Athens, W.Va., 1930-31; asst. prof. geography Pa. State Coll., 1931-37, assoc. prof., 1937-43, prof., 1943-45; prof. geography U. Hawaii, 1945-46; prof. econ. geography Grad. Sch. Geography Clark U., Worcester, Mass., from 1946, dir. Grad. Sch. Geography, 1962-65; field work in human geography, eastern Caroline Islands (as part of Coordinated Investigation of Micronesian Anthropology program of NRC in cooperation with Navy), 1947. Author: Mineral Industries of Pennsylvania, 1933; (with Marion Murphy) Pennsylvania: A Regional Geography, 1937, Pennsylvania Landscapes, 1938, rev. edit., 1952; World Survey, 1947; Central Business District Studies, 1955; asst. editor Econ. Geography, 1946-49, editor, 1949-62, from 1963, mng. editor, 1962-63; contbr. articles to profl. jours. Fellow Am. Geog. Soc.; hon. fellow Royal Scottish Geog. Soc.; mem. AAUP, Assn. Am. Georgaphers, Nat. Coun. Geog. Edn., Sigma Xi, Gamma Alpha. *

MURPHY, ROBERT FRANCIS, anthropologist, educator; b. Rockaway Beach, N.Y., Mar. 3, 1924; s. John E. and Marion (Nolan) M.; m. Yolanda Bukowska, Apr. 1, 1950; children: Pamela Ann, Robert Steven. B.A., Columbia U., 1949, Ph.D. in Anthropology, 1954. Rsch. assoc. U. Ill., Urbana, 1953-55; asst. prof. dept. anthropology U. Calif., Berkeley, 1955-61, assoc. prof., 1961-63; prof. Columbia U., N.Y.C., 1963-90, chmn. dept. anthropology, 1969-72. Author: The Trumai Indians of Central Brazil, 1956, Mundurucu Religion, 1958, Headhunter's Heritage, 1960, The Dialectics of Social Life, 1971, Robert H. Lowie, 1972, (with Yolanda Murphy) Women of the Forest, 1974, An Overture to Social Anthropology, 1979, The Body Silent, 1987 (Lionel Trilling award Columbia U.); Contbr. articles to profl. jours. Mem. Am. Anthrop. Assn., Am. Ethnol. Soc. Home: Leonia N.J. Died Oct. 8, 1990.

MURRAY, ARTHUR, dance instructor, business executive; b. N.Y.C., Apr. 4, 1895; s. Abraham and Sara (Shore) M.; m. Kathryn Kohnfelder, Apr. 24, 1925; children: Phyllis and Jane (twins). Student, Ga. Sch. Tech., 1918-21. Pres., dir. chain 450 dance schs. throughout U.S., known as Arthur Murray Dance Studios, until 1964; producer Arthur Murray TV Show. Author: How to Become a Good Dancer, 1938, Arthur Murray's Dance Secrets, 1947; contbr. dance articles to encys. including Ency. Brit. Mem. Irish Am. Hist. Soc. Clubs: Pacific, Waialai Country. Home: Honolulu Hawaii Died Mar. 3, 1991; buried Honolulu.

MURRAY, LAWRENCE N(EWBOLD), banker; b. N.Y.C., Dec. 20, 1894; s. Francis W. and Mary Gertrude (Lawrence) M.; m. Mary Brewster Trowbridge, 1918; children: Caroline L., Frank T., Margaret T. Grad., St. Paul's Sch., Concord, N.H., 1913; BA, Yale U., 1917. Asst. cashier Nat. Comml. Bank, Albany, N.Y., 1922-25; with Koppers Co., Inc., Pitts., 1925; asst. cashier Mellon Nat. Bank, Pitts., 1925-29, v.p., dir., 1929-46; pres., dir. Mellon Nat. Bank & Trust Co., Pitts., 1946-58; bd. dirs. Am. Brake Shoe Co., Alco Products Inc. Mem. Duquesne Club, Pitts. Golf Club, Rolling Rock Club of Pitts., Links (N.Y.C.), Yale of N.Y.C. Republican. Episcopalian. *

MUSCARELLE, JOSEPH LOUIS, construction and real estate company executive; b. N.Y.C., Nov. 24, 1903; s. Ciro and Cira (Spinella) M.; m. Margaret Perrapato, Oct. 26, 1930; children: Carol Infante, Marlene Flanagan, Joseph Louis. Student, Coll. William and Mary, 1923-27. Pres. Joseph L. Muscarelle, Inc., Maywood, N.J., 1926-71, chmn. bd., 1971-89; dir. Nt. Community Bank, Rutherford, N.J.; pres. Ross-Meagher, Ltd., Ottawa, Can., 1964-89, Joseph L. Muscarelle Investment Co., Maywood, 1954-89; trustee Bergen Community Coll., Paramus, N.J. Bd. govs. N.Y. Cultural Ctr.; pres. Joseph L. Muscarelle Found., Maywood. Mem. N.J. Bldg. Contractors Assn. (trustee). Home: Hackensack N.J. Died Apr. 9, 1989.

MUSCHENHEIM, WILLIAM EMIL, architect, educator; b. N.Y.C., Nov. 7, 1902; s. Frederick Augustus and Elsa (Unger) M.; m. Elizabeth Marie Bodanzky, Nov. 29, 1930; children: Carl Arthur, Anna Elizabeth Muschenheim Arms. Student, Williams Coll., 1919-21, MIT, 1921-24; MArch, Behrens Master Sch. Architecture, Acad. Fine Arts, Vienna, Austria, 1929. Archtl. designer Joseph Urban (architect), N.Y.C., 1929-33; prin. William Muschenheim, N.Y.C. and Ann Arbor, Mich., from 1934; pres. Muschenheim, Hammarskjold & Arms, Inc. (architects, planners), Ann Arbor, 1968-71; prof. architecture U. Mich., Ann Arbor, 1950-72, prof. emeritus, 1972-90. Author: Elements of the Art of Architecture, 1964, Why Architecture, 1980; contbr. articles to profl. jours.; designs include original facade New Sch. for Social Rsch., color scheme for Chgo. World's Fair, 1933, Solomon Guggenheim Mus. Non-Objective Art, Marine Transp/ Bldg. N.Y. World's Fair, 1939. Recipient gold medal Mich. Soc. Architects, 1984; Horace H. Rackham research travel grantee, 1958, 64, 72. William Muschenheim teaching fellowship established at U. Mich., 1984. Fellow AIA (edn. com. 1959-61, fgn. relations com. 1963-64); mem. AAUP, Assn. Collegiate Schs. Architecture (edn. com. 1961-63, fgn. relations com. 1964-66), Internat. Congress of Modern Architects. Home: Ann Arbor Mich. Died Feb. 1, 1990; buried Sleepy Hollow Cemetery, North Tarrytown, N.Y.

MUSE, PAUL FOREST, university administrator; b. Norwich, Dec. 5, 1905; s. John Thomas and Margaret (Allison) M.; m. Belvie Jean Spratt, Dec. 25, 1926; children: David Paul, Neil Edwin. BS in Edn., Ohio U., 1932; MA, Ohio State U., 1937, PhD, 1946. Tchr., vice prin. Mt. Vernon High Sch., 1927-38; tchr. Bowling Green State U., 1938-47; head bus. edn. dept., dean Ind. State U., Terre Haute, 1964-71; cons. in field, 1964-89. Contbr. articles to profl. jours. Recipient John Robert Gregg award, 1963, Disting. Alumnus Svc. award Ohio State U., 1970. Mem. Nat. Bus. Edn. Assn. (pres. 1963-64), Pi Omega Pi (pres. 1952-53). Home: Terre Haute Ind. Died Apr. 12, 1989.

MUSSELMAN, MERLE MCNEIL, surgeon, educator; b. Topeka, Sept. 19, 1915; s. Charles Albert and Jimmie (Drake) M.; m. Dorothy Gregg, Oct. 5, 1940; m. Charles, Ann, Jane, Mary. BS, U. Nebr., Lincoln, 1937; MD, U. Nebr., Omaha, 1939; MS in Surgery, U. Mich., 1949. Diplomate Am. Bd. Surgery (bd. dirs. 1961-67, chmn. credentials com. 1966-67). Intern L.I. Coll. Hosp., Bklyn., 1939-40; surg. intern U. Mich. Hosp., Ann Arbor, 1940-41, resident in surgery, 1946-50; dir. surgery Wayne County Gen. Hosp., Eloise, Mich., 1950-54; prof., Coll. Medicine U. Nebr., Omaha, 1954-81, chmn. dept. surgery, 1955-72, prof. emeritus, 1981-90. Mem. editorial bd. Am. Jour. Surgery, 1957-70, Jour. Trauma, 1960-77; contbr. numerous articles to med. jours. Bd. dirs. Douglas County chpt. ARC, Omaha, 1959-65; mem. bd. edn., Omaha Pub. Schs., 1963-71. Maj. M.C., U.S. Army, 1941-46, PTO. Decorated Bronze Star medal. Mem. ACS, Am. Surg. Assn., Cen. Surg. Assn., Frederick A. Coller Surg. Soc., Western Surg. Assn., Alpha Omega Alpha, Rotary. Home: Omaha Nebr. Died Nov. 1, 1990; buried Omaha, Nebr.

MYERS, FRED ARTHUR, museum director; b. Lancaster, Pa., Dec. 21, 1937; s. Joseph Arthur and Mary Carpenter (Leaman) M.; m. Mary Frances McGrann, May 6, 1961; children: Elizabeth, Benjamin, Margaret. B.A. cum laude, Harvard U., 1959, M.A., 1962. Registrar Mus. Art, Carnegie Inst., Pitts., 1962-64, asst. curator paintings, 1965-66, asst. to dir., 1967-70; dir. Grand Rapids (Mich.) Art Mus., 1970-78, Thomas Gilcrease Inst. Am. History and Art, Tulsa, 1978-91. Bd. dirs. Okla. Found. for the Humanities, 1982-88. Served with AUS, 1960. Recipient Detur prize Harvard U., 1956. Mem. Am. Mus. Assn., Mt.-Plains Mus. Assn., Assn. Art Mus. Dirs., Tulsa Country Club. Home: Tulsa Okla. Died Oct. 3, 1991; interred Lancaster, Pa.

MYERS, JACOB MARTIN, clergyman, religion educator; b. nr. York, Pa., Oct. 25, 1904; s. Harvey Allen, Sr. and Sarah Annie (Seiffert) M.; m. Mary Helen Kimmel, June 26, 1926; 1 child, Helen Elizabeth. A.B., Gettysburg Coll., 1927; B.D., Luth. Theol. Sem., Gettysburg, 1930, S.T.M., 1931; S.T.D., Temple U., 1937; Ph.D., Johns Hopkins, 1946; Litt. D. (hon.), Gettysburg Coll., 1967; D.D. (hon.), Susquehanna U., 1977. Ordained to ministry Luth. Ch., 1930; pastor Grace Parish, Gettysburg, 1930-50; supply pastor Dillsburg (Pa.) Parish, 1950-51; mem. faculty Luth. Theol. Sem., from 1937, prof., head O.T. dept., from 1942; Holman lectr. on Augsburg Confession Gettysburg Sem., 1959; guest prof. O.T. Pitts. Theol. Sem., 1965-66, 67-68. Author: The Linguistic and Literary Form of the Book of Ruth, 1955, The Layman's Bible Commentary Vol. 14 Hosea, Joel, Amos, Obadiah, Jonah, 1959, The Anchor Bible: I Chronicles, 1965, The Anchor Bible: II Chronicles, 1965, The Anchor Bible: Ezra-Nehemiah, 1965, Invitation to the Old Testament, 1966, The World of the Restoration, 1968, Anchor Bible 42: I and II Esdras, 1974, Grace and Torah, 1975; editor: Biblical Studies in Memory of H. C. Alleman, 1960, Theological and Missionary Studies in Memory of John Aberly, in 1965, (with O. Reimherr and H.N. Bream) Search the Scriptures: New Testament Studies in Honor of Raymond T. Stamm, 1969; contbr. (with O. Reimherr and H.N. Bream) introduction and the exegesis for Judges, The Interpreter's Bible, 1951; contbr. articles including In Memorium of Howard N. Bream to Luth. publs. Mem. Soc. Biblical Lit. and Exegesis, Brit. Soc. O.T. Study (asso.), Am. Inst. Archaeology, Am. Oriental Soc., Am. Acad. Religion, Phi Beta Kappa. Home: Gettysburg Pa. Deceased. †

MYERS, JOHN, business executive; b. London, Eng., Sept. 1, 1895; came to U.S., 1935, naturalized, 1942; s. Meyer and Claire (Light) M.; m. Ettie Gergman, 1918; 1 cau., Jeannette (Mrs. L. Robert Vitkin). Student pub. schs., Eng.; student, Sch. Dentistry, Paris. Practicing dentist Eng., 1921-35; gen. mgr., dir., exec. v.p. Am. Flange & Mfg. Co., Inc., from 1935; pres. John Myers Found., John Myers Gallery, John Myers Music Corp., Interplanetary Communications Assn., Inc. Exhibited paintings at Studio Club Galleries, Mt. Vernon, N.Y., Netherland Club, N.Y.C. Bd. dirs. N.Y.C. Anti-Crime Com., Inc.; hon. dep. fire chief of N.Y.C. Mem. Am. Bibl. Ency. Soc. (bd. dirs.), Am. Arbitration Assn. (panel of arbitrators), Artists Equity, Ballet Assn. Am., Palm Beach Art League, Lambs Club, Golden Bridge Hounds Club. *

MYERS, ROBERT LEE, technical consultant; b. Akron, Ohio, Feb. 28, 1923; s. Lee J. and Esther Irene (Hartz) M.; m. Alice Emily Cox, Sept. 24, 1944; children: Douglas Lee, Jeffrey Robert, Susan Deane, Laurie Alyssa. BS in Chemistry, Kent State U., 1944; PhD in Organic Chemistry, U. Ill., 1947. Research assoc. Gen. Electric, Schnectady, N.Y., 1947-55; mgr. lab. capacitor div. Gen. Electric, Hudson Falls, N.Y., 1955-60; assoc. dir. Borg Warner Research Lab., Des Plaines, Ill., 1960-63; dir. chem. research Am. Cynamid Co., Stamford, Conn., 1963-67; dir. research Lederle Labs., Pearl River, N.Y., 1967-69; v.p. research GAF Corp., N.Y.C., 1969-72; v.p. tech. St. Regis Corp., West Nyack, N.Y., 1972-85, Champion Internat., West Nyack, 1985-87; cons. Serendipity Cons., Darien, Conn., from 1987. Contbr. articles to profl. jours.; patentee in field. Trustee St. Thomas Aquinas Coll., Sparkill, N.Y., from 1981; bd. dirs. Tappan Zee Theatre Restoration, Nyack, N.Y., from 1981. Named Disting. Alumnus, Kent State U., 1960. Fellow Tech. Assn. Pulp Paper Industry (bd. dirs. 1979-82); mem. AAAS, Am. Chem. Soc., Inst. Paper Chemistry (chmn. research adv. com. 1980-86), Union League. Democrat. Methodist. Club: Rockland Country (Sparkill). Home: West Nyack N.Y. Deceased.

MYERS, VERNON C., publishing executive; b. St. Louis, Sept. 9, 1911; s. William Peter and Cora P. (Klein) M.; m. Mary Jane Martin, Feb. 12, 1938; children: Manning Martin, Melinda Beagle. BJ, U. Mo., 1932. Circulation mgr. Effingham (Ill.) Daily Record and Weekly Democrat, 1932-33; with promotion dept. Des Moines Register and Tribune, 1933-35, promotion mgr., 1935-38; dir. visual rsch. Cowles Mags., Inc., Des Moines, 1938-41; mem. N.Y. advt. staff, west coast advt. mgr., promotion mgr. Look mag., 1941-43, 46-47; asst. to pres. Cowles Mags., Inc., 1948-51, v.p., 1951-71; bd. dirs. Cowles Communications, Inc., 1952-71, pres. Look mag. div., 1967-71; pub. Look mag., 1952-67; trustee Aetna Income Shares, Aetna Fund; past chmn. Mag. Advt. Bur. Past v.p. bd. trustees Miss Hall's Sch., Pittsfield, Mass.; past trustee Automotive Safety Found. With USAAF, 1943-45. Decorated Bronze Star; recipient Disting. Svc. award U. Mo. Sch. Journalism, 1957. Mem. Soc. Profl. Journalists, Nat. Mcpl. League (exec. coun., Disting. Citizen award 1969), Am. Soc. Corp. Execs., Wee Burn Club (Darien, Conn.), Delta Beta (award), Alpha Delta Sigma, Alpha Sigma Phi. Home: Norwalk Conn. Died Jan. 25, 1990; buried Norwalk, Conn.

MYRDAL, KARL GUNNAR, economist; b. Gustafs, Sweden, Dec. 6, 1898; s. Carl Adolf and Anna Sofia (Carlson) Petterson; m. Alva Reimer, Oct. 8, 1924; children—Jan, Sissela, Kaj. Grad. Law Sch., Stockholm U., 1923; Juris Dr. in Econs., 1927; Fil.dr. (hon.), 1966; LL.D. (hon.), Harvard U., 1938, Leeds U., 1957, Yale U., 1959, Brandeis U., 1962, Howard U., 1962, U. Edinburgh, 1964, Swarthmore Coll., 1964, Sir George Williams U., 1967, U. Mich., 1967, Lehigh U., 1967, Atlanta U., 1970, U. Philippines, 1971; Litt.D. (hon.), Fisk U., 1947, Upsala Coll., East Orange, N.J., 1969; J.D. (hon.), Nancy U., 1950; L.H.D. (hon.), Columbia U., 1954, New Sch. Social Research, N.Y.C., 1956, Wayne State U., 1963, Gustavus Adolphus Coll., 1971; D. Social Sci. (hon.), U. Birmingham, 1961, U. Louisville, 1968; D.D. (hon.), Lincoln U. (Pa.), 1964; D.C.L. (hon.), Temple U., 1968; Fil.dr. (hon.), Oslo U., 1969; Dr. Sociologie h.c., Jyväskylä U., 1969; Dr. h.c., Helsinki U., 1971; D.Sc. (hon.), Dartmouth Coll., 1971, Herriot-Watt U., Edinburgh, 1979. Practiced law, Sweden; apptd. docent in polit. econs. Stockholm U., 1927; travel as Rockefeller fellow in U.S., 1929-30; asso. prof. Post-Grad. Inst. Internat. Studies, Geneva, 1930-31; apptd. acting prof. Stockholm U., 1931, apptd. to Lars Hierta chair of polit. econ. and public finance, 1933, now prof. emeritus internat. economy; Godkin lectr. Harvard U., 1938; dir. Study of Am. Negro Problem, Carnegie Corp. Am., 1938-42; vis. research fellow Center for Study Democratic Instns., Santa Barbara, Calif., 1973-74; Disting. vis. prof. City U. N.Y., 1974-75, U. Calif., Irvine, 1977, U. Wis., 1977; Slick prof. U. Tex., 1978. Active public affairs in Sweden; adv. to govt. on econ., social and fiscal policy, 1933-38; mem. Swedish Senate for Social Dem. Party, 1936-38, 43-47; bd. dirs. Swedish Bank; mem. Population, Housing and Agrl. commns., Sweden; minister of commerce Sweden, 1945-47; exec. sec. UN Econ. Commn. for Europe, 1947-57. Recipient Nobel prize for econs., 1974; Nehru award for internat. understanding, 1981. Fellow Econometric Soc.; mem. Brit. Acad., Royal Acad. Sci. in Sweden, Hungarian Acad. Sci., Am. Acad. Arts and Scis., Am. Philos. Soc.; hon. mem. Am. Econ. Assn., Ams. for Dem. Action. Author: The Cost of Living in Sweden, 1830-1930, 1933; Monetary Equilibrium, 1939; Population: A Problem for Democracy, 1940; An American Dilemma: The Negro Problem and Modern Democracy, 1944; The Political Element in the Development of Economic Theory, 1953; Development and Under-development, The Mechanism of National and International Inequality, 1956; An International Economy: Problems and Prospects, 1956; Economic Theory and Underdeveloped Regions, 1957; Value in Social Theory, 1958; Beyond the Welfare State: Economic Planning and Its International Implications, 1960; Challenge to Affluence, 1963; Asian Drama: An Inquiry into the Poverty of Nations, 1968; Objectivity in Social Research, 1969; The Challenge of World Poverty: A World Anti-Poverty Program in Outline, 1970; Against the Stream: Critical Essays on Economics, 1973; How Sweden is Governed, 1982; also several other books on econ. theory pub. in Sweden, govt. reports.Deceased. Home: Djursholm Sweden †

MYSAK, EDWARD DAMIEN, speech pathology educator, consultant; b. Bklyn., Apr. 13, 1930; s. Charles and Mary (Zytynski) M.; m. Theresa Mary Marchi, Oct. 10, 1953; children: Damien, Blaise. BA cum laude, Bklyn. Coll., 1954, M.A., 1955; Ph.D., Purdue U., 1958. Cert. in speech pathology and audiology. Asst. prof. U. Conn., Storrs, 1957-61; dir. speech edn. Newington (Conn.) Children's Hosp., 1957-61; prof. speech pathology, chmn. dept. Columbia U., N.Y.C., 1961-89; cons. speech pathology VA Hosps., N.Y.C., 1962-89, N.Y.C. Dept. Health, 1967-89 , Lenox Hill Hosp., N.Y.C., 1975-89. Author: Principles of a Reflex Therapy Approach to Cerebral Palsy, 1963, Speech Pathology and Feedback Theory, 1966, Neuroevolutional Approach to Cerebral Palsy and Speech, 1968, Pathologies of Speech Systems, 1968, Neurospeech Therapy for the Cerebral Palsied, 1980, Pathology of the Speech System, 1989. Fellow Am. Speech-Lang.-Hearing Assn., Am. Acad. Cerebral Palsy and Devel. Medicine, Am. Acad. Audiology; mem. AAUP, N.Y. State Speech-Lang.-Hearing Assn. (Disting. Achievment award 1990), N.Y.C. Speech Lang. Assn. (Profl. Achievement award 1987). Home: Riverhead N.Y. Died Dec. 13, 1989; buried St. John's Roman Cath. Cemetery, Riverhead, N.Y.

NACHTRIEB, NORMAN HARRY, chemist, educator; b. Chgo., Mar. 4, 1916; s. Norman David and Minnie (Barnard) N.; m. Marcia Binford, Aug. 22, 1953; 1 dau., Marianna C. BS, U. Chgo., 1936, PhD, 1941. Chemist Ill. Geol. Survey, Urbana, 1937-38, Pitts. Plate Glass Co., Barberton, Ohio, 1941-43; research chemist Manhattan project, U. Chgo., 1943-44; alternate group leader Los Alamos Sci. Lab., 1944-46; asst. prof. chemistry U. Chgo., 1946-48, assoc. prof., 1948-53, prof., 1953-84, prof. emeritus, 1984-91, chmn. dept., 1962-71, head phys sci. sect. coll., 1958-59, 60-62, asso dean phys. scis. div., 1973-76, master phys. scis. co legiate div., assoc. dean coll., 1973-76; vis. pro chemistry U. Ill., Chgo., 1985-91. Author: Principl and Practice of Spectrochemical Analysis, 195 Principles of Modern Chemistry, 1986, 2d edit., 199 Chemistry, Science of Change, 1989; adv. editor: Ency Brit, from 1955; assoc. editor Jour. Chem. Physic 1956-58; mem.editorial adv. bd. Analytical Chemistr 1958-61. Mem. policy bd. SPE div. NSF, 1964-6 mem. adv. bd. edn. Consol. High Sch. Dist. 230, 196 69; served on Palos Pk. Planning Commn. Recipien Quantrell award U. Chgo., 1962, 77; J.T. Baker fello analytical chemistry, 1940-41; NSF sr. postdoctora fellow, 1959-60. Fellow Am. Phys. Soc.; mem. Am Chem. Soc. (adv. bd. petroleum research fund 1967-70). Home: Palos Park Ill. Died Sept. 11, 1991; buried Palo Park, Ill.

NAD, LEON MARION, accounting firm executive; b Houston, Dec. 8, 1927; s. Irving and Esther (Atlas) N. m. Marcia Helen Damsky, Aug. 14, 1949; 1 dau. Charlotte Dale. B.A., Rice U., 1946; M.B.A., U. Pa. 1948. C.P.A., N.Y. Instr. acctg. U. Pa., Phila., 1948-51; staff acct. Ernst & Young, Phila., 1951-56; sr. tax specialist Price Waterhouse, N.Y.C., 1956, Houston 1956-58; tax mgr. Price Waterhouse, N.Y.C., 1958-64 ptnr., 1964-88, nat. dir. tech. tax services, 1978-85, assoc. vice chmn., tax cons., 1985-88; lectr. in acct Rutgers U.-Camden, 1951-56, Rutgers U.-Newark 1958-61; lectr. in taxation Seton Hall U., South Orange N.J., 1987-88; adj. assoc. prof. Fordham U., N.Y.C. 1988-91; adv. dir. Doctors Ctr. Internat. Bank, Houston, 1982-88. Chmn. bd. dirs. Wharton Bus. Sch. Club N.Y., N.Y.C., 1970-71; mem. Rice U. Fund Council, Houston, 1973-76. Mem. Am. Inst. C.P.A.s. Republican. Jewish. Clubs: Princeton, Rockefeller Ctr. Home: West Orange N.J. Died Oct. 31, 1991; buried Aheb Shalom Cemetery, West Orange, N.J.

NAGEL, CHARLES, museum director, architect; b. St. Louis, Mar. 24, 1899; s. Charles and Anne (Shepley) N.; m. Lucie Oliver, Aug. 31, 1940. B.A., Yale U., 1923, B.F.A., 1926, M.F.A., 1928; fellow, Berkeley Coll., from 1933; student, Am. Sch., Fontainbleau, 1926; D.F.A., MacMurray Coll., 1956. Architect Boston, St. Louis, 1927-30; asst. prof. history of art, curator decorative arts Yale U., 1930-36; ptnr. Nagel & Dunn (architects), St. Louis, 1936-42; dir. Bklyn. Mus., 1946-55, City Art Mus., St. Louis, 1955-64, Nat. Portrait Gallery, Smithsonian Instn., 1964-69; Mem. adv. com. on arts Dept. of State Adv. Com. to Nat. Park Service on rehab. of Independence Hall; advisor Com. on Restoration of White House. Author: American Furniture 1650-1850, 1949, (novel) Seven Letters to Counsel, 1965;, collaborator (with Russell Kettell): Early American Rooms, 1936; projects include alterations Christ Ch. Cathedral, St. Louis, 1938-42, St. Mark's Ch., 1939 (spl. award St. Louis chpt. AIA and Producer's Council 1976), Grace Ch., Clarksville, Mo., 1941, St. Michael and All Angels Ch., Cuernavaca, Mexico, 1983. Bd. dirs. City Art Mus., 1938-42, acting dir., 1942-46; trustee Carl Schurz Meml. Fund. Beaux Arts Soc. N.Y. scholar to Am. Sch., Fontainebleau, 1926; recipient N.Y. City Municipal Art Soc. prize, 1926, Stella della Solidarieta by Italian govt., 1953; Nat. Portrait Gallery medal, 1978; Benjamin Franklin fellow Royal Soc. Arts, London. Mem. Mo. Assn. Architects, Am. Assn. Museums (mem. council), Assn. Art Mus. Dirs. (pres. 1953), Internat. Council Museums, Am. Inst. Interior Designers (hon.), Yale Assos. Fine Arts (trustee), Yale Alumni Bd., Alpha Delta Phi, Pundits. Episcopalian. Clubs: Elizabethan; Cosmos (Washington). Home: Marion Mass. Died Feb. 27, 1992.

NAGLE, RAYMOND J., dentistry educator; b. Worcester, Mass., Aug. 16, 1900; s. John J. and Anna (Hayes) N.; m. Elva Pomfret, June 6, 1931. AB, St. Mary's Coll., 1920; DMD, Harvard U., 1924; ScD (hon.), Northwestern U., 1963. Diplomate Am. Bd. Oral Medicine. Asst. prof. clin. dentistry Dental Sch., Harvard U.; dean Coll. Dentistry, prof. prosthetic dentistry NYU; Edmond Noyes Meml. lectr. Northwestern U., 1963; vis. oral surgeon Boston City Hosp.; cons. prosthodontics VA at Cushing Gen. Hosp., regional clinic Bklyn., Manhattan; ctrl. office cons. VA, WAshington; chmn. subcom. to establish a med. and dental sch. at U. Mass.; chmn. subcom. on hosps. and edn. Selective Svc.; sec. Adv. Bd. for Dental Specialties; chmn. adv. bd. on cleft palate harelip N.Y.C. Health Dept.; chmn. bd. cons. Murray and Leonie Guggenheim Dental Clinic; mem. deans com. N.Y. Vets. Hosps.; mem. dental coun. N.Y. State Bd. Dental Examiners. Editor Jour. Prosthetic Dentistry. Mem. Commn. Health Svcs., N.Y.C., Nat. Adv. Dental Rsch. Coun.; pres. Fund Dental Edn. Examiner, Am. Bd. Prosthodontics, also v.p.; mem. vis. com. Harvard Med. Sch. & Sch. Dentistry, U. Pitts. Dental Sch. Fellow Internat. Coll. Dentists, Am. Coll. Dentists; mem. ADA (chmn. coun. dental edn.), Am. Assn. Dental Schs. (pres. exec. com.), Am. Acad. Dental Sci. (pres.), N.Y. Soc. Med. Rsch. (v.p.), Greater N.Y. Acad. Prosthodontics (pres.), Mass. Dental Soc. (prs.), N.Y.Inst. Clin. Oral Pathology, Sci. Rsch. Sco. Am., N.Y. Acad. Dentistry, Am. Acad. Dental Medicine (Samuel Charles Miller award 1963), Pan Am. Odontological Assn. (pres.), N.Y. Acad. Scis., Acad. Internat. Medicine and Dentistry, Dental Editors Assn., Harvard Odontological

Soc., Harriet Newall Lowell Soc. for Dental Rsch., Internat. Soc. for Dental Rsch., Bristol Premed. and Predental Soc. (hon.), Harvard Club, Univ. Club, Omicron Kappa Upsilon, Xi Psi Phi. Home: Centerville Mass. Died, 1991.

NAKASHIMA, GEORGE KATSUTOSHI, furniture designer; b. Spokane, Wash., May 24, 1905; s. Katsuharu and Suzu (Thoma) N.; m. Marion Sumire Okajima, Feb. 14, 1941; children: Mira Shizu Nakashima Yarnall, Kevin Katwuya. Diploma, Am. Sch. Fine Arts, Fontainebleau, France, 1928; BArch, U. Wash., 1929; MArch, MIT, 1930. Pvt. practice architecture and furniture design U.S., France, Japan, India, 1931-40; design and mfr. furniture, New Hope, Pa., 1943-90; pres. Nakashima, Woodworker. ltar for Peace, Cathedral St. John the Devine, N.Y.C., 1986; Prin. works include Golconda, Sri Aurobindo Ashram, Pondicherry, India, 1940, Ch. of Christ the King, Kyoto, Japan, 1965, Monstery of Christ in the Desert, Abiquiu, N.Mex., 1970, el Soledad, San Miguel de Allende, Guanajuato, Mex., 1974, exhibited in Mus. Modern Art, N.Y.C., Renwick Gallery, Washington. Decorated 3d Order of the Sacred Treasure (Japan); recipient Gold medal for craftsmanship AIA, 1952, Hazlett award, 1981, Gold medal Japanese Am. of the Biennum, J.A.C.L., 1980; named Alumnus Summa Laude Dignatus, U. Wash., 1990. Fellow Am. Craft Coun. Home: New Hope Pa. Died June 15, 1990; buried Thompson Meml. Cemetery.

NAKAZAWA, YOSHIO, architectural firm executive; b. Issaquah, Wash., Dec. 12, 1917; s. Gensei and Sei (Tashiro) N.; m. Yuri L. Takahashi, Sept. 11, 1949; children: Paul Wesley, John Warren. BS in Design, Ill. Inst. Tech., 1951. Registered architect, Ill. Project architect Pace Assocs., Chgo., 1954-58; architect mgr. Gen. Am. Transp., Niles, Ill., 1959-62; pres. Nakazawa Corp., Evanston, Ill., 1963-90. Patentee in interior modular constrn. Served to master sgt. U.S. Army, 1941-46, PTO. Recipient First Honor award, USAF, 1979, Cert. Appreciation, USN, 1965, 66, 72, Cert. Commendation USN, 1966, 67, 72, AIA Disting. Bldg. award Chgo. Assn. Commerce and Industry, 1967, Award of Merit AIA/Naval Facilities Engring. Command, 1982. Fellow AIA; mem. Nat. Fire Protection Assn., Am. Soc. Testing and Materials. Home: Wilmette Ill. Died Jan. 23, 1990.

NAKSZYNSKI, NIKOLAUS GUNTHER See **KINSKI, KLAUS**

NAMUTH, HANS, photographer, filmmaker; b. Essen, Germany, Mar. 17, 1915; came to U.S., 1941, naturalized, 1943; s. Adolph and Anna (Weiskirch) N.; m. Carmen P. de Herrera, July 17, 1943; children: Tessa, Peter. Student, Humboldt Oberrealschule, Germany, 1925-31. vis. artist Harvard U., 1981. Photographer in Paris, France and Majorca, Spain, 1935-36; Spanish Civil War for Life mag., Vu mag., Schweizer Illustrierte, 1936-37; exhbns. include Pan Am. Union, Washington, Mus. Natural History, N.Y.C., Mus. Modern Art., N.Y.C., Am. Fedn. Arts, 1947-51, Corcoran Gallery Art, Washington, 1974, Leo Castelli Gallery, N.Y.C., 1973, 75, 77, 84, 88, Washington Gallery Photography, 1976, Broxton Gallery, L.A., 1976, Pace Gallery, 1981, Modernism Gallery, San Francisco, 1984, Hunter Coll., N.Y.C., 1984, Lenbachhaus, Munich, 1986, Galerie Carla Fuehr, Munich, 1987, Rencontres Internationales de la Photographie, Arles, France, 1988, Galerie Zabriskie, Paris, 1977, 89, Musee d'Art Moderne de la Ville de Paris, 1979, Seibu Corp. Am., Tokyo, 1983, Centre Georges Pompidou, Paris, 1989, Yvon Lambert Galerie, Paris, 1989, Benton Gallery, Southampton, N.Y., 1989, Benteler-Morgan Gallery, Houston, 1990, FotoFest Gallery, Houston, 1990, Hooks-Epstein Galleries, Houston, 1990, Permanent Faces, Guild Hall, L.I., N.Y., 1991; large photog. exhbn.: Seventeen American Painters; assigned by Dept. State, U.S. Pavilion Brussels (Belgium) World's Fair, 1958; represented in permanent collections Tulane U., New Orleans, Va. Mus. Fine Arts, Richmond, Met. Mus. Art, Mus. Modern Art, N.Y.C., L.A. County Mus. Art, Cleve. Art Mus., Folkwang Mus., Essen, Fed. Republic Germany, San Francisco Mus. Fine Art; filmmaker: Jackson Pollock, 1950-51, de Kooning at the Modern, 1969, de Kooning the painter, Josef Albers: Homage to the Square, 1969, Brancusi Retrospective, 1969, de Kooning at the Modern, 1969, de Kooning the Painter, mid 1960's, Henri Matisse Centennial at Grand Palais, 1970, (with Paul Falkenberg) Calder's Universe, 1977 (recipient Pollock film award of merit Film Council Greater Boston Film Festival 1952), Louis I. Kahn: Architect, 1974, Alfred Stieglitz, Photographer (Red Ribbon award Am. Film Festival 1983), Balthus at the Pompidou, 1984, (with Georg Reisner) Spanisches Tagebuch 1936, 1986, "Jasper Johns": Take an Object, 1990; author: Fifty Two Artists, 1973, (with Brian O'Doherty) American Masters, 1973, Early American Tools, 1975, L'Atelier de Jackson Pollock, 1978, Pollock Painting, 1980, Artists 1950-1981: A Personal View, 1981, (with Georg Reisner) Spanisches Tagebuch 1936, 1986, Los Todos Santeros, 1989; contbr. to other publs. Served with French Fgn. Legion, 1939-40; with M.I. U.S. Army, 1943-45, ETO. Decorated Purple Heart; Croix de Guerre; Medaille du Maroc France; 1st award Asso. Bus. Publs., 1955; award Art Dirs. Club, 1956; Recognition of Pub. Service State Dept., 1958; certificate of merit Art Dirs. Club N.Y.C., 1959; award Art Dirs. Club, Phila., 1959; spl. citation for film Image from the Seas, 1958. Mem. Am. Soc. Mag. Photographers. Democrat. Home: New York N.Y. Died Oct. 13, 1990; buried Oakland Cemetery, Sag Harbor, N.Y.

NATHAN, WILLIAM ISRAEL, department store executive; b. Kiev, Russia, Dec. 26, 1896; came to U.S., 1906, naturalized, 1921; s. Israel and Helen (Butnitsky) N.; m. Charlotte Aarons, Dec. 16, 1925; children: Ira, Fred, Honora (Mrs. Indyke) Cynthia (Mrs. Salzhour). Ed. pub. schs., N.Y.C. Ptnr. Superior Clothing Co., N.Y.C., 1918-26; men's clothing mfr., 1926-35, ladies suit mfr., 1935-52; chmn. bd. Virginia Dare Stores Corp., N.Y.C., from 1956, Atlantic Thrift Ctrs., Inc., N.Y.C., from 1949; v.p. Animal Ins. Co., N.Y.C., from 1952. Pres. Big Bros. Lodge, Mt. Vernon, N.Y., from 1949; chmn. Mt. Vernon United Jewish Appeal Campaign, 1948; active Mt. Vernon Hosp., Mt. Vernon YMHA and YWHA, Jewish Ctr. Mt. Vernon. Mem. Hebrew Immigrant Aid Soc., Grand St. Boys Assn., B'nai B'rith, Century Club of N.Y.C., Grand Club of Mt. Vernon, Ridgeway Golf Club of White Plains. *

NEAL, WILLIAM HENRY, government official; b. Charlotte, N.C., Dec. 19, 1896; s. Frank S. and Elizabeth (Caldwell) N.; m. Jeannette Archer, Mar. 9, 1927; children: William Henry, James Archer. BA, Davidson (N.C.) Coll., 1917. Instr. Greenbrier Mil. Sch., Lewisburg, W.Va., 1917-18; asst. cashier Charlotte Nat. Bank, 1919-29; dir. pub. rels. Wachovia Bank & Trust Co., Winston-Salem, N.C., 1929-34, v.p., 1934-36, sr. v.p., 1946-60; asst. to Sec. of Treas., nat. dir. Savs. Bond div., from 1960; mem. faculty Grad. Sch. Banking, Rutgers U., 1937-56, Sch. Fin. Pub. Rels., Northwestern U.; N.C. chmn. U.S. Savs. Bond div. Treasury Dept., 1950-54; spl. rep. U. S. Treasury Dept. to Europe, 1958. Trustee Presbym. Home, High Point, N.C., St. Andrews Presbyn. Coll., Laurinburg, N.C. Recipient Exceptional Svc. award Sec. of Treasury, 1965. Mem. Winston-Salem C. of C., Fin. Advertisers Assn. Am. (pres. 1938, mem. sr. adv. coun.), N.C. Bankers Assn. (past pres.), Am. Bankers Assn., N.C. Coun. Chs., N.C. Soc. Cin., Davidson Coll. Alumni Assn., Forsyth Country Club, Civitan, Old Town Country Club. Democrat. *

NEEL, ALICE, artist; b. Merion Square, Pa., Jan. 28, 1900. Student Phila. Sch. Design for Women, 1921-25; Doctorate (hon.), Moore Coll. Art, 1971. Group shows include: Retrospectives Moore Coll. Art, 1971, Whitney Mus. Art, 1974, 77, 80, 82, Pa. Acad. Fine Arts, 1980, 81, Newport Harbor Art Mus., Newport Beach, Calif., 1981-82, Hirshhorn Mus., Washington, 1982, Met. Mus. N.Y., 1982, Robert Miller Gallery, 1982, Eleanor Ettinger, Inc., N.Y., 1982, Vanderwoude Tananbaum Gallery, 1982; represented in permanent collections Met. Mus. Art, Mus. Modern Art, Whitney Mus. Am. Art, Hirshhorn Mus., Am. Mus. Moscow, others; easel painter Fed. Works Agy., 1933-43; lectr. painting seminar U. Pa. Grad. Sch., 1971-72; lectr. Skowhegan Sch. Painting and Sculpture, summer 1972. Recipient Longview Found. award, 1962; Am. Acad. Arts and Letters award, 1969; Benjamin Altman Figure prize N.A.D., 1971. Mem. Artists Equity Assn. Deceased. Home: New York N.Y. †

NEESE, C. G., federal judge; b. Paris, Tenn., Oct. 3, 1916; s. Charles Gentry and Sarah Anna (Nunn) N.; m. Althea Debord; children: Charles Gelbert III, Gerry Jan. Student, U. Tenn., 1936; LL.B., Cumberland U., 1937, LL.D. (hon.), 1988. Bar: Tenn. 1938. Practice in Paris and Nashville, 1938-61; exec. asst. to gov. of Tenn., 1944; adminstrv. asst. to Senator Kefauver, 1949-51; U.S. dist. judge Eastern Dist. Tenn., 1961-82, sr. U.S. dist. judge, 1982-89; Past sec., gen. counsel Capitol Life Ins. Co. Tenn. Dir. primary campaigns Senator Kefauver, 1948, 54; A founder, original trustee, 1st pres. Family Clinic, Nashville; former trustee Tusculum Coll. Mem. Phi Delta Phi, SAR. Democrat. Clubs: Masons, Freolac Soc. Home: Nashville Tenn. Died Oct. 20, 1989; buried Paris, Tenn.

NEILL, ROBERT, lawyer; b. Batesville, Ark., July 23, 1908; s. Robert and Ida (Wing) N.; m. Nancy Mitchell, Aug. 5, 1939; children—Robert III, Nancy Lee. A.B., U. Mo., 1929; LL.B., Harvard U., 1932. Bar: Mo. 1932. Assoc. Thompson & Mitchell, and predecessors, St. Louis, 1932-44, ptnr., from 1944; personal counsel to adminstr. RFC, 1953; counsel Adv. Com. Financial Instrns. Act, 1956-57; adv. com. Jordan Charitable Trust, from 1958; Mem. adv. com. to comptroller currency, 1962-63; cons. Mo. Commn. Finance on New Banking Code, 1966. Bd. curators U. Mo., 1956-69, pres., 1964-67. Fellow Am. Bar Found.; mem. ABA, Mo. Bar Assn., St. Louis Bar Assn. (past v.p.), Law Library Assn. St. Louis (dir., past pres.), Phi Delta Phi (hon.). Club: Bogey (St. Louis). Home: Saint Louis Mo. Died Oct. 19, 1987; buried Bellefontaine Cemetery, St. Louis.

NEILL, THOMAS TAYLOR, government consultant; b. Washington, Dec. 4, 1903; s. Charles Patrick and Esther (Waggaman) N.; m. Helen Mitchell, June 8, 1929; children: Agnes Neill Williams, Hugh Mitchell. DBS in Mech. Engring., Cath. U. Am., 1925; MS, MIT, 1926. Mech. engr. aircraft engine rsch. lab. Nat. Bur. Standards, Washington, 1926-39; ignition engr. Wright-Patterson AFB, USAAF, Dayton, Ohio, 1939-42; asst. to dir. rsch. NACA, Washington, 1942-58, exec. sec. security classification bd., 1945-55; chmn. bd. NACA, Washington, Ohio, 1955-58; chief rsch. adminstrn. div. office dir. of advanced rsch. programs, NASA, Washington, 1958-61, chmn. security classification bd., 1958-70; chief rsch. and tech. reports div. Office Advanced Rsch. and Tech., Washington, 1961-70; cons. Nat. Air and Space Mus., Smithsonian Instn., Washington, 1971-81. Patentee synchronized street traffic control system. Mem. Soc. Automotive Engrs. (v.p. aircraft 1953). Home: Washington D.C. Died July 29, 1988; buried Mt. Olivet Cemetery, Washington, D.C.

NELSON, ERLAND NELS PETER, psychology educator; b. Ruskin, Nebr., July 28, 1897; s. Hans and Frederikke (Olsen) N.; m. Naida Editha Randall, Aug. 6, 1924; children: Isabelle Frederikke, Erland Randall. BA, Peru (Neb.) State Tchrs. Coll., 1927; MA, U. Nebr., 1930, PhD, 1937; student, U. Chgo., 1931, 33. Rural tchr. Dundy County, Nebr., 1920; supt. Comstock, 1922-24, Juniata, 1924-26; prof. commerce Dana Coll., Blair, Nebr., 1926-29, pres., 1929-36; head dept. psychology and edn. Newberry (S.C.) Coll., 1936-43; pres. Carthage (Ill.) Coll., 1943-49; prof. psychology U. S.C., from 1949. V.p. bd. edn. United Luth. Ch. in Am., 1956-60; chmn. Luth. Student Ctr., U. S.C.; bd. dirs. Richland County Mental Bd. Fellow Am. Psychol. Assn.; mem. Soc. for Psychol. Study Social Issues, S.C. Soc. Philosophy, S.C. Psychol. Assn. (pres. 1963-64), Southeastern Psychol. Assn., AAUP, Edn. Soc. N.Am., Am. Petroleum Inst., Am. Mgmt. Assn., Bankers Club Am., N.Y. So. Soc., Phi Delta Kappa, Gamma Sigma, Alpha Tau Omega. *

NELSON, HARRY WILLIAM, poet, author, artist; b. N.Y.C., June 9, 1908; s. Nels William and Alma Constance (Svenson) N.; student Brown U., 1926-28; AB cum laude, Yale, 1933; postgrad. U. N.H., summer 1939, Lafayette U., summer 1951, U. Conn., 1950-51; studied under Harve Stein, 1949-59, Clarence Brodeur, 1963-70, Beatrice Cuming, 1964-67, Art Students League, Lyman Allyn Mus., 1948-70, Robert A. Cale, 1974, 77. Tchr. English, R.E. Fitch Sr. High Sch., Groton, Conn., 1934-64, dir. dramatics, 1942-52; innovator, nat. spokesman for dramatic choric odes. Founder, 1st pres. Indian and Colonial Rsch. Ctr., Old Mystic, Conn., 1965-70, lectr. 20th ann. address, 1985. Recipient Leander Leitner award Am. Lit. Assn., 1940, Cora Smith Gould Meml. award, 1946; Monday prize Poetry Soc. Ga., 1969; Suffield (Conn.) Conf. Poetry award, 1971, 1st prize ann. contest Mass. State Poetry Soc., 1986; finalist Chase Going Woodhouse poetry competition Mohegan Coll., 1974; named Most Accomplished Poet, recipient Excellence of Performance award Greater Hartford Civic and Arts Festival Poetry Contest, 1976; hon. mention Carlisle (Pa.) Poets award, 1978; 1st award in poetry Conn. Writers Competition, Conn. Writers League, 1980, 1st prize Paul Mellon Arts Ctr., Wallingford, Conn. Spring Poetry Festival, 1981; 1st prize Mass. State Poetry Soc., 1986; State of Conn. Medal 350th Commemorative, 1985; elected to Educators' Hall of Fame, 1987. Mem. Living Heritage Guild Groton (pres. 1965-67), New London Art Students League (pres. 1965-68), Poetry Soc. Am. (nominee governing bd. preservation of soc. 1978, ind. 1980), Mystic Art Assn. (Wimpfheimer award 1979, Maxwelton award for aquamedia, 1981), Essex Art Assn. (bd. dirs. 1987, E. Gould Chalker award 1985), Conn. (publs. com. 1977 1st and 3d awards Ann. Yellow Pad Competition 1979, asso. editor Conn. River Rev. 1979-82), Pa. poetry socs., Shelley Soc. N.Y., Internat. Platform Assn., Gungywamp Soc., Chi Delta Theta. Author: Startled Flight (poems, included in spl. Am. lit. collection Beinecke Rare Book and Manuscript Library, Yale), 1930; Impelling Reminiscence (poems) (Leitner award), 1940; Ours is the Work (dramatic choric ode), 1942; The Years of the Whirlwind (poems, dramatic choric ode), 1943; The Moon is Near (also illustrator; narrative poem), 1944; Never to Forget This (dramatic choric ode), 1944; The Fever in the Drum (poems), 1945; From Moon-Filled Sky (songs), 1947; Look to the Horizon Within (dramatic choric ode), 1948; The Winter Tree (poems; 1971 Suffield Conf. Poetry award), 1972; Not of This Star Dust (poems), 1973; Blame the Skulk of Night, 1974; Wolf Stone, Wolf Stone (poems), 1976; Encounter at the Aquarium (poems), 1978; Command Performance (poems), 1980, A Catch of Creation, 1984; others; poems pub. in various lit. revs., also Hartford Courant, from 1968; poetry readings schs., colls., various orgns.; guest poet Williams Sch., 1974, 75, 78, 79, 81, Housatonic Community Coll., Bridgeport, 1980, Stamford Radio WSTC, 1981, Groton Library, 1985, Celebration of Arts program U. Conn. and Groton Arts Com., 1986. Exhibited one-man show Lyman Allyn Mus., 1968, Groton Playhouse Gallery, 1956, Hartford Nat. Bank, 1964-68, Waterford Library, 1971, Woodworth Hall, Conn. Coll., 1972, retrospective Lawrence Meml. Hosp., New London, 1973, 80, 82, 89, Groton Public Library, 1980, 87, Conn. Bank & Trust, 1983; group shows at Boston Mus. Fine Arts, Sterling Library Yale, Lyme Art Gallery, from 1968, Mystic Art Gallery, from 1950, Essex Art Gallery, from 1964, Converse Gallery, Cummings Art Center, Conn. Coll., 1973; Bicentennial Commn., Mystic Art Assn., 1976, prints exhbn., 1979, others; one-man retrospective show Liberty Bank, Old Mystic, 1977, 50th Anniversary Exhbn. The Early Years: Mystic Art Assn., 1981, Eastern Conn. Symphony Orch. Old Lyme Exhibit, 1981,

Invitational New Eng. Art Show, U.S. Coast Guard Acad., 1981, New Eng. South Shore Artists, Westerly Library, 1984; represented in permanent collections at Lyman Allyn Mus., Groton Library, pvt. collections. Recipient Silver trophy Am. Cancer Art Exhbn., Mitchell Coll., 1968, Spl. award for monotypes, 1970, Spl. prize design and graphics, 1971; 1st prize for tech. excellence U. Conn. Avery Point Art Exhbn., 1969, 1st prize unltd. media, 1971; awards East Haddam, 1969, 71, New London Mall, 1971, Southington, 1971, 1st in show, Montville, 1973, best in show, Colchester, 1974; others. Cons. art Groton Library, 1984-86; ind. film maker, showing and lecturing colls., schs., museums, orgns., from 1958; Shakespeare Celebration lectr. Groton Arts Com., Groton Library, 1981, Michelangelo, 1983, Waterford Library, 1984; films include The Research Paper, The Tall Ships, Fleet and One Tuna, Our Walden, Puppet and Camera, The Edge of Winter, The Eternal Prelude, Vain Carrousel, This Autumn Day. Died Aug. 19, 1989; buried Starr Cemetery, Groton, Conn. Home: Groton Conn.

NELSON, JOHN HERBERT, dean, educator; b. Rutherford County, N.C., July 29, 1897; s. Augustus M. and Anna (Fowler) N.; m. Kathryn Langmade, Aug. 20, 1929. AB, Wofford Coll., 1918; PhD, Cornell U., 1923. Instr. English Cornell U., 1919-25; assoc. prof. English U. Kans., 1925-30, prof., from 1930, assoc. dean Coll. Liberal Arts and Scis., 1933-41, asst. dean Grad. Sch., 1941-46, dean, 1946-63, acting chancellor, 1951; bd. dirs. Midwest Inter-Libr. Corp., 1949-52. Author: (with F.C. Prescott) Prose and Poetry of the Revolution, 1925; The Negro Character in American Literature, 1926; (with G.D. Sanders) Chief Modern Poets of England and America, 1929; Contemporary Trends, 1933. Mem. adv. com. grad. studies Inst. Internat. Edn., 1948-51; mem. adv. bd. Masaryk Inst. Mem. MLA, North Cen. Assn. (non. mem.; exec. bd. com. colls. and univs.), Phi Beta Kappa. *

NELSON, NORTON, environmental medicine educator, toxicologist; b. McClure, Ohio, Feb. 6, 1910; s. William and Bertha C. (Ballmer) N.; m. Rose S. Cohen, Sept. 3, 1936; children: Robert, Margaret, Richard. A.B., Wittenberg U., 1932, D.Sc. (hon.), 1964; Ph.D., U. Cin., 1938. Rsch. asst. Children's Hosp. Rsch. Found., Cin., 1934-38, rsch. assoc., 1946-47; biochemist May Inst. Med. Rsch., Jewish Hosp., Cin., 1938-42; asst. prof. biochemistry U. Cin., 1946-47; asso. prof. indsl. medicine NYU, 1947-53, dir. rsch. Inst. Indsl. Medicine, 1947-53, prof. environ. medicine, 1953-80; dir. Inst. Environ. Medicine, NYU Med. Center, 1954-80 (on leave 1966-67), chmn. dept. environ. medicine, 1954-80; dir. Lanza Labs., Sch. Medicine NYU, Tuxedo, 1962-66; provost University Hghts. campus NYU, 1966-67; chief chemistry dept. Armored Med. Biochemists; dir. NYU Valley Ctr., 1967-80; cons. NSF, 1971-72, 74-75, FDA, 1972-77; chmn. adv. com. on protocols for safety evaluation; mem. com. on environ. physiology NRC, chmn. com. air quality standards in space flight, mem. com. research in life sci., com. on nitrate accumulation, 1970-72; mem. Armed Forces Epidemiol. Bd., 1962-77, cons., from 1977; cons. Commn. on Environ. Health, 1962-65; mem. Mayor's Tech. Adv. Com. on Radiation, Mayor's Sci. and Tech. Adv. Council, 1966-74; mem. exec. com. N.Y.C. Health Research Council, chmn. environ. pollution working group, 1965-72; advisor in formation and mem. adv. com. Nat. Inst. Environ. Health Sci., NIH, 1967-71, 74-77, cons., 1972-80, chmn. task force on rsch. planning in environ. health sci., 1969-70, chmn. 2d task force, 1975-76; mem. Cancer Cause and Prevention adv. com. NIH, Nat. Cancer Inst., 1971-73, Carcinogenesis Program (Etiology), 1972-73, Clearinghouse on Environ. Carcinogenesis, 1976-80; mem. pesticide adv. com. HEW, 1970; mem. panel on herbicides U.S. Office Sci. and Tech., 1969, com. tech. forecasting behalf environ. health, 1970, chmn. task force on hazardous trace substances, 1970; mem. panel on chems. and health Pres.'s Sci. Adv. Com., 1970-73; mem. hazardous materials adv. com. EPA, 1970-74, cons. sci. adv. bd., 1974-75, chmn. environ. health adv. com., 1975-80; mem. roster cons. to adminstr. ERDA, 1976-78; chmn. conf. on protocols for evaluating chems. in environ. NRC, Nat. Acad. Scis., 1972; mem. White House Task Force on Air Pollution, 1969, Environ. Studies Bd., 1974-77; chmn. human ecology commn. Internat. Assn. Ecology; mem. Commn. Natural Resources, 1977-80; mem. expert panel on carcinogenicity Internat. Union Against Cancer; mem. com. motor vehicle emission WHO, 1964-68, mem. com. microchem. pollutants, 1964-68; chmn. Expert Com. Manual Toxicity of Chems., 1975-77; mem. panel U.S.-USSR Joint Commn. for Health Cooperation, from 1972, U.S.-Japan Coop. Med. Sci. Program, 1972-78; mem. subcom. toxicology of metals Permanent Commn. and Internat. Assn. Occupational Health, from 1972; vis. com. dept. nutrition and food scis. MIT, 1971-74; mem. Milbank Meml. Fund Commn. for Study Higher Edn. Pub. Health, 1972-75; mem. energy policy project adv. bd. Ford Found., 1972-74; mem. Hudson Basin Project adv. bd. Rockefeller Found., 1973-75, Pres.'s Biomed. Research Panel, chmn. subcluster on environ. health and toxicology, 1975; chmn. Bd. Toxicology and Environ. Health Hazards, Nat. Acad. Scis., 1977-80, ex-officio mem., 1981; bd. dirs. Found. for Advanced Edn. in Sci. Assoc. editor: Jour. Occupational Medicine; cons. editor: Environ. Research; mem. editorial bd.: Archives of Environ. Health, Jour. Toxicology and Environ. Health, MIT Press Series of Toxicology, from 1981. Trustee Tuxedo Meml. Hosp., 1957-75; trustee Indsl. Health Found., 1969-75, sci. adviser, from 1976; mem. vis. com. bd. overseers Harvard U. Sch. Pub. Health, 1973-76; mem. adv. com. on occupational safety and health edn. Resource Center, from 1980; chmn. med. and sci. adv. bd. Will Rogers Meml. Hosp., 1960-70, chmn., 1968-70; mem. research adv. com. Boyce Thompson Inst. Plant Research; adv. council dept. stats. Princeton U., 1973-76; bd. dirs. N.Y. Lung Assn., 1974-77; mem. biomed. and environ. sci. adv. com. Los Alamos Sci. Lab., 1976-80; chmn. panel environ. health NIH Fogarty Center, Am. Coll. Preventive Medicine, 1975; cons. NSF, 1971-72, 74-75; mem. project 4 com. Sci. Com. Problems of Environ., Internat. Council Sci. Unions, NRC, 1974-77; chmn. bd. sci. counselors Nat. Toxicology Program, from 1980; chmn. carcinogenesis adv. panel Office Tech. Assessment, U.S. Congress, 1979-81; chmn. and mem. exec. com. Sci. Group on Methodologies for Safety Evaluation of Chems., from 1979; mem. sci. com. on problems of environ. WHO, from 1979; mem. UN Environ. Programme; mem. com. health related effects of marijuana use NRC, from 1980; sr. mem. Inst. Medicine, 1981; mem. health research rev. com. State of N.Y., from 1977; co-chmn. coal techs., health and environ. effects of energy techs. Fed. Interagy. Com., Dept. Energy, Dept. Health and Human Services, EPA, 1979-80; mem. environ. research and devel. subpanel energy research adv. bd. Dept. Energy, from 1980; v.p. John B. Pierce Found., from 1983 . Served to lt. col. San. Corps, AUS, 1942-46. Recipient Nat. Health Achievement award Blue Cross and Blue Shield Assns., 1979. Mem. Am. Indsl. Hygiene Assn., Soc. Exptl. Biology and Medicine, Harvey Soc., Air Pollution Control Assn., Ecology Soc. Am., Tarrytown Hist. Soc. (pres. 1958-60), AAAS, Am. Acad. Occupational Medicine (hon.), Am. Chem. Soc., Am. Pub. Health Assn. (Com. occupational health and safety), Am. Soc. Biol. Chemists, Am. Soc. Pharmacology and Exptl. Therapeutics (com. environ. pharmacology), Soc. Occupational and Environ. Health, N.Y. Acad. Scis. (hon., life, Gordon Y. Billard award 1976), Indsl. Hygiene Round Table, Soc. Toxicology (hon.), Sigma Xi. Home: North Tarrytown N.Y. Died Feb. 4, 1990.

NELSON, ROGER MILTON, insurance company executive, lawyer; b. Detroit, Aug. 27, 1924; s. Milton and and Christine Florence (Rogers) N.; m. Nancy Marilyn Agy, Oct. 22, 1948; children—Gregory A., Halley A. B.S., Ohio U., 1948; J.D., Case-Western Res. U. Bar: Ohio bar 1950. With Shelby Mut. Ins. Co., Ohio, 1950-86, asst. gen. counsel, 1965-70, v.p., gen. counsel, 1970-74, sr. v.p., gen. counsel, 1974-81, exec. v.p., sec., gen. counsel, 1981-86. Served with USAAF, 1943-45. Decorated D.F.C., Air medal with 5 oak leaf clusters. Mem. ABA, Ohio Assn. Civil Trial Attys. (pres. 1978-79, turstee 1972-86). Republican. Home: San Marcos Calif. Died Jan. 14, 1990; buried Eternal Hills Meml. Pk., Oceanside, Calif.

NELSON, S. PAGE, banker; b. Patton, Ala., July 13, 1896; s. Robert Jr. and Elvira Ann (Clark) N.; m. Julie Murray Forrest, Sept. 25, 1920; children: Julie Murray (Mrs. Edward Munroe Williams), S. Page, Jr. Ed., Gilman Country Sch., Balt., 1912-14, Johns Hopkins U., 1914-15; night student, U. Md. Law Sch., 1915-17. Asst. treas. Johns Hopkins U., 1920-32, later trustee; v.p. The Savs. Bank of Balt., 1934-45, pres., 1945-59, chmn., from 1959; dir. Merc. Safe Deposit & Trust Co., Monumental Life Ins. Co., U.S. F. & G. Co., Balt. Equitable Soc. Trustee McDonogh Sch. Served as 1st lt., 110th F.A., World War I. Mem. Balt. Assn. Commerce (pres. 1950), Elkridge Club, Mchts. Club, Alpha Delta Phi. *

NEMEC, STANLEY S., physician; b. Yugoslavia, June 16, 1911; s. Adolf and Josefina (Koblizek) N.; M.D., St. Louis U., 1936; m. Katherine M. Vidakovich Barr, June 15, 1940; children: Edward S., Mary K., Charles S., Robert S., Louise K., Dorothy K., Barbara K. Gen. med. practice, 1936-43; radiologist, St. Louis City Hosp., 1943-46; practice medicine specializing in radiology, 1946-89; cons. radiologist Wabash R.R. Woodland Hosp., Moberly, Mo.; radiologist St. Charles Clinic, Marian Hosp.; asst. in radiology St. Louis U. Sch. Medicine. Diplomate Am. Bd. Radiology, Nat. Bd. Med. Examiners, Fellow Am. Coll. Radiology; mem. Radiology Soc. N.A., A.M.A., So. Med. Assn., St. Louis Med. Soc., St. Louis Soc. Neurology and Psychiatry. Author: History of the Croatian Settlement in St. Louis, 1931; Yugoslav Sokol Almanac, 1933. Editor: Sokol Magazine, 1931-34, The Koch Messenger, 1939. Contbr. articles to profl. jours. Died Apr. 4, 1989; buried Calvary Cemetery, Edwardsville, Ill. Home: Saint Louis Mo.

NEMEROV, HOWARD, United States poet laureate, educator, author; b. N.Y.C., Mar. 1, 1920; s. David and Gertrude (Russek) N.; m. Margaret Russell, Jan. 26, 1944; children: David, Alexander Michael, Jeremy Seth. AB, Harvard U., 1941; 13 hon. doctorate degrees including, Washington U., St. Louis, 1991. Instr. English, Hamilton Coll., Clinton, N.Y., 1946-48; mem. faculty lit. and langs. Bennington (Vt.) Coll., 1948-66; prof. English Brandeis U., 1966-69; writer-in-residence Hollins (Va.) Coll., 1962; Fannie Hurst prof. creative lit. Washington U., St. Louis, 1969, Edward Mallinckrodt disting. univ. prof. English, until 1990; cons. poetry in English to Library of Congress; vis. lectr. English, U. Minn., 1958-59; asso. editor Furioso, 1946-51. Author: (verse) Image and the Law, 1947, Guide to the Ruins, 1950, The Salt Garden, 1955, Mirrors and Windows, 1958, New and Selected Poems, 1960, Gnomes and Occasions, 1973, The Western Approaches, Poems, 1973-75, Collected Poems, 1977, Sentences, 1980, Inside the Onion, 1984, War Stories, 1987; (novels) The Melodramatists, 1949, Federigo, or the Power of Love, 1954, The Homecoming Game, 1957; (short stories) A Commodity of Dreams, 1959; (verse, including 2 plays) The Next Room of the Dream, 1962; (essays) Reflections on Poetry and Poetics, 1962, Poetry and Fiction: Essays, 1963, Figures of Thought, 1978, New and Selected Essays, 1984, The Oak in the Acorn, 1987; also author Stories, Fables and Other Diversions, 1961, The Blue Swallows, 1967, Journal of the Fictive Life, 1981; contbr. critical writings to various periodicals.Book collection of his works: A Howard Nemerov Reader, pub. 1991. Served as pilot RAF, 8th A.F., USAAF, 1942-45. Bowdoin prize essayist Harvard Coll., 1940; Kenyon Rev. fellow fiction, 1955; recipient Blumenthal prize Poetry mag., 1958, 2d prize short story competition Va. Quar. Rev., 1958, award for novel Nat. Inst. Arts and Letters, 1961, Arts award Brandeis U., 1963, St. Botolph's Club (Boston) Arts award, 1967, Theodore Roethke Meml. prize for poetry, 1968, Frank O'Hara Meml. prize Poetry mag., 1971, Nat. Book award in poetry, 1978, Pulitzer prize in poetry, 1978, Wilma and Roswell Messing, Jr. award St. Louis U., 1979, Bollingen prize for poetry, 1981, 1st Aiken/Taylor prize in poetry Sewanee Rev. and U. So., 1987, Nat. Medal Arts, 1987; Guggenheim fellow, 1968; Wallace Stevens poetry fellow Yale U., 1983; named U.S.Poet Laureate, Library of Congress, 1988, reapptd., 1989-90. Fellow Am. Acad. Arts and Scis., Acad. Am. Poets; mem. Nat. Inst. Arts and Letters, Am. Acad. Arts and Letters (vice chancellor 1987). Home: Saint Louis Mo. Died July 5, 1991; buried St. Louis.

NEMETZ, ANTHONY ALBERT, philosophy educator; b. Sheboygan, Wis., Mar. 7, 1923; s. Anton W. and Anna (Heim) N.; m. Jane Frances Maynes, Dec. 29, 1948; children—Thomas, Christine, Mary A., Clare, Margaret, Joseph, Catherine. Grad., St. Francis Sem., Milw., 1943; M.A., U. Chgo., 1948, Ph.D., 1953; L.H.D., St. Bonaventure U., 1959. Instr. DePaul U., 1949-52; from instr. to assoc. prof. Ohio State U., 1952-64; prof. philosophy U. Ga., Athens, 1964-88, prof. emeritus of religion, 1988-89; vis. prof. U. Tex., Austin, spring, summer, 1967, summer 1968; instr. Inst. Orgn. Mgmt., U.S. C. of C., 1966-88. Contbr. chpts. to books, articles to profl. jours. Mem. selection com. area VIII Woodrow Wilson Found., 1962-63; ednl. cons., tchr. summer insts. leadership tng. AFL-CIO, 1956-64. Served with AUS, 1943-46. Decorated Bronze Star; recipient Good Teaching award Ohio State U., 1955, Andrew Wright award, 1964. Mem. Am. Philos. Assn., Ga. Philos. Assn. (chmn. 1970-71), Am. Cath. Philos. Assn., AAUP (exec. com. U. Ga. 1967-69), Medieval Acad., Metaphys. Soc., Danforth Assos. Roman Catholic. Home: Athens Ga. Died Feb. 17, 1989; buried Oconee Hill Cemetery, Athens, Ga.

NES, WILLIAM ROBERT, biochemist, educator; b. Oxford, Eng., May 16, 1926; s. William Hamilton and Mary Robinson (Lineback) N. (Am. citizens); m. Estelle Jeanne Shirley, May 16, 1946; children: Shirley Anne, William David. B.A., U. Okla., 1946; Ph.D., U. Va., 1950; postgrad., Princeton U., 1954, Cancer Inst. Heidelberg, 1955, U. Wales, Swansea, 1956. Fellow Mayo Found., Rochester, Minn., 1950-51; mem. staff Nat. Inst. Arthritis and Metabolic Diseases, Bethesda, Md., 1951-58; dir. tng. program for steroid biochemistry Worcester Found. for Exptl. Biology, Shrewsbury, Mass., 1958-64; assoc. prof. biochemistry Clark U., 1958-64; prof. chemistry and pharm. chemistry U. Miss., 1964-67; W.L. Obold prof. biol. scis., dir. Inst. Population Studies, Drexel U., Phila., 1967-88; vis. prof. ob-gyn Hahnemann Med. Coll., 1970-87; participating scientist Franklin Inst. Research Labs., 1971-84; cons. to industry; mem. met. biol. panel NSF, 1966-69; mem. steroid drug panel FDA, 1974; mem. physiol. chemistry study sect. NIH, 1979-81, 84-87, ad hoc mem. endocrinology study sect., 1987, chmn. spl. study sect., 1983, mem., 1984; mem. fellowship evaluation panel in biochemistry and biophysics NRC, 1979; mem. research and pubs. com. Norristown State Hosp., 1975-77. Author: Biochemistry of Steroids and Other Isopentenoids, 1977, Lipids in Evolution, 1980; contbr. chpts. to Reproductive Biology, 1972, Advances in Lipid Research, 1977, Methods in Enzymology, 1985, others; contbr. numerous articles to profl. jours. Served to ensign USNR, 1944-46; served to lt. (j.g.) Res. Recipient Research Achievement award Drexel U., 1976, Legion of Merit Chapel of the Four Chaplains, Phila., 1981; grantee Anna Fuller Fund, 1955-56, Danforth Found., 1965-67, NIH, from 1958, Am. Cancer Soc., 1960-70, also various indsl. grants. Mem. Am. Chem. Soc., Am. Soc. Biol. Chemists, AAAS, Endocrine Soc., Phytochem. Soc., Soc. Protozoologists, Am. Pub. Health Assn., Am. Oil Chemists' Soc. Republican. Episcopalian. Home: Rose Valley Pa. Died Mar. 24, 1988; buried St. David's Cemetery, Wayne, Pa.

NESBIT, REED MILLER, surgeon; b. Concord, Calif., Dec. 8, 1898; s. Edward T. and Effie Alice (Miller) N.;

m. Mabel O. Wilkins, Apr. 7, 1928; children: Nancy A., Mary T., Mabel A. Student, U. Calif., 1917-18; AB, Stanford U., 1921, MD, 1925. Intern Fresno County Hosp., 1925; asst. resident in surgery U. Mich. Hosp., 1925-26; instr. surgery Med. Sch., U. Mich., 1926-29, asst. prof., 1929-32, assoc. prof., 1932-43, prof., from 1943; in charge urology sect., specialist in genitourinary surgery Univ. Hosp., from 1930. Author: Fundamentals of Urology, 1942, ed edit., 1948; Transurethral Prostatectomy, 1942; Prostatectomia Transuretra (Mexico City), 1946; Problems in Diagnosis, 1948; Your Prostate Gland, 1951; editor: American Lectures in Urology. Decorated Order Brilliant Star (Republic of China). Fellow ACS (regent); mem. AMA, Washtenaw County Med. Soc., Am. Urol. Assn., Am. Assn. Genito-Urinary Surgeons, Internat. Urol. Soc., Clin. Soc. Genito-Urinary Surgens, Galens Med. Soc., Am. Surg. Soc., Barton Hills Country Club, Ann Arbor Golf and Couting Club, Sigma Xi, Phi Chi, Alpha Omega Alpha. Republican. Episcopalian. *

NESBITT, JAMES COLIN, electric utility executive; b. N.Y.C., Aug. 24, 1923; s. James C. and Hazel A. (Murphy) N.; m. Betty Grace Hanson, July 6, 1946; children: James Colin III, Harry S., Judith Ann Galer. B.S. in Bus. Adminstrn, Boston U., 1947. Student trainee Narragansett Electric Co., 1947-48; acct., treasury supr. New Eng. Power Service Co., 1948-63; asst. treas. New Eng. Electric System and subs. cos., 1963-71, treas., 1971-80, v.p. fin., 1980-88; asst. treas. Yankee Atomic Electric Co., 1965-88 ; dir. Bay Bank Middlesex. Mem. fin. div., exec. com. Edison Electric Inst., 1970-88. Mem. Fin. Execs Inst., Treasurers Club Boston, Wilderness County Club (Naples, Fla.), Braeburn Country Club (Newton, Mass.), Sigma Alpha Epsilon. Home: Naples Fla. Died Oct. 31, 1988; cremated.

NESS, JULIUS B., state supreme court justice; b. Manning, S.C., Feb. 27, 1916; s. Morris P. and Raye L. N.; m. Katherine Rhoad, Jan. 25, 1946; children: Gail Ness Richardson, Richard B. BS, U. S.C., 1938, LLB, 1940, JD, 1970. Bar: S.C. 1940. Sole practice Bamberg, S.C., 1940-58; U.S. senator from S.C., 1957-58; judge S.C. Cir. Ct., 1958-74; assoc. justice S.C. Supreme Ct., 1974-85, chief justice, 1985-88, ret., 1988; with Ness Motley Loadholt Richardson & Poole, Barnwell, S.C., from 1988; instr. Nat. Coll. State Judiciary, 1971. Mem. S.C. Hwy. Commn., 1954-56, chmn., 1956. Served to capt. U.S. Army, 1941-45. Named S.C. Judge of Yr. Assn. Trial Lawyers Am., S.C. Trial Lawyers Assn., 1973, 79. Mem. S.C. Bar, ABA. Democrat. Home: Barnwell S.C. Deceased. †

NETZ, CHARLES VAIL, pharmacy educator; b. Owatonna, Minn., Oct. 13, 1897; s. Richard H.G. and Lelia (Vail) N.; m. Gladys M. Westberg, June 15, 1929. BS, U. Minn., 1922, MS, 1924, PhD in Pharm. Chemistry, 1940. With Coll. Pharmacy, U. Minn., from 1919, prof., from 1946, assoc. dean, 1960; mem. Minn. State Bd. Health, 1947-55; sec. Minn. State Pharm. Assn., 1939-48, pres., 1950-51. Mem. Am. Pharm. Assn., Am. Chem. Soc., Nat. Assn. Retail Druggists, AAUP, Sigma Xi, Phi Lambda Upsilon, Rho Chi. Republican. Lutheran. *

NEUMILLER, LOUIS BONTZ, business executive; b. Peoria, Ill., Jan. 14, 1896; s. Henry J. and Mary (Bontz) H.; m. Selma Engstrom, Apr. 23, 1930; children: Martha (Mrs. Steven Koch), Mary (Mrs. Richard Dill), Anamarie. With Caterpillar Tractor Co., from 1915, succesively clk,, drafting rm. supt., parts mgr., sales mgr., also dir. indsl. rels., v.p., pres., 1941-54, chmn. bd., 1954-62, also bd. dirs.; bd. dirs. C., R.I. & P. Ry. Comml. Nat. Bank, Peoria. Hon. trustee Knox Coll.; v.p. Proctor Community Hosp.; trustee Forest Park Found., Peoria. Mem. Chgo. Club, Union League Club, Country Club of Peoria, Creve Coeur Club of Peoria, Beta Gamma Sigma. *

NEVILLE, HARVEY ALEXANDER, university president; b. Millwood, Va., Feb. 18, 1898; s. Harvey Alexander and Mary Moffat (Drake) N.; m. Ilda Langdon, Dec. 29, 1923; children: Robert Geoffrey, Anthony Edward, Mary Alice (Mrs. Malcolm MacKenzie). AB, Randolph-Macon Coll., 1918, LLD, 1952, LHD, 1962; MA, Princeton U., 1920, Phd, 1921; LLD (hon.), Moravian Coll., 1962, Lafayette Coll., 1962, Phila. Coll. Textiles and Sci., 1965; DSc, Cedar Crest Coll., 1965, Lehigh U., 1965. Asst. in chemistry Princeton U., 1918-21; instr. chemistry U. Ill., 1921-24, assoc. in chemistry, 1924-27; asst. prof. chemistry Lehigh U., 1927-30, assoc. prof., 1930-38, prof. chemistry, head dept. chemistry and chem. engring., 1938-52, also dir. Inst. of Rsch., 1945-60, dean Grad. Sch., 1949-56, v.p., provost, 1956-61, pres., 1961-64, pres. emeritus, from 1964. Fellow Am. Inst. Chemists; mem. AAAS, Am. Chem. Soc., Am. Soc. Engring. Edn., Saucon Valley Country Club, Phi Beta Kappa, Sigma Xi, Alpha Chi Sigma, Phi Kappa Sigma, Tau Beta Pi. Episcopalian. *

NEVILLE, JAMES FRANCIS, lawyer; b. Harrison, N.Y., Sept. 10, 1907; s. Denis and Annie (Hanratty) N.; m. Mary R. Gilroy, Nov. 8, 1935; children: James Francis, Thomas Joseph, Martha Ann, Gerald Denis, Kathleen Ann. A.B., Georgetown U., 1932, J.D., 1938. Bar: D.C. 1938. With Dept. Agr., 1934-37; atty. legal div. FHA, 1938-46; asst. zone commr. FHA, Western U.S., 1947-48; dep. asst. commr. field ops. FHA, 1948-51; zone commr. FHA, Eastern U.S., 1951-54; regional dir. FHA, Southwestern U.S.; then dir. internat. div. FHA; dep. adminstr. Farms Home Adminstrn., Dept. Agr.; now nat. and internat. housing cons.; pres., dir. Indsl. Loan Corp. in, Va.; v.p. realty holding and constrn. corps. in Ohio; mgr. Navy Dept.-owned realty, Midwest, S.W., Western, Pacific areas; dir. Navy Dept. Capehart Housing Projects, 1958-59; dir. rental housing, mortgage fin. Nat. Assn. Home Builders, Washington, 1959-61; operating commr. FHA, Washington, 1961-63; pres. Skyline Plaza Corp.; mng. dir. JTJ Mut. Investments; chmn. Fairfax County Bd. Real Estate Equalization, Va.; dir. various orgns. Co-author: also articles on mortgage financing. The Apartment Plan. Trustee Man-Kan Trust. Recipient Merrick medal Georgetown U., 1932. Mem. D.C. Bar Assn., Gamma Eta Gamma. Club: Fairfax Country (Fairfax, Va.). Home: Falls Church Va. Deceased. †

NEVISON, THOMAS OLIVER, lawyer; b. Rock Creek, Ohio, Apr. 5, 1898; s. Oliver James and Ella (Bowman) N.; m. Agnes Valerie Sofko, Aug. 17, 1926; children: Thomas Oliver, William Richard Edward. Student, Ohio State U., 1918-20, LLB, 1923. Bar: Ohio 1923, Fed. 1925, U.S. Supreme Ct. 1942. Practiced law Cleve., from 1923; chief asst. U.S. atty. No. Dist. Ohio, 1929-30; ptnr. firm Jones, Day, Cockley & Reavis, Cleve., 1936-63, counsel, from 1964. Mem. ABA, Ohio Bar Assn., Cleve Bar Assn., Order of Coif, Delta Theta Phi. *

NEWELL, ALLEN, computer sciences educator; b. San Francisco, Mar. 19, 1927; s. Robert R. and Jeannette (LeValley) N.; m. Noel Marie McKenna, Dec. 20, 1947; 1 son, Paul Allen. BS in Physics, Stanford U., 1949; postgrad. in math., Princeton U., 1949-50; PhD in Indsl. Adminstrn, Carnegie Inst. Tech., 1957. Research scientist RAND Corp., Santa Monica, Cal., 1950-61; Univ. prof. Carnegie-Mellon U., Pitts., 1961-92; U.A. and Helen Whitaker U. Prof. in Computer Sci., 1976-92; cons. Xerox Corp. Author: (with G. Ernst) GPS, A Case Study in Generality, 1969, (with G. Bell) Computer Structures, 1971, (with H.A. Simon) Human Problem Solving, 1972, (with C.G. Bell and J. Grason) Designing Computers and Digital Systems, 1972. Recipient Harry Goode award Am. Fedn. Information Processing Socs., 1971; with H.A. Simon A.M. Turing award Assn. Computing Machinery, 1975. Fellow IEEE, AAAS; mem. Am. Psychol. Assn., Assn. Computing Machinery, Nat. Acad. Sci., Am. Acad. Arts and Sci. Inst. Mgmt. Sci. Home: Pittsburgh Pa. Died July 19, 1992. †

NEWELL, S(TERLING) R(UFFIN), government official; b. Falls Church, Va., Nov. 13, 1898; s. George Morgan and Elizabeth (Coghill) N.; m. Esther Williams, Sept. 8, 1926; children: Elizabeth Ann, Hildreth Adele, Sterling Ruffin. BS, U. Md., 1922; AM, Am. U., 1930; Social Sci. Rsch. Coun. fellow, Harvard U., 1930-31. Chief agrl. tng. 4th Dist., U.S. Vets Bur., 1922-24; county agt. U. Md., 1924-26; with U.S. Dept. Agr. Crop Reporting Bd., 1926-34, Market Rsch. div. Bur. Agrl. Econs., 1934-40; asst. to chief Agrl. Mktg. Svc., 1940-42; asst. dep. dir. Food Distbn. Adminstrn., 1942-44, asst. chief and chief Livestock br., 1944-46; dep. asst. adminstr. for mktg., prodn. adminstrn. U.S. Dept. Agr., 1946-50; asst. chief Bur. Agrl. Econs., also chmn. U.S. Crop Reporting Bd., 1950-53; dir. Agrl. Estimates div., chmn. U.S. Crop Reporting Bd. Agrl. Mktg. Svc., 1953-61; dep. adminstr. Statis. Reporting Svc., chmn. Crop Reprotíng Bd., 1961-62; cons. on agrl. stats. Orgn. European Cooperation and Devel., from 1963. With U.S. Army, World War I, 1918. Recipient Disting. Svc. award U.S. Dept. Agr., 1959. Mem. Am. Farm Econs. Assn., Cosmos Club (Washington). *

NEWMAN, DONALD JOSEPH, criminologist, educator; b. Janesville, Wis., June 4, 1924; s. Kendall Morton and Catherine Agnes (Mahoney) N.; m. Evelyn Shirley Zatlin, Dec. 17, 1949 (div. Mar. 1987); children: Richard Lawrence, Bethany Ann Newman Schroeder, Kendall Joseph; m. Katherine Blueglass Smith, Mar. 1988; 1 stepdaugter, Megan Smith. BS, U. Wis., Madison, 1949, MS, 1952, PhD, 1954. Prof. sociology St. Lawrence U., Canton, N.Y., 1953-60; prof. law and social work U. Wis., Madison, 1960-67; prof. criminal justice SUNY, Albany, 1967-77, 84-90, dean Sch. Criminal Justice, 1977-84; cons. U.S. Dept. Justice, Am. Correctional Assn., Ministry of Justice of Japan, Am. Bar Found. Author: Conviction: The Determination of Guilt or Innocence Without Trial, 1966, Criminal Justice Administration, 1969, 82, Introduction to Criminal Justice, 1975, 78, 86, 89, Elderly Criminals, 1984, Principles of Criminal Justice, 1984. Served with U.S. Army, 1943-46. Recipient Outstanding Contbn. to Criminal Justice Adminstrn. award Am. Soc. Pub. Adminstrn., 1986, Pres.'s award for Acad. Excellence, 1988; research grantee Ford Found., 1965-72, Law Enforcement Assistance Adminstrn., 1974-82, NSF, 1968-72, NIMH, 1975-84. Mem. Am. Soc. Criminology, Acad. Criminal Justice Sci., Soc. for Study of Sociol. Problems, Am. Sociol. Assn. Democrat. Home: Slingerlands N.Y. Died Jan 26, 1990.

NEWMAN, GERALD, restaurant franchise company executive; b. Chgo., May 26, 1931; s. Morris and Sara (Glaser) N.; m. Bobbi F. Greenblatt, Dec. 18, 1955; children: Marc, Jeffrey. Student, Chgo. City Jr. Colls., 1949-51, U. Ill., 1949, Roosevelt U., 1957. Bookkeeper Evans Fur Co., Chgo., 1951; controller Stacy Constrn. Co., Chgo., 1951-59; co-owner, accountant Met. Roofing Co., Chgo., 1959-61; with McDonald's Corp., Oak Brook, Ill., 1961-92; v.p., controller McDonald's Corp., 1969-72, exec. v.p., 1972-80, sr. exec. v.p., 1980-92, also dir.; bd. dirs. Family Foods of Holland; former chmn. bd. Golden Arches of Eng. Adv. bd. dirs. DePaul U. Sch. Acctg.; pres., chief exec. officer Ronald McDonald Children's Charities, 1984; past bd. trustees Spertus Coll. Mem. Am. Inst. Corp. Contrs. Jewish. Home: Highland Park Ill. Died Oct. 10, 1992. †

NEWMAN, JOHN ROBERT, banker; b. Dobbs Ferry, N.Y., Dec. 22, 1932; s. Edwin John and Helen Harvey (McElmeel) N.; m. Mary Doran, Aug. 27, 1960; children: John Robert Jr., James Daniel, Edward Michael, Christopher Cuddy, Maura Jeanne, Craig Doran. Student, Middlebury Coll., 1950-52; BS in Econs., U. S.C., 1954; hon. degree, Rutgers U., 1966. Asst. trust officer First Westchester Nat. Bank, Bronxville, N.Y., 1958-59; trust officer State Nat. Bank of Conn., Greenwich, 1959-64, sr. trust officer, 1964-67; sr. v.p. Merchants Bank & Trust Co., Norwalk, Conn., 1968-73, exec. v.p., 1974-80, pres., 1981-85, chmn. bd., 1985-90; state rep. Conf. State Bank Suprs., Hartford, Conn., 1985. Bd. dirs. Norwalk Hosp. Sgt. USAF, 1954-58. Named Small Bus. Adv. of Yr. 4th Congl. Dist. Washington, 1980, Small Bus. Banker of Yr. U.S. Small Bus. Adminstrn., 1981. Mem. Norwalk C. of C. (bd. dirs. 1984-88), Shorehaven Golf Club (1st v.p. 1987-89, bd. dirs. 1987-90), Pine Valley (N.J.) Golf Club. Republican. Home: Norwalk Conn. Died Aug. 18, 1990; buried St. John's Cemetery, Norwalk, Conn.

NEWMAN, LOUIS BENJAMIN, educator, physician; b. N.Y.C.; s. Morris and Mollie (Banzuly) N.; m. Rose Manilow, Jan. 21, 1951. M.E., Ill. Inst. Tech., 1921; M.D., Rush Med. Coll., 1933. Diplomate Am. Bd. Phys. Med. and Rehab. Intern Cook County Hosp., Chgo., 1932-33; practice of medicine, specializing rehab. medicine Chgo., from 1933; prof. rehab. medicine Northwestern U. Sch. Medicine, from 1946; chief rehab. medicine VA Hosp., Hines, Ill., 1946-53, VA Research Hosp., Chgo., 1953-66; cons. rehab. medicine VA hosps. and several community hosps. Chgo., from 1967; professorial lectr. rehab. medicine Coll. Medicine, U. Ill., Loyola U. Stritch Med. Sch., U. Health Scis.-The Chgo. Med. Sch.; mem. drs. adv. com. Shaare Zedek Hosp. and Med. Center, Jerusalem, Israel; cons. Loyola U. Hosp.; Mem. med. adv. and cons. bd. Armour Research Fedn. of Ill. Inst. Tech. Contbr. articles to med. jours. Health div. com. on handicapped Welfare Council of Met. Chgo.; med. adv. bd. Research Project on Rehab. Met. Chgo., Vis. Nurse Assn., United Parkinson Found., Am. Rehab. Found., Nat. Found., Inc., Am. Assn. Rehab. Therapists, Assn. Phys. and Mental Rehab., Nat. Multiple Sclerosis Soc.; Founding mem. Hebrew U. Jerusalem, from 1970; founding mem. Magen David Adom-Israeli Red Cross, from 1978; mem. Chgo. com Weizmann Inst. Sci., Rehovot, Israel, from 1970; mem. com. Israel Inst. Tech., Technion City, from 1970; v.p. Am. Mus. Phys. Medicine and Rehab., Chgo., from 1982. Served as comdr. M.C. USNR, World War II; head dept. phys. medicine and rehab. Naval Hosps., Oakland, Calif.; head dept. phys. medicine and rehab. Naval Hosps., also Seattle. Recipient B'nai B'rith award in recognition services for rehab. hospitalized vets., 1952; commendation Pres.'s Com. on Employment of Physically Handicapped, 1956; John E. Davis award for outstanding service phys. medicine and rehab. Assn. Phys. and Mental Rehab., 1956; disting. service award Ill. Inst. Tech., 1957; named Civil Servant of Year Fed. Personnel Council Chgo., 1958; meritorious service award VA, 1958; Citation Pub. Service as Useful Citizen U. Chgo., 1959; commendation from adminstr. vets. affairs for success Crusade of Mercy Drive at VA Research Hospital Chgo., 1962; Disting. Service key Am. Congress of Rehab. Medicine, 1963; Nat. Rehab. Citation for outstanding services Am. Legion, 1967; Disting. Achievement award Assn. Med. Rehab. Dirs. and Coordinators, 1967; award for outstanding devotion and achievements in rehab. Ill. and Chgo. Socs. Phys. Medicine and Rehab., 1986; Louis B. Newman Disting. Service award established by Ill. Soc. Phys. Medicine and Rehab., 1980; represented in archives Armed Forces Med. Library, 1956, 80. Fellow Am. Geriatrics Soc.; mem. Am. Congress Rehab. Medicine (v.p.; chmn. midwestern sect. 1948-49), AMA (past chmn. sect. on phys. medicine), Ill. Soc. Phys. Medicine and Rehab. (founding mem., 1st pres., recognition award 1986), Inst. Medicine Chgo. (rehab. com.), Nat. Multiple Sclerosis Soc. (med. adv. bd.), Internat. Soc. Rehab. of Disabled, World Med. Assn., Ill., Chgo. med. socs., Am. Acad. Phys. Medicine and Rehab. (pres.), Chgo. Heart Assn. (rehab. com.), Ill. Assn. Professions (charter mem.), Vis. Nurse Assn. (mem. med. adv. com. from 1967), Am. Assn. Electromyography and Electrodiagnosis, Am. Inst. Ultrasonics in Medicine. Home: Chicago Ill. Deceased. †

NEWMAN, L(OUIS) L(EON), chemical engineer; b. Dec. 16, 1898; m. Lucie Leonie Seyler, 1941. BS, Carnegie Inst. Tech., 1921, ME, 1941. Engaged in gasoline recovery from natural gas H.A. Fisher Co., Wooten-Hughes Co., 1922-24; R&D manufactured gas processes Semet-Solvay Engring. div. Allied Chem. & Dye Corp., 1925-38; asst. prof. fuel tech. Pa. State Coll., 1939-42; chief maintenance and repair sect., facilities div. chems. br. WPB, 1942-43; with Bur. of Mines, from 1943, asst. chief coal technologist, 1955-59, chief coal technologist, from 1959; mem. synthetic liquid fuels mission to Germany, Tech. Indsl. Intelligence Com., 1945; cons. synthetic ammonia prodn. ICA, from 1950; cons. com. on pub. works peat mission to USSR, U.S. Ho. of Reps., 1957; Bur. Mines liaison rep. div. chemistry and chem. tech. NRC-Nat. Acad. Scis., 1959-61. Mem. Am. Gas Assn., Inst. Gas Engrs. (Gt. Britain) Inst. Fuel (Gt. Britain) Chem. Engrs. Club of Washington, Cosmos Club of Washington, Sigma Xi. *

NEWSOM, CARROLL VINCENT, educator, academic administrator; b. Buckley, Ill., Feb. 23, 1904; s. Curtis Bishop and Mattie F. (Fisher) N.; AB, Coll. Emporia, 1924, LHD (hon.), 1957; MA, U. Mich., 1927, PhD, 1931, LLD (hon.), 1974, 23 other hon. degrees; m. Frances J. Higley, Aug. 15, 1928; children: Jeanne Carolyn (Mrs. W.A. Challener, III), Walter Burton, Gerald Higley. Mem. faculties U. Mich., U. N.M., Oberlin Coll., 1927-48; asst. commr. for higher edn. State N.Y. 1948-50, asso. commr. for higher and profl. edn., 1950-55; exec. v.p. NYU, 1955-56, pres., 1956-62; sr. v.p. Prentice-Hall, Inc., Englewood Cliffs, N.J., 1962-64, vice chmn. bd., 1962-65, pres., 1964-65; chmn. bd. Hawthorn Books, 1964-65; chmn. exec. com. Random House, Inc., 1967-70, dir., 1967-70; leader in ednl. TV; ednl. cons. RCA, 1965-66, v.p., 1966-69, dir., 1961-71; edn. cons. instns. in France, Turkey, India, Ethiopia. Mem. and mem. bds. several orgns. in field of edn., math. and internat. affairs; bd. dirs. Nat. Assn. Ednl. Broadcasters; mem., dir. N.Y. World's Fair Corp., 1959-64; bd. dirs. Guggenheim Found., 1962-76, chmn., 1974-76; mem. several other coms. and bds. Decorated chevalier Legion of Honor (France); recipient Pasteur medal. Fellow AAAS (pres. S.W. div. 1940-41, nat. coun. 1945-46); Benjamin Franklin fellow Royal Soc. Arts (London); mem. and officer several nat. profl. assns. and orgns. including Phi Beta Kappa. Author or co-author several books in field math., gen. edn.including: (with Howard Eves) Foundations and Fundamental Concepts of Mathematics, 1958, Mathematical Discourses, 1964, The Roots of Christianity, 1979, Problems are for Solving, 1984; also articles profl. jours. Contbr. yearbook Nat. Soc. for Study of Edn., 1952. Editor: A Television Policy for Education, 1952, Am. Math. Monthly, 1947-51. Died Feb. 3, 1990; buried Gerow Cemetery, nr. Fairfield, Conn. Home: Dublin Ohio

NEWSOM, LIONEL HODGE, university president; b. Wichita Falls, Tex., Nov. 11, 1919; s. Lawson J. and Georgia (McCullough) N.; m. Jane M. Emerson, June 17, 1946; 1 dau., Jacqueline Newsom Peters. AB, Lincoln (Mo.) U., 1938, LHD (hon.), 1975; MA, U. Mich., 1940; PhD, Washington U., St. Louis, 1956; LLD (hon.), Davidson Coll., 1972, Bowling Green State U., 1974, Western Mich. U., 1976, U. Miami, 1975, Wright State U., 1975, Wilberforce U., Ohio, 1984; DHum (hon.), Miami U., Oxford, Ohio, 1979; LHD (hon.), Central State U., Wilberforce, 1984; hon. degree, Barber-Scotia Coll., 1990. Instr. Lincoln U., 1946-47; assoc. prof. sociology Stowe Tchrs. Coll., 1949-51; assoc. prof. So. U., Baton Rouge, 1947-49, prof., 1951-55, head dept. sociology, 1956-60; prof., dir. Woodrow Wilson Scholarship Program Morehouse Coll., 1960-64; pres. Barber-Scotia Coll., Concord, N.C., 1964-66, Disting. prof. sociology, 1986-87; assoc. project dir. So. Regional Edn. Bd., Atlanta, 1966-68; pres. Johnson C. Smith U., Charlotte, N.C., 1969-72; pres. Central State U., Wilberforce, from 1972, pres. emeritus; civilian aide to Sec. of Army, from 1979; Past mem. adv. council Danforth Assocs.; supr. community services St. Louis Housing Authority, 1955-56. Author: The Negro in Higher Education in the South, 1967, also articles. Mem. adv. bd. to com. nat. employment Am. Friends Soc.; chmn. Ga. Council Human Relations, 1963; mem. bd. nat. missions Presbyn. Ch. U.S.A., 1970-73; mem. Nat. Mus. Afro-Am. History and Culture Planning Council, from 1973; trustee Mint Mus., N.C. Leadership Inst., Boggs Acad., Ga., Barber-Scotia Coll.; bd. visitors Davidson Coll. Served with AUS, 1943-46. Recipient Alumni Achievement award Lincoln U., 1965, Alumni citation Washington U., 1973, Presdl. award U. Cin., 1973, Brotherhood award NCCJ, Dayton, Ohio, 1984; United Negro Coll. Fund disting. scholar Barber-Scotia Coll., Concord, N.C., 1985-86. Fellow Am. Sociol. Assn.; mem. AAUP (past pres. So. U. chpt.), Nat. Council Social Studies, Inter-Univ. Council Ohio (chmn. 1975-76), So. Sociol. Assn., Assn. Social Sci. Tchrs., Ohio Coll. Assn. (pres. 1976-77), Charlotte C. of C. (bd. dirs.), Alpha Kappa Delta, Pi Gamma Mu, Alpha Phi Alpha (nat. pres. 1964-69, award of merit 1979), Sigma Pi Phi. Club: Rotarian. Home: Charlotte N.C. Died Jan. 2, 1991; buried Charlotte, N.C.

NEWSTETTER, WILBER IRVIN, social administration educator; b. Massillon, Ohio, Nov. 30, 1896; s. William Marcus and Laura (Vogt) N.; m. Jessie Hinds Hayden, Aug. 25, 1921; children: Wilber Irvin, Jessie (Mrs. K.C. Heald, Jr.), John Hayden. AB, U. Pa., 1919; AM, Western Res. U., 1922. Asst. buying agt. Glidden Co., 1919-20; social worker, dir. Woodland Ctr., Cleve., 1920-26; asst. prof. group work Western Res. U., 1926-30, assoc. prof., 1930-34, prof., 1934-38; dir. Univ. Ctrs., Cleve., 1926-38, Harkness and Wawokiye Camps, 1920-33, Camp Northland, 1934-44; dean Sch. Social Work U. Pitts., 1938-62, prof. social adminstrn., from 1938; vis. prof. U. Toronto, 1945. Author: Wawokiye Camp: A Research Project in Group Work; co-author, editor Group Adjustment: A Study in Experimental Sociology. Bd. dirs., mem. exec. com. Community Chest of Allegheny Country; mem. program com. Nat. Conf. Social Work, 1941, chmn. sect. VI, community orgn. and planning, San Francisco, 1947, mem. exec. com., 1949-51; mem. study com. Nat. Coun. on Social Work Edn., 1948-52, treas., 1952-54; bd. dirs. Health and Welfare Fedn.; mem. Gov.'s Commn. on Penal and Correctional Affairs, Pa. From pvt. to 1st lt., field arty. U.S. Army, with AEF, 1918-19. Recipient Centennial award Mich. State U., 1955. Mem. Am. Assn. Schs. of Social Work (pres. 1938-40, treas. 1941-42), AAUP, Nat. Assn. Social Workers, Phi Gamma Delta. Presbyterian. *

NEWTON, CARL ELBRIDGE, lawyer; b. Aug. 22, 1898; s. Elbridge Ward and Adelaide Louise (Veazie) N.; m. Mary Barrow, June 12, 1926; children: Sallie Barrow Newton Calhoun, William Elbridge, Thomas Vesey. Student, Tufts Coll., 1916-17; BS, Dartmouth Coll., 1920; BA in Jurisprudence, Oxford (Eng.) U., 1922, BCL (Rhodes scholar), 1923, MA (hon.), 1968; postgrad., Harvard U., 1924. Bar: N.Y. 1927. Asst. U.S. atty. So. Dist. N.Y., N.Y.C., 1925-27; barrister Inner Temple, London, 1924-89; spl. asst. atty. gen. N.Y. N.Y.C., 1928; assoc. White & Case, N.Y.C., 1929-33; mem. firm Donovan, Leisure, Newton & Irvine, N.Y.C. and Washington, 1934-42, 46-89; pres. C & O Rlwy., Cleve., also Richmond, Va., 1942-46. Dep. U.S. Coal Mines adminstr., 1943. 2d lt. U.S. Army, 1918-19. Fellow Am. Coll. Trial Lawyers; mem. ABA, SAR, Fed. Bar Coun., Mayflower Descs., Bar Assn. City N.Y., Century Assn., Explorers Club, Church Club, River Club, Masons, Phi Beta Kappa, Zeta Psi. Congregationalist. Home: New York NY Died Oct. 12, 1989.

NEWTON, MAXWELL, financial columnist, consultant; b. Perth, Western Australia, Australia, Apr. 28, 1929; came to U.S., 1980; s. George William and Norah (Christian) N.; m. Anne Kirby Robertson, 1952 (div. 1974); children: Sarah Jane, Anthony James, Penelope Anne; m. Diane Austin, Apr. 28, 1975 (div. June 1979); children: Natasha, Sally, Emma Jane; m. Valerie Olivia Waldron, Nov. 14, 1981. BA in Econs., U. Western Australia, Perth; BA, Cambridge U. Polit. corr. Sydney Morning Herald, Australia, 1957-60; editor Australian Fin. Rev., John Fairfax Ltd., Sydney, 1960-64, The Australian, News Ltd., Sydney, 1964-65; mng. dir. Maxwell Newton Publs., Melbourne, Australia, 1966-79; fin. columnist N.Y. Post, Australian, London Times, Boston Herald, South China Morning Post, Gwinette Daily News, Melbourne Herald, Dublin Sunday Post, from 1980; pres. Max News Fin. Network Boca Raton, Fla., 1983-90. Author: The Fed, 1983; pub. Fed. Fortnightly mag., 1986-90, Maxwell Newton's Daily N.Y. Money Market Report, 1982. Cambridge U. Wrenbury scholar, 1953; recipient Adam Smith prize in Econs.; Clare Coll. hon. scholar, Cambridge U., 1953. Assoc. Lehrman Inst. Died July 23, 1990.

NEWTON, NORMAN THOMAS (KING), landscape architect, educator; b. Corry, Pa., Apr. 21, 1898; s. John Peter and Jessie Bertha (King) N.; m. Lyyli E.E. Lamsa, July 20, 1966. B.S., Cornell U., 1919, Master Landscape Design, 1920; fellow, Am. Acad. in Rome, Italy, 1923-26; A.M. (hon.), Harvard, 1957. Landscape architect with Bryant Fleming, Wyoming, N.Y., 1920-23; with Ferruccio Vitale, N.Y.C., 1926-31; asso. firm Ferruccio Vitale, 1930-31; ind. practice N.Y.C., 1931-42; landscape architect for many parks, residences, instns., historic sites and other land devels.; asso. landscape architect U.S. Nat. Park Service, 1933-39; later cons.; asst. prof. landscape architecture Harvard Grad. Sch. Design, 1939-47, asso. prof., 1947-55, prof., 1955-66, Charles Eliot prof. landscape architecture, 1963-66, Charles Eliot prof. emeritus, from 1966, chmn. dept. archtl. scis., 1949-64, sec. faculty design, 1950-64; cons. Sch. Fine Arts, U. Pa., 1958; resident landscape architect Am. Acad. in Rome, Italy, 1967. Author: Structure of Design, Preliminary Notes, 1949, An Approach to Design, 1951, rev. edit., 1979, Design on the Land, the Development of Landscape Architecture, 1971, King-Rice Notes, 1976, The Forebears of George Oscar King, 1978; Editor: State Park Master Planning Manual, 1937, War Damage to Monuments and Fine Arts of Italy, 1946, Uncle Johnny, a Soldier's Journal, 1974; contbr. to profl. jours.; Lectr., critic in design at ateliers, 1927-38; exhibitions include 1920's measured drawings Gund Gallery, Harvard Grad. Sch. Design, 1988. Bd. dirs. Hubbard Ednl. Trust. Served as aviation cadet USMCR, 1918; served to lt. col. USAAF, 1942-46; sr. monuments officer Brit. 8th Army, through Italian campaign; later, dir. sub-commn. for Monuments, Fine Arts and Archives, Allied Commn. Italy, 330th Air Svc. Group, 1942-43. Awarded Rome prize in landscape architecture, 1923; decorated comdr. Sts. Maurice and Lazarus, grand officer Crown of Italy, 1946; Order Star of Solidarity Italy, 1950; recipient Disting. Mem. award Sigma Lambd Alpha, 1984, Disting. Educator award Hubbard Ednl. Trust, 1991; profiled in Landscape Architecture mag., 1989; subject of videotape biography Hubbard Ednl. Trust, 1976. Fellow Am. Acad. Rome, Am. Soc. Landscape Architects (trustee; treas. 1940-43, 46-57, nat. pres. 1957-61, Bradford Williams medal 1975, ASLA medal 1979); mem. Alumni Assn. Am. Acad. in Rome, Accademia delle Arti del Disegno (Firenze), Theta Delta Chi. Clubs: Century Assn. (N.Y.C.); Faculty (Cambridge). Home: Cambridge Mass. Died Sept. 12, 1992. †

NEWTON, ROBERT PARK, JR., engineering company executive; b. Jackson, Ga., Oct. 25, 1913; s. Robert Park and Bessie (Powell) N.; m. Elizabeth Edwards, Aug. 11, 1936; children: Nancy, Robert Park III, William Aris. B.S. in Chem. Engring, Ga. Inst. Tech., 1935. Asst. chemistry instr. Ga. Inst. Tech., 1936; research chemist Swann & Co., Birmingham, Ala., 1936-39; plant design engr. Naval Stores, Valdosta, Ga., 1940; exec. v.p. Wannamaker Chem. Co., Orangeburg, S.C., 1941-45; pres., treas. Applied Engring Co., Orangeburg, 1946-74, chmn. bd., 1974-79; chmn. bd. Autodynamics Inc., Tampa, Fla., from 1979; dir. 1st Nat. Bank, Orangeburg. Past mem. nat. adv. bd. Ga. Inst. Tech. Mem. Am. Chem. Soc., S.C. C. of C. (dir.), Phi Delta Theta, Tau Beta Pi, Alpha Chi Sigma. Clubs: Orangeburg Country; Wildcat Cliffs Country (Highlands, N.C.). Lodge: Rotary. Home: Orangeburg S.C. Died July 14, 1988; buried Orangeburg, S.C.

NEXON, HUBERT HENRY, lawyer, utility company executive; b. Boston, Mar. 4, 1917; s. Norman D. and Sadie (Sheppy) N.; m. Phyllis L. Goldstein, Aug. 3, 1942; children: David H., Norman D., Janet A. A.B., Harvard U., 1937, LL.B., 1940. Bar: N.Y. 1941, Ill. 1946. Atty. with U.S. Govt., 1941-46; pvt. practice Chgo., 1946-55; gen. counsel Commonwealth Edison Co., Chgo., 1955-82, sr. v.p., 1973-82; pres. Nuclear Electric Ins. Ltd., 1980-87, Nuclear Service Orgn., 1982-87; dir., v.p. Nuclear Mut. Ltd. Mem. Bd. Edn. Northbrook (Ill.) Elem. Schs., 1955-58; dir., v.p. Civic Fedn.; mem. bd. govs. Met. Housing and Planning Coun. Chgo. Served with AUS, 1942-45. Mem. ABA, Chgo. Bar Assn. Home: Glencoe Ill. Died Apr. 30, 1990.

NEYER, JOSEPH, educator, writer, lecturer; b. New Rochelle, N.Y., Mar. 8, 1913; s. Louis and Tillie (Berzon) N.; m. Friderika Ginsberg, July 26, 1966. A.B. magna cum laude, Harvard U., 1934, A.M., 1935, Ph.D., 1942; student, U. Paris, 1936-37. Asst. philosophy Harvard U., 1937-38, 39-40; research asst. anthropology U. Chgo., 1938-39; instr. philosophy Vassar Coll., 1940-42; Rockefeller fellow, 1946-47; mem. faculty Rutgers U., New Brunswick, N.J., 1947-89, prof. philosophy, 1963-75, prof. emeritus, 1975-89, chmn. dept., 1953-65. Author articles in social and polit. philosophy, sociology, psychoanalysis, recent Middle East history.; mem. editorial bd.: Middle East Review; adv. bd.: Jerusalem Quar. Served with AUS, 1942-46. Mem. Am. Profs. for Peace in Middle East (mem. nat. steering com.), Am. Acad. Assn. Peace in Middle East (vice-chmn. bd. dirs.), Am. Sociol. Assn., Am. Philos. Soc., Phi Beta Kappa. Home: New York N.Y. Died Sept. 14, 1989.

NICHOL, FRANCIS DAVID, editor; b. Thirlmere, New South Wales, Australia, Feb. 14, 1897; came to U.S., 1950; s. John and Mary (Fearon) N.; m. Rose Elizabeth Macklin, Aug. 11, 1919; 1 child, Virginia Marie. Student, San Fernando Acad., 1910-14, Isaacs Woodbury Bus. Coll., 1916; ThB, Pacific Union Coll., Angwin, Calif., 1920; DD, Andrews U., Berrien Springs, Mich., 1958. Assoc. editor Signs of the Times, Calif., 1921-27, Rev. and Herald, Washington, 1928-45; editor Life and Health, Nat. Health Jour., Washington, 1934-45, Rev. and Herald, from 1945; dir. Rev. and Herald Pub. Assn. Author: Creation--Not Evolution, 1926; Answers to Objections, 1932; God's Challenge to Modern Apostasy, 1935; the Answer to Modern Religious Thinking, 1936; Behold He Cometh, 1937; The Case Against Liquor, 1944; The Midnight Cry, 1944; Reasons for Our Faith, 1947; Let's Live Our Beliefs, 1947; Letters From Far Lands, 1948; Ellen G. White and her Critics, 1950; Questions People Have Asked Me, 1959; contbr. to Ency. Brit., Sci. Am., Religion in Life, others; gen. editor Bible Commentary, 1952-57. Mem. Am. Hist. Soc., AMA (com. on medicine and religion), Acad. Polit. Sci., Am. Soc. Ch. History, Acad. Religion and Mental Health. Seventh-day Adventist. *

NICHOLS, BRUCE W., lawyer; b. N.Y.C., Jan. 3, 1930; s. Frederick Willis and Marjorie B. (Lyon) N. A.B., Princeton U., 1951; LL.B., Harvard U., 1954. Bar: N.Y. 1954. Assoc. firm Davis Polk & Wardwell, N.Y.C., 1954-61, partner, 1961-89, sr. counsel, 1989-90. Mem. ABA, Assn. of Bar of City of N.Y., N.Y. State Bar Assn., N.Y. Law Inst. (chmn. exec. com. 1973-83, pres. 1983-88). Republican. Episcopalian. Clubs: Princeton of N.Y, Down Town Assn. Home: New York N.Y. Died May 17, 1990; buried Flushing (N.Y.) Cemetery.

NICHOLS, NATHAN LANKFORD, physics educator; b. Jackson, Mich., Nov. 16, 1917; s. Herbert N.T. and Louise C. McConnel N.; m. Donna Jean Martin, Apr. 5, 1941; children: Gordon Martin, Nancy Louise Elsner, Barbara Elizabeth Brundage, Cameron Bruce, Brian Mark. AB, Western Mich. U., 1939; MS, U. Mich., 1945; PhD, Mich. State U., 1953. Tchr. high sch. sci. Barnard, S.D., 1939-4, Milford, Mich., 1940-43; instr.

physics Ill. Coll., Jacksonville, 1943-44, U. Mich., Ann Arbor, 1944-45; prof., head dept. physics Alma Mich. Coll., 1949-55; prof. physics Western Mich. U., Kalamazoo, 1955-91. Mem. Am. Assn. Physics Tchrs., Optical Soc. Am., Kalamazoo Optimists pres. 1970-71 . Home: Kalamazoo Mich. Died June 17, 1991.

NICHOLS, PHILIP, JR., federal judge; b. Boston, Aug. 11, 1907; s. Philip and Mabel (Gibson) N.; m. Dorothy Jackson, Apr. 19, 1940; children: Donald, Patricia, Christopher. A.B., Harvard U., 1929, LL.B., 1932. Bar: Mass. 1932, D.C. 1954. Pvt. practice Boston, 1932-38; atty. lands div. Dept. Justice, Washington, 1938-41, Office of Gen. Counsel, WPB, 1942-43; counsel Navy Price Adjustment. Bd., 1945-46; gen. counsel War Contracts Price Adjustment. Bd., 1946; chief counsel Bur. Fed. Supply, Treasury Dept., 1946-48; asst. gen. counsel U.S. Treasury Dept., 1948-51, commr. customs, 1961-64; gen. counsel Renegotiation Bd., 1951-54; pvt. practice, 1954-61; judge U.S. Customs Ct., 1964-66, U.S. Ct. Claims, 1966-82; judge U.S. Ct. Appeals (fed. cir.), 1982-83, sr. judge, 1983-90. Served from lt. (j.g.) to lt. comdr. USNR, 1943-46. Mem. Fed., Am. bar assns. Home: Washington D.C. Died Jan. 26, 1990; cremated.

NICHOLS, ROY FRANKLIN, dean, history educator; b. Newark, Mar. 3, 1896; s. Franklin C. and Anna (Cairns) N.; m. Jeannette Paddock, 1920. AB, Rutgers U., 1918, AM, 1919; fellow, Columbia U., 1920-21, PhD, 1923; LittD (hon.), Franklin and Marshall Coll., 1937, Muhlenberg Coll., 1956; LHD (hon.), Rutgers U., 1941, PdD, 1964; MA, Cambridge U., Eng., 1948; fellow, Trinity Coll., Cambridge U., 1948-49; LLD (hon.), Moravian Coll., 1953, Lincoln U., 1959, Knox Coll., 1960; DSc (hon.), Lebanon Valley, 1961. Instr. history Columbia U., 1922-25; asst. prof. history U. Pa., 1925-30, prof., from 1930, dean Grad. Sch. Arts and Scis., from 1952, vice provost, from 1953; vis. prof. Columbia U., 1944-45, Stanford U., 1952; vis. prof. Am. history Cambridge U., 1948-49; Fulbright lectr., India and Japan, 1962. Author: The Democratic Machine (1850-54), 1923; (with others) Syllabus for History of Civilization, 1927; (with C.A. Beard and W.C. Bagley) America Yesterday and Today, 1938; (with Jeannette P. Nichols) Growth of American Democracy, 1939, The Republic of the United States: A History, 1942, A Short Story of American Democracy, 1943; Franklin Pierce, 1931; Disruption of the American Democracy, 1948; Advance Agents of American Democracy, 1959; Stakes of Power, 1845-1877, 1961, others. Trustee Rutgers U., from 1950, bd. govs., from 1958; chmn. Social Sci. Rsch. Coun. Recipient Pulitzer prize in history, 1949; Haney medal, Atheneum award, 1962. Mem. Am. Acad. Polit. and Social Sci. (dir.), Soc. Am. Studies, Presbyn. Hist. Soc. (dir.), Libr. Co. Phila. (dir.), Athenaeum Phila. (dir.), Am. Philos. Soc. (v.p. 1962), Am. Hist. Assn. (coun. 1943-47), Middle States Assn. Hi8story Tchrs. (pres. 1932-33), Pa. Hist. Assn. (pres. 1936-39), Pa. Fedn. Hist. Socs. (pres. 1940-42), Pa. Hist. Commn., Hist. Soc. Pa. (v.p.), Soc. Am. Historians, Gen. Soc. Am. (pres. 1946-57), AAUP, Am. Assn. State/Local History, The Rittenhouse Club, Franklin Inn, Lenape (Phila.), Cosmos (Washington), Authors Club (London), Century Club (N.Y.C.), Phi Beta Kappa (senator), Pi Gamma Mu. Baptist. *

NICHOLS, SHUFORD REINHARDT, corporation executive; b. Des Arc, Ark., Jan. 26, 1909; s. Henry and Grace (Reinhardt) N.; m. Laura Campbell, June 18, 1935; children: Henry Lee, Anne Robinson, Laura Patricia. B.A., Washington and Lee U., 1930; postgrad., Harvard U., 1931. Pres. So. Compress Co., North Little Rock, Ark., 1930-87; chmn. bd. Farmer & Mchts. Bank., from 1965; dir. Aberdeen Devel. Corp. Pres. bd. trustees Ark. Coll., 1966-76, trustee, from 1956; pres. Presbyterian Found. Ark./Okla., Inc., 1983-85. Recipient Ark. Coll. medal, 1984, 87. Mem. Sigma Nu, Omicron Delta Kappa. Presbyterian. Clubs: Little Rock, Little Rock Country, XV of Little Rock, Balboa Club de Mazatlan, Confrerié des Chevaliers du Tastevin. Home: Little Rock Ark. Died Mar. 27, 1989; buried Mt. Holly Cemetery, Little Rock, Ark.

NICHOLSON, DWIGHT ROY, physicist, educator; b. Racine, Wis., Oct. 3, 1947; s. Forrest Arlyn and Johanna Jacoba (Bergsma) N.; m. Jane Alice Mechling, June 14, 1969. B.S., U. Wis., 1969; Ph.D., U. Calif.-Berkeley, 1975. Research assoc. and lectr. U. Colo., Boulder, 1975-78, asst. prof., 1978; asst. prof. dept. physics and astronomy U. Iowa, Iowa City, 1978-81, assoc. prof. 1981-85, prof., 1986-91, chmn. dept., 1985-91. cons. Los Alamos Nat. Lab., 1977-91 , Sci. Applications, Inc., Boulder, 1976-78. Author: Introduction to Plasma Theory, 1983; author tech. articles. Johnson's Wax scholar, 1965-67; NSF trainee, 1969-72; univ. faculty scholar U. Iowa, 1983-85. Mem. Am. Phys. Soc., AAAS, Union Radio Scientifique Internationale, Am. Geophys. Union. Died Nov. 1, 1991. Home: Tulsa Okla. †

NICHOLSON, THOMAS DOMINIC, astronomer, museum director; b. N.Y.C., Dec. 14, 1922; s. Dominic J. and Catherine (Brown) N.; m. Branca Costa, Dec. 26, 1946; children—Lester C., Diana C., Glen C., Gail C. BS, U.S. Mcht. Marine Acad.; BA, St. John's U., 1950; MS, Fordham U., 1953, PhD, 1962; ScD (hon.), Lawrence U., 1988. Marine deck officer Moore-McCormack Lines, 1941-46; from instr. to asst. prof. nautical sci. and asst. to dept. head U.S. Mcht. Marine Acad., 1946-53; lectr., instr. dept. astronomy Hayden Planetarium, Am. Mus. Natural History, N.Y.C., 1952-53, assoc. astronomer, 1953-57, astronomer, 1957-67, chmn., 1964-67, mus. asst. dir., 1967-68, dep. dir., 1968-69, dir., 1969-89; TV weather forecaster sta. WNBC, N.Y.C., 1967-72; lectr. in astronomy U.S. Mil. Acad., Yale U., NNYU; mem. geodetic surveying expdns., Arctic, 1956, Greenland Ice Cap, 1958; mem. adv. council Astrophys. Obs., Princeton U.; mem. evaluation and testing team for hand held space sextant for Gemini XII, NASA, 1965, 66; mem. nat. adv. bd. Monell Chem. Senses Center. Author: (with J. M. Chamberlain) Planets, Stars and Space, 1957, Adventure with Stars, 1958, also numerous articles; Editor: Curator; Contbg. editor: Christian Sci. Monitor, Natural History Mag. Served with U.S. Merchant Marine, 1941-46; lt. (j.g.) USNR. Recipient Medal of Honor St. John's U., 1959, Emmy award for TV program Solar Eclipse: Darkness at Noon, 1970. Fellow AAAS, Royal Astron. Soc., Am. Astron. Assn.; mem. Inst. Nav. (past pres.), Astron. Soc. Pacific, Am. Meteorol. Soc., Am. Assn. Museums (v.p.), Assn. Systematics Collections (pres.), Assn. Nat. Scis. Instns. (founder). Home: Woodcliff Lake N.J. Died July 9, 1991; cremated.

NIEDERLEHNER, LEONARD, lawyer; b. Cin., Oct. 12, 1914; s. Louis William and Agnes (Clark) N.; m. Helen Virginia Warfield, July 2, 1948; children: James, Barbara, John. LL.B., U. Cin., 1937. Bar: Ohio bar 1937, Supreme Ct. bar 1958, D.C. bar 1967. Practice law Cin., 1937-40; sec. to congressman, 1938; with Office Gen. Counsel, FSA, 1941; counsel bur. yards and docks Navy Dept., 1946-47; munitions bd. Office Sec. Def., 1948-52, asst. gen. counsel, 1952-53; dep. gen. counsel Dept. Def., Washington, 1953-91. Served to lt. comdr. USNR, 1942-46. Recipient Dept. Def. Disting. Civilian Service medal, 1961, medal with palm, 1969, medal with double palm, 1973, medal with triple palm, 1987; Rockefeller Pub. Service award, 1961; Nat. Civil Service League Service award, 1965; Pres. medal for Disting. Fed. Civilian Service, 1979; Presdl. rank of Meritorious Exec., 1980, 85; Disting. Public Service medal Dept. Def., 1981; Silver Beaver award Boy Scouts Am., 1967. Mem. Inter-Am., Fed. bar assns., Order of Coif. Methodist. Home: Arlington Va. Died Dec. 10, 1991. †

NIELSEN, JENS RUD, physicist, educator; b. Copenhagen, Denmark, Sept. 22, 1894; came to U.S., 1922, naturalized, 1930; s. Niels F. and Marie (Johansen) N.; m. Gertrude Siegmund, Oct. 19, 1923; children: John Rud, Thomas Rud (dec.), Mary Ruth (Mrs. Lejeune Wilson). Magister scientiarum, U. Copenhagen, 1919; PhD, Calif. Inst. Tech., 1924. Instr. Royal Tech. Coll., Copenhagen, 1919-22; prof. physics Humbold State Coll., Arcata, Calif., 1923-24; asst. prof. U. Okla., 1924-26, assoc. prof., 1926-30, prof., 1930-44, rsch. prof. physics, bd. dirs., from 1944; cons. Phillips Petroleum Co., 1945-63. Assoc. editor Am. Jour. Physics, 1940-43, Jour. Chem. Physics, 1950-53; contbr. articles to profl. jours. Am.-Scandinavian Found. fellow, 1922-23, Guggenheim fellow, 1931-32, Rask-Oersted fellow, 1932-33. Fellow AAAS, Am. Phys. Soc., Optical Soc. Am. (assoc. editor jour. 1950-61); mem. Am. Assn. Physics Tchrs., AAUP (coun. 1948-50), Phi Beta Kappa, Sigma Xi. *

NIELSEN, LAWRENCE ERNIE, physicist; b. Pilot Rock, Oreg., Dec. 17, 1917; s. Hans Christian and Mable Esther (Galbreath) N.; m. Deanne May Boss, June 27, 1942; 1 dau., Linda Carolyn Nielsen Hickel. A.B., Pacific U., Forest Grove, Oreg., 1940; M.S., Wash. State U., 1942; Ph.D., Cornell U., 1945. Physicist Monsanto Co., Springfield, Mass., 1945-63; distinguished sci. fellow Monsanto Co., St. Louis, 1963-77; plastics cons. Redmond, Oreg., 1977-92; affiliate prof. Washington U., St. Louis, 1965-76. Author: Mechanical Properties of Polymers, 1962, Mechanical Properties of Polymers and Composites, 1974, Polymer Rheology, 1977, Predicting Properties of Mixtures, 1978, Pioneer Roads in Central Oregon, 1985, In the Ruts of the Wagon Wheels, 1987. Roads of Yesterday in Northeastern Oregon, 1990; also articles. Recipient internat. research award Soc. Plastics Engrs., 1981. Fellow Am. Phys. Soc.; mem. Am. Chem. Soc., Soc. Rheology (Bingham medal 1976), Am. Alpine Club. Home: Redmond Oreg. Died Feb. 15, 1992. †

NIELSEN, OTTO R., consultant, psychologist, educator; b. Omaha, Dec. 24, 1905; s. Peder and Marthina (Christiansen) N.; m. Martha Jane Butts, June 17, 1935; children: Elizabeth Carol, Patricia Jean, David Howard. AB, Tex. Christian U., 1933, BD, 1937, AM, 1940; postgrad., U. Chgo., 1933, U. Minn., 1939; PhD, U. Tex., 1942. Asst. prof. psychology Tex. Christian U., 1938-40, dean men, 1933-40, dir. pers., 1936-40, exec. v.p., 1950-52, dean Sch. Edn., dir. tchr. edn., 1952-63; dean, prof. psychology and pers. adminstrn. Tex. Coll. Arts and Industries, Kingsville, 1942-50; chief div. human resources devel. AID, Latin Am., 1963-67; prof. psychology U. Americas, Puebla, Mexico, 1967-77, exec. v.p., 1967-74; dir. rsch. Hogg Fund, 1940-42; instr. ednl. psychology, asst. to dean Coll. Arts and Scis., U. Tex., 1940-42; prof. vocat. guidance East Tex. State Tchrs. Coll., summer 1942; vis. assoc. prof. U. Chgo., summers 1947-48; cons. in field. Fellow APA; mem. NEA, Tex. Pers. Assn. (past dir.), Corpus Christi Pers. Assn. (past exec. com.), Tex. Soc. Mental Hygiene (past dir.), So. Conf. Acad. Deans (past pres.), Am. Assn. Higher Edn., So. Assn. Colls. and Secondary Schs., Tex. Assn. Coords. Vets. Coll. Edn. (past exec. com.), Am. Coll. Pers. Assn., Assn. Tex. Colls., Tex. Tchrs. Assn., Rotary (past bd. dirs.), Phi Delta Kappa. Mem. Christian Ch. Home: Dallas Tex. Died June 3, 1991; buried Greenwood Meml. Pk., Ft. Worth.

NIGHTINGALE, EARL CLIFFORD, radio commentator, writer; b. Los Angeles, Mar. 12, 1921; s. Albert Victor and Gladys Fae (Hamer) N.; m. Mary Peterson, July 21, 1942 (div. 1960); children: David Alan, Pamela; m. Lenarda Certa, May 17, 1962 (div. 1976); 1 son, Earl Clifford.; m. Diana Lee Johnson, May 15, 1982. Writer, announcer Sta. KTAR, Phoenix, 1946-49, CBS, Sta. WBBM, Chgo., 1949-50; founder, owner Earl Nightingale, Inc., Chgo., 1950, chmn. bd., 1950-59; writer, producer own radio program Sta. WGN, Chgo., 1950-56; (merged with Lloyd Conant and Splty. Mail Services), Chgo., 1959; forming Nightingale-Conant Corp., Chgo., 1959, chmn. bd., 1959-87, chmn. emeritus, 1987-89. Writer, narrator daily radio program "Our Changing World", broadcast world-wide, also on TV early 1970's; voice of Sky King, hero of adventure series, 1950-54; radio show host Sta. WGN, 1950-56; author: (personal motivational record) The Strangest Secret (Gold record), 1959, This is Earl Nightingale, 1969, (books) Earl Nightingale's Greatest Discovery: The Strangest Secret Revisited, 1987, The Winner's Notebook, 1987. Active various civic and cultural affairs; Hon. trustee Broward Community Coll., 1974-75. Served with USMC, 1938-46. Inducted into Radio Hall of Fame, 1986, Internat. Speakers Hall of Fame; recipient Gold medal for lit. excellence Napoleon Hill Found., 1987. Home: Paradise Valley Ariz. Died Mar. 25, 1989; cremated.

NIGRELLI, ROSS FRANCO, marine biologist, science director; b. Pittston, Pa., 1903; s. Castrenza and Emanuela (Franco) N.; m. Margaret Carrozza, 1927; 1 dau., Emanuela Dobrin. BS, Pa. State U., 1927; MS, NYU, 1929, PhD, 1936, postdoctoral, 1958-74. Teaching fellow biology NYU, 1927-31; resident fellow N.Y. Zool. Soc., 1931-32, 70-85; pathologist N.Y. Aquarium, N.Y. Zool. Soc., from 1934, dir. Lab. Marine Biochemistry and Ecology, 1958-63, founder, dir. Osborn Labs. of Marine Scis., 1964-73, sr. scientist, 1973-89; dir. N.Y. Aquarium, 1966-70; instr. biology Coll. CCNY, 1936-42; vis. instr. biology NYU, 1943-45, vis. asst. prof., 1945-49, adj. asso. prof., 1949-58; adj. prof. Grad. Sch. Arts and Scis., 1958-80. Author several books on diseases of fish, also numerous articles; editorial bd. Revue Internationale d'Oceanographie Medicale, Nice, France, 1967, Current Topics in Comparative Pathobiology, from 1970. Cons. U.S. Fish and Wildlife Service, 1943-48; sci. cons. Bingham Oceanographic Lab., Yale U., 1943-60; cons. U.S. Pure Food and Drug Adminstrn., 1945-85, USN Applied Sci. Lab., 1966-70; mem. tech. adv. com. Atlantic States Fisheries Commn., 1946-56; com. animals from nature Inst. Animal Resources, Nat. Acad. Sci., 1954-74; mem. panel experts fisheries div. FAO; mem. subpanel on marine biology Panel Oceanographic Pres.'s Sci. Adv. Commn., 1965-66; adv. panel for sea grant NOAA, Dept. Commerce, 1971-85; mem. Internat. Union Dirs. Zool. Gardens, 1968-70, N.Y.C. Mayor's Oceanographic Adv. Com., 1969-73; adv. council Regional Med. Library program N.Y. Acad. Medicine, 1967; adv. com. Soc. for Zool. Edn., from 1968; extramural reviewer EPA, from 1972. Recipient Order Merit, Soc. d'Encouragement pour la Recherche et l'Invention. Hon. fellow N.Y. Zool. Soc., N.Y. Acad. Scis. (life mem., chmn., sec. biology 1946-47, councillor 1948-51, 70-73, rec. sec. 1954, v.p. 1955, pres. 1957, trustee 1959, bd. govs. 1971-73), A.A.A.S. (mem. council 1951-52, 56); fellow Conservation Found., Am. Acad. Microbiology (emeritus), Royal Soc. Tropical Medicine and Hygiene, Consular Law Soc.; mem. Am. Soc. Parasitologists (emeritus), Internat. Acad. Pathology (emeritus), Am. Micros. Soc. (hon. mem.; emeritus), Am. Soc. Zoologists (emeritus), Am. Assn. Pathologists and Bacteriologists (emeritus), Am. Soc. Tropical Medicine and Hygiene (emeritus), N.Y. Inst. Ocean Resources (treas.; gov. 1970-73), Hudson River Environ. Soc. (dir. 1970-71), Soc. Exptl. Biology and Medicine (hon. mem.), Am. Assn. Anatomists (emeritus), Harvey Soc. (hon.), Bermuda Biol. Sta., Inc., Soc. Protozoologists (hon. mem., pres. 1947-49, exec. com. 1952-53), Wildlife Disease Assn., Soc. Am. Microbiologists (emeritus), Am. Assn. Cancer Research (emeritus), Soc. Systematic Zoologists, Atlantic Fishery Biologists, Am. Soc. Ichthyology and Herpetology, Internat. Soc. Toxicology (founding mem.), Royal Soc. Medicine, Soc. for Preservation Old Fishes (charter), Soc. Invertebrate Pathology, Internat. Platform Assn., Sigma Xi. Club: Explorers. Home: East Quogue N.Y. Died Oct. 4, 1989.

NISKA, MARALIN, soprano; b. San Pedro, Calif.; d. William Albert and Vera Zoe (Stott) Dice; m. William Mullen, May, 1970; stepchildren: Robert, Stuart. B.A. in Edn, Long Beach U.; M.A. in English Lit, UCLA. Leading roles in maj. opera house include: Traviata, Manon Lescaut, Madame Butterfly, Tosca, Medea, Salome; appeared in opera houses, including, Met. Opera House, N.Y.C. Opera, San Francisco Opera, Lyric Opera Chgo., Boston Opera, Houston Opera, San

Diego Opera, Ft. Worth Opera; appeared in: 1st live telecast of La Boheme, Met. Opera, 1977; created role of Emilia Marty in: 1st live telecast of The Makropoulos Affair, N.Y.C. Opera, 1970; appeared as Minnie in: radio broadcast of Fanciulla del West, N.Y. State Theatre. Named Woman of Yr. Los Angeles Times, 1967. Mem. Am. Guild Mus. Artists (bd. govs.), Young Audiences (exec. bd.). Home: New York N.Y. Deceased. †

NIXON, ELLIOTT BODLEY, lawyer; b. Balt., Aug. 21, 1921. AB, Princeton U., 1942; JD, Harvard U., 1948. Bar: N.Y. 1949, U.S. Supreme Ct. 1957. Ptnr. Burlingham Underwood & Lord and predecessor firms, N.Y.C., 1956-88, of counsel, 1989-92. Contbr. articles to encyclopaedias and profl. jours. Mem. ABA, Assn. of Bar of City of N.Y., Internat. Bar Assn., Maritime Law Assn. U.S. (editor Am. Maritime Cases 1969-92). Home: New York N.Y. Died Nov. 3, 1992. †

NIXON, LOUISE ALDRICH, librarian; b. Paradise, Kans., July 27, 1897; d. John William and Eva (Aldrich) Nixon. BA, U. Kans., 1919; MA, U. Minn., 1924, U. Denver Sch. Librarianship, 1951. Tchr. Mankato, Minn., 1919-22; teaching fellow dept. history U. Minn., 1922-24; asst. dir. Nebr. Legis. Reference Bur., 1931-39; libr. Nebr. Legis. Coun., 1939-49; exec. sec. Nebr. Pub. Libr. Commn., Lincoln, from 1950. Compiler: Nebraska Blue Book, 1932-48. Mem. ALA, Am. Assn. State Librarians, Am. Fedn. Art, Missouri Valley Adult Edn., Nebr. Art Assn., Nebr. Libr. Assn., Mountain Plains Libr. Assn., Adult Edn. Assn. U.S., LWV, Mortar Board, University Club. *

NOETHER, GOTTFRIED EMANUEL, statistics educator; b. Karlsruhe, Germany, Jan. 7, 1915; s. Fritz and Regina (Wuerth) N.; m. Emiliana Pasca, Aug. 1, 1942; 1 dau., Monica Gail. B.A., Ohio State U., 1940; M.A., U. Ill., 1941; Ph.D., Columbia U., 1949. Instr. N.Y.U., 1949-51; faculty Boston U., 1951-68, prof., 1958-68; prof. stats. U. Conn., Storrs, 1968-85, head dept., 1968-82; mem. statis. adv. com. Fed. Office Mgmt. and Budget, 1973-76; Fulbright lectr., Germany, 1957-58, Austria, 1965-66. Author: Elements of Nonparametric Statistics, 1967, Introduction to Statistics-The Nonparametric Way, 1990; editor The American Statistician, 1976-80; contbr. rsch. articles to profl. jours. Served to 1st lt. AUS, 1941-45. Fellow Am. Statis. Assn. (dir. 1971-73), Inst. Math. Statistics; mem. Internat. Statis. Inst., Math. Assn. Am., Sigma Xi, Pi Mu Epsilon. Home: Storrs Conn. Died Aug. 22, 1991; cremated.

NOLAN, JOSEPH P., government official; b. Covington, Ky., Mar. 16, 1897; s. Joseph Aloysius and Julia (Harrington) N.; m. Marguerite Ruth Haley, June 13, 1923; children: Patricia (Mrs. Lester Gottlieb), Pauline (Mrs. William P. Kelly), Marguerite (Mrs. Joseph M. Flannery), Joseph P., James A., John J. With Post Office Dept., from 1919; insp. in charge Post Office Dept., Cleve., 1944-45, Cin., 1943-60; regional dir. Post Office Dept., Cin. region, from 1961. Pres. Covington Latin Sch. PTA, 1958-59. With U.S. Army, 1918-19. Mem. Fed. Bus. Assn. *

NOLAN, THOMAS BRENNAN, research geologist; b. Greenfield, Mass., May 21, 1901; s. Frank Wesley and Anna (Brennan) N.; m. Mabelle Orleman, Dec. 3, 1927; 1 son, Thomas Brennan. Ph.B. in Metallurgy, Yale U., 1921, Ph.D. in Geology, 1924; LL.D. (hon.), U. St. Andrews, 1962. Geologist U.S. Geol. Survey, 1924-44, asst. dir., 1944-56, dir., 1956-65, research geologist, from 1965. Contbr. numerous articles, reports, bulls. to profl. and govtl. jours. Recipient Spendiaroff prize Internat. Geol. Congress, 1933; K. C. Li prize and medal Columbia, 1954; Rockefeller Pub. Service award Princeton, 1961; Silver medal Tokyo Geog. Soc., 1965; Wilbur Cross medal Yale U., 1987. Fellow Geol. Soc. Am. (pres. 1961), Soc. Econ. Geologists (pres. 1950), Am. Geophys. Union, Mineral. Soc. Am., Royal Soc. Edinburgh (hon.); mem. Nat. Acad. Scis., Geol. Soc. Washington, Am. Philos. Soc., Tokyo Geog. Soc. (hon. mem.), Internat. Union Geol. Scis., Am. Acad. Arts and Scis., Geol. Soc. London (fgn. mem.), Am. Ornithologists Union, Sigma Xi. Clubs: Cosmos (Washington); Yale. Home: Washington D.C. Died Aug. 2, 1992. †

NOLAND, JAMES ELLSWORTH, federal judge; b. LaGrange, Mo., Apr. 22, 1920; s. Otto Arthur and Elzena (Ellsworth) N.; m. Helen Warvel, Feb. 4, 1948; children: Kathleen Kimberly, James Ellsworth, Christopher Warvel. A.B., Ind. U., 1942, LL.B., 1948; M.B.A., Harvard U., 1943. Bar: Ind. 1948. Since practiced in Bloomington; partner law firm of Hilgedag and Noland, Indpls., 1955-66, 1st asst. city atty., 1956-57; dep. atty. gen. Ind., 1952; spl. asst. U.S. atty. gen., 1953; appointed Ind. State Election Commr., 1954; U.S. judge So. Dist. Ind., 1966-92, chief judge, 1984-86; Mem. com. on magistrates system Jud. Conf. U.S., 1973-81; mem. 81st (1949-51) Congress, 7th Ind., Dist.; sec. Ind. Democratic Com., 1960-66; chmn. bd. visitors Ind. Law Sch., Indpls., 1974-76; mem. com. Bicentennial of U.S. Constn., 1987-92. Served as capt., Transp. Corps. AUS, 1943-46. Mem. ABA (chmn. jud. adminstrn. div. 1984-85), Ind. Bar Assn., Ind. Assn. Trial Lawyers (pres. 1956), Nat. Conf. Fed. Trial Judges (chmn. 1981-82), Fed. Judges Assn. (bd. dirs. 1988-91), Phi Delta Phi, Phi Kappa Psi. Mem. Moravian Ch. Home: Indianapolis Ind. Died Aug. 12, 1992. †

NOLTING, FREDERICK ERNEST, JR., diplomat; b. Richmond, Va., Aug. 24, 1911; s. Frederick Ernest and Mary (Buford) N.; m. Olivia Lindsay Crumpler, Sept. 7, 1940; children: Mary Buford Nolting Bruner, Grace Lindsay, Frances Talbott Nolting Temple, Jane Underwood. BA, U. Va., 1933, MA, 1940, PhD, 1942; MA, Harvard U., 1941. Mem. investment firm, Richmond, 1934-39; country specialist, then asst. chief No. European affairs U.S. Dept. State, Washington, 1946-48, charge Swiss-Benelux affairs, coord. Far East aid programs, 1949-50, asst. to dep. under sec. state, 1950-53, spl. asst. to sec. state for mut. security affairs, 1935-55; dir. Office Polit. Affairs with personal rank min. U.S. del. to NATO, Paris, 1955-57; dep. chief mission USRO, alt. U.S. permanent rep. North Atlantic Coun., 1957-61; U.S. amb. to Vietnam, Saigon, 1961-63; mem. spl. intelligence survey U.S. Govt., 1963-64; diplomat in residence U. Va., 1973-74, prof., 1975-82, prof. emeritus Sch. Govt. and Fgn. Affairs, from 1982; mem. U.S. del. to 6th session UN Gen. Assembly, 1951; v.p. European offices Morgan Guaranty Trust Co. N.Y., Paris, 1964-69, asst. to chmn., N.Y.C., 1969-73, cons., from 1973; Olsson prof. bus. adminstrn. U. Va. Grad. Sch. Bus. Adminstrn., Charlottesville, from 1973, dir. White Burkett Miller Ctr. Pub. Affairs, from 1975. Author: From Trust to Tragedy, 1988. Charter mem. Piedmont Environ. Coun.; chmn., bd. dirs. Thomas Jefferson Meml. Found. Lt. comdr. USNR, 1942-46. Decorated Order of Orange Nassau. Mem. So. Soc. Philosophy, Coun. on Fgn. Rels., River Club (N.Y.C.), Met. Club ((Washington), Farmington Club (Charlottesville), Phi Beta Kappa, Omicron Delta Kappa, Delta Psi. Episcopalian. Home: Charlottesville Va. Died Dec. 14, 1989; buried St. Paul's Churchyard, Ivy, Va.

NORDMEYER, GEORGE, German language educator; b. Burgoerner, Germany, Jan. 11, 1912; came to U.S., 1932, naturalized, 1939; s. Wilhelm and Ida (Niemann) N.; m. Barbara S. Thommpson, Sept. 4, 1935; children: Alice Eda Nordmeyer Carroll, Mary Betsy. Student, U. Munich, 1930-32; PhD, Yale U., 1934. Rsch. asst. Yale U., New Haven, 1932-34, Sterling rsch. fellow, 1934-35, instr., asst. prof., assoc. prof. German,, 1939-62; instr., asst. prof. W.Va. U., Morgantown, 1935-39; prof. Hunter Coll., CUNY, 1962-77, prof. emeritus, 1977-90, chmn. dept., 1965-77; vis. prof. NYU, spring 1966. Author, co-author textbooks on German; also articles. Sr. faculty fellow Yale U., 1961-62. Mem. MLA, Linguistic Soc. Am., Assn. Tchrs. German. Home: Palo Alto Calif. Died Oct. 23, 1990; buried Palo Alto, Calif.

NORMAN, GEORGE EMERSON, JR., textile consultant; b. Charlotte, N.C., June 14, 1914; s. George Emerson and Lucy Bowden (Smith) N.; m. Jane Webb, June 29, 1943 (dec. 1950); children: Lane Smith, George Emerson III; m. Hilda Graham Roberts, Sept. 25, 1952; children: Vernon Roberts, Dean Graham. B.S., N.C. State Coll., 1938. With Burlington Industries, from 1938; beginning in quality control and devel. depts., successively exec. hosiery div., decorative fabrics div., asst. to pres., charge subs. Goodall Sanford, Inc., 1954-56, exec. v.p., 1956-59, pres., 1959-63; v.p. Burlington Industries, 1959-63, v.p. charge corp. research and devel., 1963-69, v.p. new bus. ventures, 1969-75, v.p. energy planning and conservation, 1975-77, v.p. public affairs, 1977-79, cons., 1979; v.p., dir., exec. com. Carlyle & Co. Jewelers, 1969-90; mem. exec. com., trustee Textile Research Inst., Princeton U., 1965-73, chmn., 1972. Mem. Greensboro Sports Council, N.C., 1972-90; mem. Greensboro (N.C.) Bd. Edn., 1959-72, chmn., 1970-72; chmn. rev. bd. Gateways, Inc., 1974-76; mem. bd. Engring. Found. N.C. State U., 1968-89, pres., 1975-77; mem. exec. com. Met. bd. YMCA, 1969-90, pres., 1978, 79; v.p., bd. dirs. Blue Ridge Assembly SE Region YMCA, 1976, pres., 1981-83, chmn. bd. trustees, from 1988; bd. dirs. United Arts Council, from 1970, pres., 1971-72; exec. com., bd. dirs. United Way of Greater Greensboro, 1971-76, campaign chmn., 1972, exec. v.p., 1973, pres., 1974-75; exec. com., bd. dirs. N.C. Symphony Soc., 1970-83, sec.-treas., 1972-77, vice chmn., 1977, chmn., 1978; exec. com., trustee Greensboro Coll., from 1971, vice-chmn., 1974-86; bd. dirs. Oak Ridge Acad., 1969-80, Am. Lung Assn. N.C., 1981-89, Greensboro Cerebral Palsy and Orthopedic Sch., 1975-81, N.C. State U. Found., 1977-81; bd. dirs. Goodwill Industries, from 1974, pres., 1978-80; trustee Research Triangle Inst., from 1973, exec. com., from 1974; bd. visitors Appalachian State U., Boone, N.C., 1974-80, Guilford Coll., Greensboro, 1975-79; bd. dirs. Eastern Music Festival, 1973-86, exec. com., 1974; mem. adv. council N.C. OSHA, 1975-84; bd. dirs. Nat. Metric Council, 1975-80, exec. com., 1978, Bell House, 1988; mem. N.C. Energy Policy Council, 1977-84; pres. Musical Arts Guild, U. N.C., Greensboro, 1978; mem. Guilford County Pvt. Industry Council, 1980-86. Served as capt. AUS, 1942-46. Recipient Community Arts award Greensboro Altrusa Club, 1979, Service to Mankind award Sertoma Club, 1979, Disting. Service award Mayor's Com. on Handicapped, 1979, Watauga medal N.C. State U., 1981; named Civic Leader Year, 1973. Mem. N.C. State U. Alumni Assn. (dir. 1968-74, exec. com. 1968, pres. 1972, chmn. 1973), Greensboro C. of C. (dir. 1972-73, Disting. Citizen award 1979), Scabbard and Blade, Pi Kappa Phi, Phi Psi. Clubs: Civitan (pres.), Greensboro Country; Country of N.C., Pinehurst Country (Pinehurst, N.C.); Beech Mountain Country (N.C.). Home: Greensboro N.C. Died Oct. 21, 1990. †

NORMAN, NORMAN B., advertising agency executive, marketing consultant; b. N.Y.C., Oct. 3, 1914; m. Gail Snyder, 1943; children—Peter, Susan. A.B., Columbia U., 1934. From advt. asst. to new bus. and account mgmt. The Biow Co., 1936-42; exec. v.p. Norman A. Mack & Co., 1945-48; with William H. Weintraub & Co., 1948-55; co-founder Norman, Craig & Kummel (now NCK Orgn.), N.Y.C., 1955, pres., chmn. bd., 1955-80, hon. chmn., 1980-91; instr. mktg. Columbia U. Sch. Bus., 1953-56; trustee exec. com. N.Y. Police Found., from 1982; bd. dirs. Assn. Better N.Y.C., from 1975. Served to lt. USNR, 1942-45. Decorated Bronze Star. Mem. Am. Assn. Advt. Agys. (dir. 1967-70). Clubs: N.Y. Yacht (N.Y.C.), Sky (N.Y.C.). Home: Key Largo Fla.

NORTH, ALEX, composer; b. Chester, Pa., Dec. 4, 1910. Student, Juilliard Sch. Music, Moscow Conservatory. Composer: opera Hither and Thither of Danny Dither; ballet American Lyric, 1937, Daddy Long Legs, Mal de siècle, Wall Street Ballet; musicals Rhapsody for piano and orch, 1941, Revue for clarinet and orch; performed by Benny Goodman, 1946, 3 symphonies, 1947, 68, 71, 3 symphonic suites from film scores, Holiday set, 1948; cantatas for chorus and orch. Morning Star, 1947, Negro Mother, 1948; film scores Streetcar Named Desire, 1951, Death of a Salesman, Viva Zapata, 1952, Member of the Wedding, The Rose Tattoo, 1955, The Rainmaker, 1957; Spartacus, 1960, Children's Hour, Cleopatra, 1963, The Misfits, The Agony and the Ecstasy, Who's Afraid of Virginia Woolf?, 1966, Shoes of the Fisherman, 1969, 2001: A Space Odyssey, Once, Upon a Scoundrel, Bite the Bullet, Shanks, Wise Blood, Carny, Dragon Slayer, Under the Volcano, Prizzi's Honor, Good Morning Vietnam, 1987, The Dead, 1987, The Penitent, 1987, The Last Butterfly, 1989, numerous others; also TV scores. Guggenheim fellow recipient Composers and Lyricists Guild award 1963, Laurel award 1956, 57, 66, 67, 69, Golden Globe award 1969, Emmy award for series Rich Man, Poor Man 1976, 15 Acad. award nominations; hon. Oscar for lifetime achievement in film music Acad. Motion Picture Arts and Scis., 1986; Golden Soundtrack award ASCAP, 1986; Career Achievement award Soc. Preservation Film Music, 1986; Golden Score award Am. Soc. Music Arrangers, 1986; ASCAP Golden Sound Track award, 1988; Magic of Music Film award Metro Phoenix, 1989. Home: Pacific Palisades Calif. Died Sept. 8, 1991; ashes to Pacific Ocean.

NORTH, EDMUND HALL, screenwriter; b. N.Y.C., Mar. 12, 1911; s. Robert and Eleanor (Hall) N.; m. Collette Ford, Oct. 11, 1947; children: Susan, Bobbie. Student, Stanford U., 1928-30. Screenwriter feature films One Night of Love, 1934, I Dream Too Much, 1935, Young Man with a Horn, 1950, The Day the Earth Stood Still, 1951, Cowboy, 1958, Sink the Bismarck!, 1960, Damn the Defiant, 1962, Patton (Acad. award Oscar), 1970, Meteor, 1979, others, from 1979; mem. numerous coms. Producer-Writers Guild Pension Plan, Los Angeles, chmn. bd., 1963-64; bd. dirs. Nat. Captioning Inst., Washington, 1979-86. Served to maj. Signal Corps, U.S. Army, 1941-45, ETO. Mem. Writers Guild Am.-West (pres. Screen br. 1956-57, Valentine Davies award 1967, Best Story and Screenplay award 1970, Morgan Cox award 1975), Acad. Motion Picture Arts and Scis. (Acad. award 1970). Home: Los Angeles Calif. Died Aug. 28, 1990; cremated. †

NORTH, HARPER QUA, physicist; b. Los Angeles, Jan. 24, 1917; s. Richard L. and Mary Elizabeth (Qua) N.; m. Frances Norris, June 14, 1969; children: Anita M., James S. B.S., Calif. Inst. Tech., 1938; M.A., UCLA, 1940, Ph.D., 1947. Research asso. Gen. Electric Co., 1940-49; dir. semiconductor div. Hughes Aircraft Co., Culver City, Calif., 1949-54; pres. Pacific Semiconductors, Inc., Lawndale, Calif., 1954-61, chmn. bd., 1961-62; chmn. bd. TRW Electronics, Lawndale, 1962; v.p. research and devel. TRW Inc., Los Angeles, 1962-69; mgr. electro-optical dept. Northrop Corp., Palos Verdes Peninsula, Calif., 1969-73; asso. dir. research in electronics Naval Research Lab., Washington, 1975-79, tech. services, 1979-81; cons. Dept. Def., 1951-75, chmn. adv. group electron devices, 1968-75. Mem. Nat. Export Expansion Council, 1962-64; Pres. Schenectady Light Opera Co., 1948-49; Bd. dirs. So. Calif. Industry Edn. Council, 1963-65, Calif. Inst. Cancer Research, 1964-69. Fellow Am. Phys. Soc., IEEE; mem. Electronic Industries Assn. (chmn. 1964-66, hon. bd. mem., recipient, medal of honor 1966), Sigma Xi. Home: San Diego Calif. Died May 13, 1989; buried El Camino Meml. Pk., San Diego.

NORTHROP, FILMER STUART CUCKOW, philosophy and law educator; b. Janesville, Wis., Nov. 27, 1893; s. Marshall Ellsworth and Ruth (Cuckow) N.; desc. Joseph Northrop who came to New Haven, 1638, founded Milford, 1639; m. Christine Johnston, Aug. 6, 1919; children: Filmer Johnston, Stuart Johnston. AB, Beloit Coll., 1915; AM, Yale U., 1919, Harvard U., 1922; PhD, Harvard U., 1924; grad. student, Freiburg, Germany, 1922-23, Trinity Coll., Cambridge U., London, 1922-23; LLD (hon.), U. Hawaii, 1949, Rollins

Coll., 1955; LittD (hon.), Beloit Coll., 1946, Pratt Inst., 1961. Engaged in social work N.Y.C., 1915-16; ednl. sec. Internat. Com. YMCA, Hong Kong, 1919-20; instr. philosophy Yale U., 1923-26, asst. prof., 1926-29, assoc. prof., 1929-32, prof. philosophy, 1932-47, also master of Silliman Coll., 1940-47, Sterling prof. philosophy and law, 1947-62, Sterling prof. emeritus; vis. prof. U. Iowa, U. Mich., U. Va., U. Hawaii, Nat. U. Mex.; prof. extraordinaire Nat. Autonomous U. Mex., from 1949. Author: Science and First Principles, 1931; The Meeting of East and West, 1946; The logic of the Sciences and the Humanities, 1947; The Taming of the Nations (Freedom House award), 1952; European Union and U.S. Foreign Policy, 1954; The Complexity of Legal and Ethical Theory, 1959; Philosophical Anthropology and Practical Politics, 1959; Man, Nature and God, 1962; editor, contbr. Ideological Differences and World Order, 1949; Epistemology in Anthropology, 1964, others; contbr. articles to jours. Bd. dirs. Sch. for Asiatic Studies; founder mem., mem. exec. com. Nat. Conf. Sci. Philosophy and Religion. Served to 2d lt., troop train comdr. Tank Corps, U.S. Army, 1918-19. Decorated Order of Aztec Eagle (Mex.); Guggenheim fellow, 1932-33. Fellow AAAS (chmn. sect. L, 1947, mem. coun.), Am. Geog. Soc., Am. Acad. Polit. and Social Sci., Am. Acad. Arts and Asi.; mem. Am. Philos. Assn., N.Y. Philosophy Club, Am. Oriental Soc., The Century Assn., Lawn Club, Grad. Club, Beaumont Club, Mory's, Elizabeth Club, Aurelian Club, Berzelius Club, Phi Beta Kappa, Sigma Xi, Delta Sigma Rho. Congregationalist. *

NORTON, VICTOR THANE, manufacturing executive; b. Ridgeway, Pa., Jan. 15, 1904; s. Homer Burdette and Gertrude Callula N.; m. Elizabeth Smith, July 2, 1932; children: Victor Thane, Nina R., Elizabeth R. BSCE, Northwestern U., 1926. Asst. to pres. Jewel Tea Co., Inc., 1927-39; v.p. Cudahy Packing Co., 1939-44, Kenyon & Eckardt, 1944-46; pres. Am. Home Foods, Inc., 1946-50; v.p. NBC, 1950-53; pres. Am. Hard Rubber Co., N.Y.C., 1953-57, Pequanoc Rubber Co., Butler, N.J., 1953-58; pres., dir., chmn. exec. com. Amerace Corp., N.Y.C., 1957-62; chmn., dir. exec. com. Amerace Corp., 1968. Mem. Univ. Club N.Y.C. , Beaverkill Club Livingston Manor, N.Y. , Riverside Yacht Club past gov. , Beta Theta Pi, Delta Sigma Rho. Home: Bowling Green Ohio Died Oct. 14, 1989.

NOSSITER, BERNARD DANIEL, journalist; b. N.Y.C., Apr. 10, 1926; s. Murry Paul and Rose (Weingarten) N.; m. Jacqueline Sarah Robinson, Dec. 3, 1950; children: Daniel, Joshua, Adam, Jonathan. AB magna cum laude, Dartmouth Coll., 1947; MA, Harvard U., 1948. Reporter World Telegram and Sun, N.Y.C., 1952-55; nat. econs. reporter Washington Post, 1955-64; European econs. corr. Washington Post, Paris, 1964-67; South Asia corr. Washington Post, 1967-68, London corr., 1971-79; UN bur. chief N.Y. Times, 1979-83; freelance writer London, 1987-92. Author: The Mythmakers: An Essay on Power and Wealth, 1964, Soft State: A Newspaperman's Chronicle of India, 1970, Britain - A Future That Works, 1978, The Global Struggle for More, 1987, Fat Years and Lean, 1990; contbr. articles to profl. jours. Served with AUS, 1944-46, to 2d lt. inf., 1950-51. Recipient Medal for Disting. Washington corr. Sigma Delta Chi, 1961, Hillman Found. award for book, 1965, Fairchild award Overseas Press Club, 1966, George Polk award, 1969; Nieman fellow, 1962-63. Mem. Coun. Fgn. Rels., Phi Beta Kappa. Jewish. Home: New York N.Y. Died June 24, 1992. †

NOVAK, MILAN VACLAV, physician, educator, dean; b. Cobb, Wis., Dec. 24, 1907; s. Philip and Barbara (Vavrina) N.; m. Dorothy Flint, July 28, 1934; children: Mary Dayle, John Lotus, Raymond William. B.A., Macalester Coll., 1929, D.Sc., 1947; M.S., U. Minn., 1930, Ph.D., 1932, B.S., 1936, M.B., 1938, M.D., 1938. Asst. prof. bacteriology U. Tenn., 1932-33; pharmacology research fellow U. Minn., 1933-34, part-time instr. bacteriology, 1934-38; chief bacteriologist, dir. blood bank U. Minn. Hosps., 1938-40, instr. in med. bacteriology, 1938-40; asso. prof. bacteriology and pub. health U. Ill., 1940-43, prof., head dept. bacteriology and pub. health, 1943-64, asso. dean Grad. Coll., 1950-68, acting dean, 1968-69, dir. Blood Bank, 1942-54; asso. internal medicine U. Ariz. Coll. Medicine, 1970-92; coordinator Ariz. Regional Med. Program in Pulmonary Diseases, 1970-92; dir. State Bank of Lombard, Ill.; Pres. Tb Inst. Chgo. and Cook County, 1960, Midwest Conf. Grad. Study, 1960; grad. div. Land Grant Colls. and State Univs., 1965. Author: Bacteriology Lab. Directions for Students of the Med. Scis; Editor: Nat. Ofcl. Handbook for Speedskating, 1960-79. Bd. dirs. Am. Lung Assn., 1956-70, Ariz. Lung Assn., from 1970. Fellow AAAS; mem. Am. Thoracic Soc., AMA, Soc. Exptl. Biology and Medicine, Soc. Am. Bacteriologists, Macalester Coll. Allumni Assn. (dir. 1960-65), Phi Beta Pi, Gamma Alpha, Sigma Xi. Presbyn. Home: Tucson Ariz. Died Jan. 5, 1992.

NOYCE, ROBERT NORTON, electronics company executive; b. Burlington, Iowa, Dec. 12, 1927; s. Ralph B. and Harriet (Norton) N.; m. Ann S. Bowers; children: William B., Pendred, Priscilla, Margaret. BA, Grinnell Coll., 1949; PhD, MIT, 1953. Rsch. engr. Philco Corp., Phila., 1953-56, Shockley Semicondr. Lab., Mountain View, Calif., 1956-57; founder, dir. rsch. Fairchild Semicondr., Mountain View, 1957-59, v.p., gen. mgr., 1959-65; group v.p. Fairchild Camera & Instrument, Mountain View, 1965-68; founder, pres. Intel Corp., Santa Clara, Calif., 1968-75, chmn., 1968-75, vice chmn., from 1979; pres., chief exec. officer Sematech, Inc. (consortium formed by the semicondr. industry, U.S. Govt. and academia), Austin, Tex., 1988-90; dir. Diasonics Inc., Milpitas, Calif. Patentee early integrated circuitry, numerous others. Pioneer in creating semicondr. industry. Trustee Grinnell Coll., 1962-90. Recipient Stuart Ballentine award Franklin Inst., 1967, Harry Goode award AFIPS, 1978, Nat. Medal of Sci. Pres. U.S. , 1979, Nat. Medal of Tech. Pres. U.S., 1987, Harold Pender award U. Pa., 1980, John Fritz medal, 1989; named to Nat. Inventors Hall of Fame, 1983, Nat. Bus. Hall of Fame, 1989. Fellow IEEE (Cledo Brunetti award 1978, medal of honor 1978, Faraday medal 1979); mem. Nat. Acad. Engring. (first Charles Stark Draper award 1989), AAAS, Nat. Acad. Sci. Home: Austin Tex. Died June 3, 1990; cremated.

NOYES, PIERREPONT T., manufacturing company executive; b. Oneida, N.Y., 1914. Grad., Colgate U., 1936. Chmn. bd., CEO Oneida (N.Y.) Ltd., 1936-92; vice-chmn. bd. Camden Wire Co.; mem. adv. bd. Liberty Mut. Ins. Co.; dir. Lincoln Nat. Bank & Trust Co. of Cen. N.Y., Lincoln First Group, Inc., Rena Ware Distbrs., Inc. Mem. Saratoga Springs Commn.; bd. dirs. N.Y. State Coun. Econ. Edn., Assoc. Industries N.Y. State, Indsl. Assn. Mohawk Valley; bd. dirs., mem. exec. com. Saratoga Performing Arts Ctr.; bd. visitors Marcy State Hosp.; trustee Oneida Improvement Assn., Colgate U. Mem. Sterling Silversmiths Guild (past pres.), Silver Users Assn. (adv. com.). Home: Oneida N.Y. Died Apr. 8, 1992.

NSUBUGA, EMMANUEL CARDINAL, archbishop of Kampala; b. Kisube, Uganda, Nov. 5, 1914. Ordained priest Roman Cath. Ch., 1946; consecrated bishop of Kampala, 1966; archbishop of Kampala, 1976-90; elevated to Sacred Coll. of Cardinals, 1976; titular ch. St. Maria Nuova; mem. Congregation of Evangelization of Peoples. Died Apr. 20, 1991; buried Nalukolongo Home for Disabled, Uganda. Home: Kisubi Uganda

NUGENT, BROTHER GREGORY, educator, university official; b. Troy, N.Y., Oct. 17, 1911; s. Harry Bartholomew and Margaret (Woods) N. Student, Manhattan Coll., N.Y.C., 1929-30; Pd.D (hon.), Manhattan Coll., 1986; A.B., Cath. U. Am., 1934, LHD, 1991; A.M., NYU, 1939, Ph.D., 1945; LL.D., Manhattanville Coll., 1963, Iona Coll., 1963; D.R.E., Providence Coll., 1971; L.H.D., Pace U., 1973; Litt. D., Coll. of Mt. St. Vincent, 1975; LHD, Cath. U. Am., 1991. Entered Inst. of Bros. Christian Schs., 1930; instr. langs. De La Salle Inst., N.Y.C., 1934-46; asst. prof. German Manhattan (N.Y.) Coll., 1946-50, asso. prof., 1950-51, prof., 1951-75, asst. dean liberal arts program, 1951-52, dean sch. arts and sci., 1952-59, acad. v.p., 1959-62, pres., 1962-75; spl. asst. to pres. Cath. U. Am., from 1975, sec. bd. trustees, 1980-92; trustee Coll. Entrance Exam. Bd., 1962-65; mem. N.Y. State Adv. Council on Higher Edn., 1963-67, Regents Regional Coordinating Council for Postsecondary Edn., N.Y.C., 1973. Author: Catholicism in Schiller's Dramas, 1949. Bd. govs. Coll. of Mt. St. Vincent, 1965-68, trustee, 1968-80; trustee Cath. U. Am., 1968-75, Manhattan Coll., 1959-75; trustee La Salle U., 1969-89, chmn., 1982-88. Recipient Mother Scholastica Meml. award Medaille Coll., 1966; Theodore M. Hesburgh award Assn. Cath. Colls. and Univs., 1988. Mem. Middle States Assn. (com. instns. higher edn., trustee), Am. Council Edn. (com. Fed. Relations), Assn. Am. Colls. (com. religion higher edn.), Council Higher Ednl. Instns. N.Y.C. (dir. 1962-64, 67-75), Assn. Colls. and Univs. State N.Y. (mem. exec. com.), Religious Edn. Assn. (dir. 1959-77), Cath. Renascence Soc. (asst. treas., bd. dirs. 1952-54), Nat. Cath. Edn. Assn. (vice pres. coll. and univ. dept. 1962-64, pres. 1964-66, mem. gen. exec. bd. 1966-73), Assn. Modern Lang. Tchrs. Middle States (pres. 1949), Christian Bros. Edn. Assn. Home: Washington D.C. Died June 20, 1992. †

NUNES, GORDON MAXWELL, painting educator; b. Porterville, Calif., Aug. 1, 1914; s. John J. and Minnie (Witt) N. With Douglas Aircraft Engring Co., 1941-45; mem. faculty UCLA, 1948-83, prof. painting., prof. emeritus, from 1983; Mem. Inst. Creative Art, 1963, 67. Creator animated cartoons, 1937-41; Paintings exhbt., throughout U.S., from 1950. Home: Los Angeles Calif. Deceased. †

NUREYEV, RUDOLF HAMETOVICH, ballet dancer, ballet company executive; b. USSR, Mar. 17, 1938; defected 1961; Student ballet, Lenigrad (USSR) Ballet Sch.; hon. doctorate, Phila. Coll. Performing Arts,, 1980; studied conducting with, Wilhelm Hübner, Varujan Kojian. Dancer Kirov Ballet, Leningrad, 1955-61, soloist, 1958-61; dancer Ballet of Marquis de Cuevas, 1961; with Ruth Page and Chgo. Opera Ballet, 1962; artistic dir. Paris Opera Ballet, 1983-89, prin. choreographer, 1989-93; prin. choreographer Palais Garnier, 1988-93. London debut (with Margot Fonteyn and Royal Ballet) Giselle, 1962; Am. debut (with Maria Tallchief) on Bell Telephone Hour; has appeared as guest artist with 25 companies including Am. Ballet Theatre, Australian Ballet, Colón Theatre Ballet, Deutsche Opera Ballet, Berlin, Dutch Nat. Ballet, Nat. Ballet Can., Paris Opera Ballet, Royal Danish Ballet, others; choreographer: (ballets) Romeo and Juliet, La Bayadere, Raymonda, Swan Lake, Tancredi, Sleeping Beauty, Nutcracker, Don Quixote, Don Juan, Giselle, Manfred, The Tempest, (films) including Evening With Royal Ballet, 1963, Romeo and Juliet, 1966, I Am A Dancer, 1972, Don Quixote, 1972, Valentino, 1977, Exposed, 1983, Washington Square, Cinderella, 1986; appeared in The King and I, O'Keefe Ctr., Toronto, 1989, also toured; appeared in ballet The Overcoat (Flemming Flindt) created for him, Cleveland San Jose Ballet, 1991. Recipient Capezio Dance award, 1987. Home: London Eng. Died Jan. 6, 1993. †

NUTE, GRACE LEE, history educator; b. North Conway, N.H., Oct. 13, 1895; d. Dexter Asbury and Mary Virginia (Eisele) Nute. AB, Smith Coll., 1917; AM, Radcliffe Coll., 1918, PhD, 1921; LittD, Hamline U., 1943. Curator manuscripts Minn. Hist. Soc., St. Paul, 1921-46, rsch. assoc., 1946-58; asst. prof. history Hamline U., St. Paul, 1927-37, assoc. prof., 1937-40, prof. Minn. history, 1940-90; lectr. U. Minn., 1939-40, extension div., 1948-52, on hist. rsch. before pub. groups; vis. prof. Macalester Coll., 1956-59. Included in 100 Living Great of Minn., by popular poll, 1949; author several books, 1931-90 including History of the Arts in Minnesota, 1958, Minnesota Heritage, 1959 (with others); mem. editorial bd. The Naturalist, Natural History Soc. of Minn.; collaborator Ency. Brit. Films prodn.: Robert Cavalier, Sieur de la Salle, 1950. Chmn. Clarence W. Alvord Meml. Commn., 1949-56. Guggenheim Found. fellow, 1934-35. Mem. Am. Hist. Assn., Miss. Valley Hist. Assn., Zonta, Pen and Brush, Phi Beta Kapp, Phi Beta Kappa Assocs., Delta Kappa Gamma. Home: Walnut Creek Calif. Died May 4, 1990.

NYE, GEORGE DEWEY, lawyer; b. Waverly, Ohio, Aug. 6, 1898; s. George B. and Cresse (Evans) N.; m. Leota Baker, Mar. 15, 1941; 1 dau. by former marriage, Marie Louise (Mrs. Paul Armour). LLB, Ohio State U., 1922. Bar: Ohio 1922. Elected pros. atty. Pike County, 1922, 24, elected common pleas judge, 1930, 32; elected lt. gov. State of Ohio, 1944, 48, 50; law practice Waverly, from 1922; owner real estate devel. Lake White, nr. Waverly. Mem. Pike County Bar Assn. (past pres.), Masons, Shriners. Methodist Episcopalian. *

OBERBECK, ARTHUR WILLIAM, army officer; b. Chgo., Jan. 13, 1912; s. Arthur Walter and Edna (Trinkaus) O.; m. Margaret Lanigan, Sept. 7, 1938 (dec. Nov. 1970); children: Donald D., Michael M.; m. Carole Kivela, June 23, 1972 (div. Dec. 1979); children: Tracy Janine, Scott Ryan. B.S., U.S. Mil. Acad., 1937; M.S. in Civil Engring, U. Calif.-Berkeley, 1940; grad., Army War Coll., 1955; J.D., U. Tex. Law Sch., 1975. Commd. 2d lt. C.E. U.S. Army, 1937, advanced through grades to lt. gen., 1969; assigned 5th Engrs. Ft. Belvoir, Va., 1937-39; assigned 3d Engrs. Hawaii and Pacific areas, 1940-44; div. engr. 24th Inf. Div., 1942-44, div. engr. Hdqrs. S.W. Pacific, 1944-45, World War II, assigned Manhattan Engring. Dist and AEC, 1945-47, asst. prof. math. U.S. Mil. Acad., 1947-51, assigned Armed Forces Spl. Weapons Project, 1951-54, mem. strategic plans group, joint staff Joint Chiefs Staff, 1955-56, dir.spl. weapons devel. USCONARC, 1956-60, dir. coordination and analysis Office Army Chief Staff, 1960-62; comdg. gen. 1st Inf. Div. Ft. Riley, Kans., 1963-64; dir. J-3 div. U.S. European Command Paris, France, 1964-66; comdr. Joint Task Force Eight and Test Command, DASA Sandia Base, N.Mex., 1966-68; comdg. gen. U.S. Army Engr. Ctr.; also comdt. U.S. Army Engr. Sch. Ft. Belvoir, Va., 1968; sr. army mem. Weapons Systems Evaluation group Washington, 1968-69; dir. Weapons Systems Evaluation group, 1969-72; legal cons. Center for Energy Studies, U. Tex., 1976-79. Decorated D.S.M., Legion of Merit with two oak leaf clusters. Mem. State Bar Tex. Club: Balcones Country. Home: San Antonio Tex. Died Sept. 7, 1989; buried Arlington Nat. Cemetery.

O'BRIAN, ROBERT ENLOW, university president, government official; b. Bryant, Ill., July 22, 1895; s. William and Mary Catherine (Laemle) O'B.; m. Mabel Day, 1920; 1 son, Edward Day. AB, DePauw U., 1918; BD, Garrett Bibl. Inst., 1920; MA, Northwestern U., 1921, PhD, 1927. DD, Wesley Coll., Grand Forks, N.C., 1931. Pres. Morningside Coll., Sioux City, Iowa, 1931-36; chmn. Mcpl. Housing Commns. of Iowa; sec. of state State of Iowa, 1937-39; pres. Tabor (Iowa) Coll., 1940-42, REO Foods, Inc., 1945-64; coord. numismatics Roosevelt U., from 1964. Sec. Democratic Nat. Com., 1940-46. Mem. Am. Legion, Phi Beta Kappa, Delta Sigma Rho. *

O'BRIEN, DALE, public relations consultant; b. Chgo., Nov. 12, 1916; s. Harold Dale and Charlotte (Klapper) O'B.; m. Helen Lundgren, June 7, 1941 (dec. Dec. 23, 1984); children: Katherine, Harold Dale, John David. A.B., U. Kans., 1937. Dir. pub. relations and advt., bd. editors Ency. Brit., Inc., 1945-49; partner Mayer & O'Brien, Chgo., 1950-52, pres., 1952-61; pres. Dale O'Brien & Co., Chgo., from 1961; exec. v.p., dir. Wis. Week-End, Inc., 1972-80; pres. Wis. Acad. Scis., Arts and Letters, 1978. Home: Fairhope Ala. Died Aug. 23, 1988.

O'BRIEN, DAVID VINCENT, federal judge; b. New Rochelle, N.Y., June 19, 1932; s. Donald R. and

Florence L. (Duffy) O'B.; m. Barbara Mett, July 7, 1956 (div. June 1974); children: Kathryn, Elizabeth, Kevin, David V., Daniel; m. Janet Burgess, July 18, 1974. B.A., U. Vt., 1956; J.D., Syracuse U., 1959. Bar: N.Y. 1960, V.I. 1971. Ptnr. Byrne, Costello & O'Brien, Syracuse, 1966-70, Merwin, Alexander & O'Brien, St. Croix, V.I., 1971-78, O'Brien & Moore, St. Croix, V.I., 1978-81; judge U.S. Dist. Ct. V.I., St. Croix, 1981-88, chief judge, 1988-89. Served with USMC, 1950-52, Vietnam. Republican. Roman Catholic. Home: Christiansted St. Croix, V.I. Died Dec. 22, 1989; buried St. Croix, V.I.

O'BRIEN, HENRY XAVIER, chief justice supreme ct. Pa.; b. Pitts., Nov. 29, 1903; s. Patrick Joseph and Delia Gertrude (Clougherty) O'B.; BS in Econs., Duquesne U., 1925, JD, 1928, LLD (hon.), 1956; LLD (hon.), St. Francis Coll., 1967, Gannon U., Erie, Pa., 1981; m. Caroline Nuttall, July 5, 1928 (dec. 1953); children: Henry Xavier, Carolyn Ann O'Brien Staley; m. Rosemary Hager, Aug. 25, 1956. Bar: Pa., 1929; Gen. practice, Pitts., 1929-47; asst. dist. atty., 1942-47; mem. faculty Duquesne U. Sch. Law, 1945-60; judge Ct. Common Pleas 5th Jud. Dist. Pa., 1947-62; justice Supreme Ct. Pa., 1962-83, chief justice, 1980-83; sr. counsel Reed, Smith, Shaw & McClay, Pitts., 1983-90. Trustee Duquesne U. Died Feb. 17, 1990; buried Calvary Cemetery, Pitts. Home: Pittsburgh Pa.

O'BRIEN, JAMES EDWARD, lawyer; b. Trinidad, Colo., Mar. 22, 1912; s. George A. and Alice A. (Lapsley) O'B.; m. Mary Louise James, Jan. 2, 1936 (dec. 1978); m. Jeanne Gilmore LaClair, 1979. AB, U. Calif., Berkeley, 1932, JD, 1935. Bar: Calif. 1935. Practice in San Francisco, 1935-66; assoc., ptnr. Pillsbury, Madison & Sutro, 1935-66; v.p., dir. Standard Oil Co. Calif., San Francisco, 1966-77; of counsel firm Pillsbury, Madison & Sutro, 1977-92; dir. W.P. Fuller & Co., El Portal Mining Co., Abercrombie & Fitch Co.; pres. bd. dirs. Stanford Hosp.; bd. dirs. Acad. for Ednl. Devel. N.Y., Nat. Fund for Med. Edn., Am. Enterprise Inst.; trustee Internat. and Comparative Law Ctr., Dallas, Southwestern Legal Found., Mills Coll., San Francisco Asian Art Commn. Chmn. Friends of Bancroft Library. Served as lt. col. USAAF, 1942-46. Decorated Legion of Merit, Bronze Star; Croix de Guerre with Silver Star. Mem. ABA, San Francisco C. of C. (past v.p., dir.), Internat. C. of C., Am. Soc. Internat. Law, Internat. Law Assn., Am. Law Inst. Clubs: Pacific-Union (San Francisco), Bohemian (San Francisco), City (San Francisco). Home: Palo Alto Calif. Died May 26, 1992. †

O'BRIEN, LAWRENCE FRANCIS, basketball commissioner, chairman Democratic National Committee; b. Springfield, Mass., July 7, 1917; s. Lawrence Francis and Myra Theresa (Sweeney) O'B.; m. Elva Brassard, May 30, 1944; 1 son, Lawrence Francis III. JD, Northeastern U., 1942; LLD (hon.), Western New Eng. Coll., 1962, Villanova U., 1966, Loyola U., 1967, Xavier U., 1971; LHD (hon.), Am. Internat. Coll., 1971, Wheeling Coll., 1971, St. Anselms Coll., 1966; D in Pub. Adminstrn. (hon.), Northeastern U., 1965, Seton Hall U., 1967; DSc in Bus. Adminstrn. (hon.), Bryant Coll., 1978; HHD (hon.), Springfield Coll., 1982. Engaged in real estate and pub. relations Springfield, Mass., 1943-60; active organizing polit. campaigns, 1938-90; dir. orgn. Dem. Congl. campaigns 2d Dist. Mass., 1946, 48, 50; adminstrv. asst. to U.S. Rep. Furcolo, 1948-50; dir. orgn. Sen. John F. Kennedy's campaign, 1952, Mass. Dem. Com., 1956-57, Sen. Kennedy's re-election campaign, 1958; nat. dir. orgn. Kennedy for Pres. campaign, 1959-60, Dem. Nat. Com., 1960, Dem. presdl. campaigns, 1960, 64, 68; spl. asst. to President Kennedy for Congl. relations, 1961-63, Pres. Johnson for Congl. relations, 1963-65; postmaster gen. of U.S., 1965-68; chmn. Dem. Nat. Com., 1968-69, 70-72; temporary and permanent chmn. Dem. Nat. Conv., 1972; pres. McDonnell & Co. Inc. (investment bankers), N.Y.C., 1969, O'Brien Assocs. (mgmt. cons.), 1969, 73-75; commr. Nat. Basketball Assn., 1975-84, sr. adv., 1984-87; bd. trustees Internat. Basketball Hall of Fame, 1975-89, pres., 1985-87. Author: The O'Brien Campaign Manual, 1960, 64, 68, 72, No Final Victories: A Life in Politics from John F. Kennedy to Watergate, 1974; contbr. articles to various newspapers. Served with AUS, World War II. Recipient Spl. Victor award, 1977, Brotherhood award NCCJ, 1977, Israel Prime Minister's medal in disting. service to democracy, 1978, John W. Bunn award for outstanding contbns. to basketball and to sports Basketball Hall of Fame, 1984; NBA world championship trophy designated Larry O'Brien trophy, 1984, others; named Sports Man of Yr. Sporting News, 1976, Man. of Yr. Basketball Weekly, 1976. Mem. U.S. internat. sports com. USIA. Roman Catholic. Home: New York N.Y. Died Sept. 28, 1990; buried Springfield, Mass.

O'BRIEN, RICHARD FRANK, college chancellor; b. Ogden, Utah, Oct. 20, 1921; s. James William and Mary Eleanor (Hinley) O'B.; m. Doris May Kirsten, Aug. 25, 1943; children: Susan Linda O'Brien Cretarolo, Cynthia Ann O'Brien Ford, Sally Jane. B.A. in History, U. Calif.-Santa Barbara, 1943; M.A. in Higher Edn., Stanford U., 1947, Ed.D., 1950. Mem. staff Stanford (Calif.) U., 1947-64, 67-69, dir. devel., campaign dir. PACE program, 1959-64, asst. to the pres., 1967-69; sec. Stanford Med. Center, 1969-70; v.p. planning and devel. U. Chgo., 1964-67; pres. Menlo Sch. and Coll., Atherton, Calif., 1970-87, chancellor, 1987-89; pres. Las Lomitas Sch. Bd., Atherton, Calif., 1955-58. Author: The University Development Program, 1958. Trustee UCSB Found., 1978-83, Westlake Sch., Los Angeles, 1980-83, Palo Alto Med. Research Inst., Assn. Ind. Calif. Colls. and Univs., Herbert Hoover Boys' Club. Served to lt. (j.g.) USNR, 1943-46; comdr. Res. Clubs: Palo Alto, Bohemian, Menlo Country, California. Home: Atherton Calif. Died Sept. 11, 1989; cremated.

O'BYRNE, ELEANOR MARY, university president; b. Savannah, Ga., Sept. 12, 1896; d. Michael A. and Marie (McDonough) O'Byrne. Student, Pape Sch., Savannah, 1902-08; BA, Manhattanville Sacred Heart, 1921; MA, Fordham U., 1926; BA, Oxford U., 1933, MA, 1936; LHD, NYU, 1953, Fordham U., 1956; LLD, U. Notre Dame, 1964. Directress of studies Convent of the Sacred Heart, Overbrook, Pa., 1924-28, Washington, 1928-29; leave of residence for study abroad, 1930-33; prof. history, warden of freshmen Manhattanville Coll. of Sacred Heart, 1933-34, dean, 1934-45, pres., from 1945; dir. Cath. Scholarships for Negroes, Inc.; trustee Coll. Entrance Exam. Bd. Mem. Nat. Cath. Edn. Assn., AAUW, Inst. Internat. Edn., Assn. Am. Colls. Roman Catholic. *

O'BYRNE, JOHN COATES, legal educator; b. Albany, N.Y., May 13, 1920; s. John C. and Katherine (Riley) O'B.; m. Marjorie Ann Hinners, Apr. 28, 1945; children: Kathleen, Stephen, Margret, Mary. AB, Syracuse U., 1941, MS in Pub. Adminstrn., 1943; LLB, Harvard U., 1948. Bar: N.Y. 1948, Iowa 1950, U.S. Supreme Ct. 1950. Sole practice Iowa City, 1950-66; prof. law U. Iowa Coll. Law, 1948-66, Northwestern U. Sch. Law, 1966-72; dir. Corp. Counsel Inst., 1966-69; dean Northeastern U. Sch. Law, Boston, 1972-77; Shackelford prof. law U. Ga. Law Sch., Athens, from 1977; vis. prof. U. Tex. Sch. Law, 1953, Boston Coll. Law Sch., 1965-66, Northwestern U. Sch. Law, 1956-57, Chgo.-Kent Law Sch., summers 1971, 74, Northeastern U. Law Sch., summers from 1978, U. Miami Law Sch., spring 1986; cons. land reform AID, 1961-67; cons. IRS, 1972-76; dir. Agrl. Law Center, U. Iowa, 1953-62; reporter Uniform Mgmt. Instl. Funds Act, 1970-72. Author: Iowa's Water Resources, 1956, Legal Economic Research, 1959, (with Davenport) Farm Income Tax Manual, 9th edit, 1988, Farmers Tax Guide, 12th edit, 1988, (with Phelan and Wulf) Workbook for Iowa Estate Planners, 1966, (with McCord) Deskbook for Illinois Estate Planners, 1969, (with Pennell) Federal Taxation of Partners and Partnerships, 1971, (with Kahn) Sum and Substance of Federal Income Tax, 2d edit, 1973; also articles. Lt. comdr. (ret.) USNR. Mem. Am. Law Inst., Phi Beta Kappa. Home: Athens Ga. Deceased. †

O'CONNELL, WALTER FRANCIS, company financial executive; b. Hartford, Conn., Aug. 29, 1913; s. Michael Timothy and Catherine (Donahue) O'C.; m. Majel E. Kehoe, July 8,, 1937 (div.); children: Michael K., Walter Francis, Edward T., Martha Ann; m. Pauline Peyton Forney, Oct. 20, 1952; children: Francis Peyton O'Connell Rust, Roberta Buchan O'Connell Gibson, Pauline Peyton O'Connell Blair. Student, Trinity Coll., 1932-33, Georgetown U., 1933-34; BCS, Columbia U., 1938; D Bus. Adminstrn. (hon.), U. S.C., Aiken, 1990. With Bur. Internal Revenue, 1938-40; ptnr. A.M. Pullen & Co., 1940-49, W.F. O'Connell & Co., 1949-52; asst. to fin. v.p. Olin Industries, Inc., 1952-54; v.p. Olin Mathison Chem. Corp., 1954, v.p. fin., 1955-61; chmn. bd. United Nuclear Corp. subs. Olin Industries, 1962-68, bd. dirs., 1964-86; chmn. bd. Milchem, Inc.; chmn. fin. com., bd. dirs. Olin Corp.; bd. dirs. Squibb Corp., Adams Express Co., Hialeah Park, Inc. Trustee John M. Olin Found., N.Y.C., Tax Found., Washington, Aiken Day Sch. Walter and Pauline O'Connell Exptl. Theater at U. S.C. Aiken Etherredge Ctr. and Walter F. O'Connell Econ. Enterprise Inst. at U. S.C. Aiken named in his honor. Mem. Met. Club (N.Y.C.), Links Club, Union League Club, Country Club Fairfield, Blind Brook Club, Jockey Club. Home: Aiken S.C. Died Sept. 27, 1991; cremated.

O'CONNOR, CLARENCE (DANIEL), special education educator; b. Pembina, N.D., Mar. 25, 1898; s. Archie M. and Amelia (Brennan) O'C.; m. Helen Pumphrey, June 30, 1941. AB, U. N.C., 1921; AM, Columbia U., 1934; LHD, U. N.D., 1941; LittD, Gallaudet Coll., 1960. Prin. Consol. Sch., Woodworth, N.D., 1917-18, McGregor, N.D., 1918-19; high sch. tchr. East Grand Forks, Minn., 1921-23; voice instr. Wesley Coll., U. N.D., 1923-25; spl. tng. to teach the deaf Clarke Sch. for the Deaf, Northampton, Mass., 1930-31; asst. to supt. Lexington Sch. for the Deaf, N.Y.C., 1931-33, prin., 1933-35, supt., from 1935; mem. faculty Columbia U., Hunter Coll., from 1935; v.p. Captioned Films for the Deaf, Inc.; adviser N.Y.C. Bd. Edn., N.Y. State Bd. Regents, from 1938; chmn. N.Y. State Spl. Schs. for the Deaf Com., from 1942; chmn. N.Y. State Com. to Study Cert. Reguirements for Tchrs. of Deaf, 1957-58; mem. adv. coun. N.Y. Mental Hygiene Clinic for Deaf; mem. com. on problems of deafness NRC; mem. subcom. on deafness N.Y. Med. Sch., from 1953; mem. tech. adv. com. on hearing and speech N.Y.C. Dept. Health, from 1953; mem. hearing conservation com., sch. health sect. Am Pub. Health Assn., from 1953; mem. Nat. Com. Competencies Tchrs. of Deaf, from 1954; dir. Program for Tng. Tchrs. of Deaf, U.S. Office of Edn., 1961-62; cons. UN Com. Deaf and Hard of Hearing. Contbr. chpt. to textbook. Recipient citation for svc. to secondary edn. Shattuck Sch., Faribault, Minn. Mem. Am. Instrs. for Deaf, Internat. Coun. for Exceptional Children, Conf. Execs. of Am. Schs. for Deaf, NEA, N.Y. Acad. Pub. Edn., Alexander Graham Bell Assn. for Deaf (pres. 1945-57), Cosmos Club of Washington, Men's Faculty Club of Columbia U., Univ. Club of N.Y.C., Phi Delta Theta. Democrat. Roman Catholic. *

O'CONNOR, JOSEPH B., government official; b. Troy, N.Y., May 20, 1896; s. Edward A. and Catherine (Kelly) O'C.; m. Virginia F. Wonycott, Dec. 21, 1918; children: Joseph B., Virginia Catherine (Mrs. Alvin D. Puth). Student, St. Laurent Coll., 1911-14, Cath. U. Am., 1915-17. Customers man Newburger, Henderson & Loeb, N.Y.C., 1917; pub. acctg. bus. Portsmouth, Va., 1918-19; spl. acct. S.A.L. Ry., 1919-20; acct. U.S. R.R. Adminstrn., 1920-25; account examiner ICC, 1925-34; dep. dir. Region II Social Security Bd., 1937-42; dep. dir. War Manpower Commn., 1943-47; regional dir. Region II Dept. Labor and U.S. Employment Svc., 1948-49, Dept. HEW (and predecessor FSA), from 1949. Chmn. local bd. O.P.A., N.Y.C., 1943; mem. exec. com. N.Y. Vets. Ctr.; mem. Vets. Employment Relief Bd. Served as ensign U.S. Navy, World War I. Mem. Internat. Assn. Pub. Employment Svcs., Am. Legion, Elks, KC. Roman Catholic. *

ODDO, THOMAS CHARLES, university president, clergyman; b. Jamaica, N.Y., June 12, 1944; s. Dominick Charles and Catherine Anna (Arthen) O. AB, U. Notre Dame, 1965, MTh, 1969; PhD, Harvard U., 1979. Ordained priest Roman Catholic Ch., 1970. Joined Congregation of Holy Cross, 1965; asst. prof. religious studies Stonehill Coll., North Easton, Mass., 1974-82; pres. U. Portland,, Oreg., 1982-89. Bd. dirs. United Way of Columbia-Williamette, 1983-89, DePaul Alcoholism Treatment Ctr., Portland, 1982-88, Ecuminical Ministries of Oreg., 1982-89, La. Pacific Corp., 1987-89, St. Edward's U., 1984, U. Notre Dame, 1989. Recipient Pres.' Medallion U. Notre Dame, 1965; fellow Harvard Div. Sch., 1970-71, Harvard U., 1971-73. Mem. Am. Acad. Religion, Coll. Theology Soc. Club: City (Portland). Home: Portland Oreg. Died Oct. 29, 1989; buried Notre Dame, Ind.

ODELL, ROBERT STEWART, business executive; b. Churdan, Iowa, Jan. 24, 1898; s. Halsey and Leona (Stewart) O.; m. Helen Pfeiffer, Apr. 7, 1917; 1 son, Robert Stewart. Pres. Allied Properties, Clift and Plaza Hotels, San Francisco, Santa Barbara Biltmore Hotel, Allied Land and Livestock Co., Elko, Nev.; bd. dirs. Wells Fargo Bank, San Francisco, Alleghany Corp., N.Y. Central. Mem. Press Club, Union League Club, Confrerie des Chavaliers du Tastevin, Coral Casino Beach and Cabana Club (pres.), Rancheros Visitadores (Santa Barbara), Menlo Circus Club (Atherton, Calif.). *

O'DELL, SCOTT, writer; b. Los Angeles, 1898; s. Bennett Mason and May Elizabeth (Gabriel) Scott; m. Jane Dorsa Rattenbury (div.); m. Elizabeth Hall; children: Susan Elizabeth Anderson, David Mason. Student, Occidental Coll., 1919, U. Wis., 1920, Stanford U., 1920-21, U. Rome, 1925. Author: Woman of Spain, 1934, Hill of the Hawk, 1947, (with William Doyle) Man Alone, 1953, Country of the Sun, 1957, The Sea is Red, 1958, Island of the Blue Dolphins, 1960 (Newbery medal 1961, Rupert Hughes award 1960, Hans Christian Andersen award of merit 1962, William Allen White award 1963, German Juvenile Internat. award 1963, Nene award 1964), The King's Fifth, 1966 (Newbery honor book 1967, German Juvenile Internat. award 1969), The Black Pearl, 1967 (Newbery honor book 1968, Phoenix award 1989), (with Rhoda Kellogg) The Psychology of Children's Art, 1967, The Dark Canoe, 1968, Journey to Jericho, 1969, Sing Down The Moon, 1970 (Newbery honor book 1971), The Treasure of Topo-el-Bampo, 1972, The Cruise of the Arctic Star, 1973, Child of Fire, 1974, The Hawk That Dare Not Hunt By Day, 1975, Zia, 1976, The 290, 1976, Carlota, 1977, Kathleen, Please Come Home, 1978, The Captive, 1979, Sarah Bishop, 1980, The Feathered Serpent, 1981, The Spanish Smile, 1982, The Amethyst Ring, 1983, The Castle in the Sea, 1983, Alexandra, 1984 (Parents' Choice award 1984, Fla. State Hist. Assn. award 1985), The Road to Damietta, 1985, Streams to the River, River to the Sea, 1986 (Parent's Choice award 1986), The Serpent Never Sleeps, 1987, Black Star, Bright Dawn, 1988, My Name Is Not Angelica, 1989; book columnist L.A. Times; book editor L.A. Daily News. Recipient Hans Christian Andersen Internat. medal, 1972, U. So. Miss. medallion, 1976, Regina medal, 1978. Mem. Authors Guild. Home: Waccabuc N.Y. Died Oct. 15, 1989; cremated.

ODIORNE, GEORGE STANLEY, business educator; b. Merrimac, Mass., Nov. 4, 1920; s. Charles Thomas and Katherine (Hosford) O.; m. Margaret J. Hanna, Apr. 3, 1943; 1 child, Robert Howard. B.S., Rutgers U., 1948; M.B.A., NYU, 1951, Ph.D., 1957; hon. doctorate, Central New Eng. Coll. Mgr. Am. Can Co., Jersey City, 1938-51; chmn. mgmt. services Rutgers U., New Brunswick, N.J., 1951-53; div. mgr. Am. Mgmt. Assn., N.Y.C., 1954-58; personnel mgr. Gen. Mills, Inc., Mpls., 1958-59; prof. indsl. relations U. Mich., Ann

Arbor, 1959-69; dean., prof. mgmt. U. Utah, Salt Lake City, 1969-74; dean U. Mass., Amherst, 1974-78, prof. mgmt., 1978-84; sr. rsch. assoc. Eckerd Coll., St. Petersburg, Fla., Harold D. Holder prof. mgmt., 1984-89; bd. dirs. MBO, Inc., George Odiorne Assocs. Author: Management by Objectives, 1965, Management Decisions by Objectives, 1969, Green Power, 1969, Training by Objectives, 1970, Personnel Administration, 1971, Management and the Activity Trap, 1973, MBO II-A System of Leadership, 1979, Personnel Effectiveness, 1979, Executive Skills, 1980, Techniques of Organizational Change, 1981, Sales Management by Objective, 1982, The Change Resistors, 1982, How Managers Make Things Happen, 1982, Management by Negotiation, 1984, Strategic Management of Human Resources, 1985, The Human Side of Management, 1988, Training and Development; A Guide for Professionals, 1988; mem. editorial adv. bd. Personnel mag., 1986; mem. editorial adv. com. Clearing House, 1986 contbr. numerous articles to profl. jours. Twp. committeeman, Bridgewater, N.J., 1956-57. Served to capt. AUS, 1942-46. Recipient NYU Founders Day award, 1957, Disting. Achievement award U. Wis., 1969, W.H. McFeely award YMCA, Pericles award Am. Employment Assn., Book award Am. Soc. Mil. Controllers, 50 yr. award of merit N.Y. Personnel Assn., 1979, Book of Yr. award Am. Coll. Hosp. Admintrs., 1985; named to Hall of Fame, Nat. Mgmt. Assn., 1986, Tng. Mag. Human Resource and Devel. Hall of Fame, 1986. Mem. Am. Econ. Assn., Am. Soc. Pers. Adminstrn., Am. Arbitration Assn., Am. Soc. for Tng. and Devel. Home: Saint Petersburg Fla. Died Jan. 19, 1992; buried Merrimac, Mass.

ODLE, STANLEY GENE, university provost; b. Caldwell, Idaho, June 30, 1926; s. Glen Burdett and Dorothy Jewell (Hudgens) O.; children: Scott David (dec.), Andrea Jean, Shawn Deemer. B.A., Coll. Idaho, Caldwell, 1950; M.A., Columbia U. Tchrs. Coll., 1951; Ed.D., Stanford U., 1955; postdoctoral fellow, U. Minn., Mpls., 1962-63; L.H.D. (hon.), Alfred U., 1982. Mem. adminstrv. staff Coll. Idaho, 1952-70, dean adminstrn., 1967-70; occasionally mem. acting presdl. team; v.p. student affairs, then v.p. acad. affairs Alfred (N.Y.) U., 1970-76, provost, three times acting pres., 1976-88; cons. in field. Author: You and Your Future Fields of Study, 1954, Barriers to Higher Education for Idaho Youth, 1955, The College of Idaho Takes Stock, 2 vols. and summary, 1969-70, also articles.; Contbg. editor: Going to College Handbook, 1968. Served with AUS, 1944-46. Decorated Bronze Star, Purple Heart, Army Combat medal, Combat Inf. badge; Security State scholar, 1949; VA trainee, 1962-63; recipient Trustee citation Alfred U., 1979. Mem. Sigma Delta Pi, Delta Mu Delta, Phi Kappa Phi. Democrat. Presbyterian. Home: Alfred N.Y. Died Oct. 24, 1990.

OELKERS, CAROL LYNN, statistics educator, consultant; b. Montreal, Que., Can., Aug. 7, 1941; d. Orwill Ernest and Evelyn Ester (Hall) Marchant; m. Herbert H. Oelkers, May 29, 1971; children: Keith Ross, Scott Carl. B.Sc., M.Sc. McGill U., Montreal, 1962, 1968; B.A., Sir George Williams Coll., 1965. Statistician, Imperial Tobacco Ltd., Montreal, 1962-68; prof. stats. Dawson Coll., Montreal, 1969-71; stats. cons. Carol Marchant, Montreal, 1968-71; spl. lectr. in econs. St. John Fisher Coll., Rochester, N.Y., 1972-89; ptnr. in statis. cons. C & H Assoc., Rochester, 1983-89; adj. faculty mem. Coll. Continuing Edn. Ctr. for Quality and Applied Stats., Rochester Inst. Tech.; mem. Rochester Philharm. Orch. Geva Theatrem. Rochester Women Network. Presbyterian. Avocations: tennis, skiing, needlework, volunteer at school. Died May 1, 1989; buried Webster Union Cemetery, Rochester, N.Y. Home: Rochester N.Y.

O'FAOLAIN, SEAN, author; b. Ireland, 1900; s. Denis Whelan; m. Eileen Gould, 1928; 2 children. Ed. Nat. U. Ireland, Harvard U. Prin. works include: There's a Birdie in the Cage, 1935; A Born Genius, 1936; Bird Alone, 1936; The Autobiography of Wolfe Tone, 1937; A Purse of Coppers, 1937; An Irish Journey, 1939; Come Back to Erin, 1940; Story of Ireland, 1943; Teresa, 1947; The Irish, 1948; The Short Story, 1948; Summer in Italy, 1949; South to Sicily, 1953; The Vanishing Hero, 1956; I Remember, I Remember, 1962; Vive Moi, 1965; The Talking Trees, 1970; And Again, 1979, A nest of Simple Folk, 1989; biographies include: Constance Markievicz: a Biography, 1934; King of the Beggars, 1938; The Great O'Neill, 1942; Newman's Way, 1952; collected short stories include: The Stories of Sean O'Faolain, 1958; The Heat of the Sun, 1966; Foreign Affairs, 1975; Selected Stories of Sean O'Faolain, 1978; Collected Stories, 1980, 83; play: She Had to Do Something, 1938; lectr. in English, Boston Coll., 1929, St. Mary's Coll., Strawberry Hill, 1929-33. Bd. dirs. Arts Council of Ireland, 1957-59. Commonwealth fellow, 1926-28; John Harvard fellow, 1928-29. Died Apr. 20, 1991. Home: Dublin Ireland

OFFIELD, WRIGLEY, advertising executive; b. Chgo., Feb. 8, 1917; s. James R. and Dorothy Wrighley O; m. Edna jean Headley, Jan. 4, 1941; children: Dorsee, James S., Paxton H. Student, Yale U., 1938. With William Wrigley Jr. Co., Chgo., 1940-66, copy dir., 1945-53, advt. mgr., 1953-6, v.p., 1960-66; engr. Douglas Aircraft, 1942-44, Memovox Inc., 1944-45; pres., founder Aims Inc., Chgo. Pres. Offield Family Found., 1980-91. Home: Chicago Ill. Died July 17, 1991.

OFFUTT, CASPER YOST, banker; b. Omaha, Oct. 30, 1893; s. Charles Lemuel and Bertha (Yost) O.; m. Mary Esterbrook Longmaid, Nov. 2, 1921; children: Mary (Mrs. Richardson Pratt, Jr.), Casper Yost, John. Grad., Lawrenceville Prep. Sch., 1911; AB, Yale U., 1915; LLB, Harvard U., 1920. Bar: Nebr. 1920. 2d sec. U.S. Embassy, Santiago, Chile, 1917-18; 1st sec., charge d'affaires U.S. Legation, Panama, 1918-19; practiced law Omaha, 1920-39; sr. v.p., trust officer, dir. U.S. Nat. Bank of Omaha, 1940-59, dir., chmn. trust com. bd. dirs., from 1959; dir. Wright & Wilhelmy Co., Omaha; lectr. Latin-Am. history U. Omaha, 1959-64, Creighton U., from 1964. Trustee Father Flanagan's Boys Home; pres. Omaha Community Chest, 1941; v.p. Munroe Home for Crippled Children. Decorated Order of Merit (Chile). Mem. Soc. Liberal Arts (trustee from 1941, pres. 1952-59, v.p. 1959-62), Jaycees (pres. 1921), Omaha Com. Fgn. Rels., Omaha Club, West Omaha Rotary (hon.), Phi Beta Kappa, Alpha Delta Phi. Republican. Presbyterian. *

O'FIAICH, TOMAS CARDINAL, archbishop of Armagh; b. County Armagh, Ireland, Nov. 3, 1923; s. Patrick and Annie (Caraher) Fee; B.A., St. Patrick's Coll., Maynooth, 1943; M.A., Univ. Coll., Dublin, 1950; Lic. Hist. Sc., Cath. U. Louvain (Belgium), 1952. Ordained priest Roman Cath. Ch., 1948; mem. faculty St. Patrick's Coll., Maynooth, 1953-77, prof. modern history, 1959-74, pres., 1974-77; consecrated Archbishop of Armagh and primate of All Ireland, 1977; created cardinal, 1979; chmn. Irish Episcopal Conf., 1977-90; archbishop of Armagh; pres. Irish Speaking Priests, 1955-67. Author: Gaelscrínte i gCein, 1960; Irish Cultural Influence in Europe, 1966; Imeacht na nIarlai, 1972; Ma Nuad, 1972; Art McCooey and His Times, 1973; Art MacCumhaidh: Dánta, 1973; Columbanus in His Own Words, 1974; Oliver Plunkett-Ireland's New Saint, 1975; Oilibhear Pluinceid, 1976; Art MacBionaid: Dánta, 1979; Gaelscrínte San Eoraip, 1986; editor: Seanchas Ardmhacha, 1953-77; also articles.Died May 8, 1990. Home: Armagh No. Ireland †

OGILBY, LYMAN CUNNINGHAM, bishop; b. Hartford, Conn., Jan. 25, 1922; s. Remsen B. and Lois M. (Cunningham) O.; m. Ruth Dale, Nov. 4, 1953; children—Peter R., Lois E., Henry A. BS, Hamilton Coll., 1943, DD, 1963; BD, Episc. Theol. Sch., 1949; DD, Trinity Coll., 1954; LLD (hon.), U. Pa., 1981; Dr Humanities (hon.), Trinity Coll., Quezon City, The Philippines, 1987. Ordained deacon Episcopal Ch., 1949, priest, 1950; chaplain, tchr. Brent Sch., Baguio, Philippines, 1949-53; asst. priest Epiphany Mission, 1950-53; suffragan bishop Philippines, 1953-57, bishop of Philippines, 1957-67; bishop coadjutor S.D., 1967-70; Procter fellow, lectr. Christian mission Episcopal Theol. Sch., Cambridge, Mass., 1970-71; asst. bishop of Pa., 1971-73; bishop-coadjutor of Pa., 1973, bishop, 1974-87; Sec. Council Ch. of S.E. Asia, 1960-67; chmn. conv. Nat. Council Chs., Philippines, 1962-63; vice chmn. Nat. Council Chs. Philippines, 1963-65; sec. S.D. Council Chs., 1968-70; bd. dirs. Overseas Ministries Study Ctr., 1975. Author articles, essays. Chmn. bd. govs. St. Luke's Hosp., Quezon City, Philippines; chmn. bd. trustees Brent Sch., Baguio, 1957-67; trustees Am. Assn. Philipines, 1960-62; chmn. bd. coun. Epis. Community Svcs., Diocese of Pa., 1974-87; alumni trustee Hamilton Coll., Clinton, N.Y., 1975-79; bd. dirs. Met. Christian Coun. Phila., 1971-87; trustee Gen. Theol. Sem., N.Y.C., 1973-79; Epis. visitor Western Mich., 1988-89. Lt. USNR, 1943-46. Home: Philadelphia Pa. Died Nov. 3, 1990; buried churchyard of Christ Ch., Phila.

OGLESBY, CLARKSON HILL, civil engineering educator, writer; b. Clarksville, Mo., Nov. 9, 1908; s. Edwin Bright Oglesby and Frances Lewis Thomas; m. Ardis May Hansen, June 8, 1938; children: Virginia Lee Hancock, Judith Lynne Donaghey, Marjorie Kay Zellner. AB in Engring., Stanford U., 1932, degree in civil engring., 1936. Registered civil engr., Calif. Draftsman to engr. State of Ariz. Dept. Transportation, Phoenix, 1928-41; constrn. engr. Vinson and Pringle, Phoenix, 1941-43; acting asst. prof. civil engring. Stanford (Calif.) U., 1943-46, asst. prof., 1946-48, assoc. prof., 1947-52, prof., 1952-74; cons. Calif. Toll Bridge Author, San Francisco, 1948; prof., cons. in constrn. mgmt. Cath. U., Chile, U. New South Wales, Australia and U. Cape Town, South Africa. Author: Highway Engineering, 1952, 4th rev. edit., 1982, Methods Improvement, 1972, Productivity Improvement in Construction, 1988; also articles. Recipient Carroll H. Dunn award of excellence Constrn. Industry Inst., 1991. Mem. ASCE (hon., Peurifory award Constrn. Rsch. 1988), NSPF (Outstanding Constrn. Educator 1984), Nat. Acad. Engring., Phi Beta Kappa, Sigma Xi, Tau Beta Pi. Democrat. Congregationalist. Home: Palo Alto Calif. Died Aug. 23, 1992. †

O'HARA, JAMES GRANT, lawyer, congressman; b. Washington, Nov. 8, 1925; s. Raphael McNulty and Neta Lloyd (Hemphill) O'H; m. Susan Pearl Puskas, Feb. 14, 1953; children: Ray, Thomas, Patrick, Brendan, Mary, Brigid, Neal. BA, U. Mich., 1954, JD, 1955; LLD, Mich. State U., 1975. Bar: Mich. 1955, D.C. 1976. Pvt. practice Detroit, 1955-59; mem. 86th-94th Congress from 12th Mich. dist., 1959-77, chmn. farm labor subcom., 1971-73, chmn. higher edn. subcom., 1973-77; ptnr. Patton, Boggs & Blow, Washington, 1977-89; chmn. Fed. Minimum Wage Study Commn., Washington, 1978-81. Chmn. Dem. Party Rules Commn., Washington, 1969-72, Rules Com. Dem. Nat. Conv., Miami Beach, Fla., 1972, Parlimentarian, 1972-76, Dem. Party Jud. Commn., Washington, 1977—. Served to sgt. U.S. Army, 1943-46, PTO. Mem. D.C. Bar Assn., Mich. Bar Assn., U.S. Internat. Tempest Assn. (pres.), Severn Sailing Assn. Democrat. Roman Catholic. Belle Haven Country (Alexandria, Va.). Home: Alexandria Va. Died Mar. 13, 1989.

OHLANDT, BEVERLY, distillery executive; b. Bklyn., Mar. 23, 1898; s. Peter and Kathryn (Dunn) O.; m. Marie Battey, June 29, 1919; 1 dau., Dorothy (Mrs. Robert Furlotte). Student pub. schs., Bklyn. Asst. sales mgr. Thomas J. Lipton, 1919-23; gen. sales mgr. R.B. Davis Co., 1923-28; pres. Grocery Products Co., 1938-44; v.p., dir. Schenley Distillers Corp., 1944-48; exec. v.p. Nat. Distillers Chem. Corp., N.Y.C., from 1948, vice chmn., from 1965, also dir.; vice chmn. Licensec Beverage Industries, Inc.; chmn. Licensed Beverage Bd., from 1961, Bourbon Inst., from 1963; bd. dirs. Distilled Spirits Inst. Served as lt., inf. U.S. Army AEF, 1916-69. *

OHRBACH, JEROME KANE, clothing chain executive; b. Bklyn., Dec. 17, 1907; s. Nathan M. and Matilda (Kane) O.; m. Gladys T. Otey, June 4, 1940 (div. 1952); children: Barbara Jane, Susan, Jeffrey; m. Marjorie Winters McGee, Oct. 1954; children: Lisa Kane, Caryl Edna; m. Ingrid Goude, 1962. AB, Cornell U., 1929. Asst. advt. dir., asst. buyer, buyer, mdse. mgr. Ohrbachs Inc., N.Y.C.; gen. mdse. mgr., 1930-39, v.p., 1940-46, pres., 1946-62, opned L.A. store, 1948; spl. ptnr. Dreyfus & Co., 1947-70, Weiss, Peck & Greer, from 1970; pres. Transpacific Equipment Corp., from 1962; prin. owner Factory discotheque, L.A., from 1967; as advt. dir. introduced new instnl. approach in retail advt. Mem. Cornell Coun., N.Y.C. Bd. Higher Edn., 1950; bd. dirs. Ctr. Theatre Group, L.A. Lt. col. USAAF, 1942-46, MTO. Mem. Explorers Club, Century Country Club, Hillcrest Country Club. Home: Los Angeles Calif. Died June 28, 1990; buried Salem Field Cemetery, N.Y.C.

OKRESS, ERNEST CARL, physicist, electrical engineer; b. Hamtramck, Mich., Mar. 9, 1910; s. Ernest Steven and Emilie (Schvanner) O. B.E.E., U. Detroit, 1935; M.Sc., U. Mich., 1940; postgrad., NYU, 1946-48, NYU, 1946-48, Poly. U., 1951-53, Schlumberger Ltd., 1972-74; D.Sc., Sussex (Eng.) Coll. Tech., 1974. Cert. profl. engr. Nat. Council Engring. Examiners; nationally registered cons. Adv. engr., mgr. Microwave Center, Westinghouse Electric Corp., Bloomfield, N.J. and Elmira, N.Y., 1940-59; sr. research engr. Sperry Gyroscope Co., Great Neck, N.Y., 1959-62; mgr. plasma physics, research div. Am. Standard, Inc., Piscataway, N.J., 1962-68; sr. engr. cons. SFD Labs., Inc. subsidiary Varian Assos., Union, N.J., 1968; sr. physicist, mem. sci. staff Brookhaven Nat. Lab., Upton, N.Y., 1968-70; sr. research scientist Cons. Seversky Electron-Atom Corp., Garden City, N.Y., 1970; sr. research physicist EMR div. Schlumberger, Ltd., Princeton, N.J., 1970-72, cons. engr., 1972-74; cons. engr. Westinghouse Electric Corp., 1972, Princeton Electron Products, 1972-74, USDA, 1968-74; sr. physicist-engr. Gen. Electric Co., Space Scis. Lab., Valley Forge Space Center, 1974-75; pvt. practice as cons. engr., 1988-89; cons. physicist Gen. Electric Co., 1975-77, Univ. City Sci. Center, 1977-78; cons., prin. scientist Franklin Research Center div. Arvin/Calspan Corp., Phila., 1978-88; tchr. U.S. Office Edn., 1943. Author, editor: Crossed Field Microwave Devices, 1961, Microwave Power Engineering, 1968; Papers examiner, book reviewer: Jour. Applied Physics, 1947, 49, 52, IEEE, 1953, 56; contbr. articles to profl. jours. Recipient Westinghouse spl. patents awards for outstanding inventions, 1945, 50, cert. commendation U.S. Office Sci. Research and Devel., 1945; cert. recognition NASA, 1976. Fellow IEEE, Am. Phys. Soc.; mem. N.Y. Acad. Sci. (invited mem.), Sigma Xi. Home: Philadelphia Pa. Died Dec. 24, 1989.

OLAV, V, King of Norway; b. Appleton House, Eng., July 2, 1903; s. King Haakon VII and Queen Maud (d. King Edward VII of Eng.); m. Princess Märtha of Sweden, Mar. 21, 1929 (dec. 1954); children: Crown Prince Harald, Princess Ragnhild (wife of Erling Lorentzen), Princess Astrid (wife of Johan Martin Ferner). Ed., Norwegian Mil. Acad., Balliol Coll., Oxford U. Comdr.-in-chief Norwegian Forces, World War II; leader govt. in exile in Eng., until 1945, when Norway was liberated; following death of father, succeeded to throne, Sept. 21, 1957. Home: Oslo Norway Died Jan. 17, 1991; interred Royal Mausoleum, Akershus Castle, Norway.

OLDS, ELIZABETH, artist; b. Mpls., Dec. 10, 1896; d. Fred Allen and Harriet (Trussell) O. Student, U. Minn., 1915-17, Mpls. Coll. Art and Design, 1918-21, Art Students League, N.Y.C., 1921-22. One-woman exhbns. ACA Gallery, 1937, 41, 50, 52, 55, 60, 63, S.I. Inst. Arts and Scis., 1969; represented in permanent collections Met. Mus., N.Y.C., Mus. Modern Art, N.Y.C., Bklyn. Mus., Phila. Mus., Nat. Mus. Am. Art Smithsonian Instn., Washington; retrospective exhbn.

118 painting, drawings, prints sponsored by RGK Found. and U. Tex., April, May, 1986; illustrator 6 books for children including The Big Fire, 1945, Riding the Rails, 1948, Feather Mountain, 1951, Deep Treasure, 1958, Plop, Plop Ploppie, Little Una (all Jr. Lit. Guild selections). Guggenheim fellow, 1926. Home: Sarasota Fla. Died Mar. 4, 1991; buried Lakewood Cemetery, Mpls.

OLFIELD, LORD ROBERT See **HAVERS, LORD MICHAEL**

OLIVE, LINDSAY SHEPHERD, botany educator; b. Florence, S.C., Apr. 30, 1917; s. Lindsay Shepherd and Sarah Carolyn (Williamson) O.; m. Anna Jean Grant, Aug. 28, 1942. A.B., U. N.C., 1938; M.A., 1940, Ph.D., 1942. Instr. botany U. N.C., 1942-44; mycologist, plant disease diagnostician Dept. Agr., 1944-45; asst. prof. botany U. Ga., 1945-46; assoc. prof. botany La. State U., 1946-49; assoc. prof. botany Columbia U., 1949-57, prof., 1957-67; prof. dept. botany U. N.C., Chapel Hill, 1968-69; disting. univ. prof. U. N.C., 1970-82, disting. univ. prof. emeritus, 1982-88. Contbr. to: Ency. Americana; contbr. chpts. to books.; Author: The Mycetozoans, 1975; also numerous articles on classification, life histories, cytology, genetics, evolution of fungi and mycetozoans. Guggenheim fellow, 1956. Fellow AAAS; mem. Nature Conservancy (hon. life mem.; former project com. chmn.), Am. Bot. Soc., Mycological Soc. Am. (pres. 1966, Disting. Mycologist award 1981), Soc. Protozoologists, Torrey Bot. Club (pres. 1962), Brit. Mycological Soc. (hon.), Nat. Acad. Scis., Phi Beta Kappa, Sigma Xi. Home: Highlands N.C. Died Oct. 19, 1988; buried Highlands Meml. Pk.

OLIVER, CLARENCE PAUL, zoology educator; b. Obion County, Tenn., Nov. 8, 1898; s. Benjamin Wesley and Mary Eunellie (Massey) O.; m. Cecile Worley, July 29, 1931; children: Peter Lee, George Benjamin. AB, U. Tex., 1925, MA, 1930, PhD, 1931. Asst. prof. zoology Washington U., St. Louis, 1930-32; from asst. prof. to prof. zoology U. Minn., 1932-46, dir. Dight Inst. Human Genetics, 1941-46; prof. zoology U. Tex., Austin, from 1946; Ashbel Smith prof. zoology U. Tex., from 1963, chmn. dept. zoology, 1947-59. Co-mng. editor Genetics, 1957-63; contbr. articles to profl. jours. Mem. AAAS, Am. Assn. Cancer Rsch., Soc. Exptl. Biology and Medicine, Am. Soc. Human Genetics (pres. 1953), Genetics Soc. Am. (pres. 1958), Am. Genetics Assn., Am. Soc. Zoologists, Am. Soc. Naturalists. *

OLIVER, GRAYDEN, petroleum engineer; b. Portland, Oreg., Sept. 23, 1894; s. Emery and Annette (Sylvester) O.; m. Mona C. Gardner, Jan. 4, 1923 (dec.); children: Suzanne (Mrs. Luis E. Benitez), Grayden E. BS, U. Calif., 1918. Master mechanic Moering Bros., Sacramento, 1916-18; field engr. Natomas Co. of Calif., 1919-20; prodn. engr. Wallace Refineries, 1920-21; gas engr., refinery supt. Pacific Gasoline Co., 1921-22; chief engr. Refiners Constrn. Co., 1922-28; tech. editor Petroleum World and Hydraulic Engring., 1926-29; cons. petroleum engr., from 1929; pres. Yuba River Sand Co., Oliver Rsch. Lab.; pres., gen. mgr. Wyandotte Orchards, Inc.; dir. Pacific Producers Inc. Served as lt., sci. and rsch. div. A.S., U.S. Army, 1917-19. Mem. ASCE, Calif. Natural Gasoline Assn., Am. Inst. Mining and Metall. Engrs., Am. Petroleum Inst., Am. Assn. Petroleum Geologists, Petroleum Oil Club (L.A.), Sutter Club (Sacramento), Commonwealth Club (San Francisco), Kappa Alpha. *

OLIVER, JOHN WATKINS, district judge; b. Cape Girardeau, Mo., Dec. 17, 1914; s. Robert Burett and Jessie (McCreery) O.; m. Gertrude Field, Jan. 24, 1940; children: John Watkins II, Gertrude, Jane, David. AB, U. Mo., 1934, LLB, 1936. Bar: Mo. 1936. Practiced in Kansas City, 1936-62; U.S. judge U.S. Dist Ct. (we. dist.) Mo., 1962-90, sr. judge; mem. Jud. Conf. U.S. Standing Com. on Adminstrn. Probaation, 1963-90, chmn. bd. of election commrs., Kansas City, 1950-54; mem. Mo. Bd. Law Examiners, 1952-62; bd. dirs. Mo. Law Sch. Found., Am. Law Inst. Mem. Kansas City Bar Assn., Mo. State Bar (gov. 1945-46), Lawyers Assn. Kansas City (bd. dirs. 1942), Am. Judicature Soc., Mo. Hist. Soc., Soc. of Friends. Home: Kansas City Mo. Died Apr. 25, 1990; interred Mt. Washington Cemetery, Kansas City, Mo.

OLIVIER, SIR LAURENCE KERR, actor, director; b. Dorking, Surrey, Eng., May 22, 1907; s. Gerard Kerr and Agnes Louise (Crookenden) O.; m. Jill Esmond, 1930 (div. 1940); 1 son, Simon Tarquin; m. Vivien Leigh, Aug. 30, 1940 (div. 1960); m. Joan Plowright, Mar. 17, 1960; children: Richard Kerr, Tamsin Agnes Margaret, Julie Kate. Student, St. Edward's Sch., Oxford, Eng.; MA (hon.), Tufts Coll., 1946; DLitt (hon.), Oxford U., U. Manchester, 1968, U. London, 1968, U. Sussex, 1978; LLD (hon.), Edinburgh U. Actor Birmingham Repertory Co., 1925-28, Old Vic Theatre Co., 1937-38, 44-46, 49; founder New Vic Theatre Co., 1944; toured Australia and N. Z., 1948; mgr., actor St. James' Theatre, 1950-51; producer, actor Festival of Britain, 1951-54; actor Shakespeare Meml. Theatre, 1955; 1st dir. Chichester Festival Theatre, Nat. Theatre Gt. Brit., 1963-73. Stage appearances include: Murder on the Second Floor; dir., actor King Lear, 1946; dir. Skin of Our Teeth, 1946; producer and dir. Born Yesterday, 1946; motion picture debut, 1930; films include: Murder for Sale, 1930, The Yellow Ticket, 1931, Friends and Lovers, 1931, Westward Passage, 1932, Perfect Understanding, 1933, No Funny Business, 1934, I Stand Condemned, 1936, As You Like It, Fire Over England, 1937, Divorce of Lady X, 1938, Wuthering Heights, Clouds Over Europe, 1939, Rebecca, 21 Days Together, Pride and Prejudice, 1940, That Hamilton Woman, 1941, Demi-Paradise, 49th Parallel, The Invaders, 1942, Adventure for Two, Henry V, 1945, Carrie, The Magic Box, 1952, Beggar's Opera, Devil's Disciple, 1959, Spartacus, 1960, The Entertainer, 1960, Term of Trail, 1963, Bunny Lake is Missing, 1965, Othello, 1965, Khartoum, 1966, Shoes of the Fisherman, 1968, Oh, What a Lovely War, 1969, Dance of Death, David Copperfield, 1970, Three Sisters, 1970, Nicholas and Alexandria, 1971, Sleuth, 1972, Lady Caroline Lamb, 1972, Marathon Man, 1975, The Seven Percent Solution, 1976, A Bridge Too Far, 1977, The Betsy, 1978, The Boys from Brazil, 1978, A Little Romance, 1978, Dracula, 1978, Clash of the Titans, 1979, Inchon, 1979, The Jazz Singer, 1980, Wagner, 1982, The Bounty, 1984, Wild Geese II, 1984; dir., producer and actor Hamlet, 1947, Venus Observed, 1950; dir., actor: Richard III, 1954, The Prince and the Showgirl, 1956, John Gabriel Berkman, 1958; TV appearances include: The Power and the Glory, John Gabriel Borkman, 1959, The Moon and Sixpence, Long Day's Journey Into Night, 1972, The Merchant of Venice, 1973, Love Among the Ruins, 1974, Jesus of Nazareth, Cat on a Hot Tin Roof, Hindle Wakes, The Collection (Emmy award), 1976, Come Back Little Sheba, Daphne Laureola, Saturday Sunday Monday, 1977, Brideshead Revisited, Granada TV, 1979, A Voyage Around My Father, 1982, King Lear, 1983, The Ebony Tower, 1984, The Last Days of Pompeii, miniseries Peter the Great, 1986; appearances with Nat. Theatre include: Uncle Vanya, The Recruiting Officer, 1963, The Master Builder, 1964, Love for Love, 1966, Dance of Death, 1966, Othello, 1963, 66, Flea in Her Ear, 1967, Home and Beauty, 1969, Merchant of Venice, 1969, John Gabriel Borkman, The Power and the Glory, World at War, 1973, Love Among the Ruins, A Voyage Round My Father, 1982, King Lear, 1982. Author: (autobiography) Confessions of an Actor, 1983, On Acting, 1986. Served with Brit. Fleet Air Army, 1940-43. Created knight by King George VI, lord by Queen Elizabeth; decorated comdr. Order Dannebrog, Denmark, officer Legion of Honour, grand officer Ordine al Merito della Repubblica, Italy, Order of Yugoslav Flag with Gold Wreath, 1971, Order of Merit, 1981; recipient Oscar award for best actor, Acad. Motion Picture Arts and Scis., 1948; award for directing, producing and acting in Hamlet, Brit. Film Industry; Emmy award for the Moon and Sixpence, 1960, For Long Day's Journey Into Night, 1973; Danish Sonning prize, 1966; Gold medallion Swedish Acad. Lit.; hon. Oscar for lifelong contbn. to art of film, 1979. Clubs: Garrick; Green Room, Marylebone Cricket. Home: Steyning Eng. Died July 12, 1989.

OLMSTED, MILDRED SCOTT (MRS. ALLEN SEYMOUR OLMSTED), social worker; b. Glenolden, Pa.; d. Henry J. and Adele Brebant (Hamrick) Scott; m. Allen Seymour Olmsted II, Oct. 30, 1921 (dec. 1977); children: Peter Scott (dec.), Enid Scott Olmsted Burke, Anthony Scott. BA, Smith Coll., 1912, LHD (hon.), 1974; certificate (Coll. Settlements' Assn. fellow), U. Pa. Sch. Social Work, 1913; LLD (hon.), Swarthmore Coll., 1987, Haverford Coll., 1988. Sec. Main Line Fedn. Chs., YMCA service in mil. camps in U.S. and France; internat. relief work Am. Friends' Service Com., France and Germany, World War I; asst. dir. White Williams Found., 1920-22; leader European and Russian Goodwill Tour, 1932; nat. exec. dir. U.S. sect. Women's Internat. League for Peace and Freedom, mem. internat. exec. com., 1935-49, exec. dir. emeritus, 1966-90; Mem. U.S. del. to internat. congresses, Prague, Grenoble, Zurich, Luhacovice, Luxembourg, Paris, Copenhagen, Birmingham, Eng., Stockholm, Asilomar, U.S., The Hague, Nyborg, Denmark, Tokyo, New Delhi; rep. UN Council Non-Governmental Orgns., 1949, Confs. Church and War, 1950, Conf. Church and Peace, 1953; organized 1st Soviet-Am. Women's Conf., Bryn Mawr, Pa., Moscow; rep. Internat. Women's Congress, New Delhi, 1970, Women, SALT and Arms Control, Washington, 1978, World Conf. Religion for Peace, from 1971; organized social service dept. Bryn Mawr Hosp., became head worker; co-founder Sch. in Rose Valley, 1929; mem. state and local bds. Nat. Youth Adminstrn., 1938-40; dir. Nat. Women's Com. to Oppose Conscription, 1942-47. Mem. Consultative Peace Council; vice chmn. Nat. Peace Conf., 1940-51, Joint Friends' Peace Com.; mem. governing bd. Post War World Council, 1944; governing council Upland Inst. Social Conflict Mgmt.; bd. Phila. Birth Control League; mem. bd. Promoting Enduring Peace; mem. exec. com. peace edn. Am. Friends Service Com.; clk. Providence Friends Meeting, from 1970; mem. Phila. Yearly Meeting Friends Commn. on Projects and Concerns, from 1974; co-chairperson Sane Peace Award Dinner, Oct. 1978. Recipient Sane Phila. Peace award, 1972, Sacco-Vanzelti award Community Ch. Boston, 1987; Disting. Alumna award Friends Central Sch., 1974; honored by Older Women's League, 1985, Grad. Sch. Social Work Alumni Assn., U. Pa., 1985, Women's Internat. League for Peace and Freedom (only life mem.), 1985, ACLU, Phila., 1985, Providence Friends Meeting, 1985. Mem. A.A.U.W., Am. Acad. Certified Social Workers, World Affairs Council, Fgn. Policy Assn., Women's Overseas Service League, Turn Toward Peace Movement (mem. council and exec. com. from 1961), Morris, Tyler arboreteums, Nat. Assn. Social Workers, ACLU (Pa. dir.), LWV, S.E. Pa. Civil Liberties Union (vice chmn.), The Nature Conservancy, Planned Parenthood, Internat. Planned Parenthood, Nat. Wildlife Fedn., Internat. Wildlife Fedn., Audubon Soc., Nat. Trust Historic Preservation. (home and garden placed on historic preservation list). Home: Rose Valley Pa. Died July 2, 1990.

OLPIN, A(LBERT) RAY, university president; b. Grove, Utah, June 1, 1898; s. Albert Henry and Alvira (Smith) O.; m. Elva Chipman, Apr. 12, 1922; children: Helen Rae Callahan, Barbara Ann Hooks, Virginia Adams, Howar Ray. AB, Brigham Young U., 1923; PhD, Columbia U., 1930; DSc, Calif. Coll. Medicine, 1960; LLD, U. Utah, 1964. Missionary in Japan, 1916-20; instr. Brigham Young U., 1922-24; asst. in physics Columbia U., 1924-25; mem. tech. staff Bell Telephone Labs., 1925-33; lectr. Bklyn. Poly., 1931-33; dir. rsch. Kendall Mills, Charlotte, N.C., 1933-39; prof., dir. indsl. rsch. Ohio State U., 1939-46; pres. U. Utah, 1946-64, pres. emeritus, from 1964. Assoc. editor Jour. Applied Physics, 1937-38; others. Ford Found. grantee, 1964. Fellow Am. Phys. Soc.; mem. AAAS, NEA, Assn. Asian Studies, Sigma Xi, others. *

OLSEN, C. ARILD, church official, educator; b. Omaha, Feb. 2, 1898; s. Ole C. and Karen (Andersen) O.; m. Elise H. Hermansen, Oct. 14, 1926; children: Lois M. Dunavan, Erik H. Grad., State Inst. Gymnastics, Copenhagen, 1922; PhB, U. Chgo., 1925, MA, 1927; LLD, Augustana Coll., 1952. Prof. history and social sci. Grand View Coll., 1925-30, dean men, 1925-26, pres., 1932-38; pres. Grand View Coll. Sem., 1932-38; supr. community svcs. & edn. FSA, Dept. Agr., Lincoln, Nebr., 1939-41; field supr. FSA, Dept. Agr., Washington, 1941-43, chief edn. & orgn. sect., 1943-45; chief evang. affairs sect. Office of Mil. Govt., Berlin, 1945-46; chief religious affairs br. Berlin, 1946-50, Office High Commr. Germany, 1950-51; assoc. exec. sec. divsn. Christian life & work, Nat. Coun. Chs. Christ in USA, 1951-54, exec. sec., 1954-64, exec. dir. dept. ch. & soc., from 1965. Deocrated Knight's Cross of Order of Merit, Germany. Lutheran. *

OLSEN, EINAR ARTHUR, college president, author; b. Gloucester, Mass., Apr. 14, 1917; s. Carl Johann and Aina Elena (Kaupilla) O.; m. Vera A. Seppala, Aug. 24, 1947; children: Donald, Stephen. BS, U. Maine, Orono, 1946, MEd, 1947; EdD, Boston U., 1952. Tchr. pub. schs. Jonesport, Maine, 1947-49; dir. health Essex County, Mass., 1952-55; assoc. prof. health Tex. Western Coll., El Paso, 1955-57; assoc. prof., then prof. health Mankato (Minn.) State Coll., 1957-67, chmn. dept. health, 1960-67; dean Farmington (Maine) State Coll., 1967-68, acting pres., 1968-69; pres. U. Maine, Farmington, 1969-81; vis. prof. U. N.Mex., Albuquerque, 1957; mem. faculty N.D. Internat. Sch. Alcohol Studies, 1965; chmn. adv. council alcohol and drug abuse Gov. of Maine, 1971-73, mem., 1971-76; mem. Nat. Commn. Allied Health Edn., 1977-79. Author: (juvenile books) Mystery at Salvage Rock, 1970, The Lobster King, 1970, Adrift on a Raft, 1970, Killer in the Trap, A(with others) Golf, Swimming, Tennis, 1961, The Foundations of Health, 1967, 2d edit., 1976, Programmed Instruction in Health Education and Physical Education, 1970. Mem. Maine Gov.'s Adv. Council Pub. Broadcasting, 1974-76; bd. dirs. Maine Lung Assn., Rural Health Assn. Franklin County; trustee Bancroft Sch.; mem. com. research and planning Maine Hosp. Assn. Served with USN, 1942-45. Recipient Presdl. citation Am. Assn. Advancement Health Edn., 1980; Teaching fellow Boston U., 1950-52; grantee Hill Found., 1965, 67, Maine Regional Med. Program, 1973. Mem. Am. Assn. State Colls. and Univs. (from rep. Maine 1971, chmn. allied health professions com. 1974-76), Am. Assn. Colls. Tchr. Edn. (Maine rep. 1971-74), Am. Assn. Higher Edn., AAHPER, Phi Delta Kappa, Eta Sigma Gamma. Home: Lincolnville Center Maine Died Dec. 15, 1985; interred Seaside Cemetery, Gloucester, Mass.

OLSEN, EUGENE FIELD, business executive; b. Rock Rapids, Iowa, May 1, 1896; s. John and Hattie (Dickson) O.; m. Florence Davenport, Feb. 20, 1918 (dec. Mar. 1920); 1 child, Gene D.; m. Gertrude Lewis, July 12, 1922 (dec. Apr. 1960); m. Cherie Wallace, Dec. 30, 1961. Student, Iowa State Coll., 1914-17; CE, MIT, 1918-19, degree in aero. engring., 1919. Pres., gen. mgr. Anchor Concrete Machinery Co., 1919-27; pres. Consol. Concrete Machinery Co., 1927-31; pres., treas., dir. Stearns Mfg. Co., 1932-48, Bassett Foundry, 1943-48; pres., dir. Ind. Limestone Co., 1945-46; active ptnr. Ida (Mich.) Mfg. Co., 1942-46; active & controlling ptnr. Purity Ice and Ice Cream Co., 1945-48; v.p., sec., dir. Euro Canning Co., Ida, 1946-54; pres., dir. Adrian Peerless, Inc., 1947-59; treas., dir. Sperti-Faraday, Inc., Adrian, 1946-48; v.p., dir. Local Loan Co., Ames, Iowa, 1940-50; others. Lt. U.S. Army. Mem. Nat. Concrete Masonry Assn., Sigma Phi Epsilon, Delta Sigma Rho, others. Republican. Episcopalian. *

OLSEN, FRANCIS RICHARD, advertising executive; b. Bklyn., Sept. 26, 1933; s. Smith and Mildred (Moisuk) O.; m. Phyllis Jean Hildenbrand, Sept. 2,

1956; children: Neil Richard, Randi Jean. B.B.A., Hofstra U., 1955; postgrad., NYU, 1958-62. Trainee-timebuyer William Esty, N.Y.C., 1955-61; planner-network negotiator Needham, Harper & Steers, N.Y.C., 1962-64, v.p., media dir., 1965-66; v.p., media dir. Ted Bates, N.Y.C., 1966-69; sr. v.p., founding ptnr. Vitt Media Internat. Inc., N.Y.C., 1969-80, vice chmn., sec., dfir., 1981-91; mem. faculty N.Y. Inst. Advt., 1969-70; lectr. St. John's U., 1972, 74, 88, St. John's U. GBA, Queens, N.Y., 1976, 78, 90, Fordham U. GBA, 1990; lectr. in field. Editor: Advertising Planning, Implementation and Control, 1980; contbr. articles to profl. jours. Cubmaster Boy Scouts Am., Sea Cliff, N.Y., 1974-76; com. chmn. Cub Scouts Am., 1976, 77-78; mem. fin.. com. Sea Cliff Meth. Ch., 1981-82. Scholar Hofstra U., 1951; recipient Cert. of Merit Advt. Club of N.Y., 1971, Recruitment award Boy Scouts Am., 1975, Media Creativity award Progressive Architecture, 1976. Mem. Media Dirs. Council, Internat. Radio and TV Execs. Soc., Nat. Assn. TV Programming Exces., Glen Players Club (Glen Head, N.Y.), Sea Cliff Yacht Club, Masons, Sons of Norway, Norseman Fedn., Delta Tau. Home: Sea Cliff N.Y. Died Sept. 24, 1991; buried Andes, N.Y.

OLSEN, MARVIN ELLIOTT, sociology educator; b. Hamilton, N.Y., Apr. 18, 1936; s. Edward Gustave and Faith Theresa (Elliott) O.; m. Katherine Irene Melchiors, Sept. 8, 1956 (div. 1978); children: Lawrence Frederick, Steven Elliott, David Edward; m. Valencia Anne Fonseca, Nov. 20, 1982. BA, Grinnell Coll., 1957; MA, U. Mich., 1958, PhD, 1965. Instr. U. Mich., Ann Arbor, 1963-65; asst. prof. Ind. U., Bloomington, 1965-69, assoc. prof., 1969-74, prof., 1974-76; affiliate prof. U. Wash., Seattle, 1974-80; sr. research scientist Battelle Human Affairs Research Ctrs., Seattle, 1974-79; prof. Wash. State U., Pullman, 1980-84; chmn. dept. sociology Mich. State U., East Lansing, 1984-90, prof. dept. sociology, 1984-92; dir. Inst. Social Rsch. Ind. U., 1970-74; vis. assoc. prof. Uppsala (Sweden) U., 1971-72; vis. rsch. fellow Internat. Inst. Environ. and Soc., Berlin, 1979, 81. Author: The Process of Social Organization, 1968, 2d edit, 1978, Participatory Pluralism, 1982, Societal Dynamics, 1990; co-author Designing a Citizen Involvement Program, 1987, Viewing the World Ecologically, 1992; editor: Power in Societies, 1979; co-editor Handbook of Applied Sociology, 1981. Pres. World Future Soc., Seattle, 1975-76; mem. Citizens' Task Force for the King County Energy Planning Project, Seattle, 1979-80, Sci. Adv. Com. to Northwest Power Planning Council, Portland, Oreg., 1981-83. Served to capt. USAF, 1958-62. Mem. Am. Sociol. Assn. (area rep. 1985-87, chmn. Environ. Sociology sect. 1983-85), Internat. Sociol. Assn., North Cen. Sociol. Assn. (pres. 1989-90), Soc. for Applied Sociology (pres. 1987-88), Coalition for Utilizing Sociology (coord. 1988-90)., Phi Beta Kappa, Phi Kappa Phi. Democrat. Unitarian. Home: Easton Wash. Died May 7, 1992. †

OLSON, ELDER JAMES, humanities educator, poet; b. Chgo., Mar. 9, 1909; s. Elder James and Hilda (Schroeder) O.; m. Ann E. Jones, Feb. 13, 1937 (div. 1948); children: Ann Olson Goldberg, Elder; m. Geraldine Hays, Sept. 17, 1948; children: Inez Olivia Olson Strong, Shelley Olson de Alereu. BA, U. Chgo., 1934, MA, 1935, PhD, 1938. Instr. Armour Inst. Tech., Chgo., 1935-42; mem. faculty U. Chgo., 1942-92, prof. English, 1954-92, Distinguished Service prof., 1971-77, Distinguished Service prof. emeritus, 1977-92; M.D. Anderson Distinguished prof. U. Houston, 1978-79; Rockefeller prof. U. Frankfurt, Germany, 1948, U. Philippines, 1966-67; vis. prof. U. P.R., 1952-53; Mahlon Powell prof. philosophy Ind. U., 1955, vis. prof. lit. criticism, 1958-59; fellow Sch. Letters, 1961, Patten lectr., 1964; vis. prof. U. N.Mex., 1982. Author: Thing of Sorrow, 1934, The Cock of Heaven, 1940, (with others) Critics and Criticism, 1952, The Poetry of Dylan Thomas, 1954, The Scarecrow Christ, 1954, Plays and Poems, 1958, Tragedy and The Theory of Drama, 1961, The Theory of Comedy, 1968; (poems) Collected Poems, 1963, Olson's Penny Arcade, 1975, On Value Judgements in the Arts & Other Essays, 1976, Last Poems, 1984; editor: American Lyric Poems, 1963, Aristotle's Poetics and English Literature, 1965, Major Voices, 1973; mem. adv. bd. Forum. Recipient Witter Bynner award, 1927; Guarantor's award Poetry mag., 1931; Tietjens award, 1953; Emily Clark Balch award Va. Quar. Rev., 1965; Quantrell award U. Chgo., 1966; Distinguished Service award U. Philippines, 1967; grantee Longview Found., 1958; award Poetry Soc. Am., 1955; award Acad. Am. Poets, 1956; award Soc. Midland Authors, 1976; Mary Elinore Smith prize, 1986. Mem. MLA, PEN, Soc. Européene de Culture, Phi Beta Kappa. Home: Albuquerque N.Mex. Died July 25, 1992. †

OLSON, JAMES CHESTER, management consultant; b. Elkhart, Ind., Jan. 11, 1907; s. Julius Axel and Chalmers Berdice (Hess) O.; m. Jean Lorraine Stewart, Apr. 7, 1945; children: James Stewart, Julia Jean (Mrs. F. Graham Luckenbill II), David Chalmers. AB, Wittenberg Coll., 1930, LLD (hon.), 1955; MBA, Harvard U., 1933. Instr. econs. and bus. adminstrn., asst. dir. admissions Wittenberg Coll., 1933-36; cons. Booz, Allen & Hamilton, N.Y.C., 1936-40, jr. partner, 1940-42, sr. partner, 1942-62, mem. exec. com., 1948-62, vice chmn., exec. com., 1960-62; dir. Booz Allen Method Systems Inc., Booz Allen & Hamilton Internat., Ltd., Booz Allen Applied Research, Inc.; v.p., dir. Booz, Allen & Hamilton, Inc., 1962-64; dir. Bancroft Racket Co. Inc. and affiliates, 1945-74, chmn. bd., 1966-74; dir. Colonial Trust Co., 1954-56, Church & Dwight Co. Inc., 1969-74, 1158 Fifth Av. Corp., 1950-52, 1115 Fifth Ave. Corp., N.Y.C., 1977-79; participant implementation of Marshall Plan during World War II; bd. mgrs. Candlewood Lake Club Owners Corp., 1962-65, pres., chmn. bd., 1970-71. Mem. U.S. Mut. Security Adminstrn. (now AID) program evaluation project Greece, 1953; trustee Wittenberg U., 1969-82, emeritus mem., 1982-92, chmn. audit com., 1971-72. Mem. Nat. Sales Execs. Inc., Phi Kappa Psi. Presbyterian. Club: Harvard (N.Y.C.). Home: New York N.Y. Died Mar. 31, 1992; buried Center Cemetery, New Milford , Conn.

OLSON, LAWRENCE, history educator; b. Memphis, May 7, 1918; s. Lawrence A. and Wanda (Liddell) O.; m. Jeane E. Noordhoff, Dec. 19, 1941; children: Alexandra Lyman, Sarah Liddell. B.A., U. Miss., 1938; M.A., Harvard U., 1939, Ph.D., 1955; M.A. (hon.), Wesleyan U., Middletown, Conn., 1969. Cultural attache Am. embassy, Manila, Philippines, 1951-52; staff assoc. Am. Univs. Field Staff, 1955-66, sr. staff assoc., 1962-66; prof. history Wesleyan U., 1966-84, prof. emeritus, 1984-92, developer univ. Asian studies program; vis. prof. Dartmouth, 1964-65; vis. fellow Coun. on Fgn. Rels., 1968-69. Author: The Cranes on Dying River and Other Poems, 1947, Dimensions of Japan, 1963, Japan in Postwar Asia, 1970, Ambivalent Moderns: Portraits of Cultural Identity, 1992. Served to lt. (j.g.) USNR, 1942-46. Recipient Japanese Order Sacred Treasure, 1987; Ford fellow, 1952-54, Rockefeller fellow, 1963, Fulbright rsch. fellow Japan, 1973-74, Woodrow Wilson Internat. Ctr. for Scholars fellow, 1979-80. Mem. Japan Soc., Assn. Asian Studies. Home: Washington D.C. Died Mar. 17, 1992.

OLSON, RICHARD HALL, manufacturing executive; b. Mazeppa, Minn., Dec. 15, 1898; s. Nels M. and Anna C. (Swenson) O.; m. Muriel P. Burdick, July 22, 1922; 1 child, Franklin Pierce. BS, U. Minn., 1919. Field svc. engr. Electric Machinery Mfg. Co., 1919-23, dist. mgr., 1924-30, Ea. sales mgr., 1930-44, v.p., dir., 1944-50, pres., gen. mgr., dir., 1950-59, chmn., 1959; group v.p. Worthington Corp., from 1959. Mem. Am. Inst. Elec. Engrs., Tau Beta Pi, Tau Kappa Epsilon. *

OLSSON, GEORGE CARL PHILLIP, farmers cooperative executive; b. Boston, Aug. 16, 1903; s. John Otto and Ida Charlotte (Carlson) O.; m. Mary Arnold Craig, Jan. 23, 1933; children: Dexter Arnold, Philip Craig. JD, Boston U., 1926. Bar: Mass. Clk. cts. Plymouth County, Mass., 1928-58; chmn. bd. dirs. Ocean Spray Cranberries, Inc., Hanson, Mass., 1958-74, v.p. govt. rels., 1974-91; dir. Plymouth Fed. Savs. & Loan Assn. Past dir. regional Boy Scouts Am.; v.p. Plymouth Plantation, hist. orgn.; chmn. Plymouth-Provinetown Pilgrim 350th Celebration Commnn.; del. Rep. nat. convs., 1936, 40. Lt. comdr. USNR, 1942-45. Mem. Nat. Canners Assn. (legis. com.), Nat. Coun. Farmer Coops. (dir.), Swedish Colonial Soc. Am., Mass. Bar Assn., Plymouth County Bar Assn., Old Colony Club (Plymouth), Masons, Lambda Chi Alpha. Congregationalist. Home: Plymouth Mass. Died Nov. 13, 1991; buried Plymouth, Mass.

OLSTEN, WILLIAM, personnel services company executive; b. 1919; m. Miriam Olsten; children: Stuart, Cheryl Olsten Ashburn. Grad., NYU, 1951. With Chevrolet div. GM, 1940-43; founder Olsten Corp., Westbury, N.Y., 1950-91, CEO, until 1990, chmn., 1990-91. With U.S. Army, World War II, ETO. Home: Old Westbury N.Y. Died Oct. 3, 1991; buried L.I., N.Y.

O'MALLEY, CHARLES ACHESON, insurance company executive; b. Island Heights, N.J., Aug. 13, 1917; s. Charles Acheson and Edna Josephine (Ill) O'M.; m. Nancy Bertelsen, May 16, 1958; children: Brooke, Barbara, Charles, Arthur, Michael. Student, Rutgers U., Bklyn. Coll. With Lethbridge-Owens & Phillips, N.Y.C., 1942-62, pres., 1955-62; merged with Fred S. James & Co., Inc., Chgo., 1963; mem. exec. com. Fred S. James & Co., Inc., 1969-82, exec. v.p., 1971-75, chmn. exec. com., from 1975, chmn. bd., 1980-85, chief exec. officer, 1981-85; pres. Fred S. James & Co., Inc. (aquired by Transam. Corp.), 1982; dir. Transam. Corp., 1982-88; bd. dirs. Wigham Poland Holdings Ltd. Trustee Coll. of Ins.; Chmn. Fund Raising for Retarded Children, 1968-69; chmn. N.Y. Zool. Soc., 1976-77. Served to 1st lt. USAAF, 1943-45. Mem. Ins. Brokers Assn. N.Y. (past dir.), Casualty and Surety Agts. Assn. Clubs: N.Y. Yacht, Chesapeake Bay Yacht, India House, Wall Street, Monroe. Home: Stuart Fla. Died Apr. 15, 1989.

O'MALLEY, COMERFORD J., priest, educator; b. Chgo., Mar. 8, 1902; s. Austin and Alice (Comerford) O'M.;. BA, St. Mary's Sem., Perryville, Mo., 1926, MA, 1927; STD, Collegio Angelico, Rome, 1929; LLD (hon.), Niagara U., 1948. Ordained priest Roman Cath. Ch., 1982. Prof. theology St. Mary's Sem., Perryville, 1929-34; prof. philosophy De Paul U., Chgo., 1934-36, dean Coll. Commerce, 1936-44, pres., 1944-64, chancellor, 1964-91, also vice chmn. bd. trustees; consultor to provincial We. Province, Congregation of Mission, 1962—. Mem. Commn. on Acceditation of Svc. Experiences of Am. Coun. Edn., Chgo. Recreation Commn., Mayor's Com. on Sch. Bd. Nominations. Mem. Chgo. Soc. Cath. Psychologists (past pres.), Blue Key, Delta Sigma Pi. Home: Chicago Ill. Died Feb. 27, 1991.

O'MEARA, EDWARD THOMAS, bishop; b. St. Louis, Aug. 3, 1921; s. John and Mary (Fogarty) O'M. Student, Kenrick Sem., 1943-46; STD, Angelicum U., Rome, 1953. Ordained priest Roman Cath. Ch., 1946. Monseignor, then ordained bishop Roman Catholic Ch., 1972; asst. pastor St. Louis Cathedral, 1952-55; asst. nat. dir. Soc. for Propagation of the Faith, St. Louis, 1956-60, dir., 1960-67; nat. dir. N.Y.C., 1967-79; archbishop of Indpls., 1980-92; apptd. titular bishop of Thisiduo and aux. bishop of St. Louis, 1972-80; pres., chmn. Cath. Relief Svcs., until 1991. Editor: World Mission mag. Home: Indianapolis Ind. Died Jan. 10, 1992.

O'MEARA, JOSEPH, academic dean, lawyer; b. Cin., Nov. 8, 1898; s. Joseph and Nancy J. (Gibson) O'M.; m. Jean Collow, June 11, 1928; children: David, Nancy Strang. AB, Xavier U., 1921; LLB, U. Cin., 1943. Bar: Ohio 1921. Assoc. Western & So. Life Ins. Co., 1926-40; mem. law firm Merland, O'Meara, Santen & Willging, Cin., 1924-53, Dargusch, Caren, Greek & King, Columbus, Ohio, 1946-53; lectr. fed. taxation coll. law U. Cin., 1943-46, Practicing Law Inst., 1943-48; dean law sch., prof. U. Notre Dame, from 1952. Contbr. articles to law jours. Mem. ABA, Am. Law Inst., Am. Judicature Soc., Ind. Bar Assn., ACLU. Democrat. Roman Catholic. *

O'MEARA, WALTER ANDREW, author; b. Mpls., Jan. 29, 1897; s. Michael and Mary (Wolfe) O'M; m. Esther Molly Arnold, Aug. 17, 1922; children: Donn, Ellen, Deirdre, Wolfe. Student, U. Minn., 1914-15; AB, U. Wis., 1920. Reporter Duluth (Minn.) News-Tribune, 1918; group head J. Walter Thompson Co., Chgo., 1920-31, creative dir., 1942-46, spl. cons., co-chmn. Rev. Bd., 1946-52, bus. cons., 1952-89; producer, police and security tng. films, 1957-89; v.p., chmn. plan bd. Benton & Bowles Inc., 1932-40; novelist, historian, 1941-89. Author: The Trees Went Forth, 1947, The Grand Portage, 1951, Short Story Collection: Tale of the Two Borders, 1952, The Spanish Bride, 1954, Minnesota Gothic, 1956, Just Looking (essays), 1956, The Devil's Cross, 1957, The Savage Country, The First Northwest Passage, 1961, The Last Portage, 1962, Guns at the Forks, 1965, The Duke of War, 1966, Daughters of the Country, 1968, Sioux are Coming, 1971, In the Country of the Walking Dead, 1972, We Made It Through the Winter: A Memoir of Boyhood in Northern Minnesota, 1974; also short stories, articles, critical revs. in nat. mags. Chief planning staff OSS, 1942-43; dep. price adminstr. OPA, 1943-44. With U.S. Army, 1918. Recipient Journalism citation U. Wis., 1957. Mem. Champlain Soc., Authors' League, Players Club (N.Y.C.), Phi Beta Kappa, Sigma Delta Chi. Democrat. Home: Cohasset Mass. Died Sept. 29, 1989; buried Cohasset Ctrl. Cemetery.

O'NEAL, FOREST HODGE, law educator; b. Rayville, La., Sept. 17, 1917; s. Forest Hodge and Nancy (Wright) O'N.; children by previous marriage-Forest Hodge III, Laurie, Mark N., Dee, Nancy, Karen; m. Barbara Schmidt McEntire, Oct. 3, 1988. Certificate, Northeast Jr. Coll., Monroe, La., 1936; A.B., La. State U., 1938; LL.B., 1940; J.S.D., Yale, 1949; S.J.D., Harvard, 1954. Bar: La. bar 1940, Ga. bar 1955, Mo. bar 1977. Asso. firm Sullivan & Cromwell, N.Y.C., 1941; asso. prof. law U. Miss., 1945-46, prof. law, 1946-47; acting dean and prof. law Walter F. George Sch. of Law, Mercer U., 1947-48, dean, 1949-56; prof. law Vanderbilt U. Law Sch., 1956-59; prof. law Duke U. Sch. Law, 1959-76, dean, 1966-68, James B. Duke prof. law, 1972-76; George Alexander Madill prof. law Washington U. Sch. Law, St. Louis, 1976-88, dean, 1980-85; vis. prof. law NYU, 1957-58, U. Minn., 1973, U. Mich., 1987, U. Fla., 1989. Author: (with Robert B. Thompson) Close Corporations: Law and Practice (2 vols.), 1958, 2d edit., 1971, Oppression of Minority Shareholders (2 vols.), 1975; (with Jordan Derwin) Expulsion or Oppression of Business Associates: Squeeze-Outs in Small Enterprises, 1961, (with Annie Laurie O'Neal) Humor, The Politician's Tool, 1964; editor in chief La. Law Rev, 1939-40; faculty adviser Miss. Law Rev, 1940-47; editor Corporate Practice Commentator, from 1959; contbr. (with Annie Laurie O'Neal) articles to law and bus. revs. Chmn. Southern Law Rev. Conf., 1948; commr. Uniform State Laws for, Ga., 1955; chmn. S. Eastern Regional Conf. Assn. Am. Law Schs., 1968-69. Served to lt. USNR, 1942-45; with U.S. Naval Base, 1945, Saipan. Sterling fellow Yale U., 1940. Mem. ABA (bd. editors jour. 1971-77), Mo. Bar Assn., La. Bar Assn., Ga. Bar Assn. (bd. govs. 1948-49, 1951-52, 1954-55), Assn. Am. Law Schs. (mem. exec. com. 1968-70), Order of Coif, Omicron Delta Kappa, Gamma Eta Gamma, Phi Kappa Phi. Baptist. Home: Sarasota Fla. Died Jan. 24, 1991.

O'NEAL, FREDERICK, actor, lecturer, director; b. Brooksville, Miss., Aug. 27, 1905; s. Ransome James and Ninnie Bell (Thompson) O'N.; m. Charlotte T. Hainey, Apr. 18, 1942. Ed., New Theatre Sch., N.Y.C., Am. Theatre Wing, N.Y.C.; also pvt. instrn.; AFD (hon.), Columbia Coll., Chgo., 1966; HHD (hon.), Lincoln U., Mo., 1976; DFA (hon.), Coll. of Wooster,

1976; DHL (hon.), St. John's U., 1981; DOH (hon.), Tougaloo Coll., 1982. Vis. prof. So. Ill. U., 1962, Clark Coll., Atlanta, 1963; founder Aldridge Players, St. Louis, 1927, Am. Negro Theatre, N.Y.C., 1940, Brit. Negro Theatre, London, 1948; pres. Inst. Study of Arts in Edn., Inc., 1980-92. Numerous theatrical appearances, U.S. and abroad, 1944-70, also motion pictures, 1949-92 , also numerous TV appearances; Author: The Negro in American Theatre, 1956. Organizer, pres. emeritus Schomburg Corp.; bd. dirs. Inst. for Adv. Studies in Theatre Arts, George Meany Labor Studies Ctr., 1990, UN Devel. Corp., Nat. Com. U.S./China Rels.; sec. Muscular Dystrophy Assn., 1980-89; mem. N.Y.C. Alliance for the Arts, 1978—, NAACP. With U.S. Army, 1942-43. Recipient Derwent award, 1945, first and 2d place N.Y. Critics poll, 1945, Donaldson award, 1945, Dutch Treat disc, 1944-45, spl. award New Eng. Theatre Conf., 1963, citation Ohio Community Theatre Assn., 1964, Hoey award Catholic Interracial Council, 1964, award Am. Jewish Congress, 1964, Canada Lee Found. Achievement award, 1954, Motion Pictures Critics award, 1957, Ira Aldridge citation Assn. Study Negro Life and History, 1963, N.Y.C. Central Labor Council award, 1967, City of St. Louis award, 1968, Nat. Urban League EOD award, 1966, Am. Vet.'s Com. George W. Norris Civil Rights award, 1970; League for Indsl. Democracy award, 1973; George M. Cohan award Cath. Actors Guild, 1980; named to Black Filmmakers Hall of Fame, 1975; Labor Recognition award N.Y. State AFL-CIO Fedns., 1985; Dem. Heritage award Am. Jewish Com., 1985; David L. Clendenin award Workers Def. League, 1987, APRI Spl. Recognition award , 1989, Disting. Am. Leadership award Black Heritage Assn., 1989, Lifetime Svc. award Sickle Cell Anemia Found. of Greater N.Y., Appreciation award Black Trade Unionists, 1991, Living Legend award Nat. Black Theatre Festival, 1991. Fellow Coll. Am. Theatre; mem. NATAS, SAG, AFTRA, ANTA, AFL-CIO (v.p. 1969-89, v.p. emeritus 1989-92), Actors Equity Assn. (pres. 1964-73, pres. emeritus 1973-92, pres. found. 1964-73), Actors and Artists Am. (internat. pres. 1970-89, pres. emeritus 1989), Actors Fund, Urban League, Cath. Interracial Coun. (pres. 1979-81), Am. Vets Com., Knights St. Peter Claver, Players Club, Lambs Club. Home: New York N.Y. Died Aug. 25, 1992. †

O'NEAL, PERRY ERNEST, lawyer; b. Rush County, Ind., Apr. 27, 1893; s. Lieu Allen and Frances (Finley) O'N.; m. Lucy Holliday, Oct. 21, 1925; children: Alice H. Dye, Perry H. Student, Wabash Coll., 1910-12; LLB, Ind. U., 1915. Bar: Ind. 1915. Practiced law Rushville, Ind., 1915-17, Inpls., from 1920; mem. firm Thompson O'Neal & Smith, from 1940; dir. Ind. Nat. Bank, Real Silk Hosiery Mills Inc. Capt. inf. U.S. Army, 1917-19. Mem. ABA, AIM, 7th Fed. Cir. Bar, Ind. Bar Assn., Inpls. Bar, , Am. Law Inst., others. *

O'NEILL, GERARD KITCHEN, physicist, educator; b. Bklyn., Feb. 6, 1927; s. Edward G. and Dorothy (Kitchen) O'N.; married, 1950 (div. 1966); children: Janet, Roger, Eleanor; m. Renate Steffen, 1973; 1 son, Edward. BA, Swarthmore Coll., 1950, ScD (hon.), 1978; PhD, Cornell U., 1954. Instr. rated pilot. Mem. faculty Princeton U., 1954-85, prof. physics, 1965-85, prof. emeritus, 1985-92; co-founder, pres. Space Studies Inst., Princeton U., from 1978; founder, pres., chmn. bd. dirs. Geostar Corp., 1983-85, also bd. dirs., 1983-91; founder, chmn. bd. dirs. OCI, Princeton, 1986-91; founder, gen. ptnr. VSE Internat., Princeton, 1991; Hunsaker prof. aerospace MIT, 1976-77; presdl. appointee Nat. Commn. on Space, 1985-86. Author pobls. on exptl. elem. particle physics, particle storage rings, nuclear physics, space devel. techniques; author: The High Frontier, 1977 (Bhi Beta Kappa Sci. Book award), (grad. textbook) Introduction to Elementary Particle Physics, 1979, 81, The Technology Edge, 1983, 2081: A Hopeful View of the Human Future, The Technology Edge: Opportunities for America in World Competition; editor: Space Manufacturing from Non-Terrestrial Materials, 1977; inventor storage ring prin. Served with USNR, 1944-46. Recipient Ann. award Assn. Space Explorers, 1986, Ann. award Ea. sect. IEEE, 1986. Fellow AIAA, Am. Phys. Soc., Phi Beta Kappa. Home: Princeton N.J. Died Apr. 27, 1992.

O'NEILL, MICHAEL C(ORNELIUS), archbishop; b. Kemptville, Ont., Can., Feb. 15, 1898; s. Peter J. and Maude (Vroom) O'N. Student, U. Toronto, 1921-24; BA, St. Augustine's Sem., 1927, LLD, U. Toronto, 1952. With Can. Explosives, Ltd., 1915-16, Can. Civil Svc., 1919-21; ordained priest Roman Cath. Ch., 1927; tchr., rector St. Joseph's Sem., 1928-39; rector St. Joseph's Cathedral, Edmonton, Alta., 1946-47; archbishop Regina, Sask., from 1948. Served with F.A., C.E.F., Can. Army, 1916-19, as chaplain, Can. Army overseas, 1939-46. Decorated Mil. Medal, Order Brit. Empire, 1943. *

O'NEILL, MICHAEL JOYCE, magazine publisher; b. Shreveport, La., Apr. 2, 1922; s. Michael Joyce and Anna (McCrea) O'N.; m. Marie Clark, Apr. 24, 1948; children: Michael, James, Kate, Clark; m. Betty Wright Landreth, Nov. 6, 1976. B.S., U. Pa., 1947. Dir. spl. events Phila. Inquirer, 1947-49, regional mgr. advt. dept., 1949-51; exec. dir. Phila. Inquirer Charities, 1951-53; advt. dir. TV Guide, Phila., 1953-62; pres. Liberty Bell Park, Phila., 1962-64; chmn. Phila. Eagles Football Club, 1962-64; v.p., dir. corp. rels. Young & Rubicam, Inc., N.Y.C., 1964-66; v.p., advt. dir. Look Mag., N.Y.C., 1966-70; v.p., pub. CBS Mags., Field & Stream mag., N.Y.C., 1970-72, Epicure mag., 1972-74; sr. v.p. for advt., group pub. CBS Mags., 1974-1976, cons., 1976-86; sr. v.p. Howard Sloan Communications Search, Inc. Trustee Annenberg Sch. Communications U. Pa. Served with USNR, 1941-45. Mem. Mag. Pubs. Assn. (dir.), Advt. Council (mag. dir.), Hunting Hall of Fame (dir.), Am. League Anglers (dir.), Pa. Soc. Clubs: University (N.Y.C.), Racquet (Phila.); Sky, Dutch Treat, African Safari. Home: New York N.Y. Died Apr. 22, 1989.

OPPENHEIM, ALFRED, retired wholesale grocery executive; b. Brockton, Mass., June 15, 1915; s. Abraham M. and Leonora (Wiscotch) O.; m. Naomi Mezoff, Oct. 30, 1942; children: Betsy, Jeffrey. Student, City U., Paris, 1945. Sales mgr. Brockton Products Co., Mass., 1934; sales supr. New Eng. Grocers Supply Co., Worcester, Mass., 1935-39; sales mgr. Silver Bros., Manchester, N.H., 1939-41; pres. Cressey Dockham & Co., Inc., Salem, Mass., 1946-51, 53-74, chmn. bd., chief exec. officer, 1975-85. Served to capt. AUS, 1942-46, 51-53. Decorated Bronze Star, Bronze Star with oak leaf cluster; Chung Moo Disting. Service medal Korea. Mem. C. of C., Nat. Wholesale Grocers Assn., Am. Wholesale Grocers Assn., New Eng. Wholesale Grocers Assn. (pres. 1963-64), Ind. Grocers Alliance (dir. 1974-85), Food Exec. Club. Jewish (dir. temple). Clubs: Dolphin Yacht (commodore 1960-61 Marblehead), Ferncroft Country (Danvers, Mass.); Boca Woods Country. Home: Danvers Mass. Deceased. †

OPPENHEIM, SAUL CHESTERFIELD, educator; b. N.Y.C., Jan. 16, 1897; s. Jacob and Julia (Jaffe) O.; m. Morgery H. Heiman, Sept. 22, 1922; 1 child, Daniel Payne. AB in Econs. & History summa cum laude, Columbia U., 1918, AM, 1920; JD, U. Mich., 1926, SJD, 1929. Bar: Mich. 1926, D.C. 1935, U.S. Supreme Ct. 1935. Instr. econs. U. Mich., 1921-26, teaching & rsch. asst. to dean law sch., 1926-27, prof. law, from 1952; prof. law George Washington U., 1927-52, univ. adviser on rsch. George Washington Patent, Trademark & Copyright Rsch. Inst., from 1957. Author: Cases on Trade Regulation, 1936, Cases on Federal Antitrust Laws, 1948, Unfair Trade Practices-Cases, Comments and Materials, 1950, National Transportation Policy and Inter-Carrier Competitive Rates, 1945, Antitrust Law: Case and Comment, 1959; also articles; editor-in-chief Trade Regulation Law series. Sgt. U.S. Army, 1918-19. Mem. ABA, Assn. Am. Law Schs., N.Y. Bar Assn., Fed. Bar Assn., Phi Beta Kappa, others. *

OPPENHEIMER, FRITZ ERNEST, lawyer; b. Berlin, Mar. 10, 1898; s. Ernst and Amalie (Friedlander) O.; m. Elizabeth Kaulia, Oct. 23, 1927; children: Ellen Ingeborg, Ernest Albert. Ed., Berlin U., 1919-20, Freiburg U., 1920-21; LLD, Breslau U., 1922, Paris U., 1924-25, London U., 1925. Assoc. with solicitors London, 1925-35; counselor in chambers of atty. gen. Eng. and Brit Treasury, 1936-40; with firm Cadwalader, Wickersham & Taft, N.Y.C., 1940-43; chief analyst Bd. Econ. Warfare, Washington, 1943; spl. asst. U.S. Mil. Govt. for Germany, 1946; spl. asst. for German-Austrian affairs Dept. State, 1946-48; legal adviser to sec. State at confs. Cooun. Fgn. Mins., Moscow, 1947, London, 1947, Paris, 1949; U.S. dep. fgn. min. on treaty for Austria, 1947; legal adviser U.S. amb. 6-Power Conf. on Germany, London, 1948; pvt. practice, N.Y., from 1948. Author various publs. on internat., corp. & tax law in English, French and German. Lt. German Army, 1915-18; lt. col. U.S. Army, 1943-45. Decorated Legion of Merit, Bronze Star. Mem. N.Y.C. Bar ASsn., Am. Soc. Internat. Law, Internat. Law Assn., Coun. Fgn. Rels. *

OPPENHEIMER, MONROE, lawyer; b. N.Y.C., Sept. 20, 1904; s. Morris and Julia Bacharach O.; m. Ruth Shapiro, Feb. 16, 1933; children: Judith, Mark. Bar: Mo. 1926. Assoc. Stern & Burnett, St. Louis, 1927-29, Lewis, Rice, Tucker, Allen & Chubb, 1929-33; chief atty. A.A.A., 1933-35; asst. gen. counsel, then gen. counsel Resettlement Adminstrn., 1935-37; head atty. Office of Solicitor, Dept. of Agr., 1937-41; gen. counsel Bd. Econ. Warfare, 1941-43. Mem. ABA, Fed. Bar Assn., Fed. Communications Bar., Yale Law Sch. Assn., Order of Coif, Phi Beta Kappa. Home: Washington DC Died Oct. 2, 1990.

OPTON, FRANK G., lawyer; b. Dusseldorf, Germany, Feb. 25, 1906; m. Eva Opton; children: Ilse Tebbetts, Dorothy Scott, Barbara Pizer, Margaret Morin. LLD cum laude, U. Cologne, 1929; LLB, N.Y. Sch. Law, 1938. Bar: N.Y. 1939. Mem. firm Lynton, Klein, Opton and Saslow, N.Y.C.; lectr. Practising Law Inst., 1942—, NYU Law Sch., 1956-62. Contbr. articles to profl. jours. Mem. ABA (mem. com. on treatment of enemy property in wartime 1962), Nat. Panel Arbitrators, Am. Arbitration Assn., Assn. Bar City N.Y. (mem. com. on adminstrv. law 1964-66), N.Y. State Bar Assn. (mem. com. internat. law 1969-89), Internat. Bar Assn. Home: Hightstown N.J. Died June 20, 1989.

ORIANS, GEORGE HARRISON, educator, author; b. Marion, Ohio, Apr. 19, 1900; s. George Joseph and Nettie Katherine (Zachman) O.; m. Dorothy Ruth Schmidlin, Aug. 29, 1941; children: Daryl Ruth, Margaret Janelle, George Randall. AB, North-Cen. Coll., 1922; AM, U. Ill., 1923, PhD, 1926; postgrad., Yale U. and Libr. Congress, 1936. Assoc. prof. English U. Idaho, 1928-29; lectr. Am. lit. U. Toledo, 1929-32, prof. English, 1934-70, prof. emeritus, 1970; dir. summer sessions, 1934-51, chmn. English dept. 1938-53; vis. prof. summers So. Meth. U., U. Colo., U. Wash.; lectr. Nat. Audubon Soc., 1947-59; vis. prof. U. Mich., 1967-68. Editorial bd. North-West Ohio Quar., The United States, 1865-1900, Hayes Meml. Found. (4 extant vols.); photographer, producer (films) Ruins of Mexico and Guatemala, Lake Erie, Glacier to Port, Feather Symphony, By Erie's Changing Shores, Great Smoky Skyland, Roanoke Northwest, Gay Wings, Finding Birds in Mexico, 1977, (antipollution film) The Fate of a River (The Maumee); author: The Indian in the American Metrical Romance, 1930, A Short History of American Literature, 1940; a series of studies in Hawthorne, 1935-44; a series of studies in American fictional motifs, 1932-38; co-author: American Local-Color Stories, 1941, The American Heritage, 2 vols., 1949, Transitions in American Literature, 1954, articles on Indian Wars, 1962-66, History of the Burt Theatre, 1962, Nine Sermons of Cotton Mather: Days of Humiliation, 1969; editor: Specimens of American Poets (1822), 1972, Theatrical Life of Otto Kruger, 1975; contbr. revs. and articles to mags., yearbooks, 1930-88. Turstee Ohioana Libr., Columbus, Ohio. Recipient Water Conservation award Nat. Wildlife Fedn. and Sear Found., 1966; named Naturalist of Yr., Toledo Naturalists Assn., 1977. Mem. MLA, AAUP, Internat. Platform Assn., Phi Beta Kappa, Phi Kappa Phi. Home: Toledo Ohio Died Apr. 14, 1985; cremated.

ORLOFF, JACK, physician, research physiologist; b. Bklyn., Dec. 22, 1921; s. Samuel and Rebecca (Kaplan) O.; m. Martha Vaughan, Aug. 4, 1951; children: Jonathan Michael, David Geoffrey, Gregory Joshua; 1 child by previous marriage, Lee Frances. Student, Columbia U., 1937-38, Harvard U., 1938-40; M.D., N.Y. U., 1943. Diplomate Am. Bd. Internal Medicine. Intern Mt. Sinai Hosp., N.Y.C., 1944; resident medicine Montefiore Hosp., N.Y.C., 1944-46; research fellow Yale Med. Sch., 1948-50; mem. sr. research staff Nat. Heart Inst., Bethesda, Md., 1950-57, dep. chief lab. kidney and electrolyte metabolism, 1957-62, chief lab., 1962-75; dir. intramural research Nat. Heart, Lung and Blood Inst., Bethesda, Md., 1974-88; professorial lectr. physiology, med. Georgetown U. Med. Sch., 1962-84; disting. alumni lectr. N.Y. U. Sch. Medicine, 1966; Del.-at-large exec. council Fedn. Am. Sci., 1962-64, exec. com., treas., 1963-64. Author: Essays in Metabolism, 1957, Metabolic Disturbances in Clinical Medicine, 1958, The Metabolic Basis of Inherited Disease, 1972, Heart, Kidney and Electrolytes, 1962, Diseases of the Kidney, 1971, Cellular Function of Metabolic Transport, 1964, Hormones and the Kidney, 1964, Nobel Symposium on Prostaglandins, 1967, Physioli of Diuretic Agents, 1966, Ocytocin, Vasopressin and their Structural Analogues, 1964; Editorial bd.: Am. Jour. Physiology, sect. editor, 1964-68, Jour. Applied Physiology, 1964-68, Renal Physiology sect. 8, Handbook of Physiology, 1973; asso. editor: Kidney Internat, 1971-87; cons. editor: Life Scis, 1973-78. Trustee Greenacres Sch., Rockville, Md., 1960-64, v.p. bd. trustees, 1962-63; Mem. sci. adv. bd. Nat. Kidney Found., 1962-71; mem. Inst. Medicine Nat. Acad. Scis. Served to capt. M.C. AUS, 1946-48. Recipient Homer Smith award N.Y. Heart Assn., 1973, Meritorious Service award USPHS, 1974, Distinguished Alumni Achievement award in basic sci. N.Y. U. Sch. Medicine, 1976; Distinguished Service medal HEW, 1977. Mem. Am. So. Clin. Investigation, Am. Physiol. Soc., Fedn. Am. Scientists (vice-chmn. 1963-64), Assn. Am. Physicians, Am. Soc. Nephrology (sec.-treas. 1970-72, pres. 1973-74), Sigma Xi, Alpha Omega Alpha. Club: Cosmos. Home: Rockville Md. Died Dec. 6, 1988.

ORMONDROYD, JESSE, educator; b. Phila., Feb. 7, 1897; s. Herbert and Jeanette Ellson (Wrighton) O.; m. Kathleen Felton, June 2, 1921; children: Edward, Ruth. AB, U. Pa., 1920. Rsch. & design engr. Westinghouse Elec. & Mfg. Co., 1920-30, mgr. exptl. divsn. turbine works, 1930-37; prof. engring. U. Mich., from 1937; chmn. dept. engring. mechs., 1963-64; egnr. on vibration problems. Author: (with Karelitz & Garrelts) Problems in Mechanics, 1939; also papers on theory of vibration in various tech. publs.; in charge of mfg. design 200-inch telescope mounting. With U.S. Army A.S., 1917-19. Mem. ASME, Am. Soc. for Engring. Edn., Franklin Inst., Newcomen Soc., Rotary, Lambda Chi Alpha, Phi Beta Kappa, Tau Beta Pi, Phi Kappa Phi, Sigma Xi. *

OROWAN, EGON, physicist, engineering educator; b. Budapest, Hungary, Aug. 2, 1902; came to U.S., 1950; s. Berthold and Josephine (Sagvari) O.; m. Yolan Schonfeld, Jan. 20, 1941 (dec.); 1 child, Susan Katherine. Diploma in engring., Tech. U. of Berlin, 1929, Engring. Dr., 1932, MA, 1948, Dr. Ing. (hon.), 1965. Asst. prof. Tech. U., Berlin-Charlottenburg, 1928-33; in charge Krypton Gas Works, United Incandescent Lamp and Elec. Co., Hungary, 1936; rsch. assoc. physics dept. U. Birmingham, Eng., 1937-39; rsch. assoc. physics dept. Cavendish Labs., U. Cambridge, Eng., 1937-39, Nuffield Rsch. fellow, 1945-47, reader in the physics of metals, 1947-50; George Westinghouse prof. mech. engring. MIT, 1951-68, sr. lectr., 1968-73, prof. emeritus,

1973; vis. Inst. prof. Carnegie Inst. Tech, 1962-63; Alcoa vis. prof. U. Pitts., 1972-73. Recipient Thomas Hawksley Gold medal Inst. Mech. Engrs., 1944, Eugene C. Bingham medal Soc. Rheclogy, 1959, Carl Friedrich Gauss medal, 1968, Vincent Bendix medal Am. Soc. for Engring. Edn., 1971, Paul Bergsoe medal Danish Metall. Soc., 1973; fellow Gonville and Calus Coll., Cambridge, Eng., 1949. Fellow Royal Soc.; mem. Am. Acad. Arts and Scis., Nat. Acad. Sci.; Acad. Sci. Gôttingen. Home: Cambridge Mass. Died Aug. 2, 1989.

OROWITZ, EUGENE MAURICE See LANDON, MICHAEL

ORR, DOUGLASS WINNETT, former psychiatrist, psychoanalyst; b. Lincoln, Nebr., Aug. 29, 1905; s. H. Winnett (M.D.) and Grace (Douglass) O.; m. Jean Walker, Mar. 28, 1931; children: Stephen Winnett, Nancy Ann (Mrs. Lee S. Adams). A.B., Swarthmore Coll., 1928; M.S., Northwestern U., 1934, M.D., 1935. Instr. English, adviser exptl. coll. U. Wis., 1928-30; intern Cook County Hosp., Chgo., 1935-36; resident psychiatry Menninger Clinic and Psychiat. Hosp., Topeka, 1937-38; mem. staff Menninger Clinic and Psychiat. Hosp., 1938-41; practice medicine specializing in psychiatry Seattle, 1941-42, 46-65; co-founder N.W. Clinic Psychiatry and Neurology, Seattle, 1946; resigned N.W. Clinic Psychiatry and Neurology, 1953; tng. analyst San Francisco Psychoanalytic Inst., 1947-65, Los Angeles Psychoanalytic Soc. and Inst., 1966-80, Joint Com. for Psychoanalytic Tng. in San Diego; tng. analyst San Diego Psychoanalytic Inst., 1974-80, ret., 1980; dir. Seattle Psychoanalytic Tng. Center, 1952-58, 62-64, Seattle Psychoanalytic Inst., 1964-65; practice psychoanalysis, La Jolla, Calif., 1966-80; clin. asso. prof. U. Wash. Sch. Medicine, 1958-64; cons. VA, Surgeon Gen. AUS, 1946-47. Author: (with Mrs. D.W. Orr) Health Insurance with Medical Care: The British Experience, 1938, Professional Counseling on Human Behavior, 1965, (with Mrs. Lee S. Adams) Life Cycle Counseling: Guidelines for Helping People, 1987; mem. editorial bd. Archives of Gen. Psychiatry, 1959-64; contbr. articles to profl. jours. Trustee Pinel Found., 1948-55, pres., 1953; trustee Seattle Psychiat. Clinic for Adults, 1953-64. Served as lt. comdr. USNR, 1942-46. Mem. Am. Psychiat. Assn. (councilor 1954-57), Am. Psychoanalytic Assn., Phi Beta Kappa, Sigma Xi, Delta Upsilon. Home: Santa Rosa Calif. Deceased. †

ORTON, WILLIAM ROLEN, JR., retired mathematics educator; b. Texarkana, Tex., May 4, 1922; s. William Rolen and Mignon Janette (Johnson) O.; m. Marion Claire Rogers, Sept. 6, 1950; children: Lori Ann, William III, Lisa Marion, Benjamin Rogers. B.A., U. Ark., 1947; M.A., U. Ill., 1948, Ph.D., 1951; postgrad., U. Paris, 1951-52, U. Wash., 1965-66. Instr. Oberlin (Ohio) Coll., 1952-53; asst. prof. math. U. Ark., Fayetteville, 1953-57; assoc. prof. U. Ark., 1957-64, prof., 1964-87, emeritus, 1987-90; dir., instr. NSF Insts. Secondary Math. Tchrs., 1960-72; dir. NSF Comprehensive Program in Math. Edn. for Ark., 1972-76; cons. NSF Found., India staff, 1967-68; dir. Internat. Conf. Secondary Sch. Math. programs, 1969. Editor proc.: Conf. Internat. Secondary Math, 1969. Served with U.S. Army, 1943-46. Fulbright scholar Iran, 1977-78; Decorated Purple Heart, Bronze Star.; NSF faculty fellow, 1965-66. Mem. Math. Assn. Am., Am. Math. Soc., Phi Beta Kappa, Sigma Xi, Pi Mu Epsilon, Omicron Delta Kappa, Kappa Sigma. Home: Fayetteville Ark. Died May 1990. †

OSBORNE, HERBERT JOHN, banker; b. Bklyn., June 11, 1897; s. Herbert S. and Margaret (O'Malley) O.; m. Helen J. Coneagh, Nov. 24, 1927: children: Robert, Alan, Donald. Student, NYU. Clk. Banker's Trust Co., 1915-20; clk. Mfrs. Hanover Trust Co. (formerly the Hanover Bank), 1920-28, asst. treas., 1929, asst. v.p., 1930-36, v.p., 1936-55, sr. v.p., 1955-62; chmn. exec. com. Summit Trust Co.; dir. Hygrade Food Products Corp., Mill Factors Corp., Boorum & Pease Co., McMillan Book Co.; dir., chmn., exec. com. Summit & Elizabeth Trust Co. Mem. NCCJ (treas. emeritus, trustee, mem. exec. & fin. coms.). *

OSSENFORT, WILLIAM FREDERICK, physician; b. Centaur, Mo., Oct. 17, 1898; s. Charles Henry and Caroline (Lenz) O.; m. Violet Marie Benson, June 20, 1928; 1 child, William Frederick. BS in Edn., S.E. Mo. State Tchrs. Coll., 1921; student, U. Mo., 1923; MD cum laude, Washington U., St. Louis, 1928. Sch. tchr. Allenton, Mo., 1917-18; high sch. prin. Crystal City, Mo., 1919-20, Charleston, Mo., 1921-24; instr. Will Mayfield Coll., 1924, 25; asst. surgeon USPHS, 1928-31, passed asst. surgeon, 1931-40, surgeon, 1940-42; asst. surgeon gen. in charge Divsn. Marine Hosps. & Relief, Washington, 1942-44; chief Divsn. Commd. Officer of Office of Surgeon Gen., 1944-46; chief med. officer U.S. Merchant Marine Acad., Kings Point, N.Y., 1948-50; chief quarantine officer Panama Canal, 1950-52; dir. Hosp. Facilities Program, Dallas, 1952-62; pvt. practice medicine, from 1963. With U.S. Army, 1918. Mem. AMA, ACP, So. Med. Assn., Am. Psychiat. Assn., Tex. Med. Assn., Sigma Xi, others. *

OSSOFSKY, JACK, voluntary agency executive, gerontologist, advocate, consultant; b. N.Y.C., Sept. 24, 1925; s. Harry and Mary (Bogomolny) O.; m. Myrel Solney, Jan. 25, 1947 (div. Oct. 1970); children: Mindy Ann, Robert Carl; m. Eula J. Wood, Feb. 15, 1975. B.S.S., CCNY, 1950. Dir. retirement and community services Retail, Wholesale Dept. Store Union, AFL-CIO, N.Y.C., 1950-65; project dir. Nat. Council on the Aging, N.Y.C., 1965-67, assoc. dir., 1967-69; dep. dir. Nat. Council on the Aging, Washington, 1969-71, exec. dir., 1971-86; pres. Nat. Council on the Aging, 1986-92; convener UN North Am. World Assembly on Aging, Washington, 1980-81; chmn. Leadership Council Aging Orgns., Washington, 1981-82, 84-85. Contbr. 40 chpts. to books, articles to profl. jours.; mem. editorial bd., Ednl. Gerontology, from 1979. Vice chmn. Sr. Citizens for Kennedy and Johnson, Washington, 1959-60; vice chmn. Sr. Citizens for Johnson and Humphrey, 1964; del. White House Conf. on Aging, 1971, 81; trustee Hobart Jackson Fellowship Fund, U. Pa., Phila., 1979-85; mem. numerous bds. and adv. cons. Served with U.S. Army, 1943-46. Recipient Cert. of Honor W.Va. Social Welfare Conf., 1977; named Hon. Citizen El Paso, Tex. and Mpls., 1978; recipient award of Appreciation U.S. Dept. Labor, 1979; Lifetime Achievement award on behalf of Aging, 1986. Mem. Nat. Assembly Social Agys. (dir. 1979-81), Nat. Social Welfare Conf., Hawaiian Pacific Gerontol. Soc. (hon.). Home: Alexandria Va. Died Sept. 4, 1992. †

OSSORIO, ALFONSO ANGEL, painter, sculptor; b. Manila, Philippines, Aug. 2, 1916; came to U.S., 1930, naturalized, 1939; s. Miguel Jose and Maria Paz Yuango O. BA, Harvard U., 1938; postgrad., R.I. Sch. Design, 1938-39. One-man shows include Wakefield Gallery, N.Y.C., 1941, 42, Mortimer Brandt Gallery, N.Y.C., 1945, Betty Parsons Gallery, N.Y.C., 1951, 53, 56, 58, 59, 61, Cordier & Ekstrom Gallery, N.Y.C., 1961, 63, 65, 67, Gallerie Fachetti, Paris, 1952, Gallerie Stadler, Paris, 1960, 61, Gallerie Cordler-Stadler, Frankfurt, Germany, 1961, Cordier and Ekstrom Gallery, N.Y.C., 1968, 69, 72; group exhbns. include Whitney Mus. Annuals, Carnegie Inst. annuals, Am. Fedns. Arts travelling exhbns., also Rome-N.Y. Art Found., 1957-59, Osaka (Japan) Art Festival, 1958, Arte Nouva, Turin, Italy, 1959, Neue Malerie, Munich, 1960, Arts of Assemblage, Mus. Modern Art, 1961, Structure e Stile, Turin, 1962, Galleries Pilotes, Lausanne, Switzerland, 1963, Artists Select, Finch Coll., N.Y.C., 1964, Contemporary Am. Art at U. Ill., 1965, at Chgo. Art Inst., 1966, Campo Vitale, Palazzio Grassi, Venice, 1967, Am. Arts 1670-1966, Whitney Mus., 1966; represented in permanent collections Met. Mus. Art, Whitney Mus., Mus. Modern Art, Phila. Mus. Art, Balt. Mus. Art, Worcester (Mass.) Mus. Art, Yale Art Gallery, NYU Art Gallery, Ateneo de Manila, Internat. Inst. Aesthetic Rsch., Turin, Museo de Arts Abstracto, Cuenca, Spain, Städtische Galerie, Munich; murals in ch. of Victorias, Negros Philippines, Washington Sq. Village, N.Y.C.; assemblage in N.Y. Hilton Hotel, 1964; co-founder, dir. Sigma Gallery, East Hampton, N.Y., 1957-60; dir. exhbns. Exec. House, N.Y.C., 1956-58. With AUS, 1943-46. Home: East Hampton N.Y. Died Dec. 5, 1990.

OSTERTAG, HAROLD C(HARLES), congressman; b. Attica, N.Y., June 23, 1896; s. Otto John and Frances (Briem) O.; m. Grace Bryson, June 25, 1919. Grad., Chamberlin Mil. Inst., 1915. State assemblyman from Wyo. County, N.Y., 1932-50; chmn. N.Y. Join Legis. Com. on Interstate Cooperation, 1936-50; chmn. bd. mgrs. Coun. State Govts., 1938, mem.-at-large, 1950-55; mem. 82d Congress 41st dist. N.Y., also 83d-87th Congresses, 39th dist., 88th Congress, 37th N.Y. Dist.; vice chmn. Nat. Rep. Congl. Com. Sgt. inf. AEF, France, World War I. Mem. Am. Legion, Attica C. of C., VFW, Nat. Rep. Club. *

O'SULLIVAN, CLIFFORD, judge; b. Chgo., Dec. 8, 1897; s. Patrick Thomas and Mary A. (Clifford) O'S.; m. Theresa A. Kearney, Feb. 4, 1928; children: Clifford Patrick, Sheila Keelan, John K., Mary A., Therese. Student, Campion Acad., Prairie du Chien, Wis.; LLB, U. Notre Dame, 1920; spl. student AEF, Univ. Coll., King's Coll., Lincoln's Inn, London. Bar: Ill. 1920, Mich. 1921. Practiced law Walsh & Walsh, Port Huron, Mich., 1920-24, Walsh, Walsh & O'Sullivan, 1926-57; assoc. Defrees, Buckingham & Eaton, Chgo., 1924-26; U.S. dist. judge Ea. Dist. Mich., 1957-60; judge U.S. Cir. Ct. Appeals (6th cir.), from 1960. Cpl. 122d F.A. U.S. Army, WWI. *

O'SULLIVAN, DANIEL EDWARD, insurance company executive; b. N.Y.C., Jan. 6, 1929; s. Michael and Nora (Walsh) O'S.; m. Rosemary E. McGuigan, Sept. 29, 1956; children: Nora, Julie, Daniel. B.S., Fordham U., 1948. Group underwriter The Union Labor Life Ins. Co., N.Y.C., 1950-57; asst. agy. mgr. western div., San Francisco The Union Labor Life Ins.Co., N.Y.C., 1958-62; 2d v.p. The Union Labor Life Ins. Co., N.Y.C., 1962-64, v.p., asst. to pres., N.Y.C., 1964-69, sr. v.p., 1969-70, exec. v.p., 1970-79, pres., 1979; pres., CEO Ullico Inc. (ins. holding co. including Union Labor Life Ins. Co.), 1984-90. Chmn. Planning Bd., Woodcliff Lake, N.J., 1970-83. Mem. Am. Coun. Life Ins. (bd. dirs.), Health Ins. Assn. Am. (bd. dirs.). Home: McLean Va. Died Nov. 25, 1990.

O'SULLIVAN, RICHARD JOHN, banker; b. N.Y.C., May 16, 1938; s. James Vincent and Nora Madeleine (Condon) O'S.; m. Jayne Helen Walls, Sept. 14, 1963; children: Tracy, Jill, Tara. B.B.A., Lehman Coll., N.Y.C., 1968. Mem. info. staff Western Electric Co., N.Y.C., 1956-68; systems mgr. Gen. Analytics, N.Y.C., 1968-71; v.p. U.S. Trust Co., N.Y.C., 1971-77; sr. v.p. computing and communications svcs. Morgan Guaranty Trust Co. of N.Y., N.Y.C., 1977-90. Served to sgt. USNG, 1956-64. Republican. Roman Catholic. Home: Hartsdale N.Y. Died Mar. 17, 1990; buried Gate of Heaven Cemetery, Valhalla, N.Y.

OSWALT, EDNA RICKEY, psychologist, educator; b. Albany, Ohio, Apr. 22, 1897; d. Fred Elza and Mary Alice (Robinett) Rickey; m. Ernest George Lotz, June 12, 1926 (dec. May 1938); m. Glen DeWitt Oswalt, Jan. 1, 1943. AB, Ohio U., 1917, BE, 1920; MA, Ohio State U., 1921, PhD, 1924. Tchr. high sch. Beverly and Jackson, Ohio, 1917-20; psychologist Bur. Juvenile Rsch., 1920-24; supervisory tchr., psychologist Colo. Normal Sch., 1924-31; dir. Colo. Sch. Ind. Instrn., 1931-34; supervisory tchr., asst. dir. psychology ednl. clinic Western State Tchrs. Coll., Kalamazoo, 1934-36; asst. prof. psychology Kent State U., 1936-37, dir. psychology clinic, 1936-46, assoc. prof. psychology, 1937-46, prof. psychology, from 1946; prof. psychology Westminster Coll., 1960-65; psychol. cons. Earle Speech Clinic, Akron, Ohio, from 1965; vis. prof. abnormal psychology Syracuse U., 1929-32. Fellow AAAS, APA, Am. Assn. Mental Deficient; mem. NEA, Ohio Edn. Assn., Ohio Probation Assn., Am. Assn. Gifted Children, Ohio Assn. Gifted Children, Am. Assn. Univ. Women, Sigma Xi, others. *

OTT, RICHARD B., judge; b. Ritzville, Wash., Mar. 19, 1897; s. Sebastian and Christina (Hege) O.; m. Allene Mills, July 18, 1926; 1 child, Patricia Hennings. LLB, U. Idaho, 1919. Bar: Idaho 1919, Wash. 1921. Gen. practice Oakley, Idaho, 1919-21, Ritzville, 1921-49; pros. atty. Adams County, Wash., 1923-31; city atty. City of Ritzville, 1925-33; judge Superior Ct. for Adams County, 1949-55; judge Supreme Ct. State of Wash., from 1955, chief justice, 1963-65. Mayor City of Ritzville, 1931-32; rep. Wash. Legislature, 1933-37. 2d lt. U.S. Army, 1918, maj. JAGD, 1946-54. Mem. ABA, Wash. Bar Assn., Am. Legion, Phi Gamma Delta, Phi Alpha Delta, others. *

OTTOMAN, RICHARD EDWARD, oncologist; b. Guthrie, Okla., Aug. 3, 1910; s. Adolph and Ferne (Christian) O.; m. Mary Elizabeth Merrill, Nov. 27, 1943; 1 adopted dau., Bonnie Ann. Student, Jackson Jr. Coll., 1932-34; M.D., U. Mich., 1941. Diplomate: Am. Bd. Radiology. Rotating intern Virginia Mason Hosp., Seattle, 1941-42; staff physician Birmingham VA Hosp., Van Nuys, Calif., 1946-47; resident radiology Birmingham VA Hosp., 1947-50, asst. radiologist, 1950; from asst. radiologist to chief therapeutic radiologist Long Beach (Calif.) VA Hosp., 1950-52, attending staff, 1952-56; vis. roentgenologist Los Angeles (Cal.) County at Harbor Gen. Hospital, 1950-56; attending staff St. John's Hosp., 1956-60, affiliate cons., 1960-70; cons. radiology and radioisotopes St. Joseph's Hosp., Burbank, Calif., 1950-60; cons. radiology Valley Hosp., Van Nuys, from 1956; now cons. oncology Valley Hosp.; individual practice medicine Los Angeles, from 1955; instr. U. So. Calif.; asst. prof. radiology UCLA, 1950-54, asso. prof., then prof. radiology and anatomy, 1954-61, 61-72, vice-chmn. dept. radiology, 1961-65, prof. emeritus, from 1980; cons. radiobiology Atomic Energy Program, 1952-64; chief radiation therapy Santa Monica (Calif.) Hosp. Med. Center, 1971-73, Valley Hosp., Van Nuys, 1973-76; mem. ednl. staff Northridge Hosp. and Med. Center, from 1975 ; cons. Los Angeles Planned Parenthood Center, 1957-66, mem. med. adv. com., 1959-62. Contbr. numerous articles to med. jours. Past trustee, past sec., treas. James T. Case Radiologic Fund. Served from 1st lt. to maj. M.C. AUS, 1942-46. Fellow Am. Coll. Radiology; mem. AAAS, AMA, Calif. Med. Assn., Am. Roentgen Ray Soc., Nat. Geog. Soc., Plato Soc. of UCLA, Phi Rho Sigma (life). Home: Santa Ynez Calif. Deceased. †

OUTLER, ALBERT COOK, clergyman, educator; b. Thomasville, Ga., Nov. 17, 1908; s. John Morgan and Gertrude Flint (Dewberry) O.; A.B., Wofford Coll., 1928, D.D., 1952; B.D., Emory U., 1933, Litt.D. (hon.), 1968; Ph.D., Yale U., 1938; D.D., Kalamazoo Coll., 1962; L.H.D. (hon.), Lycoming Coll., 1964, Ohio Wesleyan U., 1967, Duke U., 1974; LL.D. (hon.), U. Notre Dame, 1966; D.S.T. (hon.), Gen. Theol. Sem., 1967; D.H.L. (hon.), Loyola U., New Orleans, 1978, Cath. U. Am., 1979; m. Carlotta Grace Smith, Dec. 18, 1931; children: Frances Gertrude, David Stevens. Ordained to ministry Meth. Ch.; pastor, Baxley, Ga., 1928-30, Pineview, Ga., 1930-32, Gordon, Ga., 1932-34, Macon, 1934-35; instr. theology Duke U., 1938-39, asst. prof., 1939-41, asso. prof., 1941-45; asso. prof. Yale U., 1945-48, Dwight prof. theology, 1948-51; prof. theology So. Meth. U., Dallas, 1951-80, prof. emeritus, 1980-89, chmn. grad. council of humanities, 1960-63; research prof. religion Tex. Wesleyan Coll., 1983-85. Del. Meth. Ch. 3d World Council on Faith and Order, Lund, Sweden, 1952; chmn. Am. sect. FOC Theol. Commn. on Tradition; Meth. del. to 3d Assembly World Council Chs., New Delhi, 1961; vice chmn. 4th World Council on Faith and Order, Montreal, 1963; del.-observer 2d Vatican Council, 1962-65; vis. sr. fellow, Council Humanities, Princeton U., 1956-57; hon. fellow Wesley Coll., Sydney, Australia, 1980. Fellow Am. Acad. Arts and Sci.; mem. Am. Soc. Ch. History (pres. 1963-64),

World Council Chs., Am. Theol. Soc. (pres. 1960, sec. 1960-62), Acad. of Tex., Nat. Council Religion Higher Edn., Am. Cath. Hist. Assn. (pres. 1972-73), Duodecim, Phi Beta Kappa. Club: Elizabethan. Author: A Christian Context for Counseling, 1946; Colleges, Faculties and Religion, 1949; Psychotherapy and the Christian Message, 1954; The Confessions and Enchiridion of St. Augustine, 1955; The Christian Tradition and the Unity We Seek, 1957; John Wesley, 1964; Who Trusts in God, 1968; John Wesley, Sermons, I-IV; contbr. articles to profl. jours.Recipient Pax Christi award Benedictine Order, 1987. Died Sept. 1, 1989; buried Restland Meml., Dallas. Home: Bradenton Fla.

OVCHINNIKOV, YURI ANATOLIYEVICH, biochemist, educator; b. Moscow, Aug. 2, 1934; s. Anatoly and Yelena Ovchinnikov; m. 1st Tatyana Kirensky, 1956; m. Tatyana Marchenko, 1982; 4 children. Grad. Moscow State U., 1957; D.Sc. (hon.), U. Uppsala, U. Paris, U. Sofia, U. Granada, U. Gdansk, U. San Marcos, Peru, U. Ricardo Palma, Peru, Friedrich-Schiller U., German Dem. Republic. Research worker Shemyakin Inst. Bio-organic Chemistry, USSR Acad. Sci., 1960, dir., 1970; corr. mem. USSR Acad. Scis., 1968, mem., 1970, v.p., 1974, chmn. chem. tech. and biol. scis. div., from 1974; prof. Moscow U., until 1988; mem. Acad. Scis. Bulgaria, Czechoslovakia, GDR, Hungary, Spain, India; cand. mem. Central Com., CPSU, from 1981; chmn. FEBS Council, 1984-86; mem. Acad. Leopoldina. Author sci. papers, monographs; editor Bioorganitcheskaya chimia, Biologicheskie membrany and mem. editorial bds. numerous internat. jours. Recipient Lenin prize, 1978; Decorated Order of Lenin (3); Hero of Socialist Labour, 1981, State prize, 1982. Mem. USSR Acad. Scis., Ussr. Acad. Agrl. Scis., Bulgaria Acad. Scis., German Dem. Republic Acad. Scis., Czechoslovakian Acad. Scis., Hungarian Acad. Scis., Indian Nat. Sci. Acad., Royal Swedish Acad. Engring. Scis., German Acad. Natural Scis., Serbian Acad. Scis. and Arts, European Acad. Arts, Scis. and Humanities, Royal Acad. Exact, Phys. and Natural Scis., Royal Acad. Scis. and Arts of Barcelona, Acad. Agrl. Scis. German Dem. Republic, World Acad. Art and Sci., Japanese Biochem. Soc., Am. Phylosophical Soc., Cuban Chem. Soc., Biochem. Soc. German Dem. Republic, Serbian Chem. Soc. Died Feb. 27, 1988. Home: Moscow Russia

OVERDUIN, HENK, museum deputy director; b. Leiden, The Netherlands, May 1, 1943; s. Machiel and Jo (Zweegman) O.; m. Ria Matze, June 27, 1967. Grad. sociology of art, U. Leiden, 1969. Asst. curator modern art Frans Halsmuseum, Haarlem, The Netherlands, 1970-72, head dept. edn., 1972-75; head dept. edn. Haags Gemeentemuseum, The Hague, The Netherlands, 1975-82, dep. dir., from 1982; chmn. Dutch Mus. Assn., Amsterdam, from 1983. Contbr. articles on mus. policy to profl. jours.; also catalogues. Mem. Internat. Council Mus. Home: The Hague The Netherlands Died Oct. 26, 1988; buried The Netherlands.

OVERN, ALFRED VICTOR, educational consultant; b. Mpls., Nov. 28, 1893; s. Anton Gustav and Severine Mathilde (Wieding) O. AB, U. Minn., 1915, MS, 1926, PhD, 1930. Supt. schs. Hills, Minn., 1915-17, Alden, Minn., 1917-18, 19-23; prin. high sch. Hutchinson, Minn., 1923-27; instr. edn. State Coll., Brookings, S.D., 1928; head dept. edn. Augsburg Coll., Mpls., 1929-30; prof. edn. U. N.D., 1930-50, dir. grad. divsn., 1950-51; field rep. U.S. Office Edn., 1951-53, regional rep., 1953-54; spl. program advisor Cen. office U.S. Office Edn., Washington, 1954-64; ednl. cons., Mpls., from 1964; vis. prof. Duke U., U. Mich., State Coll. Pa. Author numerous publs. on edn. Mem. Internat. Platform Assn., NEA, N.D. Edn. Assn. *

OVERTON, RICHARD CLEGHORN, history educator, writer, railways consultant; b. Montclair, N.J., Nov. 9, 1907; s. Frank Carlton and Ruth (Bynner) O.; m. Sylvia Lee, 1933; 1 son, Alan Doughty; m. Cornelia Smythe, 1940; children: Elisabeth (Mrs. J.S. Gordon), Edward; m. Addie Lou Roberts, 1956. A.B., Williams Coll., 1929; Ph.D. in History, Harvard U., 1944. With Chatham-Phenix Nat. Bank & Trust Co., N.Y.C., 1930-32; instr. French Hotchkiss Sch., 1932-33; asst. econs. Williams Coll., 1933-34; instr. Am. history North Adams State Tchrs. Coll., 1933-34, Amherst Coll., 1936-38; counsellor Am. history Harvard U., 1938-39; with C.B. & Q. R.R. Co., Chgo., 1939-45, research cons., 1949-65; prof. bus. history Northwestern U., 1945-54; instr. history and geography Burr & Burton Sem., Manchester, Vt., 1955-60, tchr. social studies, 1973-82; prof. U.S. history U. Western Ont., 1961-73, emeritus, 1973-88; dir. Central Vt. Ry., 1974-78; prof. Am. history Williams Coll. Inst. Am. Studies, 1956-58; cons. Bur. Ry. Econs., 1955-58; cons. editor Macmillan Co., 1965-77, Can. Nat. Rys., 1979-82. Author: Burlington West, 1941, Gulf to Rockies, 1953, Burlington Route, 1965, Perkins/Budd, 1982; Contbr. articles to various hist. and ry. mags. Mem. Ry. and Locomotive Hist. Soc., Vt. Hist. Soc., Bus. Hist. Conf., Lexington Group, Phi Beta Kappa, Delta Sigma Rho, Theta Delta Chi. Republican. Congregationalist. Home: Manchester Center Vt. Died Sept. 30, 1988; buried Manchester, Vt.

OVERTON, WILLIAM WARD, JR., banker; b. Kansas City, Kans., Apr. 30, 1897; s. William Ward and Ella (Barnes) O.; m. Evelyn Lucas, June 30, 1924; children: Nancy Lemmon, William T., Thomas N. Student pvt. schs., Kansas City U., U. Tex. Pres. W.W. Overton & Co., 1913-61; later chmn. bd., dir. Tex. Bank & Trust Co., Dallas, from 1936, chmn. bd., from 1947, pres., from 1961; bd. dirs. numerous corps. Mem. Am. Bankers Assn., Mid-Continent Oil and Gas Assn., Newcomen Soc., others. *

OWE, AAGE WILLIAND, aluminum company executive; b. Horten, Norway, Oct. 9, 1894; s. Christofer and Inga Franziska (Jacobsen) O.; m. Marie Mathiesen, June 3, 1922. MChemE, Norwegian Inst. Tech., 1920. Tchr. high sch. Oslo, 1914-18; asst. prof. Norwegian Inst. Tech., Trondheim, 1920-23; rsch. chemist O. Mustad & Son, Oslo, 1923-27, chief chemist, 1927-35; chief engr. A/S Margarincentralen, Oslo, 1935-45, tech. dir., 1946; chmn. bd. Norsk Brenslimport A/S, 1940-42, 45-62, A/S Nordisk Lettmtall, 1945-47; dir. indsl. supply Ministry of Supply, Oslo, 1945; mng. dir., vice chmn. bd. A/S Ardal Verk, Oslo, 1947-51; dir., gen., vice chmn. bd. A/S Ardal og Sunndal Verk, 1952-64; mem. bd. O. Mustad & Son, 1957-59. Decorated Knight of Order of North Star, Sweden, knight Order of White Rose of Finland, comdr. Order of Sanct Olva, Norway; recipient Norsk Hydro prize Assn. Norwegian Engrs., 1958. Mem. Royal Norwegian Acad. Sci. & Letters in Oslo, Norwegian Acad. Tech. Sci., Norwegian Chem. Soc., Royal Norwegian Coun. fro Sci. & Indsl. Rsch., Assn. Norwegian Engrs., others. *

OWEN, JAMES CHURCHILL, lawyer; b. Cripple Creek, Colo., May 24, 1901; s. James and Winifred (Churchill) O.; m. Alice Wright Mann, Oct. 31, 1925; children: James Churchill, William Mann, Thomas Page. Student, U. Colo., 1919-20; AB, Yale U., 1923; LLB, Harvard U., 1926. Bar: Colo. 1926. Since practiced in Denver; with Holme, Roberts, & Owen (and predecessor firm), from 1926, sr. partner, 1955-86, of counsel, from 1986; legal staff WPB, Washington, 1942-45, asst. gen. counsel, 1944-45. Bd. dirs. Boys' Clubs Am., Boys Clubs Denver. Mem. ABA, Colo. Bar Assn., Denver Bar Assn. Republican. Episcopalian. Clubs: Denver, Denver Country, Cherry Hills Country, Cactus, Mile High (Denver). Lodge: Rotary. Home: Denver Colo. Deceased. †

OWENS, HUGH FRANKLIN, lawyer, former government official; b. Muskogee, Okla., Oct. 15, 1909; s. James Francis and Elizabeth (Turner) O.; m. Louise Simon, Dec. 27, 1934; 1 child, Julie. A.B., U. Ill., 1931; LL.B., U. Okla., 1934. Bar: Ill. 1934, Okla. 1934, Tex. 1952, U.S. Supreme Ct 1964. Assoc. Cummins, Hagenah & Flynn, Chgo., 1934-36, Rainey, Flynn, Green & Anderson, Oklahoma City, 1936-48; ptnr. Hervey, May & Owens, Oklahoma City, 1948-51; div. atty. Superior Oil Co., Midland, Tex., 1951-53; gen. counsel Nat. Asso. Petroleum Co., Tulsa, 1953; pvt. practice Oklahoma City, 1953-59; first adminstr. Okla. Securities Commn., 1959-64; commr. SEC, Washington, 1964-73; acting chmn. SEC, 1971; chmn., bd. dirs. Securities Investor Protection Corp., Washington, 1973-82; of counsel Andrews, Davis, Legg, Bixler, Milsten & Murrah, Oklahoma City, from 1982; mem. faculty Oklahoma City U. Law Sch., part-time 1957-64; pub. mem. Okla. Bd. Pub. Accountancy, 1985-87. Bd. dirs. Salvation Army, Oklahoma City Community Fund, 1938-41. Served to lt. comdr. USNR, World War II, PTO. Recipient Presdl. citation, 1971; named Outstanding Oklahoman Okla. Econ. Club, 1971. Mem. ABA, Okla. Bar Assn., Kan. Bar Assn. (hon. life), U.S. Jr. C. of C. (v.p. 1940-41, dir.), Oklahoma City C. of C. (bd. dirs. 1938-40), Nat. Assn. R.R. and Utility Commrs. (exec. com. 1964-73), Phi Delta Phi, Sigma Chi (Significant Sig award). Democrat. Roman Catholic. Clubs: Metropolitan, Chevy Chase (Washington); Men's Dinner (Oklahoma City); Economic. Home: Oklahoma City Okla. Deceased. †

OWENS, WILLIAM A., English language educator, writer; b. Blossom, Tex., Nov. 2, 1905; s. Charles and Jessie Ann (Chennault) O.; m. Ann Slater Wood, Dec. 23, 1946; children: Jessie Ann, David Edward. BA, So. Meth. U., 1932, MA, 1933, LittD (hon.), 1978; PhD, State U. Iowa, 1941. Tchr. Lamar County (Tex.) Schs., 1928-30, Greenville (Tex.) Pub. Schs., 1934-35; instr. English Wesley Coll., Greenville, 1935, Miss. State Coll., 1936; tchr. English Robert E. Lee High Sch., Goose Creek, Tex., 1936-37; mem. faculty Tex. A&M Coll., 1937-47, assoc. prof., 1941-47; mem. faculty Columbia U., N.Y.C., 1947-90, assoc. prof. English, 1953-66, prof., 1966-74, prof. emeritus, 1974-90, dir. summer session, 1959-69, dean summer session, 1969-72, dean emeritus, 1974-90; dir. rsch. folk materials U. Tex., 1941, dir. oral history Tex. oil pioneers, 1952-58; writer in residence Tex. A&M U., 1976; vis. prof. English U. Tex. at Austin, summer 1978. Author: Swing and Turn: Texas Play-Party Games, 1936, Texas Folk Songs, 1950, rev., 1976, Slave Mutiny, 1953 (repub. as Black Mutiny 1968), Walking on Borrowed Land, 1954, Fever in the Earth, 1958, Pocantico Hills 1609-1959, 1960, Look to the River, 1963, This Stubborn Soil, 1966 (Tex. Inst. of Letters award), Three Friends, 1969; (with Mody C. Boatright) Tales From the Derrick Floor, 1970, A Season of Weathering, 1973; (with Michael Frary) Impressions of the Big Thicket, 1973, A Fair and Happy Land, 1975, Tell Me a Story, Sing Me a Song, 1983, (with Lyman Grant) The Letters of Roy Bedichek, 1985, Eye Deep in Hell, 1989. 2d lt. AUS, 1942-45. Decorated Legion of Merit; sr. fellow NEH, 1974-75. Home: Nyack N.Y. Died Dec. 8, 1990; buried Grace Episcopal Ch., Nyack, N.Y.

OXENBURG, ALLEN SVEN, opera director; b. N.Y.C., July 10, 1927; s. William and Elisabeth (Berlin) O. Founder, Am. Opera Soc. N.Y.C., 1951, since artistic dir.; Author librettos, articles on music; also translator. Mem. English Speaking Union. Home: New York N.Y. Died July 2, 1992. †

OXTOBY, JOHN CORNING, mathematician, educator; b. Saginaw, Mich., Sept. 14, 1910; s. William Henry and Ida Jane (Corning) O.; m. Jean Ann Shaffer, June 9, 1945; children—Thomas Corning, David William, Margaret Jane. A.B., U. Calif. at Berkeley, 1933, M.A., 1934; student, Harvard U., 1934-36, jr. fellow Soc. of Fellows, 1936-39; D.Sc. (hon.), Widener U., 1980. Mem. faculty Bryn Mawr Coll., 1939-79, prof. math., 1954-79, Class of 1897 prof. math., 1975-79, prof. emeritus, 1979-91, head dept., 1948-76; research asso. Yale U., 1960-61. Author: Measure and Category, 2d edit., 1980 (numerous transls.); contbr. articles to profl. jours. Recipient Disting. Teaching award Lindback Found., 1978. Mem. Am. Math. Soc. (editorial bd. Bull. 1956-60), Math. Assn. Am. (Hedrick lectr. 1956), Phi Beta Kappa, Sigma Xi. Home: Haverford Pa. Died Jan. 2, 1991.

OZER, BERNARD, merchandising company executive; b. Bronx, N.Y., June 21, 1930; s. Hyman and Sadie (Ureysky) O. B.B.A., CCNY. Buyer Orbach's, N.Y.C., 1960-61; v.p. mktg. Assoc. Merchandising Corp., N.Y.C., 1961-91; tchr. Fashion Inst. Tech., Parsons Sch. Design, U. Ala., Kent State U. Pres. Ozerview (fashion cons. Pierre Balmain). Author: newsletter, Ozerview (nat. distrbn.). Chmn. Working Orgn. for Retarded Child, N.Y.C., from 1976; chmn. Samuel Waxman Cancer Research, 1979, City Meals on Wheels, 1983. Named Man of Yr. Working Orgn. for Retared Child, N.Y.C., 1976; named Man of Yr. Samuel Waxman Cancer Research, N.Y.C., 1979. Mem. Retailing Soc.-CCNY (pres. 1949-50). Jewish. Home: New York N.Y. Died May 12, 1991.

PABST, ADOLF, mineralogy educator; b. Chgo., Nov. 30, 1899; s. Edmund F. and Emma (Hoffman) P.; m. Gudrun-Lisabeth Berg, June 5, 1929 (dec. June 1973). AB, U. Ill., 1925; PhD, U. Calif., Berkeley, 1928. Lectr. mineralogy U. Calif., 1927-28, instr., 1929-31, asst. prof., 1931-36, assoc. prof., 1936-44, prof., 1944-67, prof. emeritus, 1967-90; disting. vis. prof. mineralogy and crystallography U. Nev., Reno, 1967-68; vis. prof. geology U. Oreg., 1968-69; vis. prof. U. Kiel, Germany, 1970-71, Tech. U. Berlin, 1971; vis. scientist Am. Geol. Inst., 1967; mem. U.S. Nat. Com. for Crystallography, 1957-59; mem. mgmt. com. Mineral. Abstracts, 1959-62; chmn. bd. editors U. Calif. Publs. on Geol. Scis., 1958-62. Author: Minerals of California, 1938, Mineral Tables, 1938; also over 100 articles. Recipient Friedrich Becke medal Austrian Mineral. Soc., 1974; fellow Am.-Scandinavian Found., Oslo, 1928-29, Guggenheim fellow, London, 1938-39; Fulbright scholar Mineral. Inst., U. Vienna, Austria, 1955-56; Fulbright grantee, 1970-71. Fellow Geol. Soc. Am., Mineral. Soc. Am. (councilor 1942-45, pres. 1951, Roebling medal 1965), Calif. Acad. Sci.; mem. German Mineral. Soc. (hon.), Phi Beta Kappa, Sigma Xi (v.p. Calif. 1944-45), Theta Tau (hon.). Home: Berkeley Calif. Died Apr. 3, 1990; buried Berkeley, Calif.

PACE, ROBERT SCOTT, college president; b. N.Y.C., July 7, 1904; s. Homer St. Clair and Mabel (Vanderhoof) P.; m. Elizabeth Josefa Neville, July 13, 1928. Pres. Pace Coll., N.Y.C., 1942-89. Home: Middletown N.J. Died Nov. 19, 1989.

PACK, ARTHUR NEWTON, forestry expert; b. Cleve., Feb. 20, 1893; s. Charles Lathrop and Alice Gertrude (Hatch) P.; m. Eleanor Brown, Dec. 18, 1919; children: Eleanor, Vernon Lathrop, Margaret; m. Phoebe Katherine Finley, June 11, 1936; children: Charles Lathrop II, Phoebe Irene. BA, Williams Coll., 1914; postgrad., Harvard U., 1914-15; DSc (hon.), U. Ariz., 1959; LLD (hon.), U. N.Mex., 1960. Dealer in standing timber, 1919-20; dir., v.p. 1st Nat. Bank Rio Arriba; then engaged in pub. & community work; spl. commr. Am. Forestry Assn., Europe, 1921. Author: Our Vanishing Forests, 1923, (with E. Laurence Palmer) The Nature Almanac--A Handbook of Nature Education, 1927, Forestry-An Economic Challenge, 1933, The Challenge of Leisure, 1934, I See 'Em at the Museum, 1954, The Ghost Ranch Story, 1960; editor Nature mag.; explorer and lectr. on natural history, 1932-42. Pres. Charles Lathrop Pack Forestry Found.; pres. emeritus Ariz. Sonora Desert Mus.; others. Mem. Am. Nature Assn., Beta Theta Pi. *

PAFFENBARGER, RALPH SEAL, educator, engineer; b. McArthur, Ohio, Apr. 25, 1894; s. Andrew W. and Ida (Seal) P.; m. Viola Link, Nov. 4, 1918; children: Ralph Seal, Tom L., Carolyn P. BEE, Ohio State U., 1915, BIE, 1928, MSc, 1930. Instr. Chillocothe (Ohio) High Sch., 1915-16; engr. Mead Pulp & Paper Co., 1916-17, Ohio Fuel Gas Co., 1917-19; instr.-prof. dept. engring., drawing Ohio State U., from 1919, dept. chmn., 1944-64; tech. advisor sound movie films, film strips McGraw-Hill Text Films. Lt. inf. U.S. Army, 1918. Mem. AAAS, ASME, Am. Soc. Engring. Edn., Am. Legion, Tau Beta Pi, Alpha Pi Mu, Phi Kappa Tau. Methodist. *

PAGE, CHARLES HUNT, educator, sociologist; b. Tonawanda, N.Y., Apr. 12, 1909; s. Ralph and Laura (Hunt) P.; m. Leonora McClure, June 15, 1936. A.B., U. Ill., 1931; Ph.D., Columbia U., 1940. Staff Birch-Wathen Sch., N.Y.C., 1931-33; instr. sociology CCNY, 1933-40; lectr. Columbia U., 1941-42; asst. prof., assoc. prof. Smith Coll., 1946-52, prof. sociology, 1953-60, chmn. dept. sociology and anthropology, 1951-52; prof. sociology, chmn. dept. sociology and anthropology CCNY, 1952-53; prof. sociology, chmn. dept. sociology and anthropology Princeton U., 1960-65, chmn. Roger William Straus Council on Human Relations, 1962-64; provost Adlai E. Stevenson Coll., prof. sociology U. Calif., Santa Cruz, 1965-68; prof. sociology U. Mass., 1968-75, Robert Morrison MacIver prof. sociology, 1973-75. Author: Class and American Sociology, 1940, Sociology and Contemporary Education, 1964, Fifty Years in the Sociological Enterprise: A Lucky Journey, 1982, (with R.M. MacIver) Society, 1949, (with John Talamini) Sport and Society, 1973; editor: (with Berger and Abel) Freedom and Control in Modern Society, 1954, Am. Sociol. Rev., 1958-60. Field sec. Nat. Refugee Service, 1940-41. Served to lt. comdr. USNR, 1942-46. Mem. Am. Sociol. Assn. (council 1958-60, 61-63, exec. com. 1958-60), Eastern Sociol. Soc. (pres. 1965-66), N. Am. Soc. Sociology of Sport, Internat. Sociol. Assn. Home: Northampton Mass. Died Feb. 9, 1992; buried Northampton, Mass.

PAGE, IRVINE HEINLY, physician; b. Indpls., Jan. 7, 1901; s. Lafayette and Marian (Heinly) P.; m. Beatrice Allen, Oct. 28, 1930; children: Christopher, Nicholas. B.A. in Chemistry, Cornell U., 1921, M.D., 1926; LL.D., John Carroll U., 1956; D.Sc. (hon.), Union U., 1957, Boston U., 1957, Ohio State U., 1960, U. Brazil, 1961, Cleve. State U., 1970; M.D. (hon.), U. Siena, Italy, 1965, Med. Coll. Ohio, 1973, Ind. U., 1975, Rockefeller U., 1977. Intern Presbyn. Hosp., N.Y.C., 1926-28; head chem. div. Kaiser Wilhelm Inst., Munich, Germany, 1928-31; assoc. mem. Hosp. of Rockefeller Inst. for Med. Research, 1931-37; dir. Lab. for Clin. Research, Indpls. City Hosp., 1937-44; dir. research div. Cleve. Clinic Found., 1945-66, sr. cons. research div., 1966-68, cons. emeritus, 1968-91; Past mem. nat. adv. heart council, USPHS; chmn. gov. bd. Methods in Medical Research; mem. subcom. shock Nat. Acad. Scis.-NRC; mem. adv. com. Whitaker Found.; mem. Nat. Acad. Scis. Author: Chemistry of the Brain, 1937, Hypertension, 1943, Arterial Hypertension-Its Diagnosis and Treatment, 1945, Experimental Renal Hypertension, 1948, Strokes, 1961, Serotonin, 1968, (with J. W. McCubbin) Renal Hypertension, 1968, Speaking to the Doctor, 1972, (with F. M. Bumpus) Anglotensin, 1974, Hypertension Mechanisms, 1987, Hypertension Research—A Memoir 1920-60, 1988; also articles.; editorial bd. various profl. jours.; editor-in-chief: Modern Medicine. Trustee Whitehead Inst. Med. Research. Recipient Lasker award Am. Heart Assn., 1958; alumni award of distinction Cornell U. Med. Coll., 1961; John Phillips Meml. award A.C.P., 1962; Gairdner award, 1963; Distinguished Service award AMA, 1964; Med. Communications award Am. Med. Writers Assn., 1965; Achievement award AMA, 1966; Oscar B. Hunter Meml. award, 1966; Passano Found. award, 1967; Sheen award AMA, 1968; Heart of the Year award Am. Heart Assn., 1969; Stouffer prize, 1970; Gifted Tchr. award Am. Coll. Cardiology, 1970, Presdl. award Nat. Hypertension Assn., 1985. Master ACP; mem. NAS, Inst. Medicine (founding), Nat. Hypertension Assn. (pres.), Am. Soc. Pharmacology and Exptl. Therapeutics (hon.), Central Soc. Clin. Rsch., Soc. for Exptl. Biology in Medicine (pres.), Am. Heart Assn. (past pres., founder and mem. coun. on high blood pressure rsch., chmn. coun. on artherosclerosis, founder coun. high blood rsch.), AMA (chmn. sci. adv. com., past chmn. sect. on exptl. med.), Am. Soc. Biol. Chem., Am. Acad. Arts and Scis., Soc. Exptl. Biology and Medicine, Am. Physiol. Soc., Am. Chem. Soc., AAAS (v.p.), Am. Acad. Arts and Scis., Am. Soc. Study Arteriosclerosis (founding mem.), German Med. Soc. (corr.), Swedish Royal Acad. Sci. (fgn.), Sigma Xi. Home: Hyannisport Mass. Died June 10, 1991; cremated.

PAGE, RUTH, dancer; b. Indpls., Mar. 22, 1899; d. Lafayette and Marian (Heinly) P.; m. Thomas Hart Fisher, Feb. 8, 1925; m. Andre Delfan, May 16, 1983. Studied under, Enrico Cecchetti, Monte Carlo, 1925; student, Tudor Hall, N.Y.C.; hon. L.H.D., Ind. U., 1983, DePaul U., Chgo., 1984, U. Ill., 1985, Lincoln Coll., 1985. Dancer, with Pavlowa at age of 15; performed leading role in J. Alden Carpenter's The Birthday of the Infanta produced by Chgo. Opera Co., 1919; later in N.Y.C.; toured U.S. as prin. dancer with Adolph Bolm's Ballet, later appeared in London, with Mr. Bolm; premier danseuse, 2d Music Box Revue, N.Y.C., 1921-23; premiere danseuse, Chgo. Allied Arts performances, 1924, 25, 26, Municipal Opera Co., Buenos Aires, Ravinia Opera Co., 1926-31; dancer with Diaghilev's Ballet Russe de Monte Carlo, 1925; guest soloist with Met. Opera Co., 1926-28; guest artist at enthronement ceremonies for Emperor Hirohito, Japan, 1928; performed series of Am. dances before Sophil Soc., Moscow, 1930; ballet dir., Chgo. Opera, 1934-37, 42-43, 45; dir., Fed. Theatre Dance Project, Chgo., 1938-39; S.Am. tour with first dance group as co-dir., Page-Stone Ballet, 1940, guest choreographer with Bentley Stone; dancer: Frankie and Johnny for Ballet Russe de Monte Carlo, 1945; guest choreographer, dancer: The Bells for Ballet, Russe de Monte Carlo, 1946, Billy Sunday, 1948, Impromptu au Bois, and Revanche, Les Ballets des Champs-Elysees, 1951, Royal Festival Ballet, Vilia, 1953; co-dir., Les Ballets Americains, Theatre des Champs Elysees, Paris, 1950; ballet mistress, Chgo. Lyric Opera, 1954-69; choreographer, dir. Ruth Page's Chgo. Opera Ballet, 1956-66, Ruth Page's Internat. Ballet, 1966-70; pres. Ruth Page Found. Sch. of Dance, Chgo., from 1971, bequeathed to City of Chgo.; choreographer: Merry Widow Ballet, 1956, Susanna and the Barber, 1957, Salome, 1957, Triumph of Chastity, 1958, El Amor Brujo, 1958, Camille, 1958, Carmen, 1959, Fledermaus, 1960, Concertino, 1961, Mefistofela, 1962, Bullets or Bon-Bons, 1965, Nutcracker, 1965-76, Carmina Burana, 1966, Bolero, 1967, Dancer's Ritual, 1968, Alice in the Garden, 1970, also Alice in Wonderland and Alice Through the Looking Glass at Pitts. Ballet Theatre, 1971, Catulli Carmina, 1973, Chain of Fools, 1973; restaged Die Fledermaus, PBS prodn., 1986; lectr. tour: Ruth Page's Invitation to the Dance, 1971-72; Author: Class, A Selection of Notes on Dance Classes Around the World, 1916-1980, 1985, Page by Page. Contbr. to mags. Subject 2 biog. TV programs shown on PBS. Recipient award Adult Council Greater Chgo., 1963, citation outstanding service Ballet Guild Chgo., Mahariski award Columbia U., 1977, Ill. Assn. Dance Cos. award for outstanding service to dance, 1978, Community Arts Found. award, 1978, Dance Mag. award, 1980, medals of merit Mayors Daley, Byrne, Chgo., Ill. Gubernatorial award, 1985, Peabody award for Merry Widow prodn., PBS, 1985, Ruth Page Week at Ravinia, 1985. Mem. Chgo. Nat. Assn. Dance Masters (hon.). Clubs: Arts (Chgo.), Friday (Chgo.), Racquet (Chgo.). Home: Chicago Ill. Died Apr. 7, 1991.

PAGET, RICHARD MOSCROP, management consultant; b. Ft. Smith, Ark., Oct. 2, 1913; s. Ernest Walter and Mildred (Moscrop) P.; m. Inez Bouvea, June 27, 1936; children—Richard James, Nancy Louise. B.S., Northwestern U., 1934. Staff mem., later partner Booz, Allen & Hamilton, Chgo. and N.Y.C., 1934-42; founder, pres., mgmt. cons. Cresap, McCormick & Paget, Inc., N.Y.C., Chgo., San Francisco, Washington, from 1946, London, Eng. and Melbourne, Australia; former bd. dirs. Ligget & Meyers Tobacco Co., Washington Post Co., Union Dime Savs. Bank. Mem. Pres.'s Adv. Council Exec. Orgn., 1969-72; trustee emeritus Met. Mus. Art, Northwestern U., Evanston, Ill., N.Y.U. Med. Center, N.Y.C. Served from lt. (j.g.) to capt. USNR, 1942-46. Decorated Legion of Merit. Mem. Assn. Cons. Mgmt. Engrs. (pres. 1958-59, 77-78, Gilbreth medal 1973, Mgmt. Cons. award 1977), Beta Gamma Sigma. Clubs: University (Washington). Home: Naples Fla. Died Jan. 5, 1991.

PAINE, RALPH DELAHAYE, investment company executive; b. Newark, Mar. 31, 1906; s. Ralph Delahaye and Katharine Lansing P.; m. Elena Dimitrievna von Hoershelman, Mar. 7, 1933 div. 1943 ; m. Nancy White Dauphinot, July 25, 1947. PhB, Yale U., 1929. Securities analyst Edward B. Smith & Co., N.Y.C., 1929-31; with Time mag., 1931-38, bus. editor, 1933-38; editorial asst. to pres. Time, Inc., 1938-39; mng. dir. March of Time, Ltd., London, 1939-40; mng. editor Fortune mag., 1941-53, pub., 1953-67; v.p. Time, Inc., 1953-67, head rsch. and devel. dept., 1964-65; pres., treas. Barton Mountain Corp. (Vt.); war corr., Pacific, 1945. 2d lt. R.O.C., F.A., U.S. Army, 1929-34. Mem. Skull and Bones, Delta Kappa Epsilon. Home: Barton Vt. Died Jan. 12, 1991.

PAINE, STEPHEN WILLIAM, college president; b. Grand Rapids, Mich., Oct. 28, 1908; s. Stephen Hugh and Mary Wilfrieda (Fischer) P.; m. Helen Lucile Paul, Aug. 17, 1934; children: Marjorie (dec.), Carolyn Esther, Miriam Ruth, Stephen William, Kathryn Elizabeth. A.B., Wheaton (Ill.) Coll., 1930, LL.D., 1939; A.M., U. Ill., 1931, Ph.D., 1933; L.H.D., Houghton Coll., 1976. Instr. classics Houghton (N.Y.) Coll., 1933-34, prof. Greek, 1934-72, dean of Coll., 1934-37, pres. coll., 1937-72, pres. emeritus, from 1972; Mem. bd. adminstrn. Wesleyan Church, 1935-68, 72-80; mem. bd. adminstrn. Nat. Assn. Evangelicals, from 1942, pres., 1948-49; mem. commn. of Christian higher edn. Assn. Am. Colls., 1955-58. Author: Toward the Mark-Studies in Philippians, 1953, Studies in the Book of James, 1955, The Christian and the Movies, 1957, Beginning Greek, 1960, 1961; mem. transl. com.: New Internat. Version Bible; contbr.: Wesleyan Advocate, United Evangel. Action. Trustee Asbury Theol. Sem., 1965-78, Houghton Coll., 1972-80, United Wesleyan Coll., 1974-80. Mem. Evangel. Theol. Soc. (pres. 1967), Classical Assn. Atlantic States, Gideons Internat., Phi Beta Kappa, Wheaton Coll. Honor Soc., Pi Kappa Delta. Home: Houghton N.Y. Died Feb. 9, 1992; buried Mt. Pleasant Cemetery, Houghton, N.Y.

PAINE, THOMAS OTTEN, engineer, space agency administrator; b. Berkeley, Calif., Nov. 9, 1921; s. George Thomas and Ada Louise (Otten) P.; m. Barbara Helen Taunton Pearse, Oct. 1, 1946; children: Marguerite Ada, George Thomas, Judith Janet, Frank Taunton. A.B. in Engring, Brown U., 1942; M.S. in Phys. Metallurgy, Stanford, 1947; Ph.D., Stanford U., 1949. Research assoc. Stanford U., 1947-49; with Gen. Electric Co., 1949-68, 70-76, GE Research Lab., Schenectady; mgr. Center Advanced Studies Santa Barbara, Calif., 1963-68; v.p., group exec. power generation, 1970-73, sr. v.p. sci. and tech., 1973-76; pres., dir. Northrop Corp., Los Angeles, 1976-82; chmn. Thomas Paine Assocs., Los Angeles, from 1982, Nat. Commn. on Space, 1984-86; dep. adminstr., then adminstr. NASA, 1968-70; dir. NIKE, Quotron Systems, Orbital Scis. Contbr. articles to tech. publs.; co-inventor lodex R magnets. Bd. dirs. Pacific Forum, Honolulu, Planetary Soc., Pasadena. Served to lt. USNR, World War II. Decorated Submarine Combat insignia with stars, USN Commendation medal; grand ufficiale della Ordine al Merito Italy; recipient Distinguished Service medal NASA, 1970, Apollo Achievement award, Disting. Pub. Service Medal, 1986, Washington award Western Soc. Engrs., 1972; John Fritz medal United Engring. Socs., 1976; Faraday medal Inst. Elec. Engrs., London, 1976; Humanitarian award NCCJ; Konstantin Tsiolkovskii medal, USSR, 1987. Fellow AIAA; mem. Nat. Acad. Engring., N.Y. Acad. Scis., Am. Phys. Soc., IEEE, U.S. Naval Inst., Am. Astronautical Soc. (John F. Kennedy Astronautics award 1987), Explorers Club (N.Y.C.), Lotos Club (N.Y.C.), Sky Club (N.Y.C.), Cosmos Club (Washington), Calif. Club (L.A.), Regency Club (L.A.), Sigma Xi. Home: Brentwood Calif. Died May 4, 1992; buried Santa Barbara Cemetery, Santa Barbara, Calif.

PALEY, WILLIAM S., broadcasting executive; b. Chgo., Sept. 28, 1901; s. Samuel and Goldie (Drell) P.; m. Dorothy Hart Hearst, May 11, 1932; children: Jeffrey, Hilary; m. Barbara Cushing Mortimer, July 28, 1947; children: William Cushing, Kate Cushing. Grad., Western Mil. Acad., Alton, Ill., 1918; student, U. Chgo., 1918-19; B.S., U. Pa., 1922; LL.D., Adelphi U., 1957, Bates Coll., 1963, U. Pa., 1968, Columbia U., 1975, Brown U., 1975, Pratt Inst., 1977, Dartmouth Coll., 1979; L.H.D., Ithaca Coll., 1978, U. So. Calif., 1985, Rutgers U., 1986, L.I. U., Southampton, 1987. Vice-pres., sec. Congress Cigar Co., Phila., 1922-28; pres. CBS Inc., N.Y.C., 1928-46, chmn. bd., 1946-83, founder chmn., 1983-86, acting chmn., 1986-87, chmn., 1987-90, also dir.; former ptnr. Whitcom Investment Co., N.Y.C., from 1982; founder, bd. dirs. Genetics Inst., from 1980, Thinking Machines Corp., from 1983—; co-chmn. Internat. Herald Tribune, from 1983. Trustee Mus. Modern Art, from 1937, pres., 1968-72, chmn., 1972-85, chmn. emeritus, 1985-90; life trustee Columbia U., 1950-73, trustee emeritus, 1973-90, bd. dirs. W. Averell Harriman Inst. for Advanced Study of Soviet Union, Columbia U.; mem. Com. for White House Conf. on Edn., 1954-56; chmn. Pres.'s Materials Policy Commn. which produced report Resources for Freedom, 1951-52; mem. exec. com. Resources for the Future, 1952-69, chmn., 1966-69, hon. bd. dirs., from 1969; chmn. N.Y.C. Task Force on Urban Design which prepared the report The Threatened City, 1967, Urban Design Council City N.Y., 1968-71; pres., dir. William S. Paley Found., Greenpark Found., Inc.; trustee North Shore Univ., Hosp., 1949-73, co-chmn. bd. trustees, 1954-73; founding mem. Bedford-Stuyvesant D and S Corp., dir., 1967-72; founder, chmn. bd. Mus. of Broadcasting, from 1976; mem. Commn. on Critical Choices for Am., 1973-77, Commn. for Cultural Affairs, N.Y.C., 1975-78; life trustee Fedn. Jewish Philanthropies of N.Y. Served as col. AUS, World War II; dep. chief psychol. warfare div. SHAEF; dep. chief info. control div. USGCC. Decorated Legion of Merit; Medal for Merit; officer Legion of Honor France; Croix de Guerre with Palm France; comdr. Order of Merit Italy; assoc. comdr. Order of St. John of Jerusalem; recipient Gold Achievement medal Poor Richard Club; Keynote award Nat. Assn. Broadcasters; George Foster Peabody award citation, 1958, 1961; spl. award Broadcast Pioneers; award Concert Artist Guild, 1965; Skowhegan Gertrude Vanderbilt Whitney award; gold medal award Nat. Planning Assn., David Sarnoff award U. Ariz., 1979, gold medallion Soc. of Family of Man, 1982, Joseph Wharton award Wharton Sch. Club N.Y., 1983, Life Achievement award TV Guide, 1984, award Ctr. for Communications, 1985; co-recipient Walter Cronkite award Ariz. State U., 1984; Medallion of Honor City of N.Y.; First Amendment Freedoms award Anti-Defamation League B'nai B'rith; Robert Eunson Distinguished Service award Assn. Press Broadcasters; named to Jr. Achievement Nat. Bus. Hall of Fame, 1984. Fellow Royal Soc. Arts; mem. Coun. Fgn. Rels., France Am. Soc., Acad. Polit. Scis., Nat. Inst. Social Scis. Clubs: River, Century Assn; The Metropolitan (Washington); Turf and Field, Nat. Golf, Meadowbrook; Economic (N.Y.); Lyford Cay (Nassau); Bucks (London). Home: New York N.Y. Died Oct. 26, 1990; buried St. John's Cemetery, N.Y.

PALFREY, THOMAS ROSSMAN, Romance languages educator; b. Vincennes, Ind., Oct. 22, 1895; s. Thomas Fairbanks Rossman and Mary (Lyon) P.; m. Magdalen Fettig, Aug. 30, 1921; 1 child, Thomas Rossman. Student, U. Toulouse, France, 1919; AB, Ind. U., 1920, AM, 1922; D of Univ., U. Paris, 1927. Instr. Romance langs. Ind. U., Bloomington, 1920; instr., assoc., asst. prof. No. Ill. U., DeKalb, 1925-30; assoc. prof., prof. Northwestern U., Evanston, Ill., 1930-62; prof. French, Ariz. State U., Tempe, from 1962; vis.

prof. summers N.Mex. Highlands U., 1936, UCLA, 1947; vis. prof. Command and Gen. Staff Sch., 1948, 49, 51, mem. ednl. survey commn., 1949; asst. comdt. Chgo. USAR Sch., 1950, comdt., 1950-53; cons. editor Rinehart & Co. Author, editor monographs and textbooks in French lang. and lit., comparative lit. and Romance bibliographer; contbr. articles to learned jours. Served on Mexican Border, 1916-17; 3d. lt. inf. U.S. Army, 1917-19, AEF in France; col. inf. G.S.C., 1942-46. Decorated Bronze Star medal, chevalier Legion of Honor, Croix de Guerre with palme (France), officer Order of Crown (Belgium). Mem. MLA, AaUP, Am. Assns. Tchrs. French, Modern Humanities Rsch. Assn., MLA Cen. West and South, Soc. Friends Nat. Bibliotheque,Internat. Assn. French Studies, Internat. Assn. Comparative Lit., Phi Beta Kappa, Phi Kappa Psi, Pi Delta Phi. Democrat. Episcopalian. *

PALMER, C. EARL, association executive; b. Erie, Pa., Mar. 9, 1897; s. George Henry and Mary Mae (Morton) P.; m. Helen Ayers, Apr. 30, 1921; children: WarrenAyers (dec.), Shirley B. Palmer Brehm. Grad. high sch. Dir. pub. rels. Celotex Corp., Chgo., 1926-32; propr. interior decorating bus., Wilmette, Ill., 1932-38; acting welfare and athletic officer USN Air Base, Glenview, Ill., 1938-41; field dir. Alaska area ARC, 1942-45; with staff procurement office Am. Nat. Red Cross, Washington, 1945-48; mfrs. rep. Pierce Wire Rec. Machines, 1948-53; sec.-treas. Am. Soc. Photogrammetry, Washington, from 1953. Mem. Am. Legion, Nat. Sojourners, Masons, Shriners. *

PALMER, GEORGE D(AVID), JR., chemistry educator; b. Helena, Ark., Dec. 7, 1897; s. George David and Sophie (Ladd) P.; m. Maude Roberts Collins, Dec. 27, 1923; 1 child, George D. BS, Clemson Coll., 1919; AM, Johns Hopkins U., 1921, PhD, 1924. Lab. asst. Bur. Standards, Washington, summer 1919; head dept. chemistry Guilford (N.C.) Coll., 1921-22; asst. prof. organic chemistry Kans. State Agrl. Coll., 1924-27; prof. chemistry U. Ala., Tuscaloosa, from 1927, head dept. organic chemistry, from 1948; chemistry cons. Swann Chem. Co., Birmingham, ala., 1942. Author: Introduction of Organic Chemistry, 1934, The Inside of the Atom or An Introduction to Atomic Structure and Radioactivity, 1936, rev. edit., 1937, Introduction to Formula System of Organic Chemistry, 1940; contbg. author: Collateral Readings in Inorganic Chemistry, 1947, Unit Processes in Organic Synthesis, rev. edit., 1947; also numerous monographs, pamphlets and articles to sci. jours.; patentee process for producing sulphur organic compounds. Fellow AAAS, Am. Inst. Chemists; mem. Am. Chem. Soc. (chmn. Ala. sect.), So. Assn. Sci. and Industry (founder, 1st pres., sec. trustee, 1st award in recognition of founding for for stimulation given establishment So. Rsch. Inst. 1947), Ala. Accad. Sci. (pres.), Ala. Edn. Assn., Tuscaloosa C. of C., C. of C. of South (hon.), Hopkins Club, Rotary (pres.), Sigma Xi, Gamma Sigma Epsilon. Democrat. Episcopalian. *

PALMER, STEPHEN EUGENE, clergyman; b. Independence, Iowa, Aug. 2, 1896; s. Alanson Llewelyn and Mary (Clark) P.; m. Katharine Hoelzel Greenslade, June 28, 1922 (dec. Feb. 1976); children: Stephen Eugene, Robert John, David Clark; m. Helen Donner Whiley, Apr. 16, 1977. AB, Coll. of Wooster, 1917; student, U. Rennes, France, 1919; M.Div., B.D. with honors, McCormick Theol. Sem., 1922; D.D., Coll. of Wooster, 1942. Ordained to ministry Presbyn. Ch., 1922; pastor First Ch., Superior, Wis., 1922-26, Waukesha, Wis., 1926-30; pastor Westminster Ch., Youngstown, Ohio, 1930-36, First Ch., Lockport, N.Y., 1936-62; interim pastor Lafayette Ave. Presbyn. Ch., Buffalo, 1962-63; interim pastor 1st Presbyn. Ch., Akron, Ohio, 1964-65, Sheridan, Wyo., 1966-67, Casper, Wyo., 1968-69, Skaneateles, N.Y., 1970-71; interim pastor Fairmount Presbyn. Ch., Cleve., 1974-75; Study and travel, Egypt, Palestine, 1928, 1936; Pres. Ministers Assn. Youngstown and Lockport. Author: Quisling and Others, 1981. Leader in orgn. of Youngstown Citizens' Assn. for Good Govt., 1933; vice moderator Gen. Assembly Presbyn. Ch. U.S.A.; also moderator Presbytery Western N.Y., 1943-44, 61-62; chmn. fgn. missions Synod of N.Y., 1950-56; bd. Fgn. Missions of Presbyn. Ch., 1946-52. Served as 1st lt. inf. U.S. Army, World War I. Fellowship visitation to Hungarian Ref. Chs. Yugoslavia, 1958; churches of twelve African nations, 1965-66; churches of fourteen nations West Africa, 1967-68; mission stas. and chs. Amazon River, 1971-72; United Ch. S. India, 1973; United Ch. S. India Far East, 1976. Mem. McCormick Theol. Sem. Alumni Assn. (pres. 1942-43), Am. Legion, Vets. Fgn. Wars. Clubs: Masons (Buffalo), Rotary (Buffalo), Torch (Buffalo) (dir.). Home: Lakeland Fla. Died June 2, 1992.

PALMER, WALTER LINCOLN, internal medicine educator; b. Evanston, Ill., June 29, 1896; s. Walter Aaron and Alice (Bonney) P.; m. Elisabeth Ricketts, May 15, 1926; children: Robert Howard, Donald Walter, Elisabeth Bonney, Henry Ricketts. Student, Colo. Coll., 1914-17; SB, U. Chgo., 1918, MS, 1919, PhD, 1926; MD, Rush Med. Coll., Chgo., 1921; DSc (honoris causa), Colo. Coll., 1965. Diplomate Am. Bd. Internal Medicine. Intern Cook County Hosp., Chgo., 1921-23, resident in internal medicine, 1924-26; intern Presbyn. Hosp., Chgo., 1923; pvt. practice, Chgo., from 1927; asst. prof. medicine U. Chgo., 1927-30, assoc. prof., 1930-41, prof., 1941-54, Richard T. Crane prof., 1954-61, Richard T. Crane prof. emeritus, from 1961; cons. in gastroenterology to surgeon gen. U.S. Army, World War II. Master ACP (bd. regents 1945-57, pres. 1956-57); mem. AMA, AAAS, Am. Clin. and Climatol. Assn., Am. Soc. for Clin. Investigation, Am. Therapeutic Soc., Am. Gastroent. Assn., Assn. Am. Physicians. *

PALMIERI, EDMUND LOUIS, federal judge; b. N.Y.C., May 14, 1907; s. John and Assunta (Soviero) P.; m. Cecile Claude Verron, Feb. 18, 1937; children: Marie-Claude Wrenn, Michelle Warren, Alain John. AB, Columbia, 1926, LLD, 1929; diploma di studio, U. Rome, 1923; cert. d'etudes francaises, U. Grenoble, France, 1925. Bar: N.Y. 1930. Law sec. to hon. Charles Evans Hughes Permanent Ct. Internat. Justice, The Hague, 1929; assoc. Hughes, Schurman & Swight, N.Y.C., 1929-31; asst. U.S. atyy. So. Dist. N.Y., 1931-34; asst. corp. counsel City of N.Y., 1934-37, Office of Mayor, 1937-40; city magistrate N.Y.C., 1940-43; pvt. practice in law, 1945-54; judge U.S. Dist. Ct. (so. dist.) N.Y., 1954-89; cons. Rockefeller Found., 1949. Past editor Columbia Law Rev. Mem. Allied Commn. to Rome; lt. col. AUS, 1943-45. Decorated Legion of Merit with battle stars. Mem. Phi Beta Kappa. Home: New York N.Y. Died June 15, 1989.

PAN, HERMES, choreographer; b. Memphis, Dec. 10, 1909; s. Pantelis and Mary (Huston) Panagiotopulos. Studies with, Miss Georgia Brown's Pvt. Sch., Nashville. Choreographer films and TV, 1933-86. Dancer Broadway musicals, 1927-30; choreographer: (mus. films) Flying Down to Rio, 1933, The Gay Divorcee, 1934, Top Hat, 1935, I Dream Too Much, 1935, Swing Time, 1936, Shall We Dance, 1937, Damsel in Distress (Oscar award), 1937, Carefree, 1938, The Story of Vernon and Irene Castle, 1939, That Night in Rio, 1941, Moon Over Miami, 1941, Rise and Shine, 1941, Song of the Islands, 1942, My Gal Sal, 1942, Sweet Rosie O'Grady, 1943, Pin-Up Girl, 1944, Irish Eyes Are Smiling, 1944, Blue Skies, 1946, The Shocking Miss Pilgrim, 1947, I Wonder Who's Kissing Her Now, 1947, The Barkleys of Broadway, 1949, Let's Dance, 1950, Excuse My Dust, 1951, Lovely to Look At, 1952, Kiss Me Kate, 1953, The Student Prince, 1954, Jupiter's Darling, 1955, Hit the Deck, 1955, Meet Me in Las Vegas, 1956, Silk Stockings, 1956, Pal Joey, 1957, Porgy and Bess, 1959, Can-Can, 1960, Flower Drum Song, 1961, My Fair Lady, 1964, Finian's Rainbow, 1968, Darling Lili, 1969, Lost Horizon, 1973, (TV spls.) An Evening With Fred Astaire (Emmy award), 1961, Sounds of America, Star-Time Academy Award of Songs, Remember How Great, Frances Langford Show. Recipient Emmy award Nat. Acad. TV Arts and Scis., 1958, 59, Nat. Film award for Achievement in Cinema, 1980, Joffrey Ballet award, 1986. Roman Catholic. Home: Beverly Hills Calif. Died Sept. 19, 1990.

PANITZ, MURRAY WOLFE, flutist; b. N.Y.C., Aug. 30, 1925; s. Julius and Rose (Polsky) P.; m. Myrna J. Rubenstein, Sept. 13, 1945; 1 dau., Amy Jo. Performer's certificate, Eastman Sch. Music, U. Rochester, 1945; B.Mus. (George Eastman scholar), Manhattan Sch. Music, 1950, Mus.M., 1950. prof. flute Temple U., Phila. Solo flutist, Nat. Symphony, Washington, 1945-61, Phila. Orch., 1961-89, appearances with, City Center Ballet Orch., Symphony of Air, Little Orch. N.Y., Columbia, RCA Victor, Capitol Records rec. orchs., 1950-61; mem., Phila. Woodwind Quintet. Served with USAAF, 1945-49. Home: Hackensack N.J. Died Apr. 1989. †

PANUFNIK, SIR ANDRZEJ, composer, conductor; b. Warsaw, Poland, Sept. 24, 1914; s. Tomasz and Matylda (Thonnes) P.; m. Camilla Jessel, 1963; 2 children. Ed. Warsaw State Conservatory and the State Acad. Music (with Felix Weingartner), Vienna, R.A.M. (hon.), 1984; D.Phil. (hon.), 1985; hon. doctorate Frederic Chopin Acad. Music, Warsaw, 1991. Condr. Cracow Philharm. Orch., 1945-46; dir. Warwaw Phil. Orch., 1946-47; v.p. Polish Composers' Union, 1948-54; vice chmn. Internat. Music Council of UNESCO, 1950-53; settled in Eng., 1954, naturalized, 1961; mus. dir. City of Birmingham Symphony Orch., 1957-59; vis. condr. leading European, N. and S. Am. orchs., 1947-91; mainly composition, 1959. Commns. from Boston Symphony Orch. (Centenary), London Symphony Orch. (3 commns.), Royal Philharmonic So., London, Sir Georg Solti and Chgo. Symphony Orch. (Centenary), Sir Yehudi Menuhin, Mistislav Rostropovitch; Compositions include: Piano Trio, 1934, Five Polish Peasant Songs, 1940, Tragic Overture, 1942, Nocturne, 1947, Lullaby, 1947, Twelve Miniature Studies, 1947, Sinfonia Rustica, 1948, Hommage á Chopin, 1949, Old Polish Suite, 1950, Concerto in Modo Antico, 1951, Heroic Overture, 1952, Rhapsody, 1956, Sinfonia Elegiaca, 1957, Polonia - Suite 1959, Concerto for Piano and Orch., 1962, Landscape, 1962, Sinfonia Sacra, 1963, Two Lyric Pieces, 1963, Song to the Virgin Mary, 1964, Autumn Music, 1965, Katyn Epitaph, 1966, Jagiellonian Triptych, 1966, Reflections for Piano, 1968, The Universal Prayer, 1968-69, Thames Pageant, 1969, Concerto for Violin and Strings, 1971, Triangles, 1972, Winter Solstice, 1972, Sinfonia Concertante, 1973, Sinfonia di Sfere, 1974-75, String Quartet, 1976, Dreamscape, 1976, Sinfonia Mistica, 1977, Metasinfonia, 1978, Concerto Festivo, 1979, Concertino, 1980, String Quartet No. 2, 1980. Paean for Queen Elizabeth, 1980, Sinfonia Votiva, 1981, A Procession for Peace, 1982, Arbor Cosmica, 1983, Pentasonata, 1984, Bassoon Concerto, 1985, Symphony No. 9, 1986, String Sextet, 1987, symphony No. 10, 1988, Harmony, 1989, String Quartet No. 3, 1990, Cello Concerto, 1991. Ballet Music: Elegy, 1967, Cain and Abel, 1968, Miss Julie, 1970, Homage to Chopin, 1980, Adieu, 1980, Polonia, 1980, Dances of the Golden Hall, 1980. Author: Composing Myself , 1987. Recipient 1st prize Chopin Competition, 1949, Banner of Labour 1st class, 1949; State prizewinner, 1951, 52; Pre-Olympic Competition 1st prize, 1952; 1st prize for mus. composition Prince Rainier III of Monaco, 1963, Sibelius Centenary medal, 1965, Knight of Mark Twain, U.S., 1966, Prix de Prince Pierre de Monaco, 1983; decorated Knight Bachelor, U.K., 1991, Knight's Cross Order of Polonia Restituta (posthomous award), 1991. Died Oct. 27, 1991; buried Richmond, Eng. Home: Twickenham Eng.

PAPADOPOULOS, DIMITRIOS (ECUMENICAL PATRIARCH DIMITRIOS I), archbishop; b. Istanbul, Sept. 8, 1914; D.Theol., Sch. of Halki, Heybeliada-Istanbul, 1937. Ordained deacon of the Eastern Orthodox Ch., 1937, priest, 1942, bishop, 1964. Sec., preacher, Edessa, Greece, 1937-38; deacon, priest, preacher, Ferikoy, Istanbul, 1939-45; priest Orthodox Community, Tehran, Iran, 1945-50; head priest Orthodox Community, Ferikoy, 1950-64; bishop of Elaia, Aux. Bishop of Patriarch Athenagoras, Istanbul; bishop, Kurtulus, Istanbul, 1964-72, Met. of Imvros and Tenedos, 1972; elected to Holy and Sacred Synod; Archbishop of Constantinople, New Rome and Ecumenical Patriarch, under the name Dimitrios I, 1972-91. Died Oct. 2, 1991. Home: Istanbul Turkey

PAPANEK, JAN, lecturer, diplomat; b. Brezovapod, Bradlom, Czechoslovakia, Oct. 24, 1896; s. Stefan and Alzbeta (Palanska) P.; m. Betka Papanek, Feb. 13, 1926. Grad., Ecole Libre des Scis. Politiques, Paris, 1921, Inst. des Hautes Etudes Internat., Paris, 1923, Acad. de Droit Internat., The Hague, 1923; LLD, Sorbonne, Paris, 1923, Charles U. Prague, 1928; LLD (hon.), Hobart Coll., 1943. With ministry fgn. affairs, 1922-24; attache Czechoslovak Legation, Budapest, 1925-26; sec. Czechoslovak Legation, Washington, 1926-31; parliamentary sec. to min. fgn. affairs, 1932-35; Czechoslovak consul Pitts., 1935-39; personal rep. Czechoslovak Pres. E. Benes, Chgo., 1939-41; min. plenipotentiary, dir. Czechoslovak Govt. Info. Svc., N.Y.C., 1942-46; ambassador, del. UN, 1946-48; del. UN Conf. Internat. Orgn., San Francisco, 1945; mem. contbns. com. UN, 1947-49, mem. adv. com. on adminstrn. and budgetary questions, 1948-50; lectr. on UN and world polit. geography NYU Grad. Sch. Govt., 1949-51; UN commentator CBC, 1950-53; pres. Am. Fund for Czechoslovak Refugees, Inc., N.Y.C., 1948-91; dir. office, Camp Pendelton, Calif., 1975. Author: La Tchecoslovaquie, L'Histoire Politique et Juridique, 1923, Czechoslovakia, World of Tomorrow, 1945, Ten Years-The Czechoslovak Question in the United Nations, 1958, Oral History to 1951; contbr. articles to profl. jours. Chmn. Internat. League Rights of Man, 1965-70; sec. Coop. Am. Relief Everywhere; mem. exec. com. Am. Coun. Vol. Agys. for Fgn. Svc.; mem. b. Am. Immigration and Citizenship Conf. 1st lt. Czechoslovakian Army, 1916-19. Decorated Czechoslovak Revolutionary medal, medal of merit Czechoslovakia; Fat.di Guerra, Italy; recipient Highest honor Pres. Vaclav Havel of Czechoslovakia, 1991. Mem. UN Corrs. Assn., Coun. Free Czechoslovakia, Czechoslovak Nat. Coun. Am., Czechoslovak Soc. Arts and Scis., Internat. Law Assn., Am. Acad. Polit. and Social Sci., Acad. Polit. Sci. Home: Scarsdale N.Y. Died Nov. 30, 1991; buried Bohemian Nat. Cemetery.

PAPEN, GEORGE WILLIAM, surgeon, educator; b. Albany, N.Y., Aug. 20, 1893; s. Theodore and Margaret (Ayen) P.; m. Helen J. Le Maistre, Oct. 20, 1920; children: George William Jr. (dec.), Francis Crandon. MD, Tufts U., 1916. Intern in surgery Boston City Hosp., 1916-17, vis. surgeon, 1924-29, surgeon-in-chief 1st surg. svc., 1949-55, cons. surgeon, from 1957; resident in surgery East Boston Relief Sta., 1917; pvt. practice, Boston, from 1919; clin. prof. surgery Tufts U., 1945-49; chief staff Parker Hill Med. Ctr., Roxbury, Mass., from 1953. Assoc. editor Mass. Physician, from 1949. Trustee Tufts U. Capt. M.C., U.S. Army, 1917-19, AEF in France. Fellow ACS; mem. AMA, Mass. Med. Soc., Norfolk Dist. Med. Soc., Boston Surg. Soc., Nat. Gastroent. Soc., Internat. Proctological Soc. (hon.), Alpha Omega Alpha. *

PAPP, JOSEPH, theater producer, director; b. Bklyn., June 21, 1922; s. Samuel and Yetta (Miritch) Papirofsky; m. Gail Bovard Merrifield, Jan. 18, 1976; children by previous marriages: Susan, Barbara, Michael, Miranda, Anthony. Grad., Actors Lab., Hollywood, Calif., 1948; D.F.A. (hon.), Columbia Coll., Chgo., 1971, Northwestern U., 1972, CUNY, 1974, Villanova U., 1976, Kalamazoo Coll., 1977, NYU, 1978, Carnegie-Mellon U., 1978, Princeton U., 1979. Founder nonprofit Shakespeare Workshop (name changed to N.Y. Shakespeare Festival 1960) including Delacorte Theater, N.Y.C., 1954, Mobile Theater, Public Theater complex (6 theaters) with prodns. on Broadway, film, TV and cable TV; Lincoln Ctr. constituent at Beaumont and Newhouse theaters, 1973-77; disting. seminar prof. L.I.U., 1965-66; adj. prof. directing Yale U. Sch.

Drama, New Haven, 1966-67; adj. prof. play directing Columbia U., N.Y.C., 1967-69; vis. fellow humanities U. Colo., 1965; resident faculty Fla. State U. Sch. Theater, Tallahassee, 1985-86. Producer, dir. 114 prodns. of Shakespeare's plays, 63 in Central Park, Delacorte Theater, 1957-87; plays include Electra, 1964, Threepenny Opera, 1977, Pirates of Penzance, 1980, Don Juan, 1982, The Golem, 1984, The Mystery of Edwin Drood, 1985, others; producer, dir. Shakespeare's plays, Mobile Theater, 1957-72, also new plays including An Evening at New Rican Village, 1978, The Mighty Gents, 1979, others; producer, dir. plays Public Theater complex, N.Y.C., from 1967; premiere prodns. of new plays including Hair, 1967, No Place to be Somebody, 1968, The Basic Training of Pavlo Hummel, 1971, Short Eyes, 1974, A Chorus Line, 1975, For Colored Girls Who Have Considered Suicide/When the Rainbow is Enuf, 1976, Runaways, 1978, A Prayer for My Daughter, 1978, I'm Getting My Act Together and Taking It on the Road, 1978, Spell 7, 1979, Sorrows of Stephen, 1980, Alice in Concert, 1981, Buried Inside Extra, 1983, The Normal Heart, 1985, Cuba and his Teddy Bear, 1986; dir., producer plays Beaumont and Newhouse Theaters including Boom Boom Room, 1973, The Taking of Miss Janie, 1975, Threepenny Opera, 1976, Streamers, 1976, The Cherry Orchard, 1977; producer Broadway prodns. including: Two Gentlemen of Verona, 1971, Sticks and Bones, 1972, That Championship Season, 1972, Much Ado About Nothing, 1972, A Chorus Line, 1975, For Colored Girls, 1976, Runaways, 1978, The Pirates of Penzance, 1980, Plenty, 1982, The Human Comedy, 1984, The Mystery of Edwin Drood, 1985, Serious Money, 1988; producer, dir. TV and film prodns. including: Much Ado About Nothing, CBS/BBC, 1973, Sticks and Bones, CBS, 1973, Wedding Band, ABC, 1974, Kiss Me Petruchio, PBS/BBC, 1979, The Haggadah, PBS, 1981, Alice at the Palace, NBC, 1981, The Pirates of Penzance, 1981, The Dance and the Railroad, 1982, Swan Lake Minnesota, 1982, A Midsummer Night's Dream, 1982, Rehearsing Hamlet, 1983, Plenty, 1985; contbr. articles on theater to mags. and books; author: (prodn. handbooks) Troilus and Cressida, Love's Labour's Lost, The Naked Hamlet. Mem. Vol. Lawyers for the Arts, 1981, Internat. Rescue Com., 1980; mem. adv. council on theater Princeton U., 1977; mem. Am. Theater Planning Bd., 1977, Lincoln Center Inc. Bd., 1973-77; mem. playwrights nominating com. Rockefeller Found., 1971; mem. nat. screening com. Fulbright-Hays awards, 1962-67; mem. adv. com. N.Y. Edn. Task Force on Performing Arts Centers, 1962; mem. bd. overseers theater arts Brandeis U.; bd. dirs. Harlem Cultural Com.; mem. Mayor's Adv. Com. for Broadway Dist., 1982, 83, Save the Morosco and Helen Hayes Theaters Campaign, 1982, Vietnam Vets., 1982. Served with USN, 1942-46. Recipient numerous awards including Tony award, 1957, 58, 72, 73, 76, 81; Spl. Tony award for Profl. Excellence and Disting. Achievement in Theater, 1973, 79, Spl. Gold Tony for A Chorus Line as longest running show in Broadway history, 1984; Drama Desk award, 1976, 79, 81, 84; Outer Circle Critics citation, 1957, 58, 68, 71, 72; Theater World award, 1976; Vernon Rice award Drama Desk, 1968; Albert S. Bard award, 1968; N.Y. Drama Critics Circle award, 1972, 74, 75, 81, 83; Los Angeles Drama Critics award, 1976; Lotos Club awards, 1968, 73; Handel medallion, N.Y.C., 1971; Obie award, 1955, 56, 75, 76, 77, 79; Am. Theater Assn. citation 1973; Richard L. Coe award, 1983; Pulitzer prize for plays 1970, 73, 76; Commonwealth award of Disting. Service (jointly with Sir Laurence Olivier), 1979; The Am. Acad. and Inst. of Arts and Letters Gold medal award for disting. service to the arts, 1981. Mem. ANTA (pres. 1969, dir. ann. award 1965), Dirs. Guild Am., Internat. Theater Inst., Actors Equity Assn., Nat. Acad. TV Arts and Scis., Sigma Alpha Delta (hon.). Home: New York N.Y. Died Oct. 31, 1991.

PARK, THOMAS, science educator, biologist; b. Danville, Ill., Nov. 17, 1908; s. Samuel Thomas and Fronie (Stealey) P.; m. Martha Alden Whitehead, July 31, 1928 (dec. June 1963); children—Sherley, Judith; m. Frances L. Lear, Apr. 18, 1969. B.S., U. Chgo., 1930, Ph.D., 1932; Sc.D., U. Ill., 1973. NRC fellow Johns Hopkins U., 1933-35, instr., asso. biology, 1935-37; instr. zoology U. Chgo., 1937-39, asst. prof., 1939-42, assoc. prof., 1942-47, prof. zoology, 1947-73, prof. emeritus, 1973-92, assoc. dean biol. scis., 1943-46; Rockefeller fellow Oxford U., Eng., 1948; sci. attache Am. embassy, London, 1949. Joint author: Principles of Animal Ecology, 1949; Contbr. articles on ecology to sci. jours.; Editor of: Ecology, 1940-50, Physiol. Zoology, 1955-73; mem. bd. editors: Ency. Brit. Mem. adv. panel NSF; mem. Ill. Bd. Natural Resources and Conservation. Fellow AAAS (life, dir. from 1954, chmn. bd. 1962, pres. 1961); mem. Ecol. Soc. Am. (pres. 1958-59, Eminent Ecologist citation 1971, life mem.), Am. Soc. Naturalists (hon.), Am. Soc. Zoologists, Soc. Study Evolution, Am. Statis. Soc., Sigma Xi, Phi Delta Theta. Club: Quadrangle (Chgo.). Home: Chicago Ill. Died Mar. 30, 1992.

PARKER, DANIEL, aviation company executive; b. Chgo., June 8, 1925; s. Kenneth Safford and Mildred (Gapen) P.; m. 1st, Sally Minor; children: Geoffrey Safford, Steven Minor, Jennifer Parker Coleon, Sarah Parker Topping; m. 2d, JoAnn Slack. BA, Milton Coll., 1947, DBA, 1968; MBA, Harvard U., 1949; LLD, Am. U., 1968. Dir. rsch. and product devel. Parker Pen Co., 1950, dir., 1950-73, 77-86, sec., 1951, exec. v.p., 1952-60, pres., 1960-66, chmn. bd., 1966-73, hon. chmn., 1977-86; chmn., chief exec. officer Omniflight, Inc., 1977-92; U.S. mem. Bus. Adv. Coun. to Internat. Fin. Corp. (World Bank), 1987-92; adminstr. AID, Washington, 1973-77; Pres.'s spl. coord. for internat. disaster assistance, 1975-77; dir. Overseas Pvt. Investment Corp., 1971-73, chmn., 1973-77; mem. Pres.'s Pub. Adv. Com. on Trade Policy, 1968-69. Mem. Republican Nat. Fin. Com., 1961-73, Wis. Rep. Fin. Com., 1961-73; hon. trustee Com. Econ. Devel., Conf. Bd., 1965-80, People to People, 1965-72, Johnson Found., 1977-80, Meridian House Internat., 1977-83; bd. dirs., exec. com. Overseas Devel. Coun., 1969-73, 78-83; hon. chmn. trustees Milton Coll., 1956-73; bd. dirs. Internat. Exec. Svc. Corps, from 1977. Served as lt. USMC, 1942-46. Mem. NAM (dir., chmn. bd. 1968, hon. v.p. 1969-92), Coun. Better Bus. Burs. (vice chmn., dir., exec. com. 1969-73), Coun. on Fgn. Rels., Internat. C. of C. (trustee U.S. coun. 1965-73, chmn. devel. policy bd. 1980-83). Clubs: Metropolitan (Washington), Capitol Hill (Washington), Chevy Chase (Washington), Cornell (N.Y.C.), Seabrook Island (S.C.), Janesville Country, James Island Yacht (Charleston). Home: Wadmalaw Island S.C. Died Jan. 28, 1992; buried Wadmalaw Island, S.C.

PARKER, DAVID STUART, engineering company executive, army officer; b. Ft. Huachuca, Ariz., Mar. 22, 1919; s. Roscoe Stewart and Marguerite Helen (Blossom) P.; m. Betty Hamilton Augur, May 2, 1942; children: David Stuart, Bruce Hamilton, Stephen Bixby, Anne Elizabeth. BS, U.S. Mil. Acad., 1940; MSCE, U. Calif., Berkeley, 1949; grad., Army War Coll., 1957. Registered profl. engr. D.C. Commd. 2d lt. U.S. Army, 1940, advanced through grades to maj. gen., 1967; command and staff assignments in U.S., 1940-44; mem. staffs Adm. Nimitz and Gen. MacArthur PTO, 1945; chief constrn. div. Office Chief Engr., Hdqrs., Tokyo, 1945-48; instr., then asst. prof. mil. topography and graphics U.S. Mil. Acad., 1949-52; asst. dist. engr. Portland, Oreg., 1954-56; chief stratetic planning Korea, 1957-60; engr. group Korea, 1960-61; with Def. Intelligence Agy., Washington, 1961-63; lt. gov. C.Z., 1963-65; v.p. Panama Canal Co., 1963-65; div. engr. N. Atlantic div. C.E., N.Y.C., 1965-66; dir. force planning analysis Office of Chief of Staff, U.S. Army, 1966-68; comdr. Engr. Troops, Vietnam, 1968-69; gov. C.Z., pres. Panama Canal Co., 1971-75; v.p. corp. planning Internat. Engring. Co., San Francisco, 1975-90. Pres. Canal Zone Boy Scout Coun., 1963-64. Mem. NSPE, ASCE, Soc. Am. Mil. Engrs., Assn. U.S. Army. Home: Alexandria Va. Died May 9, 1990; interred Arlington Nat. Cemetery.

PARKER, DAVIS RAFF, academic adminstrator; b. Cleve., Mar. 30, 1927; s. W. Mercier and Catherine (Raff) P.; m. Frances Jane Wykle, Sept. 3, 1949; children: Lynn, Elizabeth, Catherine. A.B., Princeton, 1949; M.A., Western Res. U., 1956. Tchr. French, history and Latin, coach Univ. Sch., Cleve., 1950-58; asst. headmaster Milw. Univ. Sch., 1958-61, headmaster, 1961-64, 1964-66; headmaster Haverford (Pa.) Sch., 1966-87; assoc. dean admissions Gettysburg (Pa.) Coll., 1987-89. Bd. dirs. Haverford Civic Assn.; trustee Nat. Assn. Ind. Schs.; elder Ardmore Presbyn. Ch., 1977-80, trustee, 1984-87; trustee Gettysburg Presbyn. Ch., 1988-89. Served with USNR, 1945-46. Mem. Pa. Assn. Ind. Schs. (past pres.), Headmasters Assn. (treas., v.p.), Country Day Sch. Headmasters Assn. Clubs: Princeton (Phila.), Gettysburg Country. Home: Gettysburg Pa. Died Dec. 2, 1989; buried Evergreen Cemetery, Gettysburg, Pa.

PARKER, GLENN, chief justice state supreme court; b. Murray, Iowa, Nov. 25, 1898; s. Charles and LaVanchie (Ball) P.; m. Ruth Beggs, June 8, 1924; children: William Robert, Marilyn Ruth Parker Reeder). AB, U. Wyo., 1922, LLB, 1927; postgrad., U. Chgo., 1922. Bar: Wyo. 1927. Tchr. English, Laramie (Wyo.) High Sch., 1922-23; prin., supt. suburban schs., Casper, Wyo., 1923-26; practiced in Laramie, from 1927; city atty. City of Laramie, 1930-32; county atty. Albany County, Wyo., 1932-42; judge 2d Jud. Dist. Wyo., 1949-55; assoc. justice Supreme Ct. Wyo., Cheyenne, 1955-63, chief justice, from 1963; instr., lectr. U. Wyo. Law Sch., from 1935. Regional chmn. Boy Scouts Am. Col. JAGC, AUS, 1942-46. Recipient Outstanding Alumnus award U. Wyo., 1958. Mem. ABA, Wyo. Bar Assn., Albany County Bar Assn., Patent Bar Assn., C. of C. (past bd. dirs.), Am. Legion, Masons (32d degree), Shriners, Elks, Rotary. Episcopalian. *

PARKER, JOSEPH ORVILLE, lawyer; b. Pratt, Kans., Dec. 11, 1908; s. Jackson O. and Louise (Fritsche) P.; m. Mary Louise Klose Parker, Apr. 1, 1936; 1 child, Dorothy Louise Parker Johnson. Student, Southwestern Coll., 1927-28; AB, U. Kans., 1931; LLB, Harvard U., 1934. Bar: Kans. 1935, U.S. Supreme Ct. 1947. Pvt. practice Pratt, 1935-36; atty. Office Solicitor, Dept. Agr., Washington, 1936-44; dir. mktg. investigation and counsel Com. on Agr., U.S. Ho. of Reps., Washington, 1945-46, gen. counsel, 1947-51; assoc. firm L. Alton Denslow Law Offices, Washington, 1951-71; mem. U.S. Internat. Trade Commn., Washington, 1971-91, vice-chmn., 1971-75, 76-78, chmn., 1978-80; of counsel Curtis Mallet Prevost Colt & Mosle, Washington, 1981-91; sr. cons. Select Com. on Fgn. Aid, U.S. Ho. of Reps., 1947; adv. Presdl. Commn. on Indsl. Use of Agrl. Commodities, 1956-57; U.S. del. FAO, Rome, 1955; chmn. internat. trade devel. bd. Inst. Am. Poultry Industries, 1956-71. With USN, 1944. Mem. ABA, Fed. Bar Assn., Harvard Law Sch. Assn., Nat. Grange, Bohlen Law Club, Nat. Lawyers Club, Capitol Hill Club, Delta Upsilon. Republican. Presbyterian. Home: Arlington Va. Died Dec. 30, 1991.

PARKER, RALPH DOUGLAS, mining company executive; b. Lockeford, Calif., Apr. 27, 1898; naturalized Can. citizen, 1932.; s. Joseph Douglas and Minerva (Hartley) P.; m. Mina Bayne Todhunter, Jan. 1, 1930. BSc, U. Calif., Berkeley, 1921; LLD, Laurentian U. Sudbury, Ont., Can., 1961. Asst. mine supt. McIntyre Porcupine Mines, Schumacher, Ont., 1922-28; with Internat. Nickel Co. Can., Ltd., from 1928, supt. mines, gen. supt. mining and smelting div., asst. v.p., 1947-54, asst. v.p., gen. mgr. Can. ops., 1954-55, v.p., gen. mgr. Can. ops., 1955-57, v.p. in charge Can. ops., 1958, sr. v.p., from 1960, also hon. chmn., bd. dirs.; bd. dirs. Internat. Nickel Devel. Co., Ltd., Campbell Chebougamau Mines, Ltd., Commonwealth Internat. Corp., Ltd., Commonwealth Internat. Leverage Fund, Ltd., Eriez Mfg. Co., Lakehead Pineline Co., Mond Nickel Exploration, Ltd., Mystery Lake Nickel Mines, Ltd., Can. Permanent Trust Co., Dominion Ins. Corp., Interprovincial Pipe Line Co., KVP Co., Ltd., Phillips Elec. Co., Ltd. Chmn. bd. govs. Laurentian U. Sudbury. With U.S. Army, 1917-18. Mem. AIME, Can. Inst. Mining and Metallurgy (pres. 1964-65), South African Inst. Mining and Metallurgy, Inst. Metals (London), Internat. C. of C. (Can. coun., bd. dirs.), Tech. Svc. Coun. (advisor), Instn. Mining and Metallurgy (London), Mt. Royal Club, Man. Club, Engrs. Club, York Club, Toronto Club, Toronto Hunt Club, Granite Club, Idylwylde Golf and Country Club. *

PARKER, RALPH HALSTEAD, librarian; b. Bertram, Tex., Apr. 21, 1909; s. James Francis and Rosalthe Lee (Lawhon) P.; m. Mary Kate Norman, June 23, 1935; 1 dau., Judith Kay. B.A., U. Tex., 1929, M.A., 1930, Ph.D., 1935; grad. student, U. Chgo., 1936-37. Loan librarian U. Tex., 1930-36; librarian Pomona Coll., Claremont, Calif., 1937-40; dir. libraries U. Ga., 1940-47; librarian U. Mo., 1947-67; founding dean U. Mo. Sch. Libr. and Info. Sci., 1966-74, prof., 1974-78, prof. emeritus, dean emeritus, 1978-90; Mem. Mo. Library Commn., 1946-67, pres., 1959-66. Author: Library Applications of Punched Cards, 1952; Contbr. articles to profl. jours. Served with AUS, 1943-46. U. Chgo. fellow, 1936-37. Mem. A.L.A. (chmn. library equipment com. 1942-43, financial adminstrn. sect. 1957-59), Mo. Library Assn. (pres. 1951-52), Am. Soc. for Information Sci., State Hist. Soc. Mo., Sigma Delta Chi. Democrat. Methodist. Home: Columbia Mo. Died July 1, 1990; buried Meml. Pk Mausoleum, Columbia, Mo.

PARKER, RAYMOND, artist, educator; b. Beresford, S.D., Aug. 22, 1922; s. Roscoe J. and Esther (Mork) P.; m. Denise Griffin, Mar. 30, 1954; children: Kate, Caroline. B.A., State U. Iowa, 1946, M.F.A., 1948. Mem. faculty Hunter Coll., 1955-89, prof. art, 1962-89; Mem. adv. com. Artists for CORE, from 1964; mem. Fulbright-Hays com. on awards Internat. Exchange Program. One-man exhbns. include, Walker Art Center, Mpls., 1950, Paul Kantor Gallery, Los Angeles, 1953, 56, Memphis Acad. Art, 1953, Louisville Art Center, 1954, Union Coll., Schenectady, 1955, Martin Widdifield Gallery, N.Y.C., 1957, 59, U. So. Calif., 1959, Kootz Gallery, N.Y.C., 1960-64, 66, Galerie Neufville, Paris, France, 1960, Galleria Dell Ariete, Milan, Italy, 1961, Dwan Gallery, Los Angeles, 1960, 62, Guggenheim Mus., 1961, Bennington Coll., 1961, Des Moines Art Center, 1962, 63, Dayton (Ohio) Art Inst., 1965, Gertrude Kasle Gallery, Detroit, 1966, 70, Washington Gallery Modern Art, 1966, San Francisco Mus. Art, 1967, Quay Gallery, San Francisco, 1970, 72, 74, Chgo. Arts Club, 1971, Fischbach Gallery, N.Y.C., 1970, 71, 73, Sch. Visual Arts, N.Y.C., 1971, David Berger Gallery, Pitts., 1974, Portland Center for Visual Arts, 1974, Benson Gallery, Bridgehamton, N.Y., 1974, 80, Berenson Gallery, Miami, Fla., 1974, Fischbach Gallery, N.Y.C., 1974, Am. U., Washington, 1975, Susan Caldwell Gallery, N.Y.C., 1976, 80, U. Md., 1977, Caldwell Gallery, 1977, U. Tex., Austin, 1977, Billiard Room Gallery, Cambridge, Mass., 1978, Betty Cunningham Gallery, N.Y.C., 1979, 80, The Phillips Collection, Washington, 1979, Gloria Luria Gallery, Bay Harbor Islands, Fla., 1980, Joe Grippi Gallery, N.Y.C., 1980, SUNY, Cortland, 1981, Carl Solway Gallery, Cin., 1983, Butler Inst. Am. Art, Youngstown, Ohio, 1986, Gloria Luria Gallery, Bay Harbor Islands, Fla., 1986, retrospective exhibition organized by William C. Agee Leubsdorf Art Gallery Hunter Coll., N.Y.C., 1990, others; work represented in permanent collections, Albright-Knox Art Gallery, Dayton Art Inst., Des Moines Art Center, Ft. Worth Mus., Guggenheim Mus., James A. Michener Found., Allentown, Pa., Los Angeles County Mus., Mpls. Inst. Art, Minn. Hist. Soc., Mus. Modern Art, Rose Art Mus. at Brandeis U., State U. Iowa, Tate Gallery, London, Eng., Walker Art Center, Whitney Mus., Miami (Fla.)-Dade Jr. Coll., Met. Mus., N.Y.C., Childe Hassim Found., Wadsworth Atheneum, Art Inst. Chgo., Mass. Inst. Tech., Internat. Minerals and Chems. Corp., Skokie, Ill., Larry Aldrich Old Hundred, Ridgefield, Conn., Portland (Maine) Mus., San Francisco Mus. Art., Cleve. Mus., U. Tex.,

Nat. Gallery Art, Washington, Ft. Lauderdale Mus., Fla., Hudson River Mus., Yonkers, N.Y., U. Ky. Arts Mus., Lexington, Rice U. Mus., Houston, Guild Hall, East Hampton, N.Y., Australian Nat. Gallery, Canberra Mus., Austin, U. N.Mex. Mus., Delgado Mus., New Orleans, Akron (Ohio) Mus., Phila. Mus., Am. U., Vassar Coll., Milw. Art Center, Phillips Collection, Washington, Princeton U., others. With U.S. Mcht. Marine, World War II. Recipient Ford Found. award Corcoran Biennial, 1963; award Nat. Council Arts, 1967; Guggenheim fellow, 1967, 81. Home: New York N.Y. Died Apr. 14, 1990.

PARKER, RICHARD ALEXANDER, Romance languages educator; b. Balt., Nov. 20, 1898; s. Samuel Merritt and Emma (Lawrence) P.; m. Hellen H. Hayden, Aug. 13, 1924 (dec. 1930); 1 child, Geoffrey Pierre; m. Martha Beck, Oct. 14, 1931 (div. 1947); m. Elizabeth M. Kramer, Sept. 11, 1947; 1 child, Dorothea Allegra. AB, Johns Hopkins U., 1921, PhD, 1929; diploma, U. Paris, 1934, U. Madrid, 1948. Instr. modern langs. Balt. City Coll., 1923-28; instr. French, Johns Hopkins U., Balt., 1028-29; instr. Romance langs. NYU, N.Y.C., 1929-30, asst. prof., 1930-45, assoc. prof., 1945-50, prof., from 1950, chmn. dept., from 1949, acting chmn. dept. Romance and Slavic langs. Grad. Sch., 1959; assoc. corr. Bull. Soc. for Study 17th Century. Author: Claude de L'Estoille, Poet and Dramatist, 1930; co-editor: Great Short Stories of Anatole France, 1936; editor: Contes de l'inattendu, 1959; also articles and revs. Decorated Order of Palmes Académiques. Mem. MLA, Am. Assn. Tchrs. French, Am. Assn. Tchrs. Spanish. *

PARKHURST, GEORGE LEIGH, oil company executive; b. Evanston, Ill., Jan. 10, 1907; s. George T. and Jessie (Furness) P.; m. Margaret Sarles, July 2, 1932; children—Peter, Perry, Paul. BSChemE, Armour Inst. Tech., 1927; grad. study, U. Chgo., 1927-30; JD, De Paul U., 1934. Chemist, chem. engr., sr. patent atty. Standard Oil Co. (Ind.), Whiting, Ind. and Chgo., 1927-41; asst. dir. refining, contract exec. Petroleum Adminstrn. for War, Washington, 1941-45; pres. Oronite Chem. Co., San Francisco, 1946-49, chmn. bd., 1949-55; chmn. bd. Chevron Research Corp., 1949-53, dir., 1945-71; v.p. Standard Oil Co. Calif., 1949-71, dir., 1955-71; v.p., dir. Calif. Oil Co., 1960-68; pres. Chevron Chem. Co., 1956-58, dir., from 1956; chmn. Irving Oil Co., 1962-63; dir. Arabian-Am. Oil Co., 1955-71, Trans-Arabian Pipe Line Co., 1955-71; cons., from 1972; dir. Fisher Berkeley Corp., Natomas Co. Contbr. articles to tech. publs. Bd. dirs. Coll. Prep. Sch., 1973-77. Fellow AAAS (v.p. 1954), Am. Inst. Chemists; mem. Am. Chem. Soc. (emeritus mem., chmn. Chgo. sect. 1941, trustee Calif. sect. 1969-81), San Francisco Com. Fgn. Relations, Alpha Chi Sigma, Tau Beta Pi, Phi Lambda Upsilon, Delta Theta Phi. Clubs: World Trade, Bohemian (San Francisco); Chemists (Chgo. and N.Y.C.); University (N.Y.C.). Home: San Mateo Calif. Died Mar. 30, 1990.

PARKINSON, THOMAS FRANCIS, English language educator, author; b. San Francisco, Feb. 24, 1920; s. T. F. and Catherine (Green) P.; m. Ariel Reynolds, Dec. 23, 1948; children: Katherine, Chrysa. A.B. summa cum laude, U. Calif. at Berkeley, 1945, M.A., 1946, Ph.D., 1948. Asst. prof. English U. Calif., Berkeley, 1948-53, assoc. prof., 1953-60, prof. English, 1960-91, spl. asst. to chancellor, 1979-81; vis. asst. prof. Wesleyan U., Conn., 1951-52; Fulbright prof. U. Bordeaux, France, 1953-54, U. Frankfurt, Germany, 1954, Nice and Grenoble, France, 1965-66; vis. prof. U. Wash., Seattle, 1968; vis. lectr. Oxford (Eng.) U., 1969; vis. prof. U. York (Eng.), 1970; mem. lit. panel Nat. Endowment for Arts, 1971-74; vis. sr. research fellow St. John's Coll., Oxford U., 1984-85. Author: Men, Women, Vines, 1959, A Casebook on the Beats, 1961, Thanatos, 1965, rev. edit., 1975, Protect the Earth, 1970, Homage to Jack Spicer, 1970, W.B. Yeats, Self-Critic and the Later Poetry, 2 vols, 1971, (verse drama) What the Blind Man Saw, 1974, (verse) The Canters of Thomas Parkinson, 1977, Hart Crane and Yvor Winters: Their Literary Correspondence, 1978, (verse) From the Grande Chartreuse, 1980, Crane and Winters, 1982, Poets, Poems, Movements, 1987, paper edit., 1988 (Am. Book award 1988), Verse Poems New and Selected, 1988; editor: Masterworks of Prose, 1961, Robert Lowell, 1969. Served with USAAF, 1943. Recipient Berkeley Citation, U. Calif., 1991; Guggenheim fellow, 1957-58; Inst. Creative Art fellow, 1963-64; Am. Philos. Soc. Travel grantee, 1957, 68; Humanities research prof., 1969-70, 80-81; sr. fellow NEH, 1984-85; Am. Council Learned Socs. grantee, 1985. Mem. AAUP (pres. Berkeley chpt. 1962-63), MLA. Democrat. Roman Catholic. Office: Univ Calif Dept English Berkeley CA 94720 Died Jan. 15, 1992; buried Berkeley, Calif.

PARKS, BERT, entertainer; b. Atlanta, Dec. 30, 1914; s. Aaron and Hattie (Spiegel) Jacobson; m. Annette Liebman, June 8, 1943; children—Jeffrey, Joel, Annette. Student, Marist Coll., Atlanta, 1926-32. Radio announcer radio sta. WGST, Atlanta, 1932; staff announcer CBS, N.Y.C., 1933-39; master of ceremonies Break the Bank (radio and TV), 1946-56, Stop the Music (radio and TV), 1947-55, Double or Nothing (TV), 1953-55, Miss America Pageant, 1956-79, numerous other beauty pageants and TV spls. Appeared in: starring role The Music Man on Broadway, 1960-61; TV appearances include: Yours for a Song, 1961-63, guest on Burke's Law, Ellery Queen, The Bionic Woman; appeared in film The Freshman, 1990. Served with AUS, 1942-45, CBI. Decorated Bronze Star medal; recipient Poor Richard award, 1957, City of Hope award, 1958, TV Forecast award, 1950, March of Dimes Man of Year award, 1963. Home: Los Angeles Calif. Died Feb. 2, 1992.

PARKS, ED HORACE, III, lawyer; b. Tulsa, Apr. 11, 1948; s. Ed H. Jr. and Nancy D. (Dickson) P. BS in Philosophy, Okla. State U., 1972; JD, U. Tulsa, 1975. Bar: Okla. 1975, U.S. Dist. Ct. (no. and we. dists.) Okla. 1975, U.S. Ct. Appeals (10th cir.) 1975, U.S. Supreme Ct. 1980. Assoc. Boyd & Parks, Tulsa, 1975-79; ptnr. Parks & Buck, Tulsa, from 1980. Bd. dirs. Okla. Health Systems Agy., Oklahoma City, 1978-86, vice chmn., 1986. Served with Okla. N.G., 1969-75. Mem. ABA, Okla. Bar Assn., Tulsa County Bar Assn. (chmn. grievances com. from 1989), Assn. Trial Lawyers Am., Okla. Trial Lawyers Assn., Utica Square Club, Lions (pres. Tulsa 1976), Phi Alpha Delta. Democrat. Baptist. Home: Tulsa Okla. Deceased.

PARKS, HENRY GREEN, food company executive; b. Atlanta, Sept. 29, 1916; s. Henry Green and Gainelle (Williams) P.; children: Grace Johnson, Cheryl V. BA, Ohio State U.; LLD, Temple U., 1975. Sales rep. Pabst Brewing Co., N.Y.C., 1940-42; pntr. W.B. Graham & Assocs., Inc., N.Y.C., 1942-48; founder H.G. Parks, Inc., Balt., 1951-89; dir. Tuesday Publs., Inc., First Pa. Corp., W.R. Grace & Co.; mem. Balt. City Coun., 1963-70; treas. Balt. Dem. Cen. Com., 1970-72; bd. dirs. Boys' Town Homes of Md., World Health adminstrv. Svcs. Bd. advisers Black Enterprise mag., 1970—. Vice-chmn. Vol. Coun. on Equal Opportunity, 1963. Named hon. col. Ft. McHenry Guard, 1973; recipient hon. citation award for outstanding leadership United Negro Coll. Fund, 1972. Home: Baltimore Md. Died Apr. 24, 1989.

PARR, ALBERT EIDE, marine researcher; b. Bergen, Norway, Aug. 15, 1900; came to U.S., 1926, naturalized, 1932; s. Thomas and Helga (Eide) P.; m. Ella Hage, Dec. 31, 1925; children: Hedvig, Gifford Nils, Thomas, Victoria-Johanne. Student, Royal U., Oslo, 1921-25; DSc, Yale U., 1946, Colby Coll., 1956. Asst. zoology Bergen Mus., 1918-19; asst. Bur. Fisheries, Norway, 1924-26, N.Y. Aquarium, 1926; curator Bingham oceanographic collection Yale U., 1927-42, asst. prof. zoology, 1931-37, assoc. prof., 1937-38, prof. ocenaography, 1938-42, sci. dir. oceanographic expdns., 1931-37, dir. marine rsch., 1937-42; dir. Peabody Mus., 1938-42; dir. Am. Mus. Natural History, N.Y.C., 1942-59, sr. scientist, 1959-68, dir. emeritus, 1968-91. Trustee Woods Hole (Mass.) Oceanographic Inst. Contbr. articles to profl. jours. Home: Wilder VT Died July 17, 1991.

PARRY, ALBERT, educator, writer, lecturer; b. Rostov on-the-Don, Russia, Feb. 24, 1901; came to U.S., 1921, naturalized, 1926; s. Joseph and Elizabeth (Blass) P.; m. Louise Emily Goodman, Oct. 25, 1941 (div. 1971); children—James Donald, Thomas Hugh. Student, Columbia U., 1925-26; A.B., U. Chgo., 1935, Ph.D., 1938. Newspaper and mag. free-lance writer, 1921-37; editor Consol. Book Pubs., Inc., Chgo., 1937-41; asst. div. social scis. U. Chgo., 1939; research dir. radio broadcasts Chgo. Sun, 1941-42; information officer OSS, Washington, 1942-45; exec. bd. Chgo. Council Fgn. Relations, 1943-47; asso. prof. polit. sci. Northwestern U., 1946-47; prof. Russian civilization and lang. Colgate U., 1947-69, prof. emeritus, 1969-92, head dept. Russian studies, 1947-69; dir. Russian Area and Lang. Insts., 1961-66; prof. Russian civlization and lang., chmn. Slavic studies Case Western Res. U., 1969-71, emeritus; program cons. Radio Free Europe, N.Y.C., 1950-52; vis. lectr., cons. U.S. Army War Coll., 1958-72; cons. Spl. Ops. Research Office, Dept. Army, 1960; vis. lectr. Inter-Am. Def. Coll., 1962-68; vis. scholar Radio Liberty, Munich, 1967-68; Exec. officer Com. to Defend Am. by Aiding Allies, 1940-41, Fight for Freedom Com., 1941. Author: Garrets and Pretenders, a history of bohemianism in America, 1933, rev. edit., 1960, Tattoo, 1933, Whistler's Father, 1939, Riddle of the Reich, (with Wythe Williams), 1941, Russian Cavalcade, a military record, 1944, Korea, an annotated bibliography of Russian publications, (with John T. Dorosh and Elizabeth G. Dorosh), 1950, Russia's Rockets and Missiles, 1960, The New Class Divided, Science and Technology Versus Communism, 1966, America Learns Russian, 1967, The Russian Scientist, 1973, Twentieth-Century Russian Literature, (with Harry T. Moore), 1974, Terrorism: From Robespierre to Arafat, 1976; Full Steam Ahead! The Life of Peter Demens, Founder of St. Petersburg, Florida, 1987; column Soviet Affairs in Missiles and Rockets mag, 1957-63; contbr. to Some Historians of Modern Europe, 1942; translator Building Lenin's Russia (Liberman), 1945, The Moscow Puzzles (Kordemsky) 1972; translator, editor Peter Kapitsa on Life and Science, 1968; frequent contbr. to profl. and popular jours. Grantee Am. Council Learned Socs., 1961, U.S. Office Edn., MLA, 1965-66. Mem. Am. Assn. Tchrs. Slavic and East European Langs. (nat. pres. 1961), Phi Beta Kappa. Home: Los Angeles Calif. Died May 4, 1992.

PARSHALL, DOUGLASS EWELL, artist; b. N.Y.C., Nov. 19, 1899; s. DeWitt and Carrie (Ewell) P.; m. Barbara Cowles, Jan. 11, 1938; 1 dau., Cecilia Pruter. Student, Thachter Sch., 1917-19. One-man shows include Cowie Galleries, Challis Galleries, Laguna Beach, Calif., Gallery de Silva, Montecito and Santa Barbara, Calif., Santa Barbara Mus.; numerous group shows; represented in permanent collection Santa Barbara Mus. Art, de Young Mus., San Francisco, Guggenheim Mus., N.Y.C. Mem. Nat. Water Color Soc., West Coast Water Color Soc. Republican. Episcopalian. Home: Santa Barbara Calif. Died Aug. 29, 1990.

PARSONS, HAYWARD TREAT, lawyer; b. Bucksport, Maine, Sept. 4, 1893; s. Arthur Lincoln and Annie (Treat) P.; m. Mary Bradstreet, Nov. 28, 1942. AB, Bowdoin Coll., 1916; LLB, Harvard U., 1919. Bar: R.I. 1920. Ptnr. Hinckley, Allen, Salisbury & Parsons, Providence, from 1925; U.S. concilliation comr. Providence and Bristol cos., 1934-46; bd. dirs., sec. Baltic Mills Co.; sec. Baltic Water Co., Sprague Warehouses, Inc.; bd. dirs. Nicholson File Co., Nicholson File Co. Can., Ltd., Nicholson File Export Co., Title Guarantee Co. R.I., Smith Estates, Inc., Inc. Estates. Trustee Maine Cen. Inst.; bd. dirs. Providence Athenaeum, 1951-55; mem. fin. com. R.I. Assn. for Blind. Mem. ABA, R.I. Bar Assn. (exec. com., treas. 1947-56), Hope Club, Agawam Hunt Club, Turks Head Club, Harvard Club, Bowdoin Club. *

PARSONS, JAMES GRAHAM, foreign service officer; b. N.Y.C., Oct. 28, 1907; s. James Graham and Adelaide Douglas (Smyth) P.; m. Margaret Josephine Boulton, Sept. 25, 1936 (dec. 1987); children: Margaret Parsons Hallett, Jane I. Parsons Lyons. BA, Yale U., 1929; postgrad., NYU, 1931-32. Pvt. sec. to U.S. amb. to Japan, Am. Embassy, Tokyo, 1932-36; vice consul Am. Embassy, Havana, Cuba, 1936-38, Mukden, Manchuria, 1938-40; 3d sec., vice consul Am. Embassy, Ottawa, Ont., Can., 1940-43; assigned Dept. State, Washington, 1943-47, asst. chief div. Brit. commonwealth affairs, 1945-47; asst. to personal rep. of Pres. of U.S. to Pope, The Vatican, 1947-48; 1st sec., consul Am. Embassy, New Delhi and Kathmandu, Nepal, 1948-50; assigned to Nat. War Coll., 1950-51; dep. dir. Office European Regional Affairs, Dept. State, 1951-53; dep. chief mission, min. Am. Embassy, Tokyo, 1953-56, amb. to Kingdom of Laos, Vientiane, 1956-58, to Sweden, Stockholm, 1961-67; dep. asst. sec. state Dept. State, 1958=59, asst. sec. for Far Ea. affairs, 1959-61, sr. fgn. svc. insp., 1967-69, adv. to Indsl. Coll. Armed Forces, 1969-70, cons., 1972-74; dep. chmn. US. SALT del., Vienna and Helsinki, 1970-72; mem. Permanent Joint Bd. on Def. U.S. and Can., 1945-47. Mem. Yale Club (N.Y.C.), Met. Club (Washington), Phi Beta Kappa, Zeta Psi. Episcopalian. Home: Stockbridge Mass. Died Oct. 20, 1991; buried Stockbridge, Mass.

PARSONS, WILLIAM WALTER, educator; b. L.A., June 18, 1912; s. Hazen M. and Alice (LeSueur) P.; m. Lois G. Shattuck, Sept. 14, 1935 (dec. Dec. 1979); children—Roger Paul, Richard Walter, Arthur Shattuck.; m. Janette Rainwater, Sept. 3, 1982. B.S. magna cum laude, U. So. Calif., 1935; M.S. (fellow), Syracuse U., 1938; postgrad., Am. U., 1941-42; LL.D., Southeastern U., 1957. Mem. field staff Regent's Edn. Inquiry, Albany, N.Y., 1936; field cons. Pub. Adminstrn. Service, Chgo., 1937-40; spl. asst. N.Y. State Dept. Edn., 1940-41; budget examiner Bur. Budget, 1941-44; dep. dir. mgmt. procurement div. Treasury Dept., 1944-45; tech. asst. Office Sec. Treasury, 1945-46, adminstrv. asst. to sec. treasury, 1946-50, adminstrv. asst. sec. treasury, 1950-59; v.p. System Devel. Corp., Santa Monica, 1959-63, sr. v.p., 1963-68, v.p. adminstrn., 1968-70; v.p. bus. affairs U. Hawaii, 1970-72; spl. cons. to comptr. gen. U.S., 1972-73; asst. regional mgr. U.S. GAO, San Francisco, 1973-74, L.A., 1974-79; Disting. prof. in residence Sch. Public Adminstrn., U. So. Calif., L.A., 1979-91; on loan as asst. adminstr. mgmt. Economic Stblzn. Agy., 1950. Editorial bd. Pub. Adminstrn. Rev., 1949-52. Trustee, mem. budget com. United Community Services, Washington, 1949-52; mem. exec. com., chmn. hdqrs. com. Community Chest Fedn., 1952-56; bd. dirs., mem. exec. com. United Givers Fund, 1956-58; dir. D.C. chpt. A.R.C., 1956-58; v.p. Health and Welfare Council Nat. Capital Area., 1958-59. Mem. Am. Soc. Pub. Adminstrn. (pres. 1954, council and exec. com. 1953-56), Nat. Acad. Pub. Adminstrn., Phi Beta Phi, Beta Gamma Sigma, Beta Alpha Psi. Home: Pacific Palisades Calif. Died Sept. 28, 1991; cremated.

PARTRIDGE, DONALD BARROWS, college president; b. Canton, Maine, Jan. 17, 1917; s. Donald B. and Geneva S. (Sturtevant) P.; m. Martha B. Packard, Sept. 28, 1940; children: Margaret, Martha Jane, Donald, John, James. B.S., Bates Coll., 1938, M.Ed., 1949; postgrad., Harvard Grad. Sch. Edn.; LL.D., Phila. Coll. Textiles and Sci., 1974. Tchr. chemistry and physics high schs. Maine, Mass., 1939-45; dir. guidance Sanford (Maine) Public Sch. Systems, 1945-48; dir. admissions and placement Phila. Coll. Textiles and Sci., 1948-53, dean students, 1953-62, dean coll., 1962-66, v.p., dean, 1967-76, v.p., dir. devel., 1976-77, acting pres., 1977-78, pres., 1978-84, trustee, from 1978. Fellow Scottish Coll. Textiles (hon.); mem. Nat. Council Textile Edn. (hon. mem.; pres. 1968-69), Phi Psi Frat.

Republican. Congregationalist. Clubs: Pastorius, Masons, Phila. Rotary. Home: Hatboro Pa. Died Mar. 16, 1991.

PASANT, ATHANASE J., insurance company executive; b. Bay City, Mich., Aug. 29, 1918; s. Arthur J. and Rose M. (Novak) P.; m. Shirley K. Williston, Feb. 12, 1945; children: James, Thomas, David, Christina. B.A. in Econs., Mich. State U., 1949. Agt., brokerage mgr. Great West Life Ins. Co., Lansing, Mich., 1945-55; gen. agt. Ill. Mid-Continent Life Ins. Co., Evanston, Ill., 1955-60; pres. Apex Investments, Lansing, 1960-61; founder, pres. Jackson Nat. Life Ins. Co., Lansing, 1961-88, chmn., from 1961; pres., dir. Chrissy Corp., Wilmington, Del., 1981-88, Jackson Nat. Life of Tex., Irving, 1981-88; vice chmn. Mich. Life & Health Guarantee Assn., Lansing, 1982-85. Home: Lansing Mich. Deceased. †

PASTERNAK, JOSEPH, motion picture producer; b. Silagy-Somlyo, Rumania, Sept. 19, 1901; came to U.S., 1921, naturalized, 1927; s. Samuel and Roza Janovitz P.; m. Darrell, Jan. 9, 1942; children: Michael, Jeffrey, Peter. Began as asst. dir., 1923; motion picture producer Universal Pictures, Europe, U.S. Producer Nice Girl, The Flame of New Orleans, It Started with Eve, 1941, Seven Sweethearts, 1942, Anchors Aweigh, 1944, Thousands Cheer, Song of Russia, This Time for Keeps; for M.G.M. including The Merry Widow, Because Your're Mine, Small Town Girl, Latin Lovers, 1952, Easy to Love, Flame and the Flesh, 1953, Ask Any Girl, 1959, Please Don't Eat the Daisies, 1960, Where the Boys Are, 1961, Jumbo, 1962, A Ticklish Affair, 1963, Girl Happy, 1965, Penelope, 1966; author: Easy the Hard Way, 1956. Died Sept. 13, 1991.

PASTORE, PETER NICHOLAS, physician, educator; b. Bluefield, W.Va., Nov. 8, 1907; s. Louis and Carmela (Ricciardulli) P.; m. Julia Rourke, Sept. 14, 1939; children: Ann (Mrs. Vincent M. Cremona, Jr.), Louis (dec.), Julie, Mary (Mrs. Cyrus Dolph IV), Peter Nicholas, Jr. A.B., U. Richmond, 1930; M.D., Med. Coll. Va., 1934; M.S., U. Minn., 1939. Diplomate: Am. Bd. Otolaryngology. Intern Med. Coll. Va., 1934, resident surgery, 1935-36; fellow Mayo Clinic, 1936-39, staff assoc., 1939-42; mem. faculty Med. Coll. Va., from 1942, prof., chmn. dept. otology, rhinology, laryngology, audiology and speech pathology, 1942-76, prof. emeritus, from 1976; founder, dir. Med. Coll. Va. (Hearing and Speech Center), from 1942; chief otolaryngology McGuire VA Med. Center, Richmond, 1955-76; dir. continuing med. edn. in otolaryngology McGuire VA Med. Center, from 1980; scholar-in-residence Med. Coll. Va.-Va. Commonwealth Univ. Libraries, from 1981; cons. U.S. Naval Hosp., Portsmouth, Va., McDonald Army Hosp., Ft. Eustis, Va. Med. dir. Richmond chpt. Am. Cancer Soc., 1959-60, pres., 1961-63; bd. dirs. Richmond Children's Aid Soc., 1944-47, Va. Soc. Crippled Children and Adults, from 1954; mem. Gov. Va. Adv. Com. Handicapped Children, 1964-72; pres. Richmond Easter Seal Soc. Crippled Children and Adults, 1967-70; Mem. bd. Benedictine High Sch., Richmond, 1959-65, pres., 1964-66. Served to 1st lt., M.C. AUS, World War II. Fellow Am. Coll. Surgeons (regent 1965-69), Internat. Coll. Surgeons (pres. Va. surg. div. 1959-61), A.M.A., Am. Acad. Ophthalmology and Otolaryngology (life mem., award merit 1960); mem. Med. Soc. Va., Richmond Acad. Medicine, Va. Soc. Ophthalmology and Otolaryngology (life mem., pres. 1952-53), Richmond Eye, Ear, Nose and Throat Soc. (life mem., pres. 1945-46), Am. Otol. Soc.(life mem.), Am. Laryngol. Assn. (life mem.), Am. Laryng. Rhinol. and Otol. Soc. (life mem.), Catholic Physicians Guild (pres. 1962-65), Pan-Am. Assn. Oto-Rhino-Laryngology-Broncho-Esophagology, Tidewater Otol. Med. Soc. (hon. mem.), W.Va. Otol. Soc. (hon. mem.), Dallas Otol. Soc. (hon. mem.), Phi Beta Kappa, Sigma Xi, Alpha Omega Alpha. Club: Willow Oaks Country. Home: Richmond Va. Deceased. †

PATEE, DORIS S., children's book editor; b. Holyoke, Mass., Sept. 21, 1897; d. Fred H. and Mary (Goodenough) P. AB, Wellesley Coll., 1919. Bookseller Hampshire Bookshop, Northampton, Mass., 1920-31; dir. promotion Nat. Assn. Book Pubs., N.Y.C., 1931-33; children's book editor Macmillan Co., N.Y.C., from 1933, also bd. dirs. Mem. Children's Book Coun. (pres. 1947-49, bd. dirs. 1957-60), Am. Inst. Graphic Arts. *

PATES, GORDON, newspaper editor; b. San Francisco, Sept. 1, 1916; s. Rutherford and Louise (Ryder) P.; m. Lorraine Lindeberg, Aug. 24, 1941; children: Bonnie J., William G. B.A., U. Wash., 1939. With San Francisco Chronicle, 1939-79; successively copyboy, reporter, copyreader, desk editor, editor This World mag., successively Sunday editor, advt. research dir., promotion dir., mng. editor, 1954-77, exec. editor, 1977-79. Served as tech. sgt. USAAF, 1942-46. Recipient award for distinguished domestic news reporting Nat. Headliners Club, 1948. Home: Walnut Creek Calif. Died Aug. 29, 1988; cremated.

PATRICK, ROBERT JOHN, JR., lawyer; b. San Francisco, July 1, 1934; s. Robert J. and Marie E. (McKinnon) P.; m. Janet Mary Cline, June 13, 1959; children: John, Stewart, William. B.A., Stanford U., 1956, LL.B., 1959; M.Internat. Affairs, Columbia U., 1960. Bar: Calif. 1960, N.Y. 1961, D.C. 1976. Assoc. Cleary, Gottlieb, Steen & Hamilton, N.Y.C., 1961-66; assoc. Cleary, Gottlieb, Steen & Hamilton, Paris, 1966-69; dep., then internat. tax counsel U.S. Treasury Dept., Washington, 1969-76; ptnr. Delaney & Patrick, Washington, 1976-78; sr. tax counsel Exxon Corp., N.Y.C., 1979-81; ptnr. Jones, Day, Reavis & Pogue, Washington, 1981-83; dir. internat. tax practice Price Waterhouse, Washington, 1983-92. Contbr. articles to profl. jours. Recipient Exceptional Service award U.S. Treasury Dept., 1976. Mem. ABA, State Bar Calif., Internat. Fiscal Assn. (v.p. U.S. br. 1978). Home: Washington D.C. Died Dec. 4, 1992. †

PATTEN, DAVID L(ONGFELLOW), consulting engineer, banker; b. Westwood, Mass., Sept. 12, 1894; s. Charles Campbell and Florence (Mayhew) P.; m. Beatrice L. Allen, Apr. 2, 1918 (dec. May 1943); m. Dorothy Kendall Russell, Oct. 28, 1945. SB, MIT, 1916; cert. lang. prof., U. Paris, 1919. Engr. Stone & Webster Engring. Corp., Boston, 1920; supt. all prodn. Paramount Motion Picture Corp., N.Y.C., 1921-23; salesman Harris Forbes & Co., Boston, 1924-33; a founder, ptnr., bd. dirs. Whiting Week & Knowles (then Whiting Weeks & Stubbs, Inc.), Boston, 1933-42; cons. engr., Duxbury, Mass., 1946-48, from 1950; chief mission to Portugal, ECA, 1948-50; assoc. F.P. Morgan Co., Boston. Air raid warden Town of Brookline, Mass., 1941-42; advisor Boys Club, Boston, also mem. internat. com.; Mem. New Eng. Com. for Sales U.S. Govt. Bonds, Boston Community Fund, ARC, Boston. 2d lt. U.S. Army, 1917-19, AEF; comdr. USN, 1942-45; capt. USNR ret. Decorated Legion of Merit. Mem. Soc. Real Estate Appraisers, Soc. Real Estate Brokers, Boston C. of C., MIT Alumni Assn. Ilife), Univ. Club (Washington), Duxbury Yacht Club, Union Boat Club, Phi Gamma Delta. Republican. *

PATTERSON, CHESTER MARCH, lawyer; b. Wichita, Kans., Nov. 21, 1894; s. Alexander Clark and Ethlena (Riggs) P.; m. Georgina Castro Fernandez, Aug. 17, 1921; children: Jenane Patterson Navez), Chester March Jr. AB, U. Kans., 1917; LLB, Harvard U., 1924. Bar: N.Y. 1925. Assoc. Hall, Patterson, Taylor, McNicol & Marrett and predecessors, N.Y.C., 1924-34, ptnr., from 1934; bd. dirs. Gt. Island Holding Corp., Am. Maize Products Co., Hutting Mfg. Co. Bd. dirs. E. Matilda Ziegler Found. for Blind. 2d lt. U.S. Army, 1917-19. Mem. ABA, Inter-Am. Bar Assn., N.Y. State Bar Assn., Bar Assn. City N.Y., Harvard Club, Masons. *

PATTERSON, GEORGE STUART, petroleum company executive, consultant; b. Phila., May 10, 1909; s. George Stuart and Eleanora (Willing) P.; m. Marguerite A. Bushnell, Dec. 9, 1933; children: George Stuart, Robert Gray, Lee W.; m. Patricia Ann Cochran, Feb. 23, 1963; 1 dau., Patricia Lee. Grad., St. Paul's Sch., 1927; B.A., Yale U., 1931. With George H. McFadden & Bros. (cotton mchts.), Memphis, 1931-40; with Buckeye Pipeline Co., N.Y.C., 1940-72, exec. v.p., 1948-52, pres., 1952-70, chmn. bd., 1970-72; chmn., chief exec. officer Everglades Pipeline Co., Port Everglades, Fla., until 1989; dir. XPLOR Energy Co. past dir. N.W. Energy Co., Interlake, Inc., Howmet Corp., Bankers Oil and Gas Co.; mem. adv. bd. Chem. Bank.; life bd. dirs. Am. Petroleum Inst. Trustee L.I. U.; pres. Meadow Club, Southampton, L.I., 22 yrs. Served to 1st lt. USMCR, 1943-45, PTO. Episcopalian. Home: Gulfstream Fla. Died Sept. 24, 1989; buried Phila.

PATTERSON, JAMES OGLETHORPE, SR., bishop; b. Derma, Miss., July 21, 1912; s. William A. and Moline Terry P.; m. Deborah Indiana Mason, July 4, 1934; children: James Oglethorpe, Janet Patterson Wheeler. Th.M., Howe Sch. Religion (now LeMoyne-Owen Coll.); D.C.L., Pillar of Fire Sem., 1969; PH.D., Trinity Hall Coll., 1970. Former pastor various parishes; bishop East Tenn. jurisdiction Ch. of God in Christ, 12 yrs.; pres. bishop Ch. of God in Christ, Inc. (Pentacostal), Memphis, 1968-89; dir. Tri-State Bank Memphis. Founder Mason Found. Recipient numerous awards, honors, citations. Home: Memphis Tenn. Died Dec. 29, 1989.

PATTERSON, JOSEPH JULIAN, architect; b. Danville, Ill., May 3, 1894; s. Jesse Julian and Nancy Jane (Purkins) P.; m. Madaline Elizabeth Gammel, June 24, 1919; 1 child, Patricia Ann Patterson Sharratt. BArch, U. Ill., 1917; postgrad., Okla. A&M U., 1917-19. Assoc. prof. architecture Okla. A&M U., 1917-25; designer Wyatt C. Hedrick, 1925-32; pvt. practice, Ft. Worth, 1932-35; ptnr. Patterson & Teague, Ft. Worth, 1935-39, Wilson, Patterson, Sowden, Dunlap & Epperly and predecessor, Ft. Worth, from 1939. Prin. works include Children's Mus., Ft. Worth, bldgs. for North Tex. State U., Arlington State Coll., Abilene Chriistian Coll., San Angelo Coll., Cooke County Jr. Coll., also numerous secondary and elem. schs., chs., banks, office bldgs. Mem. Commn. on Architecture and Allied Arts, Episcopal Diocese of Dallas; mem. AIA design team Ft. Worth City Plan, from 1960; cons. Natural Sci. for Youth Found., from 1963; vestryman Episcopal Ch. 2d lt. Q.M.C., U.S. Army, 1918. Fellow AIA (pres. Ft. Worth 19509); mem. Tex. Soc. Architects (bd. dirs. from 1959), Ft. Worth C. of C. (met. plan com.), Masons, Shriners, Elks, Lions (bd. dirs. 1950-53), Alpha Rho Chi, Phi Kappa Phi, Sigma Tau, Sigma Chi. *

PATTERSON, MERRILL REEVES, retired humanities educator; b. Jersey City, Jan. 27, 1902; s. William Clifford and Maybelle Virginia (Reeves) P.; m. Dana Robinson Rymer, June 23, 1928; children: Merrill Reeves Jr., Barbara (Mrs. B.S. Nelson). BS, Wesleyan U., 1925; AM, Brown U., 1930; PhD, Yale, 1933; LittD, Marietta Coll., 1967, D of Univ. (hon.), AJO (hon.). Mng. editor New Haven (Conn.) Union, 1926-27; master Tilton Sch., N.H., 1927-28; instr. in English Wesleyan U., Middletown, Conn., 1932-34; asst. in English Conn. Coll. for Women, New London, Conn., 1933-34; instr. in English Marietta (Ohio) Coll., 1934-36, asst. prof., 1936-38, prof., 1938-39, Hillyer prof. and chmn. dept., 1939, dean of coll., 1948-67, dean emeritus, dir. acad. advising, 1967-72; cons. Parkersburg (W.Va.) Community Coll., 1972-75, Distinguished prof., chmn. humanities div., 1975-88, ret., 1988; instr. 25th Coll. Tng. Detachment (air crew), 1943-44; Pres. Nat. Stillwater (Okla.) Conf. Acad. Deans, 1958-59; commr. N. Central Assn. Commn. Colls. and Univs. Editor and author: booklet Picture of an Inauguration, 1945; Contbr. to: Dict. Am. Biography, 1931, Rhode Island Historical Collections, 1941, Eleusis of Chi Omega, 1938, 45, Ohio Farmer, 1939, Ohioana Quar., 1971, script Speaking of Shakespeare (accepted by Folger Library, Washington), 1978; other publs. Dir. pub. affairs. Marietta Civil Def. Program, 1950-51; mem. Citizens Narcotics Adv. Com. for Ohio, 1954-56; dir. Ohio Citizens Council for Health and Welfare; trustee emeritus Marietta Meml. Hosp.; Ohio chmn. dedication Wood County (W.Va.) Airport, 1946; gen. chmn. inauguration of Pres. Shimer Marietta Coll., 1945; dir. coll. activities for Ohio of Nat. Heritage Found.; mem. exec. com. Council of Affiliated Instns., Inst. European Studies, from 1968; sr. adv., charter mem. U.S. Congressional Adv. Bd., from 1981; trustee 1988 Bicentennial Steering Com. for Marietta, chmn. 1980-83. Recipient award for exceptional service Crusade for Freedom, 1955; distinguished service awards Nat. Heritage Found., 1958; distinguished service awards Inst. European Studies, Vienna, 1972; Silver Knight award Nat. Mgmt. Assn., 1967; award for work in arts and humanities Gov. Ohio, 1985; honored as human resource of U.S. Am. Heritage Research Assn., 1975; Dr. Merrill R. Patterson Bicentennial Messages (collection of addresses) pub. in his honor to commemorate Bicentennial Ordinance of 1787 and 200th birthday of Marietta, 1987-88. Mem. Modern Lang. Assn. Am., Nat. Council Tchrs. Eng. Coll. Eng. Assn., Ohio Coll. Assn. (past pres.; com. membership and inspection), Ohio Council Advanced Placement, Am. Conf. Acad. Deans (recorder, cons., group leader, exec. com., treas.from 1960), C. of C., Ohioana Library Assn. (trustee, treas.; pres. 1967-85, Martha Kinney Cooper award 1985), Oratorio Soc. (violinist, concertmaster), Fine Arts Commn. (sec.), Marietta Community Concert Assn. (dir.), Internat. Platform Assn., Omicron Delta Kappa (distinguished certificate of meritorious award 1972), Alpha Psi Omega, Delta Kappa Epsilon, Beta Beta Beta, Pi Kappa Delta, Pi Delta Epsilon. Republican. Conglist. (moderator 1963-65, 1968-70, gen. chmn. sesquecentennial observance 1946). Clubs: Mason (Shriner), Rotary (past pres., dist. gov. 1956-57, consultative com. on internat. service 1958-59, mem. internat. found. fellowships com. 1959-61, Paul Harris fellow 1973), Marietta Reading (past pres.), Marietta Country. Home: Marietta Ohio Deceased. †

PATTISON, EDWARD WORTHINGTON, lawyer, congressman; b. Troy, N.Y., Apr. 29, 1932; s. Edward Hargrave and Elisabeth (Royce) P.; m. Eleanor Copley, Nov. 23, 1951; children: Mark, Lynn, Laura, Wendy. A.B., Cornell U., 1953, LL.B., 1957. Bar: N.Y. 1957. Partner Smith, Pattison, Sampson & Jones, Troy, 1959-72; v.p. Smith, Pattison, Sampson & Jones, 1972-74, Pattison, Herzog, Sampson & Nichols, 1974; mem. 94th-95th Congresses from 29th Dist. N.Y.; com. on judiciary, banking, fin. and urban affairs com., adminstrn. com. 94th-96th Congresses from 29th Dist. N.Y.; fellow Kennedy Inst. Politics, Harvard U., 1979; sr. univ. lectr. Rensselaer Poly. Inst., 1979-80; lectr. Antioch/New Eng. Grad. Sch., 1981; Mem. Comptrollers Com. on Revision N.Y. State Real Property Tax Law, 1971-74; treas. Capital Dist. Regional Planning Commn., 1970-74, commr., 1974; mem. exec. com. Rensselaer County Inter-govtl. Council, 1972-74; chmn. Gen. Revenue Sharing Commn. Rensselaer County, 1973-74; Chmn. Town of Sand Lake Democratic Com., 1961-65; mem. exec. com. Rensselaer County Dem. Com., 1962-64; chmn. Rensselaer County Citizens for Kennedy-Johnson, 1960; Rensselaer County treas., 1969-74; candidate U.S. Congress from 30th Dist. N.Y., 1970, Rensselaer County Exec., 1973, N.Y. State Senate 41st Dist., 1980; ptnr. Pattison, Sampson, Ginsberg & Griffin, P.C., 1986-90; polit. commentator TV Channel 13, Albany, N.Y., 1987—; bd. dirs. The Eddy, Inc.;. Author: The Marketing of Property Acquired for Taxes, 1972, The Political Parties, Ralph Nader, Where Are You?, 1972, How To Conduct a Tax Sale, 1973; columnist Daily Gazette, 1988-90; commentator Sta. WNYT-TV, Sta. WQBK,. Bd. dirs. Salvation Army, adv. bd., 1964-71; bd. dirs. Family and Children's Service, Inc., 1965-73; bd. dirs. United Community Services, sec., 1966-70, mem. exec. com., 1966-72; bd. dirs. Rensselaer County Tb and Pub. Health Assn., pres., 1964-67; bd. dirs. Commn. on Econ. Opportunity for Rensselaer County Area, chmn., 1965-68; bd. dirs. Cornell U. Nat. Secondary Schs. Com., 1964-67; chmn.

Cornell Club of Albany Secondary Schs. Com., 1962-70, HSORA, Inc., 1966-74; bd. dirs. N.Y. State Environmental Health Assn., sec., 1971-74; sec. Home Aide Service of Eastern N.Y., Inc., 1972-74, Mohawk Hudson Community Found., 1971-74, WMHT (Channel 17 Ednl. TV), 1974, 79-83; trustee Hoosac Sch., 1972-79; chmn. bd. Congl. Inst. on Future, 1979-90; bd. dirs. Millay Colony for Arts, 1979-83, Legal Aid Soc. Northeastern N.Y., Howard & Bush Found., from 1987, TRIP, Inc., 1981-88; chmn. N.Y. State Office Bus. Permits, from 1982. Served to 1st lt. F.A. AUS, 1954-56. Mem. N.Y. State Bar Assn. (Elihu Root-Henry L. Stimson award 1990), Rensselaer County Bar Assn. (exec. com. 1964-67, pres. 1974), Assn. Bar City N.Y. (asso.). Home: West Sand Lake N.Y. Died Aug. 22, 1990; interred Oakwood Cemetery, Troy, N.Y.

PATTISON, JOHN NORWOOD, engineering educator; b. Cedar Rapids, Iowa, June 1, 1919; s. Warren Berry and Laura Margaret House P.; m. Shirley Vivian Abendroth, Dec. 31, 1963; children: George Edgar, Kay Louise Meister, Carol Ann Stegmiller. BS in Chemistry, W.Va. U., 1941; postgrad., U. Pitts., 1943-44; PhD, Purdue U., 1948. Chemist Am. Viscose Corp., Roanoke, Va., 1941, Mellon Inst. Indsl. Rsch., 1942; sr. rsch. chemist Koppers United Co., Kobuta, Pa., 1942-46; asst. chief chem. rsch. div. Battelle Meml. Inst., Columbus, Ohio, 1948-56; head catalyst rsch. div. Cities Svc. R&D Co., Lake Charles, La., 1956-57; mgr. R&D Girdler Catalysts, Chemetron Corp., Louisville, Newport, Tenn., 1957-61; v.p., dir. Scott Rsch. Labs., Inc., San Bernardino, Calif., 1961-64; cons.in air pollution control Pasadena, Calif., 1964-66; prof. environ. engring. U. Cin., 1967-91; chmn., pres. Environ. Rsch. Inc., Cin., 1972-74; Fulbright lectr. U. Valle, Cali, Colombia, 1974; chmn. panel testing, inspection maintenance, commn. on motor vehicle emissions NAS, 1971-73. Contbr. articles to tech. jours., chpt. to book. Pres., Sharon Heights Civic Assn., 1952-53; bd. dirs. Air Pollution Control League Greater Cin., 1978-91. With AUS, 1944-46. Mem. Air Pollution Assn. chmn. Columbus sect. 1956 , Internat. Standards Orgn. vice chmn. subcom., intersoc. com. methods air sampling and analysis 1968-91 , Soc. Automotive Engrs., Sigma Xi, Sigma Pi Sigma, Kappa Alpha. Home: Cincinnati Ohio Died Mar. 20, 1991.

PATTON, GEORGE ERWIN, landscape architect; b. Franklin, N.C., Mar. 18, 1920; s. Robert Andrew and Mamie Dickey (Slagle) P.; m. Sydney Ott Belleville, Mar. 29, 1958 (dec. 1990). B.S. in Landscape Architecture, N.C. State U., 1948. Landscape architect Simonds and Simonds (Landscape Architects), Pitts., 1948-49, 51-54; prin. George E. Patton, Inc. (Landscape Architecture and Planning), Phila., 1954-91; lectr. dept. landscape architecture Sch. Fine Arts, U. Pa., 1955-65; Mem. Phila. Art Commn., 1960-68; advisor Eastern Regional Office HUD, 1964-70. Prin. works include numerous parks, coll. campuses, other institutional and indsl. projects.including site planning and landscaping Kimball Art Mus., Ft. Worth, Phila. Mus. Art; designer Locust Walk for Quadrangle on U. Pa.; participant restoration projects for Independence and Rittenhouse Sqs., Phila.; mem. publ. bd. , contbr. Landscape Architecture, 1975-80, chmn., 1978-80; contbr. articles to Archtl. Record, Garden Design. With USMCR, 1943-46. Rome prize fellow Am. Acad. in Rome, 1949-51; Fulbright scholar, 1950-51. Fellow Am. Soc. Landscape Architects (trustee, 1st v.p. 1967-69), Pa. Hort. Soc., Am. Assn. Botanic Gardens, and Arboreta, Am. Rhododendron Soc. Clubs: Phila. Cricket, Union League. Home: Philadelphia Pa. Died Mar. 6, 1991; buried Patton Valley, Franklin, N.C.

PATTON, LESLIE K(ARR), psychology and education educator; b. Senatobia, Miss., Sept. 6, 1898; s. James Virgil and Fannie Trueheart (McKay) P.; m. Rachel Mary Cessna, June 7, 1930. BSEE, Ga. Inst. Tech., 1924; AM, Emory U., 1929; PhD, Columbia U., 1040. Instr. math. Ga. Inst. Tech., Atlanta, 1924-27; asst. dean men Emory U., 1928-32; asst. to dir. admissions Columbia U., N.Y.C., 1935-38; dir. pers., prof. psychology Coe Coll., 1943-44; dean coll., prof. edn. and psychology Tusculum Coll., 1939-43, 45-50, acting pres., 1950-51, v.p., 1951-53; dean coll. Cen. Coll., Fayette, Mo., 1953-55; assoc. prof. psychology East Tenn. State Coll., Johnson City, 1955-57, prof., chmn. edn. and psychology, 1957-64, chmn. emeritus, prof. psychology, from 1965. Author: The Purposes of Church-Related Colleges, 1940. Program dir. USO, Army-Navy YMCA, Camp Shelby, Miss., 1944-45; moderator Holston Presbytery, 1948-49. With USN, 1917-19. Mem. APA, AAUP, NEA, East Tenn. Edn. Assn. (chmn. coll. sect. 1947-48), Tenn. Coun. Ind. and Ch.-Related Colls. (sec.-treas. 1947-49), Tenn. Coll. Assn. (exe. com. 1947-48), Tenn. Edn. Assn., Am. Legion, VFW, Rotary, Phi Delta Kappa, Kappa Delta Pi, Sigma Chi. Democrat. *

PATTON, MACON GLASGOW, broadcasting company executive; b. Durham, N.C., Apr. 18, 1936; s. James R. and Bertha E. (Moye) P.; m. Josephine Reid Ward, June 18, 1960; children: Macon G., Josephine Reid. A.B., U. N.C., Chapel Hill, 1958, M.B.A., 1962. With Donaldson, Lufkin & Jenrette, Inc., N.Y.C., 1962-75; ptnr. investment banking div. Donaldson, Lufkin & Jenrette, Inc., 1971-75; chmn., chief exec. officer Cosmos Broadcasting Corp., Greenville, S.C., from 1975; also dir. Liberty Corp.; dir. Spartan Mills, Liberty Life Ins. Co., Cosmos Broadcasting Co., Atlantic Land Co., Liberty Corp., Builder Marts Am., Hatteras Income Securities, Inc., Reedy River Ventures. Trustee Converse Coll., Spartanburg, S.C., Brevard (N.C.) Music Center; bd. dirs. Bus. Found. N.C.; mem. Morehead Bus. Fellowship Com.; vice chmn. advanced gifts U. N.C.-Carolina M.B.A. Campaign. Served with M.C. U.S. Army, 1959-60. Presbyterian. Clubs: University (N.Y.C.); Greenville Country. Home: Greenville S.C. Deceased. †

PAUL, FLOYD W(ALTER), retail chain executive; b. Springville, Iowa, Jan. 20, 1893; s. Walter and Alfin Minnie (Boxwell) P.; m. Helen M. Soboda, Sept. 8, 1917. AB, Coe Coll., Cedar Rapids, Iowa, 1915, LLD, 1948; MA, Rutgers U., 1964. Tchr. pub. schs., Iowa, 1915-18; in retail bus., Cedar Rapids, 1918-25; asst. mgr. McCrory Stores Corp., West Palm Beach, Fla., 1925-27, mgr., 1927-36, dist. mgr., 1933-39, divl. mdse. mgr., 1939-44, v.p., 1944, exec. v.p., 1945, pres., 1946-59; pres., bd. dirs., mem. exec. com. McCrory-McLellan Stores, 1959-61; v.p., bd. dirs. McCrory Corp., 1960. Trustee Coe Coll., 1950. 2d lt. F.A., U.S. Army, 1918. Mem. Church Club, Nat. Arts Club, Masons, Phi Kappa Phi. Democrat. Episcopalian. *

PAULEY, CLAUDE A(RLINGTON), tire and rubber company executive; b. Toledo, Nov. 23, 1898; s. Leander J. and Catherine B. (Riehm) P.; m. Victoria E. Glenn, May 10, 1924 (dec. Sept. 1940); m. Kathryn MacCrae, Feb. 14, 1947. AB, Westeern Res. U., 1921. CPA, Ohio. Acct. Edison Lamp Works. div. GE, Harrison, N.J., 1921-22; ptnr. Wintermute, Pauley & Agler, CPA's, Cleve., 1922-27; auditor Sebring (Ohio) Pottery Co., 1927-31; acct. Firestone Tire & Rubber Co., Akron, Ohio, 1931-43, compt., 1943-62; ret., 1962. Mem. regional exec. com. Boy Scouts Am.; trustee Children's Hosp.; bd. govs. Western Res. U. Mem. AICPA, Fin. Exec. Inst., Am. Legion, Portage Country Club, Masons (32d degree), Phi Beta Kappa, Delta Upsilon. *

PAULSEN, MARTIN RAYMOND, lawyer; b. Friendship, Wis., Aug. 2, 1895; s. Paul and Julia (Jacobsen) P.; m. Mary Hazen, Dec. 18, 1920. Student, U. Dublin, Ireland, 1919; LLB, U. Wis., 1923. Bar: Wis. 1923. Practiced in Racine, Wis., until 1931, Milw., from 1931; mem. Shaw, Muskat & Paulsen, Milw.; bd. dirs., mem. exec. com. Wis. Electric Power Co.; bd. dirs. Wis.-Mich. Power Co., Wis. Natural Gas Co., Milw. Electric Ry. & Transport Co., Milw. Forge & Machine Co., Edward E. Gillen Co. Mem. Greater Milw. Com., 1952-56. With USMC, 1917-19, AEF in France. Mem. ABA, Wis. Bar Assn., Milw. Club, Univ. Club, Milw. Athletic Club, Order of Coif, Phi Kappa Phi. *

PAULSON, MOSES, physician; b. Balt., May 2, 1897; s. David and Deborah (Bogatsky) P.; m. Helen Golden, June 9, 1926. B.S., U. Md., 1917, M.D., 1921. House physician Sinai Hosp., Balt., 1921-22; chief gastroenterology Sinai Hosp., 1946-64, attending physician, from 1964; resident physician St. Agnes Hosp., 1922-23; in charge night accident service Emergency Hosp., Washington, 1923-24; resident Children's Hosp., Washington, 1923-24; gen. practice Balt., 1924-26; full-time research in digestive diseases (gastro-enterology) Johns Hopkins U., 1926-29, part time, from 1929, asst. in medicine, 1927-28, instr., 1928-33, assoc., 1933-46, asst. prof. medicine, 1946-55, assoc. prof., 1955-84, assoc. prof. emeritus, 1984-91; physician Johns Hopkins Hosp., 1930-84, hon. physician, from 1984; cons. gastroenterology Diagnostic Clinic, 1934-55; cons. pvt.-out-patient services Johns Hopkins Hosp., 1946-68, Regional Office VA, 1950; cons. gastroenterology Perry Point (Md.) VA Hosp.; practice internal medicine, specializing in gastroenterology, 1930-84; hon. vis. physician Ch. Home and Infirmary, Mercy, St. Agnes, Sinai hosps., Greater Balt. Med. Center.; Cons. Council on Drugs, A.M.A., 1958-70. Author: Gastroenterlogic Medicine, 1969; Editorial bd.: Am. Jour. Digestive Diseases, 1934-50, Gastroenterology, 1940-55; Contbr. numerous articles to med. publs. Served as hosp. apprentice 1st class USNR, 1917-21. Gastroenterology chair named in honor of Moses and Helen Paulson, Johns Hopkins U., 1983; recipient Premier Physicians award Nat. Found. for Ileitis and Colitis, 1989. Mem. Fellow ACP, Am. Coll. Gastroenterology; mem. AMA, AAAS, Am. Soc. Gastrointestinal Endoscopy, Am. Soc. Microbiology, So. Med. Assn. (citation gastroent. sect. 1983), Am. Gastroent. Assn., Am. Soc. for Rsch. in Psychosomatic Problems, Med. and Chirurg. Faculty Md., Johns Hopkins Club, Masons, Phi Delta Epsilon. Home: Baltimore Md. Died Nov. 24, 1991. †

PAXTON, ALEXANDER G(ALLATIN), cotton merchant; b. Vicksburg, Miss., Oct. 3, 1896; m. Ruth Chapman, 1923; children: Robert Gallatin, Mary Burton Paxton Glasco. Grad., Washington and Lee U., 1917. Owner, operator A.G. Paxton Co., cotton shippers, domestic export, Greenville, Miss.; pres. A.G. Paxton Co., cotton mchts.; mem. N.Y. Cotton Exch., Greenville Cotton Exec. Author: The Vicksburg Campaign—A Story of Perseverance, The Atlanta Campaign, The Retrograde of the Confederacy, The Peninsular Campaign. Mem. adv. commn. Civil War Centennial; pres. Miss. Heart Assn. Maj. gen. U.S. Army, 1940-45, 51, PTO, Korea; lt. gen. Miss. N.G. ret. Decorated Air medal, Legion of Merit, Bronze Star. Mem. Rotary. Methodist. *

PAYNE, CARR, investment banker; b. Morganton, N.C., Dec. 28, 1898; s. Bruce Ryburn and Lula (Carr) P.; m. Mary Evans Tarpley, Oct. 10, 1922; children: Bruce Ryburn II, Maxwell Carr Jr. BA, Vanderbilt U., 1919. With mcpl. dept. Caldwell & Co., Nashville, 1919-30; v.p. Cumberland Securities Corp., Nashville, from 1931. Treas., bd. dirs. Nashville Community Chest, 1942-50; bd. dirs. Nashville Vis. Nurses Assn., from 1930; chmn. bd. stewards United Meth. Ch., 1949-50. Mem. Investment Bankers Assn. Am. (chmn. So. group 1958, nat. bd. govs. 1961-63), Nashville Security Traders Assn. (pres. 1946), Cumberland Club, Belle Meade Country Club, Union League Club (Chgo.), Bankers Club (Cin.), Masons (32d degree), Shriners, Kiwanis (pres. Nashville 1941, lt. gov. 1944), Sigma Nu. *

PAYNE, MELVIN MONROE, scientific and educational society executive; b. Washington, May 23, 1911; s. Julian R. and Jeanette V. (Perry) P.; m. Ethel B. McDonnell, Sept. 1, 1938; children: Melvin Monroe (dec.), Frances, Nancy Jeanette. Student, Nat. U., 1929-30; J.D., Southeastern U., 1939; D.Sc., S.D. Sch. Mines and Tech., 1962, Iowa Wesleyan Coll., 1969; LL.D., U. Miami, 1973. Bar: D.C. bar 1941. With N.Y. Sun, 1927; asst. to sec. Ry. Accounting Officers Assn., 1930-32; with Nat. Geog. Soc., Washington, 1932-87, pres., chief exec. officer, 1967-76, chmn. bd., 1976-87, chmn. emeritus, 1987-90, also trustee, chmn. emeritus com. rsch. and exploration; adv. dir. Washington Mut. Investors Fund. Trustee emeritus Fed. City Council; trustee, v.p. U.S. Capitol Hist. Soc.; trustee White House Hist. Assn., Inst. Nautical Archaeology; mem. internat. adv. council Louis Leakey Meml. Inst. for African Prehistory, program rev. coun. Jane Goodall Inst. Wildlife Research, Edn., and Conservation, adv. bd. Gorilla Found. Recipient Conservation Svc. award U.S. Dept. Interior, 1974, Grosvenor award Nat. Geog. Soc., 1982. Mem. Am. Assn. Geographers, AAAS, Supreme Ct. Hist. Soc. (v.p., trustee, exec. com.). Clubs: Alfalfa, Cosmos (Washington), Burning Tree (Bethesda). Home: Bethesda Md. Died Oct. 6, 1990.

PEACOCK, NEAL DOW, horticulture educator; b. Kokomo, Ind., Jan. 27, 1897; s. Jason L. and Amy (Hobson) P.; m. Tacie Thomas, July 12, 1921; children: Margaret Ellen Peacock Noyes, Joseph Neal. BS, Purdue U., 1010, D Agr. (hon.), 1965; MS, U. Tenn., 1923; PhD, Mich. State U., 1936. Instr., then asst. prof. horticulture Ga. State Coll. Agr., 1919-21; field rep. Tenn. Hort. Soc., 1921-23; assoc. prof., then prof. U. Tenn., Knoxville, 1923-48, head dept., 1923-48, vice chmn. Coll. Agr., 1948-57, dean resident instrn., from 1957. Mem. Sigma Xi, Phi Kappa Phi, Alpha Zeta, Gamma Sigma Delta, Omicron Delta Kappa. Mem. Soc. of Friends. *

PEAKE, KIRBY, consumer products company executive, business consultant; b. Detroit, Feb. 19, 1915; s. Robert Louis and Christina Josephine (DeBolt) P.; m. Jessie Charlotte Barnecott, Nov. 18, 1939 (div.); children—Nancy Peake Aupperle, Jonathan, Robert, Sarah; m. Hanna Mayer Johnson, Nov. 26, 1976. A.B., Colgate U., 1937. Reporter Binghamton (N.Y.) Press, 1935-38; with Vick Chem. Co. div. Richardson-Merrell, Inc., 1938-59, pres., 1948-59; adminstrv. v.p. Carter-Wallace, Inc., N.Y.C., 1959-61, pres., chief exec. officer, 1961-72, chmn. bd., chief exec. officer, 1972-74, dir., 1960-75; chmn. bd., dir. Frank W. Horner, Ltd., Montreal, Que., Can., 1962-74; chmn. bd. Millmaster Onyx Corp., 1963-69. Chmn. N.Y. State Commn. for Catskills, 1972-75; Bd. dirs. Proprietary Assn., until 1971, Am. Found. for Pharm. Edn., 1965-72, Vis. Nurse Service N.Y., 1969-74; trustee Colgate U., 1962-72; chmn. Maroon Council, Colgate U., 1975-85. Mem. N.Y. Yacht Club, Indian Creek Yacht and Country Club (Kilmarnock, Va.), Phi Beta Kappa. Republican. Presbyterian. Home: Irvington Va. Died July 9, 1991; cremated.

PEARCE, JAMES WISHART, lawyer; b. Cin., Apr. 10, 1916; s. Charles Tabb and Jean (Wishart) P.; m. Helen deKay Thompson, Sept. 26, 1942; children: James W., Paula Carroll, Jeanne Tabb; m. Emma Chambers Wuerdeman, Apr. 13, 1985; m. Ruth E. Pearce. BS, MIT, 1937; LLB, U. Va., 1941. Bar: Ohio 1942. Atty. Atlantic Refining Co., 1941-42; assoc. Wood, Arey, Herron and Evans, 1945-47, Zugelter and Zugelter, Cin., 1947-59; ptnr. Pearce and Schaeperklaus, Cin., 1959-81, of counsel, 1982-89; ret., 1989. Hon. bd. dirs. YMCA of Cin. and Hamilton County. Served with USNR, 1942-45. Mem. Cin. Patent Law Assn. (pres. 1969-70), Cin. Bar Assn. Episcopalian. Home: Cincinnati Ohio Died Jan. 18, 1992. †

PEARLMAN, HENRY BERNARD, otolaryngology educator; b. Russia, July 15, 1901; came to U.S., 1905, naturalized, 1923; s. Hessel and Sarah Dolgin P.; m. Dorothy Zimmerman, Aug. 9, 1931; children: Daniel, Robert. BA, U. Wis., 1923; MD, Rush Med. Sch., Chgo., 1926. Diplomate Am. Bd. Otolaryngology. Intern L.A. Gen. Hosp., 1925-26, St. Mary's Hosp., Madison, Wis., 1926; pvt. practice Belville, Wis., 1926-30; sr. intern otolaryngology U. Chgo. Med. Sch., 1931-32, mem. faculty, 1932-91, prof. otolaryngology, 1952-91. Mem. AMA, Ill. Med. Soc., Chgo. Med. Soc., Am. Otol. Assn., Am. Laryngol., Rhinol. and Otol. Soc.,

Chgo. Laryngol. and Otol. Soc., Soc. Univ. Laryngologists, Sigma Xi. Home: Chicago Ill. Died 1991.

PEARSON, DONALD STUART, mathematics, engineering educator; b. Cleve., Feb. 19, 1905; s. David Browne and Dorothy Mathilda (Oehlhoff) P.; m. Doris Marion White, Apr. 1, 1985. B.S., Case Western Res. U., 1929, M.S., 1933; Ph.D., St. Andrews U., 1958, LL.D., 1968; Ed.D. (hon.), Phila. Coll., 1973. Registered profl. engr., surveyor, Ariz., Ohio, Pa. chartered engr., London. Prof., chmn. elec. engring. dept. Ohio No. U., 1938-43; design engr. Westinghouse Electric Corp., 1944-45; mem. grad. faculty Mich. State U., 1945-49; mem. grad. faculty Pa. State U., 1949-65, research supr., 1957, emeritus prof., 1965-89; prof. math. Lorain County Community Coll., 1965-76, chmn. dept. math., 1971; voluntary prof. Ariz. State U., 1980-85; alumni ednl. adviser Case Western Res. U., from 1972; adviser Engring. Coll. Mag. Associated, 1964; examiner Ohio State Bd. Profl. Engrs., 1939-53; founder OHIO-MATYC, U. Cin., 1972; research project supr. Boeing, 1957. Author: Creative Image, 1959, Creativeness for Engineers, 4th edit, 1961, Basic Energy Converters, 1962, Reflections, 1981, Meaning of Time, 1982, Living Today, 1983, The Great Spirit, 1987, Ethics, 1988; contbr. articles profl. jours.; regional editor: MATYC jour., 1970-75. Mem. Environ. Protection Bd., Olmsted Falls, Ohio, 1972-75; charter mem. Engrs. Found. Ohio, Columbus, 1970. Recipient Army-Navy E award, 1944, Lee Gold medal research award, 1958, cert. Nat. Council Engring. Examiners, 1970, Community Leader of Am. award, 1972, Outstanding Educator of Am. award, 1973, citation 88th Congress Invention and Patent System, Library of Congress, 1964, LCCC cert. of recognition, 1975; fellow Ohio No. U., 1957; fellow St. Andrews Res., 1958. Fellow Instn. Elec. Engrs. (London) (life), Royal Soc. Arts (London), Intercontinental Biog. Soc., Am. Soc. Engring. Edn. (life; br. chmn. 1949), Worldwide Acad. of Scholars (life); mem. IEEE (life sr. mem., br. counselor, chmn. Central Pa. sect. 1953), AAUP (emeritus mem.), Ohio Ret. Tchrs. Assn. (life), Math. Assn. Am., Planetary Soc., Newcomen Soc., Franklin Inst., Ohio Soc. Profl. Engrs., AAAS, Amateur Yacht Research Soc. (London), Lloyds Register Am. Yachts, Sun City Engrs., Tau Beta Pi (eminent mem.; founder, pres. Sun City alumnus chpt. 1981-83), Eta Kappa Nu (life, benefactor), Phi Delta Kappa, Pi Mu Epsilon (hon.), Theta Chi, Ariz. State Poetry Soc. Clubs: Masons, Shriners, Kiwanis (dir. 1940), Bay View Boat (life mem.), Sun City Scots, Amateur Radio, University, Statesman's. Home: Winter Park Fla. Died Feb. 10, 1989; buried Aurora Cemetery, Aurora, Ohio.

PEARSON, JIM BERRY, historian, educator; b. Gilmer, Tex., Jan. 3, 1924; s. John Henry and Vera Louisa (Berry) P.; m. June Louise Young (dec.); children—Jim Berry, Terry Lee; m. Mary Frances Shields, June 1972. B.A., North Tex. State U., Denton, 1947, M.A., 1949; Ph.D., U. Tex., 1955. Asst. prof., then prof. Midwestern U., Wichita Falls, Tex., 1949-55; assoc. prof. Arlington (Tex.) State U., 1955-58; asst. prof., then assoc. prof. U. Tex., Austin, 1968-71, asst. dean, 1961-66, asst. v.p. acad. affairs, 1970-71; assoc. v.p. acad. affairs, prof. history and edn. North Tex. State U., Denton, 1971-73; dean Coll. Arts and Scis., 1973-81, prof. history, 1973-90; project dir. Council of Chief State Sch. Officers, Washington, 1966-68; cons. in field; tchr. Tex. Consortium's Malaysia Program, 1986-87;. Author: The Maxwell Land Grant, 1961 (Theta Sigma Phi award); co-author: Texas: The Land and Its People, 3d edit, 1986; The Red River & Twining Area: A New Mexico Mining Story, 1986; Co-editor: Education in the States: Historical Developments and Outlook, 1969, Education in the States: National Development Since 1900, 1969; Book rev. editor: Southwestern Hist. Quar, 1969-72; adv. editor: Tex. Council Jour, 1968-78. Mem. Austin Com. Human Relations.; Active local YMCA, United Neighbors. Served with AUS, 1943-46, CBI. Recipient Outstanding Tchr. award U. Tex. Student Assembly, 1964; Disting.Svc. award Council Chief State Sch. Officers, 1968, Outstanding Svc. awad. U. North Tex., 1989, Disting. Alumnus award (posthumous), U. North Tex., 1991. Mem. Orgn. Am. Historians, Southwestern Social Sci. Assn., Western Hist. Assn., Tex. Hist. Assn. (chmn. com. teaching 1969-72, 2d v.p., 1986-87, 89-90, pres.-elect 1990), Toastmasters, Alpha Phi Omega. Home: Denton Tex. Died June 18, 1990.

PEARSON, OLOF HJALMER, physician; b. Boston, Feb. 7, 1913; s. Nils August and Esther (Peterson) P.; m. Barbara Farr, Dec. 30, 1942; children—Jane, Alan. John, Thomas. A.B. magna cum laude, Harvard, 1934, M.D. cum laude, 1939. Asst. physiology Harvard U., 1935-37, instr., 1945-48; faculty Cornell U. Med. Coll., 1949-60, asso. prof. medicine, 1952-60; asso. mem. Sloan Kettering Inst., N.Y.C., 1948-60; prof. medicine Case Western Res. U. Sch. Medicine, Cleve., 1968-73; Am. Cancer Soc. prof. oncology Western Res. U. Sch. Medicine, Cleve., 1973-83, prof. emeritus, 1983-90, head sect. endocrinology dept. medicine, 1963-70; dir. clin. labs. U. Hosps. Cleve., 1960-63, asso. attending physician, 1960-67, attending physician, from 1967. Author: (with C.C. Thomas) Hypophysectomy, 1957; also numerous articles.; Editor: (with C.C. Thomas) Dynamic Studies of Metabolic Bone Disease, 1964. Recipient Sloan award for cancer research Sloan Kettering Inst., 1955. Fellow A.C.P.; mem. Assn. Am. Physicians, Am. Assn. for Cancer Research, Am. Fedn. for Clin. Research, Am. Soc. for Clin. Investigation, Am. Soc. Biol. Chemists, Harvey Soc., Central Soc. for Clin. Research. Home: Scarborough Maine Died May 25, 1990; buried Scarborough, Maine.

PEARSON, WALLACE M., osteopathic medicine educator; b. Eaton County, Mich., July 12, 1895; s. Miles and Rebecca (Reed) P.; m. Ethel Newman, Sept. 25, 1921 (dec.); children: Wallace G., Jackie Pearson Lewis; m. Dorothy S. Lewis, Dec. 29, 1952; 1 stepchild Jackie Weyman. AB, Albion Coll., 1917; DO, Kirksville Coll. Osteopathy, 1929. Chemist, bacteriologist City of Flint, Mich., 1919-20; instr. chemistry Albion Coll., 1920-21; cashier, v.p. Comml. State Bank, Fowlerville, Mich., 1921-25; prof. chemistry Kirksville (Mo.) Coll. Osteopathy and Surgery, 1925-29, prof. osteo. prins. and practice, from 1947; chief staff Kirksville Osteo. Hosp., from 1956; prin. investigator teaching grant in phys. medicine and rehab. HEW. Translator book on Strasser Pigeons. Mem. Kirksville Charter Commn.; mem. Mo. Ho. of Reps., 1947-56; bd. dirs. Adair County United Fund. With U.S. Army, 1917-19. Mem. Am. Osteo. Assn. (pres. 1963-64), Mo. Rabbit Breeders Assn. (past pres.), Nat. Strasser Pigeon Club, Masons, KT, Shriners, Kiwanis, Delta Tau Delta, Psi Sigma Alpha. *

PEASE, HOWARD, author; b. Stockton, Calif., Sept. 6, 1894; s. Isaac Newton and Stella (Cooley) P.; m. Pauline Nott, Nov. 4, 1927 (dec.); 1 child, Philip Howard; m. Rossie Ferrier, Sept. 1956. AB, Stanford U., 1923. Tchr. pub. and pvt. schs., Calif., 1924-25, 28-34; instr. English, Vassar Coll., Poughkeepsie, N.Y., 1926-27. Author numerous books, including The Jinx Ship, 1927 (also fgn. edits. in English, Danish, French, Czechoslovakian, Dutch, Belgian, Italian), The Black Tanger, 1941, Night Boat, 1942, Thunderbolt House, 1944 (silver medal Commonwealth Club Calif.), Heart of Dancer, 1946 (award Child Study Assn., medal Boy's Clubs Am.), Bound for Singapore, 1948, The Dark Adventure, 1950, Captain of the Araby, 1953, Shipwrectk, 1957, Mystery on Telegraph Hill, 1961; contbr. to ednl. mags. and books. Sgt. U.S. Army, 1918-19, AEF. Mem. PEN. Democrat. *

PECCORINI, FRANCISCO LETONA, philosopher, educator; b. San Miguel, El Salvador, Nov. 27, 1915; came to U.S., 1962, naturalized, 1976; s. Miguel Vinerta and Julia (Letona) P.; m. Teresa Samayoa; 1 stepdau., Teresa Moran Enneman. Ph. Licentiate, Colegio de San Francisco Javier, Burgos, Spain, 1943; Ph.D., Pontifical U. Comillas, Santender, Spain, 1958. Tchr. San Jose High Sch., San Salvador, 1943-47; writer Estudios Centro Americanos, San Salvador, 1947-52, editor mag., 1952-55; prof. philosophy U. Deusto, Bilbao, Spain, 1956-58, Nat. U., San Salvador, 1959-62; asst. prof. U. San Diego, 1963-66; mem. faculty Calif. State U., Long Beach, 1966-86, prof. philosophy, 1972-86, prof. emeritus, 1986. Author: A Method of Self-Orientation to Thinking, 1970, La Voluntad del Pueblo en la Emancipación de El Salvador, 1972, From Gentile's "Actualism" to Sciacca's "Idea," 1981, On to the World of Freedom. A Kantian Meditation on Finite Selfhood, 1982, Selfhood as Thinking Thought in The Work of Gabriel Marcel, 1987; also articles. Mem. Nat. Acad. Historia of San Salvador, Acad. Lang. El Salvador, Medieval Acad. Am., Medieval Assn. Pacific, Am. Philos. Assn., Inst. for Ency. of Ultimate Reality and Meaning (Toronto). Home: Long Beach Calif. Died Mar. 15, 1989; buried San Salvador, El Salvador.

PECHILLO, JEROME ARTHUR, bishop; b. Bklyn., May 16, 1919; s. Arthur Salvatore and Catherine Murphy. B.A.-Philosophy. Ed. Cath. U., Washington, 1947. Ordained priest S.T.B. Roman Catholic Ch., 1947; ordained titular bishop of Novasparsa and prelate of Coronel Oviedo, Paraguay, 1966-90; aux. bishop of Newark, 1976-90; held several positions Franciscan Prep. Sem., Hollidaysburg, Pa. until 1961; apptd. Vatican rep. to Missionaries in Paraguay, 1961; treas. N.E. Cath. Pastoral Ctr. Hispanics for Nat. Coun. Cath. Bishops; mem. Latin Am. com. Nat. Conf. Cath. Bishops. Died Jan. 1, 1991. Home: Jersey City N.J.

PECHMAN, JOSEPH AARON, economist; b. N.Y.C., Apr. 2, 1918; s. Gershon and Lena (Pechman) P.; m. Sylvia Massow, Sept. 29, 1943; children: Ellen Massow, Jane Elizabeth. B.S., CCNY, 1937; M.A., U. Wis., 1938, Ph.D., 1942, LL.D. (hon.), 1978. Statistician Nat. Research Project, Phila., 1937; research asst. econs. U. Wis., 1937-38, research assoc., 1939-41; asst. dir. Wis. income tax study Wis. Tax. Commn., 1938-39; economist OPA, 1941-42; tax adv. staff Treasury Dept., 1946-53; assoc. prof. finance Sch. Indsl. Mgmt., MIT, 1953-54; economist Council Econ. Advisers, 1954-56, Com. Econ. Devel., 1956-60; exec. dir. studies govt. finance Brookings Instn., 1960-69, sr. fellow, 1960-88, sr. fellow emeritus, 1988-89, dir. econ. studies, 1962-83; Arnold Bernhard vis. prof. Williams Coll., 1988; Irving Fisher research prof. Yale, 1965-66; cons. Council Econ. Advisers, Treasury Dept., 1961-68; fellow Center for Advanced Study in Behavioral Scis., 1975-76. Author: Federal Tax Policy, 5th edit., 1987, (with Henry Aaron and Michael Tausig) Social Security: Perspectives for Reform, 1968, (with Benjamin Okner) Who Bears the Tax Burden?, 1974, (with George Break) Federal Tax Reform: The Impossible Dream?, 1975, Who Paid the Taxes, 1966-85, 1985, Tax Reform, The Rich and the Poor, 2d edit., 1989; author, editor: The Role Economist in Government, An International Perspective, 1989; contbr. numerous articles, reports in field. Served with AUS, 1942-45. Fellow Am. Econ. Assn. (bd. editors 1960-63, exec. com. 1972-74, v.p. 1978, pres. 1989, Disting. Fellow 1985); mem. Am. Acad. Arts and Scis., Phi Beta Kappa. Home: Bethesda Md. Died Aug. 19, 1989; buried Bethesda, Md.

PECK, DAVID WARNER, state justice, lawyer; b. Crawfordsville, Ind., Dec. 3, 1902; s. Dumont M. and Juliet (Warner) P.; m. Elizabeth Saville, Jan. 30, 1929; children—David W., Morgan Scott. A.B. with disting. honors, Wabash Coll., 1922, LL.D., 1954; LL.B., Harvard, 1925; D.J.S., Suffolk U., 1952; LL.D., Union Coll., Albany, N.Y., 1953. Asst. U.S. atty. N.Y., 1925-28; partner firm Sullivan & Cromwell, N.Y.C., 1934-43, 58-77; of counsel Sullivan & Cromwell, 1978-80; justice Supreme Ct. N.Y., 1943-45; assoc. justice appellate div. Supreme Ct., 1st dep., 1945-47, presiding justice, 1947-57; mem. Permanent Internat. Ct. Arbitration, 1957-63. Author: (TV drama) The Greer Case, 1955, Decision at Law, 1961. Mem. task force on legal services and procedure 2d Hoover Commn.; chmn. N.Y. State Commn. on Revision and Simplification of Constn., 1959-61; adv. trustee Vincent Astor Found.; hon. trustee Wabash Coll.; trustee Greenwich Svs. Bank, Vincent Astor Fund, NYU Law Ctr. Found. Mem. ABA, N.Y. Bar Assn. (pres. 1962), Assn. Bar City N.Y., Am. Arbitration Assn. (chmn. bd. dirs. 1965-69), Chevaliers du Tastevin, Ind. Acad., Met. Opera Assn., N.Y. County Lawyers Assn. Clubs: Quaker Hill Country (Pawling, N.Y.); Century Assn. (N.Y.C.); Muirfield (Scotland). Died Aug. 23, 1990; buried Quaker Hill Cemetery, Pawling, N.Y.

PECK, FREDERIC C(ARLETON), retail chain executive; b. N.Y.C., June 28, 1894; s. George Farmer and Emma Jane (Pratt) P.; m. Edna Coldwell Hartley, Sept. 25, 1920; children: Anne Peck Cumpston, Jane Peck Haisell, Judith Peck Erdman. Student, Yale U., 1915-18. Treas., v.p., bd. dirs. Peck & Peck, Inc., N.Y.C., 1927-55, pres., from 1955; bd. dirs. 1722 Chestnut Street Corp., 7734 Forsyth Boulevard Corp., Raymond Fulton Corp., 48th Street-Park Avenue Corp. Mem. Aviation Commandery Naval Order U.S., Berzelius Club (Yale), Racquet and Tennis Club, Yale Club, Round Hill Club. *

PEDERSEN, CHARLES J., chemist, researcher; b. Fusan, Republic of Korea, Oct. 3, 1904; came to U.S., 1922; naturalized, 1953; widowed; 2 children. MS, MIT, 1927. Research chemist E.I. du Pont de Nemours and Co., Wilmington, Del., 1927-69. Recipient Nobel Prize in Chemistry, 1987. Home: Salem N.J. Died Oct. 26, 1989; buried Salem, N.J.

PEEK, MILTON LEROY, publisher; b. Arkansas City, Kans., Aug. 1, 1897; s. Frank M. and Ada Bell (McComas) P.; m. Marion Lee Green, Oct. 23, 1930; children: Janet Lee Peek Clancy II, Nancy Pilat Peek Heck. Student, Kans., 1915-21. With Leavenworth (Kans.) Times, 1918-19; city editor Madison (Wis.) Capital Times, 1919-20; with Capper Publs., 1921-28, successively advt. solicitor in Topeka, farm paper rep. in Kansas City, Chgo., N.Y.C., ea. mgr. Household mag.; with Curtis Pub. Co., from 1928, successively advt. solicitor, publ. mgr. Ladies Home Jour., publ. mgr., sales mgr. Country Gentleman, 1928-54, v.p., advt. dir. Better Farming, from 1954; Pacific Coast mgr. Sat. Eve. Post, Curtis Pub. Co., v.p., mgr. Detroit office, from 1960. Mem. Pa. Fish Commn. 2d lt. F.A., U.S. Army, World War I. Mem. Masons. *

PEELER, JOSEPH DAVID, lawyer; b. Nashville, Sept. 29, 1895; s. Joseph David and Virginia (McCue) P.; m. Elizabeth F. Boggess, Apr. 27, 1927; children: Stuart Thorne, Joyce Woodson. AB, U. Ala., 1915; LLB cum laude, Harvard U., 1920. Bar: Ky. 1920, Calif. 1929. Practiced in Louisville, 1920-29, L.A., from 1929; mem. Musick, Peeler & Garrett, L.A.; bd. dirs. Cypres Mines Corp., Basic Vegetable Products. Mem. U.S. teams Internat. Tuna Tournament, 1939, 47, 48, 55; bd. fellows Claremont Coll. Capt. USAC, World War I; lt. col. USAAF, World War II. Mem. ABA, Calif. Bar Assn., L.A. Bar Assn., Calif. Club, Bolsa Chica Gun Club, Tuna Club (past pres.), L.A. Club, Wilshire Country Club, Thunderbird Country Club, Connetquot River Club, Phi Beta Kappa, Delta Kappa Epsilon. Republican. Congregationalist. Died Oct. 15, 1991.*

PEELING, JAMES HEDLEY, history and sociology educator; b. Windsor Twp., Pa., Mar. 6, 1896; s. John and Malinda (Stein) P.; m. Florence Marks, June 17, 1926 (dec. 1950); 1 child, Marjorie Helene Peeling Johnson; m. Ruth S. Thies, Aug. 3, 1951. AB, Gettysburg Coll., 1920, AM, 1923; PhD, U. Chgo., 1929. Tchr. Nazareth Hall Mil. Acad., 1920-21, Storm King Sch. for Boys, Cornwall, N.Y., 1921-24, U. Chgo. High Sch., 1927-28; chmn. dept. social sci. Indpls. Tchrs. Coll., 1928-30; assoc. prof. history and sociology Butler U., Indpls., 1930-37, acting head dept. sociology, 1937-46, prof., head dept., from 1946; spl. lectr. Marion County Gen. Hosp. Nursing Sch., 1937-60; lectr. Meth. Hosp. Nursing Sch., 1945-50. Contbr. to Dictionary of American Biography and articles to profl. jours. Active

Indpls. Redevel. Commn., 1951-62; cons., adviser to civic, religious and welfare agys., Indpls.; bd. dirs. Indpls. Family Svc. Assn.; mem. adv. coun. Indpls. Met. YMCA; mem. rsch. com. Indpls. Health and Welfare Coun., 1948-52. Sgt. U.S. Army, 1917-18. Fellow Am. Sociol. Assn.; mem. AAUP, Nat. Coun. Family Rels., Ind. Coun. Family Rels. (past pres.), Ind. Acad. Social Scis. (past officer, bd. dirs.), Torch Club (past pres. Indpls.), Phi Beta Kappa, Phi Kappa Phi, Kappa Delta Rho. *

PEERY, THOMAS MARTIN, pathologist, educator; b. Lynchburg, Va., Aug. 24, 1909; s. John Carnahan and Alean Emma (Martin) P.; m. Eleanor Bishop, Oct. 9, 1936; children: Eleanor Peery Russell, Sue Peery Moore, Linda Peery Markin. B.A., Newberry Coll., 1928, D.M.S. (hon.), 1966; M.D., Med. Coll. of S.C., 1932. Diplomate: Nat. Bd. Med. Examiners, Am. Bd. Pathology. Intern Met. Hosp., N.Y.C., 1932-33, resident physician, 1933-34; asst. pathologist Roper Hosp., Charleston, S.C., 1934-38; faculty pathology George Washington U., from 1938, prof., 1950-74, chmn. dept., 1954-74, prof. emeritus, 1974-92, dir. postgrad. instrn., 1945-56; chief dept. pathology U. Hosp., 1947-74; pathologist Alexandria Hosp., 1941-47; dir. Technicon Corp., Tarrytown, N.Y., 1963-80, cons., 1980-83. Sr. author: Pathology, 2d edit., 1971, Design for Med. Education, 1965; Editorial bd.: Med. Annals of D.C., 1945-70, Pathologist, 1977-83; Contbr. articles to profl. jours.; Pathology cons.: Random House Dictionary of English Language, from 1964. Mem. Bd. Health Alexandria, Va., 1944-46. Mem. Am. Assn. Pathologists, Coll. Am. Pathologists (chmn. com. internat. exchange pathologists 1958-60, advisor to com. on anatomic pathology 1976-80), AMA (chmn. sect. pathology and physiology 1959, exec. com. 1958-63, chmn. exhibit lab. 1961-64), Am. Soc. Clin. Pathologists (exec. com. 1955-58, bd. schs. med. tech. 1958-61, pres. 1968-69, award for outstanding investigation 1958, award for exhibit lab. 1964, Ward-Burdick award for meritorious contbns. to clin. pathology 1974, mem. archives com. 1976-82, mem. Pan Am. com. 1977-85), Internat. Acad. Pathology, Am. Heart Assn., Soc. Exptl. Biology and Medicine, AAAS, Wash. Acad. Medicine, Washington Soc. Pathologists (pres. 1940-41), Sigma Xi, Alpha Omega Alpha. Clubs: Cosmos, Belle Haven Country. Home: Alexandria Va. Died May 7, 1992.

PEGLER, (JAMES) WESTBROOK, newspaperman; b. Mpls., Aug. 2, 1894; s. Arthur James and Frances (Nicholson) P.; m. Julia Harpman, Aug. 28, 1922 (dec. 1955); m. Pearl Pegler, 1959 (div. 1961); m. Maud Toward, 1961. Ed., parochial sch., Chgo.; LLD, Knox Coll., 1943. Corr. European staff UP, 1916-18, corr. with AEF, 1917-18; sports editor United News, N.Y.C., 1919-25; Ea. sports corr. Chgo. Tribune, 1925-33; with N.Y. World-Telegram, Chgo. Daily News, other newspapers,, 1933-44; columnist King Features Syndicate, from 1944. Author: '/Tain't Right, 1936, Dissenting Opinions of Mister Westbrook Pegler, 1938, George Spelvin, American, 1942. With USN, 1918-19. Recipient Pulizter prize for reporting, 1941, gold medal Nassau County Bar Assn., 1944, award Am. Legion, 2 awards for achievement in journalism Nat. Headliners Club. Mem. Chgo. Press Vets., Silurians, Jonathan Club (L.A.), Nat. Press Club (Washington), Tucson Country Club, Old Pueblo Club (Tucson), Dutch Treat. *

PELL, WILLIAM HICKS, mathematician; b. Lewisport, Ky., Oct. 15, 1914; s. William Clay and Florence Beulah (Hicks) P.; m. Dorothy Small, Aug. 23, 1939. B.S., U. Ky., 1936, M.S., 1938; Ph.D., U. Wis., 1943. Grad. asst. math. U. Ky., 1936-38, U. Wis., 1938-42; instr. Math. Brown U., 1943; research aerodynamicist Bell Aircraft Corp., 1943-47; research assoc. div. applied math. Brown U., 1947-48, asst. prof., then asso. prof., 1948-56; prof., head math. dept. U. Ky., 1952-53; mathematician Nat. Bur. Standards, Washington, 1956-58, acting chief, then chief math. physics sect., 1958-65; program dir. applied math. and statistics NSF, 1965-67, head math. scis. sect., 1967-80, spl. projects program, from 1980, Cons., 1981-83; vis. prof. U. Md., from 1983. Assoc. editor: Jour. Research, sect. B, Nat. Bur. Standards, 1961-65, Soc. Indsl. and Applied Math. Jour. Applied Math, 1962-68. Postdoctoral fellow Sch. Applied Math., Brown U., 1942-43; postdoctoral fellow Inst. Fluid Dynamics and Applied Math., U. Md., 1955-56. Fellow AAAS (sect. com. math.); mem. Am. Math. Soc., ASME, Soc. Indsl. and Applied Math., Math. Assn. Am., Am. Acad. Mechanics, Soc. Natural Philosophy, Phi Beta Kappa, Sigma Xi, Omicron Delta Kappa. Home: Lewisport Ky. Died Mar. 14, 1988; buried Owensboro, Ky.

PELLETIER, WILFRID, symphony conductor; b. Montreal, Que., Can., June 30, 1896; s. Elzear and Zelire Pelletier; m. Rose Bampton, May 24, 1937; children: Camille, Frank. Student, Philipp, Rousseal, Widor; MusD (hon.), U. Montreal, 1936, Laval U., N.Y. Colll. Music. Asst. condr. French and Italian repertoire Met. Opera Assn., N.Y.C., from 1917; condr. Ravinia Opera Co., Chgo., 9 summers, San Francisco Opera Co. 10 yrs., N.Y. Philharm. Children's Concerts, N.Y.C., 1953-56; dir. Conservatory Music and Drama, Montreal, from 1943; condr. orchs. on several radio programs; dir. Met. Opera Auditions of Air, 12 yrs.; dir. Orch. Symphonique dQue.; gen. dir. music teaching, Que. Decorated Legion of Honor (France), comdr. Order St. Michael and St. George (Eng.), Christian den Tiendes Friheds Meds (Denmark). *

PENDERGRASS, EUGENE P., radiology educator; b. Florence, S.C., Oct. 6, 1895; s. Edward J. and E. Ethel (Smith) P.; m. Rebecca Barker, Sept. 9, 1922; children: Henry Pancoast, Jane Barker, Margaret Bradford, Huston. Student, Wofford Coll., 1912-14, DSc (hon.), 1959; student, U. N.C., 1914-16; MD, U. Pa., 1918. Diplomate Am. Bd. Radiology. Intern U. Pa. Hosp., Phila., 1918-19, assoc. dir. dept. radiology, 1922-39, dir., 1939-61, pres. med. staff, 1949-53; asst. prof. Grad. Sch. Medicine, U. Pa., 1928-37, prof. radiology, from 1937—, prof. Sch. Medicine, 1931-61, prof. emeritus, 1961-64, Dr. Matthew J. Wilson prof. rsch. radiology, from 1964, dir. bicentennial observance Sch. Medicine, 1962-65; cons. 2d Army Area; resident cons. Armed Forces Inst. Pathology spl. med. adv. group VA; spl. cons. USPHS, also mem. pneumoconiosis com.; dir. Picker Found., 1959; chmn. vis. com. Brookhaven Nat. Labs., 1959; mem. cancer control chmn., bd. sci. counsellors Nat. Cancer Inst.; mem. Biking Safety Commn., 1946; mem. war commn. on safety Code Am. Standards Assn.; sec.-gen. Inter-Am. Congress Radiology, Washington, 1955; mem. adv. com. SSS; investigator OSRD; mem. com. on radiology NRC; also others. Author: (with Philip J. Hodes and J. Parsons Schaeffer) The Head and Neck in Roentgen Diagnosis, 1956; author: Pneumoconiosis, 1959; assoc. editor: The Cyclopedia of Medicine, 1940; also articles. Lt. M.C., USNRF, 1918-19; lct. comdr. M.C., USNR, 1935-51. Fellow ACP; mem. AMA (gold medal 1929), Am. Coll. Radiology (pres. 1948-49, chnn. bd. chancellors 1944-48), Am. Roentgen Ray Soc. (award 1935, 44), Radiol. Soc. N.Am. (pres. 1954, award 1944, 46), Am. Cancer Soc. (exec. com., dir., pres. 1958-59), Philadelphia County Med. Soc. (pres. 1943-44), Phila. Reontgen Ray Soc. (pres. 1928), Phila. Coll. Physicians, Am. Trudeau Soc., Mexican Soc. Radiology, Franklin Inst., Phila. Art Alliance, Phila. Country Club, Merion Cricket Club. *

PENDLETON, RALPH COOPER, physician, surgeon; b. Salt Lake City, June 14, 1895; s. Andrew Jackson and Elizabeth Ann (Cooper) P.; mm. Frances W. Johnson, Aug. 15, 1922; children: Mary Barbara, Ralph Brian. SB, U. Utah, 1917; MD, U. Pa., 1919. Intern Bklyn. Hosp., 1919-21; pvt. practice, Salt Lake City, from 1921; instr. surg. anatomy, asst. clin. prof. surgery U. Utah, Salt Lake City, from 1923; mem. staff dept. surgery Holy Cross Hosp.; attending surgeon VA Hosp., Salt Lake City; speaker on burns to med. socs., CD groupw, U.S. Army, USN, med. pers. Contbr. articles to sci. jours.; recorded effectiveness of paraffin wax open air spray method to treat burns. Mem. med. com. Nat. Ski Patrol. With U.S. Army, 1917-18, mem. USAR, 1925-30; capt. M.C., USNR, 1931-41. Fellow ACS; mem. AMA, Utah Med. Assn., Salt Lake County Med. Assn., Southwestern Surg. Soc., Salt Lake City Surg. Soc., VFW, Am. Legion, Salt Lake Country Club, Masons, KT, Shriners, Phi Beta Pi, Sigma Chi. *

PEPONIS, JAMES ARTHUR, communications company executive; b. Chgo., Sept. 28, 1934; s. Arthur H. and Ethel A. (Karambis) P.; B.S., Northwestern U., 1956, M.B.A., 1979; m. Catherine Coulolias, Aug. 22, 1959; children—Nancy Ellen, Arthur James. With Linde div. Union Carbide Corp., Chgo., 1956-59, Plaza Cleaners & Dyers, Inc., Chgo., 1959-62; div. mgr. Ill. Bell Telephone Co., Chgo., 1962-83; area mgr. AT&T Communications, 1984-86, div. mgr. Network Field Ops., 1986-87, div. mgr. mktg. support, 1987—. Dist. chmn., exec. bd. Chgo. council Boy Scouts Am., 1965-68; mem., bd. dirs. archdiocesan council Greek Orthodox Archdiocese of N. and S.Am., 1977—; mem. exec. com. United Hellenic Am. Congress, 1979—; gen. chmn. Greek Heritage Week, 1980; bd. dirs. Wilmette Baseball Assn., 1980, Hellenic Mus. and Cultural Ctr., 1988—; mem. alumni bd. J.L. Kellogg Grad. Sch. Bus., Northwestern U., 1981-84, 1986-87, mem. parents council, 1982-84; Archon of Ecumenical Patriarchate of Constantinople of Greek Orthodox Ch., 1982; pres. Annunciation Greek Orthodox Cathedral of Chgo., 1985-86; bd. dirs. Hubbard St. Dance Co., 1986—, v.p., 1987—. Served with inf. U.S. Army, 1958-59, to lt. USNG, 1958-66. Recipient Erickson tDied Oct. 21, 1992.rophy Army N.G. Bur. of U.S., 1961, award of Merit, Boy Scouts Am., 1968; Knight of Holy Sepulcher of Ecumenical Patriarchate of Jerusalem, Greek Orthodox Ch., 1984. Mem. Western Soc. Engrs., Northwestern Mgmt. Club of Chgo. (v.p. 1985-86, pres. 1986—), Northwestern Exec. Masters Alumni Assn. (bd. dirs. 1985-86), Am. Mktg. Assn., League of Greek Orthodox Stewards (nat. chmn. 1986—). Home: Wilmette Ill. †

PEPPER, CLAUDE DENSON, congressman; b. Dudleyville, Ala., Sept. 8, 1900; s. Joseph Wheeler and Lena (Talbot) P.; m. Irene Mildred Webster, Dec. 29, 1936 (dec. 1979). AB, U. Ala., 1921; JD, Harvard U., 1924; LLD, McMaster U., 1941, Toronto U., 1942, U. Ala., 1942, Rollins Coll., 1944; DSc, U. Miami, 1974. Bar: Ala. 1924, Fla. 1925. Instr. law U. Ark., 1924-25; sole practice Perry, Fla.; mem. Fla. Ho. Reps., 1929; sole practice Tallahassee, 1930-37; mem. Fla. Bd. Pub. Welfare, 1931-32, Fla. Bd. Law Examiners, 1933; U.S. senator from Fla., 1936-51; mem. coms. on Fgn. Relations, on mil. affairs, on small bus., on edn. and labor chmn. subcom. on wartime health and edn., 78th congl reorgn. Senate Fgn. Relations Com.; mem. 88th-89th congresses from 3d dist. Fla., 1962, 90th congress from 11th dist. Fla., 1966, 93d congress from 14th dist. Fla., 1972, 98th-100th congresses from 18th dist. Fla., 1982-89; chmn. com. on crime, chmn. Fla. del. Dem. Nat Conv., 1940-44, del., 1948, 52-56, 60-64, 68, 72, 76, 80. Contbr. articles to periodicals. Vice chmn. nat. bd. dirs. Nat. Parkinson Found. Recipient Mary and Albert Lasker Pub. Service award, 1967, Eleanor Roosevelt Humanities award, 1968, Ballington and Maud Booth award Vols. of Am., 1978, Hubert H. Humphrey Statesmanship award Fla. Dem. Party, 1979, Andrus award Nat. Ret. Tchrs. Assn., 1980, Ze'ev Jabotinsky Centennial award, 1980, Man of Yr. award Fla. Gold Coast C. of C., 1981, others. Mem. Internat. Bar Assn., Inter-Am. Bar Assn., ABA, Fla. Bar Assn. (exec. com.), Tallahassee Bar Assn., Miami Beach Bar Assn., Coral Gables Bar Assn., Dade County Bar Assn., Bar City of N.Y., Western C. of C. of the Americas, Fla. State U. Alumni Assn., Fla. State Soc., Am. Legion, Jasons, Fla. Blue Key, Phi Beta Kappa, Omicron Delta Kappa, Phi Alpha Delta (Outstanding Alumnus award U. Fla. chpt. 1975), Sigma Upsilon, Kappa Alpha. Baptist. Clubs: Harvard U. (Washington, Miami, Fla.); Jefferson Island, Army and Navy (Washington); Coral Gables (Fla.) Country; Miami Shores Country, Miami, Jockey, Bankers, Palm Bay (Miami); La Gorce Country (Miami Beach, Fla.); Columbia Country (Chevy Chase, Md.); Burning Tree (Bethesda, Md.). Lodges: Masons, Shriners, Elks, Optimists, Moose, Kiwanis, Woodman of World. Home: Miami Fla. Died May 30, 1989.

PERCY, WALKER, author; b. Birmingham, Ala., May 28, 1916; s. Leroy Pratt and Martha Susan (Phinizy) P.; m. Mary Bernice Townsend, Nov. 7, 1946; children: Mary Pratt, Ann Boyd. B.A., U. N.C., 1937; M.D., Columbia U., 1941. Intern Bellevue Hosp., N.Y.C., 1942; writer, 1943-90. Author: The Moviegoer, 1961 (Nat. Book award 1962), The Last Gentleman, 1966, Love in the Ruins, 1971, (essays) The Message in the Bottle, 1975, Lancelot, 1976, The Second Coming, 1980, Lost in the Cosmos, 1983, The Thanatos Syndrome, 1987; Contbr. philos., critical and med. essays to jours., mags. Recipient award NEH, Dr. Jefferson lectr. Fellow Am. Acad. Arts and Scis.; mem. Nat. Inst. Arts and Letters. Roman Catholic. Home: Covington Ky. Died May 10, 1990.

PEREGRINE, DAVID, ballet dancer; b. Llay, Wales, Sept. 19, 1954; s. George and Joyce (Shefield) Evans. Student, Nesta Toumine Sch., Ottawa, Banff Sch. Fine Arts. Mem. corps de ballet Royal Winnipeg Ballet Sch., 1975-78, soloist, 1978-80, prin. dancer, 1980-89. Dancer with San Francisco Ballet, 1984-86; guest artist Dutch Nat. Ballet, 1982, Boston Ballet, 1986, Scottish Ballet, 1986; appearances in galas in Can., U.S., Eng., Japan, Netherlands; acting debut as Smike in Nicholas Nickelby, Man. Theatre Ctr. Recipient Bronze medal Japan Ballet Competition, 1980, Bronze medal Varna Ballet Competition, 1980; decorated Order of Can.; Royal Winnipeg Ballet scholar, 1972-75. Mem. Can. Actors Equity, Assn. Can. TV and Radio Artists (award 1983). Home: Winnipeg Man., Canada Died June, 1989.

PEREZ SANCHEZ, EZEQUIEL, bishop; b. San Luis Potosi, Mexico, Apr. 9, 1911. Ordained priest Roman Cath. Ch., 1936. Named bishop of San Luis Potosi, 1973—. Home: San Luis Potosi Mex. Died Nov. 13, 1986; buried Cathedral San Luis Potosi, Mex.

PERKINS, ANTHONY, actor; b. N.Y.C., Apr. 4, 1932; s. Osgood and Janet (Rane) P.; m. Berinthia Berenson, 1973; children: Osgood, Elvis. Student, Rollins Coll., 1951-53, Columbia U., 1954. First profl. engagement, Brattleboro, Vt., 1946; TV appearances on Alcoa, U.S. Steel and Armstrong hours; actor: (TV film) Les Miserables; (films) The Actress, 1953, Friendly Persuasion, 1955, The Lonely Man, 1956, Fear Strikes Out, 1956, The Tin Star, 1956, This Bitter Earth, The Sea Wall, 1957, Desire Under the Elms, 1957, The Matchmaker, 1957, Green Mansions, 1958, On The Beach, 1959, Tall Story, 1959, Psycho, 1959, Goodbye Again, 1960, Phaedra, 1961, Five Miles to Midnight, The Trial, Two are Guilty, 1962, The Fool Killer, 1963, The Adorable Idiot, 1964, Is Paris Burning?, 1965, The Champagne Murders, 1966, Pretty Poison, 1967, Catch 22, 1968, Ten Days Wonder, WUSA, 1968, Someone Behind the Door, 1970, The Life and Times of Judge Roy Bean, 1972, Play It As It Lays, 1972, Lovin' Molly, 1974, Murder on the Orient Express, 1974, Mahogany, 1975, The Black Hole, 1979, Double Negative, 1980, Ffolkes, 1980, Twice a Woman, 1981, Psycho II, 1983, Crimes of Passion, 1984, For the Term of His Natural Life, The Thrill of Genius, Shadow of Death, Destroyer, 1988, Edge of Sanity, 1989, Enid's Sleeping, Love at Large; (plays) The Star-Spangled Girl, 1966, Steambath, 1972, Winterkills, 1977, Remember My Name, 1977, The Black Hole, 1978; (Broadway plays) Tea and Sympathy, 1954 (Theatre World award), Look Homeward Angel, 1957, Greenwillow, 1960, Harold, 1962, Equus, 1976-77, Romantic Comedy, 1979-80, (TV miniseries) Napolean and Josephine: A Love Story, 1987; actor, dir.: (film) Psycho III, 1986; actor (TV movie) Psycho IV: The Beginning, 1990; dir.: Lucky Stiff. Home: Los Angeles Calif. †

PERKINS, GILBERT HAROLD, banker; b. N.Y.C., Sept. 14, 1896; s. James E. and Ella (Case) P.; m. Virginia A. Van Houten. With Chem. Bank & Trust Co., N.Y.C., 1913-63, asst. cashier, 1927, v.p., 1933-51, exec. v.p., 1951-56, vice chmn., 1956-63; dir., mem. exec. com. McCrory Corp., N.Y.C., from 1964; mem. adv. com. to bd. Chem. Bank N.Y. Trust Co.; bd. dirs., mem. exec. com. Assoc. Spring Corp., Foster Wheeler Corp., Glen Alden Corp., 1st Nat Bank Jersey City. Mem. Links Club, Montclair Golf Club. *

PERKINS, JAMES ALFRED, university president; b. Phila., Oct. 11, 1911; s. H. Norman and Emily Cramp (Taylor) P.; m. Jean E. Bredin, June 20, 1938; children: Barbara Ann Perkins Tinker, Joan Bredin Perkins Saalfield, John, David, Tracy. AB, Swarthmore Coll., 1934; MA, Princeton U., 1936, PhD, 1937; LLD, various colls. and univs. Instr. polit. sci. Princeton (N.J.) U., 1937-39, asst. dir. Sch. Pub. and Internat. Affairs, 1939-41; dir. pulp and oper div. OPA, Washington, 1941-43; asst. to adminstr. FEA, Washington, 1943-45; v.p. Swarthmore (Pa.) Coll., 1945-50; exec. assoc. Carnegie Corp., 1950-51, v.p., 1951-53; pres. Cornell U., Ithaca, N.Y., from 1963; chmn., bd. dirs. Cornell Aero. Lab. Cornell U., Ithaca, from 1963; trustee RAND Corp., from 1961; gen. gen. adv. com. ACDA; chmn. Presdl. adv. panel Nat. Acad. Fgn. Affairs, from 1962; chmn. Presdl. Gen. Adv. Com. on Fgn. Assistance Programs, from 1965; mem. Presdl. panel cons. on fgn. policy, President's Spl. Com. on Nuclear Proliferation, edn. adv. com. Dept. Def., Com. for Improvement Mgmt. in Govt., Nat. Citizens Commn. for Internat. Cooperation; trustee Ednl. Testing Svc., from 1964, Tchrs. Ins. and Annuity Assn., from 1957, Inst. Def. Analyses, 1958-61. Sec. Carnegie Found. for Advancement Teaching, 1954-55, v.p., 1955-63; trustee Meml. Sloan-Kettering Cancer Ctr., N.Y.C., from 1963; chmn. N.Y. State Regents Adv. Com. on Ednl. Leadership. Mem. Coun. Fgn. Rels. (trustee), Am. Polit. Sci. Assn., Coun. Higher Edn. Am. Republics, Am. Acad. Arts and Scis., Century Club, Coffee House, Cosmos Club (Washington, Phi Beta Kappa (hon.). Mem. Soc. of Friends. *

PERKINS, JAMES ELIAB, physician; b. St. Paul, Minn., July 17, 1905; s. Frederick Eliab and Lulu Maud (Shadie) P.; m. Anna Frances Diehl, June 20, 1934; children: Ann Adele, William Eliab, Melinda Louise. BS, U. Minn., 1927, MD, 1930; MPH, Johns Hopkins U., 1931, D of Pub. Health, 1934. Epidemiologist Minn. State Dept. Health, 1930-33; epidemiologist N.Y. State Dept. Health, 1934, dist. state helath officer, 1935-38, dir. div. communicable diseases, 1938-45, dep. commr., 1946-47; mng. dir. Nat. Tuberculosis Assn., 1948-90; as sr. surgeon, USPHS Res., sent to Italy, 1945; as mem. Med. Nutrition Mission to Italy, 1945; mem. U.S. delegation to World Health Assembly of UN, 1948, 50, 61; mem. Pub. Health Planning Team, Western Germany, 1951; pres. Nat. Citizens Com., WHO, 1956-58, mem. expert com. Tb, 1959, 64; pres. Nat. Health Coun., 1960; vice-chmn. Nat. Commn. on Community Health Svcs., 1962-90; mem. nat. adv. health coun. USPHS, 1963-66. Contbr. articles to profl. jours. Fellow N.Y. Acad. Medicine, Am. Pub. Health Assn.; mem. Internat. Union Against Tb (exec. com.), Am. Epidemiol. Soc., Univ. Club (N.Y.C.), Phi Beta Theta, Nu Sigma Nu, Delta Omega. Home: Bronxville NY Died Mar. 25, 1990.

PERLIS, ALAN J., computer science educator; b. Pitts., Apr. 1, 1922; s. Louis Phillip and Zelda Anne (Gilfond) P.; m. Sydelle Gordon, Oct. 28, 1951; children—Mark Lawrence, Robert Gordon, Andrea Lynn. BS in Chemistry, Carnegie Inst. Tech., 1943; postgrad., Calif. Inst. Tech., 1946-47; MS, MIT, 1950, PhD in Math, 1950; DSc (hon.), Davis and Elkins Coll., 1968, Purdue U., 1973, Waterloo U., 1974, Sacred Heart U., 1979. Asst. prof. math., dir. computer center Purdue U., 1952-56; mem. faculty Carnegie Inst. Tech., 1956-71, prof. math., dir. computer center, 1960-65, head dept. math., 1961-64, head dept. computer sci., 1965-71; Eugene Higgins prof. computer sci. Yale U., 1971-90, chmn. dept., 1976-90; Gordon and Betty Moore vis. prof. engring. Calif. Inst. Tech., 1977; mem. NSF computer com. Nat. Joint Computer Com., 1954-56, Gov. Pa. Council Sci. and Tech., from 1963; com. computers research NIH, 1965-71; mem. computer sci. and engring. research bd. Nat. Acad. Sci., from 1968; mem. Assembly of Engring., NRC, from 1978, bd. trustees Computer Aided Programming, NRC, from 1988; advisor Multi-Machine Computing Lab., Aberdeen Proving Ground, Md. Served to 1st lt. USAAF, 1942-45, ETO. Mem. Nat. Acad. Engring., Assn. Computing Machinery (pres. 1962-64, editor-in-chief jour. Communications 1958-62, A.M. Turning prize 1966), Soc. Indsl. and Applied Math., Am. Math. Soc., Math. Assn., Am. Acad. Arts. and Scis., Conn. Acad. Sci. Engring. Home: Woodbridge Conn. Died Feb. 7, 1990; buried Washington, D.C. area.

PERRIN, RICHARD WILLIAM EDMUND, architect; b. Milw., Mar. 14, 1909; s. Richard and Emily (Tischer) P.; m. Adeline Pucyloski, Oct. 22, 1932. Student, U. Wis., 1927-29, Layton Sch. Art, 1929-31, Beaux Arts Inst. Design, 1934-35. Apprentice architect Richard Philipp, Milw., 1927-34; supr. Hist. Am. Bldgs. Survey Milw., 1934-35; practice architecture with Elliott B. Mason, Milw., 1934-42, Smith, Hinchman & Grylls, Detroit, 1942-43; cartographic engr. U.S. Army Mapping Service, 1943-44; asst. dir. Housing Authority City Milw., 1944-46, exec. dir., 1946-71; exec. dir. Milw. Redevel. Authority, 1961-71; exec. sec. City Plan Commn., also; commr. dept. city devel., 1961-71; historic Am. bldgs. survey adv. bd. Dept. Interior; bd. dirs. Wis. Archtl. Archive. Author numerous articles; also books. Mem. Wis. Com. Historic Sites Preservation, 1968-74, Wis. Historic Preservation Rev. Bd.; chmn. Milw. Landmarks Commn., 1964-71; mem. Wis. Capitol and Exec. Residence Bd., 1966-74; hon. curator history Milw. Pub. Mus. Recipient numerous citations, awards. Fellow AIA (vice chmn. nat. com. historic bldgs. preservation 1961); mem. Nat. Assn. Housing Ofcls. (life), Soc. Archtl. Historians, Wis. Acad. Scis., Arts and Letters (v.p. arts, pres. 1973), Internat. Council Monuments and Sites (U.S. com. 1968-73), Arbeitskreis für Hausforschung (Germany). Home: Milwaukee Wis. Deceased. †

PERRY, HAROLD R., bishop; b. Lake Charles, La., Oct. 9, 1916. Grad., St. Augustine Sem., St. Mary's Sem. Ordained priest Roman Catholic Ch., 1944. Assoc. pastor various parishes, La., Ark., Miss.; rector Divine Word Sem., Bay St. Louis, Miss., 1958-63; apptd. provincial of so. province of Soc. of the Divine Word, 1964; consecrated bishop Roman Cath. Ch., 1965; aux. bishop of New Orleans, 1965-91. Home: New Orleans La. Died July 17, 1991.

PERRY, NORMAN L., plastics company executive; b. N.Y.C., July 2, 1928; s. Joseph and Bella Perlmutter; m. Estelle Siegal, May 31, 1953; children—Gilbert, Stephen. B.Ch.E., Cooper Union, 1949. Tech. sales dir. Argus Chem. Co., 1954-64; tech. sales mgr. Colorite Plastics Co. div. Plastic Spltys. and Techs., Inc., Ridgefield, N.J., 1964-72, v.p., 1972-80, exec. v.p., 1980-88, pres., 1988-90; mem. tech. adv. coun. Polymer Processing Inst. of Stevens Inst. Tech., Hoboken, N.J., 1984-90; lectr. on vinyl compounding Newark Coll. Engring. Author: The Compounding of Polyvinyl Chloride, chpt. 1, Encyclopedia of PVC, 2d edit.; patentee in field. Pres. Wayne Dem. Club, N.J., 1975-77; mem. Passaic County Cem. Mcpl. Com. and Exec. Com., N.J., 1977-90. Mem. Soc. Plastics Engrs. (pres. Palisades chpt. 1972-74), Am. Chem. Soc., ASTM. Home: Wayne N.J. Died Jan. 15, 1990; buried Mt. Nebo Cemetery, Totowa, N.J.

PERRY, PAUL, flavor chemist; b. N.Y.C., May 12, 1926; s. Samuel J. and Gertrude (Fishoff) P.; m. Leatrice Oster, Sept. 12, 1948; children: Gail Madelaine, Lisa Randie. B.S. in Chemistry, L.I. U., 1949; M.S. in Chemistry, Poly. Inst. Bklyn., 1953; B.S. in Chem. Engring., Poly. Inst Bklyn., 1953; Ph.D. in Chemistry, Poly. Inst. Bklyn., 1957; postdoctoral, Pa. State U., 1958. Chemist L. Baron Co. (Yonkers), N.Y., 1949-51; chief flavor chemist Globe Extract Co., Bklyn., 1951-58; v.p. flavors V&E Kohnstamm Co., Bklyn., 1958-65; dir. research and devel. Fries & Fries Co., Cin., 1965-70; dir. flavor dept. Warner-Jenkinson Inc., St. Louis, from 1970; pres. Perry Assocs. Ltd., St. Louis; sr. scientist 7-Up; vis. prof. U. Mo.; cons. Orthodox Union. Contbr. numerous articles to profl. jours.; patentee in field. Served with AUS, 1943-46. Decorated Purple Heart; decorated D.S.C. Mem. Chem. Sources Assn. (pres. 1978), Am. Assn. Cereal Chemists (pres. 1976-77), Inst. Food Technologists (chmn. 1958-59), Flavor Chemists Soc., Am. Chem. Soc., Candy Tehcnologists Assn., Am. Soc. Enologists, Soft Drink Technologists Assn., Flavor and Extract Mfrs. Assn., Essential Oil Assn., Am. Jewish Congress, Jewish Fedn., Christian and Jewish, Anti-Defamation League, NAACP. Lodge: B'nai B'rith. Home: Saint Louis Mo. Died Mar. 26, 1988; buried Ladue, Mo.

PERRY, RUSSELL H., lawyer, consultant; b. Cornell, Ill., Nov. 8, 1908; s. Walter O. and Mabel (Hilton) P.; m. Phoebe Sherwood, June 2, 1956. Student, N.Y. U., 1937; J.D. cum laude, Bklyn. Law Sch., 1940; D.C.L., Atlanta Law Sch., 1973; hon. doctor Civil Law, Dallas Bapt. U. Northwood Inst., 1986. Bar: N.Y. bar 1941, Tex. bar 1963. Clk. Chgo. Fire & Marine Ins. Co., 1925-32; underwriter Republic Ins. Co., N.Y.C., 1934-38; charge Republic Ins. Co. (Eastern dept. underwriting), 1939-42, asst. to v.p., 1942-43; spl. agt. L.I., Westchester, 1943-44; mgr. L.I. (Eastern dept.), 1945-47, resident sec., 1947-49, v.p., 1949-59, exec. v.p., 1959-61; pres., chief exec. officer, dir. Republic Financial Services, Inc., Republic Ins. Co. Group, 1961-71, chmn. bd., pres., chief exec. officer, 1971-72, chmn. bd., chief exec. officer, 1972-84, chmn. bd., 1985-Apr. 87; ptnr. Rubinstein & Perry, Dallas, 1987-88; mem. found. community adv. bd. KERA-TV, Dallas; dir. Taca, Inc., Dallas; alt. bd. dirs. USA Cafes, Inc., Dallas, Ins. Information Inst., Celtic Internat. Ins. Co., Navigators Ins. Co.; adv. dir. Met. Fin. Savs. & Loan Assn.; chmn., chief exec. officer Union Bank & Trust Co. Mem. exec. com. Assn. Tex. Fire-Casualty Cos.; mem. adv. council Airline Passengers Assn.; bd. dirs., past chmn. Tex. Good Rds. Transp. Assn.; mem. Dallas Bapt. Coll. Devel. Bd.; bd. dirs. Tex. Soc. to Prevent Blindness.; mem., former chmn., nat. adv. bd. Salvation Army Adv. Bd., Dallas; chmn. emeritus Dallas Council on World Affairs; adv. dir. Am. Cancer Soc.; bd. dirs. Tex. Research League; Nat. Devel. Council mem. Big Bros./Big Sisters Am., Hon. bd. govs. Citizen's Choice, Washington; dir. Tex. Assn. Taxpayers, Nat. Legal Center for Public Interest, Washington; past chmn. Landmark Legal Found., Kansas City, Mo.; pres. Trinity Improvement Assn.; dir., past pres. Tex. Bur. Econ. Understanding; past chmn. Bus.-Industry Polit. Action Com.; chmn. Nat. Ctr. For Policy Analysis. Recipient G. Mabry Seay award Dallas Assn. Ins. Agts., 1970; Headliner of Year award Press Club of Dallas, 1975; Person of Vision award Tex. Soc. Prevention of Blindness, 1977; Linz award for Dallas civic service, 1978; Torch of Liberty award Anti-Defamation League, 1979; Horatio Alger award, 1981; others. Mem. U.S. C. of C. (mem. public affairs com.), E. Tex. C. of C. (dir., past chmn.), N.Y. C. of C., Am. Ins. Assn. (alternate dir.), La. Ins. Adv. Assn. (exec. com.), Philonomic Soc., Am., N.Y. bar assns., State Bar Tex., Newcomen Soc. N.Am., Delta Theta Phi. Clubs: New York University, Insurance, Dallas Petroleum, Dallas Country, Dallas Knife and Fork (dir., mem. exec. com.), Rock Creek Barbecue, Austin. Lodge: Rotary. Home: Dallas Tex. Died Apr. 10, 1988; buried Dallas. †

PERRY, WILLIAM COX, lawyer; b. Franklin, Tex., July 10, 1917; s. William Charner and Elizabeth Ola (Cox) P.; m. Nancy Palmer Little, Oct. 26, 1944; children—Adele Perry Hart, Nan Perry Nelson, Mary Perry Ellis. B.A., Rice U., 1938; LL.B., U. Tex., 1941. Bar: Tex. 1941. Assoc. Butler & Binion, Houston, 1945-49, ptnr., 1949-78, mng. ptnr., 1978-82, ptnr., 1982-85, of counsel, 1986-88; vis. lectr. polit. sci. Rice U., Houston, 1946-55. Bd. dirs. Legal Found. Am., from 1983. Served to lt. USN, 1942-45; PTO. Fellow Am. Bar Found.; mem. ABA (editor Natural Resources Lawyer 1973, chmn. sect. natural resources law 1973-74), State Bar Tex., Houston Bar Assn. (v.p. 1947-48), Order of Coif, Phi Beta Kappa, Phi Delta Theta, Phi Delta Phi. Baptist. Club: Houston Country (dir. 1978-81). Home: Houston Tex. Died July 3, 1988; buried Forest Pk., Lawndale, Houston.

PERTINI, SANDRO, president of Italy; b. Stella, Italy, 1896; grad. in law, social and polit. scis.; married. Trained as journalist; served as lt. 1st World War; joined Socialist Party, 1914; arrested for anti-fascist publ., 1925; imprisoned, 1926; emigrated to France; arrested for polit. disturbances and anti-fascist activities; returned secretly to Italy, 1927; imprisoned, 1928-35; in polit. detention camp, 1935-43; mem. exec. council Italian Socialist Party, 1943; fought against German troops Porta San Paolo, Rome, arrested but escaped, 1944; sec. Socialist Party in occupied Italy; organized insurrections, No. Italy, 1945; mem. Socialist Party Adminstrn. until 1948; mem. Constituent Assembly, 1946; life senator, 1948—; chmn. Socialist Parliamentary Group; mem. Chamber Deps., 1953-76, dep. speaker, 1963-68, speaker, 1968-76; mng. editor Avanti, 1945-46, 50-52, Il Lavoro nuovo, 1947; pres. Italian Rep., 1978-85. Decorated Gold medal for mil. valor in partisan activities. Died Feb. 24, 1990; cremated. Home: Rome Italy

PERYAM, DAVID ROGER, psychologist; b. Encampment, Wyo., Mar. 22, 1915; s. George G. and Marguerite (Knopf) P.; m. Margaret Gail Terwilliger, Jan. 2, 1935 (dec. Apr. 1976); children: David B., Mary L., Kenneth F., Laura J.; m. Nancy Jo Peryam, June 18, 1978; children: Eugene, Christine Weidner. BA, U. Wyo., 1939; MA, Ohio State U., 1940; PhD, Ill. Inst. Tech., 1961. Lic. psychologist, Ill. Rsch. supr. Joseph E. Seagram & Sons, Louisville, Ky., 1940-44; warehouse supt. Calvert Distilling, Relay, Md., 1947-48; chief food acceptance dept. Armed Forces Food and Container Inst., Chgo., 1949-63; tech. dir. Peryam & Kroll Rsch., Chgo., 1963-84, sr. psychologist, 1985-92. Pres. Suburban Community Chest Council, Berwyn, Ill., 1958-59; bd. dirs. United Way Park Forest, Ill., 1953-86, Rich E. High Sch., Park Forest, 1957-60. Fellow ASTM (merit award 1985), Am. Psychologist Assn. (sec. div. 23 1967-70); mem. Inst. Food Technologists, Am. Mktg. Assn. Home: Park Forest Ill. Died Nov. 13, 1992. †

PETER, CARL JOSEPH, clergyman, theology educator; b. Omaha, Apr. 4, 1932; s. Carl Joseph and Anne Marie (Schinker) P. S.T.D., Pontifical Gregorian U., Rome, 1962; Ph.D., Univ. Thomas Aquinas (Angelicum), Rome, 1963; D.D. (hon.), Creighton U., 1978. Ordained priest Roman Catholic Ch., 1957. Assoc. pastor St. Patrick's Ch., Fremont, Nebr., 1958-60; asst. vice rector N.Am. Coll., Rome, 1960-64; asst. prof. Sch. Theology Cath. U. Am., Washington, 1964-67, assoc. prof., 1967-72, prof. systematic theology, 1972-91, chmn. dept. theology, 1975-77, dean Sch. Religious Studies, 1977-85; vis. lectr. Princeton Theol. Sem., N.J., 1974, 76; mem. Presbyn.-Roman Cath. Dialogue USA, 1967-72, Luth.-Roman Cath. Dialogue USA, from 1972, Roman Cath.-Jewish Dialogue nat. capital area, 1986-91, Faith and Order Commn., Nat. Council Chs., 1971-72. Author books; contbr. over 200 articles and revs. to profl. jours. Trustee Washington Theol. Consortium, 1977-85, Pontifical Coll. Josephinum, Columbus, Ohio, 1976-85, St. Mary's Sem. and Univ., Balt., 1988-91; mem. Pope's Internat. Theol. Commn., 1980-91. Named resource person to U.S. Del. to Synod of Bishops, 1971, 83, 85, Peritus to Synod of Bishops by Pope John Paul II, 1983. Mem. Cath. Theol. Soc. Am. (John Courtney Murray award for Distinction in Theology 1975, pres. 1971-72). Democrat. Home: Washington D.C. Died Aug. 20, 1991; buried Omaha, Nebr.

PETER, LAURENCE JOHNSTON, educator, author; b. Vancouver, B.C., Can., Sept. 16, 1919; s. Victor C. and Vicenta (Steves) P.; m. Irene J. Howe, Feb. 25, 1967; children: John, Edward, Alice, Margaret. B.A., Western Wash. State Coll., 1957, M.Ed., 1958; Ed.D., Wash. State U., 1963; LH.D. (hon.), Heidelberg Coll., Tiffin, Ohio, 1982. Tchr. B.C., 1941-47; instr. B.C. Prison, Burnaby, 1947-48; guidance counselor Vancouver, 1948-64; instr. U. B.C., 1964; asst. prof. U. So. Calif., L.A., 1964-66, assoc. prof., 1966-69, prof., 1969-70; dir. Evelyn Frieden Center for Prescriptive Teaching, 1967-70; ind. research and writing projects, 1970-90; adj. prof. U. Calif., Turlock.; Panel mem. rev. bd. HEW, 1969-70. Author: Prescriptive Teaching, 1965, (with Raymond Hull) The Peter Principle: Why Things Always Go Wrong, 1969, The Peter Prescription: How to Make Things Go Right, 1972, The Peter Plan: A Proposal for Survival, 1975, Competencies for Teaching, 4. vols., 1975, Peter's Quotations: Ideas for Our Time, Peter's People and Their Marvelous Ideas, 1979, Peter's Almanac, 1982, (with Bill Dana) The Laughter Prescription, 1982, Why Things Go Wrong or The Peter Principle Revisited, 1984, The Peter Pyramid or Will We Ever Get the Point, 1985, Processes of Teaching, 1985. Vice pres. B.C. div. Canadian Mental Health Assn., 1959-61; Bd. dirs. Big Bros. Greater Los Angeles. Recipient Phi Delta Kappa research award U. So. Calif., 1970; Canadian Univs. Assn. Alumni award; Disting. Alumnus awards Western Wash. State Coll.; Disting. Alumnus awards Wash. State U.; Will Rogers Top Hand award, 1979, Noble Prize Assn. for the Promotion of Humor in Internat. Affairs, 1984. Mem. AAUP, P.E.N., AFTRA, Authors Guild, Phi Delta Kappa. Home: Palos Verdes Estates Calif. Died Jan. 12, 1990; cremated.

PETERING, RALPH EDWIN, electrical manufacturing company executive; b. LaPorte, Ind., Apr. 26, 1908; s. George H. and Magdalena (Droege) P.; m. Ernestine Hohengarten, Oct. 14, 1939; children: Nancy Jane, Elizabeth Anne, Robert R. B.S., U. Ill., 1931; postgrad., Loyola U., Chgo., 1938; LL.D., Christ Sem., St. Louis, 1980. C.P.A., Ill. Sr. accountant Lybrand, Ross Bros. & Montgomery, Chgo., 1931-33, 35-42; comptroller Silver Fleet Motor Express, Inc., Louisville, 1933-35; auditor Fed. Res. Bank, Chgo., 1935; comptroller Emerson Electric Co. (formerly Emerson Electric Mfg. Co.), St. Louis, 1942-46, comptroller, asst. sec., 1946-50, comptroller, asst. sec., asst. treas., 1950-51, v.p., asst. treas., 1951, v.p., treas., 1952-65, sr. v.p., 1965-73, also dir., 1951-72. Mem. Am. Inst. C.P.A.s (Elijah Watts Sells Gold medal 1938), Ill. Soc. C.P.A.s (Gold medal 1938), Beta Gamma Sigma. Home: Saint Louis Mo. Died June 10, 1990; buried Bellefontaine Cemetery, St. Louis.

PETERMAN, MYNIE GUSTAV, pediatrian; b. Merrill, Wis., Mar. 5, 1896; s. Albert Frederick and Ida (Braatz) P.; m. Mildred Mackenzie, Sept. 29, 1924; children: Albert Frederick, Mary Jean. ScB, U. Wis., 1918; AM, Washington U., St. Louis, 1920, MD, 1921. Diplomate Am. Bd. Pediatrics. Chief resident City and County Hosp., St. Paul, 1921-22; fellow, 1st asst., assoc. in pediatrics Mayo Found. and Clinic, Rochester, Minn., 1922-25; practiced in Milw., from 1925; dir. labs. and rsch. Milw. Children's Hosp., 1925-53; former head dept. Milwaukee County Hosp.; med. officer Bur. Medicine, FDA, Washington, from 1964; introduced new treatment for epilepsy in childhood, 1924, new test for syphilis, 1927, classification for convulsions, 1933. Editor English transl. Diseases of Children, 5 vols., 1935; contbr. articles to med. jours., chpts. to books. Col. USAR ret. Fellow Am. Acad. Neurology; mem. AMA, Internat. Congress Pediatrics, Am. Acad. Pediatrics, Cen. Soc. for Clin. Rsch., Am. Assn. for Rsch. in Nervous and Mental Diseases, Wis. Med. Soc., Milwaukee County Med. Soc., Am. Epilepsy Soc., Milw. Pediatric Soc., Osler Soc., Madrid Pediatric Soc., Sigma Xi, Phi Sigma. *

PETERS, WILLIAM WESLEY, archiect, planner; b. Terre Haute, Ind., June 12, 1912; s. Frederick Romer and Clara (Margedant) P.; m. Svetlana Wright, Apr. 1, 1935 (dec. Sept. 1946); children: Brandoch, Daniel (dec.); m. Svetlana Allilueva, Apr. 7, 1970 (div. May 1973); 1 child, Olga Margedant. Student, Evansville Coll., 1929-30, DSc (hon.), 1971; student, MIT, 1930-32; DFA (hon.), Centre Coll. Ky., 1973. Pvt. practice Evansville, Ind., 1936; with Frank Lloyd Wright Found., Taliesin, Spring Green, Wis., 1936-91; with Frank Lloyd Wright Found., Taliesin West, Scottsdale, Ariz., 1936-91, sec.-treas., 1943-59, v.p., 1959-91; chief architect Taliesin Assoc. Architects, 1959-91; mem. ednl. staff Frank Lloyd Wright Sch. Architecture; structural engr. Guggenheim Mus., N.Y.C., Adminstrn. and Rsch. Tower, Johnson Wax Co., Racine, Wis., Price Tower, Bartlesville, Okla. Completed works designed by Frank Lloyd Wright: Beth Sholom Synagogue, Phila., Annunciation Greek Orthodox Ch., Milw., Marin County Civic Ctr., San Raphael, Calif., Grady Gammage Auditorium, Tempe, Ariz.; designing architect San Jose (Calif.) Community Theater, Lewis and Eugenia van Wezel Performing Arts Hall, Sarasota, Fla., Vets. Meml. Auditorium, San Raphael, Calif., Music bldg. Ariz. State U., Tempe, Ascension Luth. Ch., Scottsdale, Lincoln Income Life Ins. Office Bldg. and Bank, Louisville, Thorpe Inst. Design Bldg., Monona Basin Master Plan, Madison, Wis., Golden Rondelle for S.C. Johnson & Son, Racine, feasibility study and projection for Island of Minoo, Imperial Govt. Iran Palace at Mehrdasht nr. Tehran, and residential complex in Chalus nr. Caspian Sea for Her Imperial Highness Princess Shams Pahlavi of Iran, Ascension Luth. Ch., Scottsdale, St. Mary's Roman Cath. Ch., Alma, Mich., Bank of Spring Green, Wis., Mt. Damavand Coll., Tehran, Our Lady of Fatima Ch., Tucson, Ariz. Biltmore restoration, Phoenix, Regional Art Ctr., Centre Coll., Danville, Ky., master plan and recreational devel. for Ricardo Bordallo, Agana, Guam, master plan Bartlesville (Okla.) Community Ctr. Peforming Arts Ctr. and Community Ctr. Hall, Bartlesville, Performing Arts Ctr., Clearwater. Home: Scottsdale Ariz. Died July 17, 1991; buried Spring Green, Wis.

PETERSEN, FORREST SILAS, businessman, naval officer; b. Holdrege, Nebr., May 16, 1922; s. Elmer Louis and Stella Bell (Nickels) P.; m. Jean Baldwin Carter, June 17, 1978. Student, U. Nebr., 1939-40; B.S., U.S. Naval Acad., 1944; B.S. in Aero. Engring, U.S. Naval Postgrad. Sch., 1952; M.S. in Engring, Princeton U., 1953. Commd. ensign USN, 1944, advanced through grades to vice adm., 1976; designated naval aviator, 1947, assigned fighter squadrons, 1947-50, 53-56; instr. Naval Test Pilot Sch., 1956-58; research pilot X-15 plane, 1958-62; comdg. officer Fighter Squadron 154, 1962; with naval reactors br. AEC, 1963; exec. officer U.S.S. Enterprise, 1964-66; with Office Chief Naval Operations, Washington, 1966-67; comdg. officer U.S.S. Bexar, 1967-68, comdg. officer U.S.S. Enterprise, 1969-71; asst. dir. strategic and support systems test and evaluation DDR&E, Dept. Def., 1972-74; comdr. attack carrier striking forces 6th Fleet, 1974-75; vice chief Naval Material, 1975-76; dep. chief naval ops. (air warfare), 1976, comdr. Naval Air Systems Command, 1976-80; pres. Petersen Baldwin Enterprises, Inc. Georgetown, S.C., 1980-90. Decorated D.S.M., Legion of Merit, D.F.C., Bronze Star medal; recipient Disting. Service medal NASA, 1962, Collier trophy Look mag., 1962; named to Carrier Aviation's Mat. Meml. Hall of Fame, 1991, to Test Pilot's Hall of Honor, 1991. Fellow AIAA; mem. Soc. Exptl. Test Pilots, Nat. Soc. Aerospace Profls. (Montgomery award 1962), Nat. Aero. Assn. Home: Georgetown S.C. Died Dec. 8, 1990; buried Arlington Nat. Cemetery.

PETERSON, HAROLD OSCAR, radiologist, educator; b. Dalbo, Minn., Apr. 13, 1909; s. Adolph Oscar and Hulda (Forslund) P.; m. Margaret Dorothy Ferris, Sept. 22, 1934; children: John F., Judith Ann Peterson Lyons, Richard H., James R. BS, U. Minn., 1930, MD, 1933. Diplomate Am. Bd. Radiology (trustee 1959-65, 65-71). Intern Kansas City (Mo.) Gen. Hosp., 1933-34; resident radiology Mass. Gen. Hosp., Boston, 1935-36; from mem. faculty to prof. emeritus radiology U. Minn. Med. Sch., 1937-92, chmn. dept. radiology, 1957-70; radiologist, head dept. Charles T. Miller Hosp., St. Paul, 1941-57, Children's Hosp., St. Paul, 1948-57; radiologist Bethesda Hosp., St. Paul, 1941-44, St. Joseph's Hosp., St. Paul, 1941-43, Interstate Clinic, Red Wing, Minn., 1940-57; chief staff U. Minn. Hosp., 1966-68; prof. radiology emeritus U. Minn., 1989-92; Pancoast lectr., Phila., 1956; cons. Mpls. Gen. Hosp., 1958; Friedman lectr. U. Cin., 1959; Caldwell lectr. Am. Roentgen Ray Soc., 1961 (gold medal); Hodges lectr., Ann Arbor, Mich., 1962; Carmen lectr. St. Louis Med. Soc., 1962; ann. lectr. Canadian Assn. Radiologists, 1962; Manville lectr. La. Med. Soc., 1961; Golden lectr. N.Y. Roentgen Soc., 1964; Rigler lectr., Tel Aviv, 1965; Holmes lectr. New Eng. Roentgen Ray Soc., 1965; Kirklin Weber Meml. lectr. Mayo Clinic, 1965; Dyke lectr. Columbia, 1971; Stauffer lectr. Temple U., 1972; Rigler lectr. U. Minn., 1972; vis. prof. U. Tex. Med. Br., Galveston, 1979-80, 81, U. Tex. Health Sci. Center, San Antonio, 1980-81, 82-83, 84-85. Sr. author: Introduction to Neuroradiology, 1972; contbr. numerous articles to profl. jours. Margaret F. and Harold O. Peterson Professorship in Neuroradiology established at U. Minn., Minn. Med. Found., 1989. Fellow Am. Coll. Radiology (chancellor 1958-62, 65-69, v.p. 1963-64, chmn. com. tech. affairs 1965-69, gold medal St. Louis meeting 1971), Am. Coll. Chest Physicians; mem. Am. Roentgen Ray Soc. (dir. instructional courses 1957-76, exec. council 1954-57, chmn. council 1956-57, pres. 1964), Am. Soc. Neuroradiology (charter, founding mem., pres. 1967), AMA, Minn., Ramsey County Med. Socs., Minn. Radiol. Soc., Minn. Trudeau Soc., Radiol. Soc. N. Am., AAUP, Am. Trudeau Soc., AAAS, Assn. Am. Med. Colls., Minn. Soc. Neurol. Scis., Am. Soc. Pediatric Radiology (charter, founding mem.), Pan Am. Med. Assn., Minn. Acad. Medicine, Am. Acad. Neurology, Sigma Xi; hon. mem. numerous med. socs. Republican. Methodist. Club: Midland Hills Country (St. Paul). Home: Saint Paul Minn. Died July 22, 1992. †

PETERSON, MARTIN SEVERIN, physical scientist; b. Salem, Oreg., Apr. 21, 1897; s. Axel and Matilda (Collinson) P.; m. Wilma Loomis, Aug. 21, 1926; 1 child, Tom Loomis. AB, Reed Coll., 1920; MA, U. Nebr., 1929, PhD, 1932. Dir. Meml. Settlement House, Englewood, N.J., 1921-23; instr. English, Iowa State U., 1923-25; asst. prof. U. Nebr., 1926-46; tech. editor Western Regional Rsch. Lab., USDA, 1946-47; chief tech. svcs. office Q.M. Food and Container Inst., Chgo., 1947-62; gen. phys. scientist U.S. Army Rsch. and Engring. Labs., Natick, Mass., from 1962; vis. prof. English, U. Mont., summer 1935; Rockefeller fellow U. Chgo., 1925-26. Author: Joaquin Miller: Literary Frontiersman, 1937, Using Better English, 1937, Scientific Thinking and Scientific Writing, 1961; editor: (with D.K. Tressler) Food Technology the World Over, vol. 1, 1963, Food Tech., 1951-61; assoc. editor Prairie Schooner, 1928-46; editor-in-chief Food Rsch., 1952-61. Mem. Inst. Food Tech., Packaging Inst., Q.M. Assn. Episcopalian. *

PETERSON, PAUL MURREY, law educator; b. Lockwood, Mo., June 5, 1897; s. James M. and Mary E. (Neale) P.; m. Mildred E. Koblank, July 30, 1927; 1 child, Murrey. Student, Westminster Coll., Fulton, Mo., 1915-17; LLB, U. Mo., 1922. Bar: Mo. 1922. Practiced in Columbia, Mo., from 1922; atty. State Bar Mo., Columbia, 1936-38; prof. law U. Mo., Columbia, from 1942, gen. counsel to curators, from 1954. Author: (with Willard L. Eckhardt) Possessory Estates, Future Interests and Conveyances in Missouri, Missouri Legal Forms with Suggestions on Drafting. Mem. Selective Svc. Bd., World War II. With U.S. Army, 1917-19, AEF. Mem. ABA, Nat. Assn. Coll. and Univ. Attys. (past pres.), Am. Judicature Soc., Mo. State Bar, Boone County Bar Assn. (past pres.), Am. Legion (past comdr.), Order of Coif, Phi Alpha Delta. Democrat. Presbyterian. *

PETERSON, ROBERT DONALD, building materials distribution company executive; b. Mpls., Mar. 20, 1919; s. Swan Peter and Bertha Tina (Larson) P.; m. Belva LaPriel Haynie, June 21, 1942 (dec. 1956); children: Lynn Douglas, Janice Alda; m. Emma Jean Emery, Aug. 8, 1959. B.S. in Forest Product, U. Minn., 1941; M.S., U. Wash., 1942. Salesman Palmer G. Lewis Co., Inc., Seattle, 1946-52, sales mgr., 1952-60, gen. mgr., exec. v.p., 1960-67; pres., chief exec. officer Palmer G. Lewis Co., Inc., Auburn, Wash., 1967-79, chmn., chief exec. officer, 1979-85, chmn., 1985-90, also bd. dirs.; dir. CAPRI NW, 1983. Served to 1st lt. U.S. Army Air Force, 1943-46. Agnes Healy Anderson fellow U. Wash., 1941-42. Mem. Bldg. Material Distbn. Assn. (pres. 1970-71), Xi Sigma Phi, Alpha Zeta, Gamma Sigma Delta, Sigma Xi. Clubs: Washington Athletic, Overlake Golf and Country, Seattle Lumbermen's (pres. 1957-58). Lodge: Rotary (Seattle). Home: Bellevue Wash. Died Jan. 9, 1990; buried Bellevue, Wash.

PETERSON, SPIRO, educator; b. New Haven, Dec. 25, 1922; s. Walter and Anastasia (Morris) P.; m. Yerevan Sarkisian, June 10, 1951; children: Ellen Dorothea, Anastasia Lynne, Andrew Townsend. AB, Trinity Coll., Hartford, 1944; MA, Harvard U., 1947, PhD, 1953. Mem. faculty Miami U., Oxford, Ohio, 1952-87; assoc. prof. Miami U., 1958-62, prof., 1962-87, chmn. dept. English, 1964-73, dean Grad. Sch. and Research, 1972-82. Editor, annotator: The Counterfeit Lady Unveiled and Other Criminal Fiction of Seventeenth-Century England, 1961; author: Daniel Defoe: A Reference Guide 1731-1924, 1987. Mem. Woodrow Wilson Fellowship Selection Com., 1964-71. Served with inf. AUS, 1943-46. Decorated Bronze Star; recipient Benjamin Harrison award Miami U., 1987. Mem. Coll. English Assn. Ohio (pres. 1971-72, exec. council), MLA, Am. Soc. 18th Century Studies, Phi Beta Kappa, Phi Kappa Phi. Home: Oxford Ohio Died June 11, 1992. †

PETREE, NEIL, merchant; b. Norborne, Mo., Mar. 18, 1898; s. Louis E. and Kittie (Neil) P.; m. Vera Thomas, May 1919. AB in Econs., Stanford U., 1919. Salesman Weinstock Lubin and Co., Sacramento, 1919, then buyer, group buyer, mdse. mgr. apparel group; div. mdse. mgr., then sales mgr., gen. mdse. mgr. Hale Bros., San Francisco, 1925-28, mdse. mgr. for 6 dept. stores in Calif., 1928-29; v.p. Assoc. Dry Goods Corp. N.Y., 1929; pres., bd. dirs. Barker Bros., L.A., 1938-59, vice chmn. bd., chmn. exec. com., from 1959; pres. James McCreery & Co., 1931-38; pres., bd. dirs. W. & J. Sloane, Inc., 1957-59; v.p., bd. dirs. Larchfield Corp., Marshall-Wells Co., K-H-T Corp., N.Y.C.; bd. dirs. Investment Co. Am., So. Calif. Gas Co., Bank Am., Pacific Mut. Lfie Ins. Co., Douglas Aircraft Co., Inc., Gladding McBean & Co. State dir. for So. Calif., OPA, L.A., 1942-43; pres. L.A. War Chest, 1945; chmn. Met. Traffic and Transit Com., Hollywood Bowl Assn., 1953-54. Ambulance driver, aviator French Army, World War I; lt., aviator U.S. Army, World War I. Recipient Cavalier award as outstanding mcht. who did most for country, 1942, award L.A. Realty Bd., 1953, western achievement award for furniture industry, 1968. Mem. Downtown Business men's Assn. (bd. dirs.), L.A. C. of C. (bd. dirs.), Calif. C. of C. (pres. 1952-53), Stanford U. Alumni Assn. (pres.), Automobile Club So. Calif. (bd. dirs.), Calif. Club, Bel Air Bay Club, L.A. Country Club, Delta Tau Delta. *

PETRIE, JOHN DANIEL, insurance company executive; b. McLouth, Kans., June 26, 1936; s. Daniel C. and Mildred (Means) P.; m. Joyce Shannon, Apr. 3, 1955; children: Michael, Patrick, Kristy, Susan. Grad. high sch., McLouth, 1954. Sr. v.p. Kansas City (Mo.) Life Ins. Co., from 1954. Home: Shawnee Kans. Deceased.

PETTIT, ARTHUR EDWIN, lawyer; b. Stuttgart, Ark., Dec. 29, 1896; s. Edwin and Anna (Means) P.; m. Mary Mabel Long, Mar. 21, 1926; children: Jeffrey, Arthur Gerald. AB, Columbia U., 1917, LLB, 1921. Bar: N.Y. 1921. Practiced in N.Y.C., from 1921; mem.

Winthrop, Stimson, Putnam & Roberts, N.Y.C., from 1942; bd. dirs. Singer Mfg. Co. Bd. dirs., v.p., trustee N.Y. Law Inst. With USNRF, 1918-19. Mem. Down Town Assn., Rumson Club. *

PETTIT, MANSON BOWERS, psychiatrist; b. Waco, Tex., May 26, 1902; s. Benjamin Franklin and Nancy (Phillips) P.; m. Dagny Rudback, Mar. 26, 1930; children: Marjorie Pettit James, John Whitney.; m. Louise K. Graves, May 19, 1984. A.B., Trinity U., 1923; M.D., Vanderbilt U., 1928. Diplomate: Am. Bd. Psychiatry and Neurology. Intern Meth. Hosp. So. Calif., 1928-29; rotating gen. intern St. Elizabeth's Hosp., Washington, 1930-31; resident psychiatry St. Elizabeth's Hosp., 1931-33, staff psychiatrist, 1933-58, clin. dir., 1958-60; med. supt. State Hosp. Number 2, St. Joseph, Mo., 1960-66; supt. Southwestern State Hosp., Thomasville, Ga., 1966-73; cons. clin. psychiatry Community Mental Health Center, Archbold Meml. Hosp., Thomasville, 1974-79; psychotherapist Washington Inst. Mental Hygiene, 1930-58; organizer Arlington County Mental Hygiene Center, 1947-60; Lectr. mental health, hygiene asso. clin. prof. psychiatry Georgetown U., 1941-60. Contbr. to: articles, book revs. to profl. jours. Biol. Abstracts. Mem. St. Joseph Community Welfare Council, from 1960. Fellow Am. Psychiat. Assn.; mem. Interprofl. Inst., AMA, Buchanan County Med. Soc. Methodist. Clubs: Mason (Shriner), Kiwanis, Shriners. Home: Silver Spring Md. Deceased.

PETUCHOWSKI, JAKOB JOSEF, clergyman, research educator; b. Berlin, July 30, 1925; came to U.S., 1948, naturalized, 1954; s. Siegmund and Lucie Recha (Loewenthal) P.; m. Elizabeth Rita Mayer, Nov. 28, 1946; children—Samuel Judah, Aaron Mark, Jonathan Mayer. B.A. with honors, U. London, 1947; B.H.L., Hebrew Union Coll., 1949, M.A., 1952, Ph.D., 1955; Fellow Humane Letters, Maimonides Coll., Winnipeg, Man., Can., 1959; Dr.phil.h.c., U. Cologne, Fed. Republic Germany, 1978; D.Lit. (hon.), Brown U., 1979. Ordained rabbi, 1952. Rabbi Beth Israel, Washington, Pa., 1955-56; asst. prof. Rabbinics Hebrew Union Coll.-Jewish Inst. Religion, Cin., 1956-59, assoc. prof., 1959-63, prof., 1963-65, prof. Rabbinics and theology, 1965-74, rsch. prof. Jewish theology and liturgy, 1974-91, Sol and Arlene Bronstein prof. Judaeo-Christian studies, 1981-91; vis. prof. philosophy Judaeo-Christian studies, 1981-91; vis. prof. philosophy, religion Antioch Coll., Ohio, 1961; vis. prof. Jewish philosophy Te.-Aviv U., 1971, vis. prof. Judaic studies Harvard U. Div. Sch., 1985; vis. prof. Ariz. State U., 1990; dir. Jewish studies Hebrew Union Coll., Jerusalem, 1963-64; rabbi Temple B'nai Israel, Laredo, tex., part-time, 1956-91. Author: The Theology of Haham David Nieto, 1954, 70, Ever Since Sinai- A Modern View of Torah, 1961, 68, 79, Prayerbook Reform in Europe, 1968, Heirs of the Pharisees, 1970, 2d edit., 1986, Contributions to the Scientific Study of Jewish Liturgy, 1970, Understanding Jewish Prayer, 1972, Beten im Judentum, 1976, Es Lehrten unsere Meister, 1979, Theology and Poetry, 1978, Ferner Lehrten unsere Meister, 1980, Die Stimme vom Sinai, 1981, Gottesdienst des Herzens, 1981, Wie unsere Meister die Schrift erklären, 1982, Our Masters Taught, 1982, Feiertage des Herrn, 1984; co-author: Lexikon der Jüdisch-Christlichen Begegnung, 1989; editor: New Perspectives on Abraham Geiger, 1975, When Jews and Christians Meet, 1988; co-editor: Versoehnung in der Jüdischen und Christlichen Liturgie, 1990; mem. editorial bd. Hebrew Union Coll. Ann.; contbr. articles to profl. jour. Decorated Order of Merit 1st class (Fed. Republic Germany); Heinsheimer Meml. fellow Hebrew Union Coll., 1952-55. Fellow Am. Acad. for Jewish Research; mem. Assn. Jewish Studies. Home: Cincinnati Ohio Died Nov. 12, 1991; buried Cin.

PFISTER, MURRAY CHARLES, interior designer; b. Santa Rosa, Calif., Dec. 10, 1939; s. Charles Rudolf and Elinor (Murray) P. With Skidmore, Owings and Merrill, San Francisco, 1965-81, assoc. ptnr., 1974-81; prin. The Pfister Partnership, San Francisco, from 1981; trustee San Francisco Mus. Modern Art; former trustee Univ. Art Mus., U. Calif., Berkeley; bd. dirs. Am. Coun. Arts. Prin. works include Deutsche Bank, Frankfurt, Fed. Republic Germany, Royal Dutch Shell Hdqrs., The Hague, The Netherlands, The 21 Club, N.Y.C., Plaza Las Fuentes Hotel, Pasadena, Calif., Empress Place Mus., Singapore, Grand Hotel, Washington, others. Recipient Product Design award for Pfister Wall Bracket, Resources Coun. Inc., 1982, Silver award Inst. Bus. Designers and Contract mag., 1983, Achievement of Excellence in Interior Architecture award for Grand Hotel, Washington chpt. AIA, 1985, Design Excellence in Interior Architecture award for Royal Dutch Shell Hdqrs., San Francisco chpt., 1986-87, Designer of Yr. award Interiors mag., 1986; honored in Salute to Timeless Design, Omega Watch Corp., 1986; named to Hall of Fame Interior Design mag., 1986; design recipient Exceptional Lighting Design award for Deutsche Bank Illuminating Engring. Soc. N.Am., 1986-87. Mem. Am. Soc. Interior Designers, Met. Club of N.Y., Arts Club Chgo., Villa Taverna Club (San Francisco). Home: San Francisco Calif. Died Oct. 1, 1990, San Francisco. †

PFUND, HARRY WILLIAM, educator; b. Phila., Jan. 3, 1900; s. William J. and Anna M. (Erb) P.; m. Friederike Marie Haufe, July 4, 1931; children: Peter Harry, Helga Friederike (Mrs. Helmut Gutmann). A.B., Haverford Coll., 1922; A.M., Harvard U., 1926, Ph.D., 1931; postgrad. univs., Munich, Berlin, Heidelberg. Instr. German Harvard U., 1924-26; instr., tutor Harvard U., Radcliffe Coll., 1928-30; instr. German Haverford Coll., 1926-27, asst. to assoc. prof., 1930-48, prof., 1948-67, prof. emeritus, from 1965, chmn. dept. German, 1955-65; Exchange lectr. German univs., summer 1966; Ottendorfer traveling fellow N.Y. U., 1927-28; Vis. lectr. U. Colo., summer 1954, West Chester (Pa.) State Coll., 1967-72, Villanova U., 1972-73. Author: Studien zu Wort und Stil bei Brockes, 1935, A History of the German Society of Pennsylvania, 1944, rev. edit., 1964; co-editor: Studies in Honor of John Albrecht Walz, 1941; founder, mem. editorial bd.: Am.- German Rev, 1934-70; contbr. articles, revs. to mags. Asst. sec. Carl Schurz Meml. Found., Phila., 1931-33, dir., mem. exec. com., 1946-49, v.p., 1949-56, pres., 1956-62; Relief work Am. Friends Service Com. (Quakers), Germany, also head mission, French Zone, 1946-47. Named hon. citizen Freiburg, Germany, 1949; decorated Officer's Cross, Order of Merit Republic Germany). Mem. Am. Assn. Tchrs. German (pres. Phila. chpt. 1968-70), MLA, German Soc. Pa. (past v.p.), Nat. Carl Schurz Assn. (pres. 1962-71), Phi Beta Kappa. Home: Kennett Square Pa. Deceased. †

PHELPS, MALCOM ELZA, physician, surgeon; b. El Reno, Okla., Oct. 16, 1905; s. James I. and Lydia (Malcom) P.; m. Maxine Hicks, Mar. 22, 1925; children—James V., Joseph M. Student, U. Okla., 1922-26; M.D., State U. Ia., 1929. Intern U. Okla. Hosp., 1929-30, resident surgeon, 1930-31; asst. in urology Dr. W.J. Wallce, Oklahoma City, 1932-33; practice medicine El Reno, 1931-68; founder Phelps Clinic, El Reno, 1948; cons. surgeon U.S. Indian Hosp., Concho, Okla., 1938-50; chief of staff El Reno Sanitarium, 1945-54; mem. staff Park View Hosp., El Reno, from 1954; div. surgeon, examiner C.R.I.&P. R.R., from 1953; mem. Nat. Adv. Com. Poliomyelitis Vaccine, 1955-57; mem. adv. com. dependents med. care Dept. Def., 1956-68; spl. adviser to surgeon gen. army, 1957, 59; mem. adminstrs. med. adv. com. FAA, 1960-66; field dir. AMA Vol. Physicians Vietnam, 1966-67; dir. Supporting Assistance Health Office AID, Dept. State, 1968-74; clin. prof. family practice and community medicine U. Okla. Sch. Medicine, Oklahoma City, from 1974; cons. U.S.S.W. Reformatory (Bur. Prisons), USPHS. Editorial Bd.: Worldwide Abstracts of Gen. Medicine. Licensed judge Am. Kennel Dog Show, 1945; trustee, pres. Shepherd Found.; bd. dirs. Am. Bd. Family Practice, 1968-72, treas., 1972-74. Decorated Medal of Health 1st class Vietnam; named to Okla. Hall of Fame, 1967. Founding mem., life fellow S.W. Surg. Congress; mem. A.M.A. (poliovaccine com. 1957, com. preparation gen. practice 1957-58, v.p. 1967-68), So. Med. Assn., Okla. Med. Soc. (v.p. 1950), Am. Acad. Gen. Practice (founding mem., v.p., chmn. bd. 1952-56, pres. 1957, treas. 1962-66, pres. Family Health Found. Am. 1958-62), Am. Med. Writers Assn., Am. Soc. Clin. Hypnosis, Am. Assn. Physicians and Surgeons, Am. Assn. Ry. Surgeons, Flying Physicians Assn. (founding mem.), Delta Tau Delta, Phi Chi. Mem. Christian Ch. Clubs: Mason, Elk, Oklahoma City Kennel (pres. 1945-56), Bulldog of America (pres. 1958-60). Home: El Reno Okla. Died Mar. 29, 1991.

PHILIPP, CYRUS L., transportation company executive; b. Milw., Mar. 28, 1898; s. Emanuel L. and Bertha S. Philipp; m. Mary Edwards, Oct. 3, 1925 (dec. Feb. 1965); children: Emanuel II, Mary Philipp Baur, Patricia (dec.). BA, U. Wis., 1920. With Union Refrigerator Transit Co., Milw., from 1920, pres., from 1936; v.p., bd. dirs. Gen. Am. Transp. Corp., Chgo., from 1937; bd. dirs. 1st Wis. Nat. Bank, Milw., 1st Wis. Trust Co., Milw., Wis. Bank Shares, Milw., Perfex Corp., Milw.; trustee, mem. fin. com. Northwestern Mut. Life Ins. Co., Milw. Trustee Milw. Downer Sem.; v.p., mem. corp. bd., pres. aux. bd. Milw. Hosp.; mem. Rep. Nat. Com. for Wis., 1944-52; former chmn. Wis. Rep. Cen. Com.; mem. fin. com. Milw. County Rep. Com.; former mem. exec. com. Rep. Nat. Com. Mem. Milw. Club, Milwaukee Country Club, Wis. Club, Milw. Athletic Club, Univ. Club, Chgo. Club, Union League Club (Chgo.), Attic Club (Chgo.), Tavern Club (Chgo.). *

PHILIPS, IRVING, psychiatrist; b. Hartford, Conn., Oct. 5, 1921; s. Simon and Sarah (Berkovitz) P.; m. Mary Gray Philips, June 10, 1949; children: Laura, Daniel, Donald. A.B., Oberlin Coll., 1943; M.D., U. Ill., 1948. Intern Michael Reese Hosp., 1948-49, resident, 1949-52; resident Menninger Sch. Psychiatry, 1952-53, Langley Porter Inst., 1955-57; dir. mental retardation U. Calif., 1957-75; prof. psychiatry, dir. child and adolescent psychiatry U. Calif.-San Francisco, 1972-92. Author: Prevention and Treatment of Mental Retardation, 1966, Child Psychiatry: A Plan for the Coming Decades; book review editor: Am. Jour Child Psychiatry, 1972-82 . Served to capt. U.S. Army, 1943-46, 53-55. Fellow Am. Acad. Child Psychiatry (pres. 1985-87), Am. Orthopsychiat. Assn., Am. Psychiat. Assn. (trustee 1966-73, Royer ward 1987), Am. Coll. Psychiatrists; mem. AMA, Group for Advancement Psychiatry, Calif. Med. Assn., No. Calif. Psychiat. Soc., Internat. Assn. Child and Adolescent Psychiatry and Allied Professions (treas. 1983—). Home: San Francisco Calif. Died Aug. 30, 1992. †

PHILLIPS, JAY, corporate executive; b. Minsk, Russia, Mar. 22, 1898; came to U.S., 1900; s. Edward Phillips; m. Rose T. Ebin, Aug.7, 1917. Pres. Ed. Phillips & Sons Co., Mpls.; chmn. bd. Century Metalcraft Corp., L.A.; bd. dirs. Nat. Presto Industries, Inc., Eau Claire, Wis. Trustee, v.p. Nat. Soc. Crippled Children and Adults; pres. Mt. Sinai Hosp., Mpls.; bd. dirs. Mpls. Symphony Orch., Mpls. Fedn. Jewish Svc., Mpls. coun. Boy Scouts Am. Fellow Brandeis U. Mem. Wine and Spirits Wholesalers Am. (bd. dirs.), Mpls. C. of C. (bd. dirs.), Hillcrest Country Club (L.A.), Westview Country Club (Miami, Fla.), Variety Club N.W. *

PHILLIPS, JOHN GOLDSMITH, former art curator; b. Glens Falls, N.Y., Jan. 22, 1907; s. John Goldsmith and Mary Agnes (O'Connor) P.; m. Giovanna Sodi, Oct. 2, 1937; children: Anthony V., Beatrice M., Guy L. AB, Harvard U., 1929. Mem. staff Met. Mus. Art, N.Y.C., 1929-71, assoc. curator, 1934-50, curator Renaissance art, 1957-61, curator Western European arts, 1962-67, chmn. Western European arts, 1967-71, emeritus, 1971-92. Author: Early Florentine Designers and Engravers, 1955, China-Trade Porcelain, 1956; contbr. articles to mags., bulls. Guggenheim fellow, Italy, 1961. Mem. Century Assn. Club. Home: Palm Beach Fla. Died Feb. 17, 1992.

PHILLIPS, NATHANIEL POPE, lawyer; b. Pointe Coupee Parish, La., Aug. 24, 1898; s. Nathaniel P. and Lula (Torras) P.; m. Eleanor Kelleher, May 6, 1933; 1 child, Nathaniel Pope. BS, La. State U., 1921; LLB, Tulane U., 1924. Bar: La. 1924. Practiced in New Orleans, from 1924; mem. Chaffe, McCall, Phillips, Burke, Toler & Hopkins, New Orleans, from 1940. With U.S. Army, World War I; lt. USNR, World War II. Mem. ABA, La. Bar Assn., New Orleans Bar Assn., Boston Club (pres. 1956-58), Lake Shore Club, Petroleum Club, Phi Delta Phi. *

PHILLIPS, RALPH WILBUR, dental educator; b. Farmland, Ind., Jan. 12, 1918; s. J. Stanley and Effie Mae (Berger) P.; m. Dorothy E. McCleaster, Aug. 21, 1943; 1 dau., Cheryl D. (Mrs. William J. Dale). B.S., Ind. U., 1940, M.S., 1950; D.Sc., U. Ala., 1960. Mem. faculty Ind. U. Sch. Dentistry, Indpls., from 1940; research prof. dental materials Ind. U. Sch. Dentistry, from 1962, asst. dean research, 1966-74, assoc. dean research, from 1974; assoc. dir. Oral Health Research Inst., from 1974; vis. prof. U. Calif. at San Francisco, U. Tenn., La. State U.; mem. rev. com. research grants Am. Fund Dental Health, from 1979; cons. bioengring. programs Rensselaer Poly. Inst., U. Va., N.Y. U.; Past chmn. dental study sect. Nat. Inst. Dental Research, chmn. bio-materials research adv. com., from 1962; mem. dental panel FDA, from 1977, chmn., from 1978. Author: Skinner's Science of Dental Materials, 8th edit, 1982, Elements of Dental Materials for Dental Hygienists and Assistants, 4th edit, 1984, also articles, sects. in books; co-author: Materials for the Practicing Dentist, 1969, Modern Day Practice in Crown and Bridge, 4th edit, 1986, Text on Operative Dentistry, 1981, 85, Review of Dentistry, 1981; pub. over 300 papers; Editorial bds. numerous dental jours. Recipient Callahan award Ohio Dental Assn., 1964; research award Chgo. Dental Soc., 1948, 54; gold medal research award Alumni Assn. Columbia Dental Sch., 1960; distinguished citation Washington U., St. Louis, 1958; ann. recognition award Ind. U. Student Union Bd., 1959; Hollenback award Am. Acad. Operative Dentistry, 1977; Spanedel award N.Y. Dental Assn., 1977; Internat. Research award Mass. Dental Assn., 1979; Gold Medal award Pierre Fauchard Acad., 1979; also 1st Internat. Nakayama Meml. award Japanese sect., 1981; G.V. Black award Washington U., 1982; Schweitzer award N.Y. Acad. Prosthodontics, 1988. Fellow Am. Coll. Dentists (Gies award 1976), Internat. Coll. Dentists, AAAS (past dir. dentistry sect.), Am. Acad. Gen. Dentistry (hon. fellowship, recognition award 1981); hon. mem. Am. Acad. Restorative Dentistry, Am. Dental Assn.; mem. Internat. Assn. Dental Research (past pres., Souder award 1964), Am. Chem. Soc., Am. Assn. Dental Schs., Am. Assn. Dental Editors, Belgian Dental Assn. (hon.), Indpls. Dental Soc., Ind. Acad. Sci., Ind. U. Alumni Assn. (dir.), Sigma Xi, Omicron Kappa Upsilon, Phi Lambda Epsilon, Alpha Chi Sigma, Phi Eta Sigma. Home: Indianapolis Ind. Deceased. †

PHILLIPS, SAMUEL COCHRAN, air force officer; b. Springerville, Ariz., Feb. 19, 1921; s. Clarence A. and Mabel (Cochran) P.; m. Betty Anne Brown, Aug. 15, 1942; children: Dana Stabile, Janie Culpepper, Kathleen. BSEE, U. Wyoming, 1942, LLD (hon.), 1963; MSEE, U. Mich., 1950. Commd. 2d lt. U.S. Army, 1942; advanced through grades to maj. gen. USAF, 1968; combat tours with 8th Air Force World War II; assigned theatre hdqrs. Frankfort, Germany, 1945-47; dir. ops. Armament Labs; B53 project officer, chief air def. missiles div. Wright-Patterson AFB, 1955-56; chief logistics, dir. material 7th Air div. SAC, Eng., 1956-69; program dir. Minuteman, later vice comdr. Ballistic Systems div., Calif., 1959-63; dir. Apollo program NASA, 1964-69; comdr. Air Force Space and Missile System Orgn., 1969-72; dir. Nat. Security Agy., 1972-73, chief cen. svc. security, 1973; comdr. USAF Strategic Air Command, 1973-75; ret., 1975. Decorated DFC with oak leaf cluster, air medal with 7 oak leaf clusters, Legion of Merit, Croix de Guerre (France).

Mem. IEEE, Kappa Sigma, Alpha Kappa Psi (hon.). Home: Washington D.C. Died Jan. 31, 1990.

PHILLIPS, VELMA, home economics educator; b. Knox County, Ill., Oct. 28, 1894; d. William T. and Sarah Dell (Maxey) P. PhB, Knox Coll., Galesburg, Ill., 1914; AM, U. Chgo., 1915; PhD, Columbia U., 1927. Instr. home econs. Lenox Coll., Hopkinton, Iowa, 1915-16, Baker U., Baldwin, Kans., 1916-17; home econs. asst. Horace Mann High Sch., N.Y.C., 1917-18; dir. home econs., dean women Mont. State Normal Coll., 1918-24; ednl. advertiser Abraham and Straus, Inc., Bklyn., 1924-28; dir. home econs. Ohio U., Athens, 1929-39; dean Wash. State U. Coll. Home Econs., Pullman, 1939-61; prof. San Fernando State Coll., Calif., from 1961; rep. Internat. Fedn. Univ. Women, Stockholm, 1939, Internat. Congress Home Econs., Copenhagen, 1939, White House Conf. on Children and Youth, 1950; del. Internat. Congress Home Econs., Stockholm, 1949; chmn. Wash. State Nutrition Com., from 1941. Author: Evidences of Need of Education for Efficient Purchasing, 1931, Consumer Buying, 1951, Careers for You in Home Economics, 1957, (with Mildred Graves Ryan) Clothing, 1947, (with Walter J. Willis) Consumer Buying, 1958. Mem. AAAS, AAUW, Bus. and Profl. Women, Kappa Delta Pi, Phi Upsilon Omicron, Omicron Nu. Methodist. *

PHILPOTT, ALBERT LEE, state legislator; b. Philpott, Va., July 29, 1919; s. John Elkania and Mary Gertrude (Prillaman) P.; m. Katherine Apperson Spencer, 1941; children—Judy Philpott Divers, Albert Lee. B.A., U. Richmond, 1941, J.D., 1947, LLD (hon.), 1978. Bar: Va. 1947. Commonwealth's atty. Henry County, 1952-57; mem. Va. Ho. of Dels., 1958-91, speaker, 1980-91; practice law, 1947-91; bd. dirs. Bassett Furniture Industries, Blue Ridge Airport Authority; adv. bd. dirs. Dominion Bank; mem. Jud. Coun. Dist. Cts. Com., Va. Code Commn., exec. com. So. Legis. Conf., Coun. of State Govts. Mem. Bassett Meml. Libr. Bd.; trustee Jamestown, Yorktown Found. 1st. lt. USAAF, 1941-45. Named Legislator of Yr. Va. Assn. Local Exec. Constl. Officers, 1990; recipient Disting. Svc. award Am. Legion, 1977, Alumni Disting. Svc. award, U. Richmond, 1977, Va. Cultural Laureate award for Statesmanship, 1977, Disting. Svc. award Va. Trial Lawyers, 1979, Disting. Virginian award Va. Exchange Clubs, 1980. Mem. ABA, Va. State Bar, Va. State Bar Assn., Martinsville-Henry County Bar Assn., Elks, Moose, KP, Lambda Chi Alpha, ODK, Delta Theta Phi. Home: Richmond Va. Died Sept. 28, 1991; buried Martinsville, Va.

PHLEGER, ATHERTON MACONDRAY, lawyer; b. San Francisco, Feb. 5, 1926; s. Herman and Mary Elena (Macondray) P.; m. Jean Cameron, Apr. 19, 1980; children: Michael Atherton, Elena Dean, Peter Macondray, Mariana, Kelley, Cameron. A.B., Stanford U., 1949; LL.B., Harvard U., 1952. Bar: Calif. 1953. Assoc., then partner Brobeck, Phleger & Harrison, San Francisco, 1958-88; Dir. Wells Fargo & Co., Wells Fargo Bank. Trustee Childrens Hosp., San Francisco, William G. Irwin Charity Found. Served with USMCR, 1943-46. Mem. ABA, Calif. Bar Assn. Clubs: Pacific-Union (San Francisco), Bohemian (San Francisco); Burlingame Country. Home: San Francisco Calif. Died Nov. 6, 1988; buried Cypress Lawn Cemetery, Calif.

PICKER, ARNOLD MELVILLE, motion picture company executive; b. N.Y.C., Sept. 29, 1913; s. David Victor and Celia Charlotte (Weinberg) P.; m. Nettie Ray Cohen, Jan. 14, 1937; children: Carol D. Picker Frank, Phyllis B. Picker Dessner. BS, Coll. City N.Y., 1935. V.p. Columbia Pictures Internat. Corp., 1945-51; asst. chief, then chief distbn. div., motion picture bur. overseas div. OWI, 1942-45; with United Artists Corp., N.Y.C., 1951-89; exec. v.p. United Artists Corp., 1961-67, chem. exec. com., 1967-89; chem. exec. com., v.p. entertainment svcs. Transam. Corp. Mem., sec. Commerce travel adv. com. U.S. Travel Svc.; mem. U.S. Adv. Commn. on Internat. Ednl. and Cultural Affairs; mem. adv. coun., trustee Am. Film Inst.; mem. bd. dirs. Joint Commn. Mental Health Children, Inc.; standing com. motion pictures U.S.-USSR Cultural Exch. Agreement; ofcl. del. U.S. Govt. film festivals at Cannes, Karlovy Vary, others.; mem. bd. dirs. City Coll. Fund; chmn. bd. Found. Child Mental Welfare. Decorated knight officer Order Merit (Italy). Mem. Motion Picture Export Assn. Am. (bd. dirs.). Home: Boston Mass. Died Oct. 8, 1989.

PICKETT, WILLIAM FRANCIS, horticulture educator; b. Kansas City, Mo., Nov. 25, 1894; s. Clarkson Cook and Evalena (Jenkins) P.; m. Alva Lee Cooper, July 31, 1918; 1 child, Robert Cooper. BS, Kans. State U., 1917, MS, 1923; PhD., Mich. State U., 1935. Asst. in horticulture Kans. State Coll., 1917; asst. prof. Tarlton (Tex.) Agr. Coll., 1917-18; mem. faculty Kans. State U., Manhattan, from 1918, prof., from 1936; head dept. horticulture, horticulturist Kans. Agrl. Expt. Sta., 1938-60, acting dir., 1956; state forester State of Kans., 1932-55; liaison officer fgn. agrl. affairs, 1952-60; campus coord. ICA-India-Kans. State U. team, 1956-62, chief party, from 1962. Copntbr. articles to profl. jours. Fellow AAAS; mem. Kans. Hort. Soc. (pres. 1938-40), Am. Soc. for Hort. Sci., Am. Pomological Soc., Kiwanis, Sigma Xi, Kappa Sigma, Gamma Sigma Delta, Phi Sigma, Phi Kappa Phi, Alpha Zeta. Republican. Baptist. *

PIERCE, LOUIS, chemist, educator; b. Ely, Minn., May 22, 1929; s. John and Angela (Bolka) P.; m. Geraldine Caroline Ustar, May 29, 1954; children: Nancy, Louis, Jerome, John, Susan. B.S., Western Res. U., 1951, M.S., 1952, Ph.D., 1954. Research fellow Harvard, 1954-56; asst. prof. U. Notre Dame, 1956-59, asso. prof., 1959-62, prof. chemistry, from 1962; asst. and acting dir. U. Notre Dame (Computing Center), 1962-64. Alfred P. Sloan Found. fellow, 1961-65; NSF Sr. Postdoctoral fellow, 1965-66. Mem. Am. Chem. Soc., Am. Phys. Soc. Home: South Bend Ind. Deceased. †

PIERRE, WILLIAM HENRY, soil science educator; b. Brussels, Wis., Aug. 2, 1898; s. Alice Oerkwitz, Oct. 16, 1928; children: Mary Frances, Louise Joanne, Nancy Jean. BS, U. Wis., 1921, MS, 1923; PhD, 1925. Soil surveyor S.D. State Coll., 1921-22; asst. soil chemist Ala. Poly. Inst., 1925-29; assoc. prof. agronomy W.Va. U., Morgantown, 1929-36, prof., from 1938, head dept. agronomy and genetics, 1936-38; head dept. agronomy Iowa State U., Ames, 1938-64; lectr. U. Chgo., summer 1941; U.S. del. 2d Inter-Am. Conf. on Agr., Mexico City, 1942; mem. FAO mission to Uruguay, 1950, to Brazil, 1951; mem. agrl. bd. NRC, NAS, 1955-62; AID cons. U. Republic of Uruguay, 1965-66. Contbr. articles to sci. and popular jours. Fellow AAAS, Am. Soc. Agronomy (pres. 1947, nitrogen rsch. award 1931); mem. AAUP, Soil Sci. Soc. Am. (pres. 1940), Internat. Soc. Soil Scientists, Henry Newman Hon. Soc., KC, Rotary, Sigma Xi, Phi Kappa Phi, Phi Sigma, Alpha Zeta, Gamma Sigma Delta, Delta Theta Sigma. Roman Catholic. *

PIERSON, EARL WENDELL, accountant; b. Elgin, Ill., July 15, 1910; s. Per Algot and Emma (Johnson) P.; m. Hazel C. Nelson., Nov. 29, 1934; 1 son, Earl Wendell. B.A., U. Wis., 1933. With Arthur Andersen & Co. (C.P.A.'s), Chgo., 1933-37; With Arthur Andersen & Co. (C.P.A.'s), Houston, 1937-73, partner, 1949-73, adv. group, 1956-65, Chmn., 1957-58, partner charge Houston office, 1961-68, partners bd., 1968-69, with firm, until 1973; past pres., dir. HCRC Corp. Past pres., dir. River Oaks Property Owners; treas., mem. exec. com. Houston Assn. Retarded Children, 1965-66; life mem., past chmn. bd. govs. Center for Retarded, Inc., Houston; past trustee, treas. Mus. Fine Arts; mem. U. Wis. Found.; Life mem. bd. dirs. St. Joseph Hosp. Found.; past trustee St. Joseph Hosp.; past mem. Houston Crime Commn. Mem. Am. Inst. C.P.A.'s (hon.), Tex. Soc. C.P.A.'s, Beta Gamma Sigma, Alpha Kappa Psi, Beta Alpha Psi. Methodist (past bd. adminstrn.). Clubs: River Oaks Country (past trustee, treas.), Ramada, Coronado (past dir.). Home: Houston Tex. Died May 11, 1989; buried Elgin, Ill.

PIERSON, ELMER F., business executive, lawyer; b. Kansas City, Mo., Aug. 27, 1896; s. John G. and Anna L. Pierson; m. Marie Walton Kahmann, Dec. 27, 1922; children: Marilyn Cecilia, Martha Ann. LLB, Kansas City Sch. Law, 1919. Bar: Mo. 1991. Chmn. bd., pres. The Vendo Co., Kansas City; bd. dirs. 1st Nat. Bank Kansas City;bd. dirs., v.p. Assoc. Industries Mo. Vice chmn. bd. trustees U. Kansas City; trustee Philharm. Assn., Art Inst., Midwest Rsch. Inst., Kansas City Mus.; pres. Real Estate Bd., 193-34; mem. adv. com. Trinity Luth. Hosp.; chmn. 4th War Loan Drive, Kansas City; bd. dirs. Boy Scouts Am. Lt. inf. U.S. Army, World War I. Mem. NAM (bd. dirs.), U.S. C. of C. (past v.p., bd. dirs.), Kansas City C. of C. (prs. 1946, bd. dirs.), Inst. Dirs. (London), Nat. Automatic Merchandising Assn. (past pres.), Native Sons Orgn. Kansas City, Kansas City Club, River Club, Augusta Nat. Golf Club (Ga.), Mission Hills Country Club, Mercury Club (past pres.), Meridian Club (past pres.), Lions (past pres.), Phi Alpha Delta. *

PIGA, FRANCO, government official; b. Rome, Mar. 18, 1927; m. Teresa di Macco; 4 children. Law degree. Pres. Disezione del Consiglio di Stato, Rome, from 1973; minister Industry, Commerce and Agrl., Rome, 1987; pres. Comm. Nat. Soc. e Borsa, Rome, 1984-88. Author: Pubblico e Privato Nella Dinamica Delle Istituzioni, 1985. Named Cavaliere di Gran Croce. Home: Rome Italy Died Dec. 26, 1990.

PIGFORD, ROBERT LAMAR, chemical engineer, educator; b. Meridian, Miss., Apr. 16, 1917; s. Lamar and Zula Vivian (Harrington) P; m. Marian Gray Pinkston, Aug. 30, 1939; children: Nancy Marie, Robert Harrington. BS, Miss. State Coll., 1938; MS, U. Ill., 1940, PhD, 1942. Rsch. engr. exptl. sta. E.I. DuPont de Nemours & Co., Inc., Wilmington, Del., 1941-47; Allan P. Coburn prof. chem. engring., chmn. dept. U. Del., 1947-66, Univ. prof., 1975-1984, Univ. Rsch. prof., 1984-88; prof. chem. engring. U. Calif., Berkeley, 1966-75; vis. prof. U. Wis., 1957, Cambridge U., 1959; part-time cons. indsl. chem. cos., from 1946; mem. sci. adv. bd. USAF, 1956-60. Author: (with W.R. Marshall Jr.) Applications of Differential Equations to Chemical Engineering Problems, 1946, (with T.K. Sherwood) Absorption and Extraction, 1951, (with T.K. Sherwood and C.R. Wilke) Mass Transfer, 1975; (with A.P. Coburn) contbr. sects. on diffusional ops., gas absorption and distillation in J.H. Perry's Chemical Engineers Handbook; mem. numerous edit. adv. bds. Recipien Francis Alison award U. Del., 1979. Mem. NAS, Am Inst. Chem. Engrs. (Profl. Progress award 1955, William H. Walker award 1958, W.K. Lewis award 1970 Founders award 1973), Nat. Acad. Engring., Am Chem. Society (emeritus, editor Jour. Indsl. and Engring. Chemistry Fundamentals 25 yrs.), Sigma Xi, Tau Beta Pi. Home: Newark Del. Died Aug. 4, 1988; cremated.

PIGOTT, JAMES M., investment banker; b. Bethel Springs, Tenn., Sept. 12, 1894; s. John T. and Dona (Hendrix) P.; m. Fredericka Blankenship, Sept. 26, 1925; 1 child, Mary Fredericka Pigott Kostner, Jr. Student pub. schs., Jackson, Tenn. Bond salesman, sales mgr., v.p. Cen. Republic Co. (consolidated with Dean Witter & Co.), Chgo., 1926-52, exec. vp., 1952-54, pres., 1954-57, bd. dirs., 1949-57; lit. ptnr. Dean Witter & Co., Chgo.; bd. dirs. Ins. Exch. Bldg. Corp. Trustee Graham Found. Advanced Studies in Fine Arts. Mem. Bond Club, Chgo. Athletic Assn. *

PIKARSKY, MILTON, civil engineering educator, consultant; b. N.Y.C., Mar. 28, 1924; s. Abraham J. and Celia (Kaufman) P.; m. Sally Nesel (div.); children—Joel Jay, Amy Jo; m. Christine Mickelson Johnson. B.C.E., CCNY, 1944; postgrad. DePaul U. Law Sch., 1959-60; M.C.E., Ill. Inst. Tech., 1969. Registered profl engr., Ind., Ill., Mich., Ohio, Mo., N.Y., Tex. Structural designer, field engr. N.Y. Central R.R., 1944-56; cons. engr. Plumb, Tuckett and Pikarsky, 1956-59; project coordinator Blue Island R.R. Group, 1959-60; engr. pub. works City of Chgo., 1960-63, commr. of pub. works, 1964-73; chmn., chief exec. officer Chgo. Transit Authority, 1973-75; Regional Transp. Authority, 1975-78; adj. prof. U. Ill.-Chgo., 1976-84; dir. Transp. Rsch. Inst., Ill. Inst. Tech., Chgo., 1979-84, rsch. prof. Ill. Inst. Tech., 1979-84; Disting. Prof. civil engring. dir. Inst. Transp. Systems, CCNY, from 1984; dir. engring. studies Nat. Council on Pub. Works Improvement, from 1986; chmn. state and regional planning panel Energy Engring. Bd., Nat. Rsch. Council, 1987-88; mem. adv. council on sci. and engring. CCNY, from 1980, U. Pa., 1974-83, U. Ill.-Chgo., from 1984; mem. MIT Ctr. for Transp. Studies; dir. for Chgo. area TRUST project, 1984-85. tech. advisor on pub. transp. systems for several fgn. govts. Co-author: Chicago Public Works: A History, 1973; Urban Transportation Policy and Management, 1976. Contbr. numerous articles to profl. jours. Mem. exec. com. Chgo. South Side Planning Bd., 1980-85; trustee Children's World Montessori Sch. of Park Ridge, Ill., Inventors' Council of Chgo., 1983-87. Served with USN, 1944-46. Recipient Townsend Harris medal CCNY, 1968. Fellow AAAS, ASCE (control group of transp. rsch. council, James Lurie prize 1977, Civil Govt. award 1973, Civil Engr. of 1970 award); mem. Nat. Acad. Engring. (membership com. 1984-87), NRC (exec. com. from 1982, Am. Ry. Engring. Assn., Am. Pub. Works Assn. (1 of 10 Pub. Works Men of Yr. 1969), Am. Road and Transp. Builders Assn., Nat. Soc. Profl. Engrs. (past dir.), Ill. Soc. Profl. Engrs. (past dir.), Western Soc. Engrs. (chmn. transp. div. 1980-85), Ill. Univs. Transp. Rsch. Consortium (chmn. exec. com.), Sigma Xi, Tau Beta Pi, Chi Epsilon. Clubs: Ground Hog (Chgo.), Economic. Died June 15, 1989; buried Riverside Meml. Pk., Rochelle, N.J. Home: Yonkers N.Y.

PILIÉ, LOUIS M., accountant; b. New Orleans, Dec. 13, 1898; s. Giles Gustave and Emma (Roubion) P.; m. Amelie Jeanne Andrieu, Apr. 14, 1921; children: Lucille Pilié Sarrat, Louis Andrieu, Roland Joseph, Martin Arnaud, Noel Francis. Student, Loyola U., New Orleans. CPA, La. Clk., asst. bookkeeper Tenn. Coal, Iron & R.R. Co., 1916-18; jr., then sr. acct. Albert J. Derbes, CPA's, New Orleans, 1918-25, sr. ptnr., 1925; founder, ptnr. Barton & Pilié, CPA's, New Orleans, from 1933; ptnr. Peat, Marwick, Mitchell & Co., New Orleans; mem. faculty evening div. Loyola U. Contbr. articles to profl. jours., chpt. to handbook. Mem. Orleans Parish Sch. Bd., 1941-52, also past v.p.; mem. Nat. Citizens Coun. for Better Schs., 1957-59; pres. New Orleans Tchrs. Retirement Fund; chmn. fund raising Loyola U. Program Progress; mem. exec. com. Tulane U. Tax Inst.; bd. dirs. New Orleans Opera House Assn., House of Good Shepherd, New Orleans. Mem. AICPA, past v.p., pres., mem. coun., trial bd., rep. Internat. Congress Accts., Amsterdam 1957), La. Soc. CPA's (past pres.), Am. Acctg. Assn., Cath. Accts. Guild New Orleans (founder, past pres.), Serrra Club, KC, Blue Key, Beta Alpha Phi (hon.), Beta Gamms Sigma, Pi Kappa Epsilon, Sigma Lambda Epsilon. *

PILPEL, HARRIET FLEISCHL, lawyer; b. N.Y.C.; d. Julius and Ethel (Loewy) Fleischl; m. Robert Pilpel, 1933 (dec. 1987); children: Judith Ethel (Mrs. Alan Appelbaum), Robert Harry; m. Irvin B. Schwartz, 1989. B.A., Vassar Coll.; M.A. in Internat. Relations and Pub. Law; LL.B. (Kent scholar), Columbia U.; D.H.L. (hon.), Queens Coll., Charlotte, N.C., 1981. Bar: N.Y. 1936. Research asst. Columbia Law Sch., 1934-35; practice in N.Y.C., from 1934; sr. partner Greenbaum, Wolff & Ernst.; counsel Weil, Gotshal & Manges, 1982-91; past mem. Citizen's Adv. Com. to N.Y.C. Dept. Correction; spl. counsel U.S. Govt. com. for Oliver Wendell Holmes Devise; panel expert U.S. Govt. Copyright Office; cons. Spl. Com. Divorce and Marriage Laws of Nat. Conf. Commrs. Uniform State

Laws; mem. adv. bd. Arthur and Elizabeth Schlesinger Library on History of Women in Am.; cons. Women's Bur. U.S. Dept. Labor, 1965-76; gen. counsel UCLS, 1979-86; mem. com. on polit. and civil rights Pres. Kennedy's Commn. on Status Women; mem. spl. task force on status women Pres. Johnson's Citizens' Adv. Com.; project dir. HEW Study on Family Planning, Contraception, Vol. Sterilization and Abortion; gen. counsel Planned Parenthood-World Population; counsel Assn. for Voluntary Surgical Contraception; mem. bd. visitors Columbia U. Sch. Law; mem. com. on law, social action and urban affairs Am. Jewish Congress; bd. dirs. Population Resource Center; mem. adv. com. New Women's Career Program; mem. Women's Forum; mem. N.Y. core group of nat. bd. YWCA; co-chmn. Nat. Coalition v. Censorship; chair panel law and planned parenthood Internat. Planned Parenthood Fedn., 1970-78; trustee N.Y. Ethical Culture Soc., chairperson devel. law and policy program Columbia U. Ctr. Population and Family Health, co-chairperson Nat. Coalition Against Censorship; President's disting. visitor Vassar Coll., 1985. Author: (with Theodora Zavin) Your Marriage and the Law, 1952, 64, Rights and Writers, 1960, (with Morton D. Goldberg) A Copyright Guide, 1960, (with Minna Post Peyser) Know Your Rights, 1965; Writer, lectr. TV and radio appearances on marriage and family law, lit. and entertainment law, constl. law, civil liberties, birth control, abortion, and related subjects, status of women, problems of sr. citizens and legal profession.; contbg. editor Entertainment Law and Fin.; mem. adv. bd. Media Law Reporter. Recipient SIECUS award, 1973; Margaret Sanger award, 1974; Louise Waterman Wise Laureate award, 1978; Earl Warren Civil Liberties award, 1978; ann. medal for excellence Columbia U. Law Sch. Alumni Assn., 1980; Allard K. Lowenstein award, 1981; award U. Conn. Law Sch., 1983. Mem. ABA, Am. Assn. Marriage Counselors (affiliate), Am. Acad. Matrimonial Lawyers, Copyright Soc. U.S.A. (past trustee), Assn. Bar City N.Y., N.Y. State Bar Assn., ACLU (vice chmn. nat. adv. council), Lawyers Alliance for Nuclear Arms Control (exec. bd. N.Y. chpt.), Am. Law Inst., Columbia U. Law Sch. Alumni Assn., Authors League Am., PEN Club, Am. Soc. Journalists and Authors, Phi Beta Kappa. Home: New York N.Y. Died Apr. 23, 1991; buried Pleasantville, N.Y.

PIMEN, PATRIARCH (SERGEY MIKHAILOVICH ISVEKOV), Russian ecclesiastic; b. Bogorodsk, Moscow Region, July 1910. Became monk, 1927; ordained priest, 1932. Bishop of Odessa, 1957, archbishop, of Leningrad, 1960-63; archbishop of Krutitsky and Kolomna, 1963-71, patriarch Metropolitan of Moscow and All Russia, 1971-90. Decorated Grand Cordon, Order of the Cedar of Lebanon, 1972; Order of St. Sergius of Radonezh, USSR, 1979, Order of Friendship of the Peoples, 1980. Died May 3, 1990. Home: Moscow Russia

PIMENTEL, GEORGE CLAUDE, chemistry educator; b. Rolinda, Calif., May 2, 1922; s. Emile J. and Lorraine Alice (Reid) P.; m.; children: Anne Christine, Tess Loren, Janice Amy. AB, UCLA, 1943; PhD in Chemistry, U. Calif., Berkeley, 1949; PhD (hon.), U. Ariz., 1986, Colo. Sch. Mines, 1987, U. Rochester, 1988. From instr. to assoc. prof. chemistry U. Calif., Berkeley, 1949-59, prof., 1959-89; assoc. dir. Lawrence Berkeley (Calif.) Lab., 1980-88; dep. dir. NSF, Washington, 1977-80; mem. Lunar and Planetary Missions Bd., 1967-70; chmn. Opportunities in Chemistry com. NRC; participant U.S.-Japan Eminent Scientists Exch. Program, 1973-74. Editor: Chem. Study Project, 1960; author 12 sci. books; contbr. over 200 papers to profl. jours. Served with USNR, 1944-46. Guggenheim fellow, 1955; recipient Campus Teaching award U. Calif., Berkeley, 1968, Coll. Chemistry Teaching award Mfg. Chemists Assn., 1971, Joseph Priestley Meml. award Dickinson Coll., 1972, Spectroscopy Soc. Pitts., 1974, Alexander von Humboldt Sr. Scientist award, 1974, Pauling medal, 1982, Wolf prize, 1982, Debye award, 1983, Madison Marshall award, 1983, Nat. Medal of Sci. award, 1985, August-Wilhelm-von Hofmann-Denkumnze medal, 1985, William Proctor prize, 1985, Robert A. Welch award, 1986, Maurice F. Hasler award, 1987, Gold medal Am. Inst. Chemistry, 1988, Donald Noyce Edn. award, 1989, Berkeley citation, 1989. Fellow AAAS, Am. Acad. Arts and Sci., Royal Soc. Chemistry (hon.); mem. Nat. Acad. Scis., Royal Instn. (hon.), Am. Philos. Soc., Am. Chem. Soc. (pres. 1986-89, Precision Sci. award 1959, Priestley medal 1989, Chem. Edn. award 1990), Am. Phys. Soc. (Earle K. Plyer prize, Lippincott medal 1980), Optical Soc. Am., Phi Beta Kappa, Sigma Xi, Phi Eta Sigma, Phi Lambda Epsilon, Alpha Chi Sigma. Home: Kensington Calif. Died June 18, 1989; buried Kensington, Calif.

PINES, NED LEWIS, publishing and insurance company executive; b. Malden, Mass., Dec. 10, 1905; s. Joseph and Dora (Goldes) P.; m. Jacquelyn Sangor, Aug. 29, 1938 (div. 1959); children: Judith Ann (Mrs. Judith P. Bernard), Susan Jane; m. Maxine Firestone, Nov. 19, 1967. Student, Columbia U., 1923-24. Pres. Pines Publs., Inc., 1928-61; pres. Popular Library, Inc., 1942-66, chmn., 1966-68; chmn. bd., dir. mem. finance and exec. coms. Eastern Life Ins. Co. N.Y., 1949-71; cons. U.S. Life Corp., N.Y.C., 1971-76; Mem. coordinating com. Columbia U. Inst. Research, 1945-47. Contbr. articles on Paris restaurants to Avenue Mag., 1985-86. Bd. dirs. Jewish Guild for Blind, 1950-73; life trustee Fedn. Jewish Philanthropies N.Y., 1968; mem. nat. judging com. Boys' Clubs Am.; adv. com. Commentary mag., 1970-90; bd. dirs. Merce Cunningham Dance Found., 1970-74, Am. Friends of Israel Mus., Jerusalem, from 1976; Founder United Jewish Appeal, 1940. Recipient U.S. Treasury award, 1945; award Bur. Intercultural Edn., 1949; Nat. Mass Media award Thomas Alva Edison Found., Inc., 1956; gold medallion and certificate Boys' Clubs Am., 1956. Clubs: Harmonie (N.Y.C.); Noyac Golf (Sag Harbor, N.Y.); Southampton (N.Y.) Golf; American (Paris). Home: New York N.Y. Died May 14, 1990.

PINGER, HENRY AMBROSE, bishop; b. Lindsay, Nebr., Aug. 16, 1897; s. John and Elizabeth (Kraus) P. Student, Franciscan Sem., Cleve., 1919-21, Franciscan Theol. Sem., St. Louis, 1925. Ordained priest Roman Cath. Ch., 1924. Missionary to China, Shantung Province, 1926; apptd. vicar apostolic of Chowtsun, Shantung, China, 1937; consecrated bishop, Chgo., 1937; in Japanese concentration camp, China, 1943-45; bishop Diocese of Chowtsun, from 1946; prisoner of Chinese communists, 1951-56, excelled from China,, 1956; chaplain Little Sisters of Poor, Indpls. *

PINKERT, JOSEPH S., steel industry executive; b. Chgo., June 22, 1908; s. Simon and Ida (Graff) P.; m. Clare Bloomberg, Mar. 1, 1936 (dec. 1975); children: Stuart, Dale, Ralph; m. Rebecca K. Rosenberg, Sept. 12, 1976. B.A., U. Chgo., 1930. V.p. Peoples Iron & Metal Co., Chgo., 1930-45; sr. ptnr. Consol. Mill Supply Co., 1945-60; pres. Peoples Iron & Metal Co., Chgo., 1945-65, Continental Debanding Corp., Chgo., 1945-50, Peoples Iron & Metal Co., Chgo., 1950-75; pres. Scrap Corp. Am., Northbrook, Ill., 1965-75, chmn. bd., 1975-82; chmn. bd. Control Metals Corp., Northbrook, 1982-86; bd. dirs. Chgo. City Bank & Trust Co.; cons. Iroquois Foundry Co., Browntown, Wis., Scrap Mgmt., Chgo. Former bd. dirs. Mt. Sinai Hosp., Chgo., Woodlawn Hosp., Chgo. State Ill. Task Force Environ. Control; past pres. Congregation Rodfei Zedek; bd. dirs. Chgo. S.E. Commn., 1970-87; trustee Spertus Coll. Judaica; active United Jewish Fund, former chmn. metals div. Mem. Inst. Scrap Iron and Steel (former pres. Chgo. chpt., chmn. nat. com. fair trades and practices, nat. dir.-at-large). Home: Northbrook Ill. Died Aug. 20, 1990.

PINKERTON, HENRY, pathology educator; b. Bklyn., June 13, 1897; s. Harry William and Helen S. (White) P.; m. Dorothy Blake Wright, May 20, 1927. BS, MIT, 1918; MD, Harvard U., 1924. Instr., then asst. prof. pathology Harvard U. Med. Sch., Boston, 1927-39; prof. pathology, dir. dept. St. Louis U. Sch. Medicine, from 1939; pathologist-in-chief St. Mary's Group Hosps., St. Louis, from 1939; Mem. ARC Typhus Expdn. to Poland, 1991, Harvard Expdn. to Peru, 1937; cons. Armed Forces Inst. Pathology, from 1944; area cons. in pathology VA, from 1948; Christian Fenger lectr. Chgo. Inst. Medicine, 1952. Contbr. chpts. to textbooks. With U.S. Army, 1917-18, AEF in France. Mem. Am. Assn. Cancer Rsch., Soc. Exptl. Biology and Medicine, Am. Coll. Pathologists, Am. Assn. Pathologists and Bacteriologists, Am. Soc. Exptl. Pathology, Am. Acad. Tropical Medicine, Pathol. and Surg. Soc. St. Louis, Sigma Xi. *

PINNELL, GEORGE LEWIS, office equipment company executive; b. Caterville, Mo., Mar. 2, 1921; s. George Lewis and Elma (Fly) P.; m. Joan Russell, Jan. 31, 1942; children: Richard Vance, James Lunsford. Student, Eastern Okla. Coll. Edn., 1943. Partner Jaynes Bus. Machines, Walla Walla, Wash., 1945-50; owner Pinnell Office Machines, Yakima, Wash., 1950-87; bd. dirs. Pinnell, Inc., Yakima, Pinnell Cash Register Co. Pres. United Good Neighbors, Yakima, 1962, Oreg.-Wash.-B.C. Community Chests and Councils, 1963, United Way Yakima, 1970; campaign chmn. for Congresswoman Catherine May, 1958; bd. govs. Am. Nat. Red Cross, 1966-72. Served with AUS and USAAF, 1942-45. Recipient Disting. Service award U.S. Jr. C. of C., 1953. Mem. Nat. Office Machine Dealers Assn. (bd. dirs. 1949), N.W. Office Machine Dealers (pres. 1947). Republican. Clubs: Rotary (pres. 1965-66), Cameratta (pres. 1952) (Yakima). Home: Yakima Wash. Deceased. †

PINNELL, WILLIAM GEORGE, university administrator; b. Clarksburg, W.Va., Sept. 6, 1922; s. George Mason and Anna (Wagner) P.; m. Dorothy Elizabeth Graham, June 25, 1946; 1 child, Georgia Pinnell Stowe. A.B., W.Va. U., 1950, M.A., 1952; D.B.A., Ind. U., 1954. Asst. dean Ind. U. Sch. Bus., Bloomington, 1954-56, assoc. dean, then acting dean, 1956-63, dean, 1963-71, univ. v.p., treas., 1971-74, exec. v.p., 1974-88, exec. v.p. emeritus, 1988-91; pres. Ind. U. Found., 1983-88; dir. Kroger Co., Pub. Service Co. Ind., Consolidated Products, Inc. Author: An Analysis of the Economic Base of Evansville; co-author: Case Study of a Depressed Area; contbr. articles to profl. jours. Bd. dirs. Ind. U. Found. Served to lt. (j.g.) USNR, 1942-47. Mem. Am. Econ. Assn., Am. Fin. Assn., Internat. Bus. Edn. Assn., Regional Sci. Assn., Midwest Econ. Assn., Midest Bus. Adminstrn. Assn., Beta Gamma Sigma, Beta Alpha Psi, Sigma Iota Epsilon, Alpha Kappa Psi, Pi Alpha Alpha. Methodist. Home: Bloomington Ind. Died Mar. 18, 1991; buried Valhalla Meml. Garden, Bloomington, Ind.

PIOTROVSKY, BORIS BORISOVICH, Soviet museum director, historian, educator; b. 1908. Ed. Leningrad State U.; Dr. (hon.), U. Delhi. Sci. worker, head sect. State Acad. Material Culture (now Inst. of Archaeology), USSR Acad. Scis., 1929-53, dir. Leningrad br. Inst. Archaeology, 1953-54, academician, from 1970, sci. collaborator, sci. dir. Eastern dept. and dep. dir. for sci. matters State Hermitage Mus., Leningrad, 1931-61, dir., 1961-90, prof., 1968-90; mem. CPSU, from 1945; mem. Presidium, from 1980; research on history and archaeology of Ancient East and Caucasus; in charge of excavations at Urart Fortress, Erevan (Armenia), from 1939; dir. USSR Acad. Scis. archaeol. expdn. in Nubia, Egypt, 1960-62. Author: History and Culture of Uraratu, 1946 (State Prize). Contbr. articles to profl. jours. Named honored art worker of Armenia, 1961; recipient State prize, Red Banner of Labour (3), Hero of Socialist Labour, 1983, Order of Hammer and Sickle, 1983. Mem. Prehistory and Protohistory Soc. Florence (hon.), Brit. Acad. Sci. (hon., corr. mem.), French Acad. Sci. (hon.), others. Died Oct. 15, 1990. Home: Saint Petersburg Russia

PIPER, SIR DAVID TOWRY, museum director, author; b. London, July 21, 1918; s. S.H. and Mary P.; m. Anne Richmond, 1945; 4 children. Student Clifton Coll., St. Catharine's Coll., Cambridge. Asst. keeper Nat. Portrait Gallery, London, 1946-64, dir. 1964-67; Slade prof. fine art Oxford U., 1966-67; dir. Fitzwilliam Mus., Cambridge, Eng., 1967-73, Ashmolean Mus., Oxford, Eng., 1973-85; Clark lectr. Cambridge U., 1977-78; fellow Worcester Coll. Oxford, 1973-85; mem. Royal Fine Art com. Author: The English Face, 1992, Catalogue of 17th Century Portraits in the National Portrait Gallery, 1963; Companion Guide to London, 1964, Painting in England, 1500-1880, 1965, Shades, 1970, London (World Cultural Guide series), 1971, The Treasures of Oxford, 1977, Kings and Queens of England and Scotland, 1980; novels (as Peter Towry) include: It's Warm Inside, 1953, Trial By Battle, 1959; editor: Enjoying Paintings, 1964, The Genius of British Painting, 1975. Served with Indian Army, 1940-45; Japanese POW, 1942-45. Died Dec. 29, 1990. Home: Oxford Eng.

PIPER, HARRY CUSHING, securities industry executive; b. Mpls., Oct. 14, 1917; s. Harry C. and Louise (Gillette) P.; children: Harry III, Addison, David. B.A., Princeton U., 1940; postgrad., U. Minn., Mpls., 1941, United Theol. Sem., Mpls., 1971-73. With Piper, Jaffray & Hopwood, Mpls., 1946-87, chmn., 1982-87, chmn. emeritus, 1987-90; chmn. Inst. Ecumenical and Cultural Research. Bd. dirs. YMCA, Mpls., Tentmakers Found., Plymouth Music Series; bd. regents St. Olaf Coll; trustee Breck Sch. Wih U.S. Army, 1943-45. Republican. Home: Wayzata Minn. Died Aug. 19, 1990.

PIPKIN, FRANCIS MARION, physicist, educator; b. Marianna, Ark., Nov. 27, 1925; s. Larry Stewart and Augusta Pearl (Hill) P.; m. Phyllis Burr, June 14, 1958; children—Jane, Augusta. Student, U. Kan., 1943-44, Morningside Coll., Sioux City, Ia., 1946-47; B.A., State U. Ia., 1950; M.A., Princeton, 1952, Ph.D., 1954. Jr. fellow Soc. Fellows, Harvard U., 1954-57, mem. faculty, from 1957, prof. physics, 1964-76, Baird prof. sci., 1976-88; assoc. dean Harvard and Radcliffe colls., 1974-77; helped plan and oversee Cambridge Electron Accelerator; researcher particle physics Fermi Nat. Accelerator Lab., Batavia, Ill., Synchroton Lab., Cornell U. Author research papers. Served with U.S. Army, 1944-46. Alfred P. Sloan fellow, 1959-63. Mem. Am. Phys. Soc., Am. Acad. Arts and Scis., Sigma Xi. Home: Belmont Mass. Died Jan. 5, 1992; buried Sioux City, Iowa.

PIPPY, CHESLEY ALWYN, railway system executive; b. St. John's, Nfld., Can., Nov. 9, 1894; s. William George and Jessie (Lindsay) P.; m. Edna Maud Hill, July 3, 1919; children: Chesley Alwyn, Douglas John. Student, St. John's Meth. Coll., St. John's Bonaventure Coll. Pres. Nfld Tractor & Equipment Co. Ltd., North Star Cement, Ltd., Nfld. Cement Co., Ltd., Peerless Equipment Co., Ltd., Hill Realty, Ltd., United Cotton Mills, Ltd., Nfld. Fibrply, Ltd., Nfld. Hardwoods, Ltd.; chmn. Job Bros. & Co., Ltd., Northantic Fisheries, Ltd., Blue Peter S.S.'s, Ltd.; bd. dirs. Can. Nat. Rys., Royal Bank Can., Tedcap Equipment Co., Ltd., Nfld. Trawling Co., Ltd., Nfld. Dehydrating Process Co., Ltd.; mem. Nfld. adv. bd. Montreal Trust Co. Bd. dirs. Nfld. Tb Assn.; serving bro. Venerable Order of Hosp. of St. John of Jerusalem. Recipient Disting. Svc. Cross, Salvation Army; named hon. lt. col. 56th Ind. Field Squadron R.C.E., Can. Army. Mem. Nfld. Yachting Club, Masons, Odd Fellows. *

PIRLOT, PAUL LEON, emeritus educator, biologist; b. Mettet, Belgium, Mar. 17, 1920; s. Leon and Frumence (Quinet) P.; children: Marie-Antoinette, Jean-Paul, Brigitte. Licence, Philosophie et Lettres, Brussels, 1942; Licence Sci., U. Louvain, 1946, Agrege Enseignement, 1949; Ph.D. In Zoology, U. London, 1949, D.Sc., 1959. Research assoc. Inst. Recherche Scientifique Afrique Centrale, Zaire, 1949-57; assoc. prof. U. Montreal, 1958-63, prof. vertebrate biology, 1963-85, prof. emeritus, from 1985. Author 5 books in field;

contbr. articles on comparative neuromorphology and theoretical biology to profl. jours. Mem. Soc. Scientifique de Bruxelles, N.Y. Acad. Sci., Soc. Study of Evolution, Can. Soc. History and Philosophy of Sci., Nat. Geographic Soc., Assn. Ecrivains de Langue Francaise. Roman Catholic. Home: Brome County Can. Deceased. †

PISACANO, NICHOLAS JOSEPH, physician, educator; b. Phila., June 6, 1924; s. Joseph Harry and Rafaella (Saquella) P.; m. Virginia Leigh Burleson; children: Toni Ann, Nicki Rae, Dean Alan, Don Arlie, Lorie Sue, Elizabeth Patterson. B.A., Western Md. Coll., 1947; M.D., Hahnemann Med. Coll., 1951; D.Sc. (hon.), Western Md. Coll., 1980. Intern Stamford (Conn.) Hosp., 1951-52, resident, 1952-53; gen. practice medicine South Royalton, Vt., 1953-55, Phila., 1955-62; asst. prof. medicine Med. Sch., U. Ky., Lexington, 1962-65, asso. prof., 1965-66, assoc. prof. biology, 1966, dir. continuing med. edn., 1962-66; asst. dean Coll. Arts and Scis., U. Ky., 1966; asst. v.p. U. Ky. Med. Center, from 1968, prof., chmn. dept. allied health edn. and research, 1971-90; exec. dir., sec. Am. Bd. Family Practice, 1969-90, sec., 1990; med. dir. Phila. div. Am. Cancer Soc., 1958-62. Pres. Ky. Mental Health Assn., from 1977; trustee U. Ky., 1987; sec. Internat. Ctr. Family Medicine, from 1988; bd. mem. Internat. Med. Scholars Program, from 1988. With U.S. Army, 1943-46. Recipient Most Popular Prof. award, 1965; Distinguished Teaching award U. Ky., 1967; Spl. Recognition plaque Student Am. Med. Assn., 1967; Spokewheel award, 1968; Spl. Recognition for Family Practice Edn. Ky. Acad. Family Physicians; Max Cheplove M.D. award N.Y. Acad. Family Physicians, 1975; U. Ky. fellow, 1975; Outstanding Alumnus of Yr. award Hahnemann Med. Sch., 1979. Mem. AAAS, Am. Acad. Family Physicians (Thomas Johnston award 1877, John G. Walsh award 1987), Pan Am. Med. Soc., So. Med. Soc., Ky. Med. Soc., Can. Coll. Family Physicians (hon., W. Victor Johnson orator 1977), N.Y. Acad. Scis., Assn. Am. Med. Colls., Soc. Health and Human Values. Home: Lexington Ky. Died Mar. 11, 1990; buried Lexington Cemetery, Lexington, Ky.

PISK, PAUL AMADEUS, music educator, composer; b. Vienna, Austria, May 16, 1893; came to U.S., 1926, naturalized, 1943; s. Ludwig and Eugenie (Pollock) P.; m. Martha Marie Frank, Nov. 15, 1919; 1 child, George Michael. Student, Vienna Conservatory Music; condr. diploma, State Music Tchrs. Austria; studied composition with Franz Schreker, Arnold Schoenberg; studied piano with S. Epstein. Music editor Anbruch, periodical and Arbeiterzeitung, Vienna, 1925-32; head music dept. Vienna People's Mcpl. U., 1922-34, New Vienna Conservatory, 1925-26, Austro-Am. Summer Conservatory, 1931-33; prof. music U. Redlands, Calif., 1913-51, dir. Sch. Music, 1948-51; prof. music U. Tex., Austin, 1951-63, Washington, St. Louis, from 1963; vis. prof. Boston U., Ariz. State U., U. Calif., Berkeley, U. So. Calif., L.A. Composer in all fields of music; contbr. articles in field and biog. sketches. Recipient composition prize City of Vienna, 1925, prize Tex. Composers Guild, 1953, 55, 57, 58. Fellow MacDowell Colony; mem. Am. Renaissance Soc., Am. Musicology Soc., Am. Composers Alliance, Nat. Assn. Composers, Music Tchrs. Nat. Assn., Masons, Phi Mu Alpha, Pi Kappa Lambda. Democrat. Presbyterian. *

PITTS, THOMAS JEFFERSON, lawyer; b. Charleston, S.C., Sept. 17, 1895; s. William McGill and Martha Matilda (Cox) P.; m. Mertie Mable Teats, Sept. 18, 1920 (dec. Dec. 1958). Student, Northeastern State Coll.; LLB, Chgo. Law Sch., LLM, 1930; LLD, Howard Payne Coll., 1947. Asst. to supt., chen chief clk. gen. claim dept. M.P. R.R. Co.; practiced in Eastland County, Tex., 1922-32; practiced in Gregg County, Tex., 1933-37, Odessa, Tex., from 1938; spl. judge county and dist. cts.; del. to Inter-Am. Bar Conf., Lima, Peru, 1945, Internat. Bar Conf., Montevideo, Uruguay, 1951, London, 1956; chmn. adv. com. State Bd. for Vocat. Edn., 1945-52. Mem. bd. editors State Bar Jour.; editor Jud. Dist. Bar News; contbr. to various legal publs. Del. Dem. Nat. Conv., Presdl. elector, 1944, 48; chmn. Electoral Coll. Tex., 1944; mem. spl. com. 3 electoral colls. U.S.; chmn. Ector County Dem. Exec. Com.; past congl. dist. chmn.; hon. pres. Tex. Dem. Conv., 1950; Dem. chmn. senatorial dist., 1954-55; chmn. dist. Dem. exec. com. of county chmn., from 1954; trustee Howard Payne Coll.; mem. exec. com. Nat. Found. Infantile Paralysis. Mem., officer numerous legal assns., KP, Lions, Order of Coif, Cap and Gown, Phi Delta Phi. Baptist. *

PIZER, IRWIN HOWARD, medical librarian; b. Wellington, N.Z., Oct. 16, 1934; s. Harry and Cecelia (Cohen) P. BS, Antioch Coll., Yellow Springs, Ohio, 1957; MS, Columbia U., 1960. Librarian, assoc. prof. med. history Upstate Med. Ctr., SUNY, Syracuse, 1964-69, dir. biomed. communication network, 1966-70; assoc. dir. librs. SUNY, Buffalo, 1969-71; univ. libr. health scis., prof. libr. adminstrn. U. Ill. at Chgo., 1971-89, prof. emeritus, 1990-91; libr. cons., 1989-91; dir. Region 3 Regional Med. Libr., Nat. Libr. Medicine, 1980-89, chmn. BRS User Adv. Bd., 1977-78, 82-83; mem. Biomed. Communication Network, 1981-89, chmn. 1982-83; chmn. 5th Internat. Congress on Med. Librarianship, Tokyo, 1981-85, 6th Congress, New Delhi, 1985-90; peer reviewer U.S. Dept. Edn. Office Edn. Rsch. and Improvement, from 1987; chmn. Ill. statewide libr. and preservation adv. coun. Ill. State Libr., from 1988. Developer world's first online biomed. info. system, The SUNY Biomed. Communications Network; author articles in field, chpts. in books.; editorial bd. INSPEL-Internat. Jour. Spl. Libraries, 1981-85. Bd. dirs. Ranch Triangle Conservation Assn., Chgo., 1971-74, pres., 1973; bd. dirs. Lincoln Park Conservation Assn., 1972-73. Fellow Med. Libr. Assn. (bd. dirs. 1975-78, chmn. nat. program com. 1986-89, editor Bull. Med. Libr. Assn. 1988-91, Murray Gottlieb prize 1964, Ida and George Eliot prize 1966, Janet Doe lectr. 1984, Archives award 1985, Pres.'s award 1986, Frank Bradway Rogers Info. Advancement award 1987, Marcia C. Noyes award 1991), Acad. Health Info. Profls. (Disting. mem. 1989-91), Upstate N.Y.-Ont. Med. Libr. Assn. (hon.); mem. ALA, AAUP, Internat. Fedn. Libr. Assns. and Instns. (chmn. sect. biol. and med. scis. librs. 1977-83, sec., 1983-85, standing com. 1983-87, chmn. div. spl. librs. 1981-85, mem. profl. bd. 1981-87, chmn. 1985-87, exec. bd. 1985-87, mem. program mgmt. com. 1985-87, chmn. 51st coun. theme com., chmn. conf. programs coms., standing com. sect. on conservation from 1987, chmn. publs. com. from 1989), Health Sci. Librs. Ill., Spl. Librs. Assn., Soc. of Scholarly Pub., Sigma Xi. Home: Chicago Ill. Died July 8, 1991; buried N.Y.C.

PLATT, HARRISON GRAY, writer, editor; b. Portland, Oreg., Apr. 27, 1902; s. Harrison Gray and Nelly (Durham) P.; m. Rhoda Failing Burpee, Aug. 19, 1925; children: Harrison Gray III, William Brewster; m. Mary Alice Kaye, Dec. 30, 1943. Grad., Punahou Acad., Honolulu, 1920; B.A., Reed Coll., 1925; postgrad., Yale U., 1925-26; M.A., Harvard U., 1927, postgrad., 1928-30. Faculty dept. lang. and lit. Reed Coll., 1927-28; dept. English Brown U., 1930-38; editor Reilly & Lee Co., 1941-43; assoc. editor Bobbs Merrill Co., Inc., 1944-54, editor gen. pub. dept., 1954-60; tech. editor C.L. Barnhart (Reference Books), 1960-61, mng. editor, 1961-63; chief dictionary editor for Harcourt Brace Jovanovich, N.Y.C., 1963-78; ret. Harcourt Brace Jovanovich, 1978; free-lancer writer, editor, 1978—. Author: (with Porter G. Perrin) Current Expressions of Fact and Opinion, 1941; other books and articles.; exec. editor: Dictionary of Army Terms, 1944, World Book Ency. Dictionary, 1963; editor in chief: Harcourt Brace School Dictionary, 1968, HBJ Sch. Dictionary, 1977, Harcourt Brace Intermediate Dictionary, 1968; contbr.: American College Dictionary, 1947. Democrat. Episcopalian. Home: New York N.Y. Died Sept. 17, 1992. †

PLATT, JAMES WESTLAKE, oil company executive; b. Magilligan, North Ireland, June 13, 1897; s. William Thomas and Elizabeth (Lucas) P.; m. Veronica Norma Hope Arnold, July 11, 1927; children: Anthony Michael, Brian Arnold, Colin Peter Sherard, Desmond Christopher St. Martin. Student, Oxford (Eng.) U., 1919-21. Joined Royal Dutch Shell Group, 1921, served in China,, until 1938; gen. mgr. mktg. interests Royal Dutch Shell Group, AArgentina, 1938-44; mng. dir. Eagle Oil & Shipping Co. Ltd., 1944; mng. dir., bd. dirs. Shell Petroleum Co. Ltd.,, 1949-57, Bataatsce Petroleum Maatschappij N.V., 1949-57; bd. dirs. Shell Transport & Trading Co. Ltd. Hon. mem. Co. Master Mariners; chmn. Hong Kong Salaries Commn., 1959, U.K. Adv. Coun.. Edn. for Mgmt., from 1960; chmn. Found. Mgmt. Edn., 1960; mem. governing body Sch. Oriental and African Studies, from 1962. With New Zealand Div., 1914-18. Decorated comdr. Order of Brit. Empire; hon. fellow Balliol Coll., Oxford U., 1963. *

PLATT, KENNETH ALLAN, physician; b. Denver, Oct. 14, 1923; s. Ralph Briton and Myrtle Marie (Reed) P.; m. Margaret Elizabeth Sullenberger, Sept. 14, 1947; children: Carolyn, Susan, Gregory. Student, Ohio State U., 1944-46; M.D., U. Colo., 1950. Intern Denver Gen. Hosp., 1950-51; gen. practice medicine Westminster, Colo., 1953-88; med. dir. Colo. Found. for Med. Care, Denver, 1972-88, pres., 1971-72; mem. Nat. PSRO Council, 1978-80; v.p. Citizens Bank, Westminster. Pres. Sch. Bd. Dist. 50, 1964-72; Chmn. bd. St. Anthony's Hosps., Denver, 1982-84. Served with U.S. Army, 1943-46, 51-53. Decorated Bronze Star, Army Commendation medal.; Recipient awards Westminster Rotary, 1970, awards C. of C., 1971, awards Dist. 50 Edn. Bd., 1972. Mem. AMA, Colo. State Med. Soc. (pres. 1971-72), Clear Creek Valley Med. Soc., Nat. Acad. Scis., Inst. of Medicine. Republican. Presbyterian. Clubs: Lakewood Country, Ranch Country, Am. Sportsmans. Home: Denver Colo. Died July 2, 1988; interred Fairmount Mausoleum, Denver.

PLATTEN, DONALD CAMPBELL, banker; b. N.Y.C., Sept. 18, 1918; s. John Homer and Katherine Campbell (Viele) P.; BA, Princeton U., 1940; grad. Advanced Mgmt. Program, Harvard U., 1966; m. Margaret Leslie Wyckoff, June 24, 1940; children: Katherine L. Platten Tyson, Peter W., Alison C. Platten Vanderbilt. With Chem. Bank N.Y.C., 1940—, sr. v.p., 1964-67. exec. v.p., 1967-70, 1st v.p., 1970-72, pres., 1972-73, chmn. bd., 1973-83; chmn. bd. Chem. N.Y. Corp., 1973-83, chmn. exec. com., 1983-89; honorary dir., chmn. emeritus, 1989-91. Reader's Digest Assn. Inc., Thomson Newspapers, Inc. Bd. dirs. Goodwill Industries Greater N.Y., Charles A. Dana Found.; trustee Collegiate Sch., N.Y.C., Presbyn. Hosp., Am. Mus. Natural History, Am. U. Beirut; emeritus trustee Princeton U.; mem. Pres. Carter's Commn. on Nat. Agenda for 80s. 1st lt. AUS, 1944-46. Mem. Coun. Fgn. Rels. Clubs: Univ., Blind Brook. Died Aug. 25, 1991 Home: New York N.Y.

PLAUT, WALTER SIGMUND, zoology educator; b. Darmstadt, Germany, Nov. 21, 1923; came to U.S., 1939; s. Adolf and Gerty (Pfaelzer) P.; m. Nicole Colen, Aug. 16, 1953; children: Andrea, Eric, Miriam, Jessica. B.A., Rutgers U., 1949; M.S., U. Wis., 1950, Ph.D., 1952. Research assoc. U. Calif.-Berkeley, 1954-56; asst. prof. botany U. Wis., Madison, 1956-60, assoc. prof. zoology, 1960-65, prof., 1965—, chmn. zoology, 1978-86, chmn. biology core curriculum, 1970—. Served with U.S. Army, 1942-45, ETO. NIH postdoctoral fellow London, 1952, Lund, Sweden, 1953; vis. prof. Ford Found., Lima, Peru, 1970, U. Sao Paulo, Ribeirao Preto, Brazil, 1974. Mem. Am. Soc. Cell Biology. Home: Madison Wis. Deceased. †

PLESSET, MILTON SPINOZA, physicist, fluid dynamicist, educator; b. Pitts., Feb. 7, 1908; s. Benjamin Milton and Anna (Schwartz) P.; m. Isabel Avis Rosanoff, Mar. 28, 1934 (dec. Aug. 1985); children—Michael Rosanoff, Jean Ann Gray, Marjorie Leva, Judith Else. B.S., U. Pitts., 1929, M.S., 1930; Ph.D., Yale U., 1932. Instr. theoretical physics U. Rochester, N.Y., 1935-40; head analytical group research lab. Douglas Aircraft Co., Santa Monica, Calif., 1942-45; prof. Calif. Inst. Tech., Pasadena, 1963-78, prof. emeritus, 1978-91; adj. prof. UCLA, from 1976; researcher Bohr Inst., Denmark; cons. to dir. Naval Ordance Test St., Pasadena, 1945-48; cons. Gen. Motors Research Lab., Detroit, 1955-70, Electric Power Research Inst., Palo Alto, Calif., 1971-75, U.S. Nuclear Regulatory Commn., Washington, from 1983. Editor: Transient Two-Phase Flows-OECD Conf., 1981; contbr. articles to profl. jours. Mem. sci. adv. bd. U.S. Air Force, Washington, 1951-53; mem. sci. adv. council State of Calif., Sacramento, 1959-61; mem. adv. panel in mechs. Nat. Bur. Standards, Washington, 1959-63, mem. adv. com. reactor safeguards U.S. Nuclear Regulatory Commn., Washington, 1975-82, chmn., 1980. Fellow Am. Phys. Soc. (mem. exec. com. fluids dynamics div. 1963-72), ASME (chmn. exec. com. 1965-67, chmn exec. com fluids engring. div. 1971-72); mem. Am. Nuclear Soc., Nat. Acad. Engring. Democrat. Home: San Marino Calif. Died Feb. 19, 1991; buried Mt. Sinai Meml. Pk., L.A.

PLUMMER, GLADYS EMILY SERENA, religious organization executive; b. N.Y.C., May 17, 1894; d. Carl and Elena (De La Pena) Mueller; m. George W. Plummer, Dec. 25, 1936 (dec. Jan. 1944). Student, Columbia U., 1927. Sec.-gen. Soc. Rosicruciana in Am. (Soc. Rosicrucians, Inc.), N.Y.C., 1933-44, pres. for life, also pres. Met. Consistory, from 1944; lectr. on Christian mysticism and metaphysics; mem. Sem. Bibl. Rsch., N.Y.C. Author books, pamphlets and lessons on Rosicrucian philosophy. Trustee Holy Orthodox Ch. in Am. *

POBOISK, DONALD PAUL, agricultural products company executive; b. St. Paul, Apr. 24, 1926; s. David Peter and Daphne (Mulvaney) P.; m. JoAnn Amunson, July 26, 1952; 1 son, David Arthur. BA, U. Minn., 1951; MA, Fletcher Sch. Law and Diplomacy, 1953; postgrad., NYU Grad. Sch. Bus. Administrn., 1954. Fgn. affairs officer Dept. State, Washington, 1951-52; financial analyst Standard Oil Co. (N.J.), N.Y.C., 1953-56; asst. sec., asst. treas. Minn. & Ont. Paper Co., Mpls., 1956-64; mgr. internat. devel. Boise (Idaho) Cascade Corp., 1964-66; asst. treas. Archer Daniels Midland Co., Mpls., 1966-68; treas. Archer Daniels Midland Co., Decatur, Ill., 1969-89, also v.p., 1973-86, treas., chief fin. officer, 1986-89, also chmn. audit com., bd. dirs.; bd. dirs. Magna Group, Inc., Millikin Nat. Bank. Served with CIC AUS, 1945-47. Mem. Phi Beta Kappa, Phi Delta Theta. Clubs: Decatur, Decatur Country, Southside Country. Home: Decatur Ill. Died Mar. 17, 1989.

POELKER, JOHN HENRY, mayor; b. St. Louis, Apr. 14, 1913; s. John G. and Anna (Bongner) P.; m. Ruth Cambron, Oct. 19, 1940; children: John S., Susan M., Kathy M. Student, St. Louis U., 1930-34. Sales corr., asst. to div. sales mgr. Nat. Ammonia div. E.I. duPont de Nemours Co., Inc., St. Louis, 1930-42; spl. agt. FBI, 1942-53; city assessor City of St. Louis, 1953-56, city comptr., 1957-73, mayor, 1973-77. Mem. Internat. Assn. Assessing Officers, Mcpl. Fin. Officers Assn., Nat. Assn. Accts. Democrat. Home: Saint Louis Mo. Died Feb. 9, 1990.

POISTER, R(ALPH) S(EYMOUR), steel company executive; b. Kent, Ohio, Mar. 2, 1893; s. Frederick Emil and Carrie (Seymour) P.; m. Beatrice Jeavons, Nov. 3, 1915 (dec.); children: John J., Patricia. Student, Case Sch. Applied Sci., 1915. Dir. Chromium Mining and Smelting Corp. Ltd., Montreal, Que., Can.; v.p., bd. dirs. Salem Brosius Co., Carnegie, Pa. Mem. Am. Iron and Steel Inst., Iron and Steel Inst. Eng., 1st Iron Works Assn., Newcomen Soc. Eng. (Am. branch), Duquesne Club (Pitts.), Edgeworth Club, Sigma Alpha Epsilon. Republican. *

POLAND, REGINALD, museum director; b. Providence, Sept. 28, 1893; s. William Carey and Clara (Harkness) P.; m. Mary Helen Bare, Oct. 28, 1922. AB,

Brown U., 1914, DFA (hon.), 1949; MA, Princeton U., 1915, Harvard U., 1917. Dir. Denver Art Assn., 1919-21; ednl. dir. Detroit Inst. Arts, 1921-25; dir. San Diego Art Gallery, 1926-50, Norton Gallery, 1952-54; dir. museums Atlanta, 1954-63, emeritus, from 1963. Bd. dirs. Spanish Village, San Diego, 1939-50, pres., 1941-45; bd. dirs. San Diego Mus. of Man, San Diego Symphony Assn.; bd. dirs. Globe Theatre, pres., 1946-50; v.p. Atlanta Civic Ballet; bd. dirs. Atlanta Festival of Arts, 1962-64. Decorated Royal Order Kingdom of Spain; recipient gold medal Calif. Pacific Internat. Expn., 1935; Carl Schurtz fellow, 1936, fellow for study in Germany, 1958. Mem. Am. Assn. Art Mus. Dirs., Western Assn. Art Mus. Dirs. (past pres.), Atlanta Art Assn. (sec.), San Diego Art Guild, La Jolla Art Ctr., Phi Beta Kappa. *

POLK, JAMES HILLIARD, consultant, military officer; b. Philippine Islands, Dec. 13, 1911; s. Harding and Esther (Fleming) P.; m. Josephine Leavell, Nov. 7, 1936; children: Josephine W. Polk Schwartz, Jr., James Hilliard III. BS, U.S. Mil. Acad., 1933; grad., Nat. War Coll., 1952. Commd. 2d lt. U.S. Army, 1933, advanced through grades to gen., 1967, comdr. armored regt. in (Patton's 3rd Army), WWII, 1951; staff officer U.S. Army, Korea, 1951, mem., 1957-59; U.S. comdt. in Berlin during Autobahn crisis U.S. Army, 1963; comdg. gen. U.S. Army, Frankfurt, Germany, 1964-66, Heidleberg,, Europe, 1966-71; ret. U.S. Army, 1971; cons. industry and rsch. agys. including Army Materiel Command System Analysis Agy. Pres. Army Emergency Relief Soc., 1971-92. Decorated D.S.M. with oak leaf cluster, Silver Star with oak leaf cluster, Bronze Star, Legion of Merit with two oak leaf clusters; comdr. Legion of Honor, Croix de Guerre, France, Grand Cross, Germany. Mem. Soc. Cincinnati, Order Carabao, Washington Inst. Fgn. Affairs, Army War Coll. Alumni Assn., U.S. Horse Cavalry Assn. (pres. 1977), Chevey Chase (Md.) Club, Army-Navy Club (Washington). Home: Washington D.C. Died Feb. 17, 1992.

POLLACK, HERBERT, physician, educator, consultant in bio-electromagnetics; b. N.Y.C., June 29, 1905; s. Isaac and Mary (Luntz) P.; m. Ruth Brill, Nov. 14, 1946; children: Jane Sobol, Constance Cohen. B.A., Washington and Lee U., 1925; M.D., Cornell U., 1929; Ph.D., U. Minn., 1933. Diplomate: Am. Bd. Internal Medicine, Am. Bd. Nutrition. Research asst. Wood's Hole Marine Biol. Lab., 1926, 27, 28; instr., research asst. physiology Cornell U. Med. Coll., N.Y.C., 1928, instr. medicine, 1934-40; house officer in pathology New Eng. Deaconess Hosp., 1929-30; Littauer fellow, asst. pathology London Hosp., 1929; house officer in medicine U. Chgo., 1931-32; fellow in medicine Mayo Clinic, 1932-34; asst. physician Mt. Sinai Hosp., N.Y.C., 1934-37, physician in charge metabolism clinic, 1937-40, assoc. physician for metabolism, from 1940; lectr. Columbia Coll. Physicians and Surgeons, N.Y.C., from 1940; sole practice medicine N.Y.C., 1934-60; vis. physician Bellevue Hosp., N.Y.C., 1954; assoc. attending physician Univ. Hosp., N.Y.C., 1954; assoc. prof. clin. medicine NYU Med. Sch., 1954; clin. prof. medicine George Washington U. Med. Sch., Washington, 1964-70, emeritus, 1970-90; chmn. med. adv. com. FAA; cons. in medicine and bio-electromagnetics to numerous orgns. and govtl. agys. Author: Modern Diabetic Care, 1940, Your Diabetes, 1951; assoc. editor: Metabolism Jour., from 1951; mem. editorial bd.: Diabetes Jour., from 1953; mem. editorial: Jour. Nutrition; contbr. articles to profl. jours. Trustee, U.S. Naval Acad. Found. Decorated Bronze Star, Purple Heart; recipient Outstanding Civilian Service medal (2), Dept. Army. Fellow Am. Pub. Health Assn., ACP, N.Y. Acad. Medicine, Am. Heart Assn. (dir. 1956-66); mem. Aerospace Med. Assn., AMA, AAAS, Am. Soc. Clin. Investigation, Am. Inst. Nutrition, Am. Physiol. Soc., Soc. Exptl. Biology and Medicine, Am. Diabetic Assn. (dir.), N.Y. Diabetic Assn. (pres.), Federated Socs. Exptl. Biology (chmn. life scis. adv. com. 1972), Bioelectromagnetics Soc. (charter), Phi Beta Kappa, Sigma Xi. Clubs: Overseas Press (N.Y.C.), Harmonie (N.Y.C.); Cosmos (Washington), Metropolitan (Washington), Army-Navy (Washington); Chevy Chase (Md.); Washington Inst. Fgn. Affairs. Home: Washington D.C. Died Jan. 2, 1990; buried Long Island, N.Y.

POLLARD, BRAXTON, educator, advertising executive; b. Hannibal, Mo., Oct. 8, 1908; s. William Braxton and Nancy Elizabeth (Robinson) P.; m. Maj-Britt Larsson, May 29, 1963 (div. 1974); children: Elizabeth Kristina, Braxton Erik W. Student, Washington U., St. Louis, 1926-27; B.J., U. Mo., 1930. Mem. research dept. D'Arcy Advt. Co., 1930-33; dir. publicity Nat. Mark Twain Centennial, 1934-35; writer Selznick Internat. Pictures, Inc., 1935-36; theatre reviewer, feature writer N.Y. Sun, 1936-37; advt. mgr. A.P. Green Co., 1938-47; mem. central advt. dept. Monsanto Chem. Co., 1947-54, mgr. internat. advt., 1954-65, mgr. advt. media, 1965-68, mgr. advt. design and prodn., 1968-69, mgr. corporate promotion, 1969-71; prof. internat. advt. Sch. Journalism, U. Mo., Columbia, from 1971; founder, editor-in-chief Monsanto Internat. mag., 1948-65; condr. workshops for Assn. Nat. Advertisers, also; Am. Mgmt. Assn.; instr. Inst. Advt., St. Louis U., 1951-52. Author: A Basic Guide to International Advertising, 1959, also articles; contbr. to: International and Intercultural Communications, 1976, International Advertising: Practical Considerations, 1986. Publicity chmn. Fgn. Trade Bur., St. Louis C. of C., 1950-60; mem. advt. activities com. 50th Anniversary Celebration, U. Mo. Sch. Journalism, 1959; panel judges McKinsey Found. award Harvard Bus. Rev., 1963; Distinguished lectr. U. Mo. Sch. Journalism 50th Anniversary Celebration, 1959. Recipient Best Mag. Advt. in Japan award, Japan Advt. Assn., 1959. Mem. Internat. Advt. Assn. (Internat. Advt. Man of Year award 1962, Best Chem. advt. award 1954), Assn. Nat. Advertisers, Indsl. Advertisers Assn. (past pres. St. Louis), Hist. Soc. Mo., Municipal Theatre Assn. St. Louis, Kappa Sigma, Kappa Tau Alpha. Baptist. Home: Saint Louis Mo. Deceased. †

POLLARD, WARREN RANDOLPH, transportation company executive; b. Jersey City, 1898; s. Charles Edwin and Addie Drake (Moore) P.; m. Margie Belle Taylor, June 22, 1920; children: Warren Randolph, Charles Alec. BSEE, Ga. Inst. Tech., 1920. Student engr. GE, Schenectady, 1920-22; engr. Ga. Power Co., Atanta, 1922-33; supr. automobile equipment Ga. Power Co., Atlanta, 1933-38; mgt. transp. in charge streetcar and bus svc. Ga. Power Co., Atlanta, Augusta, Macon, Columbus, Rome, Ga., 1938-46; chmn. bd. Va. cos., from 1964; pres., bd. dirs. United Transit Co.; bd. dirs. Cen. Nat. Bank Richmond, Va., Am. Transp. Enterprises. Co-chmn. campaign ARC, Atlanta, 1945, gen. campaign, Richmond, 1949; pres. Community Chese, 1951. Recipient Silver Beaver award Boy Scouts Am. Mem. Am. Transit Assn. (pres. 1948-49, bd. dirs.), U.S. C. of C., Richmond C. of C. (past bd. dirs.), Va.'s Sr. Golf Assn., Commonwealth Club, Country Club Va., Masons, Chi Phi. Episcopalian. *

POLLEY, JOSEPH CRAWFORD, mathematics educator; b. Cheshire, Conn., Aug. 17, 1897; s. James Clarence and Lillie Harkness (Jimmerson) P.; m. Mildred Miles Richardson, Sept. 8, 1923; children: Barbara Miles Polley Smith, Elizabeth Anne Polley Martin. AB, Yale U., 1921, AM, 1923; PhD, Cornell U., 1929. Tchr. math. Roxbury Sch., 1921-22, West Haven (Conn.) High Sch., 1922-23, Cascadilla Sch., Ithaca, N.Y., 1927-28; instr. Yale U., New Haven, 19222-23, Colgate U., 1923-27, Cornell U., Ithaca, 1928-29; prof. math Wabash Coll., Crawfordville, Ind., from 1929, head dept., 1929-63; prof. Biarritz (France) Am. U., 1945-46; asst. chief reading U.S. Armed Forces Inst., Frankfurt, Germany, 1946; chmn. Ind. Sch. and Coll. Com. on Math., 1959-63. Elder Presbyn. Ch. Fellow AAAS, Ind. Acad. Sci.; mem. Math. Assn. Am. (past bd. govs.), Am. Math. Soc., Ouiatenon Club, Masons, Sigma Xi, Lambda Chi Alpha. *

POLLOCK, DAVIS ALLEN, insurance company executive; b. Douds, Iowa, Aug. 31, 1942; s. David Edwin and Bertha Dorothy (Barker) P.; children: Eric, Kirsten. BS, Drake U., 1964; exec. program, Stanford U., 1984. Various positions Cen. Life Assurance Co., Des Moines, 1964-73, asst. actuary, 1973-77, v.p., 1977-79, v.p. corp. planning, 1979-82, v.p. corp. devel., 1989; sr. v.p. group Cen. Life Assurance Co., Madison, Wis., 1982-87, exec. v.p. employee benefits, 1987-89; bd. dirs. Meriter Health Enterprises, Inc., Elderhouse, Health Care Assocs. Chmn. visioning com. Methodist Ch., Des Moines, 1978-79, pastor parish com., 1980; coach various youth sports; tutor for underprivileged children. Fellow Soc. Actuaries (edn. com. 1975-79); mem. Am. Acad. Actuaries, Des Moines Actuaries Club (pres. 1980), Phi Eta Sigma, Omicron Delta Kappa, Kappa Mu Epsilon. Republican. Lodge: Masons. Home: Madison Wis. Died Sept. 28, 1990; buried Zion Luth. Cemetery, Douds, Iowa.

POMUS, DOC (JEROME SOLON FELDER), songwriter, performer, record producer, journalist; b. Bklyn., June 27, 1925; s. Morris and Millie (Goldstein) Felder; m. Wilma Rose Burke, June 27, 1957 (div. 1967); children: Sharyn Ruth, Geoffrey John. Student, Bklyn. Coll., 1942-45. Rec. artist After Hours, Coral, Savoy, Derby, Chess labels, 1943-55; ind. songwriter, 1955-91. Co-editor: Whiskey, Women and, 1984-91; songwriter: Teenager In Love, Hushabye, Save the Last Dance for Me (Broadcast Music, Inc. award), This Magic Moment (Broadcast Music, Inc. award), Can't Get Used to Losing You (Broadcast Music, Inc. award), His Latest Flame, Little Sister, Surrender, Suspicion, Sweets for My Sweet, others. Bd. of govs. R&B Found., Washington. Named Songwriter of Yr. Acad. of Blues, 1980, 81; inducted into Hall of Fame, N.Y. Music Awards, 1985; winner Grammy award, 1981; recipient numerous awards Broadcast Music, Inc. Mem. Nat. Acad. Rec. Arts and Scis. (bd. govs. Hall of Fame 1985-87). Democrat. Home: New York N.Y. Died Mar. 14, 1991. †

POOLE, JOHN BAYARD, broadcasting executive, lawyer; b. Chgo., May 17, 1912; s. John Eugene and Edna (Carpenter) P.; m. Evelyn Singer, Apr. 10, 1979; 1 child, Leah Kathleen. Student, U. Chgo., 1929-32; LL.B., Detroit Coll. Law, 1936, J.D., 1968. Bar: Mich. 1936. Partner Poole, Littell & Sutherland, Detroit, 1936-76; of counsel Butzel, Long, Gust, Klein & VanZile, 1976-79, 84; chmn. exec. com. Capital Cities Communications, 1960-64; chmn. Poole Broadcasting Co. (WJRT-TV), Flint, Mich., WPRI-TV, Providence, WTEN-TV, Albany, N.Y.; sec., v.p., dir. Storer Broadcasting Co., Detroit, 1945-55; dir. Knight Ridder Newspapers, Inc., 1978-84, Mich. Nat. Bank of Detroit, 1964-82, dir. Mich. Nat. Corp., 1972-82. Pres., chmn., trustee William Beaumont Hosp., 1960-84; trustee U. Chgo., from 1974, Cranbrook Ednl. Community, 1976-79. Fellow Am. Bar Found.; mem. ABA, Detroit Bar Assn., Mich. Bar Assns., Am. Judicature Soc. Episcopalian (vestryman 1959-62). Clubs: Bloomfield Hills Country (bd. govs., pres.); Indian Creek Country, Surf (Miami). Home: Bloomfield Hills Mich. Died Apr. 14, 1989; buried White Chapel Cemetery, Troy, Mich.

POOLEY, ROBERT C(ECIL), English language educator; b. Bklyn., Mar. 25, 1989; s. Cecil Silas Webb and Charlotte Lillian (Groser) P.; m. Lucile Mae Setzler, Aug. 29, 1927; children: Robert Neville, Alan Setzler. Student, Gen. Theol. Sem., 1922-24; AB, Colo. Coll. Edn., 1926, AM, 1927; PhD, U. Wis., 1932. Teaching fellow Colo. Coll. Edn., 1926, asst. prof., 1927-31; asst. prof. English, U. Wis., Madison, 1931-35, assoc. prof., 1935-40, prof., from 1940, chmn. dept. integrated liberal studies, 1947-63, dir. Wis. English curriculum project, from 1963; spl. cons. on English preinduction tng. br. Army Svc. Forces, 1941-43; chmn. Nat. Com. on Gen. Edn., 1949-50; curiculum cons. Lebanon Valley Coll., Jamestown Coll., Beloit Coll. Author: Teaching English Usage, 1946, Teaching English Grammar, 1957; editor: America Reads; contbg. editor Lit. and Life; also articles to profl. jours. and encys. Recipient W. Wilbur Hatfield award, 1952. Mem. Nat. Conf. on Rsch. in English (pres. 1938), Nat. Coun. Tchrs. English (pres. 1941, dir. publs. until 1952), Am. Dialect Soc., Wis. English Tchrs. Assn. (pres. 1936), Univ. Club, Phi Kappa Phi, Phi Delta Kappa, Pi Kappa Delta, Phi Kappa Tau. Episcopalian. *

PORTER, DAVID STEWART, federal judge; b. Cin., Sept. 23, 1909; s. Charles Hamilton and Caroline (Pemberton) P.; m. Marjorie Bluett Ellis, July 26, 1956; children by previous marriage—Mary Stewart, Margaret Lee, Elizabeth Sue. A.B., U. Cin., 1932, J.D., 1934. Bar: Ohio bar 1934. Practice in Troy, 1936-49; judge Common Pleas Ct., Miami County, Ohio, 1949-66; U.S. dist. judge So. Dist., Ohio, 1966-79, sr. dist. judge, from 1979; Active Ohio Jud. Conf.; past pres. Ohio Common Pleas Judges Assn.; faculty adviser Nat. Coll. State Trial Judges, 1964-65. Past bd. dirs. Ohio Blue Cross, Dettmer Hosp., Troy; elder Presbyn. Ch. Mem. Am., Ohio, Cin. and Miami County bar assns., Am. Judicature Soc. Home: Cincinnati Ohio Died Jan. 5, 1989; Riverside Cemetery, Troy, Ohio.

PORTER, ELIOT FURNESS, photographer; b. Winnetka, Ill., Dec. 6, 1901; s. James Foster and Ruth Wadsworth (Furness) P.; m. Marian Brown, 1927 (div. 1934); children: Eliot Furness, Charles Anthony; m. Aline Kilham, May 8, 1936; children: Jonathan, Stephen, Partick Eliot. BS, Harvard U., 1924, MD, 1929; DFA (hon.), Colby Coll., 1969; LittD (hon.), U. Albuquerque, 1974; DFA (hon.), U. New Mex., 1987. Tchr. biochemistry and bacteriology Harvard, also Radcliffe Coll., 1929-39; engaged in photography, from 1939; Asso. fellow Morse Coll., Yale, 1967; bd. dirs. Sierra Club, until 1971. Exhbns. include Stielglitz's An Am. Place, 1939, Mus. Modern Art, 1943, 52, George Eastman House, Rochester, N.Y., 1960, Art Inst. Chgo., 1953, Nelson Gallery, Kansas City, Mo., 1959, Met. Mus. Art, N.Y.C., 1979, N.Y.C., 1986, numerous others.; published books include: In Wildness is the Preservation of the World, 1962, The Place No One Knew-Glen Canyon on the Colorado, 1963, Forever Wild—The Adirondacks, 1966, Summer Island, 1966, Baja California—the Geography of Hope, 1967, Galapagos, The Flow of Wildness, 1968, Down the Colorado, 1969, Appalachian Wilderness, 1970, (with Peter Matthiesson) African Experience, The Tree Where Man was Born, 1972, Birds of North America—A Personal Selection, 1972, Moments of Discovery, Adventures with American Birds, 1977, Antarctica, 1978, Intimate Landscapes, 1979, (with Peter Levi) The Greek World, 1980, (with Wallace Stegner) American Places, 1981, (with Jonathan Porter) All under Heaven, 1983, Eliot Porter's Southwest, 1985, Maine, 1986, Eliot Porter, 1987, (with Ellen Auerbach) Mexican Churches, 1987, The West, 1988, (with Jonathan Porter) Iceland, 1989, (with James Gleick) Nature's Chaos, 1990, (with Auerbach) Mexican Celebrations, 1990, (with Wilma Stern) Monuments of Egypt, 1990; also contbr. books ornithology, natural history. Recipient Conservation Service award U.S. Dept. Interior, 1967; Maine Commn. on Arts and Humanities award, 1968; Disting. Son of Maine award, 1969; Newhouse citation Syracuse U., 1973; Gov.'s award N.Mex. Arts Commn., 1976; Kulturpreis Deutschen Gesellschaft für Photographie, 1982; Guggenheim fellow, 1941, 46. Fellow Am. Acad. Arts and Scis.; mem. Am. Ornithol. Union, Cooper, Wilson ornithol. socs., Sierra Club. Home: Corrales N.Mex. Died Nov. 2, 1990; cremated.

PORTER, JOHN BYRON, paper manufacturing company executive; b. West Swanzey, N.H., Aug. 17, 1896; s. John Byron and Flora M. (Ball) P.; m. Elisabeth Malvessi, Jan. 1, 1925; 1 child, John Ball. BCS cum laude, NYU, 1923. Asst. sec. Union Bag & Paper Corp., 1930-39, asst. compt., 1939-50, budget dir., 1949-50, compt., 1950-56, v.p., from 1956. Lt. U.S. Army, 1917-19. Mem. Fin. Execs. Inst., Nat. Assn. Cost Accts., Masons, Delta Mu Delta. *

PORTER, ROBERT WILLIAM, federal judge; b. Monmouth, Ill., Aug. 13, 1926; s. William Benson and Vieva Laurel (Drew) P.; m. Lois Virginia Freeman, July 4, 1956; children: Robert William, William Benson, John David. A.B. cum laude, Monmouth Coll., 1949; J.D., U. Mich., 1952. Bar: Tex. 1953. Home office counsel Res. Life Ins. Co., Dallas, 1952-54; assoc. and ptnr. Thompson, Coe, Cousins, & Irons, Dallas, 1954-74; judge U.S. Dist. Ct., No. Dist., Dallas, 1974-89, chief judge, 1987-89; now sr. status, 1990; spl. counsel County of Dallas, 1972-74; lectr. Robert A. Taft Inst. of Govt., U. Tex., Arlington, 1972-73. Vice chmn. bd. trustees Lamplighter Sch. Inc., 1967-74, councilman, Richardson, Tex., 1965-66, mayor pro tem., 1966, mayor, 1967; pres. Tex. Assn. Mayors, Councilmen and Commrs., 1965-66, Greater County League of Municipalities, 1966-67; mem. exec. com. N. Central Tex. Council of Govts., 1966-67, 70-72, regional citizen rep., 1967-72; mem. Dallas County Election Bd., 1972-74; original conferee Goals for Dallas, chmn. neighboring communities com., mem. task force com., vice chmn. task force on transp. and communications, chmn. achievement com. for transp. and communications, 1965-74; mem. State Rep. Exec. Com., 1966-68; chmn. Task Force on Modernization of State and Local Govts., 1967; dep. state chmn. Rep. Party of Tex., 1969-71; Dallas County Rep. chmn., 1972-74; mem. adv. council S.W. Center Advanced Study, 1966-69; trustee Lamplighter, 1977-85. Served in USN, 1944-46, PTO. Recipient Disting. Alumni award City of Richardson, 1967, Disting. Citizen's award North Cen. Tex. Coun. of Govts., 1972. Mem. Tex. Bar Assn., Barristers Soc., U. Mich. Law Sch. Alumni Assn., Delta Theta Phi (Disting. Sv. Award 1974), Alpha Tau Omega. Presbyterian. Home: Dallas Tex. Died Nov. 1991. †

PORTER, SYLVIA, author, columnist; b. Patchogue, L.I., N.Y., June 18, 1913; d. Loius and Rose (Maisel) Feldman; m. Reed R. Porter, 1931; m. Sumner C. Collins, 1943; 1 child, Cris Sarah; 1 stepson, Sumner Campbell Collins; m. James F. Fox, 1979. BA magna cum laude, Hunter Coll., 1932; postgrad., NYU, 1933; 16 hon. degrees. Founder weekly news letter (Reporting on Govts.), 1934; columnist N.Y. Post, 1935-77; columnist Your Money N.Y. Daily News, from 1978; syndicated columnist L.A. Times Syndicate; chmn. Sylvia Porter Orgn., Inc., 1987-91. Editor in chief: Sylvia Porter's Personal Fin. mag., 1983-89; author: How to Live Within Your Income, 1984, Sylvia Porter's Income Tax Guide, 1960—, How to Get More for Your Money, 1961, Sylvia Porter's Money Book-How to Earn It, Spend It, Save It, Invest It, Borrow It, and Use It to Better Your Life, 1975, paperback edit., 1976, Sylvia Porter's New Money Book for the 80's, 1979, paperback edit., 1981, Sylvia Porter's Your Own Money, 1983, Love and Money, 1985, Your Financial Security, 1988, Sylvia Porter's Your Finances in the 1990s, 1990. Named one of Am.'s 25 Most Influential Women World Almanac, 1977-82; Woman of the Decade Ladies Home Jour., 1979. Mem. Phi Beta Kappa. Home: Pound Ridge N.Y. Died June 6, 1991; cremated.

PORTER, VERNON CARROLL, artist, educational administrator; b. Cleve., Aug. 6, 1896; s. James and Anna (Brockman) P.; m. Beata Beach, Sept. 39, 1937. Student, Art Students League, 1926-34, Art Sch. Paris, 1926, Bklyn. Poly. Inst., 1941. Freelance artist designer, N.Y.C., 1925-32; asst. to dir. Whitney Mus. Am. Art, N.Y.C., 1932-35; gallery dir. Am. Fine Arts Soc., N.Y.C., 1935-38; dir. Riverside Mus., N.Y.C., 1938-48; asst. dir. Art Students League N.Y., N.Y.C., 1949-50; dir. Nat. Acad. Sch. Fine Arts, NAD, N.Y.C., from 1950; pioneer 1st outdoor art exhbn. in U.S., Washington Square, N.Y.C., 1932. Author mus. notes, catalogue forwards and critical revs. Chmn. Artists Aid Com. Mem. Am. Fine Arts Soc. (trustee), Art Students League (life). *

PORTERFIELD, JAMES H., public relations company executive; b. Willow Bend, W.Va., Sept. 21, 1910; s. Isaac L. and Roxie L. (Fisher) P.; m. Irene Smith, Oct. 4, 1930; children: Christopher, Karen. B.A. in Journalism, W.Va. U., 1936. Reporter Morgantown (W.Va.) Post, 1936-37; city editor-mng. editor Morgantown Dominion-News, 1937; successively reporter, writer, state editor AP, Phila., 1937-43; writer-editor AP, N.Y.C., 1943-47; account exec., then v.p., account exec. Carl Byoir & Assos., Inc., N.Y.C., 1947-65; exec. v.p. Carl Byoir & Assocs., Inc., 1965-83; also dir. Author articles, detective stories. Recipient Perley Isaac Reed achievement award W.Va. U., 1977. Mem. Pub. Relations Soc. Am. (chmn. counselors sect. 1977, citation meritorious service counselors sect. 1976, chmn.'s citation 1977). Episcopalian. Home: Fort Myers Fla. Died Sept. 24, 1989; cremated.

POSSUM, PETER EVER, physics educator; b. Meridean, Wis., Aug. 30, 1895; s. Ole Johnson and Lena (Nelson) F.; m. May Battles, Aug. 16, 1925 (dec. 1936); 1 child, James Richard; m. Almeda Anderson, June 30, 1937; children: John Anthony, Steven Paul. AB, St. Olaf Coll., Northfield, Minn., 1919; AM, U. Wis., 1923. Asst. prof. St. Olaf Coll., 1923-30, assoc. prof., 1930-42, prof., 1942-65, dept. chmn., 1945-65, dean of coll., 1951-52; lectr. Waterloo (Ont., Can.) U., 1965-92; lectr. physics U. Minn., 1943-44. Author: Laboratory Physics, 1927. Mem. Northfield City Coun., 1940-44, Sch. Bd., 1945-57. Mem. Am. Phys. Soc., Am. Assn. Physics Tchrs., Optical Soc. Am., Minn. Acad. Sci., Rotary, Sigma Xi, Gamma Alpha. Lutheran. *

POST, L(EON) ABBETT, steel fabricating company executive; b. N.Y.C., July 24, 1897; s. Andrew Jackson and Mary Briggs (Abbett) P.; m. Elsie Rosalie Morrill, Sept. 2, 1922; children: Leon Abbett, Priscilla Elsie. ME, Stevens Inst. Tech., 1918. Assoc. Post and McCord, steel constructors, N.Y.C., 1919-41; with constrn. div. WPB, Washington, 1941-42; exec. v.p. Am. Inst. Steel Constrn., Inc., N.Y.C., 1942-62; v.p. Burrell Tripp Corp., N.Y.C., 1962-63, Allmetal Fabricators, Inc., N.Y.C., fromm 1963. Ensign, naval aviator USNR, 1918-19. Mem. Univ. Club, Chi Chi. Republican. Episcopalian. *

POSTON, GRETCHEN, public relations executive, conference and special events planner; b. Mpls., Feb. 14, 1932; d. George and Katharene (Walsh) Houselander; m. Raymond L. Poston, Jr., Dec. 30, 1960; children: Jeffrey, Carol, Ramsey , Katharene. BS, St. Mary's Coll., Leavenworth, Kans., 1952. Sch. tchr. Mo., France, Germany and Va., 1952-60; co-founder, spl. events organizer WashingtonInc., 1965-89; co-founder Wonderful Weddings, Inc., 1965-77; social sec. to White House, Washington, 1977-81; organizer social events Dem. Nat. Convs., 1964, 72, 76; spokesperson Ky. Fried Chicken, Spiegel Catalogue. Author: (with others) The Wonderful Wedding Workbook, 1966. Bd. dirs. St. Mary's Coll.; spokesperson Distilled Spirits Coun. Roman Catholic. Home: Washington D.C. Died Jan. 6, 1992; buried Arlington Nat. Cemetery.

POTTER, CHARLES JACKSON, coal mining company executive; b. Greenfield, Mo., July 16, 1908; s. Henry Arthur and Effie May (Evans) P.; m. Jane Elizabeth Griffith, Jan. 24, 1948; children: Susan, Charles, Carolyn. B.S., U. Mo.-Rolla, 1929, M.S., 1930; Ph.D., W.Va. U., 1932; D.Eng. (hon.), U. Mo., 1950; LL.D. (hon.), Indiana U. Pa., 1982. Combustion engr. Continental Coal Co., Fairmont, W.Va., 1934-38; chief mktg. div. Dept. Interior, Washington, 1938-40; with Rochester & Pittsburgh Coal Co., Indiana, Pa., 1940-89, chmn., 1970-89; dep. adminstr. Solid Fuels Adminstrn., Washington, 1943-46; dir. Savs. & Trust Co. of Pa., Rochester & Pittsburgh Coal Can., United Eastern Coal Sales Corp. Trustee Indiana U. Pa.; bd. govs. Pa. System Higher Edn. Recipient Merit medal Pres. Truman; named hon. comdr. Order British Empire. Mem. Am. Inst. Mining and Metall. Engrs. (Erskine Ramsay medal 1975, Howard N. Eavenson award 1976). Republican. Home: Indiana Pa. Died June 10, 1990.

POTTER, RUSSELL SHERWOOD, architect; b. Union, N.J., Aug. 20, 1897; s. David Magie and Rowena (Johnson) P.; m. Louise Erna Burdorf, Dec. 31, 1923; children: Ann Sherwood Potter Pedley), Helen Elizabeth Potter Davis. BS in Architecture, U. Pa., 1918, U. Pa., 1920-21; postgrad., U. Grenoble, France, 1919. With Russell S. Potter,, Cin., 1928-33; ptnr. Potter, Tyler, Martin Y Roth, architects, Cin., from 1933; prof. in charge dept. architecture Miami U., Oxford, Ohio, 193-47; mem. Oho Bd. Examiners Architects, 1948-56. Prin. works include Naval Sci. Bldg., Miami U., 1947-49; East Green Dormitory project Ohio U., 1950-60, West Green Dormitory project, 1960-63, Coll. Edn. Bldg., 1959-61, Space Arts Bldg., 1959-61; Barrows and Bascomb halls Oberlin (Ohio) Coll., 1954-55, East Hall, men's dormitory, South Hall Girls Dormitory and dining facility, 1960-63. With USMC, 1918-19. Fellow AIA; mem. Architects Soc. Ohio (pres. 1947-48). *

POTTS, JAMES MANNING, clergyman; b. Como, N.C., July 14, 1895; s. Reginald Harrell and Annie Christian (Moore) P.; m. Agnes Wilson Wright, Dec. 23, 1961; children: Anne Wilson (dec.), Reginald Harrell, James Manning Jr., Joseph Christian, Katherine Coleman (dec.), Agnes Withers. BA, Randolph-Macon Coll., 1917, Randolph-Macon Coll., 1920; DD, Randolph-Macon Coll., 1935; ThB, Princeton U., 1924, ThM, 1925; postgrad, U. Va., U. Chgo.; Litt.D., Ewha Woman's U., Seoul, Korea, 1961. Ordained to ministry Meth. Ch., 1927. Tchr. John Marshall High Sch., Richmond, Va., 1917-19; fellow in apologetics and Christian ethics Princeton (N.J.) U. Theol. Sem., 1925; pastor Berryman Ch., Richmond, 1926-30, Trinity Ch., Petersburg, Va., 1930-32, Barton Heights Ch., Richmond, 1932-35; poastor Greene Meml. Chl, Roanoke, Va., 1940-44; dist. supt. Richmond dist. Meth. Ch., 1935-40; assoc. dir., also editor publs. Crusade for Christ, Chgo., 1944-48; editor The Upper Room Pulpit, 1948-56, The Upper Room and Upper Room Radio and TV Parish, from 1948; mem. exec. com. TV, Radio and Film Commn., Meth. Ch., 1952-64, missionary sec. Va. Conf., 1932-35, mem. bds. and coms., 1940-48; exec. sec. Meth. Advance, 1938-50; mem. gen. bd. Nat. Coun. Chs. Christ, 1952-55, mem. broadcasting and film commn., 1952-65; del. World Coun. Chs. and World Christian Broadcasting Assn., New Delhi, 1961; mem. Meth. Gen. Confs., 1938, 40, 44, chmn. Va. del., 1940, 44; Va. chmn. Uniting Conf. Meth. Ch., 1939, Copenhagen, 1939, Oxford, 1951; numerous others. Editor: Prayers of the Early Church, Prayers of the Middle Ages, The Letters of Francis Asbury; assoc. editor: The JOurnal of Francis Asbury; mem. editorial bd. Selections from Letters of John Wesley, Francis Asbury, John Woolman, History of American Methodism, Listening to the Saints, Grace Sufficient; contbr. articles on early Va. Methodism and devetional lit. Trustee Randolph-Macon Coll. Fellow Internat. Meth. Hist. Soc. (v.p., exec. com.); mem. Am. Acad. Polit. and Social Sci., Southeastern Jurisdictional Hist. Soc. (pres.), World Meth. Coun. (exec. com.), Nat. Coun. on Family Rels., Nat. Midcentury Com. for Children and Youth, Wesley Hist. Soc. (London), Assn. Meth. Hist. Socs. (exec. com.), Adv. Coun. on Naval Affairs, Tau Kappa Alpha, Omicron Delta Kappa, Theta Phi, Kappa Alpha. *

POUDER, GEORGE HARRY, editor; b. Balt., May 11, 1896; s. George H. and Ellen Jane (Owens) P.; m. Elizabeth Cabell Noland, Oct. 6, 1928 (dec. Sept. 1956); m. Joanna Douglas Coulter, June 1, 1957. BS, Johns Hopkins U., 1926. Instr. fgn. trade and ocean shipping Johns Hopkins U., Balt.; reporter, spl. writer Balt. Sun and Evening Sun, 1920-30; dir. export and import bur. Balt. Assn. Commerce, 1926-49, exec. v.p., 1930-61; drama critic Gardens, Houses and People mag., 1943-59; editor Balt. mag., 1949-64; trade adviser Nat. Fgn. Trade Coun.; compt. Vagabond Theatre, Balt. sect. Citizens Emergency Relief Com., 1931; mem. Nat. Adv. Com. on Fgn. Svc., 1933. Author poems, articles, essays, and book revs. Treas. Balt. Emergency Commn., 1933-36; mem. Balt. Aviation Commn., 1938-44; chmn. info. Balt. Civilian Moblzn.; chmn. Balt. Emergency Port Commn., 1942-45; chmn. commerce and industry Balt. CD Com., 1944-45; dir. Employers Adv. Coun., 1945-47; chmn. Balt. Home Md., from 1962; treas. United Seamen's Svc., 1942-46; truste Balt. Mcpl. (Peale) Mus.; consul of Denmark, 1949-54. With U.S. Army, 1917-19, AEF in France. Recipient Outstanding Mgmt. award Soc. for Acvancement Mgmt., 1958. Mem. Md. Hist. Soc. (chmn. maritime collection), Balt. Soc. Consuls, Am. Assn. Port Authorities, SAR, Charcoal Club (pres. from 1943), Balt. Country, Johns Hopkins Club. Baptist. *

POULSON, DONALD FREDERICK, research biologist, educator; b. Idaho Falls, Ida., Oct. 5, 1910; s. Christian Frederick and Esther (Johnson) P.; m. Margaret Judd Boardman, June 18, 1934; children: Donald Boardman, Christian Frederick II. B.S., Calif. Inst. Tech., 1933, Ph.D., 1936; M.A., Yale U., 1955. Teaching fellow biology Calif. Inst. Tech., 1934-36, Gosney research fellow biology, 1949; research asst. dept. embryology Carnegie Inst. Washington, 1936-37; instr. biology Yale U., 1937-40, asst. prof., 1940-46, asso. prof., 1946-55, prof., 1955-81, prof. emeritus and sr. rsch. biologist, 1981-89, chmn. dept. biology, 1962-65; rsch. collaborator Brookhaven Nat. Lab., 1951-55; Fulbright com. NRC, 1958-60; Central qualifications bd. Nat. Insts. Health, 1961-63. Author: The Embryonic Development of Drosophila Melanogaster, 1937; contbr. Biology of Drosophila, 1950; Contbr. articles sci. jours. Citizen amb. genetics del. People to People, People's Republic of China, 1987. Fellow Calhoun Coll., Yale U., 1954; Fulbright sr. research scholar Commonwealth Sci. and Indsl. Research Orgn., Canberra, Australia, 1957-58, 66-67; Guggenheim fellow, 1957-58; Japan Soc. Promotion of Sci. fellow, 1979. Fellow AAAS (council 1960-62); mem. Internat. Soc. Developmental Biologists, Am. Soc. Naturalists (treas. 1951-53), Am. Soc. Zoologists, Genetics Soc. Am., Soc. Developmental Biology, Conn. Acad. Arts and Scis., Sigma Xi. Home: Orange Conn. Died Dec. 7, 1989; cremated.

POUSETTE-DART, RICHARD, artist; b. St. Paul, June 8, 1916; s. Nathaniel and Flora Pousette-D.; m. Evelyn Gracey, June 2, 1946; children: Joanna, Jonathan. Student, Bard Coll., 1934, L.L.D. (hon.), 1965. lectr. Boston Mus. Sch. Fine Arts, 1959, Mpls. Inst. Fine Arts, 1965; instr. painting New Sch. Social Research, 1959-61; prof. art Sarah Lawrence Coll., 1971-74; guest critic Columbia, 1968. Represented in permanent collections Mus. Modern Art, Met. Mus. Art, Pasadena Mus. Art, Whitney Mus. Am. Art, Addison Gallery, Albright-Knox Art Gallery, Buffalo, Hirschhorn Mus. and Sculpture Garden, Washington, Ringling Mus., Sarasota, Fla., U. Nebr., Lincoln, Smithsonian Mus., Washington, Corcoran Gallery Art, Washington, Indpls. Mus. Art, Phillips Collection, Washington, , The Phillips Collection, Washington, The Detroit Mus. Art, also pvt. collections; one-man exhbns. include Artists Gallery, N.Y.C., 1939, Marion Williard Gallery, 1941, 42, 44, 45, Peggy Guggenheim Gallery Art of This Century, 1946, Betty Parsons Gallery, 1948-52, 55, 58, 59, 61, 67, Obelisk Gallery, Boston, 1970, Whitney Mus. Am. Art, 1963, 74-75, Harkus, Krakow, Rosen, Sonnabend Gallery, Boston, 1974, 75, Edwin A. Ulrich Mus. Art, Wichita, Kans., 1975, Allentown (Pa.) Art Mus., 1975, Andrew Crispo Gallery, N.Y.C., 1976, 78, Arts Club Chgo., 1978, Marisa del Rey Gallery, N.Y.C., 1981, 83, 86 Schweyer-Galdo Gallery, Birmingham, Mich., 1982-83, Hope Makler Gallery, Phila., 1984, Virginia Miller Gallery, Coral Gables, Fla., 1985, 86, Mus. of Art, Ft. Lauderdale, Fla., 1986, ACA Galleries, N.Y.C., 1990, Recent Works, 1991, Le Marie Tranier Gallery, Washington, 1992, ACA Gallery,, N.Y.C., 1992; group exhbns. include Pa. Acad. Ann., 1947-48, Whitney Mus. Ann., 1950-51, 53, 56, 57-58, 78, Toledo Mus., 1950-54, Corcoran Gallery, Va. Mus. Fine Arts, Detroit Inst., Chgo. Art Inst., Whitney Mus., 1959, 78, Brooks Meml. Art Gallery, Memphis, John

Heron Art Inst., Indpls., St. Louis City Art Mus., Mus. Legion of Honor, San Francisco, Mus. Modern Art, N.Y.C., 1969, Mpls. Art Mus., Cornell U., Carnegie Internat. Exhbn., Nat. Gallery Art, Washington, 1974, Allentown (Pa.) Art Mus., 1975, Ulrich Mus. Art, Wichita, Kans., 1975, Andrew Crispo Gallery, 1975, 76, 77, 78, 79, Herbert F. Johnson Mus. Art, 1978, Seibu Mus., Tokyo, 1978, Vatican Mus., Rome, 1980, Terra Mus., Evanston, Ill., 1980, Mus. of Art, Uffizzi Mus., Florence, Italy, 1982, Mus. Art Ft. Lauderdale, 1986, Newport Harbor Mus., Newport Beach, Calif., 1986, Los Angeles County Mus. Art, 1986, Solomon R. Guggenheim Mus., N.Y., 1985-87, Met. Mus., N.Y., 1987, Piemonte Dioce, Italy, 1992; decade exhbn., Whitney Mus. of Am. Art, 1973; retrospective exhbn. Whitney Mus. of Am. Art, 1963, Haus der Kunst, Munich, Germany, 1981-82, Los Angeles County Mus. Art, 1982, Indpls. Mus. Art, 1990, Detroit Inst. Art, 1991, Columbus Mus., Ga., 1991, The Phillips collection, Washington, 1991, others, Germany, Japan, S. Am., Rome; travelling exhbn., Mus. Modern Art, 1968-70; mural commn., East Bronx Hosp., 1970, North Bronx Hosp., 1974; selected group show Nat. Gallery Art, 1973, Whitney Mus. Am. Art, Ciba-Geigy Collection Contemporary Paintings, U. Art Mus., U. Tex., Austin, Marisadel Re Gallery, N.Y.C., 1990, ACA Galleries, N.Y.C., 1990, 91, Le Mariē Tranie Gallery, Washington, 1992, Phillips Collection, Washington, 1992, Columbus Mus., Ga., 1991. Recipient Comstock prize Art Inst. Chgo., 1961, silver medal award Corcoran Biennial, Washington, 1965, Nat. Arts Council award, 1966, also others; Guggenheim Found. grantee, 1951; Ford Found. grantee, 1959. Home: Suffern N.Y. Died Oct. 25, 1992. †

POWELL, BENJAMIN HARRISON, IV, corporation executive; b. Huntsville, Tex., Feb. 2, 1915; s. Benjamin Harrison and Marian Leigh (Rather) P.; m. Kitty King Corbett, Aug. 5, 1939; children: Nancy (Mrs. Harvin C. Moore III), Marian (Mrs. James E. Osborne), Benjamin Harrison V, Katherine (Mrs. Archibald Hill IV). B.A., Va. Mil. Inst., 1936; LL.B., U. Tex., 1939; LL.M., Harvard U., 1940. Bar: Tex. bar 1939. With firm Powell, Wirtz, Rauhut & McGinnis (and predecessor), Austin, 1940-41, 46-55; partner Powell, Wirtz, Rauhut & McGinnis (and predecessor), 1947-55; asso. prof. bus. law U. Tex., 1940-41; exec. v.p., dir., gen. counsel Brown & Root, Inc. (and domestic and fgn. subsidiaries), Houston, 1955-80; pres. Bonito Offshore, Inc., 1980-82; sr. chmn. bd. dirs. Am. Nat. Bank, Austin. Trustee George C. Marshall Found. Served to lt. col. U.S. Army, 1941-45. Decorated Legion of Merit. Mem. Phi Delta Phi, Phi Delta Theta, Friars. Episcopalian. Club: Lion (past dir.). Home: Houston Tex. Died Aug. 23, 1989; buried Oakwood Cemetery, Huntsville, Tex.

POWELL, CLILAN BETHANY, physician; b. Suffolk, Va., Aug. 8, 1894; s. Everett and Eliza (Lundy) P.; m. Lena A. Dukes, Oct. 9, 1938. Grad., Va. Normal Coll., 1913; MD, Howard U., 1920. Roentgenologist, 1922; x-ray specialist, N.Y.C., 1922-33; 1st v.p. Victory Mut. Life Ins. Co., 1933, pres., 1940-59; pres. Personal Loan Co., 1935-59; pres., editor N.Y. Amsterdam News, Community Fin. Corp.; chmn. bd. Unity Funeral Homes, N.Y.C., Bklyn., Bronx. Mem. N.Y. State Commn. World's Fair, 1964, 65, N.Y. State Athletic Commn., NAACP, Boys of Yesteryear, also others; asst. publicity dir. Nat. Rep. Campaign Com., 1944. Mem. Omega Psi Phi. *

POWELL, JULIUS CHERRY, university president; b. Harriman, Tenn., Jan. 23, 1926; s. Julius K. and Lucille L. (Cherry) P.; m. Elizabeth D. Case, Nov. 22, 1950; children—Karen, Julia. B.A., U. Ky., 1950, D.Ed., 1970; M.Ed., U. Louisville, 1952. Tchr. Louisville Pub. Sch. System, 1950-57; with Ky. Dept. Edn., 1957-60; exec. asst. to pres. Eastern Ky. U., Richmond, 1960-62, dean bus. affairs, 1962-65, exec. dean, 1965-69, v.p. for adminstrn., 1969-76, pres., 1976-84, pres. emeritus, 1984-88; Mem. Council on Pub. Higher Edn. Served with AUS, 1944-47. Mem. Phi Delta Kappa, Kappa Delta Pi. Democrat. Club: Rotary. Home: Richmond Ky. Died Mar. 16, 1988.

POWERS, ODELL EUGENE, business executive; b. Peoria, Ill., May 2, 1928; s. Clarence O. and Beulah (Fernandez) P.; m. Elizabeth Marie Johnson, Mar. 12, 1950; children: Mark Daniel, Kristin Lynne, Julianne Lynne, Elizabeth M. BS, Bradley U., 1952. Mng. dir. Caterpillar Mitsubishi, Inc., Tokyo, Japan, 1963-67; dir. internat. fin. and adminstrn. Honeywell, Inc., Mpls., 1967-69; v.p. Honeywell, Inc. (Honeywell-Europe), Brussels, 1969-71, exec. v.p., 1971-73; pres., chief exec. officer Turbodyne Corp. div. Studebake-Worthington, Inc., Mpls., 1973-76, chmn. bd., chief exec. officer, 1976-78; chmn. bd., chief exec. officer Worthington Compressors, Inc., Holyoke, Mass, 1976-78; pres., chief operating officer McGraw-Edison Co., Rolling Meadows, Ill., 1979-81, also bd. dirs.; pres., chief operating officer S.J. Groves & Sons Co., Mpls., 1981-83; bd. dirs. Nicolet Instrument Corp., Madison, Wis., from 1983, pres., from 1988, chmn. bd., until 1991; bd. dirs. Internat. Multifoods, Mpls. Trustee emeritus Bradley U.; trustee, treas. YMCA, Mpls. Served with AUS, 1946-47. With U.S. Army, late 1940's. Republican. Presbyterian. Clubs: Mpls.; Met. (N.Y.C.) ; Tucson Country, Tucson Nat.; Minikahda Country (Minn.); Maple Bluff Country, Madison (Madison, Wis.). Home: Minnetonka Minn. Died Dec. 11, 1991; buried Lakewood Cemetery, Mpls.

POWERS, SAMUEL JOSEPH, JR., lawyer; b. Ellicott City, Md., July 26, 1917; s. Samuel J. and Irene (McDonald) P.; m. Marion W. Locke, Jan. 15, 1945 (dec. 1979); children: Richard S., Thomas E.; m. Lillian R. Rooney, Oct. 21, 1981. AB, Loyola Coll., Balt., 1939; JD, Cath. U. Am., 1942. Bar: Fla. 1946, D.C. 1972. Pvt. practice law Miami, Fla.; of counsel Blackwell & Walker, 1946-85; mcpl. judge City North Miami, 1952-53; asst. atty. gen., 1969-70; counsel to Pres. Nixon in case Hon. John J. Sirica, U.S. Dist. Ct., D.C. vs. Richard M. Nixon, Pres. of U.S., 1973. Lt. with USNR, 1942-45. Fellow Am. Coll. Trial Lawyers, Am. Coll. Probate Counsel, Am. Bar Found.; mem. ABA, Fla. Bar Assn. (chmn. bar grievance com. 1957), D.C. Bar Assn., Fed. Bar Assn., Dade County Bar Assn. (pres., past dir., mem. exec. com.), Internat. Assn. Def. Counsel (pres. 1970), Am. Judicature Soc., Am. Law Inst., Def. Rsch. Inst. (regional v.p. 1965-66, bd. dir. 1966, 69-71), Fla. Coun. Bar Assn. Pres., S. Fla. Inter-Profl. Coun. (charter), Dade County Def. Bar Assn. (pres. 1965-66), Fla. Soc. Prevention Blindness (chmn. Dade County com. 1966). Lodge: Kiwanian (bd. dir. Miami 1963-65, pres. 1968). Home: Miami Beach Fla. Died Mar. 29, 1991.

PRALL, BERT R., business executive; b. Cheyenne, Wyo., Mar. 6, 1895; s. Edward James and Naomi (Apperson) P.; m. Luella Powell, June 16, 1919; 1 child, Bert Apperson. Buyer Montgomery Ward & Co., Chgo., 1919-27, mgr. tire dept., 1927-39, mdse. mgr. hard lines, 1939-42, v.p., gen. operating mgr., bd. dirs., 1942-45; exec. v.p., bd. dirs. Dayton (Ohio) Rubber Mfg. Co., 1946-47; v.p., bd. dirs. Butler Bros., 1948-49, pres., bd. dirs., 1949-56; v.p., bd. dirs. Scott Burr Stores Corp., 1949-56; bd. dirs., dept. chmn. Fed. Res. Bank Chgo., 1953-55, chmn., 1955-60; chmn. bd., pres. H.L. Green Co., Inc., N.Y.C., 1960-61; chmn. bd. Met. Stores Ltd., London, Ont., Can., 1960-61; chmn., bd. dirs. Phillips & Buttorff Mfg. Co., Nashville, 1956-57; treas. Midwest Variety, Inc.; chmn. fin. com., bd. dirs. Universal Variety, Inc.; chmn. fin. com., bd. dirs. Universal Oil Products Co., Des Plaines, Ill.; v.p., bd. dirs., mem. exec. com. McCrory Corp., N.Y.C.; chmn. Chgo.-Tokyo Bank Chgo.; dir. Chicagoland Commerce and Industry Expn., Inc. Dir. merchandising Chgo. Internat. Trade Fair, from 1961; mem. adv. com. Civic Fedn. Chgo., Jr. Achievement; v.p., bd. dirs. Goodwill Industries Chgo. With USNR, World War I. Mem. Chgo. Assn. Commerce and Industry (v.p., bd. dirs.), Japan Am. Soc. Chgo. (v.p., bd. dirs.), Newcomen Soc., Chgo. Club, Westmoreland Country Club, Execs. Club, Bankers Club, Mid-Am. Club, Masons. Republican. *

PRATT, CARROLL CORNELIUS, psychology educator, musicologist; b. North Brookfield, Mass., Apr. 27, 1894; s. Dana Joseph and Sara (Nutting) P.; m. Marjory Bates, June 14, 1923; children: Dana Joseph, Anita Caroline. AB, Clark Coll., 1915, AM, 1916, PhD, 1921, ScD (hon.), 1948. Instr. exptl. psychology Clark U., 1922; instr., asst. prof. psychology Harvard U., Cambridge, Mass., 1923-37, acting organist and choirmaster, 1925; prof., head dept. Rutgers U., 1937-45; lectr. Princeton (N.J.) U., 1939-42, chmn. dept., 1947-53, prof., 1953-62, prof. emeritus, from 1962; acting head dept. philosophy, psychology and sociology U. Ankara, Turkey, 1945-47; prof., chmn. dept. psychology Rider Coll., from 1963; dir. Army pers. psychology Harvard U., 1943, mem. vis. com. to dept. psychology, 1956-63; broadcaster on psychology Sta. WMCA, N.Y.C., 1944-45; vis. prof. U. Calif., Berkeley, 1959; mem. emergency com. on psychology NRC; mem. com. on musicology Am. Coun. Learned Socs. Author: The Meaning of Music, 1932, The Logic of Modern Psychology, 1939, Psychology: The Third Dimension of War, 1942, Some Aspects of Musicology, 1957; editor: Military Psychology, 1942, Psychol. Rev., 1948-54; also articles. With Signal Corps, U.S. Army, 1917-19, AEF. Guggenheim fellow U. Berlin, 1931. Mem. APA, Am. Acad. Arts and Scis., Soc. for Asian Music (bd. dirs. from 1962), Soc. Exptl. Psychologists, Am. Soc. Aesthetics (pres. 1950-52), Am. Musicological Soc., Phi Beta Kappa (hon.), Sigma Xi. *

PRATT, WALDO ELLIOTT, JR., business executive; b. Chelsea, Mass., Dec. 31, 1895; s. Waldo Elliott and Ina (Angus) P.; m. Helen Virginia Stanley, Feb. 15, 1923; children: Nancy Virginia Pratt Rhoads, Waldo Elliott 3d, Stanley Edward. Grad., Amherst Coll., 1918. With Lockwood, Gren & Co., 1920-27; with Eaton & Howard, investment mgrs., Boston, from 1928, treas., 1932-42, also bd. dirs.; dir. Wellesley (Mass.) Trust Co., 1931-42, treas., 1938-42; bd. dirs. United Elastic Corp., Easthampton, Mass., from 1932; bd. dirs. Hollingsworth & Whitney Co., Boston, 1939-54, asst. treas., 1945-51, treas., 1951-54, v.p., 1952-54; asst. treas. Scott Paper Co., 1954-55. Trustee Eaton & Howard Balanced Fund, Eaton & Howard Stock Fund; trustee Newton-Wellesley Hosp.; chmn. budget com. United Ch. of Christ, 1961-63; bd. dirs. United Ch. Bd. for World Ministries, 1955-63; treas. Mass. Congl. Christian Conf., Mass. Congl. Fund. 2d lt. F.A., U.S. Army, 1917-19; capt. USAAF, 1942-45. Mem. Soc. Mayflower Desc., Brookline Country Club, Duxbury Yacht Club. Republican. *

PREBLUDA, HARRY JACOB, consulting chemist; b. Fall River, Mass., May 19, 1911; s. Barney and Esther (Chernock) P.; m. Renetta Berkman, June 16, 1946; children: Jeffrey Lee, Ellen (Mrs. Jonathan Chilton). B.S. magna cum laude, U. R.I., 1932, M.S., 1933; Ph.D. in Biochemistry (Eli Lilly fellow), Johns Hopkins U., 1937. Instr. organic chemistry U. R.I., Kingston, 1933-35; cons. chemist U.S. Indsl. Alcohol Co., Balt., 1937-38; devel. biochemist U.S. Indsl. Chems. Co., Balt., 1938-44; mgr. spl. products div. Nat. Distillers & Chem. Corp., N.Y.C., 1944-52, mgr. spl. products sales, 1952-61; cons. chemist Miami, Fla., 1961-90; assoc. Roger Williams Tech. and Econ. Services, Inc., Princeton, N.J., 1973-75, project leader, 1975-85, dir., 1979-85; dir. R.I. Found., pres. Option Fund, 1964-75. Author: Introduction to Organic Chemistry, 1936, The Newer Knowledge of Animal Nutrition, 1978; contbg. author CRC Handbook Chemistry and Physics; editor: Chemurgic Digest, from 1963; adv. panel: Chemtech., 1978-88, chmn. adv. panel, 1980; mem. E.V. McCollum Commemorative Com., from 1979, contbr. articles to profl. jours.; patentee in field. Mem. Forward Trenton Com., 1972-73. Research Corp. fellow, 1937-38. Fellow Inst. Chemists (life), AAAS, N.Y. Acad. Scis.; mem. Nat. Farm Chemurgic Council (dir., sec.), Am. Chem. Soc. (Disting. Service award Agrl. and Food Chem. div. 1987), World Poultry Sci. Assn., Am. Inst. Food Technologists (past pres.), Animal Nutrition Rsch. Coun., Assn. Cons. Chemists and Chem. Engrs., Fla. Inst. Chemists (pres. 1982-85), Sigma Xi, Phi Kappa Phi. Clubs: Johns Hopkins Faculty, Chemists. Lodge: Masons. Home: Miami Beach Fla. Died July 21, 1990; buried Trenton, N.J.

PRESENT, ARTHUR JEROME, physician, educator; b. Rochester, N.Y., May 24, 1905; s. Morris and Sarah (Straws) P.; m. Barbara Kennard, Oct. 7, 1961. B.A., Yale U., 1927, M.D., 1932; Sc.D. in Medicine, Columbia U., 1937. Surg. intern Duke Hosp., Durham, N.C., 1932-33; med. intern Strong Meml. Hosp., Rochester, 1933-34; resident radiology Presbyn. Hosp., N.Y.C., 1934-37; assoc. radiologist Scripps Meml. Hosp. and Scripps Clinic, La Jolla, Calif., 1937-40; pvt. practice radiology Tucson, 1946-70; assoc. prof. radiology Coll. Medicine, U. Ariz., 1970-71, prof., 1971-86, prof. emeritus, 1986-89; cons. Tuscon Med. Center, St. Mary's Hosp., St. Joseph's Hosp., VA Hosp. Tucson, USAF Hosp. Tucson. Vice pres. Tucson Festival Soc., 1958-61, pres., 1961-62; pres. Ariz. Corral Theatre, 1958-63. Served to lt. col. U.S. Army, 1940-46. Fellow Am. Coll. Radiology (chmn. bd. chancellors 1960-61, pres. 1962-63, Gold medal 1975); mem. Am., Ariz. med. assns., Radiol. Soc. N.A., Am. Roentgen Ray Soc., AAAS, Am. Cancer Soc. (pres. Ariz. 1958-59, nat. bd. dirs., exec. com. 1963-67), Sigma Xi. Club: Old Pueblo (Tucson). Home: Tucson Ariz. Died Sept. 22, 1989; cremated.

PRESGRAVE, RALPH, business educator, consultant; b. London, July 31, 1898; s. Alfred Woodward and Ada Augusta (Jenner) P.; m. Marjorie Jean Morrison, Apr. 15, 1924; children: Ian Hamilton, Sheila Presgrave Cooney, Roger. B Applied Sci., U. Toronto, Ont., Can., 1921. With York Knitting Mills Ltd., Toronto, from 1921, v.p., from 1950; co-founder, cons. ptnr. Woods, Gordon & Co., bus. cons., from 1932; prof. U. Toronto Sch. Bus., from 1959; v.p. Thomson Rsch. Assocs.; ind. arbitrator labor-mgmt. disputes; chmn. Pub. Svc. Grievance Bd. Ont. Recipient Gilbreth award, 1951. Fellow Am. Inst. Indsl. Engrs.; mem. Can. Mfrs. Assn. *

PRESTON, JEROME, business executive; b. Woburn, Mass., Dec. 23, 1898; s. Elwyn Greeley and Emily (Brown) P.; m. Iva H. Stone, Jan. 3, 1922; children: Jerome, Priscilla, Nathaniel Stone. Grad., Harvard U., 1919. With Blyth, Witter Co. (Blyth & Co.), 1920-32; gen. ptnr. Preston, Moss & Co., 1932-56, ltd. ptnr., from 1956; bd. dirs. Mississippi River Fuel Corp., Gilchrist Co.; trustee, v.p. Home Savs. Ban, Boston. Trustee, mem. adv. com. Mass. Hosp. Assn.; pres. Mass. Meml. Hosps.; chmn. Boston U. Med. Ctr.; bd. dirs. World Peace Found.; trustee, mem. exec. com. Boston U. Col. USAAF, 1942-45. Mem. Coun. on Fgn. Rels., Union Club, St. Botolph Club, Harvard Club, Harvard Club (N.Y.C.). *

PRESTON, JOHN FREDERICK, JR., telephone company executive; b. Missoula, Mont., June 18, 1917; s. John Frederick and Maud (Hunicke) P.; m. Barbara Pogue, Aug. 19, 1942 (dec. Aug. 1963); children: John Frederick, Thomas Pogue; m. Sue Marshall Schell, Nov. 28, 1964. B.A., Washington and Jefferson Coll., 1938; J.D., Georgetown U., 1947. Bar: D.C. 1941, Md. 1955, N.Y. 1959. Spl. agt. FBI, 1942-47; counsel Joint Congl. Com. Labor-Mgmt., 1947-49; trial counsel NLRB, 1949-52; atty. Chesapeake & Potomac Telephone Companies, 1952-55; gen. atty. Chesapeake & Potomac Telephone Co. Md., 1955-58; atty. A.T.&T., 1958-61, gen. atty., 1963-74, gen. solicitor, 1974-76, asso. gen. counsel, 1976-82; v.p., gen. counsel Ohio Bell Telephone Co., 1961-63. Mem. Am., N.Y. State, N.Y. County, Fed. Communications bar assns., Am. Judicature Soc., Phi Beta Kappa, Phi Gamma Delta. Home: Vero Beach Fla. Died Aug. 11, 1988; buried Lewes, Del.

PRICE, HAROLD ARCHIBALD, lawyer, judge; b. Morristown, N.J., July 13, 1893; s. Archibald and Jane

(Babbitt) P.; m. Elizabeth Reed, Apr. 5, 1926 (dec. 1989); children: Charlton R., Jane Willsea, Miriam Patten. LLB, NYU, 1916. Bar: N.J. 1916. Practice in Morristown, 1916-56, 63-85; ptnr. Schenck, Price, Smith & King (and predecessors), 1963-85; judge Superior Ct. N.J., 1956-63; presiding judge part B appellate div., 1958-63; apptd. by N.J. Supreme Ct. to investiage, Twp. Lodi, N.J., 1930, City Newark, 1936, dep. atty. gen., N.J., 1947; vice chmn. N.J. Joint Legis. Commn. (to study capital punishment), 1964. Pres. Morristown YMCA, 1948-50; trustee Morristown chpt. ARC, 1941-45, chmn. 1943-45; trustee Community Chest and Coun. Morris County, 1949-50, Morristown Meml. Hosp., 1943-58; com. mgrs. Morristown Meml. Hosp., 1943-58, v.p., 1958; pres. bd. trustees Presbyn. Ch., 1934-35, 36-38. Fellow Am. Bar Found., Am. Probate Counsel; mem. ABA, N.J. Bar Assn., Essex County Bar Assn., Morris County Bar Assn., Am. Coll. Trial Attys., Am. Judicature Soc. (dir. 1966-90), Inst. Practicing Lawyers (founder, trustee 1941-90), Washington Assn. N.J. (trustee 1948-66, pres. 1948-53, 63-66), NYU Law Alumni Assn. (dir. 1964-67), Masons. Home: Morris Twp. N.J. Died Sept. 26, 1990.

PRICE, PHILIP, lawyer; b. Phila., Mar. 13, 1898; s. Eli K. and Evelyn (Taylor) P.; m. Sarah Meade Harrison, June 10, 1922; children: John Sergeant 3d, Sarah M. Pricee Parker, Evelyn T. Price Scott, Nancy M. Price Hiestand, Philip Jr. AB, U. Pa., 1919, LLB, 1922. Bar: Pa. 1922. With Dechert Price & Rhoades and predecessors, Phila., 1928-42, sr. ptnr., 1942-70. Treas., v.p. Fairmont Park Commn.; mem. Phila. Art Commn., 1953-68; mem. bd. Greater Phila. Movement; trustee Phila. Mus. Art; pres. Fairmont Park Art Assn., 1954-69; bd. mgrs. Children's Hosp. Phila.; bd. dirs. Overbrook Sch. for Blind, 1933-77. With USNRF, 1918; lt. USCGR, 1945. Mem. ABA, Pa. Bar Assn., Phila. Bar Assn., Soc. Colonial Wars, 1st Troop Phila. City Cav., Pa. N.G. (hon.), Swedish Colonial Soc., Phila. Club, Rittenhouse Club, St. Anthony Club, Univ. Barge Club, Legal Club, Phi Beta Kappa. Home: Philadelphia Pa. Died May 9, 1989; buried The Woodlands Cemetery.

PRICE, THOMAS ROWE, investment counselor; b. Glyndon, Md., Mar. 16, 1898; s. Thomas Rowe and Ella S. (Black) P.; m. Eleanor B. Gherky, Sept. 18, 1926; children: Richard B., Thomas R. BA, Swarthmore Coll., 1919. Asst. supt. Ft. Pitt Stamping & Enameling Co., 1919; chemist D.I. Du Pont de Nemours & Co., 1919-21; salesman Smith, Ockhardt & Co., brokers, Balt., 1921-22, Jenkins, Whedbee & Poe, bonds, Balt., 1923-24; mgr. investment dept., dir. investment mgmt. dept. Mackubin, Legg & Co., Balt., 1925-37; chmn., bd. dirs. T. Rowe Price & Assocs., Inc., investment rsch. and counsel, Balt.; pres., bd. dirs. T. Rowe Price Growth Stock Fund, Inc., Balt., from 1950, Rowe Price Mgmt. Co., Balt., from 1960, Rowe Price New Horizons Fund, Inc., Balt., from 1960; bd. dirs. Md. Fine & Splty. Wire Co.; mem. sr. adv. coun. McCormick & Co. Author: Change—The Investor's Only Certainty, 1937, Picking Growth Stocks (series articles), 1939, What Makes a Growth Stock Grow, 1956; also others. Mem. Nat. Assn. Investment Cos. (bd. govs.), N.Y. Soc. Security Analysts, Investment Counsel Assn. Am. (bd. govs.), Md. Club, Balt. Country Club, Mchts. Club, Pinnacle Club (N.Y.C.), Delta Upsilon. *

PRIMEAU, ERNEST JOHN, clergyman; b. Chgo., Sept. 17, 1909; s. Ernest and Angelina (LaVigne) P. Student, Loyola U., Chgo., 1926-28; STD, St. Mary of the Lake Sem., Mundelein, Ill., 1936; licentiate canon law, Lateran U., Rome, 1948. Ordained priest Roman Cath. Ch., 1934. Prof. math. and physics Quigley Prep. Sem., Chgo., 1937-46; rector Collegio S. Maria del Lago, Rome, 1946-58; pastor Our Lady of Mt. Carmel Parish, Chgo., 1949; bishop Manchester, N.H., 1959-89. Mem. South Congregation of Holy Office. Home: Manchester N.H. Died June 15, 1989.

PRINDEVILLE, CHARLES TREGO, meat packing company executive; b. Chgo., Dec. 8, 1896; s. Charles Henry and Estelle (Trego) P.; m. Dorothy Black, July 22, 1926. AB, Harvard U., 1918. With Swift & Co., Chgo., 1921-89, v.p., 1941-89, dir., 1953-89. Mem. W.P.B., 1942; chief fats and oils br. War Food Adminstrn., Washington, 1943. Lt. col. U.S. Army, mem. Gen. Staff and SOS, 1942. Mem. Nat. Plant Food Inst. (pres. 1956-57). Home: Vienna Va. Died Sept. 4, 1989.

PRITCHARD, CLAUDIUS HORNBY, clergyman; b. Blacksburg, Va., Nov. 21, 1896; s. Samuel Reynolds and Mary (Aiken) P.; m. Katherine Ellison, Aug. 13, 1924; children: Claudius Hornby Jr., Mary Grace. BS, Va. Poly. Inst., 1918, MS, 1919; BD, Union Theol. Sem., Richmond, Va., 1924; DD (hon.), Hampden-Sydney Coll., 1937. Ordained to ministry Presbyn. Ch., 1924. Instr. physics and math. Va. Poly. Inst., Blacksburg, 1919, asst. prof. physics, 1921; student engr. GE, 1920; mission pastor Bream Meml. Presbyn. Ch., Charleston, W.Va., 1924-26; pastor Lydia Robson Meml. Ch., Charleston, 1926-30, Oakhurst Presbyn. Ch., Decatur, Ga., 1930-35; ednl. sec. Gen Assembly's Home Mission Com., Atlanta, 1935-44, exec. sec., 1944-49; sec. div. home missions Bd. Ch. Ext., 1949-63; chmn. Gen. Commn. Chaplains and Armed Forces Pers., Washington, from 1963. Author: Living Epistles, 1959; editor: Why Stand Ye Idle, 1941. *

PRITCHARD, SIR JOHN (MICHAEL), conductor; b. London, Feb. 5, 1921. Staff mem., asst. condr. Glyndebourne Festival, 1947; debut Vienna State Opera and Royal Opera, Covent Gardens, 1952; Am. debut Pitts. Symphony Orch., 1953; music dir. Royal Liverpool Philharm. Orch., 1957-63, London Philharm., 1962-66; chief condr. Cologne Opera, 1978-89; mus. dir. Theatre de la Mannaie, Brussels, 1981-86, BBC Symphony Orch., 1982-89, San Francisco Opera, 1986; music dir. Glyndebourne Festival Opera, 1969-77; active Musica Viva concerts, Liverpool and London; condr. final concert night The Proms, BBC summer series at Royal Albert Hall, London, 1989. Decorated knight, Eng., 1983. Home: San Francisco Calif. Died Dec. 5, 1989.

PROFFITT, CHARLES G., book publisher; b. N.Y.C., Apr. 28, 1896; s. Charles C. and Lucy G. (Mooney) P.; m. Ruth C. Lohman, Oct. 22, 1927; 1 child, Ruth S. AB, Columbia U., 1917, postgrad., 1924-27. Alumni sec., editor Columbia Alumni News, Columbia U., N.Y.C., 1920-24; mgr., asst. dir., assoc. dir. Columbia U. Press, 1927-46, dir., sec., treas., 1946-58, pres., dir., from 1958, trustee, from 1956; trustee Greenwich Savs. Bank, N.Y.C. Bd. dirs. Morningside Heights, Inc.; trustee Cathedral St. John the Divine. Lt. F.A., U.S. Army, 1917-19. Mem. Columbia Coll. Alumni Assn. (sec. 1927-43, treas. 1943-50), Soc. Older Grads. Columbia U. (bd. dirs.), Am. Inst. Graphic Arts, Pilgrims, Century Assn., Columbia U. Club, Columbia U. Faculty Club (treas. 1933-62, Ch. Club N.Y., Gipsy Trail Club (Carmel, N.Y.), Pubs. Lunch Club. Republican. Episcopalian. *

PROSHANSKY, HAROLD MILTON, psychologist, university president, educator; b. N.Y.C., Sept. 16, 1920; s. Samuel and Rose (Enteles) P.; m. Etta Weissman, Sept. 19, 1942; children: Eric Jay, Ellen Jane. B.S., CCNY, 1941; M.A., Columbia U., 1942; Ph.D., NYU, 1952. Asst. prof. psychology Bklyn. Coll., CUNY, 1953-59; spl. research fellow NIMH; asso. prof. psychology U. Mich., Ann Arbor, 1959-61; asso. prof. Bklyn. Coll., 1961-66, prof., from 1966; exec. officer Ph.D. program psychology Grad. Sch. and Univ. Center, CUNY, 1966-68, dean grad. sch., 1968-70, provost, 1971-72; pres. Grad. Sch. and Univ. Center, CUNY (Grad. Sch. and Univ. Center), 1972-90; cons. in field; mem. profl. adv. com. Cooper-Hewitt Mus.; bd. dirs. Sector Investment Fund; mem. adv. com. Pratt Inst. Author, contbg. author books.; Contbr. articles to profl. jours. Bd. dirs. Catalyst., Nat. Sports Art Mus., Inst. Responsive Edn., Phipps Housing Found., 1985-89, Bryant Park Restoration Com. of N.Y. Pub. Library, Project Return.; trustee L.I. U., 1986-89. Sgt. AUS, 1942-46. NIMH research grantee, 1960-67, 67-74; NIMH spl. research fellow Univ. Coll., London, 1969-70. Fellow Am. Psychol. Assn., AAAS, Soc. Psychol. Study Social Issues (pres. 1972-73); mem. NAS, Environ. Design Research Assos. Home: New York N.Y. Died Dec. 13, 1991; buried N.Y.C.

PROSSER, ELEANOR ALICE, retired dramatic literature educator; b. Pasadena, Calif., Sept. 1, 1922; d. Norman Isbel P. and Alice Bertha (Austin) McGuffin. Jr. cert., Pasadena Jr. Coll., 1941; A.B. in Speech and Drama, Occidental Coll., 1950; M.A. in English, Stanford U., 1957, Ph.D. in English, 1960. Acting instr. speech, dir. drama Occidental Coll., Los Angeles, 1950; from teaching asst. to acting instr. English Stanford U., (Calif.), 1953-56, from assoc. prof. drama to prof., 1966-81, Margery Bailey Prof. dramatic lit., 1981-84; from asst. prof. to prof. English San Jose State Coll., Calif., 1956-66; mem. acting co. Oreg. Shakespearean Festival, Ashland, 1952-54. Author: Drama and Religion in the English Mystery Plays, 1961, Hamlet and Revenge, 1967, 2d edit., 1971, Shakespeare's Anonymous Editors: Scribe and Compositor in the Folio Text of 2 Henry IV, 1981. Recipient Walter J. Gores award Stanford U., 1981. Mem. Shakespeare Assn. Am. (trustee 1975-78). Democrat. Home: Los Altos Calif. Deceased. †

PROUTY, MORTON DENNISON, JR., natural gas pipeline company executive; b. Chgo., Mar. 18, 1918; s. Morton Dennison and Flora Harriett (Houghton) P.; m. Elsie Shipman, Nov. 4, 1945; children: Catherine Prouty Horn, Carol Prouty Ostberg. BS, U. Ill., 1939; postgrad., Northwestern U., 1946-47. CPA, Ill. Auditing staff Arthur Andersen & Co., Chgo., 1939-41, 45-49; corp. officer Ala.-Tenn. Natural Gas Co., Florence, Ala., 1949-78; pres. Ala-Tenn. Natural Gas Co., Florence, Ala., 1978-82; pres. Ala-Tenn Resources, Inc., Florence, 1982-84, chmn. bd., 1984-91, chmn. emeritus, from 1991. Author: (poems) Sparks on the Wind, 1961, Footsteps on the Mountain, 1969, The Pharisee, 1974, To a Young Mariner, 1983, The Edge of Time, 1988. Served to capt. U.S. Army, 1941-45, ETO. Named Poet Laureate of Ala., 1987-91. Mem. Nat. Assn. Accts., Rotary. Presbyterian. Home: Florence Ala. Deceased. †

PRUGH, DANE GASKILL, child psychiatrist, pediatrician; b. Phila., June 3, 1918; s. Wallace Eby and Esther Ann (Gaskill) P.; m. Anne Davison, Feb. 27, 1943 (dec. 1983); children: Joan Elizabeth, Wallace Dane; m. Elizabeth Stiles, 1984 (dec. 1988). B.A., Miami U., Oxford, Ohio, 1940; M.D., Harvard U., 1943. Intern Children's Hosp., Boston, 1943; resident in pediatrics Children's Hosp., 1944; gen. practice medicine Dayton, Ohio, 1946-47; Commonwealth Fund fellow in psychiatry Strong Meml. Hosp., Rochester, N.Y., 1947-48; in pediatric psychiatry N.Y. Hosp., N.Y.C., 1948-49; instr. Harvard U. Med. Sch., Boston, 1949-51; asst. prof. pediatrics, psychiatry and public health Harvard U. Med. Sch., 1951-55; dir. psychiat. div. med. service Children's Hosp., Boston, 1949-55; assoc. prof. psychiatry and pediatrics Rochester Sch. Medicine and chief child psychiatry div. Strong Meml. Hosp., 1955-63; prof., chief child psychiatry U. Colo. Med. Center, 1963-70; prof. psychiatry and pediatrics, dir. tng., child psychiatry and pediatric-psychiat. liaison U. Colo. Health Scis. Center, 1970-85, prof. emeritus, from 1986; clin. prof. psychiatry and pediatrics U. Calif., Irvine Sch. Medicine, from 1988; lectr. Sch. Social Work, Denver U., 1964-70; field instr. Sch. Profl. Psychology, Denver U., 1980-85; cons. in field; various vis. professorships including vis. prof. child health U. Otago Sch. Medicine, Dunedin, N.Z., 1969; various meml. lectureships; mem. Colo. Gov.'s Commn. on Children, Denver, 1977-80; mem. Task Panel on Pres.'s Commn. on Mental Health, 1977-78. Author: The Psychosocial Aspects of Pediatrics, 1983; contbr. numerous articles, chpt. to profl. publs.; editor: (with H. Stuart) The Healthy Child: Physical, Psychological and Social Development, 1960. Mem. subcom. Denver Mayor's Com. on Urban Renewal, 1967-69; chmn. East Arapahoe Human Relations Council, Denver, 1968-70. Served with M.C., U.S. Army, 1944-46. Recipient Whitehead award ACLU, 1970, Hannah Solomon award Nat. Council Jewish Women, 1970. Fellow Am. Orthopsychiat. Assn. (life; pres. 1968-69), Am. Acad. Pediatrics (life, chmn. sect. child devel. 1967-68), Am. Acad. Child Psychiatry (life; chmn. com. on liaison, primary care 1978-81), Am. Acad. Child and Adolescent Psychiatry (recipient Simon Wile award child psychiatry consultation, liaison, pediatrics 1988), Am. Psychiat. Assn. (life, chmn. com. on standards for children's facilities 1969-72), Am. Psychosomatic Soc. (council 1954-57); mem. Boston Psychoanalytic Soc., Western N.Y. Psychoanalytic Soc., Denver Psychoanalytic Soc., Group Advancement of Psychiatry (chmn. com. child psychiatry 1962-66), Soc. Pediatric Research, Am. Pediatric Soc., N.Y. Acad. Scis., Boylston Med. Soc., Phi Beta Kappa, Sigma Xi. Home: Pomona Calif. Deceased. †

PUCCI, EMILIO (MARCHESE DI BARSENTO), fashion designer; b. Naples, Italy, Nov. 20, 1914; s. Orazio and Augusta (Pavoncelli) Pucci; m. Cristina Nannini, Feb. 7, 1959; children: Alessandro, Laudomia. Student, U. Milan, Italy, 1933-35, U. Ga., 1935-36; MA in Social Scis., Reed Coll., Portland, Oreg., 1937; Dr. Polit. Sci., U. Florence, Italy, 1941. Fashion creator, pres. Casa di Alta Moda Emilio Pucci Srl, Florence, 1951-92; pres. Antico Setificio Fiorentino, 1958, Emilio Pucci Ltd., N.Y.C. Producer collections for fashion show in Florence, Jan. and July 1950; with other fashion designers showed collection Italian fashions in Russia, 1958. Mem. Italian Parliament for Florence, 1963-72; counsellor Florence City Coun., 1964-90. Lt. col. Italian Air Force, 1941-52. Recipient Neiman Marcus Fashion award, 1954, Burdines Sunshine award, 1955, Sports Illustrated Sporting Look Designers award, 1961; medallion Harper's Bazaar. Mem. Associazone Proprieta' Edilizia (pres.), Consul Fashion Designers of Am. (award 1990), Società di San Giovanni Battista (pres.), Società di San Giovanni di Dio (pres.), Italian Pvt. Sector Initiative, Italian Stylists Assn. (hon. pres.), Cavaliere del Lavoro, Circolo Unione Club, Circolo del Golf Club, Tennis Club, Florence Club, Circolo della Caccia (Rome), Eagle Ski Club (Gstaad, Switzerland), Corviglia Club (St. Moritz), Rotary. Home: Florence Italy Died Nov. 29, 1992. †

PUGH, EMERSON MARTINDALE, physics educator; b. Ogden, Utah, July 19, 1896; s. William and Hattie Fox (Martindale) P.; m. Ruth Hazel Edgin, Sept. 18, 1920; children: George Edgin, Emerson William. BS, Carnegie Inst. Tech., 1918; postgrad., Stevens Inst. Tech., 1918-19; MS, U. Pitts., 1927; PhD, Calif. Inst. ech., 1929. Cashier Uinta County State Bank, 1919-20; mem. faculty dept. physics, fellow Petroleum Inst. and NRC, Carnegie Inst. Tech., Pitts., from 1920, prof., assoc. head dept., from 1960; dir. rsch. projects USNR, 1941-43, OSRD, 1943-45, U.S. Army Ordnance, 1945-62. Author: (with Emerson W. Pugh) Principles of Electricity and Magnetism, 1960, (with G.H. Winslow) Physical Measurements, 1965. Ensign USN, 1918-19. Fellow Am. Phys. Soc.; mem. AAUP, Am. Soc. Physics Tchrs., Sigma Xi, Pi Mu Epsilon, Tau Beta Pi, Phi Kappa Phi, Delta Tau Delta. Presbyterian. *

PULITZER, MRS. RALPH See LEECH, MARGARET KERNOCHAN

PULITZER, SAM CLARENCE, manufacturing executive; b. New Orleans, Sept. 15, 1905; s. Simon and Clara (Klingsberg) P.; m. Syliva Copeland, Oct. 4, 1932; children: Sidney, Melanie, Arthur. Owner, pres. Wembley, Inc., New Orleans, 1925-89. Organizer La. Orgn. for Retarded Children; bd. dirs. Touro Infirmary. Mem. Nat. Men's Tie Found. (pres.). Home: New Orleans La. Died Oct. 20, 1989.

PUMPHREY, FRED HOMER, university dean; b. Dayton, Ohio, July 31, 1898; s. Elgar Grant and Ella (Rhoades) P.; m. Gladice Eno, June 20, 1922; children: Betty Ruth, Pattie Evelyn, James Eno, Margaret

Elaine. AB, Ohio State U., 1920, BEE, 1921, EE, 1927, DSc (hon.), 1962. With Dayton Power & Light Co., 1921-22; gen. meter supt. Kans. Gas & Electric Co., 1922-24; tech. engr. S.I. (N.Y.) Edison Corp., 1924-27; instr. State U. Iowa, 1927-28; prof. elec. engring. Rutgers U., 1928-45; engr. ednl. svc. div. GE, Schenectady, 1945-56; prof., head dept. elec. engring. U. Fla., 1946-58; dean engring. Auburn (Ala.) U., from 1958. Author: Electrical Engineering: Essential Theory and Typical Applications, rev. edit., 1953, Fundamentals of Electrical Engineering, rev. edit., 1959; co-author: Fundamentals of Radio, rev. edit., 1959. Lt. F.A., U.S. Army, 1918; lt. col. Signal Corps, AUS, 1942-44. Fellow IEEE; mem. NSPE, Ala. Soc. Profl. Engrs., Am. Soc. Engring. Edn. (chmn. elec. engring. com. 1947, ednl. methods div. 1952, mem. project operating unit from 1963), Masons, Kiwanis, Phi Beta Kappa, Sigma Xi (pres. Fla. chpt. 1953-54), Tau Beta Pi, Eta Kappa Nu, Phi Eta Sigma, Omicron Delta Kappa. *

PURCELL, ROBERT W., corporation executive; b. Watertown, N.Y., Oct. 24, 1911; s. Francis and Ella (Conger) P.; m. Hazel Becker, Oct. 14, 1939 (dec. 1978); m. Wendy Bowern, July 4, 1979. A.B., Cornell U., 1932, LL.B., 1935. Asso. White & Case, N.Y.C., 1935-38; practice law Cleve., 1938-40; office counsel Alleghany Corp., 1940-53, v.p., 1945-53, dir., 1946-53, vice chmn., 1947-53; gen. counsel C. & O. Ry., 1943-53, v.p., gen. counsel, 1945-53, v.p. charge law, dir., mem. retirement, finance com., 1946-53, vice chmn., 1947-53; chmn. bd. Pathe Industries, Inc., 1945-50, dir., 1941-53; v.p., dir. White Sulphur Springs Co., 1946-53; dir. Cleve. Cliffs Iron Co., 1946-53; chmn. bd. Investors Diversified Services, Inc., Mpls., 1953-57; bus. cons. Rockefeller Family & Assos., 1955-79; dir. Internat. Basic Economy Corp., 1955-80, chmn. bd., 1958-68; dir. Basic Resources Internat. S.A., 1972-81, chmn. bd., 1972-80; dir. C.I.T. Fin. Corp., 1967-81, Seabd. World Airlines, Inc., 1963-80, Bendix Corp., 1965-81, Internat. Minerals & Chem. Corp., 1961-85, Investors Group, 1949-82, Pittston Co., Caneel Bay, Inc., 1958-86, Rockefeller Center, Inc., 1976-82, K mart Corp., 1971-84. Life gov. N.Y. Hosp.; trustee emeritus Cornell U., chmn. bd. trustees, 1968-78; hon. trustee Internat. House. Mem. Psi Upsilon. Clubs: New York Yacht (N.Y.C.), Cornell (N.Y.C.), University (N.Y.C.). Home: New York N.Y. Died Aug. 9, 1991.

PURVIN, ROBERT LEMAN, chemical engineer; b. Farmersville, Tex., June 5, 1917; s. Julius L. and Adelaide F. (Mittenthal) P.; m. Maria Czartoryski Chajecki, Feb. 1972; children: James Kenneth, Laura Jill Purvin Zinner, Duane Emory, Robert Leman, Jeffrey Leon, Lisa Purvin Oliner. BA with highest honors, U. Tex., 1937, BS with highest honors, 1938; DSChemE, MIT, 1941; LLD (hon.), Manhattan Coll., 1981. Engr. refinery tech. service Humble Oil & Refining Co., 1941-46; cons., 1946-50; cons. sr. partner Purvin & Gertz, Inc., 1946-57; pres., dir. Purmil Corp., 1953-90; exec. v.p., dir. Foster Grant Co., Inc., 1957-62, cons., 1962-70; v.p., dir. TransAtlantic Trading Ltd., 1965-66; mgr. TransAtlantic Gas Assocs., 1963-69; sub. dir. gen. Fertilizantes Fosfatados Mexicanos (S.A. de C.V.), 1965-67, cons., 1962-70; exec. v.p., dir. Distrigas Corp., 1969-70; chmn. bd. Purvin & Lee, Inc., 1970-75; pres., chief exec. officer Barber Oil, 1975-78; cons., 1978-91; dir. Oxford Energy Corp., Santa Rosa, Calif., 1986-91; Consultor Manhattan Coll., 1967-81. Recipient Disting. Engring. Grad. award U. Tex., 1969. Fellow Am. Inst. Chem. Engrs.; mem. Am. Chem. Soc., Nat. Soc. Profl. Engrs., Soc. Gas Operators, Ind. Petroleum Assn. Am., Phi Beta Kappa, Sigma Xi, Phi Lambda Upsilon, Tau Beta Pi. Club: Sky (N.Y.C.). Lodges: Masons, Shriners. Home: Mamaroneck N.Y. Died June 19, 1991; buried Temple Emanuel Cemetery, Dallas, Tex.

PUTMAN, DWIGHT FREDERICK, clergyman, church official; b. Trent, Pa., Sept. 3, 1898; s. William Bruce and Caroline (Shaulis) P.; m. Agnes Rebecca Kelly, Aug. 18, 1924; children: Dwight, Kathryn, Carolyn. BA, Gettysburg Coll., 1920, MA, 1923; diploma, Theol. Sem., 1923, DD, 1943; postgrad., Union Theol. Sem., 1926-29; LLD, Muhlenberg Coll., 1953. Ordained to ministry Luth. Ch., 1923. Pastor Somerset County, Pa., 1023-26, Hudson Heights, N.J., 1927-30, Gettysburg, Pa., 1930-48; pres. Cen. Pa. Synod, Luth. Ch. Am., Harrisburg, Pa., from 1948; mem. bd. social missions United Luth Ch., from 1954, mem. exec. bd., 1950-58; pres. Pa. Coun. Chs., 1952-53; mem. exec. coun. Luth. Ch. Am., from 1962. Republican. *

QUANBECK, MARTIN, education educator; b. McVille, N.D., Jan. 10, 1905; s. Thor S. and Bergit Overbo Q.; m. Esther M. Goodrich, July 26, 1931; children: Paul M., David H. BA, Augsburg Coll., 1929; MA, U. Minn., 1933, PhD, 1952. Tchr. ungraded rural sch. Nelson County, N.D., 1923-25; prin. high sch. Mantorville, Minn., 1929-31, supt. schs., 1931-36; tchr. Waldorf Coll., Forest City, Iowa, 1936-38; prof. edn. Augsburg Coll., Mpls., 1938-70, prof. emeritus, 1970-91, dean, 1950-65; part time supr. student teaching several colls., 1970-91. Mem. Nat. Soc. Study Edn., Phi Delta Kappa. Lutheran. Home: Minneapolis Minn. Died Sept. 22, 1991.

QUARLES, JOHN RHODES, lawyer; b. Louisa County, Va., June 8, 1897; s. John Rhodes and Emma (Wheeler) Q.; m. Josephine Franklin, Sept. 15, 1928; children: Barbara Jean Quarles Harper, Elizabeth Ann Quarles Glennon, John Rhodes Jr. AB, U. Va., 1917; MA, Harvard U., 1918, LLB, 1928. Bar: Mass. 1929. Assoc. Ropes & Gray, and predecessors, Boston, 1928-37, mem., from 1937; bd. dirs. William Carter Co., Boston Safe Deposit & Trust Co., Singing Needles, Inc., Thomas Long Co.; trustee Bingham (Maine) Assoc. Fund. Mem. adminstrv. bd. Tufts-New Eng. Med. Ctr.; trustee Affiliated Hosps., Inc., Social Law Libr., Garland Jr. Coll., Boston Floating Hosp., Episcopal Theol. Sem., Cambridge, Mass., Harvard Med. Ctr., Boston; past pres., trustee Boston Lying-In Hosp.; chmn., trustee Wellesley Coll.; sec., trustee New Eng. Ctr. Hosp.; mem. nat. commn. ch. unity Episcopal Ch. 2d lt. inf., U.S. Army, World War I. Fellow Am. Bar Assn.; mem. Mass. Bar Assn., Boston Bar Assn., Bar Assn. City N.Y., Union Club, St. Botolph Club, St. Bernard Fish and Game Club (Que., Can.), Raven Soc., Phi Beta Kappa, Delta Sigma Rho. *

QUAYLE, SIR (JOHN) ANTHONY, theatre director, actor; b. Ainsdale, Lancashire, Eng., Sept. 7, 1913; s. Arthur and Esther Overton; ed. Rugby, Royal Acad. Dramatic Art; m. Hermione Hannan (div.); m. 2d, Dorothy Hyson, 1947; children: Rosanna, Jenny, Christopher. First appeared as straight man to a comic in vaudeville; stage appearance O Theatre, 1931; joined Old Vic Co., 1932; first stage appearance, N.Y.C., 1936; dir., actor, producer numerous films and plays in Eng., also ran Stratford-on-Avon theatre, 1948-56; producer Harvey, London, 1948, dir., 1975; on stage in Henry VIII, 1949; Henry IV, 1950; Volpone, 1952; Titus Andronicus, 1955; View from the Bridge, 1956; Galileo, 1967; Sleuth, 1970; The Idiot, 1970; The Headhunters, 1974; You Turn Somersaults, 1977; Hobson's Choice, 1982; toured England in King Lear, 1980; dir., co-star The Firstborn, 1958; motion pictures Saraband for Dead Lovers, 1949; Hamlet, 1950; Woman in a Dressing Gown, 1957; Pursuit of Graf Spee, 1958; Ice Cold in Alex, 1958; Guns of Navarone, 1961; Lawrence of Arabia, 1962; Fall of the Roman Empire, 1964; Operation Crossbow, 1965; A Study in Terror; Anne of the Thousand Days; Q.B. VII, 1971; Bequest to the Nation; The Tamarind Seed; 21 Hours at Munich, 1976; The Eagle Has Landed, 1977; Murder by Decree, 1978; Dial M for Murder; dir. Tiger at the Gates, 1968; actor, dir. Clarence Brown Co., Tenn., from 1975; numerous radio and TV appearances including Q.B. VII, Moses, 1974, Great Expectations, 1974, Benjamin Franklin, 1974, David and Saul, 1975, Ice Age, Henry IV, Masada, The Manions of America, The Tempest, King Lear, Oedipus at Colonus; producer, dir. Caesar and Cleopatra NBC; producer The Idiot, 1970; dir. plays Harvey, 1975, Rip Van Winkle, 1975, The Old Country, 1978, The Rules of the Game, 1982. Author: Eight Hours from England, 1945; On Such a Night, 1947. Decorated knight Brit. Empire. Deceased. Home: London Eng.

QUEENAN, JOHN WILLIAM, accountant; b. Aurora, Ill., Jan. 11, 1906; s. William and Mary (Dalton) Q.; m. Alice Thomas, June 15, 1927; children: Joan Queenan McClellan, Alice Jane Queenan Coenen, John T., Charles W. BS, U. Ill., 1927. With Haskins & Sells, N.Y.C., 1927-70, mem. firm, 1939-70, mng. ptnr., 1956-70; mem. Fed. Price Commn., 1971-73; vice chmn., mem. Fin. Acctg. Standards Bd., 1973-74. Mem. Am. Acctng. Assn., AICPA (past pres.), Ill., N.Y. socs. CPAs, Accts. Am. Club, Fifty Club, Illini Club, The Blind Brook Club (portchester, N.Y.), Board Rm. Club, Greenwich Country Club, Indian Harbor Yacht Club, Skytop (Pa.) Club, Jupiter Hills (Fla.) Club, Tequesta Country (Fla.) Club. Home: Greenwich Conn. Died Feb. 7, 1992.

QUIGLEY, JOSEPH MILTON, energy holding company executive; b. Belle Plaine, Iowa, Dec. 2, 1922; s. Lee L. and Emma (Polichek) Q.; m. Margaret M. Scriven, Feb. 26, 1946; children: Joseph B., Mark W., Lisa Ann, Susan. Student, Loras Coll., Dubuque, Iowa, 1940-42, DePaul U., 1943; B.S.C., State U. Iowa, 1950, M.A., 1951. Audit mgr. Arthur Andersen & Co., 1951-59; auditor State U. Iowa, 1959-61; with No. Ill. Gas Co., 1961-83, treas, 1964-70, v.p., sec.-treas., 1970-71, fin. v.p., sec., treas., 1971-73, financial v.p., sec., 1973-81, sr. v.p., sec., 1981-83; financial v.p., sec. NICOR Inc., 1976-81, sec., 1981-83; v.p. gas utility No. States Power Co., 1983-85; bd. dirs. Harris Bank-Naperville; past mem., fin. coun. Am. Mgmt. Assn. Served with AUS, 1943-46. Decorated Bronze Star medal. Mem. Chgo. Tax Club, Am. Gas Assn., Am. Soc. Corp. Secs., Fin. Execs. Inst., Ill. C. of C., St. Paul C. of C., Economic Club, Utility and Telecommunications Securities Club, Executives Club of Chgo., Naperville Country Club. Home: Aurora Ill. Died Sept. 9, 1990; buried Marshalltown, Iowa.

QUINN, BAYARD ELMER, engineering educator; b. Phila., May 10, 1915; s. Bayard Elmer and Martha (Engle) Q.; m. Charlotte Louise Benedict, June 30, 1945; children: Bayard Paul, James Benedict. B.S., Drexel Inst. Tech., 1937; M.S., Cornell U., 1942, Ph.D., 1945. Registered profl. engr., Ind., Pa. Draftsman RCA Mfg. Co., Camden, N.J., 1934-37; engr. Gen. Electric Co., Schenectady, 1937-40; asst. prof. Cornell U., 1940-46; prof. Purdue U., Lafayette, Ind., 1946-81; prof. emeritus Purdue U., from 1981, dir. grad. programs, continuing engring. edn., 1979-81. Mem. pavement condition evaluation com. Transp. Research Bd., NRC, 1968-75, mem. surface properties-vehicle interaction com., 1973-78; cons. Boeing Airplane Co., Gen. Motors Corp., AEC, NSF, Hwy. Research Bd., Am. Assn. State Hwy. Ofcls. Road Test.; Dist. commr. Boy Scouts Am., 1965-74. Mem. Am. Soc. Mech. Engrs., Am. Soc. Engring. Edn., Sigma Xi, Pi Tau Sigma, Tau Beta Pi. Presbyn. (elder). Clubs: University, Sailing, Wabash Valley Torch (Lafayette) (pres. 1966). Home: West Lafayette Ind. Died July 22, 1990. †

QUINN, EDWARD JAMES, banker; b. N.Y.C., Apr. 2, 1911; s. Edward M. and Mary M. (Schneider) Q.; m. Marie A. Stafford, Apr. 22, 1939 (dec. 1972); children: Mary Ann Brown, James E., Patrick M., Sheila G.; m. Margaret B. O'Neill, Nov. 4, 1982. Student, Hofstra Coll., 1946-52; grad., Am. Inst. Banking, 1932-39, Grad. Sch. Banking at Rutgers, 1955-57. Messenger J.S. Bache & Co., N.Y.C., 1926-27; bookkeeper Nassau-Suffolk Bond & Mortgage Guaranty Co., Mineola, N.Y., 1928; sr. v.p. European-Am. Bank & Trust Co., from 1928. Chmn. investment com. United Fund L.I., 1968-71; treas. Nassau County Boy Scouts Am., 1936-39, Nassau County March Dimes, 1947-48, Nassau County Easter Seal Appeal, 1948-55, Suffolk County Cancer Soc., 1955-57, Union Free Sch. Dist. 22, Farmingdale, 1948-57; mem. U.S. Savs. Bond Com., Nassau County, 1952-65; bd. regents Royal Arcanum, 1938-39, grand committeeman, 1940-41; Mem. Bd. Appeals Village Farmingdale, 1941-56. Served with Med. Detachment AUS, 1943-46. 1st Sgt. Army Commendation ribbon, 1986. Mem. Mcpl. Forum N.Y., Mcpl. Finance Officers Assn. U.S., L.I. Bankers Assn. (chmn. check clearing com. 1955, legis. com. 1965-71), Nat. Assn. Accts., Am. Legion. Clubs: St. George's Golf and Country (Stony Brook, N.Y.); Southward Ho Country (Brightwaters, N.Y.); Atlantis (Fla.) Country. Home: Greenlawn N.Y. Deceased. †

QUINNEY, SEYMOUR JOSEPH, lawyer; b. Logan, Utah, May 12, 1893; s. Joseph Jr. and Ida B. (Theurer) Q.; m. Jessie S. Eccles, Aug. 17, 1917; children: David E., Janet Quinney Lawson. BS, Utah State U., 1916; LLB, Harvard U., 1919. Bar: Utah 1919. Practiced in Salt Lake City, from 1919; ptnr. Ray, Quinney & Nebeker, from 1940; gen. counsel 1st Security Corp. and affiliates; gen. counsel, bd. dirs. 1st Security Investment Co. and affiliates; bd. dirs. Eccles Investment Co., Anderson Lumber Co., 1st Security Life Ins. Co. Tex.; pres., dir. Salt Lake City Winter Sports Assn.; operator Alta Ski Area. Adviser to Utah gov. on coordination state instns. higher edn., 1921-22, on taxation reforms, 1921; mem. Utah Ho. of Reps., 1921; mem. exec. com., bd. dirs. Utah State Symphony. With U.S. Army, 1918-19. Mem. ABA, Utah State Bar, Alta Club (bd. dirs.). Republican. *

RABE, WILLIAM GEORGE, food company executive; b. Bklyn., 1896. Treas., chmn. exec. com., bd. dirs. Hershey Creamery Co.; pres., bd. dirs. 1st Geneva Corp.; bd. dirs. Technicolor, Inc., N.Y. Cen. R.R. Co., Beech-Nut Live Savers, Inc.; hon. bd. dirs. Mfrs. Hanover Trust Co., N.Y.C. *

RABORN, WILLIAM FRANCIS, JR., naval officer, government agency administrator, corporation executive; b. Decatur, Tex., June 8, 1905; s. William Francis and Cornelia Victoria (Moore) R.; m. Mildred T. Terrell, Apr. 5, 1955; children: Barbara Raborn Richardson, William Francis III. B.S., U.S. Naval Acad., 1928; student, Naval War Coll., 1951-52. Commd. ensign USN, 1928, advanced through grades to vice adm., 1960; designated naval aviator, 1934, assigned battleships, destroyers, aircraft carriers, 1928-40; established Aviation Gunnery Sch., Barbers Point, Pearl Harbor, T.H., 1940-42; exec. officer U.S.S. Hancock, Fast Carrier Task Forces Pacific, 1943-45; chief staff Comdr. Task Force 77, Comdr. Carrier Div. 2, Western Pacific, 1945-47; ops. officer Comdr. for Naval Air West Coast, 1947-49; research and development guided missiles Bur. Ordnance, 1949-50; dep. dir. guided missile div. Office Chief Naval Ops., 1952-54; comdg. officer U.S.S. Bennington, 1954-55; asst. chief staff (ops.) CINCLANT Atlantic Fleet, 1955; 1st dir. Navy's Fleet Ballistic Missile Program; dir. Office of Spl. Projects, Polaris Program; then dep. chief naval ops. (devel.) USN, 1963; corp. v.p. program mgmt. Aerojet-Gen. Corp., Azusa, Calif., 1963-65; v.p., gen. rep. Aerojet-Gen. Corp., 1967-70; dir. CIA, 1965-67; pres. W.F. Raborn, Co., Inc., 1970-86. Decorated D.S.M.; recipient Robert J. Collier Trophy Nat. Aero. Assn., 1961, Presdl. Nat. Secuity medal, 1966, James V. Forrestal award Nat. Security Indsl. Assn., 1966. Baptist. Club: Mason (33 deg.). Home: McLean Va. Died Mar. 7, 1990.

RACKER, EFRAIM, biochemist; b. Nowy Sacz, Poland, June 28, 1913; came to U.S., 1941, naturalized, 1947; m. Franziska Weiss, Aug. 25, 1945; 1 child, Ann Racker Costello. MD, U. Vienna, Austria, 1938; DSc (hon.), U. Chgo., 1968, U. Rochester. Rsch. asst. biochemistry Cardiff (South Wales) Mental Hosp., 1938-40; rsch. assoc. dept. physiology U. Minn., 1941-42; intern, resident Harlem Hosp., N.Y.C., 1942-44; asst. prof. microbiology NYU Sch. Medicine, 1944-52; asst. prof. biochemistry Yale U., 1952-54; chief div. nutrition and physiology Pub. Health Rsch. Inst., N.Y.C., 1954-66; Albert Einstein prof. biochemistry Cornell U., Ithaca, N.Y., 1966-91; mem. biochemistry study sect. div. rsch. grants NIH, 1957-70; chmn. bd. sci. counselors Cancer Inst., 1975-76; 73d Christian A. Herter lectr., 1975; 10th Sir Frederick Gowland Hopkins Meml. lectr., 1975; Walker-Ames lectr., 1977. Author: Mechanism in Bioenergetics, 1965, A New Look at Mechanisms in Bioenergetics, 1976; editor: Membranes of Mitochondria and Chloroplasts, 1970, Energy Transducing Mechanisms, 1975; editorial bd. Jour. Biol. Chemistry, 1959-72. Recipient Warren Triennial prize Mass. Gen. Hosp., 1974, Nat. Medal Sci., 1976. Mem. AAAS, NAS, Am. Soc. Biol. Chemists, Harvey Soc., Brit. Biochem. Soc., Am. Acad. Arts and Scis. Home: Ithaca N.Y. Died Sept. 9, 1991; buried Lakeview Cemetery, Ithaca, N.Y.

RADCLIFFE, HARRY SOUTHLAND, trade association executive; b. Cornwall-on-Hudson, N.Y., Nov. 30, 1894; s. Harry Richardson and Mary Anna (Ehlers) R.; m. Sarah E. Randall, July 2, 1917; children: Byron Mason, Margaret Jane Radcliffe Jacobus. Student, Phila. Optical Coll., 1915-16, NYU, 1936-37. Stock clk., then salesman M.N. Trafford Co., importers, 1912-15, ptnr., 1919-30; pres. Harry S. Radcliffe, Inc., 1928-32; registrar N.Y. Coll. Chiropractic, 1932-34; asst. dir. Book Mfrs. Inst., 1935-36; exec. sec. Lace and Embroidery Assn. Am. Inc., 1936-50, exec. dir., from 1950; exec. sec. Nat. Coun. Am. Importers, Inc., 1936-50, v.p., from 1950; sec. Linen Trade Assn., Inc., from 1936; mem. bus. adv. com. Inter-Am. Comml. Arbitration Commn., from 1941; import cons. OPA, 1942-46; mem. import adv. com. Dept. Commerce; mem. adv. com. on comml. activities of Fgn. Svc., Dept. State and Dept. Commerce, 1946-50; mem. fgn. trade comm. Com. Econ. Devel., 1945; lectr. on transp. and fgn. trade Columbia U., 1945; lectr. mktg. and fgn. trade NYU, 1947-56. Author: The American Tariff on Alcoholic Beverages, 1933; editor Am. Importer, 1936-49; contbr. articles on import trade in export trade publs., also newspapers. 1st lt. USMC, 1917-19; capt. Naval Militia, 1922-24. Decorated officer Order du Merite Comml. (France), chevalier Ordre de Couronne (Belgium), hon. officer Order Brit. Empire, officer Order Orange-Nassau (Netherlands), officer Order of Merit (Italy); recipient award World Trade Writers Assn., 1953, medal of honor Am. C. of C. in France, 1954. Mem. Internat. C. of C. (com. on formalities in internat. trade from 1948), U.S. C. of C. (fgn. commerce dept. com. 1952-59), Am. Arbitration Assn. (natl panel from 1928), Madison Golf Club. Methodist. *

RADCLIFFE, JANETTE See ROBERTS, JANET LOUISE

RADCLIFF-UMSTEAD, DOUGLAS, Romance languages educator; b. Silver Spring, Md., Jan. 10, 1944; s. Henry Raymond and Lula Louisa (De Carlo Ey) R.; m. Eleonora Della Fugata (dec.). A.B., Johns Hopkins U., 1960; Ph.D., U.Calif.-Berkeley, 1964. Asst. prof. French and Italian U. Calif.-Santa Barbara, 1964-68; assoc. prof. French and Italian, dir. Ctr. Medieval and Renaissance Studies U. Pitts., 1968-76, prof. French and Italian, 1976-77; prof. romance langs., chmn. dept. romance lang. Kent State U., Ohio, 1977-92; cons. NEH and other founds. Author: Birth of Modern Comedy in Renaissance Italy, 1969, Ugo Foscolo, Biographical and Critical Study, 1971, The Mirror of our Anguish, A Study of Pirandello's Narrative, 1977, The Exile into Eternity, A Study of Bassani's Narrative, 1987, Little Girl, Wait for Me!, 1989; contbr. articles to profl. jours. Guggenheim fellow, 1974; grantee NEH, Woodrow Wilson Found., NDEA, Lilian Schermer Found.; Fulbright fellow. Mem. MLA, Am. Assn. Univ. Profs. Italian. Home: Kent Ohio Died Mar. 22, 1992.

RADNER, GILDA, comedienne; b. Detroit, June 28, 1946; m. G.E. Smith, Apr., 1980 (div.); m. Gene Wilder, 1984. Ed., U. Mich. With Second City company, Toronto, Ont., Can.; appeared in Can. performance of Godspell; also various CBC prodns.; wrote and performed Nat. Lampoon Radio Hour; appeared Nat. Lampoon Show, off-Broadway, 1974; regular on NBC's Saturday Night Live, 1975-80; theatre appearances include: Broadway, 1977, Lunch Hour, 1980; Broadway debut in Live from New York, 1979; films include: Mister Mike's Mondo Video, 1979, Gilda Live, 1980, First Family, 1981, Hanky Panky, 1982, It Came from Hollywood, 1982, Woman in Red, 1984, Movers and Shakers, 1985, Haunted Honeymoon, 1986. Recipient Emmy award as outstanding actress in variety series. Mem. AFTRA. Jewish. Died May 20, 1989. †

RADTKE, SCHRADE FRED, engineering company executive; b. Mpls., Aug. 21, 1919; s. Fred August and Adelheld Isabel (Schrade) R.; m. Genevieve Nix, Apr. 18, 1942; children—Schrade Fred, Mark Lane. B.S., MIT, 1940, Ph.D., 1949. Registered profl. engr. Ill., Va., Del. Instr. MIT, Cambridge, 1946-49; research supr. DuPont Co., Newport, Del., 1949-53; dir. research Reynolds Metals Co., Richmond, Va., 1953-58; pres., chief exec. officer Internat. Lead Xinc Research Orgn. Inc., N.Y.C., 1958-83; pres. Cosmos Engring. Inc., New Canaan, Conn., 1983-88; cons. Frankford Arsenal, Phila., 1955-75. Author: Cooperative Research and Development, 1984; contbr. articles to profl. jours.; patentee in field. Commr. Boy Scouts Am., Richmond, 1954-58; trustee R.I. Sch. Design, Mus. Transp., Boston. Served to lt. col. U.S. Army, 1943-46; mem. USAR (ret.). Recipient Freedom House award Wendell Wilkie Found., 1949; award Mass. Com. Catholics, Protestants and Jews, 1949; U.S. Rubber fellow, 1948. Fellow Am. Chem. Soc., AIME; mem. Am. Ceramics Soc., Am. Soc. Metals, Inst. Metals, Am. Die Casting Inst. (Doehler award), Am. Hot Die Galvanizers Assn. (Role of Honor award), Am. Welding Soc., Nat. Acad. Sci. (adv. bd. 1958-63), AAAS, Sigma Xi, Tau Beta Pi. Republican. Presbyterian. Club: Cosmos (Washington). Home: New Canaan Conn. Died Apr. 9, 1988; inurned; Mt. Auburn Cemetery, Berwyn, Ill.

RAFFMAN, RELLY, music educator, composer; b. New Bedford, Mass., Sept. 4, 1921; s. Joseph and Mary Alice (Worswick) R.; m. Rita LaPlante, Feb. 14, 1951; children: Diana, Nancy. B.A., Dartmouth, 1947; M.A., Columbia, 1949; postgrad., Ind. U., 1950-51. Instr. music S.W. Mo. State Coll., 1949-50; prof. music, then George N. and Selma Jeppson prof. music Clark U., Worcester, Mass., 1954-88. Composer: The Friendly Beasts, 1956, Triptych, 1957, Fye in Sinful Fantasy, 1959, In the Beginning, 1960, Shal I Compare Thee?, 1961, The Passionate Pilgrim, 1962, Farewell, Thou Art Too Dear, 1964, Jubilate Deo (Psalm 100), 1966, Matins, 1970, Sweet Was The Song, 1970, Virtue, 1975, The Three Ravens, 1975, Fü Eliot, 1980. Served to comdr. USNR, 1942-45, 51-54. Decorated D.F.C. with gold star, Air medal with 6 gold stars; recipient Ernest Bloch award, 1959. Home: Worcester Mass. Died Mar. 6, 1988; cremated.

RAFTERY, LAWRENCE M., labor union executive; b. St. Louis, Feb. 27, 1895; s. Sylvester T. and Rosa (Winterbauer) R.; m. Enid Veil King, Oct. 19, 1916; children: Josephine, Sylvester, John, Lawrence, Eugene, Donald, Mary Raftery Hartrum, Linda Raftery Bratton, Eloise Raftery March. Student, Christian Bros. Coll. Paperhander, painter, 1913-23; trustee, bus. agt. local 115, Painters Union, 1919-23, sec., bus. agt. dist. coun., 1925, del. bldg. trades dept. nat. conv., from 1926; v.p. Brotherhood Painters, Decorators and Paperhangers Am., 1937-52, gen. pres., 1952-65, pres. emeritus, from 1965; mem. adv. bd. Unemployment Bur. Mo., from 1929. Mem. Grand Jury, St. Louis, 1936. Roman Catholic. *

RAGAN, ROY ALLEN, editor; b. Indpls., Sept. 9, 1929; s. Paul Elden and Nora Elvira (Merritt) R.; m. Frankie M. Jones, Dec. 11, 1974; children: Paul Allen, Kevin Linder, Sheryl Ann, Mark Ray, Gregory Reese. B.A. in Sociology, Ind. U., 1956. Agt., Lincoln Nat. Life Ins. Co., Indpls., 1957-60; asst. editor Rough Notes Pub. Co., Indpls., 1960-64, mng. editor, 1967-70, editor, 1970-89, editor life and health ins. publs., 1981-89; tchr. 6th grade pub. schs. Indpls., 1964-67; freelance copywriter, editor.; Vice pres., bd. dirs. PSI, Indpls., PSI (extrasensory perception and other parapsychol. phenomena.). Author: 161 Direct Mail Letters, 1980. Active local Boy Scouts Am., 1968-78. Served with AUS, 1948-52. Mem. Nat. Assn. Life Underwriters, Gen. Agts. and Mgrs. Assn., Nat. Assn. Health Underwriters, Indpls. Mus. Art, Indpls. Zoo, WFYI Channel 20, Nat. Writers Club. Republican. Presbyterian. Clubs: Masons, Toastmasters. Home: Indianapolis Ind. Died Oct. 28, 1989; buried Maple Hill Cemetery, Plainfield, Ind.

RAGATZ, ROLAND ANDREW, chemical engineering educator; b. Prairie du Sac, Wis., Dec. 1898; s. John Jacob and Anna (Tarnutzer) R.; m. Nancy Gertrude Hansen, Mar. 15, 1930; children: Helen Karen, Andrew Roland. BSChemE, U. Wis., 1920, MS, 1923, PhD, 1931. Instr. chem. engring. U. Wis., Madison, 1920-26, asst. prof., 1926-29, 30-37, assoc. prof., 1937-42, prof., from 1942, chmn. dept., 1941-46, 49-51, 55-64; rsch. engr. A.O. Smith Corp., Milw., 1929-30. Collaborator: Applications of Chemical Engineering, 1940; co-author: Chemical Process Principles, Vol I, Material and Energy Balances, Vo. II, Thermodynamics, Chemical Process Principles Charts. Recipient Benjamin Smith Reynolds award, 1959. Mem. AICE, Am. Chem. Soc., Am. Soc. for Engring. Edn. (chmn. chem. engring. div. 1947-48, bd. dirs. 1948), Am. Soc. for Metals, Sigma Xi, Tau Beta Pi, Phi Lambda Upsilon, Alpha Chi Sigma. Lutheran. *

RAGLAND, JAMES BLACK, wholesale food distribution company executive; b. Murfreesboro, Tenn., Jan. 28, 1917; s. Charles Burton and Bess (Black) R.; m. Evelyn Claire Kingins, Nov. 14, 1940; children: Evelyn Claire Ragland McKnight, James Black Jr. BA, Vanderbilt U., 1938. With C.B. Ragland Co., Nashville, 1938-91; pres. C.B. Ragland Co., 1961-84, chmn., 1984-91; dir. 3d Nat. Bank Nashville. Served with USNR, 1942-45. Mem. Nat.-Am. Wholesale Grocers' Assn., Tenn. Wholesale Grocers Assn., Nashville C. of C. Methodist. Club: Belle Meade Country. Lodge: Rotary. Home: Nashville Tenn. Died Aug., 1991. †

RAHMAN, FAZLUR, philosophy educator; b. Seraisaleh, Pakistan, Sept. 21, 1919; came to U.S., 1969; d. Shihab and Wafadar (Qazi) Din; m. Bilqees Rafiq Rahman, Jan. 25, 1950; children: Mahmood, Khaliq, Salma, Laiq, Shafiq, Atiq. BA, U. Punjah, Pakistan, 1940, MA, 1942; DPhil, Oxford U., 1950. Lectr. in Persian studies and Islamic philosophy U. Durham, Eng., 1950-58; assoc. prof. Inst. Islamic Studies, McGill U., Montreal, Can., 1958-61; vis. prof. Islamic Research Inst., Karachi, Pakistan, 1961-62; dir. Islamic Research Inst., Islamabad, Pakistan, 1962-68; prof. Islamic Thought U. Chgo., from 1969, Harold H. Swift Disting. Service Prof. of Islamic Thought, from 1986; vis. prof. UCLA, 1969; cons. to U.S. State Dept., Washington, 1979-80, Govt. of Indonesia for Higher Islamic Studies, 1985. Contbr. numerous articles to profl. jours., author numerous books. Home: Chicago Ill. Died July 26, 1988.

RAHN, HERMANN, physiologist; b. East Lansing, Mich., July 5, 1912; s. Otto and Bell S. (Farrand) R.; m. Katharine F. Wilson, Aug. 29, 1939; children: Robert F., Katharine B. AB, Cornell U., 1933; student, U. Kiel, 1933-34; PhD, U. Rochester, 1938, DSc (hon.), 1973; Docteur honoris causa, U. Paris, 1964; LLD (hon.), Yonsei U., Korea, 1965; Titulo de Profesor Honorario U. Peruana Cayetano Heredia, Peru, 1980; MD (hon.), U. Bern, Switzerland, 1981. NRC fellow Harvard U., 1938-39; instr. physiology U. Wyo., 1939-41; asst. physiology Sch. Medicine, U. Rochester, 1941-42, instr., 1942-46, asst. prof., 1946-50, asso. prof., vice chmn. dept., 1950-56; Lawrence D. Bell prof. physiology, chmn. dept. Sch. Medicine, U. Buffalo (now SUNY-Buffalo), 1956-73; distinguished prof. physiology Sch. Medicine, U. Buffalo, from 1973; vis. prof. Med. Faculty San Marcos U., Lima, Peru, 1955, Dartmouth Med. Sch., 1962, Lab. de Physiologie Respiratoire, CNRS, Strasbourg, France, 1971, Max-Planck-Inst. für experimentelle Medizin, Göttingen, Fed. Republic Germany, 1977; mem. adv. com. biol. sci. Air Force Office Sci. Research and Devel., 1958-64; mem. physiol. study sect. NIH, 1958-62; mem. working committee space sci. bd. Nat. Acad. Sci.-NRC, 1962-65; mem. gen. med. research program project com. NIH, 1964-67; mem. research career award com. Nat. Inst. Gen. Med. Scis., 1968-72; cardiopulmonary adv. com. Nat. Heart Inst., 1968-71; mem. nat. adv. bd. R/V Alpha Helix, 1968-71; chmn. com. on underwater physiology and medicine NRC, 1972-74. Author: (with W.O. Fenn) A Graphical Analysis of the Respiratory Gas Exchange, 1955, (with others) Blood Gases: Hemoglobin, Base Excess and Maldistribution, 1973; editorial bd.: Am. Jour. Physiology, Jour. Applied Physiology, 1953-62, sect. editor for respiration, 1962, bd. publ. trustees, 1959-62; editor: (with W.O. Fenn) Handbook of Physiology-Respiration, Vols. I, II, 1964-65, Physiology of Breath-Hold Diving and the Ama of Japan, 1965, (with G. C. Whittow) Seabird Energetics, 1984, (with O. Prakash) Acid-Base Balance and Body Temperature, 1985. Recipient Sr. U.S. Scientist award Alexander von Humboldt Found., 1976. Mem. Am. Inst. Biol. Sci. (adv. com. physiol. 1957-64, adv. panel 1967-71), Am. Physiol. Soc. (council 1960-65, pres. 1963-64), Nat. Acad. Sci., Inst. Medicine, Nat. Acad. Sci., Harvey Soc. (hon.), Soc. Exptl. Biology and Medicine, Internat. Union Physiol. Scis. (council 1965-74, U.S. nat. com. 1966-74, v.p. 1971-74, exec. com. 1971-74), Am. Soc. Zoologists, Am. Acad. Arts and Sci., Sigma Xi. Home: Buffalo N.Y. Died June 23, 1990. †

RAINS, ALBERT, lawyer, bank executive, congressman; b. DeKalb County, Ala., Mar. 11, 1902; m. Allison Blair, Dec. 29, 1939. Student, Snead State Jr. Coll., Boaz, Ala., Jacksonville State Coll., U. Ala.; LLD, Jackson State U. Bar: Ala. 1928. Mem. firm Rains & Rains, Gadsden, Ala., 1928-91; dep. solicitor Etowah County, Ala., 1930-35; city atty. Gadsden, 1935-44; mem. House of Reps., Ala. Legislature, 1942-44, 79th yo 89th Congresses, 5th Ala. Dist.; mem. at large 88th Congress from Ala.; chmn. Housing subcom. Banking and Currency Com., joint Com. Def. Prodn.; chmn. bd. dirs. First City Nat. Bank; bd. dirs. First Ala. Bank, First Ala. Bancshares, Inc. Author: With Heritage So Rich. Trustee Athens Coll., Judson Coll. Democrat. Home: Gadsden Ala. Died Mar. 22, 1991; buried Gadsden, Ala.

RAJCHMAN, JAN ALEKSANDER, electronics engineer; b. London, Aug. 10, 1911; came to U.S., 1935, naturalized, 1940; s. Ludwik Witold and Marija Clotylda (Bojanczyk) R.; m. Ruth Vi Teitrick, June 30, 1944; children: Alice Rajchman Hammond, John A. Grad., Coll. of Geneva, 1930; MEE, Swiss Fed. Inst. Tech., Zurich, 1938. Engr. RCA Mfg. Co., 1935-36; with RCA Labs., 1936-76, dir. computer rsch. lab., 1961-67, staff v.p. data processing, 1967-71, staff v.p. info. scis., 1971-76; vis. Mackay prof. U. Calif., Berkeley, winter 1977; mem. user grantee group in optical communication NSF, from 1969; mem. advanced memory adv. com. Advanced Rsch. Project Agy., 1975, cons., 1977-89. Author, patentee infield; chmn. editorial adv. bd. RCA Rev., 1969-76. Co-recipient Leval medal Franklin Inst., 1947; recipient Harold Pender award U. Pa., 1977. Fellow IEEE (chmn. Liebman award com. 1970, chmn. awards fields com. 1971-73, Liebman Meml. award 1960, Edison medal 1974), Am. Phys. Soc.; mem. AAAS, NAE (peer rev. com. 1975-77), Am. Optical Soc., N.Y. Acad. Scis., Sigma Xi (chpt. pres.). Home: Princeton N.J. Died Apr. 1, 1989; buried Princeton, N.J.

RAMAGE, LAWSON PATERSON, naval officer; b. Monroe Bridge, Mass., Jan. 19, 1909; s. Lawson and Edith Mary (Ramage) R.; m. Barbara Alice Pine, Nov. 2, 1935; children: Joan Ramage Mitchell, James, Alfred, Virginia Ramage Ross. BS, U.S. Naval Acad., 1931; grad., U.S. Naval Postgrad. Sch., 1939, Armed Forces Staff Coll., 1950, Naval War Coll., 1955. Commd. ensign USN, 1931, advanced through grades to vice adm.,

1963; various assignments in ships and submarines, 1931-45; pers. officer, staff comdr. submarines Pacific Fleet, 1945-46; comdr. Submarine Div. 52, 1946-47; project officer Regulus guided missile Office Asst. Chief Naval Ops., 1947-50; readiness and new devel. officer, staff comdr. submarines Atlantic Fleet, 1950-51, chief staff, aide to comdr. submarine force, 1955; comdr. Submarine Squadron 6, 1951-53, USS Rankin, 1953-54; spl. asst. to chief naval ops. Navy Dept., 1955-56; dir. surface type warfare div. Office Chief Naval Ops., 1956-58, dir. anti-submarine and submarine warfare div., 1959-61, asst. chief naval ops. for fleet ops. and readiness, 1961-62, dep. chief naval ops., 1963-64; comdr. Cruiser Div. 2, Cruiser Force, Atlantic Fleet, 1958-59, dep. comdr. submarines, 1962-63; comdr. 1st Fleet, 1964-66; dep. comdr.-in-chief U.S. Pacific Fleet, 1966-67; comdr. Mil. Sea Transp. Svc., 1966-67. Decorated Medal of Honor, Navy Cross with gold star, Silver Star medal, Bronze Star medal, D.S.M. with gold star. Mem. Medal of Honor Soc., Army and Navy Legion of Valor, Mil. Order World Wars. Home: Washington D.C. Died Apr. 15, 1990; buried Arlington Nat. Cemetery.

RAMSAY, MARION LIVINGSTON, newspaperman; b. Balt., Aug. 12, 1897; s. William Breckinridge and Elizabetrh Burke (Rosan) R.; m. Alma Claire Gaines, June 30, 1924; 1 stepchild, William Galt; children: Jeanne Breckinridge, Andrew Clement. Student, Johns Hopkins U., 1920-23, George Washington U., 1926, Nat. U., 1928. Telegrapher, 1913-17; reporter, copyreader, rewrite man Balt. Star, 1920; reporter, polit. writer Balt. Sun, 1920-23; reporter Balt. Am., 1923, 24, city editor, 1925; corr., specializing in econ. and pub. utility subjects Universal Svc., Washington, 1925-35; dir. info. and rsch. REA, 1035-41; dir. info., advisor on Chgo. PWA subway and traction unification project Fed. Works Agy., 1941-44; mem. bd. editors U.S. News and World Report, 1944-63; freelance writer, from 1963; temp. spl. asst. chmn. FCC, 1938-39. Author: Pyramids of Power, 1937. Sgt. Signal Corps, U.S. Army, 1917-19, AEF. Mem. Nat. Press Club, Chgo. Press Club, Detroit Press Club. Democrat. *

RANARD, DONALD LOUIS, foreign service officer; b. Taunton, Mass., Jan. 13, 1917; s. Louis D. and Fannie (Delmont) R.; m. Virginia Celia Adams, Aug. 23, 1941; children: Patricia L., Donald A., Andrew B., John K., Amy S. AB, Brown U., 1940. Polit. sci. intern War Dept., Washington, 1941; chief classification OQMG, 1941-44; asst. chief, chief classification Dept. State, Washington, 1944-49; chief student and trainee sect., edn. exch. svc., 1949-50, asst. br. chief staff analyst, 1950-51, acting chief program devel. staff edn. exch. svc., 1950-51, chief leaders and specialist div., 1951-52; cultural attache, dir. ednl. exch. program Am. Embassy, Tokyo, 1952-55; sec., consul Diplomatic Svc., 1956-74; fgn. svc. inspector Fgn. Svc. Insp. Corps, 1956; consul, Penang, Malaya, 1956-59; 1st sec., counselor polit. assairs Am. Embassy, Seoul, 1959-62; dir. Office Far Ea. Programs, Dept. State, Washington, 1962-64; assigned Nat. War Coll., 1964-65; dep. chief mission, counselor, consul-gen. Am. Embassy, Rangoon, Burma, 1965-69, Canberra, Australia, 1969-70; country dir. for Korea, State Dept., 1970-90; cons. UNESCO, Paris, 1951; chmn. U.S. Ednl. Commn., Japan, 1952-55; spl. asst., mem. promotion. Mem. Washington Brown Club (past, sec., pres.), Internat. Club (Washington), Phi Sigma Kappa. Home: Vienna Va. Died July 27, 1990.

RANKIN, KARL LOTT, foreign service officer; b. Manitowoc, Wis., Sept. 4, 1898; s. Emmet Woollen and Alberta (Lott) R.; m. Pauline Jordan, Oct. 3, 1925 (dec.); m. Ruth Thompson, Mar. 6, 1978. Grad., Mercerburg Acad., 1916; student, Calif. Inst. Tech., 1917-19, Fed. Polytechnic, Zürich, 1920-21; C.E., Princeton, 1922; LL.D., Bowdoin Coll., Bates Coll. Constrn. supt. Nr. East Relief, Caucasus, 1922-25; mgr. of real estate devel. co. Linden, N.J., 1925-27; entered U.S. Govt. service, 1927; assigned as asst. trade commr. Prague, Czechoslovakia; comml. attaché Prague, 1929, Athens and Tirana, 1932, Brussels and Luxembourg, 1939; comml. attaché, consul Belgrade, 1940; comml. attaché Cairo, 1941; interned by Japanese in Manila before reaching Egypt, 1942-43; comml. attaché Cairo, 1944; counselor of embassy for econ. affairs Athens and Belgrade, 1944; chargé d'affaires a.i., Athens, 1946; counselor of legation Vienna, 1946-47; counselor of embassy Athens, 1947; chargé d'affaires a.i., 1947-48, apptd. career minister, 1948; consul gen. Canton, 1949, Hong Kong and Macau, 1949; minister and chargé d'affairs Taipei, 1950-53; ambassador Nat. Govt. Chiang Kai-shek, Taiwan, China, 1953-57, to Yugoslavia, 1958-61. Author: China Assignment, 1964. Hon. trustee Am. Coll. Greece, Athens. Served on active duty USN, 1918; lt. comdr. Res. 1937. Decorated Grand Cordon Order Brilliant Star (China). Mem. ASCE (life), Am.-Hellenic C. of C. (hon. pres.), Phi Kappa Sigma, Dial Lodge (Princeton). Congregationalist. Clubs: Cosmos (Washington); Princeton (N.Y.C.); Burnt Store Country, Isles Yacht (Punta Gorda, Fla.). Home: Kennebunkport Maine Died Jan. 15, 1991; cremated.

RANKIN, RAYMOND COILE, college president, clergyman; b. Greeneville, Tenn., Mar. 16, 1894; s. Thomas Samuel and Mary (Coile) R.; m. Katherine Peyton, May 12, 1924; children: Mary Ellen Rankin Cowles, Virginia Rankin Schaeffer, Jane Rankin Herring. AB, Tusculum Coll., 1914, DD, 1927; grad., McCormick Theol. Sem., 1917; LLD, King Coll., Bristol, Tenn., 1962. Ordained to ministry Presbyn. Ch., 1917. With YMCA, 1917-18; rural life worker Presbyn. Ch., 1918-23; assoc. pastor 1st Presbyn. Ch., Wichita, Kans., 1923-28, Watauga Avenue Presbyn. Ch., Johnson City, Tenn., 1931-44, Lindsay Meml. Presbyn. Ch., Memphis, 1944-51; exec. min. Fort Street Ch., Detroit, 1928-30; pres. Tusculum Coll., Greeneville, from 1951, trustee, 1942-51; chmn. week-day bd. religious edn., Wichita, 1924-25; mem. spl. race rels. com. Presbyn. Ch., 1947-49; pres. Johnson City Ministerial Assn., 1935, Mins. Assn. Memphis, 1947-48. Contbr. articles to ednl. and religious jours. Pres. Community Chest, Johnson City, 1932-33; chmn. dept. social svc. Coun. of Chs., Detroit, 1930. Mem. Ch. and Profl. Social Workers (pres. 1950-51), Cross Cut Club (pres. 1948-49), Civitans, Phi Delta Alpha. *

RAPAPORT, WALTER, hospital administrator, psychiatrist; b. nr. Carmel, N.J., Aug. 8, 1895; s. Charles and Reba (Sverlof) R.; m. Sadye Robin, Aug. 2, 1919; children: Janet Rapaport Einstoss, Robert, Shirley Rapaport Donovan. BS, Georgetown U., 1917, MD, 1919. Intern Washington Asylum, 1919-21; pvt. practice psychiatry, Washington, 1921022, Oakland, Calif., 1929-34; med. dir., supt. Mendocino State Hosp., Talmage, Calif., 1939-47, Agnews State Hosp., San Jose, Calif., 1947-53, from 1957; dir. mental hygiene State of Calif., 1953-57. Bd. regents U. Santa Clara, Calif. Capt. M.C., USNR, 1941-46. Fellow Am. Psychiat. Assn.; mem. AMA, Calif. Med. Soc., Assn. Mil. Surgeons U.S., Commonwealth Club Calif., Masons (32d degree), Shriners. *

RARICK, JOSEPH FRANCIS, SR., lawyer, educator; b. Bartonville, Ill., July 6, 1921; s. Orville Rufus and Jessie Sally (Boman) R.; m. Louise Lucille Strickfaden, Sept. 12, 1946; 1 son, Joseph Francis. B.A. with highest honors, U. Ill., 1943, J.D., 1948, LL.M. (Regent fellow), 1949; J.S.D., Columbia U., 1956. Bar: Ill. 1948, Okla. 1956. Asst. prof. law U. Minn., 1949-53; asso. prof. U. Okla., 1953-57, prof., 1957-67, David Ross Boyd prof. law, 1967-84, Alfred P. Murrah prof. law, 1984-89; cons. in field; adv., mem. legis. coms. Okla. Water Resources Bd. Author: The Right to Use Water in Oklahoma, 1975, Problems in Lands Allotted to American Indians, 1980; contbr. articles to law revs. and jours. Served to capt. U.S. Army, 1943-46. Recipient cert. meritorious service Okla. Water Users Assn., 1970, cert. meritorious service Okla. Water Resources Bd., 1971, cert. meritorious service Okla. Water Pollution Control Bd., 1979, Water Pioneer award Gov. of Okla., 1987; Kerr Found. grantee, 1968, 70, 72; Rocky Mountain Mineral Law Found. grantee, 1978; grantee several oil corps., 1980; named Father of Okla. Water Law, Okla. Ho. of Reps., 1983. Mem. Okla. Bar Assn., Order of Coif, Phi Beta Kappa, Phi Kappa Phi, Omicron Delta Kappa, Phi Delta Phi. Democrat. Anglican. Home: Norman Okla. Died Jan. 14, 1989; inurned; St. John's Episc. Ch. Columbarium, Norman, Okla.

RARIG, FREDERICK JOHN, lawyer, farmer; b. Mpls., July 3, 1915; s. Frank Miller and Eta C. (Galbreath) R.; m. Reva M. Schoenberg, June 26, 1938; children: Elizabeth Ann (Mrs. Chester J. Tyson III), Alice Jane, Susan Joanna (Mrs. Paul Todd Makler, Jr.), Frederick John. B.A. cum laude, U. Minn., 1935; LL.B., Cornell U., 1939. Bar: Minn. 1940. Spl. asst. to atty. gen. Dept. Justice, 1940-46, chief Los angeles office Anti-Trust div., 1944-46; v.p., asso. gen. counsel Rohm and Haas Co., Phila., 1974-80, ret. Mem. Devon Breeders Assn. N.Am., Adams County Fruitgrowers Assn. Democrat. Mem. Soc. of Friends Internat. House. Home: Orrtanna Pa. Deceased. †

RASHID BIN SAID AL-MAKTUM, SHEIKH See **AL-MAKTUM, SHEIKH RASHID IBN SAID**

RASMUS, HENRY IRVING, JR., clergyman; b. Spokane, Wash., Mar. 30, 1894; s. Henry Irving and Anna Margaret (Sniff) R.; m. Beulah Mae Bryum, Feb. 20, 1919. AB, U. So. Calif., 1917, BD, 1925, DD (hon.), 1938; postgrad., Boston U., 1917-18. Pastor, La Mesa, Calif., 1919-22; assoc. min. 1st Ch., Glendale, Calif., 1922-26, El Monte, Calif., 1926-28; assoc. min. Mt. Olive Ch., Hollywood, Calif., 1928-32, 1st Ch., Pomona, Calif., 1932-35, Univ. Ch,, L.A., 1935-36, 1st Ch., Pasadena, 1936-37, Central Park Ch., Buffalo, 1938-56; min. Community Meth. Ch., Balboa Island, Calif.; interim min. 1st Meth. Ch., Fullerton, Calif., 1959; on sabbatical leave, 1956-57; pres. Gen. Ministerium Buffalo and Erie County, 1951-52; mem. Commn. on World Svc. and Fin., Genesee Conf., Meth. Ch., 1948-56, also mem. bds. ministerial tng., conf. rels., 1938-56; pres. Buffalo Meth. Ministerium, 1948-49; trustee Buffalo Coun. of Chs., 1946-48. Author: Ministry of Symbolism. Spl. lectr. on Abraham Lincoln to clubs, schs. and chs. With OTC, 1918. Mem. Masons, Rotary, Phi Kappa Phi, Kappa Alpha. *

RATCLIFFE, MYRON FENWICK, investment management executive, banker; b. Evanston, Ill., June 5, 1902; s. James Lewis and Jean (Gardner) R.; m. Margaret Archibald, May 5, 1945; 1 dau., Elizabeth Robertson (Mrs. Robert W. Heinze). B.S., U. Ill., 1925, LL.B., 1927. With firm Goldman, Sachs & Co., N.Y.C., 1925-33; adminstr. financial codes NRA, 1934-35; syndicate mgr. Lehman Bros., N.Y.C., 1936-49; partner Bache & Co., Chgo., 1949-56; pres. Miami Corp., Chgo., 1956-77; dir. Miami Corp., 1956-83; pres. Cutler Oil & Gas Corp., Chgo., 1956-77; dir. Cutler Oil & Gas Corp., 1956-83; chmn. bd., dir. Nat. Blvd. Bank, Chgo., 1956-80; hon. chmn. Nat. Blvd. Bank, 1981-87; former dir. Nat.-Standard Co., Niles, Mich. Bd. govs. Midwest Stock Exchange, 1949-56; trustee Children's Home and Aid Soc. Ill.; former pres. Chgo. Curling Club. Served as lt. col. AUS, 1942-46. Decorated Legion of Merit. Clubs: Bond, Casino, Chicago, Mid-America (Chgo.); Indian Hill Country (Winnetka, Ill.); Old Elm Country (Fort Sheridan, Ill.); Birnam Wood Golf (Santa Barbara, (Calif.). Lodge: Masons. Home: Winnetka Ill. Died Mar. 9, 1991; buried Meml. Pk., Skokie, Ill.

RATH, EDWIN R(OSCOE), electrical engineer, business executive; b. Pleasanton, Nebr., Apr. 20, 1895; a. John and Lucretia (Lewis) R.; m. Geneva A. Bliss, June 19, 1917. BS, U. Pitts., 1017, EE, 1921. Instr., asst. prof., assoc. prof. elec. engring. U. Pitts., 1918-26; prof. math. and physics St. Vincent's Coll., Latrobe, Pa., 1918-26; with sales and promotion depts. Philip Carey Co., Cin., 1926-32; in charge indsl. rsch., prof. Engring. Expt. Sta., U. N.H., 1932-38; v.p., chief engr. Poser Transmission Coun., Inc., N.Y.C., from 1938; exec. v.p., sec. Nat. Indsl. Leather Assn., N.Y.C., from 1938; exec. sec. Fluid Controls Inst., Inc., from 1959. Mem. IEEE, Am. Soc. for Engring. Edn., Masons. *

RATH, THEODORE AUGUST, clergyman; b. Balt., July 2, 1904; s. Christian Gottlob and Lydia Friedericke (Pfost) R.; m. Lottie Grace Mahoney, Aug. 15, 1931; children: Donald Wilbert, Robert Earl, Janet Mabel Garrison, Lois Evelyn King. BD, Union Theol. Sem., 1930, STM, 1945; DD, Bloomfield Coll. and Sem., 1960. Ordained to ministry Evang. Ch., 1931. Min. Bklyn., 1931-33, Queens Village, N.Y., 1933-37, Clinton, N.J., 1937-46; assoc. exec. town and country chs. Presbyn. Ch. U.S.A., Synod, N.J., 1946-51; min. West Milford (N.J.) Presbyn. Ch.; founder Ringwood Presbyn. Ch. W. Milford, Ringwood and Oak Ridge Parish, 1951-56; synod exec. Synod, N.J., 1956-60; pres. Bloomfield Coll., 1960-69, pres. emeritus, 1969; interim pastor Webb Horton Meml. Presbyn. Ch., Middletown, N.Y., 1970-72, Westminster United Presbyn. Ch., Lakeland, 1975-76; 2d pastor First Presbyn. Ch., Port Jervis, N.Y., 1972-73; chaplain N.J. Reformatory Women, 1938-46. Chmn. com. ministry to migrants N.J. Coun. Chs., 1948-51, chmn. dept. rsch. and ch. devel., 1958-59, pres. coun., 1959-61, dir. town and country dept., 1945-47; mem. dept. ministerial rels. United Presbyn. Ch., 1959-64; bd. home missions Presbyn. Ch. U.S.A., 1959-61; chmn. Jud. Commn., Synod of N.J.; pres. N.J. Commn. Against Discrimination Housing, 1963-66; mem. Bloomfield Devel. com., 1961-65; bd. dirs. Blair Acad., Bloomfield Coll.; pres N.J. Coll. Fund Assn.; mem. N.J. adv. com. Salvation Army; trustee Alexander Linn Hosp., Sussex, N.J. Mem. N.J. Assn. Colls. and Univs. (pres. 1965-67), Newcomen Soc. N.Am. Home: Lakeland Fla. Died Nov. 17, 1989.

RATNER, MILTON DUNNE, transportation executive, artist; b. Oak Park, Ill., Mar. 1, 1918; s. Harry and Sadie (Kane) R.; m. Audrey Slater Muss, Sept. 27, 1980; children: John, Gary, Francine. B.S., Northwestern U., 1939, M.D., 1943. Intern Cook County Hosp., Chgo., 1939; co-founder to chmn. bd. Midwest Emery Freight System, Inc., Chgo., 1945-80; Chmn. bd. Rentar Industries, Inc.; dir. Rentar Trailer and Container Leasing Co. Artist collages, boxes and sculptures; exhbns. include Klein Gallery, No. Ill. U. Gallery. Bd. overseers Jewish Theol. Sem. Am.; bd. dirs. Am. Israel Cultural Found., N.Y.C., Spertus Coll. of Judaica, Chgo., Chgo. Med. Sch., Joslyn Art Museum, Omaha, Indpls. Mus. Art, Mus. Contemporary Art, Chgo.; trustee Roosevelt U., N.Y.C. Opera; mem. governing bd. Art Inst. of Chgo.; commr. Mus. African Art, Smithsonian Mus. Served to capt. M.C. U.S. Army, 1942-45. Mem. Am. Trucking Assn. (com. chmn.), Irregular Common and Contract Carriers Assn. (pres. 1959-65), Internat. Inst. Refrigeration, Alpha Omega Alpha. Jewish. Home: Chicago Ill. Died July 10, 1991.

RAUH, JOSEPH L., JR., lawyer; b. Cin., Jan. 3, 1911; s. Joseph L. and Sara (Weiler) R.; m. Olie Westheimer, Sept. 1, 1935; children: B. Michael, Carl S. BS, Harvard U., 1932, LLB, 1935; LHD (hon.), Hebrew Union Coll., 1978; LLD (hon.), Georgetown U., 1990. Bar: D.C. 1946. Law sec. supreme ct.justices Cardozo and Frankfurter, 1936-39; counsel various govt. agys., 1935-42; since practiced in Washington; gen. dep. housing expediter Vets. Emergency Housing Program, 1946-47; mem. Rauh & Levy, Washington, 1947-61, Rauh & Silard and successor firms, 1961-87; Washington counsel UAW, 1951-63, 66-87, gen. counsel, 1963-66; gen. counsel Leadership Conf. on Civil Rights, 1940-92; emeritus, 1992—; gen. counsel Miners for Democracy, 1970-72; Wayne Morse chair U. Oreg., 1989; regents' lectr. U. Calif.-San Diego, 1990. Author articles civil rights and liberties. Trustee Antioch Law Sch. and successor D.C. Sch. Law, 1980—; nat. bd. dirs. NAACP; vice chmn. D.C. Dem. Com., 1952-64, chmn., 1964-67, del. Dem. Nat. Conv., 1948, 52, 60, 64, 80. Lt. col. AUS, 1942-45. Decorated Legion of Merit, Disting. Service Star P.I.; recipient Civil Rights award Am. Jewish Congress, 1963, Florina Lasker Civil Liberties award, 1965, Oliver Wendell Holmes award ACLU, 1967, Isaiah award Am. Jewish Com., 1972, Nat. Congress Hispanic Citizens award, 1976, Four Freedoms award, 1983, Leadership Conf. Humphrey Civil Rights award, 1984, Bearer of Light award Union Am. Hebrew Congregations, 1985, Eugene V. Debs Found. award, 1986, Marshall-Wythe medallion William and Mary Coll., 1987, Common Cause award, 1987, Alliance for Justice award, 1987, ACLU Medal of Liberty, 1987, Antioch Law Sch. award, 1988, Mass. Sr. Action Council award, 1988. Cin. ACLU award, 1988, LDF award NAACP, 1989, Am. Assn. for Affirmative Action award, 1990, Pro Bono award NAACPLDF, 1990, Martin Luther King award B'nai B'rith, 1991; fellow Brandeis U., 1969—; hon. fellow U. Pa. Law Sch., 1970; John F. Kennedy Meml. fellow N.Z., 1974. Mem. Ams. for Dem. Action (chmn. exec. com. 1947-52, vice chmn. 1952-55, 57—, nat. chmn. 1955-57). Home: Washington D.C. Died Sept. 3, 1992. †

RAULT, CLEMENS V., naval officer, dentist; b. New Orleans, Aug. 11, 1896; s. Joseph E. and Sophie (Umbach) R.; m. Violet Engler. DDS, Loyola U., New Orleans, 1918; MSD, Northwestern U., 1937; DSc (hon.), Georgetown U., 1959. Commd. 2d lt. (j.g.) USN, 1918, advanced through grades to read adm., 1947; asst. chief Bur., chief Dental divsn. Bur. Med. & Surgery, ret., 1950; dean Georgetown U. Sch. Dentistry, from 1950; cons. NIH, clin. ctr., USPHS. Contbr. articles to profl. jours. Decorated D.S.M. Fellow Am. Coll. Dentists, Internat. Coll. Dentists, AAAS; mem. Internat. Assn. Dental Rsch., Am. Dental Assn., N.J. Dental Assn., Am. Assn. Dental Schs., others. *

RAUNIKAR, ROBERT, agricultural economist, educator; b. McAlester, Okla., June 13, 1931; s. Ed and Frances (Videgar) R.; m. Mary Angelum Leggett, Dec. 20, 1958; children: Robert Austin, Jane R. Miller, Frank Edwin. Student, Eastern Okla. State Coll., 1949-50; B.S., Okla. State U., 1956, M.S., 1958; Ph.D., N.C. State U., 1963. Research asst. N.C. State U., Raleigh, 1958; asst. prof. U. Ga., Griffin, 1962-69, assoc. prof., 1969-77, prof. agrl. econs., 1977-90, head dept., 1988-90. Contbr. articles to profl. jours. Served with USAF, 1951-55. Mem. Am. Agrl. Econs. Assn., So. Agrl. Econs. Assn. (pres. 1982-83), Internat. Agrl. Econs. Assn., Northeastern Agrl. Econs. Council, Agrl. Econs. Assn. Ga., Pi Gamma Mu, Gamma Sigma Delta. Home: Griffin Ga. Died Aug. 9, 1990; buried Oakhill Cemetery, Griffin Ga.

RAUSHENBUSH, STEPHEN, author, educator; b. N.Y.C., May 12, 1896; s. Walter and Pauline (Rother) R.; m. Josephine Joan Burns, Jan. 25, 1936; children: Stephanie, Burns; children by previous marriage: Roger, Carl. BA, Amherst Coll., 1917; student, U. Rennes, France, 1919, George Washington U., 1939. Labor rels. mgr. clothing industry Rochester, N.Y., 1919-20; engaged in travel and oil industry Venezuela and Mexico, 1920-22; staff mem. Bur. Indsl. Rsch., N.Y.C., 1923-25; sec. Nat. Com. on Coal and Power, 1926-29; asst. prof. Dartmouth Coll., 1929-30; chief investigator Legislative Inquiry on Pub. Utilities, Pa., 1931; dir. Indsl. Rels., Pa., 1931-34; chief investigator Legislative Inquiry on sub-Standard Industries, Pa., 1934; chief investigator, sec. U.S. Senate Munitions Inquiry, 1934-36; lectr. Pendel Hill Postgrad. Sch., 1938-39; cons. on resources UN, 1947-50, also Pub. Affairs Inst. Author: The Power Fight, 1932, The March of Fascism, 1939, Our Conservation Job, 1949; (with Josephine Raushenbush) The Final Choice, 1937; editor: The Future of Our Natural Resources, 1952, Pension in the Economy, 1955, Productivity and Employment, 1956; contbr. articles to profl. jours. Co-chmn. U.S. Food for Peace Misison, S.Am., 1961. With A.E.F., France, World War I. Mem. Am. Legion, Phi Beta Kappa, Alpha Delta Phi. Democrat. Baptist. Home: Sarasota Fla. Died July 4, 1991.

RAVER, LEONARD, musician, educator; b. Wenatchee, Wash., Jan. 8, 1927; s. Floyd M. and Ruth Elizabeth (Markham) R. B.Mus., U. Puget Sound, 1951; M.Mus., Syracuse U., 1952; D.Sacred Music, Union Theol. Sem., 1957. Organ faculty Juilliard Sch. Music, N.Y.C., 1975-90, U. Dubuque, Iowa, 1952-54, Bates Coll., 1960-61, Pa. State U., 1961-66, Gen. Theol. Sem., 1966-71, Hartt Sch. Music, Yale U., 1971-75, 1974-77. Organist, N.Y. Philharm., 1977-92, Orch. de Paris, 1978, Musica Aeterna Orch., N.Y.C., 1976-81, Internat. Congress of Organists, 1977, Radio City Music Hall with Am. Symphony Orch., 1981, Am. Guild Organists, 1984, Internat. Orgn. Festival, Netherlands, 1985; guest artist, Chamber Music Soc. of Lincoln Ctr., 1978; recs. with N.Y. Philharm.; rec. artist: Prayer and Toccata (Gail Kubik), A Quaker Reader (Ned Rorem), Constellations (Dan Locklair), Blessings (Daniel Pinkham), Suite for Organ (G. Read); repertory included modern Am. works, music for organ, electronic sounds and percussion, mixed new works with Baroque and Romantic scores; gave premier performances of Quaker Reader and Organbook by Ned Rorem, Organ Concerto by Daniel Pinkham, Auden Variations by Vincent Persichetti, King of Instruments by William Albright, Phantasmagoria and Galactic Novae by Gardner Read, Symphony for Organ by David Diamond. Served with U.S. Army, 1946-48. Fulbright scholar The Netherlands, 1958-60. Mem. Am. Guild Organists, Music Library Assn., Phi Mu Alpha Sinfonia. Home: Bayside N.Y. Died Jan. 29, 1992.

RAVIOLA, D'ELIA GIUSEPPINA, anatomist, physician, educator; b. Arona, Italy, Aug. 30, 1935; came to U.S., 1970; d. Giovanni and Milena (Di Toma) d'Elia; M.D. summa cum laude, U. Pavia (Italy), 1959; Ph.D. in Anatomy, 1968; m. Elio Raviola, Mar. 24, 1960; 1 child, Giuseppe James. Resident in oncology U. Pavia, 1964-68, asst. prof., 1960-70; asst. in opthalmology Harvard U. Med. Sch., Cambridge, Mass., 1970-71, lectr. opthalmology, from 1978; assoc. prof. anatomy Boston U. Med. Sch., 1972-78, prof., 1979-85; research prof. physiology, 1985-86. Fulbright scholar, 1964; recipient award New Eng. Ophtholmological Soc. Mem. Am. Soc. Cell Biology, Am. Assn. Anatomists, Assn. Research in Vision and Opthalmology, Internat. Soc. Eye Research. Club: Harvard. Died Oct. 30, 1986; buried Newton, Mass. Home: Newton Highlands Mass.

RAVITCH, MARK MITCHELL, surgeon, educator; b. N.Y.C., Sept. 12, 1910; s. Mitchell M. and Annette (Manevitch) R.; m. Irene Ravitch, Feb. 27, 1932; children: Nancy Ravitch Schwentker, Michael Mark, Mary Robin. A.B., U. Okla., 1930; M.D., Johns Hopkins U., 1934. Diplomate: Am. Bd. Surgery, Am. Bd. Thoracic Surgery. Resident Johns Hopkins Hosp., 1934-43, dir. blood bank, 1939-52; from instr. to asso. prof. surgery Johns Hopkins Med. Sch., 1941-52, asso. prof., then prof. surgery, 1956-66; clin. prof. surgery Columbia Coll. Physicians and Surgeons, 1952-56; dir. dept. surgery Mt. Sinai Hosp., N.Y.C., 1952-56; surgeon in chief Balt. City Hosps., 1956-66; prof. surgery U. Chgo. Med. Sch., 1966-69, prof. pediatric surgery, head div., 1966-69; surgeon in chief Montefiore Hosp., Pitts., 1969-86; prof. surgery U. Pitts. Med. Sch., 1969-89; Hon. asso., cons. surgeon Guy's Hosp., London, 1949; Felton Bequest vis. prof. surgery Royal Children's Hosp., Melbourne, Australia, 1968. Author 22 med. texts including: Intussusception, 1959, Alfred Blalock-1899-1964, 1966, Repair of Hernias, 1969, Congenital Deformities of the Chest Wall and Their Operative Correction, 1977, A Century of Surgery, 1880-1980, 2 vols., 1981, Atlas of General Thoracic Surgery, 1987, also contbr. 100 chpts. to books, over 400 monographs, articles; editor: The Papers of Alfred Blalock, 2 vols., 1966, Pediatric Surgery, 2 vols., 4th edit., 1986, Stapling in Surgery, 1984, Principles and Practice of Surgical Stapling, 1986, Second Thoughts of a Surgical Curmudgeon, 1986; editor-in-chief: Current Problems in Surgery, 1964-88, Surg. Rounds, from 1977. Served to maj. M.C., AUS, 1943-46. Decorated comdr. Order of the Couronne de Chene of the Grand-Ducy of Luxembourg; recipient medal Vishnevskii Inst. Surgery, Moscow, 1960; Roswell Park medal, 1984; McGraw medal, 1986; Service award Johns Hopkins U. Med. Alumni; U. Pitts. Rare Book Med. Libr. dedicated in his honor, 1992; repository of all his writings added to Nat. Med. Libr., Bethesda, Md., 1992. Fellow N.Y. Acad. Medicine, Royal Coll. Physicians and Surgeons (hon.) (Glasgow), Royal Australasian Coll. Surgeons (Melbourne) (hon.); mem. Am. Assn. Thoracic Surgery, Soc. Univ. Surgeons, Internat. Cardiovascular Soc., ACS (1st v.p. 1977, pres. S.W. Pa. chpt. 1977-78), Brit. Assn. Pediatric Surgeons (hon.), So. Thoracic Surg. Soc. (hon.), Soc. Vascular Surgery, Am. Surg. Assn. (1st v.p. 1973-74, pres. 1983-84, named Ofcl. Historian), So. Surg. Assn., Western Surg. Assn., Central Surg. Assn., Am. Acad. Pediatrics (pres. surg. sect. 1967-69, Ladd medal 1972), Am. Assn. Pediatric Surgery, Internat. Soc. Surgery, Soc. Clin. Surgeons (hon.), Acad. St. Chiara (Italy), Johns Hopkins Soc. Scholars, Can. Assn. Pediatric Surgeons (hon.), French Assn. Surgery (hon.), Phi Beta Kappa, Alpha Omega Alpha; hon. mem. Halsted Soc., Korea Surg. Soc., Surg. Research Soc. Australia. Home: Pittsburgh Pa. Died Mar. 1, 1989; buried West Tisbury, Mass.

RAWLINGS, CALVIN W(ILLIAM), member Democratic National Committee, lawyer; b. Provo, Utah, 1895; s. William S. and Margaret Ann Rawlings; m. Ruth Candland; children: Elaine, Joyce. LLB, U. Utah, 1919. Bar: Utah 1919. Mem. Rawlings, Wallace, Robert & Black, Salt Lake City, from 1919. Utah chmn. Dem. Nat. Com., 1932-36, mem. from Utah, from 1948; mem. exec. com. Boy Scouts Am., Salt Lake City. 1st lt. F.A., U.S. Army, 1917-18. Mem. ABA, Utah Bar Assn., Salt Lake County Bar Assn., Nat. Conf. Commrs. Uniform State Laws (life). Mem. LDS Ch. *

RAWLINGS, NORBORNE L., corporate executive; b. Lawrenceville, Ga., June 18, 1894; s. James and Jennie Gee (Meredith) R.; m. Lucy Dabney Hix, June 8, 1921; children: Dabney Hix Holloway, Norborne. BS, U.S. Naval Acad., 1917; MS, MIT, 1921. Commd. ensign USN, 1917, advanced through grades to rear adm., 1943; various positions, then head shipbldg. divsn. Bur. Ships Navy Dept., Washington, 1939-42; comdr. U.S. Naval Drydocks, 1943-45; vice chief material divsn. Sec. Navy, Navy Dept., until 1947; spl. rep. Newport News Shipbldg. & Dry Dock Co., 1947-49, asst. gen. mgr., 1949-50, gen. mgr., from 1950, v.p., 1952-53, exec. v.p., 1953-60, v.p. nuclear power activities, 1960, ret., then dir., chmn. exec. com. Decorated Legion of Merit (2). Mem. U.S. Naval Inst., Soc. Naval Architects, Marine Engrs., Soc. Naval Engrs. *

RAWSON, KENNETT LONGLEY, publishing company executive; b. Chgo., 1911; s. Frederick Holbrook and Edith (Kennett) R.; m. Eleanor MacMannis, 1954; children: Linda Kennett, Kennett Longley. Student, Phillips Acad., Andover, Mass., 1926-29; A.B., Yale, 1933. Mem. Arctic expdns. led by Comdr. Donald MacMillan, 1925, 26, 27, 29; navigator 2d Byrd Antarctic Expdn., 1933-35; editorial dept. G.P. Putman's Sons, 1936, editor firm, 1938-41, editor, 1945, v.p., editor in chief, dir., 1947-50; pres. David McKay Co., Inc., N.Y.C., 1950-74, Rawson, Wade Pubs., Inc., N.Y.C., 1974-81, Rawson Assocs. div. Scribner Book Co., N.Y.C., 1981-86; also sr. v.p. Scribner Book Cos.; chair publs. com. Rawson Assocs. div. Macmillan Publ. Co., N.Y.C., 1987-91. Author: A Boy's Eye View of the Arctic, 1926. Bd. dirs. emeritus Mather Hosp., Port Jefferson, N.Y.; former pres. Greenwich House, N.Y.C. Served as lt. comdr. USNR, 1941-45; communications, navigating officer, comdg. officer. Decorated Navy Cross. Mem. Century Assn. Clubs: Yale (N.Y.C.); Oldfield, Setauket Yacht. Home: East Setauket N.Y. Deceased. †

RAWSON, RALPH WILLIAM, military officer, manufacturing company executive, city manager; b. Cass City, Mich., May 21, 1916; s. William Audley and Mary Lena (Day) R.; m. Julie Cabanne Parker, June 1, 1941; children: William A., Julie M., Richard L., Nancy A. BS in Elec. Engring, U.S. Naval Acad., 1939; MS in Aero, Mass. Inst. Tech., 1946; grad., Advanced Mgmt. Program, Harvard, 1963. Commd. ensign USN, 1939; advanced through grades to rear adm. USNR, 1959; designated naval aviator USN, 1942, prin. assignments as aero. engring. duty officer, 1946-55; with Fansteel Metall. Corp., 1955-64, v.p., gen. mgr. chem. and metall. div., 1962-64; pres. Firth Sterling, Inc., Pitts., 1964-67, chmn., chief exec., 1967-68; pres. Vasco (a Teledyne Co.), Latrobe, Pa., 1968-70, Am. Gage and Machine Co., Elgin, Ill., 1970-72; city mgr. Madeira Beach, Fla., 1973-86. Decorated D.F.C. Mem. Harvard Bus. Sch. Club (Central Fla.), Gulf Beachs Rotary Club. Home: Madeira Beach Fla. Died Aug. 3, 1991; buried Fla. Nat. Cemetery, Bushnell.

RAY, SATYAJIT, film producer, director; b. Calcutta, India, May 2, 1921; s. Sukumar and Suprabha (Das) Ray; studied Ballygunge Govt. Sch., also Presidency Coll., Calcutta; B.A., U. Calcutta, 1974; D.Litt. (hon.), Royal Coll. Art, London, 1974, Oxford U., 1981; m. Bijoya Das, 1949; 1 son. Visualizer, D.J. Keymer & Co., advt. firm, 1943, art dir., 1949-56; film producer dir., 1953-92; produced first feature film Pather Panchali, 1955 (Cannes Spl. award 1956, San Francisco Best film, 1957, 15 other internat. awards); other films include Aparajito (Venice Grand Prix 1957, San Francisco best direction); Jalsaghar, 1958, Devi, 1959, Apur Sansar, 1959 (Selznick award, Sutherland trophy 1960), Teen Kanya, 1961, Kanchanjangha, 1962, Two Daughters, 1963, Mahanagar, 1964, Charulata, 1964, The Coward and the Holy Man, 1965, The Hero, 1965, The Adventures of Goopy and Bagha, 1968, Days and Nights in the Forest, 1969, The Adversary, 1970, Company Limited, 1971, Distant Thunder, 1973 (Berlin Film Festival Prize 1973), Golden Fortress, 1974, The Middle Man, 1975, The Chessplayers, 1977, The Kingdom of Diamonds, 1980, Pikoo, 1982, Enemy of the People, 1989, Descendents, 1990, The Stranger, 1991. Founder Film Soc., Calcutta, 1947. Decorated Order Yugoslav Flag, 1971, Legion of Honour, France; recipient Hon. Acad. award, 1992. Composer background music for own films, from 1960. Editor Sandesh, children's mag., from 1961. Author: (essays) Our Films, Their Films, 1976; (with Sukumar Ray) Nonsense Rhymes, 1975, also novels, short stories, film articles. Died Apr. 23, 1992. Home: Calcutta India

READ, HAROLD E., banker; b. Hartford, Conn., Sept. 8, 1898; s. Wallace F. and Dorothy (Cossey) R.; m. Margaret Gray Rodgers; 1 child, Harold E. Ed., Hartford High Sch. With Conn. Bank & Trust Co., from 1916, 1st v.p., dir.; bd. dirs. Nat. Fire Ins. Co. Hartford, Dunham Bush, Inc., West Hartford, Baxley & Henry, Inc., East Hartford. Trustee Soc. for Savs., Hartford. Mem. Conn. C. of C., NCCJ, Conn. Bankers Assn. *

REAM, NORMAN JACOB, management consultant; b. Aurora, Ill., June 20, 1912; s. Edward Franklin and Margaret E. (Colbert) R.; m. Eileen Margaret Bouvia, May 24, 1952; children: Judith Ellen (Mrs. William B. Miles), Patricia Margaret (Mrs. Paul W. Michel), Norma Jane (Mrs. Robert Yamaguchi), John Patrick. B.S. in Accountancy, U. Ill., 1934; postgrad., Northwestern U., 1940-41. C.P.A., Calif., Ill., N.Y. Mem. controllers staff Pure Oil Co., 1934-41; accountant Touche, Niven & Co. (C.P.A.'s), Chgo., 1941-42; sr. cons. George Fry & Assos., Chgo., 1942-47; dir. accounting research IBM Corp., 1947-50; asst. treas. Lever Bros., 1950-53; corp. dir. systems planning Lockheed Aircraft Corp., 1953-65; dir. Inst. Computer Scis. and Tech., Nat. Bur. Standards, 1965-66; spl. asst. to sec. navy, also mem. navy secretariat, 1966-69; prin. S.D. Leidesdorf & Co., 1969-71; chmn. Jamerica Cons. Group, from 1971; guest lectr. Japan Mgmt. Assn., Japan Productivity Center, 1963-67, Japan Acad. Sci., Hiroshima, 1965; Mem. U.S. del. UN Conf. Application Sci. and Tech. for Benefit Less Devel. Areas, Geneva, Switzerland, 1963; speaker Internat. Mgmt. Congress CIOS XV, Tokyo, Japan, 1969, Constl. Assembly of Inter-Am. Center Tax Adminstrn., 1967, 1st Internat.

Conf. on Communications, Tokyo, 1972. Contbr. articles to profl. jours. Gen. chmn. Incorporation City of Downey, Calif., 1954-56. Recipient Disting. Civilian Svc. medal USN; named to Resources Mgmt. Hall of Fame, 1989. Mem. Am. Inst. C.P.A.'s (hon.), Calif. Soc. C.P.A.'s, N.Y. Soc. C.P.A.'s, Am. Accounting Assn., IEEE (life), Inst. Mgmt. Scis., Am. Mgmt. Assn. (sr. planning council from 1962). Home: San Clemente Calif. Deceased. †

REAMEY, GEORGE SPOTTSWOOD, clergyman; b. Leatherwood, Va., Nov. 4, 1895; s. Henry Dupuy and Elsie (Gravely) R.; m. Mutie Moyler Owen, Apr. 27, 1922; m. Elizabeth Dudley Dratt, Aug. 30, 1960. AB, Randolph Macon Coll., 1917, DD (hon.), 1946; BD, Emory U., 1920-22; PhD, Yale U., 1932. Ordained to ministry Meth. Episc. Ch., 1922. Pastor Gladys Charge, 1922-26, Cradock Ch., 1926-28, Appomattox, 1928-29, Highland Springs Ch., Va., 1932-34, Byrd Park Ch., Richmond, 1934-35, Fulton Hill Ch., Richmond, 1935-38; editor Richmond Christian Adv., 1938-39, Va. Meth. Adv., from 1939. Author: Do You Know Your Bible?, Daily Devotional Readings in the Gospels of Matthew, Mark, Luke, John and Book of Acts, Strength for Today series, What Can I Believe About God?; also articles. Mem. Conf. Hist. Soc., Nat. Meth. Press Assn., Phi Beta Kappa. *

REARDON, JOHN EDWARD, mayor; b. Kansas City, Kans., Aug. 23, 1943; s. Joseph E. and Helen (Cahill) R.; m. Helen Kasick, June 18, 1966; children—Joseph, Kathleen. B.S. in History and Govt, Rockhurst Coll., Kansas City, Mo., 1965. Tchr., head social studies dept. Arrowhead Jr. High Sch., Kansas City, Kans., 1966-72; register of deeds Wyandotte County/Kansas City, Kans., 1972-75; mayor of Kansas City, Kans., from 1975; mem. Kansas City Devel. Corp. Bd. dirs. Kansas City United Way. Recipient Loyalty Day award VFW; named Outstanding Young Kansan Jaycees, 1978, also numerous certificates of appreciation. Mem. U.S. Conf. Mayors, Kans. League Municipalities (v.p.), Kansas City C. of C. Democrat. Roman Catholic. Club: Central Ave. Optimists. Home: Kansas City Kans. Deceased.

REASONER, HARRY, television news reporter; b. Dakota City, Iowa, Apr. 17, 1923; s. Harry Ray and Eunice (Nicholl) R.; m. Kathleen Ann Carroll, Sept. 7, 1946 (div. Apr. 1981); children—Stuart, Ann, Elizabeth, Jane, Mary Ray, Ellen, Jonathan; m. Lois Parker Weber, May 28, 1988. Student, Stanford U., U. Minn., 1942; BJ, U. Minn., 1989. Reporter, drama critic Mpls. Times, 1942-43, 46-48; asst. dir. publicity Northwest Airlines, 1948-50; newswriter radio sta. WCCO, Mpls., 1950-51; editor regional prodn. center USIA, Manila, Philippines, 1951-54; news dir. sta. KEYD-TV, Mpls., 1954-56; reporter, corr. CBS News, from 1956, reporter, corr., regular mem., co-editor weekly show "60 Minutes", 1968-91; former reporter, corr. ABC News. Author: (novel) Tell Me About Women, 2d edit., 1964; (collected essays) The Reasoner Report, 1966; (memoirs) Before the Colors Fade, 1981. Served with AUS, 1943-46. Recipient 3 Emmy awards including for news documentary, 1967-68, outstanding news broadcasting, 1974; Peabody award, 1967; U. Mo. honor medal, 1970. Home: Westport Conn. Died Aug. 6, 1991.

RECKNAGEL, RICHARD OTTO, physiology educator; b. Springfield, Mo., Jan. 11, 1916; s. Emil and Ella (Moench) R.; m. Maesine G. Recknagel, June 19, 1943; children—Frank Otto, Judith Susan. B.S., Wayne State U., 1939; Ph.D., U. Pa., 1949; A Laurea Honoris Causa, U. Turin, Italy, 1992. Asst. prof. physiology Sch. Medicine, Case Western Res. U., 1956-60, asso. prof., 1960-65, prof. physiology and biophysics, 1965-86, prof. emeritus, 1986-91, dir. dept. physiology, 1978-86. Served to 1st lt. USAAF, World War II. Recipient Kaiser-Permanente Teaching award, 1977; NIH grantee, 57-86. Home: Cleveland Ohio Died Dec. 2, 1991; buried Paint Creek Cemetery, Lake Orion, Mich.

REDDALL, H(ENRY) HASTINGS, business executive; b. Bloomfield, N.J., Nov. 8, 1893; s. John William and May Eloise (Smith) R.; m. Janet Ewing, Oct. 15; 1925. B.S., Colgate U., 1918; postgrad., U.S. Naval War Coll., 1932, 33, Rutgers U., 1955. Joined Western Electric Co., N.Y.C., 1913 (on leave 1915-19); auditor assigned No. Electric Co., Montreal, Que., Can., 1919-22; asst. cashier Western Electric, 1922, asst. treas., 1922-31, 32-41, 46; treas. subsidiary Nassau Smelting & Refining Co., Inc., Tottenville, N.Y., 1931-32; chief corp. accountant parent co. Western Electric Co., 1941-43, chief factory auditor, 1943-45; chief field auditor Nassau Smelting & Refining Co., Inc., 1945-46, treas., 1946-58, 1946-58; treas. Weco Corp., 1946-58, dir., 1947-58. Contbr.: crossword puzzles to N.Y. Times; others. Chmn. fin. com., treas. St. James Episcopal Ch., Brookhaven, also; del. diocesan convs., bd. dirs. Colgate Alumni Corp., 1937-40, 43-46; trustee Dodge Fund Colgate U., 1950-60; pres., trustee Brookhaven Free Library., 1959-75, trustee emeritus, 1975-89. Lt. (j.g.) USNR, 1917-36. Recipient Alumni award for distinguished service to Colgate U., 1945; Commodore's Meml. Sailing award, 1965; Bishop's Cross Episcopal Diocese L.I., 1971. Mem. Mil. Order Fgn. Wars, Soc. Colonial Wars, Loyal Legion, Vet. Corps. Artillery, Mil. Soc. War of 1812, SAR, Bellport-Brookhaven Hist. Soc. (trustee, treas., chmn. bldg. com. 1966-84, hon. trustee 1984, trustee meml. fund), Stamford Geneal. Soc., Soc. for Preservation L.I. Antiquities, Suffolk Marine Mus. N.Y., Great South Bay Yacht Racing Assn., Telephone Pioneers Am., Descs. Washington Army at Valley Forge, Phi Beta Kappa, Delta Kappa Epsilon (hon. 1987). Republican. Clubs: Bellport Bay (N.Y.); Yacht (comdr. 1946-47, 59-60, hon. trustee 1960-89); Quantuck Beach (Westhampton, N.Y.). Home: Brookhaven N.Y. Died Oct. 28, 1989; buried Woodland Cemetery, Bellport, N.Y.

REDER, BERNARD, sculptor, graphic artist; b. Czernowitz, Austria; came to U.S., 1943, naturalized, 1948; s. Jakob and Hinde (Gingold) R.; m. Gusti Korn, Sept. 1924. Student, Acad. Fine Arts, Prague, 1920. One-man shows Prague, 1928, 35; retrospective exhbn. Wildenstein Gallery, Paris, 1940; exhibited Galerie de Berri, Paris, 1940, Grace Borgenichg Gallery, N.Y.C., 1951-53, Art Inst. Chgo., 1953, World House Galleries, N.Y.C., 1959, 61, also Whitney Mus. Modern Art, Norton Gallery and Sch. Art, Mpls. Inst. Arts, Marion Koogler McNay Art Inst., San Antonio; group exhbns. Mus. Modern Art; represented in permanent collections Mus. Modern Art, Whitney Mus. Am. Art. Ford Found. grantee for sculpture, 1959; recipient award for sculpture Am. Acad. Arts & Letters, 1962. *

REED, GEORGE FRANKLIN, investment executive, lawyer; b. Beaver, Pa., Jan. 19, 1935; s. Harold Francis and Mary Lou (Eckles) R.; m. Anne Stewart Dixon, May 5, 1962; children: George Franklin, Peter, Carolyn. BA, Princeton U., 1956; JD, U. Pa., 1959. Bar: Pa. 1960. Assoc. Morgan Lewis & Bockius, Phila., 1960-67; gen. counsel Pa. Dept. Ins., Harrisburg, 1967-69; ins. commr. Commonwealth of Pa., Harrisburg, 1969-71; sr. v.p., counsel Am. Gen. Corp., Houston, 1971-79, vice-chmn. bd., 1979-83; chmn. bd. Am. Capital Mgmt. & Rsch. Inc., Houston, 1976-90, pres., 1976-87; bd. dirs. 30 registered investment cos. managed by Am. Capital Mgmt. and Rsch. Chmn. state employees div. Tri-County United Fund, Harrisburg, 1969, bd. dirs., 1970-71; mem. Pa. Gov.'s Cabinet, 1969-71; bd. regents Mercersburg Acad., from 1971; trustee Retina Rsch. Found., from 1979, Salvation Army, from 1978, St. Joseph Hosp., 1980-88; bd. dirs. Houston Symphony Soc., 1982-88, Am. Cancer Soc., from 1987. With U.S. Army, 1959-60, Pa. N.G., 1960-65. Recipient Disting. Service award Harrisburg Jaycees, 1969. Mem. ABA, Tex. Bar Assn., Pa. Bar Assn. (chmn. young lawyers sect. 1968-69), Phila. Bar Assn. (sec. jr. bar conf. 1962-63), Houston Bar Assn., Houston C. of C. (bd. dirs. 1974-75), Investment Co. Inst. (bd. govs. 1977-88, chmn. 1984-86), Lakeside Country Club (Houston), Princeton Club (N.Y.C.). Republican. Presbyterian. Home: Houston Tex. Deceased. †

REED, PHILIP DUNHAM, corporation executive; b. Milw., Nov. 16, 1899; s. William Dennis and Virginia Brandreth (Dunham) R.; m. Mabel Mayhew Smith, July 16, 1921 (dec.); children: Philip Dunham, Kathryn Virginia. B.S. in Elec. Engring, U. Wis., 1921, LL.D., 1950; LL.B. cum laude, Fordham U., 1924; LL.D., Union Coll., 1941, Bklyn. Poly. Inst., 1942, Swarthmore Coll., 1954; D.C.S., N.Y. U., 1950; E.D., Rensselaer Poly. Inst., 1941. With law firm Pennie, Davis, Marvin & Edmonds, 1921-22; v.p., patent counsel Van Heusen Products, Inc., 1922-26; with law dept. Gen. Electric Co., 1926-37, asst. to pres. and dir., 1938-39, chmn. bd., 1940-42, 45-58, chmn. fin. com., 1946-59, dir. emeritus, 1968-89; dir. Fed. Res. Bank of N.Y., 1959-65, chmn. bd., 1960-65; past dir. Am. Express Co., Bankers Trust Co., Cowles Broadcasting, Inc., Bigelow-Sanford Inc., Eurofund Internat. Inc., Elfun Trusts, Kraft Corp., Met. Life Ins. Co., Otis Elevator Co., Scott Paper Co., Tiffany & Co.; sr. cons. to dir. of priorities Office Prodn. Mgmt., 1941, dept. dir. materials div., July-Dec. 1941; chief bur. industries WPB, Jan.-July 1942; dep. chief of U.S. Mission for Econ. Affairs, London, Eng., 1942-43, chief of mission with rank of minister, Oct. 1943-Jan. 1945; cons. U.S. del. Conf. on World Orgn., San Francisco, 1945. Vice chmn. bus. adv. council Dept. Commerce (now Bus. Council), 1951-52, mem., from 1940, mem. U.S. adv. com. on info., 1948-61; chmn. U.S. del. Anglo-Am. Council on Productivity, 1948-52; trustee Com. for Econ. Devel., mem. research, policy com., 1946-75, chmn., 1948-49; bd. dirs. Internat. Exec. Service Corps., 1964-86, chmn. exec. com., 1966-74; trustee Eisenhower Exchange Fellowships, 1953-75, vice chmn., 1955-75, chmn. fin. com., 1956-58; trustee Winston Churchill Found. of U.S., 1970-75; former dir. Carnegie Endowment for Internat. Peace; former v.p. Met. Opera Assn. Recipient President's Certificate of Merit award, 1947; decorated officer Legion of Honor, France, 1947, comdr., 1951. Mem. Internat. C. of C. (exec. com. U.S. council from 1945, chmn. 1945-48, pres. chamber 1949-51, hon. pres., until 1989), Council on Fgn. Relations (dir. 1946-69, dir. emeritus 1969-89). Republican. Conglist. Clubs: University (N.Y.C.), Links (N.Y.C.); Apawamis (Rye, N.Y.); Blind Brook (Port Chester, N.Y.); Bohemian (San Francisco); Mill Reef (Antigua, W.I.). Home: Rye N.Y. Died Mar. 10, 1989; buried Christ's Ch., Rye, N.Y.

REED, WILLIAM DOYLE, entomologist; b. Eupora, Miss., Sept. 25, 1897; s. James William and Ophelia Caroline (Riddell) R.; m. Agnes Louise Pope, May 29, 1926. BS, Miss. State Coll., 1922; postgrad., Cornell U., 1923-24. Prof. zoology and entomology Clemson Coll., 1922-25; entomologist U.S. Dept. Agr., B.E. & P.A., 1925-42; inf. res. U.S. Army, 1922-37; entomologist, chief insect & rodent control sect. Office Chief Engrs., Washington, 1946-62; ret. Contbr. articles to profl. jours. Mem. A.C.I.R.C., Am. Soc. Mil. Engrs., AAAS, Entomol. Soc. Am., Entomol. Soc. Wash., Am. Assn. Econ. Entomologists, APHA, Va. Acad. Scis., Wash. Acad. Scis., others. *

REES, ALBERT (EVERETT), economist; b. N.Y.C., Aug. 21, 1921; s. Hugo R. and Rosalie (Landman) R.; m. Candida Kranold, July 15, 1945; 1 son, David; m. Marianne Russ, June 22, 1963; children: Daniel, Jonathan. B.A., Oberlin Coll., 1943; M.A., U. Chgo., 1947, Ph.D., 1950. Instr. Roosevelt Coll., Chgo., 1947-48; asst. prof. econs. U. Chgo., 1948-54, assoc. prof., 1954-61, prof., chmn. dept., 1961-64; prof. econs. Princeton U., 1966-79, chmn. dept., 1971-74, provost, 1975-77; pres. Alfred P. Sloan Found., N.Y.C., 1979-89; sr. rsch. economist Princeton U., N.J., 1989-92; chmn. Math. Policy Rsch. Inc., 1989-92; past dir. Nabisco Brands, Inc.; staff Coun. Econ. Advisors, 1954-55; dir. Council on Wage and Price Stability, 1974-75. Author: Real Wages in Manufacturing, 1890-1914, 1961, The Economics of Trade Unions, 1962, (with George P. Shultz) Workers and Wages in an Urban Labor Market, 1970, The Economics of Work and Pay, 1973, Striking a Balance, 1984, (with Sharon P. Smith) Faculty Retirement in the Arts and Sciences, 1991; editor Jour. Polit. Economy, 1954-59. Trustee Oberlin Coll., from 1986. Mem. Am. Econ. Assn. Home: Princeton N.J. Died Sept. 5, 1992. †

REESE, CHARLES LEE, JR., publisher, editor; b. Wilmington, Del., Apr. 7, 1903; s. Charles Lee and Harriet Stedman (Bent) R.; m. Harriet Hurd Curtis, Oct. 2, 1926 (dec. 1971); children: Charles Lee (dec. 1985), Sara C. Pryor, Peter A. Karthaus (dec. 1976); m. Annette Mason Bush, Sept. 16, 1972. Grad., Wilmington Friends Sch., 1920; B.A., U. Va., 1924; grad. study, Cambridge U., Eng., 1924-25; LLD (hon.), U. Del. Mng. editor Popular Radio, N.Y.C., 1925-26; mem. editorial staff Time (mag.), 1927; with News-Journal papers, since 1927, editor, 1934-47, exec. editor, v.p., 1947-55; pres. News-Jour. Co., 1955-68, chmn. bd., 1966-72, vice chmn. bd., 1972-78. Author: (with Charles M. Curtis) Old Swede's Church, 1698-1938, (with Alfred E. Bissell) Further Notes on the Pursuit of Salar, The Horse on Rodney Square; editor Delaware History mag., 1946-70, (memoir) Farwell Christima; editor: The Autobiography of Christopher L. Ward. Dir. emeritus Wilmington Med. Ctr.; chmn. Lalor Found.; hon. dir., past pres. Wilmington Music Sch.; past pres. Hist. Soc. Del.; hon. trustee Wilmington Soc. of Fine Arts (past pres.). Recipient Gov.'s award for Outstanding Contbn. in History and Culture. Clubs: Wilmington, Greenville Country. Home: Hockessin Del. Died Aug. 16, 1989; buried Smyrna, Del.

REESE, HARRY BROWNE, lawyer, educator; b. Feb. 11, 1926. s. Harry Benson and Dorothy (Browne) R.; student Ohio Wesleyan U., 1943-44, B.A. summa cum laude, Ohio State U., 1947; LL.B. magna cum laude, Harvard U., 1950; m. Nancy Lea Wonders, Sept. 6, 1947; children: Ellyn Browne, David Wonders, Susan Elisabeth, Gwendolyn Alma, John Benson. Bar: Ohio 1950, Ill. 1954. Law clk. to judge, U.S. Ct. Appeals (2d cir.) 1950-51; asst. prof. law, Ohio State U., Columbus, 1951-53; asst. prof. Northwestern U., Chgo., 1953-55, assoc. prof., 1955-57, prof., 1957-75, William Wirt Gurley prof. law, 1975-91; cons. Pres.'s Commn. Gov. Security, 1957-58. Trustee Law Sch. Admission Coun., 1961-78, pres., 1969-72; Ill. commr. Nat. Conf. Commrs. on Uniform State Laws, from 1973; one of six law profs. to appear in film series "Great Law Teachers" to demonstrate teaching techs., 1967. Served with USNR, 1943-45. Mem. Assn. Am. Law Schs. (exec. com. 1976-80), Siot and Cynwydd Soc. (pres. 1964), Phi Beta Kappa, Phi Delta Theta, Phi Delta Phi. Republican. Episcopalian. Died Sept. 5, 1991; buried Ridgewood Cemetery, Wellston, Ohio. Home: Winnetka Ill.

REESE, KENNETH WENDELL, diversified manufacturing company executive; b. Orange, Tex., Aug. 1, 1930; s. Richard W. and Florence (Mulhollan) R.; m. Mary A. Broom, Aug. 22, 1955; children: Jimmy, Michael, Gary. BBA, U. Houston, 1954. Asst. treas. Firestone Tire & Rubber Co., Akron, Ohio, 1968-70, treas., from 1970, v.p., 1973-75, exec. v.p. finance, 1975; sr. v.p. fin. Tenneco Inc., Houston, 1975-78, exec. v.p., 1978-90, vice chmn., from 1990, also bd. dirs.; bd. dirs. Tex. Commerce Bancshares Inc., Fleming Cos., Inc., Tex. Med. Ctr. Bd. dirs. Cotton Bowl Athletic Assn.; mem. adv. bd. Coll. Bus. Adminstrn., U. Houston. 1st lt. AUS, 1954-56. Mem. U. Houston Athletic Lettermans Assn. Baptist. Clubs: Heritage, Houston City, Ramada, River Oaks Country, Forum (bd. dirs.). Home: Houston Tex. Died Nov. 1991. †

REESE, WILLIS LIVINGSTON MESIER, legal educator; b. Bernardsville, N.J., June 16, 1913; s. William Willis and Augusta (Bliss) R.; m. Frances Gallatin Stevens, June 26, 1937; children: William Willis, Frances Gallatin, John Rathbone, George Bliss, Alexander Stevens. Grad., St. Paul's Sch., N.H., 1931; AB, Yale U., 1935, LLB, 1938; LLD, U. Leuven, Belgium, 1972, Trinity Coll., 1979. Bar: N.Y. 1938, U.S. Supreme Ct. 1945. Law clk. Judge Thomas Swan, 1938-39; assoc.

Winthrop, Stimson, Putnam & Roberts, N.Y.C., 1939-41; from asst. prof. to Charles Evans Hughes prof. law Columbia U., 1946-81, emeritus, 1981-90, dir. Parker Sch. Fgn. and Comparative Law, 1955-80; Lectr. Hague Acad. Internat. Law, 1964, 76, mem. curatorium, from 1975; mem. Inst. Internat. Law, from 1971, adv. com. on pvt. internat. law Sec. of State, from 1964; U.S. del. Hague Conf. Pvt. Internat. Law, 1956, 60, 64, 68, 72, 76, 80, 84, 85, ; reporter restatement (2d) conflict laws Am. Law Inst. Author: (with Rosenberg) Cases and Materials on Conflict of Laws, 1984. Bd. dirs. Episc. Ch. Found., from 1979, N.Y. Legal Aid Soc., 1951-71; chmn. Community Action for Legal Services, 1967-70; former mayor Hewlett Bay Pk., L.I.; mem. N.Y. Law Revision Commn., 1973-83; Pres. bd. trustees Millbrook Sch., 1968-77; pres. Five Towns United Fund, 1959, chmn. bd., 1958, 60. Served as capt. AUS, 1941-46. Mem. Am. Assn. Comparative Study Law (sec., dir. 1955-80), Joint Conf. Legal Edn. (1st v.p.), Assn. of Bar of City of N.Y., Internat. Law Assn. (Am. br.), Am. Bar Assn., Am. Soc. Internat. Law, Am. Fgn. Law Assn. (pres. 1964-67), Am. Assn. UN (pres. Five Towns chpt. 1962-63, 77-81), Acad. Polit. Sci. (life), Inst. Internat. Law, Phi Beta Kappa, Order of Coif. Episcopalian (sr. warden, sec. standing com. Diocese N.Y. 1963-65). Clubs: Century, Rockaway Hunting, Union. Home: Hughsonville N.Y. Died July 9, 1990; buried Wappingers Falls (N.Y.) Cemetery.

REESING, JOHN PALMER, JR., English language educator; b. Gatesville, Tex., Sept. 15, 1920; s. John Palmer and Anne (Baines) R. B.A., Baylor U., 1941; M.A., Tulane U., 1942; Ph.D., Harvard U., 1954. Mem. faculty George Washington U., Washington, 1946-49, 54-87, prof. English, 1962-87, chmn. dept., 1963-70, 75-83, acting chmn., 1972-73; instr. English Oberlin Coll., 1953-54. Author: Milton's Poetic Art, 1968. Served to 1st lt. AUS, 1942-46. Mem. MLA, Modern Humanities Rsch. Assn. (Am. sec. 1984-90), Internat. Assn. Univ. Profs. English, Renaissance Soc. Am. Episcopalian. Clubs: Cosmos, Harvard (Washington). Home: Arlington Va. Died July 15, 1990; buried Masonic Cemetary, Gatesville, Tex.

REF-REN See KONARSKI, FELIKS

REGAN, PURDY C., steel engineer; b. Catawba, Ky., July 5, 1897; s. William L. and Maude L. (Purdy) R.; m. Jean Seaman, May 1, 1942; children: William M., Don S., Blair S., Betty J. Grad., Pitts. Tech. Inst., 1916. Steel mill worker, 1911-16; with sales dept. Andrews Steel Corp., 1919-37; organized P.C. Regan Co. metall. cons., sales engrs., Cin., 1937, pres., from 1937; v.p., dir. Columbus Anvil & Forging Co., from 1947. Mem. Am. Soc. Steel Treaters, Am. Soc. Steel Engrs. *

REGESTER, JOHN DICKINSON, college dean; b. Duquesne, Pa., Oct. 20, 1897; s. Enos Dickinson and Vernetta Belle (Steffy) R.; m. Frances Willard Andrews, Mar. 29, 1923; children: John Andrews, Adda Elizabeth. AB, Allegheny Coll., 1920; STB, Boston U. Sch. Theology, 1922; PhD, Boston U., 1928; postgrad. Harvard U., U. Edinburgh, U. Basel, U. Chgo. Prof. philosophy U. Puget Sound, from 1924, dean, 1936-58, dean faculties, 1958-60, dean grad. sch., from 1960; prof. philosophy Boston U., summer 1934. Author: Albert Schweitzer: The Man and His Work; contbr. to Albert Schweitzer Sein Denken und Sein Weg, 1962. Hosp. corpsman USNR, 1917-19. Borden P. Bowne fellow Boston U., 1922-23, 27-28, Jacob Sleeper travelling fellow Boston U., 1923-24. Mem. Am. Philos. Assn., N.W. Coll. Pers. Assn., Phi Beta Kappa, others. *

REHFUSS, WALTER GUY, life insurance company executive; b. Wadena, Minn., Nov. 8, 1936; s. Kenneth Edward and Selma Eldora (Reinsvild) R.; m. Camille Grace Dziedzic, June 20, 1959 (div.); m. Susan Keyser, Dec. 21, 1985; children: Peter, Kenneth, Kay, Sue Ellen. BS in Psychology and Math., Carroll Coll., 1958. Actuary Old Line Ins. Co., Milw., 1958-69; v.p. life systems Network Data Processing, Cedar Rapids, Iowa, 1969-71; v.p. Am. Defender Life, Raleigh, N.C., 1971-74; sr. v.p. adminstrn. Ky. Cen. Life Ins. Co., Lexington, from 1974; adv. bd. Space Design Internat., Cin., from 1987. Vice chmn. United Way, Lexington, 1977; bd. dirs. Lexington Transit Authority, 1977-78, Jr. Achievement, Lexington, 1984-86, Lexington Sister Cities Internat., from 1988. Fellow Life Office Mgmt. Assn.; mem. CLU Assn. (CLU award 1978). Republican. Episcopalian. Home: Lexington Ky. Deceased. †

REICHELDERFER, F(RANCIS) W(ILTON), meterological consultant; b. Harlan, Ind., Aug. 6, 1895; s. Francis Allen and Mae (Carrington) Lynde; m. Beatrice Hoyle, June 19, 1920; 1 child, Bruce Allen. AB in Sci., Northwestern U., 1917, DSc (hon.), 1939; postgrad., Harvard U., 1918, Geophys. Inst., Bergen, Norway, 1931. Apptd. naval meterol. officer, 1918; meteorologist 1st trans-Atlantic flight, internat. aviation races, spl. assignments, news svcs., U.S. Weather Bur., 1938-64; cons. internat. meteorol. orgns., from 1964. Contbr. articles to profl. jours. Fellow AAAS, Inst. Aero. Scis.; mem. Wash. Acad. Scis., NAS, Am. Meteorol. Soc., Internat. Meteorol. Orgn., World Meteorol. Orgn., Nat. Adv. Com. for Aeronautics, Am. Geophys. Union, Philos. Soc. Wash., Internat. Geophys. Year, others. *

REICHHOLD, HENRY, business executive; b. Berlin, July 31, 1901; came to U.S., 1924, naturalized, 1937; s. Carl and Lina (Petersen) R.; m. Ilse Breuer, may 1, 1930; children: Dieter, Ingrid. Student, Univs. Berlin and Vienna, 1908-19. Lab. asst. Ford Motor Corp., Detroit, 1924-27; founder and pres. Reichhold Chemicals, Inc. (former subs. Beck, Koller), Ferndale, Mich., 1927-42; chmn., bd. dirs. Reichhold Chemicals, Inc., Ferndale, Mich., 1942-89, chmn. exec. com., 1956-85, then pres., gen. mgr., chmn. exec. com., to chmn., CEO, 1963-85. Mem. N.Y. Athletic Club, Whippoorwill Country Club. Home: Chappaqua N.Y. Died Dec. 11, 1989.

REID, ROSS, lawyer, business executive; b. Spokane, Wash., Mar. 9, 1917; s. William George and Margaret (Gamble) R.; m. Sara Falknor, Dec. 31, 1940 (div.); 1 dau., Heather (Mrs. Edmund A. Schaffzin); m. Marney Sick Meeker, Jan. 19, 1966. A.B., Whitman Coll., 1938; student, U. Wash. Sch. Law, 1938-40; J.D., Northwestern U., 1942; LLD (hon.), Whitman Coll., 1988. Bar: Ill. 1941, N.Y. 1943, D.C. 1960. Assoc. firm Root, Clark, Buckner & Ballantine, N.Y.C., 1942-53; mem. firm Dewey, Ballantine, Bushby, Palmer & Wood (and predecessors), N.Y.C., 1954-62; v.p., dir., gen. counsel Beechnut Life Savers, Inc., 1962-68; sr. v.p., dir., gen. counsel, exec. com. Squibb Corp., 1968-83, dir. exec. com., 1983-84; dir. Allegheny Power System, Inc.; trustee Emigrant Savs. Bank; mem. N.Y State Lawyers Com. to Support Ct. Reorgn., 1958-60. Chmn. bd. Am. Heart Assn., 1972-74; chmn. N.Y. Heart Assn., 1964-72, exec. com.; bd. dirs. Internat. Cardiology Found.; bd. mem. 1st v.p. Internat. Soc. and Fedn. Cardiology; trustee Whitman Coll., Robert A. Taft Inst. Govt., Food and Drug Law Inst.; chmn. The 50 Million Dollar Campaign for Whitman, 1980-87. Served with USAAF, 1945. Recipient Gold Heart award Am. Heart Assn., 1970. Fellow Am. Bar Found.; mem. ABA, N.Y. Bar Assn., Assn.of Bar of City of N.Y. (chmn. membership com. 1961-64, exec. com. 1962-66), Jud. Conf. Second Circuit (exec. sec. plans com. 1960-64), Am. Judicature Soc., Order of Coif, Beta Theta Pi, Delta Sigma Rho, Delta Theta Phi. Clubs: University (N.Y.C.), West Side Tennis (N.Y.C.), Union; Coral Beach and Tennis (Bermuda); Seattle Tennis. Home: New York N.Y. Died Oct. 9, 1989; buried N.Y.C.

REID, WILLARD MALCOLM, parasitologist, educator; b. Ft. Morgan, Colo., Oct. 9, 1910; s. Willard and Caroline (Riggs) R.; m. Janet Helen Sharp, Sept. 4, 1937; children: Caroline (Mrs. Ted R. Ridelhuber), Donald Malcolm, Willard Sharp, Nancy Jane (Mrs. Jerry Robbins), Judith Ann (Mrs. Roy Graves). B.S., Monmouth Coll., 1932, D.Sc., 1960; postgrad., Heidelberg (Germany) U., 1933; M.S., Kan. State Coll., 1937, Ph.D., 1941; postgrad., Brown U., 1937-38, U. Mich., 1939. Instr. Assiut (Egypt) Coll., 1933-35; prof. biology, dept. head Monmouth Coll., 1937-51; Fulbright research prof. U. Cairo, Egypt, 1951-52; head poultry unit U.S. State Dept. AID, 1952-55; parasitologist poultry sci. dept. U. Ga., Athens, from 1955; Distinguished Alumni Found. prof. U. Ga., 1964-78, Disting. Alumni Found. prof. emeritus, from 1978; poultry cons. Eli Lilly Co., Mathtech; internat. cons. on poultry disease control, coccidiosis. Author textbook on sci. writing, also numerous articles. Mem. Am. Soc. Parasitologists, Poultry Sci. Assn., Am. Assn. Avian Pathologists, Am. Soc. Protozoologists. Home: Athens Ga. Deceased. †

REIDY, EDWARD MICHAEL, lawyer; b. Cambridge, Mass., Sept. 18, 1897; s. David Joseph and Margaret (Geary) R.; m. Florence R. Hanrahan, Apr. 21, 1924; children: Elizabeth Ann Callaghan, Jean Marie McLoone, Edward J., Florence Kapusta. LLB, Georgetown U., 1920, MPL, 1921, LLM, 1921. Bar: D.C. 1920, U.S. Supreme Ct., 1928. Various positions, 1913-22; atty. ICC, Washington, 1922-28, asst. chief counsel, 1928-48, assoc. chief counsel, 1948-52, chief counsel, from 1952, gen. counsel, 1954-55; gen. atty. So. Pacific Co., Washington, 1955-62; pvt. practice Washington, from 1962. Contbr. articles to profl. jours. Sgt. U.S. Army, 1918. Mem. Am. Legion, Cath. War Vets. *

REIFEL, BEN, banker, former congressman; b. Parmelee, S.D., Sept. 19, 1906; s. William and Lucy Lily Burning (Breast) R.; m. Alice Janet Johnson, Dec. 26, 1933 (dec. Feb. 1972); 1 child, Loyce Nadine Anderson; m. Frances Reifel; 1 stepdau. Carol Honstead. BS, S.D. State U., 1932; MPA, Harvard, 1950, DPA, 1952; D Humanities, S.D. U., 1971. With Bur. Indian Affairs, 1933-60, reservation supt., 1946-49, 52-54, area dir., 1955-60; mem. 87th-91st congress 2d Dist. S.D.; pres. Arrow, Inc.; chmn. bd. Am. Indian Nat. Bank, Washington. 1st v.p. Nat. Easter Seal Bd.; mem. adv. bd. Nat. coun. Boy Scouts Am.; mem. Nat. adv. Coun. for Edn. Disadvantaged Children; bd. dirs. regional program bicentennial Am. Issues Forum, Denver; former trustee Huron (S.D.) Coll., Freedom Found., Valley Forge, Pa. With AUS, WWII. Recipient Outstanding Am. Indian award, 1956, Indian Coun. Fire Honor award 1960, Silver Antelope award Boy Scouts Am., 1960, Disting. Svc. award Dept. Interior, 1961. Mem. Masons, Rotary, Elk. Republican. Home: Aberdeen S.D. Died Jan. 2, 1990.

REILLY, WILLIAM PATRICK, advertising executive; b. Norfolk, Va., Nov. 22, 1917; s. Charles Francis and Mary (Miney) R.; m. Anne Waite, May 16, 1953; 1 child, Patricia Mary. Student, Coll. William and Mary, 1935. With Stds. Brands, Inc., 1936-41, 46-53, Young & Rubicam, Inc., 1953-91; v.p. Young & Rubicam, Inc., San Francisco, 1958-64, sr. v.p., 1964-68, dir. domestic brs., 1967-68; vice chmn., gen. mgr. Young & Rubicam, Inc., N.Y.C., 1968-91; chmn. bd. subs. J.K. Gill, Ltd., Portland, Oreg., 1971-91. Active local Community Fund; bd. dirs. Advt. Coun. Mem. Am. Mktg. Assn., Am. Assn. Advt. Agys., Nat. Assn. Outdoor Advertisers (exec. com.), Wee Burn Country Club, Union League Club (N.Y.C.). Home: Chevy Chase Md. Died Oct. 7, 1991.

REINEKE, HAROLD GEORGE, physician; b. New Ulm, Minn., July 30, 1897; s. George Frederick and Louisa Augusta (Remund) R.; m. Ruth Catherine Olsen, Jan. 24, 1922. Student, Carleton Coll., 1915-17; BS, U. Minn., 1921, MB, 1922, MD, 1923. Diplomate Am. Bd. Radiology. Postgrad. medicine Cin. Gen. Hosp., 1924-25, resident, 1926-29, asst. dir. dept. radiology, 1934-51; instr. radiology U. Cin., 1929-34, asst. prof., 1934-47, assoc. prof., 1947-53, prof. clin. radiology, from 1953; radiologist various hosps.; jr. mem. Drs. Doughty, Bader & Reineke, 1939-46, sr. mem. Drs. Reineke, Hawley, Brown & White. With U.S. Army, World War I. Fellow Am. Coll. Radiology, Acad. Internal Medicine; mem. Cin. Acad. Medicine, Ohio State Med. Assn., AMA, Ohio State Radiol. Assn., Cin. Radiol. Soc., Archeol. Inst. Am., Hist. & Philos. Soc. Ohio, Radiol. Soc. N.Am., Am. Roentgen Ray Soc., others. *

REINSCH, JAMES LEONARD, cable company executive; b. Streator, Ill., June 28, 1908; s. Henry Emil and Lillian (Funk) R.; m. Phyllis McGeough, Feb. 1, 1936; children: Penelope Luise, James Leonard. B.S., Northwestern U., 1934. With radio sta. WLS, Chgo., 1924; former chmn. bd. Cox Broadcasting Corp.; chmn. bd. Sunbelt Cable Co., 1983-86; pres. Nat. Cable Communications Inc., from 1986; former dir. 1st Nat. Bank Atlanta; also cable cons. Former chmn. U.S. Adv. Commn. Information; radio adviser to White House, 1945-52; TV and radio cons. Democratic Nat. Com.; exec. dir. Democratic Nat. Conv., 1956, 60-64, also arrangements dir., 1968, TV-radio dir. Dem. presdl. campaign, 1960; mem. Carnegie Commn. on Future Public Broadcasting. Author: Radio Station Management, 1948, rev. edit., 1960, Getting Elected, 1987. Bd. dirs., exec. com. Am. Cancer Soc. Recipient D.F. Keller award Northwestern U., Disting. Bus. Mgmt. award Emory U., 1968, award Am. Women in Radio and TV, 1975, Disting. Svc. award Nat. Assn. Broadcasters, 1978, Peabody award, 1990. Mem. Atlanta Art Assn., Internat. Radio and TV Soc. (gold medal 1973), Cable Pioneers, Capital City Club (Atlanta), Peachtree Golf Club (Atlanta), Burning Tree Club (Washington), Broadcast Pioneers (N.Y.C.), Nat. Capital Dem. (Washington), Palm Beach Polo and Country Club, Palm Beach Yacht Club, Wellington Club, Rotary, Delta Chi, Di Gamma Kappa. Home: Marietta Ga. Died May 9, 1991; buried Arlington Meml. Cemetery, Atlanta.

REISCHAUER, EDWIN OLDFATHER, East Asian historian, diplomat; b. Tokyo, Japan, Oct. 15, 1910; s. August Karl and Helen (Oldfather) R.; m. Adrienne Danton, July 5, 1935; children—Ann Heinemann, Robert Danton, Joan Simon; m. Haru Matsukata, Jan. 6, 1956. A.B., Oberlin Coll., 1931; A.M., Harvard U., 1932, Ph.D., 1939; student, U. Paris, 1933-35. Studies abroad on Harvard-Yenching Inst. fellowship in France, Japan, China, 1933-38; instr. Harvard U., 1939-42, asso. prof. Far Eastern langs., 1946-50, prof., 1950-61, Univ. prof., 1966-81; dir. Harvard-Yenching Inst., 1956-61; sr. research analyst Dept. State, summer 1941, War Dept., 1942-43; chmn. Japan-Korea Secretariat; and spl. asst. to dir. Office of Far Eastern Affairs, Dept. of state, 1945-46; mem. Cultural Sci. Mission to, Japan, 1948-49; U.S. ambassador to Japan, Tokyo, 1961-66; Chmn. bd. trustees Harvard-Yenching Inst., 1970-83. Author: Japan, Past and Present, 1946, rev. edit., 1963, The United States and Japan, 1950, rev. edit., 1957, 90, Wanted: An Asian Policy, 1955, Ennin's Diary: The Record of a Pilgrimage to China in Search of the Law, 1955, Ennin's Travels in T'ang China, 1955, (with J.K. Fairbank) East Asia, The Great Tradition, 1960, (with Fairbank and Craig) East Asia: The Modern Transformation, 1965, Beyond Vietnam: The United States and Asia, 1967, Japan: The Story of a Nation, 1970, rev. edits., 1981, 89, (with Fairbank and Craig) East Asia: Tradition and Transformation, 1973, Toward the 21st Century: Education for a Changing World, 1973, The Japanese, 1977, My Life between Japan and America, 1986, The Japanese Today: Change and Continuity, 1988. Served as lt. col. Mil. Intelligence Service, War Dept. Gen. Staff, 1943-45. Awarded Legion of Merit. Mem. Assn. for Asian Studies (pres. 1955-56), Japan Acad. (hon.), Phi Betta Kappa. Home: La Jolla Calif. Died Sept. 1, 1990; cremated.

REISLER, RAYMOND, SR., lawyer, arbitrator, judge, hearing officer; b. Bklyn., Nov. 28, 1907; s. Frank O. and Fannie R.; m. Harriet Spitzer, Sept. 10, 1933; children: Nancy, Raymond. B.A., Cornell U., 1927, postgrad. in law, 1926-27; J.D., Columbia U., 1929; postgrad. (fellow), Nat. Coll. Judiciary, 1975. Bar: N.Y. 1930, U.S. Supreme Ct. 1957. Assoc. firm Ruston & Snyder, Bklyn., 1930-34, partner, 1934-36; prin. firm

Raymond Reisler (successor firm to Ruston & Snyder), 1936-67; judge Criminal Ct. N.Y.C., 1967-78; acting justice N.Y. State Supreme Ct., 1977-78; counsel firm Buchman, O'Brien & Williams, N.Y.C., from 1978; jud. hearing officer N.Y. State; adminstrv. law judge N.Y. State Dept. Health, Dept. Agriculture and Markets; referee N.Y. State Commn. on Jud. Conduct; appellate div. N.Y. State Supreme Ct.; hearing officer state and city govt. agys.; trial officer N.Y.C. Housing Authority; trial examiner N.Y.C. Bd. Edn.; arbitrator Am. Arbitration Assn., Cir. Ct. of City of N.Y.; dep. asst. atty. gen. State of N.Y., 1952-65; lectr. St. Johns' U. Law Sch., 1957-62; mem. faculty Bklyn. Law Sch., 1963-68; speaker in field. Contbr. articles to profl. jours. Life mem. emeritus Cornell U. Council. Fellow N.Y. Bar Found.; mem. ABA (chmn. nat. joint conf. lawyers, ins. cos. and adjusters 1963-67, chmn. nat. conf. unauthorized practice law 1961, com. unauthorized practice of law), N.Y. State Bar Assn. (exec. com. 1951-63, chmn. com. unlawful practice law 1955-64, plaque for service 1964, resolution of appreciation 1964), Bklyn. Bar Assn. (pres. 1960-61, mem. trustee council from 1961, Scroll of Appreciation 1961, 72, Gold Medal award 1973), Queen's County Bar Assn. (jud. council), Assn. Bar City N.Y., Fed. Bar Assn., Fed. Bar Council, Cornell Law Alumni Assn., Columbia Law Alumni Assn., Judges Assn. of Criminal Ct. City N.Y., Iota Theta (hon.), Sigma Alpha Mu (nat. pres. 1959-61). Clubs: Princeton, Cornell, Cornell Alumni of N.Y. (pres. 1967-69); Tennis (Palm Springs) (hon.); Williamsburg (hon. v.p.). Lodges: K.P. (dep. grand chancellor 1941-42, hon. life. mem. 1979-92, Meml. award 1979), Lions (hon. pres., life mem.). Home: Neponsit N.Y. Died Apr. 2, 1992.

REISS, RAYMOND HENRY, manufacturer; b. Chgo., June 29, 1897; s. Jacob L. and Mary (Detmer) R.; m. Ruth Ann Kransz, Sept. 16, 1924 (dec. 1935); children: Raymond Henry, Rita Gorman, Ruth Clifford, Theodore J., Lucy R. Mullen. BS, Georgetown U., 1919, PhD, 1933; LLD, Fordham U., 1938; PhD, St. Michael's Coll., 1950. With Ronthor Reiss Corp., from 1919, v.p., 1924-28, exec. v.p., 1928-55, pres., chmn., from 1955; bd. dirs. Reiss Steamship Co., C. Reiss Coal Co., others. Mem. pres.'s coun. Georgetown U. Decorated Knight of Malta, Knight Comdr. Equestrian Order Holy Sepulchre of Jersusalem. *

REMICK, LEE (MRS. WILLIAM RORY GOWANS), actress; b. Quincy, Mass., Dec. 14, 1935; d. Frank E. and Margaret (Waldo) R.; m. William A. Colleran, Aug. 3, 1957 (div. 1969); children: Kate, Matthew; m. William Rory Gowans, Dec. 18, 1970. Student, Barnard Coll., 1953. Broadway debut in Be Your Age, 1953; other plays include: Anyone Can Whistle, 1964, Wait Until Dark, 1966, Bus Stop, London, 1974, Agnes of God, 1982, I Do, I Do, 1983, Follies in Concert, 1985; films include: A Face in the Crowd, 1956, The Long Hot Summer, 1957, Anatomy of a Murder, 1959, Wild River, 1959, Sanctuary, 1960, Experiment in Terror, 1961, Days of Wine and Roses, 1961 (Acad. award nomination), The Wheeler Dealers, 1962, Baby The Rain Must Fall, 1963, Hallelujah Trail, 1965, No Way to Treat a Lady, 1967, The Detective, 1968, Hard Contract, 1969, Loot, 1972, A Delicate Balance, 1973, Hennessy, 1974, The Omen, 1976, Telefon, 1977, The Europeans, 1979, The Competition, 1980, Tribute, 1980; appeared in TV prodns.: Jennie, Lady Randolph Churchill, 1975, (mini-series) Wheels, 1978, Ike, 1979, Haywire, 1980, The Women's Room, 1981, The Letter, 1982, Mistral's Daughter, 1984, Rearview Mirror, 1984, The Snow Queen, 1985, Toughlove, 1985, Follies in Concert, 1986, Of Pure Blood, 1986, Eleanor in Her Own Words, 1986, (mini-series) Nutcracker: Money, Madness, Murder, 1987, Money, Murder, Madness, 1987, The Vision, 1988, A Bridge to Silence, 1989, Around The World in 80 Days, 1989, Dark Holiday, 1989. Home: Los Angeles Calif. Died July 2, 1991.

RENAUD, PIERRE JEAN MARIE, civil engineer; b. Paris, June 18, 1894; s. Jules and Valentine (Philippe) R.; m. Antoinette Trevoux, Oct. 1, 1923; children: Helene Wolfe, Didier. Ed., Poly. Sch., Paris, 1913. Engr. Civil Dept. Bridges & Hwys., Rouen, France, 1920-31; chief engr., dir. Harbour of Algier, 1932-41; gen. dir. works Lyon, France, 1942-44, gen. insp. bridges & hwys., 1948, commr. reconstrn., 1949; gen. sec. Nat. Def., 1949, gen. commr. pub. works & bldgs., 1951; pres. Dept. Gen. Counsel Bridges & Hwys., 1957, hon. pres., 1963; v.p. Counsel of Adminstrn. Soc. Nat. Les Chemnius de Fen Francais, 1958; pres. counsel adminstrn. Compagnie Gen. Transatlantique, 1963-64. With French Army, 1914-18. Decorated Mil. Cross 1914-18 with 5 citations; comdr. Legion of Honor, Equatorial Africa; recipient grand prize city planning World Exhbn., Paris, 1937. *

RENICK, RALPH APPERSON, journalist; b. N.Y.C., Aug. 9, 1928; s. Ralph Apperson and Rosalie (Dwyer) R.; m. Elizabeth Jane Henry, June 5, 1949 (dec. July, 1964); children: Patricia Garrard, Kathryn MacParland, Ralph A., Susan Joseph, Pamela, Michele. A.B., U. Miami, Fla., 1949. News dir. TV Sta. WTVJ, Miami, 1950-58, v.p. for news, 1958-85; v.p. Wometco Enterprises, Miami, 1959-77; v.p. in charge Wometco Broadcast News Ops., 1977-85; commentator CBS Sta. WCIX, Miami, 1989-90; instr. TV news reporting U. Miami, 1952-58. Mem. Fla. Trust for Hist. Preservation, 1987-91. Recipient Radio-TV Mirror award, 1967. Mem. Radio Television News Dirs. Assn. (nat. pres. 1958-59), AP Broadcasters Assn. (pres. 1979-81), Nat. Press Club, Radio-TV Corrs. Assn., Iron Arrow, Confrerie de la Chaine des Rotisseurs, Soc. Profl. Journalists (chpt. pres. 1958-59). Lodge: Knights of Malta. Home: Miami Shores Fla. Died July, 1991; buried Miami, Fla.

RENNER, JOHN WILSON, retired physical science educator; b. DeSmet, S.D., July 25, 1924; s. Harry Milton and Maude E. (Callahan) R.; m. Carol Jean Fennel, June 19, 1948; children: Mary Joanne, Michael John, David Joseph. B.A., Huron (S.D.) Coll., 1945, U. S.D., 1946; M.A., U. S.D., 1948; Ph.D., State U. Iowa, 1955. Sci., math. tchr. Elk Point (S.D.) High Sch., 1946-47; physics instr. Moorhead (Minn.) State Tchrs. Coll., 1948-49; instr. physics U. S.D., 1949-52; phys. sci. supr. Lab. High Sch., State U. Iowa, 1952-55; asst. prof. sci. edn., physics instr. Univ. High Sch., U. Ill., 1955-56; dir. Radiol. Def. Sch., Fed. Civil Def. Adminstrn., 1956-58; asst. prof. physics and edn., acting head dept. physics Creighton U., Omaha, 1958-59; asso. exec. sec. Nat. Sci. Tchrs. Assn., 1959-62; prof. sci. edn. U. Okla., Norman, 1962-87; prof. emeritus sci. edn. U. Okla., from 1987, adj. prof. physics, 1979-87, dir. sci. curriculum improvement study Okla. Trial Ctr.,, 1964-73, assoc. disting. lectr., 1985-87; cons. sci. curriculum improvement study U. Calif.-Berkeley, 1964-73; sci. edn. cons. Educator's Progress Service, Randolph, Wis.; dir. tchr. services Frontiers Sci. Found. Okla., Inc., 1962-65; adv. bd. Sci. World mag., 1962-66. Author: (with Harry B. Packard) Experiments and Exercises in Physics, 1961, Investigations in Physics, 1974, (with Stafford and Ragan) Teaching Science in the Elementary School, 1968, 3d edit., 1979, (with others) Guiding Learning in the Secondary School, 1972, Guiding Learning in the Elementary School, 1973, (with Don G. Stafford) Teaching Science in the Secondary School, 1972, (with D.G. Stafford, Vivian Coulter) The Learning Science Program, Grades K-6, 1977, (with D.G. Stafford, John J. Rusch) Physical Science: Inquiry and Investigation, 1977, (with Edmund A. Mark) The Learining Cycle and Elementary School Science Teaching, 1988; also films, film strips.; contbr. articles profl. jours.; cons., contbr.: World Book Ency. Served with USNR, 1943-44. Named Tchr. of Yr. U. Okla., 1966; recipient Regents award for superior teaching, 1971, Benjamin J. Dasher Outstanding Paper award IEEE, 1978, Disting. Svc. citation Huron Coll., 1980, Alumni Achievement award U. S.D., 1986, Disting. Contbn. to Sci. Edn. Through Rsch. award U. S.D., 1988. Mem. NEA, Nat. Sci. Tchrs. Assn. (dir. Sci. Teaching Leaflet Series 1961-66, Robert H. Carleton award), Nat. Assn. Rsch. in Sci. Teaching (pres. 1979-80), Phi Beta Kappa, Sigma Xi, Sigma Pi Sigma, Phi Delta Kappa. Home: Norman Okla. Deceased. †

RENTZEL, DELOS WILSON, government official; b. Houston, Oct. 20, 1909; s. William Frederick and Sarah (Enloe) R.; m. Janice P. Rentzel, Oct. 1972; children by previous marriage: Delos Wilson, Thomas Lance, Christopher Horton. Student, Tex. Agrl. and Mining Coll., 1929. Dir. communications Am. Air Lines, Inc., 1931-43; pres. Aero. Radio, Inc., 1943-48, Aero Radio de Mexico, 1944-47; adminstr. CAA, 1948-50; chmn. CAB, 1950; under sec. commerce for transp., 1951-52; v.p. indsl. dept. W.R. Grace & Co., 1952-53; pres. Auto Transport, Inc., Tex. Audo Transport, Inc.; chmn. bd. Slick Airways, Inc., 1954-65, mem. exec. com., pres., also dir., 1957; v.p., dir. Martin-Marietta Corp., 1965-91, pres. lime & cement div., 1965-91; chmn. Air Coord. Com.; chmn. Radio Tech. Planning Bd.; mem. NACA, 1948-51; cons. Sec. of Commerce and Def. Mobilizer, 1953. Recipient Ann. award Air Force Assn., 1950, Gold medal Dept. Commerce, 1951. Mem. Nat. Def. Transp. Assn. (life mem., hon. pres. Oklahoma City chpt.), Am. Legion, N.Y. Presbyn. Club, Burning Tree Club (Washington). Home: Oklahoma City Okla. Died Sept. 6, 1991.

REQUA, ELOISE GALLUP, library director; b. Chgo., Dec. 1, 1902; d. William Bruyn and Susan Eloise (Gallup) ReQua. A.B., Bryn Mawr Coll., 1924; student, Sch. Internat. Studies, Geneva, Switzerland, 1928; postgrad. fgn. trade and langs., Bryn Mawr Coll., U. Chgo. Founder Library Internat. Relations, Chgo., 1932, dir., 1932-89; trustee, founder The Story Cove, the Children's Internat. Library at Century of Progress Expn. (and later given to U. Chgo.), 1933-34; on leave, as asst. in publicity office Bryn Mawr Coll., Pa., 1934-35; as exec. sec. of ann. benefit Ill. Soc. Mental Hygiene, 1936; organizer World Trade Reference Library for Internat. House of New Orleans, 1946; bd. govs. Internat. House, Chgo., 1959-74. Editor: (with Jane Statham) The Developing Nations: A Guide to Information Sources, Concerning Their Economic, Political and Social Problems, 1965. Recipient plaque of recognition, 1968; medal Eloy Alfaro Internat. Found., 1959; Cert. of Merit, Mayor Richard J. Daley, 1973. Mem. Spl. Libraries Assn. (chmn. pub. relations com. 1945-46), Am. Polit. Sci. Assn., Ill. LWV, Nat. Soc. Colonial Dames. Republican. Clubs: Fortnightly, Bryn Mawr Coll., Arts (Chgo.). Home: Chicago Ill. Died Sept. 26, 1989.

RESO, SIDNEY J(OSEPH), oil company executive; b. New Orleans, La., Feb. 12, 1935; s. James Anthony and Josephine (Shindler) R.; m. Patricia Marie Armond, Aug. 20, 1955; children: Robin M., Cyd N., Gregory S. (dec.), Christopher M., Renee E. B.S. in Petroleum Engring, La. State U., 1957; grad. exec. program, U. Va., 1971. With Humble Oil and Refining Co. (now Exxon Co., U.S.A.), 1957-65, 69-72, 73-75; div. mgr. Humble Oil and Refining Co. (now Exxon Co., U.S.A.), Houston, 1973-74; mgr. prodn. dept. ops. Exxon Co. U.S.A., 1974-75; chief engr. prodn. dept. Esso Standard Oil (Australia) Ltd., Sydney, New South Wales, 1965-67; mgr. natural gas dept. Esso Standard Oil (Australia) Ltd., 1967-69; dir. Esso Australia, Ltd., Sydney, 1972-73; v.p. Esso Europe Inc., London, 1975-78, Exxon Corp., N.Y.C., 1978-80, Exxon Co. U.S.A., Houston, 1980-81; sr. v.p. Exxon Co. U.S.A., 1981-85; exec. v.p. Exxon USA, 1985-86, Exxon Co. Internat., 1986-87; pres. Exxon Co. Internat., Florham Park, N.J., 1988-92. Mem. Am. Petroleum Inst., Soc. Petroleum Engrs., Tau Beta Pi, Pi Epsilon Tau. Roman Catholic. Clubs: River Oaks Country (Houston), Spring Brook Country (Morristown, N.J.). Home: Morristown N.J. Died May 3, 1992. †

RESTEMEYER, WILLIAM EDWARD, electrical engineer, educator; b. Cin., Apr. 28, 1916; s. William Edward and Lillian A. (Schmidt-Goesling) R.; m. Virginia Lee Harris, Apr. 21, 1943; children—William E., Virginia Lee. E.E. with honors, U. Cin., 1938, M.A. with honors, 1939; postgrad., UCLA, 1960, U. Mich., 1961; D.Sc. (hon.), Capitol Inst. Tech., 1976. Teaching fellow U. Cin., 1939-40, instr., 1940-42, asst. prof., 1942-52, assoc. prof., 1952-61, prof., from 1961, adminstrv. aide, 1968-69, asst. dept. head dept. elec. and computer engring., 1976-77, adminstrv. assoc., 1987-89; vis. scientist Ohio Acad. Sci.; visitor Accreditation Bd. for Engring. and Tech.; cons. Avco, Gen. Electric Co., NRL, N.Y. State Edn. Dept., NASA, NATO, NSF. Contbr. articles to profl. jours. Chmn. bd. mgmt. Campus YMCA. Served to lt. (j.g.) USN, 1945. Schmitt scholar, 1984, 85. Mem. Am. Soc. Engring. Edn. (nat. officer), AAAS, IEEE (sr.), Math. Assn. Am., Internat. Math. Union, Sigma Xi, Omicron Delta Kappa, Tau Beta Pi, Eta Kappa Nu, Phi Eta Sigma, Alpha Sigma Lambda, Pi Kappa Alpha. Lodges: Masons, Scottish Rite. Home: Cincinnati Ohio Died Jan. 4, 1989; buried Vine St. Hill Cemetery, Cincinnati.

RETTGER, ROBERT ERNEST, petroleum geologist; b. Terre Haute, Ind., Apr. 6, 1897; s. Louis J. and Mina (Gard) R.; m. Ima Winchell, Dec. 28, 1922; children: Robert W., Priscilla Bell. Student, Wabash Coll., 1915-16; AB, U. Wis., 1920, MA, 1922. Asst. prof. geology Cornell U., 1922-25; geologist Sun Oil Co., 1925-49, geophys. coord., 1949-57, asst. chief geologist S.W. divsn., 1957-61, chief geologist, 1961-62, ret., 1962. With U.S. Army, 1917-18. Mem. Am. Assn. Petroleum Geologists, Dallas Geol. Soc., Beta Theta Pi, Sigma Gamma Epsilon. *

REUBEN, ALLAN HERBERT, lawyer; b. Pitts., June 24, 1931; s. Monte M. and Miriam (Barthfeld) R.; m. Gladys Winkler, May 25, 1956; children: John David, Patricia Anne, Catherine Ellen. B.A. summa cum laude, U. Pitts., 1953; LL.B. magna cum laude, Harvard U., 1956. Bar: Pa. 1957. Law clk. to judge U.S. Ct. Appeals (3d cir.), 1956-57; asso. firm Wolf, Block, Schorr & Solis-Cohen, Phila., 1957-65; partner Wolf, Block, Schorr & Solis-Cohen, from 1965; lectr. Banking Law Inst., 1969. Mem.: Harvard Law Rev, 1954-56. Trustee Lawyers Com. Civil Rights Under Law, from 1976; chmn., mem. governing bd. employment discrimination referral project Phila. Bar Assn.-Lawyers Com. Civil Rights Under Law, 1971-75; bd. dirs. Pub. Interest Law Center Phila., from 1975; mem. S.E. regional planning council Pa. Gov.'s Justice Commn., 1973-78, exec. com., 1974-78; mem. exec. com. S.E. regional adv. com. Pa. Com. on Crime and Delinquency, 1979-80; trustee Community Legal Services Phila., 1971, 1980-82; bd. dirs. Pa. Legal Services Center, 1978-80, chmn. evaluation com.; bd. commrs. Cheltenham Twp., Pa., 1972-87, chmn. health and sanitation com., 1980-87; chmn. Shopping Center Task Force, 1981-87; vice chmn. Parks and Recreation Com., 1980-87 ; bd. dirs. Phila. Am. Jewish Com., from 1965, v.p., 1973-77; mem. Jewish Community Relations Com., Phila., from 1965, bd. dirs., from 1973, chmn. civil rights com., from 1975; bd. govs. Renal Youth Rehab. Program, 1976-80. Mem. Am. Judicature Soc., ABA, Fed. Bar Assn., Pa. Bar Assn., Phila. Bar Assn. (co-chmn. subcom. riots in N. Phila. 1965, chmn. subcom. invasion of privacy by electronic means 1966-70, 72-78, chmn. speakers Law Day 1966, chmn. speakers bur. 1967, chmn. civil rights com. 1971, 1980-82, chancellor's commn. on abortion 1971-72, public relations com. from 1965, speakers panel from 1965, mem. sect. corp., banking and bus. law from 1965, chmn. com. fin. 1966-67, exec. com. 1969-70, 72, 83, sec. 1973, editor Phila. Lawyer 1969-74, co-chmn. editorial bd. from 1974), Phi Beta Kappa. Home: Philadelphia Pa. Deceased. †

REVELLE, ROGER RANDALL DOUGAN, public policy educator; b. Seattle, Mar. 7, 1909; s. William R. and Ella R. (Dougan) R.; m. Ellen Virginia Clark, June 22, 1931; children—Anne Revelle Shumway, Mary Ellen Revelle Paci, Carolyn Revelle Hufbauer, William Roger. B.A., Pomona Coll., 1929; Ph.D., U. Calif.-Berkeley, 1936; Sc.D. (hon.), Pomona Coll., Carlton Coll., Colby Coll., Dartmouth Coll., Bucknell U., U. Mass., Utah State U., U. Miami, Old Dominion U., U.

R.I.; L.H.D. (hon.), Williams Coll.; LL.D. (hon.), Carnegie-Mellon U.; M.A. (hon.), Harvard U. Research asst., instr. to prof., dir. Scripps Instn., La Jolla, Calif., 1931-64; Richard Saltonstall prof. population policy, dir. Ctr. Population Studies Harvard U., Cambridge, Mass., 1964-78; prof. sci. and pub. policy U. Calif.-San Diego, from 1976, Univ. dean of research, 1963-64; sci. adv. to sec. U.S. Dept. Interior, Washington, 1961-63; chmn. bd. sci. and tech. in devel. NRC, 1961-65; U.S. del. UNESCO Gen. Conf., 1963, 79, UN Conf. Sci. and Tech., 1978; mem. U.S. Nat. Commn. for UNESCO, 1958-64, vice-chmn., 1970-76; chmn. U.S. del. Intergovtl. Oceanographic Commn., UNESCO, Paris, 1962, 63; chmn. Com. on Climatic Changes and the Ocean, Intergovl. Oceanographic Commn./Sci. Com. on Ocean Rsch., 1978-83. Author: Land and Water Development in the Indus Plain, 1964; editor: Consequences of Rapid Population Growth, 1972, (with Hans Landsberg) America's Changing Environment, 1969, (with David Glass) Population and Social Change, 1974; contbr. over 200 articles to profl. jours. Bd. fellows Claremont Univ. Ctr., Calif., from 1978; hon. bd. dirs. La Jolla Chamber Music Soc., Calif., from 1978; trustee Theatre and Arts Found. San Diego County, LaJolla, from 1958, Woods Hole Oceanographic Instn., Mass., from 1960; mem. Commn. on Arts and Culture, City of San Diego, from 1988. Served to comdr. USNR, 1941-48. Recipient Sittara y Imtiaz, Govt. of Pakistan, 1964, Tyler prize, 1984, Balzan prize, 1986, Vannevar Bush award Nat. Sci. Bd., 1984, medal New Eng. Aquarium Soc., 1981, Nat. medal Sci., 1990; named Mr. San Diego, 1987, Alumnus of Yr. U. Calif.- San Diego, 1989, Revelle Coll. Fellow AAAS (pres. and chmn. 1973-75), Am. Acad. Arts and Scis. (v.p. 1970-74), Am. Geophys. Union (sect. pres. 1959-61; Bowie medal 1968); mem. Nat. Acad. Scis. (council 1961-64, 71-74; Agassiz medal 1958), Am. Philos. Soc., Council Fgn. Relations, Internat. Assn. Phys. Scis. Ocean (pres. 1964-68). Democrat. Clubs: Cosmos (Washington); Century Association (N.Y.C.); Bohemian (San Francisco); Tavern, Saturday (Boston). Home: La Jolla Calif. Died July 15, 1991; cremated.

REVERE, ANNE, actress; b. N.Y.C., June 25, 1903; d. C.T. and Harriette (Winn) R.; m. Samuel Rosen, 1935. BA, Wellesley Coll., 1926; student, Am. Lab. Sch., N.Y.C. Actress motion pictures, including: song of Bernadette, National Velvet, Sunday Dinner for a Soldier, Fallen Angel, Dragonwyck, Gentlemen's Agreement, Place in the Sun, Great Missouri Raid; also roles in theatre prodns.: Double Door, Children's Hour, Cue for Passion, Toys in the Attic; TV shows include: Search for Tomorrow, Six Million Dollar Man, Baretta, Sesame Street. Recipient Academy award as best supporting actress, 1945, Tony award for performance Toys in the Attic, 1960. Home: New York N.Y. Died Dec. 18, 1990.

REVILLE, EUGENE THOMAS, educational administrator; b. Buffalo, Jan. 9, 1932; s. James and Agnes (Murphy) R.; m. Joan Schmelzinger, Aug. 18, 1956; 4 children. BS in Elem. Edn., N.Y. State Coll. Tchrs. at Buffalo, 1953; MEd. in Adminstrn., U. Buffalo, 1961. Prin. Buffalo Bd. Edn., 1962-66, adminstr. chief project, 1966-71, assoc. supt. instructional service, 1971-75, supt. schs., from 1975. Contbr. articles to profl. jours. Home: Cleveland Ohio Deceased. †

REYBURN, HAROLD ORBRA, accountant; b. Granby, Mo., May 3, 1915; s. Robert D. and Nettie (Burnett) R.; m. C. DeLyte Tallman, Dec. 3, 1938 (div.); children: A. Kim, Donna DeLyte (Mrs. Michael G. Griffith), Thomas M.; m. Linda K. Terrill, Apr. 16, 1970. B.C.S., Okla. Sch. Accountancy, 1939. C.P.A., Okla., Tex. Accountant St. Louis Mining & Smelting Co., 1933-34, Shell Oil Co., 1934-40; with Frazer & Torbet (C.P.A.'s), Tulsa, 1940-44; partner Nicholson, Reyburn & Co. (C.P.A.'s), Tulsa, 1944-57, Coopers & Lybrand, Tulsa, 1957-78; instr. Okla. Sch. Accountancy, nights 1940-54; pres. Caywood Oil & Gas Co., 1951-58; adv. dir. Utica Nat. Bank & Trust Co., 1979-88; dir. Nash Oil Co., 1949-59, Consol. Oil Co., 1949-86, Bovaird Supply Co., 1978-86; v.p. Microfilm Service, Inc., 1950-58; Chmn. mayor's adv. com. City of Tulsa, 1966-67; treas., dir. Skelly Stadium Corp., Tulsa, 1965-75; trustee, mem. exec. com. Tulsa Psychiat. Center, 1959-85; treas., 1959-73, pres., 1973, chmn. bd., 1974-77; treas., dir. Tulsa Sci. Center, 1969-76. Contbr. to profl. jours. Named to Okla. Acctg. Hall of Fame, 1990. Mem. Am. Inst. C.P.A.'s, Okla. Soc. C.P.A.'s (pres. 1953-54), Tulsa C. of C. (dir. 1970-76), Nat. Assn. Accountants (pres. Tulsa 1953-54). Baptist (treas. to 1986, mem. finance com. to 1986, brotherhood deacons 1941-87). Club: Southern Hills Country (Tulsa). Home: Tulsa Okla. Deceased. †

REYNOLDS, JAMES A., magazine editor; b. Tulsa, Feb. 5, 1929; s. Leslie Bruce and Anna Lear (Williams) R.; m. Anne Prisco, May 3, 1953; children: Jan Reynolds Bodanyi, Bruce M. B.A., Okla. A&M Coll., 1949; M.S., Syracuse U., 1954. Legis. correspondent United Press, Albany, N.Y., 1950-54; news editor Congl. Quarterly, Washington, 1954-55; Washington correspondent The Wall St. Jour., Washington, 1955-59; editorial staff Nat. Geographic, Washington, 1959-63; mng. editor, Washington editor, exec. editor Med. Econs., Oradell, N.J., 1963-80; editor Home Mag., Oradell, 1980-82, RN Mag., Oradell, 1983-87; dir. spl. projects Med. Econs., Oradell, N.J., from 1987. Served to cpl. U.S. Army, 1951-53. Recipient Jesse H. Neal Editorial Achievement award Assn. Bus. Pubs., 1974, 84, 85, 86, 87. Mem. Nat. Press Club, Am. Soc. Mag. Editors, N.Y. Bus. Press Editors, Soc. Profl. Journalists (life). Club: Bicycle USA-League of Am. Wheelmen (v.p. 1982-84). Home: Oradell N.J. Deceased. †

REYNOLDS, JOSEPH BERCHMANS, investment banker; b. Cin., Aug. 20, 1896; s. Edmund B. and Anastasia (Broderick) R.; m. Aimee E. Brown, June 26, 1937; children: Joseph Martin, James Broderick. Student, Xavier U., Marquette U. Officer SS Bermudian, Furness With, Ltd., 1915-16; account exec. W.A. Daniels & Co., 1920-22; ptnr. Van Leunen-Reynolds, 1922-25; treas. Reynolds, Brett & Ernst, Inc., 1925-32; ptnr. Benj. D. Bartlett & Co., Cin., from 1947; chmn. Vulcan Corp., Cin.; dir., chmn. fin. com. U.S. Shoe Corp., Cin.; mem. exec. com. Midwest Stock Exch., 1955-58, vice chmn., 1965; chmn. bd. dirs. Cin. Stock Exch., 1945-49. Trustee Legal Aid Soc. Cin. and Hamilton County; mem. pres.'s coun. Xavier U., 1962. Lt. U.S. Army, 1917-19. *

REYNOLDS, RUSSEL BURTON, army officer writer; b. Dundee, Mich., Dec. 24, 1894; s. Sydney Howard and Nellie (Johnson) R.; m. Florine Janney, Jan. 12, 1918; 1 child, Russel Burton. Student, U. Wis., 1913-15, 17; grad., Inf. Sch., 1922, Command & Gen. Staff Sch., 1938. Commd. 2d lt. U.S. Army, 1917, advanced through grades to maj. gen., 1944; asst. prof. mil. sci. & tactics U. Pa., 1925-29, Ripon Coll., 1936-37; instr. Inf. Sch., 1929-33, Med. Field Svc. Sch., 1938-41, Gen. Staff Corps, 1942-44; dir. mil. pers. divsn. Army Svc. Forces, 1942-44; comdg. gen. 6th Svc. Command, Chgo., 1944-45; mem. staff U.S. Army Forces, Western Pacific, 1945-46; chief spl. svcs. Dept. Army, 1946-49. Decorated DSM with oak leaf cluster. *

RHEA, CLAUDE HIRAM, JR., academic administrator; b. Carrollton, Mo., Oct. 26, 1927; s. Claude Hiram Sr. and Cecile Virginia (Walden) R.; m. Carolyn Priscilla Turnage, Aug. 26, 1951; children: Claude H. III, Charles Randall, Margaret Elizabeth. BA, William Jewell Coll., 1950; B of Music in Edn., Fla. State U., 1953, M of Music in Edn., 1954, EdD, 1958; postgrad., U. Rochester, 1960. Dean, prof. Sch. of Ch. Music New Orleans Bapt. Theol. Sem., 1954-63; adminstrv. v.p., prof. Houston Bapt. Coll., 1963-67; cons. music and mass media So. Bapt. Fgn. Mission Bd., Richmond, Va., 1967-69; dean Sch. Music Samford U., Birmingham, Ala., 1969-82; pres. Palm Beach Atlantic Coll., West Palm Beach, Fla., from 1982; vis. prof. Internat. Bapt. Theol. Sem., Zürich, Switzerland, summers 1959, 60; chmn. bd., chief exec. officer Palmetto Broadcasters Inc., West Palm Beach, from 1983, Keys Broadcasters Inc., Key West, Fla., 1984, Cen. Fla. Educators Broadcasters Inc., Leesburg/Orlando, Fla., 1985, Jacksonville Educators Broadcastors Inc., 1986-89; sec., dir. Interactive Video Resources Inc., West Palm Beach, 1987-89. Recording artist LP record albums: Claude Rhea Sings, 1957, Creation, 1958, Majestic Themes, 1959, Radiance of Christmas, 1963; author, composer (with wife) song books: A Child's Life in Song, 1963, Sing While you Grow, 1965; author, editor: (cook book) Lottie Moon Cookbook, 1965; author: With My Song I Will Praise Him, 1977; contbr. articles to music jours., 1957-76. Pres. Downtown Assn., West Palm Beach, from 1985; mem. Econ. Coun. of the Palm Beaches, from 1983. With U.S. Army, 1945-47, ETO. Recipient Good Shepherd's award Nat. Boy Scouts Am., 1988. Fellow Royal Soc. of Arts (London); mem. Fla. Ind. Colls. and Univs. Fund (bd. dirs., sec. 1987-88), Ind. Colls. and Univs. of Fla. (bd. dirs.), Am. Coun. Edn., Coun. Ind. Colls., Downtown Rotary (chorister from 1982), Palm Beaches C. of C. (bd. dirs.), Gov.s Club, Exec. Club (founding dir. from 1987), Bear Island Country Club. Republican. Home: West Palm Beach Fla. Died Sept. 19, 1990. †

RHOADS, ESTHER BIDDLE, organization official; b. Phila., Nov. 26, 1896; d. Edward G. and Margaret Ely (Paxson) R. BS, Earlham Coll., 1921, LHD, 1960; LLD, Drexel Inst. Tech., 1962. Tchr. Friends Sch., Tokyo, 1917-18, 21-40, 1947-60; work with Am. Friends Svc. Com. with Japanese Evacuees, Calif. & Ariz., 1942-45; relief worker, presenter internat. seminars Japan, 1946-60; tutor to crown prince, other mems. Japanese Imperial family, 1950-60; relief worker Tunisia, 1960-61; mem. bd. Am. Friends Svc. Com., from 1962, vice chmn., from 1963. Trustee Friends Sch., Tokyo, Tsudo Coll., Tokyo, Internat. Christian U., Japan. Mem. Asiatic Soc., Japan Am. Soc. *

RHODES, GEORGE MILTON, congressman; b. Reading, Pa., Feb. 24, 1898; s. George Mifflin and Catherine (Fessler) R.; m. Margie Seiverling, June 11, 1921. Ed. pub. schs., Reading. Formerly printer, editor, labor rep.; mem. from 13th Pa. dist., then 14th Pa. dist., 6th Pa. dist. U.S. Ho. of Reps.; mem. War Manpower Com., Civilian Def. Com.; mem. bd. Reading Housing Authority. With U.S. Army, World War I. Mem. Am. Legion. *

RHODES, KENT, publishing company executive; b. Bklyn., Feb. 5, 1912; s. Clarence and Louise (Rhodes) Klinck; m. Christina Riordan, July 19, 1952; children: David Christian, Jean Louise, Brian Mark. B.S., Amos Tuck Sch., Dartmouth, 1933; L.H.D. (hon.), Mercy Coll., 1978. Editor, pub. Dartmouth Pictorial, 1931-33; with Time Inc., 1933-44; with Reader's Digest Assn., Inc., Pleasantville, N.Y., 1944-78, dir., 1965-78, exec. v.p., 1970-75, pres., 1975-76, chmn. bd., 1976-78; bd. dirs. Mag. Pubs. Assn., N.Y.C., 1956-78, chmn., 1958-60, pres., 1979-82. Bd. dirs. Reader's Digest Found., 1970-86, pres., 1974-86; chmn. Reader's Digest Fund for Blind, 1973-86; trustee Outward Bound, 1966, pres., 1971-72, chmn. bd., 1973; trustee Hurricane Island Outward Bound Sch., Maine, 1971-77, Harvey Sch., Katonah, N.Y., 1966-77, Internat. Exec. Svc. Corps., 1973-78, Internat. House, from 1977, Inst. Internat. Edn., from 1978, Taft Inst. for Two-Party Govt., from 1986, Thompson Island Outward Bound Ctr., from 1987; bd. dirs. Advt. Coun., 1986-89, Nat. Accreditation Coun., 1986-89; mem. Presdl. Commn. on Postal Svc., 1976-77. Recipient William Caxton Human Relations award Am. Jewish Com., 1965. Mem. Assn. Publ. Prodn. Mgrs. (founder, 1st pres. 1939), Nat. Inst. Social Sci., Westchester County Assn. (bd. dirs. 1972-83, vice chmn. 1975-77, chmn. 1978), Direct Mail Mktg. Assn. (bd. dirs. 1964-72, vice chmn. 1971), Pilgrims of U.S., Zeta Psi. Clubs: Knickerbocker, Dartmouth, University, N.Y. Athletic (N.Y.C.); Fishers Island (N.Y.). Home: Fishers Island N.Y. Died Dec. 20, 1991; buried St. John's Cemetery, Fisher's Island, N.Y.

RHODES, WILLARD, ethnomusicologist, educator; b. Deshler, Ohio, May 12, 1901; s. John Osborne and Lula (Sheely) R.; m. Lillian Hansen, July 6, 1940; 1 dau., Joy Cooper. A.B., B.Mus., Heidelberg Coll., 1922; student, Wittenberg Coll., 1922-23; M.A., Columbia, 1925; student, Mannes Sch. Music., 1923-25, Ecole Normale de Musique, Paris, 1925-27. Dir. music Pub. Schs., Bronxville, N.Y., 1935-37; asso. music Columbia, 1937-46, asst. prof., 1946-49, asso. prof., 1949-54; prof. music Columbia U., 1954-69, prof. emeritus music, 1969-92; Edn. specialist, music cons. Bur. Indian Affairs, from 1938; collector, editor Music North Am. Indian Library Congress, 1952; vis. prof. U. Hawaii, 1970; vis. research prof. Centre for Nigerian Cultural Studies, Ahmadu Bello U., Zaria, 1974. Conductor, chorus master, Am. Opera Co., 1927-30, asst. conductor, Cin. Summer Opera Co., 1928-33; pianist-accompanist on concert tours, pvt. teaching, Chgo., 1930-35; Author: (with others) Musikgseschicte in Bildern, (with R. Gordon Wasson) Maria Sabena and Her Mazatec Mushroom Velada, 1974; Editor, annotator: (with R. Gordon Wasson) Ethnic Folkways Library; Contbr. (with R. Gordon Wasson) articles to profl. jours. Fulbright sr. research fellowship S. Rhodesia, 1958-59; Am. Inst. Indian Studies research grantee for research in carnatic music India, 1965-66. Fellow African Studies Assn., Am. Inst. Indian Studies; mem. Internat. Inst. for Comparative Music Research and Documentation (mem. scientific bd.), Am. Anthrop. Soc., Am. Musicol. Soc., Am. Folklore Soc., African Music Soc., Am. Ethnol. Soc. (councilor 1959), Music Library Assn., Soc. Ethnomusicology (pres. 1955-57), Soc. Asian Music (hon. pres.), Internat. Folk Music Council (pres. 1967). Congregationalist. Home: Sun City Ariz. Died May 15, 1992.

RICCIARDI, FRANC MARIO, business executive; b. Montclair, N.J., Aug. 21, 1923; s. John J. and Rose Marie (Codella) R.; m. Rosemarie Stivaly, Aug. 24, 1944; children: April, Johanna, Francesca. A.B., Rutgers U., 1946, M.A., 1947. Asst. prof. fin. U. Vt., 1947-51; asst. dir. N.Y. Stock Exchange Inst., N.Y.C., 1951-53; v.p. charge divs. Am. Mgmt. Assn., 1953-58; dir. planning Monroe Calculating Machine Co. (div. Litton Industries), 1959-61, v.p., 1961-64; pres. Kimball Co., 1961-64; exec. v.p., dir. Kidde, Inc., Clifton, N.J., 1964-66, pres., 1966-69; chmn., pres., chief exec. officer Richton Internat. Corp., N.Y.C., 1969-89; bd. dirs. Internat. Am. Homes Inc. Served with AUS, 1942-44. Recipient Medallion of Achievement award Golden Sq. Club Phila., 1968; named Man of Yr., Boys' Towns Italy, 1971. Mem. Theta Chi. Clubs: Tiro A Segno of N.Y.; Ridgewood (N.J.) Country; The Leash, Clay Hill Shooting, Metropolitan, Doubles (N.Y.C.); Dutchess Valley Rod and Gun, Mashomack Fish and Game Preserve (N.Y.); Mount Kenya Safari (Kenya, E. Africa); Wildlife Research Co. (Locust Valley, N.Y.); Annabel's (London); Bonnette Hunting and Fishing (Fla.). Home: Ridgewood N.J. Died May 8, 1989; buried Monclair, N.J.

RICE, LOUIS ALBERT, educator; b. Frederick, Md., July 9, 1895; s. Lewis A. and Susan Addie (Blumenauer) R.; m. Elizabeth Johnson Michael, Aug. 20, 1919; children: Ralph Michael, Joseph Albert. BCS, NYU, 1921, BS, 1927, AM, 1930. Tchr. various high schs., 1913-16; prin. Balt. YMCA Bus. Sch., 1916; office mgr. Frederick, 1916-17; tchr. Roselle Park (N.J.) High Sch., 1917-18, U.S. Army, 1918; head comml. dept. Cranford (N.J.) High Sch., 1918-21; tchr. Sr. High Sch., Montclair, N.J., 1921-22; office mgr. NYU, 1924-27; asst. supr. high schs. N.J. State Dept. Edn., 1927-36; vice prin. Packard Sch., N.Y.C., 1936-38; prin. Packard Sch., 1938-49; pres. Packard Jr. Coll., 1949-54; supr. instrn. evening divsn. Fairleigh Dickinson U., 1954, assoc. dean coll., charge adminstrn. Teaneck campus, 1955-58; prof. Fairleigh Dickinson U., from 1958; lectr. bus. edn. NYU, 1928-41, 48, also other univs. Mem. NEA, Ea. Comml. Tchrs. Assn., N.J. Coun. Edn., AAUP, Am. Assn. Jr. Colls., others. *

RICE, PHILIP JOSEPH, JR., consulting physicist; b. Middletown, Conn., Feb. 28, 1917; s. Philip Joseph and Sarah (Moran) R.; m. Jean Ann Mattern, Apr. 7, 1956; children—Monica, Adrienne. A.B., Brown U., 1940; M.S., Case-Western Res. U., 1942, Yale, 1946; Ph.D., Yale, 1948. Mem. tech. staff Radiation Lab., Mass. Inst. Tech., 1942-45, Bell Telephone Labs., 1948-52; mgr. electron devices lab. SRI Internat., Menlo Park, Calif., 1952-62, mgr. phys. electronics lab., 1962-66, program mgr., engring. scis. and indsl. devel., 1966-83, gen. mgr. tech. innovation, 1971, lab. dir., 1976-83; pvt. cons., 1983-89. Author tech. papers, articles. Trustee Western Electronic Edn. Fund. Mem. IEEE (sr. mem., V. K. Zworykn award 1963), Am. Phys. Soc., Sigma Xi. Home: Atherton Calif. Died May 10, 1989.

RICHARD, WILLIAM RALPH, JR., research chemist; b. Bklyn., Oct. 13, 1922; s. William Ralph and Helen (Brodie) R.; m. Joan Coombs, Aug. 23, 1947; children: Carol Lucile, Suzanne Louise, Janet Elizabeth. AB in Chemistry, Amherst Coll., 1943; MS in Chemistry, U. Mich., 1947, PhD in Chemistry, 1950. Rsch. chemist Monsanto Chem. Co., Springfield, Mass., 1943-46; DuPont fellow U. Mich., Ann Arbor, 1948-50; group leader rsch. engring. div. Monsanto, Dayton, Ohio, 1950-63, mgr. rsch. and devel. organic div., St. Louis, 1963-74; dir. rsch. and devel. Monsanto Indsl. Co., St. Louis, 1974-90, dir. rsch. and devel. splty. chems., 1985-90; pres. Delos Inc., Kirkwood, Mo., 1985-90; mem. indsl. adv. bd. Coll. Engring. and Tech. So. Ill. U., Carbondale, environ. risk com. Chem. Mfgrs. Assn., Washington, 1980-83. Contbr. articles to profl. jours. Patentee in field. Bd. dirs. Dayton Civic Ballet, 1959-61. Mem. Am. Chem. Soc., AAAS, Soc. Risk Analysis, Nat. Conf. Advancement of Rsch. (bd. dirs. 1982-90), Soc. Rsch. Adminstrs. (indsl. div. pres. 1982, Hartford-Nicholson award 1981). Presbyterian. Avocations: tennis, sailing. Died July 16, 1990. Home: Saint Louis Mo. †

RICHARDS, ARTHUR LINCOLN, organization executive; b. Emmett, Idaho, June 21, 1907; s. Arthur Allen and Sedenia (Dunford) R.; m. Ida Elizabeth Parker; children: Herbert Miles, Sarah Elizabeth, John Miles. Student, Pasadena City Coll., 1925-28, George Washington U., 1929-30, Nat. War Coll., 1948-49. Clk. Am. consulate, Guadalajara, Mexico, 1930; fgn. svc. officer Dept. State, 1930; 3d sec., vice consul Tehran, Iran, 1931-34; vice consul Jerusalem, 1934-35, Cairo, 1935-38, Cape Town, South Africa, 1938-42; 2d sec. Am. legation Pretoria, South Africa, 1942-45; asst. chief Brit. Commonwealth div. Dept. State, 1945-45; counselor of embassy, dept. chief mission Tehran, Iran, 1949-52; dir. Office Greek, Turkish and Iranian Affairs, Dept. State, 1952; Am. consul gen. Istanbul, Turkey, 1954-56; ops. coord. Dept. State, 1956-58, spl. asst. to under sec. state for law of sea, 1958-60, amb. to Ethiopia, 1960-62; dep. rep. U.S. on Disarmament Conf. Geneva, 1963-64; chief examiner Dept. State, 1964-66; exec. dir. Nat. Coun. for Community Svcs. to Internat. Visitors, 1966-68, Washington Internat. Ctr., 1968-73; sec. to U.S. delegation to Internat. Telecommunications Conf., Cairo, 1936; advisor U.S. delegation to South Seas Conf., Canberra, Australia, 1946; vice chmn. U.S. delegation Law of Sea Conf., Geneva, 1960; v.p. Meridian House Found., Washington, 1968-73. Home: Bethesda Md. Died Feb. 23, 1991.

RICHARDS, ATHERTON, business executive; b. Honolulu, Sept. 29, 1894; s. Theodore and Mary (Atherton) R.; m. Helen Dulany, Jan. 27, 1938 (div.). AB, Wesleyan U., 1915. With Bur. Mcpl. Rsch., N.Y.C., 1915-16; staff mem. San Francisco Bur. Govtl. Rsch., 1916-17; treas. Castle & Cooke Ltd., Honolulu; pres., dir. Hawaiian Pineapple Co., 1932-41; bd. dirs. numerous cos.; spl. asst. to Coord. Info., Washington, 1941; pres. Fijelen R & D Co., from 1945; pres. Film N File, Inc.; trustee B.P. Bishop Estate, Kamehameha Schs.; pres. bd. trustees Bishop Mus. 1st lt. inf. U.S. Army, 1917-18, lt. col., then. col., 1942-43. Mem. Psi Upsilon. *

RICHARDS, ROBERT L(AURENCE), corporate executive; b. Phila., Nov. 5, 1898; s. John Franklin and Mary Alice (Young) R.; m. Julie M. Vance, Apr. 17, 1926; children: Julie Ziegler, Robert L., Mary A. Wright, Jane. BS, U. Pa., 1922. With E.I. du Pont de Nemours and Co., Wilmington, Del., 1923-35, 41 on, supr. rayon & cellophane ops., 1923-35, asst. mgr. cellophane divsn., 1944, mgr. nylon divsn., 1945, asst. gen. mgr. textile fibers dept., 1947, gen. mgr., 1949, v.p., 1954-61, also bd. dirs., from 1954; plant mgr., asst. gen. mgr., dir. Ducilo S.A. Productora de Rayon, Buenos Aires, 1935-41. Assoc. trustee U. Pa. Mem. Theta Chi, Alpha Chi Sigma. *

RICHARDS, WILLIAM GEORGE, savings and loan executive; b. Lockhart, Tex., Feb. 20, 1920; s. Cyrus F. and Gussie (Baldridge) R.; LL.B., U. Tex., 1948; m. Winnifred Adams, Nov. 23, 1940 (dec. May 1969); children: Bettye Ann (Mrs. Rogers), Mark Andrew; m. 2d, Corrie Marsh, Mar. 29, 1972. Admitted to Tex. bar, 1948; practiced law with father, Lockhart, 1948-55; v.p., atty., dir. Lockhart Savs. & Loan Assn., 1948-55; exec. v.p. Benjamin Franklin Savs. & Loan Assn., 1955-64, pres., 1964-74, vice-chmn. bd., 1974-75; chmn. bd., chief exec. officer Surety Savs. Assn., Houston, 1975-78; trustee Savs. & Loan Found., Inc., 1957-59. Mem. Tex. Ho. of Reps., 1947-50; mayor of Lockhart, 1954-55. Mem. adv. com. Coll. Bus. Adminstrn. U. Houston, 1966-70. Served with USNR, 1942-45. Mem. Nat. League Insured Savs. Assns. (exec. com. 1962-66), Houston C. of C. (dir. 1966, 68-73), Tex. Savs. and Loan League (dir. 1953-63, 63-66; pres. 1967-68), Phi Delta Phi. Democrat. Episcopalian. Clubs: Onion Creek, Austin (Austin).Died Feb. 28, 1992. Home: Austin Tex. †

RICHARDS-BRANDT, MARY ROBINSON, physician, medical consultant, writer; b. Chgo., Sept. 26, 1921; d. Russell Dean and Anna Elizabeth (Isham) Robinson; m. Joseph Samuel Richards, Dec. 18, 1943 (div. 1968); children: Anne Leslie, Kathleen Elizabeth; m. Melville Steven Brandt, Dec. 27, 1982. B.S. cum laude in Chemistry, Purdue U., 1944; M.D., U. Ill., Chgo., 1947. Diplomate Am. Bd. Pediatrics. Intern Cook County Hosp., Chgo., 1947-48; resident Mcpl. Contagious Hosp., La Rabida Hosp., Children's Meml. Hosp., Chgo., 1948-50; clin. fellow Babies Hosp., N.Y.C., 1952-54; practice medicine specializing in pediatrics Glenview, Ill., 1950-52, Tenafly, N.J., 1957-63; writer, researcher Med. Economics, Oradell, N.J., 1964; group med. dir. Sudler & Hennessey, N.Y.C., 1964-69, v.p., sr. v.p., group med. dir., 1971-85; assoc. med. dir. Syntex Labs. Palo Alto, Calif., 1969-71. Author articles, med. brochures, reports and booklets in field. Mem., Alpine Bd. Edn., N.J., 1956-59; mem. bd. health, recreation com., Alpine, 1959-63. Fellow Am. Acad. Pediatrics; mem. Babies Hosp. Alumni Assn., Kappa Kappa Gamma, Am. Med. Writers Assn., Pharm. Advt. Council, Alpha Omega Alpha. Episcopalian. Clubs: Englewood Field (N.J.); Knickerbocker Country. Home: Fort Lee N.J. Deceased. †

RICHARDSON, CARLOS ALBERT, lawyer; b. Mohawk, N.Y., Sept. 30, 1895; s. Charles D. and Jennie (Richardson) T.; m. Dorothea U. Whitney, June 1, 1919; children: Carlos Albert, Robert W., Frances L. Student, Boston U., 1914-15, Northeastern U., 1915-17; LLB, Denver U., 1922. Bar: Colo. 1923, Conn. 1930. Mem. firm Hoffman & Richardson, Denver, 1923-30, Camp, Williams & Richardson, New Britain, Conn., from 1930. Sgt. engrs. AEF, 1917-19; 1st lt. Colo. N.G., 1923. Mem. Conn. Soc. Crippled Children, VFW, Mil. Order Purple Heart. *

RICHARDSON, TONY, stage and film producer; b. Shipley, Yorkshire, Eng., June 5, 1928; came to U.S., 1974; s. Clarence Albert and Elsie Evans (Campion) R.; m. Vanessa Redgrave, 1962 (div. 1967); children: Natasha, Joely, Katharine Grimond. B.A., Wadham Coll. Oxford U. (Eng.), 1950. Dir. BBC, 1953-55; assoc. artistic dir. the joint artistic dir. English Stage Co.-Royal Ct. Theatre, 1956-64; dir. Woodfall Film Prodns. Ltd., London, Eng., from 1958; plays: (produced or directed) Look Back in Anger (Royal Ct. Theatre, also Broadway, 1957), The Chairs, Pericles and Othello (Stratford), The Entertainer, Luther, The Seagull, St. Joan of the Stockyards, Hamlet, Threepenny Opera, I Claudius, Arturo Ui, A Taste of Honey, Lady From the Sea, As You Like It (L.A.); films: (produced or directed): Look Back in Anger, 1958, The Entertainer, 1959, Sanctuary,1961, A Taste of Honey, 1961, The Loneliness of the Long Distance Runner, 1962, Tom Jones (recipient Acad. award), 1963, The Loved One, 1964, Mademoiselle, 1966, The Sailor from Gibraltar, 1967, Red and Blue, 1967, Charge of the Light Brigade, 1968, Laughter in the Dark, 1969, Hamlet, 1970, Ned Kelly, 1970, A Delicate Balance, 1973, Dead Cert 1973, Joseph Andrews, 1977, Death in Canaan, 1978, The Border, 1981, The Hotel New Hampshire, 1984, Penalty Phase, 1986, Antony and Cleopatra, 1987, Shadow in the Sun, 1988, Phanton of the Opera, 1989, Hills Like White Elephants, 1989, Blue Sky, 1991. Died Nov. 15, 1991. Home: Los Angeles Calif.

RICHEY, HERMAN G(LENN), educator; b. Cray County, Ind., Nov. 4, 1897; s. George Willard and Susan May (Bennett) R.; m. Marie Magdalena Rousseau, Aug. 9, 1923; 1 child, Herman Glenn. AB, Ind. State Tchrs. Coll., 1920; PhM, U. Wis., 1924; AM, U. Chgo., 1927, PhD, 1930. High sch. prin. North Terre Haute, Ind., 1920-26; rsch. sec. Lab. Schs. U. Chgo., 1928-33; instr. edn. U. Chgo., 1930-35, asst., then assoc. prof., 1935-48, prof., from 1948, sec. dept., from 1942, dean student Grad. Sch. Edn., 1947-48; dept. grad. studies Coll. Edn. U. P.R., 1965. Author: (with Newton Edwards) The School in the American Social Order, 1947, The Extent of Equalization Secured through State School Funds, 1938, The Relation of Accelerated, Normal and Retarded Puberty on Height and Weight of School Children, 1937; editor: Child Psychology, 1963, The Improvement and Impact of School Testing Program, 1963, Theories of Learning, 1964, Behavioral Science and Educational Administration, 1964; deptl. editor Ency. Britannica, from 1951. Mem. NEA, Am. Ednl. Rsch. Assn., Am. Assn. Coll. Tchrs. Edn., Comparative Edn. Soc., Phi Delta Kappa. *

RICHMOND, ISIDOR, architect; b. Chelsea, Mass., Dec. 2, 1893; s. Hyman and Lena (Tanzer) R.; m. Anne Bovarnick, Nov. 30, 1933; 1 child, Jean. Student, MIT, 1923, Am. Acad. Rome. Formerly with Cram & Ferguson, Bellows & Aldrich, Guy Lowell; established ind. practice, 1925; assoc. architect Newtowne Ct. Housing project, Cambridge, Mass.; instr. architecture MIT; founder Isidor Richmond & Carney Goldberg, 1946. Bldgs. designed include Lamson & Hubbard, Boston, chapel Isabella Thoburn Coll., Lucknow, India, indsl. bldgs. Dennison Mfg. Co., Framingham, various housing projects, Brookline, Mass, also coll. bldgs., librs., temples, synagogues. Trustee Boston Arts Festival; mem. Beacon Hill Archtl. Commn. Lt. (j.g.) USN, World War I, comdr. Res. Recipient Harleston Parker Gold Medal, Boston Soc. Architects, 1949, AIA Award of Merit, 1954. Fellow AIA; mem. Boston Archtl. Ctr., Boston Soc. Architects. *

RIDDEL, JOSEPH NEILL, English educator; b. Grantsville, W.Va., Sept. 11, 1931; s. James F. and Selma (Stump) R.; m. Virginia Lee Johnson, Apr. 17, 1957 (div. 1987); children: Kevin Joe, Valerie Anne, Vanessa Lee. A.B., Glenville State Coll., W.Va., 1953; M.S., U. Wis., 1956, Ph.D., 1960. Instr., later asst. prof. Duke U., 1960-64; vis. asst. prof. U. Calif., Riverside, 1964-65; assoc. prof., then prof. SUNY, Buffalo, 1965-72; prof. English UCLA, from 1973; faculty Sch. of Criticism and Theory, Northwestern U., summer 1981; dir. Ctr. for Critical Studies and the Human Scis., UCLA, from 1988; vis. Longstreet prof. Emory U., 1990. Author: The Clairvoyant Eye: The Poetry and Poetics of Wallace Stevens, 1965 (Explicator Prize 1965), republished, 1990, C. Day Lewis, 1971, The Inverted Bell: Modernism and the Counterpoetics of William Carlos Williams, 1974, republished, 1990. Served with AUS, 1953-55. Guggenheim fellow, 1976; sr. fellow Center for Twentieth Century Studies, U. Wis., Milw., 1977. Mem. Modern Lang. Assn., English Inst., Internat. Assn. Univ. Profs. of English. Democrat. Home: Los Angeles Calif. Deceased. †

RIDDER, WALTER THOMPSON, newspaper correspondent; b. N.Y.C., Apr. 1, 1917; s. Victor Frank and Marie (Thompson) R.; m. Marie Stix Wasserman, May 22, 1948; children: Ellen, Stephanie, Victor F. II, Pamela. Student, Columbia U., 1934-36; B.S., Harvard, 1939; PhD in Physiol. Optics, U. Houston, 1989. Reporter Duluth Herald-News-Tribune, 1940-41; Washington corr. St. Paul Pioneer Press-Dispatch, 1941-42, 1944-45, from 46; war corr. St. Paul, Duluth newspapers and N.Am. Newspaper Alliance in, ETO, 1945-46; fgn. corr. St. Paul, Duluth newspapers and N.Am. Newspaper Alliance in, 1947-48; chief field br., info. div. OSR, ECA, 1950-52; Washington corr. Ridder Publs., Inc.; also dir.; pub. Gary (Ind.) Post-Tribune, 1966-72; dir. Knight-Ridder Newspapers. Contbr. to nat. mags. Served as tech. sgt. AUS, 1942-43. Decorated Award of Merit, War Dept.; St. Olav's Medal from King Haakon of Norway; Order Merit W. Ger.). Mem. Overseas Writers, Delta Psi, Sigma Delta Chi. Unitarian. Clubs: Metropolitan, National Press (Washington); Burning Tree, Newport (R.I.) Country, Gridiron, N.Y. Yacht. Home: Mc Lean Va. Deceased. †

RIDDLE, JOHN PAUL, aviation consultant; b. Pikeville, Ky., May 19, 1901; s. Tandy M. and Bessie (Ferrell) R.; m. Adele Goeser, July 31, 1948; children: James Pardee III, Robert Strickler Pardee, Christopher Pardee, Adele Pardee, Tandy Miles, John Paul. Grad., Pikeville Coll. Acad., 1920, USAF Mechanics Sch., 1921, USAF Flying Sch., 1922. Pres. Airport Office Bldg Corp., Kendall Lakes Corp.; aviation cons. Coral Cables, Fla. Home: Coral Gables Fla. Died Apr. 6, 1989.

RIDING, LAURA **See JACKSON, LAURA**

RIEGEL, ROBERT EDGAR, educator, author; b. Reading, Pa., Dec. 4, 1897; s. Lewis Edgar and Florence Edna (Wetherhold) R.; m. Mary Mabel Cowden, June 21, 1923. Student, Lawrence Coll., 1915-16; AB, Carroll Coll., 1919, LLD, 1946; AM, U. Wis., 1920, PhD, 1922; AM, Dartmouth Coll., 1936. Prof. history Dartmouth Coll., from 1922; summer sch. tchr. various univs.; mem. faculty U. Calif., 1954-55, Tex. Western Coll., 1964-65. Author: The Story of the Western Railroads, 1926, America Moves West, 1930, rev. edit., 1947, Young America, 1830-1840, 1949, (with David F. Long) The America Story (2 vols.), 1955, American Feminists, 1963; also textbooks; contbr. articles to profl. jours.; editor: An Introduction to the Social Sciences (2 vols.), 1941, Dictionary of American Biography. Recipient Guggenheim grant, 1960-61. Mem. Am. Hist. Assn., Miss. Valley Hist. Assn., Soc. Am. Historians, Nat. Coun. Social Studies, Am. Assn. Univ. Profs., Social Studies Assn. *

RIES, HERMAN ELKAN, JR., physical chemist; b. Scranton, Pa., May 6, 1911; s. Herman Elkan and Henrietta (Brenner) R.; m. Elizabeth Hamburger, Aug. 17, 1940 (dec. July 1979); children: Walter Elkan, Richard Alan; m. Mildred Small Allen, May 8, 1981. B.S., U. Chgo., 1933; Ph.D., 1936. Head lab. instr. phys. chemistry U. Chgo., 1934-36; head phys. chemistry sect. Sinclair Refining Co. Research Labs., 1936-51, asst. dir. catalysis research div., 1948-50; research assoc. Standard Oil Co., Ind., Whiting, 1951-72; vis. prof. Inst. for Chem. Research, Kyoto U., Japan, 1972-74; research assoc. dept. biology U. Chgo., 1974-91; cons. in surface chemistry, 1972-91; faculty participant in research Argonne Nat. Labs., 1978; cons. petroleum and water pollution UN Indsl. Devel. Orgn., from 1973; lectr. Institut Francais du Petrol, Paris, 1951-57; vis. scientist Cavendish Lab., U. Cambridge,

Eng., 1964; vis. research assoc. Physico-Chimie des Surfaces et des Membranes CNRS U. Paris, 1984; assoc. sec. 1st Internat. Congress on Catalysis, 1956; coordinator critical data on monolayers Nat. Acad. Sci.-NRC-Nat. Bur. Standards, from 1965; lectr. World Congress on Surface Chemistry, London, 1957, Brussels, Belgium, 1964, Barcelona, Spain, 1968, Zurich, Switzerland, 1972, Moscow, USSR, 1976, Internat. Conf. on Surface and Colloid Sci., Jerusalem, 1981, Internat. Conf. on Surface and Colloid Sci., Paris, 1983, Potsdam, N.Y., 1985, Hakone, Japan, 1988; plenary lectr. Chem. Soc. Japan, 1973, Internat. Conf. on Transferred Films, Susono City, 1988; Welch Found. lectr., 1978-79. Author: Structure and Sintering Properties of Cracking Catalysts and Related Materials, 1952, Physical Adsorption, 1953, Monomolecular Films, 1973, Direct Measurement of Adsorption of Radiostearic Acid onto Vapor-Deposited Metal Films, 1964, Electron Microscope Studies of Monolayers of Lecithin, 1975, Monolayers of Lipids and Polymers, 1988; mem. editorial bd., reviewer: Jour. Colloid and Interface Sci, 1970-73; mem. editorial bd.: Advances in Colloid and Interface Sci, from 1981; contbr. articles to profl. jours. Recipient Ipatieff award Am. Chem. Soc., 1950, certificate of merit div. colloid and surface chemistry, 1975. Fellow AAAS; mem. Am. Chem. Soc. (nat. awards com. 1965-68, 73-75, co-chmn. phys. chemistry group Chgo. sect. 1948-49, coms. continuing edn., environment Chgo. sect. 1970-71, reviewer Jour. Phys. Chemistry from 1960, Jour. Am. Chem. Soc., Jour. Chem. Physics, Langmuir, exec. com. petroleum div. 1951-52, adv. com. colloid div. from 1956, exec. com. div. colloid and surface chemistry 1964), AAAS (adv. bd. Gordon Research Confs. 1947-51, program com. Gordon Research Conf. from 1960, chmn. Gordon Research Conf. on Interfaces 1960), Faraday Soc. (London), Chem. Soc. Japan, Am. Inst. Chemists, Am. Soc. Lubrication Engrs. (fundamentals com. 1960), N.Y. Acad. Scis., Internat. Union of Pure and Applied Chemistry (affiliate), Sigma Xi, Phi Beta Kappa. Clubs: Catalysis (Chgo.), Quadrangle (Chgo.). Home: Chicago Ill. Died Oct. 3, 1991; buried Rosehill Cemetery, Chgo.

RIESENBERGER, FRANK RALPH, business executive; b. Union City, N.J., Feb. 13, 1897; s. Adam and Sophia (Werner) R.; m. Dorothea Woodfin, Mar. 4, 1963. ME, Stevens Inst. Tech., 1918. Profl. engr., 1919-21; efficiency engr. Julius Kayser & Co., 1922; v.p. Van Realte Co., Inc., N.Y.C., 1933-48, pres., 1948-61, chmn. bd., CEO, from 1961. Mem. Tau Beta Pi, Beta Theta Pi. *

RIGGINS, JOHN ALFRED, JR., lawyer; b. Phoenix, June 9, 1912; s. John Alfred and Hattie Alice (Harrah) R.; m. Elaine Eleanor Stambaugh, Sept. 20, 1947; children—Kristi Anne, John Alfred, III. LL.B., U. Ariz., 1936. Bar: Ariz. 1936, U.S. Supreme Ct. 1957, D.C. 1969. Sole practice, to 1946; ptnr. Jennings, Strouss & Salmon, Phoenix, 1946-70, sr. ptnr., 1970-82, of counsel, 1982-86. Pres. Ariz.-Mexico Commn., 1970-80; chmn. bd. dirs. Ariz. State U. Found. Served with U.S. Army, Mem. ABA, Nat. Water Resources Assn. (past pres., dir.). Presbyterian. Died July 4, 1986; cremated. Home: Phoenix Ariz.

RIGHTER, RICHARD SCOTT, lawyer; b. Topeka, Aug. 3, 1894; s. William Henry and Ida May (Scott) R.; m. Kathryn Harford, Feb. 21, 1931; 1 child, William H. AB, Washburn Coll., 1916; LLB, Harvard U., 1920. Bar: Mo. 1920. Practiced law Kansas City, Mo., from 1920; ptnr. Lathrop, Righter, Gordon & Parker, Kansas City, from 1928. Mem. Mo. Constl. Conv., 1943, 44. Mem. C. of C., Lawyers Assn. Kansas City, ABA, Kans. Bar Assn. *

RIGLER, LEE GEORGE, radiologist; b. Mpls., Oct. 16, 1896; s. Harris and Rose (Rabinowitz) R.; m. Matil Sprung, Sept. 8, 1920; children: Stanley Paul, Nancy Judith, Ruth Margaret. BS, U. Minn., 1917, MB, 1919, MD, 1920. In gen. practice, 1920-22, fellow in internal medicine, 1922-23; roentgenologist Mpls. Gen. Hosps., 1923-26; formerly chief dept., spl. cons. USPHS; assoc. prof. radiology U. Minn., 1927-29, prof., 1929-57, head dept., 1923-57; prof. radiology UCLA; former exec. dir. Cedars Lebanon Hosp., Mt. Sinai Hosp. Recipient Caldwell medal Am. Roentgen Ray Soc., Crookshank medal Brit. Faculty Radiologists, Grubbe award. Fellow Am. Assn. Chest Physicians, Am. Coll. Radiology; mem. AMA, AAAS, Am. Cancer Soc., Am. Bd. Radiology, Minn. Radiol. Soc., Am. Roentgen Ray Soc., many others. *

RINDLAUB, JEAN WADE, advertising agency executive; b. Lancaster, Pa., Feb. 9, 1904; d. Robert M. and Lola (Hess) Wade; m. Willard W. Rindlaub, Mar. 15, 1930 (dec. 1983); children: John Wade, Anne Wade Rindlaub Dow. Sec. to advt. mgr., later head co. publs. Armstrong Cork Co., Lancaster, 1925-30; various positions to copy group head Batten, Barton, Durstine & Osborn, N.Y.C., 1930-46, v.p., from 1946, bd. dirs., from 1954; adviser Tobé-Coburn Sch. for Fashion Careers. Bd. dirs., vice chmn. Nat. Safety Coun.; mem. N.Y. State Coun. Women; co-founder Sr. Svcs. Ctr., Teaneck, N.J.; chmn. Friendship House; mem. Adv. Bd. on Sr. Citizens, Adv. Bd. on Community Rels.; vol. tchr.'s asst.; newsletter columnist Nat. Coun. Women. Named Woman of Yr., Am. Advt. Fedn., 1951, to Hall of Fame, 1989; Teaneck (N.J.) Citizen of Yr., 1981. Mem. Advt. Women N.Y. (bd. dirs.), Fashion Group (bd. dirs.), Gamma Alpha Chi (hon. v.p.). Episcopalian. Home: Stamford Conn. Died Dec. 19, 1991; buried Landes Valley, Pa.

RINEY, RICHARD THOMAS, corporate executive; b. West Louisville, Ky., Dec. 11, 1896; s. Richard T. and Mary V. (Blandford) R.; m. Hannah C. Mathews, Nov. 22, 1923. Student, Lockyear's Bus. Coll., 1916. With Sterling Brewers, Inc., Evansville, Ind., from 1917, pres., gen. mgr., from 1934, then chmn. Sec. bd. dirs. U.S. Brewers' Found., Inc. Mem. Evansville C. of C., Ind. Brewers Assn., Evansville Mfrs. Assn., Evansville Employers' Assn., Am. Legion. *

RINSLEY, DONALD BRENDAN, psychiatrist; b. N.Y.C., Jan. 31, 1928; s. Louis and Annamay (Hindle) R.; m. Charlotte Anne Trowbridge; 1 child, Eve Anne. A.B. with honors, Harvard U., 1949, postgrad., 1949-50; M.D., Washington U., St. Louis, 1954; diploma in child psychiatry (hon.), Menninger Found., 1975. Diplomate Am. Bd. Psychiatry and Neurology, Am. Bd. Med. Psychotherapists (fellow). Intern in pediatrics St. Louis Children's Hosp., 1954-55; fellow in psychiatry Menninger Found., Topeka, 1955-56, 58-60; staff psychiatrist Dept. Justice, U.S. Med. Center for Fed. Prisoners, Springfield, Mo., 1956-58; resident psychiatrist Topeka State Hosp., 1955-56, 58-60, asst. chief adolescent unit, childrens sect., 1960-68, chief, 1968-70, dir. sect., 1970-75; asso. chief psychiatry edn. Colmery-O'Neil VA Med. Center, Topeka, 1975-89; cons. psychiatrist C.F. Menninger Meml. Hosp., 1976-89; cons. psychiatrist children's div. Menninger Found., 1981-89, Skillman prof. child psychiatry, 1983-84; asst. in pediatrics Washington U. Sch. Medicine, St. Louis, 1954-55; faculty gen. psychiatry Karl Menninger Sch. Psychiatry and Mental Health Scis., Topeka, from 1960, faculty child psychiatry, from 1968, exec. com. faculty in child psychiatry, 1969-75, 77-79; asso. clin. prof. psychiatry U. Kans. Sch. Medicine, 1970-77, clin. prof., 1977-89; sr. asst. surgeon to surgeon USPHS, 1956-80; affiliate prof. psychiatry Oral Roberts U. Sch. Medicine, 1987-89; Arthur B. Richter vis. prof. of child psychiatry, U. Ind. Sch. Medicine, 1988. Author: Treatment of the Severely Disturbed Adolescent, 1980; Borderline and Other Self Disorders, 1982, Development, Dynamics and Treatment of Borderline and Narcissistic Personalities, 1989; mem. editorial bd. Internat. Jour. Med. Psychotherapy, Adolescent Psychiatry; cons. editor Bull. Menninger Clinic; hon. cons. editor: Argentine Jour. Child and Adolescent Psychiatry and Psychology; contbr. articles to profl. jours. Recipient Edward A. Strecker Meml. award Inst. Pa. Hosp., 1968; William C. Menninger award Menninger Found., 1982; Spencer Found. fellow in advanced studies Menninger Found., 1976-79; fellow in interdisciplinary studies, from 1979. Fellow Am. Psychiat. Assn. (br. chmn. com. research 1964-65), Am. Coll. Psychoanalysts, Royal Soc. Health, AAAS, N.Y. Acad. Scis., Am. Soc. Adolescent Psychiatry, Am. Assn. Childrens Residential Centers; mem. Assn. for Research Nervous and Mental Disease, Soc. for Acad. Psychiatry, Am. Acad. Psychoanalysis, Canadian Psychiat. Assn. (corr.), Am. Assn. Psychiat. Services for Children, Sigmund Freud Soc. (Vienna), Argentine Assn. Child and Adolescent Psychiatry and Psychology (hon.), Sigma Xi (zone cons. to chpt. at large 1969-71, mem. com. on membership at large 1972-75). Club: Harvard-Radcliffe of Kansas City. Home: Topeka Kans. Died Dec. 23, 1989; buried Mt. Calvary, Topeka, Kansas.

RINZLER, CAROL GENE EISEN, lawyer, writer; b. Newark, Sept. 12, 1941; d. Irving Y. and Ruth (Katz) Eisen; m. Carl Rinzler, July 21, 1962 (div. 1976); children: Michael Franklin, Jane Ruth Amelia. AB, Goucher Coll., 1962; JD, Yale U., 1980. Bar: N.Y. 1981, U.S. Supreme Ct. 1984. Editor Charterhouse Books, Inc., N.Y.C., 1971-73, pub., 1973-74; articles editor Glamour mag., N.Y.C., 1974-77; assoc. Cahill Gordon & Reindel, N.Y.C., 1980-86; of counsel Rembar & Curtis, N.Y.C., 1986-90; pvt. practice law, 1990. Author: Frankly McCarthy, 1969, Nobody Said You Had to Eat Off the Floor, 1971, The Girl Who Got All the Breaks, 1980, Your Adolescent: An Owner's Manual, 1981, How to Set Up for a Mah-jongg Game and Other Lost Arts (with J. Gelman), 1987; contbg. editor: Pubs. Weekly, 1983-90; book critic, columnist Mademoiselle mag., 1981-86, Cosmopolitan mag., 1983-87; contbr. articles, columns and revs. to various publs. Mem. Friends of Scarlett O'Hara, Women's Media Group (pres. 1984-85), Nat. Book Critics Circle., PEN (exec. bd. 1986-90), Assn. Bar City N.Y. (com. copyright and intellectual property 1984-87). Jewish. Club: Cosmopolitan (N.Y.C.). Home: New York N.Y. Died Dec. 6, 1990; buried Rutland Jewish Cemetery, East Clarendon, Vt.

RIPPEL, JULIUS ALEXANDER, business and foundation executive; b. Newark, July 22, 1901; s. Albert A. and Caroline (Greig) R.; B.S., Dartmouth Coll., 1923; L.H.D. (hon.), Med. Coll. Pa., 1972, Upsala Coll., 1977; Sc.D. (hon.), Georgetown U. Sch. Medicine, 1977; m. Carol W. Richards, 1924; children: Susan J., Eric R. With J.S. Rippel & Co., Newark, 1923-38, v.p., 1933-38; pres. Julius A. Rippel, Inc., Newark, 1938-55, Rippel & Co., Newark, 1955-82; dir. emeritus NUI Corp. Pres., dir., chmn. Fannie E. Rippel Found., 1953-83, trustee, 1953-91. Recipient Outstanding Citizen award Advt. Club Newark, 1943; Hosp. Achievement award N.J. Hosp. Assn., 1969; Heart award N.Y. Cardiology Soc., 1969; spl. citation United Hosps. of Newark, 1969; Disting. Service award Am. Heart Assn., 1970; Dignity-of-Man award Kessler Inst. Rehab., 1971; Merit citation Upper N.J. chpt. Nat. Multiple Sclerosis Assn., 1971; Man of Yr. award Mt. Carmel Guild N.J., 1972; spl. award Columbus Hosp., Newark, 1973; cert. of Achievement, Assn. Advancement Med. Instrumentation, 1974; Thanks award St. Michael's Med. Center, Newark, 1974; Citizens award Acad. Medicine N.J., 1976; achievement award Ariz. State U., 1977; Dartmouth Coll. Alumni award, 1980; Albert Gallatin fellow NYU, 1977. Mem. Am. Hosp. Assn. (hon.), Investment Bankers Assn., Nat. Assn. Securities Dealers, Phi Beta Kappa Assos., Kappa Sigma. Clubs: Baltusrol Golf (Springfield, N.J.); Morris County Golf (Convent, N.J.); Essex (Newark). Died Dec. 30, 1991. Home: Madison N.J.

RITCHIE, JOHN, lawyer; b. Norfolk, Va., Mar. 19, 1904; s. John and Edith (Kensett) R., Jr; m. Sarah Dunlap Wallace, Apr. 20, 1929; children: John, Albert. B.S., U. Va., 1925, LL.B., 1927; J.S.D., Yale U., 1931; LL.D. (hon.), Coll. William and Mary, 1979. Bar: Nebr. 1927, Ill. 1957, Va. 1942, Mo. 1952, Wis. 1953. With Ritchie, Chase, Canaday & Swenson, Omaha, 1927-28; asst. prof. law Furman U., 1928-30, U. Wash., 1931-36; Sterling fellow Yale U., 1930-31; prof. law U. Md., 1936-37; prof. law U. Va., 1937-52, asst. dean, 1941-49; dean law sch., Kirby prof. law Washington U., 1952-53; prof., dean Sch. Law, U. Wis., 1953-57, Law Sch., Northwestern U., Chgo., 1957-72; John Henry Wigmore prof. Law Sch., Northwestern U., 1966-72, emeritus prof. and dean, 1972; prof. law U. Va., 1972-74, scholar-in-residence, from 1974; vis. distinguished prof. U. Tenn., 1974, U. Okla., 1975, Coll. William and Mary, 1976; Tucker lectr. Washington and Lee U.; Detocqueville lectr. Marquette U.; bd. dirs. First Nat. Bank and Trust Co., Evanston, 1963-72. Co-author: Decedent's Estates and Trusts, 1955, 6th edit., 1982; author: The First Hundred Years: A Short History of the School of Law of the University of Virginia for the Period 1826-1926, 1978; Editorial bd., Found. Press.; Contbr. various legal publs. Mem. Ill. Jud. Adv. Council, 1964-68; bd. dirs. Am. Council on Edn., 1965-68, First Nat. Bank and Trust Co., Evanston, Ill., 1963-72, United Charities Chgo., 1966-72. Served to col. U.S. Army, 1942-45. Decorated Bronze Star, Army Commendation medal. Fellow Am. Bar Found., Va. Law Found., Va. Bar Found.; mem. ABA (ho. of dels. 1957-71), Ill. Bar Assn., Chgo. Bar Assn., Assn. Am. Law Schs. (pres. 1964), Law Club Chgo., Judge Advs. Assn. (pres. 1951-52), Order of Coif (nat. pres. 1952-55), Raven Soc., Phi Beta Kappa, Omicron Delta Kappa, Phi Kappa Psi, Phi Delta Phi. Episcopalian. Clubs: Wayfarers, Colonnade, Greencroft, Law Club of Chgo. Home: Charlottesville Va. Died Mar. 4, 1988; buried Mt. Olive Cemetery, Frederick, Md.

RITT, MARTIN, director, actor; b. N.Y.C., Mar. 2, 1914; s. Morris and Rose R. Student, Elon Coll., DFA (hon.), 1989; student, Group Theatre, N.Y.C.; DFA (hon.), Am. Film Inst., 1989. Bd. govs. Acad. Motion Pictures Arts and Scis., 1980. Broadway appearances include Golden Boy, 1937, Plant in the Sun, 1938, The Gentle People, 1939, Two on an Island, 1939, They Should Have Stood in Bed, 1942, The Eve of St. Mark, 1942, Winged Victory, 1943; also on tour Men of Distinction, 1953, Maya, 1953, The Flowering Peach, 1954, Born Yesterday, Phila., 1955; motion picture appearances in Winged Victory, 1944, End of the Game, 1976, Hollywood on Trial, 1977, Slugger's Wife, 1984; Broadway prodns. directed include: Mr. Peebles and Mr. Hooker, 1946, Yellow Jack, 1947, The Big People, Conn. and Mass., 1947, Set My People Free, 1948, The Man, 1950, Cry of the Peacock, 1950, Golden Boy, Boy Meets Girl, The Front Page, all Phila., 1954, A View From the Bridge, 1955, A Memory of Two Mondays, 1955; motion pictures directed include: Edge of the City, 1957, The Long Hot Summer, 1958, The Sound and the Fury, 1959, The Black Orchid, 1959, Five Branded Women, 1960, Paris Blues, 1961, Adventures of a Young Man (Hollywood Fgn. Press award), 1962, The Outrage, 1964, The Spy Who Came in from the Cold, 1966 (Photoplay, Film Daily, Brit. Film Acad., Soc. Film and TV Arts and Scis. awards), Hombre, 1967, The Brotherhood, 1968, Sounder, 1972 (Christopher award, DCA award Outstanding Dir. Achievement), Pete 'n' Tillie, 1972, Casey's Shadow, 1978, Norma Rae, 1979 (German Film Critics award), Cross Creek, 1982, Murphy's Romance, 1985, Nuts, 1987, Stanley & Iris, 1989; co-producer, dir.: Hud, 1963 (Motion Picture Herald award, Cleve. Critics Best Picture award, Best dir. award Hollywood Fgn. Press, Dirs. Guild Am. award), The Molly Maguires, 1970, The Great White Hope, 1970, Backroads, 1980, Murphy's Romance, 1985; dir., producer: Conrack, 1974 (Box Office Blue Ribbon award, Czechoslovakia award), The Front, 1976 (5h Tehran Internat. award); dir. TV series Danger; also plays for U.S. Steel Hour, Playwrites Theatre, Actors Studio Theatre; TV appearances in Danger, Starlight Theatre. Served with USAAF, World War II. Recipient numerous awards including Peabody award, Actors Studio award, Jean Renoir award, 1984, Upton Sinclair award Dirs. Guild Am., Disting. Alumnus award Elon Coll., 1980, Norma Rae German Film Critics award, 1981, citation N.Y.C., ACLU award,

1982, Boston U. Lifetime Achievement award, 1988. Mem. Screen Directors Guild, AFTRA, Actors Equity Assn., Screen Actors Guild. Home: Pacific Palisades Calif. Died Dec. 7, 1991; cremated.

RIVER, LOUIS PHILIP, surgeon; b. San Francisco, Mar. 12, 1901; s. Louis Philip and Amy (Hopkins) R.; m. Elizabeth Lambert, Sept. 18, 1928; children: Louis, George, Amy (Mrs. T. Valenzuela), Valerie (Mrs. A.W. Vaughan III). S.B., U. Chgo., 1922, M.D., 1925. Diplomate: Am. Bd. Surgery. Intern Presbyn. Hosp., Chgo., 1924-25; pvt. practice Oak Park, Ill., 1925-72; attending surgeon Oak Park Hosp., 1928-77, Cook County Hosp., Chgo., 1937-74; clin. prof. surgery Stritch Med. Sch., Loyola U., Chgo., from 1952; prof. surgery Cook County Postgrad. Med. Sch., 1937-72. Contbr. articles to surg. jours. Served to lt. col. M.C. AUS, 1942-46, ETO. Fellow ACS, Internat. Coll. Surgeons (pres. U.S. sect. 1974, internat. corp. sec. 1973-77), Ill. Surg. Soc. (pres. 1968), Chgo. Med. Soc. (Pub. Svc. award 1978). Home: Oak Park Ill. Died Jan. 24, 1991.

RIVERS, G(EORGE) L(AMB), lawyer; b. Charleston, S.C., May 26, 1896; s. Moultrie Rutledge and Eliza Ingraham (Buist) R.; m. Ethel Pinckney Rutledge, Nov. 20, 1930; children: George Lamb Buist, Thomas Rutledge. AB, Coll. Charleston, 1916, AM, 1916; ed., Harvard U. Law Sch., 1916-17, 19. Bar: S.C. 1919. Asst. U.S. dist. atty. Ea. Dist. S.C., 1922; mem. Hagood, Rivers & Young, from 1920; pres. Cen. R.R. of S.C.; chmn., dir. counsel 1st Fed. Savs. & Loan Assn. Charleston, numerous other corp. directorships. Mem. S.C. Ho. of Reps., 1924-28, Senate, 1930; trustee bd. visitors S.C. Mil. Coll., 1930; pres. bd. trustees Coll. Charleston. 1st lt. AEF, World War I. Decorated D.S.C., 1918. Mem. ABA, S.C. State Bar Assn., Charleston County Bar Assn., St. Georges Soc., St. Andrews Soc., Footlight Players, S.C. Soc., St. Cecilia Soc., Alpha Tau Omega. *

RIZZO, ANTHONY AUGUSTINE, clinical periodontist, government official; b. Birmingham, Ala., June 8, 1928; s. John and Josephine Elizabeth (Giattina) R.; m. Betty Krueger, June 24, 1955 (dec. Feb. 1971); children: David, Patricia; m. Teresa Hamm, Aug. 25, 1973; children—Michael, Jonathan, Daniel. A.B., Birmingham-So. Coll., 1951; D.M.D., U. Ala., 1956, M.S., 1956. Resident in periodontology U. Ala., 1956-57; prin. investigator Nat. Inst. Dental Research, NIH, Bethesda, Md., 1957-68, chief biomaterials program, 1968-71, chief periodontal disease program, 1971-73, spl. asst. for program coordination, 1973-84, dep. assoc. dir. extramural programs, 1984-85, chief periodontal and soft tissue disease program, from 1985; vis. lectr. Dental Sch., Howard U., Washington, 1965-67; staff periodontist NIH Commd. Officers Clnic, Bethesda, Md., 1981-86. Contbr. articles to profl. publs., 1959-89. Recipient Commendation medal USPHS, 1977, Outstanding Service medal USPHS, 1988. Mem. Internat. Assn. Dental Research, Am. Assn. Dental Research, Delta Sigma Delta, Omicron Delta Kappa. Democrat. Roman Catholic. Home: Kensington Md. Died Apr. 20, 1991. †

RIZZO, FRANCIS LAZZARO, former mayor; b. Phila., Oct. 23, 1920; s. Raffaele and Theresa (Erminio) R.; m. Carmella Silvestri, 1942; children: Francis Silvestri, Joanna Ellen. Patrolman City of Phila., 1943-51, sgt., 1951-54, capt., 1954-59, insp., 1959-64, dep. police commr., 1964-67, police commr., 1967-71, mayor, 1972-80; chmn. Delaware Valley Regional Planning Commn., 1972-91. Recipient Phila. Crime Commn. award for lowest crime rate among ten largest cities, 1969, J. Edgar Hoover award VFW, 1969, Honor award U.S. Secret Svc., 1969, numerous civic and regional awards. Mem. S.E. Pa. Police Chiefs Assn., Fraternal Order Police, Sons of Italy, Lions. Republican. Roman Catholic. Home: Philadelphia Pa. Died July 16, 1991.

ROBB, DAVID METHENY, art historian, educator; b. Tak Hing Chau, South China, Sept. 19, 1903; s. John Knox and Maude (Lawson) R.; m. Jane Elizabeth Robb; children: Howard, Martha, Elizabeth, David Metheny, Sara M. AB, Oberlin Coll., 1926, AM, 1927; MFA, Princeton U., 1935, PhD, 1941. Assoc. prof. fine arts Colgate U., 1930-35; assoc. prof. fine arts U. Minn., 1935-39, prof. art history, 1939; chmn. dept. art history U. Pa., 1939-55, chmn. art dept., 1965-66; vis. prof. U. Del., 1967-68; Charles Beebe Martin lectr. in classics Oberlin Coll., 1970. Author: (with J.J. Garrison) Art in the Western World, 1942, The Harper History of Painting, 1951, The Art of the Illuminated Manuscript, 1973; contbr. articles and revs. in art and hist. jours. Guggenheim fellow, 1956-57, Fulbright rsch. scholar, 1956-57, 63-64. Mem. Coll. Art Assn. Am. (pres. 1960-62), Mediaeval Acad. Am., Archaeol. Inst. Am., Soc. Archtl. Historians, Soc. for Am. Studies, Art Alliance Club, Franklin Inn Club, Athenaeum Club (Phila.), Tau Sigma Delta, Phi Beta Kappa. Home: Merion Station Pa. Died Apr. 9, 1990.

ROBB, JOHN DONALD, composer, educator; b. Mpls., June 12, 1892; s. John G. and Harriet A. (Gay) R.; m. Harriet F. Block, Sept. 24, 1921; children—Priscilla (Mrs. Sanford N. McDonnell), John Donald, Nancy Gay (Mrs. William C. Briggs). A.B., Yale, 1915; student law, U. Minn., 1916-17, Harvard, 1920-22; grad. student music, Juillard Sch., N.Y.C.; M.A., Mills Coll., 1950; DMus. (hon.), U. N.Mex., 1986. Bar: N.Y. bar 1923. Practiced in N.Y.C., until 1941; prof. music, head dept. U. N.Mex., 1941-42; acting dean U. N.Mex. (Coll. Fine Arts), 1942-46, dean, 1946-57, emeritus, 1957-89; vis prof., nat. Conservatory Music, El Salvador, 1962; condr. in U.S.A., S.Am., C.Am., 1963-64; chmn. com. copyright revision Nat. Assn. Schs. Music, 1957-58; Republican candidate congressman at large, N.Mex., 1960; bd. regents Highlands U., Las Vegas, N.Mex., 1960-72, pres. bd., 1966-70; dir. Rio Grande Electronic Music Lab., Albuquerque; bd. dirs. Community Concerts Assn. Albuquerque, 1941-73, pres., 1967-68. Author: Hispanic Folk Songs of New Mexico, 1954, Hispanic Folk Music of New Mexico and the Southwest, 1980, also articles.; Compositions include Little Jo; opera, piano concerto, 4 symphonies, more than 100 other mus. compositions, including electronic music. Recipient Achievement and Excellence award N.Mex. Arts Commn., 1975; Rockefeller Fund grantee; Nat. Endowment for Arts Grantee. Mem. ASCAP, Kappa Kappa Psi, Pi Kappa Lambda, Tau Kappa Alpha, Alpha Delta Phi, Delta Sigma Rho. Clubs: Elihu, Yale. Home: Albuquerque N. Mex. Died Jan. 16, 1989.

ROBBIE, JOSEPH, lawyer, professional football team executive; b. Sisseton, S.D., July 7, 1916; s. Joseph and Jennie (Ready) R.; m. Elizabeth Ann Lyle, Dec. 28, 1942; children—Diane Robbie Truly, David (dec.), Janet Robbie Hancock, Joseph Michael, Kathleen (dec.), Lynn, Deborah Robbie Huggins, Timothy, Brian, Daniel, Kevin. A.B., U. S.D., 1943, J.D., 1946; LL.D., Biscayne Coll., 1970, U. S.D., 1979; D. Arts and Scis. (hon.), Mt. Marty Coll., 1979; H.H.D. (hon.), St. Leo Coll., 1982. Bar: S.D. 1946, Minn. 1951. Practice in Mitchell, S.D., 1948-53, Mpls., from 1953; founder, pres., mng. gen. ptnr. Miami Dolphins, Ltd., 1965-90; Mem. Fla. Bd. Bus. Regulation, 1977; mem. exec. com. Hubert H. Humphrey Inst. Pub. Affairs, from 1977; regional counsel, acting regional enforcement dir. OPS, Mpls., 1951-52, regional dir., 1952-53; 1st chmn. commn., 1959-65; regional v.p. Nat. Municipal League, 1977; charter mem., sec.-treas. Twin Cities Met. Planning Commn., 1957-65; spl. counsel com. for hearings to create Dept. Urban Affairs U.S. Senate, 1961; exec. dir., legal counsel Commn. Municipal Annexation and Consol. Minn. Legislature, 1961-63; asst. prof. econs. Dakota Wesleyan U., 1946-48; spl. instr., debate coach Coll. St. Catherine, St. Paul, 1953-54. Author: Minn. Municipal Commn. Act, 1959-60. Chmn. Harry S. Truman Library Fund Drive, 1956; v.p., presiding officer Am. Lebanese Syrian Associated Charities, 1966-68, bd. dirs., from 1959; chmn. Community Relations Bd. Dade County, 1973; mem. tourist devel. adv. council Bd. Broward County Commrs., 1977; chmn. nat. alumni fund drive Dakota Dome, U. S.D., 1972; co-chmn. fund drive Curley High Sch., Miami, 1973, Gesu Ch., 1973; hon. chmn. Century of Service Fund campaign, Yankton, S.D., 1978; com. to raise funds Carleton Coll., Northfield, Minn., 1973; mem. S.D. Legislature, 1949-51, joint caucus leader; chmn. S.D. Democratic Party, 1948-50; candidate gov., S.D., 1950, U.S. Congress from Minn., 1956, 58; v.p. Catholic Charities, Archdiocese of Miami; bd. govs. St. Jude Children's Research Hosp., Memphis, 1959-80; bd. dirs. Boys Town Miami, from 1969, Operation Self-Help, 1969-71, United Fund, from 1972, Am. Health Found., from 1975, Dakota Dome Devel. Corp.; mem. steering com. Friends of Religion, U. Miami, from 1979; mem. adv. bd. Fla. Meml. Coll., Miami, from 1967; trustee Biscayne Coll., 1970-71, 76-81, trustee emeritus, 1981-90 , chmn. devel. bd., 1976, mem. adv. com. sports adminstrn.; trustee Dade Found., 1972-75; trustee Pub. Health Trust, Jackson Meml. Hosp., 1973-79, from 1981; chmn. bd. dirs. Cath. Service Bur., Archdiocese of Miami, 1977-79; mem. citizens' bd. U. Miami; mem. adv. council Coll. Arts and Letters, U. Notre Dame, 1973; mem. council advisors Fla. State U. System, from 1975; incorporator Sunshine State Games Found., 1980; bd. dirs. USO, from 1976, Jesuit Program for Living and Learning, from 1978. Served with USNR, 1941-45. Decorated Bronze Star; recipient Nathan Burkan Meml. award for essay copywright law, 1946; J. Ernest O'Brien Commendation award Nat. Assn. Tobacco Distbrs., 1966; Good Samaritan award Variety Club Miami, 1971; Alumni award excellence No. State Coll., 1971; Outstanding Alumnus award Sisseton (S.D.) High Sch., 1971; Silver Medallion award Fla. Region NCCJ, 1973; Citation for meritorious pub. service Dept. of Navy, 1974; Horatio Alger award, 1979; Humanitarian award Big Bros./Big Sisters of Greater Miami, 1982; CHIEF award Ind. Colls. and Univs. of Fla., 1981; named Pro Football Exec. of Year L.I. Athletic Club, 1973, Pop Warner Football Father of Yr., 1976; named to U. S.D. Hall of Fame, 1982; Miami Dolphins winners Nat. Football League World Championship, 1972-73; Hon. fellow Hebrew U., 1973. Mem. No. State Coll. Alumni Assn. (nat. fund raising chmn.), Miami C. of C. (gov.). Clubs: Kiwanian, LaGorce Country, Miami, Ocean Reef, Palm Bay, Tiger Bay. Lodge: Knights of Malta. Home: Miami Shores Fla. Died Jan. 7, 1990.

ROBBINS, CHARLES EDWARD, business association executive; b. Perry, Okla., July 19, 1906; s. William Marion and Mary (Swan) R.; m. Pauline Frederick, Mar. 29, 1969; 1 child by previous marriage, Charles Edward. Student, U. Okla., 1924; B.A., DePauw U., 1928; postgrad., U. Cin., 1930-31, U. Chgo., 1938-39. Reporter Indpls. Star, 1928-29; reporter Wall St. Jour., Cin., 1929-34; mng. editor Wall St. Jour., N.Y.C., 1934-35; Midwest mgr. Wall St. Jour., Chgo., 1935-41; with bus. dept. N.Y. Times, 1941-49; v.p. Bozell & Jacobs, N.Y.C., 1949-53; exec. mgr., founding mem. Atomic Indsl. Forum, N.Y.C., 1953-72, pres., 1972-74, dir., 1973-89; cons. and lectr. internat. bus. and energy, from 1974; ofcl. rep. UN World Energy Conf., from 1980. Served to lt. USNR, 1943-46. Mem. Am. Nuclear Soc., UN Assn., Fgn. Policy Assn., N.Y. Soc. Profl. Journalists, Phi Gamma Delta, Sigma Delta Chi. Episcopalian. Home: Sarasota Fla. Died Aug. 9, 1989.

ROBBINS, ROSSELL HOPE, English language educator, mediaevalist; b. Wallasey, Eng., July 22, 1912; came to U.S., 1937, naturalized, 1944; s. Rossell Casson and Alice (Hope) R.; m. Helen Ann Mins, June 9, 1939. BA with honours, U. Liverpool, Eng., 1933, diploma in edn., 1934; PhD, Cambridge (Eng.) U., 1937; licentiate, Guildhall Sch. Music, London, 1932, Matthay Sch. Music, Liverpool, 1935. Dir. studies Cambridge U., 1935-37; instr. Bklyn. Coll., CUNY, 1942; staff cons. Nat. Inst. Social Rels., Washington, 1946; asst. prof., assoc. prof. Bklyn. Poly. Inst., 1946-54; vis. prof. U. N.C., Chapel Hill, 1958, Duke U., Durham, N.C., 1965, Sir George Williams U., 1968; Can. Coun. prof. Mt. Allison U., 1965; Internat. prof. English, SUNY, Albany, 1969-82; Beckman prof. U. Calif., Berkeley, 1966, Regents' prof., Riverside, 1968-69; vis. scholar Univ. Ctr. in Va., Richmond, 1966, California (Pa.) State Coll., 1969; 1st Thomas Kirby lectr. La. State U., 1976; vis. lectr. throughout U.S., Can., Europe, Japan, 1957-82, including Brit. Univ. Tchrs. English, 1962; overseas speaker Brit. Assn. Advancement Sci., 1963, Humanities Assn. Can., 1966, 69, Internat. Musicology Soc., Ljubljana, 1967, also others. faculty assoc. Columbia U., 1956-66. Author: (with C. Brown) The Index of Middle English Verse, 1943, (with J. Cutler) Supplement to the Index, 1966; author: Christopher Marlowe: Dr. Faustus, 2d edit., 1967, The T.S. Eliot Myth, 2d edit., 1964, Secular Lyrics of the XIV and XV Centuries, 2d edit., 1955, Historical Poems of the XIV and XV Centuries, 1959, Encyclopedia of Witchcraft and Demonology, 16th edit., 1982, The Hundred Tales, 2d edit., 1962, Early English Christman Carols, 1961, The Chaucerian Apocrypha, 1973, Poems Dealing with Contemporary Conditions, 1975, Chaucer at Albany, 1975, Witchcraft: Introduction to the Literature, 1978, also numerous articles; gen. editor: Old English and Middle English, Lexikon des Mittelalters, 1975, Middle English Texts & Contexts, 1975; hon. gen. editor: The Index of Middle English Prose, 1978; mem. editorial bd. Medievalia of Humanistica, Vita etc in Chaucer and Middle English Studies in Honour of Rossell Hope Robbins, 1974. With AUS, 1943-46. Commonwealth Fund fellow NYU, 1937-39, Noble fellow U. Liverpool, 1939-40, Guggenheim fellow, 1955-56, rsch. fellow SUNY, 1971, 72, sr. fellow Inst. Humanistic Studies, 1977; Ford vis. fellow Harvard U., 1958, 59. Fellow Royal Soc. Lit.; mem. AAUP, MLA (chmn. Mid. English bibliography com. from 1959, chmn. div. 22, 1975-78), Renaissance Soc., Internat. Assn. Univ. Profs. English, Modern Humanities Rsch. Assn., Anglo-Norman Text Soc., Early English Tex. Soc., N.Y. Folklore Soc., Internat. Ct. Lit. Assnn., New Chaucer Soc., Mid. English Tex. Soc. (U.S. bd. dirs.), Medieval Club N.Y. (pres. 1977-79), Soc. Rencesvals. Home: Saugerties N.Y. Died Mar. 5, 1990.

ROBERTON, KENNETH BAILLIE, manufacturing company executive; b. Montreal, Que., Can., Dec. 4, 1895; s. George Edwin and Isabel (Baillie) R.; m. Carol Paterson; children: Irvine Baillie, Douglas Paterson, Sonia Roberton Wight. BSc, McGill U., Montreal, 1920. Chmn. Dominion Oilcloth & Linoleum Co. Ltd., Congoleum Can., Ltd., McFarlane Son & Hodgson, Barry & Staines Linoleum (Can.) Ltd.; bd. dirs. Caledonian-Can. Ins. Co., Guardian Ins. Co., Ltd., Nairn & Williamson (Holdings) Ltd., London, Michel Nairn Investments, Ltd.; trustee Guardian Assurance Co., Ltd., London. Lt. Royal Arty., Can. Army, 1914-17. *

ROBERTS, CARROLL CURTIS, clergyman; b. Chico, Calif., Sept. 10, 1896; s. Burma L. and Annie Laurie (Ferguson) R.; m. Ruth Ellen Williams, June 22, 1920; children: Rosemary Ann, Wayne Williams. AB, N.W. Christian Coll., Eugene, Oreg., 1920; DD, Lynchburg Coll., 1944; student, U. Oreg., 1916-20, Union Theol. Sem., N.Y., 1933, Coll. of the Bible, Lexington, Ky., 1935, Union Theol. Sem., Richmond, Va., 1936-38. Ordained to ministry Disciples of Christ Ch., 1918. Min. various chs. Oreg., Idaho, Calif., South Africa, N.C., Va., Washington, 1919-59; instr. ch. adminstrn. N.W. Christian Coll., Eugene, 1950-54, field rep., 1959-63; min. Garfield Park Christian Ch., Santa Cruz, Calif., from 1963; mem. numerous coms., commns., couns. Disciples of Christ. Del. Nat. Coun. Chs. Christ, U.S., 1954-56, 60. Mem. Nat. Evang. Assn. Disciples of Christ, Theta Sigma. *

ROBERTS, FRANK LESTER, physician, university dean; b. Miles City, Mont., Sept. 8, 1895; s. Henry and Florence (Sipes) R.; m. Jane Taylor, Nov. 19, 1924; children: Henry (dec.), Sally Roberts Cobb, Anne Roberts Johnson. BA, U. Minn., 1918, MA, 1919, BM, 1921, MD, 1922; DPH, Johns Hopkins U., 1936. Intern Northwestern Hosp., Mpls., 1922-23; county health officer Tenn. Dept. Health, 1923-37; mem. faculty U. Tenn. Coll. Medicine, Memphis, from 1937—, assoc. dean, from 1953; adviser on med. edn. Govt. of Iran, 1958-60. Rsch. on vital capacity of children, changes in mammary glands during pregnancy, growth of children, epidemiology of syphilis in rural areas. Fellow ACP, APHA; mem. Sigma Xi, Alpha Omega Alpha. Democrat. *

ROBERTS, JANET LOUISE (JANETTE RADCLIFFE), author, librarian; b. New Britain, Conn., Jan. 20, 1925; d. Walter Nelson and Marjorie Mae (Miller) R. B.A., Otterbein Coll., 1946, H.H.D., 1979; M.S.L.S., Columbia U., 1966. Reference librarian Dayton and Montgomery County (Ohio) Public Library, 1966-78. Author: numerous books including Jewels of Terror, 1970, The Weeping Lady, 1971, Ravenswood, 1971, Love Song, 1971, Dark Rose, 1971, The Devil's Own, 1972, The Curse of Kenton, 1972, Marriage of Inconvenience, 1972, Rivertown, 1972, My Lady Mischief, 1973, The Dancing Doll, 1973, The Dornstein Icon, 1973, The Golden Thistle, 1973, Isle of the Dolphins, 1973, La Casa Dorada, 1973, The Cardross Luck, 1974, The First Waltz, 1974, Castlereagh, 1975, Jade Vendetta, 1976, Wilderness Inn, 1976, Island of Desire, 1977, Black Pearls, 1979, Golden Lotus, 1979, Silver Jasmine, 1980, Flamenco Rose, 1981, Forget Me Not, 1982, Scarlet Poppies, 1983; under pseudonym Rebecca Danton: Sign of the Golden Goose, 1972, Black Horse Tavern, 1972, Fire Opals, 1977, Amethyst Love, 1977, Ship of Hate, 1977, Star Sapphire, 1979, Ruby Heart, 1980, French Jade, 1982, White Fire, 1982; under pseudonym Louisa Bronte: Lord Satan, 1972, Her Demon Lover, 1973, Greystone Tavern, 1975, Gathering at Greystone, 1976, The Vallette Heritage, 1978, The Van Rhyne Heritage, 1979, The Gunther Heritage, 1981; pseudonym Janette Radcliffe: The Blue-Eyed Gypsy, 1974, The Moonlight Gondola, 1975, Gentleman Pirate, 1975, The Heart Awakens, 1977, Scarlet Secrets, 1977, Hidden Fires, 1978, Stormy Surrender, 1978, American Baroness, 1980, The Court of the Flowering Peach, 1981. Mem. ALA, Ohio Library Assn., Authors Guild. Home: New York N.Y. Deceased.

ROBERTS, JOHN C(URTIS), textile company executive; b. Portsmouth, Va., June 30, 1895; s. Eugene Curtis and Mary Louise (Sykes) R.; m. Reta Grace Brantley, Jan. 30, 1925; 1 child, John Curtis Jr. LLD, Belmont Abbey Coll., 1964. CPA, N.C. Chmn. Textiles, Inc., Gastonia, N.C., from 1952, Threads, Inc., Gastonia; sec.-treas. Comml. Resl Estate & Investment Co.; v.p. Wix Corp. Treas., trustee Gaston Meml. Hosp., Inc., 1946-57; chmn. bd. trustee Sims Legion Park, 1947-56. 2d lt. inf., U.S. Army, World War I. Mem. NAM, N.C. Traffic League (pres.), N.C. Textile Mfrs. Assn. (pres.), Gastonia C. of C. (past pres.), Combed Yarn Spinners Assn. (past pres.), Am. Cotton Mfrs. Inst., Cotton Textile Inst. (past bd. dirs.), Am. Legion, Masons, Shriners, Elks, Kiwanis (past pres.). Methodist. *

ROBERTS, JOHN MILTON, anthropology educator; b. Omaha, Dec. 8, 1916; s. John Milton and Ruth (Kohler) R.; m. Marie Louise Kotouc, May 22, 1941; children: Tania, Andrea; m. Joan Marilyn Skutt, Oct. 22, 1961; children: James, John. A.B., U. Nebr., 1937; student, U. Chgo., 1937-39; Ph.D., Yale U., 1947. Asst. prof. anthropology U. Minn., 1947-48, Harvard U., 1948-53; asso. prof., then prof. U. Nebr., 1953-58; prof. Cornell U., 1958-71; Andrew W. Mellon prof. anthropology U. Pitts., 1971-87, prof. emeritus, 1987-90; prof. comparative cultures Naval War Coll., 1969-70; Commn. on Behavioral and Social Scis. and Edn.—NRC. Author: Three Navaho Households, 1951; co-author: Zuni Law, 1954, Studies of an Elementary Game of Strategy, 1967; Contbr. articles to profl. jours. Served as officer AUS, 1942-45. Decorated Silver Star, Bronze Star.; fellow Center Advanced Study Behavioral Scis., 1956-57. Fellow Am. Acad. Arts and Scis.; mem. Nat. Acad. Scis., Am. Anthrop. Assn., Am. Ethnological Soc. (past pres.), Am. Sociol. Assn., Am. Psychol. Assn., Linguistic Soc. Am., Royal Anthrop. Inst., Soc. Am. Archaeology, Northeastern Anthrop. Assn. (past pres.), Soc. Cross-Cultural Research (past pres.), Anthrop. Assn. Study of Play (past pres.), Phi Beta Kappa, Sigma Xi. Home: Pittsburgh Pa. Died Apr. 2, 1990; buried Pitts.

ROBERTS, KENNETH ALLISON, former congressman; b. Piedmont, Ala., Nov. 1, 1912; s. John Franklin and Josephine (Burton) R.; m. Margaret McMillian, Sept. 22, 1953; children: Margaret, Allison. Student, Samford Coll., 1929; LLB, U. Ala., 1935. Bar: Ala. 1936. Atty. Anniston, Ala., 1935, 45-50, Talladega, Ala., 1937-42; abstractor Dept. Agr., Ala., 1935-37; pres. Piedmont Devel. Co., Inc.; senator State of Ala., 1942; mem. 82d-87th Congresses from 4th Ala. dist.; rep.-at-large 88th Congress State of Ala.; mem. gen. counsel Vehicle Equipment Safety Commn. Mem. Nat. Hwy. Safety Adv. Com., Interstate and Fgn. Commerce Com. Served as lt. USNR, 1942-45, Atlantic and Pacific theaters of ops.; lt. commdr. Res. ret. Mem. VFW, Am. Legion, 40 and 8, Masons, Lions (dist. gov. 1940), Alpha Tau Omega, Phi Alpha Delta, Blue Key. Home: Rockville Md. Died May 9, 1989.

ROBERTS, NORBERT JOSEPH, physician; b. Alabama, N.Y., June 6, 1916; s. Cory Rudell and Bertha (McTigue) R.; m. Winifred Irene Dolan, Oct. 23, 1943; children: Norbert Joseph, Jerome M., Kevin J., Beth Ann, Mary Ann. Student, Canisius Coll., Buffalo, 1934-36; M.D., U. Buffalo, 1940; M.S., U. Minn., 1949. Diplomate Am. Bd. Preventive Medicine (vice-chmn. 1978-85), Am. Bd. Internal Medicine. Intern Buffalo Gen. Hosp., 1940-41, resident pathology, 1941-42; fellow internal medicine Mayo Found. for Med. Edn. and Research, 1946-49; sr. physician Exxon Corp., N.Y.C., 1949-52, assoc. dir. medicine, 1955-74, dir. medicine, 1974-81, v.p. medicine and environ. health, 1981; dir. medicine Pa. R.R., 1952-55; asst. prof. dept. community medicine Sch. Medicine, U. Pa., 1953-73; assoc. clin. prof. dept. community medicine Mt. Sinai Med. Sch., N.Y.C., 1974-82; lectr. NYU Inst. Environ. Medicine, 1955-87; chmn. Residency Rev. Com. Preventive Medicine, 1979-85. Contbr. articles to profl. jours. Bd. dirs., mem. exec. com. Nat. Assn. Drug Abuse Problems, from 1972; bd. dirs. N.Y. League for Hard of Hearing, 1974-81, Nat. Fund for Med. Edn.; trustee Exxon Edn. Found., 1976-81. Served from 1st lt. to maj. USAAF, 1942-46, ETO. Fellow ACP, Am. Coll. Preventive Medicine, N.Y. Acad. Scis. (v.p. 1981-85), Am. Coll. Occupational Medicine (past pres.); mem. West Side Clin. Soc. N.Y.C. (past pres.), N.Y. Acad. Medicine (pres. 1981-83), Soc. Occupational and Environ. Health (v.p., dir. 1978-81), Med. Execs. (past pres.), Soverign Mil. Order Malta (master knight). Roman Catholic. Club: University (N.Y.C.). Home: Bradenton Beach Fla. Deceased. †

ROBERTS, WALTER ORR, solar astronomer; b. West Bridgewater, Mass., Aug. 20, 1915; s. Ernest Marion and Alice Elliott (Orr) R.; m. Janet Naomi Smock, June 8, 1940; children—David Stuart, Alan Arthur, Jennifer Roberts McCarthy, Jonathan Orr. A.B., Amherst Coll., 1938, D.Sc. (hon.), 1959; M.A., Harvard, 1940, Ph.D., 1943; D.Sc. (hon.), Ripon Coll., 1958, Colo. Coll., 1962, C.W. Post Coll. of L.I. U., 1964, Carleton Coll., 1966, Southwestern at Memphis, 1968, U. Colo., 1968, U. Denver, 1969, U. Alaska, 1975. Operator High Altitude Obs., Climax, Colo., 1940-47, dir., 1940-60; dir. charge solar research program High Altitude Obs., Boulder, Colo., 1947-50; instr. Harvard U., 1947-48, Radcliffe Coll., 1947-48; research asso. Harvard Coll. Obs., 1948-73; founder, dir. Nat. Center for Atmospheric Research, 1960-68, research assoc., from 1975; prof. astro-geophysics U. Colo., Boulder, 1957-88, prof. emeritus astrophys., planetary and atmospheric scis., 1988-90; dir. program in food, climate and world's future Aspen (Colo.) Inst. Humanistic Studies, 1974-81; trustee Univ. Corp. Atmospheric Research, 1959, pres., 1960-73, pres. emeritus, 1980-90, pres. Found., 1986-87; trustee Mitre Corp., 1960-87, Upper Atmosphere Research Corp., 1971-74; chmn. com. on arctic sci. and tech. NAS, 1972-73, mem. com. on internat. environ. programs, 1971-77; mem. com. cons. Report on State of Human Environment, UN Stockholm Conf., 1972; mem. U.S. Nat. Commn. for UNESCO, 1964-67; mem. def. sci. bd. Dept. Def., 1972-75; mem. adv. panel for NSF Journalistic History, 1972; mem. adv. com. World Meteorol. Orgn., 1963-68; mem. bur. com. effects solar terrestrial disturbances in lower atmosphere Spl. Com. Solar-Terrestrial Physics, 1972-77; mem. subcom. U.S.-USSR coop. program man's impact on environment Dept. State, 1973-80; mem. visiting com. Smithsonian Astrophys. Obs., 1975-78; mem. founding bd., chmn. task force sci. and tech. Civilian/Mil. Inst., Air Force Acad., 1975-83; mem. Council on Sci. and Tech. for Devel., 1977-84; pres. U. Corp. for Atmospheric Research Found., 1986-87; bd. dirs. Weather Techs. Inc. Asso. editor: Jour. Geophys. Research, 1960-64; editorial bd.: Science, 1970-72, Jour. Planetary and Space Sci. Trustee Max C. Fleischmann Found., 1967-80, Charles F. Kettering Found., 1964-70, Amherst Coll., 1964-70; mem. Am. council UN U.; trustee Aspen Inst. for Humanistic Studies, 1970-90; sec. Marconi Internat. Fellowship Council, 1974-86; trustee Internat. Fedn. Insts. Advanced Study, 1971-81, chmn. program com.; bd. dirs. Internat. Inst. Environment and Devel., 1971-76, Worldwatch Inst., 1975-85. Recipient Hodgkins medal Smithsonian Instn., 1973, Mitchell Prize award, 1979, Internat. Environ. Leadership medal UN, 1982, Man Sci. award Achievement Rewards for Coll. Scientists Found., 1986, Sci. award Bonfils-Stanton Found., 1986, Pacesetter award Boulder County, 1986, U. Colo. medal, 1988, Rsch. award Eleanor Roosevelt Inst. for Cancer, 1988, N.Am. Leadership award UN Environ. Program, 1989; named Man of Sci., ARC Found., 1986. Fellow AAAS (dir. 1963-70, pres. 1967, mem. com. on arid lands 1973-83), Am. Acad. Arts and Scis., Royal Astron. Soc.; mem. Acad. Ind. Scholars, Aspen Soc. Fellows, Am. Rocket Soc., Am. Astron. Soc. (mem. council), Am. Meteorol. Soc., Internat. Astron. Union, Colo.-Wyo. Acad. Sci., Am. Geophys. Union, Am. Philos. Soc., Fedn. Am. Scientists, AIAA, Internat. Acad. Astronautics , Council Fgn. Relations, Royal Soc. Arts, Explorers Club, Sigma Xi, Phi Beta Kappa, Sigma Pi Sigma. Club: Rocky Mountain Harvard. Home: Boulder Colo. Died Mar. 12, 1990; buried Boulder, Colo.

ROBERTSON, DURANT WAITE, JR., language professional, educator; b. Washington, Oct. 11, 1914; s. Durant Waite and Emma (Jones) R.; m. Betty McLean Hansen, July 17, 1937; children: Susanna, Durant Waite III, Douglas. BA, U. N.C., 1935, MA, 1937, Ph.D., 1945; DHL, U. N.C., Greensboro, 1982; DLitt, Villanova U., 1973; DHL, Princeton U., 1987. Instr. U. Md., 1938-42, U. N.C., 1942-44, Yale U., 1945-46; from instr. to prof. English Princeton U., 1946-92, Murray prof. English lit., 1970-80, prof. emeritus, 1980-92; vis. prof. Duke U., 1982, 83, 84. Author: (with B.F. Huppe) Piers Plowman and Scriptural Tradition, 1951, A Preface to Chaucer, 1962, (with B.F. Huppe) Fruyt and Chaf, 1963, Chaucer's London, 1968, The Literature of Medieval England, 1970, Abelard and Heloise, 1972, Essays in Medieval Culture, 1980, (with others) The Meaning of Courtly Love, 1968, Signs and Symbols in Chaucer's Poetry, 1981, Theolinguistics, 1981, Chaucer and Scriptural Tradition, 1984, The Pupular Literature of Medieval England, 1985, Social Unrest in the Late Middle Ages, 1986, Essays in Honor of Edward B. King, 1991; translator: St. Augustine, On Christian Doctrine, 1958; contbr. articles to learned jours. Fellow Am. Coun. Learned Socs., 1945-46; Guggenheim fellow, 1957; Nat. Humanities Ctr. fellow, 1980-81. Fellow Mediaeval Acad. Am.; mem. New Chaucer Soc., Renaissance Soc. Am. Home: Chapel Hill N.C. Died July 26, 1992. †

ROBERTSON, ELGIN BARNETT, electrical engineer; b. Meridian, Tex., June 4, 1893; s. Ephraim Barnett and Fanny Lee (Farabee) R.; m. Willie Cassidy; children: Mary Lee, Marian Robertson Joy, Elgin. EE, U. Tex., 1915; DEng, So. Meth. U., 1954. Registered profl. engr., Tex. Design engr. Westinghouse Electric & Mfg. Co., 1915-20; chief elec. engr. Ry. & Indsl. Engine Co., 1920-24, midwest mgr., 1924-28; pres. Elgin B. Robertson, Inc., Dallas, 1928-64; chmn. bd. Elgin B. Robertson, Inc., from 1964; pres. :lastics Mfg. Co., 1939-64, chmn. bd., from 1964; bd. dirs. Oak Cliff Bank & Trust Co.; regional utilities engr., regional mgr. prodn. dept. WPB, Dallas, 1942-45. Councilman, mayor pro tem City of Dallas, 1959-63; bd. dirs. Red Bird Indsl. Park. Recipient Disting. Engring. Grad. award U. Tex., 1960. Fellow IEEE (hon., past bd. dirs., pres. 1953-54); mem. NSPE (bd. dirs. 1951-53), Tex. Soc. Profl. Engrs. (bd. dirs. 1940-44, pres. 1945), Oak Cliff C. of C. (pres. 1958-59), Dallas C. of C. (bd. dirs. 1960-63), Tex. Hist. Assn., Dallas Hist. Soc., Engrs. Club, Elecric Club, Oak Cliff Country Club, Masons (32d degree), Shriners, Eta Kappa Nu, Theta Xi. Methodist. *

ROBERTSON, LAWRENCE MARSHALL, electric utility executive, consulting engineer; b. Denver, Jan. 20, 1900; s. Hugh Lawrence and Grace (Worden) R.; m. Mildred Eleanor Blackwood, Nov. 15, 1924 (dec. 1971); 1 son, Lawrence Marshall Jr. B.S.E.E. with honors, U. Colo., 1922, E.E., 1927, M.S.E.E., 1938, D.Engring. (hon.), 1938; D.Engring. (hon.), U. Colo., 1955; J.D., U. Denver, 1979. Profl. engr., Colo., Calif., Wash., Wyo., Ill., N.Y. Engr. to chief elec. engr. Pub. Svc. Co. Colo., Denver, 1922-53, chief elec. engr., mgr. engring., 1953-59, mng. engr., v.p. engring., 1959-68; cons. engr. elec. utilities Colo., Wash., Ill., Argentina, Dominican Republic, from 1968, U.S. Bur. Reclamation, Denver, 1969, Pub. Utilities Dist., Wenatchee, Wash., 1975-79, Power Authority, Buenos Aires, 1969, Dominican Republic, 1981. Contbr. chpts. to books, articles to publs. Chmn. Solid Waste Disposal Denver Region, 1968-73; mem. Fed. Power Commn. Adv. Com., Washington, 1962-67; mem., pres. Colo. State Bd. Registered Profl. Engrs., 1957-69. Served with U.S. Army, 1918. Named Disting. Engring. Alumnus, U. Colo., 1968; recipient Gold Medal award Colo. Engring. Coun., 1954. Life fellow IEEE (v.p. 1945, dir. 1956, Habirshaw award 1963, Centennial award 1984); mem. Profl. Engrs. Colo. (A.J. Ryan award 1969), Conference Internationale (Paris, Attwood award 1982), Denver C. of C. (dir. 1949), Sigma Xi, Tau Beta Pi, Eta Kappa Nu, Sigma Tau, Sigma Delta Kappa, Alpha Tau Omega, Masons, Shriners. Republican. Methodist. Home: Denver Colo. Died July 23, 1988; buried Crown Hill Cemetery, Jefferson County, Colo.

ROBEY, MARGARET DURHAM, college president; b. Gastonia, N.C., Apr. 14, 1898; d. Robert Lee and Mary Willie (Craton) Durham; m. Harry Russell Robey, Sept. 12, 1922. AB cum laude, Duke U., 1917; MEd, U. Va., 1952, Mary Washington Coll. Instr. French and English lit. Martha Washington Coll. and So. Sem.; pres. So. Sem. Jr. Coll., Buena Vista, Va.; jr. coll. rep. com. women in coll. and def. Nat. Com. on Edn. and Def.; speaker on internat. rels. and world orgn. at ednl. meetings in east and south. Local chmn. ARC, Children's Home Soc.; state chmn. internat. rels. Va. Fedn. Women's Clubs, 1936, 69, 40, state chmn. scrapbooks, 1944-47; chmn. 7th congl. dist. Va., Women's Action Com. for Victory and Lasting Peace; pres. Rockbridge Hist. Soc., 1948-51. Named hon. citizen Boy's Town. Mem. So. Assn. Jr. Colls. (exec. bd. from 1964), Internat. Platform Assn., Marathons (state chmn.), Nat. Com. on Cause and Cure War, AAUW (state chmn. internat. rels. 1939-40), Adminstrv. Women in Edn. (Va. coun.), Nat. Coun. Women U.S., Assn. Va. Colls. (v.p. 1958-59), Am. Assn. Jr. Colls. (chmn. women's div. 1944-45, mem. commn. on adminstrn. 1960-63), Am. Acad. Polit. and Social Sci., DAR, E-Ko-L, Kappa Delta. *

ROBINSON, DWIGHT PARKER, JR., executive; b. Seattle, Jan. 15, 1900; s. Dwight Parker and Mary Elizabeth (Stearns) R.; m. Mary Helen Gass, Sept. 22, 1943. Student, Noble and Greenough Sch.; AB, Harvard U., 1920, MBA, 1925. Salesman Amory,

Browne & Co., 1923-24; statistician Lee Higginson & Co., 1926-29, asst. trust office, 1929-31; with Mass. Investors Trust, 1932, trustee, 1937, chmn., 1954-65, adv. bd., 1965-89; chmn., dir. Mass. Investors Growth Stock Fund, until 1965, adv. bd., 1965-89; dir. Texaco, Inc., Depositors Fund Boston, Inc., Exch. Fund Boston, Inc., Ctrl. and S.W. Corp., John Hancock Mut. Life Ins. Co., Boston Safe Deposit & Trust Co., Diversification Fund, Inc., Am. R & D Corp.; mem. corp. Boston Five Cents Savs. Bank, Suffolk-Franklin Savs. Bank. Overseer Boys Clubs Boston; bd. dirs. Salsburg Seminar Am. Studies; mem. various vis. coms. Harvard Coll.; ind. mem. corp. United Community Svcs.; trustee Northeastern U. Mass. Gen. Hosp., Denison House, Mus. Sci. Served as civilian Office of Procurement, Dept. Navy, World War II. Fellow Am. Acad. Arts and Scis.; mem. Harvard Club, Somerset Club, Union Club, The Country Club, River Club, Links Club. Republican. Unitarian. Home: Brookline Mass. Deceased.

ROBINSON, EARL HAWLEY, composer, writer, singer, conductor, educator; b. Seattle, July 2, 1910; s. Morris John and Hazel Beth (Hawley) R.; m. Helen Wortis, Feb. 17, 1937 (dec. June 1963); children: Perry Morris, James; m. Ruth Martin, May 5, 1965 (div. 1975). MusB, U. Wash., 1933; studies with Aaron Copeland, Met. Music Sch., N.Y.C., 1935-39; studies with Hanns Eisler, L.A., 1945-47. Lectrs. and concerts in U.S., Can., Europe; entertainer White House, Washington, 1942-44. Wrote music for Fed. Theater shows, N.Y.C., 1936-39, (including Processional, Life and Death of an American, Sing for Your Supper); condr.: American Peoples chorus, 1937-42; Guggenheim fellowship and renewal to make mus. setting of: The People, Yes (by Carl Sandburg), 1940-41; music dir., Elisabeth Irwin High Sch., N.Y.C., 1957-65; condr., Extension Chorus, UCLA, 1967-68; tchr. sound and music for film and theatre, UCLA extension, 1969-71, U. Wash. extension Songs of the Working People, From the American Revolution to the present, 1989, music for radio, theater, films, TV, also singing on radio and TV; composer: cantatas Ballad for Americans, Lonesome Train, Tower of Babel, Illinois People (commd. by State of Ill. for Sesquicentennial Year 1968), Strange Unusual Evening, In the Folded and Quiet Yesterdays, Garden of Eden, Building the Pyramid, Grand Coulee Dam; A Concert for Francis, Ride the Wind, Song dance cantatas for children, Good Morning, Come Along, When We Grow Up; songs for children's mus. Gingerbread John; composer of score for L.A. Coronet Theatre Prodn. of Dark of the Moon; ballet score, Bouquet for Molly; folk operas Sandhog, David of Sassoun; symphonic poem with tenor voice A Country They Call Puget Sound, Concerto for Five String Banjo; Song of Atlantis, a music drama; piano concerto A New Human, (musicals) Earl Robinson's America, I Been Thinkin' about J.C., Listen for the Dolphin; songs Once upon a Soon Time, The House I Live In (Oscar award 1947), Black and White, Joe Hill, Abe Lincoln, John Brown, Free and Equal Blues, Same Boat Brother, Now, Build Fun City, Four Hugs A Day, He Built the Road, Hurry Sundown, Suppose, All the Words are New, Logan's Lament, Message From a New Address, Planet Earth Real Estate Company, The World is My Garden, I Choose Wilderness; author songs Folk Guitar in 10 Sessions, 1965; mus. editor: Young Folk Song Book, 1963, Songs of the Great West, 1967, Songs of Brecht and Eisler, 1966; songs for, 20th Century-Fox film, Walk in the Sun, Paramount film, California, MGM, film Romance of Rosie Ridge; songs and background score for documentary film The Roosevelt Story, Eagle Lion film, Texas Story, Gen. Motors, indsl. film, Giants in the Land; composed, sang, narrated, Fox, short film, Muscle Beach; score and songs for, Universal NBC film, The Great Man's Whiskers, ABC Movie of the Week, Maybe I'll Come Home in the Spring, 1971, Adventures of Huckleberry Finn, ABC-TV, 1975, The Pumpkin Who Couldn't Smile, CBS, 1979. Recipient Hall of Fame award Nat. Acad. Rec. Arts and Scis., 1980. Mem. Authors League, Screen Actors Guild, Dramatists Guild, Am. Fedn. Musicians, ASCAP (Gold Record 1976), Song Writers Guild. Home: Seattle Wash. Died July 20, 1991; buried Seattle, Wash.

ROBINSON, HAROLD NYLE, financial executive; b. McCorkle, W.Va., Mar. 8, 1925; s. Richard Moses and Emmer (McClure) R.; m. Mary Lou Williams, Aug. 26, 1949; children: David Lynn, Diane Susan, R. Gregory. BSBA, W.Va. U., 1950. CPA, Pa. With Ernst & Ernst, CPA's, Pitts., 1949-59; with Robertshaw Controls Co., Richmond, Va., 1959-85, contr., 1963-85, v.p., 1978-85, also bd. dirs. Dist. treas. Robert E. Lee coun. Boy Scouts Am., 1963-66, asst. scoutmaster, from 1964, mem. exec. bd., from 1969; pres. Huguenot High Sch. PTA, 1968-70; mem. budget and allocations com. United Way Greater Richmond; mem. Southampton Recreation Assn., Richmond. With USNR, 1943-46. Mem. AICPA, Inst. Internal Auditors (pres. Richmond chpt. 1963-64), Planning Execs. Inst. (pres. Richmond chpt. 1965-66), Fin. Execs. Inst. (pres. Va. chpt. 1969-70), Va. Soc. CPA's, Execs. Club (treas. 1966-68, bd. dirs. 1966-69, pres. 1968-69), Willow Oaks Country Club, Tau Kappa Epsilon, Alpha Kappa Psi. Republican. Methodist. Home: Richmond Va. Died Oct. 25, 1985; buried Westhampton Meml. Pk., Richmond, Va.

ROBINSON, JOHN EDMUND, dentist; b. Kearny, N.J., Nov. 27, 1924; s. John Edmund and Norma (McDonald) R.; m. Mary Bellinger, Nov. 23, 1956. D.D.S., SUNY, Buffalo, 1952. Practice dentistry, specializing in maxillofacial prosthetics North Syracuse, N.Y., 1952-56; instr. dental surgery Zoller Dental Clinic, U. Chgo. Hosps. and Clincs, 1957-58, asst. prof. dental surgery, 1958-64, asso. prof., 1964-70, prof., 1970-80, prof. emeritus, 1980-89, head unit maxillofacial prosthetic rehab., 1964-80; cons. U. Ill. Center for Craniofacial Anomalies, 1968-89, VA Hosp., Bay Pines, Fla., 1980-89, Asheville, N.C., 1983-88. Served with USNR, 1943-46, PTO. Recipient Ackerman award in maxillofacial prosthetics, 1981. Fellow Am. Coll. Dentists, Midwest Acad. Prosthodontists, Am. Acad. Maxillofacial Prosthetics (pres. 1970-71), Fedn. Prosthodontic Orgns. (pres. 1973-74). Home: Sun City Fla. Died Nov. 9, 1989; cremated.

ROBINSON, KINSEY MAXFIELD, corporate executive; b. Mankato, Minn., Feb. 5, 1895; s. Henry W. and Anna (Maxfield) R.; m. Ruth Hamby; children: Robert Maxfield Jr., Kinsey William, Ann Elizabeth Robinson Croyle, Ruth Robinson Vitus, Zoe Robinson Kelm. Grad. prep. dept., Coll. of Idaho, 1914. Teamster, wireman, foreman inside wiring, groundman Idaho-Oreg. Light & Power Co., 1911-14; lineman Idaho Power Co., 1914-16, local mgr., 1916-21, div. engr., 1921-27, div. mgr., 1927-29, asst. gen. mgr., 1929-33, v.p., gen. mgr., 1933-34, pres., gen. mgr., 1934-38; pres., bd. dirs. Wash. Water Power Co., Spokane, 1938-60; chmn. bd. Wash. Water Power Co., from 1960; pres. Limestone Co., from 1952; chmn. bd. Spokane Indsl. Park, Inc., from 1960; pres. Pacific N.W. Power Co., 1954-57, chmn. bd., from 1957; pres. Wash. Irrigation and Devel. Co., from 1952; bd. dirs. Bunker Hill Co. Mem. Gov.'s Sch. Adv. Coun.; mem. exec. com. Gov.'s Employ Handicapped Com. Mem. NAM (past bd. dirs.), Am. Mining Congress, Assn. Edison Illuminating Cos., Inland Empire Indsl. Rsch. (chmn.), Nat. Assn. Electric Cos., High Temperature Reactor Devel. Assocs. (trustee from 1958, v.p. from 1960), Newcomen Soc, Masons, Shriners, Elks, Hayden Lake Country Club, Spokane Country Club, Spokane Club, Wash. Athletic Club. Presbyterian. *

ROBINSON, RICHARD EARL, federal judge; b. Omaha, Feb. 3, 1903; s. Richard and Jane (Hanna) R.; m. Florence Rich, May 22, 1929 (dec.); children: Thomas E., John L. LL.B., Creighton U., 1927. Bar: Nebr. 1927. Practiced in Omaha, until 1956; U.S. dist. judge for Dist. Nebr., from 1956; chief judge, 1957-72, now sr. judge. Mem. Omaha Airport Commn., 1950-51, finance commr., Omaha, 1951. Recipient Brandeis award Brandeis U. Club of Omaha, 1957; Alumni Merit award Creighton U., 1967; Man of Yr. award Omaha Club, 1986. Home: Omaha Nebr. Deceased. †

ROBINSON, ROBERT ALEXANDER, orthopaedic surgeon; b. Rochester, N.Y., Jan. 9, 1914; s. Robert Clarence and Anna (Bill) R.; m. Beatrice Clark, June 21, 1941; children—Ann, Barbara, Robert Alexander, Elizabeth. Student, Harvard U., 1932-35; M.D., Columbia Coll. Physicians and Surgeons, 1939. Diplomate: Am. Bd. Orthopaedic Surgery. Rotating intern Bklyn. Hosp., 1939-41, resident gen. surgery, 1941-42; asst. resident orthopaedics Strong Meml. Hosp., Rochester, 1946, resident orthopaedics, 1947-48; resident orthopaedics Rochester Gen. Hosp., 1946-47; house surgeon Robert Jones and Agnes Hunt Orthopaedic Hosp., Oswestry, Eng., 1948-49; instr. orthopaedic surgery Sch. Medicine and Dentistry, U. Rochester, 1949-51, asst. prof., 1951-53; prof. orthopaedic surgery Johns Hopkins U.; also orthopaedic surgeon in charge Johns Hopkins Hosp., 1953-79, Disting. Service prof., 1977-79; emeritus dir. dept. orthopedic surgery Johns Hopkins U. Sch. Medicine, from 1979; pvt. practice, from 1979; trustee Orthopaedic Research and Edn. Found., 1970-74, pres., 1975-77. Trustee Easter Seal Research Found., 1975-77. Served in M.C. AUS, 1942-46; sta. and field hosps., comdg. officer, chief surgery 90th Field Hosp. 1946, Tacloban, Leyte, Philippines. Fellow Am. Acad. Orthopaedic Surgeons, A.C.S.; mem. Soc. Univ. Surgeons, Am. Orthopaedic Assn., Brit. Orthopaedic Assn. (corr.), Am. Surg. Assn., Société Internationale de Chirugie Orthopedique et de Traumatologie. Home: Baltimore Md. Died Aug. 16, 1990.

ROBINSON, STEPHEN BROOKS, oil company executive; b. Lincoln, Nebr., Aug. 20, 1896; s. Frederick A. and Minnie Irene (Ellis) R.; m. Jane Holloway Stephens, Jan. 26, 1950; children: Stephen Charles, Marguerite Mae. Acct., Wichita, Kans., 1937-45; internal auditor Kerr-McGee Oil Industries, Oklahoma City, 1945-51, asst. sec.-treas., 1951-58, sec., 1958-64, adminstrv. asst. to pres., from 1964; sec. Triangle Refineries, Inc., from 1962, Kermac Nuclear Fuels Corp., from 1961, Downtown Airpark, Inc., from 1952, West Cen. Broadcasting Co., Peoria, Ill., from 1953, Cimarron TV Corp., from 1961, Knox Industries, from 1961, Tascosa Gas Co., from 1959. Mem. Am. Soc. Corp. Secs., Ind. Petroleum Assn. Am., Oklahoma City Petroleum Club, Masons. Mem. Christian Ch. *

ROBY, DOUGLAS FERGUSSON, business executive; b. Pomfret, Md., Mar. 24, 1898; s. Edwin and Mary (Fergusson) R.; m. Ruth Clippert, Nov. 23, 1926; children: Hermine R. Klingler, Douglas Fergusson Jr., Ruth R. Glancy. AB, U. Mich., 1923. With Am. metal Products Co., Detroit, 1934-92, v.p., 1936-46; treas. Am. metal Products Co., 1939-46, exec. v.p., 1946-54, pres., 1954-58, chmn. bd., 1958-60; dir. Borroughs Mfg. Co., Kalamazoo, Gen. Spring Products, Kitchner, Ont., Can., Briggs Mfg. Co., Kelsey Hayes Co., Braun Engring. Co., 1st Fed. Savs. & Loan Assn. of Detroit. Mem. Internat. Olympic Com., 1952-92; v.p. Amateur Athletic Union of U.S., 1951-53; mem. art commn. City of Detroit, 1957-92; trustee Grace Hosp., Detroit, Detroit TB Sanatorium. Mem. U.S. Olympic Com. (v.p., mem. exec. bd.), N.Am. (dir. 1956-59), Mason (K.T.), Phi Delta Theta. Episcopalian. Home: Ypsilanti Mich. Died Mar. 31, 1992; interred Woodlawn Cemetery.

ROBY, FRANK HELMUTH, electric company executive; b. Indpls., May 5, 1911; s. William E. and Gertrude L. (Hellmuth) R.; m. Mary Jane Rogo, May 18, 1950; children: Joan Alan and Joan Ellen (twins). BSEE, Purdue U., 1933. With Square D Co., 1933-58, v.p. mktg., bd. dirs., 1950-58; exec. v.p. Fed. Pacific Electric Co., Newark, 1958-64, pres., 1964-65, also bd. dirs. Contbr. articles to profl. publs. Active Boy Scouts Am., local pres., 1964-65. Mem. IEEE, Am. Standards Assn. (pres. 1962-64), Nat. Elec. Mfrs. Assn. (bd. govs., chmn. planning com. 1964), Electronic Industries Assn. (bd. dirs.). *

ROCKEFELLER, BLANCHETTE HOOKER, organization executive; b. N.Y.C., Oct. 2, 1909; d. Elon Huntington and Blanche (Ferry) Hooker; m. John D. Rockefeller 3d, Nov. 11, 1932 (dec. July 1978); children: Sandra Ferry, John Davison IV, Hope Aldrich, Alida R. Messinger. A.B., Vassar Coll., 1931. Mem. Nat. Council on the Humanities, 1974-79. Trustee Mus. Modern Art, 1953-92, pres., 1959-62, 72-85, pres. emeritus, 1986-92, chmn., 1985-87; mem. Am. adv. com. to Japan Found., 1972-81, N.Y. State Council on Arts, 1979-86; pres. JDR 3d Fund, 1978-92, Asian Cultural Council, 1980-92; trustee Community Service Soc., 1933-57, vice chmn., 1952-57; trustee Brearly Sch., 1947-56, Vassar Coll., 1949-56, Juilliard Sch., 1973-92; bd. dirs. Lincoln Ctr. Theater, 1985-89. Mem. Japan Soc., Asia Soc., Philharmonic Symphony Soc., Friends of Japan House Gallery, Friends of Asia House Gallery. Clubs: Cosmopolitan, River. Home: New York N.Y. Died Nov. 29, 1992. †

ROCKEFELLER, WILLIAM, lawyer; b. N.Y.C., Dec. 4, 1918; s. William Avery and Florence (Lincoln) R.; m. Mary D. Gillett, July 3, 1947; children: Mary Gillett Fogarty, Edith McKee Laird, Sarah Stillman Bogdanovitch. Grad., St. Paul's Sch., 1936; A.B., Yale U., 1940; student, U. Wis., 1940-41; LL.B., Columbia U., 1947. Bar: N.Y. 1948. Asso. firm Dorr, Hammond, Hand & Dawson, 1947-55, Shearman & Sterling, N.Y.C., 1955-57; ptnr. Shearman & Sterling, from 1957; bd. dirs. Indian Spring Land Co., Conn., Cranston Print Works, Oneida Ltd. Trustee, sec. bd. Meml. Sloan-Kettering Cancer Ctr.; bd. dirs. ASPCA, pres., 1956-64; pres. Met. Opera Assn., 1973-78, chmn., 1978-86; chmn. Met. Opera Guild; bd. dirs. Lincoln Ctr.; chmn. Geraldine R. Dodge Found., until 1990; trustee Paul Smith's Coll.; chmn. Oldfields Sch.; chmn. coun. James Baker Inst., Cornell U., until 1990; pres. Am. Dog Mus.; chmn. coun. James A. Baker Inst.; dir. Coun. Bd. Govs. N.Y. Colls.; chmn. Yale Alumni Bd., late 1960's-70's; former pres. Wesminster Kennel Club, Am. Kennel Club. Served to lt. comdr. USNR, 1941-46. Decorated Bronze Star; recipient gold medal Nat. Inst. Social Sci., 1977, Yale Medal, 1987; decorated Order of St. John of Jerusalem. Fellow ABA; mem. N.Y. Bar Assn., Assn. Bar City N.Y., Am. Yacht Club (Rye), N.Y. Yacht Club, St. Regis Yacht Club, Links Club, Anglers Club, Met. Opera Club, Racquet and Tennis Club, The Brook Club, River Club (N.Y.C.), The Farmers Club, Pilgrims of U.S., Phi Delta Phi. Episcopalian. Home: Rye N.Y. Died Mar. 16, 1990; buried Tarrytown, N.Y.

ROCKEY, KENNETH HENRY, business executive; b. N.Y.C., June 25, 1894; s. Walter S. and Maud (Harter) R.; m. Isabelle Angermeier, Dec. 1, 1917 (dec. Feb. 1946); m. Edna Angermeier, Dec. 23, 1953. LittB, Princeton U., 1916. With Nat. Bank Commerce, N.Y.C., 1916-19; rep. Nat. Bank Commerce, London, 1919-22; nat. bank examiner, N.Y.C., 1922-24; ptnr. Huth & Co., 1924-30; pres., mng. dir. Portero Sugar Co., 1930-31; exec. ofcl., dir. assoc. firms Chilean nitrate industry, 1931-40; pres., chmn. bd. Chilean Nitrate Sales Corp., 1932-40, Rio Blanco Copper Corp., N.Y.C., 1940-60; chmn. bd. Arma Corp., 1945-46, pres., bd. dirs., 1952-54; pres., chmn. bd. Trebor Mines, Ltd., Toronto, Ont., Can., 1948-50; v.p., bd. dirs. Brit. Industries Corp., N.Y.C., 1948-55; treas., bd. dirs. 1060 Fifth Avenue Corp.; hon. bd. dirs. Universal Oil Products Co., Des Plaines, Ill.; bd. dirs. emeritus Philip Morris & Co., Ltd., Inc.; chmn. price adjustment bd. Navy Dept., Washington, 1942-44. Treas., bd. dirs. Fountain House Found., Inc. Mem. Princeton Club, Univ. Club, Bankers Club, Grolier Club, Anglers Club. Baptist. *

ROCKWELL, WILLARD FREDERICK, JR., manufacturing company executive; b. Boston, Mar. 3, 1914; s. Willard Frederick and Clara (Thayer) R.; m. Constance Templeton, July 16, 1942; children—Patricia Lynne Rockwell Boorn, Willard Frederick III, Steven Kent, George Peter, Russell Alden. B.S., Pa. State U., 1935, I.E., 1955; LL.D., Grove City Coll., Lambuth

Coll.; D.Eng. (hon.), Tufts U., Carnegie-Mellon U., Washington and Jefferson Coll. Registered profl. engr., Pa., Calif. Cost acct. Pitts. Equitable Meter Co., 1935-36, mgr. engring., 1937-39, v.p., controller, 1939-43, v.p., gen. mgr., 1945-47; asst. to controller Timken-Detroit Axle Co., 1936-37; pres. Rockwell Mfg. Co., Pitts., 1947-64; vice chmn. bd., chief exec. officer Rockwell Mfg. Co., 1964-71, chmn. bd., 1971-73, also dir.; pres. Rockwell-Standard Corp., 1963-67, dir., 1942-67; chmn. bd., chief exec. officer N.Am. Rockwell Corp., 1967-73; chmn. bd. Rockwell Internat., 1973-79, chmn. exec. com., dir., from 1979; chmn., chief exec. officer Astrotech Internat. Co., Pitts.; dir. the El Paso Co., Mellon Bank N.A., Mellon Nat. Corp., Lone Star Industries, Inc., Planning Research Corp., Magic Chef, Inc., Pitts. Athletic Co., Inc. (Pitts. Pirates), El Paso Products Co. Mem. Greater Pitts. Airport Adv. Bd.; trustee Am. Enterprise Inst. for Pub. Policy Research, Aerospace Edn. Found., U. So. Calif., Grove City Coll., Pa., Point Park Coll., Carnegie Mus. Natural History; chmn. exec. com. Tax Found., Inc.; bd. dirs. World Affairs Council Pitts.; chmn. bd. govs. Ford's Theatre, Washington. Served to capt., ordnance corps, AUS, World War II. Fellow Royal Soc. Arts; mem. Natural Gas and Petroleum Assn. Can., Am. Petroleum Inst., Engrs. Soc. Western Pa., Gas Appliance Mfrs. Assn. (pres. 1956, bd. dirs.), ASME, Am. Inst. Indsl. Engrs., Am. Ordnance Assn., Am. Water Works Assn., Soc. Automotive Engrs., Conf. Bd., Internat. C. of C. (trustee U.S. council), Mil. Order World Wars, Pa. C. of C. (past pres. bd. dirs.), Smithsonian Assocs., Pa. Soc., SAR, Omicron Delta Kappa, Kappa Sigma, Delta Sigma Pi. Clubs: Pitts. Athletic Assn., Duquesne, University, Long Vue (Pitts.); University (N.Y.C.); Laurel Valley Golf, Rolling Rock (Ligonier, Pa.); Bath, Indian Creek (Miami Beach, Fla.); Chicago; Detroit Athletic; California (Los Angeles); Cat Cay (Bahamas). Home: Pittsburgh Pa. Died Sept. 24, 1992. †

RODALE, ROBERT DAVID, editor, publisher; b. N.Y.C., Mar. 27, 1930; s. Jerome Irving and Anna Apollonia (Andrews) R.; m. Ardath Harter, June 23, 1951; children: Heather, Heidi, David, Maria, Anthony. Student, Lehigh U., 1947-52. Chief exec. officer Rodale Press, Inc., Emmaus, Pa., 1949-90, editor mags. Organic Gardening and Farming, Prevention, Runner's World, Backpacker, The New Farm, Rodale's Practical Homeowner, others, 1952-90; adj. prof. Pa. State U. Author: Sane Living in a Mad World, 1972, The Best Health Ideas I Know, 1974; author/editor: Our Next Frontier, 1981; editor: The Challenge of Earthworm Research, 1961, The Basic Book of Organic Gardening, 1971. Chmn. Lehigh County Velodrome Commn., Emmaus, Pa., from 1974, Rodale Inst., Emmanus, 1987-90; Friends of the Parks, Allentown, Pa. Recipient Disting. Internat. Shooter badge Dept. Def., 1963. Home: Emmaus Pa. Died Sept. 20, 1990; buried Emmaus, Pa.

RODDENBERRY, EUGENE WESLEY (GENE RODDENBERRY), writer, producer; b. El Paso, Tex., Aug. 19, 1921; s. Eugene Edward and Caroline Glen (Golemon) R.; m. Majel Leigh Hudec, Aug. 6, 1969; children—Darleen, Dawn Alison, Eugene Wesley Jr. A.A., Los Angeles City Coll.; student, U. Miami, Columbia U., U. So. Calif.; D.H.L. (hon.), Emerson Coll., 1973; DLitt (hon.), Union Coll., 1977; DSc (hon.), Clarkson Coll., 1981. Pilot Pan Am. World Airways, 1945-49; sgt. Los Angeles Police Dept., 1949-53; freelance TV and motion picture writer, 1953-62; pres. Norway Prodns., Inc. Producer TV and motion pictures, 1962-91; writer, producer: movie Pretty Maids All in a Row, 1970, Star Trek - The Motion Picture, 1979; creator, producer: movie Genesis II, Star Trek, The Lieutenant, Questor Tapes, Planet Earth; co-author: The Making of Star Trek, 1968, Star Trek - The Motion Picture: A Novel, 1979; exec. cons. Star Trek II: The Wrath of Khan, Star Trek III: The Search for Spock, Star Trek IV: The Voyage Home, Star Trek V: The Final Frontier, Star Trek VI: The Undiscovered Country; creator, exec. producer TV series Star Trek: The Next Generation (Peabody award). Served with USAAF, 1941-45. Decorated D.F.C., Air Medal.; recipient writing and prodn. awards Writers Guild Am., writing and prodn. awards Nat. Acad. TV Arts and Scis., writing and prodn. awards other TV orgns. Mem. ACLU, Writers Guild Am. (past mem. exec. council), TV Acad. Arts and Scis. (past gov.), Am. Humanist Assn. Clubs: Explorers (N.Y.C.); Bel-Air Country, La Costa Country. Home: Los Angeles Calif. Died Oct. 24, 1991; cremated.

RODDIS, LOUIS HARRY, JR., naval officer, consulting engineer; b. Charleston, S.C., Sept. 9, 1918; s. Louis Harry and Winifred Emily (Stiles) R.; married. B.S., U.S. Naval Acad., 1939; M.S., MIT, 1944. Registered profl. engr., Pa., D.C., N.Y., N.J., S.C. chartered engr., U.K. Commd. ensign USN, 1939, advanced through grades to capt., 1957; various assignments, sea duty, 1939-41, Pearl Harbor, 1941; assigned Phila. Naval Shipyard, 1944, staff of comdr. Joint Task Force I, atomic weapons tests, Bikini, 1946, assigned Clinton Labs., Manhattan Engring. Dist. (now Oak Ridge Nat. Lab.), 1946; staff bur. ships Dept. Navy Washington; staff bur. ships, nuclear ship propulsion program AEC, assisted nuclear reactor design U.S.S. Nautilus Dept. Navy, 1947-55; dep. dir. div. reactor devel. AEC, 1955-58; pres., dir. Pa. Electric Co., Johnstown, 1958-67, chmn., 1967-69; dir. nuclear power activities Gen. Pub. Utilities Corp., N.Y.C., 1967-69; vice chmn. Consol. Edison Co. N.Y., 1969, 73-74, pres., 1969-73, also trustee; pres., chief exec. officer John J. McMullen Assos., Inc., N.Y.C., 1975-76; asso. co. Panero-Tizian Assos., Inc., 1975-76; cons. engr., from 1976; bd. dirs. Detroit Edison Co., Inc.; mem. Pres.'s Adv. Coun. on Energy Rsch. and Devel., 1973-75; cons. U.S. Dept. State Disarmament Commn., 1960-61, U.S. Maritime Adminstrn., 1959-62; chmn. maritime rsch. adv. com. Nat. Acad. Scis.-NRC, 1958-60; mem. Gov.'s Com. of 100 for Better Edn., 1962-64, Gov.'s Coun. Sci. & Tech., 1963-65, Pa. Indsl. Devel. Authority, 1961-68; pres. Atomic Indsl. Forum, 1962-64; adv. com. Rockefeller U., 1972-86; mem. energy rsch. adv. bd. Dept. Energy, 1978-85, chmn. Author tech. articles on nuclear power and energy subjects. Bd. dirs. Mercy Hosp., Johnstown, 1959-67, Metal Properties Council, 1970-74. Recipient Outstanding Service award AEC, 1957; Arthur S. Flemming career award Washington C. of C., 1958; Outstanding Citizen award Johnstown Inter-Service Club Council, 1963, Exceptional Service award U.S. Dept. Energy, 1984. Fellow Royal Instn. Naval Architects; mem. ASME (Fellowship award), IEEE, Am. Nuclear Soc. (pres. 1969-70, Fellowship award 1970), Soc. Naval Engrs., Am. Soc. Naval Architects and Marine Engrs., Nat. Acad. Engring., Nat. Soc. Profl. Engrs., ASHRAE, N.Y. C. of C., Newcomen Soc. N.Am., Edison Electric Assn. (dir. 1969-73), Human Factor Soc., Am. Gas Assn. (dir. 1973-74), Commerce and Industry Assn. N.Y. (dir. 1969-74), Sigma Xi, Tau Beta Pi. Clubs: Army Navy (Washington); Rotary (Charleston). Home: Charleston S.C. Died Sept. 15, 1991; cremated.

RODGERS, JAMES A(LEXANDER), manufacturing company executive; b. St. Louis, July 24, 1898; s. James A. and Emily (Masehmeyer) R.; m. Margaret M. Combs, Oct. 27, 1925; children: James A., Margaret M., Jean F. EE, Washington U., St. Louis, 1920. Chief engr. Emerson Electric Mfg. Co., St. Louis, 1920-37; pres., bd. dirs. White Rodgers Co., St. Louis, from 1937, chmn. bd., from 1963; mem. St. Louis Electric Bd. Trade. Mem. ASHRAE, AIM, Nat. Electric Mfrs. Assn., Am. Gas Assn., Engrs. Club, Union League Club (Chgo.). *

RODMAN, ROLAND VERE, oil company executive; b. Blair, Nebr., Sept. 23, 1897; s. Walter Benton and America (Robertson) R.; m. Marjorie May Leach, Aug. 10, 1922; children: Priscilla Jean Rodman Wandel, Marjorie Ann Rodman Scott, Mary Louis Rodman Davis. LLB, U. Nebr., 1919; LLD, Oklahoma City U., 1963. Bar: Nebr. 1919, Colo. 1937. Pvt. practice, Nebr., 1922-37; gen. counsel Bay Petroleum Corp., Denver, 1937-39, v.p., gen. mgr., 1939-46, pres., 1946-47; pres., bd. dirs. Anderson-Prichard Oil Corp., 1947-61, Anderson-Prichard Pipe Line Corp., 1947-61; pres., bd. dirs. Apco Oil Corp., Oklahoma City, 1961-65, chmn., from 1965; bd. dirs. Norgren Co., Denver. Past pres. Frontiers Sci. Found. Okla.; bd. dirs. Oklahoma City U., St. Anthony Hosp. Decorated Bene Merenti medal Pope Pius XII, 1957. Mem. ABA, Nebr. Bar Assn., Am. Petroleum Inst. (bd. dirs.), Ind. Petroleum Assn. Am. (bd. dirs.), Nat.o Petroleum Refiners Assn. (v.p.), Nat. Petroleum Coun., Oklahoma City C. of C., Am. Legion, Cherry Hills Country Club (Denver), Gold and Country Club, Masons, Shriners, Phi Delta Phi. *

ROE, KENNETH ANDREW, engineering company executive; b. Perry, N.Y., Jan. 31, 1916; s. Ralph Coats and Esther (Bishop) R.; m. Hazel Winifred Thropp, Feb. 22, 1942; children: Ralph C., Randall B., K. Keith, Hollace L., W. Barton. BA, Columbia U., 1938; BSChemE, MIT, 1941; MSME, U. Pa., 1946; certificate in naval architecture, U.S. Naval Acad., 1942; PhD in Mech. Engring. (hon.), Stevens Inst. Tech., 1978; hon. degree, Manhattan Coll., 1989. Registered profl. engr., Pa., Calif., Conn., Mich., Wash., Fla., Nebr., N.J., N.Y. Engr. Burns and Roe Enterprises, Inc., Oradell, N.J., 1938-41, exec. adminstrv. officer, 1945-54, exec. v.p., 1945-63, pres., 1963-84, chmn., chief exec. officer, 1971-91; bd. dirs. T. Y. Lin Internat., San Francisco, Polar Molecular Corp., Saginaw, Mich.; presenter numerous papers and addresses to profl. socs. Chmn. Engring. Fund Columbia U., mem. engring. coun., engring. coun. acad. adv. com., trustee ad hoc com. for univ. alumni; former trustee, vice chmn. bd. trustees Manhattan Coll.; mem. bd. overseers Coll. Engring. and Applied Sci., U. Pa.; trustee Stevens Inst. Tech., mem. exec. com.; bd. dirs. Polymer Processing inst., Stevens Inst. Tech.; past chmn. N.J. Conf. for Promotion of Better Govt.; past trustee British-Am. Edn. Found.; dir. Bergen County C. of C., 1973-75; pres. 400 Assn. Inc., Palm Beach, Fla. Lt. comdr. USN, 1941-45. Recipient Edwin F. Church medal ASME, 1979, Svc. to Constrn. Industry citation Engring. News-Record, 1980, Carl Kayan award Columbia U., 1977, Pupin medal Columbia U., 1983, Stevens Honor award Stevens Inst. Tech., 1981, John Fritz medal, 1984, Hoover medal, 1984, Moles award, 1985, Corp. Leadership award MIT, 1987, D. Robert Yarnall award U. Pa. Engring. Alumni Soc., 1985; named Disting. N.J. Civil Engr. by N.J. Sect. ASCE, 1982, Eminent Engr. by N.Y. chpt. Tau Beta Pi, 1987, Pres.'s award ASCE posthumously, 1992. Fellow AAAS, Am. Inst. Chem. Engrs., Inst. Engrs. (Australia), Inst. Mech. Engrs. (Eng.), ASME (hon. mem., pres. 1971-72, Centennial award Met. Sect. 1980, Centennial Hon. Medallion 1980, Engring. award of Outstanding Leadership 1965); mem. Am. Chem. Soc. (sr.), AIAA, Am. Nuclear Soc., IEEE, NSPE (NSPE award 1981, mem. engrs. roundtable), N.J. Soc. Profl. Engrs. and Land Surveyors (Engr. of Yr. 1980), Bergen County Soc. Profl. Engrs. (Engr. of Yr. 1980), Ky. Soc. Profl. Engrs., Soc. Petroleum Engrs. of AIME, Am. Assn. Engring. Studies (1st chmn. and acting pres. bd. govs. 1980, chmn. bd. govs. exec. com. 1980-81, industry adv. com. 1982-83, mem. coms.), Am. Nuclear Energy Coun. (bd. dirs.), NAE (mem. coms.), MHD Indsl. Forum (mem. adv. com. 1982), Nat. Coun. Synthetic Fuels Prodn. (mem. exec. com. 1980-82, bd. dirs. 1980-82), Engrs. Joint Coun. (chmn. 1978-80, dir. 1976-80), U.S. Nat. Com./ World Energy Conf. (chmn. investment adv. com., mem. exec. com., bd. dirs., mem. membership com., planning and adv. com.), Columbia Engring. Affiliates, Soc. Columbia Grads., Thomas Egleston Assocs.(Egleston medal com. 1981-83), John Jay Assocs., Sch. Engring. and Applied Sci. Alumni Assn. (bd. mgrs.), Metropolitan Club (bd. govs. 1984-88), Order of the Founders and Patriots of Am. (gov. N.J. Soc. 1984-86), SAR. Home: Palm Beach Fla. Died June 3, 1991.

ROESCH, RAYMOND AUGUST, university president, clergyman; b. Jenkintown, Pa., Sept. 16, 1914; s. Aloysius Adam and Anna Estelle (Fleck) R. B.A., U. Dayton, 1936; M.A., Cath. U. Am., 1945; postgrad., Columbia U., 1949; Ph.D., Fordham U., 1954; D. Pedagogy (hon.), Coll. of Steubenville, 1976; H.H.D. (hon.), Wright State U., 1979; P.H.L. (hon.), U. Dayton, 1982. High sch. tchr. Cathedral Latin Sch., Cleve., 1936-41; ordained priest Roman Cath. Ch., 1944; guidance dir. Chaminade High Sch., Mineola, N.Y., 1945-49; parish priest St. Mary's Ch., Mt.Vernon, N.Y., 1949-51; prof. psychology, chmn. dept. U. Dayton, 1951-59, pres., 1959-79, pres. emeritus, 1979-91, spl. asst. to univ. pres., 1989-91; pres. Chaminade U. of Honolulu, 1982-89; dir. Kukui Gardens Corp., 1985-89; pres. Dayton-Miami Valley Consortium, 1968-78. Sec. bd. trustees Ohio Higher Edn. Assistance Commn.; mem. Ednl. Commn. of States, 1969-79; mem. adv. council ROTC Affairs, 1963-66; mem. Ohio Higher Edn. Facilities Commn., 1968-82; bd. dirs. Serenity Found., Dayton, Dayton Met. YMCA, 1975, Dayton APC, 1979; chmn. bd. Ohio Found. Independent Colls., 1976-78; trustee Good Samaritan Hosp., Dayton, Mary Manse Coll., Toledo; mem. gov.'s bd. Ohio Scholarship Fund; mem. Dayton Area Progress Council, 1979; bd. dirs. Dayton chpt. NCCJ, from 1980, Dayton chpt. ARC, from 1980; mem. Hawaii Ednl. Loan Program Council, from 1984. Recipient Disting. Civilian Service award, 1969, Outstanding Service to Civic Affairs award Am. Soc. for Pub. Adminstrn., 1972, Disting. Alumnus award, 1973, NCCJ award, 1982; named to U. Dayton Hall of Fame, 1979; honoree Alzheimer Assn. Miami Valley Chpt., 1990. Mem. AAAS, Am., Am. Cath. psychol. assns., N.E.A., Ohio Coll. Assn. (pres. 1967-68), Assn. Am. Colls. (mem. commn. faculty and students 1965), Ind. Colls. and Univs. Ohio (v.p. 1968), Assn. Urban Univs. (v.p. from 1976), Hawaii Assn. Ind. Colls. and Univs. (chmn. 1984), Phi Delta Kappa, Tau Alpha Pi. Lodge: Rotary. Home: Dayton Ohio Died July 7, 1991; buried Queen of Heaven Cemetery, Beavercreek, Ohio.

ROGERS, CHARLES B., artist, gallery executive; b. Gt. Bend, Kans., Jan. 27, 1911; s. Walter and Sarah (Schoonoever) R.; m. Ruth Estella Walker; 1 son, Robert C. Student (Volker grantee), Nat. Acad. Art; B.F.A., Bethany Coll., 1942; M.F.A., Calif. Coll. Arts and Crafts, 1947. Head Sch. Art Bethany Coll., 1947-53; mgr. Huntington Hartford Found., Pacific Palisades, Calif., 1954-66; asst. dir. Huntington Hartford Found., 1954-66; head Sch. Art Kans. Wesleyan U., 1966-67; dir. Rogers House Museum Gallery, Ellsworth, Kans., 1968-87. Author, illustrator: Quill of the Kansan, 1970, The Great West, 1973, Images of the American West, 1975, Country Neighbor, 1977, Art Observations, 1980, The Essence of Drawing, 1986; exhibited in more than 100 one-man shows including, Mus. N.Mex., Santa Fe, Inst. Tech., Rochester, N.Y., Smithsonian Instn., Disney Studios; exhibited in more than 250 group shows including, Denver Art Mus., Derby Gallery, London, Eng., Chgo. Art Inst., Fuji Daimaru Gallery, Kyoto, Japan; represented in permanent collections, Library of Congress, Met. Mus. Art, N.Y.C., Phila. Mus. Art, U. Kans., Kans. State U., Instituto Mexicano; works include murals at U.S. Post Office, Council Grove, Kans., Britton Meml., Ellsworth. Served with USN, 1942-46. Tiffany Found. grantee, Huntington Hartford Found. grantee; recipient numerous awards including Mikami award Japanese Brush Painting, awards from Kansas City Art Inst., Painters and Sculptors, Los Angeles, Topeka Ann., Nat. Vets. Art, Santa Monica, Calif. Fellow Am. Inst. Fine Arts; mem. Soc. Am. Graphic Artists, Kans. Fedn. Art (pres.), St. Mary's Coll. (hon.). Home: Ellsworth Kans. Died Dec. 10, 1987; buried Ellsworth, Kans.

ROGERS, GEORGE EDWARD, headmaster; b. Manchester, Conn., June 8, 1897; s. William and Helena (McMurray) R.; m. Lillian Ruth Biggin, Aug. 24, 1927; 1 child, Beverly Tiffany. Grad., Huntsinger Bus. Coll., 1916; AB, Tufts U., 1924, EdD, 1957. Pvt. sec. Aetna Life Ins. Co., Hartford, Conn., 1916-19, Cheney Bros., Manchester, 1919-20; tchr. Williston Acad., 1924-26;

submaster Goddard Sem., 1926-27, headmaster, 1927-29; tchr. Northwood Sch., Lake Placid Club N.Y., 1929-35; headmaster Monson (Mass.) Acad., FROM 1935; TRUSTEE mONSON sAVS. bANK. Sec. Monson Free Libr.; trustee Wing Meml. Hosp., Palmer, Mass. With Battery F, 41st C.A., World War I. Mem. Rotary, Phi Beta Kappa, Delta Upsilon. Republican. Congregationalist. *

ROGERS, LOCKHART BURGESS, chemist, educator; b. Manchester, Conn., July 16, 1917; s. William Lockhart and Mabel (Burgess) R.; m. Eleanor Greene Smith, Sept. 6, 1952; children: Eleanor Rogers Johnson, Winslow S. A.B., Wesleyan U., Middletown, Conn., 1939; A.M., Princeton U., 1940, Ph.D., 1942. Instr., then asst. prof. Stanford U., 1942-46; group leader Oak Ridge Nat. Lab., 1946-48; from asst. prof. to prof. M.I.T., 1948-61; prof. chemistry Purdue U., 1961-74; Graham Perdue prof. chemistry U. Ga., Athens, 1974-86, prof. emeritus, 1986-92, interim head dept., 1982-85; Mem. adv. com. NSF, NIH, EPA, Army Research Office, Durham, USAF Office Sci. Research; mem. adv. com., analytical div. Oak Ridge Nat. Lab., Lawrence Livermore Lab., Nat. Bur. Standards; mem. commn. equilibrium data Internat. Union Pure and Applied Chemistry, 1967-73, 77-79; mem. U.S. nat. com., 1968-71; chmn. Gordon Conf. Analytical Chemistry, 1954; mem. com. on analytical chemistry NRC. Editorial adv. com.: Jour. Electrochem. Soc., Analytical Chemistry, Separation and Science Technology. Recipient Dal Nogare award Chromatography Forum; 100th Anniversary award Assn. Analytical Chemists; Benedetti-Pichler award Am. Microchem. Soc. Mem. Am. Chem. Soc. (emeritus; awards for Chromatography, analytical chemistry, excellence in teaching, Herty award Ga. sect.; chmn. Northeastern sect. 1959, nat. councilor Northeastern sect. 1957-59, Purdue sect. 1967-74, sec.-treas. analytical div. 1959-61, chmn. 1961), Electrochem. Soc. (chmn. Boston sect. 1959, nat. councilor 1960), Am. Acad. Arts and Scis., Soc. Analytical Chemists Pitts. (Pitts. Analytical Chemistry award 1989), Chgo. Chromatography Discussion Group (Merit award), Phi Beta Kappa, Sigma Xi, Phi Lambda Upsilon (hon.), Alpha Chi Sigma, Delta Tau Delta. Home: Athens Ga. Died Mar. 31, 1992; buried Manchester, Conn.

ROGERS, NAT STEWART, wholesale executive; b. Portland, Ore., Mar. 23, 1898; s. Manford Gross and Emma A. (Wilmot) R.; m. Marian Esther Wurzbacher, Dec. 14, 1922; children: Robert S., Ann (Mrs. James H. Wiborg), N. Stewart. BS, U. Wash., 1943. Mgr. Kaseno Product Co., 1921-24; exec. v.p., dir. Van Waters & Rogers, Inc., Seattle, 1923-62, chmn., dir., 1962-67; chmn. exec. com., dir. VWR United Corp., 1967-70; dir. Olympic Steamship Co., John Fluke Mfg. Co. Past pres. Seattle Found., Seattle Symphony. Served with USNRF, World War I. Mem. C. of C. (past pres.), Masons, Rotary (past pres.), Arctic Club (past pres.), Rainier Club (past pres.). Republican. Congregationalist. Home: Mercer Island Wash. Died Feb. 6, 1990.

ROGERS, ROBERT FRANCIS, television producer; b. Washington, Apr. 4, 1931; s. Robert Francis and Margaret Katherine (McLaughlin) R.; m. Elizabeth Hunter Buck, Jan. 24, 1953; children—Eileen Margaret, Christopher Thomas, Timothy Francis. Student, The Citadel, 1949-50; B.A., Georgetown U., 1953. Commd. 2d lt. U.S. Army, 1953, advanced through grades to capt., 1959, resigned, 1961; free lance writer, 1961-62; asso. producer, writer NBC News, Washington, 1962-67; producer, writer, dir. documentaries NBC, Washington, 1967-80, sr. producer documentaries, 1980-85, sr. producer, mgr. news documentaries, 1985-89. Contbr. articles and stories to mags. Programs recipient Alfred I. duPont-Columbia U. award, Am. award Overseas Press Club award. Mem. Nat. Acad. TV Arts and Scis., Writers Guild Am., Dirs. Guild Am., Sigma Delta Chi. Roman Catholic. Club: Kenwood Golf and Country. Home: Bethesda Md. Died Sept. 24, 1989.

ROGERS, ROBERT WENTWORTH, humanities educator, dean; b. Boston, Dec. 1, 1914; s. Lester Frances and Elizabeth (Gill) R.; m. Jeanne Francis Way, May 18, 1946 (dec. 1955); foster children—Susan Way, Sarah Wentworth; m. Elizabeth Belcher Yudkin, Nov. 23, 1956; one son, John Parker; foster children—Michael Yudkin, David Yudkin. A.B., U. Mich., 1936; M.A., Harvard, 1937, Ph.D., 1942. Instr. English, sr. tutor Dunster House, Harvard, 1946-48; asst. prof. English U. Ill., Champaign-Urbana, 1948-51, asso. prof., 1951-55, prof., 1955-79, exec. sec. dept. English, 1953-57, acting head, 1956-57, head dept., 1957-64, dean Coll. Liberal Arts and Scis., 1964-79, dean and prof. English emeritus, 1979-92; Mem. Commn. on Arts and Scis., Nat. Assn. State Univs. and Land Grant Colls., 1972-74. Author: The Major Satires of Alexander Pope, 1955; also articles, revs.; Editorial bd.: jour. English and Germanic Philology, 1954-66. Bd. dirs. Center Research Libraries, 1964-67. Served from ensign to lt. (s.g.) USNR, 1942-46. Guggenheim fellow, 1957-58. Mem. Modern Lang. Assn., Nat. Council Tchrs. English (adv. council 1960-62), Midwest Modern Lang. Assn. (pres. 1960-61), AAUP, Nat. Assn. Chmn. Depts. English (sec.-treas. 1963-64), Council Colls. Arts and Scis. State Univs. and Land Grant Colls. (pres. 1972), Assn. Am. Colls. (dir. 1977-80), Pilgrim Soc. (dir.), Phi Beta Kappa, Phi Kappa Phi, Psi Upsilon. Home: Champaign Ill. Died Feb. 24, 1992; buried Plymouth, Mass.

ROGERS, VIRGIL MADISON, university dean; b. Moore, S.C., Oct. 15, 1898; s. James and Catherine (McCravy) R.; m. Helen Blackstock (dec. 1931); 1 child, Virginia; m. Julia Chaine, Sept. 1, 1933; children: Bruce, Julia. AB, Wofford Coll., 1921, LLD, 1954; AM, We. State Coll., 1924; EdD, Columbia U., 1944. Tchr., prin. pub. schs. Delta, Colo., 1921-26; dir. secondary edn. We. State Coll., Colo., 1926-29; supt. schs. Gunnison, Colo., 1929-34, Boulder, Colo., 1934-40, River Forest, Ill., 1940-45, Battle Creek, Mich., 1945-53; dean sch. edn. Syracuse (N.Y.) U., 1953-64; dir. ednl. implications automation project NEA, 1963-66; mem. group sch. adminstrs. vis. schs. USSR, fall 1959, 61, summer, 1966; lectr. ednl. adminstrn. various colls. and univs.; cons. for Peace Corps, Nyassaland, fall 1962; ednl. cons. Field Enterprises Ednl. Corp., 1968-74. Author: (with others) Practical Applications of Democratic Adminstration, 1951; contbr. articles to ednl. jours. Group leader Mid-Century White House Conf. on Youth and Children, 1950, cons., 1960; mem. N.Y. Gov.'s Commn. Youth, 1963-65; mem. human resources study bd. FAA, 1964-65; mem. edn. mission War Dept. to Germany for survey German sch. system, 1947. With F.A., U.S. Army, 1918. Mem. NEA (mem., chmn. ethics com. 1943-46, mem. commn. on def. democracy through edn. 1948-54, dir. from N.Y. State 1956-63), Am. Assn. Sch. Adminstrs. (pres. 1952-53), Colo. Edn. Assn. (pres. 1939-40), Nat. Soc. Study Edn., Colo. Mountain Club (pres.), Phi Delta Kappa. Home: Syracuse N.Y. Died Mar. 3, 1990.

ROIZIN, LEON, neuropathologist, neurotoxicologist; b. Dubossare, Russia, Dec. 31, 1912; s. L. and S. (Akerman) R.; m. Evelyn Iannoni, June 21, 1941; children: Diane, Laurie. M.D. summa cum laude, U. Milan, Italy, 1936; cert. lab. dir., N.Y. State Dept. Health, 1971. Diplomate Am. Bd. Psychiatry and Neurology, Am. Bd. Pathology. Am. Bd. Gen. Toxology. Asst. Neuropsychiat. Clinic, Royal U. Pavia, Italy, 1936-39; extraordinary asst. Med. Sch. Sao Paulo, Brazil, 1939-40; asst. dept. neuropathology and neurotoxicology N.Y. Psychiat. Inst., N.Y.C., 1940, dir. dept. neuropathology and neurotoxicology, 1965-87, researcher Neurotoxicology Svc. and Rsch. Unit of Inst., until 1991; successively asso., prin., chief psychiat. research, chief dept.; prof. neuropathology Coll. Physicians and Surgeons, Columbia U., prof. emeritus, 1987-91; cons. in field. Contbr. numerous articles, chpts. to profl. publs.; chief editor: Neurotoxicology, vol. I; editorial bd.: Acta Neurologica. Recipient Thorton Willson award Eastern Psychiat. Assn., 1962; Disting. Service citation N.Y. State Dept. Mental Hygiene, 1969; NIH grantee; Nat. Mental Health Assn. grantee. Fellow Am. Acad. Neurology, Am. Psychiat. Assn., N.Y. Acad. Scis., Am. Coll. Pathologists; mem. Internat. Brain Research Orgn., Internat. Soc. Neuropathology, World Fedn. Neurology (chmn. research group on neurotoxicology and occupational neurology), Sezione di Neuropathologia, Societe Italiana di Neurologia. Home: Bronx N.Y. Died Mar. 6, 1991.

ROKAHR, THEODORE, banker; b. N.Y.C., July 6, 1896; s. Ernst and Margaret (Raab) R.; m. Geraldine M. Proulx, Nov. 20, 1922; 1 child, John Ernst. Grad., Rutgers U. Grad. Sch. Banking, 1937. Various positions to asst. to v.p. charge bus. devel. Irving Trust Co. N.Y. (formerly Irvine Nat. Bank), 1914-19; from chief clk. to exec. v.p. Utica (N.Y.) Nat. Bank & Trust Co., 1926-30; v.p. Citizens Trust Co. Utica, 1930-31; v.p., treas. 1st Bank & Trust Co. Utica, 1931-49, pres., bd. dirs., 1949-58; chmn. bd., CEO, bd. dirs. Marine Midland Trust Co. Mohawk Valley, Utica, from 1958; clk. Nat. Nassau Bank N.Y., 1918-14; mem. adv. bd. Marine Midland Corp.; bd. dirs. Utica Fire Ins. Co., Oneida County, Inc. Author pamphlets on banking. Bd. dirs. Better Bus. Bur., Utica, Hosp. Plan, Inc., Utica; trustee Utica Coll. Found. Named hon. alumnus Utica Coll., 1965. Mem. Am. Bankers Assn., N.Y. Bankers Assn., Madison-Oneida-Herkimer Bankers Assn., Am. Inst. Banking, Utica C. of C. (bd. dirs.), Mcpl. Rsch. Bur. (bd. dirs.), Ft. Schuyler Club, Yahnumdasis Golf Club, Masons, Shriners. *

ROLVAAG, KARL FRITJOF, former financial executive, former governor; b. Northfield, Minn., July 18, 1913; s. Ole Edvart and Jennie (Berdahl) R.; m. Florence A. Boedeker, Aug. 28, 1943; children: Paul F., Kristin V. BA with spl. honors, St. Olaf Coll., 1941; postgrad., U. Minn., 1945-46; LLD, St. Mary's Coll., Winona, Minn., 1963. Lt. gov. State of Minn., 1954-63, gov., 1963-67; U.S. ambassador to Iceland, 1967-69; rep. Dept. State Cultural Exch. Prog. to Scandinavian Countries, 1961; mem. Minn. Pub. Svc. Commn., 1972-90; chmn. Minn. Dem. Farm Labor Party, 1950-54. Capt. AUS, 1941-47. Decorated Silver Star, Purple Heart (U.S.); comdrs. cross Order St. Olav (Norway); Am. Scandinavian Found. scholar U. Oslo (Norway), 1947-48. Mem. Minn. Hist. Soc., Am. Scandinavian Found., V.F.W., D.A.V. Lutheran. Home: Northfield Minn. Died Dec. 20, 1990.

ROMAN, HERSCHEL LEWIS, geneticist; b. Szumsk, Poland, Sept. 29, 1914; came to U.S., 1921, naturalized, 1927; s. Isadore and Anna R.; m. Caryl Kahn, Aug. 11, 1938; children—Linda, Ann. AB, U. Mo., 1936, PhD, 1942; hon. doctorate, U. Paris, 1986, U. Mo., 1989. Instr. U. Wash., Seattle, 1942-46, asst. prof., 1946-47, assoc. prof., 1947-52, prof., 1952-83, prof. emeritus, 1983-89, chmn. dept. genetics, 1959-80; vis. investigator Carlsberg Lab., Copenhagen, 1960; vis. prof. Australian Nat. U., Canberra, 1966; cons. in field. Editor: Ann. Rev. Genetics, 1965-84, rsch. publs. on maize genetics, yeast genetics. Served with AC U.S. Army, 1943-46. Guggenheim fellow, 1952, Fulbright fellow, 1956; recipient Merit citation U. Mo., 1973, Gold medal Emil Christian Hansen Found., Copenhagen, 1980. Mem. AAAS, Nat. Acad. Scis., Genetics Soc. Am. (pres. 1968, T.H. Morgan medal 1985). Home: Seattle Wash. Died July 2, 1989.

ROMIG, LLEUELLEN DEWIGHT, utility executive; b. Ulrichsville, Ohio, May 7, 1897; s. Charles G. and Adeline (Lleuellen) R.; m. Katharine M. Fralick, July 31, 1926; 1 child, George C. BS, U. Ill., 1922. With So. Calif. Gas Co., L.A., 1922-65, treas., 1945-65. With AC, U.S. Army, 1918. Mem. Am. Gas Assn., Pacific Coast Gas Assn., Tax Execs. Inst. (pres. L.A. chpt. 1950). *

ROOD, PAUL, physics educator; b. Lawton, Mich., May 3, 1894; s. Harry Lincoln and Mary (Rose) R.; m. Josephine Connable, Oct. 6, 1928; children: Ellen, Jean, Peggy, Jonathan. AB, Albion (Mich.) Coll., 1916; AAM, U. Mich., 1921, PhD, 1938. Mem. faculty physics dept. Western Mich. U., Kalamazoo, 1916-64, prof., 1937-64, head dept., 1944-64; ret., 1964; instr. Naval V-12 Unit, 1943-45; rsch. on photoelectric effect Rsch. Lab, GE, Schenectady, 1926-27. With USN, 1918-19. Mem. AAAS, Am. Phys. Soc., Am. Optical Soc., Am. Assn. Physics Tchrs., Mich. Edn. Assn., Torch Club, Masons, Kiwanis, Sigma Xi. *

ROOSEVELT, ARCHIBALD BULLOCH, JR., banker; b. Boston, Feb. 18, 1918; s. Archibald Bulloch and Grace Stackpole (Lockwood) R.; m. Selwa Showker, Sept. 1, 1950; 1 son, Tweed. Grad., Groton Sch., 1936; B.A., Harvard, 1939. Newspaperman, 1939-42; joined U.S. Fgn. Service, 1947, Central Intelligence Group (later CIA), 1947; attache Am. embassy, Beirut, Lebanon, 1947-49; chief Near East sect. Voice of Am., 1949-50; consul Istanbul, Turkey, 1951-53; assigned Dept. State, 1953-58; 1st sec., spl. asst. to ambassador to Spain Madrid, 1958; attaché, spl. asst. Am. Embassy, London, Eng., 1962-66; assigned Dept. State, 1966-74; v.p., dir. internat. relations Chase Manhattan Bank, 1975-90. Author: For Lust of Knowing-Memoirs of an Intelligence Officer, 1988. Served from 2d lt. to capt. AUS, 1942-47. Mem. F Street Club. Home: Washington D.C. Died May 31, 1990; buried Oyster Bay, N.Y.

ROOSEVELT, ELLIOTT, writer, rancher; b. N.Y.C., Sept. 23, 1910; s. Franklin Delano (31st Pres. of the U.S.) and Anna Eleanor R.; m. Elizabeth Donner, 1931 (div. 1933); 1 son William Donner; m. Ruth Josephine Googins, July 22, 1933; children: Ruth Chandler, Elliott, David Boynton; m. Faye Emerson 1944 (div. 1950); m. Minnewa Bell, 1951; m. Patricia Whitehead, '60. Engaged in advt., editing, radio work, 1929-41; pres., dir. Dalco Uranium, Inc., 1957-90. Author: As He Saw It, 1946; co-author: (with James Brough) An Untold Story: The Roosevelts of Hyde Park, 1973, The Roosevelts of the White House: A Rendezvous with Destiny, 1975; editor: F.D.R., His Personal Letters, Early Years: F.D.R., His Personal Letters, 1905-28; F.D.R., His Personal Letters, 1928-45 (2 vols.). Mayor of Miami Beach, Fla., 1965-69; bd. dirs. Tex. Agrl. and Mech. Coll., 1937-39; v.p. Aeronaut. C. of C. of Am., Inc., 1934-35. Brig. gen. USAAF, 1940-45. Decorated Legion of Merit, D.F.C. (2), Air medal (2); comdr. Order Brit. Empire; Legion of Honor, Croix de Guerre with palm (2) (French); comdr. Order Assoum Alacuite. Mem. Denver Country Club, Phoenix Country Club, Paradise Valley Racquet Club (Scottsdale, Ariz.), Mason. Home: Meeker Colo. Died Oct. 27, 1990.

ROOSEVELT, JAMES, business consultant; b. N.Y.C., Dec. 23, 1907; s. Franklin Delano (31st pres. U.S.) and Anna Eleanor (Roosevelt) R.; m. Betsey Cushing (div. 1940); children: Sara Wilford, Kate Roosevelt Whitney; m. Romelle Schneider (div. 1955); children: James, Michael, Anne Johnston; m. Gladys Irene Owens, July 9, 1956 (div. Sept. 1969); 1 child, Hall Delano; m. Mary Lena Winskill, Oct. 3, 1969; 1 child, Rebecca Mary. Student, Harvard U., 1930; LL.D. (hon.), Woodbury U., 1977; Ph.D. (hon.), Calif. Western U.; B.S., Chapman Coll., 1985. Ins. broker, 1930; organizer Roosevelt & Sargent, Inc., Boston; pres. Roosevelt & Sargent, Inc., until 1937, resigned, 1938; in motion picture industry, 1938-40; reentered Roosevelt & Sargent, Inc.; as exec. v.p. establishing west coast office, 1946; pres. James Roosevelt & Co., Corona Del Mar, Calif.; mem. 84th-89th congresses from 26th Calif. Dist., 1954-65; U.S. rep. to ECOSOC, 1965-66; with Internat. Overseas Svcs. Mgmt. Co., 1966-70, pres., 1970-71, bus. cons., 1970-90; pres. IOS Devel. Co. Ltd.; exec. dir. Enterprise Inst. Chapman Coll.; lectr. Soc. Ecology, U. Calif. at Irvine, Chancellors Club; lectr. polit. sci. Woodbury U., Chapman Coll., others. Author: Affectionately, F.D.R, 1959, My Parents, 1976, A Family Matter, 1979. Democratic nat. committeeman, 1948-52, Dem. candidate for gov., Calif., 1950; v.p. Eleanor Roosevelt Cancer Found.; bd. dirs. Nat. Found.-March of Dimes; trustee Chapman Coll., Orange, Calif.; participant Arm and Hammer Peace and Human Rights Confs., 1979, 80, 81; mem. Orange County Transp. Commn., from 1979, chmn., 1985-86; chmn. Nat. Com. to Preserve Social Security and Medicare, Washington. Served from capt. to col. USMCR, 1940-45, PTO; brig. gen. Res. Decorated Navy Cross, Silver Star; recipient Humanitarian award NCCJ, 1981, Nat. Americanism award Anti-Defamation League of B'nai Brith. Club: Metropolitan (N.Y.C.); Center (Costa Mesa, Calif.); Balboa Bay (Newport Beach, Calif.). Home: Newport Beach Calif. Died Aug. 13, 1991.

ROOT, BLAKE SMITH, educator; b. Sparland, Ill., July 2, 1905; s. Wilbur Stowell and Minnie (Smith) R.; m. Irene Lerch, Aug. 16, 1933; children: Betty Irene (Mrs. David Biren), Majorie Kay (Mrs. Frank Sands), Joan Marie (Mrs. Stewart Rhodes), Roberta Jane (Mrs. John Monacelli), Robert Blake. BS, Monmouth Coll., 1927; MA, U. Ill., 1931; postgrad., Midland Coll., 1935; extension student, Ind. U., U. Neb., 1935-36; EdD, George Washington U., 1948. Tchr. social studies, coach Fremont (Nebr.) Sr. High Sch., 1927-36; tchr. Pekin, Ill., 1936, Anacostia Jr.-Sr. High Sch., Washington, 1937; tchr. Western Sr. High Sch., Washington, 1937-42, chmn. social studies, 1939-41, asst. prin., 1942-43, 44-45; tng. specialist WPB, 1943; indsl. analyst War Food Adminstrn., 1943; head profl. and tech. tgn. sect. OPA, 1945-48; assoc. prof. edn. George Washington U., 1948-52, prof., 1953-71, chmn. dept., asst. dean Sch. Edn., 1956-71, acting dean Sch. Edn., 1957, 63, 67-68, prof. emeritus, 1971-90; farmer, Victoria, Ill., 1941-62. Recipient Disting. Alumni award Monmouth Coll., 1963, Dr. Edn. Alumni Recognition award George Washington U., 1968. Mem. AAUP, NEA, Am. Soc. Tng. Dirs. (chmn. profl. standards com. 1959-60, rsch. com. 1960-61), Nat. Assn. Secondary Sch. Prins., Nat. Coun. Social Studies, Nat. Sch. Pub. Rels. Assn., Tng. Ofcl. Conf. Washington, Fed. Sch. Men D.C., Nat. Collegiate Players, Theta Chi, Phi Delta Kappa (pres. Beta Gamma chpt. 1948-49). Congregationalist. Home: Arlington Va. Died Jan. 25, 1990.

ROOTS, JOHN MCCOOK, author, lecturer, foreign correspondent; b. Hankow, China (parents Am. citizens) Oct. 27, 1903; s. Logan Herbert and Eliza Lydia (McCook) R. B.A. cum laude, Harvard Coll., 1925. Contbr. New York Times, Herald Tribune, Atlantic Monthly, Asia, Pace, Look, Reader's Digest, Time, Saturday Rev., others, from 1927; traveling rep., dir. Moral Re-Armament teams, S. Africa, 1929-31, U.S., 1932, Great Britain, France, Switzerland, The Netherlands, Germany, Italy, Can. Belgium, East Africa, Greece, Middle East 1932-68; lectr. U.S. and Can., 1964-81; fgn. corr. various publs., numerous countries including China, Egypt, Israel, Jordan, Lebanon, Syria, Saudi Arabia, Indonesia, Iran, 1927-80; assoc. Up With People orgn., 1968-88; author: Chou: a Biography of China's Legendary Chou En-lai, 1978. Recipient Washburn Prize for History, Harvard Coll., 1925. Clubs: Harvard (N.Y.C.), Army and Navy (Washington). Died July 26, 1988; buried Mackinac Island, Mich. Home: Saint Ignace Mich.

ROPP, CLARENCE DANIEL LUTHER, university dean; b. Martinsburg, W.Va., May 22, 1788; s. George Luther and Mattie Ellen (Shotts) R.; m. Emily May Morrisey, Nov. 7, 1945. AB, W.Va. U., 1918, AM, 1923; PhD, NYU, 1925; LLD, U. Bridgeport, 1963. Chemist E.I. Du Pont Co., Pompton Lakes, N.J., 1918; acct. Thorn Lumber Co., Martinsburg, 1919; teaching fellow in chemistry NYU, N.Y.C., 1923-25; instr. chemistry Washington Square Coll., N.Y.C., 1925-28, premed. advisor, 1927-28; prof. Jr. Coll. Conn., 1928-47; prof. U. Bridgeport, Conn., from 1947, dean Coll. Arts and Sci., 1947-64, dean emeritus, from 1964. Contbr. articles to chem. jours. Mem. Kiwanis, Phi Beta Kappa, Phi Lambda Upsilon, Phi Theta Kappa, Pi Delta Epsilon, Pi Gamma Mu, Delta Tau Kappa, Aristeia. *

ROSA, CLARENCE HENRY, architect; b. Lansing, Mich., July 13, 1912; s. George Henry and Eva (Blum) R.; m. Marcella Vonda Orr, Dec. 31, 1937 (dec. May 1967); children: Tadd Henry, Zosia Eve, Krisia Marie; m. Clarice Carr Dawson, Oct. 18, 1975. B.S. in Arch, U. Mich., 1936. Dep. dir. Mich. Bldg. Div., 1941-69; pvt. practice Lansing, 1969-88. Assoc. dir. architecture and engring.: Northville (Mich.) State Hosp, 1948-56, Steven T. Mason bldg, Lansing, 1952, State Capitol Complex, Lansing, 1962-69; dir. architecture and engring.: Central Mich. U, Mt. Pleasant, 1950-66, Medium Security Correctional Inst, Ionia, Mich., 1958-62, Mich. Secondary Facilities Center, Lansing, 1966-69. Mem. Lansing Urban Redevel. Bd., 1962-78, chmn., 1967-69; mem. Lansing Model Cities Policy Bd., 1968-72; mem. Lansing Symphony Bd., 1974-80, v.p., 1977-80; mem. Lansing Bd. Edn., 1955-72, pres., 1959-61, 70-72; mem. Mich. Commn. Architecture, 1971-72; charter bd. dirs. Lansing Arts Council/Center, 1975-86, pres., 1976-78; charter bd. dirs. Lansing Library, 1978-85, R.E. Olds Mus., 1979-85; chmn. Mich. Council Ret. State Employees, 1983-87; mem. exec. com. Mich. Coun., 1987-89; mem. Lansing Pub. Svc. Bd., 1984-89. Fellow AIA (pres. Mid-Mich. chpt. 1946, regional dir. 1972-75); mem. Mich. Soc. Architects (exec. v.p. 1972-76, Gold medal 1972), Mich. Assn. Professions (treas. 1973-78). Unitarian. Lodges: Masons, Shriners, Civitan (past pres. Lansing). Home: Lansing Mich. Died Nov. 23, 1990; buried East Lansing, Mich.

ROSE, ALBERT, consulting physicist; b. N.Y.C., Mar. 30, 1910; s. Simon and Sarah (Cohen) Rosenblum; m. Lillian Loebel, Aug. 25, 1940; children: Mark Loebel, Jane Susan. AB, Cornell U., 1931, PhD, 1935; PhD (hon.), Rochester Inst. Tech., 1989. Mem. tech. stafff, researcher RCA Labs., Princeton, N.J., 1935-75; dir. research Labs. RCA Ltd., Zurich, Switzerland, 1955-58; vis. scientist Exxon Labs., 1979-86; mem. planning com. Internat. Confs. on Semiconductors, Internat. Conf. on Photoconductivity, Internat. Conf. on Electrophotography; vis. prof. Stanford U., 1976, Hebrew U., Jerusalem, 1976-77, Boston U., 1977, 78, Poly. Inst., Mexico City, 1978, U. Del., 1979; vis. scientist Chronar Corp., 1983. Author: Concepts in Photoconductivity, 1963, Vision: Human and Electronic, 1974, Electron Phonon Interactions, 1989; editorial bd.: Phys. Rev, 1956-58, Advances in Electronics, 1948-75, Jour. Physics and Chemistry of Solids, 1958-75; contbr. articles to profl. jours. Patentee in field; Inventor image orthicon TV camera tube. Recipient certificate of merit USN, 1946, TV Broadcasters award, 1945, David Sarnoff Gold medal Soc. Motion Picture and TV Engrs., 1958; Mary Shephard Upson distinguished prof. Cornell U., 1967; Fairchild distinguished scholar Calif. Inst. Tech., 1975; recipient Leo Friend award in chem. tech., 1982. Fellow Am. Phys. Soc., IEEE (Morris Liebman award 1945, Edison medal 1979); mem. Nat. Acad. Engring., Société Suisse de Physique, Soc. Photog. Scientists and Engrs. (hon.). Home: Princeton N.J. Died July 26, 1990.

ROSE, AUGUSTUS STEELE, neurologist; b. Fayetteville, N.C., July 14, 1907; s. Augustus S. and Jean (Evans) R.; m. Grace Duncan, June 24, 1932; children: Ann Duncun (Mrs. Bruce F. Davie), Augustus Steele III, Charles Duncan, Jane Evans. Student, Davidson Coll., 1924-25; BS in Medicine, U. N.C., 1930; MD, Harvard U., 1932. Teaching fellow anatomy U. N.C. Sch. Medicine, 1928-30, Harvard Med. Sch., 1931-32; med. intern Mass. Gen. Hosp., Boston, 1932-34, asst. neurology, 1937-39; jr. physician McLean Hosp., Waverly, Mass., 1934; assoc. prof. anatomy U. N.C., 1934-37; asst. to chief dept. therapeutic rsch. Boston Psychopathic Hosp., Waverly, Mass., 1939-51; instr. neurology and psychiatry Harvard Med. Sch., 1939-51; prof. neurology UCLA, 1951-74, prof. emeritus, 1974-89; chmn. dept. neurology, dir. Reed Neurol. Rsch. Ctr., 1970-74; disting. physician VA, 1974-89; mem. staff U. Calif., Harbor Gen., VA, St. John's hosps.; dir. Am. Bd. Psychiatry and Neurology, 1960-68, v.p., 1968; adv. bd. Med. Spltys.; mem. Nat. Adv. Neurol. Disease and Stroke Coun., 1968-72; v.p. 9th Internat. Neurol. Congress, 1969; mem. med. adv. bd. psychiatry and neurology svcs. VA Ctrl. Office. Editor: (with C.M. Pearson) Mechanism of Demyelination, 1963. Dir. Epilepsy Found. Am.; mem. med. adv. bd. Nat. Multiple Sclerosis Soc., 1952-89, chmn., 1955-60; mem. adv. bd. Myasthenia Gravis Found., Calif. Epilepsy Soc., Parkinson's Diseases Found.; mem. nat. coun. Pomona Coll. Recipient Disting. Svc. award U. N.C. Sch. Medicine, 1962. Fellow AMA (chmn. residency rev. com. 1968), Am. Psychiat. Assn.; mem. Am. Neurol. Assn. (pres. 1968-69), Am. Acad. Neurology (pres. 1959-61), Am. Epilepsy Soc. (coun. 1962-64), Brit. Assn. Neurologists (hon. fgn.), Western Assn. Physicians, World Fedn. Neurology, Alpha Omega Alpha. Presbyterian. Home: Beverly Hills Calif. Died June 24, 1989.

ROSE, DAVID, composer, conductor; b. London, June 24, 1910; came to U.S., 1914; s. Meyer and Eva Rose; m. Betty Jane Bartholomew, Dec. 28, 1948; children: Melanie, Angela. Student, Chgo. Coll. Music. Pianist, Ted Fiorito Orch., 1933-35; staff arranger, pianist, NBC, Chgo., 1935-38, musical dir. Calif. Melodies series, NBC, 1938-42; mus. dir. and condr., composer, from 1946; orch. condr., mus. dir. radio and TV programs: Red Skelton Show, 20 yrs., Bob Hope Show, 1959-62, also Bonanza, 14 yrs., The Loneliest Runner, NBC; movie Little House on the Prairie, NBC-TV.; Composer: The Stripper, Moss Hart Prodn.; composer USAAF benefit show Winged Victory, on Broadway, 1943; composer: scores for motion pictures including The Wonder Man, 1945 (Oscar nomination), Texas Carnival, Rich, Young and Pretty, 1951, The Clown, Bright Road, Jupiter's Darling, Port Afrique, 1956, Never Too Late, Please Don't Eat The Daisies, 1960, Hombre; scored: movie Suddenly Love, Sam's Son, 1984; TV spl. Dear Mr. Pres., 1983, 3 Little House on the Prairie spls.; mus. dir. TV series Highway to Heaven; condr., composer music more than 50 record albums, scores for 36 films, 24 TV series. Sgt. USAAF, 1942-45. Recipient Emmy awards for Fred Astaire Program, 1959, Bonanza, 1971, Craftsman episode Little House on the Prairie, 1979, He Was Only 12, 1982; 22 Grammy awards. Mem. ASCAP. Home: Sherman Oaks Calif. Died Aug. 24, 1990.

ROSE, FRANK ANTHONY, university administrator, public affairs consultant; b. Meridian, Miss., Oct. 16, 1920; s. Frank Anthony and Susan Clare (Cooper) R.; m. Tommye Stewart, Oct. 16, 1942; children—Susan Rose Dabney, Frank Anthony, Julian, Elizabeth. A.B., Transylvania U., 1942, LL.D., 1958; B.D., Lexington Sem., 1946; LL.D., Lynchburg Coll., 1951, U. Cin., 1958, U. Ala., 1958, Samford U., 1960; D.H.L., St. Bernard Coll., 1964; D.Sc. W. Va., U., 1965; D.Hum., Am. U.-Mexico, 1965, Bapt. Coll. Charleston, 1970; D.Litt., Central Meth. Coll., 1977. Dir. admissions, prof. philosophy Transylvania U., Lexington, Ky., 1943-48, advisor to pres., 1948-51, pres., 1951-58; pres. U. Ala., 1958-69; chmn. bd. Univ. Assocs., Inc. (later merged with Cassidy & Assocs.), Washington, from 1969, sr. cons., until 1991; nat. chmn. for planning and devel. Salk Inst., 1970-74; mem. bd. control, exec. com. So. Regional Edn. Bd., 1958-68; mem. Commn. on Higher Edn. Opportunity in the South, 1964-68. Chmn. bd. trustees Am. Univs. Field Staff, 1968-74; bd. curators Transylvania U.; chmn. Ala. March of Dimes, 1958-65, regional chmn., 1965-69; trustee Salk Inst. Biol. Studies, Nat. Found.; mem. Nat. Citizen Com. on Public TV; mem. adv. panel ROTC affairs, U.S. Army, 1964-68; chmn. bd. visitors U.S. Mil. Acad., West Point, 1968-69; bd. govs. Air Univ., 1960, chmn., 1962; mem. exec. com., trustee March of Dimes, from 1975; chmn. bd. govs. Georgetown U. AIMS Med. Sch. Program, from 1982; mem. Alexander Graham Bell Centennial Bd., 1984; cons. Georgetown U. Med. Ctr, Washington, from 1982, Mt. Sinai Med. Ctr., from 1985, White House Staff on Edn. and Minority Affairs, from 1965; del. U.S. Com. to Atlantic Congress, NATO, 1959; exec. com. Reading is Fundamental, from 1969; mem. Nat. Commn. States Desegregation of Schs., 1976-78; nat. adv. com. Council on Med. Health Professions Edn., 1977-81; chmn. bd. Christian Ch. Found., 1977-79; mem. policy bd. TACTICS. Recipient Tutwiller award for contbn. to Am. higher edn., 1980. Mem. Nat. Assn. State Univs. and Land Grant Colls. (exec. com. 1965), Cosmos Club, Phi Beta Kappa, Alpha Omega Alpha, Omicron Delta Kappa (nat. pres. 1968), Kappa Alpha (pres., trustee scholarship fund 1988-91, Disting. Svc. award 1988). Democrat. Died Feb. 1, 1991; buried Lexington, Ky. Home: Lexington Ky.

ROSE, HORACE CHAPMAN, lawyer; b. Columbus, Ohio, Feb. 11, 1907; s. Henry Nelson and Grace (Chapman) R.; m. Katherine Cast, Oct. 1, 1938; 1 son, Jonathan Chapman. A.B., Princeton U., 1928; LL.B., Harvard U., 1931. Bar: Ohio 1933, D.C. 1946. Sec. to Oliver Wendell Holmes (assoc. justice Supreme Ct. U.S.), 1931-32; assoc. Jones, Day, Cockley & Reavis (formerly Tolles, Hogsett & Ginn), Cleve., 1933-38; ptnr. Jones, Day Reavis & Pogue, Cleve., Washington, 1939-42, 46-52, 56-76, of counsel, 1977-82; dir. Office of Contract Settlement, Washington, 1946; asst. sec. treasury, 1953-55, undersec. treasury, 1955-56. Trustee Cleve. Orch., Cleve. Council World Affairs; bd. dirs. Atlantic Council, Washington; trustee emeritus Princeton U., Brookings Instn. Served to col. AUS, 1942-45. Decorated Legion of Merit. Mem. Am., Ohio, Cleve. bar assns., Am. Law Inst. (council), Phi Beta Kappa. Republican. Episcopalian. Clubs: Union (Cleve.), Tavern (Cleve.), Kirtland Country (Cleve.); Princeton (N.Y.C.); Metropolitan (Washington), Burning Tree (Washington), Chevy Chase (Washington). Home: Washington D.C. Died Feb. 17, 1990; buried Greenlawn Cemetery, Columbus, Ohio.

ROSE, JAMES V., manufacturing executive; b. Detroit, Nov. 10, 1925; s. Martin William and Charlotte Eleanor (Gurnsey) R.; m. Sue Rose; children: Patricia, Martin, Katherine. BA, Mich. State U., 1952, MBA, 1970. Gen. prodn. supr. Chrysler Corp., Detroit, 1962-66; dir. Chrysler Corp., Venezuela, 1966-69; mgr. Hamtramck assembly Chrysler Corp., Detroit; v.p. U.S. indsl. truck mfg. Hyster Co., Danville, Ill., 1975-80, sr. v.p., gen. mgr., 1980-89. Bd. dirs. Danville Area Labor-Mgmt. Council, 1985-89, Danville Area Econ. Devel., 1983-89, Danville Area Community Coll. Found. Bd., 1987-89. Served with USN, 1942-46, PTO. Mem. Ill. C. of C. (bd. dirs. 1985-89). Episcopalian. Home: Danville Ill. Died May 30, 1989.

ROSE, JERZY EDWIN, neurophysiologist; b. Buczacz, Poland, Mar. 5, 1909; came to U.S., 1940, naturalized, 1943; s. Henryk and Regina (Deiches) R.; m. Hanna Maria Sobkowicz, Mar. 14, 1972. M.D., Jagiellon U., Cracow, Poland, 1934. Fellow Emperor William Inst. Brain Research, Berlin and German Inst. Brain Research, Neustadt, 1936-38; sr. asst. in neurology and psychiatry Stefan Batory U., Wilno, Poland, 1938-39; research assoc. Henry Phipps Psychiat. Clinic, Johns Hopkins U., 1940-43; asst. prof., assoc. prof. psychiatry and physiology Johns Hopkins U., Balt., 1946-60; prof. neurophysiology U. Wis., Madison, 1960-79, prof. emeritus, 1979-92. Served with M.C. AUS, 1943-46. Mem. NAS, Am. Assn. Anatomists, Am. Physiol. Soc., Internat. Brain Research Orgn. Jewish. Home: Madison Wis. Died June 1, 1992. †

ROSE, WILLIAM, corporate lawyer; b. 1928. BA, Emerson Coll.; LLB, Fordham U. Assoc. Levin, Rosmarin & Schwartz, 1957-65; with Callaway Mills Inc., 1965-68, Indian Head Inc., 1968-74; v.p., gen. counsel Beaunit Corp., 1974-79; with Avnet Inc., N.Y.C., 1979-80, v.p. gen. counsel, from 1980. Home: Great Neck N.Y. Deceased. †

ROSECRANCE, FRANCIS CHASE, education educator; b. Ogle County, Ill., Nov. 8, 1897; s. Frank Edwin and Stella Kate (Chase) R.; m. Marjorie Dell Newton, July 22, 1922; 1 child, Richard Newton. BA, Lawrence Coll., 1920; postgrad., U. Chgo., 1927-28;

PhD, Northwestern U., 1936. High sch. tchr., supr. street trades, dir. life advisement Milw. Pub. Schs., 1920-34; instr., then assoc. prof., prof. edn. Northwestern U., Evanston, Ill., 1934-46; assoc. dean Sch. Edn., prof. NYU, N.Y.C., 1946-56, dir. Ctr. Community and Field Svcs., 1950-54; dean Coll. Edn., prof. Wayne State U., Detroit, 1956-64; disting. prof. edn. Fla. Atlantic U., Boca Raton, from 1964; cons. U.S. Office Edn., 1937, W.K. Kellogg Found., 1937, Commn. Tchr. Edn., 1940-42, War Dept., 1943; vice chmn., chmn. Nat. Com. on The People Act, 1950-53; mem. adv. com. on colls. and bd. Christian Edn. United Presbyn. Ch. U.S.A., 1950-53; chmn. adv. coun. Presbyn. Synod of N.C., 1953-56; chmn. study commn. Presbyn. Synod Va., 1954-56;; chmn. adv. com. Presbyn. Synod of Mo., 1960-62. Author: (with others) General Education in the American High School, 1942, Creating an Industrial Citilization, 1952, Your and Your Community, 1954, Our Community; author: The American College and Its Teachers, 1962, (with V. Hayden) School Guidance and Personnel Services, 1960. Dir. Am. com. project Fund for Adult Edn., Ford Found., 1953-56; trustee Alma Coll., 1962-64; bd. visitors Davidson Coll. Mem. AAUP, NEA (commn. profl. rights and responsibilities 1957-63), Soc. for Advancement Edn., Am. Assn. Sch. Adminstrs., Mich. Assn. Sch. Adminstrs., Holland Soc., Nat. Planning Assn., Masons, Phi Beta Kappa, Phi Delta Kappa, Tau Kappa Alpha, Sigma Phi Epsilon. *

ROSECRANCE, RALPH CLAYTON, manufacturing company executive; b. Monroe Center, Ill., Apr. 17, 1893; s. Frank Edwin and Stella Kate (Chase) R.; m. Winifred LeRoy Smith, Sept. 11, 1920; children: Robert Bruce, Marjorie Ann Rosecrance Wright. BA, Hillsdale (Mich.) Coll., 1916; LLD, Hillsdale Coll., 1959; postgrad., U. Mich., 1917. Various positions to dir. sales and v.p. J.L. Clark Mfg. Co., Rockford, Ill., 1919-52, pres., gen. mgr., 1952-64, chmn. bd., from 1964, also bd. dirs.; bd. dirs. Ill. Nat. Bank & Trust Co., Felsenthal Plastic div. J.L. Clark Mfg. Co. Chmn. Winnebago County chpt. ARC, 1942-49, nat. chmn. conv. com., 1946, hon. life mem. bd. dirs., 1964; bd. dirs. Rockford Jr. Achievement, from 1959; mem. Rockford Hosp. Commn., 1945-53; trustee J.L. Clark Mfg. Co. Found.; chmn. Rockford Adv. Com., pres., from 1958; chmn. can industry Multiple Sclerosis Hope Chest DrIve, 1961; chmn. bd. trustees Hillsdale Coll.; vice chmn. bd. trustees Rockford coll.; trustee Rockford Symphony Orch. Assn., pres., 1962. Sgt. maj. U.S. Army, 1917-18. Mem. Can Mfrs. Inst. (nat. pres. 1949-50, 63-64), Ill. C. of C. (bd. dirs., v.p. 1952-58, mem. spl. bd. com. on r.r. transp. 1958), Rotarian (pres. 1949-50). Congregationalist (past trustee). *

ROSEN, LEO, lawyer; b. Kaunas, Lithuania, Nov. 25, 1906; came to U.S., 1909, naturalized, 1915; s. Paul and Lina (Tubin) R.; m. Lucille Grullow, June 24, 1931; children: Elizabeth, Michael, Charles. A.B. cum laude, Washington U., St. Louis, 1926; LL.B. cum laude, Yale U., 1929. Bar: N.Y. 1931. Practiced in N.Y.C., from 1931; with firm Greenbaum, Wolff & Ernst, 1936-82, ptnr., 1945-82; of counsel Wolf, Haldenstein, Adlen, Freeman & Herz, 1982-89; Mem. N.Y.C. advisory council State Commn. on Human Rights, 1951-71; chmn. law com. Am. Ethical Union, 1956-76. Trustee, v.p. Hudson Guild; bd. dirs., v.p. Brotherhood in Action; bd. dirs. Riverdale Neighborhood House. Mem. Am., N.Y. State bar assns., N.Y. County Lawyers Assn., Assn. Bar City N.Y. (admissions, arbitration, corp. law coms.), Phi Beta Kappa, Order of Coif. Home: New York N.Y. Died June 21, 1989; cremated.

ROSEN, MORTIMER GILBERT, obstetrics and gynecology educator; b. Bklyn., Dec. 31, 1931; m. Lynn Schwartz, Mar. 31, 1955; children: Robert, Brad. BS, U. Wis., 1951; MD, NYU, 1955. Diplomate Am. Bd. Ob-Gyn. (examiner, mem. bd./examiner div. maternal-fetal medicine), Nat. Bd. Medical Examiners. Intern in medicine and surgery Bellevue Hosp., NYU Med. Sch., 1955-56, asst. resident ob-gyn., 1956-57; asst. resident ob-gyn. The Genesee Hosp. U. Rochester, 1959-60, assoc. resident ob-gyn., 1960-61, chief resident, 1961-62; from instr. to sr. instr. ob-gyn. U. Rochester Sch. Medicine and Dentistry, 1962-65, asst. prof., 1965-68, assoc. prof., dir. rsch., 1968-73; prof. reproductive biology Case Western Res. U. Sch. Medicine, 1973-85, dir. perinatal rsch. unit Clin. Rsch. Ctr. NIH, 1973-81, 83-85; Willard C. Rappleye prof. ob-gyn., chmn. dept. Columbia U. Coll. Physicians and Surgeons, from 1985; dir. obstet. and gynecol. svc. Presbyn. Hosp. in City of N.Y., from 1985; dir. dept. ob-gyn., dir. Maternity and Infant Care Project, Cleve. Met. Gen. Hosp., 1973-85; mem. ad hoc com. sci. evaluation br. Nat. Inst. Neurol. and Communicative Disorders and Stroke NIH, Gen. Clin. Rsch. Ctrs. br. NIH; dir.-at-large Assn. Program Dirs. Gen. Clin. Rsch. Ctr.; chmn. mental retardation rsch. com. Nat. Inst. Child Health and Human Devel., mem. consensus panel on fetal monitoring, panel on prenatal and perinatal factors associated with brain disorders, chmn. consensus panel on caesarian childbirth; chmn. obstetrics and perinatology forward planning com., mental retardation and devel. disabilities bd., Nat. Inst. Child Health and Human Devel./NIH; chmn. prenatal care panel Nat. Inst. Child Health and Human Devel./PHS, 1987-89. Contbr. numerous articles to profl. jours.; editor Obstetrics and Gynecology; mem. editorial bd. Jour. Perinatal Medicine; cons. Am. Jour. Diseases Children, Am. Jour. Ob-Gyn. Maj. USAF, 1957-59. Recipient Solomon A. Berson Med. Alumni Achievement award NYU Med. Sch., 1983. Fellow N.Y. Obstet. Soc.; mem. AMA, Am. Coll. Obstetricians and Gynecologists, Am. Acad. Pediatrics (com. on fetus and newborn Ohio chpt.), Acad. Medicine of Cleve., N.Y. Acad. Scis., Royal Soc. Medicine, Soc. Neurosci., Soc. for Psychophysiol. Rsch., Perinatal Rsch. Soc., Cen. Assn. Obstetricians and Gynecologists (adv. bd. Design Rsch. Ctr.), Assn. Profs. Ob-Gyn., Cleve. Soc. Obstetricians and Gynecologists (chmn. maternal health com.), Ohio Perinatal Soc., Soc. Perinatal Obstetricians (bd. dirs.). Home: Bronx N.Y. DIed Aug. 27, 1992. †

ROSENBAUM, NATHAN, banker; b. Russia, Aug. 15, 1897; came to U.S., 1903, naturalized, 1907; s. Morris and Anna (Shatz) R.; m. Elizabeth Scher, May 27, 1923; children: Arthur S. and J. Paul (twins). Student, Temple U., 1916-18. Mem. staff Phila. Inquirer and Evening Ledger, 1917-24; mortgage broker, 1924-29; pres. Colonial Trust Co., Wilmington, Del., 1930-31; head Rosenbaum & Co., comml. bankers, Phila., from 1932. Author: Songs and Symphonies, 1919, Each in His Time, 1925, My Hand and Seal, 1947, A Man from Parnassus, 1951, Create the World, 1956. Mem. Am. Poetry League, Zionist Orgn. Am., Phila. Bd. Realtors, Poetry Soc. Am., Temple U. Mid-Town Club, B'nai B'rith. *

ROSENBERG, GEORGE, hospital administrator; b. N.Y.C., Sept. 2, 1896; s. Maxwell and Lena (Silberman) R.; m. Clara Vogel, Nov. 4, 1928; children: David, Judith Rosenberg Bernstein. Student, NYU, 1919-21; MD, Boston U., 1925; postgrad., Allgemeine Krankenhaus, Vienna, Austria, 1928. Diplomate Am. Bd. Psychiatry and Neurology. Intern Binghamton (N.Y.) Hosp., 1926-27, Bayonne (N.J.) Gen. Hosp., 1927-28; pvt. practice, N.Y.C., 1928-41; med. officer VA Hosp., Alexandria, Va., 1942-44; chief acute svc. VA Hosp., Murfreesboro, Tenn., 1944-51; chief staff VA Hosp., Montrose, N.Y., 1956-61; chief acute svc. VA Hosp., Canandaigua, N.Y., 1952-56; dir. VA Hosp., Jefferson Barracks, Mo., 1961-63; area chief psychiatry VA, St. Louis, 1963; dir. VA Hosp., Lyons, N.J., from 1963; instr. Vanderbilt U., Nashville, 1944-51, Cornell U., 1956-61, Washington U., St. Louis, 1961-63; lectr. Willard (N.Y.) State Hosp., 1952-53 clin. prof. psychiatry N.Y. Med. Coll., Flower and Fifth Avenue Hosp., N.Y.C., from 1963. Contbr. articles to med. jours. Fellow Am. Psychiat. Assn., Am. Geriatric Soc.; mem. AMA, Cen. EEG Soc., Am. Psychotherapeutic Soc., Am. Hosp. Assn., Masons (32d degree). *

ROSENBLATT, LEONARD, chemical company executive; b. N.Y.C., Oct. 20, 1929. BBA, CCNY, 1953; grad. Advanced Mgmt. Program, Harvard U., 1973. Gen. mgr. div. Witco Chem., N.Y.C., 1949-63; various positions including exec. v.p. constn. products div. W.R. Grace & Co., Mass., 1963-81; pres., chief exec. officer Ausimont Compo NV, Waltham, Mass., 1981-89, also bd. dirs. Bd. dirs. The League Sch. of Boston; trustee Outwardbound; adv. bd. Suffolk U., Fla. Govs. Council of 100. Served to sgt. USAF, 1947-49. Home: Boston Mass. Died July 19, 1990.

ROSENQUIT, BERNARD, artist; b. Hotin, Romania, Dec. 26, 1923; s. Eli and Ida (Schotkin) R. Student (Monitor scholar), Art Students League, N.Y.C., 1947-50; student (Mrs. John D. Rockefeller III scholar), Atelier 17, N.Y.C., 1955-56; student (Fulbright grantee), Fotainbleau Sch. Fine Arts, France, 1947; student (Monitor scholar), Bklyn. Mus. Sch. Fine Arts, 1955-56, Inst. Art and Archaeology, Paris, 1958-59. Instr. painting and drawing Five Towns Music and Art Found., N.Y.C. and Cedarhurst, N.Y., Bronx House Community Ctr., 1961-62, Riverdale (N.Y.) Neighborhood and Lit. Assn., also Fieldston Sch. Arts Center, 1962-64. Artist woodcuts and oil painting; one-man exhbns. include Roko Gallery, N.Y.C., 1951-71; group exhbns. include Honolulu Acad. Fine Arts, Boston Mus. Fine Arts, Bklyn. Mus. Fine Arts, Newark Mus. Art, Toronto Mus. Fine Arts, Oakland (Calif.) Art Mus., U.S. Nat. Mus., Washington, Seattle Mus. Fine Arts, Mus. Modern Art, N.Y.C., New Sch. Social Research, U. So. Ill., others; represented in permanent collections Met. Mus. Art, Bklyn. Mus. Fine Arts, Victoria and Albert Mus., London, Smithsonian Instn., Bryn Mawr Coll., U. Kans. Mus., Dallas Art Assn., Long Beach (N.Y.) Pub. Library, Peabody Coll. Mus., N.Y. Pub. Library, San Diego Mus. of Art; works reproduced book rev. sect. N.Y. Times. Grantee Louis Comfort Tiffany Found., 1959. Mem. Artists Equity Assn., Art Students League., Phila. Print Club. Home: New York N.Y. Died Mar. 8, 1991.

ROSENSTEIN, CLAUDE HOUSTON, lawyer; b. Gonzales, Tex., Aug. 31, 1893; s. Robert Edward and Mary Effie (Gould) R.; m. Helen S. Fist, Jan. 31, 1916; children: Robert H., Mary Helen Rosenstein Zeligson, Daniel L. LLB, U. Okla., 1913. Bar: Okla. 1913. Practiced in Tulsa, from 1915; mem. Rosenstein, Mesirow & Fist; atty. Tulsa Bd. Edn.; pres., bd. dirs. Oil Producing, Inc., 15th & Frisco Bldg. Co.; chmn. bd. Crane Carrier Industries, Inc. Bd. dirs. YMCA, Tulsa, 1935-54. Fellow Am. Coll. Trial Lawyers; mem. ABA, Okla. Bar Assn., Tulsa County Bar Assn. (past pres.), Petroleum Club Tulsa, Meadowbrook Country Club, Masons (33d degree), Order of Coif, Phi Delta Phi. *

ROSLER, LEE, publishing company executive; b. N.Y.C., Nov. 2, 1923; s. Julius and Ethel (Agid) R.; m. Elaine Rhodes, Sept. 20, 1945; children: David, Michael, Donald. BSS, CCNY, 1948. Sales promotion specialist Prudential Ins. Co. Inc., 1952-55; cons. advt. and promotion, 1955-58; successively dir. publs., v.p., pres. Farnsworth Pub. Co. Inc., Rockville Centre, N.Y., 1958-88; pres. Narwood Assoc., from 1988; direct mail cons. to advt. agys. Author: Opportunities in Life Insurance Selling; contbr. numerous articles on direct mail and promotion to profl. jours. With USAAF, 1942-45. Mem. L.I. Direct Marketers Assn. Home: Massapequa N.Y. Deceased. †

ROSS, ALEXANDER, artist; b. Dunfermline, Scotland, Oct. 28, 1908; came to U.S., 1912, naturalized, 1921; s. James and Elizabeth (Anderson) R.; m. Helen R. Connelly, June 30, 1932; children: Robert Alexander, Arlene, Wendy, Alan. Student, Carnegie Tech., 1930-32; M.A. (hon.), Boston Coll., 1953. Co-juror 11th Ann. Western Fedn. Watercolor, Houston, 1986. Profl. artist, Pitts., 1934-40, advt. artist, N.Y.C., 1940-42, editorial artist, 1942-65, portrait commns., from 1958; painter mag. covers monthly Good Housekeeping, 1941-54; dir. creative painting seminar, Cath. U. Workshop, 1954; illustrator mags.; book Rifle and Plow (50 books of year award), Saints: Adventures in Courage, 1963, Fr. Gilbert's Book of Prayer; others; one-man shows, Eric Gallery, N.Y.C., 1973, Carlson Gallery of U. Bridgeport, 1974, Demers Gallery, Hilton Head, S.C., 1972-73, 74, 76, 77, Tenn. Fine Arts Gallery, Nashville, 1974, Thompson Gallery, Phoenix, 1975, Palm Beach (Fla.) Galleries, 1976, Naples (Fla.) Art Gallery, 1978-79, others; represented in permanent collections USAF Acad., represented, USAF Hist. Soc.; also pvt. collections.; contbr. articles to various publs., nat. mags.; narrator film New Directions in Watercolor. Recipient 1st prize water color New Canaan Outdoor Show, 1964; award Excellence Soc. Illustrators Show, 1964; Dixie prize Conn. Watercolor Soc., 1964, 71; Ranger Fund Purchase award, 1964; Alexander Crane award, 1965; Sage Allen award, 1967; Adolf and Clara Obrig award NAD, 1972, 80; Merit award NAD, 1973; Walter Biggs Meml. award Nat. Acad., 1975. Mem. NAD (assoc.), Silvermine Art Guild, Am. Water Color Soc. (Ford Times award 1973, 76, Marthe T. McKinnon award 1974, Lena Newcastle award 1982). Home: Ridgefield Conn. Deceased. †

ROSS, DAVID WILLIAM, II, public relations executive; b. Manhasset, N.Y., Sept. 16; s. David William and Agnes Davis (Stokes) R.; m. Joan Rodgers, Feb. 22, 1958 (dec. Aug. 1984); children: David William III, Tracy Elizabeth, Hilary Chipmen. B.S., Syracuse U., 1956; postgrad., Hofstra U., 1957. Mgr. publicity Allied Corp., N.Y.C., 1958-62; dir. communications Combustion Engring. Corp., N.Y.C., 1962-66, Singer Co., N.Y.C., 1966-70, Wheelabrator-Frye, N.Y.C., 1970-73, Gen. Instrument, N.Y.C., 1973-75; exec. v.p. Baron/Canning & Co., Inc., N.Y.C., 1975-87; v.p. A.L. Williams Corp., Duluth, Ga., from 1987; faculty Parson's Sch. Design, N.Y.C., 1982-83; dir. Adams & Amundsen, Inc., Cleve. Served with USAF, 1950-54, ETO. Home: Duluth Ga. Deceased. †

ROSS, HAROLD TRUSLOW, speech educator; b. Rochester, Ind., Oct. 27, 1895; s. Omer Tyra and Adelaide (Truslow) R.; m. Rosella Stoner, June 29, 1921; children: John Stoner, Patricia Jean. AB, DePauw U., 1918; postgrad., U. Liverpool, Eng., 1919; AM, Columbia U., 1924; PhD, State U. Iowa, 1932. Head English dept. Elkhart (Ind.) High Sch., 1920-23; English master Cutler Sch., N.Y.C., 1923-24; instr. Iowa State U., 1924-27; instr., asst. prof., assoc. prof. speech DePauw U., 1927-36, prof., head dept., dir. Little Theater, 1936-60, prof. emeritus, from 1960, dir. radio studio, 1945-60, asst. dean univ., 1964-65, dir. grad. studies, from 1964; vis. prof. U. Denver, summers 1939-48, 50. Author: (with C.C. Shoemaker) Speech in a Democracy, 1942, (with D. Gooch) Manual for Radio, (with O.M. Peterson and A.W. Shumaker) Basic Principles of Communication, 1953; editor The Footlight, 1925-29, Ind. Speech News, 1931-39; contbr. to History and Criticism of American Address, 1942, Ency. Americana, 1954, American Public Address, 1961; also articles on Am. oratory. Mem. State Supt.'s Com. on Ednl. TV, 1958-62. Sgt. U.S. Army, World War I, AEF. Mem. AAUP, Assn. Coll. Honor Soc. (coun. 1955-63, exec. com. 1959-60), Speech Assn. Am. (chmn. com. on nomenclature in discussion 1938-40), Ind. TV Coun. (chmn. 1953-56), Cen. States Speech Assn. (bd. dirs. 1948-49), Ind. Speech Assn. (bd. dirs. 1932-42, pres. 1948-49, 57-58), Ind. Coll. Speech Conf. (chmn. 1948-49), Nat. Assn. Study Comm., DePauw U. Alumni Assn. (nat. v.p. 1955-58), Nat. Collegiate Players, Masons, Kiwanis, Delta Sigma Rho (pres. 1958-63), Sigma Upsilon, Sigma Nu. Republican. Methodist. *

ROSS, JAMES BRENT, publishing company executive; b. Williamstown, W.Va., June 12, 1925; s. Claget Howard and Hazel (Bailey) R.; m. Alma Eugenia Lowe, Dec. 26, 1947; children—Anna Elizabeth, William Brent. A.B., W.Va. U., 1949; M.S., U. Pitts., 1950. Editor W.B. Saunders Co., Phila., 1951-57; mgr. coll. textbook dept. Reinhold Pub. Corp., N.Y.C., 1957-62, gen. mgr. book div., 1962-67, v.p., 1965-68; pub., dir. Chapman-Reinhold Book Corp., 1968; exec. v.p., pub.

Pergamon Press, Inc.; pres. Pergamon Pub. Co., N.Y.C., 1968-69, Hutchinson Ross Pub. Co. (formerly Dowden, Hutchinson & Ross, Inc.), Stroudsburg, Pa., from 1970; owner James B. Ross & Assos. (pub. cons.), 1969-89. Trustee, Open Space Inst., Inc., N.Y.C., 1966-72, pres., 1968-70, chmn., 1970-72; bd. govs. Nature Conservancy, Inc., 1952-65, pres., 1958-60, gov. emeritus, 1978-89, trustee Eastern Pa. chpt., 1976-89. Served with USNR, 1943-46. Recipient Green Leaf Conservation award Nature Conservancy, 1960. Fellow AAAS; mem. Am. Inst. Biol. Sci. (bd. govs. 1966-71, bd. mem.-at-large 1973-77), Ecol. Soc. Am., Am. Chem. Soc. (life), Am. Ornithologists Union, Sigma Xi. Clubs: Mason (32 deg., Shriner), Elk, Torch. Home: Stroudsburg Pa. Died Sept. 3, 1989; cremated.

ROSS, JOHN RAYMOND, architect; b. Mpls., Mar. 27, 1923; s. Christian and Pearl (Le Bresh) R.; m. Elizabeth Conroy, Jan. 13, 1968; children—John T., Scott A., Dennis F., Michael E., Timothy J. B.Arch., U. So. Calif., 1949. Prin. John R. Ross & Assos. (Architect), San Jose, Calif., 1956; partner Holdredge & Ross Architects, San Luis Obispo, Calif., 1956-57; prin. John R. Ross & Assocs. (Architects), San Luis Obispo, 1956-60, John R. Ross & Assocs., Inc., 1960-65; partner Ross & Levin Architects, 1965-75; prin. Ross Levin Macintyre (Architects), San Luis Obispo, 1975-87; pvt. cons. architect San Luis Obispo, 1987-90; dir., sec. Swift Aire Lines, Inc., San Luis Obispo; lectr. Calif. Poly. State U., 1956-66; mem. Calif. Bd. Archtl. Examiners, 1968-76, pres., 1970-71; dir. Nat. Council Archtl. Registration Bds., 1972-74, v.p., 1978-79, pres., 1979-80. Chmn. San Luis Obispo County Republican central com., 1968-70; mem. Calif. Rep. central com., 1967-70. Served to lt., inf. U.S. Army, 1942-46, PTO; to capt. C.E. 1950-52, Korea. Fellow AIA; mem. Am. Arbitration Assn. (nat. arbitrator 1970—), Alpha Rho Chi (nat. pres., pres. Alpha Rho Chi Found. 1989-90). Republican. Roman Catholic. Club: Caballeros de San Luis Obispo. Home: Arroyo Grande Calif. Died June 6, 1990; cremated.

ROSS, RANDALL AUSTIN, paper manufacturing company executive; b. Cleve., Feb. 7, 1895; s. Thomas Waller and Mary Sackett (Austin) R.; m. Cornelia Van Dyke Jones, Oct. 5, 1929; children: Harriet Cary, Cornelia Ann. Student, Williams Coll., 1918. Purchasing agt., sales mgr., v.p., gen. sales mgr. Cornell Paperbd. Products Co. div. St. Regis Paper Co., Milw., 1920-55, sr. v.p., 1955-62. Bd. dirs. Chgo. Symphony Assn. of Milw., YMCA, Columbia Hosp., Milw.; trustee Milw. Downer Sem. Mem. Milw. Club, Milw. Country Club (past bd. dirs., pres.), Milw. Univ. Club (past bd. dirs., pres.), Tavern Club (Chgo.), Williams Club (N.Y.C.). *

ROSS, STANLEY, editor, publisher; b. N.Y.C., Jan. 18, 1914; s. Harry Paul and Bella R.; m. Eleanore Lyle, July 1, 1948 (dec. Feb. 1960); 1 child, Michael Stanley; m. Countess Margarita Theresa Parravicini. Student, CCNY, 1932-36, U. Caracas, Venezuela, 1941-43. Editor The Argus, 1932-34; owner of 9 weeklies under corporate name Stanley Ross Assos., 1936; N.Y. Times corr. Venezuela and other S.Am. countries, 1940-43; pub. relations adviser to Pres. of Venezuela, 1941-43; traveled widely through Latin and S.Am. for U.S. mags., 1940-47; AP and NBC corr. Argentina, 1943-45; organized Latin Am. Press Syndicate (serving 700 Latin Am. papers), 1946; founder, pub., editor El Caribe and El Urgente (daily papers), Dominican Republic, 1947-49; pub., editor The Star, Wilmington, Del., 1948-50; editor N.Y. Amsterdam News, 1951; editor in chief, assoc. pub. El Diario de Nueva York (daily newspaper), 1955-62; editor-in-chief Bklyn. Eagle, 1962-63, La Prensa (daily), 1961-62; editor, pub. El Tiempo, N.Y.C., 1963-69, 73-75, El Mundo, N.Y.C., 1969-71; also editor in chief L.I. (N.Y.) Post; internat. editor ABC of the Americas and, Madrid; cons. on Latin Am. Affairs Dept. Justice; lectr. Latin Am. affairs, throughout U.S., 1948. Author semi-weekly articles appearing in 245 Latin Am. papers.; Author: Communism in Latin America, 1947, The War for Trade in Latin America, 1947, Axel Wenner-Gren, The Sphinx of Sweden, 1948. Decorated comdr. Order Ruben Dario (Nicaragua). Mem. Assn. de Escritores Americanos (1st U.S. citizen elected pres. 1946, 47), Nat. Soc. Prevention Juvenile Delinquency (hon. pres.), N.Y. Advt. Club. Republican. Clubs: Masons, Overseas Press. Home: Washington D.C. Died Sept. 20, 1992. †

ROSS, WALTER MARION, banker; b. Oskaloosa, Iowa, Nov. 19, 1903; s. Rufus Cyrus and Anna Pearl (Jones) R.; m. Virginia Cooke McGehee, Nov. 14, 1931; 1 child, Virginia Antoinette Barker Ross; m. Lovene Fisher Strotz. Student, Knox Coll., 1921-23. With Globe Superior Corp., 1923-26, Rollins Hosiery Mills, 1926-28, Gen. Motors Acceptance Corp., N.Y.C., 1928-42; v.p. First Nat. Bank, Louisville, 1946-50; exec. v.p. Chem. Bank, N.Y.C., 1950-68, dir.; mem. exec. and audit coms. ISI Corp., San Francisco. Lt. col. AUS, 1942-46. Decorated Bronze Star; recipient Commendation award OSS, Rumania, 1945. Mem. Greenwich Country Club, Filson Club (Louisville), Thunderbird Country Club (Palm Springs, Calif.), Beta Theta Pi. Home: Indian Wells Calif. Died Nov. 10, 1990.

ROSSER, JOHN BARKLEY, mathematician, rocket ballistician; b. Jacksonville, Fla., Dec. 6, 1907; s. Harwood and Ethel (Merryday) R.; m. Annetta L. Hamilton, Sept. 7, 1935; children: Edwenna Merryday, John Barkley. B.S., U. Fla., 1929, M.S., 1931, D.Sc. (hon.), 1970; Ph.D., Princeton U., 1934; D.Sc. (hon.), Otterbein Coll., 1971. Procter research fellow Princeton U., 1933-35, lectr., 1939-40; NRC fellow Harvard U., 1935-36; instr. math. Cornell U., 1936-39, asst. prof., 1939-40, assoc. prof., 1940-43, prof., 1943-63, chmn. dept., 1961-62; prof. math. and computer scis. U. Wis., Madison, 1963-78; dir. Math. Research Ctr. U. Wis., 1963-73; ballistician Allegany Ballistics Lab., 1944-46; dir. research Inst. Numerical Analysis, Nat. Bur. Standards, 1949-50, mem. com. for evaluation, 1953; dir. ART project Army Ordnance, 1951-52; mem. Stewart Com. (monitoring U.S. space satellite), 1955-58; dir. FOCUS project Inst. Def. Analyses, 1959-61, SCAMP project, summers 1962-63; cons. rocket ballistics govt. agys. and industries; pres. CO- OP, 1959-60; chmn. math. div. NRC, 1960-62; chmn. Conf. Bd. Math. Scis., 1963-65. Author: (with R. R. Newton and G. L. Gross) Mathematical Theory of Rocket Flight, 1947, Theory and Application of Various Integrals, 1948, (with A. R. Turquette) Many-Valued Logics, 1952, Logic for Mathematicians, 1953, 2d edit., 1978, Deux Esquisses de Logique, 1955, Simplified Independence Proofs, 1969, (with Carl de Boor) Pocket Calculator Supplement for Calculus, 1979; author research papers math., computers, mil. rocket development. Guggenheim and Fulbright research fellow U. Paris, 1953-54; recipient Presdl. Cert. of Merit, 1948; Dept. Navy commendation, 1960; Distinguished Civilian award Dept. Army, 1974. Mem. Am. Acad. Arts and Scis., Soc. Indsl. and Applied Math (pres. 1964-66), Am. Math. Soc. (council 1948-51), Math. Assn. Am., Assn. Symbolic Logic (exec. com. 1935-37, 41-44, pres. 1950-53), Assn. Computing Machinery (council 1954-56), Sigma Xi, Phi Kappa Phi. Presbyterian. Clubs: Madison; Cosmos (Washington). Home: Madison Wis. Deceased. †

ROSSETTI, LOUIS, architect; b. Paris, May 6, 1895; s. Noel and Adele (Voetter) R.; m. Anita Castellucci, May 5, 1926; children: Dorothea, Carl, Louis A., Angela. Grad. in archtl. engring., Engring. Coll., Rome, 1920, D Engring., 1922. Registered architect, Mich., also 32 other states; registered Nat. Coun. Archtl. Registration Bds. With Giffels & Rossetti, architects and engrs., Detroit, 1928-57, ptnr., from 1957. Prin. works include Terminal Bldg. at Detroit Met. Airport, IBM Airborne Computer Plant, Owego, N.Y., North Campus Labs., U. Mich., U.S. Post Office, Detroit, GE Electronics Park, Syracuse, N.Y., ITT Microwave Tower and Labs., Nutley, N.J., Conv. Exhibit Bldg., Detroit. Mem. Mich. Cultural Commn. Traveling scholar, U.S., 1924. Fellow AIA (chmn. com. on edn., civic design Detroit chpt., nat. and chpt. honor awards); mem. Mich. Soc. Architects. *

ROSSITER, FRANK RAYMOND, historian; b. Abington, Pa., Dec. 21, 1937; s. Frank Augustus and Dorothy Anna (Weiss) R. A.B., Harvard U., 1959; M.S. in Edn, U. Pa., 1964; Ph.D., Princeton U., 1970. Tchr. social studies Springfield Twp. Sr. High Sch., Montgomery County, Pa., 1963-66; asst. prof. history U. Mich., Ann Arbor, 1970-75; asso. prof. history and Am. studies U. Tex., Dallas, 1975-89. Author: Charles Ives and His America, 1975. Served with USN, 1959-62. Woodrow Wilson fellow, 1966-67; Nat. Endowment for the Humanities fellow, 1973-74, 79, 85; ASCAP-Deems Taylor award, 1976. Mem. Am. Hist. Assn., Orgn. Am. Historians, Am. Studies Assn. Democrat. Home: Dallas Tex. Died Jan. 15, 1989; buried Montgomery County, Pa.

ROTH, GEORGE FREDERIC, JR., architect, architectural historian, consultant; b. Covington, Ky., Jan. 18, 1905; s. George Frederic and Matilda (Tieke) R.; m. Ruth Irene Marley, Dec. 22, 1937; 1 son, George Frederic III. B.S. in Architecture, U. Cin., 1927, M.S., 1929. Sole practice architecture Cin., 1931-89; adj. prof. U. Cin., 1929-65; lectr. and writer. Chmn. zoning and planning City of Lakeside Park, Ky., 1959-62; chmn. Cin. Archtl. Rev. Bd., 1972-77; v.p. Miami Purchase Assn., 1968-81; mem. Covington Bd. Edn., Ky., 1941-52; dir. No. Ky. U. Found. Recipient Gold medal Architects Soc., Ohio, 1982; named hon. Ky. Col. Fellow AIA (pres. Cin. chpt. 1939-41); mem. Archtl. Found. Cin. (bd. dirs.), Cin. Engring. Soc. Republican. Episcopalian. Club: Filson (Louisville). Lodges: Masons; Shriners. Home: Pittsburgh Pa. Died Oct. 22, 1989.

ROTH, PHILIP A., manufacturing company executive; b. N.Y.C., 1896. Student, Columbia U., 1917. Exec. v.p., treas., bd. dirs., mem. exec. com. Gen. Indsl. Enterprises; pres. Ramco Enterprises, Inc. (formerly S. Stroock & Co.)ú; vice chmn., bd. dirs. Loew's Inc.; vice chmn., trustee Title Guarantee Co.; bd. dirs. Trade Bank & Trust Co., Collins & Aikman Corp., F.H. McGraw & Co., Best & Co., Inc. *

ROTHMAN, FRED BERNARD, publishing company executive; b. N.Y.C., Sept. 25, 1908; s. Benjamin and Yetta (Blumenfeld) R.; m. Dorothy Regosin, Feb. 21, 1935; 1 son, Paul A. B.S., NYU, 1928, LL.B., 1929, M.Ed., 1933; B.L.S., Columbia U., 1936. Library asst. NYU, 1926-38; law librarian NYU Sch. Law, 1939-45; pres. Fred B. Rothman & Co., Littleton, Colo., 1945-85. Contbr. articles to profl. jours. Mem. Bibliog. Soc. Am., Am. Assn. Law Libraries. Jewish. Home: Littleton Colo. Died Apr. 23, 1988; buried Wellwood Cemetery, Pine Lawn, N.Y.

ROTHSCHILD, V(ICTOR) HENRY, II, lawyer; b. N.Y.C., Apr. 4, 1908; s. Victor Sidney and Lily (Sulzberger) R.; m. Ann Eleanor Hatfield, May 29, 1939 (div.); children: Thomas Adams, V. Henry III; 1 stepchild, Cameron; m. Jacqueline Dury Roy; stepchildren: Michel, Serge, Christian Roy. A.B. with honors, Cornell U., 1929; LL.B. with honors, Yale U., 1932. Bar: N.Y. 1934. Since practiced in N.Y.C.; assoc. Root, Clark, Buckner & Ballantine (now Dewey, Ballantine, Bushby, Palmer & Wood), N.Y.C., 1932-40; mem. Rothschild & Salwen, N.Y.C., 1955-81; counsel Lord Day & Lord, Barrett Smith, N.Y.C., from 1981; mem. Salary Stblzn. Bd., 1951-52, chief counsel, 1951, vice chmn., 1952; lectr. Practising Law Inst., NYU Inst. Fed. Taxation. Author: (with William J. Casey) Pay Contracts with Key Men, 1952; (with J.K. Lasser) Deferred Compensation for Executives, 1955, Compensating the Corporate Executive, 1962; (with George Thomas Washington), 3d edit., 1962; (with Myer Feldman) Executive Compensation and Federal Securities Legislation, 1957, Financing Stock Purchases, 1957, Expense Accounts for Executives, 1958, Business Gifts as Income, 1961, The New Stock Option, 1965, Top Management Compensation Outlook, 1966, The Restricted Stock Arrangement, 1968; (with Peter Miller) Employee Stock Options and the New Maximum Tax Rate on Earned Income, 1971, Stock Option Plans in France, 1972; (with Jack B. Salwen) Stock Option Plans in Transition, 1973, Regulation of Deferred Compensation for Executives by the Pension Reform Act, 1975, Funding Deferred Compensation Arrangements, 1976; (with Robert J. Salwen) Protecting the Executive against Inflation, 1980; (with Arthur D. Sporn) Executive Compensation, 1984, 2d edit.; contbg. author: Executive Compensation, a Road Map for the Corporate Advisor, 1984; contbr. articles to legal and non-legal publs.; editor: Yale Law Sch. Jour., 1930-32. Hon. trustee Asso. YM-YWCA Greater N.Y. Mem. ABA (mem. sect. corp., banking and bus., com. on employee benefits, tax), N.Y. State Bar Assn. (chmn. com. on employee benefits 1968-70, chmn. com. retirement plan 1971-76), N.Y.C. Bar Assn., Am. Pension Conf. (steering com. 1966-70), Phi Beta Kappa, Phi Kappa Phi, Pi Lambda Phi. Clubs: Sky (N.Y.C.), Yale (N.Y.C.). Home: New York N.Y. Deceased. †

ROTKO, BERNARD BENJAMIN, physician, hospital executive; b. Rovno, Poland, May 23, 1908; came to U.S., 1921, naturalized, 1925; s. Benjamin and Rose (Tabachnick) R.; m. Bessie Goldberg, Sept. 4, 1933; children: Michel, Judith. B.S., Villanova Coll., 1931; M.D., Jefferson Med. Coll., 1935. Intern St. Josephs Hosp., Phila., 1936-37; practice medicine specializing in internal medicine Phila., 1937-83; med. dir. Rolling Hill Hosp., Elkins Park, Pa., 1953-80, pres., 1953-80, exec. dir., 1980-83; chmn. bd. R.H. Med. Services, 1969-80, Mediq, Inc., from 1980. Mem. Cheltenham Twp. Bd. Health, Pa., 1959-83. Served to lt. comdr. War Shipping Adminstrn. USN, 1943-46. Mem. AMA, Pa. Med. Soc., Philadelphia County Med. Soc. Home: Pennsauken N.J.

ROUDEBUSH, GEORGE M., lawyer; b. Newtonsville, Ohio, Jan. 25, 1894; s. George Milton and Rosalind (Patchell) R.; m. Harriett McCann, June 28, 1924; children: George Milton, Jane Roudebush Daganhardt, Thomas M. A.B., Denison U., 1915; LL.B., U. Cin., 1917. Bar: Ohio 1917. Practice in Cleve., 1919-92; partner firm Roudebush, Brown, Corlett & Ulrich (and predecessors, merged with Arter & Hadden in 1986), 1919-92; dir. corps. Trustee Denison U., from 1940, chmn. fin. com., 1940-73. Served to capt., inf. U.S. Army, 1917-19; served to capt., inf. AEF, in France. Named to Athletic Hall of Fame Denison U., 1975; recipient alumni citation. Mem. Am., Ohio, Cleve. bar assns., Cleve. C. of C. (chmn. fin. com., mem. 100 year club), SAR, Beta Theta Pi. Baptist. Clubs: Cleve. Athletic, Mayfield Country, Midday. Home: Cleveland Ohio Died Feb., 1992. †

ROUSSO, ELI L., clothing company executive; b. N.Y.C., Nov. 3, 1920; s. Louis E. and Dora (Cohen) R.; m. Julia Saporta, Nov. 15, 1941; children: Doris (Mrs. Albert Taxin), Louis, Susan (Mrs. Edward Tawil). Student, Fashion Inst. Tech., N.Y.C., 1946, Chic's Sch. Pattern Making, N.Y.C., 1947. Founder, 1946; since pres. Russ Togs, Inc., N.Y.C. Active Anti-Defamation League, Hebrew U., Jerusalem, Five Towns Community Chest; hon. chmn. bd. overseers Albert Einstein Coll. Medicine; past chmn. bd. Sephardic Home for Aged; founder Sephardic Temple, Cedarhurst; pres. Prime Ministers' Club State of Israel Bonds; bd. dirs. Hebrew U., Yeshiva U., Misgav Ladach Hosp. Served with USNR, 1942-45. Named Ky. col., 1964. Clubs: Friars (N.Y.C.); High Ridge Country (West Palm Beach, Fla.); Seawane Country (Hewlett Harbor, N.Y.); Masons. Home: Hewlett N.Y. Deceased. †

ROUTH, JOSEPH P., business executive; b. N.Y.C., 1893. Student, Cornell U., 1917. Chmn. bd., CEO, Pittston Co.; chmn. bd., bd. dirs. U.S. Trucking Corp., Sheridan-Wyo. Coal Co., Inc., Baker and Willaims; bd. dirs. Pittston Clinchfield Coal Sales Corp., Amigo Smokeless Coal Co., Raleigh S.S. Agy., Inc., Brink's, Inc. *

ROVE, OLAF N(ORBERG), geologist; b. Milw., Feb. 11, 1898; s. Olaf and Emma (Norberg) R.; m. Dorothy Haessler, Sept. 6, 1925 (div. 1937); m. Elin S. Phinney, Dec. 18, 1939; stepchildren: Eric, Stephen, Alan, Frank. BS, U. Wis., 1922, MS, 1925; postgrad., U. Oslo, 1923-24; PhD, M IT, 1939. Mine geologist Phelps Dodge Corp., Ariz., 1926-29; resident geologist Empire Zinc Co., N.Mex., 1929-31; geologist N.J. Zinc Co., 1931-35; teaching fellow MIT, Cambridge, 1935-38; assoc. geologist Nfld (Can.) Geol. Survey, 1939; mining engr. U.S. Bur. Mines, Washington, 1940; geologist U.S. Smelting, Refining and Mining Co., Boston, 1940-42; chief manganese and chrome ore sect. WPB, Washington, 1942-44, cons. geologist, 1944-46; geologist U.S. Geol. Wurvey, 1946, chief mineral deposits br., 1947-53, acting asst. chief geologist, 1953-54; geologist mineral exploration ore div. Union Carbide Corp., 1954, chief geologist, 1956-63; cons. mining geologist, N.Y.C., from 1963. Fellow Geol. Soc. Am.; mem. IAME, Soc. Econ. Geologists (pres. 1962), Cosmos Club (Washington). *

ROWAN, PELHAM AGEE, corporate executive; b. Anniston, Ala., Dec. 27, 1931; s. Peyton and Caroline (Agee) R.; m. Charlotte Ann Davis, May 3, 1978; children: David, Sherry Mills, Pelhan Agee Jr. BS, U. Ala.; postgrad., LaSalle Extension U. Sr. v.p. fin., treas., sec., bd. dirs. Motion Industries, Inc., Birmingham, Ala., until 1983. With USAAF, 1954-57. Mem. Rotary. Episcopalian. Home: Birmingham Ala. Died July 2, 1983; buried Forest Crest Cemetery, Birmingham, Ala.

ROWE, DONALD EDWARD, transportation executive; b. St. Petersburg, Fla., Feb. 17, 1929; s. George Welsh and Eleanor (Barsantee) R.; m. Marjorie Bidwell, Mar. 6, 1954; children: Richard, Sandra, David. Student, Joplin Bus. Coll., 1948-49. Founder Imperial Internat. Inc., Corte Madera, Calif., from 1953, chmn., pres., 1953-85; founder Rowe & Co. Info. Services Internat., Hammond, La., from 1987, United Nat. Internat. Lines, Inc., Yokohama, Japan, from 1987; chmn., pres. subs. Thru-Container Services GmbH, Bremerhaven, Fed. Republic Germany, subs. Thru-Container Internat., Ltd., Hong Kong. Served with U.S. Army, 1945-46; with USAF, 1946-48. Recipient Spl. Recognition, U.S. Ho. of Reps., 1978. Mem. Nat. Defense Transp. Assn. (nat. v.p. 1972-73, Disting. Service award 1979). Republican. Home: Friendswood Tex. Deceased. †

ROWLAND, DONALD WINSLOW, history educator; b. Mariposa, Calif., Jan. 12, 1898; s. Thomas Burdine and Miriam Isabel (Gallison) R.; m. Eunice Wachter; 1 child, Dare Rowland Doolittle. AB, U. Calif., Berkeley, 1925, AM, 1926, PhD, 1931. Teaching asst. U. Calif., 1926-27, 28-29, vis. prof., summer 1935; asst. prof. history U. Hawaii, Honolulu, 1930-35, vis. prof., summer 1941, 55; asst. prof., assoc. prof. U. So. Calif., L.A., 1935-39, prof., from 1939, head dept.., 11938-44, 46-55; vis. prof. U. Oreg., summer 1933, Am. U., fall 1945, U. Mich., summer 1957; sr. polit. analyst, head polit. analysis sect. Office Coord. Inter-Am. Affairs, 1944-46. Author: History of the Office of the Coordinator of Inter-American Affairs, 1949; contbg. author: New Spain and the West, 2 vols., 1932; bd. editors Pacific Hist. Rev., 1951-55; contbr. articles on L.Am., Spain and Hawaii to profl. jours. With F.A., U.S. Army, 1917, AEF, 1918-19. Native Sons Golden West rsch. fellow, Spain, 1927-28. Mem. Am. Hist. Assn., Western Coll. Assn. (joint commn. on improvement tchr. edn. in Calif. 1961-62), Am. Assn. Colls. Tchr. Edn., Conf. L.Am. History, Pacific Coast Conf. L.Am. Studies, Phi Kappa Phi, Phi Alpha Theta. *

ROWLEY, WORTH, lawyer; b. Boston, Aug. 14, 1916; s. Clarence Worth and Catherine Agnes (Foley) R.; m. Jacqueline Magrath, May 4, 1940 (div.); children: Jonathan M., Susannah W., Belinha P., Joshua F.; m. Jane Pedersen, Apr. 1, 1972; children—Clarence Worth III, Eliza Ann. J.D., Northeastern U., 1938. Bar: Mass. 1938, D.C. 1958. Practice law with father Boston, 1938-41; with Antitrust Div., U.S. Dept. Justice, Washington, 1945-58; sole practice Washington, 1958-69; ptnr. Rowley & Watts, Washington, 1969-88. Served as lt. (j.g.) USNR, 1942-45. Mem. ABA, Am. Law Inst., D.C. Bar Assn. Democrat. Unitarian. Clubs: Nat. Press, Internat., University (Washington); Hyannis Port Yacht, West Beach, Hyannis Port (Hyannisport). Home: Washington D.C. Died Aug. 23, 1988; interred Pine Grove Cemetery, South Yarmouth, Mass.

ROYALTY, ROBERT MALCOLM, lawyer; b. Danville, Ill., Jan. 7, 1933; s. Gerald Loren and Virginia Ellen (Davis) R.; m. Patricia Eileen Ruth Clark, July 16, 1954; children: V. Beth Royalty, Robert M., John G. (dec.), Patricia M., Sarah E. B.A., Beloit Coll., 1954; J.D., Harvard U., 1959. Bar: Ill. 1959, Ga. 1962, D.C. 1962. Assoc. Crowell & Leibman, Chgo., 1959-62; ptnr. Sutherland, Asbill & Brennan, Atlanta, from 1968. Mem. nat. bd. trustees Cystic Fibrosis Found., 1982-84, pres. Ga. chpt., 1979-82. Served with U.S. Army, 1954-56. Mem. ABA (mem. council sect. corp., banking and bus. law 1982-86, chmn. state regulation of securities com. 1973-80), Ga. Bar Assn., Atlanta Bar Assn., D.C. Bar Assn., Lawyers Club Atlanta, Cherokee Town and Country Club, Commerce Club, Peachtree Club. Republican. Roman Catholic. Home: Atlanta Ga. Deceased. †

ROYSE, JOHN ANTHONY, lawyer; b. Indpls., Jan. 18, 1898; s. Harry Edgar and Sarah Catherine (O'Brien) R.; m. Gertrude Catherine Hanf, June 22, 1921; 1 child, John Anthony. LLB, Ind. U., 1922. Bar: Ind. 1922. U.S. collector of customs, Ind., 1922-27; practiced in Indpls., from 1927; chmn. bd. Smith-Alsop Paint & Varnish Co.; bd. dirs. Union Mortgage Co.; greeder pure-bred Jersey cattle and Arabian horses. Mem. ABA, Ind. Bar Assn., Indpls. Bar Assn., Internat. Arabian Horse Assn., Am. Jersey Cattle Club, Am. Legion (founder). *

ROZSNYAI, ZOLTAN FRANK, composer, conductor; b. Budapest, Hungary, Jan. 29, 1927; came to U.S., 1961, naturalized, 1967; s. Laszlo Lesly and Francisca (Molnar) R.; 1 dau. from previous marriage, Christine Monica; m. Susan C. Daily, Nov. 29, 1971; children: Susanna Francesca, Dorothy-Katherine. Ed., Franz Liszt Acad. Music; Ph.D. in Music, Pazmany Peter U., 1949; postgrad., U. Vienna, 1959-61. artistic head music div. U.S.Internat. U. Sch. Performing Arts, 1968-71; acoustical expert, cons. concert hall, theater and studio; partner cAc; owner, chief cons. TAc. Concert pianist, 1942-52, organist, 1940-50, music dir., Miskolc Philharmonic Orch., 1949-50, Debrecen Opera, 1950-52, regular condr., Hungarian Nat. Philharmony, 1952-56, founder, 1st music dir., Philharmonia Hungarica, Vienna, 1956-60, music dir., Continental Cinecraft Motion Picture Co., 1961-63, asst. condr., N.Y. Philharmonic Orch., 1962-63, music dir., Cleve. Philharmonic and Utica Symphony Orch., 1963-67, San Diego Symphony Orch., 1967-71, Knoxville Symphony, 1978-85; artistic dir., So. Calif. Philharmonic Soc., San Diego, from 1971; recs. with Columbia, Vox, Qualiton, Direct-to-Disk, others.; founder U.S. Internat. U. Orch., chmn. music dept., 1967-71; composer numerous pieces, orchestrations, transcriptions, film scores. Recipient diploma and prize Internat. Condrs. Competition in Rome, Italy, 1956, Cultural Merit star Hungary, Golden Key of Detroit, Spl. Peace Bell with citation from Willy Brandt, Berlin, citation of recognition City of N.Y. from Mayor Robert Wagner. Home: San Diego Calif. Died Sept. 10, 1990.

RUBENDALL, HOWARD LANE, college president; b. Williamstown, Pa., May 14, 1910; s. Charles Wesley and Charlotte (Rowe) R.; m. Carolyn Dennett, Apr. 3, 1935; children: Linda Rubendall Shanklin, Suzanne Rubendall Lauber. BA, Dickinson Coll., 1931, DD, 1945; MDiv, Union Theol. Sem., 1937; LHD, Trinity Coll., 1957; LLD, U. Pa., 1966, Dickinson Sch. Law, 1966. Ordained to ministry Congl. Ch., 1937. Tchr. Am. U., Cairo, 1931-34, The Hill Sch., Pottstown, Pa., 1937-41; pastor First Presbyn. Ch., Albany, N.Y., 1941-44; headmaster Mt. Hermon (Mass.) Sch. for Boys, 1944-59; pres. Northfield Schs., 1955-61, Dickinson Coll., Carlisle, Pa., 1961-75. Past trustee Harrisburg Acad., Williston Acad.; past pres. Coun. Religion Ind. Schs.; past dir. Mass. Higher Edn. Assistance Corp.; past pres. Ind. Schs. Found. of Mass., Inc.; hon. v.p. Am. Friends of Coll. Cevenol, Inc.; past trustee Dickinson Coll.; past dir. Union Theol. Sem. Mem. Headmasters Assn., Century Assn., Univ. Club (N.Y.C.), Omicron Delta Kappa, Phi Kappa Sigma. Home: Naples Fla. Died Apr. 13, 1991; buried Orleans, Mass.

RUBIN, ABE, college president, podiatrist; b. Winnipeg, Man., Can., Aug. 14, 1911; s. Burrows and Lily R. (Adilman) R.; m. Doris Silvia Miller, July 8, 1949; children: Mark B., Hollis Beth. Student, U. Man., 1928-32; DPM, Ill. Coll. Podiatric Medicine, 1937, EdD, 1967; postgrad., U. Chgo., 1952-55; LittD, Ohio Coll. Podiatry, 1968. Assoc. prof. anatomy Ill. Coll. Podiatric Medicine, 1937-42, dir. clinics, head orthopedic dept., 1947-55; exec. sec. Am. Podiatry Assn., Washington, 1955-62, editor assn. jour., 1955-70; exec. dir. Coun. Podiatric Edn., 1962-70; pvt. practice, 1938-42; v.p., dean Ohio Coll. Podiatric Medicine, Cleve., 1970-71, pres., 1971-85, pres. emeritus, 1985-90; cons. N1H, Nat. Acad. Scis., Inst. of Medicine, others. Contbr. articles med. jours. encys.; co-editor: The Podiatry Curriculum; mem. editorial adv. bd.: Jour. Am. Podiatry Assn. Capt. USAAF, 1942-46. Recipient Gold award Wm. J. Stickel Ann. awards rsch. podiatry, 1954. Fellow Am. Coll. Foot Orthopedists (past pres.), Am. Med. Writers Assn. (chpt. pres.), AAAS; mem. Am. Podiatry Assn., Am. Assn. Colls. Podiatric Medicine (pres. 1970), Am. Pub. Health Assn., Gerontol. Soc., Am. Inst. Parliamentarians. Home: Silver Spring Md. Died Mar. 11, 1990; buried Judean Gardens, Md.

RUBIN, ALVIN BENJAMIN, federal judge; b. Alexandria, La., Mar. 13, 1920; s. Simon and Frances (Prussack) R.; m. Janice Ginsberg, Feb. 19, 1946; children: Michael H., David S. B.S. in Bus. Adminstrn, La. State U., 1941, LL.B., 1942; LLD, Loyola U., 1990, La. State U., 1990. Bar: La. 1942. Ptnr. Sanders, Miller, Downing, Rubin & Kean, 1946-66; U.S. dist. judge Eastern Dist. La., 1966-77; U.S. circuit judge 5th Circuit Ct. Appeals, 1977-89, sr. judge, 1989-91; adj. prof. law La. State U., 1946-89; vis. lectr. Law Sch. So. U., 1985-89, Law Sch. Duke U., 1985-89; lectr. taxation Am. Law Inst., Tulane U. Tax Inst., Ga. Tax Inst., La. State U. Mineral Law Inst., ABA seimnars, others; artibtaror Fed. Mediation and Conciliation Svc., 1964-66; bd. dirs. Fed. Jud. Ctr., 1986-89, co-chmn. Author: (with McMahon) Louisiana Pleadings and Judicial Forms Annotated, (with Janice G. Rubin) Louisiana Trust Handbook, (with Gerald LeVan) Louisiana Wills and Trusts, (with Anthony D. Leo) Law Clerk's Handbook, (with Laura B. Bartell) 2d edit. Law Clerk's Handbook; bd. editors: Manual for Complex Litigation, 1983-90, Manual on Judicial Writing. Chmn. Baton Rouge Zoning Study Com.; mem. La. Legislative Adminstrv. Procedure Com. Sec. Baton Rouge United Givers Fund, 1954-66; bd. dirs. Council for Legal Edn. in Profl. Responsibility, 1970-80, 86, Cornell U., 1980-86, New Orleans Jewish Welfare Fedn., 1972-76; mem. vis. com. Law Sch., U. Chgo., 1972-75, U. Miami, 1974-80, Harvard U., 1975-82, disting. jud. visitor U. Notre Dame, 1980, U. Iowa, 1983, U. Conn., 1984; past bd. dirs. Baton Rouge chpt. Girl Scouts Am., Mental Health Guidance Center, Community Chest, Community Services Council, Nat. Assn. Crippled Children and Adults; past adv. bd. local Salvation Army, YWCA, Blundon Orphanage; trustee Temple B'nai Israel, 1966-74, Temple Sinai, 1973-76. Served to capt. AUS, 1942-46, ETO. Recipient Golden Deeds award, 1964, Brotherhood award NCCJ, 1968, Disting.Alumnus award La. State U., 1982, 1st Disting. Alumnus award Law Sch. La. State U., 1988, ACLU award, 1989. Fellow Am. Acad. Arts Scis.; mem. ABA (bd. editors jour. 1976-82, task force competency in legal edn. 1978-80, chmn. estate and gift tax com. 1964, chmn. sect. bar activities 1963, chmn. lawyer referrral com. 1969-72, task force on Habeas Corpus in Capital Cases 1989), Am. Law Inst., La. Bar Assn. (chmn. sect. trust estates, probate and immovable property law 1961, chmn. labor law sect. 1957, jr. bar sect. 1955, com. on ct. adminstrn. Jud. Conf.), Nat. Acad. Arbitrators, am. Arbitration Assn., La. Law Inst., Order of Coif, Blue Key (hon.), Masons (32 degree), Phi Beta Kappa (hon.), Phi Delta Phi, Omicron Delta Kappa. Lodge: Mason (32 deg.). Home: Baton Rouge La. Died June 11, 1991.

RUBIN, WLADYSLAW CARDINAL, cardinal; b. Toki, Lwow, Poland, Sept. 20, 1917. Student St. Joseph U., Beirut. Ordained priest Roman Cath. Ch., 1946. Served as chaplain for Polish community and Polish refugees in Italy, 1953-58, rector Polish Coll., Rome, 1964; titular bishop of Serta and aux. bishop for Gniezno, 1964-79; sec. gen. Synod of Bishop, 1967-79; elevated to Sacred Coll. Cardinals, 1979; prefect Sacred Congregation for Eastern Chs., 1980-85; mem. Sacred Congregations for Doctrine of Faith and for Causes of Saints; mem. Supreme Tribunal for Apostolic Signature; sec. for Promoting Christian Unity, Pontifical Com. for Rev. of Oriental Canon Law, Sacred Congregation for Doctrine of Faith, for Religious and Secular Insts., for Evangelization of People, for Causes of Saints, for Cath. Edn., Supreme of Apostolic Signature; sec. for Christian Unity, Pontifical Com. for Revision of Codex of Eastern Canonical Law; deacon of St. Maria in Via Lata. Died Nov. 28, 1990. Hôme: Rome Italy

RUBINSTEIN, LUCIEN JULES, neuropathologist, educator; b. Antwerp, Belgium, Oct. 15, 1924; s. Emile and Diane (Silberfeld) R.; m. Dorothea Elizabeth Lunzer, 1950; children: Marion Harriet, Edmund John, Francis Marcel; m. Mary Margaret Herman, 1969. L.R.C.P., M.R.C.S., M.B., B.S. (hon.) with distinction in medicine and forensic, U. London (Eng.), 1948, M.D., 1952. House surgeon, house physician, casualty officer London Hosp., 1948-49, pathology asst., demonstrator chem. pathology, 1949-52; lectr., sr. lectr. morbid anatomy Med. Coll. London Hosp., 1954-61; vis. asst. prof. neuropathology U. Minn., 1959-60; vis. scientist NIH, 1960; attending neuropathologist Montefiore Hosp., N.Y.C., 1961-64; assoc. prof. neuropathology Columbia U., 1961-64; prof. pathology (neuropathology) Stanford U. Sch. Medicine, 1964-81; prof. pathology, dir. div. neuropathology U. Va. Sch. Medicine, Charlottesville, 1981-90; adviser WHO, Geneva; adv. cons. Nat. Inst. Neurol. Diseases and Stroke, NIH, Bethesda, Md. Author: (with D.S. Russell) Pathology of Tumors of the Nervous System, 1959, 5th edit., 1989, Tumors of the Central Nervous System, 1972, supplement, 1982, also chpts. for 12 books; mem. editorial bd.: Neuropathology Applied Neurobiology, Acta Neuropathologica, Cancer, Clin. Neuropathology, Glia, Jour. Neuro-Oncology. Contbr. 140 articles to profl. jours. Served with M.C. Brit. Army, 1952-54. Recipient T.A.M. Ross prize in clin. medicine and pathology London Hosp., 1948, Farber award for brain tumor research, 1982. Mem. Am. Assn. Neuropathologists (pres. 1970-71, council mem. 1966-74, Disitng. Contbns. award 1989), Internat. Acad. Pathology, Brit. Neuropath. Soc., Mexican Assn. Pathologists (hon.), World Fedn. Neurology, Australian and New Zealand Soc. Neuropathology (hon.). Home: Alexandria Va. Died Jan. 22, 1990; buried Charlottesville, Va.

RUCCIUS, FREDERICK EDWARD, JR., banker; b. Wyndmoor, Pa., Feb. 29, 1928; s. Frederick Edward and Dorothy Mae (Maust) R.; m. Ruth Louise Lowe, Aug. 13, 1949; children: Frederick Edward III, William L., Ann L., Karen L. Student, Muhlenberg Coll., 1945-46, U. Pa., evenings 1950-56; grad., Stonier Grad. Sch. Banking, Rutgers U., 1962. Vice pres. Continental Bank, Norristown, Pa., 1948-68; sr. v.p. Bank of Pa., Reading, 1968-74, pres., 1974-78, chmn. bd., chief exec. officer, dir., 1978-88; chmn. bd., dir. Fin. Realty Co.; vice chmn., dir. Dauphin Deposit Corp.; dir. Dauphin Life Ins. Co. Bd. dirs., past chmn. Camp Fire, Inc.; treas. N.E. Pa. synod Luth. Ch. Am.; bd. dirs. Greater

Berks Devel. Fund, Reading Ctr. City Devel. Fund, Community Gen. Hosp., Caron Found., Highlands at Wyomissing; chmn., vice chmn. Berkshire Health System; trustee Reading Mus. Found., Muhlenberg Coll. Bd. Assocs.; pres. council Albright Coll. Mem. Berks County C. of C., Pa. Bankers Assn. Republican. Lutheran. Clubs: Wyomissing, Berkshire. Home: Wyomissing Pa. Died May 22, 1988; buried Forest Hills Meml. Pk., Reading, Pa.

RUCKS, JOSEPH GIBSON, lawyer; b. Guthrie, Okla., Jan. 7, 1913; s. William Ward and Martha (Gibson) R.; m. Mary E. Durand, Mar. 25, 1937 (dec. 1989); children: Marthe Victoria, Charles Durand. A.B., U. Okla., 1934, LL.B., 1936. Bar: Okla. 1936. Practice law Oklahoma City, from 1936; mem. firm Fowler, Rucks, Baker, Jopling, Gramlich & Mee, 1952-71, McAfee, Taft, Mark, Bond, Rucks & Woodruff, 1971-80, McAfee & Taft, 1980-88. Pres. Areawide Health Planning Orgn. of Central Okla., 1971-74; mem. Oklahoma City Appeals Rev. Bd., 1965-75; mem., treas. Community Council, 1975-77, v.p., 1978-81, pres., 1982-83; bd. dirs. Okla. State Fair; chmn. Gov.'s Adv. Council on Capital Expenditures, 1967, mem. town council, Nichols Hills, Okla., 1962-65, mayor, 1964-65. Served to lt. col. AUS, World War II, ETO. Decorated Bronze Star; Croix de Guerre (France). Fellow Am. Bar Found.; mem. ABA, Okla. Bar Assn. (bd. govs. 1965-67), Oklahoma County Bar Assn. (pres. 1955, dir. 1977-80), Okla. Heart Assn. (pres. 1959), Oklahoma City C. of C. (dir.), Phi Gamma Delta, Phi Delta Phi. Presbyterian (elder). Club: Rotary. Home: Oklahoma City Okla. Died Apr. 13, 1988; buried Rose Hill Cemetery, Oklahoma City.

RUDD, HUGHES DAY, journalist; b. Wichita, Kans., Sept. 14, 1921; s. Hughes Day and Gladys (Burdett) R.; m. Anna Greenwood, Apr. 10, 1956; 1 son, Jon D. Student, U. Mo., 1938-40, U. Minn., 1951-52, Stanford, 1952-55. With Kansas City (Mo.) Star, 1946-50, Mpls. Tribune, 1950-51; mem. staff CBS News, 1959-79; bur. chief CBS News, Moscow, USSR, 1965-66, Central Europe, Bonn, W.Ger., 1966-67; anchorman Morning News, 1973-77; with ABC News, N.Y.C., from 1979. Author: My Escape From the CIA and Other Improbable Events, 1966; also numerous articles, stories. Served with F.A. AUS, 1941-45, ETO. Decorated Silver Star, Purple Heart, Air medal with 6 clusters.; recipient Emmy award, George Peabody award. Mem. Sigma Alpha Epsilon. Home: New York N.Y. Died Oct. 13, 1992. †

RUDE, CHESTER A., banker; b. Elmore, Minn., May 20, 1895; s. John and Inga (Knutson) R.; m. Lorraine Frankenfeld, Nov. 23, 1921; children: Lorraine Rude Henninger, Budd Frankenfeld, Myron Orton. Student, U. Wash., 1920-21. Bd. dirs., mem. exec. com. Security-1st Nat. Bank L.A.; bd. dirs. Pacific Outdoor Advt., N.Am. Aviation, Inc. Bd. dirs. Rose Hills Meml. Park Assn., Whittier, Calif., Ch. Div. Sch. of Pacific, Episcopal Diocesan Investment Trust; pres. bd. trustees Claremont Men's Coll.; pres. bd. dirs. Hops. of Good Samaritan, L.A. Capt. 163 inf., U.S. Army, World War I. Mem. Calif. Bankers Assn. (past pres.), Robert Morris Assocs. (past pres.), L.A. Country Club, Calif. Club. Republican. *

RUDHYAR, DANE, author, composer; b. Paris, Mar. 23, 1895; came to U.S., 1916, naturalized, 1926; s. Leon and Lucie (Bajaud) R.; m. Malya Contento, June 9, 1930; m. Eya Fechin, June 27, 1945 (div. 1954); m. Gail Tana Whittall, Mar. 27, 1964. PhB, U. Paris, 1911; student, Paris Conservatoire Music, 1912. First orchestral performances at festival abstract dance Met. Opera, N.Y.C., 1917; lectr., Europe, 1960, 62-63, U.S., summer 1964. Author: (poems) Toward Man, 1929, White Thunder, 1938; Rebirth of Hindu Music, 1928, Art as Release of Power, 1930, Liberation through Sound, 1931, Astrology of Personality, 1936, New Mansions for New Men, 1937, The Pulse of Life, 1943, The Moon: Cycles of Life, 1945, Modern Man's Conflicts, 1948, Gifts of the Spirit, 1956, Fire Out of Stone, 1959, Existence, Rhythme et Symbole; also mag. articles; composer music for Pilgrimage Play, 1920, 22, Surge of Fire, 1925, music for modern dancers. Recipient $1,000 prize for symphonic poem L.A. Philharm., 1922. Mem. Internat. Composers Guild, New Music Soc., Am. Composers Alliance. *

RUDOLF, LESLIE E., medical educator; b. Pelham, N.Y., Nov. 12, 1927. BS, Union Coll., 1951; MD, Cornell U., 1955. Diplomate Am. Bd. Surgery. Intern and resident Peter Bent Brigham Hosp., Boston, 1955-59, 60-61; asst. Harvard Med. Sch., Boston, 1959-60; instr. N.Y. Hosp.-Cornell U., 1961-63, asst. prof. to assoc. prof., 1963-72; Bruce Morton prof. surgery Sch. Medicine, U. Va., Charlottesville, from 1972, vice chmn. dept. surgery, from 1976; mem. Nat. Bd. Med. Examiners. Markle scholar in acad. medicine, 1966-71. Mem. ACS, Soc. Surgeons of Alimentary Tract, Am. Soc. Nephrology, Am. Soc. Artificial Internal Organs, Transplantation Soc. Home: Charlottesville Va. Died Oct. 16, 1990.

RULE, ELTON H., broadcasting executive; b. Stockton, Calif., 1917; m. Betty Louise Bender; children: Cindy Rule Dunne, Christie, James. Grad., Sacramento Coll. With ABC, Inc., 1952-90; gen. sales mgr. Sta. KABC-TV ABC, Inc., L.A., 1953-60, gen. mgr. sta., 1960-61, v.p., gen. mgr., 1961-68, pres. ABC-TV Network, 1968-70, group v.p., 1969-72, pres., 1970-72, pres., cEO, mem. exec. com., 1972-83, vice chmn., 1983-84, mem. bd. dirs., 1970-90, vice chmn., exec. com., from 1983; pres. Calif. Broadcasters Assn., 1966-67. Mem. adv. bd. Inst. Sports Medicine and Athletic Trauma, Lenox Hill Hosp., from 1973; bd. visitors UCLA Sch. Medicine, from 1980. Recipient Gold medal award Internat. Radio and TV Soc., 1975, award for outstanding achievement in bus. mgmt. U. So. Calif. Sch. Bus. Adminstrn., 1978, Gov.'s award Acad. TV Arts and Scis., 1981. Home: Beverly Hills Calif. Died May 5, 1990; cremated.

RUMBERGER, CALVIN LEE, food company executive; b. Warriors Mark, Pa., Sept. 1, 1898; s. George Edwin and Louella Rebecca (Wilson) R.; m. Jessie Catherine Hollinger, Sept. 19, 1923; children: Dalton L., Earl E. BS, Pa. State U., 1920. With mfg. div. H.J. Heinz Co., Pitts., 1929-33, 45-47, exec. gen. sales div., 1933-45, gen. mgr. rsch. and quality control div., 1947-51, v.p. rsch. and quality control div., 1951-62, v.p. corp. devel., 1962-64, bd. dirs., 1953-58; pres., treas., bd. dirs. Heinz Alimentos S.A., Mex., from 1963; Pres. Agrl. Rsch. Inst., 1957-58. Mem. Nat. Canners Assn. (bd. dirs. 1955-58, chmn. sci. rsch. com.), Am. Mgmt. Assn. (bd. dirs., coun.), Assn. Food and Drug Ofcls. U.S., Inst. Food Technologists, Pa. Canners Assn., Nutrition Found., Can Mfrs. Inst., Pitts. C. of C., Pa. State U. Alumni Assn., City Farmers Club (past pres.), Univ. Club, Duquesne Club, Mt. Lebanon Golf Club, Masons, Alpha Zeta. *

RUMMEL, CHARLES GARMIN, architect, engineer; b. Beaver, Pa., Feb. 29, 1912; s. William Bernard and Dora O. (Garman) R.; m. Cynthia Walker, Feb. 19, 1943; children: Cynthia Drake, Susan Garman, Sarah, McNeely, Charles Garman. BArch, U. Ill., 1933. Registered architect, engr. Architect Shaw Naess & Murphy, Chgo., 1937-47; ptnr. Naess & Murphy, Chgo., 1947-57; 1st. v.p. G.F. Murphy Assocs., Chgo., 1957-62; vice chmn. Lester B. Knight & Assoc., Inc., Chgo., 1967-86; also bd. dirs. Lester B. Knight & Assoc., Inc. Dir. numerous major archtl. and engring. projects in Chgo. area including Prudential Bldg., No. Trust Co. Bank, Richard J. Daley Ctr., Jardine Filtration Plant, O'Hare Internat. Airport, State of Ill. Ctr., Social Secuirty Adminstrn. Payment Ctr. Served to lt. col. C.E. U.S. Army, 1941-46. Plym fellow U. Ill. for European study, 1934-35. Fellow AIA; mem. Western Soc. Engrs. (pres.), Ill. Bd. Archtl. Examiners (chmn. 1947-69), Nat. Coun. Archtl. Registration Bds. Clubs: Glenview, Univ., Tavern (pres.). Home: Kenilworth Ill. Died Oct. 21, 1991; buried Christ Ch. graveyard, Winnetka, Ill.

RUSK, HOWARD A., physician; b. Brookfield, Mo., Apr. 9, 1901; s. Michael Yost and Augusta Eastin (Shipp) R.; m. Gladys Houx, Oct. 20, 1926 (dec. 1980); children: Martha Rusk Sutphen, Howard A. Jr., John Michael. AB, U. Mo., 1923, LLD, 1947; MD, U. Pa., 1925; DSc (hon.), Boston U., 1949, Lehigh U., 1956, Middlebury Coll., 1957, Trinity Coll., 1961, Women's Med. Coll., 1962, U. Portland, 1969, Hofstra U., 1972, Jersey City State Coll., 1974, Calif. Coll. Podiatric Medicine, 1976, Coll. New Rochelle, 1977, Brandeis U., 1978; LLD, Westminster Coll., 1950, Hahnemann Med. Coll., 1952, Chungang U., Korea, 1956, L.I. U., 1957, Mo. Valley Coll., 1965; LHD (hon.), Adelphi Coll., 1957; LittD, Ithaca Coll., 1961; MD (hon.), U. Rennes, France, 1965; DMSc (hon.), Brown U., 1969. Diplomate Am. Bd. Internal Medicine, Am. Bd. Phys. Medicine and Rehab. Pvt. practice internal medicine, St. Louis, 1926-42; instr. medicine Washington U., St. Louis, 1929-42; former assoc. chief staff St. Luke's Hosp., St. Louis; prof., chmn. dept. rehab. medicine NYU Sch. Medicine, N.Y.C., from 1946, founder, dir. Inst. Phys. Medicine and Rehab., 1946-78, Disting. Univ. prof., from 1978; cons. in rehab. Baruch Com. secretariat UN, N.Y.C.; chmn. health resources adv. com. ODM, 1950-57; mem. Pub. Health Coun., N.Y. Dept. Health; founder, pres. World Rehab. Fund, 1955-82; bd. dirs. Chem. Fund, Inc., Companion Life Ins. Co., Graphic Arts Mut. Ins. Co., IPCO Hosp. Supply Corp.; chmn. pub. policy com. Advt. Council; presenter to med. assns.; columnist, part-time assoc. editor N.Y. Times, 1946-69. Author: (with Eugene J. Taylor) New Hope for the Handicapped, 1949; author: Living with a Disability, 1953, Rehabilitation Medicine, 1958, 4th edit., 1977, Rehabilitation of the Cardiovascular Patient, 1958, (autobiography) A World To Care For, 1972; co-author: Cardiovascular Rehabilitation, 1958; contbr. articles to Ency. Brit. and med. jours. Trustee U. Pa., 1962-67; bd. dirs. N.Y. Found. Col. M.C., USAAF, 1943-45, brig. gen. Res. ret. Decorated D.S.M, Nat. Medal Republic of Korea, Order Jose Fernandez Madrid (Colombia), officier Legion of Honor (France); recipient Dr. C.C. Criss award, 1952, Lasker award APHA, 1952, rsch. award Am. Pharm. Mfrs. Assn., 1952, gold medal Nat. Inst. Social Sci., 1954, Internat. Benjamin Franklin Soc., 1955, Albert Lasker award for svcs. to physically disabled, 1957, 60, Gold Key award Am. Congress Phys. Medicine and Rehab., 1958, also others. Fellow ACP, Royal Coll. Physicians; mem. AMA, N.Y. Acad. Medicine, Internat. Soc. for Welfare Cripples (pres. 1954), Nat. Assn. Sci. Writers, Phi Beta Kappa, Alpha Omega Alpha, Phi Delta Theta, Nu Sigma Nu. Home: New York N.Y. Died Nov. 4, 1989; buried Brookfield, Mo.

RUSSELL, ALBERT RICHARD, association executive; b. Oxford, Miss., Apr. 11, 1915; s. Albert Edgar and Clara Marie (Graves) R.; m. Sada Frances Norris, Dec. 29, 1961. B.A., U. Miss., 1936, postgrad. law, 1937. With Americana Corp., N.Y.C., 1937-39; sec.-mgr. Delta Council, Stoneville, Miss., 1939-41; with Nat. Cotton Council Am., Memphis, 1946-83, adminstrv. v.p., 1967-68, exec. v.p., 1969-78, spl. adv. to mgmt., 1978-83; exec. v.p. Cotton Council Internat., 1969-78; bd. mgrs. N.Y. Cotton Exchange, 1982-86. Author: History National Cotton Council, 1980, Updated History, 1987. Bd. dirs. Effective Citizens Orgn., 1963-65; trustee Oscar Johnston Cotton Found., 1969-78; mem. adv. council Sch. Bus., U. Miss., 1982-86. Served as flight navigator USNR, 1942-46. Mem. U. Miss. Hall of Fame, 1937. Mem. Soc. Assn. Execs., Am. Soc. Assn. Execs., A.I.M. (pres. council 1966-78), Phi Delta Theta. Episcopalian. Home: Oxford Miss. Died Nov. 9, 1989.

RUSSELL, CHARLES HINTON, university administrator; b. Lovelock, Nev., Dec. 27, 1903; s. Robert James and Ellen Daisy (Ernst) R.; m. Marjorie Ann Guild, Mar. 19, 1939; children: Clark George, Virginia Ellen, Craig Robert, Charles David, James Todd. AB, U. Nev., 1926. Tchr., 1926-27; with mine office Ruth, Nev., 1928-29; editor The Ely (Nev.) Record, 1929-46; assemblyman Nev. State Legislature, 1935-40; state senator Nev. Legislature, 1941-46, pres. pro tempore, 1943; mem. at large 80th Congress Nev., 1947-49; gov. Nev., 1950-58; dir. U.S. Ops. Mission, Asuncion, Paraguay, 1959-63; dir. devel., asst. to pres. U. Nev., Reno, 1963-89; former agt. joint com. on Fgn. Econ. Coop., 1949-50. Mem. Masons, Shriner, Jester, KP, Elks. Republican. Episcopalian. Home: Carson City Nev. Died Sept. 13, 1989; buried Dayton, Nev.

RUSSELL, FRANCIS, author; b. Boston, Jan. 12, 1910; s. Leo Spotten and Ethel May (Kent) R.; m. Sharon Soong, Mar. 5, 1966 (div. 1981); 1 child, Sara; m. Rosalind Lawson, Mar. 16, 1984. Student, U. Breslau, Germany, 1931-32; A.B., Bowdoin Coll., 1933; A.M., Harvard U., 1937. Writer for various Irish, English and Am. publs., 1946—; author: Three Studies in 20th Century Obscurity, 1954, Am. Heritage Book of the Pioneer, The French and Indian Wars, 1961, Tragedy in Dedham, 1962, Lexington, Concord and Bunker Hill, 1963, The Great Interlude, 1964, The World of Dürer, 1967, The Shadow of Blooming Grove, 1968, The Making of the Nation, 1968, The Confident Years, 1969, Forty Years On, 1970, The Horizon Concise History of Germany, 1973, A City in Terror, 1975, The President Makers from Mark Hanna to Joseph P. Kennedy, 1976, Adams: An American Dynasty, 1976, The Secret War, 1981, Sacco-Vanzetti: The Case Resolved, 1986, The Knave of Boston, 1987; co-author: Spirit, 1960. Served to capt. Can. Army, 1941-46. Recipient Edgar award Mystery Writers Am., 1962; Guggenheim fellow, 1964, 65; recipient Friendship award Fed. Republic of Germany. Fellow Soc. Am. Historians; mem. Goethe Soc. (dir.), Black Watch Assn., Boston Authors' Club, Dorchester Hist. Soc. Episcopalian. Club: Harvard (Boston). Home: Sandwich Mass. Died Mar. 21, 1989.

RUSSELL, FRANCIS HENRY, educator, former United States ambassador; b. Cambridge, Mass., Oct. 1, 1904; s. James P. and Edith (Pratt) R.; m. Ruth Libbey, June 16, 1932; children: Paul Libbey, Alene J. (Mrs. Adam Hochschild). AB, Tufts Coll., 1926, LLD, 1959; LLB, Harvard U., 1929. Bar: Mass. 1929. Mem. firm Russell, Houston & Russell, Boston, 1929-41; chief div. world trade intelligence (econ. warfare) U.S. Dept. State, 1942-44, dir. Office of Pub. Affairs, 1945-52; chargé d'affaires Am. Embassy, Tel Aviv, 1953-54; spl. asst. sec. state, 1954-56, U.S. amb. to New Zealand, 1957-60, U.S. amb. to Ghana, 1960-62, U.S. amb. to Tunisia, 1962-69; cons. to policy planning staff, 1947; staff, U.S. delegation UN Conf., San Francisco, 1945, UN Assembly, London, 1946; U.S. del. NATO Conf. on Info., London, 1951; chmn. Nat. Conf. Am. Fgn. Policy, 1945-52; amb. in residence Fletcher Sch. Law and Diplomacy, Tufts U., 1969-89. Author Mass. group med. practice law, 1941. Mem. Tufts Alumni Coun. (past chmn.), Phi Beta Kappa, Delta Upsilon. Unitarian. Home: Belmont Mass. Died Mar. 31, 1989.

RUSSELL, JOHN, JR., lawyer; b. Phila., Jan. 24, 1894; s. John and Janet (Paton) R.; m. Barbara Macdonald Frantz, Sept. 15, 1922. AB, Princeton U., 1916; LLB, U. Pa., 1921. Bar: Pa. 1922. Pvt. practice, Phila., from 1922; mem. Morgan, Lewis & Bockius. Chmn. Lower Merion Twp. Planning Commn., Montgomery County, Pa.; mem. grad. coun. Princeton U.; bd. mgrs. Franklin Inst. 1st lt. U.S. Army, 1918-19, AEF in France. Mem. Rittenhouse Club, Princeton Club, Merion Cricket Club. *

RUSSELL, LAO (MRS. WALTER RUSSELL), philosopher, author, educator; b. Ivinghoe, Buckinghamshire, Eng.; d. Alfred William and Florence (Hills) Cook; m. Walter Russell, July 29, 1948. Ed. pvt. tutors. Founder Walter Russell Found. (now known as U. Sci. and Philosophy), Waynesboro, Va., 1948, mng. dir., from 1948, pres., from 1949. Author: God Will

Work With You But Not For You, 1955 (named one of 6 best books of year N.Y. Herald Tribune 1955), An Eternal Message of Light and Love, 1964, My Love I Extend to You, 1966, Love-A Scientific and Living Philosophy of Love and Sex, 1966, Why You Cannot Die!-The Continuity of Life-Reincarnation Explained, 1972, (with Walter Russell) One Year Home Study Course in Universal Law, Natural Science and Living Philosophy, 1950, Scientific Answer to Human Relations, 1951, Atomic Suicide?, 1957, The World Crisis-Its Explanation and Solution, 1958, The One-World Purpose-A Plan to Dissolve War By a Power More Mighty than War, 1960; executed (with husband) statue Christ of the Blue Ridge, 1948; also colossal model, 1950; presented bronze bust of George Washington (sculptured by husband) to Va. Bicentennial Commn., 1976. Founded Shrine of Beauty known as Swannanoa Palace and Sculpture Gardens, 1948; Founder Man-Woman Equalization League, 1955, Internat. Age of Character Clubs, 1966. Home: Waynesboro Va. Died May 5, 1988; buried Waynesboro, Va.

RUSSELL, PAUL LAWRENCE, ballet dancer; b. Mineola, Tex., Mar. 2, 1947; s. Dorse Edgar and Eddie Mae (London) R. Student, Pasadena City Coll., 1965-66, UCLA, 1967-68. Prin. dancer, Hartford Ballet, 1968-71, prin. dancer, Dance Theater of Harlem, 1971-77, Scottish Ballet, 1978-80, San Francisco Ballet, from 1980, guest prin. dancer throughout U.S., Europe; choreographer: Nutcracker, Garden State Ballet, 1977, Three Preludes, 1983, Chopin Images, 1984; artistic dir. Am. Festival Ballet, 1988—; TV appearances include: Monte Carlo Show; appeared in film A Piece of the Action; instr. Syracuse U., 1971. Mem. Brit. Equity, Am. Guild Musical Artists. Home: Boise Idaho Died Feb. 15, 1991.

RUSSELL, R. DANA, geological consultant; b. Pomona, Calif., Nov. 15, 1906; s. Henry Edison and Ann Beatrice (Rolph) R.; m. Mary Flower Pugh, June 2, 1933; children: Nancy Beatrice (Mrs. Theodore D. Graves), Richard Dana. A.B., Pomona Coll., 1927; Ph.D., U. Cal. at Berkeley, 1931. From instr. to asso. prof. geology La. State U., 1931-42; research asso., oceanographer, div. war research U. Calif., 1942-46; from mgr. publs. dept. to sr. cons. geophysics (Navy Electronics Lab.), 1945-55; mgr. geol. research, then asso. dir. exploration research Marathon Oil Co., 1955-70, cons., 1970-71; ind. cons., from 1970; lectr. Calif. Inst. Tech., 1948, Scripps Instn. Oceanography, 1949-55; Mem. Bikini Sci. Resurvey team, 1947; mem. com. sedimentation NRC, 1932-46; mem. hon. com. Centre de Recherches et d'Etudes Oceanographiques, 1949-72; mem. U.S. Nat. Com. Geology, 1973-77. Contbr. to profl. jours., books. Recipient commendation meritorious service U.S. Navy, 1947, 55. Fellow Geol. Soc. Am. (chmn. nominating com. 1964, bldg. com. 1969-72, hdqrs. adv. com. 1972-75); mem. Am. Geol. Inst. (dir., pres. 1973), Am. Petroleum Inst., Am. Assn. Petroleum Geologists (chmn. research com. 1956-58, trustee research fund 1960-62), Soc. Econ. Paleontologists and Mineralogists (v.p. 1943, pres. 1948), Am. Inst. Profl. Geologists (pres. 1969). Home: Santa Rosa Calif. Deceased. †

RUTH, EARL BAKER, congressman; b. Spencer, N.C., Feb. 7, 1916; s. Earl Monroe and Marion (Baker) R.; m. Jane Wiley, Dec. 27, 1938; children: Billie Jane Ruth Foil, Earl Wiley, Marian Ann Ruth Reber, Jacqueline Dell Ruth Burleson. BA, U. N.C., 1938, MA, 1942, PhD, 1955. Tchr., coach Chapel Hill (N.C.) High Sch., 1938-39, Piedmont Jr. High Sch., Charlotte, N.C., 1939-40; with shipping dept. McCrary Mills, Asheboro, N.C., 1940-41; asst. supt. N.C. State Parks, 1941; grad. asst. phys. edn. U. N.C., 1945-46; football coach, baseball and basketball coach, athletic dir. chmn. dept. phys. edn., dean students Catawba Coll., Salisbury, N.C., 1946-68; mem. 91st-93d Congresses 8th Dist. N.C.; gov. Am. Samoa Pago Pago, 1975-89. Mem. City Coun., Salisbury, also mayor pro tem, 1967-678; active local Boy Scouts Am.; bd. dirs. Salisbury YMCA; elder Presbyn. Ch. Lt. USNR, 1942-45. Mem. VFW, Am. Legion, Nat. Sportscasters and Sportswriters (past pres. awards program), Elks, Civitan. Republican. Home: Salisbury N.C. Died Aug. 15, 1989.

RUTLEDGE, PHILIP CASTEEN, consulting engineer; b. Champaign, Ill., Feb. 17, 1906; s. George and Rella (Casteen) R.; m. Dorothy Loomis, June 16, 1934 (dec. 1973); children: John Loomis, Cecily; m. Catherine P. Brobston, Mar. 29, 1975. SB, Harvard U., 1927, ScD, 1939; SM, MIT, 1933; DEng (hon.), Purdue U., 1957. Field engr. on constrn. Barney-Ahlers Constrn. Co. N.Y., 1928-29; structural designer Stone & Webster Engring. Co., Boston, 1929-31; instr. soil mechanics Grad. Sch. Engring. Harvard U., 1933-37; assoc. prof., prof. soil mechanics Purdue U., 1937-43; prof. civil engring. Tech. Inst. Northwestern U., Evanston, Ill., 1943-52; chmn. dept. civil engring. Northwestern U., Evanston, 1947-52; cons. engr., ptnr. Mueser, Rutledge, Wentworth & Johnston and predecessor firm, N.Y.C., 1952-76; mem. bd. cons. on airfield pavements Office Chief of Engrs., U.S. Army, 1943-57; chmn. bd. cons. on earth dams Calif. Dept. Water Resources, 1963-74; tech. assoc. Atlantic-Pacific Interoceanic Canal Study Commn., 1965-70; cons. heavy founds. and dams Treas. Internat. Conf. on Soil Mechanics, Cambridge, Mass., 1936; chmn. Edn. Conf. on Soil Mechanics, Purdue U., 1940, U.S. Nat. Com. on Soil Mechanics, 1947-48; mem. AEC Plowshare Adv. Com., 1959-71. Recipient War Dept. Cert. of Appreciation for svcs. during World War II. Mem. ASCE (contbr. tech. articles to procs.), Am. Inst. Cons. Engrs., Am. Geophys. Inst., Nat. Acad. Engring., Boston Soc. Civil Engrs., The Moles, Harvard Club, Engrs. Club, Wee Burn Club, Sigma Xi, Phi Kappa Sigma. Congregationalist. Home: Vero Beach Fla. Died July 14, 1990.

RUTZ, WILLIAM EDWARD, machine tools manufacturing company executive; b. Fond du Lac, Wis., Mar. 29, 1896; s. Herman and Amelia (Wambler) R.; m. Eleanor K. Bergen, June 27, 1931. Grad. pub. schs., Fond du Lac. Tool and diemaker Demountable Typewriter Co., Fond du Lac, 1913-23, Am. Can Co., Grand Rapids, Mich., 1913-23; tool and machine designer Demountable Typewriter co. and Teetor Adding Machine Co., Des Moines; machine and foundry supt. Giddings & Lewis Machine Tool Co., Fond du Lac, 1923-35, v.p., works mgr., 1935-53, exec. v.p., 1953-61, also bd. dirs., from 1945; v.p., bd. dirs. Tobin Tool & Die Co., Fond du Lac; bd. dirs. Giddings & Lewis-Fraser, Ltd., Arbroath, Scotland, Fawick Corp., Cleve., Fed. Res. Bank, Chgo. Mem. ASME, Am. Soc. Tool Engrs., Nat. Machine Tool Builders Assn., U.S. C. of C., Wis. C. of C. (past pres.), Fond du Lac C. of C. (past pres.), Masons (32d degree), Shriners, Rotary (past pres.). Republican. *

RUWE, LESTER NICHOLAS, ambassador; b. Grosse Pointe Farms, Mich., Sept. 22, 1933; s. Lester Frederick and Ruth M. (Devoy) R.; m. Nancy Lammerding, Feb. 13, 1975. B.A., Brown U., 1955. Mem. staff Nixon for Pres., Washington, 1960; mem. staff John Tower for Senate, Houston, 1961, Nixon for Gov., Los Angeles, 1962, Charles Percy for Gov., Chgo., 1964; mem. sr. staff Nixon for Pres., N.Y.C., 1968; asst. chief of protocol Dept. State, Washington, 1969-76; U.S. ambassador to Iceland Dept. State, Reykjavik, from 1985; mem. sr. staff Reagan for Pres., Los Angeles and Washington, 1979-80; chief of staff Office of Richard Nixon, N.Y.C., 1980-84; sr. cons. Reagan-Bush '84, Washington, 1984. Clubs: Everglades (Palm Beach, Fla.); Chevy Chase (Md.). Home: Washington D.C. Died May 2, 1990.

RYAN, HEWSON ANTHONY, political science educator; b. New Haven, June 16, 1922; s. James Patrick and Clara Hewson (Sprightly) R.; m. Helene E. Lecko, July 4, 1949; children—Alexander H. (dec.), Anthony H., Anne S. B.A., Yale U., 1946, M.A., 1948; Ph.D., U. Madrid, Spain, 1950. Instr. Spanish Yale U., New Haven, 1947-51, Sterling fellow, 1949; joined U.S. Fgn. Svc., 1951; dir. Centro Colombo Americano, Bogota, Colombia, 1951-54; cultural affairs officer Am. embassy, La Paz, Bolivia, 1954-56; info. officer Am. embassy, Santiago, Chile, 1956-58, pub. affairs officer, 1958-61; asst. dir. USIA, Washington, 1961-64, assoc. dir., 1964-66, dep. dir., 1966-69; U.S. ambassador to Honduras, 1969-73; dep. asst. sec. state Inter-Am. affairs Washington, 1975-77; diplomat in residence Fletcher Sch. Law and Diplomacy, Tufts U., Boston, 1973-74, Edward R. Murrow prof. pub. diplomacy, 1977-90, emeritus, 1990-91; adviser U.S. del. 5th meeting Fgn. Ministers Americas, 1959; U.S. observer 2d UNESCO Regional Conf. Info., 1960; cons. to UN, 1977-91; chmn. Chilean Fulbright Commn., 1958-61; dir. Nat. Endowment for Humanities Seminar for Journalists, 1978, 79, seminars for secondary tchrs., 1986-88; hon. consul of Honduras at, Boston, 1980-91; hon. prof. Northeast Normal U., China, 1988. Contbr. articles to profl. jours. Bd. dirs. Info. Inst., Santa Barbara, Calif., from 1985, Americas Found., from 1980. Served with inf. AUS, 1942-46, ETO. Decorated Bronze Star; Grand Cross of Morazan Honduras, 1973; recipient Distinguished Service award USIA, 1964. Mem. Council on Fgn. Relations, Fgn. Service Protective Assn. (pres. 1975-77), Center for Inter-Am. Relations, Council Advanced Internat. Studies (Argentina), Pan Am. Soc. New Eng. (v.p. 1978-80). Clubs: Overseas Press (N.Y.C.); DACOR (Washington); Harvard (Boston); Monday (Winchester). Home: Winchester Mass. Died Sept. 28, 1991.

RYAN, JEROME RANDOLPH, physician; b. Texarkana, Ark., Sept. 6, 1934; s. Jerome Lukeman and Marion Eileen (Hunter) R.; m. Rosemary Gullett, June 7, 1960; children: Thomas, Cathleen, John, Stephen, Joseph, Margaret. B.S., U. Notre Dame, 1956; M.D., Georgetown U., 1960. Diplomate: Am. Bd. Internal Medicine. Intern U. Tex. Med. Br., Galveston, 1960-61; resident in medicine VA Hosp., New Orleans, 1964-66; research asso., chief resident med. service VA Hosp., 1966-67; NIH trainee Joslin Clinic, Boston, 1967-68; mem. faculty dept. medicine Tulane U. Sch. Medicine, New Orleans, from 1968, prof. medicine, 1975-81, chief sect. diabetes and metabolic diseases, 1980-81, adj. prof. pharmacology, 1980-89; med. dir. Clin. Research Ctr., New Orleans, 1982-89; sr. vis. physician Charity Hosp. La., New Orleans, 1968-89; mem. staff Hotel Dieu Hosp., New Orleans, 1968-89, Tulane U. Med. Center Hosp., 1976-89; founder, med. dir. La. Camp for Diabetic Children, 1971-86; Bd. dirs. Greater New Orleans Diabetes Assn., 1970-89, v.p., 1978-79; bd. dirs. La. affiliate Am. Diabetes Assn., 1978-89, pres., 1980-81, Jerome R. Ryan Camping Program named in his honor, 1988. Contbr. articles to med. jours. Served with M.C. USN, 1961-64. Recipient Bectin Dickinson award for outstanding contbn. to camping, 1984; named Outstanding Member Diatetic Assn., 1988. Fellow A.C.P (Laureate award La. chpt. 1988); mem. Am. Fedn. Clin. Research, Soc. Soc. Clin. Investigation, AMA, Am. Soc. Clin. Pharmacology and Therapeutics (chmn. program com. 1979-80), La. State Med. Soc., So. Sugar Club, Musser-Burch Soc., New Orleans Acad. Internal Medicine, New Orleans Grad. Med. Assembly (vice chmn. program com. 1977-78). Roman Catholic. Home: New Orleans La. Died May 21, 1989; buried Westlawn Cemetery, New Orleans.

RYAN, SISTER M. PATON, college president. Pres. St. Joseph Coll., West Hartford, Conn. Home: West Hartford Conn. Died Jan. 2, 1991.

RYAN, TUBAL CLAUDE, aerospace-electronics manufacturer; b. Parsons Kans., Jan. 3, 1898; s. William Marion and Ida Frances (Ziegler) R.; m. Gladys Bowen, 1928; children: David Claude (dec.), Jerome Donald, Stephen Michael. Student, Oreg. State U., 1919; grad., USAC Pilot Sch., 1921. Founder Ryan Flying Co. and Sch. Aeronautics, 1922; founder Ryan Airlines (1st yr.-round daily scheduled passenger svc.), 1925, designer, started mfg. Ryan monoplanes, 1927; founder, chmn., CEO, Ryan Aero. Co., mfrs. personal and mil.-type planes, 1928; bd. dirs. U.S. Nat. Bank, San Diego, Emptor Corp., San Diego Gas and Electric Co; World War II ops. included volume prodn. Ryan Tng. Planes and Ryan Fireball, R-1, also operation major flight and tech. tng. ctrs. for USAAF. Ryan Airlines, Inc. manufactured Lindbergh's Spirit of St. Louis, 1927; developer world's 1st jet vertical take-off and landing airplane Ryan Vertiject, 1956, 1st jet fighter for USN. 2d lt., pilot USAC, 1921. Recipient Presdl. cert. of merit, World War II, Horatio Alger award Am. Schs. and Colls. Assn., 1958. Mem. Aircraft Industries Assn., Air Force Assn., Navy League, Inst. Aero. Scis., Soc. Automotive Engrs., San Diego Yacht Club, Cuyamaca Club. Presbyterian. *

RYERSON, MARGERY AUSTIN, painter; b. Morristown, N.J., Sept. 15, 1886; d. David Austen and Mary McIlvaine (Brown) R. A.B., Vassar Coll., 1909; studied, Art Students League, N.Y.C.; studied under Robert Henri and Charles W. Hawthorne. Painter, etcher and lithographer. Represented prints in permanent collections, Smithsonian Instn., other mus., U.S. and abroad; exhibited paintings in collections, N.J. Hist. Soc., painting in collections., Norfolk Mus. Arts and Scis., Va., prints in collections, Abbott Labs., painting in collections, NAD, paintings in collections, Vassar Coll., Philbrook Art Ctr., Tulsa, Frye Mus., Seattle, Va. State Coll., Union Theol. Sem.; contbr.: Art in Am., The Am. Scholar, Am. Artist, The Artist, N.Y. Herald Tribune, N.Y. Times Book Rev.; compiler: The Art Spirit, by Robert Henri; co-editor: Hawthorne on Painting; illustrator: Winkle Boo. Recipient 1st prize (oil) Hudson Valley Art Assn., 1956, 57, 58; recipient Gold medal for oil portrait Nat. Arts Club, 1957, 62, 69, Silver medal Nat. Arts Club, 1971, Maynard portrait prize NAD, 1959, 1st prize Balt. Water Color Club, 1960; portrait prize (oil) Silvermine Guild, 1960; recipient Hook Meml. Am. Watercolor Soc., Talens N.J. Watercolor Soc., 1963, Winsor and Newton N.J. Watercolor Soc., 1968, Stevenson prize (oil) Nat. Arts Club, 1967, Grumbacher Nat. Arts Club, 1972, Clinedinst medal Artist Fellowship, 1971, Holton Meml. Watercolor prize Knickerbocker Artists, 1974, prize for graphics Knickerbocker Artists, 1978, Dole prize Am. Artists Profl. Leauge, 1973, prize for graphics Am. Artists Profl. League, 1974, Albany Print Club prize, 1973, N.A., 1959; painter mem. Grand Central Art Galleries. Mem. Am. Watercolor Soc., Balt. Water Color Club, Knickerbocker Artists, Soc. Am. Graphic Artists, Allied Artists Am. (v.p. 1952-53), Audubon Artists (corr. sec. 1958-59), N.J. Watercolor Soc., Print Club Albany, Pen and Brush. Home: New York N.Y. Died Apr. 30, 1989. †

RYLE, WALTER HARRINGTON, college president; b. Yates, Mo., June 1, 1896; s. Walter Harrington and Kate (Stark) R.; m. Maurine Lea, June 7, 1927; 1 child, Waalter Harrington IV. BS, N.E. Mo. State Tchrs. Coll., 1919; AM, George Peabody Tchrs. Coll., 1927, PhD, 1930; postgrad., U. Wis., 1927-28. Prin. high sch., Clifton Hill, Mo., 1916-17, Palmyra (Mo.) High Sch., 1919-21; supt. pub. schs., Clifton Hill, 1917-18; supt. schs., Holden, Mo., 1921-27; instr. history Peabody Coll., Nashville, 1929-30; asst. prof. history N.E. Mo. State Tchrs. Coll., Kirksville, 1928-29, prof. social sci., 1930-37, pres., from 1937. Author: Missouri: Union or Secession, 1931, Geography of Missouri, 1934, The Story of Missouri, 1938; also articles. Col. personal staff Gov. of Mo., 1937-42; chmn. Coun. of Def.; comdr. Citizens Def. Corps; reemployment committeeman Selective Svc. Bd.; chmn. Navy Relief Fund Adair County; mem. Mo. coordinating coun. UNESCO; chmn. Kirksville Dist. coun. Boy Scouts Am., from 1944, pres. Cen. Mo. Area coun., from 1949; past mem. bd. dirs. and pres. Mo. Creation Assn.; chmn. Adair county com. Mo. Dept. Resources and Devel.; mem. Mo. Gov.'s Coun. oln Higher Edn. With inf. U.S. Army, World War I, mem. Mo. N.G. ret. Mem. NEA, Am. Hist. Assn., Mississippi Valley Hist. Assn., Mo. Hist. Assn., Mo. Tchrs. Assn. (advisor legis. com. from 1934), Am. Legion, SAR, Kirksville Country Club, Masons, Rotary (pres. 1939), Kappa Delta Pi, Phi Delta Kappa. Baptist. *

RYTAND, DAVID A., physician, educator; b. San Francisco, Nov. 4, 1909; s. Henri Garfield and Hattie (Abramson) Levy; m. Nancy Holmquist, Dec. 22, 1937; children: Sally, David Henry, William Allen. A.B., Stanford U., 1929, M.D., 1933. Intern Lane Hosp., San Francisco, 1932-33, resident, 1933-36; instr. medicine Stanford U. Sch. Medicine, Calif., 1936-38, asst. prof., 1938-48, assoc. prof., 1948-54, prof., 1954-75, Arthur L. Bloomfield prof. medicine, 1958-75, Bloomfield prof. emeritus, from 1975, exec. dept. medicine, 1954-59; chief cardiology Santa Clara Valley Med. Ctr., Calif., 1975-82. Editor: Annual Review of Medicine, 1954-62. Chmn. Stanford U. Med. Fund, 1975-78; dir. alumni relations Stanford U. Med. Sch., 1981-85. Fellow AAAS, ACP; mem. Assn. Am. Physicians, Am. Soc. Clin. Investigation, Calif. Acad. Medicine (pres. 1985), Western Soc. Clin. Research (pres. 1954), Soc. Exptl. Biology and Medicine, Am. Soc. Pharmacology and Exptl. Therapeutics, Western Assn. Physicians (pres. 1959), Stanford Med. Alumni Assn. (sec.-treas. 1964-75, pres. 1977-78). Home: Atherton Calif. Died Sept. 23, 1991; buried Alta Mesa, Palo Alto, Calif.

SABRY, H. E. ALY, government official; b. Aug. 30, 1920; married; 2 children. Grad., Mil. Acad., 1939, Air Force Acad., 1940. Tchr. Air Force Acad.; chief bur. Comdr. in Chief of Armed Forces; head Office Polit. Affairs, Pres. of Republic, 1953; minister presdl. affairs United Arab Republic, 1957, prime minister, 1964-65, v.p., 1965-67; sec. gen. Arab Socialist Union, 1965-67, 68-70; mem. Egypt's delegation Evacuation Agreement talks, 1954, Conf. Bandoeng, 1955, Brioni, 1956, UN Gen. Assembly, 1960, Casablanca, 1961, Belgrade, 1961; rep. Egypt at Security Coun. meetings concerning nationalization of Suez Canal Co., 1956; head United Arab Republic delegation to Colombo Conf., Ceylon, 1962; United Arab Republic rep. Addis-Ababa African Summit Conf., 1962, Cairo African Summit Con., 1962, 2d Non-Aligned Summit Conf., Cairo, 1964; mem. Nat. Assembly for Kanayat dist., 1957. Home: Cairo United Arab Republic Died Aug. 4, 1991.

SACHS, ALLAN MAXWELL, physicist, educator; b. N.Y.C., July 13, 1921; s. George M. and Elsa (Shenfield) S.; m. Judith Morrison, Dec. 19, 1949; children: Carolyn, George Morrison, Marjorie. Grad., Horace Mann Sch., 1938; BA, Harvard U., 1942, MA, 1947, PhD, 1949. Instr. physics Columbia U., N.Y.C., 1949-50, assoc., 1950-51, from asst. to assoc. prof., 1951-60, prof., 1960-89, chmn. dept. physics, 1967-71, chmn. exec. com. senate, 1971-74. Contbr. articles to profl. jours; rschr. on particle physics. Served to maj. USAAF, 1942-45. Decorated Bronze star. Fellow Am. Phys. Soc.; mem. Am. Assn. Physics Tchrs., Phi Beta Kappa. Home: Dobbs Ferry N.Y. Died Sept. 20, 1989.

SACKS, ALBERT MARTIN, lawyer, educator; b. N.Y.C., Aug. 15, 1920; s. Harry and Minnie (Miretsky) S.; m. Sadelle Roselyn Rader, Nov. 22, 1945; children—Margery, Janet. BBA, CCNY, 1940; LLB magna cum laude, Harvard U., 1948. Bar: D.C. 1951, Mass. 1957. Law clk. to presiding judge U.S. Ct. Appeals (2d cir.), 1948-49; law clk. to Justice Felix Frankfurter U.S. Supreme Ct., 1949-50; assoc. Covington & Burling, 1950-52; asst. prof. law Harvard U., Cambridge, Mass., 1952-55, prof., 1955-69, Dane prof. law, 1969-81, assoc. dean Law Sch., 1968-71, dean Law Sch., 1971-81; reporter U.S. Supreme Ct. Adv. Com. Fed. Rules of Civil Procedure, 1965-70; chmn. Boston Home Rule Commn., 1968-71, Mass. Atty. Gen.'s Com. on Civil Rights and Liberties, 1967-69. Author: (with Henry Hart) The Legal Process, 1958; pres. Harvard Law Rev., 1948; contbr. articles to law revs. Served with AUS, 1943-46. Mem. Am. Law Inst., Am. Acad. Arts and Scis., ABA, Assn. Am. Law Schs. (pres. 1980-81). Home: Belmont Mass. Died Mar. 22, 1991; cremated.

SAINER, LEONARD, lawyer, business executive; b. London, Oct. 12, 1909; s. Archer and Sarah (Lewis) S. Ed., Univ. Coll., London, London Sch. Econs. Formerly sr. ptnr., now cons. Titmuss Sainer & Webb, London; life pres., cons. Sears plc, London. Home: London Eng. Deceased. †

ST. JACQUES, RAYMOND, actor, director; b. 1930. Student, Yale. Stage appearances include Seventh Heaven, The Blacks, Night Life, The Cool World; asst. dir., fencing dir., Am. Shakespeare Festival, Stratford, Conn.; appeared in TV miniseries Roots, 1977, TV films Search for the Gods, 1975, Secrets of Three Hungry Wives, 1978, Superior Court, The Wild Pair, 1987, They Live, Glory, Strange Turf, also numerous guest appearances major series; film debut in Black Like Me, 1964; films include The Pawnbroker, 1964, Mister Moses, 1965, Mister Buddwing, 1966, The Comedians, 1967, The Green Berets, 1968, Uptight, 1968, If He Hollers Let Him Go, 1968, Change of Mind, 1970, Cotton Comes to Harlem, 1970, Cool Breeze, 1972, The Book of Numbers, 1973, Born Again, 1978, Eyes of Laura Mars, 1978, The Private Files of J. Edgar Hoover, 1978, Sweet Dirty Tony, 1981, The Evil That Men Do, 1984, Glory, 1989. Home: Beverly Hills Calif. Died Aug. 27, 1990.

SAKHAROV, ANDREI DIMITRIYEVICH, nulcear physicist, peace activist; b. Moscow, May 21, 1921; grad. Moscow State U., 1942; PhD 1953; hon. deg. Bologna U., 1989; m. Yelena Bonner, 1971; 2 children. Physicist, P.N. Lebedev Physics Inst., Acad. of Scis., Moscow, 1945-80; achieved important breakthrough in controlled nuclear fusion leading to devel. of Soviet hydrogen bomb; founder Human Rights Comm., 1970; active Soviet human rights campaign; in internal exile, 1980—. Decorated Order of Lenin; recipient Eleanor Roosevelt Peace award, 1973; Cino del Duca prize, 1974; Stalin prize; Reinhold Niebohr prize U. Chgo., 1974; Nobel Peace prize, 1975. Mem. Am. Acad. Arts and Scis., Nat. Acad. Scis., French Acad. Sci. (fgn. assoc.), Soviet Acad. Scis. Author: Progress, Peaceful Coexistence and Intellectual Freedom, 1968; Sakharov Speaks, 1974; My Country and the World, 1975; Alarm and Hope, 1979, Memoirs, 1990 (published posthumously), also, others. Died Dec. 14, 1989. Home: Novogorod Russia

SALBER, EVA JULIET, medical educator, author; b. Capetown, South Africa, Jan. 5, 1916; came to U.S., 1956, naturalized, 1961; d. Moses and Fanny (Srolowitz) S.; m. Harry Tarley Phillips, Nov. 1, 1939; children: David, Mark, Rosalie, Philip. M.B., Ch.B., U. Capetown, 1938, D.P.H., 1945, M.D., 1955. Intern Provincial Hosp., Port Elizabeth, South Africa, Elliot Sir Henry Hosp., Umtata, South Africa; resident Capetown Free Dispensary and Queen Elizabeth Hosp. for Children, London, 1940-44; rsch. assoc. epidemiology Harvard Sch. Pub. Health, Boston, 1959-61, sr. rsch. assoc., 1961-66; dir. Martha Eliot Family Health Center, Boston, 1967-69; sr. assoc. Harvard Center Community Health and Med. Care, Boston, 1969-70; prof. community and family medicine Duke U., Durham, N.C., 1971-82, prof. emeritus, 1982-90; cons. in field.; Milton rsch. assoc. Harvard Sch. Pub. Health, Boston, 1957-58; lectr. Harvard Med. Sch., 1967-70, U. N.C., 1972-78. Author: Caring and Curing: Community Participation in Health Services, 1975, (with Connie Service) Community Health Education: The Lay Advisor Approach, 1977, Don't Send Me Flowers When I'm Dead: Voices of Rural Elderly, 1983, (with H.T. Phillips) Services to the Elderly in England, 1980, The Mind is Not the Heart: Recollections of a Woman Physician, 1989; contbr. numerous articles to profl. jours. Sr. bursar South Africa Coun. Indsl. and Sci. Rsch., 1950-55; bd. dirs. N.C. Student Rural Health Coalition, 1978-90, N.C. Black Ch. Project, Raleigh, 1980-90, Community Mental Health Ctr., Chapel Hill, N.C., 1981-83. Recipient Margaret Sanger award Planned Parenthood, Orange County, N.C., 1990; Radcliffe Inst. scholar, 1966-67; Sr. Internat. fellow NIH, London, 1980. Fellow Am. Pub. Health Assn.; mem. Internat. Epidemiology Assn., Am. Gerontol. Soc. Democrat. Jewish. Home: Chapel Hill N.C. Died Nov. 18, 1990.

SALET, EUGENE ALBERT, army officer, college administrator; b. Standish, Calif., May 25, 1911; s. August and Marie (Irigary) S.; BA, U. Nev., 1934, LLD (hon.), 1968; student Nat. War Coll., 1955; Advanced Mgmt. Program, Harvard U., 1958; LLD (hon.), Dickinson Law Sch., 1966; DD (hon.), Am. Theol. Sem., 1985; m. Irene Taylor, June 13, 1936; children: Suzette Taylor Salet Cook, Eugene Michael. Commd. 2d lt. U.S. Army, 1934, advanced through grades to maj. gen., 1962, ret., 1970; trust devel. officer 1st Nat. Bank & Trust Co., Augusta, Ga., 1970-73; pres. Ga. Mil. Coll., Milledgeville, 1973-85, dean dept. adult edn., 1970-73; pres. U.S. Army War Coll., 1964-67; sec. NATO mil. com., 1955-58. Decorated D.S.M., Silver Star, Legion of Merit with 2 oak leaf clusters, Bronze Star with 2 oak leaf clusters; Mil. Valor Cross (Italy), Croix de Guerre (France), Fourragère (France), others; named Disting. Nevadan, 1967. Mem. Assn. Pvt. Colls. and Schs. (pres. 1984-85), Assn. Mil. Colls. and Schs. U.S. (pres. 1983-84), 3d Inf. Div. Assn., VFW, Ret. Officers Assn., Kiwanis, Harvard Club. Republican. Roman Catholic. Died Feb. 6, 1992; buried Westover Cemetary, Augusta, Ga. Home: Augusta Ga.

SALISBURY, RICHARD FRANK, anthropologist; b. London, Dec. 8, 1926; emigrated to Can., 1962, naturalized, 1976; s. Thomas and Marjorie Beatrice (Smith) S.; m. Mary Elizabeth Roseborough, Aug. 28, 1954; children: Thomas S., John W., Catherine E. A.B., Cambridge U., 1949, M.A., 1956; M.A., Harvard U., 1955; Ph.D., Australian Nat. U., 1957. Research assoc. Harvard Sch. Public Health, Boston, 1955-56; asst. prof. Tufts U., Boston, 1956-57, U. Calif. at Berkeley, 1957-62; assoc. prof. McGill U., Montreal, Que., Can., 1962-65, prof., 1966-70, chmn. dept. sociology and anthropology, 1966-70, dir. program Anthropology of Devel., 1970-86, dir. Ctr. Developing Area Studies, 1975-78, 86, dean faculty of arts, from 1986; vis. prof. U. Papua, New Guinea, 1967, 84; mem. acad. panel Can. Council, 1974-78; cons. to Adminstr. Papua, 1971, Can. Dept. Agr., 1970, James Bay Devel. Corp., 1971-72, Indians of Que. Assn., 1972-75, Communications Can., 1974-75, James Bay Energy Corp., 1982, Lahmeyer Internat., 1984; bd. dirs. Que. Univs. Commn. Author: From Stone to Steel, 1962, Structures of Custodial Care, 1962, Behavioral Science Research in New Guinea, 1967, Vunamami, 1969, Development and James Bay, 1972, Not By Bread Alone, 1972, A House Divided, 1978, Negotiating a Way of Life, 1979, Affluence and Cultural Survival, 1983, A Homeland for the Cree, 1986. Pres. Westmount High Sch. Com., 1974-75; mem. Commn. on Future of Que. Univs., 1977-79; bd. dirs. Que. Inst. Research on Culture, 1979-84, Can. Human Rights Found., from 1980. Served with Royal Marines, 1945-48. Fellow Royal Soc. Can., Royal Anthrop. Inst., Am. Anthrop. Assn.; mem. Can. Sociology and Anthropology Assn. (pres. 1969-70), Am. Ethnol. Assn. (pres. 1979-80), Soc. Applied Anthropology, Soc. Applied Anthropology in Can. (pres. 1986). Home: Westmount Que., Can. Died June 17, 1989.

SALK, LEE, psychologist; b. N.Y.C., Dec. 27, 1926; s. Daniel Bonn and Dora (Press) S.; m. Mary Jane Salk; children by previous marriage: Eric, Pia. Student, Rutgers U., 1944, U. Louisville, 1946; A.B. in Psychology, U. Mich., 1949, M.A. in Sociology, 1950, Ph.D. in Psychology, 1954. Asst. in psychology U. Mich., 1948-50; research asst. Research Center Group Dynamics, 1949; instr. in psychology of adjustment Extension Service, 1951-54; clin. psychologist Psychol. Clinic, Inst. Human Adjustment, 1952-53; research asst. Mich. Dept. Mental Health, 1949, research program dir., 1951-52, research cons., 1953-54; researcher Lab. Group Research, 1950; research asso. Wayne U., 1950-51; chief clin. psychologist Pontiac Child Guidance Clinic, 1952; pvt. practice diagnostic cons., 1952-54; clin. psychology intern Detroit Vets. Mental Hygiene Clinic, 1952-53, Dearborn (Mich.) VA Hosp., 1953-54; research asso. dept. psychiatry Allan Meml. Inst. Psychiatry, McGill U., Montreal, Que., Can., 1954-57; instr. Indsl. Relations Centre Allan Meml. Inst. Psychiatry, McGill U., 1954-55; instr. McGill Extension Service, 1955, vis. lectr. human relations, 1957-59; pvt. practice diagnosis and psychotherapy, 1954-57; chief psychologist psychiat. cons. service Univ. Settlement House, N.Y.C., 1957-58; instr. sci. methods, resident tng. program, dept. psychiatry City Hosp., Elmhurst, N.Y., 1958-63, clin. dir. deprol research program, 1960; chief psychologist pediatric psychiatry service Lenox Hill Hosp., N.Y., 1962-66; cons. psychologist dept. pediatrics Lenox Hill Hosp., 1976-92; pvt. practice intensive psychotherapy diagnosis and cons., N.Y.C., 1957-66; chief psychologist, child psychiatry service N.Y. Hosp.-Cornell U. Med. Center, N.Y.C., 1966-67, attending psychologist in pediatrics, 1966-92, dir. div. pediatric psychology, 1968-76; attending psychologist Payne Whitney Psychiat. Clinic, 1976-92; clin. asst. prof. psychology in pediatrics and psychiatry Cornell U. Med. Coll., 1966-67, clin. asso. prof., 1968, clin. prof. psychology in pediatrics, 1971-92, clin. prof. psychology in psychiatry, 1976-92; asso. research scientist N.Y. U. Coll. Dentistry, 1971-72; lectr. in human devel. and family studies Cornell U. N.Y. State Coll. Human Ecology, 1969-72; adj. prof. Brown U., 1979—; prin. NBC-TV Nightly News Doctor's Office, N.Y.C. and Chgo., 1976—; syndicated on NBC-Radio News and Info. Service, 1975-77; Macklin Meml. lectr. U.S. Naval Med. Hosp., Portsmouth, Va., 1971; Jonas A. Berg Meml. lectr., 1973; invited speaker numerous orgns.; mem. profl. adv. bd. Floating Hosp. (formerly HOPE ship), from 1972, Internat. Childbirth Edn. Assn., from 1972; mem. adv. council, bd. dirs. Postgrad. Center Mental Health, Guanabara, Brazil, from 1973; mem. adv. bd. Found. for Edn. Human Relations, from 1976, Public Action Coalition on Toys, from 1976; mem. nat. adv. council Boys' Clubs Am. Nat. Health Project, from 1977; hon. mem. bd. dirs. Artists Family Theatre Project, Inc., 1977; bd. dirs. N.Y. State Citizens' Council for Children, Youth and Their Families, from 1977 ; mem. Head Start Child Abuse and Neglect Prevention Task Force, Agy. for Child Devel., City N.Y., from 1978; mem. nat. adv. council Nat. Orgn. for Non-Parents, from 1978; cons. in field. Author: How to Raise a Human Being, 1969, What Every Child Would Like His Parents to Know, 1972, Preparing for Parenthood, 1974, What Every Child Would Like Parents To Know About Divorce, 1978, Dear Dr. Salk, 1979, Ask Dr. Salk, 1981, My Father, My Son: Intimate Relationships, 1982, The Complete Dr. Salk: An A to Z Guide to Raising Your Child, 1983, Your Child's First Year, 1983; columnist: McCall's Mag, from 1972, Pediatric Annals, 1972-74, Talk to Dr. Salk; syndicated newspaper column, 1973-77; contbr. (with Rita Kramer) numerous articles to profl. publs.; subject of (with Rita Kramer) film features; author (with Rita Kramer) audio cassette programs. Served to s/sgt. Armored Forces, World War II. Recipient Key to City and named Ambassador Good Will City of Chattanooga, 1973; recipient Key to City City of Indpls., 1974, spl. citation ARC, 1974, Pearl Merrill award, 1974, Nat. Media award hon. mention Am. Psychol. Found., 1977, Hannah G. Solomon award Nat. Council Jewish Women, 1977. Mem. Am. Psychol. Assn. (exec. com. sect. clin. child psychology 1970-72, pres. sect. 1976-77, pres. div. child and youth services 1979-80, Disting. Profl. Contbn. in Clin. Child Psychology award 1978), AAAS, Royal Soc. Medicine, Am. Acad. Psychotherapists, World Fedn. Mental Health, N.Y. Acad. Scis., Soc. Research Child Devel., Soc. Pediatric Psychology (pres. 1970-71, 71-72, Disting. Contbns. award 1977), Harvey Soc., Soc. Psychol. Study Social Issues, Internat. Soc. Polit. Psychology, North Shore Child Guidance Assn. (hon.). Home: New York N.Y. Died May 2, 1992.

SALKO, HENRY S., textile company executive; b. N.Y.C., Feb. 24, 1925; s. Max and Louise M. (Ginsberg) S.; m. Myrna Schacht; children: Richard Michael, Karen Leslie, Amy Lynn. BS in Econs., U. Pa., 1949. With Max Salko Corp., N.Y.C., 1949-90, v.p., 1958-90; bd. dirs. Ritz Tower Hotel. Chmn. Citizens for Eisenhower; mem. Rep. Town Com., Mamaroneck, 1953-56; trustee Harrison (N.Y.) Jewish Community Ctr., 1970-73; mem. Pub. Employees Rels. Bd. Harrison, 1970-73; pres. Young Reps., 1952-54. With 75th Inf. Div., U.S. Army, 1943-45. Decorated Bronze Star, Purple Heart. Mem. N.Y. Acad. Sci., Retail Assocs. Group, Textile Sq. Club, Wharton Club, City Athletic Club, B'nai B'rith (N.Y. state regional bd. Anti-Defamation League 1979-83, nat. commr. 1989—, chmn. various coms., pres. Westchester Putman coun. 1984-85, v.p. dist. 1 N.E. U.S., pres. 1989-90, internat. bd. govs.), Delta Sigma Rho, Alpha Epsilon Pi. Home: Stamford Conn. Died June 3, 1990.

SALLER, SYLVESTER JOHN, archaeology educator, priest; b. Petoskey, Mich., Sept. 25, 1895; s. John and Mary (Hofbauer) S. AB, St. Joseph's Coll., Teutopolis, Ill., 1913; postgrad., several Franciscan monasteries, 1913-22; Lector Generalis Sacrae Scripturae, St. Anthony's Coll., Rome, 1932, Franciscan Bibl. Inst., Jerusalem, 1932. Prof. classical langs. St. Joseph's Coll., Teutopolis, 1922-27, Hinsdale, Ill., 1927-28; prof. O.T., St. Joseph Sem., 1958-60; prof. archaeology Franciscan Bible Inst., from 1932; pres. Franciscan Monastery of Transfiguration on Mt. Thabor, Palestine, 1943-44, Studium Biblicum Franciscanum, Flagellation, Jerusalem, 1945-50; dir. excavations at Bethany, Mt. Nebo (Siaghah) in Trans-Jordan, 1933, 35, 37, also numerous other Byzantine sites in Nebo region, St. John Bapt.'s 'Ein Karim, 1941-42. Author: The Memorial of Moses on Mount Nebo, 2 vols., 1941, Discoveries at St. John's 'Ein Karim,' 1941-42, 46, (with E. Testa) The Archaeological Setting of the Shrine of Bethpage, 1961, The Jebusite Burial Place, 1964; co-author: The Town of Nebo (Kiirbet-El-Mekhayyat) with brief survey of other ancient Christian monuments in Transjordan, Jerusalem, 1948; translator: (from German to English) The Bible in the Light of Modern Science, 1960; also articles. *

SALLET, DIRSE WILKIS, mechanical engineering educator; b. Washington, Aug. 10, 1936; s. Richard and Margarete Louise (Stolzenbach) S.; m. Martha Jane Obert, June 9, 1963 (div.); children: Stefan and Michael (twins), Bonnie, Johnny. B.S.M.E., George Washington U., 1961; M.S.M.E., U. Kans., 1963; Dr.Ing., U. Stuttgart, Germany, 1966. Registered profl. engr., Md. Research asso. Inst. Aero and Gas Dynamics, U. Stuttgart, 1963-66; research mech. engr. Naval Ordnance Lab., Silver Spring, Md., 1966-67; asst. prof. mech. engring. U. Md., College Park, 1967-70, assoc. prof., 1970-76, prof., 1976-90; vis. scientist Max Planck Inst. Fluid Mechanic Rsch., Götingen, Fed. Republic Germany, also Aerodynamische Versuchsanstalt Göttingen, 1973-74; vis. rsch. scientist Ctr. Nuclear Rsch. Karlsruhe (Germany) Inst. Nuclear Reactor Components, 1980-81; cons. in field; vis. prof. Tech. U. Munich, 1987, 89; chmn. Md. Bd. Boiler Rules. Contbr. articles to profl. jours. Recipient numerous research contracts Dept. Transp., numerous research contracts Dept. Def.; recipient Alexander von Humboldt Prize, 1985. Mem. ASME, Am. Phys. Soc., Washington Acad. Scis., Philos. Soc. Washington (pres. 1984-85), Gauss Gesellschaft Göttingen, Sigma Xi, Pi Tau Sigma. Home: Hyattsville Md. Died Mar. 24, 1992.

SALM, PETER, comparative litature educator; b. Hameln, Germany, Aug. 23, 1919; came to U.S., 1938; s. Uri and Heleh (Hahlo) Salm Byrns; m. June Macy, Aug. 10, 1958; 1 child, Anthony. B.A., UCLA, 1951; Ph.D., Yale U., 1958. Teaching fellow UCLA, Yale U.; asst. prof. German Wesleyan U., Middletown, Conn., 1958-63; assoc. prof. German Case Western Res. U., Cleve., 1963-65, chmn. German dept., chmn. div. modern langs. and lit., until 1976, prof. comparative lit. and German, 1976-86, prof. emeritus, 1986-90. Author: Three Modes of Criticism, 1968, German transl., 1970, The Poem As Plant, 1971, Pinpoint of Eternity, 1986; translator: (Goethe) Faust I, 1962, 3d edit., 1985. Served to tech. sgt. CIC, U.S. Army, 1942-46. Mem. MLA, Phi Beta Kappa. Democrat. Home: Cleveland Heights Ohio Died Oct. 21, 1990.

SALTER, HERBERT WILLIAM, physician; b. Ohio, Dec. 12, 1897; s. William A. and Minnie Etta (Mundhenk) S.; m. Edna K. Hastings, Dec. 24, 1936; 1 child by previous marriage, Herbert William. Student, W.Va. U., 1915-16; BS, Ohio State U., 1918; MD, Harvard U., 1922. Asst. resident in gynecology Lakeside Hosp., Cleve., 1923-24; resident in surgery Huron Road Hosp., Cleve., 1924-25; resident in obstetrics Cleve. Maternity Hosp., 1924; pvt. practice, Cleve., from 1925; intern Lakeside Hosp., Cleve., 1922-23; dir. dept. gen. practice Doctor's Hosp., Booth Meml. Hosp.; owner, operator Salter Automobile Import Co., Cleve., 1958-60. Rep. candidate for coroner, Cuyahoga County, Cleve., 1952. Comdr. USNR, 1942-45. Mem. AMA, Am. Acad. Family Practice (pres. Ohio from 1955), Cleve. Acad. Medicine (bd. dirs. 1952-58), Ohio Med. Assn., Am. Assn. Physicians and Surgeons. Congregationalist. *

SALTER, LEWIS SPENCER, academic administrator, physicist; b. Norman, Okla., Feb. 4, 1926; s. Lewis Spencer and Reaves (Alford) S.; m. Mary Anna Morse, June 19, 1950; children: David Reaves, Samuel Allen, John Michael, Andrew Lewis. BS, U. Okla., 1949; BA, Oxford U., Eng., 1953, PhD, 1956; LHD (hon.), Wabash Coll., 1987; DSc (hon.), Hanover Coll., 1988, Knox Coll., 1989. Instr. math. U. Md. Overseas Program, Eng., 1952-53; asst. prof., assoc. prof., prof. physics Wabash Coll., Crawfordsville, Ind., 1953-67; assoc. prof. physics Bandung (Indonesia) Inst. Tech., 1958-60; vis. physicist NRC, Ottawa, Ont., Can., 1963-64; cons. Argonne Nat. Lab., 1965-72; dean, exec. v.p., v.p. acad. affairs Knox Coll., Galesburg, Ill., 1968-78; pres. Wabash Coll., Crawfordsville, 1978-88, pres. emeritus, 1989, chancellor, 1988-89, prof. physics, 1989; sec. Ind. selection com. Rhodes scholarships, 1981-87; commr., exec. bd. North Central Assn., 1984-89; cons. sci. edn., Indonesia, 1972, World Bank sector survey team, 1973; cons. NSF; bd. dirs. Lubricol Corp. Mem. com. on ministry Am. Bapt. Conv., 1984-87; mem. NCAA Council, 1987-89. Served to 1st lt., inf. AUS, 1943-46. Recipient award for excellence in teaching Danforth Found., 1967. Mem. Am. Phys. Soc., Am. Assn. Physics Tchrs., Am. Sci. Affiliation, Associated Colls. of Ind. (pres.), Phi Beta Kappa, Phi Mu Alpha, Sigma Pi Sigma. Democrat. Baptist. Home: Crawfordsville Ind. Died Nov. 19, 1989; buried Crawfordsville, Ind.

SALTIEL, WILLIAM DAVID, lawyer; b. Chgo., Oct. 21, 1895; s. Leopold and Marie (Friedman) S.; m. Cicely Friedman Haas, June 21, 1932; 1 stepchild, Charles Ilaas. LLB, Chgo.-Kent Coll. Law, 1918. Bar: Ill. 1918. Practiced in Chgo.; mem. Saltiel & Saltiel; asst. corp. counsel City of Chgo., 1920-23, city atty., 1927-31; spl. atty. Bd. Edn., Chgo., 1931; spl. asst. to atty. gen. U.S., 1941-45; midwest chief small bus. sect. Dept. Justice; former master in chancery Dist. Ct.; former gen. counsel Jr. C. of C.; lectr. Henry C. Frick Edn. Commn., from 1954; also lectr. various subjects. Founder, organizer non-partisan campaign Polit. Edn. League of U.S. Jr. C. of C.; pres. Chgo. bd. Denver Sanatorium, 1945-48; mem. speakers' staff Rep. Nat. Com., Ill. Rep. Com., Cook County Rep. Cen. Com., 1920-36; v.p. Am. Citizen's Found.; sec., bd. dirs., gen. counsel Chgo. Opera Co.; v.p. Adult Edn. Coun. Greater Chgo., from 1965; mem. Ill. Human Rels. Commn.; mem. nat. bd. Vols. of Am.; mem. Welfare Coun. Met. Chgo.; pres. Am. Friends of Austria; also others. With USN, 1918-19. Decorated Gold Medal of Merit (Austria), knight Gold Medal of Honor (Italy). Mdm. ABA, Ill. Bar Assn., Chgo. Bar Assn., Mchts. and Mfrs. Club Chgo. (bd. govs.), Masons, Pi Gamma U (hon.). *

SALTONSTALL, WILLIAM GURDON, educational administrator; b. Milton, Mass., Nov. 11, 1905; s. Robert and Caroline (Stevenson) S.; m. Katharyn Watson, Sept. 22, 1941; children: Josephine Saltonstall Converse, Katharyn Saltonstall Hok, William Gurdon Jr., Samuel Stevenson, Deborah Saltonstall Twining. AB, Harvard U., 1928, MA, 1931, LLD, 1953; LHD (hon.), Williams Coll., 1947, Tufts U., 1950, Dartmouth Coll., 1952, Bowdoin Coll., 1952; LittD, Colby Coll., 1954, Princeton U., 1956; LLD, U. N.H., River Coll., 1967. Tchr. history and English, William Penn Charter Sch., 1928-30; traveled and studied in Europe, 1931-32; tchr. history Phillips Exeter Acad., 1932-40, chmn. history dept., 1940-42, prin., 1946-63; dir. in Nigeria, Peace Corps, 1963-65; program coord. Rodmann Job Corps Ctr., New Bedford, Mass., from 1965, sr. advisor, from 1966; former trustee Ednl. Testing Svc. Author: Ports of Piscataqua, 1941. Chmn. Mass. Bd. Edn., 1966-68; trustee Milton Acad., Friends Acad., New Bedford, Southeastern Mass. U., Currier Art Gallery, Colby Coll.; bd. overseers Harvard U., 1946-52, 58-64; bd. dirs. N.H. Hist. Soc., pres. bd. trustees, 1958-63; former visitor U.S. Naval Acad., Annapolis, Md. Mem. New Eng. Assn. Colls. and Secondary Schs. (pres.), Am. Acad. Arts and Scis., Colonial Soc. Mass., Assoc. Harvard Alumni (pres.), Owl Club (Harvard), Beverly Yacht Club (Boston), Tavern Club (Boston). Home: Marion Mass. Died Dec. 18, 1989; buried Salem, Mass.

SALTZBERG, BERNARD, biomathematician; b. Chgo., Apr. 21, 1919; s. David and Pearl (Weiss) S.; m. Evalyn Freidin, Oct. 17, 1942; children—Steven, Larry, Dale, Eugene, Gwen. B.S., Ill. Inst. Tech, 1952; M.S., 1953; Ph.D. in Biomed. and Elec. Engring, Marquette U., 1972. Supervising research engr. Am. Machine & Foundry Research Lab., 1952-56; sr. sci. staff Space Tech. div. TRW, 1956-60; sr. scientist Bissett-Berman Corp., 1960-65; prof. Med. Sch., Engring. Sch. Tulane U., New Orleans, 1965-75, prof. biomath., 1965-75; dir. div. biomed. computing Med. Sch., Tulane U., 1968-75; prof. U. Tex. Med. Sch., Houston, 1976-89; head Neurosci. Signal Analysis sect. U. Tex. Mental Scis. Inst., Houston, 1976-89; mem. faculty Rice U., 1977-89, Baylor Coll. Medicine, 1977-89, U. Houston, 1977-89; dir. Advanced Instruments Devel. Corp.; mem. exec. com. Inst. Comprehensive Medicine. Contbr. articles to profl. jours. Served with USAF, 1943-46. Schleider scholar, 1964-66; NIH, Office Naval Research grantee. Mem. NIH (mem. adv. study sect.), NIMH (mem. adv. study sect.), Neuroelectric Soc. (v.p.), Am. EEG Soc., Soc. Neurosci., Epilepsy Soc., Soc. Biol. Psychiatry, Soc. Psychophysiol. Research, AAAS, Biomedical Engring. Soc. Jewish. Home: Houston Tex. Died Dec. 22, 1989; buried Eden Memorial Park, Los Angeles.

SALZMAN, HERBERT, business executive; b. N.Y.C., May 2, 1916; s. William S. and Minnie (Reich) S.; m. Rita Fredricks, May 26, 1947; children: Anthony David, Jeffrey Jonathan. BA cum laude, Yale U., 1938; grad. advanced mgmt. course, Columbia U., 1954. Vice pres. Standard Bag Corp., N.Y.C., 1938-59, pres., 1959-66; asst. adminstr, in charge agys. pvt. resources div. AID, 1966-71; exec. v.p. Overseas Pvt. Investment Corp., 1971-73, dir., exec. v.p., 1973-76; U.S. permanent rep. and ambassador OECD, Paris, 1977-81; commr. N.Y.C. Office Internat. Bus. Devel., 1983-84; gen. ptnr. Bradford Assocs., Princeton, N.J., 1984-90; Mem. adv. com. on multinat. enterprises Dept. State, 1975-77. Contbr.: chpt. to The Political Economy of World Business (George Ball), 1975. Bd. dirs. Adlai Stevenson Inst. Internat. Affairs, 1968-75, Kennedy Center Prodns., from 1972; mem. vis. com. Middle East Center, U. Chgo., 1964-70, Center for Internat. Affairs, Harvard, 1975-81; vice-chmn. bd. trustees Studio Theatre, John F. Kennedy Center, 1976-79. Served to lt. comdr. USNR, 1941-46. Mem. Council Fgn. Relations. Clubs: Yale, Century (N.Y.C.). Home: New York N.Y. Died Dec. 23, 1990.

SAMMARTINO, PETER, university chancellor; b. N.Y.C., Aug. 15, 1904; s. Guy and Eva (Amendola) S.; m. Sylvia Scaramelli, Dec. 5, 1933 (dec. 1992). B.S., CCNY, 1924; M.A., NYU, 1928, Ph.D., 1931; post-grad., Sorbonne, 1931-32; Litt.D., L.I. U.; LL.D., U. Liberia, Kyung Hee U.; D.H.L., Fairleigh Dickinson U.; D.H.E., Unity Coll.; Doct. ès Lettres, U. Zaire; D.B.A., Bangkok U. Tchr. pub. schs. N.Y.C., Townsend Harris High Sch., Coll. City N.Y.; in charge lang. New Coll., Tchrs. Coll., Columbia U.; founder, 1st pres. Fairleigh Dickinson Jr. Coll., Rutherford, N.J., 1942-48, pres., 1948-56; pres. Fairleigh Dickinson U., Rutherford, 1956-67; ednl. editor United Am., also Atlantica, La Voix de France. Author: Demanage Higher Education, The President of a Small College, I Dreamed a College, Survey of French Literature, The Man Who Was William Shakespeare, 20 other books. Chmn. Econ. Devel. Participation Pres.'s Commn. on Higher Edn., White House Conf. on Edn., 1956; past pres. N.J. Assn. Colls. and Univs.; bd. chmn. Am. Inst. Italian Studies; past pres. Internat. Assn. Univ. Presidents; v.p. N.J. Constl. Conv.; mem. N.J. Bicentennial Commn.; mem. president's adv. bd. U.S. Peace Corps; mem. bd. fgn. scholarships.; Founder, pres. Restore Ellis Island Commn.; mem. bd. Friends of Cuttington Coll.; v.p. Nat. Italian-Am. Found.; pres. N.Y. Cultural Center, N.Y.C., 1969-76; dir. Tibetan Found., 1969; com. on accreditation and institutional eligibility Office of Edn., 1971; chmn. N.J. Basic Skills Task Force, 1972; Bd. dirs. Columbus Hosp., Newark; chmn. bd. trustees St. Stephens Sch., Rome; trustee N.J. Hist. Soc., N.J. State Opera; nat. chmn. Internat. Columbus Quincentennial Commn. Decorated comdr. Order des Palmes Academiques, chevalier Legion of Honor France; chevalier Order Crown of Italy; grand officer Star of Solidarity; comdr. Order of Merit Italy; Knight of Malta; grand band Star of Africa Liberia; chevalier Order of Lion Iran; comdr. L'Ordre National Ivory Coast; recipient Silver medal S.A.R., Townsend Harris medal, Gold medal U. Bologna, Brotherhood award NCCJ; named N.J. Man of Year N.J. Advt. Council, 1963; Distinguished alumni award N.Y. U., 1968; 125th anniversary medal in higher edn. U. City of N.Y.; Franklin fellow Royal Soc. Arts.; Columbus Countdown award, 1985. Mem. Alpha Phi Delta (past nat. pres.). Republican. Roman Catholic. Clubs: Salmagundi, University (N.Y.C.); Upper Montclair Country, Pot and Kettle, Bar Harbor. Home: Rutherford N.J. Died Mar. 29, 1992.

SAMMIS, WALTER HENRY, public utlities consultant; b. Hempstead, N.Y., June 28, 1896; s. Henry and Mignon Irene (Macnamee) S.; m. Zayle Donaldson Wright, Dec. 8, 1948. EE, Columbia U., 1917; LLD, Thiel Coll., U. Akron. With Bklyn. Rapid Transit and Pub. Svc. Co., N.J., 1915-16; instr. elec. engring. Columbia U., N.Y.C., 1919-20; engr. Consumers Power Co., Jackson, Mich., 1920-24; power sales and rate analysis engr. C.H. Tenney and Co., Boston, 1924-25; asst. to v.p. and gen. mgr. Consumers Power Co., Jackson, 1925-29; asst. to v.p. Allied Power & Light Corp., N.Y.C., 1929-30, Commonwealth & So. Corp. (Del. and N.Y.), 1930-35; v.p., bd. dirs. Commonwealth & So. Corp. (Del.), 1938-41; bd. dirs. Commonwealth & So. Corp. (Del.), 1949-52; dir., mem. exec. com. Ohio Valley Electric Corp. and Ind.-Ky. Electric Corp., from 1952; v.p., dir. Commonwealth & So. Corp. (N.Y.), 1938-44, dir., 1947-49; v.p., dir. Transp. Securitie s Corp., 1933-38, pres., dir., 1938-43; v.p., dir. Consumers Power Co., 1932-44; v.p., dir. Ohio Edison Co., Akron, 1933-36, 41-44, pres., 1944-64; v.p., dir. Pa. Power Co., New Castle, 1933-36, pres., 1936-50, 53-64, chmn. bd., 1950-53; dir. Nat. Assn. Electric Cos., 1945-49; mem. Coun. Electric Operating Cos., 1942-45, Electric Utility Def. Adv. Coun., 1950-53; trustee East Cen. Nuclear Group, Inc. Trustee Citizens for Progress, Akron, from 1961; trustee Columbia U., 1947-53, now life trustee, mem. adv. com. on investments, chmn. nat. com. Sch. Engring. and Supplied Sci. Devel. Foud; pres., trustee Akron City Hosp. Ensign USNRF, 1917-19. Fellow IEEE; mem. Edison Electric Inst. (bd. dirs. 1944-48, 52-59, 60-63, pres. 1953-54), Ohio C. of C. (v.p. 1949-56), Sigma Xi, Tau Beta Pi. Republican. Episcopalian. *

SAMMONS, CHARLES A., holding company executive; b. 1901; married. With Postal Mut. Indemnity Co., 1929-48; past pres., chmn. bd., dir. Res. Life Ins. Co.; now chmn. bd., dir. Sammons Enterprises Inc., Dallas. Deceased. Home: Dallas Tex. †

SAMSTAG, GORDON, artist, educator; b. N.Y.C., June 21, 1906; s. Solomon and Evelyn (Scharff) S.; m. Anne Davis, Nov. 3, 1933. Student, Nat. Acad., N.Y.C., Academie Colarossi, Paris; study tour, Europe, Singapore, Hong Kong and Iceland. instr. N.A.D. Sch., N.Y.C., 1930-33, Art Students League, 1955, 56; dir. Am. Art Sch., N.Y.C., 1958-61; sr. lectr. fine arts South Australia Sch. Art, 1961-71; pvt. instr., Cairns, Queensland. One-man show Valand Gallery, Naples, Fla., 1985. Recipient Lippincott prize PAFA, Phila.; recipient Allied Artists of Am. prize, others. Fellow Royal South Australian Soc. Art; mem. Nat. Acad. N.Y. (Clark prize), Naples Art Assn. (bd. control). Clubs: Naples Sailing and Yacht (Fla.); Mamaroneck Sailing and Beach (N.Y.). Home: Naples Fla. Deceased. †

SAMUELS, SEYMOUR, JR., lawyer; b. Nashville, Oct. 23, 1912; s. Seymour and Maud Stella (Rosenfeld) S.; m. Essie Wenar, July 7, 1937; children—Seymour Samuels, Charles W. B.A., Vanderbilt U., 1933, J.D. 1935. Bar: Tenn. 1935, U.S. Dist. Ct. (mid. dist.) Tenn. 1937, U.S. Ct. Appeals (6th cir.) 1943, U.S. Tax Ct. 1940, U.S. Supreme Ct., 1967. Sole practice Nashville, 1935-40; ptnr. Samuels & Allen, Nashville, 1940-42; area rent atty., dep. rent dir. OPA, Nashville, 1942-43; ptnr. Nashville Bag & Burlap Co., 1946-59; dep. dir. law Nashville Met. Govt., 1963-67; ptnr. Hooker & Willis, Nashville, 1967, Hooker, Hooker, Willis & Samuels, Nashville, 1968; assoc. Farris, Evans & Evans, Nashville, 1969-71; ptnr. Farris, Warfield & Samuels, Nashville, 1972-74, Schulman, Leroy & Bennett, Nashville, 1975—. Mem. Nashville Met. Traffic and Parking Commn., 1967-70, Met. Govt. Charter Revision Com., 1970-73, Met. Govt. Transit Authority, 1973-74; chmn. Davidson county Democratic Campaign Com., 1968. Served with USN, 1943-46. Mem. ABA, Tenn. Bar Assn., Nashville Bar Assn., Am. Judicature Soc., Order of Coif, Phi Beta Kappa. Club: Nashville City. Died July 20, 1992. Home: Nashville Tenn. †

SANCHINI, DOMINICK JOSEPH, aerospace company executive, lawyer; b. Raritan, N.J., Dec. 2, 1926; Enrico and Ernesta (Pesci) S.; m. Claire Rich, Oct. 17, 1953; children: Donna Claire, Diane Rae. Student, Princeton U., 1944, Tufts U., 1945; B.S. in Mech. Engring., Lehigh U., 1951; postgrad., Rutgers U. Law Sch., 1953; LL.B., U. So. Calif., 1958. Bar: Calif. Mech. engr. Exxon Corp., Linden, N.J., 1951-53; systems engr. Rockwell Internat., Canoga Park, Calif., 1953-58, assoc. program mgr. Saturn engine (F-1), 1958-68, mfg. dir. tool, engr. exptl., 1968-70, assoc. program mgr. SSME Shuttle, 1970-75, v.p. program mgr. SSME, 1975-83, exec. v.p., 1983-90. Served with USN, 1944-47. Recipient Engr. of Yr. award San Fernando Valley Engring. Council, 1980, Pub. Service award NASA, 1981. Mem. AIAA, Nat. Acad. Engrs. (award 1984), State Bar Calif. Republican. Roman Catholic. Home: Thousand Oaks Calif. Died Nov. 17, 1990.

SANDBERG, ADOLPH ENGELBREKT, geology educator; b. Mpls., Feb. 15, 1898; s. Gustaf Adolf and Tekla (Meck) S.; m. Harriet Burquist, Sept. 14, 1929 (dec. 1962); children: David Alexander, Philip Alan; m. Marian Mitchell Heiberg, Sept. 6, 1963; stepchildren: Carol Ellen Cook, Ann Phillips. AB, U. Minn., 1929; AM, U. Cin., 1931, PhD, 1937. Instr. geology U. Cin., 1929-39; geologist Panama Canal, Cocoli, C.Z., 1939-44, Socony Vacuum Oil Co. Colombia, Bogota, 1944-46, Gulf Oil Co., Managua, Nicaragua, 1947-48; prof. geology La. State U., Raton Rouge, from 1948, chmn. dept., from 1953; cons. geologist, Panema, Chile, Columbia, Minn. Fellow Geol. Soc. Am.; mem. AIME, Soc. Econ. Geologists, Am. Assn. Geology Tchrs., U.S. Naval Inst., Sigma Xi. *

SANDERS, BENJAMIN ELBERT, educator, biochemist; b. Bowersville, Ga., Oct. 19, 1918; s. C. Lamar and Christine (Hogsed) S.; m. Dorothy McIntyre, Sept. 7, 1946; children: Lamar, Marcia Jean. B.S., Wofford Coll., 1939; M.S. in Chemistry, U. Ga., 1942; Ph.D. (Am. Chem. Soc. fellow), Purdue U., 1949. Diplomate: Am. Bd. Clin. Chemistry. Research biochemist Henry Ford Hosp., Detroit, 1949-51; research asso. Sharp & Dohme Co., West Point, Pa., 1951-53, Merck, Sharp & Dohme Research Labs., West Point, Pa., 1953-58; dir. protein chemistry dept. Merck Inst., West Point, 1958-61; assoc. prof. biochemistry State U. N.Y., Buffalo, 1961-67; prof. State U. N.Y., 1967-85, prof. emeritus, 1986-92, asso. chmn. biochemistry dept., 1966-75; Research collaborator Brookhaven Nat. Lab., 1958-63. Author articles plasma protein isolation and characterization, biochemistry schizophrenia to profl. publs. Bd. dirs. North Penn YMCA, 1956-61. Served to 1st lt. AUS, 1942-46. Fellow A.A.A.S.; mem. Am. Chem. Soc., Am. Soc. Biol. Chemists, N.Y. Acad. Scis., Sigma Xi, Phi Lambda Upsilon. Presbyterian. Home: West End N.C. Died July 29, 1992. †

SANDERS, DANIEL SELVARAJAH, social work educator; b. Sri Lanka, Sept. 18, 1928; came to U.S., 1965, naturalized, 1968; s. David S. and Harriet C. (Handy) S.; m. Christobel C. Niles, Apr. 14, 1959. B.A., U. Ceylon, 1953; diploma social welfare, U. Wales, 1958; M.S.W., U. Minn., 1967, Ph.D., 1971. Assoc. dir., lectr. Ceylon Inst. Social Work, 1955-61; exec. dir., research assoc. Inst. Social Study, Ceylon, 1961-65; spl. projects cons., adminstr. Div. Child Welfare, Minn. Dept. Public Welfare, 1967-69; mem. faculty U. Hawaii, 1971-86, prof. social work, dean, dir. internat. programs, 1974-86; dean, prof., dir. Ctr. for Study Internat. Social Welfare Policiesand Svcs. U. Ill., Champaign, 1987-89; pres. Luth. Campus Ministry, Evang. Luth. Ch. Am., 1978-79, 85-86; founder, 1st pres. Interuniv. Consortium for Internat. Social Devel., 1980-89. Author: Impact of Reform Movements on Social Policy Changes, 1972, The Developmental Perspective in Social Work, 1982; co-author: Fundamentals of Social Work Practice, 1981, Education for International Social Welfare, 1984, Visions for the Future: Social Work and Pacific-Asian Perspectives, 1988, Peace and Development ; An Interdisciplinary Perspective, 1989; founder, exec. editor Ceylon Jour. Social Work, 1955-60; editorial adv. Internat. Social Work, 1976-86, Social Devel. Issues, 1984-89, Jour. Social Devel. in Africa, 1986-89; editorial bd. Law and Social Work Quar., 1980-82. Bd. dirs. Hospice Hawaii, 1982-84, Hawaii Council Chs., 1982-84. Brit. Council scholar, 1957-58; Ecumenical scholar World Council Chs., 1965-66; fellow Inst. Internat. Edn. Devel., 1966-67; fellow NIMH, 1969-71. Mem. Nat. Assn. Social Workers, Council Social Work Edn. (bd. dirs. 1983-86), Internat. Assn. Schs. of Social Work (bd. dirs. 1987-89), Internat. Soc. Community Devel., Internat. Conf. Social Welfare (U.S. com. bd. dirs. 1986-89). Home: Urbana Ill. Died Oct. 14, 1989; buried Mount Hope Cemetery, U. Ill., Champaign-Urbana.

SANDERS, DORSEY ADDREN, veterinary medicine researcher; b. Bascomville, S.C., Jan. 2, 1898; s. John Wesley and Sarah Emma (Wilson) S.; m. Grace Aurora Schwandt, June 21, 1926; 1 child, Dorsey Addren Jr. BSA, Clemson Coll., 1920; DVM, Kans. State Coll., 1923. Rsch. veterinarian U. Ky., 1923-25; mem. faculty U. Fla., Gainesville, from 1925, prof., head dept. vet. sci., 1948-57, rsch. veterinarian, from 1957; adviser coop. mut. assistance animal disease rsch. program ICA, from 1955; mem. Fla. adv. com., chmn. vet. sect. slection for doctors, dentists and veterinarians for armed forces, from 1951. With Vet. Corps, USAR, 1020-30. Mem. AVMA, Fla. Vet. Med. Assn. (pres. 1949-51), Sigma Xi, Gamma Sigma Delta. Presbyterian. *

SANDERS, RONALD, author; b. Union City, N.J., July 7, 1932; s. George Harry and Rose (Rachlin) S.; m. Beverly Helen Gingold, Mar. 19, 1967. B.A. summa cum laude, Kenyon Coll., 1954; M.A., Columbia, 1957. Lectr. history Queens Coll., Flushing, N.Y., 1958-65; assoc. editor Midstream mag., N.Y.C., 1965-73, editor, 1973-75; B.G. Rudolph chair in Jewish Studies Syracuse U., 1988-89. Author: Israel: The View from Masada, 1966, The Downtown Jews, 1969, Reflections on a Tea Pot, 1972, Lost Tribes and Promised Lands, 1978, The Days Grow Short: The Life and Music of Kurt Weill, 1980, The High Walls of Jerusalem, 1984, Shores of Refuge, 1988; co-editor: Socialist Thought: A Documentary History, 1964. Served with AUS, 1953-55. Recipient B'nai B'rith Book award, 1970, Literary Lion award N.Y. Pub. Library, 1987; Fulbright fellow France, 1960-61; NEH fellow, 1991. Jewish. Home: New York N.Y. Died Jan. 11, 1991; buried Beth Moses Cemetery, Pinelawn, N.Y.

SANDERSON, BENNETT, lawyer; b. Littleton, Mass., Oct. 31, 1893; s. George Augustus and Annie Sarah (Bennett) S.; m. Caroline Potter, Oct. 4, 1924; children: Edward Potter (dec.), David, Allen Bennett. AB, Yale U., 1916; LLB, Harvard U., 1920. Bar: Mass. 1920. Assoc. Herrick, Smith, Donald & Farley, Boston, 1920-24; asst. U.S. Atty. for Mass., 1924-26; U.S. commr. for Mass., 1926-29; ptnr. Hale & Sanderson, Boston, 1926-27, Hale, Sanderson, Byrnes & Morton, Boston, from 1927. Moderator Town of Littleton, 1921-24, town counsel, 1938-48; chmn. Littleton Fin. Com., 1938-43; pres. Mass. Assn. Town Fin. Coms., 1942-43, Littleton Lyceum, 1938; pres. Wachusett coun. Boy Scouts Am., 1944-46; mem. Mass. Conservation Coun., 1944-54, Littleton Rep. Com.; pres. Community Meml. Hosp., Ayer, Mass., 1952-55, mem. exec. com., 1955-65; trustee Social Law Libr., Boston, 1947-51, Boston Legal Aid Soc. Maj. F.A., U.S. Army, 1917-18. Mem. Mass. Bar Assn., Middlesex County Bar Assn. (past pres.), Boston Bar Assn., Boston Yale Club (past sec.), Appalachian Mountain Club. Episcopalian. *

SANFORD, JOHN ELROY See FOXX, REDD

SANSONE, ROBERT, toy manufacturing executive; b. Plainfield, N.J., Mar. 4, 1942; s. Joseph and Lucille (DeRosa) S.; m. Cynthia Sokol; children from previous marriage: Robert Blake, Susan Odette. BA, Columbia U., 1962, MBA, 1963; postgrad. advanced mgmt. program, Harvard U., 1978. Product mgr. Gen. Foods Corp., White Plains, N.Y., 1963-69; mktg. mgr. Mex. subs., Mexico City, 1970-73; gen. mgr. Venezuelan subs., Caracas, 1973-75; pres., dir. Brazilian subs., Sao Paulo, 1975-78; asst. to pres. White Plains, 1978-79, v.p., gen. mgr. pet foods div., 1979-82, v.p., gen. mgr. beverages div., 1982-85, group v.p., 1986-87; pres. Mattel U.S.A., Hawthorne, Calif., 1987-91; White House fellow U.S. Dept. Commerce, Washington, 1969-70; prof. Autonomous U. of Mex., Mexico City, 1971-73; dir. North St. Capital Corp., White Plains. Trustee bd. edn., Clarkstown, N.Y., 1967-69; bd. dirs. Vol. Ambulance Corps, Clarkstown, N.Y., 1967-69, Caracas Choral Soc., 1974-75; dir. Salvation Army Adv. Council, Westchester, N.Y., 1979-85, Coun. for the Arts, Westchester, 1979-85 , Columbia Bus. Sch. Alumni Assn., N.Y.C., from 1980, Pet Foods Inst., Washington, 1979-82; dir., pres. Am. C. of C. for Brazil, 1977-78. Bronfman fellow, 1963; Harriman scholar, 1963. Mem. White House Fellows Assn. (Washington)., Phi Beta Kappa, Beta Gamma Sigma, Sigma Nu. Republican. Roman Catholic. Home: Marina Del Rey Calif. Died July 15, 1991.

SAPHIER, A. S., manufacturing company executive; b. N.Y.C., Dec. 17, 1898; s. Sol J. and Lena (Rabiner) S.; m. Dorothy C. Kuehn, Sept. 29, 1925; children: Colette, Marlene. Ed. pub. schs., N.Y.C. Pres. Cen. Gotham Co., 1925-26; ptnr. L.S. Saphier & Co., 1926-41; dir. Gen. Bronze Corp., Garden City, N.Y., from 1937, became chmn., 1945, pres., 1946-61, now chmn. bd. and pres.; chmn., bd. dirs. United Aircraft Products, Inc. With Tank Corps, U.S. Army, World War I. Mem. NAM, Nat. Security Indsl. Assn., U.S. C. of C., Traffic Club. *

SARAFIAN, ARMEN, university president; b. Van Nuys, Calif., Mar. 5, 1920; s. Kevork and Lucy (Gazarian) S.; m. Doris Manoogian, 1941; children: Winston, Norman, Joy. A.B. magna cum laude, La Verne Coll., 1940, LL.D. (hon.), 1967; M.A., Claremont Grad. U., 1947; Ph.D., U. So. Calif., Los Angeles, 1964. Tchr. public elem. and secondary schs. Calif., 1940-47; tchr. English and Am. history and polit. sci. Pasadena (Calif.) Jr. Coll. Dist., 1947-51; mem. part-time faculty various colls. and univs. in Calif., 1947-68; coordinator secondary and jr. coll. edn. Pasadena City Schs., 1951-59; adminstrv. dean for instruction Pasadena City Coll., 1959-65, pres., 1965-76, pres. emeritus, 1976-85; supt. Pasadena Area Community Coll. Dist., 1966-76; adj. prof. community coll. adminstrn. U. So. Calif., Los Angeles, 1968-78; pres. La Verne (Calif.) Coll. (name changed to La Verne U. 1978), 1976-85, pres. emeritus, 1985-89; founder Am. Armenian Internat. Coll., 1976; interim pres. Colo. Mountain Coll., Glenwood Springs, 1986-87, pres. emeritus, 1987-89; interim chancellor Peralta Community Coll. Dist., Oakland, Calif., 1987-89; cons. to industry, govt. and bus., 1952—; dir. mgmt. reorgn. of Conn. System of Regional Community Colls., 1974-75; mem. adult and continuing edn. com. for Calif. Community Colls., 1974-75; Delta Epsilon disting. lectr. U. So. Calif., 1973; project dir., cons. joint legis. com. on higher edn. State of Alaska, 1973-77; mem. mgmt. team U. Alaska System, 1977; acad. planning specialist Mary Hardin-Baylor Coll., Belton, Tex., 1974; mem. western regional adv. bd. Coll. Entrance Examination Bd., 1971-75; mgmt. adv. to City of Pasadena Mcpl. Govt., 1972-73; founder Am. Armenian Internat. Coll., 1976; mem. Calif. State Bd. Edn., 1986-88; mem. Calif. Ednl. Tech. Com., 1986-88; chmn. Joint Vocat. Edn. Com., 1986-88; mem. Gov.'s Commn. on Ednl. Quality, 1987-88;. Mem. policy bd. Gt. Plains Nat. Instructional TV Library, 1975-79; founder and mem. exec. com. Pasadena Hall of Sci. Project, 1965-76; founder, adult adv. Pasadena Area Youth Council, 1953-66; mem. St. Luke Hosp. Adv. Bd., 1969-71, Mayor's Com. on Children and Youth, Pasadena, 1960-62; pres. Calif. Conservation Council, 1966-68; mem. nat. adv. council for nurse tng. USPHS, 1967-71; judge Los Angeles Times Scholarship Award Contest, 1974; bd. dirs. Pasadena Urban Coalition, 1973-76; trustee La Verne Coll., 1969-76. Recipient Disting. Community Service award Pasadena Edn. Assn., 1956, Conservation Merit award Calif. Conservation Council, 1960, Meritorious Service award Pasadena City Coll. Faculty Senate, 1960, Ralph Story award Pasadena City Coll. Faculty Assn., 1974, U. So. Calif. Service award, 1974, Recognition award USPHS, 1972, Others award Salvation Army, 1975, Recognition award Pasadena Arts Council, 1976; named Citizen of the Day Sierra Madre City Council, 1972, Arthur Noble disting. citizen City of Pasadena, 1976. Mem. Calif. Scholarship Fedn., Calif. Jr. Coll. Assn. (mem. legis. com. 1973-76), Pasadena Area Sch. Trustees Assn. (founder 1966), Pasadena Arts Council, Pasadena Hist. Soc., La Verne C. of C. (pres. 1978-79), Native Sons of the Golden West, Pasadena Council of Parents and Tchrs. (hon. life), Assoc. Student Body of Pasadena City Coll., Pasadena C. of C. (v.p. 1972), La Verne C. of C. (pres. 1978-79), Calif. State Bd. Edn., Calif. State Ednl. Tech. Com., Phi Delta Kappa (Spl. Recognition award 1970). Home: Oakland Calif. Died Mar. 11, 1989; buried Pasadena, Calif.

SARNOFF, STANLEY JAY, physiologist; b. Bklyn., Apr. 5, 1917; s. Jacob and Belle (Roosin) S.; m. Lili Charlotte Dreyfus, Sept. 11, 1948; children: Daniela Martha Sarnoff Bargezi, Robert Burnham Louis. Grad., Peddie Sch., 1934; A.B., Princeton U., 1938; M.D., Johns Hopkins U., 1942. Asst. resident Mass. Gen. Hosp., Boston, 1947; assoc. prof. physiology Harvard Sch. Pub. Health, 1948-57; vis. lectr. Howard U., 1957-65; med. dir. Nat. Heart Inst., USPHS, Bethesda, Md.; chief lab. cardiovascular physiology NIH, 1954-65; professorial lectr. George Washington U., 1957-64; St. Cyres and Halliburton lectr., London, 1961; chmn. bd., chief exec. officer Survival Tech., Inc., Bethesda, Md., 1969-90; mem. Army Sci. Bd., 1982-88, Joint Civilian Orientation Conf., 1982, Def. Policy Adv. Com. on Trade, from 1982. Editor: Ency. Cardiology, Am. Jour. Cardiology, 1957-65, Am. Jour. Physiology, 1958-66, Jour. Applied Physiology. Recipient Distinguished Service award Princeton U., 1938, 57, Porter travel award, 1950, Jacobs Found. award for meritorious heart research, 1957; Carl J. Wiggers award circulation group Am. Physiol. Soc., 1970; Small Businessman of Year award Washington, 1973. Mem. Am. Physiol. Soc., Nat. Security Indsl. Assn. (v.p. from 1981), Stanley J. Sarnoff Soc. Fellows for Rsch. in Cardiovascular Sci. (founder 1980), Am. Heart Assn., Princeton Club (Washington and N.Y.C.), Cosmos Club (Washington), Sigma Xi. Home: Bethesda Md. Died May 23, 1990; buried Barnard, Vt.

SATO, SHO, lawyer, educator; b. 1923. A.B., Denver U., 1944; LL.B., Harvard U., 1951. Bar: Calif. 1952. Dep. atty. gen. Calif. State's Atty. Gen.'s Office, 1952-55; acting assoc. prof. U. Calif.-Berkeley, 1955-57, assoc. prof., 1957-59, prof. law, from 1959; Fulbright lectr. U. Tokyo, 1966, Fulbright researcher, 1981; Fulbright resident U. Kobe, Japan, 1970; vis. scholar Nihon U., Japan, 1977; mem. Gov.'s Commn. on Law of Preemption, 1966-67; mem. Calif. Law Rev. Commn., 1960-69, vice-chmn., 1965-67, chmn., 1967-69. Author: (with Van Alstyne) State and Local Government Law, 2d edit., 1977. Home: Berkeley Calif. Deceased. †

SATTEE, ANDREW L., construction company executive; b. Trenton, Oct. 11, 1920; s. Anthony and Civita S.; m. Emily Ozdonsky; 1 son, Drew. Grad., Wharton Sch., U. Pa., 1944. C.P.A., N.J. Founder, partner Sattee Clayton & Co., C.P.A.s, 1944-63; gen. mgr., exec. v.p., dir. Maule Industries, Inc., 1965-76; pres. Sattee Assos. (merger and acquisitions), from 1978; chmn. bd. Continental Cement Co. (U.S. subs. Scancem A.B.); founder, dir. Burlington Concrete & Associated Cos., 1954-63; former chmn. bd. Continental Cement Co. of Fla.; bd. dirs. Bermuda Cement Co., Hamilton. Former mem. Fla. Council of 100; former mem. exec. bd. South Fla. council Boy Scouts Am. Mem. AICPA, Fla. Inst. CPAs. Home: Fort Lauderdale Fla. Deceased. †

SATTERTHWAITE, JOSEPH CHARLES, United States ambassador; b. Tecumseh, Mich., Mar. 4, 1900; s. Joseph Newton and Eva (Perry) S.; m. Leyia Ilbars, Dec. 18, 1945; 1 child, Ruth Eva. AB, U. Mich., 1923, AM, 1924, LLD, 1958. Fgn. svc. clk. Stuttgart, Germany, 1924; fgn. svc. officer Dept. State, Washington, 1926-27; vice consul Guadalajara, Mexico, 1927-29; 3d sec. Am. Embassy, Mexico City, 1929-34; sec. Am. delegation North and Cen. Am. Regional Radio Conf., Mexico City, 1933; 3d sec. Am. Embassy, Buenos Aires, 1934, 2d sec., 1935-36; sec. Am. delegation Inter-Am. Conf. for Maintenance of Peace, Buenos Aires, 1936; 2d sec. Am. Embassy, Ankara, Turkey, 1940; 1st sec. Am. Embassy, Ankara, 1941; 1st sec. of legation and consul Damascus, 1944; asst. chief Div. Near Eastern Affairs State Dept., 1945, spl. asst. to dir. Office Near Eastern and African Affairs, acting chief Div. Rsch. for Near East and Africa, 1946-47, dep. dir., 1947-48, dir., 1948; apptd. A.E. & P. to Cylon, 1949; diplomatic agt., min. Tangier, Morocco, 1953; amb. to Burma, 1955; dir. gen. Fgn. Svc., 1957-58; asst. sec. of state for African affairs, 1958-61, amb. to Republic of South Africa, 1961-65; presdl. rep. with rank of min. and chief of spl. diplomatic mission to Kingdom of Nepal, negotiating 1st agreement of commerce and friendship with that country, 1947; presdl. rep. with rank of minister and chief of spl. diplomatic mission to Kingdom of Nepal, negotiating 1st agreement of commerce and friendshp with that country, 1947. With U.S. Army, 1918-19. Mem. Am. Fgn. Svc. Assn. (pres. 1959), Diplomatic and Consular Officers Ret. (pres. 1974-75), Middle East Inst., Met. Club, Army and Navy Club (Washington), Phi Beta Kappa. Mem. Soc. of Friends. Home: Washington D.C. Died Dec. 19, 1990; buried Rock Creek Cemetery.

SATTERTHWAITE, LINTON, archaeologist; b. Trenton, N.J., Feb. 8, 1897; s. Linton and Florence Willis (Hibbs) S.; m. Margaret Elizabeth Conway, May 21, 1930. BA, Ya.e U., 1920; PhD, U. Pa., 1943. Bar: N.J. 1923. Reporter, 1920-23, practiced law,, 1924-28, archaeol. rschr.,, from 1929; rsch. in Mayan ruins in Brit. Honduras, Guatemala, also in Tex., W.Va., Wyo., Calif.; curator U. Pa. Mus.; prof. anthropology U. Pa. Author reports on expdns. and on Mayan epigraphy. 2d lt. RAF, 1918-19. Mem. various profl. socs. *

SAUGUET, HENRI, composer; b. Bordeaux, France, May 18, 1901; s. Auguste Poupard and Elizabeth Sauguet. Disciple, Erik Satie. pres. Comite Nat. del la Musique, 1966-89. Composer numerous ballets, including Les Mirages, Les Forains, La Rencontre, La Chatte, La Nuit, La Dame aux Camelias, Paris, L'Imposteur; operas include La Charteuse de Parme, Les Caprices de Marianne, Le Plumet du Colonel, La Gageure Imprevue, La Contrebasse, Les Paindes Autres; symphonies, concerts, quartets, trios, songs, cantatas, incidental music. Decorated officer Legion of Honor, comdr. Ordre Nat. du Merite. Mem. Com. Arts and Letters, Acad. Beaux-Arts. Home: Paris France Died June 22, 1989.

SAUNDERS, JOSEPH BENJAMIN, JR., petroleum executive; b. Hillsboro, Tex., July 25, 1901; s. Joseph Benjamin and Irene Imogene (McQuatters) S.; m. Gladys LaVerne Edmondson, Oct. 9, 1926 (dec. Apr. 1966); children: Eleanor Suzanne Saunders Inkley, Joseph Benjamin; m. Georgia J. Comegys, Mar. 30, 1968 (div. Feb. 1979); m. Georgia J. Hazen, Oct. 10, 1986. Grad., Chillicothe (Mo.) Bus. Coll., 1923; LL.D., Oklahoma City U., 1967; D.Hum., Okla. Christian Coll., 1975. Various positions oil industry, 1923-37; founder Triangle Refiners, 1936-46; partner, pres., dir. Triangle Refineries, Inc., Houston, 1946-64; chmn. bd. Triangle Refineries, Inc., from 1964; pres., dir. Withers & Wellford Oil Co., Memphis, to 1950; v.p., dir. Transcentral Oil Corp., Chgo., to 1952; v.p., dir., chmn. Triangle Pipeline Co., Shreveport, La., to 1954; chmn. bd. Triangle Realty Co., Houston, to 1972; vice chmn. bd. Kerr-McGee Corp., Oklahoma City, to 1972, dir. emeritus, from 1972; chmn. bd. petroleum products terminals, Atlanta, Birmingham, Chattanooga, LaGrange, Mo., Louisville, Mobile, Ala., Nashville, St. Louis, Niceville, Fla., Anniston and Montgomery, Ala., to 1972; dir., mem. exec. com. First State Bank & Trust Co., Oklahoma City, to 1983, J.R. Butler & Co., Houston. Trustee Oklahoma City U., Oklahoma City Community Found., until 1979; trustee, exec. com., pres., hon. past chmn. Nat. Cowboy Hall Fame; v.p., trustee Mummers Theatre, to 1972; v.p., dir., exec. com. Oklahoma City Symphony Soc.; pres. bd. Okla. Christian Coll. Recipient hon. citations NCCJ, 1972, hon. citations Oklahoma City Symphony, 1974, hon. citations Nat. Cowboy Hall of Fame, 1977; named to Okla. Hall of Fame, 1974; Hall of Fame for Gt. Westerners, 1979; named Grand Old Man of Refining, 1976. Mem. Oklahoma City C. of C. (v.p., dir. 1974), Am. Petroleum Inst. (life mem. gen. com. from 1972), Nat. Petroleum Refiners Assn., Ind. Petroleum Assn. Am. Clubs: Masons, Shriners, KT, Legion of Honor, River Oaks Country, Lakeside Country, Houston, International, Petroleum, Coronado (Houston); Petroleum, Beacon (Oklahoma City); Petroleum (Dallas); Seigniory (Que., Can.); Mo. Athletic (St. Louis), St. Louis; Chicago, Chgo. Oil Men's; Balboa de Mazatlan (Mexico). Home: Houston Tex. Died Nov. 26, 1989; buried Oklahoma City, Okla. †

SAUVÉ, MAURICE, economist, government official, academic administrator; b. Montreal, Que., Can., Sept. 20, 1923; m. Jeanne Benoit, 1948; 1 child, Jean-François. B.A., U. Montreal, 1944, LL.B., 1948; Ph.D. in Econs., U. Paris, 1952. Corporate dir. Can. and Cath. Confedn. of Labour, 1952-55; asst. sec. Royal Commn. on Can.'s Econ. Prospects, 1955-58; officer Que. Liberal Party, 1958-62; mem. Can. Parliament for les Iles-de-la-Madeleine, 1962-68; minister of forestry and rural devel. Govt. of Can., 1964-68; exec. v.p. Consol. Bathurst Co. Ltd., 1968-81; chancellor U. Ottawa, 1985-91; dir. Andres Wines Ltd., Automobiles Renault Can. Ltee, Barclays Can. Ltd., Benson & Hedges (Can.) Ltd., Comml. Life Assurance Co. of Can., Halifax Ins. Co., Can. Occidental Petroleum. Home: Montreal Que., Can. Died Apr. 13, 1992.

SAVAGE, ERNEST C., insurance broker; b. Phila., Apr. 17, 1897; s. Charles Chauncey and Anne Vandervoort (King) S.; m. Jane Bell Yeatman, June 28, 1922; children: Ernest C., Jane Bell Savage Clement, Anne L. Savage Barnum. AB, Princeton U., 1919. Formed Lukens, Savage & Co., ins. brokerage, Phila., 1922; ptnr. Lukens, Savage & Washburn, ins. brokerage, N.Y.C. and Phila., from 1925. Trustee Princeton U., Presbyn. Hosp., Phila.; bd. dirs. Union Theol. Sem. 2d lt. U.S. Army, 1918, AEF. Mem. Am. Hist. Assn., Phila. Club. Presbyterian. *

SAWARD, ERNEST WELTON, physician; b. N.Y.C., Oct. 14, 1914; s. Ernest Welton and Alice Virginia (Knorr) S.; m. Virginia Wagner, Sept. 1, 1938 (dec. 1982); children: Thomas, Susan, Lawrence; m. Elizabeth Katherine Meik, Aug. 14, 1982. AB, Colgate U., 1936; MD, U. Rochester, 1939. Diplomate Am. Bd. Internal Medicine, 1946. Medical house officer Barnes Hosp., St. Louis, 1939-41; resident Peter Bent Brigham, Boston, 1941-42; chief of medicine Manhattan Project, Hanford, Wash., 1943-45; med. dir. Kaiser-Permanente Program, Portland, 1945-70; prof., assoc. dean U. Rochester (N.Y.) Med. Sch., 1970-85, emeritus prof., 1985-89; cons. Blue Cross, Rochester, from 1970; bd. dirs. Group Health Assn., Rochester, from 1973, Health Systems Agy., Rochester, from 1975, Hosp. Rev. and Planning Council, Albany, 1975-87. Contbr. articles to profl. jours. Recipient Svc. awards War Dept., 1945, HEW, 1975, HHS, 1978, Gov. N.Y., 1986; recipient Justin Ford Kimball award Am. Hosp. Assn., 1988. Fellow AAAS; mem. Group Health Assn. Am. (bd. dirs. from 1972), State Communities Aid Assn. (bd. dirs. from 1986), Nat. Inst. Medicine (founder, council 1970, Gustave O. Lienhard award with Nat. Acad. Scis. 1987), Nat. Acad. Scis., Nat. Profl. Standards Rev. Council (chmn. 1973-76). Home: San Jose Calif. Died June 6, 1989.

SAWYER, HORACE A(DALL), business executive; b. Fate, Tex., Apr. 11, 1894; s. Drew and Maude Agnes (Keyes) S.; m. Mary Jessie Shiels, Dec. 9, 1924; children: Horace Adall Jr., Mary Rozell Sawyer Middleton. Student, Rockwall (Tex.) Coll., 1912-13; BS, Tex. A&M Coll., 1916. Various engring. positions, 1916-17; dist. commr., acting dist. commr. gen., agt. U.S. Dept. State, Liberia, 1919-21; assoc. Nagle, Witt, Rollins Engring. Co., Dallas, 1922-23; field engr. Portland Cement Assn., Dallas and Abilene, Tex., 1923-25; svc. engr. Lone Star Cement Corp., Dallas, 1925-26; asst. sales mgr. Lone Star Cement Corp., N.Y.C., 1926-31; v.p., mgr. La. div. Lone Star Cement Corp., New Orleans, 1931-52; pres. Lone Star Cement Corp., N.Y.C., 1952-61, chmn., 1959-64, mem. exec. com., bd. dirs., 1952-64; bd. dirs. So. Materials Co.; pres. Cuban Portland Cement Corp., 1955-58, chmn., 1958-59; pres. Cia Argentina de Cemento Portland, 1956-64, Cia Uruguaya de Cemento Portland, 1957-63; chmn. bd. dirs. Pioneer Sand & Gravel Co., 1959-64; trustee Dry Dock Savs. Bank, N.Y.C. Mem. bd. commrs. Port of New Orleans, 1948-51, pres., 1951; vice chmn. New Orleans R.R. Terminal Bd., 1949-52; bd. dirs. McGehee's Sch. for Girls, 1944-51. Capt. C.E., U.S. Army, 1917-19. Mem. ASCE (assoc., pres. La. sect. 1937), ASTM, Concrete Inst., Portland Cement Assn. (past bd. dirs.), Pan Am. Soc. U.S., Siwanoy Country Club, Boston Club, Country Club (New Orleans), Union League Club, Am. Yacht Club (Rye, N.Y.), Blind Brook Club (Port Chester, N.Y.), Masons (32d degree), Shriners, Tau Beta Pi. Presbyterian. *

SAWYER, WARREN ALLEN, librarian, educator; b. Bay Shore, N.Y., June 22, 1937; s. George John and Thelma Jacqueline (Caldwell) S.; m. Judith Alvord Littlepage, Jan. 25, 1958; children—Anne, Angus. B.S., Hampden-Sydney Coll., 1959; M.S.L.S., U. N.C., 1966. Asst. prof., dir. library Coll. Charleston, S.C., 1966-68; asst. prof., dir. library Med. U. S.C., Charleston, 1968-76, assoc. prof., 1976-84, prof., 1984-89, dir. edn. service, 1976-78, dir. libraries and learning resource ctrs., 1978-89; Mem. biomed. library rev. com. NIH, 1976-80; mem. long range planning panel Nat. Library Medicine, 1985; vis. research assoc. Inst. for the History of Medicine, Johns Hopkins U., 1986. Contbr. articles to profl. jours. Bd. dirs. Coll. Prep. Sch., Charleston, Shamrock House, Charleston. NIH grantee, from 1969. Mem. Assn. Acad. Health Scis. Library Dirs. (edn. bd. 1982-84), Med. Library Assn., Waring Library Soc. (pres. 1983-84), Consortium So. Biomed. Libraries (pres. 1982), S.C. Health Info. Network (exec. com. from 1985), Am. Assn. for the History of Medicine. Democrat. Episcopalian. Home: Charleston S.C. Died Nov. 23, 1990; buried Charleston., S.C.

SAYE, ALBERT BERRY, political science educator; b. Rutledge, Ga., Nov. 29, 1912; s. William Bibb and Suvinnie (Whitten) S.; m. Ruth Kendrick, Dec. 20, 1939. Student, Emory U., 1930-32; A.B., U. Ga., 1934, M.A., 1935; diplome de francais, degre superieur, U. Dijon, France, 1938; Ph.D., Harvard U., 1941; postgrad., Cambridge U., 1939. Instr. history U. Ga., 1934-36, asst. prof. history, 1939-41, asst. prof. polit. sci., 1941-43, assoc. prof., 1943-47, prof., 1947-57, prof. law and Alumni Found. Disting. prof. polit. sci., 1957-80, Richard B. Russell prof. polit. sci., 1975-80, prof. emeritus, 1980-89; Fulbright prof. India, 1982. Author 12 books including American Constitutional Law, 3d edit., 1979, Principles of American Government, llth edit., 1989, A Constitutional History of Georgia, 1970, Georgia Government and History, 3d edit., 198l, A List of the Early Settlers of Georgia, 1983, Handbook on the Constitutions of the U.S. and Georgia, 1983, New Viewpoints in Georgia History 1732-1789, 1943; editor: Walter McElreath, 1985, Abraham Baldwin, 1987. Trustee Found. for Ga. Legal History, 1986, mem. Bicentennial Council of 13 Original States, 1987. Recipient Lewis H. Beck scholarship, 1936, M.G. Michael research award, 1942, Abraham Baldwin award, 1979, Blue Key award, 1981. Mem. Internat., Am., So. polit. sci. assns., Ga. Bar Assn., Ga. Hist. Soc., Demosthenian Lit. Soc. Baptist. Home: Athens Ga. Died Mar. 28, 1989; buried Rutledge (Ga.) City Cemetery.

SCANLON, CHARLES JOSEPH, banker; b. Chgo., July 14, 1915; s. Charles J. and Mary J. (Clark) S.; m. Margaret Hemmens, May 14, 1938; children: Barbara J. (Mrs. Stephen Brodt), Lisbeth C. (Mrs. Kent Fairfield). Student, Northwestern U.; grad., Rutgers U. Grad. Sch. Banking, 1949; LL.D., North Central Coll., 1963; D.B.A., Western Mich. U., 1964. With Fed. Res. Bank Chgo., 1933-70, chief examiner, 1955-59, 1st v.p., 1959-62, pres., 1962-70; v.p. Gen. Motors Corp., N.Y.C., 1970-80; dir., pres., chief exec. officer UBAF Arab-Am. Bank, N.Y.C., 1981-82, chmn. exec. com., 1980-85; dir. United Student Aid Funds, Inc., Essex Land Conservation Trust; vice chmn. bd. W.P. Carey & Co., Inc., N.Y.C.; lectr. Inter-Agy. Bank Examination Sch., 1953-57, Grad. Sch. Banking U. Wis.; banking cons. Republic Liberia, 1961. Trustee Com. Econ. Devel., St. Lukes-Roosevelt Hosp. Ctr.; mem. Bd. of Fin., Essex, Conn. Episcopalian. Clubs: Economic, Bankers, Union League (Chgo.); Essex Yacht; Blooming Grove Hunting and Fishing (Hawley, Pa.). Home: Essex Conn. Died Nov. 15, 1990; buried Riverview Cemetery, Essex, Conn.

SCARTH, JOHN CAMPBELL, paper company executive; b. Sherbrooke, Que., Can., July 5, 1924; s. Hubert Ashley and Christine (McIntosh) S.; m. Ellen Marion Frazar, June 3, 1948; children: Ian, Jane. B.Sc., U. Bishops Coll., Lennoxville, Que., 1945. With KVP Co. Ltd., Can., 1948-61, v.p. sales, 1958-61; asst. to pres. KVP Sutherland Paper Co. subs. Brown Co., Kalamazoo, 1961-63; v.p. KVP Sutherland Paper Co. subs. Brown Co., 1963-68; pres. Deerfield Glassine Co., Monroe Bridge, Mass., 1968; exec. v.p. E.B. Eddy Paper Co. (name now E.B. Eddy Forest Products, Ltd.), Hull, Que., Can., 1968-72; pres. E.B. Eddy Paper Co. (name now E.B. Eddy Forest Products, Ltd.), 1972-88, chief exec. officer; chief exec. officer Eddy Paper Co. Ltd., Ottawa, Ont., Can., from 1988. Home: Ottawa Can. Deceased. †

SCELBA, MARIO, Italian government official; b. Sept. 5, 1901. JD, U. Rome; hon. degree, U. Ottawa, Ont., Can., Columbia U., Fordham U. Founder, pres. Italian People's Party, 1919; pvt. practice, 1926-91. Founder, Christian Dem. Party and newspaper Il Popolo, 1941; minister for posts and telecommunications, 1945-47, minister interior, 1947-53, 60-62, 54-55; prime minister, 1954-55; mem. Chamber of Deps.; dep. to European Parliamentary Assembly, 1958-91; pres. nat. coun. Christian Dem. Party, 1966-91. Home: Rome Italy Deceased.

SCHACHTEL, HYMAN JUDAH, rabbi; b. London, Eng., May 24, 1907; came to U.S., 1914, naturalized, 1921; s. Bernard and Janie (Spector) S.; m. Barbara H. Levin, Oct. 15, 1941; children—Bernard, Ann Mollie. BA, U. Cin., 1928; B of Hebrew, Hebrew Union Coll., 1931, DD (hon.), 1958; postgrad., Columbia Tchrs. Coll., 1933-37; EdD, U. Houston, 1948; DHL (hon.), Southwestern U., 1955. Ordained rabbi, 1931; rabbi West End Synagogue, N.Y.C., 1931-43; chief rabbi Temple Beth Israel, Houston, 1943-75; tchr. philosophy U. Houston, 1950-55; lectr. theology, history, philosophy St. Mary's Cath. Sem., Houston; adj. prof. religion Inst. Religion, from 1973; lectr. Judaism U. Houston, 1974, U. St. Thomas, 1973-90. Author: Real Enjoyment of Living, 1954, The Life You Want to Live, 1956, The Shadowed Valley, 1964, Aspects of Jewish Homiletics, 1964, How to Meet The Challenge of Life and Death, 1974. Chmn. subcom. edn. Gov.'s Commn. Human Relations, 1970-90; pres. Tex. Kallah Rabbis, 1962, Houston Rabbinical Assn., 1960; mem. exec. bd. Central Conf. Am. Rabbis, 1965-67; v.p., sec.-treas. Southwest region, from 1966; chaplain Variety Club, Houston, from 1955, Houston Fire Dept., from 1964; delivered inaugural prayer for Pres. Lyndon Johnson, 1965; v.p. N.Y. Bd. Rabbis, 1942-43; exec. com. Houston Met. Ministries. Pres., Harris County Mental Health Assn., 1960; mem. bd. Houston Symphony Soc., from 1955, San Harris County Mental Health Assn., 1960, Houston Symphony Soc., from 1955, San Jacinto council Girl Scouts, from 1962, Houston Heart Assn., from 1964, Houston Crime Commn., 1962-65; mem. nat. planning bd., trustee United Fund Harris County, from 1965; bd. overseers Hebrew Fund Harris County, 1965-90, Hebrew Union Coll.-Jewish Inst. Religion, 1961-65; trustee Houston Salvation Army, Houston chpt. ARC, Inst. Religion, Houston, DePelchin Faith Home, Harris County Mental Health Assn., bd. dirs. Houston Grand Opera, Nat. Found. Ileitis and Colitis; mem. adv. council Harris County Restitution Ctr.; v.p. Nat. Assn. Ret. Reformed Rabbis; mem. Houston/Harris County Sesquicentennial Com. Recipient Coronat medal St. Edward's U., Austin Tex., 1963, award NCCJ, 1975, Human Relations award Houston chpt. Am. Jewish Com., 1975, Humanitarian award B'nai B'rith, Houston, 1975, Disting. Alumnus award U. Houston, 1977, I.M. Hogg award, 1987. Mem. Tex. Philos. Soc., Nat. Orgn. Ret. Reform Rabbis (pres. 1986), Phi Delta Kappa, Phi Epsilon Pi (hon.). Club: Kiwanis. Home: Houston Tex. Died Jan. 11, 1990; buried Cong. Beth Israel Cemetery, Houston.

SCHAEFER, JACK WARNER, writer; b. Cleve., Nov. 19, 1907; s. Carl Walter and Minnie Luella (Hively) S.; m. Eugenia Hammond Ives, Aug. 26, 1931 (div. Dec. 1948); children—Carl Walter, Christopher Pomery, Susan Hammond, Jonathan Ives; m. Louise Wilhide Deans, 1949. AB, Oberlin Coll., 1929; postgrad., Columbia U., 1929-30; LittD (hon.), Oberlin Coll., 1989. Reporter and office man U.P., 1930-31; asst. dir. edn. Conn. State Reformatory, 1931-38; asso. editor New Haven Jour. Courier, 1932-39, editor, 1939-42; editorial writer Balt. Sun, 1942-44; asso. editor Norfolk Virginian-Pilot, 1944-48; editor The Shoreliner, 1949; asso. Lindsay Advt. Co., New Haven, 1949; editor and pub. Theatre News, 1935-40, The Movies, 1939-41. Author: (novels) Shane, 1949 (transl. 35 langs., Finest Western Novel award Western Writers Am.), First Blood, 1953, The Canyon, 1953, Company of Cowards, 1957, Old Ramon, 1960, Monte Walsh, 1963, The Great Endurance Horse Race, 1963, Stubby Pringle's Christmas, 1964, Heroes Without Glory, 1965; (short stories) The Big Range, 1953, The Pioneers, 1954, The Kean Land and Other Stories, The Plainsmen, 1963, Heroes Without Glory, 1965, Collected Stories, 1966, Mavericks, 1967, New Mexico, 1967, Collected Short Novels, 1967, An American Bestiary, 1975, Conversations with a Pocket Gopher . . . and Other Outspoken Neighbors, 1978; also stories in nat. mags. Home: Santa Fe N.Mex. Died Jan. 24, 1991.

SCHAEFER, W(ILLIAM) STANLEY, publishing company executive; b. Adams, N.Y., Mar. 31, 1907; s. William and Katherine (Lehman) S.; m. Marthe Marschall, Feb. 16, 1934; children: Ann (Mrs. Donald Pease), Katherine. A.B. (State N.Y. scholar), Cornell U., 1931, student Law Sch., 1929-31. Mgr. Cornell U. Press, 1931-40, dir., 1940-43; mgr. Comstock Pub. Co., 1931-43; Univ. pub. Cornell U., 1940-43; v.p. W.H. Freeman & Co., San Francisco, 1949-62; pres. W.H. Freeman & Co., 1962-69, 71-73, chmn., 1962-74, chief exec. officer, 1962-73, editor-in-chief, 1962-69, 71-73; former dir. W.H. Freeman & Co., Ltd., Oxford, Eng., Sci. Am., Inc., N.Y.C. Club: Cercle de l'Union (San Francisco). Home: Los Altos Calif. Died Feb. 1, 1989.

SCHAFER, EDWARD HETZEL, scholar, author; b. Seattle, Wash., Aug. 23, 1913; s. Edward Hetzel and Lillian (Moorehead) S.; m. Phyllis Brooks, Sept. 7, 1971; children from previous marriage: Tamlyn, Julian, Kevin. A.B. in Anthropology, U. Calif., Berkeley, 1938, Ph.D. in Oriental Langs, 1947; M.A., U. Hawaii, 1940; postgrad., Harvard U., 1940-41. Lectr. in Oriental langs. U. Calif., Berkeley, 1947; asst. prof. Oriental langs. U. Calif., 1947-53, asso. prof., 1953-58, prof., 1958-69, Agassiz prof. Oriental langs. and lit., from 1969. Author: The Empire of Min, 1954, Tu Wan's Stone Catalogue of Cloudy Forest, 1961, The Golden Peaches of Samarkand, 1963, Ancient China, 1967, The Vermilion Bird, 1967, Shore of Pearls, 1970, The Divine Woman, 1973, Pacing the Void, 1977, Mirages on the Sea of Time, 1985; Editor: Jour. Am. Oriental Soc, 1958-64; Contbr. articles to profl. jours. Served with USNR, 1941-46. Decorated Bronze Star; Guggenheim fellow, 1953-54, 68-69. Mem. Am. Oriental Soc. (past pres.). Home: Berkeley Calif. Deceased. †

SCHAFFER, ROSE NUSSBAUM, artist, lecturer, tour guide; b. Newark; d. Adolph and Carrie (Kolber) Nussbaum; m. Jacob Schaffer, June 4, 1923; children—Judith Schaffer Howard, Ruth Ann. Student, NYU, 1919-20, Art Students League, 1931-34, Pratt Graphic Center, 1958; pvt. study with, Bernard Karfiol, Morris Davidson, Sol Wilson, Antonio Frasconi, Seong Moy. Exhibited various one-woman shows including, Barzansky Galleries, N.Y.C., Rossmoor Gallery, 1987, group shows, Nat. Acad., Audubon Artists, Nat. Assn. Women Artists, ACA Gallery, N.Y.C., Argent Gallery, N.Y.C., Library of Congress, Washington, Smithsonian Instn., Washington, Montclair Mus., Newark Mus., Jersey City Mus., Delgado Mus., New Orleans, Boston Mus., Wichita Mus., Bklyn. Mus., Rochester Meml. Gallery, Conn. Acad., Cape Cod Gallery, Provincetown Gallery, Albany Print Club, Henry Clews Found., Napoule, France, Casino Municipal, Cannes, France, retrospective, Rossmoor Galleries, Jamesburg, N.J., 1981; represented in permanent collections, Smithsonian Instn., Montclair (N.J.) Mus., Tenn. Fine Arts Center, Nashville, Art Assn. Richmond (Ind.), Chryster Mus., Norfolk, Va., Rutgers Coll. Mus., Springfield (Mass.) Art Mus., J.F. Kennedy Library, Newark and West Orange (N.J.) Libraries, Daus. of Israel, Pleasant Valley Home, West Orange, Burpee Art Mus., Rockford, Ill., others. Vice pres. Newark sect. Nat. Council Jewish Women, 1945; founder Essex unit Nat. Assn. Retarded Children, 1948; founder, sec. Occupational Center Essex County, 1950-69; bd. dirs. Essex County (N.J.) Women's Com. for Brandeis U., 1960-70, also life mem. com.; founder Curative Workshop (now N.J. Rehab. Com.), Newark, 1923; pres. Sisterhood Temple Israel, South Orange, N.J. Recipient Ida Wells Stroud award Am. Artists Profl. League, 1951, award Painters and Sculptors Soc. N.J., 1956, award Ross Gallery, 1932, award Art Center of Oranges, 1947, award Terry Nat., 1935, award Short Hills at Mall, 1969, award Seton Hall U., 1956, award New Haven Paint and Print Club, 1958, award South Orange-Maplewood Gallery, 1958, award L. Bamberger & Co., 1960, purchase awards Overlook Hosp., 1961, 62. Mem. Am. Fedn. Arts, Art Students League (life mem.), Nat. Assn. Women Artists, Artists Equity, United Order True Sisters (pres. 1931). Home: West Orange N.J. Died Oct. 23, 1989; buried Beth Israel Cemetery, Woodbridge, Conn.

SCHAFFNER, FRANKLIN JAMES, director, producer; b. Tokyo, May 30, 1922; s. Paul Franklin and Sarah (Swords) S.; m. Helen Jean Gilchrist, Apr. 17, 1948; children: Jenny, Kate. A.B., Franklin and Marshall Coll., 1942. pres. Gilchrist Prodns., 1962-68, Franklin Schaffner Prodns., Beverly Hills, Calif., 1969-89. TV dir.: Studio One, 1948-51, 52-56, Ford Theater, 1951-52, Person to Person with Edward R. Murrow, 1956-58, Playhouse 90, 1958-60; producer, dir.: Kaiser Aluminum Hour, 1958, Dupont Show of Week, 1963-65; dir.: plays including Twelve Angry Men, 1954, Caine Mutiny Court Martial, World's Greatest Robbery, The Army Game, Cruel Day; Broadway play Advise and Consent, 1960 (recipient Best Direction award Variety Critics Poll); movies including The Stripper, 1963, Best Man, 1964 (diploma Kalrovy Vary Festival), War Lord, 1965, Double Man, 1966, Planet of the Apes, 1968, Patton, 1971 (Dirs. Guild Am. award, Acad. Motion Picture Arts and Scis. Oscar), Nicholas and Alexandra, 1972, Papillon, 1973, Islands in the Stream, 1976, The Boys From Brazil, 1978, Sphinx, 1981, Yes, Georgio, 1982, Lionheard, 1987, Welcome Home, 1989; Recipient Emmy awards 1954, 55, 62. Served to lt. USNR, 1942-46. Recipient Sylvania award, 1953, 54, Trustee award for documentary Tour of the White House Am. Acad. TV Arts and Scis., 1962. Mem. Dirs. Guild Am. (nat. bd. dirs. 1960-61, 62-63, 64-65, 73-74), Nat. Acad. TV Arts and Scis., Acad. Motion Pictures Arts and Scis., Phi Beta Kappa. Clubs: Players (N.Y.C.); Riviera Tennis (Los Angeles); Waramaug Country (New Preston, Conn.); Reform (London). Home: Santa Monica Calif. Died July 2, 1989.

SCHANCK, FRANCIS RABER, JR., investment banker; b. Los Angeles, Oct. 22, 1907; s. Francis Raber and Florence Ethel (Carr) S.; m. Kathryn Sterling Short, June 10, 1933 (dec. Mar. 1989); children: Jordan Thomas, Susan Fawcett, Peter Carr; m. Katharine Sanders Maley, Nov. 10, 1989. Student, Stanford, 1926-29. Successively with E.A. Pierce & Co., Anderson & Fox Co., C.F. Childs & Co., 1927-30; office and dept. mgr. First Boston Corp., Portland, Ore., San Francisco, Los Angeles and Chgo., 1930-42, 46-48; dept. mgr., partner Bacon, Whipple & Co., Chgo., 1948-62, mng. partner, 1962-76, sr. partner, 1977-82, adv. dir., 1983-87; expert witness mcpl. fin. for various Congl. Coms. Former mem. bds. edn. Community Consol. Sch. Dist. 181 and High Sch. Dist. 86, DuPage-Cook County, Ill.; former trustee Village Hinsdale, Ill. Served to comdr. USNR, World War II, PTO. Mem. Investment Bankers Assn. Am. (chmn. central states group 1962-63, nat. bd. govs., v.p. 1964-65, 1st v.p. 1966-67, pres. 1967-68), Municipal Bond Club Chgo. (past pres.), Security Industry Assn. (chmn. governing council 1972), Bond Club Chgo. (past pres.), Zeta Psi. Clubs: Chicago, Commercial, Union League, Attic (Chgo.); Hinsdale Golf (Ill.). Home: Hinsdale N.Y. Died Nov. 1, 1991.

SCHANG, FREDERICK C., JR., concert manager; b. N.Y.C., Dec. 15, 1893; s. F.C. and Blanche Elizabeth (Mock) S.; m. Emily Sterz, Sept. 1920; children: Rosalind, Frederick C. III. LittB, Columbia U., 1915. Reporter N.Y. Tribune, 2 yrs.; press agt. Diaghileff Ballet Russe; sec., bd. dirs. Met. Mus. Bur., mgrs. Caruso; ptnr. Schang, Doulens & Wright, Inc., N.Y.C.; chmn., bd. dirs. Columbia Artists Mgmt. Inc. Contbr. articles on music to trade press. Maj. USAC, 1942-44. Decorated Knight of Danebrog (Denmark), Order of Vasa (Sweden). Mem. Westhampton Country Club, N.Y. Athletic Club. Unitarian. *

SCHAPIRO, ARENHOLD COHEN, lawyer; b. Portsmouth, Ohio, Feb. 25, 1893; s. Abraham and Cecelia (Schloss) S.; m. Regina Hall, Sept. 28, 1920; 1 child, Felice Schapiro Klein. LLB, Ohio State U., 1914. Bar: Ohio 1914. Practiced in Portsmouth, from 1914; mem. Kimble, Schapiro, Stevens, Harsha & Harcha; asst. city solicitor, Portsmouth, 1930-35; bd. dirs. Ohio Bar Title Ins. Co.; mem. Commn. on Grievance and Discipline, Supreme Ct. Ohio, from 1962. With U.S. Army, 1917-19. Fellow Am. Bar Found.; mem. AMA, Ohio Bar Assn. (exec. com. 1952-56, pres. 1957-58, past chmn. local bar activities, bd. dirs. Found. from 1963), Portsmouth Bar Assn. (pres. 1945-46), Masons, Elks, B'nai B'rith, Zeta Beta Tau. *

SCHAPIRO, RUTH GOLDMAN, lawyer; b. N.Y.C., Oct. 31, 1926; d. Louis Albert and Sarah (Shapiro) Goldman; m. Donald Schapiro, June 29, 1952; children: Jane Goldman, Robert Andrew. A.B., Wellesley Coll., 1947; LL.B., Columbia U., 1950. Bar: N.Y. 1950, D.C. 1978. Asst. to reporters Am. Law Inst. Fed. Income Tax Statute, N.Y.C., 1950-51; assoc., then ptnr. Proskauer Rose Goetz & Mendelsohn, N.Y.C., 1955-91; mem. nominating commn. U.S. Tax Ct., 1978-81. Notes editor: Columbia Law Rev., 1949-50; editor: Tax Shelters, Practising Law Inst., 1983; contbr. articles to legal jours. Vice-chmn. adv. com. NYU Inst. Fed. Taxation, 1979-85; mem. adv. com. NYU-IRS Continuing Legal Edn. Project. Fellow Am. Bar Found., N.Y. Bar Found.; mem. ABA, N.Y. State Bar Assn. (chmn. tax sect. 1981-82, exec. com. 1982-84, ho. of dels., 1981-84, 89-91, chmn. fin. com. 1984-87, chmn. spl. com on Women in the Crts. 1986-89), Assn. Bar City N.Y. (taxation com. 1972-75, 78-79, chair personal income tax com. 1990—), N.Y. County Lawyers Assn., Am. Coll. Tax Counsel, Am. Judicature Soc., N.Y. Wellesley Club. Jewish. Home: New York N.Y. Died Aug. 26, 1991; buried Queens, N.Y.

SCHECHTER, ABEL ALAN, broadcasting consultant; b. Central Falls, R.I., Aug. 10, 1907; s. George and Celia (Riven) S.; m. Fritzi B. Breger, July 24, 1941 (dec. 1989). Grad., Boston U., 1929. Reporter Providence (R.I.) Jour., N.Y. World, A.P.; organizer, 1st dir. news NBC, N.Y.C., 1932-42; pub. relations cons. War Dept., 1941; v.p. MBS, 1945-50, Crowell Collier Pub. Co., 1950-51; 1st exec. producer Today show NBC, 1951-52; chmn. A.A. Schechter Assos., Inc. (pub. rels. firm), 1952-73; dir. Hill and Knowlton, 1973-89, Hill & Knowlton, Inc., 1975-79. Author: Go Ahead Garrison, 1940, I Live On Air, (with Edward Anthony), 1941. Served as lt. col. USAAF, 1942-43, Washington; in charge radio and press communications for war corrs., 1943-45, G.H.Q., Southwest Pacific area. Decorated Legion of Merit. Mem. Sigma Delta Chi. Clubs: Overseas Press (N.Y.); Dutch Treat (N.Y.C.); Nat. Press (Washington). Home: Palm Beach Fla. Died May 24, 1989.

SCHEETZ, HENRY FRANKLIN, JR., financial executive; b. Ambler, Pa., Apr. 9, 1898; s. Henry Franklin and Lillie (Freed) S.; m. Hazel Caroline Knight, May 28, 1932; children: Henry Franklin III, Thomas S. Student, Lehigh U., 1916-17; grad., Carnegie Inst. Tech. Pres., dir. Fuller Label & Box Co., Pitts., 1923-57; v.p., dir. Bradley & Gilbert, Louisville, 1942-57, Gebhart Folding Box Co., Dayton, Ohio, 1946-57; asst.

to chmn. bd. Brown Co., Boston, 1958-59, chmn. bd., 1960, also bd. dirs.; ptnr. Penn Pacific Co., Pitts., from 1958. *

SCHEIE, HAROLD GLENDON, ophthalmologist; b. Brookings, S.D., Mar. 24, 1909; s. Lars T. and Ella Mae (Ware) S.; 1 child, Harold Glendon Jr.; m. Mary Ann Tallman, Nov. 1, 1951; children: Eric Glendon, Nancy Ware. BS, U. Minn., 1931, MD, 1935, LHD (hon.), 1989; DSc, U. Pa., 1940, LLD (hon.), 1978; DMedSci (hon.), Villanova U., 1968. Diplomate Am. Bd. Ophthalmology (mem. bd.). Intern U. Pa. Hosp., Phila., 1935-37; instr. ophthalmology U. Pa., 1940-45, asst. prof., 1945-49, prof., 1953-60, Norris and de Schweinitz prof. ophthalmology, chmn. dept., 1960-75, prof. emeritus, 1977-90; chief Phila. Gen. Hosp., Children's Hosp. Phila., 1960-75; founding dir. Scheie Eye Inst., Presbyn. Med. Ctr. Phila., 1972-77. Author: (with M. Weiner) Surgery of the Eye, 1952, (with Daniel M. Albert) Textbook of Ophthalmology, 8th edit., 1969 (with Daniel M. Albert, 9th edit., 1976; author: A History of Ophthalmology at the University of Pennsylvania, 1965; mem. editorial bd. Archives of Ophthamology, 1954-64, Jour. Pediatric Ophthalmology; also over 200 articles. Trustee Minn. Med. Found.; bd. dirs. Nat. Soc. for Prevention Blindness, Inc., 1968-77, mem. exec. com., 1970-77, v.p., 1972-73; trustee Episcopal Acad. Maj. M.C., U.S. Army, 1942-46, CBI, brig. gen. Res. ret. Decorated Legion of Merit, Order Brit. Empire; recipient Howe award AMA, 1964, gold medal U. Buffalo, 1964, Am. Ophthal. Soc., 1984, Derrick T. Vail gold medal Internat. Eye Found., 1980, 3 Lucien Howe medals for disting. svc. to ophthalmology. Fellow ACS (regent 1964-70); mem. AMA, Pa. Med. Soc., Philadelphia County Med. Soc. (Strittmatter award), Am. Assn. Ophthalmology (3d v.p. 1970), Am. Ophthal. Soc. (coun. 1965-70, pres. coun. 1970), Am. Acad. Ophthalmology (1st v.p. 1960-61), Cons. to Armed Forces, Coll. Physicians Phila. (v.p. 1958-59), Pa. Acad. Ophthalmoology and Otolaryngology (pres. 1968), Soc. for Contemporary Ophthalmology (bd. govs. 1970, Disting. Svc. award 1974), Jules Gonin Soc., Ophthal. Soc. U.K., Burma Star Assn. *. Home: Philadelphia Pa. Died Mar. 5, 1990.

SCHELL, JOHN LE ROY, public relations executive; b. Mpls., June 30, 1919; s. Arvid and Svea (Johnson) S.; m. Marjorie Eddy, Oct. 19, 1950. Student, U. Minn., 1938-41. Joined N. Am. Newspaper Alliance, N.Y.C., 1946; editor N. Am. Newspaper Alliance, 1951-55, exec. v.p., asst. to chmn. bd., 1953-55; promotion dir. Bell Syndicate, Inc., Asso. Newspapers, Inc., Consol. Newspaper, McClure Newspaper Syndicate, 1952-55; dir. pub. relations Gen. Foods Co., 1955-62; pub. relations cons., 1962-65; v.p., dir. pub. relations Armour & Co., 1965-70; in charge N.Am., Neilson McCarthy Internat., from 1971; Chmn. pub. relations com. 5th Internat. Food Conf. and Exhbn., 1960-62. Served as lt., fighter pilot USN, 1941-46. Decorated D.F.C. with gold star, Air medal with 2 gold stars; World War II Ace. Club: Dutch Treat. Home: Miami Fla. Deceased. †

SCHERAGO, MORRIS, bacteriology educator; b. Roman, Romania, Dec. 25, 1895; came to U.S., 1989, naturaliized, 1916; s. Israel and Bessie (Jacobs) S.; m. Jane Stone, Sept. 5, 1920; children: Emily Stone Scherago Rubin, Earl James. BS, Cornell U., 1917, DVM, 1919. Diplomate Am. Bd. Microbiology. Asst. pathologist and bacteriologist Cornell U., 1918-19; instr. bacteriology U. Ky., Lexington, 1919-20, asst. prof., 1920-21, assoc. prof., 1922-24, prof., from 1924, acting head dept., 1922-23, head dept., from 1924, mem. rsch. com., dir. Rsch. Found.; vis. prof. Washington U. Sch. Medicine, St. Louis, assigned to Bangkok, 1951-52; bacteriologist Life Ext. Inst., N.Y.C., summer 1919; lab. asst. USPHS, U.S. Marine Hosp., S.I., N.Y., summer 1918; asst. bacteriologist N.Y. State Dept. Health, Albany, summer 1920. Asst. editor Rev. Allergy and Applied Immunology, Annals Allergy, from 1949—; editor allergy sect. Biol. Abstracts; contbr. articles to profl. jours. Chmn. budget com. Lexington Community Chest, 1931-34. Co-recipient King award Ky. Acad. Sci., 1941; rsch. grantee Nat. Heart Inst., 1955-57, Nat. Inst. Allergy and Infectious Diseases, 1958-64. Fellow APHA, AAAS, Am. Coll. Allergists (chmn. adv. bd. and standardization com., rsch. grantee 1947-48), Am. Acad. Microbiology, Am. Soc. Clin. Pathologists (assoc.); mem. AAUP (pres. U. Ky. chpt. 1959-60), Am. Soc. Microgioloby (pres.-Ky.-Tenn. br. 1940-41, councilor 1942-46), Am. Assn. Immunologists, Am. Soc. Profl. Biologists (past exec. sec.), Ohio Valley Allergy Soc., Ky. Acad. Sci. (pres. 1948-49), Lions (past pres.), B'nai B'rith (pres. Ky. chpt. 1956-57), Sigma Xi, Omicron Delta Kappa. *

SCHERER, GORDON HARRY, lawyer, congressman; b. Cin., Dec. 26, 1906; s. John E. and Minnie (Kuehnle) S.; m. Virginia E. Mottern, Feb. 18, 1933; children: Gordon Mottern, Suzanne Virginia (Mrs. Michael Kitei). Student, U. Cin.; LL.B., Salmon P. Chase Coll. Law, 1929; LL.D., Institutum Divi Thomae, 1961. Bar: Ohio 1929. Pvt. practice Cin., from 1929; asst. pros. atty. Hamilton County, Ohio, 1933-41; dir. safety City of Cin., 1943-44; mem. Planning Commn. Cin., 1946-47; mem. 83d-87th Congresses from 1st Dist. Ohio, mem. un-Am. activities com., pub. works com.; mem. U.S. nat. commn. UNESCO, 1970-73; U.S. mem. exec. bd. UNESCO, Paris, 1974-75; U.S. del. UNESCO Internat. Conf. on Programs for Devel. of Communications, Acapulco, Mex., 1982; U.S. rep. to UN, 1972-73; dir. Universal Guaranty Life Ins. Co. of Ohio, 1965-80; chmn. bd. Gentile Bros. Co., 1969-82; pres. bd. trustees Cin. So. Ry., 1968-81; Mem. Ohio Supreme Ct. Bd. Commrs. on Grievances and Discipline, 1970-76; Mem. bd. visitors USAF Acad., Colorado Springs, Colo., 1971-75; chmn. Republican Party of Hamilton County, 1962-68; mem. Ohio Rep. State Central and Exec. coms., 1964-70; mem. bd. elections, Hamilton County, 1968-78. Trustee Ams. for Constl. Action; mem. Cin. City Council, 1945-49. Recipient Patriotic Service awards Coalition Am. Patriotic Socs., Am. Legion, DAR; Disting. Service award Negro Citizens Cin. Mem. Am., Ohio, Cin. bar assns., Order of Curia, Phi Alpha Delta. Club: Mason (33 deg.). Home: Cincinnati Ohio Died Aug. 13, 1988; inurned; Spring Grove Mausoleum, Cincinnati.

SCHIEFFELIN, WILLIAM JAY, III, business executive; b. N.Y.C., Feb. 9, 1922; s. William Jay, Jr. and Annette (Markoe) S.; m. Joy Williams Proctor, June 19, 1947; children: Hope Williams, Timothy Proctor, Andrew Lawrence, Michael Markoe. B.A., Yale U., 1945. With Schieffelin & Co. (later known as Schieffelin & Somerset Co.), N.Y.C., 1948-86, v.p. charge pharm. labs. div., 1949-62, chmn., chief exec. officer, 1962-83; cons. Schieffelin & Somerset Co. div. parent co. LVMH Moet Hennessy-Louis Vuitton, N.Y.C., 1983-86; former chmn. Almay, Inc., N.Y.C.; chmn. Almay Inc., Simi Winery; dir. Baccarat, Inc., N.Y.C., Centennial Ins. Co., Atlantic Mut. Ins. Co.; Bd. dirs. Drug. Chem. and Allied Trades Assn., 1955-62, pres., 1961-62; bd. dirs. Econ. Devel. Council N.Y., 1974-79; mem. exec. com. Nat. Assn. Beverage Importers, Inc., 1973-83; mem. adv. bd. La Maison Francaise, 1964-83; mem. adv. com. European Inst. Bus. Adminstrn., 1965-77; past dir. N.Y. Bd. Trade, 1955-63. Served to capt., 612th F.A. Bn. (Pack) AUS, 1942-46, CBI. Decorated chevalier Ordre National du Mérite, Legion of Honor France; comdr. Order of Merit (Italy). Mem. Am. Pharm. Assn. (life), Hundred Year Assn. N.Y. (pres. 1968-70), N.Y. Offshore Power Boat Racing Assn. (hon. life), Commerce and Industry Assn. N.Y. (past chmn. 1972-73), N.Y. Chamber Commerce and Industry (exec. com.), French C. of C. of U.S. (exec. v.p. 1968-80, councillor 1980-89), Brit.-Am. C. of C. (dir. 1971-89), Commanderie de Bordeaux (comdr. 1966), Pilgrims U.S., Beta Theta Pi (past pres. Phi Chi chpt.). Clubs: N.Y. Yacht, Yale, Union (N.Y.C.). Home: Mount Ksico N.Y. Died Mar. 23, 1989; buried St. Matthew's Cemetery, Bedford, N.Y.

SCHIFF, ALBERT, shoe company executive; b. Lithuania, Nov. 14, 1893; came to U.S., 1912, naturalized.; s. Hyman Herschel and Ethel (Schlessinger) S.; m. Ethel Zox, Nov. 19, 1920; 1 child, Elaine Schiff Milstein. Grad., Rabbinical Sem., Telshia, Lithuania, 1911. V.p. Shoe Corp. Am., Columbus, Ohio, from 1947, also bd. dirs. Hon. pres. Jewish Nat. Fund Am.; mem. adminstrv. com. Zionist Orgn. Am., from 1950; bd. dirs. Nat. Jewish Welfare Bd., Am. Israel Cultural Found. Mem. Cavendish Club, Lotos Club. *

SCHIFF, DOROTHY, publisher; b. N.Y.C., Mar. 11, 1903; d. Mortimer L. and Adele A. (Neustadt) S.; m. Richard B. W. Hall, Oct. 17, 1923; children: Mortimer W., Adele T.; m. George Backer, Oct. 21, 1932; 1 child, Sarah Ann; m. Theodore Olin Thackrey, July 29, 1943; m. Rudolf Sonneborn, 1953. Student, Brearley Sch., N.Y.C., 1912-20, Bryn Mawr Coll., 1920-21. Majority stockholder N.Y. Post, 1939-42, pres., pub., 1942, owner, pub., 1943-89. Mem. Ellis Island Investigating Com., 1934; bd. dirs. Henry St. Settlement, Mt. Sinai Hosp., 1934-38, Woman's Trade Union League of N.Y., 1939, N.Y.C. Bd. of Child Welfare, 1937-39. Decorated Légion d'Honneur (France). Mem. Am. Soc. Newspaper Editors, Washintgon Press Club. Democrat. Home: New York N.Y. Died Aug. 30, 1989.

SCHILLER, WILLIAM EDWARD, chocolate manufacturing company executive; b. Sydney Mines, N.S., Can., Feb. 15, 1909; m. Mary Lambie (dec. Dec. 1957): children: Kathryn Schiller McCarthy, Carl Frederick, Eileen; m. Mary McClure, Apr. 7, 1962. AB, MBA, U. Mich., 1933. Acct. Arthur Andersen & Co., CPA's, Chgo. and N.Y.C., 1933-47; contr. Hershey (Pa.) Foods Corp., 1947, treas., 1948-65, v.p., 1956-65, chmn. bd., 1965-74, also bd. dirs.; bd. dirs. Hershey Trust Co., Hershey Bank. Bd. dirs. Milton Hershey Sch., M.S. Hershey Found. Mem. Pa. C. of C. (past chmn.). Home: Hershey Pa. Died May 2, 1990; buried Hershey, Pa.

SCHIRMER, EDWARD ADOLPH, advertising executive; b. Mt. Vernon, N.Y., Mar. 1, 1901; s. Edward Adoph and Martha (Armstrong) S.; m. Grace Emerson, 1924; 1 child, Edward Emerson; m. Frances Hamilton, Aug. 19, 1937; children: Michael Wheeler, Robert Hamilton. Grad., Lawrenceville Sch., 1918; student, Princeton U., 1918. Assoc. Hanover Nat. Bank, 1919-25, U.S. Pub. Assn., 1925-30; dir. Crowell-Collier Pub., San Francisco, 1930-35, Detroit, 1935; v.p., dir. Crowell-Collier Pub., 1935-50; exec. v.p. Crowell-Collier Pub., N.Y.C., 1950-53; sr. v.p., dir. Campbell-Ewald Co., Detroit, 1953-89; dir. Goebel Brewing Co. Trsutee Lawrenceville (N.J.) Sch.; mem. Wayne County Salvage Com., 1941-89, past chmn. scrap metal drive, waste paper campaign; mem. advt. com. 5th war bond drive U.S. Treasury Dept.; co-chmn. war advt. coun. Mich. sponsorship com., World War II. Mem. Adcraft Club (v.p., dir. 1941-43, pres. 1944-45), Econ. Club, Detroit Athletic Club, Detroit Club, Bloomfield Hills (Mich.) Country Club, Bloomfield Open Hunt Club. Republican. Episcopalian. Home: Palm Springs Calif. Died Mar. 21, 1989.

SCHISLER, J(OHN) HARRY, insurance company executive; b. Balt., Nov. 14, 1893; s. John H. and Linnie (Scheffer) S.; m. Mildred H. Hawkins, Jan. 9, 1926; 1 child, John Gardner. Student, Balt. City Coll., 1906-10; LLB, U. Md., 1914. Bar: Md. 1915. With Fidelity & Deposit Co. Md., Balt., from 1914, exec. v.p., dir., from 1950; with Am. Bonding Co. Balt., 1914-57, exec. v.p., dir., 1950-57; pres., dir. East End Loan & Savs. Assn., from 1920. Trustee Goucher Coll., Meth. Home for Aged, Lovely Lane Meth. Ch., Patterson Meml. Assn., Balt. Conf. Pensions Fund, Inc., Md. Gen. Hosp. Lt. (j.g.) USNR, 1917-19. Mem. ABA, Md. Bar Assn., Balt. Bar Assn., Internat. Assn. Ins. Counsel, Balt. Country Club, Mchts. Club, Masons, Shriners. *

SCHLOSSMAN, NORMAN JOSEPH, architect; b. Chgo., Mar. 13, 1901; s. Isaac and Augusta (Hess) S.; m. Carol Rosenfeld, Dec. 20, 1927 (dec. 1968); 1 child, John Isaac; m. Bertha Holzheimer Loewenthal, Jan. 21, 1969 (dec. 1989). B.S. in Architecture, Armour Inst. (now Ill. Inst. Tech.), 1921. Designer Coolidge & Hodgdon, Chgo., 1923-25; co-founder Loebl & Schlossman also Loebl, Schlossman & Demuth, Chgo., 1925-46; ptnr., co-founder Loebl, Schlossman & Bennett, Chgo., 1946-65, Loebl, Schlossman, Bennett & Dart, Chgo., 1965-76, Loebl, Schlossman & Hackl, Chgo., from 1976; mem. exec. com. Bldg. Research Adv. Council, Nat. Acad. Sci., D.C., 1959-62; mem. New Constrn., Planning and Procurement Commn., State of Ill., 1965-67. Prin. works include town plan, dwellings, schs., bus. ctr., Park Forest, Ill., Temple Sholom, Temple Emanuel, Chgo., Congregation Solel, Highland Park, Ill., Louis A. Weiss Hosp., Michael Reese Med. Ctr., Chgo., Old Orchard, Oakbrook, River Oaks and Hawthorn shopping ctrs., Ill., Prairie Shores apts., 1350-60 Lake Shore Dr. apts., Chgo., Winton Place, Lakewood, Ohio, Highland Park High Sch., Ill., Deerfield High Sch., Ill., Water Tower Place, Chgo. Civic Ctr. (with others). Chmn. Bldg. Code Com., Highland Park, Ill., 1947-50; Chmn. Plan Commn., Highland Park, 1954-61; chmn. Downtown Redevel. Commn., Highland Park, 1978-81; bd. overseers Coll. Architecture, Ill. Inst. Tech., from 1983; life mem. nat. commn. Anti-Defamation League. Fellow AIA (pres. Chgo. chpt. 1946-50, nat. first v.p. 1953-54, chancellor Coll. Fellows 1966-68). Clubs: Tavern, Arts, Carlton (Chgo.); Northmoor Country (Highland Park); Lake Shore Country (Glencoe). Home: Winnetka Ill. Deceased. †

SCHMALZ, CARL NELSON, department store executive; b. Huntley, Ill., Jan. 4, 1898; s. Otto Henry and Eunice Hattie (Howe) S.; m. Esther Dorothy Fowler, June 22, 1923; children: Carl Nelson, Robert Fowler, David Harrison. AB cum laude, Harvard U., 1919, MBA, 1921. Rsch. dir. Rike-Kumler Co., Dayton, Ohio, 1922-25; asst. prof. U. Mich. Sch. Bus. Adminstrn., Ann Arbor, 1925-29; asst. prof., chief Bur. Bus. Rsch., Harvard U. Grad. Sch. Bus. Adminstrn., Cambridge, Mass., 1929-39; with R.H. Stearns Co., Boston, from 1939—, pres., from 1946, also bd. dirs.; v.p., bd. dirs., mem. exec. com. Frederick Atkins, Inc., N.Y.C., from 1947—; mem. Boston Retail Trade Bd. Bd. dirs. New Eng. Coun., Boston Mcpl. Rsch. Bur.; chmn. United Fund Campaign Greater Boston, 1962; mem. corp. United Fund Greater Boston, Mass. Meml. Hosp., Boston; mem. adv. com. Simmons Coll. Sch. Bus., Boston. Mem. Nat. Retail Mchts. Assn. (bd. dirs. from 1941, v.p. 1961, chmn. exec. com. 1962-63, chmn. contrs. congress 1956-46, pres. from 1964), Boston Mail Users Coun. (pres. from 1963), Union Club, Comml. Club, Harvard Club, Harvard Faculty Club. Republican. *

SCHMID, JOHN HAVILAND, lawyer; b. N.Y.C., Jan. 5, 1896; s. George Frederick and Maude Augusta (Burke-Kellock) S.; m. Esther Margaret Winslow, Dec. 7, 1918; children: Katharine Schmid Maxon, John H., Helen Schmid Ketcham. LL.B., Cornell U., 1919. Bar: N.Y. 1020, N.J. 1926. Pvt. practice, 1920-29; mem. Burke & Burke, N.Y.C., from 1929, Bourne, Schmid, Burke & Noll, Summit, N.J., from 1942; bd. dirs. Atlantic Casting & Engring. Corp., O.S. Tyson & Co., Inc., Frazar & Co., Inc. Aviator USN, 1918-19. Mem. Bar Assn. City N.Y., Upper Montclair Country Club, Wall Street Club, Phi Kappa Psi, Phi Delta Phi. Congregationalist. *

SCHMIDT, ALEXANDER MACKAY, health services executive, university administrator; b. Jamestown, N.D., Jan. 26, 1930; s. Theodore G. and Marion W. (MacKay) S.; m. Patricia Ann White, June 27, 1952; children—Susan Jane, Sarah Ann. BS, Northwestern U., 1951; MD, U. Utah, 1955. Intern medicine U. Utah Affiliated Hosps., 1955-56, resident, 1958-60; USPHS rsch. fellow in cardiology U. Utah Coll. Medicine, 1960-62, from instr. medicine to asst. dean, 1962-68; dir. U. Utah Coll. Medicine Cardiovascular Rsch. and Tng. Ctr., 1966-67; chief edn. and tng. br. Regional Med. Programs Svc., HEW, Washington, 1967-68; commr. FDA, HEW, Washington, 1973-76; exec. assoc. dean, assoc. prof. medicine U. Ill. Coll. Medicine, Chgo., 1969-70; dean, prof. medicine Abraham Lincoln Sch. Medicine, U. Ill., 1970-73; vice chancellor health svcs., acad. affairs, health affairs U. Ill., Chgo., 1977-87; prof. health policy and social medicine Inst. Govt. and Pub. Affairs, U. Ill., 1987-88; v.p., dir. Tech. Advancement Ctr. Univ. Hosp. Consortium, Oakbrook Terr., Ill., 1988-89; co-chmn. rev. com., div. regional med. programs Health Services and Mental Health Adminstrn., 1970-73; dir. Am. Cyanamid Co. Contbr. articles to profl. jours. Trustee Food and Drug Law Inst., from 1974; mem. Oak Park-River Forest Sch. Bd., from 1983. Served with AUS, 1956-58, ETO. Markle scholar academic medicine, 1966; named Best Tchr., Class of 1968 U. Utah; recipient Disting. Svc. medal USPHS, 1976, Disting. Svc. medal HEW, 1976. Fellow Inst. of Medicine Chgo.; mem. Am. Fedn. Clin. Rsch., Am. Thoracic Soc., Utah Thoracic Soc., AMA, Utah Med. Soc., AAAS, Am. Soc. Internal Medicine, Utah Soc. Internal Medicine, N.Y. Acad. Sci., Alpha Omega Alpha. Home: Oak Park Ill. Died Jan. 28, 1991; buried Chapel Hill Gardens, Oak Brook, Ill.

SCHMIDT, FRED HENRY, physics educator; b. Detroit, Sept. 12, 1915; s. Hugo W. and Maude (Schmidt) S.; m. Margaret Cresswell, Sept. 5, 1939; children: Karla Schmidt Steel, Kurt. B.S. in Engring, U. Mich., 1937; M.A., U. Buffalo, 1940; Ph.D., U. Cal. at Berkeley, 1945. Engr. Am. Tel. & Tel. Co., Denver, 1937-39; physicist Manhattan Project, Berkeley, Oak Ridge and Los Alamos, 1942-45, Radiation Lab., U. Calif., Berkeley, 1945-46; mem. faculty U. Wash., Seattle, 1946-86, prof. physics, 1956-86, prof. emeritus, 1986-91. Author: (with others) The Energy Controversy: The Fight Over Nuclear Power, 1976; Contbr. (with others) articles to physics jours. Guggenheim fellow Amsterdam, Geneva, 1956-57; NSF Postdoctoral fellow, Geneva, 1963-64. Fellow Am. Phys. Soc.; mem. Sigma Xi. Home: Seattle Wash. Died Jan. 17, 1991; buried Seattle.

SCHMIDT, GEORGE PAUL, history educator; b. St. Louis, Feb. 26, 1894; s. Charles Christopher and Marianna (Stockhardt) S.; m. Irma Gotch, Mar. 20, 1921; children: George Paul Jr., Marianne Elizabeth. AB, Washington U., St. Louis, 1918, AM, 1919; PhD, Columbia U., 1930. Mem. faculty Concordia Coll., Ft. Wayne, Ind., 1920-30, Douglass Coll., New Brunswick, N.J., 1930-60, Am. Army U., Biarritz, France, 1945-46; dean internat. studies seminars, summer 1949, 50; Whitney vis. prof. Thiel Coll., 1960-61; prof. history Cape Cod Community Coll., Hyannis, Mass., 1961-89. Author: The Old Time College President, 1930, The Liberal Arts College, 1957; contbr. articles to profl. jours. Mem. AAUP, Am. Hist. Assn., Phi Beta Kappa. Home: Princeton NJ Died May 22, 1989.

SCHMIDT, HAROLD ROBERT, lawyer; b. Braddock, Pa., Sept. 4, 1913; s. Abraham I. and Gustella (Frankle) S.; m. Bernice V. Williams, June 24, 1941; children: Barbara N. Schmidt Wickwire, Edward C., Gordon W. AB, U. Mich., 1934; LLB, U. Pitts., 1937. Bar: Pa. 1937, D.C. 1976. Sr. ptnr. in charge litigation Rose, Schmidt, Hasley & DiSalle, Pitts., Washington, Ann Arbor, Mich. and Washington, Pa., from 1946; co-chmn. Lawyers Non-Partisan Com. to Secure Additional Judges for Ct. Common Pleas, Allegheny County, 1963; chmn. Com. to Modernize Jury Selection Procedures, Allegheny County, 1965; permanent mem. Jud. Conf. 3d Circuit; former govt. appeal agt. local bd. 19, SSS, Pitts.; panel participant 1st Internat. Med.-Legal Seminar Pitts. Inst. Legal Medicine, U. Rome, 1965; lectr. 3d seminar U. London Med. Coll., 1967; lectr. short course on antitrust law So. Meth. U., 1979, 80, 82-83. Author: Handbook and Guide to the Federal Coal Mine Health and Safety Act of 1969 and Related State Statutes, 1970; contbg. author: Antitrust Law and the Coal Industry, 1983; editor-in-chief: U. Pitts. Law Rev., 1936-37. Chmn. exec. com. Pitts. chpt. Am. Jewish Com.; emeritus bd. dirs. ann. giving fund U. Pitts.; bd. visitors Sch. Law, from 1978; mem. Ft. Pitt Mus. Assocs.; ann. fund leadership com. U. Mich.; mem. Gov.'s Trial Ct. Nominating Commn. of Allegheny County, Pa., 1979; chmn. Appellate Ct. Nominating Commn. Pa., from 1985; bd. visitors So. Meth. U. Sch. Law, 1984-87. Served to capt. AUS, World War II. Fellow Internat. Acad. Trial Lawyers (bd. dirs., dean acad. 1983, pres.-elect 1986, pres. 1987); mem. World Assn. Lawyers (founder, life mem.), ABA (mem. council sect. antitrust law 1984-85, vice chmn. civil practice and procedure com. sect. antitrust law 1980-82), Pa. Bar Assn., Allegheny County Bar Assn., Supreme Ct. Hist. Soc., Nat. Assn. R.R. Trial Counsel, JAG Assn., Acad. Trial Lawyers Allegheny County (past pres.), U. Pitts. Law Sch. Alumni Assn. (past pres.), Am. Law Inst., World Peace through Law Ctr., Am. Judicature Soc., Internat. Soc. Barristers (past gov.), Soc. Mining Law Antiquarians, Pa. Inst. Legal Medicine, Pa. Def. Inst., Def. Research Inst., Res. Officers Assn. U.S., Pa. Soc., Order of Coif, Phi Beta Kappa, Phi Kappa Psi, Phi Eta Sigma. Clubs: Duquesne, Concordia, U. Michigan (past pres.). Lodge: Masons. Home: Pittsburgh Pa. Deceased. †

SCHMIDT, LEON HERBERT, pharmacologist, educator; b. Huron, Ohio, June 28, 1909; s. Herbert H. and Amelia Margaret (Baehr) S.; m. Ida Theresa Genther, July 28, 1931; children: Nancy Jeanne, Richard Allen. BA, DePauw U., 1929; PhD, U. Cin., 1932; ScD (hon.), DePauw U., 1968. Rsch. assoc. Christ Hosp. Inst. Med. Rsch., Cin., 1932-36, dir., 1936-63; instr. biol. chemistry Coll. Medicine U. Cin., 1938-41, from asst. to assoc. prof., 1941-50, rsch. prof., 1950-63; dir. Nat. Ctr. for Primate Biology U. Calif., Davis, 1963-68, prof. pharmacology Sch. Medicine, 1968-69; assoc. dir. chemotherapy rsch. So. Rsch. Inst., 1969-76; prof. pharmacology U. Ala. Med. Ctr., Birmingham, 1969-76, sr. scientist, 1967-89; Charles Francis Craig lectr. Am. Soc. Tropical Medicine, 1957; John Blair Barnwell Meml. lectr VA Conf. on Pulmonary Diseases, 1971; dir. Commn. Malaria, Armed Forces Epidemiol. Bd., 1964-65; cons. USPHS, NRC, 1946-67; mem. adv. coun. Nat. Inst. Allergy and Infectious Diseases, 1962-66, Nat. Inst. Child Health and Human Devel., 1967-71; mem. Drug Safety Commn., WHO (expert adv. panel malaria); mem. adv. com. Wis. Regional Primate Ctr.; adv. med. bd. Leonard Wood Meml. Hosp.; exec. com. VA Com. on Chemotherapy of Tb; mem. com. on med. rsch. Nat. Tb Assn. Mem. editorial bd. Am. Rev. Tb, Jour. Nat. Malaria Soc., Jour. Pharmacology and Exptl. Therapeutics, Am. Jour. Tropical Medicine and Hygiene; bd. editors Infection and Immunity, 1970-74, Antimicrobial Agts. and Chemotherapy, 1970-89. Recipient Trudeau medal Am. Thoracic Soc., 1967. Fellow AAAS, Am. Soc. Tropical Medicine and Hygiene, N.Y. Acad. Scis.; mem. Am. Trudeau Soc. (hon.), Am. Soc. Pharmacology and Exptl. Therapeutics, Am. Chem. Soc., Soc. Am. Bacteriologists, Am. Soc. Biol. Chemists, Am. Acad. Microbiology, Am. Assn. Cancer Rsch. Home: Birmingham Ala. Died May 14, 1989.

SCHNEIDER, ELISABETH WINTERSTEEN, English language educator; b. Salt Lake City, Sept. 7, 1987; d. Anton and Mary (Robinson) S. AB, Smith Coll., 1920; AM, U. Pa., 1926, PhD, 1933; postgrad., Oxford (Eng.) U., 1930-31. Instr. English, Temple U., Phila., 1926-33, asst. prof., 1933-39, assoc. prof., 1939-45, prof., 1945-64; prof. U. Calif., Santa Barbara, from 1964. Author: The Aesthetics of William Hazlitt, 1933, Aesthetic Motive, 1939, (with A.L. Walker and H.E. Childs) The Range of Literature, 1960; editor: Samuel Taylor Coleridge: Selected Prose and Poetry, 1951, Coleridge, Opium, and Kubla Khan, 1953, Poems and Poetry, 1964; also articles and revs. Mem. MLA, AAUP, Modern Humanities Rsch. Assn., Coll. English Assn. (past pres.), Phi Beta Kappa. Democrat. Presbyterian. *

SCHNEIDER, FREDERICK H., banker; m. Ruth Oswald; children: Edith Schneider Roshe, Frederick H. Jr. Grad., U. Pa., 1939; LLB, St. John's U., 1947. Trustee Roosevelt Savs. Bank, Bklyn., 1951-83, v.p., 1963-67, pres., 1967-83, ret., 1983; mem. Nassau adv. bd. Mfrs. Hanover Trust, 1971-81. Bd. dirs. Ottilie Home for Children, 1952-77, pres., 1961-63; trustee Village of Garden City, N.Y., 1963-69, mayor, 1969-71; bd. dirs. Swedenborg Found., Inc., 1981-91. With USNR, World War II. Mem. Nassau Bar Assn., Savs. Bank Assn. of N.Y. State (pres. 1973-74, bd. dirs.), Nat. Assn. Mut. Savs. Banks (bd. dirs. 1973-79), L.I. Assn. (bd. dirs. 1975-80), Garden City C. of C., Rotary, Masons. Home: La Canada Calif. Died Aug. 12, 1991.

SCHNEIDER, MELVIN, business executive; b. Austria, 1914. BA, Northwestern U., 1934, LLB, 1937. Pres., CEO Martin-Brower Corp., Chgo.; chmn. Comet Packaging Corp.; pres., CEO Prince Castle Inc.; pres., dir. 4800 S. Austin Corp.; dir. M-B Cartage Co. Pres., bd. dirs. Robert E. Schneider Found., MEP Found. Home: Wilmette Ill. Died Sept. 19, 1990.

SCHNEIDERMAN, HOWARD ALLEN, science educator, zoologist; b. N.Y.C., Feb. 9, 1927; s. Louis and Anna (Center) S.; m. Audrey MacLeod, Sept. 16, 1951; children: Anne Mercedes, John Howard. A.B., Swarthmore Coll., 1948; M.A. in Zoology, Harvard U., 1949, Ph.D. in Physiology, 1952; D.Sc. (hon.), La Salle Coll., 1975, Swarthmore Coll., 1982; DSc (hon.), U. Toledo, 1984, U. Mass., 1986, Washington U., St. Louis, 1989; LLD, Clemson U., 1989. AEC predoctoral fellow Harvard U., 1949-52, Univ. research fellow, 1952-53; asst. prof. zoology, then asso. prof. Cornell U., 1953-61; prof. biology, chmn. dept. Case Western Reserve U., Cleve., 1961-66, Jared Potter Kirtland Disting. prof. biology, 1966-69, co-dir. Devel. Biology Ctr., 1961-69; prof. biol. sci., dean sch., dir. Ctr. Pathobiology, U. Calif., Irvine, 1969-79, chmn. dept. developmental and cell biology, 1969-75; sr. v.p. R & D, Monsanto Co., St. Louis, from 1979, chief scientist, until 1990, mem. exec. mgmt. com., 1983-90; cons. Gen. Med. Sci. Inst., Nat. Inst. Child Health and Devel., NIH, 1961-79; instr. invertebrate zoology Marine Biol. Lab., Woods Hole, Mass., 1956-58, trustee, mem. exec. com., 1966-72; spl. research, devel., genetics, insect hormones, and insect physiology; bd. dirs. G. D. Searle and Co. Editorial bd.: Results and Problems of Cell Differentiation; contbr. over 200 articles to profl. jours. Adv. commr. Marshall Scholarship Commn., 1973-77, chmn., 1976-77; trustee Mo. Bot. Garden, from 1981. Served with USNR, 1945-46. Recipient U. Calif. Irvine medal, 1989; NSF sr. fellow Cambridge (Eng.) U., 1959-60. Fellow AAAS, N.Y. Acad. Scis.; mem. Nat. Acad. Sci. (assembly life scis. from 1975), Am. Acad. Arts and Scis., Soc. Exptl. Biology (Eng.), Am. Soc. Zoologists, Entomol. Soc. Am., Lepidopterist Soc., Corp. Marine Biol Lab., Am. Soc. Naturalists, Soc. Developmental Biology (pres. 1965-66), Internat. Soc. Developmental Biology (dir. from 1981), Genetics Soc. Am., AAUP, Am. Inst. Biol. Scis., Soc. Chem. Industry, Am. Soc. Cell Biology, Japanese Soc. Developmental Biology, Nat. Sci. Bd., Phi Beta Kappa, Sigma Xi. Home: Saint Louis Mo. Died Dec. 5, 1990; cremated.

SCHOB, ANTHONY JOHN, corporate executive; b. Phila., Mar. 10, 1898; s. Frank and Marie (Vorel) S.; m. Lillian Ramsey, mar. 10, 1933. BS, U. Pa., 102-. Pres. HonorBilt Products, Inc., Phila., 1924-36; assoc. Nachman Corp., Chgo., 1936, exec. v.p., 1936-47, pres., 1947-56, chmn. bd., 1956-65, chmn. exec. and fin. com., from 1965. Mem. Furniture Club Am., Tucson Country Club, Oak Park Country Club (Ill.). *

SCHOCKEN, GERSHOM GUSTAV, publisher, editor; b. Zwickau, Germany, Sept. 1912; arrived in Israel, 1933. Ed. U. Heidelberg, London Sch. Econs. Joined staff Haaretz daily newspaper, Tel Aviv, 1937, pub., editor, 1939-90; dir. Schocken Pub. House Ltd.; mem. Knesset, 1955-59. Named Internat. Editor-of-Yr., World Press Rev., 1983. Died Dec. 22, 1990; buried Tel-Aviv, Israel. Home: Tel Aviv Israel

SCHOTTE, OSCAR EMIL, biology educator; b. Minsk, Russia, Dec. 21, 1896; came to U.S., 1932, naturalized, 1937; s. Richard and Emily (Leisten) S.; m. Anna Pearce Munsell, June 16, 1939; children: Anna Tilghman Munsell, Richard Theodore; 1 foster child, Mrs. James Eells. Lic. es scis., U. Geneva, 1920, PhD, 1925; MA, Amherst Coll., 1944. Instr. biology U. Geneva, 1922-28; fellow Rockefeller Found., Freiburg, Germany, 1928-32; Sterling fellow in zoology Yale U., New Haven, 1932-34; tchr. biology Marine Biol. Lab., Woods Hole, Mass., 1933-44; asst. prof. Amherst (Mass.) Coll., 1934-37, assoc. prof., 1937-44, prof., 1944-48, Rufus Tyler Lincoln prof., from 1948, chmn. dept., 1944-46. Rsch. in exptl. embryology, regeneration and endocrinology. Fellow AAAS; mem. Soc. Helvetic Sci., Am. Soc. Zoologists, Am. Soc. Anatomists, Am. Soc. Naturalists, Woods Hole Corp., Soc. for Growth and Devel., Am. Acad. Arts and Scis. *

SCHOTTENSTEIN, JEROME M., retail company executive; b. 1926; married. With Schottenstein Stores Corp., Columbus, Ohio, 1972-92, chmn., chief exec. officer; chmn. Retail Ventures, Inc., 1980-92; pres. Nat. Industries Inc.; v.p., dir. Shonac Corp.; pres., chmn., dir. Valley Fair Corp., Little Ferry, N.J., 1979-92; chmn. L.F. Widman, Inc., 1979-92. Home: Columbus Ohio Died Mar. 10, 1992. †

SCHRAER, ROSEMARY S. J., university chancellor; b. Ilion, N.Y., Aug. 1, 1924; d. Ulysses Sidney and Rose Katherine (Ortner) Schmidt; m. Allan Gramlick Jenkins, May 3, 1946 (dec. Aug. 13, 1947); 1 child, David; m. Harald Schraer, June 12, 1952. AB, Syracuse U., 1946, MS in Zoology, 1949, PhD in Biochemistry, 1953. Vis. research assoc. Harvard Med. Sch., Boston, Mass., 1967-68; vis. scientist Radcliffe Inst. Ind. Study, Cambridge, Mass., 1967-68; acting head dept. computer sci. Pa. State U., University Park, 1973-74, assoc. dean for research, 1973-78, prof. biochemistry, 1975-86, assoc. provost, 1981-85; exec. vice chancellor U. Calif., Riverside, 1986-87, chancellor, 1987-92; fellow Cavendish Coll., Cambridge U., Eng., 1987; bd. dirs. Am. Coun. on Pharm. Edn., Chgo., 1983-88, Accrediting Commn. for Sr. Colls. and Univs., Oakland, Calif., 1988-91, Presley Inst. of Corrections Rsch. and Tng., Sacramento, Calif., 1988-92; bd. visitors Southwestern U. Sch. Law, L.A., 1988-92. Mem. Monday Morning Group, Riverside, 1987-92, Coun. on Competitiveness, Washington, 1988-90, adv. bd. dirs. Nat. Prepaid Tuition Plan, Overland Park, Kans., 1988-91; bd. dirs. Inst. for Evaluating Health Risks, San Francisco, from 1988, Community Health Corp., 1988-91, Riverside Land Conservancy, 1988-92—; co-chair United Way Indland Valleys, 1990; mem. Riverside County Office Edn. Commn. on Edn., 1992. Univ. fellow Syracuse U., 1951-52. Mem. AAAS, Am. Chem. Soc., Am. Inst. Chemists, Am. Soc. Cell Biology, Am. Soc. Biol. Chemists, Am. Physciol. Soc., Phi Beta Kappa. Home: Moreno Valley Calif. Died Apr. 10, 1992.

SCHROEDER, CHARLES ROBBINS, zoo director; b. N.Y.C., July 29, 1901; s. Charles and Antoinette (Adametz) S.; m. Margaret Wolf, Nov. 5, 1931 (dec.); children: Mary Ann, Charles Randolph; m. C. Maxine Christenson Dawson, 1967. BS, Wash. State Coll., 1929, D.V.M., 1929. vet. Lederle Antitoxin Labs., Pearl River, N.Y., 1929-32; vet. San Diego (Calif.) Zool. Gardens, 1932-37, 39-41, dir., 1953-72, dir. emeritus, 1972-91; vet. N.Y. Zool. Park, 1937-39; prodn. mgr. Lederle Lab. div. Am. Cynamid Co., 1941-53. Fellow N.Y. Acad. Scis. (chmn. biology sect. 1948-49), Am. Pub. Health Assn., Calif. Acad. Scis., Am. Assn. Zool. Parks and Aquariums, San Diego Soc. Natural History; mem. N.Y. Zool. Soc., Am., N.Y.C. (sec.-treas. 1941-53) vet med. assns., Internat. Union Dirs. Zool. Gardens (pres. 1969), Masons, Rotary, Sigma Xi, Phi Kappa Phi, Alpha Psi. Republican. Presbyterian. Home: San Diego Calif. Died Mar. 21, 1991; cremated.

SCHULLIAN, DOROTHY MAY, librarian, historian; b. Lakewood, Ohio, May 19, 1906; d. Joseph Gustave and Louise (Knippel) S.; m. Howard Bernhardt Adelmann, July 6, 1978. A.B., Western Res. U., 1927;

Ph.D., U. Chgo., 1931. Fellow Am. Acad., Rome, 1931-34; instr. ancient langs. Albion Coll., 1939-44; asst. curator, curator, asst. chief, then chief history medicine div. Nat. Library of Medicine, Cleve., 1944-61; curator History of Sci. Collections, Cornell U. Library, 1961-72; Garrison lectr. Am. Assn. History Medicine. Author: (with Marbury B. Ogle) Rodulfi Tortarii Carmina, 1933, (with Max Schoen) Music and Medicine, 1948, (with Francis E. Sommer) Catalogue of Incunabula and Manuscripts, 1950, (with Luigi Belloni) Carlo Francesco Cogrossi, New Theory of the Contagious Disease Among Oxen, 1953, Tortellii de Medicina et Medicis, Iac Bartholoti de Antiquitate Medicinae, 1954, Alessandro Benedetti, Diaria de bello Carolino, with Latin text, English translation, commentary, 1967, The Baglivi Correspondence from the library of Sir William Osler, 1974; Editor: Notes and Events in Jour. of History of Medicine and Allied Scis, 1952-84; contbr. articles to profl. periodicals. Fellow Internat. Acad. History of Med.; mem. Am. Assn. History Medicine, History of Sci. Soc., Bibliog. Soc. Am., Am. Philol. Assn., Mediaeval Acad. Am., Am. Classical League, Classical Assn. of the Atlantic States, Phi Beta Kappa. Methodist. Home: Ithaca N.Y. Died Apr. 1, 1989; buried Lakewood Park Cemetery, Rocky River, Ohio.

SCHULZ, ERNST (BERNHERD), political science educator; b. Cleve., Nov. 1, 1896; s. Ernst Paul and Agnes Hermina (Krause) S.; m. Catherine L. Illie, June 21, 1921; children: Robert, Constance, Dorothy, Mary. Student, Case Inst. Tech., 1915-18; BS, U. Mich., 1920, AM, 1921, PhD, 1927. Mem. staff Detroit Bur. Govtl. Rsch., 1921; sec. Bur. Govt., U. Mich., Ann Arbor, 1921-22, 23-24, instr. polit. sci., 1924-27; instr. U. Cin., 1922-23; asst. prof. Lehigh U., Bethlehem, Pa., 1927-31, assoc. prof., 1931-45, prof., from 1945. Author: Government, A Phase of Social Organization, 1929, American City Government, 1949, Essentials of Government, 1958, Democracy, 1964, (with W.L. Godshall and others) Principles and Functions of Government in the United States, 1948. Mem. Am. Polit. Sci. Assn., Nat. Mcpl. League, Am. Acad. Polit. and Social Sci., Tau Beta Pi, Kappa Sigma. *

SCHUMACHER, ROBERT KENT, lawyer; b. Omaha, Nov. 29, 1924; s. William Alfred and Doris (Scroggin) S.; m. Margaret Clary Stocks, Dec. 23, 1949; children: Doris Ann Schumacher McMorrow, Richard Wendell, John William. S.B. in Elec. Engring, MIT, 1947; J.D., Harvard U., 1950. Bar: Okla. 1952, Ill. 1961. Sec. patent atty., mgr. legal and patents Well Surveys, Inc., Tulsa, 1950-61; assoc. Fitch, Even, Tabin and Flannery, Chgo., 1961-63; ptnr. Fitch, Even, Tabin and Flannery, from 1963. Served with AUS, 1944-46. Mem. ABA, Chgo. Bar Assn., Am. Intellectual Property Law Assn., Intellectual Property Law Assn. Chgo., Sigma Xi. Home: Winnetka Ill. Deceased. †

SCHUMAN, WILLIAM HOWARD, composer, administrator, educator; b. N.Y.C., Aug. 4, 1910; m. Frances Prince, Mar. 27, 1936; children—Anthony William, Andrea Frances. BS, Columbia U., 1935, MA, 1937, MusD, 1954; pvt. study, Max Persin, Charles Haubiel, Roy Harris; MusD (hon.), Chgo. Mus. Coll., 1946, U. Wis., 1949, Phila. Conservatory Music, 1952, Cin. Coll. Music, 1953, Hartt Coll. Music, 1956, Allegheny Coll., 1961, N.Y. U., 1962, Oberlin Coll., 1963, U. R.I., 1965, Peabody Conservatory, 1971, U. Rochester, 1972, N.C. U., 1980, New Eng. Conservatory Music, 1981, SUNY, 1986, Yale U., 1988; DFA (hon.), Adelphi Coll., 1963, Northwestern U., 1963, U. N.Mex., 1964, SUNY, 1974; DJ (hon.), Bates Coll., 1966; LHD (hon.), Colgate U., 1960, Brandeis U., 1962, Dartmouth Coll., 1962, N.Y. U., 1962, Fordham U., 1970, Ashland Coll., 1970, The Johns Hopkins U., 1985, The Juilliard Sch., 1987. Dir. chorus, mem. faculty Sarah Lawrence Coll., Bronxville, N.Y., 1935-45; dir. publs. G. Schirmer, Inc., N.Y.C., 1944-45; spl. publs. cons., 1945-52; pres. Julliard Sch. Music, N.Y.C., 1945-62, pres. emeritus, 1962-92; pres. Lincoln Center Performing Arts, N.Y.C., 1962-69; emeritus Lincoln Center Performing Arts, 1969-92; mem. adv. com. cultural info. USIA; vice chmn. U.S. delegation UNESCO Internat. Conf. Creative Artists, Venice, Italy, 1952; cons. in field. Recipient numerous awards including 1st Town Hall-League of Composers award 1940, N.Y. Music Critics Circle award 1941-42, award of Merit Nat. Assn. Am. Composers and Condrs. 1941-42, 1st Pulitzer prize for music, 1943, award Nat. Inst. Arts and Letters 1943, N.Y. Music Critics Circle award 1950-51, Columbia U. Bicentennial Anniversary medal 1957, 1st Brandeis U. Creative Arts award in music 1957, Citation of Merit State U. N.Y. 1963, Gold Medal Honor for music, Nat. Arts Club 1964, Ann. Composer's Award, Lancaster Symphony Orch. 1965, Brandeis medal for disting. svc. to higher edn. 1965, certificate of Merit Sigma Alpha Iota 1967, Concert Artists Guild award 1967, Mark M. Horblit prize for composition Boston Symphony Orch. 1980, Gold medal Am. Acad. Arts and Letters, 1982, Nat. Medal Arts, 1987, Kennedy Ctr. Honors award, 1989; prin. compositions include: (orchestral works) 10 symphonies, Three Colloquies for French horn and orch., New England Triptych, numerous others; (choral works) cantatas including A Free Song (first Pulitzer prize given for music), numerous shorter works such as Carols of Death; (band works) George Washington Bridge, 1950, overture Chester, 1956; (chamber music) 5 string quartets In Sweet Music; (piano compositions) Voyage, 1953; (score for film) Steeltown; (opera) The Mighty Casey; recs. Evocation-To Thee Old Cause; prin. commns. include, Elizabeth Sprague Coolidge Found. in Library of Congress, The Koussevitzky Music Found., Inc., Dallas Symphony League, Louisville Philharmonic, Ballet Theatre, U.S. Nat. Commn. for UNESCO through Dept. of State, Andre Kostelanetz, Samuel Dushkin, St. Lawrence U., Ford Found., Chamber Music Soc. Lincoln Center, N.Y. Philharmonic (3), Boston Symphony Orch., Nat. Symphony Orch., St. Louis Symphony Orch., Broadcast Music, Inc., Van Cliburn Internat. Piano Competition; composer (collaboration with Richard Purdy Wilbur) On Freedom's Ground: An American Cantata, 1985, commd. for 100th anniversary of Statue of Liberty. Chmn. bd. judges Student Composers Awards of Broadcast Music, Inc.; bd. dirs. Nat. Ednl. TV Bd., Film Soc. Lincoln Ctr., Charles E. Ives Soc., Koussevitzky Music Found., Walter Naumberg Found. (past pres.), Composers Forum; dir. Nat. Ednl. TV, Nat. Humanities Ctr.; music panel NEA; adv. coun. N.C. Sch. Arts.; adv. panel U.S. cultural Presentation Programs; Music Adv. U.S. Info. Agy.; chmn. Norlin Found., MacDowell Colony, NET Coun. on Programs; vice chmn. U.S. Del. UNESCO Internat. Conf. for Creative Arts, Chamber Music Soc. Lincoln Ctr.; active Creative Awards Commn., Brandeis U., U.S.-Japan Com. for Ednl. and Cultural Cooperation of U.S. Dept. State; vis. com. Boston U. Sch. Arts, Harvard U. Dept. Music; coll. of electors Hall of Fame for Great Ams.; bd. overseers Hopkins Ctr. of dartmouth Coll.;. Guggenheim fellow, 1939-41; recipient First Town Hall League of Composers award, 1940, N.Y. Music Critics Circle award, 1942, Nat. Medal Arts, 1987, Kennedy Ctr. Honors award, 1989. Fellow Nat. Inst. Arts and Letters, Am. Acad. and Inst. Arts and Letters, Royal Acad. Music (hon.), others. Clubs: Century (N.Y.C.), Lotos (N.Y.C.). Home: New York N.Y. Died Feb. 15, 1992.

SCHUR, MILTON OSCAR, chemical engineer, business executive; b. Boston, Sept. 5, 1895; s. Eugene Harry and Martha (Reinherz) S.; m. Etta Ruth Levine, Sept. 2, 1917; 1 child, Bertram H. BS, MIT, 1916. Rsch. chemist MIT, Cambridge, 1916-17, U.S. Bur. Mines and C.W.S., U.S. Army, 1918-19; chem. engr. Chem. Products Co., Washington, 1917-18; with Brown Co., Berlin, N.H., 1919-44; dir. rsch. Brown Co., Berlin, 1940-44; dir. R & D, Ecusta Paper Corp. (now div. Olin Mathieson Chem. Corp., Piscag Forest, N.C., 1944-60; v.p. packaging div. Olin Mathieson Chem. Co., from 1960; mem. paper industry tech. adv. com. WPB, World War II. Patentee in field. Fellow AAAS, Am. Inst. Chemists, N.Y. Acad. Scis.; mem. AICE, TAPPI, Am. Chem. Soc., Rsch. Soc. Am., Can. Tech. Assn. Pulp and Paper Industry, Soc. Chemical Industry, Forest Products Rsch. Soc., Chemists Club (N.Y.C.). *

SCHUSTER, FRANKLIN PHILLIP, otolaryngologist; b. El Paso, Tex., Jan. 4, 1895; s. Michael Phillip and Eugenia (Monyay) S.; m. Hallie Jarratt Morton, Oct. 11, 1924; children: Franklin Phillip Jr., Jarratt. BS, U. Chgo., 1916; MD, Rush Med. Coll., Chgo.., 1918. Diplomate Am. Bd. Otolaryngology, Nat. Bd. Med. Examiners. Intern Presbyn. Hosp. and Cook County Hosp., Chgo., 1918-19, resident in ear, nose and throat, 1919-20; pvt. practice, El Paso, from 1921; specialist So. Pacific R.R. and Tex. & Pacific R.R., from 1926; v.p., bd. dirs. El Paso Med. Ctr.; cons. William Beaumont Army Hosp., El Paso, VA Hosp., Ft. Bayard, Tex.; med. examiner aeronautics br. U.S. Dept. Commerce, 1927-37; lectr. U. Tex. Postgrad. Sch. Medicine. Contbr. articles to med. jours. Mem. med. adv. bd. SSS, Tex. With Med. Res. Corps, U.S. Army, 1917-19, lst lt. Res., 1930-36. Fellow ACS; mem. AMA, Am. Bronchoesophagological Assn., Am. Acad. Otolaryngology-Head and Neck Surgery, Am. Laryngol., Rhinol. and Otol. Soc., Tex. Med. Soc., El Paso County Med. Soc. (past pres.), Country Club El Paso, Coronado Country Club, Masons, Rotary, Alpha Omega Alpha, Nu Sigma Nu. Democrat. Presbyterian. *

SCHUSTER, MAX LINCOLN, publisher, editor; b. Kalusz, Austria, Mar. 2, 1897; (parents Am. citizens); s. Barnet and Esther (Stieglitz) S.; m. Ray Haskell. BLitt, Columbia U., 1917. Mem. staff UP Assns., Washington; chief publ. sect. Bur. War Risk Ins., U.S. Treasury Dept.; N.Y. corr. Boston Evening Transcript; assoc. in journalism Columbia U. Grad. Sch. Journalism; co-founder, ptnr. Simon & Schuster, Inc., N.Y.C., from 1924, pres., editor-in-chief, chmn. editorial bd.; assoc. Pocket Books, Inc., N.Y.C. Author: Eyes on the World: A Photographic Record of History in the Making, 1935; editor: A Treasury of the World's Great Letters, 1940; editor-in-chief: The Inner Sanctum Library of Living Literature; contbr. to mags. Trustee Montefiore Hosp., N.Y. Jewish Hosp. Fellow Am. Geog. Soc.; mem. Friends of Scripta Mathematica, Bibliog. Soc. Am., Shakespeare Fellowship, Three Hours for Lunch Club, Soc. for Prevention Cruelty to Gentle Readers (founder), Wednesday Culture Club That Meets on Fridays, Downing Street Young Men's Marching Club, Columbia U. Pulitzer Sch. Journalism Alumni Assn., High Fidelity Friends of WQXR, Lotos Club, Dutch Treat Club, Rockefeller Center Luncheon Club, Book Table, Sea Cliff Garden Club. *

SCHUTTE, CHARLES FREDERICK, lawyer; b. Honolulu, May 29, 1921; s. Charles Frederick and Genevieve (Murphy) S.; m. Kathleen McCall, Nov. 5, 1942 (dec. June 1979). B.A., U. Hawaii, 1943, M.A., 1947; J.D., Columbia U., 1950. Bar: N.Y. 1950, Hawaii 1953. Lectr. govt. U. Hawaii, 1947, 52-53; asso. Root, Ballantine, Harlan, Bushby & Palmer, N.Y.C., 1950-51; asso. Smith, Wild, Beebe & Cades (name changed to Cades Schutte Fleming & Wright), Honolulu, 1952-53, partner, 1954-88; bd. dirs. First Hawaiian Bank. Served to capt. AUS, 1942-46. Decorated Bronze Star. Fellow Am. Bar Found.; mem. ABA, Am. Law Inst., Hawaii Bar Assn. (pres. 1976), Assn. Bar City N.Y. Clubs: Pacific (Honolulu) (pres. 1970-71), Oahu Country (Honolulu), Plaza (Honolulu) (chmn. 1981-83). Home: Kailua Hawaii Died Apr. 7, 1988; buried Honolulu.

SCHUYLER, JAMES MARCUS, poet, author; b. Chgo., Nov. 9, 1923; s. Marcus James and Margaret (Connor) S. Student, Bethany (W.Va.) Coll., 1941-43, U. Florence, 1947-48. Mem. staff Mus. Modern Art, N.Y.C., 1957-61; critic Art News mag. Author: poetry Salute, 1962, May 24th or So, 1966, Freely Espousing: Poems, 1969, The Crystal Lithium, 1972, A Sun Cab, 1972, Hymn to Life: Poems, 1974, The Home Book: Prose and Poems, 1951-70, 1977, The Morning of the Poem, 1980, A Few Day, 1985, Selected Poems, 1988; fiction Alfred and Guinevere, 1958, (with John Ashbery) A Nest of Ninnies, 1969, What's For Dinner, 1978, Early in '71, 1982, libretto A Picnic Cantata, 1955. Recipient Longview Found. award, 1961; Frank O'Hara prize Poetry mag., 1969; Nat. Inst. Arts and Letters award, 1976; Pulitzer prize for poetry, 1981; Nat. Endowment Arts grantee, 1971, 72; Guggenheim fellow, 1981. Fellow Am. Acad. Am. Poets. Home: New York N.Y. Died Apr. 12, 1991; buried Little Portion Friary, Mt. Sinai, N.Y.

SCHWADA, JOHN, former university president; b. Tyrone, Okla., Sept. 23, 1919; s. William and Grace (Foster) S.; m. Wilma Ruth Webster, May 24, 1947; children: John Webster, Ann. B.S., N.E. Mo. State Coll., 1941; M.A., U. Mo., 1947; Ph.D., U. Tex., 1951. Teaching fellow U. Tex., 1947-50; prof. polit. sci. U. Mo., Columbia, 1951-71; chancellor U. Mo., 1964-71; pres. Ariz. State U., Tempe, 1971-81. Comptroller, budget dir., State of Mo., 1958-61; bd. fellows Am. Grad. Sch. Internat. Mgmt.; bd. dirs. Pub. Broadcasting Service, 1974-80; mem. Ariz. State Bd. Edn., 1975-79. Served to capt. USAAC, 1942-46. Home: Phoenix Ariz. Deceased. †

SCHWANTES, ARTHUR (JOHN), agricultural engineering educator; b. Kewaunee Wis., Feb. 25, 1896; s. Charles and Alvina (Tess) S.; m. Laura Streu, May 8, 1918; children: Jean Schwantes Fay, John, Robert (dec.), Marilyn Schwantes Wandke. BS, U. Minn., 1925; MS, U. Wis., 1930. Registered profl. engr., Minn. Salesman, demonstrator land clearing machinery A.J. Kirstin Co., Escanaba, Mich., 1917-21; asst. prof. agrl. engring. U. Minn., St. Paul, 1921-28, assoc. prof., head power and machinery sect., 1928-40, prof., head dept. agrl. engring., 1940-64, prof. emeritus, from 1964; mem. bd., cons. Experience, Inc., Mpls., from 1964; cons. Fish, Richardson & Neave, patent attys., N.Y.C., 1948-52; engring. advisor on farm mechanization Tech. Coop. Adminstrn., Dept. State, Egypt, 1952-53. Sgt. U.S. Army, 1918-19. Lutheran. Fellow AAAS, Am. Soc. Agrl. Engrs. (nat. pres. 1948-49); mem. Am. Soc. Engring. Edn. (pres., sec. Minn. sect.), Nat. Safety Coun. (bd. dirs., mem. farm safety conf.), Engrs. Club, Gamma Sigma Delta. Lutheran. *

SCHWARTZ, ABBA PHILIP, lawyer; b. Balt., Apr. 17, 1916; s. Harry and Fannie (Berman) S. B.S. in Fgn. Service, Georgetown U., 1936; LL.B., Harvard U., 1939. Bar: D.C. 1940. Ofcl. Intergovtl. Com. on Refugees, London, Eng., 1946-47; reparations dir. UN Internat. Refugee Orgn., Geneva, Switzerland, 1947-49; partner law firm Washington, 1949-62; adminstr., asst. sec. Bur. Security and Consular Affairs, State Dept., 1962-66; practice law Washington, 1967-89; U.S. rep. 18th Session, Council Intergovtl. Com. on European Migration, Geneva, 1962, 18th Session, Council Intergovtl. Com. on European Migration (20th-24th sessions), 1963-65; U.S. del., vice chmn. 20th Internat. Conf. Red Cross, Vienna, Austria, 1965; chief White House Mission to Vietnam, 1965; spl. asst. to sec. def. on prisoners of war in Vietnam, from 1967; spl. counsel to Intergovtl. Com. on Migration, from 1968. Author: The Open Society, 1968, paperback, 1969; Contbr. articles on immigration and refugees to periodicals. Bd. govs. ARC, 1963-66; mem. N.Y. State Commn. To Commemorate Centennial of Franklin Delano Roosevelt, 1982; mem. adv. com. to U.S. Commn. for Eleanor Roosevelt Centennial, 1984. Served with U.S. Mcht. Marines, 1942-44; to lt. USNR, 1944-46. Decorated Order Orange Nassau (The Netherlands). Mem. ABA, Fed. Bar Assn., D.C. Bar Assn., PEN, Franklin and Eleanor Roosevelt Inst. (bd. dirs.), Reform Club (London), Nat. Capital Democratic Club, Harvard Club (N.Y.C., Washington). Home: Washington D.C. Died Sept. 12, 1989; buried Arlington Nat. Cemetery.

SCHWARTZ, ALVIN, author; b. Bklyn., Apr. 25, 1927; s. Harry and Gussie (Younger) S.; m. Barbara Carmer, Aug. 7, 1954; children: John H., Peter H., Nancy H., Elizabeth O. AB, Colby Coll., 1949; MS,

Northwestern U., 1951. Reporter Binghamton (N.Y.) Press, 1951-55; sr. writer Prudential Ins. Co., 1956-57, Doremus & Co., 1956-57, Nat. Found., 1957-58; dir. comms. Opinion Rsch. Corp., Princeton, N.J., 1958-63; author juveniles, 1964-92. Author juv. books including: The Unions: What They Are, How They Came to Be, How They Affect Each of Us, 1972, A Twister of Twists, A Tanlger of Tongues, 1972, Central City/Spread City: The Metropolitan Regions Where More and More of Us Live, 1973, Tomfoolery: Trickery and Foolery with Words, 1973, Witcracks: Jokes and Jests from American Folkore, 1973, Cross Your Fingers, Spit in Your Hat: Superstitions and Other Beliefs, 1974, Whoppers: Tall Tales and other Lies, 1975, The Rainy Day Book, 1968. Home: Princeton N.J. Died Mar. 14, 1992.

SCHWARTZ, ARTHUR HARRY, judge; b. N.Y.C., Nov. 18, 1903; s. Louis and Ida (Rothstein) S.; m. Dorothy Blaine, Aug. 5, 1928 (dec. 1956); children: Anne, Lois; m. Betty Spare, Feb. 14, 1958. AB, Columbia U., 1923, LLB, 1926. Asst. dept. govt. Columbia, 1922-25; asst. U.S. atty. So. Dist. N.Y., 1926-33, chief asst. charge prohibition div., 1931-33; counsel N.Y. State Joint Legislative Com. Legislative Practices, 1944-46; rep. campaign mgr. N.Y. State, 1944; counsel N.Y. State Rep. Com., from 1944, Temp. Commn. Need for a State U., 1946-48, N.Y. Temp. Commn. on Coordination State Activities, 1948-59, Rep. State Campaign mgr., 1948-52; apptd. justice N.Y. State Supreme Ct., 1952; mem. com. on character and fitness 1st Jud. Dept., 1948, vice chmn., from 1977; lectr. law Pace Inst. Accountancy, 1928-35; ptnr. Schwartz & Frohlich, N.Y.C., 1935-70, Schwartz, Burns, Lesser & Jacoby, N.Y.C., 1970-74; counsel Burns, Jackson, et al, from 1975; disting. lectr. law Pace Law Sch., White Plains, N.Y., 1979; mem. N.Y. State Law Revision Commn., 1960-74, N.Y. State Commn. Jud. and Legislative Salaries, 1972-74; chmn. N.Y. State Bd. Elections, 1974-76; asst. counsel N.Y. State Task Force on Parimutuel Revenue and the Breeding Industry, 1982-83; asst. counsel to Com. on Sports and Industry N.Y. State, 1984-85; research assoc. Senate Com. on Voting Machines and Registration, 1986. Editor-in-chief Columbia Law Rev., 1925-26; bd. editors N.Y. Law Jour, from 1976. Recipient Alumnus medal Columbia Coll., 1957; fellow Brandeis U. Mem. ABA, Fed. Bar Assn., N.Y. Bar Assn., Assn. Bar City N.Y. (past v.p.), Am. Coll. Trial Lawyers, N.Y. County Lawyers Assn. (past pres.), Legal Aid Soc. N.Y. (past bd. dirs.), Columbia Law Alumni Assn., Columbia Coll. Alumni Assn., Soc. Am. Magicians, Phi Beta Kappa. Club: University. Home: Dobbs Ferry N.Y. Died Oct. 8, 1990.

SCHWARTZ, DAVID, lawyer, arbitrator, mediator, judge; b. N.Y.C., July 7, 1916; s. Hyman and Nettie (Strauss) S.; m. Louisa Van Wezel Stone, June 15, 1968; children by previous marriage: Jonathan, Joanna Kyd. AB cum laude, NYU, 1936; LLB magna cum laude, Harvard U., 1939. Bar: N.Y. 1940, D.C. 1965, U.S. Supreme Ct. 1946, U.S. Ct. Claims 1954, U.S. Tax Ct. 1954. Assoc. Karelsen & Karelsen, N.Y.C., 1939-40; spl. asst. to atty. gen. Dept. Justice, Washington, 1941-42, chief trial atty. antitrust and enemy property div. Immigration Service, 1945-56; law clk. to Justice Stanley F. Reed U.S. Supreme Ct., 1942-43; legal adviser Greece and Balkan missions UNRRA and predecessor Dept. State, 1943-45; counsel Devel. & Resources Corp., N.Y.C., 1956-57; ptnr. Stroock & Stroock & Lavan, N.Y.C., 1957-68; trial judge U.S. Ct. Claims Washington, 1968-82; sole practice law and alternative dispute resolution services, Washington, 1982-89; sr. adviser U.S. Claims Ct. Adv. Coun., 1982-86; adj. prof. law Georgetown U., 1981-88; adj. asst. prof. NYU Law Ctr., 1957-68; adj. prof. U. Pa. Law Sch., 1984; vis. prof. U. Wis. at Madison Law Sch., summers 1976, 78, U. San Diego Law Sch., summers 1977, 79-81, Inst. Internat. and Comparative Law (U. San Diego), London, summers 1983, 85, Hastings Coll. of Advocacy, summers 1975, 77, 79. Co-author: Government Litigation-Cases and Notes, 1963, Litigation with the Federal Government, 2d edit., 1983; bd. editors Harvard Law Rev., 1937-39. Mem. D.C. Consumer Claims Arbitration Bd., 1987-89. Recipient John D. Rockefeller III Pub. Service award, 1955. Mem. ABA, Fed. Bar Assn., D.C. Bar Assn. (chmn. fee arbitration bd. 1983-88, hearing panel profl. responsibility bd. 1983-86), Assn. Bar City N.Y., Am. Law Inst. (bd. advisers restatement of contracts second). Democrat. Jewish. Died Dec. 21, 1989. Home: Washington D.C.

SCHWARTZ, DONALD EDWARD, lawyer, educator; b. Bklyn., Aug. 21, 1930; s. Harry and Esther (Goldman) S.; m. Ann Roberta Sher, June 23, 1968; children: Pamela Bonnie, Abigail Jane. A.B., Union Coll., 1952; LL.B., Harvard U., 1955; LL.M., N.Y. U., 1966; LL.D. (hon.), Georgetown U., 1983. Bar: N.Y. bar 1956, D.C. 1960. Mem. staff Office of Opinion Writing, SEC, 1957-59; counsel, sec. Columbia Fin. Corp., Washington, 1959-61; asso. firm Brinsmade & Schafrann, N.Y.C., 1961-62; partner Brinsmade & Schafrann, 1962-64; asso. firm Hill, Betts, Yamaoka, Freehill and Longcope, N.Y.C., 1964-66; of counsel firm Williams & Connolly, from 1979; mem. faculty Georgetown U. Law Center, Washington, from 1966; prof. Georgetown U. Law Center, from 1969, asso. dean, 1979-83; vis. prof. N.Y. U. Law Sch., 1973-74; cons. Bur. of Nat. Affairs, Inc., Washington; mem. legal adv. com. N.Y. Stock Exchange; dir. Project on Corp. Responsibility, Inc. Author, editor books on corp. law.; Contbr. articles to profl. jours. Served with U.S. Army, 1955-57. Mem. ABA (com. on corp. laws, com. on fed. regulation of securities), Fed. Bar Assn. (mem. exec. council of fed. securities law com.), Assn. Bar City N.Y. (corp. laws com.), Am. Law Inst. Democrat. Jewish. Home: Bethesda Md. Deceased. †

SCHWARTZ, HAROLD, investment company and publishing executive; b. N.Y.C., Oct. 27, 1920; s. Max and Toby (Hornstein) S.; m. Leatrice Kornhauser, Sept. 17, 1948 (div. Nov. 1972); children—Peter, William; m. Penelope Carnahan Welcher, Dec. 7, 1972; children—Margaret, Hilary. Student, U. Mo., 1938-40; B.A., N.Y. U., 1946. Mag. editor Street & Smith, N.Y.C., 1946-48; v.p., editorial dir. Juvenile div. Parents Mag. Enterprises, N.Y.C., 1949-67; co-founder Greenwood Press, Inc., Westport, Conn., 1967, pres., 1967-72; founder Blue Hill Trading Co., North Brooklin, Maine, 1972, pres., 1972-75; co-founder, chmn. bd. Winslow Investment Co., Bangor and Portland, Maine, 1981-90; founder, bd. dir. F.L. Putnam/Winslow, 1990. Served with USAAF, 1942-46. Home: South Portland Maine Died Dec. 23, 1990.

SCHWARTZ, THOMAS D., lawyer; b. Carbondale, Ill., Apr. 1, 1932; s. Walker and Mabel (Smith) S.; m. Kathryn Ann Hooker, Mar. 16, 1957; children: Patricia Ann, Thomas Andrew. B.A., So. Ill. U., 1956; J.D., U. Chgo., 1961. Bar: Ill. 1961, U.S. Fed. Ct. 1961, U.S. Supreme Ct. 1974, U.S. Tax Ct. 1984. Lectr. bus. law and govt., asst. legal counsel So. Ill. U., Carbondale, 1961-62; practice law Carbondale, 1962-63; trust officer, v.p. First Nat. Bank & Trust Co., Mt. Vernon, Ill., 1963-65; asst. to pres. Alton Box Board Co., Ill., 1965-66; corp. sec. Alton Box Board Co., 1966-83; v.p. adminstrn. Alton Packaging Corp., 1978-83; pres. Smurfit Pension Mgmt. Svcs., 1980-83; ptnr. Feirich, Schoen, Mager & Green, Carbondale, Ill., from 1983; bd. dirs. First Nat. Bank & Trust, Carbondale, from 1974; pres. So. Bancshares Ltd., Carbondale. Mem. adv. bd. St. Anthony's Hosp., Alton, Ill., 1973-83, pres., 1980-83; elder First Presbyn. Ch., Alton, from 1970, chmn. bd. trustees, 1972-76; bd. dirs. Pride, Inc.; bd. dirs. Jr. Achievement, pres., 1979-81; founder, bd. dirs. River Bend Civic Progress Assn., Alton, 1980-83 . Served with AUS, 1956-58. Mem. ABA, Ill. Bar Assn., Jackson County Bar Assn., St. Louis Bar Assn., Southwestern Ill. Indsl. Assn. (founder, 1st chmn. 1974), Ill. Mfg. Assn. (dir., chmn. So. div. 1977-79). Home: Carbondale Ill. Deceased. †

SCHWARZ, RALPH JOSEPH, investment company executive; b. Rutland, Vt., Jan. 31, 1898; s. Louis and Lisetta (Stein) S.; m. Mathilde Levy, Jan. 23,1932; children: Katharine L. Schwarz Bradford, Suaan Schwarz Babbin, Thomas. Grad. high sch., Mt. Vernon. V.p. Artcraft Silk Hosiery Mills., 1919-39; pres. Sapphire Corp., Quakertown, Telford, Pa., 1940-63, Em El Es Corp., investments, N.Y.C., from 1963. With USN, World War I. *

SCHWEIGERT, BERNARD SYLVESTER, food science educator; b. Alpha, N.D., Mar. 29, 1921; s. John Sylvester and Barbara (Busche) S.; m. Dianne Cave, Mar. 22, 1989; children from previous marriage: James Bernard, John Frederick. BS, U. Wis., 1943, MS, 1944, PhD, 1946. Research and teaching asst. U. Wis., Madison, 1942-46; assoc. prof. Tex. A&M U., College Station, 1946-48; from asst. prof. to assoc. prof. U. Chgo., 1948-60; prof., chmn. dept. food sci. Mich. State U., East Lansing, 1960-70; prof. food sci. U. Calif., Davis, 1970-89, chmn. dept., 1970-88; bd. dirs. Universal Foods Corp., Milw.; mem. sci. adv. coun. Nutrasweet Corp.; chmn. dietary guidelines adv. com. USDA and HEW, Washington, 1983-89; mem. bd. agriculture and renewable resources Nat. Acad. Scis., 1979-82, research adv. com. AID, 1971-84, sci. adv. com. Nutrition Found. Inc., 1965-70, 73-87, sci. adv. com., bd. govs. Refrigeration Rsch. Found., from 1971, bd. trustees Food Processors Inst., 1973-86. Co-editor: Science of Meat and Meat Products, 1971, 3d edit., 1987, Food Sci. and Tech. Monograph Series, Advances in Food Research; sci. editor emeritus Food Sci. and Tech. and Nutrition; contbr. numerous articles to profl. jours. Nat. Livestock and Meat Bd. fellow, 1943-45; recipient Underwood-Prescott award MIT, 1969. Mem. AAAS, Am. Chem. Soc., Am. Dairy Sci. Assn., Am. Inst. Nutrition, Am. Meat Sci. Assn. (Signal Service award 1963), Am. Soc. Animal Sci., Inst. Food Technologists (pres. 1978-79, rep. bd. dirs. nat. nutrition consortium 1979-82, del. to internat. union food sci. and tech. 1982-87; Babcock-Hart award 1974, Nicholas-Appert award 1981, Carl R. Fellers award 1985), Internat. Union Food Sci. and Tech., Internat. Union Nutritional Scis., Am. Council Sci. and Health (bd. advisors 1980-89), Am. Dietetic Assn. (adv. com. 1979-82). Home: Redding Calif. Died Oct. 7, 1989; cremated.

SCHWEIKER, MALCOLM ALDERFER, tile company executive; b. Shippack, Pa., Feb. 27, 1895; s. George W. and Alice M. (Alderfer) S.; m. Blanche R. Schultz, Apr. 3, 1920; children: Malcolm Alderfer Jr., Richard Schultz, Sylvia Schultz. LLB, Ursinus Coll. Gen. contractor, indsl. exec. various cos.; chmn. bd. Am. Olean Tile Co., Langdale, Pa., from 1960; pres. Keller Pottery Co., North Wales, Pa., from 1958; bd. dirs. Nat. Gypsum Co., Buffalo. Trustee, v.p. Schwenkfelder Libr.; trustee Perkiomen Sch., Pennsburg, Pa. Mem. SAR, Mfrs. Golf and Country Club (Oreland, Pa.), Masons. Republican. *

SCHWEITZER, GERTRUDE HONIG, artist; b. N.Y.C.. DFA (hon.), Pratt Inst. chmn. arts and skills corps N.Y. chpt. ARC, Ft. Jay Regional Hosp., WWII, Governor's Island, N.Y. One-woman shows include Montclair (N.J.) Art Mus., Washington Water Color Club, Cayuga Mus. History and Art, Auburn, N.Y., Potsdam Gallery Art, Currier Gallery Art, Manchester, N.H., Bevier Gallery, Rochester (N.Y.) Inst. Tech., Erie (Pa.) Pub. Mus., Cortland Libr., N.Y.C., Norton Gallery and Sch. Art, West Palm Beach, Fla., Galerie Charpentier, Paris (1st. Am.), Hanover Gallery, London, Gallery L'Obelisco, Rome, Galleria Al Cavallion, Venice, Italy, Galleria Il Naviglio, Milan, Italy, High Mus., Atlanta, Worth Ave. Gallery, Palm Beach., Fla., Fla. So. Coll., Lakeland, Witte Meml. Mus., San Antonio, Phila. Art Alliance, Hokin Gallery, Palm Beach, Pratt Manhattan Ctr., N.Y.C., New Britain Mus. Am. Art; exhibited at Corcoran Gallery, Washington, Art Inst. Chgo., R.I. Sch. Design, Denver Art Mus., Sarasota Art Mus., NAD, N.Y.C., Audubon Soc., N.Y.C., L.A. County Fair, U. Minn., U. Ill., Ball State Tchrs. Coll., Muncie, Ind., Newark Art Club, Mus. Art, Santa Fe, N.Mex., Mus. Legion of Honor, San Francisco, Menina, Siclily, 200 Yrs. Am. Watercolors Met. Mus. Art, N.Y.C.; represented in permanent collections including Albi Mus., France, Bklyn. Mus., Toledo Mus., Met. Mus. Art, N.Y.C., Walker Art Mus. of Bowdoin Coll., Whitney Mus. Am. Art, N.Y.C., Mus. of Palm Beaches and Norton Gallery and Sch. Art, West Palm Beach, Montclair Art Mus., Witte Meml. Mus., San Antonio, Atlanta Art Assn. Galleries, Art Inst. Chgo., Mus. Modern Art, Paris, Albi Mus., France, Hackley Art Gallery, Muskegon, Mich., Davenport (Iowa) Mcpl. Art Gallery, Canajoharie (N.Y.) Libr. and Art Gallery, Rochester (N.Y.) Meml. Art Gallery, New Britain Mus. Am. Art, NAD, Neuberger Mus. SUNY, Soc. Four Arts, Palm Beach, Fla., Mus. N.Mex., also numerous pvt. collections. Recipient Am. Water Color Soc. medal, Am. Artists Profl. League medal for water color State of N.J., Phila. Water Color prize Pa. Acad. Fine Arts, 1st prize Norton Gallery and Sch. Art, Soc. Four Arts, Grand Nat. Exhbn., Miami, Fla., 1st prize, best woman painter N.J. State Exhbn., N.Y. State award Am. Artists Profl. League, Nat. Arts Club, also Pauline Wick award, 1st prize, medal award Seton Hall U., 1st Grumbacher Purchase award Audubon 17th Ann. Exhbn.; Crumbacher award 27th Ann. Exhbn.; Honor Roll award Am. Artist Profl. League; 27th Ann. N.J. State Exhbn. Eleanor S. Higgins award; Alumni medal Pratt Inst. Mem. Am. Water Color Soc., Fla. Artists Group, Soc. Four Arts (award), Audubon Soc., N.J. Water Color and Sculpture Soc. Home: Palm Beach FL Died Nov. 10, 1989.

SCHWENDEMAN, J(OSEPH) R(AYMOND), geography educator; b. Waterford, Ohio, May 11, 1897; s. Francis John and Margaret (Tornes) S.; m. Eithnea O'Donnell, Oct. 12, 1921; children: Elaine, Marion, Gerald, Joseph, Francis, Beth Ann. BS, Ohio U., 1926; AM, Clark U., 1927, PhD, 1941; postgrad., U. Minn., 1927-28. Part-time instr. U. Minn., Mpls., 1927-28; head dept. geography State Tchrs. Coll., Moorehead, Minn., 1928-44; prof., head dept. geography U. ky., Lexington, from 1944; vis. lectr. summers Columbia U., 1927, State Tchrs. Coll., Spearfish, S.D., 1928, Ohio U., 1941, St. John's U., Collegeville, Minn., 1943; worked on preparation of land use suitability maps, atlas and state base maps for Ky.; organizer, condr. expdn. for study of weather on volcano Orizaba, Mex., 1949; dir. student travel groups in Europe, Can., U.S., Mex. Author publs. in field; compiler: (with Irwin Sanders) Societies around the World, 2 vols., 1948, rev., 1956, Geography of Kentucky, 1958, rev., 1963; editor, pub: Director of College Geography of U.S., vols. 1-16, 1949-65; contbg. author: Regional Geography of North American Midwest, 1956, World Political Geography; revised geog. sect. Lincoln Libr., 1952 edition.; patentee in field; holder copyrights; inventor Geomatic World Map Projection, 1963. Mem. Cath. Commn. on Intellectual and Cultural Affairs, Ky. Econ. Devel. Bd. Fellow Nat. Coun. Geography Tchrs.; mem. AAUP, Ky. Acad. Sci., Assn. Am. Geographers, Kiwanis. Roman Catholic. *

SCIASCIA, LEONARDO, writer; b. Recalmuto, Italy, Jan. 8, 1921. Ed., Inst. Magistrale Caltanissetta. Dep. for Radical Party, European Parliament. Author: Le parrocchie di Regalpetra, 1956, Gli zii de Sicilia, 1958, Il giorno della civetta, 1961 (Mafia Vendetta 1963), Pirandello e la Sicilia, 1961, Il consiglio d'Egitto, 1963, A ciascuno il suo, 1963, Morte dell'inquisitore, 1964, Feste religiose in Sicilia, 1965, Recitazione della controversia liparitana, 1969, El contesto, 1971, Il mare colore del vino, 1973. Recipient numerous prizes, including Premio Crotone, Premio Libera Stampa Lugano, Premio Prato. Home: Palermo Italy Died Nov. 20, 1989. †

SCISSON, SIDNEY E., retired engineering company executive, engineer; b. Danville, Ark., Feb. 4, 1917; s. Eugene and Arvie (Keathley) S.; m. Betti Shumaker,

Sept. 8, 1942; children: Jane Scisson Grimshaw, Judith Scisson Fererri. Student, Ark. Tech. U., 1934-36; B.S. in Gen. Engring, Okla. State U., 1939. Registered profl. engr., Ill., Ky., Ohio, Okla., R.I. Civil engr. U.S. C.E., Tulsa, 1939-42; civil engr. Pate Engring. Co., Tulsa, 1945-48; a founder and with Fenix & Scisson, Inc. (engring. and constrn. services for govt. and industry), Tulsa, from 1948; dir. Atlas Life Ins. Co. Treas.-pres. Tulsa Civic Ballet, 1965. Served with USNR, 1942-45. Named Disting. Alumnus Okla. State U., Stillwater, Disting. Alumnus Ark. Tech. U., Russellville. Mem. Nat. Acad. Engring., AIME, ASCE, Okla. Soc. Civil Engrs., Nat. Soc. Profl. Engrs., Okla. Soc. Profl. Engrs., Am. Gas Assn., Natural Gas Processors Assn., Associated Gen. Contractors Am. Clubs: So. Hills Country; Tulsa (Tulsa). Home: Tulsa Okla. Deceased. †

SCOTT, FREDERICK BARTLETT, supply company executive; b. Syracuse, N.Y., May 29, 1894; s. Frederick B. and Isabel (Hawley) S.; m. Laura Beecher, Nov. 17, 1923; children: Phyllis Beecher Scott Eliot, Caroline Scott Turner. ME, Cornell U., 1918. With maintenance div. Hammond Steel Co., Solvay, N.Y., 1919-20; product supr. machine tool div. Syracuse Supply Co., 1920-21, mgr., sales engr. Rochester (N.Y.) Office, 1921-27, v.p., mgr. machine tool div., 1927-39, pres., 1939-62, chmn. bd., from 1962, also mem. exec. com.; bd. dirs. Marine Midland Trust Co. Cen. N.Y.; tech. adviser, cons. Office Price Moblzn. and WPB, 1941-43. Mem. Am. Machine Tool Distbrs. Assn. (past pres., exec. com.), Onondaga Golf and Country Club, Century Club. *

SCOTT, HOMER VERLYN, business executive; b. Chgo., Dec. 26, 1896; s. John Franklin and Carrie (Ogard) S.; m. Dorothy Justine McNeil, Dec. 31, 1923; children: Justine Vallee, Carol Ann. Student, Northwestern Sch. Commerce, Chgo., 1919. Chief clk. master mechanics dept. Chgo. North Shore Electric Co., 1916-17; with Adams and Westlake, Chgo., 1919-20, Splitdorf Electric Co., Chgo., 1920-25; pres. Homer V. Scott Co., mfrs. reps., Chgo., from 1925, Distbrs. Warehouse, Inc., Chgo. 2d lt. Ill. N.G., 1915-19. Mem. Ill. Athletic Club, Lake Shore Club, Execs. Club, Mpls. Athletic Club, Masons, Shriners, Elks. Republican. Episcopalian. *

SCOTT, LELAND WAKEFIELD, lawyer; b. Amherst, Wis., Mar. 19, 1893; s. Frank Edward and Clara Matilda (Lombard) S.; m. Winifred S. Crowther, July 18, 1917; 1 child, Donald James. LLB, St. Paul Coll. Law, 1917. Bar: Minn., U.S. Supreme Ct. Sec. to gov. State of Minn., 1916-21; asst. U.S. atty., Minn., 1921-27; atty. Office Gen. Counsel, Bur. Internal Revenue, 1927-28; ptnr. Dorsey, Owen, Barber, Scott & Barber, Mpls., 1928-60; of counsel Dorsey, Owen, Marquart, Windhorst & West, Mpls., from 1960; gen. counsel Mayo Clinic, Rochester, Minn., 1960-62. Mem. ABA, Fed. Bar Assn., Minn. Bar Assn., Nat. Lawyers Club, Mpls. Club, Univ. Club, Masons. *

SCOTT, SIR PETER (MARKHAM), artist, ornithologist; b. Sept. 14, 1909; s. Robert Falcon Scott and Kathleen Bruce Young; m. Elizabeth Jane Howard, 1942 (div. 1951); 1 daughter; m. Philippa Talbot-Ponsonby, 1951; 2 children. MA, U. Cambridge; student, Munich State Acad., Royal Acad. Schs., London; LLD (hon.), U. Exeter, 1963, U. Aberdeen, 1963, U. Birmingham, 1974, U. Bristol, 1974, U. Liverpool, 1984; DSc., U. Bath, 1979, U. Guelph, 1981, U. Ulster, 1987. Chmn. World Wildlife Fund Internat., 1961-82, chmn. council, 1983-85, hon. chmn., 1985-89; chmn. Survival Service Commn. IUCN, 1962-81, Falkland Islands Found., 1979-89; trustee emeritus World Wildlife Fund U.K., chmn. yachting com., 1947-48; internat. jury for yachting, Olympic Games, Melbourne, 1956, Naples, 1960, Tokyo, 1964; chancellor Birmingham U., 1974-83; rector Aberdeen U., 1960-63; leader ornithological expeditions to Cen. Highlands, Iceland to mark wild geese, 1951, 53, expeditions to Australiasia Galapagos Islands, Seychelles and Antarctic; represented Great Britain in Olympic Games in single-handed sailing, 1936; explored unmapped Perry River area in Can. Arctic, 1949; speaker nature feature programmes on TV. Author: Morning Flight, 1935, Wild Chorus, 1938, The Battle of the Narrow Seas, 1945, Portrait Drawings, 1949, Key to Wildfowl of the World, 1949 (Coloured Key 1958), Wild Geese and Eskimos, 1951; (with James Fisher) A Thousand Geese, 1953; (with Hugh Boyd) Wildfowl of the British Isles, 1957; (with Philippa Scott) Animals in Africa, 1962; (with the Wildfowl Trust) The Swans, 1972, Fishwatchers' Guide to West Atlantic Coral Reefs, 1972, Observations of Wildlife, 1980, Travel Diaries of a Naturalist, vol. I, 1983, vol. II, 1985, vol. III, 1987; (autobiography) The Eye of the Wind, 1961; illustrator books A Bird in the Bush, Grey Goose, Through the Air, The Snow Goose, Adventures Among Birds, Handbook of British Birds, vol. III, Waterfowl of the World, Birds of the Western Palearctic, vol. I, The Wildfowl of Britain and Europe; oil paintings exhibited at London and N.Y.C. Chmn. The Otter Trust, Inland Waterways Assn., Winston Churchill Meml. Trust; mem. council Boy Scout Assn., 1945-73. Served with Brit. mil., 1939-45. Decorated Icelandic Order of the Falcon, 1969, Comdr. Dutch Order of Golden Ark, 1976; recipient Internat. Gold badge for gliding, 1958, Internat. Diamond badge, 1963, Nat. Gliding Championship award, 1963, Cherry Kearton medal RGS, 1967, Albert Medal RSA, 1970, Bernard Tucker medal BOU, 1970, Arthur Allen medal Cornell U., 1971, Gold medal N.Y. Zoolog. Soc., 1975, Internat. Pahlavi Environment prize U.N., 1977, IUCN John Phillips medal, 1981, World Woldlife Fund 20th Anniversary Spl. award, 1981, Founder's medal, 1983, Gold medal Phila. Acad. of Natural Scis., 1983, RSPB Gold award, 1986, J.P. Getty prize, 1986. Mem. Soc. of Wildlife Artists (pres. 1964-78), Fauna and Flora Preservation Soc. (pres. 1981-89), Glos Assoc. of Youth Clubs, Internat. Yacht Racing Union (pres. 1955-69), Glos Trust for Nature conservation, Brit. Butterfly Conservation Soc., Brit. Gliding Assn. (v.p., chmn. 1968-70), Inland Waterways Assn., Camping Club of Great Britain, Bristol Gliding Club. Clubs: Royal Thames Yacht, Explorers (N.Y.C.). Home: Gloucester Eng. Died Aug. 29, 1989. †

SCOTT, STUART NASH, lawyer; b. Madison, Wis., Dec. 6, 1906; s. William Amasa and Nellie Irene (Nash) S.; m. Katherine L. Miller, Sept. 5, 1928; 1 dau., Susan Miller Scott Porter. B.A., Yale U., 1927; LL.B. magna cum laude, Harvard U., 1930. Bar: N.Y. 1932, D.C. 1947. Asst. prof. Harvard U. Law Sch., 1930-31; asso. Dewey, Ballantine, Bushby, Palmer & Wood (and predecessor), N.Y.C., 1931-41, partner, 1941-87, of counsel, 1987-92; counsel French Purchasing Commn., 1939-40, Bur. Aeros., Navy Dept., 1941-44; gen. counsel Surplus War Property Adminstrn., 1944; chmn. N.Y. State Temp. Commn. to Study Govt. Ops. in N.Y.C., 1971-73; U.S. ambassador to Portugal, 1974-75. Editor: Harvard Law Rev., 1928-30. Former bd. dirs. Wooster Sch., Columbia Sch. Social Work, The Hudson Fund. Recipient Disting. Civilian Service medal Navy Dept., 1944. Mem. ABA (ho. dels. 1971-74), N.Y. State Bar Assn. (pres. 1970-71), Assn. Bar City N.Y. (chmn. exec. com. 1967-68). Clubs: Century Assn. (N.Y.C.). Home: New York N.Y. Died Feb. 26, 1992.

SCOTT, WILLIAM GEORGE, artist; b. Greenock, Scotland, Feb. 15, 1913; s. William John and Agnes (Murray) S.; m. Hilda Mary Lucas, May 19, 1937; children: Robert, James. Student, Belfast (Northern Ireland) Sch. Art, 1929, Royal Acad. Art, London, 1931; DrRCA (hon.), Royal Coll. Art, London, 1975; DLitt (hon.), Queens U., Belfast, 1976, Trinity Coll., Dublin, Ireland, 1977. Works exhibited Leger Gallery, 1942, 44, 46, Leicester (Eng.) Gallery, 1948, 51, Hanover (Fed. Republic of Germany) Gallery, 1953, 56, 61, 63, 65, 67, Martha Jackson Gallery, N.Y.C., 1954, 58, 73-74, Venice (Italy) Bienale, 1958, São Paulo (Brazil) Bienal, 1953, 61, Tate Gallery, 1972, 86, Gimpel Fils Galley, 1974, 76, 78, 80, 85, 87, Moos Gallery, Toronto, Can., 1975, 82, Kasahara (Japan) Gallery, 1976, Ulster Arts Council, 1979, 86, Imperial War Mus., 1981, Gimpel Weidenhofer Gallery, N.Y.C., 1983, Nat. Gallery Scotland, 1986, Mus. Modern Art, St. Ettienne, France, 1987, Victoria and Albert Mus., also Paris, N.Y., Toledo, Republic of South Africa, Can., Australia, S.Am.; contbr. (film): Every Picture Tells a Story, 1987. Decorated CBE, Royal Academician; recipient Silver and Bronze awards for Achievement. Club: Chelsea (Eng.) Arts (hon. life). Home: London Eng. Died Dec. 28, 1989. †

SCOULAR, FLORENCE ISABELLE, nutrition educator, college dean; b. Iron Ridge, Wis., Nov. 17, 1987; d. John David and Nellie Louise (Thomas) S. BS, Stout Inst., Menomonie, Wis., 1919; MS, Iowa State Coll., 1929; PhD, U. Iowa, 1937. Instr. home econs. River Falls State Coll., 1919-20; supr. home econs. Ironwood (Mich.) Pub. Schs., 1920-22; instr. foods and nutrition Stout Inst., 1922-27; instr. sci. nutrition Buffalo State Coll., 1928-30; asst. prof. foods and nutrition Purdue U., West Lafayette, Ind., 1930-31, Okla. A&M Coll., 1931-33; rsch. asst. in nutrition Iowa Child Welfare Rsch. Sta., U. Iowa, 1933-36; acting head dept. home econs. Skidmore Coll., 1936-37, Ea. Ill. State Coll., 1937-38; prof., dean Sch. Home Econs., North Tex. State Coll., Denton, from 1938; chmn. Tex. Nutrition Coun. Contbr. articles to profl. jours. Fellow Tex. Acad. Sci.; mem. AAAS, NEA, AAUP, Am. Home Econs. Assn., Tex. Home Econs. Assn. (pres.), Tex. Tchrs. Assn., Am. Vocat. Assn., Tex. Vocat. Assn., Coll. Classroom Tchrs. Assn., Dallas Clin. Diabetes Assn., Am. Chem. Soc., Royal Soc. for Promotion Health, Am. Dietetic Assn., Am. Inst. Nutrition, AAUW, Sch. Food Svc. Assn., Tex. Dietetic Assn. (pres.), Royal Soc. Health, Coun. Adminstrs. Home Econs., Sigma Xi, Delta Kappa Gamma, Iota Sigma Pi, Phi Upsilon Omicron. *

SCRIBNER, ALLISON KENNETH, chemical company executive; b. Boston, Sept. 9, 1898; s. Corey A. and Anna A. (Field) S.; m. Marie Scribner, Nov. 10, 1923; 1 child, Allison Kenneth Jr. AB in Chemistry cum laude, Harvard U., 1920. With Va. Chems., Inc., and predecessor, West Norfolk, from 1921, bd. dirs., from 1948, v.p., gen. mgr., 1950-57, pres., from 1957; bd. dirs. Norfolk, Franklin & Danville Ry. Chmn. bd. trustees Portsmouth (Va.) Supplemental Retirement System, 1953-57; mem. Portsmouth Sch. Bd., 1949-51; v.p., trustee Tidewater Va. Devel. Coun., 1957-61; former v.p. Portsmouth Area Community Chest; bd. visitors Old Dominion Coll., Norfolk, from 1963, chmn. edn. com., from 1963. Mem. Am. Assn. Textile Chemists and Colorists, Am. Chem. Soc., Va. Mfrs. Assn. (pres. 1957-58), Va. C. of C., Portsmouth C. of C., Execs. Club (pres. 1955-56), Hampton Roads Engrs. Club (Norfolk), Rotary (pres. 1934-35). Methodist. *

SCRIPPS, JOHN P., newspaper publisher; b. Cleve., Oct. 5, 1912; s. John Paul and Edith (McRae) S.; m. Elizabeth Field McClannahan (div. 1938); 1 child, Edith; m. Edythe Henderson; children: Peter Montague, Paul Kenneth, Barbara Victoria. Student, U. So. Calif. Chmn. bd. John P. Scripps Newspapers; pub. Ventura Star Free Press, Watsonville Register Pajaronian, Redding Record-Searchlight, San Luis Obispo Telegram-Tribune, Morro Bay Sun-Bull., Tulare Advance-Register, Thousand Oaks News Chronicle (all Calif.), Bremerton (Wash.) Sun; dir. San Diego Trust & Savs. Bank. Bd. dris. Del Mar Charities, Zool. Soc., San Diego. Mem. Internat. Wine and Food Soc., San Diego Club, San Diego Yacht Club, Long Beach Yacht Club, Transpacific Yacht Club, Cruising of Am. Club. Home: LaJolla Calif. Died Mar. 15, 1989.

SEALS, WOODROW, judge; b. Bogalusa, La., Dec. 24, 1917; s. Charles Bradley and Ruby (Hughey) S.; m. Sarah Elizabeth Newman, June 1, 1942; 1 son, Bradley Newman. J.D., U. Tex., 1949. Bar: Tex. 1949. U.S. atty. So. Dist. Tex., 1961-66; U.S. dist. judge, 1966-82, sr. U.S. dist. judge, 1982-90. Dem. presdl. campaign mgr., 1960. Served to lt. col. USAF. Recipient Papal medal for work with needy, 1979, World Meth. Peace award, 1987,. Home: Houston Tex. Died Oct. 27, 1990; cremated.

SEALY, DONALD FARRINGTON, educator; b. Newark, Feb. 28, 1897; s. Frank Linwood and Emma Grace (Farrington) S.; m. Elizabeth Varick Howell, June 7, 1938. BA, Columbia, 1918, MA, 1920, LLB, 1923; SJD, St. Lawrence U., 1943. Bar: N.Y. 1923, U.S. Ct. Appeals 1945. With Bklyn. Law Sch., from 1924; successively instr., asst. prof., assoc. prof., prof. law, Grad. Sch., Bklyn. Law Sch., from 1946. Author: Text on Persons and Domestic Relations, rev. edit., 1936, Text on Torts, 1939; compiler, editor casebooks. With USNRF, WWI. Mem. ABA, N.Y. State Bar Assn., Assn. Bar City N.Y., S.R., Sigma Chi, Phi Delta Phi, Delta Theta Phi, Columbia U. Club (N.Y.C.). *

SEALY, TOM, lawyer; b. Santa Anna, Tex., Feb. 18, 1909; s. Thomas Richard and Elizabeth (Harper) S.; m. Mary Velma McCord, Jan. 16, 1936 (dec. June 1990); 1 child, Nancy. LLB, U. Tex., 1931. Bar: Tex. 1931. Practice in Midland, 1935-89; mem. firm Stubbeman, McRae, Sealy, Laughlin & Browder, 1936-89; hon. dir. First City Nat. Bank, Midland; past dir. First Savs. and Loan Assn., Tex. Land & Mortgage Co., Midland, Champlin Petroleum Co., Tex.-N.Mex. Ry. Co. Past mem. city council, Midland.; Past chmn. bd. regents U. Tex., past. chmn. devel. bd.; mem., former chmn. coordinating bd. Tex. Coll. and U. System; past trustee Tex. Presbyn. Found., Presbyn.-Austin Theol. Sem.; hon. trustee Southwestern Legal Found.; past chmn., dir. Tex. Research League; past pres. U. Texas Law Sch. Found., bd. govs. Midland Meml. Found., 1984-88. Lt. col. USAAF, World War II. Recipient Disting. Alumnus award U. Tex., 1966, Outstanding Alumnus award U. Tex. Law Sch., 1970; Tom Sealy research professorship in energy law established in his honor at U. Tex. Law Sch. Atlantic Richfield Co. Fellow Am. Bar Found., Tex. Bar Founds. (50-Yr. award 1985); mem. ABA, State Bar Tex., Midland C. of C. (past pres.), Tex. Assn. Def. Counsel (past pres.), Am. Assn. Petroleum Landmen (hon.), Midland Petroleum Club (past pres.), Plaza Club (vice chmn. bd. govs.), Midland Country Club, Phi Delta Phi. Presbyterian. Home: Midland Tex. Died Apr. 27, 1992. †

SEARS, ERNEST ROBERT, geneticist, emeritus educator; b. Bethel, Oreg., Oct. 15, 1910; s. Jacob Perlonzo and Ada Estella (McKee) S.; m. Caroline F. Eichorn, July 5, 1936; 1 son, Michael Allan; m. Lotti Maria Steinitz, June 16, 1950; children: John, Barbara, Kathleen. B.S., Oreg. State Agrl. Coll., 1932; A.M., Harvard U., 1934, Ph.D., 1936; D.Sc., Goettingen U. Agt. Dept. Agr., 1936-41, geneticist, 1941-80; research assoc. U. Mo., Columbia, 1937-63; prof. U. Mo., 1963-80, prof. emeritus, 1980-91; Hannaford research fellow, Australia, 1980-81, Einstein research fellow, Israel, 1981, Agrl. Research Council fellow, Eng., 1982; Michael vis. prof., Israel, 1985; vis. prof. U. Stellenbosch, South Africa, 1985. Contbr. articles to tech. jours. Fulbright research fellow Germany, 1958; Recipient Stevenson award for research in agronomy, 1951, Hoblitzelle award for research in agrl. sci., 1958, Disting. Service award Oreg. State Agrl. Coll., 1973; Nat. Agr.-Bus. award, 1981; Wolf prize for agrl. sci., 1986, Agronomic Rsch. Award Am. Soc. Agronomy, 1991A; named to Agr. Research Service Hall of Fame U.S. Dept. Agr., 1987; named Sesquicentennial Prof., U. Mo., 1990. Fellow Agronomy Soc. Am., AAAS, Indian Soc. Genetics and Plant Breeding (hon.), Japanese Genetics Soc. (hon.); mem. Am. Acad. Arts and Scis., Nat. Acad. Scis., Bot. Soc. Am., Genetics Soc. Am. (pres. 1978-79), Am. Soc. Naturalists, Genetics Soc. Can. (Excellence award 1977), Am. Inst. Biol. Scis., Am. Assn. Cereal Chemists (hon.), Sigma Xi (chpt. research award 1970), Phi Kappa Phi, Alpha Zeta, Gamma Sigma Delta (Distinguished Service award 1958), Alpha Gamma Rho. Home: Columbia Mo. Died Feb. 15, 1991. †

SEARS, ROBERT RICHARDSON, psychology educator; b. Palo Alto, Calif., Aug. 31, 1908; s. Jesse Brundage and Stella Louise (Richardson) S.; m. Pauline Kirkpatrick Snedden, June 25, 1932; children—David O'Keefe, Nancy Louise. A.B., Stanford U., 1929; Ph.D., Yale U., 1932. Instr. psychology U. Ill., Chgo., 1932-35, assoc., 1935-36; research asst. prof. Inst. Human Relations, Yale U., 1936-37, asst. prof. psychology, 1937-42, assoc. prof., 1942; prof. child psychology, dir. Child Welfare Rsch. Sta. U. Iowa, 1942-49; prof. edn. and child psychology, dir. lab. human devel. Harvard Grad. Sch. Edn., 1949-53; prof. psychology, head dept. Stanford U., 1953-61, dean Sch. Humanities and Sci., 1961-70, David Starr Jordan prof. psychology, 1970-73; clin. psychologist Inst. Juvenile Rsch., Chgo., 1932-36; lectr. psychology Wesleyan U., Conn., spring 1937; vis. asst. prof. Stanford U., summer 1941. Author: (with others) Frustration and Aggression, 1939, Objective Studies of Psychoanalytic Concepts, 1943, Patterns of Child Rearing, 1958, Identification and Child Rearing, 1965; Contbr. (with others) tech. articles to psychol. jours. Trustee Center Advanced Study Behavioral Scis., 1953-75, fellow, 1968-69. Mem. Am. Philos. Soc., Am. Acad. Arts and Scis. Am. Psychol. Assn. (pres. 1950-51), Western Psychol. Assn. (pres. 1964), Soc. Research Child Devel. (editor monographs 1971-75, pres. 1973-75), NRC (chmn. com. child devel. 1947-50, div. anthropology and psychology 1945-48), Social Sci. Research Council (vice chmn. bd. dirs. 1950-53), Sigma Xi. Home: Stanford Calif. Died May 23, 1989; buried Menlo Park, Calif.

SEARS, WILLIAM GRAY (WILL SEARS), lawyer; b. Houston, Oct. 18, 1910; s. William Gray and Betty Bringhurst (Gaines) S.; m. Maurine Rawlings, Sept. 14, 1935; children: Betty Sears Munson), William Gray III (dec.), Charles R. Student, Rice U., 1927-29; JD, South Tex. Coll. Law, 1935. Bar: Tex. 1935. Atty. Fed. Land Bank of Houston, 1935-38; asst. city atty. Houston, 1938-40; 1st asst. city atty., 1946-48, city atty., 1948-56; ptnr. Hofheinz, Sears, James & Burns, Houston, 1956-61; ptnr. Sears & Burns, Houston, 1962-90, ret., 1985. Trustee Retina Research Found. Maj. AUS, 1940-46. Decorated Purple Heart with oak leaf cluster; recipient certificate of Meritorious Service SSS, 1970. Fellow Tex. Bar Found. (life); mem. ABA, Fed. Bar Assn., Houston Bar Assn., Am. Judicature Soc., Nat. Inst. Municipal Law Officers, Tex. State Bar, Am. Hist., Southwestern Hist. Assn., Philos. Soc. Tex., Nat. Trust Hist. Preservation, Am. Heritage Assn., Ret. Officers Assn., Delta Theta Phi (scholarship key). Home: Houston Tex. Deceased. †

SEBRELL, WILLIAM HENRY, JR., physician, foundation executive; b. Portsmouth, Va., Sept. 11, 1901; s. William Henry and Millicent J. (Overton) S.; m. Margaret Shirley Bruffey, June 16, 1926 (dec. 1945); children: Betty Clark, William Henry; m. Eloise Hopkins Glover, May 13, 1950 (dec. 1973); m. Helena Braddock Lemp, Sept. 29, 1978; 1 step-son, Page Glover. M.D., U. Va., 1925; postgrad., George Washington U., 1928-30; grad., USPHS Officers Sch., 1926; ScD., Alfred U., 1955, Rutgers U., 1956. Intern Marine Hosp., New Orleans, 1925-26; commd. officer USPHS, 1925, advanced through grades to asst. surgeon gen., 1950; various assignments, 1926-43, chief div. physiology, 1943-48; dir. Exptl. Biology and Medicine Inst., 1947-50, NIMH, 1950-55; instnl. research grants Am. Cancer Soc., 1955-57, research cons., 1955-57; dir. inst. human nutrition Columbia, 1957-70, Robert R. Williams prof. nutrition, 1961-70, prof. emeritus, 1970-92; med. dir. Weight Watchers Internat., 1972-79; exec. dir. Weight Watchers Internat. Found., 1971-92; past chmn. Williams-Waterman Fund Rsch. Corp.; past dir. Nat. Health Coun.; past mem. or mem. internat. commns. on health, nutrition, 1935-92; mem. Food and Nutrition Bd.; exec. com., 1956-70, NRC, Nat. Vitamin Found.; pres., 1955; chmn. protein adv. group UNICEF, WHO, FAO, 1964. Contbr. numerous articles to med. jours., texts. Recipient Mead Johnson prize, 1940; Research medal So. Med. Assn., 1946; Legion of Merit, 1946; Joseph Goldberger award AMA, 1952; Disting. Service award Food and Nutrition Council Greater N.Y., 1968. Fellow A.C.P., Am. Pub. Health Assn., AAAS, Am. Inst. Nutrition (pres. 1955); mem. Am. Soc. Clin. Nutrition (Conrad Elvehjem 1968, pres. 1963), Internat. Union Nutrition Scis. (chmn. U.S. nat. com. 1963, chmn. com. recommended dietary allowances 1968), fgn., nat. and local med. and profl. assns. or orgns., Phi Beta Kappa, Sigma Xi, Alpha Omega Alpha, Phi Tau Sigma. Episcopalian. Clubs: Cosmos (Washington); Century (N.Y.C.). Home: Pompano Beach Fla. Died Sept. 29, 1992. †

SEDGWICK, ELLERY, JR., manufacturing executive; b. Boston, Sept. 8; s. Ellery and Mabel (Cabot) S.; m. Elizabeth Wade, May 5, 1940; children: Ellery, Irene, Walter, Theodore. Grad. Harvard U., 1932; grad., Harvard Bus. Sch., 1934. Asst. bank examiner Fed. Res. Bank of Cleve., 1934-35; various positions, including v.p. Nat. City Bank of Cleve., 1935-40, 45-52; pres. Medusa Corp., 1952-65, chmn., CEO, 1965-81, chmn., exec. com., 1976-79; dir. Cleve. Trust Co., Eaton Co., Oglebay Norton Co.; trustee Beechbrook. Trustee Univ. Hosps.; trustee, hon. mem. bd. govs. Case-Western Res. U.; trustee Lake View Cemetery Assn.; Hawken Sch., Com. Econ. Devel. (hon.). Home: Gates

Mills Ohio Died Sept. 8, 1991; buried Stockbridge, Mass.

SEED, HARRY BOLTON, civil engineering educator; b. Bolton, Eng., Aug. 19, 1922; came to U.S., 1947, naturalized, 1966; s. Arthur Bolton and Annie (Wood) S.; m. Muriel Johnson Evans, Dec. 29, 1953; children: Raymond Bolton, Jacqueline Carol. B.Sc. in Engring, Kings Coll., London U., 1944, Ph.D., 1947; S.M., Harvard, 1948. Asst. lectr. King's Coll., 1945-47; instr. Harvard U., 1948-49; found. engr. Thomas Worcester Inc., Boston, 1949-50; mem. faculty U. Calif. at Berkeley, 1950-89, prof. civil engring., 1960-89; cons. U.S. Bur. Reclamation, 1965-89, sec. interior, 1966-69, NASA, 1966-68, AEC, 1973-89, C.E., U.S. Army, 1967-89, Calif. Dept. Water Resources, 1963-89, U.S. Navy, 1972, Aswan Dam, Egypt, 1981, Alaska Pipeline Project, also dams in Pakiston, Calif., engring. cos.; Terzaghi lectr., 1967, Rankine lectr., 1979, Nabor Carillo lectr., 1986; mem. Calif. Seismic Safety Commn., Presdl. Panel on Safety Fed. Dams. Recipient Croes medal ASCE, 1960, 62, 72, Middlebrooks award, 1958, 64, 66, 71, Wellington prize, 1968, Rowland prize, 1961, Research prize, 1962, Norman medal, 1968, 77, Karl Terzaghi award, 1973, Vincent Bendix award, 1976, T.K. Hsieh award, 1980, Lamme award, 1983, Disting. Engring. Achievement award, 1983, Kevin Nash Gold medal, 1985, Nat. medal of Sci., 1987. Mem. ASCE (hon.), Earthquake Engring. Research Inst., Hwy. Research Bd., Nat. Acad. Engring., Nat. Acad. Scis., Seismol. Soc. Am., U.S. Com. on Large Dams, Structural Engrs. Assn. Calif. Home: Orinda Calif. Died Apr. 23, 1989.

SEEMAN, BERNARD, author, editor; b. N.Y.C., Oct. 19, 1911; s. William J. and Lena (Kerner) S.; student pub. schs.; m. Geraldine Adele Micallef, Jan. 19, 1933. Freelance writer Ken mag., 1938-39; mil. writer, Far East specialist Friday mag., 1939-40; Latin Am. corr. Click mag., 1940-41; war corr. Far East Theatre, 1945 for Readers Scope, Internat. Digest; asso. editor Mag. Digest, also med. and sci. editor, Hillman Publs., 1946-54; exec. editor Internist Observer, Inc., 1958-76; exec. v.p. Sci. & Medicine Pub. Co., 1976-78; editor, spl. editorial cons. Science & Medicine Pub. Co., 1978-81. Spl. cons. on Japan OWI, 1944. Mem. Nat. Assn. Sci. Writers, Acad. Polit. Sci., Fedn. Am. Scientists, Nat. Acad. Rec. Arts and Scis., Authors League Am., Authors Guild, AAAS, Mus. Modern Art, Astron. Soc. Pacific, Leakey Found. Author: Enemy Japan, 1945; The River of Life, 1961 (winner Howard W. Blakeslee award Am. Heart Assn.); Man Against Pain, 1962; The Story of Electricity and Magnetism, 1962; (with Lawrence Salisbury) Cross-Currents in the Philippines, Inst. of Pacific Relations, 1946; (with Dr. Henry Dolger) How to Live with Diabetes, 1958, 5th edit., 1985; Your Sight, 1968. Died, Dec. 20, 1990. Home: Brookfield Center Conn. †

SEGAL, BERNICE G., chemistry educator; b. Bklyn., Sept. 5, 1929; d. Louis and Lillian (Rosenblatt) Ginsberg; m. Norman M. Segal, Dec. 21, 1952; children—Elizabeth Carol, Daniel Alan. BA summa cum laude, Radcliffe Coll., 1950; MA, Columbia U., 1952, PhD, 1955. Postdoctoral fellow Columbia U., N.Y.C., 1955-57; instr. Barnard Coll., N.Y.C., 1958-64, asst. prof., 1964-69, assoc. prof., 1969-75, prof. chemistry, 1975-89, chair dept., 1973-83, 86-87; Mem. advanced placement devel. com. Coll. Bd. and Ednl. Testing Service, Princeton, N.J., 1975-80, chmn., 1980-83, mem. chem. adv. com. Coll. Bd., N.Y.C., 1976-80. Author: Chemistry, Experiment and Theory, 1985; contbr. articles to profl. jours. Mem. Am. Chem. Soc., Am. Phys. Soc., AAUP, Phi Beta Kappa, Sigma Xi. Home: Tenafly N.J. Died Apr. 9, 1989.

SEGAL, HARRY LOUIS, internist, gastroenterologist, educator; b. Phila., Jan. 13, 1900; s. Morris and Bertha Segal. BS, Syracuse U., 1922, MD, 1924. Intern in pathology Michael Reese Hosp., Chgo., 1924-25, intern in medicine, 1925-26, chief resident in medicine, 1926-27; asst. in medicine Sch. Medicine and Dentistry, U. Rochester, N.Y., 1929-32, instr. medicine, 1932-49, assoc. in medicine, 1949-51, asst. prof., 1951-56, assoc. prof., 1956-58, clin. assoc. prof., 1958-60, clin. prof., 1960-65, prof., 1965-70, prof. emeritus, 1970-90; pvt. practice, Rochester, 1929-72; physician-in-chief Genesee Hosp., Rochester, 1956-67; physician-in-chief emeritus, 1967-90; vis. prof. U. Lagos, 1962-63, 64, external examiner in medicine, 1967, vis. prof., 1968, 70, 72, 73; guest lectr. West African Soc. Gastroenterology, 1980, U. Ilorin, Nigeria, 1980. Contbr. numerous articles to profl. jours. Recipient award of merit U. Rochester, 1956, Albert D. Daiser award, 1959, Alumni citation, 1973; Schindler award Am. Gastroscopic Soc., 1959; Centennial award Syracuse U., 1970. Fellow AMA, ACP; mem. AAUP, Am. Heart Assn., Am. Soc. Gastrointestinal Endoscopy, Am. Gastroent. Assn., N.Y. Acad. Scis., AAAS, Am. Psychosomatic Soc., Assn. Am. Med. Colls., Monroe County Med. Soc., Rochester Acad. Medicine, West African Soc. Gastroenterology (hon.), Sigma Xi, Alpha Omega Alpha. Co-developer gastroscopic color photographic system; originator tubeless gastric analysis with cation exchange resins. Died June 4, 1990. Home: Brighton N.Y.

SEGEL, RONALD GEORGE, publishing company executive, accountant; b. Cambridge, Mass., Aug. 26,

1935; s. Joseph Robert and Sally Mary (Smith) S.; m. Roberta Weinberg, Aug. 31, 1958; children: Beverly, Maxine, Mark. A.B., Harvard Coll., 1957; M.B.A., Harvard Bus. Sch., 1959. CPA, Mass. Acct. Touche Ross Bailey & Smart, N.Y.C., 1959-63; fin. v.p. Rose Jewelers, Detroit, 1963-67, Eastco., Westwood, Mass., 1967-71; fin. v.p. Reed Publishing (U.S.A.), Boston, 1971, chmn., CEO, 1977-91; chmn., CEO Cahners Pub. Co., 1977-91; dir. Deerfield Splty. Papers, Wellesley, Mass., 1978; dir. and chmn. Internat. Computaprint Corp., Ft. Washington, Pa., 1982-91. Trustee Temple Beth Elohim, Wellesley, Mass., 1980-81; treas. Harvard Class of 1957, from 1973. Mem. Mass. CPA Soc. Jewish. Club: Pine Brook Country (Weston, Mass.) (dir. 1981-83). Home: Weston Mass. Died Aug. 30, 1991.

SEGHERS, PAUL D'OTRENGE, lawyer; b. New Orleans, June 9, 1897; s. Edward Domenic and Mary Eleanora (Elder) S.; m. Marie Louise Lebrun, 1923; 1 child, Mary Louise Mastai; m. May Towles Kirk; 1 child, Paul D'Otrenge; m. Bronislawa Zaleska, May 8, 1943 (dec. Mar. 1958); m. Mary Dyezynski, Feb. 1960. BCS, Southeastern U., 1923; LLB, NYU, 1952. Bar: N.Y. 1952. With tax dept. Barrow, Wade, Guthrie & Co., N.Y.C., 1931-36, 37-40; assoc. editor Fed. Tax Svc., Prentice-Hall, Inc., N.Y.C., 1936-37; pvt. practice CPA N.Y.C., 1940-49; tax dept. Garey & Garey, N.Y.C., 1949-52; pvt. practice law N.Y.C., from 1953; pres. Inst. on U.S. Taxation of Fgn. Income, Inc.; lectr. on fed. taxation. Author: Essentially Equivalent to a Dividend, 1960; editorial adv. bd.: Jour. Taxation; contbr. articles to profl. jours. Founder, pres. Fed. Tax Forum, Inc. Mem. ABA, N.Y. State Bar Assn., Assn. Bar City of N.Y., N.Y. State Soc. CPA's (past chmn. fed. tax com.), Suffolk County Bar Assn., Am. Inst. Accts., Huntington C. of C (past chmn. com. on rev. town expenditures), Soc. War 1812 (La.), Fed. Bar Assn. N.Y., Fed. Bar Assn. N.J., Fed. Bar Assn. Conn., Consular Law Soc., Nat. Assn. Accts., N.Y. Bd. Trade (chmn. internat. sect. 1958-60), SAR, VFW, Am. Legion, Huntington Lawyers Univ. Club, Lawyers Club (N.Y.C.). *

SEGOE, LADISLAS, city planner, consulting engineer; b. Debreczen, Hungary, Aug. 17, 1894; came to U.S., 1921, naturalized, 1926; s. Adolph and Leona (Kohn) S.; m. Vilma Czittler, Mar. 24, 1926. Diploma in engring., Tech. U. Budapest, 1919. Town planning projects Yugoslav Govt., 1920-21; resident city planner Tech. Adv. Corp. of N.Y., 1921-24, jr. mem. of firm, 1924-26; planning engr. and sec. in charge of staff Cin. City Planning Commn., 1926-28; planning cons. in pvt. practice as head Ladislas Segoe & Assocs., Cin., from 1928; planning cons. Detroit, Cin., Pitts.; mem. state planning bds., fed. planning and housing agys.; lectr. on city planning Post-Grad. Sch., Tng. for Pub. Svc., U. Cin., 1930-42; lectr. Sch. City Planning, Harvard U., U. Calif., Carnegie Inst. Tech.; pres. Alfred Bettman Found. for Community Planning; bd. Greater Cin. Better Housing League. Prin. author: Local Planning Administration, 1941; co-author: Urban Government, 1939, Urban Planning and Land Politics, 1939, Our Cities, Their Role in the National Economy, 1937; contbr. articles to profl. jours. U.S. del. to 2d Interamerican Congress of Municipalities, Santiago, Chile, 1941; dir. Urbanism Com. to Natural Resources Com. in charge of nationwide study of Am. Cities, 1935-38. Recipient Disting. Svc. award Am. Inst. Planners, 1957. Mem. NRC, Internat. Fedn. Housing and Town Planning, Am. soc. Planning Ofcls., Am. Inst. Cons. Engrs., Inst. Traffic Engrs., Am. Soc. C.E., A. Inst. Planners. *

SEGRÈ, EMILIO, physicist, educator; b. Tivoli, Rome, Italy, Feb. 1, 1905; came to U.S., 1938, naturalized, 1944; s. Giuseppe and Amelia (Treves) S.; m. Elfriede Spiro, Feb. 2, 1936 (dec. Oct. 1970); children: Claudio, Amelia, Fausta; m. Rosa Mines, Feb. 12, 1972. Ph.D., U. Rome, 1928; D honoris causa, U. Palermo, Italy, Gustavus Adolphus Coll., St. Peter, Minn., Tel Aviv U., Hebrew Union Coll., Los Angeles, U. Genova, Italy. Asst. prof. U. Rome, 1932-36; dir. physics lab. U. Palermo, Italy, 1936-38; research asst. U. Calif.-Berkeley, 1938-43, prof. physics, 1945-72, emeritus, 1972-89, group leader Los Alamos Sci. Lab., 1943-46; hon. prof. San Marcos U., Lima; vis. prof. U. Ill., Purdue U.; prof. physics U. Rome, 1974-75; lectr. in field. Author: several books including Enrico Fermi, Physicist and 2 vols. on history of physics. Recipient Hofmann medal German Chem. Soc., Cannizzaro medal Accad. Lincei; Nobel prize in physics, 1959; decorated great cross merit Republic of Italy; Rockefeller Found. fellow, 1930-31; Guggenheim fellow, 1959; Fulbright fellow, 1951. Fellow AAAS, Am. Phys. Soc.; mem. Nat. Acad. Scis., Am. Philos. Soc., Am. Acad. Arts and Scis., Heidelberg Akademie Wissenschaften, European Phys. Soc., Acad. Scis. Peru, Soc. Progress of Sci. (Uruguay), Società Italiana di fisica, Accad. Naz. Lincei (Italy), Accad. Naz. XL (Italy), Indian Acad. Scis. Bangalore, Internat. Acad. History of Scis., others. Home: Lafayette Calif. Died Apr. 22, 1989; buried Oakmont Meml. Pk., Lafayette, Calif.

SEIBERT, FLORENCE BARBARA, educator, biochemist; b. Easton, Pa., Oct. 6, 1897; d. Geroge Peter and Barbara (Memmert) S. AB, Goucher Coll., 1918, LLD, 1938; PhD, Yale, 1923; postgrad., U. Chgo., 1923-24, ScD, 1941; ScD, U. Pa., 1945, Lafayette Coll., 1947, Woman's Med. Coll., 1950. Chemist Hammersley

Paper Mill, 1918-20; instr. pathology and asst. Sprague Meml. Inst., Chgo., 1924-28, asst. prof. biochemistry and assocs., 1928-32; asst. prof. biochemistry Henry Phipps Inst., U. Pa., Phila., 1932-37, assoc. prof., 1937-55, prof., 1955-59, prof. emeritus, 1959-91; spl. cons. USPHS, 1958-73; dir. Cancer Rsch. Lab. Mound Park Hosp. Found., St. Petersburg, Fla., 1964-66; cons. VA, Bay Pines, 1963-91; exptl. work on protein and distilled water pyrogens, 1922-24, on chemistry and immunology of Tb Com. on Med. Rsch. of Nat. Tb. Assn., 1924-59; preparation Nat. Standard for Tuberculins, 1939, Internat. Standard for WHO, 1952; exptl. work cancer, 1954-58, 64-91. Author: Pebbles on the Hill of a Scientist, 1968; also sci. articles and revs. Am. Physiol. Soc. Porter fellow, Yale U., New Haven, 1922-23, Porter fellow U. Chgo., 1923-24; recipient Ricketts prize Chgo., 1924, Trudeau medal Nat. Tb Assn., 1938, First Achievement award AAUW, 1943 (named endowed fellowship 1963), Nat. Achievement award, 1944, Gimbel Phila. award, 1946, John Scott award, 1947, Disting. Dau. Pa., 1950, 1962; Guggenheim fellow U. Uppsala (Sweden), 1937-38. Fellow AAAS; mem. Am. Assn. Blood Banks (hon., John Elliott award 1962), Trudeau Soc. (hon.), N.Y. Acad. Scis., Am. Assn. Biol. Chemists, Am. Chem. Soc. (Garvan gold medal 1942), Phi Beta Kappa, Sigma Xi, Iota Sigma Pi (hon.), Sigma Delta Epsilon (hon.). Presbyn. Home: Saint Petersburg Fla. Died Aug. 23, 1991.

SEIDENBAUM, ART DAVID, journalist; b. Bronx, N.Y., May 4, 1930; s. William G. and Lida (Aretsky) S.; children: Kyle Scott, Kerry Kai. B.S., Northwestern U., 1951; postgrad., Harvard U., 1951-52. Reporter Life mag., N.Y.C., 1955-59; corr. Life mag., Los Angeles, 1959-61; W. Coast bur. chief, contbg. editor Saturday Evening Post, Los Angeles, 1961-62; columnist Los Angeles Times, 1962-78, editor book review sect., 1978-85, editor opinion pages, from 1985. Author: Los Angeles 200: A Bicentennial Celebration (Harry Abrams), 1980. Home: Los Angeles Calif. Deceased. †

SEIFERHELD, DAVID FROEHLICH, textile company consultant; b. N.Y.C., Sept. 20, 1904; s. Sigmund and Gertrude (Froehlich) S.; m. Jeanne Lucienne Longuet, Oct. 13, 1964. B.A., Yale, 1926. With N. Erlanger, Blumgart & Co., Inc., 1926-92, dir., 1932-92, v.p., 1937-43, pres., 1943-59, chmn. exec. com., 1959-69, cons.; Adviser, cons. NRA, 1933; dir. Youth Builders, Inc., 1939-42; founder, treas. Internat. Coordination Council, 1939; dir., treas. Shortwave Research, Inc., 1940-42; treas., dir. Emergency Rescue Com., 1940-44; dir. Internat. Rescue Com., 1945-59; dep. dir. counter intelligence OSS, 1942-43; dir. Overseas News Agy., 1944-45; cons. OPA, 1946-47, OPS, 1951. Bd. dirs. Wiltwyck Sch. for Boys, 1960-69. Home: Grasse France Deceased. †

SEIFERTH, SOLIS, architect; b. New Orleans, Feb. 13, 1895; s. Herman Joshua and Cecelia (Cohen) S.; m. Helen B. Stern, Feb. 7, 1923; 1 child, Celia Kornfeld. BArch, Tulane U., 1915. Ind. practice architect New Orleans, from 1920; architect Seiferth & Gibert, from 1960; chief archtl. supr. for La., FHA, 1934-36; pres. La. Bd. Archtl. Examiners, 1930-38, Nat. Coun. Archtl. Registration Bds., 1945-48; chmn. zoning and major st. plan coms. New Orleans City Planning and Zoning Commn., 1923-30. Prin. works include La. State Capitol, Baton Rouge, 1930, various bldgs. La. State U., 1932-59, Southeastern La. Coll., 1934-38, Charity Hosp., New Orleans, 1938, Touro Infirmary, New Orleans, 1938-61, IBM bldg., New Orleans, 1956, also various schs., hotels, stores and residences. Pres. New Orleans Cultural Ctr. Commn., from 1961, Jewish Children's Home, New Orleans, 1950-58; sec., trustee Newman Sch., New Orleans, from 1940. Capt. U.S. Army, 1917-19, maj. AUS, 1942-45. Fellow AIA (pres. New Orleans 1928-30, 58-60); mem. La. Architects Assn., La. Landmarks Soc. (bd. dirs.), Nat. Trust Historic Preservation, La. Engring. soc., La. Hist. Soc., La. Hist. Assn. *

SEIXAS, FRANK ARCHIBALD, physician; b. N.Y.C., Oct. 5, 1919; s. Archibald Sousa and Ethel Miriam (Isaacs) S.; m. Judith Sartorius, Sept. 29, 1946; children: Peter, Abigail Seixas Horowitz, Noah. B.A., Cornell U., 1939; M.A., Columbia U., 1940, M.D., 1951; postgrad., Rutgers U., 1966, Am. Coll. Physicians, 1970. Diplomate: Am. Bd. Internal Medicine. Intern Montefiore Hosp., Bronx, N.Y., 1951-52; resident Roosevelt Hosp., N.Y.C., 1952-54; fellow in psychiatry Mt. Sinai Hosp., 1954-55; practice medicine, specializing in internal medicine N.Y.C., from 1955; mem. staff N.Y. Cardiac Center, Yonkers, 1956-65, Roosevelt Hosp., from 1955, N.Y. Hosp., from 1955; clin. asst. prof. medicine Cornell U. Med. Coll., from 1966, clin. asso. prof. pub. health, from 1975; med. dir. Nat. Council on Alcoholism, 1968-78, Norwood Hosp. Comprehensive Alcoholism Program, 1979-80; physician Appleton Alcoholism Treatment Center, 1981-83; clin. asst. prof. medicine Harvard Med. Coll., from 1981; adminstr. Support Program for Alcoholism Research-NCA, 1973-78; med. dir. ACCEPT, 1965-70; rep. to UN for ICAA, from 1966. Editor-in-chief: Physicians Alcohol Newsletter of A.M.S.A, 1965-78; editor: Annals of N.Y. Acad. Scis., Vols. 178, 197, 215, 233, 252, from 1968; editor: Alcoholism Clin. and Exptl. Research, 1977-79; editor emeritus, from 1979, editorial bd., from 1980; editor: Currents in Alcoholism, 1977-79; chmn. bd., Shipping Digest, to 1978. Sec., bd. dirs. Nat. Alliance on Shaping Safer Cities, 1973-75; bd. dirs. N.Y. Assn. for New Ams., to 1980, Lower East Side Service Center, to 1980, Westchester Council on Alcoholism, from 1986; mem. adv. council on alcoholism Dept. Mental Health and Mental Retardation Services of N.Y.C., to 1980. Served to lt. comdr. USNR, 1940-45. Fellow ACP; mem. Pan Am. Med. Assn. (pres. alcoholism div. Western Hemisphere), SAR. Clubs: Cornell U. (Boston), Med. Faculty (Boston), Cornell Alumni (Boston). Home: Hastings Hdsn N.Y. Died May 8, 1992. †

SELDERS, GILBERT VIVIAN, educational administrator; b. Alliance, N.J., Jan. 3, 1893; s. George S. and Anna (Saphro) S.; m. Alice Wadhams Hall, June 21, 1924 (dec.); children: Timothy, Marian. AB, Harvard U., 1914. Music critic Phila. Evening Ledger, 1914-16; newspaper corr. abroad during WW, polit. corr. L'Echo de Paris, Washington, 1918; assoc. editor Colliers, 1919; assoc. to mng. editor The Dial, 1920-23; dramatic critic Dial-N.Y. Evening Graphic, 1929; columnist N.Y. Jour., 1931-37; dir. tv programs CBS, 1937-45; prof., dean The Annenberg Sch. Communications, U. Pa., 1959-63. Author: Seven Lively Arts, 1924, The Stammering Century, 1928, The Great Audience, 1950, The Public Arts, 1956; author: (play) Lysistrata, 1930, (hist. motion picture) This Is America, 1933; co-author: (play) Swingin' the Dream, 1939; editor: Portable Ring Lardner, 1946. Sgt. U.S. Army, 1918. Mem. Nat. Inst. Arts and Letters, Phi Beta Kappa, Century Club (N.Y.C.). *

SELFE, ROBERT W., physician; b. Richmond, Va., Apr. 27, 1943; s. Robert W. and Alta Belle (Fields) S.; m. Bonnie Lou Henry, June 12, 1965 (div.); 1 child, Sean Daris. Student, Muskingum Coll., 1961-63; BA, Ohio State U., 1965, MD, 1968. Diplomate Am. Bd. Otolaryngology. Otolaryngologist-in-chief N.Y. Hosp., N.Y.C., from 1981; prof. clin. otorhinolaryngology, chmn. dept. otorhinolaryngology Cornell U. Med. Coll., N.Y.C., from 1981. Served to lt. comdr. USN, 1975-77. Home: New York N.Y. Deceased. †

SELIKOFF, IRVING JOHN, physician, researcher, educator; b. Bklyn., Jan. 15, 1915; s. Abraham and Tilli (Katz) S.; m. Celia Shiffrin, Feb. 4, 1946 (dec. 1986). B.S., Columbia U., 1935; M.D., Anderson Coll. Medicine, U. Melbourne, Australia, 1941; Sc.D. (hon.), Tufts U., 1976, Bucknell U., 1979, N.J. State Coll., 1980, CUNY, 1984, U. N.J., 1987. Diplomate: Am. Bd. Preventive Medicine. Intern Newark Beth Israel Hosp., 1943-44; asst. morbid anatomy Mt. Sinai Hosp., N.Y.C., 1941; resident Sea View Hosp., N.Y.C.,, 1944-46; founding dir. div. environ. and occupational medicine, Mt. Sinai Med. Ctr., N.Y.C., 1966-85; emeritus prof. Mt. Sinai Sch. Medicine, CUNY; researcher, until 1992; cons. medicine Barnert Meml. Hosp., Paterson, N.J.; mem. Nat. Cancer Adv. Bd., 1979-84; pres. Collegium Ramazzini, 1982; cons. WHO, other agys., bus. and unions. Author: The Management of Tuberculosis, 1956, Biological Effects of Asbestos, 1965, Toxicity of Vinyl Chloride and Polyvinyl Chloride, (with D.H.K. Lee) Asbestos and Disease, 1978, Health Hazards of Asbestos Exposure, 1979, AIDS, 1985, (with C. Maltoni) Living in a Chemical World, 1988; also over 350 articles profl. jours.; editor 11 books; editor-in-chief Am. Jour. Indsl. Medicine, from 1980, Environ. Research, 1970-87. Recipient Lasker award in Medicine, 1955; Ann. Research award Am. Cancer Soc., 1976; Edwards medal Welsh Nat. Sch. Medicine, 1977; award in sci. and tech., CUNY, 1986, other awards Am. Cancer Soc., AFL-CIO. Fellow Royal Soc. Edinburgh, Am. Pub. Health Assn. (award), Am. Coll. Chest Physicians (pres. N.J. chpt. 1954-55); mem. N.Y. Pub. Health Assn. (Haven Emerson award 1975), N.Y. Acad. Scis. (pres. 1969-70, bd. govs. from 1970, Poiley award and medal 1974), Inst. Medicine Nat. Acad. Scis., Soc. Occupational and Environ. Health (pres. 1973-74), Am. Coll. Toxicology (pres. 1980). Home: Ridgewood N.J. Died May 20, 1992.

SELL, STEPHEN, orchestra executive; b. Newark, Oct. 4, 1941; s. Edward and Rose (Rizk) S.; children: Lisa, Jesse. A.B., Rutgers U., 1963. Mgmt. intern Cleve. Orch., 1963-64; adminstrv. asst. Carnegie Hall Corp., N.Y.C., 1964-65; asst. mgr. Pitts. Symphony, 1965-69; gen. mgr. St. Paul Chamber Orch., 1969-73; dir. spl. projects Nat. Endowment for Arts, Washington, 1973-75; exec. dir. Minn. State Arts Bd., Mpls., 1975-78; exec. v.p. Atlanta Symphony, 1978-82; exec. dir. Phila. Orch., 1982-89; chmn. Nat. Assembly of State Art Agys., Washington, 1977-78; treas. Am. Arts Alliance, Washington, 1982-84; chmn. Maj. Orch. Mgrs. Conf., 1983-85. Home: Philadelphia Pa. Died May 26, 1989.

SELLERS, JAMES MCBRAYER, military academy president; b. Lexington, Mo., June 20, 1895; s. Sandford and Lucia Valentine (Rogers) S.; m. Rebekah Hall Evans, Dec. 28, 1925; children—Stephen Wentworth, James McBrayer, Frederick Evans. A.B., U. Chgo., 1917. Asst. comdt. and instr. Wentworth Mil. Acad., Lexington, 1920-24, comdt., 1924-33, supt., 1933-60, pres., from 1967. Served from 2d lt. to capt., 6th Regt. USMC, 1917-20. Decorated D.S.C., Navy Cross, Silver Star, Purple Heart; Croix de Guerre. Mem. Mil. Schs. Assn. (past pres.), Phi Beta Kappa, Sigma Xi., Beta Theta Pi. Presbyterian. Lodge: Masons (K.T., grand comdr. 1951-52, grand master 1953-54). Home: Lexington Mo. Deceased. †

SELLERS, RICHARD MORGAN, insurance company executive; b. Beeville, Tex., Aug. 14, 1913; s. Richard and Lena Lee (Morgan) S.; m. Lucille Marshall, Mar. 22, 1941; 1 child, R. Marshall. A.B., So. Methodist U., 1934; M.A., U. Mich., 1936. With Commonwealth Life Ins. Co., Louisville, 1936-62, 70-78; pres. Commonwealth Life Ins. Co., 1970-73, vice chmn. bd., 1973-78, dir., 1950-62, 70-84; sr. v.p. U.S. Life Ins. Co., N.Y.C., 1962-70; dir. Capital Enterprise Ins. Group, 1960-62, 70-84. Contbr. articles to profl. jours. Bd. dirs. Greater Louisville Fund for Arts. Mem. Soc. Actuaries, Phi Beta Kappa. Clubs: Louisville Country, Wynn Stay; Princeton, Cavendish (N.Y.C.). Home: Louisville Ky. Died Jan. 24, 1989; buried Louisville, Ky.

SELZER, ARTHUR, cardiologist, educator; b. Lwow, Poland, July 3, 1911; came to U.S., 1938, naturalized, 1943; s. Martin and Janina (Lam) S.; m. Jadwiga Winkler, July 31, 1936; children: Martin Arthur, Peter Michael. M.D., U. Cracow, 1936; postgrad., U. London, 1936-38. Diplomate Am. Bd. Internal Medicine. Intern Univ. Hosp. Lwow, 1935-36; vol. asst. Hammersmith Hosp., also Nat. Heart Hosp., London, 1936-38; practice medicine specializing in cardiology San Francisco, 1941-59, cons. in cardiology, from 1959; mem. faculty Stanford U. Med. Sch., 1941-76, clin. prof. medicine, 1957-76, emeritus, 1976-91; clin. prof. medicine U. Calif. Med. Sch., San Francisco, from 1960; mem. staff Presbyn. Hosp., San Francisco, from 1959, chief cardiology, 1959-84; chmn. San Francisco Community Chest Health Council, 1953-55. Author: The Heart: Its Functions in Health and Disease, 1965, Principles of Clinical Cardiology, 1975, 83; also articles. Fellow Am. Coll. Cardiology; master ACP; mem. Calif. Acad. Medicine (pres. 1972-73). Home: Burlingame Calif. Died Nov. 26, 1991.

SELZER, CHARLES LOUIS, retired educational administrator; b. Homestead, Iowa, Dec. 21, 1914; s. Louis Carl and Caroline (Shoup) S.; m. Louise Kippenhan, Mar. 9, 1935; 1 dau., Patricia Madelyn Selzer Carstensen. BA cum laude, Coe Coll., 1935; MA, State U. Iowa, 1950, postgrad., from 1951. Notary public. Tchr., prin., coach Amana (Iowa) High Sch., 1935-50; supt. Amana Community Schs., 1950-83; guest lectr. U. Iowa, summers 1977-79; bd. dirs. Amana Telephone Co., Amana Woolens, Inc. Contbr. to Amana News Bull.; translator Amana documents and testimonies; author: Amana Coop. Edn. Plan; TV appearance: (Amana segment) 60 Minutes. Former justice of peace, Iowa County; mem. Iowa County Crime Commn.; pres. Amana Community Chest, 1951-53; mem. adv. bd. Kirkwood Coll., Amana Service Co.; mem. Iowa County Soc. Aging, Area X Grant Wood Spl. Edn. Bd., Amana Travel Council, Amana Hist. Landmark Charter and Constn. Commn., from 1977; pres. Amana Bicentennial; mem. bicentennial com. Coe Coll. Mem. Am. Assn. Sch. Adminstrs., Iowa Assn. Sch. Adminstrs., NEA, Iowa Edn. Assn., Amana Young Men's Bur. (hon. past pres.), Iowa Poweshiek County Supts. Assn., Sr. Supts. Iowa, Joint County Area X Supts. Assn. (legis. com.), Iowa Benton Supts. Assn. (legis. com.), Amana Soc. (bd. dirs.), Iowa Peace Officers Assn., Amana Hist. Soc., Nat. Notary Assn., Amana Men's Chorus, Iowa County Hist. Soc. (pres. 1965-67), Iowa County Schoolmasters Assn. (past pres.), Amana Landmark Soc. (mem. constn. com.), Coe Coll. Alumni Assn., U. Iowa Alumni Assn., Phi Beta Kappa. Mem. Amana Ch. Soc. (trustee, elder, pres. from 1971). Clubs: Elks, Masons (32 deg.), Shriners, El Kahir, Homestead Welfare (past pres., sec.), Cedar Rapids Toastmasters (hon.). Home: Homestead Iowa Deceased. †

SELZNICK, IRENE MAYER, theatrical producer; b. N.Y.C., Apr. 2, 1907; d. Louis B. and Margaret (Shenberg) Mayer; m. David O. Selznick, Apr. 29, 1930 (div. Jan. 1948); children: Lewis Jeffrey, Daniel Mayer. Ed. pub. schs., Brookline, Mass.; ed., Holywood Sch. Girls, Calif. With Selznick-Internat. Pictures, Inc., Culver City, Calif., 1936-40, Vanguard Films, Calif., N.Y.C., 1941-49; mng. dir. Irene M. Selznick Co., N.Y.C., from 1946. Produced Tennessee Williams' A Street Car Named Desire, N.Y.C., 1947, London, 1949, John von Druten's Bell, Book and Candle, 1950, George Tabori's Flight Into Egypt, 1952, Enid Bagnold's The Chalk Garden, N.Y.C., London, 1955, The Last Joke, London, 1960, Graham Greene's The Complaisant Lover, N.Y.C., 1961; author: A Private View, 1983. Home: New York N.Y. Died Oct. 10, 1990.

SENDON, ANDRES RODRIGUEZ, foreign language educator; b. La Coruna, Spain, Oct. 13, 1894; came to U.S., 1914, naturalized, 1942; s. Manuel and Dolores (Rodriguez) S.; m. Mary Kemendo, May 25, 1922; children: Dolores Morse, Andrea Mildenberger. AB, Baylor U., 1920, MA, 1922; postgrad., Columbia U., 1923-24, U. Tex., 1929, 31. Buyer bananas and Mexican handwork for export, 1912-14; stock agt. Eagle Oil Co., Tampico, Mexico, 1912-14; efficiency dept. Dodge Bros., Detroit, summers 1917-18; faculty Baylor U., from 1919, prof. Spanish, chmn. dept., from 1948. Active pub. rels. activities with Mexican population, Waco, Tex. Mem. AAUP, Modern Lang. Assn., Am. Assn. Tchrs. Spanish and Portuguese, South Ctrl. Modern Lang. Assn., Pi Alpha Lambda (founder-sponsor), Sigma Delta Pi (founder), Sigma Alpha Epsilon. Baptist. *

SENN, MILTON JOHN EDWARD, pediatrician, child psychiatrist; b. Milw., Mar. 23, 1902; s. John and Louise (Rosenkranz) S.; m. Blanche Forsythe, Sept. 8, 1932; 1 child, Corelyn F. BS, U. Wis., 1925, MD, 1927; MA (hon.), Yale U., 1948. Intern Columbia Hosp., Milw., 1927-29; resident Children's Hosp., Milw., 1927-28; fellow, instr. pediatrics Washington U., St. Louis, 1929-33; assoc. in pediatrics Cornell U. Med. Coll., N.Y.C., 1933-39, Commonwealth Fund fellow in psychiatry, 1937-39, prof. pediatrics and psychiatry, 1948-49; asst., assoc., later attending pediatrician N.Y. Hosp., N.Y.C., 1933-49; Sterling prof. pediatrics and psychiatry Yale U. Med. Sch., New Haven, 1948-70, prof. emeritus, 1970-90, dir. Child Study Ctr., 1948-66; pediatrician-in-chief Grace-New Haven Community Hosp., 1951-58. Sr. author: The Newborn: Experiences of 8 American Families, Problems of Child Behavior and Development; author: Insights on the Child Development Movement: Speaking Our for America's Children; also articles. Bd. dirs. Field Found. Mem. Am. Pediatric Soc., Am. Acad. Pediatrics, Am. Orthopsychiat. Assn., N.Y. Acad. Medicine. Home: Southbury Conn. Died June 8, 1990; cremated.

SENSENBRENNER, MAYNARD E., mayor; b. Circleville, Ohio, Sept. 18, 1902; s. Edward and Anna (Lama) S.; m. Mildred Sexauer, Oct. 8, 1927; children: Edward, Richard. Student pub. schs., Circleville. Investigator, clk. Ohio Civil Svc. Commn., 1934-53; mayor City of Columbus, Ohio, 1954-91. V.p. Boy Scouts Am., 20 yrs. recipient Silver Beaver; v.p. Camp Fire Girls; mem. Big Bro. Assn.; elder Presbyn. Ch. Mem. Kiwanis. Democrat. Home: Columbus Ohio Died Aug. 2, 1991.

SERKIN, RUDOLF, pianist; b. Eger, Bohemia, Mar. 28, 1903; s. Mordko Serkin and Augusta (Schargl) S.; m. Irene Busch; children: Ursula, Elisabeth, John, Peter, Judith, Marguerite. Studied piano with Richard Robert, studied composition with J. Marx and Arnold Schoenberg; MusD, Curtis Inst. Music, Williams Coll., Temple U., U. Vt., Oberlin (Ohio) Coll., U. Rochester, Harvard U., 1973, Marlboro Coll.; MusD (hon.), New Eng. Conservatory Music, 1985. Apptd. dept. piano Curtis Inst. Music, Phila., 1939-75, dir., 1968-75; founding mem., artistic dir., pres. Marlboro Music Sch. and Festival, Vt.; former mem. Nat. Coun. on Arts, Carnegie Commn. Report. European concert debut as guest artist with Vienna Symphony Orch., 1915; began concert career in solo, concerto and chamber music recitals, Europe, 1920; appeared with Adolf Busch in series of sonatas for violin and piano, with Busch Chamber Players in the Bach suites and Brandenburg concertos; debut in Am., Coolidge Festival, Washington, 1933; launched concert career in U.S. with N.Y. Philharm. under Toscanini, 1936; played a series of Mozart and Beethoven, with Nat. Orch. Assn., 1937; with Adolf Busch; played complete series of Beethoven piano and violin sonatas, N.Y.C., 1938; made ann. concert tours in U.S. since, 1934; recent appearances include Carnegie Hall Concert, N.Y.C., 1987, performance of Beethoven's Emperor Concerto with Chgo. Symphony Orch., Cleve. Orch., 1988; frequent participant Casals Festival, from 1950; numerous recs.; performances at The White House, 1966, 70; considered child prodigy at age of 4. Decorated grand officiale del Ordina, Orden pour le Merite (Fed. Republic of Germany), Cross of Honor for Scis. and Artist (Austria), comdr's. cross Icelandic Order of Falcon; recipient Presdl. medal of freedom, 1963, Honors medal Kennedy Ctr., 1981, Ernst von Siemens Musikpreis, 1978, Nat. medal of arts, 1988. Fellow Am. Acad. Arts and Scis.; mem. Acad. Nationale di Santa Cecilia (Rome) (hon.), Verein Beethoven Haus (Bonn), Neue Bachgesellschaft (Bonn), Philharm. Symphony Soc. N.Y., Am. Philos. Soc., Riemenschneider Bach Inst. Home: Brattleboro Vt. Died May 8, 1991; buried Vt.

SETON, ANYA, author; b. N.Y.C.; d. Ernest Thompson and Grace (Gallatin) S.; children: Pamela Cottier Forcey, Seton Cottier (dec.), Clemency Chase Coggins. Ed. pvt. tutors in, Spence Sch., N.Y.C. Author: My Theodosia, 1941, Dragonwyck, 1944 (made into movie), The Turquoise, 1946, The Hearth and Eagle, 1948, Foxfire, 1950 (made into movie), Katherine, 1954, The Mistletoe and Sword; juvenile, 1955, The Winthrop Woman, 1958, Washington Irving, 1960, Devil Water, 1962, Avalon, 1965, Green Darkness, 1973, Smouldering Fires, 1975; (all translated into many langs), also short stories mags. Recipient Medal of Honor Soc. Colonial Wars, 1958. Mem. League Am. Penwomen, Pen and Brush Club (hon.), P.E.N. Home: Old Greenwich Conn. Died Nov. 8, 1990.

SETTLEMYER, CLAUDE HAROLD, retail textile executive; b. Lancaster, S.C., Oct. 9, 1912; s. Arthur Frank and Cornelia Ethel (Dabney) S.; m. Helen M. Grady, June 27, 1942; children: William Boyd, Anita Lynn, Susan Elizabeth. Student, Wingate Jr. Coll., 1928-31; A.B., Duke, 1934. With Cannon Mills Co., Kannapolis, N.C., 1934-37; with Cannon Mills, Inc., N.Y.C., 1937-77, v.p., 1956-59, exec. v.p., 1961-73, sr. v.p., 1973-77. Served from lt. (j.g.) to lt. comdr. USNR, 1942-45. Mem. Phi Delta Theta. Clubs: Sea Pines Golf, Water Gap (Pa.) Country. Home: Hilton Head Island S.C. Died Dec. 12, 1988; buried Six Oaks Cemetery, Hilton Head Island, S.C.

SEUSS, DR. See **GEISEL, THEODOR SEUSS**

SEYBOLD, LAWRENCE F., utilities executive; b. Forest Junction, Wis., May 16, 1897; s. William and Mary (Dunker) S.; m. Marie W. Broecker, Sept. 4, 1926; children: Alice Marie, Janet, Erwin. BS, U. Wis., 1918. Student engr. Commonwealth Edison Co., Chgo., 1917; inspector Bur. of Steam Engring., U.S. Navy Dept., 1919; sr. engr. Milw. Electric Rlwy. and Light Co., 1919-26, asst. rsch. engr., 1926-29; rsch. engr. Wis. Electric Power Co., Milw., 1929-41, v.p., 1938-47, dir., from 1931, exec. v.p., 1947-56, pres., 1956-62, chmn. bd., from 1962; v.p., dir. Milw. Electric Rlwy. and Transport Co., 1938-56, pres., 1956-62, chmn. bd., 1962-64; chmn. bd. Wis. Natural Gas Co.; with Wis.-Mich. Power Co., from 1940, pres., 1956-62, chmn. bd., from 1962; dir. Badger Auto Svc. Co., from 1946, pres., 1956-62, chmn. bd., from 1962; dir. 1st Wis. Nat. Bank of Milw., First Wis. Trust Co., 1st Wis. Bankshares Corp., Bradley Wash. Fountain Co., Milw., Forge & Machine Co. Ensign USNRF, 1918-19. Mem. Eta Kappa Nu, Athletic Club, Milw. Club, Milw. Engrs. Club, Mason. Methodist. *

SEYFARTH, HENRY EDWARD, lawyer; b. Blue Island, Ill., Apr. 16, 1908; s. Ward Richard and Florence Louise (Klein) S.; m. Elizabeth Ellis, Feb. 15, 1965; children: B. Marie, Victoria Fesmire, Richard R. Parkin. B.A., U. Ill., 1928; J.D., U. Chgo., 1930. Asst. State's Atty. Cook County, Ill., 1930-35; ptnr. Pope & Ballard, Chgo., 1935-45; founder, ptnr. Seyfarth, Shaw, Fairweather & Geraldson, Chgo., 1945-87, cons., 1987-91; chmn. bd. dirs. Gt. Lakes Fin. Resources, Inc., 1st Nat. Bank of Blue Island, Ill.; bd. dirs. Community Bank of Homewood-Flossmoor (Ill.), Naples (Fla.) Community Hosp.; chmn. bd. Union Nat. Bank Chgo.; counsel Tribune Co., Chgo., 1980's. Trustee Northwestern Meml. Hosp., Chgo., North Cen. Coll., Naperville, Ill. Mem. Chgo. Bar Assn., Ill. Bar Assn., Bar Assn. Washington, Assn. for Modern Banking in Ill. (founder, chmn. 1965-75). Republican. Episcopalian. Clubs: Chicago, University; Barrington Hills (Ill.) Country, Naples (Fla.) Yacht, Port Royal, Royal Poinciana Golf. Home: Naples Fla. Died Aug. 16, 1991; buried Mt. Greenwood Cemetery, Chgo.

SEYMOUR, ERNEST RICHARD, retired naval officer, consultant; b. Syracuse, N.Y., Oct. 6, 1931; s. Willard Renwick and Virginia (Smith) S.; m. Virginia Ann Metzler, Feb. 6, 1954; children: Ernest Richard, Deborah L., Stephen E. B.S., U.S. Naval Acad., 1953, U.S. Naval Postgrad. Sch., 1961; Aero. E., Calif. Inst. Tech., 1962. Commd. ensign U.S. Navy, 1953, advanced through grades to vice adm.; naval aviator, 1955-89; asst. program mgr. for logistics A-7 aircraft Naval Air Systems Command, Washington, 1968; later project mgr., then dep. comdr. plans and program tour as mem. staff chief naval ops.; exec. asst. to vice chief naval ops., asst. dep. chief naval ops. (air warfare), vice chief naval material, comdr. Naval Air Systems Command., ret., 1983; cons., 1983-89. Decorated D.S.M., Silver Star, Legion of Merit (3), D.F.C., Bronze Star, Air medal (23). Episcopalian. Home: Vienna Va. Died May 17, 1989. †

SEYMOUR, RAYMOND BENEDICT, chemistry educator, chemical engineer, author; b. Boston, July 26, 1912; s. Walter A. and Marie E. (Doherty) S.; m. Frances B. Horan, Sept. 16, 1936; children: David Ray, Susan Seymour Smith, Peter, Phillip Alan. BS, U. N.H., 1933, MS, 1935; PhD, U. Iowa, 1937. Registered profl. engr., Tex., Ohio. Instr. chemistry U. N.H., Durham, 1933-35, U. Iowa, Iowa City, 1935-37; rsch. chemist Goodyear Tire & Rubber Co., Akron, Ohio, 1937-39; chief chemist Atlas Mineral and Chem. Products, Mertztown, Pa., 1939-41; exec. v.p., gen. mgr., tech. dir. Atlas Mineral Products divsn. Electric Storage Battery Co., Mertztown, Pa., 1949-54; pres., also bd. dirs. Atlas Mineral Products div. Electric Storage Battery Co., Mertztown, Pa., 1954-55; rsch. group leader Monsanto Co., Dayton, Ohio, 1941-45; dir. rsch. U. Chattanooga, 1945-48, Johnson & Johnson, New Brunswick, N.J., 1948-49; pres., tech. dir. Loven Chem. of Calif., 1955-58; pres. Corrosion Resistant Products, Inc., 1956-57; pres., chmn. bd. Alcylite Plastics & Chem. Corp., 1958-60; prof. chemistry, dean sci. div. Sul Ross State U., 1959-64; assoc. chmn. chemistry dept. U. Houston, 1964-66, coord. polymer chemistry, 1964-76, assoc. prof. chemistry, 1964-69, prof., 1969-76, prof. emeritus, 1976-91, assoc. dir. research, 1966-68; adj. prof. polymer sci. U. So. Miss., Hattiesburg, 1974-76, disting. prof., 1976-91; cons. edn. AID, U.S. Dept. State, East Pakistan, 1968; dir. NSF Inst. 1965; NAS vis. prof. fgn. countries, 1976-79; chair Tamkang U., Taiwan, 1978; plenary speaker Plastec Internat., Zagreb, Yugoslavia, 1986, Plastique Modernos, Madrid, 1987, R.B. Seymour Recognition Day at Tamkang U., Taiwan, 1991; U.S. del. Internat. Union Pure and Applied Chemistry, Jerusalem, 1987; chmn. Experimat 87, Bordeaux, 1987; Fred Garland Meml. lectr., 1988; Carl Marvel Meml. lectr. U. Rio de Janeiro, 1989. Author numerous books including: Hot Organic Coatings, 1959, Introduction to Polymer Chemistry, 1971, General Organic Chemistry, 1971, Modern Plastics Technology, 1975, Polymer Chemistry: An Introduction, 1981, Conductive Polymers, 1981, History of Polymer Chemistry, 1981, 2d edit. 1988, Plastics vs. Corrosives, 1982, Macromolecular Solutions, 1982, Structure-Property Relationships in Polymers, 1983, History of Polyolefins, 1985, Pioneers in Polymer Science: Selected Biographies, 1986, Advances in Polyolefins, 1986, Origin and Development of High Performance Polymers, 1986, Polymers for Engineering Applications, 1987, Origin and Development of Polymer Composites, 1987, New Advances in Polyolefins, 1987, Applications of Polymers, 1987, Engineering Polymers Sourcebook, 1987, Eminent Polymer Scientists, 1987, Polymer Composites, 1987, Polymer Chemistry: An Introduction, 1988, Organic Coatings Handbook, 1989, Origin and Development of Organic Coatings, 1989, Origin and Development of Man Made Fibers, 1990, Giant Molecules, 1990, Man Made Fibers Handbook, 1990, Modern Plastic Composite Technology, 1990, History of Rubber, 1990, Rubber Handbook, 1990, Polymer Science for Chemists and Engineers, 1990, Handbook of PolyoleFins, 1991, Polymer Science Pioneers, 1991; contbr. 2,000 articles to profl. jours.; patentee in field. Recipient Opdycke, 1933, Chem. Engring. Plastics award, 1953, Western Plastics award, 1960, Teaching Excellence award U. Houston, 1975, Catalyst Excellence in Teaching award Chem. Mfrs. Assn., 1976, So. Chemists award, 1981, Silver plaque Plasticos Modernos, 1987, Outstanding Alumnus award U. Iowa, 1990; named Western Plastics Pioneer, 1977, Outstanding Chemist in Miss., 1986; elected to Western Plastics Hall of Fame, 1981, Internat. Plastics Hall of Fame, 1988, and numerous otehr awards. Fellow AAAS, Am. Inst. Chemists (honor scroll 1980, Chemist Pioneer award 1985), Tex. Acad. Sci.; mem. AAUP, Am. Inst. Chem. Engrs., Am. Chem. Soc. (Southeastern Tex. ann. award 1972, Charles Herty award 1985, plenary speaker R.B. Seymour Recognition Day 1987), Soc. Plastics Industry, Nat. Assn. Corrosion Engrs., Am Soc. Oceanography, Soc. Plastics Engrs. (internat. edn. award 1982, Internat. Plastics award 1989), Plastics Pioneers Assn., Miss. Acad. Sci., Sigma Xi, Phi Kappa Phi, Alpha Chi Sigma, Gamma Sigma Epsilon. Club: Hattiesburg Country. Lodge: Rotary. Home: Hattiesburg Miss. Died Nov. 15, 1991. †

SHAABER, MATTHIAS ADAM, English language educator; b. Reading, Pa., Dec. 13, 1897; s. Harry Christopher and Emma Fredericka (Moyer) S.; m. Margaret Livingston Donaldson, June 17, 1933. AB, U. Pa., 1918, AM, 1924, PhD, 1928. Instr. English U. Pa., 1919-20, 22-34, asst. prof., 1934-39, assoc. prof., 1939-42, prof., from 1942, John Welsh centennial prof. English history and lit., from 1958, chmn. dept. English, 1957-62; vis. lectr. U. So. Calif., 1939, Columbia U., 1948, 52-53, Duke U., 1950. Author: Some Forerunners of the Newspaper in England, 1476-1622, 1929, The Art of Writing Business Letters, 1930, (with Matthew W. Black) Shakespeare's Seventeenth-Century Editors, 1937; editor: The Second Part of Henry IV (New Variorum Shakespeare), 1940, Studies in the Renaissance, from 1955, Seventeenth-Century English Prose, 1957. With U.S. Army, WWI. Mem. Phi Gamma Delta. *

SHADEGG, STEPHEN, author; b. Mpls., Dec. 8, 1909; s. Jacob Carl and Katherine (Barden) S.; m. Eugenia Kehr, Feb. 14, 1939 (dec. 1988); children: Cynthia, Eugenia, Stephen David, John Barden. Student, Pasadena (Calif.) Community Playhouse Sch. Theatre, 1931-32. Writer for radio, 1936-38, writer for pulp mags., 1939-45; pres. S-K Rsch. Labs. (pharmaceuticals), Phoenix, 1941-77, Stephen Shadegg Assocs., Inc. (advt. and pub. rels.), 1963-90; adj. lectr. Ariz. State U., 1981-84. Author: Barry Goldwater: Freedom is His Flight Plan, 1962, How to Win an Election, 1964, What Happened to Goldwater ?, 1965, The Remnant, 1968, Winning's a Lot More Fun, 1969, Clare Boothe Luce, 1971, (unattributed) With No Apologies, 1979 (Book of the Month Club), Miss Lulu's Legacy, 1984, Arizona Politics: The Struggle to End One-Party Rule, 1986; contbr. nat. mags.; author spl. publs. : Arizona: An Adventure in Irrigation, presented to U.S. Congress for Cen. Ariz. Project, 1949, The Phoenix Story: An Adventure in Reclamation, 1958, Century One (growth and devel. in Salt River Valley, 1959); contbr.: Left, Right and Center, 1965, Modern American History, 1969; writer, prod. radio programs Stas. KTAR and KOY, CBS, 1934-36; screenwriter RKO Pictures, 1939-40. Pres. Phoenix Little Theatre, 1949, 52; gen. fund chmn. Phoenix chpt. ARC, 1952; chmn. Ariz. crusade Am. Cancer Soc., 1957-60; mem. nat. coun. Protestant Episcopal Ch., 1961-90; gen. mgr. senatorial campaign Barry Goldwater, 1952, 58, 74, Paul Laxalt (Nev.), 1974; cons. to Nat. Rep. Senatorial Campaign Com., 1959-60; chmn. Ariz. Rep. Party, 1960-62; Western regional dir. Goldwater for Pres. Com., 1964, Rep. Nat. Com., 1961-62; gen. campaign mgr. Gov. Jack Williams, 1966, 68, 70, Sen. Paul Fannin, 1970, Eldon Rudd for Congress, 1976, 78, 80, 82, 84. Named Phoenix Man of Yr. Phoenix Advt. Club, 1951. Mem. Edmund Burke Soc. Am. Elk, Kiwanis, Press Club, Ariz. Country Club (pres. 1956). Home: Phoenix Ariz. Died Apr. 16, 1990; buried Meml. Garden Christ Ch. of the Ascension, Paradise Valley, Ariz.

SHAFFER, CLYDE H(OOVER), ice cream manufacturer; b. Hooversville, Pa., Jan. 12, 1900; s. Robert Stuart and Martha Jane (Hoover) S.; m. Elizabeth Carins Smith, Oct. 9, 1931; children: Clyde Hoover, Diane Elizabeth (Mrs. Bruce R. Castor). BA, Pa. State U., 1925. From trainee to plant mgr. Breyer Ice Cream

Co., N.Y.C.; v.p. Breyer Ice Cream Co., Phila.; regional v.p. Breyer Ice Cream Co., N.Y.C.; v.p., treas. Breyer Ice Cream Co., Phila., 1925-41, pres., 1941-90; v.p. Sealtest Foods; bd. dirs. Nat. Dairy Products Corp. Served with U.S. Army, 1918. Republican. Home: Pompano Beach Fla. Died Aug. 3, 1990.

SHAFROTH, WILL, lawyer; b. Denver, July 10, 1894; s. John Franklin and Virginia (Morrison) S.; m. Janet Durrie, Nov. 25, 1924; children: Stephen Morrison, Sylvia. AB, U. Mich., 1914; JD, U. Calif., 1916. Pvt. practice Denver, 1916-17, 24-34; commd. 2d lt. U.S. Army, 1917, advanced through grades to capt., 1918, served in France with 78th F.A., 6th div.; mem. Am. Mil. Mission to Hungary, 1919; relief work with Am. Relief Adminstrn., 1920-22; chief div. procedural studies and stats. Admisntrv. Office, U.S. Cts., 1940-60, dep. dir., 1960-64; counsel Lambert, Furlow, Elmore & Heidenberger, 1965-75; in charge food distbn. Dist. Samara, Russia, famine of 1922, also relief work in Constantinople. Mem. ABA (adviser to sect. legal edn. 1930-34, 35-40), Am. Law Inst., Fed. Bar Assn., Am. Judicature Soc., Am. Relief Adminstrn. Assn., Chevy Chase Club, Cactus Club (Denver), Phi Delta Theta, Phi Delta Phi. Democrat. Home: Springmoor N.C. Died Aug. 23, 1991.

SHANLEY, BERNARD MICHAEL, lawyer; b. Newark, 1903; s. Bernard Michael and Regina (Ryan) S.; m. Maureen Virginia Smith, Aug. 1, 1936 (dec.); children: Maureen S. Kirk, Seton, Kevin, Brigid Shanley Lamb, Brendan. Student, Columbia U., 1925, Fordham U. Law Sch., 1928. Bar: N.J. 1929, U.S. Supreme Ct. 1950, D.C. 1960. Founder, sr. ptnr. Shanley & Fisher, P.C., Newark, 1934-92; advisor Gen. Eisenhower's personal staff, 1952 campaign; on leave from firm to act as dep. chief staff and spl. counsel to Pres. U.S., 1953-55; sec. to Pres., 1955-57; bd. dirs. Pub. Svc. Electric and Gas, Chubb Corp.; counsel N.J. C. of C. Former chmn. N.J. Rep. Fin. Com., vice-chmn. Northeast; mem. exec. com., rules com., coun. legal advisors; Rep. Nat. Committeeman for N.J., 1960-64, 68-92; Rep. candidate for U.S. Senate, 1964; mem. adv. bd. St. Benedict's Prep. Sch.; trustee Victoria Found., Ch. of Our Lady of Perpetual Help, Bernardsville, N.J.; bd. dirs. Tri-County Scholarship Fund. Diocese of Paterson, N.J.. Served with AUS, 1942-45. Designated knight St. Gregory the Great (Pope John Paul II); recipient Medal of St. Benedict, 1990, War Dept. citation. Fellow Am. Bar Found. (life); mem. ABA, N.J., Essex County, Somerset County Bar Assn., Am. Judicature Soc. Clubs: Two Hundred (Somerset County); Essex (Newark); Metropolitan, Capitol Hill (Washington); Nat. Golf Links Am. (Southampton, N.Y.); Roxiticus Golf (pres. emeritus) (Mendham, N.J.), Morris County Golf. Home: Bernardsville N.J. Died Feb. 25, 1992.

SHANNON, DAVID ALLEN, history educator; b. Terre Haute, Ind., Nov. 30, 1920; s. John Raymond and Esther (Allen) S.; m. Jane Short, Aug. 31, 1940; children: Molly Shannon Osborne, Sarah Shannon Olson. B.S., Ind. State Coll., 1941; M.S., U. Wis., 1946, Ph.D., 1951. Instr. history Carnegie Inst. Tech., 1948-51; asst. prof., then asso. prof. Columbia Tchrs. Coll., 1951-57; faculty U. Wis., 1957-65, prof. history, 1960-65; prof., chmn. dept. history U. Md., 1965-68, Rutgers U., 1968-69; prof. history, dean faculty arts and scis. U. Va., Charlottesville, 1969-71, v.p., provost, 1971-81, Commonwealth prof. history, from 1975, prof. emeritus, until 1991; tchr. U. Calif. at Berkeley, 1957, U. Stockholm, 1959, U. Lund, Sweden, 1960, U. Aix-Marseille, France, 1962-63; Thomas Jefferson vis. fellow Downing Coll., U. Cambridge, Eng., fall 1976. Author: The Socialist Party of America: A History, 1955, The Decline of American Communism, 1959, Twentieth Century America, 1963, Between the Wars, 1965, 2d edit., 1979; co-author: A History of Teachers College Columbia University, 1954; editor: The Great Depression, 1960, Beatrice Webb's American Diary, 1898, 1963, Progressivism and Postwar Reaction, 1966. Served with USAAF, 1943-45. Mem. Orgn. Am. Historians (past exec. com.), Va. Hist. Soc. (trustee 1981-91), Am. Hist. Assn., So. Hist. Assn. Home: Charlottesville Va. Died Nov. 8, 1991; buried U. Va. Cemetery, Charlottesville, Va.

SHANTARAM, VANKUDRE, motion picture director, producer, actor; b. Nov. 18, 1901; student Kolhapur High Sch. Founder, mem. Prabhat Film Co., Poona; former chief producer Govt. India Films Div.; mem. Censor Bd., Film Adv. Bd., Film Enquiry Com.; dir., producer numerous films, including King of Ayodhya, Chandrasena, Duniya-na-mane, Shakuntala, Ramjoshi, Amar Bhoopali, Jhanak Jhanak Payal Baaje, Do Ankhen Barah Haath. Recipient Berlin Gold Bear award. Internat. Catholic award, Hollywood Fgn. Press award. Died Oct. 28, 1990; cremated. Home: Bombay India

SHAPIRO, HARRY LIONEL, physical anthropologist, educator; b. Boston, Mar. 19, 1902; s. Jacob and Rose (Clemens) S.; children—Thomas C., Harriet R., James E. A.B., Harvard U., Cambridge, Mass., 1923, A.M., 1925, Ph.D., 1926. Asst. curator Am. Mus. Natural History, N.Y.C., 1926-31, assoc. curator, 1931-42, curator, 1942, chmn., 1942-70, chmn. emeritus, 1970-90; prof. phys. anthropology Columbia U., N.Y.C., 1938-73; scientific resident Lehman Coll., N.Y.C., from 1979. Author: Heritage of the Bounty: The Story of the Pitcairn Island Through Six Generations, 1936, Migration and Environment, 1939, Aspects of Culture, 1956, The Jewish People: A Biological History, 1960; editor: Man, Culture and Society, 1956; Peking Man, 1975. Bd. dirs. cons. Louise Wise Services for Children, N.Y.C., 1985-90. Recipient Theodore Roosevelt Disting. Service medal, 1964; Contbn. to Sci. award N.Y. Acad. Scis., 1977; Research in Forensic Anthropology award Am. Acad. Forensic Scis., 1983; named hon. assoc. Bernice P. Bishop Mus., Honolulu. Mem. Am. Anthrop. Assn. (pres. 1948), Am. Ethnol. Soc. (pres. 1942-43), Am. Eugenics Soc. (pres. 1955-62), Nat. Acad. Scis., Am. Acad. Arts and Scis., N.Y. Acad. Scis. (anthropology chmn.). Home: New York N.Y. Died Jan. 7, 1990; buried Pine Plains, N.Y.

SHAPIRO, MOSES, electronics manufacturing company executive; b. N.Y.C., Nov. 30, 1910; s. Samuel and Rachel (Gochberg) S.; m. Barbara Ann Hewson, Dec. 27, 1970; children by previous marriage—Robert B., Susan J., William B. Student, Fordam U., 1929; LL.B., St. Lawrence U., 1932. Bar: N.Y. bar 1933. Pvt. practice labor law, 1933-1953, indsl. relations cons., 1934-52, impartial chmn., labor arbitrator for numerous nat. industries, 1936-45; exec. v.p. Gen. Instrument Corp., N.Y.C., 1955-60, pres., 1960-68, vice chmn., 1968-69, chmn., chief exec. officer, 1969-76, chmn. exec. com., dir., 1977-88, dir. emeritus, 1988-90; mgmt. cons., 1976-90; Disting. adj. prof. bus. N.Y. U.; lectr. Practising Law Inst., CCNY; dir. Toys R Us, Inc., Welbilt Corp., Century Communications. Contbr. articles on indsl. relations to profl. jours. Bd. dirs. Theatre Devel. Fund; mem. Pres.'s Task Force Tech. Transfer, Nat. Planning Assn., CAMRAND Com., N.Y. Mayor's Contingency Task Force. Decorated commendatore dell Ordine della Stella della Solidarieta Italiana, Italy; decorated by Govt. of the Republic of China. Jewish. Home: Bellport N.Y. Died Mar. 19, 1990.

SHARFMAN, HERBERT, judge; b. Northampton, Pa., July 29, 1909; s. Meyer and Minnie (Caplan) S.; m. Dorothy Muriel Cohen, Feb. 8, 1932 (dec. 1987); children—Richard M., Jo-Ellen Crews. A.B., U. Pa., 1930; LL.B., Columbia U., 1933. Bar: Pa. 1933, U.S. Dist. Ct. (ea. dist.) Pa. 1935, U.S. Supreme Ct., 1945. Sole practice, Lehigh and Northampton Counties, Pa., 1933-44; atty.-adv. pub. utilities br. OPA, Washington, 1944-46, FCC, Washington, 1946-52; adminstrv. law judge FCC, Washington, 1952-74, Postal Rate Commn. Washington, 1974-76, part-time adminstrv. law judge, 1976. Mem. ABA, Pa. State Bar Assn., Lehigh County Bar Assn. Jewish. Died May 19, 1992. Home: Orlando Fla.

SHARKEY, JOSEPH THOMAS, banker; b. Bklyn., Jan. 12, 1895; s. Thomas J. and Catherine T. (Siebert) S.; m. Helen A. Flaherty, Feb. 11, 1935; children: Joan C. Sharkey Farrell, Catherine H. Sharkey Caulfield, Hlen T. Student, NYU. Acct. U.S. Govt., 1918-23; bus. acct. U.S. Civil Svc., 1923-33; alderman, councilman City of New York, 1933-66, akprotu leader, 1940-61, pres., 1949-51; exec. mem., leader 4th Assembly Dist., Bklyn., 1943-59; chmn. exec. com., leader Kings County, 1953-61; chmn., pres., CEO Dime Savs. Bank, Williamsburg, Bklyn.; pres. Export-Import Devel. Corp., N.Y.C. Author: Sharkey, Kent Laws, Sharkey Brown, Isaacs Law, numerous others. Pres., chmn. bd. Seneca Dem. Club, Bklyn., 1943-59; del. Dem. Nat. Conv., 1956-60; trustee Little Sisters of Sick Poor, Angel Guardian Home. Mem. Emerald Assn. L.I. (past pres.), St. Patrick's Soc. (past pres. Bklyn.), Friendly Sons St. Patrick K.C., Elk, Bklyn. Club, Bankers Club, Montauk, Downtown Athletic Club (N.Y.C.), Cathedral Club. Home: Brooklyn N.Y. Died Jan. 1, 1991.

SHARP, THELMA PARKINSON, committeewoman; b. Vineland, N.J., May 12, 1898; d. James Casper and Ina (Fenton) Parkinson; m. William Howard Sharp, June 29, 1941 (dec., 1957). Tchr. Vineland (N.J.) High Sch., 1922; mem. Cumberland County Tax Bd., 1923-26, pres., 1926-29; mem. N.J. State Bd. Tax Appeals, 1932-44; committeewoman Dem. Nat. Com., from 1954; mem. Assay Commn., 1936; pres. Civil Svc. Commn. of N.J.; mem. women's adv. com. World's Fair, N.Y.; del. White House Conf. on Edn.; organized March of Dimes Com. for Cumberland County, 1937; mem. Cumberland County coun. Girl Scouts, Am. Dem. State Committeewoman from Cumberland County, from 1922, vice-chair, 1948-56; N.J. del.-at-large Dem. Nat. Conv., 1924-56, mem. platform com., 1952, co-chmn., 1956. Mem. Bd. Visitors Vineland Tng. Sch.; v.p. bd. dirs. Roosevelt Pk. Colony for Aged; trustee Meth. Home for Aged, N.J. Welfare Coun.; adv. coun. Grad. Sch. Social Studies Rutgers U. Mem. Woman's Soc. Christian Svc. (past pres.), Am. Assn. UN (trustee N.J. br.), Am Assn. U. Women (past pres. Cumberland br., past state divsn. 2nd v.p., state legis. chair), United Coun. Ch. Women (past regional v.p.), Acad. Polit. and Social Scis., Am. Legion Aux., Newcomb Hosp. Aux., Cumberland County Hist. Assns., N.J. Art League, Vineland Little Theatre, N.Y. State Grange, N.J. Welfare Coun. *

SHATTUCK, CHARLES HARLEN, language professional, educator; b. Belvidere, Ill., Nov. 23, 1910; s. Deazro Harlen and Katherine Margaret (Hines) S.; m. Susan Elizabeth Deuel, Nov. 24, 1936; children—Kate Shattuck Green, Judith. A.B., U. Ill., 1932, M.A., 1934, Ph.D., 1938. Asst. in English U. Ill., Urbana, 1934-38, instr., 1938-43, asst. prof., 1943-48, assoc. prof., 1948-58, prof., 1958-79, emeritus, 1979-92, ann. humanities lectr., 1981, dir. U. Theatre, 1943-63, mem. Center for Advanced Study, 1961-62, 66; Henry Noble MacCracken Chair of English, dir. exptl. theatre Vassar Coll., Poughkeepsie, N.Y., 1948-49; vis. prof. U. Tenn., 1979, Lindsay Young vis. prof., 1981; vis. Disting. prof. SUNY, Plattsburgh, 1980; vis. prof. Ind. U., 1990; Folger Shakespeare Birthday lectr., 1983; dir. Folger Inst. Seminar, 1985; lectr. Mid-Am. Theatre Conf., 1984, W.Va. Shakespeare Conf., 1986, Ohio Shakespeare Conf, 1987, Skidmore Coll. Shakespeare Birthday, 1987. Author: Bulwer and Macready, 1958, William Charles Macready's King John, 1962, Mr. Macready Produces As You Like It, 1963, The Shakespeare Promptbooks, 1965, The Hamlet of Edwin Booth, 1969, John Philip Kemble Promptbooks, 1975, Shakespeare on the American Stage, vol. 1, 1976, vol. 2, 1987; Editor: Accent, 1940-60, Accent, An Anthology, 1973. Recipient George Freedley award for best book on theatre, 1969, 76, 87, Bernard Hewitt award for best book on theatre, 1988; Folger Shakespeare Library fellow, 1959, 61, 74, 78; Guggenheim fellow, 1961-62, 68-69. Mem. Soc. Theatre Research, Am. Soc. Theatre Research (dir. 1968), Shakespeare Assn. Am. (pres. 1979). Home: Urbana Ill. Died Sept. 21, 1992. †

SHAW, ARNOLD, author, composer, educator; b. N.Y.C., June 28, 1909; s. David and Sarah (Coller) S.; m. Ghita Milgrom; children—Mindy Sura, Elizabeth Hilda. M.A., Columbia U., 1931. Exec. editor Musette Pubs., N.Y.C., 1941; dir. pub. rels., advt. Big Three Music Corp., 1944; editor Swank mag., 1945; dir. pub. rels., advt. Leeds Music Corp., 1946; v.p., gen. profl. mgr. Duchess Music Co., 1949, Hill & Range Songs, 1953, Edward B. Marks Music Corp., 1955-66; Lectr. Juilliard Sch. Music, 1945, New Sch., 1957; Fairleigh Dickinson U., 1964-65, U. Nev., Reno, U. Okla., 1971, U. Nev., Las Vegas, from 1977; Mem. nat. adv. bd. inst. for rsch.for black music Fisk U.; dir. Popular Music Rsch. Ctr. U. Nev., Las Vegas, 1985-89. Pianist on radio, 1926; orch. leader, 1932; TV producer-narrator-writer-composer: series Curtain Time-Gt. Musicals; host: series Window on the Arts, 1972-73; author: The Music Scene in the New Book of Knowledge, 1970-89, Lingo of Tin Pan Alley, 1950, The Money Song, 1953, Belafonte, 1960, Sinatra: 20th Century Romantic, 1968, The Rock Revolution: What's Happening in Today's Music, 1969, The World of Soul, 1970, The Street that Never Slept: N.Y.'s Fabled 52d St, 1971, The Rockin' '50s, 1974, 2d edit. 1987, 52d St.: The Street of Jazz, 1977, Honkers and Shouters: The Golden Years of Rhythm & Blues, (ASCAP-Deems Taylor award), 1978, 87, Music Scene, New Book of Knowledge Annuals, 1970-87, Sinatra: The Entertainer, 1982, Dictionary of American Pop/Rock, 1982 (Amb. of Honor award English Speaking Union), Black Popular Music in America, 1986, The Jazz Age: Popular Music in the 1920's, 1987 (ASCAP-Deems Taylor award 1988); Let's Dance: Popular Music in the 1930's; editor: Mathematical Basis of the Arts by Joseph Schillinger, 1948; co-editor: Schillinger System of Musical Composition, 1946; composer: Sing a Song of Americans, 1941, A Man Called Peter and Other Songs, 1956, Mobiles for Piano, 1966, Stabiles for Piano, 1968, Plabiles for Piano, 1971, One Finger Piano, Kiss Me Another, Night Lights, A Whirl of Waltzes for Piano, 1974, The Mod Moppet: 7 Nursery Rip-Offs for Piano, 1975, They Had a Dream: An American Musical Odyssey, 1975-76, The Bubble-Gum Waltzes, 1977, An American Sonata, 1978, Snapshots of Three Friends, 1980, The Lights of Christmas/Chanukah, 1980, Felicidad!, 1981, The Promise of Easter/Passover, 1981, Snapshot of Guido, 1985, The IASPM Preludes, 1986, Snapshot of Leonard, 1987, The Desert Suite, 1987, The Argentinian Suite, 1988, Biographics and a Certain Lady, 1988. Mem. Authors Guild, Am. Musicological Soc., ASCAP (Deems Taylor award 1968, 79, 89), Am. Guild Authors and Composers, Nat. Acad. Rec. Arts and Scis., Nat. Soc. Lit. and the Arts, Nat. Music Tchrs. Assn., Nev. Music Tchrs. Assn. (Nev. Composer of Yr. award 1973), Las Vegas Music Tchrs. Assn. (pres. 1975-77, founder, chmn. Bolognini scholarship awards 1976-89), Sonneck Soc., Univ. Music Soc. of U. Nev. Las Vegas (pres. 1980), Internat. Assn. Study Popular Music (co-chmn. Am. br. 1984-88). Home: Las Vegas Nev. Died Sept. 26, 1989; buried Las Vegas, Nev.

SHAW, (BENJAMIN) CHANDLER, history and political science educator; b. Ormond Beach, Fla., Apr. 19, 1896; s. Hiram B. and Susie (Andrews) S.;m. Lucile Byrd, June 16, 1939; children: Martha Alice, Anne Chandler. AB, Rollins Coll., 1919; PhD, U. N.C., 1935; grad. study, Am. Acad., Rome, 1931, Royal U., Perugia, Italy, summers 1932, 33, 36. Instr. U. N.C., 1932-35; mem. faculty Bethany (W.Va.) Coll., from 1935, head dept.history and polit. sci., from 1946; George T. Oliver prof. history and polit. sci.; vis. prof. W.Va. U., 1952-60. Author: Etruscan Perugia, 1939, Seven Centuries that Rocked the World, 1950, Nebuchadnezzar to Chirst, 1957. Helenistic and Roman Civilization, 1961. Johns Hopkins U. fellow, 1937. *

SHAW, JAY SADLER, business company executive; b. Chgo., Oct. 17, 1897; s. Solomon Benjamin and Etta (Sadler) S.; m. Cornelia Flood, Mar. 23, 1921; children: Jay Flood, Howard Gordon. Salesman Brown & Bigelow, St. Paul, 1921-24, dist. sales mgr., 1924-28, asst. sales mgr., 1928-32, gen. sales mgr., 1932-33, v.p.sales, 1933-40; chmn., dir. Shaw-Barton, Inc., Coshocton; dir. Coshocton Nat. Bank, Edmont, Inc., Ohio State Life Ins. Co. Chmn. Coshocton County Rep. Com. Mem. Ohio C. of C. (dir.), Town and Country Club, Athletic Club, Mason 32 degree. Unitarian. *

SHAW, WALTER RICE, political science educator; b. Greenwood, Ind., Jan. 25, 1896; s. Orien Bass and Margaret Estelle (Rice) S.; m. Doris West Bepler, July 6, 1922; children: Alice Louise, Norman Vincent. AB, Wabash Coll., 1917, LLD, 1964; postgrad, Yale U., 1919-20, U. Strasbourg, summer 1920, London Sch. Econs., winter 1922; Dr. en droit, U. Bordeaux, France, 1922. Asst. prof. history Washington and Lee U., 1922-23; instr. polit. sci. U. Wis., 1923-24, asst. prof., 1924-27, assoc. prof., 1927-32, prof., 1932-40; prof. and chmn. dept. govt. CCNY, N.Y.C., 1940-51; prof. polit. sci. and dir. grad. studies, internat. rels. Yale U., New Haven, Conn., 1951-64, prof. polit. sci. emeritus, from 1964; sec. Fellowships for Social Scis. Rsch. Coun., N.Y.C., 1929-32; vis. prof. Harvard U., 1934-35; head rsch. analyst divsn. polit. studies Dept. of State, Washington, 1942-43; tech. program expert Office Fgn. Relief and Rehab. Operations, 1943; assoc. Internat. Adminstrn. Columbia U. Naval Sch. Mil. Govt., 1944-45; chief orgnl., planning UN Interim Commn. on Food and Agrl., 1944-45; sec-gen. Conf. on Food and Agrl. Orgn. of UN, Que., 1945; adminstrv. cons. World Health Orgn., 1946-48; internat. study project dir. UNESCO, 1948-50; spl. cons. Mutual Sec. Agy., 1952; co-dir. UN Egyptian Inst. Pub. Adminstrn., Cairo, 1954-55; program staff U.S. Nat. Commn. UNESCO, 1964-65. Author and co-author of books on polit. sci.; contbr. articles to profl. jours. Capt. U.S. Army, 1917-19. Fellow AFS, Social Sci. Rsch. Coun., Guggenheim Found.; mem. Am. Polit. Sci. Assn., Phi Delta Theta, Phi Beta Kappa. *

SHAW, WOODY HERMAN, jazz trumpeter, composer; b. Laurinburg, N.C., Dec. 24, 1944; s. Woody Shaw and Rosalie Pegues S.; m. Maxine Gree; 1 son, Woody Louis Armstrong. Leader Woody Shaw Quintet, from 1975, performed in concert halls, colls., night clubs, community centers throughout, U.S., Can., Mex., Latin Am., Caribbean, Europe, Japan, Australia; toured Europe with Art Blakey's Jazz Messengers; albums include Blackstone Legacy, 1970, Song of Songs, 1972, The Moontrane, 1974, Love Dance, 1975, Little Red's Fantasy, 1976, Live at Berlin Festival, 1976, Rosewood, 1978, Stepping Stones, 1979, Woody 3, 1979, For Sure, 1980, Iron Men, 1981, United, 1981, Night Music, 1984; recs. with Eric Dolphy, Horace Silver, Art Blakey, Jackie McLean, Hank Mobley, Mc Coy Tyner, Dexter Gordon, Booker Ervin, Larry Young, Archie Shepp, Lionel Hampton. Named Number 1 Jazz Trumpeter, Downbeat Readers Poll 1978, 80; recipient N.Y. Jazz award, 1979; named Number 1 Jazz Album Rosewood Downbeat Readers Poll 1978; Nat. Endowment Arts grantee for composition 1977, nominated for Grammy award (2), 1978. Home: New York N.Y. Died May 9, 1989.

SHAWN, WILLIAM, editor; b. Chgo., Aug. 31, 1907; s. Benjamin W. and Anna (Bransky) Chon; m. Cecille Lyon, Sept. 1, 1928; children: Wallace, Allen, Mary. Student, U. Mich., 1925-27. Reporter Las Vegas Optic, 1928; Midwest editor Internat. Illustrated News, Chgo., 1929-33; reporter, then assoc. editor New Yorker mag., 1933-39, mng. editor, 1939-52, editor, 1952-1987; editor Farrar, Straus & Giroux, N.Y.C., 1987-92. Recipient Poses Creative Arts medal Brandeis U., 1985. Home: New York N.Y. Died Dec. 8, 1992. †

SHCHERBITSKY, VLADIMIR VAILIYEVICH, Soviet government official; b. Dnepropetrovsk Oblast, Ukraine, Feb. 17, 1918. Grad. Dnepropetrovsk Chem. Engr. Inst., 1941. Instr. Young Communist League Dist. Com., 1934-35; mem. Communist Party Soviet Union, 1941-90, Urkaine Supreme Soviet, 1935; engr. Dneprodzerzhinsk, 1945-46; head dept. orgn. and instrn. Dneprodzerzhinsk City Com., Ukrainian Communist Party, 1948, 2d sec., 1948-51, 1st sec., 1952-54, mem. auditing com., 1952-54, candidate mem. Cen. Com., 1954-56, mem., 1956-90, 2d sec., 1954-55, 1st sec. Dnepropetrovsk Oblast Com., 1955-57; dep. Supreme Soviet, Ukrainian Soviet Socialist Republic, 1955-90; mem. cen. auditing com. Communist Party Soviet Union, 1956-61; mem. Presidium, then Politburo, Ukraine Communist Party, 1957, sec. Cen. Com., 1957-61; chmn. Council of Ministers of Ukraine, 1961-63, 65-72; cand. mem. Presidium of Cen. Com., Communist Party Soviet Union, 1961-63, 65-66, mem. Cen. Com., 1961-90, cand. mem. Politburo, 1966-71, mem., 1971-89; 1st sec. Dnepropetrovsk Indsl. Regional Com., Communist Party of Ukraine, 1963-65, 1st sec. Dnepropetrovsk Regional Com., 1964-65, 1st sec. Cen. Com., 1972-89; dep. to USSR Supreme Soviet, 1958-90; mem. Presidium of USSR Supreme Soviet, 1972-90. Served with Soviet Army, 1941-45. Decorated Order of Lenin (6), Order of October Revolution, Hero of Socialist Labour (2) and others.Died Feb. 6, 1990. Home: Moscow Russia †

SHEA, FRANCIS MICHAEL, lawyer; b. Manchester, N.H., June 16, 1905; s. Michael Francis and Margaret (Muldoon) S.; m. Hilda Droshnicop, July 22, 1936; 1 child, Richard. A.B., Dartmouth Coll., 1925; LL.B., Harvard U., 1928. Bar: N.Y. 1930, D.C. 1946. Staff research project for Bernard Flexner, N.Y., 1928-29; asso. Slee, O'Brian, Hellings and Ulsh, Buffalo, 1929-33; chief of opinion sect., legal div. A.A.A., 1933-35; specialist, legal div. SEC, Feb.-July 1935; gen. counsel P.R. Reconstrn. Adminstrn., 1935-36; dean and prof. law U. Buffalo Law Sch., 1936-41; on leave of absence, July 1939-Feb. 1941, asst. atty. gen. of U.S., 1939-Oct. 1945, asso. counsel for the prosecution of major Axis war criminals, 1945; sr. ptnr. Shea & Gardner, Washington, 1947-89; Chmn. Atty. Gen.'s Com. on Bankruptcy Adminstrn., 1941-45, Jud. Conf. Com. Laws Pertaining Mental Disorders; dir. Joint Conf. Legal Edn., N.Y. State; exec. com., 1936-40. Contbr. to law jours. Mem. ABA, New York State Bar Assn., D.C. Bar Assn., Assn. Bar City N.Y., Maritime Law Assn., Am. Law Inst. (life). Democrat. Roman Catholic. Clubs: Metropolitan, Cosmos (Washington). Home: Alexandria Va. Died Aug. 8, 1989.

SHEA, WILLIAM ALFRED, lawyer; b. N.Y.C., June 21, 1907; s. Ashley P. and Olive L. (Martin) S.; m. May Nora Shaw, Sept. 16, 1937; children: William A. Jr., Kathy Ann Anfuso, Patricia A. Ryan. LLB, Georgetown U., 1931, LHD (hon.), 1971; LHD (hon.), St. Johns U., 1973, St. Francis Coll., 1974; LLD (hon.), L.I. U., 1986. Bar: D.C. 1931, N.Y. 1932. Ptnr. Shea & Gould, N.Y.C.; counsel liquidation bur. N.Y. State Banking Dept., 1934-36; asst. gen. counsel to supt. ins. N.Y. State, 1936-41; mem. N.Y. State Ins. Bd., 1956; trustee emeritus, sec., gen. counsel Cross Land Savs., FSB; dir., gen. counsel Interboro Mut. Indemnity Ins. Co., N.Y.C.; bd. dirs. Nat. Benefit Life Ins. Co., N.Y.C., Companion Life Ins. Co. Vice chmn. bd. Benjamin N. Cardozo Sch. Law, N.Y.C., North Shore Univ. Hosp., Manhasset, N.Y., Taft Inst. Two-Party Govt. Mem. ABA, Fed. Bar Assn., N.Y. State Bar Assn., Assn. of Bar City of N.Y., N.Y. County Lawyer's Assn., Bklyn. Bar Assn., Lawyer's Club of Bklyn., Sands Point Golf Club, Sky Club, University Club. Home: New York N.Y. Died Oct. 3, 1991; buried Trinity Ch. Cemetery, N.Y.C.

SHEATSLEY, PAUL BAKER, survey research director; b. N.Y.C., Aug. 30, 1916; s. Paul Weidner and Nina Genevieve (Baker) S.; m. Priscilla Ward Jones, May 25, 1940 (div. 1947); children: Pamela, Jo Ann (Mrs. Norman Cope); m. Natalie Bennett, May 31, 1947; 1 dau., Victoria. A.B., Princeton U., 1936. Editor Boonton (N.J.) Tribune, 1937-39; pub. relations dir. Newark Internat. Baseball Club, 1939; dir. field staff Audience Research Inst., 1940-42; Eastern rep. Nat. Opinion Research Center, U. Chgo., 1942-63, dir. survey research service, 1963-76, acting dir., 1970-71, sr. survey dir., 1977-86, cons., 1986-89; dir. field work wartime morale studies for OWI, 1942-44; studies Am. attitudes toward fgn. policy issues for State Dept., 1945-57; dir. nat. ambulatory med. care survey Nat. Ctr. for Health Stats., 1973-85. Editorial staff: Record Research, from 1961; co-editor: Blues Research, 1959-74; asso. editor: Am. Sociol. Rev., 1967-68; contbr. articles to profl. jours., Ency. Americana. Bd. dirs. Roper Center for Pub. Opinion Research. Paul B. Sheatsley Library dedicated at Nat. Opinion Rsch. Ctr., U. Chgo., 1986. Mem. Am. Assn. Pub. Opinion Research (pres. 1967-68, Disting. Achievement award 1982), World Assn. Pub. Opinion Research, Soc. Psychol. Study Social Issues, Am. Sociol. Assn., Am. Pub. Health Assn. Home: Chicago Ill. Died Jan. 15, 1989.

SHEEDY, HERMAN JAMES, investment banker; b. Fairview, Ind., Oct. 24, 1898; s. James and Roberta (Rush) S.; m. Lois Barbara Blout, Sept. 1, 1921; 1 child, H. James. With McDonald & Co. and predecessors, Cleve., from 1927, sr. ptnr., from 1944; dir. Educator & Exec. Co., Columbus, Ohio, Educator & Exec. Insurers, Educator & Exec. Life Co.; mem. bd. govs. Investment Bankers Assn. Am., 1962-65, Midwest Stock Exchange, 1955-58, vice-chmn., 1961-62; mem. Am. Stock Exchange. Active Butler U., Hiram (Ohio) Coll., Doctors Hosp., Cleve., Ohio Soc. Christian Chs., trustee, vice-chmn. Pension Fund Christian Chs., v.p., dir. Ohio Disciples Extension Corp. Mem. Union Club, Cleve., Athletic Club, Cleve., Shaker Heights (Ohio) Country Club, Delta Tau Delta. *

SHEEHAN, JOHN CLARK, chemistry educator; b. Battle Creek, Mich., Sept. 23, 1915; s. Leo Clark and Florence B. (Green) S.; m. Marion M. Jennings, June 2, 1941; children—John Clark, David E., Elizabeth Sheehan Watkins. BS, Battle Creek Coll., 1937; MS, U. Mich., 1938, PhD in Organic Chemistry, 1941; DSc (hon.), U. Notre Dame, 1963; DEng (hon.), Stevens Inst. Tech., 1980. Research assoc. Nat. Def. Research Com. Project, U. Mich., Ann Arbor, 1941; sr. research chemist Merck & Co., Inc., Rahway, N.J., 1941-46; asst. prof. chemistry MIT, Cambridge, 1946-49, assoc. prof., 1949-52, prof. organic chemistry, 1952-77, prof. emeritus, sr. lectr., 1977-92; Reilly lectr. U. Notre Dame, 1953; Swiss-Am. Found. lectr., Zurich, Basel and Bern, 1958; McGregory lectr. Colgate U., 1958; Bachmann Meml. lectr. U. Mich., 1959; A.H. Robins Meml. lectr., Richmond, Va., 1975; sci. liaison officer Am. Embassy Office Naval Research, London, 1953-54; cons. Pres.'s Sci. Adv. Com., 1961-65; chmn. Pres.'s Sci. Adv. Com. Chemistry and Biology; mem. Pres.'s Sci. Adv. Com. Ltd. War Panel, 1961-65; nat. counselor Gordon Research Confs., NIH; Blicke Meml. lectr., 1981. Author: The Enchanted Ring: The Untold Story of Penicillin, 1982, also over 150 sci. publs.; editor-in-chief: Organic Synthesis, 1958; past assoc. editor Organic Reactions; editorial bd. Jour. Organic Chemistry, Antimicrobial Agts. and Chemotherapy; holder 90 patents including basic patent on medically important semi-synthetic penicillin. Recipient John Scott award City of Phila., 1964; medal Synthetic Organic Chem. Mfrs. Assn., 1969; Outstanding Achievement award U. Mich., 1971; Oesper award for contbns. of hist. importance to chemistry, 1982. Fellow Am. Acad. Arts and Scis., N.Y. Acad. Scis., Chem. Soc. (London), Royal Inst. Chemists (London); mem. NAS, Am. Chem. Soc. (Pure Chemistry award 1951, Organic Chemistry award 1959, chmn. organic div. 1959-60, bd. dirs. 1966-69, 71-76, past chmn. grants and fellowships com., chmn. internat. activities com., nat. dir.), Sigma Xi. Home: Lexington Mass. Died Mar. 21, 1992; interred Battle Creek, Mich.

SHEEHY, JOSEPH E., government official; b. Washington, Conn., Jan. 2, 1898; s. John and Ellen (Kenny) S.; m. Madeline McGrath, Oct. 12, 1926. LLB, Georgetown U., 1924. Bar: D.C. 1924. With Fed. Trade Commn., Washington, from 1925; dir. Bureau Restraint of Trade, Washington, from 1950; adj. prof. grad. sch. law Georgetown U., 1959-64. Mem. ABA, Fed. Bar Assn. *

SHEETS, MILLARD OWEN, artist; b. Pomona, Calif., June 24, 1907; s. John Jasper and Millie (Owen) S.; m. Mary Baskerville, Apr. 25, 1930; children: Millard Owen, Carlyn Owen Towle, David, John Anthony. Student, Chouinard Sch. Art, 1929; M.F.A. Hon., Otis Art Inst., Los Angeles, 1963; LL.D. Hon., Notre Dame U., 1964; D.F.A. (hon.), Otis-Parsons Inst. Design, New Sch. Social Research, 1984. Dir. art dept. Scripps Coll., Claremont, Calif., 1932-55, dir. art dept. grad. sch., 1938-55; dir. Los Angeles County Art Inst. (now Otis Parson Art Inst.), 1953-59; pres. Millard Sheets Designs, Inc., Claremont, from 1954; artist, war corr. Life Mag., India-Burma, 1943-44; mem. U.S. Dept. State Specialist program, Turkey-Russia, 1960-61; guest U.S. Mus. Dirs., W.Ger., 1958; mem. conf. on humanities Am. Council Learned Soc., Corning, N.Y., 1951; works include Library Tower Christ the Tchr., U. Notre Dame, 1964; works include mosaic dome and chapel Nat. Shrine, Washington, 1968, 70; mosaic facade Detroit Pub. Library, 1960; two tile murals-facade Los Angeles City Hall E, 1972; one man shows U.S. and abroad. Author: Your Drawing is a Measure of Your Mind, 1983, subject: Milard Sheets: One - Man Renaissance, 1983; murals include Rainbow Tower, Honolulu, numerous bldgs., Calif., Tex., 17 USAF tng. schs. Recipient Grand award Artists Guild of Chgo., 1951; recipient award for contbn. to profession Am. Inst. Bldg. Design, 1964, Cert. of Achievement Bicentennial City of Los Angeles, 1981; named Guest of Honor Internat. Watercolor Exhbn., Art Inst. Chgo., 1938. Mem. NAD, Nat. Watercolor Soc. (pres. citation distinctive achievements), Calif. Watercolor Soc., Am. Watercolor Soc. (Dolphin medal 1986), San Diego Watercolor Soc. Home: Gualala Calif. Died Mar. 31, 1989; buried Gualala, Calif.

SHEFELMAN, HAROLD S., lawyer; b. N.Y.C., Apr. 15, 1898; s. Joseph and Henrietta (Lovett) S.; m. Madolene Whitehead, Aug 12, 1924 (dec. June 1955); children—Thomas Whitehead, June Henderson; m. Sylvia Rogers, 1958 (div.); m. Nona Proctor Church, 1977. Ph.B., Brown U., 1920; LL.B., Yale, 1925; LL.D., Seattle Pacific U., Brown U. Bar: Wash. bar 1926. Since practiced in Seattle; mem. Roberts, Shefelman, Lawrence, Gay & Moch, until 1978; counsel Roberts and Shefelman, from 1978; lectr. Sch. Law, U. Wash., 1930-57; Mem. Seattle City Planning Commn., 1948-71, chmn., 1950-52, 54-56; mem. interim com. nation-wide conf. on met. area problems, Lansing, Mich., 1957; chmn. Wash. Child Welfare Adv. Com., 1949-51; mem. Wash. State Bd. Edn., 1951-57; chmn. Wash. delegation White House Conf. on Edn., 1955; chmn. com. State Govt. Orgn., 1951-55; exec. com. Seattle Health and Welfare Council, 1950-52; chmn. State Citizens' Com. (survey state's pub. welfare problems), 1949-50, Seattle Civic Center Commn., 1956-72; pres. Seattle Municipal League, 1956-58; mem. adv. council Bonneville Power Authority, 1940-45. Mem. council Nat. Municipal League, 1955-75, Gov.'s Constl. Revision Commn., 1968-69; chmn. Wash. State Tax Adv. Council, 1957-59; bd. regents U. Wash., 1957-75, past pres.; trustee emeritus Brown U.; trustee Pacific Sci. Center Found., also pres., chmn.; hon. life mem. exec. com., past v.p. Yale Law Sch. Assn.; trustee Century 21 Expn. Served with U.S. Army, World War I. Recipient citation of honor Wash. State chpt. AIA, 1955, Disting. Citizen award Nat. Mcpl. League, 1961; Outstanding Citizen award Seattle Mcpl. League, 1961; Others award Salvation Army, 1963; Bishop's cross Diocese Olympia, 1956; Outstanding Alumnus award Brown U., 1970; Recognition award U. Wash., 1977; knight Order of Hosp. of St. John of Jerusalem; named Hon. Tex. Citizen, 1966. Fellow Am. Bar Found.; mem. ABA (ho. of dels. 1938-40, 54-56, past council on legal edn., council mcpl. law sect. 1948-61, chmn. sect. 1952-54), Wash. Bar Assn., Seattle Bar Assn. (pres. 1937-38), Am. Law Inst. (life mem.), Am. Judicature Soc. (past dir.), Am. Soc. Planning Ofcls. (dir. 1957-62, pres. 1959-61), Mcpl. Forum (N.Y.C.), Acad. Polit. Sci., Order of Coif, Phi Beta Kappa Assos., Phi Beta Kappa. Episcopalian (chancellor Diocese of Olympia 1952-80). Clubs: Mason (Seattle) (Shriner), College (Seattle), Washington Athletic (Seattle). Home: Seattle Wash. Deceased. †

SHELFER, A. GORDON, JR., transportation services company executive; b. Fort Benning, Ga., Dec. 4, 1943; s. Angus G. and Betty (Lewis) S.; m. Margo Lynn Carr, Jan. 12, 1963; children: Tad Douglas, Roger Adam, Andrew Gordon. B.S.B.A., U. Fla., 1965. Personnel mgr. Unijax, Inc. subs. IU Internat. Corp., Jacksonville, Fla., 1967-74; v.p.-personnel and indsl. relations Viands, Inc. subs. IU Internat. Corp., Jacksonville, 1974-76; v.p.-adminstrn. Pacific Intermountain Express subs. IU Internat. Corp., Walnut Creek, Calif., 1976-82; sr. v.p.-human resource Saunders System, Inc., Birmingham, Ala., 1982-84; exec. v.p.-ops. Saunders System, Inc., 1984-85, pres., chief exec. officer, 1985-86; sr. v.p. human resources Ryder Truck Rental, Inc., 1987-89; sr. v.p. Ryder Distbn, Resources, Ryder Transp. Resources, from 1989. Mem. U. Fla. Alumni Band, 1853 Soc., U.S. Soccer Fedn. (referee grade 7), Birmingham Track Club, 1853 Soc., MENSA. Republican. Presbyterian. Home: Birmingham Ala. Deceased. †

SHELMIRE, BEDFORD, dermatologist; b. Zachary, La., Jan. 19, 1894; s. Jesse Bedford and Mary Lousie (Christian) S.; m. Mabel Battle Bunch, Apr. 25, 1925; children: Jesse Bedford, William Overton, David Sutton. BS, U. Tex., 1918; MD, Columbia U., 1920; postgrad., Paris and Vienna, 1923-24. Diplomate Am. Coll. of Physicians. Intern Bellevue Hosp., N.Y.C., 1920-22; instr. dept. dermatology Baylor U. Sch. Medicine, Dallas, 1923, prof. dermatology, 1928-42; prof. dermatology U. Tex., 1942-52; mem. consulting staff Parkland Hosp., Tex. Children's Hosp., Dallas. Contbr. articles to profl. jours. Mem. AMA (chmn. sect. dermatology), Am. Dermatol. Assn., Am. Soc. for Study of Allergy, Am. Soc. Investigative Dermatology (pres.), Tex. State and Dallas County med. socs., Idlewild Club, Dallas Country Club. *

SHELY, BENJAMIN L., manufacturing executive; b. Chaplin, Ky., Aug. 18, 1933; s. Clarence Willis and Dorothy (Hurst) S.; m. Janet Lucille Wilson; children: Scott, Todd. BS, U. Ky., 1955; MS, Ind. U., Bloomington, 1957. Successively chemist, rsch. specialist, sr. rsch. specialist 3M Co., St. Paul, 1957-69, applied rsch. mgr., 1969-71, lab. mgr., 1971-73, tech. dir., 1973-77, group internat. mktg. dir., 1977-81, internat. exec. dir., 1981-82, gen. mgr., 1982-83, div. v.p., 1983-85, group v.p., from 1985. Contbr. articles to profl. jours.; holder 15 patents imaging related. 2d lt. Signal Corps, U.S. Army, 1955-59. Mem. Nat. Assn. Printers and Lithographers (bd. dirs. 1984-89, Appreciation award 1989), Nat. Assn. Photographic Mfrs., Inc. (bd. dirs. 1985-87), Nat. Printing Equipment and Supply Assn., Inc. (bd. dirs. 1985-87), Graphic Communications Assn., Internat. Assn. Photoplatemakers, Carlton Soc. Republican. Methodist. Home: Stillwater Minn. Died March 8, 1990, Stillwater, Okla. †

SHEMIN, DAVID, biochemist, educator; b. N.Y.C., Mar. 18, 1911; s. Louis and Mary (Bush) S.; m. Mildred B. Sumpter (dec. 1962); children: Louise P., Elizabeth; m. Charlotte Norton, Mar. 1963. BS in Chemistry, CCNY, 1932; AM in Chemistry, Columbia U., 1933, PhD in Biochemistry, 1938. Asst. prof. biochemistry Columbia U., 1945-49, assoc. prof., 1949-53, prof., 1953-68; prof. biochemistry Northwestern U., Evanston, Ill., 1968-79, emeritus, 1979-91, chmn. dept. biochemistry and molecular biology, 1974-79; dep. dir. Cancer Ctr. Northwestern Med. Sch., Evanston, Ill., 1975-87; mem. Marine Biol. Lab., Woods Hole, Mass.; invited lectr. numerous seminars, symposiums, univs., world-wide, including Internat. Cong. Biochemistry, Brussels, 1955, Harvey Soc., 1955, Oak Ridge Nat. Lab., Brookhaven Nat. Lab., Weizmann Inst. and Hadassah Med. Sch., Israel, 1965, Royal Soc. London, 1975, Japanese Biochem. Soc., Tokyo, 1975, N.Y. Acad. Sci., 1978; Albert Noyes lectr. U. Ill., 1956; vis. prof. Karolinska Inst., Stockholm, 1947, Pasteur Inst., Paris, 1958-59, Weizman Inst., Israel, 1970, 72; exch. prof. Japanese Soc. Promotion of Sci., 1975; mem. rsch. coun. Pub. Health Inst., City of N.Y., 1963-68; mem. external adv. com. Worcester Found., 1972-79; bd. visitors Boston U., 1978-91; mem. adv. coun. chemistry and chem. engring, CCNY, 1980-91; adv. com. Searle Scholars Program, 1981-91, chmn., 1982-91; Camille and Henry Dreyfus Disting. lectr. Editor Physiol. Rev., 1950's, Biochem. Preparations, 1952-62, editor-in-chief Vol. 5, Jour. Biol. Chemistry, 1960-65, Archives Biochemistry and Biophysics, 1967-71; contbr. articles to sci. publs. Recipient Pasteur medal Pasteur Inst., 1951, Stevens award Columbia U., 1952, Townsend Harris medal CCNY, 1982; Guggenheim fellow, 1956; Commonwealth fellow, 1965; Rockefeller Found. fellow, Bellagio, Italy, 1987; Fogarty Internat. scholar NIH, 1979-85; grantee NIH, 1948-83, NSF, 25 yrs., Am. Cancer Soc., 18 yrs. Fellow NAS, Am. Acad. Arts and Scis; hon. mem. Japan Biochem. Soc., Swiss Biochem. Soc. Home: Woods Hole Mass. Died Nov. 26, 1991; buried Woods Hole (Mass.) Village Cemetery.

SHENKER, MORRIS ABRAHAM, lawyer, hotel executive; b. Kalius, Russia, Jan. 10, 1907; s. Abraham and Tziporah (Meshurith) S.; m. Lillian Rose Koplar, Dec. 23, 1939; children: Morris Arthur, Patricia Ann. A.B., St. Louis U., 1932; J.D., Washington U., St. Louis, 1932. Bar: Mo. 1932, U.S. Dist. Ct. 1936, U.S. Circuit Ct. Appeals 1939, U.S. Supreme Ct. 1940. Sole practice Las Vegas, 1975-84; part-owner Dunes Hotel and Casino, Las Vegas, 1975-85, chmn. bd., until 1984; parent corp. M & R Investment Corp., 1975-84, Vegas Village, Inc., 1975-79, Sierra Charter Corp., L.A.; chmn. exec. com. M & R Investment Corp., from 1975; bd. dirs. Continental Connector Corp., chmn. bd., 1977; pres., dir. I. J. K. Nev., Inc.; bd. dirs. Royal Bank of Mid-County, Aptos Seascape Inc.; v.p., dir. Nat. States Ins. Co., St. Louis; lectr. Washington U. Sch. Law, St. Louis U., Mo. U., Law Sci. Inst. of U. Tex.; mem. faculty Nat. Coll. Criminal Def. Lawyers and Public Defenders, from 1972, also regent; prof. charter session Nat. Coll., 1972. Contbr. articles to mags. and profl. jours. Pres., bd. dirs. Max and Thelma Manne Found., St. Louis, Morris and Lillian Shenker Found.; sec., bd. dirs. Sam and Janet Koplar Found.; bd. dirs. Israel Investors Corp., N.Y.C., Bd. Jewish Edn., 1954-64, Jewish Hosp. St. Louis, 1964-66, Am. Friends of Hebrew U., from 1964, Am. Friends of Tel Aviv U., from 1965, St. Louis Heart Assn., 1965-70, Council of Jewish Fedns. and Welfare Funds, Inc., 1969-73, Jewish Community Center Assn., 1970-75; hon. chmn. Nat. Meml. Day Observance for John F. Kennedy, Nov. 22, 1964; hon. bd. govs. Hebrew U. Jerusalem, 1973; cons., adv. to Pres. John F. Kennedy, 1960, 62; Mo. coordinator Johnson-Humphrey campaign, 1964; former mem. Democratic Com. of Mo.; del. Dem. Nat. Conv., 1948, 52, 64, 68, former Democratic committeeman, mem. nat. exec. council Am. Jewish Com., bd. govs., 1970, mem. exec. com., 1963, 64; life mem. bd. dirs. Jewish Fedn. St. Louis, pres., 1966-68; chmn. St. Louis Commn. Crime and Law Enforcement, 1969-72; asso. chmn. bequest and legacy com. Nat. Jewish Hosp., 1964; mem. nat. cabinet United Jewish Appeal, 1970-73; del. 1st constituent assembly Jewish Agy. for Israel, 1971; mem. nat. steering com. Washington U., 1966-68; internat. bd. govs. Hebrew U., 1965-73; bd. govs. Devel. Corp. Israel, 1959-77, Child Center of Our Lady of Grace, 1964-68, Technion, 1970-80; trustee United Israel Appeal, Inc., 1966; mem. adv. bd. Am. Jewish Congress, from 1964; bd. overseers Jewish Theol. Sem. Am., from 1964; mem. cabinet Midwest Leadership Inst., United Jewish Appeal, 1969, mem. nat. cash com., 1971; mem. bd. nat. adv. council of Am. com. Weizmann Inst. Sci., from 1967; bd. regents Congregation of B'nai Amoona; mem. adv. bd. Am. Med. Center, 1953-66; mem. adv. com. United Way Las Vegas, 1976, chmn. corp. gifts, 1975; founder Dismas House. Recipient citation City of St. Louis March of Dimes Telethon, 1960; Merit award Cardinal Glennon Meml. Children's Hosp.; Louis Marshall award Jewish Theol. Sem. Am., 1963; Human Relations award St. Louis U., 1964; Disting. Service award Am. Jewish Com., 1965; Nat. award Sertoma; Merit award Louisville Bar Assn., 1965; Honor award Lawyers Assn. St. Louis, 1966; Disting. Alumni award Washington U., 1967; cert. of merit Nat. Coll. Criminal Def. Lawyers and Public Defenders, 1974; Guardian of Menorah award B'nai B'rith Found. U.S., 1975; David Ben-Gurion award Israel Bonds, 1975; Humanitarian award Nat. Jewish Hosp. and Research Center, 1977; Keser Torah award St. Louis Rabbinical Coll., 1979; Human Relations award Inst. Human Relations of Am. Jewish Com., 1979; sect. of Little City dedicated in his honor, 1979; award Boys' Clubs Am., 1980. Fellow Nat. Coll. Criminal Def. Lawyers and Public Defenders; mem. Am. Bar Assn., Nat. Assn. Def. Lawyers in Criminal Cases (dir. from 1961, pres. 1968), Lawyers Assn. St. Louis (v.p. 1958, 59), Mo. Bar Assn., Bar. Assn. St. Louis, Order of Coif, Alpha Kappa Psi. Home: Saint Louis Mo. Died Aug. 8, 1989.

SHENON, PHILIP JOHN, mining geologist; b. Salmon, Idaho, Sept. 19, 1897; s. Philip and Mary (McKinney) S.; m. Marian Moyle, Aug. 22, 1929; children: Philip Michael, Patricia May, Marian Elizabeth. BS in Mining, U. Calif., 1922; MS in Metallurgy, U. Idaho, 1924; PhD in Geology, U. Minn., 1926. Geologist San Francisco Mines of Mexico, 1927-28; asst. prof. Mont. Sch. Mines, 1928-30; assoc. geologist U.S. Geol. Survey, 1930-38, regional geologist, 1942-44; asst. chief geologist Internat. Nickel Co., 1938-41, cons. geologist, 1941-42; chief civilian engring. and terrain intelligence team, Ctrl. Pacific U.S. Army, 1944-45; cons. geologist, ptnr. Shenon and Full, Spokane, Idaho, 1946-49, Salt Lake City, from 1952; head dept. mining U. Utah, 1949-52; vis. lectr. Stanford U., 1959-60; mem. Nat. Minerals Adv. Coun., 1950-51, Pres. Materials Policy Commn., 1950-51; com. on nonfuel minerals Resources for the Future, 1953; earth sci. sect. Nat. Sci. Found., 1954-56; U.S. nat. com. Internat. Union Geol. Scis., from 1961.; dir. Day Mines, Inc. Contbr. articles to profl. jours. Mem. AIME (past dir.), Geol. Soc. Am. (past counsilor), Am. Geol. Inst., Internat. Union Geol. Scis., Soc. Econ. Geologists (pres. 1961), Canadian Inst. Mining and Metallurgy, Atla Club (Salt Lake City), Spokane Club. *

SHEPARD, A. COURTENAY, consumer products company executive; b. N.Y.C., Apr. 19, 1939; s. Donald and Suzanne (Mercadier) S.; m. Faith Eland (div. 1980); children: David C., Scott B., Andrew M.; m. Belinda Kirby, Sept. 17, 1982. B.A., Brown U., 1961. With Procter & Gamble Co., Cin., 1961-68, Philip Morris Inc., N.Y.C., 1968-71; gen. mgr. R.J. Reynolds Foods, N.Y.C., 1971-73; mktg. and gen. mgmt. Colgate Palmolive Co., Brazil, Venezuela, Fed. Republic Germany, Can. and U.S.A., 1973-81; corp. v.p., pres. Colgate U.S.A., N.Y.C., 1981-89; mgmt. cons., 1989-91. Mem. Soap and Detergent Assn. (chmn. dir.), Grocery Products Mfrs. Can. (dir. 1980-81). Home: Westport Conn. Died July 10, 1991; buried Kennebunk, Maine.

SHEPARD, ALLAN GUY, state supreme court chief justice; b. Gardner, Mass., Dec. 18, 1922; s. Guy H. and May (Kendall) S.; m. Donna K. Soderlund; children: Lynn Kendall, Paul Vernon, Ann Kendall, Matthew Dean Soderlund, Christopher Nelson Soderlund. Student, Boston U., 1942-43; B.S., U. Washington, 1948, J.D., 1951; LL.M., U. Va., 1984. Bar: Idaho 1951. Asst. atty. gen. Idaho, 1951-57; chief counsel Idaho Dept. Hwys., 1952-57; pvt. practice Boise, 1957-63; mem. Idaho Ho. of Reps. from Ada County, 1958-63; atty. gen. Idaho, 1963-69; justice Idaho Supreme Ct., 1969-89, chief justice, 1974-76, 78-80, 87-89; Mem. Western States Hwy. Policy Com., 1959-63. Mem. youth and govt. com. YMCA Idaho, from 1953, chmn., 1969; adv. bd. Booth Meml. Hosp., Boise. Mem. Am., Idaho, 3d Dist. bar assns., Western Assn. Attys. Gen. (chmn. 1965-66), Nat. Assn. Attys. Gen. (pres. 1968), Delta Theta Phi. Republican. Episcopalian. Home: Boise Idaho Died May 27, 1989; buried Dry Creek Cemetery, Boise.

SHEPARD, FRANK PARSONS, investment company executive; b. St. Paul, May 16, 1895; s. Frank Parsons and Anna Walker (McMillan) S.; m. Katherine White McMillan, Oct. 11, 1919; children: Frank Parsons (dec.), Margaret McMillan (Mrs. Philip M. Harder), James Renwick. AB, Yale U., 1917. With Guaranty Co. of N.Y., 1919, v.p., 1929-34; v.p. Bankers Trust Co., 1934-60; mem. bd. trustees Robert Coll., Istanbul, Turkey. Mem. bd. trustees Inst. for Crippled and Disabled; dir., chmn. fin. com. Union Theol. Sem., N.Y.C. 1st lt. F.A., U.S. Army, 1917-19. Mem. Coun. Fgn. Rels., Century Assn., Yale Club, Down Town Assn. (N.Y.C.), Nat. Golf Links of Am. (Southampton, N.Y.), Maidstone (Easthampton, N.Y.). Presbyn. *

SHEPARD, HAROLD, legal educator; b. Paris, Idaho, Nov. 28, 1897; s. Joseph Russell and Rose (Budge) S.; m. Eleanor Stahman, June 9, 1921 (dec.); m. Marian Graham McCracken, Feb. 18, 1959. AB, Stanford U., 1919, JD, 1922; LLD, Tulane U., 1946. Prof. law, deanlaw sch. U. Wyo., 1922-23; assoc. prof. law Stanford U., 1923-26, prof. law, 1926-30, 49-61, William Nelson Cromwell prof. law, prof. law emeritus, from 1961; prof. law U. Chgo., 1930-31; prof. law and dean law sch. U. Wash., 1931-36; Wald prof. of contracts U. Cin., 1936-39; prof. law Duke U., 1940-42, dean law sch., 1947-49; vis. prof. law Columbia U., summer1929, U. Chgo., 1929-30, U. Minn., summer 1930, Stanford U., 1932; vis. prof. Duke U., 1939-40; vis. law prof. U. Utah, 1961-62; sec. Assn. Am. Law Schs., 1937-40, pres., 1941. Author: Cases and Materials on Contracts, (with H. Wellington) Contracts and Contract Remedies, 1957, (with Bill Sher) Introduction to Freedom of Contract, 1960. 2nd lt. U.S. Army, World War I.; served as maj., lt. col. and col. World War II; chief contract termination br., later of legal divsn., Office Chief Ordinance. Mem. ABA, Wyo. Bar Assn., Wash. Bar Assn., Ohio Bar Assn., Phi Beta Kappa, Order of Coif (nat. pres. 1959-61), Phi Alpha Delta, Theta Chi. *

SHEPHERD, SAUNDRA DIANNE, pediatrician, educator, consultant; b. N.Y.C., July 16, 1945; d. Archibald Ethelbert and Sylvia Marguerite (Allman) Shepherd; m. Peter John Payne Finch, Nov. 24, 1973; 1 dau., Abi Jean Shepherd-Finch. B.S., CCNY, 1968; M.A., Hunter Coll., 1971; M.D., Yale U., 1975. Intern NYU/Bellevue Pediatrics, 1975-76, resident, 1976-78, fellow, 1978-79; fellow in pediatric hematology and oncology, Bellevue Hosp., N.Y.C., 1978-79, Columbia-Presbyn. Med. Ctr., N.Y.C., 1979-80, staff assoc. responsible for pediatric sickle cell clinic, Columbia-Presbyn. Med. Ctr., 1980-81, clin. instr. pediatrics, 1981-84; attending physician St. Luke's Roosevelt Hosp. Ctr., 1980-90, Harlem Hosp. Ctr., N.Y.C., 1982-84; dir. pediatric tng. residency program in social medicine, 1986—; asst. prof. pediatrics and community medicine residency program in social medicine Montefiore Hosp., 1984-86; mem. adj. faculty Sophie Davis Sch. Biomed. Edn., CCNY, 1980—; adj. lectr. Fordham U. Grad. Sch. Social Work, 1982-86; social medicine residency program preceptor Martin Luther King Health Ctr., N.Y.C.; cons. physician Family Ct., N.Y.C., 1972—; cons. pediatrician Legal Aid Soc., 1972—, advisor for project for homeless familiesDied Oct. 8, 1992., 1983—; cons. pediatrician Legal Service Corp., N.Y.C.; mem. Emergency Com. to Aid Lebanon; vol. physician, El Salvador; delivered med. aid to Mozambique, 1986; mem. First U.S.-Nicaragua Colloquium on Health, 1983. Bd. dirs. United Meth. City Soc., advisor on med. aid for Mozambique, 1986; mem. pres.'s adv. com. for housing plans for homeless Borough of Bronx. Regents Coll. scholar, 1963, Woods Found. scholar, 1963, Nat. Med. Fellowship award, 1971-73, NIH Postdoctoral Tng. grantee, 1978, 79; recipient Luth. Brotherhood award, 1963, Fannie Lou Hammer award Fannie Lou Hammer Ednl. Organ. and Women for Racial and Econ. Equality, 1989, 90. Mem. Physicians for Social Responsibility, Am. Acad. Pediatrics, N.Y. Acad. Scis., Am. Med. Women's Assn., Am. Pub. Health Assn., Pub. Health Assn. NYC, Am. Orthopsychiat. Assn., N.Y.

Acad. Scis., Ambulatory Pediatrics Assn. Home: New York N.Y. †

SHEPPERD, JOHN BEN, insurance, banking and petroleum consultant; b. Gladewater, Tex., Oct. 19, 1915; s. Alfred Fulton and Berthal (Phillips) S.; m. Mamie Strieber, Oct. 6, 1938; children: Alfred Lewis, John Ben Jr. (dec.), Marianne and Suzanne (twins). LL.B., U. Tex., 1941; LL.D. (hon.), North Tex. State Coll., 1951, Chapman Christian Coll., Los Angeles, 1953, Southwestern U., 1955. Bar: Tex. 1941. Sec. State of Tex., 1950-52, atty. gen., 1952-56; ptnr. Shepperd and Meacham, Pub. Relations Cons., Shepperd and Rodman, Attys.; dir. Tex. Commerce Bank-Odessa, First State Bank-Gladewater, Blue Cross-Blue Shield, Dallas. Author: The President's Guide to Club and Organizations Management and Meetings. Former mem., chmn. Tex. Econ. Devel. Commn., Tex. Civil War Centennial Commn., Tex. Hist. Commn., Tex. Arts Commn.; mem. Tex. State Library and Archives Commn. Mem. Nat. Assn. Attys. Gen. (pres. 1956), W. Tex. C. of C. (pres. 1966), Tex. Jaycees (pres. 1941), U.S. Jaycees (pres. 1947). Democrat. Mem. Christian Ch. Home: Gladewater Tex. Died March 8, 1990; buried Gladewater, Tex. †

SHER, JOANNA RUTH HOLLENBERG, physician; b. Winnipeg, Man., Can., May 23, 1933; came to U.S., 1949, naturalized, 1958; d. Joseph and Dorothy Hollenberg; m. Norman Sher, Dec. 28, 1955; children: Jonathan Aaron, Katherine Amy. AB, U. Chgo., 1952, BS, 1956, MD, 1956. Rotating intern Kings County Hosp., Bklyn., 1956-57, resident pathology, 1957-58; fellow pathology Kings County Hosp., SUNY Downstate Med. Center, Bklyn., 1960-62; Nat. Inst. Neurol. Diseases spl. fellow in neuropath. SUNY Downstate Med. Center, 1962-64; asst. neuropathologist Kings County Hosp., Bklyn., 1964-70, dir. neuropath. lab., 1970-92; prof. clin. pathology, SUNY Health Sci. Ctr., Bklyn., 1977-87, asst. dean, 1977-83, disting. service prof., 1987-92; cons. depts. pathology Brookdale Hosp. and Med. Center, Bklyn., Maimonides Hosp. and Med. Center, Bklyn., Bklyn. Hosp., L.I. Coll. Hosp. Diplomate Am. Bd. Pathology. Fellow Am. Soc. Clin. Pathologists, Coll. Am. Pathologists; mem. Internat. Acad. Pathology, Am. Acad. Neurology, Am. Assn. Neuropathologists, Phi Beta Kappa, Sigma Xi, Alpha Omega Alpha. Editor: (with D. Ford) Primary Intracranial Neoplasms, 1979, (with M. Adachi) Neuromuscular Disease, 1990; author: (with R. Lechtenberg) Aids in the Nervous System, 1988; contbr. articles to profl. jours. Recipient Jean Redman Oliver Master Tchr. award SUNY Alumni, 1988, Alumni Disting. Svc. award U. Chgo., 1991. Died July 4, 1992. Home: Brooklyn N.Y. †

SHERER, CHARLES ROBERT, mathematician, educator; b. Red Cloud, Nebr., Jan. 3, 1895; s. Tracey J. and Sophia (Bradshaw) S.; m. U. Mirth Walker, July 20, 1917; 1 child, C. Richard. BA, U. Nebr., 1917, MA, 1921. Tchr. math. Blair (Nebr.) High Sch., 1917-18, Hastings (Nebr.) Coll., 1918-19, U. Nebr., 1918-28; prof. math. Tex. Christian U., from 1928, chmn. math. dept., 1928-62. Mem. Math. Assn. Am., Tex. Acad. Scis., Sigma Xi. *

SHERF, ARDEN FREDERICK, former plant pathology educator; b. Brooklyn Center, Minn., Aug. 7, 1916; s. Fred Elmer and Alice (Stubbs) S.; m. Jean Marian Voigt, Jan. 25, 1942; children: Carol (Mrs. Herbert Flower, Jr.), David, Stephen, Andrea (Mrs. Dale Smith). B.S., U. Minn., 1939; Ph.D., U. Nebr., 1948. Research asst. plant pathologist U. Minn., 1937-39; research asst. plant pathologist, then asst. plant pathologist U. Nebr., 1939-49; asso. prof. Iowa State U., 1949-54; mem. faculty Cornell U., from 1954, asso. prof. plant pathology, 1954-59, prof., 1959-81, prof. emeritus, from 1981, dept. extension leader, 1965-81; lectr. U. Calif.-Davis, 1961; cons. to Brit. Ministry Agr., 1968; cons. New South Wales Dept. Agr., Australia, 1975. Co-author: Vegetable Diseases and Their Control, 1960, 2d edit., 1986; Contbr.: articles to profl. jours. Served with USNR, 1942-46; comdr. Res. (ret.). Fellow AAAS, Am. Phytopath. Soc.; mem. Ret. Officers Assn., Sigma Xi, Gamma Sigma Delta. Methodist. Home: Ithaca N.Y. Deceased. †

SHERIDAN, HARRIET WALTZER, university dean; b. N.Y.C., July 21, 1925; d. Ben and Mildred (Wolff) Waltzer; m. E.P. Sheridan, June 30, 1950; children: Alison, Ruth. A.B. (Helen Gray Cone fellow 1945-46), Hunter Coll., 1944; M.A. (Trustee fellow 1944-45, Marjorie Hope Nicholson fellow 1945-46), Smith Coll., 1945; Ph.D. (Univ. fellow 1946-47), Yale, 1950; D.H.L., Rush U., 1980. Instr. English Hunter Coll., 1947-49; asst. to asso. prof. English and edn. Carleton Coll., Northfield, Minn., 1953-67, prof., 1967-81, Andrew W. Mellon prof. humanities, 1974-81, dean, 1976-79, acting pres., Jan.-Aug., 1977, chmn. faculty, 1971-73, chmn. English dept., 1973-75; dean of Coll., prof. English Brown U., Providence, from 1979; dir. Northwest Bancorp.; Field reader curriculum improvement program U.S. Office Edn., from 1963; tchr. NDEA Inst. in English, summer 1965, dir., summer 1966. Author: Structure and Style: An Analytical Approach to Prose Writing, 1966; Editor: Minn. English Jour, 1966-72. Mem. Gov. Minn. adv. council Minn. Right to Read Program; mem. Sloan Commn. on Higher Edn. and Govt.; mem. fellowships adv. council Danforth Found., 1974-80; mem. nat. bd. consultants Nat. Endowment for Humanities; mem. bd. Minn. Humanities Commn., 1977-79, mem. exec. com., 1978-79; mem. corp. bd. Bishop Whipple Schs., 1977-79; trustee Breck Sch., 1977-79; commr. Commn. on Instns. of Higher Edn., New Eng. Assn. Schs. and Colls., from 1980; bd. dirs. Butler Hosp., from 1980. Louis W. and Maud Hill Family Found. Research grantee, 1962-64. Mem. Nat. Council Tchrs. English., Minn. Council Tchrs. Egnlish (chmn. editorial bd. 1973-75), Internat. Reading Assn., AAUP, AAUW, MLA (exec. com. 1975-78, chmn. com. on public literacy 1978-80, mem. com. on teaching and profl. activities Assn. of Depts. English from 1980), Orton Soc., Assn. Minn. Dept. English Chairmen (chmn. 1973-77), Phi Beta Kappa. Home: Barrington R.I. Died Sept. 8, 1992. †

SHERMAN, HIRAM, actor; b. Boston, Feb. 11, 1908; s. Clifford L. and Gwendolen (Lawrence) S. Student, U. Ill., 1926-27, Goodman Meml. Theatre, Chgo., 1929-30. Asst. in drama dept. NYU, 1934-35, also tchr. other drama schs. Mem. Goodman Meml. Repertory Theatre, 1927-30; appeared summer theatre in N.Y. and R.I., 1931, 32; Broadway prodns. include Horse Eats Hat, 1936, The Cradle Will Rock, 1937, Julius Caesar, 1937, The Shoemaker's Holiday, 1938, Sing Out the News, 1938, Very Warm for May, 1939, The Contrast, 1940, The Winter's Tale, 1940, Boyd's Daughter, 1940, Mum's The Word, 1940, The Talley Method, 1941, Cyrano de Bergerac, 1946, ANTA, Album, 1948, The Alchemist, 1948, Town House, 1948, Four Twelves are 48, 1951, Two's Company, 1952, 3 for Tonight, 1955, Goodbye Again, 1956, Orpheus in the Underworld, 1956, Measure for Measure, 1957, The Merry Widow, 1957, International Soiree, 1958, The Killer, 1960, Mary, Mary, 1962, Where's Daddy?, 1966, How Now, Dow Jones, 1967-68, Anne of Green Gables (New Theatre, London), 1969; appeared with Am. Shakespeare Festival, nat. cos., London prodns. and summer stock; motion pictures included One Third of a Nation, 1939, The Solid Gold Cadillac, 1956, Mary, Mary, 1963, Oh Dad, Poor Dad, Mama's Hung You in the Closet and I'm Feeling So Bad, 1966; TV appearances, 1951—. With USNR, 1941-46. Recipient Tony award, 1953, also 1967-68 for best supporting mus. actor. Mem. AFTRA, SAG, Actors Equity Assn. (coun. 1939-70, 3d v.p. 1959-61), Am. Guild Variety Artists, Am. Guild Mus. Artists, Coffee House Club (N.Y.C.). Home: Springfield Ill. Died Apr. 11, 1989.

SHERMAN, JONATHAN GOODHUE, clergyman; b. St. Louis, June 13, 1907; s. Stephen Fish and Marion Louise (Goodhue) S., Jr.; m. Frances Le Baron Casady, Jan. 1, 1938; children—Thomas Oakley, Sallie Goodhue, Marilyn Nancy, Jonathan Goodhue. Student, Kent Sch., Conn., 1921-25; A.B., Yale U., 1929; S.T.B., Gen. Theol. Sem., 1936, S.T.D., 1949; D.C.L., Nashotah House Sem., 1971; L.H.D., Adelphi U., 1980. Fellow and tutor Gen. Theol. Sem., 1933-35; ordained priest Episcopal Ch., 1934; priest in charge St. Thomas's Ch., Farmingdale, N.Y., 1935-38; rector St. Thomas Ch., Bellerose, N.Y., 1939-49; suffragan bishop Episc. Diocese, L.I., 1949-66, bishop, 1966-77; instr. Holy Scripture George Mercer Jr. Meml. Sch. Theology, from 1956; Protestant chaplain Creedmoor State Hosp., 1940-49; sec. Trustees of Estate Belonging to Diocese of L.I., 1945-48; mem. nat. council Episcopal Service for Youth, 1945-56, pres., 1952-56; pres. Ch. Mission of Help of Diocese of L.I., 1944-51, Episc. Ch. Bldg. Fund, 1955-82; chmn. Joint Comm. Ch. Architecture and Allied Arts, 1956-65; mem. Standing Liturgical Commn., 1965-71; pres. 2d Province, 1970-73; mem. Dept. Christian Edn., 1937-44, dir., 1956-60; visitor Poor Clares of Reparation, 1966-85; mem. Anglican-Orthodox Consultation, 1968-77; vice chmn. Ho. of Bishops, 1974-76; dean Diocesan Leaders' Conf., 1938, 45, 46; chmn. Commn. on Relations with Eastern Chs., 1972-77. Author: The Christian Faith, 1935, The Spirit of Knowledge, 1961; Editor: Tidings, 1943-45. Mem. exec. council C.W. Post Coll., 1964-70; Trustee Ho. of Redeemer, from 1949, Gen. Theol. Sem., 1961-76, Walter H.D. Killough Estate, from 1966. Mem. Anglican Soc. (pres. 1953-62), Nat. Assn. Episcopal Schs. (gov.), Phi Beta Kappa. Clubs: Union League (N.Y.C.); Kiwanis, University of L.I. Home: Simsbury Conn. Died Oct. 27, 1989.

SHERRILL, FRANK ODELL, university trustee; b. Madison, N.C., Apr. 4, 1894; s. Charles Fletcher and Nannie Jane (Swaim) S.; m. Ruth Jenkins, Dec. 14, 1921; children: Frank, Jane, Ruth, John Charles, Rufus. Organizer, pres. S & W Cafeterias, Charlotte, N.C., from 1920, Select Foods, Inc., Charlotte, from 1942; dir. Liberty Life Ins. Co., Greenville, S.C., N.C. Nat. Bank, Charlotte, Am. Comml. Agy., Inc.; adviser on feeding naval pers. to sec. navy; spl. adviser comdr. 4th Army Command, 1940-45; mem. health bd., Charlotte, 1938-46. Dir. YMCA's of Carolinas; trustee Duke U. Recipient Bronze award Am. Restaurant Hall of Fame, 1951. Mem. Nat. Restaurant Assn. (pres. 1936-37), Charlotte C. of C., Omicron Delta Kappa. Methodist. *

SHERRILL, FRED GLOVER, corporate executive; b. East Hampton, N.Y., Dec. 9, 1894; s. Abram Elisha and nettie Irene (Glover) S.; m. Martha Griffin Arterburn, Feb. 2, 1920; children: Susan V., Peter N., Stephen M. BS, U.S. Mil. Acad., 1918. With J.G. Boswell Co., Ariz., 1926-42, 45-59; cons. J.G. Boswell Co., from 1959; chmn. bd. L.A. br. Fed. Res. Bank, San Francisco, 1946-52; pres. Western Cotton Shippers, 1950-51; dir. Tulare Lake Basin Water Storage Dist., from 1946, Farmer's Investment Co., from 1949, Citizen's Comml. Trust and Savs. Bank, Pasadena, Calif., from 1953, Gen. Dynamics Corp., 1960-62; adviser on cotton export to sec. of agr., 1946-49. Bd. dirs. John Tracy Clinic, from 1951. Commd. 2d lt. U.S. Army 1918, advanced through grades to col. 1943. Decorated Disting. Svc. medal. *

SHERRILL, HELEN HARDWICKE, dean; b. Sherman, Tex., June 24, 1898; d. George and Mattie (Cunningham) Hardwicke; m. Lewis Joseph Sherrill, May 12, 1921; children: John, Mary Durham. AB, Hollins Coll., 1920; MSW, Kent Sch. Social Work, 1942. Rschr. positive mental heatlh, rschr. in schs., therapist Child Guidance Clinic, Louisville, 1943-50, 57-62; rschr. accidents in children Presbyn.-Columbia Hosp., N.Y.C., 1951; lectr., counsellor students Barnard Coll., 1952-57; dean women Union Theol. Sem., N.Y.C., from 1962. Author: (with Lewis Sherrill) Becoming a Christian, 1943, Sex Education Through Family Living, 1954, The Child in Crisis, 1956, Christian Parenthood, 1964; contbr. articles to profl. jours. Mem. NASW, Am. Orthopsychiat. Assn. *

SHERRY, ARTHUR HARNETT, legal educator; b. Berkeley, Calif., Mar. 10, 1908; s. Arthur Valentine and Cecilia Delphine (Harnett) S.; m. Barbara Hurley, Nov. 7, 1934 (dec. 1945); children—Suzanne, Judith; m. Mary Ellen Leary, July 25, 1949; 1 child, Virginia. A.B., St. Mary's Coll., Moraga, Calif., 1929; J.D., U. Calif.-Berkeley, 1932. Bar: Calif. 1932, U.S. Supreme Ct. 1951. Asst. dist. atty. Alameda County, Calif., 1933-50; asst. chief counsel Crime Study Commn., Calif., 1950-51; chief asst. atty. gen. State of Calif., 1951-53; Walter Perry Johnson prof. law U. Calif.-Berkeley, 1953-75, prof. emeritus, 1975-86; prof. law Hastings Coll. of Law, San Francisco, 1975-85; chmn. adv. com. on criminal stats., Calif. Dept. Justice, 1951-60; dir. study commn. Insanity and criminal offenders Calif. Gov's. Office, 1960-62; dir. Calif. penal code rev. legis. project, 1964-69. Author: Administration of Criminal Justice in the United States, 1955; California Criminal Procedure, 1950. Contbr. articles to profl. jours. Bd. dirs. Hanna Boys Ctr., Sonoma, Calif., 1964-69; active Pub. Safety Commn., Piedmont, Calif., 1978-79. Served to lt. col. USAAF, 1942-45, ETO, NATOUSA. Decorated Bronze Star; recipient Signum Fedei award St. Mary's Coll., 1968. Mem. Am. Law Assn. (adv. com. model penal code project 1951-62), ABA (project dir. survey adminstrn. of criminal justice 1954-58), Calif. State Bar Assn., Calif. Peace Officers Assn., St. Mary's Coll. Alumni Assn. (pres. 1963-65), U. Calif.-Berkeley Sch. Law Alumni Assn. (Alumnus of Yr. 1975). Roman Catholic. Clubs: Bohemian (San Francisco); Faculty (U. Calif.-Berkeley). Died June 29, 1986; buried St. Dominic's Cemetery, Benicia, Calif. Home: Piedmont Calif.

SHERWOOD, DONALD, business executive; b. Watervillet, Mich., Oct. 16, 1897; s. Robert H. and Mary V. (Brown) S.; m. Frances Wellington, Oct. 19, 1922; children: Donald Henry, Arthur W., Frances W. BS, Purdue U., 1920. With Elliott Machine Corp., Balt., v.p., from 1945; also dir.; dir. Ellicott-Brandt, Balt., McConway-Torley, Pitts., Timberland-Elliott, Can., Mercantile Safe Deposit & Trust Co., Balt., Chesapeake & Potomac Telephone Co., Wilmington Truck Rental Co. *

SHIELDS, WILLIAM MAURICE, wood products company executive; b. Vancouver, Wash., Feb. 24, 1937; s. Marshall Joseph and Pearl Elizabeth (Wardle) S.; m. Catherine Diane D'Orsa, June 16, 1962; children: Debi, Janelle, Jackie. B.S. in Bus. Adminstrn., U. Oreg., 1959. Prodn. supt. Willamette Industries, Inc., Lebanon, Oreg., 1970-71, prodn. mgr., 1971-73; gen. prodn. mgr. Willamette Industries, Inc., Albany, Oreg., 1973-76; sr. v.p. Willamette Industries, Inc., Ruston, La., 1976-80; exec. v.p. Willamette Industries, Inc., Portland, Oreg., 1980-91; with Weyerhaeuser, Washington, from 1991. Served to 1st lt. U.S. Army, 1960-62. Mem. Nat. Forest Products Assn. (bd. govs., chmn. bd. dirs.), Western Wood Products Assn. (bd. dirs. from 1982). Republican. Home: Kent Wash. Deceased. †

SHIELY, ALBERT RAYMOND, JR., air force officer; b. St. Paul, July 14, 1920; s. Albert Raymond and Helene (Paulet) S.; m. Edith C. Morrison, Sept. 9, 1944; children: Diane M., Albert Raymond III, Barbara J. B.S., U.S. Mil. Acad., 1943; M.S., U. Ill., 1947; grad., Indsl. Coll. Armed Forces, 1962. Served with Minn. N.G., 1938-40; commd. 2d lt. Air Corps, U.S. Army, 1943; advanced through grades to maj. gen. USAF, 1970; exchange officer with RAF, 1949-51; research and devel. engr., program dir. for devel. Air Def. Systems and Air Traffic Control Systems, 1951-65; vice comdr. electronic systems div. Air Force Systems Command, 1965-67; comdr. European comm. area Air Force Comm. Svc., 1967-69, vice comdr., 1969-71; comdr. electronics systems div. L.G. Hanscom Field, Bedford, Mass., 1971-74; selectman Town of Barrington (N.H.), 1978-81. Commr. Little League, Syosset, N.Y., 1955-57; commr. Rhineland Dist. Boy Scouts Am., 1967-69; mem. Okaw Valley council, from 1969.

Decorated D.S.M., Legion of Merit with 3 oak leaf clusters, Air medal, Air Force Commendation medal.; recipient Disting. Alumnus award U. Ill. Elec. Engring. Alumni Assn., 1976. Mem. Air Force Assn., Ret. Officers Assn., Sigma Nu. Roman Catholic. Club: Kiwanis. Home: Barrington N.H. Died Feb. 27, 1989; buried U.S. Mil. Acad., West Point, N.Y.

SHIMER, WILLIAM ALLISON, educator; b. Freed, W.Va., May 17, 1894; s. Elgridge Ellsworth and Celestine (Elliott) S.; children: Adair, Ellot Richmond; m. Dorothy E. Blair. Diploma, Glenville (W.Va.) Tchrs. Coll., 1914; AB, Harvard, 1918, AM, 1925, PhD, 1925; AM, U. Rochester, 1922; Harvard fellow, U. Paris, 1925-26; LLD, George Washington U., 1938. Began as tchr. W.Va. rural schs., 1910; sec. Student Y.M.C.A., Rochester, 1919-22; exec. sec. Harvard Grad. Schs. Soc., 1923-25; instr. philosophy Ohio State U., 1926-29, asst. prof., 1929-30; gen. sec. Found. Moral Leadership, N.Y.C., 1930-32; pres. philosophy and psuchology sect. Ohio Coll. Assn., 1927-30; asst. sec. United Chpts. Phi Beta Kappa Found., 1930-31, sec., 1931-43; founder and editor The Am. Scholar, 1931-43; editor The Key Reporter, 1935-42; dean faculty, John Howard Harris prof. of Philosophy Bucknell U., 1940-43; pres. Marietta Coll., 1945-47; librn. Maunaolu Coll., Maui, Hawaii, from 1960; vis. sr. prof. philos. U. Hawaii, 1947-51; exec. officer U.S. Ednl Commn. for France, 1949-50. Contbr. to periodicals, including Internat. Jour. of Ethics, The Personalist, The Monist, The Am. Scholar. Co-dir. Asia-Pacific div. World Brotherhood, 1951-58, Hawaii chpt., 1958-60, edit. and studies sec., 1958-60; chmn. World's Sunday Sch. Assn., 1941-45; mem. Internat. Coun. Religious Edn.; com. acad. freedom Assn. Am. Colls.; com. accrediting procedure North Ctrl. Assn. Colls.; com. accreditation Ohio Coll Assn. Lt. USNR. Fellow AAAS; mem. AAUP, Am. Philos. Assn., Am. LEgion, Phi Beta Kappa, War Work Coun. (religious and ednl. sec.), Rotary, Harvard Club. *

SHIPLEY, JAMES ROSS, designer, educator; b. Marion, Ohio, Dec. 26, 1910; s. Jay R. and Anna M. (Bolley) S.; m. Dorothy J. Elliott, May 29, 1941; children—Ann, Robert E. and David E. Diploma, Cleve. Inst. Art, 1935; B.S., Western Res. U., 1936; grad. student, U. So. Calif., summer 1940; A.M., U. Ill., 1949. Artist J.H. Maish Advt. Agy., 1929-31; designer styling sect. Gen. Motors Corp., 1936-38; salesman Procter and Gamble Co., 1938-39; instr. art, charge curriculum indsl. design U. Ill., Urbana, 1939-41, assoc., 1941-45, asst. prof., 1945-48, assoc. prof., 1949, prof., 1949-78, prof. emeritus, 1978-90, head dept. art and design, 1956-77; prof., acting head dept. art Pa. State U., University Park, 1978-79; art dir. VioBin Corp., 1944-54; design cons., from 1944; acad. dir. advanced studies for designers. Inst. Contemporary Art, 1958. Exhibited paintings Cleve. Mus. Art, Detroit Inst. Arts, designs, Automobile and Culture-Detroit Style, Detroit Inst. Arts, 1985. Mem. visual arts com. Festival of Americas, Chgo., 1959; mem. Exploratory com. visual arts Am. Council Learned Socs., 1949, Ill. Bd. Higher Edn. com. Z on grad. and profl. edn. in humanities and arts, 1969-70; mem. visual arts panel Ill. Arts Council, 1971-76; cons. Ind. Commn. for Higher Edn., 1976. Fellow Nat. Assn. Schs. Art (v.p. 1960-61, pres. 1961-63, major writer standards, procedures and manuals for accrediting profl. programs in art); mem. Am. Soc. Indsl. Designers (ednl. sec. 1959-61), Indsl. Design Edn. Assn. (pres. 1959-61), Indsl. Designers Inst. (chmn. edn. com.; vice chmn. Midwest chpt. 1949), Citizens Ednl. Coun., Midwest Coll. Art Conf. (pres. 1961- 62), Marion Country Archers (pres. 1929-31), Dial Club, Kiwanis, Alpha Beta Delta (pres. 1933-34). Presbyterian. Home: Champaign Ill. Died Jan. 10, 1990.

SHIRKY, SAM(UEL) B(RYAN), chemistry educator; b. Norborne, Mo., Oct. 9, 1896; s. Gideon Bowman and Eugenia (Mansur) S.; m. Frances Marguerite Forbes, June 6, 1918; 1 child, Frances Marguerite (Mrs. Norman D. Asel). BS, U. Mo., 1918, MA, 1919. Asst. dept. agrl. chemistry U. Mo., 1918-19, supt. short courses, asst. to dean and dir., asst. prof. of agr. Coll. Agr., 1920-29, assoc. prof., 1929-40, prof. agr., from 1941, assoc. dean faculty Coll. Agr., 1946-62, assoc. dean emeritus, from 1962, assoc. dir. agrl. expt. sta., 1948-62, assoc. dir. emeritus, from 1962, dir. Tech. Edn. Svcs., from 1962; operated farm near Richmond, Mo., 1920; sec.-treas. U. Mo. Coll. Agr. Found., 1941-63. Fellow AAAS; mem. NEA, Kiwanis (pres. 1934), Kappa Sigma, Gamma Sigma Delta (nat. pres. 1950-52), Alpha Zeta, Gamma Alpha. Methodist. *

SHIRLEY, DAVID ALLEN, chemist, educator; b. Knoxville, Tenn., Sept. 15, 1918; s. John Fletcher and Tennie Marie (Beets) S.; m. Ruth Charlotte Wright, Aug. 30, 1941; children: Carolyn R., Allen C., Robert E., Elizabeth M. B.S. in Chemistry, U. Tenn., 1939, M.S., 1940; Ph.D., Iowa State U., 1943, postdoctoral research fellow, 1943-44. Research chemist E.I. duPont de Nemours & Co., Inc., 1944-47; asst., then assoc. prof. Tulane U., 1947-53; mem. faculty U. Tenn., Knoxville, 1953-79, prof. chemistry, 1955-79, head dept., 1962-79. Author: Preparation of Organic Intermediates, 1951, Organic Chemistry, 1964; Assoc. editor: (Gilman): Organic Chemistry-An Advanced Treatise, vols. III and IV, 1953; (Adams), Organic Reactions, Vol. VIII, 1954; Contbr. articles to profl. jours. Recipient Chancellor's Citation for extraordinary svc. U. Tenn., 1979. Mem. Am. Chem. Soc. (emeritus, chmn. E. Tenn. sect. 1959), Chem. Soc. (London, Eng.), AAUP, Tenn. Acad. Sci., Phi Beta Kappa (pres. U. Tenn. chpt. 1976-77), Sigma Xi (pres. U. Tenn. chpt. 1960), Phi Kappa Phi. Home: Knoxville Tenn. Died Aug. 25, 1988; buried Greenwood Cemetery, Knoxville, Tenn.

SHOCH, DAVID EUGENE, physician, educator; b. Warsaw, Poland, June 10, 1918; s. Henry and Hannah (Dembina) S.; m. Gertrude Amelia Weinstock, June 10, 1945; children: James, John. B.S., Coll. City N.Y., 1938; M.S., Northwestern U., 1939, Ph.D., 1943, M.D., 1946. Diplomate: Am. Bd. Ophthalmology (dir., vice chmn. 1978, chmn. 1979). Intern Cook County Hosp., Chgo., 1945-46, resident ophthalmology, 1948-52; practice medicine, specializing in ophthalmology Chgo., 1952-90; asst. prof. ophthalmology dept. Northwestern U., Chgo., 1952-66, prof., 1966-90, head dept. ophthalmology, 1966-83; head ophthalmology dept. Northwestern Meml. Hosp., 1966-83, Childrens Meml. Hosp., 1966-83 VA Lakeside Hosp., 1966-84. Editorial cons. in ophthalmology: Postgrad. Med; abstract editor: Am. Jour. Ophthalmology; author numerous articles and book chpts. V.p Nat. Soc. to Prevent Blindness, 1982-84; trustee Assn. U. Profs. (pres. 1973). Ophthalmology; bd. dirs., sec. Heed Ophthalmic Found. Served to capt., M.C. AUS, 1946-48. Recipient Merit award Northwestern U., 1974, Svc. award, 1986, Alumni medal, 1990. Fellow ACS; mem. AMA, AAAS, Am. Acad. Ophthalmology (sec. for instrn. 1972-78, pres. 1981, Honor award 1975, Guest of Honor 1988), Assn. Rsch. in Vision and Ophthalmology, Chgo. Ophthalmol. Soc. (past pres.), Am. Ophthalmol. Soc. (coun. 1982-85, chmn. 1985, pres. 1989, Lucien Howe medal 1990). Home: Glencoe Ill. Died May 8, 1990; buried, Chgo., Ill.

SHOCK, NATHAN WETHERILL, gerontologist; b. Lafayette, Ind., Dec. 25, 1906; m. Margaret B. Truman, Sept. 9, 1928; children: Joseph B., John H. B.S., Purdue U., 1926, M.S., 1927, D.Sc. (hon.), 1954; Ph.D., U. Chgo., 1930; L.H.D. (hon.), Johns Hopkins U., 1981. Research asso. dept. pediatrics, instr. physiology U. Chgo., 1930-32; research asso. Inst. Child Welfare; asst. prof. physiology U. Calif. at Berkeley, 1933-41; with Nat. Inst. on Aging NIH, 1941-76; sci. dir. Nat. Inst. Aging, NIH, 1975-76, scientist emeritus, 1977-89; chief Gerontology Research Center NIH and Balt. City Hosps., 1941-76; vis. physiologist Francis Scott Key Med. Ctr. from 1941. Author: Trends in Gerontology, rev. edit, 1957, A Classified Bibliography of Gerontology and Geriatrics, vol. I, 1951, vol. II, 1957, vol. III, 1963, (with George T. Baker III) The Internat. Assn. of Geronotlogy, 1986, (with D. Ingram, G.T. Baker III) The Potential for Nutritional Modulation of Aging Processes, 1991; editor: Biol. Aspects of Aging, 1962, Perspectives in Experimental Gerontology, 1966; Editor-in-chief: Jour. Gerontology, 1963-69; editor gerontology section: Biol. Abstracts, 1953; editor: Conf. on Problems of Aging, Josiah Macy Found, 1950-54. Mem. Md. Commn. on Aging, 1967-75; mem. North Am. com. First Pan-Am. Gerontol. Congress, Mexico City, 1956, Am. com. 4th Internat. Congress on Gerontology, Merano, Italy, 1957. Recipient Ciba travel award 3d Internat. Gerontol. Congress, London, 1954, award Gerontol. Research Found., St. Louis, 1956; Modern Medicine achievement award, 1960; Willard O. Thompson award Am. Geriatrics Soc., 1965; 1st Ann. Research award Gerontol. Soc., 1965; 1st Brookdale award, 1979; Superior Service award HEW, 1965; Disting. Service award, 1976; Disting. Service award Am. Heart Assn., 1965; Chancellor's medal Syracuse U., 1977; Ollie A. Randall award Nat. Council on Aging, 1977; Kasten Meml. award U. So. Calif., 1978; Disting. Achievement award Am. Coll. Nutrition, 1981. Fellow N.Y. Acad. Scis., Am. Psychol. Assn. (pres. maturity and old age div. 1952-53, chmn. research com. 1958-64), Am. Heart Assn. (council circulation), Am. Physiol. Soc., Gerontol. Soc. (sec. 1951-58, pres. 1960, chmn. publs. com. 1969-75); mem. Internat. Assn. Gerontol. Socs. (governing bd.; pres. 1969-71), Soc. Exptl. Biology and Medicine (chmn. Md. sect. 1956), Am. Inst. Biol. Scis. (chmn. com. basic biol. research on aging 1955), Am. Geriatric Soc., Soc. Research Child Devel., Psychometric Soc., AAAS (v.p. sect. N-med. sci. 1959); hon. mem. Socidad Argentina de Gerontología y Geriatria, Brit. Soc. Research on Aging. Home: Baltimore Md. Died Nov. 12, 1989.

SHOCKLEY, WILLIAM BRADFORD, physicist, educator; b. London, Feb. 13, 1910; (Am. parents); s. William Hillman and May (Bradford) S.; m. Jean A. Bailey, 1933 (div. 1955); children: Alison, William Alden, Richard Condit; m. Emmy Lanning, 1955. B.S., Calif. Inst. Tech., 1932; Ph.D., M.I.T., 1936; Sc.D. (hon.), Rutgers U., 1956, U. Pa., 1955, Gustavus Adolphus Coll., Minn., 1963. Teaching fellow M.I.T., 1932-36; mem. tech. staff Bell Telephone Labs., 1936-42, 45, dir. transistor physics research, 1954; dir. Shockley Semicondr. Lab.; pres. Shockley Transistor Corp., 1958-60; cons. Shockley Transistor unit Clevite Transistor, 1960-65; lectr. Stanford U., 1958-63, Alexander M. Poniatoff prof. engring. sci. and applied sci., 1963-75, prof. emeritus, 1975-89; exec. cons. Bell Telephone Labs., 1965-75; dep. dir. research, weapons systems evaluation group Dept. Def., 1954-55; expert cons. Office Sec. War, 1944-45; vis. lectr. Princeton U., 1946; vis. prof. Calif. Inst. Tech., 1954-55; sci. adv., policy council Joint Research and Devel. Bd., 1947-49; sr. cons. Army Sci. Adv. Panel, 1951-63; dir. research Anti-submarine Welfare Ops. Research Group USN, 1942-44; researcher on energy bands of solids, ferromagnetic domains, plastic properties of metals; semicondr. theory applied to devices and device defects such as disclosations; fundamentals of electromagnetic energy and momentum; mental tools for sci. thinking, ops. research on human quality problems. Author: Electrons and Holes in Semiconductors, 1950, (with W.A. Gong) Mechanics, 1966; editor: Imperfections of Nearly Perfect Crystals, 1952; holder over 90 patents; inventor junction transistor. Recipient medal for Merit, 1946; Air Force citation of honor, 1951; U.S. Army cert. of appreciation, 1953; co-winner (with John Bardeen and Walter H. Brattain) Nobel Prize in Physics, 1956; Wilhelm Exner medal Oesterreichischer Gewerbeverein Austria, 1963; Holley medal ASME, 1963; Calif. Inst. Tech. Alumni Disting. Service award, 1966; NASA cert. of appreciation Apollo 8, 1969; Public Service Group Achievement award NASA, 1969; Cert. Establishment of Bardeen, Brattain, Shockley Fellowship by Semicondr. Equipment and Materials Inst., Inc., 1977; Meritorious Inventors of 20th Century award L.A. Patent Law Assn., 1984; named to U.S. Inventor's Hall of Fame, 1974, Calif. Inventor's Hall of Fame, 1983, Infomart Info. Processing Hall of Fame, Dallas, 1988. Fellow AAAS; mem. Am. Phys. Soc. (O.E. Buckley prize 1953), Nat. Acad. Sci. (Comstock prize 1954), IEEE (Morris Liebmann prize 1952, Gold medal, 25th anniversary of transistor 1972, Medal of Honor 1980), Sigma Xi, Tau Beta Pi. Home: Stanford Calif. Died Aug. 12, 1989; buried Alta Mesa Meml. Pk., Palo Alto, Calif.

SHOCKLEY, WOODLAND GRAY, civil engineer; b. Crisfield, Md., June 3, 1914; s. Wilson Gray and Mary Ann (Woodland) S.; m. Tinia Hope Wise, July 9, 1939; children: William Gray, Rebecca Shockley McDougal. BS with honors, Antioch Coll., 1936. Registered profl. engr., Miss. Civil engr. U.S. Army Engrs., Little Rock, 1938-46; various positions Waterways Exptl. Sta. U.S. Army Engrs., Vicksburg, Miss., 1946-81; cons. Vicksburg, 1980-91; mem. Tech. Studies Adv. Com., Washington, 1957-68; chmn. Com. Residential Slabs on Ground, Washington, 1978-79. Contbr. articles to profl. jours. Mem. ASCE (hon.), ASTM (hon.) (Merit award 1979, W.T. Kavanaugh award 1991), NSPE, Internat. Soc. Soil Mechanics and Found. Engring. Presbyterian. Home: Vicksburg Miss. Died Aug. 2, 1991; buried Green Acres Meml. Pk., Vicksburg, Miss.

SHOEMAKER, VAUGHN, cartoonist, painter, lecturer; b. Chgo., Aug. 11, 1902; s. William Henry and Estella Jane (Vaughn) S.; m. Evelyn Marian Arnold, July 3, 1926; 1 son, Vaughn Richard, Jr. Grad. high sch., Chgo., 1922; student, Chgo. Acad. Fine Arts; LittD (hon.), Wheaton Coll. (Ill.), 1945. With art dept. Chgo. Daily News, 1922, chief cartoonist, 1925-52; editorial cartoonist N.Y. Herald Tribune, 1956-61, 70; chief cartoonist Chgo. Am. and Chgo. Today, 1961-71; creator cartoon figure John Q. Public, 1930; syndicated Des Moines Register and Tribune, Nat. Newspaper syndicate, Chgo. Tribune, N.Y. News, 1930-71; instr. Chgo. Acad. Fine Arts, 1927-42. Author: The Best of Shoemaker Cartoons, 7 books, 1938-66; Permanent Editorial Cartoon Collection, Huntington Library, San Marino, Calif.; Permanent Editorial Cartoon Collection, Syracuse (N.Y.) U., U. Mo., Wheaton (Ill.) Coll., Chgo. Hist. Soc.; one-man water color exhbn., Obrien Galleries, Chgo., 1935, 36, Marshall Field Galleries, 1938, one-man oil exhbn., Masters Gallery, Carmel, Calif., 1973, El Prado Gallery, Sedona, Ariz., 1984; first telecasting of cartoons in Chgo., Sta. W9XAP, 1930; TV shows Over Shoemaker's Shoulder, WBKB, NBC, ABC, 1949-50. Recipient Pulitzer prize in cartooning, 1938, 47; Nat. Headliner's award Atlantic City, 1943; Nat. Safety Council Grand award, 1946, 49; Outstanding Achievement award, 1952, 53, 58; Sigma Delta Chi awards, 1945, 50; Freedom Found. Gold medals Valley Forge, 1949 through 1969; Christopher Gold Medal award, 1957; Lincoln Nat. Life Found. awards, 1955, 66, 68. Mem. Christian Bus. Men's Com., The Gideons; mem. Nat. Cartoonist Soc. N.Y., Assn. Am. Editorial Cartoonists, Soc. Western Artists San Francisco, Sigma Delta Chi. Clubs: Palette and Chisel Acad. Fine Art (Chgo.) (hon.), Ill. Athletic (Chgo.), Jackson Park Yacht (Chgo.) (dir. 1948), Great Lakes Cruising (Chgo.) (commodore 1949), Chgo. Press (Chgo.), Chgo. Headline (Chgo.); San Francisco Press (San Francisco), Marine's Memorial (San Francisco); National Press (Washington, D.C.). Home: Carol Stream Ill. Died Aug. 18, 1991; buried Elm Lawn Meml. Park, Elmhurst, Ill.

SHOPE, LESLIE REED, public relations executive; b. Halifax, Pa., June 26, 1894; s. Charles R. and Frances D. (Behm) S.; m. Eleanor Hudders, Sept. 24, 1920; 1 child, Roger H. AB, Neff Coll., 1917; postgrad., Ecole de Aeronautique, 1919, New Sch. Social Rsch., 1926. Sales, advt. mgr. Glenn L. Martin Co., 1919-22; account exec. M.P. Gould Advt. Agy., 1922-26; prin. owner advt. agy. N.Y.C., 1926-34; dir. sales promotion Equitable Life Assurance Soc. U.S., 1934-42, head advt., pub. rels., 1946-60; cons. human comm., from 1963. Pres. Radio Free Europe Fund, N.Y.C., 1961-63. Capt. Air Corps., U.S. Army, 1917-19; col. USAAF, 1942-46. Decorated Legion of Merit, Croix de Guerre with palm (France). Mem. Internat. Soc. Gen. Semantics, Res.

Officers Assn., 50th Aero. Squadron Assn., Am. Legion, Army and Navy Club (N.Y.C.). *

SHORELL, IRVING DANIEL, plastic surgeon; b. N.Y.C., Aug. 29, 1898; s. Jacobus Myron and Fannie (Feiner) S.; m. Minna Weisenberg, July 20, 1920 (dec.); children: Irma Loraine, Joan Beverly; m. Marre Farrow Goodwin, Dec. 31, 1948 (div.). BS, Princeton U., 1918; MA, Columbia U., 1919; MD, Georgetown U., 1923; postgrad., Johns Hopkins U., Mayo Clinic, various hosps. in Vienna, Austria, Heidelberg and Berlin, Germany, Paris and London. Physician, surgeon Washington, 1923; house surgeon Georgetown Hosp., Washington; mem. staff Garfield Hosp., Galliger Meml. Hosp. and Emergency Hosp., Washington, Johns Hopkins U., N.Y. Hosp., Ruptured and Crippled Hosp., Hosp. for Joint Diseases, Polycline Hosp., N.Y.C.; prin., from 1924; chief plastic surgeon N.Y. Plastic Surgery Hosp.; founder, chmn. bd. The League to Prevent Accidents (now inc. with Nat. Safety Coun.), from 1936; organized and sent ambulance corps to France before German invasion, 1939-40; negotiated with U.S. Govt. to send ships for wounded and mutilated British citizens and soldiers, 1940; mem. commn. to negotiate for German refugees who were accepted by Dominican Republic; called by authorities to organize and plan for facially deformed victims Texas City disaster, 1947. Contbr. articles on sinus diseases and plastic surgery in med. jours. Adv. to State Dept. on S.Am. Affairs, from 1958. Decorated Legion of Honor (France), Commr. Order White Rose (Finland), Knight of Danneborg (Denmark). Mem. AMA, Washington Med. Assn., N.Y. County Med. Assn., N.Y. State Med. Assn., Golf of Paris Club (hon.). *

SHORT, LLOYD MILTON, educator; b. Knoxville, Ill., Feb. 3, 1897; s. James Francis and Ada Carlotte)Palmquist) S.; m. Bessie Alice Thayer, Sept. 6, 1924; children: Marjorie Lucile, Wlizabeth Ann. AB, Knox Coll., 1919, LLD (hon.), 1947; MA, U. Ill., 1920, PhD, 1922; LLD, Sioux Falls Coll., 1958. Inst. polit. sci. U. Akron, 1922-23; asst. prof. polit sci. and pub. law U. Mo., 1923-27, assoc. prof., 1927-29, prof. polit. sci. and asst. dean grad. sch., 1929-35, prof., 1935-65; dir. pub. adminstrn. ctr. U. Minn., 1935-61, chmn. dept. polit. sci., 1952-61; prof. pub. affairs Lincoln U. Pa., 1965-66; mem. staff Inst. fot Govt. Rsch. Brookings Inst., 1921-23. Author: The United States Steamboat Inspection Service, 1922, The Development of National Administrative Organization in the United States, 1923, (with C.W. Tiller) The United States Bureau of Navigation and Finance, 1942, (with C. Peniman and F. Flom) The Minnesota Department od Taxation, 1955; contbr. articles to polit. sci. jours. Sr. review and negotiations officer U.S. Civic Svc. Commn., 1942; chmn. spl. examining coms., Minn. Civil Svc. Dept., 1939, 42, 45, 55, St. Paul Civic Svc. Bur., 1944; chmn. adv. com. social sci. personnel U.S. Civil Svc. Commn., 1944-50; chmn. Minn. constitutional commn., 1944-48; chmn. Task Force on Overall Structure Minn. Self-Survey, 1955-56. 2d lt. USO, 1919-24. Mem. AAUP, Am. Polit. Sci. Assn. (exec. coun. 1935-37, v.p. 1951-52), Internat. City Mgrs. Assn., Midwest Conf. Polit. Scientists (pres. 1960-61), Pub. Personnel Assn., Am. Soc. Pub. Adminstrsn. (pres. 1960-61), Tau Kappa Epsilon, Phi Beta Kappa, Delta Sigma Rho. Baptist. *

SHORT, WILLIAM HOSLEY, architect; b. Warren, Mass., May 29, 1924; s. Walter Edwin and Mary Allen (Hosley) S. AB, Princeton U., 1949, MFA, 1952. Registered Architect, N.J., N.Y., Mass., Conn., Maine, Fla., Md. Apprentice Holden Egan Assocs., N.Y.C., 1952-55, Kenneth Kassler Architect, Princeton, 1955-56; supr. constrn. Solomon R. Guggenheim Mus., N.Y.C., 1956-60; ptnr. Venturi-Short Architects, Phila., N.Y.C., 1960-63; propr. William H. Short Architect, Princeton, 1963-74; ptnr. Short & Ford Architects, Princeton, 1974-91. Prin. works include: Guernsey Hall Condominiums, Princeton, 1974 (AIA award of merit 1975), Sandanwede residence, Nantucket, Mass., 1976 (AIA honor award 1978), addition to Woodrow Wilson Sch. and Library, Princeton U., 1980, Lawrenceville Sch. Master planning and new bldgs., 1985-90, Nassau Presbyn. Ch. addition, 1988, restoration Drumthwacket (N.J. gov.'s madnsion). Bd. advisors Nat. Trust Hist. Preservation, 1983-91; mem. Hist. Sites Commn. Princeton, 1970-85, N.J. State Rev. Com. Hist. Sites, 1980-82. With USAAF, 1943-46, ETO. Fellow AIA; mem. N.J. Hist. Soc. (bd. govs. 1987-91), N.J. Soc. Architects (hist. resources chmn. 1991), Hist. Soc. Princeton, Nassau Club. Home: Princeton N.J. Died Feb. 20, 1991.

SHRADY, FREDERICK CHARLES, sculptor; b. East View, N.Y., Oct. 22, 1907; s. Henry Merwin and Harrie (Moore) S.; married; 1 child, Henry Merwin; m. Maria Louise Likar-Waltersdorff, July 9, 1946; children: Alexander, Maria, Theresa, Marie Antoinette, Marie LouiseMaria Christina, Nicholas. Grad., Choate Sch., 1928; student, Oxford U., Eng., 1931; DFA (hon.), Holy Cross Coll., 1969; DHL (hon.), Sacred Heart U., Fairfield, Conn., 1988. Sculptor Descent from The Cross, St. Stephen's Cathedral, Vienna, 28 ft. statue Peter the Fisherman, Fordham U., main doors Life of Mary, Basilica of Annuniciation, Nazareth in Holy Land, Christ the Tchr., Fairfield U., 16 foot bronze Vets. Meml., Bridgeport, Conn., 18 foot aluminum statue Benedict the Moor, Pitts., Dionysius and Apollo, Bridgeport U., statues, Chgo., Washington, Pitts., Rochester, N.Y., Hartford, Conn., 10 foot statue St. Ann, Stanford U., St. Elizabeth Seton Shrine, St. Patrick's Cathedral, N.Y.C., 6 foot bronze triad Gen. Electric Hdqrs., Fairfield, Conn., 6 foot Risen Christ bronze Archdiocese Hdqrs., N.Y.C., 15 foot bronze FBI Hoover Meml., Washington, Christ, Rosary Hill Hosp., Hawthorne, N.Y., 12 foot marble Our Lady of Fatima, Vatican Gardens, Vatican City, 3 foot bronze St. John, Montgomery, Ala., bronze head St. Francis, Vatican City, 7 foot bronze Virgin and Child, Sarasota, Fla., 10 foot bronze Urban Builder, Stamford, Conn., 7 foot St. Francis,. Greenwich, Conn., 9 foot bronze St. Camilous, Stamford, statue of Lazarus, Resurrection Cemetery, Pitts.,other bronzes; represented Met. Mus., N.Y.C., Joseph Hirshhorn Collections, Vatican Mus., also others; also numerous portraits and small bronzes. Decorated Legion of Honor France, Knight Equestrian Order Holy Sepulchre of Jerusalem. Roman Catholic. Club: Century Assn. (N.Y.C.). Home: Easton Conn. Died Jan. 20, 1990; buried Resurrection Cemetery, Pittsburgh.

SHRODES, CAROLINE, English literature educator; b. Madison, Minn.; d. George H. and Clara (Blasing) S. PhB, U. Chgo., 1928, MA, 1934; PhD, U. Calif., 1949. Teaching asst. U. Wis., 1937-39; instr. Stockton (Calif.) Coll., 1939-46; prof. San Francisco State U., from 1946, chmn. English dept., 1964-73; core faculty Union Grad. Sch., from 1973. Author: (with Campbell, Van Gundy) Patterns for Living, 1940, Psychology Through Literature, (with Husband, Van Gundy), 1943, English at Work, (with Grant, Van Gundy), 1943, Approaches to Prose, (with Van Gundy), 1959, (with Josephson, Wilson) Reading for Rhetoric, 1962, 67, 75, 79, (with Van Gundy, Dorius) Reading for Understanding, 1968, (with Finestone, Shugrue) The Conscious Reader, 1974, 78, 85, 88, 91; editor: Studies in Language and Literature, 1973-75, Calif. Council for the Humanities in Pub. Policy, 1977-78. Mem. Am. Psychol. Assn., Nat. Council Tchrs. English, Assn. Depts. English (pres. 1969-70), Modern Language Assn. Home: Sausalito Calif. Died Mar. 18, 1991; cremated.

SHRUM, GORDON MERRITT, utility executive; b. Smithville, Ont., Can., Jan. 14, 1896; s. William Burton and Emma Jane (Merritt) S.; m. Oenone Ballie, May 30, 1929; children: Gordon Ballie, Laura Jane; m. Meda KEator, June 15, 1941. BA, U. Toronto, 1920, MA, 1921, PhD, 1923; DSc, U. B.C., 1961. With U. B.C., 1925-61, successively staff physics dept., dir. dept. univ. edn., 1925-53, dean faculty grad. students, 1956-61; chmn., pres. officer B.C. Electric Co. Ltd., 1961-62; chmn. B.C. Hydro and Power Authority, from 1962; chancellor Simon Fraser U., from 1963; dir. Atomic Energy Can., Ltd. Chmn. B.C. Energy Bd., Royal Commn. on B.C. Power Commn.; chmn. adv. com. rsch. and devel. Glassco Royal Commn.; head Can. del. 7th PAcific Sci. Congress, N.Z., 1949, 8th Pacific Sci. Congress, Manila, 1953. With Can. F.A., 1916-19, as lt. col. B.C. contingent Can. Officer Tng. Corps, 1938-46. Decorated Order Brit. Empire; recipient Mil. medal; silver medal in math. U. Toronto, 1920. Fellow Royal Soc. Can., Am. Phys. Soc.; mem. B.C. Rsch. Coun., Can. Assn. Physicists (pres. 1952-53), Beta Theta Pi, Univ. Club. *

SHUBSDA, THADDEUS A., bishop; b. Los Angeles, Apr. 2, 1925. Grad., St. John's Sem. Ordained priest Roman Catholic Ch., 1950. Ordained titular bishop of Trau and aux. bishop of Los Angeles, 1977-82; apptd. bishop of Monterey Calif., 1982-91. Home: Monterey Calif. Died Apr. 26, 1991; buried Monterey, Calif.

SHUGART, KENNETH LAVERNE, naval officer; b. Cheyenne, Wyo., Nov. 3, 1925; s. Kenneth Laverne and Helen Maude (Ladely) S.;m. Muriel Mary McDermott, June6, 1948; children: Kenneth Blair, Daniel William, Paul Mary. BS, US Naval Acad, 1947. Commd. ensign USN, 1947, advanced through grades to rear adm.; instr. U.S. Naval Acad., 1947-48, 53-56; chief staff comdr. Carrier Group I, 1972-74, Naval Air Force, U.S. Pacific Fleet, 1975-76; comdr. Tng. Command, U.S. Atlantic Fleet, 1976-83; chief naval edn. 2d tng. NAS, Pensacola, Fla., 1976-83; asst. to pres. Bapt. Care Inc., Pensacola, 1983-85. Decorated Legion of Merit (2), DFC (4), Bronze Star, DSM, Air medal (17), Joint Svc. Commendation medal, Navy Commendation medal. Home: Pensacola FL Died June 19, 1985; buried Barrancas Nat. Cemetery, Pensacola, Fla.

SHUMWAY, FRANK RITTER, corporate executive; b. Rochester, N.Y., Mar. 27, 1906; s. Robert Crittenden and Adelina (Ritter) S.; m. Hettie Beaman Lakin, Sept. 8, 1930; children: Mary Ellen Shumway Gaylord, Frank Ritter, Charles Lakin. AB, Princeton U., 1928; MA, Univ. Coll., Oxford U., England, 1931. With Sybron Corp. (formerly Ritter Co., later Ritter Pfaudler Corp.), 1934-92, sec., 1936-53, treas., 1940-53, v.p., 1939-53, pres., 1953-65, chmn., 1965-71, hon. chmn., 1971-76, hon. dir., from 1976; mem. adv. bd. Security Trust Co. Mem. adv. bd. United Community Chest; past pres., mem. adv. bd. Rochester YMCA; mem. adv. com. Ctr. for Strategic and Internat. Studies, Georgetown U.; trustee Rochester Ctr. for Govtl. and Community Rsch., Inc., Rochester Boys Club, Rochester Area Found., Project Hope, Nat. Fund for Med. Edn., Am. Fund for Dental Health; exec. com., trustee Rochester Inst. Tech.; pres. Family Svc. of Rochester, 1943-46; asst. Presbyn. pastor Larchmon (N.Y.) Ave. Ch. Mem. NAM (bd. dirs. 1952-53, 60-61), U.S. C. of C. (pres. 1970-71), Empire State C. of C. (pres. 1950-53, 64-66, chmn. bd. 1966-68, bd. dirs.), Rochester C. of C. (trustee, past pres.), U.S. Power Squadrons (chief comdr. 1948-49, mem. governing bd.), U.S. Figure Skating Assn. (pres. 1961-63, hon. mem. exec. com.), Am. Dental Trade Assn. (pres. 1968-70), Country Club of Rochester (pres. 1946), Rochester Yacht Club (commodore 1951-53), Genesse Valley Club, Great Lakes Cruising Club (commodore 1972-73, bd. dirs.), Skating Club (past pres.). Home: Rochester N.Y. Died Mar. 9, 1992.

SHUMWAY, LOWELL, publisher, consultant; b. New Brunswick, N.J., Feb. 22, 1894; s. Edgar Solomon and Florence (Snow) S.; m. Ruth Dwight Fuller, Mar. 4, 1918 (dec. July, 1950); m. Katherine Van Benschoten Cairns, June 27, 1957. AB, Amherst Coll., 1914. Clk. Nat. City Bank, 1914-15; asst. subscription sales mgr. Butterick Pub. Co., 1915-17; with McCall Corp., N.Y.C., 1919-59, asst. subscription sales mgr., subscription sales mgr., circulation mgr., 1941-49, v.p. charge circulation, 1949-57, circulation cons., 1957-59, pub. cons., from 1959; dir. Ctrl. Registry, 1944-55, chmn., 1953-55; dir. S-M News, 1951-57, sec., 1954-57; dir. Nat. Mag. Svc., 1955-57. Dir. Nat. Better Bus. Bureau, from 1950, treas., 1957-64. 1st lt., inf. U.S. Army, World War I. Recipient Amherst Coll. medal, 1954. Mem. Amherst Club (v.p. 1945-47), Bronxville Field Club (gov. 1953-57), Theta Xi. *

SHUTZ, BYRON THEODORE, realtor, mortgage banker; b. New Philadelphia, Ohio, June 26, 1899; s. George E. and Millie (Auman) S.; m. Maxine Christopher, Dec. 27, 1924; children: Byron Christopher, Laura Ann Shutz Cray, Susanne Shutz Curry. Student, U. Kans., 1917-18. With Herbert V. Jones & Co., 1919, jr. partner, 1924; jr. partner Herbert V. Jones & Co. (co. became inc.), 1934, exec. v.p., 1939-44, pres., 1944-72; chmn. Byron Shutz Co., from 1973; pres. Companion Investments, Inc.; adv. dir. Boatmen's First Nat. Bank Kansas City; bd. dirs. Farm & Home Savs. Assn.; advt. dir. Real Estate Bd., Kansas City, 1927-30, pres., 1934-35; apptd. by Gov. F.C. Donnell as 1 of 3 original Mo. real estate commrs., 1941-45; bd. dirs. First Nat. Bank. Chmn. War Fund Campaign of Kansas City-Jackson County chpt., ARC, 1944, mem. chpt. bd. dirs., 1945-46, chpt. chmn., 1945, 46, chmn. nat. nominating com., 1948, mem. Midwestern area adv. council, hon. mem. chpt. bd. dirs.; Bd. govs. Am. Royal Live Stock and Horse Show; bd. dirs. Starlight Theatre Assn.; soc. fellows Nelson Gallery Found.; trustee Andrew Drumm Inst., Jacob L. Loose and Ella C. Loose Charity Funds, U. Kans. Endowment Assn.; hon. dir. Rockhurst Coll. Mem. Mo. Real Estate Assn. (organizer 1936, past pres.), Mortgage Bankers Assn. Am. (pres. 1939-40, life mem. bd. govs., mem. past pres. adv. council; trustee Research and Ednl. Trust Fund), Kansas City C. of C. (past dir.), Bankers Assn. of Am. (past pres.), U.S. C. of C., Friends of Art, Am. Soc. Real Estate Counselors, Midwest Research Inst. (dir., trustee, adv.), Phi Kappa Psi. Mem. Christian Ch. Clubs: Kansas City, Kansas City Country, University, River, Mercury (Kansas City, Mo.); Flat Rock (Mack's Inn, Idaho). Lodges: Masons, Jesters. Home: Kansas City Mo. Died Nov. 26, 1988; buried Kansas City, Mo.

SHYRE, PAUL, playwright, director, actor, educator; b. N.Y.C., Mar. 8, 1926; s. Louis Phillip and Mary (Lee) S. Student, U. Fla., Gainesville, 1945, Am. Acad. Dramatic Arts, N.Y.C., 1946-47. Prof. dept. theatre arts Cornell U., 1980. Adapted for stage: The Child Buyer, 1964, A Whitman Portrait, 1967, Ah Men!, 1981; adapted for stage, dir., co-producer: (Sean O'Casey novels) Pictures in the Hallway, 1956, I Knock At The Door, 1957, Drums Under the Windows, 1960, (John Dos Passos anthology) U.S.A., 1959; adapted, dir.: (plays) Will Rogers USA, 1972; adapted, dir., performed: Blasts and Bravos: An Evening with H.L. Mencken, 1975, Paris Was Yesterday, 1980; author: Carl Sandburg: Echos and Silences, PBS Am. Playhouse series, 1982, Eugene O'Neill: A Glory of Ghosts, PBS; Hizzoner!, PBS, 1985 (Emmy award 1986), Broadway premiere, 1988; actor: play Absurd Person Singular, St. Joan, California Suite. Recipient N.Y. Drama Desk award, 1957, Obie award, 1957, Creative Arts award Brandeis U., 1958, Tony award, 1958, San Francisco Internat. Film Festival Spl. Jury award, 1986, Emmy award. Mem. Actors Equity Assn., Writers Guild, Dramatists Guild, Soc. Dirs. and Choreographers, AFTRA, Screen Actors Guild. Home: New York N.Y. Died Nov. 19, 1989.

SIBLEY, WILLIAM HART, lawyer; b. Union Point, Ga., Aug. 4, 1898; s. Samuel Hale and Florence Weldon (Hart) S.; m. Patricia Wilson, Aug. 14, 1929; children: Josiah Wilson (dec.), William Hart (dec.), Samuel Hale II. AB, U. Ga., 1920; BL, Harvard U., 1923. Bar: Ga. 1922. Assoc. Alston, Alston, Foster & Moise, Atlanta, 1922-31; ptnr. Alston, Foster, Moise & Sibley, Atlanta, 1931-42, Alston, Sibley, Miller, Spaun & Shackelford, 1942-62; of counsel Alston, Miller & Gaines, from 1962; bd. dirs. Citizens & So. Emory Bank. With USN, 1918. Mem. ABA, Ga. Bar Assn., Atlanta Bar Assn. (pres. 1939), Chi Phi, Piedmont Driving Club, Capital City Club (Atlanta). Democrat. *

SIDDALL, CECIL JAMES, justice; b. Sanford, Maine, Mar. 2, 1894; s. Thomas and Lillie (Sutcliffe) S.; m. Miriam Nealley, Nov. 20, 1934; children: Patricia, Shirley. LLB, U. Maine, 1917; LLD, Nasson Coll., Springvale, Maine, 1958. Bar: Maine, 1916. Ptnr. Titcomb & Siddall, 1938-53; register of probate York County, 1925-29; justice Maine Superior Ct., 1953-58, Maine Supreme Jud. Ct., 1958-65; mem. Maine Ho. of Reps., Sanford, 1923-25. Mem. ABA, Maine Bar Assn. *

SIEGEL, BENJAMIN M., physics educator; b. Superior, Wis., Mar. 26, 1916; s. Aaron and Pauline (Josephs) S.; m. Rachel Josefowitz, June 15, 1944; children: Charles E., H. Barry, Ruth V. B.S., Mass. Inst. Tech., 1938, Ph.D., 1940. Vis. fellow Calif. Inst. Tech., 1940-41; research assoc. Mass. Inst. Tech., 1941-42, 44-46, 48-49, Harvard U., 1942-44; assoc. Weizman Inst. Sci., 1946-48; assoc. prof. engring. physics Cornell U., Ithaca, N.Y., 1949-59, prof. applied and engring. physics, 1959-86, prof. emeritus, 1986-90; vis. prof. exptl. physics Hebrew U., Jerusalem, Israel, 1962-63; vis. fellow Salk Inst. Biol. Studies, La Jolla, Calif., 1971. Author: Modern Developments in Electron Microscopy, 1964; Editor: Physical Aspects of Electron Microscopy and Microbeam Analysis, 1975; contbr. numerous articles to profl. jours. Mem. Am. Jewish Com., Am. Friends Hebrew U., Am. Jewish Congress., Am. Jewish League for Israel, Electron Microscopy Soc. Am. (pres. 1973, past dir., disting. investigator in phys. scis. 1982), Am. Phys. Soc., Am. Vacuum Soc., Am. Profs. Peace in Middle East, AAAS, Fedn. Am. Scientists, AAUP, Union Concerned Scientists, Sigma Xi, Sigma Alpha Mu. Jewish. Home: Ithaca N.Y. Died Mar. 22, 1990; buried Ithaca, N.Y.

SIEGEL, DON, film director; b. Chgo., Oct. 26, 1912; m. Carol Rydall. Ed., Jesus Coll. Cambridge (Eng.) U. Films include Hitler Lives, 1946 (2 Acad. awards), Star in the Night, 1945, The Verdict, 1946, Night unto Night, 1949, The Big Steel, 1949, Duel at Silver Creek, 1952, No Time for Flowers, 1952, Count the Hours, 1953, China Venture, 1953, Riot in Cell Block Eleven, 1954, Private Hell, 36, 1954, An Annapolis Story, 1955, Invasion of the Body Snatchers, 1956, Crime in the Streets, 1956, Baby-Face Nelson, 1957, Spanish Affair, 1957, The Line-up, 1958, The Gun Runners, 1958, Hound-Dog Man, 1959, Edge of Eternity, 1959, Flaming Star, 1960, Hell is for Heroes, 1962, The Killers, 1964, The Hanged Man, 1964, Madigan, 1968, Stranger on the Run, 1967, Coogan's Bluff, 1969, Two Mules for Sister Sara, 1970, The Beguiled, 1971, Dirty Harry, 1971, Charley Varrick, 1973, Black Windmill, 1974, The Shootist, 1976, Telefon, 1977, Escape From Alcatraz, 1979, Rough Cut, 1980; dir., actor: Films include Play Misty for Me, 1971, Jinxed, 1982; actor: Films include Invasion of the Body Snatchers, 1978 (remake); appeared with Royal Acad. Dramatic Arts, London, Contemporary Theatre Group, Hollywood, Calif. Home: Nipomo Calif. Died Apr. 20, 1991.

SIEGMEISTER, ELIE, composer, writer, music educator; b. N.Y.C., Jan. 15, 1909; s. William and Bessie (Gitler) S.; m. Hannah Mersel, Jan. 15, 1930; children: Willa, Miriam, Nancy. B.A., Columbia U., 1927; studied with, Nadia Boulanger, Paris, 1927-32; diploma, École Normale de Musique, Paris, 1931; fellow, Juilliard Grad. Sch. Music, 1935-38. prof. music Hofstra U., 1949-76, composer-in-residence, 1966-76; condr. Hofstra Symphony Orch., 1953-65, Pro Arte Symphony Orch., 1965-66; founder Am. Composers Alliance, 1938; organized Am. Ballad Singers, 1939, dir. numerous concerts including Town Hall, 1939, 40, 41, 45, 46, made nation-wide tours, 1942-44; vis. lectr. U. Minn., 1948; expert cons. to War Dept., 1945. Composer orchestral and stage works on Am. themes, performing and publicizing Am. music, 1931-1952; composer numerous musical works in various, abstract forms, including; for orch. Ozark Set, 1943, Wilderness Road, 1944, Prairie Legend, 1944, Western Suite, 1945, Sunday in Brooklyn, 1946, Symphony No. 1, 1947, From My Window, 1949, Symphony No. 2, 1950-71, Divertimento, 1953, Clarinet Concerto, 1956, Symphony No. 3, 1957, Theater Set, 1959, Flute Concerto, 1960, Dick Whittington and His Cat, 1966, Five Fantasies of the Theater, 1967, The Face of War, 1968, Symphony No. 4, 1970, Symphony No. 5, 1971, Piano Concerto, 1974, Shadows and Light, 1975, Fables from the Dark Wood, 1976, Double Concerto for violin, piano and orch, 1976, Violin Concerto, 1978, Fantasies in Line and Color, 1981, Symphony No. 6, 1983, From These Shores 1986, Symphony No. 7, 1986, Symphony No. 8, 1988, Figures in the Wind, 1990; for Symphonic band Prarie Legend, 1944, Five American Folk Songs, 1949, Deep Sea Chanty, 1951, Riversong, 1951, Hootenanny, 1955, Front Porch Saturday Night, 1977, Celebration, 1977 and others; for chorus: Abraham Lincoln Walks at Midnight, 1937, The New Colossus, 1949, In Our Time, 1965, I Have A Dream, 1967, A Cycle of Cities, 1974, Scenes of the Big Town, 1987, others; operas include Darling Corie, 1952, The Plough and the Stars, 1969, Miranda and the Dark Young Man, 1955, The Mermaid in Lock No. 7, 1958, Night of the Moonspell, 1976, The Marquesa of O, 1982, The Lady of the Lake, 1985, Angel Levine, 1985; Broadway musical Sing Out, Sweet Land, 1944; film score They Came to Cordura, 1959; chamber music String Quartet No. 1, 1935, String Quartet No. 2, 1960, String Quartet No. 3 (on Hebrew Themes), 1973, Piano Sonata No. 1, 1944, Piano Sonata No. 2, 1964, Piano Sonata No. 3, 1979, Piano Sonata No. 4, 1980, Piano Sonata No. 5, 1987; Sextet for Brass and Percussion, 1965, Violin Sonata No. 2, 1965, Violin Sonata No. 3, 1966, Violin Sonata No. 4, 1971, Violin Sonata No. 5, 1972, Violin Sonata No. 6, 1988, Songs of Experience for voice, viola and piano, 1977, Ways of Love, for voice and chamber ensemble, 1983; Five Langston Hughes Songs for Voice and Chamber Ensemble, 1983, Ten Minutes for Four Players, 1988, Violin Sonata No. 6, 1988; over 100 concert songs, 1927-90. Author or co-author: several books relating to music including: (with Olin Downes) A Treasury of American Song, 1940, 82, 86; Music Lover's Handbook, 1943, Invitation to Music, 1959, Harmony and Melody, 2 vols., 1965-66, The New Music Lover's Handbook, 1976, 83; contbr. to: Musical America, Musical Quar., Keynote, N.Y. Times; Works have been performed by, Toscanini, Stokowski, Mitropoulos, Maazel, Commissiona, et al.; and by N.Y. Philharmonic, NBC, Phila., Cleve. and other symphony orchs., also in Germany, France, Italy, Norway, Israel, USSR, Mexico, Eng., Australia. Founder Am. Composer's Alliance, 1937, Am.-Soviet Music Soc., 1945, Kennedy Ctr. Black Music Competition, 1977-79. Recipient 38th ann. Acad.-Inst. award Am. Acad. and Inst. Arts and Letters, 1978; Guggenheim Found. fellow, 1978; composer-in-residence Rockefeller Found. Ctr. Bellagio, Italy, 1983. Mem. ASCAP (bd. dirs. 1972-91, chmn. symphony and concert com. 1987-90, asst. sec. 1989), Am. Acad. and Inst. Arts and Letters, Am. Music Ctr., Coun. Creative ARtists, Librs. and Mus. (founder, chmn. 1971—). Home: Great Neck N.Y. Died Mar. 10, 1991; buried Mt. Hebron Cemetery, Flushing, N.Y.

SIFFORD, DARRELL CHARLES, journalist; b. Moberly, Mo., Sept. 19, 1931; s. Charles Dewey and Hazel Odell S.; m. Marilyn Gray Oakley, June 16, 1977; children: Jay, Grant. B.J., U. Mo., 1953. Mng. editor News Tribune, Jefferson City, Mo., 1955-62; night city editor Courier Jour., Louisville, 1962-66; exec. editor Charlotte (N.C.) News, 1966-76; syndicated columnist Phila. Inquirer, 1976-92; bd. mng. editors AP, 1974-76; pres. news council N.C. AP, 1974. Author: A Love of the Land, 1980, Father and Son, 1982, The Only Child, 1989. Served with AUS, 1953-55. Recipient Journalism award Am. Osteo. Assn., 1977, writing award Nat. Epilepsy Found., 1971, Ann. award Phila. Soc. Clin. Psychologists, 1980, Robert T. Morse award Am. Psychiat. Assn., 1980, Spl. Presdl. citation Am. Psychiat. Assn., 1988, ann. award Am. Mental Health Fund, 1988, Pa. Psychol. Assn., 1989. Mem. Hershey's Mill Golf Club, Vesper Club. Home: West Chester Pa. Died Mar. 6, 1992. †

SIGMIER, CHARLES C., manufacturing executive; b. Louisville, Nov. 14, 1898; s. Lee and Lille (Billings) S.; m. Marcella Haas, Jan. 27, 1920; 1 child, Mary Jean. Student pub. schs., Cleve. Teller Union Trust Co., Cleve., 1915-21, br. mgr., 1921-23; with Midland Bank, from 1923, asst. cashier, 1926-29, asst. v.p., 1929-32, pres., from 1932; v.p. Cleve. Trust Co., 1939-51; chmn. bd. Parker-Hannifin Corp. (formerly named Parker Appliance Co.), 1951-62, chmn. fin. com., from 1963; dir. Reliance Electric & Engring. Co., Osborn Mfg. Co. (Mantua, Ohio). Hon. trustee Cleve. Area Heart Soc., Euclid-Glenville Hosp., Cleve. Mem. Shaker Heights Country Club, Cleveland Athletic Club, Union Club. *

SILLCOX, LEWIS KETCHAM, engineering educator; b. Germantown, Pa., Apr. 30, 1886; s. George Washington and Georgiana (Parker) S.; m. Edna May Harris, Sept. 14, 1918 (dec. Feb. 1961); children: Elsie Winifred (Mrs. Donald G. Bridge), Esther Harris (Mrs. Stanley L. Whittemore), Enid Burnham (Mrs. Fred E. Brown), Edith May (Mrs. Conrad F. Reiman), Robert Lewis. Student, Trinity Sch., N.Y. and L'Ecole Polytechnique, Brussels, 1903; D.Sc., Clarkson Coll., 1932; D.Eng., Cumberland U., 1941, Purdue U., 1951; LL.D., Syracuse U., 1948, Queen's U., 1955; D.H.L., Norwich U., 1963. Machinist apprentice N.Y.C. & H.R. R.R., High Bridge, N.Y., 1903-07; foundry apprentice McSherry Mfg. Co., Middletown, Ohio, 1907-09; shop. engr. Canadian Car & Foundry Co., Montreal, Que., Can., 1909-12; mech. engr. Canadian No. Ry., Toronto, Ont., 1912-16, I.C. R.R., 1916-18; gen. supt. motive power C.,M. & St.P. Ry., Chgo., 1918-27; asst. to pres., exec. v.p., vice chmn. bd. N.Y. Air Brake Co., N.Y.C., 1927-59; first dir. Office of Transp. Exec. Dept. State of N.Y., Albany, 1959-60; prof., lectr. engring. Purdue U., from 1946; lectr. transp. various colls., univs. Author: Mastering Momentum, 1941; Contbr. to tech. publs. Chmn. mech. engring. adv. com. Princeton, 1938- 58; vis. com. dept. mech. engring. Mass. Inst. Tech., 1955-57; trustee, gen. chmn. vis. coms. Norwich U.; hon. curator Baker Library, Harvard, from 1935; mem. Alfred Noble Joint Prize Com., 1943-78; Ret. trustee Hosp. Rev. and Planning Council Central N.Y., Inc.; mem. adv. bd. Salvation Army. Recipient gold medals ASME, gold medals Inst. Mech. Engrs., George Washington Honor medal, 1954, Freedoms Found. award, 1955; first recipient Transp. Research Forum award, 1977. Fellow Inst. Mech. Engrs., IEEE, AAAS; hon. mem. ASME (past pres.), A.R.E.A., Engring. Inst. Can.; mem. ASCE (life, past pres.), Am. Inst. Mining and Metall. Engrs. (life), other nat., state, local profl. engring. socs., Sigma Xi, Pi Tau Sigma, Tau Beta Pi. Episcopalian. Clubs: Mason (Boston) (32 deg., K.T., Shriner), Harvard (Boston); University (N.Y.C., Chgo.); Black River Valley (Watertown, N.Y.); Seigniory (Can.). Home: Watertown N.Y. Died Mar. 3, 1989.

SILVER, HENRY K., pediatrician, educator; b. Phila., Apr. 22, 1918; s. Samuel and Dora (Kreitzer) S.; m. Harriet Ashkenas, June 15, 1941; children: Stephen, Andrew. B.A., U. Calif., Berkeley, 1938, M.D., 1942. Diplomate: Am. Bd. Pediatrics. Intern U. Calif. Hosp., San Francisco, 1941-42; resident Children's Hosp., Phila., 1942-43; instr., then asst. prof. pediatrics U. Calif. Med. Sch., San Francisco, 1946-52; asso. prof. Yale Med. Sch., 1952-57; prof. pediatrics U. Colo. Med. Sch., Denver, 1957-91; asso. dean admissions U. Colo. Med. Sch., 1977-91; clin. prof. nursing U. Colo. Sch. Nursing, 1976-91. Co-author: Healthy Babies-Happy Parents, 1958, Current Pediatric Diagnosis and Treatment, 9th edit., 1986, Handbook of Pediatrics, 15th edit., 1986. Rosenberg Found. fellow, 1945-47; recipient George Armstrong award Ambulatory Pediatric Assn., 1972; Martha May Eliot award Am. Pub. Health Assn., 1974; Eleanor Roosevelt Humanitarian award Denver chpt. Hadassah, 1973; Outstanding Physician Asst. Educator award Assn. Physician Asst. Programs, 1984; award for outstanding service to the profession Am. Acad. Physician Assts., 1984; Thomas Jefferson award U. Colo., 1985; award Nat. Primary Care Nurse Practitioner Symposium, 1985. Mem. Inst. of Medicine Nat. Acad. Sci., Am. Acad. Pediatrics, Western Soc. Pediatric Research (Ross award in edn. 1962), Soc. Pediatric Research, Am. Pediatric Soc., Sigma Xi, Alpha Omega Alpha. Home: Denver Colo. Died Jan. 13, 1991. †

SILVERSTEIN, ELIZABETH BLUME, lawyer; b. Newark, Nov. 2, 1892; d. Selig and Goldie (Arahowitz) Blume; m. Max Silverstein, Aug. 23, 1934 (dec. 1955); 1 son, Nathan Royce. LL.B., N.J. Law Sch. (now Rutgers U. Sch. Law), 1911. Bar: N.J. 1913, U.S. Supreme Ct. 1921, U.S. Tax Ct. 1960. First woman lawyer in N.J. in practice law, 1913, 1st woman in N.J. to represent defendant, unassisted in homicide case, 1916, 1st woman on legal adv. bd. of Draft Bd. during World War I, Essex County, N.J. Founding mem., del. First Am. Jewish Congress, 1916, 23, exec. bd. dirs., mem. immigration com., 1923, del. 1st World Jewish Congress, 1936; leader Balfour parade, Newark. Mem. Woman's Lawyers Assn. (v.p. 1920s), ABA, Essex County Bar Assn., Am. Judicature Soc., N.J. State Bar Assn., Nat. Assn. Women Lawyers (N.J. state del.). Republican. (del. Republican conv. 1932). Club: Heinberg Rep. (pres. 1920's). Lodges: Ind. Order Brith Abraham (1st woman to serve nat. order exec. positions, asst. to Grand Master, chmn. Jewish rights, chmn. com. on disability), Louis D. Brandies Lodge (pres. 1920s). Died Feb. 3, 1991; buried Mt. Hebron Cemetery, Flushing, N.Y.. Home: Newark N.J.

SILZ, WALTER, educator; b. Cleve., Sept. 27, 1894; s. Max Alexander and Friederike Caroline (Lieb) S.; m. Frieda R. Osgood, June 23, 1922 (dec.); m. Priscilla M. Kramer, June 24, 1939. AB summa cum laude, Harvard, 1917, AM, 1918, PhD, 1922; student, U. Heidelberg, U. Munich, 1920-21. Prof. German Harvard and Radcliffe, 1922-36; prof. and head German dept. Washington U., 1936-39, Swarthmore Coll., 1939-48; prof., head Germanic sect. Princeton, 1948-54; Gebhard Prof. Germanic langs., lits. Columbia, from 1954; Guggenheim fellow, 1926-27, 60-61; Harvard exchange prof. to western colls., 1929-30; vis. prof. Princeton, 1947-48, U. Calif. at Berkeley, summer 1949, Ind. U., 1965. Author: H.v. Kleist's Conception of the Tragic, 1923, Early German Romanticism, 1929, German Romantic Lyrics, 1934, Realism and Reality, 1954, H.v. Kleist, 1961; editorial bd.: Germanic Rev., from 1954, Modern Lang. Assn. Publ., from 1956; contbr. to jours. Mem. Modern Lang. Assn., Am. Assn. Tchrs. German, AAUP, Phi Beta Kappa. *

SIM, JOHN CAMERON, journalism educator; b. Grand Forks, N.D., Feb. 7, 1911; s. John Cameron and Katherine Gertrude (Mason) S.; m. Mary L. Hanson, Sept. 10, 1946; children: Erin Terese, John Cameron III. BA, U. N.D., 1932; MA, U. Minn., 1940. Mng. editor East Grand Forks Record, 1931-39, editor, co-pub., 1946-56; instr. journalism U. N.D., 1934-40, U. Ala., 1940-41; univ. editor U. N.H., 1941-42; mem. faculty U. Minn., Mpls., from 1956, prof. journalism, from 1967; asst. dir. Sch. Journalism and Mass Communication, Mpls., from 1970; editor Assoc. Coll. Press Bus. Rev., 1960-66, conf. mgr., 1960-66; pres. Red River Valley Editorial Assn., 1949-50; dir. Minn. High Sch. Press Assn., from 1964; nat. conf. mgr. Nat. Sch. Press Assn., 1959-61; cons. on scholastic press, also mass media teaching UNESCO, 1975. Author: The Grass Roots Press: America's Weekly Newspapers, 1969. With AUS, 1942-46. Recipient Towley award Journalism Edn. Assn., 1978; grantee U. Minn. Grad. Sch., 1970. Mem. AAUP, Soc. Profl. Journalists, Minn. Press Assn. (hon.), Minn. Press Club, Campus Club, Phi Beta Kappa, Kappa Tau Alpha. Home: Minneapolis Minn. Died Sept. 25, 1990; cremated.

SIMENON, GEORGES, novelist; b. Leige, Belgium, Feb. 13, 1903; s. Desire and Henriette (Brull) S.; grad. Coll. Saint-Servais, Liege, 1917; m. Regine Renchon (div.); m. 2d, Denise Ouimet, June 22, 1950; children: Marc, Jean, Marie-Georges, Pierre. Novelist, Paris, from 1921; creator detective Inspector Maigret, 1929, writer

80 Maigret novels; author more than 200 novels under 17 different pseudonyms, author 131 non-detective novels; works translated into 55 langs.; 50 novels adapted into films; non-fiction works include When I was Old; Letter to my Mother, 1974; Mé moires Intimes, 1981; 21 vols. daily recs. of thoughts, memoirs, souvenirs. Died Sept. 4, 1989; cremated. Home: Lausanne Switzerland

SIMEONE, FIORINDO ANTHONY, surgeon, educator; b. St. Ambrose, Italy, Jan. 20, 1908; came to U.S., 1914, naturalized, 1930; s. Antonio and Antonia (Rivera) S.; m. Martha Toothill, Aug. 16, 1941 (dec.); children: Timothy A., Maria Antonia, Francesca Angelica, Martha Christina, Walter John; m. Margaret Jacoy, June 15, 1972. A.B., Brown U., 1929, Sc.M., 1930, Sc.D. (hon.), 1954; M.D., Harvard, 1934; perpetual student, St. Bartholomew's Hosp. Med. Sch., London. Diplomate: Am. Bd. Surgery, Am. Bd. Thoracic Surgery. Intern Mass. Gen. Hosp., 1934-36, surg. resident, 1938-40; G.U. surg. resident Peter Bent Brigham Hosp., 1940-41; NRC fellow Harvard U., 1936-38; asst. prof. surgery Harvard Med. Sch., 1946-50; prof. surgery Western Res. U., also dir. surgery Cleve. Met. Gen., 1950-67; prof. med. sci. Brown U., from 1967; surgeon-in-chief Miriam Hosp., Providence, R.I., 1967-77, surgeon-in-chief emeritus, 1977-90; spl. asst. for cancer control to gov., State of R.I.; cons. to Surgeon Gen., U.S. Army, from 1946; mem. bd. cons. Mass. Gen. Hosp., Boston. Author: (with J. C. White and R. H. Smithwick) The Autonomic Nervous System, 1952, (with J. B. Kinmonth and C. G. Rob) Vascular Surgery, 1962; Contbr. (with J. B. Kinmonth and C. G. Rob) articles to profl. jours. Served from capt. to col. M.C. AUS, 1942-46, ETO. MTO. Decorated Comdr. Nat. Order of Cedars Republic of Lebanon, Legion of Merit; recipient Verrazzano Day award, 1973, W.W. Keene award Brown U., 1976; Disting. Service award Hosp. Assn. R.I., 1978; Disting. Service award Am. Heart Assn. R.I. affiliate, 1979; William S. Stone Lectureship award Am. Trauma Soc., 1981; named to R.I. Hall of Fame, 1973. Fellow ACS, AAAS, N.Y. Acad. Sci., Internat. Coll. Surgeons (hon.); mem. AMA, Am. Surg. Assn., Soc. U. Surgeons, Central Surg. Soc., Cleve. Surg. Soc. (pres.), New Eng. Surg. Soc. (pres. 1982-83), Cleve. Area Heart Soc. (pres.), Soc. Exptl. Biology and Medicine (pres. chpt.), U.S. Med. Cons. World War II, Phi Beta Kappa, Sigma Xi (pres.), Alpha Omega Alpha. Home: North Providence R.I. Died June 13, 1990; buried Cranston, R.I.

SIMKIN, WILLIAM E., labor arbitrator; b. Merrifield, N.Y., Jan. 13, 1907; s. Alfred E. and Florence (Manchester) S.; m. Ruth Commons, Aug. 31, 1929; children: Thomas, Peter. BS, Earlham Coll., 1927, LLD, 1963; postgrad., Columbia U., 1928-30, U. Pa., 1937-39. Prin. Cen. High Sch., Sherwood, N.Y., 1928-30; sci. tchr. Bklyn. Friends Sch., 1930-32; field rep. in W.Va. Am. Friends Svc. Com., 1932-37; instr. industry Wharton Sch. Fin. and Commerce U. Pa., 1937-39, labor arbitrator, 1939-61, 69-92; impartial chmn. Full Fashioned Hosiery Industry, 1939-42, 51-61; assoc. impartial chmn. Phila. Men's Clothing Industry, 1940-61, Phila. Dress Industry, 1947-61, Honeywell, Inc., 1970-92; umpire Goodyear Tire & Rubber Co., 1945-51, 55-59, Crucible Steel Co., 1952-61, Bethlehem Steel Co., Shipbldg. div., 1945-50, 52-55, Nat. Can. Corp., 1954-61; spl. mediation rep., assoc. pub. mem. Nat. War Labor Bd., 1942-43, chmn. shipbldg. commn., 1943-45; dir. Fed. Mediation and Conciliation Svc., 1961-69; chmn. labor rels. panel FRS, 1970-92; chmn. Fgn. Svc. Grievance Bd., State Dept. 1971-76; lectr. Sch. Bus. Adminstrn., Harvard, Kennedy Sch. Govt., 1971-73; other. Author: Mediation and the Dynamics of Collective Bargaining, 1970. Mem. Nat. Acad. Arbitrators (pres. 1950), Indsl. Rels. and Rsch. Assn. Home: Tucson Ariz. Died Mar. 4, 1992.

SIMMONS, CARROLL DAY, banker, accountant; b. Liberty Hill, Tex., Sept. 30, 1896; s. Isaac Isaiah and Ida (Stanford) S.; m. Bernice Lee, May 26, 1917; 1 child, Jean. Student, North Tex. Tchrs. Coll., 1915-16, 19-20; BBA, MBA, U. Tex., 1924. CPA Tex. 1929. Tchr. rural schs. Tex., 1913-15, Pearsall (Tex.) High Sch., 1916-17; supt. London Sch., Nuuces County, 1920-23; statis. asst. to registrar U. Tex., 1924-25, sec. bd. regents, 1925-19, assoc. prof. bus. adminstrn., 1927-29, prof. bus. statistics, 1929-53, investment officer, 1931-41, acting controller, assoc. controller, controller, 1937-49, v.p., 1947-50, vice chancellor bus., fin., 1950-52; v.p., sr. trust officer First City Nat. Bank, Houston, 1953-64; adj. prof. bus. adminstrn. U. Tex., 1925-27. Contbr. articles to profl. jours. Asst. sec.-treas. Tex. Med. Ctr., Inc. 1st lt. WWI. Mem. Am. Statis. Assn. (dist. rep. 1927-39), Beta Gamma Sigma, Beta Alpha Psi, Rotary, Masons, Forty Acres Club, Houston Club. Democrat. Baptist. *

SIMMONS, EDWARD DWYER, university administrator; b. North Dighton, Mass., Aug. 29, 1924; s. Percy Briggs and Anna Cecilia (O'Connell) S.; m. Marguerite Mary Scheibelhut, Aug. 12, 1950; children: Kathleen, Marguerite, Edward, Patricia, Thomas, Mary, Susan, Timothy, Martha, Carol, Michael, Jeanne. Student, St. Charles Coll., 1942-44; A.B., St. Mary's U., 1945, S.T.B., 1947; M.A., U. Notre Dame, 1949, Ph.D., 1952. Instr. U. Notre Dame, 1950-52; mem. faculty Marquette U., Milw., from 1952, prof., from 1965, chmn. dept. philosophy, 1966-68; acting grad. dean Marquette U. (Grad. Sch.), 1967-68, assoc. v.p. for acad. affairs, 1968-74, v.p. for acad. affairs, from 1974. Author: The Scientific Art of Logic, 1961; Editor: Essays on Knowledge and Methodology, 1965; Contbr. chpts. to books, articles, papers to profl. lit. Bd. dirs. Trinity Meml. Hosp., Cudahy, Wis., 1969-86, chmn., 1970-84; bd. overseers St. Francis Sem., Milw., 1977-82; bd. dirs. St. Mary's Acad., 1976-82. Mem. Am. Philos. Assn., Jacques Maritain Assn., Metaphys. Soc. Am., Am. Philos. Assn., Am. Cath. Philos. Assn. (exec. council 1960-63), Nat. Cath. Ednl. Assn. (exec. com. coll. and univ. dept. 1969-72), Am. Assn. Higher Edn., AAUP (v.p. Marquette U. chpt. 1965-66). Home: South Milwaukee Wis. Died Nov. 12, 1987.

SIMMONS, GLENN BALLARD, educator; b. Ponce de Leon, Fla., Apr. 9, 1897; s. Jesse Asbury and Lillian Cornella (Ballard) S.; m. Evalyn Louise McNeil, DEc. 31, 1923; children: Glenn Ballard, Evalyn Louise. AB in Edn., U. Fla., 1922, MA in Edn., 1929; PhD, Johns Hopkins U., 1933. Supv. prin. Panama City (Fla.) Pub. Schs., 1922-25, Brookville City Schs., 1926-27, Tallahassee City Schs., 1927-28; asst. prof. edn. Coll. Edn. U. Fla., 1928-29; asst. dean Lab. Sch. Coll. Edn., 1928-41, prof. edn., dir., 1935-49, acting dean, 1941-49, dir. dept. off-campus instrn., 1949-62; dir. instl. rels. Fla. Atlantic U., 1962-63; dean Coll. Edn., from 1963; state coord. tchr. recruitment, 1951-63. Mem. adv. coun. Fla. Citizens Com. Edn. Mem. NEA, Fla. Edn. Assn. (pres. 1941-42, v.p. 1942-44, bd. dirs. 1930-31, 40-41), Am. Legion, Fla. Continuing Edn. Coun, C. of C., Kappa Delta Pi, Phi Delta Kappa, Phi Kappa Phi, Kappa Phi, Pi Gamma Mu Alumni Assn. *

SIMMONS, RICHARD SHERIDAN, banker, lawyer; b. N.Y.C., Sept. 28, 1928; s. William and Mary E. (Sheridan) S.; m. Margaret Patricia Casey, June 30, 1955; 1 son, William. B.A. summa cum laude, Princeton U., 1951; LL.B., Yale U., 1954. Bar: N.Y. 1956. Mem. firm Cravath, Swaine & Moore, N.Y.C., 1956-85, ptnr., 1963-85; vice chmn. Chem. Banking Corp. and Chem. Bank, N.Y.C., 1985-90; Dep. supt. Banks of State of N.Y., 1959-60. Editor: Yale Law Jour, 1954. Served with U.S. Army, 1954-56. Mem. Internat. Bar Assn., ABA (chmn. banking com. 1970-75), N.Y. State Bar Assn., Assn. Bar City of N.Y., Council on Fgn. Relations, Soc. Colonial Wars, St. Nicholas Soc., SAR. Mem. Dutch Reformed Ch. Clubs: University, Links, North Hempstead Country, Sailfish Point Golf. Home: New York N.Y. Died Feb. 10, 1991.

SIMMS, LEROY ALANSON, retired newspaper executive; b. Emelle, Ala., Sept. 17, 1905; s. John Thomas and Minnie Epes (Thomas) S.; m. Virginia Hammill, June 30, 1926 (dec.); m. Martha Alice Holliman, May 17, 1969; 1 dau., Lucie Grey Simms Grubbs (dec.). Student, U. Ill., 1924-25; L.H.D. (hon.),, U. Ala., 1982. Reporter, Birmingham (Ala.) News, 1924-26; Reporter Tampa (Fla.) Morning Tribune, 1926-27; city editor Birmingham Post, 1927-28, mng. editor, 1929-31; asst. editor Newspaper Enterprise Assn., Cleve., 1931-32; day editor AP, Birmingham bur., 1933-38, Ala. corr., 1938-58; mng. editor Birmingham News, 1959-61; editor Huntsville (Ala.) Times, 1961-86, v.p., dir., 1963-88, pub., 1964-85, chmn. bd., 1985-88; v.p. Huntsville Indsl. Expansion Com. 1966-70, pres., 1970-71. Author: Road to War: Alabama Leaves the Union, 1960. Mem. Am., So. newspaper pubs. assns., Ala. Press Assn. (dir. 1964-66), Ala. A.P. Assn. (pres. 1965-66), Am. Soc. Newspaper Editors, C. of C. (dir.), Sigma Delta Chi (chmn. Ala. 1960), Theta Chi. Clubs: Rotary, Heritage. Home: Huntsville Ala. Died 1992. †

SIMON, ARTHUR EMIL, lawyer; b. Milw., Sept. 16, 1895; s. Arthur and Hilda Amanda (Simon) S.; m. Victoria McLean, Aug. 20, 1924. AB summa cum laude, U. Wash., 1917; LLB cum laude, Harvard U., 1920; LLD (hon.), Whitworth Coll., 1964. Bar: Wash. 1920. Assoc. Charles H. Winders, Seattle, 1920-22, Bausman, Oldham, Bullitt & Eggerman, Seattle, 1922-26; asst. U.S. atty. Western Dist. Wash., 1926, chief asst. U.S. atty., 1927; asst. Western counsel N.P. Ry., 1927-29; mem. firm Revelle, Simon & Coles, Seattle, 1929-37, Harman, Hartman, Simon & Coles, Seattle, 1937-42, Wright, Innis, Simon & Todd, Seattle, from 1942; spl. asst. U.S. atty. gen., 1953-55. Trustee King County Hosp. System, 1954-6-, pres., 1956-57. With U.S. Army, 1918-19. Mem. ABA, Wash. State Bar Assn., King County Bar Assn., Am. Judicature Soc., Am. Legion, others. *

SIMON, CHARLIE MAY (MRS. JOHN GOULD FLETCHER), author; b. Monticello, Ark., Aug. 17, 1897; d. Charles W. and Mary (Jackson) Hogue; m. John Gould Fletcher, Jan. 18, 1936. Art student, Chgo. Art Inst., Grande Chaumiere, Paris. Tchr. Japan Women's U., Tokyo. Author: Joe Mason, 1946, The Royal Road, 1948, Johnswood, 1954, All Men Are Brothers, biography of Albert Schweitzer, 1958, A Seed Shall Serve, biography pf Toyohiko Kagawa (Albert Schweitzer book prize Kindler Verlag, Munich), 1958, Sun and the Birch, 1960, The Andrew Carnegie Story (biography), 1965. *

SIMON, KATE GROBSMITH, writer; b. Warsaw, Poland, Dec. 5, 1912; d. Jacob and Lina (Babiez) Grobsmith. BA, Hunter Coll., 1935. Former book reviewer New Republic, Nation, Book of Month Club; freelance editor A.A. Knopf Co., 1952-55. Author: New York Places and Pleasures, rev. edit., 1964, Mexico Places and Pleasures, 1962, (with Andreas Feininger) New York, 1964, Italy: The Places in Between, Kate Simon's Paris: Places and Pleasures, London: Places and Pleasures; contbr. articles to popular mags. Mem. Authors League. Home: New York NY Died Feb. 4, 1990.

SIMON, RAOUL BERNARD, import/export company executive; b. Constitucion, Chile, July 14, 1893; s. Pacific and Louisa (Bernard) S.; m. Sara Brand, Mar., 1919; children: Raoul, Eliana. CE, U. Chile, 1917. Registered Civil Engr., Chile. Civil engr. Chilean State Rys., 1918-27; dir. Bur. Budget Chilean Govt., 1927-31; dir. Ctrl. Bank of Chile, 1928-31; pres. Grace & Co. (Chile), S.A., consignees of Graceline and Panamerikan Grace Airways, Santiago, 1931-39; mgr. Grace & Co. (Chile), S.A., consignees of Graceline and Panamerikan Grace Airways, from 1940; v.p. W.R. Grace & Co., N.Y.C., from 1946; pres. Inst. Civil Engrs. of Chile. Academic mem. U. Chile. Mem. Econ. Club. of League of Nations, Club de Golf Los Leones, Club de la Union (Santiago). *

SIMONDS, BRUCE, pianist, educator; b. Bridgeport, Conn., July 5, 1895; s. Henry Dwight and Fannie Abigail (Tibbals) S.; m. Rosalind Olive Brown, June 30, 1922; children: Elisabeth Treat Simonds Burns, Rogert Tyrrell. AB, Yale U., 1917, AM, 1938, MusB, 1918; student, Schola Cantorum, Paris, 1919-21. Instr. Yale U., 1921-24, asst. prof., 1924-30, assoc. prof., 1930-38, prof., 1938-64; dean Yale Sch. Music, 1941-54; dir. Norfolk Music Sch. of Yale, 1941-59; supr. music Westover Sch., 1928-89. Debut as pianist, London, Paris, 1921; appeared with leading orchestras in Boston, Cleve., Phila., Mpls., New Haven, and in various cities and colls., 1921-89; composer Two Organ Preludes on Gregorian Themes, 1930, Habanera for Violin, 1933. Recipient Chappell gold medal Matthay Piano Sch., London. Mem. Am. Mattay Assn. (1st pres.), Am. Acad. Arts and Scis., Graduates Club, Lawn Club, Elizabethan Club (New Haven), Century Assn. (N.Y.C.), Phi Beta Kappa, Zeta Psi. Home: Hamden Conn. Died June 30, 1989.

SIMONS, HOWARD, newspaper editor, foundation administrator; b. Albany, N.Y., June 3, 1929; s. Reuben and Mae (Chesler) S.; m. Florence Katz, Nov. 11, 1956; children: Anna, Isabel, Julie, Rebecca. B.A., Union Coll., Schenectady, 1951, Litt.D., 1973; M.S. in Journalism, Columbia, 1952. Writer, editor Sci. Service, Washington, 1954-59; Am. corr. New Scientist, London, 1964-67; with Washington Post, 1961-84, mng. editor, 1971-84; curator Nieman Found., Harvard U., 1984-89; M. Lyle Spencer vis. prof. Syracuse U., 1975; Intellectual Interchange scholar, Japan, 1975; disting. vis. prof. U. S.C., 1984-87; mem. Pulitzer Prize bd., 1987-89. Free-lance writer, 1959-61; author: (with Joseph A. Califano, Jr.) The Media and the Law, 1976, (with Joseph A. Califano, Jr.) Business and Media, 1979, Simons' List Book, 1977, (with Haynes Johnson) The Landing, 1986. Served with AUS, 1952-54. Recipient AAAS/Westinghouse Electric Corp. Sci. writing award, 1962, 64, Raymond Clapper Journalism award, 1966; Nieman fellow Harvard, 1958-59. Mem. Overseas Writers, Council Fgn. Relations. Home: Cambridge Mass. Died June 13, 1989.

SIMONS, THOMAS CUNNINGHAM, financial services holding company executive; b. Pasadena, Calif., Nov. 12, 1928; s. Seward Churchyard and Evelyn (Cunningham) S.; m. Joan Gardiner, Sept. 16, 1950; children: Thomas Seward, Martha Simons Dale, Sarah Simons Rivers, John Caldwell. Grad., Thacher Sch., Ojai, Calif., 1946; A.B., Harvard U., 1950. C.L.U. With Conn. Gen. Life Ins. Co., 1953-78; mgr. Conn. Gen. Life Ins. Co., Los Angeles, 1960-63, v.p. agy. dept., 1963-69, v.p., 1969-71, sr. v.p., 1971-76, exec. v.p., 1976-78; chmn. bd. Capital Holding Corp., Louisville, from 1978, chief exec. officer, 1978-88; bd. dirs. Citizens Fidelity Corp., Louisville, BF Goodrich Co., Citizens Fidelity Bank and Trust Co., Louisville, Champion Internat. Corp., PNC Fin. Corp. Bd. dirs. Louisville Fund for Arts; trustee Thacher Sch., Ojai, Calif.; v.p. Louisville/Jefferson County Downtown Devel. Corp. Served to lt. (j.g.) USNR, 1950-53. Clubs: Louisville Country, Jefferson, River Valley. Home: Louisville Ky. Died Aug. 17, 1988; buried South Londonderry, Vt.

SIMONSON, HUGH MELVIN, state official; b. Pittsville, Wis., Apr. 2, 1917; s. Carl Sigrid and Leah Leonore (Lewis) S.; children—Mark W., Lynne M. Acct. Consol. Papers, Wisconsin Rapids, Wis., 1937-40; with Wisconsin Rapids Police Dept., 1940-53; with Wis. Nat. Guard, 1947-79, chief auditor, 1953-59, dep. adj. gen., 1969-77; adj. gen. dept. mil. affairs State of Wis., 1977-79. Served with AUS, 1942-46. Recipient Meritorious Service award Nat. Guard Assn. U.S., 1975; decorated Legion of Merit with oak leaf cluster. Mem. Nat. Guard Assn. U.S. Lutheran. Clubs: Masons, Shriners. Home: Madison Wis. Died Oct. 30, 1987; buried Camp Williams Cemetery, Camp Douglas, Wis.

SIMPSON, JOHN DUNCAN, engineering executive; b. Chgo., Mar. 7, 1937; s. Duncan Ross and Josephine (Gleeson) S.; m. Elli Hatcher, Feb. 1, 1964; children: Heather, Sean. B.S., U.S. Mil. Acad., 1959; M.S.,

Princeton U., 1962, M.P.A., 1969. Commd. 2d lt. U.S. Army, 1959, advanced to lt. col., 1972; spl. asst. to U.S. comdr. Berlin, 1964-66; asst. prof. econs. and public policy U.S. Mil. Acad., 1968-71, exec. asst. Office Emergency Preparedness, spl. asst. to chmn. Pres.'s Oil Policy Com., 1971-72; dep. commr. EPA, N.Y.C., 1972-73; exec. dir., gen. mgr. Regional Transp. Dist., Denver, 1973-79; pres. Value Capture Opportunities, Inc., Denver, 1976-79; exec. dir. Met. Transp. Authority, L.I. R.R. Co., N.Y.C. Transit Authority, Metro Suburban Bus Authority, Triborough Bridge and Tunnel Authority, Metro Airports, N.Y.C., 1979-80; pres., chief operating officer N.Y.C. Transit Authority, Manhattan and Bronx Surface Transit Operating Authority, S.I. Rapid Transit Operating Authority, S. Bklyn. R.R. Co., 1981-83; pres. Fluor Transp. and Infrastructure Inc., Irvine, Calif., 1983-86, Fluor Daniel Venture Group, Inc., 1986-88. Served with USMC, 1954-55. Decorated Bronze Star (3), Air medal, Meritorious Service medal. Mem. Am. Public Transit Assn. (v.p., dir. 1974-83), West Point Soc. Club: Army-Navy (Washington). Home: Laguna Beach Calif. Died Aug. 21, 1989; buried U.S. Mil. Acad., West Point, N.Y.

SIMS, ERNEST THEODORE, JR., horticulturist, educator; b. Atlanta, Aug. 29, 1932; s. Ernest Theodore and Alice Louise (Miller) S.; m. Margaret Elizabeth Richter, Dec. 28, 1963; children: Ernest Theodore III, John Christopher Richter. B.S.A., U. Ga., 1954; M.Sc., Ohio State U., 1959, Ph.D., 1962; diploma, Oak Ridge Inst. Nuclear Studies, 1965. Pomologist Sims Fruit Farms, Conyers, Ga., 1956-57; grad. research asst. Ohio State U., Columbus, 1957-62; asst. prof. horticulture Clemson (S.C.) U., 1962-67, assoc. prof., 1967-72, prof., 1972-88, acting head dept. horticulture, 1981-88, mem. faculty senate, 1969-71, 85-86, mem. commn. on faculty affairs, 1986-87, chmn. faculty devel. com., 1986-87; cons. State of S.C. Dept. Edn., 1980, Southeast Consortium Internat. Devel., 1986-87, Caribbean Agrl. Research and Devel. Inst., 1986-87; collaborator Agy. Internat. Devel., 1987. Contbr. articles to profl. jours. Active Boy Scouts Am., 1967-69, 78-79. Served with U.S. Army, 1954-56. Decorated Army Commendation medal; recipient Meritorious Service medal, 1986. Mem. Am. Soc. Hort. Sci. (co-chmn. program com. 1980-81, Carroll R. Miller award 1975, co-recipient L.M. Ware disting. research award So. Region 1984), Internat. Soc. Hort. Sci., Am. Soc. Plant Physiologists, Fla. State Hort. Soc., Produce Mktg. Assn., Nat. Peach Council, S.C. Acad. Sci., S.C. Hort. Soc. (charter), Nat. Assn. Colls. and Tchrs. Agr., Nat. Council Therapy and Rehab. Through Horticulture, Res. Officers Assn. U.S., Civil Affairs Assn., Sigma Xi, Phi Kappa Phi, Gamma Sigma Delta, Alpha Zeta. Home: Clemson S.C. Died June 3, 1988; buried Arlington Nat. Cemetery.

SINGER, ISAAC BASHEVIS, writer; b. Radzymin, Poland, July 14, 1904; came to U.S., 1935, naturalized, 1943; s. Pinchos Menachem and Bathsheba (Zylberman) S.; m. Alma Haimann, Feb. 14, 1940; 1 son, Israel Zamir. Student, Rabbinical Sem., Warsaw, Poland, 1920-27; DHL (hon.), Hebrew Union Coll., Cin., 1963; LittD (hon.), L.I. U., 1979. With Hebrew and Yiddish publs. in Poland, 1926-35, Jewish Daily Forward, N.Y.C., 1935-85. Author: Satan in Goray, 1935, The Family Moskat, 1950, The Magician of Lublin, 1960, The Spinoza of Market Street, 1961, The Slave, 1962, Short Friday, 1964, In My Father's Court, 1966, The Manor, 1967, The Seance, 1968, The Estate, 1969, A Friend of Kafka, 1970, Enemies: A Love Story, 1970 (film version 1989), A Crown of Feathers, 1973, Passions, 1976, A little Boy in Search of God, A Young Man In Search of Love, 1978, Shosha, 1978, Old Love, 1979, Lost in America, 1981, The Collected Stories of Isaac Bashevis Singer, 1982, The Golem, 1982, Yentl, the Yeshiva Boy, 1983, Love and Exile, 1984, The Image and Other Stories, 1985, Gimple, The Fool, 1987, The Death of Methuselah and Other Stories, 1988, The King of the Fields, 1989, also books for children including A Day of Pleasure, 1970 (Nat. Book award), Stories for Children, 1987; appearance in PBS prodn. American Masters: Isaac in America, 1987. Recipient Epstein Fiction award, 1963, Playboy award for best fiction/short story, 1967, Poses Creative Arts award, 1970, Nat. Book awards, 1970, 74, Nobel Prize for Lit., 1978, Handel medallion, 1986, Gold medal Acad. Arts and Letters, 1989. Fellow Jewish Acad. Arts and Scis., Nat. Inst. Arts and Letters, Polish Inst. Arts and Scis. in Am.; mem. Am. Acad. Arts and Letters. Club: PEN (N.Y.C.). Home: Surfside Fla. Died July 24, 1991; buried Beth-El Cemetery, N.J.

SINGER, SAMUEL BENJAMIN, merchant; b. Indpls., Nov. 21, 1895; s. Jacob and Sarah (Cohen) S.; m. Corinne Shweig, July 8, 1919; children: Morton J., Salley Stein. BSEE, Purdue U., 1917. Pres. Schweig-Engel Co., St. Louis, from 1939. Active local Jewish Community Ctrs. Mem. Nat. Assn. Radio and TV Dealers (sec. 1958-64), B'nai B'rith. *

SINGHER, MARTIAL, baritone, educator, stage director; b. Oloron St.-Marie, France, Aug. 14, 1904; s. Joseph-Paul and Marie (Dubourg) S.; m. Eta Busch, Jan. 10, 1940; children: Charles-Michael, Jean-Pierre, Philip. Ph.D., Normal Superior Sch., St. Cloud, Seine, France, 1927; Mus.D. (hon.), Met. Sch. Music, 1950; Dr. honoris causa, Chgo. Mus. Coll., 1954. Dir. opera dept., vocal instr. Curtis Inst. Music, Phila., 1955-68; dir. voice and opera dept. Music Acad. West, Santa Barbara, Calif., 1962-81; chancellor's artist-in-residence U. Calif., Santa Barbara, 1985-89. Leading baritone, Paris Grand Opera, 1930-40, Teatro Colon, Buenos Aires, 1936-43, Met. Opera, N.Y.C., 1943-60; recitalist and concert singer throughout Europe and Am.; soloist, N.Y. Philharmonic, Phila., Cleve., Nat., Mpls., Chgo., Balt., Boston, St. Louis symphony orchs.; leading baritone Chgo. Civic Opera Co., Rio de Janeiro Teatro Mcpl., San Francisco Opera and others; recorded with RCA Victor, Columbia, Decca, Vanguard, Arch Records.; author: An Interpretive Guide to Operatic Arias: A Handbook for Singers, Coaches, Teachers and Students, 1983; study tapes for singers: Martial Singher recites French poems set to music by French composers, 1990. Decorated officer Legion of Honor (France), 1982. Roman Catholic. Home: Santa Barbara Calif. Died Mar. 10, 1990; cremated.

SIRI, GIUSEPPE CARDINAL, archbishop; b. Genoa, May 20, 1906; s. Nicolo Siri and Giulia Bellavista. Ed. Episcopal Sem., Genoa and Pontifical Gregorian U., Rome. Ordained priest, Roman Cath. Ch., 1928; consecrated bishop; elevated to Sacred Coll. of Cardinals, 1953; Titular Bishop of Livias, 1944; archbishop of Genoa, 1946-87; proclaimed cardinal 1953; pres. Episcopal Dir. Com., Italian Cath. Action, Episcopal Conf. of Italy (C.E.I.), 1959-61; chmn. Italian Episcopal Conf., 1955-65; Apostolic adminstr. of Bobbio, from 1983; mem. Sacred Congregations of Sacraments of the Council and of Seminaries and Univs. of Study. Author: Corso di Teologia per Laici, 1942, La Strada passa per Cristo, 1985, Getsemani, Riflessioni sul Movimento teologico contemporaneo, 1980, La giovinezza della Chiesa, 1983, Il primato della verita, 1984. Died May 3, 1989. Home: Genoa Italy

SIRICA, JOHN J., judge; b. 1904; m. Lucile M. Camalier, Feb. 26, 1952; children: John J. Jr., Patricia Anne, Eileen Marie. LL.B., Georgetown U., 1926; hon. degrees, Coll. New Rochelle, N.Y., Brown U., New Eng. Sch. Law, Boston, Fairfield (Conn.) U., CUNY, Duke U., Georgetown U. Former mem. firm Hogan & Hartson, Washington; judge U.S. Dist. Ct. for D.C., 1957-92, chief Judge, 1971-74, sr. judge, 1977-92. Author: To Set the Record Straight, 1979. Recipient numerous awards and honors including being named Time Mag. Man of Yr., 1973. Mem. ABA, Bar Assn. D.C. (hon.). Clubs: Congressional Country, Nat. Lawyers, Lido Civic. Home: Washington D.C. Died Aug., 1992. †

SISKIND, AARON, photographer; b. N.Y.C., Dec. 4, 1903; m. Sidonie Glaller, 1929. B in Social Sci. in Lit., CCNY, 1926. Instr. English, various pub. schs. N.Y.C., 1926-49; profl. free-lance phototgrapher, 1932—; mem. Film and Photo League, N.Y., 1932-35, 36-41; instr. photography Trenton Coll., 1950, Black Mountain Coll., Beria, N.C., 1951; prof. photography Inst. Design, Ill. Inst. Tech., Chgo., 1951-71, head dept. photography, 1961-71; adj. prof. R.I. Sch. Design, Providence, 1971; vis. lectr. Harvard U., Cambridge, Mass., 1973; mem., trustee Gallery Contemporary Art Chgo. One man shows Egan Gallery, N.Y.C., 1947, Inst. Design, Ill. Inst. Tech., Chgo., 1949, Internat. Mus. Photograph, George Eastman House, Rochester, N.Y., 1954, 63, 65, Art Inst. Chgo., 1955, 64, 75, Centre Culturel Am., Paris, 1957, The Cliff Dwellers, Chgo., 1960, Mus. Modern Art, N.Y.C., 1965, Portland U., Oreg., 1970, Milw. Art Ctr., 1971, Art Mus., R.I. Sch. Design, Providence, 1972, Fogg Art Mus., Harvard U., Cambridge, Mass., 1973, Friends of Photography, Carmel, Calif., 1973, Washington Gallery Photography, 1974, Smart Gallery, U. Chgo., 1975, Vision Gallery, Boston, 1976, Light Gallery, N.Y.C., 1978, Chrysler Mus., Norfolk, Va., 1979, Chgo. Ctr. Contemporary Photography, 1981, U. Ariz. Mus. Art, Tucson, 1982, Royal Palm Gallery, Palm Beach, Fla., 1982, G.H. Dalsheimer Gallery, Balt., 1982, Susan Harder Gallery, N.Y.C., 1982, Mus. Fine Arts, St. Petersburg, Fla., 1984, L.A. County Mus. Art, 1986; numerous group shows including Barbican Art Gallery, London, 1985; represented in permanent collections Ctr. Creative Photography Siskind Archive, U. Ariz., Tucson, Mus. Modern Art, N.Y.C., Met. Mus. Art, N.Y.C., Internat. Ctr. Photography, George Eastman House, Rochester, N.Y., Carpenter Ctr. and Fogg Art Mus., Harvard U., Cambridge, Mass., Art Inst. Chgo., Mpls. Inst. Art, Mus. Fine Arts, Houston, Nat. Gallery Can., Ottawa, Ont., Bibliotheque Nationale, Paris, co-editor, Choice poetry and photographer mag., 1961-70; subject numerous publs. Recipient Disting. Career in Photography award Friends of Photography, 1981; gold award of merit Phila. Coll. Art; Guggenheim fellow, 1966. Mem. Soc. Photog. Edn. (founder). Home: Providence R.I. Died Feb. 8, 1991.

SISLER, GEORGE FREDERICK, state legislator, business consultant; b. Andrew, Iowa, Nov. 25, 1896; s. Charles N. and Sara (Glade) S. AB, U. Dubuque, 1916; MA, U. Chgo. MAster Lake Forest Acad., 1921-23; engaged in advt., 1924-26, in real estate bus., 1927-30; with 1st NAt. Bank Chgo., 1931-62, v.p., 1955-62; pres. Ch. Fedn. of Greater Chgo., 1962-63; bus. cons. Mem. Ill. LEgis.; dir. U. Dubuque. Mem. Immigrants Svcs. League (past pres., dir.), Coun. Fgn. Rels., UN Assn. Ill (pres. 1965), Coun. Profit Sharing Industries (trustee), English Speaking Union (treas.), Rotary (past pres., dir.), Univ. Club, Fin and Feather Club. Presbyterian. *

SISSON, THOMAS RANDOLPH CLINTON, physician; b. Winnipeg, Man., Can., Jan. 22, 1920; s. Lorne Randolph Clinton and Edna Marie (Wilson) S.; m. Anne Robson, May 5, 1945; children: Geoffrey Rhawn Lorne, Peter Alexander Wilson, Paul Cleeland Robson. A.B., Colgate U., 1941; M.D., Temple U., 1944. Diplomate Am. Bd. Pediatrics. Intern St. John's Riverside Hosp., Yonkers, N.Y., 1944-45; resident U. Rochester Med. Ctr., N.Y., 1946-48, N.Y. Hosp.-Cornell U. Med. Ctr., 1948-50; sr. instr. pediatrics, obstetrics U. Rochester, 1953-60; assoc. prof. pediatrics Albert Einstein Coll. Medicine, 1960-65; co-dir. clin. research Geigy Medicine, 1965-67; prof. pediatrics, assoc. prof. obstetrics, dir. perinatal research Temple U. Sch. Medicine, Phila., 1967-78; clin. prof. pediatrics U. Medicine and Dentistry N.J. Rutgers Med. Sch., from 1978; chmn. dept. pediatrics Raritan Bay Med. Ctr., N.J., 1978-84; dir. neonatal research Newark Beth Israel Med. Ctr., 1984-87; prof. N.J. Med. Sch., from 1987; mem. com. photobiology NRC/Nat. Acad. Sci., 1972-76, adv. bd. Inst. Infant Services, from 1975; cons. Bur. Radiation Health, FDA, Nat. Inst. Heart Disease and Stroke, from 1972, Nat. Inst. for Child Health and Human Devel., from 1980; research assoc. neonatology Pa. Hosp., from 1987; clin. prof. pediatrics U. Pa., from 1988;. Contbr. articles to profl. jours. Served with M.C., USNR, 1945-46, 50-51. Buswell faculty fellow U. Rochester Sch. Medicine and Dentistry, 1956-59; grantee NIH, 1967-77, Ross Labs., 1976-77, Ortho Research Found., 1968-69. Fellow Am. Acad. Pediatrics, Internat. Soc. Hematology, Am. Coll. Nutrition; mem. Soc. Pediatric Research, Am. Fedn. Clin. Research, Am. Inst. Nutrition, Am. Soc. Photobiology, AAAS, AMA, Pan-Am. Med. Soc., N.Y. Acad. Scis., Med. Soc. N.J., Soc. Behavioral Pediatrics, Delta Upsilon, Alpha Omega Alpha, Phi Chi. Episcopalian. Home: Bryn Mawr Pa. Deceased. †

SISTRUNK, JAMES DUDLEY, educator, clergyman, librarian; b. Jayess, Miss., Aug. 13, 1919; s. James Cannon and Amelia Frances (Smith) S.; m. Helen Anna Wilson, Dec. 19, 1942; children: James Dudley, Richard Stanley. Student, La. State U., 1945-46, Clarke Meml. Coll., 1951-52; B.A., Baylor U., 1954; B.D., Southwestern Bapt. Theol. Sem., 1957, M.Div., 1972; B.S. in L.S, North Tex. State U., 1959; postgrad., U. N.C., 1960. With Interstate Oil Pipe Line Co., Natchez, Miss., 1946-51; ordained to ministry Bapt. Ch., 1952; pastor Belfalls (Tex.) Bapt. Ch., 1952-54, Fairview Bapt. Ch., Valley Mills, Tex., 1955-57, Tolarsville Bapt. Ch., N.C., 1969-82; circulation librarian Southwestern Bapt. Theol. Sem., 1957-59; adminstrv. librarian Southeastern Bapt. Theol. Sem., 1959-64; librarian, mem. faculty Campbell U., Buies Creek, N.C., 1964-85; prof. Campbell U.; ret., 1985; Mem. Harnett County Public Library Bd. Author: The History of Carrie Rich Memorial Library from 1887 to 1966. Served with USAAF, 1940-45. Mem. ALA, Southeastern, N.C. library assns., Am. Theol. Library Assn. Club: Lion (dir., membership chmn. pres.). Home: Sanford N.C. Deceased. †

SITTERLY, CHARLOTTE MOORE, physicist; b. Ercildoun, Pa., Sept. 24, 1898; d. George Winfield and Elizabeth Palmer (Walton) Moore; m. Bancroft Walker Sitterly, May 30, 1937. AB, Swarthmore Coll., 1920, DSc (hon.), 1962; PhD, U. Calif., 1931; Hon. Dr., U. Kiel, U. Mich., 1968, 71. Computer specialist Princeton Obs., 1920-25, 28-29, rsch. asst., 1931-36, assoc., 1936-45; computer specialist Mt. Wilson Obs., 1925-28; physicist Nat. Bur. Standards, 1945-70; rsch. physicist (part-time) Naval Rsch. lab., Washington, 1971-90. Author: Atomic Lines in the Sun Spot Spectrum, 1932, A Multiplet Table of Astrophysical Interest, 1945, Atomic Energy Levels (3 vols.), 1949, 52, 58, An Ultraviolet Multiplet Table, 5 sects., 1950, 52, 62, Selected Tables of Atomic Spectra, 7 sects., 1965-76, Bibliography on Analyses of Optical Atomic Spectra, 4 sects., 1968, 69, Ionization Potentials, 1970; co-author: The Masses of the Stars, 1940, The Infrared Solar Spectrum, 1947, The Solar Spectrum 2935A to 8770A, 1966. Recipient U.S. Dept. Commerce Exceptional Svc. award, 1960, Fed. Woman's award 1961, Annie Jump Cannon Centennial medal, 1963, Career Svc. award Nat. Civil Svc. League, 1966, William F. Meggers award Optical Soc. Am., 1972. Fellow Optical Soc. Am., Am. Phys. Soc., AAAS (v.p. 1952); mem. Royal Aston. Soc. (fgn. assoc.), Am. Astron. Soc. (v.p. 1958-60), Soc. Applied Spectroscopy (hon.), Internat. Astron. Union (pres. commn. on fundamental spectroscopic data 1961-67), Soc. Royale des Sciences de Liege (corr.), Phi Beta Kappa, Sigma Xi. Home: Washington D.C. Died Mar. 3, 1990.

SITTON, FRED MONROE, speech and drama educator; b. Pyote, Tex., Mar. 27, 1924; s. Fitzhugh Lee and Aurie Hester (Hutchison) S.; m. Kathryn Irene Means, July 19, 1947. B.A., Tex. Western Coll., 1943, M.A., 1951; M.F.A., U. Tex., 1954; L.D.A., U. N.C., 1959; Ph.D., Northwestern U., 1962. Tchr. pub. schs. Pecos, Tex., 1947-52, Charlotte, N.C., 1954-58; instr. U. N.C., Chapel Hill, 1957-59; prof. speech and drama Valparaiso (Ind.) U., 1961-83, prof. emeritus, 1983-89, chmn. dept. speech and drama, 1970-81; producer, dir. Summer Stock Theatre, Pocono Pines, Pa., 1962-67; dir. Profl. Stock, Valparaiso, 1968-72; founder Children's

Theatre, Valparaiso, 1963. Served with U.S. Maritime Service, 1943-46. U. N.C. grantee in theatre, 1958-59. Mem. Am. Theatre Assn., Children's Theatre Assn., Pi Kappa Alpha. Democrat. Home: Pyote Tex. Died Oct. 17, 1988; buried Pyote (Tex.) Cemetery.

SKILLING, HUGH HILDRETH, electrical engineering educator; b. San Diego, Sept. 2, 1905; s. William Thompson and Bird (Hildreth) S.; m. Hazel Dillon, June 21, 1932; 1 child, Ann Katherine. Student, Sant Diego State Coll., 1922-24; AB, Stanford U., 1926, MSEE, 1927, PhD, 1931; SM, MIT, 1930. Registered profl. engr., Calif. Elec. engr. So. Calif. Edison Co., L.A., 1927-29; instr. elec. engring. Stanford U., 1929, 31-35, asst. prof., 1935-39, assoc. prof., 1939-42, prof., from 1942, acting head dept., 1941-44, exec. head, 1944-64, acting dean Sch. Engring., 1944-46, assoc. dean, 1952-54; Fulbright prof. elec. engring. Cambridge U., England, 1951-52, vis. prof., 1965; lectr. electric power transmission MIT, 1934; lectr. Madrid, 1952, U. Chile, Santiago, 1957; cons. elec. engring. edn. Dartmouth Coll., 1958, U. Hawaii, 1958, U. Alaska, 1964; cons. editor John Wiley & Sons, Inc., 1951-71; mem. rev. team U. Philippines, 1953. Author: Transient Electric Currents, 1937, Fundamentals of Electric Waves, 1942, 2d edit., 1948, Prelude to Bikini, 1947, Exploring Electricity, 1948, Electric Transmission Lines, 1951, Electrical Engineering Circuits, 1951, 2d edit., 1965, A First Course in Electromechanics, 1960, Electromechanics, 1962, Do You Teach?, 1969, Electric Networks, 1974, Teaching: Guidance by Distinguished Teachers, 1977; work transl. into Spanish, Russian, Polish, Vietnamese, Thai; contbr. articles to McGraw-Hill Ency. Sci. and profl. jours. Supr. U.S. Army Signal Corps Radio Tng. Program, Stanford, 1942-43; expert cons. Army Svc. Forces, 1944; ofcl. investigator Nat. Def. Rsch. Com., 1942-44; sci. observer atomic bomb tests, Bikini Atoll, 1946. Fellow IEEE (medal for edn. 1964), AAAS; mem. Phi Beta Kappa, Sigma Xi. Home: Stanford Calif. Died Oct. 23, 1990; buried Palo Alto, Calif.

SKINNER, BURRHUS FREDERIC, psychologist, educator; b. Susquehanna, Pa., Mar. 20, 1904; s. William Arthur and Grace (Burrhus) S.; m. Yvonne Blue, Nov. 1, 1936; children—Julie (Mrs. Ernest Vargas), Deborah (Mrs. Barry Buzan). A.B., Hamilton Coll., 1926, Sc.D., 1951; M.A., Harvard U., 1930, Ph.D., 1931, Sc.D., 1985; Sc.D., N.C. State U., 1960, U. Chgo., 1967, U. Mo., 1968, Alfred U., 1969, U. Exeter, Eng., 1969, Ind. U., 1970, McGill U., 1970, C.W. Post Center L.I. U., 1971, Dickinson Coll., 1972, Lowell Technol. Inst., 1974, Nasson Coll., 1976, Colby Coll., 1984; Litt.D. (hon.), Ripon Coll., 1957, Tufts U., 1977, SUNY-Buffalo, 1986; L.H.D., Rockford Coll., 1971, Framingham (Mass.) State Coll., 1972, U. Md.-Balt. County, 1973, New Coll., Hofstra U., 1974, Exptl. Coll. Inst. Behavioral Research, 1974, Johns Hopkins U., 1979, SUNY, Buffalo, 1986; LL.D., Ohio Wesleyan U., 1971, Hobart and William Smith Coll., 1972, Western Mich. U., 1976, Ball State U., 1983; D.Soc.Sci., U. Louisville, 1977, D.Laws, Keio U., Tokyo, 1979. Research fellow NRC, Harvard, 1931-33; jr. fellow Harvard Soc. Fellows, 1933-36; instr. psychology U. Minn., Mpls., 1936-37; asst. prof. U. Minn., 1937-39, assoc. prof., 1939-45; conducted war research sponsored by Gen. Mills, Inc., 1942-43; prof. psychology, chmn. dept. Ind. U., 1945-48; William James lectr. Harvard U., 1947, prof. psychology, 1948-57, Edgar Pierce prof., 1958-74, prof. emeritus, 1974-90. Author: Behavior of Organisms, 1938, Walden Two, 1948, Science and Human Behavior, 1953, Verbal Behavior, 1957, (with C.B. Ferster) Schedules of Reinforcement, 1957, Cumulative Record, 1959, rev. 1961, 72, (with J.G. Holland) The Analysis of Behavior, 1961, The Technology of Teaching, 1968, Contingencies of Reinforcement: A Theoretical Analysis, 1969, Beyond Freedom and Dignity, 1971, About Behaviorism, 1974, Particulars of My Life, 1976, Reflections on Behaviorism and Society, 1978, The Shaping of a Behaviorist, 1979, Notebooks, 1980, A Matter of Consequences, 1983, (with M.E. Vaughan) Enjoy Old Age, 1983, Upon Further Reflection, 1986, Recent Issues in the Analysis of Behavior, 1989. Recipient distinguished sci. contbn. award, 1958, Nat. medal Sci., 1968, Gold medal Am. Psychol. Assn., 1971, Joseph P. Kennedy, Jr. Found. award, 1971; award for excellence in psychiatry Albert Einstein Sch. Medicine, 1985; President's award N.Y. Acad. Scis., 1985; Guggenheim fellow, 1944-45. Fellow Royal Soc. Arts; mem. Am. Psychol. Assn., Swedish Psychol. Soc., Brit. Psychol. Soc., Spanish Psychol. Soc., AAAS, Nat. Acad. Sci., Am. Acad. Arts and Scis., Am. Philos. Soc., Phi Beta Kappa, Sigma Xi. Home: Cambridge Mass. Died Aug. 18, 1990; buried Mt. Auburn Cemetery, Mass.

SKINNER, JOHN LLEWELLYN, architect; b. Cleve., Aug. 20, 1893; s. William Charles and Clara Charlotte (Coulton) S.; m. Leone Hardy Mines, Dec. 16, 1924; 1 child, John Llewellyn. BA, U. Tornoto, 1916; MArch, Harvard, 1920. Prof., head dept. architecture Ga. Tech., 1922-25; architect Miami, Fla., from 1925; ptnr. Steward-Skinner. Prin. works include Jackson Meml. Dr.'s Mercy Hosp., Miami, Palmer Eye Inst., Miami, Holy Cross Hosp., Ft. Lauderdale, Fla., U. Miami Med. Sch., Med. Rsch. Bldg., MArine Lab., main libr., bus. sch. math. , meteorology bldgs. of Fla. State U., Dade County Auditorium, Miami Pub. Libr., Miami Internat. Airport, Internat. Terminal, Bogota, Columbia, Miami Seaquarium, Torpical Park Race Corps Tng. Ctr., Miami, Miami Cancer Inst.; one-man watercolor shows include U. Fla., Ga. Inst. Tech., others. Bd. dirs. Little Switzerland Assn., Inc. Nelson Robinson Travelling Rsch. fellow, Europe, 1920-22, Affiliated felloe Am. Acad. Rome, 1921-22. Fellow AIA (Wade lectr. 1940, pres. So. Fla. chpt., bd. dirs.), Am. Artists Profl. League (pres. Miami chpt.), Beta Theta Pi, Phi Kappa Phi, Masons, Rotary. Clubs: Biscayne Bay Yacht (vice comdr.), Harvard, Houghton Fortnightly (Miami). Republican. *

SKINNER, SHERROD E., automotive manufacturing executive; b. Britain, Conn., Oct. 19, 1896; s. Edward J. and Lillie (Buritt) S.; m. Abigail Leete, May 28, 1921; children: Martha L., Shirley Y., Sherwood E., Jr. (killed in Korean are, Oct. 26, 1952), David. ME, Rensselaer Polytech Inst., 1920. With Landers, Frary & Clark Co., New Britain, 1920-30, advancing to asst. gen. supt.; chief. engr. Ternstedt Mfg., div. of Gen. Motors Corp., Detroit, 1930-35, gen. mgr., 1935-40; became gen. mgr. Oldsmobile div. Gen. Motors Corp., 1942-59, exec. v.p., 1959-61, group exec. accessory divs., 1950-61, past dir., mem. ops. policy com.; mem. bd. dirs. Continential Can Co., Inc., Chmn. Aerospace Inc., L.A. Trustee Rensselaer Poly Inst. With USN, WWI. Recipient Exceptional Civilian Svc. award U.S. Army, 1945. Fellow Am. Soc. Mech. Engrs.; mem. Soc. Automotive Engrs., Chi Phi, Sigma Xi, Tau Beta Pi. Clubs: Detroit Athletic, Detroit, Bloomfield Hills Country, Recess, Shuttle MEadow Country (New Britian). *

SKLAR, RICHARD J., broadcast executive; b. Bklyn., Nov. 21, 1929; s. William and Cecile F. (Fox) S.; m. Sydelle Helfgott, July 8, 1954; children: Scott Richard, Holly. BS, NYU, 1953. Announcer, copywriter Sta. WPAC, Patchogue, N.Y., 1954; program dir. Sta. WINS, N.Y.C., 1955-61, Sta. WMGM, N.Y.C., 1961-62, Sta. WABC, N.Y.C., 1962-77; v.p. programming ABC Radio div., N.Y.C., 1977-84; pres. Sklar Communications, Inc., N.Y.C., from 1984; ptnr. Bowen Sklar Programming, Eng.; adj. prof. St. Johns U., N.Y.C., 1975-92; v.p. Interep Radio Store, N.Y.C., 1991-92, Stratosphere Broadcasting, 1991-92, Music Net, 1992. Author: Tom Swift and His Giant Robot, 1954, Rocking America: How the All-Hit Radio Stations Took Over America, 1984; contbr. articles to profl. jours. Mem. Internat. Radio and TV Soc. (mem. bd. govs. 1974-84), Broadcast Pioneers. Club: N.Y. Road Runners. Home: New York N.Y. Died June 22, 1992.

SKLARE, MARSHALL, sociology educator; b. Chgo., Oct. 21, 1921; s. Irving and Bee (Lippman) S.; m. Rose Bernards, June 8, 1947; children—Daniel Avram, Judith Eve, Joshua Mayer. Student, Northwestern U., 1938-39, 40-43; diploma, Coll. Jewish Studies, Chgo., 1943; M.A. in Sociology, U. Chgo., 1948; Ph.D., Columbia U. (in Sociology), 1953. Lectr. dept. sociology and anthropology CCNY, 1952-53; study dir. to dir. Div. Sci. Research, Am. Jewish Com., 1953-66; lectr. Wurzweiler Sch. Social Work, Yeshiva U., 1960-66, Stern Coll. for Women, 1963-64; prof. sociology Wurzweiler Sch. Social Work and Ferkauf Grad. Sch. Humanities and Social Sci., 1966-70; Fulbright lectr. Hebrew U. of Jerusalem, 1965-66; vis. lectr. Princeton Theol. Sem., 1968-69; vis. prof. Am. Jewish sociology Brandeis U., Waltham, Mass., 1969-70, prof. Jewish studies and sociology, 1970-79, Klutznick Family prof. Am. Jewish studies and sociology, 1979-91, emeritus, 1992; dir. Center for Modern Jewish Studies Brandeis U., 1980-86; vis. prof. sociology Clark U., 1970-72, SUNY, Albany, 1983; sr. fellow Nat. Endowment for Humanities, 1972-73; chmn. award com. Fred Sherrow Meml. Prize; cons. Max Weinreich Center for Advanced Jewish Studies, YIVO Inst. for Jewish Research.; Adviser univ. nominations com. Tel Aviv U. Author: Conservative Judaism: An American Religious Movement, 1955, rev. edit., 1972, (with M. Vosk) The Riverton Study: How Jews Look at Themselves and Their Neighbors, 1957, The Jews: Social Patterns of an American Group, 1958, 77, (with J. Greenblum) Jewish Identity on the Suburban Frontier: A Study of Group Survival in the Open Society, 1967, 2d edit., 1979, (with J. Greenblum and B.B. Ringer) Not Quite at Home: How an American Jewish Community Lives with Itself and its Neighbors, 1969, America's Jews, 1971, The Jew in American Society, 1974, The Jewish Community in America, 1974, Understanding American Jewry, 1982, American Jews: A Reader, 1983; Contbr. articles to profl. jours.; Mem. editorial bd.: Am. Jewish History. Mem. Assn. for Sociol. Study of Jewry (pres., chmn. com. on curriculum and resources), Am. Jewish Hist. Soc. (mem. acad. adv. council, library com.), Assn. for Jewish Studies (dir., sec./treas.), Am. Sociol. Assn. (program organizer). Home: Newton Centre Mass. Died Mar. 1, 1992.

SKOURAS, SPYROS P., motion pictures; b. Skourobonion, Greece, Mar. 28, 1893; Became naturalized citizen of U.S., 1913; m. Saroula Bruiglia; children: Daphne Dolores, Spyros, Diana, Plato. Began as busboy in St. Louis hotels; organized chain of theatres in St. Louis (sold to Warner Bros.); successively gen. mgr. Warner Bros circuit; assoc. with Paramount Pictures; pres. Nat. Theatres Amusement Co.; pres. 20th Century-Fox Film Corp., 1942-62, now chmn. bd.; chmn. Skouras Lines. *

SLAUGHTER, WILLIAM EDWARD, JR., petroleum company executive; b. Chgo., Dec. 5, 1908; s. William Edward and Maggie (Fergusson) S.; m. Betty Helen Pesch, Dec. 27, 1961 (dec. 1984); children: Gloria, William Edward IV, Kent. Student, Northwestern U., 1927-28, Detroit Inst. Tech., 1931-33. Various sales, mktg. positions in oil industry, 1929-32; co-founder, pres., dir. Aurora Gasoline Co., 1932-61; v.p., dir. Marathon Internat. Oil Co., 1961-65; v.p. gen. services Marathon Oil Co., 1965-70, ret. Mem. businessmen's adv. com. Wayne State U. Religious Ctr., 1960-70; chmn. Mich. Turnpike Authority, 1953-55; pres. Boys Clubs Met. Detroit, 1970-71, vice chmn., 1971, chmn., 1972-73, mem. exec. com., 1974-75, trustee, 1975-87, bd. dirs., 1958-75; trustee Boys and Girls Clubs Southeastern Mich., 1985-90, Detroit Osteo Hosp. Corp., 1951-73; trustee, pres. William E. Slaughter Jr. Found. Inc., 1957-90; bd. dirs. Jr. Achievement Northwestern Ohio Inc., 1965-70, Boys Clubs Broward County (Fla.), from 1974, The Opera Guild Inc., Ft. Lauderdale. Mem. Am. Petroleum Inst., NAM, Assn. Petroleum Industries Mich. (chmn. 1956-61), Mich. C. of C. (charter, bd. dirs.). Clubs: 100 Detroit, Detroit Athletic; 100 Broward County; 100 South Palm Beach County; Oakland Hills Country; Boca Raton Hotel and Beach (Fla.). Home: Birmingham Mich. Died June 8, 1990.

SLAWSON, JOHN, organization executive, psychologist; b. Russia, Apr. 16, 1898; came to U.S., 1904, naturalized, 1991; s. Samuel and Fanny (Tarsy) S.; m. Ada Schupper, Dec. 22, 1937; children: June Slawson Kopilow, Judith Barbara, Ruth Ann Slawson Kaufman. BS, Columbia U., 1919, MA, 1920, PhD, 1927; DHL (hon.), Hebrew Union Coll.-Inst. Rel., 1962. Instr. CCNY, 1919-20; investigator, psychologist N.Y. State Dept. Welfare, 1920-24; asst. dir. Cleve. Jewish Welfare Fedn., 1924-28; exec. dir. Detroit Jewish Welfare Fedn., 1928-32, Jewish Bd. Guardians, N.Y.C., 1932-43; exec. v.p. Am. Jewish Com., N.Y.C., 1943-67, exec. v.p. emeritus, 1967-89; lectr. U. Mich., 1930-31, New Sch. for Social Rsch., 1966-69; lectr. Columbia U., 1966-69, adj. prof., 1973-74; adj. assoc. prof. Hunter Coll. Social Work, CUNY, 1972-73; cons. wartime delinquency U.S. Children's Bur., Social Security bd., FSA, 1942-44; spl. adviser to President's Com. on Juvenile Delinquency and Youth Crime, 1962; Am. Jewish Com. del. Paris Peace Conf., 1946; mem. com. human rights Commn. To Study Orgn. Peace; mem. U.S. com. for UNESCO, 1952-54, mem. exec. com., 1954-58. Author: The Delinquent Boy, 1926, reissued 1975, The Role of Science in Intergroup Relations, 1962; also articles, chpts. to books. Bd. dirs. Hebrew U. Jerusalem, Interracial Colloquy, Am. Assn. for Jewish Edn., Nat. Commn. against Discrimination in Housing. Fellow APA, Am. Orthopsychiat. Assn.; mem. NASW, Am. Sociol. Assn., Soc. Psychol. Study Social Issues, Nat. Assn. Human Rights Workers, Nat. Conf. on Social Work, Assn. Jewish Community Rels. Workers, Coun. on Fgn. Rels. Home: New York N.Y. Died Dec. 12, 1989; buried Beth Moses Cemetery, L.I.

SLEIGHT, JESSIE ADELE, editor; b. Stony Brook, N.Y., May 8, 1896; d. Charles Mills and Adella Abigail (Bayles) S. Student, pub schs., L.I. and Bklyn.; pvt. study piano and organ. Staff Musical Am.; asst. to A. Walter Kramer, 1920-21; asst. to editor The George Matthew Adams Svc., N.Y.C.; newspaper syndicate, 1922-34, editor, from 1935. Organist St. James Episcopal. Ch., 1942-55. Mem. Authors LEague Am., Inc., Woman Pays Club. *

SLICHTER, WILLIAM PENCE, research chemist, business executive; b. Mar. 31, 1922; s. Sumner Huber and Ada (Pence) S.; m. Ruth Kaple, June 17, 1950 (dec.); children: Nancy (dec.), Carol, Catherine, Margaret. BA in Chemistry, Harvard U., 1944, MA in Physics, 1949, PhD in Chem. Physics, 1950. Mem. tech. staff Bell Telephone Labs., Murray Hill, N.J., 1950-87, head chem. phys. dept., 1958-67, chem. dir., 1967-73; exec. dir. rsch. materials sci. and engring. div. AT&T Bell Labs., Murray Hill, 1973-87; mem. Nat. Materials Adv. Bd.; chmn. study on engring. rsch. ctrs. for NSF; mem. human rights com. NAS; Charles Hurd lectr. chemistry dept. Northwestern U., 1976. Mem. editorial bd. Science mag., Jour. Polymer Sci., Advances in Polymer Sci. Served to 1st lt. AUS, 1943-46, PTO. Fellow AAAS, Am. Phys. Soc. (High Polymer Physics prize 1970), Am. Acad. Arts and Scis.; mem. NAE, Am. Chem. Soc., Electrochems. Soc., Materials Rsch. Soc., Minerals, Metals and Materials Soc. Home: Chatham N.J. Died Oct. 25, 1990; buried Madison, Wis.

SLOAN, JOHN ELLIOT, JR., association executive; b. Nashville, Nov. 6, 1936; s. John E. and Margaret (Howe) S.; m. Delphine Oman, Apr. 4, 1964; children: Elliott, Delphine, Oman, Catherine. B.A. cum laude, Vanderbilt U., Nashville, 1958; student, Stonier Grad. Sch. Banking, Rutgers U., 1969-71. Vice pres. First Am. Bank, Nashville, 1961-72; pres. Harpeth Nat. Bank, Franklin, Tenn., 1972-75; pres., chief exec. officer First Tenn. Bank, Nashville, 1976-83, Nat. Fedn. Ind. Bus., San Mateo, Calif., from 1983; dir. Am. Health Corp., Nashville. Pres. Nashville Jr. C. of C., 1962-71; pres., bd. dirs. Nashville Boys Club, from 1965; mayor, commr. City of Brentwood, Tenn., 1969-73; chmn. state adv. council to SBA, 1977-83; chmn. nat. adv. council U.S. SBA, 1981-83; commr. Williamson County, 1978-82; mem. U.S. C of C Small Bus. Council, 1981-83;

mem. Tenn. Bd. Equalization, 1972-83; bd. dirs. Nat. Alliance of Bus., 1984, Jr. Achievement, 1985, Boys Clubs Am., 1985, Montgomery Bell Acad., 1978, Nashville Symphony Assn., 1970; trustee King Coll., Bristol, Tenn., 1982. Served to lt. j.g. USN, 1958-61. Named advocate of Yr., SBA, 1981; Disting. fellow Shavano Inst. for Nat. Leadership, Hillsdale Coll., Mich., 1984. Mem. Chief Exec. Officer's Club. Home: Franklin Tenn. Died Nov. 10, 1991. †

SLOAN, WILLIAM BOYD, judge; b. Gainesville, Ga., July 9, 1895; s. Wilford Baker and Angeline (Reed) S.; m. Jessie Lea Jackson, Sept. 6, 1923. Student, North Ga. Coll., 1912-13; studies law in father's law office. Bar: Ga. 1915. Rep. Ga. State Gen. Assembly, 1927-31; asst. atty. gen. Ga., 1932; judge City Ct., Hall County, Ga., 1934-45, Superior Cts. Northeast Dist. Ga., 1945-48, U.S. Dist. Ct. (no. dist.) Ga., from 1951. Mem. ABA, Ga. State Bar Assn. *

SLOSBERG, SAMUEL LOUIS, shoe manufacturing company executive; b. Chelsea, Mass., Mar. 30, 1897; s. Jacon A. and Bessie (Abromovitz) S.; m. Helen Sagoff, May 30, 1925; children: Flroence, Edna. AB cum laude, Harvard, 1917. With Green Shoe Mfg. Co., Boston, from 1919, chmn. bd., from 1968. Pres. Beth Israel Hosp., Boston, from 1964; trustee Children's Hosp., Boston, Brandeis U. With USN, WWI. Mem. Nat. Shoe Mfrs. Assn. (past pres.). *

SMALLWOOD, JOHN WILLIAM, investment banker; b. Paterson, N.J., June 24, 1893; s. John William and ELizabeth (Bonney) S.; m. Carolyn Naudorf Linkroum, Nov. 25, 1914; children: Miriam Elsie, John William, Carolyn Elizabeth, Franklin. Student, pub. schs., N.J. Reporter Wall St. Jour., 1911-15; oil securities analyst Carl H. Pforzheimer & Co., 1915-25, ptnr., from 1925; pres., dir. Petroleum & Trading Corp. Pres., dir. Carl and Lily Pforzheimer Found., Inc.; trustee, chmn. fin. com. Ridgewood Hosp. Assn. (Valley Hosp.). Mem. Am. Petroleum Inst., City Mid Day Club. Bond Club, Ridgewood Club. Presbyterian. *

SMALLWOOD, JOSEPH ROBERTS, premier of Newfoundland; b. Dec. 24, 1900; s. Charles and Minnie Smallwood; m. Clara Isobel Oates; 3 children. Began as newspaperman; active in bringing Nfld. into Can. union; leader Liberal Party; now premier and minister of econ. devel.; mem. Privy Coun. Mem. United Ch. of Can. Home: Saint Johns NF Can. Died Dec. 17, 1991.

SMELZER, DONALD CAMPBELL, physician, hospital director; b. Montreal, Can., Jan. 7, 1896; came to U.S., 1922, naturalized 1930; s. John Hamilton and Lillian (Campbell) S.; m. Ethel Proper, Dec. 8, 1924; children: Martha Ann, Barbara Campbell, Diane Claire. MD, C.M. McGill U., 1918. Asst. supt. Montreal Gen. Hosp., 1921-23; also supt. Buffalo Gen. Hosp., 1923-25; dir. Charles T. Miller Hosp., St. Paul, 1925-30; dir. grad. hosp. U. Pa., 1930-41; dir. Germantown Dispensary and Hosp., 1941-48; trustee Am. Hosp. Assn., 1939-41, pres., 1944-45; past pres. Phila. Hosp. Assn.; pres. Hosp. Assn. Pa., 1943-44; trustee AHA, 1945-46; pvt. hosp. cons., from 1964. Contbr. articles on hosp. adminstrn. Mem. Nat. Rehab. Adv. Coun. Fed. Security Agy.; chmn. adv. com. Phila. Hosp. Coun., 1946-48; chmn. Coun. Internat. Rels. ANA, 1946-48; exec. dir. Hosp. Planning Adv. Citizens Conf., from 1952, Lancaster (Pa.) Gen. Hosp., 1952-64; U.S. del. to Internat. Hosp. Congress, Amsterdam, Holland, 1949, Brussels, 1951. Served as lt. Med. Corps Can. Army, 1918-19; capt. Med. Corps, 1919-21. Fellow AMA, Am. Coll. Hosp. Adminstrs. (charter); mem. Minn. Hosp. Assn. (hon.), Med. Soc. Pa., Phila. Coll. Physicians, Am. Pub. Health Cons., St. Andrews Soc. Phila., Soc. Med. Adminstrs., Lancaster County Med. Soc., Alpha Kappa Kappa, Alpha Omega Alpha, Hamilton Club. Republican. Presbyterian. *

SMILEY, JOSEPH ROYALL, university president, educator; b. Dallas, Mar. 17, 1910; s. S. Lehman and Mabel (Royall) S.; m. Mary Fincher, May 25, 1935 (dec. Jan. 1981); children: Stephen, Mary. A.B., So. Meth. U., 1931, A.M., 1932, LL.D., 1964; Ph.D., Columbia, 1947; LL.D., U. Denver, 1966. Instr. Ark. A&M Coll., Magnolia, 1934-35; instr., asst. prof., assoc. prof. North Tex. State Coll., Denton, 1935-38, 40-43, 46-47; lectr. Columbia U., 1938-40; asst. prof. U. Ill., 1947-49, asst. dean grad. coll., 1949-50, assoc. dean, 1950-51, prof. French, 1951-58, head dept., 1952-54, dean coll. liberal arts and scis., 1954-58; pres. Tex. Western Coll., U. Tex., 1958-60; v.p., provost U. Tex., Austin, 1960-61, pres., 1961-63; pres. U. Colo., Boulder, 1963-69; pres. U. Tex., El Paso, 1969-73, pres. emeritus, H.Y. Benedict prof. modern langs., 1973-80, prof. emeritus, 1980-90; Vis. prof. U. Colo., 1974; Mem. bd. advisers Mountain States Telephone; dir. El Paso Electric Co. Commr. Western Interstate Commn. on Higher Edn., 1963- 67, exec. com., 1965-67; chmn. U.S. Adv. Commn. on Internat. Ednl. and Cultural Affairs, 1966-69; mem. Govt. Adv. Com. Internat. Book Programs, 1966-68; chmn. Boulder Housing Authority, 1966-68; mem. adv. com. for instl. relations NSF, 1967-69; Mem. bd. Asso. Rocky Mountain Univs., 1963, sec.-treas., 1965-66, vice chmn., 1966-67; Fulbright research fellow, France, 1953-54; mem. President's Commn. on White House Fellows. Author: Diderot's Relations with Grimm, 1950; Bd. editors: Tex. Western Press, 1973-78; Contbr. articles to profl. jours. Bd. dirs. East-West Center, Honolulu, 1966-69; bd. visitors Air U., 1968-71. Served as lt. USNR, 1943-46. Decorated chevalier Legion of Honor France; recipient U. Colo. medal, 1987. Mem. Phi Kappa Phi, Kappa Alpha, Phi Beta Kappa. Episcopalian. Home: El Paso Tex. Died May 25, 1990; buried El Paso, Tex.

SMITH, ALBERT BARNES, JR., university president emeritus; b. Pitts., Apr. 21, 1915; s. Albert Barnes and Valeria (Fetterman) S.; m. Lucile Nevin, June 22, 1940; children: Albert Barnes III, Sandra Lucile, Deborah Ann. B.B.A., Westminster Coll., 1937; M.Litt., U. Pitts., 1938; Pd.D., Westminster Coll., 1956; LL.D. hon., Seton Hill Coll., 1980. With U. Pitts., from 1938, beginning as research asst. Sch. Retailing, successively sr. fellow research, asst. prof. retailing, assoc. prof., asst. dir., 1938-53, prof. retailing, 1951-61; dean U. Pitts. (Grad. Sch. Retailing), 1953-61, dir. devel., 1959-62, prof. bus. adminstrn., from 1961, assoc. dean grad. sch. bus., 1961-63, asst. to chancellor, 1962-63; pres. U. Pitts. at Greensburg, 1963-80, pres. emeritus, from 1980; Past bd. dirs. WQED. Served as lt. (j.g.), Supply Corps USNR, 1944-46. Mem. Alpha Sigma Pi, Eta Mu Pi. Presbyterian (elder). Lodge: Rotary. Home: Omaha Nebr. Deceased. †

SMITH, ALPHEUS, educator; b. Lake Arrowhead, Calif., Mar. 29, 1898; s. Albert William and Ruby Hazel (Green) S.; m. Lauretta Hessin Nichols, Sept. 8, 1922; 1 child, Strether. AB, Cornell U., 1919; PhD, Harvard U., 1932. Exec. Standard Oil Co. of N.Y., Turkey, Greece, 1919-21; teaching asst., assoc. prof. English Northwestern U., 1927-46; vis. prof. U. Nebr., 1933, 36; ednl. broadcaster Chgo., 1933-42; prof. N.Y. State Sch. Indsl. and Labor Rels. Cornell U., from 1946, prof. in charge of extension, 1947-48, 54-56, dir., 1956-60, sec., from 1960; vis. lectr. U. Hawaii, 1960. 2d. lt. U.S. Army, 1818-19; lt. col. U.S. Army, 1942-46. Awarded Legion of Merit. Mem. AAUP, Indsl. Rels. Rsch. Assn., Theta Delta Chi. *

SMITH, ANTHONY WAYNE, lawyer, consultant, environmentalist; b. Pitts.; s. Anthony Woodward and Janey Mulhern (Coard) S.; m. Anya E. Freedel, June 20, 1930. B.A. with high honors, U. Pitts.; J.D., Yale U., 1934. Bar: N.Y. State 1935, U.S. Supreme Ct. 1940, D.C. 1947. Sec. to gov. Pa., 1932-33; with firm Donovan, Leisure, Newton & Lumbard, N.Y.C., 1934-37; pvt. practice law Washington, from 1949; asst. gen. counsel CIO, Washington, 1937-56, asst. dir. state and city indsl. union councils, 1941-55, exec. sec. housing com., 1937-39, 41-42, asst. sec. Latin Am. com., 1939-40; observer UN, 1954-56; atty. polit. edn. com. AFL-CIO, 1956-58; pres., gen. counsel Nat. Parks and Conservation Assn., 1958-80, spl. counsel, 1980-92; comml. farmer, Franklin County, Pa., 1954-92; exec. committeeman Emergency Com. on Natural Resources, 1952-53, Citizens Com. on Natural Resources, 1953-78, C & O Canal Assn., 1954-71, Little Cove Assn., from 1971; del. various gen. sessions Internat. Union for Conservation of Nature, from 1952; pres. South Cen. Pa. Citizens Assn., from 1962; gen. counsel Citizens Permanent Conf. Potomac River Basin, from 1968; chmn. Environ. Coalition for N.Am., from 1970; co-chmn. Everglades Coalition, from 1969; observer to UN Conf. on Human Environ., Stockholm, Sweden, 1972, UN Environ. Programme, Geneva, Switzerland, 1973; mem. adv. com. to sec. state on UN Conf. on Human Environment, 1972; mem. adv. com. to sec. state UN Conf. Law of Sea, 1972-83; mem. U.S. Delegation, 1973-83; mem. adv. com. to Coun. on Environ. Quality on U.S.-USSR Sci. Exch., 1974; mem. steering com. The Unfinished Agenda (Laurance S. Rockefeller Report on Environ.), 1976-77; bd. dirs. Coun. on Ocean Law, 1982; mem. steering com. intensive timber harvest N.Y. State Andirondack Park Agy., 1980-82; spl. counsel Chesapeake Bay Found., 1980, Negative Population Growth, 1981-92; mem. steering com. OSHA Environ. Network, indsl. union dept. AFL-CIO, 1980-87; chmn. cons. group on norms and incentives for population stabilization, 1982; cons. Scholastic Mags., from 1981; spl. cons. Solarex Corp., 1982-86, population internat. security U. Pitts., 1988, chair cons. group Ecol. Forest Mgmt., from 1990; initiated legislation resulting in establishment of Atomic Energy Commn., 1945. Bd. editors Yale Law Jour. 1931-34; co-author Nat. Labor Relations Act, Fair Labor Standards Act; contbr. numerous articles to profl. jours. Served as 2d lt. AUS, 1926-30. Recipient Bicentennial Medallion of Distinction, U. Pitts., 1987. Mem. Am. Farm Bur. Fedn., Pa. County Farmers Assn., Franklin County Farmers Assn., Nat. Concord Granges, Pa. Concord Granges, Nat. Lawyers Club, Bar Assn. D.C., Assn. of Bar of City of N.Y., Delta Tau Delta, Phi Mu Sigma, Delta Sigma Rho, Omicron Delta Kappa. Club: Yale (N.Y.C.). Home: Mercerburg Pa. Died Feb. 29, 1992.

SMITH, ARTHUR HENRY, management consultant; b. Milw., Mar. 11, 1912; s. Charles Arthur and Margaret (Duckart) S.; m. Isabelle Marie Skarolid, June 1, 1940; children—Gary Arthur, Virginia Isabelle, Judy Anne. B.A., U. Wis., 1936; grad., Advanced Mgmt. Program, Harvard, 1952. C.P.A., Wis. Within Gen. Mills, Inc., 1936-60, dir. mgmt. analysis, 1954-60; v.p., dir. Midwest Tech. Devel. Corp., Mpls., 1960-63; pres., dir. Turbomatic, Inc., Mpls., 1962-63; dir. Dynasonics Corp., 1960-62, Electra Sci. Corp., 1961-63; controller Hunt Foods & Industries, Inc.; dir. finance Hunt Foods & Industries, Inc. (Hunt-Wesson foods div.), 1963-65; mgmt. cons. Price Waterhouse & Co., 1965-66; v.p., controller Libby, McNeill & Libby, 1966-67; fin. v.p., treas. Internat. Industries, Inc., 1967-71; also dir.; pres. A. Smith & Assos., 1971-88; pres. Solar Conversion Corp. Am., Van Nuys, Calif., 1975-76. Contbr. articles to profl. jours. Treas. Stuart Cameron McLeod Soc. Mem. Calif. Soc. C.P.A.'s, Nat. Assn. Accountants (past pres. Mpls. chpt., past nat. dir. and v.p.), Harvard Bus. Sch. Assn. (past mem. nat. exec. council), Phi Beta Kappa. Home: Rocklin Calif. Died Dec. 10, 1988; buried Calvary Cemetery, Citrus Heights, Calif.

SMITH, BRYAN, insurance executive; b. Easton, Ill., Jan. 21, 1897; s. James H. and Nancy (Street) S.; m. Elizabeth H. Stoufer, June 16, 1934; children: Charles B., Susan J. BS, MA, U. Minn., 1925. Instr. econs. River Falls (Wis.) Normal Sch., 1925-26; with Liberty Mut. Ins. Co., from 1926; successively salesman mgr. Worcester, Duluth, St. Paul, Pitts.; div. v.p. Worcester, Phila., N.Y.C.; adminstrv. v.p. Worcester, Boston; exec. v.p. Worcester, 1955-56, pres., 1956-62, chmn. bd., from 1962; also dir., chmn. bd., dir. Liberty Mut. Fire Ins. Co.; dir. Nat. Shawnut Bank of Boston, Liberty Life Assurance Co.; trustee Am. Inst. Property and Liability Underwriters, Inc. Mem. bd. govs. Mass. Safety Coun. Mem. Greater N.Y. Safety Coun. (dir., chmn. exec. com. 1950-52), Ins. Inst. Am. (bd. govs.), Health Ins. Assn. Am. (dir.), Theta Chi, Delta Sigma Pi. *

SMITH, BUNNIE OTHANEL, retired educator; b. Clarksville, Fla., May 29, 1903; s. Isma Isaac and Lula (Cox) S.; m. Tommie Naomi Harkey, Aug. 29, 1929; children: Norman Harkey, Hamilton Othanel. B.S., U. Fla., 1925; M.A., Columbia U., 1932, Ph.D., 1938; LittD (hon.), Hofstra U., 1986. Asst. prin. Panama City, Fla., 1925-26; sci. tchr. Brooksville, Fla., 1926-27; high sch. prin., supervising prin. Tallahassee, 1927-30; asst. prof. U. Fla., 1930-37; mem. faculty U. Ill., 1937-70, prof. history and philosophy edn., 1945-70, chmn. dept. history and philosophy of edn., 1966-70, prof. emeritus, from 1970; prof. edn. U. South Fla., Tampa, 1970-75; prof. emeritus U. South Fla., from 1975; vis. prof. U. Fla., summer 1940, Columbia, summer 1945; mem. internat. group to prepare manuscript on curriculum devel. for UNESCO, 1955; adv. edn. editor Rand McNally and Co., 1953-80; chmn. grad. records exam. in edn. Ednl. Testing Service, 1967-73; mem. Nat. Inst. Advanced Study Teaching Disadvantaged Youth, 1966-68; chmn. adv. council Associated Orgns. Tchr. Edn., 1963; mem. Ill. Council Econ. Edn., 1968; dir. Leadership Tng. Inst., U.S. Office Edn., 1970-75; co-dir. Tchr. Evaluation and Assessment Ctr., 1980-85. Author: Logical Aspects of Educational Measurement, 1938, (with others) The Improvement of Practical Intelligence, 1950, Fundamentals of Curriculum Development, 1950, Social Foundations of Education, 1956, (with Robert H. Ennis) Language and Concepts in Education, 1961, (with Milton Meux) A Study of the Logic of Teaching, 1962, (with others) Democracy and Excellence in Secondary Education, 1963, A Study of the Strategies of Teaching, 1967, (with Donald Orlosky) Socialization and Schooling, 1975, Curriculum Development: Concepts and Issues, 1978, (with others) A Design for a School of Pedagogy, 1980; Mem. editorial bd.: Ency. Ednl. Research, 1960, 70, Jour. Tchr. Edn, 1959-62; editor: Progressive Education, 1947-52, Research in Teacher Education: A Symposium, 1971; asst. editor: Curriculum Jour, 1934-40. Recipient Centennial award U. Fla., 1953, Disting. Alumnus award, 1975, Phi Delta Kappa and Coll. Edn. Lifetime of Excellence award, 1986; citation Nat. Tchr. Corps, 1977; award for excellence in profl. writing Am. Assn. Colls. for Tchr. Edn., 1981, Outstanding Achievement award John Dewey Soc., 1990; medal for disting. svc. Columbia U. Tchrs. Coll., 1981. Mem. AAAS, ASCD, NEA (life), Nat. Acad. Edn., Philosophy Edn. Soc. (pres. 1956-57, exec. com. 1957-58), Nat. Soc. Coll. Tchrs. Edn. (pres. 1949, exec. com. 1948), Am. Ednl. Research Assn. (v.p. 1967-69, mem. at large exec. bd 1970-73, Div. B award 1981), Nat. Soc. Study Edn., John Dewey Soc. (award 1975), Phi Kappa Phi, Phi Delta Kappa, Kappa Delta Pi, Chi Phi. Democrat. Home: Clearwater Fla. Deceased. †

SMITH, CHARLES F., corporation executive; b. Boise, Idaho, Apr. 14, 1895; s. Nathan Lockwood and Ella (Avery) S.; m. Helen Williams, Dec. 3, 1932. Pres., dir. F.I.F. Mgmt. Corp., Denver, 1932-61; dir. Fin. Indsl. Fund Inc., 1935-60, chmn. bd.; chmn. bd. Fin. Indsl. Income Fund Inc.; dir. FIF Assocs., Inc. Mem. Nat. Assn. Security Dealers, Bond Club Denver, Nat. Assn. Investment Cos., Rotary, Cherry Hills Country Club, Denver Athletic Club. *

SMITH, CYRUS ROWLETT, business executive; b. Minerva, Tex., Sept. 9, 1899; s. Roy Edgerton and Marion (Burck) S.; m. Elizabeth L. Manget, Dec. 29, 1934 (div.); 1 child, Douglas Manget. Ed., U. Tex., 1920-24. Pub. acct. Peat, Marwick Mitchell & Co., Dallas, 1924-26; asst. treas. Tex.-La. Power Co., Ft. Worth, 1926-28; v.p. Tex. Air Transport, Inc., Ft. Worth, 1929-30, Am. Airways, Inc., Ft. Worth and St. Louis, 1930-33, Am. Airlines, Inc., Ft. Worth, 1934; pres. Am. Airlines, Inc., Chgo. and N.Y.C., 1934-42, chmn. bd., 1946-68, chmn., chief exec. officer, 1973-74; U.S. sec. commerce, 1968-69; ptnr. Lazard Freres & Co., 1969-73. Served from col. to maj. gen. USAAF, 1942-45; dep. comdr. Air Transport Command 1942-45. Decorated D.S.M., Legion of Merit, Air Medal U.S.; comdr. Order Brit. Empire; named to Aviation Hall of Fame, 1974; Bus. Hall of Fame, 1975; recipient Wright Bros. award, Billy Mitchell award. Democrat. Baptist. Club: Metropolitan (Washington). Home: Washington D.C. Died Apr. 4, 1990. †

SMITH, DAVID BEACH, electrical engineer researcher; b. Newton, N.J., Dec. 3, 1911; s. George Abram and Klara (Frank) S.; m. Emma Bailey Hoffer, Aug. 15, 1942 (dec. Dec. 4, 1988); children: Josephine, David, George, Peter, Susan. BEE, MIT, 1933, MS, 1934. Patent solicitor Philco Corp., Phila., 1934-49, dir. rsch., 1939-45, v.p. rsch., 1945-46, v.p. rsch. & engring., 1946-58, v.p. tech. affairs, 1958-61; v.p. R & D Philco-Ford, Phila., 1961-64; prof., grad. group chmn. systems engring., lectr. Moore Sch. U. Phila., 1965-67, 69-72; pres. HRB-Singer, State Coll., Pa., 1967-68; prof. & dir. engring. mgmt. program Drexel U., Phila., 1972-78, prof., lectr., emeritus prof., 1978-90, 90-92; mem., 97th chmn. Sci. & Arts Com. Franklin Inst., Phila., 1969-88. Author: (with George Roland) Systems Engineering and Management, Vol. 8; editor: Advances in Modern Engineering, 1974; contbr. articles to profl. jours. Pres. The Meadowbrook (Pa.) Sch., 1951-62; charter vestryman Ch. Constrn. Com. St. John's Episcopal Ch., Huntingdon Valley, Pa., 1952-54; trustee Abington (Pa.) Meml. Hosp., 1960-63. Named Fellow AIEE, 1955, Inst. Radio Engrs., 1955. Fellow IEEE; mem. Sigma Xi, Franklin Inst. Home: Gladwyne Pa. Died Dec. 3, 1992. †

SMITH, EARL E. T., financier; b. Newport, R.I.; s. Sydney J. and Fannie Bogert (Tailer) S.; m. Consuelo Vandebilt, Jan. 7, 1926; children—Iris (Mrs. Donald Christ), Virginia (Mrs. Edwin Burke); m. Florence Pritchett, July 12, 1948 (dec. 1965); 1 son, Earl E.T.; m. Lesly Stockard Hickox, 1968. Student, Taft Sch., 1922, Yale, 1926. Mem. N.Y. Stock Exchange, 1926-91; founding mem., ptnr. then sr. ptnr. Paige, Smith & Remick (investment brokers), 1930-39; amb. to Cuba, 1957-59; mayor of Palm Beach, Fla., 1971-77; dir. Bank of Palm Beach & Trust Co., U.S. Sugar Corp., N.Y. Cen. R.R., N.Y. Dock Corp., Lionel Corp., CF and I Steel Corp., Sotheby's; mem. War Prodn. Bd., 1940"s; mem. Rep. Nat. Finance Com., 1954-56; del. from Fla. to Rep. Nat. Conv., 1952, 56, 60, 80, mem. platform com., 1960, 80; chmn. Fla. State Rep. Finance Com., 1954-56; mem. Presdl. Commn. on Broadcasting to Cuba. Author: The Fourth Floor, 1962, 2d edit., 1991. Trustee John F. Kennedy Meml. Library.; chmn. bd. Preservation Found. of Palm Beach, Inc. Served to lt. col. AUS; Served to lt. col. USAAF, World War II. Recipient Freedom award Order of Lafayette, 1963; George E. Sokolsky Meml. award Am. Jewish League Against Communism, 1963; Earl E.T. Smith Park named in his honor, Palm Beach, 1989. Clubs: Mason. (N.Y.C.), Brook (N.Y.C.) (gov.), Racquet and Tennis (N.Y.C.), Deepdale Golf (N.Y.C.); Seminole Golf (Palm Beach), Everglades (Palm Beach) (gov.); Nat. Golf Links of America. Home: Palm Beach Fla. Died Feb. 15, 1991; buried Palm Beach, Fla.

SMITH, EDGAR PICHARD, corporate executive; b. N.Y.C., June 19, 1920; s. Edgar W. and Marthe (Troqueme) S.; m. Margaret Myrtle Love, June 17, 1942; children: Suzanne Love Smith Talbott, Marthe Michelle, Deborah Hawkins, Elizabeth Pichard. AB, Princeton U., 1942. Mng. editor Princeton Tiger, 1942; mem. staff Fortune mag., 1946-57, assoc. editor, 1947-52, asst. mng. editor, 1953; mng. editor Archtl. Forum, 1957-58; corp. staff Time, 1959-62; v.p. Time-Life Broadcast, 1962-73, dir. spl. projects, 1973-75, cons., from 1975. Served from 2d lt. to capt. inf. AUS, 1942-46; active duty M.I., 1951-52. Decorated Croix de Guerre (France). Mem. Univ. Club (N.Y.C.), Morris County Golf Club, Princeton Club, Somerset Hills Country Club. Home: Far Hills N.J. Died Oct. 10, 1989; buried New Vernon (N.J.) Cemetery.

SMITH, FREDERICK BUREN, educator; b. Hartwell, Ga., July 11, 1896; s. Henry Harrison and Laura (Buffington) S.; m. Marjorie Nichols Willsie, Oct. 18, 1923. BS, U. Ga., 1922; MS, Iowa State Coll., 1923, PhD, 1926. Prin. rural graded schs. of Oconee County, near Walballa, S.C., 1915-17; instr. chemistry and biology Vivian (La.) High Sch., 1923-24; rsch. fellow Iowa State Coll., 1924-26; asst. prof. agronomy Colo. State Coll., 1926-27; asst. chief soil chemistry and bacteriol. Iowa State Coll., 1927-32; prof. soils and microbiol. U. Fla., 1937-44, microbiol. and head dept. soils, 1944-65, microbiologist, from 1965. Contbr. articles to various tech. jours. and expt. sts. bulls. Seaman USN, 1918-19. Fellow AAAS, Am. Inst. Chemists, Am. Soc. Agronomy; mem. Internat. Soc. Soil Sci. (sec.-treas. 1937-38), Am. Soc. Agronomy (sec.-treas. 1932, 37, 38), Soil Sci. Soc. Am. (sec. 1937-38), Soil Sci. Soc. Fla. (pres. 1941), Fla. State Hort. Soc., Fla. Acad. Scis., Am. Legion (adj. 1943-44), Sifma Xi. (pres. Fla. chpt. 1948-49), Alpha Zeta Gamma, Sigma Delta, Phi Sigme, Phi Kappa Phi, Masons. Democrat. Presbyterian. *

SMITH, GEORGE FREDERICK, business executive; b. Chgo., Mar. 16, 1897; m. Estelle Taylor, Sept. 20, 1919; children: Dorothy, Patricia Ann. DS, Phila. Coll. Pharmacy and Sci.; LLD, Rutgers U., Seton Hall U. Began as salesman R.M. Hollingshead Co., San Francisco; becoming v.p., gen. mgr. R.M. Hollingshead Co., 1930; with Johnson & Johnson, from 1933, pres., 1943-60; ret., dir.; dir. MEad Johnson Co., Am. Telephone & Telegraph, United N.J. R.R. and Canal Co.; del. River Basin Rsch., Inc., Triangle Conduit and Cable Corp.; mem. bd. mgrs. New Brunswick Savings Instn. Contbr. articles to various trade publs. and periodicals. Dir., past chmn. Health Info. Found.; chmn. N.J. com. Regional Plan Assn.; pres. N.J. Bd. Edn.; chmn., bd. trustees N.J. Coll. Medicine and Dentistry; past vice chmn. N.J. Turnpike Authority; chmn. N.J. State Water Resources Adv. Com.; pres. Nat. Fund Grad. Nursing Edn.; mem. N.J. State Tercentenary Commn.; pres. N.J. Orgn. Better State; trustee, past chmn. Health News Inst.; trustee Nat. Fund Med. Edn., Com. Econ. Devel.; del. N.J. Constrn. Conv., 1919, pres., 1955, 56; trustee Tchrs. Coll. Columbia U., Nat. Jewish Hosp., Denver. Served with AUS, World War I, with AEF to lst. lt. Recipient Outstanding Citizen N.J. award N.J. Advt. Club, 1955, N.J. Bus. Statesman of Yr., Sales Execs. Club No. N.J., 1958. Mem. World Med. Assn. (dir. U.S. com.), N.J. State C. of C. (v.p.), Pharm Mfrs. Assn. (past pres. dir.) New Brunswick C. of C. (pres. 1942-44), Am. Drug Mfrs. Assn. (v.p.), N.J. Acad. Polit. Sci., COnstitutional Conv. Assn. (pres. 1955-56). Clubs: Union, Plainfield, Country, Pine Valley Country, Skytop, Essex, Seaview Country. *

SMITH, GREGORY, priest; b. Mar. 25, 1898; s. Edward F. and Annie E. (Feeney) S. AB, St. Francis Coll., 1928, AM, 1930; LittD, St. Thomas Sem., 1948, PhD, 1956. Ordained priest Roman Cath. Ch., 1922, domestic prealte, 1949, protonotary apostolic, 1959. Began as asst. pastor St. Francis de Sales Ch., Denver, 1922-28; pastor St. May's Ch., Littleton, Colo., 1928-32, St. John Evangelsit Ch., Denver, 1932-40, St. Francis de Sales Ch., from 1940; supt. St. Francis de Sales High Sch., from 1940; diocean dir. Soc. Propagation of Faith, from 1927, Confreternity of Christian Doctrine, from 1935; also chmn. nat. com. adult religious discussion clubs, 1935-61; cons. Archdiocese of Denver, from 1948, vicar gen., from 1954. Contbr. numerous religious discussion texts. *

SMITH, H. SHELTON, educator; b. McCleansville, N.C., May 8, 1893; s. Henry Brooks and Lula Jane (Wyrick) S.; m. Alma Bowden, May 27, 1918; 1 child, Richard Bowden. AB, TLon Coll., 1917; PhD, Yale U., 1923; DD (hon.), Defiance Coll., 1926; LittD (hon.), Elon Coll., 1940. Dir. leadership edn. Internat. Coun. Religious Edn., 1923-28; assoc. prof. religious edn. Tchrs. Coll., Columbia U., 1928-29, Yale U., 1929-31; assoc. prof. religious edn. Duke U., 1931-40, prof. Christian ethics, dir. grad. studies in religion, 1940-45, prof. Am. religious thoughts, 1945-62, James B. Duke prof. Am. religious thought, from 1962, dir. grad. studies in religion, 1940-45, chaplain, 1917-18; mem. exec. com. N.C. Coun. Chs., Am. Ch. Hist. Soc., NAt. Coun. Chs., Christ U.S.A., Am. Theol. Soc.; lectr. in field. Author: Faith and Nuture, 1941, Changing Conceptions of Original Sin: A Study in American THeology Since 1750, Am. Christianity, 1620-1820, 1960, American Christianty 1820-1960, 1963. Mem. Am. Soc. Ch. History (pres. 1957), Am. Theol. Soc. (pres. 1958-59). *

SMITH, HARLAN JAMES, astronomer, educator; b. Wheeling, W.Va., Aug. 25, 1924; s. Paul Elder and Anna Persis (McGregor) S.; m. Joan Greene, Dec. 21, 1950; children: Nathaniel, Sara (dec.), Julia, Theodore, Hannah. AB, Harvard U., 1949, MA, 1951, PhD, 1955; DPhys. Sci. (hon.), Nicholas Copernicus U., Torun, Poland, 1973, Denison U., 1983. Rsch. asst. astronomy, teaching fellow and rsch. fellow Harvard U., Cambridge, Mass., 1946-53; from instr. to assoc. prof. astronomy Yale U., New Haven, 1953-63; prof. astronomy, chmn. dept. U. Tex., Austin, 1963-78, dir. McDonald Obs., 1963-89, mem. team constrn. 107 inch McDonald reflector telescope; mem. Space Sci. Bd., 1977-79; Edward Randall Jr. Centennial prof. astromony U. Tex., Austin, 1985. Co-editor: Astron. Jour., 1960-63. Served as weather observer USAAF, 1943-46. Recipient Disting. Svc. medal NASA, 1991; George R. Agassiz research fellow Harvard Obs., 1952-53. Fellow AAAS; mem. Am. Astron. Soc. (acting sec. 1961-62, chmn. planetary div. 1974-75, coun. 1975-78, v.p. 1977-79, Masursky award div. planetary scis. 1993), Royal Astron. Soc., Am. Geophys. Union, Assoc. Univs. Rsch. in Astronomy (chmn. bd. dirs. 1980-82), Internat. Astron. Union, Sigma Xi. Home: Austin Tex. Died Oct. 17, 1991; buried Mt. Auburn Cemetery, Cambridge, Mass.

SMITH, HAROLD COLBY, retired printing and publishing executive; b. Clifton, Ill., Aug. 28, 1903; s. Weldon Charles and Alice Mary (Colby) S.; m. Maude Adams, May 9, 1930; children: Lewis Adams, Carolyn Colby (Mrs. Harold C. Ochsner Jr.), Miriam Goodale. A.B., U. Ill., 1927. With advt. dept. Chgo. Tribune, 1927-30; with J.J. Little & Ives, N.Y.C., 1930-31, Colonial Press, Inc., Clinton, Mass., 1931-73; pres., dir. Colonial Press, Inc., 1937-72, C.H. Simonds Co., 1943-61, Colonial Offset, Inc., Clinton, 1961-68; v.p., dir. Victoreen Leece Neville, Inc., Cleve., 1967-73; treas., dir., exec. com. Rex. Corp., West Acton, Mass., 1955-59; cons. Am. Enka Corp., Ashville, N.C., 1957-67; dir., treas. Nashoba Engring. Co., Inc., Gilbert Harold, Inc.; mem. adv. com. Worcester County Nat. Bank, 1962-68; dir. Freeman, Cooper & Co., San Francisco, 1971-87, Colorcon, Inc., West Point, Pa., 1972-78. Editor, pub.: The Colby Family in Early America, 1970. Mem. Concord Players, 1938-47; mem. fin. bd. Town of Concord, 1950-57, bd. selectmen, 1957-61, chmn., 1958-61; trustee Clinton Hosp. Assn., 1948-70, v.p., 1950-70; trustee Mus. of Sci., Miami, Fla., 1973-78. Served as pvt. Q.M.C. U.S. Army, 1918-19, AEF. Mem. Asso. Industries Mass. (dir. 1960-70), Am. Inst. Graphic Arts, Worcester Metal Trades Assn. (dir. 1947-49), Soc. Colonial Wars, Soc. of Cincinnati, SAR, Phi Kappa Sigma. Republican. Clubs: Rotary (Clinton) (hon., pres. 1944); Social Circle, Concord Country (Concord, Mass.); Bass River Yacht (gov. 1961-65); Key Biscayne Yacht (Fla.). Home: South Yarmouth Mass. Deceased. †

SMITH, JACQUELINE SARAH, television executive; b. Phila., May 24, 1933; d. Percy and Gertrude (Elman) Feldenkreis; children: David Anthony, Elinor Sara. Student, Antioch Coll., 1950-54. Producer, writer children's program Sta. KPIX, San Francisco, 1956-58; dir. on-air-promotion Sta. WPIX, N.Y.C., 1960-63; exec. producer children's program CBS-TV Network, 1964-69, dir. spl. programs, 1973-77; dir. spl. projects Warner Bros. TV, 1969-73; v.p. daytime programs ABC Entertainment, N.Y.C., 1977-87, cons., 1987-88, in charge daytime programming, 1989-91; pres. Pygmalion Prodns., 1989. Inducted into YWCA Acad. Women Achievers, 1981. Home: Santa Monica Calif. Died June 3, 1992.

SMITH, JAMES HENRY, insurance executive; b. Chestertown, Md., Mar. 29, 1910; s. Tilghman and Clara (Murray) S.; m. Roberta Foard, July 4, 1931; children: Warren F., Wendell M., Janet F. Smith Dann, Robert H. BA, U. Del., 1930, LLD, 1968; LLD, Alfred U., 1967, Rider Coll., 1972. With Equitable Life Assurance Soc. U.S., N.Y.C., 1930-34, 42-90, v.p., assoc. actuary, 1953-57, underwriting v.p., 1958-65, v.p., actuary, 1965-67, pres., 1967-69, pres., CEO, 1969-73, chmn., CEO, 1973-75, also dir., 1966; with Travelers Ins. Co., Hartford, Conn., 1935-42; dir. Colgate Palmolive Co., Uniroyal Inc.; past chmn. Helath Ins. Coun., Health Ins. Assn. Am.; mem. HEW Adv. Coun. on Social Security. Bd. dirs. N.Y. Urban Coalition, Meth. Hosp. Bklyn., Drug Abuse Coun.; trustee Alfred U., nat. trustee YMCA. Fellow Soc. Actuaries (past gov.); mem. Am. Acad. Actuaries, Internat. Congress Actuaries, N.Y. Chamber Commerce and Industry (vice-chmn. econ. devel.), Univ. Club, Links Club, Sky Club (N.Y.C.), Rock Spring Club (West Orange, N.J.). Home: Maplewood N.J. Died Jan. 10, 1990.

SMITH, JESSICA, author, editor; b. Madison, N.J., Nov. 29, 1895; d. Walter and Jessie May (Stout) S.; m. Harold M. Ware, Jan. 1925 dec. Aug. 1935) 1 child, David Ware; m. John Abt, Mar. 1937. AB, Swarthmore Coll., 1915. Writer Phila. N.Am., 1911-12; organizer, speaker Woman's Suffrage Movement; famine relief work and publicity Am. Friends Svc. Com. in Russia, 1922-24; mem. Russian Reconstrn. Farms (Am.), USSR, N. Caucasus, 1926-28; editor: Soviet Union Review, Washington, 1929-33; tour USSR, 1935, 45, 61, 65; editor: Soviet Russia Today (Am. mag.), 1936-50, New. World Review, from 1950. Author: Woman in Soviet Russia, 1928, (with Bayer and Brody) War and Peace in Finland, 1940, Jungle Law or Human Reason, 1949, Negotiations the Way to PEace, 1954, The American People Want PEace, 1955; translator: Over the Polem by George Baidukov, 1938. *

SMITH, JOHN EDWIN, nuclear engineering plant executive; b. Charlotte, N.C., June 14, 1924; s. Wilburn J. and Banna Dale (Oastwalt) S.;m. Mary Elizabeth Shelton, Aug. 16, 1947; children: Shelley Hobson, Dale Henslee, Jed. B Mech. Engring., N.C. State U., 1949; M Nuclear Engring., U. S.C. Sch. Reactor Tech., Oak Ridge, Tenn., 1961. Test man Buck Steam Sta. Duke Power Co., Spencer, N.C., 1949-50; test man Dan River Steam Sta. Duke Power Co., Draper, N.C., 1950-51; shift supr., asst. plant mgr. Lee Steam Sta. Duke Power Co., Pelzer, S.C., 1951-55; plant engr. Cliffside (N.C.) Steam Sta. Duke Power Co., 1955-60; sta. mgr. Oconee Nuclear Sta. Duke Power Co., Seneca, S.C., 1968-84; asst. to v.p. nuclear prodn. Duke Power Co., Charlotte, 1984-86; shift supr., ops. engr. plant supr. Carolinas-Va. Tube Reactor, Parr, S.C., 1961-67; pres. J. Ed's Nuclear Svc. Corp., Central, S.C., 1986-92; cons. safety rev. bd. Duke Power Co., Charlotte, 1986-92, co. nuclear rev. bd. Davis Besse Nuclear Plant, Port Clinton, Ohio, 1986-92, nuclear safety adv. bd. Riverbend Nuclear Sta., St. Lawrenceville, La., 1986-92. Contbr. International Nuclear Safety Guide, 1988. Pres. Pickens County Habitat for Humanity, Clemson, S.C., 1986-89. With U.S. Army, 1943-46, ETO, PTO. Recipient George Westinghouse Gold medal ASME, 1989. Mem. Am. Nuclear Soc., Rotary (pres. Clemson club 1976), Men's Fellowship Club (Clemson). Republican. Baptist. Home: Central S.C. Died July 28, 1992. †

SMITH, JOHN LEWIS, JR., federal judge; b. Washington, Sept. 20, 1912; s. John Lewis and Claribel (Cassin) S.; m. Madeline Cotter, Oct. 3, 1940 (dec. 1967); children: John Lewis III, Madeline Smith Lynn, Joseph Cotter, Janet Ambler Smith Garabrant, Barbara Cassin Smith Fennell; m. Louise Tompkins Parker, Feb. 15, 1974. A.B. cum laude, Princeton U., 1935; LL.B., Georgetown U., 1938, LL.M., 1939, LL.D. (hon.), 1985. Bar: D.C. 1938, U.S. Supreme Ct 1943. Asst. U.S. Atty.'s Office, Washington, 1940-46; pvt. practice Washington, 1946-56; mem. D.C. Pub. Utilities Commn., 1956-57; assoc. judge D.C. Ct. Gen. Sessions, 1957-59, chief judge, 1959-66; judge U.S. Dist. Ct. D.C., 1966-82, chief judge, 1981-82, sr. active judge, from 1983; presiding judge U.S. Fgn. Intelligence Surveillance Ct., from 1982; Chmn., Republican Vets Com. for D.C., 1952; Chmn. Vets. Com. for Eisenhower-Nixon Inaugural, 1953, 57; pres. Rep. Club D.C., 1955-56. Trustee Boys Club Washington, from 1965; bd. dirs. D.C. chpt. ARC, from 1957, Washington Heart Assn., from 1967. Served to col. AUS, World War II. Decorated Army Commendation medal; recipient 1st scholarship prizes Georgetown U. Law Sch., 1936, 37, Princeton Class award, 1959, Georgetown U. Alumni Achievement award, 1960. Fellow Am. Bar Found.; mem. Am. Bar Assn., Bar Assn. D.C., Lawyers Club, The Barristers, Am. Judicature Soc., Mil. Order World Wars (gen. staff emeritus). Clubs: Nat. Lawyers (founder mem.), Princeton, Vinson (Washington); Chevy Chase (Md.); Rehoboth Beach (Del.) Country. Home: Bethesda Md. Deceased. †

SMITH, KENNETH, bass-baritone; b. Leeds, Eng., Aug. 26, 1920; came to U.S., 1924, naturalized, 1931; s. Thomas Henry and Ada (Sedgewick) S.; m. Marguerite Prentice, Mar. 3, 1945; 1 son, Eric. Student, Manhattan Sch. Music, 1945-46, N.Y. Coll. Music, 1946-49. prof. voice, chmn. voice dept. U. Kans., 1965-83, prof. emeritus, from 1983, chmn. dept. performance, 1976. N.Y.C. debut, NBC-TV, Opera Down in the Valley, 1950; with New Eng. Opera Co., 1950; concert debut Town Hall, 1951, Central City Opera, 1953, Chgo. Lyric Opera, 1955-58, N.Y.C. Opera, 1956, 60, Washington Opera, 1959; also festivals, various cities; appeared: Am. premiere Billy Budd, NBC-TV, 1951, Gloriana, Cin. May Festival, 1956, Tempest, N.Y. C. Opera Co., 1956, War and Peace, NBC-TV, 1957; world premiere Life of the Mission, San Antonio, 1959; debut with Met. Opera Co., 1963, San Francisco Opera, 1966; with N.Y. Philharmonic, symphony orchs., various cities U.S., also Symphony of the Air; recordings, Columbia, RCA-Victor, Concert Hall Soc. records; world premiere opera Cyrano, U. Colo., 1965; world premiere Carry Nation, 1966, My Heart's in the Highlands,; world premiere Nat. Ednl. TV, 1970; 1st performance with L'Orqueta Sinfonica Nacional de Venezuela, Caracas, 1968. Served from 2d lt. to 1st lt. USAAF, 1942-45. Decorated D.F.C., Air medal with clusters. Mem. Actors Equity, AFTRA, Am. Guild Mus. Artists, Screen Actors Guild, Pi Kappa Lambda. Home: Cambridge Md. Died Dec. 28, 1989.

SMITH, LARKIN, congressman; b. Poplarville, Miss., June 26, 1944. BA, William Carey Coll. Police chief City of Gulfport, Miss., 1977-83; sheriff Harrison County, 1984-89; mem. 101st Congress from 5th Miss. dist., 1989. Home: Washington D.C. Died Aug. 13, 1989. †

SMITH, LEONARD CHARLES, biochemistry educator; b. Spokane, Wash., Jan. 31, 1921; s. Leonard Charles and Edith (McLellan) S.; m. Mary Elaine Rush, Oct. 1, 1945; children: David Evan, Lynn Frederic, Steven Mark, Peter Douglas, Andrew Ian. A.B., U. Mont., 1943; Ph.D., U. Ill., 1949. Instr. biochemistry Northwestern U. Med. Sch., Chgo., 1949-56; asso. prof. biochemistry U. S.D., Vermillion, 1956-61, prof., 1962-66; prof. chemistry Ind. State U., Terre Haute, 1966-90; adj. prof. biochemistry Terre Haute Center for Med. Edn., Sch. Medicine, Ind. U., 1972-80; vis. lectr. Glasgow (U.K.) U., 1961-62; Research biochemist Hines (Ill.) VA Hosp., 1949-56. Mem. Am. Chem. Soc., Soc. Exptl. Biology and Medicine, Chem. Soc. (U.K.), AMA (affiliate), Sigma Xi, Pi Mu Epsilon, Phi Sigma. Home: Terre Haute Ind. Died Jan. 18, 1990; buried Wood Wreath Cemetery, New Berlin, Ill.

SMITH, MORTON, historian, educator; b. Phila., May 28, 1915; s. Rupert Henry and Mary (Funk) S. A.B. magna cum laude, Harvard Coll, 1936; S.T.B. cum laude, Harvard U., 1940; Ph.D. in Classics, Hebrew U., 1948; Th.D. in O.T., Harvard U., 1957. Instr. Biblical lit. Brown U., Providence, 1950-51, asst. prof., 1951-55; vis. prof. history of religion Drew U., Madison, N.J., 1956-57; asst. prof. ancient history Columbia U., N.Y.C., 1957-60, assoc. prof. ancient history, 1960-62, prof., 1962-85, prof. emeritus, 1985-91, spl. lectr. religion, 1986-88, assoc. prof. religion, 1988-91; ann. lectr. religion Am. Council Learned Socs., N.Y.C., 1961-62; mem. Sch. Hist. Studies Inst. for Advanced Study, Princeton, N.J., 1966-67. Author: The Ancient Greeks, 1960, Palestinian Parties & Politics That Shaped the Old Testament, 1971, Clement of Alexandria, 1973, Jesus the Magician 1978 (Lionel Trilling award Columbia U.), Hope and History, 1980. Recipient Ralph Marcus Centennial award Soc. Bibl. Lit., 1980; fellow Guggenheim Found., 1955-56, Bollingen Found., 1964. Mem. Am. Acad. Jewish Research, Am. Acad. Arts & Scis., Assn. Ancient Historians, Assn. Internationale de Papyrologues, Studiorum Novi Testamenti Soc. Home: New York N.Y. Died July 11, 1991; buried Phila.

SMITH, NEAL AUSTIN, electrical engineer, educator; b. Norwich, Ohio, Feb. 10, 1919; s. Miner Francis and Bessie Lillian (Shuman) S.; m. Faye Louise Schlupe, June 7, 1942. B.E.E., Ohio State U., 1941, M.Sc., 1947. Elec. engr. Fed. Machine & Welder Co., Warren, Ohio, 1941-43, asst. chief elec. engr., 1943-44; instr. elec. engring. Ohio State U., 1947-54, asst. prof., 1954-60, assoc. prof., 1960-65, prof., 1965-84, prof. emeritus, 1984-89; cons. in elec. power systems, electric shock, fires of elec. origin. Contbr. articles to profl. jours. Served as lt. j.g. USNR, 1944-46. NSF grantee, 1961-62. Mem. Am. Legion (past post comdr.), Eta Kappa Nu, Tau Beta Pi. Clubs: Mason, Ohio State U. Faculty. Home: Columbus Ohio Died July 15, 1989; buried Oak Hill Cemetery, Millersburg, Ohio.

SMITH, PAUL KIMBRELL, educator; b. Lancaster, S.C., Dec. 3, 1895; s. Edward Emerson and Fannie Wells (Young) S.; m. Ray Gandy, July 25, 1923; children: Paul Kimbrell, Benjamin Carmichael. BS, U. S.C., 1916, MA, 1917; MA, U. Chgo., 1925; PhD, U. Ill., 1931. Adj. prof. math. U. S.C., 1919-22; asst. prof. math. A&M Coll. Tex., 1922-24, No. Ill. State Tchrs. Coll., DeKalb, 1925-26; prof. math. Miss. Woman's Coll., 1926-28, West Tenn. State Tchrs. Coll., 1931-28, La. Poly Inst., 1932-59, U. S.C., from 1959; also head dept. Author: (with Henry F. Schroeder) College Mathematics for Freshman, 1948. Mem. AAUP, Mat. Assn. Am., Am. Legion, NAt. Coun. Tchrs. Math., Tau Kappa Epsilon, Pi Mu Epsilon, Phi Kappa Phi, Masons. *

SMITH, PAUL SAMUEL, college administrator; b. Richmond, Ind., July 3, 1897; s. Harry J. and Louise (Wolfe) S.; m. Lillian E. McMinn, Aug. 28, 1923; 1 dau., Eleanor Patricia. A.B., Earlham Coll., 1919; LL.D.; A.M., U. Wis., 1922, Ph.D., 1927; L.H.D., Calif. Coll. Medicine; LL.D., Whittier Coll. Fellow in history U. Wis., 1919-20, teaching asst., 1920-22; prof. Am. history Whittier (Calif.) Coll., from 1923, dir. summer session, 1939-51, coll. pres., 1951-69, chancellor, from 1969, emeritus, until 1991; Pres. Western Coll. Assn., 1958-59; Lectr. on problems on constl. govt. Radio lectr. in series of discussions on problems of democratic govt. Author: booklet American Political Institutions and Social Idealism, 1928, A New Approach to the American Constitution, 1931, New Approach to the Study of the American Constitution; Pamphlet, Calif. Dept. Edn., 1940, Nixon Analecs, 1975; Contbr. to: The Young Nixon, 1977. Mem. Am. Revolution Bicentennial Commn. Mem. Am. Hist. Assn., Am. Polit. Sci. Assn., Pi Gamma Mu. Mem. Soc. of Friends. Home: Brea Calif. Died May 19, 1991; buried Richmond, Ind.

SMITH, RALPH CARLISLE, educational consultant, lawyer; b. West New York, N.J., May 24, 1910; s. Alfred Thomas and Katharine (Haller) S.; m. Harriett V. Petersen, May 20, 1954. Chem.-Engr., Rensselaer Poly. Inst., 1931; J.D., George Washington U., 1939; M.A., U. N.M., 1955, Ph.D., 1962. Bar: D.C. 1940, U.S. Supreme Ct 1946; Registered profl. engr., N.Mex. Chemist E.I. duPont de Nemours & Co., Inc., 1931-35; engr. U.S. Patent Office, 1935-37, Colgate Palmolive Co., 1938-42; patent counsel Manhattan Project, Los Alamos, 1943-47; asst. dir. Los Alamos Sci. Lab., 1946-57; asst. to pres. nuclear electronic div. ACF Industries, 1957-60; mem. faculty N.Mex. Highlands U., 1961-78, prof. polit. sci., 1965-78, v.p., acad. dean, 1966-70, pres., 1970-72, counsel to pres., 1973-78; mem. law faculty U. N.M., 1950-57; cons. Teaching Machines, Albuquerque, 1961-65, Lytle Corp., Albuquerque, 1960-61, Columbia (Mo.) Coll., from 1978; County probate judge, Los Alamos, 1950-55, justice of peace, 1948-50, city magistrate, City of Las Vegas, 1977, Chmn. planning commn., Las Vegas, 1964-78. Co-author: The Effects of Atomic Weapons, 1950, History of Los Alamos Scientific Laboratory, 1961, 83; Co-editor: National Nuclear Energy Series, 1951. Editorial bd. Nat. Forum, 1984-89. PAtentee in field. Republican candidate for Congress, 1956. Served to lt. col., C.E. AUS, 1942-47. Decorated Legion of Merit, Army Commendation medal. Fellow Am. Inst. Chemists; mem. Am. Phys. Soc., Am. Nuclear Soc., Am. Inst. Chem. Engrs., Am. Intellectual Property Law Assn., Order of Coif, Sigma Xi, Tau Beta Pi, Phi Kappa Phi. Home: San Francisco Calif. Died Feb. 27, 1989; buried Presidio Nat. Cemetery, San Francisco.

SMITH, RUSSELL EVANS, federal judge; b. Butte, Mont., Nov. 16, 1908; s. Ernest Clifford and Florence (Evans) S.; m. Mary Ruth Larison, June 21, 1931; children: Sonia Lee Zenk, Russell Evans Jr. LL.B. cum laude, U. Mont., 1931, LL.D. (hon.), 1980. Bar: Mont. 1931. Marshal, law clk. Mont. Supreme Ct., 1931-33; practiced in Cut Bank, Mont., 1933-35, Missoula, Mont., 1935-42, 45-66; counsel for Mont., OPA, 1942-43; judge U.S. Dist. Ct. for Mont., from 1966, chief judge, to 1978, sr. judge, from 1978; lectr. U. Mont. Law Sch.; Mem. Mont. Bd. Bar Examiners. Served to USNR, 1943-45. Mem. Mont. Bar Assn. (past pres. 1956), Alpha Tau Omega, Phi Delta Phi. Home: Missoula Mont. Deceased. †

SMITH, SAMUEL ABBOT, ex-director Smaller War Plants Corporation; b. Arlington, Mass., Dec. 9, 1895; s. George Albert and Anna (Putnam) S.; m. Priscilla Gale, June 17, 1920; children: Anna Putnam Foote, Lyman, Gale Mayfield. Student, Milton (Mass.) Acad.; AB, Harvard U., 1918. Pres., dir., treas. Thomas Strahan Co., mfrs. wall paper, Chelsea, Mass.; dir., mem. exec. com. Sheraton Corp. of Am., Boston; dir. Federated Bus. Svcs. Inc.; dir., mem. exec. com. Am. Mut. Liability Ins. Co., Wakefield, Mass.; dir., mem. investment com. Am. Mut. Ins. Co. Boston, Wakefield, Am. Policyholders Ins. Co., Wakefield; dir. Am. Life Ins. Co. of Wakefield, Control Molding Corp.; mem. Chelsea adv. com. Nat. Shawmut Bank of Boston; trustee, mem. rsch. and policy com. Com. Econ. Devel.; mem. U.S. Senate Adv. Com. on Social Security, 1947-49. Past pres., dir. Samller Bus. Assn. of New Eng., Inc.; past pres., dir. Wall Paper Inst., N.Y.C.; trustee, chmn. fin. com. New Eng. Econ. Edn. Coun.; mem. adv. bd. small bus. Northeastern U. Recipient Justin P. Allman award Wallpaper Wholesalers Assn., 1956. Mem. Wall Paper Inst. (labor rels. com.), Wallpaper Coun. Inc. (dir.), Phi Beta Kappa. Unitarian. *

SMITH, W. ANGLE, bishop; b. Elgin, Tex., Dec. 21, 1894; s. William Angle and Mary E. (Marrs) S.; m. Bess Owens, July 20, 1920; children: William Angle, Bryant Wesley, Shelby Lee. AB, Southwestern U., 1917; MA, Columbia U., 1924; student, Perksin Sch. Theology, Vanderbilt Sch. religion, Union Theol. Sem.; DD, McMurry Coll., 1927, Centenary Coll., 1934, Southwestern U., 1937; LLD, So. Meth. U., 1945; LittD, Okla. City U., 1945, DST, 1958; DD, Central Coll., 1946. Ordained to ministry M.E. Ch., 1921. Pastor Kerrville, Tex., 1920-21, Midland, Tex., 1921-23; Pastor Tulip St. Ch., Nasjville, 1924-26, Trinity Ch., El Paso, 1926-30, 1st Ch., Shreveport, La., 1930-34, Mt. Vernon Place Ch., Washington, 1934-36, 1st Meth. Ch., Dallas, 1938-44; elected bishop of Meth. ch., 1944; chosen official rep. Coun. Bishops, The Meth. Ch., to India, Burma, Malaysia, 1946; fraternal del. Gen. Conf. Mexican MEth. Ch., 1950, Latin Am. Gen. Conf., Colivia, 1952, Mexican Gen. Conf., 1954, Hawaii, 1955; represented Coun. Bishops Gen. Conf., Brazil, 1960, 65, Latin Am. Ctrl. Conf., Lima, Peru, 1960; bishop in charge Pacific area, Latin Am., Ctrl. COnf., 1960, Hong Kong-Taiwan area, 1960-61. Pres. Centenary Coll., 1932-33, trustee, 1931-34, trustee Southwestern U., 1928-30, from 1944, Meth. Home, Waco, Okla. Meth. Children's Home; pres. bd. trustees Okla. City U., McMurry Coll., mem. bds. Evangelism Missions of Meth. Ch.; pres. gen. bd. Evangelism, div. cultivation and edn., structure Meth. ocersear; pres. Coun. Bishops og Meth. Ch., 1957-58; pres. Meth. Chaplains Commn., from 1964; exec. com., chmn. program com. World Meth. Protestant Gen. Conf., 1936. Mem. Kappa Alpha, Tau Kappa Alpha, Theta Phi, Sigma Theta, Chi ALpha, Masons (35 Shriner). *

SMITH, WILBUR STEVENSON, consulting engineer; b. Columbia, S.C., Sept. 6, 1911; s. George W. and Margaret Rebecca (Stevenson) S.; m. Sarah E. Bolick, Dec. 22, 1934; children: Sarah, Margaret, Stephanie. BS magna cum laude, U. S.C., 1932, MS, 1933, LLD, 1963; postgrad., Harvard U., 1936-37; L.H.D., Lander Coll., 1975. Registered profl. engr., 50 states, D.C. Electric hwy. engr. S.C. Hwy. Dept., 1933-34, asst. traffic engr., 1935-37, traffic engr., 1937-42; traffic cons. FBI, 1942-63; chmn., dir. Freeman, Fox, Wilbur Smith & Assos. (cons. engrs.), London, 1964-71; transp. cons. U.S. Office CD, 1942-43; assoc. dir. Yale U. Bur. Hwy. Traffic, 1943-57, research assoc., 1957-68; chmn. bd. emeritus Eno Found. for Transp., Westport, Conn.; founder, pres. Wilbur Smith & Assocs., New Haven, 1952, offices in Columbia, S.C., Richmond, Va., Falls Church, Va., Washington, San Francisco, Houston, Pitts., also 13 fgn. locations, (co. merged into Aramco, Inc., 1981), chmn. bd. until 1983, co. later returned to original name, Wilbur Smith Assocs., sr. cons., 1983-90; owner Wilbur S. Smith Mgmt., 1985-90; bd. dirs. Koger Properties, Inc., Republic Nat. Bank, Columbia, Rank Devel. Inc.; cons. Office of Comml. Programs NASA, The Harry Frank Guggenheim Found. Author: (with N. Hebden) State City Relationships in Highway Affairs, 1950, (with T. Matson, F. Hurd) Traffic Engineering, 1955; author (with T. Matson, F. Hurd) tech. bulls., reports, traffic surveys. Mem. pres.'s nat. adv. coun., U. S.C.; trustee U. S.C.-Bus. Partnership Found., S.C. Research Authority; mem. dean's coun. Sch. Engring. Duke U.; past pres. Theodore H. Matson Meml. Fund; bd. overseers Comprehensive Cancer Duke U. Med. Ctr. Recipient Disting. Alumnus award U. S.C., 1968, Disting. Alumnus award Coll. Engring. U. S.C., 1990; inducted into S.C. Bus. Hall of Fame, 1989. Mem. IEEE, NSPE (George S. Bartlett award 1985—, NSPE award 1985), Internat. Road Fedn., Inst. Engrs. Australia, Inst. Civil Engrs. (U.K.), N.Z. Instn. Engrs., Internat. Bridge, Tunnel and Turnpike Assn., Am. Inst. Cons. Engrs., ASCE (hon., past chmn. hwy. div. exec. com., Francis C. Turner Lecture award 1990), Transp. Research Bd. (Roy W. Crum award 1980), Inst. Transp. Engrs. (hon., past nat. pres.), Nat. Acad. Engring., Am. Rd. and Transp. Builders Assn. (past pres., dir.), Hong Kong Instn. Engrs., Am. Soc. Safety Engrs., S.C. Soc. Profl. Engrs. (Engr. of Yr., 1964), N.Y. Soc. Profl. Engrs., Am. Pub. Works Assn. (hon. mem. Inst. Transp.), Phi Beta Kappa, Tau Beta Pi, Phi Sigma Kappa, Chi Epsilon (hon.), Blue Key. Clubs: Forest Lake Country (Columbia, S.C.), Palmetto (Columbia, S.C.), Summit (Columbia, S.C.); Grads. (New Haven); Cosmos (Washington); Miami; Yale (N.Y.C.); St. Stephens (London); Wild Dunes (S.C.) Beach and Racquet. Home: Columbia S.C. Died July 25, 1990; buried Columbia, S.C.

SMITH, WILLIAM ARTHUR, artist; b. Toledo, Apr. 19, 1918; s. Bert Arthur and Catherine Jane (Doan) S.;

m. Mary France Nixon, Sept. 30, 1939 (div. 1946); 1 son, Richard Keane; m. Ferol Yvonne Stratton, Oct. 10, 1949; children: Kim, Kathlin Alexandra. Student, Keane's Art Sch., Toledo, 1932-36, U. Toledo, 1936-37; M.A., U. Toledo, 1954. Newspaper work, 1936-37; established studio N.Y.C., 1937; instr. Grand Central Art Sch., 1942-43; lectr. Acad. Fine Arts, Athens, 1954, U. Santa Tomas, Manila, 1955, Acad. Fine Arts, Warsaw, 1958; ofcl. del. Internat. Assn. Plastic Arts, Venice, 1954; mem. ofcl. del. to Russia under Cultural Exchange Agreement, 1958. Represented in Met. Mus. N.Y.C., Library of Congress, Washington, one-man shows Toledo Mus. Art, 1942, 52, Bucknell U., 1952, others, also many fgn. cities; artist mural Md. House, 1968; portrait of Carl Sandburg hanging in permanent collection Nat. Portrait Gallery, Washington; designed numerous U.S. postage stamps.; illustrator five books John Day Pub. Co. and others; author: Gerd Utescher; author, illustrator articles for various mags. Bd. dirs. Welcome House, v.p., 1966-73. Recipient Adolph and Clara Obrig prize for oil painting, 1953, Am. Artists Group prize for lithography Soc. Am. Graphic Artists, 1954, Knobloch prize, 1956, Winslow Homer Meml. prize, 1962, Am. Patriots' medal, 1974, Postal Commemorative Soc. prize, 1974; Dolphin fellow. Mem. Internat. Assn. Art (U.S. del. 1963, 66, 69, 73, exec. com. 1963-69, v.p. 1966-69, pres. 1973-76, hon. pres. 1976—, pres. U.S. nat. com. 1970-77, hon. pres. 1977-89), NAD (sec. 1954-55, council 1953-56, 75-78, Watercolor award 1949, 51), Am. Watercolor Soc. (trustee 1949, pres. 1956-57, hon. pres. 1957-89, Silver medal 1948, 52, 73, Stuart Watercolor prize 1954, Gold medal 1957, 65, Bronze medal 1972), Calif. Watercolor Soc., Audubon Artists, Phila. Watercolor Club, Nat. Soc. Mural Painters, Dutch Treat Club. Home: Pineville Pa. Died Apr. 27, 1989; buried New Hope, Pa.

SMITH, WILLIAM FRENCH, lawyer, United States attorney general; b. Wilton, N.H., Aug. 26, 1917; s. William French and Margaret (Dawson) S.; m. Jean Webb, Nov. 6, 1964. A.B. summa cum laude, U. Calif., 1939; LL.B., Harvard U., 1942; hon. degrees, Pepperdine U., DePaul U., U. San Diego. Bar: Calif. 1942. Atty., sr. ptnr. Gibson, Dunn & Crutcher, Los Angeles, 1946-81, 85-90; atty. gen. U.S., Washington, 1981-85; mem. Pres. Fgn. Intelligence Adv. Bd., Washington, 1985-89, Pres. Drug Adv. Com., 1989-90; bd. dirs. Crocker Nat. Bank, San Francisco, 1971-81, Pullman, Inc., Chgo., 1979-81, Pacific Mut. Life Ins. Co., L.A., 1970-81, RCA, N.Y.C., 1985-86; bd. dirs. Pacific Enterprises, L.A., 1967-81, NBC Corp., N.Y.C., 1985-90, Am. Internat Group Inc., N.Y.C., 1985-90, Pacific Telesis Group, Pacific Bell, San Francisco, 1974-81, 1985-90, Gen. Electric Co., N.Y.C., 1986-90, H.F. Ahmanson & Co., L.A., 1974-81, 1985-90, Earle M. Jorgensen Co., Los Angeles, Fisher Sci. Group Inc., La Jolla, Calif., 1986-89, Weintraub Entertainment Group Inc., L.A., 1987-90, Spectradyne, Inc., L.A., 1989-90. Mem. U.S. Adv. Commn. on Internat. Ednl. and Cultural Affairs, 1971-78, Stanton Panel on Internat. Info., Edn. and Cultural Relations, 1974-75; U.S. del. The East-West Ctr. for Cultural and Tech. Interchange, Hawaii, 1975-77; mem. adv. council Sch. Govt., Harvard U., 1977-90, mem. visiting com. Ctr. Internat. Affairs, Harvard U., 1986-90; mem. adv. bd. Ctr. for Strategic and Internat. Studies, Georgetown U., Washington, 1978-82, 85-90; mem. nat. bd. advisors Fedn. for Am. Immigration Reform (FAIR), 1985-90; mem. nat. adv. com. Internat. Tennis Found. and Hall of Fame, Inc., 1985-90, Nat. Legal Ctr. for the Pub. Interest, 1985-90; mem. exec. com. The Calif. Roundtable, 1976-81, bd. dirs. 85-90, Calif. Community Found., 1980-81, 85-90; bd. regents U. Calif., 1968-90, chmn., 1970-72, 74-75, 76; bd. dirs. Legal Aid Found. Los Angeles, 1963-72; bd. dirs. Los Angeles World Affairs Council, 1970-90, pres., 1975-78; dir. Am.-China Soc., 1987-90; trustee Claremont McKenna Coll., 1967-90, Ind. Colls. of So. Calif., 1969-74, Ctr. Theatre Group, Los Angeles Music Ctr., 1970-81, Henry E. Huntington Library and Art Gallery, 1971-90, The Cate Sch., 1971-78, Northrop Inst. Tech., 1973-75; chmn. bd. trustees The Ronald Reagan Presdl. Library Found., 1985-90; nat. trustee Nat. Symphony Orch., Washington, 1974-90; mem. bd. fellows The Inst. Jud. Adminstrn., Inc., 1981-90; chmn. Calif. Delegation to Rep. Nat. Conv., 1968, vice chmn., 1971, 76, 80, 88. Served to lt. USNR, 1942-46. Fellow Am. Bar Found.; mem. ABA (fellow sect. of litigation 1985-90, standing com. law and nat. security 1985-90), Los Angeles County Bar Assn., Am. Judicature Soc., Am. Law Inst., Calif. C. of C. (bd. dirs. 1963-80, pres. 1974-75), Order of Coif (hon.), Phi Beta Kappa, Pi Gamma Mu, Pi Sigma Alpha, Phi Delta Phi. Home: San Marino Calif. Died Oct. 29, 1990; buried Forest Lawn Meml. Pk., Glendale, Calif.

SMITH, WILLIAM WALLACE, clergyman; b. Lamoni, Iowa, Nov. 18, 1900; s. Joseph and Ada Rachel (Clark) S.; m. Rosamond Bunnell, Nov. 12, 1924; children—Rosalee (Mrs. Otto Helmut Elser), Wallace Bunnell. A.A., Graceland Coll., Lamoni, 1922, D.D. (hon.), 1970; A.B., U. Mo., 1924. Ordained to ministry Reorganized Ch. of Jesus Christ of Latter Day Saints, 1928; asso. pastor Stone Ch. Congregation, Independence, 1929-30; pastor First Ch., Portland, Oreg., 1945-46; mem. council Twelve Apostles, 1947-50; counsellor to pres. Reorganized Ch. Jesus Christ of Latter Day Saints, 1950-58, pres., 1958-78, pres. emeritus, 1978-89; asst. editor in chief Saints' Herald, 1950-58, editor in chief, 1958-78, contbg. editor, from 1979; dir. Pacific Land Devel. Assn. Mem. bd. trustees Independence Sanitarium and Hosp.; Hon. fellow Harry Truman Library Inst. for Nat. and Internat. Affairs. Mem. Mo. Hist. Soc. (trustee), Jackson County Hist. Soc., C. of C., Delta Upsilon. Club: Rotarian. Home: Independence Mo. Died Aug. 9, 1989.

SMYTH, CHARLES PHELPS, chemist; b. Clinton, N.Y., Feb. 10, 1895; s. Charles Henry and Ruth Anna (Phelps) S.; m. Emily Ellen Vezin, Feb. 12, 1955. AB, Princeton U., 1916, AM, 1917; PhD, Harvard U., 1921; DSc, U. Salford, 1970. Asst. chemist U.S. Bur. Standards, 1917; faculty chemistry Princeton (N.J.) U., 1920-63, David B. Jones prof. chemistry, 1958-63, prof. emeritus, 1963-90, sr. rsch. chemist, 1963-68; liaison scientist Office Naval Rsch., London, 1969-70, cons., 1963-69, 1971-90; lectr. Am. Chem. Soc., Inst. Chem., 1927; hon. chmn. Gordon Con. on Dielectrics, 1970; cons. on project for Rubber Res., 1941-42; chemist on Atom Bomb Project, 1943-45; expert cons. OSRD serving with U.S. Army, 1945, ETO. Author: Dielectric Behavior and Structure, 1955, Dielectric Constant and Molecular Structure, 1931; assoc. editor Jour. Chem. Physics, 1933-36, 52-54; mem. editorial bd. Annual Tables of Physical Constants, 1941-45; adv. editor Dielectrics; contbr. 300 papers and articles to Jour. Am. Chem. Soc., Jour. Chem. Physics, Philos. Mag., other sci. publs. 2d lt. O.R.C., 2d lt. Chem. Svc. sect. Nat. Army, 1st lt. Chem. Warfare Svc., U.S. Army, 1918; lt. comdr. USNR, 1937-41. Recipient medal of Freedom, War Dept., cert. merit OSRD, cert. appreciation, War Dept., cert. in recognition of pub. svc. U.S. Dept. State, 1958. Fellow Am. Phys. Soc.; mem. Nat. Acad. Scis., Am. Chem. Soc. (nichols medal 1954), Am. Philos. Soc. (coun. 1968-71), Chem. Soc. (London), Royal Instn. (London), Sigma Xi, Phi Beta Kappa, Alpha Chi Sigma. Home: Princeton N.J. Died Mar. 18, 1990.

SNAPPER, ARTHUR, manufacture packaging materials; b. Pittsburg, Kans., Feb. 26, 1898; s. George and Elizabeth (Joseph) S.; m. Albena Wittak, June 12, 1922; children: Joan, Arthur George. Grad., MArwuette U. Law Sch., 1918. Bar: Wis. 1919. Atty. ovt. practice, Milw., 1919-23; chief legal examiner securities dir. R.R. Commn., Wis., 1923-30; with Milprint Inc., Milw., from 1930; pres. Milprint Inc., from 1958, chmn. bd., from 1960, chmn. exec. com., from 1965; dir., mem. exec. com. Phillip Morris Inc. V.p. Milw. Symphony Orch., 1959-61, bd. givs., from 1956. Mem. Printing Industry Am. (past pres., union employers sect. I), Wis. Bar Assn., Milw. Bar Assn., Milw. Assn. Commerce, Masons (Shriner), KP. *

SNEDDEN, CHARLES WILLIS, newspaper publisher; b. Spokane, Wash., July 20, 1913; s. William Angus and Christine Ann (McLachlan) S.; m. Helen Elizabeth McNeel, Apr. 11, 1934; 1 son, Duane McLachlan. Student, Oreg. State Coll., U. Oreg., Wash. State Coll., 1930-33; LL.D., U. Alaska, 1967. Linotype machinist Columbian and Mergenthaler Linotype Co., Vancouver, Wash., 1933-41; pres. CWS Grinding & Machine Works, Portland, Oreg., 1935-44; supr. machinist div. Kaiser Shipyard, Vancouver, Wash., 1942-44; propr. Marshal-Wells retail hardware, Vancouver, Wash., 1943-49; ind. newspaper prodn. cons., 1945-50; pub. Fairbanks (Alaska) Daily News-Miner, from 1950, also pres.; pres. Aurora Bldg., Inc., Comml. Printing Co., Inc., Fairbanks Pub. Co., Inc.; dir. Fairbanks Econ. Devel. Corp., Wien Alaska Airlines, 1956-79; mem. Fairbanks Mcpl. Utilities Bd., 1951-54, Alaska Employment Security Com., 1954-57; nat. council Nat. Planning Assn., 1959-65. Pres. Fairbanks United Good Neighbors; pres., mem. adv. bd. St. Josephs Hosp.; bd. govs. No. Devel. Adv. Com.; trustee U. Alaska Found., 1982-90. Recipient Fairbanks George Nehrbas award, 1962; City of Fairbanks award, 1961; named Boss of Year Jr. C. of C., 1956, Alaskan of the Year award, 1987; named Laureate Alaska Bus. Hall of Fame, 1989. Mem. Fairbanks C. of C. (past dir.), Alaska C. of C. (dir., past pres.), Pacific N.W. Trade Assn. (v.p.), Inland Empire Waterways Assn. Republican. Conglist. Clubs: Mason (Shriner), Elk, Rotarian. Home: Fairbanks Alaska Died Aug. 6, 1989; buried Fairbanks, Alaska.

SNELLING, RICHARD ARKWRIGHT, governor, business executive; b. Allentown, Pa., Feb. 18, 1927; s. Walter Otheman and Marjorie (Gahring) S.; m. Barbara T. Weil, June 14, 1947; children: Jacqueline, Mark, Diane, Andrew. Student, Lehigh U., 1943; A.B., Harvard U., 1948. Chmn. bd. Shelburne Industries, Inc., Barreca Products Co., Inc., Wessel Hardware Co., from 1959; mem. Vt. Ho. of Reps., 1959-60, 72-74, 75-76; gov. State of Vt., 1977-85, 1990-91; Mem. Vt. Devel. Commn., 1960-62, Adv. Com. on Intergovtl. Relations, 1977-83; chmn. Vt. Aeros. Commn., 1968-72; mem. Presdl. Adv. Com. on Federalism, 1981-85; del. Republican Nat. Conv., 1960-68, 80; Rep. nominee for lt. gov. Vt., 1964, Rep. nominee for gov. Vt., 1966; chmn. Vt. Rep. Fin. Com., 1974-76; candidate U.S. Senate from Vt., 1986; pres. Snelling Capital Corp., from 1985; bd. dirs. New Eng. Council. Chmn. bd. dirs. Greater Burlington Indsl. Corp., 1960-62; trustee Med. Center Hosp. of Vt.; mem. steering com. Edn. Commn. of the States, 1977-85. Served with AUS, 1944-46, ETO. Mem. Nat. Govs. Assn. (exec. com. 1977-85, chmn. 1981-82), Rep. Govs. Assn. (chmn. 1980), Chief Execs. Forum, World Bus. Council (bd. dirs. 1985-91), Lake Champlain C. of C. (dir. 1962-64). Home: Shelburne Vt. Died Aug. 13, 1991.

SNYDER, DONALD B(ERTRAM), publisher; b. Wabash, Ind., Jan. 15, 1897; s. John M. and Elizabeth (Arnett) S.; m. Esther Mostrom, July 1, 1926; children: Donald Bertram, Peter G., John M. Pub., treas. Youth's Companion Perry Mason, Co., 1927-29, House Beautiful Co., 1930-33, Atlantic Monthly Mag., 1933-64; dir. AM Co. *

SNYDER, FREDERICK EDWARD, legal educator, corporate executive; b. Kingston, N.Y., Apr. 3, 1944; s. John I. and Agatha (Flick) S.; m. Jacqueline Carone, June 20, 1970 (div. 1984). AB, Georgetown U., 1966, JD, 1974; MPhil, Yale U., 1969, PhD, 1970; LLM, Harvard U., 1977. Bar: Conn. 1974, N.Y. 1976, Mass. 1981. Law clk. to chief justice Conn. Supreme Ct., 1974; assoc. Baker & McKenzie, N.Y.C., 1975-76, Bingham Dana & Gould, Boston, 1976-77; fellow in law and humanities Harvard U. Law Sch., Boston, 1977-78, asst. dean, lectr. on law, dir. clin. programs, assoc. dir. East Asian legal studies, 1978-83, asst. dean for internat. and comparative legal studies, lectr. Latin Am. law, adminstr. grad. program, assoc. dir. East Asian legal studies, 1983-90; bd. dirs. Cambridge and Somerville Legal Services; pres. Cambridge Transnat. Assocs., Inc. Playright: Six Ways to Be Left Alone, 1985; author: Law, Politics and Revolution in Latin America: A Research Guide and Bibliography, 1982, (with S. Sathirathai) Third World Attitudes Toward International Law, 1987; editor (book) Latin American Society and Legal Culture, 1985. Named Fulbright Disting. Vis. Lectr., Universidad de Los Andes, Columbia, 1987. Mem. ABA, Ateneo Mexicano de Jurisprudencia (hon.), Inst. Politics and Constl. Law of U. La Plata (hon.), Critical Legal Studies Conf., Assn. Am. Law Schs. (pres. Sect. Grad. Studies), UN Assn., Harvard Faculty Club (bd. mgrs. 1980-83). Democrat. Home: Vienna Va. Died Apr. 20, 1990.

SNYDER, MITCH, peace and justice activist; b. Bklyn., Aug. 14, 1943; s. Robert and Beatrice Snyder; divorced; children: Richard, Dean. With Community for Creative Non-Violence, Washington, 1973-90. Author: (with Mary Ellen Hombs) Homelessness in America: A Forced March to Nonwhere; subject of made-for-TV movie: Samaritan; subject of book: Signal Through the Flames; subject of documemtary: Promises to Keep (Academy award nominee). Home: Washington D.C. Died July 5, 1990; cremated.

SNYDER, NORMAN, telecommunications executive; b. Ithaca, N.Y., June 16, 1897; s. Virgil and Margarethe (Giesinger) S.; m. Valia Grodnitzky, May 20, 1933. BA, Cornell U., 1921; grad. student, Rensselaer Poly. Inst., 1938, U. Goettingen, Germany; PhD, Charles U., Czechoslovakia, 1946. Staff engr. Gen. Electric Co., RCA, 1920-38, Hammond Rsch. Corp., 1939-41; sr. engr. Signal Corps, War Dept., 1941-43; systems engr. fgn. svc. Internat. Tel. & Tel., 1943-52; tech. adviser communications Govt. Saudi Arabia, 1953; tech. cons. Haller, Raymond & Brown, Inc., 1954-57; chief telecommunications adviser Iran, 1957-64; telecommunications adviser Office U.S. Econ. Coord., Ctrl. Treaty Orgn., 1958-64; sr. staff engr. Collins Radio Internat., C.A., Beirut, Lebanon, from 1964. Mem. IEEE, U.S. Electro-Technic Soc., German-Am. Engrs., Quill and Dagger Soc., Clubs: University (State College, Pa.), Propeller (Beirut). *

SNYDER, WAHL JOHN, architect; b. Beaver, Pa., July 5, 1910; s. Wahl John and Frances (Kuhl) S.; m. Jane Roth, Apr. 6, 1946; children—Karen Lynn Fant, Deborah Denman Appleton. B.S., Pa. State U., 1932. Owner firm Wahl Snyder & Assos. (architects), Miami, Fla., 1937-89; Mem. bd. dirs. archtl. bd. Inter-Am. Center Authority; bd. dirs. Florida Architecture mag.; pres. Fla. Bd. Arch., 1968. Prin. works include Zollner residence, Golden Beach, Fla., 1954, Levitz residence, Coral Gables, Fla., 1970, Anchorage Apt, Miami Beach, 1956, Briggs residence, Nassau, 1958, Staley residence, Decatur, Ill., 1968, McArthur Engring. Bldg, U. Miami, 1959, Ski Complex, Beech Mountain, N.C., 1969, also, townhouses and condominiums. Mem. bd. appeals Bal Harbour Village, Fla. Served with C.E. AUS, 1942-44. Fellow AIA (pres. Fla. 1957, citation Lanai Apt. design 1956); mem. Fla. Assn. Architects, Com. of 100, Wine and Food Soc., Scarab, Sigma Pi. Presbyterian (elder). Clubs: Bath (Miami Beach; Symphony, Vizcayans (Miami). Lodge: Rotary (Miami Shores) (past pres. 1961-62). Home: Miami Shores Fla. Died Jan. 30, 1989; buried So. Meml. Pk., Fla.

SOBEY, WILLIAM MACDONALD, retail executive; b. New Glasgow, N.S., Can., June 9, 1927; m. Doris Cameron. D.C.L., Dalhousie U., Can. Chmn., CEO Sobey's Stores Ltd., Stellarton, N.S., 1974-85, hon. chmn., 1985-89. Home: Stellarton N.S., Can. Died May 29, 1989; buried King's Head Cemetery, Pickou County, N.S.

SODERHOLM, LARS GUSTAV, magazine editor; b. Kvillinge, Sweden, May 7, 1924; came to U.S., 1927, naturalized, 1939; s. Nils Gustav and Ebba Augusta (Stenholm) S.; m. Betty Cartwright, Nov. 22, 1951; children: Elin Ann, Robert Gustav. B.S. in Mech. Engring., Ill. Inst. Tech., 1949. Registered profl. engr., Ill., Ind., Ia., Minn., Mo., Wis. Safety engr. Am. Asso. Ins. Cos., Chgo., 1949-51; design-devel. engr. Whiting Corp., Harvey, Ill., 1951-59; Midwest editor Design News, Cahners Pub. Co., Chgo., 1959-71; editorial dir. Design News, Cahners Pub. Co., Boston, from 1971; corp. v.p. Design News, Cahners Pub. Co., from 1981; Coordinator ann. fluidic seminars Milw. Sch. Engring., 1965-68; bd. govs. Nat. Conf. Power Transmission, from 1978. Author numerous articles in field. Served with AUS, 1943-45. Recipient Master key for service, 1966, Cahners award for excellence, 1967. Mem. Nat., Mass. socs. profl. engrs., Am. Soc. Bus. Press Editors (pres. Chgo. 1966-67, nat. pres. 1969-70), Am. Bus. Press (Western editorial bd. 1970-71), Fluid Power Soc., Nat. Fluid Power Assn. (tech. rep.), Nat. Conf. on Fluid Power (exec. com. from 1975), Sigma Delta Chi. Home: Southborough Mass. Deceased. †

SOFIELD, HAROLD AUGUSTUS, orthopedic surgeon; b. Jersey city, Mar. 27, 1900; s. David and Elvaretta (Brown) S.; m. Ruth Robinson, Apr. 19, 1934; children—David, Julie (Mrs. Otis Tholander). Student, Columbia, 1918-23; M.D., Northwestern U., 1928. Diplomate: Am. Bd. Orthopedic Surgery (past pres.). Intern San Francisco Hosp., 1927-28; resident Shriners Hosp. for Crippled Children, Chgo., 1928-30, resident orthopedic surgery, 1928-35, chief surgeon, 1944-65, emeritus, 1965-87; chief cons. orthopedic surgery VA for, Ill., Ind. and Wis., from 1946; sr. cons. orthopedic surgery VA Hosp., Hines, Ill.; staff orthopedic surgery West Surburban Hosp., dir. surg. edn.; past chmn., life trustee; staff Gottlieb Meml. Hosp., Melrose Park, Ill.; asso. prof. dept. orthopedic surgery Northwestern U., 1946-50, prof., 1950-68, emeritus prof., 1968-87; cons. Norwegian Am., DuPage County Meml., Westlake Community hosps.; spl. cons. lectr. U.S. Army hosps. in, Europe, 1955; rep. adv. com. on phys. therapy edn. Council on Med. Edn. and Hosp.; sec.-treas., co-founder Orthopaedic Research and Edn. Found.; past chmn. sect. orthopedic surgery NRC, Washington; treas. Pub. Health Study and Survey Commn. Ill.; chief cons. orthopedic surgery to S. Pacific Theatre. Contbr. articles to surg. jours., books. Past chmn. bd. trustees Easter Seal Research Found.; trustee Lincoln (Ill.) Acad.; past chmn. exec. com. orthopedics overseas div. Medico-CARE; past med. adv. univ. senate Northwestern U. Served with USN, World War I; served as col. M.C. AUS, World War II. Decorated Bronze Star, Legion of Merit with 5 battle stars; comdr. Order Daniel Carrion Peru). Fellow A.C.S., Brit. Orthopaedic Assn. (hon.); mem. AMA (Sheen award 1981), Assn. Mil. Surgeons U.S., Clin., Chgo. Orthopedic Soc. (past pres.), Am. Orthopedic Assn. (past sec.-treas.), Ill. State med. soc. (past v.p.), Chgo. med. soc., past pres., Public Service award 1980), Ill. Assn. for Crippled children, Chgo. Inst. Medicine, Am. Acad. Orthopaedic Surgeons (pres. 1959), Soc. Med. Cons. to Armed Forces, Orthopaedic Research Soc., Australian Orthopaedic Assn. (corr.), Internat. Soc. Orthopaedic Surgery, Am. Ret. Physicians Assn. (sec.-treas. 1976-80), Am. Legion, Assn. Bone and Joint Surgeons (hon.), Soc. Orthopaedic Surgeons of Chile (hon.), Latin Am. Soc. Orthopaedic Surgery and Traumatology (hon.), Academia Nat. de Medicina of Brazil (hon.), Beta Theta Pi. Clubs: Mason (33 deg., Shriner, Jester, Red Cross of Constantine), Loyal Order of Boar, Oak Park (Ill.) Country. Home: Amherst Mass. Died Dec. 21, 1987.

SOKOL, SIDNEY S., financial consultant; b. N.Y.C., Aug. 16, 1913; s. Harry and Rose (Rosalinsky) S.; m. Evelyn Gold, Nov. 3, 1935; children: Bernice Gabrielle, Marilyn Roberta. BS, CCNY, 1934, MBA, 1941; postgrad., Columbia U., 1934-35. CPA, N.Y. With Dept. Treasury, 1935-42, 46-73, successively mem. bur. accounts, staff procurement div. Office Fiscal Asst. Sec., rep. Fed. Res. Bank of N.Y., staff bur. accounts., dep. commr. acctg. systems, to 1957, tech. asst. to fiscal asst. sec., 1957-61, fin. cons., 1973-75; chief disbursing br. Office Dependency Benefits, Dept. War, 1942-46; mem. departmental com. on pub. adminstrn. USDA Grad. Sch. Recipient Meritorious Civilian Svc. award Dept. War, 1946, Silver medal Dept. Treasury, 1956, Gold medal, 1964. Mem. AICPA, Fed. Govt. Accts. Assn., Beta Gamma Sigma. Home: New York N.Y. Died Dec. 30, 1990; buried Mt. Ararat Cemetery, Farmingdale, N.Y.

SOKOLOFF, MELVIN See LEWIS, MEL

SOKOLOW, ASA D., lawyer; b. N.Y.C., Apr. 22, 1919; s. Harry J. and Dorothy (Turkeltaub) S.; m. Phyllis E. Cahen, Jan. 31, 1943 (dec. Apr. 1982); children—Jeffrey, Judith, Jonathan; m. Renee J. Ginsberg, June 11, 1984. Grad., Phillips Acad., Andover, Mass., 1936; B.A., Yale U., 1940, LL.B., 1947. Assoc. Cahill, Gordon and Reindel, N.Y.C., 1947-59; from ptnr. to sr. ptnr. Rosenman & Colin (and predecessor firm Rosenman Colin Freund Lewis & Cohen), N.Y.C., 1960-90. Author: The Political Theory of Arthur J. Penty, 1940; co-author: Discovery Proceedings Under the Federal Rules, 1955. Past v.p., past trustee Park Ave. Synagogue, N.Y.C.; past trustee Soc. for Advancement Judaism, N.Y.C.; bd. dirs. Lawyers Com. for Civil Rights Under Law, 1965-90. Capt. U.S. Army, 1941-45; NATOUSA, ETO. Recipient Leadership award State of Israel Bonds, 1980. Mem. ABA, Assn. Bar City N.Y., N.Y. State Bar Assn. Democrat. Clubs: Morys (New Haven); Yale, Harmonie (N.Y.C.); Sunningdale Country (Scarsdale, N.Y.). Home: New York N.Y. Died June 26, 1882.

SOLFISBURG, ROY JOHN, state justice; b. Aurora, Ill., Sept. 9, 1916; s. Roy John and Helen (Iliff) S.; m. Edith Squieres, Dec. 28, 1940; children: Roy John III, Susan, Sally, Sandra, William. BA, U. Ill., 1938, LLB, 1940; LLD, Chgo. Kent Coll. Law, 1963, John Marshall Law Sch., 1963. Bar: Ill. 1940. Corp. counsel Aurora, 1949-53; commr. Ill. Ct. of Claims, 1953-54; master chancery Cir. Ct. Kane County, 1954-56; cir. judge 16th Jud. Dist. Ill., 1956-57; mem. Appellate Ct. 2d Dist. Ill., 1957-60, presiding justice, 1960; justice Ill. Supreme Ct., 1960-69, chief justice, 1962-63, 67-69.; Chmn. Met. Cts. Conf. of U.S., 1962-65. Lt. (s.g.) USNR, World War II. Mem. Am., Ill. Kane County bar assns., Am. Legion (vice-chmn. disting. guest com. 1962, judge advocate 11th dist. 1959-60), Elk (past exalted ruler Aurora), Exch. Club (pres. 1949), Union League (Aurora). Home: Aurora Ill. Died Apr. 19, 1991.

SOLOMON, BARBARA MILLER, history educator; b. Boston, Feb. 12, 1919; d. Benjamin Allen and Bessie (Pinsky) Miller Skirball; m. Peter Herman Solomon, May 13, 1940 (dec. 1987); children: Peter Herman Jr., Maida Elizabeth. AB, Radcliffe Coll., 1940; PhD, Harvard U., 1953; LittD (hon.), Regis Coll., 1986. Asst. prof. history Wheelock Coll., Mass., 1957-59; instr. Radcliffe Coll., Cambridge, Mass., 1960-61, assoc. dean, 1963-70, vis. scholar, 1989-90; lectr. history and lit. Harvard U., Cambridge, 1965-74, rsch. fellow, 1968-69, asst. dean, 1970-74, sr. lectr., 1974-85, lectr. Extension Sch., 1985-86; mem. adv. com. Arthur and Elizabeth Schlesinger Libr. for History Women Am., 1965—, chmn., 1975-76, hon. vis. scholar, 1989-91. Author: In the Company of Educated Women, 1984 (Frederick W. Ness award 1986), Ancestors and Immigrants, 1956, reprinted, 1965, 72, 89; editor: Educated Women, 12 vols., 1987. Guggenheim fellow, 1976-77; Radcliffe Mellon scholar, 1979-80. Mem. Cosmopolitan Club. Jewish. Home: Cambridge Mass. Died Aug. 20, 1992. †

SOLTERER, JOSEF, educator; b. Vienna, Dec. 28, 1897; came to U.S., 1924, naturalized, 1932; s. Carl and Maria (Widhalm) S.; m. Hortense M. McClure, June 15, 1929 (dec. Oct. 1952); 1 child, Carl F.; m. A. Elizabeth Curran, June 14, 1955; 1 child, Helen Maria. AM, Georgetown U., 1929, PhD, 1932, LLD, 1957; DSc, U. Catolica de Chile, 1955. Navigation officer KPM, Java, Dutch East Indies, 1920-23; instr. fgn. lang. So. Coll., Hattiesburg, Miss., 1924-27; instr. to prof. econs. Georgetown U., 1929-92, chmn. dept., 1940-92; cons. Credit Coops., Haiti, 1945; cons., lectr. Econ. Orgn., Instituto de Estudios Superiores, Monterey, Mexico, 1949, U. Catolica of Chile, 1954; Fulbright prof. univs. Inssbruck, Vienna, 1955. Comd. Freg. Lt., Austro-Hungarian Navy, 1917. Mem. Am., Cath. (pres. 1949-50) econ. assns., Econometric Soc., Soc. Indsl. and Applied Math., Am. Statis. Assn. Home: Washington D.C. Died Jan. 7, 1992.

SOMERS, CARIN ALMA, librarian; b. Frankfurt/Main, Ger., Mar. 18, 1934; d. Josef and Helen Josephine (Badham) Stein; m. Frank George Somers, Aug. 23, 1958. B.A., Newton (Mass.) Coll. Sacred Heart, 1955; M.A., Dalhousie U., Halifax, N.S., Can., 1956; B.L.S., U. Toronto, 1961. Registrar, then lectr. French St. Mary's U., Halifax, 1956-60; with Halifax City Regional Library, 1958-64, librarian tech. services, 1961-64; asst. librarian, then chief librarian Halifax County Regional Library, 1964-73; supr. pub. libraries N.S. Provincial Library, Halifax, 1973-74, dir., 1974-87; occasional lectr. Dalhousie U. Sch. Library Service. Contbr. articles to profl. jours. Decorated Gov. Gen.'s medal, Can. (Queen Elizabeth II) Silver Jubilee medal; grantee Province N.S., 1960-61; grantee French Govt., 1956. Mem. Can. Library Assn. (2d v.p. 1974-75), Atlantic Provinces Library Assn. (past pres.), N.S. Library Assn., N.S. Bird Soc., Can. Nature Fedn. Roman Catholic. Club: Royal N.S. Yacht Squadron. Home: Halifax N.S., Can. Died Mar. 3, 1990.

SOMOGYL, ERWIN GEORGE, research company executive; b. Budapest, July 29, 1912; s. Michael and Elizabeth (Grosz) S.; m. Florence Wray, July 3, 1937; children: Nancy Catherine Somogyi Morgan, Michael Wray. BS, U. Mich., 1935. With Monsanto Chem. Co., 1935-63, dir. rsch., 1952-60, v.p., gen. mgr. rsch. and engring. div., 1960-63; v.p. tech. Wheeling Steel Corp. (W.Va.), 1966-67; chmn. bd. Sch. Rsch. & Svc. Corp., Fullerton, Calif., 1967-90; mem. Gov. Mo. Sci. Adv. Com.; dir., chmn. fin. com. Indsl. Rsch. Inst.; adv. bd. Chem. and Engring. News. Trustee, chmn. Tarko Coll.; trustee Presbyn. Intercommunity Hosp., Whittier, Calif.; elder Presbyn. ch. Home: Fullerton Calif. Died Oct. 17, 1990.

SONNICHSEN, CHARLES LELAND, editor; b. Fonda, Ia., Sept. 20, 1901; s. Henry Matthew and Mary (Hults) S.; m. Augusta Jones, July 23, 1933 (div. 1950); children: Charles P., Mary A., Nancy L.; m. Carol Wade, Jan. 26, 1956. BA, U. Minn., 1924; MA, Harvard U., 1927, PhD, 1931. Asst. master St. James Ch., Faribault, Minn., 1924-26; instr. Carnegie Inst. Tech., 1927-29; faculty U. Tex., El Paso, 1931-72, prof. English, chmn. dept., 1933-60, dean Grad. Div., 1960-67, H.Y. Benedict prof. English, 1965-72, emeritus, 1972-91; dir. pubs. Ariz. Hist. Soc.; vis. prof. U. Tex., 1936, 38. Editor: Jour. Ariz. History; author: Billy King's Tombstone, 1942, Roy Bean: Law West of the Pecos, 1943, Cowboys and Cattle Kings, 1950, I'll Die Before I'll Run, 1951 (with William V. Morrison) Alias Billy the Kid 1955: Ten Texas Feuds, 1957, The Mescalero Apaches, 1958, Tularosa: Last of the Frontier West, 1960, The El Paso Salt War, 1961, (anthology) The Southwest In Life and Literature, 1962, Outlaw, 1966, Pass of the North, 1968, Morris Parker's White Oaks, 1971, others. Recipient Wrangler award Nat. Cowboy Hall Fame, Bowdoin prize, 1931; Rockefeller fellow U. Okla., 1948. Fellow Tex. Hist. Assn.; mem. Southwestern Am. Lit. Assn., N.Mex. Tex. (past pres.) folklore socs., Rocky Mountain Modern Lang. Assn., Western Lit. Assn. (pres. 1966), Assn. Tex. Grad. Schs. (pres. 1966), Tucson Westerner, English Westerners, Tex. Inst. Letters, Western Writers Am. (Spur award), Lambda Alpha Xi, Alpha Chi. Republican. Home: Tucson Ariz. Died June 28, 1991.

SORENSEN, VIRGINIA (MRS. ALEC WAUGH), author; b. Provo, Utah, Feb. 17, 1912; d. Claud E. and Helen El Deva (Blackett) Eggertsen; m. Frederick C. Sorensen, Aug. 16, 1933; children: Elizabeth (Mrs. David Allan Hepburn), Frederick W.; m. Alec Waugh, 1969. A.B., Brigham Young U., 1934. Author: novels A Little Lower Than the Angels, 1942, On This Star, 1946, The Neighbors, 1947, The Evening and the Morning, 1949, The Proper Gods, 1951, Many Heavens, 1954, Kingdom Come, 1960, The Man With The Key, 1974; children's book Curious Missie, 1953; The House Next Door, 1954, Plain Girl, 1955 (recipient award Child Study Assn. Am. 1955), Miracles on Maple Hill, 1956 (recipient Newbery award A.L.A. 1956); short stories Where Nothing is Long Ago, 1963; children's books Lotte's Locket, 1964, Around the Corner, 1970, Friends of the Road, 1977. Guggenheim fellow, 1946-47, 54-55. Mem. Authors Guild, P.E.N., Phi Beta Kappa. Home: New York N.Y. Deceased. †

SORENSON, HERBERT, educator; b. Dawson, Minn., Apr. 12, 1898. BS, U. Minn., 1924, MA, 1926, PhD, 1928. Tchr. rural sch., 1916-17, prin. semigrades sch., 1917, supt., 1920-22; statistician Northwestern U., 1924-25; asst., instr., asst. prof., assoc. prof. U. Minn., 1926-37; dir. adult edn. Minn., 1935-36; pres. Duluth State Tchrs. Coll., 1938-46; with Griffenhagen & Assocs., Chgo., 1946-47; prof. ednl. psychology U. Ky., 1947-50, disting. prof. ednl. psychology, from 1950; vis. prof. U. Oslo, 1950-51. Contbr. to books, workbooks and articles to profl. jours. Lt. U.S. Coast Guard res. Carnegie grantee, 1934. Fellow AAAS; mem. Am. Assn. Sch. Adminstrs., Am. Psychol. Assn., Sigma Xi, Phi Delta Kappa, Kiwanis (pres. 1945). *

SORENSON, LLOYD RAYMOND, shipbuilding company executive; b. Calais, Maine, Oct. 20, 1897; s. Soren and Annetta (Dahl) S.; m. Lucy Apkers, June 30, 1923 (dec. 1948); children: Lucy JEan, Lloyd Raymond, Sylvia Joan. BSEE, MIT, 1919. With Newport News Shipbuilding & Dry Dock Co., from 1918, asst. naval architect, 1930-42, cost engr., 1942-54, prodn. mgr., 1954-56, v.p., prodn. mgr., 1955-57, v.p., from 1957, gen. mgr., 1957-64; pres., dir. Newport News Bldg. & Loan Assn. Mem. Kiwanis (past pres.), James River Country Club (past. pres.), Propeller (past pres.). *

SOULE, ROLAND P., business executive; b. Rochester, N.Y., Jan. 17, 1896; s. Herbert C. and Ella (Wiles) S.; m. Ann Pettit, July 9, 1925; children: Barbara, Martha (dec.). BS, Rochester U., 1917; Chem. Eng., Columbia, 1920, AM, 1921, PhD, 1922. Mgr. chem. products div. Henry L. Doherty & Co., 1922-26; chief technologist Internat. Coal Carbonization Co., 1926-30; tech. economist Tri-Continental Corp., 1930-38; v.p. in charge rsch. and devel. Am. Machine & Foundry Co., 1945-49; with Irving Trust Co., from 1949, v.p. in charge rsch. and planning div., 1950-61, cons., from 1961; lectr. chem. engring. Columbia; mem. adv. com., rsch. div. NYU; dir. Am. Machine & Foundry Co., Boston Capitol Corp. Contbr. tech. publs. Mem. Am. Chem. Soc., Am. Inst. Chem. Engrs., Phi Beta Kappa, Tau Beta Pi, Sigma Xi, Phi Lambda Upsilon, Delta Upsilon, Univ. Clubs, Chemists Club. *

SOUPAULT, PHILIPPE, writer, poet; b. Paris, Feb. 10, 1895. Student, Sorbonne, Paris. mem. Dadaistic movement; one of founders of surrealism. Home: Paris France Died Mar. 11, 1990.

SOUSTELLE, JACQUES EMILE, anthropologist; b. Montpellier, France, Feb. 3, 1912; s. Jean and Germaine (Blatiere) S.; m. Georgette Fagot, Aug. 5, 1931. PhD in Philosophy, U. Lyon; HHD, Ecole Normale Superieure. Anthropologist sci. missions Cen. Am., 1932-39; dep. dir. Mus. of Man., 1938-39; lectr. Coll. de France and Colonial Sch., 1938-39; various to nat. commr. for information France, 1942; dir. spl. svcs. Algiers, 1943-44; Rep. commr. Bordeaux, France, 1944; minister of info. France, 1945, sec. colonial affairs, 1945, dep. for la Mayenne, 1945-46; chief sec. Rassemblement, France, 1947-52; French People's Assembly dep., then Social Rep. of Rhone, 1951-58; gov. gen. Algeria, 1955-56; sec. info. France, 1958-59; mem. cen. com., Rhone dep. Union New Republic, 1958; dep. min. to prime min., 1959-60; gen. del. Communal Orgn. Regions of Sahara,

1959-60; pres. Ctr. Info. on Problems Algeria and the Sahara, 1960; polit. editor bimonthly Here is Why, 1960; prof. sociology Sch. Advanced Studies, 1969-90; founder-pres. Mouvement Nat. Progrès et Liberté, 1970; mem. Nat. Coun. Sci. Rsch., 1971-90; prosecuted for plotting against authority of state, 1962; resigned from Town Counsel, Lyon, 1962, re-elected, 1971; warrant issued against him, 1962; in exile abroad, 1962-68; returned to France following gen. amnesty, 1968; mem. exec. bd. Vigilance Com. Antifascist Intellectuals; joined Gen. de Gaulle in London, 1940. Author: Against the Whole World (memories of the Free French Government), The Daily Life of the Aztecs, Beloved and Suffering Algeria, False Hope, 1962, Along a New Road, The Page is Not Turned, 1965, History of Gaullism, 1967, The Four Suns, 1967, Art of Ancient Mexico, 1967, Israel's Long March, 1968, Twenty-Eight Years of Gaullism, 1968, Les Azteques, 1970. Decorated office Legion of Honor, Rosette of the Resistance, comdr. Order Brit. Empire, comdr. Polonia Restituta; recipient medal of Freedom, U.S.A. Home: Lyons France Died Aug. 7, 1990.

SOUTHARD, FRANK ALLAN, JR., economist; b. Cleve., Jan. 17, 1907; s. Frank Allan and May Lucretia (Bowsher) S.; m. Mary Isabel Hay, Dec. 27, 1941. A.B., Pomona Coll., 1927, LL.D., 1976; Ph.D., U. Calif., 1930. Instr. U. Calif., 1930-31; asst. prof., prof. econs. Cornell U., 1931-48, chmn. dept. econs., 1946-48; researcher internat. relations Carnegie Endowment, 1934-35; sr. econ. analyst U.S. Tariff Commn., 1933; Guggenheim fellow to study fgn. exchange policy in S.Am., 1940; asst. dir. monetary research Treasury Dept., 1941-42, dir. office internat. fin., 1947-48; asso. dir. research and statis. in charge internat. sect. Bd. Govs. Fed. Res. System, 1948-49; U.S. exec. dir. IMF and spl. asst. to Sec. Treasury, 1949-62; dep. mng. dir., vice chmn. exec. bd. IMF, 1962-74; dir. Atlantic Council, from 1974; alt. gov. (U.S.), bd. govs. Internat. Bank and Monetary Fund., 1949-62. Author: American Industry in Europe, 1931, Foreign Exchange Practice and Policy, 1940, The Finances of European Liberation, 1946; co-author: Canadian American Industry, 1936, International Monetary System, 1976, The Floating Rate System, 1978, The Evolution of the IMF, 1980, The International Monetary System in Transition. Bd. dirs. Population Crisis Com. Served to comdr. USNR, 1942-46, MTO; fin. adviser Allied Force Hdqrs., 1943-45. Decorated Legion of Merit; officer Order Brit. Empire; officer Legion of Honor (France). Mem. Phi Beta Kappa Assos. Republican. Presbyterian. Home: Delray Beach Fla. Died Nov. 25, 1989; buried Washington.

SOUTHERN, SAMUEL DONALD, gas and oil industry executive; b. Plymouth, Eng., Sept. 19, 1909; m. Alexandra C. (dec.); 1 child, Ronald D. D. Engring. (hon.), Tech. U. Nova Scotia, 1983. Chmn. Atco Ltd., Calgary, Alta., Can., 1961-90; chmn. Sentgraf Enterprises Ltd. Active City of Calgary Fire Dept., 1933-51. Served with RCAF. Home: Calgary Alta., Can. Died Mar. 22, 1990; buried Calgary, Alta., Can.

SOUTHWICK, PHILIP LEE, chemist; b. Lincoln, Nebr., Nov. 15, 1916; s. Philip Orin and Dorothy (Harpham) S.; m. Helen Louise Cather, Sept. 1, 1942; 1 son, James Philip. A.B., U. Nebr., 1939, M.A., 1940; Ph.D., U. Ill., 1943. Research chemist Merck & Co., Inc., Rahway, N.J., 1943-46; faculty Carnegie-Mellon U., Pitts., 1946-92; prof. chemistry Carnegie-Mellon U., 1955-92. Mem. exec. com. Samuel and Emma Winters Found., 1962-75; chmn. organic chemistry com. Health Rsch. and Svcs. Found., 1975-85; mem. com. on awards in chemistry Fulbright Act, Nat. Acad. Scis.-NRC, 1960-63. Recipient Carnegie Teaching award, 1953. Fellow N.Y. Acad. Scis., AAAS; mem. Am. Chem. Soc., Pitts. Chemists Club, Pitts. Bibliophiles, Phi Beta Kappa, Sigma Xi, Alpha Chi Sigma. Home: Pittsburgh Pa. Died June 8, 1992. †

SPAETH, CARL BERNHARDT, lawyer; b. Cleve., May 3, 1907; s. Charles and Elizabeth (Villwock) S.; m. Sheila Grant, Sept. 25, 1931; children: Carl Grant, Laurin Sheila. AB, Dartmouth Coll., 1929, BS in Jurisprudence, 1931, BCL, 1932. Prof. law Temple U., 1933-34; assoc. prof. law Northwestern U., 1935-39, Yale U., 1939-40; v.p., gen. counsel Cia de Fomento Venezolano, Caracas, Venezuela, 1940; asst. coord. Inter-Am. affairs Office Emergency Mgmt., Washington, 1940-42; U.S. mem. Emergency Adv. Com. for Polit. Def., Montevideo, Uruguay, 1942-44; chief River Plata div. Dept. State, 1944-45; asst. diplomatic adviser UNRRA, 1945; spl. asst. to asst. sec. state for Am. Rep. affairs, 1945-46; dean Law Sch. Stanford U., 1946-62, William Nelson Cronwell prof. law, 1962-72, prof. emeritus, 1972-91, dir. Ctr. for Rsch. in Internat. Studies, 1962-72; on leave 1952-53, to serve as dir. Div. Overseas Activities, Ford Found., Pasadena, N.Y.C.; cons. legal edn. India Law Inst., New Delhi, 1959-60. Rhodes scholar Oxford U., England; Sterling fellow Yale U., 1933. Mem. Phi Beta Kappa, Psi Upsilon. Home: Stanford Calif. Died Feb. 10, 1991; buried Alta Mesa Cemetery.

SPALDING, JOHN V., judge; b. Newton, Mass., Dec. 8, 1897; s. George Frederick and Florence Alberton (Faxon) S.; m. Jacqueline Veen, Sept. 24, 1930; children: Robert Veen, Marianne. 010AB, Harvard U., 1920, LLB, 1923; JSD (hon.), Suffolk U., 1952; LLD, Northeastern U., 1955. Bar: Mass. 1923. Atty. Sotrey, Thorndike, Palmer & Didge, Boston, 1923; asst. U.S. dist. atty. Dist. Mass., 1926-29; ptnr. Hale, Sanderson, Byrnes & Morton, 1929-36, Harwood & Spalding, 1936-42; justice Superior Ct. Mass., 1942-44; Supreme judge Ct. Mass., 1944, chief justice, from 1944; lectr. in field. Mem. Mass. Judicial Coun.; chmn. NEwton (Mass.) Lic. Commn. Fellow Am. Acad. Arts ans Scis.; mem. Mass. Bar Assn., Boston Bar Assn., Union Club, Harvard Club (Boston). *

SPEAR, MICHAEL DAVID, real estate company executive; b. N.Y.C., Aug. 7, 1941; s. Juan Xavier and Beatrice (Greenspan) S.; m. Judith Sue Vogel, June 19, 1966; children: Lisa Beth, Jodi Lynn, Lara Anne, Jeni Kate. BArch, Rensselaer Poly. Inst., 1964; M in City Planning, Harvard U., 1966. Dir. research The Rouse Co., Columbia, Md., 1967-71, gen. mgr. for City of Columbia, 1971-78, exec. v.p. devel., 1978-86, pres., 1986-90; guest lectr. various univs. and colls. Bd. dirs. Howard County Gen. Hosp., Columbia, Balt. Mus. Art; mem. Harvard overseers vis. com. Grad. Sch. Design. Traveling fellow Harvard U., Cambridge, 1966. Mem. Urban Land Inst. (chmn. urban devel. council), Internat. Council Shopping Ctrs. Democrat. Jewish. Home: Ithaca N.Y. Died Aug. 24, 1990. †

SPECTRE, JAY, interior designer; b. Louisville, Oct. 6, 1929; s. Marcus J. and Mirian (Schatkter) S. Student pub. schs., Louisville. With Hubbuch in Kentucky, Louisville, 1951-55; exec. v.p. Clarence House Insternat., N.Y.C., 1985-92; pres. Jay Spectre, Inc., N.Y.C., 1960-92, J.S.p.s. Inc., 1985-92; guest lectr. Smithsonian Instn., others. Author: Point of View: Design by Jay Spectre; work featured in internat. mags. including Archtl. Digest, Abitari Connaissance des Arts, French Vogue, Italian Vogue, Paris Match and in books; established licensee program, 1985; designer furniture for Century, rugs for Louis De Poortere., fabrics for Valdese Weavers, china and crystal for Sasaki, sheets and towels for Fieldcrest, lamps for Paul Hanson, outdoor furniture for Brown Jordan, artwork for Frame Picture Enterprise, accesories for Silvestriv. Recipient Chgo. Design Fest award for design excellence, 1982, Daphne award, 1986, Spl. Daphne award, 1986, Top Interior Designer award Met. Home Design, 100, 1990, award of excellence Brides Mag., 1987; named Dean of Design, 1983, One of top 10 designers in U.S.A. Smithsonian Inst., 1979; inaugurated into Interior Design Mag. Hall of Fame, 1986; recognized in AD 100, 1990. Mem. Am. Soc. Interior Designers, Japan Soc. Home: New York N.Y. Died Nov. 16, 1992. †

SPEER, GEORGE SCOTT, psychologist; b. Oak Park, Ill., Sept. 24, 1908; s. George Scott and Dorothy May (Niver) S.; m. Jean Mainland, July 24, 1936; children: Mary Catherine, George Scott. Student, U. Wis., 1927-28; AB, Cen. YMCA Coll., Chgo., 1934; SM, U. Chgo., 1936. Diplomate in counseling and guidance Am. Bd. Examiners in Profl. Psychology. Rsch. asst. Mooseheart (Ill.) Lab. for Child Rsch., 1935-36; psychologist Berkshire Indsl. Farm, Canaan, N.Y., 1936-37, Sangamon County Child Guidance Svc., Springfield, Ill., 1937-40; asst. prof. psychology and dean students Cen. YMCA Coll., 1940-45; prof. dir. Inst. for Psychol. Svcs., Ill. Inst. Tech., 1945-74, prof. emeritus, cons., 1974-92; cons. Wurlitzer Found., 1955-92; psychologist Adj. Gen.'s Office, War Dept., Fort Sheridan and Chgo., 1942. Fellow Am. Psychol. Assn.; mem. Nat. Vocat. Guidance Assn., Nat. Assn. Remedial Tchrs., Am. Soc. Engring. Edn., Am. Personnel and Guidance Assn., Am., Midwestern psychol. assns., Am. Assn. Mental Deficiency, Nat. Soc. for Rsch. in Child Devel., Internat. Assn. Counseling Svcs. (pres.), Beta Theta Pi, Sigma Xi. Home: Oak Park Ill. Died Mar. 17, 1992.

SPEIDEL, CARL CASKEY, anatomy educator; b. Washington, Oct. 26, 1893; s. George and Emma (Caskey) S.; m. Margaret Snowles, June 17, 1920. PhB cum laude, Lafayette Coll., 1914; PhD, Princeton U., 1918; ScD (hon.), Lafayette Coll., 1942. Part-time asst. biology Princeton, 1914-16, Maule fellow biology, 1916-17; instr. zoology U. Akron, 1917-18; asst. prof. anatony U. Va. Med. Sch., 1920-22, assoc. prof., 1922-31, prof., 1931-64, prof. emeritus, from 1964, chmn. sch. anatomy, 1959-50; vis. prof. biolocy Randolph-Macon Woman's Coll., 1964-65; past trustee Marine Biology Lab. Corp., Woods Hole, Mass. Contbr. to tech. papers. Fellow AAAS; mem. Am. Assn. Anatomists (mem. exec. com. 1940-47), Am. Soc. Zoologists, Am. Soc. Naturalists, Va. Acad. Sci., L.I. Biology Assn., Phi Beta Kappa, Sigma Xi, Alpha Omega Alpha, Nu Sigma Nu, Raven Soc., Colonnade Club. Democrat. Presbyterian. *

SPELLMAN, EUGENE PAUL, federal judge; b. N.Y.C., Sept. 16, 1930; s. Michael Francis and Mary Elizabeth (Loftus) S.; m. Roberta J. Recht, July 16, 1959; children: James Kevin, Michael Patrick. AA, U. Fla., 1951, BA, 1953, JD, 1955, JD (hon.), 1967; JD (hon.), St. Thomas U. Sch. Law, 1990; LHD (hon.), Biscayne Coll., 1977. Bar: Fla. 1956, U.S. Ct. Appeals (5th cir.) 1963, U.S. Dist. Ct. So. Fla. 1956, U.S. Supreme Ct. 1971. Rsch. aide to chief judge 3d Dist. Ct. Appeals, Miami, Fla., 1957-58; asst. atty. gen. Criminal Appeals Div., Tallahassee, 1958-59, 60-61; asst. state atty. Dade County (Fla.), also head Rackets and Frauds div., 1959-61; pvt. practice law, 1961-69; apptd. spl. prosecutor Judge Curtis E. Chillingsworth murder case by Govs. Leroy Collins and Farris Bryant, 1969-70; apptd. spl. asst. atty. gen., 1969-70; gen. counsel Biscayne Coll., 1970-79; judge so. dist. Fla. U.S. Dist. Ct., Miami, 1979-91; apptd. by chief justice U.S. Supreme Ct. to Jud. Conf. Com. on Defender Svcs., 1988. Chmn. Fla. Council for Blind, 1963-65; former chmn. Gov.'s Commn. on Employment of Handicapped; former mem. Pres.'s Commn. on Employment of Handicapped; pres. Southeastern Inst. Human Devel., 1977; bd. dirs. Marian Center Inc.; Disabilities Planning Coun. Fla., 1978-80; mem. bd. adminstrn. Biscayne Coll.; apptd. to coun. advisors Mailman Ctr. for Child Devel., U. Miami, 1982; mem bd. visitors St. Thomas U. Sch. Law 1985; hon. mem. Pres.'s Circle, Barry U., 1990. Hon. mem. Order St. Augustine Rome; named a Knight of St. Gregory by Pope John Paul II, 1985; recipient Outstanding Achievement award Fla. Assn. Rehab. Facilities, 1983, Outstanding Jud. Achievement award Fla. Criminal Def. Atty.'s Assn., 1985, Nat. Assn. Criminal Def. Attys., 1990, St. Thomas Moore award Cath. Lawyers' Guild, 1988, 1st ann. Dick Moran award Miami Coalition for Care to the Homeless, 1989, award of appreciation State of Fla., award of appreciation Fla. Police Benevolent Assn., award of appreciation Dade County Police Benevolent Assn. Inc., Jud. Achievement award Nat. Assn. Criminal Def. Attys., 1990; Eugene P. Spellman Inn named in his honor St. Thomas U. Sch. Law, Phi Delta Phi, 1989; Eugene P. Spellman Inn named in his honor The Am. Inns of Ct./ U. Miami, 1990. Mem. ABA (jud. adminstrn. sect.), Fla., Dade County bar assns., Am., Fla. trial lawyers assns., Supreme Ct. Hist. Soc. (founding mem.), Am. Judicature Soc., Dade County Assn. Retarded Citizens (bd. dirs.), Nat. Assn. for Rehabilitative Facilities, Fla. Assn. Rehabilitative Facilities (Outstanding Achievement award 1978), Knights of Malta. Democrat. Roman Catholic. Home: Miami Fla. Died May 4, 1991.

SPENCER, WINTHROP W., banker; b. Cambridge, Mass., Jan. 29, 1897; s. Charles W. and Ethel M. (Wheeler) S.; m. Marigold Chandler, June 22, 1927; 1 child, George Chandler. AB, Harvard, 1918. Inspector Nat City Bank N.Y., 1919-27; v.p., treas. The Lee, Higginson Trust Co., Boston, 1927-34; v.p. The Colonial Trust Co., Waterbury, Conn., 1934-46, pres., 1946-57, chmn. bd., from 1957; also dir.; mem. stockholders adv. com. Reserve Bank of Boston, 1951-54; dir., mem. exec. com. Am. Hardware Corp., The Watertown Indsl. Devel. Corp.; dir. Hill Corps, Savage Arms Corp., Coun. Devel. Corp. (Berlin, Conn.), Peter, Paul, Inc. (Naugatuck, COnn.), Plymouth Cordage Co. (Plymouth, Mass.). Pres. Waterbury Clearing House Assn.; trustee The Waterbury Found., Conn. Pub. Expenditure Coun., Hartford; mem. exec. com., treas. Waterbury Hosp.; trustee, treas. Taft Sch., Watertown. Mem. Conn. Bankers Assn. (pres. 1950-51). Republican. Episcopalian. *

SPENGLER, JOSEPH JOHN, economist, educator; b. Piqua, Ohio, Nov. 19, 1902; s. Joseph Otto and Philomena (Schlosser) S.; m. Dorothy Marie Kress, Aug. 13, 1927. AB, Ohio State U., 1926, MA, 1929, PhD, 1930, LHD (hon.), 1965; LHD (hon.), Alma Coll., Tulane U., 1978. Scholar in econs. Ohio State U., 1926-27, asst. instr., 1927-28, instr., 1928-30; rsch. fellow Brookings Instn., 1928; asst. prof. econs. U. Ariz., 1930-32ž, assoc. prof., 1933-34; assoc. prof. econs. Duke U., 1932-33, 34-37, prof., 1937-55, James B. Duke prof. econs., from 1955; tchr. U. N.C., 1935, 72-73, U. Chgo., 1952, Kyoto U., 1952, U. Malaya, 1956, U. Pitts., 1957; cons. Nat. Resources Planning Bd., 1940-42, USDA; regional price exec. Office Price Adminstrn., 1942-43. Author: The Fecundity of Native and Foreign Born Women in New England, 1930, France Faces Depopulation, 1938, 2d edit., 1979, French Predecessors of Malthus, 1942, Indian Economic Thought: A Preface to Its History, 1971, Declaning Population Growth Revisited, 1971, Population Economics, 1972, Population Change, Modernization, and Welfare, 1974, Population and America's Future, 1975, Facing Zero Population Growth, 1978, Origins of Economic Thought and Justice; co-author: The Economics of Individual and Population Aging, 1980; editor: Natural Resources and Economic Growth, 1961, Origins of Economic Thought and Justice, 1980; co-editor: Economic Growth: Brazil, India, Japan, 1955, Population Theory and Policy, 1956, Demographic Analysis, 1956; contbr.: American Studies in Honor of William Kenneth Boyd, 1940, Evolutionary Thought in America, 1950, World Population and Future Resources, 1952, Survey of Contemporary Economics, 1952, Economic Development, Principles and Patterns, 1954, Economics and Public Policy, 1954, Economics of International Migration, 1958, Population and World Politics, 1958, Francois Quesnay et La Physiocratie, 1958, Commonwealth Perspectives, 1958, Essays in Economic Thought, 1960, Traditions, Values and Socio-Economic Development in India, 1963, Employment, Income and Retirement Problems of the Aged, 1963, Bureaucracy adn Political Development, The Population Crisis and the Use of World Resources, 1964, The South in Continuity and Change, 1965, Modernization, 1966, Aging and Social Policy, 1966, Social Aspects of Aging, 1966; contbr. over 250 articles to profl. jours. With Ohio N.G., 1922-24. Fellow AAAS, Am. Statis. Assn., History of Econs. Soc. (past pres.); mem. Am. Philos Soc., Am., World acads. art and scis., Am. Econ. Assn. (past. pres.), Am. Population

Assn. (past pres.), Atlantic Econ. Soc. (past pres.), Royal Econ. Soc., Social Sci. Rsch. Coun., Soc. Gen. Systems Rsch., Mt. Pellerin Soc., Phi Beta Kappa. Home: Durham N.C. Died Jan. 2, 1991; buried Duke U., Durham, N.C.

SPERRY, WARREN MYRON, neurochemist; b. Chili, N.Y., June 30, 1900; s. D. Carlos and Ethel (Henderson) S.; m. Olwen M. Leach, 1925 (dec. Dec. 1966); 1 child, Carl B. B in Chemistry, Cornell U., 1921; MS, U. Ill., 1922; PhD, U. Rochester, 1925, ScD (hon.), 1965. From instr. to asst. prof. biochemistry U. Rochester, 1925-30; mem. faculty Columbia Coll. Physicians and Surgeons, 1930-90, prof. biochemistry, 1954-90; chemist Babies Hosp., N.Y.C., 1930-38; head dept. biochemistry N.Y. State Psychiat. Inst., 1938-90, chief psychiat. rsch. (biochemistry), 1958-90; mem. subcom. biochem. nomenclature NRC, 1949-90; mem. Am. Bd. Clin. Chemistry, 1954-59; mem. cardiovascular study sect. USPHS, 1948-52, mem. physiol. chemistry study sect., 1961-65; mem. rsch. rev. panel Nat. Multiple Sclerosis Soc., 1953-61; mem. commn. clin. chemistry, div. biol. chemistry Internat. Union Pure and Applied Chemistry, 1952-58, pres. div. commn., 1963-67. Mem. editorial bd. Jour. Biol. Chemistry, 1949-58; mng. editor Western Hemisphere Jour. Neurochemistry; author numerous articles in field. Fellow AAAS, Am. Inst. Chemists, N.Y. Acad. Scis; mem. AAUP, Am. Chem. Soc. (councilor 1944-56, chmn. N.Y. sect. 1954-55), Am. Soc. Biol. Chemists, Am. Oil Chemists Soc., Am. Assn. Clin. Chemists (Ames award 1961), Am. Heart Assn., Assn. Rsch. Nervous and Mental Disease, Soc. Exptl. Biology and Medicine, Soc. Pediatric Rsch., Biochem. Soc. (London), Harvey Soc., Masons, Sigma Xi, Phi Kappa Phi, Alpha Chi Sigma. Democrat. Baptist. Home: Bronx N.Y. Died July 11, 1990; cremated.

SPERTI, GEORGE SPERI, research scientist; b. Covington, Ky., Jan. 17, 1900; s. George Sperti and Caroline (Speri) S. E.E., U. Cin., 1923; D.Sc. (hon.), Dayton U., 1934, Duquesne U., 1936, Bryant Coll., 1957, Thomas More Coll., 1975, Xavier U., 1978; L.H.D. (hon.), Caldwell Coll., 1974. Asst. chief Meter Labs., U.G. & E., Cin., 1922; asst. research dir. Duncan Elec. and Mfg. Co., Lafayette, 1923; research asst. U. Cin., 1924-25, research prof. and dir. research (also co-founder) Basic Sci. Research Lab., 1925-35; bd. dirs. Gen. Devel. Labs., Inc., N.Y.C., 1930-35; bd. dirs. Sperti Lamp Corp., 1930-40, dir., 1935; research prof., dir. research, trustee, bd. regents, pres. St. Thomas Inst.; prin. cons. War Production Bd., 1942; dir. Franklin Corp. Author: Probiotics, 1971; co-author: Quantum Theory in Biology, 1927, Correlated Investigations in the Basic Sciences; editor: Studies Inst. Divi Thomae. Holder 120 patents. Founding mem. Am. Soc. for Aged, mem. Med. and Sci. Com.; bd. dirs. Am. Council for Internat. Promotion of Democracy under God Inc., 1959. Recipient Catholic Action medal, 1942; Mendel medal, 1943; Christian Culture award, 1947; Star of Solidarity Third Class of the Italian Republic, 1956; Gold Medal Univ. Int. degli Studi Sociali "Pro Deo," 1958; William Howard Taft award, 1970; Cin. Scientist Engr. of Yr. award, 1970; Honor Scroll Ohio Inst. Chemistry, 1983. Mem. Pontifical Acad. Sci., AAAS, Am. Phys. Soc., Royal Soc. Arts (London), Emeritus Hall; hon. mem. Societa Italiana de Fisica; mem. Academie Internat. de Philosophie des Scis., (Brussels), Engring. Soc. Cin., Academia de Doctores (Madrid). Home: Cincinnati Ohio Died Apr. 29, 1991.

SPEWACK, BELLA COHEN, playwright, scenarist; b. Hungary (now Romania), 1899; d. Adolph and Fanny (Cohen) Loebel; m. Samuel Spewack, Mar. 18, 1922 (dec. Oct. 1971). Grad. high sch., N.Y.C. Reporter N.Y. Call, N.Y. Evening Mail, N.Y. World, N.Y. Evening World; feature writer N.Y. Herald Tribune, N.Y. Times; nat. publicity dir. Camp Fire Girls, Girl Scouts U.S.; asst. to husband, fgn. corr. N.Y. World, Russia, Europe, 1922-26. Author: (with husband, Samuel Spewack) (plays) Solitaire Man, 1926, Poppa, 1928, War Song, 1928, Clear All Wires, 1932, Spring Song, 1934, Boy Meets Girl, 1935, Leave It to Me (mus. comedy with songs by Cole Porter), 1938, Miss Swan Expects, 1939 (later pub. under Angels, 1959), Magic Nutcracker, 1961, My Three Angels, 1953, The Festival, 1955; (with Cole Porter) Kiss Me Kate, 1949; (teleplays) (with husband) Kiss Me Kate, My Three Angels, 1959, magic Nutcracker, 1961; (films) Clear All Wires, Boy Meets Girl, The Cat and the Fiddle, Rendezvous, The Nuisance, Three Loves has Nancy, My Favorite Wife, (screenplay) Week-End at The Waldorf (with husband), 1945, (play, with husband) Woman Bites Dog, 1946; also broadcast series for ABC on work of UNRRA; reporting on conditions abroad from London, Paris, Berlin, Prague and Geneva; author: (short story) The Laugh, included in Edward J. O'Brien's Best Short Stories for 1925. Pres. N.Y. Girls Scholarship Fund. Mem. Dramatists Guild, Screen Writers Guild. Home: New York N.Y. Died Apr. 27, 1990.

SPICOLA, JAMES R., grain trading company executive; b. Aitkin, Minn., June 27, 1930; s. James Anthony and Harriet Onique (Rollins) Spicola; m. Eleanor Hemingway, Jan. 6, 1951; children: Ann Spicola Jerhoff, John Allen, Thomas Anthony. B.B.A., U. Minn., 1954. With Cargill, Inc., 1954-91; trainee Mpls., 1954-55; asst. merchant Ft. Dodge, Iowa, 1955-56; account mgr. Memphis, 1956-61; adminstrv. asst. Mpls., 1961-67, dep. div. head processing and refining, 1967-68, v.p., div. head processing and refining, 1968-73, group v.p., 1973-84, also bd. dirs., pres., chief operating officer, 1984-91. Bd. dirs. YMCA, Mpls.; trustee Minn. Med. Found., Mpls. Served with U.S. Army, 1951-52. Club: Interlachen Country (treas. 1977, v.p. 1978, pres. 1979) (Edina, Minn.). Home: Edina Minn. Died Jan. 29, 1991; buried Mpls.

SPIEGELBERG, HERBERT, philosophy educator; b. Strasbourg, France, May 18, 1904; came to U.S., 1938, naturalized, 1944; s. Wilhelm and Elisabeth (von Recklinghausen) S.; m. Eldora Haskell, July 6, 1944; children: Gwen Elisabeth Spiegelberg Butler, Lynne Sylvia Spiegelberg Morgan. Student, U. Heidelberg, Germany, 1922-24, U. Freiburg, Germany, 1924-25; PhD, U. Munich, 1928; LHD (hon.), Lawrence U., 1973. Instr., rsch. assoc. Swarthmore Coll., 1938-41; mem. faculty Lawrence Coll., Appleton, Wis., 1941-63, Ingraham prof. philosophy, chmn. dept., 1954-63; prof. Washington U., St. Louis, 1963-71, prof. emeritus, 1971-90; vis. prof. U. Mich., 1951-52, U. So. Calif., 1960; Fulbright lectr. U. Munich, 1961-62. Author: Gesetz und Sittengesetz, 1935, Antirelativismus, 1935, The Phenomenological Movement, 1960, 2d edit., 1965, rev., 1980, The Socratic Enigma, 1964, Phenomenology in Psychology and Psychiatry, 1972, Doing Phenomenology, 1975; also articles. Mem. AAUP, Am. Philos. Assn., Metaphys. Soc., Phi Beta Kappa (hon.). Home: Saint Louis Mo. Died Sept. 6, 1990.

SPIEL, HILDE, writer; b. Vienna, Oct. 19, 1911; arrived in London, 1936; PhD, U. Vienna, 1936. Theater critic Welt, Berlin, Germany, 1946-48; corr. Neues Osterreich, Haagsche Post, Neue Zeitung, Suddeutsche Zeitung, Tagesspiegel, Weltwoche, London, 1949-63; corr. FAZ, Weltwoche, Vienna, 1963-90. Author: Kati auf der Brucke, 1933, Verwirrung am Wolfgangsee, 1935, Flute and Drums, 1939, Der Park und die Wildniss, 1963, Laurence Olivier, 1958, Welt im Widerschein, 1960, The Darkened Room, 1961, Fanny von Arnstein oder die Emanzipation, 1962, Richard III, 1964, Der Wiener Kongress in Augenzeugenberichten, 1965, Verliebt in Dobling, 1966, Ruckkehr nac Wien, 1968, Staedte und Menschen, 1971, Wien, Spektman einer Stadt, 1971, Die Zeitgenossiche Literatur osterreichs, 1976; editor jour., 1960. Recipient Julius Reich prize Vienna, Critic prize Salzburg; named prof., 1933, Fed. Cross of Merit, 1962; decorated Austrian Cross Arts and Lit., 1972, golden insigne Prov. of Vienna. Mem. Internat. PEN Club (gen. sec. Austria 1966-72, v.p. 1972). Home: Upper Austria Austria Died Nov. 29, 1990.

SPIELMAN, JOHN RUSSEL, chemistry educator; b. Santa Barbara, Calif., May 14, 1930; s. John von Voorhies and Helen (Sterrett) S.; m. Lois Lee Meeker, June 27, 1953; children: Katherine Jean, John Alexander, Steven Russel. BS, Stanford U., 1953; MS, U. So. Calif., 1958, PhD, 1962. Mem. faculty Calif. State U., L.A., 1961-85, prof. chemistry, 1974-85; vis. prof. Inst. Inorganic Chemistry, Philipps U., Marburg, Germany, 1969-70. Contbr. articles on boron hydrides, carboranes and organometallics to profl. jours. Mem. So. Calif. Regional Commn., United Ministries in Higher Edn., 1976-80. With U.S. Army, 1954-56. Mem. AAAS, Am. Chem. Soc. Congregationalist. Home: Arcadia Calif. Died Jan. 5, 1985; buried Live Oak Meml. Pk., Monrovia, Calif.

SPIES, EMERSON GEORGE, legal educator, dean; b. Akron, N.Y., Nov. 6, 1914. A.B., Hobart Coll., 1936, B.A. in Jurisprudence, 1938, LL.D. (hon.), 1966; B.C.L., Oxford U., 1939. Bar: N.Y. 1941, Va. 1951. Tutorial fellow U. Chgo., 1939-41; assoc. Mudge, Stern, Williams and Tucker, N.Y.C., 1941-43; asst. prof. law U. Va., Charlottesville, 1946-47, assoc. prof. law, 1947-50, prof. law, 1950-67, Joseph M. Hartfield prof. law, 1967-76, Mary & Daniel Loughran prof. law, 1976-85, prof. emeritus, 1985-90, acting dean Sch. Law, 1976, dean Sch. Law, 1976-80; vis. prof. Inst. Advanced Studies, Australia U., 1964; chmn. Law Sch. Adminstrn. Test Council, 1963-66. Bd. trustees Hobart Coll., 1969-74, William Smith Coll., 1969-74. Served to capt. JAGC, AUS, 1943-46. Fellow Am. Bar Found.; mem. Va. State Bar Assn. (chmn. com. on legal edn. and admissions to bar 1966-68), Order of Coif, Phi Beta Kappa. Home: Charlottesville Va. Died Sept. 24, 1990.

SPINNING, NORMA STOREY, university trustee; b. Rochester, N.Y., Mar. 22, 1896; d. William R. and Cora (Burns) Storey; m. James M. Spinning, Aug. 21, 1934. AB, U. Rochester, 1918. Tchr. West High Sch., Rochester, 1918-34; trustee U. Rochester, from 1950; bd. dirs. Med. Motor Svc., from 1955. Mem. AAUW, Meml. Art Gallery Rochester, Rochester Assn. UN, Rochester Civic Music Assn. *

SPRAGG, HOWARD EUGENE, church official; b. Boston, Sept. 15, 1917; s. Lee Hanford and Lillian (Hunter) S.; m. Jane Nichols, June 23, 1942; children: Susan E., Peter Hunter, Paul Alexander, Martha Ann, Deborah Townsend. A.B. summa cum laude, Tufts Coll., 1938; B.D., Chgo. Theol. Sem., 1947, D.D., 1968; D.D., Yankton Coll., 1956, Ursinus Coll., 1973, Northland Coll., 1974; L.H.D., Rollins Coll. Ordained to ministry Congl. and Christian Chs., 1942; pastor South Congl. Ch., Chgo., 1942-48; gen. dir. P.R. mission Congl. and Christian Chs., 1948-52; sec. Bd. Home Missions Congl. and Chrisian Chs., 1952-54, gen. sec. for adminstrn., 1954-58, treas., 1959-69; also treas. ten affiliated corps., including United Ch. Found. Annuity Congl. Ministers, Retirement Fund Lay Workers; treas. United Ch. Bd. Homeland Ministries, 1959-69, exec. v.p., chief exec. officer, 1969-84; fin. v.p. treas. United Church Found.; former mem. governing bd. Nat. Council Chs. Trustee Dillard U., Am. Coll., Madura, India; nat. adv. coun. Hampshire Coll.; former trustee Talladega Coll., LeMoyne Owen Coll., Tougaloo Coll., Huston-Tillotson Coll.; dir. Workplace Health Fund; v.p., trustee Amistad Research Ctr.; founding trustee New Coll., Sarasota, Fla.; propr., mem. Boston Athenaeum. Mem. Soc. Arts, Religion and Culture (v.p.), Univ. Club (N.Y.C.), Phi Beta Kappa. Home: Deering N.H. Died Feb. 26, 1991; buried Bayview Cemetery, Hatfield Point, N.B., Can.

SPRAGUE, ARTHUR COLBY, educator; b. Boston, Apr. 6, 1895; s. Philo Woodruff and Harriette Appleton (Woods) S.; m. Rosamond Mary Kent, Aug. 3, 1946. AB, Harvard U., 1921, PhD, 1925. Instr., asst. prof. English Harvard U., Cambridge, Mass., 1925-36; assoc. prof. Bryn Mawr Coll., 1936-50, prof. English lit., 1950-63, Mary E. Garrett Found. prof., 1957-63, prof. emeritus, 1963-91; Fulbright Lectr. Cambridge U., Royal U. Malta, 1951-52; hon. fellow Shakespeare Inst., Stratford-on-Avon, 1963-65; vis. prof. U. Basel, 1966, Voorhees Coll., 1968-70; mem. Jesus Coll., Cambridge. Author: Beaumont and Fletcher on the Restoration Stage, 1926, Samuel Daniel's Poems and a Defence of Ryme, 1930, Shakespeare and the Audience, 1935, Shakespeare and the Actors, 1944, Shakespearian Players and Performances, 1953, Shakespeare's Histories, 1964, (with J.C. Trewin) Shakespeare's Plays Today, 1970. Mem. Phila. Shakespeare Soc., Shakespeare Club Stratford-upon-Avon (pres. 1972-73), The Players Club (N.Y.C.). Republican. Anglican. Home: Columbia S.C. Died Sept. 17, 1991; buried Calais, Vt.

SPRAGUE, MILTON ALAN, agronomist, educator; b. Washburn, Wis., June 16, 1914; s. Monroe Horr and Daza (Glover) S.; m. Margarete Hardegen, May 20, 1944; children—Monroe A., Katherine A., Lowell H, Barbara H. A.B., Northland Coll., 1936; M.S., U. Wis., 1938, Ph.D., 1941. Research, teaching forage crop physiology and weed control U. Ark., 1940-42, 46; mem. faculty Rutgers U., 1946-84, chmn. dept. farm crops, 1955-61, Disting. prof. and research specialist, 1974-84, prof. emeritus, 1984-91; agr. cons. to Peru, Yucatan, 1965-72, Quintana Roo, 1981; agrl. cons. to Am. Heritage Dictionary, 1971; contbr. to Internat. Grassland Congress, 1952, 60, 65, 66, 70, 74, 81. Contbg. author: Field Crop Production for the Northeast, 1947, rev. edit, 1952, Grasslands, 1959, Forages, 1951, rev. edit., 1966; author, co-editor: No-tillage and Surface-tillage Agriculture, 1986; contbr. rsch. papers to profl. jours., agrl. experiment sta. bulls. Del. People to People, Australia, New Zealand, 1988. Lt. USNR, 1942-46; ret. Res. Recipient Merit certificate Am. Forage and Grassland Council, 1966; No-Till Pioneer award, 1976. Fellow Am. Soc. Agronomy (dir. 1956-59, 74-77, sec.-treas. N.E. br. 70, Rsch. award 1977); mem. Am. Grassland Coun. (dir. 1958-61, 1969-72), Am. Soc. Plant Physiology, Am. Soc. Dairy Sci., Crop Sci. Soc. Am., Soil Sci. Soc. Am., Naval Inst., Sigma Xi. Home: Chico Calif. Died Mar. 2, 1991.

SPRAGUE, ROBERT CHAPMAN, electric components company executive; b. N.Y.C., Aug. 3, 1900; s. Frank Julian and Harriet Chapman (Jones) S.; m. Florence Antoinette van Zelm, May 24, 1921 (dec. June 1987); children: Robert Chapman Jr. (dec.), John Louis. Grad., Hotchkiss Sch., 1918; B.S., U.S. Naval Acad., 1920; grad., U.S. Naval Postgrad. Sch., 1922; S.M., MIT, 1924; D.Engring. (hon.), Northeastern U., 1953; D.Sc. (hon.), Williams Coll., 1954, Lowell Tech. Inst., 1959, North Adams State Coll., 1972, U. Mass., 1975; LL.D (hon.), Tufts U., 1959, U. N.H., 1967. Commd. lt. USN, 1922, resigned, 1926; Founder Sprague Electric Co. (originally Sprague Spltys. Co.), Quincy, Mass., 1926, pres., 1926-53, chmn., chief exec. officer, 1953-71, treas., 1954-65, hon. chmn., chmn. exec. com, 1971-76, hon. chmn., dir., 1976-91; dir. Draper Lab. Div. (now Charles Stark Draper Lab. Inc.), 1970-78, mem. emeritus, 1979-91; dir. security resources panel (Gaither Com.) of sci. adv. com. Office Def. Moblzn., 1957-58; mem. various govtl. coms.; trustee MITRE Corp., 1958-81, chmn., 1969-72, hon. trustee, 1981-91. Former sr. warden St. John's Episcopal Ch., Williamstown, Mass., sr. warden emeritus, 1968-91; chmn. Pine Cobble Sch., Williamstown, 1942-68, trustee emeritus, 1968-91; trustee Hudson Inst., 1961-71; mem. corp. MIT, 1953-55, life mem., 1955-75, life mem. emeritus, 1975-91; mem. corp. Northeastern U., from 1953; bd. govs. Mass. Sci. and Tech. Found., 1970-78. Recipient Man of Yr. award Hotchkiss Alumni Assn., 1958, New Eng. Council, 1965; North Adams State Coll. award, 1972, Francis Hayden award, 1983, Ephraim Williams medal of Honor Williams Coll., 1991. Fellow IEEE (sr. mem., life fellow), Am. Acad. Arts and Scis.; mem. Assoc. Industries Mass. (bd. dirs. 1945-73, hon. chmn. 1973-91, mem. exec. com. 1957-73, pres. 1951-53), Electronic Industries Assn. (pres. 1950-51, bd. govs. 1943-80, chmn. 1950-52, 53-54, hon. gov. 1980-91, medal of honor 1954, 1978), Nat. Acad. Engring. Clubs: Algonquin, Union (Boston); Metropolitan (Washington).

Home: Williamstown Mass. Died Sept. 27, 1991; buried Williamstown, Mass.

SPRINGER, WILLIAM LEE, government official, former congressman; b. Sullivan, Ind., Apr. 12, 1909; s. Otha Lee and Daisy Ellen (Tucker) S.; m. Elsie Cora Mattis, May 9, 1942; children: Katherine Curtis, Anne (Mrs. Paul McKnight), Georgia Mattis (Mrs. William Finger). B.A., DePauw U., 1931, LL.D. (hon.), 1972; LL.B., U. Ill., 1935; LL.D. (hon.), Millikin U., 1953, Lincoln Coll., 1966, Eastern Ill. U., 1976. Bar: Ill. bar 1935. Assoc. Busch & Harrington, Champaign, Ill., 1936-39; states atty. Champaign County, 1940-42, county judge, 1946-50; mem. 82d-92nd Congress from 22d Ill. Dist., 1951-73, ranking minority mem. com. on interstate and fgn. commerce, subcoms. on transp. and aeronautics, communications and power, pub. health and environment, 1964-72, Congl. rep. internat. confs. trade, space communications and energy; mem. Fed. Power Commn., 1973, vice-chmn., 1974-75; mem. Fed. Election Commn., 1976-79. Contbr. treatises law to profl. jours. Served to lt. USNR, 1942-45. Mem. Am., Champaign County bar assns., Am. Juridical Soc., Champaign County Country Club, Kiwanis. Republican. Presbyterian. Home: Champaign Ill. Died Sept. 20, 1992. †

SPROUL, ALLAN, banker; b. San Francisco, Mar. 9, 1896; s. Robert and Sarah Elizabeth (Moore) S.; m. Marion Meredith Bogle, Apr. 2, 1921; children: Allan, Gordon John, David Saffell. BS, U. Calif., 1919; LLD, NYU, 1947, Columbia U., 1956, Colgate U., 1956, U. Calif., Berkeley, 1963. Head div. analysis and rsch. Fed. reserve Bank San Francisco, 1920-24, asst. fed. agt. and sec., 1924-30; asst. dep. gov., sec. Fed. Reserve Bank N.Y., 1930-34, asst. to gov., sec., 1934-36, dept. gov., 1936, 1st v.p., 1936, pres., 1941-56; dir. Kaiser Aluminum & Chem. Corp., Wells Fargo Bank, San Francisco; chmn. war fin. com. 2d Frd. Res. Dist., 1942-43; mem. N.Y. State War Fin. Com., 1943-45; chmn. PResdl. Com. Balance of Payments of U.S., 1961. Served as pilot AS, U.S. Army, 1918. Mem. Com. Econ. Devel. (trustee), St. Andrew's Soc., Alpha Delta Phi, Century Assn. Club, Bohemian Club. *

SPUHLER, JAMES NORMAN, anthropologist, educator; b. Tucumcari, N.Mex., Mar. 1, 1917; s. Frank Jacob and Hettie (Aylesworth) S.; m. Helen Margaret McKaig, Sept, 14, 1946; 1 child, Derek Drake. B.A., U. N.Mex., 1940; M.A. (Cutting scholar), Harvard U., 1942, Ph.D. (Nat. scholar), 1946; M.A., Oxford U., 1962. Instr. anthropology and zoology Ohio State U., 1946-47, asst. prof., 1947-50; faculty U. Mich., 1950-68, prof. anthropology and human genetics, 1960-68, chmn. dept. anthropology, 1959- 67, adj. prof., 1984-86; Leslie Spier prof. anthropology U. N.Mex., 1967-84; Leslie spier prof. emeritus, 1984—; rsch. fellow Oxford U., 1962-63; vis. prof. anthropology and zoology, numerous univs.; U. Cons. NIH, 1955-60, NSF, 1965-67; dir. child health survey Atomic Bomb Casualty Commn., 1959; affiliate genomics and structural biology group Los Alamos Nat. Lab. Author: Genetic Diversity and Human Behavior, 1968; editor and contbr.: Natural Selection in Man, 1958, Evolution of Man's Capacity for Culture, 1959, Yearbook of Physical Anthropology, 1952, (with others) Race Differences in Intelligence, 1975; editor (with others) Jour. Anthrop. Research, 1975-80; assoc. editor (with others) Am. Anthropologist, 1954-55, Human Biology, 1953-74, Am. Jour. Human Genetics, 1955-58, Evolution, 1960-63, Am. Jour. Phys. Anthropology, 1969-73, Am. Naturalist, 1978-80, Anthropol. Linguistics, 1983—. Served to lt. (s.g.) USNR, 1942-46, 51-52. Recipient award for sci. reviewing NAS, 1990; fellow Ctr. Advanced Study in Behavioral Scis., 1955-56, 71-72. Fellow Am. Anthrop. Assn. (exec. bd. 1958-60), N.Y. Acad. Scis., Explorers Club; mem. Genetics Soc. Am., Biometric Soc. (adv. bd. 1951-54), Am. Assn. Phys. Anthropologists (exec. com. 1954-55, sec.-treas. 1955-58, pres. 1975-77), Am. Soc. Human Genetics (dir. 1951- 53, 63-65), Am. Soc. Naturalists, Soc. Study Evolution, Sigma Xi. Home: Santa Fe N.Mex. Died Sept. 2, 1992; buried Santa Fe Cemetery. †

SPURR, STEPHEN HOPKINS, ecology educator; b. Washington, Feb. 14, 1918; s. Josiah Edward and Sophie Clara (Burchard) S.; m. Patricia Chapman Orton, Aug. 18, 1945; children: Daniel Orton, Jean Burchard. BS with highest honors, U. Fla., 1938, DSc (hon.), 1971; MF cum laude, Yale U., 1940, PhD, 1950. Instr., asst. prof., acting dir. Harvard Forest, Harvard U., 1940-50; assoc. prof. U. Minn., Mpls., 1950-52; prof. U. Mich., Ann Arbor, 1952-71, asst. to v.p. acad. affairs, dean Sch. Grad. Studies, 1962-65, v.p., 1969-71; prof. botany and pub. affairs U. Tex., Austin, 1971-83, pres., 1971-74; Albright lectr. U. Calif., 1966; vis. scholar Ctr. for Advanced Studies in Behavioral Scis., 1966-67; George S. Long lectr. U. Wash., 1975; mem. President's Adv. Panel on Timber and Environ, 1971-73; bd. dirs., v.p. Capital Broadcasting Co.; chmn. Grad. Rec. Exam. Bd. and Coun. Grad. Schs., 1969-71; mem. Commn. on Non Traditional Study, 1971 ; mem. Nat. Bd. Grad. Edn., 1971-75; trustee Ednl. Testing Svc., Carnegie Coun. for Policy Studies in Higher Edn., Inst. Internat. Edn., 1972-77. Author: Aerial Photographs in Forstry, 1948, Forest Inventory, 1952, Photogrammetry and Photo-Interpretation, 1960, Forest Ecology, 1962, Academic Degree Structures, 1970, American Forest Policy in Development, 1976; founding editor Forest Sci., 1955-60; inventor photogrammetric devices. Trustee Carnegie Found. for Advancement Teaching, Nature Conservancy; mem. coun. Yale U. from 1978. Recipient Wilber Cross medal Yale U., 1978; Oberlaender Trust fellow Yale U., 1050, sci. faculty fellow NSF, 1957-58; Fulbright rsch. scholar, New Zealand and Australia, 1960. Fellow Soc. Am. Foresters (coun., founding chmn. div. forest mgmt., v.p.); mem. New Zealand Inst. Foresters (hon.), Am. Forestry Assn. (bd. dirs. 1972-75), Ecol. Soc. Am., Conf. Biol. Editors (exec. com.), Lake States Forest Tree Improvement Com. (chmn.), Orgn. for Tropical Studies (pres. 1967-68), Mich. Acad. Sci., Arts and Letters (pres. 1968-69), Mich. Soc. Fellows (sr. fellow 1970-90), Philos. Soc. Tex., Phi Beta Kappa, Sigma Xi, Phi Eta Sigma, Phi Kappa Phi. Unitarian. Home: Austin Tex. Died, 1992; buried East Alstead, N.H.

STACEY, CHARLES PERRY, history educator; b. Toronto, Ont., Can., July 30, 1906; s. Charles Edward and Pearl (Perry) S.; m. Doris Newton Shiell, Aug. 26, 1939 (dec. 1969); m. Helen Kathleen Allen, Oct. 3, 1980. B.A., U. Toronto, 1927, LL.D., 1980; B.A., M.A., Corpus Christi Coll., Oxford (Eng.) U., 1929; A.M., Princeton, 1931, Ph.D., 1933; LL.D., Mount Allison U., 1959, York U., 1973, U. Toronto, 1980; D.Litt., U. N.B., 1967, Carleton U., 1974, U. Western Ont., 1977; D.Sc. Mil., Royal Roads Mil. Coll., 1978. Instr., then asst. prof. history Princeton U., 1934-40; commd. maj. Canadian Army, 1940, advanced through grades to col., 1944; hist. officer Canadian Mil. Hdqrs., London, Eng., 1940-45; dir. hist. sect. Canadian Army, 1945-59; faculty dept. history U. Toronto, from 1959, univ. prof., from 1973; sr. fellow Massey Coll., 1973. Author: Canada and the British Army, 1846-1871, 1936, The Military Problems of Canada, 1940, The Canadian Army, 1939-1945, An Official Historical Summary, 1948, Six Years of War, 1955, Records of the Nile Voyageurs, 1959, Quebec, 1759: The Siege and the Battle, 1959, The Victory Campaign, 1960, Arms, Men and Governments, 1970, The Arts of War and Peace, 1914-1945, Vol. 5 of Historical Documents of Canada, 1972, A Very Double Life: The Private World of Mackenzie King, 1976, Mackenzie King and the Atlantic Triangle, 1976, Canada and the Age of Conflict: A History of Canadian External Policies, Vol. I, 1977, Vol. II, 1981, (with Ken Bell) The Royal Canadian Regiment, 1883-1983, 1983, A Date with History, Memoirs of a Canadian Historian, 1983, (with Barbara M. Wilson) The Half-Million: The Canadians in Britain, 1939-1946, 1987. Pres. Can. Writers' Found., 1958-59. Decorated officer Order of Can., officer Order Brit. Empire, Canadian Forces Decoration; recipient Gov. Gen. Can. award, 1948. Mem. Royal Soc. Can. (Tyrrell medal, hon. sec. 1957-59, pres. sect. II 1968-69), Can. Hist. Assn. (pres. 1952-53). Club: Royal Canadian Mil. Inst. (Toronto). Home: Toronto Ont., Can. Died Nov. 17, 1989; buried Toronto.

STACK, LEE PRATHER, business executive; b. Danbury, N.C., Aug. 31, 1893; s. A.M. and Charity (Prather) S.; m. Mildred McIntyre, July 19, 1917; children: Lee P., Stephen A., Allen M. Grad., Trinity Coll., 1915. With Seaboard Ry, 1915-21, Wood Struthers & Co.; mem. N.Y. Stock Exch., N.Y.C., 1921-33; asst. treas. John Hancock Mut. Life Ins. Co., Boston, v.p., 1941-58, dir., 1954-58; gen. ptnr. Paine, Webber, Jackson & Curtis, from 1958; dir., chmn. exec. com. Boston & Maine R.R. Co.; dir. McDonald's Corp., Chgo., Mass. Small Bus. Investments Co., Boston, Mass. Bus. Devel. Corp.; trustee Shawnut Assn., Provident Instn. Savs. of Boston. Mem. Beacon Soc. Clubs: Comml., Algonquin, Univ., Union (Boston), Quinnpiack (New Haven), Chgo. *

STAGGERS, HARLEY ORRIN, SR., congressman; b. Keyser, W.Va., Aug. 3, 1907; s. Jacob Kinsey and Frances Winona (Cuberledge) S.; m. Mary Veronica Casey, Oct. 4, 1943; children: Margaret Ann, Mary Katherine, Frances Susan, Elizabeth Ellen, Harley Orrin, Daniel Casey. AB, Emory and Henry Coll., 1931, LLD, 1953; postgrad., Duke U., 1935; LLD, Davis and Elkins Coll., 1969, W.Va. U., W.Va. Wesleyan Coll., 1971. Coach, tchr. sci. Norton High Sch., Va., 1931-33; head coach Potomac State Coll., Keyser, 1933-35; sheriff Mineral County, Keyser, 1937-41; right-of-way agt., Va. dir. Office Govt. Reports Later OWI, 1942; mem. 81st-96th congresses from 2d W.Va. Dist., 1948-80; chmn. house interstate and fgn. commerce com., 1966. Lt. comdr. AC USNR, 1942-46; ATP, PTO. Mem. W.Va. Farm Bur., Am. Legion, VFW, DAV, Amvets, K.P.; Elks; Moose; Lions. Democrat. Methodist. Died Aug. 20, 1991; interred Keyser, W.Va. Home: Keyser W.Va.

STAIR, HENRY BOWEN, business executive; b. Brodhead, Wis., June 12, 1903; s. Lewis J. and Nellie (Bowen) S.; m. Helen C. Callsen, Sept. 17, 1927; children: Margaret Stair Anderson, Holly Stair Greer, Catherine Stair Snyder. AB, U. Wis., 1925. Account clk. Ill. Bell Telephone, 1925-30, statistician, 1930-45, gen. acctng. mgr. state area, 1945-49, asst. v.p., 1949, v.p., treas., 1952-56, dir., 1956-92, v.p. ops., 1956-65, exec. v.p., 1965-92; asst. v.p. AT&T, N.Y.C., 1949, asst. treas., 1950-52; dir. 1st Nat. Bank of Highland Park. Bd. dirs., v.p. Chgo. Boys Clubs; dir. Children's Meml. Hosp. Mem. Chgo. Assn. Commerce and Industry (dir.), Investment Analysts Soc., Armed Forces Comms. and Electronics Assn., Western Soc. Engrs., Newcomen Soc., Attic Club, Comml. Club, Econ. Club, Univ. Club (Chgo.), Exmoore Country Club (Highland Park). Home: Highland Park Ill. Died Jan. 18, 1992.

STALEY, MARTHA MCHENRY GREEN (MRS. WALTER G. STALEY), civic worker; b. Kirkwood, Mo., Oct. 22, 1905; d. Allen Percival and Josephine (Brown) Green; A.A., Hardin Coll., 1925; postgrad. Art Student's League N.Y.C., 1925-28, 50, Acad. Julian, Paris, 1950; m. Walter Goodwin Staley, Dec. 25, 1928; children: Martha Staley Marks, Walter Goodwin, Allen Percival Green. First v.p. Mo. Assn. Mental Health, 1960-64, bd. dirs., 1958-64; v.p. East Central Mo. Mental Health Assn., from 1969; v.p. Presbyn. Home for Children Mo., 1962-63, bd. dirs., 1968-71; chmn. Audrain Fine Arts Council, 1965-70; pres. Audrain County Hist. Soc., 1965-70; mem. advisory council Mo. Arthritis Center, from 1971. Bd. dirs. Allen P. and Josephine B. Green Found; trustee Mexico-Audrain County Library, 1959-66. Life mem. St. George Village Bot. Garden of St. Croix, Landmarks Soc. of St. Croix, Island Center of St. Croix; mem. Nat. Soc. Colonial Dames Am., Nat. Soc. Magna Charta Dames, Daus. Brit. Empire, Huguenot Soc. S.C. Presbyterian. Died Apr. 15, 1987; buried East Lawn Meml. Pk., Mexico, Mo. Home: Mexico Mo.

STALEY, SEWARD CHARLE, educator; b. Sprakers, N.Y., Aug. 1, 1893; s. Alfred and Amy (Plank) S.; m. Helen Croft Johnson, Dec. 24, 1949; 1 stepchild, Harian Warren Johnson. BPE, Springfield Coll., 1917, DS, 1952; MA, Clark U., 1920; PhD, U. Ill., 1929; student phys. edn., sports, fgn. countries, 1921, 1929-30, 1936, 1956. Asst. dir. physical edn. Y.M.C.A., Memphis, 1911-12; dir. Y.M.C.A., Lockport, N.Y., 1912-13; asst. dir. Y.M.C.A., Holyoke, Mass., 1913-14; dir. Y.M.C.A., Holyoke, 1916-17; dir. athletics U.S. Army Camp, Syracuse, N.Y., 1917, Greek Army, Aisa Minor, 1920-21; dir. playgrounds Northampton, Mass., 1916, Alton, 1917; asst. dir. athletics Camp Gordon, Ga., 1918; asst. dir. phys. edn. Clark U., 1919-20; vis. prof. physical edn. No. Ill. U., 1961-63. Author books relating to field, latest publ.: Physical Exercise Programs; contbr. articles to profl. jours. Cons. phys. tng. U.S. Army and USN, 1942-45; past pres. Ill. State Phys. Edn. Assn.; founder, past chmn. annual conf. Big Ten Tchrs. of Phys. Edn., 1935, annual conf. Ill. Coll. and Univ. Tchrs. of phys. Edn. and Athletic Coaches, 1939. Recipient William H. Anderson award. Fellow Ill. Assn. Health Phys. Edn., Safety Am. Assn. Health Phys. Edn. and Recreation, Am. Acad. Physical Edn. (past pres.); mem. Coll. Phys. Edn. Assn. (pres. 1954), Delta Theta Epsilon, Phi Delta Kappa, Kappa Delta Pi, Phi Kappa Phi. Methodist. *

STALNAKER, JOHN MARSHALL, educational corporation administrator; b. Duluth, Minn., Aug. 17, 1903; s. William Edward and Sara (Tatham) S.; m. Ruth Elizabeth Culp, July 29, 1933 (dec. Apr. 1968); children: John Culp, Robert Culp, Judith S. Aycock.; m. Edna Remmers, Aug. 21, 1969. B.S. with honors, U. Chgo., 1925; A.M. in Psychology, 1928; LL.D., Purdue U., 1956, Centre Coll., 1960. Tchr. rural sch. Hardisty, Alta., Can., 1922; tchr. math., sci. Harvard Sch. for Boys, 1925-26; instr. psychology, spl. research asst. to pres., 1926-30; asst. prof. edn. and psychology (on leave) Purdue U., 1930-31; dir. attitude measurement, athletic survey U. Minn., 1930-31; examiner (instr.) bd. exams. U. Chgo., 1931-36, asst. prof., 1936-37, assoc. prof., 1937-44; prof. Princeton U., 1944-45; research assoc. Coll. Entrance Exam Bd., 1936-37, cons. examiner, 1937-42; assoc. sec., 1942-45, dir. Navy test research unit, 1942-45; contractor's tech. rep. for N.D.R.C. project N-106, 1942-45; dir. Army-Navy Coll. Qualifying Test, 1943-45; dean students, prof. psychology Stanford, 1945-49; prof. psychology, coordinator psychol. scis. and services Ill. Inst. Tech., 1949-51; cons. Fund for Advancement Edn., 1952-55, NSF, 1952-56; dir. studies Assn. Am. Med. Colls., 1949-55; pres. Nat. Merit Scholarship Corp., 1955-69, pres. emeritus, hon. dir., 1969-90; mem. bd. North Shore Mental Health Assn., 1967-70; mem. Northfield Twp. Mental Health Adv. Bd., 1978-79, Ill. Bd. Higher Edn., 1969-75; trustee, dir. Pepsi-Cola Scholarship Bd., 1945-54; mem. adv. com. Fgn. Service Exam. Dept. State, 1941-51; sci. adv. bd. to Chief of Staff, USAF, 1950-53; mem. bd. fgn. scholarships Dept. State, 1962-67, chmn., 1962-65. Contbr. articles to ednl., psychol. jours. Bd. dirs. Sarasota (Fla.) Inst. Lifetime Learning, 1982-86; bd. dirs., treas. Jefferson Ctr. (HUD pub. housing project), 1986-87. Recipient Certificate Merit Pres. U.S., 1948, Distinguished Civilian Service award Sec. Navy, 1946; citation for outstanding contbn. to edn. Nat. Assn. Secondary Sch. Prins., 1970; Distinguished Service medal Coll. Entrance Exam. Bd., 1976. Fellow Am. Psychol. Assn.; mem. Psychometric Soc., Am. Edn. Research Assn., Phi Beta Kappa, Sigma Xi, Tau Kappa Epsilon. Home: Sarasota Fla. Died Aug. 20, 1990; buried Sarasota, Fla.

STAMPER, WILLSON YOUNG, III, artist; b. N.Y.C., Jan. 5, 1912; s. Willson Young and Marguerita (Malcolm) S.; children: Kimon, Allen, Robin. Student, Art Students League, 1934. Conservator art Cin. Art Mus., Taft Mus., 1936-43; conservator art Honolulu Acad. Art, 1945-62; instr. Cin. Art Mus., 1936-43, Carnegie Found. art course, 1936-39; dir. Art Sch., Honolulu Acad. Art, 1945-62. Works reproduced in numerous books and mags.; one-man exhbns. include,

Cin. Art Mus., 1946, 50, Honolulu Art Acad., 1948, Contemporary Arts Center of Hawaii, 1963, Down Town Gallery, 1977, Manuge Galleries, Halifax, N.S., Can., 1981, Albright Knox Art Gallery, Buffalo, Zwicker Art Gallery, Halifax, from 1985, Honolulu Acad. Arts, 1987; exhibited in group shows, Carnegie Internat., 1952, World's Fair, 1939, Stanford U. Art Gallery, 1958, various mus. and galleries; represented in permanent collections, Cin. Art Mus., Mus. Modern Art, Honolulu Acad. Art, ceramic mural commd. by, State of Hawaii, 1975; painted portrait of, Hawaii Supreme Ct. Chief Justice William Richardson. Recipient 15 1st prizes for nat. mus. exhbns. Home: Lake Mary Fla. Deceased. †

STANGEL, ARTHUR GEORGE, wholesale executive; b. Kewamee, Wis., May 31, 1897; s. Jacob John and Mary A. (Krema) S.; m. Jane A. Menten, May 16, 1936. Student, pub. schs. With J.J. Stangel Hardware Co. Manitowac, Wis., from 1917; v.p., gen. mgr Manitowac, 1929-48, pres., treas., 1948-63, chmn.-treas., from 1963; also dir.; dir. Sentry Life Ins. Co., Hardware Mut. Casualty Co., Hardware DEalers Mut. Fire Ins. Co. (Stevens Point, Wis.), Sentry Life Ins. Co., 1st Nat. Bank (Manitowoc). Served Med. Transport WW I. Mem. Wis. Good Rds. Assn. (dir., exec. com.), Rotary, Serra Internat. *

STANTON, ROGER, editor, publisher, sports broadcaster; b. Mpls., Dec. 31, 1928; s. M.E. and Pearl (Lind) S.; m. Pamela Elizabeth Kornmeier, Dec. 19, 1970. B.A., U. Mich., 1951. With advt. pub. relations dept. Fed. Dept. Stores, Detroit, 1951-54; sales promotion mgr. Wolf Detroit Envelope Co., 1954-56; editor employee publs. Nat. Bank Detroit, 1956-64, coordinator employee recreation program, 1957-64; pres. editor, pub. Football News, Detroit, from 1962; pub. Basketball Weekly, from 1967, Big Ten Report, 1972-77; Sports dir. Sta. WDTM, Detroit, Sta. WXON-TV; instr. writing pub. relations Sta. YMCA, Detroit, 1960-62; chmn. indsl. publs. for Mich. Week, 1958-63. Bd. dirs. Mich. chpt. Nat. Football Found. and Hall of Fame.; Mem. speakers bur. United Found.; Active in pub. relations work; mem. exec. bd. Detroit Area council Boy Scouts Am., from 1977; bd. govs. U. Mich., 1983-88; del. Mich. Republican Com. Mem. Nat. Sportswriters and Sports Broadcasters Assn., Basketball Writers Assn., Coll. Football Writers Assn., Pro Football Writers Assn., Coll. Sports Info. Dirs. Assn., Sigma Delta Chi. Clubs: Adcraft (publicity chmn.), U. Mich. (mem. bd. govs.), Economic (publicity com.), Lochmoor, Press, Detroit (Detroit); Palm Bay (Miami, Fla.), Racquet (Miami, Fla.); Carlton (Chgo.); St. George's (Bermuda). Home: Grosse Pointe Mich. Deceased. †

STANWYCK, BARBARA (RUBY STEVENS), actress; b. Bklyn., July 16, 1907; d. Byron and Catherine (McGee) Stevens; m. Frank Fay, Aug. 26, 1928 (div. 1935); m. Robert Taylor, May 14, 1939 (div. 1951); 1 son. Ed. pub. schs., Bklyn. Began as chorus girl; later scored success in Burlesque, prod. by Arthur Hopkins; 82 motion pictures include Meet John Doe, 1941, The Great Man's Lady, The Gay Sisters, 1942, Double Indemnity, 1944, My Reputations, 1945, Christmas in Connecticut, Two Mrs. Carrolls, 1946, The Bride Wore Boots, Strange Love of Martha Ivars, 1947, Cry Wolf, The Other Love, B.F.'s Daughter, 1948, Sorry Wrong Number, File on Thelma Jordon, The Lady Gambles, The Lie, East-Side, West-Side, The Furies, 1949, To Please a Lady, 1950, The Man in the Cloak, 1951, Clash by Night, 1951, Jeopardy, 1952, Titanic, 1952, Executive Suite, Witness to Murder, Escape to Burma, 1955, Cattle Queen of Montana, There's Always Tomorrow, 1956, Maverick Queen, 1956, These Wilder Years, 1956, Crime of Passion, 1957, Trooper Hook, 1957, Walk on the Wild Side, 1962, Roustabout, 1964, The Night Walker, 1965; TV shows The Barbara Stanwyck Theater, NBC-TV, 1960-61, The Big Valley, ABC-TV, The Colbys, 1985-87; appeared in: TV movie The Letters, 1973; TV mini-series The Thorn Birds; guest star numerous TV shows. Recipient Emmy award, 1960-61, 66, 83, hon. Acad. award, 1982, Am. Film Inst. award, 1987. Home: West Hollywood Calif. Died Jan. 20, 1990.

STAPLES, JACK ROBISON, investment banker; b. Scranton, Pa., Apr. 29, 1911; s. Reuben and Ann (Williams) S.; m. Leah Virginia Gentle, Oct. 23, 1937; children—Jill (Mrs. Duke Winston Thomas), Judith (Mrs. Frederick Standish C. Perry), James George, Jack Robinson Jr. (dec.). A.B., Ohio Wesleyan U., 1934. Salesman Maynard H. Murch & Co., Cleve., 1934-43, partner, 1945-50; partner Fulton, Reid & Co., Cleve., 1950-56; exec. v.p., dir. Fulton, Reid & Staples, Inc. (formerly known as Fulton, Reid & Co., Inc.), Cleve., 1956-71, pres., chief operating officer, from 1971, vice-chmn., 1975; ptnr. Roney & Co. (merger with Fulton, Reid & Staples, Inc.), Cleve., until 1990; pres., chmn. bd. Cascade Industries. Bd. govs. Midwest Stock Exchange, 1965-66, 73-77; Capt. United Appeal, Cleve., 1952-55; mem. Juvenile Delinquency Prevention Com., from 1961; treas. Jimmie Lee Found. Served to lt. USNR, World War II. Mem. Securities Industry Assn. Am. (past chmn. No. Ohio Group), Nat. Assn. Securities Dealers (past com. chmn.), Bond Club Cleve. (dir. 1965-68, pres 1967), Newcomen Soc. N. Am., Alpha Sigma Phi. Clubs: Union, Cleve. Athletic (past pres.), Cleve. Skating (past pres.). Home: Beachwood Ohio Died Apr. 17, 1990; buried Knollwood Cemetery, Mayfield Hghts., Ohio.

STARCH, ELMER, consultant; b. West Concord, Minn., Aug. 1, 1898; s. Stephen and Frances (Kumerth) S.; m. Karen Buck, July 20, 1927; children: Eleda, Karl, Marshall. BA, U. Minn., 1926; student, Harvard, 1932. Pres. Riggin-Starch Corp., 1929-49; mng. dir. Fairway Farms Corp., 1933-41; head econs. dept. Mont. State Coll., 1933-39; dir. Gt. Plains region Resettlement Adminstrn.; coord. Office SEc. Agr. Adviser agrl. programs Trukish Govt., 1950-53; agrl. adviser Tnuisia, 1957-60; leader Econ. Explorations, Inter-River Plain Somalia, 1960-61; devel. cons. Morocco, Tchad, Congo, Gabon, 1961-62; cons. UN Sel. Conf., 1962-63; pvt. cons. econ. devel., from 1963. Contbr. numerous articles in resource devel. and mgmt. Mem. Farm Econs. Assn., Range Mgmt. Assn., Alpha Zeta. *

STARKEY, ROBERT LYMAN, microbiology educator; b. Fitchburg, Mass., Sept. 27, 1899; s. Charles W. and Etta C. (Howes) S.; m. Florence Tenney, 1928. B.S., Mass. Agr. Coll., 1921; M.S., Rutgers U., 1923, Ph.D., 1924. Instr. bacteriology U. Minn., 1924-26; assoc. prof. soil microbiology Rutgers U., 1926-44, prof. microbiology, 1944-65, emeritus prof., from 1966, head dept. agrl. microbiology, 1954-65; assoc. soil microbiologist N.J. Agr. Expt. Sta., 1926-44, research specialist, 1944-65; Participant 1st Internat. Congress Soil Sci., Wash., 1927, 2d Congress, Russia, 1930; sec. sect. agrl. and indsl. microbiology 3d Internat. Microbiology Congress, N.Y.C., 1939; v.p. sect. agrl. microbiology 6th Congress, Rome, Italy, 1953; focal topic chmn. 8th congress, Montreal, Can., 1962; v.p. sect. microbiology, chmn. symposium 9th Internat. Bot. Congress, Montreal, 1959; rep. Soc. Am. Bacteriologists on NRC, 1956-59. Co-author: The Soil and the Microbe; Contbr. articles on soil microbiology and microbiol. physiology and indsl. microbiology to profl. jours. Served with SATC, World War I. Rockefeller fellow, 1937-38; Recipient Distinguished Research award adv. bd. Research Council Rutgers U., 1958, certificate Office Naval Research, 1967, award Alumni Assn. U. Mass., 1969; Charles Thom award Soc. for Indsl. Microbiology, 1976; Robert L. Starkey professorship named in honor at Waksman Inst. Microbiology, 1983, Starkey Apts. at Rutgers U., 1981. Fellow AAAS; mem. Am. Soc. Agronomy (exec. com., mem. bd. govs. 1957-58), Theobald Smith Soc. (1st pres. 1941-42), Am. Soc. Microbiology (pres. 1962-63, hon. mem.), Can. Soc. for Microbiology (hon.), Associacion Mexican de Microbiologia (hon.), Sigma Xi, Phi Kappa Phi, Phi Sigma Kappa. Republican. Unitarian. Home: Jamesburg N.J. Deceased. †

STARKOFF, BERNARD JULIUS, publisher; b. Cleve., Aug. 6, 1917; s. Jack and Rea (Aronowitz) S.; m. Florence C. Friedman, Oct. 14, 1944; children: Jay, Earl, Barbara. B.A., U. Cin., 1940; M.H.L., Hebrew Union Coll., 1943. V.p. Chem. Rubber Co., Cleve., 1947-62, pres., 1963-73; pres. CRC Press, Inc., Boca Raton, Fla., 1973-86, chmn., 1973-86, dir. pub., 1987-90; mng. ptnr. Starkoff Assocs., Boca Raton, 1978-91; pres. Supersearch, Inc., Boca Raton, 1982-91; dir. Imreg Corp., New Orleans, Boca Bancorp. Bd. regents Coll. of Boca Raton, 1982-85; bd. dirs. Found. Fla. Atlantic U., Boca Raton, 1982-91, Temple Beth El, 1981-86, United Way, 1980-91, Kravis Performing Arts Ctr., 1987-91. Jewish. Home: Boca Raton Fla. Died Sept. 15, 1991; buried Boca Raton, Fla.

STARR, EUGENE CARL, consulting engineer; b. Falls City, Oreg., Aug. 6, 1901; s. Harie Eugene and Loretta Alice (Hart) S.; m. Oma Mae Herald, Sept. 11, 1950. B.S. in Elec. Engring, Oreg. State U., Corvallis, 1923, E.E., 1938. Registered profl. engr., Oreg. High voltage research engr. Gen. Electric Co., 1923-27; instr. elec. engring. Oreg. State U., 1927-33, asso. prof., 1934-39, prof., 1939-54; coordinator aircraft precipitation static research OSRD, 1942-45; cons. Bonneville Power Adminstrn., Portland, Oreg., 1939-54, chief engr., dir. div. engring., 1954-61, cons. engr., from 1962; civilian sci. observer Bikini atom bomb tests, 1946; cons. indsl. power AEC, 1953-65; mem. adv. panel on electricity Nat. Bur. Standards, Nat. Acad. Scis.-NRC, 1961-64; mem. U.S. nat. com., U.S. rep. study com. 14 Internat. Conf. Large High Voltage Electric Systems, 1962-78; mem. adv. group tech. coms. 8, 28, 30 Internat. Electrotech. Commn., from 1954; mem. adv. coms. Fed. Power Commn., 1965-67; mem. task force on nuclear safety research Electric Power Research Inst., 1969-75. Author: Electric Power Generation sect. McGraw-Hill Ency. of Sci. and Tech.; contbr. articles to profl. jours. Mem. Portland Mayor's Utility Underground Conversion Com., 1972-74. Recipient Disting. Service award and Gold medal U.S. Dept. Interior, 1958; Engr. of Yr. award Profl. Engrs. Oreg., 1965; Disting. Service award Oreg. State U., 1976. Fellow IEEE (life, mem. editorial bd. 1965-66, dir. 1963-64, Habirshaw medal and award 1968, Lamme medal 1980, Centennial medal 1984), AAAS; mem. Am. Nuclear Soc., Nat. Soc. Profl. Engrs., Nat. Acad. Engring., Sigma Xi, Tau Beta Pi, Sigma Tau, Eta Kappa Nu, Phi Kappa Phi. Home: Portland Oreg. Died Feb. 5, 1988. †

STARR, ISAAC, therapeutic research educator; b. Phila., Mar. 6, 1895; s. Isaac and Mary Savage (Barclay) S.; m. Edith Nelson Page, Apr. 22, 1922; children: Isaac, Vidal Davis Staff Hoyt, Lynford Lardner, Harold Page. BS magna cum laude, Princeton U., 1916; MD, U. Pa., 1920. House officer Mass. Gen. Hosp., Boston, 1920-22; instr. pharmacology U. Pa., 1922-28, asst. prof. clin. pharmacology, 1928-33, assoc. in medicine, 1928-33, Hartzell rsch. prof. therapeutics, 1933-45, 48-61, emeritus prof. therapeutic rsch., 1961-89, prof. therapeutic rsch., dean Sch. Medicine, 1945-48; cons. cardiovascular disease Selective Svc. of Pa.; mem. revision com. U.S. Pharmocopea, 1930-50; mem. com. on drug addiction and narcotics NRC, 1947-89, chmn., 1947-60, mem. com. on problems of alcohol, 1949-89; chmn. Office of Naval Rsch. Adv. Group on Burn Program, 1951; cons. U.S. Naval Air Devel. Ctr., 1951-64. Author: Physiologic Therapy for Obstructive Vascular Disease; mem. editorial bd. Circulation, 1949-53, 55-60, Am. Heart Jour., 1938-50. Recipient Selective Svc. medal. Mem. AMA (chmn. coun. on drugs 1959-62), Am. Soc. Clin. Investigation (pres. 1939), Assn. Am. Physicians, Am. Physiol. Soc., Am. Soc. Pharmacology and Exptl. Therapeutics, Am. Heart Assn. (Albert Lasker award 1957), Coll. Physicians of Phila., Phila. Club, Princeton of Phila. Club. Home: Roxborough Pa. Died June 22, 1989.

STARRY, LEO JOSEPH, surgeon; b. Dodgeville, Wis., May 13, 1894; s. John T. and Bridget C. (McGilligan) S.; m. Marie Patch, June 21, 1922; 1 childm Helen Kathryn. BS, U. Wis., 1917; MD, Washington U. St. Louis, 1919. Intern St. Anthony Hosp., Oklahoma City, 1919-20; surgeon pvt. practice, Oklahoma City, from 1920; chmn. surg. dept. Okla Med Ctr., 1948-52, prof. surgery, 1948-60, prof. emeritus, from 1960; pres. of staff St. Anthony Hosp., from 1963; attending staff St. Anthony Bapt., Mercy, Crippled Children's Univ. Hosps. Decorated Knight of Holy Scripture, Grand Cross. Mem. Internat. Coll. Surgeons (v.p.), A.C.S., AMA, Oklahoma City Surg. Soc. (past pres.), Oklahoma City Acad. Medicine (past pres.), Okla. Surg. Soc., Southwestern (past pres.), Southeastern Surg. COngresses, Phi Beta Pi, Sigma Sigma, Theta Kappa Phi (hon.), KC (4*). Clubs: Mens Dinner. *

STEAKLEY, ZOLLIE COFFER, JR., lawyer, state justice; b. Rotan, Tex., Aug. 29, 1908; s. Zollie Coffer and Frances Elizabeth (McGlasson) S.; m. Ruth Butler, June 4, 1939. B.A., Hardin-Simmons U., 1929, LL.D., 1959; J.D., U. Tex., 1932; LL.D., U. Corpus Christi, 1958. Bar: Tex. bar 1932. Pvt. practice law, 1932-39, 46-57; asst. atty. gen. Tex., 1939-42, sec. state, 1957-60; justice Supreme Ct. of Tex., Austin, 1961-80; spl. asst. to atty. gen. State of Tex., 1987-92. Home: Austin Tex. Died Mar. 24, 1992. †

STEARNS, BETTY JANE, public relations executive; b. St. Paul. Ph.B., U. Chgo., 1945, M.A., 1948; cert. advt. studies, U. London, 1949. Editor Chgo. Stagebill, 1948-49; sec. U. Chgo. Cancer Research Found., 1949; writer Chas. A. Stevens & Co., 1949-50; account exec. The Pub. Relations Bd., Chgo., 1950-53, v.p., 1953-63, sr. v.p., 1963-78, mng. ptnr., 1978-85; exec. v.p. Porter Novelli (formerly Pub. Rels. Bd./Needham), Chgo., 1985-88, sr. counselor, 1989-91; chmn. bd. dirs. Sta. WBEZ, Chgo., 1980-84, now dir.; dir. Chgo. Apparel Industry Bd. Author, editor: Careers in Music, 1976, Winning The Money Game, 1979; editor-writer, producer: book, radio series Instrumental Odyssey, 1970. Bd. dirs. Bus. Vols. for Arts. Recipient Golden Trumpet award Publicity Club of Chgo., 1959, 64, 68-70, 72-73, 76-79, 84, 85. Mem. Pub. Relations Soc. Am. (Silver Anvil award 1972, 76, 82), Home Fashions League, The Fashion Group of Chgo. (pres. 1967-68), Com. of 200, Chgo. Network (dir. 1982-85, 1989—), Arts Chgo. Club. Home: Chicago Ill. Deceased.

STEBER, ELEANOR, soprano; b. Wheeling, W.Va., July 17, 1914; d. William Charles and Ida A. (Nolte) S. MusB, New Eng. Conservatory Music, 1938; MusD (hon.), Bethany Coll., U. W.Va., Fla. So. Coll., Temple U., Ithaca Coll., Marshall Coll.; L.H.D. (hon.), Wheaton Coll., 1966; DFA, U. Oklahoma City.; DFA (hon.), U. Charleston. Head vocal dept. Cleve. Inst. Music, 1963-73; voice faculty Juilliard Sch. Music, 1971-85, New Eng. Conservatory Music, 1971-89, Phila. Music Acad., 1975, Bklyn. Coll., 1980's; Bd. dirs. Bklyn. Opera Co., Opera Soc., Washington; founder, pres. Eleanor Steber Music Found., 1975-90. Singer (1935); winner Met. Auditions of Air, spring 1940; with Met. Opera Co., 1940-66, San Francisco Opera Co., 1945, Central City Opera Festival, 1946, Cin. Summer Opera, 5 summers; appeared with Met., all maj. Am. opera cos., and all maj. European festivals including Glyndebourne, 1948, Bayreuth, 1953, Florence, Italy, 1954, Salzburg, 1959, sang with 7 opera cos. in Yugoslavia, 1955, Vienna Staatsoper, 1956; sang title role world premier and rec. Samuel Barber's Vanessa, 1958; commd. and sang world premier Barber's Knoxville, Summer of 1915, 1948, also in Chgo., 1980; soloist with N.Y. Philharmonic, NBC, Boston, Mpls., Chgo., Cin., Kansas City, Denver, Montreal, Phila. Symphony orchs., others; radio and TV appearances; star of: TV's Voice of Firestone, 10 yrs; Concert tours throughout, U.S., Can., Europe, Orient; duo recitals with Blanche Thebom, 1970's; 3 solo recitals Alice Tully Hall, N.Y.C., 1973; recorded over 100 albums. Mem. Delta Omicron, Pi Kappa Lambda. Lutheran. Home: Port

Jefferson N.Y. Died Oct. 3, 1990; buried Wheeling, W.Va.

STEDMAN, JOHN PORTERFIELD, banker; b. Oxford, N.C., Sept. 17, 1894; s. John Porterfield and Laura (Cordon) S.; m. Laurie Branch, Apr. 6, 1922 (dec.); 1 child, John Branch; m. Victoria Pringle Earle, Feb. 14, 1926; 1 child, Victoria E. Student, U. N.C., 1912-14. Asst. cashier Bank of Washington (N.C.), 1918-26; v.p. N.C. Bank & Trust Co., 1926-31; exec. v.p. Regional Agrl Corp. of Raleigh (N.C.); also Albany, N.Y., 1932-34; asst. treas. F.S. Royster Guano Co., Norfold, Va., 1934-39; chmn. bd., pres. Scottish Bank, Lumberton, N.C., 1939-63; pres., dir. Protective Agy., Inc., from 1941, Protective Realty, Inc., from 1954; chmn. bd. Bus. Devel. Corp. N.C., from 1956, 1st Union Nat. Bank N.C., Charlotte, from 1963. Pres. Robeson County chpt. ARC, 1941-43, treas., 1932; trustee U.N.C., from 1945, East Carolina Coll., 1952-56; bd. dirs. Merit System of N.C., 1950-52. 2d lt. U.S. Army, 1917-18. Mem. N.C. Bankers Assn. (pres. 1952-53), C. of C. (pres. 1953-54), Am. Legion (past comdr.), Hist. Soc. Va., Hist. Soc. N.C., Elks, Rotarian (pres. 1945). Epsicopalian. *

STEEFEL, LAWRENCE D., JR., art historian; b. Mpls., Mar. 20, 1926; s. Lawrence D. and Genevieve Rose (Fallon) S.; m. Marion Hildur Charlson, Aug. 10, 1950; children: David Simon, Carl Iver, Sarah Christine. B.A., Haverford Coll., 1946; M.F.A., Princeton U., 1956, Ph.D., 1960. Instr. to asst. prof. Lawrence Coll., Appleton, Wis., 1956-64; asso. prof. U. Wash., Seattle, 1964-67; Steinberg prof. art history Washington U., St. Louis, 1967-89, emeritus, from 1989. Author: The Position of Duchamp's Glass in the Development of His Art, 1977. Served with AUS, 1949-50, 51-53. Home: Saint Louis Mo. Deceased. †

STEEL, CHARLES LOWNDES, III, electric utility executive; b. Colon, Panama Canal Zone, Mar. 22, 1924; s. Charles and Katharine (Porter) S.; m. Janet Shearer Smith, Oct. 1, 1944; children: Charles Lowndes, Natalie, Christopher Allen. BS in Engring., U.S. Mil. Acad., 1944; MS, Harvard U., 1950; MS in Polit. Sci., George Washington U., 1961; postgrad., U.S. Army War Coll., 1961. Registered profl. engr., Mass., Ark. Commd. 2d lt. U.S. Army C.E., 1944; advanced through grades to col., 1966; nuclear weapons officer Manhatten Engring. Dist., Sandia Base, N.Mex., 1946-49; mem. faculty U.S. Army War Coll., 1961-64; spl. asst. to supreme comdr. SHAPE, Paris, 1964-66; ret., 1970; dir. pub. affairs Ark. Power & Light Co., Little Rock, 1970-75, v.p. pub. affairs, 1975-79, v.p., asst. to pres., 1979-81, sr. v.p., 1981-85, exec. v.p., 1985-88; ret., 1988. Mem. task force Presdl. Task Force on Nat. Water Policy, 1979-81; pres. Ark. Better Bus. Bur., 1977-78, Ark. Basin Assn., from 1981; bd. dirs. U.S. Indsl. Coun., 1972-86; chmn. Ark. Nature Conservancy, 1983-89; mem. Little Rock Port Authority, from 1981. Decorated Legion of Merit (3); decorated Joint Svc. Commendation medal; named Disting. Engr. Little Rock Dist. U.S. C.E., 1967-70; decorated Disting. Svc. medal Korea. Mem. Ark. Fedn. Water & Air Users (pres. 1974, 75), Soc. Am. Mil Engrs. (pres.), Nat. Soc. Profl. Engrs., Ark. Soc. Profl. Engrs. Episcopalian. Home: Herber Springs Ariz. Deceased. †

STEEN, MELVIN CLIFFORD, lawyer; b. Mpls., Feb. 16, 1907; s. Erick and Annie (Running) S.; m. Dorothy M. Wagner, Nov. 4, 1932; m. Florence W. Rollins, Sept. 13, 1952; children: Gordon R., Leslie A., Deborah R., Erick R. JD, U. Minn., 1929. Bar: Minn. 1931, N.Y. 1931, D.C. 1947. Assoc. Root, Clark, Buckner & Ballantine, N.Y.C., 1929-44, ptnr., 1944-45; founding ptnr. Cleary, Gottlieb, Steen & Hamilton, NYC, Washington, Paris, Brussels, London, Hong Kong, Tokyo, Frankfurt, 1946-92. Decorated chevalier de la Legion d'Honneur; recipient Outstanding Achievement award U. Minn., 1975; Melvin C. Steen Fellowship Fund of Legal Aid Soc. established in his name by Cleary Gottlieb et al, 1990. Mem. ABA, Internat. Law Assn., N.Y. State Bar Assn., Assn. of Bar of City of N.Y., Am. Bar Found., N.Y. County Lawyers Assn., Order of Coif, Delta Theta Phi. Clubs: India House (N.Y.C.), Sky (N.Y.C.); Siwanoy Country (Bronxville, N.Y.); Minnesota (Mpls.). Home: Bronxville N.Y. Died June 28, 1992.

STEER, CHARLES MELVIN, obstetrics educator; b. Midvale, N.J., Feb. 13, 1913; s. Charles Henry and Augusta (Smith) S.; m. Catherine Quinn, June 29, 1945; children: Elizabeth Miller, Ann. AB, Columbia U., 1933, MD, 1937, D Med. Sci., 1942. Resident in ob-gyn Presbyn. Hosp., N.Y.C., 1939-43; pvt. practice, N.Y.C., 1946-82; mem. faculty dept. ob-gyn Columbia U. Coll. Physicians and Surgeons, N.Y.C., 1946-82, prof. emeritus, 1982-90, acting chmn. dept., 1968-71. Author: Evaluation of the Pelvis in Obstetrics; contbr. articles to med. jours. Maj. M.C., U.S. Army, 1943-46. Fellow ACS, Am. Coll. Ob-Gyn, N.Y. Obstet. Soc., Siwanoy Club. Home: Bronxville N.Y. Died Feb. 22, 1990.

STEFFEN, REY JOHN, hotel and corporate officer; b. Milw., Apr. 13, 1894; s. George John and Emily (Volkman) S.; m. Charlotte Eitel, June 14, 1923. Student, U. Wis. Newspaper reporter, advt. writer Milw. Jour., 1914; advt. and mdse. counselor Critchfield & Co., Chgo., 1919-22; v.p., gen. mgr. Hough Mfg. Corp., 1923-33; mng. dir. Bismark Hotel, 1933-40; exec. v.p. Albert Schwill & Co., 1940-44; Pres. LaSalle-Madison Co., from 1944; pres. LaSalle Hotel, from 1944; v.p. Hough Mfg. Co., from 1923; chmn. Nat. Hotel Industry Avd. Com. to OPA, 1945. Lt. U.S. Army, 1918-19. Mem. Chgo. Hotel Assn. (chmn. bd.), Ill. Hotel Assn. (dir.), Nat. Restuarant Assn., Am. Legion, Montecito Country Club. *

STEIGER, FREDERIC, artist; b. Solwutz, Austria, Oct. 21, 1905; s. Michael and Ida (Schaeffer) S.; m. Netty Meth, Aug. 5, 1922 (div.); m. Ruby Eleanor Fevens; children—Trudi Kearns, Linda. Student, Olmouc (Austria) U. One man exhbns. include, Carroll Galleries, Nfld. Toronto, Indsl. Trade Fair, 1949, Roberts Art Gallery, Toronto, Ont., Can., 1950, Odeon Theatre Gallery, Toronto and Ottawa, 1950, Victoria Coll., Univ. Toronto, 1954, Ho. of Assembly, St. John's, Nfld., Can., 1960, Arts Club, Montreal, Que., Can., 1957, L'Art Francaise Art Gallery, 1957, Upper Can. Coll., 1959, Simpsons Art Gallery, 1961, North York Pub. Art Gallery, 1962, Richview Pub.Libr., 1968, Eaton Art Gallery, Toronto, 1972, 79, Galerie Lyson, Toronto, 1980-81, Ont. Inst. Studies in Edn., 1986, Karney-Daniels Art Gallery, 1986, Brampton Art Gallery, 1978, 1987; exhibited in group shows at Vancouver Art Mus., 1939, travelling exhbn. Nat. Gallery, 1938, 40, 41, 42, Royal Can. Acad., Montreal and Toronto, 1941, 45, Montreal Mus. Art, 1941, Ont. Soc. Artists, Art Gallery Toronto, 1938-40, Eaton's Art Gallery, 1944, Continental Art Gallery, Montreal, 1945, Cummerford Gallery, N.Y.C., 1962, Edn. Centre, Toronto, 1963, Linchrist Gallery, 1985, O'Keefe Centre Art Gallery, Toronto, Agnes Etherington Art Gallery, Kingston, Ont., Art Loan Soc., Ont.; represented in permanent collections, IBM, 40 portraits, Nfld. Parliament Bldg., Meml. U. Nfld., St. John's, Hallmark Collection Can. Art, Imperial Oil Ltd., Toronto, Met. Toronto Pub. Library, Wellesley Hosp., Toronto, Royal Ins. Co., Toronto, Etobicoke Hydro-U. of Saskatchewan; also pvt. collections; portrait of King Peter of Yugoslavia, 1974, Hon. William G. Davis, Premier of Ont, 1976, Hon. John C. Crosbie, M.P., 1983; work included in "Many Faces, Many Spaces," Artists in Ont., 1987; subject article (in Discovery mag.) Ruby Steiger-Cataloguing a Life's Work by Diana McLaren. Recipient Bronze medal IBM Corp. Unitarian. Home: Islington Ont., Can. Died Aug. 4, 1990; cremated.

STEIN, RICHARD GEORGE, architect; b. Chgo., Aug. 23, 1916; s. Julius J. and Minnie (Gartenzaun) S.; m. Ethel Levy, June 10, 1940; 1 child, Carl J. Cert. in Design, Cooper Union, 1937; B.Arch. magna cum laude, NYU, 1937; M.Arch., Harvard U., 1939. Draftsman, designer firm Gropius & Breuer, Cambridge, Mass., 1939-41; designer Edward D. Stone, N.Y.C., 1941, Tuttle, Seelye, Place & Raymond, N.Y.C., 1941-43; partner Katz, Waisman, Blumenkranz, Stein, Weber, N.Y.C., 1946-60; propr. Richard G. Stein & Assos., N.Y.C., 1960-76; partner Richard G. Stein & Partners, 1977-78, The Stein Partnership, 1978-90; instr., adj. prof. Cooper Union, from 1946; guest critic Syracuse U., 1961; mem. N.Y. State Bd. Examiners Architecture, 1964-74, chmn., 1970-72; chmn. joint com. on N.Y.C. community dists. of Citizens' Union-Citizens' Housing and Planning Council, 1968-73; prin. investigator NSF funded research on energy utilization in schs. (through N.Y.C. Bd. Edn.); mem. Nat. Bur. Standards Task Force on Illumination Performance Standards, 1977. Architect for pub. facilities including Rochdale Park, Queens, N.Y., 1971, Manhattan Children's Treatment Ctr. Wards Island, N.Y., 1971, Eleanor Roosevelt campus, Wiltwyck Sch. Boys, Yorktown Heights, N.Y., 1966, master plan and facilities planning for N.Y.C. Community Coll., 1973-78, master plan and projects for Bronx River restoration, from 1977, Co-generation plant, Trenton, combined police and fire dept. facility, N.Y.C. (Mcpl. Art Soc. award 1984), biotech. start-up labs. for Columbia U., new combined police and fire facility and restoration of historic facades E. 67th St., N.Y.C., 1984, hostel for mentally retarded adults New Castle, N.Y., 1985, new firehouse Rescue Co. 1, N.Y.C., 1986, restoration of deteriorated terra cotta Gothic towers Shepard Hall, CCNY, 1986, new adminstrn. bldg. Mid-Hudson Psychiat. Ctr., New Hampton, N.Y., 1987, Women's Rights Nat. Hist. Pk., Seneca Falls, N.Y., 1988, housing for homeless, 1989, new 41st precinct Police Sta., Bronx, N.Y., 1987, renovation 22d precinct, Central Pk., N.Y.C., 1987; author: Architecture and Energy, 1977; contbr. articles to profl. jours., also studies, handbooks for fed., state and local govts.; retrospective exhbn., Arthur A. Houghton Jr. Gallery, Cooper Union, N.Y.C., 1980, Urban Ctr., N.Y.C., 1981, U. N.Mex., 1985, U. Ky., 1986. Chmn. Croton Planning Bd. Served with C.E. AUS, 1943-46, PTO. Recipient cert. of commendation Parks Assn. N.Y.C., for Stephen Wise Plaza, 1965, Design Steel award for Central Park Music Festival N.Y.C., 1967, citation Indsl. Design Rev. for Inwood Park, 1970; Merit award N.Y. State Assn. Architects; Merit award AIA for Rochdale Park, 1971; 1st place competition for affordable house N.J. Dept. Community Affairs, 1978; Arnold W. Brunner scholar, 1962, 72. Fellow AIA (mem. task force on energy conservation 1972-74, pres. N.Y. chpt. 1976-77, chmn. fellowship com.; chmn. regional devel. and natural resources com., chmn. Delano and Aldrich Emerson fellowship com. from 1965, 1981 Medal of honor N.Y. chpt.), Architects, Designers and Planners for Social Responsibility (exec. com. 1982-85). Home: Croton-On-Hudson N.Y. Died Apr. 18, 1990; buried Bethel Cemetery, Croton, N.Y.

STEIN, SYDNEY, JR., investment counsellor; b. Chgo., Oct. 24, 1901; s. Sydney and Clara (Meyer) S.; m. Jeannette Shambaugh, Jan. 7, 1936 (div. 1972); children: Nancy Stein Seasholes, Susan Stein Elmendorf, Edith Carol Stein; m. Nancy Lilley, Sept. 28, 1983. Ph.B., U. Chgo., 1923. With A.G. Becker & Co. (investment bankers), 1923-32; founder, investment counsel Sydney Stein, Jr. & Assos. (now Stein Roe & Farnham), 1932-late 70's; cons., adminstrv. and orgn. problems war supply and internat. relations Fed. Bur. Budget, Washington, 1941-45; chmn. bd., treas. Leich Electric Co., Genoa, Ill., 1945-50; dir. Stein Roe & Farnham Balanced Fund, Inc., 1948-76, Stein Roe & Farnham Capital Opportunities Fund, 1954-76, Stein Roe & Farnham Stock Fund, Inc., 1963-76; cons. to Pres. and dir. Bur. Budget on structure and ops. govt., 1961-67; Mem. Adv. Com. Pvt. Enterprise in Fgn. Aid, 1964-65; mem. Pres.'s Spl. Panel Fed. Salaries, 1965, Randall Adv. Panel on Fed. Pay Systems, 1961-63. Life trustee U. Chgo.; trustee Brookings Instn., Washington, 1960-91, vice chmn. bd., 1967-71. Sydney Stein Jr. Chair in Internat. Security established in his honor Brookings Inst. Mem. Phi Beta Kappa. Clubs: Tavern (Chgo.), Quadrangle (Chgo.), Attic (Chgo.), Standard (Chgo.), Mid-America (Chgo.), Commercial (Chgo.), Arts (Chgo.), Chicago (Chgo.); Cosmos (Washington). Home: Chicago Ill. Died Oct. 2, 1991; cremated.

STEINER, RICHARD LEWIS, urban planner; b. Balt., Nov. 4, 1913; s. Bernard Christian and Ethel (Mulligan) S.; m. Madeline Kelser Sadler, Jan. 17, 1969 (wid. Aug. 1988); children by former marriage: David, Roland, Carol, Stephen (dec.). BCE, Yale U., 1936; M in City Planning, MIT, 1939; postgrad., Harvard U., Johns Hopkins U. Registered profl. engr., Md. Cons. Town Planning Bd., Lexington, Mass., 1938; rural rd. inventory and traffic analyst Conn. Hwy. Dept., Hartford, 1938; project planner U.S. Housing Authority, Washington, 1938-41; dir. Balt. Redevel. Commn., 1946-54; dep. commr. Urban Renewal Adminstrn. HHFA, Washington, 1954-57, commr., 1957-59; dir. Balt. Urban Renewal and Housing Agy., 1959-67; spl. cons. to sec. HUD, 1967-68; prof. city planning Howard U., Washington, 1968-70; vis. prof. community planning Sch. Social Work and Community Planning U. Md. at Balt., 1970-74, planning asst. to univ. chancellor, 1974-78, urban cons., 1968-82; past mem. Mt. Vernon Pl. Archtl. Adv. Commn.; vis. lectr. city planning and urban renewal U. Pitts., Johns Hopkins U., U. N.C., MIT, Md. Inst. Art, Grad. Sch. U.S. Dept. Agr., NYU, Practicing Law Inst. Past bd. dirs. Nat. Housing Conf., Union Meml. Hosp., Balt.; past v.p. Balt. Neighborhoods, Inc.; past v.p. and bd. dirs. Transitional Living Council Cen. Md.; v.p., bd. dirs. Family and Children's Services of Cen. Md., Balt.; past mem. planning adv. com. U. Md. Hosp., Balt.; mem. Sherwood Gardens Com., Guilford Assn., Balt.; bd. dirs., past pres. Md. Ptnrs. of the Alliance; past mem. housing com. Md. Commn. on Aging; past mem. Balt. Mayor's Task Force on Population Migration, Balt. Area Housing Council; former mem. adv. commn. Problems Met. Soc. United Presbyn. Ch. of U.S.A.; emeritus mem. bd. visitors, past 1st v.p., chmn. exec. com. Md. State Sch. Deaf; hon. trustee Balt. Mus. Art, pres., 1969-71; past pres., hon. bd. mem. Md. Sch. for Deaf Found.; mem. Annapolis, Md. Power Squadron; elder, former deacon and trustee First and Franklin St. Presbyn. Ch., Balt. Served from ensign to lt. comdr. C.E.C., USNR, 1941-45. Fellow ASCE (pres. Md. sect. 1965); mem. Engring. Soc. Balt., Md. Assn. Engrs., Am. Inst. Cert. Planners (past pres. Washington and Balt. chpts., Disting. Service award 1977), Nat. Assn. Housing and Redevel. Ofcls. (past gov., M. Justin Herman Disting. Service award 1975), Am. Planning Assn., MIT City Planning Alumni Assn. (past pres.), Tau Beta Pi, Lambda Alpha, Sigma Xi (assoc.). Clubs: 14 W. Hamilton St., Ctr. (Balt.); Mory's (New Haven); Johns Hopkins. Home: Baltimore Md. Died Dec. 13, 1989; buried Mt. Olivet Cemetery, Frederick, Md.

STEINGUT, STANLEY, state legislator; b. Bklyn., May 20, 1920; s. Irwin and Rae (Kaufman) S.; m. Madeline Fellerman, May 30, 1943; children: Robert, Theodore, Ilene. Student, Union Coll., 1943; LLD, LLB, St. John's U., 1948. Bar: N.Y. Pvt. practice law Bklyn.; mem. N.Y. State Assembly, 1953-89, minority leader, 1969-74, Speaker of the Assembly, 1975-78; sr. patnr. Berger & Steingut, Manhattan; lectr. Union Coll.; chmn. exec. com. Kings County Dem. Com., 1962-69. Bd. dirs. Bklyn. Jewish Ctr.; trustee Unity Club Bklyn, Bklyn. Jewish Med. Ctr. Served in USN. Chubb fellow Yale, New Haven. Mem. Nat. Conf. Legis. Leaders, N.Y., Bklyn. bar assns., Jewish War Vets, Madison, Nat. Dem. clubs. Home: Brooklyn N.Y. Died Dec. 8, 1989.

STEINKE, PAUL KARL WILLI, microbiologist; b. Friedeberg, Germany, July 13, 1921; came to U.S., 1925, naturalized, 1932; s. George Willey and Selma Ida (Hartel) S.; m. Alma Louise Winkler, Aug. 17, 1944; children: Kristine, Lynda, Mark. Student, Purdue U., 1943; B.S., U. Wis., 1947, M.S., 1948, Ph.D., 1951. Research asst. U. Wis., 1947-49, teaching asst., 1949-50; food bacteriologist Chain Belt Co., Milw., 1951-56; dir. microbiol. Paul-Lewis Co., Milw., 1956-62; mgr. tech.

services Pfizer Inc., N.Y.C., 1962-64, mgr. market devel., 1964-72; tech. dir. Pfizer Inc., Milw., 1972-86. Served with USNR, 1943-46. Mem. Master Brewers Assn. Ams., Am. Soc. Brewing Chemists, Am. Soc. Microbiology. Lutheran. Home: Milwaukee Wis. Died Apr. 25, 1989; buried Milwaukee, Wis.

STEINKRAUS, WARREN EDWARD, philosophy educator; b. Boston, Feb. 14, 1922; s. John Herman and Florence Louise (Rabe) S.; m. Barbara Annette Morris, July 15, 1948; 1 dau., Elizabeth. A.B., Baldwin-Wallace Coll., 1943, L.H.D., 1975; S.T.B., Boston U., 1946, Ph.D. (Jacob Sleeper fellow), 1952; postgrad., U. Iowa, 1957, Harvard U., 1961, Cambridge U., Eng., 1970, 84-85. Instr. English lit. Emerson Coll., 1946-49; instr. philosophy Cornell Coll., Mt. Vernon, Ia., 1949-50; instr. Depauw U., 1950-52, asst. prof., 1952-56; assoc. prof., chmn. dept. philosophy Iowa Wesleyan Coll., 1956-59; prof., head dept. philosophy Union Coll., Barbourville, Ky., 1959-64; prof. philosophy SUNY, Oswego, 1964-87, Faculty Exch. prof., 1975-87; vis. hon. prof. philosophy Benaras Hindu U., Varanasi, India, 1977-78; cons. Kraus Reprints, N.Y.C., 1966-68, Choice, 1968-90. Author: (with G. R. Malkani) Discussion of Karma, 1966, Philosophy of Art, 1974, reprinted 1984; contbg. author: Ency. of Philosophy, 1967, The Critique of War, 1969, Hegel & The Philosophy of Religion, 1970, The Abdication of Philosophy, 1976, Creativity in Art, Religion and Culture, 1985, Possibility of the Aesthetic Experience, 1986, Religion and Philosophy in the U.S.A., 1987, others; editor: (with K. Schmitz) Art and Logic in Hegel's Philosophy, 1980; music editor Motive Mag, 1943-46; editor Philos. Forum, 1947; editor and contbr.: New Studies in Berkeley's Philosophy, 1966, reprinted 1981, Representative Essays of Borden Parker Bowne, 1980; editor: New Studies in Hegel's Philosophy, 1971; lit. editor then rev. editor: Idealistic Studies, 1974-89; editorial bd. Jour. Social Philosophy, 1981-89, The Personalist Forum, 1985-89; co-editor: (with R. N. Beck) Studies in Personalism, 1988; contbr. numerous articles to profl. jours. Active Oswego Civic Orch. and Chorus, 1964-89.. SUNY summer research fellow, 1966, 67; SUNY grantee, 1965, 68, 75; Am. Council Learned Socs. Travel grantee, 1972, 75; NEH vis. philosopher grantee, 1972, 73. Mem. Am. Philos. Assn., Metaphys. Soc. Am., Hegel Soc. Am. (v.p. 1968-70, mem. exec. council 1976-78), Am. Aesthetics Soc., Fellowship of Reconciliation, Gandhi-King Soc. (co-chmn., co-founder, editor newsletter 1980-89)., Phi Mu Alpha Sinfonia. Democrat. Mem. Troy Conf. United Methodist Ch. Home: Oswego N.Y. Died Feb. 19, 1990; buried Riverside Cemetery, Oswego, N.Y.

STEINLE, JOHN GERARD, lawyer, health organization executive, executive; b. Havre, Mont., Nov. 8, 1916; s. Francis X. and Ada L. (de Lorimier) S.; BS, St. Mary's Coll., 1936; MA, U. So. Calif., 1937; LLB, St. Louis City Coll. Law, 1941; MS, Syracuse U., 1947; m. Joan E. Sinnott, Aug. 14, 1945, (div. June 1972); children: Susan Bebko, Elizabeth McFarland, Gretchen Prater, Jacquelynn Leisos, Abbe Anne Finn, Robyn; m. Bianca Santisteban, July 15, 1972. Adminstr. St. Louis City Infirmary, 1939-42; chief hosp. adminstrn. sect. USPHS, Washington, 1947-51, hosp. program dir., N.Y.C., 1951-54; pres. John G. Steinle & Assocs., Garden City, N.Y., 1954-70, Health Orgns., Systems and Planning Corp., Garden City, 1970-75, John G. Steinle and Assocs., Inc., 1975-90; gen. counsel Face Up Profl. Skin Care Ctrs., Inc., Newport Beach, Calif., 1985-90. Lectr. hosp. adminstrn. Columbia, 1952-59. Trustees Adelphi U., Garden City, 1953-62; chmn. bd. Madison Park Hosp., Bklyn., 1955-61. Served with AUS, 1942-46. Decorated Silver Star, Purple Heart. Mem. Assn. Med. Colls., AIA, Acad. Hosp. Cons. (pres. 1964-66), Internat. Hosp. Assn., Princeton Club (N.Y.C.). Author: (with Ivan Belknap) The Community and Its Hospitals, 1963; contbr. numerous articles to profl. jours.; editor: Health and Hosp. Encys., 1974; cons. editor Hosp. Topics Mag. Died Sept. 19, 1990 Home: Fort Lee N.J.

STENHOUSE, EVANGELINE E., physician; b. LaSalle, Ill., May 15, 1893; d. Thomas and Hannah (Ulrich) S. PhB, U. Chgo., 1916; MD, Rush Med. Coll., 1931; postgrad., U. Chgo., 1932-35. Diplomate Nat. Bd. Med. Examiners, AM. Bd. Dermatology and Syphilology. Tchr. home econs. Twp. High Sch., Grand Rapids, Minn., 1916-18; edn. sec. ctrl. bd. Y.W.C.A., Chgo., 1919-21; dir. Putnam Sch. Y.W.C.A., Grand Rapids, 1921-25; intern Swedish Covenant Hosp., Chgo., 1931-32; dermatologist student health svcs. U. Chgo., 1935-40; dermatologist, syphilologist pvt. practice, from 1935; instr. dept. dermatology U. Chgo., 1940-43; cons. in field; dermatology clinic staff mem. MAry Thompson Hosp., pres. med. staff, 1958-59. Mem. AMA, Am. MEd. Women's Assn. (pres.), Acad. Dermatology and Syphilology, Soc. Investigative Dermatology, Sigma Delta Epsilon. Baptist. *

STEPHAN, ROBERT DOWNS, construction supplies company executive; b. Chgo., Feb. 8, 1905; s. John Edward and Lettie A. (Downs) S.; m. Virginia Delehanty, Oct. 19, 1929; children—Roxanne (Mrs. R.R. O'Brien), Ellen Virginia (Mrs. R.A. Hunziker), Patricia (Mrs. Lynn Harshbarger), Mary Bob, Penelope (Mrs. Anthony Cuttone). A.B., U. Notre Dame, 1927. With U.S. Gypsum Co., Chgo., 1934-71, from credit mgr to dist. mgr., 1939-41, div. sales mgr., 1941-44, mdse. mgr., 1944-48, dealer sales mgr., 1948-53, v.p., 1953-71; Cons. in field, from 1971. Author: Selling Large Accounts. Mem. McGraw Wildlife Found. Clubs: Union League (Chgo.), Notre Dame (Chgo.); Barrington (Ill.) Hills Country. Home: Barrington Ill. Died Oct. 21, 1989.

STEPHENSON, CLARENCE BRUCE, banker; b. Portland, Oreg., May 25, 1895; s. George C. and Mary E. (Bruce) S.; m. Catherine Vernon Slaighter, June 12, 1924; children: Barbara Vernon, Dorothy Elizabeth, MArjorie Jean. LLB, U. Oreg., 1917; postgrad., HArvard U., 1921-22. Bar: Oreg. 1920. Assoc. Prescott Cookingham Atty.; atty. Ladd & Tilton Bank, Portland, 1920-21, asst. to sr. v.p., 1923-25, mgr. liquidation, 1925-28; spl. agt. New England Mut. Life Ins. Co., Portland, 1928-29; exec. v.p. Security Savings & Trust Co., Portland, 1930-32; v.p. 1st Nat. Bank Oreg., Portland, 1932-53, pres., 1953-60, chmn. bd. dirs., from 1960; dir. Oreg. Portland Cement Co. Former dir. United Fund, past pres., past dir., 1938; ca,paign chmn. Portland Community Chest; trustee Reed Coll. With A.E.F., WW I. Named Portland's Sr. 1st Citizen, 1953. Mem. Oreg. Hist. Soc. (dir.), Libr. Assn. Portland (past pres.), Oreg. Heart Assn., Rotary (past pres.), City Club (past. pres.), Arlington Club (past dir.), Waverly Country Club (Portland). Republican. Presbyterian. *

STERN, ARTHUR CECIL, environmental engineer, educator; b. Petersburg, Va., Mar. 14, 1909; s. Harry Abraham and Marie Leah (Rosenstock) S.; m. Dorothy Henrietta Anspacher, 1937 (dec. 1975); children—Richard Cecil, Elizabeth Ann Stern Grenwold, Robert Cecil; m. Katherine Humphrey Barbour Perlman, Oct. 30, 1976. M.E., Stevens Inst. Tech., Hoboken, N.J., 1930, M.S., 1933, D.Engring. (hon.), 1975. Registered prof. engr., N.C.; diplomate Am. Bd. Indsl. Hygiene, Am. Bd. Environ. Engring. Instr. Stevens Acad. Tech., 1930-33; supt. air pollution survey N.Y.C. Dept. Health, 1933-35; chief engr. N.Y. State Dept. Labor, N.Y.C., 1940-55; asst. dir. USPHS, Washington, 1955-68; prof. U. N.C. Chapel Hill, 1968-78; prof. emeritus Chapel Hill, 1978-92; Mem. environ. awards panel Am. Paper Inst., N.Y.C., from 1980; exchange scientist Czechoslavak Acad. Scis., Prague, 1982, 83. Co-author: Fundamentals of Air Pollution, 1984; editor: Air Pollution, 1977, 86. Recipient C.E. Barthel award Internat. Union Air Pollution Prevention Assns., 1983, Lynan Ruppertau award Am. Waste Mgmt. Assn., 1991. Fellow Air Pollution Control Assn. (pres. 1975-76, R.B. Mellon award 1970); mem. ASME (emeritus), Am. Acad. Environ. Engrs. (hon. diplomate, Gordon M. Fair award 1983), Tau Beta Pi (Eminent Engr. award 1991). Home: Chapel Hill N.C. Died Apr. 17, 1992.

STERN, MILTON H., lawyer, business consultant; b. Newark, Mar. 27, 1924; s. Louis Stern and Sabina (Goldenberg) Lieberman; m. Susanne Hannoch, Mar. 27, 1947 (div. May 1972); m. Joan Helen Curran, Aug. 17, 1972; children: Andrew, Kenneth, Thomas, Patricia, Ellen. AB, Lafayette Coll., 1943; LLB, Columbia U., 1948. Bar: N.J. 1948, U.S. Tax Ct. 1951. Tax specialist J. K. Lasser & Co., N.Y.C., 1948-52; ptnr. Hannoch Weisman, Roseland, N.J., from 1953; bd. dirs. Value Realty Co.; trustee Laurie Found., New Brunswick, N.J. Author: Inside the Family-Held Business, 1986, Inside the Family-Held Insurance Agency, 1989; contbr. numerous articles to profl. jours. Chmn. Essex County chpt. Am. Jewish Com., Millburn, N.J., 1970-71; v.p. Mental Health Assn. Essex County, East Orange, N.J. Harlan Fiske Stone scholar, 1947, 48. Mem. ABA, N.J. State Bar Assn., Essex County Bar Assn. Jewish. Home: Livingston N.J. Deceased. †

STERN, PHILIP MAURICE, author, philanthropist; b. N.Y.C., May 24, 1926; s. Edgar Bloom and Edith (Rosenwald) S.; m. Helen Phillips Burroughs Sedgwick, Aug. 30, 1957; children: Henry D., Michael P., Helen P., David M., Eve; m. Nellie L. Gifford, June 14, 1975; m. Helen Markel, Feb. 9, 1980. A.B. magna cum laude, Harvard, 1947; postgrad., Georgetown U. Law Center, 1975-76; L.H.D. (hon.), Colgate U., 1974. Reporter, editorial writer New Orleans Item, 1948; legislative asst. U.S. Rep. Henry M. Jackson, 1949-50, U.S. Senator Paul Douglas, 1951-52; personal asst. Wilson W. Wyatt, campaign mgr. to Adlai E. Stevenson, 1952; dir. research Democratic Nat. Com., also sr. editor Dem. Digest, 1953-56; editor No. Va. Sun, Arlington, 1957-60, editor, pub., 1960; dep. asst. sec. of state for pub. affairs, 1961-62, mag. writer, author, 1962-92; spl. assignment reporter, nat. staff Washington Post, 1974-75; founder Fund for Investigative Journalism, 1968, Stern Community Law Firm, Stern Concern., 1970, Ctr. for Pub. Financing of Campaigns, 1975-76, Citizens for Common Sense in Nat. Def., 1982, Ams. for Fair Elections, 1983, Project for Investigative Journalism on Money in Politics, 1983; founder, co-chmn. Citizens Against PACs, 1984; Commentator In the Public Interest, 1979-85, Nat. Pub. Radio, 1985. Author: The Great Treasury Raid, 1964, (with George de Vincent) The Shame of a Nation, 1966, (with Helen B. Stern) Oh, Say Can You See: A Bifocal Tour of Washington, 1966, The Oppenheimer Case: Security on Trial, 1969, The Rape of the Taxpayer, 1973, Lawyers on Trial, 1980, The Best Congress Money Could Buy, 1988, also numerous articles various publs. including N.Y. Times, Washington Post. Del. Democratic Nat. Conv., 1968; dir. Council on Founds., 1964-69; Pres. Stern Fund, 1963-76, Philip M. Stern Family Fund., 1969-92. Rockefeller fellow, 1948-49. Mem. Phi Beta Kappa. Home: Washington D.C. Died June 1, 1992.

STERNE, EMMA GELDERS, author, editor; b. Birmingham, Ala., May 13, 1894; d. Louis and Blanche (Loeb) Gelders; m. Roy M. Sterne, Mar. 7, 1917; children: Ann, Barbara. BA, Smith Coll., 1916; student, Grad. Sch. Columbia, 1922, 29. Author: White Swallow, 1927, Blue Pigeons, 1929, Loud Sing Cuckoo, 1930, No Surrender, 1932, Amarantha Gay, M.D., 1933, The Calico Ball, 1934, Drums of Monmouth, 1935, Far Town Road, 1935, Miranda is a Princess, 1936, Some Plant Olive Trees, 1937, European Summer, 1938, The Pirate of Chatham Square, 1939, America Was Like This, 1941, We Live to be Free, 1942, Incident in Yorkville, 1943, Printer's Devil, 1952, Long Black Schooner, 1953, Let The Moon Go By, 1955, Golden Book adaptations of Moby DIck and Little Women, 1956, Biography of Mary McLeod Bethune, 1958, Blood Brothers, from Harvey to Drew, 1959, Balboa, 1961, (with Barbara Lindsay) The Sea, 1959, Stories from Old and New Testament, 1959, King Arthur Legends, 1962, They Took Their Stand, 1964, I Have A Dream, 1965; also short stories and plays. Recipient $500 prize for children's play, 1931. Democrat. *

STETTEN, DEWITT, JR., biochemist; b. N.Y.C., May 31, 1909; s. DeWitt and Magdalen (Ernst) S.; m. Marjorie Roloff, Feb. 7, 1941 (dec. 1983); children: Gail, Nancy, Mary Stetten Carson, George; m. Jane Klein Lazarow, Aug. 5, 1984; stepchildren: Normand H. Lazarow, Paul B. Lazarow. BA, Harvard U., 1930; MD, Columbia U., 1934, PhD, 1940; DSc (hon.), Washington U., St. Louis, 1974, Coll. Medicine & Dentistry N.J., 1976, Worcester Found. for Exptl. Biology, 1979. Intern 3d med. div. Bellevue Hosp., N.Y.C., 1934-37; instr., asst. prof. biochemistry Columbia U. Coll. Physicians and Surgeons, N.Y.C., 1940-47; assoc. in medicine Peter Bent Brigham Hosp., Boston, 1947-49; asst. prof. biol. chemistry Harvard U. Med. Sch., Boston, 1947-48; chief div. nutrition and physiology N.Y.C. Pub. Health Rsch. Inst., 1948-54; assoc. dir. in charge rsch. Nat. Inst. Arthritis and Metabolic Diseases, NIH, Bethesda, Md., 1954-62; dean Rutgers Med. Sch., New Brunswick, N.J., 1962-70; dir. Nat. Inst. Gen. Med. Scis., NIH, Bethesda, 1970-74; dep. dir. for sci. NIH, Bethesda, 1974-79, sr. sci. adv. to dir., 1979-86, emeritus dep. dir. for sci., 1986-90; mem. subcom. liver diseases NRC, 1948-49, panel intermediary metabolism, com. on growth, 1948-52, chmn. panel, 1950, mem. exec. bd. div. med. scis., 1965-69; cons. Walter Reed Army Med. Ctr., 1948-53; chmn. rsch. com. N.Y. Diabetes Assn., 1951-52; cons., mem. study com. NIH, 1952-53; mem. adv. com. health rsch. facilities and resources; mem. adv. coun. dept. biology Princeton U.; chmn. nat. adv. com. Okla. Found. Med. Rsch., 1966; chmn. nat. sci. adv. com. Roche Inst. Molecular Biology, 1966-70. Author: (with others) Principles of Biochemistry, 1954, 2d edit., 1959; mem. editorial bd. Sci. and Perspectives in Biology and Medicine; also articles. Trustee N.J. Mental Health R & D Bd.; bd. dirs. Found. for Advanced Edn. in Scis., pres., 1973; mem. vis. com. Oklahoma City Campus, U. Okla.; bd. visitors Grad. Sch. Pub. Health, U. Pitts. Recipient Joseph Mather Smith prize Columbia U., 1943, Alvarenga prize Phila. Coll. Physicians, 1954, Banting medal Am. Diabetes Assn., 1957, gold medal for disting. achievement in medicine Columbia U. Coll. Physicians and Surgeons, 1974, Superior Svc. award HEW, 1976; Woodrow Wilson fellow, from 1979. Mem. NAS (coun. 1976-79), AAAS (chmn. sect. on medicine and v.p. 1962), Am. Acad. Arts and Scis., Am. Chem. Soc., Am. Soc. Biol. Chemists, N.Y. Acad. Scis., Harvey Soc., Soc. Exptl. Biology and Medicine (pres. 1977-79), Washington Acad. Medicine, Med. Soc. N.J., Phi Beta Kappa, Sigma Xi, Alpha Omega Alpha. Home: Bethesda Md. Died Aug. 28, 1990; buried Ch. of Messiah, Woods Hole, Mass.

STEVENS, AMES, textile executive; b. Lowell, Mass., May 31, 1897; s. Charles Brooks and Edith (Ames) S.; m. Phyllis Broosk, June 25, 1921; children: Edward Brooks, George, Priscilla, Ames Jr. AB, Harvard, 1919. Textile mfg., from 1919; pres., treas. Ames Worsted Co., Lowell; chmn., treas. Ames Textile Corp., N.Y.C.; pres. Whittier Mills Co., Chattahoechee, Ga.; treas. Maine Spinning Co., Skowhegan; v.p. Lawrence Mfg. Co., Lowell; asst. dir. of wool div. W.P.B., 1944; wool cons. O.P.A., 1942-46, O.P.S., 1951, O.Q.M.G., 1951; mem. wool com. Munitions Bd., from 1948; chmn. wool com. Q.M. Assn., from 1947. Mem. bus. com. Boy Scouts Am. Decorated Army medal of Freedom. Mem. Nat. Assn. Wool Mfrs. (dir.). *

STEVENS, EDMUND WILLIAM, journalist; b. Denver, July 22, 1910; s. Edmund William and Florence (Ballance) S.; m. Nina Andreyevna Bondarenko, Mar. 14, 1935; children: Edmund, Anastasia (Marchesa Ferrari di Collesape). BA, Columbia U., 1932, postgrad. govt. internat. law, 1932-33; student Russian, Moscow U., 1934. Translator Moscow pub. house, 1935-37, Am.-Russian C. of C.; fgn. corr. Manchester Guardian Daily Herald, London, 1937-39, Reuters, summer 1938; Moscow rep. Cunard-White Star Line, 1938; fgn. corr. Christian Sci. Monitor, Riga, Latvia, 1939; covered

Finnish War, invasion of Norway, Rumania, 1940, Italo-Greek War, 1940-41; Ethiopian campaign with Wingate, Haile Selassie, 1941; with Brit. 8th Army in Western Desert, 1942-43; accompanied Churchill and Harriman to Moscow as spl. adviser to Gen. Russell Maxwell, Aug. 1942, Wendell Willkie through Mideast, 1942; war corr. in Russia, 1943-44; Moscow corr. Christian Sci. Monitor, 1946-49; chief Mediterranean News Bur., Hdqrs. in Rome, 1949-55; China corr. Look mag., 1954-56; chief Moscow bur. Time, Inc., 1956-63; syndicated columnist Newsday; also spl. corr. Soviet affairs Saturday Evening Post, 1963-68; corr. Sunday Times, London, 1964, London Times, 1973, Giornale nuovo, Milan, die Weltwoche, Zurich, 1978; radio reporter NBC News, 1971; sr. mem., dean of fgn. corrs. in Moscow for London Times, Giornale, Milan, Italy, other papers. Author: Russia is No Riddle, 1945, This is Russia Uncensored, 1950, North Africa Powder Keg, 1954, Living the History of Modern Russia, 1989. Decorated Africa Star Brit. War Office, 1939-45; Star, George medal King George VI, Eng., 1945; recipient citiation U.S. War Dept., 1943, Pulitzer prize for internat. reporting, 1950, citation for excellence Overseas Press Club, 1956-58, George Polk Meml. award L.I. U., 1958. Mem. Overseas Press Club, Associazione della Stampa Estera (Rome), Delta Phi. Home: Moscow Russia Died May 24, 1992; inurned; Peredelkino, Russia.

STEVENS, EDWARD JOHN, JR., artist; b. Jersey City, Feb. 4, 1923; s. Edward John and Genevieve (Grosel) S.; m. Joan V. Fox, July 27, 1982. B.A., State Tchrs. Coll., Newark, 1943; M.A., Tchrs. Coll. Columbia U., 1944. Instr. Newark Sch. Fine and Indsl. Art, 1947-59, dir., 1959-88. One-man shows including, Weyhe Gallery, N.Y.C., Honolulu Acad. Arts, Balt. Mus. Art, Whitte Mus., Tex.; represented in permanent collection, Whitney Mus. Am. Art, N.Y.C., Chgo. Art Inst., also 45 other museums. Mem. Audubon Artists. Home: Wood Ridge N.J. Died Nov. 17, 1988.

STEVENS, HOLLY, author, editor; b. Hartford, Conn., Aug. 10, 1924; d. Wallace and Elsie Viola (Kachel) S.; m. John Martin Hanchak, Aug. 5, 1944 (div. Sept. 1951); 1 son, Peter Reed Hanchak; m. Duncan Stephenson, Aug. 24, 1957 (div. Dec. 1965). Student, Vassar Coll., 1941-42, U. Conn., 1951-53. Fire underwriter Aetna Life Affiliated Cos., Hartford, 1942-46; purchasing asst. Trinity Coll., Hartford, 1955-64; sec. Yale U., 1966-68; advt. mgr. Yale Rev., 1968-69, bus. mgr., 1969-77; cons. Conn. Public Radio, 1979; founder, dir. New Eng. Poetry Circuit, 1963-68; founder, dir. Conn. Poetry Circuit, 1968-72, mem. selection com., from 1972; founding mem. Poetry Center Trinity Coll. Author: Souvenirs and Prophecies: The Young Wallace Stevens, 1977; editor: Letters of Wallace Stevens, 1966, 67, The Palm at the End of The Mind: Selected Poems and a Play by Wallace Stevens, 1971; contbr. to So. Rev., Hudson Rev., others. Bd. dirs. New Haven Symphony Orch., 1975-85, asst. sec., 1980-83. Timothy Dwight Coll. fellow, 1971; fellow Pierpont Morgan Library, 1979-82; Ingram Merrill Found. grantee, 1964; Supplemental award, 1965; Nat. Endowment for Humanities sr. fellow, 1972-73. Clubs: Elizabethan, Mory's (Yale). Home: Guilford Conn. Died Mar. 4, 1992.

STEVENS, PRESTON STANDISH, architect; b. Pike County, Miss., Jan. 28, 1896; s. Augustin Washburn and Caroline (Ulmer) S.; m. Hermoine Ross Walkr, Dec. 10, 1928; 1 child, Preston Standish. Student, Miss. Coll., 1913-15, Ga. Inst. Tech., 1919. Pvt. practice Atlanta, 1919-89; hon. chmn. fin. com. Stevens & Wilkinson, architects and engrs., Inc. Prin. works include Ga. Bapt. Hosp., Atlanta, 1920-89, Rich's Inc., Richway Stores, 1950-89, E. Rivers Elem. Sch., Atlanta, 1950, Ga. Ctr. for Continuing Edn., Athens, 1958; architect Techwood Housing Project, Atlanta, 1st slum clearance project in U.S., 1935, Citco office bldg., Tulsa, 1973, Tower Pl., Atlanta, 1975, Bapt. Village, Waycross, Canterbury Ct., Atlanta; contbr. articles to profl. jours. Fellow AIA; mem. Capital City Club (life), Peidmont Driving Club. Home: Atlanta Ga. Died Aug. 29, 1989.

STEVENS, RUBY See STANWYCK, BARBARA

STEWART, DONALD OGDEN, author, actor; b. Columbus, Ohio, Nov. 30, 1894; s. Gilbert Hollans and Clara Lanfon (Ogden) S.; m. Beatrice Amos, July 24, 1926 (div. Sept. 1938); children: Ames Ogden, Donald Ogden Jr.; m. Ella Winter Steffens, Mar. 4, 1939. Appeared in Holiday, N.Y.C., 1928-29, Rebound, 1930; author of numerous books, from 1921, 3 plays and musical comedy; screen plays include Life With Father, Without Love, Cass Timberlane, Edward My Son, The Kidders, 1951 (play prod. London 1957, 58, Hamburg 1958, Acad. award Winner Best Screenplay 1971). Seaman USN, WW I. Mem. Delta Kappa Epsilon. *

STEWART, HAROLD JULIAN, physician; b. Accomac, Va., Feb. 17, 1896; s. Preston Savage and Catherine Sarah (Williams) S. AB, Johns Hopkins, 1915, AM, 1923, MD, 1919. Diplomate Am. Bd. Internal Medicine. Intern, resident house physician St. Luke's Hosp., 1919-21, Bingham fellow in medicine, Johns Hopkins, 1921-22; asst. physician Johns Hopkins Hosp., 1921-22; asst. resident physician Hosp. of Rockefeller Inst. for Med. Rsch., 1922-28, resident physician, 1928-29, asst. in medicine, 1922-29, assoc. in medicine, 1929-32, heart specialist, from 1922; mem. faculty Cornell Med. Coll., from 1932; attending physician N.Y. Hosp., 1932-61, cons. physician, from 1961; chief Cardiac Clinic, 1932-61; head cardiac div., dept. medicine Cornell Med. Coll., head cardiac div., dept. medicine Cornell Med. Coll.-N.Y. Hosp. Ctr., 1932-61; prof. of clin. medicine Cornell U. Med. Coll., 1959-61, prof. emeritus, from 1961; formerly cons., prin. scientist, med. dept. Brookhaven Nat. Labs. Assn. Univs., assoc. chief examiner Nat. Bd. Med. Examiners. Author: Cardiac Therapy, 1952, Cardiac Arrhythmias in Cecil and Loeb's Textbook of Medicine, 1955, Chronic Constrictive Pericarditis in Nelson's Loose Leaf Medicine, 1951, Chronic Constrictive Pericarditis in Disorders of the Heart and Circulation, edited by Levy, 1952, Mitral Valvulotomy (with Stewart and Glenn), 1959; sci. com. ACTA Cardiologica; contbr. sci. articles to profl. publs. Fellow ACP, AMA; mem. Am. Heart Assn., N.Y. Heart Assn. (dir.), N.Y. State Med. Soc., N.Y. County Med. Soc.s., N.Y. Acad. Medicine, Nat. Inst. Social Scis., N.Y. Clin. Soc. (pres. 1958-59), N.Y. Med. and Surg. Soc. (pres. 1963-64), Phi Beta Kappa, Nu Sigma Nu, Clubs: Contemporary, Century Assn., Union, The Pilgrims. *

STEWART, IRVIN, public administration educator; b. Fort Worth, Oct. 27, 1899; s. William Henry and Sarah Aline (Howell) S.; m. Florence E. Dezendorf, July 31, 1926; 1 son, Richard Edwin. Student, U. Okla., 1917-19; LL.B., U. Tex., 1920, A.B., A.M., 1922; Ph.D., Columbia, 1926; LL.D., Waynesburg, 1946, W.Va. Wesleyan, 1948, W.Va. State Coll., 1948, Marshall Coll., 1953; Litt.D., Bethany Coll., 1954. Instr. govt. U. Tex., Austin, 1922-25, adj. prof., 1925-26, assoc. prof., 1928-29; asst. solicitor U.S. Dept. State, Washington, D.C., 1926-28; prof., head dept. govt. Am. U. Grad. Sch., Washington, 1929-30; tchr. summer sessions Duke U., Durham, N.C., Columbia U., N.Y.C., UCLA; in charge elec. communications, treaty div. Dept. State, Washington, 1930-34; mem. Am. delegations internat. radio confs. Washington, 1927, Copenhagen, 1931, Madrid, 1932, Mexico City, 1933; to Pan-Am. Comml. Conf., Washington, 1931, Internat. Telegraph Conf., Madrid, 1932; mem. FCC, Washington; chmn. telegraph div. FCC, 1934-37, vice chmn. commn., 1935-37; dir. Com. on Sci. Aids to Learning, 1937-46; exec. sec. Nat. Def. Research Com., 1940-45, OSRD, Com. on Med. Research (Office for Emergency Mgmt.), 1941-45; dep. dir. OSRD, 1946; pres. W.Va. U., Morgantown, 1946-58, prof. govt., 1958-67; cons. Nat. Acad. Pub. Adminstrn., from 1967; on leave as dir. telecommunications mgmt. Exec. Office Pres., 1962-63; Chmn. Pres.'s Communications Policy Bd., 1950; nat. com. Devel. Scientists and Engrs., 1956; nat. adv. com. for Rural Def., 1956; chmn. Am. delegation Internat. Conf. on Orgn. and Adminstrn. Applied Research, 1956; mem. W.Va. Commn. on Constl. Revision, 1957-62. Author: Consular Privileges and Immunities, 1926, Organizing Scientific Research for War, 1948; Editor: Radio, 1929. Mem. Bd. Edn. Am. Bapt. Conv., 1952-58. Recipient Pres.'s Medal for Merit, 1948; Humanities award W.Va. B'nai B'rith. Mem. Am. Assn. Land Grant Colls. and State Univs. (pres. 1956), Am. Soc. Pub. Adminstrn., Am. Polit. Sci. Assn., Phi Beta Kappa, Phi Delta Phi, Pi Sigma Alpha. Democrat. Baptist. Clubs: Century (N.Y.C.); Cosmos (Washington). Home: Washington D.C. Died Dec. 26, 1990; cremated.

STEWART, ISAAC MITTON, lawyer, former chemical company executive, rancher; b. Salt Lake City, Dec. 30, 1904; s. Charles Biekley and Katherine (Romney) S.; m. June Woodruff, Dec. 16, 1927; children: Isaac Mitton, Charles Owen, June, Helen (Mrs. Richard B. Bennett), Wilford. Student, UCLA, 1923-24; J.D. with honors, George Washington U., 1928. Bar: Utah 1931, D.C. 1933. Adminstrv. asst. to Hon. Reed Smoot, U.S. senator from Utah, 1928-32; spl. asst. U.S. Senate Com. Finance, 1926-32; practiced law Washington, 1933-36; v.p. Union Carbide Corp., 1949-67, cons., 1967-81; dir., officer various corps.; dir. Consol. Freightways, Inc., 1958-83, cons., 1983-84; Owner Stewart Ranch, Kamas, Utah. Pres. Salt Lake (Mormon) Tabernacle Choir, 1962-75; Mem. adv. com. Senate Interstate and Fgn. Commerce Com. in a study fgn. trade; chmn. bus. and industry com. Nat. Citizens Commn. on Internat. Cooperation. Recipient George Washington U. Alumni Achievement award in law and pub. service, 1965. Mem. Am. Pioneer Trails Assn., Inc. (mem. adv. council), Am. Mothers Com., Inc. (adv. board), Phi Alpha Delta. Mem. LDS Ch. Home: Midway UT Deceased. †

STEWART, JAMES, insurance executive; b. Germany, Nov. 25, 1912; s. Cecil Parker and Reine Marie Melanie (Tracy) S.; m. Martha Stewart, May 18, 1970; children: Tracy, James Cecil, Reine Elizabeth, Barry, China. Student, Harvard U., 1931. Salesman Electrolux Co., Los Angeles, Qui Soit Perfume, N.Y.C.; runner, stock clk. statis. dept. Bancamerica Blair Corp., N.Y.C., 1932-33; with classified advt. dept. New York Times; longshoreman Houston, Los Angeles, San Francisco, 1934; with publicity dept., cruise dir. French Line, N.Y.C., 1934-36; asst. marine mgr., br. mgr., br. supt., supt. ins. Am. Asiatic Underwriters, Shanghai, 1936-37, Hanoi and Saigon, 1938-39; sec., dir., supt. ins. Cie Franco-Americaine D'Assurances, 1936-39; embassy corr. for Paris-Soir, 1939; v.p. Frank B. Hall & Co., Inc., N.Y.C., 1939-42, ptnr., v.p., sec., chmn. and chief exec. officer, chmn. exec. com., 1945-78, also bd. dirs., 1945-84; bd. dirs. Am. Mcht. Marine S/S Corp., Am. Homestead, Inc. Served with AUS, 1942; to lt. (s.g.) USNR, 1942-45. Decorated Shanghai medal, Asiatic Pacific medal. Mem. Assn. Average Adjusters U.S., Am. Shipping Soc., Racquet and Tennis Club, The Brook Club, India House, Deepdale Golf Club, Everglades Club, Bath and Tennis Club, Sunningdale Golf Club, Lyford Cay Club, Southampton Club, The Bathing Cup of Southampton Club, Nat. Golf Links Am. Club. Republican. Home: New York N.Y. Died Sept. 15, 1991.

STEWART, MAXWELL SLUTZ, editor, economist; b. Johnstown, Pa., July 4, 1900; s. John Vincent and Maud (Slutz) S.; m. Marguerite Ann McKlveen, Aug. 17, 1928; 1 child, Luther Maxwell. AB, Allegheny Coll., 1921, LittD, 1940; postgrad., Norwestern U., 1921, Boston U., 1922-23; MA, Columbia U., 1926. Instr. Columbia Coll., Milton, Ore., 1921-22, Shanghai (China) Am. Sch., 1923-25, Yenching U., Peking, China, 1926-30; economist rsch. staff Fgn. Policy Assn., 1931-34; lectr New Sch. Social Rsch., 1935; assoc. editor The Nation, 1934-47; editor Pub. Affairs Pamphlets, 1935, editorial cons., 1970-90; sec. Pub. Affairs Com., 1951-90; editor pamphlet series Am. Coun., Inst. Pacific Rels., 1942-43, 46-48; lectr. econs. CCNY, 1938-41. Author: Social Security, 1937, rev. edit., 1939, (with Walter E. Meyer, William B. Brown) America in a World at War, 1942, Building for Peace at Home and Abroad, 1943, How Can We Stay Prosperous, 1958, The Taxes We Pay, 1959, That No Man Shall Hunger, 1960, Investing in Income and Security, 1961, the European Common Market and the United States, 1962, Finding Able Men and Women for City Careers, 1964; The Poor Among Us, 1964, Can We Save Our Cities?, 1965, A New Look at our Crowded World, 1966, What Inflation and Tight Money Means to You, 1968, Your 1970 Census, 1969, A Chance for Every Child, 1970, Money for Our Cities: Revenue Sharing the Answer, 1971, When People Need Help, 1973, Housing—A National Crisis, 1973, Food for the World's Hungry, 1974; editor: The Growing Family, 1955, Problems of Family Life and How to Meet Them, 1956; also series reports Fgn. Policy Assn., pamphlets Pub. Affairs Com.; contbr. articles to profl. jours. Cons. War Manpower Commn., 1943-44; mem. com. of experts Campaign for World Cooperation, 1938-39. Served with USMC, AEF, 1918-19. Recipient Disting. Svc. medal Tchrs. Coll., Columbia, 1974. Mem. Soc. of Friends. Home: Annandale NJ Died Mar. 27, 1990.

STEWART, ROBERT MCLEAN, business executive; b. Aylmer, Que., Can., 1895; Came to U.S., 1927, naturalized, 1937; s. Robert William and Henrietta (McLean) S.; m. Ruby Maud Moorman, July 18, 1942; children: MAry Elizabeth, Margaret Jean. Asst. sec. dept. soldiers civil re-establishment Govt. Can., 1918-27; investment banker Nat. City Co., Montreal, Que., Can.; also N.Y.C., 1927-34; v.p., dir. Harriman & Co., Inc., 1934-46; pres., dir. S.A. Mines Co., Inc. (ans assoc. firms), 1946-51; ptnr. William A. M. Burden & Co., 1949-62; mng. ptnr. Stewart, Fox & Winthrop, Houston, from 1957; ptnr. Fox., Wells and Rogers, from 1963; chmn., chief exec. officer Oil Participations, Inc., Austral Oil Co., Inc. (both Houston and N.Y.C.), Mine Mgmt. Inc., de Vegh Mut. Fund, Inc. Served with Can and British forces, 1914-18; exec. dir. pilot tng. C.A.A., Washington, 1942-44. Mem. Investment Bankers Assn. (former gov. and chmn. com. om securities act of 1933, indsl. securities), Coun. Fgn. Rels., Inc., Union League Club, Down Town Assn., Met. Club, Can. Club, Mining Club, Petroleum Club, Ramanda Club, River Oaks Club. *

STIGLER, GEORGE JOSEPH, economist, educator; b. Renton, Wash., Jan. 17, 1911; s. Joseph and Elizabeth (Hungler) S.; m. Margaret Mack, Dec. 26, 1936 (dec. Aug. 1970); children: Stephen, David, Joseph. BBA, U. Wash., 1931; MBA, Northwestern U., 1932; PhD, U. Chgo., 1938; ScD (hon.), Carnegie Mellon U., 1973, U. Rochester, 1974, Helsinki Sch. Econs., 1976, Northwestern U., 1979; LLD (hon.), Brown U., 1980; DHL (hon.), Columbia U., 1990. Asst. prof. econs. Iowa State Coll., Ames, 1936-38; asst. prof. U. Minn., Mpls., 1938-41, assoc. prof., 1941-44, prof., 1944-46; prof. Brown U., Providence, 1946-47; prof. econs. Columbia U., N.Y.C., 1947-58; Walgreen prof. Am. instns. U. Chgo., 1958-91, dir. ctr. study economy and the state, 1977-91; lectr. London Sch. Econs., 1948; vice chmn., bd. dirs. Securities Investor Protection Corp., 1971-74; bd. dirs. Chgo. Bd. Trade, 1980-83; mem. atty. gen.'s com. for study of antitrust laws; mem. Blue Ribbon Def. Panel. Author: Production and Distribution Theories, 1940, The Theory of Price, 1946, Trends in Output and Employment, 1947, Five Lectures on Economic Problems, 1949, (with K. Boulding) Readings in Price Theory, 1952, Trends in Employment in the Service Industries, 1956, (with D. Blank) Supply and Demand for Scientific Personnel, 1957, The Intellectual and the Market Place, 1964, 84, Essays in the History of Economics, 1965, The Organization of Industry, 1968, (with J.K. Kindahl) The Behavior of Industrial Prices, 1970, The Citizen and the State, 1975, The Economist as Preacher, 1982, The Essence of Stigler, 1986, Memoirs of an Unregulated Economist, 1988; Editor: Chicago Studies in Political Economy, 1988; editor Jour. Polit.

Economy, 1972-91; contbr. articles to profl. jours. Trustee Carleton Coll., Northfield, Minn.; bd. dirs. Lynde and Harry Bradley Found., 1986-89, Duff-Phelps Selected Utility Fund, 1987-89. Recipient Nobel prize in econs., 1982, Nat. Medal of Honor, 1987; Guggenheim fellow, 1955; fellow Ctr. for Advanced Study in Behavioral Scis., 1957-58. Fellow Am. Acad. Arts and Scis., Am. Statis. Soc., Econometric Soc., Nat. Acad. Sci.; mem. Am. Econ. Assn. (pres. 1964), Royal Econ. Soc., Am. Philos. Soc., History of Econs. Soc. (pres. 1977), Mt. Pelerin Soc. (pres. 1977-78). Home: Chicago Ill. Died Dec. 1, 1991.

STILL, BAYRD, historian, educator; b. Woodstock, Ill., July 7, 1906; s. Guy E. and Carrie (Bayrd) S. A.B., U. Wis., 1928, A.M., 1929, Ph.D., 1933. Asst. prof. history U. Wis., Milw., 1932-38; assoc. prof. history Duke U., 1938-47; prof. history N.Y. U., 1947-74, head history dept., 1955-70, acting dean Coll. Arts and Sci., 1958-60, acting dean Grad Sch. Arts and Sci., 1971, dir. Archives Office, 1974-84; Vis. prof. history Columbia U., 1966-67. Author: Milwaukee: The History of a City, 1948, rev. edit., 1965, Mirror for Gotham: New York as Seen By Contemporaries from Dutch Days to the Present, 1956, The West: Contemporary Records of America's Expansion across the Continent, 1607-1890, 1961, Pionniers vers l'Ouest, 1965, 73, New York City, a Student's Guide to Localized History, 1965, Urban America: A History with Documents, 1974, (with Joseph J. Roberto) Greenwich Village: A Brief Architectural and Historical Guide, 1975, rev. edit., 1981; contbr. to: New York: The Centennial Years, 1976, Essays in the History of New York City, 1978, (with others) New York University: One Hundred and Fifty Years, 1981, Around the Square, 1992; co-author, participant: (with others) CBS-TV series America in the Making, 1954-55; Editor: (with John T. McCoy) The Official Pictorial History of the A.A.F, 1947; mem. editorial bd.: N.Y.C. Almanac and Guide, 1957, Jour. Urban History, 1973-86; contbr. articles to profl. jours., mags. Mem. Landmarks Preservation Commn., N.Y.C., 1962-65, Task Force Municipal Archives, 1966-92; N.Y. coordinating com. Sr. Fulbright Hays Program for Vis. Guest Scholars, 1971-92; trustee Inst. Early N.Y.C. History; chmn. bd. adv. Bklyn. Rediscovery, 1976-92; arts and humanities editorial policy bd. Inst. Sci. Info., 1979-82; adv. bd. Hist. Records of N.Y. County Clk., 1980-92. Served as 1st lt. to lt. col. USAAF, 1942-46. Decorated Legion of Merit.; Pintard fellow N.Y. Hist. Soc.; Gallatin fellow N.Y. U.; asso. Columbia U. Seminar on the City. Mem. Am. Hist. Assn. (chmn. local arrangements com. ann. conv. 1954), Orgn. Am. Historians, Soc. Am. Historians, Urban History Group, Urban History Assn., Phi Beta Kappa, Phi Kappa Phi, Delta Upsilon. Home: Woodstock Ill. Died Nov. 19, 1992. †

STILLE, JOHN KENNETH, chemistry educator; b. Tucson, May 8, 1930; s. John Rudolph and Margaret Victoria (Sakrison) S.; m. Dolores Jean Engelking, June 7, 1958; children: John Robert, James Kenneth. B.S., U. Ariz., 1952, M.S., 1953; Ph.D., U. Ill., 1957. Instr. organic chemistry U. Iowa, Iowa City, 1956-59, asst. prof., 1959-63, asso. prof., 1963-65, prof., 1965-77; prof. Colo. State U., Ft. Collins, 1977-86, univ. disting. prof., 1986-89; guest prof. Royal Inst. Tech., Stockholm, 1969; cons. E.I. duPont de Nemours & Co., Inc. Author: Introduction to Polymer Chemistry, 1962, Industrial Organic Chemistry, 1968; Editor: Condensation Monomers (vol. 27 High Polymers), Jour. Am. Chem. Soc., 1982-87; Asso. editor: Macromolecules, 1968-82; editorial bd.: Jour. Macromolecular Sci; adv. bd.: Jour. Polymer Sci. Served to lt. comdr. USNR, 1953-55. Fellow Chem. Soc. London; mem. Am. Chem. Soc. (chmn. polymer div. 1975, award in polymer chemistry 1982, Colo. sect. award 1988, Arthur Cope award 1989), Phi Lambda Upsilon, Alpha Chi Sigma, Soc. Sigma Xi. Home: Fort Collins Colo. Died July 19, 1989; buried Ft. Logan Nat. Cemetery, Denver, Colo.

STILLMAN, W. PAUL, banker; b. Newark, Sept. 17, 1897; m. Louise Stillman. LLD (hon.), Rider Coll., 1950, St. Lawrence U., 1964, Seton Hall U., 1967, Drew U., 1971, Rutgers U., 1975, Monmouth Coll., 1976. Bd. dirs. Mut. Benefit Life Ins. Co., Newark, 1938, chmn. bd., CEO, 1946-78; Chmn. bd., CEO 1st Nat. State Bank of N.J. (formerly Nat. State Bank, Newark), until 1978; chmn. bd. 1st Nat. State Bancorp., Newark; dir., mem. exec. com. Union Camp Corp.; dir. Tri-Continental Corp., Food Fair Stores, Inc., C.F. Mueller Co., Becton-Dickinson & Co. Commr. Port Authority of N.Y. and N.J., 1960-89, vice chmn., 1974-77; active in preservation and rehab. of downtown Newark; trustee United Hosps. Newark; bd. overseers Found. for Advancement Grad. Study in Engring.; chmn. Cancer Inst. N.J.; trustee N.Y. U.; adv. council dept. politics Princeton U.; chmn. N.J. Tercentenary Fund, 1962; pres. N.J. Electoral Coll., 1952; del.-at-large Republican Nat. Conv., 1956; founder N.J. Heart Assn. Mem. SAR, N.J. C. of C. (treas., dir.). Co-founder W. Paul Stillman Sch. Bus. Adminstrn., Seton Hall U., 1973. Home: Fair Haven N.J. Died Apr. 30, 1989.

STILWELL, RICHARD GILES, government official, former army officer; b. Buffalo, Feb. 24, 1917; s. William Giles and Mina (Frazer) S.; m. Alice K. Simpson, Sept. 3, 1938; children: Ann Strong, Richard Giles, William J., Barbara Snook, Dian Shackelford. Student, Brown U., 1933-34; B.S., U.S. Mil. Acad., 1938; grad., Army War Coll., 1955; LL.D., Kyung Hee U., 1974, Myong Ji U., 1976. Commd. 2d lt. U.S. Army, 1938; advanced through grades to gen., 1973, chief ops. 90th div. XXII Corps, 1943-45; asst. mil. advisor to Sec. of State, Europe, 1945-47; spl. mil. advisor to Am. Ambassador, Italy, 1947-49; various positions CIA, 1949-52; comdr. 15th Inf. Regt., 3d Inf. Div., Korea, sr. advisor I Rep. of Korea Army Corps., 1952-53, instr. Army War Coll., 1954-56; chief of staff Presdl. Mission to Far East, 1954; chief strategic planning Supreme Hdqrs., Allied Powers Europe, 1956-58; comdr. Western Area, Germany, 1958-59; advisor Pres.'s Com. Study of Fgn. Asst. Programs, 1959; comdr. cadet regt. U.S. Mil. Acad., 1959-61, comdt. of cadets, 1961-63; chief ops. U.S. Mil. Assistance Command, Vietnam, 1963, chief of staff, 1964-65; chief Joint U.S. Mil. Adv. Group, Thailand, 1965-67; comdg. gen. 1st Armored Div., Fort Hood, Tex., 1967-68; dep. comdg. gen. III Marine Amphibious Force; comdg. gen. XXIV U.S. Army Corps, 1968-69; dep. chief of staff mil. ops. U.S. Army, also sr. Army mem. U.S. delegations Mil. Staff Com. UN, 1969-72; comdg. gen. 6th U.S. Army, San Francisco, 1972-73; comdr.-in-chief UN Command, comdr. U.S. Force, Korea, and comdg. gen. 8th U.S. Army, 1973-76; ret., 1976; dep. under sec. for policy Dept. Def., Washington, 1981-85; chmn. Def. Security Rev. Commn., 1985-86, Presdl. Korean War Vets. Meml. Bd., 1987-91; pres. Stilwell Assocs., Arlington, Va. Pres. Army War Coll. Alumni Assn., 1979-85; mem. Atlantic Council, Council Fgn. Relations, Washington Inst. Fgn. Affairs; dir. Com. on the Present Danger. Decorated D.F.C., D.S.M., Army D.S.M. with 3 oak leaf clusters, Bronze Star with 2 oak leaf clusters, Silver Star with oak leaf cluster, Air medal with 29 oak leaf clusters, Legion of Merit with 3 oak leaf clusters, Disting. Pub. Service medal, Disting. Nat. Intelligence medal, Purple Heart; Croix de Guerre with star (France); Order of White Lion 2d Class, Cross of Valor (Czechoslovakia); Order of Fatherland 1st Class Russia; Order of Leopold, Croix de Guerre with palm (Belgium); Order of Italy; Order of Taeguk (Korea); others. Mem. Assn. Former Intelligence Officers (past nat. pres.). Republican. Episcopalian. Club: Army Navy. Home: McLean Va. Died Dec. 25, 1991. †

STINEBAUGH, VIRGIL, superintendent of schools; b. Carroll County, Ind., Sept. 17, 1897; s. James Gilbert and Mary Elizabeth (Reiff) S.; m. Audra Humberd, July 31, 1918; children: Marjorie Kathryn Miller, James Richard. AB, Manchester Coll., Ind., 1921; LLD, Manchester Coll., 1945; AM, Columbia, 1927; student, Ind. U., 1924. Tchr. in rural schs. Carroll County, Ind., 1915-19; prin. Twp. High Sch., Carroll County, 1920-24, Delphi (Ind.) High Sch., 1924-28; dir. elem. and high sch. inspection Ind. State Dept. Pub. Instrn., 1928-31; dir. curriculum studies and asst. supt. of schs. Indpls., 1931-44, supt. of schs., 1944-50; prin. Paul C. Stetson Sch., 1951-63; mem. curriculum staff Tchrs. Coll., Columbia, summer 1936; lectr. Ind. State Tchrs. Coll., summer session 1938, 39, 40, Butler U., 1950, N.Y.U., 1953; vis. assoc. prof. edn. Manchester Coll., 1963-64; pres. Ind. Coun. on Religion in Higher Edn., 1954-57. Co-author: Spelling Today, 1946. Pres. bd. dirs. Indpls. YMCA, 1950-52, trustee, from 1954. Mem. Am. Assn. Sch. Adminstrs., NEA, Kiwanis, Clubs: Ind. Schoolmasters, Columbia, Meridian Hills Country. *

STIPHER, KARL JOSEPH, lawyer; b. Indpls., Oct. 23, 1912; s. Josiah C. and Clara (Fuerst) S.; m. Jean Houghteling, June 22, 1939; children—Richard, Karen (Mrs. John Irby), Stephen. Student, Harvard Law Sch., 1935-36; LL.B., Ind. U., 1938. Bar: Ind. 1938. Assoc. Gilliom & Gilliom, Indpls., 1938-45; dep. atty. gen. Ind., 1945-47; assoc. Baker & Daniels, Indpls., 1948-50, ptnr., 1950-84, of counsel, from 1984; mem. Ind. Civil Code Study Commn., 1968-71. Bd. dirs. Catholic Social Services, 1968-78, Alcoholic Rehab. Ctr., Our Lady of Grace Acad.; pres., bd. dirs. Domestic Relations Counseling Service; bd. visitors Ind. U. Law Sch., 1974-78; v.p. Greater Indpls. Progress Com.; chmn. Indpls. Mayor's Task Force on Pub. Safety and Criminal Justice; mem. Citizens Ct. Adv. Com.; pres. Ind. Lawyers Commn. Mem. ABA, Ind. Bar Assn. (pres. 1975-76), Indpls. Bar Assn. (pres. 1973), 7th Fed. Cir. Ct. Bar Assn. (pres. 1968-69), Internat. Bar Assn., Am. Bar Found., Am. Coll. Trial Lawyers, Ind. Soc. Chgo., Nat. Assn. R.R. Trial Counsel, Alumni Assn. Arsenal Tech. High Sch. (pres.). Clubs: Variety, Mud Creek Players, Indpls. Athletic, Indpls. Lit. Home: Indianapolis Ind. Died Apr. 13, 1988.

STIRLING, JAMES, architect; b. Glasgow, Scotland, Apr. 22, 1926; s. Joseph and Louisa (Fraser) S.; m. Mary Shand, 1966; children: Ben, Kate, Sophie. Student, Liverpool Art Sch., 1942; diploma of architecture, Liverpool U., 1950. Ptnr. firm James Stirling and James Gowan, London, 1956-63, James Stirling and Michael Wilford, London, 1971-92; William and Charlotte Shepherd Davenport vis. prof. archtl. design Yale U., 1967; vis. prof. Akademie der Kunste, Dusseldorf (Germany), 1976. Prin. works include engring. bldg. Leicester U., 1959-63, New Town Housing Runcorn, 1967-77, Olivetti Tng. Sch., Haslemere, Eng., 1969, Nueu Staatsgalerie, Stuttgart Art Gallery, 1977, 84, Fogg Mus., 1979-84, an extension of the Tate Gallery, London, 1980, Performing Arts Centre, Cornell U., 1983, Brera Mus. Extension, Milan, 1986, Sci. Libr., U. Calif., Irvine, 1987; exhbns. Mus. Modern Art, N.Y.C., 1969, Venice Bienale, 1976; author: James Stirling Buildings and Projects, 1976. Served to lt. 6th Airborne Div., Brit. Army, 1943-45. Decorated knight Order Brit. Empire, 1992; Recipient Burnner award U.S., 1976, Alvar Aalto medal Finland, 1978, Royal Gold medal, 1980, Pritzker Architecture prize, 1981, Thomas Jefferson medal, 1986, Premium Imperiale, Japan, 1990. Fellow AIA (hon.); assoc. Royal Inst. British Architects; mem. Akademie der Kunste Berlin (hon.). Home: London Eng. Died June 25, 1992; cremated.

STITCH, MALCOLM LANE, applied physicist; b. Elizabeth, N.J., Apr. 23, 1923; s. Max and Charlotte S.; m. Sharon Anne Fahlberg, Dec. 30, 1975; children: Andrew Bray, Campbell Muir, Stefan Andreus, Mathias Christoph, Wendy Jade, Amy Elizabeth. Student, Rensselaer Poly. Inst., 1940-43; B.A. in French, So. Meth. U., 1947; B.S. in Physics, 1947; Ph.D. in Physics, Columbia U., 1953. Instr. physics Sarah Lawrence Coll., 1948-50, Cooper Union Coll., 1951; research asst. Columbia U. Radiation Lab., 1948-50, 51-53; research physicist Varian Assos., 1953-56; with Hughes Aircraft, 1956-68, mgr. laser tech. and devel. dept., 1962-65, asst. mgr. high frequency lab., 1965-67, chief scientist lasers, 1967-68; asst. gen. mgr. Korad dept. Union Carbide Corp., Santa Monica, Calif., 1968-73; cons. in field, 1973-74; mgr. electro-optics sect. laser enrichment dept. Exxon Nuclear Co., Richland, Wash., 1974-81; engring. assoc. tech. dept. Exxon Research and Engring. Co., Florham Park, N.J., 1981-84; sr. tech. adviser SIS project Rockwell Internat., Richland, Wash., 1984-87; sr. engr.-advisor Westinghouse-Hanford Co., Richland, Wash., 1987-91; former adj. prof. elec. engring. U. So. Calif.; former cons. U.S. Naval Research Lab., Am. Nat. Standards Inst., Nat. Acad. Scis.; former chmn. laser sect. Electronic Industries Assn. Editor: Laser Handbook, Vol. 3, 1979, Vols. 4 and 5, 1985; contbr. articles to profl. jours. Served with U.S. Army, 1943-46. Fellow IEEE, Soc. Photo-Optical Instrumentation Engrs., Inst. Advancement Engring. So. Calif. (past dir.); mem. N.Y. Acad. Scis., Optical Soc. Am., Am. Phys. Soc., AAAS, Sigma Xi. Republican. Episcopalian. Club: Capital Hill (Washington). Home: Richland WA Died Dec. 25, 1991.

STIVENDER, EDWARD DAVID, conductor, chorus master; b. Milw., Sept. 6, 1933; s. Edward Herman and Frances Strauther (Stabler) S. Mus.B., Northwestern U., 1955. Compiler, editor, translator: Mascagni: An Autobiography, 1988; asst. condr., Lyric Opera Chgo., 1961-65, asst. chorus master, Met. Opera Assn., N.Y.C., 1965-73, chorus master, from 1973, condr., from 1978. Served with USN, 1955-57. Fulbright grantee Rome Opera, 1963-65. Home: New York N.Y. Deceased. †

STODDARD, GEORGE DINSMORE, educator; b. Carbondale, Pa., Oct. 8, 1897; s. Eugene Anson and Charlotte (Dinsmore) S.; m. Margaret Trautwein, Dec. 26, 1925; children: Philip Hendrick, Arthur Dinsmore, Eleanor, Carline, Alfred Eugene. AB, Pa. State Coll., 1921; diploma, U. Paris, 1923; PhD, U. Iowa, 1925; LittD, Colgate U., 1942; LLD, St. Lawrence U., 1942, Syracuse U., 1942, Hobart Coll., 1942, NYU, 1943, Skidmore Coll., 1943, Union Coll., 1944, Yeshiva U., 1946, U. of Fla., 1948, Lake Forest Coll., 1948, Washington U., 1948, U. Toledo, 1949, U. Louisville, 1952; LHD, Alfred U., 1943; DCL, Shurtleff Coll., 1952; DFA, Grinnell Coll., 1959. Assoc. in psychology and edn. U. Iowa, 1925-26, asst. prof., 1926-28, assoc. prof. psychology, 1928-29, prof., 1929-42, dir. Iowa Child Welfare Rsch. Sta., 1928-42, dean of Grad. Coll., 1936-42, head dept. psychology, 1938-39; pres., commr. edn. U. State of N.Y., 1942-45; pres. U. Ill., 1946-53; chmn. directing com. self study NYU, dean Sch. of Edn., 1956-60, chancellor, exec. v.p., from 1960, disting. prof. edn., from 1964; chmn. Am. Coun. Edn., 1946-47; dir. Ency. Britannica Films; mem. bd. Lincoln Ctr. for the Performing Arts, Am. Shakespeare Festival. Author: Iowa Placement Examinations, 1925, Tests and Measurements in High School Instruction (with G. M. Ruch), 1927, The General Shop (with L.V. Newkirk), 1928, Study Manual in Elementary Statistics (with E. F. Lindquist), 1929, Getting Ideas from the Movies (with P. W. Holaday), 1933, Child Psychology (with B. L. Wellman), 1936, The Meaning of Intelligence, 1943, Tertiary Education, 1944, Frontiers in Education, 1945, On the Education of Women, 1950, Krebiozen, The Great Cancer Mystery, The Dual Progress Plan, 1961; editor in chief New Wonder World Ency.; mem. editorial bd. Ednl. Forum. Chmn. U.S. Edn. Mission to Japan, 1946; del. UNESCO gen. confs., London, 1945, Paris, 1946, 48, 51, Mexico City, 1947, Beirut, 1949, Florence, 1950; mem. U.S. Nat. Commn. UNESCO, chmn., 1949-52; vice chmn. Nat. Com. Mid-century White House Conf. Children and Youth, 1950. 2d lt. F.A. R.C., 1918-23. Fellow AAAS; mem. APA, NEA, Soc. Advancement Edn. Coun. Fgn. Affairs, Inc., Sigma Pi, Phi Kappa Phi, Delta Sigma Rho, Phi Delta Kappa, Sigma Xi, Phi Beta Kappa, Kappa Delta Pi (laureate chpt.), Century Assn. Club. Unitarian. *

STODDARD, GEORGE EDWARD, agricultural science educator; b. Boise, Idaho, July 15, 1921; s. William R. and Estella (Hansen) S.; m. Corinne Marie Pecora, Aug. 7, 1946; children: Karalee (Mrs. M.D. Salvesen), Douglas G., Steven E., Gary W., Shauna (Mrs. Robert Reeder). B.S. in Agr, U. Idaho, 1943;

M.S., U. Wis., 1948, Ph.D., 1950. Asst. prof. Iowa State Coll., Ames, 1949-52; prof. Utah State U., Logan, from 1952; head dept. dairy sci. Utah State U., 1960-76, acad. adminstrv. asst. animal, dairy and vet. scis. dept., 1980-86, assoc. dean agr., 1981-86, prof. emeritus animal, dairy and vet. scis., from 1986; pres. Agri Mgmt. Consultants, Inc., 1972-77; mem. staff Agriservices Found., 1975-76; pvt. dairy and livestock cons., 1977—; mem. Utah Dairy Commn. Contbr. articles to profl. jours. Served with USMCR, 1943-46, PTO; now capt. Res. (ret.). Decorated Purple Heart; recipient Faculty Service award Asso. Students Utah State U., 1967, Disting. Prof. in Coll. Agr. award; named Hon. State Farmer Future Farmers of Am., Utah, 1969; Cert. of Recognition, Nat. Assn. State Univs. and Land Grant Colls., 1986. Mem. Am. Soc. Animal Scis., Am. Dairy Sci. Assn., AAAS, Utah Acad. Arts and Scis., Am. Dairy Assn. Utah (exec. com.), Utah Dairy Council (ex-officio mem.), Alpha Gamma Rho (Disting. Service award), Delta Phi Kappa (internat. exec. com.), Sigma Xi, Alpha Zeta. Mem. Ch. of Jesus Christ of Latter-day Saints (bishop). Home: Logan UT Deceased. †

STOETZNER, ERIC WOLDEMAR, newspaper publishing executive, consultant; b. Leipzig, Germany, Mar. 11, 1901; came to U.S. 1938, naturalized, 1944; s. Woldemar and Emma (Wolf) S. m. Fridel Henning-Gronau, Dec. 20, 1927 (dec. Sept. 1967); 1 child, Renee Fuller. Student, U. Leipzig, 1922; PhD in Econ. Sci., Frankfurt am Main, 1925. Advt. dir., bus. mgr., mem. bd. Frankfurter Zeitung, Fed. Republic Germany, 1930-38; bus. mgr. mag. Schurz Found., Phila., 1939-43; internat. analyst of pub. N.Y. Times, 1944-45, dir. fgn. bus. promotion, 1945-50, dir. fgn. advt., 1950-70; internat. cons., 1970-90. Subject of book by Horst Fischer; Werbung, Menschen, Politik: Die Stoetzner Story, 1986, (TV film) The Prophet of Reconcilization, 1989. Decorated Chevalier de l'ordre du Merite Comml. de la France, Officer's Cross, German Order of Merit, 1953, Grand Cross, German Order Merit, 1981; recipient hon. plaque City of Frankfurt, 1979, Disting. Internat. Recognition award Fellowship Former Overseas Residents, 1984; named Symbol of 1938 Frankfurter Allgemeine Zeitung in report, Four Dramatic Lives of a Frankfordian, 1983. Mem. Internat. Advt. Assn. (hon. life, v.p. 1956-59), Confrerie des Chevaliers du Tastevin, Rotary (Mr. internatalist N.Y. chpt.). Mem. Soc. of Friends. Home: Stamford Conn. Died Oct. 2, 1990.

STOKES, JOHN W., management consultant; b. Long Branch, N.J., Sept. 18, 1896; s. John W. and Duella (Hagerty) S.; m. Dorothy Baker, Nov. 19, 1927 (dec.); children: Janet Cobb, Mary Jean Carlstedt, Betty Ann Johnson, Dorothy Lee. Student, U. Minn., 1919-20; AB, Macalester Coll., 1925; postgrad., Boston U., 1940. Southeastern mgr. U.S. C. of C., 1926-30; with Field Mar. Merchants N. Assn. N.Y., 1930-35; pres., treas. Thompson's Spa, Inc., 1937-42, Stokes Food Svc., Inc.; pres. John W. Stokes & Co., Boston; bd. dirs. Am. Motels, Inc.; trustee Newton-Wellesley Hosp.; pres. Mass. Restaurant Assn., 1942-48; dir. Internat. Soc. Food Svc. Cons. Author: Employee Feeding, Food Service in Industry and Institution; contbr. articles to profl. jours. Mem. Execs. Club (past pres.), Algonquin Club (Boston). *

STOKES, JOSEPH, III, medical educator; b. Phila., Dec. 2, 1924; s. Joseph and Frances (Elkinton) S.; m. Ruth Whitson, June 26, 1948; children: Peter, Margaret, J. Barclay, Joseph. A.B., Haverford Coll., 1946; M.D. magna cum laude, Harvard U., 1949. Diplomate: Am. Bd. Internal Medicine, Nat. Bd. Med. Examiners. Intern Johns Hopkins Hosp., 1949-50, asst. resident, 1950-51; resident gen. medicine Mass. Gen. Hosp., 1953-54, clin. asst. medicine, 1954-55, asst. medicine, 1955-61, acting chief infectious disease unit, 1960-61; asst. medicine Johns Hopkins Sch. Medicine, 1950-51; joined USPHS, 1951, advanced through grades to sr. asst. surgeon, med. officer Nat. Heart Inst., NIH, assigned Framingham Heart Study, 1955-60; research assoc. preventive medicine Harvard Med. Sch., 1951-53, teaching fellow medicine, 1953-54, instr. preventive medicine, 1954-56, assoc. preventive medicine, 1956-61; asst. medicine Peter Bent Brigham Hosp., Boston, 1951-53; chief family health program Harvard U. Med. Sch.-Mass. Gen. Hosp., 1954-61; heart disease control officer Hawaii Health Dept., 1961-62; dir. med. edn. Queen's Hosp., Honolulu, 1962-64, asst. chief medicine, 1963-64; cons. Tripler Army Hosp., Honolulu, 1963-64; prof. medicine, dean U. Calif. at San Diego Sch. Medicine, 1964-66, prof. community medicine, 1966-81, emeritus, 1981-89, chmn. dept., 1966-75; prof. medicine sect. preventive medicine and epidemiology Boston U. Med. Center, 1981-89; prof. pub. health Boston U. Sch. Pub. Health, 1981-89; also adj. prof. dept. health scis. nutrition program Sargent Coll. Allied Health Professions, sr. rsch. assoc. Ctr. Ednl. Devel. Health Boston U.; mem. planning com. Pres.' Commn. on Health Edn., 1972; vis. lectr. preventive and social medicine Harvard U., 1979; spl. cons. Time-Life Books, 1972-74; mem. exec. coord. com. Nat. Cholesterol Edn. Program, 1985-89; mem. health risk appraisal update project Carter Ctr., Atlanta, 1986-87; mem. arteriosclerosis, hypertension and lipid metabolism adv. com.,1987-89, NIH, 1987-89;prin. investigator, Framingham Offspring/Spouse Study, 1981-89, co-prin. investigator, The Framingham Study, 1981-89; lectr., Dept. of Preventive Medicine, Harvard Med. Sch, 1981-89. Editor: Am. Jour. Preventive Medicine, 1986-89, New Eng. Jour. Medicine Progress Series, 1964-75; editorial bd. New Eng. Jour. Medicine, 1958-59, Jour. Community Health, 1974-76; contbr. articles to profl. jours. Recipient Medallion of Survival award Soc. Prospective Medicine, 1987, Swedish Med. Soc. medal, 1987, Disting. Svc. award Am. Coll. Preventive Medicine, 1989, Am. Coll. of Preventive Medicine, Disting. Svc. award Apr. 1989. Fellow ACP, Council on Clinical Cardiology, Council on Epidemiology; mem. AAAS, Mass. Med. Soc., Assn. Tchrs. Preventive Medicine (pres. 1973-74), Soc. Preventive Cardiology (1st convenor 1984), Internat. Epidemiologic Assn., Soc. Epidemiologic Research, Am. Fedn. Clin. Research, Am. Heart Assn., Soc. Gen. Internal Medicine, Physicians for Social Responsibility, Assn. Behavioral Scis. and Med. Edn. (pres. 1976-77), Harvard Med. Alumni Council, Alpha Omega Alpha; mem. Internal Soc. and Fedn. of Cardiology, 1981-89. Home: Arlington Mass. Died June 12, 1989; cremated.

STOKES, KATHARINE MARTIN, librarian; b. Hoguestown, Pa., Nov. 26, 1906; d. Charles Sumner and Georgia (Martin) S. BS, Simmons Coll., 1928; MA in Libr. Sci., U. Mich., 1945, MA, 1955, PhD, 1959. Asst. libr. Ludington Meml. Libr., Bryn Mawr, Pa., 1928-30; catalogue and circulation asst. Harrisburg (Pa.) Pub. Libr., 1930-31; circulation libr. Pa. State Coll. Libr., 1931-40, asst. libr., 1940-45; acting reference libr. Swarthmore Coll., 1940; circulation libr. U. Ill. Libr., 1945-48; libr. Western Mich. U. Libr., 1948-66, dir. libns., 1966-67; coll. and univ. libr. specialist div. libr. svcs. U.S. Office Edn., 1967-72; conf. sec. local arrangements com. on planning D.C. meeting Internat. Fedn. Libr. Assns., 1974. Editor Mich. Libr., 1949-51; contbr. articles to profl. jours. Mem. ALA, AAUP, AAUW, D.C. Libr. Assn., Beta Phi Mu. Presbyterian. Home: Alexandria Va. Died Oct. 21, 1989.

STOLLER, ROBERT JESSE, psychiatrist, educator; b. Bronxville, N.Y., Dec. 15, 1924; s. Benjamin and Bessie (Greene) S.; m. Sybil A. White, Dec. 28, 1948; children—Richard, Lawrence, Jonathan, Roger. Student, Columbia, 1942-43; B.A., U. Calif., Berkeley, 1945; M.D., U. Calif., San Francisco, 1948. Diplomate: Am. Bd. Psychiatry and Neurology. Intern San Francisco County Hosp., 1949; resident psychiatry Palo Alto (Calif.) VA Hosp., 1950, Los Angeles County Gen. Hosp., 1953, Los Angeles Psychoanalytic Inst., 1961; instr. U. So. Calif. Med. Sch., 1953-54; instr., asst. prof., asso. prof., to prof. U. Calif. Med. Sch., Los Angeles, 1954-91. Author: Sex and Gender: On the Development of Masculinity and Feminity , 1968, vol. II, 1975, Splitting, 1973, Perversion: The Erotic Form of Hatred, , 1975, Sexual Excitement: Dynamics of Erotic Life, 1979, Observing the Erotic Imagination, 1985, Presentations of Gender, 1985, (with K.M. Colby) Cognitive Science and Psychoanalysis, 1988, (with G. Herdt) Intimate Communications: Erotics and the Study of Culture, 1990, Pain and Passion, 1991, Porn, Myths for the 21st Century, 1991; also articles. Served with AUS, 1943-46; Served with USAF, 1950-53. Fellow Am. Coll. Psychiatrists, Am. Psychiat. Assn.; mem. Internat., Am. Psychoanalytic Assn., Los Angeles Psychoanalytic Soc.-Inst., Royal Coll. Psychiatrists. Home: Pacific Palisades Calif. Died Sept. 6, 1991; buried L.A.

STOLTZ, MERTON PHILIP, economics, statistics educator, academic administrator; b. Glidden, Wis., Mar. 28, 1913; s. Philip and Frances Anne (Mertig) S.; m. Margaret Ruth Wackerman, June 10, 1939; children: Frances Margaret, Elizabeth Ann. B.B.A., U. Minn., 1934; A.M., Brown U., 1936; Ph.D., U. Minn., 1941; LL.D. (hon.), Tougaloo Coll., 1977, Brown U., 1978. Instr. U. Minn., 1937-40; asst. prof. Brown U., 1940-46, asso. prof., 1946-50, prof., 1950-89, chmn. dept. econs., 1956- 64, asso. dean Grad. Sch., 1960-64, dean of univ., 1964-66, provost, 1966-78, acting pres., 1969-70, 76-77. Author: (with Richard K. Gaumnitz) Elements of Statistics, 1939, The Growth and Stability of the Rhode Island Economy, 1955; Contbr. articles to profl. jours. Trustee Tougaloo Coll. Mem. Am. Econ. Assn., Am. Statis. Assn., Econometric Soc. Home: Providence R.I. Died Aug. 7, 1989; buried Swan Point Cemetery, Providence, R.I.

STOMMEL, HENRY MELSON, oceanographer; b. Wilmington, Del., Sept. 27, 1920; m. Elizabeth Stommel; children: Abigail S. Adams, Elijah, Matthew. BS, Yale U., 1942, DSc (hon.), 1970; DSc (hon.), Gothenburg U., Sweden, 1964, U. Chgo., 1970. Instr. math. and astronomy Yale U., New Haven, Conn., 1942-44; rsch. assoc. phys. oceanography Woods Hole (Mass.) Oceanographic Inst., 1944-59, oceanographer, 1978-92; prof. oceanography Harvard U., Boston, 1960-63, MIT, 1963-78. Author numerous popular and sci. books; co-author: (with Elizabeth Stommel) Volcano Weather: The Year Without a Summer, 1983. Recipient Crafoord prize Swedish Acad. Sci., 1983, Nat. Medal of Sci., 1989. Mem. NAS, Am. Acad. Arts and Scis., Am. Astron. Soc., Royal Soc. London, Acad. Sci. France, Soviet Acad. Sci. Home: Woods Hole Mass. Died Jan. 17, 1990.

STONE, CLIFFORD FONTAINE, manufacturing company executive, consultant; b. Ashland, Wis., Aug. 20, 1894; s. James and Sophia (Fontaine) S. LLB, George WashingtonU., 1918. Mem. legal staff, officer Steel & Tube Co., Milw. Coke & Gas Co., Newport Chem. Co., 1919-21; mem. legal staff, then v.p. Goodyear Tire & Rubber Co., Akron, Ohio, 1921-29, dir., officer group investment firms and other corps., 1930-34; dir., dir. exec. com. Interchem. Corp., N.Y.C., 1938-64; dir., mem. exec. com. Christodora House, N.Y.C., 1938-64. *

STONE, FERDINAND FAIRFAX, law educator; b. Urbana, Ohio, Dec. 12, 1908; s. Samuel Lukins Pidgeon and Lutie Vella (Ivins) S. A.B., Ohio State U., 1930, L.H.D. (hon.), 1982, A.M., 1931; B.A. in Juris, (Rhodes scholar Exeter Coll.), Oxford (Eng.) U., 1933, B.C.L., 1934, M.A., 1957; D.Juristic Sci. (Sterling fellow), Yale U., 1936; Dr. h.c., U. Grenoble (France), 1966; LL.D., Tulane U., 1982. Mem. legal staff U.S. Supreme Ct. Adv. Com. on Rules Civil Proc., 1935-36; instr. law U. Wyo., 1936-37; vis. prof. law So. Meth. U., summer 1937; asso. prof. law Tulane U., New Orleans, 1937-43, prof. law, 1948-63, W.R. Irby prof. law, 1963-79, prof. emeritus, 1979-89, scholar-in-residence, 1980-89; dir. Tulane Inst. for Comparative Law, 1949-78; acting prof. law Stanford, 1947-48; prof. Asso. de la Faculté de Droit Grenoble, 1960, 66, 76, de l'Institut Universitaire d'Etudes Européenees de Turin, 1960; Fulbright lectr. law King's Coll., U. London, 1957-58; Gastprof. Rechtswissenschaftliches Fakultät U. Kö ln, 1962; Fulbright prof. law dept. U. Edinburgh, 1963; vis. Ford prof. Am. law U. London, 1972; vis. Simon prof., laws faculty U. Manchester, Eng., 1975; vis. prof. Inter-Am. U. of P.R., 1977, 79, U. Coll. Wales Sch. Law, 1978; Faculty Law U. Exeter, Eng., 1980. Author: Handbook of Law Study, 1952, Institutions fondamentales du droit des Etats-Unis, 1965, Stone on Louisiana Tort Doctrine, 1977; Contbr. articles to legal jours. Served as lt. comdr. USNR, 1943-46. Recipient medal of homage Free U. Brussels, 1958; decorated hon. officer Order Brit. Empire.; Rockefeller Found. grantee comparative law study Europe, 1955. Mem. Internat. Acad. Comparative Law, Am. Assn. for Comparative Study Law (dir.), La. Bar Assn., Order of Coif, Phi Beta Kappa, Omicron Delta Kappa, Phi Gamma Delta, Phi Delta Phi. Episcopalian. Club: Athenaeum (London). Home: New Orleans La. Died June 10, 1989.

STONE, FRANKLIN MARTIN, judge; b. Atlantic, Iowa; s. Fred Martin and Sarah A. (Russell) S.; married; 1 child from previous marriage, Franklin Martin Jr. Jr. coll. certificate, Chaffey Coll., Ontario, Calif., 1929; J.D., George Washington U., 1934. Bar: D.C. 1934, Minn. 1939, Fla. 1976, U.S. Ct. Appeals (D.C. cir.) 1940, U.S. Supreme Ct. 1943, U.S. Ct. Claims 1946, U.S. Ct. Customs and Patent Appeals 1973, U.S. Ct. Appeals (Fed. cir.) 1976. Spl. agt. FBI, 1934-44, adminstrv. asst. to dir., 1940-44; partner firm Stone & Iversen, Waseca, Minn., 1946-55; city atty. Waseca, 1948-54; gen. counsel CAB, 1955-61; trial judge U.S. Ct. of Claims, Washington, 1961-74; sr. trial judge U.S. Ct. of Claims, from 1974; judge advocate Minn. Ret. Army Officers Assn., 1948-49. Chmn. Waseca County Republican Com., 1948-54; An incorporator, past sec., dir. Minn. DeMolay Found.; bd. dirs. Mae Volen Sr. Ctr., 1982-88; Ruling elder Presbyterian Ch.; bd. dirs. Boca Raton, Fla. Presbyn. Found., 1984-90, v.p. bd. 1987-90. Served from capt. to maj. AUS, OSS, 1944-46, ETO, CBI. Recipient Legion of Honor (Order DeMolay); Alumni Achievement award George Washington U., 1946; certificate of recognition Minn. Bar Assn., 1947; Gold Good Citizenship award Nat. Soc. S.A.R., 1980. Mem. Am., Fed., D.C., Minn., Fla., Palm Beach County, South Palm Beach County bar assns., Am. Legion (past comdr.), V.F.W., Minn. Res. Officers Assn. (judge advocate 1948-49), Am. Assn. Ret. Persons (pres. Boca Raton chpt. 1979, dir. 1978-82), Delray Beach Council (past pres., dir. 1983-84), Navy League U.S. (judge advocate from 1986), Sigma Nu. Clubs: National Lawyers (Washington), Congressional Country (Bethesda, Md.), Capitol Hill (Washington); One Hundred of South Palm Beach County, Boca Del Mar Country, Golden Harbour Yacht (Boca Raton) . Lodges: Masons (past master), Shriners (pres. Waseca Club 1950, Boca Raton club 1980, bd. govs. 1980-83, pres. bd. trustees Boca Raton Club Holding Corp. from 1983, chmn. wills and endowments com. Amara Temple, 1985), Scottish Rite, KT, Jesters (bd. dirs. Billiken club 1984—, pres. 1986), Kiwanis. Home: Boca Raton Fla. Died Jan. 31, 1990; interred Boca Raton (Fla.) Mausoleum.

STONE, GRACE ZARING, author; b. N.Y.C., Jan. 9, 1896; d. Charles Wesley and Grace (Owen) Zaring; m. Ellis S. Stone, Apr. 1, 1917; 1 child, Eleanor Spencer Stone Perenyi. Student, Sacred Heart Convent, N.Y.C.; pvt. tutors, studied music and dancing in Paris. Author: Letters to a Djinn, 1922, The Heaven and Earth of Dona Elean, 1929, The Bitter Tea of General Yen, 1930, The Almond Tree, 1931, The Cold Journey, 1934, (under psuedonmy of Ehtel Vance) Escape, 1939, Reprisal, 1942, Winter Meeting, 1946, The Secret Thread, 1948, The Grotton, 1951; contbr. fiction to mags. Mem. Royal Soc. Lit. Home: Stonington Conn. Died Sept. 29, 1991.

STONE, H. LOWELL, physiology educator; b. Baton Rouge, July 22, 1936; m. Nancy Hunter, Aug. 17, 1957; children: Brenda, Sharon, Donna. BS, Rice U., 1958; MS, U. Ill., 1959, PhD, 1961. Rsch. and teaching asst. U. Ill., Urbana, 1958-61; postdoctoral fellow dept. physiology U. Miss., 1961-63, asst. prof., 1963-64; rsch.

physiologist USAF Sch. Aerospace Medicine, Brooks AFB, Tex., 1964-71; prof. physiology U. Tex. Med. Br., Galveston, 1971-77; prof., head dept. U. Okla. Health Ctr., Oklahoma City, 1977-84; cons. cardiologist Emory U., Atlanta. Contbr. over 200 articles to profl. jours. Fellow Am. Coll. Cardiology; mem. Am. Physiol. Soc., Am. Soc. Pharmacology and Exptl. Therapy, Soc. for Neurosci., Soc. Exptl. Biology and Medicine, Rotary. Home: Oklahoma City Okla. Died Nov. 16, 1984; buried Resurrection Meml. Cemetery, Oklahoma City.

STONE, I. F. (ISIDOR FEINSTEIN STONE), journalist; b. Phila., Dec. 24, 1907; s. Bernard and Katherine (Novack) Feinstein; m. Esther M. Roisman, July 7, 1929; children: Celia Stone Gilbert, Jeremy J., Christopher D. Student, U. Pa., 1924-27, B.A., 1975; L.H.D. (hon.), Amherst Coll., 1970, Reed Coll., 1976, Am. U., 1978; Litt.D. (hon.), Brown U., 1971, Colby Coll., 1982; LL.D. (hon.), New Sch. Social Research, 1978; D. Litt. (hon.), U. So. Calif., 1981. Editor, pub. The Progress, Haddonfield, N.J., 1922; reporter Haddonfield Press, Camden (N.J.) Courier-Post, Phila. Record, Phila. Inquirer, 1923-33; editorial writer Phila. Record, 1933, N.Y. Post, 1933-39; asso. editor The Nation, 1938-40, Washington editor, 1940-46; reporter, columnist, editorial writer PM, N.Y. Star, N.Y. Post, N.Y. Daily Compass, 1942-52; editor, pub. I.F. Stone's Bi-Weekly, Washington, 1953-71; Disting. scholar in residence Am. U., 1975-89. Author: The Court Disposes, 1937, Business as Usual, 1941, Underground to Palestine, 1946, This is Israel, 1948, The Hidden History of the Korean War, 1952, The Truman Era, 1953, The Haunted Fifties, 1964, In a Time of Torment, 1967, The Killings at Kent State, 1970, Polemics and Prophecies, 1971, The Best of I.F. Stone's Weekly, 1973, The Trial of Socrates, 1988; past contbg. editor: N.Y. Rev. Books. Recipient George Polk Meml. award L.I. U., 1970, Journalism award Columbia U., 1971, Medal of Liberty, ACLU, 1987; subject of film I.F. Stone's Weekly by Gerry Brock, Jr. Home: New York N.Y. Died June 18, 1989.

STONE, IRVING, author; b. San Francisco, July 14, 1903; s. Charles and Pauline (Rosenberg) Tannenbaum; stepson I. Stone; m. Jean Factor, Feb. 11, 1934; children: Paula, Kenneth. BA, U. Calif., 1923, postgrad., 1924-26; MA, U. So. Calif., 1924, LittD (hon.), 1956; DLitt (hon.), Coe Coll., 1967; LLD (hon.), U. Calif., Berkeley, 1968; DLitt (hon.), Calif. State Colls., 1971; DHL (hon.), Hebrew Union Coll., Cin., 1978. Instr. econs. U. So. Calif., Los Angeles, 1923-24, U. Calif., Berkeley, 1924-26; prof. creative writing U. Ind., 1948, U. Wash., 1961; novelist, from 1933; lectr. Calif. State Colls., 1966; art critic Los Angeles Times Mirror, 1959-60; regent's prof. UCLA, from 1984. Author: numerous books, primarily biographical novels including Pageant of Youth, 1933, Lust for Life, (Van Gogh), 1934, Dear Theo (Van Gogh), 1937, Sailor on Horseback (Jack London), 1938, False Witness, 1940, Clarence Darrow for the Defense, 1941, They Also Ran, 1943, Immortal Wife (Jessie B. Fremont), 1944, Adversary in the House (Eugene V. Debs), 1947, Earl Warren, 1948, The Passionate Journey (John Noble), 1949, We Speak for Ourselves, 1950, The President's Lady (Rachel Jackson), 1951, Love is Eternal (Mary Todd Lincoln), 1954, Men to Match My Mountains, 1956, The Agony and the Ecstasy ((Michelangelo), 1961, I, Michelangelo, Sculptor, 1962, Lincoln: A Contemporary Portrait, 1962, The Story of Michelangelo's Pieta, 1963, The Irving Stone Reader, 1963, The Great Adventure of Michelangelo, 1965, Those Who Love (Abigail Admas) 1965, There Was Light, 1970, Passions of the Mind (Sigmund Freud), 1971, The Greek Treasure (Henry and Sophia Schliemann), 1975, Irving Stone's Jack London, 1977, The Origin (Charles Darwin), 1980, Depths of Glory (Camille Pissarro), 1985; contbr. to mags. and newspapers. Chmn. Allan Nevins Meml. Fund, Huntington Library, from 1972; mem. adv. council Nat. Soc. Arts and Letters, from 1976; v.p. Eugene V. Debs Found.; adv. bd. U. Calif. Inst. Creative Arts; founder Calif. State Coll Com. for Arts; contbg. mem. Am. Sch. Classical Studies, Athens. Decorated Order of Merit, Golden Lily of Florence, Italy; recipient Gold trophy Am. Women in Radio and TV, 1968, Herbert Adams Meml. medal Nat. Sculpture Soc., 1970, Golden Plate award Am. Acad. Achievement, 1971, Alumnus of Yr. award U. Calif. at Berkeley, 1971, Author of Yr. award Book Bank U.S.A., 1976, Commendatore, Grande Ufficiale, Rep. of Italy, Hon. Citation Union of Soviet Writers, 1983, Commandeur dans l'Ordre des Arts et des Lettres French Ministry of Culture, 1984, Hon. fellow Southern Calif. Hist Soc., 1988; named Hon. citizen Athens, Greece, 1972. Mem. Authors League Am., P.E.N., Soc. Am. Historians, Acad. Motion Picture Arts and Scis., Fellows for Schweitzer (founder, pres.), Western Writers Am., Acad. Polit. Sci., Hist. Soc. So. Calif., Calif. Writers Guild (former pres.), Acad. Am. Poets (founder), Ctr. for Study of Evolution and the Origin of Life UCLA, Berkeley Fellows (charter mem.). Clubs: Bohemian (San Francisco), Calif. Writers (hon.). Home: Los Angeles Calif. Died Aug. 26, 1989.

STONE, MORRIS SAMUEL, greeting card company executive; b. Cleve., Mar. 15, 1911; s. Jacob and Jennie (Kanter) Sapirstein; m. Maxeen Myerson, May 14, 1960. Various positions to vice chmn. bd. Am. Greetings Corp., Cleve., 1928-89. Home: Shaker Heights Ohio Died June 23, 1989.

STONE, SIR (JOHN) RICHARD (NICHOLAS), finance, accounting educator, economist; b. Eng., Aug. 30, 1913; s. Gilbert Stone; m. Winifred Jenkins, 1936 (div.); m. Feodora Leontinoff, 1941 (dec. 1956); 1 daughter; m. Mrs. Giovanna Croft-Murray, 1960. MA, Cambridge (Eng.) U., 1938; ScD, Cambridge (Eng.) U., Eng., 1957. With C.E. Heath and Co., Lloyd's Brokers, Eng., 1936-39, Ministry Econ. Warfare, Eng., 1939-40, Cen. Statis. Office, Offices of War Cabinet, Eng., 1940-45; dir. dept. applied econs. Cambridge (Eng.) U., 1945-55, P.D. Leake Prof. finance, acctg., 1955-80, ret., 1980-91. Author: The Role of Measurement in Economics, 1951, Quantity and Price Indexes in National Accounts, 1956, Input-Output and National Accounts, 1961, Mathematics in the Social Sciences and Other Essays, 1966, Mathematical Models of the Economy, and Other Essays, 1970, Demographic Accounting and Model Building, 1971, Aspects of Economic and Social Modelling, 1980, several books with others; editor, author: (with others) A Programme for Growth, 1962-74; contbr. articles to profl. jours. Named Fellow King's Coll. U. Cambridge, 1945-91, hon. fellow Gonville and Caius Coll. U. Cambridge, 1976; recipient numerous hon. doctorates, Nobel prize for Econs., 1984. Mem. Internat. Statis. Inst., Econometric. Soc. (pres. 1955). Home: Cambridge England Died Dec. 6, 1991. †

STONE, SHEPARD, institute executive, journalist; b. Nashua, N.H., Mar. 31, 1908; s. Simon W. and Anna (Gold) S.; m. Charlotte Hasenclever, Aug. 15, 1933; 1 child, Margaret Ann Stone Jennings. A.B., Dartmouth Coll., 1929; postgrad., U. Heidelberg, 1930; Ph.D., U. Berlin, 1933, prof. h.c, 1978; Dr. h.c., Free U. Berlin, 1954; Dr. rer. pol. h.c, U. Basel, Switzerland, 1967. Writer fgn. affairs, 1933-42; reporter N.Y. Times, 1934-35, editorial asst. Sunday dept., 1935-42, asst. Sunday editor, 1946-49; spl. cons. to U.S. High Commr. for Germany, 1949-50, dir. Office of Pub. Affairs, 1950-52; staff Ford Found., 1953, dir. internal affairs, 1954-68; pres. Internat. Assn. Cultural Freedom, Paris, 1968-73; dir. Aspen Berlin (Germany) Inst. for Humanistic Studies, 1974-88; pres. Internat. Assn. for Cultural Freedom, 1988-90; cons. to State Dept. and ACDA, 1961; hon. chmn. McCloy Scholars Program J.F. Kennedy Sch. Govt., Harvard U., 1988-90. Author: Shadow Over Europe, 1938; Editor: (with H.W. Baldwin) We Saw It Happen, 1938. Served from lt. to lt. col., G-2 hdqrs., 1st Army AUS, 1942-46. Decorated Legion of Merit, Comdrs. Cross Order of Merit Fed. Republic Germany).; named Hon. Citizen of Berlin, 1983. Mem. Council Fgn. Relations N.Y.C. Clubs: Century (N.Y.C.). Home: Cambridge Mass. Died May 4, 1990.

STOUGHTON, RICHARD BAKER, physician, educator; b. Duluth, Minn., July 4, 1923; s. E. Zachary and Edna Marie (Baker) S.; m. Gwendolen S. Schmidt, June 10, 1946; 1 son, Roland. B.S., U. Chgo., 1945, M.D., 1947. Diplomate Am. Bd. Dermatology (pres. 1980). Resident U. Chgo. Hosp., 1948-51; instr. U. Chgo., 1951-56; assoc. prof., dir. dermatology Western Res. U., Cleve., 1957-67; mem., head div. dermatology Scripps Clinic and Research Found., LaJolla, Calif., 1967-77; prof., head div. dermatology U. Calif., San Diego, 1977-82; emeritus prof. U. Calif. at San Diego, 1982-92; chmn. tng. grants sect. for dermatology NIH, 1962-67; mem. Armed Forces Epidemiology Bd., 1968-74; chmn. med. adv. bd. Nat. Psoriasis Found., 1975-77. Contbr. articles to profl. jours. Served to capt. AUS, 1952-54. Decorated Bronze Star; recipient Profl. Achievement award U. Chgo., 1989. Mem. Soc. Investigative Dermatology (pres. 1976, dir., Rothman gold award 1983, editor jour. 1967-72), Am. Acad. Dermatology (dir. 1963-67), Am. Dermatol. Assn. (dir. 1979-85, pres. 1985), Brit. Assn. Dermatologists (hon.). Home: Rancho Santa Fe Calif. Died May 24, 1992. †

STOVALL, FLOYD, educator; b. Temple, Tex., July 7, 1896; s. Jonathon Benjamin and Henrietta Jacobine (Hock) S.; m. Maude Lambert. AB, U. Tex., 1923, MA, 1924, PhD, 1927. Asst. prof. English U. Tex., 1927-35, chmn. dept., 1933-35; head dept. English North Tex. State Coll., 1935-49, dean arts and scis., 1946-49; prof. English U. N.C., 1949-55; Edgar Allan Poe prof. english U. Va., from 1955, chmn. dept. English, 1956-61; vis. prof. Stephen F. Austin State Tchrs. Coll., Nacogdoches, Tex., 1927-32, Duke U., 1936, 50, 53, U. Tex., 1937, 40, U. Ill., 1948, U. Wis., 1963; spl. lectr. Am. Lit. Okla. U., 1942; mem. edit. bd. Am. Lit., 1959-63. Author: Desire and Restraint in Shelley, 1931, American Idealism, 1943; co-author: Transitions in American Literature, 1953; editor: Walt Whitman, Representative Selections, with Introduction, Bibliography and Notes (Am. Writers Series), 1934, The Development of American Literary Criticism, 1955, The Poems of Edgar Allen Poe, 1965; editor, co-author: Eight American Authors: A Review of Research and Criticism, 1956; co-editor: Reading Around the World, 1946; contbr. articles to profl. jours. Mem. AAUP, Modern Lang. Assn. (sec. Wordsworth Group 1936, mem. adv. coun. Am. Lit. Group 1939-41, chmn. 1952, chmn. lit. and soc. group 1949), South-Ctrl. Modern Lang. Assn. (chmn. Am. lit. sect. 1941), Nat. Coun. Tchrs. English, Phi Beta Kappa, Colonnade Club, Farmington Country Club. Democrat. Baptist. *

STOVER, MILTON EDWARD, financial consultant; b. Mechen, W.Va., Dec. 9, 1897; s. Arthur J. and Nora (Allen) S.; m. Pauline Waterman, July 26, 1924; children: Barbara, James, Mary. BS, U. Mich., 1925. With Ernst & Ernst CPA's, Detroit, 1925-33; controller, treas. Evans Products Co., Plymount, Mich., 1933-42, Gen. Cable Corp., St. Louis, 1942-43; v.p., dir. Fruehauf Trailer Co., Detroit, 1943-50; v.p. fin. CLinton Foods, Inc., N.Y.C., 1950-53; v.p. fin., dir. Mack Trucks Inc., N.Y.C., 1953-59; pres. Stover Assocs. Cons., Deerfield Beach, Fla., from 1959; dir. Gray-Wilson Co., Detroit. Mem. Controllers Inst. Am., Am. Inst. Cost Accountants. Clubs: Union League, Bankers Am. *

STOWE, WILLIAM MCFERRIN, clergyman; b. Franklin, Tenn., Jan. 28, 1913; s. John Joel and Myra Anderson (McFerrin) S.; m. Twila Farrell, July 28, 1943; children: William McFerrin, Twila Gayle Stowe Keighley, Martha Elizabeth. A.B., Hendrix Coll., Conway, Ark., 1932, D.D., 1956; B.D., Duke, 1935, D.D., 1967; Ph.D., Boston U., 1938; D.D., Oklahoma City U., 1955; L.H.D., Southwestern Coll.; LL.D., So. Meth. U., Baker U., 1966. Ordained to ministry Meth. Ch., 1937; pastor Meth. Ch., Alta Loma, Tex., 1938-40, Garden Villas Meth. Ch., Houston, 1940-44; mem. staff Bd. Edn., Meth. Ch.; dir. youth work Tex. Cont. Meth. Ch., 1940-44; dir. spl. tng. enterprises, 1944-49; sec. vocat. counsel Meth. Ch., 1946-48; pastor First Meth. Ch., Stillwater, Okla., 1949-51, St. Luke's Meth. Ch., Oklahoma City, 1951-64; elected bishop, 1964; bishop The Meth. Ch., Kansas Area, 1964-72, Dallas-Ft. Worth, 1972-80; bishop-in-residence Perkins Sch. Theology, So. Meth. U., 1980-89; vis. prof. The Iliff Sch. Theol., Denver, summer 1945-47, Scarritt Coll., Nashville, 1944-46; spl. lectr. Boston U. Sch. Theology, 1945, Perkins Sch. Theology, So. Meth. U., 1944-46, Westminster Theol. Sem., 1946-47, Grad. Sch. Religion, U. So. Cal., 1946, Gammon Sch. Theology, 1944-45; dean Okla. Meth. Pastors' Sch.; Mem. exec. com. Okla. Council Chs.; pres. Oklahoma City Council Chs., 1955-56; pres. Okla. Conf. bd. edn. The Meth. Ch., mem. exec. com. jurisdictional bd. edn., mem. co-ordinating council, del. to world conf., 1956, 61, 66, 71, 76, 81, jurisdictional conf., 1956, 60, 64, del. gen. conf., 1956, 60, 64; mem. world council; del. World Meth. Theol. Inst., Oxford, Eng., 1958, 62, 73; exec. com. Okla. Meth. Conf. Council; pres. Okla. Conf. Meth. Commn. Christian Higher Edn., 1956-60; mem. exec. com. World Meth. Council; mem. governing bd. Nat. Conf. Chs.; pres. Tex. Conf. Chs., 1976-77. Author: Characteristics of Jesus, 1962, Power of Paul, 1963, It All Began With God, If I Were a Pastor, 1983; contbr. articles to religious jours. Trustee So. Meth. U., Southwestern U., Huston-Tillotson Coll., Lydia Patterson Inst., Perkins Sch. Theology, Tex. Wesleyan Coll., 1972-80. Recipient Distinguished Alumnus award Boston U. Sch. Theology; Distinguished Service award Baker U., 1972; Recognition award Southwestern Coll., 1972. Mem. Sigma Chi (Significant Sig award 1972). Club: The Mokus (Boston). Lodge: Masons. Home: Dallas Tex. Died Nov. 24, 1988; body donated to science.

STRANG, RUTH, education educator; b. Chatham, N.J., Apr. 3, 1895; d. Charles Garrett and Anna (Bergen) S. BS, Columbia U., 1922, AM, 1924, PhD, 1926. Tchr. N.Y.C. (N.Y.) Pub. Schs., 1917-20; asst. in nutrition Tchrs. Coll., 1923-24, instr. health edn., 1924-25, rsch. fellow, 1926-27; editor Jour. Nat. Assn. Deans of Women, from 1935; prof. edn. Tchrs. Coll., Columbia U., 1935-60, prof. emeritus, 1960; prof. edn. U. Ariz., from 1960. Author: An Introduction to Child Study, 1951, The Role of the Teacher in Personnel Work, 1953, The Adolescent Views Himself, 1957, Group Work in Education, 1958, Helping Your Gifted Child, 1960, Helping Your Child Improve His Reading, 1962, Diagnostic Teaching of Reading, 1964, Helping Your Child Develop His Potentialities, 1965. Mem. Nat. Assn. Remedial Tchrs. (pres. 1955). *

STRATTON, SAMUEL STUDDIFORD, congressman; b. Yonkers, N.Y., Sept. 27, 1916; s. Paul and Ethel Irene (Russell) S.; m. Joan H. Wolfe, Dec. 17, 1947; children: Lisa (Mrs. Martin Gonzalez), Debra, Kevin, Kim, Brian. Grad., Blair Acad., Blairstown, N.J., 1933; A.B., U. Rochester, 1937; M.A., Harvard U., 1940; LL.D., Hartwick Coll., 1967, Coll. St. Rose, 1974, Union Coll., 1978. Exec. sec. to Mass. congressman, 1941-42; dep. sec.-gen. Far Eastern Commn., 1946-48; lectr. Union Coll., Schenectady, Rensselaer Poly. Inst., 1948-54; TV and radio news commentator Schenectady, 1950-56; mem. 86-87th Congresses from 32d Dist. N.Y., 88th-91st Congresses from 35th Dist. N.Y., 92d Congress from 29th Dist. N.Y., 93d-97th Congresses from 28th N.Y. dist., 1973-83, 98th-100th Congresses from 23d N.Y. dist., 1983-1989; former mem. Com. Armed Svcs.; former chmn. Subcom. on Investigations.; U.S. rep. to 2d spl. session UN Gen. Assembly on Disarmament, 1982; Hon. trustee U. Rochester. Councilman, Schenectady, 1950-56, mayor, 1956-59. Served from ensign to capt. USNR, World War II, Korea; capt. Res. ret. Mem. Res. Officers Assn., Am. Legion, V.F.W., Amvets, Navy League, Phi Beta Kappa, Psi Upsilon. Democrat. Lodge: Masons. Home: Amsterdam N.Y. Died Sept. 13, 1990.

STRAUSS, L.Z. MORRIS, business; b. Charleston, W.Va., Aug. 4, 1897; s. Lewis and Ross (Liehtenstein) S.; m. Eleanor Saks, June 2, 1921; children: L.Z. Morris, Carolyn Saks. Student, Va. Mechanics Inst., 1913-14. Engaged in capital mgmt.; dir. 1st Realty Capital Funds Corp., Polaroid Corp. V.p. Lewis and Rosa Strauss

Meml. Fund. Lt. U.S. Army, 1918. Club: Lakeside (Richmond, Va.). *

STREET, EDWARD ROBERT, construction company executive; b. Charlotte, N.C., 1938. Grad., Davidson Coll., 1959, Ga. Inst. Tech., 1962. Chmn., pres., chief exec. officer McDevitt & Street Co. subs. Street Enterprises Inc., Charlotte, 1972-84, chmn., sole owner, 1984-90. Home: Charlotte N.C. Died Apr. 5, 1990.

STREET, JABEZ CURRY, nuclear physics educator; b. Opelika, Ala., May 5, 1906; s. Jabez Curry and Anne Dunklin Street; m. Leila Fripp Tison, 1939; children—Caroline Dunklin, Curry Tison. B.S. in Elec. Engring., Ala. Poly. Inst., Auburn, 1927; Ph.D. in Physics, U. Va., Charlottesville, 1931; M.S. (hon.), Harvard U., Cambridge, Mass., 1939. Elec. engr. Bklyn. Edison Power Co., 1927-28; instr. Harvard U., Cambridge, Mass., 1932-36, asst. prof., 1936-39, assoc. prof., 1939-40, prof. physics, 1945-55, chmn. dept. physics, 1955-60, dir. Cambridge electron accelerator, 1962-63, asst. to dean faculty sci., 1966-72, Mallinckrodt prof. physics, 1968-76; staff radiation lab., head devel. group ground and ship radar systems MIT, Cambridge, 1940-44, head div. 12, 1944-45; assoc. dir. Brit. Br. Radiation Lab., Eng., 1944; Active radar panel R & D bd. USAF, 1949-53, sci. adv. bd., 1951-56, mem. Project Charles, 1950; vis. com. Brookhaven Nat. Lab., 1950-53; tech. adv. com. Lincoln Lab., 1953-54. Co-author: Physics, 1952; contbr. articles to profl. jours.; Established (with E. Stevenson) existence of fundamental particle, the Muon. Carnegie Found. grantee, 1934; recipient citation U.S. Govt., 1946; cert. of merit Office Sci. Research and Devel., Harvard U.; Guggenheim fellow, 1962. Mem. Nat. Acad. Sci., AAAS, Am. Phys. Soc., Scabbard and Blade, Sigma Xi, Tau Beta Pi, Phi Kappa Nu, Lambda Chi Alpha, Phi Kappa Phi. Republican. Episcopalian. Home: Charleston S.C. Died Nov. 7, 1989; buried Grahamville (S.C.) Cemetery.

STREETER, RUTH CHENEY, military officer; b. Brookline, Mass., Oct. 2, 1895; d. Charles Paine and Mary Ward (Lyon) Cheney; m. Thomas Winthrop Streeter, June 23, 1917; children: Frank Sherwin, Henry Schofield, Thomas Winthrop, Lillian Carpenter. Commd. maj. USMC Res., 1943, advanced through grades to col., 1945. Past mem. N.J. Tercentenary Celebration Commn.; del. N.J. Constnl. Conv., 1947; Rep. presdl. elector N.J., 1948; mem. Def. Adv. Coun. for Women to the Svc., 1951-52; foreman Fed. Grand Jury, Newark, N.J., 1953-54. Awarded Legion of Merit. Mem. Nat. Soc. Colonial Dames Am. (nat. pres. 1948-52). *

STREHLOW, ROGER ALBERT, chemist, educator; b. Milw., Nov. 25, 1925; s. Elmer John and Edna (Schmidt) S.; m. Ruby M. Miller, Aug. 21, 1948; children: John C., James E. B.S., U. Wis., 1947, Ph.D., 1950. Phys. chemist Ballistic Research Labs., Aberdeen Proving Ground, Md., 1950-58; chief physics br. Interior Ballistics Lab., 1958-60; vis. prof. aero. engring. U. Ill. at Urbana, 1960-61, prof. aero. and astronautical engring., 1961-84, prof. emeritus, from 1984; Chmn. bd. advisers Central States sect. Combustion Inst., 1966-78; bd. dirs. Combustion Inst., 1980-86, v.p., 1982-84. Author: Fundamentals of Combustion, 1968, Explosion Hazards and Evaluation, 1983, Combustion Fundamentals, 1984; dep. editor: Combustion and Flame, 1972-84, editor, from 1984. Fellow Am. Phys. Soc., AIAA; mem. Am. Chem. Soc., Am. Inst. Chem. Engring., Combustion Inst., Nat. Fire Protection Assn., Sigma Xi, Alpha Chi Sigma. Home: Champaign Ill. Deceased. †

STREIFER, WILLIAM, optical scientist, electrical engineering and physics educator; b. Poland, Sept. 13, 1936; came to U.S., 1938, naturalized, 1944; s. Joseph and Sylvia (Ast) S.; m. Shirley R. Gruber, June 1, 1958; children: Jonathan Mark, Roberta Lynn, Suzanne Beth. B.E.E., CUNY, 1957; M.S., Columbia U., 1959; Ph.D., Brown U., 1962. Prin. scientist Palo Alto (Calif.) Research Center, Xerox Corp., 1972-85, sr. research fellow, 1980-85; prof. elec. engring. and physics, dir. Ctr. for High Tech. Materials U. N.Mex., Albuquerque, 1985-86, chaired prof. microelectronics, 1985-86; research mgr. Spectra Diode Labs., San Jose, Calif., 1986-90. Editor IEEE Jour. Quantum Electronics, 1982-88. Recipient Jack Morton medal IEEE, 1985, also Centennial Service medal, Traveling lectr. award. Mem. Nat. Acad. Engring. Home: Palo Alto Calif. Died Oct. 1, 1990; buried Palo Alto, Calif.

STRNAT, KARL JOSEF, engineering company executive, consultant; b. Vienna, Austria, Mar. 29, 1929; s. Johann Anton and Maria Franziska (Matousek) S.; m. Maria Anna Luef, June 12, 1954; children: Reinhold M.W., Evelyn M.J., Martin A.P., Christina M. Ingenieur f. Maschinenbau, Technolog. Gewerbemuseum, Vienna, 1948; MS in Engring. Physics, Technische Hochschule Wien (now Tech. U. Wien), Vienna, 1953; DSc, Technische Hochschule Wien (now Tech. Universität Wien), Vienna, 1956. Asst., researcher Tech. Hochschule Wien, Vienna, 1953-57; physicist, supr. rsch. USAF Materials Lab., Wright-Patterson AFB, Ohio, 1958-68; prof., dir. rsch. lab. U. Dayton, Ohio, 1968-89, prof. emeritus, 1989-92; owner, mgr. KJS Assocs., Dayton and Fairborn, Ohio, 1989-92; ind. cons. Fairborn, part-time 1968-92; cons. cos. in U.S.A., U.K., Fed. Republic Germany, Japan, People's Republic of China, 1968-92; lectr., instr. in field. Author 19 VCR tapes; editor 6 conf. proc.; contbr. articles to profl. jours. Recipient 4 civilian svc. awards USAF, 1965-68, 4 teaching and rsch. awards U. Dayton, 1971-80, Disting. Svc. award Carnegie-Mellon U., 1990. Fellow IEEE (various coms., disting. lectr.; mem. ASTM, Tau Beta Pi (hon.). Roman Catholic. Home: Fairborn Ohio Died May 1, 1992. †

STRONG, EDWARD WILLIAM, philosophy educator; b. Dallas, Oreg., Oct. 16, 1901; s. Harold W. and Ethel (Hillman) S.; m. Gertrude L. Dowsett, Jan. 1, 1925; childen: Ann Catherine Strong Pope, Richard Devon, Douglas Hillman. AB, Stanford U., 1925; AM, Columbia U., 1929, PhD, 1937. Lectr., instr. CCNY, 1927-32; lectr. philosphy U. Calif., Berkeley, 1932-36, asst. prof., assoc. prof., 1936-47, prof., 1947-68, Mills prof. philosophy emeritus, 1968-90, chmn. dept. sociology and social instns., 1946-52, assoc. dean Coll. Letters and Sci., 1947-55, vice chancellor, 1958-61, acting chief campus officer, 1961, chancellor, 1961-65; mgr. radiation lab., Berkeley, 1943-45. Author: Procedures and Metaphysics, 1936; founder Jour. History of Philosphy. Mem. bd. advisors Inst. World Affairs; trustee World Affairs Coun. No. Calif., from 1964. Mem. Am. Philos. Assn. (exec. com. Pacific div. 1939-41, acting sec. 1950, sec.-treas. 1945-47, v.p. 1950, pres., chmn. nat. bd. officers 1952), Am. Coun. Edn. (bd. dirs. 1964-66), Bohemian Club. Home: Berkeley Calif. Died Jan. 13, 1990.

STRONG, JOHN DONOVAN, physicist, educator; b. Riverdale, Kans., Jan. 15, 1905; s. Fred and Anna Laura (Bennett) S.; m. Bethany June McLaughlin, Sept. 2, 1928; children: Patricia Ann, Virginia Marie. Student, Friends U., 1921-22; AB, Kans. U., 1926; MS, U. Mich., 1928, PhD, 1930; DSc (hon.), Southwestern at Memphis, 1962. Nat. rsch. fellow physics Rockefeller Found., Calif. Inst. Tech., 1930-32; rsch. fellow on 200-inch telescope project Palomar Mountain, 1932-37; asst. prof. physics and astrophysics Calif. Inst. Tech., 1937-42; rsch. fellow Harvard, Cambridge, Mass., 1942-45; prof. physics Johns Hopkins U., 1945-52, profl. exptl. physics, 1952-67, dir. lab. of astrophysics and phys. meteorology,, 1967-92; prof. physics and astronomy U. Mass., 1967-92; cons. Libbey-Owens Ford Corp. Author: Procedures in Experimental Physics, 1938, Concepts of Classical Optics, 1958. Fellow Franklin Inst. (Longstreth medal 1939, Levy medal 1942), Am. Acad. Arts and Scis.; mem. Soc. Royale des Scis. de Liege (corr.), Optical Soc. Am. (pres. 1959, Ives medal 1956), Internat. Acad. Astronautics, Phi Beta Kappa, Sigma Xi. Republican. Home: Amherst MA Died Mar. 21, 1992; buried Amherst, Mass.

STRONG, LEONELL C(LARENCE), cancer research scientist; b. Renova, Pa., Jan. 19, 1894; s. Clarence A. and Ella (Mead) S.; m. Katherine Bittner, June 27, 1919; children: Leonell Clarence (M.D.), Wilson W. BS, Allegheny Coll., 1917, ScD, 1939; PhD, Columbia U., 1922; MD (hon.), U. Perugia, Italy, 1957. Assoc. prof. St. Stephen's Coll., 1921-25; rsch. fellow Harvard Med. Sch., 1925-27; rsch. assoc. U. Mich., 1927-30, Roscoe B. Jackson Meml. Lab., 1930-33; rsch. assoc. cancer Yale Med. Sch., 1933-53; dir. biol. sta. Roswell Park Meml. Inst., Springville, N.Y., 1953-64; vis. fellow Salk Inst. Biol. Studies, San Diego, from 1964; Belgium-Am. Found. and Anna Fuller Fund lectr., Europe, 1948; guest lectr. Internat. Gerontology Congress, St. Louis, 1951, London, 1954, Venice and Merano, Italy, 1957, Karolinska Inst., Stockholm, 1955, San Francisco, 2d Mammary Cancer Symposium, Perugia, 1957, Internat. Cancer Congress, Atlantic City, 1939, St. Louis, 1947, London, 1958; rsch. prof. U. Buffalo Grad. Sch., from 1955. Contbr. numerous articles on cancer rsch. Mem. NRC com. gastric cancer Nat. Adv. Cancer Coun. Mem. Royal Soc. Medicine (London), Genetics Soc. Am., Am. Assn. Cancer Rsch., French Assn. Cancer Rsch. (assoc.), Sigma Xi, Phi Beta Kappa, Mason, Rotary. *

STROUD, JAMES BART, psychologist, educator; b. Hiawassee, Ga., July 5, 1897; s. William Harve and Lou (Swanson) S.; m. Coretta Teasley, June 26, 1923; children: Margaret (Mrs. Ernest Hixon), Elizabeth. AB, Lincoln Meml. U., 1920, DLitt, 1946; AM, U. Chgo., 1927, PhD, 1930. Instr. Greek and Latin Young Harris Coll., 1922-26; assoc. prof. psychology Kans. State Tchrs. Coll., 1930-34, prof., head dept., 1935; assoc. prof. edn. and psychology U. Iowa, 1938-44, prof., 1944-89. Author: Educational Psychology, 1935, Introduction to General Psychology, 1938, Reading Readiness Tests, 1951, Primary Reading Profiles, 1953, Improving Reading Ability, rev. edit., 1955, Psychology in Education, rev. edit., 1956, other psychol. texts. Fellow APA (exec. com., pres. div. ednl. psychology); mem. Am. Assn. Ednl. Rsch., Nat. Soc. Study Edn., Sigma Xi, Phi Delta Kappa. Home: Iowa City Ia Died Aug. 29, 1989.

STROUT, RICHARD LEE, newspaperman, columnist; b. Cohoes, N.Y., Mar. 14, 1898; s. George Morris and Mary Susan (Lang) S.; m. Edith R. Mayne, June 21, 1924 (dec. Jan. 1932); children: Alan Mayne, Phyllis Mayne, Nancy Ewing; m. Ernestine Wilke, Sept. 4, 1939; children: Elizabeth Wilke, Mary Newman. A.B., Harvard U., 1919, M.A., 1923; D.Litt. hon., Brown U., 1980. Began newspaper work with Sheffield (Eng.) Independent, 1919; reporter Boston Post, 1921; with Christian Science Monitor, 1921-84, Washington Bur., 1925-84; TRB column The New Republic, 1944-83. Author: (with E.B. White) Farewell to Model T, 1936. Editor: Maud, 1939, TRB: Views and Perspectives on the Presidency, 1979. Commd. 2d lt. inf. U.S. Army, World War I; war corr. World War II. Recipient George Polk award Nat. Reporting, 1958; award for journalism U. Mo., 1974; Sidney Hillman award, 1974; Fourth Estate award Nat. Press Club, 1975; Pulitzer Spl. citation, 1978; Population Action Council award, 1983; Fedn. for Immigration Reform award, 1983. Fellow Sigma Delta Chi (hon.). Clubs: National Press, Overseas Writers, Cosmos. Home: Washington D.C. Died Aug. 19, 1990; buried South Lee, N.H.

STUART, JAMES MILTON, investment banking company executive, financial consultant; b. N.Y.C., Dec. 23, 1932; s. Milton M. and Elizabeth (Lowenstein) S.; m. Ellen Menke, Feb. 20, 1962 (dec. 1974); children: James M. Jr., John E., Mary E.; m. Eve Rosenbloom, Dec. 16, 1977; children: Nina L., Kara Stern, Edwin Stern, Amanda Stern. BA, Brown U., 1954; M in Bus., Columbia U., 1958. Ptnr. Stuart Bros., N.Y.C., 1966-85; owner James M. Stuart, N.Y.C., 1985-92; bd. dirs. Warner Computer Systems, Inc., Fairlawn J.J., Ketchum & Co., Inc., Clark, N.J., Wordtronics Corp., Prospect, N.J. Trustee Hudson Guild, Inc., N.Y.C., 1971-92, Am. Shakespeare Theater, Stratford, Conn., 1986-88; bd. govs. Pathways for Youth, N.Y.C., 1966-92, John Carter Brown Libr., Brown U., Providence. With U.S. Army, 1954-56. Mem. Univ. Club, Harmonie Club, Princeton Club. Home: Purchase N.Y. Died Nov. 23, 1992. †

STUART, WILLIAM MOORE, business executive; b. Basham, Va., Sept. 13, 1896; s. Charles Wesley and Lorena J. (Moore) S.; m. Helen Raymond, June 12, 1917; children: Helen Lenore, Waren Moore, Spencer Raymond. Student, Taylor U., 1916. With U.S. Shipping Bd., abroad, 1919-20, Sherwin-William Co., 1921-31; dir.; with Martin-Senour Co., Chgo., from 1931, pres., from 1946; dir. mfrs. coun. Nat. Automotive Parts Assn., Better Govt. Assn., Chgo. Recipient Paint Industry Man of Yr. award 1958. Mem. Chgo. Assn. Commerce, Ill. Mfrs. Assn. (dir.). Clubs: Union League, Beverly Country, Executives, Lake Shore. Republican. Presbyterian. *

STUMP, FELIX BUDWELL, naval officer; b. Parkersburg, W.Va., Dec. 15, 1894; s. John Sutton and Lily (Budwell) S.; m. Myra Morgan, Dec. 22, 1923; 1 son, John Morgan; m. Elizabeth Smith, Aug. 11, 1937; children: Frances, Felix. BS, U.S. Naval Acad., 1917; MS, MIT, 1924. Commd. ensign USN, 1917, advanced through grades to adm., 1953; nav. U.S. S. Cincinnati, World War I; flight tng. Naval Air Sta., Pensacola, Fla., 1919-20; comdr. exptl. squadron Naval Air Sta., Norfolk, Va., 1921-22; with torpedo plane squadron U.S.S. Langley, 1925-27; staff Naval Air Sta., Norfolk, 1927-30; comdr. cruiser scouting squadrons, 1930-32; with bur. aero. Navy Dept., 1932-34, 37-40; comdr. dive bombing squadron U.S.S. Saratoga, 1934-36; exec. U.S.S. Enterprise, 1940-41; comdr. U.S.S. Langeley, 1941; dir. compined ops., intelligence ctr. Am., Brit., Dutch, Aus. Com. Java, 1942; capt. new U.S.S. Lexington, 1943-44; comdr. Carrier Div. 24, 1944-45; chief naval air tech. tng., 1945-48; comdr. Air Force, Atlantic Fleet, 1948-51, 2d Fleet and NATO Striking Fleet, 1951-53; comdr. in chief Pacific and U.S. Pacific Fleet, 1953-58; chmn. bd. Air Am., Inc., Air Asia Co., Ltd., from 1959. Trustee Freedoms Found. Decorated Navy Cross with gold star, DSM, Legion of Merit with gold stars, Silver Star medal, also fgn. decorations. *

STUMP, FOREST J., metal products executive; b. Akron, Ohio, July 30, 1920; s. Forest M. and Olga (Franks) S.; m. Ardelle Wimmer, June 15, 1941; children: Kristine, James. Student, Wooster (Ohio) Coll., 1946-47; BA in Bus. Adminstrn., Ashland Coll., 1948. Builder, mortgage banker, 1952-63; pres. U.S. Steel Homes div. U.S. Steel Corp., from 1963. Mem. Masons. *

STUMP, LAWRENCE M., academic principal; b. Falls City, Nebr., Nov. 27, 1898; s. Washington C. and Abbie (Melvin) S.; m. Irene J. Luitjens, 1919; children: Lois Marguarite (Mrs. Weiland Henry, Jr.), Betty Louise (Mrs. Clyde D. Bailey). AB, Pacific Union Coll., 1924; MA, U. Philippines, 1932; PhD, U. Ariz., 1946. Pres. Philippine Union Coll., Manila, 1930-44; supt. Seventh-day Adventist ednl. instns. in S.Am., 1946-50; prin. Lodi (Calif.) Acad., 1950-52; pres. Atlantic Union Coll., South Lancaster, Mass., 1960; prin. San Pasqual Acad., from 1960. Bd. dirs. Paradise Valley Hosp., National City, Calif.; mem. exec. com. S.E. Calif. Conv. Seventh-day Adventists. Mem. Kiwanis, Phi Delta Kappa. *

STURGES, JOHN ELIOT, film director, producer; b. Oak Park, Ill., Jan. 3, 1910; s. Reginald Rowe and Grace Delafield (Sturges) Carne; m. Dorothy Lynn Brooks, Jan. 5, 1945 (div.); children: Deborah Lynn, Michael Eliot. Student, Marin Jr. Coll., 1930-32; jr. cert., 1932. With art dept. RKO Studio, Hollywood, Calif., 1932-34, film editor, 1936-42; prodn. asst., David Selznick Prodns., 1934-36; film dir., Columbia Pictures,

Metro-Goldwyn-Mayer, Paramount Pictures, Warner Bros., 1945-58; producer, dir., Mirisch Co., Hollywood, Calif., 1958-70; films directed include Bad Day at Black Rock, 1954, Gunfight at the OK Corral, 1956, The Old Man and the Sea, 1958, Never So Few, 1959, Joe Kidd, 1972, The Eagle Has Landed, 1976; producer, dir.: The Magnificent Seven, 1960, The Great Escape, 1963, Trail, 1965, The Satan Bug, 1965m The Hallelujah Trail, 1965, Ice Station Zebra, 1968, Hour of the Gun, 1967, Marooned, 1969, McQ, 1974. Served to capt. USAAF, 1942-45. Decorated Bronze Star. Mem. Dirs. Guild Am. (dir.), Writers Guild Am. West, Producers Guild Am., Dramatists Guild Am., Acad. Motion Picture Arts and Scis., Brit. Acad. Film and TV Arts. Democrat. Home: San Luis Obispo Calif. Died Aug. 18, 1992. †

STURGIS, SOMERS HAYES, physician; b. Groton, Mass., Oct. 14, 1904; s. S. Warren and Edith (Barnes) S.; m. Frances Anne Sturgis, Aug. 5, 1933; children: Anne Russell, Margaret, Joan. Grad., Groton Sch., 1922; AB cum laude, Harvard U., 1927, MD, 1931. Diplomate Am. Bd. Ob-Gyn., Am. Bd. Surgery. Surg. intern Mass. Gen. Hosp., Boston, 1931-33, grad. asst., 1935-37, asst. in surgery, 1938-41, asst. surgeon, 1941-50, mem. courtesy staff, 1951-71; asst. to Dr. Henry Marble, 1934; Rockefeller rsch. fellow endocrinology Carnegie Instsn., Washington, Balt., 1942; sidney C. Graves rsch. fellow gynecology Free Hosp. for Women, Brookline, Mass., 1946; mem. faculty Harvard U., Cambridge, Mass., 1947-71; from asst. gynecology, instr. to clin. prof. gynecology Harvard U., Cambridge, 1947-56, clin. prof. gynecology, 1956-69, prof. gynecology, 1970, prof. gynecology emeritus, 1971-91; sr. assoc. surgery Peter Bent Brigham Hosp., Boston, 1951-53, gynecol. surgeon, head dept., 1953-70; cons. gynecology Children's Med. Ctr., Boston, 1952-91; gynecologist Harvard U. Health Svc., 1970-91; mem. courtesy staff Mt. Auburn Hosp., Cambridge, 1951-70. Assoc. editor: Fertility and Sterility, 1955-64, Psychosomatic Medicine, 1961-62. Pres. Planned Parenthood League Mass., 1968-71. Maj. med. corp. AUS, 1942-45. Decorated Bronze Star. Mem. A.C.S., Am. Coll. Ob-Gyn., Am. Soc. Study Sterility (pres., dir. 1955-56), Am. Gynecol. Soc., Soc. Pelvic Surgeons (pres. 1969), Soc. Gynecol. Investigation, Am. Surg. Assn., Boston Surg. Soc., Boston Obstet. Soc., New Eng. Surg. Soc. Home: Cambridge Ma. Died Apr. 3, 1991.

STURMAN, JOSEPH HOWARD, lawyer; b. Chgo., Apr. 21, 1931; s. Benjamin A. and Rose (Spitzner) S.; 1 son, Lee David. B.S., UCLA, 1953, J.D. (De Garmo scholar), 1956. Bar: Calif. 1956. Practiced in Beverly Hills, 1957-65, Los Angeles, from 1965; research asst. Calif. Supreme Ct., San Francisco, 1956-57; partner firm Balter & Sturman (and predecessor), Los Angeles, 1965-79; Murchison & Cumming, Los Angeles, 1979-81, Goldfarb, Sturman & Averbach & Sturman, Encino, Calif., from 1981; referee Calif. State Bar Ct., 1979-83, mem. resolutions com., 1987-90, vice chair, 1990-91. Mem. law rev., UCLA, 1954-56. Residential chmn. United Crusade, Monterey Park, Calif., 1967; mem. long-range planning com. City of Monterey Park, 1966-67, chmn. exec. com. teen center, 1967-68; Mem. exec. com. Calif. Democratic Central Com., 1966-68; mem. Los Angeles County Dem. Central Com., 1966-68; mem. Calif. Dem. Council, 1956-68, controller, 1965-67. Recipient Outstanding Service award United Crusade, 1967. Mem. Wilshire Bar Assn. (bd. govs. 1972-79, pres. 1978), L.A. County Bar Assn. (trustee 1990-91), San Fernando Valley Bar Assn. (trustee 1986-90, pres. elect from 1990), Am. Assn. Attys.-CPAs (dir. 1973-75), Calif. Assn. Attys.-CPAs (pres. 1977), Calif. Soc. CPAs, ACLU (dir. So. Calif. chpt. 1973-75), Order of Coif, Phi Beta Kappa, Beta Gamma Sigma. Jewish. Home: North Hollywood Calif. Deceased. †

STURZENEGGER, OTTO, chemical company executive; b. Zurich, Switzerland, Feb. 27, 1926; came to U.S., 1948; s. Otto and Julia (Oertle) S.; m. Gerd Wold, Oct. 19, 1957; children: Elsie, Thomas O. BS, Fed. Inst. Tech., Zurich, 1948; MS, Okla. State U., 1949, PhD, 1953; grad. advanced mgmt. program, Harvard U., 1969; LHD (hon.), Mercy Coll., Dobbs Ferry, N.Y., 1982. Asst. to pres. Geigy Chem. Corp., Ardsley, N.Y., 1960-63, pres. mfg. engring. div., 1963-69, pres. agr. chem. div., 1969-70; pres., chief exec. officer Ciba-Geigy Corp., Ardsley, 1970-78, chmn., chief exec. officer, 1978-86, chmn., 1978-90; dir. Ciba-Geigy A.G., Basle, Switzerland, 1986-90. Bd. dirs. United Way Tri-State, N.Y.C., 1974-75; bd. govs. Kennedy Ctr., Washington, 1981; mem. adv. coun. N.Y. Med. Coll.-Hosp. Found., Valhalla, 1983-86. Recipient Westchester Man of Yr. award Gannett Newspapers, 1982. Mem. Chem. Mfrs. Assn. (gov.), Am. Swiss Assn.(bd. dirs.), Sigma Xi. Home: Hastings on Hudson N.Y. Died June 9, 1990; buried Zurich, Switzerland.

SUGARMAN, NATHAN, chemist, educator; b. Chgo., Mar. 3, 1917; s. Barnett and Tessie (Fischer) S.; m. Goldie G. Greenberg, Aug. 22, 1940; children—Tanya, Barry. B.S., U. Chgo., 1937, Ph.D., 1941. Rsch. assoc. metall. lab. U. Chgo., 1942-45, section chief Manhattan Project, 1943, asst. prof. chemistry, 1946-48, asst. prof., 1948-52, prof., from 1952, then prof. emeritus; With Los Alamos, Sci. Lab., 1945-46. Recipient Quantrell award for excellence in undergrad. teaching U. Chgo., 1966. Mem. AAAS, Am. Chem. Soc., Am. Phys. Soc., Fedn. Am. Scientists. Home: Chicago Ill. Died Sept. 6, 1990.

SUITS, CHAUNCEY GUY, research physicist; b. Oshkosh, Wis., Mar. 12, 1905; s. Chauncey G. and Otillia M. Suits; m. Laura E. Struckmeyer, Oct. 28, 1931; children—James Carr, David Guy. A.B., U. Wis., 1927; D.Sc., Nat. Technische Hochschule, Switzerland, 1929, Union Coll., 1944, Hamilton Coll., 1946, Drexel Inst., 1955, Marquette U., 1959; D.Eng., Rensselaer Poly. Inst., 1950. Physics cons. U.S. Forest Products Lab., Madison, Wis., 1929-30; physicist, research lab. Gen. Electric Co., 1930-40, asst. to dir. reseach lab., 1940-45, v.p., dir. research, 1945-65; cons. ind. research mgmt., from 1965; mem. N.Y. State Sci. and Tech. Found., from 1967, acting chmn., from 1975; mem. Naval Res. Adv. Com., 1956-64, chmn., 1958-61; mem. research adv. com. Com. on Sci. and Astronomy, U.S. Ho. of Reps. Contbr. articles to profl. jours.; holder 77 patents on variety elec. devices. Recipient Eta Kappa Nu award as outstanding young elec. engr., 1937, U.S. Presdl. medal for merit, 1948, King's medal for Service in Cause of Freedom (Great Britain), Procter prize Sci. Research Soc. Am., 1958, Disting. Service award Am. Mgmt. Assn., 1959, Indsl. Research Inst. Fellow IEEE (Frederik Philips award 1974), Am. Phys. Soc.; mem. Nat. Acad. Scis., Soc. History Tech., Am. Philos. Soc., Am. Acad. Arts and Scis., Nat. Acad. Engring. (founding mem.), Dirs. Indsl. Research (chmn. 1962-63), NAM (research com. 1952-65), Indsl. Research Inst., Phi Beta Kappa, Sigma Xi, Sigma Pi, Phi Mu Alpha, Phi Sigma Phi. Clubs: Lake George, Mohawk Golf, Glens Fall Country. Home: Pilot Knob N.Y. Died Aug. 14, 1991.

SULLIVAN, BOLTON, manufacturing executive; b. Chgo., Feb. 7, 1896; s. Joseph William and Jennie (Bolton) S.; m. Constance McDermott, Oct. 16, 1924; children: Gierlet, John. Student, U. Minn., 1919, U.S. Naval Acad., 1920. Investment banker Mpls., 1919-24; with SKIL Corp. (formerly Skilsaw, Inc.), Chgo., 1924-90, pres., 1940-58, chmn. bd. dirs., 1958-90, chmn. exec. com.; dir. Dean Co. Mem. Knights of Malta, Knights of St. Gregory, Univ. Club, Chgo. Club, Shoreacres Club, Old Elm Club, Seminole Club, Delta Kappa Epsilon. Roman Catholic. Home: Libertyville Ill. Died July 26, 1990.

SULLIVAN, CARL ROLLYNN, JR., association executive; b. Marietta, Ohio, Feb. 20, 1926; s. Carl Rollynn and Grace Roberta (Bengel) S.; m. Dolores Marion Cortes, Sept. 12, 1950; children: Carl R., Michael D., Peter A. B.S. in Forestry, W.Va. U., 1950; M.S. in Hydrobiology, Ohio State U., 1953. Asst. chief fish div. W.Va. Conservation Commn., 1951-55; land mgr., pub. relations mgr. Ravenswood Works, Kaiser Aluminum & Chem. Corp., 1955-62; exec. dir. W.Va. Centennial Commn., 1962-63; dir. Alaska Purchase Centennial, Anchorage, 1964-67; owner, mgr. Sullivan Services Advt. and Pub. Relations, 1968-72; exec. sec. Sports Fishing Inst., 1972-75; exec. dir. Am. Fisheries Soc., Bethesda, Md., from 1975. Editor: Fisheries mag., 1976-80. Contbr. articles to profl. jours. Commnr. W.Va. Dept. Natural Resources, 1956-60, from 1980; mem. U.S. Outer Continental Shelf Policy Com., Dept. Interior; mem. vis. com. W.Va. U. Coll. Agr. and Forestry. Served with U.S. Army, 1944-46. Recipient Gulf Oil Conservation award, 1984, Spl. Conservation Achievement award Nat. Wildlife Fedn., 1989, Barbara Swain award Resource Coun. Am., 1990. Mem. Am. League Anglers and Boaters (pres.), Am. Fisheries Soc., Wildlife Soc., Am. Soc. Assn. Execs., Council Engring. and Sci. Soc. Execs., Am. Oceanic Orgn., Izaak Walton League Am., Nat. Shellfish Assn., Renewable Natural Resource Found. (chmn. 1987-89). Methodist. Home: Charles Town W.Va. Deceased. †

SULLIVAN, DENNIS EDWARD, lawyer; b. Franklin, N.H., Aug. 27, 1894; s. Dennis E. and Mary A. (Welch) S.; m. Olive E. Marshall, July 14, 1931; children: Mary K., Anne. LLB, Boston U., 1924. Bar: N.H. 1924. Gen. practice law Franklin, N.H., 1924-34; asst. U.S. atty. Dist. of N.H., 1934-45; U.S. atty., from 1945; assoc. justice N.H. Superior Ct., from 1949. Mayor, City of Franklin, N.H., 1929-31. Served with U.S. Navy, World War I. Mem. N.H. Bar Assn., Am. Legion, Elks, KC (4 deg.). Democrat. Roman Catholic. *

SULLIVAN, ELEANOR REGIS, magazine editor; b. Cambridge, Mass., Oct. 19, 1928; d. Timothy Joseph and Katherine Irene (Dowd) S. B.S., Salem State Coll., 1950. Tchr. Clinton Grammar Sch., Conn., 1950-53, Russell Sch., Cambridge, Mass., 1953-57, George Washington Sch., White Plains, N.Y., 1957-60; editorial asst. Pocket Books, Inc., N.Y.C., 1961-62; editor Charles Scribner's Sons, N.Y.C., 1962-69; mng. editor Davis Publs., Inc., N.Y.C., from 1970; editor-in-chief Alfred Hitchcock's Mystery Mag., 1975-81, Ellery Queen's Mystery Mag., 1982-91; tchr. writing workshops. Author: Whodunit: A Biblio-Bio-Anecdotal Memoir of Frederic Dannay, 1984; contbr. stories and articles to mags., newspapers, books; pen names include Lika Van Ness, Julia DeHaan, Ruth Gaviros. Vol. ARC, St. Albans Naval Hosp., Queens, N.Y., 1968-73; vol. tutor I Have A Dream Program, N.Y.C., 1986-87. Mem. Mystery Writers Am. (bd. dirs. 1974-77, 82-85, Ellery Queen award 1987), Dramatists Guild, Am. Film Inst. Democrat. Home: New York N.Y. Died July 12, 1991.

SULLIVAN, MAX WILLIAM, museum director; b. Fremont, Mich., Sept. 27, 1909; s. James Timothy and Gertrude Maude (Clark) S.; m. Jeannette Stuart Todd, June 21, 1939 (div. 1974); children: Todd, Timothy Clark, William Shaun, Michael Towle, Caleb Kendall; m. Ruth Lois Wilkins, Aug. 31, 1975. A.B., Western Mich. U., 1932; M.A. in Teaching, Harvard U., 1941; LL.D., Providence Coll., 1950. Instr. arts and crafts Cranbrook Sch., Bloomfield Hills, Mich., 1933-35; condr. summer play sch., 1933-37; instr. arts and crafts Middlesex Sch., Concord, Mass., 1935-38; head art dept. Groton (Mass.) Sch., 1938-42; cons. art edn., sch. edn. Harvard, 1940-42; dir. exhbn. contemporary N.E. handicrafts Worcester (Mass.) Art Mus., 1942-43; cons. Met. Mus., N.Y.C., 1943-44; conducted survey recreational therapy in mil. hosps.; dir. edn. Mus. of Art, R.I. Sch. Design, Providence, 1944-45; dean edn. R.I. Sch. Design, 1945-47, pres. of corp., 1947-55; dir. Portland Art Assn.-Mus. and Art Sch., 1957-60, Everson Mus. Art of Syracuse and Onondage County, 1961-71; program dir. Kimbell Art Mus., Fort Worth, 1971-74; dir. adminstrv. services Kimbell Art Mus., 1974-76; adj. prof. art, dir. Univ. Art Gallery U. Tex. at Arlington, 1976-85; exhbns. curator Sch. Architecture and Design U. Tex., Arlington, from 1985. Mem. Coun. Mus's. and Edn. in the Visual Arts, 1973-78. Mem. AIA. Home: Fort Worth Tex. Deceased. †

SULLIVAN, THOMAS MICHAEL, civil engineer; b. Wellsville, N.Y., Apr. 28, 1913; s. Daniel Vincent and Catherine Theresa (McCarthy) S.; m. Margaret Louise Neptune, Aug. 5, 1939; children: Thomas Patrick, Kathleen Ann. BArch, BS in Structural Engring., Okla. State U., 1935. Registered profl. engr., Tex. Dir. internat. properties, then asst. sec. TWA, 1940-47; asst. airport engr., then 1st dep. dir. aviation Port N.Y. Authority, 1947-68; exec. dir. Dallas/Ft. Worth Regional Airport, 1968-75; dir. mktg. ground transp. Vought Corp., Dallas, 1975-91; mem. Presdl. Aviation Adv. Commn., 1970-72, Dallas/Ft. Worth Airport Bd.; cons. airports throughout world. Contbr. articles to profl. jours. Hon. v.p. State Fair Tex. Recipient Disting. Svc. medal Port N.Y. Authority for design Kennedy Airport, 1957, Engr. of Yr. award Am. Pub. Works Assn., 1972, Headliner of Yr. award Press Club of Dallas, 1974, Safety award Air Line Pilots Assn., 1973. Mem. Airport Operators Coun. Internat. Am. Pub. Transit Assn., ASCE (James Laurie prize 1975), Am. Helicopter Soc., Tex. Soc. Profl. Engrs., Tex. Soc. Architects, Knights of Malta, K.C. Kiwanis, Northwood Club. Roman Catholic. Home: Dallas Tex. Died Apr. 7, 1991.

SULZBY, JAMES FREDERICK, JR., real estate executive; b. Birmingham, Ala., Dec. 24, 1905; s. James Frederick and Annie (Dobbins) S.; m. Martha Belle Hilton, Nov. 9, 1935; children: James Frederick III, Martha Hilton (Mrs. Robert J.B. Clark). Student, Howard Coll., Birmingham, 1925-26; AB, Birmingham-So. Coll., 1928; grad., Am. Inst. Banking, 1934; LittD (hon.), Athens Coll.; LHD (hon.), Samford U., 1988. With trust dept. First Nat. Bank of Birmingham, 1929-43; partner Sulzby Realty Co., Birmingham, 1943-88; dir. Ala. Fed. Savs. & Loan Assn.; bd. dirs. Birmingham Area Bd. Realtors, pres., 1953; pres. Norwood Gardens, Inc. (housing project). Author: Birmingham As It Was in Jackson County, 1944, Birmingham Sketches, 1945, Annals of the Southside Baptist Church, 1947, Historic Alabama Hotels and Resorts, 1960, Arthur W. Smith, A Birmingham Pioneer, 1855-1944, 1961, Toward a History of Samford University, 1986. Trustee Rushton Lectures, Birmingham Civic Symphony Assn., Oak Hill Meml. Assn.; bd. dirs. Birmingham Sunday Sch. Assn., Ala. Baptist Publ. (emeritus mem.); mem. Birmingham Planning Commn., chmn., 1948-61; mem. adv. com. Civil War Centennial Commn.; historian 75th anniversary celebration for Birmingham, 1946; mem. adv. bd. Nat. Hist. Records; treas., mem. exec. com. Southside Bapt. Ch.; pres. Ala. Bapt. Young Peoples Union, 1932-33; bd. govs. Civic Theatre Birmingham, 1946-48; bd. dirs. Ala. Hall of Fame; chmn. Jefferson County Nat. Found. Infantile Paralysis, 1951-52, Jefferson County Hist. Commn.; mem. Cahaba Hist. Commn. Recipient Lit. award A.L.A., 1962. Mem. Newcomen Soc. U.S. (mem. Ala. com.), Ala. Hist. Assn. (pres. 1947-49, sec. 1950), Ala. Bapt. Hist. Soc. (pres. 1947-49), Birmingham-Jefferson Hist. Soc., Birmingham Hist. Soc. (sec. 1945-50, trustee from 1950), Avondale Civic Assn. (pres. 1946), Am. Planning and Civic Assn. (dir.), Ala. Assn. Realtors (pres. 1952), Ala. Writers Conclave (pres. 1950), Nat. Assn. Real Estate Bds. (dir. 1952-56), Ala. Acad. Sci. (pres. 1965, trustee), Birmingham-So. Coll. Nat. Alumni Assn. (pasr pres., Disting. Alumnus award 1985), Phi Beta Kappa, Phi Alpha Theta, Omega Tau Rho, Delta Sigma Phi, Omicron Delta Kappa. Democrat. Baptist. Clubs: Filson, Mountain Brook; Univ. (Tuscaloosa, Ala.). Home: Birmingham Ala. Died Oct. 27, 1988; buried Elmwood Cemetery, Birmingham, Ala. †

SUMMERSON, JOHN NEWENHAM, architectural historian; b. Darlington, Eng., Nov. 25, 1904; s. Samuel and Dorothea (Newenham) S.; ed. Univ. Coll., London; D.Litt. (hon.), univs. Leicester, Hull, Oxford and Newcastle; D.Sc. (hon.), U. Edinburgh; m. Elizabeth Hepworth, 1938; 3 children. Served in architects' offices and tchr. Edinburgh Coll. Art, 1929-30; on staff Architect and Bldg. News, 1934-40; dep. dir. Nat.

Bldgs. Record, 1940-45; curator Sir John Soane's Mus., 1945-84; mem. Royal Commn. Hist. Monuments, Hist. Bldgs. Council; chmn. Nat. Council Diplomas in Arts and Design, 1960-69; lectr. history of architecture Birkbeck Coll., 1961-70; Slade prof. fine art Oxford U., 1958-59; Ferens prof. fine art U. Hull, 1960-61, 70-71; Slade prof. fine art Cambridge U., 1966-67; Bampton lectr. Columbia U., 1967-68. Trustee, Nat. Portrait Gallery, 1966-73. Decorated Royal Gold medal for Architecture, 1976; comdr. Order Brit. Empire, Companion of Honour, 1987. Fellow Brit. Acad., Soc. Arts; mem. Am. Acad. Arts and Scis. (hon.). Author: John Nash, 1934, Georgian London, 1945, 6th rev. edit., 1988, Heavenly Mansions, 1949, Sir John Soane, 1952, Sir Christopher Wren, 1953, Architecture in Britain, 1530-1830, 1953, 7th rev. edit., 1983, The Classical Language of Architecture, 1964, Book of John Thorpe, 1966, Inigo Jones, 1966, Victorian Architecture, 1970, The Life and Work of John Nash, 1980, The Architecture of the 18th Century, 1986, The Unromantic Castle, 1990.Died Nov. 10, 1992. Home: London England †

SUNDERLAND, THOMAS ELBERT, lawyer, corporate executive; b. Ann Arbor, Mich., Apr. 28, 1907; s. Edson R. and Hannah Dell (Read) S.; m. Mary Louise Allyn, Dec. 21, 1946; children: Louise Allyn Sunderland Gavin, Anne Read, Thomas Edson (dec.), Mary Compton Sunderland Williamson, Alice Elizabeth (dec.). Student, Eng. and Sorbonne U., Paris, 1924-25; AB summa cum laude, U. Mich., 1928; student, U. Mich. Law Sch., 1927-29; JD, U. Calif.-Berkeley, 1930; postgrad., Harvard Bus. Sch., 1948. Bar: Mich. 1930, N.Y. 1933, D.C. 1948, Ill. 1948, Mass. 1962, Ariz. 1969, U.S. Supreme Ct., 1948. Union guardian Trust Co., Detroit, 1930-31, N.Y.C., 1931-48, Chgo., 1948-60; with firm Cadwalader, Wickersham & Taft, N.Y.C., 1931-33, Milbank, Tweed, Hadley & McCloy, N.Y.C., 1933-36, Townley, Updike & Carter, N.Y.C., 1936-40; gen. counsel Pan Am. Petroleum & Transport Co., Am. Oil Co., N.Y.C., 1940-48; dir., mem. exec. com. Pan Am. Petroleum & Transport Co., Am. Oil Co., 1945-48; v.p., gen. counsel, dir. Amoco Corp. (Standard Oil Co., Ind.), Chgo., 1948-60; also bd. dirs. Standard Oil Co. (Ind.), Chgo.; pres., chief exec. officer, chmn. bd., dir. United Fruit Co., Boston, 1959-69; with firm Snell & Wilmer, Phoenix, 1969-79; dir. First Nat. Bank of Boston, Nat. Cash Register Co., Liberty Mut. Ins. Co., Johns-Manville Corp.; mem. com. on pub. affairs Am. Petroleum Inst., 1948-59. Nat. trustee Lake Forest Coll.; trustee Lawrence Hall of Sci., U. Calif. at Berkeley; Boston Hosp. for Women, Winsor Sch., Boston; mem. vis. com. Grad. Sch. Bus. Adminstrn., Law Sch. and Sch. Pub. Health, Harvard U.; mem. vis. com Law Sch. U. Chgo., Law Sch. U. Stanford; chmn. nat. com. U. Mich. Law Sch., also vis. com.; trustee Phoenix Symphony, 1971-81, pres., 1979-81; mem. corp. Northeastern U., Boston; nat. bd. dirs. Nat. Merit Scholarship Corp.; trustee Phoenix Country Day Sch. Lt. col. USAAF, 1942-46, ETO. Decorated Bronze Star. Mem. ABA (com. on jurisprudence and law reform 1940-41, nat. chmn. sect. antitrust law 1953-58), Inter-Am. Bar Assn., Am. Law Inst., Ill. Bar Assn., Ariz. Bar Assn., Assn. of Bar of City of N.Y., Chgo. Bar Assn., Coun. on Fgn. Rels., Nat. Indsl. Conf. Bd. (sr. mem.), Squadron A Assn. (N.Y.C.), Assn. Gen. Counsel (co-founder), Wianno Club, The Beach Club, Bohemian Club, Phoenix Country Club, The Country Club, Chgo. Club, Chgo. Golf Club, Glenview Club, Met. Club, Union League, Ariz. Club., Paradise Valley Club, Phi Beta Kappa, Phi Delta Phi, Phi Gamma Delta, Phi Kappa Phi. Home: Paradise Valley Ariz. Died Mar. 1, 1991; buried Christ Church yard, Winnetka, Ill.

SUNDHEIM, GEORGE MELCHOIR, lawyer; b. Chgo., Jan. 26, 1894; s. Joseph John and Margaret Catherine (Mathias) S.; m. Bertha Korup, Sept. 24, 1919 (dec. Sept. 1954); children: Dorothy Gene, Marguerite Catherine, George Melchoir; m. 2d, Blanche Paynter, Apr. 4, 1956. Grad., Lewis Inst. Tech., 1913; student, Northwestern U., 1915-16, Chgo. Kent Coll. Law, 1916, Columbia U. and Fordham U., 1917. Bar: N.Y. 1919, Ill. 1922, U.S. Dist. Ct. 1932, U.S. Supreme Ct. 1932. With Chgo. Title & Trust Co., 1911-14; atty. Nat. Biscuit Co., N.Y.C., 1916-17, 19-22; with law firm Tenney, Harding, Sherman & Rogers, Chgo., 1922-29; pvt. practice law, from 1929; gen. counsel, sec., bd. dirs. Barney Olson, Inc., Gas Equipment Maintenance Inc., Allied Mfg. & Sales Inc., Streeter-Amet Co.; gen. counsel, asst. sec., dir. Crooks Terminal Warehouses, Inc.; gen. counsel, dir. Clearing Safe Deposit Co., Grand Specialties Co., Sasgen Derrick Co., State Bank of Clearing; gen. counsel, sec. 565 W. Washington Corp.; gen. counsel Anderson Engring. Co., Brewer Sewing Supplies Co., Gt. Lakes Spring div. Rockwell Standard Corp., Sch. Dist. 110, Engine Sales, Inc.; counsel Agar Container div. Internat. Paper Co., Arkell Safety Bag, Ethican Suture div. Johnson & Johnson. Justice of peace Lyons Twp., Cook County, 1930-38; trustee Village of LaGrange, Ill., 1940-42; chmn. LaGrange Zoning Appeal Bd., Lagrange Coun.; atty. for trustees of schs. Stickney Twp. Served with naval aviation USN, World War I. Mem. ABA, Ill. State Bar Assn., Chgo. Bar Assn., Am. Legion (adj.), Masons, Union League Club, LaGrange Country Club, Big Foot Country Club (Lake Geneva, Wis.), Northwestern Univ. Club (Evanston, Ill.). Republican. Methodist. *

SUPPON, CHARLES RICHARD, fashion designer; b. East St. Louis, Ill., Jan. 12, 1949; s. Charles George and Myra Louise (Sova) S. BFA, U. Chgo. and Sch. of Art Inst., 1971. Asst. to Mr. Klein Calvin Klein, Ltd., N.Y.C., 1971-76; designer Intresport, N.Y.C., from 1976; contbr. Simplicity Designer Patterns, 1977; vis. instr. fashion Parsons Fashion Inst. Tech., 1977-79. Recipient Coty award, 1979; Menswear nomination, 1979. Mem. Fashion Coun. Am. Methodist. Home: New York N.Y. Died Mar. 21, 1989.

SUTHERLAND, ALLEN JENNINGS, banker; b. Waverly, Nebr., May 1, 1896; s. Alfred E. and Minnie (Olsen) S.; m. Estelle Warner, June 29, 1921; children: A. Paul, Barbara (Mrs. James Louis Dall). AB, U. Nebr., 1917. Cashier First State Bank, Palmer, Kans., 1920-21; mgr. Am. Bank, Oakland, Calif., 1922-24; pres. First Nat. Bank, Bakersfield, Calif., 1924-28; v.p., cashier Security Trust & Savs. Bank of San Diego, 1928-45, pres., 1945-57; chmn. bd. Fiesta del Pacifico, Inc., San Diego, from 1958; chmn. San Diego bd. Security First Nat. Bank; bd. dirs. City Transit System. Bd. dirs. The Putnam Found., San Diego. Served as ensign USN, 1917. Mem. San Diego Opera Guild, Fine Arts Soc. San Diego, Am. Legion, Masons, Elks, Town and Country Club, Yacht Club of San Diego. Presbyterian. *

SUTTON, HORACE ASHLEY, magazine editor, writer; b. N.Y.C., May 17, 1919; s. Herman and Belle (Chodorov) S.; m. Nancy Waring, May 7, 1950; 1 son, Andrew Charles; m. Patricia Anne Diamond, June 8, 1958; children: Miranda, Patrick. Student, U. Pa., 1936-38, Columbia U., 1938-41. With N.Y. Sun, 1938-39; with N.Y. Post, 1939-41, travel editor, 1946-47; travel editor Sat. Rev., 1947-61, asso. editor, 1961-72, editorial dir., 1975-81; editorial dir. World Mag., 1972-73, Saturday Rev./World, 1973-74; syndicated newspaper travel columnist Of All Places, from 1952; contbg. travel editor Sports Illustrated, 1954-61; contbg. editor McCalls mag., 1961-65, asso. editor, 1967-68, mng. editor, 1969, contbg. editor, 1971; editorial dir. Paradise of Pacific, 1963-66; contbg. columnist Bon Appetit mag., 1979-80; editor Signature mag., 1981-85; editor-in-chief Citicorp Pub. Co., 1985-87; radio-TV commentator and panelist. Author: Footloose in France, 1948, Footloose in Canada, 1950, Footloose in Italy, 1950, Happy Holiday, 1950, Footloose in Switzerland, 1951, Confessions of a Grand Hotel, 1952, Sutton's Places, 1954, Aloha, Hawaii, 1967, Travelers: The American Tourist from Stagecoach to Space Shuttle, 1980, A Palace for Potentates: The Beverly Wilshire Hotel, 1989; editorial cons. travel Endless Vacation Mag., 1987-88, exec. editor 1988-89, editorial dir., 1989-90. Served to capt. inf. AUS, 1941-46, ETO. Decorated Bronze Star U.S.; Croix de Guerre with silver star, Legion of Honor (France), Star of Solidarity (Italy); recipient Travel Journalism award Am. Soc. Travel Agts., 1951, Journalism award for mags. TWA, 1951, for newspapers 1959, for mags., 1970, Asia mag. Overseas Press Club award, 1968, French Medaille du Tourisme Nat. Fedn. Syndicate d'Initiative, 1973, French Medaille de la Connaissance, 1980, Marcia Vickery Wallace Meml. award Caribbean Tourist Assn., 1987, Gold award Pacific Asia Travel Assn., 1989, Melva C. Pederson extraordinary journalistic achievement award Am. Soc. Travel Agts., 1989, Pata Gold award, 1991. Mem. Travel Writers Assn. (past pres.). Club: Overseas Press (N.Y.C.) (bd. govs. 1960-62). Home: New York N.Y. Died Oct. 26, 1991.

SUTTON, REGINALD MILLER, transportation consultant; b. Omaha, Mar. 15, 1899; s. Robert Marshall and Edith Jane (Hearle) S.; m. Alice Stone, Mar. 18, 1920; children: Betty Jane Sutton McVicar, Alice Nancy Sutton Gilmore, Beverly Ann Sutton Ward. Student, Creighton U., 1923-24. With Union Pacific R.R., 1915-89, clk., traveling acct., chief clk., dept. and gen. auditor, 1915-55, v.p., gen. auditor, 1955-60, v.p., contr., dir., 1960-66, v.p. fin., dir., 1967-69, exec. v.p., 1969-70; mem. exec. com. Union Pacific Corp., 1967-70; dir., cons., 1971-89; dir. Union Pacific R.R. Bd. dirs. Bishop Clarkson Meml. Hosp. With USNR, World War I. Mem. Am. Legion, Assn. Am. R.R.s (past chmn. acctg. div.), Newcomen Soc., Omaha Country Club, N.Y. Athletic Club (N.Y.C.), Masons, Shriners. Episcopalian. Home: Omaha Nebr. Died Mar. 27, 1989.

SWALES, WILLIAM EDWARD, oil company executive; b. Parkersburg, W.Va., May 15, 1925; s. John Richard and Ellen (South) S.; m. Lydia Eugena Mills, Dec. 26, 1948; children: Joseph V., Susan Eugena, David Lee. BA in Geology, W.Va. U., 1949, MS in Geology, 1951; grad., advanced mgmt. program Stanford U., 1968; DSc (hon.), W.Va. U., 1986; LLD (hon.), Marietta Coll., 1986. With Marathon Oil Co. (subs. USX Corp.), Findlay, Ohio, 1954-70, 74-87, mgr. Western Hemisphere and Australia div., 1967-70; exec. v.p. Oasis Oil Co. of Libya Inc., Tripoli, 1970-72; pres. Oasis Oil Co., 1972-74; spl. asst. to sr. v.p. prodn., internat. Marathon Oil Co., Findlay, Ohio, 1974; v.p. prodn., internat. Marathon Oil Co. (subs. USX Corp.), 1974-77, sr. v.p. prodn., internat., 1977-82, also bd. dirs., 1983-84, sr. v.p. exploraton and prodn., 1984-85, pres., 1985-87, pres. Marathon Petroleum Co., 1982-83; exec. dir. USX Corp., Pitts., 1985-90, vice chmn. energy, 1987-90, ret., 1990; exec. dir. USX Corp., 1985; dir. OHM Corp. With USN, 1943-45. Mem. Am. Assn. Petroleum Geologists, Soc. Petroleum Engrs., Am. Geol. Inst., Nat. Petroleum Coun., OHM Corp., 25 Yr. Club Petroleum Industry, Findlay Country Club, Ballen Isles Country Club of JDM, Rolling Rock Club. Home: West Palm Beach Fla. Died June 13, 1992. †

SWANBERG, WILLIAM ANDREW, author; b. St. Paul, Nov. 23, 1907; s. Charles Henning and Valborg (Larsen) S.; m. Dorothy Upham Green, Mar. 21, 1936; children: John William, Sara Valborg. B.A., U. Minn., 1930; postgrad., N.Y. U., 1944. Worked as common laborer during the depression; Editor Dell Pub. Co., N.Y.C., 1935-44; field rep. OWI, Europe, 1944-45; free lance writer, from 1945. Author: Sickles the Incredible, 1956, First Blood-The Story of Fort Sumter, 1957, Jim Fisk, 1959, Citizen Hearst, 1961, Dreiser, 1965, Pulitzer, 1967, The Rector and The Rogue, 1968, Luce and His Empire, 1972 (Pulitzer prize for biography 1973), Norman Thomas: The Last Idealist, 1976 (Nat. Book award for biography 1977), Whitney Father, Whitney Heiress, 1980. Mem. Newtown Library Bd. Recipient Christopher award, 1959, Frank Luther Mott Research prize, 1962, Van Wyck Brooks award for non-fiction, 1968, Outstanding Achievement award U. Minn., Carr Van Anda award in journalism Ohio U.; Guggenheim fellow, 1960. Fellow Soc. Am Historians; mem. Authors League Am., Internat. P.E.N. Home: Southbury Conn. Deceased. †

SWANK, ARTHUR JACKSON, utility company executive; b. Colusa, Calif., Sept. 28, 1896; s. John Lois and Hattie Mae (Hart) S.; m. Jeanette Killebrew, June 27, 1923; 1 dau., Jane Elizabeth (Mrs. F. William Popp, Jr.). BS cum laude, U. Calif., Berkeley, 1918. Registered profl. engr., Calif. With Pacific Gas & Electric Co., from 1919, laborer, electrician, constrn. foreman, asst. engr., supt., also asst. dispatcher, asst. engr., asst. mgr. gen. constrn., also mgr. gen. constrn., v.p. gen. constrn., 1953-58, v.p. ops. and constrn., from 1958; v.p. Nev. Power Co., from 1963. Mem. exec. bd. San Francisco coun. Boy Scouts Am.; mem. men's adv. com. San Francisco coun. Girl Scouts U.S. Served as 2d lt. U.S. Army, 1918. Fellow Am. Inst. E.E.; mem. Pacific Coast Elec. Assn. (dir.), C. of C., Newcomen Soc., Masons, Engrs. Club, Electric Club of San Francisco, Eta Kappa Nu. *

SWANN, MICHAEL MEREDITH, university administrator, former broadcasting executive; b. Shortlands, Kent, Eng., Mar. 1, 1920; s. Meredith Blake Robson and Marjorie (Dykes) S.; M.A., Cambridge (Eng.) U., 1940, Ph.D., 1949; LL.D., Aberdeen U., 1967; D.Sc., Leicester U., 1968; D.Univ., York U., 1968, U. Edinburgh, 1983; D.Litt., Heriot Watt U., 1971; m. Teresa Ann Gleadowe, Aug. 7, 1942; children—Richard Meredith, Sylvia Swann Garnett, Catriona Swann Watson, Peter. Demonstrator, fellow Gonville and Caius Coll., Cambridge U., 1946-52; prof. natural history U. Edinburgh (Scotland), 1952-65, vice chancellor, prin., 1965-73; chmn. bd. BBC, 1973-80; chancellor U. York, 1980-90. Chmn. Scottish Health Services Sci. Council, 1971-73, Joint Com. Interdepartmental Antibiotics in Animal Husbandry, 1968-70, Joint Com. on Future Vet. Profession, 1971-75; chmn. Royal Acad. Music, London, 1983-90; mem. Med. Research Council, 1962-65, Sci. Research Council, 1970-73. Served to lt. col. Brit. Army, 1940-46. Created knight bachelor Order Brit. Empire. Fellow Inst. Biology, Royal Soc. (London and Edinburgh), Royal Coll. Physicians Edinburgh (hon.), Royal Coll. Surgeons Edinburgh (hon.). Clubs: Athenaeum (London, Eng.); New (Edinburgh).Died Sept. 22, 1990. Home: Cheltenham Eng. †

SWANSON, CARROLL ARTHUR, botanist, educator; b. Burlington, Iowa, Sept. 6, 1915; s. Frank Arthur and Fidelia (Holmen) S.; m. Betty Marker, June 15, 1941; children: Richard Marker, Nancy Joan. AB, Augustana Coll., 1937; MSc, Ohio State U., 1938, PhD, 1942. Mem. faculty Ohio State U., from 1940, prof. botany, from 1956, chmn. dept., 1967-68, chmn. faculty organismic and developmental biology, 1968-69, assoc. dean Coll. Biol. Scis., 1969-70; rsch. assoc. Manhattan Project, 1943-46, Oak Ridge Inst. Nuclear Studies, 1952, Argonne Nat. Lab., 1954; program dir. spl. projects in sci. edn. NSF, 1959-60, mem. nat. panel regulatory biology, 1964-66. Author: (with others) Laboratory Plant Physiology, 1955; mem. editorial com. Ann. Revs. Plant Physiology, 1954-60, editorial bd. Plant Physiology, from 1969; contbr. articles to profl. jours. Mem. AAAS, Am. Soc. Plant Physiologists (exec. com. from 1973), Scandinavian, Can. socs. plant physiologists, Bot. Soc. Am., Ohio Acad. Sci. (joint adminstrv. bd. from 1967), Sigma Xi. Home: Columbus Ohio Died June 9, 1991; buried Union Cemetery, Columbus, Ohio.

SWANSON, FRANK, newspaper publisher; b. Edmonton, Alta., Can., Apr. 11, 1917; s. Frank and Clara (Olson) S.; m. Vera Gowing, Dec. 2, 1944; 1 child, David. BA, U. Alta., 1937; MS, Columbia U., 1938. With London bur. Southam Newspapers of Can., 1945-48; parliamentary corr. Ottawa Citizen, 1948, 56-60, assoc. editor, 1956-60, editor, 1960-62; v.p., pub. The Calgary (Alta.) Herald, 1962-90. Served to maj. Can. Army, 1940-45. Mem. Can. War Corr. Assn., Rideau Club, Ranchmen's Club, Calgary Petroleum Club, Calgary Golf and Country Club, Glencoe Club. Home: Calgary, AB Canada Died Mar. 5, 1990.

SWANSON, H(AROLD) N(ORLING), literary agent; b. Centerville, Iowa, Aug. 28, 1899; s. Swan P. and Lillian (Norling) S.; m. Ruth Evelyn Taylor, Jan. 13, 1930 (dec. 1982); m. Norma Virginia Sherman, Jan. 10, 1984; children: Janet Shanks-Willingham, Carol Shanks-Galli, Thomas J. Shanks. BA in Humanities, Grinnell Coll., 1923. V.p. and editorial dir. Collegiate World Pub. Co., Chgo., 1923-30; editor College Humor Mag., 1923-30; producer R.K.O. Radio Pictures Studio, Hollywood, Calif., 1930-34; founder, pres. H.N. Swanson Inc., L.A., 1934-91. Author: Corn, Moods from Mid-America, 1922, They Fell in Love, 1932, Sprinkled with Ruby Dust, 1989, (screen play) Big Business Girl, 1930. Mem. Sigma Delta Chi, St. James Club (L.A.), Tavern Club (Chgo., founding mem. 1927). Home: Beverly Hills Calif. Died May 31, 1991; buried Forest Lawn Meml. Pk, Calif.

SWARTHOUT, GLENDON FRED, author; b. Pinckney, Mich., Apr. 8, 1918; s. Fred Harrington and Lila (Chubb) S.; m. Kathryn Blair Vaughn, Dec. 28, 1940; 1 son, Miles. A.B., U. Mich., 1939, A.M., 1946; Ph.D., Mich. State U., 1955. Author: Willow Run, 1943, They Came to Cordura, 1958, Where the Boys Are, 1960, Welcome to Thebes, 1962, (with Kathryn Swarthout) The Ghost and the Magic Saber, 1963, The Cadillac Cowboys, 1964, (with Kathryn Swarthout) Whichaway, 1966, The Eagle and the Iron Cross, 1966, Loveland, 1968, (with Kathryn Swarthout) The Button Boat, 1969, Bless the Beasts and Children, 1970, (with Kathryn Swarthout) TV Thompson, 1972, The Tin Lizzie Troop, 1972, Luck and Pluck, 1973, The Shootist, 1975, (with Kathryn Swarthout) Whales to See The, 1975, The Melodeon, 1977, Skeletons, 1979, (with Kathryn Swarthout) Cadbury's Coffin, 1982, The Old Colts, 1985, The Homesman, 1988; contbr.: short stories to mags. including New World Writing, Esquire. Served with U.S. Army, 1943-45, ETO. Recipient Playwriting award Theater Guild, 1947, Hopwood award in fiction 1948, O. Henry Prize Short Stories 1960, Gold medal Nat. Soc. Arts and Letters 1972, Spur award for best western novel Western Writers Am. 1975, 88, Wrangler award for outstanding western novel Western Heritage Found., 1988, Owen Wister award for lifetime achievement Western Writers Am., 1991. Home: Scottsdale Ariz. Died Sept. 23, 1992. †

SWARTHOUT, HERBERT MARION, insurance executive; b. Sioux Falls, S.D., Aug. 29, 1900; s. Earl Beagle and Jennie Laura (Aldrich) S.; m. Lila Ellen Sosamon, Dec. 21, 1926 (dec. Sept. 1985); 1 dau., Joan Swarthout Wahlstedt; m. Eleanor Replogle, Apr. 22, 1989. Student, Nebr. U., 1920-21, Washington U., 1922; grad., Am. Coll. Life Underwriters, 1942. In life ins. bus., 1928-90; specializing in estate planning; rep. Mut. Benefit Life Ins. Co. of N.J., 1947-90; founder Uniformed Services Benefit Assn., exec. dir., 1959-75; pres. Herrick Fin. Services, Inc. Sponsor activities YMCA; pres., gen. chmn. Heart Am. Meml. Torch Ceremony, 1963-64; bd. dirs. Frontier Army Mus. Assn., 1981-90. Mem. Nebr. U. Alumni Assn. (past pres. Kansas City chpt.), Life Underwriters Assn. Kansas City, Million Dollar Round Table (life and qualifying), Nat. Assn. Life Underwriters, Am. Soc. C.L.U.'s, Five Million Dollar Forum, Top of the Table, Mut. Benefit Life Nat. Assos. Hall of Fame, S.R. (pres. Kansas City 1956, pres. Mo. soc. 1958-59), S.A.R., Assn. U.S. Army (liaison chmn.), Kansas City Art Inst. Mem. Christian Ch. Clubs: Masons (Kansas City, Mo.), Shriners (Kansas City, Mo.), DeMolay (Kansas City, Mo.) (hon. legion of honor), Rotary (Kansas City, Mo.), Kansas City (Kansas City, Mo.), Carriage (Kansas City, Mo.), Eleven-Eleven (Kansas City, Mo.). Home: Kansas City Mo. Died Apr. 2, 1990; interred Forest Lawn Mausoleum, Kansas City, Mo.

SWARTZ, EDWARD M(ITCHELL), manufacturing executive; b. Russia, Apr. 2, 1896; brought to U.S., 1903, naturalized, 1917; s. Samuel and Belle (Lebow) S.; m. Gertrude W. Weisman, June 29, 1919; children: Frederick C., Robert J. Student, Lowell Inst., 1915-16, Boston U., 1917-19. Mech. engr., 1915-19; a founder Keystone Mfg. Co., Boston, 1919, pres., 1919-34/from 52, treas., from 1934; pres., treas. Keystone Camera Co., Boston. Mem. Soc. Motion Picture and TV Engrs., Nat. Assn. Photog. Mfrs. (pres., dir.), Masons, Belmont (Mass.) Country Club. *

SWEARER, HOWARD ROBERT, educational institute administrator, university president; b. Hutchinson, Kans., Mar. 13, 1932; s. Edward Mays and Elloise (Keeney) S.; m. Janet Lois Baker, June 19, 1954; children: Nicholas Baker, Howard Randolph, Richard William. AB, Princeton U., 1954; MA, Harvard U., 1956, PhD, 1960; hon. doctorate, Brown U., Princeton U., Providence Coll., Roger Williams Coll., Tougaloo Coll., Allegheny Coll. Assoc. prof. polit. sci. UCLA, 1960-67; program officer-in-charge office European and internat. affairs Ford Found., N.Y.C., 1967-70; pres. Carleton Coll., Northfield, Minn., 1970-77; pres. Brown U., Providence, 1977-89, dir. Thomas Watson Inst. for Internat. Studies, 1989-91; bd. dirs. Bolt, Beranek & Newman, SBSF Fund, Wang Labs., Inc., Keystone Provident Life Ins. Co. Bd. dirs The Salzberg Seminar, German Marshall Fund, R.I. Pub. Expenditure Coun., pres., 1986-88; trustee Brookings Instn.; exec. com. Pub. Agenda Fund. 1st lt. AUS, 1958-59. Mem. Coun. Fgn. Rels. Home: Thompson Conn. Died Oct. 19, 1991; cremated.

SWEAZEY, GEORGE EDGAR, minister; b. Salt Lake City, Mar. 17, 1905; s. George Beaty and Anna (Furry) S.; m. Mary Handy Enaminger, June 24, 1937; children: Ann Fulton Sweazey Prichard, George Edgar, Mary Handy. AB, Westminster Coll., Mo., 1927, DD, 1939; ThB, Princeton Theol. Sem., 1930; MA, Princeton U., 1930; PhD, U. Berlin, 1931; DD, Grove City Coll., 1948; LHD, Waynesburg Coll., 1970, Lindenwood Coll., 1970, Centre Coll., 1971; HHD, Westminster Coll., 1970. Ordained to ministry Presbyn. Ch., 1932. Minister 2d Presbyn. Ch., Danville, Ky., 1932-39, Tyler Pl. Presbyn. Ch., St. Louis, 1939-45, Huguenot Meml. Presbyn. Ch., Pelham, N.Y., 1953-58, Webster Groves (Mo.) Presbyn. Ch., 1959-71; prof. homiletics Princeton (N.J.) Theol. Sem., 1971-75; sec. for evangelism Presbyn. Ch. in U.S.A., 1945-53; chmn. dept. evangelism, mem. gen. bd. Nat. Coun. Chs. of Christ in U.S.A., 1952; pres. Mo. Coun. Chs., 1944; mem. Commn. on Ecumenical Mission and Rels. United Presbyn. Ch., 1959-71, chmn. gen. coun., 1969-70, moderator Gen. Assembly, 1969-70. Author: The Keeper of the Door, 1946, Effective Evangelism, 1953, The Christian Answer, 1962, In Holy Marriage, 1966, Evangelism in the United States, 1958, Preaching the Good News, 1975. Bd. dirs. St. Luke's Hosp., St. Louis; trustee Westminster Coll., Lindenwood Coll., Princeton Theol. Sem. Home: Princeton N.J. Died Jan. 23, 1992.

SWEDLOW, JEROLD LINDSAY, engineering educator; b. Denver, Aug. 31, 1935; s. Jack and Evelyn Lillian (Weinstein) S.; m. Patricia Lucille Lauer, Mar. 25, 1959; children: Jason, Pamela, Kathryn. BS, Calif. Inst. Tech., 1957, PhD, 1965; MS, Stanford U., 1960. Research engr. Ingersoll-Rand Corp., Phillipsburg, N.J., 1957-59; research fellow Calif. Inst. Tech., Pasadena, 1965-66; asst. prof. engring. Carnegie-Mellon U., Pitts., 1966-69, assoc. prof., 1969-73, prof., 1973-89, assoc. dean, 1977-79; vis. scientist U.S. Steel Research Labs., 1966; sr. vis. fellow Imperial Coll., London, 1973-74; chmn. Com. on Toughness Requirements for Materials in Weapon Systems, Washington, 1977-80. Contbr. articles to profl. jours.; editor: Reports of Current Research, Internat. Jour. Fracture, from 1969. Pres. bd. trustees First Unitarian Ch., Pitts. Recipient Philip M. McKenna Meml. award Carnegie-Mellon U., 1978; recipient Ralph Coats Roe award Am. Soc. Engring. Edn., 1983. Fellow AAAS, ASTM (award of Merit 1983), ASME; mem. Am. Acad. Mechanics, Internat. Congress on Fracture (founder). Democrat. Home: Pittsburgh Pa. Died July, 1989.

SWEENEY, HENRY WHITCOMB, government official; b. Springfield, Mass., Sept. 12, 1898; s. Anthony Joseph and E. Inez (Stacy) S.; m. Mae Edith Fichter, June 12, 1934; 1 dau., Diana Mae. BA, Columbia U., 1919, BS, 1920, MS, 1921, MA, 1924, PhD, 1936, LLM, 1960; LLB, Georgetown U., 1940. Bar: D.C. 1940, Va. 1944; CPA, N.Y., D.C., Va., N.J., La., Ark., P.R., N.J., Wiss., Ill. Tchr. acctg. U. Wis., U. Pitts., 1921-25; pub. acct. Price, Waterhouse & Co., 1925-35; fed. govt. acct., supervisory bank examiner, 1935-39; chief acct. Navy Contract Appeals Bd., 1939-43; prof. acctg. Georgetown U., 1936-44; sr. ptnr. Henry W. Sweeney & Co., CPAs, N.Y.C., also Washington, from 1943; prof. law Georgetown Law Sch., 1941-58; spl. asst. to asst. sec. Dept. Def., 1951-53, 64, dep. asst. sec. for acctg. and audit policy, from 1965; guest prof. law U. Frankfurt, Germany, 1954; adj. prof. fin. acctg. Columbia Grad. Sch. Bus., from 1956; pres. Singer & Friedlander, Inc., investment bankers, N.Y.C., from 1957. Author: Introductory Accounting, 1924; Stabilized Accounting, rev. edit., 1964; (with Houstin Shockey) Effects of Operating as a Corporation or Partnership, 1957; (with Houstin Shockey and Gerald Brady) Taxation and Business Planning, 1963. Mem. AICPA, Assn. Bar D.C., Assn. Bar City N.Y., Va. Bar Assn., Cosmos Club, Union League, Recess Club, West Side Tennis Club, Heights Casino Cub, Accts. Club, Columbia U. Club, Grolier Club, Army-Navy Country Club (Arlington, Va.), Sleepy Hollow Country Club (Scarborough, N.Y.), Alpha Kappa Psi, Beta Gamma Sigma, Pi Gamma Mu, Phi Kappa Psi, Phi Alpha Delta. *

SWENSON, BIRGER, publishing executive; b. Averstad, Skattkarr, Sweden, July 31, 1895; came to U.S., 1912, naturalized, 1918; s. Sven and Johanna (Spetz) Svensson; m. Lyal E. Westerlund, Aug. 14, 1943. A.B., Augustana Coll., 1924, LL.D., 1958; student, Theol. Sem., 1925-26, Northwestern U., summer 1923. Field rep. Augustana Book Concern, Rock Island, Ill., 1926; circulation mgr. Augustana Book Concern, 1927-42, sales mgr., 1942-44, acting mgr., 1944-45, gen. mgr., treas., 1945-62; assoc. exec. sec. Fortress Press, Bd. Publ. Lutheran Ch. Am., Rock Island, 1962-63; exec. bd. Ill. Synod Luth. Ch. Am., 1965-71; dir. Graphic Arts Industry, Mpls., 1946-66. Author: autobiography My Story, 1979; Editor: Augustana Almanac, 1930-47; co-editor: Augustana Ann, 1948-62; mem. editorial com.: Am.-Swedish Handbook, vols. 1, 2, 4, 5, 6, 7, 8. Bd. missions Augustana Luth. Ch., 1941-50; pres. Rock Island YMCA, 1957-59; Mem. Rock Island Bd. Zoning Appeals, 1965-75; Bd. dirs. Luth. Hosp., Moline, Ill., 1943-48, 63-65; trustee Augustana Luth. Found., 1930-62, Augustana Annuity Trust, 1942-83; past pres. Augustana Annuity Trust; founder Swenson Swedish Immigration Research Center, Augustana Coll. Served with U.S. Army, 1918-19, Europe. Decorated knight Order of Vasa 1st class Sweden, comdr. Order of North Star Sweden. Mem. Augustana Luther League Council (treas. 1933-37), Am. Fedn. Luth. Brotherhoods (treas. 1939-43), Augustana Coll. Alumni Assn. (pres. 1938-39), Internat. Council Religious Edn. (nat. pres. publs. sect. 1950-51), Luth. Men Am., Protestant Church-Owned Pubs. Assn. (past pres.), Nat. Council Chs. Christ U.S. (bd. mgrs. central dept. publs. and distbn. 1950-54), Augustana, Swedish Pioneer, Ill. hist. socs., Am.-Scandinavian Found., Am. Swedish Hist. Found., Am. Swedish Inst., Augustana Swedish Inst., Nat. Luth. Pubs. House Mgrs. Assn. (treas. 1933-63), Rock Island County Hist. Soc., Rock Island C. of C. (life mem.), Am. Legion. Republican. Clubs: Union League (Chgo.); Intrepids Inc, Kiwanis (life mem.), Quad City Athletic. Home: Rock Island Ill. Died Jan. 18, 1990; buried Rock Island, Ill.

SWENSON, MAY, poet; b. Logan, Utah, May 28, 1913; d. Dan Arthur and Margaret (Hellberg) S. B.S., Utah State U., 1934, LittD (hon.), 1987, PhD (hon.), 1987. Editor New Directions Press, 1959-66; mem. staff Breadloaf Writers Conf., 1976. Poet-in-residence, Purdue U., Lafayette, Ind., 1966-67, U. N.C., Greensboro, 1968-69, 75, Lethbridge U., Alta., Can., 1970, U. Calif., Riverside, 1973; Hurst prof. Washington U., St. Louis, 1982; Author: Another Animal, 1954, A Cage of Spines, 1958, To Mix with Time, 1963, Poems to Solve, 1966, Half Sun Half Sleep, 1967, Iconographs, 1970, More Poems to Solve, 1971, (translated from Swedish) Windows & Stones (Tomas Tranströmer), 1972, The Guess and Spell Coloring Book, 1976, New and Selected Things Taking Place, 1978, In Other Words, 1987, Love Poems, 1991, The Complete Poems to Solve, 1992. Recipient Nat. Inst. Arts and Letters award, 1960; Brandeis U. award, 1967; Disting. Service Gold medal Utah State U., 1967; Shelley Meml. award Poetry Soc. Am., 1968; transl. medal Internat. Poetry Forum, 1972; Bollingen prize in poetry Yale U., 1981; Guggenheim fellow, 1959; Amy Lowell Travelling scholar, 1960; Ford Found. fellow, 1965; Rockefeller Found. fellow, 1967-68; Lucy Martin Donnally fellow Bryn Mawr Coll., 1968-69, McArthur Found. fellow, 1987; Nat. Endowment for Arts grantee, 1974. Fellow Acad. Am. Poets (chancellor 1980); mem. Am. Acad. and Inst. Arts and Letters, Corp. of Yaddo. Home: Sea Cliff N.Y. Died Dec. 4, 1989; buried Logan, Utah.

SWIFT, FREDERIC FAY, college administrator, publisher; b. Auburn, N.Y., Mar. 6, 1907; s. Dr. Charles Frederic and Lucy (Williams) S.; Mus.B., Ithaca Coll., 1928; M.S., Syracuse U., 1940; Mus.D., U. Montreal, 1947; m. Ruth Ainslie, June 25, 1930 (dec. Aug. 1950); children: Nancy Ruth, Robert Frederic, David William; m. Norma C. Wood, Sept. 1951; 1 dau., Deborah Fae. Supr. music edn., Ilion, N.Y., 1928-48; sec.-treas. N.Y. State Sch. Music Assn., 1932-45; dir. Williams Music Camp, 1944-47; founder, pres. N.Y. State Music Camp, Otter Lake, 1947-84; chmn. edn. dept., dir. tchr. tng. Hartwick Coll., 1958-72, coord. student teaching, 1972-75, chmn. music dept., 1955-71, chmn. edn. dept., 1957-75, chmn. divsn. Applied Arts and Scis.; dir. music Ilion Bapt. Ch., 1928-48, Main Street Bapt. Ch., Oneonta, 1948-49, United Presbyn. Ch., Oneonta, 1950-55; dir. choirs of Delhi State Inst., 1954-56; pres. Nat. Sch. Vocal Assn., 1940-48; exec. sec. N.Y. State Sch. Music Assn., 1933-46; condr., adjudicator at more than 200 state and nat. festivals in music; mng. editor Sch. Music News, 1936-57, Woodwind World-Brass and Percussion; sec.-treas., mng. editor Swift-Dorr Publs., Inc., 1970-80; vocal editor Sch. Musician, 1948-51. Chmn. bd. dirs. Future for Oneonta Found., Inc., from 1982. Mem. Nat. Assn. Am. Composers and Condrs., ASCAP, AAUP, Greater Oneonta C. of C. (treas.), Phi Mu Alpha, Phi Delta Kappa, Oracle. Mason. Rotarian. Author: Fundamentals of Music, Easter Dawning, Christmas by Candlelight, Belwin Orchestra Folio, Class Lessons for Strings General Music (8 books). Elementary Conducting; Music Speaks For Itself (2 books); Workbook in Music Theory; A Gift for Santa, Fundamentals of Singing; Musical Homes for Boys and Girls; Story of Easter; All About Music; Everyone Can Read A Song; Our World of Music Series; Listen There's Music; James Baxter, American Pioneer Music Educator; Independent Study in Music Theory, Mini-Courses in Music, 5 vols.; Practical Suggestions for Young Teachers; History of the New York State School Music Association, 1975; (with Deborah Swift) What Everyone Should Know About Music, 1984; also numerous works for band, orch. and choir in field of music edn. Died Sept. 25, 1989; buried Glenwood Cemetery, Oneonta, N.Y. Home: Oneonta N.Y.

SWING, GAEL DUANE, college president; b. LaPorte County, Ind., Mar. 13, 1932; s. William Edward and Ruth Dorothy (Jessup) S.; m. Sandra Sue Scott, Apr. 13, 1957; children: Scott, Kristie, Janet. AB, Franklin (Ind.) Coll., 1954; MS, Ind. U., 1963; LLD, U. Indpls., 1984. Sales rep. Burroughs Corp., Indpls., 1954; successively dir. placement and admission counselor, dir. admissions, bus. mgr., v.p. devel. Franklin Coll., 1954-69; dir. spl. program services Office Devel., Washington U., St. Louis, 1969-73; exec. v.p. North Central Coll., Naperville, Ill., 1973-75; pres. North Central Coll., 1975-90; mem. Ill. Bd. Higher Edn. Non-Pub. Adv. Com.; dir. Comml. Resources Inc.; mem. univ. senate United Methodist Ch. Recipient Alumni citation Franklin Coll., 1975. Mem. Fedn. Ind. Ill. Colls. and

Univs. (exec. com.), Coll. Conf. Ill. and Wis. (chmn.), Nat. Assn. Schs., Colls. and Univs. of United Meth. Ch. (chmn. com. on ch. relations), Assoc. Colls. Ill. (bd. dirs.), Ednl. and Instl. Ins. Adminstrs. (chmn.), West Suburban Regional Acad. Consortium (bd. dirs.). Methodist. Clubs: Naperville Country; Union League (Chgo.). Home: Hudson Ind. Died May 31, 1990; buried La Porte, Ind.

SWINK, JOHN LEWIS, academic administrator; b. Rocky Ford, Colo., Aug. 16, 1914; s. Lester and Grace Hoffman (Hunsaker) S.; m. Florence Glover, Feb. 14, 1940; children: Nancy, Patricia, Annette. BS, Rutgers U., 1936; MBA, NYU, 1948. With Prudential Life Ins. Co., 1936-39; mem. faculty Rutgers U., New Brunswick, N.J., 1939-91, dean adminstrn., 1958-62, v.p., treas., 1962-74, sr. v.p., treas. emeritus, 1974-91; trustee New Brunswick Savs. Bank. Bd. mgrs. Rutgers U. Found., 1974. Maj. inf. AUS, WWII. Decorated Bronze Star with oak leaf cluster, Croix de Guerre (Luxembourg), Fourragere (Belgium). Mem. Chi Psi. Presbyterian. Home: Westfield N.J. Died Jan. 20, 1991.

SWIRE, WILLARD, theatrical executive; b. Phila., Sept. 10, 1910; s. Herbert L.R. and Lialette (Reading) S.; m. Helen Eastburn Rawlings, May 8, 1935 (div. Oct. 1941); 1 child, R. Derek; m. Janet Katherine Dickson, May 29, 1948. BS, U. Pa., 1932. Actor, from 1932; founding mem. New Stages, 1947; asst. exec. sec. Actors' Equity Assn., N.Y.C., 1948-54, 1971-77, assoc. exec. sec., 1977-80, exec. sec., 1980-81, exec. cons., 1981-91; exec. dir. Am. Nat. Theatre and Acad., 1954-63; producer Sharon (Conn.) Playhouse, 1958-61, 67-68; owner, operator Cafe Renaissance, N.Y.C., 1963-71; trustee Sharon Creative Arts Found., from 1957, pres., 1958-59, also v.p., chmn., exec. dir.; adj. prof. dept. drama U. Miami; pres. Theatre Authority. Appeared in plays including Dear Ruth, London, 1945, Lamp at Midnight, 1947, The Respectful, Prostitute, 1948; editor: Three Distinctive Plays about Abraham Lincoln, 1961. Mem. Nat. Council, USO. Served with AUS, 1943-45, ETO. Decorated Bronze Star, Purple Heart. Fellow Am. Theatre Assn.; mem. Am. Ednl. Theatre Assn. (bd. dirs.), Nat. Theatre Conf., AFTRA, Actors Fund (life), Associated Actors and Artistes Am. (treas.), Lambda Chi Alpha. Clubs: Players (bd. dirs., asst. treas.), Lambs, Coffee House (N.Y.C.); Mask and Wig (Phila.) (bd. govs.); Savage (London). Home: New York N.Y. Died Nov. 13, 1991; buried Kenisco Cemetery.

SWOYER, ANN MYRTLE See WALKER, NANCY

SYKES, WEATHERS YORK, insurance company executive; b. Pond, Miss., May 13, 1927; s. Weathers and Irene Berniece (Lehmann) S.; m. Carol Elaine Williams, Sept. 4, 1960; children: Michael Gregory, Lori Denise, Stephen York. B.S., U. Wis., 1950. Asst. claims mgr. Supreme Life Ins. Co. of Am., Chgo., 1962-65, asst. sec., mgr. actuarial dept., 1965-68, v.p. adminstrv. services, 1968-71, sr. v.p. adminstrv. services, 1971-76, also dir., 1973-76; sr. v.p. ops. Chgo. Met. Mut. Assurance Co., 1976-90, also dir., mem. exec. com.; bd. dirs. Heritage/ Pullman Bank & Trust Co.; cons. Ill. Dept. Welfare; mem. Chgo. Crime Commn., from 1974. Mem. editorial adv. bd. Chgo. Reporter, from 1975. V.p., trustee Michael Reese Research Found.; trustee, mem. exec. com. Michael Reese Med. Ctr.; trustee Ravinia Festival Assn., Community Renewal Soc.; pres. Michael Reese Health Plan, 1976-90; mem. vis. com. Div. Sch. U. Chgo., 1974-80; vice chmn. Joint Negro Appeal, 1976; bd. dirs., mem. exec. com. Mental Health Assn. Greater Chgo., 1978-80; bd. dirs. Chgo. State U. Found., Chgo. Econ. Devel. Corp., 1981-90, Com. on Decent Unbiased Campaign Tactics; deacon Chgo. United, 1981-90, prin., 1987-90; mem. council South Side Planning Bd., Chgo., from 1982. Served with AUS, 1944-46. Mem. Nat. Strategy Forum, Chgo. Forum (co-chmn. 1968-70), Sci. Research Soc. N.Am., Navy League of U.S. (dir. Chgo. council from 1983, v.p. 1985, exec. com.), Sigma Xi. Roman Catholic. Clubs: Executives (Chgo.), Original Forty (Chgo.). Home: Chicago Ill. Died Feb. 5, 1990; buried Chgo.

SYVERSON, ALDRICH, educator; b. Glenwood, Minn., Mar. 25, 1914; s. Julius and Anna (Arenson) S.; m. Eleanor Marie Wall, June 16, 1942; children: Elizabeth Anne (Mrs. Douglas Elden Shaw), William Richard. Student, U. Chgo., 1931-32; BSChemE, U. Minn., 1938, PhD, 1942. Rsch. engr. B.F. Goodrich Co., Akron, Ohio, 1942-44; mgr. organic chems. devel. B.F. Goodrich Chem. Co., Akron, 1944-45; mgr. Avon Lake (Ohio) Exptl. Sta., 1945-48; assoc. prof. chem. engring. Syracuse (N.Y.) U., 1948-50; assoc. prof. chem. engring. Ohio State U., Columbus, 1950-54, prof., 1954-59, 60-78, prof., chmn. dept. chem. engring., 1968-76, prof. emeritus, 1978-88; dir. rsch. O.M. Scott Co., Marysville, Ohio, 1959-60. Contbr. articles to profl. jours. Hormel Rsch. Found. fellow, 1942; named Tech. Man of Yr., Columbus Tech. Coun., 1974. Fellow AICE; mem. AAAS, Am. Chem. Soc., Am. Soc. Engring. Edn., Sigma Xi, Tau Beta Pi, Phi Lambda Upsilon. Lutheran. Home: Worthington Ohio Died Sept. 18, 1988.

SZLADITS, LOLA LEONTIN, librarian; b. Budapest, Hungary, Mar. 11, 1923; came to U.S., 1950, naturalized, 1956; d. Bodog and Margit (Stern) Abel; m. Charles Szladits, Oct. 9, 1950 (dec. June 1986). Ph.D., Peter Pazmany U., Budapest, 1946; postgrad., Columbia U., 1946-47, Sorbonne, U. Paris, Spring 1948; Dip. Lib., Univ. Coll., London U., 1950. Med. sec. Allied Control Commn., U.S. Forces in, Hungary, 1945-46; Oriental librarian Courtauld Inst. Art, London, 1948-50; indexer Nat. Health Council, N.Y.C., 1950-51; librarian, first asst. rare book room N.Y. Acad. Medicine, N.Y.C., 1951-55; library asst. art div. N.Y. Pub. Library, N.Y.C., 1955, first. asst. Berg Collection, 1955-69, curator Berg Collection English and Am. Lit., 1969-89; mem. council Princeton Library in, N.Y., from 1979, Rosenbach Found. Library, from 1980, Dictionary Lit. Biography, 1981-84. Author: Book Collecting: A Modern Guide, 1977; author numerous exhbn. catalogs, 1969-89 including, Independence, 1975, The Thirties in England, 1979. Fellow Morgan Library, Library Assn. Eng.; mem. Bibliog. Soc. Am. (council 1976-82), English-Speaking Union, N.Y. Hist. Soc., Keats-Shelley Assn. Am. (dir. from 1974). Lutheran. Clubs: Princeton, Hroswitha, Women's City. Home: New York N.Y. Died Mar. 30, 1990; cremated.

SZOLD, HAROLD JAMES, banker; b. Streator, Ill., Dec. 13, 1896; s. Adolph and Rachel Esther (Gumbiner) S.; m. Helen Alexander, Sept. 17, 1921; 1 dau., Sarah Margaret. AB, Knox Coll., Galesburg, Ill., 1915; student, Harvard Grad. Sch. Bus. With Lehman Bros., N.Y.C., from 1924, ptnr., from 1941; dir., mem. exec. com. Allied Stores Corp., Gimbel Bros., Inc., Interstate Dept. Stores, Inc.; dir. Bing & Bing, Inc., N.Y.C., Firth Sterling Steel & Carbide Corp., McKeesport, Pa., Climax Molybdenum Co., Gen. Cigar Co., Inc., Brunswick-Balke-Collender. Trustee Barone Hirsch Fund, N.Y.C.; bd. dirs. Bklyn. Bur. of Social Svc. and Jewish Agrl. Soc., Inc., N.Y.C. *

TABBACK, VICTOR See TAYBACK, VIC

TAGGART, KENNETH DALE, diversified company executive; b. Montclair, N.J., Oct. 10, 1935; s. John A. and Elizabeth J. (Kinley) T.; m. Mary Ellen Hickey, June 25, 1960. BBA, Rutgers U., 1957. Mgr. Arthur Young & Co., N.Y.C., 1958-68; with Thyssen-Bornemisza Inc., N.Y.C., from 1968, controller, v.p., 1973-76, corp. exec. v.p., from 1976, pres. InCon Packaging Inc. div., 1981-87, pres. TBG Info. Systems Inc. div., 1987-89; bd. dirs. Ball-InCon Glass Packaging Corp. Mem. Am. Inst. CPAs, N.J. Soc. CPAs. Club: N.Y. Athletic. Home: Essex Fells N.J. Died Feb. 14, 1989. †

TALBOT, TIMOTHY RALPH, physician, medical center administrator, educator; b. Berkeley, Calif., July 14, 1916; s. Timothy R. and Caroline E. (Lowe) T.; m. Mary Robinson, Oct. 16, 1943; children: Timothy R., Mary Talbot Havens, William R., Lucy Talbot Myers, David C. A.B., U. Pa., 1937, M.D., 1941. Nat. Cancer Inst. fellow Chester Beatty Research Inst., London, 1956-57; dir. Inst. Cancer Research, Phila., 1957-76; assoc. prof. medicine U. Pa., Phila., 1966-87; pres. Fox Chase Cancer Center, Phila., 1974-81, pres. emeritus, from 1982; vice chmn. Fox Chase Cancer Center, 1981-84; mem. Pa. Gov.'s Sci. Adv. Com., 1966-75, Pa. Gov.'s Task Force Cancer Control, 1974-78, Pa. Cancer Control Prevention and Research Adv. Bd., 1981—; chmn. cancer control grant rev. com. Nat. Cancer Inst., 1974-78. Mem. Assn. Am. Cancer Insts. (pres. 1968, dir. 1972-76, 78, chmn. 1982-83). Home: Haverford Pa. Deceased.

TALBOTT, GEORGE HAROLD, clergyman; b. Marengo, Iowa, Feb. 8, 1894; s. George Edward and Mary Elizabeth (Davis) T.; m. Barbara Baringer Stofer, June 11, 1918; children: Mary Martha (dec.), Barbara Jane (Mrs. Marcos E. Kinevan). Student, Missouri Valley Coll., Marshall, Mo., 1915-17; BA, Princeton U., 1922; BST, Princeton Theol. Sem., 1923, MST, 1923; DD, Mo. Valley Coll., 1930; LHD, Bloomfield Coll. and Sem., 1957. Ordained to ministry Presbyn. Ch., 1922. Student pastor Blairstown and Denton (Mo.) chs., 1915-17; pastor Clivedon Ch., Germantown, Pa., 1919-23, First Ch., Passaic, N.J., from 1923; chaplain Police and Fire Depts., Passaic, Gerald V. Carroll post Am. Legion; prof. pastoral theology Bloomfield Sem., from 1948, prof. eccles. polity, lectr. Christian ethics; mem. gen. assembly Presbyn. Ch. U.S.A., 1926, 33, 40, 43, 44, 45, chmn. com. on edn., 1933, com. on bill and overtures, 1943, chmn. Nat. Mission, 1945, mem. commn. of 15, Presbyn. Emergency Commn.; vice chmn. wartime svc. commn. Presbyn. Ch.; mem. exec. com. Com. on Ch. Activities; mem. Com. on Chaplains and Svc. Pers.; cooperating pastor under Presbyn. Ch., U.S. Army at Camp Croft, S.C., 1941; mem. permanent jud. com. Synod of N.J., 1936, moderator, 1937-38. Contbr. articles to periodicals. Mem. Mayor's Com. of Strike Settlement; mem. Passaic Welfare Bd.; mem. exec. com. Anti-Poverty Com., City of Passaic; bd. govs. Passaic Gen. Hosp., from 1927; sec. Princeton Thel. Sem. Alumni Assn., 1934-41, pres., 1942; pres. Princeton Theol. Sem. Alumni of N.Y. and Vicinity, 1937-38; chmn. bd. dirs. Bloomfield Coll. and Sem. Served as 1st lt., inf., AEF, World War I, 1917-19, wounded in Meuse-Argonne offensive, 1981. Decorated Purple Heart. Mem. Am. Legion, Masons (32 deg.), Friars Club (Princeton). *

TALBOTT, JOHN HAROLD, physician, editor; b. Grinnell, Iowa, July 10, 1902; s. Arthur D. and Caroline (Flook) T.; m. Mildred Cherry, Sept. 3, 1932; children: John A., Cherry Talbott Towbridge. AB, Grinnell Coll., 1924, DSc, 1946; MD, Harvard U., 1929. Intern Presbyn. Hosp., N.Y.C., 1929-31; faculty Harvard Med. Sch., 1931-46; med. staff Mass. Gen. Hosp., Boston, 1931-46; prof. medicine U. Buffalo, N.Y., 1946-59; physician-in-chief Buffalo Gen. Hosp., 1946-59; dir. div. sci. publs. AMA, 1959-69; editor Jour. AMA, 1959-69, editor emeritus, 1970-72; clin. prof. medicine U. Miami, Fla., 1971-90.; dir. U.S., Army Frostbie Commn. to Korea, 1951; chmn. Josiah Macy, Jr. Con. on Cold Injury, 1952-58; mem. sci. adv. panel Dept. Army, 1958-60; mem. sci. com. Nat. Arthritis and Rheumatism Found.; dir. Niagara Share Investment Co., 1956-70. Author: Gout, 3d edit., 1967; co-author: (with R. Ferrandis) Collagen Diseases, 1956, (with L.M. Lockie) Progress in Arthritis, 1958, A Biographical History of Medicine, 1970, Collagen-Vascular Diseases, 1974, (with T.F. Yu) Gout and Uric Acid Metabolism, 1976, Clinical Rheumatology, 1978; editor: Medicine, 1947-59, Seminars in Arthritis and Rheumatism, 1971-90, Surg. Forum of ACS, 1971; editorial bd. M.D. Mag., 1973-90, Merck Manual, 1971-90. Col. AUS, 1941-46; comdg. officer Climatic Rsch. Lab. Decorated Legion of Merit. Mem. A.C.P. (gov. Western N.Y. 1955-59), AMA, Assn. Am. Physicians, Am. Soc. Clin. Investigation. Home: Miami Fla. Died Oct. 10, 1990.

TALBOTT, PHILIP MELVILLE, bank executive; b. Arlington, Va., Feb. 12, 1896; s. Thomas M. and Annie K. (Nourse) T.; m. Delavan Redfield Thompson, May 23, 1921; children: Philip Melville, Jr., Jean Redfield. Grad., Randolph Macon Acad., Front Royal, Va., 1914. With Woodward & Lothrop, Inc., Washington, 1914-59, successively salesman, asst. buyer, floor mgr., floor supt., also asst. svc. dir., rsch. dir., asst. to gen. mgr., and 3d v.p., asst. sec., v.p. and sec., sr. v.p., 1914-50, sr. v.p., sec., 1950-59; spl. asst. to pres. Nat. Savs. and Trust Co., from 1959; chmn. bd. Potomac Small Bus. Funds, Inc., Annandale, Va.; dir. McCormick Assocs., Inc., Washington, Pepsi Cola Bottling Co., Washington, P.J. Nee Co., Potomac Electric Power Co., No. Va. Bank, Suburban Savs. and Loan Asns., Annandale. Pres. C. of C. of U.S., Washington Bd. Trade; 1st v.p., dir. exec. com. Washington Mchts. and Mfrs. Assn.; mem. nat. distbn. coun. adv. com. to Sec. Commerce; mem. exec. com. Greater Nat. Capital Com.; mem. Econ. Devel. Bd., Washington; mem. exec. com. Fed. City Coun.; mem. com. planning D.C. chpt. Nat. Found. Imfantile Paralysis; mem. awards merit com., cons. Pres.'s Com. Nat. Employment Physically Handicapped; congressional incorporator Am. Fedn. Physically Handicapped, Inc.; mem. town coun. Falls Ch., Va.; chmn. bus. adv. bd. Sch. Bus. Adminstrn. Am. U.; dir. Advance Schs. Retail Mgmt., N.Y.C.; mem. adv. bd. fin. com. Washington YMCA; dir. exec. com. United Givers Fund Nat. Capital Area, Inc., Arlington (Va.) chpt. ARC, Arlington Hosp., Med. Svc. D.C. Inc. (dir., chmn. fin. com.); mem. adv. com. extension divsn. U. Va. Served with U.S. Army, World War I; AEF, France. Recipient citation Randolph-Macon Acad., award Res. Officers Assn. Am.; Merite Award Comml. (France). Mem. AIM (assoc.), Nat. Retail Dry Goods Assn. (dir., pres.), Am. Standards Assn. (dir.), Am. Mgmt. Assn., Internat. C. of C. (trustee, U.S. Coun.), Arlington C. of C., Alexandria C. of C., Fairfax County C. of C., Falls Church C. of C., Newcomen Soc. N.Am., Am. Legion, Washington Golf and Country Club (dir.), Rotary (past pres.), Masons, Circus Saints and Sinners Club (v.p., dir. P.T. Barnum Tent), Farmington Country Club (Charlottesville, Va.), Nat. Press Club, Met. (Washington), Eta Mu Pi. *

TALLAMY, BERTRAM DALLEY, consulting engineer; b. Plainfield, N.J., Dec. 1, 1901; s. Bertram Falion and Ina (Dalley) T.; m. Doris Fisk, Nov. 3, 1927; 1 child, Bertram Fisk. C.E., Rennsselaer Poly. Inst., 1925, D Engring. (hon.), 1957. Mem. engring. firm Sheehan, Fretts & Tallamy, 1929-35; dep. chief engr. Niagara Frontier Planning Bd., 1935-37, chief engr., 1937-45; dep. supt. N.Y. State Dept. Pub. Works, 1945-47, chief engr., 1947, supt., 1948-54; chmn. N.Y. State Thruway Authority, 1950-56; fed. hwy. adminstr. Washington, 1955-61; cons. engr. U.S. rep. Pan-Am congresses, 1957-61. Recipient ann. award for engring. achievement N.Y. Soc. Profl. Engrs., citation in engring. U. Buffalo, 1955, award Am. Road Builders Assn., 1961. Mem. Am. Assn. State Hwy. Ofcls. (exec. com., pres. 1951-52), Am. Soc. C.E., Soc. Am. Mil. Engrs., Nat. Soc. Profl. Engrs., Mason, Tau Beta Pi, Chi Epsilon, Alpha Tau Omega. Mem. Dutch Reformed Ch. Home: Sand Lake NY Died Sept. 14, 1989.

TALVELA, MARTTI OLAVI, bass, opera and concert singer; b. Hiitola, Finland, Feb. 4, 1935; s. Toivo and Nelly T.; m. Anna Kaariainen, 1957; 3 children. Tchr. Lahti Music High Sch., 1958; with Royal Opera House, Stockholm, 1961-62; artistic dir. Savonlinna Opera Festival, Finland, 1972-89. Performances at Deutsche Opera, Berlin, Staatsoper, Hamburg, Germany, Vienna, Austria, Munich, Germany, Royal Opera, Covent Garden, Met. Opera, N.Y.C.; debut, Met. Opera, N.Y.C., 1968; performances, La Scala, Milan, Italy, Rome, San Francisco, Tokyo, Bayreuth, Salzburg, 1962-89; considered one of the greatest interpretors of title role Boris Gudunov, numerous recs., TV appearances. Recipient Finnish State prize, 1973. Home: Bronx N.Y. Died July 22, 1989.

TALYZIN, NIKOLAI VLADIMIROVICH, Soviet government official; b. Jan. 28, 1929, Moscow. Ed. Moscow Electrotechnical Inst. of Communications, grad. 1955. Electrician and technician-constructor 1944; engr., chief constructor, sr. scientist and dep. dir. Sci. Research Inst., 1955-65; dep. minister for Communications, 1965-75, minister, 1975-80; vice-chmn. Council of Ministers, 1980-85, 88-89, first dep. chmn., 1985-88, non-voting mem. of the Politboro, 1985-89, head state planning com. Gosplan, dep. prime min., 1985-88; chmn. Bur. for Social Devel., 1988-89. Mem. Central Com. of CPSU; dep. to Supreme Soviet of USSR (10th session); chmn. Central Bd. USSR-Finland Soc.; dr. and prof. tech. scis.; Laureate of State. Deceased. Home: Moscow Russia

TAM, REUBEN, painter; b. Kapaa, Kauai, Hawaii, Jan. 17, 1916; s. Kee Tam and Loo-See T.; m. Geraldine King, May 20, 1948. Ed.B., U. Hawaii, 1937; postgrad., Calif. Sch. Fine Arts, 1940, Columbia U., 1942-45. instr. painting Bklyn. Mus. Art Sch., 1948-74, prof. Oreg. State U., 1966; adj. assoc. prof. Queens Coll., 1973. One man shows Calif. Palace Legion Honor, 1940, Honolulu Acad. Arts, 1941, 67, 84, Downtown Gallery, 1945, 46, 49, 52, Phila. Art Alliance, 1954, Alan Gallery, 1954, 57, 59, 61, 64, 67, Portland (Oreg.) Art Mus., 1966, Oreg. State U., 1966, Wichita Art Assn., 1971, Coe Kerr Gallery, 1971, 75, 79, Sheldon Meml. Art Gallery, Lincoln, Nebr., 1976, El Paso Mus., 1978, others; group exhbns. Am. painting surveys, from 1943, including Carnegie Inst., Whitney Mus. Am. Art, Met. Mus. Art, San Francisco Mus. Art, Walker Art Center, Chgo. Art Inst., also S.Am., Australia, Europe, works in permanent collections, Mus. Modern Art, Met. Mus. Art, Wichita Art Mus., Krannert Art Mus., Albright Art Gallery, Whitney Mus. Am. Art, Bklyn Mus., Smithsonian Instn., Nat. Collection Fine Art, Hawaii State Found., others. Recipient 1st prize Honolulu Acad. Arts, 1939, 41, Golden Gate Exposition, 1940, Bklyn. Mus., 1952, NAD, 1974, 77; award Am. Acad. and Inst. Arts and Letters, 1978; Guggenheim fellow, 1948. Home: Kapaa Hawaii Died Jan. 3, 1991; buried Kapaa, Kauai, Hawaii.

TANAKA, JEFFREY SCOTT, psychologist, educator; b. L.A., Aug. 29, 1958. AB, UCLA, 1979, MA, 1980, PhD, 1984. Assoc. prof. psychology NYU, N.Y.C., 1983-90, U. Ill., Champaign, 1990-92. Contbr. book chpts./reviews in field, articles to profl. jours. Fellow Am. Psychol. Assn. (bd. ethnic minority affairs), Am. Psychol. Soc.; mem. Soc. for Multivariate Exptl. Psychology, Am. Stat. Assn., Psychometric Soc., Inst. Math. Stat. Home: Champaign Ill. Died Nov. 3, 1992. †

TANENBAUM, MARC HERMAN, clergyman; b. Balt., Oct. 13, 1925; s. Abraham and Sadie (Siger) T.; m. Helga Weiss, May 22, 1955 (div. Sept. 1977); children: Adena, Michael, Susan, Joshua; m. Georgette F. Bennett, June 6, 1982. B.A., Yeshiva U., 1945; M in Hebrew Lit, Jewish Theol. Sem. Am., 1950, DDiv, 1975. Rabbi, 1950; exec. dir. Synagogue Council Am. (nat. coordinating agy. Orthodox, Conservative and Reform rabbinic and congl. bodies of Judaism U.S.), 1954-60; dir. dept. interreligious affairs Am. Jewish Com., 1961-83, dir. dept. internat. relations, 1983-89; Editor, pub. relations counselor Abelard Schuman (pub.), 1956, Henry Schuman, Farrar, Straus & Giroux; staffer Eternal Light radio program; corr., columnist Jewish Telegraphic Agy.; TV writer and panelist WMAR-TV, Balt.; writer, narrator, dir. religious films; editor Interreligious Newsletter, Trend of Events (news weekly.). Editor: Judaism: Orthodox, Conservative and Reform; Author, co-author 7 books; contbr. articles to religious publs. Mem. exec. com. White House Conf. on Children and Youth, 1960; nat. adv. council White House Conf. on Aging, 1961; nat. vice chmn. ARC; v.p., dir. Religion in Am. Life; dir. Clergymen's Econ. Inst.; mem. council trustees United Seamen's Service; mem. religious adv. com. U.S. Com. for UN; mem. U.S. nat. commn. for UNESCO, Com. Internat. Econ. Growth; bd. dirs. Internat. Rescue Com., Am. Jewish World Svc., Nat. Peace Bd.; chmn. emeritus Internat. Jewish Com. for Interreligious Consultations with the Vatican, Covenant House Bd. Recipient Internat. Interfaith Achievement award Internat. Conf. Christians and Jews; 15 hon. doctorates. Mem. Nat. Conf. Christians and Jews, Rabbinical Assembly Am. Home: New York N.Y. Died July 3, 1992. †

TANG, ANTHONY MATTHEW, economist, educator; b. Shanghai, China, May 6, 1924; came to U.S., 1945, naturalized, 1953; s. Shu-ping and Yueh-pao (Hsu) T.; m. Jane Pentecost, Nov. 27, 1946 (dec. Sept. 1987); children: Matthew, Jeremiah, John, Lyda Anne, Arthur, Patricia. B.B.A., Loyola U., New Orleans, 1949; Ph.D., Vanderbilt U., 1955. Faculty Vanderbilt U., Nashville, 1955—, prof. econs. and bus. adminstrn., 1963-86, prof. emeritus, 1986—, chmn. dept., 1968-71, dir., grad. program in econ. devel., 1961-63, dir. East Asian studies program, 1973-76, dir. grad. studies, 1983-86; assoc. for Philippines Winrock Internat. Inst. for Agrl. Devel., 1986-88; vis. lectr. Osaka U., Japan, 1959-60; vis. prof. U. Calif.-Berkeley, 1963-64, U. Sao Paulo, Brazil, 1973, Nat. Taiwan U., 1974-75, U. Hawaii, summer 1979, 80; vis. prof. econs., chmn. dept., dean faculty commerce and social scis. Chinese U., Hong Kong, 1966-68, external examiner, 1968-70, 79-81, 84-86; vis. prof. econs. Ctr. for Chinese Studies, U. Mich., 1976-77; vis. sr. rsch. fellow Chung-Hua Instn. for Econ. Research, Taipei, summer 1981; vis. prof. agrl. econs. U. Philippines at Los Banos, 1986-88; vis. prof. econs. U. Philippines, Diliman, 1987-88, Chinese U. of Hong Kong, 1988—; lectr. East-West Ctr. for bank sr. staff tng. program, Asian Devel. Bank Manila; cons. FOA, 1954, Ford Found., 1973, Internat. Food Policy Rsch. Inst., 1978, 89, Midwest China Study Resource Ctr., 1979, UN Devel. Program, Panama, 1983, 84, 85, Astan Devel. Bank, 1989. Author: Economic Development of the Southern Piedmont, 1958, Longterm Economic Projections for Hong Kong, 1969; editor: Evolution, Welfare, and Time in Economics, 1976, Food and Agriculture in China: Trends and Projections, 1979, An Analytical and Empirical Investigation of Agriculture in Mainland China, 1952-80, 1984, Why Does Overcrowded, Resource-Poor East Asia Succeed?, 1987; contbr. to Theory and Design of Economic Development, 1966, China in Crisis, 1968, Economic Trends in Communist China, 1968, Subsistence Agriculture and Economic Development, 1969, Agrarian Policies and Problems in Communist and Non-communist Countries, 1971, Trade, Agriculture and Development, 1975, Agricultural Growth in Japan, Korea, Taiwan, and the Philippines, 1979, Modern Chinese Economic History, 1979, Asian Agricultural Development in Comparative Perspective, 1981, Papers and Proceedings of Dr. Sun Yat-sen Symposium, 1983, China: The 80s Era, 1984, Agricultural Development in the Third World, 1984, Poverty in Asia, 1987; mem. editorial bd. Hong Kong Jour. Bus. Mgmt. Mem. Am. Econ. Assn. (adv. com. U.S. Census 1960-63, mem. policy bd. for Econs. Insts. 1963-66, mem. del. to Peking, China 1981), Assn. Comparative Econ. Studies, Am. Agrl. Econs. Assn. (editorial council jour. 1968-71), Internat. Agrl. Econs. Assn., Soc. Asian Studies, So. Econ. Assn. (editor jour. 1963-66), Midwest Regional Seminar on China (exec. bd. com. on Asian Econ. Studies). Home: Dallas Tex. Deceased. †

TANNER, CHAMP BEAN, soil science and meteorology educator, researcher; b. Idaho Falls, Idaho, Nov. 16, 1920; s. Bertrand Myron and Orea (Bean) T.; m. Catherine Cox, Sept. 24, 1941; children: Bertrand, Catherine, Terry Lee, Myron, Clarke. B.S., Brigham Young U., 1942; Ph.D., U. Wis., 1950. Instr. soil sci. and meteorology U. Wis., Madison, 1950-51, asst. prof., 1951-55, assoc. prof., 1955-60, prof., 1960-88, Emil Truog prof. soil sci., 1979-88, prof. emeritus, from 1988; vis. prof. Cornell U., 1956, U. Guelph, Ont., Can., 1979; vis. scientist Commonwealth Sci. and Indsl. Research Orgn., Canberra, Australia, 1981. Served to 1st lt. U.S. Army, 1943-46. Recipient Outstanding Achievement award in biometeorology Am. Meteorol. Soc., 1980; Fulbright scholar U. Queensland, Brisbane, Australia, 1969. Fellow Am. Soc. Agronomy, AAAS, Soil Sci. Soc. Am. (soil sci. research award 1978), Crop. Sci. Soc. Am.; mem. Nat. Acad. Scis., Sigma Xi, Phi Kappa Phi, others. Mem. LDS Ch. Home: Middleton Wis. Deceased. †

TANSILL, DONALD BENDER, merchant; b. N.Y.C., May 22, 1896; s. John Fred and Sarah (Neil) T.; m. Mildred O'Connell, June 22, 1927; 1 son, Donald. Student, Columbia U., 1915-16. With Bliss, Fabyan & Co., 1916-17, 19-25; in charge sales Pepperell Mfg. Co., 1925-43, v.p., 1937-50; v.p. Burlington Mills Corp. N.Y., 1950-51; exec. v.p., pres., chmn. M. Lowenstein & Sons Co., N.Y.C., from 1951; dir. Lily of France, Inc., Mary Chess, Inc. Author: So You Are Going to Sell, 1928; contbr. articles to Sat. Eve. Post. Bd. dirs. Fedn. Protestant Welfare Agys., N.Y.C. Served as ensign USNRF, 1917-19. Mem. SAR, Columbia Univ. Club, Union League Club, Regency Club of N.Y.C., Everglades Bath and Tennis Club (Palm Beach), Creek Club of L.I. Presbyterian. *

TARJAN, GEORGE, psychiatrist, educator; b. Zsolna, Hungary, June 18, 1912; came to U.S., 1939, naturalized, 1943; s. Odon and Margaret (Kohn) T.; m. Helen E. Blome, June 11, 1941; children: Robert E., James E. Student, Tisza Istvan U., Debrecen, Hungary, 1920-32; MD, Peter Pazmany U., Budapest, 1935. Diplomate Am. Bd. Neurology and Psychiatry, Am. Bd. Child Psychiatry, Nat. Bd. Med. Examiners. Intern gen. hosps. Budapest, 1934-35, Menorah Hosp., Kansas City, Mo., 1939-40; resident internal medicine Budapest, 1935-39, Mercy Hosp., Janesville, Wis., 1940-41; resident psychiatry State Hosp., Provo, Utah, 1941-43; clin. dir. Peoria (Ill.) State Hosp., 1946-47; dir. clin. svc. Pacific State Hosp., Pomona, Calif., 1947-49, supt., med. dir., 1949-65; asst. prof. psychiatry UCLA Sch. Medicine, 1953-57, assoc. prof., 1957-60, clin. prof., 1960-65, prof., 1965-91; program dir. mental retardation and child psychiatry Neuropsychiat. Inst., 1965-91; vice-chmn. Pres.'s Panel on Mental Retardation, 1961-62; mem. Joint Commn. on Mental Health of Children, 1965-70, Pres.'s Com. on Mental Retardation, 1966-71, Pres.'s Commn. on Mental Health, 1977-78, Select Congl. Panel on Promotion of Child Health, 1979-80; cons. Pres.'s Com. on Mental Retardation, 1971-91. Capt. med. corps AUS, 1943-46; col. Res. Recipient Kennedy Found. Internat. award for disting. leadership in mental retardation, 1971, Andrés Bello award for acad. achievements, Venezuela, 1976, Merit award Pres.'s Com. on Mental Retardation, 1972, ann. award Exceptional Children's Found., 1980. Fellow Am. Psychiat. Assn. (v.p. 1967-68, pres. 1983-84, sec. 1969-72, Disting. Svc. award 1973, Seymour Vestermark award 1978, Agnes McGavin award 1978), Am. Assn. Mental Deficiency (Leadership award 1970); mem. AMA, L.A. County Med. Soc., Am. Acad. Child Psychiatry (pres. 1977-79), Group for Advancement Psychiatry (pres. 1971-73), So. Calif. Psychiat. Soc., Am. Coll. Psychiatrists. Home: Sherman Oaks Calif. Died Dec. 7, 1991.

TARRANT, JOHN EDWARD, lawyer; b. Dyersburg, Tenn., Nov. 25, 1898; s. John Morgan and Penelope A. (Fumbanks) T.; m. Mary Park Kaye, May 26, 1928; children: Mary Kaye Tarrant Durham, Eleanor Tarrant Newman, Penelope Tarrant Morton. B.S., U. Va., 1921; LL.B., Harvard U., 1923. Bar: Ky. 1923. Assoc. firm Simpson, Thacher & Bartlett, N.Y.C., 1922, Bruce, Bullitt & Gordon, Louisville, 1923-26; partner firm Bruce & Bullitt, 1926-40, Ogden, Tarrant, Galphin & Street, 1940-48, Bullitt, Dawson & Tarrant, 1948-70, Tarrant, Combs & Bullitt (and predecessor), 1970-80; ptnr. Wyatt, Tarrant & Combs, 1980-85, of counsel, 1985-90; gen. counsel Fed. Land Bank; Fed. Intermediate Credit Bank, Louisville, 1930; spl. judge Ky. Ct. Appeals, 1948; chmn. bd. dirs. Louisville Investment Co., 1958-86; dir. Churchill Downs Inc., 1969-85, dir. emeritus, 1985-90; dir. Citizens Fidelity Bank & Trust Co., 1957-69, adviser, 1969-71. Mem. Louisville Bridge Commn., 1954-57; mem. personnel bd. Ky. State Police, 1957-60; bd. dirs. Louisville Central Area Assn., 1966-68, NKC, Inc. (formerly Norton-Children's Hosps., Inc.), 1969-82; trustee YWCA, 1939-63, U. Louisville, 1966-70, Norton Meml. Infirmary, 1939-69. Served O.T.C., 1918, Camp Fortress Monroe, Va. Fellow Am. Bar Found. (life); mem. N.C. Soc. Cin., Ky. Soc. Colonial Wars, SAR, Am., Ky., Louisville bar assns., Am. Law Inst. (life), Jud. Conf. Sixth Circuit U.S. (life), Am. Judicature Soc. (life), Phi Beta Kappa, Kappa Sigma. Republican. Episcopalian. Clubs: Pendennis, Filson, Louisville Country, Jefferson (Louisville); Metropolitan (Washington). Home: Louisville Ky. Died June 27, 1990; buried Cave Hill Cemetery, Louisville, Ky. †

TATE, WILLIS MCDONALD, university administrator; b. Denver, May 18, 1911; s. Robert Spence and Grace (Brown) T.; m. Joel Estes, Dec. 24, 1922 (dec. Apr. 1, 1987); children: Willis McDonald, Joel Tate Withers; m. Marian Cleary, Jan. 1, 1988. AB, So. Meth. U., 1932, AM, 1935; postgrad., U. Chgo., 1945, U. Tex., 1946-55; LLD, Tex. Wesleyan Coll., 1951, Centenary Coll., 1954, U. Denver, 1957; LHD, Oklahoma City U., 1954. Tchr. elem. sch., prin jr. high sch. Alamo Heights, San Antonio, 1932-43; exec. asst. to pastor First Meth. Ch., Houston, 1943-45; with So. Meth. U., Dallas, 1945-89, from asst. dean students to pres., 1954-71, chancellor, 1971-76, pres., 1974-76, pres. emeritus, 1976-89. Author: (with A.Q. Sartain and W.W. Finlay) Human Behavior in Industry, 1954. Pres. Univ. Senate of Meth. Ch., Tex. Coun. Chs., 1959-60, So. Univ. Conf., 1962-63, Dallas Met. YMCA, 1958-59; chmn. Coun. Protestant Colls. and Univs., 1966-67, Gov. Tex. Adv. Com. on Edn., 1979-89; past mem. exec. com. Meth. World Coun.; mem. Gov.'s Com. on Edn. Beyond High Sch., 1963-64, Goals for Dallas Planning Com. Recipient Alexander Meiklejohn award AAUP, 1965, Disting. Am. award N. Tex. Nat. Football Found. and Hall of Fame, 1965. Fellow Am. Sociol. Soc.; mem. Am. Assn. Colls. (chmn. bd. dirs. 1971), Am. Coun. on Edn. (dir.), Nat. Assn. Schs. and Colls. Meth. Ch., Tex. Hist. Assn., Philos. Soc. Tex. (pres. 1972), So. Assn. Colls., Dallas Coun. World Affairs (pres. 1963-64), Blue Key, Lambda Chi Alpha (Order of Achievement, Grand High Beta), Alpha Kappa Delta, Alpha Phi Omega, Dallas Rotary Club (past pres.), Salesmanship Club, Town and Gown Club, Dallas Country Club, Petroleum Club, Cosmos Club. Home: Dallas Tex. Died Oct. 1, 1989; interred Hillcrest Meml. Pk., Dallas.

TAUB, ABRAHAM, consulting chemist, editor; b. N.Y.C., Sept. 21, 1901; s. Richard and Emma (Druck) T. B.S., Columbia U., 1922, A.M., 1927; Sc.D. (hon.), Coll. Pharm. Sci., 1976; postgrad., NYU, 1935-37. Chemist Schwartz Labs., N.Y.C ., 1921; instr. physics and chemistry Columbia U., N.Y.C., 1922-27, asst. prof. chemistry, 1927-37, assoc. prof., 1937-48, prof. pharm. chemistry, 1948-65, head dept. pharm. chemistry, 1959-68, Disting. Service prof., 1965-69, prof. emeritus, 1969; cons. chemist N.Y.C., from 1927. Author (with Casimir Funk and H.E. Dubin): Vitamin Manual, 1936; author(with C.O. Wilson and O. Gisvold): Organic, Medicinal and Pharmaceutical Chemistry, 1971; contbr. articles to profl. jours.; editor Bull. Nat. Assn. Pharm. Mfrs., 1984; inventor, patentee in field. V.p. Scholarship Aid Fund, Inc., Columbia U., sponsor Mt. Sinai Sch. Medicine Com. 1000, 1987; gas reconnaissance officer Civilian Def. Corps, 1942-45. Co-recipient Ebert medal Am. Pharm. Assn., 1923; recipient Bicentennial Alumni medal Columbia U., 1954, Henry Hurd Rusby award Columbia U., 1962, Man of Yr. award Nat. Assn. Pharm. Mfrs., 1968, Torch of Learning award Hebrew U. Jerusalem, 1980, Disting. Alumnus award Coll. Pharm. Sci. Columbia U., 1987. Fellow AAAS, Am. Inst. Chemists; mem. N.Y. Acad. Sci. (life), Am. Pharm. Assn. (life), Am. Chem. Soc., Sigma Xi, Rho Chi. Home: New York N.Y. Died Apr. 24, 1990.

TAYBACK, VIC (VICTOR TABBACK), actor; b. Bklyn., Jan. 6; s. Najeeb James and Helen (Hanood) Tabback; m. Sheila McKay Barnard, 1962; 1 son,

Christopher. Student, Glendale Community Coll., Frederick A. Speare Sch. of Radio and TV Broadcasting. Former bank teller and cab driver. Appeared in more than 25 stage prodns., including Stalag 17, 12 Angry Men, Death of a Salesman; films include Alice Doesn't Live Here Anymore; TV debut, 1958; regular on: TV series Griff, 1973-74, Alice, 1976-85; other TV appearances include Fantasy Island; TV films include: They Call it Murder, 1971, Partners in Crime, 1973, Portrait of a Stripper, 1979, Rage, 1980, Moviolo: This Year's Blond, 1980, Gridlock, 1980, The Night the City Screamed, 1980, Mysterious Two, 1982, The Jesse Owens Story, 1984, The Three Kings; supporting roles in motion pictures Papillon, Bullitt, The Choirboys; co-founder Company of Angels theater group, Los Angeles, (recipient Golden Globe award 1979, 80); actor numerous commls. Served with USN. Home: Glendale Calif. Died May 25, 1990.

TAYLOR, ALAN JOHN PERCIVALE, historian, author; b. Birkdale, Lancshire, Eng., Mar. 25, 1906; s. Percy Lees and Constance (Sumner) T.; 6 children; m. Eva Haraszti, 1976. Student Bootham Sch., York, Eng., Oriel Coll., Oxford U. (Eng.). Lectr. in modern history U. Manchester; lectr. in internat. history Oxford U., 1953-63, tutor modern history Magdalen Coll., 1938-63, fellow, 1938-76; Benjamin Meaker vis. prof. history, Bristol U., 1976-78. Author: The Italian Problem in European Diplomacy, 1947-49, 1934; Germany's First Bid for Colonies 1884-85, 1938; The Habsburg Monarchy 1815-18, 1941, 2d edit., 1948; The Course of German History, 1945; From Napoleon to Stalin, 1950; Rumours of Wars, 1952; The Struggle for Mastery in Europe, 1848-1918, 1954; Bismarck, 1955; Englishmen and Others, 1956; The Trouble Makers: Dissent over Foreign Policy, 1792-1939, 1957; The Russian Revolution of 1917 (TV lecture script), 1958; The Origins of the Second World War, 1961; The First World War: an Illustrated History, 1963; Politics in Wartime and Other Essays, 1964; English History, 1914-1945, 1965; From Sarajevo to Potsdam, 1966; Europe: Grandeur and Decline, 1967; War by Timetable, 1969; Beaverbrook, 1972; The Second World War: an illustrated history, 1975; Essays in English History, 1976; The Last of Old Europe, 1976; The War Lords, 1977; The Russian War, 1978; How Wars Begin, 1979; Revolutions and Revolutionaries, 1980; Policiticans, Socialism and Historians, 1980; A Personal History (autobiography), 1983, How War Ends, An Old Man's, Diary, 1984; editor: Lloyd George; twelve essays, 1971; Lloyd George, a Diary, 1971; Off the Record; political interviews 1933-43, 1973; My Darling Pussy: the letters of Lloyd George and Frances Stevenson, 1975; columnist Manchester Guardian, Sunday Express. Died Sept. 7, 1990; cremated. Home: London Eng.

TAYLOR, C(LARENCE) J(OHN), judge; b. Centerville, Utah, Nov. 13, 1893; s. Peter and Margaret (Cannel) T.; m. Vera Porter, Dec. 17, 1919; children: Ruth (Mrs. J.A. Jefferies), Jeannine (Mrs. F. McKay Smith). Student, Ricks Coll., Rexburg, Idaho, 1910-14, U. Utah, 1915-16; LLB, U. Idaho, 1919. Bar: Idaho 1919. Pros. atty. Madison County, 1921-24; dist. judge 9th Dist. Idaho, 1927-49; justice Supreme Ct. Idaho, from 1949. Served as pvt. U.S. Army, 1918. Mem. Am. Legion, Elks, Phi Gamma Delta, Phi Alpha Delta. Republican. Mormon. *

TAYLOR, CLIFFORD CURTIS, agricultural economist; b. Loveland, Colo., May 15, 1895; s. Zachary and Winona (Washburn) T.; m. Emma Marie Harned, June 1921; 1 son, Clifford Curtis. BS, Colo. State Coll., 1917; MS, Iowa State Coll., 1923; MA, Harvard U., 1926, PhD, 1930. Asst. agrl. agt. Colo., 1917; sci. rsch. asst. Office of Farm Mgmt., U.S. Dept. Agr., 1918-20; state farm mgmt. demonstrator Idaho, 1920-21; rsch. asst. Iowa State Agrl. Experiment Sta., 1921-23; head dept. agrl. econs. Va. Poly. Inst., 1923-30; agrl. attaché assigned to South Africa, 1930-33, assigned to British Isles, 1935-39, assigned to Can., 1939-46; econ. counselor Poland, 1946-47; agrl. attaché, agrl. counselor New Delhi, 1947-49; counselor of embassy at New Delhi and attaché at Nepal, 1949-55; agrl. economist for FAO of UN, Cairo, 1955-56; vis. prof. agrl. econs. U. Md., 1956-61; internat. trade agreements, Wash., 1933-35; Am. rep. Internat. Wheat Adv. Com., 1936-39; tech. adviser Interant. Sugar Conf., 1937, Coun. del., London, 1937-39. Author: Agriculture in Southern Africa, 1935. Mem. Am. Farm Econ. Assn., Alpha Zeta, Phi Kappa Phi, Pi Kappa Delta. *

TAYLOR, EDWARD PLUNKET, business executive; b. Ottawa, Ont., Can., Jan. 29, 1901; s. Plunket Bourchier and Florence Gertrude (Magee) T.; m. Winifred Thornton Duguid, June 15, 1927; children: Judith (Mrs. John Mappin), Louise (Mrs. Alan Edwards), Charles. BS, McGill U., 1922. Dir. Brading Breweries, Ltd., 1923; with investment firm McLeod, Young, Weir & Co., Ltd., 1923, dir., 1929-30; pres. Can. Breweries, Ltd., 1930-44, chmn. bd., 1944-66; dir. Argus Corp. Ltd., Toronto, Roy West Banking Corp., Ltd., Trust Corp. of Bahamas, Ltd., Royal Bank Can., Massey-Ferguson Holdings, Ltd., Abbey Internat. Ins. Co. Ltd., Royal Bank Can. Trust Corp., Ltd. (London), Massey-Ferguson, Ltd.; pres. Lyford Cay Co., Ltd., Nassau, Windfields Farm Ltd., Willowdale, Ont.; chmn. bd. New Providence Devel. Co., Nassau, Internat. Housing Ltd.; chmn. Royal Bank Can. Internat. Ltd. (Nassau); hon. chmn. Ont. Jockey Club, Toronto. Mem. exec. com. Dept. Munitions and Supply, Ottawa, 1940, joint dir.-gen. munitions prodn., 1940, exec. asst. min. munitions and supply, 1941; pres. War Supplies Ltd., Washington, 1941; pres., vice chmn. Brit. Supply Coun. N.A., 1941; dir.-gen. Brit. Ministry Supply Mission, 1942; Can. dep. mem. Combined Prodn. and Resources Bd., 1942; Can. chmn. Joint War Aid Com., U.S.-Can., 1943; bd. govs. Trinity Coll Sch., McGill U. Created companion Order St. Michael and St. George, 1946. Mem. Thoroughbred Racing Assn., Jocky Club Can. (chmn.), Toronto Club, York Club, Royal Yacht Squadron Club, Bucks Club, Turf Club, Lyford Cay Club, East Hill Club, Rideau Club, Met. Club. Mem. Anglican Ch. Home: Nassau Bahamas Died May 14, 1989.

TAYLOR, FRED MONROE, federal judge; b. Nampa, Idaho, Feb. 25, 1901; s. Robert F. and Pearl (Christine) T.; m. Gwen E. McLeod, Mar. 17, 1929 (dec. June 1977); children: Jacquelyn Rae, Marta Kaye.; m. Beatrice H. Paris, Oct. 1983. LL.B., U. Idaho, 1926. Bar: Idaho 1926. Practiced in Boise, 1938-54; pros. atty. Valley County, Idaho, 1927-33, 35-38; city atty. Boise, 1944-45; judge U.S. Dist. Ct. Idaho, Boise, from 1954; mem. U.S. Jud. Conf., 1969-72, Idaho Senate, 1943-51. Mem. Idaho Bar Assn., Am. Judicature Soc., Phi Alpha Delta, Sigma Nu. Republican. Episcopalian. Clubs: Masons, Shriners. Home: Boise Idaho Died Feb. 16, 1988; interred Boise, Idaho.

TAYLOR, HERBERT CECIL, JR., anthropology educator; b. Houston, Nov. 29, 1924; s. Herbert Cecil and Pearl (Alexander) T.; m. Ruby Emma Oncken, Oct. 7, 1948 (div.); children: Laura Helen, Herbert Cecil III; m. Carol Jean Diers, Aug. 17, 1973. Student, U. N.Mex., 1942; N.Mex. A & M Coll., 1942; B.A., U. Tex. at Austin, 1949, M.A., 1949; Ph.D., U. Chgo., 1951. Teaching asst. anthropology U. Chgo., 1949-51; mem. faculty Western Wash. U., Bellingham, from 1951; prof. anthropology Western Wash. U., 1962-87, disting. service prof. emeritus, from 1987, chmn. dept. sociology-anthropology, 1960-65, dean research and grants, 1965-75, chmn. faculty council, 1959-60; vis. asst. prof. U. B.C., 1954; vis. prof. U. Calgary, 1966, 73; Chmn. steering com. Pacific N.W. Conf. Higher Edn.; twice chmn. social studies div. N.W. Sci. Assn.; anthrop. cons. Indian Claims Cases. Author books on Northwest Indians; editor collections sci. papers.; Contbr. articles, chpts. on Mexican, Am., Greenlandic, and Canadian archaeology and ethno-history to books, profl. publs. Served with AUS, 1943-46, ETO; lt. col. USAF Res.; dir. personnel Wash. Air N.G., 1973-76. Decorated USAF Commendation medal; recipient Best Tchr. award Western Wash U., 1957. Mem. Am. Ethnohist. Soc., Canadian Studies Assn., Ret. Officers Assn., Sigma Xi. Club: Bellingham Golf and Country. Home: Bellingham Wash. Deceased. †

TAYLOR, JAMES STURDEVANT, mathematics educator; b. Danbury, Conn., May 4, 1895; s. Samuel Lyons and Anna (Murphy) T.; m. Geraldine Hayes Cotton, June 2, 1926. AB, U. Calif., 1916, MA, 1917, PhD, 1918. Postdoctoral fellow Commn. for Relief in Belgium Ednl. Found., U. Louvain, 1921-22; instr. math. MIT, 1919-24; asst. prof. math. U. Pitts., 1924-26, assoc. prof., 1926-30, prof., from 1930; head dept., 1939-60; for U. Pitts. under auspices AID at Universidad Técnical Federico Santa Maria, Valparaiso, Chile, 1965-67. Author: Essentials of Calculus, 1929; contbr. articles to profl. jours. Bd. dirs. Arts and Crafts Ctr., Pitts., 1954-58; mem., bd. dirs. Belgian Am. Ednl. Found. Served as ensign USN, 1918-19. Mem. AAUP, AAAS, Am. Math. Soc., Math. Assn. Am., Internat. Brotherhood Magicians, Soc. Am. Magicians, Authors Club (pres. 1956-58), Univ. Club of Pitts., Phi Beta Kappa, Sigma Xi. Democrat. Episc. *

TAYLOR, LISA, museum director; b. N.Y.C., Jan. 8, 1933; d. Theo and Martina (Weincerl) von Bergen-Maier; m. Bertrand L. Taylor III; children: Lauren, Lindsay. Student, Corcoran Sch. Art, 1958-65, Georgetown U., 1958-62, Johns Hopkins U., 1956-58; D.F.A. (hon.), Parsons Sch. Design, 1977, Cooper Union, 1984. Adminstrv. asst. President's Fine Arts Com., 1958-62; membership dir. Corcoran Gallery Art, 1962-66; program dir. Smithsonian Instn., 1966-69; dir. Cooper-Hewitt Mus. Decorative Arts and Design, Smithsonian Instn., 1969-87, dir. emeritus, 1987-91; mem. adv. bd. Design Mus. (London), N.Y. Hist. Soc., Katonah Gallery, Ctr. for Childhood, 1989. Co-dir. (film) A Living Museum, 1968; editor: Urban Open Spaces, 1979, Cities, 1981, The Phenomenon of Change, 1984, Housing: Symbol, Structure, Site, 1990. Recipient Thomas Jefferson award, 1976; Bronze plaque Johns Hopkins YMCA, 1958; medal of honor Am. Legion, 1951; Bronze Apple award Am. Soc. Indsl. Designers, 1977; named Trailblazer of Yr. Nat. Home Fashion League, 1981, Mcpl. Art Soc. award 1987, Joseph Henry medal, 1987, Dame of Honour Order of St. John of Jerusalem. Mem. Smithsonian Instn. (hon. life, Exceptional Service award 1969, Gold medal 1972, Women's Council award 1979), Am. Soc. Interior Designers (hon.), AIA (hon.). Home: Naples Fla. Died Apr. 26, 1991.

TAYLOR, OVERTON HUME, economist, educator; b. Craig, Colo., Dec. 11, 1897; s. David Hume and Elizabeth M. (Ellis) T.; m. Edith Meyer, Nov. 6, 1953. AB, U. Colo., 1921; PhD, Harvard U., 1928. Instr. econs. U. Colo., 1921-22; tchr. pub. schs. Belgrade, Mont., 1922-23; instr. econs. U. Pa., 1928-29; lectr. Harvard U., 1929-60, prof. econs., 1960-64, emeritus, from 1964; prof. Vanderbilt U., from 1965. Author: Economics and Liberalism, 1955; The Classical Liberalism, Marxism and the 20th Century, 1960; A History of Economic Thought, 1960. Mem. Am. Econ. Assn. *

TAYLOR, PRENTISS HOTTEL, artist; b. Washington, Dec. 13, 1907; s. John Eastlack and Beatrice (Hottel) T. Student, Art Students League, 1931-32; pupil Charles W. Hawthorne. Scenic artist, 1926, lithograph, watercolor artist, 1931-91, painter in oils, 1943-91; art therapist, psychotherapy dept. St. Elizabeth's Hosp., Washington, 1943-54; profl. lectr. Am. U.; art therapist Chestnut-Lodge, Rockville, Md., 1958-78. Work represented in Libr. of Congress, Phillips Collection, Met. Mus. Art, N.Y. Mus. Modern Art, Wadsworth Atheneum, Hartford, Conn., Addison Gallery, Andover, Mass., Whitney Mus. Am. Art, Balt. Mus. Art, Seattle Art Mus., N.Y. Pub. libr., Boston Mus. Fine Arts, Phila. Mus., Valentine Mus., Richmond, Va. Mus. Fine Arts, Yale U. Gallery, Gibbes Gallery, Charleston, S.C., Smithsonian Instn., Washington, Boston Pub. Libr., several univs.; exhibited painting in U.S., 1946-49, Carnegie Inst., Corcoran Biennial, 1949-51; established, illustrator Winter Wheat Press; established (with Langston Hughes) Golden Stair Press. Recipient Am. Artists Group lithograph prize, 1953, Cannon graphic prize NAD, 1954, purchase award lithography, nat. exhbn. DePauw U., 1959. Mem. Soc. Am. Graphic Artists, Soc. Washington Printmakers, Artists Guild Washington, Nat. Acad. of Design, Print Club of Albany, Boston Printmakers. Home: Washington D.C. Died Oct. 7, 1991; cremated.

TAYLOR, THEOPHILUS MILLS, clergyman, educator, church administrator; b. Cedarville, Ohio, June 22, 1909; s. Mills J. and Martha Slater (Dill) T.; m. Lois Dean McLaughlin, Mar. 12, 1936; children: Martha Renwick, Theophilus Mills III, Jessica Anne, Caroline Kerr. Student, Muskingum Coll., 1927-30, D.D. (hon.), 1944; B.Arch., U. Pa., 1935; M.Div., Pitts.-Xenia Theol. Sem., 1941; postgrad., U. Chgo., 1946; Ph.D. in Religion, Yale, 1956. Tchr. gen. sci., indsl. arts Woodstock Sch., India, 1935-38; ordained to ministry United Presbyn. Ch., 1941; asst. pastor First Presbyn. Ch., Crafton, Pa., 1940-41; pastor United Presbyn. Ch., Barnet Center, Vt., 1941-43; John McNaugher prof. N.T. lit. and exegesis Pitts.-Xenia Theol. Sem., 1943-59, dean dept. grad. studies, 1946-59; prof. Pitts. Theol. Sem., 1960-62; sec. gen. council Gen. Assembly United Presbyn. Ch. U.S.A., 1962-72; also chmn. Ch. Exec. Devel. Bd., 1968-74; pres. Religion in Am. Life, 1970-73, mem. corp., trustee, 1974-79, emeritus trustee, 1980-89; Asst. dir. archeol. excavations, Beitin, Jordan, 1957, 60; U.P. rep. Am. com. World Council Chs., 1946-48, del. constituting assembly, 1948; rep. to Conf. U.S.A. Mem. Chs., 1948-61; del. 16th Gen. Council of Alliance Ref. Chs., Geneva, 1948, 18th Gen. Council, Sao Paolo, 1959, 3d World Conf. on Faith and Order, Lund, Sweden, 1952, 4th conf., Montreal, 1963; del. 2d assembly World Council Chs., Evanston, Ill., 1954, adviser 3d assembly, New Delhi, 1961; mem. com. religion and pub. edn. Pa. Council Christian Edn., 1950-54; sec. joint drafting com. Conf. Ch. Union of Presbyn. U.S.A. and U.P. Chs., 1955-57; moderator gen. assembly U.P. Ch. U.S.A., 1958-59, chmn. commn. ecumenical mission and relations, 1959-62; mem. working com. Commn. Faith and Order, World Council Chs., 1952-71, mem. Commn., 1952-75, chmn. theol. commn. Holy Eucharist, faith and order, 1965-71; mem. exec. com., gen. bd., chmn. gen. constituent membership com. Nat. Council Chs., U.S.A., 1960-72; sec. Am. Council for Boys' Indsl. Home and Tech. Sch., Gujranwala, India, 1944-62. Author: Uncleanness and Purification in Paul, 1956, Survey of Theological Education (Africa, Middle-East and Asia), 1962; Assoc. editor: The United Presbyn, 1947-56; editorial council: Theology Today, Princeton, N.J., 1951-73; Contbr. editorials, articles, book revs. to religious jours.; chpts. to Stewardship in Contemporary Life, 1965, Assignment: Overseas, 1966, For Me to Live, 1972. Bd. dirs. Center for Interfaith Research on Religious Architecture; mem. corp. Nyack (N.Y.) Hosp., 1965-72; trustee Muskingum Coll., 1965-78, emeritus trustee, 1979-89. Mem. Archaeol. Inst. Am., Soc. Bibl. Lit. and Exegesis, Guild for Religious Architecture, Presbyn. Hist. Soc. (pres. 1964-71), Studiorum Novi Testamenti Societas, Internat. Assn. for a Union of Democracies (mem. council 1972—, pres. 1973-85), Am. Oriental Soc. Home: East Topsham Vt. Died May 29, 1989; buried Barnet Center, Vt.

TAYLOR, WILLIAM, federal official, banker; m. Sharon Spaven; children: Claire, Emily, William III. Grad., Cornell Coll., Mt. Vernon, Iowa, 1961. Bank examiner Fed. Res. Bank Chgo., 1961-68; v.p. in charge of lending Upper Ave. Bank, Chgo., 1968-72; office mgr. James W. Rouse and Co., Chgo., 1972-76; chief fin. instns. supervision Fed. Reserve Bd. divsn. Banking Supervision and Regulation, 1976-77, asst. div. dir., 1977-79, assoc. dir., 1979-85, dir., 1985-87, staff dir., 1987-91; chmn. FDIC, Washington, 1991-92; acting pres. oversight bd. Resolution Trust Corp., 1990. Home: Washington D.C. Died Aug. 20, 1992. †

TAYLOR, WILLIAM RANDOLPH, educator; b. Phila., Dec. 21, 1895; s. William Long and Caroline Augusta (Sower) T.; m. Jean Falconer Grant, Dec. 18, 1926; children: William Randolph, James Keith. BS, U. Pa., 1916, MS, 1917, PhD, 1920. Researcher Marine Biol. Lab., summers 1917-90, Dry Tortugas La. of Carnegie Inst., Washington, summers 1924-26; asst. prof. of botany U. Pa., 1915-17, instr., 1918-22, asst. prof., 1922-27, prof., 1927-30; prof. botany and curator algae in herbarium U. Mich., Ann Arbor, 1930-66, prof. emeritus, 1966-90; hon. rsch. assoc. Farlow Herbarium Harvard, Cambridge, Mass., 1966-90; instr. botany Marine Biol. Lab., 1918-45, charge algae course, 1928-45; rsch. assoc. Acad. Natural Sci., Phila., 1925-30; mem. Hancock Expdns. to Galapagos Islands, 1934, to Central, S.Am., W.I., 1939; sr. biologist Oceanographic sect JTFI Crossroads Atomic Bomb Expdn. to No. Marshall Islands, 1946; trustee Bermuda Biol. Sta. Corp., Marine Biol. Lab Corp., 1930-90. Author: books in field, including Plants of Bikini, 1950, Marine Algae of the Northwestern Coast of North America, rev. edit, 1962, marine Algae of the Tropical and Subtropical Coasts of the Americas, 1960; also pamphlets on rsch. in cytology, tropical and alpine algae; assoc. editor: Hydrobiologia (Den Haag, Netherlands), 1946-90, Botanica Marina (Hamburg, Germany), 1959-90. With U.S. Army, WWI. Recipient Retzius medal K. Fysiografiska Sallskapet, Lund, Sweden, 1948, Gilbert Morgan Smith medal in phycology NAS, 1979; Russel lectr. U. Mich., 1964. Fellow AAAS, Am. Acad. Arts and Scis.; mem. Phycol. Soc. Am., Bot. Soc. Am., Brit. Phycol. Soc. (hon.), Soc. Phycol. de France (hon.), Acad. Nat. Sci. Phila., Mich. Acad. Scis., Arts and Letters, Linnean Soc. Longon (fgn. mem.), Soc. de Ciencias Naturales de Venezeula (corrs.), Royal Flemish Acad. Sci., Acad. des Scis., Inst. Francais, Sigma Xi, Phi Sigma. Episcopalian. Home: Ann Arbor Mich. Died Nov. 11, 1990; buried Cemetery of the Ch. of the Messiah, Woods Hole, Mass.

TAYLOR, WILLIS H(ORR), JR., patent lawyer; b. N.Y.C., Aug. 17, 1894; s. Willis Horr and Anna Mary (McCormick) T.; children: Willis H. III, William Davis. ME, Stevens Inst. Tech., 1916, ED, 1956; post-grad., N.Y. Law Sch., 1916-17, Fordham U., 1920. Bar: N.Y. 1920, D.C. 1923. Mem. firm Pennie, Edmonds, Morton, Barrows and Taylor, N.Y.C., from 1925; dir. Farrand Optical Co., Inc., N.Y.C., Farrand Controls, Inc., N.Y., Inductosyn Corp., Nev. Chmn. bd. trustees Stevens Inst. Tech.; pres. Stevens Tuition and Scholarship Plan. Served as capt., Signal Corps, U.S. Army, 1917-19, AEF. Mem. Univ. Club of N.Y.C., Sigma Xi. Republican. Roman Catholic. *

TEAGUE, DONALD, artist; b. Bklyn., Nov. 27, 1897; s. Edwin Dawes and Frances (Irel) T.; m. Verna Timmins, July 19, 1938 (dec. 1985); children: Linda Teague Key, Hilary Teague Kitch. Student, Art Students League N.Y., 1916-17, 19-20; also studied in, London, Eng.; DFA (hon.), Pepperdine U., 1989. Began as illustrator, 1921; illus. for mags.; illustrated under pseudonym of Edwin Dawes; paintings exhibited Met. Mus. Art, Nat. Acad. Design Bklyn. Mus., Art Inst. Chgo., Toledo Mus., Royal Watercolor Soc., London, Eng., Conn. Acad., Tokyo Mus., Kyoto Mus., Mus. Watercolor, Mexico City, others; represented in, Va. Mus. Fine Arts, Richmond, Frye Mus. Seattle, Collection of State of Calif., Sacramento, Collection of USAF, Colorado Springs, Colo., Mills Coll. Art Gallery, Oakland, Calif., U. Oreg., Eugene, U. Kans., Lawrence, Nat. Cowboy Hall of Fame, Phoenix Mus. Art, several pvt. collections., invitational exhibit Salon d'Autumn, Grand Palais, Paris, Nov., 1987; recipient Isador watercolor prize 1939, Zabriskie prize Am. Watercolor Soc. 1944, Winsor & Newton prize 1954, 1st watercolor prize Nat. Acad. 1947, 49, 52, 59, 65, 1st watercolor prize Soc. Western Artists 1952, 53, 54, 1st watercolor prize Calif. State Fair 1952, Gold medal Am. Watercolor Soc. 1953, 1st watercolor prize Santa Cruz Art Assn. 1954, Silver medal of Honor Am. Watercolor Soc. 1961, Grand award and Gold medal of Honor 1964, S.F.B. Morse Gold medal for Watercolor, Nat. Acad. 1962, certificate of Merit Royal Acad. London 1963, Resolution Commendation Senate State Calif. 1964, Butler prize American Watercolor Soc. 1966, Saportas award 1967, Oehler award 1968, Jurors Spl. mention 1st Internat. Exhbn. Marietta Coll. 1968, Obrig prize Nat. Acad. 1969, Lehmann award Am. Watercolor Soc. 1969, Best in Show award Soc. Western Artists 1969, Today's Art medal of merit Am. Watercolor Soc. 1971, silver medal for watercolor Cowboy Artists of Am. 1971, William A. Paton award Nat. Acad. 1972, award for excellence Marietta Coll. 1972, gold medal for watercolor Cowboy Artists of Am. 1972, Nat. Cowboy Hall of Fame 1973, 75, gold medal for Western art Franklin Mint 1973, 74, for watercolor 1974); featured in TV film, Profiles in American Art., PBS, 1982; subject book: Donald Teague - A Life in Color (Claudia Meyer), 1988. Recipient J. Francis Murphy Meml. prize Nat. Acad., 1932; Grant prize New Rochelle Art Assn., 1935; Thumb Box prize Salmagundi Club, 1936; Newcastle Meml. award, 1955; Am. Artist Mag. medal of honor, 1957, Benjamin West Clindinst Gold medal Artists Fellowship, 1984; named to Soc. Illustrators Hall of Fame, 1991. Mem. N.A.D., Nat. Acad. Western Art (Bronze medal 1976, Silver medal for watercolor 1977, 82, 83, Gold medal for watercolor 1980, Trustee's Gold medal 1980, Gold medal for contbn. fine art 1989, named to Hall of Fame 1990), Cowboy Artists Am. (emeritus, Gold medal for watercolor 1977, Silver medal for mixed media 1978), Am. Watercolor Soc. (hon.). Republican. Clubs: Bohemian (San Francisco); Salmagundi (hon.). Home: Carmel Calif. Died Dec. 13, 1991; buried Earlham Cemetery, Richmond, Ind.

TEARE, WALLACE GLEED, architect; b. Cleve., June 5, 1907; s. George Wallace and Florence Elizabeth (Gleed) T.; m. Dorothy Gabriel Schaefer, June 24, 1933; children: Richard W., Virginia Gabriel (Mrs. Albert M. Katz). B.Arch., Western Res. U., 1929, M.A., 1933; diploma, Fontainebleau (France) Sch. Fine Arts, 1930. Partner Conrad & Teare, architects, Cleve., 1931-38; Ptnr. Joseph L. Weinberg and Conrad & Teare, assoc. architects, Cleve., 1932-36; housing planner U.S. Housing Authority, Washington, 1938-39; chief planning and research Cleve. Met. Housing Authority, 1939-44; chmn. bd. Teare, Herman, & Gibans, Inc. (ptnr. predecessor firms), Cleve., from 1946; instr. Western Res. U., 1931-38, 45-47, trustee, 1948-56; housing cons. to gov., Panama Canal, 1945; archtl. cons. Cleve. City Planning Commn., 1959, mem., from 1970, vice chmn., 1971-74, chmn., from 1975; mem. Lakewood (Ohio) City Planning Commn., 1944-60, chmn., 1952-53; mem. exec. com. Regional Planning Commn. Cuyahoga County, 1951-60, from 1975. Most important works of the firm include Lakeview Terrace, Cleve., 1937, O'Neil-Sheffield Shopping Center, Sheffield Twp., Ohio, 1954 (AIA award of merit 1955), West Shore Unitarian Ch., Rocky River, 1962; (assoc. architect with Edward D. Stone) Jewish Community Fedn. Office Bldg, Cleve., 1965; Chesterfield Apts. (Charles Luckman Assocs., Cons.), Cleve., 1968; Lakeview Tower, Cleve., 1973, other housing for elderly in Ohio, Pa., Conn., from 1954, restoration Stouffer Tower City Plaza Hotel (Preservation award Cleve. chpt. AIA 1979, honor award Architects Soc. Ohio 1981); author articles on housing for elderly. Trustee Regional Assn. Cleve., Friends of Cuyahoga Met. Housing Authority ; trustee W. Shore Concerts, Lakewood, Ohio, pres., 1954-56; trustee Koch Sch. Music, Rocky River, Ohio, chmn., 1970-71. Recipient Cleve. Arts prize, 1977, Silver Medal Alpha Epsilon chpt. Tau Sigma Delta, 1987; named to Cleve. Engring. Soc. Constrn. Hall of Fame, 1985. Fellow AIA (sec. Cleve. chpt. 1944, v.p. 1948, pres. 1949, profl. adv. from 1978, mem. nat. housing com. 1972-77, chmn. 1975, HUD/AIA liaison task force 1977-78, Cleve. chpt. award honor 1983); mem. Architects Soc. Ohio (sec. Cleve. sect. 1937, v.p. 1938, Gold medal 1983), Am. Soc. Planning Ofcls. (hon. life), Am. Planning Assn., Soc. Archtl. Historians, Western Res. Archtl. Historians, Soc. for History of City and Regional Planning, Nat. Assn. Housing and Redevel. Ofcls., Nat. Housing Conf., Internat. Assn. Housing Sci. Unitarian. Home: Cleveland Ohio Deceased. †

TEBO, JULIAN DRENNER, consulting electrical engineer; b. Harpers Ferry, W.Va., July 5, 1903; s. Elmer Edward and Mary (Pearl) T.; m. Helen Gertrude Heuser, Nov. 28, 1932; children: Jay Drenner, Robert John, Cathellen May Tebo Shick. B Engring., Johns Hopkins U., 1924, DEng, 1928. Registered profl. engr., N.Y. With Bell Telephone Labs., 1928-68; head tech. rels. dept., 1961-68, chmn. rsch. com. Engring. Found., 1965-68; spl. lectr. elec. engring. Newark Coll. Engring., 1968-69; cons. elec. engr., 1968-91; mem. adv. coun. Soc. for History Tech., 1968-91. Contbr. numerous articles to profl. jours.; patentee electrolysis protection, also inductive coordination between telephone and power lines. Mem. Verona (N.J.) Bd. Edn., 1954-57; mem. Verona Borough Coun., 1957-70, pres., 1959, 68. Named to Nat. Inventors Hall of Fame; recipient letter of appreciation Zagreb (Yugoslavia) Film Co., 1975. Fellow IEEE (life, chmn. N.Y. sect. 1950-51, nat. bd. dirs. 1955-59, cert. of appreciation Life Mem. Fund Commn. 1975, Alan Ploss award 1986); mem. AIAA, ASME, N.Y. Acad. Scis., Montclair Soc. Engrs. (pres. 1957-58), Am. Phys. Soc., Telephone Pioneers Am., Engrs. Joint Coun., Sigma Xi, Alpha Tau Omega, Eta Kappa Nu. Republican. Presbyterian. Home: Verona N.J. Died Dec. 18, 1991; buried Ctrl. Presbyn. Ch., Montclair, N.J.

TELFORD, ROBERT LEE, engineering company executive; b. Lewisberg, W.Va., May 8, 1899; s. Robert Lee and Anna Boone (Bracon) T.; m. Marie Krentz, Jan. 12, 1929 (dec.). Student, Washington and Lee U., 1922. Reseach engr. M&H Silas Co., Lexington, Ky.; exec. v.p. Silas Mason Co., 1940-76; chmn. bd. dirs. M&H Silas-Mason Co., 1976-87. Chmn. bd. dirs. Naples (Fla.) Community Hosp., 1965-70. Republican. Presbyterian. Clubs: Hole in the Wall Country (pres.), Naples Yacht (bd. dirs. 1969-72) (Naples); Shreveport (La.) Country (pres. 1948-55). Home: Naples Fla. Died May, 1989.

TELINDE, RICHARD WESLEY, gynecologist; b. Waupun, Wis., Sept. 2, 1894; s. Garret and Cora (Gerretson) TeL.; m. Catharine Davenport Long, June 1, 1927. AB, U. Wis., 1917; MD, Johns Hopkins U., 1920. Intern, resident Johns Hopkins Hosp., Balt., 1920-25, chief gynecologist, 1939-89; pvt. practice Balt., 1925-89; assoc. gynecology Johns Hopkins U., 1936-39, prof. gynecology, 1939-89; vis. gynecologist Union Meml. Hosp., Church, Home and Infirmary, and Hosp. for the Women of Md. Served in SATC, 1918. Author: Operative Gynecology, 1946; contbr. articles to profl. jours. Mem. AMA, Am. Gynecol. Soc. (pres. 1953-54), Am. Gynecol. Club, So. Med. Soc., So. Surg. Assn., Balt. Med. Soc., Phi Beta Kappa, Alpha Omega Alpha; hon. mem. Peruvian, Brazilian, Cuban gynecol. socs., Bolivian, Argentine, N.J., Pitts., Miami obstet. and gynecol. socs., Ctrl., Tex., S. Atlantic assns. obstetricians and gynecologists, Soc. Gynecology and Obstetrics El Salvadore, Acad. Nat. Medicine Peru, Soc. Francise Gynecologie, Soc. Obstetricia y Ginecologia Venezuela, Internat. Coll. Surgeons,. Presbyterian. Home: Belair Md. Died Nov. 16, 1989.

TEMMER, STEPHEN FRANCIS, communications executive; b. Vienna, Austria, May 28, 1928; came to U.S., 1939; Student, Mass. Inst. Tech. V.p., chief engr., co-owner Gotham Rec. Corp., N.Y.C., 1950-57; pres., owner Gotham Audio Corp., N.Y.C., and Glendale, Calif., 1957-85, Gotham Export Corp., N.Y.C., 1968-84, Quantum Audio Labs., Inc., Glendale, 1982-85; tech. expert to spl. advisor to the Mayor on Transp. N.Y.C., 1987; engring. coord. Transp. Office Mayor of the City of N.Y., N.Y.C., 1987-92; pres. Temmer Enterprises Inc., 1987-89; bd. dirs. Thorens-Franz AG, Wettingen, Switzerland; pres., chmn. bd. Gotham AG for Electronic Products, Regensdorf, Switzerland; music dir. Stas. WNYE-FM, WMIT, 1943-47; radio dir. The Harbor Playhouse, Marion, Mass., 1946; music librarian radio div. UN, Lake Success, N.Y., 1947-48; studio engr. ABC, Inc., N.Y.C., 1948-49; gen. mgr. Sta. WBAI-FM, N.Y.C., 1957-58; tech. advisor Watergate Spl. Prosecution Force, Washington, 1973-74, Lincoln Ctr. for the Performing Arts, N.Y.C., 1974-76; adj. prof. music, U. Iowa, Iowa City, 1983; lectr. on audio rec. various colls. Producer retrospective album of The Chgo. Symphony Orch., 1985-87; contbr. numerous articles to profl. and tech. jours. Trustee The Greenwich Village Soc. for Historic Preservation, 1980-85. Fellow Audio Engring. Soc. (v.p. internat. region 1973-75, 77-79, gov. 1980-82); mem. IEEE (sr. mem.), Soc. Motion Picture and TV Engrs., Acoustical Soc. Am., Assn. German Studio Engrs., Nat. Acad. Rec. Arts and Scis., Internat. Electro-Tech. Commn., Aircraft Owners' and Pilots' Assn. Home: New York N.Y. Died Oct. 8, 1992. †

TEMPLE, ALAN HARRISON, bank executive; b. Templeville, Md., Sept. 7, 1896; s. Harry Weston and Susan Edith (Harrison) T.; m. Annalee Herndon Vernon, Feb. 14, 1922; children: Anne Vernon (Mrs. Charles A. Crumm, Jr.), Nancy (Mrs. Robert G. Hammond), Alan Harrison. BLitt in Journalism, Columbia U., 1917. Mng. editor, editor Commerce & Fin., N.Y.C., 1919-31; pres. Theo. H. Price Pub. Corp., N.Y.C., 1928-31; fin. editor N.Am. Rev., 1928-30; statistician Nat. City Bank of N.Y., 1931-41, v.p., 1941-52, exec. v.p., 1952-58, vice chmn., 1958-61; mem. trust bd. First Nat. City Bank of N.Y. (formerly Nat. City Bank of N.Y.), from 1963; dir. Moore Corp., Ltd., Prudential Ins. Co. Gt. Britain (N.Y.), Seaboard Surety Co., Centennial Ins. Co., Hudson Ins. Co., Mead Corp., Monsanto Chem. Co., Lazard Fund, Inc.; trustee Atlantic Mut. Ins. Co. Com. Econ. Devel.; trustee Nat. Indsl. Conf. Bd., chmn., 1959-61. Trustee Whitney Mus. Am. Art, Columbia U.; pres. Scarsdale Pub. Libr. Served with Divsn. Hdqrs., 27th Divsn., AEF, 1918-19. Mem. Acad. Polit. Sci. (trustee), Shenorock Shore Club (Rye, N.Y.), Univ. Club, Blind Brook Club, Union Club, Lyford Cay Club (Nassau). *

TEODORU, CONSTANTIN VALERIU, physician, educator; b. Moreni, Romania, Feb. 14, 1915; came to U.S., 1952, naturalized, 1957; s. Mihail and Viorica (Angelescu) T.; m. Maria Mirella Ioanid, Feb. 14, 1942; children: Nicolas-Dor, Dan-Eugene, Michael-Nicholas. MD, Bucharest U., 1939. Diplomate Bd. Internal Medicine. Intern, resident Brancovenesc Hosp., Bucharest, 1936-42; practice medicine Bucharest, 1939-48; assoc. prof. physiology Bucharest U., 1939-48; head med. depts. ARC, Nat. Cath. Welfare Conf., Rumanian Red Cross, Bucharest, 1946-48; chief physiol. and pharm. research lab. Roussel Drug Co., Paris, 1949-52; rsch. assoc. charge polio project Mt. Sinai Hosp., N.Y.C., 1952-57; practice medicine Jackson Heights, N.Y., 1959-91; head applied physiology, prin. investigator I. Albert Research Inst., Bklyn., 1957-64; attending dept. medicine, chief long term med. care div. Kingsbrook Med. Ctr., Bklyn., 1964-71; vis. physician, assoc. dir. medicine NYU Med. Ctr. Goldwater Meml. Hosp., N.Y.C., 1972-76; assoc. vis. physician Kings County Hosp., Bklyn., 1961-91; clin. assoc. prof. medicine Downstate Med. Ctr. SUNY, 1961-91, NYU, 1974-91. Recipient ribbon for outstanding services ARC, 1947, medal Romanian Red Cross, 1946. Fellow ACP, N.Y. Acad. Medicine; mem. Am. Physiol Soc., Am. Rheumatism Assn., N.Y. Rheumatism Assn., Endocrine Soc., Soc. Exptl. Biology and Medicine, Gerontological Soc., Reticulo Endothelial Soc., AAAS, N.Y. Acad. Scis., Harvey Soc. Home: Jackson Heights N.Y. Died Jan. 18, 1991.

TERWILLIGER, HERBERT LEE, lawyer; b. Madison, Wis., June 22, 1914; s. Walter E. and Laura (Stone) T.; m. Catharine O'Connor, Oct. 19, 1940; children: Sara (Mrs. Mancer J. Cyr), Walter Thomas, Martha (Mrs. Craig Coburn), Mary (Mrs. Stuart Campbell). Ph.B., U. Wis., 1936, J.D., 1938. Bar: Wis. 1938. Since practiced in Wausau; assoc. firm Genrich & Genrich, 1938-42, 45-46, Terwilliger, Wakeen, Piehler,

Conway S.C., and predecessor, from 1946; spl. agt. FBI, 1943-44; mem. Gov.'s Commn. on Constl. Revision, 1960-61, 63-65, Gov.'s Com. on Eminent Domain, 1965-66, 68-69. Bd. editors: Wis. Law. Rev, 1936-38. Trustee Meml. Union, U. Wis. Mem. ABA, Marathon Bar Assn., State Bar Wis. (pres. 1959-60, treas. 1953-55, chmn. ins. sect. 1954-55, dir. corp. and bus law sect. 1956-58, 62-65), Am. Coll. Trial Layers, Wausau Area C. of C. (pres. 1973), Order of Coif, Phi Kappa Phi, Delta Upsilon. Presbyn. (elder). Clubs: Elk, Mason (Shriner), Wausau, Wausau Country. Home: Wausau Wis. Deceased. †

TERWILLIGER, ROBERT ELWIN, bishop; b. Corland, N.Y., Aug. 28, 1917; s. Melville and Ella May (Seman) T.; m. Viola Mae Terwilliger, Dec. 27, 1942; 1 dau., Anne Elizabeth. B.A. summa cum laude, Syracuse U., 1939; B.D., Episcopal Theol. Sch., Cambridge, Mass., 1943; Ph.D., Yale U., 1948; S.T.M., Gen. Theol. Sem., N.Y.C., 1949; D.D. hon., Seabury Western Theol. Sem., Evanston, 1970; D.D., U. of South, Sewanee, Tenn., 1976; postgrad., Nashotah House, Wis. Ordained deacon, Episcopal Ch., 1942 ordained priest, Episcopal Ch., 1943 consecrated bishop, Episcopal Ch., 1975. Curate All Saints Ch., Worcester, Mass., 1942-44; asst. Christ Ch. Cathedral, Hartford, Conn., 1944-47; fellow, tutor Gen. Theol. Sem., N.Y.C., 1947-49; rector Christ Ch., Poughkeepsie, N.Y., 1949-60, St. James Ch., Los Angeles, 1960-62; assoc. pastor All Saints Ch., N.Y.C., 1963-67; founding dir. Trinity Inst., N.Y.C., 1967-75; suffragan bishop Episcopal Diocese of Dallas, 1976-86; chaplain Com. of Holy Spirit, N.Y.C., 1968-75, St. Hilda's and St. Hugh, N.Y.C., 1965-67; Episcopal visitor Com. of St. Mary, Peekskill, N.Y., from 1967; adj. prof. theology Gen. Theol. Sem., 1967-75. Author: Receiving the Word of God, 1959, Christian Believing, 1973, To Be a Priest; editor, contbr.: The Charismatic Christ, 1973; co-editor: To Be A Priest, 1975. Trustee U. of South, from 1975; trustee Gen. Theol. Sem.., N.Y.C., 1977-79, Nashotah House, from 1980. Mem. Anglican-Orthodox Internat. Dialogue, Phi Beta Kappa, Phi Kappa Phi. Home: Huntington N.Y. Died June 3, 1991; interred Bishop Ctr. Mausoleum, Flower Mound, Tex. †

TESTER, ALLEN C., geologist, educator; b. New Haven, Mo., Oct. 30, 1897; s. William Henry and Virginia (Crawford) T.; m. Corinne Lesh, June 10, 1920; 1 dau., Terry Anne (Mrs. Robert W. Chesney). AB, AM, U. Kans., 1921; PhD, U. Wis., 1929. Engaged in geol. study of Rocky Mountain States, Central states in Miss.-Mo. drainage, Gt. Lakes States, from 1920; exploration for petroleum Colombia, 1938-39; asst. state geologist Iowa, 1934-37; tchr. geology U. Kans., 1921-22; tchr. geology U. Iowa, 1925, prof., from 1940; cons. and exploration geologist, ground water, materials resources, mineral exploration; mem. faculty Ariz. State U., summer 1965. Mem. Iowa City (Iowa) Planning and Zoning Commn. Served from capt. to col. C.E., AUS, 1942-46, in PTO and Japan as geologist, water supply and constrn. engr. Recipient Disting. Alumni Geology award U. Kans., 1958. Fellow AAAS, Geol. Soc. Am.; mem. Am. Assn. Petroleum Geologists, Am. Geophys. Union, Iowa Acad. Sci., Geol. Soc. Iowa (pres. 1965), Am. Inst. Profl. Geologists (v.p. 1963-65), Rotary (pres. Iowa City 1949-50), Sigma Xi, Phi Delta Theta, Sigma Gamma Epsilon. Presbyterian. *

THACKREY, RUSSELL I., journalist, educational consultant; b. Kansas City, Kans., Dec. 6, 1904; s. Samuel Isaac and Carrie May (Richards) T.; m. Emily E. Sheppeard, June 29, 1928; 1 child, Elizabeth Ann (Mrs. Hardy Berry). BS, Kans. State Coll., Manhattan, 1927, MS, 1932; postgrad., U. Minn., 1938-39; LLD, U. N.H. Newspaper reporter Memphis, Wichita, Omaha, 1927-28; instr. Kans. State Coll., 1928-32, asst. prof. journalism, newspaper corr., 1932-35, prof., head dept., 1940-44, dean adminstrn., dir. summer sch., 1944-46; editor Kans. mag., 1932-35, 41-43, A.P., Kansas City, Mo., 1935-36; legis. corr. Jefferson City, Mo., 1937; asst. prof. Sch. Journalism U. Minn., 1937-40; exec. dir. Nat. Assn. State Univs. and Land-Grant Colls., 1947-70, exec. dir. emeritus, 1970-90. Author: The Future of the State University, 1970; contbr. articles to ednl. and other periodicals. Sec., treas. Nat. 4-H Club Found., 1949-50, recipient Nat. Recognitions award 1952; chmn. policy com. Washington Internat. Ctr., 1951-56; mem. exec. com. Com. Internat. Econ. Growth, 1958-59; mem. info. adv. com. So. Regional Edn. Bd., 1959-63; adv. com. univ. relationships AID, 1964-70. Served with USNR, 1943-44. Recipient Reuben Brigham award for svcs. to agr., 1961, Presdl. citation for svc. to higher edn. Am. Coll. Pub. Rels. Assn., 1970. Mem. Am. Assn. Tchrs. Journalism, Coun. Edn. for Journalism of Assn. Schs. and Depts. Journalism, Nat. Press Club. Episcopalian. Home: Washington D.C. Died Mar. 11, 1990.

THARP, LOUISE MARSHALL HALL, author, lecturer; b. Oneonta, N.Y., June 19, 1898; d. Newton M. and Louise Buffum (Varney) Hall; m. Carey Edwin Tharp, 1925; children: Carey Edwin Jr., Marshall Allen. Student, Sch. Fine Arts, Boston, 1917-19; European travel and study, 1919-21, 25; EdD (hon.), R.I. Coll. Edn.; DLitt (hon.), Northeastern U. Active in Girl Scouts U.S.A., from 1925; editor The Trailmaker, 1925-26; mem. coun. in Rochester, N.Y., 1927-28; mem. Nat. Brownie Com., 1926-34; accredited pub. speaker for Nat. Girl Scout Orgn. Author: Lords and Gentlemen, 1940; Tory Hole, 1940; Sixpence for Luck, 1941; Down to the Sea: A Life of Nathaniel Bowditch, 1942; A Sounding Trumpet: Julia Ward Howe and the Battle Hymn of the Republic, 1944; Champlain, Northwest Voyager, 1944; Company of Adventurers: The Story of the Hudson's Bay Company, 1946; The Peabody Sisters of Salem (Book-of-the-Month), 1950; Unitl Victory: Horace Mann and Mary Peabody, 1953; Three Saints and a Sinner: Julia Ward Howe, Louisa, Annie and Sam Ward, 1956; Adventurous Alliance: The Agassiz Family of Boston, 1959; Louis Agassiz: Adventurous Scientist, 1960; The Baroness and The General, 1962; Mrs. Jack: A Biography of Isabella Stewart Gardner, 1965. Recipient ALA award, 1952, NEA award, 1953. Mem. Soc. Am. Historians, Tokeneke Club (Darien, Conn.), Delta Kappa Gamma (educator's award 1950), Theta Sigma Phi. Republican. Congregationalist. *

THAYER, WALTER NELSON, lawyer, investment and communications company executive; b. Dannemora, N.Y., Apr. 24, 1910; s. Walter Nelson and Adelaide (McDonell) T.; m. Jeanne Cooley Greeley, Dec. 27, 1945; children: Ann, Susan, Gail, Thomas. A.B., Colgate U., 1931; LL.B., Yale U., 1935. Bar: N.Y. 1935. Spl. asst. atty. gen. N.Y. State, 1935-36; with firm Donovan, Leisure, Newton & Lumbard, N.Y.C., 1936-37, 38-40; asst. U.S. atty. So. Dist. N.Y., 1937-38; atty. Lend-Lease Adminstrn., 1941-42; mem. Harriman Mission, London, Eng., 1942-45; gen. counsel Fgn. Econ. Adminstrn., 1945; partner Thayer & Gilbert, N.Y.C., 1946-55, J. H. Whitney & Co., 1955-59; pres. Whitney Communications Corp., 1960-82, chmn., from 1982; pres. N.Y. Herald Tribune, 1961-66; partner Whitcom Investment Co., from 1967; pres., dir. Internat. Herald Tribune, 1973-89. Mem. President's Commn. on Campaign Costs, 1961-62, President's Adv. Council Exec. Orgn., 1969-71; spl. cons. to Pres. Nixon, 1969-71; hon. chmn., trustee Vocat. Found., Inc.; trustee Columbia, 1965-69, Mus. Modern Art; mem. President's Council Vol. Service, 1983, Dwight David Eisenhower Centennial Commn., 1987. Mem. Com. Econ. Devel. (trustee). Episcopalian. Clubs: Links (N.Y.C.); Nat. Golf (Augusta, Ga.); University, Racquet and Tennis; Lyford Cay (Nassau, Bahamas). Home: New York N.Y. Died Mar. 4, 1989; buried Napanoch, N.Y.

THIBAUT, CHAREST DELAUZON, JR., lawyer; b. Donaldsonville, La., Jan. 6, 1922; s. Charest deLauzon and Mildred (Winship) T.; m. Lillie M. Major, May 15, 1943; children: Natalie Major (Mrs. Clifford C. Comeaux, Jr.), Charest deLauzon III, Joseph Major, Cherie Adele (Mrs. Daniel L. Songy). B.A., La. State U., 1943, J.D., 1946. Bar: La. 1946. Mem. Thibaut, Thibaut, Garrett & Bacot and (predecessor firms), Baton Rouge, 1946; gen. ptnr., counsel Tidewater Land Co. Ltd.; adj. asso. prof. law La. State U. Mem. La. State U. Found. Served with AUS, 1943. Decorated papal Knight comdr. Order Holy Sepulchre. Mem. ABA, La. Bar Assn., Baton Rouge Bar Assn., Omicron Delta Kappa, Delta Kappa Epsilon, Phi Delta Phi. Clubs: Baton Rouge Country (past pres.), Serra (past pres.), Kiwanis (past gov.). Home: Oscar La. Deceased. †

THIENES, CLINTON HOBART, medical educator, pathologist; b. Evansville, Ind., Aug. 9, 1896; s. William Christ and Sarah Ann (Stinchfield) T.; m. Ruth Susan Workman, June 20, 1923; children: Arthur Howard, Geraldine May, Paul Ehrlich. AB, U. Oreg., 1918, AM, 1923, MD, 1923; PhD, Stanford U., 1926. Diplomate Nat. Bd. Med. Examiners. Asst. in zoology U. Oreg., 1917-18, asst. and instr. anatomy, 1919-22, instr. pharmacology, 1922-25, asst. prof., 1926-29; NRC fellow Stanford U., 1925-26; assoc. prof. pharmacology U. So. Calif. Sch. Medicine, 1929-31, prof., head dept., 1931-47, 48-52, prof. emeritus; dir. Inst. Med. Rsch. Huntington Meml. Hosp., Pasadena, Calif., 1952-62; attending pathologist Los Angeles County Hosp. Author: Field Manual in Toxicology for Agricultural Workers, 1938; Clinical Toxicology, 1940; Fundamentals of Pharmacology, 1945; contbr. articles to profl. jours. Fellow AAAS, ACP, Am. Coll. Clin. Pharmacology and Chemotherapy, Am. Coll. Cardiology, N.Y. Acad. Scis., Am. Acad. Neurology; mem. Am. Indsl. Hygiene Assn., Pan Am. Med. Assn., Internat. Soc. Comprehensive Medicine (pres.), Calif. Soc. Internal Medicine, Am. Soc. Pharmacologists, Soc. Exptl. Biology and Medicine (chmn. 1939-40, nat. coun. 1939-40), AMA, Calif. Med. Assn., Los Angeles County Med. Assn., Indsl. Med. Assn., Hewlett Club of L.A., Phi Beta Kappa (pres. chpt. 1942-43, Sigma Xi, Psi Upsilon, Theta Kappa Psi (grand councillor 1938-40. edit. The Messenger 1941), Alpha Omega Alpha, Alpha Epsilon Delta. Presbyterian. *

THIGPEN, WILLIAM HENRY, lawyer; b. Mascot, Tenn., Jan. 6, 1928; s. William Marcus and Dixie Leota (Craig) T.; m. Marsha Opdycke Caldwell, Jan. 4, 1986; children: Laura Alison Thigpen Gilbert, James Cameron, Kelly Elizabeth; stepchildren: Anna Loveridge Caldwell, Abigail Lewis Caldwell. B.S., Northwestern U., 1950, M.A., 1951; J.D., Harvard U., 1958. Bar: Ill. 1958, U.S. Dist. Ct. (no. dist.) Ill. 1959, U.S. Tax. Ct. 1971. Assoc. Sidley & Austin and predecessor, Chgo., 1958-65, ptnr., 1966-89; gen. counsel Northwestern U. Mem. ABA, Am. Judicature Soc., Am. Soc. Hosp. Attys., Nat. Assn. Coll. and Univ. Attys., Ill. State Bar Assn., Chgo. Bar Assn., Chgo. Council Lawyers, Harvard Law Soc. Ill. (past pres.), Nat. Harvard Law Sch. Assn. (past v.p.). Republican. Epicopalian. Clubs: Univ., Economic, Law, Mid-Day, Northwestern (past pres.) (Chgo.). Home: Winnetka Ill. Died July 9, 1989; buried Christ Ch., Winnetka, Ill.

THOM, RONALD JAMES, architect; b. Penticton, B.C., Can., May 15, 1923. Educated Vancouver Sch. Art; LL.D. (hon.) Trent U., 1971; D.Eng. (hon.) Nova Scotia Tech. Coll., 1973. Began career as concert pianist; taught Vancouver Sch. Art and U. B.C. Sch. Architecture; ptnr. Thompson, Berwick, Pratt, Vancouver, B.C., 1958; prin. R.J. Thom Architects, Toronto, from 1963; lectr. numerous Can. univs. Contbr. articles to arts jours. Fellow Royal Archtl. Inst. Can.; mem. Royal Can. Acad. Arts, Ont. Assn. Architects, Archtl. Inst. B.C. Deceased. Home: Scarborough Ont., Can.

THOMAS, CHARLES WILLIAM, II, urban studies educator; b. Md., Apr. 26, 1926; s. Charles W. and Estella Thomas; m. Shirley Wade, Aug. 30, 1958; children: Charles William III, Shawn. BS, Morgan State Coll., 1951; MA, John Carroll U., 1955; PhD, Western Res. U., 1961. With Highland View Cuyahoga County Hosp., Cleve., 1955-63, acting dir. sheltered workshop research project, 1956-58, co-prin. investigator, dir. aging research project, until 1963; asst. prof., dir. counseling services and personnel devel. Job Corps Ctr., U. Oreg., 1963-66; evaluation design analyst, dir. edn. and tng. South Central Multipurpose Health Service Ctr., U. So. Calif., 1966-69; assoc. prof. community medicine U. So. Calif., Los Angeles, 1966-69; prin., dir. Ctr. for Study Racial and Social Issues, Los Angeles, 1969-71; prof. urban studies and planning Third Coll. U. Calif.-San Diego, La Jolla, 1977-90, coordinator urban studies and planning, 1977-82; lectr. John Carroll U., 1961-63, Calif. State Coll., Los Angeles, 1967-68, Calif. State Coll., Dominguez Hills, 1970, Claremont Coll. Black Studies Ctr., 1970-71; vis. prof. counseling psychology Ariz. State U., 1970-71; vis. scientist Am. Psychol. Assn., 1979-80, Assn. Black Psychologists, 1969-70; mem. Calif. Psychology Examining Commn.; active Calif. Bd. Edn., 1975-79; facilitator, chmn. pro tem Nat. Ad Hoc Com. on Homicidal Violence Among Blacks; facilitator for devel. Nat. Black Mental Health Workers Assn.; founder, coordinator Ann. Conf. on Issues in Ethnicity and Mental Health; speaker, cons. in field. Contbr. articles, chpts. to profl. publs., popular mags. Served with AUS, 1944-46. Recipient Father of Black Psychology award Black Students' Psychol. Assn., 1970; cert. recognition Nat. Assn. Sch. Psychologists, 1971; commendation Mayor San Diego, 1976; legis. commendation State of Ohio, 1979; Legal Aid Soc. San Diego award, 1979; Outstanding Contbn. award So. Regional Edn. Bd. Community Clin. Psychology Project, 1980; commendation Christ Ch. of San Diego, 1980; San Diego Black Achievement award in sci., 1981, in journalism, 1983; Charles W. Thomas psychology scholarship established in his honor at Morgan State U., 1976; named to Scroll of Honor for Ednl. Leadership, Omega Psi Phi, 1979; Jesse Smith Noyes fellow John Carroll U.; Cleve. Found. fellow Western Res. U.; Danforth assoc., 1979; vis. scholar Howard U. Inst. Urban Affairs, 1979-80; Spl. Achievement award Morgan State U., 1986, Disting. Alumni award Nat. Equal Opportunity Assn. for Higher Edn. Fellow Am. Psychol. Assn. (chmn. edn. and tng. bd. 1971-72, chmn. task force on master's level edn. 1973); mem. Calif. State Psychol. Assn., Nat. Acad. TV Arts and Scis., AAAS (adv. body), Council for Advancement Psychol. Professions and Scis. (gov. 1969), Assn. Black Psychologists (founding chmn. 1968, hon. nat. chmn.), Black Action Council San Diego (hon.), NAACP (pres. San Diego chpt. 1977, San Diego chpt. Outstanding Service award 1976), Nat. Acad. Black Scientists (chmn.). Republican. Home: El Cajon Calif. Died Sept. 29, 1990.

THOMAS, DANNY (AMOS JACOBS), entertainer, TV producer; b. Deerfield, Mich., Jan. 6, 1914; s. Charles and Margaret Christen (Simon) Jacobs; m. Rose Marie Cassaniti, Jan. 15, 1936; children: Margaret Julia, Theresa Cecelia, Charles Anthony. Ed. high sch.; L.H.D., Belmont Abbey, Internat. Coll., Springfield, Mass., 1970, Christian Bros. Coll., Memphis; LL.D., Loyola U., Chgo.; D.Performing Arts (hon.), Toledo U., Loyola-Marymount U. at Los Angeles. Radio work, 1934; appeared as night club master of ceremonies, 1938-40; appeared on radio, Chgo., 1940; master ceremonies, 5100 Club, Chgo. night club, 1940-43; developed own radio, TV program; appeared Oriental Theatre, Chgo., 1943, La Martinique (night club), N.Y., 1943-44, Roxy Theatre, N.Y., 1948, Ciro's, Hollywood, Calif., 1949, London Palladium, Eng., Chgo. Theatre, overseas entertainer, ETO, with Marlene Dietrich & Co., with Fanny Brice on radio, 1944; overseas entertainer with own troupe, Pacific Area; returned to Chgo. as entertainer, Chez Paree (night club), 1945-46; appeared in first motion picture The Unfinished Dance, 1946; other films include The Big City, 1947, Call Me Mister, 1948, I'll See You in My Dreams, 1951, Jazz Singer, 1952; appeared in TV shows Make Room for Daddy (Emmy awards 1953-64), Danny Thomas Spls., 1964-68, Danny Thomas Hours, 1967-68, Make Room for Granddaddy, 1970, The Practice, 1976-77, television film Side By Side, 1988; numerous engagements night clubs and theatres; guest on various TV shows including The Tonight Show, 1991; author: (with Bill Davidson) autobiography Make Room for Danny, 1991. Recipient awards NCCJ, 1957; Layman's award AMA; Better World award Ladies Aux.; Better World award VFW, 1972; Michelango award Boys Town of Italy, 1973; award Gov. of Ohio, 1975; Entertainment award White House Corrs., 1975; Humanitarian award Lions Internat., 1975; Father Flanagan-Boys Town award, 1981; Murray-Green-Meany award AFL-CIO, 1981; Hubert H. Humphrey award Touchdown Club, 1981; Am. Edn. award, 1984; recipient Humanitarian award Variety Clubs Internat., 1984; Congl. Medal of Honor, 1984; Sword of Loyola award Loyola U., Chgo., 1985; nominated for Nobel Peace prize, 1980-81; decorated Knight Malta; knight comdr. with star Knights of Holy Sepulchre Pope Paul VI. Roman Catholic. Home: Beverly Hills Calif. Died Feb. 6, 1991.

THOMAS, DUDLEY SCOTT, chemical company executive; b. Lewisham, Kent, Eng., Feb. 10, 1896; s. Harry Ralph and Isabell (Scott) T.; m. Jessie Hanson, June 24, 1930; children: Judith Joy, Hilary Joan, Roger Dudley. Student, pub. schs., Eng. With Provincial Bank of Ireland, 1913-15, Bracht & Co., London and Antwerp, 1918-20, Dorman & Co., Ltd., 1920-22, Brit. Nigerian Timber Co., Ltd., West Africa, 1922-23; with Dominion Tar & Chem. Co., Ltd., Can., from 1923, successively chief acct., asst. sec.-treas., sec.-treas., 1923-50, v.p., 1950-63. Bd. govs. Montreal Diocesan Theol. Coll.; trustee Que. 4 Br. Gt.-War Meml. Hall. Mil. Svc., 1915-18. Fellow Chartered Inst. Secretaries. *

THOMAS, JAMES GLADWYN, lawyer; b. Akron, N.Y., Oct. 5, 1901; s. James Robinson and Fannie (Wilder) T.; m. Helen H. Herrick, Aug. 19, 1925; children: Carol (Mrs. William Brigham), (dec.), Lott H. A.B., U. Ill., 1923, J.D., 1928. Bar: Ill. 1928. Asst. dean men U. Ill., Champaign, 1923-28; of counsel Thomas, Mamer & Haughey (and predecessor firms), Champaign, from 1925; part-time prof. law U. Ill. Coll. Law, 1947-65; hon. dir. First Nat. Bank of Champaign. Past pres. YMCA, Community Chest, War Chest.; Past bd. dirs. Ill. Bar Found.; past dir., pres. U. Ill. Found.; past pres., bd. dirs. Carle Hosp. Found. Fellow Am. Bar Found.; mem. ABA (ho. dels. 1956), Ill. Bar Assn. (bd. govs. 1941-58, v.p. 1953-56, pres. 1956-57), Am. Law Inst., Am. Judicature Soc., Am. Coll. Probate Counsel, Sigma Chi. Republican. Episcopalian. Home: Savoy Ill. Died Jan. 17, 1990; buried Champaign, Ill.

THOMAS, LOUIS GODFREY LEE, metals manufacturer; b. Chgo., Jan. 26, 1896; s. Richard H. and Lucille A. (Rousseau) T.; m. Florence Louise Sammons, Sept. 19, 1952. B.S., Lewis Inst., 1918; S.B. in Mech. Engring, Mass. Inst. Tech., 1920; L.H.D. (hon.), Hahnemann Med. Coll., 1972; LL.D. (hon.), Ursinus Coll., 1981. With DeLaval Steam Turbine Co., 1920-21; engr. Economy Pumps, Inc., 1921-40, exec. v.p., 1941-48; chmn. Sci. & Mechanics Pub. Co., 1940-51; v.p. Liberty Planers, Inc., 1940-48, pres., 1948-51; pres. Smith & Mills Shapers, 1940-51, Hamilton-Thomas Corp., 1948-62, C.H. Wheeler Mfg. Co., 1950-62, Klipfel Valves, Inc., 1950-62, Griscom-Russell Co., 1959-62; chmn. Smart-Turner Machine Co., Ltd., 1949-62; dir. Fischer and Porter Co. Trustee Hahnemann Medical Coll. and Hosp., 1957-70, Eastern Psychiatric Inst. Mercy Douglas Hosp., 1965-70, Am. Onconologic Hosp., 1965-68; exec. devel. com. Villanova U., 1955-63; mem. adv. com. to dean Coll. Engring., U. Cin., 1958-63; bd. dirs. Magee Meml. Hosp. for Convalescents, 1965-70, Ursinus Coll., 1976—. Served with USA, 1917-19. Mem. Inst. Mech. Engrs. London, Soc. Naval Architects and Marine Engrs., Am. Legion, ASME, Am. Soc. Naval Engrs., Hydraulic Inst. (pres. 1955), Metal Mfrs. Assn. (v.p. 1959). Republican. Clubs: Merion Golf, Union League (Phila.); Moorings Golf, Moorings Country, Collier Athletic (Naples, Fla.). Home: North Naples Fla. Deceased. †

THOMAS, RALPH, business executive; b. Roanoke, Va., Oct. 9, 1896; s. Charles Wheeler and Lilly (Loving) T.; m. Helen Hines, Oct. 19, 1922; children: Edward Wheeler, Sarah Jane, Ralph. Grad., Va. Mil. Inst., Lexington, 1919; DBA (hon.), Cleary Coll. Foundry exec. Maxwell-Chalmers Motor Co., Detroit, 1919-22; shop assembly systems Lincoln Motor Co., 1922-23; retail sales Winton-Zuver Motors, 1923-24; sales mgr. Speaker-Hines Printing Co., Detroit, 1924-28, gen. mgr., 1928-38, bd. dirs., from 1930, pres., from 1938; pres. Builders, Inc., from 1938; mem. exec. com. Joint Com. for Printing Industry, World War II; mem. com. for establishing Printing Industry of Am., Inc., Nat. Trade Assn., 1944; chmn. Mich. Liquor Control Commn., 1942-43. Trustee Arnold Home, Cleary Coll. Mem. U.S. C. of C. (mem. transp. com. 1946), Southeastern Mich. Tourist Assn. (bd. dirs., exec. com. from 1940), Mich. Tourist Coun. (mem. adv. com. 1944-46), Am. Auto Assn. (bd. dirs. from 1934, pres. 1952), Typothetae-Franklin Assn. (pres. Detroit chpt.), Detroit Execs. Assn. (pres.), SAR, Mason, KT, Shriners, Automobile Club of Mich. (pres., bd. dirs.), Rotary (past pres.), Jesters, Detroit Athletic Club, Detroit Club, Country Club of Detroit, Country Club of Lansing. Presbyterian. *

THOMPSON, BRUCE RUTHERFORD, judge; b. Reno, July 31, 1911; s. Reuben Cyril and Mabel (McLeran) T.; m. Frances Ellen Creek, Sept. 11, 1938; children: Jeffrey, Judith, Harold. AB, U. Nev., 1932; LLB, Stanford U., 1936. Bar: Nev. 1936. Pvt. practice Reno; asst. U.S. atty. Dist. Nev., 1942-52; spl. master U.S. Dist. Ct., Reno, 1952-53; judge U.S. Dist. Ct. Nev., Reno, 1963-92. Mem. Nev. State Planning Bd., 1959-92, chmn., 1960-61; bd. regents U. Nev. Mem. Am. Judicature Soc. (dir.), ABA, State Bar Nev., Am. Coll. Trial Lawyers, Am. Law Inst., Alpha Tau Omega. Democrat. Baptist. Club: Elks. Home: Reno Nev. Died Feb. 10, 1992. †

THOMPSON, DALE MOORE, mortgage banker; b. Kansas City, Kans., Nov. 19, 1897; s. George Curl and Ruth Anna (Moore) T.; m. Dorothy Allen Brown, July 2, 1921; 1 son, William Brown (dec. 1978). A.B. cum laude, U. Mich., 1920. With City Nat. Bank and Trust Co. (and predecessor), Kansas City, Mo., 1920-34; v.p. City Nat. Bank and Trust Co. (and predecessor), 1930-34; with City Bond & Mortgage Co. (now United Mo. Mortgage Co.), Kansas City, Mo., from 1934; exec. v.p. City Bond & Mortgage Co. (now United Mo. Mortgage Co.), 1943-48, pres., 1948-68, chmn. bd., 1968-74, hon. chmn., from 1974; chmn. emeritus Central Mortgage & Realty Trust, Kansas City, from 1975; dir. Regency Bldg. Co., Kansas City.; Lectr. schs. mortgage banking Northwestern U., Stanford. Mem. Mo. Bd. Edn., 1966-82, pres., 1968-69; pres. Kansas City Philharmonic Assn., 1944-54, bd. dirs., from 1943; bd. dirs., exec. com. Truman Med. Center (formerly Kansas City Gen. Hosp. and Med. Center), from 1962, treas., 1962-78; chmn. Kansas City campaign United Negro Coll. Fund, 1958-59; Trustee Childrens Mercy Hosp., U. Kansas City; former bd. dirs. Kansas City Art Inst., Conservatory Music Kansas City. Recipient Disting. Service citation Mayor Kansas City, 1955, Community Service citation Archbishop Kansas City, 1954, citation Kansas City C. of C., 1954, citation as Pioneer in Edn. State of Mo., 1982; Protestant honoree NCCJ, 1966; sch. named in his honor, 1982. Mem. Mortgage Bankers Assn. Am. (nat. pres. 1962-63, gov. from 1956, distinguished service award 1968), U. Mich. Alumni Assn. (past dir.), English-Speaking Union (pres. Kansas City br. 1966-67), Phi Beta Kappa (pres. Kansas City 1946-49), Phi Kappa Psi, Trigon. Mem. Christian Ch. Clubs: Monterey Peninsula Country (Pebble Beach, Calif.); River (Kansas City, Mo.), University (Kansas City, Mo.), Indian Hills Country (Kansas City, Mo.). Home: Kansas City Mo. Deceased. †

THOMPSON, ERNEST THORNE, artist; b. St. John, N.B., Can., Nov. 8, 1897; s. Ernest Hyacinth and Annie Louise (Thorne) T.; m. Florence Marie Paulsen, Dec. 30, 1922; 1 son, Ernest Thorne. Diploma, Mass. Sch. Art, Boston, 1920; student, Sch. Mus. of Fine Arts, Boston, 1920-21; DFA (hon.), Coll. New Rochelle, 1980. Prof. art, dir. Sch. of Fine Arts, Notre Dame (Ind.) U., 1922-29; prof. art, chmn. dept. fine arts Coll. New Rochelle, N.Y., 1929-67; dir. Huguenot Sch. Art, New Rochelle, 1947-51; v.p. Pemaquid Group of Artists, Bristol, Maine, 1950-92. One man shows include, Farnsworth Mus., Rockland, Maine, 1955, Coll. of New Rochelle, N.Y., 1955, group exhbns. include, New Rochelle Library, 1942, 50, Soc. Illustrators, N.Y.C., 1945; represented in permanent collections, U. Notre Dame, Nat. Mus., Washington, Bibliothèque Nationale, Paris. Bd. dirs. Maine Gallery, Wiscasset, Maine. Recipient Rudolf Lesch award and medal Am. Watercolor Soc., 1955, Saportas award, 1964, Charles L. Fox award Farnsworth Mus., 1974. Mem. Am. Watercolor Soc. (past dir.), Allied Artists Am. (hon. life mem., pres. 1965-67), Chgo. Soc. Etchers, Hudson Valley Art Assn., New Rochelle Art Assn., Grand Ctrl. Art Galleries. Club: Salmagundi (N.Y.C.). Home: Round Pond Maine Died June 7, 1992. †

THOMPSON, ERNEST TRICE, church historian, educator; b. Texarkana, Tex., July 2, 1894; s. Ernest and Jimmy (Graves) T.; m. Helen Marr Beall, Oct. 12, 1921; children: Helen (Mrs. Carl L. Shires), Ernest Trice. BA, Hampden-Sydney Coll., 1914; MA, Columbia U., 1915; BD, Union Theol. Sem., Richmond, Va., 1920; DLitt, Washington and Lee U., 1933. Ordained to ministry Presbyn. Ch., 1918. Contbg. editor Presbyn. Standard, 1924-31; pastor Manhattan Ch., El Paso, 1921-22; with Union Theol Sem., 1922-64, prof. ecclesiastical history and polity, 1925-64; vis. prof. St. Andrews Coll., 1964-65, Austin Presbyn. Theol. Sem., 1965-66; assoc. editor Presbyn. of the South, 1931-37, editor, 1937-44; co-editor Presbyn. Outlook, from 1944; moderator Synod of Va., 1931, 40; moderator Gen. Assembly Presbyn. Ch. U.S., 1959-60; 1st pres. Va. Coun. Chs.; delivered Stone Lectures at Princeton Theol Sem., 1943. Author: The Changing South; Presbyterian Missions in the Southern U.S.; Changing Emphasis in American Preaching: The Sermon on the Mount and Its Meaning for Today; The Gospel According to Mark and its Meaning for Today; Jesus and Citizenship; Presbyterian in The South, Vol. 1 1607-1861; Through the Ages--A History of the Christian Church; contbr. to Am. Dictionary of Nat. Biography. Trustee Hempden Sydney Coll. Served to cpl. Ambulance Co. 313, U.S. Army, 1917-18, 1st lt. and chaplain 42d Arty., C.A.C., 1918, overseas, 1918, at Base Hosp. 101, 1918-19. Hoge fellow, 1920-21. Mem. Am. Soc. Ch. History, Phi Beta Kappa, Kappa Sigma, Omicron Delta Kappa. *

THOMPSON, PAUL BRYAN, meat packing company executive; b. Lamar, Mo., 1897; s. John Perry and Ida (Warren) T.; m. Helen Perry, Aug. 2, 1924; children: Margaret, Warren, Marilyn. Student, Drury Coll., Springfield, Mo., 1 yr. With Cudahy Packing Co., Omaha, from 1925, treas., dir., exec. v.p., pres., exec. officer, from 1960, also chmn. bd.; with Am. Salt Corp., Chgo., from 1939, treas., dir., 1940; treas., dir. Dow Cheese Co., Fond du Lac, Wis.; treas., dir. Hefea Land Co., Midwest Meat Co., Phoenix, Burnett Meat Co., Kansas City, Mo., United Benefit Life Ins. Co. Mem. Newcomen Soc., Omaha Club, Omaha Country Club, Masons, Kappa Alpha. Republican. *

THOMPSON, ROY H(ERBERT), publisher; b. Toronto, June 5, 1894; s. Herbert and Alice (Coombs) T.; m. Edna Annis Irvine, 1916 (dec.); children: Kenneth Roy, Irma Jacqueline (Mrs. I.J. Brydson), Phyllis Audrey (Mrs. P.A. Campbell). Ed. pub. schs., Toronto. Chmn. bd. Thompson Co., Ltd. (name now The Thomson Newspapers, Ltd.); owned daily papers in Timmins, Kirkland Lake, Sarnia, Welland, Woodstock, Galt, Chatham, Guelph, Port Arthur, Orillia, Oshawa, Barrie, Brampton, Georgetown, Oakville, Orangebille, Pembroke, Sudbury, all Ont., also Quebec, Que. and Moose Jaw, Prince Albert, Sask., Kamloops, Kelowna, Penticton, Nanaimo, B.C., Charlottetown, P.E.I.; owner Illustrated Newspapers in London; also some 40 others in Eng., No. Ireland, Wales, Scotland and U.S.; chmn. Scottish TV Ltd., Scotsman Publs., Ltd., others. Chmn. Scottish TV Ltd., Scotsman Publs., Ltd., Edinburgh, Scotland; pres. No. Broadcasting Co., Ltd., Woodbridge Co., Ltd., v.p. Brookland Co., Ltd.; dir. Royal Bank of Can., Reuters, Abitibi Paper Co., Ltd. Past. pres. Can. Daily Newspapers Assn.; chancellor Meml. U. Nfld. Served as lt. Can. Militia, 1914-18. Mem. Sons of Eng., Masons, Elks, Albany Club, Nat. Club. Conservative. *

THOMSON, THOMAS HAROLD, petroleum executive; b. Winnipeg, Man., Can., Feb. 12, 1935; s. Harold W. and Mary Hislop (Lees) T. B in Applied Sci. (Engring.), U. Toronto, 1957; MBA, Harvard U., 1959. Sr. analyst mktg. Imperial Oil Ltd., Montreal, Que., Can., 1959; various downstream positions Imperial Oil Ltd., Toronto, Vancouver, 1959-74, sr. v.p., 1980-84, also dir.; exec. v.p. Home Oil Distbrs., Vancouver, 1974-75; with Exxon Corp., N.Y.C., 1975-76; pres., chief operating officer, dir. Suncor Inc., 1985-86, pres., chief exec. officer, dir., 1986-89, chmn., pres. and chief executive officer, 1989-91, chmn., chief exec. officer, from 1991; chmn. bd. Electrohome Ltd., from 1991. Trustee, treas. Hillcrest Hosp., Toronto, 1978-86; trustee United Way Greater Toronto, 1979-83; campaign chmn. Cystic Fibrosis Found., 1986. Mem. Assn. Profl. Engrs. Ont., Am. Petroleum Inst. Clubs: Rosedale Golf and Country, York, Muskoka Lakes Country, Toronto Badminton and Racquet, Granite; Harvard (Toronto) (dir. 1983-86). Home: North York Can. Died, Nov. 27, 1992. †

THOMSON, VIRGIL, composer, music critic; b. Kansas City, Mo., Nov. 25, 1896; s. Quincy A. and May (Gaines) T. AB, Harvard U., 1922; studied in Paris with Nadia Boulanger; AFD (hon.), Syracuse U., 1949, Roosevelt U., 1968, U. Mo., 1971; DArts, Bard Coll., 1982; LittD, Rutgers U., 1956, Emerson Coll., 1981; LHD(hon.), Park Coll., 1966, Johns Hopkins U., 1978, U. Mo., 1980, Bklyn. Coll., 1981, Manhattanville Coll., 1983; MusD, Fairfield U., 1968, NYU, 1971, Columbia U., 1978, U. Windsor, Ont., 1981, Harvard U., 1982, New Eng. Conservatory, 1986; hon. degree, U. Conn.-Storrs, 1985. Began as choirmaster and organist, King's Chapel, Boston; lived in Paris, 10 years; writer music for Boston Transcript; writer on Modern Music, N.Y. Rev. of Books; music critic, N.Y. Herald Tribune, 1940-54; composer: (opera) Lord Byron, Four Saints in Three Acts, 1934, The Mother of Us All, 1947; 5 ballets, including Parson Weems and the Cherry Tree, Filling Station; (for orch.) 3 Concertos with orchestra for cello, flute, harp, A Solemn Music and a Joyful Fugue, Eleven Chorale Preludes by Brahms, 3 Symphonies, 5 Portraits for Orch.; (choral works) Missa Pro Defunctis, Dance in Praise, Cantata on Poems of Edward Lear, Fanfare for Peace, 7 Choruses from the Medea of Euripides, Mass for Women's Voices and Percussion, Southern Hymns; composer: (chamber music) Sonata da Chiesa for 5 instruments, 4 piano sonatas, 3 string quartets, 19 Etudes for piano, more than 150 portraits including 17 Portraits for Piano, 1984; (music for motion pictures) Journey to America, The Plow that Broke the Plains, The River, Tuesday in November, Louisiana Story, The Goddess, The Day After, 1983; also many songs and selections for piano and organ.; author: State of Music, 1939, The Musical Scene, 1945, The Art of Judging Music, 1948, Music Right and Left, 1951, Virgil Thomson by Virgil Thomson, 1966, Music Reviewed, 1940-54, 1967, American Music Since 1910, 1971, A Virgil Thomson Reader, 1981, Selected Letters of Virgil Thomson, 1988, Music With Words, 1989; also numerous essays and revs. Decorated officer Légion d'Honneur; recipient Acad. medal NYU, 1961, Deems Taylor award ASCAP, 1982, Gold medal Nat. Inst. Arts and Letters, 1966, Pulitzer prize, 1949, Handel medallion City of N.Y., 1971, Creative Arts medal Brandeis U., 1968; Macdowell award, 1977, Nat. Book Critics Circle award, 1982; Guggenheim fellow, 1960; Carnegie Hall 90th Anniversary medal, 1982; Kennedy Center honors, 1983, Henry Elias Howard Mem. prize Yale Univ., 1986, Nat. Medal of the Arts, 1988. Fellow Am. Acad. Arts and Scis.; mem. Am. Acad. Arts and Letters, Académie des Beaux-Arts (Paris) (corr. mem. 1986), Academia Nacional de Bellas Artes, Buenos Aires. Home: New York N.Y. Died Sept. 30, 1989; buried Slater, Mo.

THORN, ROBERT NICOL, physicist; b. Coeur d'Alene, Idaho, Aug. 31, 1924; s. Harry Grover and Grace (Nicol) T.; m. Betty Vogel, June 15, 1948; children: Karen, Kyle, Gretchen, Robert Nicol; m. Lorraine Patten, Oct. 10, 1962; 1 child, Andrea Kay; m. Nancy MacDonald, Dec. 24, 1983. A.B., Harvard U., 1948, A.M., 1949, Ph.D. in Theoretical Physics, 1953. Mem. staff Los Alamos Sci. Lab., from 1953, div. leader theoretical design div., 1971-76, assoc. dir. for weapons, lasers, computers and reactor safety, 1976-79, acting dir., 1979, dep. dir., 1979-85, acting dir., 1985-86, sr. advisor, 1986-89; cons. Los Alamos Nat. Lab., from 1989; cons. to bus. and govt., from 1959; mem. USAF Sci. Adv. Bd., 1962; mem. sci. adv. group Def. Atomic Support Agy., 1966-72; mem. sci. adv. com. Def. Intelligency Agy., from 1971. Chmn. Los Alamos County Commn., 1958-60. Served with AUS, 1943-46, ETO. Recipient Ernest Orlando Lawrence award AEC, 1967, Disting. Assoc. award Dept. Energy, 1989. Mem. Am. Phys. Soc., AAAS, Los Alamos Ski Club (pres. 1957-58), Los Alamos Ski Racing Club (pres. 1974-76), U.S. Ski Assn. (chmn. Alpine competition com.), Phi Beta Kappa, Sigma Xi. Home: Los Alamos N.Mex. Deceased. †

THORNBURG, DICK, newspaper editor; b. St. Louis, May 27, 1904; s. George O. and Jennie (Patterson) T.; m. Edith Baier, Feb. 1, 1944. Student, Mo. U.; LittD, U Cin., 1964. Newspaperman Columbus (Ohio) Citizen, 1929-30, United Press, 1930-33; wire eidtor Ohio Scripps-howard Bu., 1933-38; Washington corr. Ohio Scripps-Howard papers, 1938-43; news editor Scripps-howard newspaper Alliance, 1943-45, mng. editor, 1945-53; editor Cin. Post, 1953-58, Cin. Post and Times-Star, 1958-69. Mem. Queen City Clubs, Nat. Press Club, Alpha Tau Omega. Home: Cincinnati Ohio Died June 30, 1990.

THORNDIKE, ROBERT LADD, psychology and education educator; b. Montrose, N.Y., Sept. 22, 1910; s. Edward Lee and Elizabeth (Moulton) T.; m. Dorothy Vernon Mann, June 10, 1933; children: Nancy Lee Thorndike Whitney, Robert Mann, Virginia Vernon. AB, Wesleyan U., 1931; AM, Columbia U., 1932, PhD, 1955. Instr., asst. prof. psychology George Washington U., Washington, 1934-36; asst. prof. Columbia U. Tchrs. Coll., N.Y.C., 1936-40, assoc. prof., 1940-48, prof. psychology and edn., 1948-76, Ralph Narch Hoe prof. emeritus edn., 1976-90, chmn. dept., 1957-64; chmn. panel on pers., com. on human resources R & D Bd., 1948-52; mem. U.S. Army Sci. Adv. Panel, 1957-59. Author: Personnel Selection, 1949, The Concepts of Over and Under-Achievement, 1964, Reading Comprehension Education in Fifteen Countries, 1973, (with Elizabeth Hagen) Measurement and Evaluation in Psychology Education, 1955, 4th edit., 1977, 10,000 Careers, 1959, Cognitive Ability Tests, 1968, 70, (with Irving Lorge) Lorge-Thorndike Intelligence Tests, 1954, (with Lorge and Hagen) multilevel edit., 1964; editor: Educational Measurement, 2d edit., 1971; also articles. Maj. USAAF, 1942-46. Recipient numerous awards, including Butler medal for outstanding svc. Columbia U. Fellow APA (bd. dirs. 1958-61, pres. div. evaluation and measurement 19549, mil. psychology div. 1956, div. ednl. psychology 1964), Am. Statis. Assn.; mem. AAAS, Psychometric Soc. (treas. 1940-53, pres. 1953), Am. Ednl. Rsch. Assn. (pres. 1974), Phi Beta Kappa Sigma Xi. Home: Lacey Wash. Died Sept. 21, 1990; cremated.

THORNTON, JOHN WILLIAM, management consultant; b. LaCrosse, Wis., May 29, 1921; s. John W. and Blanche F. (O'Donnell) T.; m. Mary A. Wilshear, Apr. 23, 1946; children: John, Elizabeth, Catherine, Thomas, Barbara. A.B., Loras Coll., 1942; LL.B., Boston Coll., 1953. Bar: Mass. 1953. With Brown Bros., Harriman & Co., Boston, 1946-54, McKinsey & Co., N.Y.C., 1954-57; v.p. mktg. Joy Mfg. Co., Pitts., 1957-61, v.p., gen. mgr. indsl. div., 1961-62; v.p. Blaw-Knox Co., Pitts., 1962-68; pres., dir. Seaport Corp., Pitts., 1968-75; dir., mem. exec. com. Brown Co., N.Y.C., 1964-68; mgmt. cons., v.p. Denney & Co., Pitts., 1975-92. Mem. bd. adminstrn. Diocese of Pitts., 1968-81; trustee Robert Morris Coll., 1965-92 . Served to lt. USNR, 1942-46, ETO, PTO. Clubs: Duquesne (Pitts.); Union League (Chgo.). Home: Pittsburgh Pa. Died July 17, 1992. †

THORP, WILLARD LONG, economist; b. Oswego, N.Y., May 24, 1899; s. Charles Nicholas and Susan (Long) T.; m. Clarice Brows, Aug. 21, 1947. AB, Amherst Coll., 1920; AM, U. Mich., 1921; PhD, Columbia U., 1924. Prof. Amherst (Mass.) Coll., 1926-33; with U.S. Govt., Washington, 1933-35; chief economist Dun & Bradstreet, N.Y.C., 1935-40; trustee Assoc. Gas & Electric Corp., N.Y.C., 1940-46; asst. sec. for econ. affairs U.S. Dept. State, Washington, 1946-52; prof., dir. Merrill Ctr. for Econs. Amherst (Mass.) Coll., 1952-65; amb., chmn. Devel. Assistance Com., Paris, 1963-67; fellow Coun. on Fgn. Rels., N.Y.C., 1968-69; acting. pres. Amherst (Mass.) Coll., 1957; staff mem. Nat. Bur. Econ. Rsch., N.Y.C., 1982-83, emeritus dir., 1956-92; mem. Pelham (Mass.) Task Force, 1978-84, treas., 1987-90. Author: The Integration of Industrial Operations, 1924, Business Annals, 1926, Economic Institutions, 1928, Economic Problems in a Changing World, 1939, Trade, Aid or What?, 1954, The Reality of Foreign Aid, 1971; co-author: The New Inflation, 1959. 2d lt. U.S. Army, 1918. Democrat. Home: Amherst Mass. Died May 10, 1992. †

THURBER, CLARENCE EGBERT, political scientist; b. Nampa, Idaho, Sept. 16, 1921; s. Clarence Howe and Alice Helen (Egbert); m. Betty Louise Phillips, Apr. 26, 1947; children: Shirley Ann, Phillip Bradford, Barbara Field, Catherine Howe. A.B. with great distinction, Stanford U., 1943, Ph.D., 1961. Research analyst Dept. State, Washington, 1945-47; research assoc. internat. studies Brookings Instn., Washington, 1947-53; exec. assoc. internat. tng. research program Ford Found., N.Y.C., 1952-62, grantee, 1963-70; assoc. prof. polit. sci. and public adminstrn. Pa. State U., 1962-66; prof. polit. sci. and internat. studies U. Oreg., Eugene, 1966-87, dep. dir. internat. studies program, 1966-71, dir. program, 1980-87; dir. div. pub. affairs and internat. devel., 1971-74; Fulbright prof. Sch. Public Adminstrn., U. Costa Rica, 1974-75; cons. in field; dir. study fellowships internat. devel., 1963-70; exec. com. Comparative Adminstrn. Group, 1962-72; chmn. Latin Am. Devel. Adminstrn. Com., 1964-70. Author: Governmental Mechanism for Conduct of Foreign Affairs, 1949, (with Redvers Opie) The Search for Peace Settlements, 1951, (with Paul T. David) The Administration of Foreign Affairs and Overseas Operations, (with Wallace S. Sayre) Training for Specialized Mission Personnel; author, editor: (with Lawrence S. Graham) Development Administration in Latin America, 1973; (with Gerald W. Fry) The Art International Consulting, 1988. Bd. dirs. Willamette World Affairs Council. Life fellow Soc. Values in Higher Edn.; mem. Am. Soc. Public Adminstrn., Am. Polit. Sci. Assn., Soc. Internat. Devel., Internat. Studies Assn. (pres. Western region 1970-71), Internat. Soc. Community Devel. (dir.), Delta Chi. Democrat. Home: Eugene Oreg. Died Dec. 16, 1988.

THURBER, CLEVELAND, lawyer; b. Washington, Apr. 12, 1896; s. Henry Thomas and Elizabeth (Croul) T.; m. Marie Louise Palms, Sept. 20, 1924; children: Cleveland Jr., Peter Palms, Julie Thurber Sutherland, Marie Archibald. BA cum laude, Williams Coll., 1918; JD, Harvard U., 1922; LLD, Wayne State U., 1960. Bar: Mich. 1922, U.S. Dist. Ct. (so. dist.) Mich. 1923, U.S. Ct. Appeals (2d and 6th cirs.) 1934. Assoc. Miller, Canfield, Paddock & Stone, Detroit, from 1922; v.p., bd. dirs. Detroit Legal News. Trustee emeritus Williams Coll., Henry Ford Hosp., McGregor Fund; pres. Katherine Tuck Fund, David M. Whitney Fund; mem. Founders Soc. Detroit Inst. Arts; bd. dirs. Greater Detroit Area Hosp. Council, Marygrove Coll. Served to lt. U.S. Army, 1917-19. Mem. ABA, Mich. Bar Assn., Detroit Bar Assn., Am. Judicature Soc., Kappa Alpha. Presbyterian. Clubs: Yondotega, Detroit, Grosse Pointe, Country of Detroit. Home: Detroit Mich. Died June 18, 1987; buried Mt. Elliot Cemetery, Mich.

TIEKEN, THEODORE DAVID, lawyer; b. Chgo., Mar. 30, 1909; s. Theodore and Elizabeth (Chapman) T.; m. Elizabeth S. Babson, Dec. 3, 1936; children: Nancy, Theodore David Jr., Elizabeth Chapman. BS, U. Chgo., 1929, JD, 1933. Bar: Ill. 1933. With firm Winston, Strawn & Shaw, Chgo., 1933-46; gen. atty. C. I. & L. Ry., Chgo., 1946-47; v.p., gen. counsel Babson Bros. Co., Chgo., 1958-64, pres., 1964-76, chmn., 1976-84; chmn. Babson Farms, Inc., Chgo., 1984-90. Trustee Chgo. Hist. Soc., former pres.; trustee Infant Welfare Soc., Chgo.; bd. dirs. Arabian Horse Registry Am. Served to lt. comdr. USNR, 1942-45. Mem. ABA, Chgo. Bar Assn. Republican. Episcopalian. Clubs: Chgo.; Racquet, Yacht (Chgo.); Shoreacres (Lake Bluff, Ill.). Home: Chicago Ill. Died Jan. 24, 1990; cremated.

TIERNEY, GENE (GENE TAYLOR TIERNEY LOJEWSKI CASSINI), actress; b. Bklyn., Nov. 19, 1920; d. Howard Sherwood and Belle (Taylor) Tierney; m. Count Oleg Lojewski Cassini, June 1, 1941; children: Daria, Christina. Student, St. Margaret Sch., Waterbury, Conn., Brillantmont, Lausanne, Switzerland; grad., Miss Porter's Sch., Farmington, Conn. Appeared on stage in Mrs. O'Brian Entertains, 1939, The Male Animal, 1940; films include: The Return of Frank James, 1940, Heaven Can Wait, 1943, Laura, 1945, Leave Her to Heaven, 1945, The Ghost and Mrs. Muir, 1947, The Iron Curtain, 1948, That Wonderful Urge, 1948, Night and the City, 1950, Advise and Consent, 1962. Episcopalian. Home: Houston Tex. Died Oct. 30, 1991.

TIERNEY, HOWARD SHERWOOD, pharmaceutical company executive; b. N.Y.C., Apr. 27, 1918; s. Howard Sherwood and Belle Lavinia (Taylor) T.; m. Jane Meldrin Hewitt, Sept. 22, 1941; children: Michele T. Eklund, Patricia (Mrs. Robert Falkenhagen), Alison, George. BA, Yale U., 1940; postgrad., Harvard U., 1941. With Bridgeport (Conn.) Brass Co., 1941-42; with E.R. Squibb & Sons, 1945-55, v.p. overseas ops., to 1955; pres., CEO, chmn. exec. com. Denver Chem. Mfg. Co., 1955-72; exec. v.p., mem. exec. com., dir. Carter-Wallace, Inc., N.Y.C., 1973-78; pres. Culbro Corp., 1978-90; dir. Lafayette Bank and Trust Co., Bridgeport, Harold B. Scott, Inc., Stamford, Conn., Syracuse Supply Co., N.Y. Served to lt (s.g.), pilot USNR, 1943-45. Mem. Country Club of Fairfield, Aubichwi Gun Club, Fairfield County Hunt Club, Jupiter Island Club, Ekwanok Country Club, Univ. Club, Phi Beta Kappa. Republican. Episcopalian. Home: Fairfield Conn. Died Apr. 23, 1990.

TIERNEY, PAUL A., newspaper editor; b. Newburg, N.Y., July 4, 1894; s. Dennis George and Mary Frances (Delaney) T.; m. Rita J. Donohue, June 6, 1923; children: Margaret Mary, Paula Anne, Paul Thomas. Grad., Christian Bros. Sch., NYU. Reporter N.Y. Globe, 1915, Bklyn. Eagle, Newark News; mng. editor Long Island Daily Press, 1923; city editor Bklyn. Standard Union, 1924-28; with N.Y. Post, 1928-49, mng. editor, 1942-47, exec. editor, 1947-49; pub. rels. officer State U. of N.Y., 1949-51; joined S.I. Newhouse Newspapers, 1952; exec. editor Newark Star Ledger, 1952-53, Staten Island Advance, 1954; editor L.I. Star Jour., L.I. City, N.Y., from 1955. Dir. Queens Borough C. of C., NCCJ, Boys Club of Queens; trustee St. John's Hosp., Long Island City. Served with U.S. Army ambulance svc. with French Army, 1917-19. Decorated Croix de Guerre. Democrat. Roman Catholic. *

TIFFANY, (LEWIS) HANFORD, botanist, educator; b. Lawrenceveille, Ill., July 29, 1894; s. Charles Edward and Mary Frances (Hull) T.; m. Loel Zehner, Sept. 10, 1921. Grad., Eastern Ill. Tchrs. Coll., 1915, PdD (hon.), 1949; BS, U. Chgo., 1920; MS, PhD, Ohio State U., 1921, 23. Tchr. pub. schs., from 1912; instr. botany Ohio State U., 1920-25, from asst. prof. to prof., 1925-37; prof. botany, chmn. dept. botany Northwestern U., 1937-49, William Deering prof. botany, 1945-62, William Deering prof. emeritus, from 1962; hon. assoc. in cryptogamic botany Chgo. Natural History Mus., from 1944; hon. life mem. Centro Italiano de Studi Anglo-Franco-Am., from 1946; prof. algology Stone Lab, sumemrs 1928-36; bus. mgr. Ohio Jour. Sci., 1929-30. Author: The Oedogoniaceae, 1930; (with Transeau and Sampson) Work Book in General Botany, 1934; Algae, The Grass of Many Waters, 1938; (with Transeau and Sampson) Text Book of Botany, 1940; The Study of Plants, 1944; (with Britton) The Algae of Illinois, 1952; (with Simpson and Pittendrigh) Life, 1957; editor: (with Brunel and Prescott) Culturing of Algae, 1951; mem. editorial bd. Econolgy, 1950-52; contbr. articles to profl. jours. Mem. Ill. Bd. Natural Resources and Conservation, vice chmn., sec.; v.p. phycology sect. 8th Internat. Bot. Congress, Paris, 1954. Served as 2d lt., field arty. U.S. Army, 1918. Fellow AAAS, Oio Acad. Sci.; mem. Am. Soc. Naturalists, Bot. Soc. Am., Ecol. Soc. Am., Am. Microscopic Soc. (pres. 1934), Limnol. Soc. Am. (pres. 1939), Am. Soc. Plant Physiology, Am. Soc. Plant Taxonomy, Chgo. Acad. Scis. (bd. govs. from 1941; hon. life mem.), Ill. Acad. Sci., Phycol. Soc. Am. (pres. 1949), Cowles Bot. Soc., Univ. Club of Evanston, Chaos Club of Chgo., Sigma Xi, Gamma Alpha. *

TILLER, CARL WILLIAM, lecturer, church official and government executive; b. Battle Lake, Minn., Sept. 25, 1915; s. Carl J(ohn) and Edith (Wells) T.; m. Olive M. Foerster, June 21, 1940; children: Robert W., Jeanne L. (Mrs. John E. Peterson). BA summa cum laude, Concordia Coll., Moorhead, Minn., 1935, LLD, 1966; MA in Pub. Adminstrn., U. Minn., 1940. Budget sec., examiner Minn., 1936-41; exec. asst. to dir. Mcpl. Fin. Officers Assn., 1941-42; with U.S. Office of Mgmt. and Budget, 1942-72, spl. adviser budgetary devel., 1967-72; adj. prof. Am. U., 1952-70; assoc. sec. Bapt. World Alliance, Washington, 1972-78; dir. Interchurch Ctr., N.Y.C., 1978-80, pres. and exec. dir., 1980-86; dir. of libr. Am. Bapt. Hist. Soc., Rochester, N.Y., 1987-88; free lance writer, lectr., 1988-91; v/p. Twin City Bapt. Union, 1937-41; moderator Twin City Bapt. Assn., 1939-41; mem. gen. bd. Nat. Coun. Chs., 1964-75, treas., 1970-75; mem. gen. coun. Am. Bapt. Conv., 1946-53, 54-60, 63-68, pres., 1966-67; Western treas. Bapt. World Alliance, 1956-72, assoc. sec., 1972-78, rep. to UN, 1981-89; sec. N.Am. Bapt. Fellowship, 1972-78, pres. D.C. Bapt. Conv., 1969-70; v.p. CARE Inc., 1972-78; mem. gen. bd. Am. Bapt. Chs. U.S.A., 1982-85, mem. com. on Christian unity, 1982-85, mem. bd. ednl. ministries, 1982-85. Author: The Twentieth Century Baptist, 1980; contbr. articles to profl. jours. Active Am. Cancer Soc.; bd. dirs. Luther Rice Coll., 1971-77, chmn., 1973-76; bd. dirs. Japan Internat. Christian U. Found., treas., 1982-85; bd. dirs. Nat. Interreligious Svc. Bd. for Conscientious Objectors, 1983-91, treas., 1988-91. Recipient with wife Olive F. Tiller, Dahlberg Peace award Am. Bapt. Chs. U.S.A., 1991. Mem. Am. Polit. Sci. Assn., Am. Soc. Pub. Adminstrn., Am. Acctg. Assn., Am. Bapt. Hist. Soc. (pres. 1982-85), Assn. Govt. Accts. Home: Mars Pa. Died July 6, 1991; buried Ft. Lincoln Cemetery, Brentwood, Md.

TILLINGHAST, CARLTON WILSON, association executive; b. Burlington, N.J., Nov. 21, 1898; s. George Suckley and Elizabeth Rodgers (Holland) T.; m. Caroline E. McIntire, Sept. 1, 1931; children: Carlton Wilson, Caroline McIntire. Grad. Nat. Sch. Comml./Trade Assn. Exec., Northwestern U., 1927. Asst. sec., treas. Nat. Assn. Comml. Orgn. Secs., Trenton, N.J., Davenport, Iowa, Sacramento, 1926-28; field rep. Regional Planning Fedn. Phila. Tri-State Dist., 1928-34; rsch. assoc. Pa. Econ. Coun., Phila., 1934-36; dir. S.E. region Pa. Economy League, Phila., 1936-48; exec. dir. N.J. Taxpayers Assn., Trenton, 1949-64, bd. dirs., mem. exec. com., from 1964; v.p. Burlington County United Fund, from 1964; pres. Trenton Symposium, 1958. Chmn. Burlington Twp. (N.J.) Zoning Bd., from 1945; mem. N.J. Commn. to Study Adminstrn. Welfare, 1951-

53; bd. dirs. Water Resources Assn. Delaware River Basin, from 1959. Mem. Govtl. Rsch. Assn. (non. life.; nat. trustee 1951-52, 53, pres. 1952-53), Am. Soc. Pub. Adminstrn., Nat. Taxpayers Conf. (mem. policy com. 1954-63, chmn. 1961-63), Tax Inst., Nat. Tax Assn., Rotary. Episcopalian. *

TIMBRELL, CLAYTON CAREY, consultant; b. Hackensack, N.J., Mar. 6, 1921; s. Clayton Carey and Esther Edith (Harding) T.; m. Jean Dohme Breeskin, May 19, 1945; children—Carey Harding, Stuart Frederick. B.A. with high honors, Brown U., 1942; postgrad., Nat. Inst. Public Affairs, 1943. Personnel officer U.S. Dept. Agr., Washington, 1943-46; with UN, N.Y.C., 1946-85, exec. officer Office Gen. Services, 1957-62, 63-69, dep. chief adminstrv. officer UN Operation Congo, 1962, dir. Office Gen. Services, 1969-77, asst. sec.-gen., 1977-85; internat. mgmt. and adminstrn. cons., 1985-88. Mem. alumni council Brown U., 1968-74. Recipient Brown Bear award Brown U., 1977; Francis Wayland scholar, 1941. Mem. Am. Mgmt. Assn., UN Assn. U.S.A., Phi Beta Kappa. Clubs: Knickerbocker Country (Tenafly, N.J.); Brown of No. N.J. (pres. 1963-67, 72-78). Home: Tenafly N.J. Died June 8, 1988; buried Tenefly, N.J.

TINGUELY, JEAN, sculptor; b. Fribourg, Switzerland, May 22, 1925; came to U.S., 1960; s. Charles C. and Jeanne (Ruffieux) T. Student, Basel (Switzerland) Sch., Fine Arts, 1941-45. Abstract paint, sculptor Basel, 1945-52, Paris, 1952-58, Dusseldorf, Germany, 1959, N.Y.C., 1960-91. Exhibited in numerous group shows U.S., fgn. countries. Home: Essones France Died Aug. 30, 1991.

TIPPET, CLARK, choreographer, ballet dancer; b. Parsons, Kans.. Began dance studies at age 5; student, Nat. Acad. Ballet, N.Y.C. With Am. Ballet Theatre, 1972-78, soloist, 1975-76, prin. dancer, 1976-78; guest artist Md. Ballet, Bat-Dor Dance Co. of Israel, West Australian Ballet Co., 1978-82; prin. dancer Am. Ballet Theatre, 1982-92. Choreographer: (ballet) Enough Said, 1986, for Ballet Theatre S.P.E.B.S.Q.S.A., Rigaudon, Some Assembly Required, other ballets for Pacific Northwest Ballet of Seattle, Kansas City Ballet; created roles include Psychiatrist in Equus (Domy Retier-Souffer), 2d male lead in Push Comes to Shove (Twyla Tharp), Oedipus in Sphinx (Glen Tetley), male role in pas de deux Transitions (John Butler), King David in Ammon V'Tamar (Martine von Hamel), leading male role in Field, Chair and Mountain (David Gordon), male role in pas de deux Walk This Way (David Parsons), one of leading male roles in Bach Partita (Twyla Tharp). Home: New York N.Y. Died Jan. 28, 1992.

TIPPIT, HASSEL, accountant; b. Legate, Tenn., Oct. 18, 1897; s. John Irving and Vedora (Edmondson) T.; m. Kittye Tucker, Dec. 20, 1916; children: Christine, Clifford Carlisle; m. Frances Ranft, Feb. 22, 1964. Corr. course, Internat. Acctg. Soc., 1919; HHD, Case Inst. Tech., 1958; LLD, Fenn Coll. CPA, Ohio and several other states. Jr. acct. Ernst & Ernst, CPAs, 1919, asst. mgr. Cleve. office, 1929-35, resident ptnr., 1935-48, mng. ptnr., 1948-64, chmn. mng. com., from 1964. Trustee Cleve. YMCA, Community Chest; life trustee Case Inst. Tch. Mem. Am. Inst. Accts., Am. Acctg. Assn., Union League Club (N.Y.C.), Union Club, Mayfield Country Club, Pepper Pike Country Club, Athletic Club (all Cleve.). *

TISHLER, MAX, chemist, pharmaceutical executive, educator; b. Boston, Oct. 30, 1906; s. Samuel and Anna (Gray) T.; m. Elizabeth M. Verveer, June 17, 1934; children—Peter Verveer, Carl Lewis. B.S., Tufts Coll., 1928; M.A., Harvard U., 1933, Ph.D., 1934; D.Sc., Tufts U., 1956, Bucknell U., 1962, Phila. Coll. Pharmacy, 1966, U. Strathclyde, Glasgow, 1969, Rider Coll., 1970, Upsala Coll., 1972, Fairfield U., 1972, Wesleyan U., 1981; D.Eng., Stevens Inst. Tech., 1966. Teaching asst. Tufts Coll., 1924; Austin teaching fellow Harvard, 1930-34, research assoc., 1934-36, instr. chemistry, 1936-37; research chemist Merck & Co., Inc., 1937-41, head sect. process devel., 1941-44, dir. devel. research, 1944-51, assoc. dir. research and devel., 1951-54, v.p. sci. activities, chem. div., 1954-56; pres. Merck, Sharp & Dohme Research Lab. div. Merck & Co. Inc.; pres. Merck Inst. Therapeutic Research div. Merck & Co. Inc., 1956-69, sr. v.p. research and devel., 1969-70; Rennebohm lectr. sch. pharmacy U. Wis., Madison, 1963; prof. chemistry Wesleyan U., Middletown, Conn., 1970-72, Univ. prof. scis., 1972-75, Univ. prof. scis. emeritus, 1975-89; chmn. dept. chemistry Wesleyan U., 1973-75; mem. vis. com. dept. chemistry Harvard U., 1965-71, Sch. Pub. Health, 1963-69; mem. vis. com. dept. chem. engring. MIT; trustee, chmn. vis. com. dept. chemistry Tufts U.; trustee Union (N.J.) Coll., 1965-70; asso. trustee sci. U. Pa., 1960-65, 70; adv. council Newark Coll. Engring., 1956-59; adminstrv. bd. Tufts New Eng. Med. Ctr., adv. bd. Coll., 1964-68; adv. com. biol. scis. Princeton U., 1972-75; Julius W. Sturmer Meml. lectr. Phila. Coll. Pharmacy, 1964; lectr. chemistry Royal Swedish Acad. Engring. Scis., 1964; Kauffman Meml. lectr. Ohio State U., 1967; DuPont lectr. Dartmouth U.; N.B. lectr. Am. Soc. Microbiology, 1974. Author: (with J.B. Conant) Chemistry of Organic Compounds, 1937, Streptomycin, (with S. A. Waksman), 1949; co-chmn. study group, author: Chemistry in the Economy, 1973; mem. editorial bd.: Organic Syntheses, 1953-61, Separation Science, Clin. Pharmacology and Therapeutics, Bioinvention; editor: Organic Syntheses, 1960-61. Bd. dirs. Merck & Co. Found.; bd. govs. Weizmann Inst.; mem. nat. adv. council Hampshire Coll., 1964-68; bd. visitors Faculty Health Scis., SUNY, Buffalo, 1965-68; trustee Royal Soc. Medicine Found., 1965-69; bd. sci. advisers Sloan Kettering Inst., from 1974. Recipient Bd. Dirs. Sci. award Merck & Co., Medal, Indsl. Research Inst., 1961, Medal Soc. Chem. Industry, 1963, Found. Patent award, 1970, Eli Whitney award Conn. Patent Law Assn., 1974, C. Chester Stock award Meml. Sloan-Kettering Cancer Ctr., 1984. Fellow AAAS, N.Y. Acad. Sci., Royal Soc. Chemistry (hon.), Chem. Soc. London, Am. Inst. Chemists (Chem. Pioneer award 1968, Gold medal, 1977, Priestley medal 1970), Soc. Chem. Industry (chmn. Am. sect. 1966, hon. v.p. 1968, Nat. Inventors Hall of Fame 1982, Nat. Medal of Sci. 1987), Acad. Pharm. Scis. of Am. Pharm. Assn. (hon. mem.), Conn. Acad. Sci. and Engring.; mem. Am. Acad. Arts and Scis., Indsl. Research Inst., Nat. Acad. Scis., Am. Chem. Soc. (chmn. dir. organic chemistry 1951, pres. 1972, bd. dirs. 1973), Swiss Chem. Soc., Conn. Acad. Scis. and Engring., Harvard Assn. Chemists, Société Chimique de France (hon.), Phi Beta Kappa, Sigma Xi, Pi Lambda Phi (Big Pi award 1951). Club: Chemists (N.Y.C.) (hon.). Home: Middletown Conn. Died Mar. 18, 1989; buried Sharon, Mass.

TOLL, MAYNARD JOY, lawyer; b. Los Angeles, Sept. 11, 1906; s. Charles Hulbert and Eleanor Margaret (Joy) T.; m. Ethel B. Coleman, Aug. 16, 1929; children: Arline Toll Kensinger, Deborah (Mrs. Russell S. Reynolds, Jr.), Janet (Mrs. Garrison H. Davidson, Jr.), Maynard Joy, Roger Coleman. A.B., U. Calif.-Berkeley, 1927; LL.B. magna cum laude, Harvard U., 1930; LL.D., Occidental Coll., 1963, Northrop U., 1975. Bar: Calif. 1930. Practice in Los Angeles, from 1930; ptnr. firm O'Melveny & Myers, 1940-80, of counsel, 1980-89; dir. Western Fed. Savs. & Loan Assn. Chmn. Los Angeles Community Chest campaign, 1953; trustee Los Angeles City Bd. Edn., 1944-49, pres., 1947-48; trustee Los Angeles County Bar Found., 1965-77, Los Angeles County Mus. Art, 1962-78; trustee John R. and Dora Haynes Found., pres., 1978-81; trustee Hosp. Good Samaritan; bd. dirs. Automobile Club So. Calif., 1970-80, v.p., 1971-73, chmn. bd., 1973-75; bd. dirs. Am. Automobile Assn., 1972-74; mem. exec. council Nat. Conf. Bar Presidents, 1968-70; bd. dirs. Council Legal Edn. Profl. Responsibility, 1973-81, Council on Founds., 1976-78. Fellow Am. Coll. Probate Counsel, Am. Bar Found. (dir., pres. 1974-76); mem. ABA, Los Angeles County Bar Assn. (pres. 1963), Inst. Jud. Adminstrn., Nat. Legal Aid and Defender Assn. (pres. 1966-70), State Bar Calif., Am. Judicature Soc. (chmn. bd. dirs. 1972-74), Western Assn. Schs. and Colls. (dir. 1981-85, pres. 1983-85, mem. accrediting com. 1979-85), Calif. Alumni Assn. (past pres.). Clubs: California (Los Angeles), Town Hall (Los Angeles) (past pres.); Salt Air (Santa Monica, Calif.). Home: Los Angeles Calif. Died Oct. 14, 1988; buried Forest Lawn Cemetery, Hollywood Hills, Calif.

TOLLEFSON, JOHN OLIVER, management educator, university dean, consultant; b. Lane County, nr. Eugene, Oreg., Mar. 24, 1937; s. George Theodore Morris and Ona Belle (Simpson) T.; m. Nona Aileen Falmlen, Aug. 27, 1961; children: John F., William G., Elizabeth C. B.S. in Forest Engring., Oreg. State U., 1958; M.S. in Indsl. Mgmt., Purdue U., 1960, Ph D. in Econs., 1966. Logging engr. Internat. Paper Co., Vaughn, Oreg., 1958-59; asst. prof. grad. sch. bus. Tulane U., New Orleans, 1963-67; asst. prof. sch. bus. U. Kans., Lawrence, 1967-70, assoc. prof., 1970-74, prof., 1974-91, assoc. dean Sch. Bus., 1974-81, dean, 1981-90; bd. dirs. Security Cash Fund, Security Income Fund, Security Tax Exempt Fund, Topeka, Kantronics, Douglas County Bank, Lawrence; adv. dir. Kans. Pub. Svc., Lawrence, 1986-91; mem. tech. adv. com. assessment sales ratio study State of Kans., from 1974. Contbr. articles to profl. jours. Mem. Am. Assembly of Collegiate Schs. Bus. (co-chmn. ann. meeting program 1983), Am. Mktg. Assn., Decision Scis. Inst., Inst. Mgmt. Scis., AAUP, Lawrence C. of C. (bd. dirs. 1982-85). Home: Lawrence Kans. Died Aug. 7, 1991.

TOLMAN, LELAND LOCKE, lawyer; b. Albany, N.Y., Nov. 1, 1908; s. Frank Leland and Hope (Mason) T.; m. Sarah Harrison, 1955; stepchildren: Clergue Jones, Clarissa Parker. PhB, U. Chgo., 1930, JD, 1933. Bar: N.Y., 1935. Assoc. Charles J. Tobin, Albany, 1934-35; spl. atty. U.S. Dept. Justice, 1935-38, spl. atty. anti-trust div., 1938-40; assigned to staff adv. com. on rules of civil procedure U.S. Supreme Ct., asst. sec. adv. com. rules of criminal procedure, 1940-42, mem., sec. adv. com. rules civil procedure, 1953-56; asst. chief div. procedural studies and stats. Adminstrv. Office U.S. Cts., 1940-49, chief bus. adminstrn., 1949-55; dep. adminstr. 1st Jud. Dept. Jud. Conf., State of N.Y., 1955-62, dir. adminstrn. of cts., 1962-73; cons. N.Y. State Legis. Com. on Ct. Reorgn., 1973-91; cons. on German occupation ct. adminstrn. and orgn. U.S. High Commr. for Germany, 1951; dir. N.Y. State Ct. Survey, Assn. Bar City N.Y., 1953-54; mem. adv. bd. Project for Effective Justice, Columbia. Co-author: (with William Hannan and Charles Tobin) Analysis of Charitable Tax Exemptions in New York State, 1935, Bad Housekeeping - The Adminstration of the New York Courts, 1954; contbr. articles and reports to legal and profl. jours. Lt. comdr. USNR, 1942-46, PTO. Mem. Inst. Jud. Adminstrn., ABA (assoc. mem. spl. com. improvement adminstrn. of justice 1939-42, sec. 1946-47, sec. Sect. Jud. Adminstrn. 1948-53, mem. coun. 1953-62, asst. to editor ABA jour. 1938-42)), N.Y. State Bar Assn., Assn. Bar City N.Y., Nat. Conf. Ct. Adminstrv. Officers, Am. Judicature Soc., Am. Law Inst. (life), Phi Alpha Delta. Democrat. Presbyterian. Home: Orland Maine Died Jan. 11, 1991.

TOMASEK, FRANTISEK CARDINAL, archbishop of Prague; b. Studenka, Czechoslovakia, June 30, 1899; s. Frantisek and Zdenka (Vavreckova) T. DD, Faculty Theology, Olomouc, 1938. Ordained priest Roman Cath. Ch., 1922, consecrated bishop, 1949. Tchr. religion, 1922-34; asst. Pedagogik-Catechetik, Theol. Faculty SS Cyril and Methodius, Olomouc, 1934-40; sch. insp. religion, 1940-46; lectr., then prof. pegadogics and catechetik Faculty of Theology, Olomouc, 1945-50; arrested, 1951-54; pastor parish Moravská Huzová, 1954-65; consecrated aux. bishop of Olomouc, 1949; apostolic adminstr. Archdiocese Prague, 1965-77; archbishop of Prague, primate of Bohemia, 1977-91; elevated to Sacred Coll. Cardinals, 1977. Author monographs, articles; editor: Letters on Education, 1934-47. Died Aug. 4, 1992. Home: Prague Czechovakia †

TOMASELLI, JULIUS LOUIS, building materials company executive; b. Teaneck, N.J., Nov. 2, 1928; s. Vincent and Beatrice (De Paoli) T.; m. Jacqueline Morino, July 26, 1952; children: Vincent, Raymond, Robert. B.A., Lehigh U., 1951; LL.B., Columbia U., 1955. Bar: D.C. 1956, N.Y. 1957. Asso. firm Pollard, Johnson, Smythe & Robertson, N.Y.C., 1956-60; patent atty. Gen. Foods Corp., White Plains, N.Y., 1960-62; with The Flintkote Co., Rochelle Park, N.J., 1962-84; patent counsel The Flintkote Co., 1962-66, asst. sec., 1966-67, dir. adminstrv. services bldg. products group, 1967-69, asst. sec., asst. gen. counsel, 1969-73, sec., gen. counsel, 1973, v.p. adminstrn., 1973-75, v.p. employee relations, 1975-80, v.p.-adminstrn., 1980-84. Vice pres. Seabrook (Md.) Civic Assn., 1956-57; bd. dirs. Citizens for Schs., Greenburgh, N.Y., 1959-60, White Plains YMCA, 1971-72. Mem. Am. Bar Assn., Am., N.Y. patent law assns., U.S. Trademark Assn., Theta Chi, Pi Gamma Mu, Phi Alpha Theta. Club: Hackensack Golf. Home: Mahwah N.J. Died Mar. 23, 1984; buried Ferncliss Cemetery, Hartsdale, N.Y. †

TOMKINS, SILVAN SOLOMON, psychologist, educator; b. Phila., June 4, 1911; s. Samuel Solomon and Rose (Novack) T.; m. Elizabeth J. Taylor, Feb. 8, 1946; 1 child, Mark Wallace. BA, U. Pa., 1930, MA, 1931, PhD, 1934. Rsch. asst. Harvard Psychol. Clinic, 1936-43; instr. psychology Harvard U., 1943-46, lectr. social rels., 1946-47; rsch. assoc. Coll. Bd., 1947-48; assoc. prof. psychology Princeton (N.J.) U., 1947-55, prof., 1955-64; rsch. prof. CUNY, 1964-69; dir. Ctr. Study Cognition and Affect, 1964-68; prof. Livingston Coll. Rutgers U., 1968-76, prof. emeritus, 1976-91; with the Ctr. for Advanced Study in Behavioral Scis., 1960-61; clin. psychologist; indsl. cons. Author: Thematic Apperception Test, 1947; co-author: (with John B. Minor) Tomkins-Hern Picture Arrangement Test, 1955, PAT Interpretaion, 1958, Consciousness, Imagery and Affect, 1960, (with others) Aspects of the Analysis of Family Structure, 1965; editor: Contemporary Psychopathology, 1943, (with Reed and Alexander) Psychopathology, 1958, (with Samuel Messick) Computer Simulation of Personality, 1963, Affect, Imagery and Consciousness, Vol. II, 1963, others. Mem. AAAS, Am. Psychol. Assn. Home: Strathmere N.J. Died June 10, 1991.

TOMKOWIT, THADDEUS WALTER, engineering company executive; b. Maspeth, N.Y., Sept. 10, 1918; s. Walter and Theodora (Dulska) T.; m. Ann D. Czyzewski, June 20, 1943; children: Barbara Ann (Mrs. William Anderson), Judith Lynn (Mrs. John Feeney), Richard T. B.S. in Chem. Engring, Columbia, 1941, postgrad. in chem. engring, 1941-42. Diplomate: Registered profl. engr., Del. With Du Pont de Nemours, 1942-82; mgr. logistics organic chems. dept. Du Pont de Nemours, Wilmington, Del., 1972-78; mgr. logistics and works supplies, chems. and pigments dept. Du Pont de Nemours, 1978-83; pres., pvt. cons. Engring. Resources, Inc., Wilmington, 1983-88; v.p. U.S. ops. P.T. Restu Svaha, Hong Kong, from 1983. Mem. dean's adv. bd. Sch. Engring., Catholic U., 1970—, also Lehigh U., U. Tex., Worcester Poly. Tech.; Pres. Civic Assn., 1966; Bd. dirs. Catholic Social Services Del. Mem. Am. Inst. Chem. Engrs. (dir., pres. 1972, founders award 1975), Am. Soc. Engring. Edn., Engrs. Joint Coun., Engrs. Coun. for Profl. Devel., Ams. Polish Descent Cultural Soc. (past pres., Achievement award 1968), Coun. Polish Clubs and Scos. in Del. (chmn. aid to poland com.), Sigma Xi. Republican. Roman Catholic. Home: Wilmington Del. Died July 25, 1989; buried St. Charles Cemetery, Farmingdale, N.Y.

TOMPKINS, ARTHUR WILSON, insurance executive; b. Wyoming, Iowa, Aug. 6, 1895; s. Albert T. and Margaret E. (Shaffer) T.; m. Dortha E. Christopher, June 30, 1920; children: Arthur W., Margery B. Welsh, Roger B. BS, S.D. State U., 1918. Emergency demonstration leader U.S. Dept. Agr., S.D., 1918; county agt. U.S. Dept. Agr., Hayti, S.D., 1919-24; exec. sec.

S.D. Farm Bur. Fedn., 1924-30; local agt. State Farm Mut. Automobile Ins. Co., Huron, S.D., 1925-27; state dir. State Farm Ins. Cos., Huron, 1927-30, S.D. and N.D., Bloomington, Ill., 1930; supt. agts. S.D. and N.D., Bloomington, 1930-34, agy. v.p., 1934-54, exec. v.p. agy., 1954-62, 1st sr. v.p., from 1962. Pvt. U.S. Army, 1918. Mem. Life Ins. Agy. Mgmt. Assn., Nat. Assn. Life Underwriters, Am. Legion., Masons, Elk, Kiwanis. Methodist. *

TOMPKINS, WILLIAM FINLEY, lawyer; b. Newark, Feb. 26, 1913; s. William Brydon and Lillian Elizabeth (Finley) T.; m. Jane Davis Bryant, Dec. 16, 1949; 1 child, William Finley, Jr. AB, Wesleyan U., 1935; LLB, Rutgers U., 1940. Bar: N.J. 1942, D.C. 1958. U.S. atty. Dist. N.J., 1953-54; asst. atty. gen. U.S., 1954-58; ptnr. Lum, Biunno & Tompkins, Newark, 1958-83, Tompkins, McGuire & Wachenfeld, Newark, 1984-89; bd. dirs. Mut. Benefit Fund, MBL Growth Fund, MAP Govt. Fund. Mem. N.J. Ho. Assembly, 1951-53; chmn. Legis. Commn. to Study Narcotics, 1951-52; chmn. N.J. Commn. to Study Capital Punishment, 1964; del. Rep. Nat. Conv., 1964; pres. bd. trustees Newark Acad., Livingston, N.J., 1962-69, chmn. bd. trustees, 1969-75. 1st lt. U.S. Army, 1943-46. Recipient Ann. Award Soc. Former Spl. Agts. FBI, 1959. Mem. Fed. Bar Assn., ABA, N.J. State Bar Assn., Essex County Bar Assn., Am. Coll. Trial Lawyers, Am. Bar Found., Baltusrol Golf Club, Essex Club (pres. 1985-89), Mid-Ocean Club (Bermuda), B'nai B'rith (First Americanism Citation for Meritorious Svc. South Mt. chpt.). Methodist. Author: (with Harry J. Anslinger) Traffic in Narcotics, 1953. Died July 6, 1989; buried Restland Meml. Pk., Hanover, N.J. Home: Maplewood N.J.

TONNDORF, JUERGEN, educator, otolaryngologist; b. Goettingen, Germany, Feb. 1, 1914; came to U.S., 1947, naturalized, 1957; s. Woldemar and Lilli (Schneidewin) T.; m. Mechtild Brandts, Mar. 27, 1940 (dec. 1986). B.S., U. Kiel, Germany, 1934, M.D., 1938; Ph.D., U. Heidelberg, Germany, 1945; M.D. (hon.), U. Goettingen. Dozent U. Heidelberg, 1945-47; mem. research staff USAF Sch. Aviation Medicine, Randolph Field, Tex., 1947-52; from asst. prof. to prof. U. Ia., 1953-62; prof. otolaryngology, dir. rsch. and tng. Columbia Coll. Phys. and Surgeons, N.Y.C., 1962-82, prof. emeritus, 1982-89; quest of honor Internat. Symposium on Tinnitus. Editor: Beltone Translation Series, 1961-80; Editorial bd.: Annals of Otology, Rhinology and Laryngology, from 1957, German Archives HNO Heilk, from 1968, Practica Otolaryngologica, from 1970, Brit. Jour. Audiology, from 1980; Contbr. articles to profl. jours. and handbooks. Served with German Navy, 1939-45. Recipient von Eicken award German Otolaryng. Soc., 1942, L. Haymann award, 1970, Guyot prize 1979, Shambaugh award 1979; Research Career award NIH, 1964; honored by Symposium on Mechanisms of Hearing, 1980; H. Fletcher award N.Y. League for Hard-of-Hearing, 1985. Fellow Acoustical Soc. Am.; mem. Am. Acad. Otolaryngology (hon.), Assn. Research in Otolaryngology (award of merit 1980), Am. Otol. Soc. (Gold medal 1979), German Otol. Soc. (hon.), Royal Soc. Medicine, Leopoldina Acad., Collegium Oto-Rhino-Laryngologicum. (v.p. 1980-81). Home: Bronx N.Y. Died Nov. 3, 1989.

TOPOLSKI, FELIKS, artist, publisher; b. Aug. 14, 1907; s. Edward and Stanislawa (Drutowska) T.; m. Marion Everall, 1944; children: Daniel, Teresa. Student, Warsaw Acad. Art. Exhibited in London, Poland, U.S., Can., Eire, France, India, Australia, Portugal, Italy, Switzerland, Brazil, Israel, Denmark, Norway, Argentina; designer theatrical settings and costumes; executed several large murals including Cavalcade of Commonwealth for Festival of Britain, 1951, Coronation for Buckingham Palace, 1958-60; interiors Carlton Tower Hotel, London, 1960; works in permanent collections Brit. Mus., Victoria and Albert Mus., Tate Gallery, Imperial War Mus., Edinburgh, Glasgow, Nottingham, Warsaw, Bklyn., Singapore, Toronto, New Delhi, Tel Aviv, Melbourne mus.; editor, pub. Topolski's Chronicle, 1953-89; ofcl. war artist, 1940-45; contbr. to numerous publs.; author: The London Spectacle, 1935, Britain in Peace and War, 1941, Russia in War, 1942, Three Coutinents, 1944-45, 1945, Portrait of G.B.S., 1946, Confessions of a Congress Delegate, 1949, 88 Pictures, 1951, Sketches of Gandhi, 1954, The Blue Conventions, 1956, Topolski's Chronicle for Students of World Affairs, 1958, Topolski's Legal London, 1961, Face to Face, 1964; illustrator G.B. Shaw's Geneva, Pygmalion, In Good King Charles' Golden Days, 20 portraits of English writers for U. Tex. Home: London Eng. Died Aug. 24, 1989.

TORKANOWSKY, WERNER, conductor, composer; b. Berlin, Germany, Mar. 3, 1926; U.S. citizen. Violin study with mem. Israel Philharm.; student with Rafael Bronstein and Pierre Monteaux. Music dir. Ballets USA, 1959-63; condr. Spoleto Festival, 1959-62; music dir., condr. New Orleans Philharm., 1961-77; now condr. Bangor Symphony Orch.; violinist New Eng. Piano Quartette; guest condr. with most maj. orch. in U.S. Works include String Quartet, 1981, Prophecies for Cello and Piano, 1981, Three Songs, 1982, Meditations for Cello, 1982, Trio, 1982, Piano Quartet, 1983, Statements for piano trio, clarinet and voice, 1984, Divertimento for piano and strings, 1987. Recipient Walter Naumburg award for Conducting, 1960.Died Oct. 20, 1992. Home: Bangor Maine †

TORRENCE, HOWARD H., environmental economist; b. Sharon, Mass., Dec. 12, 1903; s. Howard A. and Leora (Zwieber) T.; m. Muriel Stancey, Sept. 23, 1926; children: Carla, Noel, Zachary. BA in Econ., Carnegie Inst. Tech., 1924; BS Chem., MIT, 1926; posrgrad., Harvard U. With Mass. Dept. Labor and Industry, Boston, 1926-1950; with Am. Acad. Environ., 1950-80; Environ. econ. Adv. to U.S. Senate Com., 1936, bd. dirs. Doeskin Products Corp. from 1958, Mellon Indsl fellow in Econ., mem. Nat. Indsl Recovery Bd., Air Pollution Control Assn., Am. Econ. Assn. Contbr. articles to profl. jours. Recipient Tanner Award, 1957. Mem. Green Peace, Sierra Club, Rotary, Phi Kappa Phi. Lutheran. Died Jan. 24, 1990; buried Fox Run, Mass.* †

TORRES-RIOSECO, ARTURE, Latin American literature educator; b. Talca, Chile, Oct. 17, 1897; came to U.S., 1918; s. Domingo and Juana (Rioseco) T.; m. Rosalie Margaret Godt. AB, U. Chile, 1916; MA, U. Minn., 1924. Instr. Romance langs. U. Minn., 1921-24; assoc. prof. Latin Am. lit. U. Tex., 1925-28; prof. Latin Am. lit. U. Calif., from 1928, chmn. Spanish dept., from 1956; tchr. summers Columbia U., Sanford U., U. Minn., U. Tex., MIlls. Coll., U. Mexico, U. Chile; spl. Flexner lectr. Bryn Mawr Coll., 1939, 40; Rockefeller scholar in Latin Am., 1943; lectr. Casa de Estudante, Rio de Janeiro, U. Guatemala, 1947; hon. prof. U. Guatemala, 1946; Walter-Ames prof. U. Wash., 1961; John Gordon Stipe lectr. Emory U., 1962; spl. advisor state dept. meeting, UN Orgn., San Francisco, 1945. Author: World Literature, 1949, Critical Anthology of Ruben Dario, 1949, Cau Tiverio, 1956, Enshyos Literarios, 1958, Autobiographia, 1961, Gabriela Mistral, 1962, Aspects of Spanish American Literature, 1963, Precursores del Modernismo, 1963, Panorama de la Literatura Iberamericana, 1964; editor: Revista Iberoamericana. Decorated Cross of Vasco Nunez de Balboa, Panama, 1946. Fellow Philos. Soc. Am.; mem. AAUP, Acad. Letters of Panama, Modern Lang. Assn., Tchrs. of Spanish of USA, Hispanic Soc. Am., Mexican Acad. Letters, Sigma Delta Pi. *

TORTELIER, PAUL, cellist, composer; b. Paris, Mar. 21, 1914; s. Joseph and Marguerite (Boura) T.; m. Madeleine Gaston (div. 1943); 1 child, Anne; m. Maud Monique Martin; children: Pascal, Maria Tortelier de la Pau, Pomone. Grad. with honors, Conservatoire Nat. de La Musique, Paris, 1935; D of Music (hon.), Leicester (Eng.) U., 1972, Oxford U., 1975; D.H.C. (hon.), Aston U., Birmingham, Eng., 1979. 1st cellist Opera Monte Carlo, 1935-37; cellist Boston Symphony Orch., 1937-40; prof. music Conservatoire Nat. Supèrieur de la Musique, Paris, 1956-69, Folkwang Hochschule Musik, Essen, Fed. Republic Germany, 1969-75, Conservatoire Nat. de Region, Nice, 1978-80; 1st cellist Soc. des Concerts du Conservatoire, Paris, 1946-47. Composer: Spirales, 1943, Suite for Solo Cello, 1946, Symphony Israelienne, 1956, The Great Flag (Hymn for the United Nations), 1959, Violin and Piano Concerto for performance with orch., 1965, Offrande, 1970, Alla Maud, 1973, Sonata Breve "Bucephale", 1983, Romance and Dance Variations, 1985, Sonata Breve "Mon Cirque", 1987. Supporter United World Colls., 1985—. Recipient Great Prize for Recording Bach Cello Solo Suites (2). Fellow Royal College of Music; mem. Royal Acad. Music (hon.), Soc. des Auteurs et Compositeurs. Lodge: Lions (comdr. Helsinki, Finland, 1983). Home: Nice France Died Dec. 18, 1990; cremated.

TOWER, JOHN GOODWIN, senator, international business and banking consultant; b. Houston, Sept. 29, 1925; s. Joe Z. and Beryl (Goodwin) T.; m. children: Penelope (Mrs. David Cook), Marian (dec.), Jeanne (Mrs. Berry Cox). B.A., Southwestern U., Tex., 1948, also LL.D. (hon.); M.A. in Polit. Sci., So. Meth. U., 1953; postgrad., London Sch. Econs. and Polit. Sci., U. London, 1952-53; LL.D. (hon.), Howard Payne Coll., Alfred U. Radio announcer Sta. KFDM, Beaumont, Tex., 1948, Sta. KTAE, Taylor, Tex., 1948-49; ins. agt. Dallas, 1950-51; asst. prof. polit. sci. Midwestern State U., Wichita Falls, Tex., 1951-61; U.S. senator from Tex., 1961-85; chmn. com. on armed services, mem. budget com., com. on banking, housing and urban affairs, chmn. Senate Republican policy com.; U.S. negotiator on strategic nuclear arms U.S. Del. to Negotiations on Nuclear and Space Arms, Geneva, 1985-86; disting. lectr. polit. sci. So. Meth. U., Dallas, 1986-88; chmn. Tower, Eggers & Greene Cons. Inc., Dallas and Washington, 1987-90; del. Rep. Nat. Com., 1956, 60, 64, 68, 72, 80, 88, mem. platform com., 1960, 64, 68, 72, chmn. 1980; chmn., Iran-Contra Commission, 1987; chmn. bd. dirs. Brassey's Inc.; bd. dirs. Brit. Aerospace, Inc. Author: A Program for Conservatives, Consequences, A Personal and Political Memoir, 1991; chmn. bd. dirs. Armed Forces Jour. Trustee Southwestern U. Served with USN, World War II. Recipient Order of Merit (Tunisia), Knight Commdr.'s Cross Order of Merit (Fed. Republic Germany); Hon. Fellow London Sch. Econs. and Polit. Sci. Mem. Tex. Philos. Soc., Tex. Hist. Soc., Am. Legion, Kappa Sigma (past worthy grand master). Methodist. Lodges: Masons (33 degree), Shriners. Home: Dallas Tex. Died Apr. 5, 1991; buried Sparkman Hillcrest, Dallas.

TOWERS, GRAHAM FORD, banker; b. Montreal, Sept. 29, 1897; s. William Crawford and Caroline (Auldjo) T.; m. Mary Scott Godfrey, Feb. 1, 1924. BA, McGill U., Montreal, 1920; LLD, McGill U., 1944, Queen's U., 1954; DCL, Bishop's U., Lennoxville, P.Q., 1961. Economist Royal Bank of Can., Montreal, 1920; acct. Havana br. Royal Bank of Can., 1922, inspector fgn. dept., 1924-29, chief inspector, 1929-33, asst. gen. mgr., 1933-34; gov. Bank of Can., 1934-54; pres. Indsl. Devel. Bank, 1944-54; chmn. bd. Can. Fund, Inc., Can. Investment Fund, Inc.; chmn. Brit. Petroleum Ltd. Can., Can. Life Assurance Co.; mem. Can. com. Hudson's Bay Co.; dir. Bell Telephone Co. of Can., Gen. Motors Corp., Moore Corp., Royal Bank of Can.; chmn. Fgn. Exchange Control Bd., 1939-51. Lt. Can. Army, 1915-19. Author: Financing Foreign Trade, 1921. Companion of St. Michael and St. George. Mem. Rideau Club. Mem. Anglican Ch. *

TOWL, E. CLINTON, aerospace company executive; b. Bklyn., Oct. 26, 1950; s. Allan Theodore and Mabel (Louis) T.; m. Christine Koempel; children: F. Clinton, Sandra Towl Corcoran. Student, St. Paul's Sch., Garden, L.I., N.Y., Cornell U.; LLD, Adelphi U., 1967. With S.E. Burnet, Inc., investments, N.Y.C., to 1929; founder Grumman Aircraft Engring. Corp., Baldwin, L.I., 1929, asst. treas., 1937; then v.p., asst. corp. sec., pres., chmn. bd. Grumman Corp., Bethpage, N.Y., 1969-90; dir. Grumman Aerospace Corp., Grumman Data Systems Corp., Grumman Ecosystems Corp., Grumman Internat. Inc., Grumman Allied Industries, Inc., Olson Bodies, Inc., Paumanock Devel. Corp., Paumanock Leasing Svcs., Inc., Paumanock Ins. Co. Ltd., Farmhouse Diving Svcs., Inc., Calldata Systems, Inc., L.I. Lighting Co. Chmn. payroll savs. bond com. Aerospace-Aircraft Industries, 1970; chmn. Boy Scouts Century Club, 1964-67; campaign chmn. United Fund L.I., 1965-66, pres., 1966-67, chmn. bd. trustees, 1967-68, exec. com., 1968-69. Home: Stuart Fla. Died Jan. 25, 1990.

TOWNER, LAWRENCE WILLIAM, historian, librarian; b. St. Paul, Sept. 10, 1921; s. Earl Chadwick and Cornelia Josephine (Mallum) T.; m. Rachel E. Bauman, Nov. 28, 1943; children: Wendy Kay Towner Yanikoski, Kristin Anne Towner Moses, Lawrence Baumann (dec.), Elizabeth Gail Towner Jackson, Peter Mallum, Michael Chadwick. BA, Cornell Coll., Mt. Vernon, Iowa, 1942, LHD, 1965; MA, Northwestern U., 1950, PhD, 1955; LittD, Lake Forest Coll., 1965; LHD, U. Ill., Chgo., 1986, Loyola U., Chgo., 1989. History master Chgo. Latin Sch., 1946-47; instr., then asst. prof. history MIT, Cambridge, 1950-55; asso. prof. history Coll. William and Mary, Williamsburg, Va., 1955-62; editor William and Mary Quar., Williamsburg, Va., 1956-62, mem. bd. editors, 1970-71; fellow Ctr. Study History of Liberty, Harvard U., Cambridge, Mass., 1961-62; librarian Newberry Library, Chgo., 1962-86, pres., 1975-86, pres. emeritus, 1986-92; vis. prof. English, Northwestern U., 1968-70, life trustee Newberry Libr., 1989; professorial lectr. U. Chgo., 1968. Contbr. numerous articles to mags., profl. jours.; bd. editors: Am. mag., History and Life. Mem. adv. coun. Eleutherian Mills, Hagley Found., 1965-71, 77-79; trustee Grinnell (Iowa) Coll., 1966-73, Latin Sch. Chgo., 1971-73; trustee Mus. Contemporary Art, 1970-75, chmn., 1976-78; bd. dirs. Ill. Humanities Coun., 1973-79, chmn., 1976-79; mem. exec. com. Fedn. Pub. Programs in the Humanities, 1977-78; bd. govs. Henrotin Hosp., 1977-85; mem. White House Libr. Co., 1963-65; bd. dirs. Native Am. Ednl. Svcs., 1978-84. Served to 1st lt. pilot USAAC, World War II. Decorated chevalier Arts and Letters (France); recipient Cliff Dwellers Merit award, 1977; Ill. Humanities Coun. Lawrence W. Towner Annual award for Best Risk-Tking Proposal established, 1986. Mem. Am. Hist. Assn. (mem. coun. 1973-75), Orgn. Am. Historians, Bibliog. Soc. Am., Ind. Rsch. Librs. Assn. (chmn. 1975-77), Colonial Soc. Mass., Va. Hist. Soc., Mass. Hist. Soc., Modern Poetry Assn. (pres. 1967-69, trustee 1963-69), Am. Antiquarian Soc., Cosmos Club (Washington), Harvard Club (N.Y.C.), Caxton Club, Wayfarers Club (pres. 1983-84), Phi Beta Kappa. Home: Chicago Ill. Died June 12, 1992.

TOWNSEND, WAYNE LASALLE, dean; b. Cook, Nebr., Dec. 7, 1896; s. Adelbert and Anna (Cook) T.; m. Dorothy Pierce, June 7, 1922; 1 child, Nancy Pyle. BA, U. Nebr., 1918; LLB, Yale U., 1928, JSD, 1929. Asst. cashier Minatare (Nebr.) Bank, 1920-22; cashier State Bank of Minatare, Nebr., 1922-26; instr. law Yale Sch. Law, 1929-31; vis. prof. law Tulane U., 1931-32; prof. law Western Res. U., 1932-45; assoc. with firm Thompson, Hine and Flory, Cleve., 1943-45; dean sch. of law , prof. law Washington U., 1945-51, disting. svc. prof. of law, from 1951; Legion Lex disting. vis. prof. U. So. Calif., 1959-60; labor arbitrator, Cleve., St. Louis, from 1944; referee ct. of common pleas, Ohio, 1942; judge Magistrate Ct. of Jefferson County, Mo., from 1963; compliance commr. W.P.B., Cleve., 1942-44. Author, editor: Townsend's Cases and Other Select Materials on the Law of Banking, 1938, Townsend's Ohio Corporation Law, 1940. Trustee, v.p. bd. Cleve. Pub. Libr., 1942-45; chmn. McBride Lecture Found., Cleve., 1938-45; trustee Great Lakes Hist. Soc., Cleve.; pres. St. Louis Artists Guild, 1957-58, trustee, from 1958. 2d lt. F.A., USA, 1918. Fellow Am. Bar Found.; mem. Nebr. Bar Assn., Ohio Bar Assn., Mo. Bar Assn.,

Internat. Soc. Clin. Lab. Techs. (chmn. accrediting commn.), Phi Beta Kappa, Phi Alpha Delta, Alpha Theta Chi, Chi Phi, Sigma Delta Chi. *

TOY, WING NOON, electrical engineer; b. China, Feb. 3, 1926; came to U.S., 1938; s. Young and Lou T.; m. Romayne Louis, June 9, 1956; children: Liane, Arthur, Sue-lin. BS, U. Ill., 1950, MSEE, 1952; PhD in Elec. Engring., U. Pa., 1969. Mem. tech. staff Bell Labs., Murray Hill, N.J., 1952-62, Holmdel, N.J., 1962-67; supr. Bell Labs., Naperville, Ill., 1967-73; supr. Pac Switching Tech. Group Bell Labs., Naperville, 1974-89; MacKay lectr. U. Calif.-Berkeley, 1973-74. Author: Mini/Microcomputer Hardware Design, 1979, Microprogrammed Control and Reliable Design of Small Computers, 1981, Computer Hardware/Software Architecture, 1986; contbr. articles to tech. jours.; mem. editorial bd.: Computer Mag., 1983-86; holder 28 patents in field. Served with USN, 1944-46, PTO. Named Outstanding Asian-Am. Asian-Am. Heritage Council, 1982; recipient Bell Labs. fellow, 1983. Fellow IEEE (editor TC on Computers, 1986-87, computer governing bd. 1986-87, 1990-92). Home: Glen Ellyn Ill. Died Oct. 28, 1990.

TRACY, HONOR LILBUSH WINGFIELD, writer, journalist; b. Bury St. Edmunds, Suffolk, Eng., Oct. 19, 1913; d. Humphrey Tracy and Christabel May Clare Miller. Ed., Grove Sch., Highgate, London. Fgn. corr. The Observer, 1947-50; Dublin corr. Sunday Times, London, 1950; columnist Daily Telegraph, 1973-89. Author of numerous books including: (travel books) Kakemono: A Sketchbook of Postwar Japan, 1950; Mind You, I've Said Nothing! Forays in the Irish Republic, 1953; Silk Hats and No Breakfast, 1957; Spanish Leaves, 1964; Winter in Castille, 1973; The Heart of England, 1983; (fiction) The Deserters, 1954; The Straight and Narrow Path, 1956; The Prospects are Pleasing, 1958; A Number of Things, 1959; A Season of Mists, 1961; The First Day of Friday, 1963; Men at Work, 1966; The Beauty of the World (Am. title Settled in Chambers), 1967; The Butterflies of the Province, 1970; The Quiet End of Evening, 1972; In a Year of Grace, 1975; The Man From Next Door, 1977; The Ballad of Castle Reef, 1979; contbr. numerous articles to profl. jours. and popular mags. Home: Chislehurst Eng. Died June 13, 1989. †

TRAINER, JAMES EDWARD, rubber manufacturing executive; b. N.Y.C., Sept. 16, 1895; s. James W. and Rose Anna (Shevlin) R.; m. Mary Langan, June 27, 1925; children: James Edward, Thomas Weldon, Ann. Grad. in elec. engring., Pratt Inst., Bklyn., 1914; LLD, Pratt Inst., 1963; D in Engr., Akron U., 1963. Trainer, elec. engr. Barry Mech., Western Electric Co., Aetna Explosive Co., 1914-17; from master mechanic to gen. supt. Babcock & Wilcox, Barberton, Ohio, 1917-31; gen. supt. mfg. plants Babcock & Wilcox, Barberton, 1931-39; gen. prodn. mgr. Firestone Tire & Rubber Co., 1939, v.p. prodn., 1940, dir., from 1942, exec. v.p., from 1954; asst. rubber dir. WPB, 1945; dir. mfg. and installation world's largest highpressure penstocks Hoover Dam. Trustee local coun. Boy Scouts Am., Pratt Inst. Lt. U.S. Army, 1918. Recipient citations Ordnance Dept., AUS, 1944, 45, 60, cert. appreciation War Dept., 1945, citations Nat. Safety Coun., 1951, 52, spl. award of merit Pres.' Conf. Indsl. Safety, 1952. Fellow ASME (hon. life mem.); mem. U.S. C. of C., Ohio C. of C., Akron C. of C., Am. Ordnance Assn. (pres. 1961), Profl. Engrs. and Surveyors Soc. Am. Engrs., Am. Legion, Tau Beta Pi, Portage Country Club, Firestone Country Club. Republican. Roman Catholic. *

TRAVER, ROBERT See **VOELKER, JOHN DONALDSON**

TREADWELL, CARLETON RAYMOND, biochemist, educator; b. Calhoun County, Mich., Dec. 28, 1911; s. Gilbert B. and Mine (Eyre) T.; m. Gloria E. Bennett, Sept. 3, 1941; children: Gloria Ann, Carla Maxine. AB, Battle Creek Coll., 1934; MS, U. Mich., 1935, PhD, 1939. Asst. biochemistry U. Mich., 1935-39; instr. biochemistry Baylor U., 1939-41, asst. prof., 1942-43; assoc. prof. Southwestern Med. Coll., 1943-45; mem. faculty George Washington U., Washington, 1945-89, prof. biochemistry, head dept., 1959-89; cons. med. rsch. VA Ctr., Martinsburg,W.Va., 1954-89; mem. physiol. chemistry study sect. NIH, 1959-63, mem. heart program project com., 1963-67; chmn. Gordon Rsch. Conf. Lipid Metabolism, 1959-60; mem. frontiers of sci. com. Joint Sci. Bd., 1959-60. Mem. editorial bd. Jour. Nutrition, 1955-58, Arch. Biochem. Biophys., 1966-89; contbr. articles to profl. jours. Fellow AAAS; mem. AAUP, Am. Chem. Soc., N.Y. (co-chmn. conf. atherosclerosis and hormones 1958), Washington (chmn. biol. awards com. 1959-61) acads. scis., Am. Soc. Biol. Chemists, Am. Inst. Nutrition, Soc. Exptl. Biology and Medicine (Coun. D.C. 1956-58, nat. coun. 1955), Washington Acad. Medicine, Cosmos Club, Sigma Xi. Home: Annandale Va. Died Dec. 30, 1989.

TREADWELL, GRACE, artist; b. Cape Cod, Mass., 1893; d. Walter I. and Elizabeth Hand (Wilcox) Badger; m. Raymond P. Holden, 1917; children: Elizabeth (Mrs. Scudder Parker), Richard C.; m. Abbot Treadwell, Jr., May 29, 1925. Student, Miss Porter's Sch., Farmington, Conn., 1910-12, Miss May's Sch., Boston, 1912; art student, Boston Museum Sch., 1914-16, Chaumiere, Paris, 1922. Tchr., lectr. on art. Exhibited one-woman show at Erich Gallery, N.Y.C., 1923; exhibited at Mid-Town Galleries, Pen and Brush Club, N.Y., Bklyn. Mus., Atlanta Mus.; painting signed Grace Holden at Albright Art Mus.; painted murals for St. Luke's Ch., Smethport, Pa., Pacific Sch. of Prayer, Calif., St. George and St. Mark's Schs., N.Y.C.; mural for children at Bird S. Coler Hosp.; works on tour in exhibits in Can., Paris, and museums and galleries throughout U.S. Bd. dirs., dir. art therapy Bird S. Coler Hosp. Recipient 14 awards Pen and Brush Club, 1 award Miss. Art Assn. Mem. Nat. Assn. Women Artists (pres. 1946-49, mem. adv. com. and jury), Pen and Brush Club, Woman's Club of Gt. Neck. Democrat. Roman Catholic. *

TREE, MARIETTA PEABODY, urban planner; b. Lawrence, Mass.; d. Malcolm Endicott and Mary Elizabeth (Parkman) Peabody; m. Desmond FitzGerald, Sept. 2, 1939; 1 dau., Frances; m. Ronald Tree, July 28, 1947; 1 dau., Penelope. Student, La Petite Ecole Florentine, Florence, Italy, 1934-35, U. Pa., 1936-39; LL.D., U. Pa., 1964; L.H.D., Russell Sage Coll., 1962, Bard Coll., 1964, Hobart and William Coll., 1967; LL.D., Drexel Inst. Tech., 1965; LL.D. hon. degrees, Franklin Pierce Coll., Coll. New Rochelle, Skidmore Coll. With hospitality div. Office Coordinator Inter-Am. Affairs, 1942-43; researcher Life mag., 1943-45; mem. Fair Housing Practices Panel, N.Y.C., 1958; mem. bd. commrs. N.Y.C. Commn. on Human Rights, 1959-61; U.S. rep. to Human Rights Commn. of UN, 1961-64; mem. U.S. del. UN, 1961; U.S. rep. Trusteeship Council of UN with rank of ambassador, 1964-65; mem. staff U Thant, UN Secretariat, 1966-67; partner Llewelyn-Davies Assocs. (city planners), 1968-80; dir. Llewelyn-Davies, Sahni Inc., Pan Am. Airways, N.Y.C., CBS; sr. cons. Hill & Knowlton, Inc.; editor-at-large Archtl. Digest. Del. N.Y. State Constl. Conv., 1967; mem. N.Y. State Dem. Com., 1954-60; mem. civil rights com. Dem. Adv. Coun., 1959-60; founder Syndenham Hosp., N.Y.C., 1943; past bd. dirs. UN Assn., Citizens Housing and Planning Coun., Ctr. Internat. Studies-NYU; bd. dirs. Am. Coun. for Ditchley; vice chmn. Cooper-Hewitt Mus., Am. Friends of Australia Nat. Gallery; chmn. Citizens Com. for N.Y.C., Friends of Arthur Ross Gallery, U. Pa.; bd. dirs. Franklin D. Roosevelt Four Freedoms Found., Marconi Internat. Found., Coun. Am. Ambassadors, Fund for Free Expression. Mem. Pilgrim Soc. (vice chmn.), Coun. Fgn. Rels. Episcopalian. Home: New York N.Y. Died Aug. 15, 1991; cremated.

TREIMAN, JOYCE WAHL, artist; b. Evanston, Ill., May 29, 1922; d. Rene and Rose (Doppelt) Wahl; m. Kenneth Treiman, Apr. 25, 1945; 1 child, Donald. A.A., Stephens Coll., 1941; B.F.A. (grad. fellow 1943), State U. Iowa, 1943. Vis. prof. San Fernando Valley State Coll., 1968; lectr. UCLA, 1969-70; vis. prof. State U. Calif., Long Beach, 1977. One-man shows include Paul Theobald Gallery, Chgo., 1942, John Snowden Gallery, Chgo., 1945, Art Inst. Chgo., 1947, North Shore Country Day Sch., Winnetka, Ill., 1947, Fairweather-Garnett Gallery, Evanston, 1950, Edwin Hewitt Gallery, N.Y.C., 1950, Palmer House Galleries, Chgo., 1952, Glencoe (Ill.) Library, 1953, Elizabeth Nelson Gallery, Chgo., 1953, Charles Feingarten Gallery, Chgo., 1955, Cliff Dwellers Club, Chgo., 1955, Fairweather-Hardin Gallery, Chgo., 1955, 58, 73, 81, 86, Marian Willard Gallery, N.Y.C., 1960, Felix Landau Gallery, Los Angeles, 1961, 64, La Jolla (Calif.) Mus., 1962-72, Forum Gallery, N.Y., 1963, 66, 75, 81, Adele Bednarz Gallery, Los Angeles, 1969-71, 74, Palos Verdes (Calif.) Art Mus., 1976, Mcpl. Art Gallery L.A., 1978, monotypes UCLA, 1979, drawings Art Inst. Chgo., 1979, Tortue Gallery, Santa Monica, Calif., 1980, 83, 86, 88-90, Schmidt-Bingham Gallery, N.Y.C., 1986, 88, Portland (Oreg.) Art Mus., 1988, Rochester Meml. Art Gallery, 1988, U. So. Calif. L.A., 1988, U. So. Calif. Retrospective, 1987, L.A., Rochester Meml. Art Gallery, Rochester, N.Y., 1988, Portland (Oreg.) Art Mus., 1988; numerous exhbns. including Carnegie Internat., 1955, 57, Met. Mus., 1950, Whitney Mus., 1951, 52, 53, 58, Art Inst. Chgo., 1945-59, John Herron Art Inst., 1953, Library of Congress, 1954, Cocoran Gallery, 1957, Pa. Acad. Fine Arts, 1958, Mus. Modern Art, 1962, Am. Acad. Arts and Letters, N.Y.C., 1974, 75, 76, Retrospective Exhbn., Mcpl. Art Gallery, Los Angeles, 1978; represented in permanent collections Kemper Ins. Co., Chgo., Met Mus. Art, N.Y.C., Denver Mus. Art, State U. Iowa, Ill. State Mus., Long Beach (Calif.) Mus., Whitney Mus. Am. Art, N.Y.C., Tupperware Art Mus., Orlando, Fla., Art Inst. Chgo., Utah State U., Abbott Labs., Oberlin Allen Art Mus., Internat. Mineral Corp., Pasadena Art Mus., U. Calif. at Santa Cruz, Grunwald Found., UCLA, Santa Barbara Mus. Art, Calif., Oakland Mus., Calif., Security Pacific Nat. Bank, Los Angeles, Rochester (N.Y.) Art Mus., L.A. County Art Mus., Met. Mus., N.Y., Portland (Oreg.) Mus., Santa Barbara (Calif.) Mus.; pub. collections include Art Inst. Chgo., Whitney Mus., Met. Mus., Santa Barbara (Calif.) Mus., Portland (Oreg.) Mus. Recipient numerous awards including Logan purchase prize Art Inst. Chgo., 1951, Martin B. Cahn prize, 1959, 60, Pauline Palmer prize, 1953, Saratosa Am. Painting Exhbn. award, 1959, Ford Found. purchase prize, 1960, Purchase prize Ball State Coll., 1961, prize La Jolla Art Mus., 1961, Purchase prize Pasadena Art Mus., 1961; Tiffany fellow, 1947-48; Tupperware Art Fund fellow, 1955; Tamerind Lithography fellow, 1961; Nat. Endowment for the Arts Visual Artist Fellowship grantee, 1989—. Assoc. mem. Nat. Acad. Design. Home: Pacific Palisades Calif. Died June 2, 1991; buried L.A.

TREMPER, EDWARD PAYSON, accountant; b. Seattle, July 13, 1898; s. E.P. and Harriet (Arnold) T.; m. Doris Verran, Aug. 12, 1922; children: William E., John P., Harriet Ann. BBA, U. Wash., 1920. Acct. E.G. Shorrock & Co., 1921-23; ptnr. Sparling, Clark & Tremper, 1923-28, Allen R. Smart & Co., 1937-47, Touche, Ross, Bailey and Smart, Seattle, from 1947; dir. Eastside Savs. & Loan Assn.; chmn. Wash. State Bd. Accountancy. Chmn. Kirkland (Wash.) Consol. Sch. Bd; chmn., liquidating trustee Worlds Fair Com. Mem. Am. Inst. Accts., Nat. Assn. Accts., Wash. Soc. CPAs (pres.), Seattle C. of C., World Affairs Coun. Seattle, Seattle Found., Beta Alpha Psi, Beta Theta Pi. *

TREZEVANT, JOHN GRAY, publishing company executive; b. Alameda, Calif., May 21, 1923; s. Gray and Ann (Bevan) T.; m. Dorothy Jean Heath, Mar. 13, 1948; children: Robert, Richard, John. AB, U. Calif., Berkeley, 1943. Mem. editorial staff San Francisco Chronicle, 1942-55, asst. news editor, 1951-55; assoc. journalism U. Calif., 1946-48; asst. to editor in chief Crowell-Collier Pub. Co., N.Y.C., 1955-56; mng. editor Colliers mag., 1956-57; mgr. news and publs. Nat. Assn. Broadcasters, Washington, 1957-58; Sunday editor Chgo. Sun-Times, 1958-61, mng. editor, 1962-64; exec. v.p. Chgo. Sun-Times, Chgo. Daily News, 1964-77; exec. v.p., dir., mem. exec. com. Field Enterprises Inc.; chmn. Field Newspaper Syndicate; pres. Met. Printing Co., Elk Grove Village, Ill.; bd. dirs. World Book-Childcraft Internat. Inc., FSC Paper Corp., Alsip, Ill., Can. Pacific Forest Products Ltd., Toronto; cons. Creators Syndicate, 1977-84. Assoc. Northwestern U., United Charities, Chgo.; mem. citizens com. U. Ill. Lt. USNR, 1943-46. Mem. Nat. Press Club (Washington), Balboa Bay Club (Newport Beach, Calif.), Tavern Club (Chgo.), Chgo. Club, Sigma Delta Chi. Home: Tiburon Calif. Died May 9, 1991; buried Fernwood Cemetery, Mill Valley, Calif.

TRIMBLE, GILBERT KOHLER, manufacturing company executive; b. Phila., Mar. 11, 1898; s. William McClelland and Anna Frances (Quillman) T.; m. Florence Nadine Immler, Apr. 2, 1931; children: Nancy Ann, Judith Ellen. BS, Pa. State Coll., 1920. Chem. engr., from 1920; analytical chemist Columbia Chem. Co., Barberton, Ohio, 1920; process chemist Ohio Insulator Co., Barberton, 1920-23; rsch. chemist, chem. mfg. div. B.F. Goodrich Co., Akron, Ohio, 1923-25; factory chemist Seiberling Rubber Co., Barberton, 1925-28; with Midwest Rubber Reclaiming Co., East St. Louis, from 1928, successively chief chemist, v.p., exec. v.p. sales, pres., from 1953, chmn. bd., chief exec. officer, dir., from 1963; dir. Akron Rubber Reclaiming Co., Barberton, Union Nat. Bank, East St. Louis; U.S. del. Internat. Rubber Study Group, London, 1949, Brussels, 1950, Rome, 1951, Ottawa, 1952, Copenhagen, 1953. Mem. Baruch Rubber Survey Com., 1942; mgr. scrap and reclaimed rubber Office Rubber Dir. WPB, 1943-44; mem. ruber adv. com. OPA, from 1944. Mem. Rubber Reclaimers Assn. (pres. 1954-55), Am. Chem. Soc., Mo. Athletic Club (St. Louis), Sigma Pi. Republican. Presbyterian. *

TROWBRIDGE, CALVIN D., lawyer; b. Evanston, Ill., Aug. 24, 1898; s. Cornelius and Harriet (Durand) T.; m. Lillias Webster, June 19, 1930; children: Ann (Mrs. Dwight Lawrence), Calvin D., James W. Grad., Hotchkiss Sch., Lakeville, Conn., 1916; BA, Yale U., 1920; JD, Northwestern U., 1924. Bar: Ill. 1924. Practiced in Chgo.; ptnr. firm Isham, Lincoln & Beale, from 1937; city atty. Lake Forest, Ill., 1928-45. Mem. Lake County Republican Central Com., 1923-60. Served as 2d lt., F.A., U.S. Army, 1918. Mem. ABA, Ill. Bar Assn., Chgo. Bar Assn., Attic Club (Chgo.), Onwentsia Club (Lake Forest), Delta Kappa Epsilon. *

TRUDEAU, ARTHUR GILBERT, management consultant; b. Middlebury, Vt., July 5, 1902; s. Jeremiah Charles and Mary Una (Dumas) T.; m. Helene Ruddy, Aug. 30, 1924 (dec. 1965); children: Joan Ruddy Kane, Arthur Gilbert; m. Rosalie Camalier, 1965. BS, U.S. Mil. Acad., 1924; MSCE, U. Calif., 1928; LLD (hon.), Seattle U., 1958, Middlebury Coll., 1959, U. Mich., 1960, U. Akron, 1962, Norwich U., 1962; DEng (hon.), Manhattan Coll., 1958; DSc (hon.), Pa. Mil. Coll., 1962. Commd. 2d lt. U.S. Army, 1924, advanced through grades to lt. gen., 1956; asst. adminstr. WPA, N.Y.C., 1935-36; chief of staff, engr. amphibian command, 1942-43; dep. dir. mil. tng. Army Svc. Forces, 1943-45; comdg. gen. Base X, Manila, 1945-46; chief manpower control Dept. War, 1946-48; comdg. gen. 1st Constabulary Brigade, European Command, 1948-50; dep. comdt. Army War Coll., 1950-52; comdg. gen. 1st Cav. Div., 1952-53, 7th Inf. Div., Korea, 1953, 1st Corps Korea, 1956-58; chief Army Intelligence, 1953-55; dep. chief of staff Far East and UN Command, 1955-56; chief R & D Dept. Army, 1958-62; ret., 1962; pres. Gulf Rsch. & Devel. Co., 1962-68; asst. co-chmn. bd. Rockwell Internat., 1968-72; mgmt. cons., from 1968. Contbr. numerous articles to profl. jours. Trustee Norwich U.; bd. regents Georgetown U., mem. Ctr. Strategic and Internat. Studies. Decorated D.S.M. with 2 oak leaf clusters, Silver Star with oak leaf cluster, Legion of Merit, Air medal, Bronze Star; Cordon of Ethiopia;

comdr. Order of Leopold II (Belgium); grand officer Order of Boyaca (Colombia); Order of Rising Sun, 3d class (Japan); Order of Mil. Merit, Disting. Mil. Svc. medal (Taequk) with silver star (Korea); knight comdr. Order of Sword (Sweden); UN medal; officer Knights of Malta, Knights of Holy Sepulchre. Mem. Assn. U.S. Army, Soc. Am. Mil. Engrs., U.S. Mil. Acad. Assn. Grads. (past trustee), Indsl. Rsch. Inst. (dir. emeritus), Nat. Security Indsl. Assn., U.S. Armor Assn., Am. Def. Preparedness Assn. (past pres., bd. dirs.), Dupuesne Club, Longue Vue Club, Univ. Club (N.Y.C.), Army and Navy Club (Manila, Washington), Chevy Chase Club, Rolling Rock Club. Roman Catholic. Home: Chevy Chase Md. Died June 5, 1991; buried Arlington Cemetery.

TRUEX, GEORGE ROBERT, JR., banker; b. Red Bank, N.J., May 29, 1924; s. George Robert and Elsie D. (White) T.; m. Nancy Carroll Burt, May 10, 1947 (div. 1986); children: Peter Barclay, Amy Dinsmore. A.B. in Econs., Rutgers U., 1949; LL.D. (hon.), Pacific Luth. U. Sr. v.p. Irving Trust Co., N.Y.C., 1949-66; exec. v.p. Bank of Am., San Francisco, 1966-73; vice chmn. Small Bus. Enterprises Co. (subsidiary), 1968-72; chief exec. officer Rainier Bancorp., Seattle, 1973-87, chmn. exec. com., 1987-88; dir., mem. exec. com. Nat. Airlines, Inc., Miami, Fla., 1962-80, INA Life Ins. Co. N.Y., 1965-68; dir. Security Pacific Corp., Universal Furniture Ltd., Hong Kong, Seattle br. Fed. Res. Bank San Francisco. Bd. dirs. Calif. Bankers Assn., 1969-73, Wash. State China Relations Council, 1979-83; Fin. chmn. Calif. Gov.'s Task Force on Flood Relief, 1969-73; mem. fin. advisory com. CAB, 1970-71; mem. orthopaedic council Orthopaedic Hosp., Los Angeles, 1969-72; trustee Calif. Inst. Arts, 1968-72; dir., sec.-treas., mem. exec. com. Washington Roundtable, 1983-88; bd. dirs. Walt Disney Assos. for Calif. Inst. Arts, 1972-81, San Francisco Planning and Urban Renewal Assn., 1973, East-West Ctr. Found., Hawaii; bd. dirs. Jr. Achievement So. Calif., 1967-72, pres., 1968-70, Western Regional bd. dirs., 1968-72; nat. bd. dirs. Jr. Achievement, Inc., 1968-75; bd. dirs. Jr. Achievement Greater Seattle, 1976-77; div. chmn. United Way, Inc., Los Angeles, 1970, 71; asso. gen. campaign chmn. United Way of King County, 1976, 78, gen. chmn., 1979, bd. dirs., 1979-83; bd. regents Seattle U., 1976-80; bd. dirs. Virgina Mason Hosp., from 1976, treas., from 1982; trustee Seattle U., from 1980, Bank of Am. Found., 1973; mem. adv. bd. Grad. Sch. Bus. Adminstrn., U. Wash., from 1975, chmn., 1978-80; co-chmn. fin. com. Wash. State Republican Com., from 1983. Served to capt., cav. AUS, World War II, ETO. Mem. Assn. Res. City Bankers, Seattle C. of C. (trustee 1975-78). Clubs: Bankers (San Francisco), Bohemian (San Francisco); Seattle Golf, Rainier (Seattle), Broadmoor Golf (Seattle). Home: Seattle Wash. Died Aug. 24, 1988.

TRUMPLER, PAUL ROBERT, engineering executive; b. Rahway, N.J., Nov. 3, 1914; s. William Ernst and Louise (Jelinek) T.; m. Edith M. Osterman, June 7, 1938; children: Jean Elizabeth, Allan Paul, Martin Robert. B.S. in Mech. Engring. magna cum laude, Lafayette Coll., 1936; Ph.D., Yale U., 1940. Instr. heat power engring. Ill. Inst. Tech., Chgo., 1939-41, prof. mech. engring., charge machine design, 1949-57; devel. engr. Western Electric Co., Kearny, N.J., 1941-42; heat transfer develop. engr. M.W. Kellogg Co., N.Y., 1942-47; engr. centrifugal engring. dept. Clark Bros. Co., Olean, N.Y., 1947-49; dir. Sch. Mech. Engring., U. Pa., 1957-60, prof. mech. engring., 1957-69; cons. engr. turbomachinery problems.; founder, pres. Turbo Rsch., Inc., 1961-74, Trumpler Assocs., Inc., 1974-90, Turbotherm Corp., 1974-90; pres. Turbo Rsch. Found., 1966-89. Author: Design of Film Bearings, 1966; contbr. tech. articles to profl. jours. Fellow ASME (life; chmn. heat transfer 1953); mem. Am. Soc. Engring. Edn., Phi Beta Kappa, Sigma Xi, Tau Beta Pi, Pi Tau Sigma. Presbyn. Home: West Chester Pa. Died Feb. 15, 1990; buried Bryn Mawr, Pa.

TRYON, THOMAS, author, actor; b. Hartford, Conn., Jan. 14, 1926; s. Arthur Lane and Elizabeth (Lester) T.; m. Anne Lilienthal, June 1955 (div.). B.A., Yale, 1949; studied at, Art Students League. Actor with Cape Playhouse, Dennis, Mass.; prodn. asst., CBS-TV; actor: plays Richard III, Cyrano de Bergerac, Wish You Were Here; films include The Longest Day, Moon Pilot, The Story fo Ruth, Marines, Let's Go, In Harms Way, The Glory Guys, The Cardinal; author: novel and screenplay The Other, 1971, exec. producer film, 1971; author: film Harvest Home, 1973, Lady, 1974, Crowned Heads, 1976, All That Glitters, 1986, Night of the Moonbow, 1988, Opal and Cupid, 1992, Kingdom Come: The Wings of the Morning, 1990, In the Fires of Spring, 1992, also children's novel. Served with USN, 1943-46, PTO. Recipient Prix Femina de Belgique laurel, 1964, Motion Picture Exhibitors award, 1964. Democrat. Home: Hollywood Hills Calif. Died Sept. 4, 1991; cremated.

TSEDENBAL, YUMJAAGIYN, former Mongolian government official; b. Sept. 17, 1916. Educated in, Mongolia and USSR. Tchr., dep. minister, minister of fin. Govt. of Mongolia, 1939-40; sec.-gen. cen. com. Mongolian People's Revolutionary Party, 1940-54, 1st sec., 1958-81; gen. sec. Central Com., 1981-91; chmn. State Planning Commn., 1945-48; dep. chmn. Coun. of Ministers, 1948-52, chmn., 1952-74; chmn. presidium People's Gt. Hural (head of state) of Mongolia, 1974-84. Dep. comdr.-in-chief Mongolian Army, 1941-45. Decorated Order of Lenin, Order of Kutuzov 1st class, Hero of Soviet Union, Order of Suhbaatar. Mem. Acad. of Scis. (hon.). Home: Ulan Bator Mongolian Peoples Republic Died Apr. 20, 1991.

TUBBS, TALLANT, state senator; b. San Francisco, May 8, 1897; s. Austin Chapin and Anne Tallant (Brodie) T.; m. Olivia Pillsbury Gibson, Sept. 22, 1931 (div. 1937). Ed. pvt. schs., Calif.; student, Yale U., 1917-18. Dir. Tubbs Cordage Co., San Francisco; mem. Calif. State Senate, 1925-33; Rep. nominee for U.S. Senate for Calif., 1932; mem. exec. com. Calif. State Rep. Com., 1936; appt. by Gov. of Calif. Commr. Golden Gate Internat. Expn., 1937; spl. writer San Francisco Chronicle, 1935-41. Vice chmn. Calif. Vets. for Earl Warren for Gov., 1950; vice chmn. Calif. Vets. for Eisenhower-Nixon, 1952, 56; vice chmn. Calif. Vets. for Nixon-Lodge, 1960, Calif. Vets. for Nixon for Gov., 1962. Served with U.S. Army, 1918; active duty USMC, 1942-46; capt. on staff of comdr.-in-chief Pacific Fleet, 1945. Mem. Native Sons Golden West, Am. Legion (comdr. Frederick G. Bunch Post), United Vets. of the Republic, VFW, Elks, Odd Fellows, Pacific Union Club, Univ. Club, PRess Club, San Francisco Club, Golf Club (San Francisco), Sutter Club (Sacramento), Santa Barbara Club, Valley Club of Santa Barbara, Burlingame (Calif.) Country Club, The River Club, Yale Club, Knickerbocker Club, Racquet and Tennis Club (N.Y.). Episcopalian. *

TUBBY, ROGER WELLINGTON, journalist, government administrator, educator; b. Greenwich, Conn., Dec. 30, 1910; s. George Prentiss and Frances Reynolds (Kidder) T.; m. Anne Williams, Mar. 8, 1936; children: Suzanne (Mrs. L. Batra), Jean (Mrs. R. Sherwood), Peter, Brenda (Mrs. J. Chandler). Student, Choate Sch., 1923-29; A.B., Yale U., 1933; postgrad. law sch., London Sch. Econs., 1935-36. Reporter Bennington (Vt.) Banner, 1938-40, mng. editor, 1940-42; info. specialist Bd. Econ. Warfare, 1942-44; dir. info. Fgn. Econ. Adminstrn., 1944-45, asst. to adminstr., 1945; dir. info. Office Internat. Trade, Dept. Commerce, 1945-46; press officer Dept. State, 1945-49, exec. asst. press rels., 1950; asst. press sec. White House, 1950-52; acting press sec. to Pres., Oct.-Dec. 1952, press sec., Dec. 1952; personal asst. to Democratic presdl. candidate, 1956; asst. sec. for pub. affairs Dept. State, 1961-62; ambassador U.S. rep. to European office UN, other internat. agys., Geneva, Switzerland, 1962-69; co-pub. Adirondack Daily Enterprise, Saranac Lake, N.Y., 1953-70, columnist, until 1991, Lake Placid News, 1957-70; faculty Paul Smith's (N.Y.) Coll., 1959-61, dir. devel., 1972-75; dep. commr. ops. and planning N.Y. State Dept. Parks and Recreation, 1975-77; acting dean, dean acad. rels. Fgn. Svc. Inst., Dept. State, 1969-72; adj. prof. Plattsburgh State U. Del., 1981-82; mem. Gov.'s Commn. Sports and Winter Olympics; gov.'s rep. to 1980 Winter Olympics; exec. dir. North Country Econ. Council; chmn. Olympic Accommodations Corp.; dir. Key Bank, Saranac Lake, N.Y., Champlain Valley Physicians' Hosp., Plattsburgh, N.Y., Biotechnology Corp., Lake Placid; News dir. Dem. Nat. Com., 1960; Dem. candidate for Congress from 30th N.Y. Dist., 1974. Trustee Trudeau Inst., Potsdam Coll. Found.; trustee emeritus Coll. of Atlantic, Bar Harbor, Maine; chmn. Fgn. Policy Coun., Lake Placid; pres. Adirondack North Country Assn.; bd. dirs. Adirondack Conservancy; chmn. Com. on the Adirondacks; past pres., dir. Adirondack Park Assn.; chmn. adv. com. Adirondack North Country Assn.; advisor Commn. on Adirondack in 21st Century; mem. N.Y. State Com. on Acad.-Industry Rels.; chmn. Gov.'s Tourism Adv. Coun.; mem. Gov.'s Task Force on Revitalized Area Devel. Recipient Disting. Svc. awards SUNY-Plattsburg, SUNY-Potsdam, North Country Community Coll.; named to Lake Placid Hall of Fame; Paul Harris fellow Rotary Internat. Mem. Com. on the Present Danger, Am. Fgn. Svc. Assn. Home: Saranac Lake N.Y. Died Jan. 14, 1991; interred Harriet's Town Cemetery, Saranac Lake, N.Y.

TUCKER, ALLAN, higher education educator; b. Calgary, Alta., Can., Sept. 29, 1921; came to U.S., 1946, naturalized, 1952; s. Frank and Nellie (Chester) T.; m. Rebecca Cope Kimber; children: Edwin Kimber, David Gregory. B.A., U. Toronto, Ont., Can., 1943, M.A., 1946; Ph.D., U. Mich., 1952; postgrad., U. London, Eng., summer 1955; D.Sc. (hon.), Fla. Inst. Tech., 1971. Instr. biology Mich. State U., 1946-52, asst. prof., 1952-58, assoc. prof., 1958-62, prof., 1962-64, asst. dean for advanced grad. studies, 1959-64, asst. to v.p. for research, 1959-64; vice chancellor for acad. affairs State U. System of Fla., Tallahassee, 1964-75, chmn. council acad. vice presidents, 1964-75; prof. higher edn. Fla. State U., Tallahassee, 1975-92; prof. emeritus Fla. State U., Tallahassee, 1992; dir. inst. dept. leadership Fla. State U., Tallahasee, 1976-87, dir. inst. academic leadership, 1987-92; dir. dept. leadership inst. Am. Council Edn., 1979-84; Chmn. edn. com. Fla.-Colombia Alliance, 1969-75. Author: Pigment Extraction as a Method of Quantitative Analysis of Phytoplankton, 1949, The Relation of Phytoplankton Periodicity to the Nature of the Physico-chemical Environment with special Reference to Phosphorus, 1957, Attrition of Graduate Students at the Ph.D. Level in the Traditional Arts and Sciences, 1964, Decentralized Graduate Administration with Centralized Accountability, 1965, Involvement of Statewide Governing Boards in Accreditation, 1978, Presidential Evaluation: An Academic Circus, 1979, Belling the Academic Cat, 1980, Chairing the Academic Department: Leadership Among Peers, 1981, 3d edit., 1992, Academic Freedom, Tenure and Incompetence, 1982, Solving the Teacher Education Problem: A University Wide Obligation, 1984, Queuing up for Quality: The Politics of Graduate Programming, 1985, The Academic Dean: Dove, Dragon and Diplomat, 1987, 2d edit., 1991; contbr. articles to profl. jours. Mem. exec. com. Gov.'s Commn. for Quality Edn. in, Fla., 1967; mem. panel to select NATO postdoctoral fellows in sci. Nat. Acad. Scis., 1969-71; mem. steering com. Navy Campus for Achievement, 1972-73; sci. adviser U. Ryukyus on Okinawa, 1953-55, cons. to pres., 1957-59. Recipient certificate of leadership Adult Edn. Assn. U.S.A., 1971. Mem. Council Grad. Schs. U.S. (mem. grad. edn. cost com. 1968-71), Am. Council Edn. (mem. commn. on ednl. credit 1969-76), Adult Edn. Assn. U.S.A. (mem. nat. com. on external degrees 1971-72), Nat. U. Extension Assn. (mem. nat. com. on govtl. relations 1971-74), Council on Edn. for Pub. Health (v.p. 1979), Am. Assn. Higher Edn., Sigma Xi. Home: Tallahassee Fla. Died Mar. 4, 1992; buried Oakland Cemetery, Tallahassee, Fla.

TUCKER, LEM (LEMUEL TUCKER), journalist; b. Saginaw, Mich., May 26, 1938; s. Stewart Edward and Missouri (Ward) T.; m. Renay Rosenblum, July 24, 1987; 1 child, Linn Carol. B.A. in Polit. Sci, Central Mich. U., 1960, D. Pub. Service, 1981. Copy boy, adminstr. Viet Nam Bur.; reporter WNBC-TV; reporter network TV news NBC News, 1965-70; TV news dir. WOR-TV, 1970-71; reporter ABC News, N.Y.C., 1972-77, CBS News, Washington, 1977-88; cons. Ford Found., 1970. Founding mem. Reporters Com. for Freedom of Press., Asst. to auditor gen. of, Mich., 1960. Served to 1st lt. AUS, 1961-62. Recipient Emmy award for series of news stories on hunger in Am., 1968-69, for 3-part series on black Am., CBS Evening News, 1984. Mem. AFTRA. Home: Washington D.C. Died Mar. 2, 1991; cremated.

TUEMMLER, WILLIAM BRUCE, chemical company executive; b. Flushing, N.Y., Dec. 27, 1927; s. Frederick William and Marian (Major) T.; m. Josephine Marie Briggs, Apr. 6, 1950 (div. 1978); m. Pauline Marie Caron, Dec. 28, 1978. BS in Chemistry, U. Md., 1950, PhD in Organic Chemistry, 1953. Research chemist Monsanto, Dayton, Ohio, 1953-55; research chemist FMC, Balt., 1955-57, group leader, 1957-63, asst. dir. research and devel., 1963-68, dir. research and devel. organic chem. div., 1969-73; product mgr., orgn. intermediary FMC, N.Y.C., 1968-69; dir. research and devel. indsl. chem. group FMC, Princeton, N.J., 1973-77; v.p. research and devel. Occidental Chem. Corp., Irvine, Calif. and Grand Island, N.Y., 1977-84; sr. v.p. and tech. dir., mem. policy and planning coun. Pennwalt Corp., King of Prussia, Pa., 1984-89; co. rep. to Indsl. Rsch. Inst., Coun. for Chem. Rsch. Patentee in field. Mem. Am. Chem. Assn., Indsl. Research Inst., Council for Chem. Research, Great Valley Assn. (bd. dirs. 1986-89). Republican. Roman Catholic. Home: Malvern Pa. Died Sept. 7, 1989.

TUFTS, ELEANOR MAY, art historian, educator; b. Exeter, N.H., Feb. 1, 1927; d. James Arthur and Hazel (Weinbeck) T. B.S., Simmons Coll., 1949; M.A., Harvard U., 1957; Ph.D., N.Y. U., 1971. Sec. Harvard U., 1949-50; exec. sec. Boston U. travel courses, 1950-56; dir. program devel. Council on Internat. Ednl. Exchange, N.Y.C., 1957-60; assoc. sec. World U. Service, N.Y.C., 1960-64; asst. prof. art history U. Bridgeport, 1964-66; assoc. prof. So. Conn. State Coll., New Haven, 1966-74; prof. So. Meth. U., Dallas, 1974-91, chmn. div. fine arts, 1974-78, pres. Faculty Senate, 1980-81. Author: Our Hidden Heritage: Five Centuries of Women Artists, 1974, American Women Artists: A Selected Bibliographic Guide, Vol. I, 1984, Vol. II, 1989, Luis Meléndez: Spanish Still Life Painter of the Eighteenth Century, 1985; (with others) World Impressionism, 1990; organizer Meléndez exhbn. NAD, N.Y.C., 1985. Trustee Dallas Mus. Fine Arts, 1975-80. NEH grantee, summer 1974; NEH travel grantee, summer 1984; recipient Outstanding Achievement in Art History award Women's Caucus for Art, 1985, Women Helping Women award, 1986, Dallas Women's Ctr., Alumnae Achievement award Simmons Coll., 1989; Eleanor Tufts Disting. Vis. Professorship in Art History created in her honor at So. Meth. U., 1991. Mem. AAUP (v.p. 1972-74, 75-76), Coll. Art Assn. (nat. bd. 1979-83), Am. Soc. Hispanic Art Hist. Studies, Renaissance Soc. Am., Midwest Art History Soc. (bd. dirs. 1983-86), Hispanic Soc. Am. Democrat. Club: Town and Gown (pres. 1982-83). Home: Dallas Tex. Died Dec. 2, 1991; buried Sparkman-Hillcrest Cemetary, Dallas.

TUITE, JOHN FRANCIS, plant pathologist; b. Bronx, N.Y., Nov. 23, 1927; s. Patrick and Fanny (Donohue) T.; m. Camille Maloof, July 5, 1952; children—Kathy, Frances, Brian, Ann, Paul, Clare. B.A., Hunter Coll., 1951; M.S., U. Minn., 1953, Ph.D., 1956. Asst. prof. plant pathology Purdue U., West Lafayette, Ind., 1956-60, assoc. prof., 1961-69, prof., 1970-91. Author: Plant Pathological Methods: Fungi and Bacteria, 1969, (with Stroshine, Foster and Baker) Grain Drying and Storage

Self-Study Guide, 1984, Laboratory Exercises in Methods in Plant Pathology—Fungi and Bacteria, 1988, (with Frank Cantone) Teacher's Supplement, 1990. Served with U.S. Army, 1946-47. Mem. Am. Phytopath. Soc. (pres. North Central br.), Mycol. Soc. Am., Soc. Indsl. Microbiology, Sigma Xi. Roman Catholic. Home: West Lafayette Ind. Died July 7, 1991; buried St. Boniface Cemetery, Lafayette, Ind.

TULLIO, LOUIS JOSEPH, mayor; b. Erie, May 17, 1917; s. Anthony and Ersilia (Nardone) T.; B.S., Holy Cross Coll., 1939; M.Ed., Boston U., 1957; m. Mary Cecelia McHale, June 21, 1941; children: Betty Ann (Mrs. Elswerth), June Cecelia (Mrs. Geisler), Marilyn Lou. Former high sch. tchr., asst. to pres. Gannon Coll.; asst. dir. health and phys. edn. Erie City Sch. Dist., 1957-60, sec., bus. mgr., 1960-65; mem. exec. com. Erie County Democratic Com.; mayor City of Erie, 1966-90. Bd. dirs. Harborcreek Sch. for Boys, Little Gridders of Erie, Booker T. Washington Center; trustee Erie Library and Mus. Served to lt. USNR, 1943-45. Recipient Profl. Honor award Pa. Health, Phys. Edn. and Recreation; named All-Am. Coach of Year. Roman Catholic. Died Apr. 17, 1990. Home: Erie Pa. †

TUMULTY, PHILIP ANTHONY, internal medicine educator; b. Jersey City, Nov. 4, 1912; s. Joseph Patrick and Mary Alicia (Byrne) T.; m. Claire Cotter, Jan. 24, 1942; children: Claire, Philip, Cathy, Mary, Alicia. AB cum laude, Georgetown U., 1935; MD, Johns Hopkins U., 1940. Diplomate Am. Bd. Internal Medicine. Intern, then asst. resident in medicine Johns Hopkins Hosp., Balt., 1940-42, 45-46, resident physician, instr. medicine, 1946-49, asst. dir. med. clinics, then dir., 1948-53, physician-in-charge med.-surg. group clinic, 1948-53, chmn. pvt. med. svc., from 1953, physician-in-charge pvt. patient clinic, from 1956; prof., dir. dept. medicine St. Louis U. Sch. Medicine, 1953-54; asst. prof., then assoc. prof. medicine Johns Hopkins U. Sch. Medicine, 1949-53, 55-63, prof., from 1963, David J. Carver prof., from 1974; lectr. medicine Harvard Med. Sch., 1967; James Howard Means vis. physician Mass. Gen. Hosp.; physician-in-chief pro tem dept. medicine R.I. Hosp., 1957; cons. physician Balt. City Hosp.; spl. cons. in medicine NIH; cons. in medicine USPHS, VA Hosp., Balt., Walter Reed Gen. Hosp.; lectr. medicine Nat. Naval Med. Ctr., Bethesda, Md. Officer M.C., U.S. Army, 1942-45. Clin. fellow ACP, 1947-48. Mem. Am. Clin. and Climatol. Assn., Assn. Am. Physicians, Phi Beta Kappa, Alpha Omega Alpha. Home: Baltimore Md. Died Sept. 14, 1989; buried St. Mary's Cemetery, Rockville, Md.

TURCOTTE, LAWSON PHILLIPPE, pulp producer; b. Grand Mere, Que., Can., Dec. 11, 1896; s. Alex and Mary Elizabeth (Kelly) T.; m. Eva A. Pearson, Sept. 26, 1923; 1 son, Donald L. Student, Sacred Heart Coll., Grand Mere, Gabutt Bus. Coll., Lethbridge, Alta., Can., 1912-13. Acct. Stacey Lumber Co., Lethbridge, 1913-15; sec.-treas. War Vets. Assn., 1919-25; with Puget Sound Pulp & Timber Co. (merged into Ga. Pacific Corp), Bellingham, Wash., from 1926; successively sec.-treas., exec. v.p., pres. Puget Sound Pulp & Timber Co. (merged into Ga. Pacific Corp), Bellingham, 1951-63; v.p., dir. Ga. Pacific Corp., from 1963; pres. Ketchikan Pulp Co., Alaska, from 1951; dir. Van West Logging Co., Vancouver, B.C., Can., Am. Mail Lines, Seattle, Anglo-Canadian Timber Products Co., Vancouver, Eureka Sawmills Ltd., Vancouver. Pres. St. Luke's Hosp., Bellingham. Served as sgt. Can. Army, 1915-19. Mem. NAM (dir.), U.S. Pulp Producers Assn. (dir.). *

TURK, LEONARD GERALD, machinery manufacturer; b. Rochester, N.Y., July 10, 1916; s. Benjamin and Pauline (Alder) T.; m. Jayne Kaylor, June 20, 1942; children: James L., Thomas A., William R. B.S., Carnegie Inst. Tech., 1939. Registered profl. engr., Ohio. With NRM Corp., Akron, Ohio, 1946-48; owner home constrn. bus., 1948-55; asst. v.p. rubber machinery div. NRM Corp., 1955-62, v.p., gen. mgr., 1962-65, pres., chief exec. officer, 1965-76, chmn. bd., 1976-81. Mem. Soc. Plastics Industry, Akron Rubber Group, Akron Council Engring. and Sci. Socs., Machinery and Allied Products Inst., Akron C. of C., Portage Country Club, Akron City Club, Rotary. Episcopalian. Home: West Palm Beach Fla. Died Nov. 13, 1988.

TURNBULL, DOUGLAS TAYLOR, iron company executive; b. Lobo, Ont., Can., Jan. 5, 1895; came to U.S., 1922, naturalized, 1940; s. John and Anne (Douglas) T.; m. Grace Risley, Oct. 15, 1918; children: Eric W., Donald C.; m. 2d, Elizabeth Jackson, Aug. 8, 1939. Ed. high sch. Clk. Bell Telephone Co. of Can., 1914-15; acct., asst. auditor Semet-Solvay Co., 1919-33; successively asst. auditor, treas. Woodward (Ala.) Iron Co., 1933-40, sec., from 1949, v.p., from 1958. Served to lt. RAF, 1915-18. Mem. Birmingham C. of C. *

TURNER, DARWIN THEODORE TROY, English educator; b. Cin., May 7, 1931; s. Darwin R. and Laura (Knight) T.; m. Maggie Jean Lewis; children: Pamela, Darwin K., Rachon. BA, U. Cin., 1947, MA, 1949; PhD, U. Chgo., 1956; LittD, U. Cin., 1983. Asst. prof. English Morgan State Coll., Balt., 1952-57; prof., chmn. English dept. Fla. A&M State U., Tallahassee, 1957-59; prof., chmn. English dept. N.C. A&T State U., Greensboro, 1959-66, dean grad. sch., 1966-70; vis. prof. English U. Wis., 1969; prof. English U. Mich., Ann Arbor, 1970-71; vis. prof. U. Hawaii, summer 1971; prof. English U. Iowa, Iowa City, 1971-81, U. Iowa Found. Disting. prof. English and Afro-Am. Studies, 1981-91, head African-Am. world studies, 1972-91; mem. exec. com. Conf. on Coll. Composition and Communication, 1967-69; cons. in English and Afro-Am. studies for high schs., colls., pvt. founds., fed. agys., profl. socs.; mem. grad. record exams. bd., 1970-73; state chmn., mem. regional exec. com. 2d World Festival Black and African Arts and Culture, 1973-77; chmn. Iowa Colls. and Univs. Consortium for Teaching Afro-Am. Culture. Author: (poems) Katharsis, 1964; Hawthorne's Scarlet Letter, 1967, In a Minor Chord, 1971; co-author Theory and Practice in the Teaching of Literature by Afro-Americans, 1971; editor: Black American Literature: Essays, Fiction, Poetry, 3 vols., 1969, Black American Literature, combined edit., 1970, Black Drama in America—an Anthology, 1971, The Wayward and the Seeking: Selected Writings by Jean Toomer, 1980, Cane by Jean Toomer, Norton Critical Ed., 1988; co-editor: Images of the Negro in America, 1965, Voices from the Black Experience: African and Afro-American Literature, 1972, Responding—Five, 1973, The Art of Slave Narrative, 1983; compiler: a Bibliography of Afro-American Writers, 1970; contbg. editor: CLA Jour.; adv. editor: Am. Lit., 1978-80, Black Scholar, 1983—, Hampton Jour. of Ethnic Studies, 1985—, Obsidian II, 1987—, Explorations in Ethnic Studies, 1987-88. Mem. Guilford County Bicentennial Commn., 1969-70; trustee Nat. Humanities Ctr., 1978-89, trustee emeritus 1989—; mem. Rockefeller Commn. on the Humanities, 1978-80; del. African Regional Am. Studies Conf., Ivory Coast, 1976, 2d World Festival African Arts and Culture, Nigeria, 1977; bd. dirs. Iowa Humanities Bd., 1982-90, pres.-elect 1986-87, pres. 1987-88; bd. dirs. Fedn. State Humanities Councils, 1987-90. Recipient Profl. Achievement award U. Chgo. Alumni Assn., 1972, Disting. Alumnus award U. Cinn., 1982, Disting. Writer award Mid. Atlantic Writers Assn., 1986, Equiano Disting. Achievement award U. Utah Ethnic Studies, 1989, Disting. Scholar-Tchr. award Nat. Coun. Tchrs. English Black Caucus, 1989; Am. Council Learned Socs. grantee, 1965, 78; fellow Duke-N.C. Univs. Humanities Program, 1965-66; Rockefeller Found. grantee, 1972. Mem. MLA (chmn. com. on edn. of minority groups 1970-72, del. assembly 1974-77, chmn. ethnic studies div. 1978-80, chmn. so. lit. discussion group, 1985, exec. com. div. of Black Am. lit. and culture 1985-91), Coll. Lang. Assn. (pres. 1963-65), N.C.-Va. Coll. English Assn. (pres. 1964-65), Nat. Assn. Black Profls., Nat. Humanities Faculty, Nat. Council Tchrs. English (chmn. com. on lit. minority groups 1969-79, dir.-at-large 1967-70, trustee research found. 1970-73, chmn. resolutions com. 1972, dir. commn. on lit. 1982-85), Nat. Council Black Studies (exec. com. 1976-78), Coll. English Assn. (dir. 1971-74), Am. Studies Assn., AAUP (com. A. 1977-80), Am. Assn. Advancement Humanities (dir. 1981-83), Phi Beta Kappa (senate united chpts. 1985-91, trustee found. united chpts. 1988-91), Alpha Phi Alpha, Theta Alpha Phi, Lambda Iota Tau. Home: Iowa City Iowa Died Feb. 11, 1991; buried Cin.

TURNER, JUSTIN GEORGE, lawyer, investment executive; b. Chgo., Nov. 5, 1898; s. Oscar and Bessie (Tazxey) T.; m. Gertrude Levin, July 27, 1932; children: Paul, Barbara. Student, U. Chgo., 1916-18; LLB, DePaul U., 1920; LLD, Lincoln Coll., 1956; LHD (hon.), U. Judaism, 1960. Bar: Ill. Ptnr. law firm Turner & Turner, Chgo., 1921-43; ptnr. Town Investments, Chgo. and L.A., 1932-50, Turner Investments, L.A., from 1950; pres. Pickwick Realty & Investment Co.; manuscript cons. UCLA Libr.; v.p. Nat. Lincoln Civil War Coun.; chmn. libr. com. U. Judaism, L.A. Mem. editorial bd. or publ. com. Hist. Soc. So. Calif., America: History and Life, Lincoln Sesquicentannial Assn.; contbr. articles to hist. jours. Bd. dirs. Sci. and History Alliance of Los Angeles County Mus.; mem. Friends of Librs., U. So. Calif.; bd. dirs. Calif. Sch. Hebrew Union Coll.-Jewish Inst. Religion; fellow pierpont Morgan Libr., N.Y.; trustee Nat. Found. Jewish Culture, Jewish Publ. Soc. Served with U.S. Army, 1918. Recipient Lincoln diploma of honor Lincoln Meml. U., 1962. Mem. Am. Hist. Assn., Miss. Valley Hist. Assn., Hist. Soc. So. Calif. (pres.), Ill. Hist. Soc., Pacific Coast Hist. Soc., Soc. Am. Archivists, Am. Assn. State and Local History, Mus. Assn., S.W. Mus., Book Club Calif., Renaissance Soc. Am., Keats-Shelley Soc., MLA, Am. Studies Asns., Masons, Shriners, B'nai B'rith (prs. Chgo. coun.), Hillcrest Country Club, Tamarisk Country Club, Grolier Club, Lotos Club, Racquet Club (Palm Springs, Calif.). *

TUTT, WILLIAM THAYER, hotel and investment executive; b. Coronado, Calif., Mar. 2, 1912; s. Charles L. and Eleanor (Armit) T.; m. Yvonne S. McGowan, Jan. 6, 1978; 1 child, Margaret Eleanor (Mrs. McColl.). Student, Denver U. Bus. Sch., bus. coll. With Colo. Title & Trust, 1930-32; mgr. Manitou Mineral Water Co., 1932-35; pres., dir.; mgr. Manitou Mineral Water & Sales Co., 1932-35; pres. Gen. Liquors, 1935-38; partner Boettcher & Co., 1938-42; hon. chmn. bd. dirs. Broadmoor Hotel, Inc. Hon. dir. Mountain States Tel. & Tel. Co., Broadmoor Hotel; chmn. bd. Air Force Acad. Found., Sunnyrest Sanatorium; trustee El Pomar Found.; trustee emeritus Lovelace Found.; bd. dirs., exec. com. U.S. Olympic Com. Served to lt. col. AUS, 1942-46. Decorated Legion of Merit, Officer dans l'Ordre du Merite Touristique French Govt., Olympic Order; Grand Insignia for Merits for Republic Austria; named to Nat. Cowboy Hall of Fame, Colo. Sports Hall Fame, U.S. Hockey Hall Fame, Can. Hockey Hall of Fame, Colo. Golf Hall of Fame; recipient Am. Acad. Achievement Golden Plate award. Mem. Internat. Ice Hockey Fedn. (1st v.p., hon. pres.), Amateur Hockey Assn. U.S. (pres. emeritus, dir.). Republican. Clubs: Broadmoor Golf (pres., dir.), Cheyenne Mountain Country, Garden of the Gods, Cooking Club (pres., trustee), Wigwam, Country Club of Colo. Home: Colorado Springs Colo. Died Feb., 1989.

TUTTLE, HOLMES PAUL, automobile dealer; b. Tuttle, Okla., June 17, 1905; s. James Bond and Carrie (Campbell) T.; m. Virginia Harris, Aug. 7, 1934; children: Sally Tuttle Mogan, Robert Holmes. With Ford Motor Co., 1922-89; pres., dir. Holmes Tuttle Enterprises, Inc.; founder, dir. Community Banks L.A.; dir. mem. exec. com. Dart Industries, Inc.; dir. mem. audit com. TWA, Inc. Del. Rep. Nat. Conv., 1964-68; one of the founders of Harvey Mudd Coll., Claremont, Calif.; assoc. U. So. Calif., Stanford Bus. Sch. Mem. L.A. Country Club, Calif. Club, Eldorado Country Club (Palm Desert, Calif.). Home: Los Angeles Calif. Died June 16, 1989.

TWOMBLY, GRAY HUNTINGTON, gynecologist, consultant; b. Newton, Mass., Apr. 27, 1905; s. Clifford Gray and Edith (Balch) T.; m. Mary Forester Field, Mar. 22, 1934 (dec. Jan. 10, 1989); children: Robert Gray, Helen Field Twombly Watkins, Edith Balch Twombly Eddy; m. Margaret Olmsted Ford, Oct. 28, 1989. A.B., Franklin & Marshall Coll., 1925, Sc.D. hon., 1949; M.D., Harvard U., 1929. Diplomate Am. Bd. Surgery; Am. Bd. Ob-Gyn. Surg. intern Mass. Gen. Hosp., Boston, 1930-32; asst. resident Free Hosp. for Women, Brookline, Mass., 1932; intern, fellow, resident Meml. Hosp., N.Y.C., 1933-37; clin. asst., asst. surgeon Meml Hosp., N.Y.C., 1937-48; asst. prof. cancer research Columbia U., N.Y.C., 1942-48, asst. prof. ob-gyn, 1948-54; prof. gynecology Sch. Medicine, NYU, N.Y.C., 1954-73; asst. attending gynecologist Delafield Hosp., N.Y.C., 1950-54; vis. gynecologist Bellevue Hosp., N.Y.C., 1954-81; assoc. dir. gynecology Univ. Hosp., N.Y.C., 1954-70; cons. hosps. in N.Y., N.J., Conn., 1937-81. Contbr. articles to profl. jours., chpts. to books. Mem. Bd. deacons Riverside Ch., N.Y.C., 1946-56; mem., clk. Chocorua Chapel Assn., Squam Lake, N.H., 1967-81; mem., pres. Tramp & Trail Club of N.Y., N.Y., 1935-81; mem. adv. com. Planned Parenthood; founding mem., pres. Manhattanville Neighborhood Center, N.Y.C., 1946-48. Fellow Am. Gynecol. Soc., Am. Radium Soc. (v.p. 1959-61), Soc. Pelvic Surgeons (pres. 1971); mem. Am. Cancer Soc. (pres. N.Y.C. div. 1964-66 Disting. Service award), Am Cancer Soc. (life), N.Y. Cancer Soc. (pres. 1955-56), Phi Beta Kappa, Alpha Omega Alpha. Republican. Club: Century Assn. Home: Bloomfield Conn. Died May 24, 1992; interred Trinity Cemetery, Holderness, N.H.

TWYMAN, JOSEPH PASCHAL, university president; b. Prairie Hill, Mo., Nov. 21, 1933; s. William L. and Hazel (Dry) T.; m. Patricia Joanne Harper, July 26, 1953; children—Mark Kevin, Patricia Lynn. B.A., U. Mo. at Kansas City, 1955, M.A., 1959, Ph.D., 1962. Asst. prof., then asso. prof. Okla. State U., 1960-66; asso. dir. Okla. State U. (Research Found.), 1965-66; dir. research U. Mo. at St. Louis, 1966-67; v.p. U. Tulsa, 1967-68, pres., 1968-89; cons. in field, from 1960; bd. dirs. Sooner Fed. Savs. & Loan Assn., Atlas Life Ins. Co., Western Venture Capital Corp. Author: (with others) The Concept of Role Conflict, 1964; also articles. Mem. adv. panel Southwestern Coop. Ednl. Lab., 1967-68; adv. council Okla. Lung Research and Devel. Council, 1970-78; scholarship com. Skelly Oil Co., 1968-72, Marathon Oil Co., 1970-73, Gulf Oil, 1981-82, Conoco Co., 1981-87; pres. Okla. Ind. Coll. Found., 1971-74; Adv. bd. Salvation Army, from 1972, Tulsa Opera, 1968-77, St. John's Hosp., Tulsa, 1969-76; acting chmn. Tulsa Area Health Edn. Center, 1977-79; bd. dirs. Goodwill Industries, Tulsa, 1975-82, Okla Council Econ. Edn., 1968-89, Tulsa Area United Way, 1968-77, Tulsa Civic Ballet, 1968-78, Arts and Humanities Council, Tulsa, 1970-77, Thomas Gilcrease Mus. Assn., 1970-85; mem. Okla. Council Sci. and Tech.; trustee Undercroft Montessori Sch., Tulsa, 1967-72, Children's Med. Center, 1968-73, Hillcrest Med. Center, 1969-80, 81—; mem. exec. com. Okla.'s Future, Inc., from 1968; bd. dirs. Tulsa Mental Health Assn., 1967-74, 75-78, 80-85, Mid-Continent Research and Devel. Council, 1967-69; mem. commn. on instns. of higher edn. North Central Assn. Colls. and Schs., 1975-89; trustee Tech. Edn. Research Center, Inc., Cambridge, Mass., from 1977; mem. Okla. Higher Edn. Task Force, 1986-89, Met. Tulsa Econ. Devel. Found., 1987-89; pres. Tulsa Global Trade Found., from 1986. Grantee Ford Found., 1963-66, U.S. Office Edn., 1958-60, 61-62, 62-63, 64-66. Mem. AAAS, Am. Acad. Polit. and Social Sci., Young Pres.'s Orgn., Okla. Cattlemen's Assn., Internat. Brangus Breeders Assn., Okla. Brangus Breeders Assn., Phi Delta Kappa, Omicron Delta Kappa. Presbyn. Clubs: Tulsa, So. Hills, University, Summit (Tulsa). Home: Tulsa Okla.

TYLER, C(ARROLL) L(ESLIE), government official; b. Waterville, Maine, Feb. 23, 1898; s. Harry and Anna (Ford) T.; m. Harmon Spruance; m. 2d, Elaine Theresa Whitside, 1928; m. 3d, Margaret Sallee, 1953. Ed.,

Phillips Exeter Acad., 1916; grad., U.S. Naval Acad., 1920. Mgr. Santa Fe ops. office AEC, 1947-54; gen. mgr. USAF Acad. project for Skidmore Owings & Merrill Architects, 1954-58; v.p., project mgr. Reynolds Elec. and Engring. Co., from 1958. Served from ensign to capt. USN, 1920-47; asst. dir., then dir. R&D div. Bur. of Ordnance, U.S. Navy, 1942-45; spl. asst. to Vannevar Bush, chmn. Office of Sci. R&D, in charge project which developed proximity fuse; ret. U.S. Navy, 1947. Decorated Legion of Merit; Order Brit. Empire. Mem. Army and Navy Club (Washington). *

UHLMANN, RICHARD FREDERICK, grain trader; b. Chgo., May 21, 1898; s. Fred and Hattie (Abt) U.; m. Rosamond Goldman, Jan. 3, 1925; children: Janis Uhlmann Weil, Frederick G., Audrey Uhlmann Rosenheim. AB, Cornell U., 1919. Formerly with Jackson Bros. & Co., Lafayette, Ind.; chmn. bd., bd. dirs. Uhlmann Grain Co., Chgo.; bd. dirs. Chgo. Aerial Industries, Inc., Barrington, Ill.; pres. Chgo. Bd. Trade, 1948-49. Assoc. Northwestern U. Mem. Standard Club (Chgo.), Execs. Club (Chgo.), Lake Shore Country Club (Glencoe, Ill.). Republican. Jewish. Home: Highland Park Ill. Died Nov. 9, 1989; buried Rosehill Cemetery, Chgo.

ULFELDER, HOWARD, physician, educator; b. Mexico City, Aug. 15, 1911; s. Sidney and Ethel May (Housel) U.; m. Ethel Louise Huse, Aug. 18, 1932; children: Howard, John Carleton, William Harrison, Thomas Huse. Grad., Phillips Exeter Acad., 1928; AB cum laude, Harvard U., 1932, MD, 1936. Diplomate Am. Bd Gynecology, Am. Bd. Surgery. Surg. intern Mass. Gen. Hosp., Boston, 1937-39, surg. resident E. svc., 1939-41, chief gynecol. svc., 1955-76, vis. surgeon, 1955-90, dep. to dir. for cancer affairs, 1973-90; mem. faculty Harvard Med. Sch., Boston, 1940-90, clin. prof. gynecology, 1955-62, Joe V. Meigs prof. gynecology, 1962-90; chief staff Vincent Meml. Hosp. Harvard Med. Sch., 1955-76; gynecologist Pondville State Hosp., Norfolk, Mass., 1946-90; cons. gynecologist Royal Prince Alfred Hosp., Syndey Australia, Boston Lying-In Hosp., Mass. Eye and Ear Infirmary; McIlrath vis. prof. Royal Prince Alfred Hosp., 1961; mem. Cancer Rsch. Ctr. rev. com. Nat. Cancer Inst., 1971-75; dir. Westgate Corp., Va. Co-author: An Atlas of Pelvic Operations, 1953-68; author profl. papers, chpts. textbooks. Bd. dirs. Mass. div. Am. Cancer Soc., Winchester Hosp.; mem. corp. United South End Settlements Boston; pres. Children's Art Ctr., 1969-71. Lt. co. med. corps AUS, 1942-45. Fellow AMA, ACS (bd. govs. 1959-62, 66-73), N.J. Pitts. obstet. and gynecol. socs. (hon.); mem. Kansas City Gynecol. Soc. (hon.), Miami, Honolulu obstet. and gynecol. socs. (hon.), Mass. Med. Soc., Obstet. Soc. Boston (pres. 1960-61), Eastern, Boston, Spanish surg. socs., Soc. Univ. Surgeon, Soc. Pelvic Surgeons (founder, pres. 1958-59), Am. Soc. surg. assns., AAAS, Soc. Gynecologic Oncologists, Halsted Soc., New Eng. Cancer Soc. (pres. 1975-76), Mass. Med. Benevolent Soc., numerous others. Home: Duxbury Mass. Died Apr. 29, 1990; buried Darbury, Mass.

ULLSTROM, L. BERWYN, lawyer; b. Memphis, Nebr., Sept. 18, 1919; s. LeRoy and Myrtle Estella (Parrish) U.; m. Loine Evelyn Sloan, Sept. 11, 1942; children: Linda Louise Dixon, Jeanne Ann Cook, Bruce Richard. Student, Scottsbluff Coll., 1937-40; B.S., U. Mich., 1946; LL.B., U. Denver, 1948. Bar: Colo. 1948, U.S. Supreme Ct 1954; Licensed comml. pilot. Practice in Denver, 1948-51; instr. aviation law and legal subjects U. Denver, 1948-51; trial atty. CAA, 1951-54; asso. gen. counsel FCDA, 1954-56, dep. exec. asst. adminstr., 1956-58; observer Operation Redwing, Joint Task Force 7 Pacific Thermonuclear Bomb Drop Test, 1956; exec. asst. dir. Office Civil and Def. Mblzn., Exec. Office Pres., 1958-61; cons. Dept. Def., 1961; pvt. practice law Denver, 1961-89. Served to comdr., aviation USNR, 1941-45; mem. Res. Ret. Mem. ABA, Colo. Bar Assn., Denver Bar Assn., Lawyer-Pilots Bar Assn. (v.p. Rocky Mountain region chpt. 1982-86), Am., Colo. Trial lawyers assns., Nat. Transp. Safety Bd. Bar Assn. (Northwest mountain regional v.p.), Internat. Soc. Air Safety Investigators (pres. Rocky Mountain regional chpt. 1984-86), Aircraft Owners and Pilots Assn., Phi Delta Phi. Home: Golden Colo. Died July 24, 1989; buried Crown Hill Cemetery, Lakewood, Colo.

ULRICH, EDWARD HUBER, publishing executive; b. Indpls., July 11, 1897; s. Tomey Douglas and Ida Alice (Hildebrandt) U.; m. Ruth B. Crispin, Dec. 6, 1924; children: E. Huber, Janice (Mrs. David Reeves). Student, Purdue U., 1917-18; BS, U. Pa., 1922. Asst. sec. Comml. Banking Corp., 1922-24; sales exec. circulation dept. Curtis Pub. Co., Phila., 1925-33, sales promotion mgr., 1934-41, asst. to pres., 1942-54, dir. pub. rels., 1945-64, v.p., 1955-58, sr. v.p., circulation dir., 1958-62; pres., dir. Curtis Circulation Co., 1958-62, chmn. bd., chief exec. officer, 1962; dir. Bantam Books, Inc., Vacuum Concrete Corp. Am., Nat. Mag. Svc. Co. Inc., Transworld Pub. Co. Inc., Keystone Readers Svc. Inc., London, Treasure Books Inc., Wonder Books Inc. Chmn. pub. rels. Phila. Community Chest, 1951-53; pub. rels. ofcl. United Fund Phila., 1953-56. Mem. AIM, Pub. Rels. Soc. Am. (dir. 1952-53), Am. Acad. Polit. and Social Sci., Pa. C. of C. (dir. 1958-62), Phila. Com. of 70, Masons, Down Town Club (dir., pres. 1958-62), Columbia Country Club (Chevy Chase, Md.), Seaview Country Club (Absecon, N.J.), Sigma Delta Chi, Kappa Sigma. Republican. Presbyterian. *

UMSTATTD, JAMES GREENLEAF, education educator; b. Paris, Mo., Feb. 26, 1896; s. James Thomas and Mary Helena (Greenleaf) U.; m. Martha Ethel McNutt, Dec. 26, 1918; children: James McNutt, Robert Greenleaf. BS in Edn., U. Mo., 1918, MA, 1924; PhD, U. Minn., 1930; DLitt (hon.), U. Bordeaux, 1946. Tchr. Stone Sch., Marion County, Mo., 1913-15, grade, jr. and high schs., Moberly, Mo., 1915-18; supt. schs., prin. high sch. Matoaka, W.Va., 1919-24; from asst. supt. to supt. schs. Beckley, W.Va., 1924-28; extension staff in edn. Concord State Tchrs. Coll., Athens, W.Va., 1921-24; asst. in secondary edn. Coll. of Edn., U. Minn., 1928-29, from instr. to asst. prof., 1929-36; assoc. prof. secondary edn. Wayne U., Detroit, 1936-38; gen. supr. secondary edn. Detroit Pub. Schs., 1936-38; prof. secondary edn. U. Tex., from 1938; chmn. dept. curriculum and instrn., 1939-59; edn. chief Biarritz (France) Am. U., 1945, dean and acad. adviser, 1946; vis. prof. U. W.Va., 1935, U.S.D., 1936, U. Minn., 1941, 44, 47-49, Duke U., 1950, Harvard U., 1951, U. So. Calif., 1952, U. Maine, 1956, Rice U., 1965, others; coord. Tex. Study Secondary Edn., from 1942. Author books in field. Served with USN, 1918-19. Recipient Outstanding Achievement award U. Minn., 1952, Teaching Excellence awrd U. Tex., 1963. Fellow AAAS, Royal Soc. Arts; mem. AAUP, NEA, Am. Ednl. Rsch. Assn., Am. Assn. Sch. Adminstrs. (dept. secondary sch. prins.), Nat. Inst. Tchr. Placement Assocs. (pres.), Nat. Soc. Coll. Tchrs. Edn. (pres.), Nat. Soc. Study Edn., Tex. Assn. Sch. Adminstrs., Tex. Assn. Secondary Sch. Prins., Tex. State Tchrs. Assn., Masons, Rotary, Phi Delta Kappa. Democrat. Methodist. *

UPTEGROVE, DEANE, artist; b. N.Y.C., Jan. 3, 1896; s. Jerome Pierson and Florence van Maie (Palmer) U.; m. Margaret Hamilton Howard, Mar. 9, 1918; children: Deane, Neil. Grad., Newark Acad. Reporter, feature writer Newark Evening News, 1915-17, N.Y. Evening Post, 1919-23; advt. agy. writer Alley & Richards, Inc., N.Y.C., 1951-59, pres., dir., 1957-59; sr. v.p., chmn. creative bd. Reach, McClinton & Co., 1959-60; engaged in landscape painting, advt. art cons., from 1960. Painter, works exhibited in Md., Boston, N.Y.C., No. N.J.; author sect. Advt. Art, Handbook of Advt.; author articles on art and advt. Chmn. N.J. Historic Sites Com.; vice chmn. Sussex County (N.J.) Art Com.; mem. Essex County Rep. Com., 1923-44. Served as lt. (j.g.) USN, World War I. Recipient awards for layout and design Art Dirs. Club, Gold medal for package design Nat. Packaging Soc. Mem. Nat. Soc. Art Dirs. (v.p.), Am. Assn. Advt. Agys. (chmn. art com.), Pocono Mountain Art Group, Tri-State Artists, Salmagundi Club, N.Y. Art Dirs. Club (pres.). *

URBACH, EPHRAIM ELIMELECH, rabbi, historian, educator, academic administrator; b. Wloclawek, Poland, May 25, 1912; s. Israel Joseph and Haya Esther (Spiegel) U.; student Jewish Theol. Sem., Breslau, Poland and U. Breslau, 1930; D. Litt., U. Rome, 1936; Ph.D. (hon.), Weizmann Inst. Sci., Rehovot, Israel, 1980, Ben-Gurion U. of Negev, 1984; D.H.L. (hon.), Jewish Theol. Sem. N.Y., 1982, Tel Aviv U., 1986; m. Hanna Pinczower, 1944. Ordained rabbi, 1934; chaplain Brit. Army, 1941-45; sr. lectr. Jewish Theol. Sem., Breslau, 1938; tchr. Rehavia Gymnasium, Jerusalem, 1938-41; dir. Ma'ale secondary sch., Jerusalem, 1945-50; supr. secondary schs. Israel Ministry Edn., Jerusalem, 1950-53; lectr. in Talmud and Midrash, Hebrew U., 1953-58, prof. Talmud and Midrash, 1958-80, prof. emeritus, 1980-91; pres. Israel Acad. Scis. and Humanities, Jerusalem, 1980-86. Recipient prize for Jewish studies Govt. Israel, 1955; Kaplun prize Hebrew U., Jerusalem, 1969; Leib Jaffe prize Keren Hayesod, 1970; Ch. N. Bialik prize Tel-Aviv Municipality, 1982. Mem. Acad. Hebrew Lang., Am. Acad. Jewish Studies (corr.), World Union Jewish Studies (pres.). Author: The Tossaphists: Their History, Writings and Methods, 1955, 4th edit., 1980; The Sages: Their Concepts and Beliefs, 1979, paperback edit. 1987; The Halakha: The Sources and Development, 1984. Died July 2, 1991; buried Jerusalem, Israel. Home: Jerusalem Israel

URBAN, JEROME ANDREW, oncologist, surgeon; b. Bklyn., Jan. 26, 1914; s. Frank Anthony and Jeanette Eva (Blank) U.; m. Xenia N. Poloushkin, Aug. 21, 1944; children—Alexandra Elizabeth, Xenia Ann, Jere Andrew. B.A., Columbia U., 1934, M.D., 1938; D.Sc. (hon.), St. Lawrence U., 1978. Diplomate: Am. Bd. Surgery. Intern Lenox Hill Hosp., N.Y.C., 1938-40; fellow, resident in oncol. surgery Meml. Sloan Kettering Cancer Inst., N.Y.C., 1940-44, clin. asst., 1946-56, asso. attending staff, 1956-60, attending surgeon, 1960-84, acting chief breast service, 1974-76, cons. surgeon, 1986-91; emeritus mem. Meml. Sloan Kettering Hosp., N.Y.C.; mem. courtesy staff Doctors Hosp., N.Y.C., from 1954, attending surgeon, from 1984; clin. prof. surgery Cornell U. Med. Sch., 1983-88, prof. emeritus, 1988; attending surgeon St. Luke's/Roosevelt Hosp., N.Y.C., from 1984; cons. surgeon N.Y. Infirmary; mem. courtest staff Lenox Hill, Doctors hosps.; attending staff Roosevelt Hosp.; clin. prof. emeritus of surgery Cornell U. Med. Coll., 1988. Contbr. numerous articles on medicine and surgery, particularly surg. treatment and diagnosis of breast cancer, to profl. jours., chpts. to books. Served to lt. M.C. USNR, 1944-46, PTO. Recipient Redway medal and award, 1961, Ohio Oration, 1977, Lucy Wortham James award James Ewing Soc., 1975, James Ewing award Soc. Surg. Oncology, 1985. Fellow ACS, Internat. Coll. Surgeons (hon.); mem. AMA, AAAS, Am. Radium Soc., Internat. Surg. Group, Soc. Surg. Oncology, Am. Coll. Radiology, Royal Soc. Medicine, Am. Assn. Cancer Rsch., Am. Geriatric Soc., Pan-Pacific Surg. Soc. (v.p. gen. surgery 1980), Am. Soc. Clin. Oncology, N.Y. Acad. Medicine, N.Y. Cancer Soc., N.Y. Surg. Soc., hon. mem. 13 internat. surg. socs., Camp Fire Am., Larchmont Yacht Club, St. Croix Yacht Club. Republican. Lutheran. Home: Hartsdale N.Y. Died June 13, 1991; cremated.

USSACHEVSKY, VLADIMIR, composer, author; b. Hialar, Manchuria, Nov. 3, 1911; came to U.S., 1930; B.A., Pomona Coll., 1935, hon. doctorate, 1974; Ph.D., Eastman Sch. Music, 1939. Mem. faculty Columbia U., N.Y.C., 1947-80, co-founder, dir. Columbia-Princeton Electronic Music Ctr. (now Columbia U. Electronic Music Ctr.), 1974-80, pioneer in tape work, 1951; prof. music U. Utah, Salt Lake City, from 1972. Composer: (with Otto Luening) Incantation, 1953; Poem of Cycles and Bells, 1954, Concerted piece, 1960, Rhapsodic variations, 1954; (orch.) Theme and variations, 1935, Miniatures for a curious child, 1950; (chorus) Jubilee cantata with orch., 1938, Missa brevis with soprano and 10 brass instruments, 1972, Divertimento, 1980-80, Suite for 12 Trombones, 1981, Triskelion Oboe and Piano, 1982, Dialogues and Contrasts, Brass Quintet and Tape, 1984, Piano Revisited, 1984, Anniversary Variations for Brass Quintet, 1985, numerous others; (electronic) sonic Contours for tape, 1952, underwater valse, 1952 numerous others; collaborator with Otto Luening in tape music for N.Y. prodns. King Lear and Back to Methuselah, also works for tape recorder and orch. Recipient Disting. Alumnus award U. Rochester, 1973; Nat. Inst. Arts and Letters grantee, 1962; Guggenheim fellow (2), 1957, 60; Nat. Endowment Arts grantee, 1966, 74, 75, 82, 85; NEH research grantee, 1980. Home: New York N.Y. Died Jan. 4, 1990.

UTLEY, NELSON MONROE, investment banker; b. Harvey, Ill., Apr. 17, 1895; s. George C. and Stella M. (Nelson) U.; m. Marion F. Bryant, Jan. 19, 1924 (dec. Dec. 1960); 1 dau., Alice Runnells (Mrs. John Jay Markham); m. 2d, Mrs. Edgar E. Wheeler, Sept. 14, 1963. Student, U. Ill., 1914-17. With Halsey, Stuart & Co., Inc., from 1919, bd. dirs., from 1954, mgr. govt. bond dept., 1921-22, with corp. trade dept., 1922-28, gen. mgr. trading dept., 1928-45, v.p., specialist in railroad bonds, equipment trust finance, from 1945. Served with U.S. Army, Mexican Border, 1916; capt. F.A., 1918-19. Mem. Ry. and Locomotive Hist. Soc., Univ. Club (Chgo.), South Shore Country Club (Chgo.), Bond Club (Chgo.), Psi Upsilon, Alpha Kappa Psi, Theta Nu Epsilon. *

VAN BUREN, RAEBURN, illustrator; b. Pueblo, Colo., Jan. 12, 1891; s. George Lincoln and Luella (la Mar) Van B.; m. Fern Rita Ringo, Dec. 8, 1920; 1 son, Richard. Student, Central High Sch., Kansas City, Mo., 1906-09, Art Students League, N.Y.C., 1913. Sketch artist: Kansas City Star, 1909-12; free lance illustrator, from 1913;illustrated over 350 stories for the Sat. Evening Post; also regular contbr. to 350 stories for the King Features Syndicate; creator of comic strip Abbie and Slats, syndicated in over 368 daily newspapers by United Feature Syndicate; permanent collection illustrations and comic strips Boston U. Library, Syracuse U.; Recipient award as Cartoonist of Year, Phila. B'nai B'rith 1958; nominee Best Story Strip cartoonist Nat. Cartoonist Soc. 1976; named to Cartoonist Hall of Fame 1978. Served as volunteer 107th Regt., 27th Div., N.Y. N.G., in World War I, 1917-19; with AEF, 11 mos. Mem. Nat. Cartoonists Soc., Society Illustrators, Artists and Writers. Home: Great Neck N.Y. Died Dec. 29, 1987.

VANCE, ROBERT SMITH, federal judge; b. Talladega, Ala., May 10, 1931; s. Harrell Taylor and Mae (Smith) V.; m. Helen Rainey, Oct. 4, 1953; children: Robert Smith, Charles R. B.S., U. Ala., 1950, J.D., 1952; LL.M., George Washington U., 1955. Ptnr. Vance, Thompson & Brown, Birmingham, Ala., 1956-77; judge U.S. Ct. Appeals 11th Circuit, Birmingham, 1978-89; lectr. Cumberland Sch. Law, Samford U., 1967-69. Chmn., Ala. Democratic Com., 1966-67; pres. Nat. Assn. Dem. State Chairmen, 1973-75. Served to 1st lt. AUS, 1952-54. Fellow Internat. Soc. Barristers; mem. Am., Ala., Birmingham bar assns., Am. Judicature Soc., Newcomen Soc. N.Am., Omicron Delta Kappa, Beta Gamma Sigma, Delta Chi. Episcopalian. Clubs: Birmingham Kennel, Heart of Ala. Great Dane, Am. Saluki Assn. Home: Birmingham Ala. Died Dec. 16, 1989. †

VAN CLEEF, LEE, actor; b. Somerville, N.J., Jan. 9, 1925; s. Clarence LeRoy and Marion Levinia (Van Fleet) Van C.; m. Barbara Hevelone, July 13, 1976; children by previous marriage: Alan, Deborah, David. Student pub. schs., Somerville. Farm worker N.J., 1942, 46; practice acctg. Somerville, 1946-50. Motion picture actor, 1950-89; appeared in movies: High Noon, 1951, Untamed Frontier, 1952, Kansas City Confidential, 1952, The Lawless Breed, 1952, Tumbleweed, 1953, Arena, 1953, Jack Slade, 1953, White Lightening, 1953, Vice Squad, 1953, The Beast from 20,

000 Fathoms, 1953, The Nebraskan, 1953, The Bandits of Corsica, 1953, Rails into Laramie, 1954, Man without a Star, 1955, Pardners, 1956, The Gunfight at O.K. Corral, 1957, The Lonely Man, 1957, The Young Lions, 1958, Ride Lonesome, 1959, Posse from Hell, 1961, The Man Who Shot Liberty Valance, 1962, How the West Was Won, 1963, For a Few Dollars More, 1965, The Good, the Bad, the Ugly, 1966, El Condor, 1970, The Magnificent Seven Ride, 1972, Return of Sabata, 1971, The Stranger and the Gunfighter, 1976, The Octagon, 1980, Escape from New York, 1981, The Squeeze, 1982, Armed Response, 1986, Codename: Wildgeese, 1987, Cannonball Run 3 or 4, 1988, others; starred in TV movie Nowhere to Hide, 1977; appeared in TV documentary American Civil War, ABC, 1984, Carson Show, 1984, Good Morning America, 1984, When the West Was Fun, ABC, 1979, TV series or show, including The Lone Ranger, Space Patrol, Wagon Train, Lawman, 77 Sunset Strip, Phil Silvers Special, Streets of San Francisco, The Dick Cavet Show, The Twilight Zone, Have Gun Will Travel, Maverick, Hawaiian Eye, The Untouchables, Gunsmoke, Perry Mason; starred in TV series The Master, 1984. Served with USN, 1942-46. Mem. Screen Actors Guild, Acad. Motion Picture Arts and Scis. Home: Oxnard Calif. Died Jan. 16, 1989.

VANDELL, ROBERT FRANK, business administration educator; b. Bklyn., June 22, 1928; s. Frank R. and Marjorie Drew (Pritchett) V.; m. Margaret Wheeler Edwards, Sept. 4, 1954 (div. May 1984); children: Robert Charles, Barbara Drew, Warren Edwards. BS, Yale U., 1950; MBA, Harvard U., 1952, DBA, 1958. Asst. prof. Harvard Bus. Sch., Boston, 1958-61, assoc. prof., 1961-65; prof. bus. adminstrn. Darden Bus. Sch., U. Va., Charlottesville, 1965-88; bd. dirs. Landmark Communication Inc., Norfolk, Va., TeleCable, Norfolk, several Merrill Lynch mut. funds, N.Y.C.; chief investment officer VA Supplemental Retirement System, Richmond, 1984; chmn. Vantage Fin. Mgmt. Co. Served to 1st lt. U.S. Army, 1952-54. Mem. Fin. Mgmt. Assn. (v.p. program 1986). Episcopalian. Home: Charlottesville Va. Died, 1988.

VANDENBOSCH, AMRY, political scientist, educator; b. Zeeland, Mich., Dec. 14, 1894; s. Graddus and Mary (Van Ekelenburg) V.; m. Mary Belle Wilcox, Mar. 22, 1926; chldren: Robert, Margaret Anne (Mrs. Duane A. Meeter). Student, Calvin Coll., Grand Rapids, Mich., 1915-17; PhB, U. Chgo., 1920, PhD, 1926. Instr. history Pullman Free Sch. Manual Tng., Chgo., 1920-23; instr. govt. Iowa State Coll., 1924-26; asst. prof. U. Ky., 1926-27, assoc. prof., 1927-28, prof., from 1928, head dept. polit. sci., 1934-58; lectr. Sch. for Tng. in Internat. Adminstrn., Columbia U., 1943; vis. prof. U. Chgo., sumemr 1939; with Office of Strategic Svcs., 1941-42, State Dept., 1942-44; mem. secretariat UN Conf., San Francisco, 1945; mem. Brookhaven Nuclear Rsch. Ctr. Mission to Asian Colombo Plan Countries, 1956; pres. Midwest Conf. Polit. Scientists, 1959-60; dir. William Andrew Patterson Sch. Diplomacy and Internat. Commerce; fellow Social Scis. Rsch. Coun. Author: Neutrality of the Netherlands in the World War, 1927; The Dutch East Indies--Its Government, Problems and Politics, 1933, rev. edits., 1941, 42; Dutch Foreign Policy Since 1815: A Study in Small Power Politics, 1959; (with W.N. Hogan) The United Nations, 1952, Toward World Order, 1963; (with R.A. Butwell) Southeast Asia Among the Powers, 1957; (with others) New World of Southeast Asia, 1949; (with Brookes) The City of God and the City of Man, 1964; co-editor: Readings in Citizenship. Served with 328th Machine Gun Battery, U.S. Army, with AEF, 1918-19. Mem. AAUP, Am. Soc. Internat. Law, Am. Polit. Sci. Assn. (exec. coun. 1942-45), Am. Coun. of Inst. of Pacific Rels. Democrat. Presbyterian. *

VANDERPOOL, EUGENE, archaeologist; b. Morristown, N.J., Aug. 3, 1906; s. Wynant Davis and Cornelia Grinnell (Willis) V.; m. Joan Jeffery, June 11, 1935; children: Joan Vanderpool Gayley, Ann Vanderpool Levenduski, Eugene, Alice Vanderpool Evert. AB, Princeton U., 1929. Fellow Agora Excavations, Athens, 1932-49; prof. archaeology Am. Sch. Classical Studies, Athens, 1949-71, prof. emeritus, 1971-89; vis. fellow Inst. Advanced Study, Princeton, N.J., 1944, 55. Contbr. articles to profl. jours. Decorated Greek Order of Phoenix. Mem. Archaeol. Inst. Am. (gold medal for disting. achievment 1975), German. Archaeol. Inst., Archaeol. Soc. Athens, Holland Soc. N.Y. Club. Republican. Episcopalian. Home: Athens Greece Died Aug. 1, 1989.

VANDER WERF, LESTER SETH, university dean; b. Pella, Iowa, Feb. 1, 1910; s. Seth and Jessie (Moss) Vander W.; m. Mary Elizabeth Dixey, Aug. 27, 1938; children: Leslie Vander Werf Bramhall, Linda, Dixey. AB, Hope Coll., Holland, Mich., 1931; MA, Columbia U., 1938; EdD (grad. scholar 1948-49), Syracuse (N.Y.) U., 1951. Tchr. English Middleburgh, N.Y., 1934-37; chmn. English dept. Cobleskill (N.Y.) Sch., 1938-42; supervising prin. Chestertown (N.Y.) Sch., 1942-48; mem. faculty U. N.H., 1949-53, assoc. prof. edn., 1951-53; dean edn. Northeastern U., 1953-66; dean Grad. Sch. Edn. L.I. U., Brookville, N.Y., 1966-70, disting. prof., 1970-90. Fellow AAAS; mem. NEA (life), Am. Assn. Sch. Adminstrs., Nat. Soc. Study Edn., Am. Ednl. Rsch. Assn., Phi Delta Kappa, Phi Kappa Phi, Pi Delta Kappa. Conglist. Home: Sheffield Mass. Died Jan. 22, 1990.

VAN DER ZIEL, ALDERT, electrical engineering educator; b. Zandeweer, Netherlands, Dec. 12, 1910; naturalized U.S. citizen, 1955; s. Jan and Hendrika (Kiel) Van der Z.; m. Jantina J. deWit, Nov. 22, 1935; children—Jan P., Cornelia H., Joanna C. B.A., U. Groningen, The Netherlands, 1930, M.A., 1933, Ph.D., 1934. Research physicist Philips Labs., Eindhoven, Netherlands, 1934-47; assoc. prof. physics U. B.C., Vancouver, Can., 1947-50; prof. dept. elec. engring. U. Minn., Mpls., 1950-81, prof. emeritus, 1981-91; grad. research prof. U. Fla., Gainesville, 1968-89. Author 10 books in field; contbr. numerous articles to profl. jours. Recipient Vincent Bendix award Am. Soc. Engring. Edn., 1975. Fellow IEEE (Edn. medal 1980, Centennial medal 1984); mem. Am. Phys. Soc., Sigma Xi. Lutheran. Home: Minneapolis Minn. Died Jan. 20, 1991; buried Mpls.

VAN DOREN, DOROTHY GRAFFE, writer, editor; b. San Francisco, May 2, 1896; d. George and Frances R. (Lane) Graffe; m. Mark Van Doren, Sept. 1, 1922; children: Charles, John. AB, Barnard Coll., 1918. Asst. editor The Nation, 1919-26, assoc. editor, 1926-36; with U.S. Office War Info., 1942-45, U.S. Dept. Stat , Overseas Info. Svc., 1946. Author: Strangers, 1926; Flowering Quince, 1927; Brother and Brother, 1928; Those First Affections, 1938; Dacey Hamilton, 1942; The Country Wife, 1950; The Professor and I, 1959; Men, Women and Cats, 1960; editor: The Lost Art--Letters of Seven Women, 1929; (with Alfred L. Bernheim) Labor and the Government, 1935. Trustee Barnard Coll.; mem. Sch. Bd., Cornwall, Conn. *

VAN DORN, HAROLD ARCHER, political scientist, educator; b. New Hampton, Iowa, Mar. 14, 1896; s. Frederick Hiram and Fannie Jane (Archer) Van D.; m. Viretta Calhoun, Sept. 1, 1920; 1 son, Everett Archer. AB, Grinnell Coll., 1918; AM, Columbia U., 1920, PhD (Roberts fellow), 1926. Tchr. Nankai U., Tientsin, China, 1920-22, Columbia U., 1925-26, Rutgers U., 1926-42, UCLA, 1948, Am. U., 1949, Pa. State Coll., 1950; prof., head dept. polit. sci. Kent State U., from 1950; chief fgn. air transport div. Civil Aero. Bd., 1943-47. Author: Government Owned Corporations, 1926; Twenty Years of the Chinese Republic, 1932; Selected Constitutions of East Asia, 1958; A Decade of Communist Rule in China, 1964. Served as 2d lt. U.S. Army, 1918. Mem. AAUP, Am. Polit. Sci. Assn., Ohio Assn. Economists and Polit. Scientists, Masons. *

VAN DUSEN, RICHARD CAMPBELL, lawyer, government official; b. Jackson, Mich., July 18, 1925; s. Bruce Buick and Helen (Campbell) Van D.; m. Barbara Congdon, June 28, 1949; children: Amanda Van Dusen Blessing, Lisa Van Dusen Kelley, Katherine Van Dusen Joyce. BS cum laude, U. Minn., 1945; LLB, Harvard U., 1949. Bar: Mich. 1949. Assoc. Dickinson, Wright, Moon, Van Dusen & Freeman (and predecessor), Detroit, 1949-57, ptnr., 1958-62, 64-68, 73-91, chmn., 1986-91; mem. Mich. Ho. Reps., 1954-56; under sec. U.S. Dept. HUD, Washington, 1969-72; legal adviser to gov. Mich., 1963; del. Mich. Constl. Conv., 1961-62; mem. Coun. Adminstrv. Conf. U.S., 1969-81, law revision com. State of Mich.; bd. dirs. Auto Club Ins. Group, chmn., 1978-79; bd. dirs. MCN Corp., Fed. Nat. Mortgage Assn., W.S. Butterfield Theatres, Inc., CRI Insured Mortgage Assn.; vice chmn. Am. Automobile Assn. Trustee Deerfield (Mass.) Acad., 1975-80, Citizens Research Council of Mich., Kresge Found.; bd. govs. Wayne State U., from 1979; bd. dirs. Civic, Inc., United Way of S.E. Mich., Detroit Econ. Growth Corp. With USNR, 1943-46. Mem. Fed. Bar Assn., ABA, Detroit Bar Assn. (bd. dirs. 1965-69, trustee Found. 1973-82), Mich. Bar Assn., Greater Detroit C of C. (bd. dirs., chmn. 1987-89). Republican. Episcopalian. Clubs: Econ. Detroit, Automobile of Mich. (bd. dirs., chmn. 1978-79). Home: Birmingham Mich. Died June 8, 1991.

VAN FOSSAN, ROBERT VIRGIL, insurance company executive; b. Breckenridge, Minn., Sept. 24, 1926; s. Virgil R. and Marie (Hogan) Van F.; m. Mary Jane Lake, Aug. 20, 1946; children: Deborah Van Fossan Bruers, Craig, Mark. Agy. cashier Northwestern Nat. Life Ins. Co., Mpls., 1947-49, agt., 1949-51, supr. cen. div., Chgo., 1951, supt. agys. Spokane, Wash., supt. agys., v.p., agy. dir., Mpls., 1966-69, sr. v.p., agy. dir., 1969-72; pres., chief exec. officer Mut. Benefit Life Ins. Co., Newark, 1972-78, chmn. bd., chief exec. officer, 1978-89; dir. Pub. Service Electric & Gas, Amerada Hess Corp., Nova Pharm. Corp. trustee Newark Mus., Community Found. N.J.; prin. founder, former chmn. Ptnrship. for N.J.; commr. Port Authority N.Y. and N.J.; mem. Pres.'s Pvt. Sector Survey on Cost Control; chmn. Renaissance Newark, Inc., Newark Performing Arts Corp.; former chmn. N.J. Supreme Ct. Com.; mem. exec. com. NCCJ. With USMC, World War II, PTO. Home: Mendham N.J. Died Oct. 29, 1989.

VAN HEUSEN, JAMES (EDWARD C. BABCOCK), songwriter; b. Syracuse, N.Y., Jan. 26, 1913; s. Arthur E. and Ida May (Williams) Babcock; m. Josephine Brock, Aug. 20, 1966. Student piano and voice, Syracuse U., 1930-32. Announcer Sta. WSYR, Syracuse, 1928; paino player Santly's and Remick, pubs., 1934-38; composer songs and scores for motion pictures and musicals, 1940-90; prodn. test pilot Lockheed Aircraft Corp., 1942; pres. Van Heusen Music Corp., music pubs., from 1959. Composer motion picture scores Love Thy Neighbour, 1950, (with Johnny Burke) Moonlight Becomes You, 1942, Sunday, Monday or Always, 1943, It Could Happen to You, 1944, It's Always You, 1941, Going My Way, 1943, TV score Our Town, 1955; songs include Heaven Can Wait, 1939, (with Johnny Mercer) I Thought About You, 1939, Like Someone in Love, 1944, Tender Trap, 1955, Come Fly with Me, 1958 (Cash Box award for most programmed album), To Love and Be Loved, 1958. Recipient citation and plaque for svcs. in War Fin. Program, 1945, silver medal for svcs. Treasury Dept., 1946, plaque for better understanding through internat. lang. of Am. song L.A. City Coun., 1958, plaque Saints and Sinners, L.A., 1958; Acad. Awards for Swinging on a Star, 1944, All the Way, 1957, High Hopes, 1959, Call Me Irresponsible, 1963, Emmy award and Christopher for Love and Marriage, 1955; named Hon. Citizen, State of Tex., 1958. Mem. ASCAP, Composers and Lyricists Guild, Am. Guild Authors and Composers, Authors League Am., Quite Birdmen, OX-5 Club, Thunderbird Golf and Country Club, Racquet Club, Press Club (Palm Springs, Calif.). Methodist. Home: Rancho Mirage Calif. Died Feb. 6, 1990; buried Palm Springs, Calif.

VAN HORNE, EDWARD K(ELSEY), securities broker; b. Sterling, Ill., Jan. 12, 1898; s. Edward B. and Lulu Van H.; m. Mildred M. Schmitz, Aug. 12, 1922; children: Edward Kelsey, Robert T., Barbara. Joined Stone & Webster Securities Corp., N.Y.C., from 1932, dir., from 1935, pres., 1949-63, chmn. bd., from 1963. Mem. Scarsdale (N.Y.) Golf Club, Am. Yacht Club (Rye, N.Y.), Union Club, The Recess Club (N.Y.C.). Republican. Presbyn. *

VAN PELT, JOHN ROBERT, JR., university president; b. Denver, Apr. 2, 1896; s. John Robert and Ellen Russell (Warren) Van P.; m. Frances Church, Dec. 27, 1929 (dec. Aug. 1978); children: Peter, Richard Warren, Ellen Morgan (Mrs. Ivan Price). A.B., Cornell Coll., 1918, D.Sc., 1942; B.S., Mich. Coll. Mines (now Mich. Technol. U.), 1922, E.M., 1923; LL.D., Chgo. Med. Sch., 1957; grad. study geology, U. Chgo., 1926-28; hon. alumnus, Berea Coll., 1987. Registered profl. engr. Engaged in mining industry as mucker, tracklayer, motorman, surveyor, and mill hand, 1919-21; successively instr., asst. prof., prof. geology Cornell Coll., 1922-28, also exec. sec., 1922-23; ranger-naturalist Nat. Park Service, 1926; teaching fellow geology U. Chgo., 1926-28; asst. geologist Ill. State Geol. Survey, 1927, asso. geologist, 1928-29; chief div. geology, mining and metallurgy Mus. Sci. and Industry, Chgo., 1928-30, asst. dir., 1930-40, tech. dir. in charge planning and design of exhibits, 1940-45; chmn. pub. relations com. Battelle Inst., Columbus, Ohio, 1945-51, also dir. research edn. and in charge Battelle research fellowships; pres. Mont. Sch. Mines, Butte, 1951-56; dir. Mont. Bur. Mines and Geology, 1951-56; pres. Mich. Technol. U., Houghton, 1956-64, chancellor, 1965-66, pres. emeritus, 1966-91; pres. Western Soc. Engrs., 1936-37; dir. Detroit & No. Savs. & Loan Assn., 1960-72, mem. exec. com., 1968-72; mem. Mont. del. Western Interstate Commn. for Higher Edn., 1951-56; expert cons. on tech. personnel War Dept., 1942-43; chmn. Sec. Interior's Survey Com. on U.S. Geol. Survey, 1953-54; assoc. Am. adv. council UN U., Tokyo, 1984—. Author: Boston and Keweenaw, an Etching in Copper, 1945, 4th edit., 1964; also articles in ednl. and mining press. Life trustee Cornell Coll. Served pvt. to 2d lt. F.A. U.S. Army, 1918-19. J. Robert Van Pelt Libr., Mich. Technol. U., named in his honor, 1988. Fellow AAAS (past mem. council); mem. AIME (life; dir. 1941-47, v.p. 1944-47, chmn. mineral industry edn. div. 1954-55), Am. Soc. Engring. Edn., Accreditation Bd. for Engring. and Tech. (formerly Engrs. Coun. for Profl. Devel. 1954-66), Gt. Lakes Hist. Soc., Explorers Club N.Y., Phi Beta Kappa, Sigma Xi, Theta Tau, Gamma Alpha, Tau Beta Pi. Episcopalian. Club: Miscowaubik (Calumet, Mich.). Home: Sarasota Fla. Died May 3, 1991; buried Eagle Harbor, Mich.

VAN WYCK, ALLEN, corporate executive; b. Ridgefield Park, N.J., Sept. 21, 1896; s. Henry and Jessie Isabel (Allen) Van W.; m. Tilly Irene Margarita von Hollehen, Nov. 29, 1928; m. Ester Maree Hansen, Sept. 3, 1944. Ed., Phillips Exeter Acad., 1914-15; student, Princeton U., 1915-17; LLB, Columbia U., 1922. Bar: N.Y. 1923. Assoc. Sullivan & Cromwell, N.Y., 1922-33; officer, dir. various subsidieriesof The North Am. Co., 1933-42; pres., dir. Ill. Power Co., from 1940; dir. Electric Energy Inc., Nuclear Power Group, Inc., Citizens Nat. Bank of Decatur. 2nd lt. Inf., USAR, 1917-19, 1st lt., 1919; with AEF, France, 1918-19. Mem. Chgo. Club, Decatur (Ill.) Club, Delta Kappa Epsilon. *

VAUGHAN, DAVID LISLE, lawyer; b. Vancouver, B.C., Can., Feb. 15, 1922; s. William Randolph and Blanche (Park) V.; m. Mavis Anne Carter, May 20, 1944; children: Michael David, Anna Teresa, Peter Christopher. B.A., U. B.C., 1943, LL.B., 1948. Bar: Called to bar B.C. 1948, Queen's counsel 1967. Since practiced in Vancouver; assoc. Farris, Stultz, Bull &

Farris, 1948-56, partner, 1956-64; partner Farris, Vaughan, Wills & Murphy, and predecessor firm, 1964-77; assoc. counsel Boughton & Co., 1979-84, Swinton & Co., Vancouver, 1984-90; lawyer-in-residence U. B.C. Law Faculty, 1977-78; Mem., chmn. B.C. Assessment Appeal Bd., 1978-83. Dir., mem. exec. com. Festival Concert Soc., 1973; chmn. bd. dirs. Johannesen Internat. Sch. Arts, 1980-83, Victoria Internat. Festival, 1980-83, Can. Opera Piccola, 1980-83; mem. Vancouver Art Gallery; founder mem. Met. Coop. Theatre Soc.; hon. mem. Sculptors Soc. Can.; chmn. Can. Property Taxation Assn., B.C. Served to 1st lt. Can. Army, 1943-45; comdg. officer B.C. Regt., 1960-63. Mem. Royal Can. Armoured Corps Assn. (life), Can. Bar Assn., Vancouver Bar Assn. (past mem. exec. com.), Assn. Can. Pension Mgmt. (adv. council 1976). Club: Vancouver. Home: Gibsons B.C., Can. Died Sept. 14, 1990; buried Vancouver, B.C., Can.

VAUGHAN, SARAH LOIS, singer; b. Newark, Mar. 27, 1924; d. Asbury and Ada (Baylor) V.; m. Waymon Reed, 1978, 1 child, Deborah. Singer with orchestras led by Earl (Fatha) Hines, 1943-44, Billy Eckstein, 1944-45, John Kirby, 1945-46; solo performer and rec. artist, from 1946; numerous albums including Sarah Vaughan, Swingin' Easy, No Count Sarah, Send In the Clowns, The George Gershwin Songbook, One World, One Peace, 1984, The Man I Love; performer numerous nightclubs, jazz festivals, with symphony orchs. Recipient numerous Down Beat mag. awards, including Down Beat Hall of Fame, 1985 Grammy awards, 1983, 88. Home: Los Angeles Calif. Died Apr. 3, 1990.

VAUGHAN, WILLIAM ADDISON, engineer, lawyer government official; b. Richmond, Va., Apr. 19, 1935; s. William Conway and Annie Sara (Cox) V.; m. Mary Lind Groseclose, June 10, 1961; children: William Addison, Mary Hawthorne, Sara Cox. B.S.C.E. with honors, Va. Mil. Inst., 1957; M.S. in Civil Engring., Purdue U., 1964; J.D. magna cum laude, Washington & Lee U., 1970. Bar: Mich. 1971, D.C. 1986; registered profl. engr., Va., D.C. Instr. Va. Mil. Inst., 1960-64, asst. prof. civil engring., 1964-70, dep. comdt. of cadets, 1964-67; atty. Gen. Motors Corp., Detroit, 1970, atty.-in-charge environ. and energy law sect., 1971-76, dir. energy mgmt., 1976-81; asst. sec. environ. protection safety and emergency preparedness U.S. Dept. Energy, Washington, 1981-84; asst. sec. fossil energy U.S. Dept. Energy, 1984-85, asst. sec. environ., safety and health, 1985; pres. Energy and Environmental Cons., 1986-89; of counsel Sutherland, Asbill & Brennan, Washington, 1986-89; adj. prof. environ. law and energy law U. Detroit, 1976-81; dir. Va. Mil Inst. Research Labs. Contbr. articles to profl. jours. Served in U.S. Army, 1957-60; to col. Res. U.S. Army. Recipient Gen. John A. Pershing award U.S. Army Command & Gen. Staff Coll., 1967, Bd. Dirs.' Spl. Service award Nat. Energy Resources Orgn., 1986, Nat. Environ. Devel. Assn. award for Application of Sci. Knowledge in Pub. Affaris, 1986; named Man. of Yr. Modern Indsl. Energy mag., 1980; Eno Found. scholar Yale U., summer 1966; Portland Cement Assn. scholar Purdue U., summer 1961; NSF scholar Okla. State U., summer 1962; Dept. Def. scholar U. Calif.-Berkeley, summer 1963. Mem. ABA, Mich. Bar Assn., D.C. Bar Assn., Fed. Energy Bar Assn., ASCE, Soc. Am. Mil. Engrs., Inst. Traffic Engrs., Engring. Soc. Detroit, Founders Soc. Detroit Inst. Arts, Nat. Capitol Hist. Soc., Order of Coif, Omicron Delta Kappa, Kappa Alpha Order, Delta Theta Phi. Republican. Espiscopalian. Club: Capitol Hill, City (Washington). Lodges: Shriners, Hill City, DeMolay. Home: Alexandria Va. Died Mar. 19, 1989; buried Lynchburg, Va.

VAUGHN, ARKELL M., surgeon; b. Greenville, Ill., Sept. 27, 1895; s. James M. and Elvere Adele (Meyers) V.; m. Margaret Ruberry, Dec. 23, 1922 (dec.); 1 son, Joseph R.; m. 2d, Rose Noonan Hansen, Apr. 3, 1959; stepchildren: Leroy R., Joy M., Robert J. Hansen. Student, Washington U., 1916-17; BS, U. Chgo., 1921, MS, 1922; MD, Rush Med. Coll., 1924. Diplomate Am. Bd. Surgery, Nat. Bd. Med. Examiners. Interne Mercy Hosp., Chgo., 1924-25; pvt. practice surgery Chgo., from 1925; asst. in surgery Sch. Medicine, Loyola U., 1927-30, from clin. instr. surgery to clin. assoc. prof., 1930-52, prof., from 1952; from jr. to assoc. attending surgeon Mercy Hosp., 1927-39, sr. attending surgeon, from 1939; attending surgeon Cook County Hosp., from 1942; cons. surgeon various hosps. Contbr. articles to med. jours. Mem. citizens bd. Loyola Hosp.; bd. dirs. Am. Med. Ednl. Found. Served with M.C., AEF, 1917-19. Recipinet Disting. Svc. award Miss. Valley Med. Soc. Fellow ACS, Am. Coll. Gastroenterology, Hollywood Acad. Medicine (hon.); mem. AMA (alt. del. from Ill. 1963), Am. Med. Writers Assn. (pres.), Am. Goiter Soc., Western Surg. Assn., Miss. Valley Med. Soc., Ill. Med. Soc. (pres. 1954-55), Chgo. Med. Soc., Am. Soc. Indsl. Phys. and Surg., Tri-State Indsl. Soc., Chgo. Surg. Soc., Am. Geriatric Soc., Internat. Acad. Proctology, Chgo. Soc. Indsl. Surgeons, Ill. Surg. Soc. (gov.), Pan Pacific Surg. Soc., Am. Soc. Abdom. Surg., SAR, Sigma Xi, others. *

VAZQUEZ, SIRO, oil company executive; b. Caracas, Venezuela, Feb. 10, 1910; came to U.S., 1958; s. Alfredo and Belen (Madriz) V.; m. Claire Duff, June 28, 1933; children: Claire Vazquez Otaola, Wesley Vazquez Hogan, Richard Kim. Degree in civil engring., Central U. Venezuela, 1930; BS in Petroleum Engring., U. Tulsa, 1933, ScD (hon.), 1963; postgrad., Harvard U., 1952. Petroleum insp. Govt. of Venezuela, 1933-37; various positions, chief engr., prodn. mgr., bd. dirs. Creole Petroleum Corp. affiliate Exxon Corp., 1937-58; prodn. coord. Exxon Corp. (formerly Standard Oil Co. (N.J.), N.Y.C., from 1958, v.p., 1967-70, sr. v.p., 1970-75, also bd. dirs. Decorated Order of Francisco de Miranda (Venezuela). Mem. AIME, Venezuelan Coll. Engrs., Knights of Malta, Knights of Holy Sepulchre, Univ. Club (N.Y.C.), Sleepy Hollow Country Club. Home: New York N.Y. Died Feb. 19, 1990; Gates of Heaven Cemetary.

VENEZIALE, CARLO MARCELLO, biochemist, physician, educator; b. Phila., Oct. 2, 1932; s. Marcello and Mae Veneziale; m. Joyce Laubach, Jan. 15, 1959; children: Paula Joyce, Carla Jill. BA, Haverford Coll., 1954; MD, U. Pa., 1958; MS, U. Minn., 1965; PhD, U. Wis., 1969. Intern Grad. Hosp., Phila., 1958-59; resident Mayo Clinic, Rochester, Minn., 1961-65, staff cons., 1965-85, head biochemistry sect., 1983-85; prof. medicine and biochemistry Mayo Med. Sch., 1978-85. Mem. editorial bd. Proc. Soc. Exptl. Biology and Medicine, 1976—; editor: The Regulation of Carbohydrate Formation and Utilization of Mammals, 1981; rsch. in carbohydrate metabolism, male sex steroids, regulation of cell growth. With M.C., USN, 1959-61. Mem. Am. Diabetes Assn., Endocrine Soc., Am. Soc. Biol. Chemists, Am. Soc. Andrology, Soc. for Study Reprodn., Soc. Exptl. Biology and Medicine, Cen. Soc. Roman Catholic. Home: Rochester Minn. Died Apr. 2, 1985; Rochester, Minn.

VERCORS, JEAN BRULLER, author, graphic artist; b. Paris, Feb. 20, 1902; s. Louis and Ernestine (Bourbon) Bruller. Student, Ecole Alsacienne, Paris, 1980-18. del. various confs. throughout world, 1945-91; co-founder Editions de Minuit pub. house, 1941. Major works in graphic arts and engraving include 21 recettes de mort violente, 1926; Unhomme coupé en tranches, 1929, Nouvelle clé des songes, 1934, L'Enfer, 1935, Silences, 1937, La Danse des vivants, 1938, illustrations for Hamlet, 1965; author: (novels and essays) Le Silence de la Mer, 1941, La Marche a l'Etoile, 1943, Le Sable du Temps, 1945, Les Armes de la Nuit, 1946, Les Yeux et la Lumiére, 1948, Plus our moins homme, 1950, La Puissance du jour, 1951, Les Animaux dénaturés, 1952, Les pas dans le sable, 1954, Coleres, 1956, P.P.C., 1957, Sur Ce Rivage: I. Le Périple, II. M. Prousthe, III. Liberté de Decembre, 1958-60, (with P. Misraki) Sylva, 1961, Les Chemins de l'Etre, 1965, (with P. Coronel) Quota ou les Plethoriens, 1966, La Bataille du Silence, 1967, Le Radeau de la Méduse, 1969, (plays) Zoo ou l'Assassin philanthrope, 1963, Oedipe, 1967, Le Feret le Velours, 1969, Hamlet et Oedipe-Destin ou Liberté, 1970. Mem. PEN Club, Nat. Com. Writers (hon. pres.). Home: Faremoutiers France Deceased.

VERMEULEN, CORNELIUS W., physician, educator; b. Paterson, N.J., Aug. 23, 1912; s. William and Ada (Ihrman) V.; m. Ruth Van Harn, Jan. 29, 1936; 1 child, Carl. AB, Calvin Coll., 1933; MD, U. Chgo., 1937. Intern U. Chgo. Hosp., 1937-38, resident, 1938-42; assoc. prof. urol. surgery U. Ill. Med. Sch., 1946-53; prof. urol. surgery U. Chgo. Med. Sch., 1953-91, assoc. dean div. biol. scis., 1966-69, dep. dean, 1969-91. Maj. med. corps. AUS, 1942-46. Home: Flossmoor Ill. Died Feb. 1, 1991.

VERON, EARL ERNEST, federal judge; b. Smoke Bend, La., Jan. 2, 1922; s. Dyer M. and Edna (Rodriguez) V.; m. Alverdy Heyd, Oct. 10, 1948; children: J. Michael, Douglas E. B.A., McNeese State U., 1958; J.D., La. State U., 1959. Bar: La. 1959. Pvt. practice law Lake Charles, La., 1959-67; judge 14th Jud. Dist., La., 1967-77, U.S. Dist. Ct. Western Dist. La., La., 1977-90; mem. Orleans Parish Criminal Ct., 1972. Mem. ABA, La. State Bar Assn., Southwest La. Bar Assn., Am. Judicature Soc. Home: Lake Charles La. Died Aug. 28, 1990; buried Lake Charles, La.

VERRILL, HAROLD EVERETT, business executive; b. Portland, Maine, 1893; s. Frank H. and Ida M. (Ball) V.; m. Katharine B. Hall, Nov. 29, 1917; children: Katharine (Mrs. Emegy M. Nickerson), Constance E. (Mrs. Donald Reich). Grad., Bowdoin Coll., 1915. With Hornblower & Weeks, N.Y.C., from 1915, ptnr., from 1939; dir. Maine Bonding and Casualty Co. Trustee Maine Home for Boys. Mem. Cumberland Club (Portland), Alpha Delta Phi. Republican. Congregationalist. *

VESAK, NORBERT FRANKLIN, choreographer, director; b. Vancouver, B.C., Can., Oct. 22, 1936; came to U.S., 1971, naturalized, 1979; s. Frank and Norah Grace (Riley) V. Studied dance with, Josephine Slater, 1957-60, Ted Shawn, 1960-63, La Meri, 1962, Pauline Koner, 1963, Margaret Craske, 1960-63, Merce Cunningham, 1964-66, Vera Volkova, 1969-72. Master tchr. Nat. Assn. for Regional Ballet, 1974-90; co-owner The Quest- Artisan Galleries and The Stoneflower Collection, Sausalito, Calif., until 1990; jury mem. Internat. Ballet Competition, Osaka, Japan, 1983, 87; dir. Nat. Craft of Choreography Conf., 1978, 79. Resident choreographer, Playhouse Theatre, Vancouver, B.C., 1960-68, choreographer, Can. Broadcasting Co. Television, 1965-67, Royal Winnipeg Ballet, 1970-80, San Francisco Opera, 1971-74; dir. ballet, Met. Opera Co., N.Y.C., 1976-80; choreographer, Deutsche Oper, Berlin, 1975, Nat. Ballet Can., 1976, Scottish Ballet, 1976, Miami Opera, 1978-80, Joffrey II, 1975, N.C. Dance Theatre, 1973, 74, 79, dir., Forest Meadow Festival of the Arts, 1976, Teatro Municipal, Rio de Janeiro, 1981, Am. Ballet Theater II, 1982, New World Ballet, Miami, 1982, ARTS T.V., 1983, Stuttgart Ballet, 1984-86, Bayerisches Statsoper, 1983-86, Heinz Bosl Found., 1981-86, Imax Film, 1987, L'Opera Paris, 1987, New Orleans Opera, 1988, Tribute to Olga Maynard, 1989, Met. Opera, 1989.; artistic dir. Marin Ballet Ctr. for dance, 1987; stage dir. Bernstein Mass, 1974, Banff Ctr. for the Arts, 1969-76, Greater Miami Opera, 1978-84, Met. Opera, 1979, 90, 91, Newport Opera Festival, 1979, Florentine Opera, 1982, New Orleans Opera, 1988, Ballet Fla., 1990, 91, Leningrad (USSR) State Ballet, 1990, Internat. Ballet Festival, Jackson, Miss., 1990, Juilliard Sch., N.Y.C., 1990, Columbus Opera, 1991; staging assoc. to Franco Zeffirelli, 1990, 91; commd. works for Winnipeg Ballet, others; ballets include The Gray Goose of Silence, The Ecstacy of Rita Joe, What To Do Until The Messiah Comes. Recipient Double gold medal Internat. Ballet competitions Osaka, Japan and Varna, Bulgaria, 1980; Can. Council grantee; Nat. Endowment Arts grantee. Mem. Royal Acad. Dance (London), Actors Equity (Can.), Am. Guild Musical Artists, Nat. Assn. Regional Ballet, Am. Fedn. TV and Radio Artists. Roman Catholic. Home: Sausalito Calif. Died Oct. 2, 1990.

VICKERY, KATHERINE, psychology educator; b. Dahlonega, Ga., Mar. 5, 1898; d. Elias Benton and Etta (McMullan) Vickery. AB, North Ga. Coll., 1918; AM, George Peabody Tchrs. Coll., 1919, PhD, 1929; DSc, Ala. Coll., 1947. Tchr. English and Latin Millington (Tenn.) High Sch., 1919-22; asst. prof. psychology Ala. Coll., 1922-30, assoc. prof., 1930-35, prof., from 1935, chmn. dept. psychology, from 1948; vis. prof. U. Ala., summers 1940-41, 51-52, Furman U., 1947. Author ednl. articles. Chmn. edn. subcom. Ala. Gov.'s Commn. on Status of Women. Fellow AAAS (coun. 1949-51, 57-64), Ala. Acad. Sci., Am. Psychol. Assn.; mem. So. Soc. Philosophy and Psychology, Comparative Edn. Soc., Ala. Soc. for Mental Health (bd. dirs.), AAUW (pres. Ala. div. 1948-50, v.p. S.E. Cen. region from 1963), Peabody Alumni Assn. (v.p. 1963-65), Ala. Psychol. Assn. (pres. 1955-56, chmn. bd. certification 1959-61), Southeastern Psychol. Assn., Kappa Delta Pi (nat. 1st v.p. 1942-53, pres. 1953-58, exec. sounselor 1958-64, awarded honor Key, laureate). *

VICTOR, MARTIN, manufacturing executive; b. N.Y.C., Oct. 3, 1913; s. Royall and Anna (Martin) V.; m. Helene Peters, June 26, 1948; children: Amy, Helen, Martine. AB, Harvard U., 1935; LLB, Yale U., 1938. Bar: N.Y., 1939. Assoc. Sullivan & Cromwell, N.Y.C., 1938-41, 46-53; asst. to pres. Babcock & Wilcox Co., 1953-57, sec., 1957-70, v.p., sec., 1971-90; Mayor, Village of Lattingtown, N.Y., 1955-64. Lt. comdr. USNR, 1941-45. Decorated Bronze Star. Mem. Creek Club (Locust Valley, N.Y.), Yale Club (N.Y.C.). Home: Locust Valley N.Y. Died Aug. 3, 1990.

VIETH, PAUL HERMAN, clergyman, educator; b. Warrenton, Mo., Jan. 18, 1895; s. Frederick Herman and Caroline (Schroeder) V.; m. Verna Muench, June 25, 1919; children: David, Richard, Margaret (Mrs. Walter E. Grevatt Jr.). AB, Central Wesleyan Coll.; BD, Yale U. Div. Sch., 1924; PhD, Yale U., 1928; DHum, St. Paul's U., Tokyo, 1958. DD, Central Meth. Coll., Fayette, Mo., 1962. Ordained to ministry Evangel. Synod of N.Am., 1922, transferred to Congregational Ch., 1931. Field worker Mo. S.S. Coun. Religious Edn., 1917-20, gen. sec., 1920-22; asst. minister Welcome Hall Mission, New Haven, 1922-23; dir. religious edn. Ch. of the Redeemer (Conglist.), 1923-25; dir. rsch., editor Internat. Jour. Religious Edn. Internat. Coun. Religious Edn., Chgo., 1925-31; vis. prof. religious edn. Duke U., Durham, N.C., 1931; dir. field work, assoc. prof. religious edn. Yale U. Div. Sch., 1931-39, Horace Bushnell prof. Christian nurture, 1939-63, emeritus, from 1963; advisor religious edn. Supreme Command of Allies in Pacific, Japan, 1947. Fulbright scholar Internat. Christian U., Tokyo, 1954-55. Mem. Nat. Coun. Chs. of Christ in U.S.A., World Coun. on Christian Edn., Religious Edn. Assn. Republican. *

VIRTUE, WILLIAM DALE, utility executive; b. Kingston, Mo., Dec. 10, 1893; s. Thomas S. and Lulu (Brazelton) V.; m. Ellamae Tewksbury, May 29, 1926. BS, U. Mo., 1919; LLB, Denver U., 1942. With Pub. Svc. Co. Colo., from 1919, chief acct., 1928-43, v.p., sec., 1943-53, v.p., treas., 1953-58, exec. v.p., treas., 1958-65, cons., from 1965. Mem. Edison Electric Inst., Am. Gas Assn., Am. Legion, C. of C., Contrs. Inst. Am., Kiwanis, Denver Club, Cherry Hills Country Club, Denver Athletic Club. *

VISHNIAC, ROMAN, photographer; b. Pavlovski, U.S.S.R., Aug. 18, 1897; came to U.S., 1940; m. Edith V.; 2 children. Ph.D., Shanvarsky U., U.S.S.R., 1920; Student in Oriental Art, U. Berlin. Med. sci. photographer Berlin, 1920-39; freelance photographer documenting Jewish life in Germany, 1935-39; portrait and med. photographer N.Y.C., from 1940; formerly Chevron prof. creativity Pratt Inst., N.Y.C. One-man exhbns.: The Louvre, Paris, 1939, Teachers Coll.,

N.Y.C., 1941, Jewish Mus., N.Y.C., 1971, Internat. Ctr. Photography, 1972, numerous others; works in permanent collections: Mus. of Modern Art, N.Y.C., Smithsonian Inst., Library of Congress, Washington, Jewish Mus., N.Y.C. Author: A Vanished World, 1983, photographs (under same title) in various one-man exhbns.; Polish Jews: A Pictorial Record, 1942; A Day of Pleasure, 1969; Building Blocks of Life, 1971; Roman Vishniac, 1974; producer film series Living Biology. Served in Tsarist, Kerensky and Soviet Armies, 1914-17. Home: New York N.Y. Died Jan. 22, 1990.

VLASTOS, GREGORY, educator; b. Constantinople, July 27, 1907; came to U.S., 1948; naturalized, 1971; s. Kimon and Elizabeth (Dewar) V; m. Vernon Abbott Ladd, Dec. 16, 1932; children: Marion Jean, Stephen Gregory. AB, Robert Coll., Constantinople, 1925; BD, Chgo. Theol. Sem., 1929, DD (hon.), 1968. Lectr. Queen's U., 1931-33, asst. prof., 1933-36, assoc. prof., 1936-41, prof. philosophy, 1941-48, acting head dept., 1947-48; prof. philosophy Sage Sch. Philosophy/Cornell U., 1948-55; prof. philosophy Princeton (N.J.) U., 1955-56, Stuart prof. philosophy, 1956-76, chmn. dept. philosophy, 1960-64, 70-75, Stuart prof. emeritus, 1976-91; prof. philosophy U. Calif., Berkeley, 1976-91, vis. Mills prof., 1976-91; John Locke lectr. Oxford U., 1960; John Danz vis. prof. U. Wash., Seattle, 1972; hon. vis. prof. dept. Greek Univ. Coll., London, 1975-76; Paul Carus lectr. Am. Philos. Assn., 1972; mem. Inst. for Advanced Study, Princeton U., 1954-55, Nat. Book Awards Jury; trustee Nat. Ctr. Humanities. Author: Platonic Studies, 1973, Plato's Universe, 1975; editor: Canadian Affairs, 1943-44, Plato, 2 vols., 1970, The Philosophy of Socrates, 1971; editor reprint series The Philosophy of Plato and Aristotle, and History of Ideas in Ancient Greece; mem. editorial bd. Political Theory; cons. editor Jour. History of Ideas; contbr. articles to religious philol., and philos. jours. With RCAF, 1942-44. Rsch. grantee in Greek polit. theory by Social Sci. Rsch. Coun. Can., 1944-45; Guggenheim Found. fellow, 1950-51, 58-59, 59-60; fellow Ctr. for Advanced Study in Behavioral Scis., Stanford, 1968. Fellow Am. Acad. Arts Sci.; mem. Am. Philos. Assn. (pres. ea. div. 1965), Am. Philol. Assn., Coun. for Philos. Studies, Am. Coun. Learned Soc. (dir.), Soc. for Promotion Hellenic Studies, London (hon.). Home: Berkeley Calif. Died Oct. 12, 1991.

VLIET, ELMER B(ENNETT), chemist; b. Joliet, Ill., Jan. 22, 1897; s. Richard and Loretta Elma (Bennett) V.; m. Mabel L. Swanson, July 9, 1927 (dec.); children: Verna (Mrs. T.C. Bailey), Northa (Mrs. R.W. Edwards); m. 2d, Dorothy Miller Anderson, Apr. 9, 1950. BS, U. Ill., 1918, MS, 1926. Asst. rsch. chemist Fixed Nitrogen Rsch. Lab., Washington, 1919; rsch. chemist Abbott Labs., North Chicago, Ill., 1919-35, mgr. control lab., 1935-46, dir. control, 1946-52, dir., 1946-62, v.p., sci. adminstr., 1959-62, chmn., 1959-62, cons.; chmn. Abbott Labs., Ltd., Can., 1961-62; bd. dirs. Indsl. Mgmt. Inst., Lake Forest Coll., 1962-64. Mem. editorial adv. bd., sci. editor Jour. Am. Pharm. Assn., 1952-58. Trustee Carthage Coll., from 1960; trustee Lake Bluff, 1930-35, pres., 1935-37; pres. Park Bd., 1937-39, mem. Bd. Edn., 1940-49; chmn. Zoning Bd., from 1937; mem. Lake Forest High Sch. Bd. Edn., 1949-52; local coord. Lake Bluff CD, 1941-46, Served at 2d lt. rsch. div. Chem. Warfare Svc., U.S. Army, 1918. Mem. AAAS, Am. Chem. Soc., Am. Pharm. Assn., Holland Soc. N.Y. (v.p., pres. Midwest br. 1961-65), Pharm. Mfrs. Assn. (chmn. quality control sect. 1961-65, adv. com. 1965—), Navy League (pres. Lake coun. 1962-64), Sigma Xi, Phi Lambda Upsilon, Gamma Alpha, Delta Sigma Phi. Republican. Presbyterian. *

VOEGELIN, HAROLD STANLEY, lawyer, financier; b. Summit, N.J., Sept. 10, 1919; s. Frederick Ernest and Clara Aestelle (Dorland) V.; m. Winifred Nemec Martin, Dec. 24, 1962; 1 son, Frederick P.; stepchildren: Jon F. Martin, Janis L. Kingaard. B.A., U. Mich., 1942, J.D., 1948. Bar: Calif. 1949. Teaching asst. constl. law, dept. polit. sci. U. Mich., 1947-48; assoc. firm McEntee, Willis & MacCracken, Los Angeles, 1948-52; asso., partner Brady & Nossaman, Los Angeles, 1952-57; partner Wood, Voegelin & Barton, 1957-60; sr. partner Voegelin, Barton, Harris & Callister, 1960-70, Voegelin & Barton, Los Angeles, 1970-84; ptnr. Finley, Kumble, Wagner, Heine, Underberg, Manley & Casey, Los Angeles, 1984-88, Nossaman, Guthner, Knox & Elliott, 1988-89; Pres., dir. Five-Thirty Corp.; chmn. bd. West Coast Commodity Exchange, Inc., Nesbitt Food Products, Inc.; dir. Smith Internat., Inc., Newport Beach, Calif., A.J. Bayer Co., Los Angeles, Orange City Bank, Orange, Calif.; lectr. U. So. Calif. Inst. on Fed. Taxation, Title Ins. & Trust Co. Tax Forum, Internat. and Comparative Law Ctr., So. Meth. U. Vice pres., bd. dirs. United Cerebral Palsy Assn. of Los Angeles, Inc., 1958-62; bd. dirs. South Coast Child Guidance Clinic, Newport Beach; trustee Whittier (Calif.) Coll., Nesbitt Found., Los Angeles, Lluella M. Murphey Found., So. Coast Repertory Theatre, Costa Mesa, Calif.; mem. exec. com. Pres.'s Club, U. Mich.; mem. adv. bd. Internat. and Comparative Law Center, Southwestern Legal Found., Dallas; mem. state adv. council World Trade Commn.; chmn. com. internat. trade devel. City of Los Angeles Econ. Devel. Council.; chmn., pres. Los Angeles Internat. Trade Devel. Corp. Served with USNR, 1943-45, PTO. Mem. ABA (lectr. Nat. Inst. on Current Legal Aspects of Doing Bus. in Europe), Internat. Bar Assn., Inter-Am. Bar Assn., Orange County Bar Assn., Los Angeles County Bar Assn. (chmn. com. on continuing edn. of bar 1961-62, 1st prize legal essay competition 1949), State Bar Calif. (lectr. Continuing Edn. of Bar Program), Los Angeles Area C. of C. (chmn. bd., chief exec. officer), Theta Delta Chi, Delta Theta Phi. Republican. Presbyterian. Clubs: California (Los Angeles); Newport Harbor Yacht (Newport Beach); Pacific; Balboa Bay (Newport Beach); Capitol Hill (Washington). Home: Newport Beach Calif. Died Oct. 25, 1989.

VOELKER, JOHN DONALDSON (ROBERT TRAVER), judge, author; b. Ishpeming, Mich., June 29, 1903; s. George Oliver and Annie Isabella (Traver) V.; m. Grace Taylor, Aug. 2, 1930; children: Elizabeth Voelker Tsaloff, Julie Anne Voelker Cohen, Grace Voelker Wood. Student, No. Mich. Coll., 1922-24, LLD, 1958; LLB, U. Mich., 1928. Bar: Mich. 1928. Pros. atty. Marquette County, Mich., 1935-50; justice Mich. Supreme Ct., 1957-60. Author: Troubleshooter, 19r3, Danny and the Boys, 1951, Small Town D.A., 1954, Anatomy of a Murder, 1958, Trout Madness, 1960, Hornstein's Boy, 1962, Anatomy of a Fisherman, 1964, Laughing Whitefish, 1965, The Jealous Mistress, 1968, Trout Magic, 1974, People vs. Kirk, 1981; also articles, stories in mags. Home: Ishpeming Mich. Died Mar. 18, 1991; buried Ishpeming Cemetery.

VOGEL, ORVILLE ALVIN, agronomist; b. Pilger, Nebr., May 19, 1907; s. William and Emelia (Paege) V.; m. Bertha J. Berkman, July 14, 1931; children—Evelyn May, Richard Frank. B.S., U. Nebr., 1929, M.S., 1931, Ph.D. (hon.), 1970; Ph.D., Wash. State U., Pullman, 1939. With Agr. Research Service, U.S. Dept. Agr., Wash. State U., 1931-73, research agronomist, 1965-73, prof. agronomy, 1955-73. Author articles wheat breeding. Recipient Superior Service award Dept. Agr., 1962; Nat. Medal of Sci., 1976; Distinguished Alumnus award Wash. State U., 1977; Washington State Medal of Merit, 1987; named to Agrl. Research Service Hall of Fame, 1987. Fellow Am. Soc. Agronomy (Crop Sci. award 1969, Edward Browning award 1972); mem. Sigma Xi, Alpha Zeta, Gamma Sigma Delta. Republican. Methodist. Home: Panoramic City Wash. Died Apr. 12, 1991.

VOLKER, JOSEPH FRANCIS, chancellor, dean, dental educator; b. Elizabeth, N.J., Mar. 9, 1913; s. Francis Joseph and Rose G. (Hennessey) V.; DDS, Ind. U., 1936; AB, U. Rochester, 1938, MS, 1939, PhD, 1941; DSc (hon.), U. Med. Sci., Thailand, 1967; Dr. honoris causa, Lund U., Sweden, 1968, U. Louis Pasteur de Strasbourg, 1972; DSc (hon.), Ind. U., 1970, U. Ala., 1970, Coll. Medicine and Dentistry, N.J., 1973, U. Rochester, 1975, Georgetown U., 1978, Fairleigh Dickinson U., 1978, U. Ariz., 1978; Prof. (hon.), Federal do Rio de Janeiro, 1977; LLD, (hon.) Troy State U., 1980; m. Juanita Berry, Feb. 6, 1937; children—Joseph Francis, Juanita Anne, John Berry. Dental intern Mountainside Hosp., Montclair, N.J., 1936-37; Carnegie fellow in dentistry U. Rochester, 1937-41, asst. prof. biochemistry, 1941-42; prof. clin. dentistry Dental Sch., Tufts Coll., 1942-47, dean, 1947-49; dean U. Ala. Sch. Dentistry, 1948-62, dir. research and grad. studies U. Ala. Med. Ctr., 1955-65, v.p. health affairs, 1962-66, v.p. Birmingham Affairs, 1966-68, dir. Med. Ctr., Birmingham, 1966-68, exec. v.p. U. Ala. Birmingham, 1968-69, pres., 1969-76, Disting. prof., 1982-89; chancellor U. Ala. System, University, 1976-82; dir. Ariz. Med. Sch. Study, 1960-61, Dept. State teaching specialist, Thailand, 1951; mem. Unitarian Svc. committee's med. teaching mission to Czechoslovakia, 1946, Germany, 1948. Bd. regents Nat. Library Medicine, 1973-77. Decorated Order White Lion (Czechoslovakia), Most Noble Order Crown (Thailand); comdr. Order Falcon, Republic Iceland; fellow in dental surgery Royal Coll. Surgeons Eng., 1961; fellow faculty dentistry Royal Coll. Surgeons Ireland, 1973. Diplomate Am. Bd. Oral Medicine. Mem. Inst. Medicine of Nat. Acad. Scis., Soc. Exptl. Biology and Medicine, ADA, Am. Chem. Soc., Internat. Assn. Dental Research, Sigma Xi, Omicron Kappa Upsilon, Alpha Omega Alpha. Died May 3, 1989. Home: Birmingham Ala.

VONESH, RAYMOND JAMES, bishop; b. Chgo., Jan. 25, 1916; s. Otto Francis and Mary Josephine (Brennan) V. M.A., St. Mary of Lake, Mundelein, Ill., 1939, S.T.L., 1941; J.C.L., Gregorian U., Rome, 1949. Ordained priest Roman Catholic Ch., 1941; instr. religion Sacred Heart High Sch., Chgo., 1941-45, Holy Name Cathedral, Chgo., 1945-47; with Chancery office Chgo. Notary, 1949-56; procurator St. Mary of the Lake Sem., 1956-67; vicar gen. Joliet, Ill., 1967; aux. bishop Joliet, 1968-91; notary Met. Tribunal, 1949-56; defender of the bond, 1956-66, papal chamberlain, 1957, domestic prelate, 1959; pastor St. Patrick Ch., Joliet, 1970; titular bishop of Vanariona. Home: Mokena Ill. Died Aug. 16, 1991.

VON HERNRIED RITTER VON WASEL-WALDINGAU, PAUL GEORG JULIUS See HENREID, PAUL

VON HIPPEL, ARTHUR ROBERT, science educator; b. Rostock, Germany, Nov. 19, 1898; s. Robert and Emma (Bremer) von H.; m. Dagmar Franck, June 2, 1930; children: Peter H., Arndt R., Frank N., Eric A., Marianne M. PhD, U. Goettingen, Germany. Rockefeller fellow U. Calif., 1927-28; privatdozent U. Jena, 1928-29; privat dozent U. Goettingen, 1930-33; prof. U. Istanbul, 1933-34; guest prof. U. Copenhagen, 1935-36; asst. prof. MIT, 1936-40, assoc. prof., 1940-46, prof., 1947-62, Inst. prof., 1962-64, Inst. prof. emeritus, from 1964; dir. lab. for insulation rsch. MIT; chmn. conf. on elec. insulation NRC, 1952. Editor: Dielectric Materials and Applications, 1954; The Molecular Designing of Materials and Devices, 1965; contbr. articles to profl. jours. Fellow AAAS, Am. Acad. Arts and Scis., Am. Phys. Soc., Washington Acad. Scis., N.Y. Acad. Sci. *

VON KARAJAN, HERBERT, conductor; b. Salzburg, Austria, Apr. 5, 1908; s. Ernst and Martha von K.; children: Isabel, Arabel. Student, Morzarteum, Salzburg; grad. as condr., Vienna Coll. Music, 1929. Conducting debut in The Marriage of Figaro, Ulm, Germany, 1929; condr. opera, Ulm, 1929-34; gen. dir. music, Aachen, Germany, from 1935; debut with Vienna State Opera, 1937, artistic dir., 1957-64; debut in Tristan and Isolde, Berlin State Opera, 1938; staatskapellmeister, 1941-44; condr., Prussian State Orch., until 1944; a founder, London Philharmonia Orch., 1948, permanent condr., from 1950; dir. concerts Gesellschaft der Musikfreunde, Vienna, from 1949; lifetime dir. concerts Berlin Philharm. Orch., 1955-89; artistic supr., Orchestre de Paris, 1969-71; instr. Internat. Condrs.' Course, Berlin; also guest condr. concerts Vienna Symphony Orch., 1930-34; rec. artist with Deutsche Grammophon, Polydor Internat., Electric and Mus. Industries Ltd., London; numerous worldwide guest appearances including La Scala and Lucerne (Switzerland) Festival, numerous orchestral tours; in recent years with Berlin Philharm. and Vienna Singverein; U.S. tour, 1976, 82, Japan tour, 1977; condr. Salzburg Festival, 1951-89; dir. and condr. films of operas and concerts, from 1965. Recipient Mozart Ring, Vienna, 1957, Art prize City of Lucerne, 1969; Franco-German prize Aix-en-Provence, France, 1970; also Grammy awards; named Hon. Citizen City of Berlin, 1973. Roman Catholic. Home: Saint Moritz Switzerland Died July 15, 1989.

VON LOSCH, MARIA MAGDALENA See DIETRICH, MARLENE

VON SCHLEGELL, DAVID, sculptor; b. St. Louis, May 25, 1920; s. William and Alice (Anderson) Von S.; m. Susan Howe; children: Lisa, Julia, Rosemary, Anthony, Mark. Student, U. Mich., 1940-42, Art Student's League, N.Y., 1945-46. Adj. prof., dir. studies sculpture Yale U., New Haven, Conn., 1972-92. One man shows include, Pace Gallery, N.Y.C., 1974, 77, 81, Inst. Contemporary Art, Boston, 1976, Clark U., Worcester, Mass., 1978, Herron Gallery, Indpls., 1980, group exhbns. include, Whitney Ann., N.Y.C., 1964, 66, 68, 69, Primary Structures, N.Y.C., 1966, Carnegie Internat., 1967, Carnegie Internat., Belgium, 1971, Nassau County (N.Y.) Mus., 1976-77, others, permanent pub. outdoor installations in, Boston, St. Louis, Duluth, Minn., Riyadh, Saudi Arabia, Cin., Indpls., Worcester, Mass., Miami, Fla., Phila., Balt., Pitts., Tulsa, Mountainville, N.Y. 1st lt. USAAF, 1943-44. Decorated Purple Heart, Air medal; recipient Coleman award, 1964, St. Buttolf award, 1969, Skowhegan medal for sculpture, 1978; Nat. Endowment Arts grantee, 1969; Guggenheim fellow, 1974. Home: Guilford Conn. Died Oct 5, 1992. †

VOORHEES, DONALD SHIRLEY, judge; b. Leavenworth, Kans., July 30, 1916; s. Ephraim and Edna Mary (Oliphint) V.; m. Anne Elizabeth Spillers, June 21, 1946; children: Stephen Spillers, David Todd, John Lawrence, Diane Patricia, Richard Gordon. A.B., U. Kans., 1938; LL.B., Harvard U., 1946. Bar: Okla. 1947, Wash. State 1948. Practiced law Tulsa, 1946-47, Seattle, 1947-74; partner firm Riddell, Williams, Voorhees, Ivie, & Bullitt, Seattle, 1952-74; judge U.S. Dist. Ct., Western dist., Wash., 1974-86; Bd. dirs. Fed. Jud. Center., Washington, 3 yrs. Served with USN, 1942-46. Mem. ABA, Fed. Bar Assn. (honored 1988), Washington State Bar Assn., Seattle-King County Bar Assn. (Disting. Svc. award. 1988), Maritime Law Assn., Am. Judicature Soc., Phi Beta Kappa. Home: Seattle Wash. Died July 7, 1989; buried Evergreen Washelli Cemetery, Seattle, Wash.

VOORHEES, JOSEPHINE PALMER, volunteer civic worker; b. Chgo., Nov. 19, 1894; d. Robert Francis and Mary Oresta (Ludlow) Palmer; m. Tracy Stebbins, Dec. 19, 1918; children: Mary Van (Mrs. Wilson), John Schenck. Grad., Francis W. Parker Sch., Chgo.; AB, Vassar Coll., 1917. Chmn. Bklyn. women's div. United Hosp. Fund of N.Y., 1935-42, Bklyn. Civilian Def. Vol. Office, 1942-45, Civil Def. Recruiting and Pub. Info., 1950-54; mem. exec. com. Com. for Modern Cts., from 1956. Trustee Bklyn. Inst. Arts and Scis., from 1939, Bklyn. Bur. Social Svc. and Children's Aid Soc., 1947-62; mem. governing com. Bklyn. Mus., from 1939, pres. community com., from 1963; bd. regents L.I. Coll. Hosp., from 1953. Mem. Jr. League, Vassar Club (pres. 1926-28), Cosmopolitan Club (N.Y.C.), Civitas (pres. 1943-47), Heights Casino Club (Bklyn.), Profile club (pres. 1958-61), White Mountain Garden Club (pres. from 1963). *

VORIS, ANNA MAYBELLE, museum curator; b. Mt. Rainier, Md., Aug. 5, 1920; d. Bruce Harvey and Maybelle Lee (Rea) V. B.A., George Washington U., 1954; M.A., Cath. U. Am., 1958. Mem. staff Nat. Gallery of Art, Washington, from 1951, curator of Spanish Art, 1975-80, cons., 1980-89. Author: Summary Catalogue of European Paintings and Sculpture, 1965, European Paintings and Sculpture, Illustrations, 1968, European Paintings: an Illustrated Summary Catalogue, 1975. Served in USNR, 1942-45. Home: Tampa Fla. Died Dec. 2, 1989.

VOUTÉ, WILLIAM JOSEPH, financial company executive; b. N.Y.C., Dec. 19, 1938. BS, Fordham U.; MBA, NYU; LLD (hon.) Marymount Manhattan Coll., 1986. With Salomon Bros. Inc., N.Y.C., 1960-89, ltd. ptnr., 1971 ptnr., 1972, mem. exec. com., 1981-89, vice chmn., 1987-89, also bd. dirs.; dir. Phibro-Salomon Inc. (now Salomon Inc.), N.Y.C.; founding mem., chmn. Vouté, Coats, Stuart & O'Grady, Greenwich, Conn., 1989-90, merged with First Boston Corp., vice chmn. 1990; founder, owner Vouté Fin. Corp., Bronxville, N.Y., 1991-92. Bd. dirs., hon. mem. Community Fund of Bronxville-Eastchester-Tuckahoe, Inc.; former bd. dirs., mem. fin. com. Lawrence Hosp.; former vice chmn. bd. trustees, mem. fin. and investment com. Fordham U.; former vice chmn. bd. trustees, mem. fin. and investment com., chmn. capital campaign Marymount Manhattan Coll.; trustee Friends of Am. Art in Religion, Friends of N.Y. Fire Dept. Collections, Inc.; mem. adv. com. N.Y. Police and Fire Widow's and Children's Benefit Fund, Inc.; mem. adv. bd. Catholic Youth Orgn. Westchester County, N.Y.; co-chmn. exec. com. Cardinal's Com. on Laity, Archdiocese of N.Y., chmn. exec. com. Cardinal's Com. of Laity on Wall St.; gen. chmn. 1987 Covenant House Dinner.; bd. dirs. Layman's Com. for Propogation of the Faith; trustee Papal Found.; mem. Inter-Religious Task Force; trustee, mem. devel. com. Boston Coll., chmn. Wall St. coun. and N.Y. region dev. com.; chmn. Daytop's Just Say Yes to a Drug Free World campaign. Recipient Man of Yr. award Fordham U., 1981, Club of Champions Gold Medal award Cath. Youth Orgn., 1986; honoree Inner-City Scholarsgip Fund, 1984. Clubs: St. Joseph's Mens (past pres.), Siwanoy Country (past bd. dirs.). Lodges: Knights of Malta, Knights of Holy Sepulchre (bd. councilors of eastern lieutenancy). Died Mar. 17, 1992. Home: Bronxville N.Y.

VREELAND, DIANA DALZIEL, magazine editor; b. Paris, France; d. Frederick Y. and Emily Key (Hoffman) Dalziel; m. Thomas Reed Vreeland, Mar. 1, 1924 (dec. 1966); children: Thomas Reed, Frederick D. Fashion editor Harper's Bazaar, 1939-62, columnist, 1936-38; with Vogue mag., from 1962, editor-in-chief, 1962-71, cons. editor, from 1971; Creator, cons. Costume Inst., Met. Mus. Art, from 1972. Author: (with Hemphill) Allure, 1980; D.V. (Plimpton and Hemphill), 1984. Decorated Legion of Honor France; recipient award N.Y. Fashion Designers, 1963, Chevalier de L'Ordre National de la Merite, 1970, Woman of Yr. award Westchester County Fedn. Women's Clubs, 1979, Pres.' Fellow's award R.I. Sch. Design, 1979, Rodeo Dr. award, 1983, Am. Ann. award Council of Fashion Designers, 1984, Chevalier des Arts et Lettres Ministry of Culture, France, 1984, Fellow for Life award Met. Mus, N.Y.C., 1986. Home: New York N.Y. Died Aug. 22, 1989.

VUILLEQUEZ, JEAN, metals processing executive; b. N.Y.C., Mar. 7, 1911; s. Gustave and Suzanne (Veyrey) V.; m. Germaine Bardet, Oct. 9, 1937; children: Richard Jean, Diane Suzanne. Student, NYU, 1929-33. V.p., dir. sales, dir. Am. Metal Co., Ltd. (subs. Am. Metal Climax, Inc.), N.Y.C.; also v.p., parent co., v.d., dir. Am. Metal Co., Ltd., Ill.; pres., dir. Am. Metal Co. of Lan., Ltd.; v.p., dir. Southwest Potash Corp., Us. Metals Refining Co.; dir. Titan Metal Mfg. Co., Indussa Corp., Anglo Metal Co., Ltd.; Mem. exec. com. Am. Bur. of Metal Stats., Am. Zinc Inst., Inc.; dir. Lead Industries Assn. Mem. Am. Inst. Mining and Metall. Engrs., Am. Ordnance Assn., Squadron A., Downtown Athletic Club, India House Club, Copper Club, Mining Club (N.Y.C.). Home: Stamford Conn. Died Aug. 28, 1991.

WADDELL, ST. JOHN, newspaper editor; b. Memphis, July 3, 1896; s. St. John and Ada Elizabeth (McCroskey) W.; m. Pauline Townsend, July 1, 1924; 1 dau., Irma (Mrs. Erich W. Merrill). Grad., Phillips Acad., Andover, Mass., 1914; BA, Yale U., 1917. Engaged in farming Quitman County, Miss., 1919-21; reporter Memphis Comml. Appeal, New Orleans Times Picayune,, North China Press, Shanghai, 1921-23; exec. asst. to mayor, city commr. City of Memphis, 1923-28; ins. broker, 1929-33; reporter, bus. and real estate editor Comml. Appeal, 1934-41, asst. mng. editor, 1946-59, mng. editor, 1959-61, assoc. editor, from 1961; fin. cons. WPB, 1941-42. Chmn. Memphis com. Freedoms Found., from 1962. Served to 1st lt. arty. U.S. Army, 1917-19; AEF in France and Germany; served to maj. inf. AUS, 1942-46, ETO. Mem. Am. Press Inst., Mil. Order World Wars, Am. Legion, Yale Club, Press Club of Memphis, Lions (pres., dir.), Zeta Psi. Mem. Christian Ch. (Disciples of Christ). *

WADE, JOHN WILLIAM, architect, educator; b. Florence, Ala., Dec. 25, 1925; s. Alex Chisolm and Myrtle Esther (Kent) W.; m. Flora W. Fay, Mar. 1952 (div. Mar. 1960); children—Mark, Bret, Paul; m. Donna White, Sept. 30, 1965. B.A. magna cum laude, Harvard U., 1949, B.Arch., 1952; postgrad. town planning (Fulbright scholar), Univ. Coll., London, 1952-53; M.Arch., U. Pa., 1964. Registered architect, Wis., Ala., S.C. Designer Perry, Shaw & Hepburn, Boston, 1952; designer, job capt. Eero Saarinen & Assocs., Bloomfield, Mich., 1953-56; job capt. Hideo Sasaki & Assocs., Somerville, Mass., 1956-57; pvt. practice architecture Hilton Head, S.C., 1957-63; assoc. prof., head div. architecture Tuskegee (Ala.) Inst., 1964-68; dean Sch. Architecture and Urban Planning U. Wis., Milw., 1968-75, prof., 1975-77; prof. Va. Poly. Inst. and State U., Blacksburg, 1978-91; co-chmn. Wis. Exam. Bd. for Architects, Engrs., Land Surveyors and Designers, 1968-75. Author: Architecture, Problems, and Purposes, 1976. Served with USAAF, 1944-45. Recipient grant Irwin Sweeney Miller Found., 1972-73. Home: Blacksburg Va. Died May 27, 1991; buried Blacksburg, Va.

WAGEMAN, DON H(ENRY), banker; b. Manhattan, Kans., Sept. 27, 1894; s. James L. and Judith P. (Leffingwell) W.; m. Blanche Houston, Dec. 28, 1920; children: Betty Jo, Donna Jean. Student, Kans. State Coll., 1908-09. Asst. cashier First Nat. Bank, Manhattan, 1915-17, 19-21; cashier Colony (Kans.) State Bank, 1922; asst. nat bank examiner, 1923-24; auditor Am. Nat. Bank, Cheyenne, Wyo., 1924-27, caashier, 1928, v.p., 1929-46; v.p. Seattle First Nat. Bank, 1946-53, chmn. exec. com., 1954-60; instr. U. Wash., from 1959, treas., from 1961; mem. adv. coun. Pacific Telephone N.W. Mem. nat. field advisers SBA; mem. adv. com. Liquidation Reconstrn. Fin. Corp. loans; former state chmn. Wyo. War Bonds Savs. Bond Com.; trustee, treas. Wesley Gardens Retirement Home, Des Moines, Wash., Bayview Manor Retirement Home, Seattle; trustee Seattle Symphony Orch. Served as 2d lt. U.S. Army, 1918. Mem. Am. Bankers Assn., Masons. Republican. Methodist (chmn. bd. trustees). *

WAGER, WILLIS JOSEPH, English and humanities educator; b. Pittsburg, Kans., July 24, 1911; s. Holmes and Joda (Smith) W.; m. Adah Allen, June 30, 1936 (dec. June 1970); children: Holmes, Geoffrey, Joseph; m. Inez Morton, May 30, 1971. AB, Washington U., St. Louis, 1931, AM, 1932; diploma, Kroeger Sch. Music, 1933; PhD, NYU, 1943. Exch. fellow U. Frankfurt am Main, Germany, 1933-34; asst. in English and humanities Washington U., 1932-33; instr. English, NYU, N.Y.C., 1935-43; assoc. prof. Berea Coll., 1943-45; prof. English and humanities Boston U., 1945-77, chmn. dept., 1945-49, prof. emeritus, 1977-91; spl. lectr. Am. lit. King Coll., from 1977; ednl. radio broadcaster Lowell Inst. Coop. Broadcasting Coun., Boston, 1945-51; Fulbright prof. Pädagogische Hochschule, Berlin, 1963-64, Istanbul U., 1966-68, Teheran U., 1968-70. Author: From the Hand of Man, 1963, American Literature, A World View, 1968, Musician's Guide to Copyright and Publishing, 1977; co-author: Liberal Education and Music, 1962, History of Music, 1973; author sect. in Gustave Reese, Music in Middle Ages, 1940, Living History of World, 1971;; editor: Life on the Mississippi, 1943; also articles. Mem. MLA, Am. Musicological Soc., Nat. Collegiate Players, Andiron Club (N.Y.C.), Phi Beta Kappa, Sigma Chi, Sigma Upsilon, Delta Sigma Rho, Kappa Phi Sigma, Eta Sigma Phi, Sinfonia. Democrat. Presbyterian. Home: Bristol Tenn. Died Nov. 2, 1991; buried Shipley's Cemetery.

WAGLEY, CHARLES WALTER, anthropologist; b. Clarksville, Tex., Nov. 9, 1913; s. Walter Clarence and Sally (Ridling) W.; m. Cecilia Roxo, Sept. 12, 1941; children: Isabel Anne, Carlos (dec.). AB, Columbia U., 1936, PhD, 1941; Doctor honoris cause, Univ de Bahia, Brazil, 1962; LLD, Notre Dame U., 1964. Instr. Columbia U., 1940-41, asst. prof. anthropology, 1946-49, assoc. prof., 1949-53, prof., 1953-71, Franz Boas prof. anthropology, 1965-71, exec. officer dept. anthropology, 1954-59; dir. Inst. Latin Am. Studies, 1961-69; grad. rsch. prof. U. Fla., 1971-91; fellow Ctr. for Advanced Study in Behavioral Scis., Stanfor, 1957-58; dir. Bahia State-Columbia U. Rsch. Program, 1950-53; vis. lectr., curator Museu Nacional, Rio de Janeiro, 1941-42; field party to Brazil, Inst. Inter-Am. Affairs, Div. Health and Sanitation U.S. Govt., 1942-46; staff Guggenheim Found., 1946-47, Social Sci. Rsch. Coun., 1947-48, Staff Found., 1946-47, Social Sci. Rsch. Coun., 1947-48; staff UNESCO Hylean Amazon Survey, 1948; adv. Ministry Edn., Brazil, 1953; others. Author: Economics of a Guatemalan Village, 1941, Social and Religious Life of a Guatemala Village, 1949, Amazon Town: A Study of Man in the Tropics, 1953, Minority Groups in the New World (with M. Harris), 1958, Introduction to Brazil, 1963, 2d edit., 1971, The Latin American Tradition, 1968, A Welcome of Tears, 1977, others; editor: Race and Class in Rural Brazil, 1952, 64, Social Science Research on Latin America, 1964; contbr. articles and revs. to various jours. Decorated Order Southern Cross, 1946, Medalha da Guerra (Brazil). Fellow Am. Anthrop. Assn. (pres. 1970-71), Am. Ethnol. Soc. (dir. 1949-52); mem. Am. Philos. Soc., Coun. Fgn. Rels., Am. Acad. Arts and Scis. Home: Gainesville Fla. Deceased.

WAGNER, AUBREY JOSEPH, government agency executive, consultant; b. Hillsboro, Wis., Jan. 12, 1912; s. Joseph Michael and Wilhelmina Johanna (Filter) W.; m. Dorothea Johanna Huber, Sept. 9, 1933; children—Audrey Wagner Elam, Joseph Michael, James Richard, Karl Edward. B.S. in Civil Engring., U. Wis., Madison, 1933; LL.D. (hon.), Newberry Coll., S.C., 1966; D.P.A. (hon.), Lenoir Rhyne Coll., Hickory, N.C., 1970. Registered profl. engr., Tenn. Engring. aide to br. chief TVA, Knoxville, 1934-51, asst. gen. mgr. to gen. mgr., 1951-61, bd. dirs., 1961-62, chmn. bd., 1962-78; cons. energy and resource use Knoxville, 1978-85; Cons. Ford Found., Asswan, Egypt, 1964; bd. engring. adv. Tenn. Tech. U., Cookeville, 1976-90; dir. Roy F. Weston Inc., West Chester, Pa., 1978-84; arbitration bd. PG&F-Sacramento Utility Dist., 1979-82. Contbr. chpts. to books, articles to profl. jours. Active Presdl. Commns. and Councils, Washington, 1950-78; vice chmn. Breeder Reactor Corp., Tenn. Valley, 1972-78; bd. dirs. Citizens for Home Rule, Knoxville, 1980-84. Recipient Disting. Service citation U. Wis., 1962; N.W. Daugherty award U. Tenn., 1969; Order of Achievement Lambda Chi Alpha, 1970; Engr. of Distinction award Tenn. Tech. U., 1981. Mem. Nat. Acad. Engring., Nat. Soc. Profl. Engrs., Tenn. Soc. Profl. Engrs., Am. Pub. Power Assn. (hon. life mem.), Tech. Soc. Knoxville (hon. life mem.), Explorers Club. Lutheran. Home: Knoxville Tenn. Died July 14, 1990; buried Highland Meml. Cemetery, Knoxville, Tenn.

WAGNER, DOROTHY MARIE, court reporting service executive; b. Milw., June 8, 1924; d. Theodore Anthony and Leona Helen (Ullrich) Wagner; grad. Milw. Bus. U., 1944; student Marquette U., U. Wis., Milw. Stenographer, legal sec., Milw., 1942-44; hearing reporter Wis. Workmen's Compensation Dept., 1944-48; ofcl. reporter to judge Circuit Ct., Milw., 1952-53; owner, operator ct. reporting service Dorothy M. Wagner & Assocs., Milw., 1948-90; guest lectr. ct. reporting Madison Area Tech. Coll., 1981—. Recipient Gregg Diamond medal Gregg Pub. Co., 1950. Mem. Nat. (registered profl. reporter, certificate of proficiency), Wis. shorthand reporters assns., Am. Legion Aux., Met. Milw. Assn. Commerce. Roman Catholic. Died April 14, 1990; buried Resurrection Cemetery, Mequon, Wis. Home: Thiensville Wis.

WAGNER, ROBERT F., lawyer, mayor, diplomat; b. N.Y.C., Apr. 20, 1910; s. Robert F. Wagner; m. Susan Edwards (dec. 1964); 2 sons; m. Barbara Joan Cavanagh, July 1965 (div. June 1971); m. Phyllis Fraser Cerf, Jan. 1975. A.B., Yale U., 1933, LL.B., 1937; postgrad., Harvard Sch. Bus. Adminstrn., 1934; LL.D., L.I. U., Fordham U., Bklyn. Law Sch., St. John's Law Sch., others. Mem. N.Y. State Assembly, 1938-41; city tax commn. N.Y.C., 1946, commr. housing and buildings, 1947; chmn. City Planning Commn., 1948; pres. Borough of Manhattan, N.Y.C., 1949-53; mayor N.Y.C., 1954-65; U.S. ambassador to Spain, 1968-69; ptnr. Finley, Kumble, Wagner, Heine, Underberg, Manley, Myerson & Casey, N.Y.C., 1976-87; personal envoy of Pres. U.S. to Vatican, 1978-81; First v.p., del. N.Y. Constl. Conv., 1967; chmn. bd. United Neighborhood Houses; mem. Pres.'s Crime Commn., 1965-66. chmn. jud. nominating com. First Jud. Dept. N.Y. State, 1975-82; also mem. commn. on jud. nominations N.Y. State, 1978-83; vice chmn. Port Authority N.Y. and N.J. Served to lt. col. 9th Air Force, 1942-45. Home: New York N.Y. Died Feb. 12, 1991; buried Calvary Cemetery, N.Y.C.

WAGNER, VICTORIA, academic administrator; b. Berwick, Pa., Jan. 24, 1898; d. Bruce Francis and Sue (Reay) Evans; m. Waldo Wagner, June 27, 1922; 1 dau., Eve (Mrs. Peter Cooper). Cert., State Tchrs. Coll., Fredonia, N.Y., 1916; student, Goucher Coll., 1916-17, Syracuse U., 1917-18, U. Mich., 1918-19; BS, Ind. State Coll., 1922, AB, 1925; student, Oxford and Cambridge, summer 1929; AM, Columbia U., 1930. Tchr. children's lit. Highland Park Sch., Detroit, 1919-21; tchr. English high sch., Clinton, Ind., 1922-23; tchr. reading methods Ind. State Tchrs. Coll., summer 1922; tchr. Pingry Sch., Elizabeth, N.J., 1923-24; tchr. children's lit. Edgewood Sch., Scarsdale, N.Y., 1925-29; tchr. English high sch. Scarsdale, 1925-29; mem. faculty Ethical Culture Schs., from 1929; beginning as elem. assoc. Midtown Sch.; succesively sr. adviser, tchr. edn. dept., tchr. Fieldstone Lower Sch., prin. Midtown Ethical Culture Sch., 1929-53; dir. Ethical Culture Schs., from 1953; mem. tech. adv. com. guidance N.Y. State Dept. Mental Health. Mem. mgmt. com. Bronx YWCA. Mem. ASCD, Child Study Assn., Am. Coun. Edn., Headmistress Assn. of East, Comparative Edn. Soc., Women's City Club. *

WAHLBERG, KENNETH ROGER, investment company executive; b. St. Paul, Nov. 9, 1922; s. Valfred N. and Hannah S. (Chelgren) W.; m. Marlys Quarnstrom, May 7, 1949; children—Kristi L., Patti A. B.B.A., U. Minn., 1948. Vice pres. Shaughnessy & Co., St. Paul, 1948-53; with mcpl. bond dept. Piper, Jaffray & Hopwood, Mpls., 1953-54; with Investors Diversified Services, Inc., Mpls., 1954-86; sr. v.p. investment banking and brokerage Investors Diversified Services, Inc., 1971-74, sr. v.p. cert. ops., 1974-86, retired, 1986; pres., chmn. IDS Cert. Co., 1974-86; dir. Dairy Farm Leasing Co., Mpls., Groveland Fin. Corp. Served with AUS, 1943-46. Mem. Evangelical Ch. Home: Edina Minn. Died Dec. 30, 1988; buried Union Cemetery, St. Paul, Minn.

WAKELIN, JAMES HENRY, JR., physicist, oceanographer; b. Holyoke, Mass., May 6, 1911; s. James Henry and Abbie Shattuck (Hobart) W.; m. Margaret C. Smith, July 29, 1938 (dec. Apr. 1973); children: James Henry III, Alan Blanchard, David Shattuck; m. Carol Ackiss Holman, Oct. 19, 1974. A.B., Dartmouth Coll., 1932; B.A., Cambridge U., 1934, M.A., 1939; Ph.D., Yale, 1940. Sr. physicist B. F. Goodrich Co., 1939-43; dir. research Engring. Research Assocs., Inc., Washington, 1946-48; assoc. dir. research Textile Research Inst., Princeton, N.J., 1948-51, dir. research, 1951-54, research assoc., 1954-59; asst. sec. for research and devel. USN, Washington, 1959-64; with Teledyne-Ryan Aero. Co., San Diego, 1964-71, chmn. adv. bd., 1964-69; asst. sec. sci. and tech. U.S. Dept. Commerce, Washington, 1971-72; pres., chmn. bd. Research Analysis Corp., McLean, Va., 1972-78; founder Chesapeake Instrument Corp., Shadyside, Md, 1954, v.p., cons., 1954-59; ind. cons. bus., Princeton, 1954-59; chmn. interagy. com. oceanography Fed. Council Sci. and Tech., 1959-64; head U.S. delegation Intergovtl. Conf. on Oceanographic Research, Copenhagen, 1960; mem. Intergovtl. Oceanographic Commn., UNESCO, Paris, 1961, Naval Research Adv. Com., 1964-71; mem. adv. bd. Continental Motors Corp., Detroit, 1964-71; chmn bd. Oceanic Found., Honolulu, 1965-71; chmn. Pres.' Task Force on Oceanography, 1969; mem. bd. advisors to pres. Naval War Coll., 1970-73; spl. asst. to Gov. Del. for marine and coastal affairs, 1970-71; mem. vis. com. dept. ocean engring. MIT, Cambridge, 1970-73; mem. vis. com. dept. astronomy Harvard U., Cambridge, 1970-78; chmn. interagy. com. atmospheric scis. and interdepartmental com. patent policy Fed. Council Sci. and Tech., 1971-72; chmn. com. phys. scis. Yale U., New Haven, 1973-78; hon. mem. Woods Hole Oceanographic Instn. Author: (with Tompkins and Stifler, Jr.) High-Speed Computing Devices, 1950. Chmn. bd. overseers Thayer Sch. Engring., Dartmouth Coll., 1966-70; bd. dirs. Harbor Br. Found., 1973-75, Coll. of Atlantic, Bar Harbor, Maine, from 1985. Served to lt. comdr. USNR, 1943-46. Recipient Rear Adm. William S. Parsons award USN League, 1965, Wilbur Lucius Cross medal Yale U. Grad. Sch., 1976, Robert Fletcher award Thayer Sch. Engring., Dartmouth Coll., 1977. Benjamin Franklin fellow Royal Soc. Arts; mem. Am. Phys. Soc., Nat. Geog. Soc. (trustee), N.Y. Acad. Scis., Marine Tech. Soc. (hon.; pres. 1966-68), Nat. Security Indsl. Assn. (hon.), Assn. Yale Alumni, Yale Grad. Sch. Assn. (pres. 1972-74), Sigma Xi. Congregationalist. Clubs: Chevy Chase, Cosmos (Washington). Home: Washington D.C. Died Dec. 21, 1990.

WALDEN, EMORY EARL, university dean; b. Paragould, Ark., May 25, 1898; s. Edward Coleman and Martha Jane (Russell) W.; m. Ella Bragg, June 6, 1922; 1 child, William Earl. AB, Hendrix Coll., 1922; AM, U. Colo., 1925; PhD, U. Ill., 1934. Tchr. math. Hendrix (Ark.) Acad., 1922-24; prof. math., dean Lambuth Coll., Jackson, Tenn., 1924-31; grad. asst. U. Ill., 1931-34; head math. dept. Ga. State Coll., 1934-38, 40-42; vis. prof. U. Ariz., 1938-40; mem. faculty N.Mex. State U., from 1940, prof. math., head dept., 1942-58, dean Grad. Sch., from 1956. Author papers in algebraic geometry. Mem. Math. Assn. Am., Am. Math. Soc., Sigma Xi (pres. local chpt.). *

WALDMAN, JULES LLOYD, editor, publisher; b. N.Y.C., Dec. 24, 1912; s. Harry A. and Anna Waldman; m. Agnes Tolnay, Sept. 24, 1949; children: Kathleen Ellen, Kenneth Lloyd. BA, Columbia, 1932 (state scholarship, 4 yrs.), postgrad., 1934-35. Mem. staff Bklyn. Daily Eagle, L.I. Daily Press, 1932-35; dir. staff pianist Radio Caracas, Venezuela, 1941-45; dir. bookstore chain Caracas, 1941-59; editor Clave mag., 1950-60; founder Caracas Daily Jour., 1945, editor, 1945-75, dir., 1975-90, chmn. bd., 1982-90; corr. N.Y. Times, 1945-65, Time mag., 1945-48; dir., prof. Centro Venezolano-Americano, Caracas, 1945-90; prof. journalism Central U. Venezuela, 1948-50. Author: Venezuelan Sketches, 1988; pub.: Speaking of Venezuela, 1947, Caracas Everday, 1947; columnist, contbr. to mags. and newspapers. Established ann. Nat. Good Neighbor awards, Venezuela, 1947. Decorated Order Andres Bello, Order Liberator Simon Bolivar; recipient Municipal ant Nat. Newspaper prize, 1948, Order Francisco Miranda award Pres. Venezuela, 1968, Gold Key Municipal Council Caracas, 1968, Order of Merit, 1958; named Friend of Venezuela; posthumously recognized with his portrait on Venezuelan post stamp. Mem. Alumni Assn. Columbia U. in Venezuela (pres.), Venezuelan Newspaper Pubs. Assn. (bd. dirs.), Interamerican Press Assn. Club: Overseas Press (pres. Venezuela chpt.). Home: Caracas Venezuela Died July 25, 1990.

WALKER, CHARLES A., academic administrator; b. Foreman, Ark., Dec. 14, 1935; m. 1957; 3 children. BS, Ark. Agrl. Mech. and Normal Coll., 1957; MS, Wash. State U., 1959; PhD in pharmacology, Loyola U., 1969. Rsch. asst. Wash. State U., Pullman, 1957-59; asst. prof. biology Fort Valley (Ga.) State Coll., 1959-63; asst. prof. physiol. Tuskegee (Ala.) Inst., 1963-65, assoc. prof. pharmacology, 1968-71, prof. vet. pharmacology, chmn. dept. pharmacology, 1971-74, prof. pharmacology, dean Sch. Pharmacy, 1974-86; chancellor dept. pharmacology Fla. A&M U., Tallahassee, 1986-87; chancellor U. Ark. Pine Bluff, from 1987. Home: Pine Bluff Ark. Died May 16, 1992.

WALKER, DAVID HARRY, author; b. Angus, Scotland, Feb. 9, 1911; m. Willa Magee, 1939; children: David, Giles, Barclay, Andrew. Attended, Shrewsbury (Eng.) Sch., Shropshire, 1924-29; studied at, Royal Mil. Coll., Sandhurst, Surrey, Eng., 1929-30; D.Litt., U. N.B. (Can.), Fredericton, 1955. Served with Black Watch Brit. Army, 1931-47, advanced to rank of maj.; served in India, 1932-36, Sudan, 1936-38; aide-de-camp to Gov.-Gen. of Can., 1938-39; prisoner-of-war Germany, 1940-45; instr. Staff Coll., Camberley, Surrey, 1945-46; comptroller to Viceroy of India, 1946-47. Author: (novels) The Storm and the Silence, 1949, Geordie, 1950, The Pillar, 1952, Digby, 1953, Harry Black, 1956, Where the High Winds Blow, 1960, Winter of Madness, 1964, Mallabec, 1965, Come Back, Geordie, 1966, Cab-Intersec, 1968, Pirate Rock, 1969, The Lord's Pink Ocean, 1972, Black Dougal, 1974, Ash, 1976, Pot of Gold, 1977, Memoirs: Lean, Wind, Lean, A few times Remembered, 1984; (short stories) Storms of Our Journey and Other Stories, 1962; (children's books) Sandy Was a Soldier's Boy, 1957, Dragon Hill, 1962, Big Ben, 1970. Mem. Can. Council, 1957-61; Can. commr. Roosevelt Campobello Internat. Park Commn., from 1965, chmn., 1970-72; Mem. Order of Brit. Empire, 1946. Recipient Gov. Gen's. award for lit., 1953, 54. Fellow Royal Soc. Lit.; mem. Queen's Bodyguard for Scotland, Royal and Ancient Club. Home: Saint Andrews N.B., Can. Died March 5, 1992; buried Bayside Cemetery, St, Andrews N.B.

WALKER, DEAN EVEREST, academic administrator; b. Chardon, Ohio, May 18, 1898; s. Wilmer Russell and Ina May (Day) W.; m. Florence Ley, Aug. 18, 1920 (dec. 1960); children: Dean Everest, Jeannette Ann (Mrs. James Bradford); m. 2d, Dorothy L. Keister, May 28, 1962. Student, Bethany Coll., 1916-19; BA, Tri-State Coll., 1922, LittD, 1961; BD, Butler U., 1928, MA, 1930; student, U. Edinburgh, Scotland, 1933-35; DD, Milligan Coll., 1946. Ordained to ministry Christian Ch., 1926. Tchr. high sch. Ohio, Ind., 1922-28; minister Little Flatrock Christian Ch., 1926-28; prof. ch. history Butler U., 1928-50, head dept. ch. history, 1935-50; lectr. Overdale Coll. Birmingham, Eng., 1935; pres. Milligan Coll., from 1950; rec. sec. German Evangelizing Soc., 1933-43, Christian Missionary Fellowship, from 1955; pres. European Evangelistic Soc., from 1944, N.Am. Christian Conv., 1942-44, Commn. on Restudy of Disciples of Christ, 1937-49; mem. continuation com. N.Am. Christian Conv., 1936-58, from 1959; mem. exec. com. World Conv. Disciples of Christ, 1955-61; bd. dirs. Coun. Advancement of Small Colls., 1956-61, 63. Author: Adventuring for Christian Unity, 1935; The Authority of the Word, 1950; The Tradition of Christ, 1964. Served with U.S. Army, World War I. Mem. Am. Soc. Ch. History, AAUP, Tenn. Hist. Soc., Ind. Schoolmen's Club, Masons, Rotary, Sigma Nu, Phi Kappa Phi, Tau Kappa Alpha, Theta Phi. Republican. *

WALKER, JOHN THOMAS, bishop; b. Barnesville, Ga., 1925; m. Rosa Maria Flores; 3 children. B.D., Va. Theol. Sem., 1954. Ordained to ministry Episcopalian Ch.; rector St. Mary's Ch., Detroit, 1955-57; tchr. St. Paul's Sch., 1957-66, Bishop Tucker Theol. Coll., Mukono, Uganda, 1964-65; canon Washington Cathedral, 1966-71; suffragan bishop Diocese of Washington, 1971-76, bishop coadjutor, 1976-77, bishop, 1977-89; dean Washington Nat. Cathedral, 1978-89; v.p. Nat. House Bishops of Episcopal Ch.; mem. Urban Bishops Coalition, Interfaith Conf. Met. Washington., Council of Chs. of Greater Washington. Chmn. Africare; trustee St. Paul's Sch., Va. Theol. Sch.; mem. Standing Commn. on Peace of Episc. Ch., Eisenhower Found. Home: Washington D.C. Died Sept. 30, 1989; buried Washington (D.C.) Cathedral.

WALKER, NANCY (ANN MYRTLE SWOYER), actress; b. Phila., May 10, 1922; d. Dewey and Myrtle (Lawler) Barto; m. David Craig, Jan. 29, 1951; 1 dau., Miranda. Ed., Bentley Sch., Profl. Children's Sch., both N.Y.C. Actress in Broadway shows: Best Foot Forward, 1941-42, On the Town, 1944-46, Barefoot Boy with Cheek, 1947, Look, Ma I'm Dancing, 1948, Along Fifth Avenue, 1948-49, Pal Joey, 1952-53, Phoenix 55, 1955, Fallen Angels, 1956, Copper and Brass, 1957, The Girls Against the Boys, 1959, Do Re Mi, 1960, UTBU, 1966, Girl Crazy, Broadway Rhythm, films: Stand Up and Be Counted, 1972, Forty Carats, 1973, The World's Greatest Athlete, 1973, Murder by Death, 1976, Won Ton Ton, The Dog Who Saved Hollywood, 1976; dir. film: Can't Stop the Music, 1980; regular TV appearances include Mary Tyler Moore Show, McMillan and Wife, 1971-76, Rhoda, 1974-78 (Emmy nomination 1975), The Nancy Walker Show, 1976, Blanksy's Beauties, 1977, The Golden Girls, starring role True Colors, 1990; dir. TV movies with APA, N.Y.C., 1968-69; appeared in: A Funny thing Happened on the Way to the Forum, 1971, Sondheim: A Musical Tribute, 1973; TV films include Every Man Needs One, 1972, Thursday's Game, 1974, Death Scream, 1975, Human Feelings, 1978; also known for TV commls. Recipient Genii award Am. Women in Radio and TV, 1975. Home: Los Angeles Calif. Died May 25, 1992.

WALKER, OLIVER M., mortgage banker, realtor; b. Alpine, Ala., Sept. 1898; s. Samuel and Ella Belle (Mallory) W.; student U. Ala., 1917, Marion (Ala.) Mil. Inst., 1917-18; B.S., U.S. Naval Acad., 1922; m. Elizabeth Powell Dunlop, June 11, 1932; children—Elizabeth Walker Edgeworth, Ann Walker Gaffney, O. Mallory Jr. Advt. salesman Am. Bur. Trade Extension, 1922, advt. mgr., 1923; organizer Washington Concrete Products Corp., 1924, sales mgr., 1924-30, v.p., 1930-43; sec., dir. Union Market Terminal, Washington, 1928-35; organizer, pres. Walker & Dunlop, Washington and Balt., 1935—; now chmn. emeritus; dir. mem. exec. com. Title Guarantee Co., Balt., 1941-75; pres. Am. Standard Life Ins. Co., 1953-58; lectr., speaker mortgage financing. Pres., Washington Real Estate Bd., 1949-50; pres. mortgage council Nat. Assn. Real Estate Bds., 1954-55, chmn. com. real estate econs. 1956-60. Chmn. bd. zoning appeals, Montgomery County, Md., 1943-47. Trustee, pres. Whitehall Country Sch., 1944-46; trustee Landon Sch., 1950-52, Naval Acad. Found., 1968-79. Recipient Realtor of Yr. award Washington Bd. Realtors, 1967. Mem. Mortgage Bankers Assn. Am. (gov. 1952-60, v.p. 1960—, dir. 1961-69, Certified Mortgage Bankers award 1974, dir.). Clubs: Metropolitan, Chevy Chase, Army and Navy (Washington); Sulgrave, Army and Navy Country (Arlington, Va.); Rehoboth Beach Country; Balboa (Mazatlan, Mexico). Author: Servicing Mortgage Loans, 1951. Co-author: Quar. Mortgage Market Reports, Nat. Assn. Real Estate Bds., 1955-65.Deceased. Home: Washington D.C. †

WALKER, SAMUEL SLOAN, JR., publishing company executive; b. N.Y.C., Nov. 2, 1926; s. Samuel Sloan and Audrey (Riker) W.; m. Beth Bready, Oct. 28, 1961; children—Samuel Sloan III, Randolph Ramsey, Timothy Taggart. Student, Buckley Sch., 1932-39; grad. with honors Groton Sch, 1944; B.A. with honors, Yale, 1948. Vol. ambulance driver Am. Field Svc., France and Germany, 1945; war corr. N.Y. Post, Paris, 1945-46; asst. to research dir. Time, Inc., N.Y.C., 1949-51; v.p. Free Europe Com., N.Y.C.; dir. Free Europe Press, 1951-59; founder, pres. Walker & Co., N.Y.C., 1959-92. Bd. dirs., chmn. exec. com. Am. Field Svc., 1966-86. Mem. Brookfield Hist. Soc., Phi Beta Kappa. Clubs: Century (N.Y.C.), Yale (N.Y.C.). Home: New York N.Y. Died May 29, 1992.

WALLACE, CLARENCE, lieutenant governor of British Columbia; b. Vancouver, B.C., Can., June 22, 1894; s. Alfred and Eliza E. (Underhill) W.; m. Charlotte Hazel Chapman, Sept. 12, 1916; children: Richard, David. Student, St. Andrew's Coll., 1907-10. In bus., from 1916; sec.-treas. Burrard Dry Dock Co., Ltd., 1921-29, pres., from 1929; pres. Yarrows, Ltd., Victoria, B.C.; v.p. Cassiar Packing Co. Ltd.; lt. gov. of B.C., 1955-56; dir. Crown Life Ins. Co., Can. Trust Co., B.C. Telephone Co., Ltd., Evans, Coleman & Evans, Ltd., Brit. Pacific Properties, Ltd. Mem. Indsl. Def. Bd. Served as pvt. 5th bn. Canadian Army, 1914-16, hon. col. B.C. Regt. (D.C.O.) 13th Armoured Regt. Decorated comdr. Order Brit. Empire, knight St. John. Mem. Can. Indsl. Preparedness Assn. (hon. mem. coun.), Vancouver Club, Royal Vancouver Yacht Club, Vancouver Rowing Club, Capilano Golf Club, Union Club (Victoria), Racquet and Tennis Club (N.Y.), Mt. Royal Club (Montreal), Wash. Athletic (Seattle). Presbyterian. *

WALLACE, DWANE L., airplane company executive; b. Belmont, Kans., Oct. 29, 1911; m. Velma Lunt; children: Linda Jones, Karen Johnson, Diana Wilkonson, Farah Bracco. Aero. engring. degree, U. Wichita, 1933. With Walter Beech; gen. mgr. Cessna Aircraft Co., 1934-36, pres., 1936-64, chmn., 1964-75, bd. dirs., cons., 1975-83. Designer C-34 aircraft (Cessna Airmaster), recipient (3) Detroit News Air Transport Trophies. Recipient Daniel Guggenheim medal, 1975, Wright Bros. Meml. trophy 1981; bldg. named in his honor Wichita State U., 1979. Mem. Gen. Aviation Mfrs. Assn. (founder, 1st chmn.), Aviation Pioneers Hall of Fame, Soc. Exptl. Test Pilots, Quiet Birdmen. Home: Wichita Kans. Died Dec. 21, 1989.

WALLACE, IRVING, author; b. Chgo., Mar. 19, 1916; s. Alexander and Bessie (Liss) W.; m. Sylvia Kahn, June 3, 1941; children: David, Amy. Student, Williams Inst., Berkeley, Calif., 1935. Freelance writer: articles, short stories, others, 1931-53; Author: The Fabulous Originals, 1955, The Square Pegs, 1957, The Fabulous Showman, 1959, The Sins of Philip Fleming, 1959, The Chapman Report, 1960, The Twenty-Seventh Wife, 1961, The Prize, 1962 (made into movie), The Three Sirens, 1963, The Man (George Washington Carver Inst. award, Commonwealth Club of Calif. Lit. award, Nat. Bestsellers Inst. 1965, 1964, Paperback of Year award), The Sunday Gentleman, 1965, The Plot, 1967, The Writing of One Novel, 1968, rev. edit., 1986, The Seven Minutes, 1969, The Nympho and Other Maniacs, 1971, The Word, 1972, The Fan Club, 1974 (Popular Culture Assn. award of excellence), The People's Almanac, 1975, The R Document, 1976, (with others) The Book of Lists, 1977, The Two, 1978, (with others) The People's Almanac 2, 1978, The Pigeon Project, 1979, (with others) The Book of Lists 2, 1980, The Second Lady, 1980, The Book of Predictions, 1981, The Intimate Sex Lives of Famous People, 1981, The People's Almanac 3, 1981, The Almighty, 1982, (with others) The Book of Lists 3, 1983, Significa, 1983, The Miracle, 1984, The Seventh Secret, 1986, The Celestial Bed, 1987, The Guest of Honor, 1988; contbr. to Ency. Brit. Served with USAAF, Signal Corps, AUS, 1942-46. Mem. Authors Guild Am., PEN, Soc. Authors (London).

Home: Brentwood Calif. Died June 29, 1990; buried Hillside Meml. Park, Los Angeles.

WALLACE, JOHN H., JR., university official; b. Louisville, Aug. 3, 1906; s. John II and Grace Jane (Roll) W.; m. Margaret Cook, Sept. 8, 1928; children: John Duncan, William Cook, Margaret (dec.). AB, Princeton U., 1928, MS, 1929, PhD, 1932. Owner, dir. Wallace Labs., cons. chemists, N.Y.C., Jersey City, New Brunswick, N.J., 1934-42; v.p., rsch. dir., prodn. mgr. Carter Products, Inc., pharms. and cosmetics, N.Y.C., New Brunswick, 1942-47; pres. Wallace Labs., Inc., pharms., New Brunswick, Princeton, N.J., 1942-48; dir. Wallace Rsch. Labs., cons. chemists, Princeton, 1948-51; pres. Decyl Pharmacal Co., Princeton, 1949-51; sec. Standard Insulation Co., East Rutherford, N.J., 1947-50, v.p., 1950-51; adminstrv. dir. James Forrestal Rsch. Ctr., Princeton U., 1951-69; treas., bd. dirs. Princeton Inn Co., pres., 1960; bd. dirs. Applied Sci. Corp. Princeton, pres., 1959. Mem. Princeton Twp. Com., 1949-56, mayor, 1955-56; trustee Princeton Hosp. (now Princeton Med. Ctr.), pres., 1953-63. Mem. AAAS, Am. Chem. Soc., Phi Beta Kappa. Home: Princeton N.J.

WALLACE, JOHN MCCHRYSTAL, banker; b. Salt Lake City, Dec. 14, 1893; s. William Ross and Annie (McChrystal) W.; m. Glenn Walker, Sept. 18, 1920; children—Matthew Henry Walker, John McChrystal. B.A., U. of Utah, 1916; M.B.A., Harvard, 1921; LL.D., U. Utah, 1965, Westminster Coll., 1954, Brigham Young U., 1963. With Walker Bank & Trust Co., Salt Lake City, 1921-68, dir., 1921-68, pres., 1944-57, chmn. bd., 1957-66, hon. chmn. bd., 1966-67, advisory dir., from 1967; co-founder First Interstate Bank; pres., dir. United Park City Mines Co., 1955-64; v.p., dir. Banner Mining Co., 1953-71, Ariz. Ranch & Metals Co.; founder, pres. ENERCOR. Civilian aide to sec. of army, 1952-56; mem. Utah Senate, 1933-35; Mayor, Salt Lake City, 1938-39; Mem. lay adv. bd., former chmn. Holy Cross Hosp.; trustee, former chmn. bd. trustees Westminster Coll. Named Businessman of Year Harvard Bus. Sch. Club, Utah, 1966, Disting. prof. of Bus. Westminster Coll., 1987; recipient Giants in our City award Salt Lake Area C. of C., 1977. Mem. Assn. Res. City Bankers (trustee banking research fund 1950-53), Utah Bankers Assn. (pres. 1946-47), Salt Lake City C. of C., Hon. Colo. Corps, Utah Nat. Guard, Chevaliers du Tastevin, Am. Soc. Order of St. John of Jerusalem (asso. knight), Sigma Chi. Presbyterian. Clubs: Mason (Salt Lake City) (33 deg. Shriner), Alta (Salt Lake City), Cottonwood (Salt Lake City), Country (Salt Lake City); Los Angeles Country. Home: Salt Lake City Utah Died Feb. 7, 1989.

WALLACE, MARTHA REDFIELD, management consultant, foundation executive; b. Omaha, Dec. 27, 1927; d. Ralph J. and Lois (Thompson) Redfield. BA, Wellesley Coll., 1949; MA in Internat. Fin., Tufts U., 1950; LittD (hon.), Converse Coll., 1975; LLD (hon.), Occidental Coll., 1975, Pace U., 1975, Manhattan Coll., 1977. Instr. in econs., asst. to dean Fletcher Sch. Econs., Tufts U., 1950-51; economist Dept. State, Washington, 1951-53; with RCA Internat., 1954-55; mem. editorial staff Fortune mag., 1955-57; with IBM, 1960-61; asst. dir. corp. devel. Time, Inc., 1963-67; dir., bd. dirs. Henry Luce Found., Inc., N.Y.C., 1967-83; pres. Redfield Assocs., N.Y.C., 1983-89; bd. dirs. Chem. Banking Corp., Am. Express Co., Bristol-Myers Co.; bd. dirs. N.Y. Stock Exchange, 1977-83, mem. surveillance com., 1985-89; mem. Conf. Bd., from 1974, Nat. Com. on U.S.-China Relations, from 1975, Temp. Commn. on City Fins., 1975-77, Brit.-N.Am. Com., from 1976, Trilateral Commn., 1978-84; chmn., trustee Trust for Cultural Resources City N.Y., 1977-81; mem. adv. Com. on Adminstrn. Justice, 1981-82, social svcs. vis. com. dept. polit. sci. MIT, 1986-88, U. Chgo., 1980-84, others. Trustee Williams Coll., 1974-86, trustee emeritus, 1986-89, citizens budget commn., 1976, Internat. House, 1984-89, Greater N.Y. coun. Boy Scouts Am.; bd. dirs. Am. Coun. on Germany, Greater N.Y. Fund/United Way, 1974-86, Legal Aid Soc., Regional Plan Assn., 1985-88, Citizens Crime Commn., N.Y.C., Inc., 1983—, N.Y.C. Partnership, 1980-85, Coun. Fgn. Rels., Inc., 1972-82; chmn. N.Y. Rhodes Scholars Selection Com., 1983-86, membership coun. Whitney Mus.; mem. Bretton Woods Com., 1987. Wellesley Coll. Durant scholar, 1949. Mem. Am. Judicature Soc. (bd. dirs. 1978—, v.p., exec. com. 1978-81, chmn. 1981-83), Council on Founds. (bd. dirs. 1971-77), Found. Ctr. (bd. dirs. 1971-77), Japan Soc. (bd. dirs. 1975-87, hon. dir. 1989—, chmn. 75th Anniversary Fund 1982-83), Am. Council on Germany (bd. dirs. 1980—), Asia Soc. (mem. pres.'s council, mem. Asian agenda adv. group), N.Y. Racing Assn. (bd. dirs. 1976—), Acad. Polit. Scis., Saratoga Reading Rooms, Inc., Fairbank Ctr. for East Asian Studies, Bus. Coun. for Internat. Understanding (founding mem., hon. bd. trustees 1989—), Phi Beta Kappa Assocs.(founding mem., hon. bd. trustees 1989, Phi Beta Kappa. Clubs: River, Bd. Room, Economic, Wellesley. Home: New York N.Y. Died Nov. 24, 1989; buried Williams Coll. Cemetery.

WALLER, ELLIS J., manufacturing company executive; b. Kewanee, Ill., Nov. 12, 1896; s. Peter A. and Carrie C. (Peterson) W.; m. Barodel Gould, Dec. 29, 1925; children: Harriet C., Peter W., John E. BS, Princeton U., 1919. Salesman The Boss Mfg. Co., N.Y.C., 1921-24, head sales corr. dept., gen. office, from 1924, dir., from 1929, v.p., 1930-39, exec. v.p., 1939-45, pres., 1945-61, chmn. bd., 1961-65, chmn. fin. com., from 1965; treas., dir. Kewanee Mfg. Co.; dir. Peoples Nat. Bank of Kewanee, Gen. Telephone Co. Ill. Mem. Am. Legion, Univ. Club (N.Y.C.), Princeton Club (N.Y.C.), Union League Club (Chgo.), Midland Country Club (Kewanee), Glen Arven Country Club (Thomasville, Ga.), Masons, Elks. Congregationalist. *

WALSH, JAMES AUGUSTINE, judge; b. Westfield, Mass., Sept. 17, 1906; s. Thomas and Hannah (Shea) W.; m. Mary Ficca, Feb. 17, 1930 (dec. Dec. 1966); children: James, Georgeanne, Geraldine, Thomas, Michael. Student, St. Anselm's Coll., Manchester, N.H., 1923-24; LLB, Georgetown U., 1928. Bar: D.C. 1928, Ariz. 1928. Practice law Mesa, Ariz., 1928-41; city atty. City of Mesa, 1936-40; asst. U.S. atty. Dist. Ariz., 1943; co. atty. Maricopa County, Ariz., 1943-44; judge Superior Ct., 1945-47; mem. firm Snell & Wilmer, Phoenix, 1947-52; chief counsel Ariz. Code Commn., 1951-52; U.S. dist. judge, 1952-91. Mem. Ariz. Bar Assn. Home: Tucson Ariz. Died May 1, 1991.

WALT, LEWIS WILLIAM, foundation executive, marine corps officer; b. Harveyville, Kans., Feb. 16, 1913; s. Albert Miller and Estella May (Shields) W.; m. Nancy Mary Sheehan, June 10, 1944; children: Lewis William, Lawrence Cecil, Mary Katherine; m. June B. Jacobsen, Aug. 27, 1971. BA in Chemistry, Colo. State U., 1936, LLD, 1967; grad., Marine Corps Sch., 1937, Marine Corps Command and Staff, 1950, Nat. War Coll., 1960; LLD (hon.), Barry Coll., 1967. Commd. 2d lt. USMC, 1937, advanced through grades to gen., 1968; various assignments U.S., China, Guam, 1936-42; comdr. Co. A. 1st Marine Raider Bn., Solomon Islands, 1942; regtl. ops. officer, then comdg. office 2d Bn. 5th Marine Regt., 1942-43; regtl. exec. officer 5th Marines, 1943-44; chief tactics Officer Candidates Sch., Quantico, Va., 1945-46; bn. landing team instr., troop tng. unit Pacific Marine Corps Base, San Diego, 1946-47; asst. chief staff G-3 1st Marine Brigade and 1st Marine Div., Camp Pendleton, Calif., 1947; ops. and tng. officer 1st Provisional Marine Brigade, Guam, 1947-49, chief staff, 1949; comdr. spl. tng. regt. Marine Corps Schs., 1949, chief tactics sect. S-3, 1950-51; exec. officer Basic Sch., 1951-52; asst. chief staff mil. ops. Amphibious Forces, Pacific Fleet, 1952; comdg. officer 5th Marines, 1st Marine div., asst. chief staff G-3, chief staff 1st Marine div. Korea, 1952-53; dir. advanced base problem sect. Marine Corps Ednl. Ctr., Quantico, Va., 1953-54, comdg. officer officers basic sch., 1954-56, mem. advnaces rsch. group, 1956-57; head detail br., pers. dept. Hdqrs. USMC, 1957, asst. dir. pers., 1957-59; Marine Corps rep. joint advance study group Joint Chiefs of Staff, 1960-61; asst. div. comdr. 2d Marine div., 1961-62; dir. Marine Corps Landing Force Devel. Ctr., Quantico, 1962-65; comdg. gen. 3d Marine Amphibious Force 3d Marine Div., Naval Components comdr., 1965-67; sr. adviser I Corps Mil. Assistance Command, Vietnam, 1965-67, dir. pers., dep. chief staff for manpower, 1967-68; asst. comdt. USMC, Washington, 1968-71; dir. U.S. Senate Investigation on Internat. Narcotics Traffic, 1972; sr. mil. mem. Presdl. Clemency Bd., 1974-75. Exec. dir. U.S. Marines Youth Found., 1972. Decorated Navy Cross (2), DSM (2), Silver Star, Legion of Merit with combat V, Bronze Star with combat V, Purple Heart (2), Ulchi medal, Ulchi medal with silver star, Disting. Svc. medal 2d class (Republic Korea), Svc. medal, Nat. Order medal 3d and 4th class, 1st Order Merit, Gallantry Cross with palm (Vietnam). Mem. Elks, Rotary. Methodist. Home: Gulfport Miss. Died Mar. 26, 1989.

WALTERS, DONALD E., college president; b. Feb. 22, 1934; m. Mary Clifford; 6 children. A.B., Catholic U. Am., 1962; J.D., U. Md., 1969. Asst. to pres. Mt. St. Agnes Coll., Balt., 1962-64; dir. estate planning Johns Hopkins U., Balt., 1964-65; asst. to pres. Johns Hopkins U., 1965-67; exec. asst. to chancellor state colls., dir. planning and devel. R.I. System Higher Edn., 1967-70; dep. provost Mass. State Coll. System, 1970-74, acting provost, dir., 1974-75; exec. dir. bd. govs. Ill. State Colls. and Univs., 1975-84; pres. Montclair State Coll., N.J., 1984-88; chmn. Ill. Ednl. Consortium, 1978-79; cons. U. Man. (Can.), Winnipeg, 1974, Cal. State U. System, 1974; lectr. in field. Contbr. articles to profl. jours. Mem. adv. com. Hubert H. Humphrey Fellowship Program, 1979-82. Eucharist min., lector Holy Redeemer Ch., Chatham, Mass., 1984-90. Served with USAF, 1953-56. Mem. Acad. Acad. Personnel Adminstrn. (pres. 1974-75), Am. Acad. Polit. and Social Scis., Acad. Polit. Sci. Home: Cape Cod Mass. Died Dec. 23, 1990.

WALTERS, WALTMAN, surgeon; b. Cedar Rapids, Ia., July 29, 1895; s. Frank and Mellie (Phipps) W.; m. Phoebe (d. Dr. Willian James Mayo), Feb. 5, 1921; children—Pheobe Mayo, Joan (dec.), Waltman Mayo, James Mayo, Carolyn Damon. B.S., Dartmouth, 1917; M.D., Rush Med. Coll., 1920; M.Sc. in Surgery, U. Minn., 1923; D.Sc. (h.c.), Dartmouth, 1937; LL.D., Hahnemann Med. Coll., Phila., 1942. Diplomate Am. Bd. Surgery, Am. Bd. Urology. Asst. surgeon Mayo Clinic, 1922-24; surgeon, head of a div. surgery, 1924-60, ret.; asso. prof. surgery Mayo Found., U. Minn., 1930-36, prof. surgery, 1936-60, prof. surgery emeritus, 1960-89; mem. adv. panel med. scis. research and Engring. Office Asst. Sec. Def., 1954-60; cons. D.C. Balfour lecture, Toronto, 1949, Lord Moynihan lecture, Leeds, Eng., 1951; Bevan lectr., Chgo., 1953; John Stewart lectr. Dalhousie U., 1954; Walter Estelle Lee lectr. U. Pa., 1955; Phi Beta Pi lectr. U. Miami, 1956; W.J. Mayo lectr. U. Mich.; C.H. Mayo lectr. Northwestern, 1960; Frank H. Lahey lectr., 1959, Roy McClure lectr., 1963. Author several books, spl. chpts. in books on surgery, articles in profl. jours.; Chief editor: A.M.A. Archives of Surgery, 1938-62; editor-in-chief: Lewis-Walters' Practice of Surgery, 1936-62. Life trustee Rush U., 1982-84. Rear adm. M.C., USNR, 1955-57; ret., chief surg. and exec. officer USN Hosp. 1942-44, Corona, Calif.; chief surgery USN Hosp. 1945, Phila.; inactive duty 1945. Recipient commendations Navy; Gold Medal award AMA, 1941; Gold Medal award Miss. Valley Med. Soc., 1954; certificate of Merit AMA, 1955; A.C.S. award for films, 1958; Commendation award U. Chiba, Japan, 1959; Disting. Surgeons award Am. Soc. Abdominal Surgeons, 1969; Disting. Alumnus award Dartmouth, 1950; Disting. Alumnus award Rush Med. Coll., 1970. Fellow A.C.S., Am., So., Central, Western surg. assns., Internat. Soc. Surgery, Soc. Clin. Surgery, AMA (chmn. sect. surgery, gen. and abdominal 1956, chmn. exec. com. surg. sect. 1958), German Surg. Soc., German Acad. Natural Scis., Czechoslovak Med. Soc. (hon.); mem. or hon. mem. numerous profl., med., surg., sci. socs. and assns. Congregationalist. Clubs: University (Chgo. and Rochester); Rochester Country, U.S. Senior Golf Assn. Home: Rochester Minn. Died Aug. 5, 1988; buried Rochester, Minn.

WALTON, SAM MOORE, retail executive; b. Kingfisher, Okla., 1920; m. Helen Walton; 4 children. BA, U. Mo., 1940. With J. C. Penney Co., Des Moines, 1938-42; franchise owner, operator Ben Franklin Stores, 1945-62; co-founder Wal-Mart Stores, Bentonville, Ark., 1962, chmn., chief exec. officer, 1974-88, chmn., until 1992, also bd. dirs. Served with U.S. Army, 1942-45. Recipient Presdl. Medal of Freedom, 1992. Home: Bentonville Ark. Died Apr. 5, 1992.

WALTON, THOMAS BARDEEN, investment banker; b. Butler, Mo., Dec. 28, 1896; s. Gentry Thomas and Ella (Bardeen) W.; m. Gladys Ellett, Mar. 17, 1920. Student, Westminster Coll., Fulton, Mo., 1918. Stockbroker William H. Colvin & Co., Chgo., 1928-30, Blair & Co., Chgo., 1931, Swift & Co., Chgo. and Boston, 1932-33, Jackson & Curtis, Chgo., 1933-34, James H. Oliphant & Co., Chgo., 1935-47; gen. ptnr. charge Chgo. office Fahnestock & Co., from 1947; dir. Gun Traders Ltd., London; mem. Midwest Stock Exch., Chgo. Bd. Trade, Chgo. Merc. Exch., Winnipeg Grain Exch. Mem. Chgo. Club, Attic Club, Shoreacres Club, Execs. Club, Bond Club. *

WALTS, ROBERT WARREN, English language educator; b. New Albany, Ind., Apr. 1, 1921; s. William H. and Alma Ethel (Hixon) W.; m. Gloria Halsey Denton, Jan. 22, 1944; children: Robert Denton, Anne Sawyer, Caroline Burns. A.B., Rutgers U., 1950, A.M., 1951, Ph.D. (Queens fellow), 1953. Mem. faculty U. Mo., Columbia, 1952-53, U. Ga., Atlanta, 1953-56, Ga. State Coll., Atlanta, 1953-59; prof. English S.W. Tex. State U., San Marcos, from 1959, chmn. dept., 1965-72; Piper prof. State of Tex., 1982. Author: William Dean Howells And The House Of Harper, 1957, Study Guide: The Rise Of Silas Lapham, 1963; editor: The American Southwest: Cradle of Literary Art, 1981; contbr. articles on Howells and Shakespeare to profl. jours. Commr. urban renewal, San Marcos, 1963-69. Served with USNR, 1942-45. Mem. AAUP, MLA, South Central Modern Lang. Assn., Conf. Coll. Tchrs. English (councillor), Coll. English Assn. Lodge: Kiwanis (pres. 1967). Home: Wimberley Tex. Died July 18, 1990.

WANG, AN, office automation systems company executive; b. Shanghai, China, Feb. 7, 1920; came to U.S., 1945, naturalized, 1955; s. Yin Lu and Zen Wan (Chien) W.; m. Lorraine Chiu, July 10, 1949; children: Frederick A., Courtney S., Juliette L. B.S., Chiao Tung U., 1940; M.S., Harvard U., 1946, Ph.D., 1948; D.Sc. (hon.), Lowell Inst. Tech, 1971; D.Comml. Sci. (hon.), Suffolk U., 1980; D.Sc. (hon.), Southeastern Mass. U., 1981; D. Engring. (hon.), Poly Inst. N.Y., 1982; D.Sc. (hon.), Syracuse U., 1982; LL.D. (hon.), Emmanuel Coll., 1982; D.Sc. in Bus. Adminstrn. (hon.), Bryant Coll., 1982; L.H.D. (hon.), Fairleigh Dickinson U., 1982; D. Bus. Econs. (hon.), Tufts U., 1982; D.Sc. (hon.), U. Hartford, 1983; LL.D. (hon.), Boston Coll., 1983; D of Univ. (hon.), U. Stirling, Scotland, 1983; D.Sc. (hon.), Northeastern U., 1984; D.Engring. Sci., Merrimack Coll., 1984; D.Sc. (hon.), Brown U., 1985; D.Sc., U. Mass., Amherst, 1986; D of Engring. (hon.), Worcester Poly. Inst., 1987; LL.D, Harvard U., 1987; DSc (hon.), Boston U., 1988; D Engring. (hon.), Rensselaer Poly. Inst., 1988; HHD (hon.), N.E. Sch. Law, 1988; DSc (hon.), Williams Coll., 1988; D of Engring. (hon.), Chiao Tung U., 1988. Tchr. Chiao-Tung U., China, 1940-41; engr. Central Radio Works, China, 1941-45, Chinese Govt. Supply Agy., Ottawa, Ont., Can., 1946-47; research fellow Harvard, 1948-51; owner Wang Labs., Cambridge, Mass., 1951-55; chmn. bd., chief exec. officer, dir. Wang Labs., Inc., Lowell, Mass., 1955-90. Patentee in field. Trustee Northeastern U., Mus. Sci. Fellow IEEE, Am. Acad. Arts and Scis.; mem. Nat. Acad. Engring., Sigma Xi. Home: Lincoln Mass. Died Mar. 24, 1990; buried Lincoln, Mass.

WARBURG, ERIC MAX, investment banker; b. Hamburg, Germany, Apr. 15, 1900; came to U.S., 1923, naturalized, 1938; s. Max M. and Alice (Magnus) W.; m. Dorothea Thorsch, Feb. 14, 1946; children: Marie, Max, Erica. Student, Hamburg and Berlin U. With Disconto-Gesellschaft, Berlin, 1919-20, I. Dreyfus & Co., Frankfurt, Germany, 1920-21, N.M. Rothschild & Sons, London, 1922-23, Kuhn, Loeb & Co., N.Y.C., 1923, Internat. Acceptance Bank, N.Y.C., 1925-26, 1st Nat. Bank, Portland, Oreg., 1924; ptnr. M.M. Warburg & Co., Hamburg, 1929-38, Warburg & Co., Amsterdam, 1929-39, M.M. Warburg-Brinckmann, Wirtz & Co., Hamburg, 1956-90; mem. Verwaltungsrat Effekten bank Warburg A.G.; chmn. E.M. Warburg & Co., Inc., N.Y.C., 1941; dir. S.G. Warburg & Co., Ltd., London. Mem. Coun. on Fgn. Rels., N.Y.C. Served with USAAF, 1942-46. Decorated Legion of Merit (U.S.); named to Order Brit. Empire, Croix de Guerre (France), White Rose (Finland), Bundesverdienstkreuz (Germany). Mem. Wall Street Club. Home: Hamburg-Blankensee Germany Died July 9, 1990.

WARD, J. BASIL, business executive; b. Bklyn., Mar. 19, 1893; s. P. Valentine and Charity Wilson (Lyon) W. Student, pub. schs., Evanston, Ill. Salesman Addressograph Co., Chgo., 1912-13; agt. Addressograph Co., Cin., 1913-29; asst. gen. sales mgr. U.S. and Can. Addressograph Co., Chgo., 1929, gen. sales mgr., 1929-32, agt., 1932-44; v.p. distbn. Addressograph-Multigraph Corp., Cleve., 1944-50, v.p., gen. mgr., 1950-52, pres., from 1952; pres., dir. Vari-Typer Corp., Newark, also pres. or chmn. and dir. numerous subsidiary and affiliated corps. Served as ordnance sgt. 322d F.A., U.S. Army, overseas, World War I. Mem. Cleve. C. of C., Newcomen Soc., Fifty Club, Chagrin Valley Hunt Club, Union Club, Mayfield Country Club, Cleve. Athletic Club. *

WARD, JOHN CARLTON, JR., industrialist; b. Bklyn., Jan. 21, 1893; s. John Carlton and Florence Gannon (Hanfield) W.; m. Laura Willett Pickford, Feb. 12, 1934; children: John Carlton III, Robert Pickford (stepson; 2d lt. USAAF; killed in combat 1944). ME, Cornell U., 1914. Devel. engr. Internat. Paper Co., 1914; asst. to works mgr. Niles Tool Works div. Niles-Bement-Pond Co., 1915-17; prodn. engr. U.S. Ordnance Dept., Watervliet (N.Y.) Arsenal, 1918; works mgr. Pratt & Whitney div. NMiles-Bement-Pond Co., 1919-25; v.p., gen. mgr., dir. Hartford Machine Screw Co., 1926-29; gen. works mgr. Gen. Cable Corp., 1929-34; v.p. Rome Co. Inc., 1934-35; v.p., gen. mgr., dir. Pratt & Whitney Aircraft div. United Aircraft Corp., 1935-40; in charge adv. mission to French Govt. on airplane prodn., 1940; pres. Fairchild Engine and Airplane Corp., 1940-47, chmn., 1948-49; chmn. bd. Thompson Industries, Inc., 1950-53, Vitro Minerals Corp.; pres., dir. Vitro Corp. Am., 1953-59, chmn. bd., 1960-61; bd. dirs. Sheer-Korman Assocs., U.S. Manganese Co. Stanrock Uranium Mines, Ltd.; mem. WPB Mission Gt. Britain, 1942; pres. Aircraft War Prodn. Coun. East Coast Inc., 1943; exec. mem. bd. govs. Aircraft Industries Assn; chmn. adv. bd. Indsl. Coll. Armed Svcs.; chmn. Conn. Nuclear Ctr. for Rsch. and Tng., from 1962; mem. Bus. Coun.; mem. Nat. Def. com. Commn. for Reorgn. Exec. Br. Govt.; mem., chmn. Sec. Navy's Adv. Bd. Ednl. Requirements, 1961-62. Contbr. articles to profl. jours. Bd. dirs. Flight Safety Found.; trustee Cornell U., 1948-53, dir. Aero Lab., dir. Atomic Indsl. Forum, chmn. engring. coun. Fellow ASME; mem. AAAS, AIAA, USAF Aid Soc., Air Force Assn., Def. Orientation Conf., Am. Ordnance Assn., Newcomen Soc., Cornell Soc. Engrs., U.S. Navy League, Masons, Univ. Club, Cornell Club, Norfolk Curling Club, Farmington Country Club, Tau Beta Pi. *

WARD, NORMAN, political science educator; b. Hamilton, Ont., Can., May 10, 1918; s. Arthur Bramwell and Rachel (McQueen) W.; m. Betty Edith Davis, Sept. 11, 1943; children: Nora Ward Russell, Nancy Ward Johnson, Rick, Donald, Colin, Michael. B.A., McMaster U., 1941, LL.D., 1974; M.A., U. Toronto, 1943, Ph.D., 1949; LL.D., Queen's U., 1977. Mem. faculty U. Sask., 1945-85, assoc. prof., 1951-55, prof. polit sci., 1955-85, prof. emeritus, 1985-90; free lance writer, broadcaster, 1941-90, also editor, publisher's reader, pub. affairs commentator. Author: The Canadian House of Commons: Representation, 2d edit, 1963, Government in Canada, 2d edit, 1964, The Public Purse: A Study in Canadian Democracy, 1960, Mice in the Beer, 2d edit, 1970, 3d edit., 1986, The Fully Processed Cheese, 1964, Her Majesty's Mice, 1977; co-author: A Party Politician: The Memoirs of Chubby Power, 1966, Bilingualism and Biculturalism in the Canadian House of Commons, 1970, The Government of Canada, 6th edit, 1987, Democratic Government in Canada, 5th edit, 1989, (with David Smith) Jimmy Gardiner; Relentless Liberal, 1990; Editor: The Politician (by James G. Gardiner), 1975; co-editor: Politics in Saskatchewan, 1968; mem. nat. adv. bd. Can. Ency., 1982-85. Vice chmn. Sask. Electoral Boundaries Commn., 1964-66, 72-73, 74-75, 82-83, mem. until 1986; mem. Sask. Archives Bd., 1961-83, chmn., 1983-85; mem. adv. com. Election Expenses, 1964-66; mem. Saskatoon adv. bd. Soc. Study Heritage of Can.; mem. Can. Council, 1974-80. Recipient Leacock medal, 1961; decorated officer Order Can.; Skelton Clark fellow, 1958-59. Fellow Royal Soc. Can., Can. Polit. Sci. Assn. Home: Saskatoon Sask., Can.

WARD, PAUL WILLIAM, philosophy educator; b. Indpls., June 27, 1893; s. Albert Luther and Rosalie (Wolff) W.; m. Louise Best Wilcox, Sept. 15, 1922; children: Charles Seabury, Bruce Wilcox. AB, Butler U., 1914; diploma, Union Theol. Sem., 1917; AM, Columbia U., 1916, PhD, 1928. student London Sch. Econs. and Polit. Sci., 1920-21. Lectr. Redpath Chautauquas, 1920-22; instr. philosophy Syracuse U., 1922-24, asst. prof., 1924-29, assoc. prof., 1929-37, prof., chmn. dept., 1937-59, prof. emeritus, from 1959; mem. N.Y. State Adv. Bd. on Pub. Work, from 1959. Author: Sovereignty: A Study of a Contemporary Political Notion, 1928; Intelligence in Politics, 1931; A Short History of Political Thinking, 1939; co-author: The Fields and Methods of Knowledge, 1929; contbr. articles to ednl. jours. Commd. 2d lt. pursuit pilot U.S. Air Svc., 1918, later capt. Air Corps Res.; comdg. officer 826th Guard Squadron, Provost Marshall, Mitchel Field, 1942, grad. Army Air Forces Intelligence Sch., Harrisburg, Pa., 1943; with 5th Air Force, S.W. Pacific, in New Guinea, N. East Indies and Philippine campaigns. Fellow AAAS; mem. Am. Philos. Assn., Am. Polit. Sci. Assn., Acad. Polit. Sci., Am. Acad. Polit. and Social Sci., AAUP (assoc. sec. 1939-40, chmn. com. on coll. and univ. govt. 1938-58, coun. 1941-43), Faculty Club (Syracuse), Cosmos Club (Washington), Phi Delta Theta, Tau Kappa Alpha. *

WARDLAW, FRANK HARPER, JR., former publisher; b. Indiantown, S.C., Aug. 16, 1913; s. Frank Harper and Margaret Whitefield (Hudgens) W.; m. Jane Wallace Williamson, Aug. 10, 1940 (dec. 1969); children: Frank Patterson, Harriet Ervin, George Williamson, Margaret Caroline; m. Rosemary Leonard Boynton, 1970. Student, U. S.C., 1931-33. Reporter Columbia (S.C.) Record, 1933-36, A.P., Charlotte, N.C., 1936-37; dir. news svc., instr. journalism U. S.C., 1938-44, assoc. prof. journalism, 1944-50; mng. editor U. S.C. Press, 1945-49, dir., 1949-50; dir. U. Tex. Press, 1950-74, Tex. A&M U. Press, 1974-78; mem. exec. bd. Centro Interamericano de Libros Academicso, Mexico City; mem. adv. com. on publs. Winterthur Mus., Wilmington, Del. Bd. dirs. Franklin Book Program. Fellow Tex. Inst. Letters (pres. 1958-60), Tex. Hist. Assn.; mem. Assn. Am. U. Presses (pres. 1961-63), Philos. Soc. Tex., S.C. Hist. Soc., Town and Gown Club, Blue Key, Block C, Alpha Tau Omega, Sigma Delta Chi. Presbyterian. Home: Fripp Island S.C. Died June 26, 1989.

WARKANY, JOSEF, pediatrician, researcher; b. Vienna, Austria, Mar. 25, 1902; came to U.S., 1932, naturalized, 1938; s. Jacob and Hermine (Buchwald) W.; m. Suzanne Blanche Buhlman, Apr. 24, 1937 (dec.); children—Joseph Henry, Stephen. M.D., U. Vienna, 1926; D.Sc. (hon.), Thomas Jefferson Med. Coll., 1974, U. Ill., 1975. Diplomate Am. Bd. Pediatrics. Intern Children's Clinic, Vienna, 1926-27; asst. Reichsanstalt for Mothers and Children, 1927-31; scholar Children's Hosp. Research Found., Cin., 1931-34, fellow, 1935; asst. attending pediatrician Children's Hosp., Cin., 1934-35, attending pediatrician, from 1935; founder Human Genetics div. Children's Hosp.; attending pediatrician, pediatric and contagious divs. Cin. Gen. Hosp., from 1935, dir. mental retardation research Inst. for Devel. Rsch., 1966-77; prof. research pediatrics U. Cin. Coll. Medicine, from 1953. Author: Congential Malformations, 1971. Recipient Mead-Johnson award, 1944; Borden award, 1950; award medal Am. Assn. Plastic Surgeons, 1962; Distinguished Achievement award Modern Medicine, 1964; Honors award Am. Cleft Palate Assn., 1966; Max Weinstein-Cerebral Palsy award United Cerebral Palsy Assns., 1969; Charles H. Hood Found. award, 1972; Research award Am. Assn. Mental Deficiency, 1976; Recognition award Cin. Pediatric Soc., 1976; George Rieveschl Jr. award U. Cin., 1976; Daniel Drake medal, 1985. Mem. Am. Pediatric Soc. (Howland award 1970), Soc. Pediatric Research, Ohio Med. Assn., Acad. Medicine Cin., Am. Acad. Pediatrics (hon.), Harvey Soc., Teratology Soc. (founder, 1st pres. 1960), Soc. de Pédiatrie (Paris), European Teratology Soc. (hon.), Japanese Teratology Soc. (hon.). Home: Clifton Ohio Died June 22, 1992.

WARMBOLD, THEODORE FREDRICK, II (TED WARMBOLD), newspaper editor; b. St. Louis, Dec. 10, 1943; s. Arthur John and Frances America (Hendel) W.; m. Carolyn Nizzi, Jan. 28, 1967. B.J., U. Mo., Columbia, 1966. Reporter, columnist Rochester (N.Y.) Times-Union, 1966-68; reporter Cocoa (Fla.) Today, 1967; asst. mng. editor Rochester Democrat and Chronicle, 1969-70; mng. editor San Bernardino (Calif.) Sun-Telegram, 1972-75; features editor Dallas Times Herald, 1975-76; exec. editor D mag., Dallas, 1976-77; mng. editor Los Angeles Herald Examiner, 1977-79, exec. editor, 1979-81; exec. editor San Antonio Light, 1981-86, editor, 1986-89; Kilgore counselor DePauw U., Greencastle, Ind., 1972; lectr. Am. Press Inst., 1975. Mem. Sigma Delta Chi, Kappa Tau Alpha. Roman Catholic. Home: San Antonio Tex. Died Feb. 25, 1990; buried Calvary Cemetery, St. Louis, Mo.

WARNER, JOHN CHRISTIAN, chemist, educator; b. Goshen, Ind., May 28, 1897; s. Elias and Addie (Plank) W.; m. Louise Hamer, June 17, 1925; children: William Hamer, Thomas Payton. AB, Ind. U., 1919, AM, 1920, PhD, 1923; postgrad., U. Mich., summer 1933; DSc (hon.), Northeastern U., 1951, Ind. U., 1954, Bucknell U., 1955, U. Md., 1955, Worcester Poly. Inst., 1956, Duquesne U., 1963, Grove City Coll., 1964; LLD (hon.), U. Pitts., 1953, Washington and Jefferson Coll., 1965; LHD (hon.), Youngstown U., 1959, Geneva Coll., 1964; D of Engring. (hon.), U. Toledo, 1960; DSc, Carnegie-Mellon U., 1965; LHD (hon.), Rose Poly. Inst., 1965. Rsch. chemist Barrett Co., Phila., 1918, Cosden Co., Tulsa, 1920-21; instr. chemistry Ind. U., 1921-24; rsch. chemist Wayne Chems. Corp., Ft. Wayne, Ind., 1925-26; instr. chemistry Carnegie Inst. Tech. (now Carnegie-Mellon U.), 1926-28, asst. prof., 1928-33, assoc. prof. theoretical chemistry, 1933-36, assoc. prof. metallurgy, 1936-38, prof. chemistry, 1938-65, head dept. chemistry, 1938-50, on leave to Manhattan Project, 1943-45, dean grad. studies, 1945-50, pres., 1950-65, pres. emeritus, 1965-89; Perrin Meml. lectr., India, 1950-51; chmn. Ednl. Projects, Inc., 1965-75; cons. ednl., indsl. problems; mem. gen. adv. com. AEC, 1952-64; mem. policy adv. bd. Argonne Nat. Lab., 1953-64; dir. Jones & Laughlin Steel Corp., 1951-70, Regional Indsl. Devel. Corp., PPG Industries, Inc., 1965-69, Magnetics, Inc., 1964-70, Dravco Corp., 1961-65, Eriez Mfg. Co., 1965-69, Cyrus W. Rice Co., 1967-69, Spange & Co., 1970-73; mem. rsch. adv. com. Cities Svc. Co., 1968-71; dir. Pitts. br. Fed. Res. Bank, 1954-60, chmn., 1957-60; mem. adv. com. Oakland br. Mellon Nat. Bank. Editor, co-author: Leighhou's Chemistry of Engineering Materials, 4th edit., 1942; author: (with T.P. McCutcheon and H. Seltz) General Chemistry, 3d edit., 1939; (with J.E. Vance) Uranium Technology, 1951; co-author, asst. editor: Chemistry, Metallurgy and Purification of Plutonium, 1945; co-author, editor Metallurgy of Uranium and Its Alloys, 1953; contbr. articles to profl. jours. Trustee Carnegie-Mellon U., Carnegie Inst., Argonne Univs. Assn., Univs. Rsch. Assn.; bd. dirs. Vocat. Rehab. Ctr. Fellow N.Y. Acad. Scis.; mem. AAAS, AIME, Am. Chem. Soc. (councilor, chmn. Pitts. sect. 1941-42, Pitts. award 1945, pres. 1956), Nat. Acad. Scis., Am. Inst. Chemists (gold medal 1953), Electrochem. Soc. (pres. 1952-53), Am. Soc. Engring. Edn., Pitts. Chemists Club (pres. 1941-42), Univ. Club, Duquesne Club (Pitts.), Cosmos Club (Washington), Pike Run Country Club (Jones Mills, Pa.), Phi Beta Kappa, Sigma Xi, Phi Kappa Phi, Tau Beta Pi, Delta Upsilon, Alpha Chi Sigma. Home: Pittsburgh Pa. Died Apr. 12, 1989.

WARNER, WELLMAN JOEL, social psychologist, educator; b. Lyndonville, Vt., Jan. 13, 1897; s. George A. and Rose Mary (Monahan) W.; m. Miriam Saint, Nov. 26, 1930; children: Wellman Joel, Linda. Cert., U. Grenoble, France, 1919; A.B., George Washington U., 1921; B.D., Yale, 1924; Ph.D., U. London, 1929. Ordained to ministry Meth. Ch.; dir. field work Yale, 1922-24; prof. social ethics Ohio Wesleyan U., 1930-38; prof. sociology, head dept. social scis. Dickinson Coll., Carlisle, Pa., 1938-46; prof. sociology U. Coll., head all-univ. dept. sociology and anthropology N.Y. U., 1946-59; prof. sociology and anthropology N.Y. U. (Grad. Sch. Arts and Scis.), 1959-63, emeritus prof. sociology and anthropology, 1963-90; vis. prof. U. So. Calif., 1955; Chmn. bd. dirs. Pub. Affairs Com. N.Y., 1962-70; then dir.; pres. Internat. Congress for Group Psychotherapy, Toronto, Can., 1954; then dir.; chmn. 2d Internat. Congress, Zurich, 1957, Internat. Council for Group Psychotherapy, 1954-62; cons. Dept. Instns., N.J., 1949-56, Vt., 1966-69. Author: The Wesleyan Movement in the Industrial Revolution, 1930; contbr. articles to profl. jours. and books. Pres. bd. trustees Moreno Inst. Served with U.S. Army, 1917-19; Served with AEF, France. Hooker-Dwight fellow Yale, London, Eng., 1924-26. Fellow AAAS, Am. Soc. Group Psychotherapy, Am. Anthrop. Assn., Am. Sociol. Assn. (sec. 1954-58), Soc. Sci. Study Religion; mem. ACLU (acad. freedom com.), Eastern Sociol. Soc. (Merit award), Soc. Psychol. Study Social Issues, Casa Meterna Soc. (v.p.). Home: Shelton Conn. Died Aug. 20, 1990; buried Munson, Mass.

WARREN, CHARLES MARQUIS, author, director, producer, screenwriter; b. Balt.; s. Charles and Beatrice (Porter) W.; m. Anne Crawford Tootle (dec.); m. Mildred C. Lindeberg, 1990. Grad., McDonogh Sch., Md., Balt. City Coll. pres., exec. producer Comdr. Films Corp., Beverly Hills, Calif., CMW Prodns., Beverly Hills, Emirau Prodns., Beverly Hills, CMW, Inc., Beverly Hills, MW Prodns., Agoura Hills, Calif., 1990. Dir., writer: (motion pictures) Little Big Horn, 1951, Hellgate, 1952, Arrowhead, 1953, Flight to Tangier, 1954; dir.: (motion pictures) Seven Angry Men, 1955, Tension at Table Rock, 1956, Trooper Hook, 1956, Black Whip, 1957, Copper Sky, 1957, Blood Arrow, 1956, Desert Hell, 1957, Back from the Dead, 1957, Ride a Violent Mile, 1957, Unknown Terror, 1957, Without Incident, 1957, Cattle Empire, 1958; dir., producer, writer: (motion pictures) Charro!, 1970, Down to the Sea, 1972, Hunter, 1978, The Final Day, 1988, The Missionist, 1989; creator, producer, dir.: (TV series) Gunsmoke, 1955, Rawhide, 1958, The Virginian, 1962; producer Iron Horse, 1966; author: Wilderness, 1940, History of American Dental Surgery, 1941, Only the Valiant, 1943, Valley of the Shadow, 1948, Deadhead, 1950; screenplays Beyond Glory, 1948, Redhead and the Cowboy, 1949, Streets of Laredo, 1949, Oh, Susanna, 1951, Woman of the North Country, 1951, Fighting U.S. Coast Guard, 1951, Springfield Rifle, 1952, Pony Express, 1952, The Greenhorns, 1964; contbr. short stories, serials nat. mags. Comdr. USNR,

1942-46, PTO. Decorated Purple Heart, Bronze Star; recipient Screenwriters Guild award 1955, Emmy award nomination, 1955, Brit. Critics award 1956, Western Heritage award 1959. Mem. Acad. Motion Picture Arts and Scis. (award nominee 1949), Screen Dirs. Guild, Writers Guild Am., Screen Producers Guild. Republican. Episcopalian. Home: Agoura Hills Calif. Died Aug. 11, 1990; buried Arlington Nat. Cemetery.

WARREN, FLETCHER, former ambassador; b. Wolfe City, Tex., Mar. 3, 1896; s. Moses Abraham and Mary Elizabeth (Wilson) W.; m. Wilhelmina Kuenstler, Nov. 224, 1921. AB, U. Tex., 1921; LLD, U. Andes, 1956. Supr. students Tex. Sch. for Deaf, 1921; vice consul, then consul Havana, Cuba, 1921-25; assigned to Dept. State, Washington, 1925-29, exec. asst. to asst. sec. state, 1938-42, 44-45, dir. Office S.Am. Affairs, 1950; consul, Barranquilla, Colombia, 1929-31, Budapest, Hungary, 1931-34; cons., 2d sec., Managua, Nicaragua, 1934-36; cons., 2d sec., then 1st sec. Riga, Latvia, 1936-38; counselor of embassy, Bogota, Colombia, 1942-43; amb. to Nicaragua, Managua, 1945-47, to Paraguay, Asuncion, 1947-50, to Venezuela, Caracasm 1851-56, to Turkey, Ankara, 1956-60. Served with U.S. Army, 1918-19. Mem. Am. Fgn. Svc. Assn., Am. Club (Caracas), Army and Navy Club (Washington), Pi Sigma Alpha. Home: Greenville Tex. Died Jan. 8, 1992; buried Mt. Carmel Cemetery.

WARREN, JAMES VAUGHN, physician, educator; b. Columbus, Ohio, July 1, 1915; s. James Halford and Lucile (Vaughn) W.; m. Gloria Kicklighter, May 27, 1954. B.A., Ohio State U., 1935; M.D., Harvard, 1939; D.Sc., Emory U., 1974; DSc, Med. Coll. of Ohio, 1986. Diplomate: Am. Bd. Internal Medicine (sec.-treas. 1970-71, vice chmn. 1971-72). Med. house officer Peter Bent Brigham Hosp., 1939-41, asst. resident medicine, 1941-42; research fellow medicine Harvard U., 1941-42; med. investigator problems of shock and vascular injuries OSRD, 1942-46; instr. medicine Emory U. Med. Sch., 1942-46, asso. prof. medicine, prof. physiology, chmn. dept. physiology, 1947-51, prof. medicine, 1951-52; asst. prof. medicine Yale Med. Sch., 1946-47; prof. medicine Duke Sch. Medicine, 1952-58; prof. medicine, chmn. dept. internal medicine U. Tex. Sch. Medicine, 1958-61; prof. medicine Ohio State U. Med. Sch., 1961-87, prof. emeritus, 1988-90, chmn. dept. medicine, 1961-79; Mem. cardiovascular sect. USPHS, 1952-56; mem. tng. grant com. Nat. Heart Inst., 1961-64; mem. Nat. Acad. Medicine-Inst. Medicine, 1971; part-time study dir. Inst. Medicine, 1987-88. Author: Cardiovascular Physiology, 1975; Editorial bd.: jour. Med. Opinion, 1971; Contbg. author: jour. Pre-Eclamptic and Eclamptic Toxemia of Pregnancy, 1941, Methods in Medical Research, vol. VII; Contbr. numerous articles to profl. publs. Recipient Disting. Alumnus award Duke U. Med. Ctr., 1970, Columbus Mayor's award for vol. svc., 1978, Christopher Columbus award Columbus area C. of C., 1988, Disting. Svc. award Div. Fire, Columbus, 1990. Master A.C.P.; mem. AMA (chmn. sect. internal medicine 1964-65), Assn. Profs. Medicine (pres. 1967-68, Williams disting. chmn. medicine award 1979), Am. Clin. and Climatol. Assn. (pres. 1986), Soc. Univ. Cardiologists, Am. Heart Assn. (pres. 1962-63, Gold Heart award, James B. Herrick award 1976), Am. Soc. Clin. Investigation, Am. Fedn. Clin. Research (nat. pres. 1952-53), Am. Physiol. Soc., Osler Soc., Soc. Exptl. Biology and Medicine, Assn. Am. Physicians, So., Central socs. clin. research, Sigma Xi, Alpha Omega Alpha. Conglist. Clubs: Cosmos, Explorers, Harvard. Home: Dublin Ohio Died Feb. 14, 1990; buried Union Cemetery, Columbus, Ohio.

WARREN, LUCIAN CRISSEY, journalist; b. Jamestown, N.Y., Feb. 12, 1913; s. Lucian Jason and Bernice (Scofield) W.; m. Katherine Smith, June 17, 1939; children—Sylvia, Lucian James, Katherine, Nancy. A.B., Denison U., 1936. Reporter Jamestown (N.Y.) Evening Jour., 1929-31, 34; reporter Chautauquan (N.Y.) Daily, 1935-37, editor, 1938-39; reporter Buffalo Courier-Express, 1937-43, chief Washington bur., 1945-68; chief Washington bur. Buffalo Evening News, 1969-78; Washington corr. Frederick (Md.) News-Post, from 1979, Roanoke (Va.) Time & World-News, 1979-82; pub. relations dir. Colonial Radio Corp., Buffalo, 1944; editor World Hwys., 1966-71; free-lance writer, lectr. Contbr. articles to mags. Recipient Disting. Alumnus citation Denison U.; Hall of Fame award Soc. Profl. Journalist. Mem. Overseas Writers of Washington, Standing Com. of Corrs. Washington (chmn. 1967), Phi Beta Kappa Assos., Phi Beta Kappa, Sigma Delta Chi, Phi Gamma Delta (editor 1961-62), Omicron Delta Kappa. Clubs: Gridiron (Washington) (pres. 1975, sec. from 1980), Nat. Press (Washington) (pres. 1955). Home: Issue Md. Died Oct. 12, 1988; buried Bemus Poiny Cemetery, Bemus Point, N.Y.

WARREN, ROBERT PENN, writer, poet, educator; b. Guthrie, Ky., Apr. 24, 1905; s. Robert Franklin and Anna Ruth (Penn) W.; m. Emma Brescia, Sept. 12, 1930 (div. 1950); m. Eleanor Clark, 1952; children: Rosanna, Gabriel Penn. B.A. summa cum laude, Vanderbilt U., 1925; M.A., U. Calif., 1927; postgrad., Yale U., 1927-28; B.Litt. (Rhodes scholar), Oxford U., 1930; Litt.D., U. Louisville, Colby Coll., U. Ky., Swarthmore Coll., Harvard U., Yale U., Fairfield U., Wesleyan U., Southwestern Coll. at Memphis, U. South, U. New Haven, Johns Hopkins U., Ariz. State U., Dartmouth Coll., Monmouth Coll., 1971, NYU, 1983, Oxford U., 1963; L.H.D., Kenyon Coll.; LL.D., U. Bridgeport. Mem. Fugitive Group of Poets, 1923-25; asst. prof. English, Southwestern Coll., Memphis, 1930-31; acting asst. prof. Vanderbilt U., 1931-34; asst. prof. La. State U., 1934-36, asso. prof., 1936-42; prof. English, U. Minn., 1942-50; prof. playwrighting Yale U., 1951-56, prof. English, 1961-73, prof. emeritus, 1973-89; chair of poetry Library of Congress, 1944-45, cons. in poetry, 1986; mem. staff Writer Conf. U. Colo., 1936, 37, 40, Olivet Coll., 1940; vis. lectr. U. Iowa, 1941; Jefferson lectr. NEH, 1974. Author: novel World Enough and Time, 1950; poem Brother to Dragons, new version, 1979; novel Band of Angels, 1955, Segregation, 1956; poems Promises, 1957; Selected Essays, 1958; poems The Cave, 1959; poetry You, Emperors and Others, 1960, The Legacy of the Civil War, 1961; novel Wilderness, 1961, Flood, 1964; Who Speaks for the Negro, 1965, Selected Poems New and Old, 1923-1966, 1966; poems Incarnations, 1968; poetry Audubon: A Vision, 1969, Homage to Theodore Dreiser, 1971; Author of: Meet Me in The Green Glen; Author: Or Else-Poem/Poems 1968-74, 1975, Democracy and Poetry, 1975, Selected Poems: 1923-75, 1977; novel A Place To Come To, 1977; Now and Then: Poems 1976-79, Being Here: Poems, 1978-79, 80, Rumor Verified, Poems, 1981, Chief Joseph of the Nez Perce, a poem, 1983, New and Selected Poems 1923-1985, 1985; editor or co-editor other books; a founder and editor: The So. Rev., 1935-42. Poet laureate of U.S., 1986—; recipient Houghton Mifflin Lit. Fellowship award, 1936, Levinson prize Poetry: A Mag. of Verse, 1936, Caroline Sinkler prize Poetry Soc. S.C., 1936, 37, 38, Guggenheim fellow in writing, 1939-40, 47-48, Shelley prize for poetry, 1942, Pulitzer prize for fiction, 1947, Robert Meltzer award Screen Writers Guild, 1949, Sidney Hillman award, 1957, Pulitzer prize in poetry, 1957, 81, Edna St. Vincent Millay prize Am. Poetry Soc., 1958, Nat. Book award for poetry, 1958, Irita Van Doren Lit. award N.Y. Herald Tribune, 1965, Bollingen prize in poetry Yale U., 1967, Van Wyck Brooks award for poetry, 1970, Nat. medal for Lit., 1970, award for Lit., U. S.C., 1973, Emerson-Thoreau award Am. Acad. Arts and Scis., 1975, Copernicus prize Am. Acad. Poets, 1975, Harriet Monroe award for poetry, 1979, Presdl. Medal of Freedom, 1980, Common Wealth award, 1980, Gold medal for poetry Am. Acad. and Inst. Arts & Letters, 1985, Prize fellowship McArthur Found., 1981, Nat. Medal of Arts, 1987. Mem. Am. Acad. Arts and Letters, Acad. Arts and Scis., Am. Philos. Soc., Acad. Am. Poets (chancellor). Home: Cambridge Mass. Died Sept. 15, 1989.

WARREN, W. DEAN, surgeon, educator; b. Miami, Oct. 28, 1924. MD, Johns Hopkins U., 1950. Intern Johns Hopkins U., 1950-51; asst. resident Univ. Hosp., Ann Arbor, Mich., 1951-52; asst. resident Barnes Hosp., St. Louis, 1952-54, resident, 1954-55; chief surgeon Jackson Meml. Hosp., Miami; instr. dept. surgery U. Va., 1955-56, asst. prof. surgery, 1957-60, assoc. prof., 1960-63; prof., chmn. dept. surgery U. Miami, 1963-67, 69-71, dean sch. medicine, 1967-68, v.p. med. affairs, 1968-69; prof., chmn. dept. surgery Emory U., Atlanta, 1971-88. Fellow Am. Coll. Surgeons (pres. 1986-87); mem. AMA, Am. Surg. Assn. (former pres.), Pan Am. Med. Assn., Soc. Clin. Surgery, Soc. Univ. Surgeons, Soc. Vascular Surgeons, So. Soc. Clin. Surgeons, So. Surg. Assn. (former pres.), Soc. Univ. Chmn. (former pres.), Whipple Soc. (former pres.). Home: Decatur Ga. Died May 10, 1989; cremated.

WARRINER, FREDERIC FREEMAN, actor; b. Pasadena, Calif., June 2, 1916; s. Frederick Earl and Hildreth Vivian (Vail) W. Ed., Pasadena City Coll., 1938. Dir. Barter Winter Tours, 1946-50. Appeared in: Broadway plays Speak of the Devil, 1939, Oscar Wilde, 1940, King Lear, 1950; Braodway plays Mr. Pickwick, 1950; Broadway plays Taming of the Shrew, 1951, Getting Married, 1951, A Pin to See the Peepshow, 1953; Broadway plays St. Joan, 1954-55; appeared in: Broadway plays The Wayward Saint, 1954, Major Barbara, 1956-57, Time Remembered, 1957-58, Caligula, 1959, Oliver!, 1962, Portrait of A Queen, 1969; Braodway plays Two Gentlemen of Verona, 1971-73; Phoenix Theatre, N.Y.C. Dark Lady of the Sonnets, 1937, The Octoroon, 1937, She Stoops to Conquer, 1973, Androcles and the Lion, 1973, The Plough and the Stars, 1973, Hamlet, 1973, Six Characters in Search of an Author, 1973, The Carefree Tree, 1973, The White Devil, 1973, The Doctor's Dilemma, 1973 (TV film), The Story of a Patriot, 1955; repertory-stock and off Broadway plays various N.Y. Shakespeare Festival plays under aegis of Joseph Papp; rd. shows A Man For All Seasons, 1963, The Royal Hunt of the Sun, 1963-64, R & G Are Dead, 1968, Hamlet, 1968. Winner Los Angeles-Allied Arts Contest, 1934; winner Shakespeare Contest, 1936, 37, 38. Mem. Actor's Equity Assn. (Clarence Denwent award 1951), AFTRA, Screen Actor's Guild, Am. Guild Musical Artists. Home: Old Saybrook Conn. Died Nov. 10, 1992. †

WARTELS, NAT, publishing company executive; b. N.Y.C., Jan. 19, 1902. Grad., Columbia U., Wharton Sch., U. Pa. Ptnr., pub. Crown Pubs., Inc., N.Y.C., 1936, chmn., until 1988; former prin. Outlet Book Co., Pubs. Central Bur., Living Lang. record courses. Home: New York N.Y. Died Feb. 7, 1990. †

WARTERS, D(ENNIS) N(OEL), insurance executive; b. Birmingham, Eng., Dec. 18, 1896; came to U.S., 1920, naturalized, 1926; s. William J. and Mary E. (Birch) W.; m. Lurene A. Leeds, June 30, 1923; children: Mary Ellen, William D. AB, U. Man. (Can.), 1917. Actuarial student Gt. West Life Ins. Co., Winnipeg, Man., 1917-20; asst. actuary Bankers Life Co., Des Moines, 1921-34, assoc. actuary, 1934-41, v.p., assoc. actuary, 1941-42, v.p., actuary, 1942-46, exec. v.p., 1946-56, pres., 1956-61, chmn. bd., from 1961, also dir.; dir. Ctrl. Nat. Bank & Trust Co. Contbr. articles to ins. and commerce publs. Mem. pension rsch. coun. Wharton Sch. U. Pa.; bd. dirs. Des Moines Bur. Mcpl. Rsch.; trustee Drake U.; chmn. S.S. Huebner Found.; mem. Des Moines City Park Bd. Fellow Soc. Actuaries (pres. 1960-61, gov.), Nat. Assn. Life Underwriters; mem. Life Office Mgmt. Assn. (pres.), Life Ins. Assn. (dir.), Inst. LIfe Ins. (dir.), C. of C. (dir.), Des Moines Pow Wow Club, Wakonda Club. *

WASHBURN, PAUL, bishop; b. Aurora, Ill., Mar. 31, 1911; s. Eliot Arthur and Lena (Buhrnsen) W.; m. Kathryn Elizabeth Fischer, Jan. 12, 1937; children: Mary Kathryn Washburn Smith, Jane Anne Washburn Eigenbrodt, Frederick Paul, John Arthur. B.A., N. Central Coll., Naperville, Ill., 1936, L.H.D., 1970; B.D., Evang. Theol. Sem., 1938; D.D., Ind. Central Coll., Indpls., 1954, Wiley Coll., Marshall, Tex., 1975, Garrett-Evang. Theol. Sem., 1983; D.C.L., Westmar Coll., LeMars, Iowa, 1972. Teller, bookkeeper First Nat. Bank, Aurora, 1929-32; ordained to ministry Evang. Ch., 1938; pastor in Chenoa, Ill., 1934-39, Rockford, Ill., 1939-52, Naperville, 1952-64; exec. sec. EUB Commn. Ch. Union, 1964-68; bishop United Meth. Ch., Mpls., 1968-72, Chgo. area, 1972-80; mem. exec. com. World Meth. Council, 1971-81; mem. United Meth. del. to gen. bd. Nat. Council Chs., 1970-74; pres. Bd. Global Ministries, United Meth. Ch., 1972-76. Author: An Unfinished Church, 1984; also articles. The United Methodist Primer. Pres. Council Social Ags., Rockford, 1948-49, Family Service Orgn., 1948-50; mem. exec. com. and plan Union Commn. Consultation Ch. Union; trustee Garrett-Evang. Theol. Sem., Evanston, Ill., from 1972, N. Central Coll., Naperville, Kendall Coll., Evanston, 1972-80, Northwestern Meml. Hosp., Chgo., 1972-86. Home: Lombard Ill. Died May 6. 1989; buried Naperville (Ill.) Cemetery.

WASHINGTON, BENNETTA BULLOCK, government agency official; b. Winston-Salem, N.C., May 1, 1918; d. George Oliver and Rebecca (Burgess) Bullock; m. Walter Edward Washington, Dec. 26, 1941; 1 dau., Bennetta Bullock Washington Jules-Rosette. A.B., Howard U., 1937, M.A., 1939; Ph.D., Cath. U. Am., 1951; LL.D., Wilson Coll., 1969, Smith Coll., 1970, Rider Coll., 1974, Trinity Coll., Washington, 1974; L.H.D., Dunbarton Coll., 1970, Mt. Vernon Coll., 1977. Tchr., counselor, prin. pub. schs. Washington and Balt., 1939-64; initiator, dir. Women's Center, Job Corps, OEO, 1964-70; assoc. dir. women's programs and edn. Job Corps, U.S. Dept. Labor, Washington, 1970-73, spl. asst. to asst. sec. for employment and tng., 1974-80, advisor and cons., from 1980; vis. prof. counseling and guidance NYU, 1952-63; dir. Cardozo Project in Urban Edn. Pres.'s Commn. Juvenile Delinquency, 1960-64, mem. commn., 1962-64; mem. Mayor N.Y.C. panel for decentralization of schs., 1966-67; dir. NYU Inst. Tchrs. and Counselors, V.I., 1967; selected to attend Brookings Inst. Conf. Fed. Execs., 1967; prof. Washington Sch. Psychiatry, 1968; mem. White House Conf. on Food Nutrition and Hunger, 1969, White House Conf. on Children, 1970, White House Conf. on Youth, 1971, Pres.'s Commn. Employment of Handicapped, from 1969; Martin Luther King scholar in residence Rutgers U., 1969; mem. steering com. Nat. Reading Council, from 1970; mem. nat. com. Radcliffe Coll.; govt. rep. on diplomatic missions to, Japan, Russia, France, Eng., 1969, Africa, 1971, Mex., 1973, Jamaica, 1974; cons. and lectr. on edn. and inter-group relations. adv. council midwifery program Georgetown U. Sch. Nursing, from 1976. Author: Background Factors and Adjustment, 1951, Youth in Conflict, 1963, Colored by Prejudice, 1964, Counseling the Disadvantaged Girl, 1968; contbr. articles to profl. jours. Bd. dirs. Internat. Student House; bd. dirs. Sex Info. and Edn. Council U.S., Nat. Symphony Bd., Washington Opera Soc., Mt. Vernon Coll., Ch. Youth Research, Population Reference Bur., from 1983; trustee Henry M. Strong Found., Trinity Coll., D.C., Am. Field Service, 1969-70, Meridian House Internat., 1967-81, Am. U., from 1970; founder, exec. Women in Govt., 1974; active Prevention of Blindness Soc., Florence Crittendon Home, United Fellowship of Chs. Recipient awards and citations for achievement in community service D.C. unit Nat. Council Jewish Women, 1964, awards and citations for achievement in community service Nat. Assn. Negro Bus. and Profl. Women's Clubs, 1965, awards and citations for achievement in community service Roosevelt U., 1966, awards and citations for achievement in community service P.O.E., 1966; alumni achievement award Howard U., 1969; alumni achievement award Am. U., 1974; alumni achievement award Cath. U., 1974; Human Rights and Fundamental Freedoms award, 1978; named D.C. Mother of Yr., 1978. Mem. Consortium of Univs., Women's Nat. Democratic Club (bd. govs. 1982), Alpha Kappa Alpha. Home: Washington D.C. Died May 28, 1991.

WASSON, ALEXANDER VERNER, banker; b. Pitts., Apr. 13, 1896; s. Henry Grant and Rhea (Verner) W.; m. Marion Ellen Beeson, Apr. 17, 1928. AB, Colgate U., 1918; student law, U. Pitts., 1920-22. Bar: Pa. 1923. Trust officer Union Nat. Bank of Pitts., 1929-46; v.p., trust officer First Nat. Bank of Santa Fe, 1947-52, pres., dir., 1952-62, chmn. bd., from 1962. Dir. Santa Fe Sinfonietta and Choral Soc., 1952-56, Santa Fe Community Fund, 1955-56; pres. bd. regents Mus. of N.Mex., 1955-59, bd. dirs., from 1959. Served with U.S. Army, 1917-19; from 2d lt. to maj. AUS, 1942-45. Mem. Am. Bankers Assn., N.Mex. Bankers Assn., Santa Fe County Bar Assn., N.Mex. Bar Assn. (dir. from 1958), AIM (charter mem. pres.'s coun.), Opera Assn. N.Mex. (dir. 1957-60), S.W. Monuments Assn., Rotary, Garden of Gods Club (Colorado Springs), Delta Kappa Epsilon, Phi Delta Phi. Episcopalian. *

WATERS, AARON CLEMENT, geologist, consultant; b. Waterville, Wash., May 6, 1905; s. Richard Jackson and Hattie (Clement) W.; m. Elizabeth Pearl von Hoene, June 10, 1940; adopted children: Susan Margaret, Sharon Christine. BS, U. Wash., 1926, MS, 1927; PhD, Yale U., 1930. Instr. geology Yale U., 1928-30; prof. Stanford U., 1930-42, 45-51, Johns Hopkins U., 1952; prof., founder earth scis. program U. Calif., Santa Cruz, 1967-early 70's; tchr. U. Tex., El Paso, 1979-82; cons. Los Alamos (N.Mex.) Lab., 1982-84; cons., geologist U.S. Geol. Survey, 1930, 42-45, 51-52; cons. to various firms and municipalities, from 1926; condr. geol. tng. for astronauts NASA, mid-1960's. Contbr. articles on structural geology and petrology to sci. publs. Guggenheim fellow, 1937-38. Fellow Geol. Soc. Am. (Penrose medal 1982); mem. NAS, Mineral Soc. Am., Internat. Geophys. Union, Geol. Soc. London. Democrat. Home: Tacoma Wash. Died May 18, 1991.

WATERS, EDWARD NEIGHBOR, musicologist, librarian; b. Leavenworth, Kans., July 23, 1906; s. Charles Andrew and Emma Louise (Neighbor) W.; m. Carrie Wales Baird, Nov. 29, 1928 (dec. July 1961); children: Hugh Richard, Lois Elaine (Mrs. David Jerome Affholder); m. Lilly Lesin Kay, Sept. 27, 1962. MusB, U. Rochester, 1927, MusM, 1928; MusD, Cleve. Inst. Music, 1973. Pvt. tchr. music, organist Palmyra, N.Y., 1923-30; tchr. piano Juniata Coll., 1930-31; with div. music Libr. of Congress, Washington, 1931-76, from asst. chief. to chief, 1938-76. Author: Victor Herbert, A Life in Music, 1955, Frederic Chopin by Franz Liszt, 1963; contbr. articles to profl. jours. Chmn. bd. dirs. U.S. Book Exch., 1958-62; bd. dirs. Washington Performing Arts Soc., hon., 1976-91; mem. Heineman Found. for Rsch., Ednl. and Sci. Purposes, Inc. Fulbright sr. rsch. fellow, 1962-63, Ford Found rsch. fellow, 1962-63, Chapelbrook Found. fellow, 1968. Mem. Music Libr. Assn. (pres. 1941-46), Internat. Assn. Music Librs., Am. Musicol. Soc. (sec. 1947-48), Manuscript Soc., Coun. Nat. Libr. Assn. (chmn. 1946-47), D.C. Libr. Assn. (pres. 1967), Cosmos Club. Home: Washington D.C. Died July 27, 1991.

WATKINS, CHARLES EUGENE, JR., lawyer; b. Rutherfordton, N.C., Jan. 26, 1930; s. Charles Eugene and Jacqueline (MacMillan) W.; m. Isabelle Mary Young, Dec. 6, 1952; children—Elise Marie, Charles Eugene III, James Alexander, Henry MacMillan. A.B., Duke U., 1952; J.D., Emory U., 1961. Bar: Ga., U.S. Dist. Ct. (no. dist.) Ga., U.S. Ct. Appeals (5th cir.), U.S. Ct. Appeals (11th cir.), U.S. Supreme Ct. Mng. ptnr. Hansell & Post and predecessor, Atlanta, from 1961. Editor-in chief Emory U. Jour. Pub. Law, 1960-61; contbr. articles to profl. jours. Mem., past chmn. Emory U. Law Sch. Council, Atlanta. Served to lt. USN, 1952-56; Korea. Fellow Am. Coll. Trial Lawyers; mem. ABA, Ga. Bar Assn., Atlanta Bar Assn. (v.p., chmn. jud. selection and tenure com.). Clubs: Capital City, Atlanta City, Lawyers (Atlanta). Lodge: Lions (pres. local club 1973-74). Home: Atlanta Ga. Deceased.

WATSON, ALFRED NELSON, business executive lawyer; b. Columbus, Ohio, Nov. 22, 1910; s. Alexander Livingston and Adaline (Kershner) W.; m. Elizabeth Dixon, Sept. 15, 1934; children—Keith Stuart, Andrew Graham. A.B., Ohio State U., 1931, M.S., 1932; Ph.D., 1934; LL.B., J.D., Capital U., 1955; Social Sci. Research Council fellow, U. London, Eng., 1937-38. Bar: Ohio bar 1955, U.S. Supreme Ct. bar 1958. Econ. and statis. research positions U.S. Govt., 1934-39; with Curtis Pub. Co., 1940-52; pres. market research subsidiary Nat. Analysts, Inc., 1946-52; bus. cons., pvt. practice law, 1953-58; pres. Bus. Investment Corp., Columbus, 1955-88; also bd. dirs.; v.p. Alfred Politz Research, Inc. Bus. Investment Corp., N.Y.C., 1958-61; v.p. U.S. Rubber Co., N.Y.C., 1961-63; bd. dirs. Pathe Industries, Inc., 1963-65; bd dirs. Lionel Corp., 1963-67; bd. dirs. ABC Industries, Inc., 1965-67; chmn., chief exec. officer, bd. dirs. Living Care Centers, Inc., 1968-88; pres. Northland Terr. Convalescent Ctr., Inc., 1978-88; Prof. bus. Columbia Grad. School Bus., 1963-65; cons. WPB, 1941-42; chief statistician SSS, 1942. Contbr. articles to profl. publs. Pres., bd. dirs. N.Y. Fertility Research Found.; pres. N.Y. chpt. Epilepsy Found. Am., also nat. bd. dirs.; trustee Children's Hosp., Columbus. Served to maj. USAAF, 1943-45. Fellow AAAS, Am. Statis. Assn. (v.p. 1942), Am. Coll. Nursing Home Adminstrs.; mem. Am. Mktg. Assn., Am., N.Y.C. bar assns., Market Research Council N.Y. Home: Columbus Ohio Died June 14, 1988; buried Bronxville, N.Y.

WATSON, JESSE PAUL, economist; b. Oakdale, La., Apr. 7, 1896; s. Isaiah and Sarah Elizabeth (Golemon) W.; m. Elizabeth Joyce, June 18, 1927 (dec.); 1 dau., Sonya Joyce; m. Mary Inzer Davis, June 28, 1941; 1 dau., Anne Davis. AB, U. Tex., 1922, AM, 1924; PhD, Robert Brookings Grad. Sch., 1929. Tutor in econs. U. Tex., 1922-24, instr., summer 1924; study of Bur. of the Mint Inst. for Govt. Rsch., Washington, summer 1925; rsch. in econs. and govt. The Ohio Inst., 1926-30; condr. econ. rsch. Bur. of Bus. Rsch., U. Pitts., from 1930, asst. dir., 1930-39, dir., 1942-54, prof. econ. rsch.; part-time tchr. econs. U. Pitts., from 1937; part-time spl. study of water power Nat. Resources Com., 1938-39. Co-author: Energy Resources and National Policy, 1939; contbr. articles to profl. jours. Mem. City Planning Commn., Pitts., 1942-59, chmn., 1954-59. Mem. Phi Beta Kappa, Delta Sigma Rho. *

WATTS, MAY PETREA THEILGAARD, naturalist; b. Chgo., May 1, 1893; d. Hermann and Claudia (Anderson) Theilgaard; m. Raymond Watts, Dec. 27, 1924; children: Erica, Tom, Nancy, Peter. BS, U. Chgo., 1918. Staff naturalist Morton Arboretum, Lisle, Ill., 1942-61, naturalist emeritus, from 1961; lectr. TV programs. Author: Reading the Landscape, 1957; Trees, 1964; also handbooks. Hon. mem. Friends of our Native Landscape, from 1950. Recipient Douglas medal for conservation edn. Garden Club Am., 1954; May Theilgaard Watts Reading Garden named for her Morton Arboretum, 1963l Du Page Audubon Soc. Pres.'s award, 1965. Mem. Nat. Assn. Biology Tchrs. (hon.), Garden Club Ravinia and Naperville (hon.), Phi Beta Kappa. *

WATTS, OLIN E(THREDGE), lawyer; b. Bartow, Fla., Aug. 27, 1899; s. Olin Ethredge and Frances (Allen) W.; m. Cornelia Colson, June 23, 1926; children: Margaret Cornelia (Mrs. H. Darby Perry), Frances Eloise (Mrs. Edgar W. McCurry, Jr.), Jane. AB, U. Fla., 1925, LLB, 1928, JD (hon.), 1928. Bar: Fla. 1928. Mem. Jennings, Watts, Clarke & Hamilton, Jacksonville, Fla., from 1931; mem. circuit ct. Commn. Duval Co., 1942-48; dir. Barnett Nat. Bank, Jacksonville, Fla., Fidelity Federal Savs. & Loan Assn., Jacksonville; chmn. Fla. Bd. Examiners, 1949-56. Mem. welfare bd. Duval Co., 1942-45; bd. trustees U. Fla. Law Rev. Mem. ABA (chmn. sect. legal edn. and admissions to bar); mem. Am. Law Inst., Am. Judicature Soc., Nat. Conf. Bar Examiners (past chmn.), Fla. Bar Assn., Jacksonville Bar Assn., Jacksonville Symphony Assn. (past pres.), U. Fla. Alumni Assn., Newcomen Soc. Eng., Blue Key Soc., Order of Coif, River Club, Ponde Vedra Club, Rotary, Yacht Club, Phi Delta Theta, Phi Delta Phi, Phi Kappa Phi, Phi Beta Kappa. *

WATTS, OTTO O(LIVE), chemistry educator; b. Brentwood, Ark., Mar. 21, 1893; s. J(ohn) C(layton) and Lillian Harriett (Olive) W.; m. Lela May Shaw, Sept. 12, 1919; 1 dau., Helen Florence (Mrs. George A. Campbell, Jr.). AB, Simmons Coll., (now Hardin Simmons U.), Abilene, Tex., 1913, Rice Inst., Houston, 1916; AM, U. Colo., 1923; PhD, Stanford U., 1932. postgrad. U. Mich., 1927. Tchr. high sch., Westbrook, Tex., 1913, Mart, Tex., 1914; prin. high sch., Groveton, Tex., 1916, Austin, Tex., 1919; prof. chemistry Hardin-Simmons U., from 1920, head dept., 1920-64, chmn. grad. studies, 1938-52; instr. chemistry U. Colo., 1922-24; teaching fellow, acting asst. prof. chemistry Stanford U., 1930-32; vis. prof. chemistry Tex. Western Coll., El Paso, summers 1936, 37, 39, S.F. Austin State Coll., Nacogdoches, Tex., summer, 1938. Author: (with W.H. Clark and others) General Chemistry, 1926; contbr. revs. and articles to periodicals. Served as radio sgt. 1st class, 90th div. U.S. Army, 1917-19, later instr. chemistry dept. AEF U., Beaune, France. Fellow AAAS, Tex. Acad. Sci. (hon. life; 1st v.p. 1937, treas. 1940-42); mem. Am. Chem. Soc., Tex. Archeol. and Paleontol. Soc. (dir., sec. treas.), Tex. Archeol. Soc. (life), Sigma Xi, Phi Lambda Upsilon, Alpha Chi (pres. 1950, exec. sec.-treas. Region I). Baptist. *

WAUGH, FREDERICK VAIL, agricultural economist; b. Burlington, Vt., June 11, 1898; s. Frank Albert amd Mary Alice (Vail) W.; m. Irma Louise Wilcox, Oct. 18, 1924; children: Margaret Alice, Prudence, Douglas Wilcox. BSc., Amherst Coll., 1922; MS, Rutgers U., 1924; grad. study, Harvard U., 1926-27; PhD, Columbia U., 1929; postgrad. study, European Univs., 1932-33. Splist. agrl. rsch. N.J. Dept. Agr., 1922-25; extension economist Conn. Agr. Coll., 1925-27; dir. Mass. Divsn. Mkts., 1927-28; exec. sec. New Eng. Rsch. Coun. on Mktg. and Food Supply, 1928-32; with Divsn. Statistics and Hist. Rsch. Bur. Agr. Econ., 1933-35, in charge Divsn. Mktg. and Transp. Rsch., 1935-41; asst. adminstr. Agrl. Mktg. Adminstrn. USDA, 1941-43, chief program appraisal br. Food Distbn. Adminstrn., 1943-45; agr. advisor Office of War Mobilization and Reconversion, 1945-46; economist Coun. on Econ. Advisors, 1946-51; asst. chief Bur. of Agrl. Econ., 1951-53; dir. agrl. econ. divsn. Agrl. Mktg. Svc., 1953-61; dir. econ. and statis. analysis divsn. Econ. Rsch. Svc., 1961-64, rsch. advisor, from 1964. Author: Quality as a Determinant of Vegetable Prices, 1929, Trade and Commerce, 1942, Readings on Agricultural Marketing, 1953, (with others) Marketing Policies for Agriculture, 1960, Managing Farm Surpluses, 1962; contbr. articles to profl. mags. With Ambulance Svc., U.S. Army Unit 539; attached to 5th divsn. of French Army, 1917-19, World War I. Decorated Croix de Guerre (France); recipient Sr. Rsch. award govtl. affairs Soc. Sci. Rsch. Coun., 1960-61, USDA Disting. Svc. award, 1961; European fellow Soc. Sci. Rsch. Coun, 1932-33. Fellow Am. Statis. Assn. (v.p. 1941), Am. Farm Econ. Assn. (v.p. 1939, pres. 1946), Econometric Soc.; mem. Am. Econ. Assn., The Yellow Dogs Club, Kappa Sigma. Conglist. *

WAWZONEK, STANLEY, chemistry educator; b. Valley Falls, R.I., June 23, 1914; s. John and Sophie (Krol) W.; m. Marian L. Matlock, Sept. 2, 1943; children—Ann Elizabeth, Lucile Kay, Mary Louise. B.S., Brown U., 1935; Ph.D., U. Minn., 1939. Chemist U. Minn., 1939-40; NRC fellow, 1940-41; instr. U. Ill., 1941-43, U. Tenn., 1943-44; asst. prof. State U. Iowa, 1944-47, assoc. prof., 1947-52, prof., 1952-84, prof. emeritus, 1984-88, chmn. dept. chemistry, 1962-68. Divisional editor: Jour. Electrochem. Soc; mem. editorial bd.: Organic Prep. Proc. Internat. Recipient Iowa award, 1960, Outstanding Achievement award U. Minn., 1975, Midwest award, 1976. Mem. Am. Chem. Soc., Electrochem. Soc., Am. Assn. Advancement Sci., Iowa Acad. Sci. (Disting. fellow 1979, pres. 1971-72), Phi Lambda Upsilon, Alpha Chi Sigma. Congregationalist. Lodge: Rotary. Home: Iowa City Iowa Died Jan. 6, 1988; buried Pavillion Cemetery, Yorkville, Ill.

WEAVER, EARL, dairy husbandry educator; b. Brazil, Ind., July 27, 1893; s. John and Anna (Cox) W.; m. Helen Mary Searles, June 8, 1920; children: John Searles, Harold Searles, Marianna, Ruth Marie. BS, Okla. A&M Coll., 1913; MS, Iowa State Coll., 1917; PhD, U. Minn., 1938. Tchr. high sch. Graceville, Minn., 1914-16; assoc. prof. dairying U. Minn., 1917-18; chief in dairy husbandry Iowa State Coll., 1919-29; head dairy dept. Okla. A&M Coll., 1929-37; head dairy dept. Mich. State U., 1937-55, prof. dairy dept., 1959-62, cons., 1962-63, prof. emeritus, from 1963; tech. advisor to Nat. Facultad de Agronomia, Medellin, Colombia, 1955-58; civilian instr. U.S. Army Shrivenham (Eng.) Am. U., 1945. Co-author: Successful Dairying, 1924; Agriculture for Secondary Schools, 1934; Agriculture for High Schools, 1934. Served with U.S. Marine Corps, with AEF, 1918-19. Recipient Mich. State U. Disting. Prof. award, 1962. Mem. Am. Dairy Sci. Assn. (dir. 1936-38, 39-50, pres. 1938-39, Assn. award 1957, Master Teaching award 1960), Am. Soc. Animal Prodn., Nat. Dairy Shrine Club (dir. 1949-55, pres. 1953-54), Masons, Univ. Men's Club (East Lansing, Mich.), Sigma Xi, Alpha Zeta, Phi Kappa Phi, Gamma Sigma Delta, Pi Kappa Alpha. Mem. Peoples Ch., East Lansing. *

WEAVER, THOMAS ARTHUR, printed circuit company executive; b. Indpls., Dec. 15, 1951; s. Joseph B. and Elizabeth S. (Sherman) W.;m. Denise A. Wiley, Mar. 1, 1975; children: Emily Elizabeth, Karen Marie. Student, Rose Hulman Inst., Terre Haute, Ind., 1970-72; BS in Mgmt., Ind. U., Indpls., 1976. Engr. Photos by Weaver, Noblesville, Ind., 1975-77; sec., co-founder Printed Wiring, Inc., Fishers, Ind., 1977-80, gen. mgr., 1980-84; pres. Printed Wiring, Inc., Indpls., 1984-90, also dir., vice chmn., pres. prototype & tech., 1991; nat. adv. bd. Rose Hulman Inst. Tech., Terre Haute. Dir. tng. video Tradition of Quality, 1988. Coun. mem. Town Coun., Fishers, 1988-91; chmn. Staff Parish Com. Ch., Fishers, 1987-90. With U.S. Army, 1972-74. Recipient Entrepreneur award, Jobs Creation award State of Ind., Indpls., 1988. Mem. Am. Electro Platers (wastewater operator), Phi Gamma Delta. Republican. Methodist. Home: Fishers Ind. died August 8, 1991. †

WEAVER, WINSTON ODELL, construction company executive; b. Harrisonburg, Va., Dec. 15, 1921; s. Marion Ralston and Annie (Shank) W.; m. Phyllis Livengood, July 18, 1942; children: Winston Odell, M. Steven, M. Gregory. Student, Eastern Mennonite Coll., 1939-41; B.A., Bridgewater Coll., 1947, L.H.D., 1975. With Rockingham Constrn. Co., Inc., Harrisonburg, from 1946; pres., gen. mgr. Rockingham Constrn. Co., Inc., 1956-82, chmn., from 1982; owner Mariann Meadows Farms; dir. Mennonite Broadcasts, Inc., Harrisonburg, 1957-67, v.p., 1962-67; adv. bd. Va. Nat. Bank, Harrisonburg, 1970-79, vice chmn., 1975-79; dir. First Nat. Bank, Harrisonburg, 1958-70, vice-chmn. World Vision U.S., 1982-86, chmn., 1987. Pres. Harrisonburg-Rockingham chpt. Mental Health Assn., 1960-61; chmn. Cancer Crusade, Harrisonburg, 1966; nat. alumni fund chmn. Bridgewater (Va.) Coll., 1966, 67, also trustee, mem. exec. com.; bd. dirs. World Vision U.S., 1978-89, vice chmn., mem. exec. com., 1979-89; mem. exec. com. World Vision Internat., Los Angeles, 1972-89, sec., 1982, bd. dirs., 1964-89, project dir. design and constrn. hosp., Cambodia, 1972-75; bd. visitors James Madison U., Harrisonburg, 1973-80; campaign chmn. Harrisonburg/Rockingham United Way, 1976, pres., 1977, bd. dirs., 1979-81; trustee, exec. com. Bridgewater Coll., 1963-89. Recipient Distinguished Service awards Mental Health Assn., 1961, Distinguished Service awards Cancer Crusade, 1966; named Alumnus of Year Bridgewater Coll., 1968; Outstanding Service award World Vision Internat., 1970; Harrisonburg-Rockingham C. of C. Businessman of Year award, 1977; Paul Harris fellow Rotary Club.

Mem. Am. Fedn. Small Bus. (dir. 1981-85), Internat. Platform Assn. Club: Capitol Hill (Washington). Lodge: Rotary Internat. (v.p. Harrisonburg 1974-75, pres. Harrisonburg 1975-76, Rotarian of Yr. 1987, Paul Harris fellow). Home: Harrisonburg Pa. Died Apr. 9, 1989; buried Weavers Cemetery, Harrisonburg, Va.

WEBB, JAMES EDWIN, lawyer; b. Granville County, N.C., Oct. 7, 1906; s. John Frederick and Sarah (Gorham) W.; m. Patsy Aiken Douglas, May 14, 1938; children: Sarah Gorham, James Edwin Jr. AB, U. N.C., 1928, LLD, 1949; postgrad., George Washington U., 1933-36; LLD (hon.), Syracuse U., Colo. Coll.; ScD (hon.), U. Notre Dame, 1961, Brown U., 1976; also other hon. degrees. Bar: D.C. 1936. Exec. asst. to undersec. treasury, 1946; dir. Bur. of Budget, 1946-49; undersec. of state, 1949-52; pres., gen. mgr. Republic Supply Co., 1953-58, chmn. bd., 1958; asst. to pres., bd. dirs. Kerr-McGee Oil Industries, Inc., Oklahoma City, 1952-61, 69-78; adminstr. NASA, 1961-68; pvt. practice law Washington, 1968-78. Mem. Govt. Procurement Commn., 1972-73, Comptr. Gen.'s Cons. Panel; bd. regents Smithsonian Instn., 1970-82; bd. dirs. Kerr Found., Inc., from 1977, chmn., 1980-81. Lt. col. USMCR, 1944-45. Recipient Robert J. Collier trophy, 1966, Disting. Svc. medal NASA, 1968, Presdl. Medal of Freedom, 1968, Goddard Meml. trophy, 1971, N.C. Pub. Svc. award, 1971, Bennett Svc. award Okla. State U., 1973, Gen. Acctg. Office award, 1973, Langley Gold medal Smithsonian Instn., 1976, Sylvanus Thayer award Assn. Grads. U.S. Mil. Acad.; named to Okla. Hall of Fame, 1967. Mem. ABA, D.C. Bar Assn., Nat. Planning Assn., Nat. Geog. Soc. (trustee 1966-81, Hubbard medal 1979), Marine Corps Res. Officers Assn., Am. Soc. Pub. Adminstrn. (pres. 1966-67), Nat. Acad. Pub. Adminstrn. (treas. 1969-73), Univ. Club (N.Y.C.), Chevy Chase Club, Met. Club, Alfalfa Club, Nat. Aviation Club, Nat. Space Club, Masons, Phi Beta Kappa, Phi Delta Phi. Democrat. Presbyterian. Home: Washington D.C. Died Mar. 27, 1992; buried Arlington Nat. Cemetery.

WEBBER, EVERARD LELAND, museum director; b. Chgo., Jan. 27, 1920; s. Leland Bacon and Harriet Gaylord (Peck) W.; m. Ellen Gowen Duer, Mar. 30, 1946 (dec. 1974); children: Leland Duer, James Randall, Ellen Robinson; m. Joan Wray Malloch. B.B.A., U. Cin., 1942; L.H.D., DePaul U., 1980. C.P.A., U. Ill., 1949. With Procter & Gamble Co., Cin., 1939-42, Ernst & Ernst (C.P.A.s), Chgo., 1945-50; with Field Mus. Natural History, Chgo., 1950-83, exec. asst., 1951-60, asst. dir., 1960-62, dir., 1962-80, trustee, 1966-81, pres., 1976-81, pres. emeritus, 1981-90. Trustee Savs. and Profit Sharing Fund Sears Employees, Sears Roebuck & Co., from 1980; dir. Growth Industry Shares, William Blair Ready Reserves, Inc.; mem. Nat. Council on Arts, 1970-76, Nat. Mus. Services Bd., 1977-81; Mem. Nat. 4H Service Com., 1972-76; bd. dirs. YMCA Hotel, Chgo., 1954-78, chmn., 1961-62; bd. dirs. Ill. State Mus., 1965-70; bd. dirs. Field Found. of Ill., 1982-90, chmn., 1983-90; interim pres. United Way/Crusade of Mercy, 1985-86; bd. govs. Ill. State Colls. and Univs., 1967-75. Served to lt. USNR, 1942-45. Mem. Am. Assn. Museums (v.p. 1966-70), Beta Theta Pi. Episcopalian. Clubs: Tavern, University, Attic, Caxton, Michigan Shores, Commercial, Economic (Chgo.). Home: Wilmette Ill. Died Jan. 7, 1990; buried Ch. of the Holy Comforter, Kenilworth, Ill.

WEBBER, ROBERT, actor; b. Santa Ana, Calif., Oct. ; s. Robert and Alice W.; m. Miranda Jones, Oct. 1, 1953 (div.); m. Del Mertens, Apr. 23, 1972. Student, Compton Jr. Coll., 1946. Acting debut in high sch. prodn. A Night at an Inn, 1941; profl. stage debut in Ah, Wilderness!, 1947; Broadway debut in Two Blind Mice, 1949; other stage appearances Goodbye, My Fancy, 1949, The Royal Family, 1951, No Time for Sergeants, 1955, Orpheus Descending, 1957, Wonderful Town, 1958, Fair Game, 1958, A Loss of Roses, 1959, A Period of Adjustment, 1960; films include Highway 301, 1950, 12 Angry Men, 1957, The Stripper, 1963, The Sandpiper, 1965, Harper, 1966, The Silencers, 1966, The Hired Killer, 1967, Dead Heat on a Merry-Go-Round, 1966, Don't Make Waves, 1967, The Dirty Dozen, 1967, The Great White Hope, 1970, Dollars, 1971, Midway, 1976, The Choirboys, 1977, Revenge of the Pink Panther, 1978, 10, 1979, Bring Me the Head of Alfredo Garcia, 1974, Casey's Shadow, 1978, Private Benjamin, 1980, S.O.B., 1980, Wrong Is Right, 1982, The Final Option, 1983, Wild Geese II, 1985, NUTS, 1987; numerous TV guest appearances; (TV movies) The Movie Murderer, 1970, Thief, 1971, Cutter, 1972, Double Indemnity, 1973, Murder or Mercy, 1974, Death Stalk, 1975, The Streets of L.A., 1979, Not Just Another Affair, 1982, Starflight, 1983, Shooting Stars, 1983, Getting Physical, 1984, No Man's Land, 1984, (TV series) Moonlighting, TV miniseries 79 Park Avenue, 1977, Invader, 1988. Served in USMC, 1943-45. Mem. Actors Equity Assn., AFTRA, Screen Actors Guild. Home: Malibu Calif. Died May 17, 1989; cremated.

WEBER, BERTRAM ANTON, architect; b. Chgo., Oct. 1, 1898; s. Peter Joseph and Bertha M. (Werkmeister) W.; m. Dorothea Brammer, May 9, 1928; children: Dorie W. Hechler, John B. Student, Northwestern, 1916-18; B.S., Mass. Inst. Tech., 1922. Independent practice architecture, 1923; ptnr. White & Weber, 1924-36; propr. Bertram A. Weber (architect), 1936-73, Weber & Weber Architects, gen. practice, 1973-87; assoc. architect Julia Lathrop Housing Project, Chgo.; ptnr. Cen. States Architects & Engrs., Kropp Forge Aviation Corp., 1942. Works include pvt. residences, devels., comml. bldgs., chs., hosps., schs., multiple housing Georgian Ct. Apts., Barrington, Inverness Countryside, Palatine, Ill., Julia Lathrop Apt., Chgo., DeKalb Pub. Library, Highland Park Pub. Library, Oak Park (Ill.) Post Office, YMCA, Winona, Minn. and Aurora, Ill., Doctors Hosp., Columbus, Ohio, Osteo. Hosp. of York, Pa., Chgo. Osteo. and Coll. Hosp. and Sci. bldgs., Detroit Osteo. Hosp. and Doctors Office Bldg, Riverside Osteo. Hosp, Trenton, Mich., Bi-County Community Hosp. and Med. Office Bldg., Warren, Mich., Bapt. Retirement Home, Maywood, Ill., St. James Episcopal Ch. at, Northbrook, Ill., Highland Park Presbyn. Ch, Trinity Ch., Highland Park, Deerfield Presbyn. Ch., St. Gregory's, Deerfield, St. Timothy's, Griffith, Ind., Ill. All Saints Ch., Western Springs, Ill., St. Davids Episcopal Ch., Glenview, Ill., Kildeer Sch., Long Grove, Ill., Lake Forest Acad., Highland Park Dists. 107, 108, Highland Park Hosp. nurses residence, Deerfield State Bank, Nat. Bank North Evanston, Duraclean Internat. Co. plant and office bldgs., Deerfield, Am. Legion and Recreation Bldgs., Ravinia Festival bldgs., Highland Park, Ill., Officers Quarters Glenview Air Base, 1943, Scholl Mfg. Co, Chgo., Standard Am. Ins. Co. Bldg, Park Ridge, Ill., Gen. Fin. Corp. Home Office Bldg., Calumet and Hecla office Bldg, Evanston, Ill., Evans Scholars Found. Bldg, Golf, Ill., Exmoor Country Club, Prestwick Country Club, Inverness Country Club, Aurora Country Club; others. Bd. dirs. Highland Park Hosp., Ravinia Festival Assn.; mem. Highland Park Park Dist. Bd., 12 yrs, pres., 3 yrs; mem. Highland Park Plan Commn., 8 yrs. Served with R.O.T.C., 1918, Ft. Sheridan; Served with S.N.T.C., 1918. Fellow AIA, Ill. Soc. Architects; mem. Delta Tau Delta, Scarab. Presbyn. Clubs: Exmoor, Executive, Builders, Adventurers, Dairymen's Country, Safari Internat, Anglers of Chgo. Home: Highland Park Ill. Died Dec. 17, 1989; buried Forest Home Cemetery, Forest Park, Ill.

WEBER, HENRY GEORGE, conductor; b. Berlin, Germany, Dec. 9, 1900; came to U.S., 1901; s. George and Ida (Sohr) W.; m. Marion Claire, Jan. 21, 1929; 1 child, Henry George. Student, Acad. Music, Vienna, 1911-19, 21-23, U. Chgo., 1919-20, U. Vienna, 1921-23. Condr. Mcpl. Opera Co., Bremen, Germany, 1919, Chgo Civic Opera Co., 1924-29, Florence, Italy, 1929; dir. music Sta. WGN Radio, 1934-91; dir. music Chgo. City Opera Co.; choral dir. (ann.) Chicagoland Festival. Mem. Cliff Dwellers. Republican. Home: Lake Bluff Ill. Died Jan. 14, 1991.

WEBSTER, ARCHIBALD WILSON, priest; b. Bloomington, Ind., July 2, 1897; s. John Hunter and Lora (Wilson) W.; m. Marjorie Elizabeth Flynn, Sept. 22, 1928 (dec.); 1 child, John Hunter (dec.). BA, Princeton U., 1921; MA, Washington U., St. Louis, 1926; BTh, Xenia Theol. Seminary, St. Louis, 1925, MTh, 1930; DD, Sterling (Kans.) Coll., 1941. Ordained to ministry Presbyn. Ch., 1928. Pastor 1st United Presbyn. Ch., Salinas, Calif., 1928-37, Pasadena, Calif., 1937-43, Monmouth, Ill., 1944-51, Wheeling, W.Va., 1951-62; asst. pastor Grace Presbyn. Ch., Jenkintown, Pa., 1962-66; moderator Calif. Synod United Presbyn. Ch., Salinas, 1930, 31, Ill. Synod, Evanston, 1951; mem. United Presbyn. Ch. Bd. Christian Edn., Phila., 1952-62. Author pamphlets and articles in field. Mem. Phi Beta Kappa. Lodge: Rotary (various offices, chpts.). Home: Jenkintown Pa.

WEBSTER, BETHUEL MATTHEW, lawyer; b. Denver, June 13, 1900; s. Bethuel Matthew and Anna Laura (Davidson) W.; m. Eleanor Ashton Wilson, Mar. 16, 1929 (dec. June 28, 1967); children: Elizabeth Webster Hogeland, Anna Clarissa Webster Atkinson, Eleanor Webster Shakin; m. Elizabeth W. Case, Nov. 1969. Grad., Culver Mil. Acad., 1918; A.B., U. Colo., 1922, LL.D., 1972; LL.B., Harvard U., 1925; L.H.D. (hon.), Bard Coll., 1980. Bar: N.Y. State 1927, D.C. 1929. Asst. U.S. atty. So. Dist. N.Y., 1926-27; spl. asst. to atty. gen. U.S. antitrust div., Dept. of Justice, 1927-29; gen. counsel Fed. Radio Commn., 1929; cons. U.S. High Commr. for, Germany, 1949, 51; practicing lawyer N.Y.C., from 1930; founder, mem. Webster & Sheffield, and predecessor firms, 1934-84, sr. counsel, 1984-89; served as mem. Permanent Ct. Arbitration (under the Hague Convs.), 1959-65; mem. com. sci. aids learning NRC, 1937-47; mem. com. internat. rules of jud. procedure, 1961; asst. to Dr. Vannervar Bush; dir. OSRD; report to Pres. of U.S. on postwar research, July 1945; mem., cons. Com. Scientists Supporting Bush Report; chmn. adv. com. project effective justice; mem. Armstrong research project Columbia Law Sch.; mem. mgmt. and selection coms. Arthur Goodhart Vis. Professorship in Legal Sci., Cambridge U.; mem. com. role patents indsl. research NAS-NRC; chmn. pub. health service. hosp. study com. Office Sci. and Tech., Exec. Office of Pres., 1965; ambassador representing U.S.A. to mediate dispute between U.K. and Guatemala over Brit. Honduras, 1965-68. Trustee Ford Found., 1961-70, William Nelson Cromwell Found., N.Y. Pub. Library (hon.), Inst. Pub. Adminstrn.; dir. Overbrook Found.; mem. overseers com. to visit Harvard Library; chmn. Drug Abuse Council; dir. Inst. Philos. Research; counsel N.Y. State Soc. Med. Research; deptl. com. on ct. adminstrn, 1st dept. jud. conf. of, New York, N.Y.C. Health Research Council; mem. N.Y.C. Municipal Art Commn., 1960-64, Mayor's Com. on Judiciary, 1962-65. Served as 2d lt. inf. U.S. Army, 1918-19. Recipient Norlin award U. Colo., 1968. Fellow Am. Coll. Trial Lawyers, Am. Bar Found., Aspen Inst. Humanistic Studies; mem. Assn. Bar City of N.Y. (pres. 1952-54), Am. Law Inst., N.Y. Co. Lawyers Assn., Am., N.Y. State bar assns., Am. Arbitration Assn. (dir.), Am. Judicature Soc., Fed. Bar Assn. N.Y., N.J. Bar Assn., Conn. Bar Assn. (hon.), Harvard Law Sch. Assn. of N.Y.C. (pres. 1948-49), Harvard Alumni Assn. (dir. 1952-54), Pub. Edn. Assn. (chmn. bd. of trustees 1954-58), Council on Fgn. Relations, Pilgrims of U.S. Clubs: Century, Harvard, Metropolitan (Washington). Home: New York N.Y. Died Mar. 31, 1989; buried Norfolk, Conn.

WEBSTER, BURNICE HOYLE, internist; b. Leeville, Tenn., Mar. 3, 1910; s. Thomas Jefferson and Martha Anne (Melton) W.; B.A. magna cum laude, Vanderbilt U., 1936, M.D., 1940; D.Sc., Holy Trinity Coll., 1971; D. of Humanities, Geneva. Theol. Coll., 1960, Ph.D., Fla. Research Inst., 1973; D of Therapeutic Philosophy, World U., 1985; m. Georgia Kathryn Foglemann, May 6, 1939; children: Brenda Kathryn, Phillip Hoyle, Adrienne Elise. Intern St. Thomas Hosp., Nashville, 1940-42, resident, 1942-43; practice medicine, specializing in chest disease, Nashville, 1943-85 ; mem. staff St. Thomas, Bapt., Nashville Gen., Westside hosps.; clin. prof. allied health Trevecca Coll.; cons. VA Hosp.; assoc. in medicine Vanderbilt Med. Sch., 1943-90 ; med. dir. Nashville Health Care Corp., Univ. Health Care Corp.; prof. anatomy Gupton-Jones Sch. Mortuary Sci., 1941-43, Homes. Inc., Tenn. Squire. Pres., Middle-East Tenn. chpt. Arthritis Found.; crusader Soc. Descendants Latin Kingdom of Jerusalem. Served to med. dir. USPHS. Decorated baliff grand cross Hospitaller Order St. John of Jerusalem; chevalier Sovereign Mil. Order Temple of Jerusalem recipient Disting. Service award Arthritis Found. Fellow Am. Coll. Chest Physicians, Am., Internat. colls. angiology, Royal Soc. Health, Internat. Biog. Assn. (life); mem. Am. Cancer Soc. (dir., past pres. Nashville), AMA, Am. Thoracic Soc., So. Med. Soc. (life), Tenn. Med. Assn., Nashville Acad. Medicine, SCV (surgeon-in-chief), Order St. John of Jerusalem, Royal Soc. Medicine, Tenn. Assn. Long Term Physicians (past pres.), Phi Beta Kappa, Alpha Omega Alpha, Delta Phi Alpha. Lodge: Order of Descendants of Ireland. Research in mycotic and parasitic diseases. Died 1991. Home: Nashville Tenn.

WEBSTER, REGINALD HOWARD, business executive; b. Que., Can., 1910; s. Lorne Campbell and Muriel Warren (Taylor) W. BA, McGill U., 1931; postgrad., Babson Inst. Hon. chmn. Toronto (Ont., Can.) Globe & Mail, 1980-90; pres., dir. Detroit Marine Terminals, Inc.; hon. chmn. bd. Toronto Blue Jays; pres. Imperial Trust Co., Durand Corp. Decorated Order of Canada. Home: Ile Bizard Que., Can. Died Aug. 19, 1990; buried Montreal, Que., Can.

WEBSTER, REX, advertising agency executive; b. Gatesville, Tex., May 29, 1918; s. Roscoe and Fannie (Hooser) W.; m. Madge Malone, June 1, 1941; children: Len Rex, Robin Webster Bass. BA, Tex. Tech U., 1938, MA, 1939. Program dir., comml. mgr. Sta. KFYO, Lubbock, Tex., 1935-47; ptnr. Buckner, Craig & Webster Advt. Agy., 1947-52, Craig & Webster Advg. Agy., Lubbock, 1952-59, Webster, Harris, Welborn Advt. Agy., Lubbock, 1959-72, Webster & Harris Advt. Agy., Lubbock, 1972-85, Rex Webster Assocs., 1985-89; v.p., dir. pub. relations Gt. Plains Life Ins. Co., Lubbock, 1955-57; advt. and pub. relations cons.; instr. Tex. Tech U., 1953-71. Pres. Lubbock council Camp Fire Girls, 1960, Lubbock Better Bus. Bur., 1965; v.p. South Plains council Boy Scouts Am., 1958-59; chmn. bd. dirs. Lubbock Symphony Orch., 1949-50, vocal soloist, string bass charter mem., dir. Pops Nite Chorus, 1963-71; charter mem. Lubbock Symphony Orch., 1946-78; chmn. bd. dirs. Lubbock Cerebral Palsy Treatment Ctr., 1962-63, 72-74; bd. dirs. Goodwill Industries, Lubbock; pres. Lubbock Area Extended Rehab. Services, 1983; trustee Wayland Baptist U., Plainview Tex., 1983-89; bd. dirs. Lubbock Area Found., 1987-89; chmn. bd. deacons 1st Bapt. Ch., Lubbock, 1972-73; mem. exec. com. Bapt. Gen. Conv. Tex., 1968-74. Served as lt. USNR, 1943-45. Recipient Disting. Service award Lubbock Jr. C. of C., 1955. Mem. Am. Assn. Advt. Agys. (chmn. S.W. council 1957-58), Southwestern Assn. Advt. Agys. (pres. 1955-56), Lubbock Advt. Club (pres. 1954-55, silver medal 1967), Am. Automobile Assn. (Tex. adv. bd. 1988-89), Panhandle Plains Automobile Club (v.p. 1971-78), Tex. Pub. Relations Assn. (bd. dirs. 1958-60). Lodges: Masons (32d degree), Rotary (pres. Lubbock 1947-48, dist. gov. 1956-57, bd. dirs. 1967-69, v.p. 1968-69, found. trustee 1981-84). Died Sept. 1, 1989; buried Resthaven Meml. Pk., Lubbock, Tex. Home: Lubbock Tex.

WECKER, WALTER ANDRE, manufacturing company executive; b. Peru, Ill., June 29, 1895; s. August and Josephine (Leyes) W.; m. Minnie I. Ramey, Aug. 24, 1920. Student pub. schs., LaSalle County, Ill. Invoice clk. Marquette Cement Mfg. Co., LaSalle, 1914-15, asst. credit and collection dept., 1915-16, travelling collector, 1916-18, sec., 1919-23, treas., 1923-32, v.p., 1932, pres., 1933-63, chmn. bd., from 1963, also dir.;

dir. Poor & Co., Chgo. Served with U.S. Army, World War I. Mem. Chgo. Club, Mid-Day Club, Exmoor Country Club. *

WEDEMEYER, ALBERT COADY, army officer, industrialist, author; b. Omaha, July 9, 1897; s. Albert Anthony and Margaret E. (Coady) W.; m. Elizabeth Dade Embick, Feb. 5, 1925; children: Albert Dunbar, Robert Dade. B.S., U.S. Mil. Acad., 1919; grad., Gen. Staff Sch., Ft. Leavenworth, 1936, German War Coll., Berlin, 1938; LL.D. (hon.), Rollins Coll., DePauw U., U. Pa., Creighton U., U. San Francisco, U. So. Calif.; L.H.D., Temple U.; Ph.D., China Acad. Commd. 2d lt. U.S. Army, 1919, advanced through grades to gen., 1954; served, India, China, Philippines, Europe (War Dept. Gen. Staff), 1941-43; dep. chief of staff (SE Asia Command); comdr. (China Theater), 1944-46; also chief staff to (Generalissimo Chiang Kai-Shek), 1947; made survey for Pres. U.S., rank of ambassador China and Korea, 1947; comdg. gen. (2d Army), 1946-47; dir. plans and ops. div. (Gen. Staff), 1947-48, dep. chief of staff for plans and combat ops., 1948; comdg. gen. (6th Army, Presidio), San Francisco, 1949-51; ret. from active service, 1951; exec. v.p., dir. Avco Mfg. Corp., 1951-56, Rheem Mfg. Co., 1956-59; dir. Nat. Airlines, Inc. Author: Wedemeyer Reports. Decorated Presdl. Medal of Freedom, D.S.M. with 2 clusters, D.F.C., comdr. Order of Bath (Eng.) Brit., White Sun and Blue Sky (China), grand cross Order of Phoenix (Greece), Restitude Comdrs. Cross (Poland), Order of Mil. Merit (Brazil). Clubs: Army and Navy (Washington), Chevy Chase (Washington); Bohemian (San Francisco); Metropolitan (N.Y.C.), Dutch Treat (N.Y.C.). Home: Fort Belvoir Va. Died Dec. 17, 1989; buried Arlington Nat. Cemetery.

WEDER, ERWIN HENRY, corporate executive; b. Highland, Ill., Dec. 13, 1904; s. August and Julia (Brunner) W.; m. Florence Louise (Graham), July 19, 1938; children: Mary Kay, Dona Lee, Donald Erwin, Wanda May, Janet Marie. Office work Highland Dairy Farms, 1923-25; detective Fla. East Coast Hotel Co., 1927-29; auto salesman, broker L.E. Anderson Co., 1930-32; salesman Metal Goods Corp., 1933-41; product devel., sales mgr., pres., then chmn. bd. Highland Supply Corp., 1941-91; pres., then chmn. bd., sales and products mgr. Highland Products, Inc., 1948-89 , Highland Mfg. Co., 1944-89; mng. partner, sales and products mgr. Highland Mfg. & Sales Co., 1952-90; pres., then chmn. bd. Weder Farms, Inc., 1950-90, Quality Motors, Inc., 1946-89 ; sr. ptnr., then chmn. bd. Seven W. Enterprises, 1958-91; chmn. bd. Life Extender Corp.; dir. Inland Valley Engring. owner, operator Six Bar X ranch, Jordan, Mont. Mem. St. Louis Media Club. Republican. Clubs: DX-5; Mo. Athletic; Capitol Hill; Masons. Died 1992. Home: Highland Ill.

WEED, HERBERT M., metal company executive, consultant; b. Houghton, Mich., 1921. B.A., Washington and Lee U., 1942. With The Anaconda Co., N.Y.C., 1946-82; v.p. mktg. The Anaconda Co., 1966-82; dir. United Park City Mining. Served with USNR, 1942-46. Home: Englewood Colo. Died Oct. 10, 1989; buried Denver.

WEEDEN, NORMAN DEXTER, investment banker; b. Havre, France, June 19, 1898; s. Henry Frank and Alice Mary (Dexter) W. Student pub. schs. Ptnr. Weeden & Co., San Francisco, 1922-27, v.p., dir., from 1927. Served with U.S. Army, 1918, with USAAF, 1942-45. Mem. English Speaking Union. Episcopalian. *

WEEKS, CHARLES CARSON, consultant; b. Sault Ste. Marie, Ont., Can., June 19, 1914; s. Charles Alexander and Stella Mabel (Watson) W.; m. Mildred Frances See, Jan 2, 1936; 1 dau., Mildred Sharon. Grad. high sch. With Algoma Steel Corp., Ltd., Sault Ste. Marie, Ont., 1937-85; mgr. sales Algoma Steel Corp., Ltd., 1948-57, v.p. sales, 1957-73, sr. v.p., 1973-79; pres. Carmish Cons.' Corp., Sault Ste. Marie. Mem. Am. Iron and Steel Inst. Home: Sault Sainte Marie Can. Died 1991.

WEEKS, EDWARD AUGUSTUS, editor, writer; b. Elizabeth, N.J., Feb. 19, 1898; s. Edward Augustus and Frederika (Suydam) W.; m. Frederica Watriss, May 28, 1925 (dec. July 1970); children: Sara Thompson Weeks Peabody, Edward Francis; m. Phoebe Adams, Feb. 19, 1971. Student, Cornell U., 1915-17; BS, Harvard U., 1922; postgrad., Cambridge (Eng.) U., 1922-23; LittD (hon.), Northeastern U., 1938, Lake Forest U., 1939, Williams Coll., 1942, Middlebury Coll., 1944, U. Ala., 1945, Dartmouth Coll., 1950, Bucknell U., 1952, U. Richmond, 1957, Pomona Coll., 1957, NYU, 1958, U. Akron, 1961; LHD (hon.), Hobart and William Smith Coll., 1956, Clark U., 1958; LLD (hon.), Boston U., 1953, Washington and Jefferson Coll., 1962; LHD (hon.), U. Pitts., 1959, Northwestern U., 1961; DLitt (hon.), Emerson Coll., 1959, Rutgers U., 1962; DCL (hon.), Union Coll. Manuscript reader, book salesman Horace Liveright, Inc., N.Y.C., 1923; assoc. editor Atlantic Monthly, Boston, 1924-28, editor, 1938-66; editor Atlantic Monthly Press, 1928-37, sr. cons., from 1966; trustee Colonial Williamsburg, Inc., 1958-69. Author: This Trade Writing, 1935, The Open Heart, 1955, In Friendly Candor, 1959, Breaking into Print, 1962, Boston: Cradle of Liberty, 1965, The Lowells and Their Institute, 1966, Fresh Waters, 1968, The Moisie Salmon Club: A Chronicle, 1971, My Green Age, a memoir, 1974, Myopia: 1875-1975, 1975; editor: Great Short Novels, 1941, The Picket Atlantic, 1946, (with E. Flint) Jubilee: 100 Years of the Atlantic, 1957; also essays, articles and book revs. to mags. Chmn. Mass. Com. To Reform Book Censorship, 1929, 30; bd. overseers Harvard U., 1945-51; life trustee Am. Field Svc.; trustee Wellesley Coll., 1947-65; mem. corp. Northeastern U., from 1950; bd. dirs. United Negro Coll. Fund; hon. trustee U. Rochester. With field svc. French Army, 1917; ambulance driver U.S. Army, attached to French Div., 1917-19. Decorated Vols. medal, Croiz de Guerre; recipient Henry Johnson Fisher award, 1968, Irita Van Doren award, 1970. Fellow Am. Acad. Arts and Scis.; mem. Mag. Pubs. Assn. (bd. dirs. 1960-65), Tavern Club (Boston), Anglers Club (N.Y.C.), Myopia Hunt Club (N.Y.C.), Century Club (N.Y.C.), Phi Beta Kappa, Zeta Psi. Democrat. Episcopalian. Home: Thompson Conn. Died Mar. 11, 1989.

WEEKS, OLIVER DOUGLAS, political science educator; b. Marion, Ohio, Sept. 4, 1896; s. Dana Oliver and Gertrude (Douglas) W.; m. Julien Elizabeth Devereux, June 21, 1927; children: Sarah Jane (Mrs. Theo L. Hills), Julien Devereux. AB, Ohio Wesleyan U., Delaware, 1918; AM, U. Wis., 1919, PhD, 1924. Asst. prof. history and polit. sci. Morningside Coll., Sioux City, Iowa, 1920-22; teaching asst. in polit. sci. U. Wis., 1922-24; instr. in govt. U. Tex., 1924-25; asst. prof. polit. sci. Western Res. U., 1925-26; assoc. prof. govt. U. Tex., 1926-33, prof., from 1933, chmn. dept. govt., 1936-47, 50-57; br. head polit. sci. Shrivenham (Eng.)-Am. U., 1945-46, mem. polit. sci. faculty Biarritz (France)-Am. U., 1945-46. Author: The Democratic Victory of 1932, 1933; Two Legislative Houses or One, 1938; Research in the American State Legislative Process, 1947; Texas Presidential Politics in 1952, 1953; Texas One-Party Politics in 1956, 1957; Texas in the 1960 Presidential Election, 1961; Texas in 1964: A One-Party State Again?, 1965; book rev. editor Southwestern Social Sci. Quar., 1926-45; contbr. articles to profl. jours., revs. and encys. Chmn. Austin (Tex.) Pub. Libr. Commn. Mem. Am. Polit. Sci. Assn., Southwestern Polit. Sci. Assn. (pres. 1963-64), S.W. Social Sci. Assn., So. Polit. Sci. Assn., Fortnightly Club, Town and Gown Soc. (Austin), Phi Kappa Psi, Pi Sigma Alpha. Presbyterian. *

WEEMS, FRANK TAYLOR, manufacturing executive; b. Birmingham, Ala., Dec. 26, 1924; s. Ben Carpenter and Gladys (Taylor) W.; m. Kirsten Lee Borgen, Sept. 10, 1949 (dec. Feb. 23, 1985); children: Barbara Lee, William Taylor, Robert Chipley. BS ChemE, U. Ala., 1944; SM ChemE, M.I.T., 1950. Sales engr. Dorr Co., 1948-52; tech. dir. Eimco Corp., 1952-55, regional mgr., 1955-62, mgr. indsl. sales, 1962-66, mktg. dir., 1966-68, v.p. mktg., 1968-70, pres., 1970-72; exec. v.p., pres. Air Quality Control Group, Envirotech Corp., Menlo Park, Calif., 1972-82; exec. v.p., dir. Mountain States Mineral Enterprises, Tucson, 1982-89; pres., dir. A.H. Ross & Assocs., Inc., Toronto, Ont., Can., 1982-86; v.p., dir. Mountain States Synfuels Corp., 1983-86; pres., chief fin. officer, chief exec. officer Cochlea Corp., 1984-89, also bd. dirs.; chmn. Cochlea S.A., Aubange, Belgium; bd. dirs. Granger Assocs., Santa Clara, Calif.; chmn. bd. Chem. Engring. Corp. of Tokyo, 1976-80, Bahnson Co. Inc., Winston Salem, N.C., 1976-81. Active Little League Baseball, Weston, Conn.; trustee Rowland Hall-St. Marks Sch., Salt Lake City. Served with USNR, 1943-46. NRC fellow. Mem. AIME, Am. Inst. Chem. Engrs., Mining and Metall. Soc., Tau Beta Pi, Theta Tau. Republican. Episcopalian. Clubs: Mining (N.Y.C.), Chemists (N.Y.C.); Alta (Salt Lake City); Los Altos Golf and Country; Old Pueblo (Tucson). Home: Los Altos Calif. Deceased.

WEEMS, KATHARINE LANE, sculptor; b. Boston, Feb. 22, 1899; d. Gardiner Martin and Emma Louise (Gildersleeve) Lane; m. F. Carrington Weems, Nov. 15, 1947. Prep. edn., May Sch., Boston; art edn., Sch. of Museum of Fine Arts, Boston; pupil of Charles Grafly; pupil of, Anna Hyatt Huntington, George Demetrios, Brenda Putnam. Mem. Mass. Art Commission, 1941-47. (recipient bronze medal Sesqui-Centennial Exposition, Phila. 1926, Widener Meml. gold medal Pa. Acad. Fine Arts 1927, honorable mention Paris (France) Salon 1928, Joan of Arc gold medal Nat. Assn. Women Painters and Sculptors 1928, hon. mention Grand Central Galleries, N.Y.C. 1929, bronze medal Boston Tercentenary Fine Arts Exhbn. 1930, Anna Hyatt Huntington prize Nat. Assn. Women Painters and Sculptors 1931, Speyer prize NAD 1931, 63, 73, 75, Barnet prize 1932, hon. mention Archtl. League of N.Y. 1942, Anonymous prize Nat. Assn. Women Artists 1946, Saltus gold medal for merit Nat. Acad. Design 1960, Lindsey Morris Meml. prize Nat. Sculpture Soc. 1960, Kalos Kagathos Found. sculpture prize 1981, gold medal Nat. Arts Club, N.Y.C. 1961); Prin. works include Dog Narcisse Noir, Museum Fine Arts, Boston, and Reading (Pa.) Mus.; Kangaroo, Pa. Acad. Fine Arts; 12 foot bronze group Dolphins of the Sea, Water Plaza, New Eng. Aquarium, Boston; rep. permanent collection Greek Horse, Balt. Mus. Art, Bear, Spee Club, Harvard, Whippet, Glenbow Found. Mus., Whippet and Fox, Colby Coll. Art Mus., Waterville, Maine, brick carvings and entrance doors, and 2 bronze rhinoceroses, Inst. of Biology, Harvard; sculpture on Lotta Fountain, Boston; small bronzes in pvt. collections, permanent exhbn., Weems Gallery Animal Sculpture, Mus. Sci., Boston; sculptor: Goodwin medal, Mass. Inst. Tech.; sculptor for Fincke Meml. medal, Groton Sch. Decorated chevalier L'Ordre Nat. Merit France; Nat. Academician. Fellow Nat. Sculpture Soc. (council 1949); mem. Guild Boston Artists, Nat. Assn. Women Artists, Nat. Inst. Arts and Letters, Grand Central Art Galleries, Archtl. League, Am. Artists Profl. League, N. Shore Arts Assn., Huguenot Soc., Lords of Colonial Manors., Mass. Soc. Colonial Dames Am. Allied Artists Am. Clubs: Chilton (Boston); Cosmopolitan (N.Y.C.), Pen and Brush (N.Y.C.); Catherine Lorillard Wolfe. Home: Boston Mass. Died Feb. 11, 1989; buried Hollywood Cemetery, Richmond, Va.

WEGLOSKI, DANIEL JOSEPH, hydroelectric engineer; b. Chgo., July 11, 1949; s. Joseph Paul and Elenor (Shatkowski) W.; m. Madonna Marie Meller, Aug. 14, 1971. BSCE, Ill. Inst. Tech., 1971; MBA, Loyola U., Chgo., 1977. Registered profl. engr., Ill., N.Mex. Mem. engring. team Harza Engring., Chgo., 1971-81; project engr. Daverman & Assocs., Syracuse, N.Y., 1981-84; owners rep. Dept. Pub. Utilities, Los Alamos, N.Mex., 1984-88. Presenter in field. County of Los Alamos Elvado Hydroelectric Plant dedicated in his memory. Mem. ASCE. Home: Los Alamos N.Mex. Died Mar. 28, 1988; buried N.Mex.

WEIDNER, CHARLES KENNETH, consulting engineer; b. Narcissa, Pa., Sept. 25, 1904; s. Charles Leonard and Sarah (MacNair) W.; ed. pub. schs.; m. Garnett Valentine Leyman, June 22, 1929; children: Wynn, Charles Leyman, Sarah Weidner Byrd. Constrn. foreman, then supt. heavy constrn. Wills Constrn. Co. and N.P. Ry., 1925-31; designer, engring. dept. Boeing Aircraft Co., 1931-34; instr. physics, supt. bldgs. and grounds Whitman Coll., 1934-36; asst. supt. bldgs. and grounds U. Wash., 1936-41; cons. engr., prof. U. Oreg., 1946-47; chief engr. charge design and constrn. Argonne Nat. Nuclear Research Lab., U. Chgo., 1947-51; prof. engring., also dean Sch. Engring. and Architecture, Am. U. Beirut, 1951-62, emeritus, 1962; gen. mgr. African ops. Contracting & Trading Co., 1962-65; pres. Am. Internat. Constrn. Co., 1965-67; cons. engr., 1967-79 ; dir. Middle East Export Press, 1956-66. Devel. cons., Jordan, Syria, Saudia Arabia, 1952-60, Haiti, 1966-79 ; edn. and tng. cons. U.S. Navy, 1947, U.S. Air Force, 1947, Aramco, Bapco, 1952-60. Vice pres. restoration Whitman Historic Sites, Walla Walla, Wash., 1934-36; v.p. West Surburban Symphony Assn., LaGrange, Ill., 1947-50. Served from lt. to capt. USNR, 1941-46. Decorated Bronze Star (2), medal Edn. Order of Cedars (Lebanon), Hashemite Order Independence (Jordan); recipient George Washington Honor medal. Fellow ASCE (life), Soc. Am. Mil. Engrs. (life); mem. ASME, IEEE (life), Nat. Soc. Profl. Engrs. (life), Am. Soc. Naval Engrs. (life), U.S. Naval Inst., SAR. Deceased. Home: Colorado Springs Colo.

WEIER, T. ELLIOTT, botany educator; b. N.Y.C., Jan. 4, 1903; s. John Edward and Edna Rebecca (Hammill) W.; m. Katherine Irene Schmid, Aug. 18, 1927 (dec. Mar. 1977). AB, Hope Coll., 1926; PhD in Botany, U. Mich., 1929. Fellow Commn. for Relief in Belgium, Louvain, 1929-30, NRC, Cornell U., Ithaca, N.Y., 1930-31; instr. botany Oreg. State Coll., Corvallis, 1934-36; from asst. prof. to prof. U. Calif., Davis, 1936-65, prof. emeritus, 1965-91; founder, active U. Calif. Arboretum, 1936-91, faculty rsch. lectr., 1968. Author: Introduction to Plant Biology, 6 edits., 1950-80; contbr. numerous rsch. articles on chloroplast structure, ultrastructure and cellular activity, taxonomy of crustous lichens. Recipient Disting. Alumnus award Hope Coll., Holland, Mich., 1978, Award of Merit Bot. Soc. Am., 1986. Mem. AAAS, Sigma Xi. Republican. Home: Davis Calif. Died Oct. 14, 1991.

WEIGEL, WILLIAM FREDERICK, lawyer; b. N.Y.C., Sept. 26, 1923; s. Elmer Peter and Sara Madeline (Westerbeke) W.; m. Frances B. Perry, Feb. 14, 1952 (div.); children: Madeleine Weigel Ludlow, Amy Weigel Minor, Patricia Weigel Blank, William Breck. Grad., Lawrenceville Sch., 1941; student, Princeton U., 1941-43; B.S. magna cum laude, Lehigh U., 1949; J.D., N.Y. U., 1951. Bar: N.Y. 1951, D.C. 1978. Assoc. firm Rogers Hoge & Hills, N.Y.C., 1951-59, ptnr., 1959-70, sr. ptnr., 1970-87; assoc. gen. counsel Proprietary Assn., 1960-71; sec., counsel Am. Found. Pharm. Edn., from 1971, Council Family Health, from 1972; of counsel Abelman, Frayne, Rezac & Schwab, N.Y.C., 1987-90; atty. Village of Pelham, N.Y., 1964-65, trustee, 1965-67, mayor, 1967-70; del. Westchester County Jud. Conf., 1965-71; instr. law Bernard Baruch Sch., CCNY; lectr. NYU Grad. Sch. Law, Practising Law Inst. Contbr. 26 articles on trademark and food and drug law to profl. jours.; mem. editorial adv. bd. Food Drug Cosmetic Law Jour. Served with USNR, 1942-46. Mem. ABA, N.Y. State Bar Assn. (chmn. food, drug and cosmetic law sect. 1978-81), Am. Bar Assn. N.Y. State Bar Assn. (ho. of dels. 1978-82), N.Y. State Bar Found., N.Y.C. Bar Assn., N.Y. State Conf. Bar Leaders, Internat. Acad. Law Sci. Republican. Clubs: Union League (N.Y.C.); Saratoga Reading Rooms. Home: New York N.Y. Died July 13, 1990.

WEIGHARDT, PAUL, artist, art educator; b. West Germany, 1897; m. Melli Bar. Studnet, Fine Arts Sch.,

Cologne, Paul Klee Acad. Fine Arts, Dresden. Artist Paris, 1931-39; prof. Sch. Art Inst., Chgo., 1946-63; chmn. fine arts dept. Sch. ARt Inst., Chgo., 1960-63, prof. emeritus, from 1963; tchr. architecture dept. Ill. Inst. Tech., from 1950, Evanston (Ill.) Art Ctr., from 1948. Works exhibited Salon d'Automne, Salon des Tuilerles, Salon des Independants, French Gdoup Expn. Internat., 1931-39; one-man shows Berkshin Mus., Harvars, St. Paul Gallery Fine Arts, Phillips Meml. Gallery, Knoedler Galleries, Art. Inst. Chgo., Ill. Inst. Tech., Syracuse U., Carlen Gallery, Charles Feingarten Gallery; exhibited in group shows at Phila. Acad. Fine Arts, Art. Inst. Chgo., Soc. Contemporary Art, U. Ill. and others; represented in permanent collections Albright Adr Gallery. Mem. Lambda Chi ALpha, MAsons (dist. gov. 1960-61). Republican. Congregationalist. *

WEIL, KURT HERMANN, mechanical engineer, educator; b. Germany, Nov. 26, 1895; came to U.S., 1938, naturalized, 1946; m. Charlotte Garris, Mar. 1, 1932; 1 dau., Kathleen (Mrs. Donald Posner). Dipl. Ing., Tech. U. Aachen, Germany, 1922, postgrad. Lic. prof. engr., N.Y. Engr. Junkers Corp., Germany, 1923-33; founder, mng. dir. 1st unsubsidized airline systems Junkers Airlines Persia, Iran to Iraq, 1927-33; indsl. adviser Shah Rheza Pahlevi of Iran, King Faisal I of Iraq; cons. engr. Eng., 1934-38; cons. engr., prin. cons. Bd. Econ. Warfare, 1938-42; with Eastern Aircraft div. Gen. Motors Corp., 1942-45; cons. engr. Def. Dept. for Berlin Airlift; cons. for indsl. projects in China Kicheng Bank of Shanghai; designer 3-engine all-metal cargo plane, also transport plane; devel. of hydrogen engine; cons. Safari aircraft project for underdeveloped countries, 1946-56; ptnr. Am. Devel. Assocs., N.Y.C., 1950-55; prof., head dept. mech. engring. Stevens Inst. Tech., Hoboken, N.J., from 1957; guest prof. Tech. U. Berlin. Contbr. articles to English, German and French publs. Mem. Afghan-Am. steering com. U. Kabul. Served as bomber pilot German Air Force, World War I. Decorated by Germany, Iran, Turkey. Mem. ASME, AIAA, Soc. Automotive Engrs., Am. Soc. Engring. Edn., Royal Aero. Soc., Royal Aero. Club, Soc. German Engrs., Sci. Soc. Aviation (Germany), Sigma Xi. *

WEINBERG, ELBERT, sculptor; b. Hartford, Conn., May 27, 1928; s. Hyman Phillip and Rose May (Apter) W.; divorced; 1 dau., Julia Davenport. B.F.A., R.I. Sch. Design, 1951; M.F.A., Yale U., 1955. Instr. Cooper Union Art Sch., 1956-59; vis. prof. sculpture Dartmouth Coll., 1969; vis. assoc. prof.sculpture Tyler Abroad, Temple U., 1969-70; vis. assoc. prof. sculpture Tyler Abroad, Temple U., Rome, 1974-76; artist-in-residence Union Coll. Schenectady, N.Y., 1976-80; vis. assoc. prof. Boston U., 1980-81, 84-87, prof., from 1988; instr. drawing R.I. Sch. Design, 1983-81. Exhbns. include Borgenicht Gallery, N.Y.C., 1959, 62, 66, 69, 75, 83, 86, Alpha Gallery, Boston, 1966, 69, 71, Mus. Modern Art, N.Y.C., 1959, 75, Guggenheim Mus., 1962; represented permanent collections Mus. Modern Art, Whitney Mus., N.Y.C., Bklyn. Mus., Jewish Mus., N.Y.C., Boston Mus. Fine Arts, Hirshhorn Collection, Washington, Phoenix Mus. Fine Arts, Wadsworth Atheneum, Hartford, Conn. Recipient Prix de Rome, 1951, Guggenheim award for sculpture, 1959, Am. Inst. Arts and Letters sculpture award, 1968, Elizabeth N. Watrous Gold medal for sculpture NAD, 1989, Maurice B. Hexter prize Nat. Sculpture Soc., 1991. Home: Avon Conn. Died Dec. 27, 1991.

WEINFELD, MARSHA ELAINE, lyricist, poet, music publisher; b. St. Louis; d. Sol and Rose (Manewitz) Katzman; m. B. Kash, Dec. 1961 (div. Oct. 1969); children: Maila Suzann, Shera Felice; m. David Colman Weinfeld, July 14, 1979. Grad. high sch., Ladue, Mo. Ind. poet, 1960-90, ind. lyricist, 1977-90; publisher, writer Pollyseeds Pub. Co., Yarmouthport, Mass., 1979-90. Writer, pub.: (song lyrics) Early Morning Man, 1985, Love Makes the Difference, 1988, Changes in the Dark, 1988; contbr. articles to St. Louis Post Dispatch, 1967-68, The Third Eye, 1977; numerous works of poetry pub. U.S. and Eng., 1973-79. Recipient 11 awards for poetry, 1973-79, 4 awards for radio copywriting, 1980-83, 42 awards for songs and lyrics, Los Angeles and Nashville, 1979-90. Mem. ASCAP, Nat. Acad. Songwriters, Poets and Writers. Home: Raleigh N.C. Deceased.

WEINSTEIN, ISRAEL, commissioner of public health; b. N.Y.C., May 26, 1893; s. David and Frieda (Chester) W. AB, CCNY, 1913; AM, Columbia U., 1916; ScD, NYU, 1917; MD, Columbia U., 1926, PhD, 1930. Tchr. biology N.Y.C. high schs., 1914; instr. physiology Coll. Phys. and Surg., Columbia U.; assoc. with Dr. William Park N.Y.C. Health Dept. Rsch. Labs., 1914, bacteriologist; asst. prof., Biggs prof. preventive medicine NYU Med. Sch., 1933-37; with N.Y.C. Dept. Health, from 1924; commr. of pub. health N.Y.C., 1946-47; dir. Bur. Health Edn. Dept. Pub. Health, N.Y., 1947-49. Editor Neighborhood Health, bi-monthly publ. N.Y.C. Health Dept., 1936-42; contbr. numerous articles to profl. jours. Enlisted as pvt. U.S. Army, World War I; commd. 1st lt. San. Corps; served overseas; maj. med. corps U.S. Army, 1942, advanced to lt. col.; divsn. med. insp. 71st Inf., France, Germany and Austria, World War II. Decorated Purple Heart, Bronze Star medal. Mem. AMA, N.Y. Acad. Medicine, Am. Pub. Health Assn., N.Y. State Med. Soc., Med. Soc. County of N.Y., Phi Beta Kappa, Sigma Xi, Alpha Omega Alpha. *

WEINTRAUB, EUGENE, publisher, editor; b. Kiev, Russia, Mar. 10, 1904; came to U.S., 1906; s. Louis and Rose (Kupchin) W.; m. Lilien Jacobs, Oct. 18, 1947; 1 son, David. Grad. Juilliard Sch., 1938. Dir. Am-Rus Music Corp., N.Y.C., 1940-50; editor-pub. Weintraub Music Co., N.Y.C., 1950-92; editor Music Sales Corp., N.Y.C., 1960-92. Contbr. articles to newspapers, profl. jours. Jewish. Home: New York N.Y. Died Nov. 19, 1992. †

WEINTRAUB, LOUIS, public relations executive; b. Montreal, Que., Can., June 4, 1922; came to the U.S., 1923; naturalized, 1946; s. Samuel and Bella (Silverman) W. Grad. high sch., N.Y.C.; m. Renee Arum, Nov. 4, 1951; children: Joel, Judy. Washington bur. mgr. Pix, Inc., 1940-41; asst. to picture editor Washington Post, 1940-41; news photographer Office War Information, 1941-42; picture editor Keystone Pictures, Inc., N.Y.C., 1947-49; asst. to pub. N.Y. Age, 1949-50; dir. News Press Svc., 1950-54; dir. pub. rels. Pavelle Color and Pavelle Labs., Inc., 1951-57; pres. Weintraub & Fitzsimons, Inc., pub. rels. counsel, N.Y.C., 1958-90; pres. Photo Communications Co., Inc., visual cons., N.Y.C., 1958-90. Pub. rels. adviser Hon. W. Averell Harriman, 1954-60, N.Y. gov. N.Y. State Goodwill Am., Brussels World's Fair, 1958; mem. Pres. Com. on Employment of People with Disabilities, 1958-90; trustee Citizen's Budget Commn., 1967-90. Cpl., Signal Corps, AUS, 1942-45. Decorated Croix de Guerre with Palms (France). Recipient Medal, City of Orleans, France, 1948, Pub. Svc. award Philippines Lions Internat., 1959, New Yorker of the Year Bowling Green Assn., 1987. Mem. Pub. Rels. Bowling Green Assn., 1987. Mem. Pub. Rels. Soc. Am., Silurians, Fgn. Press Assn. (disting. svc. award 1983, life), Am. Legion, VFW, Nat. Press Photographers Assn. (charter, life), N.Y. Press. Photographers Assn., N.Y. Press Club, Overseas Press Club, B'nai B'rith, K.P. Died Sept. 13, 1991.

WEIR, GORDON BRUCE, consulting meteorologist; b. Galesburg, Ill., July 20, 1919; s. Gordon Wayne and Alta Marie (Johnson) W. BS in Geology, Calif. Tech. Inst., Pasadena, 1940, MS, 1941. Forecaster Krick Weather Service, Pasadena, 1946-48, Nat. Weather Inst., Los Angeles, 1948-75, Allied Weather Cons., Los Angeles, from 1975. Served to lt. col. USAF, 1941-46. Fellow AAAS; mem. Am. Meteorol. Soc. (T.V. Seal of Approval 1960), Am. Geophys. Union. Republican. Congregationalist. Club: Athenaeum (Pasadena). Home: Los Angeles Calif.

WEISBLAT, DAVID IRWIN, pharmaceutical company executive; b. Coshocton, Ohio, Aug. 11, 1916; s. Morris and Yetta (Laddin) W.; m. Edna Christine Hawkinson Weisblat, Apr. 11, 1942; children: Ann Weisblat Ford, Sara Weisblat Schastok, David. B.A. summa cum laude, Ohio State U., 1937, Ph.D., 1941, postgrad., 1941-43; M.D. (hon.), Karolinska Institutet, Sweden, 1980. With Upjohn Co., Kalamazoo, 1943-81; dir. biochem. research Upjohn Co., 1962-68, v.p. pharm. research and devel., 1968-81, dir., 1973-81; mem. chemistry panel Cancer Chemotherapy Nat. Service Center.; mem. sci. rev. com. Neogen Corp., 1981-90; mem. WHO Onchocerciasis Chemotherapy Project Working Group, 1981-82. Contbr. sci. articles to profl. jours. Chmn. library com. Western Mich. U., 1958-64, mem. chemistry adv. com., 1958-68; mem. sci. adv. com. Pharm. Mfrs. Assn. Found., 1976; mem. molecular biology com. Mich. High Tech. Task Force, 1981-82; pres. Galesburg-Augusta Community Sch. Bd., 1960-62; trustee Charlestown Twp. Bd., 1959-63, Kalamazoo Sci. Found., 1974-90; trustee Kalamazoo Symphony Soc., Inc., 1968-77, pres., 1971-73; bd. dirs. Reproductive Health Care Ctr./Planned Parenthood South Central Mich., 1981-87; sec. Charleston Twp. Planning Commn., 1979-90; Planned Parenthood Fedn. Am. Great Lakes Region Exec. Com., 1987-89. Recipient Disting. Service award Western Mich. U., 1968. Fellow AAAS, Intra-Sci. Research Found. (hon.); mem. Am. Chem. Soc. (asso. editor Chem. Revs.), Pharm. Mfrs. Assn., Phi Beta Kappa, Sigma Xi, Phi Lambda Upsilon. Home: Galesburg Mich. Died Apr. 21, 1990, cremated.

WEISS, DUDLEY ALBERT, lawyer, trustee; b. Boston, May 17, 1912; s. William Jacob and Esther (Herman) W.; m. Thelma G. Akabas, June 9, 1940 (dec.); 1 child, Eleanor Weiss Angoff. BA, Harvard U., 1934, JD, 1937. Bar: Mass. 1937, U.S. Dist. Ct. Mass. 1938, U.S. Ct. Appeals (1st cir.) 1939, U.S. Supreme Ct. 1979. Sr. ptnr. Weiss, Angoff, Coltin, Koski & Wolf P.C., Boston, 1937—; atty., economist Office Price Adminstrn., World War II, economist, Korean War; exec. dir., gen. counsel Library Binding Inst., 1950-82, exec. dir. emeritus, 1982—. Trustee Frank M. Barnard Found., Am. London Symphony Orch. Found.; nat. panelist Am. Arbitration Assn.; bd. dirs. Maurice F. Tauber Found. Lab. Dudley A. Weiss Book Testing Lab. at Rochester Inst. Tech. named in his honor, 1982. Mem. ABA, Mass. Bar Assn., Mass. Bar Found. (life), Boston Bar Assn., Norfolk County Bar Assn., Middlesex County Bar Assn., Am. Judicature Soc., Phi Beta Kappa. Club: Harvard of Boston. Home: Boston Mass.

WEISS, JOSEPH JOHN, railway official; b. Bklyn., Feb. 11, 1895; s. Joseph and Vanderbilt (Fiedler) W.; m. Jennette Gilbert DePew, June 10, 1922. Grad., Comml. High Sch., Bklyn., 1911. Stenographer, clk. Erie R.R. Co., N.Y.C., 1911-16; from sec. to chmn. bd. to v.p. Kansas City So. Ry. Co., from 1916, also sec., asst treas., officer several subsidiaries; v.p., dir., sec. Kansas City So. Industries, Inc. Lutheran. *

WEISS, LAWRENCE ROBERT, investment banking executive; b. Pasadena, Mar. 8, 1937; s. Joseph B. and Elsie (Shaw) W.; BS in Applied Physics, UCLA, 1959; MS in Mgmt. Sci., U. So. Calif., 1974; m. Elaine Saxon, June 23, 1963; children: Jeffrey Arthur, Jason Ashley. Electronic systems engr., N.Am. Aviation, Inc., L.A., 1960-62, Litton Systems, Inc., 1962-63; group head Hughes Aircraft Co., Culver City, Calif., 1963-67, group head, sales rep., br. sales mgr., 1967-70; with Sci. Data Systems, Systems Engring. Labs., Gen. Automation, Inc., Interdata Corp., Applied Digital Data Systems, Inc., 1973-80; co-founder, chmn., pres. Health-tronics Labs. Inc., Rochester, N.Y., 1970-72, Cal-trend Personality Systems, Inc., L.A., 1973-85; co-founder, chmn. bd., v.p. Evolution Computer Systems Corp., (name changed to Evolution Techs., Inc. 1981), Irvine, Calif., 1980-82; co-founder, chmn., pres. Capital Tech. Group Inc., Irvine, 1981-83; co-founder, pres. Tek-Net Funding Corp., Irvine, 1984-85; fin. cons. Shearson Lehman Bros., Inc., Orange, Calif., 1985-86; v.p. investments Drexel Burnham Lambert Inc., Newport Beach, Calif., 1986-87; chmn. Covest Holdings, Inc., 1987-88; v.p. Wedbush-Morgan Securities, Inc., Newport Beach, 1988-89; pres. Pub. Equities Planning Corp., 1989—. Mem. Planetary Soc., U.S. Naval Inst., Am. Def. Preparedness Assn., Mensa.Deceased. Home: Dana Point Calif. †

WEISS, LEO ABRAHAM, management consultant; b. Bklyn., Dec. 6, 1918; s. Samuel A. and Carrie (Berkowitz) W.; m. Mildred Hope Ramsay, Feb. 5, 1944; children: Steven, Randolph, Robin, Scott. Student, MIT, 1935-36; BS in Aero. Engring., U. Mich., 1939. Chief engr. Simmonds Precision Products, Cambridge, Mass., 1941-42, Queens, N.Y., 1942-47; asst. to chmn. Lear, Inc., Grand Rapids, Mich., 1947-48; pres. Avien, Inc., Queens, 1948-75, Am. Scientific Enterprise, Inc., Kings Point, N.Y., 1975-81, Bus. Devel. Corp. Am., Alexandria, Va., 1981-86; chmn. Venture Clinic, Inc., Alexandria, 1986-91; cons., bd. dirs. various start-up bus., 1983-89; adv. bd. Templeton Group, N.Y.C., 1963-66, Nat. Planning Assn., Washington, 1961-62, New Dominion Mag., Arlington, 1989-91. Producer: (TV series) The Venture Game, 1989-91; columnist Wash. Bus. Jour., 1990-91; contbr. articles to profl. jours. Founding dir. MIT Enterprise Forum Washington-Balt. Inc., 1981-86; founding dir. Long Island Forum for Tech., Mineola, 1976-79. Named Man of Yr. Nat. Conf. Comml. Fin. Cos., 1958, Entrepreneur of Yr. Ernst & Young, 1989. Fellow AIAA (assoc.); mem. Am. Inst. Entrepreneurs (life), U. Mich. Alumni Assn., MIT Alumni Assn., Young Pres. Orgns. (v.p. 1960-61). Home: Alexandria Va. Died Dec., 18, 1991.

WEISS, MYRON, editor, publisher; b. Cleve., July 14, 1894; s. Alexander and Rose (Katz) W.; m. Lucie Wiese, June 22, 1928. Student, Cleve. Law Sch.; student in, France; ArtsD (hon.), Staley, 1937. Assoc. editor Time Mag., N.Y.C., 1925-38; editorial cons., from 1938; established Myron Weiss, Pub., N.Y.C., 1939; founder Casting Rsch. Info. Office, 1954, Metals Info. Libr., 1957; founder, editor, pub. Rsch., Engring. & Devel. Info. Indicator, 1956; counsel Metal Info. Libr., 1958; pub., editor Engrs. Joint Coun. Engr., 1959. Compiler, editor: Casting-Design Process (bibliography), In Defense of Love (psychoanalysis), Bedside Guide for the Management of the Heart Patient. Del. Internat. Hygenic Cong., Dresden, Germany, 1930, Nat. Health Conf., Washington, 1938, Am. Scientific Cong., 1940, Nat. Health Assembly, 1948, World Metall. Cong., 1957, Conf. Dental Journalism; mem. bd. reference Staley Coll., Boston; concillor Pan-Am. League. Mem. AAAS, Am. Pub. Health Assn., Am. Genetic Assn., Am. Arbitration Assn. (panel), Am. Med. Writers Assn., Am. Soc. Metals, Pan-Am. Med. Assn. (hon.), Nat. Press Club, Acad. Polit. Scis., Soc. History Metals, Tech. Writers Assn., Spl. Librs. Assn. *

WEISS, PAUL ALFRED, biologist; b. Vienna, Austria, Mar. 21, 1898; came to U.S., 1931, naturalized, 1939; s. Carl S. and Rosalie M. (Kohm) W.; m. Marie Helen Blaschka, Jan. 30, 1926. PhD, U. Vienna, 1922; MD (hon.), U. Frankfort, Germany, 1949; D in Natural Scis. (hon.), U. Giessen, 1957; Dr. Med. and Surg. (hon.), U. Helsinki, 1966; ScD (hon.), U. Notre Dame, 1972; MD (hon.), U. Vienna, 1974. Asst. dir. Biol. Rsch. Inst. Acad. Scis., Vienna, 1922-29, Rockefeller fellow, 1927-29, 35-37; fellow Kaiser Wilhelm Inst., Berlin, 1929-30; Sterling fellow Yale U., 1931-33; from asst. prof. to prof. zoology U. Chgo., 1933-54, chmn. div. biology master's program, 1948-54; head lab. devel. biology, prof. Rockefeller Inst. Med. Rsch., N.Y.C., 1954-64; founder, dean Grad. Sch. Biomed. Scis. U. Tex., Houston, 1964-66, prof., 1964; prof. emeritus Rockefeller U., 1954-89; Mellon lectr. U. Pitts., 1964; disting. vis. prof. Tex. A&M U., 1966-67; vis. scholar Pratt Inst., N.Y.C., 1964; vis. prof. Washington U., 1947, U. Frankfort, 1948, U. Nebr., 1951, MIT, 1956-57, NYU, 1960, U. Santander (Spain), 1963; Hopkins lectr., vis. prof. Stanford U., 1950; disting. vis. lectr. SUNY, Buffalo, 1967; lectr. numerous other univs., orgns., U.S. and

Europe. Author 11 books, over 350 papers; editor Quar. Rev. Biology, others. Ofcl. investigator charge Govt. War Rsch. Project, 1942-45; spl. cons. U.S. High Commn., Germany, 1951; chmn. U.S. del. Internat. Union Biol. Scis., 1953, 55, 58, 61, Internat. Coun. Sci. Unions, 1961; chief sci. adviser U.S. commn. gen. Brussels World's Fair, 1957-58; mem. adv. bd. Inst. Basic Rsch., U. Calif.; sci. adv. bd. Mass. Gen. Hosp., 1952-55; mem. sci. adv. bd. Pacific Sci. Ctr., 1963-89; mem. internat. cell rsch. orgn., UNESCO; chmn. div. biology and agr. NRC, 1951-55, chmn. biol. coun. also Merck fellowship bd.; mem. Fulbright com., 1949-51; trustee Fund for Neurobiology; mem. corp. Marine Biol. Lab., Woods Hole, Mass., Bermuda Biol. Sta.; mem. sci. adv. com. to Pres. U.S., 1958-60, cons. Office Sci. and Tech., 1960-89; coun. indsl. R & D Gov. N.Y. State, 1960-64; sci. adv. bd. Seattle 1961 World's Fair; mem. adv. bd. Coun. Advancement Med. Communication; assoc. neuroscis. rsch. program MIT; mem. adv. bd. Mt. Sinai Hosp. and Sch. Medicine; mem. bd. Lecomte de Nouy Found., 1968-89. Recipient numerous honors and awards; decorated grand medal Geoffroy St. Hilaire (France). Fellow AAAS (v.p. 1952-53), Internat. Inst. Embryology (v.p. 1949-55); mem. Am. Acad. Arts and Scis., Am. Soc. Naturalists, Am. Assn. Anatomists, Am. Soc. Zoologists, Harvey Soc. (pres. 1962-63), Growth Soc. (pres. 1941-42), Internat. Soc. Cell Biology (pres. 1965-68), Internat. Union Biol. Scis. (chmn. policy bd.), Nat. Acad. Scis. (mem. coun., governing bd. 1964-67), Soc. Study Growth and Devel. (pres. 1941-42), Royal Swedish, Serbian acads. sci., German Acad. Sci. Leopoldina, Max-Planck Soc., Am. Philos. Soc. (Lewis prize 1971, Lashley award 1975), Am. Physiol. Soc., Am. Soc. Cell Biology, Assn. Rsch. Nervous and Mental Diseases, Club of Rome, Literary Club, Cosmos Club, Phi Beta Kappa (hon.), Sigma Xi. Home: New York N.Y. Died Sept. 8, 1989.

WEISS, RAYMOND LEE, development officer; b. Cleve., Jan. 3, 1955; s. Raymond and Georgia Ellen (Baker) W.; B.S. in Sociology, Capital U., 1983. Child care worker Parmadale Children's Village, Parma, Ohio, 1976-79, asst. dir. edn., 1981-83, asst. dir. research and devel., 1983-87 ; cons. St. Charles Group, Lakewood, Ohio, 1983, 84, 85. Mem. adv. bd. Parma City Schs., 1983-87 ; trustee No. Ohio chpt. Nat. Hemophilia Found., 1984-87 . Mem. Ohio Council Fund Raising Execs. Avocations: photography; fishing. Home: Cleveland Ohio

WEISS, ROGER WILLIAM, social sciences educator; b. N.Y.C., Jan. 10, 1930; s. Nicholas and Irene (Roth) W. MA, U. Chgo., 1951, PhD, 1955. Asst. prof. econs. Vanderbilt U., Nashville, 1953-57; pres. N. Weiss and Co., Chgo., 1957-63; asst. prof., assoc. prof. social scis. U. Chgo., from 1963; Bd. dirs. Ill. Packing Co., Chgo., other firms. Bd. dirs. Urban Gateways, Chgo., Merit Music Program, Chgo., Music of the Baroque, Chgo. Mem. Ref. Club (London), Cliff Dweller. Home: Chicago Ill.

WEISS, THEODORE S., congressman; b. Hungary, Sept. 17, 1927; came to U.S., 1938, naturalized, 1953; s. Joseph and Pearl (Weiss) W.; m. Sonya M. Hoover; children: Thomas D., Stephen R. B.A., Syracuse U., 1951, LL.B., 1952. Bar: N.Y. 1953. Asst. dist. atty. for N.Y. county, 1955-59; mem. 95th-102nd Congresses from 17th N.Y. Dist., 1977-92; mem. edn. and labor com. 95th-101st Congresses from 17th N.Y. Dist., 1977-92, mem. govt. ops. com., 1977-92, mem. fgn. affairs com., mem. com. on children, youth and families, 1983-92, chmn. subcom. on human resources and intergovtl. relations, 1983-92, mem. banking fin. and urban affairs com., 1990-92; chmn. congl. arts caucus U.S. Ho. of Reps., Washington, 1991-92; sec. N.Y. State Cong. Delegation, 1987-92. Served with AUS, 1946-47. Mem. NAACP, ABA, ACLU, Ams. for Dem. Action (pres. 1986-89), New Dem. Coalition, N.Y. County Lawyers Assn. Jewish. Home: New York N.Y. Died Sept. 14, 1992. †

WEISSBLUTH, MITCHEL, applied physics educator, researcher; b. Yampol, Russia, Jan. 7, 1915; came to U.S., 1922, naturalized, 1928; s. Elias and Miriam (Saltzman) W.; m. Margaret Hochhauser, Feb. 25, 1940; children: Stephen, Marc, Thomas. B.A., Bklyn. Coll., 1936; M.A., George Washington U., 1941; Ph.D., U. Calif.-Berkeley, 1950. Radio engineer Crosley Radio Corp., Cin., 1941-42; sr. research engr. Jet Propulsion Lab., Pasadena, Calif., 1942-46; asst. prof. radiology Stanford U., Calif., 1954-67, assoc. prof. applied physics, 1967-76, prof. applied physics, from 1976, emeritus, until 1990; dir. biophysics lab. Stanford U., Caif., 1964-68; liaison scientist Office Naval Research, Tokyo, 1978-79, London, 1967-68; vis. lectr. U. Paris, 1965. Author: Hemoglobin, 1974, Atoms and Molecules, 1978, Photon-Atom Interactions, 1989; editor: Molecular Biophysics, 1965, Quantum Aspects of Polypeptides and Polynucleotides, 1964. Fulbright research scholar, Israel, 1960-61. Mem. Internat. Soc. Quantum Biology (pres. 1971-73), Div. Atomic and Molecular Physics, Div. Biol. Physics (exec. com. 1973-76), Am. Phys. Soc., N.Y. Acad. Sci. Jewish. Home: Stanford Calif. Died Apr. 19, 1990; buried Stanford, Calif.

WEISSLER, GERHARD LUDWIG, physicist, educator; b. Eilenburg, Germany, Feb. 20, 1918; came to U.S., 1939; naturalized, 1944; s. Otto and Margaret (Wendt) W.; m. Claire Markoff, Aug. 15, 1953; children: Roderick A., Robert E., Mark (dec.). BS, Tech. U., Berlin, 1938; MA, U. Calif., Berkeley, 1941, PhD, 1942. Cert. x-ray, radium physicist Am. Bd. Radiology. Instr. radiol. physics Med. Ctr. U. Calif., San Francisco, 1942-44; asst. prof. physics U. So. Calif., 1944-48, assoc. prof., 1948-52, head dept. physics, 1951-56, prof., 1952-89; cons. radiation physics. Contbr. articles to sci. jours. Fellow Am. Phys. Soc. (chmn. div. electron physics 1964), Optical Soc. Am.; mem. AAUP, Sigma Xi. Home: Encino Calif. Died June 13, 1989.

WEIST, DWIGHT WILSON, actor, announcer; b. Palo Alto, Calif., Jan. 16, 1910; s. Dwight Wilson and Harriet Faye (Thompson) W.; m. Elizabeth Maxwell, Oct. 19, 1934 (div.); children: Gretchen Weist Stephens, Richard; m. Avery Hathaway, Apr. 15, 1957 (div.); children: Charles, Andrew, Bart. BA, Ohio Wesleyan U., 1931. Network radio actor and announcer, 1930-60; with NBC Radio News, 1960-63; announcer Search for Tomorrow CBS-TV, 1963-80; co-owner, tchr. Weist-Barron Sch. TV, 1957-88, dir., 1988-91; narrator Path Newsreel, 1942-55. Author: On Camera, 1983; film narrator: Golden Age of Comedy, When Comedy Was King, Name of the Rose; appeared in films Zelig, Radio Days, 9 1/2 Weeks. Mem. Screen Actors Guild (bd. dirs., pres. N.Y. chpt.), AFTRA. Home: Block Island R.I. Died July 16, 1991.

WEITZEN, EDWARD H., corporate executive; b. N.Y.C.; m. Roslyn K. Weitzen; children: Rita Haves, Ide Weitzen, Rochelle Weitzen. Grad., CCNY. V.p. Bulova Watch Co., N.Y.C.; pres., CEO Gruen Industries, N.Y.C.; v.p. mktg. Am. Machine and Foundry Corp., N.Y.C.; chmn. Gen. Battery Co., Reading, Pa.; pres. Internat. Banknote Co., N.Y.C., also bd. dirs. Lt. col. U.S. Army, WWII. Home: New York N.Y. Died Sept. 30, 1991.

WELCH, BETTY JO, communications educator, consultant; b. Nashville, Mar. 7, 1934; d. Nathan Robert Hyde and Ruth (Kemp) Patterson; m. Alan Fox Welch, Sept. 14, 1957; children: Lisa Claire, Laura Brittain, Allan Neil. BS, Middle Tenn. State U., 1956, MA, 1957; EdS, George Peabody Coll., 1963; PhD, Vanderbilt U., 1980. Instr. George Peabody Coll., Nashville, 1967-70; from asst. prof. to prof. communications U. N.C., Wilmington, 1970-88; chmn. U. N.C. Faculty Assembly, Chapel Hill, 1986-87; cons. in field, 1980-88. Author: Complement to Basic Speech, 1976, 2d rev. edit., 1979; contbr. articles to profl. jours. Chmn. bd. dirs. Wilmington Civic Ballet, 1981-88; bd. dirs. Hospitality House Wilmington, 1985-88; com. chmn. Zonta Southeastern N.C., Wilmington, 1985-88. Mem. Southern Speech Communication Assn. (states adv. chair 1986-87), Speech Communication Assn. (vice chmn. sr. coll. and univ. sect. 1985-86). Republican. Episcopalian. Home: Wilmington N.C. Died 1988.

WELCH, EARL ELLIS, publishing company executive; b. Strawberry Point, Iowa, July 29, 1901; s. Oscar E. and Nora (Stalnaker) W.; m. Kathryn Phoebe Johnston, Aug. 19, 1926; children: Barbara Kay, Cynthia Sue. 010BA, State U. Iowa, 1925; PhM, U. Wis., 1933. Supt. schs. Elberon, Iowa, 1921-24; asst. prin. jr. and sr. high schs. Beaver Dam, Wis., 1927-29; prin. Stoughton, Wis., 1929-35, Austin, Minn., 1935-37; dir. secondary edn. rsch. Silver Burdett Co., N.Y.C., 1937-39; editor-in-chief Silver Burdette Co., N.Y.C., 1939-56, exec. v.p., 1956-60; pres. Morristown, N.J., 1960-63; audiovisual cons. book div. Time, Inc., Madison, N.J., 1963-90; pres. Wel-Kids, Inc., Madison, N.J., 1967-90. Co-author: (with Joseph I. Arnold) Challenges to American Youth, 1940. Mem. Soc. Curriculum Study, Am. Assn. Sch. Adminstr., Am. Assn. Prins. Secondary Schs., Nat. Coun. Social Studies, Phi Delta Kappa. Home: Madison N.J. Died Feb. 10, 1990; buried Chatham, N.J.

WELCH, JAMES MONROE, personnel consultant firm executive; b. Chattanooga, June 4, 1916; s. Benjamin H. and Laura (Gill) W.; m. Elizabeth DeMars, Dec. 24, 1936; children—Suzanne, James M. Grad. McKenzie Coll., 1934; student U. Chattanooga, 1936-39. Tech. sec., drafting instr., elec. engr. TVA, Chattanooga, 1936-43, recruiter sci. personnel-indsl. relations counselor, 1943-45; asst. to v.p., dir. research Tenn. Eastman Co., Oak Ridge and Kingsport, 1945-64, mgr. adminstrv. services and research, 1964-81; owner, pres. Appalachian Mgmt Assistance, Kingsport, 1981—. Pres. Kingsport Symphony Orch. Assn., 1949-51, Kingsport Coll. Found., 1959—, East Tenn. State U. Found., 1980-81; chmn. Tenn. March of Dimes, 1956; bd. dirs. Kingsport Community Chest, 1947-61. Named Hon. Alumnus, East Tenn. State U., 1979. Mem. Adminstrv. Mgmt. Soc. (area dir. 1964-66, Ambassador award 1985), Am. Mgmt. Assn. (planning council, gen. services div. 1970-81), Internat. Platform Assn., Jaycees (Outstanding Young Man 1948; life mem.), Am. Legion (Disting. Service award 1971) Methodist. Club: Ridgefields Country (Kingsport). Lodge: Kiwanis. Contbr. articles to publs. Home: Kingsport Tenn.

WELCH, RICHARD EDWIN, JR., history educator; b. Newburyport, Mass., June 16, 1924; s. Richard Edwin and Helen (Hale) W.; m. Christina S. Marquand, Sept. 4, 1948; children—Catherine Helen, Richard Edwin III, Christina S., Elizabeth M., Margaret Curzon. A.B., Dartmouth Coll., 1948; M.A., Harvard U., 1949, Ph.D., 1952. Instr. history Colgate U., 1952-53; asst. prof. Va. Mil. Inst., 1953-58; asst. prof. Lafayette Coll., Easton, Pa., 1958-62, assoc. prof., 1962-70, prof. Am. history, 1970-78, Charles A. Dana prof., 1978-89. Author: Theodore Sedgwick, Federalist: A Political Portrait, 1965, George Frisbie Hoar and the Half-Breed Republicans, 1971, Imperialists vs. Anti-imperialists: The Debate Over Expansionism in the 1890s, 1972, Response to Imperialism: The United States and the Philippine-American War, 1899-1902, 1979, Response to Revolution: The United States and the Cuban Revolution, 1959-1961, 1985, also numerous articles. Served with AUS, 1942-46. Mem. Am. Hist. Assn., Orgn. Am. Historians, Soc. Historians of Am. Fgn. Relations. Home: Newburyport Mass. Died June 17, 1989.

WELCH, RICHARD ENLOW, manufacturing company executive; b. Chgo., Oct. 13, 1895; s. William M. and Jeanette (Dupuis) W.; m. Eleanor Francis Holbrook, July 2, 1921; children: Barbara (Mrs. Gordon Osterstrom), Richard Enlow, Eleanor (Mrs. Michael Wampler). BS, U. Mich., 1919. With Welch Sci. Co., Chgo., from 1918, exec. v.p., 1938-64, pres., 1964-65, chmn., CEO, from 1965; dir., v.p., treas. News Map of the Week, Inc., from 1938. Mem. Sci. Apparatus Makers Assn. (chmn. lab. apparatus sect. 1942-43, 47-48, pres. 1957-58, dir. 1947-51, 54-61), University Club, Mid-Am. Club (Chgo.), Exmoor Club (Highland Park, Ill.). Presbyn. *

WELLER, AUGUSTUS BOOKSTAVER, bank executive; b. Bklyn., Feb. 17, 1894; s. Hervey and Isabella (Bookstaver) W.; m. Lilyan Collins, Sept. 23, 1919, 1 child, Don Gardiner. BA, Yale U., 1915. With Reid Ice Cream Co., 1915-16; with investment banking firms, 1916-29; pres. MotologueAdvt. Corp., 1929-34; past pres., chmn. bd., chmn. exec., bond and fin. coms. Meadowbrook Nat. Bank of Nassau County (formerly First Nat. Bank of Merrick), West Hempstead; pres. Nassau County Clearing House Assn. Rationing adminstr. Nassau County, 1941-46; past pres. Merick Bd. Edn. Adv. Bd. L.I. Assn.; dir. Nassau-Suffolk YMCA; adv. bd. Nassau-Suffolk Better Bus. Bur.; N.Y. State Adv. Bd. Salvation Army; adv. com. N.Y. State Citizens Coun. Traffic Safety; trustee, vice-chmn. Hofstra U. Recipient Nassau Rev. medallion for most outstanding pub. svc., 1944. Mem. Yale Alumni Club, Mason (33 deg., Shriner), Rotary (hon. life), Elk, Merrick Sqaure Club, Spartan Fellowcraft Club, Hempstead Golf Club, Beta Theta Pi, Gamma Delta Psi. Republican. Presbyn. *

WELLER, EDWIN ESTABROOK, lawyer, life insurance company executive; b. Montour Falls, N.Y., Feb. 12, 1909; m. Virginia Edmondson, Oct. 22, 1932; 1 child, Daniel T. BA, U. Pa., 1931, LLB, 1934. Bar: Pa. Sr. v.p., gen. counsel Provident Mut. Life. Ins. Co., Phila., 1936-74. Died 1991.

WELLES, EDWARD RANDOLPH, bishop; b. Cin., Apr. 20, 1907; s. Samuel Gardner and Mabel (De Geer) W.; m. Catharine Van Alstyne, June 2, 1931 (dec. 1983); children: Katrina (Mrs. G.G. Swanson), Harriet (Mrs. B.C. Foresman), Edward III, Peter.; m. Martha Borland Willis, Jan. 23, 1984 (dec. Apr. 1984); m. Ferne Bingham Malcolm, Nov. 2, 1984. A.B., Princeton, 1928; B.A., Oxford U., 1930, M.A., 1934; S.T.B., Gen. Theol. Sem., 1932, S.T.D., 1950; D.D., Nashotah House, 1950, Missouri Valley Coll., 1950. Ordained priest Episcopal Ch., 1931; rector Trinity Church, Woodbridge, N.J., 1931-34; chaplain St. Mark's Sch., Southborough, Mass., 1934-36; dean All Saints Cathedral, Albany, N.Y., 1936-40; rector Christ Ch., Alexandria, Va., 1940-44; dean St. Paul's Cathedral, Buffalo, N.Y., 1944-50; bishop of West Mo. Episcopal Diocese, 1950-72; bishop Manset, Maine, 1973-90. Author: Ardincaple Castle, 1930, The Christian in World at War, 1940; autobiography The Happy Disciple, 1975; columnist: Nat. Cath. Reporter, 1978-91. Pres. bd. dirs. St. Luke's Hosp., Kansas City, 1950-69, chmn. bd., 1969-72; Episcopal visitor Community of the Transfiguration, Ohio, 1950-73. Dies 1991.

WELLS, CARD OVREY, university dean; b. Spivey, Kans., Mar. 14, 1897; s. Thomas Monroe and Cora (Parsons) W.; m. Opal Guthridge, Aug. 5, 1923. AB, U. Kans., 1922; MA, U. Chgo., 1925, PhD, 1942. High sch. prin. Nashville, Kans., 1922-24; asst. prin. jr high sch. Wis. State Tchrs. Coll., Whitewater, 1925-27; prin. Wis. State Tchrs. Coll., 1927-32, prof. edn. and psychology, 1932-43, registrar and dean instrn., 1946-60; became Wis. State U.; v.p. instructional affairs, bd. dirs. Wis. State U. Found. With USN, 1918-19, 1st lt. comdr., 1943-46. Mem. NEA, Wis. Edn. Assn., Wis. Acad. Sci., Phi Delta Kappa, Kiwanis (gov. Wis.-Upper Mich. dist. 1964). Republican. Methodist. *

WELLS, JOEL REAVES, JR., bank executive; b. Troy, Ala., Nov. 14, 1928; s. Joel Reaves and Julia (Talley) W.; m. Betty Stratton, June 27, 1953; children: Linda, Martha, Joel. B.S.B.A., U. Fla., 1950, J.D., 1951. Bar: Fla. Ptnr. Maguire, Voorhis & Wells, Orlando, Fla., 1956-75; pres. Major Realty Co., Orlando, 1972-75; exec. v.p. SunBanks, Inc., Orlando, 1975-76, pres., 1976-84, chmn., chief exec. officer, 1982-89; pres. SunTrust Banks, Inc., Atlanta, 1985-90, chmn., 1990-91, also bd. dirs.; bd. dirs. SunBank, N.A., SunBanks, Inc.,

Coca-Cola Enterprises, Inc., Atlanta, Columbian Mut. Life Ins. Co., Binghamton, N.Y. Mem. Fla. Coun. of 100, from 1975; pres. Cen. Fla. Devel. Com., 1965; chmn. Mcpl. Planning Bd., Orlando, 1962, 63; pres. United Appeal Orange County, 1960; trustee Berry Coll., Rome, Ga. Recipient Disting. Service award Orlando Jaycees, 1960. Mem. Orlando C. of C. (pres. 1970), Atlanta C. of C. (past bd. dirs.). Methodist. Clubs: Rotary (pres. 1966-67), Univ., Citrus, Country (Orlando). Home: Atlanta Ga. Died Feb. 2, 1991.

WELLS, JOSEPH M(ERTON), lawyer, energy company executive; b. East Chicago, Ind., Jan. 14, 1922; s. Samuel Ralph and Helen Beatrice (Kester) W.; m. Eileen Agnes Ponsonby, Sept. 1, 1972; 1 child, R. Dodge. SB cum laude, Harvard U., 1943, LLB, 1952. Bar: Ill. 1953. Assoc., then ptnr. Ross & Hardies, Chgo., 1952-64; sec. Peoples Gas Light and Coke Co., Chgo., 1963-67, v.p., 1966-69; v.p. Peoples Energy Corp., Chgo., 1969-72; v.p., gen. counsel Peoples Gas Light and Coke Co., Chgo., 1972-81; v.p., gen. counsel MidCon Corp., Lombard, Ill., 1981-84, vice chmn., 1984-89; v.p. Occidental Petroleum Corp., L.A., 1986-89. Bd. dirs. Coun. Community Svcs. Met., Chgo., 1966-77, pres., 1970-72. Capt. U.S. Army, 1943-49. Mem. The DuPage (Oakbrook Terr., Ill.). Home: Santa Fe N.Mex. Died Apr. 24, 1991.

WELLS, ORIS VERNON, agricultural economist; b. Slate Springs, Miss., Dec. 18, 1903; s. William Allen and Annie May (Putnam) W.; m. Frances Ingram, May 28, 1930; children: Frances Jean, William Allen. BS, N.Mex. State U., 1928, LLD, 1952; postgrad., Harvard U., 1931-32; ScD (hon.), Mont. State Coll., 1950. Economist USDA, Washington, 1929-61; statis. advisor War Food Adminstrn., Washington, 1942-45, 45-46; mem. program com. USDA, 1953-59, chief Bur. Agrl. Econs., 1946-53, adminstr. agrl. mktg. svc., 1953-61; statis. adviser FAO, 1945-46; asst. dir.-gen. FAO, Rome, 1961-63, dep. dir.-gen., 1963-71; mem. gen. adminstrn. bd. USDA Grad. Sch., 1946-61; bd. dirs. CCC, 1951-61; liaison rep. USDA to food and nutrition bd. NRC, 1951-61; FAO del. UNCTAD III, Santiago, 1972, UN Conf. on Environ., Stockholm, 1972; advisor U.S. del. FAO Conf., 1946, 48, 49, 51, 55, 57; vis. lectr. U. Wis., 1949; Regents lectr. U. Calif., Berkeley, spring 1973; cons. on food info. systems Ford Found., 1973-75. Decorated grand ufficiale Ordine al Merito della Republica (Italy); recipient Disting. Svc. award USDA, 1954, Disting. Alumni award N.Mex. State U., 1964, Presdl. citation for pioneering farm policy activities, 1968. Fellow Am. Farm Econ. Assn. (pres. 1949), Am. Statis. Assn.; mem. Agrl. Hist. Soc., Soc. Internat. Devel., Internat. Conf. Agrl. Economists, Cosmos Club (Washington), Alpha Zeta. Home: Alexandria Va. Died Oct. 23, 1986; buried Mt. Comfort Cemetery.

WELLS, PETER BOYD, JR., lawyer; b. Austin, Tex., Sept. 30, 1915; s. Peter Boyd and Eleanor (Henderson) W.; m. Betty Louise Perkins, May 26, 1951; children: Peter Boyd, Elizabeth Wells Howell. B.A., U. Tex., 1936; LL.B., Harvard U., 1940. Bar: Tex., 1941. Assoc., Benckenstein, Wells & Duncan, Beaumont, Tex., 1946-58; sole practice, Beaumont, 1958-61; ptnr. Wells, Duncan & Beard, Beaumont, 1961-70, Wells, Peyton, Beard, Greenberg, Hunt & Crawford, Beaumont, 1970-92; speaker estate planning. Former treas. Tex. Hist. Found. Served to maj. insp. gen. AUS, 1941-45; ETO. Decorated Bronze Star; cert. in estate planning and probate law. Mem. ABA, Tex. Bar Found., Tex. Philos. Soc., Phi Beta Kappa, Phi Kappa Psi. Presbyterian. Clubs: Tower, Beaumont, Beaumont Rotary, Knights of San Jacinto, Sons Republic of Tex. Avocations: collecting early Tex. maps and signatures of Pres. of Republic of Tex., Bible study, rose gardener. Died 1992.

WELS, RICHARD HOFFMAN, lawyer; b. N.Y.C., May 3, 1913; s. Isidor and Belle (Hoffman) W.; m. Marquerite Samet, Dec. 12, 1954; children: Susan, Amy. A.B., Cornell, 1933; LL.B., Harvard U., 1936; postgrad., U. Ariz., 1944. Bar: N.Y. 1936. Spl. asst. dist. atty. N.Y. Co., 1936-37; assoc. Handel & Panuch, N.Y.C., 1937-38; mem. legal staff, asst. to chmn. SEC, Washington, 1938-42; spl. asst. atty. gen. U.S. and spl. asst. U.S. atty., 1941-42; spl. counsel Com. Naval Affairs, U.S. Ho. of Reps., 1943, Sea-Air Commn., Nat. Fedn. Am. Shipping, 1946; trustee, sec. William Alanson White Inst. Psychiatry, N.Y.C., from 1946; vice. chmn., dir. Am. Parents Com.; mem. Moss & Wels, 1946-57, Moss, Wels & Marcus, 1957-68, Sulzberger, Wels & Marcus, 1968-72, Moss, Wels & Marcus, 1972-78, Sperry, Weinberg, Wels, Waldman & Rubenstein, 1979-84; ptnr. Wels & Zerin, 1985-90; gen. counsel Bowling Proprs. Assn. Am., 1956-67, N.Y. State Bowling Proprs. Assn., Am. Acad. Psychoanalysis; commr. Interprofl. Comn. on Marriage and Div.; lectr. Practising Law Inst.; dir. H-R Television, Inc., Belgrave Capital Corp., Broadcast Data Base, Inc., Belgrave Securities Corp.; chmn. bd. govs. Islands Research Found.; bd. govs., chmn., trustee Daytop Village, Inc.; chmn. bd. trustees Bleuler Psychotherapy Center; trustee N.Y. State Sch. Psychiatry, Margaret Chase Smith Library, Skowhegan, Maine. Co-author: Sexual Behavior and the Law; bd. editors Family Law Quar.; contbr. articles to profl. jours. Vice chmn. Am. Jewish Com., mem. nat. exec. bd., until 1990. Served from ensign to lt. USNR, 1942-46; mem. staff Under Sec. Forrestal, 1943-44; in 1944-46, P.T.O. Mem. ABA (fin. officer, mem. council Am. family law sect.), N.Y. State Bar Assn. (chmn. family law sect.), N.Y. City Bar Assn., Am. Acad. Matrimonial Lawyers (gov.), Am. Legion, Naval Order U.S., Mil. Order World Wars, Fed. Bar Assn., Res. Officers Assn., Assn. I.C.C. Practitioners, Fed. Communications Bar Assn., Pi Lambda Phi, Sphinx Head. Clubs: Harmonie (gov.), Harvard, Cornell (N.Y.C.); Nat. Lawyers (Washington); Sunningdale Country (Scarsdale, N.Y.), Statler (Ithaca, N.Y.). Home: New York N.Y. Died Jan. 4, 1990; buried Mt. Hope Cemetery.

WELSH, EDWARD CRISTY, economist, consultant; b. Long Valley, N.J., Mar. 20, 1909; s. Edward Cristy and Florence E. (Delp) W.; m. Carolyn B. White, June 15, 1935. AB magna cum laude, Lafayette Coll., 1930, Litt.D., 1963; MA, Tufts Coll., 1932; PhD, Ohio State U., 1940; LLD, Clark U., 1965. Tchr. econs. several univs., 1930-42; economist Nat. Resources Com., 1937, Temporary Nat. Econ. Com., 1940; regional price exec. OPA, Mich., Ohio, W.Va., Ky., Ind., 1942-44; dir. price ops. all regions U.S. OPA, 1944-46, dep. adminstr., 1946; also asst. commr. O.T.C.; chief anti-trust and cartels div. Dept. Army, G.H.Q., Japan, 1947-50; asst. to chmn., econ. adv. Nat. Security Resources Bd., 1950-51; asst. to adminstr., econ. adv. RFC, 1951-53; mem. Fgn. Investment Bd., Japan, 1949-50; legis. asst. to Sen. Symington, 1953-61; exec. sec. Pres.'s Aero. and Space Coun., 1961-69; pvt. bus. cons. Honored by Army for maj. contbn. to development pvt. enterprise in Japan; recipient Arnold Air Soc. ann. award, 1962, 68, Press award Nat. Space Club, 1968; named Man of Yr. in Letters, Air Force Assn., 1969. Fellow Am. Astronaut. Soc., AIAA; mem. Internat. Acad. Astronautics, Aerospace Med. Assn., Air Force Assn., Phi Beta Kappa (hon.), Beta Gamma Sigma (hon.), Pi Delta Epsilon (hon.). Home: Arlington Va. Died Mar. 25, 1990.

WELTNER, CHARLES LONGSTREET, state supreme court justice; b. Atlanta, Dec. 17, 1927; s. Philip W. and Sally (Cobb) Hull; m. Betty Jean Center, Sept. 16, 1950 (div. 1972); children: Elizabeth Shirley, Philip, Susan Martin, Charles L.; m. Anne Fitten Glenn, Mar. 22, 1978; children: June Spalding, Anne Glenn. AB, Oglethorpe U., 1948; LLB (hon.), Columbia U., 1950; LLD (hon.), Tufts U., 1967; MA, Columbia Theol. Sem., 1983; LLM, U. Va., 1986; MLitt, Trinity Coll., Dublin, Ireland, 1990; DHL (hon.), Oglethorpe U., 1991. Bar: Ga. 1949. Sole practice Atlanta, 1950-92; mem. U.S. Congress from 5th dist. Ga., 1963-67; judge Superior Ct. Atlanta Jud. Cir., 1976-81; presiding justice Supreme Ct. Ga., Atlanta, 1991-92; chmn. jud. council Ga., 1980-81. Author: Process of Service, 1962, Southerner, 1966, John Willie Reed, 1970. Dep. chmn. Dem. Nat. Com., Washington, 1967. Served to 1st lt. U.S. Army, 1955-57. Recipient Profile in Courage award John F. Kennedy Meml. Found., 1991; fellow Inst. Politics, Harvard U. Fellow Am. Law Inst. Presbyterian. Home: Atlanta Ga. Died Aug. 31, 1992. †

WENDEL, WILLIAM HALL, manufacturing company executive; b. Johnstown, Pa., Nov. 15, 1914; s. Daniel Hall and Edna Pearl (Wendell) W.; m. Louise Davis, June 22, 1940; children: William Hall, Jeffrey Philip, Christine. B.S., U.S. Naval Acad., 1936; M.B.A., Harvard U., 1940; LLD, Niagara U., 1964; DSc, Clarkson Coll. Tech., 1971. Asst. to pres. United Engring. Co., 1946; asst. to pres. Carborundum Co., Niagara Falls, N.Y., 1947, mgr. coated products div., 1948-52, v.p. coated products div., 1952-57, group v.p. charge of four divs., 1957-59, exec. v.p., 1959-62, pres., 1962-78, also dir.; pres. Kennecott Corp., N.Y.C., 1978-79, vice-chmn., dir., cons., 1979-80; chmn. bd. dirs. Polaris Industries Inc., 1981-86; vis. prof., exec.-in-residence, enterprise chair Cornell U., 1980. Bd. dirs. Roger Tory Peterson Inst. Served to comdr. USN, 1940-45. Mem. Am. Soc. Corp. Execs. Clubs: Buffalo, Niagara, Country of Buffalo, Niagara Falls Country, Chatham, The Landings. Home: Buffalo N.Y. Died Dec. 3, 1990.

WENDEN, HENRY EDWARD, educator; b. N.Y.C., Nov. 24, 1916; s. Henry Edward and Eileen Mary (Crowley) W.; m. Beatrice Gertrude Wilson, May 25, 1943; children: Sylvia, Mark, Elaine, Rebecca. BS, Yale U., 1938; postgrad., U. Ariz., 1946-47, Wash. State Coll., 1940-41; MA, PhD, Harvard U., 1950, 58. Instr. Boston U., 1949-53; asst. prof. Tufts U., Medford, Mass., 1953-57; prof. mineralogy Ohio State U., Columbus, 1957-91. Patentee in field. With USAAF, 1941-45. Recipient Neil Miner award for Disting. Teaching, 1962, Alumni award for disting. teaching, 1964, Boyer award for disting. teaching, 1969. Fellow Mineral. Soc. Am., Ohio Acad. Sci.; mem. Mineral. Soc. Can., Nat. Assn. Geology Tchrs., Internat. Mineral. Assn. (chmn. teaching commn.), Rushlight Club, Sigma Xi. Home: Worthington Ohio Died Dec. 13, 1991.

WENG, ARMIN GEORGE, clergyman; b. Oshkosh, Wis., Oct. 9, 1897; s. George M. and Jennie F. (Hillemann) W.; m. Helga F. Westerberg, June 21. 1924 (dec. 1946); children: Elizabeth Jean, Armin george; m. Marjory P. Ruth, Sept. 6, 1947 (dec. Aug. 1964). BA, Wartburg Coll., 1919; MA, U. Pa., 1922; BD, Phila. Luth. Theol. Sem., 1923; PhD, Yale U., 1927; DD, Cathage Coll., 1940. Ordained to ministry Luth. Ch., 1922. Pastor 1st English Ch., Bridgeport, Conn., 1922-27, Immanual Ch., Phila., 1927-30, Holy Trinity Luth. Ch., Elgin, Ill., 1930-39; part-time pres. Ill. Synod of United Luth. Ch. in Am., 1937-39, full-time pres., 1939-48; pres. :uth Sch. Theology, Maywood, Ill., 1948-64, adminstrv. v.p., from 1964; prof. ch. history and acting pres. Chgo. Luth. Theol. Sem., 1941-42, spl. lectr. in ch. policy and adminstrn. Contbr. articles to profl. jours. Chmn. bd. Mins. Life and Casualty Union, Mpls.; commr. Nat. Luth Coun., chmn. commn. on student work; sec. Nat. Luth. Svc. Commn.; chmn. Bd. of Publ. United Luth. Ch., 1948-60. Awarded Cosmopilitan medal for distinguished svc., 1934. Mem. Am. Soc. Ch. History, Chgo. Ch. History Soc. Clubs: Kiwanis (hon. mem., pres. 1936), Cosmopolitan (hon. mem.). *

WENZEL, LEE BEY, lawyer; b. Edgeley, N.D., July 1, 1930; s. Russell Henry and Dorothy Kay (Greene) W.; m. Barbara Knoll, Apr. 18, 1953; children: Teresa Zinn, Mark, Neil, Christy Bradford, Dean, Julie Cressman, Lisa Sumner, Kent, Todd. B.S., UCLA, 1952, LL.B., 1957. Calif. 1957, U.S. Dist. Ct. (no., cen. and so. dists.) Calif. 1957, U.S. Supreme Ct. 1966. Dep. city atty. Los Angeles City, 1957-59; assoc. firm Jarrett & Morgan, Los Angeles, 1959-61; ptnr. Morgan, Wenzel & McNocholas, Los Angeles, 1961-90. Bd. regents U. Calif., 1979-80. Diplomate Am. Bd. Trial Attys., 1964. Fellow Internat. Acad. Trial Attys.; mem. Am. Coll. Trial Lawyers, UCLA Alumni Assn. (gen. counsel 1971-74, pres. 1978-80). Republican. Roman Catholic. Clubs: Jonathan Wilshire Country. Avocations: golf, tennis. Died 1990. Home: Northridge Calif.

WERNER, ANTHONY MATTHIAS, lawyer, business executive; b. Kewaskum, Wis., Feb. 19, 1894; s. Anton and Emma (Deutsch) W.; m. Dorothy Elizabeth Bowler, Oct. 15, 1924; children: Davis Anthony, Mary Ellen, Timothy Bowler, Anthony Matthias, John Mark. Student, U. Mich., 1917; LLB, Marwuette U., 1919. Bar: Wis. 1919. Post office clk., 1912; ptnr. Werner & Clemens, from 1919; pres., dir. Crystal Lake Crushed Stone Co., Bowler Security Co.; editor, publisher Sheboygan Press, 1951-64; pres., treas. Press Pub. Co., 1951-64, chmn. bd., from 1964; v.p., dir. Comml. Engraving Co.; dir. Union Trust Life Ins. Co.; state dir. NRA, Fed. Housing Adminstrn., Nat. Emergency Coun.; gen. counsel Allenb Property Custodian, 1942-44; mem. bd. regents U. Wis.; mem. bd. adv. Edgewood Coll., Madison, Wis. City atty. Sheboygan. 1923-29; mem. Police and Fire Commn., Sheboygan, 1933-43, chmn., 1938-40, 54-63; appointed col. staff Gov. Al G. Schmedeman, 1933; col. on staff Gov. Julius P. Heil, 1939. del. to Dem. NAt. Conv., Chgo., 1932. With USN, 1917-19. Mem. Wis. State Bar Assn, Sheboygan Bar Assn., Am. Legion, Alpha Gamma Phi. Elks, KC, Cath. Order Foresters, Frat Order Eagles. Clubs: Milw. Press, Pine Hills Country, Sheboygan Yacht, Nat. Press. *

WERNER, (ROBERT) MORT, television producer and executive; b. San Francisco, May 5, 1916; s. Harold John and Carolyn (Abrams) W.; m. Martha Wilkerson, Mar. 18, 1939; children: Carole Werner Teig, Jill Werner Kahan. Student, San Mateo Coll., 1932-34. Announcer Sta. KJBS, San Francisco, 1934-37; with Phil Harris Orch., Hollywood, Calif., 1937-39; freelance radio producer, 1939-42; co-owner, operator Sta. KUEN, Ventura, Calif., 1947-51; producer NBC, N.Y.C., from 1951, v.p. nat. programs, 1956-61; v.p. programs and talent NBC-TV Network, N.Y.C., from 1961, sr. v.p. program planning, from 1972; v.p. Kaiser Industries, 1957-60, sr. v.p., 1960-61; v.p., dir. radio and TV dept. Young & Rubicam, Inc., 1959; dir. programs OWI Pacific Bur., 1942-44. Producer Today Show, Home Show, Tonight Show with Jack Paar; exec. producer Maverick. With AUS, 1944-47. Mem. NATAS (pres. 1963, nat. coun., pres. internat. coun. 1974-76). Home: Pukalani Hawaii Died Apr. 14, 1990; buried Maui, Hawaii.

WESSEL, HAROLD COSBY, accountant, business consultant; b. Joplin, Mo., Nov. 28, 1916; s. Harold Owen and Myrtle (Cosby) W.; m. Geraldine Audrey Ringius, June 28, 1940; children: Alice Merry (Mrs. Bruce Mutchler), Robert William. Student, U. Mich., 1936-38, Walsh Sch. Bus. Adminstrn., Detroit, 1939-42. With Ernst & Ernst, 1941-75; successively accountant, Detroit, Denver, mgr., Colorado Springs, mgr., Denver, partner Ernst & Ernst, Denver, 1941-59; partner Ernst & Ernst, Phila., 1959-75; ret., 1975; pres. The Wessel Corp., 1981-85; treas. Cloverlay, Inc., 1965-68, pres., 1968-70, dir., 1968-70. Bd. dirs. exec. com. Phila. Port Corp., 1970-72; bd. dirs., exec. com. Phila. Indsl. Devel. Corp., from 1966, v.p., 1969-79, treas., from 1979; chmn. Phila. Authority for Indsl. Devel., from 1979; bd. dirs. Pa. Ballet Co., 1965-73, treas., 1965-69; bd. dirs. Spring Garden Coll., 1964-70, Young Men's Inst., 1977-79, Penjerdel Regional Found., 1978-87; mem. distbn. com. Phila. Found., 1971-81, chmn., 1980; mem. Mayor's Commn. on Aging, 1979-85; trustee Thomas Skelton Harrison Found., 1982-86. Mem. C. of C. Greater Phila. (dir. from 1961, pres. 1970-71, chmn. bd. 1971-72), Am. Inst. CPA's (council 1968-70), Pa. Inst. CPA's., Pa. Hort. Soc. (council 1980-87, chmn. fin. com. 1982-87), Valley Forge Hist. Soc. (dir. 1988-89). Clubs: Union League, Midday (Phila.) (mem. bd. 1966-79, pres. 1970-72, treas. 1974-77, v.p. 1977-79); Merion Golf (treas. 1973-79), Right Angle (mem. bd. 1965-79, v.p. 1970-72, pres. 1973-74). Home: Valley Forge Pa. Died Dec. 17, 1989.

WESSEL, MILTON R., lawyer; b. N.Y.C., Aug. 19, 1923; s. Harry N. and Elsie S. (Stettiner) W.; m. Joan L. Strauss, Jan. 29, 1953; children: Douglas C., Kenneth L., Michael R. BA, Yale U., 1946; LLB, Harvard U., 1948. Bar: N.Y. State, 1949, D.C., 1983, U.S. Supreme Ct., 1956. Asst. to U.S. atty. U.S. Dist. Ct. (so. dist.) N.Y., N.Y.C., 1953-55; spl. asst. U.S. Atty. Gen. U.S. Dept. Justice, Washington, 1958-60; ptnr. Kaye, Scholer, Fierman, Hays & Handler, N.Y.C., 1960-73; gen. counsel Chem. Industry Inst. of Toxicology, Research Triangle Park, N.C., from 1974; spl. asst. to pres. ADAPSO, Arlington, Va., from 1966; gen. counsel Coun. for Chem. Rsch., Bethlehem, Pa., from 1989; adj. profl. Georgetown U. Law Ctr., Washington, from 1982; dir. Ctr. for Study of Law, Sci. & Tech. Coll. of Law Ariz. State U., Tempe, 1988-89; bd. dirs. Sungard Data System, Inc., Wayne, Pa. Author: Government Regulation, 1972, Freedoms Edge, 1974, Rule of Reason, 1976, Science and Conscience, 1980. 1st lt. U.S. Army, 1942-45, ETO. Jewish. Home: Washington D.C. Died May 27, 1991.

WESSON, ROBERT G., political scientist, educator; b. Washington, Mar. 11, 1920; s. Laurence Goddard and Elizabeth Davis (Matthews) W. AB, U. Ariz., 1940; MA, Fletcher Sch. Law and Diplomacy, 1941; PhD, Columbia U., 1961. Asst. prof. govt. Bates Coll., 1961-62, 63-64; asst. prof. polit. sci. U. Calif., Santa Barbara, 1964-66, assoc. prof., 1966-71, prof., 1971-84, prof. emeritus, 1984-91; sr. research fellow Hoover Instn., Stanford U., 1977-91. Author: Imperial Order, 1967, State Systems, 1978, Politics, Modern Government, 1988, Cosmos and Metacosmos, 1989, Beyond Natural Selection, 1991, others; contbr.: articles to Orbis, others; editor book series Politics in Latin America, Democracy World Survey. Served with USNR, 1944-46. Home: Palo Alto Calif. Died July 1, 1991.

WEST, CHARLES W., retired army officer; b. Natches, Miss., Oct. 3, 1898; s. Howell and Emmie (Whitney) W.; m. Jortense Guiteras, Sept. 22, 1955; children: Hortense, Charles, Thomas. BS, U.S. Mil. Acad., 1920; LLB, George Washington U., 1934. Commd. 2d lt. U.S. Army; officer Coast Artillery Corps, 1920-31, Judge Advocate Gen. Corps, 1931-46; chief mil. affairs div. J.A.G. Office, 1942-43; prof. law U.S. Mil. Acad., 1944-62; brig. gen. U.S. Army Ret., 1962. Mem. ABA, George Washington Law Assn., Am. Soc Internat. Law, Judge Advocates Assn. *

WEST, EDWARD NASON, priest; b. Boston, Nov. 5, 1909; s. Edward Nason and Dora daVincente Bellizia (Willey) W. BS, Boston U., 1931, LittD (hon.), 1950; B in Sacred Theology, Gen. Theol. Sem., 1934, D in Sacred Theology (hon.), 1963; DD, Ripon Coll., 1946; ThD, Russian Theol. Inst., Paris, 1953; DD (hon.), U. King's Coll., Halifax, N.S., 1975; LHD (hon.), Episc. Theol. Sem. of the SW, 1984. Ordained deacon Protestant-Episc. Ch., 1934, priest, 1935. Curate Ossining, N.Y., 1934-37, rector, 1937-41; sacrist Cath. Ch. of St. John the Divine, N.Y., 1941-43, canon residentiary, 1943-81, sub-dean of cath., 1966-81, master of ceremonies, 1981-90; dep. to gen. conv., 1969-81; lectr. liturgies Gen. Theol. Sem., 1957-60; Washburn lectr. Episc. Theol. Sch., Cambridge, Mass., 1960; lectr. edn. NYU, 1961-62; lectr. Anglican doctrine and worship Union Theol. Sem., 1965-80, Purser Shortt lectr. U. Dublin, 1971; lectr. Diocesan Inst. Theol., 1973-92; nat. chaplain Am. Guild Organists, 1944-49, 59-60, 68-70; vice chmn. Joint Commn. Ch. Architecture and Allied Arts, 1955-87; chmn. Diocesan Commn. Ch. Bldg., 1942-82; select preacher U. Dublin, 1952, 71; hon. Canon of Vt., 1975-92; cons. Trinity Corp., U.S. Mil. Acad.; warden Community of Holy Spirit; trustee St. Vladmir's Orthodox Theol. Sch. and Acad., 1946-80, Tolstoy Found., FSA, Soc. Antiquaries, London, 1986. Author: Meditations on the Gospel of St. John, 1955, Things I Always Thought I Knew, 1947, A Glossary of Architectural and Liturgical Terms, 1985, (with Norman Laberte) The History of the Cross, 1960, God's Image in Us, 1960, The Far Spent Night, 1960, Outward and Visible--The Language of Christian Symbolism, 1989, also monographs; contbr. to Ency. Americana, Funk & Wagnell's Universal Standard Ency.; designer emblem of Anglican communion. Served to maj. chaplain, USARNG, 1947-69; lt. col. N.Y. NG, 1970-92. Decorated officer Order Orange Nassau (The Netherlands), Order of Brit. Empire, chevalier Legion of Honor (France), sub-prelate Order of St. John of Jerusalem, comdr. Order of Merit (Knights of Malta), Order of Holy Sepulchre, Order of St. Gregory the Illuminator, knight comdr. Order of Polonia Restituta, comdr. Order of St. Sava; recipient State Conspicuous Svc. Cross, silver medal Red Cross Japan. Mem. Protestant-Episc. Soc. for Promoting Religion and Learning in State N.Y., Pilgrims of U.S., St. Andrews Soc., St. George Soc., Soc. of Cin. Clubs: Century, Univ., Columbia Faculty (N.Y.C.); Athenaeum (London). Died Jan. 3, 1990; buried Cathedral of St. John the Divine, N.Y., N.Y.

WEST, DOTTIE (DOROTHY MARIE MARSH), singer; b. McMinnville, Tenn., Oct. ; d. William and Pelina (Jones) Marsh; m. William West, 1952 (div. 1972); children: Morris, Kerry, Shelly, Dale; m. Byron A. Metcalf, Aug. 27, 1973 (div. 1981). B.A. in Music, Tenn. Tech. Coll., 1956. Singing debut, WEWS-TV, Cleve., 1956-60; singer 5-piece band, Cross-Country, 1966—; performances with Grand Ole Opry, 1962-91, Memphis Symphony Orch., 1973, Kansas City Symphony, 1961-74; TV appearances include: Good Ole Nashville, Eddy Arnold Spl., Country Hit Parade, Music Country U.S.A., Glen Campbell Show, Mike Douglas Show; rec. artist Staeday Records, 1959-61, Atlantic Records, 1962, RCA, from 1962; albums include: Country Singing Sensation, Greatest Hits, Sound of Country Music, Here Comes My Baby, 1964, Would You Hold it Against Me?, 1966, Forever Young, 1970, Last Time I Saw Him, 1974, All I Ever Need Is You, 1979, What Are We Doin' In Love, 1981. Recipient Grammy award female artist for Here Comes My Baby 1965; named Number One Female Writer in U.S., Billboard mag. 1974; Number One Female Performer in Eng. 1973, 74; Country Music Artist of Yr., British Country Music Assn.; Coca Cola Country Girl 1972. Home: Sherman Oaks Calif. Died Sept. 4, 1991.

WEST, EDWARD STAUNTON, educator; b. Stuart, Va., Sept. 9, 1896; s. John Thrash and Mary Ann (Jefferson) W.; m. Ruth Evelyn Hurd, May 27, 1920. AB, Randolph-Macon Coll., 1917; MS, Kans. State Coll., 1920; OhD, U. Chgo., 1923; LLD, Randolph-Macon Coll., 1965. Instr. chemistry Kans. State Coll., 1917-22; instr. medicine Washington U., 1923-27, asst. prof., 1927-30, assoc. prof., 1930-34; prof. biochemistry, head dept. Med. Sch. U. Oreg., from 1934; sr. scientist Oreg. Primate Rsch. Ctr. Author: Physical Chemistry for Students of Biochemistry and Medicine, 1942, (with W.B. Todd) Textbook of Biophysical Chemistry, 1956, 3d edit., 1963, Textbook of Biochemistry, 1951, 3d edit., 1961. Mem. AAUP, Am. Chem. Soc., Am. Soc. Biol. Chemists, Soc. Exptl. Biol. and Medicine, Phi Beta Kappa, Sigma Xi, Phi Beta Pi. *

WEST, HERBERT BUELL, foundation executive; b. Birmingham, Apr. 19, 1916; s. Edward Hamilton and Clarine (Buell) W.; AB, Birmingham-So. Coll., 1936; m. Maria Selden McDonald, Nov. 29, 1946; children: Maria Newill, Herbert Buell, William McDonald, Maria Selden, Jane Hamilton. Writer, v.p., account supr. Batten, Barton, Durstine & Osborn, Inc., N.Y.C., 1936-66; dir., mem. distbn. com. N.Y. Community Trust, N.Y.C., 1967-89; pres., dir. Community Funds, Inc., 1967-89, James Found., Inc., 1968-89, Fairfield County Coop. Found., 1984-89. Pres., chmn. bd. Am. br. Internat. Social Service, 1966-72, v.p., 1972-83, bd. dirs., 1972-88; trustee United Community Funds and Council Am., 1968-71, Fay Sch., Southborough, Mass., 1970-80; trustee NYU Med. Center, from 1973, mem. exec. com., 1979-84; chmn. bd. trustees, chmn. exec. com. The Found. Center, 1975-81; warden St. Luke's Episcopal Ch., Darien, Conn., 1976-79; chmn. joint com. United Way/Community Found. Cooperation, from 1987, com. mem. Greater N.Y. Fund/United Way, 1976-81; bd. dirs. Welfare Research, Inc., from 1972, chmn. bd. dirs., 1978-84; bd. dirs., mem. exec. com. Nat. Charities Info. Bur., Inc., 1978-89; bd. dirs. Council on Founds., 1980-87, vice chmn., 1984-87; bd. dirs. Am. Council Nationalities Service, 1983-88; pres. A Better Chance in Darien (Conn.), 1980-83, bd. dirs., 1983-85. Maj. Adjutant Gen. Corps, AUS, 1941-46. Decorated Legion Merit. Mem. N.Y. Regional Assn. of Grantmakers (v.p., dir. 1979-82), Interphil (London). Episcopalian (mem. nat. exec. council 1961-68). Clubs: Century Association, University. Died Jan. 14, 1990; buried Spring Grove Cemetery, Darien, Conn. Home: Darien Conn.

WEST, JOHN DUNHAM, manufacturing company executive; b. Chgo., May 24, 1906; s. Charles C. and Julia B. (Dunham) W.; m. Ruth Cronk St. John, June 28, 1932. Student, Beloit Coll., 1924-25, D.Sc. (hon.), 1980; M.E., Cornell U., 1932; LHD (hon.), Lakeland Coll., 1987. Pres. Manitowoc Co., Inc., Wis., 1957-81; chief exec. officer Manitowoc Co., Inc., 1981-86, chmn. bd. dirs., 1981-87; dir. emeritus Manitowoc Savs. Bank, Employers Ins. of Wausau, Wis. Recipient Disting. Service citation U. Wis. Coll. Engring., Madison, 1982. Mem. Soc. Advancement Mgmt. (Profl. Mgr. citation 1959). Home: Manitowoc Wis. Died Dec. 1, 1989; buried Evergreen Cemetery, Manitowoc, Wis.

WEST, RHEA HORACE, JR., educator; b. Loudon, Tenn., Oct. 5, 1920; s. Rhea Horace and Verna (Quillen) W.; B.S. in Accounting, U. Tenn., 1947; postgrad. (Sloan fellow, M.I.T. fellow), M.I.T., 1959-60, 63, Case Inst. Tech., summer 1960; Ph.D., U. Ala., 1964. Asso. prof. mgmt. Wake Forest Coll., 1950-51; budget and reports analyst AEC, Oak Ridge, 1951-55; teaching fellow U. Ala., Tuscaloosa, 1956-57; asst. prof. mgmt. U. Ark., Fayetteville, 1957-59; Sloan teaching intern MIT, Cambridge, 1959-60; asso. prof. econs. Carson-Newman Coll., Jefferson City, Tenn., 1960-65; prof. mgmt. Ga. State Coll., 1965-70; prof. mgmt., dir. grad. studies Auburn (Ala.) U., 1970-75; acad. dean Cooper Inst., Knoxville, Tenn., 1976-82; chmn. dept. bus. Winston-Salem (N.C.) State U., 1982-90; mgmt. cons.; cons. Cape Kennedy and Huntsville (NASA), Lockheed Aircraft Co., U.S. CSC, others; exec. v.p. Enviro South. Active Center for Study Democratic Instns., Atlanta High Mus. Art; mem. men's com. Internat. Debutantes Ball, N.Y.C., 1976-90; supr. registration U. Tenn., 1946-50. Served with AUS, 1943-46. Mem. Am. Accounting Assn., Am. Mgmt. Assn., Am. Soc. Personnel Adminstrn. (nat. dir. industry edn. com. 1958-60), Inst. Mgmt. Scis., Soc. Advancement Mgmt., Acad. Mgmt., Soc. Sloan Fellows, Opelika Arts Assn., Acad. Polit. Sci., Am. Acad. Polit. and Social Scis., AAUP, Am. Legion, Opelika C. of C., Am. Ordnance Assn., Smithsonian Assos., Am. Acad. Arts and Scis., AAAS, AIAA, Am. Inst. Decision Scis., Am. Judicature Soc., N.Y. Acad. Scis., Internat. Platform Assn., UN Assn. U.S., Newcomer Soc. N.Am., East Tenn. Personnel and Guidance Assn., Sigma Iota Epsilon, Alpha Kappa Psi (dist. dir. 1965-90), Alpha Phi Omega, Kappa Phi Kappa (pres. 1969-70), Alpha Iota Delta, Phi Beta Lambda. Baptist. Clubs: Mass. Inst. Tech., Harvard Faculty, Kiwanis (pres. 1965). Book rev. editor Personnel Adminstr., 1960-90. Contbr. numerous articles and book revs. to profl. publs. Died Jan. 26, 1990; buried Highland Meml. Cemetery, Knoxville, Tenn. Home: Knoxville Tenn.

WEST, ROBERT HUNTER, English literature educator; b. Nashville, May 20, 1907; s. Olin and Susie (Hunter) W.; m. Conn Harris, June 23, 1934; 1 child, Susan McConnell. AB, Vanderbilt U., 1929, MA, 1930, PhD, 1939. Mem. faculty Vanderbilt U., Nashville, 1933-36; asst. prof. U. Ga., Athens, 1936-47, assoc. prof., 1947-54, prof., 1954-64, Alumni Found. prof., 1964-74; vis. prof. U. Va., 1959-60. Author: The Invisible World, 1939; Milton and the Angels, 1955; Shakespeare and the Outer Mystery, 1968; Reginald Scot and Witchcraft, 1984; contbr. numerous articles on English lit. to profl. jours.; columnist Athens Observer. Mem. Fulbright com., 1969-70. Served to capt. USAAF, 1942-46. Recipient publ. prize U. Ky. Press, 1967. Mem. MLA, Milton Soc. Am. (pres. 1974), Shakespeare Assn., South Atlantic Modern Lang. Assn., Phi Delta Theta. Episcopalian. Home: Athens Ga.

WESTBROOK, PATRICK ALAN DE LUJAN, anthropologist; b. Laredo, Tex., Nov. 24, 1924; s. Samuel Albert and Mary Jo (de Lujan) W.; student No. Ariz. U., 1942-43; B.S., Ariz. State U., 1950; M.A., Vanderbilt U., 1952; M.S., U. Oreg., 1959; M.A., San Francisco State U., 1963. News editor State Press, Tempe, Ariz., 1949-50; curator anthropology, lectr. Mus. of Man, San Diego, 1953; curator anthropology, preparator Nashville Children's Mus., 1953-54; resident fellow So. Ill. U., 1954; anthrop. research, No. Sonora, Mex., from 1954; mus. preparator Mus. Anthropology, U. Calif., Berkeley, 1955 from ; curator and mus. preparator San Mateo Mus., 1955 from; asst. curator Mus. Oriental Art, U. Oreg., 1958-59; lectr. southwestern anthropology; prof. sociology, coordinator anthropology and sociology, dept. behavioral studies City Coll., San Francisco, 1968-83, faculty emeritus, 1983—; cons. analyst U. Utah project, from 1980. Served with USNR, 1942-46. Mem. AAUP, Am. Anthrop. Assn., Am. Mus. Assn., F.B. Turner Welfare Soc., Archaeol. Inst. Am., AAAS, Am. Geog. Soc., Oceanic Soc., Alliance Francaise, Goethe Inst. (Neue Ulm, Germany), Mediaeval Acad. Am., Western Assn. Univs. and Colls. (accrediting commn. from 1968), Delta Phi Alpha, Alpha Psi Omega, Kappa Alpha. Club: Vanderbilt (San Francisco). Deceased. Home: San Francisco Calif.

WESTCOTT, GEORGE LAMAR, banker; b. Chattanooga, Aug. 28, 1894; s. Russell L. and Ola C. (Smith) W.; m. Lulu P. Smith, May 28, 1919. Student, Baylor Prep. Sch., Phila. Textile Inst. Pres. Westcott Hosiery Mills., Dalton, Ga., 1917-30; treas. Cabin Crafts, Inc., Dalton, Ga., 1932-54; dir. West Point Mfg. Co., Ga.; chmn. Hardwick Bank & Trust Co. Dalton. Bd. dirs. Hamilton Meml. Hosp., Dalton; trustee Berry Schs., Rome, Ga., Agnes Scott Coll., Decatur, Ga. Clubs: Capital City, Dalton Country. *

WESTPHAL, EVERETT AUGUST, alarm company executive; b. Hankinson, N.D., May 4, 1914; s. Herman Charles and Minnie Ida (Tiegs) W.; m. Marjorie Viola Jensen, Jan. 13, 1939; children: Bruce, Roger, Linda, Chris. With Leach & Gamble, Wahpeton, N.D., 1936-37, Standard Fence Co., Los Angeles, 1937-38, U.S. Alarm Co., Los Angeles, 1938-44; ptnr. Driess Alarm Co., 1944-45; founder Bay Alarm Co., Oakland, Calif., 1946, chmn., 1973—; founder Alarm Equipment Co., Oakland, 1961, pres., 1968-88; pres. Balco Real Estate Co., Oakland, 1978-88; chmn. Security Alarm Service, Oxnard, Calif., 1980-88. Chmn. troop Boy Scouts Am., Oakland, 1954-55. Mem. Nat. Burglar and Fire Alarm Assn. (v.p. 1952), ASTM, Western Burglar and Fire Alarm Assn. (pres. 1975). Republican. Clubs: Masons; Shriners (Oakland); Rotary (Oakland); Contra Costa Country (Concord, Calif.). Patentee alarm signalling devices. Died 1988.

WETMORE, FRANK ORTON, II, lawyer; b. Chgo., Feb. 6, 1929; s. Horace Orton and Lucia Pauline (Ambrose) W.; m. Daphne Sears Hersey, Jan. 4, 1958; children: Frank Orton III, Lucia Burnet. A.B., Cornell U., 1951; LL.B., Marquette U., 1956. Bar: Ill. 1956, Wis. 1956. With Winston & Strawn, Chgo., 1956-85, ptnr., 1965-85. Trustee and v.p. John G. Shedd Aquarium, Chgo., 1970-85, governing mem., from 1970, Chgo. Zool. Soc., from 1961; gen. suburban chmn. Met. Crusade of Mercy, Chgo., 1956-72; chmn. Hinsdale United Fund, 1975. Served to 1st lt. U.S. Army, 1951-54. Home: Hinsdale Ill. Died July 18, 1989; buried Wheaton (Ill.) Cemetery.

WEXLER, JERROLD, diversified investments executive; b. 1924. With Russell Electric, Hingham, Mass., 1948-49, Allied Rdio Corp., 1949-50, George S. Lurie Corp., 1951-60; v.p., treas. Milw. Chair Co., 1968-71;

chmn. bd. Jupiter Industries Inc., Chgo., 1970-92. Home: Chicago Ill. Died Nov. 7, 1992. †

WEXLER, MAX MENDEL, electronics engineer; b. Bklyn., Feb. 21, 1946; s. Frank and Anna (Goldberg) W.; m. Cecily Rose Garnett, Mar. 26, 1967; children: Mindy, Rebecca, David. Student RCA Inst., N.Y.C., 1966; B.Tech., N.Y. Inst. Tech., 1976. Research and devel. technician RCA Microwave, Harrison, N.J., 1966-70; tech. writer Instrument Systems Corp., Huntington, N.Y., 1970-71; project engr. ADT Security Systems, N.Y.C., 1971-89 . Mem. IEEE. Avocations: videography; audio. Died 1989. Home: Brooklyn N.Y.

WEYAND, RUTH, lawyer; b. Grinnell, Iowa, Jan. 14, 1912; d. Lorenzo Dow and May (Grafton) W.; children: Perry, Sterling. Ph.B., U. Chgo., 1930, J.D. cum laude, 1932. Bar: Ill. 1933, U.S. Supreme Ct. 1936, Washington, 1981. Assoc. pvt. law firms, Chgo., 1933-38; atty. NLRB, Washington, 1938-50, asst. gen. counsel, 1948-50; mem. pvt. law firms, Chgo. and Washington, 1950-65; assoc. gen. counsel Internat. Union Elec., Radio and Machine Workers, AFL-CIO, Washington, 1965-77; supervisory trial atty. EEOC, Phila., 1977-79, atty. Balt. dist. office, 1979, equal pay act counsel, 1979-89. Co-chmn. Campaign to End Discrimination Against Pregnant Workers, 1976-78. Recipient Ann. Citation for Achievement, William Jewell Coll., 1944; Citation for Achievement, Nat. Council Negro Women, 1948; Elizabeth Boyer award Women's Equity Action League, 1985; Georgina Smith Award AAUP, 1985. Mem. ABA, Am. Trial Lawyers Assn., NAACP (mem. nat. legal com. 1945-65), Chgo. Bar Assn., Order of Coif. Died 1989. Home: Alexandria Va.

WEYLAND, LOUIS FREDERICK, business executive; b. Tacoma, Nov. 12, 1894; s. Otto H. amd Mathilda (Walther) W.; m. FLorence Haiges, Dec. 26, 1918; children: Lois Virginia, Carolyn Jean. Student, Chgo. Bus. Coll., 1913-14. Clk. Minn. Mining & Mfg. Co., Chgo., 1915-17; salesman Minn. Mining & Mfg. Co., Cin., 1919-24; div. sales mgr. Minn. Mining & Mfg. Co., Detroit, 1926-35; sales mgr. in charge automotive products, gen. mgr. Minn. Mining & Mfg. Co., 1935-46, v.p. im charge adhesives and coatings div., 1946-52, dir., 1950-63, exec. v.p., 1952-55, exec. v.p., dir. sales, 1955-60, vice chmn. exec. com., 1960-63. 1st lt. USMC, 1917-19. Mem. Detroit Grand Opera Assn. (past pres., chmn. bd.), Minn. Orch. Assn. (bd. dirs.), Met. Opera Assn., St. Paul Civic Opera Assn., MAsons (32 Shriner), Recess Club, Mthletic Club, Athletic Town and Country Club, St. Francis Yacht Club. *

WHALEY, RANDALL MCVAY, physicist, educator; b. Hastings, Nebr., Aug. 21, 1915; s. William Joseph and Kittie (McVay) W.; m. Miriam Weckessser, Aug. 25, 1939; children: Suzanne Marie, Lisbeth Ellen, Joseph Randall. Student, Ind. U., 1933-35; B.A., U. Colo., 1938, M.A., 1940; Ph.D., Purdue U., 1947; D.Sc., Phila. Coll. Pharmacy and Sci., 1972; D.H.L. (hon.), Pa. Coll. Podiatric Medicine, 1981. Grad. asst. physics U. Colo., 1938-40; grad. research asst. physics Purdue U., 1942-45, from instr. to prof. physics, 1945-56, exec. asst. head dept., 1956- 59; assoc. dean Purdue U. (Sch. Sci., Edn. and Humanities), 1959-60; tech. asst. to sales mgr. G-M Labs., Inc., Chgo., 1940-41; v.p. grad. studies and research Wayne State U., 1960-65; chancellor U. Mo. at Kansas City, 1965- 67; spl. cons. Am. Council on Edn., 1967-68; edn. cons. Cresap, McCormick & Paget, N.Y.C., 1968-70; pres. Univ. City Sci. Center, Phila., 1970-85; pres. emeritus Univ. City Sci. Center, 1985-89; pres. emeritus Uni-Coll Corp., 1971-73, vice chmn., 1973-76; pres. Trantex, Inc., 1986-89; acting dir. Purdue Rsch. Fopund., 1959-60; del. congress Internat. Sci. Film Assn., Moscow, 1958, Prague, Czechoslovakia, 1960, Paris, 1963, Athens, 1964; cons. OEEC, summer 1959; mem. State Dept. mission to Baghdad, 1960; participant USIA conf., Cairo, 1960; mem. nat. adv. coun. on nurse tng. USPHS, 1966-70; mem. pub. evaluation com. state tech. svcs. Dept. Commerce, 1966-70; bd. dirs. Xytroniyx Inc., ARC Ltd. Mem. Gov. Ind. Citizens Com. Pub. Schs., 1955-57; exec. dir. adv. bd. edn. Nat. Acad. Scis., 1957-59; trustee Cranbrook Inst. Sci., 1961-65; bd. dirs., exec. com. Met. Fund, Inc., 1963-65; trustee Council Internat. Non-Theatrical Events, 1962-69, Mich. Health and Social Security Research Inst., 1963-65, Midwest Research Inst., Harry S. Truman Library Inst., Kansas City Museum, Met. YMCA Phila., 1975-85; mem. John Scott award com. Phila. chpt. Young Audiences, Inc., 1975-80, trustee, 1977-83; bd. visitors Air U., USAF; bd. dirs. Kansas City Gen. Hosp. and Med. Center, World Affairs Council Phila., West Phila. Corp. Fellow AAAS, Coll. Physicians Phila.; mem. Internat. Sci. Film Assn. (pres.), Am. Council Edn. (commn. internat. edn.), Am. Sci. Film Assn. (pres.), Am. Phys. Soc., Am. Assn. Physics Tchrs., AAUP, Am. Soc. Engring. Edn., Nat. Sci. Tchrs. Assn., Engring. Soc. Detroit, Phi Beta Kappa, Sigma Xi (v.p. Purdue 1958-59), Sigma Pi Sigma, Phi Delta Kappa, Phi Eta Sigma. Club:; Cosmos; Union League (Phila.). Died July 23, 1989.

WHARTON, TILFORD GIRARD, lawyer; b. Paterson, N.J., Juñe 13, 1904; s. Birdell Lamont and May Stewart (McCollom) W.; m. Isabelle Helen Schillo, Oct. 23, 1931 (dec. Mar. 8, 1964); children: Nancy Jane (Mrs. Alvin E. Duryea, Jr.), Constance Sue (Mrs. Norman D. Nasson), Lucinda Wharton Kellam. BA cum laude, Rutgers U., 1925; LLB cum laude, Yale U., 1928. Bar: N.J. 1928, U.S. Dist. Ct. N.J. 1928, U.S. Supreme Ct. 1935, U.S. Ct. Appeals (3d cir.) 1940. Sole practice, 1928-41; sr. ptnr. Wharton, Stewart & Davis, Somerville, 1941-80, of counsel, 1980-86; of counsel Ozzard, Wharton, Somerville, 1987-92; asst. prosecutor Somerset County, N.J., 1931-41, prosecutor, 1946-53; vice chmn. adv. com. on profl. ethics Supreme Ct. N.J., 1963-92; mem. Gov.'s Commn. on State Adminstrv. and Profl. Compensation, 1968-69; mem, vice chmn., acting chmn. Commn. on Revision of Criminal Law of N.J., 1969-92; mem. U.S. Cir. Judge Nominating Commn., 1977-81; pres., treas., bd. dirs. Interam. Mining Corp., N.Y.C., 1959-69. Mem. bd. editors Yale Law Jour. Mem. Yale Law Sch. Assn., from 1963, vice pres., 1967-68, exec. com., 1963-68, hon. mem., from 1978; mem. Yale Law Sch. Assn. of N.J., pres., 1964-65, trustee, 1966-75; N.J. chmn. Yale Law Sch. Capital Funds Campaign, 1963-64; eastern regional vice chmn. Yale Law Sch. Fund, 1964-65, nat. chmn., 1965-67, pres., 1967-69, bd. dirs. 1967-73; bd. overseers Rutgers U. Found., from 1977; trustee Somerset Med. Ctr., Somerville, 1945-80; gen. chmn. bldg. fund Somerset Valley YMCA, 1966-72; mem. borough council Somerville, 1947-49. Recipient Herbert Lincoln Harley award Am. Judicature Soc., 1974; N.J. State Bar Found. Medal of Honor, 1986; 50 Yrs. Disting. Service award Assn. of Fed. Bar of State of N.J., 1980; Loyal Sons of Rutgers award, 1980. Fellow Am. Bar Found. (50 year award), Am. Coll. Probate Counsel; mem. ABA (ho. dels. 1970-88, state del. 1982-83, standing com. on. profl. utilization and career devel. 1972-78, 82-88, standing com. on assn. communications 1988-91), N.J. State Bar Assn. (gen. council 1948-49, from 1961, trustee 1961-65, 2d v.p. 1965-66, 1st v.p. 1966-67, pres.-elect 1967-68, pres. 1968-69; chmn. jud. and county prosecutor appointments com. 1970-73, vice chmn. 1973-82, mem. 1982-86; chmn. nominating com. 1986-87, standing com. on profl. responsibility from 1988; mem. mandatory CLE com. 1987-88, mem. com. on legal edn. from 1991, Achievement award 1979, bd. trustees resolution of appreciation 1986), Somerset County Bar Assn. (pres. 1948), Assn. Bar City N.Y., Am. Judicature Soc. (dir. 1971-75), N.J. Bar Found. (trustee 1970-86, v.p. 1979-83, medal of honor 1986), Order of Coif, Phi Beta Kappa, Chi Psi (nat. exec. council 1979-86, Albert S. Bard award 1986), Alpha Rho of Chi Psi Meml. Found. (pres., trustee from 1952), Phi Delta Phi. Clubs: Raritan Valley Country (Somerville); Eastern Shore Yacht and Country (Pungoteague, Va.); Chemists (N.Y.C.); Vesper (Phila.). Home: Somerville N.J. Died, Aug. 22, 1992. †

WHEALON, JOHN FRANCIS, archbishop; b. Barberton, Ohio, Jan. 15, 1921; s. John J. and Mary (Zanders) W. Grad., St. Charles Coll., Catonsville. Md., 1940, St. Mary's Sem., Cleve., 1945; STL, U. Ottawa, Can., 1946; SSL, Pontifical Bibl. U., Rome, 1950; MA in Edn., John Carroll U., 1957. Ordained priest Roman Cath. Ch., 1945. Asst. pastor Diocese Cleve., 1945-53; founding rector Borromeo Sem., Wickliffe, Ohio, 1953; tchr. Latin, Hebrew, Sacred Scripture Borromeo Sem., 1953-61; titular bishop Andrapa, from 1961, aux. bishop Cleve., 1961-66, bishop Erie (Pa.), 1967-68, archbishop Hartford (Conn.), 1969-91. Home: Hartford Conn. Died Aug. 2, 1991.

WHEATLAND, STEPHEN, business executive; b. Gibraltor, Mar. 29, 1897; (parents U.S. citizens); s. Richard and Mary Kemble (Robinson) W.; m. Dorothy Parker, Nov. 28, 1921; children: Richard, Sarah, Mary, Alice N. AB, Harvard, 1921. Pres. Garfield Land Co., 1933-51; trustee Eastern Trust & Banking Co., Bangor, Maine; pres., trustee Peabody Mus., Salem, Mass.; pres. U. Maine Found., 1937-47. With USN, 1918. Mem. Mass. Hist. Soc., Colonial Soc. Mass., Odd Volumes Club. *

WHEELER, JOHN WILLIAM, lawyer; b. N.Y.C.; s. John and Rosalie (Conroy) W.; m. Muriel Davis, Sept. 7, 1940; children: Richard J., Robert E. A.B., Columbia U., 1936, LL.B., 1939. Bar: N.Y. 1939, U.S. Dist. Ct. (so. and ea. dists.) N.Y., U.S. Ct. Appeals (2d cir.), U.S. Supreme Ct., U.S. Tax Ct. Assoc. Thacher, Proffitt & Wood, and predecessor firm, Barry Wainwright Thacher & Symmers, 1939-50, ptnr., 1950-74, sr. ptnr., 1974-84, counsel, 1984-91. Pres. Alumni Fedn. Columbia U., 1962-64; chmn. bd. Columbia Coll. Fund, 1966-67. Lt., USNR, 1943-46. Recipient Alumni Fedn. medal for disting. service, Columbia U., 1947. Mem. ABA (ho. of dels. 1980-82), N.Y. State Bar Assn., Nat. Assn. Coll. and Univ. Attys. (pres. 1978-79, Disting. Service award 1982), Plandome (N.Y.) Country Club, Surf Club (Surfside, Fla.), Princeton Club N.Y.C., Columbia Faculty House. Democrat. Roman Catholic. Contbr. articles to profl jours. Died June 11, 1991.

WHEELER, RUSSELL CHARLES, dentist, educator; b. Granite City, Ill., Dec. 18, 1897; s. Andrew J. and Winona (Smith) W.; m. Lucille Elizabeth Wengler, June 16, 1934; 1 child, Douglas Lamphlier. DDS, Washington U. St. Louis, 1919. Dentist pvt. practice, St. Louis, from 1919; mem faculty Washington U. Sch. Dentistry, St. Louis, 1924-36, 45-51, assoc. prof. anatomy, 1945-51, assoc. prof., chmn. dept. dental anatomy, 1937-44; bd. dirs. Washington U. Author: Tooth Form, 2d edit. 1935; Tooth Form, Drawing and Carving, 1939, Dental Anatomy and Physiology, 4th edit. 1965; Atlas Tooth Form, 3d edit. 1962; contbr. articles to profl. jours. Fellow Am. Coll. Dentists; mem. Am. Dental Assn., Mo. Dental Assn., St. Louis Dental Soc. (pres. 1946), Am. Acad. Dental Sci. (pres. 1937), Internat. Assn. Dental Rsch., Sigma Xi, Omicron Kappa Upsilon, St. Louis U. Club. Presbyterian. *

WHEELER, WALTER HALL, geology educator; b. Syracuse, N.Y., Dec. 21, 1923; s. George Carlos and Esther (Hall) W.; m. Eula Krueger, Jan. 16, 1945; children—Diana, Roger. B.S., U. Mich., 1945, M.S., 1948; Ph.D., Yale U., 1951. Cert. profl. geologist. Asst. prof. U. N.C., Chapel Hill, 1951-57, assoc. prof., 1957-68, prof. geology, 1968-86, prof. emeritus, 1986-89; vis. scholar U. Calif.-Berkeley, 1966-67. Author: A Revision of the Uintatheres, 1961; contbr. articles to profl. jours. Served to 1st lt. USAAF, 1943-46. Fellow Geol. Soc. Am.; mem. Paleontol. Soc., Am. Assn. Petroleum Geologists, Soc. Vertebrate Paleontology, Sigma Xi. Home: Chapel Hill N.C. Died Nov. 21, 1989; cremated.

WHIGHAM, THOMAS EDMONDSON, lawyer; b. Opp, Ala., Dec. 8, 1952; s. Julian Bertie and Mildred (Edmondson) W.; m. Sally Ann Oyler, Apr. 4, 1981; children: Thomas Edmondson Jr., Bert Michael. AA, U. Fla., 1974, BA, 1977; JD, Nova U., 1980. Bar: Fla. 1981, U.S. Dist. Ct. (mid. dist.) Fla. 1981, U.S. Ct. Claims 1981, U.S. Ct. Appeals (11th cir.) 1981, U.S. Supreme Ct., 1984. Ptnr. Stenstrom, McIntosh, Julian, Colbert & Whigham, P.A., Sanford, Fla., from 1980; designated atty. Personal Injury and Wrongful Death Fla., Bar Designation Program, 1985. Committeeman Seminole County Dem. Party, Sanford, 1978; del. Fla. Dem. Conv., Orlando, 1978; mem. Sch. Dividend Program, from 1983, Sanford Bd. Adjustments and Appeals, 1984-86, Seminole county Farm Bur., from 1983; Seminole High Sch. Booster, from 1971, Gator Boosters, from 1981; mem. adv. com. Sanford Youth Club, 1988. Mem. ABA, Fla. Bar Assn., Seminole County Bar Assn. (treas. 1985-86, chmn. law week 1988), Assn. Trial Lawyers of Am., Acad. Fla. Trial Lawyers, Ducks Unltd., Nat. Wildlife Fedn., Fla. Wildlife Fedn., Audubon Soc., Alpha Tau Omega, Phi Alpha Delta. Democrat. Baptist. Club: Cen. Fla. Gator Orlando. Lodge: Optimist (pres. Sanford club 1979-1980), Rotary. Home: Sanford Ill.

WHIPPLE, BARBARA, graphic artist, writer; b. San Francisco, June 16, 1921; d. George Hoyt and Katharine Ball (Waring) W.; children by previous marriage: Christine, Katharine; m. Grant Heilman, Aug. 14, 1961; 1 child, Hans. B.A., Swarthmore Coll., 1943; B.S., Rochester Inst. Tech., 1956; M.F.A., Temple U., 1961. Tchr. Elizabethtown Coll., 1973-76, Franklin and Marshall Coll., 1974-76; grad. asst. Tyler Sch. Art, 1961; graphic artist; condr. workshops Adams State Coll., 1982, Colo. Graphic Arts Ctr., 1980, 82, Sangre de Cristo Art Ctr., Pueblo, Colo., 1985. One-person shows include: Lebanon Valley Coll., 1973, Colo. Mountain Coll., 1979, Foothills Art Center, 1980, 84, Adams State Coll., 1982, 88, North Mus., Lancaster, Pa., 1988, West Nebr. Art Ctr., 1984, Western Colo. Ctr for the Arts, 1989, Rio Grande County Mus. 1989; numerous invitational and group shows; co-author: Water Media Techniques, 1984; Water Media: Processes and Possibilities, 1986; bibliography: La Revue Moderne, 1969, Am. Artist, 1980, Colorado Outdoors, 1980; contbr. Am. Artist, 1971-80, contbg. editor, 1979-85. Bd. dirs. Swarthmore Coll., 1970-76; pres. Chaffee County LWV, 1980-81. Recipient 1st prize for prints Lancaster Open Juried Show, 1964, Best of Show award Liberal Religious Art, Denver, 1967, 1st prize for drawing Phila. Watercolor Club, 1979, others. Mem. Nat. Assn. Women Artists, Women Artists So. Colo., Associated Artists of San Luis Valley, Foothills Art Center, Nat. Mus. of Women in Arts (founding), Chaffee County Council on Arts (pres. 1988). Home: Buena Vista Colo. Died Nov. 26, 1989.

WHIPPLE, TAGGART, lawyer; b. Manchester, N.H., Oct. 15, 1912; s. Stanley Cornell and Ruth Storey (Taggart) W.; m. Katharine G. Brewster, July 10, 1941; children: Christine Whipple Farrington, George S., Hugh W. A.B., Harvard U., 1934; J.D., N.Y. U., 1938. Bar: N.Y. 1938. Law clk. to v.p., gen. counsel Lehigh Valley R.R. Co., N.Y.C., 1934-38; mem., sr. counsel Davis, Polk & Wardwell, N.Y.C. Contbr. articles to profl. jours. Trustee Hall of Fame for Great Americans, 1974-77, Village of Muttontown, N.Y., 1956-80, NYU Inst. Fine Arts, 1970-92, Vassar Coll., 1973-81; trustee NYU, 1970-89, life trustee, 1989-92; trustee NYU Law Ctr. Found., 1965-89, life trustee, 1989-92; trustee emeritus Salisbury Sch.; trustee Brit.-Am. Ednl. Found., 1970-81, East Woods Sch., 1948-64; bd. dirs. Community Hosp. at Glen Cove, 1948-69, Cold Spring Harbor Lab., 1983-92, vice chmn., 1986-92; dir. emeritus Lincoln Center for Performing Arts, Inc.; bd. dirs. Repertory Theater of Lincoln Center, 1966-73, Theatre, Inc., Phoenix Theatre, 1959-64, Soc. St. Johnland, 1962-66; hon. mem. corp. Woods Hole Oceanographic Instn. Served with AUS, 1942-45. Fellow Am. Coll. Trial Lawyers, Am. Bar Found., N.Y. State Bar Found.; mem. Am. Law Inst., Am. Judicature Soc., Fed. Bar Council, Assn. Bar City N.Y. (chmn. com. trade regulation and trade marks 1953-56), ABA (council sect. antitrust law 1966-70), N.Y. State Bar Assn. (chmn. antitrust law sect. 1962-63), Council Fgn. Relations, Asso. Harvard Alumni (pres. 1968-69). Episcopalian.

Clubs: Century, Union, Down Town, Pilgrims, Piping Rock; Anglers; Met. (Washington). Home: Oyster Bay N.Y. Died Nov. 26, 1992. †

WHITAKER, HENRY PHILIP, aeronautical engineering educator; b. Penn Yan, N.Y., June 24, 1921; s. Fred C. and Adelia (Hopkins) W.; m. H. Stephanie Paige, Apr. 5, 1952; children: Robert H., Jonathan P., Charles E. B.S., MIT, 1944, M.S., 1959. Registered profl. engr., Mass. With Consol. Vultee Aircraft Corp., 1944-47; dep. assoc. dir. Instrumentation Lab. MIT, Cambridge, 1947-59, prof. dept. aeros. and astronautics, 1959-83, prof. emeritus, 1983-89; mem. guidance and control panel AGARO NATO, 1967-78. Trustee Boston Juvenile Ct. Citizenship Tng. Program. Mem. AIAA, Soc. Automotive Engrs., Mass. Jr. C. of C. (past pres.). Home: Weston Mass. Died Nov. 22, 1989.

WHITCOMB, ROBERT FAY WRIGHT, banker; b. Topeka, Feb. 8, 1896; s. George Herbert and Jessie Elvira (Wright) W.; m. Louise Brewer, Nov. 9, 1927 (dec. Jan. 1963); children: Geroge Herbert, Julia; m. Edith Ramsay, June 1964. BA, Washburn U., 1915; MA, U. Colo., 1940. With Fidelity Trust Co., Kansas City, Mo., 1916; fgn. svcs. officer 1st Nat. City Bank N.Y.; assigned Panama, Shanghai, JAva, P.I., Japan, Argentine; pvt. bus., 1933-41; fgn. funds control U.S. Treas., 1942-43; loan officer Export-Import Bank Washington, Brazil, 1943-58; fgn. svc. officer ICA, 1958-60; adviser Korean Reconstruction Bank; lectr. on devel. banking topics, various Korean univs.; econ. cons. econ. devel. and devel. banking, Ecuador, Pakistan, Cyprus, Peru, from 1961; staff Checchi & Co., Washington, from 1961; contbr. report on exporter credit fin. Senate Com. on Banking and Currency, hearings in Export-Import Bank, 83d Congress. Decorated officer Brazilian Order So. Cross. Contbr. articles to profl. jours. Mem. Kappa Sigma, Pi Gmama Mu. Epsicopalian. *

WHITE, ANNE UNDERWOOD, geographer, consultant, researcher; b. Washington, Sept. 22, 1919; d. Norman and Anne Francis (Bayard) Underwood; m. Gilbert Fowler White, Apr. 28, 1944; children: William D., Mary B., Frances A. B.A., Vassar Coll., 1941. Jr. sociology sci. analyst U.S. Dept. Agr., Washington, 1942; econ. analyst, field examiner Nat. Labor Relations Bd., Washington, 1943-44; research asst. Gilbert F. White, Chgo., East Africa, 1966-72; editor Natural Hazards Research and Info. Ctr., Boulder, Colo., 1976-78; mem. profl. staff Inst. Behavioral Sci. U. Colo., Boulder, 1979-89; cons. World Bank, Washington, 1980, U.S. AID, Nairobi, Kenya, 1982. Author: (with Gilbert F. White and David J. Bradley) Drawers of Water: Domestic Water Use in East Africa, 1972. Contbr. chpts. to books, articles to profl. jours. Mem., Boulder County Parks and Open Space Adv. Com., 1976-82, chmn., 1977; mem. Sunshine Fire Protection Dist. Bd., Boulder County, 1981-85, chmn., 1984; chairperson Boulder County Task Force on Services for Elderly, 1984; mem. Plan Boulder County Bd., 1985-88; active mem. Women's Forum of Colo., Denver, 1976-89, Women's Democratic Club, Boulder, Plan Boulder County. Mem. Assn. Am. Geographers, Soc. Women Geographers, Colo. Water Congress, Acad. Ind. Scholars. Died April 10, 1989; buried Four Mile Canyon, Boulder, Col. Home: Boulder Colo.

WHITE, CHANDLER T., corporate executive; b. Concord, N.H., Feb. 19, 1894; s. William C. and Annie L. (Tubbs) W.; m. Gertrude A. Schimpf, Apr. 15, 1922; 1 child, Elizabeth C. BS in Organic Chemistry, Dartmouth, 1916; spl. student in chemistry, MIT, 1916, 17. Asst. instr. chemistry MIT, 1917-19; chemist Einchester Repeating Arms Co., 1919-20; joined Gen. Aniline & Film Corp., N.Y.C., 1920, gen. mgr., 1947-50; v.p. Gen. Aniline & Film Corp., from 1950; v.p., gen. mgr. Dysestuff and Chem. Div., Rensselaer, N.Y., 1953-54; v.p. trade rels. N.Y.C.; cons., from 1959. Mem. Univ. Club (N.Y.C.). *

WHITE, ELWYN BROOKS, writer; b. Mount Vernon, N.Y., July 11, 1899; s. Samuel Tilly and Jessie (Hart) W.; A.B., Cornell U., 1921; Litt.D. (hon.), Dartmouth Coll., 1948, U. Maine, 1948, Yale U., 1948, Bowdoin Coll., 1950, Hamilton Coll., 1952, Harvard U., 1954; L.H.D., Colby Coll., 1954; m. Katharine Sergeant Angell, Nov. 13, 1929; 1 son, Joel McCoun. Reporter 1921; later free lance writer and contbg. editor New Yorker mag.; contbr. monthly dept. to Harper's mag., 1938-43. Served in U.S. Army, 1918. Recipient Gold Medal Am. Acad. Arts and Letters; Presdl. medal of Freedom, 1963; Laura Ingalls Wilder award children's books. 1970; Nat. medal for Lit., 1971; Pulitzer Prize spl. citation, 1978. Fellow Am. Acad. Arts and Scis.; mem. Nat. Inst. Arts and Letters. Am. Acad. Arts and Letters, Phi Gamma Delta. Author: The Lady is Cold (poems), 1929; Is Sex Necessary? (with J. Thurber), 1929; Every Day is Saturday, 1934; The Fox of Peapack, 1938, Quo Vadimus, 1939; One Man's Meat, 1942, enlarged edit., 1944; Stuart Little, 1945; The Wild Flag, 1946; Here Is New York, 1949; Charlotte's Web, 1952; The Second Tree from the Corner, 1954; revised William Strunk, Jr.'s The Elements of Style, 1959; The Points of My Compass, 1962; The Trumpet of The Swan, 1970; Letters of E.B. White, 1976; Essays of E.B. White, 1977; Poems and Sketches of E.B. White, 1981; editor: Ho Hum, 1931; Another Ho Hum, 1932; A Subtreasury of American Humor (with Katharine S. White), 1941. Died Oct. 1, 1985. Home: Brooklin Maine

WHITE, FRANKLIN MORSE, electrical company executive; b. Fairbury, Nebr., Dec. 6, 1920; s. Chesley Franklin and Nellie Blanch (Smith) W.; B.S.E.E., U. Nebr., 1943; m. Lydia Worster, Oct. 8, 1949; 1 dau., Janet Louise. Partner, gen. mgr. White Electric Supply Co., Lincoln, Nebr., 1946-65, pres., gen. mgr., 1965—; pres. Four Way Investments, Inc., 1978—. Pres., Lincoln Family Service Assn., 1962-65; mem. Lincoln Lancaster County Planning Commn., 1962-68, civil def. commn., 1959-71. Served with Signal Corps, U.S. Army, 1943-46; served to col. USAR. Mem. Nat. Assn. Elec. Distbrs. (bd. govs. 1966-71), Nebr.-Iowa Elec. Council (pres. 1980-81), Lincoln C. of C., Nebr. Assn. Commerce and Industry, Res. Officers Assn., Newcomen Soc., U. Nebr. Alumni Assn. Republican. Mem. Christian Ch. Clubs: Nebr., Mo. River (pres. 1969-70). Lodges: Elks, Sertoma. Deceased.

WHITE, GERALD TAYLOR, history educator; b. Seattle, May 14, 1913; s. Loren Festus and Cora Belle (Taylor) W.; m. Rita Elizabeth Kuffel, July 15, 1950; children: Kenneth, David, Maria, Steven, Kian. A.B., DePauw U., 1934; M.A., U. Calif.-Berkeley, 1935, Ph.D., 1938. Research assoc. U. Calif.-Berkeley, 1938-39; archivist Fireman's Fund Ins. Co., San Francisco, 1939-40; from instr. to prof. history San Francisco State Coll., 1940-68, chmn. dept. history, 1959-64; prof. history U. Calif.-Irvine, 1968-80, prof. emeritus, 1980-89, chmn. dept., 1969-71; historian RFC, 1946-47; lectr. Am. U., 1947. Author: History of Massachusetts Hospital Life Insurance Company, 1955, Formative Years in the Far West: A History of the Standard Oil Company of California and Predecessors Through 1919, 1962, 76, Scientists in Conflict, 1968, Billions for Defense: Government Financing by the Defense Plant Corporation during WWII, 1980, The United States and the Problem & Recovery after 1893, 1982, Baptism in Oil: Stephen F. Peckham in Southern California, 1865-66, 1984; editor: The Historian, 1948-53; editorial bd. Pacific Hist. Rev, 1958-61, Bus. Hist. Rev, 1957-58, 70-72. Treas., bd. dirs. Internat. Inst. San Francisco, 1946-53; bd. dirs. San Francisco Met. YMCA, 1963-64. Served with USAAF, 1943-46. Recipient grants Am. Philos. Soc., 1948, 71, Huntington Library, 1963, 66; postdoctoral fellow Grad Sch. Bus. Adminstrn., Harvard U., 1951-52. Mem. Am. Hist. Assn. (council Pacific Coast br. 1964-72, pres. 1968-69, co-chmn. conv. program com. 1973), Orgn. Am. Historians, Econ. Hist. Assn., Lambda Chi Alpha. Democrat. Episcopalian. Home: Irvine Calif. Died Dec. 15, 1989.

WHITE, HOWARD ASHLEY, university president; b. Cloverdale, Ala., Sept. 28, 1913; s. John Parker and Mabel Clara (Hipp) W.; m. Maxcine Elliott Feltman, June 17, 1952; children—Ashley Feltman, Howard Elliott. Diploma, David Lipscomb Coll., 1932; B.A., Tulane U., 1946, M.A., 1950, Ph.D., 1956. Minister Carrollton Ave. Ch. of Christ, New Orleans, 1941-52; assoc. prof. history David Lipscomb Coll., Nashville, 1953-56; prof., chmn. dept. David Lipscomb Coll., 1956-58; chmn. social sci. dept. Pepperdine U., Malibu, Calif., 1958-65, dean grad. studies, 1965-67, dean undergrad. studies, 1967-70, exec. v.p., 1970-78, pres., 1978-85, pres. emeritus, 1985-91. Mem. Am. Hist. Assn., So. Hist. Assn., Orgn. Am. Historians, Phi Alpha Theta, Phi Delta Kappa. Clubs: Calif, Lincoln, Regency, Rotary. Home: Malibu Calif. Died Feb. 1, 1991; buried Forest Lawn Cemetery, Hollywood Hills, Calif.

WHITE, ISAAC DAVIS, army officer; b. Peterborough, N.H., Mar. 6, 1901; s. Daniel Mansfield and Minnie (Osgood) W.; m. Julie Cotton, June 14, 1928. BS, Norwich U., 1922, M in Mil. Sci. (hon.), 1951, LLD, 1957; D in Mil. Sci., U. Md., 1958; grad., Cav. Sch., troop officers course, 1928, Command and Gen. Staff Sch., 1939. Commd. 2d lt U.S. Army, 1923, advanced through grades to gen., 1955; formerly comdg. gen. U.S. Constabulary, Germany, X Corps, Korea; comdg. gen. 4th Army, Ft. Sam Houston, Tex.; past comdg. gen. Army Forces Far East, Eighth U.S. Army; comdr.-in-chief U.S. Army Pacific, 1957-61. Alumni trustee Norwich U. Decorated D.S.M with two oak leaf clusters, Silver Star with oak leaf cluster, Legion of Merit with 2 oak leaf clusters, Bronze Star with oak leaf cluster, Officer Legion of Honor, Croix de Guerre with Palm (France), Fourragere of Croix de Guerre (Belgium); named to Order of the Red Banner (Russia), Grand Officer, Order of Orange Nassau (Netherlands), Chief Comdr. Philippine Legion of Honor, Mex. Mil. Merit, 1st Class, Order of Cloud and Banner (China), Order of Merit Nat. Found. Tanjang (Korea), Korean Taeguk Disting. Svc. medal with silver star, Order Mil. Merit Toeguk with gold star (Korea), Order of Rising Sun (Japan), Knight Grand Cross Most Noble Order of Crown of Thailand. Mem. U.S. Cavalry Assn. (pres. 1946-47), S.A.R., Newcomen Soc., Phi Kappa Delta. Home: Honolulu Hawaii Died June 11, 1990.

WHITE, KEITH MERRILL, dance critic; b. Albany, Ga., Oct. 25, 1951; s. Jack C. and Juanita (Swindle) W. Studies with Jean Spear, Trinette Singleton, Sarasota, Fla., 1970-73; BFA, Ringling Sch. Art, Sarasota, 1973; studies with David Howard, Finis Jhung, Robert Blankshine, Nancy Bielski, N.Y.C., 1973-80. Dance critic Bay Area Reporter, San Francisco, 1981-90; cons. N.Y. State Counsel on the Arts, N.Y.C., 1976-80. Editor, researcher The Joffrey Ballet, 1976-79; contbr. San Francisco Chronicle Rev. Home: San Francisco Calif. Died 1991.

WHITE, LOWELL SMILEY, banker; b. St. Louis, Dec. 6, 1897; s. Coliver Hadley and Laura (Smiley) W.; m. Honora Patton, Feb. 2, 1929. Student, Park Coll., 1921. With 1st Nat. Bank, San Antonio, from 1939; chmn., exec. com. 1st Nat. Bank, from 1960; also dir. Mem. Assn. Res. City Bankers, San Antonio Club, San Antonio Country Club. *

WHITE, PATRICK, author; b. London, May 28, 1912; s. Victor and Ruth (Withycombe) W.; B.A., Kings Coll., Cambridge U., 1935. Author: Happy Valley, 1939, The Living and the Dead, 1941, The Aunt's Story, 1948, The Tree of Man, 1955, Voss, 1957, Riders in the Chariot, 1961, The Burnt Ones, 1964, The Solid Mandala, 1966, The Vivisector, 1970, The Eye of the Storm, 1973, The Cockatoos, 1974, A Fringe of Leaves, 1976, The Twyborn Affair, 1979, Memoirs of Many in One, 1986, Three Uneasy Pieces, 1989; (self-portrait) Flaws in the Glass, 1981; (plays) The Ham Funeral, 1947, The Season at Sarsaparilla, 1961, A Cheery Soul, 1962, Night On Bald Mountain, 1962, Big Toys, 1977, Signal Driver, 1981, Netherwood, 1983, Shepherd on the Rocks, 1987; (screenplay) The Night The Prowler, 1978; (stories) Three Uneasy Pieces, 1987. Served with RAF, World War II. Recipient Nobel prize in lit., 1973. Died Sept. 30, 1990; buried Sydney, Australia. Home: Sydney Australia

WHITE, ROBERT I., former college president; b. Elgin, Ill., Dec. 28, 1908; s. Robert I. and Fannie Temple (Goodenow) W.; m. Edna E. McCormick, June 7, 1930; 1 child, Ronald Edward. PhB, U. Chgo., 1929, MA, 1935, PhD, 1945; postgrad., Stanford U.; LLD (hon.), U. Akron, 1963, Sung Kyun Kwan U., Seoul, 1968, Walsh Coll., 1969; HHD (hon.), U. of Ams., Mex., 1968; LHD (hon.), McKendree Coll., 1969. Tchr. elem. sch., Thornton, Ill., 1929-31; prin. elem. and high sch., Orland Park, Ill., 1931-32; tchr., dir. student activities, asst. prin. Parker High Sch., Chgo., 1932-37; prin. sr. high sch. and jr. coll., Burlington, Iowa, 1938-46; dean Coll. Edn., Kent (Ohio) State U., 1946-58, v.p., 1958-63, pres., 1963-71, disting. prof. ednl. adminstrn., from 1971; vis. lectr. U. Chgo., 1946; vis. disting. prof. Cen. Mich. U., 1972; trustee Am. Coll. Testing Program, 1964-71, chmn. bd., 1967-71; mem. exec. com. Nat. Commn. Accrediting; chmn. Ohio Sch. Survey, 1955. Author: The Feasibility of 6-4-4 Reorganization in School Systems, 1946, American Government: Functions and Structures, 1959, Democracy at Work, 1961; also articles and monographs. Mem. NEA, Am. Assn. Higher Edn., Am. Assn. Sch. Adminstrs., S.E. Iowa Tchrs. Assn. (past pres.), North Cen. Assn. (commn. colls. and univs.), Am. Assn. Colls. (state dir. tchr. edn.), Rotary, Phi Beta Kappa, Phi Delta Kappa, Omicron Delta Kappa, Kappa Delta Pi, Sigma Nu. Congregationalist. Home: Kent Ohio Died Oct. 10, 1990; buried Standing Rock Cemetary.

WHITE, WILLIAM HENRY, editor, publisher, author; b. Glendale, Calif., Sept. 9, 1924; s. William Henry and Esther Ruth (Engel) W.; m. Virginia S. Stockton, Jan. 27, 1950 (div. 1982); children: Victoria, Deborah. Student, U. Mo., 1942; B.A., Columbia U., 1948, M.S. in Journalism, 1949. Reporter N.Y. Times, 1948-49; book editor Look, Quick, Flair mags., Cowles Mags., Inc., 1949-51; med. and sci. editor Look mag., N.Y.C., 1951-54; med. editor Sports Illustrated, 1954-55; mng. editor Med. News, 1956-59; exec. editor Med. World News, 1959-68; pres., editor Family Health mag., 1969-74; editorial dir. Med. Opinion mag., 1974-77; pres. Newspaperbooks, 1974-78, Scarsdale Inquirer, from 1980, Hartsdale Inquirer, 1981-86, Hasting Enterprise, from 1984, W.H. White Publs., Inc.; pub. Cost Containment Newsletter, 1978-86, P.C. Advisor, 1981-89, Tufts U. Diet and Nutrition Letter, from 1983, Cornell U. Animal Health Letter, Am. Cancer Soc. Jour. Ca.; internat. exec. editor World Medicine, Eng. also; Medicine Mondiale, France; free-lance writer in field medicine and sci.; writer with d Am. Karakoram Expdn., Pakistan, 1953. Assoc. Commonwealth Fund, 1955-56; Bd. dirs., v.p. World Rehab. Fund; bd. dirs. White Plains Hosp. Med. Center; treas. Royal Soc. Medicine Found., The Eye-Bank. Mem. Nat. Assn. Sci. Writers, Sigma Delta Chi, Phi Kappa Psi. Clubs: Scarsdale Golf; Royal and Ancient Golf. (St. Andrews, Scotland). Home: New York N.Y. Died Apr. 10, 1989.

WHITE, WINIFRED DEMAREST (MRS. HERBERT A. WHITE), editor; b. N.Y.C.; d. Peter Edward and Margaret (McLaughlin) Demarest; m. Joseph S. Gifford, Aug. 29, 1925 (dec. Feb. 1948); m. Herbert A. White, Nov. 14, 1964 (dec. Oct. 1972). A.B., Coll. New Rochelle, 1914; postgrad. in journalism, Columbia U. Extension, 1916-18. Tchr. English, speech Bryant High Sch., N.Y.C., 1914-17; asst. to bursar Rockefeller Inst. Med. Research, N.Y.C., 1917-26; asst. editor, asst. to exec. sec. AIME, N.Y.C., 1947-59, editor, 1960-92; exec. sec. Soc. Women Engrs., N.Y.C., 1961-73, assoc. life mem., 1973-92; cons. copy editor IEEE, 1981-92; freelance editor miscellaneous papers, 1959-90; editorial proofreader, 1978-91. Editor: Ironmaking Proc., Open Hearth Proc., Honors Book, 1950-63, Proc. Conf. on Women, 1971; copy editor

Trans. of ASHRAE, 1976-81. Recipient Ursula Laurus citation Coll. New Rochelle, 1977, Angela Merici gold medal, 1984; cert. of recognition and White Glove award Soc. Women Engrs. Home: New York N.Y. Deceased.

WHITEBROOK, ROBERT BALLARD, author; b. Seattle, Oct. 25, 1917; s. Irvin Arthur and Eugenie (Leahy) W.; m. Betty Ann Mehl, Sept. 19, 1942; 1 child, Nancy Elizabeth Nottage. AB cum laude, Stanford U., 1941; MA, U. Wash., Seattle, 1963; PhD, U. Wash., 1968. Sr. ptnr. Blyth & Co., Seattle, 1946-65; asst. prof. history U. Hawaii, Honolulu, 1967-70; freelance author, 1959-91; newspaper columnist Calif., 1984-91. Author: Aleutian Years, 1959, Coastal Exploration of Washington, 1959 (State of Wash. Centennial award 1989), Millennium Compact, 1984 (Stanford award 1989), By Cape Horn & Plain, 1988 (L.A. award 1988), Measure Of Men, 1991. Eisenhower del. to nat. conv. Rep. Party, Chgo., 1952. Lt. comdr. USNR, 1942-45. Decorated Purple Heart, Navy , 1943; recipient Time mag. award, 1953, Merit award Rounce & Coffin Club, L.A., 1960, Cert. of Merit, Seattle Hist. Soc., 1961. Mem. Explorers Club N.Y.C., Stanford U. Alumni Club Northern San Diego (pres. 1987-89), U. Wash. Alumni Assn., Shriners, Masons. Republican. Episcopalian.

WHITEHEAD, BARRY, thoroughbred racing official; b. San Francisco, Dec. 26, 1910; s. Samuel Barry II and Norine Imelda (Conway) W.; student U. San Francisco, 1929-33; m. Fritzi-Beth Bowman, Nov. 10, 1935; children—Peter Barry, David Barry. Corr. to Thoroughbred Record, Lexington, Ky., 1930; thoroughbred owner and breeder, 1932-36; racing ofcl. tracks from 1934; dir. Sullivan-Greely Corp., Weightform Corp. Asst. sec. Calif. Thoroughbred Breeders Assn., 1937; dir. Soc. N.Am. Racing Ofcls., 1955. Col., a.d.c. gov.'s staff State of La. Bd. dirs. Calif. Racing Hall of Fame, 1968, also bd. dirs. found.; bd. dirs., v.p. William P. Kyne Meml. Library, 1974. Served with AUS, World War II. Mem. Friends Bancroft Library, Calif. Hist. Soc., Thoroughbred Club of Am., Press Club of San Francisco. Contbr. to thoroughbred publs., chiefly on hist. or tech. background of racing. Has racing library. Deceased.

WHITEHEAD, MATTHEW JACKSON, educator; b. Rocky Mount, N.C., May 18, 1908; s. James Henry and Nellie Gray (Thomas) W.; m. Thelma Ray Reid, Apr. 20, 1935; children: Jocelyn Eleanor, Matthew Jackson II. AB, Johnson C. Smith U., 1930; MA, Columbia U., 1937; EdD, NYU, 1944. Head dept. English, asst. prin Highland High Sch., Gastonia, N.C., 1930-37; prof. edn., dir. summer sch. Elizabeth City (N.C.) State Tchrs. Coll., 1937-44; Gen. Edn. Bd. fellow NYU, 1943-44; assoc. prof. edn., asst. univ. registrar Howard U., Washington, 1944-51; prof., chmn. div. edn. Miner Tchrs. Coll., Washington, 1951-53, pres., 1953-58, dean grad. sch.; dean D.C. Tchrs. Coll.; chief-of-party Fed. Advanced Tchrs. Coll., Lagos, Nigeria, 1962-64. Mem. AAUP, NAACP, NEA, Am. Assn. Coll. Tchr. Edn., D.C. Writers Club, Assn. Student Teaching, Phi Delta Kappa, Kappa Delta Pi, Omega Psi Phi. Presbyterian. Home: Washington D.C. Died May 18, 1990.

WHITEHORN, JOHN CLARE, psychiatrist; b. Spencer, Nebr., Dec. 6, 1894; s. Geneo W. and Laura E. (Smith) W.; m. Jeannette Miller, June 22. 1921; children: Richard Miller, Alfred Jean (killed in action, Germany Nov. 1944), Joanne. AB, Doane Coll., 1916, LHD, 1947; MD, Harvard, 1921; ScD (hon.), U. Nebr., 1955. Asst. physiol. chem. McLean Hosp., Waverley, Mass., 1921-23; physiol. chemist McLean Hosp., 1923-38, dir. labs., 1930-38; rsch. fellow psychiatry Mass. Gen. Hosp., 1935, also psychiatrist, 1936-38; spl. instr. in social psychiatry Simmons Coll., Boston, 1936-38; instr. psychiatry Harvard U. Med. Sch., 1936-38; prof. Washington U., St. Louis, 1938-41; psychiatrist-in-chief Barnes Hosp. and assoc. hosps., St. Louis, 1938-41; head psychiatric svcs. Washington U., Malcolm A. Bliss Psychiat. Inst. of St. Louis City Hosp., 1939-41; Henry Phipps prof. psychiatry, dir. dept. psychiatry Johns Hopkins U., 1941-60, prof., psychiatrist-in-chief emeritus, from 1960; psychiatrist-in-chief Johns Hopkins Hosp., 1941-60; cons. V.A. Hosp., Perry Point, Md.; hon. assoc. physician Guy's Hosp., London, from 1948; Jacob Gimbel lectr. on sex psychology Stanford U., 1949; Samuel W. Hamilton lectr., 1953; Karen Horney Meml. lectr., 1954, Salmon lectr. N.Y. Acad. Medicine, 1955; mem. Nat. Rsch. Coun. div. med. scis., 1932-38, 38-40, 43-46, 53-57, exec. com., 1953-57. Contbr. to profl. jours. Pres. Am. Bd. Psychiatry and Neurology, 1946, 48, 49, dir., 1943-49; chmn. Md. State Mental Health adv. bd., 1950-60; mem. exec. com. Med. Care Com. State of Md., from 1953; mem. Nat. Adv. Mental Health Coun., USPHS, 1954-58, 59-63; vice chmn. Md. Bd. Health and Mental Hygiene, from 1961. Fellow AMA, AAAS (Gutheil medal 1961), Am. Coll. Psychiatrists (pres. 1965-66), Am. Psychiat. Assn. (pres. elect 1949-50, pres. 1950-51, mem. coun. from 1951); mem. Nat. Assn. Mental Health (past dir.), N.Y. Acad. Sci., Am. Chem. Soc., Ctrl. Neuropsychiatric Assn., Balt.-Washington Psychoanalytic Soc. (hon.), Assn. Rsch. in Nervous and Mental Disease (v.p. 1951, 53), Hist. Sci. Soc., Boylston Med. Soc., Alpha Omega, Phi Rho Sigma, Alpha Omega Alpha, Sigma Xi. *

WHITELEY, WILLIAM RICHARD, SR., construction executive, antique dealer; b. Chgo., July 13, 1940; s. Thomas Clayton and Arline Gladys (Meader) W.; m. Jean Dellora Olson, July 18, 1964; children: William Richard Jr., Gayle Lynn. Constrn. laborer Palmer Bros. Carpentry, Chgo., 1955-59, carpenter, 1959-64, carpenter foreman, 1964-69; carpenter supt. Loyalty Carpentry, Chgo., 1969-73; asst. project mgr. Camosy Inc., Gurnee, Ill., 1973-77; project mgr. Shaf Homes, Skokie, Ill., 1977-79, Gordon Condominiums, Chgo., 1979-85; constrn. mgr. Oak Creek Custom Homes, Wauconda, Ill., 1985-88; gen. supt. Norcon Constrn., Chgo., 1988-90. Candidate Rep. committeeman, Wauconda, 1986-90; bd. dirs. Rep. Assn., Wauconda, 1986; campaign mgr. Citizens for Open Govt., Wauconda, 1988; vice chmn. Wauconda Twp. Rep. Party, 1987-89. Recipient numerous awards Wauconda JayCees, Wauconda Boosters, Knights of Columbus. Mem. Am. Assn. Polit. Consultants, Wauconda Boosters Inc. (cert. appreciation 1986), Wauconda Rep. Assn., Wauconda Twp. Hist. Soc., KC (Knight of the month 1986). Republican. Roman Catholic. Home: Wauconda Ill. Died Oct. 31, 1990.

WHITENER, BASIL LEE, lawyer, former congressman; b. York County, S.C., May 14, 1915; s. Levi and Laura (Barrett) W.; m. Harriet Morgan, Sept. 26, 1942; children: John Morgan, Laura, Basil Lee, Barrett. Grad., Rutherford Jr. Coll., 1933; student, U.S.C., 1933-35; LL.B., Duke U., 1937; LL.D., Belmont Abbey Coll., 1960, Pfeiffer Coll., 1965. Bar: N.C. 1937. Pvt. practice Gastonia, N.C., 1937-88; mem. N.C. Ho. of Reps., 1941 Session, N.C. Gen Statutes Commn., 1945-46; dist. atty. 14th Jud. Dist., 1946-56; mem. 85th-87th congresses, 11th N.C., 88th-90th Congresses, 10th N.C. Dist.; Mem. Commn. Improvement of Adminstrn. of Justice, 1947-49. Del. Democratic Nat. convs., 1948, 60; former chmn. bd. trustees Belmont-Abbey Coll., Belmont, N.C. Served to lt. USNR, 1942-45. Mem. Am. N.C., Gaston County bar assns., Jr. C. of C. (pres. 1940), N.C. Jr. C. of C. (pres. 1941-42), Am. Legion, V.F.W., 40 and 8, Phi Delta Phi, Omicron Delta Kappa. Methodist (former steward). Clubs: Mason (32 deg., Shriner), Elk, Kiwanian, Young Democrats of N.C. (pres. 1946-47), Young Democratic Clubs Am. (chmn. adv. com. 1950-51, chmn. bd. regional dirs. 1951). Home: Gastonia N.C. Died Mar. 20, 1989.

WHITESELL, FARIS DANIEL, clergyman, educator; b. Vigo County, Ind., Aug. 11, 1895; s. Charles Clark and Eva (Pennington) W. AB, William Jewell Coll., 1921, DD, 1936; BD, No. Bapt. Theol. Sem., 1923, ThD, 1931. Ordained to Bapt. ministry, 1920. Pastor 1st Ch., Decatur, Ind., 1921-25; prof. evangelism No. Bapt. Theol. Sem., 1925-44, prof. practical theology and homiletics, from 1944, prof. preaching, from 1963; acting pastor Covenant Ch., Chgo., 1933-41; also conductor evangelistic campaigns. Author: Sixty-Five Ways to Give Evangelistic Invitations; Evangelistic Preaching and the Old Testament; The Art of Biblical Preaching, 1949; Basle New Testament Evangelism, 1949; How to Solve Your Problems, 1953, Evangelistic Illustrations from the Bible, 1954; Vestry Into Your Preaching, 1954; Let's Study, 1954; Preaching on Bible Characters, 1955; Great Personal Workers, 1956; Power in Expository Preaching, 1963, Great Expository Sermons, 1964. With U.S. Army, 1918. Republican. *

WHITLEY, JOSEPH EFIRD, medical educator; b. Albemarle, N.C., Mar. 22, 1931; s. John Efird and Ola Mae (Huneycutt) W.; m. Nancy O'Neil, Dec. 20, 1958; children: John O'Neil, Catherine Anne. B.A. magna cum laude, Wake Forest U., 1951; M.D., Bowman Gray Sch. Medicine, 1955. Intern Pennsylvania Hosp.; Phila. resident N.C. Babtist Hosp., Winston-Salem; asst. prof. Bowman Gray Sch. Medicine, Winston Salem, N.C., 1962-65; asso. prof. Bowman Gray Sch. Medicine, 1965-69, prof. dept. radiology, 1969-78; prof., chmn. dept. diagnostic radiology U. Md. Sch. Medicine, Balt., from 1978; Cons. NIH, Nat. Inst. Neurol. Diseases Stroke, 1969-79. Author: (with Nancy O. Whitley) Angiography, Techniques and Procedures, 1971. Bd. dirs. James Picker Found., 1974-80. Fellow Am. Coll. Radiology; mem. Am. Roentgen Ray Soc. Radiologic Soc. N. Am., Assn. Univ. Radiologists (pres. 1979-80, Gold medal 1989), Soc. Chmn. Acad. Radiology Depts. (pres. 1987-88), Phi Beta Kappa, Alpha Omega Alpha. Home: Baltimore Md. Died Apr. 24, 1989; buried Albemarle, N.C.

WHITLOCK, FOSTER BRAND, pharmaceutical company executive; b. Highland Park, N.J., Oct. 27, 1914; s. Frank Boudinot and Rosena (Foster) W.; m. Edna Gertrude Evans, Jan. 26, 1945; children: Charlane Whitlock Mowery, Frances Whitlock Edmondson, Janet Whitlock Wise, Brand. Student, Rutgers U., 1932-33, L.H.D. (hon.); student, U. Wis., 1934-36, Columbia U., 1954; LL.D. (hon.), Phila. Coll. Pharmacy. Engr., clk. RCA Communications, Inc., 1936-39; salesman Johnson & Johnson, New Brunswick, N.J., 1939-40; from salesman to div. mgr., sales mgr., pres., chmn. bd. Ortho Pharm. Corp. (subs. Johnson & Johnson), Raritan, N.J., 1940-64; pres., dir. Johnson & Johnson, 1958-77, mem. exec. com., 1964-77, vice chmn., 1973-77; pres., vice chmn. bd. Johnson & Johnson Internat., 1974-78; pres. Am. Found. Pharm. Edn., 1972-73; mem. Joint Commn. on Prescription Drug Use, 1976-79. Bd. dirs. Project HOPE.; Trustee, bd. govs. Rutgers U., 1968-77; pres. Rutgers U. Found., 1975-76; chmn. bd. Overlook Hosp., Summit, N.J., 1977-78; trustee Maine Coast Meml. Hosp., Elssworth; trustee Overlook Hosp. Found., from 1975, Robert Wood Johnson Found., from 1979; dir., v.p. Wendell Gilley Mus. Bird Carving, Southwest Harbor, Maine, from 1978. Served to capt. USAAF, 1942-46. Decorated Bronze Star medal, Croix de Guerre (France), Legion d'Honneur (France). Mem. Pharm. Mfrs. Assn. (dir., chmn. 1973-74), Internat. Fedn. Pharm. Mfrs. Zurich. (pres. 1974-76), S.A.R., Chi Psi. Presbyterian. Clubs: N.Y. Yacht (N.Y.C.); Ocean Reef (Fla.); Baltusrol Golf, Key Largo (Fla.) Anglers. Home: Southwest Harbor Maine Died May 24, 1991, buried Elmwood Cemetery, New Brunswick, N.J.

WHITMAN, ANN C., federal official; b. Perry, Ohio; d. Willis Wood and Esther (Few) Cook; m. Clarence Willard Moore, 1933 (div.); m. Edmund S. Whitman, Sept. 19, 1941 (div. 1961). Student, Antioch Coll.; grad., Spencerian Bus. Sch. With Com. for Free Europe, 1950; personal sec. Pres. Dwight D. Eisenhower, from 1951; also chief of staff to V.p. Nelson A. Rockefeller; ret., 1977. Home: Washington D.C. Died Oct. 15, 1991.

WHITMAN, FREDERIC BENNETT, railroad executive; b. Cambridge, Mass., Sept. 1, 1898; s. Edmund Allen and Florence Josephine (Lee) W.; m. Gertrude Bissel, June 13, 1927; children: Russell Allen, HArriet Lee. AB, Harvard, 1919, MBA, 1921. With Ft. Worth & Denver City R.R. Co., 1919; With CB&Q R.R. Co., 1921-47, supt. western dist., 1947-48; mem. Western Carriers Conf. Com., 1947-48; exec. v.p., dir. W.P. R.R. Co., San Francisco, 1948-49; pres., dir. W.P. R.R. Co., from 1949, Oakland Terminal Ryy., Salt Lake City; v.p., dir. Standard Realty & Devel. Co., Alameda Belt Line; sir., mem. exec. com. Tidewater Southern Ry.; dir. Ctrl. Cal. Traction Co., Fireman's Fund Inc. Co.; chmn. and fed. res. agt. Fed. Res. Bank San Francisco, 12th dist.; trustee Equitable Life Ins. Co. Iowa. Trustee San Francisco Bay Area Area Coun.; pres., dir. Rosenberg Found. 2d lt. U.S. Army, 1918-19. Mem. Pacific-Union Bohemian (San Francisco), Links. *

WHITMORE, EDWARD HUGH, mathematician; b. Ottawa, Ill., Feb. 26, 1926; s. Chester Teal and Maude (McCullough) W.; m. Bertha Harper, June 11, 1949; children: Stephen Harper, Ann Elizabeth. Student, U. Pa., 1944, U. Notre Dame, 1946; B.S., Ill. State U., 1949, M.S., 1951; Ph.D., Ohio State U., 1956. Instr. math. Clinton (Ill.) Community High Sch., 1949-51; grad. asst., asst. instr. math. Ohio State U., 1952-54; asst. prof. math. No. Ill. U., Dekalb, 1955; asst. prof. math. San Francisco State Coll., 1956-59, asso. prof., 1960-65; chmn. dept. math. Central Mich. U., Mt. Pleasant, 1965-74, 76-82; prof. Central Mich. U., 1965-87, ret., 1988; acting dean Central Mich. U. (Sch. Arts and Scis.), 1968-69; cons. sch. systems, Calif., Mich.; mem. Calif. Adv. Com. Math., 1962-64, Mich. Math. Curriculum Com., 1966-67. Author: Modern Mathematics, Book 1, 2d edit, 1971, Book 2, 2d edit., 1971; dept. editor: The Math. Tchr, 1967-70. Served to lt. (j.g.) USNR, 1944-47. Mem. Nat. Council Tchrs. Math. (past com. chmn.), Math. Assn. Am., Kappa Mu Epsilon, Phi Delta Kappa, Phi Eta Sigma. Home: Pickerington Ohio Died June 12, 1992. †

WHITNEY, CORNELIUS VANDERBILT, corporate executive; b. N.Y.C., Feb. 20, 1899; m. Marie Louise Hosford, Jan. 24, 1958; 5 children. B.A., Yale U., 1922; Degree in Aero. Sci. (hon.), Embry-Riddle Aero. U., 1978; L.H.D. (hon.), U. Fla., Gainesville, 1983. Founder Pan Am. Airways, 1927, chmn. bd., until 1941; founder Hudson Bay Mining and Smelting Co., 1928, chmn. bd., until 1964, dir., until 1974; pres. Whitney Industries, Inc., 1931-89; founder Marineland of Fla. Inc., 1937, chmn. bd., until 1984; asst. sec. USAAF, 1947-49; undersec. commerce, 1949-50; spl. envoy of Pres. to, Eng., Luxembourg, Italy, Spain, 1950; rep. of Pres. at funeral of King Frederick of Denmark, Jan. 1972; Dir. Churchill Downs. Co-producer motion pictures: Gone with the Wind, Rebecca, A Star Is Born, 1930-85; Author: autobiography Lone and Levels Sands, Live a Year With a Millionaire. High Peaks, The Owl Hoots Again, First Flights. Bd. dirs. Saratoga Performing Arts Ctr., Nat. Mus. of Dance; past trustee Whitney Mus. Am. Art, Am. Mus. Natural History; founder Whitney Gallery of Western Art, Cody, Wyo., 1958, dir., 1958-92; founder Nat. Mus. of Racing, Saratoga, N.Y., 1950; dir. emeritus Buffalo Bill Hist. Found., Cody, Wyo.; past mem. Ky. Gov.'s Econ. Commn. Gov. Rockefeller's adv. com. on the future of the Adirondack region. Served to 2d lt., A.C. U.S. Army, World War I; to col. USAAF, 1941-46. Decorated D.S.M., Legion of Merit with 2 battle stars; Breeder of the Yr. award N.Y. Turf Writers, 1960; spl. racing award 1985; Man of the Yr., Thoroughbred Club Am., 1966; rec. Eclipse award, 1985. Clubs: Angler (N.Y.C.), River (N.Y.C.), Brook (N.Y.C.), Jockey (N.Y.C.), Turf and Field (N.Y.C.). Home: Saratoga Springs N.Y. Died 1992. †

WHITNEY, HASSLER, mathematician; b. N.Y.C., Mar. 23, 1907; s. Edward Baldwin and A. Josepha (Newcomb) W.; m. Margaret R. Howell, May 30, 1930; children: James Newcomb, Carol, Marian; m. Mary Barnett Garfield, Jan. 16, 1955; children: Sarah Newcomb, Emily Baldwin; m. Barbara Floyd Osterman, Feb. 8, 1986. PhB, Yale U., 1928, MusB, 1929, ScD (hon.), 1947; PhD, Harvard U., 1932. Instr. math. Harvard U., Cambridge, Mass., 1930-31, 33-35, NRC fellow math., 1931-33, asst. prof., 1935-40, assoc. prof., 1940-46, prof., 1946-52; prof. Inst. Advanced Study, Princeton, N.J., 1952-77, prof. emeritus, 1977-89; chmn. math. panel NSF, 1953-56; exchange prof., France, 1951-52; Fulbright exchange prof. Coll. de France, 1957; mem. com. support of research in math. scis. NRC, 1966-67; pres. Internat. Commn. Math. Instrn., 1979-82; research math. Nat. Def. Research Com., 1943-45; cons. sch. math. Recipient Nat. Medal of Sci., 1976, Wolf prize Wolf Found., 1983. Mem. NAS, Am. Math. Soc. (Colloquium lectr. 1946, v.p. 1948-50, editor Am. Jour. Math. 1944-49, editor Math. Revs. 1949-54, chmn. com. vis. lectureship 1946-51, com. summer insts. 1953-54, Steele prize 1985), Math. Assn. Am., Nat. Council Tchrs. Math., Swiss Math. Soc. (hon.), Am. Philos. Soc., London Math. Sci. (hon.), Académie des Scis. (fgn. assoc.), N.Y. Acad. of Scis. Club: Am. Alpine (N.Y.C.). Home: Princeton N.J. Died May 10, 1989; buried Mont Dents Blanches, Switzerland.

WHITNEY, WILLIAM KUEBLER, artist: b. New Orleans, July 6, 1921; s. Percy Macklin and Elizabeth (Kuebler) W.; m. Charlotte Armide Lamm; children: Charlene, Alice. B.F.A., Cranbrook Acad. Art, 1949, M.F.A., 1958. Owner, mgr. Whitney Silver Shop, Birmingham, Mich., 1950-58; from instr. to assoc. prof. art Olivet Coll., Mich., 1959-63, prof. 1973-79. Exhbns. include: Corcoran Biennial Am. Art, 1945; Octagon House, Washington, 1972; Detroit Inst. Art, 1949; one-man show: McNeese State Coll., 1984, Battle Creek Sister City exhbn., Takasaki, Japan, 1984. Served to with U.S. Army, 1942-45, PTO. Recipient Bronze medal for Still Life Soc. Washington Artists, 1942; Merit award Mich. Acad. Sci. Arts and Letters, Ann Arbor, 1950. Mem. Mich. Soc. Archtl. Historians, Battle Creek Artists Guild, AAUP., Eaton Art League (v.p. 1984). Avocations: photography. Died Oct. 7, 1985; buried Olivet (Mich.) Cemetery. Home: Olivet Mich.

WHITTAKER, ALFRED HEACOCK, surgeon; b. Portsmouth, Oreg., Sept. 30, 1894; s. Alfred M. and Annie M. (Heacock) W.; m. Margaret E. Evans, July 16, 1917; children: Alfred E., Hilary E., Joyce E., Jeanne E., James E. MD, Ohio State U., 1918; ArtsD, Wayne State U., 1957. House surgeon Roosevelt Hosp., N.Y.C., from 1918; resident Cornell U. div. Bellvue Hosp., N.Y.C., 1919, Indsl. Hosp., Detroit, 1920; jr. attending surgeon Bellevue Hosp.; also surgeon outpatient dept. Roosevelt Hosp., 1921-22; practice gen. surgery Detroit, from 1922; surgeon Harper Hosp., 1925-53, Children's Hosp. of Mich., 1930-45, Detroit Meml. Hosp., from 1943, Deaconess Hosp., from 1922; cons. surgeon Cottage Hosp., Grosse Pointe, Mich. Contbr. numerous articles to profl. jours. Bd. dirs. Mich. Med. Svcs.; past commr. Detroit City Plan Commn.; pres. Future Detroit Inc.; med. advisor Franklin Settlement; v.p. Detroit and Mich. Artists Meml. Corp.; mem. Mayor's Com. Civic Design, 1952-53; chmn. maypr's com. Detroit 250th Anniversary Celebration Com., 1950-51; v.p. Detroit Corp. Housing Aged; v.p. Minute Men of Mich.; Mich. area chmn. Ohio State U.; mem. bd. govs. Wayne State U.; mem. med. adv. com. Nat. Fund Med. Edn. Dir. Community Fund Detroit, 1945-53, Detroit Met. Rehabilitation Inst., from 1951, Detroit chpt. ARC, from 1953; past v.p. Friends Grosse Pointe Pub. Libr.; adminstr. Nat. Med. Shrine, Beaumont Meml. on Mackinac Island; mem. bipartisan Mackinac Island State Park Commn., from 1957. Fellow AMA (recipient exceptional merit award in hist. medicine 1945), ACS, Internat. Coll. Surgeons (chmn. sect. occupational surgery 1951-53); mem. Am. Assn. Surgery Trauma, Acad. Surgery Detroit (past pres.), Am. Assn. Hist. Medicine, Mich. Assn. Indsl. Medicine and Surgery, Indsl. Med. Assn. (pres. 1949-50, chmn. med. hist. com.), Mich. Med. Soc. (chmn. Beaumont com. 1951-52), Wayne County Med. Soc., Detroit Indsl. Physicians Club, Detroit Soc. Surgery Trauma (trustee), Detroit Hist. Soc. (pres. 1946-50, trustee 1944-53), Detroit Philos. Soc., Ohio State U. Med. Alumni Assn. (past pres.), Detroit Surgical Soc., Alumni Assn. Roosevelt Hosp., Am. Legion, Kappa Sigma, Alpha Kappa Kappa. Republican. Episcopalian. Clubs: Economic, University, Boat, Detroit, Detroit Athletic, Players, Detroit Country, Harmonic (pres. 1953), University (Chgo., N.Y.C.), Faculty (Ohio State U.). *

WHITTELSEY, STUART GORDON, JR., financial executive, management consultant; b. Berkeley, Calif., Oct. 6, 1929; s. Stuart Gordon and Lucille (Crenshaw) W.; m. Peggy Porter, (div. June 1972); children: Susan, Linda; m. Clara Starin Stucky, June 25, 1972 (dec. Nov. 1986); children: Carol, Richard, Robert, Barbara, James, Jane; m. Carleen Store Cox, Oct. 11, 1987; children: Robert, William, David, m. Carleen Stone Cox, Oct. 11, 1987; children: Robert, William, David. BA, Stanford U., 1951; MBA, Harvard U., 1953. Treas., adminstrv. dir. Watkins-Johnson Co., Palo Alto, Calif., 1960-76; prin. cons. Whittelsey Assocs., Woodside, Calif., 1976-92; v.p., CFOStanford Telecom., Inc., Santa Clara, Calif., 1981-85; v.p. Informix Corp., 1986-89;. v.p. Acurex Environ., 1990-92 bd. dirs. Innowave Inc., Applied Signal Tech., Inc. Trustee Peninsula Meml. Blood Bank, 1964-92; mem. Mounted Patrol of San Mateo County, 1970-92. Deceased 1992. Home: Redwood City Calif.

WHITTEMORE, ROBERT CLIFTON, philosophy educator; b. Lockport, N.Y., Feb. 1, 1921; s. Clifton Houghton and Zelia Florence (Duke) W.; m. Dorothy Jane Gordon, June 15, 1959 (div. Jan. 1983); m. Emily Antoinette Bryant, Jan. 30, 1983. B.A., Yale U., 1949, M.A., 1951, Ph.D., 1953. Instr. Yale U., New Haven, 1951-52; instr., asst. prof., assoc. prof., prof. dept. philosophy Tulane U., New Orleans, 1952-85, dir. Am. Studies, 1983-87, prof. emeritus, 1988; state chmn. La. Endowment Humanities, 1975-78; dir. So. Assembly, New Orleans, 1968-78. Author: Makers of American Mind, 1964; Transformation of the New England Theology, 1986; author and editor: Ideology and the American Experience, 1986; editor Tulane Studies in Philosophy, from 1974. Served with AUS, 1942-45, ETO. Fellow Lilly Found., 1964-65. Fellow Am. Philos. Soc.; mem. Southwestern Philos. Soc. (pres. 1968), Hegel Soc. Am., Soc. Philosophy of Religion. Presbyterian. Home: New Orleans La. Died Oct. 1, 1988.

WHITTIER, SARAJANE, social studies educator; b. North Manchester, Ind., Dec. 17, 1912; d. Charles and Ethel Clo (Free) Leckrone; m. C. Taylor Whittier, June 18, 1934; children: Chip, Tim, Cece, Penny. BA, U. Chgo., 1934, MA, 1946. Rsch. sec. Oriental Inst., Chgo., 1935-39; tchr. pub. schs., Flossmoor, Ill., 1939-41, Sta. WSUN-TV, St. Petersburg, Fla., 1955-56, Sta. GWETA-TV, Washington, 1961-62; substitute tchr. pub. schs., Fla. and Md., 1962-89; tchr. music Gretna United Meth. Pre-sch., 1989-91. Co-author: Pasture Trails, 1941; asst. monthly newsletter Supt.'s Digest, 1983-85. Pres., PTA, St. Petersburg, 1960's; Kans. chmn. Friends of J.F.K. Ctr., Topeka, 1969-75, Tex. chmn., San Antonio, 1975-82; teaching music in pre-sch., 1989-91; also Apollo Music Club Chgo., 1933-35; guardian Camp Fire Girls, Chgo., 1936-41, bd. dirs. Camp Fire Kans., Tex., La. Gaithersburg, Md., 1958-64; Sunday sch. tchr. Christian Ch., Chgo., 1926-34, chmn. Westbank Forum Ch. Women United. St. Petersburg, 1950-57, pianist, San Antonio, 1975-82. U. Chgo. scholar, 1933-34 Mem. AAUW (past pres., life mem., pres. Algiers/Westbank), Chgo. Apollo Music Club (alto singer 1932-34). Republican. Clubs: Capital Speakers (Washington). Avocations: acting, music, directing little theatres, photography, world traveling. Died Dec. 16, 1991. Home: Gretna La.

WHITTINGTON, HARRY BENJAMIN, author, director, producer; b. Ocala, Fla., Feb. 4, 1915; s. Harry Benjamin and Rosa Elizabeth (Hardee) W.; m. Kathryn Lavinia Odom, Feb. 9, 1936; children—Harriet Kathryn Whittington Beebe, Howard Hardee. Student in English and humanities various colls. Advt. copywriter Griffith Advt. Agy.; asst. mgr. advt.-publicity Capitol Theatre, St. Petersburg, Fla.; with U.S. Post Office, St. Petersburg, 1934-47; lectr. colls., seminars, confs. Freelance writer, 1948-89, screenwriter, Warner Bros., Burbank, Calif., 1957; editor-writer REA, Washington, 1968-75; author: 100 hist. novels, including Panama, 1979 (Porgy award), Rampage, 1979 (Porgy award), Saddle the Storm, 1954 (Western Writers Am. award), Heritage of Blackoaks, 1981, Embrace the Wind, 1982; also short stories, articles. Served with USN, 1945-46. Mem. Mystery Writers Am (regional dir. 1952-54), Authors Guild, Western Writers Am. Episcopalian. Home: Indian Rocks Beach Fla. Died June 11, 1989.

WHITTINGTON, VERLE GLENN, petroleum company executive; b. Fairfield, Iowa, Dec. 2, 1929; s. Harold William and Grace Marie (Wilson) W.; m. Pauline Curran, Oct. 31, 1952; children: Kathleen Ann, James Edd, Mark Steven, Carol Lynn, John Joseph, Michael Aaron. B.A., Parsons Coll., Fairfield, 1952; J.D., U. Iowa, 1955. With Shell Oil Co., 1955-88; mgr. non-exempt employee relations and indsl. safety Shell Oil Co., N.Y.C., 1968-70; mgr. indsl. relations, employee relations orgn. Shell Oil Co., Houston, 1970-73; treas. Shell Oil Co., 1973-75, v.p. employee relations, 1975-88; chmn. Conf. Bd.'s Human Resource Mgmt. Com.; bd. dirs. R&F Coal Co., Turris Coal Co., Triton Coal Co., Marrowbone Coal Co., Wolf Creek Coal Co., Shell Mining Co., Shipyard River Coal Terminal Co., Scallop Corp., Pike County Coal Co.; chmn. trustees Shell Pension Fund, Provident Fund. Bd. dirs., Jr. Achievement SE Tex.; mem. Houston Loaned Exec. Com.; sec./treas. Exec. Service Core Houston; trustee Nat. Ctr. Occupational Readjustment. Mem. ABA (trustee), Iowa Bar Assn., Houston Bar Assn., Labor Policy Assn. (chmn. exec. com., dir.), Unemployed Benefits Assn. (bd. dirs.), Bus. Roundtable (exec. com. and employee relations com.), Petroleum Club Houston. Roman Catholic. Club: Elk. Club: River Plantation Country (Conroe). Home: Conroe Tex. Died Oct. 30, 1988.

WIBLISHAUSER, ELMER HUBERT, lawyer; b. St. Paul, July 12, 1910; s. Joseph and Magdalena (Mahowald) W.; m. Regina M. Wiblishauser; children: Thomas Frederick, Carole Jean, Lois Ann. B of Laws, St. Paul Coll. Law, 1937; JD, William Mitchell Coll. Law, 1937. Assoc. Sterling & Wiblishauser, St. Paul, 1939-40; pvt. practice St. Paul, 1940-42, 46-88. Councilman Maplewood City Council, Minn., 1962-67. Capt. U.S. Army, 1942-46. Mem. Minn. Bar Assn. (treas. 1959-63), Ramsey County Bar Assn., Am. Legion, Phi Beta Gamma. Republican. Roman Catholic. Home: Saint Paul Minn. Deceased.

WICK, GIAN CARLO, physicist, educator; b. Torino, Italy, Oct. 15, 1909; Came to U.S., 1946; naturalized, 1955.; s. Federico Carlo and Barbara (Allson) W.; m. Antonella Civalleri, Dec. 4, 1943; children: Lionel Anthony, Julian Charles; m. 2d, Vanna Chirone. Dr. Physics, U. Turin, Italy, 1930. Assoc. prof. physics U. Palermo, Italy, 1937-38, U. Padova, Italy, 1938-40; prof. physics U. Rome, 1940-45, U. Notre Dame, 1946-48, U. Calif., Berkeley, 1948-50; prof. Carnegie Inst. Tech., 1951-58; sr. physicist Brookhaven Nat. Lab., 1958-65; prof. physics Columbia U., 1965-77; mem. Inst. Advanced Study, Princeton U., 1953. Fellow Am. Phys. Soc.; mem. NAS, Am. Acad. Arts and Scis. Home: Turin Italy Died Apr. 20, 1992.

WICKENS, ARYNESS JOY, economist, statistician; b. Bellingham, Wash., Jan. 5, 1901; d. Oliver Hodgson and Elizabeth (Chapman) Joy; m. David Lawrence Wickens, June 29, 1935; children—David Elder (dec.) Donaldson. A.B., U. Wash., 1922; A.M., U. Chgo., 1924. Instr., then asst. prof. econs. and sociology Mt. Holyoke Coll., 1924-28; research asst. div. research and statistics Fed. Res. Bd., 1928-1933; chief statistician Office Econs. Adviser, Nat. Emergency Council, 1933-35; chief statistician, chief economist U.S. Central Statis. Bd., 1935-37; asst. to commr. Bur. Labor Stats., 1938-40, chief, prices and cost of living br., 1940-45, asst. commr. for program ops., 1945-49, dep. commr. of Bur., 1949-54, acting commr., 1954-55, dep. asst. sec. labor for manpower and employment, 1956-59; econ. adviser to sec. of labor, 1959-62, consumer program adviser, 1962-69, spl. asst. to asst. sec. labor for manpower, 1967-68; dir. Office of Manpower Mgmt. Data Systems, Manpower Adminstrn., 1968-70, cons. to manpower adminstr., 1970-71; pvt. cons., from 1971; statistician Commn. on Fed. Paperwork, 1976-77; mem. adv. bd. Export Import Bank U.S., 1976-77; dir. Washington-Lee Savs. & Loan Assn., McLean, Va., 1965-73, dir. emeritus, 1974-91; adviser to U.S. del. 30th and 31st sessions Internat. Labor Conf., 1947, 1948; U.S. del. to 1st gen. assembly Inter-Am. Statis. Inst., 1947; adviser to U.S. del. Econ. and Social Council of UN, 1951, 52, 60, 61. Bd. dirs. Am. Nat. Standards Inst., 1967-69; mem. Consumer Standards Bd., 1963-66, Consumer Council, 1966-69, 70-76. Recipient Distinguished Service award U.S. Dept. Labor, 1955, Fed. Woman's award, 1961. Fellow Am. Statis. Assn. (pres. 1952); mem. Am. Econ. Assn., Nat. Economists Club, Phi Beta Kappa, Kappa Kappa Gamma. Home: Jackson Miss. Died Feb. 2, 1991; buried Arlington Nat. Cemetery.

WICKER, JAMES CALDWELL, educator; b. Balt., Dec. 8, 1895; s. John Jordan and ELizabeth (Pumphrey) W.; m. Lula Jones Puckett, Nov. 20, 1917; children: John Tivis, Ruth Ann, James C. Jr. AB, U. Richmond; ThB, Southern Bapt. Theol. Sem., 1931; DD, U. Richmond, 1946. Ordained to ministry Bapt. Ch. Engaged in banking and real estate, 1919-28; pastor 1st Bapt. Ch., Elizabeth City, N.C., 1931-33, Northside Bapt. Ch., Richmond, Va., 1933-43; pres. Fork Union (Va.) Mil. Acad., from 1945. Served as USN aviator, WWI, USN chaplain, WWII. Mem. Assn. Mil. Colls. and Schs. of U.S. (pres.), Va. Mil. Schs. League, Univ. Richmond Gen. Alumni Assn. (pres.), Am. Legion, Phi Kappa Sigma, Masons, Kiwanis. Democrat. *

WIDENER, HERBERT LLOYD, physician, medical administrator; b. Abingdon, Va., Nov. 2, 1941; s. Hunter Felix and Margaret (Williams) W.; m. Marilyn Jewett Widener, Apr. 27, 1964; children: Wendy Lee, Ashley Ellyn, Charles Hunter. BA, Randolph Macon Coll., 1964; MD, Med. Coll. Va., 1968. Med. intern Med. Coll. Va., Richmond, 1968-69, resident in internal medicine, 1972-74, chief resident in internal medicine, 1974-75; cons. rheumatolgist Nalle Clinic, Charlotte, N.C., from 1977, physician, dir. quality assurance, from 1984, asst. med. dir., from 1987; mem. speaker's panel CIBA-Geigy Corp., Summit, N.J., 1988-89, Smith-Kline Beechum Labs., Phila., from 1987, mem. managed care adv. coun., from 1989. Maj. USAF, 1969-72. Mem. ACP, Am. Coll. Physician Execs., Am. Rheumatism Assn., Arthritis Found. (adv. bd. from 1984), N.C. State Med. Soc., Mecklenburg County Med. Soc. Republican. Episcopalian. Home: Charlotte N.C.

WIDENGREN, ULF NILS JOEL, pharmaceutical company executive; b. Soderhamn, Sweden, Oct. 20, 1931; s. Rudolf Lars Gustav and Edith Ingeborg Lindstrom) W.; m. Harriet Margareta Holmbom, Sept. 3, 1973; children: Marcus, Louise; m. Britt Englund, 1962 (dec. 1972); children: Staffan, Claes, Joel. Chem. Engr., 1952; B.Sc. in Econs., Stockholm Sch. Econs., 1961. Investment and ops. contractor AB Granges Liberiaforvaltning, Liberia, 1958-63; adminstrv. mgr. Gylling & Co., Stockholm, 1964-67; mgmt. specialist H.B. Maynard & Co., Stockholm, 1968; adminstrv. mgr., div. mgr. KemaNobel AB, Stockholm, 1969-76; pres. AB Astra, Sodertalje, Sweden, 1977-87 ; dir. AB Astra and its subsidiaries, Sodertalje, Skandifond AB, Stockholm, FinansSkandic AB, Stockholm. Served to capt. Swedish Army. Died Nov. 18, 1987. Home: Stockholm Sweden

WIDMOYER, FRED BIXLER, horticulturist, educator; b. Grandfield, Okla., Nov. 25, 1920; s. Fred B. and Sara D. (Popham) W.; m. Genevieve Jean Jonas, June 26, 1961; children: Cathryn Jean, Timothy Fred, Ann Louise. B.A., Tex. Tech. U., 1942, M.S., 1950; Ph.D., Mich. State U., 1954. Biology asst. Tex. Tech.

U., Lubbock, 1940-42; instr. botany Tex. Tech. U., 1946-50; adviser program instr. Philmont Scout Ranch, Cimarron, N.Mex., 1951-53; greenhouse asst. Iowa State U., Ames, 1951-53; asst. prof. Mich. State U., East Lansing, 1954-60; assoc. prof. U. Conn., Storrs, 1960-63; prof. horticulture N.Mex. State U., Las Cruces, 1963-87, prof. horticulture, emeritus, 1987-91, head dept. horticulture, 1963-82; prin. horticulturist Dept. Agr., Sci. and Edn. Adminstrn. Co-op Research, Washington, 1977-78; horticulture cons., 1986-91; adv. council Nat. Arboretum, 1970-80; tech. advisor Internat. Boundry and Water Commn. U.S.-Mexico, 1987-91. Contbr. articles on hort. sci. to profl. jours.; author, editor manuals and guides in field. Mem. Republican County Central Com., Dona Ana County, Las Cruces, 1975-77, trustee, Mesilla, N.Mex., 1982; chmn. Dona Ana County Rep. Party; vice chmn. N.Mex. 2d Congl. Dist. Served with USNR, 1942-46, PTO. Named hon. Am. Farmer and State Farmer, Future Farmers Am., Gold medal Mass. Hort. Soc.; recipient Esther Longyear Murphy medal Mich. Hort. Soc.; Paul Harris fellow Las Cruces Rotary Club, 1989. Fellow Am. Soc. Hort. Sci.; mem. Soc. Am. Florists, Garden Writers Assn., Am. Assn. Bot. Gardens and Arboretums (hon.), Am. Hort. Soc. (Scientist citation), Nat. Council Therapy Through Horticulture, N.Mex. Landscape Assn., N.Mex. Nursery Industries. Roman Catholic. Home: Las Cruces N.Mex. Died June 19, 1991; buried Ft. Bliss Nat. Cemetery, El Paso, Tex.

WIDUTIS, FLORENCE, educator, author; b. Phila., May 29, 1912; d. Elmer Russell Alburger and Josephine (Reid) Weber; m. Albert Brownell, June 1931 (div. 1934); 1 child, Barbara Dell; m. George W. Widutis, Apr., 1940 (dec. 1959); 1 child, Josephine Puckett. BS magna cum laude, NYU, 1956; MEd, U. Md., 1961; postgrad., St. Louis U., U. Ghana, U. Mexico, Opinion analyst UN Info. Office, N.Y.C., 1943; editor, exec. dir. Program Info. Exchange, N.Y.C., 1944-47; faculty Arcane Sch. Meditation, N.Y.C., 1950-53; tchr. secondary schs. N.J. and D.C., 1957-76; editor, pub. Pilgrims, Somerville, NJ, 1956-60, Beautiful Day Books, College Park, Md., from 1976; freelance writer, workshop facilitator, symposium coordinator, lecturer various orgns., various states, from 1976; Editor Internat. Inst. Transpersonal Diplomacy Bd., Hamilton, Va., 1985-87; bd. dirs. Planetary Citizens, NYC, 1978-81, William Penn House, Washington, 1983-84. Author: Here's How It's Done, 1945, Yours Is the Power, 1977, The True Path, 1979; (with Catherine H. Clark) Books for New Age, Children and Youth, 1976, (curriculum) The Person and the Planet, 1980; contbr. various poems, articles on hunger, population, peace, education, smoking and health to profl. jours. Vol. Society Friends Com. on Nat. Legis., 1978, World Hunger Edn. Service, Washington, 1979. Democrat. Mem. Society of Friends. Clubs: Wayfarers, B and B Square Dance (Washington). Home: Bethesda Md. Deceased.

WIEDEMAN, GEORGE HENKINS, psychiatrist, educator; b. Moscow, Russia, June 27, 1912; came to U.S., 1939, naturalized, 1944; s. Vincent and Helen (Abramovich) W.; m. Rachel Henkins, Apr. 25, 1939; 1 son, Michael. Student, Med. Schs. U. Berlin and Frankfort, Germany, 1931-33; M.D., U. Prague, Czechoslovakia, 1937. Diplomate: Am. Bd. Neurology and Psychiatry in psychiatry. Intern Wesson Meml. Hosp., Springfield, Mass., 1939-41; gen. practice medicine Leominster, Mass., 1941-44; fellow psychiatry, psychiat. resident Menninger Sch. Psychiatry, Topeka, 1946-48; staff psychiatrist VA Mental Hygiene Clinic, Newark, 1949-50; psychoanalytic tng. N.Y. Psychoanalytic Inst., 1949-55; pvt. practice psychiatry and psychoanalysis N.Y.C., 1950-91; lectr. N.Y. Sch. Social Work, Columbia, 1958-62, Marion Kenworthy prof. psychiatry, 1962-80; spl. lectr. Sch. Social Work, Columbia U., 1980-87; psychiat. cons. Community Service Soc. N.Y., 1952-71; sr. lectr. div. psychiat. edn. dept. psychiatry Downstate Med Center, State U. N.Y., 1972-79, tng. and supervising analyst, from 1974; mem. faculty Psychoanalytic Inst. N.Y. U. Med. Center, from 1979. Author, editor: Personality Development and Deviation, 1975; Contbr. articles to profl. jours. Served to capt. M.C. AUS, 1944-46. Mem. A.M.A., Am. Psychiat. Assn., Am. Psychoanalytic Assn., Am. Orthopsychiat. Assn., AAAS, Psychoanalytic Assn. N.Y., Med. Soc. County and State N.Y. Home: New York N.Y. Died Dec. 27, 1991; interred Ferncliff Cemetery Mausoleum.

WIESE, CLAUS, television station executive; b. Oslo, Norway, Mar. 1, 1924; came to U.S., 1951; s. Peter Olav and Gerd (Halvorsen) W.; m. Anna Joan Trapp, Aug. 12, 1950; children: Joan Gerd Wiese Saunders, Kristin, Peter Olav, II. Artium, Oslo Kathedralskole, 1944; student Nat. Theater Sch., Oslo, 1947. Actor, Det Nye Teater, Oslo, 1945-51; film editor WNAC-TV, Boston, 1952-54; prodn. mgr. WMTW-TV, Poland Spring, Maine, 1954-75, ops. mgr., 1975-82, station mgr., Auburn, Maine, from 1982. Pres. Sunday River Skiway Corp., Bethel, Maine. Served to lt. Norwegian Underground, 1942-45. Recipient Best Actor in Films award Norwegian Govt., 1950. Mem. Maine Assn. Broadcasters (pres. from 1985). Lutheran. Avocations: skiing; sailing; art. Deceased.

WIJERATNE, RANJAN, member of parliament, foreign and state minister; b. Colombo, Sri Lanka, Apr. 4, 1931; s. George Hercules Wijeratne and Maria (Rosalind) Senanayake; married, Dec. 10, 1954; 1 child, Rohan Nissanka. Student, St. Thomas' Coll., Mt. Lavinia and Gurutalawa. Tea planter, 1951-71; mgr. Demodera Group Tea Plantation, Sri Lanka, 1968-71; min. of fgn. affairs Colombo, 1989-90; dir. Whittalls Estates & Agys., 1971-78; chmn. Pelwatte Sugar Co., Ltd., 1981-91, Sir Lanka State Plantations Corp., 1984-91, Rajarata Food Grain Processing Co., Ltd., 1984-91; mem. Sri Lanka Tea Bd., 1984-91; sec., chmn. State Plantations, 1984, 87. Sec. Ministry of Agrl. Devel. and Rsch., 1978-82; chmn. Agrl. Devel. Authority, 1978-87, Land Reform Commn., 1982-87; mem. Rural Credit Adv. Com., 1978-91, Steering Com. of Dairy Devel. Bd., 1986-91, Land Commn., 1985-91; chmn. Coun. Agrl. Rsch. Policy, 1987, United Nat. Party, 1988, gen. sec., 1989. Lt. col. Sri Lanka Rifle Corps. Mem. Ceylon Planters' Soc. (chmn. 1967-68), Trade Union of Plantation Chmn., Planters' Assn. of Ceylon (chmn. 1970-71), Assn. of Producers of Plantation Crops, Agy. sect. of The Planters' Assn. of Ceylon (chmn. 1974-75), Colombo Tea Traders' Assn. (chmn. 1974-76), Ceylon Inst. Planting (v.p. 1972-74), Nat. Inst. Plantation Mgmt. (bd. govs. 1984). Buddist. Home: Colombo Sri Lanka

WILBUN, MARCUS, musician; b. Little Rock, Feb. 4, 1921; s. Matthew Mark and Claudia Lucille (Shepperson) W.; m. Lillie Blondell Bruce, Dec. 3, 1948; children: Marcus, Jr., Nancy. BA, Philander Smith Coll., 1943. Pianist, popular music N.Y.C., 1943-85, pianist, ch. music, from 1985. Fellow Am. Fedn. Musicians; mem. Omega Psi Phi. Republican. Methodist. Home: Scranton Pa. Deceased.

WILDE, BERTRAM MERBACH, investment banker; b. Phila., Dec. 28, 1898; s. James Taylor and Anna (Pressler) W.; m. Florence Louise Deal, Oct. 5, 1940; 1 child, Louise P. Student, pub. schs., Pa. With Janney Battles & E.W. Clark Inc. and predessor films), Phila., from 1915; successively office, cashier, asst. treas., sec./ treas., v.p Janney Battles & E.W. Clark Inc. and predessor films), 1915-43, pres., from 1943; dir. Luth. Brotherhood Life Ins. Pres. bd. publ. of Luth Ch. Am., also mem. bd. common investing fund; trustee Gettysburg Coll. Mem. Assn. Stock Exch. Firms (bd. govs.), Merion Cricket Club, Union League Club, Bond Club (past pres.), Racquet Club, Rittenhouse Club, Seaview Country Club, Rolling Green Golf Club. Republican. *

WILDE, CORNEL LOUIS (BÉLA LOUIS WILDE), actor, producer, director; b. Budapest, Hungary, Oct. 13, 1915; s. Beéla Louis and Renee (Vid) W.; m. Patricia Knight, Sept. 3, 1938 (div. Sept. 1951); 1 child, Wendy; m. Jean Wallace, Sept. 4, 1951 (div. 1980); 1 child, Cornel Jr. Student, Inst. Art, Budapest, Columbia U., 1934-35; BS, CCNY, 1937; student of, Lee Strasberg, Leo Bulgakov, Michael Chekhov. Theatrical appearances include Noon over Mulberry Street, Love Is Not So Simple, Daughters of Atreus, Having Wonderful Time; appeared as Tibault in Romeo and Juliet (with Sir Laurence Olivier and Viven Leigh), staged dueling scenes; motion pictures include High Sierra, 1941, Wintertime, A Song to Remember (Acad. award nomination, 1945), The Perfect Snob, A Thousand and One Nights, Leave Her to Heaven, Bandit of Sherwood Forest, 1946, Centennial Summer, 1946, Forever Amber, 1947, The Home Stretch, 1946, It Had to Be You, 1947, Walls of Jerico Roadhouse, 1948, Four Days Leave, Two Flags West, 1950, Greatest Show on Earth, 1952, At Swords Point, 1952, Saadia, 1953, Passion, 1954, Woman's World, 1954, Big Combo, Scarlet Coat, 1955, Hot Blood, Star of India, Beyond Mombassa, Omar Khayyam, Constantine the Great, The Fifth Musketeer (co-screenwriter 1978); actor, producer, dir. motion pictures including Storm Fear, 1956, Devil's Hairpin (co-author 1957), Maracaibo, 1958, The Sword of Lancelot (screenwriter film festival Gold Prize 1963), The Naked Prey, 1966, Beach Red, 1967, The Norseman; producer, dir., co-screenwriter No Blade of Grass, 1970; producer, dir., writer, actor (motion picture) Sharks' Treasure, 1975, My Very Wilde Life, 1987; illustrator book on fencing; patentee in field. Recipient James K. Hackett award, 1974, Bijou Film Soc. award, 1975; mem. Saber Squad U.S. Olympic Team. Home: Los Angeles Calif. Died Oct. 16, 1989.

WILES, EUGENE F., lawyer; b. Presho, S.D., Dec. 18, 1922. Student, Boise Jr. Coll., U. Idaho; JD, U. San Francisco, 1952. Bar: Oreg. 1952, Alaska 1961, U.S. Dist. Ct. Alaska 1961, U.S. Ct. Appeals (9th cir.) 1961, U.S. Supreme Ct. 1971. Atty. advisor Dept. Interior, Portland, Oreg., 1952-55; field solicitor Dept. Interior, Anchorage, 1956-59, asst. regional solicitor, 1960-61; ptnr. Delaney, Wiles, Hayes, Reitman & Brubaker, Inc., Anchorage, 1961-90; mem. Alaska Jud. Coun., 1972-75. Mem. ABA, Alaska Bar Assn. (gov. 1964-67, 1st v.p. 1965-66, pres 1966-67), Oreg.Bar Assn., Am. Judicature Soc. Home: Anchorage Alaska Died Oct. 19, 1990; buried Ft. Richardson Nat. Cemetery, Anchorage, Alaska.

WILKIE, JOHN, utility executive; b. N.Y.C., Jan. 4, 1904; s. John Lincoln and Edith Blake (Brown) W.; m. Dorothea Woodruff Jones, June 29, 1932 (div.); children—Dorothea Rehn (Mrs. D. Lieber), John McNeil, Peter Lex, Edith Blake Wilkie Edwards; m. Margot Loines Morrow, June 30, 1954; stepchildren—Stephen Morrow, Faith (Mrs. Stephen Williams), Constance (Mrs. Michael Fulenwider). A.B., Harvard U., 1923, M.B.A., 1925; student, Columbia, 1925-26. Dir. Cen. Hudson Gas and Electric Co., Poughkeepsie, N.Y., 1925-87, statistician, 1926, successively, asst. treas., treas., v.p., treas., 1936-60, vice chmn. bd., chief fin. officer, 1960-64, chmn. bd. and chief fin. officer, 1964-68, chmn. bd., chief exec. officer, 1968-75, chmn. fin. com., audit com., 1975-86, vice chmn. exec. com., 1986-87. Sr. mem. Conf. Bd.; past chmn. Hudson River Conservation Soc., Dutchess County War Council; dir. emeritus Regional Plan Assn., N.Y.; trustee emeritus, former chmn. bd. Vassar Coll. Mem. Am. Gas Assn., Edison Electric Inst., Newcomen Soc. Eng., Pilgrims of U.S., Delta Psi. Clubs: Downtown Assn., Harvard, Century Assn. (N.Y.C.); Harvard (Boston); Amrita (Poughkeepsie); Edgartown (Mass.) Yacht. Home: Katonah N.Y. Died Aug. 10, 1991; buried Woodlawn Cemetery, New Windsor, N.Y.

WILKINS, JAMES RAYMOND, insurance consultant; b. Nipawin, Sask., Can., Nov. 27, 1928; s. Walter Earl and Emma Virginia (DeRosier) W.; m. Frances W. Tait, Oct. 6, 1961; children: James Matthew, Mary Ellen. Grad., Ins. Inst. Am., 1952, Ins. Inst. Can., 1958. With Reed Stenhouse Ltd. (and predecessors), 1946-85, sr. ptnr., 1966-85, sr. v.p., regional dir., 1968-76, exec. v.p., 1976-83, pres., 1983-85, also dir.; dir., co-owner Internat. Warranty Co. Ltd.; chmn. bd., dirs. Imperial Lumber Co. Ltd.; pres. Wilkins Investments Ltd., Lazy J. Ranch, Ltd., pres. Davray Devels. Ltd.; sec., dir., past pres. Edmonton Eskimo Football Club; now mem. bd. govs. Past pres. Western Football Conf. Mem. Ins. Brokers Assn. Alta. Provincial Conservative. Roman Catholic. Clubs: Mayfair Golf and Country (Edmonton), Edmonton Centre (Edmonton) (founding); Ironwood Golf and Country (Palm Desert, Calif.). Deceased.

WILKINSON, PETER BARR, advertising agency executive; b. Zurich, Switzerland, May 7, 1924; parents Am. citizens; s. James Richard and Ora Signe (Eimon) W.; m. Nancy Fitts, 1949 (div. 1977); children: Ellen Wilkinson Landau, Thomas Gregg, George Geoffrey; m. Judith Mary Drew, Dec. 3, 1977; stepchildren: Peter Drew, Signe Clare, Warren Hunter, Julia Lee. B.S., Emory U. Bus. Sch., 1948. Salesman, Hughes Tool Co., Wichita Falls, Tex., 1949-50, real estate cos., Atlanta, 1950-52, Pitts. Steel Co., 1952-55; acct. exec. N.W. Ayer & Son, Phila., 1955-64; pres., chief exec. officer P.B. Wilkinson, Inc., Paoli, Pa., Easton, Md., 1964-89. Contbr. mktg. articles to profl. jours. Bd. suprs. Willistown Twp., Pa., 1963-69; chmn. Chester County Devel. Council, Pa., 1973-75; squadron exec. officer CAP, Chester County, 1975-76, Served to lt. USAF, 1944-45. Republican. Unitarian. Mem. Phi Delta Theta. Died 1989. Home: Easton Md.

WILKINSON, WILLIAM SCOTT, lawyer; b. Coushatta, La., Feb. 5, 1895; s. John D. and Alice M. (Scott) W.; m. Margaret West, Apr. 9, 1919; children: Susybelle Wilkinson Lyons, Margaret Wilkinson Wilson. B.A., La. State U., 1915, LL.B., 1917, J.D., 1960. Bar: La. 1917, U.S. Supreme Ct. 1923. Mem. firm Wilkinson & Carmody and predecessor firms, Shreveport, La., 1919-89; spl. asst. atty. gen. State of La., 1955-65; v.p., dir. Hunter Co., Shreveport, 1946-89; dir. La. div. Mid-Continent Oil & Gas Assn.; chmn. emeritus Lee Nat. Life Ins. Co.; lectr. Inst. Mineral Law of La. State U., Tulane U. Chmn. adv. council Shreveport YWCA, 1950-89; chmn. Shreveport Housing Authority, 1940-41; dir. Am. Cancer Soc., N.W. La. div. Arthritis Found., La. State U. Found., Frost Found.; mem. La. Ho. of Reps., 1920-24. Served to capt. arty. USAR, World War I, to col., AUS, World War II. Fellow Am. Coll. Trial Lawyers; mem. Internat. Bar Assn., ABA, La. Bar Assn., Fed. Power Bar Assn., Shreveport Bar Assn., Am. Judicature Soc., La. Law Inst., Blair Soc. Edinburgh, Selden Soc. London, Shreveport C. of C. (pres. 1947-48), Res. Officers Assn., SR, Am. Legion, VFW, Soc. War 1812, Sigma Nu, Omega Delta Kappa. Clubs: Shreveport Country, Demoiselle, Masons, Rotary, Univ. Died 1989.

WILKS, DICK LLOYD, banker; b. Taumarunui, N.Z., May 17, 1923; s. Mathew Harold and Annie Isobel (Parker) W.; student N.Z. schs.; B.A. in Econs., U. N.Z., 1949; m. Josephine Leslie Rantin, Sept. 25, 1934; children: Anne Leslie, Christopher Lloyd, Jeremy John. With Res. Bank N.Z., Wellington, from 1950, dep. sec., dep. chief cashier, chief cashier, exec. adviser, then dep. gov., 1977-82, gov., from 1982. Served with N.Z. Army, 1941-46. Deceased. Home: Wellington New Zealand

WILLCOX, BERTRAM FRANCIS, educator; b. Ithaca, N.Y., July 11, 1895; s. Walter Francis and Alice Elouise (Work) W.; m. Katherine Webster, Sept. 20, 1934; children: David Land, Alice Whitney, Mary MacMillan. Student, Hill Sch., 1909-13; AB, Cornell, 1917; LLB cum laude, Harvard, 1922. Bar: N.Y. 1923. Atty. Hughes Rounds Schurman & Dwight and successor firms, N.Y.C., 1923-28; ptnr. Schurman, Wiley & Willcox and successor firms, 1928-43; assoc. prof. law sch. Cornell, 1946-48, prof., 1948-63, McRoberts prof., adminstrn. of law, 1954-63, emeritus, from 1963; vis. prof. Indian Law Inst., from 1963; mem. faculty N.Y. State Sch. Indsl. & Labor Rels., Cornell; a pub. mem. appeals com. NAt. War Labor Bd., Washington, 1944-

45; per diem trial examiner for N.T. State Labor Rels. Bd., 1940-43; labor arbitrator, from 1946. Author: (with prof. Arthur E. Sutherland) Case Book on Commercial Transactions, 1951; contbr. articles in field of labor law to profl. jours. Mem. bd. editors labor law teaching materials; mem. labor law round table of Assn. Am. Law Schs., 1947-50, chmn., 1949; mem. bd. editors Indsl. and Labor Rels. Review, 1947-50, 53-56. Sec. Am. Commn. to Negotiate Peace, 1918-19. Am. field svc., France, 1917, capt. ARC, France, 1917-18, aspirant 18th Regt. French Fiedl Arty., 1918. Fulbright grantee rsch. labor rels. in nationalized gas industry London Sch. Econs., 1952; Adolf Meyer and Henry Wisner Miller awards, 1963. Mem. N.Y. State Bar Assn., N.Y.C. Bar Assn., Tompkins County Bar Assn., Lawyers Guild, Psu Upsilon, Century City Assn. (N.Y.C.). *

WILLENS, RITA JACOBS, broadcasting executive; b. Chgo., June 13, 1927; d. Bernard M. and Ruth L. (Kaplan) Smith; m. Bernard Jacobs, June 25, 1950 (dec. 1975); m. David L. Willens, July 17, 1966 (dec. 1986); children: Noah Ben Jacobs-Willens, Daniel, Deborah Riley, Carolyn Willens. B.A., Roosevelt U., Chgo., 1948. Co-founder Fine Arts Sta. WFMT, Chgo., 1951, v.p., 1951-68; editor, assoc. pub. sta. mag. Perspective on Ideas and the Arts, 1961-64; cons. fine arts broadcasting, 1968-90; pres./producer Gamut Prodns., Inc. and Living Archives Ltd., Barrington, Ill., 1974-90; producer/host weekly program Saturday Night Midnight Spl., WFMT, 1972-82; media adviser NEH. Mem. selection com. 4th Ann. Gov.'s Awards for Arts in Ill., 1981-82. Co-recipient Friends of Lit. award, 1953, George Foster Peabody award, 1961, Alfred I. duPont award, 1957, 60, Ohio State U. award, 1959, Thomas Alva Edison award, 1959; recipient Ohio State U. and 1st place Maj. Armstrong award for Gamut: The Great Idea of Man, 1975 and The Follies of '52 or Were Those Really the Days, 1977; Maj. Armstrong award, Gabriel award, Ohio State U. award for Rozhinkes mit Mandlin documentary, 1979, The Edward J. Sparling Alumni award Roosevelt U., 1988. Mem. Art Inst. Chgo., Smithsonian Instn. (com. on French Revolution), Roosevelt U. Alumni Assn. (bd. govs.). Clubs: Hadassah, ORT, B'nai B'rith, Chicago Press. Home: Barrington Ill. Died June 9, 1990; buried Westlawn Cemetery, Chgo.

WILLENSKY, ELLIOT, architect; b. Bklyn., July 11, 1933; s. Morris and Fannie (Eisenstein) W.; (div.); children: Marc Isaac, Diana Gwen. Cert. Architecture, Cooper Union, 1953; MArch, Yale U., 1955. Assoc. prof., dir. N.Y.C. program Cornell U., 1963-68; dep. adminstr. N.Y.C. Parks Recreation and Cultural Affairs Adminstrn., 1968-70; dir. High Rock Park Environ. Ctr., S.I., N.Y., 1971-76; cons. architect Elliot Willensky Architect, N.Y.C., 1976-90; adj. prof. architecture Columbia U., 1981-83; vice chmn. N.Y.C. Landmarks Preservation Commn., 1984-90, commr. 1979-90. Author: When Brooklyn Was the World, 1920-57, 1986; co-author: (with Norval White) AIA Guide to New York City, 1968, rev. 1978, 88; contbr. articles to profl. jours. Historian, Borough of Bklyn., N.Y.C., 1979-90. Recipient Awards of Merit, Mcpl. Art Soc. N.Y., 1968, 76, 78; Internat. Coun. Mus. fellow. Fellow AIA; mem. Soc. Arch. Historians, Soc. Indsl. Archeology, Frederick Law Olmsted Assn., Urban History Assn. Home: Brooklyn N.Y. Died May 26, 1990.

WILLHELM, DONALD S., energy company executive; b. Houston, July 4, 1927; s. William L. and Lucille T. (Dyar) W.; m. Nell Boyd, Mar. 2, 1951; children: James, Beth, Amy. B.S.M.E., U. Houston, 1950. Registered profl. engr., Tex. Engring. design and constrn. staff Transcontinental Gas Pipe Line Corp., Houston, 1950-56; supt. plant constrn. Transcontinental Gas Pipe Line Corp., 1956-60, various positions in engring. and operating depts., 1960-66, v.p. ops. and engring., 1966-69, sr. v.p. energy projects, 1969-89; pres. Transco Energy Co., Houston, 1971-82, Transco Devel. Co., Houston, 1982-87; ret., 1987; Mem. industry tech. adv. com. Gas Research Inst., 1976-89; bd. dirs. Dixie Pipeline Co., GDC, Inc., Western Bank-Westheimer, Kaneb Services, Inc., Immudyne, Inc., chmn. Bd. dirs. Juvenile Diabetes Found. Mem. NLPGA. Republican. Clubs: University (bd. govs. 1985-89), Lakeside Country, Houston (membership com. 1985), Petroleum. Home: Houston Tex. Died May 31, 1989.

WILLIAMS, ALBERT J., JR., engineering consultant; b. Media, Pa., Feb. 28, 1903; s. Albert J. and Rose (Cleeland) W.; A.B. in Elec. Engring., Swarthmore Coll., 1924; postgrad. U. Pa., evenings 1927-30, U. Calif. at Los Angeles, 1963; m. Phyllis Helen Zinke, Dec. 20, 1937; children: Albert J. III, Robert Ernest. Transformer engr. Bell Telephone Labs., N.Y.C., 1924-27; test engr. Leeds & Northrup Co., Phila., 1927-29, research engr., 1929-34, chief, elec. div. research dept., 1934-51, asso. dir. research, R&D dept., 1951-55, sci. adviser R&D dept., North Wales, Pa., 1955-67, sci. adviser corp. research dept., 1967-68, mem. devel. adv. com. co., 1959-68. Registered profl. engr., Pa. Fellow IEEE (recipient Morris E. Leeds award 1968), Franklin Inst. (Wetherill medal 1952), ASME (Rufus Oldenburger medal 1972); mem. Am. Phys. Soc., AAAS, Sigma Xi. Clubs: Old York Road Country (Spring House, Pa.); One Club Golf Association (Washington). Patentee in field. Contbr. articles to profl. jours. Died 1980. Home: Falmouth Mass.

WILLIAMS, ARNOLD K., education supervisor; b. Chgo., Feb. 19, 1928; s. George B. and Leola A. (Sunday) W.; m. Amy C., Aug. 26, 1950; 1 child, Patricia E. BS, U. Ill., Urbana, 1949, MS, 1950. Cert. tchr. (life), music edn. Dir. instrumental music Gary (Ind.) Community Schs., gen. supr. Pres. Greater Gary Arts Coun.; minister of music St. Timothy Community Ch. Master sgt. US Army, 1950-52. Recipient Black Music Caucus Distinguished Svc. award, Post Tribune Community Svc. in Arts award. Mem. Gary Schs. Adminstrn. Assn. (past pres.), Multi Cultural Awareness (past chmn.), Ind. Music Edn. Assn., MENC, ASCD, Phi Delta Kappa (svc. award),. Home: Gary Ind.

WILLIAMS, ARTHUR, engineering consultant; b. Swindon, Eng., July 29, 1904; came to U.S., 1926, naturalized, 1942; s. Joseph and Emily (Chirgwin) W.; m. Ellen M.I. Cullingford, Apr. 8, 1929; children: Valerie (Mrs. Robert C. Norcross), Brian R. Student, Swindon Coll. Engring. Sch., 1921-26, Harvard U. Bus. Sch., 1955. Chief engr. Superheater Co., East Chicago, Ind., 1927-42, v.p., 1946; v.p. Combustion Engring., Inc., 1949-58; v.p., sec. Submerged Combustion, Inc., 1958-65; cons. Selas Corp. Am., 1965-66; cons. engr., from 1966. Episcopalian. Home: Asheville N.C. Died.

WILLIAMS, BRIAN DAVID, lawyer; b. Indpls., Jan. 5, 1960; s. Carl Edward and Marilyn Sue (Kelly) W.; m. Kelly Anne Baker, Apr. 26, 1986 (div. Oct. 1988); 1 child, Zachary Michael. BS cum laude, Butler U., 1982; JD, Ind. U., Indpls., 1985. Bar: Ind. 1986, Fla. 1986, U.S. Dist. Ct. (no. and so. dists.) Ind. 1986, U.S. Ct. Appeals (7th cir. ct.) 1986. Assoc. Coons, Saint & Bishop, Indpls., from 1985; ptnr. Williams & Jacobs, Indpls., from 1988; v.p., bd. dirs. Old Northside, Inc., Indpls., from 1987. Mem. ABA, Ind. State Bar Assn., Indpls. Bar Assn., Assn. Trial Lawyers Am., Columbia Club. Republican. Presbyterian. Home: Indianapolis Ind. Died.

WILLIAMS, CARROLL MILTON, biology educator; b. Richmond, Va., Dec. 2, 1916; s. George Leslie and Jessie Ann (Hendricks) W.; m. Muriel Anne Voter, June 26, 1941; children: John Leslie (dec.), Wesley Conant, Peter Glenn (dec.), Roger Lee. S.B., U. Richmond, 1937, D.Sc. (hon.), 1960; A.M., Harvard U., 1938, Ph.D., 1941, M.D. summa cum laude, 1946. Asst. prof. Harvard U., 1946-48, assoc. prof. zoology, 1948-53, prof., 1953-66, Benjamin Bussey prof. biology, 1966-87, Bussey prof. emeritus, 1987-91, chmn. dept. biology, 1959-62; chief scientist phase C of Alpha Helix Expdn. to Upper Amazon, 1967. Trustee Radcliffe Coll., Boston Mus. of Sci., 1989-91. Recipient Newcomb Cleveland prize AAAS, 1950, Boylston prize and medal Harvard Med. Sch., 1961, George Ledlie prize Harvard U., 1967, Howard Taylor Ricketts award U. Chgo., 1969; Guggenheim fellow, 1955-56. Fellow AAAS (coun. 1952-54), Am. Acad. Arts and Scis. (coun. 1954-57, 73-77), Entomol. Soc. Am.; mem. Nat. Acad. Sci. (chmn. sect. zoology 1970-73, coun. 1973-76, 85-88, chmn. biol. sci. 1982-85), Inst. Medicine, Am. Soc. Zoologists, Am. PHysiol. Soc., Am. Philos. Soc., Soc. Devel. Biology, Harvey Soc., Lepidopterists Soc., Sigmet Soc., Cambridge Entomol. Club (pres. 1987-91), Examiner Club (v.p. 1986-91), Phi Beta Kappa, Sigma Xi. Home: Lexington Mass. Died Oct. 11, 1991; cremated.

WILLIAMS, CLYDE ELMER, industrial advisor; b. Salt Lake City, Sept. 8, 1893; s. Thomas J. and Ellen (Eoeles) W.; m. Martha Barlow, 1919; children: Clyde E., Samuel B., Thomas J. BS, U. Utah, 1915, DS, 1946; DS, Case Inst. Tech., 1945, Ohio State U., 1951; ED, Mich. Coll. Mining and Tech., 1949; LLD, Marietta Coll., 1955. Chemist U.S. Smelting Co., 1915-16; grad. fellow U. Utah, U.S. Bur. Mines, 1916; chemist Santa De Copper Co., 1916-17, U.S. Bur. Mines, Cornell U., 1917-18; rsch. chemist Hooker Electro-Chem. Co., Niagara Falls, N.Y., 1918-20; supt. N.W. Expt. Sta U.S. Bur. Mines, 1920-24; metallurgist Govt. Arentine on commn. to study iron, steel, fuel resources of Argenitna, 1924-25; chief metallurgist Columbia Steel Corp., San Francisco, 1925-29; asst. dir. Battelle Meml. Inst., Columbus, Ohio, 1929-34; dir. Battelle Meml. Inst., 1934-57, trustee, 1951-59, pres., 1953-58; pres. Clyde Williams and Co., from 1958, Clyde Williams Investment Mgmt. Co.; chmn. Techno Fund, Inc.; chmn., pres. CLyde Williams Corp., from 1951; v.p., dir. Borne Chem. Co., 1957-61; dir. The CLaycraft Co., F.W. Bell Inc. Mem. adv. groups, commns., bds. govtl. and pvt. orgns. normally in metall. fields; mem. adv. com. A.E.C.; mem. com. on. aircraft constrn. N.A.C.A. Recipient Presdl. Citation medal for Merit. CLubs: Rsch. Dirs., Rotary, Engrs., Mining, Cosmos, Faculty, Sicotto, Columbus (Ohio). Republican. *

WILLIAMS, DAVID LEE, financial executive, marine transportation company executive; b. Logansport, Ind., Oct. 16, 1947; s. L. Paul and Eva Marie (Richards) W. BA, Manchester Coll., Ind., 1968; MBA, Vanderbilt U., 1982. Staff acct. Ernst & Whinney, Indpls., 1968-69; dir. operational acctg. Genesco, Inc., Nashville, 1969-78; pres. Ingram Book Co., Nashville, 1978-83; sr. v.p. fin. and adminstrn. Ingram Barge Co., Nashville, from 1983; instr. Belmont Coll., Nashville, 1970-71, U. Tenn. Nashville, 1971-74, Tenn. Soc. CPAs, 1983-84; adj. lectr. Vanderbilt U., Nashville, 1983-85. Treas. Nashville City Ballet, 1985. Served to sgt. 1st class U.S. Army, 1969-74. Mem. Fin. Execs. Inst. (bd. dirs., treas. 1986), Am. Inst. CPAs, Inst. Mgmt. Acctg. (cert.). Republican. Roman Catholic. Died. Home: Nashville Tenn.

WILLIAMS, ERNEST Y., neurologist, psychiatrist, educator; b. Nevis, British West Indies; m. Matilda Herbert; children: Shirley, Joan Thomas, Ernest Y. Jr. Grad., Howard U. Med. Sch. Intern in neurology and psychiatry Bellevue and Columbia Presbyn. Hosps., Manhattan, 1930-34; mem. faculty Howard Med. Sch., 1934-80, founder dept. psychiatry and neurology, 1940, chmn. dept. psychiatry and neurology, 1940-70; pvt. practice, until 1985. Author 2 books in field; contbr. over 300 articles to profl. jours. Home: Washington D.C. Died Feb. 12, 1990.

WILLIAMS, FRANKLIN HALL, foundation executive, lawyer, ambassador; b. Flushing, N.Y., Oct. 22, 1917; s. Arthur Lee and Alinda (Lowry) W.; m. Shirley Broyard, May 27, 1944; children: Franklin Hall Jr., Paul Anatole. AB, Lincoln U., Pa., 1941; JD, Fordham U., 1945. Bar: N.Y. 1945, Calif. 1951, U.S. Supreme Ct. Asst. spl. counsel nat. office NAACP, 1945-50, West Coast regional dir., 1950-59; dir. univ., pvt. and internat. orgn. div. Peace Corps, 1961-62, dir. African Regional Office, 1963; U.S. rep. ECOSOC of UN, 1964-65; U.S. amb. to Ghana, 1965-68; dir. Urban Ctr., Columbia U., N.Y.C., 1968-70; pres. Phelps-Stokes Fund, N.Y.C., 1970-90; bd. dirs. Chem. Bank, N.Y.C., U.R.S. Inc., Consol. Edison, Inc., Borden, Inc., Am. Stock Exch. Chmn. N.Y. State adv. com. to U.S. Civil Rights Commn.; bd. dirs. Spencer Found.., ACLU, N.Y.C. Opera, Coun. Fgn. Rels., Nat. Newspaper Coun., Resources for Future; chmn. bd. trustees Barnes Found., Lincoln U.; chmn. N.Y. State Jud. Commn. on Minorities, 1987. Mem. Fordham U. Alumni Assn., Century Assn. Home: New York N.Y. Died May 20, 1990; buried N.Y.C.

WILLIAMS, GLENN CARBER, chemical engineer, educator; b. Princeton, Iowa, Oct. 9, 1914; s. H. Lurie and Jessie Elizabeth (Hire) W.; m. Dorothy Cleo Bryan, Aug. 27, 1939; children: Glenn Lurie, Cheryl. BS, U. Ill., 1937, MS, 1938; ScD, MIT, 1942. Rsch. engr., engring. expt. sta. U. Ill., 1937-38; asst. MIT, 1938-40, from instr. to assoc. prof., 1940-54, prof., from 1954; pres., dir. Combustion Inst., Nat. Def. Rsch. Com., 1942-45; mem. sub-com. on combustion NACA, 1946-59, com. on chem. energy conversion, 1960-63; mem. panel on heat div. Nat. Bur. Standards, 1959-63; panel on propulsion NRC, 1949-50; adv. com. Army Ordnance Rsch. and Devel.; mem. com. on motor vehicle emissions NAS, 1971-74. Author: (with H. C. Hottel, C. N. Satterfield) Thermodynamics of Combustion Processes, 1949. Recipient Naval Ordnance Devel. Award. Mem. AICE, Am. Chem. Soc., Combustion Inst. (pres., Egerton medal 1980), Inst. Aero Scis., Am. Acad. Arts and Scis., Sigma Xi, Alpha Chi Sigma, Omega Chi Epsilon, Kappa Kappa Sigma, Delta Sigma Phi, Tau Beta Pi. Unitarian. Home: Lexington Mass. Died July 2, 1991.

WILLIAMS, HAROLD MCNEAL, psychiatrist; b. Trenton, N.J., Feb. 21, 1932; s. McNeal and Elizabeth (Carroll) W.; BS in Chemistry, Howard U., 1954, M.D., 1958; m. Beverly Arlene Eason, Sept. 19, 1959; children: Harold Michael, Steven Craig, Timothy Martin, Robert Matthew, Elizabeth Carroll Ann. Intern, Northwestern Hosp., Mpls., 1958-59; resident psychiatry N.J. State Hosp., Trenton, 1959-62; organizer, a developer Fresno (Calif.) County Dept. Mental Health, from 1964; with Fresno County Gen. Hosp., from 1964; chief psychiatry Fresno County Dept. Mental Health, 1964-65, program chief, 1964-65, acting dir., 1966-67, chief outpatient psychiat. services, from 1967; pvt. practice medicine specializing in psychiatry, Fresno, from 1969; mem. staffs Fresno Community Hosp., Valley Med. Center, Fresno. Acting mil. cons. psychiatry March AFB, 1963-64; cons. psychiatry VA Hosp., Fresno, from 1969, Westview Convalescent Hosp., Fresno, from 1969; vis. lectr. Grad. Sch. Social Work Fresno State Coll., 1965-68. Mem. interfaith adv. coun. Fresno Community Hosp., from 1965; mem. profl. adv. com. Fresno County Mental Health Assn., 1965-66; mem. adv. bd. KJEO TV, from 1969; v.p. Profl. Svcs. Exchange Corp., from 1980. Bd. dirs. Goodwill Industries San Joaquin Valley, adv. com., Fresno, 1970-78; bd. dirs. Family Svc. Ctr. Fresno, Ctrl. Calif. Blood Bank, from 1981; trustee Fresno Found. Med. Care, from 1977, Ctrl. Calif. Health Systems Agy., 1977-78; exec. bd. Bullard High Sch. PTA, from 1977. Served to capt. M.C., USAF, 1962-64. Recipient Outstanding Achievement award in psychiatry Howard U. Med. Coll., 1958. Fellow AAAS, Acad. Psychosomatic Medicine; mem. Am. Psychiat. Assn., Ctrl.Calif. Psychiat. Soc., AMA, Calif. (alt. del. ann. conv. 1979-80, del. 1980-82, 82-84), Nat. med. assns., N.Y. Acad. Scis., Am. Geriatrics Soc., Fresno Madera Med. Soc. (gov. 1975-77, pres. 1979), Golden State Med. Assn., Calif. Psychiat. Assn., Kappa Alpha Psi, Beta Kappa Chi. Methodist. Died. Home: Fresno Calif.

WILLIAMS, HERBERT HOOVER, social worker; b. Detroit, July 20, 1929; s. Mervin Boyd and Mabel Vane (Beelman) W.; m. Shirley Loraine Bruns Hayes, Aug.

20, 1950 (div. Sept. 1963); children: Deborah Johnson, George Hayes, Dennis Hayes; m. Grace Elaine Kibler, Dec. 21, 1980; children: Debra Boehm, Larry Litke. BS, Manchester Coll., 1953; MDiv, Bethany Sem., 1956; MSW, U. Ill., 1962. Lic. ind. social worker, Ohio, diplomate clin. social work. Chief social services Ill. Youth Commn., Geneva, Ill., 1962-64; dir. social services Masonic Med. Ctr., Chgo., 1964-74; cons. numerous agencies, Chgo., 1974-77; exec. dir. Uptown Chgo. Commn., Chgo., 1977-80; pvt. practice Austinburg, Ohio, 1980-82; exec. dir. Ashtabula (Ohio) County Family Services Agy., 1982-86; pvt. practice Ashtabula Counseling Services, Austinburg, 1986-90. Chmn. bd. Old Town Players, Chgo., 1964-73, Greene Sr. Ctr., Chgo., 1966-67; pres. Jane Addams Sch. Social Work Alumni Assn., Chgo., 1966-68, Winona-Foster-Carmen-Winnemac Block Club, Chgo., 1975-76; bd. dirs. Metro-Help, Inc., Chgo., 1974-78. Mem. Nat. Assn. Social Workers, Acad. Cert. Social Workers. Democrat. Mem. Ch. of the Brethren. Lodges: Kiwanis (pres. North Shore, Chgo., 1979-80, Ashtabula, 1985-86). Home: Austinburg Ohio. Died Oct., 1990.

WILLIAMS, JOHN CARL, educator, researcher; b. Sedalia, Mo., Feb. 19, 1952; s. Frank and Kathleen W. BA, Columbia (Mo.) Coll., 1979; MEd, U. Mo., 1981, EdS, 1984; postgrad. N.E. Mo. State U., Cen. Mo. State U., U. Ariz., U. Mo.-Columbia, U. Mo.-St. Louis, Nova U., Goddard Coll., U. Fla.-Gainesville. Elem. tchr. Jamestown (Mo.) Pub. Schs., 1979-80; tchr. California (Mo.) Pub. Schs., 1980-84, elem. curriculum coordinator, 1982-84; instr. Math, faculty officer Admiral Farragut Acad., St. Petersburg, Fla., 1985-91, chmn. maths. dept., 1989-91, dir. Lower Sch. Studies, 1987-89; dir. lower mid. sch., 1989-90, head lower and middle schs., 1990-91; with Gansert, Inc., Madiera Beach, Fla., from 1985; cons. Statewide Testing and Evaluation Service, 1984-85. Mem. Assn. Supervision and Curriculum Devel., Mo. State Tchrs. Assn., NEA, Mo. NEA, Optimists, Masons, Order Ea. Star, Pi Lambda Theta, Phi Delta Kappa. Contbr. articles to profl. jours. Died. Home: Pinellas Park Fla.

WILLIAMS, JOHN WOODBRIDGE, lighting designer, educator; b. Kansas City, Mo., Apr. 16, 1950; s. Robert Keck and Betty May (Smith) W.; m. Diane Louise Ferry, Aug. 17, 1985. BS, Northwestern U., 1972, MFA, 1974. Asst. prof. Northwestern U., Evanston, Ill., 1974-80, assoc. prof. lighting design, 1980-92; dir. theater Nat. High Sch. Inst., Evanston, 1976-82; resident designer WAA-MU Show, Evanston, 1979-86, Summer Drama Festival, Evanston, 1980-86, Mariott Theatre, Lincolnshire, Ill., 1985-88. Deacon St. Thomas A. Becket Episc. Ch., Evanston, from 1989; mem. leadership coun. Evanston Episc. Parishes, 1989. Mem. United Scenic Artists Am. (bd. dirs. 1980-82), US Inst. Theatre Tech. (bd. dirs. 1986-89, exhbn. selection 1986, 88, commr. 1987-90), N.Am. Assn. Diaconate. Home: Evanston Ill. Died Oct. 12, 1992. †

WILLIAMS, JUANITA HINGST, clinical psychologist, educator; b. Jackson, Miss., Dec. 17, 1922; d. Henry Christian and Anna (Bryant) Hingst; m. James Brooks Williams, Aug. 29, 1942; children: Karen, Anita, Gretchen, Laura. BA, Rutgers U., 1957; MA, Temple U., 1959, PhD, 1963. Lic. psychologist, Fla. Psychologist VA, Bay Pines, Fla., 1963-64; asst. prof. U. South Fla., Tampa, 1966-70, assoc. prof., 1970-77, prof., 1977-85, emeritus prof., from 1985. Author: (book) Psychology of Women, 1977, 3d edit., 1987; contbr. articles to profl. jours. Mem. NOW, 1987—. Recipient Award of Distinction Athena, 1982, Woman of Distinction Soroptomist, 1987. Fellow Am. Psychol. Assn. Democrat. Home: Tampa Fla.

WILLIAMS, KENNETH RAYNOR, university president; b. Norfolk, Va., Aug. 16, 1912; s. Kenneth Raynor and Vandelia (Perry) W.; m. Edythe Williams, June 7, 1938; children—Kenneth Raynor III, Ronald, Norman. A.B., Morehouse Coll., 1933; D.H.L.; M.A., Boston U., 1936, S.T.B., 1952, Ph.D., 1962; LL.D. (hon.), Wake Forest Coll., 1963; LL.D., So. Ill. U. Ordained to ministry Baptist Ch., 1936; pastor Winston-Salem, N.C., 1936-64; instr. history and religion Winston-Salem State U., 1936-61, pres., 1961-89, chancellor, 1972-77. Former mem. bd. Citizens Coalition; mem. Winston-Salem Bd. Aldermen.; Bd. dirs. Forsyth County A.R.C. Served as chaplain AUS, 1942-46. Mem. Am. Assn. Colls. Tchr. Edn. (rep. 1964-66, dir.), Nat. Council for Tchr. Edn. (dir. 1968—), Winston-Salem C. of C. (dir.). Club: Rotarian. Home: Winston-Salem N.C. Died Dec. 31, 1989; buried Evergreen Cemetery, Winston-Salem, Mass.

WILLIAMS, MALCOLM DEMOSTHENES, educator; b. Warsaw, N.C., Sept. 26, 1909; s. Holly and Martha Eliza (Williams) W.; m. Rosa Lee Kittrell, 1 child, Frances E. Diploma, Fayetteville State Tchrs Coll., 1933; BS with honors, Hampton Inst., 1938; MA, Columbia Tchrs. Coll., 1944, EdD, 1951. Tchr., prin., supr. pub. schs. N.C., 1928-52; dir. audio-visual aids Shaw U., 1952-55; faculty Tenn. State U., Nashville, 1955-75; dean edn. Tex. So. U., 1954-55, dean emeritus, 1975-91; tchr. Hampton Inst., summer, 1949, Tex. So. U., 1954-55. Bd. dirs. Louisville Presbyn. Theol. Sem.; mem. of U.S.A. and U.S. Chs. Unification Com. of 32; pres. Frontiers Internat., Inc. Recipient Silver Beaver award Boy Scouts Am. Mem. Nat. Soc. Study Edn., NEA, Phi Delta Kappa, Kappa Delta Pi. Home: Nashville Tenn. Died Nov. 8, 1991.

WILLIAMS, MARTIN TUDOR, editor, music critic, author; b. Richmond, Va., Aug. 9, 1924; s. John Bell and Rebecca (Yancey) W.; children from former marriage: Charles, Frederick, Frank. BA, U. Va., 1948; MA, U. Pa., 1950; postgrad., Columbia U. Lectr., instr. Columbia U., N.Y.C., 1952-56; editor Macmillan Co., N.Y.C., 1955; free-lance writer N.Y.C., 1956-71; editor Americana, N.Y.C., 1959-60; dir. jazz program Smithsonian Instn., Washington, 1971-81; co-editor Smithsonian Collection Newspaper Comics, Smithsonian Books of Comic Book Comics, then editor Smithsonian Instn. Press, Washington, 1971-91; former jazz critic Saturday Rev., Evergreen Rev., N.Y. Times, Down Beat; lectr. numerous ednl. instns. Author: The Jazz Tradition, 1970-83, Jazz Heritage, 1985, Jazz in Its Time, 1989, Jazz Changes, 1991, other Jazz titles; Griffith: First Artist of the Movies, TV: The Casual Art; author articles on children's lit. and films. Recipient Deems Taylor award in music criticism ASCAP, 1971, 86; Guggenheim Found. fellow, 1978. Home: Washington D.C. Died, 1992.

WILLIAMS, RICHARD EATON, lawyer; b. Worcester, Mass., Nov. 19, 1930; s. Charles Frederick and Alice Marian (Eaton) W.; m. Karla Donna Lothrop (div. Dec. 1981); children: Kelly Jean, Lael Marian; m. Geraldine Ruth Edwards. AB, Syracuse U., 1952; LLB, Boston U., 1957. Bar: Wash. 1957, Mass. 1984, U.S. Ct. Appeals (9th cir.), U.S. Dist. Ct. (we. dist.) Wash., U.S. Dist. Ct. Mass. From assoc. to ptnr. Perkins Coie, Seattle, from 1957. Sr. editor Boston U. Law Rev., 1953. Served to lt. USNR. Mem. ABA, Wash. State Bar Assn., Seattle-King County Bar Assn., Mass. Bar Assn., Boston Bar Assn., Ranier Club (Seattle). Republican. Home: Seattle Wash. Deceased.

WILLIAMS, RICHARD LIPPINCOTT, writer, editor; b. Seattle, Nov. 28, 1910; s. Charles Richard and Dolly DeMaris (White) W.; m. Dorothy Mahone (dec. 1957); children: Diane Louise, Julie Demaris; m. Maria Teresa McGee; children: Richard, David, Robert, Mary, Virginia. B.A., U. Wash., 1933. With Seattle Times, 1933-41, Wash. State Def. Council, 1941-44, Boeing Aircraft Co., 1944-45; corr., writer Time, Inc., 1945-52; editor Dell Pub. Co., 1953-60; series editor Time-Life Books, Foods of the World, Life Library of Photography, others, 1962-73; freelance editor, 1973-75; bd. editors Smithsonian mag., from 1975. Author: The Loggers, The Northwest Coast, The Cascades. Mem. Time-Life Alumni Assn., Alpha Delta Sigma, Sigma Delta Chi, Tau Kappa Epsilon. Club: Overseas Press (N.Y.C.). Home: Saint Petersburg Fla. Died Nov. 5, 1989; buried Seattle.

WILLIAMS, ROBERT HOPE, JR., lawyer; b. Balt., June 28, 1910; s. Robert Hope and Jennie (Homan) W.; m. Louise Winslow, April 15, 1950. Student, Johns Hopkins, 1929-31, St. John's Coll., Annapolis, Md., 1932-33; LL.B., U. Md., 1937. Bar: Md. 1938, U.S. Dist. Ct. Md., U.S. Ct. Appeals (4th cir.). Practiced law, 1938-39, admiralty practice, 1939-41, 46-57; ptnr. Niles, Barton, Yost & Dankmeyer, Balt., 1957-61, Niles, Barton, Gans & Markell, Balt., 1961-67, Niles, Barton & Wilmer, Balt., 1968-91. Served to maj. JAG Dept. AUS, 1941-46. Mem. Barristers' Club Balt. (pres. 1967), Am., Md. bar assns., Maritime Law Assn. U.S., Bar Assn. Balt. City, Judge Advs. Assn., Am. Judicature Soc., Md. Hist. Soc., Star-Spangled Banner Flag House Assn., Balt. Mus. Art, Newcomen Soc. N.Am., So. Md. Soc., Walters Art Gallery, U. Md. Law Sch. Alumni Assn., Johns Hopkins Alumni Assn., Sigma Alpha Epsilon (alumni pres. 1953). Democrat. Episcopalian. Clubs: Rotarian. (Balt.), Maryland; Johns Hopkins (Balt. and N.Y.C.); St. John's Coll. Alumni (Annapolis, Md.). Home: Baltimore Md. Died Dec. 5, 1991.

WILLIAMS, SAMUEL RILEY, industrial executive; b. Francisville, La., Oct. 9, 1895; s. Harrison M. and Lintot (IHarolsen) W.; m. Andree Vignant, Aug. 2, 1919; children: Jack Riley, Gerard Harolson. BS, La. State U., 1916. With Worthington Pump Corp., from 1920; begining as mgr., dir. Bombas Worthington S.A., Madrid, Spain; successively gen. European mgr. Madrid; asst. v.p. ops. Harrison, N.J., 1920-46; exec. v.p. fgn. bus., from 1946; v.p., cons. internat. ops. Worthington Corp.; dir. Andersen, Meyer & Co., Ltd., Bombas Construs., Worthington S.A., Spain, Le Bourget, France, Mexico, Nigata Worthington, Japan, Societa Iraliana Pompe Compressori, Milan, Italy, Worthington Simpson, Ltd., England; pres. Worthington (Can.) Ltd., Toronto, 1955. 1st lt. U.S. Army, WWI. Mem. N.A.M., Nat. Fgn. Trade Coun., Am. Mgmt. Assn., Baltursol Golf Club, Essex Club (Newark). *

WILLIAMS, THOMAS (ALONZO), author, educator; b. Duluth, Minn., Nov. 15, 1926; s. Thomas Alonzo and Charlotte Clara (Marvin) W.; m. Elizabeth Mae Blood, May 26, 1951; children—Peter Alonzo, Ann Joslin. Student, U. Chgo., 1945, 48-49; B.A., U. N.H., 1950, M.A., 1958; postgrad, U. Paris, 1950-51, U. Ia., 1956-58. Prof. English U. N.H., Durham, 1958-90. Author: (novels) Ceremony of Love, 1955, Town Burning, 1959, The Night of Trees, 1961, Whipple's Castle, 1969, The Hair of Harold Roux, 1974 (Nat. Book award), Tsuga's Children, 1977, The Followed Man, 1978, The Moon Pinnace, 1986, (short stories) A High New House, Leah, 1992. Served to cpl. U.S. Army, 1944-46. Guggenheim fellow, 1963; Dial fellow Fiction, 1963; recipient Roos/Atkins Literary award, 1963, Rockefeller grantee Fiction, 1969. Mem. Authors Guild, AAUP. Democrat. Home: Durham N.H. Died Oct. 23, 1990; cremated.

WILLIAMS, WILLIAM APPLEMAN, history educator; b. Atlantic, Iowa, June 12, 1921; s. William Carleton and Mildrede (Appleman) W.; m. Wendy Williams; children: Ward, Kyenne, Savoy Jade. BS, U.S. Naval Acad., 1944; postgrad., U. Leeds, Eng., 1948; MA, U. Wis., 1948, PhD, 1950. Commd. ensign USN, 1944; resigned, 1947; mem. faculty, prof. history U. Wis., Madison, 1957-68; prof. Oreg. State U., Corvallis, 1968-86, prof. emeritus, 1986-90; Fulbright scholar U. Melbourne, Australia, 1977; James Pinckney Harrison prof. Coll. William and Mary, 1980; instr. maritime history Oreg. Coast Community Coll., 1989. Author: American-Russian Relations, 1784-1947, 1950, The Shaping of American Diplomacy, 1763-1970, 1956, The Tragedy of American Diplomacy, 1960, The Contours of American History, 1961, The United States, Cuba and Castro, 1962, The Great Evasion, 1964, The Roots of the Modern American Empire, 1969, Some Presidents: From Wilson to Nixon, 1972, History As A Way of Learning, 1975, American Confronts a Revolutionary World: 1776-1976, 1976, Americans in a Changing World, 1978, Empire as a Way of Life, 1980, also articles to mags. and newspapers. Active civil rights movement, 1946-47. Mem. Orgn. Am. Historians (pres. 1980-81). Home: Waldport Oreg. Died Mar. 5, 1990.

WILLIAMS, WILLIAM THOMAS, JR., city manager; b. Angleton, Tex., June 3, 1908; s. William Thomas and Nannie (Borum) W.; m. Valerie Clotilde Mansbendel, Feb. 14, 1933 (dec.); children: William Thomas III, Valerie Clotilde (Mrs. Sidney C. Brown); m. Helen Steck Malone, Jan. 1, 1977. Student, Univ. Afloat, 1926-27; LLB, U. Tex., 1930. Bar: Tex. 1930. Practiced in Austin, 1930-40, asst. city atty., 1940-42, 46-47, 1949-51; city atty., 1951-55; tax assessor-collector Austin, 1947-49, city mgr., 1955-67; exec. v.p. Walter Carrington Enterprises, 1967-69; v.p. Nash Phillips-Copus Co., 1969-81. Pres. McCallum High School PTA, 1956-57; pres. Laguna Gloria Art. Mus.; bd. dirs. Tex. Fine Arts Assn.; former mem. dist. bd. dirs. Am. Cancer Soc.; bd. advisors Fine Arts Assn. Served to capt. AUS, 1942-46, ETO; col. Res. ret. Decorated Bronze Star Medal. Mem. Austin C. of C. (dir. 1971-74), Tex. Bar Assn. (life), Res. Officers Assn. (pres. Austin 1946-47), Assn. U.S. Army, Ret. Officers Assn., Delta Theta Phi. Episcopalian (exec. bd. diocese Tex. 1972-74). Club: Lion (Austin) (pres. North Austin 1948-49). Home: Austin Tex. Died July 28, 1989; buried Oakwood Cemetery, Austin, Tex.

WILLIAMSON, GEORGE FRANKLIN, lawyer; b. Mpls., Oct. 29, 1897; s. James Franklin and Emma Felice (Elmore) W.; m. Mary Salina Stevenson, Apr. 10, 1928; 1 child, Ann Felice. Grad., Blake Prep. Sch., 1915; AB, Princeton, 1920; LLB, U. Minn., Minn. Coll. Law, 1923. Bar: Minn. 1928. Law clk., draftsman Williamson & Merchant, James F. Williamson, Mpls., 1916-22; ptnr. Williamson, Reif & Williamson, 1925-32; sr. ptnr. Williamson & Williamson, 1934-52, Williamson & Palmatier and predecessor frims, Mpls., from 1952; specializing in patent law. Chmn. regional citizens com. Minn. Homecrafters, Inc., 1936-51; dir. Mpls. Civic Coun., 1937, 38; del. Dem. Nat. Conv., 1936, 40; 1st state pres. Young Dems., 1933-35. Served with USN, WWI. Mem. ABA, Minn. Bar Assn., Minn. Patent LAw Assn. (pres. 1950-51), Princeton Alumni Assn. (past officer), Delta Kappa Epsilon (past sec.), Univ. Club (Mpls.), Charter Club (Princeton). Episcopalian. *

WILLINGHAM, BEN HILL, textile company executive; b. Hagan, Ga., June 1, 1914; s. Ben Kirby and Katrina (Shields) W.; m. Dorothy Wells, Feb. 17, 1936 (div. 1969); children: Ben Hill Jr., Susan Willingham Simons. Student, Vanderbilt U. Various positions to mdse. mgr. Gen. Shoe Corp. (became Genesco Inc. 1959), Nashville, 1933-44, br. mgr., 1944-48, gen. sales mgr., 1944-48, v.p. sales dept., 1950-56, corp. v.p., 1956-58, pres., 1958-69, chief exec. officer, 1959-69, bd. dirs., 1953-69; v.p. corp. planned Burlington Industries, N.Y.C., 1969-75; pres. Burlington Internat., Inc., N.Y.C., 1970-75; corp. counselor to cos. in Europe and U.S.; bd. dirs. 3d Nat. Bank Nashville, S.H. Kresge & Co., Tiffany & Co., N.Y.C. Mem. adv. coun., trustee Fashion Inst. Tech.; bd. dirs. Nashville Symphony Assn., Tenn. Mental Health Assn.; trustee United Givers Fund Nashville and Davidson Cunty, Found. for Rsch. in Human Behavior; steward, mem. bd. publs. United Meth. Ch. Mem. Am. Soc. Sales Execs., Nat. Assn. Shoe Mfrs. (bd. dirs.), Newcomen Soc. N.Am., Belle Meade Country Club, Cumberland Club, Bluegrass Club, Exch. Club, Colemere Country Club, Econ. Club, Fifth Avenue Club. Home: Savannah Ga. Died Oct. 27, 1991; Thomson, Ga.

WILLOUGHBY, ALFRED, political economist; b. Elkhorn, Wis., Dec. 2, 1898; s. LeRoy and Cora (Valentine) W.; m. Frances Cassell (div.); children: Alice (dec.), Richard, Peter, Stephen; m. Olga McLaney. AB, U. Wis., 1927; student mcpl. adminstrn., Columbia,

1937-38. Engaged as reporter for Daily News Sentinel, Milw., 1917-19, Wis. State Jour., Madison, 1919-23; rewrite man Am., Balt., 1923-24; city editor and new editor Press, Evansville, Ind., 1924-25; chief, rewrite desk Am., Balt., 1925-26; Sunday editor, editor state govt. sect. Wis. State Jour., 1927-28; mgr. direct advt. div. Dem. Printing Co., Maidson, 1928-37; asst. sec. Nat Mcpl. League, 1937-39, exec. sec., 1940-47, sec., from 1947; edit. writer Nat. Civic Review, from 1938, acting editor, 1942-47, editor, from 1947; planning cons. N.Y. State Dept. Commerce, 1943-46. Author: (with others) Tax Relations Among Governmental Units, 1938; contbr. pamphlets and studies on problems of govt. and citizenship. Mem. governing bd. Pub. Adminstrn. Svc., from 1943; mem. Am. Com. Internat. Mcpl. Coop., Census Adv. Com. on state and local govt. statis. With USN, WWI. Mem. Nat. Assn. Civic Secs., Govt. Rsch. Assn., Mcpl. Forum (N.Y.C.), Citizens Union (N.Y.C.), Polit. Sci. Assn., Sigma Delta Chi, Phi Sigma Alpha, Internat. City Mgrs. Assn. (hon.). *

WILLSON, MARION ELAINE, nursing educator; b. Whitaker, Pa., May 20, 1939; d. Marion M. and Anna M. (Rehburg) Stuart; m. Donald M. Willson, May 19, 1961; children: Clinton, Ross. B.S.N., Slippery Rock U., 1978; M. Edn., Westminster Coll., 1983. Staff nurse Children's Hosp., Pitts., 1960-63, 66-67, Columbia Hosp., Pitts., 1969; office nurse Drs. Shaffer & Mansell, M.D.s, New Wilmington, Pa., 1972-74, Dr. Carlos Flores, New Wilmington, 1979-80; project coordinator Westinghouse Health Systems, Balt., 1979; nursing instr. Saint Francis Hosp., New Castle, Pa., from 1980; faculty MSHAHEN State Bd. Rev., Youngstown, Ohio, 1982-86. Active Am. Heart Assn., Am. Cancer Soc., New Wilmington Presbyn. Ch. Recipient Vol. of Yr. award Midwest Pa. Heart Assn., 1979. Mem. Nat. League Nursing. Republican. Deceased. Home: New Wilmington Pa.

WILSON, ALLAN CHARLES, biochemistry educator; b. Ngaruawahia, New Zealand, Oct. 18, 1934; came to U.S., 1955; s. Charles and Eunice Boyce (Wood) W.; m. Leona Greenbaum, Sept. 13, 1958; children: Ruth, David. BS, U. Otago, New Zealand, 1955, DSc (hon.), 1989; MS, Wash. State U., 1957; PhD, U. Calif., Berkeley, 1961. Postdoctoral fellow Brandeis U., Waltham, Mass., 1961-64; asst. prof. U. Calif., Berkeley, 1964-68, assoc. prof., 1968-72, prof. biochemistry and molecular biology, 1972-91, Faculty Rsch. lectr., 1989-90; Steinhaus lectr. U. Calif., Irvine, 1983, Bonner lectr. Calif. Inst. Tech., 1984, Baumgartner lectr. U. Kans., 1986, Karling lectr. Purdue U., 1988; Freiberg vis. prof. Washington U., St. Louis, 1988; Art Stern Meml. lectr. Wistar Inst., 1988; Mayer lectr. MIT, 1990; Boyce Thompson lectr. Cornell U., 1990. Editor nonmammalian biochem. sect. Chem. Abstracts, 1969-70; assoc. editor Biochem. Genetics, 1976-91, Jour. Molecular Evolution, 1978-91; edit. bds. Biochem. Genetics, 1971-76, Evolution, 1978, Genetical Rsch., 1987-91, Genomics, 1987-91, New Biologist, 1989-91, others; Contbr. numerous articles to profl. jours. and books. Recipient Disting. Achievement award Washington State U., 1990; Fellow Guggenheim Meml. Found., Weizmann Inst., Israel, U. Nairobi, Kenya, 1972-73, Harvard U., 79-80, Am. Acad. Arts and Scis., 1983, Royal Soc., 1986, MacArthur Found., 1986-91; Evans fellow U. Otago, 1989. Mem. Am. Soc. Biol. Chemists (3M Life Scis. award 1991), Human Genome Orgn. (elected mem.). Home: Berkeley Calif. Died July 21, 1991; buried Berkeley, Calif.

WILSON, SIR ANGUS (FRANK JOHNSTONE), writer, educator; b. Eng., Aug. 11, 1913; s. William Frederick and Maud Ellen (Caney) W. Grad., Westminster Sch., Oxford (Eng.) U.; LittD, U. Leicester (Eng.), 1977, U. East Anglia (Eng.) and U. Liverpool, 1979, U. Sussex, 1981, U. Sorbonne, 1984. Prof. English U. East Anglia, 1966-78; dep. supt. reading room British Mus.; vis. prof., lectr. various Am. Univs., U.K. Fgn. Service (Intelligence), 1942-45; chmn. Nat. Book League, Eng., 1971-74. Author: 50 novels including Hemlock and After, No Laughing Matter, The Naughty Nineties, Such Darling Dodos, Setting the World on Fire, Anglo Saxon Attitudes, 1956, As If By Magic, 1973, The Strange Ride of Rudyard Kipling, 1977; author (biography) The World of Charles Dickens, 1970. Named Comdr. Order British Empire, 1968, Chevalier de l'Order des Arts et des Lettres, 1972, Knight Her Majesty The Queen, 1980, Fgn. Hon. Memer Am. Inst. Arts and Letters, 1980. Fellow Royal Soc. Lit. (pres. 1982-88); mem. Powys Soc. (pres. 1970-80), Dickens Fellowship (pres. 1974-75), Kipling Soc. (pres. 1980-88). Club: Athenaeum (London). Home: Bury Saint Edmunds Eng. Died May 31, 1991; cremated.

WILSON, EDGAR HUNTER, law educator; b. Asheville, N.C., Feb. 2, 1923; s. Edgar Hunter and Ethel Lee (Lunsford) W.; m. Carolyn Eskridge Gibbs, Sept. 10, 1946; 1 dau., Dorothy D. Student, Wake Forest U., 1940-41, Biltmore Coll., 1941-42, George Washington U., 1942-43; LL.B., Duke, 1948, LL.M., 1948, S.J.D., 1954. Bar: N.C. bar 1948, Ga. bar 1955, Okla. bar 1970. Prof. law Mercer U., Macon, Ga., 1948-68; dean Mercer U. (Sch. Law), 1972-77, Macon prof. law, 1977-90; exec. dir. Fla. Law Revision Commn., Gainesville, 1968-69; prof. law U. Fla., 1968-69; dean Coll. Law, U. Tulsa, 1969-72. Co-author: Georgia Insurance Code, 1960, Georgia Criminal Code, 1968, Florida Criminal Procedure Code, 1970. Rep. Ga. Gen. Assembly, 1956-60; mayor, Macon, 1960-64; Mem. Bibb County Bd. Edn., 1959-63; mem. Macon Hosp. Commn., 1960-64; v.p. Ga. Municipal Assn., 1962-63; vice chmn. Middle Ga. Goliseum Authority, 1962-66; spl. hearing officer Dept. Justice, 1965-67; Chmn. Macon-Bibb County Water and Sewer Authority, 1974-90; Bd. dirs. Macon-Bibb County Indsl. Authority, 1959-63. Served with USAAF, 1943-46. Mem. Order of Coif, Phi Delta Phi. Home: Macon Ga. Died Nov. 14, 1990; buried Riverside Cemetery, Macon, Ga.

WILSON, GROVER CLEVELAND, JR., pastor; b. Hazard, Ky., Aug. 24, 1922; s. Grover Cleveland and Agnes Kathleen (Garrow) W.; m. Mary Starke Higgenbotham, Sept. 3, 1949 (div. Aug. 1978); children: Scott, Karen Adair, Grover III. BS, Miami U., Oxford, Ohio, 1947; BD, Yale U., 1951, MDiv, 1963. ordained to ministry Presbyn. Ch. Asst. pastor Huguenot Meml. Ch., Pelham Manor, N.Y., 1951-55; assoc. pastor 1st Presbyn. Ch., Stamford, Conn., 1958-70; exec. dir. Council of Chs., Stamford, 1971-78; with Maumee Valley Presbytery, Findlay, Ohio, 1978-80; pastor Presbyn. Chs., Lemoyne and Keystone, Nebr., 1983-86, Milan and Green City, Mo., from 1986. Contbr. articles to profl. jours. Co-organizer Friendship House, Stamford, 1960, Community Return, Stamford, 1970, Council of Chs. and Synagogues, Stamford, 1975; v.p., bd. dirs. NAACP, Stamford, 1970-78; bd. dirs. Vets. of HECUS, Bridgeport, Conn., 1970-78. Served to cpl. U.S. Army, 1942-45, ETO, Prisoner of War, France and Germany. Decorated Purple Heart, Bronze Star. Democrat. Home: Milan Mo. Died Jan. 1987.

WILSON, JAMES BOYD, real estate investment company executive; b. Boston, July 19, 1942; s. Clinton Boyd and Florence Louise (Forsythe) W.; m. Frances E.B. Burke, May 9, 1964 (div. June 1986); children: Sharon Elizabeth, Patricia Ann, Debra Louise. BMus in Composition, Berkeley Coll., 1971; MEd, Boston State U., 1974; postgrad., Harvard U., 1975, U. Md., 1983. Prin. Wilson Real Estate Co., Boston, 1976-80; asst. crew mgr. Wilder Assocs., Boston, 1980-83; loan officer, fin. VA, Washington, 1983-85; prin. Boyd Assocs., Alexandria, Va., 1985-88; mem. The Conservative Network, Washington, 1985-88; bd. dirs. W&J Investment Firm, Alexandria. Mem. Greater Boston Real Estate Bd., Rental Housing Assn. Republican. Mormon. Home: Alexandria Va.

WILSON, JAMES EDWARD, judge, barrister; b. Winnipeg, Man., Can., May 29, 1914; s. James and Catherine (Price) W.; m. Florence Margaret Sadler, Jan. 5, 1940; children: Wendy, Peter, Jennifer. BA, Man. U., 1936, LLB, 1946, LLD, 1987. Sole practice Winnipeg, 1946-65; judge Ct. of Queen's Bench Province of Man., Winnipeg, from 1965. Sec. Man. Med. Sci. Found.; v.p. Def. Found.; mem. Can. Pension Appeals Bd., from 1987; pres. Man. Paraplegia Found.; hon. council Misericordia Gen. Hosp.; chmn. Westminster Found., Man. div. Can. Corpsof Commrs.; sec. bd. trustees Westminster Ch. Served to lt. col. Can. Army. Decorated Can. Forces decoration, Order of British Empire. Mem. Can. Bar Assn., Man. Bar Assn., Can. Judge's Council, Can. Assn. Adminstrn. of Justice. Home: Winnipeg, Man. Can. Deceased.

WILSON, JEAN SPANN, real estate executive; b. Murray, Ky., Dec. 29, 1929; d. Cross and Gladys (Miller) Spann; m. Beck B. Wilson, May 26, 1969; m. James F. Williams Jr., Feb. 12, 1949 (dec. 1968); children: James F. III, Johnny W. Student, Murray (Ky.) State Coll. Pvt. practice land developer, 1969-79; broker Lake Barkley Realty, Cadiz, Ky., from 1979; bd. dirs. Anderson Shores Corp., Murray, Spann Enterprises, Murray, Pennyrile Bd. Realtors, Princeton, Ky. Exec. com. Ky. Dem., 1987, 1988. Mem. Trigg County C. of C., Am. Assn. Ret. Persons (legis. com. Ky. chpt.). Democrat. Baptist. Home: Cadiz Ky. Deceased.

WILSON, JOHN ALAN, lawyer; b. Glen Ridge, N.J., Sept. 1, 1917; s. Robert and Adelaide Anna (Streubel) W.; m. Dorothy Francisco, Aug. 9, 1947 (dec. Oct. 1982); children: Robert Alan, Anne Elizabeth.; m. Carol A. Somers, Nov. 5, 1983. Grad., Deerfield (Mass.) Acad., 1935; A.B., Princeton U., 1939; LL.B., Yale U., 1942. Bar: Ohio 1950, S.C. 1983. House counsel Dresser Industries, Inc., 1949-50; sec. Affiliated Gas Equipment, Inc., 1950-55; dir. law Diamond Shamrock Corp. (formerly Diamond Alkali Co.), Cleve., 1956-61; sec. Diamond Shamrock Corp. (formerly Diamond Alkali Co.), 1961-79, 80-82, gen. counsel, 1964-81, v.p., 1967-82; dir. Eltech Systems Corp., Boca Raton, Fla., 1982-87, chmn., 1983-87; Legis. asst. to Senator Robert Taft, 1946-49. Served with AUS, 1942-45. Mem. ABA, Fed. Bar Assn., S.C. Bar Assn., Am. Soc. Corp. Secs. Clubs: Hilton Head Yacht, Sea Pines (Hilton Head Island, S.C.). Home: Hilton Head Island S.C. Died Dec. 2, 1991; buried Hilton Head Island, S.C.

WILSON, JOHN FLETCHER, speech professional; b. Keyser, W.Va., June 1, 1923; s. James Vincent and Susan May (Patton) W. BA, Wayne State U., 1947, MA, 1948; PhD, U. Wis., 1955. Instr. speech Monmouth (Ill.) Coll., 1948-50; instr. to asso. prof. Cornell U., Ithaca, N.Y., 1953-67; assoc. prof. speech Herbert H. Lehman Coll., CUNY, Bronx, 1967-71, prof., 1971-89, ret., 1989, chmn. dept. speech and theatre, 1979-85; cons. in field. Author: (with Carroll C. Arnold) Public Speaking as a Liberal Art, 1964, 6th edit. (with Molly Meijer Wertheimer), 1990. Served with USAAF, 1943-46, USAF, 1950-51. Mem. AAUP, Speech Communication Assn., Am. Forensic Assn., Eastern Communication Assn. (pres. 1977-78), N.Y. State Speech Communication Assn. (pres. 1968-69), N.Y. State Forensic Assn. (pres. 1956-57), Rhetoric Soc. Am., Tau Kappa Epsilon. Republican. Presbyterian. Home: New York N.Y.

WILSON, JOHN TRUESDELL, banker; b. Faubush, Ky., July 23, 1898; s. William Floyd and Doretta (Combest) W.; student Jefferson Sch. Law, 1929-31, Stonier Grad. Sch. Banking, Rutgers U., 1956-68; m. Evangeline Cooper, Apr. 28, 1917 (dec.); children: John Dave (dec.), James Truesdell (dec.), Eva Elizabeth (Mrs. Ollie Caplin, Jr.); m. Mary C. Pierce, Mar. 1938. Partner Truesdell Wilson Sales & Service, Somerset, Ky., 1945-52; farmer, Ky., 1921-49; salesman Swift & Co., Somerset, 1923-24; plant mgr., engr. Wood-Mosiac Co., Monticello, Ky. and Louisville, 1931-35; with First Farmers Nat. Bank, Somerset, 1933-85, pres., 1961-73, chmn., 1973-84, also dir.; dealer Chevrolet Co., Somerset, 1937-39, Chrysler Co., Somerset, 1945-52; owner, pres., operator Ky. Oil Co., Somerset, 1935-52. Dir., pres. Farmers Tobacco Warehousing Corp., from 1948, Peoples State Bank, Monticello, Ky., 1934-35. Mgr. various Democratic campaigns, 1935-58. Bd. dirs. Somerset-Pulaski County Airport, 1948-85, chmn., 1952-85. Mem. Am., Ky. bankers assns., Ky. (dir. 1950-69), Somerset-Pulaski County (pres. 1957) chambers of commerce. Clubs: Masons, Kiwanis (pres. 1955, lt. gov. 1958). Author: History of Banking in Pulaski County, 1970. Deceased. Home: Somerset Ky.

WILSON, LOGAN, association executive; b. Huntsville, Tex., Mar. 6, 1907; s. Samuel Calhoun and Sammie (Logan) W.; m. Myra Marshall, Dec. 27, 1932; children: Marshall, Reed Calhoun. Student, Sam Houston Coll., 1923-26; AM, Harvard U., 1938, PhD, 1939; LLD, Tulane U., 1953. Asst. prof. English East Tex. State Tchrs. Coll., Commerce, 1928-30, 32-36; rsch. assoc. Mass Community Project, 1936-37; assoc. prof. sociology U. Md., 1939-41; prof., head sociology dept. Tulane U., New Orleans, 1941-43, dean Newcomb Coll., 1944-51; prof., head sociology dept. U. Ky., 1943-44; v.p., provost Consol. U. N.C., 1951-53; pres. U. Tex., 1953-60, chancellor, 1960-61; pres. to pres. emeritus Am. Coun. Edn., 1961-71, 72-90; chmn. Am. Conf. Acad. Deans, 1950-51; mem. Nat. Commn. Accrediting, 1954-55; mem. com. Fund for Republic, Ford Found. 1953-54, Coll. Grants Adv. Com., 1955-56, com. Utilization of Coll. Teaching Resources, Fund for Advancement Edn., 1955-56; trustee Ctr. Advanced Study in Behavioral Scis., 1956-75, Carneigie Found. Advancement Teaching, 1958-61; adv. com. social scis. NSF, 1959-62; adv. com. study govt. and higher edn. Carnegie Found., 1960-62; mem. nat. rev. bd. East-West Ctr., 1964-68, others. Author: The Academic Man, 1942, Twentieth Century Sociology (contbr. to symposium), 1945, Sociological Analysis (with W.L. Kolb), 1949, Shaping American Higher Edn., 1972; editor: The State University, Emerging Patterns in American Higher Edn.; editor, contbr. The College and the Student; contbr. Education in the Nation's Service, The Graduate Jour., The Ednl. Record, also numerous publs. and periodicals. Recipient Disting. Svc. medallion Assn. Tex. Colls. and Univs., 1966, hon. citation Am. Alumni coun., 1968, Centennial award U. Akron, 1970; named Disting. Alumnus award Sam Houston State U., 1974. Fellow AAAS; mem. So. Univ. Conf., Assn. Am. Colls. (com. liberal edn.), State Univs. Assn. (exec. com.), Nat. Assn. State Univs., Am. Coun. Edn. (problems and policies com. 1957-61, chmn. com. 1960-61), Am. Sociol. Soc., Com. Econ. Devel., Philos. Soc. Tex. (hon. trustee), Inst. Internat. Edn., Coun. So. Univs. (pres. 1953-54), So. Assn. Colls. (commn. higher ins.), Phi Beta Kappa (senator at large 1964-90), Alpha Kappa Delta, Sigma Tau Delta, Alpha Tau Omega, others. Home: Austin Tex. Died Nov. 7, 1990; interred Wilson Cemetery, Huntsville, Tex.

WILSON, NAHUM THOMAS, IV, lawyer; b. Wenatchee, Wash., Oct. 24, 1953; s. Nahum T. and Belva Elizabeth (Hilscher) W. III; m. Deborah Faye Turney, July 1, 1978; children—Rebecca Marie, Margaret Rose. Student Universita di Perugia, Italy, 1973, Universita di Santa Maria, Rome, 1973; B.A., Notre Dame U., 1975; J.D., U. Oreg., 1979. Bar: Oreg. 1979, U.S. Dist. Ct. Oreg. 1980. Assoc. Eckley & Assoc., Salem, Oreg., 1979-81; ptnr. Anson, Depenbrock & Wilson, Salem, 1981—. Author (legal phamphlet): Landlord Tenant Handbook, 1975. Columnist (newsletter): The Dissent, 1977-79. Legal counselor Oreg. Jaycees, Salem, 1983-84. Recipient Am. Jurisprudence award Bancroft Whitney, Eugene, Oreg., 1977; Brownfield Meml. award Salem Jaycees, 1980-81; Individual Devel. Project of Yr., Salem Jaycees, 1982-83. Mem. Oreg. State Bar, ACLU (pres. chpt. 1977-79), Oreg. State Bar Assn., Marion County Bar Assn., Pi Sigma Alpha. Republican. Roman Catholic. Club: Notre Dame. Lodges: Elks, K.C. (Notre Dame program dir.). Home: Salem Oreg.

WILSON, PHYLLIS STARR, magazine editor; b. New Orleans, Feb. 11, 1928; d. Daniel Davis and Anita (Garripy) Starr; m. Hugh Hamilton Wilson, Dec. 24,

1958. B.A. in English, Tulane U., 1949. Receptionist, asst. house organ Coca-Cola Co., New Orleans, 1949; sec., editor Weird Tales mag., N.Y.C., 1950; sec. Conde Nast Publs., N.Y.C., 1951-55; researcher, writer Vogue mag., 1955-62; writer Glamour mag., 1962-67, sr. editor copy and features, 1967-71, mng. editor, 1971-77; founding editor, editor-in-chief Self mag., N.Y.C., from 1978; editorial dir. Conde Nast collections, N.Y.C., from 1987. Freelance writer, editor, from 1955; Editor, researcher: The Artist in His Studio (Alexander Liberman), 1960, Moments Preserved (Irving Penn), 1960; editor: Glamour's Health and Beauty Book, 1972. Recipient J.C. Penney U. Mo. Journalism award for med. article, 1969, award as one of outstanding women who have contbd. most to mag. pub. March of Dimes, from 1982. Mem. Am. Soc. Mag. Editors. Democrat. Home: New York N.Y.

WILSON, PORTERFIELD, automotive executive; b. Nashville, July 12, 1933; s. Monroe and Willie Mae (Sellers) W.; m. Barbara Jean Fuller Wilson, June 2, 1962; 1 child, Porterfield Christopher. Grad. high sch., Nashville. Automobile salesman Bill Snethkamp, Highland Park, Mich., 1963-70, Porterfield Wilson Pontiac, Detroit, 1970-78, Porterfield Wilson Pontiac, GMC Truck, Detroit, from 1978, Porterfield Wilson Mazda, Detroit, from 1979, Ferndale (Mich.) Honda, from 1979; land developer Porterfield's Marina Village, Detroit, from 1987; dir. First Independence Nat. Bank, Detroit, from 1982, Dunbar Meml. Hosp., Detroit, from 1980; mem. adv. bd. United Found., Detroit. Commr. Civil Svc. Commn., City of Detroit. Named to Top 100 Black Enterprise Mag., Regional Retail Firm of Yr. U.S. Dept. Commerce, Washington 1987; recipient spl. citation Bus. Acumen Pres.of U.S.A., Washington, 1978. Mem. Booker T. Washington Bus. Assn., NAACP (life), Assn. Minority Dealers (past pres.), Detroit C. of C., Detroit Boat Club, Renaissance Club, Motor City Yacht Club, Turnberry Yacht Club. Home: Detroit Mich. Deceased.

WILSON, WILLIAM LEWIS, financial company executive; b. Phila., Aug. 21, 1910; s. Charles Rea and Caroline Tilton (Imlay) W.; m. Edna F. Molineux, June 15, 1940; children: William Lewis Jr., Thomas C. AB, Dartmouth Coll., 1931; postgrad., U. Pa., 1931-32. With various newspapers, Phila., 1931-39; dir. pub. rels. Republic Aviation Corp., Farmingdale, N.Y., 1939-41, dir. indsl. rels., 1941-43; v.p., sec. Kellett Aircraft Corp., Phila., 1943-46; v.p. pub. rels. C.I.T. Fin. Corp. and subs., N.Y.C., 1946-75; bd. dirs. C.I.T. Bldgs. Corp., 1961-75. Author: Full Faith and Credit: The Story of C.I.T. Financial Corporation 1908-1975, 1975. Mem. Princeton Twp. (N.J.) Bd. Edn., 1954-60, pres., 1957-59; mem. Princeton Twp. Local Governing Body, 1962-70; mayor Princeton Twp., 1964-65; v.p., sec., bd. dirs. C.I.T. Found., 1953-75; elder Presbyn. Ch. Mem. Beden's Brook Club, Springdale Golf Club, Phi Beta Kappa. Home: Princeton N.J. Died Oct. 22, 1990; Princeton, N.J.

WILTSE, DORR NORMAN, insurance executive; b. Caro, Mich., Sept. 20, 1911; s. Norman Anson and Evie Markham (McCartney) W.; student Eastern Mich. U., 1931-33; teaching cert. Central Mich. U., 1933-37; m. Gladys May Garner, Nov. 11, 1932; children: Dorr Norman, Saire Christina. Tchr., Tuscola County (Mich.) Public Schs., 1931-42; br. mgr. Mich. Mut. Ins. Co., Caro, 1942-75; city assessor, Caro, from 1964, also casualty ins. cons., Caro, 1975-79. Vice pres. Caro Devel. Corp., 1975-79, pres., 1983-89; adv. bd. DeMolay Found. of Mich., 1965-67; founder, pres. Watrousville-Caro Area Hist. Soc., 1972-75, 78; pres. Caro Hist. Commn., 1975-79; chmn. bd. Caro Community Hosp. Endowment Found., from 1982; chmn. Caro Bicentennial Commn., 1975-76; mem. Com. to Elect Pres. Gerald R. Ford, 1975-76; mem. Indianfields-Caro-Almer Planning Commn., 1972-79; co-chmn. Mich. Sesquicentennial for Tuscola County, 1986-87. Named Citizen of Yr. Caro C. of C., 1975, Patriotic Citizen VFW, 1988. Mem. Mich. Assessors Assn., Caro Masonic Bldg. Assn., Inc. (pres. 1974-79), Nat. Trust Hist. Preservation, Nat. Hist. Soc., Hist. Soc. Mich., Huguenot Soc. Mich., Saginaw Geneal. Soc., Mich. Archaeol. Soc. Democrat. Presbyterian (elder). Clubs: Caro Lions (pres. 1946), Mich. Mut. Quarter Century, Masons (past master), Shriners. Author: The First Hundred Years, 1978; The Hidden Years of the Master, 1976; The Wiltse Saga, 1980; A Look in Your Own Backyard, 1983. Died Apr. 14, 1989; buried Indianfields Twp. Cemetery, Caro, Mich. Home: Caro Mich.

WINANS, JOHN GIBSON, physics and astronomy educator; b. Mexico, Mo., July 2, 1902; s. Theodore H. and Kate (Lewis) W.; m. Marion Frances Napper, June 20, 1928; children: Theodore Roland, Lelia Evelyn. BA magna cum laude, Colo. Coll., 1923; MA, Dartmouth Coll., 1924; PhD, U. Wis., 1927. NRC fellow Princeton (N.J.) U., 1927-28; Internat. Edn. fellow U. Göttingen, Germany, 1928-29; from instr. to assoc. prof. U. Wis., Madison, 1930-62; prof. physics and astronomy SUNY, Buffalo, 1962-72, prof. emeritus, 1972-90; Fulbright lectr. Internat. Christian U., Mitaka, Japan, 1958-59, India, 1959, Nat. Taiwan U., Taipei, 1959-60; Fulbright lectr. Banares Hindu U., Varanasi, India, 1968-69, vis. prof., 1969; aero. rsch. engr. Langley Aero. Lab., Hampton, Va., 1957; rsch. physicist Sylvania Electric Products Co., Flushing, N.Y., 1945. Author: Introductory General Physics, 1952, Everyday Physics, 1952; also articles; demonstrated circular tethered take-offs and landings for light airplanes, 1955. Sec.-treas. Wis. Com. Against Peacetime Conscription, 1955; pres. Madison Coun. Chs., 1945-46. Fellow Am. Phys. Soc.; mem. AIAA, Optical Soc. Am., Am. Assn. Physics Tchrs. (exec. com. 1951-52), Aurora Aero. Club (West Seneca, N.Y., pres. 1965-67), Phi Beta Kappa, Sigma Xi. Mem. United Ch. of Christ. Home: Buffalo N.Y. Died Jan. 1, 1990; interred Roselawn Meml. Pk., Madison, Wis.

WINBERG, CLAES ULRIK, management executive; b. Copenhagen, Sept. 23, 1925; s. Karl and Nellie (Moller) W.; M.S., Tech. U. Denmark, 1952; m. Ebba Kristina Bergenstrahle, Apr. 9, 1952; children: Ulrik, Flemming, Christer. Engr., Husqvarna Vapenfabriks AB, Sweden, 1952-53; engr. Sundstrand Machine Tool Co., Rockford, Ill., 1953-55; sales engr., Sundstrand, Paris, 1955-57; export mgr. A/S Atlas, Copenhagen, 1957-60; pres. A/S Soren Wistoft & Co., Fabriker, Copenhagen, 1960-62; asst. mgr. AB Svenska Flaktfabriken, Stockholm, 1962-66; pres. Hexagon AB, Stockholm, 1966-71; v.p. AB Bofors, Sweden, 1971-72, pres., 1972-84; bd. dirs. Hasselfors AB, other cos. and orgns. Decorated comdr. Order of Vasa, comdr. Order of Vita Ros (Finland), King's medal. Mem. Royal Patriotic Soc. Deceased. Home: Stockholm Sweden

WINDFOHR, ROBERT FRALRY, oil producer; b. Quantico, Md., Jan. 27, 1894; s. George and Lillian (Clute) W.; m. Anne Burnett, Dec. 8, 1942. LLB, U. Md., 1916. Bar: Md. 1916. Ptnr. oil producing firms Nash & Windfohr, from 1921, Nash Windfohr & Brown, from 1937; v.p., dir. Ft. Worth Air Terminal, Inc., from 1949; dir. 1st Nat. Bank of Ft. Worth, from 1943, Gen Dynamics Corp., from 1954, Champlain Oil & Refining Co., from 1955; dir. Southwestern Exposition and Fat Stock Show, from 1949. Trustee Lovelace Found. MEd. Edn. and Rsch. Recipient Disting. Svc. award Tex. Mid-Continent Oil and Gas Assn., 1957. Mem. Am. Petroleum Inst. (dir., mem. exec. com.), Tex. Mid-Continent (pres. 1951-53), Mid-Continent Oil and Gas Assn. (pres. 1953-55), Ft. Worth Art Assn. (chmn.), Nat. Petroleum Coun. Clubs: Ft. Worth, River Crest Country, Augusta Nat Golf (gov.). *

WINDLE, JOHN TAYLOR, museum director; b. West Lafayette, Ind., June 13, 1901; s. Allen Jay and Pearl Binford (Taylor) W.; m. Ann Steinbrecher, Apr. 17, 1937. A.B., U. Ill., 1925; M.A., U. Chgo., 1942; LL.D. (hon.), Hanover Coll., 1976. Reference asst. Newberry Library, Chgo., 1928-29, chief reference librarian, head of research, 1930-48; owner, dir. Shrewsbury House Mus., Madison, Ind., from 1948; founder Hist. Madison, Inc., 1960, pres., 1960-81, emeritus, from 1981; restorer hist. bldgs., Madison, 1948-73; cons. hist. preservation. Mem. exec. bd. Chgo. Civic Music Assn., 1946-48, pres., 1947-48; pres. Madison-Jefferson County Community Council, 1952-54; dir. Madison-Jefferson County Pub. Library, 1955-79. Recipient Community Service award Madison Area C. of C., 1964, citation for archtl. restoration Ind. U., 1975, Don E. Gibson Meml. award Ind. Soc. Architects, 1975, 1st Guardian of Our Heritage award Jefferson County Hist. Soc., 1982; inducted to Ind. Acad., 1978, Sagamore of the Wabash, 1981. Mem. Nat. Trust for Hist. Preservation (bd. advisers Ind. sect. 1973-79; Honor award 1984), Hist. Landmarks Found. Ind. (bd. dirs. 1972-80, adv. council, from 1980), Ind. Hist. Soc. (bd. dirs. 1972-81), Ind. Library Trustees Assn. (bd. dirs. 1955-56, 66-67). Republican. Quaker. Clubs: Caxton, Cliff Dwellers (Chgo.); Indpls. Athletic; Madison Country. Deceased. Home: Madison Ind.

WINESANKER, MICHAEL MAX, musicologist, educator; b. Toronto, Ont., Can., Aug. 7, 1913; came to U.S., 1945, naturalized, 1951; s. Samuel and Ida (English) W.; m. Esther Frumhartz, Dec. 12, 1937; children—Miriam Ruth, Rebecca Ann. Student composition with, Healey Willan, 1931-36; B.Mus., U. Toronto, 1933; M.A., U. Mich., 1941; L.Mus., Trinity Coll., London, 1940; Ph.D., Cornell U., 1944. Pvt. tchr. piano and theory Toronto, 1933-39; tchr. piano and theory Hambourg Conservatory, Toronto, 1940-42; prof. music history and theory Bayview Summer Coll., Mich., 1945; prof. musicology U. Tex., 1945-46, summer 1946; mem. faculty Tex. Christian U., 1946-83, prof. musicology, 1949-83, Piper prof., 1976, prof. emeritus, 1983-89, chmn. dept. music, 1956-81; spl. tchr. in honors humanities program Tex. Christian U., 1986-87, 87-88, 88-89; bd. dirs., v.p. Van Cliburn Internat. Piano Competition, Fort Worth Symphony Assn; interim prof. grad. musicology, Tex. Christian U., 1987-89. Author: A List of Books on Music, 1977, Books on Music, A Classified List, 1979; contbr. articles profl. jours.; debut as concert pianist performing own composition, Eaton Auditorium, Toronto, 1937. Past pres. Fort Worth Youth Symphony Orch. Grantee Am. Council Learned Socs., 1943, Tex. Christian U.-Carnegie Found., 1948, Tex. Christian U. Research Com., 1953. Mem. Am. Musicological Soc. (pres. Tex. chpt. 1950-52, 56-58, council 1958-60), Music Tchrs. Nat. Assn. (chmn. editorial and publs. com. 1961-65, chmn. musicology com. from 1968), Tex. Assn. Music Schs. (pres. 1960-61), Fort Worth Music Tchrs. Assn. (pres. 1963-65), Nat. Assn. Schs. Music (chmn. library com.), Pi Kappa Lambda, Phi Mu Alpha. Home: Fort Worth Tex. Died Mar. 4, 1989; buried Ft. Worth, Tex.

WINKEL, NINA (CATHERINE MARIA JOHANNA WINKEL), sculptor; b. Germany, May 21, 1905; d. Ernst and Augustine (Bauer) Koch; came to U.S., 1942, naturalized, 1945; student Staedel Mus. Art Sch., 1929-31; DFA (hon.), SUNY, 1985; m. George J. Winkel, Dec. 15, 1934. Trustee, Sculpture Ctr., Inc., N.Y.C. 1946-69, pres., 1970-73, pres. emeritus, trustee, 1974-90; one-man shows: Notre Dame U., 1954, Sculpture Ctr., N.Y.C., 1944, 47, 58, 72, Adirondack Mus., Elizabethtown, N.Y., 1976, Ctr. Music Drama Art, Lake Placid, N.Y., 1977, Nat. Savs. Bank, Plattsburgh, N.Y., 1979, Carpenter and Painter Gallery, Elizabethtown, 1982, Allentown (Pa.) Art Mus., 1982, SUNY-Plattsburgh, 1983, 84, SUNY-Albany, 1984, Sculpture Ctr. Inc., N.Y.C., 1984; group shows: Met. Mus., Whitney Mus., Pa. Acad., San Francisco Mus., Va. Mus.; hon. adj. prof. SUNY-Plattsburgh, 1983. Juror for sculpture competition Winter Olympics 1980 in Lake Placid, 1978; trustee Keene Valley Library Assn., from 1967, chmn. bi-centennial com., 1973-77; trustee Adirondack Mus., Elizabethtown, N.Y., from 1978. Recipient Samuel F.B. Morse Gold medal NAD, 1964, Artists Fund prize, 1979, Gold medal, 1982; Founders prize, Mrs. Louis Bennett prize Nat. Sculpture Soc.; Pen's Brush award Pen's Brush club, 1982, Disting. Service award SUNY-Plattsburgh, 1987. Fellow Nat. Sculpture Soc. (sec. 1965-68, Bronze medal 1967, 71, Purchase prize 1981, Medal of Honor 1988); mem. Nat. Acad. Design (E. Watrous Gold medal 1945, 78, 83), Sculptors Guild, Ctr. Music, Drama and Arts-Lake Placid, Omicron Delta Kappa (hon.). Winkel Sculpture Court, SUNY-Plattsburgh, dedicated Oct. 1987, contains over 50 pieces of her sculpture. Died May 24, 1990. Home: Keene Valley N.Y.

WINNET, NOCHEM SAMUEL, lawyer; b. Russia, Aug. 6, 1898; s. Charles and Rose (Metzger) W.; m. Alma Goldstein, Mar. 10, 1929; children: Martha, Donald. A.B., Harvard U., 1920, LL.B., 1923; LL.D. (hon.), Antioch Coll., 1967, Pa. Coll. Optometry, 1976, LaSalle Coll., 1981, U. Pa., 1984, Beaver Coll., 1987; D.C.L. (hon.), Temple U., 1986. Bar: Pa. 1923. Practice law, 1923-40, asst. dir. pub. safety City of Phila., 1940; judge County Ct., 1940-50; ptnr., then sr. ptnr. Fox, Rothschild, O'Brien & Frankel, Phila., 1950-90. Contbr. articles to law jours., newspapers, popular mags. Hon. pres. Crime Prevention Assn. (pres. 1940-60); campaign chmn. Citizens Com. for Home Rule Charter, 1951, State constl. amendment, 1952; pres. Fedn. Jewish Agys. Greater Phila., 1962-65, trustee, from 1950; mem. exec. com. United Fund (v.p. 1961-65); dir. Greater Phila. Movement, 1951-69, Phila. Housing Assn., Jr. Achievement Delaware Valley, Inc., Assn. Jewish Children; v.p. Am. Joint Distbn. Com.; dir. Council Jewish Fedns.; mem. exec. com. Blue Cross Greater Phila.; mem. Jewish Agy. Assembly, Israel, 1972; exec. vice-chmn. Eisenhower-Nixon Campaign for S.E. Pa., 1952; pres. Samuel S. Fels Fund, from 1962; chmn. bd. trustees Beaver Coll.; assoc. trustee U. Pa., 1964-67; chmn. adv. bd. Pa. Sch. Social Work, 1959-62. Served with U.S. Army, 1918; compliance commr. World War II, 1945-46. Recipient Famous Fifty Philadelphians award, 1959; Citizens award United Fund, 1975; Golden medallion B'nai B'rith, 1975. Mem. ABA, Pa. Bar Assn. (spl. achievement award 1978), Phila. Bar Assn. (Fidelity Bank award 1977, Gold medal 1989), Am. Coll. Trial Lawyers, Am. Law Inst., World Affairs Council Phila. (v.p. 1963-69), Lawyers Club Phila. (pres. 1965-67, dir.). Home: Philadelphia Pa. Died Mar. 14, 1990.

WINOKUR, STEPHEN CHARLES, insurance company executive; b. N.Y.C., June 16, 1941; s. Morris and Muriel Lee (Roche) E.; m. Saundra Sue Copeland, Dec. 18, 1970. BA, CCNY, 1962; PhD, U. Minn., 1967; MBA, U. Chgo., 1982. Asst. prof. U. Minn., Mpls., 1967-68; prof. Tex. Christian U., Ft. Worth, 1968-81; cons., dir. Met. Life Ins. Co., N.Y.C., 1982-85, asst. v.p., 1986-87, mng. officer, 1987-88, asst. to chmn. bd. dirs., 1988-89; cons. USAF. Alamogordo, N.Mex., 1967-68, Police Dept., Dallas, 1976-78; vis. prof. U. Minn., 1971-72, Calif. State U., Hayward, 1972, 75, 77. Author: A Primer of Verbal Behavior, 1976; editor: Minnesota Studies in the Philosophy of Science Vol. IV. Clubs: Chgo. Bus., Nat. Arts. Home: New York N.Y. Died Dec. 19, 1988; cremated.

WINSHIP, HENRY DILLON, JR., transportation executive; b. Macon, Ga., July 27, 1929; s. H. Dillon and Anne (Chichester) W.; m. Patricia Cortelyou; children: Dillon III, Adrian, Blanton. BS in Transp., U. Tenn., 1952. V.p. Transus, Atlanta, 1956-66, pres., chmn., 1966-89; chmn. Winship Group, Atlanta, 1988-89; chmn. Regulatory Common Carrier Conf., Washington, 1970. Trustee Wesleyan Coll., Macon, 1985-87; bd. visitors Oglethorpe U., Atlanta, 1983-84; elder Northwest Presbyn. Ch., Atlanta, 1970-89; mem. Bus. Coun. Ga. Sgt. U.S. Army, 1953-55. Mem. Am. Trucking Assn. (chmn. 1974), Georgia Motor Trucking Assn. (pres. 1965), World Bus. Coun., Chief Execs. Forum, Capital City Club, Cherokee Club. Republican. Home: Atlanta Ga. Died Dec, 13, 1989; buried Atlanta, Ga.

WINSLOW, DICK (RICHARD WINSLOW JOHNSON), entertainer; b. Jennings, La., Mar. 25, 1915; s. Sidney Kenneth and Wynonah (Breazeale) Johnson; m. Alice Tyrrell; 1 child, Wynonah Georgette; remarried Shirley Meleese; children: Judith Wynne, Kellie Robin, Dick Winslow Jr., Kevin Durand. Student high sch., Los Angeles. Actor MGM Studio, Culver City, Calif., 1935-37; one-man-band Disneyland, Anaheim, Calif., 1964-76, Knott's Berry Farm, Buena Park, Calif., 1976-82, Live Wires, Hollywood, Calif., 1974-85; writer, actor, musician various studios, TV commls., Calif., from 1937; gag and script writer Disney Studio, Burbank, Calif., 1937-80; actor Disney Studio, Burbank; Minstrel Vikings of Scandia, Hollywood, from 1966. Republican. Mem. Ch. of the Nazarene. Home: Studio City Calif. Deceased.

WINSOR, RALPH EVERETT, food company executive; b. Binghamton, N.Y., 1936. B.S.in Agr., Cornell U., 1957; m. Susanne Swalm; children: Carolyn, Alan, Glenn. With Curtice Burns, Inc., Rochester, N.Y., 1973-89, chmn. bd., 1980-89, also dir.; dir. Agway, Inc., Pro-Fac Co-Op Inc. Died May 25, 1989; buried Harpursville, N.Y. Home: Harpursville N.Y.

WINTER, ALDEN RAYMOND, educator; b. Bridgeport, W.Va., Mar. 23, 1897; s. Samuel J. and Claudis (Martin) W.; m. Ethel Fisher, Sept. 2, 1926 (dec. 1960); m. Cora P. Fisher, 1960. BA, W.Va. U., 1920; MS, Ohio State U., 1921, PhD, 1929. Asst. nutrition chemist Ohio Agrl. Experiment Sta., Wooster, Ohio, 1920-26; asst. prof. poultry sci. Ohio State U., 1926-33, assoc. prof., 1934-45, prof., 1945-55, prof., chmn. dept., 1955-64, part time instr. microbiology, 1932-35, 43-44; rsch. assoc. Iowa Agrl. Expt. Sta., 1944-45; AID poultry advisor in India, from 1964. Co-author: Poultry Science and Practice, 1960; assoc. editor Poultry Sci., 1954-63. Recipient Christie award, 1953. Mem. AAAS, Am. Chem. Soc., Soc. Am. Microbiology Inst. Food Tech., Poultry Sci. Assn., Indian Poultry Sci. Assn., World Poultry Sci. Assn. *

WINTER, HARRISON L., federal judge; b. Balt., Apr. 18, 1921; s. J. George and Bessie (Biden) W.; m. Gladys Woolford, June 28, 1947; children—Barbara B., Anne B. A.B., Johns Hopkins U., 1942; LL.B., U. Md., 1944. Bar: Md. bar 1945. Asso. firm Miles, Walsh, O'Brien & Morris, 1946-51, partner, 1951-53; partner Miles & Stockbridge, 1953-59; asst. atty. gen. Md., 1948-51, dep. atty. gen., 1954-55; city solicitor Balt., 1959-61; judge U.S. Dist. Ct. of Md., Balt., 1961-66; U.S. circuit judge U.S. Ct. Appeals (4th cir.), Richmond, Va., 1966-90, chief judge, 1981-89. Trustee Johns Hopkins U., vice chmn. bd., 1968-81; trustee Peabody Inst., 1959-85, chmn. bd. 1967-77; bd. dirs. Evergreen House Found. Fellow Am. Bar Found.; mem. ABA, Md. Bar Assn., Am. Law Inst., Inst. Jud. Adminstrn., Am. Coll. Trial Lawyers, Am. Judicature Soc., Order of Coif, Omicron Delta Kappa. Episcopalian. Clubs: Md. (Balt.), 14 W. Hamilton St. (Balt.), Elkridge (Balt.). Home: Baltimore Md. Died Apr. 10, 1990; buried Druid Ridge Cemetery, Baltimore, Md.

WIRGES, MANFORD FRANK, energy company executive; b. Beatrice, Nebr., Jan. 18, 1925; s. Frank Jessie and Leta Irene (Coon) W.; m. Joan Audrey Kelly, Sept. 3, 1949; 1 dau., Kelly Marie. BSChemE, U. Okla., 1944, MS, 1945. With Cities Service Co., 1946-81; mgr. corporate planning, then v.p. research and corporate planning Cities Service Co., Tulsa, 1965-72; v.p. research and tech. div. Cities Service Co., 1972-81; energy cons. Am. Productivity Ctr., Houston, 1981-82; exec. v.p. Flexivol, Inc., Houston, from 1982; mem. adv. bd. Coll. Engring., U. Okla. Standard Oil Devel. Co. fellow, 1944-45. Mem. Am. Inst. Chem. Engrs., Am. Petroleum Inst., Inst. Mgmt. Scis., 25 Year Club Petroleum Industry. Home: Tulsa Okla. Died July 9, 1992. †

WIRKKALA, TAPIO, artist, designer; b. June 2, 1915; s. Ilmari and Selma Wirkkala; m. Rut Bryk, 1945; 2 children. Ed. Indsl. Art Inst., Helsinki; Dr. honoris causa, Royal Coll. Art, 1971; Art dir. Indsl. Art Inst., 1951-54; Smithsonian Instn. travelling mus. exhbns., U.S., 1956-58, 71-73; one-man exhbns. in numerous countries including Stedilijk Mus., Amsterdam, 1976, Venezia Biennale Invitation Exhbn., 1976; designer interior Finnish Pavilion, Brussels World Fair, 1958; represented in permanent collections Europe, U.S., Australia; jury mem. numerous internat. competitions; chmn. Govt. Indsl. Art Commn., Finland, 1968-73. Named hon. royal designer of Industry, London, 1964, hon. assoc. Worshipful Co. of Goldsmiths, London, 1971; recipient seven Grandes Premios gold medals, silver medal in Triennales, Milan; Lunningprize, 1951; Most Beautiful Object of Yr. award, 1951; four prizes for designing Olympic Games stamps, 1952; S.I.A. Medal of Yr., London, 1958; Golden Obelisk Domus Milano, 1963; 5 gold medals Faenza Internat. Ceramic Competitions, 3 internat. prizes Vicenza Internat. Ceramic Competitions; hon. prize, Culture Found. Finland, 1968; decorated knight White Rose of Finland. Deceased. Home: Espoo Finland

WISBERG, AUBREY LIONEL, screenwriter, production company executive; b. London, Oct. 20; came to U.S., 1921; s. Phillip and Cynthia (Shuman) W.; m. Barbara Duberstein. Writer Columbia Pictures, Hollywood, Calif., RKO Pictures, Hollywood, 20th Century-Fox, Hollywood, Paramount Pictures, Hollywood, Universal-Internat. Pictures, Hollywood, Allied Artists Pictures, Hollywood; co-founder Am. Pictures Corp., Hollywood, Mid-Century Films, Hollywood; assoc. producer Edward Small Prodns., Hollywood; founder, exec. producer Wisberg Prodns., Hollywood. Screenwriter: The Burning Cross (Internat. Unity award) and 41 other films; playwright numerous prodns. Mem. Writers Guild Am. West, Dramatists Guild, Am. League Am., Dirs. Guild Am. Home: New York N.Y. Died Mar. 14, 1990.

WISE, BASIL FRED, dean, singer; b. Winfield, Iowa, Dec. 14, 1894; s. George Morgan and Ora (Wilson) W.; m. Ione Mary Sirts, June 22, 1921. MusB, Parsons Coll., 1918; PhB, U. Chgo., 1920; studies in Paris, 1928; LHD, Eureka Coll., 1958. Lectr. art Roosevelt U., 1942-47; dir. music Internat. Conv. Disciples of Christ, 1934-43; tchr. voice Am. Conservatory Music, Chgo., dean faculities, from 1953; dir. Music Festival of Faith, World Coun. Chs., 1954. Concert, oratoric singer; appeared with Chgo. Symphony Orch., other oratorio groups Mid. West; singer radio sta. WGN, 1926-31, NBC, 1926-31, NBC, 1926-31; editor Christian Worship, hymnal Am. Bapt., Disciples of Christ Chs.; contbr: articles in field. Mem. Chgo. Singing Tchrs. Guild (pres. 1949-52), Soc. Am. Musicians (pres. 1949-52), Hymm Soc. Am., Am. Soc. Aesthetics, Am. Musicology Soc., NAt. Assn. Tchrs. Singing (pres. 1960-61), Masons (32). Clubs: CLiff Dwellers (pres. 1954-56), Quadrangle, U. Chf., Arts. *

WISE, GEORGE SCHNEIWEIS, university chancellor; b. Pinsk, Poland, Apr. 7, 1906; came to U.S., 1926, naturalized, 1939; s. Noah and Chaya (Rabinowitz) Schneiweis; m. Florence Rosenberg, Dec. 8, 1933. B.S. summa cum laude, Furman U., 1928, LL.D., 1973; M.A., Columbia, 1930, Ph.D., 1950, LL.D., 1981; Ph.D. (hon.), Hebrew U., 1957, Tel Aviv U., 1972, Bar Ilan U., 1976; LL.D., U. Miami, 1977, Yeshiva U., 1983; H.L.D., U. Fla., 1977. Assoc. dir. Bur. Applied Social Research, Columbia, 1949-52, lectr. sociology, 1950-52; vis. prof. U. Mexico, 1956; pres. Tel-Aviv U., 1963-71, Chancellor for life, 1971-87; dir. Ctr. for Advanced Internat. Studies, U. Miami, 1978-81; Disting. prof. emeritus of internat. affairs U. Miami, 1981-87; dir. postgrad. med. edn. Mt. Sinai Med. Ctr., Miami Beach, 1978-81; Pres. Inter-Am. Paper Corp., Fabricas de Papel Tuxtepec, Mex., 1955-63; pres., chmn. Clal Israel Latin Am. Devel. Co., 1962-69; dir., exec. Israel Corp., Ltd.; dir. Indsl. Devel. Bank Israel, Israeli Paper Mills, Hadera. Author: Caudillo, 1951, Mexico de Aleman, 1952; editor: Middle East Perspectives: the next 20 years, 1981. Chmn. bd. govs. Hebrew U., 1953-62; chmn. Jewish Telegraphic Agy., 1951-55; trustee Mt. Sinai Med. Ctr., Miami, 1977—, U. Miami, 1981-86. Decorated Order of Aguila Azteca (Mex.); Order of Cultural Merit (France); Order of Andrew Bello (Venezuela). Fellow Am. Sociol. Soc.; mem. Israel Am. Soc. (pres.), Israel Am. C. of C. Clubs: Yale (N.Y.C.), Columbia U. (N.Y.C.); Univ. (Mex.); Bankers (Miami), Standard (Miami), Westview Country (Miami). Home: Miami Beach Fla. Died July 2, 1987; buried Beth David Cemetery, Elmont, N.Y.

WISE, WATSON WILLIAM, oil and gas company executive; b. Findlay, Ohio; s. William Alfred and Nella Jane (Watson) W.; m. Emma Foote. Ph.B., Yale U.; D.Letters, Ambassador Coll.; PhD, Oxford (Eng.) U. Adv. dir. First RepublicBank Tyler N.A. Bank, Tex.; dir. Tex. Research League, Austin, Nat. Civil Service League, Washington; prof. Salzburg Seminar in Am. Studies, Austria, 1963; spl. counsel, Schuman Plan NATO; del. 13th Gen. Assembly UN, 1958-59; U.S. del. Atlantic Congress, London, 1962, NATO, Luxembourg, Lisbon, 1968, Washington, The Hague, 1970, Brussels, London; mem. UN del., 1969-70; lectr. Salzaburg (Austria) Seminar; mem. coord. bd. Tex. coll and univ. system, Austin; bd. dirs. Peoples Nat. Bank, Tyler, Tex. Rsch. League, Austin, Tex.; exec. com. Lone Star Steel Co. Chmn. Good Neighbor Commn. of Tex., 1957-63; trustee George Washington U., 1958, Briarcliff Coll., Briarcliff Manor, N.Y., 1961-70, Southwestern Med. Found., Dallas, 1964, Tex. Chest Found., Atlantic Jr. Coll., from 1977, Tyler Jr. Coll., 1950-70, pres. bd. trustees; mem. Tex. Commn. Higher Edn., Austin, Tex. A & M Coun., College Station, Coun. on Goals for Dallas; pres. Tex. Rose Festival; chmn. Tex. Highway Coun.; bd. dirs. Nat. Civil Svc. League, Washington; mem. devel. bd., donor med. rsch. libr. U. Tex. Health Ctr., Tyler; dedicated Watson W. Wise Emergency Pavilion George Washington U. Hosp., Watson W. and Emma Wise Cultural Arts Ctr. Tyler Jr. Coll., statue Harry S. Jenkins pres.; donor Watson Wise Dialysis Ctr. Med. Ctr. Hosp., Tyler, Scott & White Hosp., Temple, Wadley Meml. Hosp., Texarkana, Tex., Texoma Med. Ctr., Denison, Tex., Valley Bapt. Med. Ctr. Found., Harlingen, Tex., St. Joeeph's Hosp., Paris, Severence Hosp., Seoul, Republic Korea; donor Watson W. Wise '23 Reading Room to Yale U., Seeley G. Mudd Library Donor Wise Auditorium Tyler Jr. Coll. Recipient T.B. Butler award as outstanding citizen of Tyler.; Hon. mem. Acad. Econ. and Social Soc., Trieste, Italy. Mem. Coun. Internat. Rels., Ind. Petroleum Assn. Am. (exec. com.), Southwest Ctr. Advanced Studies, Mid-Continent Oil and Gas Assn. (bd. dirs, past v.p.)., Am. Assn. Petroleum Geologists, Tex. Ind. Producers and Royalty Owners, East Tex. Ind. Producers and Royalty Owners. Clubs: Metropolitan (Washington); Dallas Petroleum; Yale, Explorers (N.Y.C.); Rolling Rock (Ligonier, Pa.). Home: Tyler Tex. Died Sept. 9, 1989; buried Tyler, Tex.

WITMER, WILLIAM KERN, petroleum company executive; b. Bartlesville, Okla., June 16, 1926; s. Russell Rudolph and Crystal Orien (Kern) W.; m. Joan Curtis, Nov. 17, 1950; children: Diane, Joanne Witmer Contreras, Marianne, Robert. BS, Okla. State U., 1949; postgrad., Harvard U., 1973. With Cities Svc. Oil Co., Bartlesville, 1949-58, mgr. budget dept., 1956-58; with Cities Svc. Co., N.Y.C., 1958-71, mgr. investor rels., 1964-66, staff v.p., 1966-68, gen. mgr. real estate, 1968-71; treas. Cities Svc. Co., Tulsa, 1975-87; v.p. fin., treas. Cities Svc. Gas Co., Oklahoma City, 1971-75. With USNR, 1944-46. Mem. Fin. Execs. Inst. (bd. dirs. Okla. chpt.), Am. Petroleum Inst., Newcomen Soc., Summit Club, Masons, Beta Alpha Psi, Kappa Sigma. Home: Tulsa Okla. Died June 15, 1987; buried Memorial Cemetery.

WITTENBERG, PHILLIP, lawyer; b. Bklyn., Apr. 4, 1895; s. William and Elizabeth (Plesetzkaya) W.; m. Ruth Budinoff, Nov. 22, 1919; children: Jonathon B., Susanna. LLB, N.Y. Law Sch., 1916. Bar: N.Y. 1916. Organizer, dir. New Playwrites Theatre, 1927-34; exec. bd. Nat. Injuction Com., 1927-31; exec. com. Internat. Jud. Assn., 1931-34; lectr. New Sch. Social Rsch., Columbia; also Cooper Union, N.Y.C., from 1939; Counsel Mystery Writers Am., Bill of Rights Fund. Author: Lit. Property, 1938, Guilty Men, 1940, Dangerous Words, 1947 (trans. Japanese 1954), The Law of Literary Property; contbr. articles reviews and mags. Trustee Am. Acad. Dramatic Arts, Sopywrite Soc. U. S. *

WITTENSTEIN, ARTHUR, lawyer; b. Bklyn., Feb. 14, 1926; s. Martin and Esther (Katz) W.; m. Aileen Classon, June 29, 1950; children: Andrew, Kate, Jessica. A.B., Columbia U., 1948; J.D., Harvard U., 1951; M.B.A., NYU, 1957. Bar: N.Y. 1952; C.P.A., N.Y. Assoc. Coopers & Lybrand, N.Y.C., 1951-58, Stroock & Stroock & Lavan, N.Y.C., 1958-60; ptnr. Stroock & Stroock & Lavan, 1961-89. Contbr. various profl. jours. With U.S. Army, 1945-46. Mem. ABA, N.Y. State Bar Assn., Assn. of Bar of City of N.Y., AICPAs, N.Y. State Soc. CPAs, Authors Guild, Heights Casino Club, India House Club. Democrat. Home: New York N.Y. Died Aug. 21, 1989; buried N.Y.C.

WOERNER, FRED F., JR., army officer; b. Phila., Aug. 12, 1933; s. Frederick Frank and Mary Ann (McCabe) W.; m. Gennie Ehrhorn, Jan. 21, 1956; children—Fred F. III, Charles, Robert, Michael. B.S., U.S. Mil. Acad., 1955; M.A. in History-Latin Am., U. Ariz., 1965; exchange student, Mil. Inst. Superior Studies, Montevideo, Uruguay. Commd. 2d lt. U.S. Army, 1955, advanced through grades to gen., 1987; aide de camp to comdg. gen. 25th Inf. Div., 1958-59; co. comdr. 2d Battle Group, 23d Inf, 2d Inf. div., Fort Benning, Ga., 1961-62; advisor Mil. Adv. Assistance Group, Vietnam, 1962-63; civic action officer U.S. Mil. Group, Guatemala City, Guatemala, 1966-69; comdg. officer 1st Bn., 6th Inf. Div., Vietnam, 1970-71; staff office Office of Asst. Chief of Staff for Force Devel., Washington, 1971-72; dir. Latin Am. Studies U.S. Army War Coll., Carlisle Barracks, Pa., 1973-77; comdr. 3d Basic Combat Tng. Brigade, Fort Leonard Wood, Mo., 1977-79; chief staff 24th Inf. Div., Fort Stewart, Ga., 1979-80; dir. Echelon Above Corps study U.S. Combined Arms Ctr., Fort Leavenworth, Kans., 1980, dep. comdr. Combined Arms Tng. Devel. Activity, 1980-82; comdr. 193d Inf. Brigade, Fort Clayton, Panama, 1982-86; comdg. gen. 6th U.S. Army, San Francisco, 1986-87; gen., comdr. in chief U.S. So. Command, Quarry Hts., Panama, 1987-89. Decorated D.S.M. with 1 oak leaf cluster, Legion of Merit with 2 oak leaf clusters, Bronze Star with 1 oak leaf cluster, Meritorious Service medal, Air medal, Commendations medal, Nat. Def. Svc. medal with 1 oak leaf cluster, Vietnam Cross of Gallantry with Gold Star, Guatemalan Cross of Mil. Merit-1st Class, Vienam Svc. medal with 4 bronze stars, Armed Forces Expeditionary medal, P.R. N.G. Disting. Service medal, Gold medal for merit (El Salvador), Disting. Service medal 1st class (Panama), Star of Carabobo (Venezuela), Order of May for merit (Argentina). Home: Philadelphia Pa. Died May 2, 1990.

WOHL, JOSEPH GENE, research company executive; b. Chgo., May 8, 1927; s. Max and Frieda (Friedmann) W.; m. Carol Weiss, June 26, 1949; children—David, Michael, Nancy, Betsy. B.S. in Physics and Math, U. Wis., 1949; postgrad., U. Md., George Washington U., Mass. Inst. Tech. Scientist U.S. Naval Research Lab., 1948-52, Office Naval Research, 1952-54; sr. engr. Sperry Gyroscope Co., 1954-57; v.p. Dunlap & Assocs. Inc., Darien, Conn., 1957-69; cons. Infoton, Inc., mfr. electronics, Burlington, Mass., 1969-71; dir. systems analysis Addressograph Data Systems Tech. Center, Cambridge, Mass., 1971-72; head dept. advanced planning (Mitre Corp.), Bedford, Mass., 1972-81; sr. v.p. Alphatech, Inc., Burlington, from 1981, also bd. dirs.; adj. asso. prof. Columbia U., 1958-66; program chmn. NATO Agard Simulation Symposium, Paris, 1979. Mem. editorial bd. Ergonomic Abstracts, 1971-85; patentee in field. Mem. fin. com. Plainview (N.Y.) Sch. Bd., 1955-56. Served with USNR, 1945-46. Fellow

AAAS (gov. council 1971), IEEE (chmn. man-machine systems group 1969-71, program chmn. Man-Machine Systems Symposium, Cambridge, Eng. 1969), Systems, Man and Cybernetics Soc. (v.p. 1980-85); mem. Sigma Xi. Home: Wayland Mass. Died Feb. 23, 1989; buried North Cemetery, Wayland, Mass.

WOHL, KNUT GETZ, economist, banker; b. Verdal, Norway, Aug. 3, 1915; s. Trygve and Ella (Getz) W.; grad. econs. U. Oslo (Norway), 1939; postgrad. U. Stockholm (Sweden), 1940-41; m. Astrid Margit Graver, Dec. 23, 1948; children: Bjorn Kjetil, Marit, Ellen. Adv. to Norwegian Ministry Fin., London, 1941-45, Oslo, 1945-46; under-sec. Ministry Social Affairs, Oslo, 1946-48; dir. fgn. trade div. Ministry Commerce, Oslo, 1948-58; dep. gov. Bank of Norway, Oslo, 1958-70, gov., 1970-85. Mem. bd. mgmt. European Payments Union, 1951-58, Monetary Agreement, 1958-69; dir. Alcan Aluminium Ltd., Montreal, Que., Can., 1967-71; chmn. econ. com. EFTA, 1967-71. Decorated comdr. Order St. Olav (Norway); Order Dannebrog (Denmark); Order Falcon (Iceland). Fellow Royal Econ. Soc. (London, Eng.). Author: Kosthold og levestandard, 1941; Plan for velstand T.V.A. og Norge, 1946; Levestandardens okonomi, 1949; Okonomisk styring i et fritt samfunn, 1975. Died 1988. Home: Oslo Norway.

WOLF, EDWIN, II, librarian; b. Phila., Dec. 6, 1911; s. Morris and Pauline (Binswanger) W.; m. Margaret Gimbel Dannenbaum, July 2, 1934 (dec. June 1964); children: Ellen R. Wolf Gettleman, Anthony E., Mary Wolf Hurtig; m. Mary Paxson Matthews, Nov. 16, 1965; stepchildren: Sandra M. Wolf Korb, Barbara M. Wolf Milic, Ann M. Wolf Massaro. Grad., William Penn Charter Sch., Phila., 1927, Bedales Sch., Eng., 1930; D.H.L. (hon.), Coll. Jewish Studies, Chgo., 1965; L.H.D. (hon.), LaSalle U., Phila., 1981; LL.D. (hon.), U. Pa., 1982. Cataloger, bibliographer, mgr. Rosenbach Co. (rare books and manuscripts), 1930-52; lectr. bibliography Bryn Mawr Coll., 1941-42; curator Library Co. of Phila, 1953-55, librarian, 1955-84; Rosenbach fellow in bibliography U. Pa., 1964; Lyell reader in bibliograpy Oxford U., 1985-86. Author: Descriptive Catalogue of the Lewis Collection of European Manuscripts, 1937, William Blake, A Descriptive Catalogue of an Exhibition, (with Elizabeth Mongan), 1939, Doctrina Christiana, the First Book Printed in the Philippines, 1947, Franklin's Way to Wealth as a Printer, 1951, William Blake's Illuminated Books, (with Geoffrey L. Keynes), 1953, History of the Jews of Philadelphia, (with Maxwell Whiteman), 1956, Rosenbach: A Biography, (with John F. Fleming), 1960, American Song Sheets, 1950-1870, 1963, Negro History: 1553-1903, An Exhibition, 1969, James Logan, 1674-1751, Bookman Extraordinary, an Exhibition, 1971, The Library of James Logan of Philadelphia, 1974, Philadelphia: A Portrait of an American City, 1975, At the Instance of Benjamin Franklin, 1976, A Flock of Beautiful Birds, 1977, Quarter of a Millennium, Library Company of Philadelphia, 1731-1981, (with Marie E. Korey), 1981; editor: Legacies of Genius, 1988; assoc. editor: Philadelphia: 300 Year History, 1982, The Book Culture of an Early American City, 1988, From Gothic Windows to Peacocks: American Embossed Leather Bindings, 1825-1855, 1990; contbr. articles to profl. jours. Pres. Fedn. Jewish Charities Greater Phila., 1959-62; pres. Nat. Found. Jewish Culture, 1960-65, Jewish Exponent, 1966-68, Greater Phila. Cultural Alliance, 1977-78, Fellows in Am. Studies, 1976-77; mem. Mayor's Cultural Adv. Com., 1984-86. Served with AUS, 1943-45; Served with M.I. Corps.; French mil. intelligence interpreter in Belgium; spl. agt. C.I.C., Germany. Guggenheim fellow, 1961; recipient Athenaeum Lit. award, 1961, Penn Club award, 1979, Phila. award, 1982, Am. Printing Hist. Assn. award, 1988, Hyde award Princeton U., 1988; named Disting. Pennsylvanian, 1982. Mem. MLA, Am. Philos. Soc., Am. Antiquarian Soc., Hist. Soc. Pa., Bibliog. Soc. Am. (past pres.), Inst. Early Am. History and Culture (past mem. council), Mass. Hist. Soc., Jewish Publ. Soc. Am. (past pres.), Friends U. Pa. Library (past pres.), Athenaeum of Phila. Jewish. Clubs: Philadelphia (Phila.), Franklin Inn (Phila.) (past pres.); Grolier (N.Y.C.). Home: Philadelphia Pa. Died Feb. 20, 1991.

WOLF, GEORGE ANTHONY, JR., physician, educator; b. East Orange, N.J., Apr. 20, 1914; s. George Anton and Jane Agnes (Devine) W.; m. Marguerite Girton Hurrey, Aug. 2, 1939; children: Patricia, Deborah. BA, NYU, 1936; MD, Cornell U., 1941; DSc (hon.), Union U., 1966, U. Vermont, 1986. Diplomate: Am. Bd. Internal Medicine. Teaching fellow biology NYU, 1935-36; intern N.Y. Hosp., 1941-42, asst. resident, 1942-43, resident physician, 1943-44, physician out-patient dept., 1944-49, asst. attending physician, 1949-52, dir. personnel health services, 1948-50; asst. anatomy Cornell U. Med. Coll., 1939-41, asst. medicine, 1942-43, instr., 1944-49, Com. Med. Research research fellow, 1944-46, asst. prof. clin. medicine, 1949-52, asst. prof. pub. health and preventive medicine, 1948-50; prof. clin. medicine U. Vt. Coll. Medicine, 1952-61, also dean; v.p. for med. and dental affairs, prof. medicine Tufts U., 1961-66; exec. dir. Tufts New Eng. Med. Center, 1961-66; dean, provost, prof. medicine U. Kans. Med. Center, 1966-70; prof. medicine U. Vt., Burlington, 1970-79, prof. emeritus medicine, 1979-90, prof. nursing, 1978-81; cons. Vt. Dept. Social Welfare, 1982-85. Author: Collecting Data from Patients, 1977, also articles in med. jours. Fellow ACP; mem. Vt. State Med. Soc. (life;

Disitng. Svc. award 1988), Chittenden County Med. Soc., N.Y. Acad. Medicine, Harvey Soc., Assn. Am. Med. Colls. (pres.), Cornell Med. Coll. Alumni Assn. (Award of Distinction 1990), Phi Beta Kappa, Zeta Psi, Alpha Omega Alpha, Phi Chi. Home: Jericho Center Vt. Died June 15, 1990; buried Jericho, Vt.

WOLF, GEORGE VAN VELSOR, lawyer; b. Balt., Aug. 10, 1908; s. Stewart George and Angeline Perkins (Griffing) W.; m. Alice Roberts Kimberly, Feb. 3, 1940; children: Constance, Van Velsor, Timothy. Student, Ecole Alsacienne, Paris, France, 1925, Andover Acad., 1926; A.B., Yale, 1930; LL.B., Harvard, 1933. Bar: Md. 1933. With Piper & Marbury (and predecessor firms), Balt., from 1933; partner Piper & Marbury (and predecessor firms), 1940-76, counsel, 1976-81, ret. ptnr., 1981; asst. atty. gen. Md., 1944-45; Mem. character com. Md. Ct. of Appeals, 1949-56; mem. Pub. Service Law Revision Commn., 1951-53, Commn. to Create An Hist. Trust for Preservation Md. Antiquities, 1959-61, Commn. To Study and Revise Testamentary Laws Md., 1965-70, Legis. Commn. on Nursing Issues, 1981-83, Md. State Bd. Med. Examiners, 1980-83. Author, lectr. on estate planning. Trustee Children's Hosp., Balt., 1954-79, v.p., 1962-71; trustee Kent and Queen Anne's Hosp., Chestertown, 1971-80, pres., 1978-80; mem. Kent County Ethics Commn., 1983-88; mem. bd. Salvation Army, pres., 1947-49. Fellow Am., Md. bar founds.; Am. Coll. Probate Counsel (regent 1972-78); mem. Md. Soc. Med. Research (pres. 1951-53), Am. Bar Assn. (chmn. real property, probate and trust law sect. 1970-71), Md. Bar Assn. (chmn. estate and trust law sect. 1961-65), Baltimore City Bar Assn. (exec. com. 1956-59). Clubs: 14 W. Hamilton St. (Balt.). Home: Sykesville Md. Deceased.

WOLF, HOWARD M., business equipment company executive; b. 1925. With United Stationers Supply Co., Des Plaines, Ill., 1946-63, pres., 1963-77, chmn. bd., chief exec. officer, 1981-88, chmn. emeritus, 1988-89. Home: Des Plaines Ill. Died, 1989.

WOLF, WILLIAM JOHN, theology educator, clergyman; b. Hartford, Conn., Jan. 17, 1918; s. William Henry and Mabel Bodine (Griggs) W.; m. Eleanor Hale Dun, Aug. 10, 1946; children: Edwin Mershon, John de Nervaud (dec.), Stephen Hale (dec.). A.B., Trinity Coll., 1940; B.D., Episcopal Theol. Sch., 1943; S.T.M., Union Theol. Sem., N.Y.C., 1944, Ph.D., 1945; D.S.T., Kenyon Coll., 1959, Trinity Coll., 1960; D.D., Gen. Theol. Sem., 1973. Ordained to ministry P.E. Ch., 1943; asst. minister Grace Ch., N.Y.C., 1943-45; faculty Episcopal Div. Sch., Cambridge, Mass., 1945-85, prof. emeritus theology, Howard Chandler Robbins chmn., 1951-90; pastor St. Elizabeth's Ch., Sudbury, 1947-51; Acting dir. laymen's inst. World Council Chs., Switzerland, 1952; rep. P.E. Ch., Faith and Order Commn., Evanston assembly World Council Chs.; del. observer of Episcopal Ch. to 2d Vatican Council; rep. P.E. Ch. Joint Commn. on Ecumenical Relations, Consultation on Ch. Union; mem. Interorthodox and Pan-Anglican Joint Doctrinal Commn., Anglican-Roman Cath. Commn. Author: Man's Knowledge of God, 1955, No Cross, No Crown, 1957, The Almost Chosen People, 1959, The Religion of Abraham Lincoln, 1963, The Thought of Frederick Maurice, 1963, A Plan of Church Union, Catholic, Evangelical and Reformed, 1965, Thoreau: Mystic, Prophet, Ecologist, 1974, Freedom's Holy Light, 1977, Benedict Arnold: A Novel, 1990; editor: Protestant Churches and Reform Today, 1964, The Spirit of Anglicanism, 1979, Anglican Spirituality, 1982, An Abridgment of Maurice's Kingdom of Christ, 1983; contbr. The Theology of Reinhold Niebuhr, 1955, Calvinism and Political Order, 1965, The Second Vatican Council, 1967, Church Union at Midpoint, 1972. Mem. Am. Theol. Soc. Home: Heath Mass. Died June 6, 1990.

WOLFE, RAPHAEL DAVID, business executive; b. Toronto, Ont., Can., Aug. 3, 1917; s. Maurice and Tillie (Manovitz) W.; m. Rose Senderowitz; children—Jonathan, Elizabeth. BA, U. Toronto, 1939; PhD (hon.), U. Haifa, Israel, 1988. Chmn., chief exec. officer Oshawa Group Ltd., Toronto, 1958-90; pres. Can. Jewish News; hon. bd. dirs. Bank of Nova Scotia; bd. dirs. Confedn. Life Ins. Co., Food Mktg. Inst. Trustee Toronto Gen. Hosp. Found.; bd. govs. Mt. Sinai Hosp.; hon. pres., Bd. dirs. Can. Firends Haita U.; bd. dirs. Can. Coun. Christians and Jews, Baycrest Ctr. for Geriatric Care, Coun. for Can. Unity, Nat. Ballet Can., Can. Technion Soc. With RCAF, 1943-46. Decorated Order of Can., 1980; recipient Human Rels. award Can. Coun. Christians and Jews, 1968; Ben Sadowski Award of Merit, 1975; named Can. Retailer of Yr., 1987. Mem. Can.-Israel C. of C. and Industry (hon. chmn.). Clubs: Montefiore, Oakdale, Primrose. Home: Willowdale Ont., Can. Died Jan. 16, 1990.

WOLFSON, SIR ISAAC, foundation executive; b. Sept. 17, 1897; s. Lord Wolfson; m. Edith Specterman, 1926 (dec. 1981); 1 son. Student, Queen's Park Sch., Glasgow, Scotland; DCL (hon.), U. Oxford, 1963; LLD (hon.), U. London, 1958, U. Glasgow, 1963, U. Cambridge, 1966, U. Manchester, 1967, U. Strathclyde, 1969, Brandeis U., 1969, U. Nottingham, 1971; PhD (hon.), U. Jerusalem, 1970. Joined The Great Universal Stores Ltd., 1932, joint chmn., then hon. life pres., from 1987; hon. pres. Weizmann Inst. Sci. Found., trustee Religious Ctr., Jerusalem; trustee Wolfson Found., from

1955; mem. Worshipful Co. of Pattenmakers. Mem. grand council Cancer Research Campaign; patron Royal Coll. Surgeons. Fellow Weizmann Inst. Sci., Israel, St. Edmund Hall, Oxford, Jews' Coll., Lady Margaret Hall, Oxford, Wolfson Coll., Oxford; recipient Einstein award, U.S., 1967, Herbert Lehmann award, U.S., 1968; named Freeman City of Glasgow, 1971.

WOLLET, ROBERT JAMES, lawyer; b. Williamsport, Pa., July 17, 1927; s. Harold E. and Sarah Margaret (Snyder) W.; m. Marguerite DiSalvo, Apr. 19, 1952; children: Nancy Lee, Robert James Jr., Christine Marie, Kimberly Ann. BS, Bucknell U., 1953; JD, U. Pa., 1956. Bar: Pa. 1958, U.S. Dist. Ct. (mid. dist.) Pa. 1959, U.S. Supreme Ct. 1988. Pvt. practice Williamsport, 1957-79, 88—; ptnr. Wollet & Anderson, Williamsport, 1980-81; judge Ct. Common Pleas Lycoming County, Williamsport, 1982-88; libr. Lycoming County, Williamsport, 1959-63; solicitor for sheriff, Lycoming County, Williamsport, 1959-63; spl. asst. atty. gen. Pa. Liquor Control Bd., 1963-71; solicitor for Lycoming County Commrs., Williamsport, 1972-76, 80-81. Sec. Lycoming County Rep. Com., 1968-80. With USAF, 1944-51. Mem. ABA, Pa. Bar Assn., Pa. Conf. State Trial Judges, Lycoming Law Assn., Wheel Club, Ross Club, Antlers Club, Masons, Shriners. Home: Williamsport Pa. Died May 1990.

WOLLSTADT, PAUL, petroleum consultant; b. Rockford, Ill., July 28, 1910; s. John and Hilda (Ekstrom) W.; m. Elzada Elizabeth Rogers, June 19, 1934 (dec. Apr. 1974); children—Roger Davis, David Carl, Loyd James; m. Elizabeth Peters, Apr. 25, 1975. A.B., U. Ill., 1932. Reporter, editorial writer, editor editorial page Rockford Register-Republic, 1932-45; mng. editor Nat. Petroleum News and Platt's Oilgram, 1945-51; asso. mgr. pub. relations dept. Mobil Oil Corp., 1951-58, asst. to chmn., 1958-59, v.p., 1959-62, sr. v.p., 1962-69; dep. asst. sec. def., 1969-71, petroleum industry cons., 1971-88; Mem. Am. Petroleum Inst. Recipient Disting. Civilian Service medal, 1971. Republican. Presbyterian. Home: Fort Pierce Fla. Died Apr. 2, 1987.

WOOD, EMMA LOU, real estate executive; b. Jasonville, Ind., Sept. 29, 1935; d. Leo William and Elizabeth (White) Warrick; student Ind. U., 1957-72; m. C.J. Wood, Jan. 31, 1966 (dec.); children: Elizabeth Marie, Charles John; m. Thomas B. McNolty, Sept. 4, 1985. Bookkeeper, Place & Co., South Bend, Ind., 1959-65; pres. C.J. Wood, Inc., South Bend, from 1976. Mem. South Bend C. of C. Clubs: Knollwood Country (Granger, Ind.); Orchard Hills Country (Niles, Mich.). Home: Niles Mich.

WOOD, HARLAND GOFF, biochemist, educator; b. Delavan, Minn., Sept. 2, 1907; s. William C. and Inez (Goff) W.; m. Mildred Lenora Davis, Sept. 14, 1929; children: Donna (dec.), Beverly, Louise. A.B., Macalester Coll., 1931, D.Sc. (hon.), 1946; Ph.D., Iowa State Coll., 1935; D.Sc., Northwestern U., 1972, U. Cin., 1982, Case Western U., 1991. Fellow NRC, biochem. dept. U. Wis., 1935-36; asst. prof. bacteriology dept. Iowa State Coll., 1936-43; assoc. prof. physiol. chemistry dept. U. Minn., 1943-46; prof., dir. biochemistry dept. Case Western Res. U., Cleve., 1946-65, prof. biochemistry, 1965-78, dean scis., 1967-69, Univ. prof., 1970-78, Univ. prof. emeritus, 1978-91; chmn. isotope panel com. on growth NRC, 1947-48; adv. council Life Ins. Med. Research Fund, 1957-62; mem. tng. grant com. NIH, 1965-69; adv. bd. Case Inst. Tech., 1971-78; adv. com. div. biology and medicine U.S. AEC, 1957-62; mem. Presdl. Sci. Adv. Com., Washington, 1968-72; mem. physiol. chemistry study sect., 1973-77; Wellcome vis. prof. in basic med. scis., St. Louis U., 1989. Recipient Eli Lilly research award in bacteriology, 1942, Carl Neuberg award Nat. Acad. Scis., 1953, Glycerine award, 1954, Modern Med. award for disting. achievement, 1968, Lynen lectr. and medal, 1972, Humbolt prize as sr. U.S. scientist W. Ger., 1979, Selman A. Waksman award in microbiology, 1986, Rosenstiel Med. Research award, 1987, Michelson-Morley Achievement award, 1987, Disting. Achievement Citation Iowa State U., 1989, Pres.'s Nat. Medal of Sci., 1989, William C. Rose award, 1990; Fulbright fellow, 1955; Guggenheim fellow, 1962. Mem. Nat. Acad. Scis. Am. Acad. Arts and Scis., Am. Heart Assn. (research com. 1949), Am. Chem. Soc., Am. Soc. Biol. Chemists (pres. 1959), N.Y. Acad. Scis., Am. Cancer Soc. (adv. bd. 1965-69), Internat. Union Biochemistry (mem. council 1967-76, sec. gen. 1970-73, pres. 1982-85), Soc. Am. Bacteriologists, Biochem. Soc. Japan (hon.); corr. mem. Der Bayerischen Akademie der Wissenschaften. Methodist. Home: Cleveland Heights Ohio Died Sept. 12, 1991; buried Mankato, Minn.

WOOD, HORACE WALTER, JR., educator; b. St. Joseph, Mo., Feb. 2, 1894; s. Horace Walter and Mary Jane (Vance) W.; m. Elevra Wilander, June 26, 1926. BS in Engring., U. Mo., 1925, CE, 1925; MS U. Mich., 1938. Registered profl. engr. Mo. Rsch. engr. Nat. Lime Assn., 1925-27; cons. Mo. Hydro Electric Co., 1927-28; field engr. Portland Cement Co., 1929; chief engr. Cement Inst. Ctrl. Div., 1930, Current River Power Co., Gasconade River Power Co., 1929-43; assoc. prof. engring mechanics, chmn. dept. U. Mo., 1931-35, assoc. prof. civil engring., 1935-42, prof. civil engring., from 1942, chmn. dept., 1956-64; hydro-electric studies and devel. Ozark region. Author: Flood Flow on Missouri Streams, 1946, Fund of Hydraulic Machinery, 1950, rev. edit. 1957; contbr. Mo. Its Resources, People and Institutions. Dir. hydraulic rsch. projects for USAF and Mo. Hwy. Commn.; mem. Mo. Basin Rsch. and Devel. Coun. 2d lt. USAC, 1917-19. Fellow Am. Soc. Civil Engrs. (pres. Mid-Mo. 1942); mem. Am. Soc. engring. Edn. (pres. Mo. sect. 1943-46, gen. coun. 1946-47, chmn. applied hydraulics com. 1948-49), Mo. Hist. Soc., Am. Geophys. Union, Nat. Soc. Prof. Engrs., Mo. Soc. Profl. Engrs., Sigma Xi, Delta Tau Delta, Tau Beta Pi, Pi Mu Epsilon, Chi Epsilon, Kiwanis. Republican. *

WOOD, J. FRANK, lawyer; b. Chester, Pa., Aug. 1, 1908; s. J. William and Sarah (Black) W.; m. Ann Budd, Feb. 4, 1939; children—John Frank, Lydia A. Wood Sargent, Susannah Wood Tavernier, Sarah Morton Wood Lewis, William Howard. A.B., Harvard U., 1930, Sheldon travelling fellow, 1930-31, J.D., 1934. Bar: N.Y. 1935. Asso. atty. Barry, Wainwright, Thacher & Symmers, N.Y.C., 1934-37; trust rep., trust officer Chem. Bank & Trust Co., N.Y.C., 1937-43; dep. supt., counsel N.Y. State Banking Dept., 1943-44, 45-50; sr. v.p., trustee Dollar Savs. Bank, N.Y.C., 1951-54; partner firm Thacher, Proffitt & Wood (and predecessor firm), N.Y.C., 1954-74; counsel Thacher, Proffitt & Wood, N.Y.C., from 1974; trustee Savs. Banks Life Ins. Fund, N.Y.C., 1953-54; dir., mem. exec. com. Instl. Investors Mut. Fund, Inc., N.Y.C., 1953-54; counsel N.Y. State Harness Racing Commn., 1954; trustee Franklin Savs. Bank, N.Y.C., 1956-78; Mem. N.Y. State Pension Commn., 1954-60; mem. adv. council pensions N.Y. State Civil Service Dept., 1960-69, chmn., 1967-69. Bd. dirs., mem. exec. com. Allergy Found. Am., 1956-72; Mem. N.Y. N.G., 1935-38. Served to capt. USMCR, 1944-46. Mem. Am. Bar Assn., Assn. Ex-Mems. Squadron A., Descs. Signers Declaration Independence, The Pilgrims, Phi Beta Kappa. Republican. Presbyterian. Clubs: Down Town Assn. (N.Y.C.), Harvard (N.Y.C.), Union (N.Y.C.). Home: Buck Hill Falls Pa. Died Dec. 28, 1989; buried Media (Pa.) Cemetery.

WOOD, VICTOR LOUIE, insurance consultant; b. Saint Jo, Tex., Nov. 9, 1913; s. Louie Edwin and Mary Emma (Foster) W.; student public schs.; m. Ida Mae Greer, June 20, 1935; children: Vern L., Charles Edward, Sue Eileen. Salesman, Pioneer Am. Life Ins. Co., Ft. Worth, 1938-47; organizer, operator Western Fidelity Life Ins. Co., Ft. Worth, 1947-52, N.Mex. Life Ins. Co., Albuquerque, 1952-64, Gt. Western Assurance Life Co., Albuquerque, 1964-70, Western Educators Life Ins. Co., Albuquerque, 1970-74, Future Security Life Ins. Co., Albuquerque, 1974-77; organizer, operator N.Mex. Investors Life Ins. Co., Albuquerque, 1977-81, cons., from 1981. Republican. Clubs: Four Hills Country, Masons. Deceased. Home: Albuquerque N.Mex.

WOODBRIDGE, JOHN SYLVESTER, airways executive; b. Shanghai, China, Jan. 27, 1897; (parents U.S. citizens); s. Samuel I. and Jeanie Wilson (Woodrow) W. AB, Princeton, 1918. Treas., asst. comptroller Pan Am. World Airways, Inc., N.Y.C., 1929-40, comptroller, from 1940; treas. Pan Am.-Grace Airways, Inc., from 1929, The Liberia Co., Liberian Devel. Corp., from 1952; dir. Am. Internat. Life Assurance Co., Fairfield Securities, Inc., Am. Home Assurance Co., Internat. Products Co. Treas. Liberian Found., Inc. Served as ambulance driver French Army, 1917-18. Decorated Purple Heart, Croix de Guerre (twice). Mem. N.Y. Soc. CPA's. *

WOODRUFF, JUNE YVONNE, insurance agency executive; b. Bellflower, Calif., Jan. 26, 1930; d. Archie Leo and Virginia (Walton) Herrick; m. Ervin Dee Woodruff, Sept. 9, 1951; 1 child, Ervin Dee. A.A., Santa Ana Coll., 1950; B.A., Loma Linda U., 1951; Tchr., Rogue River Acad., Medford, Oreg., 1958-65; asst. librarian So. Oreg. Coll., 1966; sec. Sch. Dist. 549C, Medford, 1967-69; ins. agt. AAA of Oreg., Coos Bay, 1970-75; pres., ins. agt. Woodruff & Assocs., Inc., North Bend, Oreg., from 1978. Mem. Ind. Ins. Agts. S.W. Oreg., Ind. Agts. Oreg., Nat. Ind. Agts., Am. Bus. Women's Assn. (past treas., past chmn. edn. com.), Phi Beta Psi (past treas.). Republican. Lutheran. Club: Soroptomists (chmn. UN affairs from 1981, chmn. edn. com. from 1983, Easter Seal telethon com.). Deceased. Home: Coos Bay Oreg.

WOODS, CLIFFORD CURTIS, physician, hospital director; b. Ashland, Ky., Aug. 27, 1898; s. Thomas W. and Adelaide (Crowe) W.; m. Beatrice Hammond, Mar. 23, 1945; 1 child, Thomas. MD, Vanderbilt U., 1923; postgrad., U. Pa., 1929, NYU, 1951. Intern Nashville City Hosp., 1923-24; physician surgery pvt. practice, Ashland, Ky., 1925-40; chief surgeon VA Ctr., Bay Pines, Fla., 1946-51; chief planning div., surgery VA, Washington, 1951-54; mgr. VA Hosp., Omaha, 1954-56, Kennedy VA Hosp., Memphis, 1956-61; dir. VA Med. Teaching Group Hosp., Memphis, from 1961; mem. dean's com. VA U. Tenn. Med. Sch. Mem. City-County Def. Commn., 1956-63; bd. dirs. Tri-State chpt. ARC; mem. bd. Family Svc. of Memphis. col. AUS, WWI. Fellow ACS, Southeastern Surg. Assn.; mem. AMA, Am. Hosp. Assn., Fed. Execs. Assn. Greater Memphis (pres.), Am. Coll. Hosp. Adminstrs., Soc. Med. Cons. to Armed Forces, Am. Paraplegic Soc., Am. Assn. Med. Colls., MAsons (Shriner), Odd Fellows Club. Presbyterian. *

WOODS, LESLIE VICTOR, optometrist; b. L.A., Dec. 26, 1925; s. Kenneth Campbell and Ada Lucille (Meyers) W.; student U. B.C., 1944-46; BS, Pacific U., 1948, OD, 1949; m. Noreen Ellen Barry, Nov. 23, 1950; children: Deirdre Ann, Megan Louise. Individual practice optometry, Sedro Wooley, Wash., 1949, Spokane, 1950, from 1965, Chelan, Wash., 1951-65; optometrist dept. ophthalmology Pacific Med. Ctr.; mem. faculty Columbia-Pacific U., advisor to faculty Coll. Optometry; mem. optometric faculty Spokane Community Coll., 1975-78. Chmn. optometric affairs State and County CD, 1958-65; dir. Chelan CD, 1951; mem. Wash. Welfare Med. Care Com., 1958-66; councilman, Chelan, 1952; trustee Fort Wright Coll. of the Holy Names, Spokane; vice-chmn. bd. trustees Ft. Wright Coll., 1978-79; mem. adv. bd. Pacific U. Coll. Optomotry, Forest Grove, Oreg., 1989. Co-author Intra-ocular Lenses, 1989. Mem. Wash. Optometric Assn. (pres. Inland Soc. 1975-77), North Cen. Wash. Optometric Soc. (pres. 1954-56, 63-64, state trustee 1954-56, 63-64), Calif. Optometric Assn., Am. Optometric Assn., Omega Delta, Delta Upsilon. Democrat. Roman Catholic. Club: Lions (dir. N. Spokane 1975-76, v.p. 1976, pres. 1977-78). Deceased. Home: San Francisco Calif.

WOODS, PAUL HARLOW, banker; b. Kingman, Kans., July 9, 1906; s. Paul S. and Grace (Harlow) W.; m. Wilda Cline, May 24, 1930; children: Harlow Verne, Paula, Michael. B.S., U. Kans., 1928. Teller First Nat. Bank, Wichita, Kans., 1928-29, asst. v.p., 1938-42, 44-48, v.p., 1948-55, exec. v.p., 1955-58, pres., 1958-71, also bd. dirs.; asst. cashier First Nat. Bank, Kingman, Kans., 1929-34; sec. Fed. Intermediate Credit Bank, Wichita, 1934-38; chmn. bd. dirs. Energy Reserves Group, Inc., 1973-82. Pres. bd. edn., Wichita, 1951-52, mem., 1950-61; Pres. United Fund Wichita and Sedgewick County, 1968; chmn. bd. St. Joseph Hosp. and Med. Center, 1976-78. Served to maj. AUS, 1942-44. Mem. Delta Tau Delta. Mem. Christian Ch. Club: Wichita. Home: Wichita Kans. Died June 17, 1989; buried Kingman, Kans.

WOODS, THOMAS COCHRANE, JR., communications company executive; b. Lincoln, Nebr., May 4, 1920; s. Thomas Cochrane and Sarah (Ladd) W.; m. Marjorie Jane Jones, June 1, 1943; children: Thomas Cochrane III, Avery Ladd. BA, U. Nebr., 1943. Asst. advt. mgr. Addressograph-Multigraph Corp., Cleve., 1947-58; pres. Nellewood Corp., Lincoln, 1961-85, T-V Transmission, Inc., Lincoln, 1966-75; chmn. Lincoln Telecommunications Co., from 1980, Lincoln Telephone Co.; v.p. Lincoln Devel. Co., 1958-80, W.K. Realty Co., Lincoln, 1958-80; chmn. bd., dir. Sahara Coal Co., Chgo.; dir. Woodmen Accident & Life Co., Lincoln; dir., mem. trust and loan rev. coms. FirsTier Bank, Lincoln. Pres. Woods Charitable Fund, Inc., Lincoln and Chgo., 1968-89; mem. State Bldg. Commn., Lincoln, 1966-80; mem. exec. com. Bryan Meml. Hosp., 1962-66; mem. Lincoln City Park and Recreation Adv. Bd., 1962-72, Lincoln Ctr. Devel. Assn., 1967-83; trustee Nebr. Human Resources Rsch. Found., 1968-85, U. Nebr. Found., 1961-85, Joslyn Liberal Arts Soc., Omaha, 1964-80, Nebr. Ind. Coll. Found., 1965-73; hon. trustee Joslyn Liberal Arts Soc. 1st lt. AUS, 1943-46. Mem. U.S. C. of C., Lincoln C. of C., SAR. Congregationalist. Clubs: Lincoln Univ., Lincoln Country, Nebr. (Lincoln); Chicago. Home: Lincoln Nebr. Died Dec. 7, 1989; buried Lincoln, Nebr.

WOODSIDE, EDMUND RECTOR, Greek linguist, educator; b. Lodi, Calif., Nov. 22, 1921; s. Homer Henry and Mary Augusta (Rector) W.; B.A., U. Redlands, 1946, M.A., 1950; postgrad. U. So. Calif., 1950-52; Ph.D., Kensington U., 1977; m. Dorothy Ann Wells, Feb. 14, 1981. Freelance ednl. and acad. researcher linguistics, Bible and Bibl. Greek, Pasadena, Calif. and La Verne, Calif., from 1952; adj. prof. Bibl. Greek, Calif. Center for Bibl. Studies, Culver City, 1972-83. Mem. acad. adv. council Kensington U. Served with USAAF, 1942-45. Fellow Victoria Inst., Inst. Bible Research; mem. Soc. Bibl. Lit., Internat. Orgn. for Septuagint and Cognate Studies, Am. Sci. Affiliation, AAAS, N.Y. Acad. Scis., Interdisciplinary Bibl. Research Inst., Evangel. Theol. Soc., Phi Delta Kappa. Author: A Programmed Guide to Philippians, 1968; Matthew 13, 1971; Six Parables of the End, 1972; (with J.W. McMillan) Bible Doctrine, 1969, Earthly Life of the Lord Jesus, 1975. Deceased. Home: LaVerne Calif.

WOODWARD, CHARLES NAMBY WYNN, merchandising executive; b. Vancouver, Can., Mar. 23, 1924; s. William Culham and Ruth Wynn (Johnson) W.; m. Rosemary Jukes, Jan 7, 1947; children: Wynn, John, Robyn, Christopher. Student, St. George's Sch., Vancouver U., B.C., 1940-42. With mdse. dept. Woodward Stores (Capilano), Ltd., 1945-50, store mgr., 1950-54; store mgr. Woodward Stores (Westminster), Ltd., 1954-55; gen. mgr. Woodward Stores, Ltd., 1955-57; now chmn., bd. dir. Woodward Stores (Edmonton), Ltd., Woodward Stores (Port Alberni), Ltd., Woodward Stores (Capilano), Ltd., Woodward Stores (Victoria), Ltd., Woodward Stores (Westminster), Ltd.; chief exec. officer, pres. Woodward Stores Ltd., until 1988; pres., dir. Douglas Lake Cattle Co., Ltd., Montreal Trust Co. Bd. dirs. Salvation Army, Boy Scouts, Girl Guides, G. F. Strong Rehab. Centre. Served as lt. B.C. Regt., Can. Army, 1942-45. Clubs: Univ. (Vancouver); Capilano Golf and Country, Shaughnessy Golf and Country. Deceased.

WOOLSON, KENNETH HAZEN, business executive; b. Springfield, Vt., June 18, 1897; s. William Dickinson and Frances M. (Hazen) W.; m. Dorothy M. Van Wie, Dec. 12, 1924; 1 child, Lawrence B. AB, Williams Coll., 1920. Vice chmn., dir. Jones & Lamson Machine Co.; dir. Ctrl. Vt. Pub. Svc., Inc., Springfield Terminal, Ry, Conn., Valley Electric Co. Served with flying corps, USMC, 1918-19. Mem. Sigma Phi, St. Bernard Club. Republican. Congregationalist. *

WORKMAN, WILLIAM DOUGLAS, JR., journalist; b. Greenwood, S.C., Aug. 10, 1914; s. William Douglas and Vivian (Watkins) W.; m. Rhea Thomas, June 10, 1939; children: William Douglas III, Dee. AB, The Citadel, 1935, LittD, 1969; grad. student, George Washington U., 1935-36; LittD (hon.), Newberry Coll., 1969. Reporter News and Courier, Charleston, S.C., 1936-39; mgr. sta. WTMA, Charleston, 1939-40; capital corr. News and Courier, 1946-61, Greenville (S.C.) News, 1956-62; columnist Hall Syndicate, N.Y.C., 1960-62; assoc. editor The State, Columbia, S.C., 1963-66; editor The State, 1966-73, editorial analyst, 1973-79, editorial cons., 1980-81; News analyst sta. WIS, Columbia, 1950-62; news analyst, panelist sta. WIS TV, 1953-62; rsch. fellow Inst. for So. Studies, U. S.C. Author: The Case for the South, 1960, The Bishop from Barnwell, 1963, (with others) This is the South, 1959, With all Deliberate Speed, 1957, Southern Schools, Progress and Problems, 1959; co-author: Charles E. Daniel, His Philosophy and Legacy, 1981. Republican nominee U.S. Senate, 1962; Republican nominee for Gov., 1982; bd. dirs. James F. Byrnes Found., pres., 1973-84. Served with AUS, 1940-45; to col. Res. (ret.). Decorated Legion of Merit; recipient Concurrent Resolution of Commendation S.C. Gen. Assembly, 1960, Conservation Communications award Nat. Wildlife Fedn., 1975, Editorial citation Nat. Physicians Edn. Network, 1977. Mem. Assn. Citadel Men (life, pres. 1952-53), S.C. Press Assn. (pres. 1971), Univ. South Caroliniana Soc. (pres. 1974-78), Greater Univ. S.C. Alumni Assn. (hon. life). Home: Greenville S.C.

WORSTER, KENNETH BERKLEY, lawyer; b. Covington, Ky., Dec. 29, 1937; s. Kenneth Elsworth and Anne Lucille (Foster) W.; m. Elizabeth P. Worster, Sept. 9, 1961; 1 dau., Helen S. B.S., U. Ky., 1959; J.D., Chase Coll., 1968. Bar: Ohio, U.S. Dist. Ct. (so. dist.) Ohio. Ptnr., Brumbaugh, Engelken, Worster & Amick, Greenville, Ohio, currently; judge County Ct., 1972-80; vice chmn. 2d Nat. Bank, Greenville, from 1971; instr. Edison State Coll., 1977-79. Bd. dirs. Darke County Republican Men's Club, 1979; mem. Rep. Party Central Com., 1973-78. Mem. ABA, Darke County Bar Assn., Ohio Bar Assn., Assn. Trial Lawyers Am. Presbyterian. Clubs: Elks, Kiwanis. Deceased. Home: Greenville Ohio

WORTHINGTON, WILLIAM BOWMAN, computer professional; b. Uvalde, Tex., Feb. 3, 1911; s. George Morris and Clara Ann (Bowman) W.; m. Elizabeth Rankins Frost, Feb. 22, 1936; children: George Rhodes, William Bowman Jr. Student, Rice U., 1927-30; BS, U. Va., 1932; MBA, U. Ariz., 1968, PhD, 1979. Cert. computer profl.; cert. systems profl. With Texaco, N.Y.C., 1932-33; salesman computer equipment IBM Corp., N.Y.C., Omaha, Louisville, Atlanta, Pitts., 1933-42; indsl. engr. Elliot Co., Jeanette, Pa., 1942-44; supr. systems Am. Hard Rubber, N.Y.C., 1946-51; mgmt. council Engerson Engrs., Saudi Arabia, 1951-52; with computing Hughes Aircraft, Tucson, 1952-55; project dir., combat developer U.S. Army, Ft. Huachuca, Ariz., 1955-66; instr. U. Ariz., Tucson, 1966-70; owner Limousin Cattle Breeding, Quitman, Ga., 1970-81; investments broker Tucson, from 1981. Contbr. articles to profl. jours. Bd. dirs. Tucson Boys Chorus, 1953-57, Alcohol Council of Tucson, from 1980, The Haven, Tucson, from 1980, Campus Ministry Found., Tucson, from 1984, Nat. Tchrs. Edn. Program, Durham, N.C., from 1968. With USN, 1944-46, PTO. Mem. Assn. Systems Mgmt. (bd. dirs. 1952-58, Disting. Service award 1985), Nat. Cattlemens Assn. (bd. dirs. 1979-81), N. Am. Limousin Fou. (nat. dir. 1975-81), Tucson Country Club, Pres.'s Club of Tucson, The Jefferson Soc., Masons, Shriners. Democrat. Episcopalian. Home: Tucson Ariz. Deceased.

WRATHER, JOHN DEVERAUX, JR., oil producer, motion picture producer, financier; b. Amarillo, Tex., May 24, 1918; s. John D. and Mazie (Cogdell) W.; m. Bonita Granville, Feb. 5, 1947; children—Molly, Jack, Linda, Christopher. A.B., U. Tex., 1939. Ind. oil producer Tex., Ind., Ill.; pres. Evansville (Ind.) Refining Co., 1938-40, Overton Refining Co., Amarillo Producers & Refiners Corp., Dallas, 1940-49, Jack Wrather Pictures, Inc., 1947-49, Freedom Prodns., Inc., 1949-84, Western States Investment Corp., Dallas, 1949-84, Wrather Television Prodns., Inc., 1951-84, Wrather-Alvarez Broadcasting, Inc., The Lone Ranger, Inc., Lassie, Inc., Disney-land Hotel, Anaheim, Calif., R.M.S. Queen Mary and Howard Hughes' Flying Boat Spruce Goose, L'Horizon Hotel, Palm Springs, Calif.; owner KFMB, KERO and; KEMB-TV, San Diego, KOTY-TV, Tulsa; part owner WNEW, N.Y.C.; pres. Sgt. Preston of the Yukon, Inc.; chmn. bd. Muzak, Inc., Ind. Television

Corp. and Television Programs of Am. Inc., Stephens Marine, Inc.; pres. Balboa Bay Club, Inc., Kona Kai, Inc.; pres., chmn. bd. Wrather Corp.; dir. TelePrompTer Corp., Continental Airlines, Transcontinent. Television Corp., Jerold Elec. Corp., Capitol Records, Inc.; Bd. dirs. Community Television of So. Calif.; Am. Found. Religion and Psychiatry, Corp. for Pub. Broadcasting. Motion pictures produced include The Guilty, 1946, High Tide, Perilous Water, 1947, Strike It Rich, 1948, Guilty of Treason, 1949, The Lone Ranger and The Lost City of Gold, 1958, The Magic of Lassie, 1978, The Legend of the Lone Ranger, 1981, others. Mem. devel. bd. U. Tex., vice chmn. chancellor's council; mem. advisory council Ariz. Heart Inst.; bd. counselors for performing arts U. So. Calif.; Commr. Los Angeles County-Hollywood Mus.; mem. adv. bd. Los Angeles Rams. Served to major USMC Res., 1942-53. Mem. Ind. Petroleum Assn. of Am., Internat. Radio and Television Soc., Acad. Motion Pictures Arts and Scis., Nat. Petroleum Council. Clubs: Dallas Athletic, Dallas Petroleum; Cat Cay Yacht (Bahamas); Players (N.Y.), Hemisphere (N.Y.), Skeeters (N.Y.); Marks (London), Bucks (London), White Elephant (London), Harry's Bar (London). Home: Los Angeles Calif.

WRAY, CHARLES WILLIAMSON, JR., advertising agency executive, investor, consultant; b. Raleigh, N.C., May 29, 1933; s. Charles Williamson and Adna Jones (Howell) W.; m. Edna Jacquelyn Steed, Oct. 4, 1957; children: Charlie, Susan. AB, Duke U., 1955. Trainee GE, Schenectady, 1955-56; advt. specialist GE, Plainville, Conn., 1956-57; advt. dir. Drexel Enterprises, N.C., 1957-66; account exec. Cargill, Wilson & Acree Inc., Charlotte, N.C., 1966-67, v.p., 1968-69, sr. v.p., 1970-71, exec. v.p., 1971-72, pres., 1973-75, vice chmn., 1976-77; pres. Wray-Ward-Laseter Advt., Inc., Charlotte, 1977-91; pvt. investor, cons., 1991-92; bd. dirs. E.I.C. Corp., PMC Inc. Mem. Advt. Club Charlotte (pres. 1974), Am. Advt. Fedn., Newcomen Soc., Kappa Sigma. Republican. Baptist. Lodge: Rotary. Home: Charlotte N.C. Died June 17, 1992. †

WRAY, FRANK JUNIOR, history educator; b. Camden, Ind., Apr. 29, 1921; s. Benjamin Franklin and Bessie Leanore (Ayres) W.; m. Betty Marie Binkley, Dec. 28, 1946; children: William Franklin, James Edward, Thomas Frederick, Ellen Elizabeth. A.B. with high honors, Ind. U., 1946, M.A., 1947; Ph.D., Yale U., 1954. Instr. history U. S.D., 1947-49, U. Conn., 1952, U. Vt., 1953; faculty Berea (Ky.) Coll., 1953-91, prof. history, 1964-91, William J. Hutchins Alumni prof., 1976-91, prof. emeritus, 1991, chmn. dept. history, 1983-90. Contbr. sect. to: Mennonite Ency. II, 1956, Reformation Studies, 1962, articles, revs. to profl. jours. Served with AUS, 1942-46. Am. Council Learned Socs. grantee, 1964; recipient Seabury award for Excellence in Teaching, 1967; Southeastern Inst. Medieval and Renaissance Studies fellow, 1968. Mem. Am. Hist. Assn., Soc. for Reformation Research, Am. Soc. Ch. History, Medieval Acad. Am., Renaissance Soc. Am. Republican. Baptist. Club: Masons. Home: Berea Ky. Died Feb. 11, 1992; buried Berea, Ky.

WRIGHT, CHRISTOPHER, environmental scientist; b. Chgo., Oct. 31, 1926; s. Quincy and Louise Maxey (Leonard) W.; m. Anne Carolyn McCoy, Sept. 15, 1956 (div. Apr. 1981); children—Malcolm Morehead, Diana Sewall; m. Diana Gilliland Hanson, Apr. 1, 1988. Student, U. Chgo., 1944; A.B. magna cum laude, Harvard Coll., 1949; A.B. Fulbright grantee, Oxford (Eng.) U., 1949-51; A.M., Harvard U., 1974. Exptl. physicist Manhattan Project, Los Alamos, 1944-46; instr. philosophy Williams Coll., 1954; research assoc. U. Chgo. Law Sch., 1956-58; exec. dir. Council for Atomic Age Studies, Columbia U., 1958-66; dir. Inst. for Study of Sci. in Human Affairs, 1966-72; staff natural and environ. scis. div. Rockefeller Found., N.Y.C., 1972-75; profl. staff for research and devel. policies and priorities Office Tech. Assessments, U.S. Congress, 1976-79; mem. staff for sci. policy and instn. devel. Carnegie Inst., Washington, 1979-83; sr. sci. policy advisor Washington Resources, Inc., 1984-89. Author: The Prospective Role of an Arboretum, 1972; Author, editor: Scientists and National Policy Making, 1964, Science Policies of Industrial Nations, 1975; Contbr. articles to profl. jours. Mem. Commn. to Study Orgn. of Peace, from 1971, Commn. on Year 2000, Am. Acad. Arts and Scis., 1967-72; cons. Brookings Instn., 1960, Carnegie Endowment for Internat. Peace, 1961-63, Fgn. Service Inst., Dept. State, 1964-65, Holden Arboretum, 1970-72, Josiah Macy, Jr. Found., 1975. Served with AUS, 1945-46. Resident scholar Villa Serbelloni, Rockefeller Found., 1966, 69. Fellow AAAS. Home: Washington D.C. Died May 9, 1989; cremated.

WRIGHT, HAROLD DALE, minister; b. Hackberry, La., Jan. 16, 1935; s. Cecil Earl and Lucette (Lejeune) W.; m. Barbara Jean Cockrell, Sept. 26, 1955. BA, La. Coll., 1955; BD, New Orleans Bapt. Theol. Sem., 1959, ThD, 1964. Pastor Harmony Bapt. Ch., Deville, La., 1953-54, Lakeshore (Miss.) Bapt. Ch., 1959-65; assoc. dir. dept. pastoral care So. Bapt. Hosp., New Orleans, 1965-74; dir. dept. pastoral care Bapt. Med. Ctr., Kansas City, Mo., 1975-88; mem. supplementary faculty Notre Dame Sem., New Orleans, 1971-75; contract tchr. William Carey Coll., Hattiesburg, Miss., 1971-75; supr. pastoral and ednl. ministry Midwestern Bapt. Theol. Sem., Kansas City, 1975-85. Contbr. articles to profl. jours. Mem. instl. rev. bd. Kansas City Clin. Oncology Program, 1985-88. Recipient Cert. Merit, Greater New Orleans Fedn. Chs., 1970. Fellow Coll. of Chaplains Am. Protestant Health Assn. (pres. 1982); mem. Protestant Health and Welfare Assembly (chmn. 1985-86), Assn. Clin. Pastoral Edn., Inc. (cert. supr.), Mo. Chaplains Assn., La. Chaplains Assn. (hon. life) (pres. 1972-74, Outstanding Service award, commendation, 1975). Democrat. Lodges: Kiwanis, Masons. Home: Kansas City Mo.

WRIGHT, JERAULD, U.S. ambassador; b. Amherst, Mass., June 4, 1898; s. William Mason and Marjorie R. (Jerauld) W.; m. Phyllis B. Thompson, July 23, 1938; children: Marion, William Mason. Grad., U.S Naval Acad., 1917; DS (hon.), Rose Polytech Inst.; LLD, Coll. William and Mary. Commd. ensign USN, 1917, advanced through grades to admiral, 1954; assigned to U.S.S. Castine, 1917-18, destroyers Dyer and Reid, 1918-22, U.S.S. John D. Ford, 1922-24; assigned to presdl. yacht U.S.S. Mayflower and naval aide to Pres. Calvin Coolidge, 1924-26; assigned to U.S.S. Md., 1926-29; attached to Bur. Ordinances Navy Dept., Washington, 1929-31; naval aide to Pres. Herbert Hoover; 1st lt. U.S.S. Salt Lake City, 1931-32, gunnery officer, 1932-34; exec. staff U.S. Naval Acad., 1934-35, 1939-41; aide to asst. sec. navy, 1935-36; with Bur. Ordnance, 1936-37; comdr. U.S.S. Blue, 1937-39; exec. officer U.S.S. Mississippi, 1941-42; assigned to hdqs. comdr. in chief U.S. Fleet, and staff of comdr. Naval Forces Europe; staff of comdr. Allied Expeditionary Force; staff English Adm. of Fleet, 1943; asst. chief of staff to comdr. Naval Forces N.W. Africa, 1943; comdr. cruiser Sante Fe, 1944; with Amphibious Group 5, 1944-45, cruiser div. 6, 1945; head operational readiness sect. Office of Chief Naval Ops., 1945-49; comdr. amphibious force Atlantic Fleet, 1949-51; U.S. mem. NATO NATO standing group, Washington, 1951-52; comdr. in chief U.S. Naval Forces Eastern Atlantic and Mediterranean, 1952-54; supreme allied comdr. Atlantic, comdr. in chief Western Atlantic area NATO; comdr. in chief Atlantic Fleet, 1954-60; Bd. of Nat. Intelligence Estimates, U.S. Navy, 1961-63; U.S. amb. to China, from 1963. Awarded D.S.M., Legion of Merit, with Gold Star, Bronze Star medal, Silver Star medal (U.S.), Chevaller Legion Honor (France). *

WRIGHT, JOHN BACON, lawyer; b. Oshkosh, Wis., Dec. 22, 1920; s. Merton LaMont and Doris Hamlin (Bacon) W.; m. Elizabeth D. Anderson, June 2, 1946; children: Richard, David, Mary Ann. B.S., Mich. State U., 1942; J.D., Columbia U., 1948. Bar: Md. 1949, D.C. 1950. Sole practice, Annapolis, Md., 1952-74; ptnr. Wright & Wright, Annapolis, 1974-86; ptnr. Wright, Wright & Sussman, Annapolis, 1986; city atty., Annapolis, 1953-57. Legal csl. St. John's Coll., Annapolis, 1958-84. Mem. Anne Arundel County Bd. Edn., 1963-74; mem. Anne Arundel County Adv. Commn. Adequate Pub. Facilities, 1975-76. Served to capt. Chem. Warfare and JAG Corps, U.S. Army, 1942-45, 50-52. Decorated Bronze Star medal. Mem. Am. Trial Lawyers Assn., Md. Trial Lawyers Assn. (pres. 1961), Anne Arundel County Bar Assn. (pres. 1968), Md. Bar Assn. Democrat. Methodist. Club: Yacht (Annapolis). Deceased. Home: Annapolis Md.

WRIGHT, MYRON ARNOLD, oil field equipment and forging manufacturing company executive; b. Blair, Okla., Apr. 9, 1911; s. Charles Edgar and Hattie Susan (Dillingham) W.; m. Izetta Chattin, June 4, 1935 (dec.); 1 dau., Mary Judith (Mrs. Sidney Reid, Jr.). Student, Northwestern State Tchrs. Coll., 1928-30; B.S., Okla. State U., 1933; D.Sc. (hon.), U. Tulsa; LL.D. (hon.), Okla. Christian Coll.; D. Eng. (hon.), Worcester Poly. Inst. Various engring. positions Carter Oil Co., Tulsa, 1933-43; chief petroleum engr. Carter Oil Co., 1943-44, asst. mgr. prodn., 1944-46; exec. asst. producing dept. Standard Oil Co. of N.J., N.Y.C., 1946-49, dep. coord., 1949-51; exec. v.p. Internat. Petroleum Co., Ltd., Coral Gables, Fla., 1951-52; exec. v.p., dir. Carter Oil Co., Tulsa, 1952-54; producing coord. Standard Oil Co., N.J., 1954-58, dir., 1958-60, exec. v.p., mem. exec. com., 1960-66; chmn., chief exec. officer Exxon Co. USA, 1966-76; exec. v.p., dir. Exxon Corp., 1958-66, 73-76; chmn., pres., chief exec. officer Cameron Iron Works, Inc., Houston, 1977-81, chmn., chief exec. officer, 1981-85, chmn. bd., 1986-87, dir., 1987-89; dir., mem. exec com. 1st City Bancorp. Tex., Inc., 1971-85; dir., mem. exec. com., audit com. Am. Gen. Ins. Co., 1976-83; former dir. Evans Products Co.; bd. govs. U.S. Postal Service, 1971-80, chmn., 1974-80. Mem. council overseers Jesse H. Jones Grad. Sch. Adminstrn., Rice U., bd. dirs. Rice Ctr., 1981-92. Mem. Am. Inst. Mining, Metall. and Petroleum Engrs., Am. Petroleum Inst. (dir.), NAM (dir. 1979-87), U.S. C. of C. (pres. 1966-67, chmn. 1967-68), Houston C. of C. (dir. 1978-84), Nat. Wildlife Fedn. (mem. bd. 1969-75), Tau Beta Pi, Sigma Tau Gamma, Sigma Tau, Phi Kappa Phi, Lambda Chi Alpha. Clubs: Balboa Bay (Newport Beach, Calif.); River Oaks Country, Houston, Petroleum, Ramada, Met. Racquet (Houston); Garden of Gods (Colorado Springs, Colo.). Home: Houston Tex. Deceased. †

WRIGHT, RUTH CALDWELL, educator; b. Sheldon, Ill., Sept. 18, 1898; d. John Leroy and Carolyn (Rudin) Caldwell; m. Russell P. Wright, Feb. 1, 1930. BS, U. Ill., 1927; AM, Columbia, 1935, EdD, 1942. Bus. mgr., tchr. Teintsin (China) Women's Hosp., 1922-27; asst. dean women U. Ill., 1927-30; adv. to women CCNY, 1930-36, dean women, 1936-42, dean students, 1942-63; dir. Baruch Student Ctr., 1959-63, Bi-Nat. Ctr., Veintiane, 1963-65, Taipel, Taiwan, from 1965; attache Am. India, 1952-53; cons. U.S. Tech. Coop. Mission in India, 1952-55, Visitation Univs. of India, 1949-50; cons. India Inter-U. Sem., 1950. Mem. AAUW, NEA, Am. Personnel Guidance Assn., Asia Soc., Alpha Gamma Delta, Beta Gamma Sigma, Kappa Delta Pi, Pi Lambda Theta, Pilot Club, Nat. Arts CLub. Methodist. *

WU, SHIEN-MING, mechanical engineer; b. Chekiang, China, Oct. 28, 1924; naturalized, 1970; m. Daisy T. Wu, Oct. 3, 1959; 1 child, Elaine. M.B.A., U. Pa., 1956; Ph.D., U. Wis., 1962. Prof. mech. engring. U. Wis., 1968-92, research prof. mfg. engring., 1981-92; J. Reid and Polly Anderson prof. mfg. tech., prof. mech. engring. and applied mechanics U. Mich., Ann Arbor, 1988-92; Fulbright disting. prof., Yugoslavia, 1975, USSR, 1988. Contbr. numerous articles to profl. jours. Recipient Jennings award Am. Welding Soc., 1968. Fellow Academia Sinica; mem. ASME (Blackall award 1968, C.R. Richards Meml. award 1981), Soc. Mfg. Engrs. (Nat. Edn. award 1974). Home: Ann Arbor Mich. Died Oct. 28, 1992. †

WUNDERLE, ROBERT E., economist, public affairs executive; b. Canton, Ohio, Apr. 20, 1944; s. Harold William and Helen (Ready) W.; m. Sue Anita Sutton, Nov. 17, 1966; children: Max, Sam. BS, Rutgers U., 1967; MS, Cornell U., 1968, PhD, 1971. Rsch. specialist Cornell U. Grad. Sch. Nutrition, Ithaca, N.Y., 1970-71; dir. econ. rsch. Nat. Broiler Coun., Washington, 1971-74; economist, v.p. pub. affairs Supermarkets Gen. Corp., Woodbridge, N.J., from 1974. Mem. N.Y. Nutrition Watch Commn., Albany, 1980-81; bd. dirs. Community Food Bank N.J., Newark, from 1982; chmn. N.J. Alliance for Action, Edison, from 1985; mem. N.J. Job Tng. and Coord. Commn., Trenton, from 1987. Mem. Food Mktg. Inst. (chmn. communications com. from 1986), N.Y. State Food Mchts. Assn. (bd. dirs. from 1974). Roman Catholic. Home: Westfield N.J. Deceased.

WURSTER, STEPHEN HARRY, college president, educator; b. Williamsport, Pa., Feb. 19, 1941; s. Clyde Herbert and Grace Anna (Stevens) W.; m. Jean Elizabeth Miller, June 18, 1966; children: Gregory Stephen, Mark Andrew, Elizabeth Ann. A.B., Ursinus Coll., 1963; M.Div., Drew U., 1967; M.A., U. Iowa, 1970, PhD, 1972; postdoctoral study higher edn. mgmt., Harvard U., 1980. Teaching assoc. U. Iowa, Iowa City, 1969-70; asst. to acad. v.p., asst. prof. history Ball State U., Muncie, Ind., 1971-75; dean acad. planning, faculty devel. Ball State U., 1975-81; prof. religion and history, pres. Catawba Coll., Salisbury, N.C., 1981-92; dir. NCNB Nat. Bank, Salisbury, N.C. Contbr. articles to profl. publs. Pres. Muncie Assn. Retarded Citizens, 1977-80; bd. dirs. Salisbury Symphony Soc., N.C., 1981-92; trustee N.C. Ind. Coll. Fund, Winston-Salem, 1981-92, treas., 1985-92; chmn. team examiners Hardbarger Jr. Coll. Wesley Found. fellow United Meth. Ch., 1965-66; Woodrow Wilson Found. fellow, 1970; Paul Harris fellow, 1982; named Lions Man of Yr. in Salisbury, 1987. Mem. Am. Soc. Ch. History, Soc. Coll. and Univ. Planning, Am. Assn. Higher Edn., Am. Hist. Assn., Assn. Study Higher Edn., N.C. Assn. Ind. Colls. and Univs. (bd. dirs. 1983-92. chmn. com. on grad. off-campus programs), N.C. Assn. of Coll. and Univs. (nominating com.), Salisbury Country Club, Seven Lakes Country Club, Rotary. Democrat. Mem. United Ch. of Christ. Home: Salisbury N.C. Died Aug. 28, 1992. †

WURSTER, WILLIAM WILSON, architect; b. Stockton, Calif., Oct. 20, 1895; s. Frederick William and Maude Evelyn (Wilson) W.; m. Catherine Bauer, Aug. 13, 1940 (dec. Nov. 1964); 1 child, Sarah. AB, U. Calif., 1919, LLD, 1964. Began as office boy E.B. Brown, Stockton, Calif., 1910; with John Reid Jr., San Francisco, 1920; assoc. with Charles Dean on Sacramento filtration plant, 1921-22; with Delano & Aldrich, N.Y.C., 1923-24, East Bay Water Co. filtration plant, 1924-25; architect pvt. practice, 1926-43; dean sch. arch. and planning MIT, 1944-50; dean sch., now coll. arch. U. Calif., Berkeley, 1950-59; dean Coll. Environ. Design, 1959-63, dean emeritus, 1963-64, acting dean, from 1964; arch. ptnr. Theodore C. Bernardi and Donn Emmons. Prin. works include Golden Gate Redevel. Project, San Francisco, Ctrt. Advanced Study in Behavioral Scis., Palo Alto, also office bldgs. Mem. Capitol Park and Planning COmmn., 1948, chmn., 1949-50; mem. Capitol Bldg. and Planning Commn., State of Calif., from 1959. Harvard U. Grad Sch. Design fellow, 1943. Fellow Am. Acad. Arts and Scis., Royal Acad. Fine Arts, Copemhagen, AIA; mem. Royal Inst. British Architects (corr. mem.), Am. Inst. Planners (affiliate), Tay Beta Pi. *

WYAND, ROBERT RICE, II, investment company executive; b. Hagerstown, Md., Jan. 6, 1938; s. Robert Rice and Ruth (Knadler) W.; divorced; children: Robert Rice III, Abigail; m. Anne Lewis Robison, Mar. 9, 1989. BA in Econs., Franklin & Marshall Coll., Lancaster, Pa., 1959; MA in Econs., Pa. State U., 1961. Fin. economist, bd. govs. Fed. Res. System, Washington, 1962-64; asst. to pres. Fed. Res. Bank Atlanta, 1964-68; economist, securities analyst Montag &

Caldwell, Atlanta, 1968-70, prin., 1978-84; economist Abbey Internat. Corp., Atlanta, 1970-71; economist, investment mgr. Ga. Internat. Corp., Atlanta, 1971-73; first v.p. Schroder, Naess & Thomas, Atlanta and Washington, 1973-78; portfolio mgr. Fidelity Mgmt. and Rsch. Investment Mgmt. Svc., Boston, 1978; prin. Seawell, Wyand, Murray & Stewart, Inc., Atlanta, 1984-87; pres. Strategic Portfolio Mgmt., Inc., Atlanta, from 1987; also bd. dirs. Strategic Portfolio Mgmt., Inc.; chmn. bd. dirs. Summa Capital Corp, Atlanta; bd. dirs. various entrepreneurial cos., Atlanta; lectr. Ga. Inst. Tech., Atlanta, from 1988. Contbr. articles to profl. publs. Served to 1st lt. U.S. Army, 1961. Fellow Fin. Analysts Fedn.; mem. Atlanta Soc. Fin. Analysts. Club: Beech Aero (Atlanta). Methodist. Home: Atlanta Ga. Died Oct., 1991.

WYSS, WALTHER ERWIN, lawyer; b. Medford, Wis., Feb. 17, 1909; s. John and Gertrude (Walther) W.; m. Caroline Benedict, July 6, 1935; children: Mary Beth Wyss Huttenlocher, Trudy Wyss Wood, Becky Wyss Watt, John, Wendy. BS, U. Wis., 1933, MS, 1934; JD, George Washington U., 1939. Bar: D.C. 1938, N.Y. 1941, Ill. 1946. Tchr. pub. schs., Medford, 1925-29; engr. GE, 1934-35, with patent dept., 1935-45; ptnr. Mason & Wyss, Chgo., 1946-48; founder, ptnr. Mason, Kolehmainen, Rathburn & Wyss, Chgo., 1948-90. Former leader Cub Scouts Am., Kenilworth, Ill.; former coach Little League, also youth football, Kenilworth. Fellow Am. Coll. Trial Lawyers; mem. ABA (spl. com. on complex and multi-dist. litigation 1968-73, coun. patent, trademark and copyright law sect. 1968-72, chmn. 1974-75), 7th Fed. Cir. Bar Assn., Chgo. Bar Assn., Chgo. Patent Law Assn. (pres. 1971), Am. Patent Law Assn., Nat. Lawyers Club, Kenilworth Club (pres. 1970-71), Skokie Country Club, Michigan Shores Club, Union League Club, Tower Club, Chgo. Curling Club (pres. from 1975), Order of Coif, Tau Beta Pi, Phi Delta Phi, Phi Eta Sigma, Phi Kappa Phi, Eta Kappa Nu. Home: Evanston Ill. Died Aug. 26, 1990; body donated to sci.

YAFFE, JOSEPH X., lawyer, civic leader; b. Phila., May 6, 1913; s. Samuel and Rose (Schaffer) Y.; m. Silvia F. Fishbein, July 21, 1940; children: Roy, Peter, Lisa Jo. A.B., U. Pa., 1933; J.D., Temple U., 1936. Bar: Pa. 1937. Spl. dep. atty. gen. Commonwealth of Pa., 1937-54; partner firm Yaffe and Gould, Phila., 1954-81; of counsel firm Gould Yaffe and Golden, Phila., 1981-89; pres. Commonwealth Insular Devel. Inc. Counsel, dir. Police Athletic League, 1948—; counsel, dir. Elder Craftsmen Phila., from 1959, pres., 1965-66, chmn. bd. dirs., 1966-67; mem. exec. com. Nat. Community Relations Adv. Council, 1956-64, treas., 1960-64; pres. Jewish Community Relations Council Greater Phila., 1956-59, hon. pres., 1959-89; mem. Pa. Fair Employment Practices Commn., 1960-61; mem. Phila. Fellowship Commn., 1956-76, v.p., 1960-63; mem. Pa. Human Relations Commn., 1961-86, vice chmn., 1968-74, chmn., 1974-86; counsel, dir. Soc. Handicapped Children and Adults Phila., from 1949, pres., 1962-63; dir. Pa. Easter Seal Soc. Handicapped Children and Adults, 1969-72; nat. council Jt. Distbn. Com., 1964-77; v.p. Internat. Assn. Ofcl. Human Rights Agys., 1967-68, counsel, 1973-76. Served as ensign USCGR, 1942-45. Recipient Pres. medallion Easter Seal Soc., 1965; Founder's award Police Athletic League, 1966; Distinguished Service award, 1970; Humanitarian award Salem Bapt. Ch., 1968; Service award Pa. Ho. of Reps., 1971; Distinguished Merit award NCCJ, 1976; Dr. Martin Luther King Jr. human rights award Salem Bapt. Ch., 1980; Bronze Medallion award Chapel of Four Chaplains, 1981; 25-Yr. Service award Pa. Human Relations Commn., Citation for Civic Service, City of Phila.; elected to Hall of Fame Police Athletic League, 1980. Mem. Am., Pa., Phila. bar assns., Pa. Soc. Clubs: Masons, Meadowlands Country (gov. 1963-86, v.p. 1965-71, pres. 1971-73, hon. pres. 1973-86). Home: Wyncote Pa. Died Dec. 13, 1989; buried Roosevelt Meml. Cemetery, Philadelphia.

YANCEY, ROBERT EARL, executive consultant, oil company executive; b. Cleve., July 15, 1921; s. George Washington II and Mary (Gutzwiller) Y.; m. Mary Estelline Tackett, July 25, 1941; children: Robert Earl, Susan Carol. B.E., Marshall U., 1943. With Ashland Oil Inc., Ky., 1943-82, successively process engr., project engr., operating supt., coordinator sales and refining, gen. supt. refineries, 1943-56, v.p. in charge mfg., 1956-59, adminstrv. v.p., 1959-65, dir., 1964-82, sr. v.p., 1965-72, pres., 1972-82, chief operating officer, from 1972; pres. Ashland Chem. Co., 1967-69, Ashland Petroleum Co., 1969-72; dir. Ashland Oil Inc.; exec. cons.; dir. 3d Nat. Bank, Ashland; past bd. dirs. Spindletop Rsch. Ctr., Lexington, Ky. Bd. advisors Marshall U., Huntington, W.Va., 1977. Mem. Nat. Petroleum Refiners Assn. (dir. from 1965, pres. 1969-70, chmn.), Nat. Petroleum Assn. (mfg. com.), Nat. Petroleum Council, Am. Petroleum Inst. (dir.), Ky. Soc. Profl. Engrs. (dir. from 1970). Protestant. Home: Ashland Ky. Died Jan. 27, 1991; buried Bellefonte Meml. Gardens, Ashland, Ky.

YANUCK, MARTIN, social science educator; b. Newark, Mar. 28, 1936; s. Benjamin and Rose (Borsky) Y. B.A., Rutgers U., 1958; M.A., U. Chgo., 1961, Ph.D., 1973. Asst. bibliographer South Asia U. Chgo. Librs., 1966-68; asst. prof. U. Ga., Athens, 1968-73; asst. prof. Spelman Coll., Atlanta, 1973-75, assoc. prof., chmn. history dept., from 1975; instr. Peace Corps, Chgo., 1966; dir. South Asia Microform Project, 1968-73. Editor: South Asia Library Resources, 1974. Vice-pres. Response, Inc., Athens, 1969-73; trustee Atlanta Coun. for Internat. Visitors, 1979-82; mem. coun. Internat. Magnate High Sch., Atlanta, from 1982; v.p. Congregation Beth Shalom, Atlanta, 1982-84, pres., from 1984. Mem. Assn. Asian Studies (com. South Asia librs. and documentation 1968-73), World History Assn. (steering com. 1982-83, coun. 1983-84), Am. Hist. Assn., So. Ctr. for Internat. Studies, Ga. Hist. Assn., Atlanta Com. on Fgn. Rels. Home: Tucker Ga. Died Sept., 1988.

YASEEN, LEONARD CLAYTON, real estate executive, consultant; b. Chicago Heights, Ill., June 27, 1912; ed. U. Ill.; m. Helen M. Fantus, July 29, 1934; children—Roger, Barbara. With Fantus Co. (later sold to Dun & Bradstreet), 1934, former chmn. bd.; trustee Hirshhorn Mus. Smithsonian Inst.; founder Yaseen Studies in Modern Art, Met. Mus. Art, N.Y.C., Yaseen Lectures Neuberger Mus.; former dir. Witco Chem. Co.; bd. dirs. Purchase Coll. Found.; former nat. chmn. interreligious affairs commn. Am. Jewish Com. Author: Plant Location, 1956; A Guide to Facilities Location, 1971; Direct Investment in the United States, 1974; Industrial Development in a Changing World, 1975; The Jesus Connection, 1985. Clubs: Century, Sky. Died Oct. 8, 1989. Home: Larchmont N.Y.

YASSKY, HAROLD, real estate developer; b. N.Y.C., Oct. 28, 1930; s. Morris and Bess (Goldman) Y.; m. Dolores Goldstein, Dec. 28, 1950; children: Charles, Marc, Robert, Susie. BS, Syracuse U., 1950; AA, Am. Inst. LDY, Joliet, Ill., 1951; postgrad., N.Y. State Coll. Arts/Scis., N.Y.C., 1952, Hofstra U., 1955. Cert. valuer, Internat. Real Estate Inst., 1984. V.p. Yassky Hotels, N.Y.C., 1951-55; pres. The Yassky Corp., N.Y.C., 1956-68, Assocs. Servicing Corp., N.Y.C., 1960-68, Sutton Plaza Hotel, Inc., N.Y.C., 1956-68, Seaway Idlewild Hotels, Inc., N.Y.C., 1960-64, Shopco Devel. Corp., N.Y.C., 1968-84; gen. ptnr. The Shopco Co., N.Y.C., 1968-86, The Shopco Group, N.Y.C., 1986-92, The Shopco Mgmt. Corp., N.Y.C., 1992; bd. dirs. L. Luria & Co., Am. Stock Exch., Miami, Fla. Editorial bd. Nat. Mall Monitor mag., 1980-84, Shopping Ctr. World mag., Atlanta, 1988-92; contbg. author real estate devel. manual. Chmn. bd. trustees Beth Jacob Schs., N.Y.C., 1974-92; bd. dirs. Bar Ilan U., Weizmann Inst. of Sci.; chmn. United Jewish Campaign, Rye Town, N.Y., 1968; trustee Congregation K.T.I., Portchester, N.Y., 1958-64, Aventura (Fla.) Turnberry Jewish Ctr., 1990-92. Recipient Heritage award State of Israel, 1989, Prime Ministers Club award, 1988, Chairmen's award, United Jewish Appeal Fedn., 1979. Mem. Williams Island Club, Turnberry Isle Club (Miami, Fla.). Democrat. Jewish. Home: Miami Fla. Died Dec. 5, 1992. †

YATES, ALDEN PERRY, engineering and construction company executive; b. Los Angeles, July 12, 1928; s. John Perry and Sybill Norma (Kerr) Y.; m. Dawn Blacker, Dec. 16, 1950; children: Stephen, Michael, Karen, Jeffrey, Russell, Patricia. B.S.C.E., Stanford U., 1951. Field engr. Bechtel Corp., San Francisco, 1953-70; v.p. Bechtel Power Corp., San Francisco, 1970-75; v.p., dep. div. mgr. Internat. Bechtel, Inc., Kuwait City, Kuwait, 1975-78, Bechtel Overseas Corp., London, 1978-80; pres. Bechtel Petroleum, Inc., Houston, 1980-83; pres. Bechtel Group, Inc., San Francisco, 1983-89, vice-chmn., 1989; dir. 1st City Bancorp. of Tex., Inc.; chmn., dir. Bechtel Western Power Corp., Bechtel Eastern Power Corp., Bechtel Inc., Bechtel Nat. Inc., Bechtel Civil Inc. Bd. dirs. San Francisco Opera, SRI Internat., United Way of Bay Area, Bay Area Coun., Nat. Action Coun. for Minorities in Engring.; trustee Pacific Presbyn. Med. Ctr.; chmn. San Francisco Bay Area Sci. Fair, 1988-89; mem. adv. coun. Stanford Sch. Engring. Served to lt. j.g. USCG, 1951-53. Republican. Clubs: Pacific Union (San Francisco); San Francisco Golf; Cypress Point (Pebble Beach, Calif.); Thunderbird Country (Rancho Mirage, Calif.); The Links (N.Y.C.); Menlo Circus (Atherton, Calif.). Home: San Francisco Calif. Died Apr. 12, 1989; buried Napa, Calif.

YATES, JOHN SELLERS, engineer, lawyer, business executive; b. Washington, Aug. 16, 1923; s. Mark Reid and Natalie Sellers (Barnes) Y.; m. Marguerite Kaye Tabor, June 17, 1950; children: John Sellers, Marguerite T., Christopher M.R., Jeremy S., Natalie M. B.M.E., U. Va., 1948; LL.B., U. Mich., 1951; M.Litt., Cambridge U. (Eng.), 1953. Bar: N.Y. 1954. Assoc. firm Cahill, Gordon, Reindel & Ohl, N.Y.C., 1953-57; with Mark Wood Internat., Inc., N.Y.C., from 1957; founder, pres., dir. Contemporary Products, Inc., N.Y.C., from 1962, Hypertronics Corp., from 1970, Interlicense, Inc., from 1975, Single Screw Compressor, Inc., from 1978. Chmn. Stevenson-for-Pres. Com., Richmond County, N.Y., 1956. Served to 1st lt. U.S. Army, 1943-46. Episcopalian. Deceased. Home: New York N.Y.

YAWKEY, JEAN R., baseball club executive; b. Bklyn., 1909; m. Tom Yawkey, 1944 (dec. 1976). Fashion model N.Y.C., 1934-44; majority owner, former pres., chairwoman bd. dirs. Boston Red Sox, Am. League, 1976-92. Trustee Yawkey Found.; past chmn. bd. and trustee Jimmy Fund Sidney Farber Cancer Inst. Home: Boston Mass. Died Feb. 26, 1992.

YAZEL, EUGENE ALLEN, lawyer; b. Marion, Ohio, Oct. 20, 1924; s. William M. and Dorothy Gay (Jones) Y.; m. Joan Regina Smith, Mar. 22, 1958; children: Jennifer Jill, Kathryn Kay, Laura Lynn. B.S. in Civil Engring., Case Inst. Tech., 1949; LL.B., Ohio State U., 1953; postgrad. U. Tenn., 1950. Bar: Ohio 1953. Atty. City of Marion, 1962-65, mayor, 1966-71; sole practice law, 1972-81, from 1983; judge Common Pleas Ct., 1980, 81; part time asst. judge Mcpl. Ct., 1972-81. Served with USAAF, 1943-45. Mem. Ohio Bar Assn., Marion County Bar Assn. Republican. Avocation: golf. Deceased. Home: Marion Ohio

YEAGER, JOHN SPENCER, bank executive; b. Cin., Apr. 24, 1940; s. B. John and Sara Lee (Roberson) Y.; m. Cecile Denise Fields; children: John, Stephen, Michael. BS, Northwestern U., 1962; MBA, U. Cin., 1963. Exec. v.p. Star Bank N.A., Cin., 1984-90, Star Banc Corp., 1990-92; bd. dirs. Carr Tool Co., Cin., The Hill & Griffith Co., Cin., Southwestern Ohio Steel, Hamilton, Ohio, Safeguard Corp., Covington, Ky., SOS Holding Corp. Chmn. spl. gifts Bus. Mobilized for Xavier U., Cin., 1983-84; chmn. corp. gifts div. Fine Arts Fund Drive, Cin., 1981; trustee Cin. Assn. Blind, 1980-86; vice chmn. corp. div. United Appeal Fund Drive, Cin., 1976; mem. adv. coun. Cin. Zoo, Bethesda Hosp., Inc.; mem. Fine Arts Fund Allocation Com., 1991-92; capt. capital campaign Boy Scouts Am., 1990. Mem. Cin. C. of C. (mem. edn. com. 1978-80). Republican. Methodist. Clubs: Queen City, Commonwealth (exec. com. 1984), Coldstream Country. Home: Cincinnati Ohio Died Aug. 1, 1992. †

YEAGER, LELAND E., corporation executive; b. Chgo., Aug. 10, 1896; s. Everett E. and Grace H. (Caldwell) Y.; m. Alice M. Bennett, June 7, 1922. AB, U. Ill., 1918. With Dillon, Read & Co., Chgo., San Francisco, 1919-23; v.p., dir. A.C. Allyn & Co., Inc., Chgo., N.Y.C., 1923-42; v.p. Standard Dredging Corp., N.Y.C., 1942-51, exec. v.p., 1951-52, pres., from 1952, dir., from 1934; chmn. of bd., dir. Great Lakes Terminal Warehouse Co., Toledo; dir. Iowa Pun. Svc. Co. (Sioux City), Quaker City Colg Storage Co. (Phila.), Atlantic Bank (N.Y.C.). Mem. Phi Beta Kappa, Phi Kappa Tau. *

YEAGLEY, J. WALTER, judge; b. Angola, Ind., Apr. 20, 1909; s. John George and Alice (Bailey) Y.; m. Dorothy Brown, June 27, 1942; children—John R., William J., Richard A.; m. Gail M. McKean, May 14, 1982. A.B., U. Mich., 1931, J.D., 1934. Bar: Ind. 1934. Practice in South Bend, 1934-42; spl. agt. FBI, 1942-48; dir. security and investigation div. ECA, 1948-51; asso. gen. counsel RFC, 1952-53; dep. asst. atty. gen. Dept. of Justice, 1953-59, asst. atty. gen., 1959-70; assoc. judge D.C. Ct. Appeals, 1970-79, sr. judge, 1979-85; Chmn. interdeptl. com. on internal security Nat. Security Council, 1954-59, atty. gen.'s observer on planning bd., 1958-61; chmn. Personnel Security Adv. Com., 1958-61. Mem. Am., D.C. bar assns., Bar U.S. Supreme Ct., Soc. Ex-FBI Agts., Ind. Soc., Alpha Sigma Phi. Presbyterian. Club: J.D.M. Country (Palm Beach Gardens, Fla.). Home: Riviera Beach Fla. Died Apr. 28, 1990.

YEH, WALTER HUAI-TEH, educator, composer; b. Shanghai, China, Jan. 7, 1911; came to U.S., 1944, naturalized, 1955; s. Ziang Tsung and Pei-Yu (Huang) Y.; A.B., St. John's U. (China), 1933; grad. summa cum laude Nat. Conservatory of Music (China), 1935; M.A. and Mus. M., Eastman Sch. Music, U. Rochester, 1945; A.M., Harvard, 1948, researcher, 1951-54; Ph.D., U. Rochester, 1949; m. Moong Yue, Aug. 8, 1942; children: Peter Wen-chun, Arthur Cho-chun. Prof. flute Nat. Conservatory of Music, China, 1940-44; prof. music, chmn. joint music dept. Allen U and Benedict Coll., Columbia, S.C., 1954-81, prof. music Allen U., 1954-85, chmn. humanities div. Allen U., 1957-60, 63-79, chmn. div. fine arts and drama Benedict Coll., 1968-71, 72-74, interim pres. Allen U., 1973. Bd. dirs. Columbia Lyric Theatre, 1972-75. Fellow Internat. Inst. Arts and Letters. Club: Rotary. Composer: Concerto Grosso in F for Oboe, String Quartet and Harp with String Orchestra, 1944; Symphony in D, 1944; Chinese Suite, 1945; Chinese Symphony, 1948; (madrigal) Come Away, Come Away, Death!, 1957; The Cuckoo Chorus, 1958; Hymn for Peace, 1960; And Ruth Said: Entreat Me Not to Leave Thee, 1962; The Solitary Reaper, 1964; She Never Told Her Love, 1965; This Glorious Christmas Night, 1967; Gloria Patri and Kyrie, 1968; The Pattering Rain, 1968; The Lord's Prayer, 1969; We Shall Overcome, 1970; A Tombstone Epitaph, 1971; Alleluia, May Peace Be on Earth, 1972; Farewell for Ever!, 1972; All Glory, Praise and Honor, 1973; Echoes from on the Great Wall, 1974; He Who Loves God Loves All People, 1975; Last Night, 1975; Oh Slide and Stamp!, 1976; For Dust Thou Art, and Unto Dust Shalt Thou Return, 1977; Think! Think! Think!, 1977; Long, Long Ago, 1977; Farewell Alma Mater Dear! God Be With You Till We Meet Again, 1977; Concerto Ecclesiastico, 1979; Orientalia string quartet, 1980; A Song for the Chinese People, 1981; A Japanese Song, 1982; Doxology in Chinese Style, 1983; Oriental Theme and Variations for String Quartet or String Orch., 1985; Author: An Application of Ancient Chinese Medical Practices to Modern Disease: VD-HIV (AIDS), Cancer, etc. with

Nature-made, Controlled and Variable Quasi-live Virocine, 1986. Deceased. Home: Columbia S.C.

YELLEN, JACK, songwriter; b. Poland, July 6, 1892; came to U.S., 1898; s. Abraham and Beth Bess (Wallens) Y.; m. Sylvia Stiller (div. Aug. 1944); children: Beth Yellen Wilcove, David M.; m. Lucille Hodgeman, 1944. AB and MA, U. Mich., 1913. Music pub. Ager, Yellen & Bornstein, N.Y.C. and Chgo., from 1922; screenwriter with various studios including 20th Century-Fox, RKO, Warner Bros., Hollywood, Calif., 1927-40; owner, farmer Melody Meadows, Springville, N.Y., 1929-68; dir., writer N.Y.C., 1951-69. Songwriter, lyricist: Alabama Jubilee, 1920, Are You From Dixie?, 1920, Ain't She Sweet, 1926, Happy Days Are Here Again, 1929 (4 ASCAP awards 1984, 85, 86, 87), What's in a Name George White Scandals, 1939, Hellzapoppin, Ziegfled Follies, I Wonder What's Become of Sally, Happy Feet, Big Bad Bill is Sweet William, Are You Having Any Fun?, Life Begins at 40, Mr. Segal You Gotta Make it Legal, You've got to be Loved to be Healthy, My Fifty Golden Years, Somebody to Love, Sing Baby Sing, My Yiddshe Momme, others. Served as pfc. cav. U.S. Army, 1914-18. Mem. ASCAP (bd. dirs. 1951-69), Friars Club, Songwriters Hall of Fame (founder 1969), Songwriters Guild Am. (founder 1969). Republican. Jewish. Club: Profs. Lodge: Mason. Died Apr. 17, 1991; buried Beth Israel Cemetery, Buffalo, N.Y.

YERBY, FRANK, novelist; b. Augusta, Ga., Sept. 5, 1916; s. Rufus Garvin and Willie (Smythe) Y.; m. Flora H. Claire Williams, Mar. 1, 1941 (div.); children: Jacques Loring, Nikki Ethlyn, Faune Ellena, Jan Keith; m. Blanquita Calle-Perez, 1956. A.B., Paine Coll., Augusta, 1937; M.A., Fisk U., 1938; postgrad., U. Chgo. Tchr. Fla. A. and M. Coll., Tallahassee, 1939-40, So. U., Baton Rouge, 1940-41; war work Ford Motor Co., Dearborn, Mich., 1942-44, Ranger Aircraft, Jamaica, N.Y., 1944-45. Author: The Foxes of Harrow, 1946, The Vixens, 1947, The Golden Hawk, 1948, Prides Castle, 1949, Floodtide, 1950, A Woman Called Fancy, 1951, The Saracen Blade, 1952, The Devil's Laughter, 1953, Bride of Liberty, 1953, Benton's Row, 1954, The Treasure of Pleasant Valley, 1955, Captain Rebel, 1956, Fair Oaks, 1957, The Serpent and the Staff, 1958, Jarrett's Jade, 1959, Gillian, 1960, The Garfield Honor, 1961, Griffin's Way, 1962, The Old Gods Laugh, 1964, An Odor of Sanctity, 1965, Goat Song, 1967, Judas, My Brother, 1968, Speak Now, 1969, The Dahomean, 1970, The Girl from Storyville, 1971, The Voyage Unplanned, 1974, Tobias and the Angel, 1975, A Rose For Ana Maria, 1976, Hail the Conquering Hero, 1977, A Darkness at Ingraham's Crest, 1979, Western: A Saga of the Great Plains, 1982, Devilseed, 1984, McKenzie's Hundred, 1985; contbr.: short stories to Harper's mag. Recipient O. Henry Meml. award for best first short story, 1944. Home: Madrid Spain Died Nov. 29, 1991.

YLVISAKER, PAUL NORMAN, political science educator, foundation executive; b. St. Paul, Nov. 28, 1921; s. Sigurd Christian and Norma M. (Norem) Y.; m. Barbara Edwards Ewing, Sept. 7, 1946 (dec. 1991); children: Jane Elizabeth, Mark Ewing, Peter Lauritz, David Christian. A.A., Bethany Luth. Jr. Coll., 1940; B.S., Mankato State U., 1942; postgrad., U. Minn, 1942-43; M.P.A. (Littauer fellow), Harvard, 1945, Ph.D., 1948; L.H.D. (hon.), N.Y. Med. Coll., 1967, Jersey City State Coll., 1968, Princeton, 1970, Luther Coll., 1980, Rutgers U., 1981, New Eng. Coll., 1985; LL.D. (hon.), St. Peters Coll., N.J., 1968, Bloomfield Coll., 1968, Upsala Coll., 1969, Swarthmore Coll., 1978, Bryant Coll., 1982, SUNY-New Paltz, 1983. Instr. Bethany Coll., 1943-44; staff Blue Earth County Council on Intergovtl. Relations, 1943-46; tutor, teaching fellow Harvard U., Cambridge, Mass., 1945-47, instr., 1948, vis. prof., 1968-69, prof., from 1982, dean Grad. Sch. Edn., 1972-82; asst. prof. Swarthmore Coll., 1948-53, assoc. prof. dept. polit. sci., 1953-55, dir. inter-univ. case program, 1953-54; exec. sec. to mayor of Phila., 1954-55; exec. assoc. pub. affairs program Ford Found., 1955-58, assoc. dir., 1958-59, dir., 1959-67; commr. N.J. Dept. Community Affairs, 1967-70; vis. prof. Woodrow Wilson Grad. Sch., Princeton, 1961-62, 66-69, prof. pub. affairs and urban planning, 1970-72; vis. lectr. Yale U., 1970; cons. dir. Dayton-Hudson Corp.; sr. cons. Council on Founds. Author: Intergovernmental Relations at the Grassroots, 1955, Battle of Blue Earth County, rev. edit., 1955, The Role of Private Philanthropy in Public Affairs, 1975, Foundations and Non-Profit Agencies, 1987; contbr. articles to profl. jours. Mem. Hispanic Policy Devel. Project, UN Tec. Assistance Mission to Japan, 1960-62, 64, USPHS Health Exch. Mission to USSR, 1964; chmn. Pres.'s Task Force on Cities, 1966-67; dep. chmn. task force on land use and urban growth Citizen's Adv. Com. on Environ. Quality, 1972-73; chmn. task force on legalized gambling 20th Century Fund; cons. Commn. on Pvt. Philanthropy and Pub. Needs; chmn. urban policy com. Nat. Acad. Sci., 1982-85; bd. dirs. Mary Reynolds Babcock Found., Families USA Found., Jobs for the Future Inc., Bernard Van Leer Found., 1976-86, Outward Bound; mem. Mass. State Bd. Regents, 1984-86; chmn. Access, Families U.S.A.; chmn. Ctr. Psychosocial Rsch., Assn. Governing Bds. Future Issues Panel. Sr. Fulbright rsch. scholar U.K., 1951-52; recipient Disting. Grantmakers award, 1990. Mem. Nat. Acad. Pub. Adminstrn. Home: Cambridge Mass. Died Mar. 17, 1992; buried Bear Island, Meredith, N.H.

YODER, CHARLES WILLIAM, civil engineer; b. Pottstown, Pa., June 15, 1911; s. Clinton Umstead and Lula Augusta (Beadenkopf) Y.; m. Josephine Maybelle Wormley, Nov. 4, 1939; children—C. Neal (dec.), Janica J. B.S. in Civil Engring, Pa. State U., 1932. Registered profl. engr., Wis., Pa., Ohio, Ill., Minn., Iowa. Draftsman Phila., 1933-34; with maintenance dept. Keystone Pipe Line Co., 1934; dock supt. Pa. Shipping Co., Phila., 1935-36; field engr. Bethlehem Steel Co., 1936-37, Empire Constrn. Co., 1937; jr. engr. U.S. Soil Conservation Service, 1938-39, Washington office C.E., 1939-40; asst. engr. Office Chief Engrs., 1941-42; structural engr. Pa. R.R., Phila., 1942-45; dist. structural engr. Portland Cement Assn., Milw., 1945-53; cons. engr. Charles W. Yoder & Assos., Milw., 1953-87; Lectr in field. Prin. works include: Automated Concrete Products plant Best Block Co, Milw., 1956, Dane County Meml. Coliseum, Madison, Wis., 1967 (Outstanding Civil Engring. Achievement in Wis.), home office bldg, Oilgear Co., Milw., 1973, can handling bldg, Pabst Brewing Co., 1968, tank storage bldg, 1964, distbn. center, 1975, new press bldg., Milw. Forge, 1977, office and plant facilities, Geiser's Potato Chip Co., 1979, tng. facilities center Miller Brewing Co., 1981, Milw. Quaker Meeting House, 1983. 1st chmn. Nat. Constrn. Industry Council, 1975; chmn. Zoning and Planning Commn. Erin Twp., Washington County, Wis., 1971-80; mem. Wis. Bldg. Code Rev. Bd., 1964-75; Supporter Milw. Pub. Mus., Milw. Performing Arts Center. Recipient Disting. Service citation U. Wis., 1974; named Outstanding Alumni Pa. State U. Coll. Engring., 1974, Alumni fellow, 1975, Community Service award Allied Constrn. Employers Assn., 1975, Engr. of Yr. Engrs. and Scientists of Milw., 1976. Fellow Am. Soc. C.E. (pres. Wis. sect. Wis. 1951, chmn. dist. council 1950-53, dist. dir. 1961-64, zone v.p. 1968-69, nat. pres. 1974, life mem.); mem. Am. Cons. Engrs. Council, ASTM, Am. Concrete Inst., Constrn. Specification Inst., Engrs. Joint Council (dir. 1975-78), Cons. Engrs. Council Wis., Am. Arbitration Assn. (nat. panel arbitrators), Chi Epsilon (hon.). Mem. Soc. Friends. Club: Kiwanian (past dir.). Home: Hartford Wis. Died Apr. 22, 1988.

YODER, FRANKLIN DUANE, medical educator; b. Cheyenne, Wyo., July 25, 1913; m. Catherine Will; children: Diane Janson, Jean Willemin, Mary F. BS, Northwestern U., 1935, MD, 1939; MPH, U. Calif., Berkeley, 1948. Intern Mercy Hosp., Chgo., 1938-39, resident in ob.-gyn., 1939-40; chief of staff Laramie County Meml. Hosp., Cheyenne, 1940-47; dir. Wyo. Dept. Health, Cheyenne, 1948-59, Ill. Dept. Pub. Health, Chgo. and Springfield, 1961-73, Weld County Health Dept., Greeley, Colo., 1973-79; pvt. cons., from 1979; affiliate prof. U. No. Colo. Sch. Nursing, from 1976; pvt. cons. Preventive Med. and Environ. Health, Greeley, Colo., from 1979; lectr. Northwest U., prof. pub. health; sr. mem. Ill. Ctr. Zoonoses Rsch., U. Ill.; prof., Ill. Sch. Pub. Health, 1972; clin. assoc., So. Ill. U., from 1971; clin. assoc. prof., U. Colo., from 1974; clin. prof. preventive med., U. Wyo., from 1985; lectr. U. Ill. Sch. Pub. Health, from 1972; mem. Nat. Com. Accreditation Coun. for Continuing Med. Edn. Chmn. Ohio River Valley Sanitation commn., from 1968. Served as flight surgeon with USAAF, 1942-45. Recipient Alumni Merit award Northwestern U., 1965. Mem. AMA (exec. staff, dir. environ. med. 1959-61, chmn. residency rev. com. for preventive medicine 1977), Am. Assn. Pub. Health Physicians (pres. 1963-64, Disting. Svc. award 1967), Assn. State and Territorial Health Ofcls. (sec., treas. 1954-56, pres. 1957), State and Provincial Health Auths. of N.Am. (conf. participant, hon. life pres. 1968-69), Am. Pub. Health Assn. (governing council 1969-70, 73-77, 79-80, vice-chmn. health adminstrn. sect. 1971-73, chmn. 1973-74), Colo. Med. Soc. (mem. jud. coun. 1988, mem. com. for rev. and recognition, coun. on profl. edn. from 1988), Accreditation Coun. for Continuing Med. Edn. (com. for review and recognition). Home: Greeley Colo. Died Jan. 13, 1992.

YOST, CHARLES WOODRUFF, diplomat; b. Watertown, N.Y., Nov. 6, 1907; s. Nicholas Doxtater and Gertrude (Cooper) Y.; m. Irena Oldakowska, Sept. 8, 1934; children: Nicholas, Casimir, Felicity. Grad., Hotchkiss Sch., 1924; BA, Princeton U., 1928, LLD (hon.); student, U. Paris, 1928-29; LLD (hon., St. Lawrence U., Hamilton Coll.; Dr. Social Sci. (hon.), U. Louisville. Entered Fgn. Service, Dept. State, 1930; vice counsul Fgn. Service, Dept. State, Alexandria, Egypt, 1931-32, Warsaw, 1932-33; minister-counselor Am. Embassy Fgn. Service, Dept. State, Athens, 1950-53; asst. to chmn. U.S. delegation San Francisco Conf. Fgn. Service, Dept. State, 1945, sec. gen. U.S. delegation Potsdam Conf., 1945; charge d' affaires U.S. Legation Fgn. Service, Dept. State, Bangkok, 1945-46; polit. advisor U.S. delegation UN Gen. Assembly Fgn. Service, Dept. State, 1946; 1st sec. Am. embassy Fgn. Service, Dept. State, Prague, Czechoslovakia, 1947; counselor Am. Legation Fgn. Service, Dept. State, Vienna, Austria, 1947-49; spl. asst. ambassador-at-large Council Fgn. Ministers and UN Gen. Assembly Fgn. Service, Dept. State, N.Y.C., 1949; dir. Office Eastern European Affairs Fgn. Service, Dept. State, 1949-50; minister-counselor Am. Embassy Fgn. Service, Dept. State, Athens, 1950-53; dep. high commr. to Austria Fgn. Service, Dept. State, 1953-54, U.S. minister to Kingdom of Laos, 1954-55; minister Am. embassy Fgn. Service, Dept. State, Paris, 1956-58; U.S. ambassador to Syria Fgn. Service, Dept. State, 1958, U.S. ambassador to Morocco, 1958-61, U.S. dep. rep. to UN, 1961-66, chief U.S. rep. to UN, 1969-71; sr. fellow Council Fgn. Relations, N.Y.C., 1966-69, Brookings Inst., 1975; disting. lectr. Sch. Internat. Affairs, Columbia U., 1971-73; counselor UN Assn., 1971-73; pres. Nat. Com. on U.S.-China Relations, 1973-75; spl. advisor Aspen Inst., 1976—. Author: The Age of Triumph and Frustration: Modern Dialogues, 1964, The Insecurity of Nations: International Relations in the Twentieth Century, 1967, The Conduct and Misconduct of Foreign Affairs, 1972, History and Memory, 1980. Recipient Rockefeller Pub. Service award, 1964. Mem. Council Fgn. Relations, AAAS. Died May 21, 1981; buried Watertown, N.Y.

YOST, L. MORGAN, architect; b. St. Marys, Ohio, Oct. 12, 1908; s. Lloyd and Gertrude (Morgan) Y.; m. Winogene Springer, Sept. 11, 1936; children: Elyn (Mrs. Douglas D. Mulder), Karyl (Mrs. Robert L. Thorsen), Chari (Mrs. David H. Binstadt), Owen. Student, Northwestern U., 1925-29; B.Arch., Ohio State U., 1931. Practice architecture Kenilworth, Ill., 1932-52, 60—; partner Yost & Taylor, 1952-60; exec. dir. Chgo. Architecture Found., 1967-70; architect residential and indsl. bldgs., churches, banks; designer pvt. and mil. communities.; Pres. Assn. N. Shore Architects, 1943-51. Co-author: The Packard Car and the Company, 1975; Cons. architect to: Household mag, 1945-58; cons.: Plumbing and Heating Bus, 1946-57; Assoc. editor: Am. Lumberman, 1942-52; architect-editor: Small Homes Guide, 1943-47; Contbr.: articles to others. Trustee Chgo. Architecture Found. Fellow Lake Forest Found. for Architecture and Landscape Architecture, 1931. Fellow A.I.A. (pres. Chgo. chpt. 1950-52, chmn. nat. com. on home bldg. industry); mem. Soc. Automobile Historians, Soc. Archtl. Historians, S.A.R., Alpha Rho Chi, Tau Sigma Delta. Clubs: Westmoreland Country, Kenilworth, Antique Automobile Am. (pres. Ill. region), Classic Car of Am, Cliff Dwellers. Home: Cherokee Village Ark. Died May 6, 1992. †

YOST, ROBERT LLOYD, international affairs consultant, foreign service officer; b. Kirkland, Wash., Sept. 8, 1922; s. Bartley Francis and Irma (Cleopha) Y.; m. June Horsley, Sept. 2, 1945; children: Barbara June, Elizabeth Anne, John Bartley. BA in Econs., UCLA, 1942; postgrad., Harvard U., 1952-53; MS in Internat. Rels., George Washington U., 1968. Fgn. svc. officer Dept. State, 1946; 3d sec. Madrid, 1946-49; vice consul Antwerp, Belgium, 1949-52; consul Leopoldville, 1953-55; rsch. specialist Dept. State, Washington, 1958-58; officer-in-charge OEEC affairs, 1958-59; consul, prin. officer Cebu, P.R., 1959-62; 1st sec., fin. adviser U.S. del. to OECD Paris, 1962-65; also U.S. mem. com. invisible transactions and alt. U.S. rep. bd. mgmt. European Monetary Agreement; spl. asst. to asst. sec. of State for European Affairs, 1965-67; assigned to Nat. War Coll., 1967-68; counselor, dep. chief mission Am. embassy Addis Ababa, Ethiopia, 1968-72; amb. to Burundi Bujumbura, 1972-74; dep. insp. gen. Fgn. Svc., Washington, 1974-78; ambassador to Dominican Republic Santo Domingo, 1978-82; internat. affairs cons. Dept. State, Washington, 1982-89. With AUS, 1942-46. Mem. Am. Fgn. Svc. Assn., Nat. War Coll. Alumni Assn., World Affairs Coun. of No. Calif., Fedn. for Am. Immigration Reform (mem. nat. bd. advs.), Dacor Bacon House Found. (bd. govs.), Alliance Francaise de San Francisco (bd. dirs.), Fgn. Svc. Assn. No. Calif. (chmn. steering com.), Commonwealth Club. Home: Oakland Calif. Died May 29, 1990; inurned Mountain View Cemetery, Oakland, Calif.

YOUEL, KENNETH, public relations consultant; b. Doon, Iowa, May 19, 1901; s. Blaine T. and Jennie (Hancock) Y.; m. Frances E. Rose, June 10, 1930 (dec.); children: Adele Frances (Mrs. Russell N. Chappell, Jr.), John Kenneth; m. Jan V. DiMarco, Apr. 16, 1963. B.A., U. Oreg., 1923. News staff The Oregonian, Portland, Oreg., 1923-25, Bklyn. Eagle, 1925-27; financial writer N.Y. Evening Post, 1927-31; asst. dir. communications Gen. Motors Corp., Detroit, 1931-61; pub. relations cons., from 1961; cons. USIA, Washington, 1962-69; pub. mem. U.S. Dept. State Fgn. Service Inspection Corps, Washington, 1966. Mem. Pub. Relations Soc. Am. (founder, pres. Mich. 1958, nat. pres. 1960, Disting. Svc. award 1964), Pub. Mem. Assn. (pres. 1970-73), S.A.R., Sigma Delta Chi, Phi Kappa Psi. Republican. Presbyterian. Clubs: Univ. (N.Y.C.); Farmington (Charlottesville, Va.); Everglades (Palm Beach, Fla.). Home: Earlysville Va. Died Dec. 30, 1990; buried Monticello Meml. Gardens, Charlottesville, Va.

YOUNG, ALEXANDER STUARD, JR., lawyer; b. Washington, Aug. 27, 1921; s. Alexander Stuard and Gertrude Louise (Parsons) Y.; m. Mary Elizabeth Primm, Oct. 25, 1945; children: Alexander Stuard III, A. Suzanne Young Wieland, A. Steven, A. Stanley. BS in Econs, U. Pa., 1942; JD, Georgetown U., 1950. Bar: D.C. 1950, Pa. 1951, U.S. Supreme Ct 1953. Commd. 2d lt. U.S. Army Air Force, 1942; advanced through grades to col. U.S. Air Force, 1966; service in N. Africa and Italy, 1943-45; sta. at Hdqrs. Washington, 1946-50, 51-52; with Mil. Intelligence Res., Phila., 1953-56; dist. comdr. OSI Res., 1956-65; assoc. firm Stradley, Ronon, Stevens & Young, Phila., 1950-51, 52-56, partner, 1957-88; dir. Vestaur Securities, Inc. Author: The Rights and Liabilities of Shareholders—United States, 1977, also articles; editorial asst. in transl.: W. Ger. Fgn. Investment Co. Laws, 1971, W. Ger. Domestic Investment Co. Laws, 1981; contbr.: chpt. to Practical Guide for Investments in the U.S, 1979, 2d edit., 1982. Bd. dirs., sec.-treas. Binder Schweitzer Amazonian Hosp. Found., Inc., N.Y.C., 1961-70; mem. Branford (Conn.) Electric Ry. Assn., 1969-88, Pop Warner Little Scholars, Phila., 1975-88; bd. dirs. World Affairs Council of Phila., 1984-88, adv. bd. 1988. Decorated Bronze Star, Air Force Commendation ribbon. Mem. Am. Bar Assn., Pa. Bar Assn., Phila. Bar Assn., D.C. Bar Assn., Asia-Pacific Lawyers Assn., Inter-Am. Bar Assn., Internat. Bar Assn. (mem. council bus. law sect. 1986-88), Fed. Bar Assn., Am. Law Inst., Am. Judicature Soc., Internat. Fiscal Assn., Nat. Lawyers Club, Union Internat. des Avocats, Phi Alpha Delta, Lambda Chi Alpha. Republican. Episcopalian. Clubs: Inst. Dirs. (London), Pen and Wig (London); Officers Open Mess of McGuire (N.J.) AFB; Penn; Union League (Phila.); Army-Navy (Washington). Lodge: Masons. Home: New Hope Pa. Died Nov. 30, 1988; buried Arlington Nat. Cemetery.

YOUNG, DAVID ELWYN, publisher's consultant; b. Somerville, Mass., Sept. 22, 1915; s. Elwyn Lawrence/Kimball and Henrietta Ella (Kuhn) Y.; m. Eleanor Ruth Brown, June 28, 1936; children: Joan (Mrs. George Ladenburg), Nancy (Mrs. John O'Pezio), Paul. Grad., Burdett Coll., 1933. Circulation dir., v.p., chmn. exec. com. KABLE News Co., N.Y.C., 1950-60; v.p. sales Grove Press, Inc., 1960-63, Paperback Library, 1963-68; pres. Olympia Press, N.Y., 1968-71, Manor Books, Inc., 1972-76, David E. Young, Inc., from 1976. Pres. East Meadow Blood Bank, 1952-57. Mem. Distripress. Presbyterian (elder 1953-87). Clubs: Tenn. Squires, Mt. Kenya Safari. Lodge: Masons. Home: Westbury N.Y. Died Oct. 12, 1987.

YOUNG, DAVID LINCOLN, landscape architect, educator; b. Hyannis, Mass., May 12, 1929; s. Benjamin Lee and Katherine (Watson) Y.; m. Elaine Wilson, Aug. 19, 1961; children: Katherine, Cynthia, Sarah, Arthur. BS in Landscape Arch., U. Mass., 1951, BLA, 1957; MLA, Harvard U., 1961. Staff designer Fay, Spofford & Thorndike, Eng., Boston, 1957; assoc. Shurcliff & Merrill (Landscape Architects), Boston, 1957-67; assoc. prof. landscape architecture La. State U., 1967-72; prof. landscape architecture Pa. State U., 1972-89, dept. head, 1972-84; bd. dir. Landscape Architecture Found., pres., 1979-82; bd. dir. Hubbard Ednl. Trust. With USAF, 1951-55. La. State U. Teaching Improvement grantee, 1978, Nat. Endowment for Arts grantee, 1971, 74, 77, 79. Fellow Am. Soc. Landscape Architects; mem. Coun. Educators in Landscape Architecture. Home: South Yarmouth Mass. Died Aug. 1, 1991; interred S. Yarmouth, Mass.

YOUNG, GEORGE BERKELEY, lawyer; b. Madison, Wis., July 27, 1913; s. Karl and Frances Campbell (Berkeley) Y.; m. Mary Seymour Adams, Mar. 24, 1944; children—Mary, George. A.B., Yale, 1934, A.M., 1937, Ph.D., 1939; J.D., Northwestern U., 1948. Bar: Ill. bar 1948. Asso. Isham, Lincoln & Beale, Chgo., 1948-50; mem. firm Isham, Lincoln & Beale, 1950-54; v.p. Field Enterprises, Inc., Chgo., 1954-64; pres. Field Enterprises, Inc., 1964-66, chmn., 1966-68, dir., 1952-69; instr. hist. Barnard Coll., Columbia, 1939-41; lectr. property law Northwestern U. Law Sch., 1951-53; dir. CNA Income Shares, Inc. Author: (with J.A.S. Grenville) Politics Strategy and American Diplomacy, 1966; also articles in law revs. Trustee Rush-Presbyn.-St. Luke's Med. Ctr.; v.p., trustee Art Inst. Chgo., from 1953; trustee Newberry Libr., Chgo. Served at lt. OSS USNR, 1943-45. Mem. Chgo. Bar Assn., Phi Beta Kappa, Order of Coif. Clubs: Chicago (Chgo.), Casino (Chgo.), Wayfarers (Chgo.), Commercial Commonwealth (Chgo.); Onwentsia (Lake Forest, Ill.), Shorearcres (Lake Forest, Ill.); Graduates (New Haven), Elizabethan (New Haven); Brook and Century (N.Y.C.). Home: Chicago Ill. Died Jan. 29, 1988; buried Graceland Cemetery, Chgo., Ill.

YOUNG, HERRICK BLACK, foundation administrator; b. Marshfield, Wis., Feb. 8, 1904; s. James Franklin and Charlotte (Black) Y.; m. Charlotte Elizabeth Young, June 1, 1928; children: Herrick Jackson, Charlotte Joanne, Roderick McCune, Malcolm Black. AB, Ind. U., 1925; MA, Columbia U., 1928; postgrad (Harrison fellow), U. Pa., 1935; LLD (hon.), Centre Coll. Ky., 1954; LHD (hon.), Miami U., Oxford, Ohio, 1965. Instr. Alborz Coll., Teheran, Iran, 1925-27, prof. lit., 1928-35; exec. sec. charge pers. Presbyn. Bd. Fgn. Missions, 1935-50; chmn. com. missionary pers. Fgn. Missions Conf. N.A., 1946-50; exec. dir. Internat. House Assn., 1950-54; lectr. field internat. rels.; pres. We. Coll. for Women, 1954-69; cons. to pres., contr. Tunghi U., Taichung, Taiwan, 1969-72; pres. Nr. East Found., N.Y.C., 1972-90; dir. summer seminars, S.Am., 1955, 63, Mid. East, 1956, 60, 64, Far East, 1957, 61, 65, Africa, 1985, 62, 66, Ctrl. Am. and Caribbean, 1959. Author: One Great Fellowship, 1937, Moslem Editors Say, 1937, Hemisphere Neighbors, 1940, Tuesdays at Kumler Chapel, 1963, Strange Lands and Wonderful People, 1975. Chmn. com. internat. rels. Coun. Protestant Colls.; exec. com. Internat. Com. YMCA; mem. Coun. Evaluation Fgn. Student Credential; mem. Presbyn. Commn. on Nat. Capitol Ctr.; chmn. bd. trustees Welfare of Blind; elder Presbyn. Ch. Decorated Order of Homayun (Iran), 1962; named Ky. col. Fellow Royal Geog. Soc., Royal Ctrl. Asian Soc.; mem. Assn. Am. Colls. (commn. liberal learning), Am. Coun. Edn., Nat. Assn. Fgn. Student Advisers, Newcomen Soc., Ohio Coll. Assn. (exec. com.), St. Andrews Soc., Phi Delta Kappa, Sigma Delta Chi, Masons, Univ. Club (N.Y.C.), Cosmos Club (Washington), Fort Henry Club (Wheeling, W.Va.). Republican. Home: Washington D.C. Died Feb. 15, 1990.

YOUNG, JAMES ALLEN, lawyer; b. Dayton, Ohio, Apr. 24, 1932; s. J. Otis and Gladys (Riffle) Y.; m. Sally Kimmel, Oct. 23, 1954; children: James A. Jr., Jeffrey, Karen, Gregory. BA, Ohio Wesleyan U., 1954; MA in Fgn. Affairs, George Washington U., 1958; JD, Case Western Res. U., 1960. Bar: Ohio 1960. Assoc., Hahn Loeser & Parks, Cleve., 1960-67, ptnr., from 1967; dir. OLDCO Diversified, Inc., Garco Machinery, Inc., Cleve. Editor-in-chief Case Western Res. Law Rev., 1959-60. Trustee, sec. Goodwill Industries, Cleve., from 1974; pres. Nat. Jr. Tennis League, Inc., N.Y.C., 1975-79; founder, chmn. bd. Nat. Jr. Tennis League of Cleve., from 1973, vice chmn. USTA/NJTL com., 1985-87, chmn., from 1988; trustee Ohio Wesleyan U., from 1972, vice chmn. bd., 1984-86, chmn., from 1986; founding trustee, bd. dirs. Shaker Schs. Found., Cleve., from 1982; trustee Ch. of the Saviour, Cleve., 1973-83, from 1985; chmn. Ch. of the Saviour Found., from 1989; trustee, sec., v.p. Ohio East area United Meth. Found., from 1986; mem. adv. coun. Cleve. chpt. "I Have a Dream" Found., from 1987; mem. Citizens League Greater Cleve., from 1970; mem. Coun. for Small Enterprises; dir. Superannuates Fund Assn. N.E. Ohio Ann. Conf. of United Meth. Ch., from 1987; mem. Conf. of Bd. Chmn., from 1986; bd. dirs. Austin Manor, from 1987; founder, mem. Bishop Backers of Cleve., from 1986. Served with U.S. Army, 1954-56. Recipient Alumni award Ohio Wesleyan U., 1964; Applause award Cleve. Jaycees-Jr. League, 1976; Wolcott fellow George Washington U., 1958. Mem. Cleve. Bar Assn. (past chmn. young lawyers sect.), Ohio Bar Assn., ABA, Ohio Wesleyan U. Alumni Assn. (nat. pres. 1970-73), Order of Coif, Growth Assn. of Greater Cleve., U.S. Tennis Assn. (edn. and recreation tennis coun. from 1988, Jr. tennis subcom. from 1988), Omicron Delta Kappa. Republican. Methodist. Clubs: Mid Day, Play House, Cleve. City, University (Cleve.); Park East Racquet. Lodge: Masons. Avocations: tennis, reading, coaching youth sports. Deceased. Home: Cleveland Ohio

YOUNG, JOSEPH SAMUEL, cement company executive; b. Allentown, Pa., June 15, 1898; s. Edward Mark and Kate (Anewalt) Y.; m. MArion I. Johnson, Sept. 16, 1926; 1 child, William Johnson. AB, Princeton, 1919; LLB, Columbia U., 1923; LLC, Muhlenberg Coll., 1956. With Lehigh Portland Cement Co., 1923, v.p., asst. to pres., 1926-32, pres., 1932-63, chmn. exec. com., from 1963; dir. Pa. Power and Light Co., Bell Telephone Co., Pa., also Arnstrong Cork Co. Chmn. boar trustees Trexler Found. Clubs: Saucon Valley Country, Livingston Lehigh Country, Princeton. Republican. Presbyterian. *

YOUNG, PHILIP PRATT, American literature educator, author; b. Boston, May 26, 1918; s. Roswell Philip and Katharine (Pratt) Y.; m. Caroline Anderson (dec. 1967); 1 child Jeffrey Anderson (dec. 1988); m. Katherine Hambrecht; 1 child Rosalie. BA, Amherst Coll., 1940; PhD, U. Iowa, 1948; LHD (hon.), Westminster Coll., 1970. Instr., adj. prof. NYU, 1948-53; assoc. prof. Kansas State U., Manhattan, 1953-58; prof. Pa. State U., Univeristy Park, 1959-80, Evan Pugh Prof., 1980-88, prof. emeritus, 1988-91; Fulbright lectr., 1963-64; lectr. USIA, 1957. Author: Ernest Hemingway, 1952, rev. edit. under title Ernest Hemingway: A Reconsideration, 1966, Three Bags Full..., 1972, Revolutionary Ladies, 1977 (Am. Revolution Round Table Best Book Yr. 1978), Hawthorne's Secret, 1984, The Private Melville, 1991. 1st lt. U.S. Army, 1942-46. Democrat. Episcopalian. Home: State College Pa. Died Oct. 4, 1991; buried State Coll., Pa.

YOUNG, RICHARD ALLEN, packaging company executive; b. Carthage, Mo., June 8, 1915; s. Howard I. and Myrtle Lee (Mason) Y.; m. Janice Westmoreland, Dec. 8, 1945; children: Harriette Louise, Richard Allen, Alfred Westmoreland. B.S. in Chem. Engring, Washington U., St. Louis, 1936; M.B.A., Harvard U., 1938. With Am. Zinc Co., Ill., 1938-50; v.p. Am. Zinc Co., 1944-50; with Am. Zinc, Lead & Smelting Co., St. Louis, 1950-70, exec. v.p., 1963-64, chmn. bd., 1965-70, also dir.; exec. v.p., dir. Uranium Reduction Co., St. Louis, 1955-62; pres. Bemis Co., Inc., Mpls., 1971-76, chmn., chief exec. officer, 1976-78, also dir.; dir. Harbour Group, St. Louis; Industry adviser U.S. del. on lead and zinc UN Conf., 1958-70; mem. UN Lead-Zinc Study Group, 1958-70. Trustee, chmn. St. Louis Ednl. TV Commn., 1959-71; dir., chmn. Bus.-Industry Polit. Action Com., 1976-79. Recipient Alumni Chem. Engring. award Washington U., 1960, 77. Mem. AIME, Mining and Metall. Soc. Am. Home: Saint Louis Mo. Died May 17, 1992. †

YOUNG, ROBERT AARON, art dealer; b. N.Y.C., Dec. 7; s. Jack and Ruth (Rosenberg) Y.; m. Ethel Greenbaum, Sept. 30, 1956; children—Aaron, Claudia. B.S., Syracuse U., 1954. Exec. v.p. Harvey Probber Furniture, N.Y.C., 1958-63; prin. Robert Aaron Young, Inc., Art Dealer and Pub., N.Y.C., 1963—; founder Ctr. for African Art. Producer video tapes on art related subjects. Founding soc. Lenox Hill Hosp.; mem. Am. Ballet Theatre. Home: New York N.Y.

YOUNGBLADE, CHARLES JOHN, naval officer; b. Sioux City, Iowa, Sept. 2, 1926; s. Amil Charles and Mary Ella (Manning) Y.; m. Monika Erika Hechler, Oct. 15, 1977. Student, Iowa State Coll., 1943-44; B.S., U.S. Naval Acad., 1949; M.S. in Internat. Affairs, George Washington U., 1967. Commd. ensign U.S. Navy, 1949, advanced through grades to rear adm., 1975; various squadron and adminstrv. staff positions, 1950-69; comdr. officer U.S.S. Patcatuck (AO-108), 1969-70; exec. asst. to dep. chief naval ops. for fleet ops. and readiness, 1970-71; comdg. officer U.S.S. Roosevelt (CVA-42), 1971-73; chief of staff for comdr. Naval Air Forces Atlantic, 1973-75; dep. dir. reconnaissance Joint Chiefs of Staff, Washington, 1975-76; dep. comdr. Naval Forces, So. Europe, 1976-78; comdr. Naval Safety Center, Norfolk, Va., 1978-79; v.p., gen. mgr. Eastern Dist. PRC, Norfolk, 1979-82; dir. Sci. Support Lab. CDEC, Ft. Ord, Calif., 1982-84; v.p. PRC SS, McLean, Va., 1984-90. Decorated Legion of Merit, Bronze Star, Air medal, Joint Service Commendation medal, Navy Commendation medal. Mem. Assn. Naval Aviation. Home: Chantilly Va. Died June 10, 1990; buried Arlington Nat. Cemetery.

YOUNGER, EVELLE JANSEN, lawyer, state official; b. Nebr., June 19, 1918; s. Harry C. and Maebel (Jansen) Y.; m. Mildred Eberhard, July 3, 1942; 1 son, Eric. A.B., Nebr. U., 1940, also; LL.B.; student criminology, Northwestern Law Sch., Chgo., 1940. Bar: Calif. 1946. Spl. agt. FBI, N.Y.C., also Washington; supr. nat. def. sect., 1940-46; dep. city atty. criminal div. Los Angeles, 1946-47; city pros., 1947-50; pvt. practice law Los Angeles, 1950-53; judge Municipal Ct., Los Angeles, 1953-58, Superior Ct., 1958-64; dist. atty. Los Angeles County, 1964-70; atty. gen. Calif., 1970-78; mem. firm. Buchalter, Nemer, Fields and Younger, 1979-89; instr. criminal law Southwestern U., Los Angeles, 1948; chmn. Pres. Reagan's Task Force on Adminstrn. of Justice, 1981. Contbr. articles to profl. jours. Served to maj. AUS, 1942-46; to lt. col. USAF, 1951-52; maj. gen. USAF Res. Ret. Fellow Am. Coll. Trial Lawyers; mem. Am. Bar Assn. (chmn. criminal law sect. 1962, past chmn. traffic and magistrates cts. com.), State Bar of Calif., Nat. Dist. Atty.'s Assn. (v.p.), Am. Legion, Soc. Former FBI Agts. (past chmn.), Los Angeles Peace Officers Assn. (past pres.), Council Mexican-Am. Affairs, Air Force Assn., Alpha Tau Omega Alumni Assn. (past pres.). Episcopalian. Clubs: Mason (Shriner), Elk, Trojan (dir.). Home: Los Angeles Calif. Died May 4, 1989.

YOUNGREN, HARRISON, educator; b. Altona, Ill., Nov. 27; s. David N. and Esther F. (Quick) Y.; m. Margaret Rue Stansfield, June 24, 1972. AB, Knox Coll., 1936; MA, So. Ill. U., 1967, PhD, 1975. Sales and market researcher Wander Co., 1936-41; commd. 1st lt. U.S. Army, 1941, advanced through grades to lt. col., ret., 1962; editor Mt. Carmel (Ill.) Daily Rep. Register, 1962-64; mem. faculty dept. journalism U. Wis.-Oshkosh, 1969-73; prof. journalism Angelo State U., San Angelo, Tex., from 1973, head dept., 1973-74, 78-79; reporter Branch-Smith Pub. Co.; adviser in mass communications Republic of Korea, 1956-57, Laos, 1958-61; cons. in field. Bd. dirs. Wabash Valley Coll. Found.; mem. Knox Coll. Alumni Adv. Com., from 1962. Mem. Assn. Edn. in Journalism, Tex. Journalism Edn. Council (treas.), San Angelo Press Club (bd. dirs.), Kappa Tau Alpha, Sigma Delta Chi (dir. San Angelo chpt.). Democrat. Lutheran. Deceased. Home: Mount Carmel Ill.

YOUNT, FLORENCE JANE, lawyer; b. Enid, Okla., Dec. 13, 1926; d. William Edward and Florence Evelyn (McCully) Y. B.A., State U. Iowa, 1948; J.D., S. Tex. Coll. Law, 1958; certificate, Parker Sch. Fgn. and Comparative Law, Columbia U., 1976. Bar: Tex. bar 1958. Atty. Ginther, Warren & Co., Houston, 1959-70; supr. internat. contracts Ea. Hemisphere div. CONOCO, Inc., N.Y.C., Stamford, Conn., 1970-75; sr. atty. Cities Service Co., Houston, 1975-83; contracts supr. Marathon, Houston, 1984-91; adviser to Internat. Law Socs. of three Houston law schs.; bd. dirs. South Tex. Law Jour., Inc., 1959-88, v.p., 1969, 77, 84-87, pres., 1970, 78, 79. Contbr. articles to law jours. Bd. dirs. Park Ave. Christian Ch., N.Y.C., 1971-73, First Christian Ch., Houston, 1977-78; active Vols. of Shelter, N.Y.C., 1973-75; precinct chmn., asso. legal counsel, chmn. rules com. Harris County (Tex.) Republican Com., 1958-68. Recipient Distinguished Alumnus award South Tex. Coll. Law, 1976, Houston Matrix award, 1978, award Bus. and Profl. Women's Club Houston, 1976; named One of 100 Top Corporate Women Bus. Week, 1976. Mem. ABA, Tex. Bar Assn. (contbg. editor Internat. Law Newsletter), Houston Bar Assn., S. Tex. Coll. Law Alumni Assn. (dir. 1977-80), Zool. Soc. Houston. Mem. Christian Ch. Home: Houston Tex. Died Aug. 13, 1991; cremated.

YOUNT, STANLEY GEORGE, paper company executive; b. Ketchum, Idaho, Feb. 15, 1903; s. George and Cansada (Smith) Y.; student U. Nev., 1924; m. Agnes Pratt, Feb. 17, 1944; children—Ann E., George S. Div. sales mgr. Crown Zellerbach Corp., 1926-40; pres. Southland Paper Converting Co., 1940-56; pres.

Fortifiber Corp. and affiliates, Los Angeles, 1956-77, chmn., 1977—, also dir.; dir. Stanwall Corp. Served with U.S. Army, World War I; AEF in France. Mem. Nat. Flexible Packaging Assn. (pres. Indsl. Bag and Cover div. 1954-56), Barrier Paper Mfrs. Assn. Mason (Shriner). Clubs: Jonathan (Los Angeles), Rotary. Home: Los Angeles Calif.

YOUNTS, CHARLES REIPHI, retried petroleum executive; b. Pineville, N.C., July 7, 1895; s. William E. and Eunice (Bell) Y.; m. Willie Camp, Mar. 12, 1930. Grad., Bairds U., 1912; LHD (hon.), Erskine Coll., 1962. Assoc. Standard Oil Co. of N.J., from 1912; pres. Plantation Pipe Line Co., Atlanta, 1941-59, chmn. bd. dirs., 1960, retired, 1960. Dir. Blue Ridge (N.C.) Assembly; pres. Atlanta Chs. Home for Bus. Girls; dir., past chmn. Atlanta chpt. ARC, treas.; So. area coun. YMCA's; trustee Atlanta Met. YMCA; bd. trustees, treas. Erskine Coll., Due West, S.C. 1st sgt. U.S. Army, 1917-19. Mem. So. Indsl. Rels. Conf. (past chmn. bd.), Atlanta C. of C., Newomen Soc., SAR, Masons, Rotary. Clubs: Capital City, Peidmont Driving, Univ. Yacht. Presbyterian. *

YOUNTS, JACK SPURGEON, broadcasting executive; b. Greensboro, N.C., Nov. 21, 1917; s. Millard and Maude Ethel (Murray) Y.; student Duke U., N.C. State U., Indsl. Coll. Armed Forces, 1967; m. Elizabeth Mendenhall, Dec. 5, 1942; children: Sandra Louise, Millard Stephen, Gerlind Elizabeth. Dir. ground ops. Am. Overseas Airlines, LaGuardia Airport, N.Y.C., 1944-47; pres., gen. mgr. Sta. WEEB, Southern Pines, N.C., 1947-81, chmn. bd., 1947-81; exec. v.p. Sta. WAKN, Aiken, S.C., 1949-55; pres., gen. mgr. Sta. WUSM, Havelock, Cherry Point, N.C., 1962-70; chmn. bd. Friendship Broadcasters, 1962-70; v.p., dir. Sandhills Cablevision, 1970-87; chmn. bd. Sandhill Community Broadcasters, 1947-81; pres. Satellite Services, 1980-82; dir. Pinehurst Airlines, Inc.; mem. affiliates adv. com. Mut. Network, 1953-56; mem. ABC Network Affiliate Bd., 1960-66; mem. nat. def. exec. res. FCC, 1963-70; advisor on Dept. State U.S.-Mex. Broadcast Allocations Conf., 1960-63. Mem. N.C. Gov.'s Communications Study Commn., USS N.C. Battleship Commn., Gov.'s Exec. Com. for Traffic Safety, 1962-65, chancellors pub. relations com. N.C. State U.; bd. dirs. N.C. State U. Edn. Found. Named to Broadcasting Hall of Fame. Served with USNR, World War II. Mem. Broadcast Pioneers, Soc. of So. Broadcast Execs. (chmn. 1978-87), Nat. Assn. Broadcasters (dir. 1958-62, 66-70, 74-78, chmn. membership com. 1975-78), Nat. Daytime Broadcasters Assn. (pres. 1959-61), Sandhills Area C. of C. (chmn. transp. bd. 1972-81), N.C. Assn. Broadcasters (sec.-treas. 1948-54), N.C. Assn. Press Broadcasters (pres. 1969-70), Nat. Communications Clubs, Am. Legion, VFW, SAR (state sec.), Mu Beta Psi, Kappa Kappa Psi, Sigma Nu. Clubs: Country of N.C. (Pinehurst); Beech Mountain Country; Overseas Press (N.Y.C.); Spooners Creek Yacht; Morehead City (N.C.). Lodges: Elks, Kiwanis. Died Dec. 18, 1987, interred Old Bethesda Cemetery, Aberdeen/Southern Pines, N.C. Home: Southern Pines N.C.

YTTERBERG, CARL FREDERICK, business executive; b. Chgo., Dec. 9, 1896; s. Charles and Mary (Myren) Y.; m. Ruth O. Nordquist, Sept. 10, 1921; children: Marcia Ruth, Robert Frederick. Student, Northwestern U. Dist. mgr. Kalman Floor Co., 1924-33, pres., from 1933; pres. Dominion Kalman Floor Co. of Can., from 1933, Kalman Labs., Inc.; splty. concrete floors, bldg. constrn. floors, concrete; designer in field. Served with U.S. Army, WWI. Mem. Union League Club. Republican. Baptist. *

YU, PAUL NANGAN, physician, educator; b. Kiangsi, China, Nov. 7, 1915; came to U.S., 1947, naturalized, 1952; s. Y.S. and L.H. (Yang) Y.; m. Iling Tang, June 4, 1944; children: Pauline R., Diane C., Lorraine M., Corrine M. M.D., Nat. Med. Coll., Shanghai, China, 1939. Intern First Red Cross Hosp., Shanghai, 1938-39; asst. and chief resident in medicine Central Hosp., Chungking, China, 1940-43; asst. resident in medicine Strong Meml. Hosp., Rochester, N.Y., 1947-48; practice medicine specializing in cardiology Rochester, 1952-82; asst. prof. medicine U. Rochester Med. Sch., 1954-59, asso. prof., 1959-63, prof., 1963-69, Sarah McCort Ward prof., 1969-82; head cardiology unit U. Rochester Med. Center and Strong Meml. Hosp., Rochester, 1957-82. Author: Pulmonary Blood Volume in Health and Disease; Editor: (with J.F. Goodwin) Progress in Cardiology, from 1972, Modern Concepts of Cardiovascular Disease, 1976-78. Brit. Council scholar, U.K. Mem. Assn. Am. Physicians, Am. Clin. and Climatol. Assn., Assn. Univ. Cardiologists, Am. Coll. Cardiology, ACP, Am. Physiol. Soc., Am. Heart Assn. (pres. 1972-73), Sigma Xi, Alpha Omega Alpha. Home: Tapei Taiwan Died Oct. 8, 1991.

YUDKIN, HOWARD LOUIS, electrical engineer, business executive; b. Phila., June 22, 1936; s. William and Jeanne (Livingstone) Y.; m. Judith Ann Sussman, June 7, 1959; children: Laurie Sue, Debra Robin. B.S.E.E., U. Pa., 1957; M.S., M.I.T., 1959, Ph.D., 1965. Asst. engr. U.S. Army Frankfort Arsenal, Phila., 1955; engr. Product Devel. Lab., IBM, Glendale, N.Y., 1956, Lincoln Lab., M.I.T., Lexington, 1957-68; asst. group leader Lincoln Lab., M.I.T., 1968-69, group leader, 1969-70; asst. dir. for info. and communications Office of Dir. Def. Research and Engring., Pentagon, Washington, 1970-72; dep. asst. sec. for telecommunications Dept. Def., 1972-74; v.p. Computer Sci. Corp., Falls Church, Va., 1974-77; pres. systems div. Computer Sci. Corp., 1977-80, v.p. planning systems group, 1980-81; v.p. Booz, Allen & Hamilton Inc., Bethesda, Md., 1982-86; pres., chief exec. officer Software Productivity Consortium, Reston, Va., 1986-89; tchr. M.I.T., Northeastern U., others; cons. Contbr. articles to profl. jours. Bd. dirs. Temple Beth Am, Framingham, Mass., 1968-70; pres. Temple Beth Ami, Rockville, Md., 1974-76. Recipient Meritorious Civilian Service medal Dept. Def., 1974. Mem. Armed Forces Communications and Electronics Assn., Nat. Security Industry Assn., IEEE. Home: Rockville Md. Died May 23, 1989; buried King David Cemetery, Falls Church, Va.

YUSPEH, SONIA ELIZABETH, marketing and advertising executive; b. Syracuse, Feb. 1, 1928; d. Fareed B. and Nancy (Mandour) NeJame; m. Michel H. Yuspeh, Nov. 2, 1955; children: Leonid, Denise. B.A., Syracuse U., 1951; M.A., Cornell U., 1953. Sr. project dir. Audits & Surveys, N.Y.C., 1954-56; group head Grey Advt., N.Y.C., 1956-60, asso. research dir., 1962-67, exec. research dir., 1969-72; sr. project dir. McCann-Erickson Advt., N.Y.C., 1960-62; market research dir. D'Arcy Advt., N.Y.C., 1967-69; sr. v.p. in charge of research and planning J. Walter Thompson, N.Y.C., 1972-83, dir., 1980-83; pres. Sonia Yuspeh, Inc., 1983-90; dir. Mktg. Rev. mag. Contbr. articles to mktg. jours. Mem. Am. Mktg. Assn., Advt. Research Found., Mktg. Research Council, Copy Research Council, Advt. Research Council, Phi Beta Kappa. Home: New York N.Y. Died Sept. 30, 1990.

ZALKIND, NORMAN, academic administrator; b. Fall River, Mass., Dec. 2, 1914; s. Samuel and Besse Frances (Dondis) Z.; m. Esther Fay Yamins, Oct. 27, 1940 (dec. Aug. 1975); children: Michael, Shelley; m. Pauline Anne Melanson, Feb. 16, 1986. AB, Brown U., 1935; LHD (hon.), Southeastern Mass. U., 1981. Mgr., trustee Whipple Realty Trust, Fall River, 1946-60; mng. ptnr. Wolfson-Zalkind & Co., Fall River, 1960-76; exec. dir. Office Econ. Devel. City of Fall River, 1976-84; exec. dir. Southeastern Mass. U. Found., North Dartmouth, 1984-87; asst. to pres. Southeastern Mass. U., North Dartmouth, 1987-90; bd. dirs. So. New Eng. Sch. of Law, New Bedford, Mass. Mem. Fall River Pvt. Industry Coun., 1976-84; commr. Gov.'s Commn. Future of Mature Industries in Commonwealth, Boston, 1982-85, Edn. Commn. of States, Denver, 1984-90; founding mem. Bd. Regents Higher Edn., Mass., 1981-84; trustee Southeastern Mass. U., 1974-81, chmn. bd. trustees, 1979-81; mem. Fall River Arts Lottery Commn., 1976-84, Mass. Coun. Arts & Humanities, 1972-74; chmn. Mass. Found. Arts and Humanities, Boston, 1974-78; chmn. bd. Police Commrs., Fall River, 1976-80; bd. dirs. Portugueses Cultural Found., Providence, 1990. Commdr. USNR, 1942-74. Named Citizen of the Decade Fall River C. of C., 1982, Outstanding Alumnus B.M.C. Durfee High Sch, Fall River, 1981. Mem. Mass. C. of C. (2d v.p. Greater Fall River chpt. 1990—), Quequechan (Fall River) (bd. dirs.) Club. Home: Fall River Mass. Died Sept. 11, 1990; buried Fall River, Mass.

ZASSENHAUS, HANS JULIUS, mathematics educator; b. Koblenz, Germany, May 28, 1905; came to U.S. 1959; s. Julius Paul and Margarete E.F. (Ziegler) Z.; m. Lieselotte M.R. Lohmann, Sept. 5, 1942; children: Michael, Angela, Hans Peter. Dr.rer.nat., Hamburg U., Ger., 1934, Dr.Habil., 1938; M.A.h.c., Glasgow U., 1949; Dr.Sc. hon. causa, Ottawa U., Can., 1966, McGill U., Montreal, 1974; DSc hon. causa, U. Saarbrücken, 1982, U. Linz, 1984. Wissenschaftlicher Hilfsarbeiter Rostock U., Ger., 1934-36; wissenschaftlicher Hilfsarbeiter Hamburg U., 1936-40, diÄtendozent, 1940-46, Aussenordentlicher prof., 1946-50; prof. math. McGill U., Montreal, 1949-59, U. Notre Dame, South Bend, Ind., 1959-64; rsch. prof. math. Ohio State U., Columbus, 1964-82, prof. emeritus, 1982-91; prof. cinquantenaire U. Montreal, 1977, 83; dir. Forschungsstelle für Praktische Mathematik, Hamburg, 1946-50, Computer Ctr., U. Notre Dame, 1963-64. Author: Second Theory of Groups, 1958, others; contbr. articles to profl. jours. Fairchild scholar, Calif. Inst. Tech., 1974-75; named Sr. Scientist, Humboldt Gesellschaft, 1979-83. Fellow Royal Soc. Can.; mem. Can. Math. Soc., Math. Assn. Am., Am. Math. Soc., Deutsche Math. Soc. Lutheran. Home: Columbus Ohio Died Nov. 21, 1991.

ZAZAS, GEORGE JOHN, lawyer; b. Indpls., Feb. 17, 1926; s. John George and Rhoda John (Giovanni) Z.; m. Hope Chandler, Feb. 21, 1947; children: James B., Robert C.; m. Sylvia Levinson, May 16, 1963; 1 stepson, Eric S. Edelson; m. 3d, Barbara J. Walker, Sept. 14, 1989. AB, Harvard U., 1947, JD, 1949. Bar: Ind., 1949, U.S. Ct. Appeals (5th, 6th, 7th cirs.). Assoc. Barnes & Thornburg and predecessor firm, Indpls., 1949-56, ptnr., 1957-90. Mem. Ind. Dem. Cent. Com., 1972-76. Lt. USNR, 1943-58. Mem. ABA (co-chmn. com. on practice and procedure under Nat. Labor Relations Act, labor and employment law sect. 1974-77, coun. mem. 1985-90), U.S. C. of C. (labor rels. coun.). Clubs: Woodstock, Lawyers. Died Oct. 4, 1990; buried Crown Hill Cemetary, Indpls. Home: Indianapolis Ind.

ZDUNCZYK, ELIZABETH ELEANOR, real estate company executive; b. Torrington, Conn., Sept. 16, 1910; d. John Walter and Rose (Kukulka) Klemba; m. Joseph Anthony Zdunczyk, Nov. 17, 1934; children: Elizabeth Ann, David Thomas (dec.). Student pub. schs. Waterbury and Southington, Conn. Mem. Conn. Ho. of Reps., 1950-54; tax collector Bd. Tax Rev., City of Southington, 1965-82; pres. E-Z Real Estate, Southington, 1960-86 ; Democratic party nominee for Conn. Sec. of State, 1955; dir. Southington Savs. and Loan Assn. Chmn. bloodmobile, vol. canteen Southington ARC, 1950-83; bd. dirs., 1960-86 ; pres. Bradley Meml. Hosp. Aux., 1957-58; chmn. jury commn. Southington, 1963-69; vice-chmn. Southington Dem. Town Com., 1964-86; mem. Dem. State Central Com., 1972-86 . Recipient Gold medal Unico Club, 1955. Roman Catholic. Died Dec. 8, 1986; interred Immaculate Conception Cemetery, Southington, Ct. Home: Southington Conn.

ZEANAH, OLIN WEATHERFORD, lawyer; b. Tuscaloosa, Ala., Oct. 26, 1922; s. James Monroe and Hattye (Weatherford) Z.; m. Dorothy Ingram, Sept. 12, 1947; children: Karen Zeanah Stokes, Terry Zeanah Pike. BS, U. Ala., 1948, JD, 1949. Bar: Ala. 1949. Ptnr. Davis & Zeanah, Tuscaloosa, 1949-55; dist. atty. 6th jud. cir. State of Ala., Tuscaloosa, 1955-59; sr. ptnr. Zeanah, Hust & Summerford, Tuscaloosa, 1960-87; bd. dirs. First State Bank of Tuscaloosa. Served to 1st comdr. U.S. Army, 1943-46, PTO. Fellow Am. Coll. Trial Lawyers; mem. ABA, Am. Arbitration Assn., Fedn. Ins. Counsel, Ala. Def. Lawyers Assn., Internat. Assn. Ins. Counsel, Ala. Bar Assn., Tuscaloosa County Bar Assn. Baptist. Club: Exchange (Tuscaloosa). Home: Tuscaloosa Ala. Died Sept., 1987; interred Tuscaloosa, Ala.

ZEBLEY, JOHN HAUSE, JR., accountant; b. Phila., Oct. 3, 1896; s. John Hause and Susan May (Seltzer) Z. Grad., Pierce Sch. Bus. Adminstrn., 1914; spl. studies in pub. acct., U. Pa., from 1917. Employment mgr., chief timekeeper Raritan Arsenal, Metuchen, N.J., 1919; with Turner, Crook, Zebley & Parry (merged with Ernst & Ernst), Phila., 1928-63; ptnr. Ernst & Ernst, Phila., from 1963. 2d lt. U.S. Army, 1918-19. Mem. AICPA (pres. 1955-56, past v.p., mem. acctg. principals bd. 1958-63, coun. mem.), Pa. Inst. CPA's (pres. 1941-42, past v.p.), Nat. Assn. Accts., Am. Acctg. Assn. (v.p. 1948-49), SAR, Beta Alpha Psi (hon.), Masons. Clubs: Union League (Phila.), Merion Cricket (Haverford, Pa.), Lafayette (York, Pa.). *

ZEISEL, HANS, law and sociology educator; b. Czechoslovakia, Dec. 1, 1905; m. Eva Zeisel, 1938; children: Jean Richards, John. Dr.Jur., U. Vienna, 1927, Dr. Rer. Pol., 1928; LLD (hon.), John Jay Coll., 1989, CUNY, 1990. Instr. stats. and econs. Rutgers U., 1942-43; dir. research devel. McCann-Erickson, 1943-50; dir. research Tea Council, 1950-52; prof. law and sociology U. Chgo. Law Sch., 1953-74, emeritus, 1974-92; past rsch. assoc. Ctr. for Studies in Criminal Justice; cons. Am. Bar Found., Austrian Ministry of Justice, Rand Corp., War Dept.; chmn. bd. Marplan Internat.; dir. Am. Assn. Pub. Opinion Research; bd. dirs. Bull Atomic Scientists; mem. adv. com. Police Found. Author: (with P.F. Lazarsfeld and M. Jahoda) Marienthal, 1932, Am. edit., 1971, Say It With Figures, 1947, 6th edit., 1984, (with H. Kalven, Jr.) Delay in the Court, 1957, 2d edit., 1978, (with Kalven) The American Jury, 1966, Juror Attitudes Toward Capital Punishment, 1968, In Defense of Shakespeare's Romeo and Juliet, 1968, (with G. Casper) Lay Judges in the Criminal Courts (German lang.), 1979, The Limits of Law Enforcement, 1982, Law-and-Order Thrust Has Failed, 1987. Bd. dirs. Austro-Am. Found. Recipient Grand Decoration of Honor Gold Insignia, Austrian Republic, 1981,Paul F. Lazarsfeld award for outstanding contributions in sociol. Meteorology ofAm. Sociol. Assn., 1992. Fellow AAAS, Am. Statis. Assn., Am. Sociol. Assn.; mem. Am. Acad. Arts and Scis. Home: Chicago Ill. Died Mar. 7, 1992.

ZEISLER, CLAIRE (BLOCK), textile artist; b. Cin., Apr. 18, 1903; children: Peter Florsheim, Thomas Florsheim. Student sculpture, Alexander Archipenko, Lazlo Moholy Nagy at Inst. Design, Chgo.; MFA (hon.), Loyola U., Art Inst. Chgo. One-person shows Chgo. Pub. Library, 1962, Renaisance Soc., U. Chgo., 1972, Richard Feigen Gallery, Chgo., 1968, 69, No. Ill. U. Dept. Art, DeKalb, 1970, Hadler Galleries, N.Y.C., 1977, Art Inst. Chgo. (retrospective), 1979, Fullerton Art Gallery, Calif. State U.-Fullerton, 1980, St. Louis Mus. Art, 1980, group shows include, Mus. Contemporary Crafts, N.Y.C., 1965, 68, Art Inst. Chgo., 1966, Ravinia Festival, Highland Park, Ill., 1967, Stedelijk Mus., Amsterdam, Netherlands, 1969, Smithosian Inst., Washington, 1969, Mus. Bellerive, Zurich, Switzerland, 1970-71, Ctr. Internat. de la Tapisserie Ancienne et Moderne, Lausanne, Switzerland, 1971,73, Denver Art Mus., 1972, Brit. Crafts Ctr., London, 1974, Govett-Brewster Art Gallery, New Plymout, N.Z., 1975, Kunstgewerbe Mus., Berlin, 1975, Mus. Contemporary Art, Chgo., 1976, Renwick Gallery Nat. Collection, Washington, 1977, Phila. Mus. Art, 1977, Nat. Mus. Modern Art, Kyoto, Japan, 1977, Cleve. Mus. Art, 1977, U. Mich. Mus. Art, Ann Arbor, 1978, Moore Coll. Art, Phila., 1979, Dayton Art Inst., Ohio, 1981-82, Akron Art Mus., Ohio, 1982; represented permanent collections, Art Inst. Chgo., Stedelijk Mus., Amsterdam, Netherlands, Milw. Art Ctr., Musee des Arts Decoratifs, Nantes, France, Mus. Contemporary Crafts, N.Y.C., Dreyfus Corp., N.Y.C., Kunstgewerbemuseum, Zurich, Switzerland, U. Chgo. Law Sch., St. Louis Art Mus., Borg-Warner Corp., Chgo.; works mainly are done in freestyle, rather than loom; produced free-standing fiber sculptures. Recipient Honor award Women's Caucus for Art, 1982. Home: Chicago Ill. Died Sept. 29, 1991.

ZEKAN, WILLIAM C., plastic manufacturing company executive; b. 1920; married. With A. Schulman, Inc., Akron, Ohio, from 1956, exec. v.p., 1956-63, pres., from 1963, also chmn. bd. dirs. Home: Akron Ohio Died Jan., 1991.

ZELENY, LESLIE DAY, sociologist, educator; b. Mpls., July 21, 1898; s. Anthony and Mattie (Day) Z.; m. Florence Kelley, June 5, 1924 (dec. 1948); children: James Anthony, Richard Day.; m. 2d, Eileen Cosgrove, Dec. 18, 1948. BS, U. Minn., 1922, PhD, 1931; MA, Columbia U., 1923; postgrad., London Sch. Econs./Polit. Sci., 1936. Prof. sociology St. Cloud (Minn.) State Coll., 1923-46, chmn. div. social studies, 1939-46; prof. sociology, chmn. div. social scis. Colo. State Coll., 1946-63; pof. sociology Wayne State Coll., 1963-65, Am. U. Cairo, from 1965; vis. instr. ednl. sociology U. Minn., summer 1930; vis. prof. edn. Stanford U. Sch. Edn., summer 1964; vis. instr. Colo. State Coll., sumemr 1965. Author: (with Ross L. Finney) An Introduction to Educational Sociology, 1934; (with D.S. Brainard) Problems of Our Times, 3 vols., 1935-37; Practical Sociology, 2d edit., 1942; also numerous articles, pamphlets, chpts. to books, encys.; editor (with Richard Gross) Educating Citizens for Democracy, 1958. Pvt. USMC, 1917-18, to capt. USAF, 1942-45. Fellow Am. Sociology Soc.; mem. Midwest Sociology Soc. (life.; pres. 1939), Nat. Coun. Social Studies, Pi Gamma Mu, Phi Alpha Theta, Phi Delta Kappa, Kappa Delta Pi. *

ZEMACH, MARGOT, illustrator, author; b. Los Angeles, Nov. 30, 1931; d. Benjamin and Elizabeth (Dailey) Z.; m. Harvey Fischtrom, Jan. 29, 1957 (dec. 1974); children: Kaethe, Heidi, Rachel, Rebecca. Fulbright scholar, Vienna (Austria) Acad. Fine Arts, 1955-56. Illustrator and/or author children's books: Small Boy Is Listening, 1958, Take a Giant Step, 1959, A Hat with a Rose, 1960, The Three Sillies, 1963, The Last Dragon, 1964, Nail Soup, 1964 (Soc. Typog. Arts award 1964, Am. Inst. Graphic Arts award 1964), The Tricks of Master Dabble, 1965, The Question Box, 1965, The Little Tiny Woman, 1965, Salt, A Russian Tale, 1965, The Speckled Hen, 1966, Mommy, Buy Me a China Doll, 1966, Too Much Nose, 1966, The King of the Hermits, 1966, When Shlemiel Went to Warsaw, 1968, Mazel and Shlimazel, 1968, The Judge, 1969 (Caldecott honor), Awake and Dreaming, 1970, A Penny a Look, 1971, Tales Told in Denmark, 1971, Alone in the Wild Forest, 1971, Simon Boom Gives a Wedding, 1972, Duffy and the Devil, 1973 (Caldecott medal 1974), The Foundling, 1973, The Princess and Froggie, 1975, Hush, Little Baby, 1976, Naftali and the Storyteller, 1976, It Could Always Be Worse, 1977 (Caldecott honor), To Hilda for Helping, 1977, The Frogs Who Wanted a King, 1977, Self Portrait: Margot Zemach, 1978 (Horn Book award), Jake and Honey Bunch Go To Heaven, 1982 (Silver Medal for lit. of Commonwealth Club), The Fisherman and His Wife, 1982, The Cat's Elbow, 1982, Come On Patsy, 1982, The Little Red Hen, 1984, The Sign in Mendel's Window, 1985, The Three Wishes, 1986, The Two Foolish Cats, 1987, The Chinese Mirror, 1988, The Three Little Pigs, 1988, The Magic Umbrella, 1988, Sing a Song of Popcorn, 1988, All Gods Critters Got a Place in the Choir, 1989. Recipient 1st prize Book Week Spring Children's Book Fesitval, 1965; U.S. nominee Hans Christian Andersen award, 1980, 88. Home: Berkeley Calif. Died May 21, 1989; buried Calif.

ZEMAN, IVO, chemist, researcher, chemical engineer; b. Lysice, Moravia, Czechoslovakia, Apr. 4, 1931; s. Jaroslav and Marie (Jakubickova) Z.; m. Danuse Bastlova, Aug. 25, 1956; children: Daniel, Iva. BS in Chemistry, Tech. Inst., Brno, Czechoslovakia, 1951; MS, Inst. Chem. Tech., Praha, Czechoslovakia, 1953, PhD in Chem. Sci., 1958. Registered profl. engr., Czechoslovakia. With Rsch. Inst. of Fat Ind., Usti n. L., Czechoslovakia, 1956-58, scientist, 1958-64; head analytical dept. Rsch. Inst. of Fat Ind., Praha, 1969-74; head analytical group Rsch. Dept. for Detergents, Rakovnik, Czechoslovakia, from 1974. Contbr. articles to profl. jours. Mem. com., sec. Trade Union Rsch. Inst., Usti n.L. and Rakovnik, 1959-63, 78-83. Mem. Czechoslovakia Sci. Tech. Soc., Czechoslovakia Chem. Soc., Czechoslovakia Commn. for Chromatography, Czechoslovakia Com. for Fats, Detergents and Cosmetics, Czechoslovakia Com. for Chemometry, Automotoclub, Crosswords and Puzzles Union. Home: Rakovnik Czechoslovakia Died Jan. 19, 1991; interred Brno, Moravia.

ZEMEK, MELVILLE MASON, engineer; b. Chgo., June 5, 1919; s. Michael Joseph and Sadie Anna (Olson) Z.; divorced; children: Michael, Karen. B.S. in Elec. Engring., Ga. Inst. Tech., 1940; M.B.A., U. Buffalo, 1948. Registered profl. engr., N.Y., N.J., Tex., Ill.; cert. safety profl. Engr. Factory Mutual, 1940-42; mgr. engr., 1946-77; asst. v.p., engr. Johnson Higgins, Dallas, 1977-82; engr. AID Cons. Engrs., Dallas, from 1982. Contbr. articles to mags. Served as maj. USAF, 1942-46, ETO. Mem. Soc. Fire Protection Engrs., Am. Soc. Safety Engrs., Soc. Wireless Pioneers, Mensa, Intertel, Eta Kappa Nu. Lodges: Masons, Shriners. Avocations: extra class amateur radio operator.Deceased. Home: Little Elm Tex.

ZENO, JOHN RICHARD, engineer, researcher; b. Boston, Apr. 10, 1954; s. John R. and Florence Z. BA magna cum laude, Harvard U., 1976. Cons. Allied-Signal Aerospace, Morristown, N.J., Bendix Aerospace, Teterboro, N.J.; sr. inventor Warner Communications Labs., N.Y.C.; sr. researcher Atari Inc., Sunnyvale, Calif.; chief product designer V.E. Systems Inc., Elmsford, N.Y. Home: New York N.Y. Deceased.

ZETLIN, LEV, civil engineer, educator; b. Namangan, Russia, July 14, 1918; s. Mark and Alexandra (Senelnikoff) Z.; m. Eve Shmueli, Jan. 24, 1946; children: Alexandra, Thalia, Michael Steven. Diploma, Higher Tech. Inst., Palestine, 1939; M.C.E., Cornell U., 1951, Ph.D., 1953. Research asso., asst. prof. civil engring. Cornell U., 1951-55; disting. prof. civil engring. Pratt Inst., N.Y.C., 1956-92; vis. prof. civil engring. Manhattan Coll., N.Y.C., 1957-59; guest lectr. Columbia, U. Minn., U. Va., 1955-63; Univ. prof. engring. and architecture U. Va., 1967; cons. engr.; pres. Zetlin-Argo Liaison & Guidance Corp., Lev Zetlin Cons., Spl. Structural Systems, Inc.; mem. Internal Bd. Engring.; cons. to James Bay Energy Corp., Can., Montreal Olympics Stadium.; mem. Concrete Industry Bd. N.Y.C.; former mem. adv. panel GSA, housing tech. joint panel Dept. Commerce-Dept. Housing and Urban Devel.; mem. planning com. bldg. research adv. bd. Nat. Acad. Scis.; past pres. Internat. Tech. Cooperation Centre. Mem. editorial adv. bd. Bldg.: Constrn. Mag, 1962-92; author: Reinforced Concrete Design, Standard Handbook for Engineers, 1968, Suspension Structures, Structural Engineering Handbook, 1968; contbr. articles to profl. jours.; chpt. on stadiums Ency. Brit. Trustee, chmn. consultor com. Manhattan Coll. Sacred Heart, N.Y.; mem. N.Y. State Council on Arts, 1978. Decorated Knight of honour Mil. and Hospitaler Order St. John of Jerusalem, Knight of Malta; recipient Prestressed Concrete Inst. award for N.Y. State Observation Towers N.Y. Worlds Fair, 1964; Gold medal Société Arts, Sciences, Lettres, 1969; named to Profl. and Exec. Hall of Fame. Fellow ASCE; mem. Soc. Am. Mil. Engrs., Internat. Assn. Bridge and Structural Engrs., Inst. Structural Engrs. (Eng.), N.Y. Acad. Scis., Am. Concrete Inst., Sigma Xi, Phi Kappa Phi, Chi Epsilon. Home: New York N.Y. Died Dec. 4, 1992. †

ZETTLEMOYER, ALBERT CHARLES, surface and colloid chemist, educator; b. Allentown, Pa., July 13, 1915; s. Fred R. and Florence (Nagle) Z.; m. Onetta Ruth Hartman, Dec. 21, 1940; children: Christopher, Nicholas, Anthony, Timothy, Nan. B.S. in Chem. Engring, Lehigh U., 1936, M.S. in Chemistry, 1938; Ph.D. in Phys. Chemistry, MIT, 1941; D.Sc. (hon.), Clarkson U., 1965; LL.D., China Acad., 1974. With Armstrong Cork Co., 1941; mem. faculty Lehigh U., 1941-83, Disting. Univ. prof. chemistry, 1960-83, emeritus, 1983-91, v.p. research, 1966-69, provost, 1969-80, researcher univ. Sinclair Lab., until 1991; cons. in field; dir. Koh-i-Noor Co. Author 8 book chpts., 230 tech. articles; editor: Advances in Colloid and Interface Sci, 1956-89, Nucleation, 1969, Nucleation Phenomena, 1977, Nucleation Phenomena II, 1978, Jour. Colloid and Interface Sci., from 1965. Holder 10 patents. Chmn. United Fund Appeal Bethlehem Area, 1962; bd. dirs. Bethlehem YMCA, from 1950, pres., 1958-59, 62-66, trustee, from 1970. Mattiello lectr., 1957; recipient Ault award Printing Ink Assn., 1961, Elmer G. Voigt award for edn., 1966, Hillman award Lehigh U., 1966, Pioneer award Nat. Assn. Printing Ink Mfrs., 1969. Fellow N.Y. Acad. Sci.; mem. Am. Chem. Soc. (chmn. Lehigh Valley sect. 1952-53, chmn. divisional officer's group 1953-54, div. paint, plastics and printing ink chemistry 1954-55, div. colloid chemistry 1956-57, councillor 1960—, vice chmn. council policy com. 1968-70, chmn. profl. rels. com. 1973-76, dir.-at-large 1978-79, pres.-elect 1980, nat. pres. 1981, Kendall award 1968, Mosher award 1986, 1st Lehigh Valley sect. div. svc. award 1990), Gordon Conf. (chmn. chemistry interfaces 1955, chmn. adhesion 1979, trustee 1960-63), AAAS, ASTM, Am. Inst. Chemists (honor scroll 1966, Mems. and Fellows lectr. 1980), Am. Oil Chemists Assn. (Bond medal 1961), TAPPI, Tech. Assn. Graphic Arts, Franklin Inst. (com. on sci. and arts from 1973, Wilbur and Emma Mosher award 1985), Sigma Xi (nat. lectr. 1958), Tau Beta Pi. Clubs: Rotary (pres. Bethlehem 1962); Chemists' (N.Y.C.); Saucon Valley Country. Home: Bethlehem Pa. Died Jan. 27, 1991; buried Nisky Hill Cemetery, Bethlehem, Pa.

ZIDEK, BERNICE LOUISE (MRS. STEPHEN P. ZIDEK), wire manufacturing executive; b. Chgo., Oct. 10, 1906; d. Albert and Bessie (Kaberna) Vonder; m. Stephen Paul Zidek, July 22, 1925; children: Louise Ann Zidek Pavlin, Charles Edward. Diploma Englewood (Ill.) Secretarial Coll., 1923. Asst. to asst. mgr. Emerson Drug Co., Chgo., 1923-24; office mgr. Van Dyke Industries, Chgo., 1936-38; ptnr. Midland Metal Products Co., Chgo., from 1941. Troop leader to leader trainer Lone Tree Area council Girl Scouts U.S.A., 1938-68; mem. Insight for the Blind, Inc., Ft. Lauderdale Oral Sch. Aux., Holy Cross Hosp. Aux. MacNeal Meml. Hosp. Recipient Thank You award Girl Scouts U.S.A., 1957. Mem. Nat., Fla. assns. parliamentarians, Am. Inst. Parliamentarians, Am. Guild Flower Arrangers, Fla. Fedn. Garden Clubs (life), Nat. Council State Garden Clubs (life), Nat. Council Flower Show Judges (master judge), Freedoms Found. at Valley Forge, Moraine Valley Parliamentary Unit (Ill.), Oriental Study Club South Fla. Republican. Roman Catholic. Clubs: Bauhinia Garden Circle (pres. 1965-67), Federated Garden Circles of Ft. Lauderdale (pres. 1974-75), Coral Springs Garden, Women's Civic, Coral Ridge Yacht (Ft. Lauderdale); Country of Coral Springs; Riverside (Ill.) Golf. Deceased. Home: Riverside Ill.

ZIEMANN, ROBERT LEWIS, accountant; b. Southwick, Idaho, Jan. 23, 1927; s. Gus H. and Wilda (Keeney) Z. Student, Oreg. State Coll., 1945-46, U. Idaho, 1948-49; U. Houston, BBA, 1952. Accountant Briscoe, House & Stovall, C.P.A.s, Houston, 1954; accountant Mattison & Riquelmy, C.P.A.s, Houston, 1954-61; Accountant Harris, Kerr, Forster & Co., C.P.A.s, Houston, 1961-65; self-employed as C.P.A. Houston, from 1965. Served with USAAF, 1946-47. Elk. Deceased.

ZIFFREN, PAUL, lawyer; b. Davenport, Iowa, July 18, 1913; s. Jacob and Bella Minnie (Rothenberg) Z.; m. Muriel Averett, May 20, 1948; children—Kenneth, Toni, Abbie, John. B.S., Northwestern U., 1935, J.D., 1938; LL.D. (hon.), Pepperdine U., 1985. Bar: Ill. 1938, Calif. 1944, U.S. Supreme Ct. 1951. Ptnr. Gottlieb & Schwartz, Chgo., 1942-46; ptnr. Loeb & Loeb, Los Angeles, 1946; sr. ptnr. firm Swartz, Tannenbaum & Ziffren, Los Angeles, 1946-50, Ziffren & Ziffren, Los Angeles, 1950-79, Gibson, Dunn & Crutcher, Los Angeles, from 1979; lectr. fed. taxation Northwestern U. Sch. Law; spl. asst. to chief counsel Bur. Internal Revenue, Chgo.; asst. U.S. atty-in-charge of tax div. Chgo. Mem. Dem. Nat. Com., 1953-60, exec. com., 1956-60; mem. Dem. Nat. Adv. Council, 1957-60; chmn. Calif. Conv. Com. for 1960 Dem. Nat. Conv.; bd. govs., mem. exec. council Performing Arts Council, Music Ctr., L.A.; bd. dirs. Music Ctr. Found.; trustee Brandeis U.; chmn. 1984 L.A. Olympic Games, chmn. Amateur Athletic Found., 1984-88; pres. St. Jude Hosp. Found., L.A.; bd. dirs. Community TV of So. Calif., KCET, Exec. Service Corps of So. Calif., William Holden Wildlife Found. Conv. Recipient CORO found. Pub. Affairs award, 1980, Northwestern U. Alumni Assn. Merit award, 1980, Earl Warren Legal Achievement award NAACP Legal Def. Fund, 1979, Mayor's Human Relations trophy, 1983; named Alumnus of Yr. for Northwestern U., Big Ten Club So. Calif., 1983, Headliner Greater Los Angeles Press Club, 1983, Bill of Rights in Action award Constl. Rights Found., 1984, Disting. Civil Leadership award Jr. Statesmen Found., 1984, Officer of First Class, King of Sweden, 1984, Olympic Order award Internat. Olympic Com., 1984, Gold Medal award N.F.I.C., U.S. Acad. Decathlon award, 1986, Hall of Honor award Davenport Cen. High Sch., 1989, Founders' award St. Jude Hosp. Found., Inc., 1990. Mem. ABA, Calif. State Bar Assn., Los Angeles County Bar Assn., Order of Coif. Clubs: Regency, Hillcrest Country (Los Angeles). Home: Los Angeles Calif. Died May 31, 1991.

ZILMER, BERTRAM GEORGE, editor; b. Monroe, Wis., Aug. 26, 1898; s. Albert William and Martha (Schneider) Z.; m. Joycelin Woody, Sept. 29, 1926; children: 1 child, Shirley Joycelin (Mrs. Schyler Metcalf Burton); m. Janice Morton, Oct. 17, 1936; 1 child, Martha Lois. BA, U. Wis., 1920. Reporter, state editor, telegraph editor Milw. Jour., 1920-24; copy editor N.Y. Evening Post, N.Y.C., 1925-26; news editor Consolidated Press Assn., 1926-34; editor N.Am. Newspaper Alliance, 1935-42; gen. news editor Bur. Nat. Affairs, Washington, 1942; mng. editor Daily Report for Execs., from 1947. Mem. White House Corr. Assn., Acad. Polit. Sci., Phi Beta Kappa, Phi Kappa Alpha, Sigma Delta Chi. *

ZIMMERMAN, AUSTIN MANLOVE, lawyer; b. Chgo., Dec. 28, 1909; s. Edward A. and Isabel (Chave) Z.; m. Elizabeth Thayer, Dec. 26, 1934; children: Edward Austin, John Jeffrey. A.B., Amherst Coll., 1931; postgrad., Nat. U. Mexico, 1931; J.D., Northwestern Law Sch., 1934. Bar: Ill. 1934. Practice in Chgo., 1934-67; partner Norman, Engelhardt, Zimmerman, Franke & Lauritzen (and predecessor firms), 1937-67; prin. Austin M. Zimmerman, Barrington Hills, Ill., from 1967; sec., gen. counsel All Am. Aviation (now U.S. Air and All Am. Engring.), Wilmington, Del., 1942-46; sec., dir. Allied Tractor Equipment Co., 1938-42, Gust Corp., Flex-O-Lace, Inc., 1940-42, Anela Distbrs., Inc., 1945-67, Wacker-Dearborn Corp., 1945-66, Midwest Electric Mfg. Corp., 1945-72, 1647 W. Walnut Bldg. Corp., 1952-72; sec., treas. Chgo. Exhibitions Corp., 1955-67; v.p., sec., gen. counsel, dir. Randall Bearings, Inc., Lima, Ohio, 1946; spl. counsel Chgo. and So. Airlines, 1946-50, United Airlines, 1947; sec.-treas., dir. Vancouver Ritz Properties, Ltd., B.C., Can., 1960-67, RBI, Inc., Springfield, Tenn., from 1977, Bearing & Bronze Warehousing, Inc., Greenbriar, Tenn., from 1977; atty. for zoning hearing Countryside Assn., 1948; chmn. annexation com. McHenry County property Village of Barrington Hills, 1957, chmn. law com., mem. finance and health coms. village bd., 1958-69. V.p. Barrington chpt. Lyric Opera Guild of Chgo.; alumni adviser admissions Amherst Coll., from 1951, mem. alumni council, 1964-69, 1931, 50th reunion gift chmn. class of 1931, 1966-73, chmn. 53d and 55th reunions; treas., bd. dirs. Contemporary Concerts, Inc., Chgo. Mem. Am. Bar Assn. (chmn. Midwest area, sect. of pub. contract law 1965-68, council 1968-70), Ill. State Bar Assn., McHenry Bar Assn., Chgo. Bar Assn., Fed. Bar Assn., Los Rancheros Vistadores, Chi Psi, Phi Alpha Delta. Clubs: Lion, Law, Legal, Literary, University, Mid-Day, Amherst (Chgo.) (past pres.); Barrington Hills Country, Lake Geneva (Wis.) Yacht. Home: Barrington Ill. Died Aug. 25, 1991.

ZIMMERMAN, GEORGE HERBERT, financial consultant; b. N.Y.C., Sept. 10, 1895; s. George Henry and Jessie (Browne) Z.; m. Mary Helen Campion, July 7, 1926; children: Doris (Mrs. Andrew G. Bato), Elaine (Mrs. Rankin Peck, Jr.), Jessie (Mrs. J. Daniel Hitchens), Georgia (Mrs. John J. Loftus), Louis. BCS, NYU, 1921; DSc. in Bus. Adminstrn., Assumption U., 1961. With N.Y. Edison Co., N.Y.C., 1911-16, Guarantee Securities Corp., N.Y.C and Montreal, Can., 1916-18, Gen. Motors Acceptance Corp., N.Y.C. and Chgo., 1919-26; v.p. Comml. Credit Co., Balt., 1926-28; exec. v.p. Universal Credit Corp., 1928-41; v.p. Universal C.I.T. Credit Corp., Detroit, 1941-50; pres., chmn. bd., dir. Mich. Bank, 1944-50; organized G.H. Zimmerman Co.; dir. C.I.T Fin. Corp., N.Y., from 1941; v.p., dir. Comml. Investment Trust, Inc.; dir. Nat. Surety Corp., nat. Surety Marine Ins. Corp., Svc. Fire Ins. Co. of N.Y., Svc. Casualty Corp. Dir. Met. Detroit Building Fund, 1954-61, mem. allocations com., 1953-54; mem. Black River Ranch, Onaway, Mich.; chmn. bldg. com. St. Paul Parochial Sch. and Convent, Grosse Pointe Farms, Mich., 1950-51. Recipient Alumni award Assumption U., 1959. Mem. AIM (charter mem., pres. coun., 1951-56), NYU Alumni of Detroit (organizer, first pres.), Country Club, Athletic Club (Detroit), Yacht Club (Grosse Pointe), NYU Club, Century Surf Club (Miami Beach, Fla.), Delta Sigma Pi. Roman Catholic. *

ZIMMERMAN, RAYMOND DALE, mechanical engineer, business executive; b. East Cleveland, Ohio, June 24, 1949; s. Julius Eugene and Shirley Ione (Carter) Z.; student math. Case Inst. Tech., 1966; BS cum laude in Mech. Engring. (scholar), U. Cin., 1972, MS, 1978, postgrad., 1978-81. Engring. trainee Arthur G. McKee & Co., Independence, Ohio, 1968-71; project engr. Structural Dynamics Rsch. Corp., Milford, Ohio, 1972-73, mem. tech. staff, 1973-76; rsch. asst. U. Cin., 1976-81; exec. v.p. Quixote Measurement Dynamics, Inc., Cin., 1981-82, chmn. bd., from 1981, pres., from 1982; cons. engr., 1976-89; lectr. modal analysis U. Cin., from 1977. Active Big Bros. Am., 1979-82. Structural Dynamics Rsch. Corp. study grantee, 1976-77; Foundry Ednl. Found. grantee, 1969-71. Mem. ASME (tech. reviewer div. dynamic systems and control from 1980), Soc. Exptl. Mechanics, Sigma Xi. Contbr. articles to profl. publs. Died June 16, 1989; buried All Souls Cemetary, Chardon, Ohio. Home: Cincinnati Ohio

ZIMMERMAN, STANLEY ELLIOT, lawyer; b. Springfield, Mass., Aug. 14, 1918; m. Edith Victoria McHutchison, Apr. 2, 1944; children—Stanley Elliot Jr., Philip Douglas, David James, Ann Victoria. B.A., Yale U., 1939; J.D., Harvard U., 1946. Bar: N.Y. 1947, Pa. 1973. With firm Donovan, Leisure, Newton, Lumbard & Irvine, N.Y.C., 1946-48, Klein, Alexander & Cooper, N.Y.C., 1948-51; with W.T. Grant Co., N.Y.C., 1951-71; atty. W.T. Grant Co., 1951-54, real estate atty., 1954-62, gen. counsel, asst. sec., 1962-64, sec., gen. counsel, 1964-71; sec., dir., mem. exec. com. W.T. Grant Fin. Corp., Wilmington, Del., 1966-71; sec. Jones and Presnell Studios, Inc., Charlotte, N.C., 1969-71; v.p., dir. devel. Food Fair Stores, Inc., Phila., 1971-73; partner firm Schnader, Harrison, Segal & Lewis, Phila., 1973-88. Class agt. Yale Alumni Fund, 1962-71; mem. lawyers com. George Jr. Republic, 1954-69; treas., troop committeeman Larchmont dist. Boy Scouts Am., 1964-71; trustee Larchmont (N.Y.) Pub. Library, 1969-71; Former sr. warden St. John's Ch., Larchmont; former rector's warden St. Christopher's Ch., Gladwyne, Pa. Served to comdr. USNR, 1941-45. Decorated Legion of Merit. Mem. Am., Pa., Phila. bar assns. Clubs: Phila. Country, Union League (Phila.). Home: Gladwyne Pa. Died Sept. 22, 1988; buried Kennebunk, Maine.

ZIMMERMAN, THOMAS FLETCHER, clergyman; b. Indpls., Mar. 26, 1912; s. Thomas Fletcher and Carrie D. (Kenagy) Z.; m. Elizabeth H. Price, June 17, 1933; children: Betty Zimmerman Tinlin, Thomas Fletcher III, David. Student, U. Ind., 1929; DD, N.W. Coll.; LLD, Cen. Bible Coll. Ordained to ministry Assemblies of God, 1936; asst. pastor Indpls., 1928-32; pastor Kokomo, Ind., 1933-34, Harrodsburg, Ind., 1934-35, South Bend, Ind., 1935-39, Granite City, Ill., 1939-42, Springfield, Mo., 1943-47, Cleve., 1951-52; asst. supt. Ill dist. Assemblies of God, 1941-43; asst. supt. So. Mo. Assemblies of God., 1944-47, sec.-treas., 1949-51; asst. gen. supt. Assemblies of God, 1952-59, gen. supt., 1960-85; first dir. Assemblies of God Radio Broadcast, 1945-49; mem. exec. com. Nat. Religious Broadcasters (Hall of Fame 1987); mem. exec. bd. Nat. Assn. Evangs., from 1957; chmn. adv. com. Pentecostal World Confs., 1970, 73, 76, 79, 82, 85, 89; mem. exec. com. Lausanne Com. World Evangelization, from 1975, pres., 1986-89; pres. Assemblies of God Grad. Sch., Springfield, 1973-85; mem. exec. com. Convocation Evangelizing Ethnic Am. Co-author: Operation Sunday School, 1958. Bd. dirs. Central Bible Coll., Springfield, 1953-85, chmn. bd., 1959-85, co-chmn., Jerusalem, 1990; bd. dirs. Evangel Coll., Springfield, 1954-85, Cox Med. Center, from 1968; chmn. bd. Maranatha Village Retirement Complex, Springfield, 1976-85; Protestant vice chmn. Year of Bible, 1983; mem. religious relationships com. Boy Scouts Am. Recipient Silver Beaver award Boy Scouts Am., 1969, William Ward Ayer award for outstanding svc. in broadcasting Nat. Religious Broadcasters, 1990; named to NRB Hall of Fame, 1987; named Teen Challenge Man of Yr., 1990. Mem. Springfield C. of C. (Springfieldian of Yr. award 1974), Am. Bible Soc. (bd. mgrs. from 1967, Religious Heritage of Am. Gold Medal award 1986). Lodge: Rotary. Home: Springfield Mo. Died Jan. 2, 1991; buried Greenlawn Cemetery, Springfield, Mo.

ZION, LETTIE BACKUS, civic worker; b. Yuma County, Colo., May 11, 1910; d. Elmer Abram and Valeria Anna (Hampton) Backus; m. Theodore Charles Zion, Aug. 17, 1947 (dec. 1976). B.A., U. Colo.-Boulder, 1932; M.A., U. Fla., 1943. Tchr., Yuma County High Sch., Colo., 1932-34, rural schs., Wray-Vernon, Colo., 1934-36, DeSoto County High Sch., Arcadia, Fla., 1936-42, Leesburg pub. schs., Fla., 1942-43, Vernon High Sch., Colo., 1943-44, St. Petersburg pub. schs., Fla., 1944-45, Lamoni pub. schs., Iowa, 1945-46, Laird pub. schs., Colo., 1946-47. Editor: East Yuma County History, 1978, Wray Centennial History, 1986; contbr. articles to profl. jours. Tchr. Vacation Bible Sch., Wray, Colo., 1932-87; precinct committeewoman Democrat Party, Yuma County, 1980-84; vol. ARC, first aid instr., 1941-87. Named Woman of the Year, Bus. and Profl. Women, Wray, Colo., 1970; mem. NEA, Colo. Edn. Assn., Ret. Tchrs. Assn. (v.p. 1983-85), Farmers Union. Mem. Reorganized Ch. of Jesus Christ of Latter Day Saints. Clubs: Extension Homemakers, Woman's Christian Temperance Union (Colo.) (v.p., pres. 1986-87). Deceased. Home: Wray Colo.

ZOLOTOW, MAURICE, writer; b. N.Y.C., Nov. 23, 1913; s. Harry and Pauline (Edelstein) Z.; m. Charlotte Shapiro, Apr. 14, 1938 (div. 1969); children: Stephen, Ellen. Student, NYU, 1932-33; B.A., U. Wis., 1936. Mem. editorial staff Billboard mag., 1936-37; publicity work for actors, theatrical personalities, 1937-39; contbr. articles N.Y. Times Sunday mag., 1939-41; drama critic, essayist, contbg. editor Theatre Arts mag., 1953-58; lectr. non-fiction writing Ind. U. Summer Writers' Workshop, 1958, 59, 63, Colo. U. Writers Conf., 1968; lectr. Writers Digest Writers' Conf., 1967; leader workshop Rocky Mt. Summer Writers Conf., 1968. Author: Never Whistle in a Dressing Room, 1944; novel The Great Balsamo, 1946, No People Like Show People, 1951, It Takes All Kinds, 1952, Oh Careless Love, 1959, Marilyn Monroe, 1960, Stagestruck: The Romance of Alfred Lunt and Lynn Fontanne, 1965, Shooting Star: A Biography of John Wayne, 1974, Billy Wilder in Hollywood, 1977; Confessions of a Racetrack Fiend, 1983; biog. studies movie, radio, TV and stage stars for nat. mags.; short stories pub. in Playboy; collaborator: with Allan Sherman) A Gift of Laughter, 1967; contbg. editor Los Angeles Mag., Reader's Digest. Mem. Am. Soc. Journalists and Authors (founder, 1st pres., 1949), PEN. Home: Los Angeles Calif. Died Mar. 14, 1991.

ZUBIN, JOSEPH, psychologist; b. Raseiniai, Lithuania, Oct. 9, 1900; came to U.S., 1909; s. Jacob Moses and Hannah Rachel (Brodie) Z.; m. Winifred M.P. Anderson, Oct. 12, 1934; children: Jonathan Arthur, David Anderson, Winifred Anne. AB, Johns Hopkins U., 1921; PhD, Columbia U., 1932; MD (hon.), U. Lund, Sweden, 1972; DSc (hon.), U. Rochester, 1976. Diplomate Am. Bd. Examiners in Psychology. Instr. psychometrics coll. physicians and surgeons Columbia U., 1932-33; instr. ednl. psychology CCNY, 1934-36; asst. psychologist mental hosp. survey com. Nat. Com. for Mental Hygiene, 1936-38; assoc. rsch. psychologist N.Y. State Psychiat. Inst. and Hosp., 1938-56; cons. nat. inst. mental health nat. rsch. coun. VA, 1956-69; prin. rsch. scientist N.Y. State Dept. Mental Hygiene, 1956-60, chief psychiat. rsch. biometric rsch. unit, 1956-76; rsch. psychologist VA Med. Ctr., Pitts., 1976-78; rsch. career scientist, coord. for rsch. and devel. Highland Dr. VA Med. Ctr., Pitts., 1978-90; attending biometrician N.Y. State Psychiat. Inst., from 1976; various teaching pos., asst. to full prof. dept. psychology Columbia U., 1939-69, prof. emeritus psychology, spl. lectr., from 1969; Disting. rsch. prof. Western Psychiat. Inst., U. Pitts., 1977-90; speaker in field. Assoc. editor Comprehensive Psychiatry, from 1963, Jour. of Psychopathology and Behavioral Assessment, 1985, Integrative Psychiatry, 1984, The Behavioral and Brain Scis., 1981, Biological Psychiatry, 1970, others; contbr. numerous articles to profl. jours. Recipient Stanley R. Dean award, 1974 Bd. of Regents of the Am. Coll. of Psychiatrists, Paul Hoch Disting. Leadership award N.Y. State Office Mental Health, 1988, Outstanding Contbn. to Sci. award Pitts. Fed. Exec. Bd., 1988, 89, Gold medal Am. Psychol. Found., 1990, numerous others; grantee NIMH. Social Sci. Rsch. Coun., N.Y. State Dept. Mental Hygiene. Fellow Am. Psychiat. Assn., Am. Assn. Mental Deficiency, Am. Statistical Assn.; mem. Am. Psychopathological Assn. (former pres., Paul Hoch award 1984, 68), N.Y. Acad. Scis. (Behavioral Scis. award 1981, hon. life), Am. Psychol. Assn. (Disting. Scientist award 1975, Cert. Merit 1968), Psychometric Soc., Harvey Soc., N.Y. Acad. Medicine (life), Assn. for Rsch. in Nervous and Mental Disease, Am. Genetic Soc., Am. Coll. Neuropsychopharmacology (pres. 1971-72), Psychonomic Soc., Ea. Psychol. Assn., Inst. Math. Statis. Home: Leonia N.J. Died Dec. 18, 1990.

ZUCHOWSKI, KENNETH RAYMOND, hospital administrator; b. Chgo., Oct. 13, 1942; s. Raymond Joseph and Charlotte (Boyda) Z.; m. Arlene Susan Wydajewski, Sept. 2, 1967; children: Lisa, Mark, Lynn, Melanie. BS in Acctg., Ill. Inst. Tech., 1968, MBA, 1969. Sr. auditor Arthur Andersen & Co., Chgo., 1969-74; asst. adminstr. Woodlawn Hosp., Chgo., 1974-80; asst. adminstr. Christ Hosp. and Med. Ctr., Oak Lawn, Ill., 1980-83, assoc. adminstr., from 1984; bd. dirs. Wholistic Health Ctr., Oak Lawn, from 1984. Mem. Frankfort (Ill.) Homeowners Assn., from 1971, pres. 1976; treas. COR Youth Group, Frankfort, from 1980; chmn. com. Boy Scouts Am., Frankfort, 1974-86. Mem. Healthcare Fin. Mgmt. Assn. (advanced), Met. Chgo. Hosp. Council, Ill. Hosp. Assn. Republican. Roman Catholic. Home: Frankfort Ill.

ZUKOWSKI, LUCILLE KATHRYN, mathematician, educator; b. Millinocket, Maine, Nov. 2, 1916; d. Percy J. and Winnifred A. (Ball) Pinette; BA cum laude, Colby Coll., 1937, MA, 1971; MA, Syracuse U., 1943; postgrad. Harvard U., 1946, Bryn Mawr Coll., 1947-48, U. Mich., Ann Arbor, 1954-55; m. Walter H. Zukowski, Dec. 26, 1955; 1 dau., Mary Lucille. Teaching asst. Syracuse U., 1941-43; prof. dept. math. Colby Coll., Waterville, Maine, 1943-44, 45-82, prof. emerita, 1982-87, chmn. dept., 1971-82; vis. prof. Robert Coll., Istanbul, Turkey, 1965-66, Iranzamin Coll., Tehran, Iran, 1972-73; prof. NSF Summer Insts., 1958-70; corporator Waterville Savs. Bank, 1980-87, People's Heritage Bank, 1980-87; chmn. adv. com. Mt. Merici Acad., 1979-87. NSF Summer Inst. fellow U. Colo., 1953. Mem. Math. Assn. Am., Soc. Indsl. and Applied Math., Phi Beta Kappa, Sigma Xi. Roman Catholic. Died Oct. 12, 1987; buried Veterans Cemetery, Augusta, Maine. Home: Waterville Maine

ZUMBERGE, JAMES HERBERT, university president, geologist; b. Mpls., Dec. 27, 1923; s. Herbert Samuel and Helen (Reich) Z.; m. Marilyn Edwards, June 21, 1947; children: John Edward, JoEllen, James Frederick, Mark Andrew. Student, Duke, 1943-44; BA, U. Minn., 1946, PhD, 1950; LLD (hon.), Grand Valley State Coll., 1970, Kwansei Gakuin U., Japan, 1979, Nebr. Wesleyan U., 1972, Hebrew Union Coll.-Jewish Inst. Religion, 1987; DSc (hon.), Chapman Coll., 1982; D in Pub. Adminstrn. (hon.), Chung-Ang U., Seoul, Korea, 1989. Instr. Duke U., 1946-47; mem. faculty U. Mich., 1950-62, prof. geology, 1960-62; pres. Grand Valley State Coll., Allendale, Mich., 1962-68; prof. geology, dean U. Ariz. Coll. Earth Sci., Tucson, 1968-72; chancellor U. Nebr. at Lincoln, 1972-75; pres. So. Meth. U., Dallas, 1975-80, U. So. Calif., L.A., 1980-92; cons. geologist ground water and non-metallic minerals, 1950-62; chief glaciologist Ross Ice Shelf Project, IGY, 1957-58; dir. Litton Industries, Pacific Enterprises, Security Pacific Nat. Bank; U.S. del., 1970-86; pres. Sci. Com. on Antarctic Research, 1982-86; chmn. Ross Ice Shelf Project NSF, 1970-73, also mem. steering group Greenland Ice Sheet Program, 1971-82; del. numerous internat. confs. on polar rsch., Moscow, 1958, Chamonix, 1958, Helsinki, 1960, Obergurgl, Austria, 1962, Poland, 1967, Oslo, 1970, Sydney, Australia, 1972, Mendoza, Argentina, 1976, Warsaw, 1978, New Zealand, 1980; mem. Nat. Sci. Bd., 1974-80, Commn. on Geoscis., Environment and Resources, NRC, 1990; nat. lectr. Natural History Mus. Los Angeles County, 1978-80. Author: The Lakes of Minnesota, 1952, Laboratory Manual for Physical Geology, 1951, 7th edit., 1988, Elements of Geology, 1963, 72, Elements of Physical Geology, 1976; numerous jour. articles and papers. Bd. overseers Hoover Instn. on War, Revolution and Peace, 1978-84; chmn. U.S. Arctic Rsch. Commn., 1984-87; mem. Nat. History Mus. of L.A. County. Recipient Antarctic Service medal, 1966; Distinguished Alumni award U. Minn., 1972; James H. Zumberge Library, Grand Valley State Coll. named in his honor, 1968; Cape Zumberge, Antarctica named in his honor, 1960, also Zumberge Coast, Antarctica, 1986. Mem. AAAS, Geol. Soc. Am., Am. Geophys. Union, Soc. Econ. Geologists, Internat. Glaciological Soc., Mich. Acad. Scis. (pres. 1967), Conf. Bd., One Hundred Club (L.A.), Sigma Xi (nat. lectr. 1978-80). Home: Pasadena Calif. Died Apr. 15, 1992.

ZURHELLEN, JOSEPH OWEN, JR., foreign service officer; b. N.Y.C., July 8, 1920; s. Joseph Owen and Dorrial Bernadette (Levy) Z.; m. Helen Audrey Millar, Dec. 19, 1942; children: Joseph Owen III, William, Robert, David, Stephanie Jo. AB, Columbia U., 1943, postgrad., 1946-47; postgrad., Harvard U., 1947-48; student, U.S. Navy Japanese Lang. Sch., 1942-43. Gen. mgr. Universal Sales Co. of N.Y. (export-import), 1946-47; joined fgn. service, 1947; vice consul Fgn. Svc., Yokohama, 1948-50; consul Fgn. Svc., Fukuoka, 1953-55; consul gen. Fgn. Svc., Yokohama, 1953-55; 2d sec. Embassy, Tokyo, 1955-56; staff asst. to asst. sec. state for Far Ea. Affairs, 1956-59; assigned to Nat. War Coll., 1959-60; dep. prin. officer Am. Consulate Gen., Munich, 1960-62; 1st sec. Am. Embassy, Toyko, 1962-63; Am.

consul gen. Kobe Osaka, Japan, 1963-64; counselor of embassy Am. embassy, Toyko, 1964-68; dep. chief mission embassy Tel Aviv, 1968-73; dep. dir. ACDA, Washington, 1973-75; dep. asst. sec. state for East Asian affairs, 1975-76; ambassador to Republic of Surinam, 1976-78; v.p. Fgn. Policy Assn., 1978-80, cons., 1980; Breman prof. polit. sci. U. N.C., 1980; vis. prof. polit. sci. Manhattanville Coll., Purchase, N.Y., 1981-90; prof. U. Hawaii, May, July, 1990. Served as capt. USMCR, 1943-46. Pulitzer scholar, 1939. Home: Putnam Valley N.Y. Died Nov. 5, 1990; buried Putnam Valley, N.Y.

ZWACH, JOHN M., congressman; b. Feb. 8, 1907; m. Agnes Schueller, 1940; 5 children. Teaching cert., Mankato State Coll., 1928; BS, U. Minn., 1933. Farmer Lucan, Minn., from 1940; mem. Minn. Ho. of Reps., 1934-46; mem. Minn. State Senate, 1946-66, majority leader, 1959-66; congressman mem. 90th-93d congresses from 6th Minn. Dist., 1966-75, mem. Agrl. and Vets. Affairs coms. Mem. Farm Bur., Nat. Farm Orgn., Farmers Union, Grange, K.C. Republican. Home: Lucan Minn. Died Nov. 11, 1990.

ZWICK, LEANDER PETER, JR., lawyer; b. Canton, Ohio, June 10, 1921; student Kent State U., 1940-42, U. Nancy (France), 1945; J.D., William McKinley Sch. Law, 1950. Bar: Ohio 1950, U.S. Supreme Ct. 1957. Staff photographer Canton Repository, 1946-50; asst. atty. gen. State of Ohio, 1951-53; ptnr. Rossetti, Hillibish & Zwick, Canton, 1953-54, Rossetti, Fluidine & Zwick, 1954-57, Zwick & Unger, 1957-72, Zwick Law Offices Co. L.P.A., 1972—; spl. asst. to atty. gen. Ohio, 1953-58; mem. presdl. campaign staff Robert A. Taft, 1951. Former pres., chmn. exec. com. Muscular Dystrophy Assn.; mem. exec. com., trustee Catholic Youth Council, 1959-60; exec. com. Henry Solomon Lear Soc. of Ohio No. U., 1976-78; active United Fund, Canton Players Guild, Cultural Center Arts; v.p., trustee Art Inst., Canton, 1980-83, pres., trustee, 1983—. Served with U.S. Army, 1943-45, ETO. Mem. ABA, Assn. Trial Lawyers Am., Ohio Acad. Trial Lawyers (legis. com.), Ohio Bar Assn., Stark County Bar Assn. (exec. com. 1964-68, 73-77, chmn. lawyers referral service 1966-76), Stark County Acad. Trial Lawyers (trustee), U.S. Power Squadron. Home: Canton Ohio

ZWICKER, RALPH WISE, army officer; b. Stoughten, Wis., Apr. 17, 1903; s. Henry and Jean (Wise) Z.; m. Dorothy Harriet Stewart, July 14, 1927 (dec. 1985); children: Ralph Lathrop, Richard Henry, Jean Stewart Zwicker Durant. Student, U. Wis., 1922-23; BS, U.S. Mil. Acad., 1927; grad., Naval War Coll., 1945, Nat. War Coll., 1947. Commd. 2d lt. U.S. Army, 1927; advanced through grades to maj. gen., 1952; comdg. gen. Camp Kilmer, N.J., 1953-54; comdg. gen. Southwestern Command, Command 8249th AU FEC, Japan, 1954-55; dep. comdg. gen. Southeastern Command, Command 8249th AU FEC, 1955-56; comdg. gen. Southwestern Command, AFFE 8th Army, 1956-57; comdg. gen. 24th Inf. Div., Korea, 1957, 1st Cav. Div., 1957-58, XX U.S. Army Corps, Ft. Hays, Ohio, 1958-60; cons. Rsch. Analysis Corp., 1961-68. Contbr. to Mil. Rev. Decorated D.S.M., Silver Star, Legion of Merit with oak leaf cluster, Bronze Star medal with 2 oak leaf clusters; Disting. Svc. Order (Gt. Britain), Legion of Honor, Crois de Guerre with palm (France), Order of Fatherland (USSR), War Cross (Czechoslovakia), Order Mil. Merit of Taeguk (Korea). Mem. Masons (32d degre), Shriners. Home: McLean Va. Died Aug. 9, 1991; Arlington National Cemetery.

ZWINGLE, JAMES L., former association executive; b. Corinth, Miss., July 13, 1906; s. Christopher Mullens and Maude (Woods) Z.; m. Blanche Young, Oct. 24, 1942; children: Christa Young Zwingle Snow, Erla Frank Zwingle St. Clair, Anne Katharine Zwingle Leps. BA, U. Tenn., 1929, MA, 1932; PhD, Cornell U., 1942; LLD, Park Coll. Ordained to ministry Presbyn. Ch. U.S.A. Instr. commerce, registrar Lincoln Meml. U., 1923-25; fellow in English U. Tenn., 1931-32; prof. English, Bethel Coll., 1932-35; mem. community orgn. and adult edn. TVA, 1933-34; instr. Cornell U., Ithaca, N.Y., 1936-38; dir. student pers. State Coll., Maryville, Mo., 1938-40; regional exec. U.S.O., Atlanta, 1942; dir. field svc. ea. U.S. U.S.O., N.Y.C., 1943-46, dir. ops. continental U.S., 1946-47; pres. Park Coll., Parkville, Mo., 1947-55; v.p. Cornell U., 1955-64; exec. v.p., then pres. Assn. Governing Bds. Univs. and Colls., 1964-73; cons. on S.E. Asia, Dept. State, 1967-68; mem. coun. Fedn. Regional Accrediting Commns. on Higher Edn., 1972-74. Author: Trustees in Higher Education, 1974, Effective Trusteeship, 1975. Mem. bd. Christian edn. Presbyn. Ch. U.S.A., 1953-55. Kent fellow Soc. for Values in Higher Edn. Mem. Mid. States Assn. (commn. higher edn. from 1972, exec. com.), Cosmos Club (Washington), Phi Beta Kappa, Pi Kappa Phi. Home: Silver Spring Md. Died Apr. 5, 1990; interred Bybees Chapel, McMinnville, Tenn.

ZWIPP, GEORGE KAZMER, structural engineer; b. Budapest, Hungary, Feb. 6, 1925; came to U.S., 1969, naturalized, 1975; s. Louis and Georgina (Littke) Z.; M.S. in Civil Engring., Tech. U. Budapest, 1951, M.S. in Archtl. Engring., 1960; m. Clara Boldog, July 10, 1948. Lectr., U. of Architecture, Budapest, 1963-65; internat. archtl. and structural engring. design practice, France, Pakistan, Greece, Italy, Eng., Egypt, Saudi Arabia, Spain, Can., U.S., 1966-79; asso. Severud-Perrone-

Szegezdy-Sturm, N.Y.C., 1980—. Registered profl. engr., N.Y. State, N.J., Pa. Mem. ASCE. Republican. Roman Catholic. Home: Fort Lee N.J.

ZYGMUND, ANTONI, mathematician, educator; b. Warsaw, Poland, Dec. 26, 1900; s. Wincenty and Antonina (Perkowska) Z.; m. Irena Parnowska, 1925; 1 child. Student, U. Warsaw; Dr. h.c., Washington U., St. Louis, U. Torun, Poland, U. Uppsala, Paris-Sud. Instr. Poly. Sch., Warsaw, 1922-29; docent U. Warsaw, 1926-30; prof. Univ. Wilno, Poland, 1930-39, Mt. Holyoke Coll., South Hadley, Mass., 1940-45, U. Pa., Phila., 1945-47; prof. math. U. Chgo., 1947-81, prof. emeritus, 1981-92. Author: (textbooks) Trigonometric Series, 1935, 59, 77, last edition, 1988; (with S. Saks) Analytic Functions, 1938, 2d edit.,1956, 4 other books; contbr. over 180 papers to profl. jours.; represented in Contributions for Fourier Analysis, 1988. Served with Polish Army, 1939. Recipient Nat. Medal of Sci., 1986. Mem. Nat. Acad. Scis., Polish Acad. Sci., Spanish Acad. Sci., London Math. Soc. (hon.), Italian Acad. Sci., Argentine Acad. Sci. Home: Chicago Ill. Died May 30, 1992; buried Chicago, Ill.